The New WEBSTER'S INTERNATIONAL Encyclopedia

The New WEBSTER'S INTERNATIONAL Encyclopedia

THE NEW ILLUSTRATED REFERENCE GUIDE

Michael D. Harkavy
Editor-in-Chief

Trident Press International

1998 Edition published by Trident Press International, and distributed exclusively by Trident Promotional Corporation
801 12th Avenue South, Suite 302, Naples, Florida 34102, U.S.A.

Printed in the United States of America by World Color Book Services

Library of Congress Cataloging-in-Publication Data
The New Webster's International Encyclopedia: the new illustrated reference guide/edited by Michael Harkavy p. cm.
Summary: A concise, general-subject encyclopedia with color and black-and-white illustrations, maps and charts.
ISBN 1-888777-75-3 Single Volume Standard Edition; ISBN 1-888777-76-1 Single Volume Deluxe Edition;
ISBN 1-888777-77-X Ten Volume Hardcover Edition; 1-888777-78-8 Ten Volume Paperback Edition;
ISBN 1-888777-83-4 Two Volume Edition
1. Children's encyclopedias and dictionaries. 2. Encyclopedias and dictionaries. [1. Encyclopedias and dictionaries.]
I. Harkavy, Michael David. II. American Booksellers Association
AG5.A57 1991
031-de20 90-23047
CIP
AG

Table of contents

* Map section is not numbered consecutively within the text and actually begins on page 1, which follows Earth Facts.

Foreword

The concept of an encyclopedia dates back to antiquity. It represents the human ambition and endeavor to amass and classify the totality of knowledge. From Aristotle to Francis Bacon to Denis Diderot we have witnessed pioneering and heroic efforts to that end.

Unfortunately, today, in the "age of information," in which we witness an unprecedented explosion of information and dramatic rates of growth in many fields of knowledge, it is virtually impossible to duplicate the great feat of Diderot's 28-volume *Encyclopédie* of 1751-72.

Curiously, in light of the fragmentation of the unity of knowledge and the advent of many specialized fields of learning, accompanied by their own subspecialties, the concept of an encyclopedia, by necessity, has been fragmented. Today, we have many encyclopedias dealing with the unity of various specialized realms of knowledge.

The New Webster's International Encyclopedia is a one-volume general reference developed especially for students as well as general readers. It has 17,000 entries, more than 7,000 cross-references, more than 3,800 four-color illustrations, an impressive map section, and it is up-to-date. It includes the new map of Germany and covers the Persian Gulf War as well.

This concise encyclopedia is remarkable for several reasons. It provides specialized as well as general knowledge. Furthermore, it has made a valiant effort to cover 5,000 years of human experience and its record.

The New Webster's International Encyclopedia dispels any commonly held impression that an encyclopedia must not be easy reading and, by definition, must be dull. It demonstrates that clarity need not be the victim of accuracy. In addition to considerations of correctness and reasonable adequacy, it provides readability.

Various entries are not only instructive, but are well within the range of appreciation of any intelligent reader as well. Facts and interpretations of facts are presented directly and in a way that attempts to be objective. The aim is not to impose opinions but to provide facts, not to provide isolated facts but general theories as well. What else can one ask for? The editorial board, headed by Jeremiah Kaplan, should be congratulated for this unique and remarkable encyclopedia.

Vartan Gregorian
Brown University

A

A, first letter of the English alphabet and others that can be traced back to Semitic roots. The letter was originally drawn to represent the head of an ox and given the name *aleph* (Phoenician "ox"). In Greek this became *alpha*. The shape of the letter changed gradually as it passed into the Hebrew, Greek, and Roman alphabets. Our capital *A* is based on the Greek form. The lower-case *a* was first used in medieval manuscripts. From the first 2 letters of the Greek alphabet, alpha and beta, we derive the word *alphabet*.

Aachen, also Aix-la-Chapelle (pop. 238,600), city and spa in North Rhine-Westphalia, Germany. A major industrial center producing machinery, textiles, and chemicals, it is also the site of mineral springs frequented since Roman times. The emperor Charlemagne built a palace and cathedral in the city.

Aardvark (*Orycteropus afer*), nocturnal African mammal. Measuring up to 6 ft (1.8 m) in length and weighing up to 150 lbs (68 kg), the aardvark has a stout body with a plump, ratlike tail, elongated piglike snout, and large ears. It feeds on ants and termites, tearing open their nests with its powerful limbs and catching them with its long, sticky tongue.
See also: Anteater.

Aaron, elder brother of Moses and first Jewish high priest. In the Old Testament (Exodus) Aaron speaks for Moses before the Israelites and in the Egyptian court, after Jehovah has commanded Moses to lead his people out of Egypt.
See also: Moses.

Aaron, Hank (Henry Louis Aaron; 1934-), U.S. baseball player. He broke Babe Ruth's record in 1974 with his 715th career home run. He retired in 1976 with 755 homers. An outfielder with the Milwaukee (later Atlanta) Braves, Aaron also set a National League record with 2,297 runs batted in. He finished his career with the Milwaukee Brewers of the American League.

Hank Aaron

Abacus

Abacá (*Musa textilis*), name of the plant, native to the Philippines, that yields Manila hemp.
See also: Manila hemp.

Abacus, or counting frame, ancient calculating instrument still widely used in Asia. It consists of a wooden frame containing a series of parallel rods strung with beads and divided into upper and lower portions. Each of the rods represents a power of 10; each of the beads on the lower portion counts for a power of 1 and the 2 on the upper portion for a power of 5 apiece. It can be used to solve addition, subtraction, multiplication, and division problems.

Abadan (pop. 295,000), Persian Gulf port city in Khuzestan province, southwestern Iran, on Abadan Island in the Shatt al Arab, the waterway formed by the confluence of the Tigris and Euphrates rivers. An important oil-refining center since 1909, Abadan was badly damaged by bombing during the Iraq-Iran war, which began in 1980 and ended in August 1988.

Abalone, or ear shell, marine mollusk (genus *Haliotis*) harvested as a popular seafood and for the colorful lining of its shell, which is used for making buttons and costume jewelry. The abalone is found in most mild and tropical waters clinging to submerged rocks by means of a muscular foot.

Abbasid, dynasty of Arab caliphs (749-1258) descended from Abbas (d. 653), uncle of Muhammad. The early years of Abbasid rule were marked by prosperity and strong government; they reached their high-water mark with the reign of the fifth caliph, Harun-Rashid (764-809). The dynasty was finally overthrown by Hulagu Khan, grandson of Genghis Khan, who sacked Baghdad in 1258.
See also: Muslims.

Abbe, Cleveland (1838-1916), U.S. meteorologist who inaugurated a system of scientific weather forecasting in the United States. After studying at the Pulkova Observatory in Russia, he became head of the Cincinnati Observatory and in 1869 began publishing official forecasts based largely on analyses of telegraphic reports on approaching storms.

Abbey, building of a monastic house or religious community, centered on a church. The cloistered life of medieval times grew out of the anchorite, or hermit, communities of Egypt and the Near East in the early Christian era. The first abbey in western Europe was established in France in 360, and the first in England, Bangor Abbey, in 560. Abbeys were centers of culture and the practical arts throughout western Europe.

Abbey Theatre, originally called Irish National Theatre. It was founded in 1902 by William Butler Yeats, Lady Gregory, and others to promote the work of Irish playwrights. The company moved to the Abbey Theatre in Dublin in 1904. It performs works in both English and Gaelic.
See also: Yeats, William Butler; Irish literature.

Abbott, Robert Sengstacke (1868-1940), journalist, editor, and publisher and founder of the *Chicago Defender*, an important newspaper in the United States. The son of former slaves, Abbott graduated from Kent College of Law in 1899, but soon left the legal profession. Utilizing previous newspaper experience he published the first issue of the *Chicago Defender* on May 15, 1905. A leading proponent of equal rights for African Americans, Abbott used the paper to encourage Southern blacks to move to the North for better jobs and opportunities during the industrial boom of World War I.

Abbott, Sir John Joseph Caldwell (1821-93), prime minister of Canada (1891-92). During his career as a lawyer he became involved in the Conservative Party and was an adviser to Sir John Macdonald, the first prime minister of Canada. Upon Macdonald's death in 1891, Abbott became prime minister, but he resigned after only 18 months.

A.B.C. Powers, loose entente between Argentina, Brazil, and Chile, initiated in

1906, taking its name from the countries' initials. The entente's mediation averted a U.S.-Mexican war in 1915. Its aims were cooperation and mutual nonaggression, but a treaty signed by the 3 countries in May 1915 had little real effect.

Abdomen, in vertebrates, large body cavity between the chest and the pelvis. It contains the stomach, intestines, liver, gallbladder (which are covered by the peritoneum, the thin membrane lining the cavity), kidneys, spleen, adrenal glands, pancreas, and, in the female, reproductive organs. In invertebrates, *abdomen* refers to the part of the body behind the thorax.
See also: Intestine; Stomach.

Abdul-Hamid, name of 2 sultans of the Ottoman Empire. **Abdul-Hamid I** (1725-89) succeeded his brother Mustafa III in 1774. Throughout his reign the power of Turkey was on the wane, weakened by internal revolt and continuing war with Russia. **Abdul-Hamid II** (1842-1918) succeeded his brother Murad V in 1876. The following year he began a disastrous war with Russia that resulted in Turkey's loss of control over her European provinces of Serbia, Montenegro, Bulgaria, Romania, Herzegovina, and Bosnia.
After some initial gestures toward reform, he ruled harshly by decree. Sometimes called the Bloody Sultan, he roused world opinion against him and his government by the massacre of Armenians (1894-96).
The Young Turks, a reform-minded political organization, forced him to accept a constitution and deposed him the following year after he attempted a counterrevolution.

Ralph D. Abernathy

Abdul-Jabbar, Kareem (Ferdinand Lewis Alcindor, Jr.; 1947-), U.S. basketball player. The 7-ft 2-in (218-cm) center is considered one of the greatest players of all time. Known for his "sky hook" jump shot, Abdul-Jabbar holds records in regular season scoring (38,387 points) and games played (1,560) and received the league's most-valuable-player award 6 times. After a successful college career at UCLA, he played for the Milwaukee Bucks and Los Angeles Lakers of the NBA (1969-1989). Abdul-Jabbar legally changed his name in 1971 after adopting the Muslim religion.
See also: Basketball.

Becket, Thomas *see:* Becket, Saint Thomas Á.

Abel, second son of Adam and Eve. His older brother, Cain, killed him in a fit of anger when God accepted Abel's offering but rejected Cain's. (Genesis 4.)
See also: Adam and Eve; Cain; Old Testament.

Abelard, Peter (1079-1142), leading medieval French scholastic philosopher and teacher. The school he founded in Paris would evolve into the University of Paris. The main thrust of Abelard's philosophy was that the power of human thinking or reason could achieve true knowledge in the natural and supernatural spheres. He excelled in his study of the nature of abstraction and in his search for the source of responsibility in human actions. The church condemned Abelard's original teachings as heretical. Abelard is probably best remembered for his love affair with Héloïse, one of his pupils. Following the birth of a child, Héloïse and Abelard married secretly, but Héloïse's vengeful uncle had Abelard castrated. After separating to take up monastic life, the couple exchanged a series of moving love letters.

Aberdeen (pop. 216,300), Scottish seaport and the most populous city of northern Scotland. Aberdeen is a shipbuilding and fishing center also known as the market center for the Aberdeen Angus cattle breed. In the 1970s it became the hub of the industries based on the exploitation of North Sea oil.

Aberdeen Proving Ground, U.S. Army test center for guns, ammunition, vehicles, bombs, and other ordnance, located in Hartford County, Md. Established in 1917, the 73,000-acre (29,200-hectare) post extends approximately 18 mi (29 km) along the upper Chesapeake Bay near the town of Aberdeen. The Army Ordnance Center, Test and Evaluation Command, Chemical Research Development, and Engineering centers as well as ordnance disposal and ballistic research and human engineering laboratories are currently located at this post.

Abernathy, Ralph David (1926-90), U.S. black civil rights leader and Baptist minister. In 1968 he succeeded the murdered Martin Luther King, Jr., as president of the Southern Christian Leadership Conference and led the Poor People's March on Washington D.C. that year.
See also: Civil rights; King, Martin Luther, Jr.

Aberration, optical, failure of a lens to form a perfect image of an object. The 2 types are chromatic aberration, where dispersion causes colored fringes to appear around the image, and spherical aberration, where blurring occurs because light from the outer parts of the lens is brought to a focus at a shorter distance from the lens than that passing through the center. Chromatic aberration can be reduced by using an achromatic lens; spherical aberration can be reduced by separating the elements of a compound lens.
See also: Lens.

Abidjan (pop. 1,423,000), largest city and former capital of the Ivory Coast, West Africa. Abidjan is a major port and railroad terminus, as well as one of the most modern cities of Africa. The city's main industries include canning, shipping, and the production of beer, margarine, and soap.

Abilene (pop. 7,000), agricultural city in central Kansas. Settled in 1856, Abilene was an important shipping point for Texas cattle brought north to the railroad over the Chisholm Trail. As marketing center for the surrounding farmlands, its chief industries are grain milling and the processing of dairy products. President Dwight D. Eisenhower lived in the town as a boy and chose it for his burial place and the site of a memorial museum.

Ability test, test to demonstrate a particular level of knowledge or skill. An individual general ability test consists of 8 small subtests: information test, analogies test, vocabulary, letter memory, number series, spatial relations, clock test, and sign language test.

Abnormal psychology, sometimes called *psychopathology*, the scientific study of disorders of the mind. Treatment for these disorders includes medication, psychoanalysis (the technique developed by Sigmund Freud), psychotherapy, and behavior modification.
See also: Mental illness.

Abolitionism, movement in the United States and other countries that aimed at abolishing slavery. The *Liberator*, an antislavery paper edited by William Lloyd Garrison, began publication in 1831. In 1833 the American Anti-Slavery Society was founded in Philadelphia. Some abolitionists used their homes as stations for fugitive slaves on the underground railroad. The movement produced much literature, including Harriet Beecher Stowe's *Uncle Tom's Cabin.* After the outbreak of the Civil War, abolitionist demands led to President Lincoln's Emancipation Proclamation (1863). The 13th Amendment (1865) completed the abolition of slavery in the United States. William Wilberforce and others led the movement in Britain to abolish the slave trade (1807) and slavery (1833).
See also: Civil War; Douglass, Frederick; Emancipation Proclamation; Slavery; Underground railroad.

Abortion, ending of pregnancy before the fetus is able to survive outside the womb. It can occur spontaneously (miscarriage), or it can be artificially induced. Spontaneous abortion may occur as a result of maternal or fetal disease or faulty implantation in the womb. Abortion may be artificially induced by surgical or medical means, depending on the stage of pregnancy and the patient's condition. Today, an early abortion performed in a modern facility by qualified health care professionals is relatively simple and safe. However, complications of abortion like uterine infection or injury can contribute to an inability to have children at a later time. Abortion has been long practiced in most cultures, but public opinion in the Western nations, combined with the opposition of religious leaders, led to restrictive legislation in the 19th century. By the second half of the 20th century, however, abortion was legalized in most of Europe, the USSR, and Japan. In 1973, the U.S. Supreme Court ruled in *Roe* v. *Wade* that abortions in the first or second trimester are legal, but the

moral and legal controversy surrounding abortion continues.
See also: Roe v. *Wade*.

Aboukir, village in Egypt situated on the Mediterranean coast between Alexandria and the Rosetta mouth of the Nile. The Battle of the Nile (Aug. 1798), in which British naval forces under Nelson defeated Napoleon's fleet, took place in Aboukir Bay. A second battle (1801) was fought on land at Aboukir, and Napoleon's forces were again beaten decisively by the British. The village is the site of ancient Canopus, a thriving port in Hellenistic times.

Abraham, first of the patriarchs (founding fathers) of the Jews; regarded as the founder of Judaism. God promised Abraham that his people would inherit Canaan through his son Isaac. As a test of faith and obedience, God commanded Abraham to slay Isaac. Abraham unquestioningly obeyed, and Isaac was spared. (Genesis 11-25.) Muslims consider Abraham an ancestor of the Arabs through another son, Ishmael.
See also: Jews; Judaism; Lot.

Abraham, Karl (1877-1925), German psychoanalyst whose most important work concerned the development of the libido, particularly in infancy. He suggested that various psychoses should be interpreted in terms of interruption of this development.

Abraham, Plains of, site of the decisive battle in the Canadian theater during the French and Indian wars, in which Gen. James Wolfe defeated the French at Quebec (1759).
See also: French and Indian wars

Abravanel (Abrabanel), Isaac (1437-1508), Jewish theologian and statesman. Born in Lisbon, he served King Alfonso V of Portugal in state and financial affairs. Forced after the king's death to flee to Spain, he was employed by Ferdinand and Isabella until the Jews were expelled from Spain in 1492. He then lived in various Italian cities, eventually becoming a minister of state in Venice, where he died. He is best known for his extensive commentaries on the Bible.

Absalom, third son of King David of Israel. Absalom fled his father's court after killing his brother Amnon. He later returned and was pardoned, but he then conspired against his father, proclaimed himself king, and was killed against David's wishes. (2 Samuel 13-19.)
See also: David.

Abscam, short for "Abdul-scam," referring to Abdul Enterprises, Ltd., fake company used by the Federal Bureau of Investigations (FBI) in a 1978-80 investigation of political corruption that resulted in the convictions of 1 U.S. senator, 6 U.S. representatives, and assorted local officials. Posing as wealthy Arabs or their representatives, FBI agents secretly videotaped meetings at which they paid tens of thousands of dollars to the politicians in return for promises of social immigration legislation, government contracts, and other favors.

Abscess, localized accumulation of pus, usually representing a response of the body to bacterial infection. The bacteria enter the skin via a natural opening or small cut, and they can pass into the intestinal mucous membrane or the respiratory system and be swept by the bloodstream to various organs of the body. The immune, or defense, system of the body possesses 2 mechanisms for destroying the penetrating bacteria: the leukocytes (white blood cells) and antibodies. If these defense mechanisms succumb to the bacteria, an abscess forms: The bacteria destroy a large number of cells, causing tissue death and the formation of an ulcer, which forms a pussy mass. Fortunately, the tissue is usually capable of stopping the destructive work of the bacteria, forming a barrier to the spread of the bacteria by building a wall of cells and connective tissue. Such an abscess may drain spontaneously; otherwise it should be incised.
See also: Carbuncle.

Absentee voting, allowing a registered voter to cast a ballot in an election when unable to appear at a polling place. The voter sends a paper ballot to the election official before voting day. All states make provisions for absentee voting, but their laws differ on the elections in which absentee ballots are permitted and the acceptable reasons for absence.
See also: Voting.

Absinthe, common European wormwood (*Artemisia absinthium*); also, bitter, green, distilled liqueur principally flavored with an aromatic oil obtained from the wormwood. Allegation that absinthe is poisonous led to the drink's prohibition in many countries, including the United States and Canada.

Absolute zero, temperature (0°K [kelvin]/ –273.15°C/–459.67°F) at which all substances have zero thermal energy and thus, theoretically, the lowest possible temperature. Originally conceived as the temperature at which an ideal gas at constant pressure would contract to zero volume, absolute zero is of great significance in thermodynamics and is used as the fixed point for the absolute, or kelvin, temperature scale. In practice the absolute zero temperature is unattainable, although temperatures within a few millionths of 0°K have been achieved in cryogenics laboratories.
See also: Gas; Temperature.

Absolution, in the Roman Catholic and some other churches, remission of sins pronounced by a priest in favor of a penitent.

Absolutism, form of government, such as a dictatorship, in which all power is held by an unchecked ruler. Monarchies in the ancient world were usually absolute. In England, in the 18th century, the Stuart attempt to rule by divine right failed, but elsewhere in Europe, especially France, absolutism flourished until the early 19th century. Examples of absolutism in the 20th century are the totalitarian governments of Adolf Hitler in Germany and Joseph Stalin in the Soviet Union.
See also: Dictatorship; Totalitarianism.

Absorption, taking in of energy or molecules by a material. While in *adsorption* molecules are attracted to the surface, in absorption the energy or molecules are distributed throughout the material.

Abstract expressionism, U.S. art movement of the 1940s and 1950s that explored the emotional, expressive power of nonfigurative painting. It was the first significant school of U.S. painting, influencing artists in other countries. Jackson Pollock, who dipped and spattered paint on the canvas, was called, along with some other members of the movement, an "action painter." Franz Kline, Willem de Kooning, Mark Rothko, Barnett Newman, and Arshile Gorky are considered leading abstract expressionists.
See also: Pollock, Jackson.

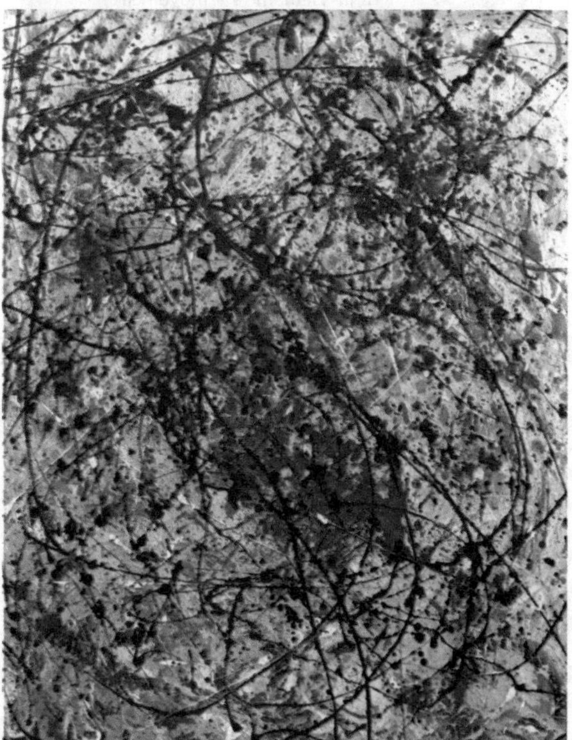

Jackson Pollock's Reflection of the Great Bear, *painted in 1947 (Stedelijk Museum, Amsterdam)*

Abu Bakr (c. A.D. 573-634), first Muslim caliph of Arabia in 632, following Muhammad's death. He ordered incursions into Syria and Iraq, thus beginning the Muslim conquests. He was Muhammad's father-in-law, as well as his closest companion and adviser.
See also: Muslims.

Abu Dhabi (pop. 243,000), largest (25,000 sq mi/64,750 sq km) of the 7 emirates that make up the United Arab Emirates (UAE),

located on the southern coast of the Persian Gulf. The land is mostly desert, with extensive oil deposits. The city of Abu Dhabi is the capital of the UAE.
See also: United Arab Emirates.

Abu Simbel, archeological site of 2 temples commissioned by Ramses II (13th century B.C.) on the west bank of the Nile, 762 mi (1,226 km) south of Cairo. The Aswan High Dam construction threatened to submerge the site, but a UNESCO project, completed in 1966, saved the temples by removing them and reconstructing them above the future waterline.
See also: Aswan High Dam.

Abydos, Greek name for a religious center in Middle Egypt inhabited since the early dynastic period (3100-2686 B.C.) and connected with the god Osiris. It is noted for its tombs of early dynastic kings and its 19th-dynasty temple (c.3100 B.C.).
See also: Osiris.

Abzug, Bella (1920-), U.S. feminist and political leader. While serving in Congress as a Democratic representative from New York (1971-77), she became a prominent spokesperson for the women's rights and anti-Vietnam War movements.
See also: Women's movements.

Acacia, any of a genus (*Acacia*) of mostly tropical trees and shrubs in the pea family. Various species produce catechu, gum arabic, and tannin. Acacia are characteristic of the savanna type of vegetation (grassland with some trees) in central and southern Africa. More than a dozen species grow in the United States. The flowers tend to be mostly yellow or white.

Academic freedom, right of members of the academic community to freedom of thought and expression. The American Association of University Professors' code of conduct proposes complete freedom of research but restricts classroom freedom to open discussion of the teacher's own subject. Despite this stand, scholastic immunity has been affected by boards of trustees, government agencies that fund some university projects, and students who object to the politics or theories of certain professors.

Academie Française (French Academy), literary and linguistic society officially recognized in 1635. Membership is limited to 40, the so-called immortals, and includes prominent public literary figures. It has been criticized for electing individuals with personal influence, while ignoring those with real merit. Molière and Emile Zola were never elected. Over the centuries, the Academy has produced the *dictionnaire*, the official arbiter of the French language.

Academy Awards®, or Oscars®, annual awards given by the Academy of Motion Picture Arts and Sciences for outstanding achievement in various branches of filmmaking. The major awards are for best leading and supporting actor and actress, best direction, best screenplay, and best film. The awards were first presented in 1928, when the best picture award was presented to *Wings*.
See also: Motion pictures.

Acadia, name given to Nova Scotia and neighboring regions of New Brunswick, Prince Edward Island, and parts of Quebec and Maine by the French colonists who settled there starting in 1604. All but Prince Edward Island and Cape Breton passed under British control by the Treaty of Utrecht (1713). The French colonists, dispersed by the British in 1755, are the subject of Henry Wadsworth Longfellow's poem *Evangeline*. Those who went to Louisiana are the ancestors of the present-day Cajuns.
See also: Cajuns; French and Indian wars; Nova Scotia.

Acadia National Park, U.S. national park covering 65 sq mi (168 sq km) in southeast Maine. The park's mountains, forests, and lakes make it an important wildlife reserve.
See also: National Park System.

Acanthus, any of a genus (*Acanthus*) of mostly tropical shrubs and herbs in the acanthus family having large, spiny leaves. Acanthus also refers to a leafy ornament used in Greek and Roman architecture.

Acanthus

Acapulco (pop. 462,100), seaport and tourist center on the Pacific coast of southern Mexico. Founded in 1550 on a natural harbor, Acapulco was a base for Spanish explorers and an important trading port. Since the 1920s it has been chiefly noted as a winter resort.

Accelerometer, device used to measure acceleration, working on the principle expressed by Newton's law: $a = F/m$, where a = acceleration, F = force, m = mass. The accelerometer measures the force expressed on a spring by an object of known mass. When acceleration takes place, the object is forced back against the spring as passengers in a car are pressed against the back of their seats. The greater the acceleration, the more the object is forced back. The distance the object moves back, measured in an electrical circuit, is a measure of the acceleration.

Accent, vocal emphasis placed on a syllable in a word. In all languages there are two kinds of accent: (1) musical chromatic or pitch accent; (2) emphatic or stress accent.

Acclimatization, process of adjustment that allows an individual organism to survive under changed conditions in its environment. In a hot, sunny climate, for example, human beings acclimatize by eating less, drinking more, and wearing lighter clothes. At higher altitudes, humans adjust to the diminished oxygen by increasing production of red blood cells.
See also: Adaptation.

Accordion, portable reed organ used for jazz and folk music. Tuned metal reeds are set in vibration by air directed at them from a central bellows through valves operated by piano-type keys on the instrument's right-hand side. Buttons on the left produce chords.
Although they were known in ancient China, the first modern accordions were built in 1829 in Vienna.

Accounting, analysis of financial records in order to reveal the financial position of an individual or firm. In the United States, an accountant who has passed a state examination becomes a certified public accountant (CPA). A financial statement is audited—that is, checked for accuracy and fairness—by an accountant who was not involved in the preparation of the statement.
See also: Audit; Bookkeeping.

Accra (pop. 965,000), capital and largest city of Ghana, on the Gulf of Guinea. The seaport, founded in the 1600s, was a center of the African slave trade until the mid-1800s. It grew in commercial importance in the 20th century after a railroad linked it with the interior.
See also: Africa; Ghana.

Acerola, commonly known as Puerto Rican, West Indian, or Barbados cherry, any of a group of subtropical and tropical trees and shrubs (genus *Malpighia*) indigenous to the West Indies, southern Texas, and parts of Mexico, Central America, and northern South America. The cherry-sized edible fruit, also called acerola, is tart, rich in vitamin C (ascorbic acid), and bright red when ripe.

Acetaminophen, common, over-the-counter pain-relieving and fever-reducing drug. It is sometimes taken instead of aspirin, which can irritate the stomach.
See also: Aspirin.

Acetic acid ($C_2H_4O_2$), colorless organic acid, the principal constituent of vinegar, used industrially in the synthesis of plastics. It was first isolated by George Stahl in 1700.
See also: Vinegar.

Acetone (CH_3COCH_3), colorless, flammable chemical used in industry as a

solvent. Because of its ability to dissolve cellulose, it is used to manufacture synthetic fibers. It is also used to make compounds. Acetone is found in large amounts in the blood and urine of diabetics. It is prepared commercially by removing the hydrogen from isopropyl alcohol or by fermenting starch.
See also: Acetylene.

Acetylene, or ethyne (C_2H_2), colorless gas that explodes on contact with air. Acetylene and oxygen are mixed and burned in the oxyacetylene torch, producing an extremely hot flame (up to 6,300°F/3,480°C) used for welding and cutting metals. Acetylene, used to make plastics, rubber, and explosive compounds, is poisonous if inhaled.
See also: Acetone; Calcium carbide.

Achaeans, people of ancient Greece identified by Homer as the Greeks who fought in the Trojan War. Some authorities believe that the Achaeans came to Greece in the 12th century B.C., briefly dominating Mycenae before being driven by the Dorians to a region in the northern Peloponnesus, which came to be known as Achaea. The Achaean cities formed the Achaean League, which opposed the Macedonians and the Romans, in the 4th century B.C. The Romans defeated the league in 146 B.C.
See also: Aeolians; Dorians; Iliad.

Achaemenids, Persian dynasty that dominated much of West Asia during the 6th-4th centuries B.C. The outstanding rulers were Cyrus the Great, Darius I, and Xerxes I. It ended when Alexander the Great defeated Darius III in 330.

Acheson, Dean Gooderham (1893-1971), U.S. diplomat who helped rebuild Europe's economic and military strength after World War II. He served Presidents Roosevelt and Truman in the State Department (1941-53), becoming secretary of state in 1949. After the war he promoted the recovery of Europe through the Marshall Plan and worked to curb Soviet expansion through the Truman Doctrine (both 1947). In 1949 he helped to formulate the North Atlantic Treaty Organization (NATO). He received the 1970 Pulitzer Prize for history for his book *Present at the Creation: My Years in the State Department.*
See also: Marshall Plan; North Atlantic Treaty Organization; Truman, Harry S.

Achilles, legendary Greek hero of the Trojan War and central figure in the *Iliad* of Homer. Dipped in the River Styx by his mother, Thetis, he was made invulnerable except at the point on his heel where she had held him. Achilles killed the Trojan hero Hector in revenge for the death of Achilles' friend Patroclus. Achilles was killed when the god Apollo guided an arrow from the Trojan warrior Paris into his heel.
See also: Trojan War; Iliad.

Achilles' tendon, tendon at the back of the ankle joining the bone of the heel to the muscles of the calf. It plays a critical role in the ability to walk, run, and stand on the toes. It is commonly injured in strenuous athletics. The name comes from the mythical Greek warrior, Achilles, who was vulnerable only in the heel.
See also: Achilles; Ankle; Tendon.

Acid, any of a class of organic or inorganic water-soluble chemical compounds that taste sour, redden vegetable substances, contain hydrogen, and readily accept electrons or give up protons. Many chemical reactions are speeded up in acid solutions, giving rise to important industrial applications. Strong acids (e.g., hydrochloric acid [HCl]), which break down easily in solution to yield hydrogen (H^+) ions, are good electrolytes (conductors of electricity). Amino acids, constitutive of proteins, are essential components of all living systems.
See also: Base.

Acidosis, medical condition in which the acid-base balance in the body fluids is disturbed in the direction of excess acidity. It can cause heavy breathing and weakness and lead to acidemia. Respiratory acidosis results from the underbreathing and consequent build-up of plasma carbon dioxide caused by lung disease, heart failure, and central respiratory depression. Metabolic acidosis may be caused by the ingestion of excess acids (as in aspirin overdose), ketosis (resulting from malnutrition or diabetes), heavy alkali loss (as from a fistula), and the inability to excrete acid (occurring in some kidney disorders).
See also: Alkalosis.

Acid rain, popular name for polluting rain or other precipitation caused by the combining of oxides of sulfur and nitrogen with atmospheric moisture. Although it is produced by naturally occurring combustion (volcanoes, forest fires), its serious increase is blamed on the burning of fossil fuels (oil, coal, natural gas) by automobiles and in industry. Acid rain may pollute water, kill vegetation, and erode buildings far from its point of origin and has thus become an international as well as a local issue.
See also: Air pollution; Environmental pollution.

Acne, common skin disease caused by inflammation of the sebaceous glands, resulting in pimples on the face and upper trunk. Acne occurs most frequently between the ages of 14 and 19 years, but cases at up to 40 years may occur. An inflamed acne lesion is preceded by a noninflamed lesion (a whitehead or blackhead), which is a plugged sebaceous gland. How these lesions form is uncertain. Blackheads become inflamed either because of local production of irritant fatty acids by bacteria or because of bacterial infection.
Patients with mild acne need only topical therapy, such as the application of a preparation containing either retinoic acid (a derivative of vitamin A) or benzoyl peroxide. Patients with more severe acne require antibiotic drugs as well as topical treatment.

Aconcagua, highest (22,834 ft/6,960 m) mountain in the Western Hemisphere, located in the Andes of northwest Argentina. It was first climbed by E.A. Fitzgerald's expedition in 1897.
See also: Andes.

Aconite, any of a genus (*Aconitum*) of flowering plants, commonly called monkshood or wolfsbane, belonging to the crowfoot family. The species *A. napellus* produces aconite, a poisonous drug.

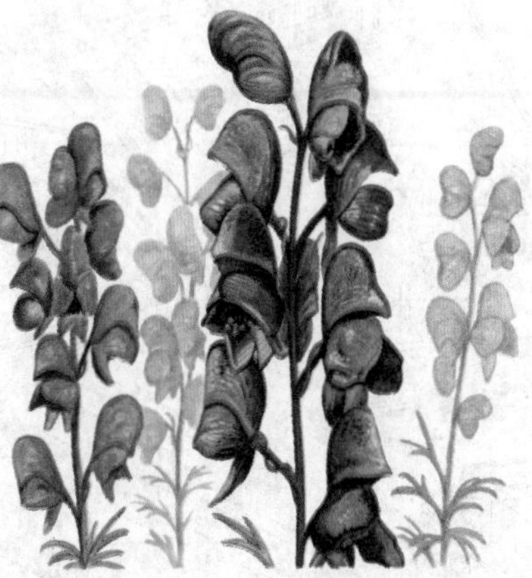

Aconite

Acorn, fruit of the oak tree, an oval nut partly encased in a hard, woody cup.
See also: Oak.

Acoustics, the science of sound, dealing with its production, transmission, and effects. Acoustics may be practically applied to, for example, the designing of auditoriums, where the audience must be able to hear the speaker or performer clearly and without echoes. This is achieved by attending to the geometry and furnishings of the hall and incorporating appropriate sound absorbing, diffusing, and reflecting surfaces.
See also: Sound.

Acquired characteristics, modifications in an organism resulting from interaction with its environment. In 1801 Jean Baptiste Lamarck proposed an evolutionary theory in which the inheritance of acquired characteristics provided the mechanism for species divergence. In later editions of *The Origin of Species*, Charles Darwin moved toward accepting this explanation along with that of natural selection, but eventually the Lamarckian mechanism was entirely discounted. Geneticists currently believe that inheritance is determined by reproductive cells.

Acromegaly, rare disease associated with the overgrowth of bone, especially in the jaws, hands, and feet. An endocrinological disorder or chronic hyperpituitarism may be the cause.

Acropolis (Greek, "high city"), fortified hilltop of an ancient Greek city, serving as its military and religious center. The most famous is the acropolis of Athens, with its many temples, including the Parthenon.
See also: Athens.

The famous Acropolis in Athens was constructed during the 5th century B.C. The largest structure on the Athenian Acropolis, the Parthenon, was dedicted to Athena, the patroness of the City. The Erechtheum was built to pay tribute to the legendary founders of Athens. The Temple of Athena Nike honored the goddess of victory.

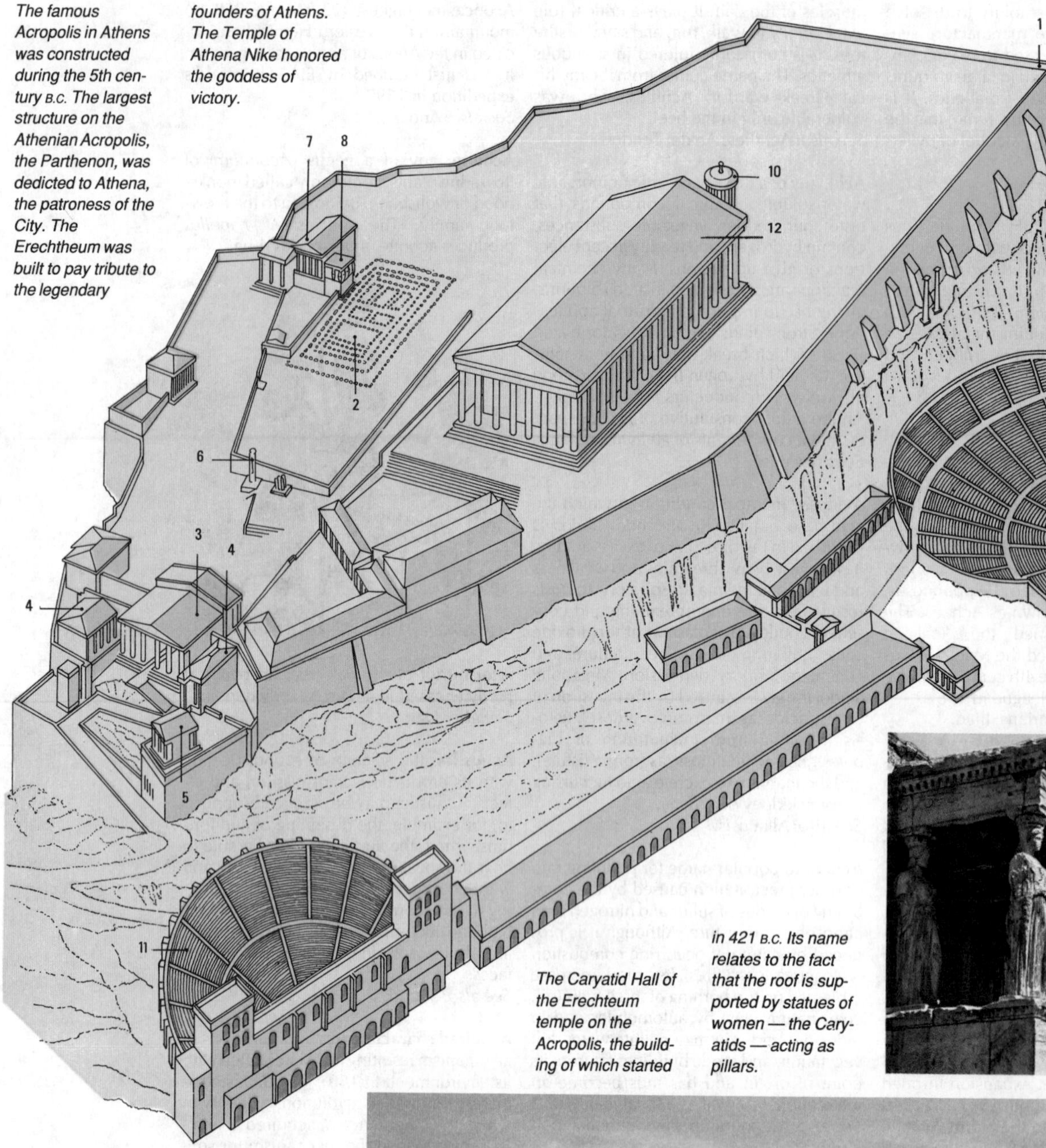

1. Pelasgian wall
2. Old temple of Athena
3. Propylaea
4. Wings with Pinakotheka
5. Temple of Athena Nike
6. Bronze statue of Athena Promachus
7. Erechtheum
8. Hall of Caryatids
9. Theater of Dionysius
10. Little temple of Rome and Augustus
11. Odeum (music hall)
12. Parthenon

The Caryatid Hall of the Erechteum temple on the Acropolis, the building of which started in 421 B.C. Its name relates to the fact that the roof is supported by statues of women — the Caryatids — acting as pillars.

The Acropolis with the Parthenon (447-438 B.C.). In the foreground are the remnants of the Odeum (music hall) of Herodes Atticus (2nd century A.D.).

Acrylic, group of versatile and durable synthetic products manufactured from petroleum as fibers, plastics, and resins for use in fabrics, glass substitutes, and protective paints. The molecules of a petroleum-based synthetic chemical or substance, acrylonitrile or acrylate, are polymerized (combined in a long, repetitive chain) to form acrylic. Orlon, Lucite, and Plexiglas are trademark names for some common acrylic products.
See also: Polymer; Polymerization.

ACTH (adrenocorticotrophic hormone), or corticotropin, hormone produced by the pituitary gland that stimulates the cortex of the adrenal gland to produce corticosteroids, which regulate many biochemical reactions in the body. Too much ACTH induces growth of the adrenal glands and provokes increased secretion of hydrocortisone. Lack of ACTH gives rise to a wasting away of the adrenal cortex; skin pigmentation is reduced, and the function of other endocrine glands, such as the thyroid, testes, and ovaries, is inhibited. The secretion of ACTH is largely controlled by the release of chemicals to the pituitary gland by the brain.
See also: Gland; Hormone.

Actinide *see:* Rare earth; Element, Chemical.

Actinium, chemical element, symbol Ac; for physical constants see Periodic Table. Actinium was discovered by André Debierne in 1899. It is radioactive and occurs naturally in minute amounts in uranium minerals. Actinium is synthesized by irradiating radium with neutrons. A reactive metal, it is obtained by reducing its fluoride with lithium vapor. It is about 150 times as active as radium and valuable in the production of neutrons. There are 26 known isotopes. Actinium-227, a beta emitter and a powerful source of alpha rays, has the longest half-life (21.77 years). Chemically, actinium is similar to lanthanum. It is the first of the actinides, a series of homologous elements analogous to the lanthanide transition series.

Actinomycosis, chronic infectious disease caused by *Actinomyces israeli*, a microorganism often (and usually harmlessly) present on the gums, tonsils, and teeth. The characteristic lesion is a hard area of multiple small communicating abscesses surrounded by granulation tissue. Other similar bacteria are usually also present.

ACTION, federal agency founded in 1971 to coordinate U.S. government volunteer programs. Over 400,000 volunteers assist seniors, residents of low income communities, and young people through food distribution, health care, drug prevention and education, and other programs. The Retired Senior Volunteer Program and Volunteers in Service to America (VISTA) are part of ACTION. The Peace Corps, which coordinates U.S. volunteers abroad, was administered under ACTION, but became independent in 1982.

Actium, now Ákra Nikólaos, promontory on the west coast of Greece. In a great sea battle fought near it in 31 B.C., Octavian's naval forces crushed those of Marc Antony and Cleopatra. Victory gave mastery of the Roman world to Octavian, who later became the first Roman emperor, Augustus.

Act of Settlement, English parliamentary act of 1701 securing the succession of the Hanoverian line. It increased parliamentary control over the monarch, who was also required to belong to the Protestant Church of England.

Act of Union, 4 acts of the British Parliament uniting England with Wales (1536), Scotland (1707), and Ireland (1801) and uniting Upper and Lower Canada (1840).

Acton, Lord (John Emerich Edward Dalberg Acton, 1st Baron Acton; 1834-1902), English historian and moralist. Lord Acton introduced German research methods into English history and launched the monumental *Cambridge Modern History* (1899-1900). He is famous for the remark, "All power tends to corrupt, and absolute power corrupts absolutely."

Actors Studio, professional workshop for actors, established in New York City in 1947; Lee Strasberg became director in 1948. The school's training, often called the Method, is based on the teachings of Constantin Stanislavski, stressing an actor's psychological interpretation of a role and emotional identification with the personality of the character.

Acts of the Apostles, fifth book of the New Testament, the only history of the early Christian Church. Probably written between A.D. 60 and 90 by the evangelist Luke, it is a continuation of St. Luke's Gospel and deals mainly with the deeds of the apostles Peter and Paul.
See also: Bible.

Acupressure (Japanese *shiatsu*), treatment system comparable to acupuncture. Pressure is applied to specific points on the surface of the body to eliminate fatigue and to stimulate natural curative abilities. Seven interrelated effects may stimulate the body to operate normally and help maintain good health: (1) invigoration of the skin, (2) stimulation of the circulation of body fluids, (3) promotion of function of striated muscles, (4) correction of disorders of the skeletal system, (5) promotion of harmonious functioning of the nervous system, (6) regulation of the operation of endocrine glands, and (7) stimulation of the normal function of internal organs.

Acupuncture, ancient Chinese medical practice in which fine needles are inserted into the body at specified points. It can be used as a pain reliever, an anesthesia, and a treatment for a variety of conditions, including arthritis, ulcers, and migraine. Research has shown that acupuncture has a specific effect on the release of certain chemical transmitters— natural painkillers known as endorphins—from nerve cells in the brain. Acupuncture is not fully accepted in the United States.
See also: Endorphin.

A.D., abbreviation for *anno Domini* (Latin, "in the year of our Lord"). The monk Dionysius Exiguus started a system of reckoning years in A.D. 532, using the year in which he believed Christ was born at the beginning of the Christian era. A.D. refers to events that took place after the birth of Christ, and B.C. (before Christ) refers to events that took place before his birth.
See also: B.C.

Adam, Robert (1728-92) and **James** (1730-94), Scottish architect brothers. Robert's studies of ancient Roman architecture helped to inspire their joint designs of graceful interiors, furnishings, and buildings, notably Syon House (1762-69) and Osterley Park House (1761-80) in London.

Adam and Eve, first man and woman, according to the Bible (Genesis 2-3). They were created in God's image and placed in the Garden of Eden to care for the earth and its inhabitants. According to the story, Adam and Eve ate the fruit from the forbidden tree of knowledge of good and evil and were exiled from Eden by God to live a mortal life. Man was destined to a life of toil and woman to the pain of childbirth, and both were subject to death.
See also: Abel; Cain; Genesis.

Adams, Abigail Smith (1744-1818), wife of John Adams, the second president of the United States, and mother of John Quincy Adams, the sixth president. Largely self-educated but highly intelligent, she wrote letters giving a lively account of contemporary society.
See also: Adams, John.

Adams, Ansel (1902-85), U.S. photographer known for his dramatic black-and-white photos capturing the beauty of California's Sierra Nevada and of the American Southwest. He founded the first college photography department in 1946 at the California School of Fine Arts (now the San Francisco Art Institute).

Ansel Adams's photograph of Hernandez, New Mexico

Adams, Brooks (1848-1927), U.S. historian, son of U.S. diplomat Charles Francis Adams, grandson of President John Quincy Adams, and brother of historian Henry Adams. He saw history as a series of economic growth cycles, a theory developed in his chief work, *The Law of Civilization and Decay* (1895).

Adams, Charles Francis (1807-86), U.S. diplomat and son of President John Quincy Adams. As minister to Great Britain (1861-68), he helped to keep Britain neutral during the Civil War. In 1871-72 he represented the United States in the Alabama Claims settlement.

Adams, Henry Brooks (1838-1918), U.S. historian, brother of Brooks Adams. His autobiography, *The Education of Henry Adams,* in which he attempted to show how ill- prepared his generation was for the 20th century, won a Pulitzer Prize in 1919. His other works include *Mount-Saint- Michel and Chartres* (1913)and the 9-volume *History of the United States* (1885-91).

Adams, John (1735-1826), second president of the United States and father of the sixth president, John Quincy Adams. Adams was a brilliant political thinker who helped lead the nation's struggle for independence.

Early life. Adams grew up on a small farm and attended Harvard University, graduating in 1755. He taught school briefly and then became a lawyer, moving to Boston in 1768. In 1764, he married Abigail Smith, the daughter of a minister.

Revolutionary leader. Adam's opposition to the British Parliament's Stamp Act of 1765 first brought him to political prominence. The Act, which imposed taxes on all printed materials, was Britain's first attempt to tax the colonies directly. Adams and others argued that the taxes were illegal since the colonists had no representation in Parliament. Adams risked political disfavor in 1770 when he acted as defense lawyer for the British captain and 8 soldiers accused of firing into the crowd in the Boston Massacre. But many admired him for his fairness, and in 1771 the people of Boston elected him to the colonial legislature.

In 1774 the First Continental Congress met in Philadelphia to protest the Intolerable Acts, further harsh laws enacted by the British government. Adams, representing Massachusetts, helped draft a declaration of rights and a petition to the king.

The following year, during the Second Continental Congress, he recommended the creation of the Continental Army, nominating George Washington as its commander-in-chief. In 1776 he served on the committee that prepared the Declaration of Independence.

Diplomat. From 1778 to 1788, with the exception of a brief return home in 1779-80, Adams lived abroad, serving the new United States in various diplomatic posts. In 1782 he helped negotiate the Treaty of Paris, which marked formal British recognition of the former colonies' independence.

President. In 1789 Adams became the nation's first vice president, serving under President George Washington for 2 terms. In 1796 he was elected president. Adams was a leader of the Federalist party, which supported strong central government. But many members of Adams's own cabinet were more loyal to another Federalist leader, Alexander Hamilton, than they were to Adams.

A split developed within Adams's administration over foreign policy. After the French Revolution, Britain and France were at war. Some U.S. leaders, including Vice President Thomas Jefferson, wanted the United States to join the war on the side of France. Others, led by Hamilton, wanted to go to war *against* France. In 1799 President Adams sent ministers to France in a successful attempt to negotiate a peace accord. Adams lost the support of his own party by seeking peace with France, and he angered the opposing Democratic-Republicans by allowing passage of the Alien and Sedition Acts, which limited the rights of both foreigners and U.S. citizens. As a result, Adams lost the 1800 election and was succeeded by Thomas Jefferson as president. A few weeks before the end of his term, in what proved to be one of his most important acts, Adams appointed John Marshall as Chief Justice of the Supreme Court. Adams lived for another 26 years. In 1825 his son, John Quincy Adams, became the nation's sixth president. John Adams died on July 4th, 1826—the 50th anniversary of the Declaration of Independence.

John Adams

2nd U.S. president

Born:	Braintree (later Quincy), Massachusetts; October 30, 1735
Term:	March 1797-March 1801
Vice President:	Thomas Jefferson
Political Party:	Federalist
Spouse:	Abigail Smith Adams
Children:	5
Died:	Quincy, Massachusetts; July 4, 1826

Adams, John Quincy (1767-1848), sixth president of the United States and son of the second president, John Adams. Adams also served as diplomat, secretary of state, senator, and representative.

Early life. As a boy, Adams accompanied his father on various diplomatic missions in Europe, where he was educated. After returning home in 1785, he studied at Harvard, graduating at the age of 19. He became a lawyer and settled in Boston to practice, but he spent much of his time writing newspaper articles on political topics.

Diplomat. In 1794 Adams was appointed ambassador to the Netherlands by President George Washington, who had been favorably impressed by Adams's political essays. He later served in diplomatic posts in London, Lisbon, and Berlin.

In 1809 President James Madison appointed Adams the first U.S. ambassador to Russia, a post he held until 1814. Adams helped to negotiate the Treaty of Ghent (1814), which ended the War of 1812 between the U.S. and Britain. From 1815 to 1817, he was ambassador to England.

Secretary of State. John Quincy Adams became secretary of state in 1817, under President James Monroe. He helped develop the Monroe Doctrine, which stated U.S. opposition to involvement by European countries in the Americas. He also negotiated the treaty with Spain (1819) that ceded Florida to the United States and established a border with Mexico.

President. Adams's presidential term (1825-29) was probably the least successful phase of his public life and certainly the unhappiest. His political enemies accused him of having made a suspicious deal with one of the other candidates, Henry Clay, in order to become president by vote of the House of Representatives. These accusations haunted him throughout his term.

As president, Adams advocated a strong national bank, protective tariffs, conservation of public lands, and protection of Native American tribes. He pushed for other national projects and improvements such as highways, canals, and railroads, but Congress rejected most of these ideas.

A tariff act passed during his term was so unpopular that it was called the Tariff of Abominations. Adams ran for reelection in 1828 but was defeated by Andrew Jackson.

Return to Congress. In 1830 Adams was elected to the U.S. House of Representatives, where he served until his death in 1848. Known as Old Man Eloquent, he fought vigorously for the right of the people to petition for the redress of wrongs, as well as against the extension of slavery. He was one of the first to claim that the federal

government could free slaves during time of war, an argument that later supported President Abraham Lincoln's Emancipation Proclamation of 1862.
Adams died at the age of 80, 2 days after suffering a stroke at his desk in the House of Representatives.

Adams, Maude (1872-1953), U.S. actress best remembered for her leading roles at the turn of the century in plays by James Barrie, Edmond Rostand, and William Shakespeare.

Adams, Roger (1889-1971), U.S. chemist and teacher whose work included research on the molecular structure and laboratory synthesis of organic compounds. He contributed to medicine and industry by determining the organic composition of gossypol, the toxic cottonseed pigment; cannabinol, a compound in marijuana; and chaulmoogric, used in treating leprosy and by developing catalytic hydrogenation, a petroleum-refining process using a platinum oxide.

Adams, Samuel (1722-1803), American Revolutionary leader and signer of the Declaration of Independence. His oratory and writings increased colonial discontent with British rule. Adams opposed the Sugar and Stamp acts (1764-65), helped organize the Boston Tea Party (1773), and urged independence at the First Continental Congress (1774). He served as governor of Massachusetts from 1794 to 1797.
See also: Boston Tea Party; Continental Congress; Intolerable Acts; Revere, Paul Stamp Act.

Adams, Samuel Hopkins (1871-1958), U.S. writer. As a newspaper and magazine journalist Adams attacked dishonesty in medicine, business, and government, and his collected articles, *The Great American Fraud* (1906), furthered the passage of the Pure Food and Drug Act. His novels include *The Clarion* (1914) and *Revelry* (1926).

Adams, Sherman (1899-1986), U.S. Republican congressional representative (1945-47), governor of New Hampshire (1949-53), and White House Chief of Staff (1953-58). Adams resigned from President Dwight D. Eisenhower's administration after political leaders condemned him for accepting gifts from industrialist Bernard Goldfine, who was under government investigation.
See also: Eisenhower, Dwight David.

Adams-Onís Treaty, or Transcontinental Treaty, U.S.-Spanish agreement (1819) defining the western boundary of the United States, negotiated by Secretary of State John Quincy Adams and the Spanish minister to the United States, Luis de Onís. Spain ceded Florida to the United States in return for the abandonment of U.S. claims to Texas.

Adaptation, an organism's adjustment to its environment in order to survive, believed to arise from transmitted genetic variations preserved by natural selection. Successful and versatile adaptation in an organism leads to widespread distribution and long-term survival. Examples include the development of lungs in amphibians and of wings in birds and insects.
See also: Acclimatization; Evolution.

Addams, Jane (1860-1935), U.S. social reformer. With Ellen Gates Starr she founded Chicago's Hull House (1889) to provide social and cultural activities for the neighborhood poor. An ardent pacifist, she served as president of the Women's International League for Peace and Freedom from 1915 to 1929 and was cowinner of the 1931 Nobel Peace Prize.
See also: Hull House; Settlement house.

Addax (*Addax nasomaculatus*), North African desert antelope of the family Bovidae. The addax stands about 3.5 feet (1 m) at the shoulder and has spirally twisted horns and broad hoofs.

Adder, common name for several species of venomous and harmless snake found in different parts of the world. Examples are the European viper (*Vipera berus*) and the puff adder (*Bitis arietans*) of Africa, deadly members of the viper family, and the hognose snake (genus *Heterodon*), a harmless species found in North America.

Adder's tongue *see:* Dogtooth violet.

Addis Ababa (pop. 1,425,000), capital of Ethiopia (since 1889). The modern city, standing on an 8,000-ft (2,438-m) central plateau, is Ethiopia's center for trade, communications, and administration and houses the headquarters of the Organization of African Unity.
See also: Ethiopia.

Addison, Joseph (1672-1719), English writer and statesman, including service as secretary of state (1717-18). Author of plays and poems, it was for his lasting contribution to the English essay form that he is best remembered, especially those essays published in the *Tatler* and the *Spectator*, which he co-founded with Sir Richard Steele.
See also: Steele, Sir Richard.

Addison, Thomas (1793-1860), English physician and teacher who described Addison's disease (atrophy of the adrenal cortex) and Addison's anemia (now *pernicious anemia*).
See also: Addison's disease; Anemia.

Addison's disease, progressive disease resulting from atrophy of the cortex (outer layer) of the adrenal glands. Deficient secretion of the hormones aldosterone or cortisol causes lowered blood volume and pressure, anemia, low blood sugar, gastrointestinal upsets, and brownish pigmentation of the skin. The cause is unknown. The disease, which occurs in all age groups and in both sexes, is often successfully treated today with adrenocortical hormones, reversing its previously fatal effects.
See also: Gland.

Ade, George (1866-1944), U.S. newspaper humorist and playwright whose *Fables in Slang* (1899) used colloquialisms and down-to-earth characters to poke fun at society.

John Quincy Adams

6th U.S. president

Born:	Braintree (later Quincy), Massachusetts; July 11, 1767
Term:	March 1825 - March 1829
Vice President:	John Caldwell Calhoun
Political Party:	Initially Federalist, later Democratic-Republican
Spouse:	Louisa Catherine Johnson Adams
Children:	4
Died:	Washington, D.C.; Feb. 23, 1848

Addis Ababa is the home of the Organization of African Unity, established in 1963. Africa Hall is the meeting place for the OAU.

Adelaide (pop. 987,100), capital of the state of South Australia in Australia. Located near the mouth of Torrens River, the city is an industrial center for automobiles and textiles and the commercial hub of a large region, exporting wool, grains, and dairy products. Adelaide accounts for almost two-thirds of the state's population and has many notable buildings and parks.
See also: Australia.

Aden (pop. 365,000), former capital and chief port of the People's Democratic Republic of Yemen (Southern Yemen), on the Gulf of Aden. Sana became the capital upon the creation of the Republic of Yemen (May 22, 1990) which merged the two Yemens. Under British rule from 1839 to 1967, it became a coaling station for ships sailing between Europe and India with the opening of the Suez Canal in 1869. Chief trade center of southern Arabia, it is also the country's industrial center, with an oil refinery.
See also: Yemen.

Konrad Adenauer

Aden, Gulf of, arm of the Arabian Sea, 550 mi (885 km) long, lying between the Republic of Yemen on the north and Somalia on the south and connected with the Red Sea by the Strait of Bab-el Mandeb. It forms part of the sea route from the Mediterranean through the Suez Canal to the Indian Ocean.

Adenauer, Konrad (1876-1967), first chancellor of West Germany (1949-63). A politician since World War I, he was twice imprisoned by the Nazis. He became leader of the Christian Democratic Union Party in 1947, and as chancellor he led West Germany through its postwar recovery into membership in the North Atlantic Treaty Organization (NATO) and the European Common Market.

Adenoids, or pharyngeal tonsils, mass of lymph tissue in the nasopharynx (above the soft palate in the back of the throat) that acts as a filter against disease. Adenoidal enlargement is the most common cause of nasal obstruction in the young and follows recurrent infections in that region.
See also: Tonsils.

Adhesion, force of attraction between surfaces of different substances, such as glue and wood or water and glass, due to intermolecular forces.
See also: Cohesion; Tissue.

Adirondack Mountains, forested range in northeast New York, source of the Hudson River, and southern extension of the Laurentian (Canadian) Shield. Mt. Marcy (5,344 ft/1,629 m), the highest peak, towers over scenic lakes and millions of acres of woodland, all contributing to make this an important resort region.
See also: New York.

Adjutant, either of 2 species of scavenger storks of India and southeast Asia. The adjutant has a naked pink neck and head, a white body, and gray wings, back, and tail. The greater adjutant (*Leptoptilos dubius*) stands about 5 ft (1.5 m) high and has a respiratory pouch hanging from the throat. The lesser adjutant (*L. javanicus*) measures about 4 ft (1.2 m).
See also: Stork.

Adler, Alfred (1870-1937), Austrian psychiatrist who founded the school of individual psychology. Adler believed that feelings of inferiority account for the maladjustment of certain individuals to society. He saw the overcoming of these feelings as the basic human drive for power.
See also: Psychology.

Adler, Dankmar (1844-1900), German-born U.S. architect and engineer whose partnership with Louis Sullivan from 1881 helped to create the famous Chicago School of Architecture. Adler's first important work was the Chicago Central Music Hall (1879).
See also: Sullivan, Louis Henri.

Adler, Felix (1851-1933), German-born U.S. educator and social reformer, founder of the Ethical Culture movement. He held professorships in Semitic literature and social and political ethics and championed educational, housing, and child-labor reforms.

Admiral, in several countries, including the United States, the highest rank in the navy. In the U.S. Navy, grades are fleet admiral, admiral, vice admiral, and rear admiral.
See also: Rank, military.

Admiralty Islands, group of about 40 volcanic and coral-reef Melanesian islands in the South Pacific, some 200 mi (320 km) northwest of New Guinea, in the Bismarck Archipelago.
See also: Bismarck Archipelago; Pacific Islands.

Adobe, Spanish name for sun-dried clay and straw bricks of Mexico and the southwest United States; also, a structure made of adobe brick. Because the brick will crumble if exposed to excessive moisture or cold, it is used for building only in hot, dry climates. Material similar to adobe has been used in arid climates throughout the world since ancient times.

Adonis and a winged Eros are depicted on this Etruscan gold ornament from the 4th century B.C. Such ornaments contained amulets and were worn on leather bands around the neck or arm.

Adolescence, period of life between childhood and full adulthood (between 12 and 20 years of age). Its physical manifestation is puberty, the development of sex characteristics, making possible sexual union and reproduction. Physical changes include the development of breasts in girls, changes in voice in boys, and the appearance of pubic hair in both. Adolescence is of psychological interest because of the changes in attitudes, emotional responsiveness, and social behavior that accompany this sexual maturation.
See also: Developmental psychology; Growth.

Adonis, in Greek mythology, beautiful mortal beloved of Aphrodite and Persephone. In an effort to resolve the problem of who would keep Adonis, Zeus commanded that he spend 6 months of every year on earth with Aphrodite, during which crops flourished, and 6 months in the underworld with Persephone, during which the earth was barren. This myth was used by the Greeks to explain the changing of the seasons. In another myth, Adonis is killed by Aphrodite's husband who is disguised as a boar.
See also: Aphrodite.

Adrenal glands, or suprarenal glands, small endocrine glands closely attached to the upper part of each kidney, each comprising a central medulla and a surrounding cortex. The adrenal medulla secretes the hormones epinephrine (adrenaline) and norepinephrine. Release of these hormones follows stress-related stimuli such as pain, emotional disturbance, hypotension (low blood sugar), exposure to severe cold, and muscular exertion. The adrenal medulla is not essential to life; a person can survive in good health after total removal of the glands if adequate substitution therapy is provided. The adrenal cortex secretes about 30 steroid hormones that are separated into 3 main groups. The glucocorticoids, including cortisol, enhance glucose formation in the tissues and cells. The mineralocorticoids, including aldosterone, are steroids that promote retention of sodium and excretion of potassium by the kidney. The androgens are sex hormones that have a weaker effect than those produced by the (male) testes and (female) ovaries. Disorders of the adrenal cortex, such as Addison's disease or Cushing's syndrome, may be due to either defective or excessive secretion of hormones.
See also: Epinephrine; Gland; Hormone.

Adrenalin *see:* Epinephrine.

Adrian IV (Nicholas Breakspear; 1100?-59), only Englishman to become pope (1154-59). He crowned Frederick Barbarossa as Holy Roman Emperor in 1155, but angered Frederick by his persistent demands for papal supremacy and also by excommunicating the crowned king of Sicily, William I the Bad. Adrian then invested William upon his pledge of allegiance and service to him. He also promised excommunication for Frederick when the latter declared himself ruler of northern Italy, but he died before carrying out his threat.

Adriatic Sea, arm of the Mediterranean Sea between Italy and Yugoslavia and Albania. The Adriatic extends for about 500 mi (800 km), with an average width of 110 mi (177 km) and a depth of up to 4,201 ft (1,250 m). The Strait of Otranto links it to the Ionian Sea to the south.

Adsorption, adhesion of molecules to a surface, to be distinguished from absorption.
See also: Absorption.

Adult education, or continuing educaton, learning undertaken by adults. Originally offering adults the educational opportunities missed in youth, adult education is now seen more as part of an ongoing process, enhancing the education already received. In the United States adult education started with the Lyceum Movement, early in the 19th century. After the Civil War, important advances were made by the Chautauqua Movement and in various federal agricultural education acts. During the Depression the Works Projects Administration (WPA) provided education programs for 2 million adults, and after World War II the G.I. Bill of Rights made advanced learning available for veterans. In the 1960s federal funds provided for basic literacy programs under the Economic Opportunity Act.

Advent (from Latin *adventus*, "arrival"), first season of the Christian church year. It begins on the Sun. nearest Nov. 30 (St. Andrew's Day) and ends on Christmas Eve. Advent has been observed since the 6th century as a period of meditative preparation for the celebration of Christ's birth and second coming.
See also: Christmas.

Adventists, members of Christian sects, mainly in the United States, who believe in the imminent second coming of Christ. Adventism grew from the teachings of William Miller (1782-1849). Members of the largest Adventist sect, the Seventh-Day Adventists, formally organized in 1863, observe Saturday as the Sabbath and support an extensive missionary program.
See also: Seventh-day Adventists.

Advertising, paid publicity designed to persuade people to buy a product or service or to adopt a viewpoint. U.S. advertising in magazines, newspapers, radio, and television provides these media with most of their income. Advertisers pay advertising agencies to conduct market research, formulate advertising campaigns, buy the necessary time or space in the medium or media chosen, and produce the actual advertisements. The United States spends more money on advertising than any other country in the world.

Aegean civilization, collective term for the Bronze Age civilizations surrounding the Aegean Sea. These cultures, which flourished from 3000 to 1200 B.C., are the Mycenaean, or Helladic, culture of the Greek mainland; the Cycladic culture of the Cyclades; the Minoan culture of Crete; and the Trojan culture. Archeological work in the area was begun in the 1870s-80s by Heinrich Schliemann, who located Troy.
See also: Crete; Mycenae; Schliemann, Heinrich; Troy.

Aegean Sea, arm of the Mediterranean Sea between mainland Greece and Turkey, the heart of the classical Greek world. About 400 mi (640 km) long and 200 mi (320 km) wide, its numerous islands, known as the Grecian Archipelago, include the Sporades, Dodecanese, and Cyclades groups. Islanders live by fishing and tourism; the Aegean also contains deposits of natural gas.
See also: Mediterranean Sea.

Aeneas, mythological Trojan prince, son of Venus and Anchises and hero of the Roman poet Vergil's *Aeneid.* After the fall of Troy he rescued his father and son and fled to Carthage and then to Italy. Rome was said to be founded by his descendants, Romulus and Remus.
See also: Aeneid; Vergil.

Aeneid, epic Latin poem, 12 books in length, depicting the life of the mythical Trojan hero Aeneas. The poem, written by Vergil between 30 and 19 B.C., describes the great achievements of Aeneas as he sought to create a new nation. Vergil selected his theme to bring glory to the emperor, Augustus, and to reconfirm the integrity of religious values in ancient Rome.

Aeneas fleeing Troy with his small son Ascanius and his blind father Anchises, portrayed in an 18th-century French painting.

Aeolian harp, ancient musical instrument, the strings of which are vibrated ("played") by the wind. It is constructed of a wooden box with 2 low wood bridges, across which the strings are loosely stretched. The harp is named for the ancient Greek god of the winds, Aeolus.

Aeolians, an ancient Greek people. They lived in east-central Greece until c.1150 B.C., when invading Dorians forced many from their land. They moved to what is now Turkey and the nearby islands of Lesbos and Tenedos.
See also: Greece, Ancient

Aerobics, exercise program specifically focused on improving physical fitness by forcing the lungs and heart to work hard for a long period, thus improving cardiovascular functioning. Running, swimming, and cycling are common aerobic activities.

Ancient and modern advertising. Such stone reliefs of the grocer at left (2nd century B.C.) were used to advertise in Roman market-places. The power of music is also used to advertise. Michael Jackson receives millions of dollars to endorse products.

Aerodynamics, branch of physics dealing with the motion of air and other gases and their flow around a body in motion, used particularly in the development of the airplane and other aircraft. Aerodynamic forces depend on the body's size, shape, and velocity and on the density, compressibility, viscosity, temperature, and pressure of the gas. At low velocities flow around the body is streamlined and causes low drag; at higher velocities turbulence occurs, with fluctuating eddies, and drag is much greater. Additional drag is created by friction. Pressure impulses radiate at the speed of sound ahead of the moving body; at supersonic velocities these impulses pile up, producing a shock wave—the "sonic boom." In airplane design all of these factors must be considered. In normal cruising flight the lift provided by the wings must equal the aircraft's weight; the forward thrust of the engine must balance the forces of drag. Lift occurs because the wing's upper surface is more convex, and therefore longer, than the lower surface, creating a difference in air speed and thus pressure, according to Bernoulli's principle.
See also: Wind tunnel.

The climate of Afghanistan is suitable for the cultivation of a great variety of fruits and nuts, apricots, pomegranates, and grapes are of special importance to the economy.

Aeronautics, technology of aircraft design, manufacture, and performance.
See also: Aerodynamics; Airplane.

Aerosol, suspension of small liquid or solid particles in a gas. Examples include smoke, fog, and clouds. Aerosol particles can remain in suspension for hours, or even indefinitely. Aerosols are also manufactured for the dispersion of insecticides, air fresheners, paints, cosmetics, etc. The use of the most common aerosol propellants, the fluorocarbons, has been curtailed because they have been implicated in the destruction of the ozone layer of the atmosphere.
See also: Fluorocarbon; Ozone.

Aertsen (Aertszen), Pieter (1508-75?), Dutch painter of finely detailed still-lifes and domestic interiors. He is regarded as one of the founders of genre painting.

Aeschylus (525-456 B.C.), earliest of the 3 great dramatists of ancient Greece, preceding Sophocles and Euripides. He is often regarded as the originator of tragedy. Only 7 of at least 80 plays survive, including *The Persians, Prometheus Bound,* and the *Oresteia*, which concerns the murder of Agamemnon by his wife, Clytemnestra, and the subsequent revenge of their son, Orestes. Aeschylus elaborated Greek dramatic form by adding a second actor (previously the poet had spoken all roles) and exploiting the dramatic possibilities of dialogue.

Aesculapius *see:* Asclepius.

Aesop, in tradition, Greek author of animal fables, said to have been a slave on 6th-century B.C. Samos, but perhaps a wholly legendary figure. Some fables attributed to Aesop are known in versions by La Fontaine and other writers.
See also: Allegory; La Fontaine, Jean de.

Affidavit, voluntary statement reduced to writing and sworn to or affirmed before an authorized magistrate or officer. Affidavits are not testimony in courts of law because the makers cannot be cross-examined, but a person who makes a false affidavit may be punished for perjury.

Affirmative action, U.S. program designed to increase the numbers of minority group members or of women in jobs or schools from which they were previously wholly or partly excluded. Affirmative action flourished in the 1960s under the leadership of Presidents Kennedy and Johnson and was institutionalized by the Equal Employment Opportunity Act of 1972. Critics have charged that the racial quotas and timetables of some affirmative action plans bring about reverse discrimination. Affirmative action was dealt a sharp blow in 1978, when the Supreme Court, in the Bakke case, ruled against the use of strict racial quotas.
See also: Bakke case.

Afghan hound, breed of dog known for speed and agility, used as a hunter in Afghanistan for centuries. It stands 24-28 in. (61-71 cm) in height at the shoulder and weighs 50-60 lb (23-27 kg), has long ears, a slim body, large feet, and a coat of long silky hair. The breed originated in Egypt c. 3000 B.C., was perfected in Afghanistan to hunt the leopard and gazelle, and was discovered by Europeans in the 1800s and brought to England after World War I.

Afghanistan, land-locked country in central Asia.

Land and climate. The high rugged mountains of the Hindu Kush cover three quarters of the country. The winters are extremely cold (as low as 15°F/–9°C) and the summers extremely hot (up to 120°F/49°C). There is very little rainfall, but the Hindu Kush is a major watershed containing fertile river valleys.

People. The majority of the people live in the fertile mountain valleys. About 2.5 million are nomadic. Islam is the most impor-

The famous Khyber Pass is located on the border between Afghanistan and Pakistan. It is a traditional route between the Middle East and the Indian subcontinent.

Afghanistan

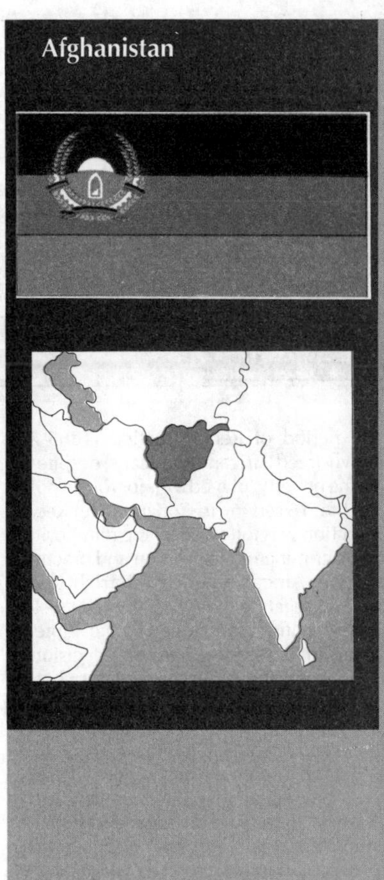

General information	
Capital:	Kabul
Area:	251,825 sq mi (652,225 sq km)
Population:	14,825,000
Official languages:	Pashto; Dari Persian
Monetary unit:	1 afghani (AF) = 100 puls
Main cities:	Kabul, Qandahar, Herat, Mazar-e Sharif
Government	
Form:	republic
Independent:	1747
Head of state:	President (elected every 7 years)
Head of government:	Prime minister (appointed by president)
Legislature:	two legislative houses (Council of Representatives; Council of Elders)
Executive:	Council of Ministers
Judiciary:	Supreme Court
Political division:	7 regions (31 provinces)
National economy	
Gross national product:	U.S. $3,520,000,000
Per capita income:	U.S. $230
Agriculture:	wheat, corn, grapes, rice, potatoes
Livestock:	sheep, cattle, goats
Fisheries:	1,500 metric tons
Mining:	natural gas, coal, lapis lazuli, barite, talc, salt
Industries:	cotton textiles, leather, plastics, fertilizers
Main exports:	carpets and rugs, fruit and vegetables, natural gas
Transportation:	no railroads; 13,670 mi (22,000 km) of roads; 2 international airports
Trading partners:	USSR, Pakistan, Japan, India, Germany
People	
Urban:	18%
Ethnic composition:	Pashtun 53%, Tadzhik 20%, Uzbek 9%, Hazara 9%
Birth rate:	47.5 per 1,000 population
Death rate:	22.5 per 1,000 population
Infant mortality:	44 per 1,000 live births
Life expectancy:	male 40.6 years, female 48.6 years

tant factor in the everyday life of the country.

Economy. Less than 25% of the country is good for cultivation. Main crops are wheat, corn, barley, rice, and fruits. Sheep are also raised. Fruits, wool, skins, and various handicrafts are important sources of foreign exchange. Coal and salt have been mined for some years, and the country has long been famous for its lapis lazuli. Iron ore is plentiful, and vast deposits of natural gas have been exploited. The lack of an infrastructure is a major obstacle to economic development; there are few paved roads, and there is no railroad.

History. Afghanistan was conquered by Alexander the Great in 330 B.C. and thrived as the Kingdom of Bactria (250-150 B.C.). The Arabs conquered Afghanistan in the 7th century, and Islam took root. Genghis Khan and Tamerlane invaded, and Babur (1143-1530) used Kabul as his base for establishing the Mogul Empire in India. Afghanistan became a united state under Ahmed Shah in 1747. Amanullah (1919-29) seized control of foreign policy from the British, began modernizing, and proclaimed a monarchy in 1926. The last king, Mohammed Zahir Shah, was overthrown in 1973 by Lt. Gen. Sardar Mohammed Daud Khan, who became president and prime minister of the new republic. Daud was overthrown in 1978 and replaced by the pro-Soviet government of Noor Mohammed Taraki. Taraki was overthrown by Hafi-zullah Amon, who was in turn overthrown by Babrak Karmal. In December 1979, 100,000 Soviet troops invaded. The forces remained through 1989 but eventually withdrew in the face of a stiff Muslim insurgency.

AFL *see:* American Federation of Labor and Congress of Industrial Organizations.

Africa, world's second-largest continent, 11,672,639 sq m (30,232,135 sq km). Africa includes Madagascar and many smaller offshore islands. With the completion of the Suez Canal in the 19th century, Africa was severed from Asia and is completely surrounded by water. Its coastline has few indentations, bays, or inlets, thus, few good harbors. From narrow coastal plains the land rises steeply to form the immense African plateau about 2,000 ft (610 m) above sea level. Apart from the coastal plains, the Congo Basin is the only sizable lowland region. The Atlas Mountains form the continent's major system, including Africa's highest peak, Mt. Kilimanjaro (19,340 ft/5,895 m) in Tanzania. The Ruwenzori chain (the Mountains of the Moon) are in east Central Africa, and the Drakensberg Mountains are in the southeast.

The Great Rift Valley of East Africa is the continent's major geological feature, with its long narrow depressions forming some of the world's largest lakes: Lake Victoria (26,828 sq mi/69,485 sq km), third largest lake in the world; Lake Tanganyika (5,715 ft/1,742 m deep), the largest freshwater lake in the world; and Lake Nyasa (360 mi/579 km long and 50 mi/80 km wide). The great rivers of Africa include the Nile (4,157 mi/6,690 km), the world's longest; the Niger; the Congo; and the Zambesi, which has been dammed at the Kariba Gorge, where it forms a lake 120 mi (193 km) long.

The great mass of Africa lies within the tropics, but contains a variety of climates.

The waterfalls of the Zambesi River in central Africa.

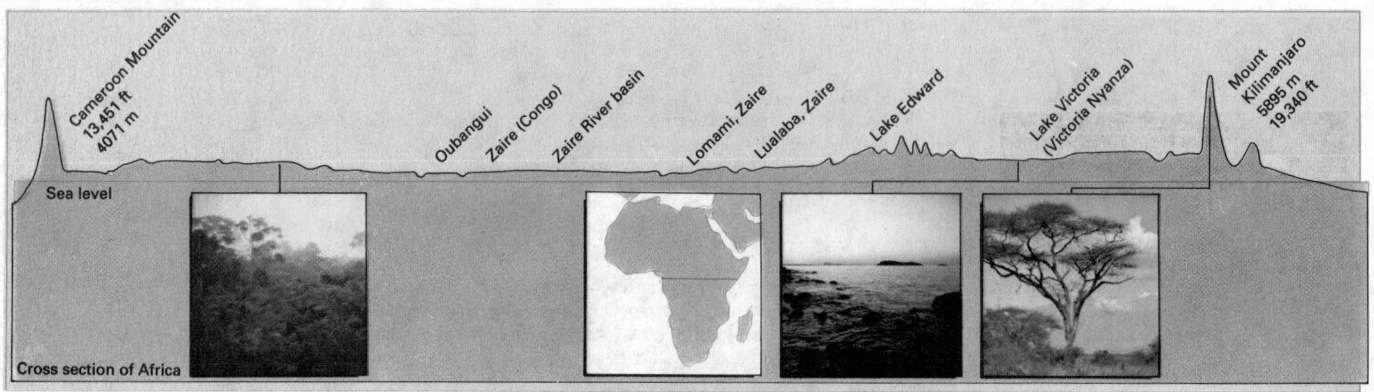

The equatorial rain forest of the Congo Basin, which receives up to 200 in. (508 cm) of rain per year, and the tropical rain forest along the Gulf of Guinea and in west Central Africa account for 20% of the continent. The humid subtropical regions have up to 43 in (109 cm) of rainfall per year. Temperate grasslands known as savannah or veldt cover 40% of Africa and usually have one dry and one rainy season per year with 20-50 in (51-127 cm) annual rainfall. The deserts cover more than 40% of the continent and include the Sahara, the world's largest, in the north and the Kalahari in the south. Finally, Africa's Mediterranean coast and the area south and southwest of Cape Province enjoy the most moderate climate, with average annual rainfall of 15-30 in (38-76 cm), hot summers, and warm pleasant winters.

Cecil Rhodes's imperialistic politics greatly influenced the history of the African continent in the 19th century.

Africa's richly varied animal life is largely preserved in national parks. Poaching, the increase in human populations, and economic development have reduced the animal population, leading to the extinction of many species and threatening more.

Africa's population consists of many distinct peoples and cultures. The northern part of the continent, from Morocco in the west to Egypt in the east, is primarily Arab, with minorities of Berbers and Tuaregs. South of the Sahara the population is overwhelmingly black. Excluding European languages introduced by colonizers, there are nearly 1,000 different languages or distinct dialects. Most people in North Africa speak Arabic; major languages in black Africa include Swahili, Hausa, Yoruba, Xhosa, and Amharic. Besides those who practice the native religions of the black African majority, there are more than 100 million African Muslims and about 35 million Christians, 5 million of them belonging to the ancient Coptic church of Egypt and Ethiopia.

Jomo Kenyatta was an important leader in the establishment of African independence movements in the 20th century.

The countries of Africa are Algeria, Angola, Benin, Botswana, Burkina Faso, Burundi, Cameroon, Cape Verde, Central African Republic, Chad, Comoros, Congo Republic, Djibouti, part of Egypt, Equatorial Guinea, Ethiopia, Gabon, Gambia, Ghana, Guinea, Guinea-Bissau, Ivory Coast, Kenya, Lesotho, Liberia, Libya, Madagascar, Malawi, Mali, Mauritania, Mauritius, Morocco, Mozambique, Niger, Nigeria, Rwanda, São Tomé and Principe, Senegal, Seychelles, Sierra Leone, Somalia Republic, Republic of South Africa, Sudan,

African wildlife

Swaziland, Tanzania, Togo, Tunisia, Uganda, Zaïre, Zambia, and Zimbabwe.

African Americans, preferred term to designate Americans of African descent, who account for about 12 percent of the U.S. population, a major minority group in society. Most African Americans live in the South and in the large cities of the North, in many of which they constitute a large portion, or even a majority, of the population.

The first African Americans were brought to North America as indentured servants, under contract to work for a particular master for a specified period, after which they were free. But from the early 1600s, the expansion of the slave trade brought larger and larger numbers of Africans who were forced to work on the expanding plantations in the South.

The institution of slavery was recognized by the U.S. Constitution, and the importance of slaves increased after 1793, when the invention of the cotton gin gave southern plantations a new financial viability. Conflict between slave society in the South and industrial development in the North led eventually to the Civil War, which ended slavery in the United States. During the period of Reconstruction (1865-77), newly freed African Americans, despite extreme poverty, played a major role in political life, 16 serving in Congress. But Reconstruction was followed by the reimposition of discriminatory legislation and practices, denying African Americans the right to vote and segregating them socially. The system of segregation, sanctioned by the Supreme Court in its *Plessy* v. *Ferguson* decision of 1896, kept the African American population in conditions of social, economic, and political oppression. That system began to break down only after World War II. In 1954 the Supreme Court outlawed "separate but equal" facilities in its historic *Brown* v. *Board of Education* decision. The struggle for equal rights and the abolition of segregation soon took a new turn.

In the 1950s and 1960s African Americans developed a broad-based civil rights movement to end discrimination in education, jobs, public facilities, and voting rights. The successes of this movement eliminated most formal barriers to the incorporation of African Americans into U.S. society, but socioeconomic discrimination remained; the gap between white and black average incomes, for example, widened during the 1980s, despite the emergence of an African American middle class. African Americans have made major contributions to U.S. society in many areas. They fought in all the nation's wars, though in integrated units only after World War II. Notable African American historical figures include Frederick Douglass and George Washington Carver, who made significant contributions to politics and science in the 19th century. In the early 1900s, Booker T. Washington, W.E.B. DuBois, and Marcus Garvey were major political leaders. The towering figures of the 1950s and 1960s included Martin Luther King, Jr., and Malcolm X. More recently, African Americans have made their mark in the political sphere (Mayor David Dinkins in New York City), the military (General Colin Powell, Chairman of the Joint Chiefs of Staff), and as members of federal, state, and local legislatures. They have achieved nationwide recognition for outstanding contributions in literature, the arts, sports, entertainment, business, and education.

African Methodist Episcopal Church (A.M.E.), black Protestant denomination akin to, but separate from, white Methodist

denominations. Founded in Philadelphia (1815) by the Rev. Richard Allen, it is the largest black Methodist body, with about 6,000 churches and 2,000,000 members.
See also: Allen, Richard.

African Methodist Episcopal Zion Church (A.M.E. Zion), independent Methodist denomination founded in New York City in 1796 by blacks disaffected by white prejudices. The church has over 1,000,000 members.

African National Congress, black African organization devoted to the "creation of a united democratic South Africa" and the political empowerment of blacks. Founded in 1912 as the Native National Congress, the organization encouraged passive resistance to the "pass" laws and other instruments of apartheid. After an outbreak of violence, it was banned in 1961 by the government of South Africa. Its leader, Nelson Mandela, was sentenced to life imprisonment, but he was released Feb. 1990.
See also: Apartheid; Mandela, Nelson; South Africa.

African violet, any of a genus (*Saintpaulia*) of perennial herbs with velvety heart-shaped leaves and purple, pink, or white violetlike flowers, native to tropical East Africa. The species *S. ionantha* is widely cultivated as a houseplant.

Afrikaans, one of the 2 official languages of South Africa. English is the other. Afrikaans evolved from the form of Dutch spoken by 17th-century Boer settlers, but incorporates Bantu, Khoisan, Malayo-Portuguese, and English words.

Afrikaners *see:* Boers.

AFS Intercultural Programs, nonprofit organization providing student exchange programs to promote living and learning experience in foreign countries. Founded in 1914 as the American Field Service and originating as a volunteer ambulance corps during World War I, the AFS became a student exchange program in 1947. Active in about 70 countries, its programs primarily involve high school age students and young professionals who are placed with host country families and attend host country schools.

Afterbirth *see:* Placenta.

Aga Khan, spiritual leader of the Ismaili sect of Shi'te Muslims; a hereditary title. His millions of followers are dispersed through the Near East, India, Pakistan, and parts of Africa and are descended from 14th-century Hindus converted by Persian Ismails. **Aga Khan I** (Hasan Ali Shah; 1800-81), a Persian provincial governor who emigrated to India in 1840, was invested as leader of the sect in 1866. **Aga Khan II** (Ali Shah) held the title from 1881 until his death in 1885. **Aga Khan III** (Sultan Sir Mahomed Shah; 1877-1957) represented British India at numerous conferences and as first president of the All-Indian Muslim League worked for Indian independence. **Aga Khan IV** (H.H. Shah Karim; 1936-) inherited the title in 1957.
See also: Islam.

Agamemnon, in Greek legend, son of Atreus and king of Mycenae who organized the expedition against Troy recounted in Homer's *Iliad.* Before setting sail he was forced to sacrifice his daughter Iphigenia. He was murdered on his return home by his wife Clytemnestra and her lover, his cousin Aegisthus. His death was avenged by his son, Orestes, and his daughter Electra.
See also: Iliad; Mycenae; Trojan War.

Agana (pop. 900), capital and political center of the island of Guam, a U.S. territory in the western Pacific Ocean.

Agassiz, Louis (Jean Louis Rodolphe Agassiz; 1807-73), Swiss-American naturalist, geologist, and educator who first proposed (1840) that large areas of the northern continents had been covered by ice sheets in the geologically recent past. He is also noted for his studies of fishes. He became a professor of zoology and geology at Harvard in 1848, where he founded the Museum of Comparative Zoology in 1859.

Agate, variety of the quartz chalcedony, found chiefly in Brazil and Uruguay. Agates form as layers in the cavities of older rocks, creating characteristic bands of colors. Semiprecious stones, they are used to make ornaments and grinding equipment.

Agave, any of a genus (*Agave*) of economically important U.S. tropical plants of the amaryllis family. Different species are used to produce soaps, foods, and drinks.

Agee, James (1909-55), U.S. writer whose works include *Let Us Now Praise Famous Men* (1941), a portrayal of Depression-era white sharecroppers done in collaboration with photographer Walker Evans, and a partly autobiographical novel, *A Death in the Family* (1957), which won a Pulitzer Prize. Agee was an influential film critic and also wrote screenplays, including *The African Queen* (1951) and *The Night of the Hunter* (1955).

Agency for International Development (AID), U.S. government agency formed in 1961 to administer nonmilitary foreign aid. It promotes long-range economic programs that help developing countries become self-sufficient, chiefly in the areas of health, education, and agriculture.

Agent Orange, herbicide used by the United States during the Vietnam War to defoliate the jungle. Agent Orange was contaminated with dioxin, a substance discovered to be toxic to human beings and animals. Use of the chemical was abandoned in the late 1970s. In postwar years, 60,000 veterans complained to the Veterans Administration that they had suffered lasting damage from Agent Orange poisoning. In 1984 the manufacturers of Agent Orange created a relief fund for the victims of Agent Orange.
See also: Chemical biological warfare; Vietnam War.

Agent Orange was used as a defoliant during the Vietnam War. Because of its toxic nature many Vietnam veterans and their children now suffer from serious diseases such as cancer.

Age of Reason, or the Enlightenment, a period in history in which accepted social, political, and religious doctrines were challenged by a new, rational view of the universe. Beginning in the 1600s and lasting until the late 1700s, the movement was led by such philosophers as, in France, René Descartes, Denis Diderot, Jean Jacques Rousseau, and Voltaire, and, in England, John Locke. Scholars of the period produced many breakthroughs in the fields of anatomy, astronomy, chemistry, mathematics, and physics. Their ideas about human dignity and progress influenced the future leaders of the French Revolution.
See also: Rousseau, Jean J. ; Locke, John.

Aggression, behavior characterized by physical or verbal attack. Aggression is defined by psychoanalysts as a manifestation of the will to have power over other people (Alfred Adler) or as a projection of the death impulse (Sigmund Freud). Unable to find a satisfactory explanation for the human readiness for hatred and aggression, Freud believed that it may be instinctual. Thus, the violent and strenuous behavior shown by infants may not be oriented toward a goal. Still, in many instances aggression that serves no apparent goal is associated with emotional disorder.
See also: Psychology.

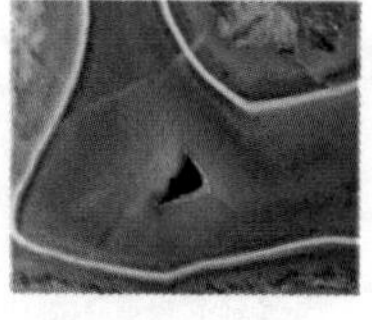

Agate

Agincourt, now Azincourt, village in northwest France, scene of a decisive battle in the Hundred Years' War. On Oct. 25, 1415, English forces under Henry V routed the French under Claude d'Albret, demonstrating the power of the English longbow over a heavily armored enemy. The French lost over 7,000 men, the English only a few hundred.
See also: Hundred Years' War.

Agnes, Saint, 4th-century virgin martyr of the Roman Catholic Church and patron saint of young girls. For refusing to sacrifice to pagan gods, she was disgraced, miraculously saved, and martyred. On her feast day, Jan. 21, the pope blesses 2 lambs in the church of St. Agnes; their wool is used to weave palla (items of ceremonial dress) for archbishops.

Agnew, Spiro Theodore (1918-96), U.S. vice president under Richard Nixon (1969-73). Agnew was elected Republican governor of Maryland (1966) and gained a reputation as a moderate liberal, though he later took a conservative stand toward civil rights demonstrations and urban unrest. He resigned from the vice presidency in 1973 following revelations of political corruption in his Maryland administration and pleaded no contest to a charge that he had failed to report income from payoffs by Maryland business people, for which he was fined $10,000. A Maryland court later fined him $248,000 for taking bribes while in office.
See also: Nixon, Richard Milhous.

Agnon, Shmuel Yosef (Samuel Josef Czaczkes; 1888-1970), Israeli writer remembered for his novels and stories of Jewish life in his native Galicia and in Palestine. In 1966 he shared the Nobel Prize for literature (with Nelly Sachs of Sweden) for works that include *The Bridal Canopy* (1937) and *The Day Before Yesterday* (1945).

Agnosticism, doctrine that one cannot know about things beyond the realm of one's experience, in particular about God. Unlike atheism, which is a rejection of divine order, agnosticism is a skeptical holding back of judgment in the absence of proof.
See also: Atheism.

Agra (pop. 891,800), historic city in the northern Indian state of Uttar Pradesh, which is situated on the Jumna River, 110 mi (177 km) southeast of Delhi. An important military and commercial center, it produces cotton, grain, raw silk, sugar, and rugs. It was the capital of the Mogul empire during the late 16th and the first half of the 17th centuries. The city has several beautiful and important Mogul buildings, including the Taj Mahal, built by Shah Jahan.
See also: Taj Mahal.

Agribusiness, the business of agriculture, extended to include supply, management, information, and machine services, as well as processing and distribution. A rapidly growing industry in the United States, agribusiness employs about one-fourth the U.S. work force.

Agricola, Gnaeus Julius (A.D. 37-93), Roman general. As proconsul of Britain (77-84) he defeated the Caledonians and extended Roman rule into Scotland. His son-in-law, the historian Tacitus, wrote the famous biography of Agricola.

Agriculture, science and practice of farming, including the production of crops, the rearing of livestock, and the care of soil. The storing and sowing of seeds, central to agriculture, developed in the Neolithic period. Tools and techniques developed gradually over the centuries. The organization of farming, especially the ownership of land, was crucial in determining the prevailing social, economic, and political structures of civilizations as diverse as those of Egypt and Babylonia, China, Rome, and Japan. In medieval Europe the self-contained manorial system shaped the agricultural village. Late in the Middle Ages communal subsistence farming gave way to farms organized to produce salable surpluses. The agricultural revolution of the 16th and 17th centuries saw advances in horticultural techniques, and by the dawn of the industrial revolution, farming was concentrated in fewer hands and was geared to feeding the cities and supplying raw materials for manufactures. During the 19th century the United States led the world in agricultural development. The transportation revolution, new machines such as McCormick's reaper, the introduction of artificial fertilizers, and increased specialization all helped raise productivity. In the late 20th century agriculture in most industrialized countries is highly specialized and relies upon pesticides, growth-stimulating antibiotics for livestock, fertilizers, and artificial insemination. By contrast, agriculture in much of the Third World is not mechanized, crop yields are not high, and famine still occurs.

Agriculture, U.S. Department of, executive department of the U.S. government concerned with the promotion and regulation of agriculture. Established in 1862, the department operates research, credit extension, conservation, crop control, distribution, and other programs.

Agricultural education as an organized field of study began only at the end of the 18th century, when a number of agricultural societies grew up in the United States and Great Britain. In the United States the first steps on the national level began with the Morrill Act (1862), which gave grants of land to the states to assist them in setting up colleges for mechanical and agricultural training. In 1917 the federal government also began to sponsor agricultural education in secondary schools. The Future Farmers of America and 4 H clubs have also been developed to encourage agricultural interest among boys and girls.

Agrimony, any of a genus (*Agrimonia*) of woodland plants of the rose family, native to Europe, Asia, North America, and the Andes Mountains of South America. The agrimony plant has featherlike hairy leaves and clusters of small yellow flowers on long spikes; the fruit is a cone-shaped burr.

Agrippa, Marcus *see:* Augustus.

Agrippina The Younger (A.D. 15-59), mother by her first marriage, of Nero and second wife of the Roman emperor Claudius. Agrippina persuaded Claudius to adopt Nero as his son and heir and then poisoned the emperor. When she interfered with Nero's rule, he had her murdered.
See also: Claudius; Nero.

Agronomy, branch of agricultural science dealing with production of field crops and management of the soil. The agronomist studies crop diseases, selective breeding, crop rotation, and climatic factors and also tests and analyzes the soil, investigates soil erosion, and designs land reclamation and irrigation schemes.

Aguinaldo, Emilio (1869-1964), leader of the Philippine independence movement. After helping the United States capture the Philippines during the Spanish-American War (1898), he led Filipino guerilla warfare against U.S. occupation. He was defeated in 1901.
See also: Philippines.

Ahmadabad, or Ahmedabad (pop. 2,800,000), capital of the state of Gujarat in northwest India, situated on the Sabarmati River, north of Bombay. One of the largest and most important cities of India in Mogul times, Ahmadabad was ceded to the British in 1818. The modern city is an important trade center, particularly for cotton textiles, and a railway junction.
See also: India.

Ahmad Shah (1724-73), Afghan ruler who founded the Durrani dynasty. Through several successful invasions of India he acquired a huge empire. Although unable to hold his empire together, he succeeded in strengthening and uniting Afghanistan and is thus often thought of as founder of the modern nation.

Ahura Mazda *see:* Zoroastrianism.

AIDS (Acquired Immune Deficiency Syndrome), viral disease that compromises the body's immune system, leaving the victim susceptible to dangerous diseases and infections. The virus, known as HIV (human immunodeficiency virus), uses certain white blood cells, known as T-helper cells, as hosts and eventually destroys them. Those with AIDS are likely to suffer from Kaposi's sarcoma (a rare and usually fatal skin cancer), *pneumocystis carinii pneumonia* (a lung infection caused by parasites), chronic herpes simplex (a virus that can cause ulcerating anal and oral herpes), as well as infections that attack the bone marrow, liver, or brain. Early flu-like symptoms of AIDS are fatigue, fever, night sweats and chills, and weight loss. During the next stage, patients display symptoms specific to diseases that appear with the breakdown of the immune system. Later symptoms are likely to include skin lesions, shortness of breath, seizures, and mental disorientation. Those currently at highest risk of infection in the United States are homosexuals and bisexuals, intravenous drug users, prostitutes, hemophiliacs and others who have required repeated transfusion, and babies of infected women. The virus is transmitted in blood and semen. Saliva, tears, and urine also contain the virus, but so far have not been found to be effective vectors. Preventive measures include avoiding sexual contact with those who are infected, using condoms, using only sterilized needles and not sharing them with anyone, and avoiding contact with blood or sores of those infected. The education of children and adults is an important preventive measure in the battle against the disease. There is at present no cure for AIDS, but since its detection in 1981, care of AIDS patients has improved. AZT (azidothymide) has proven the most effective drug to date in inhibiting the virus's ability to reproduce, but it is a retardant, not a cure, and its side effects can include anemia, dementia, and blindness. Research for effective treatment and cure continues.

Aiken, Conrad Potter (1889-1973), U.S. writer. His *Selected Poems* (1929) won a Pulitzer Prize (1930). His critiques and essays on poetry were published in *A Reviewer's ABC* (1958). Other prose works include the novel *Great Circle* (1933) and his autobiography, *Ushant* (1952).

Ailanthus, any of a genus (*Ailanthus*) of tropical-looking deciduous trees native to Asia and Australia but now widely cultivated in Europe and North America. The best-known species, *A. altissima*, grows up to 60 ft (18 m) high and thrives in polluted urban conditions in almost any kind of substrate.

Ailey, Alvin (1931-89), U.S. dancer and choreographer. Ailey was a pupil of Lester Horton, with whom he made his debut in 1950. He began choreographing in 1953 and formed his own company, the Alvin Ailey American Dance Theater, in 1958. *Creation of the World* (1954), *Blues Suite* (1958), and *Revelations* (1960) are among his most noted works.

AIM *see:* American Indian Movement.

Ainu, Japanese aborigines, possibly of Caucasoid descent, distinguished by stockiness, pale skin, and profuse body hair. Most Ainu live on Hokkaido, the northernmost of Japan's major islands. Ainu speech, little used today, bears no relation to any other language. The Ainu are few in number, many having been assimilated into Japanese society.
See also: Japan.

Air, heterogeneous mixture of tasteless, odorless, colorless, and invisible gases surrounding the earth, consisting of about 78% nitrogen, 21% oxygen, and 1% argon, carbon dioxide, hydrogen, krypton, neon, helium, and xenon. Air is what we breathe and what is essential to all plant and animal life. It is kept close to the surface of the planet by the force of gravity.
See also: Air pollution; Climate; Gas; Nitrogen; Oxygen; Weather.

Airborne troops, or paratroops or sky soldiers, soldiers brought into a combat area by parachute drop or airplane. Airborne troops have been a part of military strategy since World War II, often figuring in surprise attacks. After landing behind enemy lines, the troops may be used to destroy bridges, communications, and supplies or for hand-to-hand combat.
The airborne troops of the U.S. Army are all volunteers.
See also: Parachute.

Airbrush, pencil-like painting tool that uses compressed air to apply a fine spray. A smaller, more delicate version of the spray gun, the airbrush is often used to shade drawings, retouch photographs, or accent highlights in prints. The operator creates different effects by varying the air pressure passing through the brush.

Air compressor, device used to compress air, which is then used to power air brakes, pneumatic tools, and other machinery. Commonly, air compressors work like a piston pump, with a cylinder moving within to compress air and force it into a closed chamber.
See also: Pump; Turbine.

Air conditioning, regulation of the temperature, humidity, circulation, and composition of the air in a building, room, or vehicle. In warm weather an air-conditioning plant, working like a refrigerator, cools, dehumidifies, and filters the air. In colder weather it may be reversed to run as a heat pump.

Aircraft *see:* Airplane; Airship; Autogiro; Balloon; Glider; Helicopter; Rocket.

Aircraft, military, airplanes, helicopters, and other flying machines used for military purposes: to attack enemy forces, transport troops and supplies, and defend territory. Aircraft range in size from small electronically powered devices to huge transport planes designed to carry tanks or trucks. Speeds can reach as high as 2,000 mph (3,200 kmph). Varieties include bombers, fighters, reconnaissance aircraft, transports, special-mission aircraft, and helicopters.

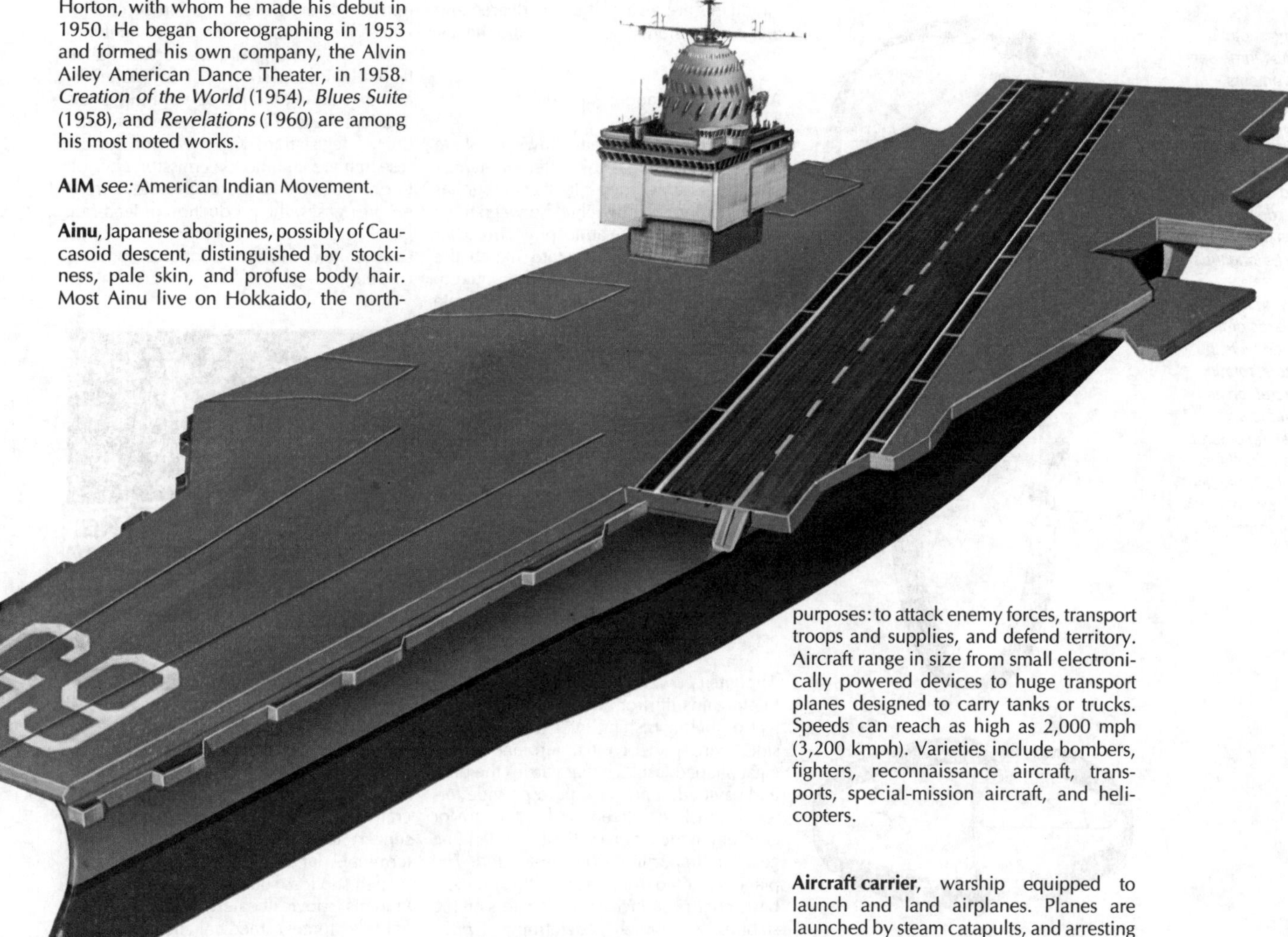

Aircraft carriers entered the nuclear age with the launching of the nuclear-powered U.S.S. Enterprise *in 1961. The ship has a flight deck of 1,123 x 257 ft (342 m x 78 m) and can carry over 50 jet aircraft. It has cruised over 200,000 miles (320,000 km) without refueling.*

Aircraft carrier, warship equipped to launch and land airplanes. Planes are launched by steam catapults, and arresting

cables are used to bring landing aircraft to a halt. Each ship is equipped with antiaircraft guns and missiles and is protected by its own planes and sister ships. The U.S. Navy's first aircraft carrier went into service in 1922. The U.S. Navy's first nuclear-powered aircraft carrier is the *Enterprise,* launched in 1961, which can carry about 50 airplanes.
See also: Navy; Navy, United States.

Air cushion vehicle (ACV), or hovercraft or ground effect machine, vehicle that rides on a cushion of compressed air. ACVs have fans that pull air inside and then force it beneath the vehicle, trapping the air between the ground surface and a rubberized skirt on the ACV. This invisible, compressed air cushion enables the ACV to maneuver over rough terrain smoothly because it eliminates friction between the craft and the surface. Though some can reach speeds of over 100 mph (160 kmph), ACVs are designed for short distances. ACVs are most often used to transport passengers and heavy freight over land or water like the one in service across the English Channel.
See also: Ship.

Airedale terrier, breed of large terriers. Weighing from 50 to 60 lb (23 to 27 kg), the Airedale was first bred in England in the 1880s. Considered to be fearless and loyal to their owners, Airedales are commonly used as watchdogs.

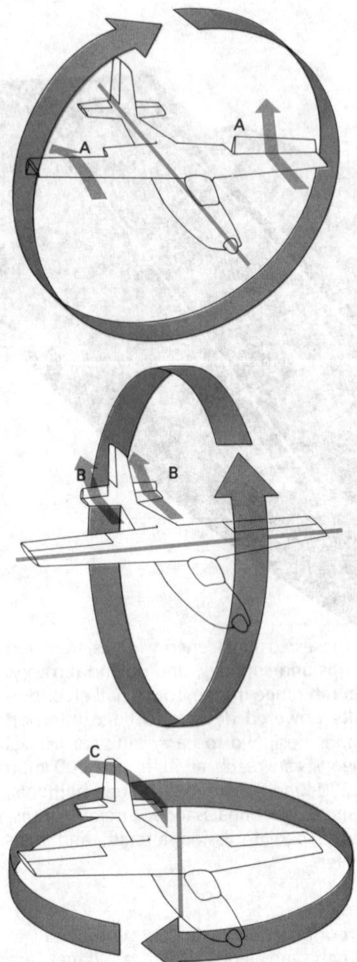

Airplane controls comprise three sets of movements. A.Moving the control column, or stick, to one side deflects the aileron on one wing up and the other aileron down, which causes the aircraft to roll on its longitudinal axis. B. Moving the stick backwards or forwards deflects the elevators, rotating the aircraft on its transverse axis. C. Pushing one rudder pedal deflects the rudder, causing the aircraft to rotate on its vertical axis.

Air Force, U.S., branch of the Department of Defense responsible for air warfare and defense and military space research. Prior to 1947 it was a branch of the U.S. Army. Air force personnel are organized into different commands. Among those responsible for actual fighting are the Strategic Air Command (SAC), which is the long-range bombardment and reconnaissance force, and the Tactical Air Command (TAC), which supports land and sea forces in action. Other commands are devoted to communications, intelligence, and training.
See also: Aircraft, military; Defense, Department of.

Air Force, U.S. Department of the, division of the U.S. Department of Defense that controls U.S. military aviation, including missile and aerospace programs.
See also: Air Force, U.S.; Defense, Department of.

Air Force Academy, U.S., center that trains students to become officers in the U.S. Air Force. Established in 1954, it is located in Colorado Springs, Colo. Graduates are awarded a B.S. degree and are commissioned as officers in the air force.

Airline *see:* Aviation; Airport.

Air lock, mechanism that allows people to pass between areas of different atmospheric pressures. The air lock chamber has 2 airtight doors sandwiched between the 2 pressure regions. The atmosphere in the air lock is gradually adjusted to match the pressure of the next space to be entered. Air locks are used when transferring people between the outside air and compressed air spaces such as underground tunnels and pneumatic caissons (watertight chambers) and between space vehicles in outer space.
See also: Bends.

Airmail, the transporting of mail by aircraft. A revolutionary 20th-century postal development, airmail is used for almost all first-class mail traveling more than 200 mi (320 km). The first official U.S. airmail delivery was in 1911, from Garden City to Mineola, N.Y.; regular airmail service began in 1918.
See also: Postal Service, U.S.

Airplane, powered heavier-than-air craft that obtains lift from the aerodynamic effect of the air rushing over its wings. Besides wings, the typical airplane has a cigar-shaped fuselage that carries the pilot and payload, a power unit to provide forward thrust, stabilizers and a tail fin for controlling the plane in flight, and landing gear for supporting it on the ground. The plane is piloted using the throttle and the 3 basic control surfaces: the elevators on the stabilizers, which determine *pitch* (whether the plane is climbing, diving, or flying horizontally), the rudder on the tail fin, which governs *yaw* (the rotation of the plane about a vertical axis), and the ailerons on the wings, which control *roll* (the rotation of the plane about the long axis through the fuselage). In turning the plane, both the rudder and the ailerons must be used to *bank* the plane into the turn. The airplane's control surfaces are operated by moving a control stick or steering column (elevators and ailerons) in conjunction with a pair of footpedals (rudder).
See also: Aerodynamics; Aviation; Wright brothers.

Air pollution, contamination of the atmosphere by harmful vapors, aerosols, and dust particles, resulting principally from the activities of humans, but to a lesser extent from natural processes. Natural pollutants include pollen particles, salt-water spray, wind-blown dust, and fine debris from volcanic eruptions. Pollution attributable to humans includes the products of fossil fuel combustion (from municipal, industrial, and domestic furnaces and automobiles): carbon monoxide, lead, oxides of nitrogen and sulfur dioxide, and smoke particles; crop spraying; and atmospheric nuclear explosions. Most air pollution arises in the urban environment, with a large portion coming from the automobile. Pollution control involves identifying the sources of contamination, developing improved or alternative technologies and sources of raw materials, and persuading industries and individuals to adopt these, if need be under the sanction of legislation. Key areas for current research are automobile emission control, the recycling and thorough oxidation of exhaust gases, the production of lead-free gasoline, and the development of alternatives to the conventional internal combustion engine.

Air pollution is one of the most serious environmental threats of our time.

Airport, site where airplanes and other aircraft take off and land. Consisting of passenger terminals, hangars, and cargo terminals, large-city airports also include related services such as shops, hotels, restaurants, movie theaters, police and fire-fighting forces, medical facilities, and

sewage plants. Although many small airports in the United States are privately owned, most large ones are owned by cities or public corporations. The Federal Aviation Administration (FAA) licenses aircraft, establishes requirements for pilots, and determines safety regulations. The International Civil Aviation Organization (ICAO) establishes airport operation and air-traffic-control standards for its 150 member countries, which include the United States and Canada.
See also: Air traffic control; Aviation.

Air rights, rights to the use of building space above a piece of property, especially railroad tracks, highways, and bridge and tunnel approaches. As urban land has grown scarcer, such rights have become increasingly valuable for housing developments and office construction.

Airship, or dirigible, lighter-than-air, self-propelled balloon whose buoyancy is provided by hydrogen or helium. The internal gas pressure causes the nonrigid type of airship, or blimp, to maintain its form. The first successful airship was designed by Henri Giffard, a French engineer, in 1852. In 1900 Count Ferdinand von Zeppelin of Germany built the first rigid airship. It used hydrogen, which is flammable, as the lifting gas and had a metal-lattice frame that held its shape. The vulnerability of rigid airships in storms and a series of spectacular fires, including the *Hindenburg* disaster in 1937, brought an end to their use.
See also: Zeppelin, Ferdinand von.

Air traffic control, system by which airplanes are monitored and guided. Relying on radar and other electronic equipment, air traffic controllers on the ground instruct pilots on landing and take-off patterns and on use of runways for taxiing.

Aisne River, northeastern French river that rises in the forests of Argonne near Vaubecort and flows northwest and west to join the Oise river near Compiègne. The Aisne is about 180 mi (290 km) long. The valley of the Aisne was the scene, during World War I, of prolonged trench warfare and was crossed in World War II by the U.S. Army during its Aug. 1944 offensive.
See also: World War I; World War II.

Aix-en-Provence (pop. 124,600), city in southern France, in the department of Bouches-du-Rhône, about 20 mi (32 km) north of Marseilles. As the Roman settlement Aquae Sextiae, it was colonized by the proconsul C. Sextius Calvinus in 123 B.C. Known from antiquity for its mineral baths, in medieval times Aix became the capital of the region of Provence, as well as a famous literary center. In 1536 it was the temporary residence of the Holy Roman Emperor Charles V.
Present-day industries include the production of olive oil, food processing, the mamunfacture of textiles, and the milling of flour.

Aix-la-Chapelle *see:* Aachen.

Aix-la-Chapelle, Congress of, meeting (1818) of the rulers of Austria, Prussia, and Russia and representatives from Great Britain and France at Aachen (Aix-la-Chapelle), Germany, after the Napoleonic Wars. The nations sought to preserve the peace established by, and resolve problems arising from, settlements made at the Congress of Vienna (1814-15).
See also: Vienna, Congress of.

Ajax, the name of 2 figures in Greek mythology. Ajax the Greater was the son of King Telamon and one of the greatest Greek heroes of the Trojan War. Informed that the arms of the slain Achilles had been awarded to Odysseus, Ajax went mad and committed suicide. The Greek warrior Ajax the Lesser also fought in the Trojan War. As punishment for raping Cassandra in Athena's temple, Ajax was shipwrecked and then killed.

Akbar (1542-1605), greatest of the Mogul emperors of India (1556-1605). He extended Mogul power over most of Afghanistan and India. An excellent administrator, he pursued a policy of religious toleration and also improved social laws, commerce, and transportation.
See also: India.

Akhenaton, or Ikhnaton, title taken by Amenhotep IV, king of Egypt (c. 1379-50 B.C.). Akhenaton started the cult of the sun god Aton, despite the opposition of the priesthood of Amon-Ra. He moved the capital from Thebes, city of Amon, to Akhetaton (now Tell el-Amarna), where he fostered a naturalistic school of art and literature. After his death the old religion was reestablished. Akhenaton was married to Nefertiti.
See also: Egypt, Ancient.

Akihito (1933-), emperor of Japan (1989-). He married a commoner, Michiko Shodo, in 1959, the first member of the royal family to do so.

Akita, powerful hunting dog originating in northern Japan in the 17th century. Standing 20-27 in (51-69 cm) high at the shoulder and weighing 75-110 lbs (34-50 kg), the Akita possesses a solid body and a short, stiff coat. Sometimes called the royal dog of Japan, the Akita is considered a symbol of good health and has been designated a national treasure by the Japanese government.

Akiva Baer ben Joseph (c. A.D. 50-135), Jewish rabbi, one of the greatest compilers of Hebrew Oral Law, whose work later formed the basis of the Mishnah. The Mishnah is part of the Talmud, a collection of writings constituting Jewish civil and religious law. After supporting a revolt against the Romans, he was executed as a rebel
See also: Talmud.

Akron (pop. 657,575), industrial city, seat of Summit County, Ohio, located on the Cuyahoga River, 36 mi (58 km) south of Cleveland. Akron was settled early in the 19th century and incorporated in 1865. Among the city's historical buildings is the home of John Brown, the abolitionist. B.F. Goodrich founded his pioneer rubber factory in Akron in 1870. With the invention of the automobile, Akron developed some of the world's largest tire and automobile plants. In addition, the city manufactures aircraft, matches, plastics, and clay and wood products.

The hydrogen-filled airship Hindenburg on fire in 1937

Akutagawa, Ryunosuke (1892-1927), Japanese writer of short stories, poetry, and plays. From medieval themes he turned to autobiographical subjects. His work's fantastic and morbid nature reveals susceptibilities that led to his suicide. His most famous story is *Rashomon* (1915).

Alabama, state in the southeast United States; bordered by Tennessee in the north, Georgia in the east, Florida and the Gulf of Mexico in the south, and Mississippi in the west.
Land and climate. The Appalachian Mountain chain ends in northern Alabama, where it forms a plateau covering a third of the state. The rest of the state is largely lowland plains, the most important of which is the famous Black Belt. Forests cover more than 60% of Alabama's land surface. Among the most important rivers are the Tennessee, the Tombigbee, the Alabama, the Coosa, the Black Warrior, and the Chattahoochee. Alabama has a generally moderate climate. Principal cities are Birmingham, Mobile, and Montgomery.
Economy. Manufacturing is the largest contributor to Alabama's economy. Leading goods are paper products, chemicals, and steel. Coal, natural gas, petroleum, and limestone are the state's most valuable minerals. Although cotton, which once ruled Alabama's 1-crop economy, is still an important crop, livestock, poultry, soybeans, and peanuts have supplanted it in revenue earned. Alabama's forests support a large lumber industry.

Akihito

Alabama

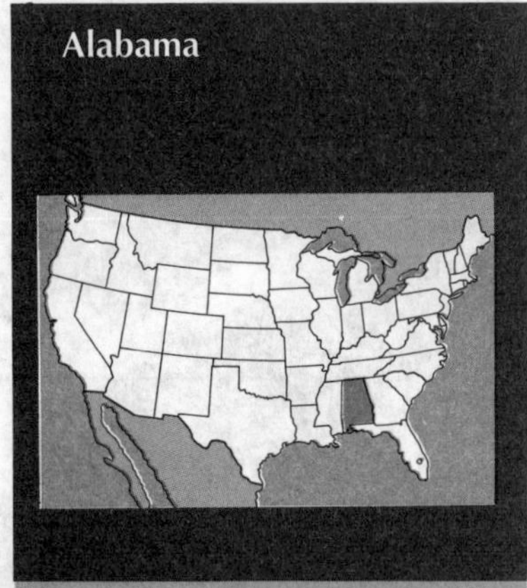

Capital:	Montgomery
Statehood:	Dec. 14, 1819 (22nd state)
Familiar name:	Heart of Dixie
Area:	51,705 sq mi (133,915 km^2; ranks 29th)
Population:	4,062,608 (1990; ranks 22nd)
Elevation:	Highest—2,407 ft (734 m), Cheaha Mountain Lowest—sea level
Motto:	Andemus jura nostra defendere (We Dare Defend Our Rights)
State flower:	Camellia
State bird:	Yellowhammer
State tree:	Southern pine
State song:	"Alabama"

Government. Alabama's constitution was adopted in 1901. The governor serves a 4-year term. The state legislature is composed of a senate of 35 members and a house of representatives of 105 members elected for 4-year terms. Alabama sends 7 representatives and 2 senators to the U.S. Congress.

History. Choctaws, Creeks, and other members of the Five Civilized Tribes originally peopled Alabama. Spain's Hernando De Soto explored the region in 1540, and France's Sieur de Bienville founded the first permanent European settlement in the Mobile area in 1702. The defeat of the Creeks by Andrew Jackson at the Battle of Horseshoe Bend (1814) opened south Alabama to settlers, who developed a slave-based plantation economy. At the outbreak of the Civil War Montgomery became the first Confederate capital. Alabama was readmitted to the Union in 1868.

One-crop farming and the sharecropping system brought widespread agricultural depression and poverty, accentuated during the early 20th century by the infestation of the cottonfields by the boll weevil. Tennessee Valley Authority projects (begun in 1933) and World War II boosted industry. The 1954 Supreme Court decision outlawing school segregation led to a period of racial tension. In 1965, black civil rights leader Dr. Martin Luther King, Jr., led a march from Selma to Montgomery in protest of voter discrimination. Alabama suffered financially in the 1970s and 1980s, although industry continues to grow.

Alabama, Confederate warship built in England (1862) for use in the U.S. Civil War. Under the command of Capt. Raphael Semmes, the *Alabama* attacked, captured, or destroyed over 60 Union commerce ships, before being sunk near Cherbourg, France (June 19, 1864) by the U.S.S. *Kearsarge*, commanded by Capt. John Winslow.
See also: Washington, Treaty of.

Alabaster, soft, usually white, semitransparent variety of the mineral gypsum, used to make decorative objects. Gypsum is composed of calcium sulfate. The alabaster used in ancient times is composed of calcium carbonate and is harder than gypsum.
See also: Gypsum.

Aladdin, boy hero of one of the stories of the *Thousand and One Nights*, a collection of folk tales from the Middle East preserved in Arabic in the 16th century. Aladdin, the son of a poor widow, comes into possession of a magic ring and lamp. As the master of the lamp and of the 2 genies, or jinns, who reside within, Aladdin amasses great wealth and becomes a sultan.
See also: Arabian Nights.

Alain-Fournier (Henri Alban Fournier; 1886-1914), French writer whose one novel, *The Wanderer* (1913), is the haunting tale of a boy's attempt to rediscover the dreamlike setting of his meeting with a beautiful girl.

Alamo, Spanish mission fortress in San Antonio, Tex. It was the site of a heroic defense (1836) by fewer than 200 Texans in the struggle for independence from Mexico. All the defenders, including Davy Crockett and Jim Bowie, died in a lengthy siege by 4,000 Mexicans under Gen. Santa Anna. The famous phrase "remember the Alamo" refers to the siege.
See also: Texas.

Alamogordo, (pop. 27,600) town in south-central New Mexico, seat of Otero County. It is the center of an agricultural, timber, and recreation area that includes the White Sands National Monument and Lincoln National Forest. The first atomic bomb was exploded near Alamogordo in a test on July 16, 1945.
See also: Nuclear weapon.

Alanbrooke, Lord (Alan Francis Brooke, 1st Viscount; 1883-1936), one of the leading British military strategists of World War II and chief of the Imperial General Staff (1941-46).

Alarcón, Pedro Antonio de (1833-91), Spanish regional writer best known for his novel *The Three-Cornered Hat* (1874). His work is distinguished by sharp realistic observation and picturesque effects.

Alaric, name of 2 Visigothic kings. **Alaric I** (c. A.D. 370-410) was commander of the Visigothic auxiliaries under the Roman Emperor Theodosius, upon whose death Alaric was proclaimed king of the Visigoths. After invading Greece and northern Italy, he captured and sacked Rome in 410. **Alaric II** (d. 507), ruled Spain and South Gaul from 484 and in 506 issued the Breviary of Alaric, a Visigothic code of Roman law, for his Roman subjects. He was slain in battle by Clovis I, king of the Franks.
See also: Goths.

Alaska

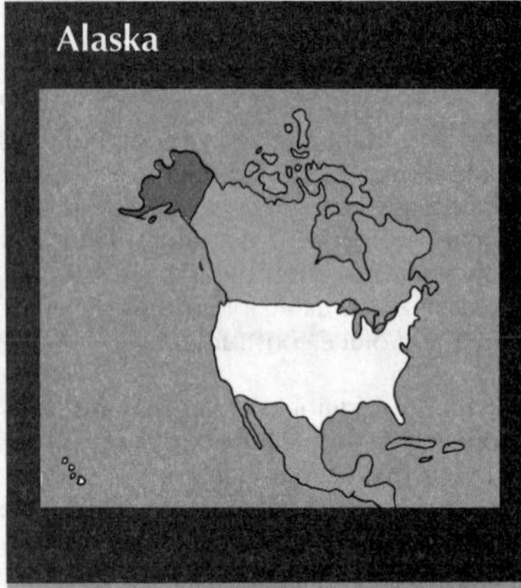

Capital:	Juneau
Statehood:	Jan. 3, 1959 (49th state)
Familiar name:	Last Frontier
Area:	591,004 sq mi (1,530,700 km^2; ranks 1st)
Population:	551,947 (1990; ranks 49th)
Elevation:	Highest —20,320 ft (6,194 m), Mt McKinley Lowest—sea level
Motto:	North to the Future
State flower:	Forget-me-not
State bird:	Willow ptarmigan
State tree:	Sitka spruce
State song:	"Alaska's Flag"

Alaska, largest state in the United States, located at the extreme northwest corner of North America, separated from the rest of the continental United States by northwest Canada; bordered by British Columbia and Yukon Territory in the west, the Pacific Ocean in the south, the Bering Sea in the west, and the Arctic Ocean in the north.

Land and climate. Alaska's general coastline is 6,640 mi (10,686 km) long, longer than the coastlines of the other 49 states combined. In the southeastern part of the Alaskan mainland is the mountainous Panhandle region, which is paralleled by the Alexander Archipelago. The Alaska Range, in the south-central part of the state, contains the highest peak in North America, Mt. McKinley. Extending southwest from the Alaska Range are the Alaska Peninsula and the Aleutian Islands. The Aleutian Range, which extends over the peninsula to Attu Island, near the Asian continent, has many active volcanoes. Between the mountain chains along the Pacific Coast and the Brooks Range, an extension of the Rockies, lies the central plateau of Alaska, crossed by the Yukon River. Alaska's northernmost settlement is Point Barrow, lying in the frozen tundra of the Arctic Coastal Plain. Southern Alaska has a relatively mild

Alaska's Mount Deborah, surrounded by snow-capped peaks

An Eskimo demonstrates the construction of a traditional igloo. The snow used in the construction has been strengthed by wind and snow and is carved with a special snow knife.

climate, with brief but hot summers. Winters are much colder in central Alaska. Principal cities are Anchorage, Fairbanks, and Juneau.

Economy. Oil is Alaska's most valuable natural resource. Prudhoe Bay, on the Arctic Coastal Plain, is believed by engineers to be the largest oil field in North America. Alaska's other major mineral products are gold, sand and gravel, and natural gas. Alaska's fishing industry is the largest in the United States. Salmon is the most important catch. Alaska's leading manufactures are food, petroleum, and paper products. Furs were the original motive for Alaska's colonization and are still important.

Government. Alaska's constitution was adopted in 1956. The governor is elected for a 4-year term. The state senate has 20 members elected for 4-year terms, and the house of representatives is composed of 40 members serving 2-year terms. Alaska sends 1 representative and 2 senators to the U.S. Congress.

History. Russia claimed Alaska after Vitus Bering sighted it in 1741. Gregory Shelikof founded the first permanent white settlement in 1784 on Kodiak Island. U.S. Secretary of State William H. Seward bought Alaska in 1867 for $7.2 million—about 2 cents an acre. Economic growth remained slow until the 1896 Klondike gold rush in the Yukon and after subsequent deposits were discovered in Nome in 1899 and Fairbanks in 1902. Alaska was established as a U.S. territory in 1912. World War II brought economic change to Alaska, with the United States sending thousands of workers to the territory to build defense installments and the Alaska Highway.

In 1942 the Japanese occupied the Aleutian Islands of Agattu, Attu, and Kiska, the only part of North America to be invaded during the war. In 1968 the Prudhoe Bay oil field was discovered, transforming the economy. The Trans-Alaska Pipeline, which carries petroleum from Prudhoe Bay to the port of Valdez, was completed in 1977. In 1980 the federal government, which controls most of the state's land, set aside more than 104 million acres 42 million hectares) for wilderness areas, wildlife refuges, and national parks and preserves. In 1989 the Exxon *Valdez* accidentally discharged 10 million gal (39 million l) of oil into Prince William Sound, in North America's worst oil spill.

Part of the gigantic oil works near Prudhoe Bay. The oil industry has attracted many people to Alaska because of the high-paying jobs.

Alaska Boundary Dispute, disagreement concerning the demarcation of the border between the Alaska Panhandle and Canada, which arose in 1898 during the Klondike gold rush. Skagway and the head of the Lynn Canal, through which supplies reached the Yukon, were claimed as Canadian territory. The question was settled in favor of the United States by a joint U.S.-British commission in 1903.

Alaska Highway, road extending 1,422 mi (2,288 km) from Delta Junction, Alaska, to Dawson Creek, British Columbia. It was built by the United States as a strategic all-weather military route in 1942. In 1946 Canada took control of the 1,221 mi (1,965 km) passing through its territory.

Alaskan malamute, strong sled dog developed by the Malemiut Eskimos. The malamute's thick coat is gray or black with white markings and a bushy tail curls across its back. Weight ranges from 75 to 85 lb (34 to 39 kg).

Alaska pipeline, oil pipeline running 789 mi (1,270 km) from Alaska's Prudhoe Bay to the port of Valdez. Finished in 1977, it was bitterly opposed by environmentalists for adversely affecting the ecology.
See also: Petroleum; Pipeline.

Al-Azhar University, in Cairo, Egypt, one of the world's oldest universities (founded in c. A.D. 970) and a major center of Islamic learning. Women gained admittance in 1962.

Alba, Duke of *see:* Alva or Alba, Fernando Alvarez de Toledo, Duke of.

Alban, Saint (d. c. 304), first Christian martyr in Britain. Martyred during the persecutions of the Emperor Diocletian, he is said to have performed many miracles. A monastery was built in his memory in 795 by the king of Mercia, near the presumed place of his execution. St. Alban's feast day is celebrated on June 22 by Roman Catholics and on June 17 by the Church of England.

Albania (People's Socialist Republic of Albania), the smallest country in the Balkans, 210 mi (338 km) long, and less than 100 mi (161 km) wide.

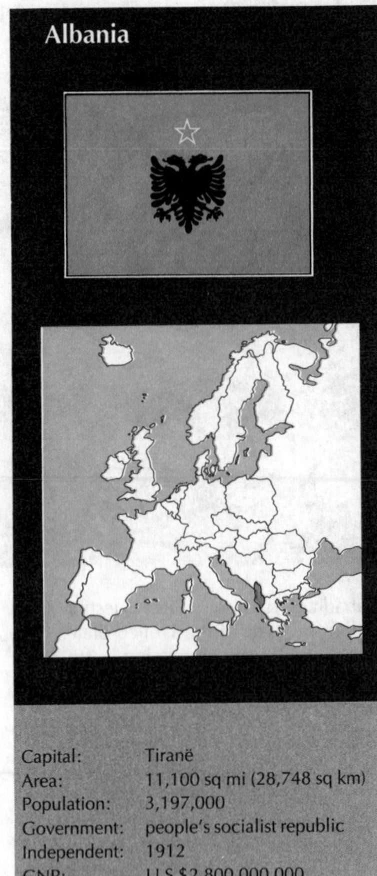

Capital:	Tiranë
Area:	11,100 sq mi (28,748 sq km)
Population:	3,197,000
Government:	people's socialist republic
Independent:	1912
GNP:	U.S.$2,800,000,000
Per capita:	U.S. $930

Land. The country is mountainous, with isolated fertile basins and a narrow coastal plain. The climate is Mediterranean, but summers can bring prolonged droughts and winters can be harsh.

People. Though officially an atheist country, Albania's population is largely Muslim, with a Roman Catholic and Greek Orthodox Christian minority.

Economy. Albania is poor and underdeveloped. Farming yields grapes and olives as well as grains, fruits, tobacco, and cotton. Albania is rich in chromium, copper, nickel, and coal, and mining provides most of the country's income. Industries produce food and petroleum products, textilesand building materials.

History. As part of ancient Illyria, Albania was successively under Greek, Roman, and Byzantine influence and control. In succeeding centuries it was invaded by Goths, Bulgars, Slavs, and Normans. Later, the national hero Scanderberg (1403?-68) delayed but failed to stop Ottoman Turkish conquest. Turkish rule Islamized Albania and suppressed nationalist aspirations until the First Balkan War (1912). Occupied in World War I, ruled by the self-proclaimed King Zog I (1928-39), then annexed by Italy and occupied in World War II, Albania regained independence under the anti-fascist guerilla leader Enver Hoxha, a Communist, who proclaimed a republic in 1946. In 1985 Hoxha died and was succeeded by Ramiz Alia.

Edward Albee

Albany (pop. 874,304), capital of New York since 1797 and seat of Albany County, located on the west bank of the Hudson River about 145 mi (233 km) north of New York City. An important industrial center, Albany's products include chemicals, paper, and textiles. Many people are also employed in state and county government offices. The opening of the Erie and Champlain canals in the 1820s and the first railroad connection with Schenectady in 1831 established Albany's position as a commercial and shipping center.
See also: New York.

Albany Congress, meeting (1754) of 25 representatives from 7 British colonies at Albany, N.Y., aimed at conciliating the Iroquois and improving the common defense of the colonies against the French. The congress adopted a plan, chiefly designed by Benjamin Franklin, providing for greater colonial unity, one of the first significant attempts at colonial cooperation. The colonial governments later rejected the plan.
See also: Revolutionary War in America.

Albany Regency, group of politicians with headquarters in Albany who controlled the New York State Democratic party (1820-54), with the first U.S. political machine. Among its members were Martin Van Buren, William L. Marcy, Silas Wright, and John A. Dix. Marcy's slogan, "To the victors belong the spoils," was its guiding principle; it rewarded the party faithful with government jobs. Starting in 1842, opposition groups (Barnburners and Hunkers) developed similar strategies, ultimately having a divisive effect on the party and diminishing the prestige of the Albany Regency.

Al Basrah, or Basra (pop. 616,700), second-largest city in Iraq and an important port, lying on the Shatt al Arab River approximately 55 mi (90 km) from the Persian Gulf. Arabs founded Al Basrah in A.D. 636, after which it became a trade center. Under Ottoman rule (1534-1918) the city declined in importance. From 1918 to 1932, the years Great Britain ruled Iraq, Al Basrah served as a military center. Located near major oil fields, it became a center for oil refining and export. Because it was the site of heavy fighting, the city's importance as a port decreased during the Iran-Iraq War of 1980-88.
See also: Persian Gulf War

Albatross, any of 14 species of large, long-winged, gliding, hook-billed seabirds forming the family Diomedeidae. Two species form the genus *Phoebetria*, the other 12 the genus *Diomedea*. Most albatrosses are white with darker markings on the back, wings, and tail. The wandering albatross (*D. exulans*) has the broadest wingspan of any living bird —up to 12 ft (3.7 m).

Albee, Edward Franklin (1928-), U.S. playwright who gained international fame with *Who's Afraid of Virginia Woolf?* (1962), a penetrating look at contemporary American marriage. His other plays include *The Zoo Story* (1958) and *The American Dream* (1961), both one-act plays, and *Tiny Alice* (1964). He won Pulitzer Prizes for *A Delicate Balance* (1966) and *Seascape* (1975).

Albéniz, Isaac (1860-1909), Spanish composer and pianist. He is best remembered for his later piano works, including the suite *Iberia* (1906-9), which is based on Spanish folk themes and popular music forms.

Albert I (1875-1934), king of the Belgians (1909-34); nephew and successor of Leopold II. During World War I Albert commanded the armed forces. He did much to improve conditions in the Belgian Congo, and he strengthened national defense and the merchant fleet and introduced social reforms in Belgium.

Albert, Carl Bert (1908-), Oklahoma Democrat, Speaker of the U.S. House of

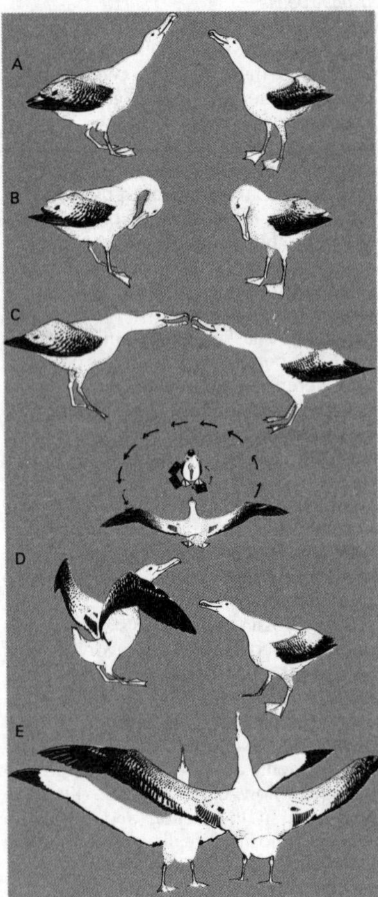

The courtship of the albatross includes a complicated dance accompanied by clattering beaks.
A. Initial neckstretching and bill clapping
B. Head bowing
C. Mutual bill clapping and nibbling
D. Male circles female with open wings. Female turns on spot always facing male.
E. Final mutual head raising and wing opening preceding mating

Representatives (1971-77). Albert graduated from the University of Oklahoma in 1931, after which he studied at Oxford University in England on a Rhodes scholarship, earning 2 law degrees. After practicing law for 6 years, he served in the U.S. Army (1941-46). A member of the U.S. House of Representatives (1947-77), Albert served as majority whip (1955-62). He was platform chair of the 1964 Democratic National Convention and chair of the 1968 Democratic National Convention. In the mid-1960s Albert supported President Lyndon Johnson's civil rights proposals despite opposition from his district.

Albert, Prince (Francis Charles Augustus Albert Emmanuel; 1819-61), prince consort of Great Britain, husband of Queen Victoria. German-born son of the Duke of Saxe-Coburg-Gotha, he married Victoria in 1840 and served as her trusted adviser. He was active in promoting fine arts.

Alberta, westernmost of Canada's Prairie Provinces; bordered by Saskatchewan (in the east), the Northwest Territories (in the north), British Columbia (in the west), and the U.S. state of Montana (in the south).
Land and Climate. Alberta is a plateau sloping gradually upward and westward to the Rocky Mountains and the Continental Divide. The south is treeless prairie, the central region is partly wooded, and the north is densely forested. The prairie is drained by the Athabasca, Saskatchewan, and Slave rivers, among others. Temperatures range from an average of 59°F (15°C) in summer to 5°F (–15°C) in winter.
People. About half of Alberta's inhabitants live in the metropolitan areas of Edmonton and Calgary. There are also some 300,000 Native Americans, three-quarters of whom live on reservations. The largest religious denomination is the United Church of Canada.
Economy. Alberta's principal crops are wheat and sugar beets; livestock raising, dairying, logging, fishing, and fur trapping also contribute to the province's wealth. Petroleum, natural gas, and coal have made Alberta one of Canada's richest provinces. The Leduc oil field was discovered in 1947, and the province contains about half of Canada's reserves of coal. Since the 1960s the leading industries have been in mineral exploitation.
History. In 1670 unexplored Alberta was granted to the Hudson's Bay Company. Few European settlers arrived until after 1869, when the Canadian government bought the land. The arrival of the Mounties (1874) and the completion of the Canadian Pacific Railway (1885) encouraged immigration. Alberta became a province in 1905.

Alberti, Leon Battista (1404-72), Italian Renaissance scholar, architect, painter, and art theorist. His architectural works include the Palazzo Rucellai in Florence and the church of San Francesco in Rimini. Alberti is noted for his literary contributions during the Italian Renaissance, including *Della pittura*, the first formulation of the aesthetic and scientific attitudes of Renaissance painting; it idealized the imitation of nature and served as a foundation for modern perspective. His architectural influence was presented in his treatise *De re aedificatoria*, which provided the Renaissance with an original program for architectural design. Alberti also wrote on a variety of subjects involving domestic animals, religion and the priesthood, jurisprudence, politics, government, mathematics, mechanics, literature, and language. He was the prototype of the Renaissance man.

Albertus Magnus, Saint (1206?-80), German scholastic philosopher and scientist and teacher of St. Thomas Aquinas. He helped establish Aristotelianism and the study of the natural sciences in Christian thought, and he was possibly the first to isolate arsenic.

Albigenses, members of a heretical sect that flourished in the 12th and 13th centuries in southern France. The Albigenses believed that the principles of good and evil are in constant struggle and that matter is evil and only the human spirit is good. A crusade proclaimed by Pope Innocent III in 1208 broke the hold of the heresy, and a special inquisition was created in 1233 to convert the Albigenses.

Albino, organism lacking normal pigmentation. The skin and hair of albino animals (including humans) is uncolored, and the irises of the eyes appear pink. Albinism, which may be total or only partial, is generally inherited. Because albino plants contain no chlorophyll and thus are unable to perform photosynthesis, they rapidly die.

Albright, Ivan Le Lorraine (1897-1983), U.S. painter of microscopically detailed canvases that focus on decay and human dissolution. His works include *That Which I Should Have Done I Did Not Do* (1941) and a series of paintings for the film *The Picture of Dorian Gray* (1944).

Albumin, protein that occurs in its most well-known state in the white of an egg. Albumin appears in animal and plant tissues. It is the primary constituent of the protein in blood serum. Albumins are used in the dyeing industry and in making photographic chemicals.

Albuquerque (pop. 480,577), largest city in New Mexico and seat of Bernalillo County, situated on the Rio Grande. Founded in 1706, it is an important commercial and industrial city, a center for nuclear energy and defense research, and a transcontinental air and land route hub. Its dry, sunny climate and nearby mountains and Native American reservations have made it a popular tourist center.

Alcan Highway *see:* Alaska Highway.

Alcatraz, rocky island in San Francisco Bay, famous as the site from 1933 to 1963 of a federal maximum security prison, nicknamed "the Rock." It is now part of the Golden Gate National Recreation Area.

Saint Albertus Magnus in a fresco by Tommasso da Modena (Seminary of Treviso)

Alchemy, blend of philosophy, mysticism, and chemical processing that originated before the Christian era. Practitioners sought the conversion of base metals into gold using the "philosopher's stone." Other goals were the prolongation of life and the secret of immortality. Alchemy began in Hellenistic Egypt and passed through the writings of the great Arab alchemists to the Latin West. In the early 16th century Paracelsus set alchemy on a new course toward chemical pharmacy, although other alchemists—including John Dee and Isaac Newton— continued to work along quasi-religious lines.
See also: Chemistry; Metallurgy.

Alcibiades (c. 450-404 B.C.), Athenian statesman and general, nephew of Pericles, and student of Socrates. He fell in and out of favor with the Athenian people during the era of the Peloponnesian War. He was eventually exiled and assassinated.
See also: Peloponnesian War.

Alcindor, Lew *see:* Abdul-Jabbar, Kareem.

Alcock and Brown, pioneer British aviators, who made the first nonstop flight across the Atlantic Ocean in 1919. Pilot Sir John William Alcock (1892-1919) and navigator Sir Arthur Whitten Brown (1886-1948) began their transatlantic flight near St. John's, Newfoundland, in a twin-engine, converted bomber, landing in a bog near Clifden, Ireland, the next day, having traveled 1,950 mi (3,138 km).

Alcohol, class of compounds containing a hydroxyl group bonded by a carbon atom. Alcohols occur widely in nature and are used as solvents and antifreezes and in chemical manufacture. They are obtained by fermentation, by oxidation or hydration of alkenes from petroleum and natural gas, and by reduction of fats and oils. The simplest alcohols are methanol and ethyl alcohol, or ethanol (the intoxicating constituent of alcoholic beverages); others include benzyl alcohol, ethylene glycol, and glycerol.
See also: Solvent.

Jean le Rond d'Alembert

Alcoholics Anonymous (A.A.), international organization founded in 1935 to help people suffering from alcoholism overcome their addictions. The practice of sharing recovery experiences among its members is a successful part of the treatment plan.

Alcoholism, chronic illness marked by compulsive drinking of alcohol, leading to physical and psychological addiction. Alcohol is a depressant that acts on the central nervous system to reduce anxiety and inhibition. It is a potent and addictive substance that impairs physical coordination, judgment, and perception and, in sufficiently high dosages, can cause unconsciousness or death. Alcohol is nearly unique among potent drugs in that moderate, self-induced levels of intoxication are socially acceptable. Because alcohol is so readily available and its use so generally accepted, its abuse remains by far the most serious drug problem in the United States. Alcohol abuse is the direct cause of crime, delinquency, and accidents that cost billions of dollars, as well as considerable physical and psychological suffering and loss of life.
Prolonged alcohol abuse causes cirrhosis of the liver, damages other organs, including the brain and heart, and may contribute to cancer of the esophagus. Drinking during pregnancy is harmful to the fetus. For the severely addicted alcoholic, withdrawal from alcohol is more dangerous and potentially more life-threatening than withdrawal from heroin and must be done under medical supervision. Treatment most often includes individual or group psychological counseling, but may also include prescriptions of Antabuse (disulfiram), which causes unpleasant physical responses, such as nausea, in patients who drink alcohol while they are taking the drug. Research continues into the causes of alcoholism, including findings that indicate a genetic component in the disease suggesting heredity.
See also: Alcoholics Anonymous; Drug abuse.

Buzz Aldrin

Alcott, (Amos) Bronson (1799-1888), U.S. educator, philosopher, and author, father of Louisa May Alcott. Founder of the progressive Temple School in Boston, his teaching methods were too advanced to be popular. A leading transcendentalist along with Ralph Waldo Emerson and Henry David Thoreau, his writings include *Concord Days* (1872) and *Table Talk* (1877).
See also: Transcendentalism.

Alcott, Louisa May (1832-88), U.S. author; daughter of Bronson Alcott. Her best-known work is the autobiographical *Little Women* (1869). Another important work, *Hospital Sketches* (1863), was based on her experiences as a Union nurse in the Civil War.

Alcuin, or Albinus (c. A.D. 735-804), English prelate and educator whose scholarship influenced medieval teaching of the liberal arts. He supervised Charlemagne's program of ecclesiastical and educational reform.

Aldehyde, any of a class of highly reactive organic chemical compounds characterized by a CHO group; especially, acetaldehyde (C_2H_4O). Formaldehyde (CH_2O) is a pungent gaseous aldehyde used commonly as a disinfectant and preservative and in making resins and plastics.
See also: Formaldehyde.

Alden, John (1599-1687), one of the leaders of Plymouth Colony. He is best known through Henry Wadsworth Longfellow's fictional poem *The Courtship of Miles Standish* (1858), in which Alden courts Priscilla Mullens on behalf of Standish but marries her himself.

Alder, any of a genus (*Alnus*) of shrubs and small trees of the birch family. Found in moist, temperate regions at high altitudes, they are indigenous to the Americas, Asia, and North Africa. One variety, the red alder (*A. rubra*), is used commercially as timber.

Aldridge, Ira Frederick (1805-67), first African American to achieve fame as an actor in the Western Hemisphere. Because of limited opportunities in the United States due to racial prejudice, he was forced to go to Europe, where he became known for his bold interpretations of Lear, Othello, and Macbeth.

Aldrin, Buzz (Edwin Eugene Aldrin, Jr.; 1930-), U.S. astronaut. Aldrin was the second man to walk on the moon, during the Apollo 11 space flight in 1969. In 1966 he was the pilot of the Gemini 12 flight, which included rendezvous maneuvers and his record 5-hour space walks.

Aldus Manutius (Teobaldo Mannucci or Manuzio; 1450-1515), Venetian founder of the Aldine Press, whose scrupulous editions of Greek and Roman classics (including the works of Aristotle) advanced Renaissance scholarship. He was the first to use italic type (1501) to produce cheap, pocket-sized editions of the Latin classics.

Aleatory music (from Latin *alea*, "dice"), music dependent on chance, applied to the post-1950 tendency of composers, such as John Cage, to leave elements in their work to the performer's decision or chance.

Aleichem, Sholem *see:* Sholem Aleichem.

Aleixandre, Vicente (1898-1984), Spanish poet. His collections of poetry include *Destruction or Love* (1935) and *Shadow of Paradise* (1944). He won the 1977 Nobel Prize for literature.

Alembert, Jean le Rond d' (1717-83), French philosopher, physicist, and mathematician, a leading figure in the French Enlightenment, and coeditor with Denis Diderot of the *Encyclopédie.* His early fame rested on his formulation of d'Alembert's principle in mechanics (1743). His other works treat calculus, music, philosophy, and astronomy.

Aleppo (pop. 961,000), second-largest city of Syria. It flourished in Byzantine times as a trade center on the caravan route to Baghdad. An important manufacturing center, its industries include textile- and carpetmaking. The cultural center of Syria, Aleppo contains the National Museum, a medieval citadel, and numerous mosques with many fine examples of Islamic art.

Aleut, native of the Aleutian Islands and western Alaska. Descended from an Eskimo people, Aleuts have their own language. Traditionally, Aleuts hunted land animals, such as caribou and bear, and sea animals, such as whales and seals. They traveled in skin-covered kayaks, made spears and fishhooks, and dressed in parkas made from animal furs and skins. Under Russian domination, which began in the 18th century, the Aleutian population dropped dramatically, dropping further with Japanese occupation of the Aleutians during World War II. Through the Alaska Native Claims Settlement Act of the U.S. Congress (1971), the Aleuts won the rights to their homeland.

Aleutian Islands, chain of rugged Alaskan islands of volcanic origin, extending westward 1,200 mi (1,900 km) from the Alaska Peninsula and separating the Bering Sea from the Pacific. Fishing is the chief occupation. During World War II the Japanese occupied the islands Agattu, Attu, and Kiska.
See also: Alaska.

Alewife (*Alosa pseudoharengus*), fish in the herring family. Alewives travel in large schools along the Atlantic coastline of the United States. They grow up to 15 in (38 cm) in saltwater and, in the freshwater of the Great Lakes, up to 6 in (15 cm). After maturity, saltwater alewives travel from the Atlantic to freshwater, where they lay their eggs.

Alexander I (1888-1934), king of Yugoslavia from 1921 to 1934. Yugoslavia, which has been formed as a country in 1918, was home to several peoples, including Serbs, Croats, and Slovenes. To ensure Serb dominance, Alexander declared himself dictator in 1929. He was assassinated by a Croatian terrorist in 1934.

Alexander III (Orlando Bandinelli; d. 1181), pope (1159-81). He continued a longstanding conflict with the Holy Roman Emperor Frederick I. Opposed also by 3 antipopes, he was victorious over Frederick at the Battle of Legano in 1176. He convened the Third Lateran Council (1179) and forced King Henry II of England to recognize papal supremacy.

Alexander VI (Rodrigo Borgia; 1431-1503), pope (1492-1503). The most notorious of the Renaissance popes, he directed his efforts at increasing the temporal power of the papacy and creating great hereditary domains for his children, among them Cesare and Lucrezia Borgia.

Alexander, name of 3 Russian tsars. **Alexander I** (1777-1825) succeeded his father, Paul I, in 1801. In 1805 he joined England and Austria against Napoleon. After French victories Napoleon proposed Franco-Russian domination of Europe, but mutual mistrust came to a head, and Napoleon invaded Russia in 1812. The French were defeated, and in 1815 Alexander formed a coalition with Austria and Prussia, the Holy Alliance. At his death, Russia faced economic ruin and rebellion. **Alexander II** (1818-81) succeeded his father, Nicholas I, in 1855. He was responsible for the emancipation of the serfs in 1861, but he was assassinated when his domestic reforms did not satisfy populist groups. In foreign policies he was a moderate, making peace in the Crimea and extending Russian power in the Far East as well as in Central Asia. **Alexander III** (1845-94) succeeded his father, Alexander II, in 1881. He discarded the latter's proposals for moderate reform in favor of rigid repression and persecution of minorities.

Alexander, Grover Cleveland (1887-1950), U.S. baseball player. One of the greatest right-handed pitchers in baseball history, in 1916 he set the major league record for shutouts in a season (16). Third on the career win list with 373, Alexander's 90 career shutouts are the second most in major league history. Alexander played with the Philadelphia Phillies, Chicago Cubs, and St. Louis Cardinals from 1911 to 1930. He was inducted into the National Baseball Hall of Fame in 1938.

Alexander Archipelago, group of more than 1,100 islands lying along the coastline of the Alaska Panhandle. They are the peaks of a submerged coastal range. Sitka, on the island of Baranof, was once capital of Alaska. The islands were discovered by Vitus Bering in 1741 and were acquired by the United States as part of the Alaska purchase in 1867. Fish, furs, gold, and timber are important items in their economy.

Alexander of Tunis, 1st Earl (Harold Rupert Leofric George Alexander; 1891-1969), last British-born governor of Canada (1946-52). He was known for his military achievements in both world wars and, in 1944, was named commander in chief of all Allied forces for Italy. Knighted (1942) and made Viscount Alexander of Tunis (1946), he then served as minister of defense for Britain (1952-54).

Alexander the Great, or Alexander III (356-323 B.C.), king of Macedonia (336-323 B.C.). At 20 Alexander succeeded his father, Philip II of Macedon, and executed Philip's plans for freeing the Greeks of Asia Minor from Persian rule. After his defeat of the Persian king Darius III at Issus in 333, Alexander subdued Phoenicia and Egypt, founding Alexandria. In 331 Alexander again defeated Darius in the battle of Gaugamela, after which the principal cities of the Persian Empire fell easily to his attack. He was proclaimed king of Asia and moved on eastward. He intended to conquer India, but his soldiers refused to follow him. Though he lived to be only 33, he conquered the greatest empire yet known in Western civilization and prepared the way for the Hellenistic Age.

Alexandria (pop. 105,000), city and port of entry in Virginia, located on the Potomac River. The home of Robert E. Lee, the city was, in part, designed by George Washington. From 1791 to 1846 it was part of the capital district. The Lee home, Arlington House, is now the site of Arlington National Cemetery. Predominantly a residential suburb of the nation's capital, Alexandria also has railroad yards and produces structural steel, chemicals, and fertilizers.

Alexandria (pop. 2,821,000), chief port and second-largest city of Egypt. Founded by Alexander the Great c. 332 B.C., it was the capital of Ptolomaic Egypt and a center of trade and learning in the Hellenistic and Roman worlds. The city has grown into Egypt's principal channel for foreign trade.
See also: Seven Wonders of the Ancient World.

Alexandrian Library, in antiquity, the greatest collection of manuscripts, first assembled in the 3rd century B.C. The library, containing more than 400,000 scrolls, was housed in Alexandria, Egypt. It was probably destroyed in stages during sieges starting with Julius Caesar's in 47 B.C.; its destruction is thought to have been complete by 400 A.D.

Alexandrite, variety of the mineral chrysoberyl, discovered in 1833 and named for Tsar Alexander II. It has brilliant luster and is predominantly green, but changes colors when viewed from different directions or in different light.

Alfalfa, or lucerne (*Medicago sativa*), legume widely grown for pasture, hay, and silage. The high protein content of this perennial makes it an excellent food for livestock, and the nitrogen-fixing bacteria on its roots are important in enriching depleted soil.

Alfonso XIII (1886-1941), king of Spain from birth until 1931. Because of the unrest during his reign, Alfonso supported Primo de Rivera's establishment of a military dictatorship in 1923. The dictator fell from power in 1930, however, and the outcome of the elections in 1931 was so pro-republican that Alfonso, although not abdicating the throne, left Spain, and a republic was established.
See also: Juan Carlos I.

Alexander the Great, depicted on a mural

Alfred the Great (A.D. 848-899), king of the West Saxons from 871. He halted the Danish invasions with his victory at Edington (878), making his kingdom of Wessex the nucleus of a unified England. He also introduced educational and legal reforms, translated Latin works into English, and began the *Anglo-Saxon Chronicle*, an important source for Anglo-Saxon history.

Algae, large and diverse group of nonvascular (rootless and stemless) aquatic plants that contain chlorophyll and carry on photosynthesis, including some of the simplest organisms known. They range in size from microscopic single-celled organisms to strands of seaweed several yards long. Most species of green algae, which are found mainly in freshwater, are microscopic. Brown algae include the familiar seaweeds found on rocky shores. Red algae, found mostly in warmer seas, include several species of economic importance. Algae are important as the basis of food chains. Many of the larger algae are used in foodstuffs, in medicine, and as manure.
See also: Eutrophication; Seaweed.

Algebra, branch of mathematics in which relationships between known and unknown quantities are represented symbolically. For a relationship to satisfy the fundamental theorem of algebra it must consist of a finite number of quantities and must have a solution. An example of such a relationship taken from elementary algebra is: $ax^n+bx^{n-1}+cx^{n-2}+ \dots +z=0$
This is an "n degree" polynomial equation (of order n). Here x is a variable denoting an unknown quantity to be found, and a, b, $c \dots z$ represent known values. Elementary algebra, the algebraic system most familiar to the general public, uses operations of arithmetic to solve equations from sets of numbers. Abstract algebra developed from elementary algebra by mathematicians attempting to solve specific problems. Mathematical structures such as fields, rings, and groups were devised. Concepts of abstract algebra have been used by theoretical physicists in the development of quantum theory as well as by digital communications engineers in the development of coding theory. Linear algebra is used to solve simultaneous linear equations and is applied extensively in economics and psychology. Manipulations of equations are accomplished through the use of matrices and vectors. Boolean algebra is a symbolic representation of classical logic developed in 1854 by George Boole. Operations such as

Tuareg craftsman trading handmade objects.

union and intersection are used. This algebraic system is used in computer science. Gradual introduction of algebraic symbols occurred between 2000 B.C. and 1550 A.D. *Arithmetica,* regarded as the first treatise on algebra, was written by Diophantus of Alexandria in the 3rd century A.D. The Arabs became leaders in the field in about the 9th century. It was not until the 16th and 17th centuries in Europe that algebra underwent a complete transformation and became almost completely symbolic, much as it is today. Abstract algebra developed in the early 19th century, with major contributions by Niels Abel and Evariste Galois.

Alger, Horatio (1834-99), U.S. author of more than 100 books whose heroes rise from rags to riches through virtue and hard work, including *Ragged Dick* (1867), *Luck and Pluck* (1869), and *Sink or Swim* (1870).

Algeria, Democratic and Popular Republic of, country in northwest Africa; bordered by Mauritania, Morocco, and Western Sahara in the west, the Mediterranean Sea

Algeria still carries the mark of its Roman conquest. The triumphal arch of the Roman Emperor Trajan (53-117 A.D.) is one of the best-preserved examples of Roman architecture.

Algeria

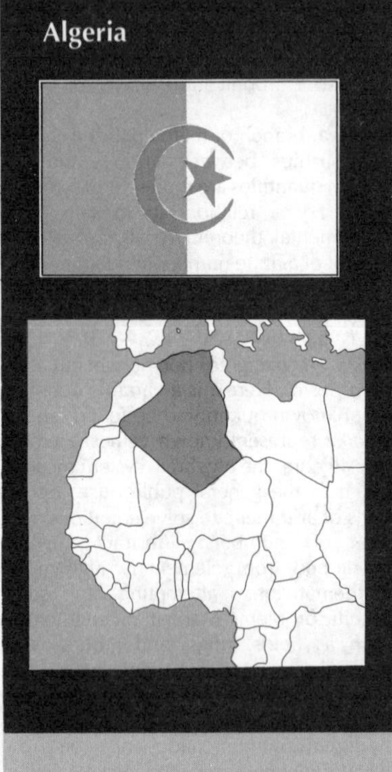

General information	
Capital:	Algiers
Area:	919,595 sq mi (2,381,741 sq km)
Population:	24,579,000
Official language:	Arabic
Monetary unit:	1 Algerian dinar (DA) = 100 centimes
Main cities:	Algiers, Oran, Constantine, Annaba
Government	
Form:	democratic and popular republic
Independent:	1962
Head of state:	President (elected every 5 years)
Head of government:	Prime minister (appointed by president)
Legislature:	one legislative house (National People's Assembly)
Executive:	Council of Ministers
Judiciary:	Supreme Court
Political division:	48 provinces (wilayas)
National economy	
Gross national product:	U.S. $58,250,000,000
Per capita income:	U.S. $2,450
Agriculture:	wheat, barley, potatoes, grapes, watermelons
Livestock:	sheep, goats, cattle
Fisheries:	70,000 metric tons
Mining:	petroleum, iron ore, phosphates, natural gas
Industries:	petroleum products, iron and steel, wine
Main exports:	petroleum, natural gas, oranges, wine, dates, phosphate
Transportation:	2,337 mi (3,761 km) of railroads; 50,734 mi (81,648 km) of roads; 5 international airports
Trading partners:	France, Germany, Italy, U.S.A
People	
Urban:	49.7%
Ethnic composition:	Arab 82%, Berber 17%, French 0.1%
Birth rate:	34.6 per 1,000 population
Death rate:	7.0 per 1,000 population
Infant mortality:	64.1 per 1,000 live births
Life expectancy:	male 61 years, female 64.1 years

in the north, Tunisia and Libya in the east, and Niger and Mali in the south. The Atlas Mountains divide the large country (919,590 sq mi/2,381,741 sq km) into the coastal region (Tell), the steppe, and the desert. Some 75% of the Algerians live in the narrow fertile coastal area. Most Algerians still live on their land, and farms yield citrus fruits, grapes, grain, and vegetables. Algeria is one of the world's most important oil-producing countries and a primary exporter of liquified natural gas. However, the economy is burdened with high levels of debt repayment.
The Phoenicians settled North Africa around 1200 B.C. The area belonged to Carthage, then to Rome, and in 201 B.C. became the Roman province of Numidia. Subsequently, Algeria was conquered by Vandals, Byzantines, and Arabs. From the 16th to the 18th centuries, Algeria was home to the Barbary pirates and the slave trade. The French took colonized Algeria (1830-1909), governing until the nationalist revolt (1954-62) led by the National Liberation Front (FLN), in which at least 100,000 Muslims and 10,000 French soldiers died. Algeria became independent on July 3, 1962. Algeria has had no diplomatic relations with the United States since the 1967 Arab-Israeli war, but in 1981 it helped negotiate the release of U.S. hostages who had been held in Iran since 1979.

Algiers (pop. 1,722,000), capital, major port, and largest city of Algeria. Founded by Berbers in A.D. 935 on the site of the Roman settlement of Licosium, it was taken by the French in 1830. The modern city lies at the base of a hill overlooking the Bay of Algiers; higher up the slope is the old Moorish city, dominated by the Casbah, a citadel built by the Turks.

Algonquins, or Algonkins, North American Native Americans. They were driven out of their territory along the St. Lawrence and Ottawa rivers by the Iroquois in the 17th and 18th centuries.

Algren, Nelson (1909-81), U.S. naturalistic novelist, best known for his fiction describing Chicago slum life. Among his works are *Never Come Morning* (1942), *The Man with the Golden Arm* (1949), and *A Walk on the Wild Side* (1956).

Alhambra (Arabic, "The Red"), 13th-century citadel and palace dominating the city of Granada, the finest large-scale example of Moorish architecture in Spain.
See also: Moors.

Ali, Muhammad (Cassius Marcellus Clay; 1942-), U.S. boxer. Ali won an Olympic gold metal in 1960 and the heavyweight championship from Sonny Liston in 1964. He was stripped of this title in 1967 by the World Boxing Association while appealing a conviction for draft evasion, later overturned. One of the greatest and most outspoken heavyweights in boxing history, he defeated George Foreman for the title in 1974, lost it in 1978 to Leon Spinks, and won it back from Spinks later that year. Larry Holmes defeated Ali in 1980. Ali changed his name after adopting the Black Muslim religion in 1964.

Ali Baba, main character in the story in *1,001 Nights*, "Ali Baba and the Forty Thieves." A poor woodcutter, he discovers that the magic words "Open, Sesame" will open the door to a secret cave containing stolen treasure. The thieves plan to kill him but are outwitted by the slave girl Morgana.

Alien and Sedition Acts, 4 unpopular laws passed by the U.S. Congress in 1798 in response to the threat of war with France. The laws empowered the president to expel or imprison aliens, made naturalization more difficult, and punished those who wrote or spoke against the government.
See also: Kentucky and Virginia Resolutions.

Alienation, one's estrangement from society and from oneself. According to the 19th-century social and economic philosopher Karl Marx, the sale of labor power and the general conditions of production and exchange under capitalism deprive the individual of his or her essential humanity.

Alimentary canal, passage from the throat to the anus functioning in digestion and absorption of food.
See also: Digestive system.

Alinsky, Saul David (1909-72), U.S. pioneer in community organization, known for his early community action work in the Chicago stockyards area (1939). He founded a school for community organization in Chicago.

Alkali, water-soluble compound of an alkali metal that acts as a strong base and neutralizes acids. Common alkalis are sodium hydroxide (NaOH), ammonia (NH_3), and sodium carbonate (Na_2CO_3). Alkalis are used to manufacture glass, soap, paper, and textiles.

Alkaloid, any of a group of organic alkali compounds found in certain plants and fungi, containing carbon, hydrogen, and nitrogen. Many alkaloids are poisonous; others, such as morphine, nicotine, and cocaine, can be addictive. Other alkaloids are caffeine and quinine. In small doses alkaloids are powerful medicines, used as analgesics, tranquilizers, and cardiac and respiratory stimulants.

Alkalosis, condition wherein the concentration of alkali in the body cells and tissues is higher than normal.
See also: Acidosis.

Allah, Arabic name (*al-ilah*) for the supreme being, used by the prophet Muhammad to designate the God of Islam.

Allahabad (pop. 619,600), city in the state of Uttar Pradesh, northern India. Situated at the confluence of the sacred rivers Ganges and Jumna, Allahabad is the goal of many Hindu pilgrims and the site of India's oldest universities.

All-American Canal, waterway, completed 1940, that brings water 80 mi (130 km) from the Imperial Reservoir on the Colorado River to irrigate 500,000 acres (200,000 hectares) of the Imperial Valley, Calif. The canal also supplies water to San Diego. A branch delivering an equal amount of water to the Coachella Valley was opened in 1958.
See also: Imperial Valley.

Allegheny Mountains, central Appalachian range extending from southwest Virginia into north-central Pennsylvania. The Alleghenies average heights of 2,000 ft (610 m) in the north and more than 4,500 ft (1,372 m) in the south.

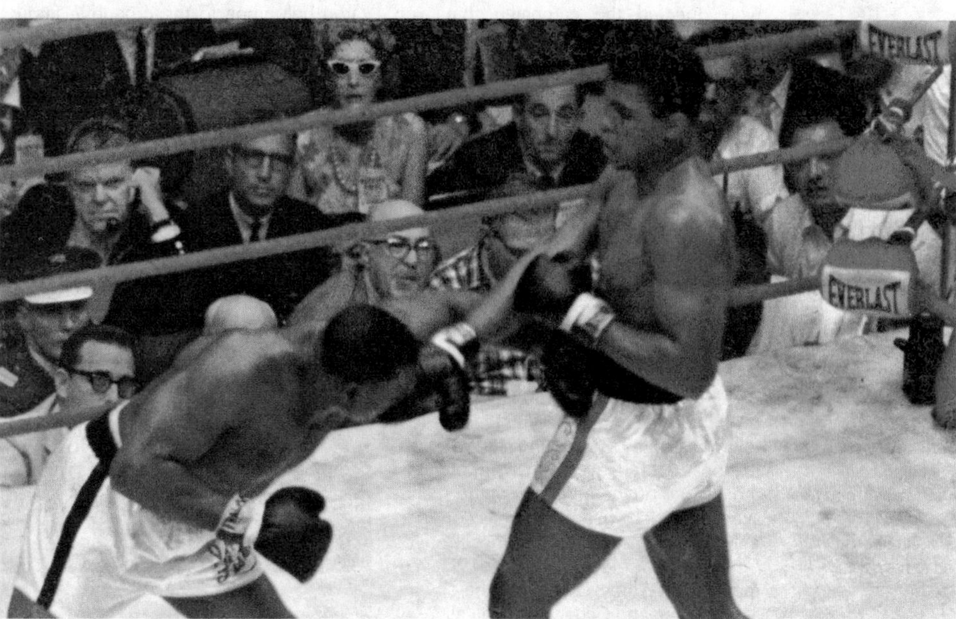

Muhammad Ali (at this time still named Cassius Clay) during his fight with Sonny Liston in 1964.

Allegheny River, river in west Pa., important transportation route before the railroads were built. In Pittsburgh, it joins the Monongahela to form the Ohio River.

Allegory, literary work in which characters and concrete images are used to represent abstract philosophical or moral notions. John Bunyan's *Pilgrim's Progress* and Edmund Spenser's *Faerie Queene* are classic English-language allegories.

Allen, Ethan (1738-89), American Revolutionary hero, leader of the Green Mountain Boys of Vermont. In 1775 he seized the British fort at Ticonderoga but was captured in an attack on Montreal. He unsuccessfully petitioned Congress for Vermont's statehood.
See also: Green Mountain Boys.

Allen, Richard (1760-1831), first bishop and founder of the African Methodist Episcopal Church. Born a slave, he was raised on a plantation in Delaware, becoming a Methodist at age 17. He bought his freedom (1786) and moved to Philadelphia, where he organized an Independent Methodist Church to better serve black people. He was ordained a minister in the Methodist Church (1799) and later founded the African Methodist Episcopal Church (1816), the first black denomination in the United States.
See also: Jones, Absalom.

Woody Allen in his film Manhattan

Allen, Woody (Allen Stewart Konigsberg; 1935-), U.S. comedian, author, and film director. A self-effacing wit established him as a major comedic talent of the 1960s and 1970s. Following a nightclub career he broke into films (1965) and wrote, directed, and starred in successes like *Bananas* (1971), the Academy Award-winning *Annie Hall* (1977), and *Crimes and Misdemeanors* (1989).

Allenby, Edmund Henry Hynman, 1st Viscount (1861-1936), British field marshal who directed the campaign that won Palestine and Syria from the Turks in World War I. From 1919 to 1925 he was British high commissioner in Egypt.

Salvador Allende in front of the Government Palace during the uprising of Chilean troops which led to his death.

Allende Gossens, Salvador (1908-73), Marxist founder of the Chilean Socialist Party, president of Chile (1970-73). His radical reform program disrupted the economy; strikes and widespread famine led to a military coup and to his death, reportedly by murder or suicide.

Allentown (pop. 686,688), commercial and industrial city in eastern Pennsylvania, seat of Lehigh County, situated on the Lehigh River about 50 mi (80 km) northwest of Philadelphia. Founded in 1762, Allentown has many Revolutionary War associations. Settled by German immigrants, the city lies on the perimeter of the "Pennsylvania Dutch" region. There is considerable light industry, and factories produce trucks, buses, electronic equipment, cement, and textiles. Located in the city are Muhlenberg and Cedar Crest colleges.

Allergy, abnormal sensitivity to specific foreign material (an allergen). The allergy sufferer produces an antibody that combines with antigens, causing certain chemicals to be released, producing allergy symptoms. In the skin, this appears as eczema or urticaria (hives); in the nose and eyes, hay fever results; in the gastrointestinal tract, diarrhea may occur. In the lungs, there may be a spasm of the bronchi (airways), leading to the wheezing and breathlessness of asthma. Common allergens include drugs (penicillin, aspirin), foods (shellfish), plant pollens, animal furs or feathers, insect stings, and the house dust mite.

Alliance for Progress, program to aid the economic and social development of Latin America, instituted by President John F. Kennedy in 1961 and brought into being when 22 nations and the United States signed the Charter of Punta del Este. The Latin American countries drew up development plans and guaranteed the larger part of capital costs, the United States meeting the remainder. Most U.S. funds are administered by the Agency for International Development, and since 1970 the Organization of American States (OAS) has also reviewed and coordinated programs.
See also: Organization of American States.

Allies, during World War I, nations bound together in opposition to the Central Powers. The Allies included the members of the Triple Entente, as well as Serbia, Belgium, Japan, Italy, and, as an "associated power," the United States. During World War II "Allies" was the popular term for some 25 nations that opposed the Axis powers. The major nations among the Allies were the United States, Britain, Russia, China, and later, the Free French. These 5 became the permanent members of the UN Security Council, established in 1945.

Alligator, either of 2 species of aquatic, carnivorous, lizardlike reptiles (genus *Alligator*) belonging to the crocodile family.

American alligator

The American alligator (*A. mississipiensis*), which lives in the southeastern United States, generally reaches a length of 9 ft (2.7 m), but the rare Chinese alligator (*A. sinensis*) is much smaller. An adult American alligator is gray and dark green in color, weighs about 500 pounds, and lives to 50 or 60 years old. The females make excellent mothers and protect the newborn for over a year. Alligators like to eat fish, frogs, turtles, birds, and small mammals.

Alliluyeva, Svetlana (1926-), daughter of Joseph Stalin and his second wife Alliluyeva. She defected from the USSR to the United States in 1966. Her *Twenty Letters to a Friend* (1967) described her life in Moscow and the reasons for her departure. *Only One Year* (1969) tells of her life after her defection. In 1984 she returned to the USSR.

Allopathy, standard form of medical practice, producing a condition incompatible with or antagonistic to the condition being treated; the opposite of homeopathy.
See also: Homeopathy.

Allotropy, occurrence of an element in 2 or more forms (allotropes) that differ in their crystalline or molecular structure. Allotropes may have strikingly different physical or chemical properties. Allotropy in which the forms are stable under different conditions and are reversibly interconvertible at certain temperatures and pressures is called anantiotropy. Notable examples of allotropy are diamond and graphite (allotropes of carbon) and oxygen and ozone.

Alloy, combination of metals with each other or with nonmetals, such as carbon or phosphorus, and formed by mixing the molten components. An alloy's properties can be adjusted by varying the proportions of the constituents. Very few metals are used today in a pure state. The most common alloys are the different forms of steel, all of which contain a large proportion of iron and small amounts of carbon and other elements. Brass and bronze, 2 well-known alloys of copper, are still used in industry.
See also: Metallurgy; Permalloy.

Allspice, dried berry of the pimento, an evergreen tree (*Pimenta officinalis*) of the myrtle family, used as a spice and for medicinal purposes.
See also: Pimento.

Allston, Washington (1779-1843), U.S. painter. After studying in London and Rome, he lived in the Boston area. He was noted for paintings on biblical and classical themes, such as *Belshazzar's Feast* and *The Deluge*. He was one of the first romantics in the United States to show a preference for classical landscapes in the style of Claude Lorrain and Salvator Rosa.

Alluvial fan, fan-shaped deposit of sediment composed of gravels, sands, and silts.

When a stream suddenly diminishes in speed before entering a large body of water or a valley, an alluvial fan is formed.

Alluvium, sand, mud, or other earthly material deposited by rivers and streams, especially in the lower parts of their courses. The deltas of some rivers, for example, the Ganges, the Nile, and the Mississippi, consist of great masses of alluvial deposits. The meadows or plains flanking many rivers have been built up of alluvium and often receive further accumulations during floods.

Almagro, Diego de *see:* Pizarro, Francisco.

Almanac, originally, a calendar giving the position of the planets, the phases of the moon, etc., particularly as used by navigators (nautical almanacs), but now any yearbook of miscellaneous information, often containing abstracts of annual statistics.
See also: Banneker, Benjamin.

Almond, tree (*Prunus amygdalus*) of the rose family, the seed of whose fruit is used as food and flavoring and for medicinal purposes. It usually grows 10-20 ft (3-6 m) high and has spear-shaped, finely serrated leaves on thorny branches. The large flowers usually occur in pairs and are rose to white in color. It is native to Asia but grows well in California and the Mediterranean region.

Aloe plant

Aloe, any of the succulent plants (genus *Aloe*), of the lily family. Aloes are natives of warm climates and especially abundant in Africa. Some aloes are used medicinally for treatment of burns, as insect repellents, and for pigment.

Alpaca (*Lama pacos*), South American hoofed herbivorous mammal, closely related to the llama. It has a long body and neck, and is about 3 ft (1 m) high at the shoulder. Its long, thick coat of black, brown, or yellowish hair provides valuable wool. All alpacas are domesticated, living in the Andes above 13,000 ft (3,962 m).
See also: Llama; Vicuña.

Alphabet (from first 2 Greek letters, *alpha* and *beta*), set of characters intended to represent the sounds of spoken language. The chief alphabets of the world are Roman (Latin), Greek, Hebrew, Cyrillic (Slavic), Arabic, and Devanagari (used for Sanskrit). Alphabets probably originated around 2000 B.C. Hebrew, Arabic, and other written languages sprang from an alphabet that appeared around 1500 B.C. Greek was derived from the Phoenician alphabet, which appeared around 1700 B.C. Roman letters were derived from Greek and from Etruscan, also a descendant of the Greek. Most of the letters used in English are from the Latin alphabet. The Cyrillic alphabet, used for Slavic languages, also derives from the Greek.

Alpha Centauri, star 4.3 light-years (about 26 trillion miles) from the earth; only the sun is nearer. It is the brightest star in the constellation Centaurus and the third brightest star in the sky.

Alpha Orionis *see:* Betelgeuse.

Alpha particle (α-, or alpha ray), one of the particles emitted in radioactive decay. It is identical with the nucleus of the helium atom, consisting of 2 protons plus 2 neutrons bound together. A moving alpha particle is strongly ionizing and so loses energy rapidly in traversing through matter. Natural alpha particles will traverse only a few centimeters of air before coming to rest.
See also: Radiation; Radioactivity; Nuclear energy.

Alphonsus Liguori, Saint (1696-1787), Italian priest who founded the Congregation of the Most Holy Redeemer (Redemptorist Order), a society of missionary preachers working with the rural poor. He was canonized in 1839.

Alps, Europe's largest mountain system, 650 mi (1000 km) long and 30-180 mi (50-290 km) wide. Its fold mountains resulted from earth movements in the Tertiary period. The Western Alps run along the French-Italian border and include Mont Blanc, the highest Alpine peak at 15,771 ft (4,807 m). The Central Alps run northeast and east through Switzerland. The Eastern Alps extend through southern Germany, Australia, and northern Italy into Yugoslavia. Peaks are snowy and etched by ice action. The Alps are known for their many glaciers, glacially deepened valleys, and magnificent scenery.

Alsace-Lorraine (pop. 4,000,000), region in northeast France occupying 5,608 sq mi (14,525 sq km) west of the Rhine. It produces grains and grapes; timber, coal, potash, and salt (Vosges Mts.); iron ore; and textiles. Metz, Nancy, Strasbourg, and Verdun are the chief cities. The people are of French and German origin. France and Germany have long disputed control of the area. In medieval times both Alsace and Lorraine were part of the Holy Roman Empire. France took Alsace after 1648 and Lorraine in 1766. Germany seized most of the region in 1871 in the Franco-Prussian War, lost it to France after World War I, regained control in World War II, then lost it again.

Alston, Walter Emmons (1911-84), baseball manager. The low-keyed man of baseball, he led the Brooklyn (later Los Angeles) Dodgers to 7 National League pennants and 4 World Series championships (1955, 1959, 1963, and 1965).

Altai Mountains, mountain system in central Asia stretching across part of the USSR and the Mongolian People's Republic. Consisting of a number of parallel ranges, the Altai region is similar in geological character to the Alps but covers a larger area. The highest peak is Mt. Belukha (15,157 ft/4,620 m). Rich in minerals (gold, silver, copper, tin, lead, zinc, iron), the Altai Mountains supply the Soviet Union with large quantities of metals, particularly lead and zinc.

Altamira, cave near Santander, northern Spain, inhabited during the Aurignacian, upper Solutrean, and Magdalenian periods

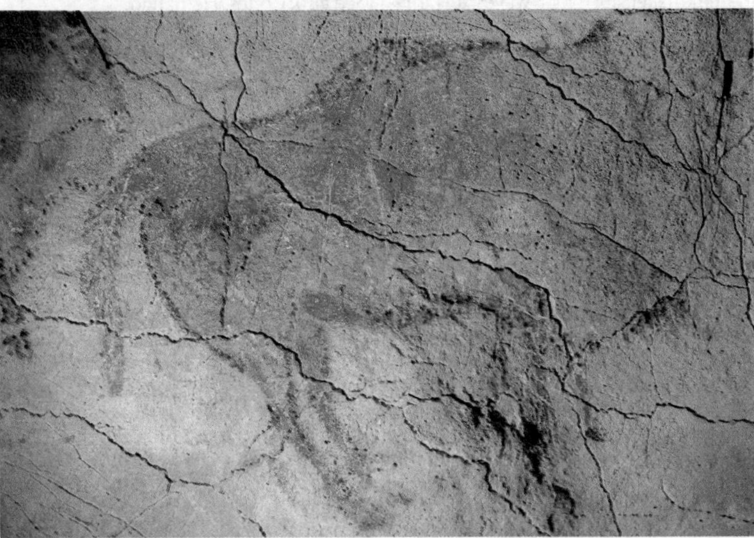

Altamira cave painting of a bison dating from 12,000 B.C.

(14,000 B.C.-10,000 B.C.). In 1879 the daughter of an amateur archaeologist discovered the striking cave paintings, believed to date from the Magdalenian period. They skillfully depict larger-than-life bulls, boars, and horses, among other paleolithic animals.

Alternating current, electrical signal that reverses direction at regular intervals. The frequency of alternation is measured in cycles per second (hertz); U.S. household current is 60 hertz.

Alternation of generations, in many lower plants and animals, alternation of 2 distinct forms. One form reproduces sexually and gives rise to the other form, which reproduces asexually. The offspring of the generation that reproduces asexually usually reproduce sexually again, but under certain conditions several asexual generations may follow each other.
See also: Plant.

Altgeld, John Peter (1847-1902), U.S. political leader and jurist who sought to defend the individual against abuses of governmental power and vested interests. As a Cook County, Ill. superior court judge, he argued that legal practice was weighted against the poor. Elected Democratic governor of Illinois (1892), he backed labor and championed reform, arousing controversy by freeing three anarchists imprisoned for Chicago's Haymarket Affair Riot of 1886 and by opposing President Cleveland's use of troops to crush the Pullman strike of 1894.

Altimeter, instrument used for estimating the height of an aircraft above sea level. Most are modified aneroid barometers and work on the principle that air pressure decreases with increased altitude, but these must be constantly recalibrated during flight to take account of changing meteorological conditions (local ground temperature and air pressure). Radar altimeters, which compute absolute altitudes (the height of the aircraft above the ground surface immediately below) by measuring the time taken for radar waves to be reflected to the aircraft from the ground, are essential for blind landings.
See also: Barometer.

Altoona (pop. 130,542), city in Blair County, south-central Pennsylvania, at the foot of the Allegheny Mountains, about 90 mi (145 km) east of Pittsburgh. First settled in 1849 as a construction camp for the Pennsylvania Railroad, it was incorporated as a city in 1868. Altoona is noted for the manufacture and repair of locomotives and railway cars. Bituminous coal deposits are found nearby.

Alum, class of double sulfates containing aluminum and such metals as potassium, ammonium, and iron.
See also: Salt, Chemical.

Alumina, or aluminum oxide, chemical compound (Al_2O_3). Found in bauxite ore, it is used in the production of aluminum, and also as an abrasive in ceramics.
See also: Aluminum.

Aluminum, chemical element, symbol Al; for physical constants see Periodic Table. Aluminum in the form of its compounds has been used for hundreds of years. Potassium aluminum sulfate, the most common alum, continues to be used in medicine as an astringent, and as a mordant in dyeing. Aluminum was first isolated by Oersted in 1825 although in an impure form. It occurs primarily in the form of complex silicates, and is the third most abundant element on earth. The principal ore of aluminum is *bauxite,* a hydrated oxide. Aluminum is a soft, tin-white, reactive, metal, the most abundant metal in the earth's crust. Aluminum is prepared by electrolysis of *alumina* (aluminum oxide) in fused *cryolite,* a procedure known as the Hall-Héroult process. Aluminum oxide occurs naturally in other important and useful forms as ruby, sapphire, corundum, and emery. Aluminum has many valuable properties which account for its wide use. It is second in malleability and sixth in ductility of all metals. It is light and a good electrical conductor. Since aluminum is soft, it is almost always alloyed with small amounts of other elements. It is the second most important metal after iron.

Alva or **Alba, Fernando Alvarez de Toledo, Duke of** (1507?-82), Spanish general who tyrannized the Netherlands. During his brutal campaign against rebellious Dutch Protestants (1567-73), he executed some 18,000 people. Hated for his atrocities and harsh taxes, and harassed by William the Silent's liberation army, Alva was recalled to Spain in 1573. In 1580 he conquered Portugal for Spain.

Alvarado, Pedro de (1485-1541), Cortés's chief lieutenant in the conquest of Mexico (1519- 21) and leader of the force that seized what are now Guatemala and El Salvador (1523-24). As governor of Guatemala he instituted forced Indian labor and founded many cities.
See also: Cortés, Hernando.

Alvarez, Luis Walter (1911-88), U.S. physicist awarded the 1968 Nobel Prize for physics for work on subatomic particles, including the discovery of transient resonance particles. He helped develop much of the hardware of nuclear physics. During World War II he worked on the development of radar and on the Manhattan (atomic bomb) Project.
See also: Bubble chamber.

Alzheimer's disease, progressive, incurable disease of the brain, the most common cause of premature senility. Its symptoms may include loss of memory, changes in personality, impaired language and motor skills, loss of control of bodily functions, and unresponsiveness. Currently it is difficult to diagnose and there is no specific treatment.
See also: Senility.

AMA *see:* American Medical Association.

Amadís of Gaul, Spanish romance of chivalry. Garci Ordóñez de Montalvo is credited with the first known version, *The Four Books of the Virtuous Knight Amadís* (1508), although some evidence suggests that the story of Amadís, the medieval knight, may have been in circulation since the late 14th century. Cervantes' *Don Quixote* owes much to *Amadís.*

Amado, Jorge (1912-), Brazilian novelist, author of *The Violent Land* (1942), *Gabriela, Clove and Cinnamon* (1958), and *Doña Flor and Her Two Husbands* (English, 1969). His books are particularly concerned with the plight of the poor.

Amalfi (pop. 6,000), seaport in the Campania region of Italy, on the Gulf of Salerno, near Naples. Built on a steep mountain slope and having a mild climate, it is a popular tourist center along the Amalfi Drive from Sorrento to Salerno. Amalfi became an important commercial and maritime center during the Middle Ages, for a time even rivaling Venice.

Amalgam, alloy of mercury with another metal, commonly used for tooth fillings.
See also: Metallurgy.

Amaranth, common name for plants of genus *Amaranthus,* including pigweed as well as plants grown as cereal and as ornamentals; also, a poetical name for a flower that never fades.
See also: Pigweed; Tumbleweed.

Amarillo (pop. 187,547), largest city and commercial center of the Texas Panhandle. Amarillo's industries include oil, natural gas, and copper refining, as well as livestock and grains. The city offers various music and art facilities and is home to several colleges and universities. Amarillo was founded in 1887 and rapidly grew in the early 1900s with the discovery of oil .

Amaryllis,family of bulbous-rooted plants with lilylike flowers. Among the best-known of the 1,200 species are the true amaryllis, the narcissus, and the snowdrop.
See also: Narcissus; Jonquil.

Amasis II (569-525 B.C.), Egyptian pharaoh of the 26th dynasty. During his long reign, he developed strong ties with Greece, using mercenaries and maintaining relations with various Greek states. Egypt prospered under his enlightened rule and skilled diplomacy. He thwarted an invasion by Nebuchadnezzar, added Cyprus to his kingdom, and through marriage became very influential in Cyrene. He was the last great Egyptian ruler before the Persian conquest, which occurred soon after his death. Amasis (or Ahmose) is also the name of the lesser-known pharaoh (c.1580-87 B.C.) who rid Egypt of the Hyksos conquerors.

Amateur Athletic Union (AAU), U.S. nonprofit organization, founded in 1888, that promotes and encourages amateur sports. The AAU sponsors the annual Junior Sports and Junior Olympic Games and other athletic competitions and presents the James E. Sullivan Award annually to the country's outstanding amateur athlete.

Amazon River, world's second-longest river (3,900 mi/6,280 km). The Amazon rises in Andean Peru near the Pacific Ocean and flows east through the world's largest equatorial rain forest to the Atlantic Ocean. It is also the world's largest river in volume and drainage area. Its basin drains 40% of South America, and it has hundreds of tributaries. Most of the Amazon is navigable, and oceangoing vessels can travel 2,300 mi (3,700 km) to Iquitos in Peru. Other ports are Belém and Manaus in Brazil. The Amazon is important for commerce in hardwoods and other forest products.
See also: Brazil.

Amazons, in Greek mythology, race of warrior women living in the Black Sea area. Their name derives from the Greek word for "breastless," due to their alleged practice of removing the right breast to aid archery. For his ninth labor, Heracles (Hercules) was required to take the girdle of the Amazonian queen Hippolyta. Amazons fought on the side of Troy in the Trojan War.

Amber, fossilized resin from prehistoric evergreens. Brownish-yellow and translucent, it is highly valued and can be easily cut and polished for ornamental purposes. Its chief scientific importance is that fossil insects up to 20 million years old have been found embedded in it.
See also: Resin.

Ambergris, waxy solid formed in the intestines of sperm whales, perhaps to protect them from the bony parts of their squid diets. When obtained from dead whales, it is soft, black, and foul-smelling, but on weathering (as when found as flotsam) it becomes hard, gray, and fragrant, and is used as a perfume fixative and in the East as a spice. The heaviest piece of ambergris found in the intestine of a sperm whale weighed 1,003 lb (455 kg).
See also: Whale.

Amberjack (genus *Seriola*), large, elongated fish found in tropical oceans. The amberjack's superior swimming and fighting abilities make it a popular game fish. Of the approximately 12 species of amberjacks, the greater amberjack (*S. dumerili*) is the largest, reaching a weight of more than 150 lb (68 kg) and a length of more than 5 ft (1.5 m).

Ambrose, Saint (c. A.D. 340-397), important Father of the Latin Church. A Roman governor who became the influential bishop of Milan, he attacked imperial moral standards and strengthened the position of the Church amid the ruins of the Roman Empire by his preaching and writing. St. Augustine was one of his converts.

Ambrosia, fabled food of the ancient Greek gods, which conferred immortality on those who partook of it; hence, anything pleasing to the taste or smell.
See also: Nectar.

Ameba, or amoeba, microscopic, one-celled organism that lives in moist earth, water, and parasitically in the bodies of animals. The ameba is a shapeless cell of jellylike material (protoplasm) encased in a thin membrane. It constantly changes shape by forming temporary projections called pseudopods (false feet) used for feeding and locomotion.
The ameba reproduces by fission (splitting). Amebas are harmless to people, except for a type that inflames the lining of the large intestine, causing a disease called amebic dysentery.

Amendment, in legislation, change in a bill or motion under discussion, or in an existing law or constitution. In the U.S. Congress a bill already passed by one house may be amended by the second house. If the first house does not agree to this amendment, a conference committee, made up of members of both houses, is called to work out a compromise.
See also: Parliamentary procedure; Bill of Rights; Constitution of the United States.

America, the 2 major continents of the Western Hemisphere, North and South America (although the name is sometimes used to mean the United States). In 1507 the German geographer Martin Waldseemüller first gave the name to the area that is now Brazil in honor of the Italian navigator Amerigo Vespucci, who supposedly discovered much of South America.
See also: Vespucci, Amerigo.

America, patriotic song written in 1832 by the Massachusetts minister, Rev. Samuel Francis Smith, to the tune of the British national anthem, "God Save the Queen (King)."

America First Committee, organization that opposed U.S. involvement in World War II. Founded in 1940, it vigorously opposed the politics of President Franklin Delano Roosevelt. Much of its support came from the Hearst newspapers and the *Chicago Tribune*. The committee advocated isolationism and neutrality in European affairs. The Japanese attack on Pearl Harbor abruptly ended support for its activities.
See also: World War II

Amebic movement caused by internal cytoplasmic streaming. The cell surface is flexible and temporary extensions, or pseudopodia (Latin, "false feet"), are formed into which the cytoplasm flows.

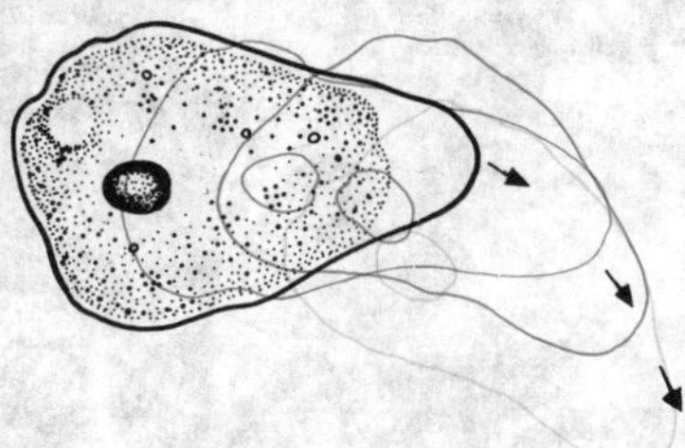

American Academy and Institute of Arts and Letters, organization to promote literature, music, and the fine arts in the United States. Based in New York City, it was formed in 1976 from the merger of the National Institute of Arts and Letters (founded 1898) and the American Academy of Arts and Letters (founded 1904). The organization, consisting of 250 members who serve for life, makes awards to American writers, artists, and composers, sponsors exhibits of their works, and purchases works to donate to museums.

American Academy in Rome, institute for independent work and advanced research in the arts, architecture, art history, and archaeology by U.S. artists and scholars in Rome, established in 1894 by the neoclassical architect Charles F. McKim as a school of architecture in Italy. By an act of Congress, the academy was officially incorporated in 1905.
See also: McKim, Charles Follen.

Statue of an Amazon

American Association of Retired Persons (AARP), private, nonprofit organization for people aged 50 and older. AARP's purpose is to improve the quality of life for the elderly through educational programs and other special services, including travel benefits, health insurance, a credit union, and pharmaceutical information. AARP, with headquarters in Washington, D.C., was founded in 1958.

American Automobile Association *see:* Automobile Association, American.

American Bar Association (ABA), voluntary national organization for members of the U.S. legal profession. Founded in 1878 at Saratoga Springs, N.Y., the group promotes the study and practice of jurisprudence and improvements in the administration of justice, and works to uphold the honor and standards of the profession. National headquarters are in Chicago. Its general policy-making body is made up of representatives from all state bar associations and acts through a board of governors. Standing committees study current legal issues. Official association publications include a legal yearbook and a monthly law journal.

American Booksellers Association (ABA), trade group primarily comprising bookstore owners and publishers, first founded in 1900 in New York City. It is active in defending First Amendment rights, providing education, research, and publications for people in the book business, as well as administering the annual ABA convention and tradeshow.

American Cancer Society *see:* Cancer Society, American.

The Amazon River meanders without restriction through a wide flood plain. These flooded areas receive rich deposits of silt from the receding waters, leaving fertile ground.

The people of the Amazon have fished for centuries in these waters. The Amazon is a freshwater home for millions of fish. The pirarucu, catfish, and the ferocious piranha are but a few of the species in the Amazon.

Deforestation in the Amazon is a direct threat to many rare animals. The "slash and burn" method to claim farmland is an environmental disaster to the "green lungs" of South America.
Projects for reforestation (top right) of the tropical rainforest cannot undo the damage against which such original inhabitants as the Kaiapo (bottom left) protest in vain.

American Civil Liberties Union (ACLU), organization founded in 1920 and dedicated to defending constitutional freedoms in the United States. Its work centers on providing legal aid in cases of violated civil liberties, especially those of political, religious, and racial minorities. From its founding the ACLU has participated in the nation's most important civil rights cases: the Scopes trial (1925), which challenged a Tennessee law barring the right to teach Darwin's theory of evolution in schools; the federal court test (1933) that ended censorship of James Joyce's *Ulysses*; and the landmark *Brown* v. *Board of Education* (1954), which successfully challenged the constitutionality of racially segregated schools. The organization generated controversy in 1978 by upholding the American Nazi Party's right to march in Skokie, Ill., and to display swastika symbols.

American Expeditionary Forces (AEF), name given to the U.S. forces serving in Europe during World War I. Its commander was General John Pershing. The first U.S. troops arrived in June 1917 and saw major action in May 1918, when they relieved the French at Château-Thierry and stopped a German advance. In June, some 6,000 U.S. marines were killed at Belleau Wood. U.S. forces were important in stemming the German counteroffensive in the second Battle of the Marne (July-Aug. 1918). By the end of the war the AEF held one-fourth of the line and had taken part in 13 battles, most of them major encounters. U.S. troops were at the front for a total of 200 days, with 1,993,000 men fighting at the end of the war. Over 100,000 members of the AEF were killed in action, a similar number died of disease (especially influenza), and more than 200,000 were wounded.
See also: Pershing, John Joseph; World War I.

American Federation of Labor and Congress of Industrial Organizations (AFL-CIO), powerful federation of labor unions created in 1955 by the merger of the AFL and CIO. Over 100 constituent unions in the United States, Mexico, Canada, and Panama represent about 15 million members. A national president, secretary-treasurer, and vice-presidents make up the executive council, which enforces policy decisions made at biennial conventions attended by several thousand delegates.
The organization's main objectives are more pay, shorter working hours, and better working conditions for employees, obtained by union-management agreements that preserve industrial harmony and prosperity. Each affiliated union conducts its own collective bargaining and determines much of its own policy. The AFL-CIO lobbies on such issues as social welfare, conservation, education, and international problems, and has backed political candidates.
The AFL, founded in 1886 under the leadership of Samuel Gompers, originally comprised only craft unions, excluding unskilled and semiskilled workers, whose numbers multiplied as mass production increased in the early 1900s. To cater to these workers, AFL dissidents in 1935 formed the Committee for Industrial Organization, later the Congress of Industrial Organizations, led by John L. Lewis. Laws hostile to organized labor led to the cooperation between and, in 1955, the merger of the AFL and CIO, with George Meany (head of AFL) as president. Despite the union membership of a large number of women, it was only in 1980 that a woman, Joyce Miller, was named to the AFL-CIO executive council.

American Indian Movement (AIM), civil rights organization in the United States and Canada, founded in 1968 to establish equal rights and improve living conditions of Native Americans. AIM has demanded the return of property rights as specified in U. S. and Canadian government treaties with various tribes, legal reform, and reform of education, employment, and health services for Native Americans.

American Labor Party, New York State left-wing political party (1936-56). Founded by labor leaders, it helped elect its member Fiorella LaGuardia mayor of New York in 1937 and 1941 and Herbert Lehman governor in 1938. In World War II it split over attitudes to the USSR: The right under David Dubinsky accused Sidney Hillman's left of being communist-controlled. The party disbanded in 1956.

American Legion, organization fostering the welfare, and protecting the rights of United States veterans of World War I, World War II, the Korean War, and the Vietnam War. Ongoing activities of the legion include building and maintaining community centers, parks, and recreation facilities; providing equipment for hospitals and other health care endeavors; care and help for disabled United States veterans; sponsorship of scout troops; annual oratory contests for high school students to promote study of the United States Constitution; and furtherance of education and employment services.

American Library Association, society "to extend and improve library service throughout the world." Founded in Philadelphia (1876) by Melvil Dewey, it is the world's oldest and largest library association and has had great influence on library development in English-speaking countries, as well as in Scan avia, the Netherlands, and Germany. With headquarters in Chicago, the organization has more than 50,000 members.

American literature see: United States literature.

American Medical Association (AMA), U.S. federation of state medical organizations. It was established in 1847 for the purpose of advancing medical knowledge, raising standards of medical education and practice, improving public health, and furthering the interests of the medical profession in general. AMA national headquarters are in Chicago Ill. Its various sections publish the weekly *Journal of the American Medical Association* (*JAMA*) and other specialized periodicals. Through its powerful national and state lobbies, the AMA has great influence on legislation.

American Museum of Natural History, institution in New York City founded in 1869 and dedicated to research and public education in anthropology and natural science. It is noted for its mounted specimens of birds and other animals from all over the world, fossil collections including dinosaur skeletons, its gem collection, and the Hayden Planetarium.

American Party, conservative U.S. political party, originally called the American Independent Party. Established in 1968, the party's purpose was to support the presidential candidacy of George C. Wallace, governor of Alabama. Wallace's platform was based largely on his opposition to desegregation of Alabama schools. The name was also used by the Know-Nothing Party of the 1850s.

American Philosophical Society, oldest surviving U.S. learned society, based in Philadelphia, where it was founded by Benjamin Franklin (1753). The U.S. counterpart of the Royal Society of London, it has nearly 600 U.S. and foreign members. It has an extensive library, much relating to Colonial science.

American Red Cross *see:* Red Cross.

American Revolution *see:* Revolutionary War in America.

American Samoa, unincorporated U.S. territory in the South Pacific, about 2,300 mi (3,700 km) southwest of Hawaii, with a total area of 76 sq mi (197 sq km). The territory consists of 7 islands: Tutuila (site of the capital, Pago Pago), the Manua group (Aununu, Ofu, Tau, Olosega), Rose, and Swains. The region is mountainous and tropical. The native Polynesians speak Samoan and English, live in villages, and practice Christianity.
The leading industry is tuna canning. Agricultural products include coconuts, bananas, and taro.
Samoa was divided between the United States and Germany, by treaty, in 1899; the eastern portion was administered by the U.S. Navy until 1951, when it passed to the jurisdiction of the Department of the Interior. American Samoans are nationals, but not citizens of the United States. They elect a governor, a legislature, and a nonvoting delegate to the U.S. Congress.
See also: Pacific Islands.

Americans for Democratic Action (ADA), independent political organization, founded in 1947, that supports liberal policies in government, promoting civil rights and opposing U.S. military involvement in developing countries. The ADA campaigns to elect liberal politicians. Its headquarters are in Washington, D.C.

American Society for the Prevention of Cruelty to Animals (ASPCA), organization founded in 1866 to prevent maltreatment of animals by enforcing laws designed to protect them, disseminating information, maintaining animal hospitals, and providing shelters and veterinary facilities. Its charter was granted by the New York State legislature and its operations are limited to that state. More than 600 organizations of a similar purpose exist in the United States.

American Society of Composers, Authors and Publishers (ASCAP), association that serves as a clearinghouse between creators and users of music. Founded in 1914, ASCAP grants licenses and collects fees to protect members from copyright infringement, covering performance as well as publication of music. The national headquarters are in New York City.

American System, term used by Henry Clay (1777-1852) for his program of economic nationalism, which provided protective tariffs and internal improvements such as roads and canals. For a time the American System had considerable support, and in President James Monroe's second term tariffs were increased and a national bank was reestablished. President John Quincy Adams's ideas went far beyond Clay's, but they antagonized westerners, who wanted the price for the public lands lowered, and Southerners, who were fearful of interference with slavery and who needed cheap imported manufactures. After Andrew Jackson became president in 1829, the provisions of the American System were not put into effect.
See also: Clay, Henry; Monroe, James.

America's Cup, international yachting trophy. The cup, the oldest trophy in international sports, was held continuously by the United States from the first race in 1851 until 1983, when the *Australia II* defeated the U.S. yacht *Liberty.* The U.S. yacht *Stars & Stripes* defeated Australia's *Kookaburra* in 1987 to regain the cup. In 1988 controversy surrounded the U.S. use of a 60-ft (20-m) catamaran, *Stars & Stripes*, which defeated the challenger, the 133-ft (44.4-m) monohull *New Zealand. New Zealand*'s team claimed the catamaran was illegal, but after several U.S. court rulings *Stars & Stripes* was awarded the cup. To avoid future controversy, all competitors will use 75-ft (25-m) monohulls with a 110-ft (36.6-m) mast in the May 1992 America's Cup competition.

America the Beautiful, patriotic song, with words written in 1893 by Katherine Lee Bates, and music by Samuel A. Ward.

Americium, chemical element, symbol Am; for physical constants see Periodic Table. Americium was synthesized by Glenn Seaborg and co-workers in 1944 by bombardment of plutonium-234 with alpha particles at the wartime Metallurgical Laboratory of the University of Chicago (now the Argonne National Laboratory). It is produced in quantity by neutron irradiation of plutonium isotopes in a nuclear reactor. Americium is a reactive, radioactive, metal, obtained by reducing its trifluoride with barium vapor. It is a member of the actinide series. The element must be handled with special care because of its great alpha and gamma activity. Americium is used in gamma radiography, glass thickness gages, and in smoke detectors. Thirteen isotopes of americium are known.

Amerigo Vespucci *see:* Vespucci, Amerigo.

Amethyst, transparent violet or purple variety of quartz, thought to be colored by iron or manganese impurities. A semiprecious gem, it is used to make jewelry. Amethysts are mined in Brazil, Uruguay, North America, and the USSR.

Amherst, Jeffrey Amherst Baron, (1717-97), British major-general who helped take Canada from the French. He commanded British forces at the capture of Louisburg on Cape Breton Island (1758), Ticonderoga and Crown Point (1759), and Montreal (1760). While governor-general of British North America (1760-63), he crushed a pro-French Indian uprising led by Pontiac.

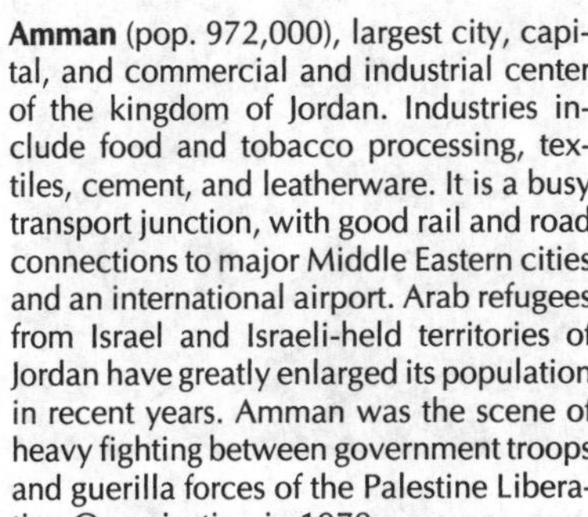

Amiens (pop. 136,400), city in northern France, capital of the Somme department on the Somme River 80 mi (130 km) north of Paris. An important trade and manufacturing center, Amiens has been noted since the 16th century for its linens, woolens, silks, and velvets. Its Cathedral of Notre Dame, begun c.1220, is one of the finest examples of French Gothic architecture.

Amin Dada, Idi (1925-), president of Uganda (1971-79). He led the military overthrow of President Milton Obote in 1971. A flamboyant and dictatorial ruler, he expelled Uganda's Asian middle class in 1972, called for the extinction of Israel in 1975, and purged many opponents. In 1975-76 he was president of the Organization of African Unity. Insurrectionists, aided by Tanzanian forces, drove out Amin in 1979. After his exile to Saudi Arabia, his whereabouts were uncertain.

Amine, chemical compound formed from ammonia (NH_3) by replacing 1 or more hydrogen atoms of the ammonia molecule with a corresponding number of hydrogen-carbon groups.

Amino acids, class of organic acids containing a carboxyl group ($COOH$) and 1 or more (NH_2) groups. Amino acids are synthesized in cells and are the basis of proteins. Amino acids are white crystalline solids that are soluble in water; they can act as acids or bases depending on the chemical environment. All amino acids (except glycine) contain at least 1 asymmetric carbon atom to which are attached the carboxyl group, the amino group, a hydrogen atom, and a fourth group that differs for each amino acid and determines its character. Amino acids can exist in 2 mirror-image forms. Generally only L-isomers (left-turning) occur in nature, but a few bacteria contain D-isomers (right-turning). Organisms link amino acids in chains called polypeptides and proteins. Digestion breaks down these linkages.
See also: Protein.

Amis, Kingsley (1922-), English novelist, poet, and critic. He emerged as a sharp satirist in *Lucky Jim* (1953), an attack on social and academic pretensions. Among his other works are *New Maps of Hell* (1960), *One Fat Englishman* (1964), *The Green Man* (1969), and *Jake's Thing* (1979).

Amethyst

Amish, conservative group of the Mennonite sect, founded by Jacob Ammann in Switzerland in the 1690s. In the 18th century members settled in what are now Indiana, Ohio, and Pennsylvania. Their farm communities reject modern life, including electricity, telephones, and cars.
See also: Mennonites; Pennsylvania Dutch.

Amman (pop. 972,000), largest city, capital, and commercial and industrial center of the kingdom of Jordan. Industries include food and tobacco processing, textiles, cement, and leatherware. It is a busy transport junction, with good rail and road connections to major Middle Eastern cities and an international airport. Arab refugees from Israel and Israeli-held territories of Jordan have greatly enlarged its population in recent years. Amman was the scene of heavy fighting between government troops and guerilla forces of the Palestine Liberation Organization in 1970.
The modern city is built on the site of the Rabbath Ammon, the capital of the ancient Ammonites. Named Philadelphia in the third century B.C., it prospered under Greek, Roman, and Byzantine rule. During the Middle Ages, after coming under Muslim control, it gradually declined to the status of a caravan village. Part of the Ottoman Empire until World War I, Amman became the capital of Transjordan, established as a British mandate in 1920. Amman remained the capital and royal residence when Jordan became independent in 1946. Its extensive Greco-Roman ruins include baths, a fortress, a temple dedicated to Hercules, a huge theater, and a Byzantine basilica.

Idi Amin Dada

Ammann, Othmar Hermann (1897-1965), U.S. engineer. He designed the George Washington Bridge in New York City (1931), the San Francisco Golden Gate Bridge (1935), and the Verrazano-Narrows Bridge in New York (1964).

Ammeter, instrument for measuring amperes of electric current. The most commonly used ammeter is of the permanent-magnet moving-coil type.
See also: Ampere; Electromagnetism.

Ammonia, chemical compound (NH_3), colorless acrid gas. Ammonia is used as a cleaning fluid (with water), as a fertilizer, a refrigerant, and to make ammonium salts, urea, and many drugs, dyes, and plastics.

Amnesia, partial or complete loss of memory. It can result from concussions, senility, severe illness, or physical or psychological trauma, and is of varying duration.

Amnesty International, organization founded in 1961 to aid political prisoners and others detained for reasons of conscience throughout the world. With thousands of members in the United States and around the world, it has advisory status with the UN and other international organizations. Amnesty International received the Nobel Prize for peace in 1977.

Poster for Amnesty International entitled The Cell *by Malsen.*

Amniocentesis, procedure of sampling the amniotic fluid surrounding a fetus by puncturing the abdomen of the pregnant woman with a very fine, hollow needle. Cells and other substances shed into the amniotic fluid by the fetus are used for detecting the presence in the fetal genes of such disorders as Down's syndrome, Tay-Sachs disease, and spinal malformations.
Amniocentesis also can be used to determine the sex of an unborn child with 98% accuracy.
See also: Genetic counseling.

Amoeba *see:* Ameba.

Amon, ancient Egyptian deity, sometimes depicted as a ram or a human with a ram's head. Chiefly worshipped in Thebes, he was identified with the sun god Re, and became known as Amon-Re, king of the gods. In Hellenistic times his temple and oracle were visited by many Greeks, who identified Amon with Zeus.

Amos (8th century B.C.), Hebrew prophet; also, a book of the Old Testament containing his life and teachings. A shepherd from Judah, Amos proclaimed that there was one God for all peoples. In neighboring Israel, he denounced corruption until expelled by the king.

Ampere (amp or A), unit for measuring the rate of flow of an electric current. One ampere is defined as the current in each of 2 parallel wires when the magnetic force between them is 2×10^{-7} newtons per meter. It is named after André Marie Ampère, the French scientist.
See also: Ammeter; Ohm's law.

Ampère, André Marie (1775-1836), French mathematician, physicist, and philosopher best remembered for many discoveries in electrodynamics and electromagnetism. He expanded Hans Oersted's experiment on the interaction between magnets and electric currents and investigated the force set up between current-carrying conductors. He also made contributions in the fields of statistics, chemistry, optics, and crystallography.
See also: Ampere; Electromagnetism.

Amphetamine, any of a group of stimulant drugs, including Benzedrine and Methedrine, derived from the chemical compound amphetamine ($C_9H_{13}N$). Amphetamines counteract fatigue, suppress appetite, speed up performance (hence the slang "speed"), and give the taker a false sense of confidence. Pronounced depression often follows use, encouraging psychological and then physical addiction. A paranoid psychosis resembling schizophrenia may result from prolonged use. Amphetamines have been used in the treatment of obesity and narcolepsy (a rare condition of abnormal sleepiness).

Amphibian, class of cold-blooded vertebrates, including frogs, toads, newts, salamanders, and caecilians. Typically they spend part of their life in water, part on land. They are distinct from reptiles in that their eggs must be laid in moist conditions, and that their soft, moist skins have no scales. The larval amphibian is usually solely aquatic; the adult is partly or entirely terrestrial, generally 4-legged, and carnivorous.

Amphibious warfare, coordinated use of land and sea forces to seize a beachhead, an area from which to carry on further military action. Although naval and ground forces have often cooperated since the earliest days of warfare, the strategy of modern amphibious military operations did not develop fully until World War II. Specially outfitted ocean vessels were constructed, and landing craft were designed, capable of making long voyages to transport troops, weapons, and supplies, and then unload them ready for combat if they met concentrated enemy opposition. Allied operations against the Japanese in the Pacific and in the landings in Italy and Normandy during World War II were typical of this strategy.

Amphibole, any of a group of silicate minerals with similar chemical compositions and characteristic optical properties. Amphiboles are usually found in lava or very old rock strata. They form long slender crystals, which in asbestos become fine fibers. Hornblende is the most common amphibole.

Amphioxus, or lancet, a small, primitive, fishlike sea animal (genus *Branchiostoma*), important as a possible descendant of the evolutionary link between invertebrates and vertebrates.

Amphitheater, open edifice built in the Roman Empire for public viewing of contests and spectacles (e.g., the Colosseum in Rome). Usually oval in form, it comprises a central arena surrounded by ascending rows of seats. Gladiators and animals used in the spectacles were held under the arena. The term is now used loosely for any large auditorium.

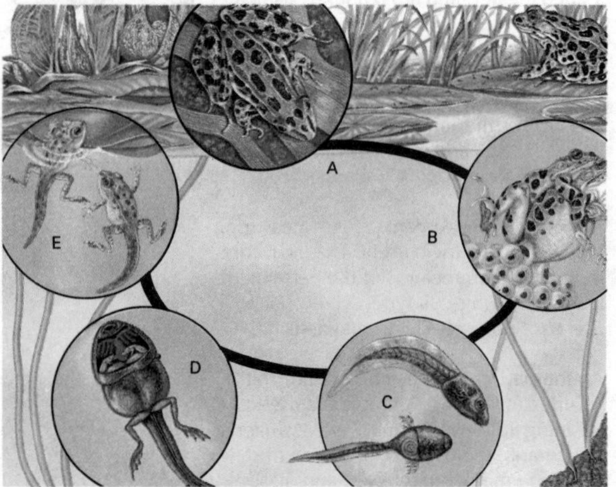

The North American leopard frog, an amphibian, lives on land in wet meadows but must remain near brooks and marshes to lay its eggs. The eggs are abandoned by the parents and left to develop into aquatic tadpoles, which after about three months, leave the water as land-living frogs.
A. Adult leopard frog in the long grass of a meadow adjacent to a marsh or pond.
B. Male (top) and female adult leopard frog during egg laying.
C. Tadpoles a few days after hatching.
D. Tadpoles eight weeks after hatching with part of ventral surface cut away to show internal gills; front limbs are still enclosed within body cavity.
E. Young frogs three months after hatching; all the limbs are developed but a tail is still present.

Ampicillin, semisynthetic antibiotic that is a derivative of penicillin, used to treat a wide range of bacterial infections. Ampicillin can kill some bacteria not effectively killed by other forms of penicillin, and is used to treat severe ear and sinus infections, meningitis in children, and various infections of the urinary, respiratory, and intestinal tracts. Among the microorganisms susceptible to ampicillin are *Salmonella*, several species of which cause a type of food poisoning, and *Salmonella typhosa*, the cause of typhoid fever. Although penicillin is still widely prescribed, its effectiveness has decreased somewhat since its introduction in 1961, because certain bacteria have begun to develop resistance to it.
See also: Penicillin.

Amritsar (pop. 594,800), city in Punjab state in northwest India. The center of the Sikh religion, it is the site of the *Amritsar* or sacred "pool of immortality" in which Sikhs immerse themselves as an act of purification. The city is also an important industrial center, known for textiles and carpets.

Amsterdam (pop. 691,700), capital and largest city of the Netherlands, and one of Europe's great commercial, financial, and cultural centers. In the province of North Holland, it lies on the IJ and Amstel rivers, at the south end of Lake IJsselmeer. The city center is built on a series of concentric semicircular canals. Other canals link it to the Rhine River and the North Sea and make Amsterdam one of Europe's major ports. It is also a major rail center and has an international airport. Amsterdam is a diamond-cutting center and produces chemicals, machinery, bicycles, electronics, beer, and textiles. It has an important stock exchange, two universities, and about 50 museums, and is home to major collections of works by Rembrandt and Van Gogh. Amsterdam grew from a medieval fishing village, becoming a major city by the 17th century. Amsterdam was under German occupation 1940-45.
See also: Netherlands

Amtrak, official nickname of the National Railroad Passenger Corp., established by Congress in an effort to halt the deterioration of railroad passenger service. Amtrak began operations on May 1, 1971, with 150 intercity trains. It improved service and increased ridership but, like the private carriers it replaced, accumulated large deficits, and has required government subsidies.
See also: Railroad.

Amundsen, Roald (1872-1928), Norwegian polar explorer. He was the first person to reach the South Pole (Dec. 14, 1911), his party beating the ill-fated Robert F. Scott expedition by one month. In the Arctic he was the first to navigate the Northwest Passage (1903-6), later crossing the North Pole in the dirigible *Norge* (1926). He was killed in the Arctic during an air search for the Italian explorer Umberto Nobile.
See also: Antarctica.

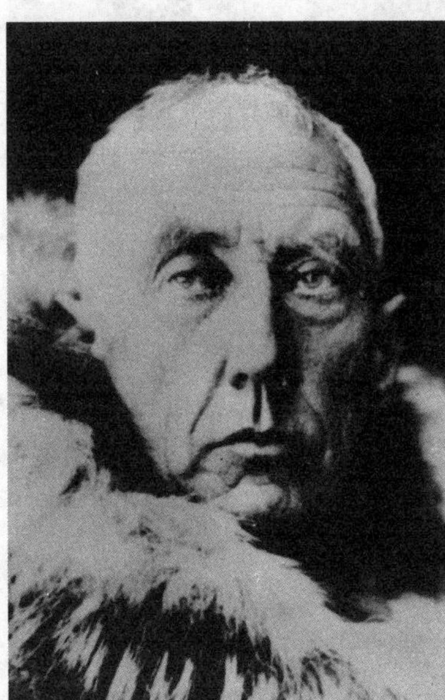
Roald Amundsen

Amur, river in northeastern Asia. Formed by the Shilka and Argun rivers in Mongolia, it flows east through the USSR for 2,700 mi (4,300 km) to empty into the Pacific. For more than half its course it forms the boundary between the USSR and China.

Amyotrophic lateral sclerosis, or Lou Gehrig's disease, progressive fatal disease in which there is degeneration of the motor nerve cells of the brain and spine, resulting in progressive muscular atrophy, paralysis, and death from asphyxiation.
See also: Gehrig, Lou.

Anabaptism, movement advocating baptism of adult believers rather than infants. The first group was formed in 1523 at Zürich by dissatisfied followers of Ulrich Zwingli. Most stressed the dictates of individual conscience, and urged nonviolence and separation of church and state. Despite widespread persecution, their doctrines spread, forming the basis of belief for the Mennonites in the Netherlands and the Hutterites in Moravia.
See also: Reformation.

Anabolic steroid, any of a group of steroids derived from the male sex hormone testosterone. They affect growth, muscle bulk, and protein buildup, and may be used in treating patients after major surgery or severe accidents or with debilitating disease, when there may be a breakdown of body protein. However, these drugs have been abused by athletes, and for this reason they are only prescribed by hospital doctors and are not available on normal prescriptions.

Anaconda, semiaquatic subfamily of the boa family. *Eunectes notaeus* is found in Paraguay and *Eunectes murinus*, probably the largest snake in the world—up to 25 ft (8 m) long and 3 ft (1 m) in circumference—throughout Brazil. Anacondas do not have a poisonous bite, but kill prey by constriction.
See also: Boa constrictor.

Anacreon (572-485? B.C.), Greek lyric poet who celebrated wine and love in mellow, simple verses. These were copied in the so-called Anacreontics, fashionable in the Hellenistic Age and again in 18th-century Europe. His main patrons were the tyrants of Samos and Athens.

Anaheim (pop. 2,410,556), city in Orange County, southern California, southeast of Los Angeles. Settled in the 1850s by German immigrant grape growers, it became a prosperous center for handling the local citrus fruit. Now a tourist center, it is home to Disneyland (built 1955), the California Angels baseball team, and the Los Angeles Rams football team. Its diversified industry includes chemicals, hardware plants, electronics, and aircraft engineering.

Analog computer, computer that operates on data by representing them with physical quantities such as voltages. Most computers are now digital rather than analog.

Anarchism, political belief that government should be abolished and the state replaced by the voluntary cooperation of individuals and groups. Like socialists, anarchists advocate the abolition of the institution of private property. But unlike socialists, they believe that government is unnecessary and intrinsically harmful. Pioneers of modern anarchism included England's William Godwin (1756-1836), France's Pierre Joseph Proudhon (1809-65), and the Russian revolutionary Mikhail Bakunin (1814-76). Emma Goldman (1869-1940) and Alexander Berkman (1870?-1936) were activeU.S. anarchists who were deported for their actions (1919). After President William McKinley was assassinated by an anarchist in 1901, anarchists were barred from entering the United States. Although anarchism is now more important philosophically than politically, it has recently become linked with student radicalism in Europe and America.
See also: Nihilism.

Anastasia (1901-18?), Russian grand duchess. Daughter of the last tsar, Nicholas II, she was probably murdered with her family during the Revolution. Several women later claimed to be Anastasia, but none could prove her identity.
See also: Russian Revolution.

Anatomy, study of the structure of plants and animals. The word is derived from a Greek verb meaning to cut up, since dissection was the main source of anatomical knowledge. Anatomy is closely related to physiology, the investigation of the functions and vital processes of living organisms. Gross anatomy is the study of the structures that can be seen with the naked eye, and microscopic anatomy, the investigation of minute parts of organs and tissues with the aid of a microscope. Comparative anatomy systematically compares the structures of different organisms.
See also: Human body.

Anaxagoras (500-428 B.C.), Greek philosopher of the Ionian school, resident of Athens, who taught that the elements were infinite in number and that everything contained a portion of every other thing. He also postulated a basic moving force of the universe, *Nous* or Mind. He was the teacher of Pericles, Euripides, and reputedly, of Socrates.
See also: Socrates.

Anaximander (611?-547? B.C.), Greek philosopher, first to give a naturalistic, rather than mythological, explanation to natural processes. He believed that the origin of all things was a formless matter, which he called "indefinite." His later works anticipated the theory of evolution and certain laws of astronomy.

Anchorage (pop. 175,000), largest city in Alaska, located in the southern part of the state at the head of Cook Inlet. Founded in 1915 as the headquarters for the Alaska Railroad and incorporated in 1920, it is now the commercial and transportation center of Alaska, serving the state's coal, gas, and oil industries. During World War II, Anchorage became an important military and air defense center. Its international airport services heavy traffic in jets bound for the Orient, Canada, and other parts of the United States and for Europe by the transpolar route. Anchorage was severely damaged by an earthquake in 1964 that killed 131 people.
See also: Alaska.

In the Andes, the llama is valued for its wool and as a beast of burden.

Anchovy, small fish of the family Engraulidae, related to the herring family, exported from the Mediterranean for use as a seasoning and garnish. It is also found on the coast of Peru.

Ancient civilization, term used to describe history and culture prior to the fall of the Roman Empire. Achievements in art, mathematics, literature, and architecture from those times still influence the modern world. The cultures of Egypt, Mesopotamia, Greece, and Rome are instances of ancient civilizations.

Hans Christian Andersen

Andersen, Hans Christian (1805-75), Danish writer, best remembered for his 168 fairy tales. Based on folklore and observation of people and events in Andersen's life, they have a deceptively simple, slyly humorous style and often carry a moral message for adults as well as children. Among his best known stories are "The Ugly Duckling," "The Emperor's Clothes," and "The Red Shoes."

Anderson, Carl David (1905-), U.S. physicist who shared the 1936 Nobel Prize in physics for the discovery of the positron (1932). Later he was codiscoverer of the first meson.
See also: Dirac, Paul Adrien Maurice.

Anderson, Dame Judith (1898-), Australian-born actress who worked in the United States. She is best known for her tragic roles in the plays of Eugene O'Neill and Shakespeare and in Robinson Jeffers's version of *Medea* (1947).

Anderson, Elizabeth Garrett (1836-1917), one of the first English women to become a doctor (1865). She helped establish the place of women in the profession and founded a women's hospital and a medical school for women.

Anderson, John Bayard (1922-), U.S. politician. He represented an Illinois district in the House of Representatives 1961-81, serving as chairman of the House Republican Conference 1969-79. Always a fiscal conservative, he gradually became a liberal on social and defense issues. After losing a bid for the Republican presidential nomination in 1980, he ran for president as an independent and polled about 7% of the popular vote.

Anderson, Marian (1902-), U.S. contralto. Overcoming the handicaps of poverty and discrimination, she became an international singing star in the 1930s. In 1939, Anderson was refused permission to perform in the DAR Constitution Hall, in Washington, D.C. Through the sponsorship of Eleanor Roosevelt and Secretary of the Interior Harold Ickes, Anderson sang from the steps of the Lincoln Memorial to a massive crowd of people of all races. She was awarded the Springarn Medal by the National Association of Colored People for the highest achievement by a black American (1939).
In 1955 she became the first African American to sing a leading role with, and be named a permanent member of, the Metropolitan Opera. She also served as alternate delegate to the UN in 1958, and won the UN peace prize in 1977.

Anderson, Maxwell (1888-1959), U.S. playwright. After early realistic plays, he concentrated on the revival of verse drama, achieving some success with such plays as *Elizabeth the Queen* (1930), *Winterset* (1935), *High Tor* (1936), and *The Bad Seed* (1954).

Anderson, Sherwood (1876-1941), U.S. writer whose novels and short stories deal largely with the rebellion of individuals against contemporary industrial society. He is best remembered for the novel *Winesburg, Ohio* (1919), which details the frustrations of small-town Midwestern life, and such story collections as *The Triumph of the Egg* (1921) and *Horses and Men* (1923). Other novels include *Poor White* (1920) and *Dark Laughter* (1925).

Andes, South America's largest mountain system, 4,500 mi (7,200 km) long and averaging 200-250 mi (320-400 km) wide, near the west coast and running almost the entire length of the continent. Aconcagua (22,835 ft/6,960 m) is the highest peak in the Western Hemisphere. The Andes rose largely in the Cenozoic era (the last 70 million years), and volcanic eruptions and earthquakes suggest the range is still rising. The South Andes divide Chile and Argentina. The Central Andes form 2 ranges flanking the high Bolivian plateau (the Altiplano), once home to the Incan civilization. The North Andes divide in Colombia and form four ranges ending in the Caribbean area. Many high Andean peaks are jagged and snowy, and glaciers fill some southern valleys. The region is an important source of copper, silver, and tin, and oil has been found in the north.

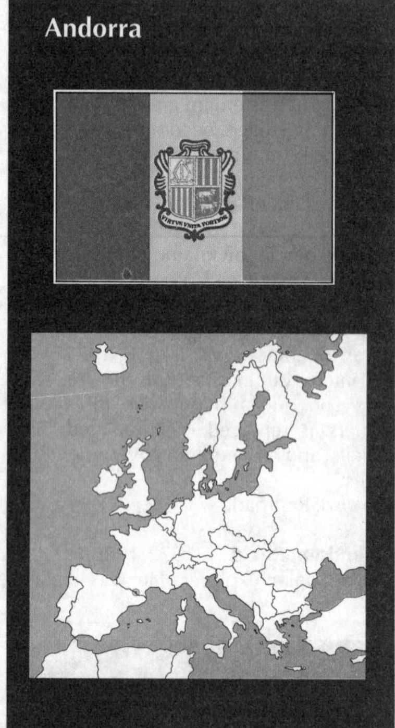

Capital:	Andorra la Vella
Area:	180 sq mi (465 sq km)
Population:	50,000
Government:	co-principality
GNP:	U.S. $340,000,000
Per capita:	U.S. $9,000

Andorra (pop. 47,000), tiny European principality (180 sq mi/465 sq km) in the eastern Pyrenees along the border between France and Spain. The Andorrans speak Catalan, French, and Spanish. Andorra uses both the French franc and the Spanish peseta as currency. The country attained autonomous status under Charlemagne, and since 1278 has been a co-principality, under the joint sovereignty of the Bishop of Urgel in Spain and, in modern times, the French chief of state. Andorra's terrain is extremely mountainous, pocketed by gorges and a few fertile valleys; the average altitude of the whole country is above 6,000 ft (1,800 m). The Valira River, flowing into Spain, has a sizable hydroelectric potential, still little exploited. Tobacco is Andorra's main money crop; rye and barley, grapes, potatoes, and sheep and cattle are also important. Other assets include iron and lead deposits, quarries, trout and lake salmon, and extensive pine woods. In recent decades tourism has brought new commercial affluence. The capital is the township of Andorra la Vella (Andorra-la-Vielle).

Clocktower in the village of Encamp in Andorra.

Andrada é Silva, José Bonifácio de (1763-1838), Brazilian geologist and statesman, known as the father of Brazilian independence. He helped create an independent monarchy under Pedro I, whom he served as prime minister (1822-23) until exiled for his democratic views. He was later tutor to Pedro II.

André, John (1750-80), English army officer, hanged as a spy by the Americans during the Revolutionary War. He secretly met Benedict Arnold behind American lines to arrange Arnold's surrender of West Point but was caught in civilian clothes, with incriminating papers.
See also: Revolutionary War in America.

Andrea del Sarto (1486-1531), leading 16th-century Florentine painter, influenced by Michelangelo and Albrecht Dürer and renowned for delicately colored church frescoes. He rivaled Raphael's classicism but foreshadowed Mannerism through his pupils Jacopo da Pontormo, Il Rosso, and Giorgio Vasari. Two of his well-known paintings are *Madonna of the Harpies* and *Holy Family.*

Andrea Doria, Italian luxury liner that sank on July 26, 1956, following an inexplicable collision with the *Stockholm,* a Swedish liner, about 45 mi (72 km) south of Nantucket Island; 51 people died. In 1981 a salvage operation run by Peter Gimbel and his wife, Elga Andersen, raised the ship's safe; further work was abandoned because of dangerous conditions.

Andretti, Mario (1940-), Italian-born U.S. race car driver. His many achievements include winning the United States Auto Club national driving championship (1965, 1966, 1969) and the Grand Prix world driving championship (1978). Andretti also finished first in the Daytona 500 (1967) and Indianapolis 500 (1969).

Andrew, John Albion (1818-67), U.S. statesman and antislavery proponent. A Unitarian, he became a staunch but moderate abolitionist and was active in organizing both the Free-Soil Party (1848) and the Republican Party (1854). He helped form the first regiment of free blacks in the North (54th Massachusetts) and ensured that black troops received the same pay as white soldiers. During Reconstruction he favored leniency toward the defeated Confederacy and opposed giving former slaves immediate citizenship.

Andrew, Saint (1st century A.D.), one of Jesus's 12 Apostles, formerly a fisherman and disciple of John the Baptist. He reputedly preached in what is now Russia and was martyred in Patras, Greece, on an X-shaped ("St. Andrew's") cross. He is the patron saint of Russia and of Scotland.
See also: Apostles.

Andrews, Charles McLean (1863-1943), U.S. historian. He stressed Colonial America's dependence upon Britain in works like *The Colonial Period of American History* (1943-41), the first volume of which won a Pulitzer Prize.

Andrews, Roy Chapman (1884-1960), U.S. naturalist, explorer, and author. From 1906 he worked for the American Museum of Natural History (later becoming its director, 1935- 41) and made important expeditions to Alaska, the Far East, and Central Asia. In Mongolia he discovered the first known fossil dinosaur eggs.

Andrews Air Force Base, headquarters for Air Force Systems Command. Established in 1943, this command, located in Camp Springs, Maryland, houses passenger aircraft for use by the president and other officials. Aircraft, missiles, and weapons systems for the United States Air Force are bought by the command at this base.

Andreyev, Leonid Nikolayevich (1871-1919), Russian novelist, short-story writer, and playwright. His work, including *The Seven That Were Hanged* (1908), reflects a basic pessimism and preoccupation with death.
See also: Russian literature.

Andric, Ivo (1892-1975), Yugoslav novelist who won the Nobel Prize for literature in 1961, largely for the epic quality of *The Bridge on the Drina.* His themes are humanity's insecurity and isolation in the face of change and death.

Androcles, in Roman legend, slave who was thrown to the wild animals in the Roman arena but was spared by a lion from whose paw he had once extracted a thorn. Amazed at the lion's behavior, the Roman officials pardoned Androcles and presented him with the lion.

Androgen *see:* Hormone.

Andromache, in Greek mythology, wife of Hector, prince and hero of Troy. After the fall of Troy, Achilles' son Neoptolemus took her as a slave to Epirus and later married her. After he divorced her, she became the wife of Hector's brother Helenus. Her farewell to Hector and mourning of his death are among the most celebrated passages in Homer's *Iliad.* Euripides also based a tragedy on her story.

Mario Andretti

Andromeda, spiral galaxy visible in the Andromeda constellation. The most distant object visible to the naked eye in northern skies, it is the nearest galaxy external to our own, but larger (120,000 light-years in diameter), and about 2 million light-years from earth.
See also: Astronomy.

The Andromeda nebula with its two elliptical companions (below and above right)

Andromeda, in Greek mythology, daughter of Cassiopeia and Cepheus, king of Ethiopia. Her mother boasted that she was more beautiful than the Nereids (sea nymphs). Out of revenge for this insult, Poseidon inundated the land and sent a sea monster to ravage the shore. Andromeda was rescued by Perseus, whom she then married.
See also: Mythology.

Andropov, Yuri Vladimirovich (1914-84), Soviet political leader, who became general secretary of the Communist party in 1982 after the death of Leonid Brezhnev and also, in 1983, chief of state. Earlier he had served as ambassador to Hungary (1954-57) and as head of the KGB, the Soviet security service (1967-82). In 1973 he became a full member of the Politburo, the governing body of the Communist party. As party leader, Andropov fought bureaucratic corruption, adopted a conciliatory attitude toward China, and tried to create a division between Western Europe and the United States on trade and military issues. After August 18, 1983, he was not seen in public.

Andros, Sir Edmund (1637-1714), British governor of New York (1674-81) and the Dominion of New England (1686-89). His attempt to curb the colonists' rights caused a rebellion. Imprisoned and sent to England for trial, he was acquitted and became governor of Virginia (1692-97).

Anemia, deficiency in the number of red blood cells or their hemoglobin content (the red substance that binds with oxygen), or both. Causes vary, but symptoms include pallor, fatigue, difficulty breathing, giddiness, heart palpitations, and loss of appetite.

Anemometer, instrument for measuring wind speed. The rotation type of mechanical anemometer estimates wind speed from the rotation of cups mounted on a vertical shaft. The sonic or acoustic anemometer depends on the velocity of sound in the wind. In laboratories, air flow is estimated from the change in resistance it causes by cooling an electrically heated wire.

Anemone, genus of wild or cultivated perennial herbs of the buttercup family (*Ranunculaceae*). Up to 3 ft (1 m) high, anemones have deeply cut, whorled leaves and white, pink, red, blue, or rarely, yellow flowers.

Anemone

Anesthesia, loss of sensation, especially the sensation of pain. The loss of sensation following injury or disease is known as pathological anesthesia, but anesthesia, either general or local, can also be drug-induced. General anesthesia is a reversible state of unconsciousness accompanied by muscle relaxation and suppression of reflexes. It is indispensable for many surgical procedures. Injections of short-acting barbiturates such as sodium pentothal are frequently used to speed the onset of anesthesia; inhaled agents, including halothane, ether, nitrous oxide, trichlorethylene, and cyclopropane, are then used to induce and maintain general anesthesia. Local anesthesia is induced by the chemical action of cocaine derivatives like novocaine or lidocaine. Regional anesthesia may be induced by blocking one or more large nerves or spinal nerve roots, as in epidural anesthesia for childbirth.
See also: Anesthesiology.

Anesthesiology, branch of medicine that deals with the administration before and during childbirth or surgery of anesthetics, drugs that dull or block sensation or anxiety. Anesthesiologists (physicians who administer anesthetics) use various techniques to anesthetize all or part of the patient's body during surgery, while monitoring and maintaining important body functions; their work may also involve resuscitation and intensive respiratory care.
See also: Anesthesia.

Aneurysm, localized dilation of a blood vessel, usually an artery, due to local fault in the wall through defect, disease, or injury, producing a pulsating swelling over which a murmur may be heard. Generally the structural integrity of the arteries enables them to resist the destructive effects of the repetitive hydraulic stress of circulation. Sometimes, however, the wall of an artery gives way, and a segment of the artery expands to form a balloon-like dilation: an aneurysm. If left untreated, the aneurysm may burst, causing death or grave disability. Even an unruptured aneurysm can lead to damage by interrupting the flow of blood or by impinging on and in some cases eroding nearby blood vessels, organs, or bone. The incidence of aneurysm rises with age.
See also: DeBakey, Michael Ellis; Stroke.

Angel, supernatural messenger and servant of the deity. Angels figure in Christianity, Judaism, Islam, and Zoroastrianism. In Christianity angels traditionally serve and praise God, but guardian angels may protect the faithful against the evil of the devil (the fallen angel, Lucifer). The hierarchy of angels is said to have 9 orders: cherubim, seraphim, thrones, dominions, virtues, powers, principalities, archangels, and angels.

Angel Falls, world's highest known waterfall (3,212 ft/979 m), on the Churin River in southeastern Venezuela, discovered by U.S. aviator Jimmy Angel in 1935. Its longest unbroken drop is 2,648 ft (807 m).

Angelfish, any of a group of freshwater tropical fish, and of several fish found in warm seas (family Chaetodontidae). The colorful freshwater angelfish is native to the Amazon basin.

Angell, Sir Norman (1874-1967), English economist and internationalist, awarded the Nobel Peace Prize in 1933. A journalist most of his life, he argued in *The Great Illusion* (1910) that war was futile and best prevented by the mutual economic interest of nations.

Angelou, Maya (1928-), U.S. author best known for her autobiographical books *I Know Why the Caged Bird Sings* (1970) and *Gather Together in My Name* (1974), which recount her struggles for identity as an African American in a hostile world.

Angevin, name of 2 medieval royal dynasties originating in the Anjou region of western France. The first ruled in parts of France and in Jerusalem and England. Henry II, son of Geoffrey of Anjou, became England's first Angevin (or Plantagenet) ruler in 1154. His descendants held power in England until 1485. The second branch, which began in 1266 when Charles, brother of Louis IX of France, became king of Naples and Sicily, ruled in Italy, Hungary, and Poland until the end of the 15th century.

Angina pectoris, severe but temporary attack of heart pain that occurs when the demand for oxygen by the heart muscle exceeds the ability of the coronary vessels to supply oxygen, due to narrowing or blockage of the vessels. The discomfort of angina pectoris, although highly variable, is most commonly felt beneath the sternum (breastbone). Pain may radiate to the left shoulder and down the inside of the left arm, straight through to the back, into the throat, the jaws, and the teeth. Anginal discomfort may be felt in the upper and lower abdomen, and occasionally in the right arm. Angina pectoris is characteristically triggered by physical activity and usually persists for no more than a few minutes, subsiding with rest.
See also: Heart.

Angiography, technique allowing visualization of blood vessels on X rays after injection of a radiopaque substance (one that shows up on X ray). It is usually performed on arteries or veins connected with organs such as the brain, heart, or kidneys, when a narrowing or blockage is suspected. Angiography is used to determine if deposits of substances such as cholesterol or calcium, known as plaque, are causing vessel narrowing, and has developed into a relatively safe and useful diagnostic technique. A typical angiographic procedure involves the passing of a catheter through the skin and into a vein or artery, where it is advanced to the structure being evaluated. Contrast material is injected into the area, making the section visible on X ray.

Angioplasty, set of techniques used in reconstructing damaged blood vessels, which may involve surgery, lasers, or tiny inflatable balloons. Usually, arteries that have become blocked by deposits of such substances as cholesterol or calcium—substances known as plaque—are reopened by inserting a catheter with an attached balloon into the diseased vessel where inflation of the balloon compresses or splits the deposits that clog the artery. Angioplasty is an important alternative to surgery for patients whose clogged coronary arteries predispose them to risk of a heart attack.

Angiosperm, member of a large class of seed-bearing plants (the flowering plants), its seeds developing completely enclosed in the tissue of the parent plant (rather than unprotected, as in the only other seed-bearing group, the gymnosperms). Containing about 250,000 species distributed throughout the world, from tiny herbs to huge trees, angiosperms are the dominant land flora. There are 2 subclasses: monocotyledons (with 1 leaf) and dicotyledons (with 2).

Angkor, extensive ruins from the ancient Khmer Empire in northwestern Cambodia, covering 40 sq mi (100 sq km). Dating from the 9th to the 13th century, the remains were found by the French in 1861. The city of Angkor Thom, with its temples and palace, is intersected by a canal system and lies within a perimeter wall. Angkor Wat, a massive complex of carved Hindu temples, is the foremost example of Khmer art and architecture.

Angle, in plane geometry, the figure formed by the intersection of two straight lines. The point of intersection is known as the vertex. If the two lines are viewed as radii of a circle of unit radius, the magnitude of an angle can be defined in terms of the proportion of the circle's circumference cut off by the two lines. Angles are measured in radians or degrees. One radian is the magnitude of an angle whose two sides cut off an arc of circumference equal in length to the radius. A degree is the magnitude of an angle whose two sides cut off 1/360 of the circumference. An angle of $\pi/2$ rad (90°), whose sides cut off one-quarter of the circumference, is a right angle, the two lines being said to be perpendicular. An angle of π rad, or 180°, whose sides cut off one-half of the circumference, is a straight angle or straight line. Angles less than 90° are termed acute; those greater than 90° but less than 180°, obtuse; greater than 180°, reflex. Pairs of angles that add up to 90° are complementary; those that add up to 180°, supplementary. In solid geometry, angles have definitions that are specific to the solids.
See also: Geometry; Trigonometry.

Angles, Germanic tribe from which England derives its name. Coming from the Schleswig-Holstein area of northern Germany, the Angles, with the Saxons and Jutes, invaded England in the 5th century and founded kingdoms including East Anglia, Mercia, and Northumbria.
See also: Anglo-Saxons.

Anglicans, community of churches developed from the Church of England. The Church of England split from the Roman Catholic Church in the 1500s, during the Reformation. It was formed by King Henry VIII, who broke with the Roman Catholic Church because he was denied permission to divorce his second wife, Anne Boleyn. The Anglican Communion is made up of the Church of England, the Anglican Church of Canada, and the Episcopal Church in the United States.

Anglo-Saxons, collective name for the Germanic peoples who dominated England from the 5th to the 11th centuries. They originated as tribes of Angles, Saxons, and Jutes who invaded England after Roman rule collapsed, creating kingdoms that eventually united to form the English nation. In modern usage, Anglo-Saxons are the English or their emigrant descendants in other parts of the world.

The Angkor Wat temple complex built in the 12th century by Suryavarman II as the center of the Khmer empire. The temple was lost in jungle growth until its rediscovery in 1860 by a French traveller.

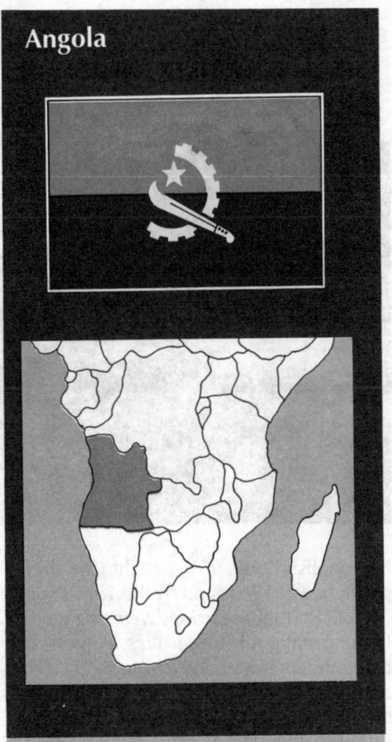

Capital:	Luanda
Area:	481,354 sq mi (1,246,700 sq km)
Population:	9,739,000
Government:	people's republic
Independent:	1975
GNP:	U.S. $6,930,000,000
Per capita:	U.S. $830

Angola, People's Republic of, independent state in southwest Africa; bordered by the Atlantic Ocean in the west, Zaire in the north, Zambia in the east, and Namibia in the south.

Land and climate. Angola is dominated by the Bié Plateau, some 4,000 ft (1,219 m) above sea level, which occasionally rises to altitudes of 8,000 ft (2,438 m) or more. To the north are tropical rain forests; to the south, semiarid or desert regions. In the east, the plateau drops off to the basins of the Zambezi and Congo rivers. The narrow coastal plain to the west, though humid, receives little rainfall. Savanna wildlife is abundant.

People. The overwhelming majority of Angolans are Africans belonging to several Bantu tribes. Bantu languages and religions predominate, although there is a significant minority of Christians, chiefly Roman Catholic.

Economy. Crude oil is Angola's principal export, followed by coffee, diamonds, and iron ore. There is also some light industry, including food processing and production of cotton, textiles, and paper.

History. Angola was a Portuguese colony from 1576 onward, and the export of slaves to Brazil caused severe depopulation. Portuguese colonization and economic development grew in the early 20th century, coupled with repression of the native peoples.

Angola's colonial history is reflected in the 17th-century church and fortress of Muxima on the Cuanza River.

Nationalists began the fight for independence in 1961, and by the 1970s some 50,000 Portuguese troops were engaged in fighting nationalist guerrillas. Angola became independent on November 5, 1975, and conflict erupted among three rival groups for control of the government. The Popular Liberation Movement (MPLA), backed by Soviet and Cuban troops, prevailed. Angola has been sympathetic to liberation groups from neighboring countries and, since 1979, has been the focus of attacks by South African troops stationed in Namibia. A 1988 accord was reached by which Cuban troops withdrew from Angola and South African troops from Namibia.

Angora *see:* Ankara.

Angora, term used for the long-haired varieties of goats, cats, and rabbits. Originally it referred to goats bred in the Angora (now Ankara) region of Turkey. The silky white hair of Angora goats has long been used for fine yarns and fabrics, especially for making mohair cloth.

Ångström (Å), unit used to measure the length of light waves and other extremely small dimensions, named for Swedish physicist Anders Jonas Ångström. It is equivalent to one ten-millionth of a millimeter (1 x 10-10m).
See also: Ångstrom, Anders Jonas.

Ångström, Anders Jonas (1814-74), Swedish physicist, one of the founders of spectroscopy (spectrum analysis) and the first to identify hydrogen in the solar spectrum (1862). The Ångström unit is named in his honor.
See also: Ångstrom.

Anguilla (pop. 7,000), island in the West Indies, 35 sq mi (90 sq km), lying 150 mi (240 km) east of Puerto Rico. Local industries include boat building, fishing, and salt. Discovered by Columbus, it became a British colony in 1650. Anguilla was part of the West Indian Associated States of St. Kitts, Nevis, and Anguilla, but it seceded in 1967 and is again under British rule.

Anhinga, also called darter, snakebird, or water turkey, large bird of the anhinga family that feeds in waters from southeast and southcentral United States to Argentina. Measuring about 3 ft (91 cm) long, it is glossy black, with silver and brown markings.
The anhinga is a strong swimmer and flier. It has webbed feet and swims mostly submerged, with its snakelike neck visible, spearing fish with its long, sharp beak. It perches in an upright position, often with wings and long fan-shaped tail spread. Similar species are the cormorant and the darters of the Eastern Hemisphere.

Anhydride, oxide that forms an acid or base when it reacts with water. Metal oxides such as calcium oxide produce hydroxides (bases) and are termed basic anhydrides. Oxides of nonmetals such as phosphorus, carbon, and sulfur produce acids on being dissolved in water and are acid anhydrides.
Organic anhydrides are used in the manufacture of solvents, paints, and dyes. Acetic anhydride is used in large quantities during the production of acetic acid and various plastics.

Anhydrous ammonia, dry or liquid form of ammonia, made by compressing pure ammonia gas (NH_3) and used as nitrogen fertilizer and as a refrigerant.
See also: Ammonia.

Ani, or tickbird, any of a genus (*Crotophaga*) of long-tailed black cuckoos native to the warm regions of the Americas. About 12 in (30 cm) in length and having flattened, blade-like beaks, anis live in flocks and build a single communal nest.

Aniakchack, volcano on the Alaska Peninsula, in the Aleutian mountain range. It is one of the largest craters in the world, with a diameter of about 6.5 mi (10.5 km). Thought to be extinct when discovered in 1922, it erupted in 1931 and is now classified as dormant.

Aniline, chemical compound ($C_6H_5NH_2$) obtained from indigo or other organic substances, or from benzol, and used in the production of dyes.
See also: Dye.

Animal, living organism distinguished from plants by locomotion, environmental reactivity, nutrient absorption, and cell structure. Animals move freely using a wide variety of mechanisms to do so, whereas plants are rooted to one place. Animals sense their environments and react to them. In the case of multicellular animals, they react by means of the nervous system; in more highly developed animals reactions to the environment are mediated by the nervous system combined with sense organs of touch, smell, taste, hearing, and sight.
Plants may react to light, chemicals, and other stimuli, but such reactions are automatic and not nervous. Plants usually contain chlorophyll, which helps them build, from inorganic material, the organic substances of which they consist. Animals must consume organic food. And while both plants and animals are made up of cells, plants have a cell wall strengthened with cellulose (a woodlike substance), but animals contain no cellulose. Other minor distinctions include the ability of plants, lacking in animals, to periodically form new organs from undifferentiated cells.

Animation, cinematographic technique creating the illusion of movement by projection of a series of drawings or photographs showing successive views of an action. The first animated cartoons were made by Emile Cohl in France in 1907. Walt Disney pioneered in the use of sound and color and in producing cartoons that aimed at suspense and drama as well as broad humor. In classic animation, drawings on transparent celluloid (cels) are superimposed to form each picture; only cels showing motion are changed from frame to frame.
See also: Disney, Walt; Schulz, Charles Monroe.

Animism, term first used by anthropologist E.B. Tylor in 1871 to designate a general belief in spiritual beings, which belief he held to be the origin of all religions. A common corruption of Tylor's sense interprets animism as the belief that all natural objects possess spirits. The psychologist Jean Piaget proposed that a growing child passes through an animistic phase.
See also: Piaget, Jean; Tylor, Sir Edward Burnett.

Anise, herb of the carrot family that yields seeds with a spicy, licorice flavor. The seeds, and the oil produced from them, are used to flavor foods, candy, and liquors like ouzo and Pernod. Anise is native to the eastern Mediterranean.

Ankara (pop. 2,235,000), capital of Turkey and of Ankara province in Asia Minor. It produces textiles, cement, flour, and beer, and trades in local Angora wool and grain. Ankara (formerly Ancyra or Angora), once a Hittite trade center, later became capital of a Roman province in 25 B.C. It replaced Istanbul as Turkey's capital in 1923.

Ankle, joint connecting the foot and the leg. Sprained ankle is a common acute injury, causing considerable discomfort and disability. The ankle joint may also be affected in rheumatoid arthritis. Pain is often due to inflammation of the sheaths of the peroneal tendon and of the bursa.
See also: Anatomy.

Anna, in the New Testament (Luke 2), Jewish prophetess, daughter of Phanuel of the tribe of Asher. Widowed at an early age, she served God in the temple by continual prayer and fasting. At the age of 84 she witnessed the presentation of Jesus in the temple.

Anna Ivanovna (1693-1740), empress of Russia from 1730. Elected puppet empress by the nobles' supreme privy council, she overthrew the council and, with German advisers, waged costly wars against the Poles and Turks and opened Russia's way to Central Asia.

Annapolis (pop. 6,813), capital of Maryland, seat of Anne Arundel County on the Severn River near Chesapeake Bay. It was settled in 1649 by Puritans from Virginia and given its present name in 1694. It is the site of St. John's College (founded 1696) and the U.S. Naval Academy (established 1845). Local industries include seafood processing and boat building.
See also: Maryland.

Annapolis *see:* United States Naval Academy.

Annapolis Convention (1786), meeting in Annapolis, Md., to discuss interstate commerce. Alexander Hamilton and James Madison wanted its scope broadened to discuss revision of the Articles of Confederation. But only 5 of the 13 states were represented, and thus a full-scale meeting was called for, leading to the Constitutional Convention at Philadelphia.
See also: Articles of Confederation; Constitution of the United States.

Annapolis Royal (pop. 630), town on the Annapolis River, west coast of Nova Scotia, near the site of the earliest permanent French settlement in Canada. The original town of Port Royal grew up around a French fort built in 1605. After nearly a century of fighting, the British finally captured Port Royal in 1710 and changed its name to Annapolis Royal in honor of Queen Anne. Until Halifax was founded in 1749, it was the capital of Nova Scotia. Today it is the center of a prosperous farming area and a summer resort.

Annapurna, Himalayan mountain in Nepal with the world's 11th-highest peak (26,391 ft/8,044 m). Its conquest in 1950 by Maurice Herzog's team was the first such success involving any great Himalayan peak.

Ann Arbor (pop. 282,937), city in southeastern Michigan, seat of Washtenaw County, and home of the University of Michigan since 1841. It is situated on the Huron River about 40 mi (65 km) west of Detroit. Once mainly a farming and fruit-growing center, Ann Arbor has also become a center of light industry since World War II. The city was settled in 1824, incorporated as a village in 1833, and given its city charter in 1851.

Anne (1665-1714), queen of Great Britain and Ireland (1702-14), last of the Stuart monarchs. Her reign was dominated by the War of the Spanish Succession, also known as Queen Anne's War in the colonies (1702-13). It also saw the Act of Union (1707), uniting England and Scotland to form the kingdom of Great Britain, and the growth of the parliamentary system.

Anne, Saint, mother of the Virgin Mary and wife of St. Joachim. Though not mentioned in Scripture, she was venerated in Early Christian times. According to an apocryphal writing of St. James, long after St. Anne had despaired of bearing a child, an angel appeared to her and foretold the birth of Mary. Often represented in art in such scenes as the Birth of the Virgin, St. Anne is the patron saint of women in labor. Her feast day is July 26.
See also: Sainte-Anne-de-Beaupré.

Annenberg, Walter (1908-), U.S. publisher. He inherited a Philadelphia-based publishing empire that included the *Philadelphia Inquirer*, founded *Seventeen* magazine and *TV Guide*, and bought the *Philadelphia Daily News*. He was appointed ambassador to Great Britain by President Richard Nixon (1969).

Anne of Austria (1601-66), queen consort and regent of France. The daughter of King Philip III of Spain, Anne married King Louis XIII of France in 1615. Her position at court was precarious because of France's involvement in the Thirty Years' War against Spain and Austria. After her husband's death in 1643, Anne served as regent for her young son, King Louis XIV, relying on Cardinal Mazarin, the successor of Cardinal Richelieu, for guidance. In 1651 she had her 13-year-old son proclaimed of age, but she remained powerful until the death of Mazarin in 1661, when Louis personally took control of the state.
See also: Mazarin, Jules Cardinal.

Anne of Brittany (1477-1514), duchess of Brittany and queen of France. Anne was married to King Charles VIII of France in 1491 and after his death became the wife of his successor, King Louis XII. Through the marriage of her daughter to the future King Francis I of France, the duchy of Brittany, the last of the great feudally held territories of France, was permanently united to the crown of France.

Anne of Cleves (1515-57), queen consort and fourth wife of England's Henry VIII. She was the daughter of a powerful German noble, and Henry married her (1540) on Thomas Cromwell's advice to forge international bonds, but 6 months later he had Parliament annul the marriage.
See also: Henry VIII.

Annexation, acquisition by a country of a territory previously outside its jurisdiction. The term is generally used to refer to the extension of a country's sovereignty by conquest or threat of force, rather than by treaty.

Anno Domini *see:* A.D.

Annual, plant that completes its life cycle in one growing season, as contrasted with biennials (two seasons) and perennials (more than two). Annuals include garden flowers and food plants such as cornflowers and tomatoes. Preventing seeding may convert an annual to a biennial or a perennial.

Annual rings, rings of dark and light wood seen across the trunk of a tree that has been cut down. The lighter rings are formed during the spring and are made up of cells with large cavities. The darker rings are formed during the summer, when less new wood is laid down and the cells have smaller cavities. In hot countries the rings represent dry and wet seasons. The size of the rings tells a great deal about the conditions under which the tree was growing, and the number of rings can be used to measure the age of the tree. The science of dating things by counting annual rings is dendrochronology.

Annuity, yearly payment a person receives for life or for a term of years, the person usually being entitled to such payment in consideration of money advanced to those who pay.

Annulment, decree to the effect that a marriage was invalid when contracted. Grounds for annulment include fraud, force, and close blood links between the parties. The Roman Catholic Church recognizes annulment but not divorce.

Annunciation, in Christian belief, the archangel Gabriel's announcement to the Virgin Mary that she would give birth to the Messiah. The Roman Catholic Church celebrates the Annunciation on March 25. The Annunciation is the theme of many Christian paintings.

Annunzio, Gabriele d' *see:* D'Annunzio, Gabriele.

Anodizing, electrolytic method of producing a corrosion-resistant or decorative layer of oxide on a metal, usually aluminum. The metal to be coated is used as an anode (positive pole), suspended in an electrolyte (usually an aqueous solution of sulfuric, chromic, or oxalic acid). When an electric current is passed through this solution, a coating of oxide builds up on the anode.
See also: Electrolysis.

Anorexia nervosa, psychological disorder characterized by a disturbed sense of body image and exaggerated anxiety about weight gain, manifested by abnormal refusal to eat, leading to severe weight loss, and, in women, amenorrhea (loss of period). The onset is usually in adolescence, and the disorder affects females predominantly; only about 5% of the cases occur in males.

Anouilh, Jean (1910-87), French playwright, whose highly theatrical dramas emphasize the dilemma of modern times, in which individuals are forced to compromise their dreams. His works include *Antigone* (1944), *The Lark* (1953), and *Beckett* (1959).

Anoxia, severe hypoxia (lowered oxygen levels in body tissues), whether due to lack of oxygen in air inhaled or lack of oxygen available in the blood or tissues. Anoxia can be of such severity as to cause permanent damage. Anemic anoxia, resulting from deficient amounts of hemoglobin in the blood, may be caused by hemorrhage or anemia or by poisoning with carbon monoxide, nitrites, or chlorates. Anoxic anoxia occurs when blood flowing through the lungs does not pick up enough oxygen, possibly caused by high altitudes or foreign gases or by abnormalities in pulmonary tissues. Stagnant anoxia, in which slow blood circulation results in loss of oxygen before the blood reaches tissues, is often associated with congestive cardiac failure or postoperative shock.

Anselm, Saint (1033?-1109), archbishop of Canterbury (from 1093), a founder of Scholasticism. He endured repeated exile for challenging the right of English kings to influence church affairs. Anselm saw reason as the servant of faith and was the author of an ontological "proof" of God's existence: the human idea of a perfect being itself implies the existence of such a being. Saint Anselm's Day is celebrated on April 21.

Ansermet, Ernest (1883-1969), Swiss orchestral conductor who directed many premieres of Stravinsky ballets. He founded the Orchestre de la Suisse Romande in 1918, conducting it until his death.

Ansky, Shloime (Solomon Samuel Rapoport; 1863-1920), Russian Yiddish author and playwright, best known for *The Dybbuk* (1916), a tragedy of demonic possession. He was active in Russian Jewish socialism, but left Russia after the Revolution and died in Poland.

Anson, Adrian Constantine, (1851-1922), U.S. baseball player, also known as "Cap" or "Pop." In 1939 he was elected to baseball's Hall of Fame as "the greatest hitter and greatest National League player-manager of the 19th century."

Ant, insect of order Hymenoptera (which also includes bees and wasps), family Formicidae, living in communities consisting of males, females, and infertile worker females. An ant colony may contain thousands and even millions of ants organized into a highly socialized community. The queen ant's function is to produce eggs. The female worker ant (there are no male worker ants) is responsible for food, protection, and building the nest. The male's singular function is to mate and die quickly. Ants are found in all parts of the planet but prefer warmer climates. An ant is usually under 1 inch (2.5 cm) in height and black, brown, or red in color. It usually lives in tunnels beneath the earth or mounds of its own making. The two antennae on the head provide the ability to hear, smell, touch, and taste, although other areas of the body can taste and touch. The ant has no ears. It has acquired a reputation for remarkable strength because it can lift 50 times its own weight. The ant produces a humming or buzzing sound capable of detection by the human ear.

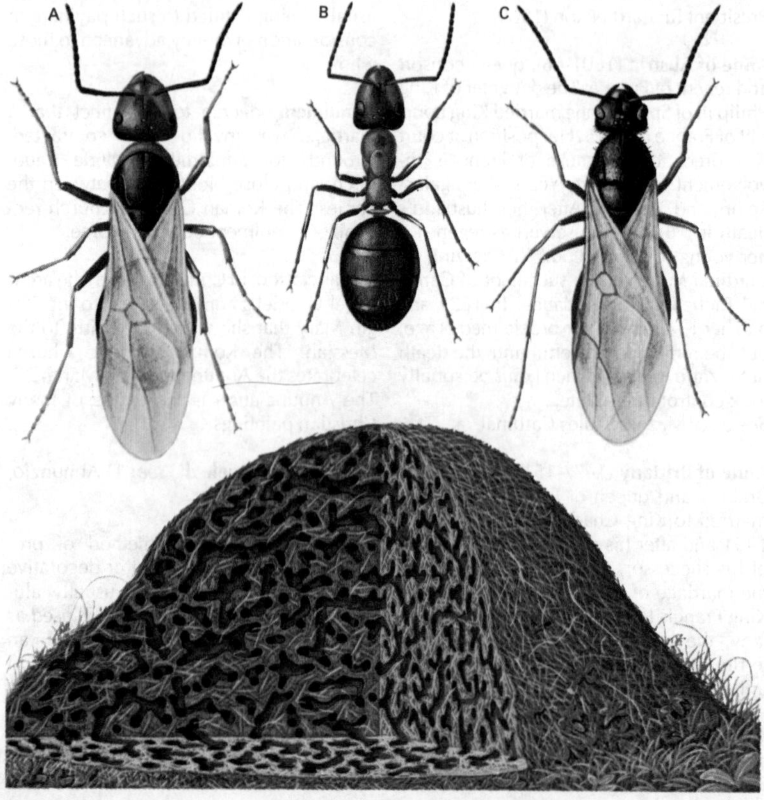

Wood ants are found primarily in pine forests, where they build pine-needle nests which can rise to a height of several feet. Each nest contains many queens (A), besides males (C) and innumerable workers (B).

Antananarivo, or Tananarive (pop. 1,050,000), capital and largest city of Madagascar. Located near the center of the island of Madagascar on a mountain ridge and linked to other areas by railroad, it is a manufacturing and communications center. The University of Madagascar and the 200-year-old palace of the Merina rulers are located in the city.

Antarctic *see:* Antarctica.

Antarctica, fifth largest continent, almost 6,000,000 sq mi (17,400,000 sq km). Antarctica is almost entirely covered by an ice cap up to 14,000 ft (4,267 m) thick except where the ice is pierced by mountain peaks.

The Vinson Massif is Antarctica's highest mountain (16,900 ft /5,150 m). The continent is circular, indented by the arc-shaped Weddell Sea (south of the Atlantic Ocean) and the rectangular Ross Sea (south of New Zealand). Pack ice virtually surrounds the rest of the continent. The western half of Antarctica, including the Antarctic Peninsula, is structurally related to the Andes; the eastern half geologically resembles Australia and South Africa. Antarctica is almost entirely within the Antarctic Circle (66°30′ S) and the climate is intensely cold, with winter temperatures as low as –80° F (–62° C), and winds up to 100 mph (161 kmph).

Capt. James Cook was the first to attempt a scientific exploration of the region (1773). The mainland was probably first sighted in 1820 by the American sea captain, Nathaniel Palmer. The Englishman James Weddell led an expedition to the area in 1823 and another Englishman, James Clark Ross, discovered the sea later named for him. The Norwegian Roald Amundsen was the first to reach the South Pole on Dec. 4, 1911 and Admiral Richard Evelyn Byrd became the first to fly over the pole on Nov. 29, 1929. Since the International Geophysical Year (1957-58), international cooperation in Antarctica has increased. On Dec. 1, 1959, 12 nations signed the 30-year Antarctic Treaty reserving the area south of 60° S for peaceful scientific investigation. In 1985, 32 nations agreed to limit access of humans to Antarctica to specific research sites. Antarctica is home to over 25 scientific installations, three of which

While some of the seas and islands surrounding Antarctica were known in the 18th century, the mainland was not explored until the 19th century.

The young of the Weddell seal (Leptonychotes weddelli) *are born on the sea ice.*

*The grey-headed albatross (*Diomedea chrysostoma) *lives on the island of South Georgia.*

Lowest on the Antarctic food chain are phytoplankton, which are eaten by zooplankton. Both are eaten by fish and baleen (toothless) whales, and fish are then eaten by birds, seals, and toothed whales.

are from the United States. During the 1980s scientists began to detect a deterioration in the ozone level above Antarctica which created great environmental concern for the region and the planet. The ozone layer protects the planet from destructive sun rays. Because of this new awareness and increasing accessibility to the region, tourism to Antarctica is rising.

Antarctic Circle, imaginary boundary, 66°30′ S lat., marking the northernmost latitude of the Antarctic region at which the sun remains above the horizon at least one day a year, the December solstice, and the southernmost latitude at which the sun is visible at the June solstice. Most of the continent of Antarctica lies within the circle.

Susan Brownell Anthony

Antarctic Ocean, ocean surrounding the Antarctic continent, also called the Southern Ocean; sometimes not considered to be a separate ocean but rather a part of the Atlantic, Indian, and Pacific oceans. Its width varies from 700 mi (1,100 km) at the tip of South America to 2,400 mi (3,860 km) off the tip of Africa. Pack ice and icebergs drift in the ocean's 29°F (–2°C) waters.

Antares, one of the brightest stars in the southern sky, in the constellation Scorpio. It is over 400 light years from earth. It is a visual binary, or double, star; the main star is a red (thus, cool) giant, 480 times the size of the sun; its companion star is blue (hot) and too small to be visible without a powerful telescope.
See also: Astronomy.

Anteater, any of 3 genera of Central and South American mammals, family Myrmecophagidae, order Edentata, including the giant anteater and the tamandua. They have long snouts, tubular, toothless mouths, and long, sticky tongues with which they catch their food, chiefly termites.
See also: Aardvark.

Antelopes

Antelope, swift-moving hollow-horned ruminant of the family Bovidae, order Artiodactyla. Common features include a hairy muzzle, narrow cheek teeth, and permanent, backward-pointing horns. Distribution is throughout Africa and Asia. Antelopes range in size from the royal antelope, probably the smallest hoofed mammal, standing about 10 in (25 cm) high at the shoulders, to the giant eland, which may be as tall as 6 ft (1.8 m).

Antenna, or aerial, component in an electrical circuit that radiates or receives radio waves. A transmitting antenna is a combination of conductors that converts AC electrical energy into electromagnetic radiation. The simple dipole consists of 2 straight conductors energized at the small gap which separates them. It can be made directional by adding electrically isolated director and reflector conductors in front and behind. Other configurations include the folded dipole, the highly directional loop antenna, and the dish type used for microwave links. A receiving antenna can consist merely of a short dielectric rod or a length of wire for low-frequency signals. For VHF and microwave signals, complex antenna configurations similar to those used for transmission must be used.

Antennae, paired sensory appendage on the head of most insects, crustaceans, and other arthropods. Nerves on the antennae are sensitive to vibrations, heat, water vapor, or chemicals. Hairs on the antennae of male mosquitoes pick up female sounds as far as one-quarter mi (0.4 km) away, while June bugs have pits in their antennae that help them smell. Most insects have 1 pair of antennae; crustaceans, such as lobsters and crabs, have 2 pairs.

Antheil, George (1900-59), U.S. composer. He studied under Ernest Bloch and brought popular motifs into serious music in works such as *Jazz Symphonietta* (1926) and the opera *Transatlantic* (1928-29). In later work he was more traditional, and after World War II he developed a neoclassical style influenced by Igor Stravinsky.

Anthemius of Tralles (d. c.534), Byzantine architect, mathematician, and physicist. With Isidorus of Miletus, he designed the Hagia Sophia in Constantinople at the order of the Byzantine emperor Justinian. It is likely that he also designed the Church of Saints Sergius and Bacchus in the same city.

Anthony, Susan Brownell (1820-1906), major U.S. leader and organizer of the fight for women's rights. A schoolteacher who backed the temperance and abolitionist movements, she later worked with Elizabeth Cady Stanton for women's suffrage and other political and economic rights. She cofounded the National Woman Suffrage Association (1868) and served as president of the National American Woman Suffrage Association (1892-1900). She also helped to write the first 3 volumes of *The History of Woman Suffrage*. In 1979, Anthony became the first woman to have her image on a coin of general circulation in the United States. The Susan B. Anthony dollar became an immediate collectible.
See also: Women's suffrage.

Anthony of Padua, Saint (1195-1231), Franciscan friar, theologian, and preacher. He was born near Lisbon but taught and preached in France and Italy. Patron saint of the poor, his feast day is June 13.

Anthony of Thebes, Saint (c.250-350), Egyptian hermit, considered the founder of Christian monasticism. He founded a desert community of ascetics near Fayum, then lived alone in a mountain cave near the Red Sea and died aged over 100. He supported St. Athanasius in the Arian controversy. His feast day is Jan. 17.

Anthrax, infectious disease affecting livestock and, more rarely, humans, causing skin pustules and lung damage. Anthrax spores, which can survive for years, may be picked up from infected animals or bone meal. It was the first disease shown (by Robert Koch in 1876) to be caused by bacteria. A vaccine effective on sheep and cattle was developed by Louis Pasteur. Anthrax is now rare in developed countries.
See also: Pasteur, Louis.

Anthropoid *see:* Primate.

Anthropology, study of the origins, evolution, and development of human beings and their various cultures and societies. Physical anthropology is concerned with human beings as physical organisms, the place of *Homo sapiens* in the framework of evolution, and the classification of early humans based upon the study of fossil remains. Cultural anthropology examines the specific knowledge, values, and behaviors that are characteristic of members of a particular society, emphasizing the uniqueness of cultures while attempting to compare them. Cultural anthropology shares with social anthropology an emphasis upon understanding behaviors within a particular context and rejects any attempt to classify or explain particular behaviors in the abstract. Social anthropology studies the structures of a society through the detailed and direct examination of patterns of relations among its classes, generations, and religious and political institutions. One of the major contributions of social anthropology has been to discredit the idea that preliterate societies are lacking in complexity or that the peoples in them lack the same intellectual abilities as peoples in industrialized societies.

Antiaircraft defense, method of protection from attack by enemy aircraft or missiles, involving early detection and interference and destruction. Radar is an early detector but can be foiled if the enemy confuses the radar by dropping metal strips called chaff. Interference with incoming missiles is accomplished with chaff, decoys, and electronic jamming devices. Radar is also used in coordination with guns or missiles on ships or on the ground to destroy the attackers. Some antiaircraft missiles use homing devices attracted to heat from enemy planes, guiding the missiles to the target.
See also: Radar.

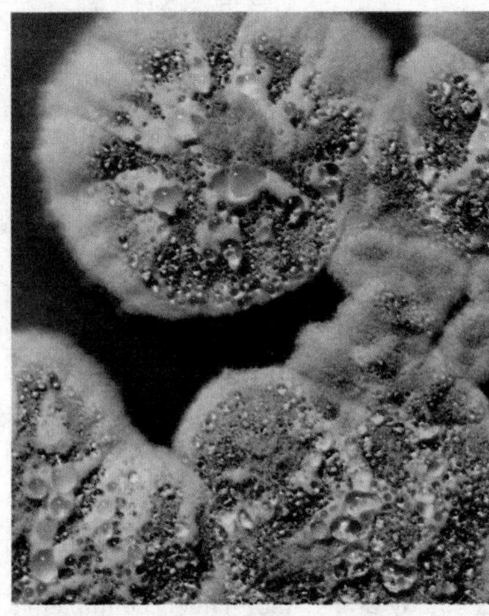

Antibiotic miracle the mold Penicillium notatum. *In 1928 Alexander Fleming discovered penicillin.*

Antibiotic, any of the substances, usually produced by microorganisms, that kill or prevent the growth of other microorganisms, especially bacteria and fungi. Louis Pasteur noted the effect in the 19th century, and in 1928 Alexander Fleming showed that the mold *Penicillium notatum* produced penicillin, a substance able to destroy certain bacteria. Other early discoveries of antibiotics include the isolation of streptomycin (by Selman Waksman), gramicidin (by René Dubos), and the cephalosporins. Semisynthetic antibiotics, in which the basic molecule is chemically modified, have increased the range of naturally occurring substances.
See also: Penicillin; Bacteria.

Antibody *see:* Immunity.

Antichrist, in Christian belief, the human antagonist of Christ. The term appears in the Epistles of St. John. While the concept is sometimes interpreted as a lawless but impersonal power, others consider the Antichrist a personal incarnation of evil. Roman Catholic writers commonly interpret the term to mean any adversary of Christ and of the Church's authority, specifically the last and greatest antagonist of the Christian Church, whose coming will precede the end of the world.

Anticoagulant, substance that interferes with blood clotting, used to treat or prevent strokes and embolism. The 2 main types are heparin, which is injected and has an immediate but short-lived effect, and the coumarins, which are taken orally and are longer lasting.
See also: Coagulant.

Anti-Defamation League *see:* B'nai B'rith.

Antidote, remedy that neutralizes a poison or counteracts its effects. A chemical antidote unites with a poison to produce a harmless chemical, a mechanical antidote prevents the absorption of a poison, and a physiologic antidote produces effects contrary to those of the given poison. Most antidotes are effective against only one kind of poison, although specific antidotes are available in less than 2% of poisonings.
See also: Antitoxin; Poison.

Antietam, Battle of *see:* Civil War.

Anti-Federalists, opponents of the ratification of the Federal Constitution of 1787. The Anti-Federalists argued that centralized power would become despotic. After Washington's inauguration, the Anti-Federalist group helped to form the Democratic-Republican Party under Jefferson.
See also: Federalist Party.

Antifreeze, substance added to a solvent to prevent it from freezing in cold weather. Antifreeze used in the cooling system of automobiles is generally made of water mixed with ethylene glycol, methanol, ethanol, or other substances that lower the freezing point.
See also: Glycol.

Antigen, foreign substance introduced into an organism, stimulating the production of antibodies that combat the intruder. Antigens may be viruses, bacteria, or the nonliving toxins they produce.

Antigone, in Greek mythology, daughter of Oedipus and Jocasta. When her brothers Eteocles and Polynices killed each other in combat, Creon, king of Thebes and Jocasta's brother, refused to allow the burial of Polynices, whom he regarded as a traitor. When Antigone defied him, Creon sentenced her to death. She is the subject of tragedies by the ancient Greek playwright Sophocles and the modern French playwright Jean Anouilh.
See also: Mythology.

Antigonid dynasty, line of kings that ruled Macedonia (northern Greece) 294 B.C.-168 B.C. **Antigonus I**, a general under Alexander the Great, was the first of the dynasty to rule Macedonia (294-283 B.C.). He was succeeded by **Antigonus II** (r. 283-239) and grandson **Demetrius II** (r. 239-229). **Phillip V**, son of Demetrius II, challenged Rome but was defeated in 197 B.C. Antigonid rule ended 168 B.C. with the defeat and capture of Philip's successor, **Perseus**.

Antigravity, hypothetical force of repulsion described in science fiction but never scientifically observed. The opposite of gravity, antigravity would cause objects to repel one another rather than to be attracted to one another. Earth's gravity pulls objects toward the planet's center, antigravity would push objects away from earth's center.

Antigua, also called Antigua Guatemala (pop. 15,800), city in south central Guatemala, once the capital. After an earthquake and flood leveled an earlier capital, Antigua was founded in 1542, quickly becoming one of the richest cities in the New World, only to be destroyed itself by an earthquake in 1773. Today Antigua is a trading and tourist center in a coffee-growing area.

Antigua and Barbuda

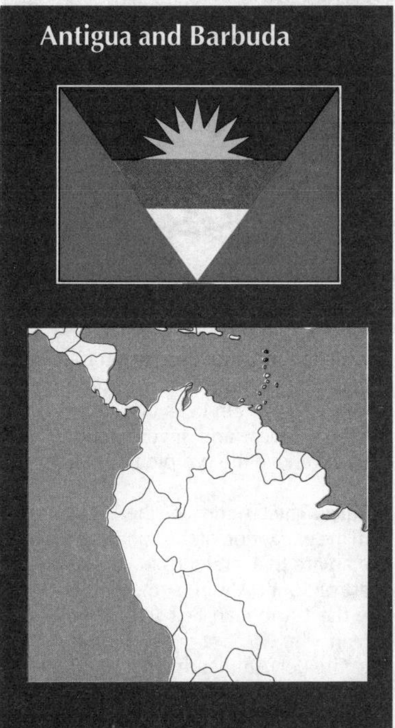

Capital:	Saint John's
Area:	170.5 sq mi (441.6 sq km)
Population:	78,400
Government:	constitutional monarchy
Independent:	1981
GNP:	U.S. $230,000,000
Per capita:	U.S. $2,800

Antigua and Barbuda, island nation in the West Indies, largest and most developed of the Leeward Islands.

Land and climate. The islands of Antigua, Barbuda, and Redonda (uninhabited), are of volcanic origin. White sandy beaches fringe the coasts; few places rise to more than 1,000 ft (2,048 m) above sea level. The climate is tropical with a dry season July-Dec.

People and economy. The population is predominantly of African and British origins. St. John's is the largest town and chief port, and tourism is the principal economic activity. In the 19th century, cotton replaced sugarcane as the main crop, and some tropical fruits are also grown. The United States maintains large naval and army bases near Parham.

History. Antigua was named by Christopher Columbus in 1493. The island passed from Spanish to French control in the 17th century and was taken over by the British in 1632. With Barbuda and Redonda as dependencies it became a self-governing West Indies Associated State in 1967 and independent in 1981.

Antigua's British past is reflected in this 18th-century harbor construction.

Antihistamine, drug used to neutralize the effects of histamine (an organic compound released by certain cells that causes tissue swelling, hives, and severe itching). It is used to relieve the symptoms of allergies.

Antilles, The, islands of the West Indies, with the exception of the Bahamas. Shaped like an arc that stretches from Cuba to the coast of South America, the Antilles separate the Caribbean Sea from the Atlantic Ocean.

The Greater Antilles include the large islands of Cuba, Jamaica, Hispaniola, and Puerto Rico. The Lesser Antilles include the Virgin Islands, the Leeward and Windward Islands, Trinidad and Tobago, Barbados, the Netherlands Antilles, and the Margarita Islands of Venezuela. Cuba, Haiti, and the Dominican Republic have long been independent nations. Three of the large islands formerly held by the British—Barbados, Jamaica, and Trinidad—gained their independence in the 1970s. All other islands of the Antilles are colonies, self-governing affiliates, or integral parts of other nations.

Anti-Masonic Party, U.S. political party (1827-36), formed to oppose Freemasons in politics. The Masons were accused, without proof, of murdering the author of a book claiming to reveal the secrets of Masonry.

The Anti-Masons held the first national nominating convention (1831) and were the first to issue a written party platform. They eventually helped form the Whig Party.

See also: Whig Party.

Antimatter, material composed of antiparticles, which are identical in mass and behavior to electrons, protons, and neutrons but have opposite electrical charges.

Matter and antimatter are both annihilated when they collide, and other particles, such as photons (quanta of energy) are released. Antimatter is rare and short-lived in our part of the universe, where matter predominates. The first antiparticle, the positron (antielectron), was discovered by Carl D. Anderson in 1932.

See also: Antigravity.

Anti-Monopoly Party, U.S. political party opposing monopolies in business in 1884. The party joined with the Greenback Party in supporting Benjamin F. Butler of Massachusetts for president, but disbanded after Butler received only 175,000 votes.

See also: Butler, Benjamin Franklin.

Antimony, chemical element, symbol Sb; for physical constants see Periodic Table. Substances containing antimony have been used for thousands of years as medicines and cosmetics. It was first characterized accurately by Nicolas Lémery in 1707. Its principal ore is stibnite, a sulfide. Antimony is obtained by roasting the sulfide to the oxide, which can be further reduced with carbon. It is an extremely brittle, bluish-white metalloid and a poor conductor of heat and electricity. Two allotropes of antimony are known. Antimony greatly increases the hardness and mechanical strength of lead. It is used in batteries, antifriction alloys, type metal, infrared detectors, diodes, and Hall-effect devices.

Its compounds are used in safety matches, flameproofing agents, paints, ceramic enamels, glass, and pottery. Antimony and its compounds are toxic.

Antioch (pop. 107,800), ancient city in Asia Minor, now known as Antakya, in southern Turkey on the Orontes River. Founded by Seleucus I in 301 B.C., it became the capital of the Seleucid Empire and was one of the great commercial centers of the ancient world. In 64 B.C. control of the city passed to Rome, which made "Antioch the Golden" capital of the empire in Asia, surpassed in splendor only by Rome and Alexandria. It was the most important center of early Christianity outside Palestine. After the decline of the Eastern Roman Empire, Antioch came under Arab and then Ottoman Turkish rule. After World War I, it was incorporated into French-administered Syria, but in 1939 it was restored to Turkey. The city is a trade and agricultural center.

Antipodes (Greek, "foot-to-foot"), 2 places exactly opposite each other on the globe, so that a straight line connecting them would pass through the center of the earth. The region around Australia and New Zealand is the antipode of England, and is thus sometimes called the Antipodes.

Antique, object that has acquired value through a combination of age, rarity, craft, and historic interest. Generally, the term applies to objects over 100 years old, though by the 1980s even those of the 1890s and early 1900s, particularly in the art nouveau style, were becoming sought-after. The U.S. 1939 Tariff Act defined antiques as "artistic antiquities" made before 1830. Certain categories of objects are favorites, notably furniture, china, rugs, and other useful and decorative articles.

Antirenters, group of tenant farmers in New York State who protested against paying rent to landlords (1839-1847). The tenant families had lived on the disputed land for generations and considered it theirs. When, in 1839, the heirs of the Dutch merchant Van Rensselaer tried to collect $400,000 in back rents. The Antirenters rose up in protest, rioting and terrorizing the landlords. In 1846, a new state constitution guaranteed ownership to the tenants.

Anti-Semitism, systematic hostility to Jews. Until the 19th century, antiJewish prejudice was basically religious in nature, stemming from the claim that the Jews were responsible for Christ's death. In the late 1800s, particularly in eastern Europe, religious hostility acquired a racist rationale, based on the idea that Jews were a distinct, and evil, race. In Tsarist Russia the Jewish population was subjected to brutal physical attacks (pogroms). Anti-Semitism became a cornerstone of the ideology of Nazi Germany under Adolf Hitler, culminating in the murder of some 6 million Jews during World War II.

See also: Concentration camp; Holocaust; Jews; Racism.

Antiseptic, substance that kills or prevents the growth of microorganisms (particularly bacteria and fungi), especially used to avoid sepsis (infection) from contamination of body surfaces and surgical instruments. Vinegar and cedar oil have been used since early times to treat wounds and for embalming. Commonly used antiseptics and disinfectants include iodine, chlorine, alcohol, isopropanol, formaldehyde, and hydrogen peroxide. Heat, ultraviolet, and ionizing radiations also have antiseptic effects.

See also: Disinfectant; Lister, Sir Joseph.

Antitoxin, antibody released into the bloodstream to counteract the poisonous products (toxins) of invading bacteria. When a small amount of a bacterial toxin is injected into the blood, the body produces its own antitoxins to combat infection. The body may also accept blood serum injected from another organism that has already formed the antitoxin. This technique is effective in fighting such diseases as diphtheria and tetanus.

Antitrust laws, legislation designed to protect competition among businesses. By preventing large firms from controlling the price or supply of goods and services, these laws work to ensure that smaller firms are not forced out of business. Congressional antitrust action includes the Sherman Antitrust Act (1890), which was used to end unfair restraint of trade practices of the Standard Oil Company and American Tobacco Company in the early 1900s. The Clayton Antitrust Act (1914) is a supplement to the Sherman Act which outlaws price discrimination, non-complete agreements, price cutting, and certain mergers. The Federal Trade Commission (FTC) was established in 1914 to enforce antitrust laws. In 1950 the Clayton Act was enhanced by the Celler-Kefauver Act. Antitrust legislation has recently been complicated by the growth of huge conglomerates that control businesses in many industries.

Anti-war movement, opposition to U.S. involvement in the Vietnam war. From a relatively small group of protesters during the Kennedy administration, the movement proliferated and gained a broad base, its popularity widely believed responsible for President Lyndon B. Johnson's decision not to run for a second term in 1968. Hundreds of thousands demonstrated their opposition in protest marches in 1968-69. Anti-war pressure intensified under President Richard M. Nixon and strongly influenced his decision to settle for peace without victory.

Ant lion, or doodlebug, larval form of any of several insects of the Myrmeleontidae family that traps ants and other prey in pits dug in sandy soil. It uses its plump, hairy body to dig by backing into the soil in a narrowing spiral path. When prey slides into the pit, the ant lion, hiding under sand at the bottom, kills the prey with its long sharp jaws, and sucks its nourishment from the victim.

Antofagasta (pop. 172,700), major Pacific seaport in northern Chile, capital of Antofagasta province. An important industrial center, it is also the shipping point for the copper, nitrates, and sulfur mined in the surrounding region, as well as being the crossroads for rail and highway connections to southern Chile and across the Andes to Bolivia and Argentina. Antofagasta was ceded to Chile by Bolivia after the War of the Pacific (1879-83).

Antoinette, Marie *see:* Marie Antoinette.

Antonioni, Michelangelo (1912-), Italian film director. His work includes *L'Avventura* (1959), *La Notte* (1961), *Eclipse* (1962), *The Red Desert* (1964), *Blow-Up* (1966), *Zabriskie Point* (1969), and *The Passenger* (1975).

Antonius Pius (A.D. 86-161), Roman emperor (138-161), tolerant of Christians, the last to achieve relative stability in the empire. Chosen consul in 120, he adopted Marcus Aurelius and Lucius Verus as successors.

Antony, Marc (Marcus Antonius; 82-30 B.C.), Roman politician and general. A member of Caesar's family, he became a tribune in 50 B.C.; after Caesar's murder in 44 B.C., Antony, then consul, joined the Triumvirate, including his brother-in-law Octavian and Lepidus, dividing the empire among them.
Antony controlled the east from the Adriatic to the Euphrates, but soon alienated Octavian by falling in love with the Egyptian queen, Cleopatra, and combining forces with her. As a result, the senate stripped Antony of his powers (32 B.C.), certain the insult would invite civil war. Octavian attacked and defeated Antony in a naval battle at Actium; Antony returned to Egypt, pursued by Octavian, and committed suicide. Cleopatra, too, died by her own hand.
See also: Rome, Ancient.

Antwerp (pop. 486,600), city and leading port, on the Scheldt River in northern Belgium. It is the capital of Antwerp province, the commercial and cultural center of Flemish Belgium, and an important manufacturing city, with oil, metal, automobile, and diamond industries. It was the center of the great Flemish school of painting: artists like Brueghel, Rubens, and Van Dyck worked there in the 16th and 17th centuries.

Anubis, ancient Egyptian god of the dead, usually portrayed as having the head of a dog or jackal. In Egyptian belief, Anubis guided the dead to the underworld, where he symbolically weighed their hearts on the scales of justice.
See also: Mythology.

Anxiety, unpleasant and disturbing emotion, ranging from ill-defined discomfort to panic or a profound sense of impending doom.
Anxious people may be irritable, restless, and agitated, or have impulses for physical activity that may be purposeless and aimless. Physical symptoms may include an increase in heart rate and blood pressure, generalized or localized muscle tension, rapid and shallow breathing, sighing or shortness of breath, dizziness, or nausea.
Anxiety may be acute, lasting a few minutes to a few hours, or chronic, with symptoms mild to moderate in intensity but almost constantly present. The chronic state may be intermittently and unpredictably accompanied by acute increases in the severity of the symptoms.
Anxiety is usually brought on by stress, which may be well defined and external or ill defined and internal. While it is often

Anti-Semitic signs worn by German soldiers outside a "Jewish" department store in Berlin in 1933. The sign at right reads: "Germans! Stand firm! Don't buy from Jews!"

thought that anxiety is always undesirable and to be avoided, human personality development studies have demonstrated that tolerable levels of age-appropriate anxiety are largely responsible for individuals' gradual establishment of sophisticated, self-reliant behavior, attitudes, and values.
See also: Phobia.

Anzio (pop. 27,100), Italian fishing port and seaside resort about 30 mi (48 km) south of Rome. As ancient Antium, it was the birthplace of the emperors Caligula and Nero. Anzio was the site of Allied landings in Jan. 1944, during World War II, leading to a bloody battle in which casualties were high.

The Star of David with the word "Jew" in the center. Patches like this had to be worn by Jewish people under Nazi domination.

Anzus Pact, treaty signed Sept. 1, 1951, by Australia, New Zealand, and the United States for mutual defense in the Pacific. The name consists of the initials of the participating countries, which meet annually.

Aorta, the body's main artery, carrying blood from the left ventricle of the heart to the branch arteries that spread throughout the body.

Apache, Native American tribe of North America's Southwest (since c.1100), from Athabascan linguistic family. Members of a nomadic hunting culture whose men lived with and worked for their wives' families, these strong fighters repelled the Spanish, only to face the Comanches and other tribes and eventually the westward expansion of the European Americans. They rejected repeated federal attempts to confine their tribes to reservations. In the bloody conflicts that followed, they were decimated, and in 1896 Geronimo, their chief, was captured. Most present-day Apaches live on 3 million acres of federal reservations in Oklahoma, New Mexico, and Arizona, supported by income from timber, tourism, cattle, and mineral resources. In 1982 the Apaches won an important Supreme Court case that tested their right to tax resources taken from their lands.

Apartheid (Afrikaans, "apartness"), policy of racial segregation as employed by the Republic of South Africa, enforced by the dominant white minority. The system separates whites from nonwhites (i.e., Coloreds, or mulattoes; Asiatics; and Africans, or Bantu), nonwhites from each other, and each individual Bantu group. The policy also involves the "separate development" of 10 Bantu homelands, where the majority of the population lives on a very small portion of poor land. Segregation and discrimination of nonwhite peoples is imposed by denying the rights to vote, own land, travel, or work without permits. In addition, workers are often separated from their families, which undermines family structure. Although dissent, led largely by the formerly outlawed African National Congress, is met with imprisonment, exile, or house arrest, resistance to apartheid continues, both inside the country (where thousands have been killed or imprisoned) and outside (in the form of nearly worldwide economic and political sanctions against South Africa). Since the 1970s and 1980s many apartheid laws have been repealed. In the early 1990s the system was completely dismantled, democratic structures were introduced, and a black majority rule was established in 1994.
See also: African National Congress; Mandela, Nelson.

Aphids on the stem of a plant

Apatosaurus see: Brontosaurus.

Ape, primate, family Pongidae, closely related to human beings. These forest dwellers, whose brain structure allows for fairly advanced reasoning, range in size from the gibbon (3 ft/0.9 m, 15 lb/6.8 kg) of southeast Asia to the gorilla (6 ft/1.8 m, 500 lb/227 kg) of Africa. The chimpanzee (5 ft/1.5 m, 150 lb/68 kg), also of Africa, is the animal most closely related to humans. It is a member of the ape family.

Apartheid and absurdity. Two bridges —one for whites and one for nonwhites—crossing the same point.

Apennines, mountain chain forming the backbone of the Italian peninsula and extending into Sicily, about 800 mi (1,287 km) long and 25-80 mi (40-129 km) wide. The predominant rocks are limestone and dolomite; sulfur and cinnabar are mined in the volcanic area near Vesuvius. Olives, grapes, and grains are widely grown, although lack of fertile topsoil prevents intensive agriculture.

Apennine Tunnel, 11.5-mi (18.5-km) train tunnel in Italy on the Florence-Bologna line; one of the longest train tunnels in the world, built from 1920-34.

Aphasia, partial or total language impairment, in which the comprehension or expression of words is diminished as a result of injury to the brain. Reeducation is the only proven treatment.

Aphid, destructive sap-feeding insect of the aphid family, also known as greenfly or plant louse. Because of the damage caused by their piercing of plant tissue and because many of the 4,000 species carry viruses, aphids are one of the world's greatest crop pests. They are an important food source for ants and other insects.

Aphrodite, in Greek mythology, goddess of love, fertility, and beauty. The daughter of Zeus and Dione in some versions, in others she is described as having risen from the sea. Her intensely sensual beauty aroused jealousy among other goddesses, particularly after the Trojan Paris chose her as the most beautiful over Hera and Athena. Wife of the crippled smith Hephaestus, she took both divine and mortal lovers, giving birth to Aeneas and Eros. The Greeks honored her with many major shrines. The Romans called her Venus.

Apia (pop. 36,000), capital and main port of Western Samoa, on the northern coast of Upolu Island. Apia's Government House was once the home of Robert Louis Stevenson, author of *Treasure Island*, who died there in 1894 and is buried nearby.

Apocalypse, prophetic revelation, usually about the end of the world and the ensuing establishment of a heavenly kingdom. Jewish and Christian apocalyptic writings appeared in Palestine between 200 B.C. and 150 A.D. and offered hope of liberation to a people under alien rule.

Apocrypha, appendix to the King James Version of the Old Testament. Protestants use the term mainly for books written in the 2 centuries before Christ and included in the Septuagint and the Vulgate, but not in the Hebrew Bible. These include Esdras I and II, Tobit, Judith, additions to Esther, the Wisdom of Solomon, Ecclesiasticus, Baruch, the Song of the Three Holy Children, Susanna and the Elders, Bel and the Dragon, the Prayer of Manasses, and Maccabees I and II.

Apollinaire, Guillaume (Wilhelm Apollinaris de Kostrowitzky; 1880-1918), influential French avant-garde poet and critic. The friend of Derain, Dufy, and Picasso, he helped to publicize Cubist and primitive art. In his lyric poems *Alcools* (1913) and *Calligrammes* (1918), he anticipated Surrealism with his use of startling associations and juxtapositions.

Apollo, in Greek mythology, the son of Zeus and Leto, twin of Artemis, and second only to Zeus in that he had the power of the sun as giver of light and life. He was the god of justice and masculine beauty, purifier of those stained by crime, divine patron of the arts, leader of the Muses, and god of music and poetry. Apollo was considered a healer who could also send disease. He spoke through the oracle at Delphi. The Romans adopted Apollo, honoring him as healer and sun god.

Apollo Project, U.S. space program initiated by President John F. Kennedy on May 25, 1961, to place a person on the moon by the end of the 1960s. The pro-

The Apollo 11 landing vehicle, or lunar module, photographed from the carrier ship. The module's task was to transport astronauts from the carrier ship to the lunar surface. The vehicle was adapted exclusively to movement in airless space.

gram's mission was accomplished (at a cost of over $24 billion) when the Apollo 11 Lunar Excursion Module (LEM) carrying astronauts Neil Armstrong and Buzz Aldrin touched down on the moon's surface on July 20, 1969. Subsequent flights allowed exploration of various areas of the moon. The program ended in 1972 with Apollo 17.
See also: National Aeronautics and Space Administration.

Apostles, the 12 disciples closest to Jesus, whom he chose to proclaim his teaching: Andrew, John, Bartholomew, Judas, Jude, the two Jameses, Matthew, Peter, Philip, Simon, and Thomas. When Judas died, Matthias replaced him. Paul and Barnabas became known as apostles for their work in spreading the gospel.
See also: Bible.

Apostles' Creed, statement of belief ascribed to Jesus's apostles and maintained in its present form since the early Middle Ages. The Roman Catholic Church uses it in the sacraments of baptism and confirmation. It is also used by various Protestant denominations.
See also: Apostles.

Apothecaries' weight, system of weights once widely used in Great Britain and the United States by druggists, now replaced by the metric system. Apothecaries' weight divides the pound into 12 ounces, the ounce into 8 drams, the dram into 3 scruples, and the scruple into 20 grains.
See also: Weights and Measures.

Appalachian Mountains, mountain system of Northeastern America, about 1,800 mi (2,897 km) long and 120-375 mi (193-603 km) wide, stretching south from Newfoundland to central Alabama. Major ranges of the north include the Notre Dame, Green, and White mountains. The central area has the Allegheny Mountains and part of the Blue Ridge Mountains. The south contains the south Blue Ridge, Cumberland, Black, and Great Smoky mountains. The highest peak is Mt. Mitchell (6,684 ft/2,037 m) in North Carolina. Appalachian forests yield much timber, and rich deposits of coal and iron have stimulated growth of industrial areas like Birmingham, Ala., and Pittsburgh, Pa. In the early years of the United States, the Appalachians were a barrier to westward expansion, but the Connecticut, Hudson, Delaware, and other rivers have cut deep gaps in the ranges.

Appalachian National Scenic Trail, longest marked hiking trail in the world, stretching over 2,000 mi (3,219 km) along the crest of the Appalachian Mountains from Mt. Katahdin in northern Maine to Springer Mountain in northern Georgia.

Appeal, in law, transfer of a case that has been decided in a lower court to a higher court for review. In most U.S. jurisdictions, if the appeals court finds that the lower court (or administrative agency) made legal errors, it may decide in favor of the party making the appeal (appellant) or order a new trial in the lower court. The highest appeals court of the land is the Supreme Court in Washington, D.C., which will only hear cases in which a substantial federal or constitutional question is involved. Otherwise, the state supreme court is the highest authority.

Appellate court *see:* Court; Trial.

Appendicitis, inflammation of the appendix, often caused by obstruction to its narrow opening, followed by swelling and bacterial infection. Acute appendicitis can lead to rupture of the organ, formation of an abscess, or peritonitis. Symptoms include abdominal pain (usually in the right lower abdomen), nausea, vomiting, and fever. Early surgical removal of the appendix is essential; any abscess requires drainage of pus and delayed removal.
See also: Appendix.

Appendix, in biology small, hollow, closed tube located where the small and large intestines meet. While it aids digestion in certain rodents, it no longer has a function in humans and is considered a vestigial organ. The disease appendicitis results when the appendix becomes inflamed.
See also: Appendicitis.

Appia, Adolphe (1862-1928), Swiss stage designer whose ideas revolutionized early 20th-century theater. He stressed the use of 3-dimensional settings and of mobile lighting with controlled intensity and color.

Appian Way, oldest Roman road, constructed by the censor Appius Claudius Caecus in 312 B.C. At first stretching from Rome to Capua (about 130 mi/209 km), by the mid-third century B.C. the road had been extended to the site of present-day Brindisi, making it the main artery to southern Italy.

Apple flower

Apple, tree (genus *Malus*) of the rose family, widely cultivated in temperate climates; also, the fruit of the tree. Over 7,000 varieties are known, but only about 40 are commercially important, the most popular U.S. variety being the Delicious. Some 15 to 20% of the world's crop is produced in the United States, mostly in the states of Washington, New York, California, Michigan, and Virginia. There are 3 main types of apples: cooking, dessert, and those used in making cider.

Apple of Sodom (*Solanum sodomeum*), spiny plant of the nightshade family, native to Palestine, that bears yellow fruit resembling small apples. It is named for the biblical apple of Sodom, which looked tempting but turned to ashes in the mouth.

Appleseed, Johnny (John Chapman; 1774-1845), U.S. folk hero. A pioneer in the Ohio River region, he wandered for 40 years, planting and tending apple orchards.

Appleton, Sir Edward Victor (1892-1965), English physicist who discovered the Appleton layer (now resolved as 2 layers, F_1 and F_2) of ionized gas molecules in the ionosphere. His work in atmospheric physics won him the 1947 Nobel Prize for physics and contributed to the development of radar. During World War II he helped develop the atomic bomb.
See also: Ionosphere.

Appolonius of Rhodes (3rd century B.C.), Greek poet, pupil of Callimachus, and later head of the library at Alexandria. In addition to shorter works, he wrote the epic *Argonautica*, describing the expedition of Jason and the Argonauts. The poem uses much of Homer's style and meter, and its portrayal of Medea is thought to have influenced the Roman poet Vergil in the creation of Dido, a character in the *Aeneid*
See also: Homer; Vergil..

Appomattox Courthouse, settlement in central Virginia where the Civil War ended with Confederate General Robert E. Lee's surrender to Union General Ulysses S. Grant on Apr. 9, 1865. The site became a national historical park in 1954.
See also: Civil War.

Apportionment, legislative, distribution of voters' representation in the lawmaking bodies. Representation can be apportioned according to population or political units. For example, although each U.S. state, whatever size, elects 2 senators, the number of seats each state holds in the House of Representatives is based on the state's population. There is a reapportionment of seats each decade when the census is taken.

Apprentice, person who works for an accomplished craftsperson to learn a trade. An apprentice normally works regular hours and earns a salary. The system of apprenticeship, begun in ancient times, reached its peak in medieval Europe with the organization of guilds representing individual crafts. Following the Industrial Revolution, guilds were gradually replaced by smaller, newer fields of apprenticeship, particularly among machine workers and electricians.
See also: Guild.

Corazon Aquino

Apricot (*Prunus armeniaca*), tree of the rose family, native to China but grown throughout temperate regions; also, the orange-colored fruit of the tree. Over 90% of the U.S. crop of apricots comes from California. They are eaten fresh or preserved by drying or canning; the kernels are used to make a liqueur.

April Fools' Day, or All Fools' Day, Apr. 1, the traditional day for practical jokes. The custom probably began in France in 1564, when New Year's Day was changed from Apr. 1 to Jan. 1. Those continuing to observe Apr. 1 were ridiculed.

Apuleius, Lucius (C.A.D. 125-185), Latin writer. His *Metamorphoses* or *The Golden Ass* is the only complete extant Latin novel. The adventures of the novel's hero, who has been turned into an ass, provide insight into Imperial Roman society.

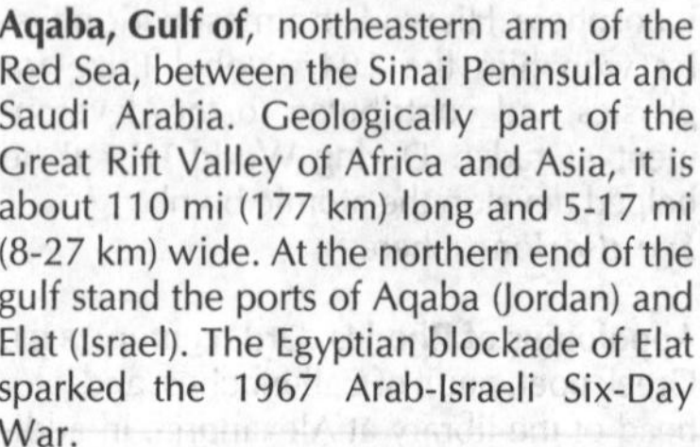

Aquamarine

Aqaba, Gulf of, northeastern arm of the Red Sea, between the Sinai Peninsula and Saudi Arabia. Geologically part of the Great Rift Valley of Africa and Asia, it is about 110 mi (177 km) long and 5-17 mi (8-27 km) wide. At the northern end of the gulf stand the ports of Aqaba (Jordan) and Elat (Israel). The Egyptian blockade of Elat sparked the 1967 Arab-Israeli Six-Day War.

Aquaculture, controlled raising of marine animals and seaweed for harvest. Aquaculture takes place in enclosures built on land or in natural bodies of water. China has practiced aquaculture for 4,000 years and is still the leading world producer of cultivated freshwater fish. Production in the United States is growing rapidly. In addition to fish, Asian sea farmers cultivate seaweed, from which are produced agar, algin, and carrageenan, used in food thickeners and in drugs.

Ancient Roman aqueducts in Spain

Aqualung *see:* Skin diving.

Aquamarine, transparent blue or pale blue-green semiprecious stone, a variety of the mineral beryl. The most important deposits are in Brazil, but aquamarine is also found in Siberia, Madagascar, and sections of the United States. Other bluish gemstones are sometimes incorrectly called aquamarine, including a blue variety of corundum called Oriental aquamarine.
See also: Beryl.

Aqua regia (Latin, "royal water"), mixture of concentrated nitric and hydrochloric acids used since the Middle Ages to dissolve gold, the "royal metal," and other substances that are difficult to get into solution.

Aquarium, tank, bowl, or pool in which aquatic animals and plants are kept. Aquariums originated in ancient Egypt and Asia. Romans used them not for decorative purposes, but as a source of fresh fish for the dinner table. The ornamental aquarium made its appearance in the West in the 18th century, when the goldfish became popular in France. The first public aquarium was opened in London in 1853, and Vienna and Paris soon followed. Today they are found in many of the major cities of the world, including, in the United States, Chicago, New York, and San Francisco. Giant aquariums, or oceanariums, large enough to hold a small whale, have been built in Los Angeles and at Marineland, Fla. These collections provide entertainment for the public as well as valuable information for students of marine life.

Aqueduct, artificial conduit for water. Ancient Rome was supplied with fresh drinking water from mountain springs by 14 aqueducts. In the south of France the Pont du Gard still stands.
The longest aqueduct today is the California State Water Project aqueduct (826 mi/1,329 km), completed in 1974.

Aquinas, Saint Thomas (1225-74), Italian scholastic theologian and philosopher. Known as the Angelic Doctor, St. Thomas reconciled Christian faith with Aristotelian reason. His teachings are basic to Roman Catholic theology. His greatest work is the *Summa Theologica* (1267-73).
See also: Scholasticism.

Aquino, Corazon (1933-), first woman president of the Philippines. The widow of slain Philippine opposition leader Benigno Aquino, she was the major opposition candidate in the 1986 presidential elections. The National Assembly—controlled by supporters of President Ferdinand Marcos—declared Marcos winner of the election, although there were major signs of fraud. After rioting broke out, Marcos left the Philippines on board a U.S. plane, and Aquino was recognized as president.

Arab, one whose language is Arabic and who identifies with Arab culture. The term originally referred to inhabitants of the Arabian Peninsula, but the Arab world today includes the countries Algeria, Egypt, Iraq, Jordan, Lebanon, Libya, Morocco, Sudan, Syria, and Tunisia. Arab culture spread after the successful campaigns of Mohammed (C.A.D. 570). In the 7th century the Arabs extended their hegemony from northwestern Africa and Spain to Afghanistan and northern India, where many non-Arabic peoples were converted to the Arabic religion of Islam. Non-Muslim peoples who are also Arabs include Palestinian, Lebanese, and Syrian Christians. In the 20th century the discovery and exploitation of petroleum in Arab lands has resulted in sudden wealth and modernization for many Arab countries. Arab hostility to the state of Israel has strengthened Pan-Arab nationalism.
See also: Islam; Middle East; Muslims.

Arabesque, elaborate decorative style characterized by curved or intertwining shapes, with grotesque, animal, human, or symbolic forms and delicate foliage.

Arabia *see:* Arabian Peninsula; Saudi Arabia.

Arabian Desert, one of the greatest desert regions in the world, comprising almost all of the deserts of the Arabian Peninsula in southwest Asia. The desert covers approximately 900,000 sq mi (2,331,000 sq km) and is surrounded by the Syrian Desert, the Persian Gulf, the Gulf of Oman, the Arabian Sea, the Gulf of Aden, and the Red Sea.

Arabian Nights, or *The Thousand and One Nights*, collection of ancient Persian, Indian, and Arabian folktales, written in Arabic and arranged in its present form during the early 16th century. The stories, which include the tales of Aladdin, Ali Baba, and Sinbad the Sailor, are linked by a framing story about Scheherazade. She marries a king who executes his wives on the second day of their marriage. Each night, she tells him part of a story but leaves the ending for the next night. The king must spare her for another day if he is to learn the ending. By the 1,001st night, the king has learned to love his wife, and Scheherazade is spared.
See also: Burton, Sir Richard Francis.

Arabian Peninsula, vast land, largely desert, in southwest Asia, surrounded by the Red Sea, the Arabian Sea, and the Persian Gulf. Saudi Arabia takes up the greatest part of land. Other countries are the Republic of Yemen, Oman, United Arab Emirates, Qatar, and Kuwait. The arid area, approximately 1,162,000 sq mi (3,009,600 sq km), is economically and politically important because of its great petroleum resources.

Arabian Sea, northwestern sea of the Indian Ocean, between India and Arabia. It is connected with the Persian Gulf by the Gulf of Oman and with the Red Sea by the Gulf of Aden. Its ports include Bombay and Karachi.

Arabic, one of the Semitic languages. The Arabic alphabet comprises 28 consonants, vowels being expressed either by positioned points or, in some cases, by insertion of the letters *alif, waw,* and *ya* where they would not otherwise occur, thereby representing the long *a, u,* and *i* respectively. Arabic is written from right to left. Classical Arabic, the language of the Koran, is used occasionally in writing, rarely in speech; a standardized modern Arabic is used in newspapers. Arabic played a large part in the dissemination of knowledge through medieval Europe because many ancient Greek and Roman texts were available solely in Arabic translation.
See also: Semitic languages.

Arabic numerals, also called Hindu-Arabic numerals, the most common symbols for numbers. These basic symbols or digits (Latin, "fingers") are: 0, 1, 2, 3, 4, 5, 6, 7, 8, and 9. The position of the digit determines its value. For example, in the Arabic numeral 846, the digit 8 has a value of 8 x 100, the digit 4 has a value of 4 x 10, and the digit 6 has a value of 6. Exactly how Arabic numerals originated is unknown. The Hindus in India probably developed 1 through 9 in about 200 B.C.; they developed zero after A.D. 600. Traders and merchants helped spread the Arabic numeral system into Europe.
See also: Numeration systems.

Arab-Israeli Wars, several conflicts between Israel and the Arabs. In 1948, when Israel was established as an independent state on what the Arabs regarded as Arab land, Egypt, Iraq, Transjordan (Jordan), Lebanon, and Syria attacked, but within a month Israel had occupied the greater part of Palestine. By July 1949, separate ceasefires were concluded with the Arab states. On Oct. 29, 1956, with the Suez Canal and Gulf of Aqaba closed to its ships, Israel invaded Egypt, which had nationalized the canal in July. British and French supporting troops occupied the canal banks but were replaced by a UN force after international furor. By Mar. 1957 all Israeli forces had left Egypt in exchange for access to the Gulf of Aqaba. In 1967 Egypt again closed the gulf to Israel, and on June 5, at the start of the Six-Day War, Israeli air strikes destroyed the Arab air forces on the ground. Israel won the West Bank of the Jordan River, the Golan Heights, the Gaza Strip, the Sinai Peninsula, and the Old City of Jerusalem. A ceasefire was accepted by June 10. On Oct. 6, 1973, Yom Kippur, Egypt and Syria attacked Israel to regain the lost territories. A ceasefire was signed on Nov. 11, 1973. Although Israeli troops penetrated deep into Syria and crossed onto the west bank of the Suez Canal, initial Arab success restored Arab confidence. Talks between Egypt and Israel led to a peace treaty in 1979. But tension ran high elsewhere, especially in Lebanon, which was used as a guerrilla base by the Palestinians and became a target for Israeli attacks. In June 1982 Israel invaded Lebanon to destroy strongholds of the Palestine Liberation Organization (PLO) guerrillas. Subsequently, under a U.S.-sponsored plan, the guerrillas left Beirut for other countries willing to accept them, and a multinational peacekeeping force, including U.S. marines, landed in Lebanon.

Satellite photo of the Sinai Peninsula

Arab League, organization promoting economic, cultural, and political cooperation among Arab states, founded in 1945. Its members include 20 of the Arab states and the PLO. In 1948 the members attacked the new state of Israel, which had been established on what the Arabs considered Arab land. The league broke with Egypt, an original member, in 1979 after the country signed a peace treaty with Israel. Egypt rejoined the league in 1989.

Arachne, in Greek mythology, mortal so expert in weaving that she challenged Athena to a contest. Arachne's tapestry, which depicted the foibles of the gods, angered the goddess, who tore it up. Arachne hanged herself in despair and was transformed into a spider.

Arachnid, insectlike arthropod of the class Arachnida. Spiders, mites, and scorpions are arachnids. While an insect's body consists of head, thorax, and abdomen, an arachnid's body has only 2 main parts: abdomen and cephalothorax, which combines head and thorax. Also unlike insects, arachnids have no wings or antennae, and they have simple rather than compound eyes.

Arafat, Yasir (1929-), Palestinian political figure. After organizing the anti-Israel Al Fatah guerrillas in the 1950s, Arafat became chairman of the Palestine Liberation Organization (PLO) in 1969. In 1974 Arafat opened a debate on Palestine at the UN, where he led the first nongovernmental delegation to take part in a General Assembly plenary session. It is generally believed that Arafat authorized terrorist actions to accomplish the goals of the PLO. In 1991, the PLO sided with Iraq in the Persian Gulf War which led to a weakening of its position. Arafat, Rabin, and Peres were awarded the Nobel Peace Prize in 1994.
See also: Palestine Liberation Organization.

Yasir Arafat

Aragón, historic region of northeastern Spain, stretching from the central Pyrenees to south of the Ebro River. The medieval kingdom of Aragón comprised what are now the provinces of Huesca, Teruel, and Saragossa, although the influence of the kings of Aragón was more extensive. King Ferdinand II of Aragón's marriage to Isabella of Castile (1479) laid the foundations of a unified Spain. Aragón's sovereignty was ended 1707-9 by Philip V during the War of the Spanish Succession (1701-14).

Aral Sea, inland sea or saltwater lake covering 24,904 sq mi (64,501 sq km) in the south of the former USSR. It is the fourth largest lake in the world and is fed by the Amu Darya and Syr Darya rivers. The sea is commercially important for its bass, carp, perch, and sturgeon.

Aramaic, Semitic language. It spread throughout Syria and Mesopotamia from the 8th century B.C. on, and was the official language of the Persian Empire. Aramaic was probably spoken by Jesus and the

apostles, and parts of the Old Testament are in Aramaic. Aramaic survives only in isolated Lebanese villages and among some Nestorians of northern Iraq and eastern Turkey.
See also: Semitic languages.

Arapaho, North American tribe of the Algonquian family. They lived as nomadic buffalo hunters on the Great Plains. Fierce enemies of European-American settlement, they were forced onto reservations at the end of the 19th century. The Arapaho are divided into 3 groups: the Southern Arapaho, the Northern Arapaho, and the Gros Ventre. Less than 5,000 Arapaho remain, mostly on reservations in Oklahoma and Wyoming.

Ararat, Mount, dormant volcanic mountain in eastern Turkey with 2 peaks, 16,950 ft (5,166 m) and 13,000 ft (3,962 m) high. According to the Bible, Noah's Ark landed on Mount Ararat (Genesis 8:4). The Armenians venerate the mountain as the "Mother of the World."
See also: Noah.

Araucanians, South American tribes famous for their resistance to the Spaniards, beginning with the 16th-century Spanish invasion of what is now central Chile. Many Araucanians crossed the Andes into Argentina on stolen Spanish horses. The tribes were defeated in the late 19th century. Today over 200,000 Araucanians live in Chile.

Arawak, group of often culturally distinct South American tribes, now living mostly in Brazil, the Guyanas, and Peru. Arawak inhabited several West Indian islands when Columbus landed in 1492. The Caribbean Arawak were wiped out by the mid-16th century by a combination of disease and forced labor brought on by Europeans.

Arc de Triomphe, illuminated for the celebration of the 200th anniversary of the French Revolution

Arbitration, process for settling disputes in which the parties submit the controversy to an impartial arbitrator. In conciliation or mediation, the impartial person tries to persuade the parties to accept a settlement; in arbitration, by prior agreement the arbitrator imposes a final and binding decision, called an award. Experienced tribunals established by trade associations arbitrate commercial disputes between business organizations. Industrial arbitration settles disputes between labor and management. Collective bargaining agreements generally provide for an impartial arbitrator to settle conflicts arising from different interpretations of the agreement. Arbitration in international affairs is one of the oldest ways of settling disputes. It was used by the Greek city-states and is today included as a provision in many treaties between nations.

Arboretum, place in which trees and shrubs are cultivated for scientific or educational purposes.

Arc, electric *see:* Electric arc.

Arc, Joan of *see:* Joan of Arc, Saint.

Arcadia, ancient Greek region in central Peloponnesus, enclosed by mountains. The simple life of its rustic inhabitants was idealized by classical pastoral poets and later writers, notably the English poet Sir Philip Sidney, as the embodiment of innocent, virtuous living.

Arcaro, Eddie (George Edward Arcaro; 1916-), U.S. jockey. The first to have won the Triple Crown twice (1941,1948) and the Kentucky Derby 5 times, and the third jockey to win more than 4,000 races. Arcaro's purses totaled more than $30 million during his career (1931-62).

Arc de Triomphe, Napoleon's triumphal arch in the Place Charles de Gaulle at the end of the Champs-Elysées, Paris. It was built 1806-36 and is 163 ft (49 m) high and 147 ft (45 m) wide. Inspired by Roman triumphal arches, it bears reliefs celebrating Napoleon's victories. The arch is also the site of the tomb of France's Unknown Soldier.

Arch, structural device to span openings and support loads. In architecture the simplest form of the arch is the round (semicircular), in which wedge-shaped stones, or voussoirs, are fitted together, receiving the stresses in the arch exerted outward onto them. Downward forces from the load combine with these to produce a diagonal force, or thrust. The voussoirs at each end of the arch are called springers; the one in the center, usually the last to be placed, is the keystone. Although the arch was known in ancient Egypt and Greece, it was not until Roman times that its use became popular.

Archaeopteryx, prehistoric feathered reptile the size of a crow, with 2 claws representing the thumb and forefinger projecting from its wing and about 20 tail vertebrae.
See also: Prehistoric animal.

Archangel (pop. 403,000; Russian, *Arkhangelsk*), city in northwestern USSR, near the mouth of the North Dvina River. Archangel is a major White Sea port, exporting lumber, resin, turpentine, and furs. Other industries include sawmilling, shipbuilding, and papermaking. Established as a trading post called Novo-Kholmogory in 1584, it later became a leading Russian port, declining after 1703, when St. Petersburg (later Leningrad) was founded. The port expanded in World War II, when it received tons of supplies shipped by the Allies.

Archbishop, metropolitan bishop of the Roman Catholic, Anglican, or Eastern Orthodox church, or of the Lutheran churches of Finland and Sweden, having jurisdiction over the bishops of a church province, or archdiocese. The archbishop consecrates bishops and presides over synods.

Archeoastronomy, study of the astronomy of ancient peoples and its relation to other aspects of culture. The field includes the work of archeologists, astronomers, historians, and anthropologists. Archeoastronomers in Great Britain have studied the circles of large stones laid more than 5,000 years ago, and believe the circles may have been calendars or a way of predicting eclipses. Also of interest are Mayan buildings, which were constructed in a direct line with Venus on the horizon.
See also: Archeology; Astronomy; Stonehenge.

Archeology, study of the past through identification and interpretation of the material remains of human cultures. Archeology uses the knowledge and techniques of such disciplines as anthropology, history, paleography, and philology. Its keystone is fieldwork. Archeology began in the early 18th century with excavations of Roman and other sites. The famous Rosetta Stone, which provided the key to Egyptian hieroglyphics, was discovered in 1799 and deciphered in 1818. In the 19th century archeology became a systematized science through the work of Heinrich Schliemann, Arthur Evans, C. L. Woolley, Howard Carter, and others. In the United States archeologists have studied the culture of early Native Americans as well as settlements of colonial America—an example of historic archeology, which deals with peoples who left behind written documents.
Suitable sites may be revealed as a result of war damage or during construction of buildings and roads. Because unusually shaped hills or mounds are sometimes artificial, they are often investigated. Ancient writings may help in locating sites. Aerial photography has sometimes revealed the existence of buried structures. The archeological team then recovers objects or fragments lying loose on the ground or inside caves, or, more often, excavates (digs) to

find the artifacts. Great care is required not to damage any object or trace of an object. Small hoes, spades, trowels, penknives, brushes, and fingers are used. Archeologists record the spatial relationships artifacts have to one another and to the layers in which they are found. Notes and drawings are made, each item is numbered, and photographs are taken.
Archeologists use 2 dating systems: absolute dating and relative dating. Early inscriptions, and especially, mention of an eclipse or other astronomical phenomena, make it easy to date a monument or site. Tree-ring chronology can help date wood remains. Pollen, an extraordinarily durable organic substance, is also a useful date indicator. Radiocarbon dating uses the known half-life of radioactive carbon-14, found in all organic matter, as a yardstick. Stratigraphy, the most important method for relative dating, uses the principle that objects found near the surface are more recent than those found lower within the ground. Because pottery styles sometimes overlap on several sites, information gained from one site can be applied to another. Chemical changes in bones can also help differentiate younger ones from older ones.

Archerfish, any of several species of Indo-Pacific fishes of the family Toxotidae with the ability to eject water from their mouths to knock insect prey to the surface; especially, *Toxotes jaculator*. The archerfish has a flat, elongated body and inhabits both fresh and salt water.

Archery, competitive and recreational sport, using bows and arrows. The three major types of archery are target, field and flight. Target and field archery involve firing arrows at set targets, while flight archery is a contest of distance shooting. An Olympic event, archery's popularity worldwide led to the formation of the International Archery Federation (1931).

Arches National Park, 82,953 acres (33,571 hectares) in eastern Utah containing natural rock arches formed by weathering and erosion. The park was established in 1929.

Archimedes (c.287-212 B.C.), Greek mathematician and physicist who spent most of his life in Syracuse, Sicily, where he was born. In mathematics he worked on the areas and volumes of conic sections, determined the value of π as lying between 3-1/7 and 3-10/71, and defined the Archimedean spiral. He founded the science of hydrostatics with his enunciation of Archimedes' principle, that the force acting to buoy up a body partially or totally immersed in a fluid is equal to the weight of the fluid displaced. He is also credited with the invention of Archimedes' screw, a machine for raising water that is still used to irrigate fields in Egypt. In physics he was the first to prove the law of the lever.
See also: Calculus; Physics.

Archipelago (Greek, "chief sea"), name originally applied to the Aegean Sea, which is studded with many small islands; by extension, any space of water interspersed with islands or the group of islands itself. The greatest archipelago is the 3,200-mile (5,100-km) crescent of more than 3,000 islands that form Indonesia.

Architecture, art or science of designing and building structures. While the beginnings of architecture are traceable to areas around the Nile, Euphrates, and Tigris rivers, the Greeks and Romans created the styles that we rely on today. Greek architecture used post-and-lintel construction: a rectangle formed by beams and columns. The Romans were the first to fully use the arch and to use concrete as a building material, making possible structures with enormous roof spans.
Byzantine architecture, which arose in the Eastern Roman Empire and later influenced Russia, introduced the dome. Islamic architecture featured interior courtyards surrounded by colonnades. At the end of the Middle Ages, European churches and monasteries were stoutly built, for defensive purposes. Starting at the end of the 12th century, stained glass, high pillars, and thin arches of Gothic architecture were held in equilibrium by exterior buttresses. The Renaissance brought a revival of classical (Greek and Roman) architecture. In the Baroque period, rich ornamentation and curves replaced the straight lines of the Renaissance. The 18th century saw a revival of classical architecture in Europe and America, and a Gothic revival began in the 19th century. Starting in the last half of the 19th century, the use of iron, steel, and reinforced concrete allowed skyscrapers to be built.

Archon, administrator of ancient Athens and other Greek city-states. Originally a life term open only to nobles, by 682 B.C. the archonship was shared by 9 members elected from the population for 1 year, and included a civil ruler, a religious head, a military commander, and 6 lawmakers. The archons lost influence with the rise of democracy.

Archimedes' screw consists of a spiral, open at the top and bottom. Water is trapped in the lowest turn of the spiral and is lifted as it rotates. Shown is a diagram of an ancient, tread-mill-driven irrigation pump.

Arc light, device in which electrical current flowing between poles or electrodes produces the electric arc, yielding an intensely bright light. Arc lights are used in searchlights and movie projectors. The mercury arc is the basis for modern fluorescent lamps.
See also: Electric light.

Arctic, region north of the Arctic Circle (66°30′ N); alternatively, regions north of the tree line.
Land and climate. The Arctic comprises the Arctic Ocean, Greenland, Spitsbergen and other islands, extreme northern Europe, Siberia, Alaska, and northern Canada. The area's central feature is the Arctic Ocean, opening south into the North Atlantic Ocean and Bering Strait. The Arctic Ocean comprises 2 main basins and has a shallow rim floored by the continental shelves of Eurasia and North America. Much of the ocean's surface is always covered with ice.
The Arctic climate is cold. In midwinter the sun never rises and the mean Jan. temperature is -33° F (-57.6° C), far lower in interior Canada and Siberia. Snow and ice never melt in the high altitudes and latitudes of the Arctic, but elsewhere the short mild summer, with 24 hours of sunlight a day, thaws the sea and the topsoil. In spring, melting icebergs floating south from the Arctic Ocean endanger North Atlantic shipping. Vegetation in the Arctic is varied but confined mainly to shrubs, flowering herbaceous plants, mosses, and lichens. Wild mammals include polar bears, reindeer, musk oxen, moose, wolves, weasels, foxes, and lemmings. Geese, ducks, gulls, cranes, falcons, auks, and ptarmigan all nest in the Arctic, and its seas harbor whales, seals, cod, salmon, and shrimp.
People. Inuits (Eskimos), Lapps, Russians, and others make up a human population of several million. Eskimos have lived in the Arctic for at least 9,000 years. Once exclusively hunters and fishers, Eskimos now also work in towns and on oil fields.
Economy. The Arctic is home to scattered agricultural, mining, and fishing industries, and the United States, Canada, and the

Archerfish

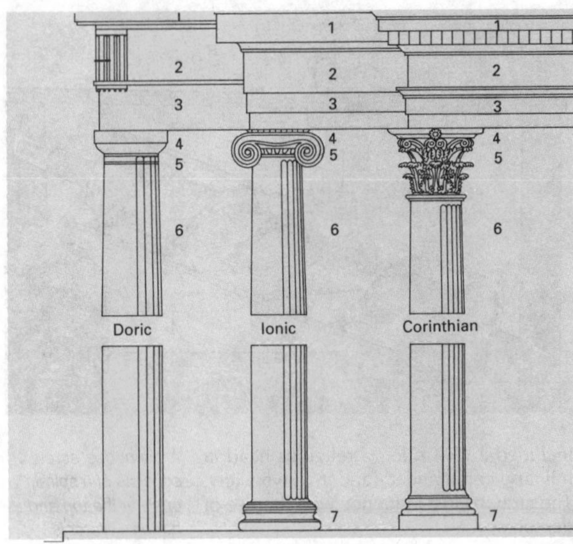

Doric, Ionic, and Corinthian columns. The Doric is the simplest and oldest of the three styles and evolved in the 7th century B.C. The Ionic style reached maturity in the 5th century B.C. and the Corinthian in the 4th century B.C. Shown are the following elements:

1. cornice
2. frieze
3. architrave
4. abacus
5. capital
6. columns with fluting
7. base

Pier Luigi Nervi's interior of the Turin Exhibition Hall.

Rome's Pantheon (c. A.D. 115-125) is the world's oldest building with its original roof intact. Shown are the following:

1. Corinthian columns of white marble
2. intermediate block leading to rotunda
3. rotunda
4. semi-domed exedra
5. marble and granite pavement
6. attic
7. hemispherical, brick and mortar dome with bronze tiles
8. central oculus, the only source of light.

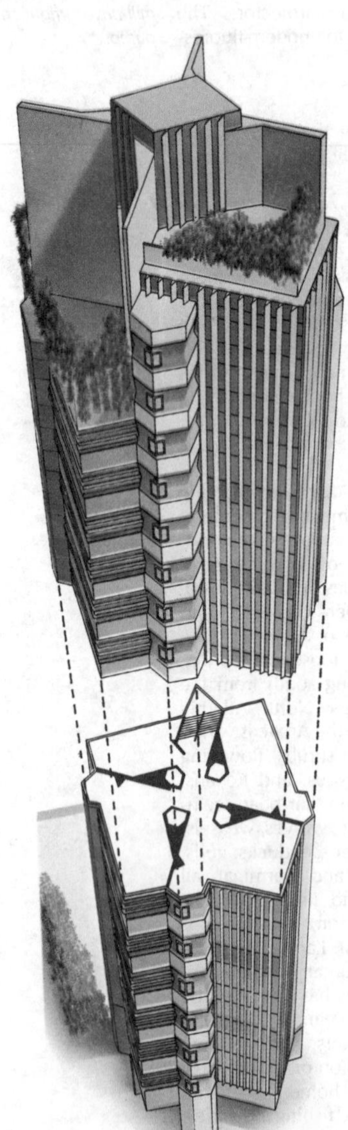

Bruno Taut's Glass Pavillion, which appeared at the Werkbund Exhibition in Cologne, Germany in 1914. Taut wrote that this was "...the lightest possible concrete structure, destined to demonstrate the use of glass in all its varied aesthetic charm...."

Frank Lloyd Wright's Price Tower in Bartlesville, Oklahoma, constructed in 1956. This illustration shows the tower dissected to reveal the plan of a typical floor. The hollow concrete cores contain elevators and service areas. The building contains business offices and duplex apartments. These are distinguished by the use of vertical louvers for the apartments and horizontal ones for the offices.

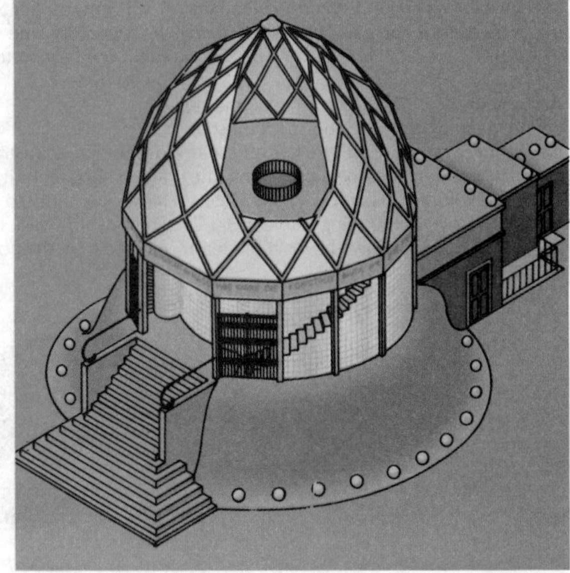

Soviet Union maintain air bases and meteorological stations there. In 1978, oil production began at Prudhoe Bay, an inlet of the Arctic Ocean in northern Alaska, the oil moving south to Valdez, Alaska, through the Alaskan Pipeline.

History. Vikings were the first recorded Arctic explorers. Norwegians visited the Russian Arctic in the 9th century and the Icelander Eric the Red established a Greenland settlement in A.D. 982. In the 16th and 17th centuries exploration was encouraged by the search for a northwest passage (a water route along the northern coast of North America, between the Atlantic and Pacific oceans) and a northeast passage (a water route between the same oceans but along the northern coast of Europe and Asia). In the 16th century Martin Frobisher reached Baffin Island, and Willem Barentz explored Novaya Zemlya and saw Spitsbergen. Henry Hudson probed eastern Greenland and the Hudson Strait in the early 17th century. But the longed-for passages remained undiscovered, and interest in Arctic exploration declined until Canadian and Russian fur traders revived it late in the 18th century. Early in the 19th century the British naval officers John and James Ross, W. E. Perry, John Rae, and Sir John Franklin traveled to unexplored areas, and James Ross discovered the north magnetic pole. N.A.E. Nordenskjöld of Sweden navigated the Northeast Passage (1878-79) and R. Amundsen the Northwest Passage (1906). In 1909 Robert E. Peary reached the North Pole. Richard E. Byrd and Floyd Bennett flew over the Pole in 1926, pioneering polar air exploration and transpolar air travel. In 1958 the U. S. nuclear submarine *Nautilus* reached the Pole.

Arctic Circle, imaginary circle at 66 30′ N lat. roughly defining the tree line and marking the southernmost point of the polar area at which the midnight sun is seen. The sun never rises on the Arctic Circle at the winter solstice on or about Dec. 21.

Arctic fox (*Alopex lagopus*), tundra dweller of the family Canidae. In summer, it is brown or gray; in winter it is white or slate blue. The Arctic fox is about 2 ft (60 cm) long, with a long tail and short, rounded ears. A true scavenger, it eats any available food and follows polar bears to eat the remains of their kills.

Arctic Ocean, the smallest ocean, centering on the North Pole and connecting with the Atlantic through the Greenland Sea and with the Pacific through the Bering Strait. It covers about 4 million sq mi (10.3 million sq km), has an average depth of 4,362 ft (1,330 m), and includes an abyss with a known depth of 17,880 ft (5,450 m) and a continental shelf extending up to 1,000 mi (1,600 km) from the coast. Most of the Arctic Ocean is frozen all year. It was probably discovered by Greek sailors around 400 B.C. and was sailed by Vikings in the 800s. Norwegian explorer Fridtjof Nansen conducted the first scientific study in 1893-96.

Arctic tern (*Sterna paradisaea*), a coast-dwelling, long-distance migrant bird of the family Laridae. The Arctic tern winters in Antarctica, then flies north to breed on Atlantic coasts from New England to the northernmost islands of the Arctic Ocean. It is about 17 in (43 cm) long, with gray, black, and white feathers and a red bill and feet.
See also: Tern.

Arctic tern

Arcturus (*Alpha Bootes*), brightest and fourth -largest star, orange-red in color. It is located in the constellation Boötes. Arcturus is about 40 light-years from earth and is moving toward earth at 3 mi (5 km) per second. Its luminosity is about 100 times that of the sun.

Ardennes, forested plateau in southeastern Belgium, northern Luxembourg, and northern France. The area is sparsely populated, with some agriculture and quarrying. It was a major battleground in World War I and World War II.
See also: Colosseum.

Arendt, Hannah (1906-75), German-born U.S. political philosopher. In 1959 she became the first woman appointed a full professor at Princeton University; she later taught at the University of Chicago and the New School for Social Research in New York. In *The Origins of Totalitarianism* (1951) she traced Nazism and Communism back to 19th-century anti-Semitism and imperialism. Her controversial *Eichmann in Jerusalem* (1963), with its theory of the "banality of evil," analyzed Nazi war crimes and the 1960 trial of Adolph Eichmann by the Israeli government.

Areopagus, small hill northwest of the Acropolis in Athens, where the supreme council of the city passed judgment on matters of state, religion, and morality. The name came to refer to the council itself. The Areopagus tried homicide cases, and it had a legislative veto and powers of impeachment.
See also: Solon.

Arequipa (pop. 302,300), city in southern Peru, capital of Arequipa department. Located at an altitude of 8,000 ft (2,400 m), between the Pacific Ocean and the Andes, Arequipa has a mild, dry climate. An important wool market and a crossroads of trade and transportation, its industries produce textiles, food, and shoes. Arequipa has frequently suffered severe damage from earthquakes.

Ares, in Greek mythology, the god of war. He was known to the Romans as Mars.

Argentina, second-largest country in South America (1,072,157 sq mi/2,776,889 sq km). Only Brazil is larger. Argentina borders on the Atlantic Ocean in the southeast; Uruguay, Brazil in the east, Paraguay in the northeast, Bolivia in the north, and Chile in the west.

Land and climate. The Andes Mountains form a natural border with Chile. The Gran Chaco region, in the north, is an extensive forested plain. Also in the north is the Paraná Plateau. The fertile Pampa in the heart of Argentina is the country's most important region economically. Semiarid Patagonia to the south yields oil. In the west, the Andes include Mt. Aconcagua (22,834 ft/6,960 m), the highest peak in South America. The climate of Argentina varies from damp and subtropical in the north to cool and dry in the south.

People. About 90% of the people are descended from Southern European immigrants, with a small Native American population. The national language is Spanish and about 90% of the population is Roman Catholic, with 70% living in urban areas like Buenos Aires.

Economy. Grain-growing and cattle-raising dominate the pampas, and agriculture is the basis of the country's wealth. Oil and other minerals come from the north and south. About 30% of the labor force works

Argentina's economy is based, in great part, on the livestock industry.

Argentina's oil-producing region of Patagonia is situated on a bleak plateau. The Limay River is in the center of the photograph.

Argentina

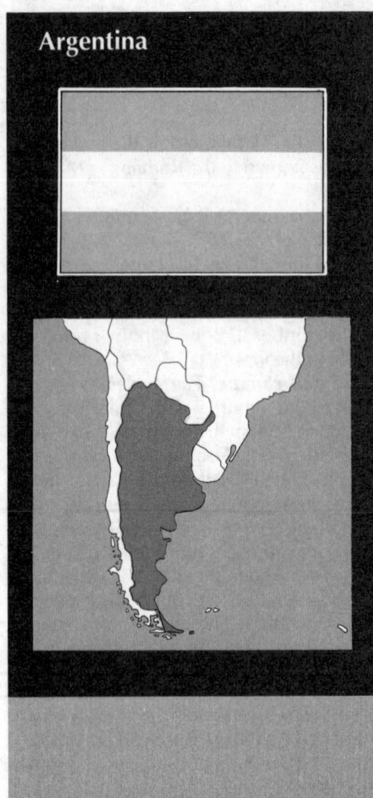

General information	
Capital:	Buenos Aires
Area:	1,068,302 sq mi (2,766,889 sq km)
Population:	32,425,000
Official language:	Spanish
Monetary unit:	1 austral = 1000 pesos
Main cities:	Buenos Aires, Córdoba, Rosario, La Plata
Government	
Form:	federal republic
Independent:	1816
Head of state:	President (elected every 6 years)
Head of government:	President
Legislature:	two legislative houses (Senate; Chamber of Deputies)
Executive:	President plus ministers
Judiciary:	Supreme Court
Political division:	22 provinces, 1 Federal District, 1 Federal Territory
National economy	
Gross national product:	U.S. $83,040,000,000
Per capita income:	U.S. $2,640
Agriculture:	sugar cane, wheat and other cereals, grapes, soybeans, sunflower seeds
Livestock:	cattle, sheep
Fisheries:	559,395 metric tons
Mining:	uranium, silver, gold
Industries:	iron and steel, motor vehicles, paper and paper products, sugar, beer
Main exports:	food and livestock, machinery and transportation equipment, iron and steel
Transportation:	21,442 mi (34,509 km) of railroads; 131,338 mi (211,369 km) of roads; 10 international airports
Trading partners:	U.S., Brazil, Germany, Netherlands
People	
Urban:	85%
Ethnic composition:	European 85%, mestizo and Indians 15%
Birth rate:	20 per 1,000 population
Death rate:	9 per 1,000 population
Infant mortality:	32 per 1,000 live births
Life expectancy:	male 67 years, female 74 years

in the country's well-developed industrial sector, much of which is located in and around Buenos Aires. High inflation is chronic and persistent.

History. Colonized by the Spanish in the 16th century, Argentina won its independence in 1816. The 19th century saw increased European immigration, economic progress, and political instability and strife with repercussions well into the 20th century. In 1944, Col. Juan Perón seized power and ruled until 1955. His dictatorship was supported by nationalists, the army, and the Roman Catholic church. However, his rule depended in large measure upon the popularity of his wife, Eva Duarte de Perón, and her death (1952), combined with a bad economy, led to Perón's ouster (1955). The Perónist movement remained popular, and in 1973 an aging Perón was restored to power. He died in 1974 and was succeeded by his wife, Isabel Perón, but the economy worsened and violence between left and right increased. Isabel Perón was overthrown in 1976, and the country was governed by military juntas for the next 6 years. In reaction to terrorism from the left, the juntas, through their agents and surrogates, kidnapped and murdered some 20,000-30,000 Argentine citizens suspected of leftist sympathies. In 1982, Argentina occupied the Falkland Islands and was defeated by Britain in the subsequent war. Gen. Leopoldo Galtieri resigned and Raúl Alfonsin was elected president of a civilian government in 1983. Nine members of the juntas stood trial for murder and human rights abuses and were sentenced to long prison terms. In 1989 Carlos Raúl Menem, a Perónist, was elected president.

Argon, chemical element, symbol Ar; for physical constants see Periodic Table. Argon was discovered by Lord Rayleigh and Sir William Ramsay in 1894. It is prepared by fractionation of liquid air, the atmosphere containing almost 1% of the element. Argon is a colorless, odorless, and chemically inert gas. It is not known to form chemical compounds, as do krypton, xenon, and radon. It is available in high purity, and is used in electric light bulbs, as a nonreactive shield in arc welding and in the production of reactive metals, and as a protective atmosphere for growing silicon, and germanium crystals.

Argonaut, or paper nautilus, small marine animal (genus *Argonauta*), a cephalopod which is native to the Mediterranean and other warm seas. Eggs are laid in a semi-transparent, papery spiral shell that can be carried by the female. The male seldom reaches an inch in length, but the female may be as long as 6 in (15 cm) or more.

Argonauts, heroes of Greek mythology who set sail in the ship *Argo* under Jason to find the Golden Fleece. With many illustrious members (Orpheus, Hercules, Castor and Pollux, Theseus), they sailed for Colchis, where the fleece was guarded by a dragon. After averting many perils, they obtained the fleece and returned home.

Argonne National Laboratory, nuclear-power research center 25 mi (40 km) south of Chicago. The University of Chicago operates it for the U.S. Energy Research and Development Administration.

Argus, or Argos, in Greek mythology, (1) the designer of the Argonauts' ship *Argo*; (2) the old dog who died after recognizing his master, Odysseus, returning in disguise to his home in Ithaca after an absence of 19 years; (3) the monster called Panoptes (the all-seeing) because of the great number of eyes in his head and over his body. He was ordered by Hera to watch Io, who had been transformed into a cow, but Hermes killed him, and by Hera's orders, Argus's eyes were sprinkled as decorations through the tail of the peacock.

Århus (pop. 253,800), port and Denmark's second largest city. Developed by the 9th century. Århus is a commercial and industrial center producing textiles, machines, beer, and timber. It is the site of the Cathedral of St. Clemens, built around 1100, and of the University of Århus, founded in 1928.

Ariadne, in Greek mythology, daughter of Minos, king of Crete. She loved the hero Theseus and gave him thread that helped him find his way out of the labyrinth. After Theseus killed the Minotaur, he married Ariadne but later deserted her. The god Bacchus gave her a crown of seven stars, which became a constellation.

Arianism, 4th-century Christian heresy founded in Alexandria by the priest Arius. He taught that Christ was not coequal and coeternal with God the Father, for the Father had created him. To curb Arianism, the Emperor Constantine called the first Council of Nicaea (A.D. 325), and the first Nicene Creed declared that God the Father and Christ the Son were of the same substance.
See also: Nicene Councils.

Arias Sánchez, Oscar (1941-), Costa Rican politician. He served as the president's financial adviser (1970-72), minister of national planning (1972-77), and president (1986-90). Arias Sánchez denied U.S.-supported Nicaraguan contras operating bases in Costa Rica, and promoted peaceful regional negotiations, for which he was awarded the Nobel Peace Prize in 1987.

Ariosto, Ludovico (1474-1533), Italian poet best remembered for the epic *Orlando Furioso* (1532), which continued the Roland legend, depicting the hero as a love-torn knight. The work greatly influenced later poets such as Edmund Spenser and Lord Byron.

Aristarchus of Samos (310-230 B.C.), Alexandrian Greek astronomer who recognized that the sun is larger than the earth. According to Archimedes, he taught that the earth orbited a motionless sun.
See also: Archimedes.

Aristides (530?-468? B.C.), called the Just, Athenian politician and general, a founder of the Delian League. He fought at the battle of Marathon (490 B.C.) and was elected archon for 489. Ostracized in 482, he was recalled in 480 and helped repulse the Persians. Later he fixed Greek cities' contributions to the Delian League.
See also: Themistocles.

Aristocracy (from Greek *aristos*, "the best," and *kratos*, "rule"), originally, the ruling of a state by its best citizens in the interest of all; used by the philosophers Plato and Aristotle in this sense. The term later came to mean a form of government dominated by a small privileged class. Today the term refers to members of a class that has hereditary privileges.

Aristophanes (450-385 B.C.), comic dramatist of ancient Greece. His works feature political, social, and literary satire, witty dialogue, vigorous rivalry, cleverly contrived comic situations, and choral lyrics. Eleven of his 40 plays survive, notably *The Frogs* (satirizing Euripides), *The Clouds* (satirizing Socrates), *Lysistrata* (a plea for pacifism), and *The Birds* (a fantasy about a sky city).
See also: Greece, Ancient; Theater.

Aristotle (384-322 B.C.), Greek philosopher, one of the most influential thinkers of the ancient world. He studied at Plato's academy in Athens in 343 B.C. and became the tutor of the young Alexander the Great. In 335 Aristotle set up his own school at the Lyceum in Athens. His works, covering a vast range of subjects, include *Physics, Metaphysics, On the Soul, On the Heavens, Poetics, Politics, Nicomachean Ethics,* and works on biology, aesthetics, rhetoric, and other subjects. Aristotle's writings reached the West through Latin translations in the 11th and 13th centuries, and had a prevailing influence on medieval and later thought. His emphasis on observation and analysis of the physical world, revolutionary for his time, underlies modern science. He developed the system of logic in use in the West until recent times.
See also: Greece, Ancient; Philosophy.

Arithmetic (Greek *arithmos*, "number"), science of numbers. Until the 16th century arithmetic was viewed as the study of all the properties and relations of all numbers; in modern times, the term usually denotes the study of the positive real numbers and zero under the operations of addition, subtraction, multiplication, and division.
See also: Mathematics.

Ariyoshi, Sawako (1931-84), Japanese writer of short stories, murder mysteries, and historical novels that explore the culture, traditions, social structure, and domestic problems of classical and modern Japan. Among her works are *Kokotsu No Hito, The Twilight Years, The River Ki, Compound Pollution, The Doctor's Wife, Diary of Princess Kazu,* and *The Curtain-Raising Bell Sounds Beautiful.*

Aristotle

Arizona

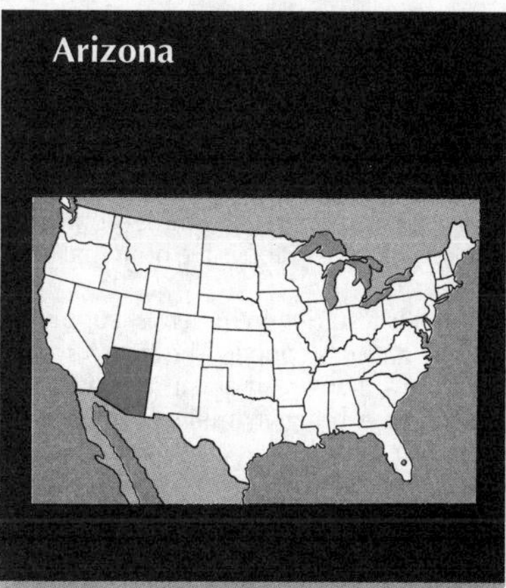

Capital:	Phoenix
Statehood:	Feb. 14, 1912 (48th state)
Familiar name:	Grand Canyon State
Area:	114,000 sq mi (295,260 km^2; ranks 6th)
Population:	3,677,985 (1990; ranks 24th)
Elevation:	Highest—12,633 ft (3,851 m), Humphreys Peak Lowest—70 ft (21 m), Colorado River
Motto:	Didat deus (God Enriches)
State flower:	Saguaro (Giant Cactus)
State bird:	Cactus wren
State tree:	Paloverde
State song:	"Arizona"

The Grand Canyon in Arizona was formed by the Colorado River over millions of years.

Arizona, state in the southwest United States; bordered by Utah in the north, New Mexico in the east, Mexico in the south, and, across the Colorado River, Nevada and California in the west.

Land and climate. The Colorado Plateau to the north contains the Grand Canyon, the Painted Desert, the Petrified Forest, and Monument Valley. A mountain chain extends northwest to southeast through the Basin and Range Region, while desert occupies the southwestern region. The most important river in Arizona is the Colorado. Although the desert climate is hot and dry, the mountain areas often have winter temperatures below 0°F (–18°C). Thirty-eight percent of all native American tribal lands are in Arizona. Principal cities are Phoenix, Tucson, and Tempe.

Economy. Manufacturing is the leading contributor to the state's wealth. The major manufactures are machinery, electronic and aeronautical products, and transportation equipment. With the aid of irrigation, Arizona's deserts become rich farmland. About 45% of farm income is from livestock products. Cotton is the principal cash crop.

Arizona is also rich in minerals, supplying half the nation's copper. The state's scenic attractions, native American reservations, and climate bring in millions of tourists each year.

Government. The state constitution, adopted in 1911, provides for an executive branch headed by a governor, who is elected for a 4-year term.

The state legislature is composed of 30 senators and 60 representatives, who serve 2-year terms. Arizona sends 2 senators and 5 representatives to the U.S. Congress.

History. Evidence of the cultures of the ancient Hohokam and Anasazi peoples is found in deserted cliff dwellings and irrigation works throughout the state.

The first European known to have visited Arizona was Marcos de Niza, a Franciscan friar, in 1539. In the late 17th century Spanish missionaries began to penetrate Arizona. Mexico gained control of the region in 1821. At the end of the Mexican War (1846-48), the terms of the Treaty of Guadalupe Hidalgo awarded Arizona north of the Gila River to the United States. The Gadsen Purchase in 1853 added the territory south of the Gila to form the present boundary between the United States and Mexico. In 1863 Arizona Territory was created. The early period of U.S. rule in Arizona was troubled by a succession of Native American wars, ending with the surrender of the Apache chief, Geronimo, in 1886. During the first third of the 20th century, a series of federal dams and irrigation systems were developed, including the Hoover Dam in 1936, but the boom following World War II (1939-45) strained Arizona's water resources. In 1974 construction began on the Central Arizona Project, which is expected to bring water to Tucson in the early 1990s.

Ark, biblical vessel Noah built for protection from the great flood (Genesis 6-9); also, the Ark of the Covenant, the sacred chest of the Hebrews representing God's presence (Exodus 25). The word can refer to a basket, box, or coffer, and in the United States, to the flat riverboats used for transport during western expansion.

See also: Noah.

Arkansas, state in the south-central United States; bordered by Tennessee and Mississippi (east), Louisiana (south), Texas and Oklahoma (west), and Missouri (north).

Land and climate. Arkansas' major rivers include the Arkansas River, which bisects the state, and the Ouachita. The Ozark Plateau, or Mountains, in the northwest and Ouachita Mountains in the west-central part of the state make up the highland region, an area of rugged hills and valleys. Between these mountains lies the Arkansas Valley, which contains Magazine Mountain. Along the Mississippi River covering the eastern third of the state is vast alluvial plain. Hot Springs National Park is a famous resort. Arkansas has a mild, rainy climate. Principal cities are Little Rock, Fort Smith, and Pine Bluff.

Economy. The most important economic activity in Arkansas, manufacturing, includes processed foods, electrical equipment, and paper and wood products. Soybeans, rice, and cotton are the principal cash crops of the state. About a third of the nation's rice is grown in Arkansas. Livestock and poultry provide the largest part of the farm income. The state's leading mineral products are natural gas, oil, and bauxite. The only active diamond field in America is at Murfreesburo.

Government. Arkansas is governed by the constitution of 1874, which provides for 35 senators serving 4-year terms and 100 representatives serving 2-year terms. The governor is elected for a 2-year term. Arkansas sends 2 senators and 4 representatives to the U.S. Congress.

History. Hernando de Soto, the first European to explore Arkansas, led an expedition into the region in 1541. René-Robert Cavelier, Sieur de la Salle claimed the entire Mississippi Valley for France during his voyage down the river in 1682. Henri de Tonti established the first permanent white settlement in the region, Arkansas Post, in 1686. The area was acquired by the United States as a part of the Louisiana Purchase in 1803. Arkansas Territory was organized in 1819. In 1861 Arkansas joined the Confederacy. A group of Arkansans formed a union government 3 years later, giving the state 2 governments. Arkansas was readmitted to the Union in 1868. Manufacturing grew after World War II (1939-45) until the income derived from it passed the state's farm income in the early 1960s. In 1957 President Dwight D. Eisenhower sent federal troops to enforce a court order to integrate Central High School in Little Rock. Today, while Arkansas faces many problems, including an unstable farm economy, it continues to attract new residents.

Arkansas

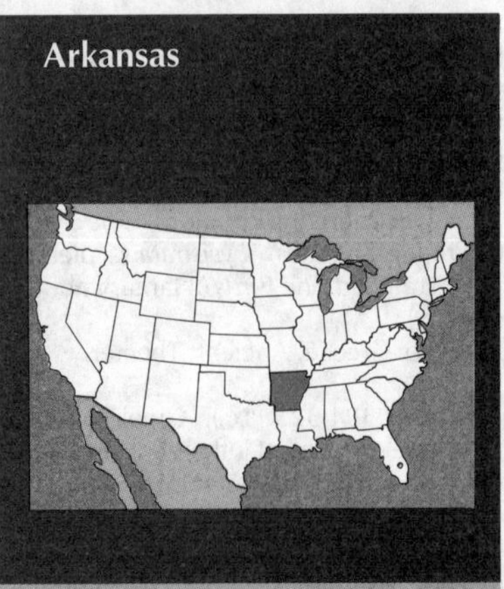

Capital:	Little Rock
Statehood:	June 15, 1836 (25th state)
Familiar name:	Land of Opportunity
Area:	53,187 sq mi (137,754 km^2); ranks 27th)
Population:	2,362,239 (1990; ranks 33rd)
Elevation:	Highest—2,753 ft (839 m), Magazine Mountain Lowest—55 ft (839 m), Ouachita River
Motto:	Regnat populus (The People Rule)
State flower:	Apple blossom
State bird:	Mockingbird
State tree:	Pine
State song:	"Arkansas"

Arkansas River, the longest tributary of the Mississippi-Missouri system, rising in the central Colorado Rocky Mountains and flowing SE 1,459 mi (2,339 km) to join the Mississippi near Greenville, Miss. The Arkansas is controlled by dams and reservoirs and is navigable to Tulsa, Okla.

Ark of the Covenant, wooden chest, overlaid inside and out with gold, containing the original Ten Commandments. The Ark was the most sacred religious object of ancient Israel, for the divine presence was believed to dwell within. It was installed in Solomon's temple but disappeared after the fall of Jerusalem and the destruction of the temple by Nebuchadnezzar in 586 B.C.

Arkwright, Sir Richard (1732-92), English industrialist and inventor of cotton carding and spinning machinery. In 1769 he patented a spinning frame that was the first machine able to produce cotton thread strong enough to use in the warp. He was a pioneer of the factory system of production, building several water- and later steam-powered mills.

Arlington National Cemetery, U.S. national cemetery in northern Virginia, established in 1864. More than 175,000 U.S. war dead and public figures are buried here. Monuments include the Tomb of the Unknown Soldier and the grave of John F. Kennedy, with its eternal flame.

Armada, fleet of armed ships, in particular Spain's "Invincible Armada," 130 ships carrying 30,000 men sent by Philip II in 1588 to seize control of the English Channel for an invasion of England. After battles with Charles Howard and Sir Francis Drake, the Spaniards took refuge off Calais. Driven out by fire ships, the surviving vessels battled storms as they attempted to return home. Only half of the ships survived.

Armadillo, armored mammals (family Dasypodidae) of the order Edentata, native to warm regions of the Western Hemisphere. There are 20 species, ranging in length from about 5 in. (12 cm) to about 5 ft (1.5 m). Largely insectivorous (insect-eating), they are usually nocturnal and live in burrows either excavated by themselves or deserted by other animals. Armadillos generally produce several identical offspring from a single fertilized egg.

See also: Edentate.

Armadillo

Armageddon, according to the Bible, the site of the world's last great battle, in which the powers of good will destroy the forces of evil (Revelation 16:16). The word derives from the name of an ancient city called "Megiddo" because of the many battles fought on its soil.

Armagnac, hilly farming area of southwestern France noted for its brandy. Count Bernard VII of Armagnac was virtual ruler of France in 1413-18. Armagnac passed to the French crown in 1607. The chief city, Auch, is a commercial center.

Armenia, republic in western Asia, bordered by Turkey, Azerbaijan, and Georgia. Armenia is mountainous and the landscape extends from subtropical lowland to snow-covered peaks. Small mountain pastures provide rich grazing for sheep and cattle, and the valleys are fertile when irrigated. Armenia is highly industrialized and mining is a chief industry. The population is mainly Armenian (90%) with minorities of Kurds, Russians, Ukrainians, Greeks and Georgians. The majority of the inhabitants is Christian. Armenia was conquered in 328 B.C. by Alexander the Great and in 66 B.C. by Rome. In A.D. 303 it became the first country to make Christianity its state religion. Later it was successively under Byzantine, Persian, Arab, Seljuk, Mongol, and Ottoman Turkish control. An Armenian republic emerged after World War I but was swiftly absorbed by the USSR. In 1991 Armenia regained its independence.
See also: Union of Soviet Socialist Republics.

Armenia

Capital:	Yerevan
Area:	11,500 sq mi (29,800 sq km)
Population:	3,499,000
Government:	republic
Independent:	1991
GNP:	U.S. $ 2,719,000,000
Per capita:	U.S. $780

Armor, protective body covering used in armed combat. The earliest armor consisted of boiled and hardened animal skins, but Roman soldiers wore armor made of iron. By the end of the 11th century, chain mail, a fabric of interlocking metal rings, was the standard form of armor. It provided poor protection against heavy blows, however, and the Middle Ages saw the development of full suits of metal plates with chain mail joints for flexibility. Full armor was used in Europe only until the 16th century. Modern armor employs nylon, fiberglass, and other synthetic materials.
See also: Knights and knighthood.

Armory Show, officially the International Exhibition of Modern Art, the first show of its kind in the United States, held at the 69th Regiment Armory, New York City, Feb.-Mar. 1913. Comprising over 1,300 works, it included a large section of paintings by contemporary Americans and works by modern European artists, including Constantin Brancusi, Georges Braque, Paul Cézanne, Marcel Duchamp, Henri Matisse, and Pablo Picasso. The avant-garde paintings caused much controversy but also the acceptance of modern art in the United States.

Arms control *see:* Disarmament; Strategic Arms Limitation Talks.

Armstrong, Anne Legendre (1927-), U.S. political figure. Appointed by President Richard M. Nixon in 1972, Armstrong was the first woman to hold the Cabinet-level position of counselor to the president, serving under Presidents Nixon and Gerald R. Ford. She was also the first woman to serve as U.S. ambassador to Great Britain, appointed by Ford in 1976 and 1977.

Armstrong, Edwin Howard (1890-1954), U.S. electronic engineer who developed the feedback concept for amplifiers (1912), invented the superheterodyne circuit used in radio receivers (1918), and perfected FM radio (1925-39).
See also: Frequency modulation.

Armstrong, Henry (1912-88), U.S. boxer. Nicknamed "Perpetual Motion" for his aggressive style, he was the only fighter to hold 3 world championships (featherweight, welterweight, and lightweight) simultaneously (1938).

Louis "Satchmo" Armstrong

Armstrong, Louis "Satchmo" (1900-71), U.S. jazz musician renowned as a virtuoso trumpeter and singer. A master of improvisation, he was one of the most important figures in the early history of jazz. Satchmo grew up in New Orleans, moved to Chicago in 1922, and by the 1930s was internationally famous. In later life he played at concerts around the world as goodwill ambassador for the U.S. State Department.
See also: Jazz.

Armstrong, Neil Alden (1930-), U.S. astronaut, first human to set foot on the moon. He studied aeronautical engineering at Purdue University (1947-55) with time out on active service in the Korean War. He joined NASA in 1962, commanding *Gemini 8* (1966) and landing the *Apollo 11* module on the moon on July 20, 1969.
See also: Astronaut.

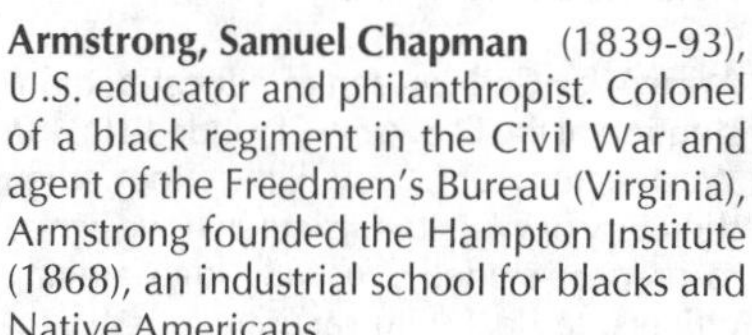

Armstrong, Samuel Chapman (1839-93), U.S. educator and philanthropist. Colonel of a black regiment in the Civil War and agent of the Freedmen's Bureau (Virginia), Armstrong founded the Hampton Institute (1868), an industrial school for blacks and Native Americans.

Armstrong, William Howard (1914-), U.S. author. Armstrong is best known for the children's novel *Sounder*, the story of an African American sharecropping family in the Depression-era South, for which he won the 1970 Newbery Medal. Other works include *Barefoot in the Grass* (1970) and *Sour Land* (1971).

Army, land fighting force of a nation; more narrowly, a large unit of ground forces under a single commander. Primitive armies consisted of raiding parties that waged individual combat using stones and clubs. Later, horses and chariots increased the mobility of armies, while the development of artillery extended their range. Formation tactics evolved with the Macedonian phalanx and Roman legion. The 20th-century army depends upon technology. Because of the ongoing development of weapons and detection systems, modern armies must be highly mobile, a need that has blurred the traditional distinctions between army, navy, and air force. Nuclear weaponry has taken the range of firepower to its limits, and the value of tactical formations has largely been eliminated by radar, making unconventional units (guerrillas, paratroops) increasingly important.
See also: Army, U.S.

Army, Department of the, division of the U.S. Department of Defense. Headed by the secretary of the Army, the department

serves as U.S. Army headquarters and directs the U.S. land forces. It is located in Washington, D.C.
See also: Army, U.S.; Defense, Department of.

Army, U.S., branch of U.S. armed forces organized to fight any war, local or global, conventional or atomic. The highest ranking officer is the chief of staff, answerable to the secretary of the army, a civilian who in turn is responsible to the secretary of defense and the president. Under the chief of staff come several major commands: the Continental Army Command, responsible for U.S. ground defense; the Air Defense Command; the Army Materiel Command, charged with procuring equipment and weapons for army units; and the Army Combat Development Command, which equips and organizes army units. The total strength of the all-volunteer U.S. Army in 1989 was 760,000. In addition, an almost equal number of men and women serve in the Army Reserve and National Guard. Members of active and reserve units were used extensively in the 1991 Persian Gulf War.
See also: Army; Army, Department of the; Defense, Department of.

Army War College, senior educational institution of the U.S. Army, founded 1901 in Washington, D.C., by Elihu Root, then secretary of War. Its curriculum is designed to prepare students, usually high-ranking officers, to deal with security issues, military strategy, war operations, and Army doctrine.
See also: Root, Elihu.

Army worm, any of several species of voracious caterpillars that travel in masses, causing severe crop damage; especially the common army worm (*Pseudaletia unipuncta*). The common army worm is the larva of a brown moth found in North America east of the Rocky Mountains. The eggs, laid in grass or on small grains, hatch into small worms that, if not controlled by parasites or pesticides, devour everything within reach and then migrate in armies to new feeding grounds.

Jean Arp's Human Concretion, *created in 1934 (Musée National d'Art Moderne, Paris)*

Arnhem (pop. 128,100), capital of the province Gelderland in the east Netherlands, located on the north bank of the Rhine River, about 60 mi (100 km) east of Rotterdam. A major river port with shipyards and a large tin refinery, Arnhem produces textiles, furniture, leather goods, and synthetic fibers. The city was seriously damaged in September 1944, when it was the site of one of the largest Allied paratroop landings in World War II.

Arnica, genus of plants of which the flowers and rootstock are used for medicinal purposes. The horizontal, dark-brown, branched rootstock of the arnica sends up a slightly hairy simple or tightly branched stem that reaches a height of 1-2 ft (30-61 cm). The basal leaves are oblong-ovate with short stems.

Arnold, Benedict (1741-1801), general and traitor in the American Revolution. He fought outstandingly for the American cause at Ticonderoga (1775) and Saratoga (1777) and in 1778 received command of Philadelphia. In 1780 Arnold assumed the command of West Point and with John André plotted its surrender to the British in revenge for past criticisms. André's capture forced Arnold to flee to the British side, and in 1781 he went into exile in London.
See also: Revolutionary War in America.

Arnold, Henry "Hap" Harley (1886-1950), pioneer aviator and U.S. Air Force general who helped build U.S. air power and develop the Air Force as a unified separate service. Arnold held several early flying records, became chief of the U.S. Army Air Corps (1938), headed the Army Air Forces in World War II, and was made general of the Army (1944), a title later changed to general of the Air Force.

Arnold, Matthew (1822-88), English poet and literary critic. His poetry, as represented by *Empedocles on Etna* (1852) and *New Poems* (1867), is mainly introspective, though Arnold also achieved a classical impersonality. Both in his poetry and in his criticism—*Culture and Anarchy* (1869), *Literature and Dogma* (1873)—Arnold showed a keen awareness of the changing cultural climate of his time.

Arnold of Brescia (c.1100-50), Italian religious reformer and political activist who strongly opposed the temporal power of the pope. He was a supporter of Peter Abelard, with whom he was condemned at the Council of Sens in 1140. In 1147 Arnold, a great orator, became leader of the rebellion that had suppressed papal authority in Rome and replaced it by a republic. On the collapse of the republic, Arnold fled to Campania but was captured, delivered to the pope by Emperor Frederick Barbarossa, and executed as a heretic.

Arno River, river in central Italy, about 150 mi (241 km) long. Its source lies in the Apennine Mountains, from which it flows through the city of Florence, emptying into the Ligurian Sea below Pisa. Much of its valley is a fertile plain where olives and grapes are grown.

Arp, Jean or **Hans** (1887-1966), French sculptor, painter, and poet. Briefly associated with the expressionist art movement Der Blaue Reiter, he was a cofounder of Dada in Zürich (1916). He was also one of the best known exponents of the surrealist movement. Starting in the 1930s he created sculptures and reliefs notable for their elemental purity and strength.
See also: Dada; Surrealism.

Arpád, dynasty of Hungarian rulers founded by Arpád (c.840-907), around whose life countless heroic legends are woven. In 890 he became chief of the Magyars and 6 years later led the conquest of Hungary and proceeded to lay the foundations for a strong, centralized state. His successors ruled as dukes of Hungary and replaced the predominantly nomadic Magyar culture by one based on agriculture and firm central rule.

Arraignment, appearance of a person in a court of law to plead guilty or not guilty to legal charges. Before or after entering this plea, the defendant may also enter various motions in his or her own behalf, such as requesting a change of venue (moving the place where the trial is to be held) or a continuance (allowing more time to prepare the case), and the defendant can even challenge the validity of the arrest and trial. If the defendant is not yet represented by a lawyer, the court may appoint one.

Arrau, Claudio (1903-), Chilean pianist. A child prodigy, he was noted throughout his long career mainly for his performances of the Romantic composers, such as Brahms.

Arrest, taking into custody of a person believed to have committed a crime. Most often an arrest is made by police or other law-enforcing officer on the strength of a warrant issued by a court and supported by evidence indicating that the named person or persons have probably committed a crime. As a general rule, and in most states, arrests may be made without a warrant only when the arresting officer has evidence that a felony (serious crime) has been committed; and on the basis of suspicious behavior, even when there is no evidence of an actual felony. A private person may sometimes make a "citizen's arrest" for a crime he or she sees committed.

Arrhythmia, irregularity in rhythm of the heartbeat, either in time or force. Arrhythmias are often extra heartbeats that cause no serious problems, although sometimes the heart rhythm can become dangerously slow or fast or is disruptive to heart function.

Arrow *see:* Archery.

Arrow, Kenneth Joseph (1921-), U.S. economist, former professor at Harvard and adviser on economic affairs to the U.S. government. In 1972 he won the Nobel Prize in economic science.

Arrowroot, plant (genus *Maranta*) native to warm, humid regions of the Western Hemisphere; also, form of starch from the rhizomes (underground stems) of the arrowroot plant and various other tropical plants. Easily digested, arrowroot is valued as a food for children and people with delicate stomachs, and is used as a thickening agent in sauces.

Arsenic, chemical element, symbol As; for physical constants see Periodic Table. Arsenic has been known since ancient times. Elemental arsenic was first described by Albertus Magnus in the 13th century. Sometimes found native, it occurs widely in the form of arsenides, from which the element is obtained as a byproduct. Arsenic is a soft and brittle gray element with a metallic luster which sublimes without melting; several other allotropic forms have been reported. The metal conducts electricity moderately well. Arsenic is used in bronzing, hardening, and improving the sphericity of metal shot, and in pyrotechnics. Compounds of arsenic are used as agricultural insecticides and poisons. Arsenic in high purity is used as a doping agent in solid-state devices. Gallium arsenide is used as a laser material to convert electricity directly into coherent light. Arsenic and its compounds are poisonous.

Artagnan, Charles d' (1620-73), French soldier whose name was immortalized by the swashbuckling character d'Artagnan in Alexandre Dumas's *The Three Musketeers*. The real d'Artagnan served bravely in the armies of Louis XIII and Louis XIV and rose to the rank of brigadier general before his death at the siege of Maastricht.

Art and the arts, skill of making or doing. The term can be used to define useful arts (beautiful objects that have functional value), decorative arts (beautiful objects that exist for their own sake), liberal arts (the study of humanities), applied arts (such as architecture), language arts (the related skills of reading, writing, speaking, and spelling), and graphic arts (such as printmaking and bookmaking). However, the term *art* is most often used to describe the fine arts, which consist of painting, sculpture, literature, dance, music, and film. Works of art can be classified as verbal (literature) or nonverbal (musical composition and visual design). Mixed arts, a combination of 2 or more basic arts, include dance, drama, and film. Theories of art which attempt to define its meaning, explain its effects, assess its worth, set guidelines for its execution, or provide a historical or social context for its interpretation have existed since the ancient Greeks and continue to be a subject of discussion among artists, scholars, and critics.

Art deco, style of design popular in the United States and Europe from the late 1920s through the 1930s. In its emphasis on geometrical shapes and simplified lines, art deco represented a radical reaction to the ornateness of Victorian design. The style was applied in architecture, interior decoration, furnituremaking, and the design of a wide range of objects from locomotives to salt-and-pepper shakers. Prime examples are the Chrysler Building and the interior of Radio City Music Hall in New York City.

Artemis, in Greek mythology, virgin goddess of the hunt. Apollo's twin, the daughter of Zeus and Leto, Artemis is usually pictured carrying a bow and arrows or a torch. She presided over wild animals and is primarily known as the goddess of the hunt. Although Artemis was a stern protector of chastity, she also watched over women in childbirth. She was worshipped as goddess of the waters; fruit, grain, and domestic animals were sacrificed to her at harvest time. Artemis is also sometimes known as the moon goddess, probably through identification with the huntress Diana, Roman goddess of the moon.

Arteriosclerosis, generic term for disease of the arteries in which their walls become thickened and rigid, and blood flow is hindered, often resulting in heart disease or stroke. The most common form of arteriosclerosis is atherosclerosis, in which fatty deposits accumulate on the artery walls, which then tend to harden.
See also: Artery.

Artery, blood vessel that carries blood away from the heart to other parts of the body. The two main arteries are the pulmonary artery and the aorta. The pulmonary artery carries blood from the right side of the heart to the lungs to be reoxygenated; the aorta, the main arterial vessel, carries oxygen-enriched blood to the body from the left side of the heart. The main arteries are quite large, the aorta being about the width of a garden hose (about 1 in/2.5 cm in diameter). Major arteries branch from the aorta to supply each limb and organ, dividing repeatedly down to the arterioles, which in turn supply the capillaries, located in body tissue. The structure of artery walls accounts for their strength and elasticity and makes them well suited to resisting the stress of the pulsating flow of blood.
See also: Arteriosclerosis.

Artesian well, well in which water rises under hydrostatic pressure above the level of the aquifer (water-bearing layer of rock) in which it has been confined. True artesian wells (named for the French province of Artois, where they were first constructed) flow without assistance.
See also: Ground water.

Arthritis, inflammation of a joint, usually accompanied by pain and frequently by changes in structure. The two most widespread arthritic disorders, osteoarthritis and rheumatoid arthritis, are usually chronic problems for which there is no cure, though modern medicine can now do a good deal to control them. Two or three times more women than men are affected by osteoarthritis, and women have the most serious form, rheumatoid arthritis, three times as often.
See also: Joint.

Arthropod, largest and most diverse phylum of the animal kingdom, containing insects, millipedes, centipedes, crustacea, arachnida, and king crabs. Arthropods are characterized by a segmented exoskeleton (external skeleton) with joined limbs that is shed at intervals, the animal emerging in a new, soft exoskeleton that has developed beneath; often this molting is followed by rapid growth. Molting may cease on attainment of adulthood, but many crustacea molt periodically throughout their lives.

Arthroscopy, technique used to visualize the interior of a joint. Using a fiber-optic endoscope (arthroscope) inserted into the joint through a small incision, a doctor can perform a thorough examination and certain surgical operations. Arthroscopy is most commonly used to treat torn cartilage in the knee, although arthroscopic procedures of the shoulder, elbow, and hip are also common. The low morbidity associated with this procedure makes it useful in a variety of joint disorders as an adjunct to diagnosis, to determine prognosis, and as a treatment.

Arthur, Chester Alan (1830-86), 21st president of the United States. Arthur was vice president under James A. Garfield and became president on Garfield's assassination. Probably his most important accomplishment as president was his support for reforms in the federal civil service system.
Lawyer. Arthur was the son of a Baptist minister and schoolteacher from Northern Ireland. He graduated from Union College in Schenectady, N.Y. in 1847 and taught school while studying law. In 1853 he joined a New York City law office and was admitted to the bar the following year. Arthur soon gained a reputation as a progressive attorney in two important civil rights cases.
Arthur opened his law firm in 1856 and became active in Republican party politics in New York State. During the Civil War he was given several honorary posts on the Republican governor's military staff.
Politician. Arthur returned to his law practice in 1863, and remained active in politics. President Ulysses Grant appointed him customs collector for the Port of New York in 1871. The customs house was notorious for being staffed with political appointees who paid part of their salaries into the party treasury. While Arthur performed his official duties conscientiously, he made little effort to change the system of rewarding party workers with government jobs. In July 1878 President Rutherford B. Hayes, seeking to reduce procedures at the customs house, had Arthur removed from his

Chester Alan Arthur

21st U.S. president	
Born:	Fairfield, Vermont; October 5, 1830
Term:	September 1881 - March 1885
Vice President:	None (Arthur succeeded to the presidency on the death of President James A. Garfield)
Political Party:	Republican
Spouse:	Ellen Lewis Herndon Arthur
Children:	2
Died:	New York City; November 18, 1886

post. Two years later the Republican party chose Arthur as its candidate for vice president, with James A. Garfield running for president.

President. Garfield and Arthur won the election of 1880, but Garfield's term as president was brief. He was shot by a disappointed office-seeker, Charles J. Guiteau, on July 2, 1881, and died on September 19. Arthur was sworn in as president the following day.

The assassination led to a widespread demand for a new system of civil service appointments. To the surprise of most people, Arthur strongly supported the proposed reforms. He signed into law the Pendleton Civil Service Act in January 1883. This law opened the way to the eventual elimination of the worst excesses of the spoils system in national politics.

Arthur sought renomination at the Republican convention of 1884, but he was defeated on the fourth ballot by James G. Blaine. After leaving the presidency, he resumed his law practice in New York City, where he died less than 2 years later.

Arthur, King, legendary British king, subject of tales and poems dating back to the 7th century. Although there are many variations of the story, which probably arose out of Irish heroic folktales, all of these have certain common elements: Arthur wins recognition as king by pulling a sword (Excalibur) from a stone; he reigns from his castle at Camelot; his Knights of the Round Table, including such heroes as Lancelot and Tristram, engage in heroic quests and illicit sexual unions.

Artichoke (*Cynara scolymus*), tall, thistle-like perennial plant of the composite family; also, its globe-shaped flower bud, the heart and spiny bracts of which are eaten as a vegetable. Native to the Mediterranean region, the artichoke is grown commercially in warm regions of the U.S.
See also: Jerusalem artichoke.

Articles of Confederation, first written constitutional structure for the United States, drafted in 1776-77, but ratified by 13 states only in 1781. The Articles established a weak national government based on a Congress, dependent on the states for funds and for executive functions. "Sovereignty, freedom, and independence" remained vested with the separate states, and there were no federal courts. The shortcomings of the Articles were recognized when the Constitutional Convention of 1787 abandoned them in favor of the present United States Constitution, which was ratified in 1789.
See also: Congress of the Confederation; Constitution of the United States; Continental Congress.

Articles of War, code adopted in 1775 by the Continental Congress to guide administration of justice and discipline in the Continental Army. The articles were based on British Army Code. Revised many times, they were replaced in 1950 by the Uniform Code of Military Justice.

Artificial insemination, introduction of sperm into the vagina by means other than copulation. The technique, widely used for breeding livestock as it produces many offspring from 1 selected male, has a limited use in treating human impotence and sterility. In humans, the procedure is timed to coincide with the woman's ovulation. If she has a regular 28-day menstrual cycle, insemination should be performed as many as 3 times between the 10th and the 14th days of the cycle.

Artificial intelligence (AI), use of computers to perform functions normally associated with human intelligence, such as reasoning, learning, and self-improvement. The question of whether it is possible to develop machines that genuinely "think" in the same sense that humans do is one of the most controversial issues in the computer sciences.

Artificial limb, device to replace missing hands, feet, arms, or legs. Prosthetics, the branch of medicine dealing with artificial limbs, has developed rapidly since World War I. Prosthetic devices are now complex mechanisms made of materials such as aluminum alloys, rubber, and plastics. Some of them are capable of mimicking the use of human limbs to a considerable extent.

Artificial organ, mechanical device designed to assume the functions of an organ of the body, particularly during surgical procedures. The 3 most commonly used artificial organs are the heart-lung machine, the artificial kidney, and (since 1985) the artificial heart, still in an experimental stage.

Artificial sweetener, synthetic substance, usually saccharin, aspartame, or acesulfame-K, used in place of sucrose (table sugar) to sweeten food and beverages. The U.S. Food and Drug Administration regulates the use of artificial sweeteners and has banned some of them as possible cancer risks.

Artificial turf, grasslike product of nylon or other synthetic material used to carpet athletic playing fields and also used in outdoor landscaping. It came into widespread use during the 1960s.

Artigas, José Gervasio (1764-1850), Uruguayan military leader who championed the cause of national independence. He joined the 1810 Argentine revolt against Spanish rule but later fought against both Portuguese and Argentine troops. He was forced into exile after Brazil occupied Montevideo in 1820. An independent Uruguay was achieved only in 1828.

Artillery, once the term for all military machinery, now applied to guns too heavy to be carried by one or two soldiers. Modern artillery had its origins in the 14th century, when weapons using gunpowder were first developed. Its use became more important as equipment became more mobile, accurate, and effective. World War II saw the development of antitank and anti-aircraft guns and the first effective use of rockets. The most modern artillery is often made of light, tough alloys, and targeting systems draw on laser and radar technology.

Art nouveau, late 19th-century art movement that influenced decorative styles throughout the West. Its themes were exotic or decadent, its characteristic line sinuous and highly ornamental. The movement aimed to reunite art and life, and so to produce everyday objects of beauty. Some notable architecture, furniture, jewelry, and book designs were produced in this style.

The graphic arts were much affected by art nouveau, as seen in the work of Aubrey Beardsley. Other notable artists were the painter Gustav Klimt, the architects Antonio Gaudi and Victor Horta, and applied artists Louis Comfort Tiffany and René Lalique.

The art nouveau "Job" poster by Alphonese Mucha. The poster was originally designed for a brand of cigarette paper.

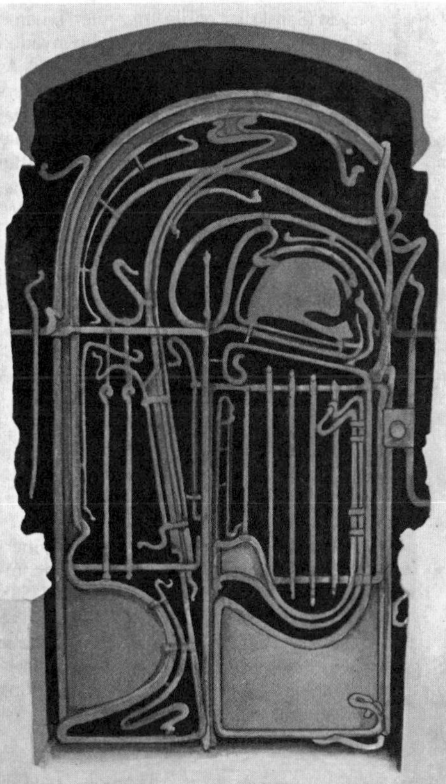

1 2

Center: Wrought iron gate set in stonework at Castle Beranger, Paris (Hector Guimard, 1894-98).
Right: Metal balustrade with leaf motif for a staircase (Louis Majorelle, 1900).

Below: fine metal-work and jewelry artifacts.
Top: Brooch of gold and translucent enamels. It typifies the art nouveau obsession with plant and insect forms (C. Dessosiers, 1901).
Bottom: Silver pillbox decorated with translucent enamel.

Art nouveau light fixtures in the Hotel Solvay in Brussels, Belgium.

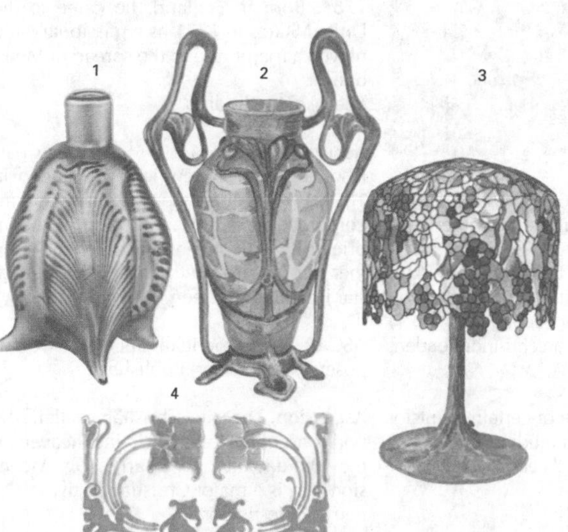

Left: Glass and ceramic artifacts.
1. *Tiffany glass bottle*
2. *Vase of green glass encased in pewter tendrils which form handles*
3. *Tiffany lamp in a tree form bearing green and purple fruit*
4. *Tile work*

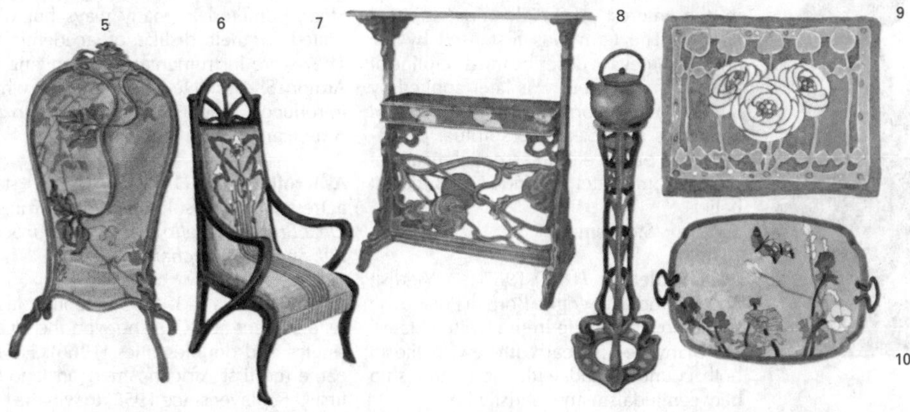

Furniture and furnishing artifacts.
5. *Firescreen of ash (Emil Galle, 1900)*
6. *Armchair (Louis Majorelle, c.1900)*
7. *Inlaid work table of ash (Emile Galle, 1900)*
8. *Copper kettle and pedestal (Reynolds)*
9. *Embroidered and appliquéd cushion cover with rose motif (Ann Macbeth)*
10. *Inlaid tray with brass handles (Louis Majorelle, 1900)*

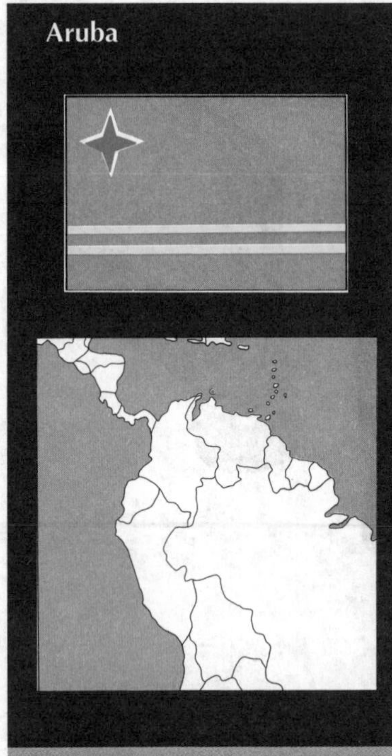

Capital:	Oranjestad
Area:	75 sq mi (193 sq km)
Population:	61,300
Government:	internal autonomy within the Kingdom of The Netherlands
Independent:	1996 scheduled
GNP:	U.S. $1,610,000,000 (incl. Netherlands Antilles)
Per capita:	U.S. $6,810

Arthur Ashe holding the 1982 Davis Cup

Aruba (pop. 67,000), island off the Venezuelan coast, part of the Netherlands Antilles, about 19 mi (30.6 km) long and 4 mi (6.4 km) wide. Its capital is Oranjestad. The chief industry is the refining of crude oil imported from Venezuela. On Jan. 1, 1986, Aruba became a semi-independent state.

Arum, common name of certain plants of the Araceae family, including lily, philodendron, and elephant's ear.

Arum

Aryan (Sanskrit, "noble" or "ruler"), name originally applied to peoples who invaded the Indus Valley in India about 1500 B.C. As a linguistic term, Aryan applies to speakers of Indo-European languages. As a racial category—used by the Nazis to designate Germans and other North Europeans—the term has no valid basis and has been discredited as an instrument of bigotry.

Asafetida, foul-smelling substance extracted from the roots of an Asian herb. Asafetida has long had a mystical significance and was often used in magical ceremonies or worn as an amulet to keep away evil spirits. It was also once used in medicine as a sedative. The plant belongs to the carrot family (Umbelliferae).

Asante *see:* Ashanti.

Asbestos, name for various fibrous minerals, such as chrysotile, used as noncombustible material. Canada and the USSR are the chief producers. It can be spun to make fireproof fabrics or molded to make tiles, bricks, and automobile brake linings. If inhaled, asbestos particles cause lung cancer and asbestosis, a serious lung disease.

Asbury, Francis (1745-1816), first Methodist bishop in the United States, elected 1784. Born in England, he came to the United States in 1771 as a missionary and played a major role in the spread of Methodism.
See also: Methodists.

Asbury Park (pop. 17,015), Atlantic Coast resort in eastern New Jersey, founded in 1871 as a religious meeting place and incorporated as a city in 1897. It is known primarily as a convention center and summer resort. It is also the birthplace of rock star Bruce Springsteen.

ASCAP *see:* American Society of Composers, Authors and Publishers.

Ascension, The, in Christian belief, the bodily ascent of Jesus Christ into heaven on the 40th day after his resurrection. Ascension Day is a major Christian festival.
See also: Jesus Christ.

Asceticism, self-denial or self-mortification in the interest of heightening spiritual powers. The term was first used by the ancient Greeks to describe the discipline of athletic training, but was later applied by Stoicists to the conquest of the body and its desires as a means to spiritual awareness. The practice is an essential means of escape from matter in Hindu and Buddhist belief
See also: Stoicism.

Asch, Sholem (1880-1957), Yiddish novelist and playwright. Born in Poland, he spent most of his life in the United States. His many books deal with Jewish life in both countries and with the relationship between Judaism and Christianity.

ASCII, acronym for American Standard Code for Information Interchange, the character code used for representing information by most non-IBM equipment.
See also: Computer.

Asclepius, in Greek mythology, the god of healing, who became so skilled that he attempted to resurrect the dead, thus angering Zeus, who struck him dead with a thunderbolt. The medical profession has adopted his symbol, a staff entwined by a snake.

Ascorbic acid *see:* Vitamin.

Asexual reproduction *see:* Reproduction.

Asgard, or Aesir, in Norse mythology, the realm of the gods. It contained many halls and palaces; chief of these was Valhalla, where Odin entertained warriors killed in battle. The only entry to Asgard was by the rainbow bridge called Bifrost.

Ash, tree or shrub (genus *fraxinus*) of the olive family. The hard, elastic wood of the white ash (*F. americana*) is used for items like mallets and baseball bats; that of the blue ash (*F. quadrangulata*) for barrel hoops, furniture veneers, and baskets.

Ashanti, or Asante, region of central Ghana, in West Africa, inhabited by the people of the same name. From the 17th century to 1902, when Britain militarily took over the region, the powerful Ashanti Confederacy linked several kingdoms under one chief. The symbol of their unity was the sacred Golden Stool.

Ashbery, John (1927-), U.S. poet of unconventional style, whose poems are experimental, fragmentary, and dreamlike. Associated with the poets of the "New York School," Ashbery is also an art critic. His *Self-Portrait in a Convex Mirror* won the Pulitzer Prize for poetry in 1975. Other works include *Some Trees* (1956), *The Tennis Court Oath* (1962), and *A Wave* (1984).

Ashcan School, or "The Eight," name given to a group of painters in New York City, formed in 1908, because they painted everyday aspects of city life. The Eight—Arthur Davies, William Glackens, Ernest Lawson, George Luks, Maurice Prendergast, Everett Shinn, Robert Henri, and John Sloan—differed in many ways but were united in their dislike of academicism. They were instrumental in organizing the Armory Show in New York in 1913, which introduced modern European art to the American public.

Ashcroft, Peggy (1907-), British stage actress. She is best known for her roles in *Dear Brutus, Othello, The School for Scandal,* and *The Merchant of Venice.*

Ashe, Arthur (1943-), U.S. tennis player. As a student at UCLA, he won the NCAA singles and doubles titles (1966). He became the first African-American (and the first U.S. player since 1955) to win the U.S.

Men's National Singles Championship (1968). He won the Australian Open (1970) and the men's singles title at Wimbledon (1975). Since 1983 he has served as nonplaying captain of the U.S. Davis Cup team.

Asheville (pop. 174,821), city and resort in the Appalachian Mountains, western North Carolina, seat of Buncombe County, near the Great Smoky Mountains National Park and the Blue Ridge Parkway. Asheville is a processing center for a rich agricultural region. Local industries produce textiles, leather goods, and wood products. Founded in 1794 and chartered as a city in 1883, it is the birthplace of the writer Thomas Wolfe and is described in his novels.

Ashkenazim, Jews whose medieval ancestors lived in Germany. Persecution drove them to spread throughout central and eastern Europe and, in the 19th and 20th centuries, overseas, notably to the United States. Their ritual and Hebrew pronunciation differ from those of Sephardim (Jews originally from Spain and Portugal). Most of the Jews in the United States and the majority of the world's Jews are Ashkenazim.

Ashland (pop. 27,064), city in northern Kentucky on the Ohio River, the seat of Boyd County. It lies in a region of coal, natural gas, and oil deposits and is an important center for iron, steel, and petroleum. The city was settled in 1815 and incorporated in 1870.

Ashton, Sir Frederick (1906-88), British dancer and choreographer. Among his influential works are *Façade* (1931) and *La Fille Mal Gardée* (1960). He was director of the Royal Ballet from 1963 to 1970.

Ash Wednesday, 40th weekday before Easter Sunday and the first day of the Christian fast of Lent. The name derives from the early practice of sprinkling penitents with ashes. Today the ash of burnt palms is used to mark the sign of the cross on the foreheads of believers.

Asia, world's largest continent, more than 17,139,000 sq mi/44,390,000 sq km (nearly 1/3 of the earth's land), with about 3.1 billion people (more than 60% of the world population). It extends from the Arctic Ocean to the Indian Ocean, and from the Pacific Ocean to the Mediterranean. Its traditional border with Europe is formed by the Ural Mountains. Asia is separated from Africa by the Red Sea and the Suez Canal. The combined land mass of Europe and Asia is sometimes treated as a single continent, Eurasia.

Asia is a continent of physical contrast, with Mt. Everest (29,028 ft/8,848 m), the world's highest mountain, and the Dead Sea (1,292 ft/394 m below sea level). At its heart is the system of mountain chains and high plateaus that includes the Karakoram Range, Himalayas, Kunlun Shan, Tien Shan, Altai Mountains, Hindu Kush, and Sulaiman Range. The major rivers include the Ob and its tributary, the Irtysh, the Yenisey, and the Lena, all flowing to the Arctic Ocean; the Indus (Pakistan), Ganges (India and Bangladesh), and Brahmaputra (China and India); and the Yellow and Yangtze rivers (China). Lake Baikal (Russian Federation) is the largest freshwater lake. Deserts include the Gobi Desert in Mongolia and the Great Sandy Desert of Arabia.

The cultural regions of the continent are East Asia (China, Korea, Japan), South Asia (India, Pakistan, Sri Lanka), Southeast Asia (Malaysia, Indonesia, etc.), and the Middle East.

The countries of Asia are Afghanistan, Armenia, Azerbaijan, Bahrain, Bangladesh, Bhutan, Brunei, Burma, Byelorussia, China, Cyprus, part of Egypt, Georgia, India, part of Indonesia, Iran, Iraq, Israel, Japan, Jordan, Kampuchea, Kazachstan, Kirghizstan, Kuwait, Laos, Lebanon, Malaysia, Maldives, Mongolia, Nepal, North Korea, Oman, Pakistan, Philippines, Qatar, Russian Federation, Saudi Arabia, Singapore, South Korea, Sri Lanka, Syria, Tadjikistan, Taiwan, Thailand, part of Turkey, Turkmenistan, United Arab Emirates, Uzbekistan, Vietnam, and the Republic of Yemen.

East Asia's port and city of Hong Kong, one of the world's great trading centers

Marco Polo's journey to Asia in the 13th century lasted over 20 years.

Ho Chi Minh was the founder of the Vietnamese independence movement in Southeast Asia.

View of the snow-covered Himalayas of Asia.

Cross section of Asia

Asia Minor, peninsula in southwestern Asia including most of modern Turkey, mountainous and surrounded on 3 sides by the Black and Mediterranean seas, bounded on the east by the upper Euphrates River. After the destruction of the Hittite empire c.1200 B.C., the land was occupied successively by the Medes, Persians, Greeks, and Romans. In the 5th century of the present era it passed to the Byzantine emperors. It was settled by Turks beginning in the 13th century and became part of the Ottoman Empire in the fifteenth. The modern Turkish state was founded in 1923.

Asimov, Isaac (1920-92), prolific (almost 400 books) U.S. author, biochemist, and educator, known for his science fiction works, including the *Foundation* trilogy (1951-53, 1982) and *The Gods Themselves* (1972), as well as for his many popular works on various fields of science and general knowledge.

Asmara (pop. 275,400), capital of Eritrea. The city is situated on a plateau about 7,000 ft (2,134 m) above sea level and has road and rail connections to the interior and to the Red Sea port of Massawa, about 40 mi (64 km) away. Industrial centre with production of textiles, soap and food. Seized by Italy in 1889, the town became the administrative seat of the colony of Eritrea in 1900. Awarded to Ethiopia by the UN in 1952, Eritrea became a province in 1962. From the 1970s the Eritrean guerillas waged a war of independence and the control of Asmara has been contested. When Asmara was captured by the Eritreans in the early 1990s independence was on its way and formally achieved in 1993.

Asoka (d.232 B.C.), third emperor of the Maurya dynasty of India, whose acceptance of Buddhism as the official religion of his vast empire contributed to that faith's predominance in Asia. He was said to have been so repelled by a particularly bloody victory of his troops over what is now Orissa that he turned to nonviolence and the Buddhist way of righteousness, and sent missionaries into Burma, Ceylon (Sri Lanka), Syria, Greece, and Egypt.
See also: Buddhism.

Asp, Egyptian cobra (*Naja haja*) of the family Elapidae, an extremely poisonous snake up to 7 ft (2 m) in length. Considered sacred in ancient Egypt, it was, according to legend, the snake that killed Cleopatra. The name is also applied to several species of vipers.
See also: Cobra.

Asparagus, garden vegetable (*Asparagus officinalis*) of the lily family, a perennial plant cultivated for its tender stalks. A well-tended asparagus bed may yield heavy crops for as long as 20 years. The main asparagus-growing areas in the U.S. are California and New Jersey. One variety of asparagus is grown for its attractive foliage alone.

Aspartame *see:* Artificial sweetener.

Aspasia (5th century B.C.), learned woman from Miletus, mistress of the Athenian statesman Pericles, by whom she had a son, Pericles the Younger. Her house was the literary and social gathering place for intellectual Athenians. She was the target of many spiteful attacks, mainly by conservatives who did not dare confront Pericles himself. Pericles was compelled to defend her against a charge of "impiety" in 432 B.C.

Aspen (pop. 3,678), town in south-central Colorado and seat of Pitkin County. In the late 19th century, Aspen (originally Ute City) was a flourishing silver-mining town, but its prosperity declined when ore deposits were exhausted. Located in the Rockies, at an altitude of 8,000 ft (2,438 m), it has become a year-round resort, with world-famous skiing facilities and a noted summer cultural festival.

Aspen, deciduous tree of the poplar genus widely distributed in north temperate regions, commercially valued as a source of pulp and matches. The best known varieties in the U.S. and Canada are the large-toothed aspen (*Populus grandidentata*) and the quaking aspen (*P. tremuloides*), a smaller tree with broad, delicate foliage that trembles with the slightest breeze..

Asphalt, tough black material made of heavy hydrocarbons and used in road paving, roofing, and canal and reservoir lining. Although natural deposits are still used, asphalt is now obtained mainly from petroleum refinery residues.

Asphodel, perennial herbaceous plant (genera *Asphodelus* and *Asphodeline*) of the lily family, with white or yellow flowers along the stalk. The yellow asphodel, or Jacob's rod, is often cultivated as an ornamental plant. Native to southern Europe and India, the asphodel was considered the flower of Hades by the ancient Greeks.

Asphyxiation, complex of symptoms resulting from a lack of oxygen or excess of carbon dioxide in the lungs. The commonest causes are drowning, suffocation or strangulation, inhalation of poisonous gases, and the obstruction of the larynx, trachea, or bronchi (as in severe cases of croup and asthma).

Aspidistra, perennial plant (*Aspidistra lurida*) of the lily family, with sturdy leaves, once a widely grown houseplant. Native to China, Java, and Japan, aspidistras bear small blue flowers close to the ground and have particularly attractive foliage.

Aspirin, or acetylsalicylic acid, effective painkiller that reduces fever and inflammation. It is useful in treating headache, minor fever, menstruation pain, rheumatic fever, inflammatory arthritis, and may help in the prevention of thrombosis (blood clots). Possible side effects include gastrointestinal irritation and hemorrhage.

Asquith, Herbert Henry, 1st Earl of Oxford and Asquith (1852-1928), English prime minister, 1908-16. His term as head of the Liberal Party was one of great activity and political reform, but his leadership foundered in Dec. 1916 over his conduct of World War I, coupled with the chaos brought about by the Easter Rising in Ireland. He resigned in favor of the rival Liberal leader, David Lloyd George.

Assad, Hafez al- (1930-), president of Syria since 1971. As minister of defense and member of the moderate wing of the Baath party, he led a coup that later made him president. A steadfast foe of Israel, Assad has supported various factions of the Palestine Liberation Organization. In 1976 he sent Syrian troops to Lebanon, where they have intervened actively in the civil war, holding power in much of the country. Assad opposed the Camp David peace treaty between Egypt and Israel. A member of the Alawi sect of Islam, Assad rules dictatorially over a population that is mostly Sunni Muslim. In the early 1990s Assad attempted to ameliorate the country's relationship with western countries, especially the United States. Assad was willing to cooperate in the Middle East peace proces.
See also: Persian Gulf War; Syria.

Assam (pop. 22,414,300), state in India located in the extreme northeast of the country and connected to the rest of India by West Bengal. To the north it is bordered by Tibet and Bhutan and to the east by Burma. The rugged land is drained by the Brahmaputra River. The climate is subtropical and rainfall varies from 70 in (178 cm) to more than 400 in (1,016 cm) per year. Tea is the main commercial product, and about 90% of the population is engaged in agriculture. Assamese is one of the official languages of India.

Assault and battery, any threatening physical act that reasonably causes another person to fear bodily harm or offensive contact. If there is actual contact, the crime is called battery. One may have assault without battery, but any case of battery necessarily includes assault. Assault and battery may be either a felony or a misdemeanor, depending on the degree of seriousness.

Assaying, method of chemical analysis used to determine the presence, absence, or quantity of a particular component of ores or alloys, used since the 2nd millennium B.C. In modern assaying, the sample is fused with a flux containing lead oxide. This produces a lead button containing the material being sought (such as gold or silver), which is heated in oxygen to oxidize the lead and other impurities. This leaves a bead of the metal sought, which is then weighed.

Assembler, computer program that converts symbolic code into binary object (machine) code for execution.
See also: Computer.

Assemblies of God, largest of the Protestant Pentecostal denominations in the United States. It was organized as a separate entity in 1914 and has about 2 million members.
See also: Pentecostal Churches.

Assembling, in computer terminology, automatic process by which a computer converts a symbolic-language program into a machine language, usually on an instruction-by-instruction basis.
See also: Assembler; Computer.

Assembly language, hardware-dependent symbolic language used in computers, usually characterized by a one-to-one correspondence of its statements with machine-language instructions.
See also: Computer.

Assembly line, production line of equipment, machinery, and workers along which successive operations are performed until the final product is complete. The modern assembly line, largely a result of innovations by Henry Ford in the automotive industry, also employs automation (machines run by machines).
See also: Mass production.

Assessment, value of property (most commonly homes, shops, and offices) for purposes of taxation, or the process of determining this value. The tax rate is generally stated as so many dollars per thousand dollars of assessed valuation. The term also refers to a demand made by a corporation for extra funds from its stockholders.

Assignment, in law, transfer of rights, especially intangible property rights: insurance policies, certificates of corporate shares, and rights to monies due or to become due. In bankruptcy, a debtor's assets may be assigned to a trustee for distribution among the creditors.

Assimilation, the process by which food is appropriated as nourishment for the body, following digestion and absorption. The food is converted into living tissues by the cells.
See also: Cell; Digestive system.

Assiniboia, 2 former, distinct districts of Canada, one formed by the Hudson's Bay Company around the Red River in 1835, incorporated in Manitoba (1870), the other, a section of the Northwest Territories (1882-1905), in the southern portion of present-day Alberta and Saskatchewan.

Assiniboine, Sioux tribe of the North American plains who left the Yanktonai Sioux to spread out from Canada across the northwestern United States. A nomadic people who lived primarily by hunting, they were greatly weakened by the extinction of the buffalo as a result of European settlements, and were placed on reservations in 1884.

Assisi, Francis of *see:* Francis of Assisi, Saint.

Associated Press (AP), oldest and one of the largest U.S. news agencies (gatherers and distributors of news). Founded in 1848 by 6 New York City newspapers, it now has offices worldwide. The AP is a nonprofit organization financed by subscriptions from member newspapers, periodicals, and broadcasting stations.

Association, in psychology, mental linking of one item with others, by similarity, contiguity, opposition, or other principles. In association tests, subjects are presented with a word and asked to respond either with a specifically related word, such as a rhyme or an antonym, or with the first word that comes to mind.
See also: Learning.

Associationism, psychological school holding that the sole mechanism of human learning consists in the permanent association in the intellect of impressions that have been repeatedly presented to the senses. Originating in the philosophy of John Locke and developed through the work of John Gay, David Hartley, James and John Stuart Mill, and Alexander Bain, the "association of ideas" was the dominant thesis in British psychology for 200 years.

Assumption of the Virgin, Roman Catholic belief (declared as official dogma by Pope Pius XII in 1950) that the Virgin Mary was "assumed into heaven body and soul" at the end of her life. Assumption Day is celebrated Aug. 15.

Assurbanipal *see:* Ashurbanipal.

Assyria *see:* Babylonia and Assyria.

Astaire, Fred (Frederick Austerlitz; 1899-1988), U.S. dancer, choreographer, and actor. First in partnership onstage with his sister Adele and later with Ginger Rogers in such films as *Top Hat* (1935) and *Swing Time* (1936), he became one of the most popular dancers and musical comedy stars, renowned for his originality and perfection. Later films, with other partners, included *Holiday Inn* (1942), *The Band Wagon* (1953), and *Funny Face* (1957).

Astarte, Phoenician goddess of love and fertility, corresponding to Babylonian Ishtar and Greek Aphrodite. In Syrian art Astarte is frequently represented with two curled ram's horns on her head.

Astatine, chemical element, symbol At; for physical constants see Periodic Table. Astatine was synthesized in 1940 by Corson, MacKenzie, and Segré at the University of California by bombarding bismuth with alpha particles. Minute quantities of astatine exist in nature as isotopes produced from uranium and thorium reacting with naturally produced neutrons. Astatine is radioactive and belongs to the halogen group of elements. It behaves chemically very much like them and is reported to be more metallic than iodine. The longest-lived isotope, astatine-210, has a half-life of 8.1 hours. Twenty-eight isotopes of astatine are known.

Assembly-line production at the Ford factory in the 1920s. The assembly line in the foreground is for the Model T.

Aster (genus *Aster*), also known as Michaelmas or Christmas daisy, perennial plant with blue, purple, white, or red flowers that bloom in autumn. The China aster (*Callistephus chinensis*), in the same family, produces bigger, almost chrysanthemum-like flowers in bright colors.

Asteria, in Greek mythology, daughter of Coeus, the Titan, and mother of Hecate. Courted by Zeus in the form of an eagle, she threw herself into the sea, where she was changed into an island, later called Delos.

Asteroid, planetoid, or minor planet of irregular shape, orbiting the sun. Ranging in diameter from a few feet (1 m) to Ceres's 470 mi (750 km), most (some 50,000 that are too small to yield to diameter measurements) lie in the asteroid belt between the orbits of Mars and Jupiter, their total mass estimated to be 0.001 that of the earth. Ceres was the first to be discovered (1801 by Giuseppe Piazzi), and Vesta is the only one visible to the naked eye. The Apollo asteroids have highly elliptical, earth-approaching orbits, and may have caused several of earth's meteorite craters. The Trojan asteroids share the orbit of the planet Jupiter.

Fred Astaire

Asthenosphere, the worldwide "soft layer" underlying the rigid lithosphere, located some 43.5-155 mi (70-250 km) below the earth's surface. Considered part of the upper mantle, the zone is characterized by low seismic velocities, suggesting that it may be partially molten. In plate tectonic theory, rigid slablike plates of the lithosphere move over the asthenosphere.

Asthma, reversible obstruction of the airways that compromises the respiratory system. Asthma attacks are typically accompanied, by coughing and wheezing.

Asthma is a chronic disorder that can be triggered by exposure to certain allergens or in response to physical or emotional stress. Therapy includes the use of steroids and bronchodilators.
See also: Allergy; Bronchitis.

Astigmatism, defect of vision caused by irregular shaping in the cornea or lens. In astigmatism, light rays do not converge evenly, some focusing behind the retina, some before it, others on it. It can be corrected by glasses or contact lenses.
See also: Eye.

Aston, Francis William (1877-1945), British physicist and chemist. At the Cavendish Laboratory, Cambridge, Aston accomplished the first artificial separation of isotopes. He was awarded the Nobel Prize for chemistry in 1922, chiefly for devising the mass spectrograph to study isotopes.

Astor, name of a prominent U.S. family involved in fur trading, real estate, and finance, as well as in U.S. and British politics. **John Jacob Astor** (1763-1848), arrived in Baltimore from Waldorf, Germany, began as a baker's boy, became a fur trader and real estate investor, and eventually amassed the fortune of the Astors. **William Backhouse Astor** (1792-1875), John Jacob's son, doubled the family's wealth. His son, **John Jacob IV** (1864-1912), an inventor and science fiction writer, died in the sinking of the *Titanic.* **William Waldorf, 1st Viscount Astor** (1848-1919), John Jacob's great-grandson, was a financier who moved to England, where he was made baron and later viscount. **Nancy Witcher (Langhorne) Astor, Viscountess Astor** (1879-1964) was the first woman to serve in the British Parliament, as Conservative member for Plymouth.

Astrakhan (pop. 487,000), capital of Astrakhan Oblast in the USSR. A port on the Caspian Sea at the mouth of the Volga River, Astrakhan handles trade in oil, fish, grain, and wood.

Astringent, substance that causes the organic tissues and canals of the body to contract, thereby checking or diminishing excessive discharges.

Astroarcheology *see:* Archeoastronomy.

Astrolabe, astronomical instrument dating from ancient times, used to measure the altitude and movements of celestial bodies. Before the introduction of the sextant, it served as a navigational aid.
See also: Sextant.

Astrology, system of beliefs based on the theory that movements of celestial bodies influence human events, which can therefore be predicted. The key factor in Western astrology is the position of the stars and planets, described relative to the 12 divisions of the zodiac, at the moment of an individual's birth.
See also: Zodiac.

Astronaut, term for U.S. test pilot or scientist chosen by NASA to crew space flights. Alan B. Shepard, Jr., made the first suborbital flight in 1961. John Glenn, Jr., orbited the earth in 1962, and Edwin E. Aldrin, Jr., and Neil Armstrong landed on the moon in 1969.

Astronautics, or astronautical engineering, scientific study of the principles of space flight, including astrodynamics, space communications, propulsion theory, astrobiology, astrogeology, and the design analysis of spacecraft.

Astronomy, study of the planets, stars, and galaxies. To most early astronomers, the earth appeared to be surrounded by a sphere that contained the stars. The high point of early astronomy was the work of the Greeks. Pythagoras (6th century B.C.), who imagined the sun, moon, and planets positioned on transparent spheres that moved along with the sphere of stars, introduced the notion of "the music of the spheres." Hipparchus (2nd century B.C.) compiled—without a telescope—an accurate catalog of 850 stars; his system of magnitude ratings is the basis for the one used today. Ptolemy (2nd century A.D.) laid out a geocentric scheme of the universe, with the earth at the center, that was regarded as gospel for 1,500 years. In 1543, the Polish mathematician Nicholas Copernicus challenged Ptolemy's theory with the idea that the sun is stationary, with everything else circling around it. In 1609, the Italian Galileo Galilei made his own telescope and confirmed Copernicus's heliocentric theory. At the same time, the German mathematician Johannes Kepler finally discredited the geocentric theory. In the late 17th century English mathematician Isaac Newton formulated laws of motion to explain why objects move as they do, how the planets stay in orbit, and why their orbits are elliptical.
Nineteenth-century astronomers analyzed the composition of stars and wondered what causes them to burn. In the early 20th century, Albert Einstein announced his theory that mass and energy are equivalent, and the idea of nuclear power was introduced. It is now known that the sun produces energy by nuclear fusion.
The branch of astronomy called cosmology seeks to find out how the universe originated. One clue discovered in the 1930s by Edwin Hubble resulted in the idea of an expanding universe and the possibility that it started off with a giant explosion—the big bang theory. An opposing idea, promoted by Fred Hoyle, the steady state theory, holds that the universe remains stable because new matter is created to fill the gaps created as galaxies expand. Space exploration and new techniques (advances in radio astronomy, and methods based on gamma, ultraviolet, and X rays) continue to expand our knowledge of the universe.
See also: Cosmology.

Astrophysics, science dealing with the physical laws governing the nature of celestial objects and events, enabling astronomers to formulate theories of stellar evolution and cosmology.
See also: Astronomy; Cosmology.

Asturias, Miguel Ángel (1899-1974), Guatemalan writer and diplomat. He won the Lenin Peace Prize in 1966 and the Nobel Prize for literature in 1967. His books *The Cyclone* (1950) and *The Green Pope* (1954) attack the exploitation of Guatemalan Indians.

Asunción (pop. 456,000), capital and largest city of Paraguay. Situated on the Paraguay River, Asunción is the main port and the industrial, transportation, and administrative center of the country. Founded in 1537 by Spanish explorers searching for a short route to Peru, Asunción was the rival of Buenos Aires until the 18th century when it was weakened by conflict between the Jesuits and their enemies.

Aswan High Dam, one of the world's largest dams, built on the Nile River in Egypt (1960-70), located 4 mi (6.4 km) south of the 1902 Aswan dam. The dam's hydroelectric generating station has a capacity of 10 billion kwh, and Lake Nasser, formed by the dam, has enough water to irrigate more than 7 million acres of farmland.

Asylum, sanctuary or place of refuge; an institution for receiving and maintaining persons suffering certain physical or mental diseases or defects.

Asyut (pop. 2,179,000), city in the eastern central region of Egypt, on the left bank of the Nile, about 250 mi (402 km) south of Cairo. A commercial and industrial center producing textiles, pottery, and ivory and wood carvings, Asyut is also the educational center of the Upper Nile Valley; its schools and institutions include the University of Asyut and the Technical and Trade School. A large community of Coptic Christians lives in the city. Asyut Barrage controls the flow of the Nile and provides water for the irrigation of Middle Egypt.

Atacama Desert, arid plateau extending from central Chile to southern Ecuador, some 600 mi (966 km) long and 2,000 ft (610 m) high. One of the driest regions on earth, it is a major source of nitrates and copper.

Atahualpa (1500-33), last Inca emperor of Peru. After holding power only in Quito, Atahualpa deposed his half brother Huascar as heir of the Inca kingdom. In 1532 the Spanish conquistadors under Francisco Pizarro executed Atahualpa for refusing to accept Christianity.
See also: Inca.

Atalanta, in Greek mythology, beautiful, swift-footed huntress who promised to marry any suitor who outran her, but to kill any she could beat. She lost to (and married) Hippomenes, who, helped by the goddess Aphrodite, had dropped 3 golden apples that Atalanta paused to pick up.

Atatürk, Kemal (Mustafa Kemal; (1881-1938), founder of modern Turkey. An army officer who gained prominence during World War I, Atatürk headed a provisional government in Ankara that opposed the Allied regime in Istanbul established after the collapse of the Ottoman Empire. In 1923 he won European recognition of the new Turkish republic. His secular regime replaced the political power of Islam and modernized the Turkish economy.

Atavism, inheritance by an individual organism of characteristics not shown by its parental generation. Once thought to be throwbacks to an ancestral form, atavisms are now known to be primarily the result of the random appearance of recessive traits, though they may result also from aberrations in the development of the embryo or from disease.

Ataxia, impaired muscular coordination resulting in unsteady gait, difficulty in fine movements, and speech disorders. Usually caused by damage to the cerebellum or the spinal cord, ataxia occurs with multiple sclerosis, syphilis, and brain tumors.

Atchison, city in northeastern Kansas, on the Missouri River. It became a trade and travel center for the opening West as a river port, Pony Express Station, and eastern terminus for the Atchison, Topeka & Santa Fe Railroad.

Atchison, David Rice (1807-86), U.S. Senator and proslavery leader of the Missouri Democratic Party. He served in the Missouri State legislature (1834-38) and was appointed to the U.S. Senate in 1843.

Athabasca, river and lake in northern Alberta and Saskatchewan, Canada. The river rises in Jasper National Park and flows to the 3,120 sq mi (8,080 sq km) lake.

Athanasius, Saint (c.297-373), early Christian theologian and Greek Father of the Church. Athanasius was elected archbishop of Alexandria in 328. He was banished to Trèves (Trier) in 335 by the emperor Constantine for his refusal to compromise with Arianism, but was restored by Constantius in 338. His writings include *On the Incarnation, Five Books Against Arius,* and *Life of St. Anthony.*

Atharva-Veda *see:* Vedas.

Atheism, denial of the existence of God, distinguished from agnosticism, which holds that the existence of God cannot be proved or disproved but does not necessarily take any position on belief.
See also: Agnosticism.

Athena (Pallas Athena), in Greek mythology, goddess of wisdom, war, and peace, who sprang fully grown from the head of Zeus. She was a patron of agriculture, arts, and the crafts of civilization. The Romans identified her with Minerva.

Athens (pop. 885,700), capital and largest city of Greece, in east central Greece. The center of ancient Greek civilization, Athens reached its political peak after the Persian wars (499-449 B.C.). Athens lost its supremacy to Sparta in the Peloponnesian War (431-404 B.C.) and later became a subject of Macedonia and then of Rome. Modern Athens, including the Aegean port of Piraeus, is the administrative, political, cultural, and economic center of Greece.

Atherosclerosis *see:* Arteriosclerosis.

Athlete's foot, popular name for a fungus infection of any area of the skin of the feet or toes, causing inflammation and itching. The fungus thrives in a warm, humid environment.
See also: Ringworm.

Athlone, Alexander Augustus Frederick William Alfred George Cambridge, 1st Earl of, (1874-1957), British army officer and member of the royal family. After a military career during the Boer War and World War I, he was governor general of the Union of South Africa (1923-31) and governor general of Canada (1940- 46).

Atlanta (pop. 2,833,511), capital and largest city of Georgia, seat of Fulton County. Founded in 1837 as the terminus of the Western and Atlantic Railroad, Atlanta was burned by Union forces under General William Sherman during the Civil War in 1864. It was rapidly rebuilt and is today the major commercial and financial center of the South Atlantic states. The city has more than 20 colleges and universities.
See also: Georgia.

Atlanta, Battle of *see:* Civil War.

Atlantic Charter, declaration of common objectives signed by U.S. President F. D. Roosevelt and British Prime Minister Winston Churchill on Aug. 14, 1941, before the United States entered World War II. It affirmed the determination of the 2 governments not to extend their territories and to promote human rights.

Atlantic City (pop. 319,416), seaside resort and convention center in southeast New Jersey. Its famous Boardwalk (built 1870) is lined by hotels, restaurants, casinos, and Convention Hall.

Atlantic Intracoastal Waterway, shallow, sheltered water route extending 1,134 mi (1,825 km) along the Atlantic seaboard from Norfolk, Va., to Key West, Fla., and serving pleasure craft and light shipping.

Atlantic Ocean, world's second-largest ocean (c.31.8 million sq mi/82.3 million sq km), separating the Americas from Europe and Africa. The North Atlantic carries the greatest proportion of the world's shipping, and about half of the world's fish come from the area.

Atlantic Provinces, the 4 Canadian provinces of Newfoundland, New Brunswick, Nova Scotia, and Prince Edward Island, the last 3 of which are sometimes called the Maritime Provinces. Comprising about 5 percent of the area of Canada, these provinces have been a fishing center since the late 1400s. Service industries, increasingly important during the 1900s, are now the leading economic activity. The majority of inhabitants are of English, Irish, Scottish, or Welsh descent.

Atlantic States, those states of the U.S. south of New England bordering on the Atlantic Ocean or closely relying on it economically. New York, New Jersey, and Pennsylvania are Middle Atlantic states. Maryland, Delaware, Virginia, North Carolina, South Carolina, Georgia, and Florida, are South Atlantic states, West Virginia occasionally considered to be part of this group as well.

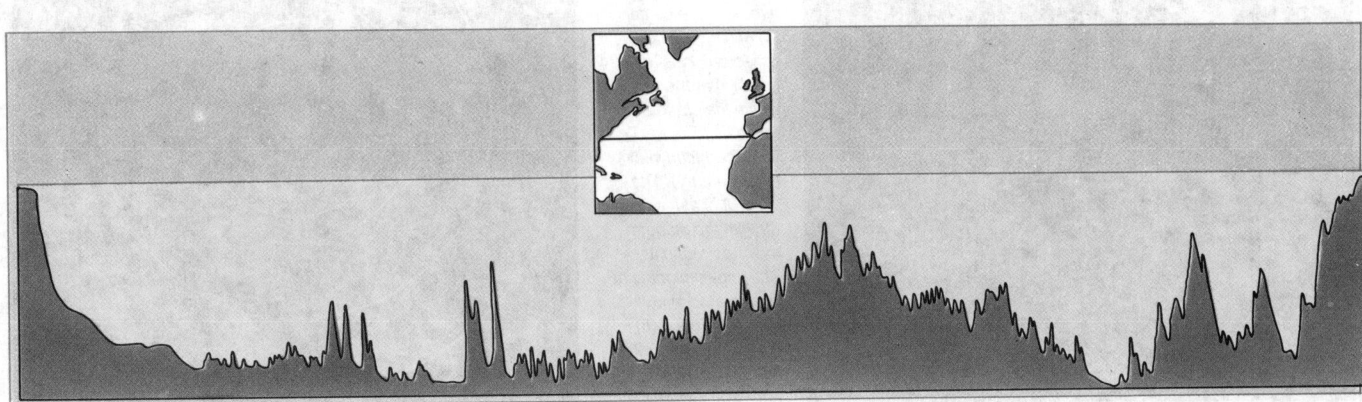

This cross-section of the Atlantic Ocean represents the ocean floor between Cape Hatteras on the American side and Gibraltar on the European side. Between the mid-Atlantic Ridge and the continental slope on the European side is the Azores-Gibraltar Ridge.

Johannes Kepler discovered the laws of planetary motion and deduced that the planets move in orbits around the Sun.

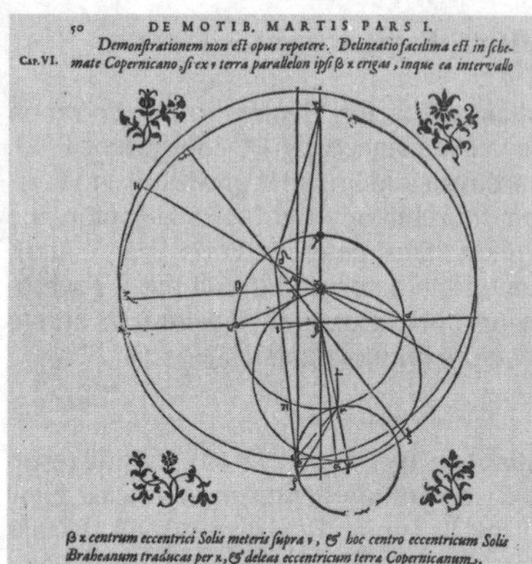

50 DE MOTIB. MARTIS PARS I.

Demonstrationem non est opus repetere. Delineatio facilima est in schemate Copernicano, si ex ν terra parallelon ipsi β κ erigas, inque ea intervallo

CAP. VI.

β κ centrum eccentrici Solis meteris supra ν, & hoc centro eccentricum Solis Braheanum traducas per κ, & deleas eccentricum terrae Copernicanum.

Drawing from Kepler's Astronomia nova which dates from 1609. In this work Kepler compared his observations with those of his former teacher Tycho Brahe.

A print from an 18th- century atlas indicating the movement of the planets around the Sun. While this observation had been made two centuries earlier by Copernicus, political and intellectual acceptance of this fact was not easily accomplished.

The rings of the planet Saturn. The outer and inner rings are separated by a dark band called the Cassini division.

An ultraviolet photograph of the comet Kohoutek made by the crew of the Skylab space station on December 25, 1973. The different colors indicate regions of different temperatures. Photographs in ultraviolet light cannot be made from the Earth because of the screening influence of the atmosphere.

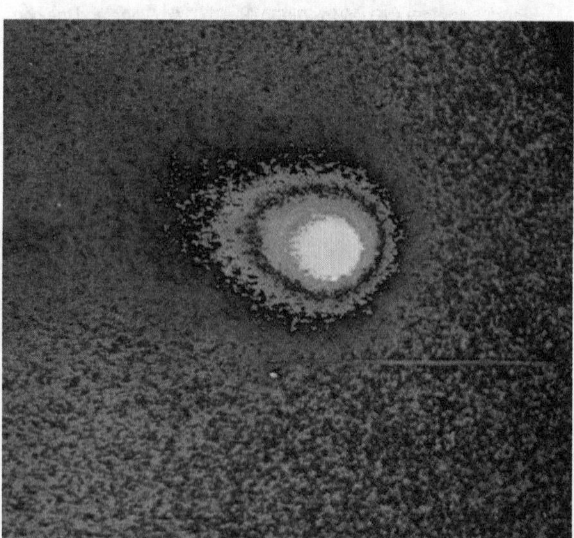

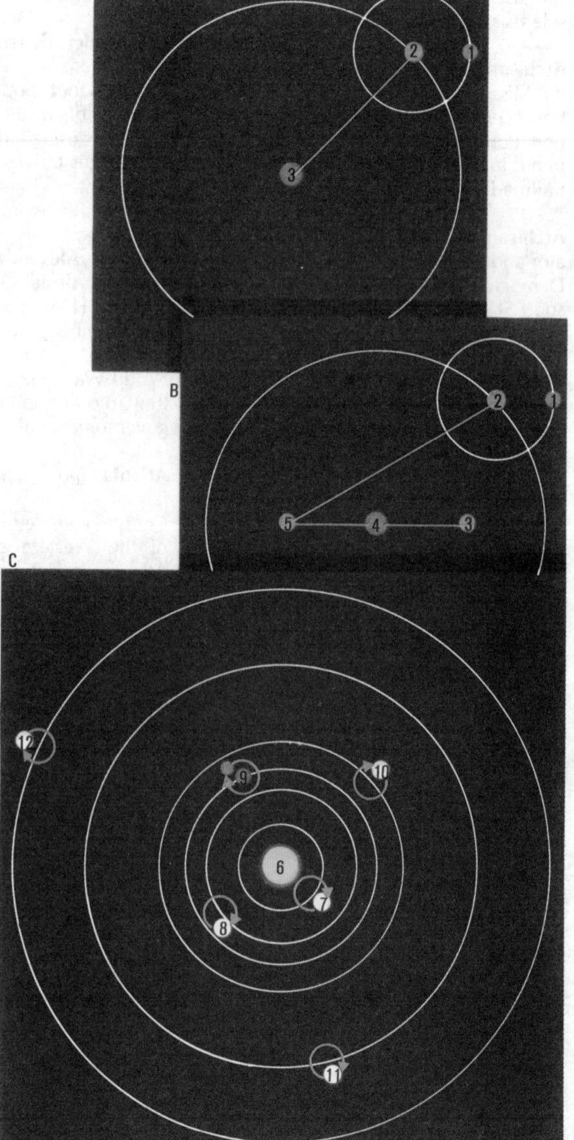

Three views of planetary motion.
A. Hipparchus' view (150 B.C.): each planet (1) moves around in a small circle (epicycle), the center of which (2) makes a larger circle around the Earth (3). Although Hipparchus' view positioned the Earth at the center at of the solar system, his calculations about the position of the planets was correct.
B. Ptolemy's view (2nd century A.D.): In the Ptolemaic system each planet (1) travels in a circle whose center (2) moves around the Earth. Ptolemy placed the Earth (3) almost at the center (4) and introduced a fictitious opposite point (5) around which the planets move.
C. Copernican view (16th century): The Sun (6) is at the center with the planets moving around it. The known planets at this time were Mercury (7), Venus (8), Earth and Moon (9), Mars (10), Jupiter (11), and Saturn (12).

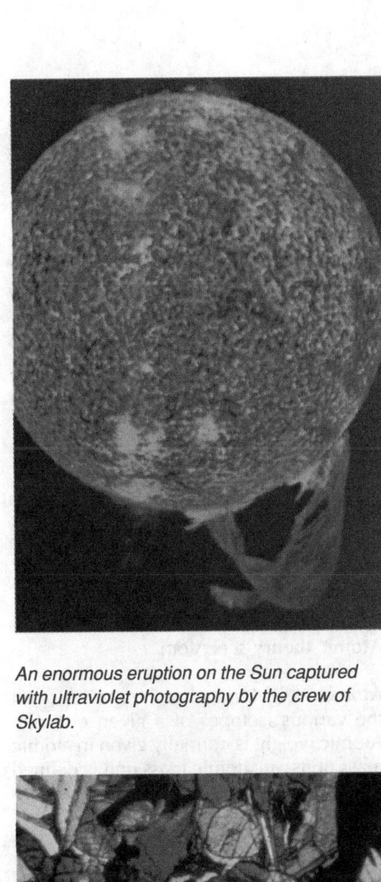

An enormous eruption on the Sun captured with ultraviolet photography by the crew of Skylab.

The fully assembled combination of service module (1), Apollo capsule (2), and lunar lander (3). The lunar lander also carried a moon jeep (4) on the last three missions.

Photograph of Halley's Comet made in 1986 by the European space probe Giotto. *Brown section (upper left) is part of the core of the planet. The various colors represent emissions of gas and dust.*

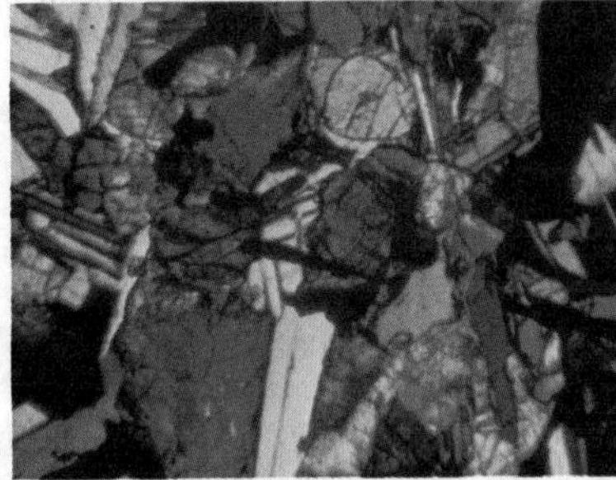

Photomicrograph of moon rocks brought back by the Apollo 12 mission. In order to reveal the structure, the photograph was taken with a polarization microscope. The colors are due to differences in thickness of the crystal layers.

Astrophysics is the study of the universe. A. Observations using gamma and X-rays of the solar corona must be made from the upper atmosphere by balloon or satellite. B. Studies of the Martian atmosphere may be made using ultraviolet radiation. Earth-based observatories or martian probes may perform the task. C. The visible spectrum. The Moon is observable from Earth. D. Infrared studies of Mars reveal surface detail. Observations may be made from telescopes on Earth or from space probes. E. Microwave radiation and radar wave lengths. Radar transmitters on Earth bounce radiation off the lunar surface to obtain profiles. F. Radio Waves. Radio telescopes map the powerful source, Centaurus A.

Atlantis, in Greek mythology, an island in the western sea (Atlantic Ocean?). Plato described it as an advanced civilization destroyed by volcanic eruptions and earthquakes. The legend has fascinated humanity since antiquity, and many have searched for the lost island. Some scholars identify Atlantis with the Mediterranean island of Thera (also called Santorini), a center of ancient Cretan civilization devastated by volcanic eruptions in 1625 B.C.

Atlas, in Greek mythology, a titan. After the titans were defeated by the Olympians, he was condemned to carry the sky on his shoulders for eternity.

Atlas Mountains, mountain system of northwest Africa. The highest peak, 13,671 ft (4,167 m), is Mount Toubkal in southwestern Morocco. The Atlas mountains are rich in coal, oil, iron ore, and phosphates.

Atmosphere, spheroidal envelope of gas and vapor surrounding a planet, retained by gravity. The composition of the earth's atmosphere and most of its physical properties vary with altitude. About 75% of the total mass of the atmosphere and 90% of its water vapor are contained in the troposphere, the lowest zone, which extends from the earth's surface to an altitude of about 5 mi (8 km) at the poles and 10 mi (16 km) at the equator. The stratosphere, where the ozone layer filters out the sun's ultraviolet radiation, extends from the troposphere to about 30 mi (50 km); the mesosphere ranges from there to about 50 mi (80 km); the ionosphere, containing electrically charged particles that reflect radio signals, goes to about 400 mi (640 km); finally, the exosphere merges into the interplanetary medium. Overall, the atmosphere is about 78% nitrogen by volume. Other major components include oxygen (21%), argon (0.93%), and carbon dioxide (0.03%).

Atoll, low-lying oval or circular coral reef, enclosing a lagoon, most prevalent in the western Pacific Ocean. Examples are the Maldive Islands, Whitsunday Island, and the Bikini Atoll.
See also: Coral.

Atom, classically, one of the minute, indivisible, homogeneous particles of which physical objects are composed; in 20th-century science, the name given to a relatively stable package of matter that is itself made up of at least 2 subatomic particles, and that defines an element. Every atom consists of a tiny nucleus (containing positively charged protons and electrically neutral neutrons) with which a number of negatively charged electrons are associated. The much smaller electrons occupy a hierarchy of orbitals that represent the atom's electronic energy levels and fill most of the space taken up by the atom. The number of protons in the nucleus of an atom (the atomic number, Z) defines the chemical element of which the atom is an example. In an isolated neutral atom the number of electrons equals the atomic number, but an electrically charged ion of the same atom has either a surfeit or a deficit of electrons. The number of neutrons in the nucleus (the neutron number, N) can vary among different atoms of the same element. Atoms with the same number of protons but different numbers of neutrons are called isotopes of the element in question. Most stable isotopes have slightly more neutrons than protons.
Although the nucleus is very small, it contains nearly all the mass of the atom—protons and neutrons having very similar masses, the mass of the electron (about 0.05% of the proton mass) being almost negligible. The mass of an atom is roughly equal to the total number of its protons and neutrons. This number, $Z + N$, is known as the mass number of the atom, A, the mass of a proton being counted as 1. In equations representing nuclear reactions, the atomic number of an atom is often written as a subscript preceding the chemical symbol for the element, and the mass number as a superscript following it. Thus an atomic nucleus with a mass number 16 and containing 8 protons belongs to an atom of oxygen-16, written ${}_8O^{16}$. The average of the mass numbers of the various naturally occurring isotopes of an element, weighted according to their relative abundance, gives the chemical atomic weight of the element. Subatomic particles fired into atomic nuclei can cause nuclear reactions that give rise either to new isotopes of the original element or to atoms of a different element. Such nuclear reactions emit alpha particles, or beta rays, sometimes accompanied by gamma rays.

Atomic bomb *see:* Nuclear bomb.

Atomic clock, precise electric device for measuring time, indirectly controlled by atomic or molecular vibration.

Atomic energy
see: Fission; Nuclear energy.

Atomic fusion *see:* Fusion; Nuclear energy.

Atomic number *see:* Atom.

Atomic particle *see:* Atom.

Atomic reactor *see:* Nuclear reactor.

Atomic theory *see:* Atom.

Atomic weight, mean of the masses of all the various isotopes of a given element. Atomic weight is normally given in atomic mass units; an atomic mass unit is defined as 1/12 of the mass of an atom of carbon-12.
See also: Atom; Periodic table.

Atom smasher *see:* Particle accelerator.

Atonement, in Christian theology, reconciliation of humanity with God through the sacrificial death of Christ. In Jewish theology, one day of the year is designated as the Day of Atonement (*Yom Kippur*).

Atreus, in Greek mythology, king of Mycenae and the father of Agamemnon and Menelaus. His brother, Thyestes, seduced Atreus's wife, Aërope, and attempted to seize the throne of Mycenae. Atreus, pretending to forgive his brother, invited him to a banquet at which he served Thyestes the bodies of his 2 sons.

Atrium, unroofed or partially roofed interior court of a Roman house, with rooms extending around it; also, entrance court of early Christian churches.

The Atlas Mountains contain oil, iron, and coal, but also have provided protection for the Berber people who have fled there during invasions.

Atrophy (Greek, "not nourished"), decrease in size and function or wasting away of any organ, tissue, or part of the body as a result of disease, malnutrition, decreased work, or normal processes of growth or body function. Among the types of atrophy are acute yellow atrophy, massive necrosis of the liver associated with severe infection; toxemia of pregnancy or ingested poisons; and progressive muscular atrophy, a motor neuron disease characterized by loss of power and wasting in the arms and legs.

Atropine, crystalline alkaloid contained in plants such as jimsonweed and deadly nightshade (belladonna), used in many gastrointestinal and ophthalmic preparations. Its chief use is as an antispasmodic to relax smooth muscles.
See also: Belladonna.

Atsina *see:* Gros Ventre.

Attachment, seizure of property by legal process, to prevent a defendant from disposing of disputed property before trial, and to guarantee payment of any judgment against him or her.

Attainder, loss of civil rights (strictly, rights of ownership and disposition of property) by someone outlawed or sentenced to death. Attainder has been almost universally abolished except in cases of treason.

Attar, fragrant, essential oil, often made from various species of roses, that forms a valuable perfume.

Attila (A.D. 406?-453), king of the Huns, who claimed domination from the Alps and the Baltic to the Caspian Sea. From 441 to 450 he ravaged the Eastern Roman Empire as far as Constantinople, and invaded Gaul in 451, this expedition earning him the title Scourge of God. He was defeated by the Romans, and subsequently invaded Italy (452), but retired without attacking Rome, apparently due to lack of supplies and sickness among his troops. He died of overindulgence at his wedding feast.
See also: Hun.

Attlee, Clement Richard, 1st Earl (1883-1967), British politician and prime minister (1945-51). Attlee led the Labour party from 1935 and served in Winston Churchill's wartime coalition cabinet before becoming prime minister. During his administration he instituted a broad program of social reforms, including the National Health Service, and nationalized many industries and the Bank of England. Also during his administration, independence was granted to India, Burma, Pakistan, Palestine, and Ceylon.

Attorney, one who is legally appointed in the place of another as an agent to transact any business for him or her; especially a lawyer.

Attorney general, chief law officer of a nation (in Canada also called minister of justice). The U.S. attorney general heads the Department of Justice, is a member of the president's cabinet, enforces federal laws, and advises the president on legal questions. Attorneys general in individual states and Canada perform similar functions.
See also: Justice, Department of.

Attucks, Crispus (c.1723-70), U.S. patriot of African and Native American parentage who was the first of 5 men to die in the Boston Massacre. It is historic irony that one of the first persons to die in the cause of American independence was an individual whose personal rights were not secure at the time of his death.
See also: Boston Massacre.

Atwood, Margaret (1939-), Canadian poet and novelist. Atwood gained prominence with a collection of poetry, *The Circle Game* (1966). Among her other works are *Bluebeard's Egg* (1983), a collection of short stories, and the novels *Surfacing* (1972), *Lady Oracle* (1976), *The Handmaid's Tale* (1985), and *Cat's Eye* (1989).

Auckland (pop. 820,754), chief port, largest city, naval base, and industrial center of New Zealand, capital of Auckland province on North Island. Founded in 1840, Auckland was New Zealand's capital until 1865, when the government was transferred to Wellington. Important industries include shipbuilding, oil refining, food processing, and automobile manufacturing. The city's War Memorial Museum contains one of the finest collections of Maori art in the world.

Auckland Islands, group of uninhabited islands, of volcanic origin, lying in the southern Pacific Ocean about 200 mi (320 km) south of New Zealand. They were used as a whaling station during the early 19th century. The islands are controlled by New Zealand.

Auden, W(ystan) H(ugh) (1907-73), Anglo-American poet and major influence in 20th century literature. In the 1930s, when he also collaborated with Christopher Isherwood on verse plays (*The Dog Beneath the Skin*, *The Ascent of F6*, and *On the Frontier*), his poetry probed pre-World War II European culture. In 1939 Auden moved to the United States, where he became a citizen in 1946. His later work, which delves into religion, psychology, and politics, includes *The Double Man* (1941), *The Age of Anxiety* (1947, Pulitzer Prize), *The Shield of Achilles* (1955), and *About the House*. He also wrote opera librettos and literary criticism.

Audiology, science of hearing; particularly, the study of hearing disorders and rehabilitation of individuals with hearing defects. Audiologists determine whether a person has a hearing deficiency by identifying and measuring hearing function loss and assessing the patient's ability to communicate. Corrective treatment may involve a hearing aid, learning to read lips, or improvement of listening skills.

Audit, in accounting, examination of accounts or dealings with money or property, performed by persons not involved in the preparation of the accounts.
See also: Accounting.

Audubon, John James (1785-1851), U.S. artist and ornithologist famous for his paintings of North American birds, reproduced in *Birds of America* (1827-38). He laborated with the Scottish naturali liam MacGillivray on an accor text, *Ornithological Biography*

Audubon drawing

Auerbach, Red (Arnold Auerbach; 1917-), U.S. basketball coach who led the Boston Celtics to 9 championships in 10 years (1957; 1959-66). He retired in 1966 after having won 1,037 professional games.

Augsburg (pop. 245,600), capital of the administrative district of Swabia in Bavaria, Germany, on the Lech River about 35 mi (56 km) from Munich. Situated on the site of a Roman colony founded by Emperor Augustus (late 1st century B.C.), it became a free imperial city (1276) and flourished as an important trade center. Augsburg lost much in power and prestige during the Thirty Years War (1618-48) and eventually was annexed by Bavaria (1806). Today it is an important commercial and rail center for south Germany. Its medieval inner quarter includes the late Gothic church of St. Ulrich and the Renaissance-style Rathaus.
See also: Augsburg Confession.

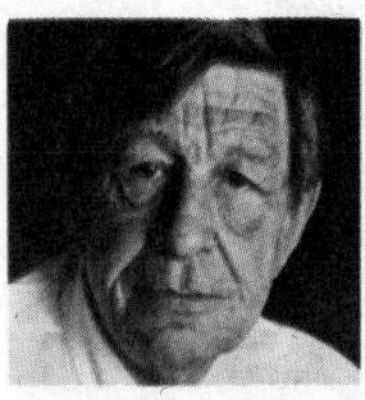

W.H. Auden

Augsburg Confession, statement of Lutheran beliefs presented to the Diet of Augsburg on June 25, 1530. The Confession, largely the work of Philip Melanchthon, was an attempt to reconcile Luther's

Augustus

reforms with Roman Catholicism. It was rejected by Emperor Charles V, which sealed the break between the Lutherans and Rome.
See also: Luther, Martin.

Augur, in ancient Rome, official who derived signs (auguries) concerning future events from the flight or other actions of birds, certain appearances in quadrupeds, lightning, or other unusual occurrences. In an elaborate ceremony, the augur would choose a spot with a clear view to wait for any signs—from thunder in the skies to the squeak of a mouse—that might indicate the "will of the gods." No important business of state could be initiated without first consulting such a diviner.

Augusta (pop. 23,000), capital of Maine and seat of Kennebec County on the Kennebec River. Among its products are textiles, shoes, paper, and foodstuffs. A Plymouth Colony trading post was established on the site in 1628, and the town grew up around Fort Western, its first permanent structure, built in 1754. Augusta became the state capital in 1831 and was incorporated in 1849.
See also: Maine.

Augusta (pop. 396,809), city in eastern Georgia on the Savannah River, seat of Richmond County. Founded as a trading post by James Oglethorpe in 1736, it was the scene of fighting during the Revolutionary War and was an important Confederate ordnance center during the Civil War. Today Augusta, a popular winter resort, houses diversified industries, the University of Georgia School of Medicine, and Woodrow Wilson's boyhood home.

Augustan Age *see:* Augustus; England; English literature; Latin literature.

Augustine, Saint (A.D. 354-430), bishop of Hippo, church father. Though raised as a Christian by his mother, St. Monica, in northern Africa, he embraced Manichaeism while in school at Carthage. Moving to Rome (383), he was influenced by Neoplatonism, but it was in Milan, where he met St. Ambrose, bishop of the city, that he was baptized a Christian (387) and took the vows of priesthood (391). In 396 he became bishop of Hippo (northern Africa). Generally acknowledged by Christians as the father of theology, he wrote many books, including the autobiographical *Confessions* and *De Civitate Dei* (*The City of God*), containing the great defense against paganism and the Christian philosophy of history. His feast day is Aug. 28.

Jane Austen

Augustine, Saint (d. A.D. 604), Italian missionary and first archbishop of Canterbury (from 601). A Benedictine monk, he was sent to England by Pope Gregory the Great to convert the populace and bring the Celtic Church under Rome's control. He was given support by King Ethelbert of Kent. His feast day is May 27 (May 26 in England and Wales).

Augustus (63 B.C.-A.D. 14), honorific title given in 27 B.C. to Gaius Julius Caesar Octavianus, adopted great-nephew and heir of Julius Caesar. With Lepidus and Marc Antony he formed a triumvirate that avenged his great-uncle's murder by defeating and destroying the main conspirators, at Philippi (42 B.C.). The deposition of Lepidus (36 B.C.) and the suicide of Antony after his defeat at Actium (31 B.C.) left Augustus sole master of the Roman world. After the ravages of 50 years of civil war, he used his power to institute religious, legal, and administrative reforms and to promote literature, the arts, and agriculture. While nominally restoring the Republic, his control of the state's finances and armed forces made him the sole ruler. He is accounted first Roman emperor (Latin, *imperator*, "commander"). He was succeeded by his stepson Tiberius. The month of August is named for him.
See also: Antony, Marc; Caesar, Julius; Cleopatra.

Auk, marine diving bird of the family Alcidae, including razorbills, puffins, and guillemots. Of the 22 species (including the extinct great auk) the smallest is the dovekie, or little auk (*Plautus alle*), which is about the size of a robin (lengths of other species are 6-30 in/15-76 cm). Auks, who seldom leave the water except to nest, usually breed in colonies, sometimes millions of individuals, and nest on high ledges or in burrows.
See also: Guillemot; Murre; Puffin.

Aurelius, Marcus *see:* Marcus Aurelius.

Aurora, display of colored lights and shimmering forms seen at night, most frequently during the equinoxes, in regions of high latitude. The aurora borealis, or northern lights, can be seen in northern Scandinavia, Canada, and Alaska, and the aurora australis, or southern lights, are seen on the borders of Antarctica in the Southern Hemisphere. Fast-moving electrons from the sun are attracted to the earth's magnetic poles, where they collide with oxygen and nitrogen ions in the ionosphere, causing them to give off energy in the form of light. The aurora most frequently appears following a major solar flare; the occurrence and intensity of the aurora is also related to the 11-year sunspot cycle.

Auschwitz, present-day Oswiecim in Poland, site of the infamous Nazi concentration camp in World War II where some 4 million inmates, mostly Jews, were murdered. The camp was opened in 1940 and run by Rudolf Hoess for 3 years. Its huge gas chambers were responsible for most deaths.

Austen, Jane (1775-1817), English novelist. Daughter of a clergyman, her novels, including *Sense and Sensibility* (1811), *Pride and Prejudice* (1813), and *Emma* (1816), vividly portray the provinciality of the English middle class of her time with ironic insight and vivid characterizations. She ultimately gave up writing, discouraged by her inability to find a publisher. Her novels were published many years after she wrote them; 2 were published posthumously. Today she is considered one of the greatest novelists in the English language, and her work is an inspiration and model for many writers.

Austerlitz (pop. 5,000), town in Moravia in southern Czechoslovakia. Currently an agricultural center, on Dec. 2, 1805 it was the site where Napoleon's army defeated the combined forces of Emperor Francis I of Austria and Tsar Alexander I of Russia in the "Battle of the Three Emperors," the beginning of Napoleon's mastery in Europe.
See also: Napoleon I.

Austin (pop. 781,572), capital of Texas and seat of Travis County on the Colorado River in south-central Texas. Founded in 1839 as Waterloo, it served as the capital of the Republic of Texas 1840-42 and was renamed in honor of Stephen F. Austin. It became state capital in 1870. Austin has seen great industrial development since the 1930s, currently is the site of extensive scientific and electronic research, and is also the center of an important agricultural, ranching, dairy, and poultry region.
See also: Texas.

Austin, Stephen Fuller (1793-1836), U.S. pioneer statesman, "Father of Texas." Upon bringing 300 families to Texas (1821), he was made the settlement's administrator. Between 1822 and 1830 he presented Texan demands for autonomy to the Mexican government, and was imprisoned for it. On his release in 1835, he joined the Texan rebellion against Mexico, and in 1836 was appointed secretary of state of the Republic of Texas.

Australia, world's largest island and smallest continent, with a total area of 2,967,877 sq mi (7,686,810 sq km). It is the only continent occupied by a single nation, the Commonwealth of Australia, a federal union comprising 6 states (the island of Tasmania, Queensland, New South Wales, Victoria, South Australia, Western Australia), the Northern Territory, and the Australian Capital Territory (Canberra). Australia has a low population density, with about 16 million people living in a country almost as large as the United States.
Geologists believe that 120 million years ago Australia was part of a vast land mass that included India, Arabia, and parts of Africa and South America. Later land bridges to Australia were destroyed by geological upheavals, leaving the continent completely isolated. This isolation accounts for the development of various species of animal life peculiar to Australia. For example, the pouched mammals (marsupials) are found mainly in Australia and neighboring islands. Australia is the world's flattest continent. Approximately 75% of its area is covered by a plateau rarely higher than 1,500 ft (4,600 m) The outstanding physical feature of the conti-

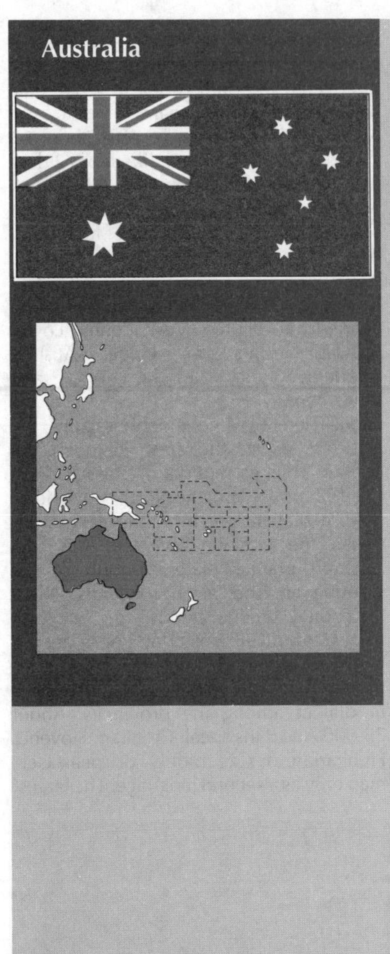

General information	
Capital:	Canberra
Area:	2,966,151 sq mi (7,682,000 sq km)
Population:	16,804,000
Official language:	English
Monetary unit:	1 Australian dollar ($A) = 100 cents
Main cities:	Sydney, Melbourne, Brisbane, Perth
Government	
Form:	constitutional monarchy
Independent:	1901
Head of state:	British monarch
Head of government:	Prime Minister
Legislature:	two legislative houses (Senate; House of Representatives)
Executive:	British monarch (represented by governor-general and the ministry)
Judiciary:	High Court of Australia
Political division:	6 states, 2 territories
National economy	
Gross national product:	U.S. $204,446,000,000
Per capita income:	U.S. $12,390
Agriculture:	sugar cane, wheat, barley, cotton, grapes
Livestock:	sheep, cattle
Fisheries:	157,100 metric tons
Mining:	gold, uranium, diamonds, bauxite, iron ore, copper
Industries:	iron and steel, nitric acid, cotton cloth, food production, machinery, motor vehicles
Main exports:	food and livestock, mineral fuels, ores, machinery
Transportation:	25,356 mi (40,807 km) of railroads; 530,009 mi (852,986 km) of roads ; 9 international airports
Trading partners:	Japan, United States, United Kingdom, Germany, New Zealand
People	
Urban:	86%
Ethnic composition:	European 95%, Asian 2%, aboriginal 1%
Birth rate:	14.9 per 1,000 population
Death rate:	7.2 per 1,000 population
Infant mortality:	8.7 per 1,000 live births
Life expectancy:	male 73 years, female 79.5 years

Captain James Cook charted the coast of Australia, called it New South Wales, and claimed it in the name of England.

nent is the Great Western Plateau, most of which is desert or semi-arid scrub country. The Great Barrier Reef, a mass of coral reefs and islands, extends for 1,250 mi (2,012 km) along its east coast.

Visited by the Dutch in the early 1600s, Australia was claimed for Britain by Capt. James Cook (1770). New South Wales, the first area settled, began as a penal colony (1788). But free settlement began in 1816, and no convicts were sent to Australia after 1840. The gold rushes (1851, 1892) brought more people to Australia, and in 1901 the 6 self-governing colonies formed an independent commonwealth.

The people of Australia are mainly of British origin, but there are some 200,000 aborigines and part-aborigines, and many immigrants from Italy, Yugoslavia, Greece, Germany, the Netherlands, and the United States. Most of the population is concentrated in the coastal cities, of which the largest is Sydney.

Australian Aborigines, earliest native inhabitants of Australia, racially distinguished by dark hair, dark skin, medium stature, broad noses, and narrow heads. Before European encroachment in the 18th and 19th centuries, they lived by well-organized nomadic food-gathering and hunting. Aborigines were enfranchised in 1962.

The kangaroo and the koala are natural symbols of Australia.

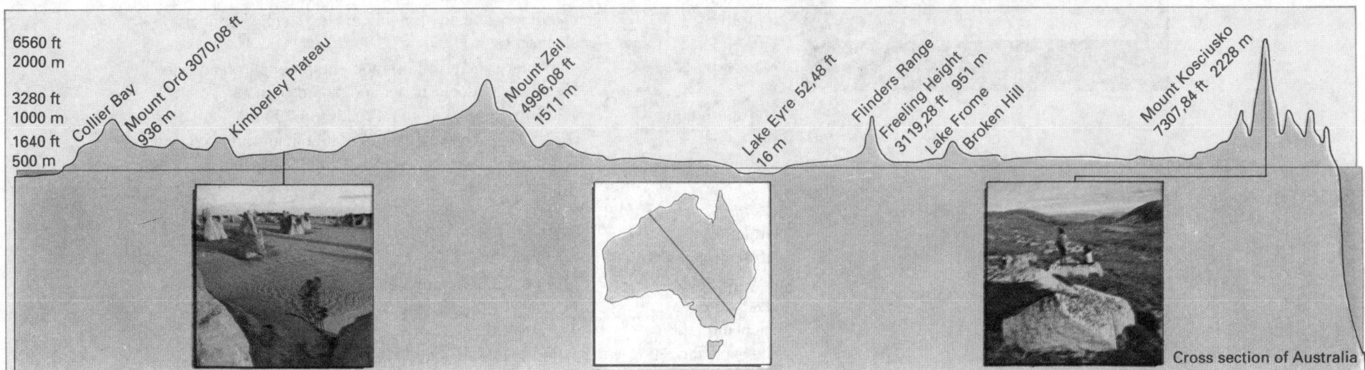

Cross section of Australia

Sydney, Australia was founded by the British captain Arthur Phillip in 1788. It was the first British penal colony in Australia.

The Australian government has attempted to integrate them into the European population, but they still face discrimination.

Australian Desert, comprises 3 deserts that cover about one-third of Australia's western and central area. They are the Great Sandy Desert, about 160,000 sq mi (414,000 sq km); the Gibson Desert, 120,000 sq mi (311,000 sq km); and the Great Victoria Desert, 130,000 sq mi (337,000 sq km).

Sydney's Opera House

Austral Islands, group of islands of volcanic origin in the South Pacific, south of Tahiti. They have a combined area of about 70 sq mi (180 sq km). The largest of the island are Rurutu and Tubuai.

Australopithecus, or "southern ape," a genus of hominids whose fossilized bones, discovered in South Africa in 1924, date back about 3 million years. Australopithecines stood erect at about 4-5 ft (120-150 cm) and walked on 2 legs without the help of their arms. Their teeth were more human than apelike, their brains about one-third those of humans in size.

Austria, federal republic in central Europe divided into 9 provinces: Vienna, Lower Austria, Burgenland, Upper Austria, Salzburg, Styria, Carinthia, Tyrol, and Vorarlberg.

Land. There are 4 geographic regions: the Austrian Alps to the West, including the country's highest mountain, Grossglockner (12,457 ft/3,797 m); the North Alpine foreland, a plateau cut by fertile valleys between the Danube and the Alps; the Austrian granite plateau, north of the Danube; and the Eastern lowlands, where the capital, Vienna, stands.

People. About 98% of today's Austrians are Germans ethnically and linguistically, although there are considerable differences in dialect among the provinces. About 75,000 Austrians speak Croatian, Slovene, Hungarian, or Czech only, or speak German only as a second language. The largest

Austria

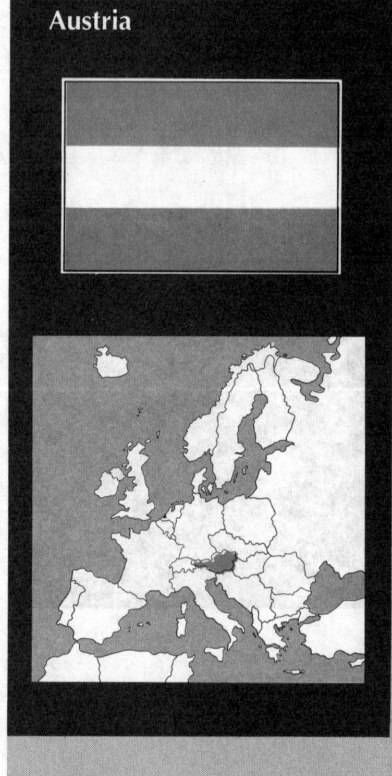

General information	
Capital:	Vienna
Area:	32,377 sq mi (83,855 sq km)
Population:	7,603,000
Official language:	German
Monetary unit:	1 Schilling (S) = 100 Groschen
Main cities:	Vienna, Graz, Linz, Salzburg
Government	
Form:	federal republic
Independent:	republic since 1918
Head of state:	President (elected every 6 years)
Head of government:	Chancellor (chosen by the President)
Legislature:	two legislative houses (Federal Council; National Council)
Executive:	Council of Ministers
Judiciary:	Supreme Court
Political division:	9 provinces
National economy	
Gross national product:	U.S. $117,644,000,000
Per capita income:	U.S. $15,560
Agriculture:	sugar beets, wheat and other cereals, potatoes, fruit
Livestock:	pigs, cattle
Mining:	iron, ore, petroleum, lignite, lead, zinc
Industries:	machinery and equipment, textiles, steel, chemicals, electronics
Main exports:	machinery and transportation equipment, iron and steel, chemical products, paper and paperboard
Transportation:	4,125 mi (6,638 km) of railroads; 66,799 mi (107,503 km) of roads; 6 international airports
Trading partners:	Germany, Italy, Switzerland, United States.
People	
Urban:	55%
Ethnic composition:	Austrians 96%, Yugoslavs 2%
Birth rate:	11.4 per 1,000 population
Death rate:	11.2 per 1,000 population
Infant mortality:	9.8 per 1,000 live births
Life expectancy:	male 71.5 years, female 78.1 years

minority group are the Croatians, who mainly live in Burgenland. Austria's cultural contributions have been noteworthy. In the 19th century Vienna was a world center for musicians and composers. Wolfgang Amadeus Mozart, Franz Joseph Haydn, Franz Schubert, Anton Bruckner, and Gustav Mahler were all Austrians, while Ludwig van Beethoven, Johann Strauss, and Franz Lehar spent most of their lives in Vienna. Sigmund Freud, the father of psychoanalysis, studied and practiced in Vienna, along with many other psychologists.

Economy. Austrian farm crops include sugar beets, potatoes, grains, grapes, fruits, tobacco, flax, and hemp; wines and beers are produced in quantity. Almost 40% of the country is forested, so wood and paper are important products. Iron ore is the primary mineral resource, but there are also deposits of lead, magnesium, copper, salt, zinc, aluminum, silver, and gypsum. Vienna, Graz, and Linz are the chief industrial centers. Tourism has helped to stimulate economic growth in recent years.

History. Inhabited from prehistoric times, settled by the Celts, and subsequently part of the Roman Empire, starting in the third century A.D. Austria was devastated by invading Vandals, Goths, Alemanni, Huns, and Avars. In 788 Charlemagne conquered Austria. The Babenberg family inherited it in 976 and retained it as duchy until 1246. In 1247 the Habsburgs acquired Austria, which became a central part of their empire until 1918. By the Treaty of Versailles, independent states (Czechoslovakia, Hungary, and Yugoslavia) were created from the old empire, while Austria itself became a republic. In 1938 Austria was annexed by Hitler's Third Reich, regaining independence following the Allied victory in 1945.

Austrian landscape

Austria-Hungary, empire formed by the union of the Kingdom of Hungary and the Austrian Empire in 1867. It was the assassination of the Archduke Francis Ferdinand, heir to the empire's throne, in 1914, by one of the many nationalist groups seeking independence that led directly to World War I. The empire, which was allied with Germany, ceased to exist at the end of World War I, and its lands were divided among the East European nations.

Authoritarianism, political philosophy based on the principle of total submission of the population to a leader or elite group that is not constitutionally responsible to the people.

Autism, impairment in the perception of and response to environmental stimuli, accompanied by absorption in self-centered mental activity. In infantile autism, the development of speech is delayed; ritualistic behavior is usual and may include abnormal routines; resistance to change, attachment to odd objects, and stereotyped patterns of play are the norm. The capacity for abstract or symbolic thought and for imaginative play is diminished. Treatment is experimental, and performance has been found to be better on tasks involving rote memory than on those requiring symbolic or linguistic skills.

Autocracy, form of government in which an individual or group has absolute power, as in Russia under the tsars and France under Louis XIV.

Autogiro or **autogyro**, rotary-wing aircraft that uses a conventional propeller to provide forward motion and an unpowered horizontal rotor for lift. Though it cannot hover or land vertically, current technology permits almost vertical takeoffs.

Automatic frequency control (AFC), circuit used in electronic devices such as radio, television, and radar to help maintain and control the frequency. The AFC circuit corrects frequency drifts (e.g., from a particular radio station) by producing a voltage that automatically reverses the drift and holds it on frequency.

Automatic pilot *see:* Giropilot.

Automation, automatically controlled operation of an apparatus, process, or system by mechanical or electronic devices (often computers) that replace constant human observation, effort, and decision.

Automobile, small, 4-wheeled vehicle that carries passengers. The 4 major components of an automobile are its power plant, drive system, control system, and body.

Power plant. Almost all automobiles are powered by internal combustion engines, usually with 4-8 cylinders attached to a crankshaft. In the internal combustion engine, gasoline from the fuel tank is mixed with air in the carburetor and fed to the cylinders. The highly explosive mixture is ignited by the spark plugs and, as it explodes, expands rapidly.

The piston within the cylinder is forced downward, turning the crankshaft. The heavy metal flywheel attached to one end of the crankshaft moves the piston back up the cylinder to its original position. The order in which the spark plugs fire is con-

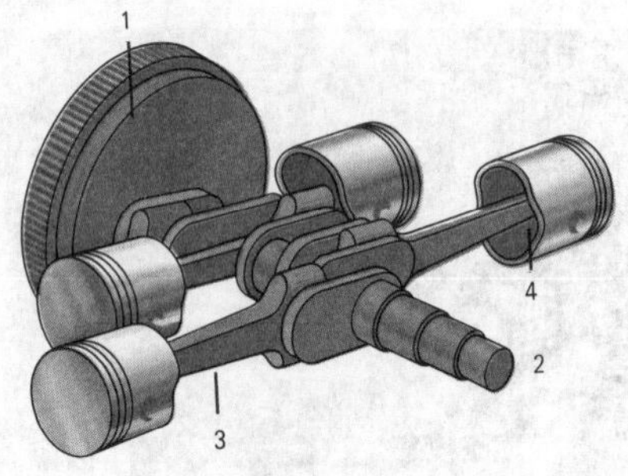

The flat four engine:
1. flywheel,
2. crankshaft,
3. connecting rod, and
4. piston.

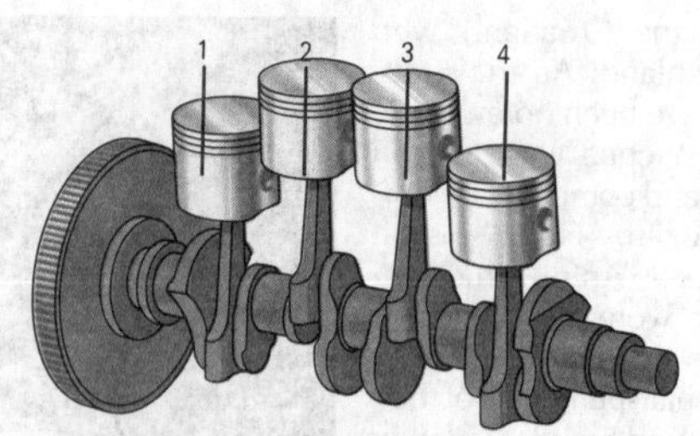

Four cylinder engine

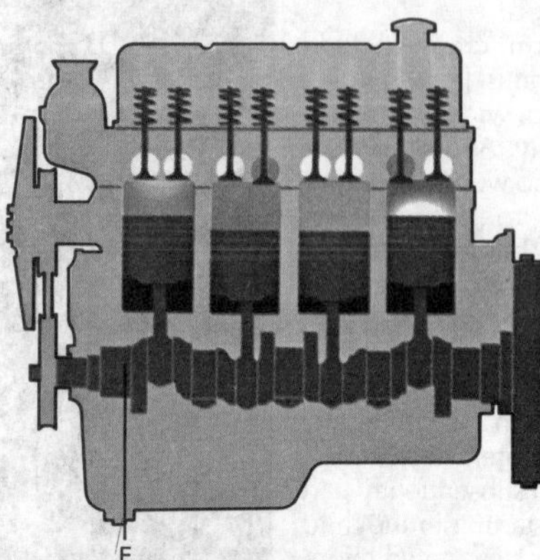

Four stroke engine: (A) both valves closed, piston is being driven down to drive crankshaft, (B) exhaust valve open, piston open to expel gases, (C) both valves closed, piston is about to compress gases, (D) intake valve open, air and fuel enter chamber as piston moves down, and (E) crankshaft.

Anatomy of a car.
1. fuel tank
2. exhaust
3. differential
4. drive shaft
5. shock absorbers
6. radiator
7. battery
8. carburetor

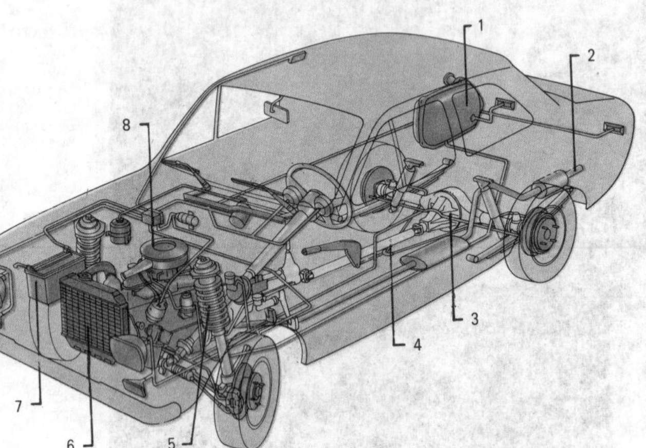

Renault 1908

Duesenberg 1929

Monocoque (one-piece frame) construction permits construction of a lighter and stronger vehicle. This method does away with the construction of the car on a separate chassis.

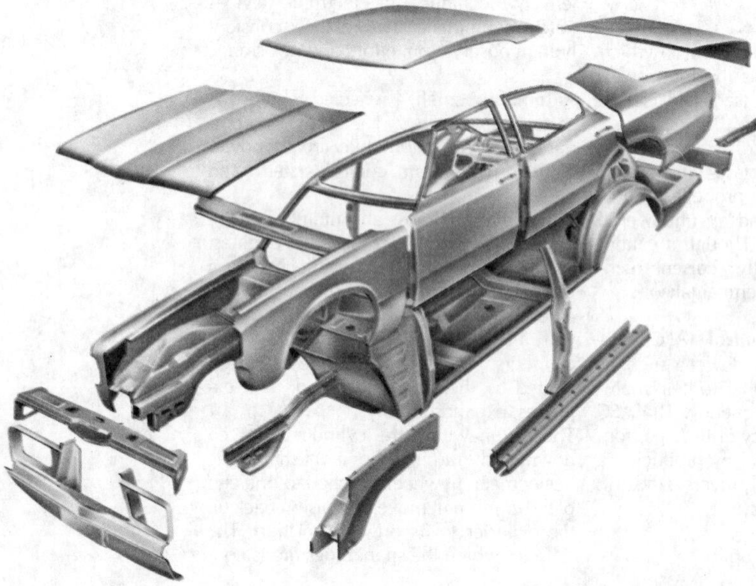

Corvette 1964

trolled by the distributor. In most engines, the gasoline vapor simply enters the cylinder through a valve at the beginning of the downstroke, but some automobiles have fuel-injection systems that greatly increase efficiency.

Drive system. In most cars, the drive is supplied by the rear wheels. The motion of the crankshaft must therefore be transmitted by a driveshaft to the rear axle, where a system of cogs turns the wheels. The rotation of the crankshaft is transmitted to the driveshaft by the clutch, which consists of 2 circular plates, one attached to the driveshaft, the other to the crankshaft. When the plates are in contact, both rotate. When one plate is drawn back, the crankshaft rotates without affecting the driveshaft, and the engine can "turn over" without moving the car. Gears alter the number of turns required from the engine to achieve a single turn of the drive wheels. The gear box also makes reverse movement possible. When cars are equipped with automatic transmission, manual control of the gears or clutch is not required.

The controls. Steering is controlled by a steering wheel, attached to horizontal track rods between the two front wheels. The movement of these rods turns the wheels. In heavy cars, power steering uses hydraulic pressure to assist the driver in turning the wheel. The pedal-operated brake system uses either the pressure of brake shoes against brake drums attached to the wheels or the more efficient disk brakes. The handbrake, which clamps onto the driveshaft or one set of wheels, is used as an emergency brake or for parking. The gas pedal is connected to the carburetor and controls the amount of gasoline vapor that enters the cylinders of the engine. The greater the quantity of vapor, the more powerful the explosion and the greater the speed of the automobile.

Body. The chassis of the car is the large steel frame that supports the engine and the control and running mechanisms. It may be a solid piece of stamped metal or a series of metal parts welded together. In cars that do not have a chassis, the body may simply be the framework that links the mechanical parts. The weight of the car is supported at the front and rear axles by metal springs, or sometimes by a hydraulic mechanism, to absorb shocks transmitted from the road and ensure a smooth ride.

Automobile Association, American (AAA), U.S.-based travel organization. Consisting of more than 800 travel agencies and 65 clubs, it has a membership of 25 million motorists throughout the United States and Canada. Among its various services are emergency road assistance, insurance, trip planning, and public education on automobile and traffic safety. The AAA was founded in 1902 and has its headquarters in Falls Church, VA.

Automobile racing, sport in which specially designed or adapted motor vehicles race indoor or outdoor courses. Dating from 1894 in France, races include the Grand Prix (worldwide series culminating in world-champion driver), stock car (special equipment on standard vehicles), midget car, sports car, and drag (acceleration competition). Major U.S. races include the Indianapolis 500 and the Daytona 500 (a stock-car race).

A monocoque construction. The car is equipped with a five-speed gear box and turbo charger. The direct surrounding of the driver are protected with rollbars and crunch zones.

Automobile Workers, United *see:* United Automobile Workers.

Autonomic nervous system, certain sections of the brain, spinal cord, and nerve pathways that govern the activity of a number of organs, making them function largely independently of conscious control. The autonomic nervous system regulates the organs of the chest (heart and lungs), the abdomen (stomach, intestine, liver, etc.), the pelvis, and many other organs and tissues of the body, including the blood vessels and skin. By contrast, the somatic nervous system comprises those parts of the brain, spinal cord, and nerve pathways that respond to the external environment, and are under voluntary control. The autonomic nervous system governs the processes that serve to maintain the individual and the species: metabolism, growth, reproduction, respiration, nutrition and digestion, the functioning of the heart and blood vessels, the excretion of waste products, temperature control, etc. An intricate system of nuclei and nerve pathways in the brain regulates the workings of the various organs. In the hypothalamus lie dozens of nuclei and pathways that exert a controlling influence over such basic life functions as eating and drinking behavior, temperature regulation, and the percentage of sugars, fats, and water in the blood. The autonomic nervous system is also involved in emotional response. Emotions can give rise to quickening of the heartbeat, changes in breathing patterns, increased secretion of gastric acid in the stomach, and alterations in the secretory pattern of the gallbladder. Malfunction of the autonomic nervous system can easily lead to serious disturbances in the functioning of an organ. Often a stomach ache is caused by the malfunction of one of the subsystems of the autonomic nervous system. The autonomic nervous system can be divided into the sympathetic and the parasympathetic systems, which in general produce opposite effects on various organs.
See also: Nervous system.

This avante-garde work by Marcel Duchamp, Bicycle on Kitchen Stool *(1913), is a reaction against the solemnity of the art establishment of his time.*

Autopsy, examination of the external structures and internal organs of a dead body for the purpose of determining the cause of death or for studying the damage done by disease; also called necropsy or postmortem examination. The law requires that every cause of death be verified by a physician or by a coroner's jury. If the cause of death is known, the death certificate is signed and no autopsy is needed, but if authorities are uncertain of the conditions leading to death, such as in a suicide or homicide, an autopsy may be indicated.

Auxin, any of several organic compounds that act as plant hormones to promote cell growth.

Avant-garde, term referring to those who experiment with new and original art forms. Used originally to describe a military unit that led the rest of the troops, *avant-garde* was first given its modern meaning by the French socialist Henri de Saint-Simon in 1825. During the 19th century, the avant-garde notion of art as a tool of social reform gave way to the idea of "art for art's sake," leading to the Dadaist and Surrealist movements of the early 20th century. Important avant-garde artists include U.S. composer John Cage (1912-) and French painter Marcel Duchamp (1887-1968).

Average, number that is typical of a group of numbers or quantities. The 3 kinds of averages—mean, median, and mode—have different statistical significance. The mean is derived by taking the sum of a group of quantities and dividing it by the number of quantities. The median divides a sampling in half; there are the same number of items above and below it. The mode is the most frequently occurring number in a group.

Averroës (Ibn-Rushd; 1126-98), Spanish-Arabian philosopher, commentator on Aristotle and Plato who exerted a great influence on the development of Latin scholastic philosophy. For him, the source of philosophic truth was reason, not faith, though he believed there was no conflict between the two.

Aviation, term referring to all aspects of building and flying aircraft. Aviation has not only changed the face of long-distance travel, but affected medical accessibility, farming practices, and the way nations wage war. The aviation industry, which includes the manufacture of aircraft and the operations of airlines, involves the work of millions of engineers, mechanics, pilots and air traffic controllers, as well as many governmental agencies. The world's first successful airplane flight was made by Wilbur and Orville Wright in 1903. Within a few years Europe and the United States had several small airplane-producing factories. Interested in developing their own air forces, various governments around the world began to purchase airplanes for military purposes. The first solo, nonstop flight across the Atlantic Ocean was accomplished by Charles Lindbergh on May 21, 1927. Amelia Earhart was the first person to fly solo from Hawaii to California in 1935. The use of commercial airplanes in the late 1930s assured the growth of aviation as an industry. The jet airliner, developed in the 1950s, gave the industry a further boost. Because of the rapid growth of civil aviation, more effective government regulation was needed. In 1958, various governmental agencies combined to form the Federal Aviation Agency (FAA), which was responsible for establishing and enforcing air traffic procedures and controls.

Avicenna (Ibn-Sina; 980-1037), Persian physician and philosopher. Of his prolific writings on theology, logic, metaphysics, and mathematics, his greatest is considered to be *The Canon of Medicine*, which remained a standard medical text in Europe until the Renaissance.

Avignon (pop. 91,500), French city on the east bank of the Rhône River in southern France, capital of Vaucluse department. During the "Babylonian Exile" (1309-78) Avignon was the papal seat. From 1378 to 1417, the city was the home of the "antipopes," rivals to the popes in Rome.

Ávila Camacho, Manuel (1897-1955), Mexican soldier and statesman. As Mexico's president (1940- 46), he supported the U.S. and promoted Latin American opposition to the Axis powers.
See also: Mexico.

Avocado (*Persea americana*), tropical evergreen tree native to the United States, Mexico, and the West Indies. The fruit, also called avocado or alligator pear, has a dark green or purple rind, bright green flesh rich in protein, vitamins, iron, and oil, and a large central seed. Avocados are also grown as house plants.

Avocet, any of several long-legged wading birds (genus *Recurvirostra*). One species flourishes in Europe, Asia, and Africa. It uses its long curving beak to sweep the water in search of the small aquatic animals on which it feeds. It has black-and-white plumage. The related American avocet has a pinkish head and breast.

Avoirdupois, English system of weight in which 1 lb contains 16 oz, in contrast to troy weight, another English system, in which 1 lb equals 12 oz. In the United States, commodities are generally weighed in avoirdupois. Most other countries use

the metric system, to which Britain is gradually converting.
See also: Weights and Measures.

Avon, name of 2 British rivers. The longer, the Upper Avon, arises in Northamptonshire and flows 96 mi (154 km) past Warwick and Stratford-upon-Avon to join the Severn at Tewkesbury. Stratford-upon-Avon was the birthplace of William Shakespeare.

AWOL (Absent Without Leave) *see:* Desertion.

Axiom, any general statement accepted as true without proof as the basis for building a logical system of other statements that are proven. These proven statements are called theorems. The axioms of a system need not be self-evident, but they must be consistent with one another.
See also: Geometry.

Axis Powers, countries allied with Nazi Germany before or during World War II. The Rome-Berlin Axis, a diplomatic agreement between Hitler and Mussolini, was formed in 1936 and reinforced by the Italian-German military pact of 1939. Japan joined the pact in 1940, and other countries followed: Hungary, Bulgaria, Romania, Slovakia, and Croatia. The Axis Powers were defeated by the Allies (or Allied Powers), led by the United States, Britain, and the Soviet Union.
See also: World War II.

Azalea, number of species of a shrub (genus *Rhododendron*), cultivated principally for ornamental purposes. Best known in the United States are the pinxter (*R. nudiflorum*), the flame azalea (*R. calendulacea*), and the rhodera (*R. canadense*).
See also: Heath.

Azazel, evil spirit thought by the early Hebrews to inhabit the wilderness. On the Day of Atonement, a goat would be sent out to the Azazel bearing the discarded sins of the people; hence the word *scapegoat.*

Azerbaijan, or Azerbaidjan, independent country on the westcoast of the Caspian Sea, bordered by Russia, Armenia and Iran. The republic consists mainly of lowlands surrounded by the Kura River and its tributary, the Araks, which forms the border with Iran. Near the Caspian coast is a fertile plain with an abundant water supply. Tea, citrus fruits, tobacco, and rice are produced there. Further inland the climate is arid, but extensive irrigation makes cultivation possible. Cotton and sheep are the basis of a large textile industry. The region is rich in minerals, notably oil and natural gas from the long-established Baku oilfields; it is one of the oldest oil-producing areas in the world. The Caucasian hills provide iron ore. The capital and chief port is Baku, and Kirovabad and Sumgait are important cities. The majority of the inhabitants is Azeri. The most important minority group is formed by the Armenians. The predominant religion among the Azeri is the Islam. Settled by Medes as part of the Persian Empire, it was periodically dominated by Romans, Arabs, Mongols, and Turks, returning to Persia in the 16th century. The Russian Tsar Alexander I annexed northern Azerbaijan in 1813. An independent republic was formed in 1918, but was conquered by the Soviets in 1920. In 1991 Azerbaijan regained its independence.
See also: Union of Soviet Socialist Republics.

Azerbaijan

Capital:	Bakoe
Area:	33,400 sq mi (86,600 sq km)
Population:	7,145,000
Government:	republic
Independent:	1991
GNP:	U.S.$6,290,000,000
Per capita:	U.S.$870

Azimuth, in navigation and astronomy, the angular distance, measured from 0 to 360°, along the horizon eastward from an observer's north point to the point of intersection of the horizon and a great circle passing through the observer's zenith and a star or planet.

Azimuth circle *see:* Navigation.

Azores (pop.252,200), 9 mountainous islands in the North Atlantic about 900 mi (1,448 km) west of Portugal. São Miguel is the largest and most populated. Colonized and under Portuguese rule since the mid-15th century, the islands enjoy considerable autonomy.

Azov, Sea of, arm of the Black Sea in southwest RF, joined to that sea by the Strait of Kerch. Maximum depth is only 50 ft (15 m); length is 200 mi (322 km), maximum width 80 mi (129 km). The Don River flows into the eastern end of the sea, known as the Gulf of Taganrog.

Aztec Ruins National Monument, site in northwestern New Mexico on the Animas River containing the excavated ruins of a 12th-century Pueblo Indian town. Mistaken for Aztec by European American settlers, the ruins include a 500-room building and many Pueblo artifacts. The monument was established in 1923.

Aztecs, pre-Columbian natives of Central Mexico, traditionally thought to have migrated from Aztlán in the north to the Valley of Mexico. A warrior tribe, they took over the cities of the Toltecs, from whom they also derived part of their culture. The Aztec empire consisted of a confederation of 3 city states, Tenochtitlán (the capital, site of present-day Mexico City), Tlacopan, and Texcoco. The empire expanded under the rule of Montezuma I, and eventually extended to present day Guatemala. Montezuma I would die defending Tenochtitlán. Religious belief contributed greatly to Aztec political and social structure. The 2 chief gods were Huitzilopochtli, god of war and the sun, and Quetzalcoatl, god of learning. Human victims were sacrificed to these and other gods. The Aztecs were superb artisans, working in gold, silver, and copper and creating fine pottery and mosaics. They are famed for their lavishly decorated temples, such as those at Tenochtitlán, Tula, Cuicuilco, Xochicalco, and Cholula. The arrival of the conquistador Hernán Cortés (1519) heralded the destruction and collapse of the Aztec empire.
See also: Mexico.

The Aztek god of revival, flowers, poetry, music, dance, and sunrise.

Azurite, blue-colored crystalline mineral once used to make artist's pigment but now mainly used in jewelry. The crystals consist of copper carbonate and water and commonly occur near the surfaces of copper mines. Large deposits of azurite are found at Chessy, near Lyons in France, in South-west Africa, and in smaller deposits in the western United States (Arizona, Utah).

Orville and Wilbur Wright were responsible for the first controlled airplane flight on December 17,1903. Their observations of a bird's flight were invaluable in understanding balance in flying objects.

Considered the best single-engined bomber of World War I, Britain's De Havilland DH-4 was of wooden construction and covered with fabric. Its armaments included forward and rear guns with bombs under each wing. After the war, more than 60 different varieties were produced and used for civil aviation.

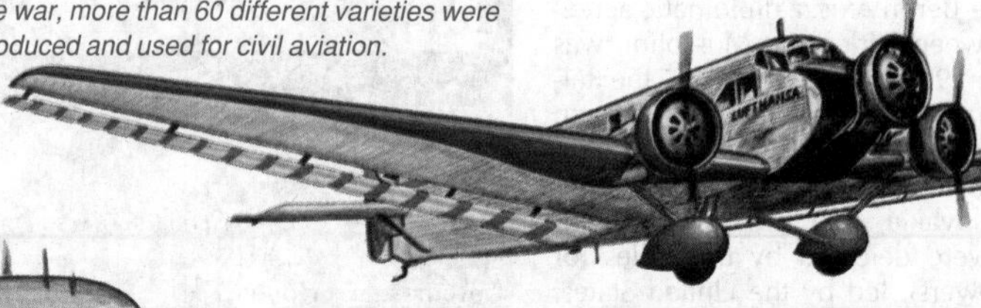

The Junkers Ju 52/3m was one of the most reliable transport aircraft ever built. Its structure was made entirely of the light alloy duralumin. Its double wing flaps were patented and its landing gears were virtually indestructible. It also had the ability to land in water and snow. More than 90% of German Luftwaffe transports were of this variety. During the 1930s, it was the leading civil airliner in Europe.

The Douglas DC-2 was first flown on May 11, 1934. It is one of the first modern airliners with cantilever wings, flaps, and retractable landing gear. The DC-2 was purchased by the American government for use in World War II.

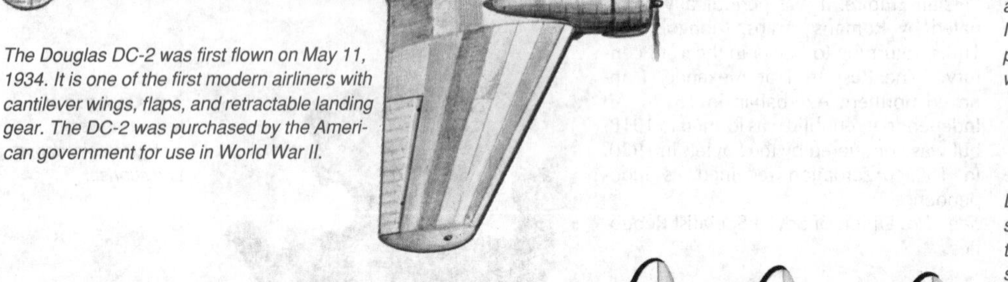

Left: The Lockheed Constellation was designed to satisfy the need for a transcontinental aircraft which would offer the ultimate in speed and luxury. Production on a civil aviation model began in 1940 but was interrupted by World War II. Flown during the war as C-69, the Constellation made its first civil, trans-Atlantic flight for TWA on Dec. 3-4, 1945. The aircraft evolved into the L-1049 Super Constellation, with increased fuel capacity and more powerful engines.

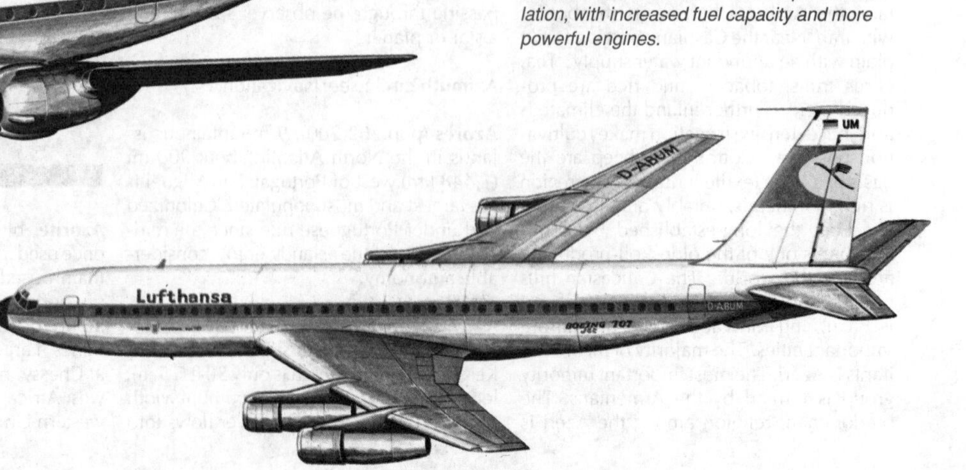

Right: In 1952 the Boeing Corporation spent $20 million to build a turbojet transport. On July 15, 1954, the now-famous Boeing 707 made its first flight. The U.S. Air Force ordered large quantities of the 707 because of its great flexibility. Both Pan American Airways and American Airlines bought the 707 for long-distance routes.

The light-as-a-feather design of this U.S. aircraft, the Voyager, made possible its 1986 flight around the world. It remained aloft 111 hours without stopping or refueling, covering 11,600 mi (18,560 km). Its shell is less than one-half inch thick with panels of Hexcel honeycomb, a paperlike polymer, covered with graphite fibers. The panels weigh 4 oz. per square foot (1 kg/sq m) but possess incredible tensile strength— a 110 -ft (33- m) wing can flex up and down more than 30 ft (90 m). The benefit of such remarkable advances in aviation materials means diminished costs, reduced friction, greater speed, and less noise and pollution.

In 1956 Britain and France began research on a supersonic transport. In 1962 a joint agreement was signed for design, development, and production. In November 1970 the British-French Concorde achieved a speed of Mach 2 (twice the speed of sound). On May 24,1976 the Concorde's trans-Atlantic service began, with a flying time of 3 1/2 hours from New York to Paris.

The Airbus A340 is scheduled to fly in 1991. It is part of a combined program with the A330 aircraft. This multi-national venture (France, Germany, Spain, Great Britain) will service long-range flights that carry as many as 440 people.

The F-117A "Stealth" fighter was a 10-year-old Pentagon secret. In April 1990 the Defense Department released, for the first time, a video of this reconnaissance-fighter aircraft. The "Stealth" project has become a controversy because of its staggering costs. The U.S. Congress has already spent $6.5 billion to acquire 59 fighters. But the Congress seems unwilling to spend another $40 billion to buy an additional 132 planes.

B

B, second letter of the English alphabet, can be traced back to ancient Semitic roots. The letter is believed to derive from the Maobite Stone hieroglyph, found in the present state of Jordan, dating from the 9th century B.C. The Hebrew letter *beth*, meaning "house," and the Greek *beta* both come from this form. The Latin is virtually the same as the Greek, and it is this latter which is still used today. The lowercase *b*, a variant in which the upper loop has disappeared through the speed of writing, appeared in the Roman period.

Baal (Semitic, "lord" or "owner"), ancient Middle East fertility god. Canaanite tablets dating from 2500 B.C. represent him combating Mot, god of drought and sterility. In Babylonia, Baal was known as Bel, and in Phoenicia as Melkart. In the Old Testament the name is used pejoratively, the cult of Baal having been denounced by the Hebrew prophets.

Ba'al Shem Tov (Israel ben Eliezer; 1700?-60), Jewish teacher and founder of the religious movement Hasidism. Ba'al Shem Tov (Hebrew: "Master of the Good Name") was considered by his followers a miracle healer. He advocated the joyous worship of God in all activities, opposing fasting and other forms of self-denial. Hasidism is now practiced by some Jews in Europe, Israel, and the United States.
See also: Hasidism.

Babar (1483-1530), also spelled Babur or Baber, Turkish prince who founded the Mogul empire in India. A descendant of Genghis Khan and Tamerlane, Babar ruled 1526-30. He defeated the forces of the Afghan sultan near Delhi and went on to conquer most of northern India.
See also: Akbar.

Charles Babbage

Babbage, Charles (1792-1871), British mathematician and inventor who devoted much labor and expense to an unsuccessful attempt to devise a mechanical calculator, his so-called "analytical engine." With J. Herschel and G. Peacock, he introduced the Leibnizian "d" notation for calculus into British mathematical use in place of the less flexible "dot" notation devised by Sir Isaac Newton.

Babbitt, Irving (1865-1933), U.S. scholar and noted opponent of Romanticism. He led the New Humanism movement in literary criticism, which stressed classical reason and restraint. His works include *The New Laokoön* (1910) and *On Being Creative* (1932).

Babbler, any of a large and varied group of birds of the Muscicapidae family found mainly in Africa, southern Asia, and Australia. Named for their loud, repeated calls, babblers are sometimes called babbling thrushes or chatterers.

Babel, Isaak Emanuilovich (1894-1941?), Russian short-story writer best known for his collections *Odessa Tales* (1923-24) and *Red Cavalry* (1926), the former describing Jewish life in the Ukraine, the latter his service with the Red Army during the Russian civil war (1918-20). Arrested 1939, he died in a Siberian prison camp.

Babel, Tower of, in the Old Testament, a tower erected to reach heaven. God punished the builders for their presumption by making them speak many mutually unintelligible languages.
See also: Old Testament.

Babirussa (*Babirussa babirussa*), wild hog of Indonesia, about 27 in (69 cm) tall and weighing about 128 lb (58 kg). The males are notable for their long tusks. A docile, night-hunting member of the pig family, it forages for fruits and vegetables in the soil near rivers and swamps.

Babi Yar, ravine near Kiev, in the Ukraine. On Sept. 29 and 30, 1941, German SS troops executed and buried more than 33,000 Soviet Jews who had been brought to the ravine on a promise of resettlement. In "Babi Yar" (1962) the Russian poet Yevgeni Yevtushenko indicted the Soviet leadership for failing to commemorate the massacre or to honor its victims.
See also: Holocaust.

Baboon, large primate monkey of the African savannas (genus *Papio*), distinguished by long muzzle and great strength. Baboons move in groups of 20 to 150 individuals. They are highly aggressive omnivores with a complex social structure. Their bodies are covered with unusually long hair, except for parts of the face and the buttocks, which may be brightly colored.
See also: Mandrill; Monkey.

The strong colors of the genital area of the baboons probably help them to impose respect upon their rivals.

Baby, infant, newborn, neonate. Babies are classified as premature, full-term, or postmature, depending on their gestational age (i.e. whether they are born early, on time, or late). Premature babies often have medical problems.

Baby boom, steep increase in the U.S. birthrate following World War II. During 1946-64, 76 million people were born, accounting for nearly one-third of the U.S. population in 1980; in the 1970s, the birthrate dropped.

Baby's breath, or babies' breath, garden plant (*Gypsophila paniculata*), known for branched clusters of tiny white or pink flowers. Most are perennials; annuals are grown from seed. Ranging from 2 to 3 ft (61 to 90 cm) in height, baby's breath is frequently used in floral bouquets.
See also: Pink.

Babylon, capital of the ancient kingdom of Babylonia, between the Tigris and Euphrates rivers (Babylon, "gate of the god"), about 55 mi (88.5 km) south of modern Baghdad. The reign of Nebuchadnezzar II (d. 562 B.C.) marked the height of Babylonian splendor. The city's Hanging Gardens were one of the Seven Wonders of the World. Cyrus of Persia captured Babylon in 538 B.C.
See also: Hammurabi; Nebuchadnezzar.

Babylonia and Assyria, ancient kingdoms of the Middle East in Mesopotamia, the fertile valley of the Tigris and Euphrates rivers. Assyria was in northern Mesopotamia, while Babylonia lay to the south. The Tigris-Euphrates Valley, along with the Nile, the Indus, and the Yellow rivers, was one of the cradles of world civilization. Agriculture and the raising of livestock may have begun in Mesopotamia earlier than anywhere else, about 8000-7000 B.C. The first urban economy was also established in Mesopotamia.
About 3000 B.C. the Sumerian civilization began to emerge in southern Babylonia. The Sumerians built an irrigation system and invented cuneiform writing. Sumer was composed of the independent and frequently hostile city-states of Lagash, Ur (where the biblical Abraham was born), Kish, Erech, and Umma. Northern Babylonia was conquered by a Semitic people from the west around 2500 B.C. and the kingdom of Akkad emerged. Its founder, Sargon (c. 2306-2250), conquered Sumer areas to the east and west, a policy of expansion that was continued by his successors. Sumerian civilization survived for a time under the kings of Ur, under whom the earliest known code of laws was compiled and work started on the great ziggurat, a tiered pyramid-shaped temple. Meanwhile an Amorite dynasty established itself in Akkad and made the town of Babylon its chief center. Southern Mesopotamia came to be called Babylonia. The sixth king of this dynasty, Hammurabi (c. 1792-1750), was an able ruler who organized his territories on imperial lines. Hammurabi's famous code divided the people into 3 classes (citizens, commoners, and slaves), and contained laws on property, inheritance, marriage, and the family. Punish-

ments for criminal offenses were usually severe, and increased with the status of the victim. About 1594 a Hittite army sacked Babylon, and the country was conquered by the Kassites, who ruled for more than 400 years, adopting Babylonian culture. By 1171 a native Babylonian dynasty had taken over, but its authority was uncertain. The 11th and 10th centuries B.C. saw the influx of Aramaean tribes from the west and Chaldean infiltration along the Persian Gulf.

The Middle Assyrian Empire began to emerge as a great military power in the 14th century B.C., reaching the height of its power around 1100. A period of decline followed, but a new Assyrian Empire rose in the 9th and 8th centuries B.C. Babylonia, Syria, and Israel fell to Assyrian arms; even Egypt was for a time under Assyrian rule. Sennacherib (705-682) made Nineveh his capital and transformed it into one of the most splendid cities of the time. During his reign Babylon revolted (689) and he destroyed the city and its inhabitants, but Babylon was in part restored by his successor, Esarhaddon.

The last great king of Assyria was Ashurbanipal (669-627?). An able general like his predecessors, he was also a devoted patron of the arts and literature. Some 25,000 tablets from the large library he assembled are now in the British Museum, London. During this period Assyria was the most powerful nation in the Middle East, but after Ashurbanipal's death it suddenly began to collapse. There was widespread revolt, and in 612 the Chaldeans of Babylonia, in alliance with the Scythians and Medes, captured and destroyed Nineveh. The last Assyrian forces were destroyed in 609.

The Assyrians decorated their buildings with glazed bricks and wall paintings. During the height of the empire the palace walls were covered with great stone reliefs that give a vivid impression of life of the time. Other remains include great statues of winged bulls and lions with human heads that once guarded the palaces.

The Neo-Babylonian Empire. After many years as a subject state of the Assyrian Empire, Babylonia recovered its independence under the Chaldean king Nabopolassar (626 B.C.). He devoted most of his reign to the destruction of Assyria, and after the fall of Nineveh brought the southern part of the empire, including Syria, Palestine, and part of southern Persia, under his control, despite the opposition of Egypt. This new Babylonian Empire, which was to enjoy immense power and prosperity, was consolidated by his son Nebuchadnezzar II (605-562).

Nebuchadnezzar continued the war against Egypt. Meanwhile, Tyre and Judah revolted. He twice captured Jerusalem, and on the second occasion (587) destroyed the city and deported most of the inhabitants of Judah to captivity in Babylon. Tyre surrendered after a siege lasting 13 years. Nebuchadnezzar made Babylon one of the most magnificent cities of ancient times. It was girdled by massive outer and inner walls with numerous gates, including the gate of Ishtar, which opened on to the great processional way that led to the temple of Marduk. The terraced Hanging Gardens overlooking the Euphrates River were one of the seven wonders of the ancient world and formed part of the imposing palace. Assassination and civil war followed his death, but prosperity returned under Nabonidus and his son Belshazzar. In 539 B.C. the ambitious Cyrus II, king of the Medes and Persians, invaded Babylonia. The Book of Daniel tells how Belshazzar was warned of the final disaster by the "writing on the wall" that mysteriously appeared during a feast the evening before Babylon fell. Babylonia now became a province of the Persian Empire, and Babylon the provincial administrative center.

Knowledge of Babylonian life comes largely from the thousands of clay cuneiform tablets that have been found at various sites, including legal and commercial records, literary and historical texts, and treatises on magic and astrology. The ancient Babylonians based their number system on 60. They separated the day into 12 double hours and the year into 12 months of 30 days each. They were the first to divide the circle into 360 degrees and the minute into 60 seconds. Their system was able to express fractions and squares and cube roots. The later Babylonians were noted astronomers, and the Chaldean priests could predict eclipses of the sun and moon.

Midway between the civilizations of the Indus and the Nile, the Babylonians acted as the great cultural intermediaries of the ancient world. Because Mesopotamia lacked such raw materials as metals, stone, and wood, the Babylonians became great merchants, trading as far as Armenia and the Red Sea. The Chaldeans, like the Assyrians before them, brought the area of the Near East known as the Fertile Crescent together under one rule, creating the first cosmopolitan society of peoples of many cultures and languages.

See also: Hammurabi; Nebuchadnezzar.

Babylonian Captivity, in Israeli history, period from the fall of Jerusalem to the Babylonians (586 B.C.) to the reconstruction of new Jewish Palestinian state (after 538 B.C.).

Bacchus, in Roman mythology, god of wine and revelry. The festivals in his honor, called *bacchanalia*, became orgies of drink and sex and were banned in 186 B.C.

See also: Dionysus.

Bach, Carl Philipp Emanuel (1714-88), German composer and musician, known as the "Hamburg Bach"; one of the sons of Johann Sebastian Bach. His *Essay on the True Art of Playing Keyboard Instruments* (1753) is still considered a valid guide to keyboard technique. From 1740 until his death he was court musician and harpsichordist to Frederick the Great.

Bach, Johann Christian (1735-82), German composer and musician, often known as the "English Bach"; youngest son of Johann Sebastian Bach. He spent many years in Italy, where he angered his family by converting to Catholicism and writing operas. He spent the last 20 years of his life in London, where he was music master to King George III.

The Ishtar Gate of ancient Babylon

Bach, Johann Sebastian (1685-1750), German composer. He composed preludes, passacaglias, toccatas, and fugues for the organ, perfecting the art of polyphony. The 48 preludes and fugues he wrote for the keyboard, published collectively as *The Well-Tempered Clavier*, are particularly renowned. Bach wrote much music for other solo instruments, notably the cello, as well as a number of concertos and orchestral suites. He also wrote hundreds of church cantatas. Among his religious compositions are the *St. John Passion*, the *Mass in B Minor*, and the *Christmas Oratorio*. His music is seen as the crowning achievement of the Baroque Age.

See also: Baroque; Cantata.

Johann Sebastian Bach

Bachelor's button, common name for several annual plants bearing small, button-shaped flowers. The cornflower is the best known.

Bachelor's degree *See:* Degree, academic.

Backbone *See:* Spine; Vertebrate.

Back swimmer *See:* Water bug.

Bacon, Francis (1561-1626), English philosopher and statesman who held various posts, finally becoming lord chancellor to James I in 1618. In 1621 he was banished from office for taking bribes and spent his last years writing. His most important contribution to philosophy was his advocacy of induction, the process of reasoning from the particular to the general, building theories on the basis of observed fact rather than making predictions from immutable general propositions. In this he was one of the founders of modern experimental science. His philosophical works were compiled in *Instauratio Magna* (1620).

Bacon, Francis (1909-), English painter. His unique style expresses the isolation and horror of the human condition, through distorted figures often conveying panic and menace.

Francis Bacon's Study after Velasquez' portrait of Pope Innocentius X *(1953)*

Bacon, Nathaniel (1647-76), leader of a popular uprising in Virginia (1676) called Bacon's Rebellion. Governor William Berkeley was driven from Jamestown by the rebels, who objected to his failure to defend European settlements from Native Americans. Bacon's death from malaria ended the revolt.
See also: Bacon's Rebellion.

Bacon, Roger (c.1214-92?), English Franciscan and scholastic philosopher renowned for his interest in science and his observation of natural phenomena. He is sometimes credited with many precocious discoveries (of the microscope, for example), but there is great doubt about the truth of these claims.

Badlands of South Dakota

Bacon's Rebellion, uprising in colonial Virginia, 1676, led by planter Nathaniel Bacon against the governor, Sir William Berkeley. Bacon led unauthorized forces against the Native Americans. Though denounced as a traitor, he briefly controlled the Jamestown colony. The civil war between his and Berkeley's forces ended shortly after Bacon's death from malaria.

Bacteria, unicellular (one-celled) microorganisms of the class Schizomycetes, existing either as free-living organisms or as parasites. Bacteria may be divided into 3 groups: aerobes, which require atmospheric oxygen to live; anaerobes, which cannot live when exposed to it; and facultative anaerobes, which can live with or without it. They also come in 3 main shapes: rod, round, and spiral, called bacillus, coccus, and spirillum respectively. Generally a bacterium has an exterior cell wall within which a membrane encloses the soft *cytoplasm*, where enzymes digest and assimilate food. The DNA in which genetic information is encoded is in a portion of the cytoplasm, but unlike that of most other cells, is not separately enclosed in a nucleus. Bacteria reproduce asexually, by fission (*mitosis*), with each cell dividing evenly in two. In certain bacteria DNA is also sometimes transferred between 2 cells (*conjugation*). Bacteria cause many different chemical reactions in their hosts. Some aid in digestion and after processes within animals, and others break down dead plant and animal material in soil to provide nutrients for new growth. Bacteria that cause disease are called pathogens.
See also: Bacteriology; Cell; Leeuwenhoek, Anton van.

Bacteriological warfare *See:* Chemical and biological warfare.

Bacteriology, science that deals with the characteristics and activities of bacteria, as related to medicine, industry, and agriculture. Bacteria were discovered in 1676 by Anton van Leeuwenhoek. Modern techniques of study began to arise around 1870, with the use of stains and the discovery of methods of growing bacteria in laboratory dishes. Much pioneering work was done by Louis Pasteur and Robert Koch.
See also: Antibiotic; Bacteria; Immunity.

Bactria, ancient Greek kingdom in central Asia, lying between the Hindu Kush Mountains and the Amu Darya River, in what is now Afghanistan and Russian Turkestan. Bactria became part of the Persian Empire and fell to Alexander the Great in 330 B.C. It became independent in 256 B.C. but fell 150 years later.

Bad Aachen *See:* Aachen.

Baden-Baden (pop. 48,700), city and spa in the German state of Baden-Württemberg. It is situated at the edge of the Black Forest in the Rhine Valley, and is famous for its warm mineral springs.

Baden-Powell, Agnes *See:* Baden-Powell, Robert Stephenson Smyth; Girl Scouts and Girl Guides.

Baden-Powell, Robert Stephenson Smyth, Lord (1857-1941), British army officer and founder of the Boy Scouts (1908) and Girl Guides (1910). His sister, Agnes Baden-Powell, was cofounder of the Girl Scouts. His published works include *Scouting for Boys* (1908) and *Girl Guiding* (1917).
See also: Boy Scouts.

Badger, any of several medium-size (about 30 lb/13.6 kg), omnivorous, burrowing mammals of the weasel family Mustelidae, distributed throughout Eurasia, North America, and parts of Indonesia. Badgers are almost always nocturnal.

Badlands, region of southwestern South Dakota, about 100 miles (160 km) long and 40 miles (64 km) wide, characterized by an almost total lack of vegetation. Heavily eroded by wind and water, the area shows rugged hills, gullied slopes, steep buttes, fluted pinnacles, and layers of multicolored shales and sandstones. The term "badlands" is also applied to similar regions in western North Dakota, eastern Arizona, northwestern Nebraska, and northern Wyoming.
See also: South Dakota.

Badlands National Park, some 243,302 acres (98,461 hectares) of badlands in southwestern South Dakota. It comprises barren ravines, ridges of multicolored shale, fossiled sandstone, and wildlife. A national monument since 1929, the area was renamed a national park in 1978.
See also: National Parks.

Badminton, game played by 2 or 4 persons using lightweight rackets and a shuttlecock or bird (a feathered ball made of cork or rubber), which is hit back and forth over a 5-foot high net that divides the court at the center. Each player "serves" by hitting the shuttlecock over the net to an opponent, who must return it before it hits the ground. The game, which probably originated in India, was introduced in the United States in the late 19th century.

Baeck, Leo (1873-1956), German rabbi and theologian of Reform Judaism. Baeck survived the Theresienstadt concentration camp. His *Essence of Judaism* (1905) interpreted Judaism as a religion devoid of mythology and concerned with the personal duty.

Baekeland, Leo Hendrik (1863-1944), Belgian-born chemist who, after emigrating to the United States in 1889, devised Velox photographic printing paper (selling the process to Eastman in 1899) and discovered Bakelite, the first modern synthetic plastic.

Baer, Karl Ernst von (1792-1876), German founder of comparative embryology. He discovered the notochord and the mammalian egg in the ovary.

Baez, Joan (1941-), U.S. singer of folk ballads and popular songs, known for her clear, expressive voice and her involvement in social and political action. Baez achieved widespread fame during the height of the Vietnam War as a performer of protest songs.

Baffin, William (c. 1584-1622), English navigator and Arctic explorer. As pilot on a vessel seeking the Northwest Passage, he is credited with the discovery of Baffin Bay (1616). Baffin Island is named after him.

Baffin Island, world's fifth-largest island, between Greenland and Canada, part of Canada's Northwest Territories, a rugged, glaciated tract 183,810 sq mi (477,906 sq km) in area with a mountain range along its east coast. The largely Eskimo population lives by fishing, trading, and whaling.
See also: Baffin, William.

Baganda *See:* Ganda.

Baghdad (pop. 2,969,000), capital and largest city of Iraq, on both banks of the Tigris River, at a point where the Tigris is only 25 mi (40 km) from the Euphrates. Founded 762 A.D., the city became the center of Arab and Muslim civilization during its golden age, in the 9th and 10th centuries. In 1258 the city was sacked by the Mongols, and in 1638 it became part of the Ottoman Empire. In 1921 it became the capital of the newly formed kingdom of Iraq. After World War II Baghdad developed into a modern metropolis. The city is a shipping and industrial center and has an international airport.
See also: Iraq; Persian Gulf War.

Bagpipe, musical wind instrument in which air is blown into a leather bag and then forced out through musical pipes. The melody is played on one or two pipes (the chanters), while drone pipes sound bass tones. The bagpipe originated in Asia but is best known as Scotland's national instrument.

Baguio (pop. 119,000), mountain resort city in Luzon in the Philippines. Baguio was developed as a modern city by William Howard Taft, then U.S. governor of the Philippines, when the country was under U.S. rule in the early 1900s. Nearly destroyed during World War II, the city was later rebuilt and is now an important gold-mining center.
See also: Philippines.

Baha'i faith, religion founded by the Persian Mirza Husain Ali Nuri (1817-92), known as Baha Ullah ("Glory of God"). The Baha'is believe in the unity of all religions and the equality of men and women. They advocate world government. The faith It has a worldwide following; its international center is in Haifa, Israel.

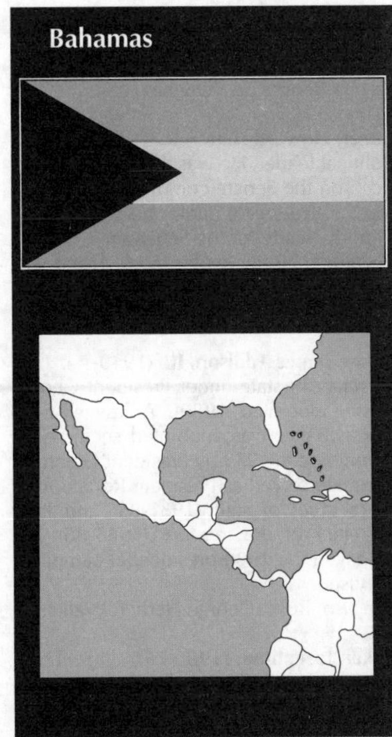

Capital:	Nassau
Area:	5,382 sq mi (13,939 sq km)
Population:	249,000
Government:	constitutional monarchy
Independent:	1973
GNP:	U.S. $2,611,000,000
Per capita:	U.S. $10,570

Bahamas, nation of some 700 subtropical islands and more than 2,000 islets, or cays, extending about 600 mi (970 km) from the coast of Florida, southeast toward Haiti. Nassau is the capital. The economy is based on tourism, fishing, and the export of wood products, cement, salt, and crayfish. Colonized by Britain in the 1640s, the islands became an independent state in 1973.
See also: Nassau.

The former governor's palace in Nassau, Bahamas. On the stairs is a statue of Columbus, who discovered the isles; in the front of the gate a typical coach.

Baha Ullah (Mirza Husain Ali Nuri; 1817-92), Persian religious leader. A disciple of Babism, a sect that split off from Islam in 1848, he was exiled to Turkey by the Persian government in 1863. In that year he proclaimed himself the Promised One awaited by the Babists. He later founded the Baha'i faith, authoring its basic text, *Kitabi Ikan*, or *Book of Certitude*.
See also: Baha'i faith.

Bahrain, independent Arab emirate consisting of Bahrain Island and a number of smaller islands, in the Persian Gulf between the Saudi Arabian coast and the Qatar peninsula. The capital is Manama.

Port of Bahrain

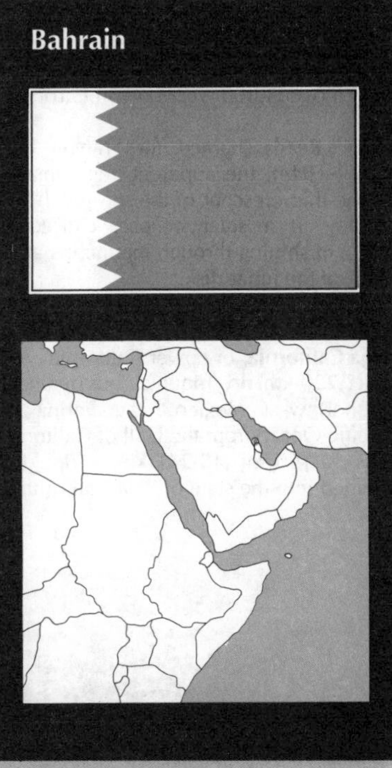

Capital:	Manama
Area:	267 sq mi (691 sq km)
Population:	489,000
Government:	monarchy
Independent:	1971
GNP:	U.S. $3,027,000,000
Per capita:	U.S. $6,610

The country has a desert climate, and the economy is based on oil drilling and refining. A trading center in ancient times, Bahrain became an emirate (monarchy) in 1783 and fell under British control in 1861. It attained independence in 1971.
See also: Arab League; Manama.

James Baker

Bail, money or property security deposited to obtain a prisoner's freedom of movement, pledging that he or she will appear before the court when called.

Bailey, Liberty Hyde (1858-1954), U.S. botanist and educator whose studies of cultivated plants linked the practice of horticulture to the science of botany. He established (1888) the country's first horticulture laboratory at what is now Michigan State University. As a professor of botany and horticulture (1888-1903), and later as dean of the College of Agriculture at Cornell University (1904-13), he pioneered agricultural education in the United States. His *Cyclopedia of American Horticulture* (1900-02) was considered a major reference work.

George Balanchine

Bailey Bridge, strong temporary or semi-permanent bridge constructed by a method suggested in 1941 by Sir Donald Bailey, then chief designer at the Royal Engineers Experimental Bridging Establishment in England. It consists of a series of mass-produced, lightweight girders that can be easily bolted together to produce the required length or to reinforce one another. Its immense flexibility and ease of construction made it immediately successful, particularly for military use. During World War II over 4,000 were built in Europe.

Baily's Beads, named for Francis Baily (1774-1844), the apparent fragmentation of the thin crescent of the sun just before totality in a solar eclipse, caused by sunlight shining through mountains at the edge of the lunar disk.
See also: Eclipse.

Baja California, or Lower California, 761-mi (1,220-km) dry, mountainous peninsula in northwest Mexico. Separating the Pacific Ocean from the Gulf of California, it is 30-150 mi (48-241 km) wide. It is divided into the state of Baja California in the north and the territory of Baja California Sur in the south.

The port of Baku in the Soviet republic of Azerbaijan. Baku is the second largest oil center of the Soviet Union.

Baker, George *See:* Divine, Father.

Baker, Howard Henry, Jr. (1925-), U.S. political leader. He was the senior Republican on the Senate committee investigating the Watergate affair and was elected minority leader of the Senate in 1977. He became majority leader in 1981 and was White House chief of staff under Pres. Ronald Reagan in 1987 and 1988.

Baker, James Addison, III (1930-), U.S. secretary of state under President George Bush (appointed 1989). A lawyer from Texas, Baker was appointed secretary of commerce in 1975 by President Gerald R. Ford. He served as President Ronald Reagan's chief of staff (1981-85) and later secretary of the treasury (1985-88). He managed the 1988 presidential campaign of Bush.
See also: Bush, George Herbert Walker.

Baker, Josephine (1906-75), U.S. born, French black singer and dancer of international fame. She was a film and stage artist, philanthropist, and social campaigner.

Baking soda *See:* Soda.

Bakke case, suit brought by Allan Bakke in 1974 against the University of California claiming that the institution's affirmative-action program had wrongfully denied him admission to medical school solely because he was white. On June 28, 1978, the U.S. Supreme Court ruled 5 to 4 in Bakke's favor, declaring that strict racial quotas to determine university admission are unconstitutional.

Baku (pop. 1,084,000), capital of the Azerbaijan Soviet Socialist Republic. On the southwest shore of the Apsheron peninsula in the Caspian Sea, Baku is the leading Soviet oil refining center as well as an important port and railroad center.
See also: Azerbaijan.

Balaklava, seaport village in the Crimean region, southwest USSR, and site of the Crimean War battle (Oct. 25, 1854) commemorated by Alfred Lord Tennyson's "The Charge of the Light Brigade" (1854).
See also: Crimean War.

Balalaika, usually 3-stringed musical instrument of ancient Slavic origin used in Russian and East European folk music. It has a triangular body and long fretted neck. Its six sizes may be combined in ensemble playing.

Balance, instrument for weighing; usually a bar with 2 matched pans suspended from each end, which pivots on a central point as weights are placed in the pans. If the weights are equal, the force of gravity on them is equal, and the balance swings level.
See also: Scale, Weighing.

Balance of nature, concept of nature as a network of relationships and interdependencies between animals and plants, all of which support and control each other in a stable and unchanging equilibrium. The concept has been greatly modified since it was first suggested in the latter half of the 19th and early 20th centuries. It is now recognized that although a degree of balance does exist, it is a highly dynamic and unstable state. The main reason for this is that animals and plants depend not only on each other but on such external factors as climate and availability of food. Where food supplies are plentiful and the range of forms of life is large, a community may achieve a fairly high degree of stability. But where the "food web" is simple, as in the northern tundras, there may be insufficient control mechanisms to prevent the periodic explosions of population that cause, for example, the self-destructive mass migration of lemmings. Many natural communities that were once stable have become unstable or have been destroyed by industry, agriculture, and disposal of sewage. Pesticides may kill beneficial insect parasites and thus lead to an uncontrollable increase in the pest population in succeeding years. Pesticides may also become concentrated in the bodies of predators at the top of the food chain. The death of hawks and owls from pesticides allows the population of rodent pests to increase. A small alteration in the balance of nature may produce unexpected consequences in some other part of the community.

Balance of payments, relation between payments in and out of a country. The figures that make up the balance of payments include trading (imports and exports), invisible earnings (insurance and banking), and capital movements (investment overseas or money from abroad). A country that persistently shows a deficit may have to devalue its currency, borrow money, or adopt strict economies. A country with a large surplus is pressured by inflation.

Balance of power, system of international relations wherein nations alter their alliances to other nations so no single nation dominates. Since World War II, the United States and the Soviet Union have emerged as superpowers, but Japan and China may, by virtue of size and military-industrial potential, demand a radically altered balance of power.
See also: International relations.

Balanchine, George (George Melitonovich Balanchivadze; 1904-83), Russian-born choreographer, founder of the School of American Ballet (1934). He worked with Sergei Diaghilev in France in the 1920s and came to the United States in 1934. In 1948 he became artistic director of the New York City Ballet.
See also: Ballet.

Balboa, Vasco Núñez de (c.1475-1519), Spanish conquistador credited as first European discoverer of the Pacific Ocean.

In 1510 he cofounded one of the first lasting European settlements on the American mainland, Antigua in Panama. Encouraged by Native American tales of a wealthy kingdom on "the other sea," in 1513 he led an expedition across the isthmus, saw the Pacific, and claimed it and all its coasts for Spain. He was later charged with treason and executed.
See also: Pacific Ocean.

Balch, Emily Greene (1867-1961), U.S. sociologist, economist, and humanitarian; joint winner of the 1946 Nobel Peace Prize. Cofounder of the Women's International League for Peace and Freedom, she was its secretary 1919-22 and 1934-35 and its honorary president from 1936.

Bald cypress, common name for a family (Taxodiaceae) of evergreens with wood cones and needlelike or scalelike leaves. The common bald cypress *(Taxodium distichum)*, the state tree of Louisiana, is prized for its wood and may be found in swamps and wetlands of the United States, from Texas to New Jersey.

Bald eagle (*Haliaetus leucocephalus*), only native North American eagle, national bird of the United States since 1782. About 3 ft (90 cm) long, with a wingspan that may reach 7 ft (2 m), it is black, with white feathers on neck, tail, and head. A member of the hawk family, it preys on fish and is protected as an endangered species in all states.

Baldness, or alopecia, lack or loss of hair, usually from the scalp, due to disease of hair follicles. Pattern baldness is an inherited tendency, often starting when a man is in his 20s. It is found in about 40% of the male population. Alopecia areata is a disease of unknown cause producing usually temporary patchy baldness, though it may be total. Prolonged fever, lupus erythematosus, ringworm, certain drugs, and poisons may lead to temporary baldness.

Baldpate *See:* Wigeon.

Baldwin, James (1924-87), African-American novelist, essayist, and playwright much of whose work deals with racial themes. His novel *Go Tell It on the Mountain* (1953) was based on his Harlem adolescence, while *Another Country* (1962) deals with sexual and racial identity. His best-known essays are collected in *Notes of a Native Son* (1955) and *The Fire Next Time* (1963). His book, *The Evidence of Things Not Seen*, about the Atlanta child murders (1985) is one of his most controversial works.

James Baldwin

Baldwin, Matthias William (1795-1866), U.S. inventor and philanthropist. *Old Ironsides*, his early locomotive (1830s), was the first of more than 1,500 locomotives designed and manufactured by Baldwin and his Baldwin Locomotive Works. His other inventions included processes for plating gold and for printing patterns on cloth. An abolitionist, he supported education for black children and founded the Franklin Institute.

Baldwin, Robert (1804-58), Canadian statesman; leader, with Louis LaFontaine, of the "Great Ministry" (1847-51). He later worked for improved relations between English and French Canadians.

Baldwin, Stanley (1867-1947), British Conservative politician, 3 times prime minister (1923-24, 1924-29, 1935-37). He led the breaking of the General Strike of 1926 and was criticized for underestimating the dangers of the rise of fascism in Europe.

Balearic Islands, Mediterranean archipelago off eastern Spain, under Spanish rule since 1349. The largest are Majorca, Minorca, and Ibiza. Products include grapes, olives, and citrus fruit.
See also: Majorca.

Baleen *See:* Whale.

Balfour, Arthur James Balfour, 1st Earl of (1848-1930), British statesman best known as author of the Balfour Declaration. He was a Conservative member of parliament 1874-1911; prime minister, 1902-05; and foreign secretary 1916-19.
See also: Balfour Declaration

Balfour Declaration, statement of British policy issued in 1917 by Foreign Secretary Arthur Balfour. It stated British support for a Jewish national home in Palestine without prejudice to the rights of the non-Jewish population.

Bali, volcanic island and province of South Indonesia, 2,171 sq mi (5,623 sq km). It is a lush, densely populated island. Industries include food processing, tourism, and handicrafts. The largely Hindu Balinese are famous for dancing, music, and decorative arts.

Baline, Israel *See:* Berlin, Irving.

Balkan Peninsula, mountainous land area in southeastern Europe, south of the Danube and Sava rivers, surrounded by the Adriatic, Ionian, Mediterranean, Aegean, and Black seas. It contains the nations of Bulgaria, Albania, Greece, European Turkey, and most of Yugoslavia.

Bald eagle

Balkan Wars, 2 wars in which the Ottoman Empire lost almost all its European territory. In the first war (1912-13) Serbia, Bulgaria, Greece, and Montenegro conquered all of Turkey's European possessions except Constantinople. In the second war (1913) Bulgaria attacked Serbia, but was itself attacked by Rumania, Greece, and Turkey. In the ensuing Treaty of Bucharest (Aug. 1913) Bulgaria lost territory to each of its enemies.

Ballad, verse narrative, often meant to be sung, usually describing an event. Traditionally ballads celebrated folk heroes or related popular romances; they were developed by European minstrels in the Middle Ages. Romantic writers, such as Sir Walter Scott, William Wordsworth, and Samuel Taylor Coleridge, adapted the form. In modern popular music the term is used loosely to apply to any kind of sentimental song, but the United States has also produced ballads of the traditional type, ranging from the anonymous "Frankie and Johnny" to the work of Bob Dylan and Joan Baez.

Ballade, verse of three 8-line stanzas concluding with a 4-line summary. The French poet François Villon (1431-63?) and the English poet Geoffrey Chaucer (c.1340-1400) used this form, which originated in 14th-century France.

Ball bearing *See:* Bearing.

Ballet, form of solo and ensemble dance meant for the stage. Ballet evolved from court entertainments of Renaissance Italy, where training in graceful movement was considered essential to a courtier's education. These entertainments were introduced into France by Catherine dé Medici, wife of King Henry II. In the courts of later kings, ballet became firmly established as an aristocratic pastime, and the kings themselves were skilled dancers. King Louis XIV established the first professional ballet school, the Royal Academy of Music and

The 18th-century ballerina Marie-Anne de Cupis Camargo. Camargo was responsible for shorter skirts, tights, and the first ballet slippers. This painting of Camargo was done by Nicolas Lancret (1690-1743).

Dance, in 1661. Charles Louis (Pierre) Beauchamp, balletmaster of the Academy, originated the 5 basic foot positions and turnout of the feet that are still fundamental to ballet technique. Early-18th-century ballet was an adjunct to opera. By mid-18th century self-contained pantomime ballets began to appear, and virtuoso dancers modified their costumes to allow more freedom of movement. Jean Georges Noverre helped establish ballet as an integral art form in which plot, music, decoration, and dance were fused into an artistic whole. The 19th-century romantic movement introduced a new emphasis on lightness and grace. Ballerinas began to dance on their toes and adopted the short, full-skirted tutu. The center of European ballet shifted to Russia with the appointment of the French dancer Marius Petipa as balletmaster of the Imperial Ballet in the 1850s. Petipa brought new standards of technical perfection, and his use of Russian folk themes and music gave ballet a wider support among the public. With his assistant Lev Ivanov, he created such classical ballets as *Swan Lake, The Nutcracker,* and *The Sleeping Beauty.*

In 1907 the visit of the U.S. dancer Isadora Duncan to St. Petersburg spurred the Russian choreographer Michel Fokine to create a new, modern ballet. Fokine joined with the Russian impresario Sergei Diaghilev to form the Russian Ballet, which opened in Paris in 1909. Diaghilev's company included some of the greatest dancers in the history of ballet: Vaslav Nijinsky, Anna Pavlova, Léonide Massine, and George Balanchine. Many of these dancers went on to found new ballet companies, thus extending Diaghilev's influence throughout the world of the dance. For the Russian Ballet Fokine created *Les Sylphides, The Firebird,* and *Rite of Spring.* From 1909 until his death, Diaghilev was the most important figure in European ballet.England's first permanent ballet company, the Vic Wells (later Sadler's Wells), was formed in 1930. Renamed the Royal Ballet in 1957, it is noted for the choreography of Frederick Ashton, and featured dancers Margot Fonteyn and Rudolph Nureyev. After the Revolution, the Russian Ballet was devoted to experimental works on political and social themes, but then returned to the classical models of Petipa. Russian dancers are acknowledged master: of the traditional style.In the United States, contemporary ballet has evolved into a distinctive form combining the modern dance of Jerome Robbins, Martha Graham, and Ruth St. Denis with the tradition of the classical ballet as adapted by Massine and Balanchine. The Ballet Theater, established in 1940, encouraged the work of new U.S. composers and choreographers, and George Balanchine's New York City Ballet has continued to add new and unorthodox works to the repertoire. Professional ballet companies have been established throughout the United States, and the popular tours U.S. companies have undertaken abroad have made this country among the most vital and influential in the dance world. Canada also has several major professional companies: Royal Winnipeg Ballet, National Ballet of Canada (Toronto), and Les Grands Ballets Canadiens (Montreal).

See also: Ailey, Alvin; Balanchine, George; Baryshnikov, Mikhail; Diaghilev, Sergei Pavlovich; Nijinski, Vaslav; Pavlova, Anna.

See also: Dance.

A. The five classical ballet positions with a sixth dancer indicating that all positions can be done on points. B. Fouette en tournant C. Brisé D. Entrechat E. Jeté

Ballistic missile *See:* Guided missile.

Ballistic Missile Early Warning System *See:* Radar.

Ballistics, science dealing with projectiles, traditionally divided into 3 parts: interior ballistics, relating to the progress of the projectile before it is released from the launching device; exterior ballistics, relating to the free flight of the projectile; and terminal ballistics, relating to the behavior of the projectile upon impact, at the end of its trajectory.

Balloon, nonpowered, nonrigid, lighter-than-air craft consisting of a bulbous envelope that holds the lifting medium and a payload-carrying basket, or "gondola," suspended below. Balloons may be captive (secured to the ground by a cable) or free-flying. Lift may be provided by a gas such as hydrogen or nonflammable helium or by heated air. Balloons are used in science (weather forecasting and astronomy), as well as for recreational purposes.

See also: Zeppelin, Ferdinand von.

The first balloon flight was accomplished by Joseph and Etienne Montgolfier on June 5, 1783 near Lyons, France. The first successful transatlantic balloon flight was accomplished in l978.

Ballot, method of registering a vote. It can be a pre-printed list of people running for office or of issues to be decided by a popular vote (referendum). In the United States, about 50% of the elections are held in a closed booth with a printed ballot mounted on a voting machine. The other type of balloting involves voters checking off their choices and depositing their ballots into a sealed box. After voting is over, the ballots are counted and the highest vote-getters are determined to be the winners.

See also: Voting.

Balm, any of various fragrant herbs of the mint family (genera *Melissa* or *Monarda*).

Used in medicinal teas and wine drinks in ancient Greece and Asia, balm is now widely used as a scent in perfume and as a food and drink flavoring.
See also: Balm of Gilead.

Balm of Gilead, liquid resinous balsam derived from an evergreen tree (*Commiphora meccanesis*). The balsam had medicinal uses in ancient times. By extension, balm of Gilead may refer to anything that soothes or heals.

Balsa, or corkwood, tropical U.S. tree (*Ochroma lagopus*), known for its extremely light wood. Ecuador is the world's largest producer of balsa wood, which is an effective insulating material and is also popular for making model airplanes and boats.

Balsam, aromatic resinous substance produced by certain plants and trees. Balsam is used in medicines, ointments, chewing gum, varnish, and perfumes.

Balsam fir (*Abies balsamea*), evergreen tree of the pine family, found in the northeastern United States and throughout much of Canada. The balsam fir makes a popular Christmas tree; its bark produces a resin called Canada balsam.

Balsam poplar *See:* Poplar.

Baltic Sea, arm of the Atlantic Ocean, extending into northern Europe. Its 163,000 sq mi (422,170 sq km) are surrounded by Sweden, Finland, the USSR, Poland, Germany, and Denmark. It is linked to the North Sea by the Skagerrak, Kattegat, and Oresund straits.

Baltic States, former Baltic coast republics of Estonia, Latvia, and Lithuania. They became independent in 1917 but were annexed by the USSR in 1940. In the late 1980s, separatist nationalist movements aimed at restoring sovereignty developed, and as of 1991 the future relationship of the Baltic states to the USSR was in doubt.
See also: Estonia; Latvia; Lithuania.

Baltimore (pop. 2,382,172), largest city in Maryland, on the Patapsco River near Chesapeake Bay. The seventh-largest city in the United States, it is one of the nation's busiest ports, an important road, rail, and air transportation hub, and a leading manufacturing center with metallurgical, electronic, and food- processing industries.
See also: Maryland.

Baltimore, Lord, collective title of 6 members of the Calvert family, founders of the colony of Maryland. **George Calvert** (1580?-1632) was granted the proprietorship of what became Maryland by Charles I of England in 1632, but died before the charter was signed. The charter rights passed to George's son **Celilius Calvert** (1605?-75), who founded the colony of Maryland in 1632. In 1691, Maryland became a royal colony, but in 1715 the Crown returned the charter to the Calverts.

Baltimore oriole (*Icterus galbula*), North American songbird about 18 in (20 cm) long, with a wingspan of about 12 in (30 cm). Males are black and bright orange; females and young are olive, yellow, and brownish. "Baltimore oriole" is now a popular term for the northern oriole because it is no longer considered a separate species but a subspecies.

Balzac, Honoré de (1799-1850), French novelist noted for social observation and sweeping vision. *The Human Comedy*, his greatest work, is a collection of novels and stories that offer a comprehensive portrait of French society. Written over a period of two decades, its best-known novels are *Père Goriot* (1835) and *Cousin Bette* (1847).

Bamako (pop. 740,000), capital of Mali, located on the Niger River in West Africa. Bamako is a trade center linked by rail to Dakar, Senegal, on the Atlantic Ocean. Factories manufacture food, textiles, and metal goods. A former French colony, Mali became independent in 1960.
See also: Mali.

Bamboo, woody plant (genus *Bambusa*) with hollow stems found in Asia, Africa, Australia, and the southern United States. Some species grow to 120 ft (27 m). In Asia the young shoots are a major foodstuff, while mature stems are used in building houses and furniture. Amorphous silica from stems is used as a catalyst in some chemical processes.

Banana, edible fruit of a large (30-ft/9-m) perennial herb that reaches maturity within 15 months from planting. Main areas of commercial cultivation are in tropical Asia, South America, and the West Indies. Only female flowers produce the banana fruit, and each plant bears fruit only once.

Banaras *See:* Varanasi.

Bancroft, George (1800-91), U.S. historian and statesman. As secretary of the navy (1845-46), he helped develop the U.S. Naval Academy at Annapolis. His 10-volume *History of the United States* (1834-74) became a standard work, though it was later criticized for its strong nationalistic bias.
See also: United States Naval Academy.

Banda, Hastings Kamuzu (1902?-), African nationalist leader, first prime minister (1964-66) and president of Malawi (from 1966). As leader of the Nyasaland nationalists and head of the Malawi Congress party (from 1960), he sought dissolution of the Federation of Rhodesia and Nyasaland.
See also: Malawi.

Bandaranaike, Sirimavo Ratwatte Dias (1916-), prime minister of Sri Lanka and the world's first woman premier. After the assassination of her husband, Prime Minister Solomon Bandaranaike, in 1959, she led his Sri Lanka Freedom party to victory in 1960, continuing his pro-Buddhist and pro-Sinhalese policies. She lost office in 1965 but was returned in 1970 with a landslide victory for her left-oriented coalition. Conservatives defeated her in 1977.
See also: Sri Lanka.

Bandicoots, any of several genera of marsupials of the family Peramelidae found in Oceania, roughly rabbit-sized with tapering snouts. There are considerable reproductive differences from other marsupials, and their fossil history is problematic, so that their relationship to other marsupials is not fully understood.

Bandung (pop. 1,463,000), capital city of West Java province, Indonesia. The third-largest city in the country, Bandung is an important industrial, educational, and tourist center.

Honoré de Balzac

Baneberry, several herbaceous plants with poisonous red, white, or black berries. Two species known as cohosh are native to the United States. Native Americans used them as emetics and cathartics.

Banff (pop. 5,200), resort town in Alberta, Canada. Situated in the Bow River Valley of the Rocky Mountains at 4,538 ft (1,383 m) altitude, its attractions are hot springs, skiing, and an abundance of wildlife.

Banff National Park, oldest park in Canada, established in 1885, located on the eastern slopes of the Rocky Mountains in southwestern Alberta. The 2,564-sq-mi (6,640-sq-km) park is characterized by glaciers, deep valleys, and mountains. There are also dense forests, alpine meadows, and many animals, including bighorn sheep, bear, and deer.
See also: National Parks.

Bangalore (pop. 2,476,000), capital city of Karnataka state, south central India. A major industrial city, it manufactures soap, telephones, machine tools, pharmaceuticals, and aircraft, along with cotton textiles and handloomed silk.

Bangkok (pop. 5,154,000), capital city of Thailand. Situated on the Chao Phraya River, about 25 mi (40 km) inland from the Gulf of Siam, Bangkok is Thailand's main port. About three-fourths of Thailand's foreign trade passes through Bangkok; principal exports include rice, teak, rubber, tin, gold, and silver. The city is also a famous jewelry trading center. In addition, almost all of Thailand's higher education institutions are located in Bangkok. Among its numerous Buddhist temples (wats) is the Wat Phra Keo, located within the Grand Palace and containing the famed "Emerald Buddha," carved from jasper.
See also: Thailand.

Bangladesh, People's Republic of Bangladesh, republic in the northeast of the Indian subcontinent, on the Bay of Bengal; formerly East Pakistan. Bangladesh is a low-lying land centered on the alluvial Ganges-Brahmaputra Delta. A tropical monsoon climate prevails, and because of

Bangladesh

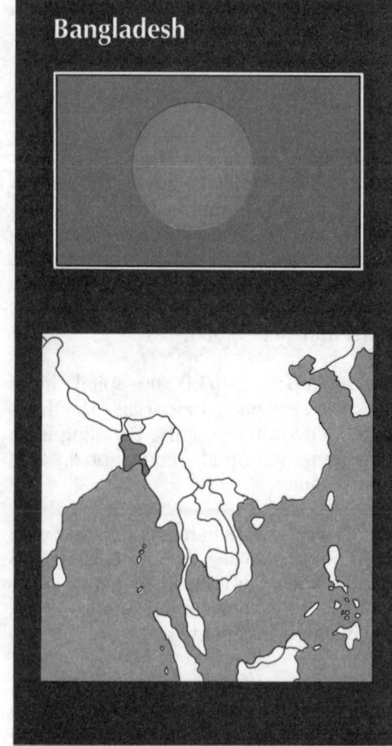

Capital:	Dhaka
Area:	55,598 sq mi (143,998 sq km)
Population:	110,290,000
Government:	republic
Independent:	1971
GNP:	U.S.$18,310,000,000
Per capita:	U.S.$170

Bangladesh is composed mostly of river deltas from the Ganges, Brahmaputra, and Meghna rivers. These waters yield over 60,000 tons of river fish annually.

heavy rains and severe cyclones, most of the country is subject to flooding. Overpopulation accentuates periodic famines and epidemics among the mainly Muslim Bengalis who constitute the great majority of the population. Bangladesh produces nearly 90% of the world's jute; tea is the other main cash crop, and sugarcane is also grown. Rice and wheat are the major subsistence crops. Natural gas is the only important mineral resource, and manufacturing is largely limited to the proceessing of raw materials. The region was created as East Pakistan (Pakistan's eastern province) in 1947. The province sought greater independence, but West Pakistan refused autonomy and troops crushed large-scale opposition in the ensuing civil war (March-Dec. 1971). Guerrilla fighting continued, Bengalis exiled in India proclaimed a Bengali republic, and Indian invasion forces overran the West Pakistani forces. A Bangladesh government was established in Dhaka in Dec. 1971.

Bangor (pop. 88,745), port city of southern Maine, at the convergence of the Penobscot and Kenduskeag rivers. Bangor is the gateway to northern and eastern Maine's resort and lumber areas and a regional commercial center producing shoes, paper, and electronic equipment.

Bangui (pop. 474,000), capital city of the Central African Republic. On the Ubangi River, it is being developed as a tourist center for the country's wildlife preserves.
See also: Central African Republic.

Banjarmasin, Banjermasin, or Bandjarmasin (pop. 381,300), capital of South Kalimantan province in Indonesia, located on an island between the Barito and Martapura rivers in southeastern Borneo. Exports include oil, diamonds, and lumber.

Banjo, stringed musical instrument with a long fretted neck and a circular frame covered by a skin resonator. Its 4 to 9 strings are played by plucking. The banjo originated among slaves in North America and may have been derived from West African instruments. It became popular in 19th-century minstrel shows, in early jazz bands, and in folk music.

Banjul (pop. 44,200), capital of Gambia in West Africa, located on St. Mary's Island where the Gambia River flows into the Atlantic Ocean. It is Gambia's only large city, its chief port and economic center. Exports include peanuts, clothing, and farm machinery. It was founded in 1816 (as Bathurst) as a British base for eliminating the slave trade. Gambia gained independence in 1965, and the city was renamed Banjul in 1973.
See also: Gambia.

Bankhead, Tallulah Brockman (1903-68), U.S. actress in plays and films. A rebel from a distinguished Southern family who made her stage debut at 16, she established herself in such plays as *Rain* (1935) and *The Little Foxes* (1939), and in films such as *Lifeboat* (1944). Her deep, cynical voice and flamboyant personality made her a successful comedienne on radio and television.

Bank holiday, day on which banks are legally closed. In England, such days are fixed annual public holidays. In U.S. history, the term refers to the 4-day period in March 1933 when President Franklin D. Roosevelt ordered all banks closed to halt panic and to assess their financial condition. More than 1,900 banks had collapsed since the beginning of the Depression in 1929.

Banking, business of dealing with money and credit transactions. The services offered by banks fall into 4 categories: safe storage, interest-bearing deposit facilities, money transfer, and loans. The nature of safe storage has changed now that most money is held in the form of bank deposits rather than gold or silver coin. Bank branches keep cash available for customers. Most banks also have safe-deposit boxes for storing valuables other than cash. The second basic service arises from the first. Since money given to a bank for safekeeping effectively amounts to a loan to the bank, the bank pays interest on it. Rates vary, depending in part on how much notice the bank requires for withdrawals. The third category of bank services, transfer of money, is carried out mainly by means of checks and credit cards. In making out checks customers authorize the bank to transfer a specified sum from their own account to someone else's (or to pay them in cash). After the check has been handed in or mailed to the bank by the payee (the person to whom the money is to be paid) it is returned to the bank of the person who has writen the check (the payor) through the clearing system run countrywide by the Federal Reserve. Credit cards, in widespread use since about 1970, allow the purchase of services and goods even in places where the bearer is not well known enough to be able to use a check. The final category of bank services, lending to customers, is the most highly developed. Although basic services are the same from one bank to another all around the world, the details and, in particular, the manner in which they are offered vary considerably. In the United States, state-chartered savings banks and state- or federally-chartered savings and loan associations originally only handled savings deposits and home mortgages, while commercial banks offered checking and a wide range of loans. Recently, however, the distinctions between these institutions have been blurred. In 1913 the Federal Reserve System was set up to strengthen the U.S. banking system. Bank failures in 1933 led to the setting up of the Federal Deposit Insurance Corporation. Since 1974 the banking industry in the

Banking was an indispensible part of the development of Europe after the Middle Ages. This portrait The Money Changer and His Wife *was painted in 1539 by Marinus van Roemerswaele.*

United States has suffered from government regulations, increased competition in financial services, and risky investments in real estate, Third World countries, and leveraged buyouts. This has resulted in the collapse of hundreds of banks in 1990 and 1991. As a result, the government has had to face great strain on its bank insurance fund. Banking and the financial services industry are now in a state of transition and restructuring to meet the financial demands of the 21st century.

Bank of Canada, central bank of Canada. It controls the amount of money available to other banks in the country. By regulating the money supply, the central bank can make sure that a stable economy and a balanced rate of growth are maintained. The central bank also issues all Canadian bank notes. It was incorporated in 1934, and, although managed by an independent governor and board of directors, it is owned by the Canadian government. The headquarters are in Ottawa.

Bank of England, central bank of the English government founded in 1694 by an Act of Parliament and Royal Charter. In 1946 it was nationalized and its stock was passed to the British Treasury. It advises the government on financial and economic conditions, facilitates the payment of government debt, services the foreign exchange markets, issues bank notes, and administers foreign exchange control.

Bank of the United States, name of 2 central banks established in the early years of the United States. In 1791 Alexander Hamilton created the first bank of the United States, chartered by Congress for 20 years. It held government deposits and had some control over the issue of paper currency and the extension of credit. But its constitutionality was questioned, and it was so strongly opposed by agrarian interests and the state banks that its charter was not renewed. A second central bank was chartered for 20 years in 1816 to help finance debts of the War of 1812, but its charter renewal was vetoed by President Andrew Jackson.

Bankruptcy, legal status of a debtor whom the courts have declared unable to pay debts. Bankruptcy is regulated by federal laws that provide for an orderly adjustment when a person or business becomes insolvent. A person or business with more debts than assets and no means of meeting debt payment may declare bankruptcy. The interest of both creditors and debtor are given consideration by the court. The Constitution gives Congress the power to establish "uniform Laws on the subject of Bankruptcies throughout the United States" (Article I, Section 8). The first bankruptcy act was passed by Congress in 1800, patterned on English law. The act on which current law is based was passed in 1898. Bankruptcy may be voluntary (filed by the debtor) or involuntary (filed by creditors). When a petition of bankruptcy is filed, the court assumes control over the assets of the debtor. A custodian or trustee is appointed to oversee the debtor's property to protect it from loss. This trustee has legal ownership of all assets of the bankrupt estate except those exempt under local law. The property of the debtor must be sold and the proceeds distributed to creditors on a percentage basis. The debtor is then legally discharged from all previous obligations.

Banneker, Benjamin (1731-1806), U.S. mathematician and astronomer, notable as the first African American to gain distinction in science. He was the author of many celebrated astronomical almanacs (1791-1802).

Bannister, Sir Roger Gilbert (1929-), British athlete, the first man to run a mile in less than 4 minutes, on May 6, 1954, in Oxford. His time was 3 min 59.4 sec.

Bannockburn, battlefield named for a village in Stirlingshire, central Scotland. Here, in 1314, Scottish forces under Robert the Bruce routed the numerically superior English army of King Edward II, assuring the throne of Scotland for Bruce and ending English rule over Scotland for a period.
See also: Bruce, Robert the.

Bannock, tribe of Native American hunters who lived in what is now eastern Idaho and western Wyoming. In 1878 some 1,500 Bannocks and Paiutes, dissatisfied with living conditions in their reservations, participated in the last Native American uprising in the Northwest.

Bantam, any of a variety of small domestic fowl, often miniatures of larger breeds.

Banting, Sir Frederick Grant (1891-1941), Canadian physiologist who, with C.H. Best, first isolated the hormone insulin from the pancreas of dogs (1921), thus providing a major breakthrough in the treatment of diabetes. For this he shared the 1923 Nobel Prize in physiology or medicine with J.J.R. Macleod, who developed the experimental facilities.
See also: Insulin.

Bantu, linguistic group of central, east, and south Africa. Bantu languages include Swahili and Zulu. The term is often used in South Africa to denote black Africans.

Bañuelos, Romana Acosta (1925-), U.S. treasurer (1971-74) under President Nixon, first Mexican-American woman to hold high government office. She began her business career in 1949 with a small tortilla stand and built it into a $5 million food company. She was the founder (1964) of the first U.S. bank owned and operated by a Mexican American, the Pan American Bank of East Los Angeles. In 1969 she established a Mexican-American student scholarship.

Banyan tree, sacred tree (*Ficus bengalensis*) of India, related to the fig. It grows up to 100 ft (30 m) high, and its branches send down aerial roots that form new trunks on reaching the soil. An individual tree can thus become a dense thicket of intertwined stems and secondary trunks covering an acre or more.

Baobab (*Adansonia digitata*), tree of tropical Africa and India with a remarkably thick trunk, reaching 30 ft (10 m) in diameter. The related Australian species is sometimes called the bottle tree for its unusual shape. The branches bear dense masses of leaves, used for medicine and condiments, white flowers, and an edible gourdlike fruit, the juice of which is made into a beverage. The bark is used to make rope, cloth, and paper, and the hollowed trunks are used for dwellings.

Bao Dai (1913-), Vietnamese emperor during the French colonial period. He was the last emperor of Annam (1926-45), until overthrown by the Viet Minh. He was later made head of state of a unified Vietnam (1949-55) created by the French in a final bid to retain Indochina, but he was forced into exile.
See also: Vietnam.

Baptism, rite of initiation into the Christian church. Some churches consider the ceremony the first step to salvation, as a symbolic purification of water. Others regard baptism as a confirmation of salvation through Christ.
See also: Christianity; John the Baptist, Saint; Roman Catholic Church.

Baptists, members of a Protestant denomination who hold that baptism is for believers only, not simply those born into the faith. Baptism, often at age 12, is by immersion. Total world membership is said to be more than 31 million, most of whom live in the United States, where they constitute the largest Protestant group. Individual churches have considerable autonomy. There is no single Baptist creed; beliefs range from fundamentalist to modernist. The evangelistic and revivalist tradition emphasizes the influence of the laity as well as ministers. The church originated with John Smyth, the leader of a group of English religious dissenters who sought refuge in Holland around 1608. The first U.S. church was founded in Providence, R.I. in 1639, by Roger Williams, and the new denomination evolved independently among the variety of Puritan dissenters. Williams later left the faith to follow his own religious vision. John Clarke in Newport, R.I. and Shubal Stearns in North Carolina were also important early leaders. The Baptist evangelical tradition began during the Great Awakening, an 18th-century U.S. religious revival, and Baptist converts spread westward along the expanding frontiers. In the 19th century the Baptists founded more than 100 colleges and universities. By 1845 the denomination had become particularly influential in the Midwest and the South. In that year a great split occurred over the slavery issue, creating Northern and Southern Baptists. After the Civil War, black churches developed an independent grouping, the National Bap-

tist Convention of America (1880). In 1915 a dispute within that membership created another major group, the National Baptist Convention, USA, Inc. In 1950 the interracial Northern Baptists formed the American Baptist Convention. The Southern Baptist Convention now includes churches beyond the borders of the historic South. U.S. Baptists are active in the World Council of Churches through the Baptist World Alliance, which was founded in 1905.
See also: Protestantism.

Bar, professional association of lawyers. Attorneys must be admitted to the bar before they can practice law in the United States. The American Bar Association, with over 90,000 members, helps to maintain the standards of the legal profession and is consulted by government on legal matters and judicial appointments.
See also: American Bar Association; Law.

Barabbas, man described in the New Testament as a bandit condemned to crucifixion at the same time as Jesus. The Roman governor Pontius Pilate agreed to spare one prisoner, and a palace crowd chose Barabbas instead of Jesus.
See also: New Testament.

Baraka, Imamu Amiri (LeRoi Jones; 1934-), African-American author and political activist whose plays, especially *Dutchman* (1964), express revulsion at the oppression of black people in white society.

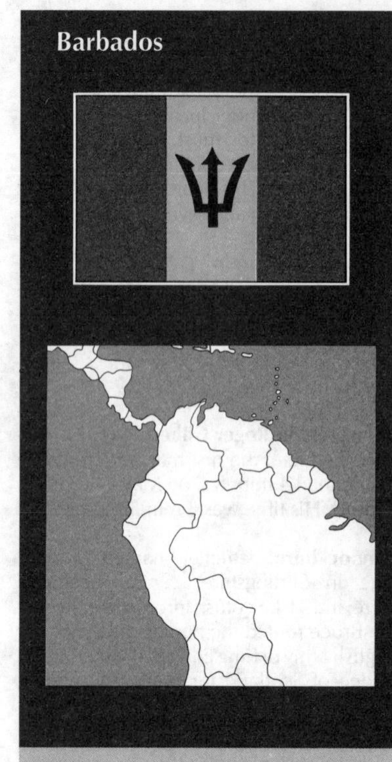

Capital:	Bridgetown
Area:	166 sq mi (430 sq km)
Population:	255,000
Form:	constitutional monarchy
Independent:	1966
GNP:	U.S.$1,530,000,000
Per capita:	U.S.$5,990

Barbados, densely populated small island in the Caribbean; a parliamentary state, part of the British Commonwealth. About 21 mi (34 km) long and 14 mi (22.5 km) wide, Barbados lies surrounded by coral reefs 250 mi (400 km) northeast of Venezuela. Bridgetown is the capital and chief business center. Carlisle Bay on the southwest coast is the only harbor. The island has no real mountains and no rivers, and water supply is from artesian wells. The mild climate makes Barbados a popular resort, but it lies in a zone of tropical storms, and destructive hurricanes are not uncommon. The soil is fertile and the whole island is cultivated. Sugarcane, introduced in the 17th century, is still the main crop, though efforts are being made to diversify agriculture and to establish light industry. Chief exports are sugar, molasses, and rum. Nearly 90% of the very dense population is of African descent. Emigrants, mainly to other West Indian islands, are numerous, and money sent home forms a useful part of the economy. Barbados was claimed by the British in 1605 and remained a colony for more than 300 years. The representative assembly was established in 1639, giving the island one of the oldest constitutions in the Commonwealth. Slavery was abolished in 1834, and full adult suffrage was granted in 1950. In 1966 the island gained independence and was admitted to the United Nations. The language is English, the Anglican church is established, and the general outlook is much influenced by a traditional image of England, though many details of life reflect historical and family links with North America.

The capital of Barbados, Bridgetown, is the only port on the island. It is vital to the tourist trade that arrives by ocean liner.

Barbarian, term originally used by ancient Greeks to denote any non-Greek-speaking people. As Greek culture spread with the conquests of Alexander the Great in Asia and the subsequent expansion of the Roman Empire in Europe, the word came to refer to peoples who lived beyond the borders of the Empire and therefore outside Greco-Roman civilization. It then took on a pejorative meaning and now refers to anyone considered uncivilized, primitive, or unsophisticated.
See also: Goths; Hun; Vandals.

Barbarossa (Khayr ad-Din; c.1483-1546), Turkish naval commander of the western Mediterranean. As high admiral of the Turkish fleet he captured Tunis and Algiers in 1518 and brought the Barbary states under Turkish sovereignty. In 1533 and 1544 he defeated Italian fleets and raided towns in Greece, Italy, France, and Spain.

Barbarossa *See:* Frederick (Holy Roman emperors).

Barbary ape, small tailless monkey (*Macaca sylvana*) of Algeria, Morocco, and Gibraltar. There is a legend that the British will lose the Rock of Gibraltar when its small colony of Barbary apes departs.

Barbary Coast *See:* Barbary States.

Barbary pirates *See:* Barbary Wars.

Barbary States, term historically applied to countries along the Mediterranean coast of North Africa, now Algeria, Tunisia, Libya, and Morocco.

Barbary Wars, 2 wars waged by the United States against African states. Barbary pirates had been attacking ships in the Mediterranean since the 16th century. In May 1801, the United States blockaded Tripoli in opposition to exorbitant payments to the Barbary States to protect its shipping. The United States won the war in 1805. The second Barbary War was fought in 1815 with Algiers. Treaties ending piracy were signed with Algiers, Tunis, and Tripoli.

Barbel *See:* Catfish.

Barber, Samuel (1910-1981), U.S. composer. Initially, he composed in a late romantic style. His music is generally tonal. Major works include two symphonies, *Adagio for Strings* (1936), and the cycle *Knoxville: Summer of 1915* (1947) for soprano and orchestra. He also wrote the operas *Vanessa* (1956) and *Anthony and Cleopatra* (1966), the latter commissioned to open the new Metropolitan Opera House in New York.

Barberry, any of several mostly evergreen, usually spiny shrubs (genus *Berberis*) having globular yellow flowers and red berries. The sour berries of the common barberry make excellent preserves, and the bark yields a yellow dye used in leather manufacture.
See also: May apple; Oregon grape.

Barbirolli, Sir John (1899-1970), English cellist and conductor, famous for his interpretations of compositions by Sibelius and other late romantics. After conducting the New York Philharmonic Orchestra (1937-42), he began a lifelong association with the Halle Orchestra in Manchester, England, and conducted the Houston Symphony Orchestra (1961-67).

Barbiturate, any of a group of drugs, derived from bituric acid, that act as seda-

tives, anesthetics, or anticonvulsants in the central nervous system by depressing nerve cell activity. Widely prescribed in the past for insomnia, their use is now discouraged because of high rates of addiction and the danger of overdose. Phenobarbital is used in the treatment of convulsions. Overdoses of barbiturates cause the deep and rapid onset of coma and can be fatal, especially when combined with alcohol.
See also: Drug.

Barbizon school: Sortie de Forêt à Fontainebleau *(Jeu de Paume, Paris), by Théodore Rousseau (1812-67)*

Barbizon school, informal group of French painters of natural and rural subjects, active c.1830-70, who frequented the village of Barbizon, near Paris. It included Théodore Rousseau, Narciso Diaz de la Peña, Jean-Baptise Corot, Jean François Millet, Jules Dupré, Constant Troyon, and Charles Daubigny.

Barbuda, island in the West Indies (62 sq mi/160 sq km), located north of the Windward group and southeast of Puerto Rico. Antigua and Barbuda form an independent nation within the Leeward Islands. Barbuda's main product is sea-island cotton.

Barcarole, or barcarolle (from Italian for "boat"), traditional boat song or musical composition of the 18th or 19th century written in that style. Barcaroles were originally sung by gondoliers in Venice. Many European composers, including Frédéric Chopin, adapted the style for their own works. Sung or played primarily in 6/8 time, barcaroles were composed as opera arias and instrumental pieces for pianos, orchestras, and choruses.

Barcelona (pop. 1,643,500), Spain's largest seaport and second largest city after Madrid. It is situated on the Mediterranean coast, in northeastern Spain, on a broad plain dotted with hills, between the Besos and Llobregat rivers. Barcelona's wide range of industries includes shipbuilding, metalworking, food processing, the manufacture of chemicals, textiles (including silk), leather goods, and glass. Agricultural commodities such as wine, olive oil, and cork are exported, and raw materials such as coal, grain, and textile fibers pass through its port. The city was founded in the 3rd century B.C. by Carthaginians. It flourished in the Middle Ages as an economic center. In 1137 it united with Aragon. Except for two brief periods of French rule (1640, 1808-14), Barcelona has been under Spanish rule ever since. Among the city's principal landmarks are the cathedral (begun 1298, completed 1498) and the Church of the Holy Family, by Antonio Gaudi, begun in 1882 and still unfinished. The center of Catalan nationalism in modern times, Barcelona was the stronghold of left-wing politics and Republican allegiance in the Spanish Civil War. It is the planned host city for the 1992 Summer Olympic Games.
See also: Spain.

Bar code, identifying code consisting of dark and light bars, designed to be read by an optical viewer. The bar code contains information about a particular product and is used primarily for inventory control.

Bard, ancient Celtic minstrel. First written of around 200 B.C., the early bards were educated poets who wielded political power in Wales, Scotland, and Ireland. Through the Middle Ages they mainly composed eulogies to their noble patrons.

Bardeen, John (1908-91), U.S. physicist noted for his studies of transistors and superconductors. He shared the 1956 Nobel Prize for physics with W. H. Brattain and W. Shockley, doing much of the research in solid-state physics that led to the development of transistorized electronic equipment. In 1972 he became the first person to win a second Nobel Prize in the same field, sharing the award with L.P. Cooper and J.R. Schrieffer for the development of their theory of superconductivity.
See also: Superconductivity.

Barenboim, Daniel (1942-), Argentine-born Israeli pianist and conductor known for his musical interpretations of Beethoven. He made his debut at the age of 7 in Buenos Aires. From 1975 to 1989 he was music director of the Orchestre de Paris.

Barents, Willem (c.1550-97), Dutch navigator, for whom the Barents Sea is named. He made 3 voyages to the Arctic in search of a northeast passage to Asia.

Barents Sea, shallow arm of the Arctic Ocean north of Norway and European Russia, bounded by Svalbard (Spitsbergen) to the northwest, Franz Josef Land to the north, and Novaya Zemlya to the east. The southwestern portion is warmed by the North Atlantic Drift and remains ice-free in winter; on its southwestern coast lies the strategic Soviet port of Murmansk.
See also: Barents, Willem.

Barge dog *See:* Schipperke.

Bar Harbor (pop .4,120), village on Mount Desert Island, eastern Maine, on the Atlantic Ocean. First settled in 1763, Bar Harbor is a popular resort near the Acadia National Park.
See also: Maine.

Bari (ancient Barium; pop. 342,100), southern Italian port on the Adriatic Sea, capital of Bari province and of the Apulia region. The city is an important agricultural, commercial, and industrial center and also has a university. Bari is the site of the Fiera del Levante, an annual trade fair highlighting the city's role as center for commercial exchanges with the Balkan countries and the Middle East. In the old quarter are the cathedral, the Church of St. Nicola (begun 1087), and the 13th-century castle of Frederick II.
See also: Italy.

Barite *See:* Barium.

Barium, chemical element, symbol Ba; for physical constants see Periodic Table. Bar-

Barcelona, Plaza de Cataluña

ium, a soft, silvery white metal, was discovered by Sir Humphrey Davy in 1808. In nature it is found chiefly as *barite* or *heavy spar* (sulfate) or *witherite* (carbonate). Barium is produced by electrolysis of its chloride and is easily oxidized. Barium sulfate (*blanc fixe*) has good covering power and does not darken in the presence of sulfides. It is used in pigments and as a filler in paper, as well as in X-ray diagnostic work and glassmaking. Other compounds of barium are used in fireworks and rat poison. Soluble barium compounds are poisonous.

Bark, outer covering of the stems and branches of woody plants. The protective outer bark usually consists of cork, while the inner bark contains food-conducting phloem and the reproductive cells of the cork cambium. Bark is usually formed in annual rings, the outer layers bursting and splitting with each new growth. Bark helps to protect the tree from extremes of climate and from various pests and diseases. Some varieties of bark have medicinal uses, others are sources of textile fibers and dyes.

Christiaan Neethling Barnard

Bark beetle *See:* Dutch elm disease.

Barkley, Alben William (1877-1956), vice president of the United States (1949-53), under Harry Truman. A Democrat from Kentucky, Barkley served in the House of Representatives (1913-27) and the Senate (1927-49). He returned to the Senate in 1954.

Barlach, Ernst (1870-1938), German expressionist sculptor, graphic artist, and playwright whose figures in bronze and wood show Gothic and cubist influences. Barlach also produced many woodcuts and lithographs, some of them to illustrate his own writings. His war memorials and other works earned him fame in the 1920s, although he fell into disfavor under Hitler and his works were removed from museums.
See also: Gothic art and architecture.

The sculpture of Ernst Barlach is characterized by its intense expression of human emotions. This work is called The Reunion.

Barley, adaptable and hardy cereal plants (*Hordeum vulgare* and *Hordeum distichon*), of the grass family, cultivated since ancient times. The USSR is the largest producer, with Canada and the United States following. Over half of the world's crop is used for animal feed, and 10% is turned into malt.

Bar mitzvah, Jewish religious ceremony marking a boy's entrance into the adult community, traditionally performed at the age of 13. The initiate is usually called upon to read part of the weekly portion of the Pentateuch or the Prophets in the synagogue. The equivalent for girls, the bas (or bat) mitzvah, was established in 20th-century Reform and Conservative Judaism.
See also: Judaism.

Barnacle, marine crustacea of the subclass Cirripedia. The shell consists primarily of calcium carbonate. Adults attach themselves to solid surfaces (even the bodies of other sea animals) and trap plankton by means of feathery organs known as cirri. There are some 1,000 species.

Barnacle goose (*Branta leucopsis*), bird that breeds in the Arctic and winters in northern Europe and occasionally North America.

Barnard, Christiaan Neethling (1922-), South African surgeon who performed the first successful human heart transplant in Dec. 1967. His autobiography *One Life* was published in 1970.

Barnard, Edward Emerson (1857-1923), U.S. astronomer who discovered Amalthea, the fifth satellite of Jupiter (1892). In 1916 he discovered Barnard's star, a red dwarf only 6 light-years from the earth, with the largest known proper motion.
See also: Jupiter.

Barnard, Frederick Augustus Porter (1809-89), president of Columbia College (1864-89), which he helped transform into a great university; and advocate of higher education for women. Barnard College (founded 1889) bears his name.

Barnard, Henry (1811-1900), U.S. educator. Instrumental in the creation of the U.S. Office of Education and first U.S. commissioner of education (1867-70), he edited and published the *American Journal of Education* (31 vol., 1855- 81).

Barnburners, radical, antislavery faction of the New York State Democratic Party in the 1840s. When the 1847 State Democratic convention defeated their resolution opposing the extension of slavery into the western territories, the Barnburners left the party and later joined with the Free Soil Party, of which Martin van Buren was the unsuccessful presidential candidate in 1848. The Barnburners then disbanded, but in the 1850s many members joined the new, antislavery Republican Party.
See also: Free Soil Party.

Barnes, Djuna (1892-1982), U.S. poet, playwright, and novelist. Her works include a collection of stories and poems entitled *A Book* (1923) and the novels *Ryder* (1928) and *Nightwood* (1936).

Barnhart, Clarence Lewis (1900-), U.S. lexicographer, editor of the *American College Dictionary* (1947), the *New Century Cyclopedia of Names* (1954), and *The World Book Dictionary* (1963). He was influenced by the linguist Leonard Bloomfield and the educational psychologist Edward Lee Thorndike.
See also: Thorndike, Edward Lee.

Barn owl, common white owl (*Tyto alba*) useful as a destroyer of rodents. It grows to a length of about 18 in (46 cm), with a white face and cinnamon-dappled white breast. It nests in cliffs, hollow trees, and buildings. Its piercing scream is probably responsible for many tales of "haunted houses."

Barn swallow (*Hirundo rustica*), common North American bird. The upper parts of the wings and head are a metallic blue, the throat is chestnut brown, and the breast is white. Barn swallows eat insects harmful to crops.

Barnum, P(hineas) T(aylor) (1810-91), U.S. impresario, showman, and publicist. The hoaxes, freaks, and curiosities exhibited in his American Museum (founded 1841) in New York included the original Siamese twins and General Tom Thumb. In 1871 he opened his famous traveling circus, which in 1881 merged with James A. Bailey's show to become Barnum and Bailey's "Greatest Show on Earth." Today there is a Barnum Museum in Bridgeport, Conn., the city of his birth.
See also: Circus.

Barometer, instrument for measuring air pressure, used in weather forecasting and for determining altitude. Most commonly encountered is the aneroid barometer, in which the effect of the air in compressing a thin corrugated metal box is amplified mechanically and read off on a scale.
See also: Altimeter.

Baron, title of nobility in Europe, indicating a powerful man, especially a business magnate.

Baroque, European style of art and architecture, and by extension, music, that flourished from the early 17th to the mid-18th century. The style in art emphasized dramatic lighting, emotional portrayal of subjects, and the illusion of depth. The direct simplicity, apparent realism, and revolutionary painting technique of the Italian artist Michelangelo Caravaggio (1573-1610) helped to spread baroque art throughout Europe. The same effects were adapted to sculpture, as seen in the works of Giovanni Lorenzo Bernini (1598-1680), whose *Ecstasy of St. Theresa* (1646) has a softness and fluidity typical of the style. From Rome baroque art spread to Naples with Luca Giordano (1632-1705) and to Venice with Giovanni Piazetta (1683-1754) and Giovanni Battista Tiepolo (1696-1770). Outside Italy the baroque was modified by national tastes and traditions. In Holland, where life was dominated by a prosperous Protestant middle class, religious and mythological subjects gave way to portraits, still lifes, interior scenes, and landscapes. Frans Hals (1580-1666), Rembrandt van Rijn (1606-69), and Jan Vermeer (1632-1675) explored techniques of light effects. In Flanders, high baroque art was epitomized in the art of Peter Paul Rubens (1577-1640). In France Caravaggio's influence can be seen in the works of Georges de la Tour (1593-1652), Louis le Nain (1593-1648), and Nicolas Poussin (1594-1665). After 1680 the impact of Rubens, who was employed at the French court, is evident. In Spain important painters of the Baroque included the court painter Diego Rodriguez de Silva y Velazquez (1599-1660) and Bartolome Esteban Murillo (1617-1682).

Music of the early Baroque was characterized by simplicity; the florid style often identified as baroque did not appear in music until around 1700. The period began around 1600 in Italy with the invention of opera, originally an attempt to reproduce the declamation of classical Greek drama, best exemplified in the music of Claudio Monteverdi (1567-1643). The Baroque also saw the cultivation of virtuoso instrumental writing and the development of the concerto by Antonio Vivaldi (c.1675-1741) and others in Italy. In France, Jean Baptiste Lully (1632-87) composed orchestral ballet music; in England, Henry Purcell (c.1659-95) wrote theater works and George Frideric Handel (1685-1759), oratorios. In Germany, church composer and organ and harpsichord virtuoso Johann Sebastian Bach (1685-1750) perfected the fugue.

Barquisimeto (pop. 682,000), capital of Lara state in northwestern Venezuela, about 220 mi (354 km) southwest of Caracas, founded in 1552. It is the commercial and agricultural center of central and western Venezuela.

Barr, Alfred Hamilton, Jr. (1901-81), U.S. art historian. Barr directed New York's Museum of Modern Art, 1929-43, organizing some of the most important shows in the history of modern art. He wrote three contemporary classics: *Cubism and Abstract Art* (1936), *Picasso* (1946), and *Matisse* (1951).

Barracuda, predatory fish (family Sphyraenidae) found in warm seas. Barracudas have elongated, cigar-shaped bodies, long snouts, and sharp teeth. They strike automatically at any gleaming object.

Barras, Paul François Jean Nicolas, Vicomte de (1755-1829), French revolutionary. At first a Jacobin, in favor of Louis XVI's execution, he later became the most powerful member of the Directory (the revolutionary government) and aided Napoleon's rise to power. He was exiled after Napoleon's coup d'état of Brumaire (1799).
See also: French language.

Barrault, Jean-Louis (1910-), French actor, director, producer, and mime. He was with the Comédie Française 1940-46 and directed the Théâtre de France 1959-68. His most famous film role was that of the mime in *Les Enfants du Paradis* (1944).

Barrie, Sir James Matthew (1860-1937), Scottish playwright and novelist best known for *Peter Pan* (1904), his play about a boy who will not grow up. His works—including *The Admirable Crichton* (1902), *What Every Woman Knows* (1908), and *Dear Brutus* (1917)—range in tone from whimsy and sentimentality to satire and pathos.

Barrett, Elizabeth *See:* Browning, Elizabeth Barrett.

Barrier reef *See:* Coral; Great Barrier Reef.

Barrios, Justo Rufino (1835-85), president of Guatemala from 1873 until his death in 1885. A dictator, Barrios dreamed of a united Central America. He died in El Salvador fighting to achieve that goal by force.
See also: Guatemala.

Barron, James (1769-1851), U.S. Navy Commodore. In 1807, Barron was ordered by a British frigate to surrender several sailors suspected of being British deserters. After being fired upon and suffering casualties, he surrendered the suspects and was court-martialed and suspended for 5 years.

Barrow, Point, northernmost point on the North American continent, at the tip of Point Barrow Peninsula on the Arctic coast of Alaska, named for Sir John Barrow, 19th-century British geographer. The city of Barrow lies some 12 mi (19 km) south.

Barry, John (1745-1803), Irish-born naval hero of the American Revolutionary War, often called "Father of the American Navy." Commander of the frigate *Lexington*, he captured the first British warship taken in combat by a regularly commissioned American cruiser.
See also: Revolutionary War in America.

Barry, Philip (1896-1949), U.S. playwright, best known for popular drawing room comedies such as *Holiday* (1928) and *The Philadelphia Story* (1939).

Barrymore, name of a noted Anglo-American theatrical family. The father was the British actor Herbert Blythe (1847-1905), who adopted the stage name **Maurice Barrymore** and came to the United States in 1875, marrying actress Georgina Drew. **Lionel Barrymore** (1878-1954), their eldest child, became an outstanding stage, radio, and film actor, continuing to perform even after arthritis had confined him to a wheelchair. **Ethel Barrymore** (1879-1959), famous for her style and wit, gave many distinctive performances on stage and screen, winning an Academy Award for her supporting role in *None But the Lonely Heart* (1944). **John Barrymore** (1882-1942) was a distinguished interpreter of Shakespearean roles, particularly *Richard III* (1920) and *Hamlet* (1922). Later he became a popular and flamboyant film actor, nicknamed "the great profile."
His children **Diana Barrymore** (1921-60) and **John Barrymore, Jr.** (1932-) also became actors.

Barter, exchange of goods or services instead of money. Many primitive economies work on this system, and barter agreements are still common in international trade. During acute inflation when the value of money changes daily, a barter system may work better.

Barth, John (1930-), U.S. novelist known for his ironic style and use of comic and elaborate allegory. His best-known works include *The Sot-Weed Factor* (1960) and *Giles Goat-Boy* (1966). Other novels include *Sabbatical* (1982) and *The Tidewater Tales* (1987).

Barth, Karl (1886-1968), Swiss theologian, one of the most influential voices of 20th-century Protestantism. He taught in Germany 1921-35, was expelled by the Nazis, and spent the rest of his life in Basel. In his "crisis theology," Barth stressed revelation and grace and reemphasized the principles of the Reformation, initiating a movement away from theological "liberalism."
See also: Protestantism.

Barthelme, Donald (1931-), U.S. short-story writer and novelist noted for his innovative techniques and surrealistic style. His works include the novels *Snow White* (1967) and *The Dead Father* (1975); the children's book *The Slightly Irregular Fire Engine or the Hithering Thithering Djinn* (1971), for which he won a National Book Award; and *Sixty Stories* (1981).

Barthes, Roland (1915-80), French philosopher, literary critic, and theorist of semiology. His works include *Writing Degree Zero* (1953), *Mythologies* (1957), *A Lover's Discourse* (1978), and his autobiography, *Roland Barthes* (1975).

Bartholdi, Frédéric Auguste (1834-1904), French sculptor, creator of the Statue of Liberty. His other monumental works include *Lion of Belfort* at Belfort, France.

Bartholomew, Saint, one of the 12 apostles. According to tradition, he preached

the Gospel in Asia Minor and India and was martyred in Armenia.
See also: Apostles.

Bartlett, John (1820-1905), U.S. editor and publisher, best known for his *Familiar Quotations*, which has gone through more than a dozen editions since its first appearance in 1855.

Bartlett, Josiah (1729-95), U.S. politician, and a signer of the Declaration of Independence. Bartlett served in the second Continental Congress (1775-76 and 1778-79) and was later chief justice (1788-90) and governor (1790-94) of New Hampshire.
See also: Continental Congress.

Bartlett, Robert Abram (1875-1946), arctic explorer who commanded the *Roosevelt* for Robert E. Perry's 1905-09 expedition. In 1913 he led his own expedition. Bartlett explored Alaska in 1925, served the U.S. government during World War II, and wrote several books.

Basalt columns form the rock formation in Northern Ireland known as the Giant's Causeway.

Barton, Clara (1821-1912), founder of the American Red Cross (1881) and its first president (until 1904). She began a lifetime of relief work by organizing care and supplies for the wounded in the Civil War. On a trip to Europe (1869-73) she became involved in the activities of the International Red Cross, working behind German lines in the Franco-Prussian War. She was later influential in extending the range of the organization's relief work.
See also: Red Cross.

Bartram, 2 American naturalists, father and son. **John Bartram** (1699-1777) planted America's first botanical garden at Kingsessing, Pa., in 1728. **William Bartram** (1739-1823), famous for his book *Travels* (1791), based on his trips with his father in the southeast United States, inspired Wordsworth and Coleridge.

Béla Bartók

Bartók, Béla (1881-1945), Hungarian composer, one of the major figures of 20th-century music, also a virtuoso concert pianist and teacher at the Budapest Academy of Music (1907-34). In 1940 he emigrated to the United States.
His work owes much to the rhythmic and melodic vitality of Eastern European folk music, on which he was an authority. Bartók's major works include his six string quartets (1908-39), *Music for Strings, Percussion,* and *Celesta* (1936), and *Concerto for Orchestra* (1943).

Baruch, Bernard Mannes (1870-1965), U.S. financier and presidential economic adviser. He was chairman of the War Industries Board in World War I, adviser to F. D. Roosevelt in World War II, and U.S. delegate to the UN Atomic Energy Commission in the 1950s, proposing the "Baruch Plan" for international control of atomic energy.

Barye, Antoine Louis (1796-1875), French painter and sculptor who specialized in animal statues. His artwork is noted for its attention to detail. Barye also painted realistic landscapes.

Baryon, in particle physics, largest class of elemental particles, including protons, neutrons, and hyperons, also called "heavy particles" because of their relatively high mass.
See also: Atom.

Baryshnikov, Mikhail (1948-), Soviet-born U.S. dancer and choreographer. He was a soloist with the Kirov Ballet, Leningrad, from 1966 until 1974, when he defected to the West, joining the American Ballet Theatre and appearing there and with other companies in modern and classical ballets. He served as director of the American Ballet Theatre 1980-89.

Barytes *See:* Barium.

Basalt, dense rock formed by the solidification of lava. It underlies ocean floors and is the basis of most oceanic islands. Frequently dark in color, its main constituents are labradorite feldspar and pyroxene. Basalt strata usually consist of hexagonal columns produced by crystallization of the molten lava during a slow cooling process, as seen in the Palisades along the Hudson River, the Devil's Postpile National Monument, Calif., and the Giant's Causeway in Ireland.

Base, in chemistry, complement of an acid. Bases are often defined as substances that react with acids to form salts, or as substances that give rise to hydroxyl (OH^-) in aqueous solutions.
See also: Chemistry.

Baseball, outdoor team sport which derives its name from the 4 bases on the playing field. Called the "national pastime" in the United States, it is also popular in Japan, Latin America, and Canada. Invented, according to legend, by Abner Doubleday in Cooperstown, N.Y. in 1839, it appears rather to have evolved from the game of rounders which was played by New England colonists. Popular with Union troops during the Civil War, it was played nationally by the late 1880s.
Baseball is played on a large field between 2 opposing teams each consisting of 9 players: a pitcher, a catcher, 4 infielders, and 3 outfielders. The field consists of the infield, outfield, and foul territory. The infield is square, with a base at each corner—home plate, first, second, and third base. The foul lines extend from home plate past first base on one side and past third on the other, separating fair (infield and outfield) from foul territory. The pitcher's mound stands near the center of the infield. The outfield is the large area between the infield and the walls or fences farthest from home plate. While one team positions itself in the field, the other team bats. The pitcher, standing on the pitcher's mound, throws the small, hard ball (about 9 in/23 cm in circumference) over home plate, within an area between the batter's knees and shoulders (the strike zone)—sometimes at speeds over 90 mph (145 kmph). The batter attempts to hit the ball with the bat, a long rounded piece of wood or metal up to 42 in (107 cm) long and 2.75 in (7 cm) in diameter. A pitch outside of the strike zone is called a ball; 4 balls pitched to the batter allow the batter to "walk" to first base. A pitch counts as a strike if the batter fails to swing at a good pitch, swings and misses, or hits the ball foul (except when there are already 2 strikes); 3 strikes and a batter is out. If the ball is hit into fair territory, the batter runs to first base. The batter is out if the ball is caught without a bounce (fly), if it is thrown to first base before the batter gets there, or if the batter is "tagged" with the ball by a fielder. As new batters walk or get hits, earlier batters move around the bases. A batter reaching home plate scores a run. When 3 batters are out, the teams switch position. When each team has had a turn at bat, an inning is complete. A team wins by scoring the most runs within 9 innings. In the case of a tie, extra innings are added.
Players in the field wear padded leather gloves to catch the ball. All players wear shoes with spiked soles so they can start and stop quickly. Batters wear plastic batting helmets to avoid injuries. Catchers wear metal face masks, padded chest protectors, and shin guards. Most major league games have 4 umpires (game officials). The home plate umpire decides whether a pitch is a ball or a strike as well as whether runners attempting to reach home plate are safe or out. The other umpires rule on plays near as well as in the outfield.
There are 2 major baseball leagues; the American League (founded 1900), with 14 teams, and the National League (founded 1876), with 12. The teams in each league are divided into Eastern and Western Divisions. These teams play a 162-game schedule between April and September. The 2 divisional champions in each league meet in a playoff after the regular season, and the first team to win 4 games in each playoff is the league champion. The American and National League champions then play in the World Series. The first team to win 4 games in this series wins the world championship.
In addition to major and minor leagues, the game is played in amateur leagues and college and high school associations, as well as by neighborhood teams of all age groups. Originally restricted to boys, baseball is now played by girls as well.

Basel (pop. 174,600), second largest city in Switzerland, capital of the half-canton of Basel Stadt. The city is Switzerland's only river port, located on the Rhine, its major trans-European railhead, and one of its most important commercial, industrial, and financial centers. Situated at the junction of the French and German borders, Basel is a key distribution center for raw materials and manufactured products between northern and central Europe. The most important industries are chemical, electrical, and machine engineering.
Founded by the Romans, Basel joined the

Layout of a major league baseball field

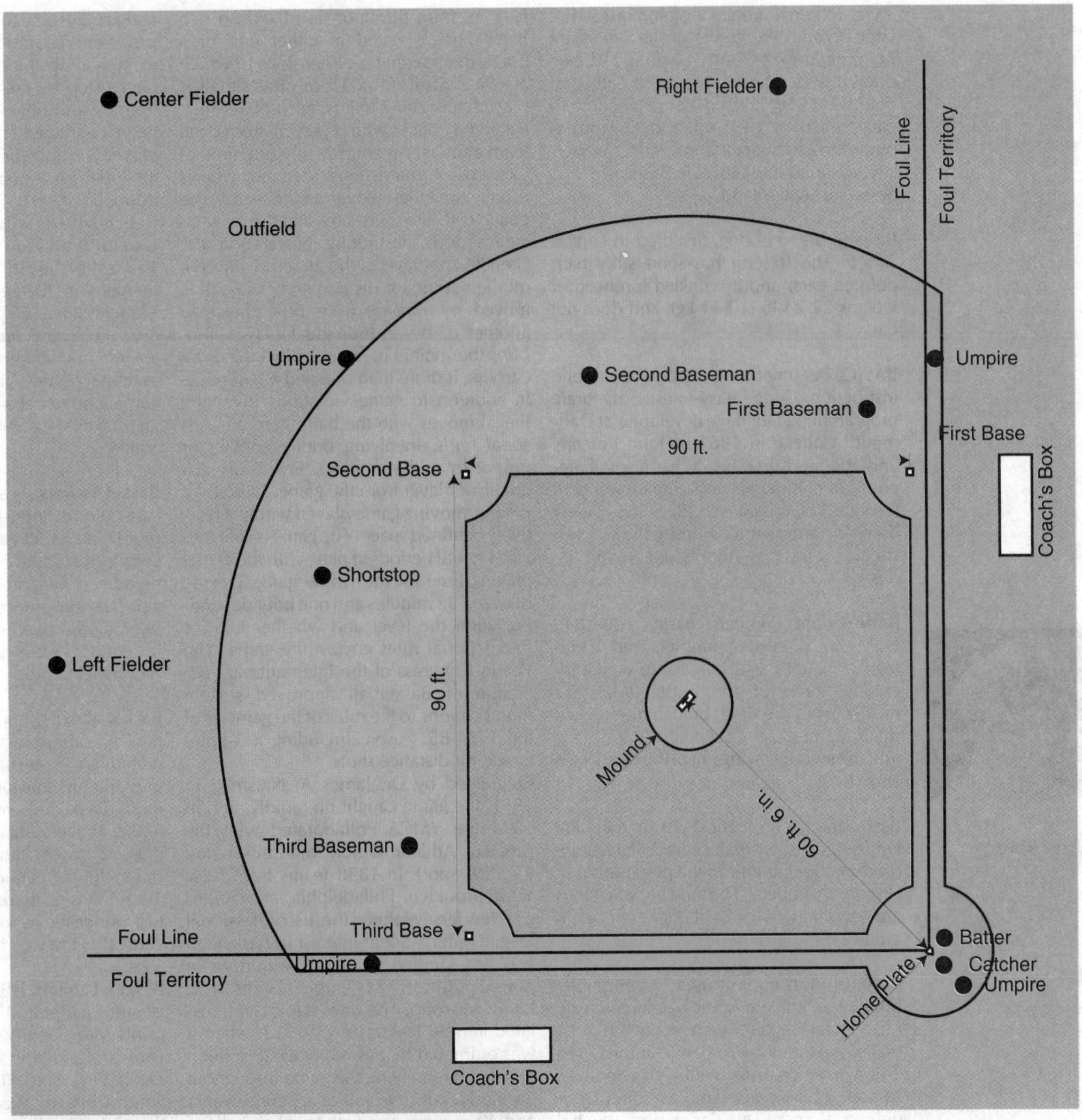

Center Fielder
Right Fielder
Foul Line
Foul Territory
Outfield
Umpire
Second Baseman
Umpire
First Baseman
First Base
90 ft.
Second Base
Coach's Box
Shortstop
Left Fielder
90 ft.
Mound
60 ft. 6 in.
Third Baseman
Third Base
Batter
Foul Line
Umpire
Catcher
Foul Territory
Home Plate
Umpire
Coach's Box

Rickey Henderson, all-time base-stealing record-holder, prepares to steal

4 ft.
4 ft.
17 in.
6 ft.
17 in.
6 ft.
8 ft.
3 ft.7 in.

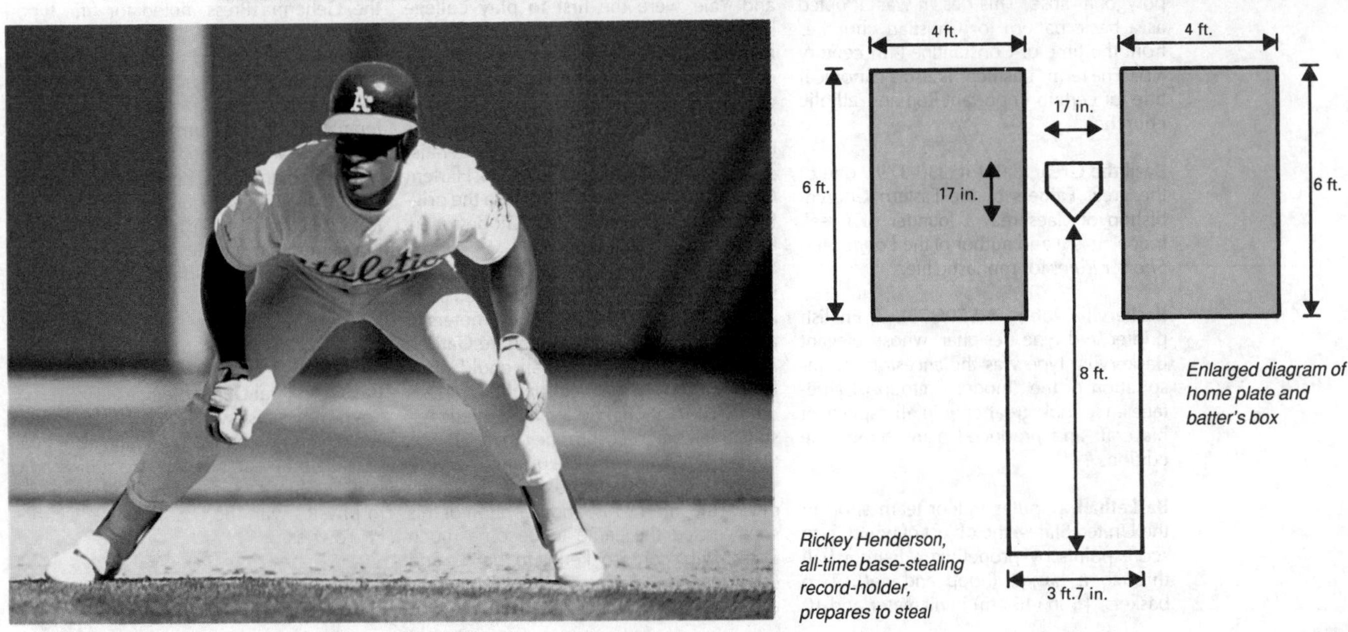

Enlarged diagram of home plate and batter's box

Swiss confederation as a canton in 1501. It later became the center of the Protestant Reformation, Luther's writings being printed here. The city's ancient cathedral (founded 1019) housed the great ecumenical council of 1431-48, and Erasmus is buried there. Switzerland's oldest university, founded in 1459, is in Basel.
See also: Switzerland.

Basenji, breed of dog, first bred in central Africa. The Basenji has short silky hair, pointed ears, and a wrinkled forehead. It weighs 22-24 lb (10-11 kg), and does not bark.

BASIC, Beginner's All-purpose Symbolic Instruction Code, easy-to-use, algebraic programming language developed at Dartmouth College in 1967 by John Kemeny and Thomas Kurtz. BASIC has a small repertory of commands and simple statement formats. For this reason, BASIC is widely used in programming instructions, personal computing, and business and industry.

Count Basie

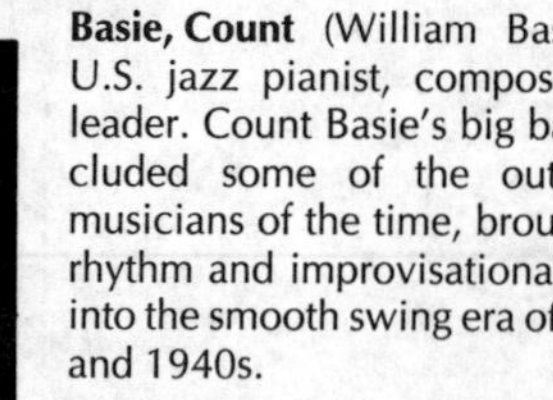

Basie, Count (William Basie; 1904-84), U.S. jazz pianist, composer, and bandleader. Count Basie's big band, which included some of the outstanding jazz musicians of the time, brought the ragged rhythm and improvisational verve of jazz into the smooth swing era of the late 1930s and 1940s.

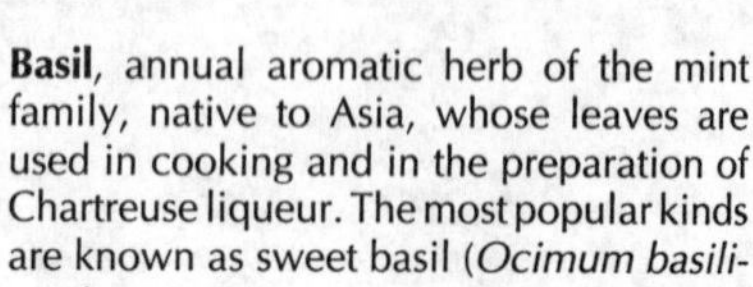

Basil, annual aromatic herb of the mint family, native to Asia, whose leaves are used in cooking and in the preparation of Chartreuse liqueur. The most popular kinds are known as sweet basil (*Ocimum basilicum*).

Basilica, in its earliest usage, large public building of ancient Rome of characteristic rectangular layout, with a central area (nave) separated by rows of columns from 2 flanking side aisles with high windows. At one or both ends was a semicircular or polygonal apse. This design was adopted as a basic pattern for Christian churches from the time of Constantine (4th century A.D.). The term "basilica" is also a canonical title for certain important Roman Catholic churches.

Basil the Great, Saint (c.330-379), one of the great Fathers of the Eastern Church, bishop of Caesarea, a founder of Greek monasticism and author of the *Longer* and *Shorter Rules* for monastic life.

Baskerville, John (1706-75), English printer and type designer, whose elegant Baskerville type was the ancestor and inspiration of the "modern" group of typefaces. He took great care in all aspects of his craft and produced many handsome editions.

Basketball, popular indoor team sport in the United States, the object of which is to score points by propelling a leather ball through a basket (hoop and net). Two baskets, 18 in (46 cm) in diameter and 10 ft (3 m) from the floor, are fixed on two backboards situated at either end of a court, the maximum dimensions of which are 94 x 50 ft (29 x 15 m). Basketball is played between 2 teams, each of 12 players and a coach, with 5 players from each team allowed on court at any one time (2 forwards, 2 guards, and a center, who is usually the tallest player on the team). The coach calls timeouts, advising the team on tactics and substituting players on the "bench" for players who are tired, injured, off their stride, or disqualified. The ball is moved by *passing* from one player to another or by an individual player *dribbling* (bouncing) it, never by kicking or by carrying it more than one and a half steps. In addition to game violations involving illegal moves with the ball, there are *personal fouls*, involving bodily contact or unsportsmanlike conduct. Five fouls disqualify a player from the game. Basketball is a fast-moving game played within a relatively confined space. The game is split into 2 or 4 equal periods of play, with the actual playing time for the whole game varying between 32 minutes and one hour depending upon the level and whether U.S. or international rules govern the game. The World Congress of the International Federation of Basketball approved several modifications to the rules of the game as of the 1984-85 season, including a 3-point basket for distance shots.
Originated by Dr. James A. Naismith in 1891, the game caught on rapidly, and in 1894 the YMCA collaborated with the Amateur Athletic Union in administering the new sport. In 1898 teams from New York, Brooklyn, Philadelphia, and Southern New Jersey formed the first professional league. International interest in basketball was first kindled by an exhibition game played at the 1904 Olympic Games in St. Louis, Missouri. The rules had been translated into 30 languages by 1913, when it was estimated that as many as 20 million people were playing the game throughout the world. The universities of Pennsylvania and Yale were the first to play college basketball, and in 1908 the National Collegiate Athletic Association was formed, establishing rules governing play in both colleges and secondary schools. The game was once dominated by New York's Celtics (1915-28), the all-black New York Renaissance (1923-40s), and the all-black Harlem Globetrotters (formed 1928). Like the original New York Celtics, the Globetrotters became an exhibition team.
Top-level college basketball was first brought to large audiences when Ned Irish, a sportswriter, convinced the promoters of athletic events at Madison Square Garden in New York that basketball could draw large crowds in a metropolitan sports arena. The National Collegiate Athletic Association championships began in 1939. A Stanford player, Hank Luisetti, demonstrated his *jump shot* to Eastern players during the late 1930s, and adoption of this shot caused the game to become much faster, with scores rocketing to the 70s and 80s. Despite many new rules designed to arrest this trend, scores have continued to rise as players become both taller and more proficient. The fast break and the technique of screening (blocking) to set up plays, backed up by tall centers to take the rebounds and other offensive tactics, have been countered by the use of player-to-player and zone defense. In 1949, the professional National Basketball League (formed in 1937) merged with the Basketball Association of America (organized in 1946). However, it was not until the 1970s that the NBA, expanded and after a merger with the new American Basketball Association (1967), became the solid crowd-drawing equivalent of professional leagues in other sports. Basketball is played in more countries than any other team ball game, and remains among the most popular player/spectator sports in the United States.

Basket Makers, prehistoric Native American culture flourishing in the Southwest more than 2,000 years ago. An agricultural people, the Basket Makers were the earliest members of a large group called the Anasazi. They developed a multi-storied dwelling called a pueblo; after about 700 A.D., the Anasazi were called the Pueblo.
See also: Pueblo.

Basket making, popular handicraft dating back to prehistoric times. It uses flexible materials to make utensils, primarily for the preparation, transportation, or storage of food. Two kinds of material are used to make baskets: hard material including grasses, leaves, and wood, and soft material including cotton, wool, and jute fiber. Two different strands are woven together to produce the basket: the warp strand runs vertically, the weft horizontally.

Baskin, Leonard (1922-), U.S. graphic artist and sculptor. His work includes the prints *Mid-Century Monster* and *The Poet Laureate* and the sculpture *Man with a Dead Bird*. Since 1953 he has taught at Smith College, Mass., where he founded the Gehenna Press, noted for fine typography.

Basking shark (*Cetorhinus maximus*), one of the largest living sharks, reaching a length of 45 ft (14 m). Found chiefly in temperate waters, the basking shark feeds only on plankton. The liver, a valuable source of oil, may account for a tenth of the total weight of the fish and provides the buoyancy that enables the shark to bask, motionless, on the surface.
See also: Shark.

Bas mitzvah *See:* Bar mitzvah.

Basov, Nikolai Gennadievich (1922-), Soviet physicist who, with his colleague Alexander Prokhorov, stated the principles of using molecular energy to amplify radio waves. They shared the 1964 Nobel Prize in physics with the U.S. physicist Charles H. Townes.

Basques, people of unique language and culture living mainly in the vicinity of the

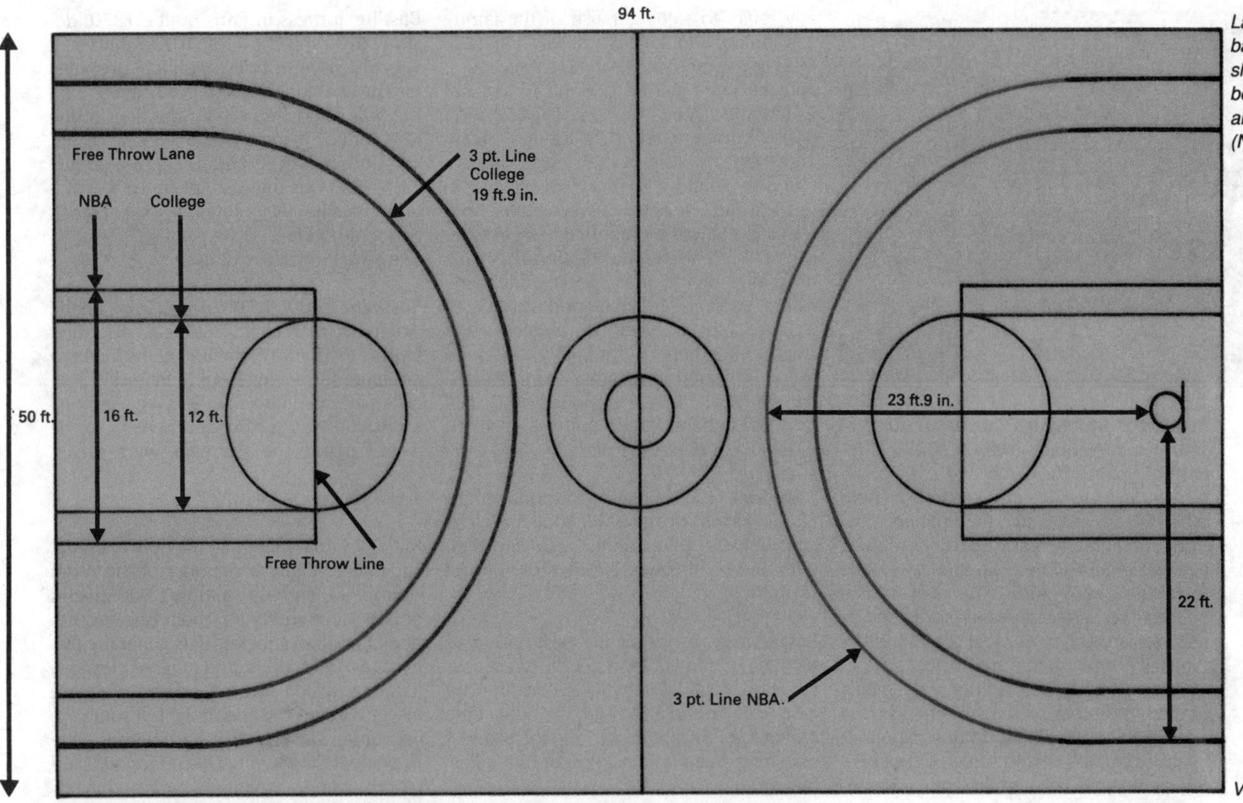

Layout of a basketball court, showing differences between collegiate and professional (NBA) measurements

View of basket area

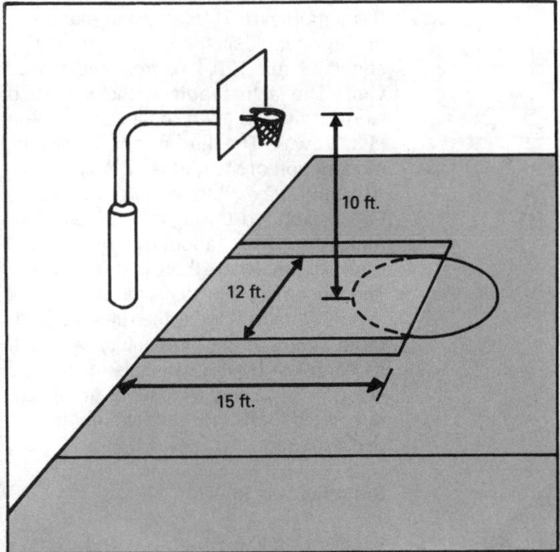

Kareem Abdul-Jabbar's skyhook and Michael Jordan on defense

The storming of the Bastille, July 14, 1789, is considered to be the beginning of the French Revolution. The Bastille, long used as a prison for political prisoners, became a symbol of political oppression.

Pyrennees Mountains (about 100,000 in southwestern France and 600,000 in northeastern Spain). Research into their blood groups indicates a long separation from other Europeans. After the Spanish Civil War, in which many Basques fought against General Franco, an effort was made to subdue the region. A surge of Basque nationalism in recent years was marked by the assassination of Admiral Luis Blanco by the Basque resistance movement ETA in 1973. In 1980 the Basques were given limited political self-determination by Spain by allowing the 3 Basque regions of Spain a parliament and some control over police, education, taxes, and other administrative procedures.

Basra (pop. 616.700), city and major port in Iraq, situated on the Shatt-al-Arab River, about 75 mi (120 km) from the Persian Gulf. The actual port is the suburb of Al'Ashr, the old town of Basra being 2 mi (3 km) away. The third part of Basra is the modern port of Ma'quil, 4 mi (6 km) above Ashr and accessible to seagoing vessels. Oil is exported through the pipeline terminus at Fao, about 4 mi (6 km) downstream, where there is also a refinery. The other main industry is the packing and export of dates. Under the rule of the Abbasid family in the 8th century, and until its conquest by the Mongols in the 13th century, Basra was a center of Arabic culture noted for its mosques and library.
See also: Iraq.

Bat

Bas relief *See:* Relief.

Bass, fish of the Serranidae and Centrarchidae families. In Europe the name usually refers to saltwater fish of the family Serranidae, popular as game fish and food. Most of them grow to 2 ft (60 cm) or more, and the giant sea bass found in tropical waters may exceed 7 ft (2 m). The European bass is common around the Mediterranean and Atlantic coasts, but related species are found in shallow tropical waters and in fresh water. In the United States and Canada, the name is applied to freshwater fish of the Centrarchidae family. The black bass, one of the most popular of game fishes, is found in lakes and streams of eastern North America. Sunfish, the smaller members of the family, are often found in aquariums. Other North American freshwater bass are spotted bass, rock bass, grass bass, largemouth bass, smallmouth bass, and silver bass.

Bass, Sam (1851-78), U.S. outlaw, the "Robin Hood" of Texas. He rode the West, first with the Joel Collins gang and then with one of his own. He died of gunshot wounds.

Bassae, site of one of the best-preserved temples of classical Greece, located near the ancient city of Phigalia in Arcadia. The temple of Apollo at Bassae was built at the end of the 5th century B.C. and its architect may have been Ictinus, builder of the Parthenon.

Bass drum *See:* Drum.

Basse-Terre (pop. 14,300), capital city of the French department of Guadeloupe in the Antilles islands in the Caribbean. Settled by the French in 1643, Basse-Terre is a transportation center exporting bananas, coffee, cocoa, and sugar.
See also: Guadeloupe.

Basset hound, short-legged, long, heavy-bodied, long-eared dog. Averaging 12-14 in (30-36 cm) in height and 45-60 lb (20-27 kg) in weight, the basset is a scent hound originally bred for hunting by the abbots of St. Hubert in France.

Bassoon, musical instrument, bass of the woodwind family, an 8-ft (2.4-m) conical tube bent double, with a double-reed mouthpiece, 8 holes, 20-22 keys, and a range of 3.5 octaves. Irrational key placement and an unstable pitch make it difficult to play.

Bass, or double bass, largest instrument of the violin family. Its form is less standardized than the other string instruments, but it usually stands about 6 ft (2 m) high and has 4 strings 42 in (108 cm) long and tuned in fourths. To increase its range a fifth low string is sometimes added. The strings are made of thick copper wire or steel cable. They are played with a bow.

Basswood, or linden, tree (genus *Tilia*) of the linden family that grows to 120 ft (37 m) in height and 3.5 ft (107 cm) in diameter. The basswood tree is valued for ornamentation and shade as well as for its soft wood and tough bark.

Bastille, fortress in Paris built c.1370, destroyed during the French Revolution. It was first used to house political prisoners by Cardinal Richelieu, in the 17th century, but was almost empty by the time of the Revolution. It remained a symbol of oppression, however, and its capture on July 14, 1789, was the first act of the Revolution. Bastille Day, July 14, is a French national holiday.
See also: French Revolution.

Bastogne (pop. 11,700), small town on the Ardennes plateau in southeast Belgium. During the Battle of the Bulge, the German counteroffensive of 1944 in World War II, an American division under Gen. Anthony McAuliffe was surrounded here for some weeks before the Germans were driven back.
See also: World War II.

Bat, nocturnal mammal, the only mammal capable of flight, a member of the order Chiroptera. There are almost 1,000 species of bats, accounting for about one-seventh of mammalian species. Bats generally live in caves, trees, roofs, and other enclosures, hanging upside down to sleep. Most are insectivorous (insect-eating), but some are vegetarian and yet others carnivorous—the 3 species of the family Desmodontidae are blood suckers, preying on birds and mammals. There are a few historical inaccuracies concerning the bat. It is not blind, it does not get tangled in hair, and it is not really aggressive. In fact, bats perform an important job by consuming insects and by depositing guano (manure), which can be used as fertilizer. Bats navigate their travel using high-frequency noises which they produce while in flight. These sounds create echoes that allow the animal to determine distance and direction, a method of navigation known as echolocation.

Bataan Peninsula, province of southwestern Luzon, the Philippines. A mountainous jungle region historically known as the last stronghold of U.S. and Philippine troops who held out 3 months against Japanese forces in 1942, during World War II. The prisoners were sent on a "death march" to a prison camp.
See also: Philippines; World War II.

Bates, Katharine Lee (1859-1929), U.S. author, best known for writing the lyrics of "America the Beautiful." She was a professor of English at Wellesley College and wrote children's literature.

Bateson, Gregory (1904-80), British-born U.S. anthropologist, best known for his study of New Guinea, *Naven* (1936; rev. 1958), and *Ecology of Mind* (1972). He wrote *Balinese Character* (1943) with his wife, Margaret Mead.

Batfish, beautifully colored marine fish of the family Ogcocephalidae, found in the Indian and Pacific oceans. Its highly compressed, almost circular body and long fins give it the appearance of a bat when swimming.

Bath (pop. 84,200), city in southwest England, on the River Avon near Bristol. Bath was founded by the Romans, who were attracted by the mineral hot springs there. In the 1700s Bath became a resort for English high society. During World War II many government services were moved there.

Bath, Order of the, British honor, established by George I in 1725 (supposedly based on an order founded in 1399). There are two divisions, military and civil, with three classes in each: knight grand cross (G.C.B.), knight commander (K.C.B.), and companion (C.B.).

Baths and bathing, historically, primarily religious, social, or pleasurable functions more often than hygienic ones. The Egyptians, Assyrians, and Greeks all used baths, but the Romans developed bathing as a central social habit, constructing elaborate public buildings, often ornately decorated and of enormous size. A Roman bath contained several rooms for disrobing, exercise, and entertainment, as well as bathing. Men and women bathed at separate times, except for one brief period in the 1st century A.D. The baths were tended by slaves. After the fall of the Roman Empire bathing declined in popularity in Europe, though it did survive as a part of monastic routine, in Jewish ritual, and in Muslim countries. In Russia and Turkey the steam bath became popular. The crusaders brought steam bathing back with them from the Middle East, but an association with immorality caused it to fall into disrepute. In the 18th century it became fashionable to spend a season at a watering- place, such as Bath, England, but only 19th-century research into hygiene made a virtue of bathing, often with primitive and usually portable cold baths at schools and institutions. Only after World War I did plumbing and bathtub production allow the bath to become a permanent installation in the home.

Bathsheba, in the Bible, wife of King David and mother of Solomon. David married Bathsheba after arranging the death of her husband, Uriah the Hittite (2 Samuel 11, 12; 1 Kings 1-20).
See also: Bible.

Bathyscaph, submersible deep-sea research vessel, invented by Auguste Piccard in the late 1940s, comprising a small, spherical, pressurized passenger cabin suspended beneath a cigar-shaped flotation hull. Before dives most of the flotation tanks in the hull are filled with gasoline, the rest with air. For dives, the air is vented and seawater takes its place; seawater is allowed to enter the gasoline-filled tanks from the bottom, compressing the gasoline and increasing the density of the vessel. To begin descent, iron ballast is jettisoned. As the vessel rises, the gasoline expands, expelling water from the flotation tanks, thus lightening the vessel further and accelerating the ascent. Battery-powered motors provide the vessel with a degree of submarine mobility.

Batik, dyeing technique in which the portions of material not to be colored are covered with wax before the fabric is dipped into dye. After the dye is dry, the wax is removed by boiling and, if necessary, the procedure is repeated for each new dye. It is an ancient Indonesian technique, introduced into Europe by Dutch traders and now also used in Africa. Imperfections caused by the breaking or melting of the wax surface are responsible for much of the accidental effect that gives batik work its character.

Batista y Zaldívar, Fulgencio (1901-73), Cuban military dictator. Becoming army chief of staff after the overthrow of the Machado government in 1933, he appointed and deposed presidents at will. He was himself president 1940-44, and took the title permanently in 1952. After his overthrow by Fidel Castro in 1959 he lived in exile in Spain.
See also: Cuba, Republic of.

Bat mitzvah *See:* Bar mitzvah.

Baton Rouge (pop. 528,264), capital of Louisiana, situated on the Mississippi River. A deepwater port and regional trade center, the city also has major oil refineries and petrochemical and aluminum factories. Founded by the French in 1719, Baton Rouge was later transferred to the British and was occupied by the Spanish from 1779. U.S.-born citizens rebelled against Spanish rule and established their independence at the battle of Baton Rouge on Sept. 23, 1810. Acquired by the United States in 1815, the city was incorporated in 1817 and became the state capital in 1849. Louisiana State University and Agricultural and Mechanical College and Southern University are both located there.
See also: Louisiana.

Battenberg, name of princely family of Germany. **Prince Alexander of Battenberg** (1857-93) was prince of Bulgaria 1879-86. **Prince (Louis) Alexander of Battenberg** became a British subject, joined the Royal Navy, married the granddaughter of Queen Victoria, and changed his name to Mountbatten in 1917.

Battering ram, ancient war machine used to break down walls and doors. Used by the Assyrians and by Alexander the Great, it was made of a beam of heavy timber with a metal tip and survived as a weapon until the 1400s, when it was replaced by the cannon.

Battery, device for converting internally stored chemical energy into direct-current electricity. The term is also applied to various other electricity sources, including the solar cell and the nuclear cell, but is usually taken to exclude the fuel cell, which requires the continuous input of a chemical fuel for operation.
See also: Electric circuit; Fuel cell.

Battle Creek (pop. 135,982), city in southern Michigan, famous as a health and sports center. John Harvey Kellogg, associated with the breakfast cereal company that bears his name, was a principal founder of the Battle Creek Health Center. The city is the world's leading producer of breakfast cereal and also produces automobile parts, electrical equipment, and machinery.
See also: Michigan.

Battleford (pop. 3,800), historic town in Saskatchewan, Canada, now a grain depot, manufacturing town, and site of the Battleford Historic Park and Fred Light Museum. Battleford was the capital of the Northwest Territories (1876-83) and of the district of Saskatchewan (1882-1905).
See also: Saskatchewan.

Battle Hymn of the Republic, U.S. patriotic song, unofficial hymn of Union troops in the Civil War. Written in 1861 by Julia Ward Howe and sung to the tune of "John Brown's Body," it later became a Protestant hymn and a protest marching song.
See also: Howe, Julia Ward.

Battle of *See:* Battles are listed under the key word, as in *Antietam, Battle of.*

Battleship, historically the largest of conventionally armed warships. Aircraft carriers superseded them during World War II as the largest fighting ships afloat. The largest battleship now is the USS *New Jersey*, with a full-load displacement of 59,000 tons (59,100 metric tons) and an overall length of 887 ft (309 m). The USS *Massachusetts* is now a floating marine museum in Fall River, MA.

Batu Khan (d. 1255 A.D.), Mongol conqueror of Russia, grandson of Genghis Khan. He ruled the westernmost part of the Mongol Empire and threatened eastern Europe from 1235 to 1242. He founded the khanate of the Golden Horde that ruled southern Russia for 200 years, isolating it from western European developments.
See also: Mongol Empire.

Baud, in computer technology, one bit per second. In general, the rate at which data is transmitted.
See also: Computer.

Baudelaire, Charles Pierre (1821-67), French poet and critic, forerunner of the Symbolists. The poems in *Les Fleurs du Mal* (*The Flowers of Evil*, 1857), with their probing of even the most bizarre sensations, outraged public opinion and led to the poet's being tried for obscenity. His later prose poems were posthumously published in *Le Spleen de Paris* (1869). He was also a critic of music and fine art, and was renowned for his translations of Edgar Allen Poe.

Baudot, Emile *See:* Telegraph.

Baudouin (1930-), fifth king of the Belgians. He spent World War II with his family in Nazi internment, and succeeded his father, King Leopold III, who abdicated

Bauxite ore was discovered in 1821 by the French chemist Paul Perthier near Les Baux in the south of France.

in 1951. In 1960 Baudouin proclaimed Congolese independence. He married a Spanish noblewoman, now Queen Fabiola.
See also: Belgium.

Bauhaus, school of design and architecture in the 20th century. Founded by Walter Gropius in 1919 at Weimar, Germany, its teachers included some of the leading artists of the time. Gropius's ideal of uniting form with function is now a universal canon of design, and the dictum "less is more" has influenced much U.S. design. The Bauhaus left Weimar in 1925 and was installed in new premises designed by Gropius in Dessau in 1927. The school was closed by the Nazis in 1933. Bauhaus teachers Gropius, Lyonel Feininger, and Ludwig Mies van der Rohe later moved to the United States.
See also: Gropius, Walter.

Baum, Lyman Frank (1856-1919), U.S. children's writer, author of 14 Oz books, including *The Wonderful Wizard of Oz* (1900), a tale of a girl carried by a cyclone to a land of adventure. The 1939 film adaptation became a motion-picture classic.

Baumfree, Isabella *See:* Truth, Sojourner.

A bayonet carried by a French soldier (c. 1760).

Bausch, name of U.S. family involved in the optical industry. **John Jacob Bausch** (1830-1926) founded Bausch and Lomb Optical Company in 1853. His 3 sons joined the company in 1875.

Bauxite, ore consisting of hydrated aluminum oxide, usually with iron oxide; the main source of aluminum. It is a claylike, amorphous material formed by the weathering of silicate rocks, especially under tropical conditions. Bauxite is used as a lining for furnaces, and is an ingredient in some quick-setting cements. Leading bauxite-producing countries include Jamaica, Australia, USSR, Suriname, Guyana, France, and the United States.
See also: Aluminum.

Bavaria (German: *Bayern*), southwest state in Germany. Its area is 27,239 sq mi (70,549 sq km) and its population exceeds 12 million. Munich is the capital and administrative center, and the site of most of the state's industry. Forestry and agriculture are also important in Bavaria. The region's borders have often changed, and it has seen many rulers, including the Romans in the 6th century B.C. and Charlemagne in the 9th century A.D. Bavaria became a kingdom in 1805 and a part of Germany in 1871. Following World War I it was a short-lived republic and then part of Germany again. After World War II Bavaria was part of West Germany.
See also: Germany.

Bavarian Succession, War of the *See:* Succession wars.

Bay, inlet of water formed along the coastline of an ocean or lake. Examples include Hudson Bay, and the Bay of Bengal.

Bayard, family name of politicians, statesmen, and U.S. senators from Delaware. **James Asheton Bayard** (1767-1815) served in the U.S. House of Representatives from 1797 to 1803 and as a U.S. senator from 1805 to 1813. His two sons, **Richard Henry** (1796-1868) and **James Asheton** (1799-1880), and his grandson, **Thomas Francis** (1828-98), also represented Delaware in the U.S. Senate. Thomas Francis Bayard served as secretary of state from 1885 to 1889 and was U.S. ambassador to Britain from 1893 to 1897. His son, also named **Thomas Francis** (1868-1942), served in the U.S. Senate in the 1920s.

Bayberry (Myricaceae), any of a family of trees and shrubs found in temperate and subtropical climates. The North American bayberry shrub (*Myrica pennsylvanica*) is found along the eastern coast from North Carolina to Nova Scotia. The waxy fruit of some species is used to make candles, scented soaps, sealing wax, and cosmetics.

Bay Colony *See:* Massachusetts.

Baylor, Elgin (1934-), U.S. basketball player and coach. Baylor, a 6 ft 5 in (196 cm) forward, played on the Los Angeles (formerly Minneapolis) Lakers of the National Basketball Association (NBA) from 1958 to 1971 and is considered one of the best all-around players in history. His achievements include being named NBA Rookie of the Year (1958-59), and scoring 71 points in a game (1960). Baylor was head coach for the New Orleans Jazz (1976-1979), and is director of basketball operations for the Los Angeles Clippers (1986-).

Bay of Bengal, wide arm of the Indian Ocean between India and Ceylon on the west, and Burma on the east. In the north, along the coast of Bangladesh, the sea is shallow because vast quantities of silt are brought down by the rivers. Further south the depth increases to a maximum of 13,020 ft (3,968 m).
The winds and surface sea currents vary with the prevailing monsoon: clockwise with the northeast monsoon and counterclockwise with the southwest monsoon. In October particularly, at the change of monsoon, very severe storms occur. The important rivers flowing into the bay are the Ganges, Brahmaputra, Godavari, Kistna, and Cauvery.
See also: Indian Ocean.

Bay of Biscay, section of the Atlantic Ocean adjoining northern Spain and part of the west coast of France. The name is a corruption of "Vizcaya," the term used by the Basques, an ethnic group populating northern Spain and southern France.
See also: Atlantic Ocean.

Bay of Fundy, funnel-shaped inlet of the Atlantic Ocean between New Brunswick and Nova Scotia in Canada. It is known for having the highest tides in the world, reaching up to 50 ft (15 m) in some parts.
See also: Atlantic Ocean.

Bay of Pigs, English name for Bahia de Cochinos (southwestern Cuba), scene of an abortive invasion of Cuba on April 17, 1961. The invaders were Cubans who had fled to the United States after Fidel Castro seized power. Although U.S. citizens were not directly involved, the CIA helped plan the invasion. The invasion was a political disaster for President Kennedy, who had approved the operation.

Bayonet, stabbing or thrusting weapon that may be fitted at the muzzle of a rifle without preventing normal firing. Usually consisting of a straight tapering blade, but sometimes a sabre or cutlass, it is used in close combat.

Bayonne (pop. 61,444), city and port in New Jersey, about 7 mi (11 km) southwest of New York City. Located on a penninsula between Newark Bay and New York Bay, it is a busy commercial port with 9 mi (14 km) of docks and large oil refineries. Other industries include the manufacture of chemicals, textiles, and electronic instruments.
See also: New Jersey.

Bayou, shallow, slow-moving creek or water channel running into a lake or a river. The word is Louisiana French, probably derived from the Choctaw (Native American) *bayuk.*

Bay Psalm Book, *The Whole Booke of Psalmes Faithfully Translated into English Metre*, first book printed in colonial America. Published in Cambridge, Mass., in 1640 as a hymnal for the Massachusetts Bay Colony, it was the work of Richard Mather, John Eliot, and Thomas Weld, and was printed by Stephen Day.

Bayreuth (pop. 71,800), industrial city in northeastern Bavaria, Germany. It is famous as the last home of Richard Wagner and as the site of his opera house, the Festspielhaus. The Bayreuth festivals, held each summer since 1876, feature Wagner's music.
See also: Wagner, Richard.

Bazooka, portable rocket launcher constructed from a smooth-bore steel tube 5 ft (1.5 m) long and open at both ends. Two people operate it: The midpoint of the tube rests on the shoulder of one person, who aims and fires the weapon while the other person loads the rockets.

BBC *See:* British Broadcasting Corporation.

B.C., "Before Christ" in the Christian (and now generally Western) system for dating events, developed by the monk Dionysius Exiguus and based on the time he believed Christ to have been born. The year of Christ's birth is considered the year 1, and the higher the number, the earlier the event. The year 100 B.C., for instance, was the year before 99 B.C. Events in the years after the birth of Christ are designated A.D. (for the Latin *Anno Domini*, "in the year of our Lord"). The expressions B.C.E. ("Before

Bauhaus group picture showing (from left to right): Josef Albers, Hinnerk Scheper, Georg Musche, Laszlo Moholy-Nagy, Herbert Bayer, Joost Schmidt, Walter Gropius,(with hat in center), Marcel Breuer, Vassily Kandinsky, Paul Klee, Lionel Feininger, Gunta Stolz, and Oskar Schlemmer.

Herbert Bayer, first a pupil and later a teacher of typography at the Bauhaus, designed this poster announcing a lecture by the German architect Hans Poelzig (New York, Museum of Modern Art).

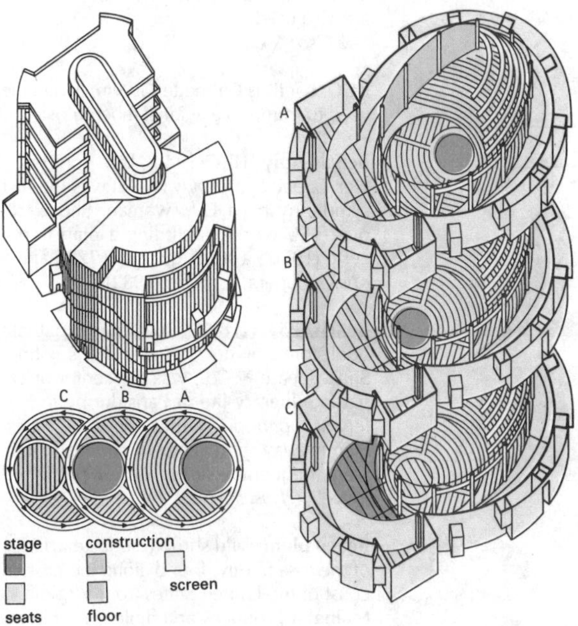

Walter Gropius designed the Total Theater in 1927 to create a flexible theater in which the audience is drawn into the drama. The stage and the surrounding seats could be revolved, even during a performance, with stage settings created primarily by projection of film and lights. The three possible positions shown create (A) a central arena, (B) a classical Greek theater, and (C) a standard theater with the stage at one end.

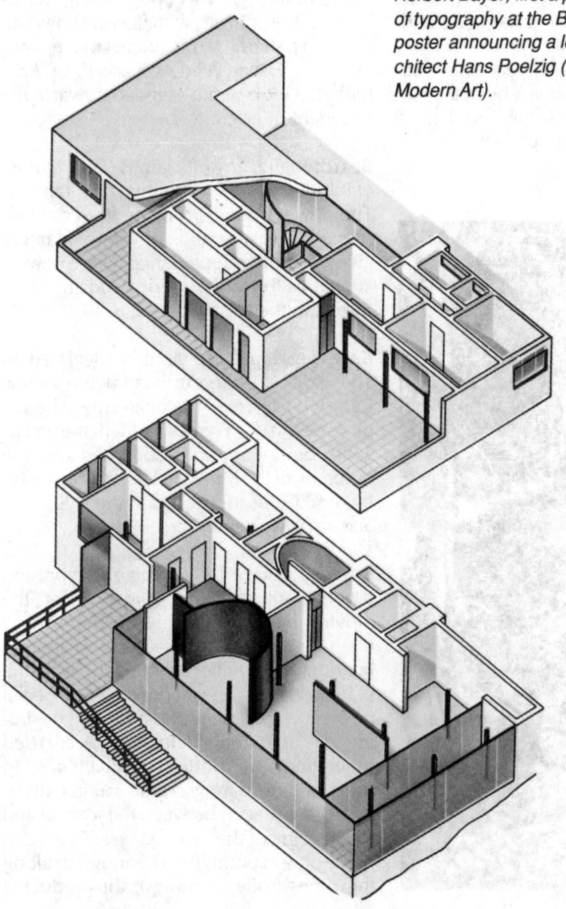

(Left) The concrete-surfaced Tugendhat House at Brno, Czechoslovakia (1930) was the last and most important European house designed by Mies van der Rohe. It particularly illustrates the made-to-measure house, with an innovative large living room area partially subdivided to fulfill various functions.

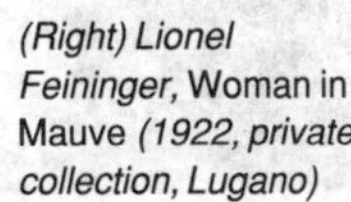

(Right) Lionel Feininger, Woman in Mauve *(1922, private collection, Lugano)*

the Common Era") and C.E. ("Common Era") are also used.
See also: A.D.

BCG, bacillus Calmette-Guérin, a vaccine used to immunize against tuberculosis.

Beach, Amy (1867-1944), U.S. composer. Her *Gaelic Symphony* (1896) was the first symphony by a U.S. woman. She wrote over 150 works, including a piano concerto (1900), a string quartet (1929), and a one-act opera, *Cabildo* (1932).

Beach, Sylvia (1887-1962), U.S. expatriate bookstore owner whose Paris shop, Shakespeare & Co., was the center of expatriate literary life in Paris during the interwar period. James Joyce, Ernest Hemingway, and other important writers were frequent visitors. Beach published Joyce's *Ulysses* (1922).

Beach plum, wild shrub (*Prunus maritima*) of the rose family, found along the eastern coast of the United States from Virginia to Maine. It produces an edible fruit, resembling a small plum, used in sauces, preserves, jellies, and pies.

Beacon, originally a warning sign or signal, for example, a fire kindled at a prominent point on the coast to warn of the approach of hostile fleets.

Beaconsfield, Earl of *See:* Disraeli, Benjamin.

Beaded lizard (*Heloderma horridum*), poisonous lizard found in Mexico, close relative of the Gila monster. It is slow-moving, with small bead-like scales and markings of alternate black and pink-orange rings, and has hooked, grooved teeth. Glands along the inside of the lower lip secrete poison.

Beads, term derived from the Saxon word *biddan*, meaning to pray. Primitive beads were made of seeds, pierced shells, teeth, and stone; later materials ranged from semiprecious stones to gold and silver. Beads have been used by humans since before history. Magical properties were assigned to them, such as the promotion of fertility and the ability to guard against evil spirits. They were often exported over vast distances by explorers for trade.

Beagle, small, short-legged hound originally bred for hunting hares. There are 2 breeds of beagle in the United States. The larger grows up to 15 in (38 cm) tall, the smaller up to 13 in (33 cm). Beagles weigh from 20 to 40 lb (9-18 kg).

Beagle *See:* Darwin, Charles Robert.

Beaked whale, any of various medium-sized toothed whales whose snouts are narrow and pointed. They feed mainly on cuttlefish and generally have 2 or 4 teeth protruding from the lower jaw. There are 15 species living in all seas.

Bean, any plant of the pulse family (especially genus *Phaseolus*), also called legumes, cultivated for its edible seeds, immature pods, or shoots. The high protein content of beans, and especially of soybeans, make them a staple item in the diets of many peoples as well as an important animal feed. Soybeans are also used for a growing range of industrial products including adhesives, plastics, and firefighting foam.

Bean, Roy (1825?-1903), U.S. justice of the peace who called himself "the only law west of the Pecos." After an early life that included arrest, jailbreak, and proprietorship of tent saloons, he settled in western Texas, where he built a combination store, saloon, and pool hall, and held court as justice and coroner. His decisions were more notable for six-gun drama and humor than legal sagacity.

Bean beetle, insect (*Epilachna varivestis*) of the order of beetles (Coleoptera), and the ladybug family (Coccinellidae). A serious pest to bean plants in Mexico, the bean beetle was accidentally introduced into Alabama around 1920, and later spread through the central and eastern United States and southern Canada.

Bean curd *See:* Tofu.

Bear, large mammal (family Ursidae), usually omnivorous, characterized by heavy build, thick limbs, small tail, and small ears. All have coarse thick hair which is, with the exception of the polar bear, dark in color. Species include the brown bear, the North American black bear, the spectacled bear, the Asiatic black bear, the sun bear, and the sloth bear. The Kodiak, a brown bear, is the largest, up to 9 ft (2.7 m) tall and 1,600 lb (730 kg).

The black bear is one of the great attractions of the national parks in Canada and the United States.

Beard, Charles and **Mary**, U.S. authors and historians who coauthored seven books, the best-known being *The Rise of American Civilization* (2 vols, 1927) and its sequels. **Charles Austin Beard** (1874-1948) taught history and political science at Columbia University from 1904 to 1917, when he resigned to protest U.S. participation in World War I. The author of more than 70 books, his most controversial was *An Economic Interpretation of the Constitution* (1913), in which he argued that the U.S. Constitution reflected the economic interests of its authors. **Mary Ritter Beard** (1876-1958), an author and leader of the women's rights movement, focused on the historical role of women.

Beard, Daniel Carter (1850-1941), painter, illustrator, and organizer of the Boy Scouts of America. As National Scout Commissioner (1910-41), he gave the movement its distinctly American character, based on Indian and pioneer lore.
See also: Boy Scouts.

Bearded collie, breed of dog distinguished by a beardlike growth of hair around its mouth. Bred in Scotland as a sheep and cattle herder, the bearded collie is a popular farm pet. It stands 20-25 in (51-56 cm) tall and weighs about 60 lb (27 kg).

Beardsley, Aubrey Vincent (1872-98), English illustrator and author. By 1894 Beardsley had become art editor of the *Yellow Book* magazine and a prolific artist. His graphic style was one of sharp black-and-white contrasts, with flowing lines and detailed patterning; his subject matter—for instance, Oscar Wilde's *Salomé*, or Aristophanes' *Lysistrata*—tended toward the decadent or erotic.

Beardtongue, any of a genus (*Pentstemon*) of tubular flowers containing five stamens. The flower derives its name from the fifth stamen, whose strands of yellow filament give a beardlike appearance. These flowers are native to North America and are widespread in the United States.

Bear Flag Republic, republic declared in 1846 by U.S. settlers in Sacramento Valley, Cal., who rejected Mexican rule. The explorer John C. Fremont aided the insurgents, but the republic collapsed after the outbreak of the Mexican War in May 1846. In 1848 California ceded to the U.S.
See also: Mexican War.

Bearing, device to minimize friction and provide support and guidance for the moving parts of a machine. There are 2 main types of bearings—plain or journal bearings, and ball or roller bearings. In the plain bearing, a sheath lined with a special metal is clamped around a turning or sliding axle or journal. Plain bearings are used in engines and industrial machines. In roller or ball bearings, small round balls or rollers are placed between the journal and the housing of the bearing case. Contact is made only at points (ball bearings) or along thin lines (roller bearings), thus reducing friction to a minimum. Ball bearings are used mainly with revolving axles such as those of cars. Roller bearings are used to carry heavy loads at relatively slow speeds. Bearings were first used in Egypt to move blocks of stone from quarries to build palaces and pyramids.

Bears and bulls, popular terms for stock and commodity investors of opposing views of market prospects. Bulls believe that stock prices will rise, bears that they will fall. Bulls therefore buy, where bears seek to sell, either to prevent a loss or to buy back at lower prices. Rising stock values are therefore referred to as a bullish market, while falling ones constitute a bearish market.
See also: Commodity exchange.

Beat generation, U.S. literary movement of the 1950s, exemplified by Jack Kerouac's *On the Road* (1956), the adventures of the original social dropout, Allen Ginsberg's long poem *Howl*, and work by such poets as Lawrence Ferlinghetti and Gregory Corso, and by novelist William S. Burroughs. The movement, a protest against complacent middle-class values, was short-lived, but influenced artistic experiments for the next 15 years.
See also: Kerouac, Jack.

Beatitudes, in the New Testament, 8 blessings pronounced by Jesus as a prologue to the Sermon on the Mount (Matthew 5:3-10), in which he calls "blessed" those who are poor in spirit, the meek, those who mourn, those who seek after holiness, the merciful, the pure in heart, the peacemakers, and those who suffer persecution for righteousness' sake.
See also: New Testament.

Beatles, English rock music group that dominated popular music in the 1960s. Guitarists and composers **John Lennon** (1940-80), **Paul McCartney** (1942-), and **George Harrison** (1943-), and drummer **Ringo Starr** (Richard Starkey; 1940-), won fame in Britain with their recording "Please Please Me" (1963). The 1964 song "I Want to Hold Your Hand" introduced them to the United States, where their concerts became scenes of mass adulation. *Revolver* (1966) and *Sgt. Pepper's Lonely Hearts Club Band* (1967) are ranked among their finest albums. The group disbanded in 1970. John Lennon's murder by a demented fan in New York City (December 1980) caused mourning around the world.
See also: Lennon, John; McCartney, Paul.

Beaton, Sir Cecil Walter Hardy (1904-80), English photographer and designer, known for his royal portraits, collections such as *Cecil Beaton's Scrapbook* (1937), and set and costume designs for shows and films such as *My Fair Lady* (stage, 1956; motion picture, 1964).

Beatrix (1938-), queen of the Netherlands (1980-), following the abdication of her mother, Juliana.
See also: Netherlands.

Beauchamp, Kathleen *See:* Mansfield, Katherine.

Beaufort scale, scale from 0 to 12 used to measure the force of wind. An 8 on the scale signifies a gale and a 12 a hurricane.
See also: Wind.

Beauharnais, Joséphine de (1763-1814), first wife of Napoleon I and empress of France. Her first husband, General Alexandre, Vicomte de Beauharnais, was guillotined in the Reign of Terror. Their son, Eugène de Beauharnais (1781-1824), was made viceroy of Italy by Napoleon. He distinguished himself in campaigns against Austria and Russia.

Beaumarchais, Pierre Augustin Caron (1732-99), French dramatist and variously an artist, litigant, and political agent. His best-known plays, *The Barber of Seville* (1775) and *The Marriage of Figaro* (1784), the basis of operas by Rossini and Mozart, ridiculed the established order and the nobility. He was instrumental in furnishing the Americans with arms and money at the outbreak of their Revolution.

Beaumont (pop. 361,226), city and major oil-refining center in east Texas, seat of Jefferson County. Beaumont was the first petroleum boom town in the United States, expanding rapidly after the first gusher, in 1901.
See also: Texas.

Beaumont, Francis (1584-1616), English Jacobean playwright. He is best known for his collaborations with John Fletcher, although Beaumont is probably the sole author of *The Woman Hater* (1607) and *The Knight of the Burning Pestle* (1607?). Beaumont and Fletcher's works include *Philaster* (1608), *The Maid's Tragedy* (1609), and *A King and No King* (1611).
See also: Fletcher, John.

Beaumont, William (1785-1853), U.S. army physician noted for his research on the human digestive system. He treated a trapper with a gunshot stomach wound; when the abdomen wouldn't close, Beaumont conducted experiments over several years to analyze the digestive process.
See also: Digestive system.

Beauregard, Pierre Gustave Toutant de (1818-93), Confederate general of the U.S. Civil War. In 1861 Beauregard commanded the attack on Fort Sumter, S.C., which opened the war. He distinguished himself at the First Battle of Bull Run, shared command at Shiloh, and held off Union naval attacks on Charleston. Joining General Joseph E. Johnston, he fell back to the Carolinas in the face of Sherman's Georgia campaign, and remained there until the end of the war.
See also: Civil War.

Beauvoir, Simone de (1908-86), French writer and a leading exponent of Existentialism and the role of women in politics and intellectual life. Her best-known works are *The Second Sex* (1953) and *The Mandarins* (1956). She also wrote an autobiographical trilogy, and a moving account of her mother's death, *A Very Easy Death* (1966). Jean-Paul Sartre was her close associate.
See also: Existentialism.

Simone de Beauvoir

Beaver, large rodent (family Castoridae), weighing up to 100 lb (45 kg) or over, of northern lands. Beavers have thick, furry waterproof coats, powerful, web-footed hindlegs, and small forelimbs with dexterous, sensitive paws. Although lissencephalic (smooth-brained), they are the most intelligent rodents, building dams and lodges (domes up to 23 ft/7 m in diameter, in which they live) from logs and mud. They use their powerful incisor teeth to fell trees and gnaw logs into shape. Their large, heavy tails are used on land for balance and in the water as rudders. Their respiratory system enables them to remain underwater for up to 15 minutes.

Beaverbrook, William Maxwell Aitken, 1st Baron (1879-1964), Canadian-born British newspaper owner and Conservative cabinet minister under Winston Churchill.

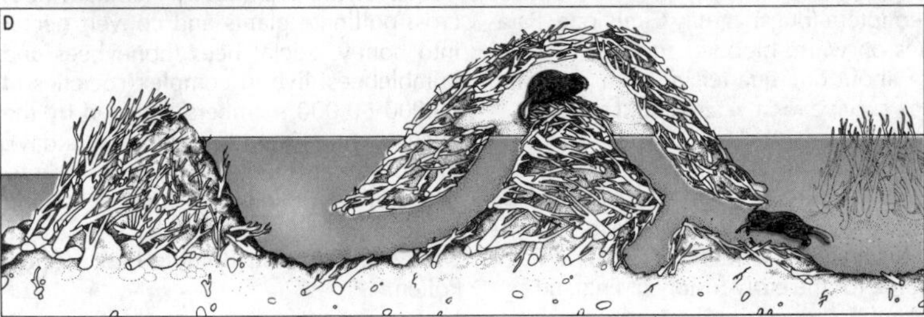

Beaver construction of a dam and lodge. A1. Skull showing incisor teeth (yellow). A2. Beaver eating inner bark of poplar twig. B. Building a dam. C. Building a lodge. D. Vertical section through dam (left), lodge (center), and food store (right).

Among his mass-circulation newspapers were the *Daily Express, Sunday Express,* and *Evening Standard.*

Bebel, August (1840-1913), leading German socialist and cofounder of the Social Democratic Party (1869). A strong antimilitarist and fighter for women's rights, his *Women and Socialism* was published in 1879.

Bebop *See:* Jazz.

Becker, Boris (1967-), German tennis player. He was the youngest winner of the men's singles title at Wimbledon (1985) and he won it again the following year. In 1988 he helped West Germany win its first Davis Cup, while winning the Masters and World Championship the same year. In 1989 he won his third Wimbledon title.

Becket, Saint Thomas à (1118?-70), martyr and archbishop of Canterbury. He first served as chancellor under Henry II, becoming a close friend. In 1162 he was appointed archbishop of Canterbury. After years of dissension with the king, in 1170 he was murdered in the cathedral of Canterbury by four knights inspired by some rash words of the king.

Beckett, Samuel Barclay (1906-89), Irish dramatist and novelist, resident in France from 1937. His work, much of it written in French, deals with habit, boredom, and suffering, and is deeply pessimistic. His novels include *Murphy* (1938) and the trilogy, *Molloy, Malone Dies,* and *The Unnameable* (1951-53). Among his plays are *Waiting for Godot* (1952) and *Happy Days* (1961). Beckett won the 1969 Nobel Prize for literature.

Beckwourth, James Pierson (1798-1867?), African-American pioneer, rancher, furtrader, and Army scout, discoverer of Beckworth Pass through the Sierra Nevada Mountains around 1850. The pass opened a direct route to California's Sacramento Valley. Believed to have been born a slave in Fredericksburg, Virginia, Beckworth grew up in St. Louis and participated in trading expeditions to the Rocky Mountains, where he encountered and lived with the Crow tribe from 1826 to 1837.

Becquerel, Antoine Henri (1852-1908), French physicist, discoverer of natural radioactivity in uranium (1896). He shared the 1903 Nobel Prize for physics with Pierre and Marie Curie.
See also: Radioactivity.

Bedbug, blood-sucking insect of the order Hemiptera (bugs), family Cimicidae. Parasites on warm-blooded animals, bedbugs are about one-quarter in (6mm) long and may survive for a year without feeding.

Bede, Saint (673?-735), known as The Venerable Bede, Anglo-Saxon monk and scholar. His *Ecclesiastical History of the English Nation,* written in Latin, is a major source for the early history of England.

Bedford, Gunning, Jr. (1747-1812), U.S. lawyer, statesman, and signer of the Constitution. Bedford attended the Constitutional Convention as a delegate from Delaware and played a major part in the drafting and ratification of the Constitution. He was appointed judge of the U.S. District Court for Delaware by George Washington in 1789.

Bedlington terrier, long-legged, fleecy-coated breed of terrier first bred in Bedlington, England, in the 19th century. It stands about 16 in (41 cm) tall and weighs 22-24 lb (10-11 kg), and was bred to fight badgers.

Bedloe's Island *See:* Liberty Island.

Bedouin, nomadic peoples of the Middle East and North Africa, especially the Syrian, Arabian, and Sahara deserts. Many bedouins have adopted non-nomadic life styles as a result of 20th-century development.

Bedouin horsemen in the Sahara Dessert

Bed sore, ulceration of the skin on the back of a person who is bedridden. Pressure of the bed against the skin first restricts the blood supply and then, by friction, breaks down the tissues into an ulcer (sore).

Bedstraw, any of a group of wild plants (genus *Galium*) found in damp woods and swamps. They have slender, square stems and fine needle-shaped leaves arranged in whorls of four to eight. The clustered flowers may be white, brown, yellow, or green. The name is derived from their former use as mattress stuffing.

Bee, any of about 20,000 species of flying insects of the superfamily Apoidae. Bees cross-pollinate plants and convert nectar into honey. Social bees (honeybees and bumblebees) live in complex societies of 10,000-50,000 members. Headed by the queen (who lays up to 2,000 eggs a day), the colony also includes female workers, who collect pollen and build cells, and fertile male bees, or drones.
See also: Beeswax; Bumble bee; Honey; Pollen.

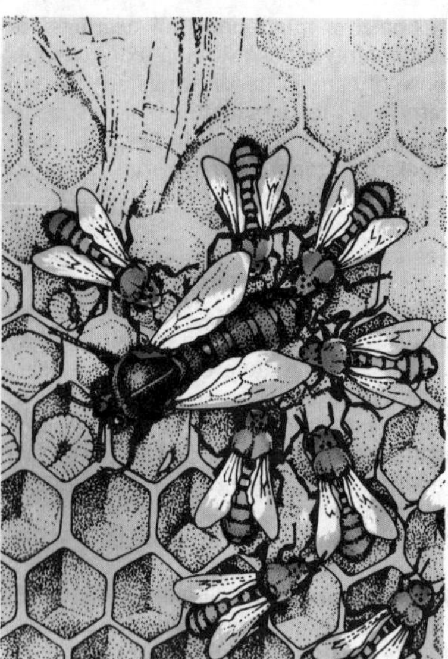

Bees swarm when a new queen matures. The new queen eventually leaves the colony with her own swarm of workers and drones to form a new colony.

Beebe, Charles William (1877-1962), U.S. naturalist best remembered for his record 3,028 ft (923 m) descent into the ocean off Bermuda in a bathysphere in 1934.

Beech, common name for a family (Fagaceae) of deciduous forest trees indigenous to the Northern Hemisphere. Featuring thin, smooth gray bark, oval leaves, and edible nuts, beech trees may grow up to 100 ft (305 m) high. The European beech is ornamental; the American beech is used for furniture and flooring.

Beecham, Sir Thomas (1879-1961), English conductor, founder of the London Philharmonic and the Royal Philharmonic orchestras.

Beecher, Catharine Esther (1800-78), U.S. educator and advocate of higher education for women. Beecher established seminaries for women in Hartford and Cincinnati. She originated the discipline of home economics and pioneered calisthenics for girls. Beecher was opposed to women's suffrage, believing that women should devote their lives to being homemakers and that the purpose of their education was to prepare them for this role.

Beecher, Henry Ward (1813-87), U.S. clergyman, orator, lecturer, author, and abolitionist. The preacher of Plymouth Congregational Church (1847-87) in Brooklyn, N.Y., he was an advocate of women's suffrage and of the theory of evolution.

Beecher, Lyman (1775-1863), U.S. clergyman and liberal theologian who helped found the American Bible Society (1816); father of Harriet Beecher Stowe. Beecher's sermons against slavery and intemperance made him one of the most influential orators of his time.

Bee-eater, any of various species of insect-eating birds (family Meropidae) living mainly in tropical Africa and Asia. They range in length from 6 to 14 in (15-36 cm), are usually green and yellow, and have long curved beaks.

Beef, the flesh of mature cattle slaughtered for food. Leading beef consuming and exporting countries include the United States, Argentina, Australia, Canada, and New Zealand.

Bee fly, insect of the family Bombyliidae that closely resembles a bee but has only one pair of wings and no stinger.

Beefwood, pine-like tree (*Casuarina equisetifolia*) native to Australia and commonly found in warm climates around the world. It thrives in sandy soil, grows to 50 ft (15 m), and is prized for its dense, hard wood.

Beekeeping practice of cultivating bees dating back over 7,000 years. In prehistoric times, people and animals collected honey from the nests of wild bees. Today the main value of the domestic honey bee is the pollination of crops.

Beelzebub, in the Bible, one of the names for the devil.

Beer, alcoholic beverage known since ancient times, made by fermenting cereals. Ale, stout, porter, and lager are varieties of beer. Today beer is produced worldwide but the beers of Germany and Holland are especially popular. In the United States the average beer consumption per person is over 20 gallons a year. The alcohol content of beer can range from 2 to 6%.

Beerbohm, Sir Max (1872-1956), English critic, satirist, and caricaturist best known for his caustic but benign characterizations of eminent Victorian and Edwardian figures, his satirical novel about Oxford, *Zuleika Dobson* (1911), and his parody *A Christmas Garland* (1912).

Beers, Clifford Whittingham (1876-1943), founder of the U.S. mental health movement. His autobiographical *A Mind That Found Itself* (1908), an account of his three years in a mental institution, informed the public of the abuses and injustices inflicted on the mentally ill.

Beersheba (pop. 112,600), chief city of the Negev Desert in southern Israel, 45 mi (72 km) southwest of Jerusalem. The city was closely associated with the biblical patriarchs Abraham and Isaac. After almost 2,000 years of somnolent existence, Beersheba was rebuilt by the Turks in the late 19th century. Since 1948 it has grown into a major industrial, trading, and transportation center.

Beeswax, yellow secretion of the glands on the abdomen of worker bees, who use it to make honeycombs. After the honey is removed, the honeycomb is melted in boiling water to yield the beeswax, which is used in such products as candles, chewing gum, cosmetics, and polishes.

Beet (*Beta vulgaris*), biennial or annual root vegetable. Red beets are edible; white-rooted sugar beets provide about one-third of the world's sugar supply; spinach beets, or chard, are used as herbs, and mangel-wurzel for fodder.

Beethoven, Ludwig van (1770-1827), German composer, recognized worldwide as one of history's greatest musicians. His progressive deafness, total by the time he reached his late 40s, never interfered with his creativity. Beethoven's work may be divided into 3 periods. During the first, ending about 1802, he was still influenced by Haydn and Mozart. The middle period, ending about 1816, was his most productive. His individual style was developed in such works as the Third (*Eroica*) and Fifth symphonies, the Fifth Piano Concerto (*Emperor*), the *Kreutzer* Violin Sonata, and his only opera, *Fidelio*. His later, more intense works include the Ninth (Choral) Symphony, the *Missa Solemnis* (Mass in D), and the late string quartets, including the Great Fugue.

Ludwig van Beethoven

Beetle, any of the more than 250,000 species of the insect order Coleoptera. Beetles are found worldwide except in oceans and have evolved adaptations to nearly all extremes of climate and environment. Beetle eggs hatch into soft, usually wormlike, larvae known as grubs. These grow and metamorphose into pupae, which are soft but resemble adult beetles in form. Pupae often live underground while they develop into adults. Adult beetles range from 1/32 in (1 mm) to over 6.5 in (16 m) in length. Their hard, protective wing cases enclose the fragile flight wings. Beetles are generally plant eaters. Many beetles, such as weevils and leaf beetles, are serious pests to crops, eating seeds or boring into roots and stems. Ladybugs are helpful to humans, feeding on other insect pests.

Beggar-tick, or stick-tight, flowering plant of genus *Bidens* of the composite family, named for the hairy, barbed seeds of its yellow flowers, which adhere to clothing or animal fur. The name is often applied to the tick trefoil, a plant of a different family (Leguminosae) but with similar barbed seeds.

Beggarweed, tall (6 ft/1.8 m), fast-growing, flowering plant (*Desmodium tortuosum*), native to the West Indies and now found in many warm climates. Beggarweed is commonly cultivated as a natural fertilizer; its roots are a source of nitrogen-fixing bacteria.

The bee-eater is a colorful tropical bird that relies on bees and wasps for most of its diet.

Begin, Menachem (1913-), Israeli prime minister, 1977-83. Begin was active in the Zionist Movement's effort to create a Jewish state in the 1930s and 1940s. He was a member and leader (1944-48) of the Irgon Zvai Leumi, an organization that fought for the creation of Israel. He fought in the Arab-Israeli war of 1948. He was elected to the Knesset (parliament) in 1948, with Israel's independence, and was an opposition leader for most of the next 30 years, pressing Israel's claim to the West Bank of the Jordan River and refusing to consider sovereignty for the Palestinians. Begin signed a peace treaty with Egypt in 1979; in 1978 he shared the Nobel Peace Prize with Egyptian President Anwar Sadat. In 1982 Begin launched a much criticized invasion of Lebanon intended to destroy command and military units of the Palestinian Liberation Organization (PLO). Israeli forces succeeded in driving out the PLO but also occupied West Beirut, a move that was very unpopular in Israel and abroad. Israeli forces were accused of allowing the massacre of Palestinian civilians in refugee camps during their occupation. The Israelis withdrew most of their forces between 1983 and 1985. Since this event Begin has remained in almost total, self-imposed seclusion and makes rare public statements.
See also: Israel.

Menachem Begin

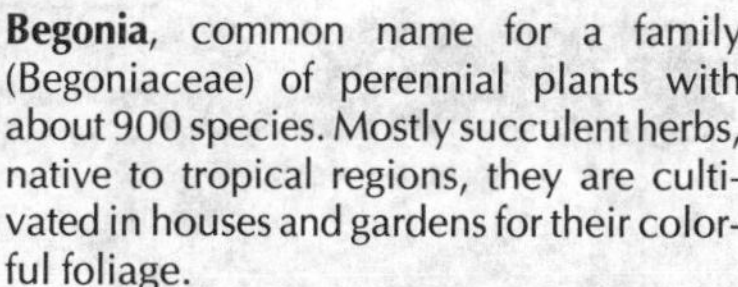

Begonia, common name for a family (Begoniaceae) of perennial plants with about 900 species. Mostly succulent herbs, native to tropical regions, they are cultivated in houses and gardens for their colorful foliage.

Behan, Brendan, (1922-64), Irish playwright and author, noted for his vivid ribaldry and satire. His works *The Quare Fellow* (1956), the autobiographical *Borstal Boy* (1958), and *The Hostage* (1959) deal largely with his experiences in the Irish Republican Army and his subsequent imprisonment.

Behavioral sciences, sciences dealing with human behavior, individually or socially, as opposed to their physiological makeup. The term embraces anthropology, psychology, and sociology.
See also: Anthropology; Psychology; Sociology.

Behaviorism, school of psychology that studies behavior exclusively in terms of objective observations of reactions to environmental stimuli. Originating with Pav-

lov's animal experiments in conditioned reflexes, behaviorism in human psychology was introduced by J.B. Watson and championed by B.F. Skinner.
See also: Pavlov, Ivan Petrovich; Skinner, B.F.; Watson, John Broadus.

Behavior therapy, methods for changing undesirable habits through learning.

Behn, Aphra (1640-89), dramatist, novelist, and poet, first professional female author in England. Her plays *The Rover* (1677) and *The Forced Marriage* (1670) and her novel *Oroonoko* (1688) show technical ingenuity and wit.

Behrens, Peter (1868-1940), German architect who pioneered a mode of functional design suited to industrial technology. His most influential work was the AEG turbine factory in Berlin (1908-09). He influenced Le Corbusier, Gropius, and Miës van der Rohe.

Behrman, Samuel Nathaniel (1893-1973), U.S. dramatist noted for his comedies of manners, including *Biography* (1932) and *No Time for Comedy* (1939). He also wrote film scripts and a biography of satirist Max Beerbohm (1960).

Beiderbecke, Bix (Leon Bismarck Beiderbecke; 1903-31), U.S. jazz musician. An accomplished pianist and brilliant cornetist, he joined the renowned Paul Whiteman band in 1928. Despite his early death through alcoholism and general ill health, he was a major innovator in the development of jazz.
See also: Jazz.

Beijing (formerly Peking; pop. 5,760,000), capital of the People's Republic of China, lying within the Hebei province, but administered directly by the central government. It is the political, commercial, cultural, and communications center of the country, and embraces a massive industrial complex. The city's rectangular layout was the work of Kublai Khan in the 13th century, and its splendors were described by Marco Polo. It became the permanent capital of China in 1421. Its occupation by French and British troops from 1860 was a contributing cause of the Boxer Rebellion (1900). In 1928 Peking (renamed Peiping) was superseded by Nanking (Nanjing), but regained its capital status and its name with the Communist victory under Mao Zedong in 1949. Beijing has two historic districts: the Inner City, enclosing the Imperial Palace and the Forbidden City, and the Outer City. In mid-1989 a massacre of demonstrators in Beijing's Tiananmen Square signaled the difficulty of China's democracy movement in the face of totalitarian authority.
See also: China

Beirut (pop. 700,000), capital city and chief port of the Republic of Lebanon, situated on the Mediterranean Sea. During early Roman times the city became famous as a center of learning. The Arabs conquered the city in A.D. 635. In 1110 it was captured by the Crusaders, who held it for two centuries. It eventually became part of the Ottoman Empire. During World War I it came under French rule and was proclaimed the capital of Lebanon in 1920. Beirut has excellent railroad connections with other nearby cities, which have enlarged the region served by its harbor. Growth of the city during the 20th century was rapid until the Lebanese civil war of 1975-76 between Muslims and Christians caused severe damage and ended Beirut's success as a financial center and tourist resort. Much of the city was left in ruins following a siege by Israeli forces in 1982, which brought about the expulsion of thousands of PLO guerrillas.

The bridges in front of the most important place of interest in Beijing, the Imperial Palace in the Forbidden City.

Béjart, Maurice (1927-), French dancer and choreographer. He danced with various companies in Europe and organized his own company in 1954. The Ballet of the 20th Century in Brussels, Belgium, which he has directed since 1959, has an international reputation.
See also: Ballet.

Bekesy, Georg von (1899-), Hungarian-born U.S. scientist who was awarded the 1961 Nobel Prize for medicine for research into the mechanism of the inner ear. A senior research fellow at Harvard University since 1947, he made discoveries about the physical mechanisms of hearing, particularly with respect to discrimination of pitch.
See also: Ear.

Belafonte, Harry (1927-), U.S. singer and actor best known for his interpretations of West Indian calypso folksongs. Belafonte is also active in many human rights causes.

Belasco, David (1853-1931), U.S. playwright and theatrical producer; famous for mounting spectacular New York productions, with lavishly detailed sets, to promote newly discovered stars.

Belém (pop. 758,100), capital of the state of Pará in northern Brazil. Situated on the Pará River, about 90 mi (145 km) from the Atlantic coast, Belém is the commercial center of the mouth of the Amazon River basin. Among its industries are tourism, rubber, timber, cacao, and Brazil nuts.
See also: Brazil.

Belfast (pop. 301,600), seaport and capital of Northern Ireland, located at the mouth of the Lagan River, an inlet of the Irish Sea. The town was populated by about 2,000 English settlers in 1613, became a county borough in 1898, and was made capital of Northern Ireland in 1920. By the end of the 18th century Belfast had become the export center for the Irish linen trade and for the developing cotton industry. The city was long known for shipbuilding, but that industry has recently declined in importance. Although newer industries, including an aircraft factory, have been established, unemployment in the area is still the highest in the United Kingdom. For the past century, Belfast has been the scene of violent conflict between the Protestant majority and Catholic minority and, recently, of guerrilla fighting between the Irish Republican Army and British troops.
See also: Ireland.

Belgian Congo *See:* Zaire.

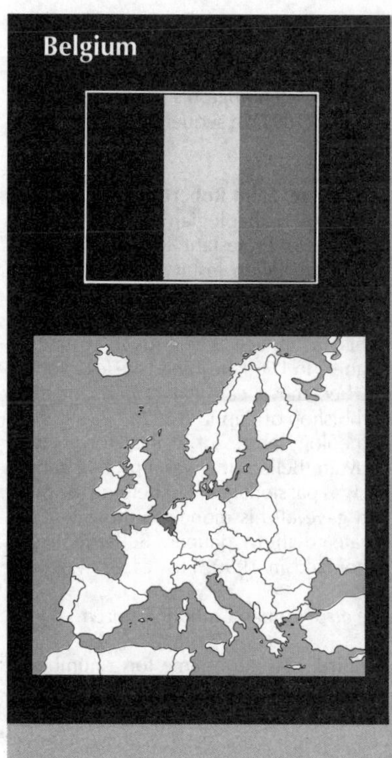

Belgium

General information	
Capital:	Brussels
Area:	11,783 sq mi (30,518 sq km)
Population:	9,878,000
Official languages:	Dutch, French, German
Monetary unit:	1 Belgian franc = 100 centimes
Main cities:	Brussels, Antwerp, Ghent
Government	
Form:	constitutional monarchy
Independent:	1830
Head of state:	Monarch
Head of government:	Prime minister
Legislature:	two legislative houses (Senate and House of Representatives)
Executive:	Belgian monarch and Cabinet
Judiciary:	highest court is Supreme Court of Justice
Political division:	9 provinces, 3 regions, 3 cultural communities
National economy	
Gross national product:	U.S.$143,560,000,000
Per capita income:	U.S. $14,550
Agriculture:	sugar beets, potatoes, wheat, barley, oats, corn
Livestock:	pigs, cattle, sheep
Fisheries:	40,370 metric tons
Mining:	hard coal, natural gas
Industries:	metal products and machinery, food, beverages, tobacco, chemicals and chemical products, iron and steel, paper, diamond cutting
Main exports:	machinery and transportation equipment, chemicals and chemical products, food and livestock, iron and steel
Transportation:	2,248 mi (3,959 km) of railroads; 79,622 mi (128,139 km) of roads; 5 international airports
Trading partners:	Germany, France, The Netherlands, United Kingdom, United States
People	
Urban:	96%
Ethnic composition:	Flemings 59.6%, Walloons 39.8%, German speaking 0.6%
Birth rate:	11.9 per 1,000 population
Death rate:	10.7 per 1,000 population
Infant mortality rate:	9.7 per 1,000 live births
Life expectancy:	male 70 years, female 77 years

Belgium, kingdom of northwestern Europe, bordered to the west by France, to the east by Luxembourg and West Germany, and to the north by the Netherlands. Belgium is one of Europe's most densely populated countries.

Land and climate. The region called Flanders borders the North Sea and is mostly flat plain with sandy beaches; further inland, the country is intensively cultivated, and is drained by the Leie, Schelde, and Dender rivers. Central Belgium consists of a low plateau that is also a rich agricultural area. At the southern end of this plateau is the Sambre-Meuse valley, the main industrial and coal-mining region. About 25% of all Belgians live in this area of only 800 sq mi (2,000 sq km). The country has a generally temperate climate.

People. Belgium is linguistically, culturally, and politically divided. A line running from east to west, just south of Brussels, divides the Flemish-speaking Flemings in the north from the French-speaking Walloons in the south. Both languages are in official use.

Economy. Belgium is not rich in natural resources, except for the coal deposits of the Sambre-Meuse valley and the Kempenland region. Its high standard of living derives from successful manufacturing industries, which account for half the gross national product. The chief commodities, about 40% of which are exported, include textiles, glass, chemicals, metal and machine goods, and diamonds; Antwerp is one of the world's leading diamond centers. Brussels (the capital), Bruges, and Mechelen are noted for lace. Belgium's numerous small farms provide about 80% of the country's food needs. Belgium's excellent system of transportation, including fine inland waterways and well-equipped ports at Antwerp and Ghent, facilitate the foreign trade that has made the country prosperous.

History. The kingdom emerged in the 1830s, when it seceded from the Netherlands, and in 1839 Belgium was recognized as a perpetually neutral sovereign state. In 1914 the Germans invaded and occupied the country for the next 4 years. In May 1940 Germany again violated Belgian neutrality, invading Belgium, the Netherlands, and Luxembourg simultaneously. Belgian forces capitulated in June 1940, but Belgian resistance forces fought alongside the Allies until the country was liberated in 1944. Belgium was a founding member of the United Nations in 1945 and a founding member of the North Atlantic Treaty Organization (NATO) in 1950. It also helped to establish the European Economic Community (EEC), which was to become part of the European Community (EC), with headquarters in Brussels.

See also: Brussels.

Ghent, Belgium: Guild Halls of the Middle Ages and Renaissance

Belgrade (pop. 1,455,000), capital and largest city of Yugoslavia, a port and industrial center at the junction of the Danube and Sava rivers. Important products include metals, chemicals, and textiles. Held in turn by the Romans, Byzantines, Bulgars, Serbs, and Ottoman Turks, the city became Yugoslavia's capital after World War I. Belgrade is known for its beautiful parks, churches, and museums.

See also: Yugoslavia.

Belisarius (c.505-565 A.D.), Byzantine general under Justinian I. He crushed the Vandals in North Africa and the Ostrogoths in Italy, taking Rome in 536. In 559 Belisarius was called from retirement to repel the Huns and Slavs from the gates of Constantinople.
See also: Byzantine Empire; Justinian I.

Alexander Graham Bell during the official inauguration of the telephone connection between New York and Chicago in October 1892

Belize (British Honduras until 1973), independent nation since 1981, on the subtropical Caribbean coast of Central America, bordered by Mexico on the north and Guatemala on the southwest. The country is densely forested. The population consists of Creoles (of mixed African and European origin), descendants of the Carib and Maya tribes, and a small minority of Europeans. Most people live on the coast. Citrus fruits, bananas, and sugarcane are the mainstay of the export-oriented economy. Fishing and livestock industries are being developed. European settlement began in the 17th century, and in the 18th century African slaves were brought in to cut mahogany. The country became a British colony in 1862 and achieved internal self-government in 1964. Disputes with Guatemala concerning the latter's claim that it had inherited Belize from Spain delayed the proclamation of independence until 1981.

Belize City (pop. 50,000), largest city and former capital of Belize, a country on the Caribbean coast. Though its proximity to the sea earned Belize City a reputation as a chief seaport, it also makes the city especially susceptible to hurricanes. Following a devastating hurricane in 1961 that destroyed the city, killed hundreds, and left thousands homeless, the capital was moved from Belize City inland to Belmopan, the current capital. For over 300 years, Belize City has been world renowned for its shipping of mahogany and logwood. The city also ships rosewood, cedar, coconuts, maize, bananas, and sugar. The British first settled Belize City in the 1600s. Now about 1 in 4 Belize citizens live in Belize City.

Belize

Capital:	Belmopan
Area:	8,867 sq mi (22,965 sq km)
Population:	185,000
Government:	constitutional monarchy
Independent:	1981
GNP:	U.S.$264,000,000
Per capita:	U.S.$1,460

Bell, metal instrument rung by a metal clapper inside. Most bells are cup-shaped, with the bottom edges tapering outward, but as musical instruments they can be pipes of varying lengths (chimes) that create different tones when struck. Bells originated in China in the 800s B.C. and were introduced to Europe in the 6th century A.D. Commonly associated with churches, where they were rung to summon people to worship, bells have also signalled emergencies or momentous events such as the independence movements in the United States and Mexico.
See also: Big Ben; Liberty Bell.

Bell, Alexander Graham (1847-1922), Scottish-born U.S. scientist and educator who invented the telephone (1876), the wax-cylinder phonograph, and various aids for teaching the deaf. He also founded the Bell Telephone Company.
See also: Telephone.

Bell, John (1797-1869), "Tennessee Bell," presidential candidate of the Constitutional Union Party (1860) who lost to Lincoln on the eve of the U.S. Civil War. As representative (1827-41) and senator (1847-59), he led a conservative group of antisecessionist southerners.

Bella Coola, tribe of Native Americans in western Canada near the North Pacific coast. The 600 Bella Coola still living reside near Queen Charlotte Sound, British Columbia, in a village on the Bella Coola River. Though they speak English and have lifestyles similar to their Canadian neighbors, they maintain their cultural heritage, lavishing gifts on guests at frequent ceremonial feasts (potlatches) and electing a band council to administer and govern the tribe. The ancestors of modern Bella Coola were successful fishermen (particularly of salmon) and woodworkers for centuries.

Belladonna, or deadly nightshade (*Atropa belladonna*), poisonous herbaceous plant of the nightshade family whose dried leaves and roots produce a crude drug of the same name. Various medicinal alkaloids, such as the muscle relaxant atropine, are produced by refining belladonna.

Bellamy, Edward (1850-98), U.S. author. His Utopian *Looking Backward 2000-1877* (1888) pictured a benevolent state socialism with worker-ownership and made him famous. His other novels include *Miss Ludington's Sister* (1884) and *Equality* (1897), a sequel to *Looking Backward.*

Bellarmine, Saint Robert Francis Romulus (1542-1621), theologian known for his opposition to Protestant Reformation doctrines. An Italian Jesuit, Saint Bellarmine was regarded by the Roman Catholic church as a key defender of the church's rights in an age when royal absolutism reigned. In 1560, he joined the Jesuit order. He became a cardinal (1599) and then archbishop of Capua (1602).
A theology professor at the University of Louvain, Bellarmine was a prolific author. He was passionate about helping the poor, and gave all his money to those less fortunate, dying a pauper. Bellarmine was canonized in 1930. His feast day is May 17.
See also: Roman Catholic Church.

Bellbird, common name for a number of bird species whose songs resemble ringing bells. The *campañero* of the South American tropical rain forest is a well-known white bellbird.

Belleau Wood, Battle of (June 6-25, 1918), part of the World War I second battle of the Marne in which a brigade of U.S. Marines, with French support, halted five German divisions. In 1923 the battlefield was dedicated as a memorial to the American dead.
See also: World War I.

Bellerophon, Greek mythological hero. Bellerophon tamed the winged horse Pegasus to aid him in the tasks set by King Iobates. He attempted to reach Olympus on his mount, but Pegasus, stung by a gadfly sent by Zeus, threw him, and Bellerophon was crippled and blinded.
See also: Mythology.

Bellflower, or bluebell, any of several species of annual, biennial, and perennial plants producing bell-shaped flowers, ranging from a few inches to more than 6 ft (1.8 m) tall, found in temperate and subtropical areas.

Bellini, family of Early Renaissance Venetian painters. **Jacopo** (c.1400-1470) evolved a much-imitated compositional technique of depicting small figures in vast, detailed architectural settings. **Gentile** (1429-1507), his elder son, is noted for his realistic portraits and his use of perspective to give a sense of spatial depth. **Giovanni** (1430-1516), the younger son, is considered the greatest Early Renaissance Venetian painter, famous for his use of light and color. His pupils, Titian and Giorgione, continued and developed his style.
See also: Renaissance.

Bellini, Vincenzo (1801-35), Italian opera composer of the bel canto school. His most popular works today are his last 3: *La*

Sonnambula (1831), *Norma* (1831), and *I Puritani* (1835).
See also: Opera.

Belloc, (Joseph Pierre) Hilaire (1870-1953), French-born English poet, essayist, and historian. An ardent Roman Catholic polemicist, his first well-known work was *The Bad Child's Book of Beasts* (1896).

Bellow, Saul (1915-), Canadian-born U.S. novelist noted for his narrative skill and his studies of Jewish-American life. His best-known books are *The Adventures of Augie March* (1953) and *Herzog* (1964). Other novels include *Dangling Man* (1944), *Henderson the Rain King* (1959), and *Humboldt's Gift* (1975). He won the 1976 Nobel Prize in literature.

Bellows, George Wesley (1882-1925), U.S. painter and lithographer, early 20th century "realist" who remained aloof from modern European influences and was influential in reviving U.S. lithography. His painting of New York City include *Forty-Two kids and Stage at Sharkey's* .
See also: Lithography.

Bell's palsy, nerve disorder that causes paralysis of one side of the face. Thought to be due to a virus infection, Bell's palsy occurs most often in young men. It begins suddenly with a dull ache behind the jaw and weakened facial muscles. The paralyzed muscles usually begin to recover within ten days or so.

Belmopan (pop. 4,000), capital city of Belize, a country on the Caribbean coast. Belmopan, the capital since 1970, is a new city built approximately 50 mi (80 km) inland from Belize City, the former capital, which was plagued by devastating hurricanes. Many of the buildings in Belmopan are adorned with ancient Mayan designs. The country's most modern hospital and many government buildings are located in the city.
See also: Belize.

Belo Horizonte (pop. 1,443,000), city in Brazil, about 220 mi (354 km) north of Rio de Janeiro. It is a fast-growing city, with heavy industry and secondary products including furniture, textiles, and footwear. The capital of Minas Gerais state, Belo Horizonte was built in 1895-97 as Brazil's first planned city. It is a center of culture and tourism.
See also: Brazil.

Belorussia *See:* Byelorussian Soviet Socialist Republic.

Belsen, German village in Lower Saxony, site of the infamous Nazi concentration camp called Bergen-Belsen, where over 115,000 people, mostly Jews, were killed.
See also: Holocaust.

Beluga, or white whale, small (13 ft/4 m) whale (*Delphinapterus leucas*) living in northern seas and prized for its skin. The sturgeon, largest Russian freshwater fish, source of caviar, is also called beluga.

Bemelmans, Ludwig (1898-1962), Austrian-American writer and illustrator of *Hansi* (1934), *My War with the United States* (1937), *Madeline* (1939), and other satiric and children's stories.

Bemis, Samuel Flagg (1891-1973), U.S. historian. A Yale professor (1935-60) and an expert on U.S. diplomatic history, his books include *A Diplomatic History of the United States* (1936) and 2 Pulitzer Prize-winning works, *Pinckney's Treaty* (1926) and *John Quincy Adams and the Foundations of American Foreign Policy* (1950).

Benares *See:* Varanasi.

Benavente y Martínez, Jacinto (1866-1954), Spanish playwright. He wrote and staged 172 comedies and helped establish the modern theater in Spain. He was awarded the 1922 Nobel Prize for literature for such popular plays as *The Bonds of Interest* (1907) and *La Malquerida* (1913).

Ben Bella, Ahmed (1918-), Algerian revolutionary who helped plan the 1954 anti-French revolt. After the post-independence power struggle, Ben Bella became president in 1962. He was ousted during Col. Houari Boumedienne's 1965 coup.
See also: Algeria.

Benchley, Robert Charles (1889-1945), U.S. writer, drama critic of *Life* (1920-29) and *The New Yorker* (1929-40). He is best known for his short humorous pieces, published in several collections—*My Ten Years in a Quandary* (1936), *Benchley Beside Himself* (1943)—and such satirical short films as—*The Treasurer's Report* (1928). His grandson, Peter Benchley (1928-), wrote the best-selling novel *Jaws* (1975).

Bendix, Vincent (1882-1945), U.S. mechanical engineer and industrialist who developed and mass-produced a 4-wheel brake system for automobiles and devised a practicable self-starter. He also had interests in aviation, and the Bendix Aviation Corporation manufactured radio and radar equipment.
See also: Automobile.

Bends, also known as caisson disease or decompression sickness, dangerous physiological reaction resulting from a rapid decrease in atmospheric pressure that may release nitrogen bubbles into the body. These can obstruct small blood vessels, collect in the joints, and damage the nervous system. Symptoms involve painful joints and muscles, convulsions, double vision, and paralysis. Divers, airplane pilots, and others working in compressed-air situations are the usual victims.

Saul Bellow

Benedict, Ruth Fulton (1887-1948), U.S. cultural anthropologist whose extensive fieldwork helped illustrate the theory of cultural relativism—what is considered deviant in one culture may be normal in another. Her classic work was *Patterns of Culture* (1934).
See also: Anthropology.

Benedictine Orders, the "Black Monks," order of monks and nuns following the rule of St. Benedict of Nursia. They believe in a combination of prayer, choral office, study, and manual labor under an abbot's supervision.
See also: Benedict of Nursia, Saint.

Benedict of Nursia, Saint (c.480-547), father of Western monasticism, whose "rule" set the pattern of monastic life from the mid-7th century. He founded the first Benedictine monastery at Monte Cassino.
See also: Benedictine Orders.

Benedict XV (Giacomo Della Chiesa; 1854-1922), Roman Catholic pope during the outbreak of World War I. Benedict was elected pope in 1914, 3 months after he was made a cardinal. His reign was punctuated by World War I and a conflict with Italy regarding Italian troops that were occupying Rome. Though Benedict tried to maintain and encourage strict neutrality,

Scenes from the life of Saint Benedict of Nursia were depicted in frescoes by the Italian painter Spinello Aretino (1373-1410). In this fresco, Benedict meets Totila, king of the Eastern Goths.

his papacy was plagued with war problems. The Allies eventually excluded him from peace negotiations. After the war, Benedict encouraged international reconciliation and endorsed the founding of the League of Nations. In 1917, he was credited with the issuance of the Code of Canon Law, a compilation of comprehensive church laws.

David Ben-Gurion arrived in Palestine in 1906 and at first worked as an agricultural laborer. Later he became one of the leaders of the Jewish Labor Movement.

Benelux, customs union formed by Belgium, the Netherlands, and Luxembourg, in 1948. "Benelux" is often used collectively for the countries themselves.

Benes, Eduard (1884-1948), co-founder, with Thomás Masaryk, of the Czechoslovak Republic. He held the posts of foreign minister (1918-35), prime minister (1921-22), president (1935-38 and 1946-48), and head of the government-in-exile (1940-45). His appeals to Great Britain and France in 1938 failed to prevent Hitler's occupation of the Sudetenland. He died after the 1948 Communist coup.
See also: Czechoslovakia.

Benét, Steven Vincent (1898-1943), U.S. poet, novelist, and short story writer, whose works center on U.S. history and tradition. His epic poems *John Brown's Body* (1928) and *Western Star* (1943) won Pulitzer Prizes. Among his most famous short stories is "The Devil and Daniel Webster" (1937).

Bengal, region including Bangladesh and northeastern India on the Bay of Bengal. Its chief city, Calcutta, was capital of British India 1833-1912, and it was an autonomous province from 1935 until the partition of India in 1947. At that time the western part became West Bengal State of India. The eastern part became a province of Pakistan, and in 1971, the independent nation of Bangladesh.

Bengal, Bay of *See:* Bay of Bengal.

Benghazi (pop. 368,000), seaport and second largest city of Libya. It is situated in northeastern Libya on the Gulf of Sidra about 600 mi (966 km) east of the capital, Tripoli. Benghazi markets and exports the products of a rich agricultural region: wool, grains, citrus fruits, dates, and olives. There is also considerable tuna and sponge fishing. Benghazi was the scene of fighting (changing hands several times) during World War II.
See also: Libya.

Ben-Gurion, David (David Grün; 1886-1973), Polish-born Israeli statesman and first prime minister of Israel. After World War I, he helped to found the Haganah, the underground Jewish army, and the Histadrut, the General Federation of Jewish Labor (1920). He became leader of the Mapai Labor Party (1930) and the World Zionist Organization (1935). As prime minister (1949-53 and 1955-63) he helped to mold the state of Israel.
See also: Israel.

Ben-Hur *See:* Wallace, Lew.

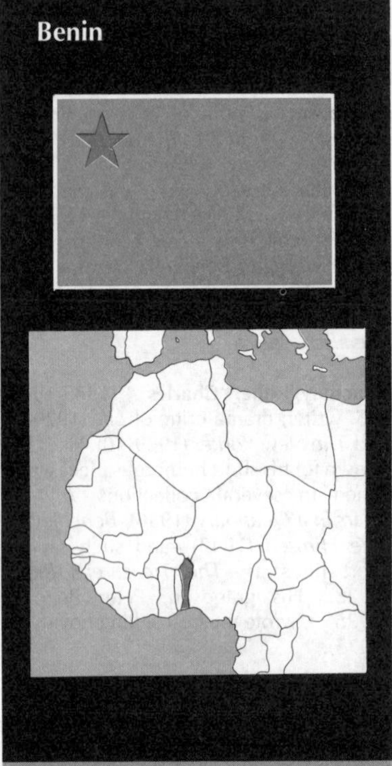

Capital:	Porto-Novo
Area:	43,450 sq mi (112,622 sq km)
Population:	4,590,000
Government:	republic
Independent:	1960
GNP:	U.S. $1,530,000,000
Per capita:	U.S. $340

Benin: In the lagoons, closed off from the sea by a levee, the houses are constructed from wood and reeds and are built on stilts. Fishing for this little village of Ganvie, north of Cotonou, consititutes an important means of livelihood.

Benin (formerly Dahomey), republic in West Africa, flanked by Togo in the west, Burkina Faso (formerly Upper Volta) in the northwest, Niger in the north, Nigeria in the east, and the Gulf of Guinea in the south.
People. The population is concentrated in the south coastal region, where Cotonou, a major port city and commercial center, and Porto-Novo, the capital, are located. There are 4 major tribes: the Fon, Adja, and Yoruba in the south and the Bariba in the northeast and central regions. There is a small European community, mostly French.
Economy. Benin is one of the world's poorer countries. Its economy is principally agricultural with most people engaged in subsistence farming. The major cash crop is the oil palm. Other exports include hides and skins, cotton, peanuts, and coffee. Benin's position as a transit point for Nigeria and land-locked Niger has provided the impetus for an expanding transport sector. Manufacturing presently accounts for less than 10% of the country's economy.
History. The independent Fon Kingdom of Dahomey emerged in the 17th century and engaged in profitable trade with the Portuguese. Known as the Slave Coast, Dahomey became one of the main slave exporting regions of West Africa. King Gezo (1818-58) raided the Yoruba for slaves and extended Dahomey's northern boundaries with the aid of its famous women soldiers. By 1850 the slave trade was declining and in 1851 the French established a trading station at Cotonou. By 1894 the French conquered the kingdom and in 1904 merged Dahomey into French West Africa. In 1960, after more than 50 years as a French colony, Dahomey became an independent republic and joined the United Nations. Plagued by economic and political instability, Dahomey witnessed a series of takeovers after independence. The first president, Herbert Maga, was toppled from power in 1963. Rivalry between President Sourow-Migan Apithy and the prime minister resulted in a coup in 1965. Following a series of unstable regimes, a 3-man Presidential Council was established in 1970 only to be overthrown by Maj. Mathiew Kerekou in 1972. In 1975 Dahomey was renamed and became the People's Republic of Benin. Since then, despite a new constitution providing for a national revolutionary assembly, Benin has been governed by President Kerekou as a 1-party military dictatorship.

Benjamin, Judah Philip (1811-84), West Indian-born U.S. politician and lawyer, called the "brains of the Confederacy." As U.S. senator from Louisiana (1853-61), he was an able advocate of the Southern cause. After secession, his friend Jefferson Davis appointed him attorney general, secretary of war, and finally secretary of state (1862-65) in the Confederate government. On the collapse of the Confederacy Benjamin fled to England, where he became a successful barrister.
See also: Civil War, U.S.

Bennett, Arnold (1867-1931), English novelist, journalist, and playwright. He is famous for his novels set in the potteries of Staffordshire: *Anna of the Five Towns* (1902), *The Old Wives' Tale* (1908), and *These Twain* (1916). He was influenced by Zola's naturalism.

Bennett, Floyd (1890-1928), U.S. aviator who piloted Richard Byrd on the first flight over the North Pole (May 9, 1926).

Bennett, James Gordon (1795-1872), Scottish-born U.S. newspaper publisher and editor, pioneer of modern news reporting. In 1835 he launched the sensationalist *New York Herald*, the first to print stock market items and use the telegraph. His son, James Gordon Bennett (1841-1918), sent H. M. Stanley to find David Livingston (1869) and founded the *New York Evening Telegram* (1869) and the *Paris Herald* (1887).

Bennett, Richard Bedford (1870-1945), prime minister of Canada (1930-35) and leader of the Conservative Party. He was created a viscount in 1941.

Bennington, town in southwestern Vermont, about 35 mi (56 km) northeast of Albany, N.Y. In 1777, during the Revolutionary War, the Green Mountain Boys defeated the British troops under General John Burgoyne in an important battle at Bennington. A granite monument just outside the town commemorates this action. Other historical landmarks are the first schoolhouse in Vermont, William Lloyd Garrison's printing shop, and several colonial buildings. The town has a historical museum. Bennington is now a manufacturing town, producing clothing, plastics, pottery, and precision machinery.

Benny, Jack (Benjamin Kubelsky; 1894-1974), U.S. comedian. Benny was known for his radio and television routines about the hilarious experiences of a miserly man. He was 17 when he made his show business debut playing violin in vaudeville shows. More than 20 films and an 18-year radio career followed. In 1950, Benny made his first television appearance using the themes that made him famous—stinginess, condemning quiet stares, and his violin playing.

Bent, William (1809-1869), U.S. fur trader and pioneer, the first permanent white resident in Colorado. He formed Bent, St. Vrain & Company, a trading firm in the upper Arkansas valley, and ran Bent's Fort, a famous trading post.

Bent grass, popular name for some grasses (genus *Agrostis*) of Europe, North America, and North Africa, widely grown for pasture cover and for hay. In the United States one widely grown species is redtop (*A. albot*). Some kinds of bent grass are suitable for lawns and golf greens.

Bentham, Jeremy (1748-1832), English philosopher, economist, and jurist, founder of Utilitarianism, a social philosophy whose aim was to achieve "the greatest happiness of the greatest number." His major work was *An Introduction to the Principles of Morals and Legislation* (1789). Bentham's ideas were influential in legal reform in the 19th century and in the thinking of John Stuart Mill and David Ricardo.
See also: Utilitarianism.

Bentley, Eric (1916-), British-born U.S. drama critic and university professor. He wrote *The Playwright as Thinker* (1946) and *What Is Theatre?* (1956). Through his translations and theater work he introduced Brecht's and Pirandello's plays to the English-speaking world.

Benton, Thomas Hart (1782-1858), U.S. statesman; great uncle of the painter Thomas Hart Benton. He represented Missouri in the U.S. Senate for 30 years (1821-51), championing the development of the West and opposing the extension of slavery. He also opposed the Mexican War. After leaving the Senate, he served one term (1853-55) in the House of Representatives.

Benton, Thomas Hart (1889-1975), U.S. painter; greatnephew of Senator Thomas Hart Benton. He was a leader of the influential 1930s regionalist school of painting, devoted to depicting the life of rural America as in his *Threshing Wheat*.

Bentonite, type of fine-grained clay that greatly increases in volume when saturated with water. It is found in rocks formed from volcanic ash. Bentonite is used in ceramics, paper manufacture, and the sealing of dams and oil wells.

Bentsen, Lloyd Millard, Jr. (1921-), U.S. Senator. As a Texas Democrat, he served 3 terms in the U.S. House of Representatives (1949-55) and won election to the U.S. Senate (1970), defeating George Bush. In 1988 he was the running mate of unsuccessful Democratic presidential candidate Michael Dukakis. Bentsen won reelection to the Senate.

Benz, Karl (1844-1929), German engineer believed to have built the first automobile (1885) with an internal combustion engine. His earliest autos had tricycle carriages and electric ignitions. His company merged with Daimler in 1926, and Daimler-Benz became the manufacturer of the Mercedes-Benz.
See also: Automobile.

Benzedrine, U.S. trade name of a drug containing amphetamine.

Benzene, colorless, flammable, toxic liquid hydrocarbon (C_6H_6) produced from petroleum and from coal gas and coal tar. Benzene is used in the manufacture of plastics and as a fuel in some engines.
See also: Aniline; Faraday, Michael.

Benzine, flammable liquid distilled from petroleum. Clear, colorless, and lighter than kerosene, benzine is a volatile mixture consisting primarily of aliphatic hydrocarbons. Benzine is often used as a drycleaning solvent, motor fuel, and to dissolve fats and oils. Benzine boils between 95° and 175F° (35°- 79°C).
See also: Petroleum.

Benzocaine, crystalline ester, used as a local anesthetic, usually in an ointment or in lozenges. It reduces pain or itching in minor wounds.
See also: Anesthesia.

Benzol *See:* Benzene.

Ben-Zvi, Itzhak (1884-1963), Russian-born second president of Israel (1952-63). Active in Jewish self-defense groups in Palestine from 1907, in 1929 he founded the National Council of Palestine Jews.

Benzyl alcohol (also called phenylcarbinol $C_6H_5CH_2OH$), colorless, aromatic alcohol found in the oils of many flowers. Ephedrine and adrenaline are derived from it. Benzyl alcohol is widely used in the perfume industry, in pharmaceuticals, and as a solvent in cellulose lacquers.

Beograd *See:* Belgrade.

Beothuk, tribe of Native Americans that once lived on the island of Newfoundland and spoke Bethukian, an independent language. Hunters by trade, the Beothuk were most likely the first people encountered by early European settlers. They had a reputation as skilled canoeists and accomplished hunters and fishermen. In 1497 the Beothuk tribe consisted of nearly 500 people, but their numbers diminished until they became extinct in 1829.

Beowulf, anonymous heroic epic poem, probably composed in the 8th century, the greatest extant poem in Old English. Using elements of Germanic legend, it is set in Scandinavia and recounts the hero Beowulf's victories over the monster Grendel and Grendel's mother, his battle with a dragon, and his death and burial.
See also: English literature.

Berbers, several culturally distinct North African peoples, usually Muslim, who speak the Hamitic Berber language or any of its main dialects. They live mainly in Algeria, Libya, Morocco, and Tunisia. Most are farmers or nomadic herders, but some are oasis-dwellers.

Berchtesgaden (pop. 8,300), small Alpine resort town in southeastern Bavaria. Nearby, Adolf Hitler built the Berghof, his fortified chalet retreat.

Berdyayev, Nikolai Aleksandrovich (187 4-1948), Russian religious philosopher. A Marxist in his youth, he later turned to Christianity and created a highly individual Christian existentialism. Expelled from the USSR in 1922, he settled in Paris.

Berg, Alban (1885-1935), Austrian composer of expressive 12-tone music. A pupil of Schoenberg, he adopted his technique in such works as his violin concerto (1935) and his operas, *Wozzeck* (1925), and the unfinished opera *Lulu*.

Bergamot (*Citrus bergamia*), fruit whose rind yields an oil used in perfumes and

Henri-Louis Bergson

George Berkeley

essences. Related to the orange, it is pear-shaped, pale-yellow or green in color, and has fragrant green pulp.

Bergen (pop. 208,900), seaport and second largest city in Norway, situated on the southwest coast on the By Fjord. From the 14th to the 16th centuries it was the northernmost member of the Hanseatic League. Several buildings from this period survive, most notably the Tyskebyggen (German House), now a museum. The central districts of the city have been destroyed by fire several times, notably in 1702, 1855, and 1916. Modern architects have used the "open plan" to create wide streets and many parks. Bergen is a major commercial and communications center for western Norway. Its shipping industry is the third largest in the country. Processing and canning of fish, shipbuilding, paper manufacture, and metalworking are its important modern industries. Bergen was the birthplace of the composer Edvard Grieg. Playwright Henrik Ibsen was manager of the National Theater there (1851-57).
See also: Norway.

Bergen-Belsen *See:* Belsen.

Berger, Victor Louis (1860-1929), first Socialist member of U.S. Congress (1911-13, 1918, 1919). Born in Austria, Berger founded and led the American Socialist Party. In World War I he was sentenced to 20 years' imprisonment for aiding the enemy, but was freed on appeal and returned to Congress (1923-29).

Bergerac, Cyrano de *See:* Cyrano de Bergerac, Savinien de.

Bergman, Ingmar (1918-), Swedish film and stage director, producer, and writer. He combines realism with imaginative symbolism to explore themes such as good and evil, love, old age, and death. Motion pictures include *The Seventh Seal* (1956), *Wild Strawberries* (1957), *Persona* (1965), *Cries and Whispers* (1972), and *Fanny and Alexander* (1982).

Ingmar Bergman

Bergman, Ingrid (1917-84), Swedish stage and screen actress. In 1936 she came to the attention of Hollywood with the film *A Woman's Face.* She went to the United States in 1939 and soon became a star. Her fresh style was shown to advantage in such films as *Intermezzo* (1939), *Gaslight* (1944), for which she won an Academy Award, and *Notorious* (1946). In 1950 her love affair with the Italian director Roberto Rossellini led to her ostracism from Hollywood. She married and later divorced Rossellini, returning to the United States with the film *Anastasia* (1956), for which she won a second Academy Award. Returning to the stage in the 1960s, Bergman was acclaimed for her performances in Turgenev's *A Month in the Country* in London and Eugene O'Neill's *More Stately Mansions* on Broadway.

Bergson, Henri-Louis (1859-1941), French philosopher. He viewed the world as containing a life-force (*élan vital*) in constant conflict with matter. Evolution, he wrote, is creative process energized by the *élan vital,* and time he saw not as a unit of measurement but as the duration of life experience. Bergson was awarded the Nobel Prize for literature in 1927.

Beriberi, disease caused by lack of vitamin B_1 (thiamine). Beriberi leaves the nerves and heart impaired. Treatment involves thiamine replacement.

Bering, Vitus Jonassen (1681-1741), Danish explorer. Sailing in the service of Russia, he explored northeast Siberia (in the 1720s) and Alaska (1741). The Bering Sea and the Bering Strait are named for him.

Bering Sea, extreme northern arm of the North Pacific Ocean, 885,000 sq mi (2,292,150 sq km) in area, bounded by East Siberia, Alaska, and the Aleutian Islands. It contains Nunivak Island, St. Lawrence Island, and the Komandorskiye Islands (USSR). The international dateline crosses it diagonally.
See also: Bering, Vitus Jonassen.

Bering Sea Controversy, Anglo-American dispute in 1886. When indiscriminate slaughter by various nations threatened seal herds in the U.S.-owned Pribilof Islands in the Bering Sea, the United States seized three Canadian ships (1886) and claimed dominion over the Bering Sea (1889). Britain objected, and in 1893 an arbitration tribunal declared the sea international.
See also: Pribilof Islands.

Bering Strait, sea-channel linking the Arctic Ocean with the Bering Sea and separating Siberia from Alaska. The channel is shallow and 55 mi (90 km) wide, covered with drift-ice from November to June.
See also: Bering, Vitus Jonassen.

Berkeley (pop. 102,724), California city on the east side of San Francisco Bay. Berkeley is the home of several renowned schools including the University of California's main campus. Incorporated in 1878, the city is named after George Berkeley, a bishop and philosopher. Its major industries include printing and chemical, equipment, and metal manufacturing. During the Vietnam War Berkeley was the site of major antiwar protests.
See also: California.

Berkeley, Busby (1895-1976), U.S. choreographer and film director who revolutionized the staging of musical production numbers in Hollywood films. He introduced lavish settings, revolving platforms, and giant staircases upon which hundreds of extras performed in such extravaganzas as *42nd Street* (1933), *Gold Diggers of 1933*, and *The Gang's All Here* (1942).

Berkeley, George (1685-1753), Irish philosopher and bishop who, rejecting the views of Locke, argued that the apparent existence of material reality was merely a projection of the mind of God.
See also: Idealism.

Berkeley, Sir William (1606-77), royal governor of Virginia, 1642-52 and 1660-77. His inability to deal with Native American frontier attacks led to Bacon's Rebellion (1676). Berkeley's harsh treatment of the rebels led to his recall to England.
See also: Bacon's Rebellion.

Berkelium, chemical element, symbol Bk; for physical constants see Periodic Table. Berkelium was discovered in Berkeley, Calif., in 1949 by S.G. Thompson, Albert Ghiorso, and Glenn Seaborg. It was synthesized initially by bombarding americium-241 with helium ions. It is produced from plutonium by multiple neutron capture in a high-flux nuclear reactor. Berkelium is a metallic element and a member of the actinide series. Several compounds of berkelium have been made, and its chemistry is analogous to that of curium. Berkelium-247 is the longest-lived isotope. It is an alpha-emitter with a half-life of 1,400 years. Ten isotopes of the element are known.

Berkman, Alexander (1870-1936), Polish-born U.S. anarchist. During a steel strike, he tried to assassinate the Carnegie Steel Co. head, Henry C. Frick (1892). He served 14 years' imprisonment. In 1917 he was imprisoned for draft obstruction, then deported to Russia in 1919.
See also: Anarchism.

Berle, Milton (Milton Berlinger; 1908-), U.S. comedian. Nicknamed "Uncle Miltie" and "Mr. Television," Berle had successful careers in vaudeville, motion pictures, stage musicals, and radio before becoming host of the "Texaco Star Theatre" on NBC (1948). For the next 6 years, his comedy show was the most frequently watched program on television and he is credited with popularizing the new medium.

Berlin (pop. 3,063,000), major city located in the eastern part of Germany on the Spree and Havel rivers. It covers 341 sq mi (883 sq km) and is at the center of a network of railroads and waterways. It was the capital

of Germany from 1871-1945. After World War II, it was divided into East Berlin (which became the capital of the communist state of East Germany) and West Berlin (a state of West Germany). In August 1961 East Germany erected the Berlin Wall to separate the 2 parts of the city. On October 3, 1990, divided Berlin was officially reunited as East Germany ceased its independent existence and became part of a unified German state. Berlin may once again become the political and spiritual capital of Germany, although details of which administrative and legislative activities of the united government will be situated there may not be worked out completely for some time.
See also: Germany.

Berlin, Congress of, international meeting of Russia, Turkey, and major European powers held in 1878 under the leadership of Otto von Bismarck to settle problems created by the 1877-78 Russo-Turkish War. The resultant Treaty of Berlin redrew boundaries in eastern Europe, generally to the advantage of Great Britain and Austria-Hungary.
See also: Bismarck, Prince Otto Von.

Berlin, Irving (Israel Baline; 1888-1989), U.S. songwriter. He wrote over 900 popular songs, including "Alexander's Ragtime Band" (1911), "God Bless America" (1918), and "White Christmas" (1942). His film scores include *Top Hat* (1935), *Annie Get Your Gun* (1946), and *Call Me Madam* (1950).

Berlin Airlift, operation by the United Kingdom and the United States to fly essential supplies into West Berlin during the Russian land and water blockade (1948-49). Its 250,000 flights and 2 million tons of supplies cost $224 million.
See also: Cold War.

Berliner, Emile (1851-1929), inventor who contributed to early telephone and phonograph developments. A year following Alexander Graham Bell's invention of the telephone, Berliner developed a powerful transmitter that enhanced the telephone receiver. He also created the flat phonograph disc, or record, and a process that employed a needle moving horizontally, thus minimizing distortion of Thomas Edison's earlier method. Berliner later produced a method for mass-duplication of records from one master disc. Born in Hanover, Germany, Berliner moved to the United States in 1870.
See also: Phonograph; Telephone.

Berlin Wall, wall 26 mi (42 km) long built in 1961 dividing East and West Berlin. Before 1961, many people fled East Germany by crossing from East to West Berlin. The wall halted this emigration. Between 1961 and 1989 over 70 East Germans were killed attempting to get past the Berlin Wall. In November 1989 the wall began to be dismantled after demonstrations for political reform erupted in East Germany.
See also: Berlin; Cold War.

Berlioz, Louis-Hector (1803-69), French romantic composer of dramatic, descriptive works. Major works include his *Symphonie Fantastique* (1830), *Requiem* (1837), the choral symphony *Romeo and Juliet* (1838-39), the oratorio *The Childhood of Christ* (1850-54), and the operas *Benvenuto Cellini* (1838), and *The Trojans* (1856-59).

Bermuda, British colony comprising about 150 coral islands of which 20 are inhabited, lying in the North Atlantic Ocean, 580 miles (933 km) east of North Carolina. The main island is Bermuda Island, with the capital, Hamilton. The climate is warm and the vegetation lush and tropical. Bermuda's first British colonists arrived in 1609. Some 60% of present inhabitants are descendants of African slaves, and the rest are mainly British. The economy depends on tourism and 2 U.S. military bases.

Bermuda Triangle, area of the Atlantic Ocean roughly bounded by Bermuda, the Greater Antilles, and the southeastern coast of the United States, in which many ships and planes are said to have vanished. Though supernatural causes have been proposed to explain the allegedly mysterious disappearances, there is no evidence of any unusual phenomena in the area at all.

Bern, or Berne (pop. 138,600), capital city of Switzerland and of Bern canton. It lies on the Aare River in German-speaking west-central Switzerland. It is an important commercial, industrial, and cultural center and the headquarters of some major international communications organizations. Bern was founded in 1191 and retains many old buildings.
See also: Switzerland.

Bernadette, Saint (Marie-Bernarde Soubirous; 1844-79), French peasant girl who claimed to have had 18 visions of the Virgin Mary in a Lourdes grotto in 1858. The grotto became a shrine, and she was beatified (1925) and canonized (1933). Her feast day is Feb. 18 in France, April 16 elsewhere.
See also: Lourdes.

Bernadotte, Jean Baptiste Jules (1763-1844), French general who founded Sweden's present royal dynasty. One of Napoleon's marshals (1804), he was elected Swedish crown prince in 1810. He fought Napoleon at Leipzig (1813) and ruled Sweden and Norway as Charles XIV (1818-44).
See also: Sweden.

Bernard, Claude (1813-78), French physiologist, one of the founders of experimental medicine. He studied the digestive process and the function of glycogen in the liver, and in 1851 he reported the existence of the vasomotor nerves.
See also: Digestive system.

Bernard of Clairvaux, Saint (1090?-1153), French theologian and mystic who was the abbot of a Cistercian monastery and inspired the Second Crusade. Founder of the Clairvaux Abbey in 1115, he was adviser to popes, kings, and bishops and was instrumental in Abelard's condemnation (1140). He was canonized in 1174.
See also: Crusades.

Louis-Hector Berlioz

Bernese mountain dog, Swiss breed of large, powerful dog. They have long black hair with russet brown spots on the legs and face and white feet and chests. The dogs typically weigh from 50-75 lbs (23-34 kg) and stand 21-27 in (53-69 cm) tall at the shoulders. Romans originally brought the breed to Switzerland more than 2,000 years ago.

Bernhardt, Sarah (Henriette Rosine Bernard; 1844-1923), French actress. Renowned for her great emotional power, she was the leading performer in classical French theater, appearing in roles created by Victorien Sardou and Edmond Rostand, among others. She made several triumphant worldwide tours.

Bernier, Joseph Elzéar (1852-1934), Canadian explorer renowned for his arctic voyages. Bernier staked Canada's claim to all the North American arctic islands, captained a dozen voyages to the arctic, and journeyed around the world several times.

Berlin Wall on the eve of demolition

Giovanni Lorenzo Bernini, a self-portrait

Bernini, Giovanni Lorenzo (1598-1680), Italian sculptor and architect who gave Rome many of its characteristic baroque features. He designed the tomb of Pope Urban VIII, the canopy over the high altar in St. Peter's, the Piazza S. Pietro, the fountain *Four Rivers* in the Piazza Navona, and the statue *St. Teresa in Ecstasy*.
See also: Baroque.

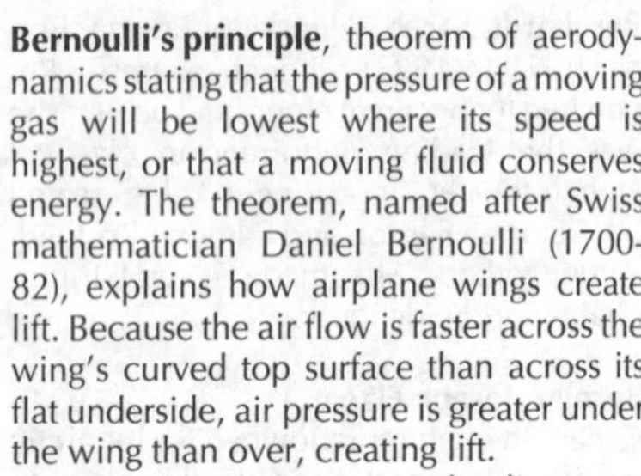

Chuck Berry

Bernoulli's principle, theorem of aerodynamics stating that the pressure of a moving gas will be lowest where its speed is highest, or that a moving fluid conserves energy. The theorem, named after Swiss mathematician Daniel Bernoulli (1700-82), explains how airplane wings create lift. Because the air flow is faster across the wing's curved top surface than across its flat underside, air pressure is greater under the wing than over, creating lift.
See also: Aerodynamics; Hydraulics.

Bernstein, Carl *See:* Watergate.

Bernstein, Leonard (1918-1990), U.S. conductor and composer, best known for his musical *West Side Story* (1957). He rose to fame as conductor of the New York Philharmonic Orchestra (1958-69). His varied works include the symphony *The Age of Anxiety* (1949), the musical *On The Town* (1944), and *The Mass* (1971).

Leonard Bernstein

Berra, Yogi (Lawrence Peter Berra; 1925-), U.S. baseball player for the New York Yankees, 1946-63. He holds the record for World Series games played (75) and greatest number of series hits (71). He won the American League's Most Valuable Player Award in 1951, 1954, and 1955.

Berrigan, Daniel and **Philip** (1922-) and (1924-), Roman Catholic priests in the pacifist "Catonsville Nine" group. In 1969, as a Vietnam War protest, the group broke into the Selective Service Office at Catonsville, Md., and poured oxblood over records and files. The Berrigans were convicted and given 3-year sentences; in 1972 Philip was tried on conspiracy charges but acquitted. In 1981 they were convicted of burglary and conspiracy after they broke into a General Electric plant and damaged 2 nuclear-missile nose cones.

Berry, Chuck (Charles Edward Anderson Berry; 1926-), U.S. rock and roll singer, songwriter, and guitarist. An influential pioneer of rock and roll music, Berry gained notoriety with white audiences and shaped blues rock and roll into his own big-beat and melodic patterned style that later influenced the Beatles and the Rolling Stones. His lyrics, loaded with ironies, spoke about the importance of rock and roll and the value of youth. Born in St. Louis, Mo., Berry played the guitar as a teenager and had his first big hit, "Maybellene," in 1955. Other hits followed: "Johnny B. Goode," "Roll Over Beethoven," "Sweet Little Sixteen," "My Ding-A-Ling," and "Rock and Roll Music."

Berryman, John (1914-72), U.S. poet, active from the 1930s. His reputation was solidified by the long poem *Homage to Mistress Bradstreet* (1956). Berryman's later work, distinguished by its black ironies and linguistic innovation, includes *His Toy, His Dream, His Rest* (1968) and *Dream Songs* (1969). He committed suicide, throwing himself off a bridge in Minneapolis.

Bertillon, Alphonse (1853-1914), French criminologist who devised a system for identifying criminals based on the body measurements. The system was adopted by the French police in 1888 and used until fingerprints became a method of identification.

Bertolucci, Bernardo (1940-), Italian filmmaker known for such films as *The Conformist* (1970), *Last Tango in Paris* (1972), *1900* (1975), and *La Luna* (1979). His films are often controversial and provocative.

Beryl, beryllium and aluminum silicate ($Be_3AP_2Si_6O_{18}$), the most common ore of beryllium. It is a transparent or translucent mineral found mainly as hexagonal crystals in granite rocks. The gem emerald is a dark green beryl containing a small amount of chromium; aquamarine is a blue-green variety of beryl. The finest varieties are found in Brazil, Sri Lanka, Siberia, and New England.
See also: Aquamarine; Beryllium.

Beryllium, chemical element, symbol Be; for physical constants see Periodic Table. Beryllium was isolated as a free metal by Friedrich Wöhler and Antoine Bussy in 1828. *Beryl* (beryllium aluminum silicate) is the commercial source of the element. The element is prepared by the reduction of beryllium fluoride with magnesium metal. Beryllium is one of the lightest and strongest of all metals and greatly increases the strength of other metals when used in alloys. Beryllium copper is extensively used for springs, electrical contacts, and nonsparking tools. Beryllium is used as a moderator in nuclear reactors. It is also used in gyroscopes, computer parts, and inertial guidance instruments. Beryllium and its salts are toxic and should be handled with the greatest of care.

Berzelius, Jöns Jakob, Baron (1779-1848), Swedish chemist who determined the atomic weights of nearly 40 elements before 1818, discovered cerium (1803), selenium (1818), and thorium (1829), introduced the terms *protein, isomerism,* and *catalysis,* and devised the modern method of writing chemical formulas (1813).

Besant, Annie (Wood) (1847-1933), British theosophist and social reformer. Besant joined the Fabian Society and was an early advocate of birth control. She became international president of the Theosophical Society (1907-33) and championed independence for India, becoming president of the Indian National Congress (1917). She published many theosophical works.
See also: Fabian Society.

Bessarabia, historic region of southeastern Europe, northwest of the Black Sea, between the Dniester and Danube rivers. After various Russo-Turkish conflicts it was ceded to Russia in 1812. After the Crimean War it passed to Moldavia (1856) but was regained by Russia (1878). Romania controlled it almost continuously from 1918 to 1944, when it joined the USSR as part of the Moldavian and Ukrainian SSR.

Bessel, Friedrich Wilhelm (1784-1846), astronomer and mathematician. Born in Germany, Bessel made the first authentic measurement of a star's distance from the earth, also called a parallax. This discovery allowed astronomers to document the earth's movement. Bessel also established a class of mathematical functions known as Bessel functions.
See also: Parallax.

Bessemer process, process of making steel from pig iron. The pig iron is loaded into a specially designed furnace or Bessemer

converter. A continuous blast of compressed air is forced through the molten metal to oxidize impurities, which are burned off or form slag. The result is molten steel. Since the 1950s, a modification of the Bessemer process, the basic oxygen process, has been in use. The Bessemer process was developed by the British inventor Sir Henry Bessemer (1813-98).
See also: Steel.

Best, Charles Herbert (1899-1978), Canadian physiologist. As a medical student at the University of Toronto, he and several colleagues isolated the hormone insulin from the pancreas and developed it as a treatment for diabetes (1921). Best's other discoveries include histaminase for the treatment of allergies, the blood-clotting agent heparin, and the vitamin choline.
See also: Insulin.

Beta-blocker, drug that affects the transmission of signals at beta-receptors, parts of the sympathetic nervous system located in the heart, lungs, kidneys, and blood vessels. Beta-blockers (or beta-adrenergic blocking agents) interfere with the stimulation of the beta-receptors. They thereby lower blood pressure and heart rate. They are used in the treatment of hypertension and cardiac arrrhythmia.
See also: Drug.

Betancourt, Rómulo (1908-81), president of Venezuela (1945-47 and 1957-63) and founder of the left-wing Acción Democrática Party (1935). Betancourt spent 1948-58 in exile after a military coup. He survived an assassination attempt in 1960.
See also: Venezuela.

Beta particle, one of the particles that can be emitted by a radioactive atomic nucleus. Most are high-speed electrons, with a mass off about $^1/_{1837}$ and a negative charge. More rarely, a beta particle can be positively charged (positron). The emission of an electron entails the change of a neutron into a proton within the nucleus. The emission of a positron is similarly associated with the change of a proton into a neutron.
See also: Radioactivity.

Betatron, apparatus designed to accelerate electrons to high velocities. Electrons are injected into a ring-shaped vacuum tube where an electromagnet running on alternating current creates a magnetic field whose polarity changes at short intervals. The electrons are accelerated around the ring by the changing magnetic field. Large betatrons can accelerate particles to energies of several hundred million electron volts.
See also: Particle accelerator.

Betel, preparation made with the seeds of the betel palm. A masticatory, betel has been chewed as a stimulant by southern Asians and eastern Africans since ancient times. Betel is made by combining slices of the betel nut seeds with lime paste and other flavorings and spreading it on a betel pepper leaf. It is then rolled and chewed.

Betelgeuse, or Alpha Orionis, second brightest star in the constellation Orion. The name was given to it by Arab astronomers (*bayt al-jawzaa*, "house of twins" in Arabic). Betelgeuse is a regular variable first magnitude red giant with a diameter up to 420 times that of the sun. It is about 500 light-years from Earth.
See also: Orion.

Bethe, Hans Albrecht (1906-), German-born U.S. theoretical physicist who proposed the nuclear carbon cycle to account for the sun's energy output (1938). During World War II he worked on the Manhattan Project. He was awarded the 1967 Nobel Prize in physics for his work on the source of stellar energy.

Bethesda (pop. 62,936), city in Montgomery County, central Maryland, a residential suburb of Washington, D.C. The U.S. Naval Medical Center is located here, as are several noted medical research centers and institutes, including the National Cancer Institute.
See also: Maryland.

Bethlehem (pop. 71,428), city in eastern Pennsylvania, 50 mi (80 km) northwest of Philadelphia, on the Lehigh River. Bethlehem was founded in 1741 by refugees from Moravia and Bohemia seeking religious freedom. The Moravian Brethren maintain a theological seminary and chapel (1803). The city is largely supported by the Bethlehem Steel Company. Bethlehem's cultural fame rests upon its patronage of music; it is the home of the Bach Choir and the annual Bach Festival.
See also: Pennsylvania.

Bethlehem (Hebrew: *Bayt Lahm*; pop. 16,300), town in Israeli-occupied West Bank, 6 mi (9.7 km) south of Jerusalem, and sacred to Jews, Christians, and Muslims. According to the Bible, it is the city where David was annointed by Samuel and the birthplace of Jesus; the traditional tomb of Rachel is outside the town. A basilica built by the Emperor Constantine over the Grotto of the Nativity (326-333) and rebuilt by Justinian I now forms the Church of the Nativity, a major attraction for tourists and pilgrims. Long contested by Christians and Muslims, it was taken by Israel during the 1967 Six-Day War.
See also: Jesus Christ; West Bank.

Bethune, Mary McLeod (1875-1955), African-American educator and civil rights activist. She founded the Daytona Normal and Industrial Institute for Negro Girls (1904), now called Bethune-Cookman College, and was Director of Negro Affairs in the National Youth Administration (1936-44) as well as President F.D. Roosevelt's special adviser on minority affairs.

Bethune, Norman (1890-1930), Canadian physician who achieved national hero status in China in 1938 for the establishment of hospitals and medical schools, and for his role as chief medical officer of the Chinese Communist Army. Bethune also achieved fame for his contribution to medicine through experiments in lung surgery and for the invention of medical instruments. He was also active in the Spanish Civil War in 1936, where he created the first mobile blood transfusion operation.

Betjeman, Sir John (1906-84), English poet laureate and architectural conservationist, often called a lyrical satirist. His works include *New Bats* in *Old Belfries* (1945), *Selected Poems* (1948), *Collected Poems* (1958), and *Victorian and Edwardian Architecture in London* (1969).

Bettelheim, Bruno (1903-90), Austrian-born U.S. psychologist who drew on his personal experience as an inmate of Nazi concentration camps to write his famous article, "Individual and Mass Behavior in Extreme Situations" (1943). His subsequent work mainly concerned the treatment of autistic and disturbed children.

Better business bureau, consumer protection organization such as exists in nearly 200 cities in the United States, Canada, and Israel. Better business bureaus answer telephone calls and written complaints from business customers who feel they have been treated unfairly. Complaints are investigated and corrective actions are recommended if the business is at fault. In cases where corrective action is not taken, the bureau can report the case to the appropriate federal agency.

Betts v. Brady *See:* Gideon v. Wainwright.

Bevatron, in physics, a 6 or more billion electron volt accelerator of protons and other atomic particles.
See also: Particle accelerator.

Beveridge, William Henry (1879-1963), British economist and social planner, director of London School of Economics (1919-37). In *Social Insurance and Allied Services* (1942), he proposed a social security system that became law. Beveridge became a knight in 1919 and a baron in 1946.

Beverly Hills (pop. 31,971), residential city in southern California, completely surrounded by Los Angeles. Formerly a Spanish ranch, it is now the home of wealthy film and television stars. The town extends into the foothills of the Santa Monica Mountains.
See also: California.

Bhagavad-Gita (*Song of God*), anonymous Sanskrit poem dating from c.200 B.C., incorporated into the Mahabharata epic, a classic work of Hinduism. It consists of a dialogue in 700 verses between Prince Arjuna and the god Krishna. The dialogue, held on the eve of a battle, covers many aspects of Hindu religious thought.
See also: Hinduism; Vishnu.

Bhopal (pop. 1,062,700), capital of Madhya Pradesh in central India. On December 3, 1984, a deadly cloud of toxic gas leaked from a Union Carbide plant, killing some 2,000 people and injuring about 200,000 others for the worst industrial accident in history. The Indian government filed lawsuits in the U.S. and in India, charging Union Carbide with negligence. Union Carbide offered a $350-million settlement over a period of 30 years, which the Indian government refused. The U.S. courts rejected the suit in 1986, but in 1989 the Indian Supreme Court ordered Union Carbide to pay $470 million in damages, which seemed to close the matter although many in India still felt the assessment was too low.
See also: India.

Bhutan

Capital:	Thimphu
Area:	18,150 sq mi (47,000 sq km)
Population:	1,497,000
Government:	hereditary monarchy
Independent:	1949
GNP:	U.S. $263,000,000
Per capita:	U.S. $180

Bhutan, kingdom on the southern slopes of the eastern Himalayas, between Tibet on the north and Bangladesh and India on the south. It is extremely mountainous, falling from 24,000 ft (7,315 m) on the northern border to 600 ft (183 m) on the frontier with India. Agriculture, limited to a few areas, is backward; terraced rice cultivation might be extended, but the cultivators lack capital. Corn, potatoes, wheat, millet, and buckwheat are grown. Fine handicrafts include wood carving, basketry, and swords and daggers with elaborately chased silver engravings. The country is slowly changing from an isolated barter system into a transitional market economy. Buddhism of the Tibetan Mahayana type mingles with propitiation of spirits.

Bhutto, Benazir (1953-), prime minister of Pakistan (1988-90, 1993-). She was the first female leader of an Islamic nation. Bhutto, a graduate of both Harvard and Oxford universities, went into exile in 1984, returned to Pakistan after 2 years, and headed the Pakistan People's Party (PPP), which her father, Zulfikan Ali Bhutto, founded. She was removed from power by political and military opponents in 1990 and reinstalled in 1993.
See also: Pakistan.

Bhutto, Zulfikar Ali (1928-79), president and prime minister of Pakistan (1971-77); father of Benazir Bhutto. He held several government posts under President Mohammad Ayub Khan, but became one of his leading opponents and was imprisoned (1968-69). He was deposed by Mohammad Zia ul-Haq in a military coup and executed 2 years later.
See also: Pakistan.

Biafra, name assumed by Nigeria's Eastern Region during its attempted secession (1967-70). Under the leadership of Colonel Ojukwu, the Ibo people of the Eastern Region declared their independence in May 1967, and the civil war, for which both sides had been preparing for some time, broke out. Outnumbered and outgunned, the Biafrans suffered heavy losses, with large numbers dying from starvation, before their final surrender. The former breakaway region was divided to form the East-Central, River, and South-Eastern states.
See also: Nigeria.

Bialik, Chaim Nachman (1873-1934), one of the greatest of modern Hebrew poets and novelists. Born in the Ukraine, he settled in Palestine in 1924. His poetry gave fiery expression to Jewish national aspirations. His publishing business in Odessa was a significant force in the revival of Hebrew language and literature.

Bible, name of the sacred writings of the Christian religion. The word "bible" is derived from the Greek *biblia*, meaning "books." A collection of writings gathered into books, the Bible consists of two main parts, the Old Testament and the New Testament. The Old Testament, written in Hebrew and Aramaic centuries before the birth of Christ, is the Christian name for the Jewish Bible. It comprises 39 books, of which the most important are the five books of the Law (Pentateuch), the Jewish Torah: Genesis, Exodus, Leviticus, Numbers, and Deuteronomy. These are followed by the books of the Prophets (Joshua, Judges, the two books of Samuel, the twelve minor prophets, and others). Finally, the Writings (Hagiographa) include Esther, Job, Psalms, Proverbs, Ecclesiastes, the Song of Songs, Lamentations, and Daniel. The New Testament, the specifically Christian part of the Bible, was written in Greek in the first 2 centuries after Christ. Of its 27 books, the 4 Gospels—of Matthew, Mark, Luke, and John—occupy the hallowed central position. These describe aspects of the life and teachings of Jesus. The remaining 23 books consist of a selection of early Christian writings that were definitively selected as canonical in the 4th century A.D.. The English translation of the Bible in widest use is the King James version (1611). In Christian doctrine, the Bible is written under the guidance of God and contains the moral and historical bases of the Christian view of the world.
See also: Christianity.

Bibliothèque nationale, national library in Paris, France. Also a depository (a library that stores copies of most printed works, especially government documents), the Bibliothèque nationale is one of the largest

Bhutan is a mountainous country. Most of the inhabitants live in the fertile river valleys.

libraries in Europe. Known more as a government archive than a public library, this expansive facility houses about 20 million printed volumes as well as numerous magazines, manuscripts, maps, engravings, coins, and medals. Many of the collections and manuscripts were once part of royal libraries.

Bicameral legislature *See:* Legislature.

Bicarbonate of soda ($NaHCO_3$), sodium bicarbonate, or baking soda, chemical compound used to relieve stomach acidity. It is also used in baking powder and fire extinguishers.

Bichat, Marie François Xavier (1771-1802), French anatomist and pathologist, founder of histology, the study of the small-scale structure of tissue. Although working without the microscope, Bichat distinguished 21 types of elementary tissues of which the organs of the body are composed.

Bicuspid *See:* Teeth.

Bicycle, 2-wheeled vehicle propelled by pedals. In the late-18th century, a device called a célérifère was demonstrated in Paris by Count Mède de Sivrac. By the early 19th century, an improved model, called a draisine, had been developed, with handlebars and a saddle. The design was further improved by Kirkpatrick MacMillan, a Scottish blacksmith, who introduced treadles that the rider moved back and forth to provide power to the rear wheels. The use of rotary pedals was incorporated by the Frenchman Ernest Michaux in his vélocipède. Popular in the 1870s was the "penny-farthing," which had a large front wheel and a much smaller rear wheel. The first bicycle with a chain-drive powering the rear wheel was made in England in 1885. Pneumatic tires were introduced soon after, and the bicycles of the 1890s were similar to those of today. Subsequent improvements include the use of gear-changing systems.

Bicycle racing, popular sport in many countries, especially in Europe. Races may take place on a special track or on open roads. Track events, which range from 140-500 m (459-1,640 ft), exercise the cyclists' tactical skills as well as testing their strength and endurance. Road races cover 50 mi (80 km) to several thousand miles. The most famous event is the Tour de France, an annual international competition that covers about 2,500 mi (4,000 km) and lasts three weeks.

Biddle, Nicholas (1786-1844), president of the second Bank of the United States (1823-36). He made it the country's first authoritative central bank, but President Andrew Jackson vetoed renewal of the bank's charter.
See also: Bank of the United States.

Bieber, Owen Frederick (1929-), president of the United Automobile Workers (UAW). The UAW, founded as a labor union in 1935, has been tainted with struggles since its beginning. Bieber, elected in 1983, is the first UAW president not involved in the union's early disputes. He initiated successful compromises between UAW and automobile manufacturers. A progressive leader, Bieber emphasized job security over pay increases and leveraged UAW interests by encouraging numerous local strikes rather than a national walkout. Bieber became a director of the Chrysler Corporation in 1984.
See also: United Automobile Workers.

Biedermeier, utilitarian middle-class style of furniture popular in Germany from about 1810 to 1850.

Bienville, Jean Baptiste le Moyne, Sieur de (1680-1768), French explorer and naval officer who founded New Orleans. Born in Canada, he helped to colonize French Louisiana, which he governed at various periods between 1701 and 1743.
See also: New Orleans.

Bierce, Ambrose Gwinett (1842-1914?), U.S. short-story writer and satirical journalist. His works include *In the Midst of Life* (1891), *Can Such Things Be?* (1893), and *The Devil's Dictionary* (1906), a compilation of sarcastic definitions. An adventurer, he distinguished himself in the Union army during the Civil War. He disappeared without trace during the Mexican Revolution of 1913-14.

Bierstadt, Albert (1830-1902), German-born U.S. landscape painter famous for his large, realistic Western scenes, including *Sierra Nevada* and *The Settlement of California*.

Bifocals *See:* Glasses.

Bigamy, in law, felony or misdemeanor of being married to 2 persons simultaneously. Ignorance of the fact that the first marriage is still valid is not an acceptable defense in most courts.

Big and Little Dippers, 2 constellations that each resemble a water dipper. The Big Dipper, located in the constellation of Ursa Major (the Great Bear), has 7 stars that are often used as reference points to find other stars. The Little Dipper, a smaller, similar grouping of stars, is fainter except for the North Star, which lies at the end of the Little Dipper's handle. The Little Dipper forms most of the constellation of Ursa Minor, the Little Bear.
See also: Constellation.

Big bang, theory that all the matter and energy of the universe was concentrated in a compact, infinitely small volume that exploded some 15 to 20 billion years ago, giving rise to the present universe, still expanding from the initial explosion. The big bang theory is the most widely accepted cosmological theory today.
See also: Cosmology.

Big Ben seen from the statue of Winston Churchill which faces the Houses of Parliament in London

Big Ben, popular name for the tower clock of the Houses of Parliament in London. It is named for Sir Benjamin Hall, the commissioner of works at the time of its installation in 1856. The bell of the clock weighs 13 tons.

Big Bend National Park, tract of mountains and desert on the Texas border with Mexico, in the Big Bend of the Rio Grande River. The park, which covers over 700,000 acres (283,500 hectares), was established in 1944 and is the last great expanse of wild land left in Texas.
See also: National Parks.

Big Five, the 5 permanent members of the UN Security Council: China, France, Great Britain, the Soviet Union, and the United States. Each of these countries has the right to veto Security Council resolutions.
See also: United Nations.

Bighorn, Rocky Mountain sheep (*Ovis canadensis*) inhabiting the higher moun-

A forerunner of the modern bicycle, the velocipede was propelled by pedals on the axis of the front wheels. It was built in the l860s by Ernest Michaux.

tain ranges of the western United States from New Mexico and southern California northward. The large horns of the male form a full circle; those of the female are smaller and upright. The bighorn stands about 3 ft (1 m) high at the shoulder.

Bighorn Mountains, range of the eastern Rocky Mountains, mainly in northern Wyoming, but extending into Montana east of the Bighorn River. The highest point is Cloud Peak (13,165 ft/4,013 m).
See also: Rocky Mountains.

Bighorn River, river in the Wind River Canyon in Wyoming and flowing through Montana, where it joins the Yellowstone River. Much of its 335 mi (539 km) course runs through deep canyons. Dams and reservoirs provide irrigation, flood control, and hydroelectric power.

Bignonia, any of several hundred species of plants of the Bignoniaceae family, native to warmer parts of the Americas. They usually have creeping or climbing stems and may reach the top of even the highest trees. One of the best known in the United States is the cross vine, which has orange-red, trumpet-shaped flowers.
See also: Calabash.

Bihzad, Kamal ad-Din (1450-1537), Persian miniature painter, famous for illustrating manuscripts such as *Timur Namah, Gulistan,* and *Khamsa.* His paintings of battle scenes and nature scenes were admired throughout the world.

Bikini, atoll in the Marshall Islands in the central Pacific Ocean. It was the site of U.S. nuclear bomb tests in the 1940s and 1950s. Inhabitants evacuated during the tests began to return in the early 1970s, but the island was again declared uninhabitable because of dangerously high radiation levels in 1978.
See also: Marshall Islands.

Bilbao (pop. 378,200), major seaport in northern Spain and former capital of a once autonomous Basque region. The town is built on both sides of the Nervión River, 8 mi (13 km) from the Bay of Biscay. The banks of the Nervión below the city are lined with shipyards, blast furnaces, and factories, for Bilbao is one of Spain's leading centers of heavy industry. The good harbor and rail connections have helped make the city the most important port on Spain's Atlantic coast. Iron ore, lead ore, and steel products rank high among its exports. Also important are wine, olive oil, and canned fish. The 14th-century city on the right bank has provisions for drainage, ventilation, and orderly pedestrian traffic that were advanced for their time.
See also: Spain.

Billiards at the court of Louis XIV, from a 17th-century engraving by Trouvain

Bile, yellow or greenish fluid secreted by the liver which aids in digestion and absorption, particularly of fatty foods. It contains water, lecithin, cholesterol, bile salts, and the pigments bilirubin and biliverdin. When needed, it is discharged through the common bile duct into the small intestine, where it breaks down fats and enables them to be absorbed through the intestinal wall. Bile is also a route of excretion for cholesterol and various drugs.
See also: Digestive system.

Bilharziasis *See:* Schistosomiasis.

Bilirubin *See:* Bile; Jaundice.

Bill, term for various written documents in politics, law, banking, commerce, and so forth. In politics, it is the draft of a statute submitted to the legislature for debate and eventual adoption as law. In the courtroom it was formerly applied to the written statement of a plaintiff's case, now usually referred to as a writ or statement of claim. Bills of attainder, passed by the English parliament and some American colonial legislatures, meted out penalties for certain political crimes but were later abolished as unconstitutional. In the commercial field, a bill of sale is a document transferring ownership of goods or property, sometimes used to secure a debt. In international trade, a bill of lading is a receipt given by a public carrier, agreeing to convey goods to a stated destination. In banking, a bill of exchange is a negotiable document, guaranteeing payment by the drawer to the payee, a form of promissory note or check. A bill of health is a document given to a ship's captain by a local authority, signifying absence of infectious or contagious disease on board.

Billiards, any of several indoor games in which balls set on a felt-covered rectangular table with cushioned edges are struck by the end of a long tapering stick (the cue). Billiards was popular in France and England as early as the 14th century. In most forms of the game, the table has 6 pockets, one in each corner and one midway along each of the longer sides. The object is to sink balls into the pockets by playing one ball off another or, in games played without pockets, to hit the balls against each other successively. *Carom billiards* and *English billiards* feature 2 white cue balls and 1 red ball. *Snooker* has 1 white cue ball, 15 red balls, and 6 balls of other colors. *Pool* (or pocket billiards), as played in the United States, has 1 white cue ball and 15 numbered colored balls and is the country's most popular billiard game.

Billings (pop. 113,419), largest city in Montana, seat of Yellowstone County, located in the south central part of the state. Billings was founded in 1882 during construction of the Northern Pacific Railroad and became a shipping and fur trading center. Major industries today include oil and sugar refining, meat packing, and flour milling.
See also: Montana.

Billings, William (1746-1800), first professional composer and musician born in the American colonies. He was noted for his simple, lively styles in hymns, psalms, and anthems.

Bill of exchange, negotiable instrument used in commerce that is drawn up and signed by one person to direct another person to pay a certain sum of money at a certain time to the bearer or to the party named on the bill. Parties involved in this transaction are frequently banks and businesses; the bill is a convenient means of transferring funds.

Bill of rights, constitutional document that defines the rights of a people; safeguarding them against undue governmental interference. In the United States these rights and safeguards are embodied in the first 10 amendments to the Constitution. After the American Revolution there was great popular demand for constitutionally defined rights to limit the power of the new government. Bills of rights were drafted in 8 states between 1776 and 1781, but when the Constitution was drawn up in 1787 no such bill was included, and ratification by the states lagged until promises were made that a bill of rights would be added. When the first Congress met in 1789, James Madison presented one containing 12 amendments, 10 of which were accepted. On Dec. 15, 1791, Secretary of State Thomas Jefferson proclaimed the Federal Bill of Rights in full force. The bill guarantees freedom of speech, of the press, and of religion. It protects against arbitrary searches and self-incrimination. It sets out proper procedures for trials, giving to all the right to trial by jury and to cross-examination of witnesses. In addition to these rights, the 5th Amendment provides that no person shall "be deprived of life, liberty, or property, without due process of law." Between 1798 and 1971, the states ratified 16 additional amendments to the Constitution.
See also: Constitution of the United States.

Billy the Kid (William H. Bonney; 1859-81), U.S. outlaw. Notorious in New Mexico as a cattle thief, he was sentenced to hang. In 1878 he escaped from jail by killing 2 guards, and was tracked down and killed by Sheriff Pat Garrett.

Biloxi (pop. 197,125), second largest city in Mississippi, a summer and winter resort located on the southern coast along the Gulf of Mexico. Fishing and boat building are major industries. The name Biloxi comes from the Sioux word for "first

people." French Old Biloxi, founded 1699, was the first European settlement in the lower Mississippi Valley.
See also: Mississippi.

Bimetallism, economic term for the use of 2 metals (usually gold and silver) to back a country's currency, making every coin and bill in circulation related to a definite value of both gold and silver. Nearly all countries now use currency based only on gold (monometallism).

Binary numbers, system of designating numbers using only the digits 0 and 1, widely employed in digital computers. Each digit in the binary system represents a successive power of 2, just as digits in the decimal system represent successive powers of 10. For example, in the binary system, the number 110 represents: $(1 \times 2^2) + (1 \times 2^1) + (0 \times 2^0)$, which equals (in the decimal system) 4 + 2 + 0, or 6. While this system may appear cumbersome, it is easily adaptable to electronic circuits, where the 2 digits (0 and 1) can be represented by the 2 states of a switch: open or closed.

Binary star, or double star, pair of stars that orbit around their common center of gravity. Though some binaries can be observed separately without a telescope, in most cases the stars are so close together that they appear to be a single star. A great number of binaries are too close to be seen separately by even the most powerful optical telescopes and are detected by studying the spectral lines of the stars.
See also: Black hole; Nova; Pulsar.

Bindweed, common name for a weedy plant (genus *Convolvulus*) of the morning-glory family, Convolvulaceae. Bindweeds have long twining stems, arrow-shaped leaves, and white or pink funnel-shaped flowers that often open only in the morning.
See also: Morning-glory.

Binet, Alfred (1857-1911), French psychologist who pioneered methods of mental testing. He collaborated with Théodore Simon in devising the Binet-Simon tests, widely used to estimate intelligence.
See also: Intelligence quotient; Psychology.

Bing, Sir Rudolf (1902-), Austrian-born British opera impresario. An opera administrator in Germany, he emigrated to Britain when the Nazis came to power, headed the Glyndebourne Opera (1935-49), and helped organize the Edinburgh Festival (1947). As general manager of New York's Metropolitan Opera (1950-72), he introduced black singers and presided over the company's move to Lincoln Center.
See also: Opera.

Bingham, George Caleb (1811-79), U.S. genre painter noted for his midwestern river scenes, such as *Fur Traders Descending the Missouri* (1845) and *Raftsmen Playing Cards* (1846). He also treated political subjects with warmth and humor, as in *Canvassing for a Vote* (1851), He served in the Missouri state legislature in 1848, and later held other state offices.

Binoculars, optical instrument consisting of a pair of compact telescopes mounted side by side. Since both eyes are used, the magnified image of distant objects appears to be in 3 dimensions. The magnifying power of a pair of binoculars and the diameter of the object lens (front lens) are engraved on the instrument. Binoculars marked 10 x 50, for example, will make objects appear 10 times closer and have object lenses that are 50 mm (about 6 in) in diameter. Binoculars can be adjusted to focus the image, to move the two telescopes nearer or farther apart to fit the eyes, and to remove double images.

Biochemistry, study of the substances occurring in living organisms and the reactions in which they are involved. It is a science on the border between biology and organic chemistry. The main constituents of living matter are water, carbohydrates, lipids, and proteins. The total chemical activity of the organism is known as its metabolism. Landmarks in biochemistry include the synthesis of urea by Friedrich Wöhler (1828), the pioneering research of Von Liebig, Pasteur, and Bernard, and, more recently, the elucidation of the structure of DNA by James Watson and Francis Crick (1953).
See also: Biology; Chemistry.

Biofeedback, method of electronically monitoring various specific biological functions, such as blood pressure, with the aim of helping a person gain greater control of otherwise unconscious physiological processes. Biofeedback techniques have been used with some success in the treatment of hypertension, chronic headaches, epilepsy, and other disorders.

Biogenesis, origin and evolution of living forms. The law of biogenesis is the principle that all living organisms are derived from a parent or parents.
See also: Reproduction.

Biological clock, mechanism that controls the rhythm of various activities of plants and animals. Some activities, such as mating, migration, and hibernation, have a yearly cycle; others, chiefly reproductive functions (including human menstruation), follow the lunar month. But the majority have a period of roughly 24 hours, called the circadian rhythm. Although related to the day/night cycle, circadian rhythms are not directly controlled by it. Many organisms in unvarying environments will continue to show 24-hour rhythms, but the pattern can be changed and the clock "reset."

Biological warfare, war waged with microorganisms and their toxins against people, animals, and plants. The United States, USSR, Great Britain, and more than 100 other countries signed an agreement in 1972 to prohibit the development, production, and stockpiling of biological weapons.

Biology, science of living things. The most important subdivisions of biology are zoology, the study of animals, and botany, the study of plants. Advances in scientific knowledge have led to an increase in the number of fields of biological study. Some biologists study subdivisions of the animal and plant kingdoms: entomology (the study of insects), mycology (fungi), paleontology (fossils), and microbiology (microorganisms). The they were mainly interested in anatomy, still an important field of study. As early biologists accumulated information about plants and animals, they noticed that some closely resembled others. Such observations were the basis for a system of classification. The Swedish naturalist Carolus Linnaeus devised a method of classifying living things, called taxonomy, in which each plant and animal is assigned a unique name. Physiology is the study of the workings of organs and how they are affected by disease. The study of diseases themselves is called pathology. Biology is also connected with other scientific disciplines. Biochemistry is the application of chemistry to biology, and biophysics is the application of physics to biology. The study of animal behavior often employs the techniques of psychology. Molecular biology studies biological processes at the level of the molecule. The study of genetics, dealing with heredity, has become increasingly important. Genetic engineering is now making possible the production of substances by means of intervention in genetic processes.

Bioluminescence, the production of nonthermal light by living organisms, such as fireflies, many marine animals, bacteria, and fungi. The effect is an example of chemiluminescence. In some cases its utility to the organism is not apparent, though in others its use is clear: In the firefly, the abdomen of the female glows, enabling the male to find her; similarly, luminescence enables many deep-sea fish to locate each other or to attract their prey. The glow in a ship's wake at night is due to luminescent microorganisms.

Biome, major ecological unit that is relatively stable, widespread, and well-defined. An example would be a savanna, a tropical grassland with a characteristic range of interlocking plant and animal forms.
See also: Ecology.

Biomedical engineering, application of principles of engineering to biology and medicine, usually involving collaboration between engineers and biological scientists. There are a number of specialty areas in the field. Bioinstrumentation is the use of electronic measuring devices to monitor, diagnose, and treat diseases; biomechanics is the study of effects of various forces on the body, such as gravity. The development of appropriate materials that can be implanted inside the human body is the province of biomaterials, and systems physiology aims at an integrated understanding of living organisms. Clinical engineering involves the development of computer instruments in hospitals, and rehabilitation engineering develops devices and procedures to expand the capabilities of disabled people.

Bionics, science of designing artificial systems that apply the principles that govern the functioning of living organisms. These may be simple imitations of nature or systems that embody laws learned from nature. An example of the latter would be radar, inspired by the echolocation systems of bats.

Biophysics, branch of biology in which the methods and principles of physics are applied to the study of living things. It has grown up in the 20th century alongside the development of electronics. Its tools include the electroencephalograph and the electron microscope. Its techniques include those of spectroscopy and X-ray diffraction. Its field of study deals with such questions as nerve transmission, bioluminescence, and materials transfer in respiration and secretion.
See also: Biology; Physics.

Biosphere, the part of the earth inhabited by living things. It forms a thin layer around the earth, including air, water, and land.

Biosynthesis, biochemical reactions by which living cells build complex molecules from simple ones.
See also: Biochemistry; Cell.

Biotechnology, industrial application of biological knowledge, in particular through the alteration of genes, called genetic engineering. Alteration of genes has been used to create new drugs, chemicals, and animal growth hormones, as well as therapies to repair genetic defects. Ethical and safety concerns about the uses of genetic engineering have generated many legal and moral conflicts in recent years.
See also: Genetic engineering.

Biotite *See:* Mica.

Birch, name for various deciduous trees and shrubs of the family Betulaceae, characterized by their smooth, white outer bark, which sometimes peels off in layers. The heart-shaped leaves have saw-tooth edges. Birch grows widely in the cooler parts of the Northern Hemisphere. The close-grained timber is used for furniture, the bark for tanning and thatching. Among the best-known species are the paper birch of North America, used by Native Americans to make canoes and tents; the silver birch, a native of Europe, widely used in the USSR for roofing material, containers, and in processing leather; and the yellow birch, which makes up some 75% of the American harvest of birchwood.

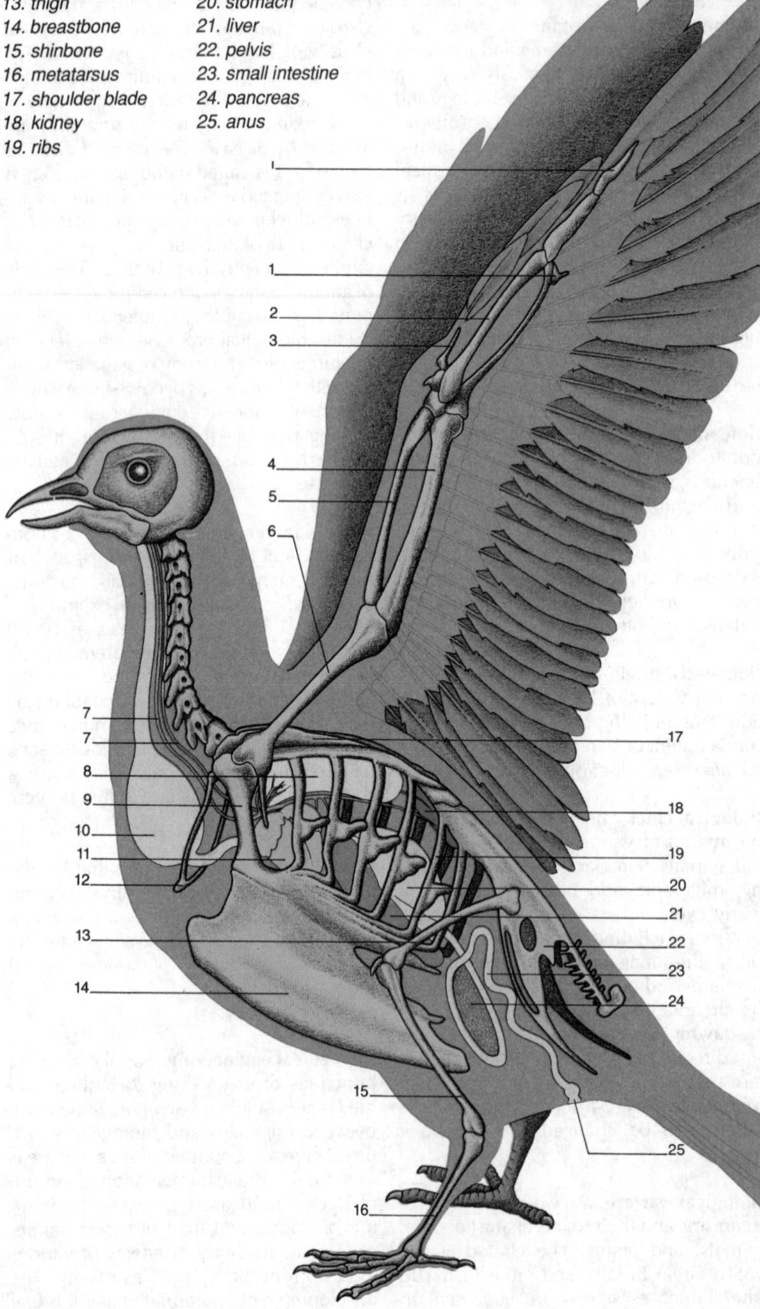

The parts of a bird.
1. finger
2. middle handbones
3. thumb
4. ulna
5. radius
6. humerus
7. bloodvessels
8. lung
9. raven's bill collarbone
10. crop
11. heart
12. connate collarbone
13. thigh
14. breastbone
15. shinbone
16. metatarsus
17. shoulder blade
18. kidney
19. ribs
20. stomach
21. liver
22. pelvis
23. small intestine
24. pancreas
25. anus

Bird, animal adapted for flight and unique in its body covering of feathers. There are more than 8,500 species. Birds are warm-blooded descendants of reptiles of the dinosaur group. They developed feathers from scales (still evident on their legs) and became two-legged as their forelimbs became wings. Their teeth disappeared, replaced by a horny bill used for feeding and performing complicated tasks, such as nest-building. The bird's body has been adapted for flight. The feathers, an efficient and light body covering, streamline the body and extend the flight surfaces: wings and tail. The skeleton is light, and the bones are hollow. Large breast muscles provide power for flight. The heaviest flying bird is the trumpeter swan of North America, which can weigh up to 38 lb (17 kg). At the other end of the scale, the bee hummingbird is about 2.5 in (6 cm) long and weighs 1/10 oz (3 g). Flightless birds can be much larger. The ostrich stands up to 8 ft (2 1/2 m) and can weigh 300 lb (136 kg). Flightless birds are mainly adapted for running or swimming. Runners have strong legs, like the ostrich; swimmers have wings that are modified as flippers, as in penguins. But some flying birds are also powerful runners, or swimmers. All birds reproduce by laying eggs that must be kept warm for correct development.

Bird, Larry (1956-), U.S. basketball player. Known for his excellence in all phases of the game, he is considered one of the best players of all time. The 6-ft 9-in (206-cm) forward joined the Boston Celtics of the

National Basketball Association (NBA) in 1979 and was named the NBA Rookie of the Year. Bird's other achievements include winning 6 NBA Most Valuable Player (MVP) awards—3 regular season (1984, 85, 86), 2 playoff (1984, 85), and 1 All-Star (1982)—and leading the Boston Celtics to 3 NBA Championships (1981, 84, 86).

Bird of paradise, any of more than 40 species of brilliantly colored, plumed birds of the family Paradiseidae, found in eastern Australia, the Moluccas, and New Guinea.

Bird of paradise, plant (*Strelitzia reginae*) named for the colorful bird which its flowers resemble. Native to South Africa, this perennial herb grows to a height of 3 to 4 ft (0.9 to 1.2m) and has long-stalked leaves. Several showy flowers, with orange sepals and blue-purple petals, rise from each of the boat-shaped bracts that tip the flowering stalks.

Birdseye, Clarence (1886-1956), U.S. inventor and industrialist who, having observed during fur-trading expeditions to Labrador (1912-16) that many foods keep indefinitely if frozen, developed a process for freezing food. In 1924 he founded General Foods to market frozen produce.
See also: Food, frozen.

Birmingham (pop. 1,008,000), second-largest city in England, about 200 mi (161 km) northwest of London. Birmingham is known as the steel city, producing everything from pins to automobiles. In ancient times a Saxon settlement existed in this area, and by 1166 the site had become a busy market village trading in small metal goods made in nearby Staffordshire, where iron and coal were plentiful. By the late 16th century the population was manufacturing metal products, from swords and cutlery to guns, buckles, jewelry, and plate. In the 17th century Birmingham became a center for scientific ideas and innovation in industry. Scientists and inventors established the Lunar Society there, its members including James Watt, Matthew Boulton, and Joseph Priestley. By 1800 Birmingham was one of the major industrial towns in Britain, but its rapid growth caused deplorable living and working conditions, resulting in riots (1839). The modern city is a center for the machine and tool industries; other products include armaments, toys, and electrical equipment.
See also: England.

Birmingham (pop. 907,810), largest city in Alabama, situated in the Jones Valley and protected by mountains to the southeast and northwest. Located in a region rich in coal and iron, it manufactures numerous iron and steel products, including pipes, stoves, cotton gins, diesel engines, and electrical equipment. Birmingham was founded and incorporated in 1871, on a site where railroads from 4 directions met in a cotton field. It is now an important rail and air terminus and has a port of entry accessible from the Gulf of Mexico through a channel. The city is also an important educational center, being the site of Miles College, Howard College, Birmingham-Southern College, and the University of Alabama Birmingham (UAB).
See also: Alabama.

Birney, James Gillespie (1792-1857), U.S. abolitionist. Birney, who came from an old slave-owning family, freed his slaves in 1834. He launched the abolitionist newspaper the *Philanthropist* in 1836, became executive secretary of the American Anti-Slavery Society in 1837, and founded the Liberty Party, standing as its presidential candidate in 1840 and 1844.
See also: Abolitionism.

Birth, the climax of gestation (the development of a child or other baby mammal within its mother's body) and the beginning of an independent life. In humans, a normal birth proceeds in 3 stages. Mild labor pains caused by contractions of the muscles of the uterus are usually the first sign that a woman is about to give birth. The contractions push the baby downwards, usually head first, which breaks the membranes surrounding the baby, causing the amniotic fluid to escape. In the second stage of labor, stronger contractions push the baby through the cervix and vagina, or birth canal. This is the most painful part and usually lasts less than 2 hours. Anesthetics and analgesics are commonly administered at this time, and delivery is aided by hand or with obstetric forceps. In some cases, the baby must be delivered by a surgical procedure called cesarean section. As soon as the baby is born, its nose and mouth are cleared of fluid and breathing starts, whereupon the umbilical cord is cut and tied. In the third stage of labor, the placenta is expelled from the uterus and bleeding is stopped by further contractions.The exact mechanism by which labor is initiated remains unknown; however, recent research indicates that hormones both from the placenta and from the mother's pituitary gland play important roles in the onset of labor.
See also: Reproduction.

Birth control, prevention of conception in order to avert unwanted births. There are various contraceptive, or birth-control, devices, including condoms, spermicidal jellies, diaphragms, intrauterine devices, and pills taken by women. Surgical sterilization (for men: vasectomy; for women: tubal ligation) is also possible. Diverse methods of birth control have become increasingly widespread in the 20th century, especially in industrialized countries.

Birth defect, congenital anomaly; structural or severe functional defect present at birth. Birth defects cause about 10% of neonatal deaths. A major anomaly is apparent at birth in 3-4% of newborns; by the age of 5, up to 7.5% of all children manifest a congenital defect. The incidence of specific congenital anomalies varies with a number of factors: (1) Individual defect (common malformations such as cleft lip and cleft palate occur in 1 in every 1,000 births). (2) Geographical area (because of factors such as differences in the genetic pool or the environment). For example, the occurrence of spina bifida is 3-4 in every 1,000 births in areas of Ireland, but under 2 in 1,000 in the United States. (3) Cultural practices: where marriages between relatives are frequent, the incidence of certain defects increases. (4) Certain prenatal problems. Scientists estimate that about 2.5-3% of infants born annually in the United States begin life with major birth defects; counting minor types of defects, the percentage increases to 7-10%.

Birthmark, skin blemish, usually congenital. There are 2 main types: pigmented nevuses or moles, which are usually brown or black and may be raised or flat; and vascular nevuses or hemangiomas, local growths of small blood vessels, such as the "strawberry mark" and the "portwine stain." Although harmless, they are sometimes removed for cosmetic reasons or if they show malignant tendencies.
See also: Mole.

Birthstone, gemstone associated with a month. The ancients allotted a birthstone to each month and believed that it would influence anyone born in that month. The stones and the qualities they were thought to impart are: *January*, garnet (loyalty); *February*, amethyst (sincerity); *March*, bloodstone (courage); *April*, diamond (innocence); *May*, emerald (love); *June*, moonstone (health); *July*, ruby (contentment); *August* sardonyx (married happiness); *September*, sapphire (clear thinking): *October*, opal (hope); *November*, topaz (faithfulness); *December*, turquoise (prosperity).

Bishop, Elizabeth (1911-79), U.S. poet and translator of Brazilian poetry, widely acclaimed for her succinct style and lyricism. Her books include the Pulitzer Prize-winning *North and South—A Cold Spring* (1955), *Questions of Travel* (1965), and *Geography III* (1976).

Bishop, Billy (William Avery Bishop; 1894-1956), Canadian military flier, credited with shooting down 72 German airplanes in World War I. In 1917 he was awarded the Victoria Cross, Britain's highest military decoration, and the Distinguished Service medal.
See also: World War I.

Bismarck, one of the most powerful German battleships of World War II. It had a speed of 30 knots, carried eight 15-in (38.1-cm) guns, and displaced more than 45,000 long tons (45,700 m tons) of water. It was sunk in May 1941 after eight different British ships bombarded it about 600 mi (970 km) off the French coast. A 1989 inspection of the sunken ship by U.S. researchers indicated that the Germans might have caused it to go down themselves to prevent its capture.
See also: World War II.

Bismarck (pop. 83,831), capital of North Dakota and seat of Burleigh County, on the Missouri River. In the mid-19th century, the original settlement was a busy river port and fortified center for the region. It had a brief boom as a supply depot for the Black Hills gold rush of the 1870s, and was the western terminus of the Pacific Railroad until 1879. The city became territorial capital in 1883, and in 1933, its skyscraper capitol was completed. There are rich lignite and petroleum deposits in the vicinity. Bismarck is also a market for grain and livestock.
See also: North Dakota.

Otto von Bismarck

Bismarck, Prince Otto von (1815-1898), German political leader who was instrumental in creating a unified German state. Born of Prussian gentry, he entered politics in 1847 and became premier of Prussia in 1862. In 1866 he defeated Austria in the Austro-Prussian War, creating the North German Federation, which excluded Austria. The Franco-Prussian War (1870-71) resulted in the defeat of France and the creation of a German empire under Prussian hegemony. Bismarck was made imperial chancellor and prince (1871). Although Wilhelm I was nominally the kaiser (emperor), Bismarck held real power and ruled as a virtual dictator. Under his regime, the German economy flourished, and German power expanded internationally. He was forced to resign in 1890 after the accession of Kaiser William II.
See also: Germany.

Bismarck Archipelago, group of mountainous islands in the Pacific Ocean, northeast of New Guinea, comprising New Britain, New Ireland, the Admiralty Islands, and many smaller islands. During World War II the Japanese captured the islands and made the area their center of defense in the southwest Pacific. After the war the islands were handed back to Australia and are currently administered from New Guinea. Most of them are covered with jungle vegetation and some have active volcanoes.

The American bison

Bismuth, chemical element, symbol Bi; for physical constants see Periodic Table. Bismuth was known to the ancients and in early times was confused with tin and lead. It was shown to be distinct from lead in 1753 by Claud J. Geoffroy. Bismuth is sometimes found native, as the minerals *bismite* and *bismuthinite*. It is obtained as a byproduct of the refining of lead, copper, and tin. Bismuth is a grayish-white, hard, brittle, low-melting metal. It is the most diamagnetic of all metals and has the highest Hall effect of any metal. It has a low thermal conductivity and a high electrical resistance. Bismuth forms low-melting alloys that are widely used in fire detection and fire extinguishing systems. Bismuth and its compounds are used in powerful magnets and, in medicine, as antisyphilitics and anti-infectives.

Bison, any of several species (genus *Bison*) of ox-like animals of the family Bovidae. Bison may weigh half a ton and stand 6 ft (1.8 m) tall. The American bison, often miscalled the buffalo, once grazed the plains and valleys of Mexico to Canada in herds of millions and was economically vital to Native Americans. Hunted ruthlessly by European Americans, it was almost extinct by 1900. There are still a few herds in U.S. and Canadian national parks and population calculations determine that there are about 15,000 bison in the United States and an equal number in Canada.

Bissau (pop. 109,000), capital, largest city, and major port of Guinea-Bissau. It is located at the mouth of the Geba River on the West African coast. Its main exports include coconuts, rice, peanuts, hardwood, palm oil, and shellfish.
See also: Guinea-Bissau.

Bithynia, ancient country of Asia Minor, in what is now Turkey. The Persians conquered Bithynia in the 600s B.C., but the country became independent after Alexander the Great's destruction of the Persian empire. Bithynia was independent from the 3rd century B.C. until 74 B.C. when Rome annexed it. It declined in the 2nd century A.D.

Bitterling, minnowlike fish of the family Cyprinidae, found in the fresh waters of Europe and Asia Minor. It is remarkable for its association with freshwater mussels. In the breeding season the female develops a 2-in (5-cm) tube with which she deposits her eggs inside a mussel. The milt (sperm), deposited by the male near the mussel, is drawn in through the mussel's respiratory siphon to fertilize the eggs. Meanwhile the mussel releases its larvae, which cling to the skin of the female bitterling and are carried around before dropping to the bottom.

Bittern, any of several species of migratory birds of the heron family. The U.S. bittern ranges from 2 to 3 ft (61 to 91 cm) tall. Its brownish color blends into marshland reeds, allowing it to feed upon its diet of fish, frogs, mice, and insects.

Bitternut, medium to large-sized tree (*Carya cordiformis*) of the walnut family, which grows mostly in low wet woods. Its name is derived from the tree's bitter-tasting nuts. Thin-shelled and cylindrical in shape, they contain a fat white kernel. Bitternut wood is used for making wooden crates and furniture.

Bitter root, any of several small perennial plants of the family Portulacaeae, with long edible roots. It is also called tobacco root because of the tobacco odor generated when cooked. Bitter root has a fat stalk and produces a single rose-colored or white flower. It is the state flower of Montana.

Bittersweet, either of 2 unrelated woody vines: U.S. bittersweet (*Celastrus scandens*) and European bittersweet (*Solanum dulcamara*). The U.S. bittersweet grows up to 20 ft (6 m) in height, and has tiny greenish flowers and a woody stem. In late autumn yellow pods split open, displaying red and yellow waxen berries. European bittersweet is rarely more than 8 ft (2.4 m) high. Its flowers vary from violet to light blue and sometimes white. The vine produces poisonous berries and leaves. It is native to Europe and Asia.

Bitumen, general term for naturally occurring hydrocarbons (compounds of hydrogen and carbon). It commonly refers to solid or semisolid compounds like pitch, tar, and asphalt. Bitumen products are widely employed to coat timber to protect it from water, and to seal roofs, arches, walls and floors.
See also: Coal; Hydrocarbon.

Bituminous sands, sands containing natural bitumen deposits. The heavy oil extracted from these sands is converted to synthetic crude oil by refining.
See also: Coal.

Bizet, Georges (1838-75), French composer, best known for his opera *Carmen* (1875), one of the most popular in history. He also wrote symphonies and incidental music for other operas.

Björling, Jussi (1911-1960), Swedish operatic tenor who specialized in Italian opera, especially works by Verdi and Puccini.
See also: Opera.

Bjørnson, Bjørnstjerne Martinius (1832-1910), Norwegian poet, critic, novelist, dramatist, and politician, winner of the Nobel Prize in literature (1903). Initially concentrating on themes of Norwegian history, he later wrote about modern social problems. Among his writings was the novel *Flags Are Flying in Town and Port* (1884).

Black, Davidson (1884-1934), Canadian anthropologist who discovered the early

human species later known popularly as Peking man. He was professor at Peking Union medical college in China until his death.
See also: Anthropology.

Black, Hugo Lafayette (1886-1971), U.S. politician and jurist, associate justice of the Supreme Court (1937-71). A supporter of the New Deal, Black was appointed to the Supreme Court by President Franklin D. Roosevelt. Although he was a former Ku Klux Klan member, he became a leader of the Court's efforts to extend civil rights.
See also: Supreme Court of the United States.

Black, Joseph (1728-99), Scottish physician and chemist. He investigated the properties of carbon dioxide, discovered the phenomena of latent and specific heats, distinguished heat from temperature, and pioneered the techniques used in the quantitative study of chemistry.
See also: Chemistry; Heat.

Black Americans *See:* African Americans.

Blackbeard (d. 1718), English pirate whose real name was probably Edward Teach or Thatch. A privateer in the War of the Spanish Succession, he later turned to piracy in the West Indies and along the Atlantic coast, until he was killed by the British.

Blackberry, prickly bramble (genus *Rubus*) of the rose family, native to north temperate regions of the world, that produces an edible fruit. Some varieties, including the loganberry and boysenberry, are cultivated to be sold fresh, frozen, or canned, and are used in beverages, liqueurs, and preserves.

Blackbird, any of several dark-colored perching birds of the family Icteridae, including the red-winged blackbird and the yellow-headed blackbird. Blackbirds may survive temperatures as low as 20°F (–6°C). They travel in huge flocks (as many as 5 million birds) and eat fruit, insects, and worms, and often do serious damage to crops.

Blackbuck (*Antilope cervicapra*), antelope of India and Pakistan. Once numbering millions, there are now only a few thousand left in the plains and woodlands where they live in herds. The females and young are yellow-fawn with a white eye-ring; the adult males are dark brown, stand about 32 in (81 cm) tall at the shoulder, and bear spiral horns up to 2 ft (60 cm) long. Blackbuck are very swift and used to be hunted with cheetahs.

Black Codes, laws enacted after the Civil War in the states that had formed the Confederacy. These codes were aimed at preserving white supremacy after the demise of slavery. Some codes persisted into the 20th century, despite constitutional amendments guaranteeing equal rights for former slaves.
See also: Civil War, U.S.

Black Death, common name for an epidemic of bubonic plague that swept through Asia and Europe in the mid-14th century, perhaps halving the population of Europe. Caused by a bacterium, the disease was carried by flea-infected rats. Its economic effects were far-reaching, among other things fanning flames of superstition and religious prejudice.
See also: Bubonic plague.

Black-eyed pea *See:* Cowpea.

Black-eyed Susan, hardy annual or biennial coneflower (*Rudbeckia hirta*), the state flower of Maryland. Sometimes called yellow daisy, it bears 20 to 40 orange-yellow ray flowers around a group of darker brown florets.

Blackfish, common name given to any of various dark-colored fishes, including the black sea bass found along the Atlantic coast of the United States, the Alaska blackfish found in streams and ponds in Alaska and Siberia, and the tautog, found in the Atlantic Ocean from New Brunswick, Canada, to South Carolina.

Blackfoot tribes, North American plains tribes of the Algonquin linguistic family. The Blackfoot, named for their black-dyed moccasins, were originally hunters and trappers in what is now Montana and the Canadian provinces of Alberta and Saskatchewan. The disappearance of the bison (killed off by white settlers), a smallpox epidemic, and wars with whites reduced the Blackfoot population. Blackfoot today are farmers and ranchers in Montana and Alberta.
See also: Algonquin.

Black Forest, wooded mountain range in the province of Baden-Württemberg, southwestern Germany. An area of great scenic beauty, it is an important tourist attraction, with lumber, clock, and toy industries.

Black Friday, term referring to 2 particular financial disasters that occurred on Fridays. The most famous was Sept. 24, 1869, when speculators Jay Gould and James Fisk tried to corner the gold market with the connivance of government officials. The market collapsed, and many were ruined. The second Black Friday was Sept. 19, 1873, when a collapse of the New York Stock Exchange led to a panic.
See also: Cornering the market; Stock exchange.

Black haw, small tree or shrub (*Viburnum prunifolium*) of the eastern and southern United States. It grows up to 15 ft (4.6 m) high. After a frost, its bluish-black berries can be eaten.

Black Hawk (1767-1838), Native American leader of the Sauk tribe, who opposed the movement of European settlers westward to Illinois. A treaty had been signed by the Sauk and Fox tribes in 1804 ceding lands east of the Mississippi River to the United States, but Black Hawk declared that the Sauk had been tricked and that the contract was invalid. In 1832, he and his warriors fought to regain their land. Black Hawk and his 2 sons were captured in 1833 and moved to a reservation near Fort Des Moines.
See also: Indian wars.

Blackhead *See:* Acne; Pore.

Black Hills, mountain range in South Dakota and Wyoming, famous for the Mount Rushmore National Memorial. Here, the heads of 4 past U.S. presidents are carved out of the mountainside. The Black Hills are rich in minerals, including gold. Their highest point is Harney Peak (7,242 ft/2,207 m).
See also: Mount Rushmore National Memorial.

Black hole, according to current astrophysical theory, the final stage of evolution for very massive stars following complete gravitational collapse. In theory, a star with a mass more than 3 times that of the sun could collapse to an indefinitely small size. The gravitational field of such an object would be so powerful that not even electromagnetic radiation (including visible light) could escape. Black holes, if they exist, would have to be detected by their gravitational effects on other bodies and by the emission of X- and gamma rays by objects falling into them. A black hole would therefore bear some resemblance to the initial state of the universe in the big bang theory.
See also: Astronomy; Big Bang; Star.

Black Hole of Calcutta, prison cell in which 146 British captives were incarcerated on the night of June 20, 1756, after a battle between British and Indian troops during which the Indian forces captured a British fort. Some of the prisoners suffocated in the 14 ft (4.3 m) by 18 ft (5.5 m) room. John Holwell, a British survivor, alleged that 123 of the 146 had died, but subsequent research suggests that there were probably about 15 deaths.

Black Kettle (1803?-68), Cheyenne chief known for his efforts to live peacefully with European settlers. Despite this, his people were subjected to unprovoked attacks by U.S. troops. In Nov. 1864 nearly 300 men, women, and children in southeastern Colorado were massacred by troops led by Col. John Chivington. Black Kettle escaped and moved to a settlement in what is now Oklahoma. In Nov. 1868 General George A. Custer led an attack that killed Black Kettle, along with as many as 100 of his people.

Blacklist, list of persons, companies, or organizations who are disapproved of and are to be boycotted.

Black lung, disease caused by inhaled dust which collects in the lungs and may eventually destroy them. Black lung has two forms, simple and complicated, and is found among coal miners and sandblasters. Symptoms are wheezing, coughing, and a higher incidence of lung infection.

Black market, illicit dealing in scarce commodities or currencies, in defiance of rules for rationing and price restrictions. In the United States, black market operations did not appear on a large scale until strict price controls and rationing were introduced during World War II. After the war, black market operations ceased for the most part as government controls were lifted. A black market also operates in countries where there is a shortage of reliable foreign currencies such as dollars or marks and people are prepared to pay above the official exchange rate to obtain them.

Black Mountains, range of the Blue Ridge Mountains in western North Carolina and highest of the Appalachians. Their highest point is Mount Mitchell (6,684 ft/2,037 m).
See also: Blue Ridge Mountains.

Blackmun, Harry Andrew (1908-), U.S. lawyer named to the U.S. Court of Appeals in 1959 and appointed Supreme Court justice by President Nixon in 1970. Blackmun has upheld liberal positions on civil and reproductive rights while remaining conservative in other respects.

Black Muslims, popular name of a U.S. black nationalist movement (originally called the Nation of Islam) founded in Detroit in 1930 by Wali Farad, who rejected racial integration and advocated thrift, hard work, and cleanliness. Under Elijah Muhammad (1934-75), the Black Muslims became a major force in the African-American community, demanding the formation of an independent Black nation in the United States. In the 1960s a split between Elijah Muhammad and Malcolm X, a Black Muslim minister and the group's most prominent leader, undermined the strength of the Nation of Islam. Malcolm X was assassinated in 1965, and when Wallace Muhammad succeeded his father as leader of the group in 1975, he turned the organization into a non-political association whose beliefs are closer to those of orthodox Islam, changing its name to the American Muslim Mission. A splinter group bearing the original name, the Nation of Islam, continues to uphold Elijah Muhammad's teachings.
See also: Malcolm X; Muhammad, Elijah.

Black Panther Party, U.S. black political movement founded in Oakland, Calif. in 1966, advocating self-defense of the African-American community and revolutionary change in the United States. Under the leadership of Eldridge Cleaver, Huey P. Newton, Bobby Seale, and others, the Panthers opened community centers and bookshops as well as doing legal battles with the authorities. Their often violent rhetoric was used to justify armed attacks that resulted in the death of many Panther leaders, such as Fred Hampton in Chicago. The influence of the party was weakened by internal factional disputes in the early 1970s, and by the 1980s its influence in the black liberation movement had ended.

Black Power, slogan coined in the mid-1960s by militant black activists, particularly Stokely Carmichael of the Student Non-violent Coordinating Committee (SNCC), to give voice to and inspire a growing black pride and aspiration for political power. A significant turning point in the history of Black Power occurred at the 1968 Summer Olympics when U.S. athletes receiving medals for their victory raised their fists in sympathy for this movement. It has evolved a multiplicity of meanings ranging from awareness of African-American economic potential to cultural and political organization.
See also: African Americans; Carmichael, Stokely.

Black Prince *See:* Edward, the Black Prince.

Black Sea, tideless island sea between Europe and Asia, bordered by Turkey, Bulgaria, Romania, and the USSR, and linked to the Sea of Azov and (via the Bosporus) to the Mediterranean. It covers 181,000 sq mi (468,790 sq km) and is up to 7,250 ft (2,210 m) deep. The Danube, Dniester, Bug, Don, and Dnieper rivers all flow into the sea, which is vital to Soviet shipping. The chief ports are Odessa, Sevastopol, Batumi, Constanta, and Varna. The USSR's Black Sea coast is an important resort area.

Black September, name applied to various armed groups within the Palestine Liberation Organization. Named for the civil war in Jordan in Sept. 1970 that led to the expulsion of all Palestinian guerrilla groups from the country by King Hussein, groups called Black September claimed responsibility for or were implicated in many violent acts in the 1970s, including the killing of 11 Israeli athletes at the 1972 Olympic Games in Munich.
See also: Arafat, Yasir; Palestine Liberation Organization.

Black Shirts, nickname given to Fascist Party activists in Italy. They were organized by Benito Mussolini in 1919 and seized control of the Italian government in 1922, forcing King Victor Emmanuel III to appoint Mussolini as leader.
See also: Mussolini, Benito.

Blacksnake (*Coluber constrictor*), non-venomous snake common in almost every part of the United States. One of the largest North American snakes, it is 4-7 ft (120-210 cm) long. The adult is a deep slate-black color, while the young are pale gray with grayish-brown patches. Sometimes known as the "racer," this snake can move along the ground as fast as a running human can run and can climb trees with ease. Its food consists mainly of lizards, frogs, mice, and birds. The eggs, usually a dozen or more, are encased in a leathery shell. Also referred to as blacksnakes are the pilot black snake (*Elaphe obsoleta*) of North America and various black snakes of Australia (genus *Pseudeschis*).

Black Sox Scandal, ironic name for 1919-20 baseball scandal that led to radical reorganization in the administration of the sport. It broke out when Edward Cicotte of the Chicago White Sox confessed to accepting a bribe to influence the outcome of the 1919 World Series. He named 7 other team members allegedly involved. All 8 were suspended for a season but were cleared of fraud.

Blackstone, Sir William (1723-80), English jurist, author of *Commentaries on the Laws of England* (1765-69). Educated at Oxford, Blackstone was admitted to the bar in 1746 and in 1758 became the first holder of the new chair in English law at Oxford. The *Commentaries*, whose influence was considerable in the United States as well as England, forms a compendium of English law up to the 18th century.

Black studies, in U.S. education, program of study of the culture, history, and literature of African Americans, initiated to correct the omission of such information from traditional scholastic disciplines. These courses were added to high-school and university curricula as a result of black protests of the 1960s.

Blackwell, Antoinette Brown (1825-1921), U.S. social reformer and Congregationalist minister. A graduate of the theological seminary of Oberlin College, she became an itinerant preacher. In 1853 the Congregational church in South Butler, N.Y., made her its pastor. She thus became the first woman in the country to be formally appointed pastor of a church. Blackwell was a writer as well. Her best-known book was *The Sexes Throughout Nature* (1875).

Blackwell, Elizabeth (1821-1910), English-born U.S. physician, first woman to be granted a medical degree in the United States. Refused admission to various medical schools, she graduated from the Geneva (N.Y.) Medical College in 1847. In 1857 she and her sister opened the New York Infirmary for Women and Children, which was entirely staffed by women, and in 1868 she helped found its Women's Medical College. Returning to England, she taught at the London School of Medicine for Women.

Black widow, poisonous spider (genus *Latrodectus*) of the Americas. Adults are black and have red or orange hourglass-shaped marks on their abdomens. The adult female is 0.5 in (1.3 cm) long and often devours the smaller male during mating. The bite of the black widow can cause considerable pain, swelling, and nausea, but is rarely fatal to healthy adults.

Bladder, muscular sac in the lower abdomen of all mammals that stores urine produced by the kidneys. Urine is carried to

the bladder through 2 tubes called ureters and is emptied through the urethra by the contraction of a sphincter muscle. The term is also used to designate any similar organ in plants or animals; for example, the swim bladder in fish and the vesicles in some seaweeds.
See also: Kidney; Urine.

Bladder, gall *See:* Gall bladder.

Bladderwort, aquatic plant (genus *Utricularia*) found in tropical and temperate zones that traps insects, larvae, small worms, and protozoa in air-filled sacs attached to its stems and roots. In medical history, the plant has been used for the treatment of eczema and other allergic skin conditions.

Blaine, James Gillespie (1830-93), U.S. politician. He served as U.S. representative (1863-76) and senator (1876-81) from Maine, and as secretary of state under Presidents James A. Garfield (1881) and Benjamin Harrison (1889-92). He was the Republican candidate for president in 1884, losing to Grover Cleveland in a campaign in which he refused to repudiate a supporter's description of the Democrats of New York as the party of "rum, Romanism, and rebellion."

Blair, U.S. family influential in 19th-century politics and the formation of the Republican Party. **Francis Preston Blair** (1791-1876) of Abington, Va. founded the *Washington Globe* and was a member of President Andrew Jackson's Kitchen Cabinet. He later helped to found the new Republican Party. His eldest son, **Montgomery Blair** (1813-83), was the lawyer who defended Dred Scott before the Supreme Court in 1857 and was postmaster general under Lincoln (1861-64). Another son, **Francis Preston Blair, Jr.** (1821-75), was instrumental in keeping Missouri from seceding when the Civil War broke out. He was a general in the Union army and was a senator from Missouri in 1871-73.
See also: Republican Party.

Blair, Anthony Charles Lynton (Tony) (1953-), British Prime Minister of the Labour Party since 1997. Blair attended public school in Scotland and studied law in Oxford. In 1983 he became an MP; in 1994 he succeeded John Smith as Party leader and as Leader of the Opposition. Under Blair Labour's politics shifted to the center, resulting in a landslide victory in the 1997 general election.

Blair, Eric *See:* Orwell, George.

Blair, Henry (19th-century), U.S. slave and inventor. He became the first black to hold a patent when he obtained patents for a corn harvester (1835) and a cotton planter (1836). In 1858, however, it was ruled that slaves could not hold federal patents; this situation prevailed until after the Civil War.

Blair, John (1732-1800), U.S. jurist who served on the committee that drafted Virginia's constitution (1776). A delegate to the Constitutional Convention (1787), Blair sat on the general court and the first court of appeals and was an associate justice of the U.S. Supreme Court (1789-96).
See also: Supreme Court of the United States.

Blair House, official guest house of the U.S. government, on Pennsylvania Ave. in Washington, D.C. It was used as a temporary White House by President Truman (1948-52). The house, built in 1824, was named for its second owner, Francis Preston Blair, whose family sold it to the government in 1942.

Blake, Eubie (James Hubert Blake; 1883-1983), African-American ragtime pianist and composer of the Broadway musical *Shuffle Along* (1921) and the songs "I'm Just Wild About Harry" and "Memories of You." He was still performing publicly in his 90s.

Blake, William (1757-1827), English poet and painter. With the help of his wife, Catherine Boucher, he developed a printing process that he used to illustrate and publish his own works, including *Songs of Innocence* (1789) and *Songs of Experience* (1794), collections of lyrics that contrast natural beauty with humanity's material world. Blake was a revolutionary in both politics and religion, which is reflected in his art, particularly in the powerful "Prophetic Books," in which he created a mythology of his own. The most famous of his Prophetic Books are *The Marriage of Heaven and Hell* (c.1790) and the epic *Jerusalem* (1804-20). Blake's work was largely ignored by his contemporaries, and his reputation grew significantly after his death.

Blanc, Mont, highest peak (15,771 ft/4,807 m) in the European Alps, in southeastern France on the border with Italy. One of the world's longest vehicular tunnels (7.5 mi/12 km), exceeded in Europe only by the 10.2 mi (16.4 km) St. Gotthard (1980), was constructed through Mont Blanc's base in 1965.

Blanchard, Jean Pierre François (1753-1809), French balloonist who made the first aeronautical crossing of the English Channel (1785) and the first balloon ascent in America (1793). He also invented the parachute (1785).

Bland, James A. (1854-1911), African-American composer. In the late 1800s he helped popularize "minstrel music" and was an accomplished banjo player. Among the songs he wrote were "Carry Me Back to Old Virginny" (1878), "Oh, Dem Golden Slippers" (1879), and "In the Evening by the Moonlight" (1879).

Blank verse, unrhymed verse in iambic pentameter (lines consisting of 5 short-long feet, totaling 10 syllables). The most common English meter, it was used to great effect by Marlowe, Shakespeare, and Milton.

Black widow

Blarney stone, stone of Blarney Castle, Ireland. In legend it has the magical power to confer the gift of eloquence on those who kiss it.

Blasco Ibáñez, Vicente (1867-1928), Spanish antimonarchist politician and novelist. His naturalistic novels include *Reeds and Mud* (1902), *Blood and Sand* (1909), and the World War I novel *The Four Horsemen of the Apocalypse* (1916). He was imprisoned dozens of times for his political activities.

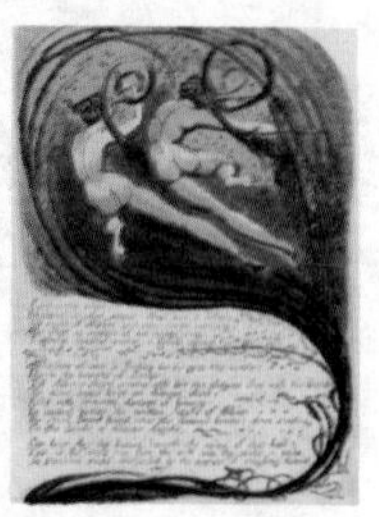
A page from Europe: A Prophesy *(1794) by the English poet and painter William Blake, who illustrated his own handwritten texts, producing a decorative harmony.*

Blatch, Harriot Eaton Stanton (1856-1940), U.S. suffragist; daughter of Elizabeth Cady Stanton and Henry B. Stanton. Blatch formed the Equality League of Self-Supporting Women (1907) and was a member of the National Woman's Party. Her books include *Mobilizing Woman Power* (1918), *A Woman's Point of View* (1920), a biography of her mother (1921), and *Challenging Years* (1940).
See also: Woman suffrage.

Blazing star, or gay feather, any of about 30 species of perennial North American wildflowers of the family Asteraceae, found in prairies and woodlands. The blazing star grows 1 to 6 ft (30 to 180 cm) high, with clusters of purple or pink blossoms surrounded by bracts (leaflike structures the same color as the flowers).

Bleaching, the process of whitening materials, usually with chemicals that reduce or oxidize color. Textiles, flour, oil, and sugar are often bleached.

Bleeding heart, garden plant (*Dicentra spectabilis*) with drooping, heart-shaped flowers, native to China and Japan. The bleeding heart vine of the verbena family is from West Africa.

Blenheim, Battle of, decisive battle in the War of Spanish Succession. On Aug. 13, 1704, troops of the Grand Alliance (England, Austria, and the United Provinces), commanded by the Duke of Marlborough and Prince Eugene of Savoy, triumphed over the Franco-Bavarian soldiers under

Marshall Tallard. Fought on the Danube between the Bavarian villages of Blindheim and Hochstadt, Blenheim saved Vienna from the forces of King Louis XIV, consolidated the Grand Alliance, and ended French occupation of Germany.
See also: Spanish Succession, War of the.

Blériot, Louis (1872-1936), French pioneer aviator and inventor. In 1909 he became the first to fly a heavier-than-air machine across the English Channel.

Bligh, William (1754-1817), reputedly cruel British naval officer, captain of the *Bounty* at the time of the now-famous mutiny (1789). In 1805 he became governor of New South Wales and was subsequently imprisoned by mutinous soldiers (1808-10).

Blindness, partial or complete loss of vision, caused by injury to the eyes, congenital defects, or diseases such as cataracts, diabetes, glaucoma, and hypertension. Infant blindness can result if the mother had rubella (German measles) early in pregnancy; malnutrition (especially vitamin A deficiency) may cause blindness in children. There are many ways for blind people to overcome their disability, including Braille (a method of reading with the fingers by touching raised dots), books on tape, and optical scanners generating speech. The use of a cane, guide dog, and sonar devices on glasses all contribute in assisting the blind. The first U.S. school for the blind was the Perkins School for the Blind (1832) in Boston.

Blindworm, legless European lizard (*Anguis fragilis*), found in meadows and woodlands. The adult is about 1 ft (30 cm) long, brownish in color, with smooth scales. The blindworm eats snails and slugs. It is believed to be blind.

Blitzkrieg (German, "lightning war"), originally used to describe the sudden German mechanized warfare attacks on Poland and France in World War II, now applied to any rapid, forceful military advance, such as the 1944 sweep through France by the U.S. Army under Patton.
See also: World War II.

Blitzstein, Marc (1905-64), U.S. composer and librettist. He wrote the texts and music for the òperas *The Cradle Will Rock* (1937) and *Regina* (1949). His greatest achievement was his translation and adaption of the English text for the 1954 New York state production of *The Threepenny Opera*, by Kurt Weil and Berthold Brecht.

Blixen-Finecke, Karen *See:* Dinesen, Isak.

Blizzard, snowstorm with high velocity winds, temperatures well below freezing, and visibility less than 500 ft (152.4 m). Such storms are common on the Great Plains east of the Rockies in the United States and Canada, in polar regions, and in parts of Europe and Asia.
See also: Snow.

Bloch, Ernest (1880-1959), Swiss-American classical composer. He was greatly influenced by traditional Jewish music, as evidenced in his symphonic poem *Israel* (1916), *Sacred Service* (1930-33), and *Three Jewish Poems* (1913). He also wrote concertos, chamber music, and suites for piano and strings.

Bloch, Konrad Emil (1912-), U.S. biochemist. His studies of animal cells resulted in the discovery of cholesterol, a fatty substance produced from acetic acid. In 1964 he shared the Nobel Prize for physiology or medicine.
See also: Biochemistry; Cholesterol.

Block, Herbert Lawrence (1909-), U.S. political cartoonist. His dry and witty cartoons have been appearing under the signature Herblock in the *Washington Post* since 1943. He was awarded the Pulitzer Prize in 1942 and 1954.

Blockade, maneuver normally imposed by means of seapower, designed to cut an enemy's supply routes and force a surrender. The objective may also be to capture an enemy port.

Blockhouse, small log or stone fortification, usually temporary and built to defend newly won territory. Common in frontier America, blockhouses were used by settlers as a gathering place to protect themselves from Native American attacks.
See also: Pioneer life in America.

Bloemfontein, capital of the Orange Free State and judicial capital of South Africa. First settled by Dutch farmers in 1846, it is now a rail and industrial center. Harvard University and the University of Michigan maintain astronomical observatories in the city.
See also: South Africa.

Blood, thick red fluid pumped by the heart and flowing throughout the body in the blood vessels of the circulatory system. The blood serves many functions in the body, but principally it carries nutrients to and waste away from individual cells and helps regulate the body's metabolism. It carries oxygen from the lungs to the tissues, and carbon dioxide from the tissues to the lungs. It transports hormones to tissues that need them, carries nutrients absorbed from the intestine, and bears away the waste products of metabolism to the organs of excretion—the lungs, the kidneys, the intestines, and the skin. Blood also defends the body against infection, and the clotting mechanism minimizes the loss of blood after an injury.
Seen with the naked eye, the blood appears opaque and homogeneous, but upon microscopic examination it is seen to consist of cells. The most numerous are red corpuscles (erythrocytes), which normally outnumber white cells (leucocytes) by 500 to 1. Also present in the blood are minute circular bodies known as platelets, or thrombocytes, necessary for clotting. The blood cells subsist in an intercellular liquid called plasma. The volume of cells and plasma is approximately equal. Blood plasma itself is a complex fluid; 90% of it is water, but the balance consists of proteins, electrolytes, other minerals, and nutrients needed by the body's cells.
Common blood disorders are leukemia (excess white blood cells or leucocytes) and anemia (a lack of red blood cells). For medical purposes, principally transfusion, blood is usually categorized into one of 4 groups, A, B, AB, and O.
See also: Blood transfusion; Blood type; Circulatory system.

Blood count, number of blood cells found in a standard volume of blood; also, the test used to determine that number.
See also: Blood; Hemoglobin.

Bloodhound, breed of dog of European origin, often used for tracking because of its acute sense of smell. Full-grown bloodhounds stand about 2 ft (0.61 m) high at the shoulder and weigh up to 110 lb (50 kg).

Bloodless Revolution *See:* Glorious Revolution.

Blood poisoning, or septicemia, invasion of the bloodstream by toxic microorganisms from a local infection. Symptoms include chills, fever, and prostration.
See also: Blood.

Blood pressure, pressure of the blood upon the walls of the arteries as it is pumped from the heart. The pressure is strongest at the left ventricle of the heart but can be felt pulsing at various points on the body. The pulsing corresponds to the force and rhythm of the heart's pumping action, and it can be measured to determine blood pressure. An instrument called a sphygmomanometer is used to ascertain the pressure at the brachial artery of the forearm, just above the elbow.
Blood pressure is recorded by 2 figures written as a fraction. The numerator indicates the systolic, or maximum, pressure produced by the heart; the denominator indicates the diastolic, or lower, pressure produced by the heart, which results in the least pressure upon the artery. "130/90," for example, is read as "130 over 90." Hypertension and stroke are disorders accompanied by high blood pressure.
See also: Blood.

Bloodroot (*Sanguinaria canadensis*), spring-flowering North American perennial. The blossom is white with 8 to 12 petals and is about 2 in (5 cm) across on a reddish stalk. Native Americans used the red sap as a paint and dye.

Bloodsucker *See:* Leech.

Blood transfusion, transfer of blood or components of blood from one person or animal to another. Transfusions are used to replace blood loss due to hemorrhaging, severe burns, or shock, and in such disorders as hemophilia. They are also used regularly in surgical procedures. Blood

must be tested for compatible classification (blood group and Rh factor) to prevent rejection reactions by the recipient. Plasma, the fluid part of blood, is often given when whole blood is not needed or is unavailable.
See also: Blood; Plasma.

Blood type, classification of an individual's blood by group—A, B, AB, or O—and Rh-factor (negative or positive). People with blood group AB can receive blood from all other groups; those with group O can donate to all other groups.
See also: Blood.

Blood vessel *See:* Artery; Blood; Capillary; Vein.

Bloody Sunday *See:* Lenin, V.I.; Union of Soviet Socialist Republics.

Bloomer, Amelia Jenks (1818-94), U.S. social reformer. She edited (1848-54) *The Lily*, a journal advocating temperance and women's rights. In a search for more practical clothes for women, she introduced the baggy pantaloons that came to be known as bloomers.
See also: Woman suffrage.

Bloomfield, Leonard (1887-1949), U.S. linguist whose book *Language* (1933) was the chief text of the structuralist school of linguistics, the scientific study of the form and pattern of language. Bloomfield taught at Illinois and Ohio State universities and was Sterling professor of linguistics at Yale after 1940.
See also: Linguistics.

Bloomsbury group, influential coterie of writers and artists who met in Bloomsbury Square, London, in the early 20th century. Influenced by G. E. Moore, the group included Virginia Woolf, Leonard Woolf, Clive Bell, Vanessa Bell, E. M. Forster, V. Sackville-West, Roger Fry, Duncan Grant, J. M. Keynes, and Lytton Strachey.

Bloor, Mother (Ella Reeve Bloor; 1862-1951), U.S. radical activist. She participated in the temperance and women's suffrage movements and was a Socialist Party organizer (1902-19) before cofounding the U.S. Communist Party (1919). Called the "Matron Saint" of the party, she served on its national committee (1932-48).
See also: Woman suffrage.

Blount, William (1749-1800), U.S. politician and a signer of the Constitution. President Washington appointed him governor of the Tennessee territory, and in 1796 he was elected to the Senate from the new state. Blount was expelled from the Senate the next year for aiding the British in their plot to seize Spanish Florida.

Blow fly, any of various flies of the family Calliphoridae. The best known of these 2-winged flies is the bluebottle (*Calliphora vicina*). Blowflies lay eggs in carrion, excrement, or open wounds.

Blücher, Gebhard Leberecht von (1742-1819), Prussian general, made a field marshal after helping to defeat Napoleon in the Battle of Leipzig (1813). A year later he led Prussian troops into Paris, and in 1815 the timely intervention of his troops was important in Wellington's victory over Napoleon at Waterloo.
See also: Napoleonic Wars.

Blue baby, infant with a blueness of skin usually caused by a congenital heart defect leading to a mixture of venous and arterial blood.
See also: Cyanosis.

Bluebeard, villain of a traditional tale in which a rich man's seventh wife disobeys him and finds the murdered bodies of former wives. She is saved by her brothers. Maeterlinck based a play on the legend.

Bluebell, any of various wild perennial plants with blue bell-shaped flowers. The term also refers to the Scottish bluebell or harebell of the bellflower family, most commonly the English bluebell, California bluebell, and Virginia bluebell.

Blueberry, any of several hardy deciduous shrubs (genus *Vaccinium*) bearing a blue-black fruit, many species of which are found in North America. The high-bush blueberry (*V. cerymbosum*), which may reach 15 ft (4.6 m) in height, and the low-bush blueberry (*V. augustifolium*) are the two most commonly cultivated. A popular component of jellies, jams, and pastry fillings, blueberries are frequently canned and frozen.

Bluebird, any of several species (genus *Sialia*) of migratory songbirds of the thrush family, related to the robin but with blue above a red breast. Bluebirds often nest near human habitations.

Bluebonnet (*Lupinus subcarnosus*), annually blooming, low-growing lupine (with edible, bean-like seeds). It is the state flower of Texas.

Blue crab, any of several edible, soft-shell crabs (*Callinectes sapidus* and *C. hastatus*) that inhabit Atlantic coastal shores and estuaries. The shell is green-brown and about 6 in (15 cm) wide; the legs are bluish. The blue crab is a scavenger, feeding on dead animals.

Bluefish (*Pomatomus saltatrix*), voracious fish of the family Pomatomidae, found in the Atlantic and Indian oceans and the Mediterranean Sea. It can grow to a length of about 4 ft (1.22 m) and attain a weight up to 30 lb (13.6 kg), though it normally averages 30 in (.75 m) in length and 10-12 lb (4.5-5.5 kg) in weight. A popular game fish resembling the pompano and related to the sea bass, the bluefish is caught commercially for food.

Bluegrass, traditional, instrumental country music, played on unamplified string instruments (banjo, fiddle, mandolin, and guitar). The style, highly improvisational with close harmonies, was developed in the late 1930s by Bill Monroe and his Blue Grass Boys and by the banjo player Earl Scruggs.

Bluegrass State *See:* Kentucky.

Blue jay, crested bird (*Cyanocitta cristata*) widespread in the eastern half of the United States and Canada. The adult is 1 ft (30 cm) long with pale gray underparts and a black necklace. Upperparts are blue with black and white markings.

Blue law, U.S. state law regulating public and private behavior in accordance with criteria of "public morality." The term, derived from the blue paper on which some were printed, was first used to describe 17th-century laws of the New Haven Colony that prohibited dancing, card playing, and drunkenness and were particularly restrictive concerning activities that could be engaged in on Sundays. The most famous blue law (ultimately repealed) was the 18th amendment to the Constitution (1919), which made the manufacture, transport, and sale of alcoholic beverages illegal. Some states still enforce blue laws today, mostly those which regulate business and public events on Sunday. Some laws have been found to be unconstitutional under the First Amendment.

Blue Nile *See:* Nile River.

Blue Ridge Mountains, eastern range of the Appalachians extending southwest 600 mi (960 km) from Pennsylvania to northern Georgia. Grandfather Mountain, at 5,964 ft (1,818 m), is the tallest peak. The Blue Ridge Mountains are pre-Cambrian metamorphic rock with igneous intrusions. Constituent ranges include the Great Smoky Mountains and the Black Mountains.
See also: Appalachian Mountains.

Blue crab

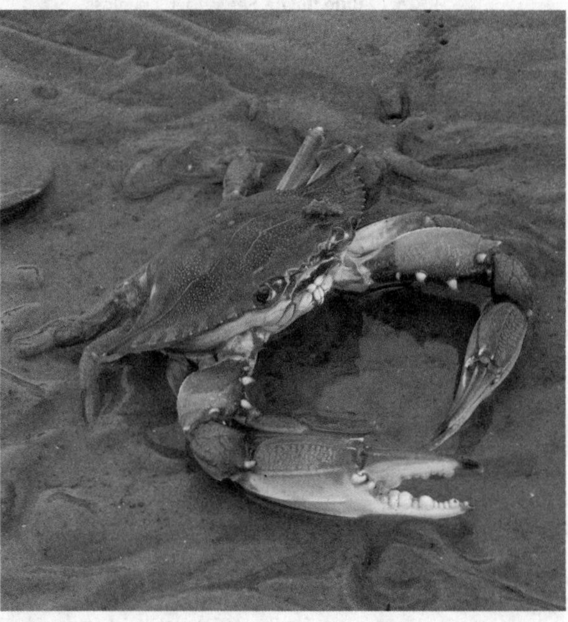

Blues, U.S. musical form derived from the work songs, spirituals, and "field hollers" of African Americans of the South, characterized by the use of flattened "blue notes." The blues, which came to be the principal basis of the jazz idiom, has the characteristic pattern of a 12-bar structure, with distinctive harmonies, most probably of African origin. What began as songs, many about despair and cynicism, accompanied by guitar, harmonica, or piano, has expanded to include a purely instrumental form. The blues were first popularized by W.C. Handy ("Memphis Blues" and "St. Louis Blues"); early blues artists include Ma Rainey, Bessie Smith, and Blind Lemon Jefferson.

Blues composer W.C. Handy at the age of 19. Handy was a songwriter, cornet-player, and bandleader. His best-known compositions are "Memphis Blues" (1912) and "St. Louis Blues" (1914), which have been recorded numerous times by Louis Armstrong among others.

Bluet, North American wildfower (*Houstonia caerula)* having 4 bluish lobes with a yellow center.

Blue thistle *See:* Viper's bugloss.

Blue vitriol *See:* Sulfate.

Blue whale, member (*Balaenoptera musculus*) of the rorqual family of baleen whales. The blue whale is the largest animal that has ever lived—up to 100 ft (30 m) in length and 220 tons (200 metric tons) in weight. Baleen whales have no teeth. Instead, thin plates in their mouths (called baleen) strain out tiny organisms, called plankton, on which the whales feed. Blue whales live in all oceans, but breed in warm waters. Like other whales, they are mammals; they bear live young and suckle them on milk. A newborn blue whale may be over 20 ft (6.1 m) long and weigh 3 tons (2.7 metric tons). Today, the blue whale is an endangered species because of excessive whaling.

Bluford, Guion Stewart, Jr. (1942-), U.S. astronaut. In 1983, Bluford made a 6-day voyage on the space shuttle *Challenger*, becoming the first African American to travel in space.

Blum, Léon (1872-1950), creator of the modern French Socialist party, and the first socialist and the first Jewish person to become premier of France. As premier in 1936-37, he led the Popular Front, a coalition of Socialists and Radicals opposed to fascism. Blum was imprisoned by the Germans, 1940-45. He became premier again in 1946-47.

Blume, Judy (1938-), U.S. author. Her best-known works are in the "young adult" genre and deal with experiences of teenagers and preteens as they grow toward maturity. Her books in this vein include *Are You There, God? It's Me, Margaret* (1970), *Then Again, Maybe I Won't* (1971), and *Forever* (1975). Adult novels include *Wifey* (1978) and *Smart Woman* (1983).

Blushing, sudden, brief redness to the face and neck that occurs when capillaries, tiny blood vessels in the skin, swell with blood.

Bly, Robert (1926-), U.S. poet and translator whose works deal with American themes. *Silence in a Snowy Field* (1962) explores his native state of Minnesota and concepts of solitude and silence. *The Light Around the Body* (1967) is an anti-Vietnam War statement. He has also translated and printed works of foreign poets including Rilke. He was the recipient of the National Book Award in 1968.

Bly, Nellie (Elizabeth Cochrane; 1867-1922), U.S. reporter. She pretended to be insane to gain entry to an insane ward to report on treatment of the insane (1888). In 1889 she beat the record of the Jules Verne character Phileas Fogg (*Around the World in Eighty Days*), traveling around the world in 72 days, 6 hours, 11 minutes, and 14 seconds.

B'nai B'rith, Jewish service organization founded in New York in 1843. B'nai B'rith supports hospitals and orphanages and offers vocational guidance and disaster relief. Branch organizations include the Hillel Foundation, for Jewish university students and faculty; B'nai B'rith Youth; and the Anti-Defamation League (founded 1913) to combat discrimination.

Boa constrictor (*Constrictor constrictor*), nonpoisonous snake of the family Boidae (which includes pythons and anacondas), mostly found in the tropics of the Americas. The live-bearing boa constrictor, 10-18 ft (3-5 m) in length, suffocates its prey (birds and mammals) by squeezing.

Boadicea, or Boudicca (d. A.D. 61), British queen of the Iceni of Norfolk. In A.D. 60 she led a revolt against the Romans, sacking Camulodunum (Colchester), Londinium (London), and Verulamium (St. Albans) before being defeated. She took poison to avoid capture.

Boar, wild, either of 2 species of wild pig, the Eurasian *Sus scrofa* and the Indian *S. cristatus.* The wild boar stands about 3 ft (91 cm) at the shoulder and has stiff bristles over a short gray-black undercoat. It has 2 tusks in the lower jaw and broad feet, adaptations to the marshy areas it inhabits. The wild boar is omnivorous.
See also: Peccary.

Boas, Franz (1858-1942), German-born U.S. anthropologist and ethnologist, leader in establishing the cultural-relativist school of anthropology in the English-speaking world. One of the earliest to use statistical

Blue whale

Boa constrictor

methods in his field, he was an authority on Native American languages, the first professor of anthropology at Columbia University (1899-1936), and the author of more than 30 books, including *The Mind of Primitive Man* (1911) and *Anthropology and Modern Life* (1928).
See also: Anthropology; Ethnography.

Boat *See:* Boating; Ship.

Boating, popular pastime using waterborne craft for pleasure. Boats can be propelled by small motors, sails, or paddles (oars). They vary from 1- and 2-person kayaks, canoes, and rowboats to yachts ranging from 30 to 120 ft (9 to 36.5 m). There are more than 14 million pleasure boats in the United States, used primarily for sports fishing and cruising inland waterways.

Bobcat (*Lynx rufus*), ferocious North American spotted lynx (wild cat), named for its short (6 in/15.2 cm) tail. A nocturnal animal, the bobcat grows to a length of about 3 ft (0.9 m) and has a brown and white coat with black spots and stripes.

Bobolink (*Dolichonyx oryzivorus*), North American migratory songbird. Also called ricebird (for feeding on rice crops during southern migration), it has a dull plumage, except in spring, when the male acquires white and yellow patches. Once hunted but now protected, the bobolink breeds in the United States and southern Canada, migrating to South America for the winter.

Bobsledding, winter sport pitting 2- or 4-person sleds against each other down a steep incline. Capable of traveling at 90 mph (145 kmph), bobsleds negotiate a twisting course with steep embankments ranging from 1,312 yards (1,200 m) to 1,640 yards (1,500 m) long. The team posting the fastest times after 4 runs is the winner. Bobsledding was invented in Switzerland around 1890.

Bobwhite, any of several North American gamebirds (genus *Colinus*)of the pheasant family, often called quail or partridge. About 10 in (25 cm) long and reddish-brown in color, the bobwhite is named for the sound of its mating call and feeds on insects and seeds. Bobwhites travel and sleep in groups, called coveys.

Boccaccio, Giovanni (1313-75), Italian writer and humanist, whose work had a lasting influence on European literature and was used as a source by such writers as Chaucer and Shakespeare. A classical scholar and friend and admirer of Petrarch, he is the author of *Amorous Fiammetta* (1343-44), the first modern psychological novel, and the *Decameron* (1348-53), a collection of 100 short and often ribald tales set against the background of a plague epidemic in Florence. The latter work was the first literary expression of Renaissance humanist realism. He also produced important works in mythology, anthropology, and biography.
See also: Renaissance.

Boccherini, Luigi (1743-1805), Italian composer and cellist, noted for his chamber music. His more than 400 works, including string quartets and quintets and cello concertos, have been compared to those of Haydn, his contemporary.
See also: Chamber Music.

Boccioni, Umberto (1882-1916), Italian painter and sculptor. A pioneer of futurism, he tried to capture the movement, speed, and sensations of modern life by using dynamic forms.
See also: Futurism.

Bode's law, or Titius-Bode law, a statement of the relative mean distances of the planets from the sun. The formula begins with the numbers of the series, 0, 3, 6, 12, 24 (each new number being twice the previous one). If each number is increased by 4 and divided by 10, the series becomes 0.4, 0.7, 1.0, 1.6, 2.8, 5.2, 10.0, 19.6, 38.8. The law holds that these numbers express the relative mean distances of the planets from the sun, the earth's distance being the standard: 1.0. The German mathematician Johann Titius discovered this relationship in 1766; the German astronomer Johann Bode published it in 1772. It holds fairly well for the planets known at the time and for Uranus and the asteroid belt (both discovered later), but not for Neptune and Pluto.
See also: Astronomy.

Bodhisattva, in Mahayana Buddhism, spiritual being on the path to enlightenment. A bodhisattva delays entrance into the state of nirvana until all others have entered the same state. Bodhisattvas are worshiped and can respond to prayer; their exemplary lives are the subject of many Buddhist legends.
See also: Buddha, Gautama; Buddhism.

Bodhi tree *See:* Bo tree; Buddha, Gautama.

Bodin, Jean (1530?-96), French political philosopher who argued that stable government required a moderate absolutism founded on divine right but subject to divine and natural law. He advocated religious toleration as necessary in a just state.
See also: Philosophy.

Bobcat

Bodleian Library, the library of Oxford University in Britain. It was established in 1602 by the English diplomat Sir Thomas Bodley to replace an earlier library, dating back to the 14th century, that had been destroyed. Its collection includes 2.5 million books, including many Oriental manuscripts.
See also: Oxford University.

Bodoni, Giambattista (1740-1813), Italian printer. The Bodoni typeface, with its sharp contrast between thick and thin strokes, has been widely used in modern printing.
See also: Printing.

Boehmeria, any of about 100 species of perennial plants of the nettle family. One variety, called *false nettle*, grows as a wild flower in the Eastern United States. Another kind, *ramie*, native to China and Japan, has been cultivated for fiber since prehistoric times. Ramie is used in industrial sewing thread, packing materials, and fishnet.
See also: Ramie.

Humphrey Bogart

Boeing, William Edward (1881-1956), U.S. industrialist and founder of the Boeing Aircraft Company, a firm specializing in large commercial and military aircraft. Boeing helped carry the world's first international airmail in one of his planes in 1919. In the post-World War I and World War II periods, his company gained worldwide importance with the development of various kinds of military aircraft. The company currently produces some of the most widely used jet aircraft in commercial aviation, including the Boeing 707 and the famous jumbo jet, the Boeing 747.

Boeotia, region of ancient Greece, north of the Gulf of Corinth in central Greece. The area of 1,100 sq mi (2,850 km) was rich farmland. The chief city, Thebes, dominated the Boeotian League, formed to protect the area from encroachment by other city-states. The home of the poets Hesiod and Pindar, Boeotia later became part of the modern Greek state.
See also: Thebes.

Bogotá is the modern business center of Colombia.

Boers (Dutch, "farmers"), term applied to South African inhabitants of Dutch, German, and French Huguenot descent who settled in the region beginning in 1652. Now called Afrikaners, they speak their own language (Afrikaans). Their racial attitudes were responsible for the rise of apartheid.

Boer War, or South African War, fought between the British and the Boers (settlers of Dutch descent) from 1899 to 1902. The Boers resented British territorial expansion from their Cape of Good Hope colony, while the British aimed at a united South Africa and complained of the harsh treatment of immigrant British gold prospectors by Boers. Well-equipped by Germany, the more numerous Boer forces took the offensive in 1899, but the arrival of British reinforcements turned the tide, and by late 1900 the Boers had to resort to guerrilla tactics. The war ended with the Treaty of Vereeniging in 1902, a British victory that shifted the conflict into the political arena.
See also: South Africa.

Boethius, Anicius Manlius Severinus (c. 480-525), Roman philosopher and statesman whose works profoundly influenced medieval thought. A high official under Theodoric the Great, he was accused of treason and executed. While in prison, he wrote his great work, *The Consolation of Philosophy*.
See also: Philosophy.

Bog, spongy, waterlogged ground composed chiefly of decaying vegetation. Often formed in stagnant lakes, bogs are mainly produced by sphagnum (bog moss), from which peat is formed. Their acidity makes bogs good natural preservers, and in Europe and America they have yielded plant and animal remains from earlier ages.

Bogart, Humphrey DeForest (1899-1957), U.S. film actor, famous for his screen image as the cool, tough anti-hero. Among his most notable films are *The Maltese Falcon* (1941), *Casablanca* (1942), and *The African Queen* (1951), for which he won an Academy Award as best actor.

Bogotá (pop. 3,983,000), capital and largest city of Colombia. Founded by the Spanish in 1538 on the site of Chibcha settlement, it is a commercial and cultural center, with several universities (the oldest from 1573). Its climate is mild because of its altitude of over 8,500 ft (2,591 m), at the edge of an Andean plateau.
See also: Colombia, Republic of.

Bohemia, historic region in central Europe. It was once part of the Austro-Hungarian Empire. In 1918, after a war-torn history, it became a province in the republic of Czechoslovakia, of which its chief city, Prague, became the capital. In 1949 it lost its separate provincial status. The area is rich in minerals and fine agricultural land.

Bohr, Niels Henrik David (1885-1962), Danish physicist who proposed a model of the atom in 1913, suggesting that the hydrogen atom consisted of a single electron orbiting around a central proton (the nucleus), and that the electron could carry only certain well-defined quantities of energy. This theory accounted both for the atom's stability and for its characteristic radiation and absorption of energy. In 1927 Bohr proposed the complementarity principle to account for apparent paradoxes in the wave and particle approaches to describing sub-atomic particles. Although he helped develop the atomic bomb, he was always deeply concerned about implications for humanity. In 1922 he received the Nobel Prize in physics.
See also: Atom; Physics.

Boileau-Despréaux, Nicolas (1636-1711), French poet, satirist, and critic. His insistence on classical standards, expressed in the didactic poem *L'Art poétique* (1674), influenced literary taste in France and England in the 18th century.

Boiler, device for heating water to produce steam. The 2 main types of boiler are the fire-tube, in which hot gases are passed through tubes surrounded by water, and the water-tube, in which water is passed through tubes surrounded by hot gases. Fuels include coal, oil, gas, and nuclear energy.

Boise (pop. 205,775), largest city and capital of the state of Idaho, located in the lower Boise River valley. Named by French-Canadian settlers Boisé (meaning wooded), it provided a resting place for travelers from the heat of the Snake River Plains. The modern city was founded in 1863. The influx of Basque shepherds in the early 20th century turned the area into a center for wool production. Products today include the famous Idaho potatoes, sugar beets, alfalfa, fruits, and dairy products, as well as steel products, furniture, and electrical equipment. The city is a center for the insurance and construction trades. There are several hot springs nearby, and the region is a vacation area.
See also: Idaho.

Boito, Arrigo (1842-1918), Italian poet and composer. His own operas include *Mefistofele* (1868; revised 1875) and *Nerone* (1918), though he is best known as the librettist of Verdi's *Otello* (1887) and *Falstaff* (1893) and of Ponchielli's *La Gioconda* (1876).
See also: Opera.

Bok, Edward William (1863-1930), Dutch-born U.S. editor. As editor of *The Ladies' Home Journal* (1889-1919), he used the magazine to campaign for good causes. In his retirement he wrote the Pulitzer Prize-winning *The Americanization of Edward Bok* (1920).

Bola (Spanish, "ball"), weapon used for hunting by native South American tribes. It consists of round leather-covered stone or iron weights connected by cords or leather thongs up to 8 ft (2.4 m) long. There may be 2 or 3 such covered balls, each with its own cord connected to a common center. The bolas are whirled overhead to gain momentum and then hurled at quarry. On contact the balls wind around the animal's legs and prevent it from fleeing. Argentinean gauchos still use bolas for catching cattle, and Eskimos in the Arctic hunt with a similar weapon.

Bolero, type of Spanish folk dance and the music that accompanies it. The bolero is performed in 3/4 time. It is often accompanied by castanets, guitars, and tambourines. Dancers perform solo or as couples. *Bolero* (1928), a 1-act ballet composed by Maurice Ravel, helped popularize the dance and musical form.

Boleyn, Anne (1507-36), second wife of Henry VIII and mother of Elizabeth I. Henry's first queen, Catherine of Aragon, had failed to produce a son, and he divorced her to marry Anne in 1533. Elizabeth was born later that year, but Anne bore no living son either. She was beheaded after being convicted of dubious charges of adultery and incest.
See also: Henry (Kings of England).

Bolingbroke, Henry St. John, 1st Viscount (1678-1751), English statesman and historian. A Tory, as secretary of state he successfully handled the negotiations for the Treaty of Utrecht (1713). He lost office on the death of Queen Anne, and sought exile in France (1715-25).
See also: Utrecht, Peace of.

Bolívar, Simón (1783-1830), South American soldier and statesman responsible for several liberation movements against Spanish authority. After several abortive attempts during the 1810s, he led the liberation of Venezuela in 1821 and created the federal state of Greater Colombia, including what is now Venezuela, Colombia, and Ecuador. He went on to liberate Peru (1824) and to form the republic of Bolivia (1825). Bolívar envisaged a united South America, but secessionist movements arose, and Peru and Bolivia turned against him in the 1820s. Venezuela and Ecuador seceded from Greater Colombia in 1829, and in the following year Bolívar resigned as president. Today he is regarded as the liberator of South America, one of the great heroes of its history.
See also: Venezuela.

Bolivia, landlocked South American republic, bordered by Brazil in the north and east, Paraguay in the southeast, Argentina in the south, and Peru and Chile in the west.
Land and climate. The 3 distinct regions of Bolivia are the Oriente (east), the Montañas (center), and the Altiplano (west). The Oriente is a low alluvial plain containing tropical forest and extensive swamps. The Montañas consists of the Cordillera Oriental mountain range, whose eastern slopes shelter fertile valleys. It is Bolivia's largest cultivated area with peaks over 21,000 ft (6,400 m) high and valleys that fall to 6,000 ft (1,929 m). The windswept Altiplano, a broad plain between 2 high Andes ranges, is the most populous area and the highest inhabited area in the world, most of it over 12,000 ft (3,658 m). It is home to more than half the population. Lake Titicaca on the Peruvian border is the highest navigable lake in the world (12,507 ft/3,812 m). The climate varies from the steady cold of the Altiplano to jungle heat in the Oriente.
People. More than half of Bolivians are Native Americans, with another one-third being mestizo (Native American and Caucasian) and about 15% Caucasians of Spanish descent. Spain's colonial policy prevented Native Americans from learning Spanish, so less than 40% of the population speak it. Most Caucasians speak at least 1 Native American language. About 95% of the people are Roman Catholic. Sucre is Bolivia's capital, but La Paz is its major city.
Economy. About two-thirds of Bolivians work subsistence farms and wheat and rice must be imported to meet basic needs. The animals of the highlands (llamas, alpacas, and vicuñas) furnish high-grade wool, a leading source of income in certain areas.

Simón Bolívar

Bolivia

General information	
Capital:	Sucre (official), La Paz (actual)
Area:	424,164 sq mi (1,098,581 sq km)
Population:	7,193,000
Official languages:	Spanish, Aymara, Quechua
Monetary unit:	1 peso boliviano = 100 centavos
Main cities:	La Paz, Santa Cruz, Cochabamba
Government	
Form:	republic
Independent:	1825
Head of state:	President (elected every 4 years)
Head of government:	President
Legislature:	two legislative houses (Chamber of Senators, Chamber of Deputies)
Executive:	President and Cabinet
Judiciary:	highest court is Supreme Court
Political division:	9 departments
National economy	
Gross national product:	U.S. $3,930,000,000
Per capita income:	U.S. $570
Agriculture:	sugarcane, potatoes, corn, bananas, cassava, rice, coffee
Livestock:	sheep, cattle, goats
Fisheries:	4,800 metric tons
Mining:	zinc, antimony, lead, tin, tungsten
Industries:	food products, nonferrous metals, beverages, textiles, chemicals
Main exports:	minerals, natural gas, coffee
Transportation:	2,264 mi (3,643 km) of railroads; 25,468 mi (40,987 km) of roads; 2 international airports
Trading partners:	Argentina, United States, Brazil, United Kingdom, Germany
People	
Urban:	49%
Ethnic composition:	mestizo 31%, Quechua 25%, Aymara 17%, European 14.5%
Birth rate:	42.8 per 1,000 population
Death rate:	14.1 per 1,000 population
Infant mortality rate:	110 per 1,000 live births
Life expectancy:	male 51 years, female 55.5 years

Lake Titicaca, on the border of Bolivia and Peru, is the highest navigable lake in the world and the largest freshwater lake in South America.

Bolivia's annual output of over 20,000 tons of tin ranks it third in world production. It is also third in its production of antimony ore. Oil has been a major export since 1967. Despite its mineral wealth Bolivia remains a comparatively poor country.

History. Before being conquered by Gonzalo and Hernando Pizarro (1538), Bolivia was home to an advanced Ayamará civilization around Lake Titicaca that was subjugated by the Incas. The Spanish exploited Bolivia's wealth with forced Indian labor. The country won its independence in 1825 after long campaigns led by José de Sucre, but over the next 100 years Bolivia lost much valuable territory in wars with Brazil, Chile, and Paraguay. The Nationalist Revolutionary Movement (MNR), a pro-miner organization, came to power in 1952 but was overthrown by the military in 1964. In 1980, after nearly 20 years of unstable military regimes, a civilian government came to power under President Hernán Siles Zuazo. Zuazo resigned in 1985 and was succeeded by Paz Estenssoro.

Böll, Heinrich (1917-85), German author and winner of the Nobel Prize for literature in 1972. His books are bitterly satiric, exploring themes of despair and love in post-World War II Europe. Important among his works are *Billiards at Half Past Nine* (1959) and *The Clown* (1965).

Boll weevil (*Anthonomus grandis*), most damaging cotton pest in the United States. The beetle, 1/4 in (6 mm) long, lays eggs in cotton buds and fruit and feeds on the bolls and blossoms, causing estimated losses of $200 million a year.

Bologna (pop. 455,900), Italian city 51 mi (82 km) north of Florence at the foot of the Apennines. It is an ancient Etruscan and Roman city, with a university founded in 1088, many medieval buildings, and Renaissance paintings and sculptures. Capital of the Emilia Romagna region, it is an agricultural and industrial center, producing farm machinery and chemicals.
See also: Italy.

Bolometer, in physics, instrument used to measure minute differences of radiant energy by changes in the electrical resistance of a *thermistor*, a form of conductor exposed to the energy. Biometers can measure the radiation from stars.
See also: Physics.

Bolsheviks, proponents of the wing of the Russian Social Democratic Labor Party (RSDLP) led by Lenin. The name originated in 1903 when the Central Committee of the RSDLP split over the criteria of party membership. Lenin called his followers *Bolsheviks* (from the Russian word for *majority*) and his opponents *Menshevik* (from the word for *minority*). The party seized state power in the revolution of Oct. 1917. In March 1918 the name was changed to Russian Communist Party. The Bolsheviks later founded the Third (Communist) International, while the Mensheviks remained affiliated to the Second (Socialist) International.
See also: Communism; Lenin, V.I.; Mensheviks.

Bolshoi Ballet, the foremost ballet company of the USSR. The Moscow company (established 1825) was overshadowed by the more traditional St. Petersburg companies until the early 20th century, when it was taken over by Alexander Gorsky, who reshaped the Bolshoi. It has been one of the world's leading companies since the late 1950s.
See also: Ballet.

Bolshoi Theater, Russian theater, ballet, and opera house, with one of the largest stages in the world. It is the home of the Bolshoi Ballet, and its productions have a worldwide reputation.
See also: Bolshoi Ballet.

Boltzmann, Ludwig (1844-1906), Austrian physicist who made fundamental contributions to thermodynamics, classical statistical mechanics, and kinetic theory. His Stefan-Boltzmann Law states that the total energy radiated from a body is proportional to the fourth power of the temperature.
See also: Thermodynamics.

Bomb, in computer technology, major failure in a program. A computer system is said to be "bombed" when it is significantly disrupted by a faulty program.
See also: Computer.

Bomb, explosive weapon that injures and kills on detonation. World War I bombs dropped by aircraft weighed as much as 660 lb (300 kg). During the late 1960s, the United States built bombs weighing 15,000 lb (6,800 kg) for use in the Vietnam War. The development of the atomic bomb enormously increased explosive power. In 1952, the United States exploded an even more destructive (10.4 megaton) hydrogen bomb, with an explosive force equivalent to 10.4 million tons of TNT. Hydrogen bombs with an explosive power of up to 100 million tons of TNT have been built since then. The so-called "smart bomb" was developed in the 1980s and used extensively in the Persian Gulf War of 1991. These bombs contain electronic mechanisms that guide the trajectory and have remarkable pinpoint accuracy. The use of cameras located in the "nose" of the bombs have provided excellent photographs of such hits.
See also: Explosive.

Bombay (pop. 8,227,000), large seaport in western India, capital of Maharashtra state, on the Arabian Sea. Bombay was built on several small islands, now joined to each other and to the mainland, forming an area of 25 sq mi (65 sq km). Its large harbor deals with the bulk of India's imports, notably wheat and machinery, and exports such as cotton, rice, and manganese. Local industries include textiles, leather goods, and printing. Bombay is an important cultural center, with a university founded in 1857. The city is overcrowded, with a fast-growing, mainly Hindu population. The site was ceded to the Portuguese in 1534 and passed to Great Britain in 1661. The city was headquarters of the British East India Company (1668-1856).
See also: India.

Bombay's Gate to India, built in 1911

Bonaparte, family name of the Emperor **Napoleon I**. The Italian spelling, Buonaparte, was general until Napoleon adopted the French form in 1796. The family emigrated to the island of Corsica in the 16th century, and Napoleon was born there in 1769. His older brother, **Joseph** (1768-1844), was king of Naples (1806-08) and of Spain (1808-13); his youngest brother, **Jérôme** (1784-1860), held the throne of Westphalia (1807-13). Napoleon's son by Empress Marie Louise of Austria was hailed by supporters as **Napoleon II** (1811-32) and king of Rome (1811-14), but he never reigned in France. **Napoleon III** (Louis Napoleon Bonaparte; 1808-73), the son of Napoleon I's brother Louis, became emperor of France after a coup in 1852, establishing the Second Empire. He was deposed in 1870.
See also: Napoleon I; Napoleon II; Napoleon III.

Bonaparte, Napoleon *See:* Napoleon.

Bonaventure, Saint (1221-74), Italian medieval scholastic philosopher and theologian. He taught at Paris and later became Master General of the Franciscan order. He distinguished between philosophy, based on humanity's natural knowledge, and theology, which attempts to understand the Christian mysteries.
See also: Scholasticism.

Bond, chemical, link that holds atoms together in compounds. The theory that atoms consist of electrons orbiting in shells around the nucleus led to an explanation of chemical bonding, which had first been noted in the nineteenth century. Atoms combine to achieve highly stable filled outer shells containing 2, 8, or 18 electrons, either by transfer of electrons from one atom to the other (ionic bond) or by the sharing of one electron from each atom such that both electrons orbit around both nuclei (covalent bond). The energy and length of chemical bonds, as well as the angles between them, may be investigated by spectroscopy and X-ray diffraction.
See also: Atom; Chemistry.

Bond, Julian (1940-), U.S. civil rights leader, Democratic member of the Georgia House of Representatives 1965-75, and state senator 1975-87. In 1965, after Bond's election to the Georgia state legislature, fellow members refused him his seat because they objected to his opposition to U.S. involvement in the Vietnam War. In December, 1966, the U.S. Supreme Court ruled in Bond's favor. At the 1968 Democratic National Convention, Bond became the first African American to have his name placed in nomination for Vice-President, but he was too young to qualify. In 1971 Bond helped found the Southern Poverty Law Center, which helps protect the legal rights of poor people of all races.
See also: Civil Rights.

Bone, hard tissue that forms the skeleton. Bone supports the body, protects its organs, acts as an anchor for muscles and as a lever for the movement of limbs, and is the main reserve of calcium and phosphate in the body. Bones have a compact, hard shell surrounding a porous, spongy bone inner layer. Human bones are classified as long bones (mostly in the arms and legs) and short bones (e.g., the skull, pelvis, and vertebrae). A hollow cavity in long bones contains marrow, which helps to form blood cells. Broken bones (fractures) mend by the production of new cartilage and its gradual replacement by new bone. Insufficient calcium, phosphate, or vitamin D causes soft bones (rickets). Other disorders include osteoporosis (loss of bone density, common in old age) and osteoarthritis.
See also: Skeleton.

Bonefish, or ladyfish, herringlike fish (*Elops saurus*) named for the large numbers of fine bones that make it tedious to eat. A popular game fish nonetheless, the bonefish is found in the West Indies and along the coast of Mexico.

Boneset, perennial plant (*Eupatorium perfoliatum*) with hairy leaves, native to wet areas of the United States. This bitter herb grows from 2 ft to 6 ft (.5 m to 2 m) high and bears small white flowers in numerous heads. Tea made from the leaves makes people sweat and is used as a tonic.

Bonheur, Rosa (1822-99), French artist famous for paintings of animals. She made her reputation with *The Horse Fair* (1853), a scene full of vigor and grace. Much of her work can be seen in England and America.

Bonhoeffer, Dietrich (1906-45), German Lutheran pastor and theologian, author of many books on Christianity in a secular world. A prominent anti-Nazi, he was arrested in 1943 and executed two years later.
See also: Theology.

Bonhomme Richard *See:* Jones, John Paul.

Boniface, Saint (c.672-754?), English missionary, called the Apostle of Germany. Backed by the Frankish rulers Charles Martel and Pepin the Short, he organized the German church, reformed the Frankish clergy, and advanced the conversion of the Saxons.

Boniface VIII (1235-1303), pope 1294-1303. He asserted papal authority over the political leaders of Europe. His bull (decree) *Unam Sanctam*, which called for the subjugation of political leaders to the pope, led to a clash with Philip IV of France. In 1303 the king's emissaries attacked Boniface in his palace at Anagni, Italy. He died three weeks later in Rome and was succeeded as pope by Benedict XI.

Bonifácio, José *See:* Andrada é Silva, José Bonifácio de.

Bonington, Richard Parkes (1802-28), English artist noted for his watercolor landscapes and genre subjects. He spent most of his brief career in France; among those he influenced were Delacroix and Corot.

Bonin Islands, group of volcanic islands about 500 mi (802 km) southeast of Japan. In all there are 27 islands with some 200 inhabitants. They were administered by the United States from 1945 to 1968, when they were returned to Japan.

Bonito, 3 types of fish resembling bluefin tuna, but rarely more than 30 in (76 cm) long. The striped bonito is found in all warm oceanic waters. The Atlantic bonito flourishes in the Mediterranean and warm sections of the Atlantic. The Pacific bonito is found in and near the Indian Ocean. They are strong swimmers and congregate in schools. Bonito, which average 6 lbs (2.7 kg), are valuable food fish.

Bonn (pop. 290,800), historic city on the Rhine River in North Rhine-Westphalia, founded in the 1st century A.D. by the Romans. It was the birthplace of Beethoven and from 1238 to 1794 served as the residence of the electors of Cologne. In 1949 it became the de facto capital of West Germany (Berlin was always considered the de jure capital). As such it served as the administrative center of the German Federal Republic. With the unification of the Federal Republic and the East German communist People's Democratic Republic in October 1990 into a single German state, Bonn's status as capital is now an important issue in Germany because there is strong support for making Berlin the capital of the reunited country.
See also: Germany.

Bonnard, Pierre (1867-1947), French artist whose style gave sparkling life and color to the sunny interiors he favored (*The Breakfast Room*). With Maurice Denis and Jean Vuillard, he formed the group known as the Nabis.

Bonneville Dam, large hydroelectric dam spanning the Columbia River between Oregon and Washington. It is 2,690 ft (820 m) long, 197 ft (60 m) high, and 1,250 ft (177 m) wide. Built 1933-43 as part of the New Deal Program, it is used for navigation, flood control, and power production.
See also: Water power.

Bonneville, Benjamin Louis Eulalie de (1796-1878), French-American soldier and pioneer. He explored the far west (1832-35) and fought in the Mexican War (1846-48). He is remembered largely because of Washington Irving's romanticized *The Adventures of Captain Bonneville* (1837).
See also: Pioneer life in America.

Bonney, William H. *See:* Billy the Kid.

Bonsai, ancient Oriental art of growing dwarf trees. Trees are kept small by pruning roots and branches and by restricting growth in trays or pots. The modern enthusiast may spend many years cultivating a miniature tree. Plants that can be dwarfed include the cedars, myrtles, junipers, oaks, cypresses, pyracanthas, and pines.

Bontemps, Arna Wendell (1902-73), African-American author of more than 30 books on black culture, including biographies, children's stories, history, literary criticism, novels, and poetry. He and Countee Cullen, a novelist and poet, adapted his *God Sends Sunday* (1931) into a musical comedy, *St. Louis Woman* (1946). An earlier novel, *Black Thunder* (1936) describes a slave revolt in Virginia. *Drums at Dusk* (1938) deals with a slave revolt in Haiti. Bontemps was a public school teacher and principal 1924-38. From 1943 until his death, he was a college professor and librarian.

Book page from the breviary of Jeanne of Evreux, dating from the mid-14th century; a fine example of Gothic book illumination, with decorated initials, ornamental frames, and sprouting leaves. Depicted are the resurrection of Christ and Mary Magdalene meeting the resurrected Lord.

Bonus Army March *See:* Hoover, Herbert Clark.

Booby, large fish-eating bird of the Sulidae family, so named because it is unwary and easily captured. Boobies have straight, sharp bills, long wedge-shaped tails, short, stout legs, and long tapered wings. Excellent fliers, boobies live mainly in tropical and subtropical regions.

Boogie-woogie *See:* Jazz.

Book, medium of communication consisting of written, printed, or blank sheets of a material, usually paper, bound together into a volume. Ancient Assyrian and Babylonian clay tablets, incised when wet, then baked until hard, are the earliest form of books. The Egyptians further developed books by changing their materials. From papyrus they made paper, which they inscribed with reed pens and ink. The ancient world adopted the Egyptian innovations, and portable rolls of sheets joined together to form scrolls were at one time the most common form of books. But animal skins were also used and eventually led to a new form. Sheets of animal skin were much stronger than papyrus; they could be sewn together and folded to form rectangular pages. Pressed tightly between wooden boards to make up a book or "codex," these were prototypes of modern books. The Chinese discovered the art of making paper in the 2nd century. Paper reached Europe in the 12th century, and by the 15th century it had almost entirely replaced all kinds of parchment in the making of books. Then, around 1436 or 1437, Johann Gutenberg of Mainz perfected movable type and produced the first mechanically printed books. The history of books since the 15th century is the story of innovations and advances in materials, techniques, and technology, which continues with today's computerized type setting, automated presses, and a wide variety of photographic and other reproduction processes.

Booby

Bookbinding, craft of gathering the pages of a book into a volume with a protective cover. Bookbinding began after papyrus gave way to parchment, sheets of which could be sewn together, glued, and secured with leather thongs and protective boards. Leather was used for bookbinding for many centuries but is now reserved for special editions. Printing and the use of paper made the production of smaller books possible. During the 19th century, new cover materials were introduced.
See also: Book.

Bookkeeping, systematic recording of financial transactions. The single-entry system consists of a single account that shows the debts owed to and by the firm. The double-entry system, more detailed, enters debit and credit items in a journal and then classifies them in a ledger. In the monthly system, a number of separate daybooks are kept, and monthly totals are posted to the ledger accounts.
See also: Accounting.

Book of Changes *See:* I Ching.

Book of Common Prayer, name of the official liturgy of the Church of England, including the services of Morning and Evening Prayer and of Holy Communion, and the Psalter, Gospels, and Epistles.
See also: Church of England.

Book of the Dead, collection of prayers, hymns, and spells brought into the object-laden tombs of the ancient Egyptians, the earliest of which dates to the 16th century

B.C. These writings, which were either inscribed on the walls of the tomb or collected in a text, served as a guide for the soul's journey in the afterlife and a protection against evil.

Book of Hours, collection of prayers to be said at canonical hours, widely used by laymen during the late Middle Ages. Illuminated editions were often masterpieces of the miniaturist's art. Ffamous are the Rohan and the de Berry Hours.

Book of Kells, illuminated manuscript of the Gospels dating from the late 8th or early 9th century, probably produced by monks of Kells in County Meath, Ireland. Its rich decoration makes it one of the finest examples of medieval manuscript decoration. It is exhibited in the library of Trinity College, Dublin.

Book of Mormon *See:* Mormons; Smith, Joseph.

Book of the Dead *See:* Egypt, Ancient.

Boomerang, throwing weapon developed in Australia. Precisely bent and balanced, it follows a curved path when thrown, such that it comes back to the thrower.

Boone, Daniel (1734-1820), American pioneer and hunter. Beginning in 1767 he made a series of trips into what is now Kentucky and in 1775 built a fort there, called Boonesboro. In 1778 he was captured by the Shawnee, who were allied with the British against the American revolutionaries. Boone escaped to warn settlers at Boonesboro of a planned attack, which they successfully resisted. He moved to Missouri in 1799, after his land titles in Kentucky were overturned.
See also: Pioneer life in America; Wilderness Road.

Boorstin, Daniel Joseph (1914-), U.S. historian, 12th Librarian of Congress (1975-87). He was, by virtue of an Act of Congress (July 1987), designated Librarian of Congress Emeritus. Dr. Boorstin's tenure was characterized by greater public visibility for the library. He is responsible for the establishment of the Center for the Book in the Library of Congress (1977) and the Council of Scholars (1980). A significant highlight of his era was the passage of the revision of the Copyright Law (1976), of which he was a strong supporter. Boorstin is known for his insightful interpretations of U.S. history. He is the author of *The Genius of American Politics* (1958); the widely acclaimed trilogy *The Americans* (1958, 1965,1973), for which he received the Bancroft Prize and the Francis Parkman Prize; and *The Discovers* (1983).

Boötes, constellation of the Northern Hemisphere, easily recognizable because it contains Arcturus, one of the brightest orange stars in the sky. Boötes is also known as The Huntsman or the Bear Driver.
See also: Arcturus.

Booth, Edwin Thomas (1833-92), U.S. actor, famous on the New York and London stage. His Shakespearean roles, particularly Hamlet, were considered theatrical landmarks. He retired briefly in 1865, because of the scandal surrounding his brother, John Wilkes Booth, who assassinated President Lincoln.

Booth, John Wilkes (1838-65), U.S. actor who assassinated Abraham Lincoln. A son of the actor Junius Brutus Booth, he was a Confederate sympathizer; eager to avenge the South's defeat, he shot President Lincoln during a performance at Ford's Theater, Washington, D.C., on April 14, 1865. Booth, breaking a leg, escaped but was finally trapped in a barn near Bowling Green, Va., where he either was shot or shot himself.

Bop, or bebop, style of jazz developed toward the end of World War II, so named in imitation of its basic rhythmic feature. Under the inspiration of musicians like Dizzy Gillespie and Charlie Parker, bop broke with the blues tradition, and carried jazz forward into new harmonic and rhythmic fields, opening the way for a more intellectual kind of jazz.

Boracic acid *See:* Boric acid.

Borax, common name for a hydrated form of sodium borate or sodium tetraborate, a white powder that becomes transparent and glasslike when heated. Borax is used in glazes and in the manufacture of ceramics and heat-resistant glass. In metallurgy it is used to remove oxide slags. Borax "beads" are used as a test for metals in chemical analysis. Large quantities of borax in the form of the mineral tincal come from Searle's Lake, Ca.
See also: Boric acid; Boron.

Bordeaux (pop. 208,200), city in southwestern France and capital of Gironde department, on the Garonne River. It is France's third-largest port and chief center for the French wine trade. Bordeaux also has canning and shipbuilding industries. The city dates from Roman times.
See also: France.

Borden, Lizzie Andrew (1860-1927), U.S. woman accused of murdering her father and stepmother with an ax on Aug. 4, 1892. She was acquitted but remained popularly condemned. The murder became part of American folklore.

Borden, Sir Robert Laird (1854-1937), Canadian prime minister (1911-20) who helped his country gain an independent voice in world affairs. Borden became Conservative leader in 1901. He was a vigorous World War I prime minister, forming a Union Party government with proconscription Liberals in 1917, and securing separate representation for Canada at the peace conference and in the League of Nations.
See also: Canada.

Border Patrol, United States, uniformed enforcement agency of the Immigration and Naturalization Service, which attempts to prevent the unlawful entry of non-citizens into the United States through coastal areas of Florida and the Gulf of Mexico.

Borg, Björn (1956-), Swedish tennis player and the only player in modern tennis history to win the men's singles title at the Wimbeldon Championships in five consecutive years, 1976-80. Earlier, as a 19-year-old, he led Sweden to its first Davis Cup victory. Borg retired from tournament tennis in 1983 and made a comeback in 1991.

Borges, Jorge Luis (1899-1986), Argentine poet and prose writer. At first influenced by the metaphorical style of Spanish *ultráismo*, he later developed a unique form between short story and essay, the "fiction." Some of the best examples are in his *Ficciones* (1944) and *El Aleph* (1949).

Jorge Luis Borges

Borgia, powerful Italian family descended from the Borjan of Valencia in Spain. **Alfonso de Borja** (1378-1458) became Pope Calixtus III. By bribery, his nephew **Rodrigo Borgia** (1431-1503) became Pope Alexander VI in 1492 and worked to enrich his family by crushing the Italian princes. His son, **Cesare Borgia** (1476-1507), used war, duplicity, and murder to seize much of central Italy. Alexander's notorious daughter, **Lucrezia Borgia** (1480-1519), was probably a pawn in her family's schemes. As duchess of Ferrara, she generously patronized the arts and learning.

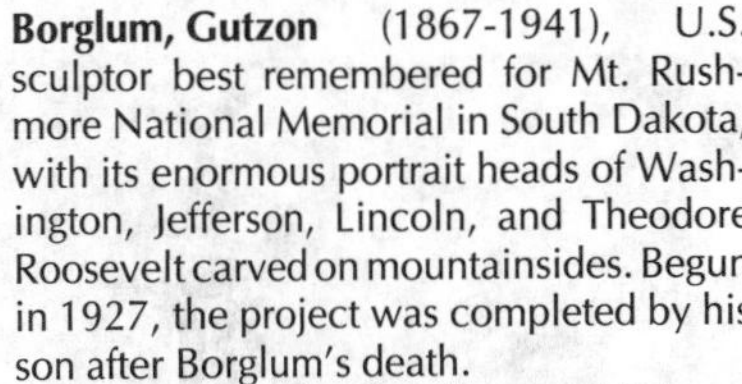

Borglum, Gutzon (1867-1941), U.S. sculptor best remembered for Mt. Rushmore National Memorial in South Dakota, with its enormous portrait heads of Washington, Jefferson, Lincoln, and Theodore Roosevelt carved on mountainsides. Begun in 1927, the project was completed by his son after Borglum's death.
See also: Mount Rushmore National Memorial.

Boric acid, white crystalline acid (H_3BO_3) occurring in nature or prepared from borax and used as a weak antiseptic.

Borlaug, Norman Ernest (1914-), U.S. agricultural scientist who was awarded the 1970 Nobel Peace Prize for his part in the development of improved varieties of cereal crops that are important in the green revolution in the developing nations of the Third World.

Borman, Frank (1928-), U.S. astronaut. After joining the Manned Spacecraft Center of NASA in 1962, Borman became command pilot on the 14-day orbital *Gemini 7* flight in December 1965. Along with James Lovell and William Anders, Borman participated in the *Apollo 8* flight, the first humans to voyage around the moon. In 1970, Borman retired from NASA and entered commercial aviation.
See also: Astronaut.

Bormann, Martin Ludwig (1900-45), German Nazi politician, Hitler's deputy from 1941. Though he vanished in 1945, he was sentenced to death for war crimes at the Nuremberg Trials in 1946. It is now thought he was killed as Berlin fell.
See also: Nazism; Nuremberg Trials.

Born, Max (1882-1970), German theoretical physicist active in the development of quantum physics. His probabilistic interpretation of the Schrödinger wave equation provided a link between wave mechanics and the quantum theory. Sharing the Nobel Prize for physics with W. Bothe in 1954, he devoted his later years to the philosophy of physics.

Born-again Christians, fundamentalist Christians who feel themselves regenerated through the experience of being "born again" (John 3:3). Related to the Calvinist doctrine of election, the experience today assumes a revivalist character. In the late 1970s, citing a decline in morality, Born-again Christians became active in U.S. politics through such organizations as the Moral Majority, led by Rev. Jerry Falwell.

Borneo, largest island of the Malay Archipelago and third largest in the world (280,100 sq mi/725,459 sq km). It contains the Indonesian province of Kalimantan, the sultanate of Brunei, and the Malaysian states of Sabah and Sarawak. Borneo is a mountainous equatorial island largely clad in tropical rain forest, and drained by several major rivers. Its highest point is Mt. Kinabalu (13,455 ft/4,101 m).
See also: Brunei; Indonesia; Malaysia.

Borodin, Aleksandr Porfirevich (1833-87), Russian chemist and composer of the group known as the Five. His musical works include the opera *Prince Igor*, completed after his death by Aleksandr Glazunov and Nikolai Rimsky-Korsakov.

Boron, chemical element, symbol B; for physical constants see Periodic Table. Boron is not found free in nature, but its compounds have been known for thousands of years. The most important source of boron is the mineral *kernite* (sodium borate). A nonmetal, boron is prepared by the vapor phase reduction of boron trichloride with hydrogen on electrically heated filaments. It is similar to carbon in that it forms stable, covalently bonded molecular networks. Compounds of boron are used in the manufacture of fiberglass, bleach, laundry products, flame retardants, antiseptics, and borosilicate glasses. Boron-10 is used as a control in nuclear reactors. Filaments of boron are lightweight and strong and are used for aerospace structures.

Bosch, Hieronymus (c.1450-1516), Dutch painter whose work features grotesque fantasy. In paintings like the *Haywain* (1485) and *The Garden of Earthly Delights* (1500) he used part-human, part-animal, part-vegetable forms to express symbolically his obsessive vision of worldly sin and eternal damnation.

Bosch, Juan *see:* Dominican Republic.

Bosnia and Hercegovina, independent country in southeastern Europe, bordering Croatia and the Federal Republic of Yugoslavia, formerly one of the 6 states of Yugoslavia. The population of over 4,000,000 consists of Serbian Orthodox, Croatian Roman Catholics, and Turkish Muslims. Before the war that ensued independence, the economy was largely based on agriculture, with wheat, maize, sugar, meat and milk the most important products. However, the war caused an economic standstill in the early 1990s, and the population became almost completely dependent on foreign-relief aid.
When Yugoslavia disintegrated, Bosnia Hercegovina became an independent state. The Bosnian Serbs opposed independence from Serbian-dominated Yugoslavia and started to expand the area under their control. Despite international intervention, the war between the Muslims, Croatians and Serbs continued into the mid-1990s.
See also: Yugoslavia.

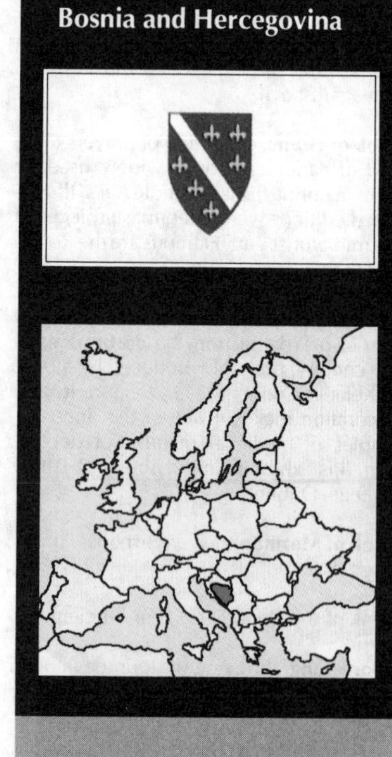

Capital:	Sarajevo
Area:	20,452 sq mi (51,129 sq km)
Population:	4,383,000
Government:	republic
Independent:	1991
GNP per capita:	U.S. $1,600

Boson, one of the 4 major classes of elementary particles (the others being the leptons, mesons, and baryons). The bosons have no mass. They include photons, gluons, and, hypothetically, the graviton. Bosons were named for the Indian physicist Satyendranath Bose, who with Albert Einstein developed a statistical theory of the behavior of these particles in the 1920s.
See also: Particle physics.

A section from Bosch's Garden of Earthly Delights *(Prado)*

Bosporus, Turkish strait 19 mi (30.6 km) long and about 0.5-2.5 mi (0.8-3.6 km) wide connecting the Black Sea and the Sea of Marmara (which is connected to the Aegean arm of the Mediterranean by the Dardanelles strait). Historically important as the sole sea link between the Black Sea and the Mediterranean, it was bridged in 1973.
See also: Turkey.

Bossuet, Jacques Bénigne (1627-1704), French prelate and historian renowned for his eloquence as an orator, especially his *Funeral Orations* (1689). He was bishop of Condom (1669-71) and of Meaux (from 1681). He wrote the famous *Discourse on Universal History* (1681) and *Treatise of the Knowledge of God and One's Self* (1722).

Boston (pop. 3,200,000), capital and largest city of Massachusetts, seaport on Massachusetts Bay. It is the most populous state capital, New England's largest city, and the nearest major U.S. seaport to Europe. It is also a major commercial, financial, manufacturing, and cultural center. Boston's industries include shipbuilding, electronics, chemicals, plastics, rubber products, and printing. The city's wool market is the nation's largest. Historic buildings include the Old State House, Paul Revere House, Christ Church, and Faneuil Hall. Boston has many notable educational institutions, and nearby Cambridge has Harvard University and the Massachusetts Institute of Technology. Settled by English Puritans in 1630, Boston became the capital of Massachusetts Bay Colony. In the Boston Massacre and Boston Tea Party the city led colonial unrest that erupted into the Revolutionary War. Modern Boston shares the acute urban problems of most large U.S. cities.
See also: Massachusetts.

Boston Massacre, incident March 5, 1770, in which some 60 Bostonians, enraged by the presence of British soldiers in Boston, harassed a British sentry, and British troops fired on the mob, killing 5 people.

Boston Tea Party, incident at Boston on Dec. 16, 1773, in protest against the tea tax and British import restrictions. A party of colonial patriots disguised in Native American dress boarded three British East India Company ships and dumped their cargo of tea into the harbor.
See also: Intolerable Acts; Revolutionary War in America.

Boswell, James (1740-95), Scottish writer and lawyer, most famous for his *Life of Samuel Johnson* (1791). In his journals he recorded his life and times with great zest. From them he culled the accounts of his travels in Corsica and elsewhere, and the brilliant conversations that distinguish the portrait of his friend Samuel Johnson.
See also: Johnson, Samuel.

Botany, the study of plants. Botany has several closely related branches. *Plant morphology*, the study of plant structure, has 2 subdisciplines: (1) plant anatomy deals with the gross structure of the plant—the shapes of the roots, stems, and leaves and the organization of the flowers; (2) plant histology deals with the structure and arrangement of the cells and tissues inside the plant. *Plant physiology* is concerned with how the plant works—how it gets its water from the soil, how the water passes up the stem, how the plant grows and moves, how its flowers open, and so on. *Biochemistry* deals with the chemical reactions going on in the plant. *Cytology* is the study of the cell protoplasm and its contents, including the nucleus. *Plant breeding* helps to produce bigger and better crops. Plants have been bred for thousands of years, but it was not until the present century, when Gregor Mendel's work in the 19th century was rediscovered, that scientists understood how characteristics are passed on from parent to offspring. By cross-pollinating selected plants, 2 or more desirable features can be combined into 1 variety. *Plant pathology* deals with plant diseases and their control. *Plant ecology* deals with the relationships between plants and their surroundings and is concerned especially with why plants grow where they do. *Plant taxonomy* deals with the naming and classification of plants. The Swedish naturalist Carolus Linnaeus (1707-78) put forward the idea of the species as the smallest unit and the genus as a group of closely related species, giving species a generic name and a specific name. For example, the plant whose common name is ragwort is scientifically known as *Senecio jacobaea*. Taxonomy is designed to show the relationships between living things, drawing information from morphology, physiology, and other branches of botany. Species with many features in common are grouped into a genus, genera with common features are grouped into a family, and families with common features are grouped into an order. If relationships exist, they may be discovered by specialists in *paleobotany*, the study of fossil plants.

Botfly, family of flies (order Diptera) whose larvae are parasitic in the tissues and cavities of humans and other mammals. The name is generally given in the United States to the horse botfly, a yellowish-brown insect about 1/2 in (13 mm) long. It lays eggs in the mane and on the legs and belly of horses. When these are licked off and swallowed, they are carried to the stomach, where they hatch. The larvae attach themselves to the lining of the stomach. Within a year, the mature larvae are discharged in the feces; they pupate in the ground and change into flies. The flies have virtually no mouth parts and do not feed during their short adult life.

Botha, Pieter Willem (1916-), South African politician who became the first executive president under a new constitution (1984-89). He entered Parliament in 1948, becoming defense minister in 1966 and prime minister in 1978. He came to recognize the importance of political change and the need to win over the loyalty and cooperation of the country's black majority.
See also: South Africa.

Boston skyline

Bothwell, James Hepburn, 4th Earl of (1536-78), Scottish nobleman who married Mary Queen of Scots in May 1567, after helping to murder her husband, Lord Darnley. In June he fled Scotland, and later died in a Danish prison.

Botswana

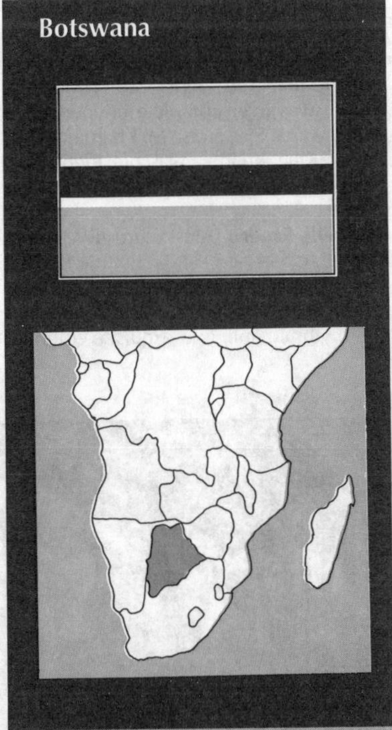

Capital:	Gaborone
Area:	224,607 sq mi (582,000 sq km)
Population:	1,373,000
Government:	republic
Independent:	1966
GNP:	U.S. $3,797,000,000
Per capita:	U.S. $2,790

Botswana (formerly Bechuanaland), landlocked republic in southern Africa, enclosed by South West Africa, Zimbabwe, and the Republic of South Africa. Its capital is Gabarone.

Land and climate. Botswana is divided into 3 main regions: the Okavango Swamp to the north, the Kalahari Desert in the south and southwest, and the mountainous areas to the east. Most of Botswana is an arid plateau some 3,000 ft (914 m) above sea level, and lack of water makes farming difficult.

People. The majority of the people are Iswana. Both English and Iswana are the official languages. Most of the people adhere to traditional African religions.

Economy. Botswana is rich in mineral resources, principally diamonds, but also manganese, asbestos, copper, nickel, and coal. Because Botswana is landlocked, it is dependent upon its neighbors, South Africa and Zimbabwe. Diamonds are the principal export. Botswana also exports its labor: considerable numbers of men move into South Africa for at least part of each year to work in the larger mines.

History. The San Bushmen, original inhabitants of Bechuanaland, were replaced by the Iswana in the 19th century. Under the leadership of King Khama in the early 1800s, the Iswana maintained their independence against invasions by Zulu and Ndebele warriors. By the mid-19th century Boers of the Transvaal sought to annex portions of Bechuanaland for its gold deposits. Bechuana sought British protection and by 1885 had become a British protectorate. On Sept. 30, 1966, the country was given complete independence as Botswana. Sir Seretse M. Khama, grandson of King Khama, was president from 1965 until his death in 1980.

Botticelli, Sandro (Alessandro di Mariano Filipepi; c.1444-1510), Florentine Renaissance painter. His work is noted for superb draftsmanship, the use of sharp yet graceful and rhythmic line, and exquisite coloring. Among his most famous works are the allegorical tableaux on mythological subjects, *Spring* and *The Birth of Venus*.
See also: Renaissance.

The Birth of Venus
by Sandro Botticelli

Bottle tree, Australian tree (*Brachychiton rupestris*) of the chocolate family, with a trunk resembling a round bottle. Although the main trunk is short and thick, the trees may grow to 60 ft (18 m). A related tree, the baobab of Africa, is also sometimes called a bottle tree.

Botulism, acute type of food poisoning, often fatal, caused by a toxin produced by the anaerobic bacteria *Clostridium botulinum* and *C. parabotulinum*, which normally live in soil but may infect poorly canned food. The toxin paralyzes the nervous system. Thorough cooking destroys both bacteria and toxin.
See also: Toxin.

Boucher, François (1703-70), French painter whose work (e.g., *The Sunrise* and *The Sunset*) epitomizes the rococo taste of 18th-century France. Influenced by Tiepolo, he painted airy, delicately colored portraits and mythological scenes. He also designed Gobelin tapestries and decorated interiors.
See also: Rococo.

Boucicault, Dion (1822?-90), Irish-born actor and playwright active in London and New York. The 150 plays that he wrote or adapted, including *London Assurance* (1841) and *The Shaughraun* (1874), ranged from light social drama to melodrama.

Boudicca *See:* Boadicea.

Bougainville, largest of the Solomon Islands, a part of the independent nation of Papua-New Guinea. Bougainville produces cacao, copra, and gold.
See also: Solomon Islands.

Bougainvillea, ornamental tropical and subtropical flowering vine (genus *Bougainvillaea*) named for the French navigator and explorer, Louis Antoine de Bougainville. The flower clusters are white or creamy-colored, each surrounded by three large floral bracts that may range from crimson or purple to yellow or white.

Boulder, city in north-central Colorado, 30 mi (48 km) northwest of Denver and the seat of Boulder County. The University of Colorado is located in the city. Glaciers, forests, and Rocky Mountain National Park make Boulder a popular resort. Local industries include space and research.
See also: Colorado.

Boulder Dam *See:* Hoover Dam.

Boulding, Kenneth Ewart (1910-), British-born U.S. economist who proposes a social science unifying economics, politics, and sociology. He is the author of more than 15 books, including *A Reconstruction of Economics* (1950), *Economics as a Science* (1970), and *A Primer on Social Dynamics* (1970).

Boulez, Pierre (1925-), French composer and conductor, noted for his extension of 12-tone techniques to rhythm and dynamics in such works as *Le Marteau sans maître* (1951) and *Pli selon pli* (1960). He was music director of the New York Philharmonic (1971-77), and has conducted many of the world's leading orchestras.

Bounty, Mutiny on the *See:* Bligh, William; Nordhoff and Hall.

Bourbon, powerful family that for generations ruled France, Naples and Sicily (the Two Sicilies), Parma, and Spain; named for the castle of Bourbon northwest of Moulins. Bourbons became part of the French ruling house when a Bourbon heiress married **Duke Robert**, Louis IX's sixth son, in 1272. In 1589 their descendant, **Henry of Navarre**, founded France's Bourbon dynasty as Henry IV. Bourbon rule in France was interrupted with Louis XVI's execution in 1793, was restored in 1814 under **Louis XVIII**, and finally ended with the deposition of **Charles X** in 1830. In Spain, Louis XIV's grandson came to the throne in 1700 as **Philip V**. In Italy, cadet branches of his family ruled Parma (1748-1860) and Naples and Sicily (1759-1861). Bourbons ruled Spain until 1931, when Alfonso XIII abdicated. In 1947 Spain was again declared a monarchy, and in 1975 **Prince Juan Carlos** of Bourbon succeeded the head of state, General Franco.

Bourgeoisie *See:* Communism.

Bourguiba, Habib Ben Ali (1903-), Tunisian nationalist politician and Tunisia's first president (1957-87). He led the campaign for independence from the 1930s onwards and was imprisoned by the French several times. He was ousted in 1987.
See also: Tunisia.

Bourke-White, Margaret (1906-71), U.S. photographer and war correspondent who covered World War II and the Korean War for Time-Life, Inc. Her coverage of India's independence movement and its leader, Mohandas Gandhi, is famous.

Bowditch, Nathaniel (1773-1838), self-taught U.S. mathematician and astronomer remembered for his *New American Practical Navigator* (1802), "the seaman's bible," later made standard in the U.S. navy. He also translated and annotated Laplace's *Celestial Mechanics* (1829-38).

Bowdoin, James (1726-90), U.S. revolutionary leader. Bowdoin served in the Massachusetts legislature (1753-76) and supported the patriots' cause. A conservative, as governor of Massachusetts (1785-87), he suppressed Shays' Rebellion. He was first president of the American Academy of Arts and Sciences.
See also: Shays' Rebellion.

Bowell, Sir Mackenzie (1823-1917), Canadian prime minister (1894-96). Elected to the House of Commons from Ontario in 1867, he held 3 cabinet-level positions under 3 successive prime ministers. On December 21, 1894, he was chosen prime minister following the death of Sir John Thompson, but his refusal to act decisively in several provincial disputes cost him the support of Parliament and his cabinet. He resigned on April 27, 1896 and remained in the Senate until 1906.
See also: Canada.

Bowen, Elizabeth (1899-1973), English-Irish novelist, whose works are distinguished by their meticulous style and emotional sensitivity. They include *The Death of the Heart* (1938), *The Heat of the Day* (1949), and *Eva Trout* (1969).

Bowerbird, forest-dwelling bird (family Ptilonorhynchidae) native to Australia and New Guinea that builds "bowers" of sticks decorated with bones, shells, berries, and flowers. Males fight and court in the bowers; the birds mate in the bower, but nest in a nearby tree. The largest of these birds, the great or red-crested bowerbird, may grow 14 in (36 cm) long.

Bowfin, large freshwater fish (*Amia calva*) of eastern North America, also known as the grindle, mudfish, or freshwater dogfish. It is sometimes referred to as a "living fossil" because it resembles a type of fish that can be traced back 130 million years. Its body may reach a length of 30 in (76 cm). Because it eats large numbers of valuable food fish, it is sometimes regarded as a pest.

Bowie, James (1796-1836), Kentucky-born frontier hero who reputedly invented the bowie hunting knife. He grew rich by land speculation and slave trading. Bowie joined the Texan fight for independence from Mexico and was one of the leaders at the Alamo, where he died.
See also: Alamo.

Bowles, Paul (1910-), U.S. author and composer living in Morocco. He is known for his exotic novels and short stories of alienation, despair, and psychological horror. His works include *The Sheltering Sky* (1949) and *Collected Stories: 1939-1976* (1979). His wife, **Jane Auer Bowles** (1917-73), was also a writer. Her works include the novel *Two Serious Ladies* (1943) and the play *In the Summer House* (1954).

Bowles, Samuel (1826-78), U.S. newspaper editor and political leader. Born in Springfield, Mass., Bowles inherited the *Springfield Republican* at age 25 and made it one of the most influential papers in the United States. He assisted the antislavery movement and helped found the Republican Party in New England.

Bowling, indoor sport that involves rolling a ball to knock down wooden pins. In tenpin bowling, the most popular form in the United States, players aim a large heavy ball down a long wooden lane at 10 pins set in a triangle. The number of pins felled determines the score. Bowling became popular in 14th-century Europe, and was brought to America by the Dutch in the 17th century. Tenpin bowling was standardized by the American Bowling Congress, founded in 1895.

Boxelder, or ash-leaf maple (*Acer negundo*), deciduous tree native to North America. It grows up to 70 ft (20 m) high and has compound leaves and grooved bark. The greenish-yellow flowers are unisexual and are borne on separate trees. The sap is sometimes tapped for its sugar.

Boxer, medium-sized dog first bred in Germany in the 1800s. The stocky, muscular dog has been used as a guide dog for the blind. Its short, shiny coat is sometimes striped or caramel-colored. It measures 21-24 in (53-61 cm) in height at the shoulder and weighs about 60-75 lb (27-34 kg).

Boxer Rebellion, violent uprising in China in 1900 directed against foreigners and instigated by the secret society "Harmonious Fists" (called Boxers by the Europeans). Encouraged by the Dowager Empress Tz'u Hsi, the Boxers showed their dislike of growing European influence and commercial exploitation in China, attacking missionaries and Chinese converts to Christianity. Troops sent to protect European nationals at Peking were repulsed. The German minister in Peking was murdered and foreign legations were besieged for nearly 2 months until relieved by an international force. Boxer violence was the pretext for Russian occupation of South Manchuria. On Sept. 7, 1901, China was forced to sign the humiliating Boxer Protocol, in which it promised to pay a huge indemnity to the United States and the European powers concerned.
See also: China; Open-Door Policy.

Boxing, sport of skilled fist-fighting. Two contestants wearing padded gloves attack each other by punching prescribed parts of the body, while avoiding or blocking their opponent's punches. Boxing contests are arranged between opponents in the same weight division or class; there are 10 classes ranging from flyweight to heavyweight. Fights take place in a square roped-off ring and consist of a number of 2- or 3-minute rounds. Scoring is usually made by a referee and 2 judges.
A win can occur by a knockout, if a boxer legitimately knocks down his opponent and the man cannot regain his feet in 10 sec. A fight may also end in a technical knockout if the referee decides that a boxer is physically unfit to go on fighting. If a contest goes its full length, the contestant awarded the most points or rounds wins by a decision.
Boxing can be traced back to the Olympic Games of ancient Greece, and to Roman gladiatorial contests. Modern boxing has its roots in 18th-century English fairground fights between bare-knuckled pugilists, who battered each other for bets until one could no longer continue.

Boxing matches in the past had no limit on the number of rounds to be fought. On April 5, 1917, champion Jack Johnson was defeated by Jess Willard in the 26th round.

Heavyweight championship bout between Evander Holyfield and James "Buster" Douglas

Boxwood, or box, several species of evergreen shrubs and trees (genus *Buxus*), native to tropical and subtropical parts of the Old World and Central America, but widely introduced elsewhere. They have small glossy leaves and are excellent hedge plants, rarely exceeding 12 ft (4 m) in height. Boxwood grows slowly. Its yellow, finely grained wood is used for musical instruments and wood engraving.

Boyd, Belle (1843-1900), Confederate spy in the American Civil War. An actress, she lived in Virginia and passed military information to the South. Caught in 1862, she was released for lack of evidence in 1863. She wrote *Belle Boyd in Camp and Prison* (1865).
See also: Civil War, U.S.

Boyle, Robert (1627-91), British natural philosopher, often called the father of modern chemistry for his rejection of the theories of the alchemists and his espousal of atomism. He discovered what is called Boyle's Law for Gases: At a constant temperature the volume of a given quantity of gas varies inversely to the pressure to which the gas is subjected.
See also: Chemistry; Philosophy.

Boyne, Battle of the, battle on the River Boyne in East Ireland on July 12, 1690, which ended James II's attempt to regain the English throne. William III's 35,000 troops decisively defeated the Catholic Jacobites' 21,000. Northern Ireland's Protestants celebrate the victory to this day.

Boy Scouts, international boys' organization founded in 1908 by Sir Robert Baden-Powell to develop character, initiative, and good citizenship. The organization is nonsectarian, nonpolitical, and nonmilitary. The Boy Scouts are organized in about 100 countries, and worldwide membership is approximately 8 million. Scouting emphasizes outdoor knowledge and skills, including nature lore and woodcraft. The Boy Scout program includes Cubs (8-10 years old), Scouts (11-13), and Explorers (14 years and older). Other senior scout groups are the Sea Scouts and Air Scouts. To achieve higher ranks, Scouts must pass tests for merit badges in various fields. In the United States, where the movement was incorporated in 1910, the scouting program is administered by a National Council, with headquarters in New Brunswick, NJ. The standard troop, led by a volunteer adult scoutmaster, has 32 members and is divided into 4 patrols of 8 Scouts. Boy Scouts have been active in safety campaigns, and conservation programs, and other community service.
See also: Baden-Powell, Robert Stephenson Smyth.

Detail of the tombstone of Tycho Brahe in the Tyn church in Prague

Boysenberry , variety of blackberry (*Rubus ursinus*) that grows on a trailing plant. The tart, dark-red to black fruits are made up of clusters of drupelets. Boysenberries grow best in mild climates and can be eaten fresh or in pies, jams, and jellies.

Boys Town, village near Omaha, Neb., founded in 1917 as a community for homeless and abandoned boys by Father Edward J. Flanagan and governed by the boys.
See also: Flanagan, Edward Joseph.

Bozeman Trail, route between Wyoming, and Montana used as a short-cut during the 1860s to reach gold fields in Montana and Idaho. The trail, named for John M. Bozeman, covered 600 mi (970 km). Native American attacks, protesting rampant European immigration, closed the trail in the late 1860s.
See also: Gold Rush.

Brace, Charles Loring (1826-90), U.S. social reformer who worked to improve conditions for poor children and helped organize the Children's Aid Society in New York City in 1853.

Braces *See:* Orthodontics.

Bradbury, Ray (1920-), U.S. science-fiction writer, whose short stories deal with moral dilemmas. Among his best-known science fiction works are *The Martian Chronicles* (1950) and *Fahrenheit 451* (1953).

Braddock, Edward (1695-1755), commander-in-chief of British forces in North America, who was disastrously defeated in the French and Indian Wars. His 1755 expedition against Fort Duquesne (on the site of present-day Pittsburgh), ran into a French and Indian ambush. Braddock was fatally wounded and his men were routed. Among the survivors was a Virginian officer, George Washington.
See also: French and Indian Wars.

Bradford, family name of prominent U.S. printers and editors. **William Bradford** (1663-1752) set up Philadelphia's first printing press and began New York's first newspaper, the *Gazette,* in 1725. His son, **Andrew Bradford** (1686-1742), started the first newspaper in Philadelphia, the *American Weekly Mercury,* in 1719. **William Bradford, III** (1722-91), grandson of William Bradford and nephew of Andrew Bradford, established the *Pennsylvania Journal* in 1742. Through this newspaper he fought for freedom of the press and became printer to the First Continental Congress.
See also: Printing.

Bradford (pop. 463,500), city and parliamentary borough of Yorkshire, England, in the Aire valley, 9 mi (14 km) from Leeds. It was concerned with the wool trade during the Middle Ages, and by the end of the 15th century had become an important center of the industry. The Bradford Exchange is a major international wool market, and the Bradford Institute of Technology is world famous for its textile design.
See also: England.

Bradford, William (1590-1657), Pilgrim Father who helped to establish Plymouth Colony and governed it most of his life (reelected 30 times from 1621). He described the *Mayflower's* voyage and the colony's first years in his *History of Plymouth Plantation.*
See also: Pilgrims.

Bradley, James (1693-1762), British astronomer. His 2 great discoveries were the aberration of light (1729) and the nutation (nodding motion) of the earth's axis (1748). Just before his death he published a catalog listing more han 60,000 stars.
See also: Astronomy.

Bradley, Omar Nelson (1893-1981), U.S. general. In 1944-45 he led the 12th Army Group (1 million men in 4 armies) in Europe. He was chief of staff of the U.S. Army (1948-49) and first chairman of the joint chiefs of staff (1949-53).
See also: World War II.

Bradley, Thomas (1917-), U.S. public official, mayor of Los Angeles. A former college track star and Los Angeles policeman who was admitted to the bar in 1956, he was elected to the Los Angeles city council in 1963. In 1973 Bradley became the city's first black mayor. He was California's Democratic gubernatorial candidate in 1982 but lost in a close race; he continued as mayor.

Bradstreet, Anne Dudley (c.1612-72), English-American colonial poet. She began writing after her emigration to Massachusetts in 1630. Her poems deal with personal reflections on the Puritan ethic. Her collection, *The Tenth Muse Lately Sprung Up in America,* was published in England in 1650.

Brady, Mathew B. (1823-96), U.S. photographer of historic events and eminent people, including 18 U.S. presidents. He spent his fortune in hiring 20 teams of photographers to take over 3,500 shots covering almost every big battle of the Civil War, a project that bankrupted him. His most famous photographs are those of Lincoln and of the battles of Bull Run and Gettysburg.

Bragg, Braxton (1817-76), Confederate Civil War general. He led the Army of Tennessee to defeat William S. Rosencrans at Chickamauga (1863), but soon lost to Ulysses S. Grant at Chattanooga, after which he forfeited his command.
See also: Civil War, U.S.; Fort Bragg.

Bragg, Sir William Henry (1862-1942), British physicist who shared the 1915 Nobel Prize in physics with his son, **Sir William Lawrence Bragg** (1890-1971), for the deduction of the atomic structure of crystals from their X-ray diffraction patterns (1912).
See also: Physics.

Brahe, Tycho (1546-1601), Danish astronomer, the greatest exponent of naked-eye positional astronomy. Johannes Kepler, who became his assistant in 1601, postulated an elliptical orbit for Mars based on his confidence in Brahe's data. Brahe's "Tychonic system," in which the planets circled the sun, which in turn orbited a stationary earth, was the principal 17th-century rival of the Copernican hypothesis. Brahe observed a supernova with the naked eye in 1872.
See also: Astronomy.

Brahmanism, Indian religion based on belief in Brahma. It developed about 500 B.C. from Dravidian and Aryan beliefs. Its ritual, symbolism, and theosophy came from the *Brahmanas*, sacred writings of the priestly caste, and from the Upanishads. It developed the "divinely ordered" caste system and gave rise to modern Hinduism.
See also: Hinduism.

Brahmans *See:* Hinduism.

Brahmaputra River, river that rises in the Himalayas and flows about 1,800 mi (2,897 km) through Tibet, northeastern India, Bangladesh, and south to the Ganges, forming the Ganges-Brahmaputra delta on the Bay of Bengal. A holy river to the Indians, its name means "son of Brahma."

Brahms, Johannes (1833-97), major German Romantic composer. Though strongly influenced by Beethoven and the Romantic movement, he developed his own rhythmic originality and emotional intensity, while using classical forms. He lived largely in Vienna from 1863. His major works include four symphonies, two piano concertos, a violin concerto, a double concerto for violin and cello, piano and chamber works, songs, part-songs, and choral works—notably, *A German Requiem* (1868) and the *Alto Rhapsody* (1869).
See also: Schumann, Clara.

Johannes Brahms

Braille, system of writing for the blind developed by Louis Braille, employing patterns of raised dots that can be read by touch. Braille typewriters and printing presses allow the mass production of books for the blind.
See also: Braille, Louis.

Braille, Louis (1809-52), French inventor of braille. Accidentally blinded at the age of 3, he conceived his raised-dot system at 15, while at the National Institute for the Blind in Paris. In 1829 he published a book explaining how his system could be used, not only for reading but also for writing and musical notation.
See also: Braille.

Brain, complex organ coordinating nerve activity and responsible for thought in higher animal forms. Invertebrates have only a rudimentary brain, most highly developed in the octopus. Vertebrates have brains more fully differentiated, consisting of forebrain, midbrain, and hindbrain. In highly developed vertebrate animals, the forebrain has developed into a large and highly differentiated *cerebrum*. The human brain is composed of some billions of interconnecting nerve cells and many more supporting cells (neuroglia). Together with the spinal cord, the brain makes up the central nervous system (CNS), which governs and coordinates the operations of all tissues and organs and is the physical basis of all mental activities: consciousness, sensation, thought, speech, memory, emotion, character, and skill.
The nervous system carries information in the form of electric signals. All the outlying nervous pathways—the peripheral nervous system, or PNS—converge on the CNS. Nerve fibers conduct in 1 direction only: Those that carry information from the sensory organs to the CNS are called afferent, or sensory pathways; those that carry impulses outward from the CNS to the muscles and glands are called efferent, or motor, pathways. Nervous pathways are made up of separate units—nerve cells known as neurons. The main parts of the neuron are the cell body, the axon, and the dendrites. Dendrites generally carry an impulse toward the cell body, and the axon carries it away from the cell body to another cell. The ends of the axon lie adjacent to, but not quite touching, the dendrites or cell bodies of other neurons; the region where the 2 nearly touch is called a synapse. Electrical impulses cannot cross synapses; the transfer is made by chemical substances called neurotransmitters. These substances have become extremely important because of the part they play in the pharmacological treatment of some psychiatric and neurological conditions. The full-grown brain is described as having 3 parts.
(1) The *brain stem* is chiefly a relay station for nervous pathways between the higher parts of the brain and the rest of the body; if it is damaged, sensory and motor functions are greatly impaired. It is also responsible for subvoluntary activities like digestion and respiration.
(2) The *cerebellum*, divided into hemispheres, each controlling a side of the body, is responsible for the coordination of voluntary muscular movements and for posture.
(3) The *cerebrum*, the highest center of the brain and the latest in evolutionary development, is responsible for sensation, thought, and the initiation of voluntary motor activity. It, too, is divided into hemispheres, each consisting of 2 main parts: (1) the *basal ganglia*, made up of a complicated collection of bunches of gray matter that clusters about the top of the brain stem, and (2) the *cerebral cortex*, also made of gray matter, separated from the basal ganglia by tracts of white matter. The cerebrum is customarily divided into 4 lobes: (1) The *frontal lobe (lobus frontalis)* controls voluntary motor patterns, the organization of the motor units necessary for speech, original thinking, and the evaluation of ideas. (2) The *parietal lobe (lobus parietalis)* is mainly concerned with the reception of body sensations and memory in regard to language and learning. The region also has a role in spatial organization. (3) The *temporal lobe (lobus temporalis)* receives auditory sensations (the sense of hearing), participates in speech through auditory monitoring, plays a role in spatial organization, and is a memory mechanism. The temporal lobe has also been variously claimed to be concerned with memory and dreams. (4) The *occipital lobe (lobus occipitalis)*, in the back of the head, is the primary center for vision. The limbic system contains components of the frontal, parietal, and temporal lobes, and controls behavioral reactions to the external environment, possibly influenced by the internal environment, which may alter the excitability of the nervous system. It seems to operate in preserving the individual (feeding, fleeing, or fighting) or the species (reproduction).
The *corpus callosum*, a large white bundle of fibers that connects the cerebral hemispheres, appears concerned with the transfer of learning from 1 hemisphere to another. The functions of the *corpus callosum* include (1) correlation of images in the left and right halves of the visual field, (2) integration of sensations from paired limbs or for learning that requires motor coordination of the limbs, and (3) unification of cerebral processes of attention and awareness. The absence of a *corpus callosum* slows down the rate of learning.

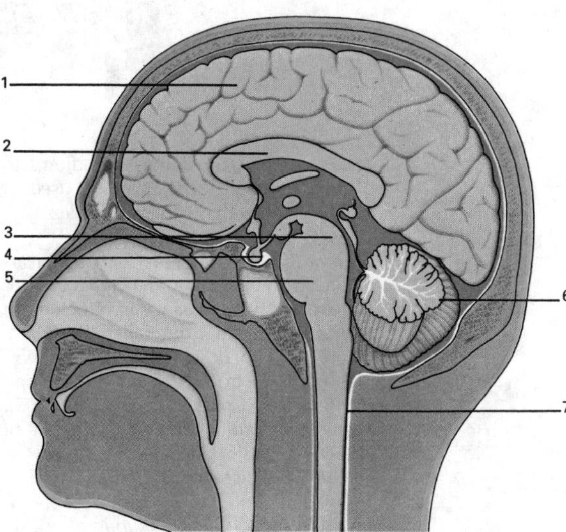

A section of the brain. The cerebrum (1) consists of two large folded lobes which enclose the ventricles (2). In these cavities the cerebrospinal fluid is produced. This fluid provides a protecting cushion round the brain and spinal cord. The medulla oblongata (7), the pons (5), and the midbrain (3) connect the spinal cord and the cerebrum. The cerebellum (6) is situated behind these structures. The pituitary gland (4) is located in a protective bony socket at the base of the brain behind the nose.

Brainwashing, manipulation of an individual's will, generally without his or her knowledge and against his or her wishes. Most commonly, it consists of a combination of isolation, personal humiliation, disorientation, systematic indoctrination, and alternating punishment and reward.

Brake, device for slowing or halting motion, usually by conversion of kinetic energy into heat energy via the medium of friction. Most airplane, automobile, and railroad brakes are mechanical drum or disk brakes, applying friction directly to some portion of the wheel or of a drum rotating with the wheel. Mechanically operated brakes cannot always be used, as when a single control must operate on a number of wheels simultaneously and equally. Hydraulic, vacuum, and air

Automobile brake
1. Pedal
2. Master cylinder and piston
3. Hydraulic pipe
4. Brake shoe with lining
5. Brake drum
6. Slave cylinder piston
7. Drum brake on
8. Drum brake off
9. Disc brake on
10. Disc brake off
11. Disc pad
12. Disc

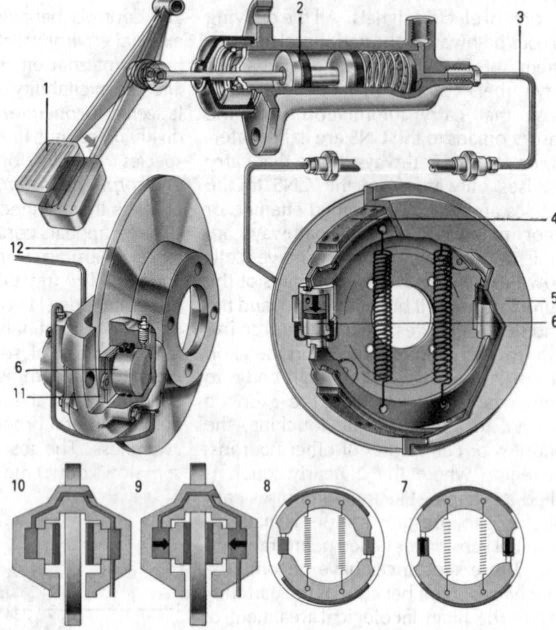

brakes, which use different mediums to distribute the pressure, may be used in combination with mechanical brakes.

Bramante, Donato (1444-1514), Italian architect who developed the classical principles of High Renaissance architecture. In 1499, he moved from Milan to Rome, where his major designs included the Tempietto of S. Pietro in Montorio (1502) and the Belvedere Court at the Vatican (1505). His greatest project, the reconstruction of St. Peter's, was not realized.
See also: Renaissance.

Bramble, any of a genus (*Rubus*) of prickly shrubs of the rose family. Several of the more than 300 species produce edible berrylike fruits, including blackberries, raspberries, and boysenberries.

Bran, husk of cereal grains (e.g., wheat, rye, or corn), removed from the flour during milling. Bran is ground and used as cattle fodder and is also mixed with cereals and other foods for human consumption, to add roughage and some nutritional elements to the diet. Certain bran extracts are also used in cleaning and dyeing compounds.

Brancusi, Constantin (1876-1957), Romanian sculptor famous for his simple, elemental, polished forms. Living in Paris from 1904, he rejected Rodin's influence, turning to abstract forms and the example of primitive art. Among his best-known works are *The Kiss* (1908) and *Bird in Space* (1919).

Brandeis, Louis Dembitz (1856-1941), U.S. jurist, influential in securing social, political, and economic reforms, especially while an associate justice of the Supreme Court (1916-39). As a lawyer he crusaded for organized labor against big business interests. Brandeis was an active Zionist. Brandeis University was named in his honor.
See also: Supreme Court of the United States.

Brandenburg, historic region in central East Germany. Formerly the central province of Prussia, it was divided by the Allies at the end of World War II between Poland and East Germany. In 1952 the German state of Brandenburg was abolished and divided into the districts of Frankfurt, Potsdam, and Cottbus.
See also: Germany.

Brand name *See:* Trademark.

Brando, Marlon (1924-), U.S. stage and screen actor. Brando's first great success was his portrayal of Stanley Kowalski in the Broadway production of Tennessee Williams's *A Streetcar Named Desire*, the film version of which (1951) brought him international fame. Although widely acclaimed as one of the greatest actors of his time, he has appeared in relatively few parts, particularly in recent years. He won Academy Awards for *On the Waterfront* (1954) and *The Godfather* (1972).

Brandt, Willy (Karl Herbert Frahm; (1913-), Social Democratic chancellor of West Germany 1969-74, whose *Ostpolitik* (Eastern policy) marked a major step towards East-West detente in Europe. He opposed Hitler, fleeing to Norway (1933) and returning after World War II to become mayor of West Berlin (1957-66). As chancellor, he secured friendship treaties with Poland and the USSR (1970), with East Germany (1972), and with Czechoslovakia (1974). Brandt's initiative won him the 1971 Nobel Peace Prize. Forced to resign in 1974 over a spy scandal in his own administration, he returned to political life in 1975.
See also: Germany.

Brandy, alcoholic drink of distilled wine, usually matured in wood casks. Brandies include cognac, made from white grapes of the Charente district in France, kirsch (made from cherries), and slivovitz (made from plums).

Brandywine, Battle of, British victory in the American Revolutionary War. On Sept. 11, 1777, at Brandywine Creek, Pa., Gen. William Howe's 15,000 British troops surprised the right flank of Washington's 11,000 men protecting Philadelphia. Washington retreated to Germantown, and Howe went on to take Philadelphia.
See also: Revolutionary War in America.

Brant, any of several North American wild geese (genus *Branta*) which breed in the Arctic and fly southward to Eurasia and North America for the winter.

Brant, Joseph (Thayendanegea; 1742-1807), Mohawk chief, Episcopal missionary, and British army colonel. He served with the British forces in the French and Indian Wars and in the American Revolutionary War, participating in the Cherry Valley Massacre (1778).
See also: French and Indian Wars; Revolutionary War in America.

Braque, Georges (1882-1963), French painter and sculptor. From fauvism he went on, together with Pablo Picasso, to evolve cubism and to be among the first to use collage. Among his major works are *Woman with a Mandolin* (1937) and the *Birds* series (1955-63).
See also: Collage; Cubism; Fauves.

Brasília (pop. 1,568,000), federal capital of Brazil since 1960, located on the Paraná River, 600 mi (966 km) northwest of the old coastal capital, Rio de Janeiro. It was built to help open the immense Brazilian interior. Its cross-shaped plan was designed by Lúcio Costa, while such major buildings as the presidential palace and the cathedral are the work of Oscar Niemeyer.
See also: Brazil.

Brass, alloy of copper and zinc, known since Roman times and widely used in industry and for ornament and decoration. Up to 36% zinc forms "alpha" α-brass, which can be worked cold; with more zinc a mixture of α and "beta"-brass is formed, which is less ductile but stronger. Brasses containing more than 45% zinc (white brasses) are unworkable and have few uses. Some brasses also contain other metals: lead for machinability, aluminum or tin for corrosion resistance, and nickel, manganese, or iron for strength.
See also: Alloy.

Bratislava (pop. 409,100), third-largest city of Czechoslavavkia. The capital of Slovakia, Bratislava is a port city on the Danube River. Its industries include mechanical engineering, oil refining, petrolem products, and cloth.
See also: Czechoslovakia.

Brattain, Walter Houser (1902-), U.S. physicist who helped invent the transistor. He shared the 1956 Nobel Prize in physics with William Shockley and John Bardeen for this invention, and for the research into the electrical properties of semiconductors that made it possible. All 3 men worked at the Bell Telephone Laboratories—Brattain from 1929—where the transistor was first announced in 1948.
See also: Physics; Transistor.

Braun, Eva (1912-45), mistress (from 1930) and later wife of Adolf Hitler. On April 29, 1945, a few days before Germany's defeat in World War II, they were married. The next day both Braun and Hitler committed suicide.
See also: Hitler, Adolf.

Braun, Wernher von (1912-77), German-American rocket pioneer. He designed most of the rockets that powered the U.S. space program, including the Jupiter rocket that launched the first U.S. satellite, *Explorer 1*, in 1958. Von Braun was born in Wirsitz, Germany (now Wyrzysk, Poland). He studied engineering at Berlin and Zürich, and in 1936, became director of the Peenemünde rocket research station. During World War II he developed the V-2 rocket, more than 4,000 of which were fired against Britain. Von Braun surrendered to the U.S. forces at the end of the war, and went to work in the United States, becoming a U.S. citizen in 1955.
See also: Rocket.

Braxton, Carter (1736-97), American political leader during the Revolutionary War period. He was a signer of the Declaration of Independence and served in the House of Burgesses, the Continental Congress, and the Congress of the Confederation.

Brazil, fifth largest country in the world and largest in South America, constituting nearly half the continent's land area. Brazil shares borders with all South American countries except Ecuador and Chile. It is the only Latin American country whose official language is Portuguese.
Land and climate. Most of Brazil falls within 2 major geographical regions: the lowlands of the Amazon River system and the plateau. Drained by the Amazon River and its tributaries, the Amazonian lowlands form the world's most extensive tropical rain forests. The climate is not excessively hot, but rainfall is as much as 80 in (203 cm) annually. The Brazilian plateau, rising to 1,000 to 3,000 ft (305 to 914 m) above sea level, is studded with occasional mountain ranges. About 40% of the population lives in the southerly part of the plateau, known as the "heartland," which contains some of the country's most productive farmland and valuable mineral deposits.
Economy. Agriculture is the traditional mainstay of Brazil's economy. Exports include cattle, coffee, cotton, sugarcane, cocoa, tobacco, soybeans, citrus fruit, and bananas. Industry has also developed; particularly iron and steel, motor vehicles, textiles, and machinery. Brazil's vast natural resources have yet to be fully developed. Rich oil deposits have been found, as well as, iron, manganese, coal, chromium, quartz, uranium, and industrial grade diamonds. The exploitation of the Amazon basin has posed a threat to the tropical rain forest, creating a major point of controversy, within Brazilan politics.
History. Portuguese colonists under Pedro lvarez Cabral claimed Brazil in 1500, and colonization began in 1532. Slaves were extensively used by plantation owners. The country remained a colony until winning its independence in 1822, as a monarchy. Slavery was abolished in 1888, and Brazil became a republic in 1889. Military re-

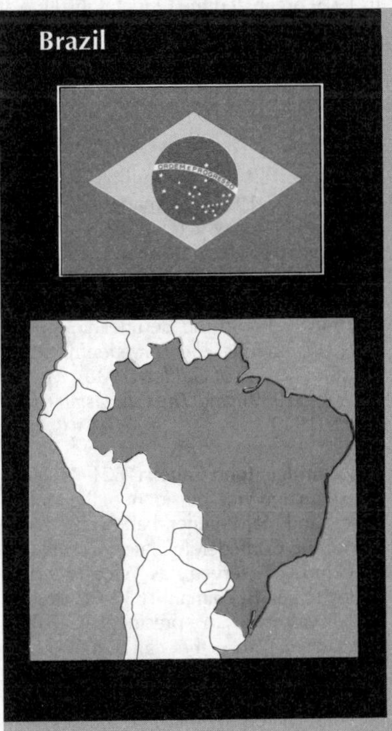

Brazil

General information	
Capital:	Brasília
Area:	3,286,488 sq mi (8,511,965 sq km)
Population:	147,404,000
Official language:	Portuguese
Monetary unit:	1 new cruzado = 100 centavos
Main cities:	São Paulo, Rio de Janeiro, Brasília
Government	
Form:	federal republic
Independent:	1822
Head of state:	President (elected every 5 years)
Head of government:	President
Legislature:	two legislative houses (Federal Senate and Chamber of Deputies)
Executive:	President and Cabinet
Judiciary:	highest court is Supreme Federal Court
Political division:	23 states, 3 territories, 1 federal district
National economy	
Gross national product:	U.S.$328,860,000,000
Per capita income:	U.S.$2,280
Agriculture:	coffee, sugarcane, corn, cassava, oranges, soybeans, rice
Livestock:	cattle, pigs, sheep
Fisheries:	840,000 metric tons
Mining:	iron ore, silver, crude petroleum, gold, coal
Industries:	chemicals, food products, iron and steel and other worked metals, machinery, transportation equipment
Main exports:	food and livestock, mineral products, machinery and mechanical appliances
Transportation:	18,526 mi (29,814 km) of railroads; 932,280 mi (1,500,319 km) of roads; 21 international airports
Trading partners:	United States, Germany, Japan, The Netherlands, Italy
People	
Urban:	74.5%
Ethnic composition:	European 53%, mulatto 22%, mestizo 12%, African 11%
Birth rate:	28.6 per 1,000 population
Death rate:	7.9 per 1,000 population
Infant mortality rate:	63 per 1,000 live births
Life expectancy:	male 62 years, female 67.5 years

Left: harbor and business center of Rio de Janeiro.
Right: the future of Brazil includes the development of the Amazon. Highways and potential building sites are well under way.

gimes prevailed until the accession of President Getúlio Vargas in 1930. A military coup overthrew the leftist civilian government of João Goulart in 1964. Often accused of torture and other human rights violations, the military continued to rule through a succession of generals who served as president. The first presidential election with civilian candidates in 20 years was held in Jan. 1985. Civilian rule was restored in the late 1980s.

Brazil nut, South American tree (genus *Bertholletia*) of the Amazon and Negro rivers. The tree grows to 160 ft (50 m), bearing very hard 6 in (15 cm) fruit containing 10 to 20 nuts. The nuts are used as food and for lubricating oil. The trees are also used for hardwood lumber.

Brazilwood, heavy wood of various trees (genus *Caesalpinia*). Extracts from this wood produce bright crimson and deep purple colors. Once an important source of dye, it is still used for making violins and in cabinetwork.

Bertolt Brecht

Brazzaville (pop. 596,200), river port and capital of the Republic of the Congo, situated below the Stanley Pool on the right bank of the Congo River. Kinshasa lies on the other side of the pool. Brazzaville was formerly the capital of the French Equatorial Africa. It was the headquarters of the Free French in Africa during World War II and gained independence in 1960. Brazzaville has always been primarily a center of government and education, although since 1945 industries such as brewing, matchmaking, and sugar refining have become established. Contributing to this industrial development is the hydroelectric plant at the nearby Djoué Falls. The the Center for Administrative and Advanced Technical Studies is located in Brazzaville.
See also: Congo.

Bread, one of humanity's earliest and most important foods, made of baked dough—a mixture of flour and water. In developed western societies, wheat flour is most commonly used and the dough is leavened (i.e., increased in volume by introducing small bubbles of carbon dioxide throughout) using yeast.

Breadfruit (*Artocarpus altilis*), tree of the mulberry family, whose fruit is the staple diet in the South Pacific. Breadfruit trees are now seen in much of tropical America. The fruit is melonlike, 8 in (20 cm) across, and is protected by a thick rind that can be woven into cloth. The pulp, which tastes like potato meal, is eaten cooked, and may be ground to make a flour.

Breakbone fever *See:* Dengue.

Breakwater, timber, masonry, or stone barrier constructed to give protection from heavy seas. Breakwaters built at right angles to the shore are called *jetties*; those built parallel with the shore (providing additional protection for a harbor), with a wharf on the sheltered side, are called *moles*.

Bream, any of a variety of European freshwater fishes of the carp family, growing up to 17 lb (8 kg). The freshwater sunfishes of the United States and the marine porgies and wrasses are also known as bream.

Breast, front of the chest; especially in female mammals, the modified cutaneous, glandular structure it bears—the mamma or mammary gland. In humans, each breast consists of 15 to 20 branching ducts surrounded by connective tissue that acts as a supporting framework. The larger partitions between the lobes form strands that extend from the skin to the underlying deep fascia. At puberty in the female, fat accumulates in the connective tissue of the breast and the overlying skin. The skin of the areola, the disk-shaped area surrounding the nipple, contains modified sweat glands and sebaceous glands. The breasts usually secrete a small quantity of fluid, or colostrum, from early pregnancy onwards, and for 2-3 days after childbirth. Milk begins about 3 days after childbirth, increasing to an average rate of about 28 fl oz (850 ml) per day. The principal constituents of breast milk are water, lactose, fat, and protein. The ejection of milk is stimulated by sucking and by the release of the pituitary hormone oxytocin.
See also: Mammary glands.

Breast cancer, malignant growth in the breast or mammary gland. Breast cancer—carcinoma of the breast—is the most common malignancy among women and has the highest fatality rate of all cancers affecting them. The annual mortality rate since 1950 has remained at about 25 in every 100,000 women. Breast cancer in men is rare and tends not to be recognized until late, thus the results of treatment are poor. In women, breast carcinoma is rarely seen before the age of 30, and the incidence rises rapidly after menopause.
See also: Cancer.

Breasted, James Henry (1865-1935), U.S. archaeologist and historian, who advanced archaeological research in Egypt and western Asia. He specialized in Egyptology, and in 1919 organized the Oriental Institute at the University of Chicago, subsequently sponsoring expeditions at Megiddo and Persepolis.
See also: Archaeology.

Brecht, Bertolt (Eugen Berthold Friedrich Brecht; 1898-1956), German Marxist playwright and poet, who revolutionized modern theater with his production techniques and concept of epic theater. He left Nazi Germany in 1933, returning to East Berlin in 1948 to found the Berliner Ensemble. His plays include *The Threepenny Opera* (1928), *The Life of Galileo* (1938), *Mother Courage* (1939), and *The Caucasian Chalk Circle* (1949).

Breckinridge, John Cabell (1821-75), congressman and vice-president of the United States, and major-general and secretary of war of the Confederate States of America. Breckinridge served as vice-president under James Buchanan 1857-61. During the 4-way race for president in 1860, Breckinridge was the candidate of the Southern Democrats on a pro-slavery, pro-Union platform, polling 18% of the popular vote. When Kentucky voted to remain in the Union, Breckinridge left his Senate seat, becoming brigadier-general and later, secretary of war for the Confederacy. When the South surrendered, he fled to Britain, but returned to the United States in 1868.
See also: Civil War, U.S.

Breckinridge, Sophonisba (1866-1948), U.S. pioneer teacher of social work. She wrote *The Delinquent Child and the Home* (1912) and *The Family and the State* (1934). She believed the government should play a key role in helping the needy.

Breedlove, Craig (1937-), U.S. racing-car driver. He set many records in *Spirit of America,* a car he designed and built himself. In 1963 he was the first U.S. driver since 1928 to hold the world land speed mark, achieving an average velocity of 407.45 mph (655.73 kph). Breedlove broke the 600 mph (966 kph) mark in the jetpowered *Spirit of America-Sonic I,* reaching 600.6 mph (966.6 kph) in 1965.

Breed's Hill *See:* Bunker Hill, Battle of.

Bremen (pop. 526,400), city in northwest Germany, situated on the Weser River, 38 mi (61 km) from Bremerhaven on the estuary. Founded by Charlemagne in A.D. 787, Bremen became a major medieval trading center, controlling its own small state within the Holy Roman Empire (from which it broke free in 1646), and acting as a leading force in the Hanseatic League of city-states. From 1806 to 1815 Bremen was in French hands. After the Congress of Vienna, it became one of the independent German states, and in 1871 merged with Bismarck's Germany. Commercial fishing, truck farming, and cattle raising are the main occupations in the rural areas surrounding the city. In the city itself, which retains much of its medieval character, the main occupations are shipbuilding and import and export shipping.
See also: Germany.

Brendan, Saint (C.A.D. 484-c.578), Irish monk, founder of Clonfert and other monasteries. Tales of his travels are recorded in the 8th-century *Voyages of St. Brendan,* and he is sometimes honored as having reached America 900 years before Columbus.

Brennan, William Joseph, Jr. (1906-), U.S. Supreme Court associate justice 1956-90, appointed by Eisenhower. He became leader of the court's liberal wing, and was a champion of civil rights, free speech, and labor relations.
See also: Supreme Court of the United States

Brenner Pass, important pass across the Alps, in the Tyrol, linking Innsbruck in Austria with Bolzano in Italy. The first good road along this ancient route was completed in 1772, and the railroad was built from 1864 to 1867.
See also: Alps.

Breslau *See:* Wroclaw.

Bresson, Robert (1907-), French film director, noted for the austere, penetrating quality of his work. His films include *Diary of a Country Priest* (1950), *The Trial of Joan of Arc* (1962), and *Lancelot of the Lake* (1976).

Brest (pop. 156,100), seaport and naval station in Finistère department, northwest France. It is built on two hills overlooking an island harbor linked with the Atlantic Ocean by a natural 6-mi (9.7-km) channel. Brest is a commercial port, but important primarily as a naval base. During World War II the base was used by German submarines and was largely destroyed by Allied bombing.
See also: France.

Brethren, Children of the, Baptist sect organized in Germany in 1708. Following persecution, the church was reorganized in 1719 in Germantown, Pa., eventually spreading its doctrine of pacifism and simple living to the Pacific coast. Headquarters in Elgin, Ill., the church sponsors mission work around the world and operates six colleges and a seminary.
See also: Baptists.

Breton, André (1896-1966), French poet and critic, a founder of surrealism. Associated at first with Dada, he broke with it and in 1924 issued the first of three surrealist manifestos, becoming the new movement's chief spokesperson. Among his works is the poetic novel, *Nadja* (1928).
See also: Surrealism.

Bretton Woods Conference, international gathering at Bretton Woods, N.H., in July 1944, at which 44 members of the United Nations planned to stabilize the international economy and national currencies after World War II. They also established the International Monetary Fund and the World Bank.
See also: United Nations; World Bank.

Breuer, Marcel (Lajos) (1902-81), Hungarian-born U.S. architect. A student and teacher at the Bauhaus 1920-28, in 1937 he moved to Harvard and continued working with Walter Gropius. A pioneer of the international style, he collaborated in the design of the UNESCO headquarters, Paris (1953-58).
See also: Bauhaus.

Brewing, process of making beer from cereal grains, usually barley. Brewing is a major industry in the United States, with a total annual production of about 125 million barrels. In the first step of brewing, malting, cleaned barley is soaked in water 2-3 days, allowed to germinate, and dried in a kiln. The malt is stored for several weeks while the malt flavor develops and various enzymes are produced. In the next stage, mashing, the ground malt is mixed with water, maintained at a warm temperature, and stirred constantly. During this process the enzymes break down the insoluble starch into soluble carbohydrates. The liquor containing these substances is filtered out (the remaining solid mash is used as animal feed) and boiled to stop enzyme activity and sterilize the brew. Hops are added at this stage to impart their characteristic flavor. Yeast is then added for about 8 days of fermentation.
See also: Beer; Fermentation.

Brewster, William (1567-1644), leader of the Plymouth Colony in New England. He sailed with the Pilgrims on the *Mayflower* in 1620. Brewster played a major part in regulating the civil and religious affairs of the Plymouth Colony.
See also: Pilgrims; Plymouth Colony.

Brezhnev, Leonid Ilyich (1906-82), USSR political leader, who became first secretary of the Communist Party and effective head of the Soviet government in 1964. He first became a member of the party central committee in 1952, and was chairman of the Presidium of the Supreme Soviet 1960-64. Brezhnev, Aleksei Kosygin, and Nikolai Podgorny took control when Nikita Khrushchev was ousted in 1964. Brezhnev assumed the additional office of chief of state in 1977. He pursued a policy of détente with the West while overseeing a massive Soviet military buildup.
See also: Union of Soviet Socialist Republics

Brian Boru (941-1014), king of Ireland from 1002. His reign marked the end of Norse domination, but unified rule ended when he was murdered after his victory against the Danes at Clontarf.
See also: Ireland.

Briand, Aristide (1862-1932), French politician, lawyer, and socialist leader who was 11 times premier of France. As foreign minister (1925-32), he was the author of the Kellogg-Briand Pact (1928). He was awarded the Nobel Peace Prize in 1926.
See also: Kellogg-Briand Peace Pact.

Briar *See:* Brier.

Briard, sheepdog first bred in France in the twelfth century. Used for herding and police work, the briard is strongly built and usually black, grey, or tawny in color. It stands 22 to 27 in (56 to 69 cm) and weighs about 70 to 80 lb (32 to 36 kg).

Brice, Fanny (Fannie Borach; 1891-1951), U.S. popular singer and performer of musical comedy. Acclaimed for her radio series in which she portrayed "Baby Snooks," she was also known for her satirical sketches and her long association with the *Ziegfeld Follies.*

Brick, building material made of clay, sometimes reinforced with straw, shaped into rectangles and hardened by heat. Sundried bricks were used as a building material at least 6,000 years ago in Mesopotamia. The discovery of the technique of firing clay in kilns enabled hard durable bricks to be made. Examples of fired bricks have been found in excavations at the city of Ur that are at least 5,000 years old. The Greeks used bricks, and the Romans made an art of brick masonry in their large-scale constructions. After the fall of Rome, bricks were not used again on a large scale until the 12th and 13th centuries.
Although bricks are important in the construction industry, concrete, plastics, and light alloys have taken over some of their functions. Modern bricks include: *common brick,* used for ordinary building purposes; *face brick,* used to resist erosion or

for decoration; *firebrick* (refractory brick), which can withstand the high temperatures found in furnaces and kilns; *paving brick*, larger, harder, and more water-resistant than the common brick; and *insulating brick*, a porous type that insulates against extremes of temperature.

Bridge, card game developed from whist. Contract bridge, the form now universally adopted, was perfected by Harold S. Vanderbilt in 1925-26. It is played by 2 pairs of partners, who make bids according to how many tricks (rounds of cards played) they calculate they can win. Demanding great skill, bridge has become immensely popular as a social and competitive game, with international championships controlled by the World Bridge Federation.

Bridge, structure that spans an obstacle and permits traffic across it. The *beam* (or girder) *bridge* consists of a rigid beam resting at either end on piers. A development of this is the *truss bridge*, with a metal framework designed for greatest strength at those points where the load has greatest moment around the piers. Where piers are impracticable, a *cantilever bridge* may be built on beams (cantilevers) extending from each side. An *arch bridge* consists of one or more arches. A *suspension bridge* comprises two towers that carry one or more flexible cables that are firmly anchored at each end; the roadway is suspended by means of vertical cables. *Movable bridges* include the *swing bridge*, pivoted on a central pier; the *bascule* (a descendant of the medieval drawbridge), whose cantilevers are pivoted inshore so that they may be swung upward; the *vertical-lift bridge*, a pair of towers between which runs a beam that may be winched vertically upward; and the *retractable bridge*, whose cantilevers may be run inshore on wheels. Temporary bridges include the pontoon or floating bridge, in which floating structures support a continuous roadway.

The Sharestan bridge over the Zaindeh River near Isfahan, Iran

Pier in Brighton

Bridge of Sighs, landmark bridge in Venice, Italy. Spanning the canal between the Doges' Palace and the state prison, its name derives from the "sighs" of the unhappy prisoners who had to cross it. Renowned for its beauty, it was designed by Italian architect Antonio Contino and completed c.1600.

Bridgeport (pop. 141,686), city in southwestern Connecticut, about 65 mi (105 km) from New York City. Products include electrical and metal goods, sewing machines, munitions, airplanes, textiles, and clothing. It is the home of the Barnum Institute of Science and History and the University of Bridgeport, founded in 1947.
See also: Connecticut.

Bridger, James (1804-81), U.S. trader, explorer, and army scout. He traded in the unexplored American West and Southwest. He discovered Great Salt Lake (1824), and founded Fort Bridger, Wy.
See also: Western frontier life.

Bridges, Harry (Alfred Bryant Renton Bridges; 1901-90), U.S. labor leader, Australian- born. He helped form the International Longshoremen's and Warehousemen's Union (ILWU) in 1937, and as its president (until 1977) fought to improve dockworking conditions. Until 1955 there were many government attempts to deport him as a communist.

Bridgetown (pop. 7,500), capital and only port of Barbados. It is a crowded and attractive tourist center, with public buildings made of coral. It was founded in 1628, and then named Indian Bridge, from a crude structure over the creek. Its modernized port now handles sugar, molasses, and rum.
See also: Barbados.

Bridgman, Laura Dewey (1829-89), first blind and deaf child to be successfully educated in the United States. She was taught the names of objects by raised letters pasted onto the objects themselves and eventually learned finger-spelling, thus paving the way for the education of other deaf-blind youths such as Helen Keller.

Brier, shrubby plant (*Erica arborea*) of the heath family, known for its fragrant, white, globe-shaped flowers. Its thick roots are used in making pipes.

Bright, Richard (1789-1858), English physician who first identified the kidney disorder known as Bright's Disease, now called nephritis.
See also: Nephritis.

Brighton (pop. 143,000), popular English seaside resort on the south coast, 51 mi (82 km) south of London. The town first gained popularity when an 18th-century doctor claimed its seawater had curative power. In 1783 the Prince of Wales (later George IV) visited the town. The onion-domed Royal Pavilion was built to his orders. Originally in classical style, it was rebuilt in 1815 by John Nash, in the exotic style of Indian Mogul architecture.
See also: England.

Brisbane (pop. 1,038,000), city and seaport in eastern Australia, capital of the state of Queensland. The city is built on both banks of the navigable Brisbane River, about 15 mi (24 km) from the outlet to the Pacific Ocean. The area was a penal settlement in 1824, then in 1838 became a city. Queensland became a separate colony in 1859.
See also: Australia.

Bristlecone pine, evergreen tree (*Pinus aristata*) native to the Rocky Mountains of the United States. Some bristlecone pines are thought to be more than 4,000 years old, possibly the oldest living things on earth. The long life of the needles helps the tree survive years of harsh weather, when few new needles can grow.

Bristol (pop. 393,800), large city and port in southwestern England, situated at the confluence of the Avon and Frome rivers, 6 mi (9.7 km) from the mouth of the Avon. First a Saxon settlement called Brycgstowe ("the place of the bridge"), by Norman times it had become a wool center and the chief port for trade with Ireland. The textile

trade flourished and in 1540 Bristol became a city. In the 17th and 18th centuries, when new trade routes had been established, Bristol shipowners engaged in "the triangular trade of the Atlantic," dealing in sugar, slaves, and tobacco. Another source of prosperity in the 18th century was the development of the city as a fashionable spa, making use of the hot mineral springs. There are some fine historic buildings and a famous suspension bridge (1864) that spans the precipitous Avon gorge.
See also: England.

Bristol Channel, inlet of the Atlantic Ocean between Wales and southwestern England. Extending 80 mi (130km) from the sea to the River Severn, it separates the heavily industrialized southwestern Wales from largely agricultural southwestern England.

Britain, modern form of the ancient name for the island now comprising England, Scotland, and Wales. The Romans referred to the 1st century B.C. Celtic inhabitants as Pritani, hence their own name for the island, Britannia.

Britain, Battle of, air battle of World War II from Aug. 8 to Oct. 31, 1940, between the British Royal Air Force (RAF) and the German Luftwaffe. The Germans intended to weaken British defenses and morale before invading the country. The Luftwaffe forces were much larger than those of the RAF, but the latter proved technically and tactically superior. The Germans bombed shipping and ports, then airfields and Midland industries, and finally, London. Daylight raids proving too costly, the Germans turned to night attacks. At the end the RAF had lost some 900 planes, the Germans over 2,300, causing Hitler to postpone his projected invasion indefinitely, thus tacitly admitted failure.
See also: Churchill, Sir Winston Leonard Spencer; World War II.

British Broadcasting Corporation (BBC), publicly financed company that runs all radio and 2 of the 3 television networks in Britain. The BBC first went on the air in 1922. Regular television programs, which began in 1936, were interrupted by World War II, but resumed in 1946. The BBC provides a wide range of news programs, documentaries, plays, comedies, concerts, and school programs, and is known for the excellence of its panel programs and educational broadcasts. The BBC has a considerable overseas audience.

British Cameroons, former UN trust territory on the west coast of Africa in what is now Nigeria and Cameroon. After World War I the former German colony of Cameroons was divided between France and Britain. After World War II both became UN trust territories. In 1960, French Cameroons became independent, and in 1961 the southern part of British Cameroons joined it to form the Republic of Cameroon. The northern part was incorporated into Nigeria.

British Columbia, westernmost of Canada's provinces, bordered by Alberta on the east, Montana, Idaho, and Washington on the south, the Pacific Ocean and Alaska on the west, and the Yukon and Northwest Territories on the north. Alberta is dominated by two mountain chains, the Coast Mountains in the west and the Canadian Rocky Mountains in the east. The 700-mi (1,127-km) coastline is broken by fjords. Vancouver Island and the Queen Charlotte Islands are the most important of the offshore chains. About 75% of the population lives in the relatively mild southwest corner of the province. Greater Vancouver alone accounts for about one-half of the total population. The provincial capital is Victoria. Forestry is the mainstay of British Columbia's economy and accounts for the province's major industries. Mining is second, including zinc, lead, silver, gold, and iron ore.
See also: Canada.

British Commonwealth of Nations *See:* Commonwealth of Nations.

British Empire *See:* Great Britain.

British Guiana *See:* Guyana.

British Honduras *See:* Belize.

British Indian Ocean Territory, British dependency in the Indian Ocean, about 1,180 mi (1,900 km) northeast of Mauritius. Consisting of the Chagos Archipelago Island group, it covers a land area of about 30 sq mi (78 sq km) and has a population of about 2,500 people. The United States maintains a naval base on the main island, Diego Garcia.

British Isles, island group bounded by the English Channel, the Strait of Dover, the North Sea, and the Atlantic Ocean. The British Isles consist of the island of Great Britain (England, Scotland, and Wales), Ireland, and about 5,500 small islands and inlets.

British Library, national library of Great Britain, one of the largest research libraries in the world. Located in London, it was originally a part of the British Museum. Its collection of rare books and manuscripts includes *Beowulf* and the Magna Carta. The library is also a depository for copyrights.

British Museum, national museum of antiquities and ethnography in London. Founded in 1753, when the British government acquired the art collection and library of Sir Hans Sloane, it opened to the public in 1759. Its present neoclassical premises were built 1823-47 and its natural history section was separated 1881-83. The museum has one of the world's foremost collections, including the Elgin Marbles.

British North America Act, act passed by the British Parliament in 1867 to create the Dominion of Canada, uniting Canada (Quebec and Ontario), New Brunswick, and Nova Scotia under a federal government. The act served as Canada's constitution until 1982; under it, amendments had to be submitted to the British Parliament for formal approval. The Constitution Act, 1982, superseded the earlier law (now also known as the Constitution Act, 1867), thus "patriating" the constitution.
See also: Confederation of Canada.

British thermal unit (BTU), quantity of heat required to raise the temperature of one pound of water 1°F at, or near, its point

In the Battle of Britain, the German Stukas (Ju-87 B1), so successful as tactical bombers, were used as pursuit planes, but they were no match for British Spitfires and Hurricanes.

The Battle of Britain brought German air raids on London. The population flocked into stations of the underground (subway) for shelter.

of maximum density (39.1°F). The BTU is equivalent to 0.252 kilogram-calorie.
See also: Calorie.

British West Indies, collective name for islands in the Caribbean Sea that are or have been dependencies of Great Britain, including Anguilla, the Bahamas, Barbados, Bermuda, Grenada, Jamaica, Trinidad and Tobago, and the British Virgin Islands. Although the British West Indies is not a political entity, the islands have formed such organizations as the West Indies Federation (1958-62) and Caricom, or the Caribbean Community, an alliance based on foreign policy and economic cooperation (1973).

Brittany, breed of hunting dog with a short, thick coat, white with orange or red-brown markings. Brittanies average 35-40 lbs (16-18 kg) and stand 18-20 in (45-50 cm) at the shoulder. A breed with a long history in France and Spain, the Brittany has the build of a spaniel but points at its quarry.

Brittany (French: *Bretagne*), historic peninsular region of northwestern France. The Romans conquered the area in 56 B.C. and named it Armonica. It was settled about 500 A.D. by Celtic Britons fleeing the Anglo-Saxon invasion. After struggles for independence from the Franks and from Normandy, Anjou, England, and France in turn, it became a French province in 1532. The Bretons retain their own cultural traditions and language.
See also: France.

Benjamin Britten

Britten, Benjamin (1913-76), British composer. His works include the operas *Peter Grimes* (1945), *Billy Budd* (1951), *The Turn of the Screw* (1954), and *Death in Venice* (1973), as well as such instrumental and choral works as the *Variations on a Theme by Frank Bridge* (1937) and *War Requiem* (1962).
See also: Opera.

Brittle star, marine invertebrate (class Ophiuroidea), 5-armed relative of starfish found in seas all over the world. The button-shaped body grows up to 2 in (5 cm), and the flexible arms, which break off readily but are regrown, grow to 2 ft (60 cm). Brittle stars feed by trapping minute particles in mucus on the arms and passing them to the mouth on the underside of the disk, or by holding animals or carrion in an arm and pushing them into the mouth. Eggs are fertilized after being released into the sea or retained in the female, where larval development takes place, the young being released as small adults.

Brno (formerly Brünn; pop. 383,400), city in central Czechoslovakia, chief city of Moravia. It was founded in the 9th century, flourishing as a free city within the kingdom of Bohemia in the 13th-14th centuries. In the 18th-19th centuries its Spielberg castle was used as a Hapsburg prison. Situated on the Svratka and Svitava rivers, Brno is a manufacturing center for cars, machinery, textiles, and other products, and is the seat of the Czechoslovak supreme court.
See also: Czechoslovakia.

Broad bean, Windsor bean, or horse bean (*Vicia faba*), annual plant producing seed pods up to 1 ft (30 cm) long, containing large edible beans. An important food in early civilizations of North Africa and southwest Asia, it is one of the most widely cultivated beans in Europe and Latin America, and is also grown for fodder.

Broadcasting *See:* Journalism; Radio; Television.

Broccoli, form of cabbage, a branching cauliflower (*Brassica oleracea botytis*), grown for the immature flowers. Originating in Italy, it is grown in Europe and America, where green-sprouting broccoli is the most popular variety.

Broglie, Louis Victor, Prince de (1892-1987), French physicist, awarded the 1929 Nobel Prize in physics for his suggestion that subatomic particles would display wave-like properties under appropriate conditions. The prediction was borne out experimentally, and de Broglie's theories led to the branch of quantum mechanics called wave mechanics.
See also: Physics; Quantum theory.

Bromegrass, any of about 60 kinds of grass of genus *Bromus*, found mostly in the Northern Hemisphere and including both weed grasses and grasses valuable as pasturage and soil binders. Plants have flat thin leaves 12-40 in (30-100 cm) tall, often with drooping flower clusters. Rescue grass (*B. unioloides*) and smooth brome (*B. inermis*) are the most economically important varieties. Some weed varieties, such as ripgut grass (*B. rigidus*) and foxtail brome (*B. rubens*), have spines on the flower clusters that can cause serious internal and external injury to grazing animals.

Bromeliad, large family of tropical plants, mostly native to the Americas, including the pineapple and epiphytes (air plants) such as Spanish moss. Most bromeliads have spike-shaped leaves that form a tight cluster, with flowers in the cluster or on spikes; the cup-shaped cluster holds water, allowing the plants to survive droughts.

Bromide, salt of hydrobromic acid, especially potassium bromide, that acts as a depressant of brain function and the heart and is used in medicine as a sedative and a hypnotic.

Bromine, chemical element, symbol Br; for physical constants see Periodic Table. Bromine was discovered by Antoine J. Balard in 1826. It belongs to the halogen group of elements and is obtained from natural brines and sea water by displacement with chlorine. Bromine, a heavy red-dish-brown liquid, is the only nonmetallic element that is liquid at room temperature. It produces irritating red fumes at room temperature and produces painful sores on skin contact. Bromine is less active than chlorine. The major use of bromine is in the production of ethylene dibromide, a lead scavenger used in making gasoline antiknock compounds. It is also used in making fumigants, flameproofing agents, water purification compounds, dyes, medicinals, sanitizers, and photographic chemicals.

Bronchitis, inflammation of the bronchi, the main branches of the windpipe, caused by viruses or bacteria or by the inhalation of smoke. Coughing, fever, and chest pains are common symptoms.

Brontë sisters, 3 English novelists and poets, daughters of an Anglican clergyman. The isolated life of the Yorkshire moors, their mother's early death, and the dissipations of their brother, Branwell, informed much of their work. **Charlotte Brontë** (1816-55) published the partly autobiographical novel *Jane Eyre* (1847) under the name Currer Bell and met with immediate success. Together with *Shirley* (1849) and *Villette* (1853), it represents an important advance in the treatment of women in English fiction. **Emily Brontë** (1818-48), using the name Ellis Bell, published a single novel, *Wuthering Heights* (1847), a masterpiece of visionary power. **Anne Brontë** (1820-49) published two novels, *Agnes Grey* (1847) and *The Tenant of Wildfell Hall* (1848), under the name Acton Bell.

The Brontë sisters, Anne, Emily, and Charlotte (left to right), painted by their brother, Branwell (National Portrait Gallery, London)

Brontosaurus, large, plant-eating, four-legged dinosaur whose fossilized skeletons have been found in the western United States. With its long neck and tail, small head, and huge body (about 68 ft/28 m long, weighing 35 tons), the brontosaurus was probably the largest land animal in the earth's history.

See also: Dinosaur.

Bronx, The, one of the 5 boroughs of New York City, the only one situated on the mainland, separated from Manhattan Island by the Harlem River. Jonas Bronck

purchased the area from the Native Americans in 1639.
See also: New York City.

Bronze, corrosion-resistant alloy of copper and tin, used for machine parts, marine hardware, and casting statues. Aluminum, iron, lead, zinc, and phosphorus are often added to bronze to harden it.
See also: Alloy.

Bronze Age, phase of history in which metal was first used to make tools and weapons. Copper and bronze were used interchangeably in the first stage, called the Copper Age. Bronze casting began in the Middle East about 3500 B.C. and in the Americas, about 1100 A.D.

Brooke, Rupert (1887-1915), English poet whose patriotic war sonnets were widely popular during World War I, author of *Poems* (1911) and *1914 and Other Poems* (1915).

Brook Farm (1841-47), Utopian community, founded at West Roxbury, Massachusetts, by Unitarian minister George Ripley. The aim was to create an egalitarian community of workers and thinkers; many leading intellectuals were attracted, including the author Nathaniel Hawthorne, who was a member, and Horace Greeley, Margaret Fuller, and Ralph Waldo Emerson, who visited.

Brookhaven National Laboratory, center for nuclear research in Upton, Long Island, N.Y. Founded in 1947 under the aegis of the U.S. Atomic Energy Commission, it has facilities for medical and agricultural research.

Brookings Institution, public service corporation founded in 1927 in Washington, D.C., for research and information on government and economic issues.

Brooklyn, one of the 5 boroughs of New York City, situated at the southwest extremity of Long Island. First settled in 1636 by Dutch farmers, Brooklyn was chartered as a city in 1834 and gradually absorbed the surrounding communities until it became a borough of New York (1896). Though its large area is primarily residential, it also has a considerable business and industrial area and the port handles a great share of New York's oceangoing traffic. Brooklyn's facilities for higher education include Pratt Institute, Polytechnic University, Brooklyn College, and parts of Long Island University (LIU). The Brooklyn Museum, located on the edge of Prospect Park, has a fine collection of Egyptian and primitive art and a notable group of 18th-century and 19th-century American paintings. The Institute of Arts and Sciences, the Brooklyn Philharmonic Orchestra, and the Brooklyn Academy of Music have international reputations.
See also: New York City.

Brooklyn Bridge, world's first steel-wire suspension bridge. It spans 1,595 ft (486 m) over the East River and joins the boroughs of Brooklyn and Manhattan. Built 1869-83 by J. A. Roebling and his son, W. A. Roebling, it was the largest suspension bridge in the world at the time of its completion.

Brooks, Gwendolyn Elizabeth (1917-), U.S. poet. She was the first African American to win the Pulitzer Prize (1949), for her semiautobiographical *Annie Allen* (1949). Her books of poems include *Bronzeville Boys and Girls* (1956), *Selected Poems* (1963), *In the Mecca* (1968), and *To Disembark* (1981).

Brooks, Van Wyck (1886-1963), U.S. critic. In *America's Coming of Age* (1915), he saw the 19th-century United States as torn between the idealistic and the materialistic. He wrote critical biographies of Mark Twain, Henry James, and Emerson. His series *Makers and Finders: A History of the Writer in America, 1800-1915*, included the Pulitzer Prize-winning *The Flowering of New England* (1936).

Broom, any of various European and Asian leguminous shrubs with yellow flowers that "explode" when bees land on them. The seeds develop in pods that twist open suddenly, throwing the seeds out with an audible crackle.

Broom, Robert (1866-1951), Scottish anatomist and paleontologist, discoverer of fossils of the humanlike *Australopithecus*. From 1903 he lived in South Africa, where he taught at Victoria College and studied the fossils, important for their bearing on human evolution. His writings include *Mammal-Like Reptiles of South Africa* (1932) and *The South African Fossil Ape-men* (1946).
See also: Paleontology.

Broun, Heywood Campbell (1888-1939), U.S. journalist. His column, "It Seems to Me," published in the *New York Tribune* (1912-21), *New York World* (1921-28), and *New York Telegram* (1928-39), was widely read for its liberal political and social views; he also wrote for the *Post* and *The New Republic*. His views, as in his defense of Sacco and Vanzetti, brought him into frequent conflict with his publishers. He ran for Congress as a Socialist (1930), and established the American Newspaper Guild (1933), serving as president until his death.
See also: Journalism.

Browder, Earl Russell (1891-1973), U.S. Communist party secretary-general 1930-44 and president of the Communist Political Association 1944-45. He was also the Communist presidential candidate in 1936 and 1940, but was expelled from the party in 1946 for advocating greater cooperation between the Soviet Union and the West.

Brown, Charles Brockden (1771-1810), one of the first U.S. professional novelists. Influenced by William Godwin, his *Alcuin: A Dialogue* (1798) and novel *Edgar Huntly* (1799) plead for social reform. *Wieland* (1799) is an outstanding Gothic novel.
See also: Communism.

Brown, Jim (1936-), U.S. football player. A running back for the Cleveland Browns (1957-65), he was one of the greatest players in National Football League (NFL) history. Brown's achievements include winning a record 8 league rushing titles and placing second among all-time leading rushers (12,312 yards). Brown was inducted into the football Hall of Fame in 1971.

Brown, John (1800-59), U.S. abolitionist. After supporters of slavery burned down the town of Lawrence, Kansas, Brown retaliated by murdering five proslavery men at Pottawatamie Creek. In October 1859 Brown seized the government arsenal at Harper's Ferry, Virginia, attempting to ignite a massive slave insurrection. Troops under Robert E. Lee stormed the arsenal and captured Brown. He was tried for treason and hanged on Dec. 2, 1859.
See also: Abolitionism.

Brown, Robert (1773-1858), Scottish physician and botanist. Brown discovered the natural continuous random movement of microscopic particles now known as Brownian motion (1827), and identified the nucleus as a constituent of nearly all living plant cells (1831). Brown studied and collected specimens of flora in Australia and Tasmania. He identified the two plant groupings of gymnosperms (conifers) and angiosperms (flowering plants), and otherwise elaborated the system of plant classification. He was also a pioneer in the microscopic examination of plant fossils.
See also: Botany.

Brown, Sir Arthur Whitten *See:* Alcock and Brown.

Brownian motion *See:* Brown, Robert; Einstein, Albert.

Brownie, in British folklore, small creature that lives with a household and helps with chores while a family sleeps. It looks like an ugly, shaggy man and usually dresses in a brown cloak. The brownie, who accepts no pay, may also cause mischief. The name is also used for the youngest group (6-8 years) of the Girl Scouts.

Brownies *See:* Girl Scouts and Girl Guides.

Browning, Elizabeth Barrett (1806-61), English lyric poet best known for *Sonnets from the Portuguese* (1850), inspired by her husband, Robert Browning, who had "rescued" her from illness and family tyranny in 1846. Other works include *Casa Guidi Windows* (1851) and *Aurora Leigh* (1857), a novel in verse.

Browning, Robert (1812-89), English poet. He perfected the dramatic monologue in "Andrea del Sarto" and "My Last Duchess." His masterpiece is *The Ring and the Book*

(4 vols., 1868-69), a 17th-century Roman murder story told from different viewpoints. His psychological insight and colloquial language profoundly influenced 20th-century poets.

Brown lung, or byssinosis, lung disease caused by inhaling of cotton dust. Symptoms include difficulty in breathing, a tight feeling in the chest, and coughing. Because cotton dust can permanently harm workers' health, the governments of many countries have set limits on their exposure to it.

Brown recluse, poisonous spider (*Loxosceles reclusa*) of the southern United States, member of the family of brown spiders (Loxoscelidae). It is about 3/8 in (1 cm) long, with a dark violin-shaped patch on its back and 6 eyes in 2 rows. The spider's poisonous bite, used to paralyze insects it eats, leaves a deep and long-lasting sore in humans, and may produce severe reactions, even death.

Brownsville (pop. 260,120), city in southern Texas near the mouth of the Rio Grande River. Named after Major Jacob Brown, who died defending the settlement from Mexican troops in 1846, Brownsville was incorporated in 1850. Brownsville is a busy port on the Gulf of Mexico and a major industrial center producing chemicals, clothing, and petroleum products. The largest city in the Rio Grande Valley, Brownsville has a tropical climate. Its population is predominantly Latin American in origin although there has been an influx of Anglo Americans since World War II.
See also: Texas.

Anton Bruckner

Brown-tail moth (*Nygmia phaeorrhoea*), member of the family of tussock moths (Liparidae, which also includes the gypsy moth), native to the northeastern United States, whose caterpillar is a serious pest to fruit and shade trees. The hairs of the caterpillars and female moths can be irritating to human skin. The moth is white with a brown abdomen, and a wingspan of about 1.5 in (3.8 cm). The female lays about 300 eggs, which hatch into hairy brown caterpillars with orange, white, or other markings. All summer the caterpillars eat leaves, spinning silk tents to winter over and emerging in spring to continue eating. Grown caterpillars spin cocoons and pupate, maturing by July.

Hunters in the Snow of January *is the name of this large painting by Pieter Bruegel the Elder (c. 1525-1569).*

Brown thrasher (*Toxostoma rufum*), bird of the mockingbird family (Mimidae), of the eastern United States and Canada. It is about 11.5 in (29 cm) long, with red-brown head and back, white-and-brown striped breast, long tail, and yellow eyes. The thrasher lives in brush and shrubs and eats insects. Its musical song, like the mockingbird's, resembles that of a variety of other birds.

Brown University, private coeducational school in Providence, R.I., established 1764. Its programs include undergraduate arts and sciences, a graduate program, and a medical school, and it awards bachelor's, master's, and doctoral degrees.

Brown v. Board of Education of Topeka, historic 1954 case in which the U.S. Supreme Court, influenced greatly by Chief Justice Warren's determination to provide a clear signal, unanimously held that racial segregation in public schools is unconstitutional. The Court thereby reversed the 1896 "separate but equal" case of *Plessy* v. *Ferguson.* The decision helped to stimulate the civil rights movement.
See also: Segregation.

Brubeck, Dave (1920-), U.S. pianist and composer in the classical and jazz idioms. He studied composition with Darius Milhaud and Arnold Schoenberg. His jazz quartet, founded in 1951 and active through the 1960s, featured alto saxophonist Paul Desmond. During the 1970s and 1980s Brubeck often performed with his three sons. His compositions, known for complex cross-rhythms and baroque counterpoint, include "Blue Rondo a la Turk" and "Take Five."

Bruce, Blanche Kelso (1841-98), public official, the first African American to serve a full term as a U.S. senator (1875-81). Born a slave in Virginia, he was educated on the plantation, then ran away in 1861 after the beginning of the Civil War. After founding schools for blacks in Kansas and Missouri and attending Oberlin College 1866-68, he became a wealthy planter in Mississippi. As a Republican senator from Mississippi, he was an advocate of civil rights for racial minorities, but also opposed discrimination against former rebels. With the end of Reconstruction, he was not reelected, but served as registrar of the U.S. Treasury under presidents James A. Garfield (1881-85) and William McKinley (1897-98).

Bruce, Robert the (1274-1329), claimant to the Scottish throne, which Edward I of England awarded to John de Baliol instead. In 1314 his forces defeated the English in the battle of Bannockburn, briefly interrupting English rule over Scotland.

Bruce, Sir David (1855-1931), British physician and bacteriologist, specialist in tropical diseases. Born in Melbourne, Australia, he studied in Edinburgh and Berlin. In Malta he discovered the bacillus causing brucellosis (1886) and its transmission in goat's milk; in Africa he discovered the organism causing sleeping sickness and its transmission by the tsetse fly (1903-10). An expert on trench fever and tetanus, he also studied the connection between human and animal diseases.
See also: Bacteriology.

Brucellosis, undulant fever, or Malta fever, infectious diseases of vertebrate animals, caused by any of a genus (*Brucella*) of bacteria. Symptoms are chills, fever, profuse sweating, slow pulse and, finally, enlargement of the spleen. Cattle, sheep, goats, and swine can pass the disease on to humans through contaminated meat, milk, and cheese, or by direct contact.

Bruch, Max (1838-1920), German composer and conductor. His best-known works are his Violin Concerto No. 1 in G minor (1868), *Scottish Fantasy* for violin and orchestra (1880), and *Kol Nidrei* for cello and orchestra (1881), based on a traditional Hebrew liturgical melody and written for the Jewish community of Liverpool, England (although Bruch himself was Protestant). He taught at the Berlin Academy of Arts 1891-1910.

Bruckner, (Josef) Anton (1824-96), Austrian composer, noted for his 9 symphonies and his choral music—Masses in D Minor (1864), E Minor (1866), and F Minor (1867-71). Richard Wagner greatly influenced Bruckner.

Bruegel, family of Flemish painters. **Pieter Bruegel the Elder** (c.1525-69) was a great painter of landscapes and allegories: *Peasant Wedding, Fall of Icarus.* Influenced by Bosch (*The Fall of the Rebel Angels*), his works are profoundly marked by his views of the human condition. **Pieter Bruegel the Younger** (1564-1637), also called Hell Bruegel, worked in his father's manner, often with an emphasis on the grotesque. **Jan Bruegel** (1568-1625), also called Velvet Bruegel, the second son, painted landscapes and still lifes with great subtlety and delicacy. He often collaborated with Rubens.

Brugge, or Bruges (pop. 117,800), well-preserved medieval city in northwestern Belgium. Once a center for wool trade, in the 15th century it was home to a school of painting led by the van Eycks and Hans Memling. Its commercial interest revived in the 19th century when the Zeebrugge Canal to the North Sea was opened. It manufactures lace and textiles.
See also: Belgium.

Bruhn, Erik (1928-86), Danish ballet dancer. He debuted with the Royal Danish Ballet in 1947 and became a soloist in 1949. For his roles in *Giselle*, *Swan Lake*,

and *La Sylphide*, Bruhn is considered one of the greatest classical dancers of his time.
See also: Ballet.

Brulé, Étienne (1592?-1633), French-born Canadian explorer. He came to Quebec around 1608, and was sent by Samuel de Champlain to live with the Algonquins (1610) and the Hurons (1611), studying their language and becoming an interpreter. On another mission for Champlain, he was the first European to reach Lake Ontario (1615), and also explored the valley of the Susquehanna River. When Quebec was seized by the English (1629) he fled to the Hurons; according to some accounts, he was later killed by the Hurons.

Brummell, Beau (George Bryan Brummell; 1778-1840), English dandy, friend of the Prince of Wales (later George IV), and an arbiter of fashion in Regency society. The "Beau" window is named after him.

Brunei

Capital:	Bandar Seri Begawan
Area:	2,226 sq mi (5,765 sq km)
Population:	251,000
Government:	monarchy (sultanate)
Independent:	1984
GNP:	U.S.$3,317,000,000
Per capita:	U.S.$14,120

Brunei, sultanate on the north coast of the island of Borneo, on the South China Sea. It has a humid tropical climate that supports dense forests. Malay is the chief language, Islam the official religion. Rubber and timber were superseded as main products after petroleum was found in 1929. Petroleum and natural gas are now extracted both on and off shore. A local sultanate, established in the 15th century, controlled all of Borneo during the 16th century. It became a British protectorate in 1888, and a 1959 constitution gave it domestic autonomy. Brunei received full independence in 1984.
See also: Borneo.

Brunel, Sir Marc Isambard (1769-1849), French-born British engineer and inventor who built the world's first underwater tunnel (Thames Tunnel, 1825). His son, **Isambard Kingdom Brunel** (1806-59), a civil engineer, designed the Clifton suspension bridge at Bristol, England, and built iron-hulled steamships, including the giant *Great Eastern* (1858).

Brunelleschi, Filippo (1377-1446), first great Italian Renaissance architect. One of the first practitioners of linear perspective, he was influenced by classical Roman and 11th-century Tuscan Romanesque architecture. His masterpiece is the dome of the Florence cathedral (1420-36).
See also: Renaissance.

Brunhild, Brünnehilde, or Brynhild, heroine of German and Scandinavian mythology dating back to A.D. 400. In the oldest Scandinavian version, Sigurd rescues her from a deep sleep imposed by Odin. In the medieval epic, she loves and is deserted by Sigurd, whose death she contrives, destroying herself on his funeral pyre. As Brünnhilde, the Valkyrie, she is the subject of German composer Richard Wagner's opera *Ring of the Nibelungs*.
See also: Nibelungenlied.

Bruno, Giordano (1548-1600), Italian philosopher. A Dominican who was expelled from the order for heresy, he held that the universe was infinite and that there is no absolute truth. He also defended the Copernican hypothesis. His major works were *On the Infinite Universe and Worlds* and *The Infinite* (both 1584). Brought to trial by the Inquisition, he refused to recant and was burned at the stake. His ideas later influenced Leibniz and Spinoza, making him an important philosophical influence on early modern science.
See also: Philosophy.

Brunswick (German: *Braunschweig*), descendants of the Wolf family. Great Britain's present line of monarchs are descendants of Brunswick dukes of Hanover, Germany. The duchy of Brunswick-Luneburg was established by Frederick II in 1235 and given to Otto, grandson of the Wolf family's founder, Henry the Lion. In 1714, Elector George Louis of Hanover succeeded to the throne of Britain as George I. A reduced duchy of Brunswick existed as a separate state and after 1735 was associated with Prussia under the House of Brunswick-Beven. Brunswick remained a constituent state of Germany from 1871 to 1946.

Brussels (pop. 137,700), Belgian capital city, headquarters of the European Common Market and NATO. First commercially important in the 12th century, it was granted a ducal charter in 1312. From the 16th to the 19th centuries it was subject successively to Spain, Austria, and France. It manufactures textiles, lace, and furniture and is a transport center.
See also: Belgium.

Brussels griffon, breed of toy dog developed in 19th-century Belgium. The Brussels griffon may be reddish brown, black, or a combination of the two. It comes in two varieties, one rough and wiry and the other, called Brabançon, having a smooth coat. Standing about 10-12 in (25-30 cm) and weighing 8-10 lb (3.6-4.5 kg), it is noted for its intelligent and affectionate nature.

Brussels sprouts, variety of cabbage first grown on the outskirts of Brussels. The edible buds on the stem are best eaten after being touched by frost.

The symbol of Brussels is the Manneken Pis created by Frans Duquesnoy in the 17th century.

Brutus, Marcus Junius (85?-42 B.C.), Roman statesman who led the assassination plot against Julius Caesar. He committed suicide after being defeated by Mark Antony and Octavian at Philippi.
See also: Anthony, Mark; Caesar, Julius; Philippi.

Bryan, William Jennings (1860-1925), U.S. political leader, orator, and lawyer. After serving in Congress in 1891-95, he ran unsuccessfully as Democratic candidate for president in 1896, 1900, and 1908. He was secretary of state under Woodrow Wilson in 1913-15. His famous "Cross of Gold" speech at the 1896 Democratic convention defended free silver. A Christian fundamentalist, he assisted in the prosecution at the Scopes Trial in 1925, when John Scopes was convicted for teaching evolution in public schools in Dayton, Tenn. Bryan was also a supporter of the income tax and of women's suffrage.
See also: Darrow, Clarence S.; Scopes trial.

Giordano Bruno

Bryant, Paul "Bear" (1913-83), U.S. football coach. The all time winningest coach in Division I-A football, Bryant compiled a record of 323 wins, 85 losses, and 17 ties while coaching at Maryland (1945), Kentucky (1946-53), Texas A & M (1954-57), and Alabama (1958-82). Bryant won or shared six national championships at Alabama (1961, 64, 65, 73, 78, 79).

Brunei's gold-domed Omar Ali Saifuddin Mosque dominates the townscape of the capital Bandar Seri Begawan (formerly Brunei Town). The mosque is situated on the bank of the Brunei River, which flows through the capital.

Bryant, William Cullen (1794-1878), U.S. poet and journalist. Editor of the New York *Evening Post* (1826) and later part owner (1829-78), he campaigned against slavery and for free speech. He wrote the pastoral odes "Thanatopsis" (1817) and translated the *Iliad* (1870) and the *Odyssey* (1872).

Bryce, James, 1st Viscount (1838-1922), British politician and historian. A professor of law at Oxford, he wrote *History of the Holy Roman Empire* (1864) and *The American Commonwealth* (1888). He was British ambassador to the U.S. 1907-13.

Bryce Canyon National Park, area of 5,835 acres in southwest Utah, created as a park in 1924. Its extraordinary formations in limestone and sandstone are the result of erosion.
See also: National Parks.

Brynhild *See:* Brunhild.

Bryophyte, most primitive division of land plants, including liverworts and mosses. The life-cycle of bryophytes has two stages: the gametophyte, a sexual stage, and its offspring, the sporophyte, an asexual spore-bearing stage.

James Buchanan

15th U.S. President	
Born:	Near Mercersburg, Pa., Apr. 23, 1791
Term:	Mar. 1857-Mar. 1861
Vice President:	John Cabell Breckinridge
Political Party:	Initially Federalist, later Democratic
Spouse:	None
Children:	None
Died:	Lancaster, Pa., June 1, 1868

Bryozoan, freshwater and marine moss animals living in colonies encrusting seaweeds, stones, or the hulls of ships and sometimes forming lacy fans. Each colony is made up of minute, tentacled polyps.

Brzezinski, Zbigniew (1928-), Polish-born U.S. political scientist and national security adviser (1977-81), who advocated more vigorous anticommunist policies.

BTU *See:* British thermal unit.

Bubble chamber, device invented by Donald Glaser (1952) to observe the paths of subatomic particles. The particles are shot through pressurized liquefied gas; they create strings of tiny bubbles, leaving "tracks" of their path.
See also: Wilson Cloud Chamber.

Buber, Martin (1878-1965), Jewish philosopher, born in Austria. Editor of a major German-Jewish journal, *Der Jude*, 1916-24, he was a leading educator and scholar of Hasidism. He was forced to leave Germany in 1938 and moved to Jerusalem. His central philosophical concept, the direct relationship between God and the individual, is expressed in *I and Thou* (1923).
See also: Hasidism.

Bubonic plague, disease transmitted to humans by fleas from infected rats. One form of the plague called Black Death swept through Europe and parts of Asia in the 1300s, killing three-quarters of the population in 20 years. Symptoms include fever, chills, and enlarged, painful lymph nodes (buboes), particularly in the groin. In its black form, hemorrhages turn black. The antibiotics tetracycline and streptomycin as well as rat control and sanitation have greatly reduced the mortality rate.
See also: Epidemic.

Buchan, John, 1st Baron Tweedsmuir (1875-1940), Scottish author and politician. He wrote a four-volume history of World War I (1920-21), biographies (of Julius Caesar, 1932), and classic adventure stories (*The Thirty-Nine Steps*, 1915). From 1935 he was governor-general of Canada.

Buchanan, James (1791-1868), 15th president of the United States. Buchanan held office during the years of mounting crisis that led up to the Civil War. The bitter divisions between North and South over the issue of slavery intensified during Buchanan's administration. When he left office in Mar. 1861, 7 slave states had already seceded from the Union and the nation was on the verge of war.
Early life. Buchanan was born in a pioneer settlement near Mercersburg, Pa. He was graduated in 1809 from Dickinson College, studied law, and then served in the War of 1812. He became a state legislator (1814-16) and later a U.S. representative from Pennsylvania (1821-31). Initially a Federalist, Buchanan switched to the Democratic party after the Federalist party dissolved in the 1820s. After serving as U.S. minister to Russia (1832-33), Buchanan became a U.S. senator (1834-45). In 1845 President James K. Polk appointed him secretary of state, a position he held until 1849.
Buchanan's diplomatic career resumed in 1853, when President Franklin Pierce named him minister to Great Britain. In 1854 Buchanan, along with the U.S. ministers to France and Spain, formulated the Ostend Manifesto, which stated that the United States should try to purchase the island of Cuba from Spain but also suggested that the United States might, under certain circumstances, be justified in using force to "wrest" the island away from Spain.
President. In 1856 the Democratic party nominated Buchanan for president. He won the election, defeating two opponents from the Republican and Native American, or "Know-Nothing," parties. Although he opposed slavery on moral grounds, Buchanan felt that it was an issue for each state or territory to decide. One such territory was "Bleeding Kansas," which had been the scene of virtual civil war between proslavery groups and abolitionists.
Buchanan endorsed the principle of popular sovereignty, which would allow the people of Kansas to vote whether to enter the Union as a slave or a free state. He submitted to Congress the proslavery state constitution drawn up at Lecompton, Kans., in Sept. 1857. However, this constitution was not approved by antislavery forces in Kansas, and the U.S. House of Representatives rejected it. Buchanan's action on the Kansas issue and his endorsement of the Supreme Court's Dred Scott decision angered the North, and the 1858 elections returned majorities hostile to the president in both houses of Congress. The financial panic of 1857 further weakened confidence in Buchanan's administration.
In 1860 the nation elected Abraham Lincoln, a Republican, as president. In the months preceding his inauguration, 7 Southern states seceded from the Union, establishing the Confederate States of America.
Although war was imminent, Buchanan tried to maintain peace. A U.S. steamer attempting to bring supplies to U.S. troops at Fort Sumter, S.C., was fired upon by a Southern battery, but since no blood was shed, Buchanan chose not to regard this as an act of war. The nation he handed over to Lincoln was still precariously at peace.
In his last annual message to Congress, On Dec. 4, 1860, Buchanan asserted that no state could secede from the Union. He professed that he knew of no legal authority to prevent it, but he said, "Secession is neither more nor less than revolution," and he supported the Union during the Civil War.

Bucharest (pop. 1,990,000), capital of Romania, on the Dîmbovita River. A medieval fortress, it became the residence of the princes of Walachia in 1459 and the capital when the new Romania was formed in 1861. It produces pharmaceutical and electrical goods, machinery, and automobiles. Bucharest was the site of violence

during the 1989 overthrow of the communist government of Nicolae Ceausescu.
See also: Romania.

Buchenwald, Nazi concentration camp set up near Weimar, Germany in 1937 to hold political and "non-Aryan" prisoners. More than 100,000 (mostly Jews) died there through starvation, extermination, and medical experimentation.
See also: Holocaust.

Buchman, Frank Nathan Daniel (1878-1961), evangelist and founder of the Moral Re-Armament movement (1938), commonly known as the MRA, an anticommunist grouping that grew rapidly and spread to over 50 countries.

Büchner, Georg (1813-37), German dramatist, forerunner of expressionism. His *Danton's Death* (1835) and *Woyzeck* (1837) use colloquial language and sometimes sordid settings to trace the powerlessness of isolated individuals against historical forces of society. Woyzeck, for example, is a soldier pressured into murdering his unfaithful mistress. *Lenz,* an unfinished work, is about a dramatist on the verge of madness.

Buchwald, Art (1925-), U.S. political columnist. Known primarily for his satires, Buchwald began his column with the *International Herald Tribune* in 1949. Later syndicated, it appeared in more than 500 newspapers. Buchwald won a Pulitzer Prize in 1982. He remains an active columnist.

Buck, Frank (1884-1950), U.S. wild-animal authority and collector. In childhood he collected and maintained small birds and other animals. In 1911 he sailed to South America, where he bought birds to sell at considerable profit. He traveled to Africa, South America, Asia, and Australia, acquiring a financial fortune and a wide reputation while capturing for zoos and circuses everything from tiny birds to elephants. Buck came to public attention in 1930 with publication of his first book, *Bring 'Em Back Alive,* which was subsequently made into a successful motion picture in which he starred. He had exhibits at the Century of Progress Exposition in Chicago in 1933 and the New York World's Fair in 1939 and was associated with the Ringling Brothers-Barnum and Bailey circus in 1937-38.

Buck, Pearl Sydenstricker (1892-1973), U.S. author. Most of her novels are set in China, where she lived until 1934. She won the Pulitzer Prize in 1932 for *The Good Earth* (1931), and the 1938 Nobel Prize in literature.

Buckeye *See:* Horse chestnut.

Buckingham Palace, London residence of the British royal family since 1837, built in 1703 and bought by George III from the Duke of Buckingham in 1761. Queen Victoria was the first monarch to use it as an official residence.
See also: London.

Buckingham, George Villiers, 1st Duke of (1592-1628), English nobleman whose influence over James I and Charles I inflamed antimonarchical feeling. He promoted costly and unsuccessful military ventures, notably the expedition to relieve the Huguenots of La Rochelle. Charles, however, shielded him from impeachment. He was eventually assassinated.

Buckley, William F(rank), Jr. (1925-), U.S. author, editor, and lecturer. He founded the weekly *National Review* (1955) to voice his often controversial conservative views. He ran unsuccessfully for mayor of New York City as a Conservative in 1965, and served as a UN delegate in 1973.

Buckner, Simon Bolivar (1823-1914), U.S. politician and Confederate general. Taken prisoner by General Grant, Buckner was released in a prisoner exchange and was commander of the District of Louisiana when the war ended. He then edited the *Louisville Courier* and served 1 term as governor of Kentucky (1887-91).
See also: Civil War, U.S.

Bucktails, political group active in New York (1816-30). They sought to keep New York City in control of state politics and opposed reforms desired by rural districts. Bucktails were so called because members wore hats with a buck's tail emblem.
See also: Tammany, Society of.

Buckthorn, common name for thorny shrub (*Rhamnus cathartica*) of the family Rhamnaceae. It has oval leaves and small, green flowers that grow in clusters. Its fruit resembles small black berries. Buckthorns are sometimes grown to form hedges and may reach a height of 12 ft (3.7 m). The bark is used to produce a yellow dye. Buckthorns are found in Europe and the United States.

Buckwheat, any of a genus (*Fagopyrum*) of common weeds, including dock and sorrel and a few tropical trees. The name applies particularly to species *F. esculentum* and *F. tartaricum,* cultivated for seeds used as cereal grain and cattle fodder.

Budapest (pop. 2,105,000), capital of Hungary, on the Danube River. Two settlements, Buda on the right bank and Pest on the left, date from Roman times but were destroyed by Mongol invaders in 1241. Buda became Hungary's capital in 1361. Both cities declined under the Turks but revived under the Hapsburgs and were united in 1873. Textiles are the main industry. The city was virtually destroyed in World War II. It was the center of the Hungarian uprising in 1956.
See also: Hungary.

Budd, Lanny *See:* Sinclair, Upton.

Buddha, Gautama (c.563-c.483 B.C.), founder of Buddhism. He was born Siddhartha Gautama, son of the raja of Kapilavastu, India, near Nepal. At the age of 29, confronting human misery for the first time, he set out to find the path to peace and serenity. For 6 years he studied under Brahman teachers, living as a hermit. Enlightenment came to him while seated under a *bodhi* or pipal tree. Thereafter he preached and gathered disciples as Buddha ("The Enlightened One").
See also: Buddhism.

Buddhism, religion and philosophy originating in India in the 6th century B.C., based on interpretations of the teaching of Siddhartha Gautama, called the Buddha, or "Enlightened One." His first disciples became the Sangha, or original Buddhist monastic order, men (and later women) who gave up home and family, shaved their heads, dressed only in rags, and devoted their lives to practicing and spreading his philosophy of Enlightenment.

In the 5th century B.C. a council in Rajagaha resulted in the Pali Canon, a body of scriptures from the oral tradition of the Buddha's teaching, together with his rules for monastic life, a collection of his sermons, and a metaphysical analysis of his concepts. From a second council, held in Vesali in the 4th century B.C., there emerged 2 separate schools of thought, the Hinayana ("Small Vehicle," surviving as Theravada, "Doctrine of the Elders"), which elected to adhere to strict monastic rules, and the Mahayana ("Large Vehicle"), which adopted a more flexible approach. As a result of a third council, in the 3rd century

One of the oldest and largest Buddha statues is in the Wat Trimitr temple in Bangkok, Thailand.

B.C., called by the Indian emperor Asoka, an ardent convert to Buddhism, missionaries were sent throughout India, as well as to Syria, North Africa, Greece, and Ceylon (now Sri Lanka). From Ceylon, in the 4th century A.D., Buddhism reached Burma, and in the 7th century it reached Tibet, where it combined with existing beliefs to become Lamaism. It made a deep mark on Chinese thought in the 4th and 5th centuries A.D. In 630 an Indian Buddhist living in China, Bodhidarma, introduced his method of meditation and direct or "spontaneous" enlightenment, which led to the dominant School of Ch'an (Zen, in Japanese). Buddhism spread to Korea in the 4th century A.D., and from there in the 6th century it entered Japan. Eventually Buddhism declined in China, but more from its ever-tolerant absorption of other philosophies, which often blurred its intrinsic character, than from the failure of its teaching. By the 7th century, Buddhism had begun to recede from India itself and, by the year 1000, except in Nepal, Buddhist sects had been almost entirely absorbed back into the Brahman religion.

Today the world of Buddhism has 2 main divisions, Theravada, the Southern School, covering Sri Lanka, Burma, Thailand, and Cambodia, and Mahayana, the Northern School, covering Nepal, Korea, China, and Japan. In the 2 schools can be counted 300-500 million followers, and there are many millions more who practice the teaching alone, for Buddhism has no service, ritual, or church in the Western sense. It is a lone process of self-awareness and self-development aimed at the ultimate enlightenment known as nirvana, a state beyond intellect, words, and form. This attainment, Buddhism holds, is the sole means by which one can be liberated from the "wheel of life," the continual cycle of birth, death, and suffering. Human beings are bound to this cycle by the cause-effect of karma, in which present circumstances and experience are the result of past thoughts and actions, and present thoughts and actions are creating those of the future. Through Buddhist teaching and the use of meditation, one can begin to purify one's thoughts and thus improve one's destiny. Buddhist teaching uses the Pali Canon as its scriptural authority, Buddha's Four Noble Truths as its main premise, and the Noble Eightfold Path as its manual.

The Four Noble Truths are (1) suffering is omnipresent; (2) its cause is wrongly directed desire; (3) remove the wrong desire and the cause for suffering is removed; (4) the Noble Eightfold Path leads to the end of suffering. The Noble Eightfold Path consists of (1) right understanding, (2) right thought, (3) right speech, (4) right action, (5) right means of livelihood, (6) right effort, (7) right concentration, (8) right meditation.

Budge, Donald (1915-), U.S. tennis player. His team won the Davis Cup in 1937, and in 1938 he was the first player to win 4 top world championships (U.S., British, Australian, and French), now referred to as the Grand Slam.

Budget, document designed to estimate income and expenditures over a certain period of time, usually 1 year. The most important budget in the United States is the federal budget, prepared annually by the executive branch of government, and transmitted to the Congress, usually in January. Most aspects of the budget must be approved by Congress.

Budgie *See:* Parakeet.

Buenos Aires (pop. 2,908,000), capital of Argentina. On the Rio de la Plata, it is a port for Argentine agricultural products, meat, hides, wool, and cereals. It has several universities and an opera house (Teatro Colón), and is the world's leading Spanish-language publishing center. Industries include food processing, textiles, automobiles, and chemical manufacturing. Founded in 1536, it became the capital of Rio de la Plata viceroyalty in 1776. An impressive economic growth after 1850 attracted many immigrants.
See also: Argentina.

This poster of Buffalo Bill compares him to Napoleon.

Buffalo, any of several humpbacked fishes (genus *Ictiobus*) of the sucker family. Related to the carp, buffalo are large freshwater fishes that inhabit the bottom of lakes and rivers and feed by sucking up tiny plant organisms. Some grow to 3 ft (91 cm) long and weigh 73 lbs (33 kg). Buffalo are fished for food.

Buffalo, any of several species of wild ox, members of the bovid family. The domesticated Indian water buffalo or carabao is used as a draft animal and for milk. It weighs about a ton, is 5 ft (1.5 m) high, and has large curved horns. Other types of Asiatic buffalo are the Philippine tamarau and the small anoa of Celebes. Cape buffaloes are dangerous big-game animals living in herds. The American bison is also incorrectly called a buffalo.

Buffalo (pop. 357,850), second largest city in the state of New York, situated at the eastern end of Lake Erie near Niagara Falls, in western New York. Buffalo was incorporated in 1832. Buffalo is at a natural junction point for lake, rail, and road transportation and is a hub of rail transport. The completion of the Erie Canal in 1825 was a turning point in the city's development. Buffalo is one of the United States' major centers of grain distribution and a leading flour-milling center and steel producer. Among the important institutions located in Buffalo are the Albright-Knox Gallery and one of the campuses of the State University of New York.
See also: New York.

Buffalo Bill (William Frederick Cody; 1846-1917), U.S. scout and showman. He claimed to have killed 4,280 buffalo to feed the builders of the Kansas Pacific Railway. He rode with the pony express in 1860, and during the Civil War was a scout in Tennessee and Missouri for the Union army. From 1872 he toured the United States and Europe with his Wild West Show.

Buffalo grass, low-growing grass (*Buchloë dactyloides*) that was once abundant on the central plains of North America and a main food of the bison and pronghorn.

Buffon, Georges Louis Leclerc, Comte de (1707-88), French naturalist who was the first modern taxonomist of the animal kingdom. He led the team that produced the 44-volume *Histoire Naturelle* (1749-1804).

Bug, name commonly given to all insects but properly applied to the order Hemiptera. These insects have pointed beaks with which they suck juice from plants or blood from animals, including humans.

Buganda *See:* Uganda.

Bugbane, any of several tall plants (genus *Cimicifuga*) of the buttercup family. They have broad leaves that divide into thin leaflets. Their small white flowers grow in branched clusters. Bugbanes are perennials that grow in mild climates. It was once thought that their unpleasant smell repelled bugs.

Bugging *See:* Wiretapping.

Bugle, wind instrument of the brass family, made of either copper or brass, with a conical bore and a cupshaped mouthpiece. The sound it produces is clear and penetrating. The bugle can produce only 7-8 different pitches; only 5 are needed in the military calls for which it is used. An instrument of great antiquity, it is mentioned in the Old Testament description of the siege of Jericho.

Buick, David Dunbar (1855-1929), Scottish-born U.S. plumber turned automobile maker. His Detroit manufacturing company produced the first Buick automobile in 1903. Money problems forced Buick to sell his interest in the company in 1906.

Building *See:* Architecture.

Bulb, short, underground storage stem composed of many fleshy scale leaves that are swollen with stored food and an outer layer of protective scale leaves. Bulbs are a means of overwintering; in the spring, flowers and foliage are rapidly produced when growing conditions are suitable. Examples of plants producing bulbs are the daffodil, tulip, snowdrop, and onion.

Bulbul, any of various species of tropical songbirds of the family Pycnonotidae, native to Africa and southern Asia. About 7 to 10 in (18 to 25 cm) long, bulbuls have plain, fluffy feathers and a slim, notched beak designed for eating fruits and insects. They tend to travel in noisy flocks and can cause damage to orchards and crops.

Bulfinch, Charles (1763-1844), U.S. architect. He designed the Massachusetts statehouse, Boston (1800); University Hall, Harvard University (1815); and the east portico of the Capitol, Washington, D.C. (1818). He emphasized the neoclassical style in U.S. civic architecture.

Bulganin, Nikolai Alexandrovich (1895-1975), Soviet leader. With the support of Nikita Khrushchev, he succeeded Georgy Malenkov as premier in 1955. He was expelled from the central committee when Khrushchev became premier in 1958.

Bulgaria, country in eastern Europe, in the Balkan mountains; bordered on the east by the Black Sea, on the west by Yugoslavia, on the south by Greece and Turkey, and on the north by Rumania, the Danube River forming the border.

Land and climate. The climate is continental in the north, with cold winters and hot summers, temperate continental in the center, and mediterranean south of the Rhodope Mountains and along the Black Sea coast. The country's capital is Sofia.

People. Nearly 90% of Bulgarians are descendants of the Bulgars, a migratory people of Mongol origin. About a tenth of the population is ethnically Turkish.

The monastery high on the slopes of the Rila Mountains is the most treasured monument of Bulgarian architecture and painting.

Bulgaria

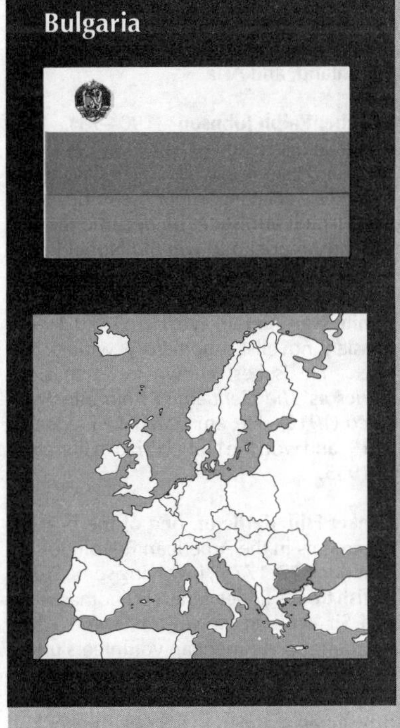

General information	
Capital:	Sofia
Area:	42,855 sq mi (110,994 sq km)
Population:	8,987,000
Official language:	Bulgarian
Monetary unit:	1 lev = 100 stotinki
Main cities:	Sofia, Plovdiv, Varna
Government	
Form:	socialist republic
Independent:	1908
Head of state:	President
Head of government:	Prime minister
Legislature:	one legislative house (National Assembly)
Executive:	President and Council of Ministers
Judiciary:	highest court is Supreme Court
Political division:	8 provinces, 1 city commune
National economy	
Gross national product:	U.S. $67,600,000,000
Per capita income:	U.S. $7,510
Agriculture:	wheat, corn, barley, grapes, sugar beets, tomatoes
Livestock:	poultry, sheep, pigs
Fisheries:	110,500 metric tons
Mining:	coal, iron ore, crude petroleum, lead, salt
Industries:	cement, crude steel, pig iron, nitrogenous and phosphate fertilizers, sulfuric acid
Main exports:	machinery and equipment, foodstuffs, beverages and tobacco products, fuels, mineral raw material and metals
Transportation:	2,672 mi (4,300 km) of railroads; 23,555 mi (37,908 km) of roads; 3 international airports
Trading partners:	USSR, Germany, Czechoslovakia, Libya, Poland
People	
Urban:	66.5%
Ethnic composition:	Bulgarian 85%, Turkish 8.5%, Gypsy 2.6%, Macedonian 2.5%
Birth rate:	13.0 per 1,000 population
Death rate:	12.0 per 1,000 population
Infant mortality rate:	14.7 per 1,000 live births
Life expectancy:	male 68 years, female 74.5 years

Bulgarian is a southern-Slavic language similar to Russian.
Economy. Though agriculture still employs the majority of the work force, it accounts for only 35% of the national income. Modern industries produce trucks, ships, transistors, chemicals, cement, porcelain, and glass. Lead, zinc, iron ore, copper, and manganese are mined. There are also deposits of oil and natural gas.
History. In the 17th century, the Eastern Bulgars conquered and merged with the Slavic population and adopted their language and customs. Between the 7th and 14th centuries, Bulgarian empires were major participants in Balkan political life, but in 1396 the country was occupied by the Ottoman Empire, which ruled Bulgaria for nearly 500 years. The Congress of Berlin (1878) restricted Turkish hegemony and in 1908 Bulgaria proclaimed its independence under Ferdinand I of Saxe-Coburg-Gotha. Bulgaria supported Germany in World War I and World War II. In 1944 the USSR occupied the country; in 1946 the monarchy was abolished and a republic proclaimed, under the control of the Communist party. In the upheavals of 1989, the Bulgarian Communist party changed its name to the Socialists and won control of the parliament in the first free elections.

Bulge, Battle of the, last major western counteroffensive by the Germans in World War II. They planned to capture Liège and Antwerp, thus dividing the Allied armies. The German assault in the Ardennes began on Dec. 16, 1944, and create a huge "bulge" in the Allied lines. Although suffering about 77,000 casualties, the Allies stopped the German advance by Jan. 16, 1945.
See also: World War II.

Bulimia, eating disorder characterized by insatiable appetite; eating binges are generally followed by self-induced vomiting. It is related to anorexia nervosa. Often observed in psychotics, it also commonly affects adolescent girls.
See also: Anorexia nervosa.

Bull, John *See:* John Bull.

Bulldog, medium-sized, low-slung dog originally bred in England for bullbaiting and related sports (outlawed in 1835). It has a massive head with an undershot jaw, broad shoulders, and strong legs. It weighs 40 to 50 lb (18 to 23 kg).

Bullfighting, Spanish national sport and spectacle, also popular in Latin America. Probably developed by the Moors, it was taken over by aristocratic professionals in the 18th century. The modern bullfight stresses the grace, skill, and daring of the *matador.* After a procession, the bull is released. Two mounted *picadors* jab the bull's neck with lances to lower its head for the matador's capework. Then three *banderilleros* thrust decorated wooden goads into the bull's back. The matador, after using his cape to make daring and graceful passes at the bull, kills it with a swordthrust between the shoulders. In Portugal, the matador is on horseback and does not kill the bull.

Bullfinch, any of several species of small songbirds native to Europe and Asia, named for their short, stout bill. The common bullfinch (*Pyrrhula pyrrhula*) is a popular cage bird that can be taught to sing tunes. The bullfinch's diet is mostly berries and seeds.

Bullfrog, large North American frog (*Rana catesbeiana*) named for its booming call, which is made by passing air up and down the windpipe, the swollen airsacs acting as resonators. Bullfrogs grow up to 8 in (20 cm) long and live near water, where they feed on many kinds of animals, including small snakes and alligators. They hibernate under logs or in holes, emerging in spring to lay up to 25,000 eggs.
See also: Frog.

Bullhead, North American freshwater catfish (genus *Ictalurus*) with broad head and tapering tail. Bullheads grow up to 1 ft (30 cm) long and weigh 2 lb (1 kg). Bullhead is also a name for a marine fish of the southern United States, and for the miller's thumb, a European freshwater fish.
See also: Catfish.

Bullmastiff, breed of dog obtained by crossing the bulldog and the mastiff. Standing about 24 to 27 in (61 to 69 cm) and weighing 100 to 130 lb (45 to 59 kg), this agile, powerful dog is used as a watchdog and bodyguard.

Bull Moose Party *See:* Progressive Party.

Bull Run, Battles of, 2 clashes in the American Civil War around Manassas Junction near Bull Run Creek, 25 mi (40 km) southwest of Washington, D.C. In the First Battle of Bull Run, July 1861, Union general Irvin McDowell was sent against Confederates led by P.G.T. Beauregard, but was repulsed by them. Gen. "Stonewall" Jackson was so nicknamed for his tenacity in this battle. In the Second Battle of Bull Run, Aug. 1862, Jackson attacked Union general John Pope and forced his retreat.
See also: Civil War, U.S.

Bull terrier, muscular dog that combines the strength of the bulldog and the speed and intelligence of the white English terrier, the 2 breeds from which it was first developed in 1835. The bull terrier has an oval head, pointed ears, a straight tail, a smooth white or brindled coat, and weighs 30-36 lb (13.5-16 kg).

Bulrush, any of a genus (*Scirpus*) of sedges growing in water or marshes, up to 6 ft (2 m) high, with narrow leaves and spiky flowers. Bulrushes grow from rhizomes, which help to anchor debris accumulating in the water, hastening the natural drying out of swamps. Bulrushes are used by Peruvian Indians to make boats.

Bulwer, Sir Henry *See:* Clayton-Bulwer Treaty.

Bulwer-Lytton, Edward George Earle Lytton, 1st Baron Lytton (1803-73), English author and politician. His best-known works include the historical novels *The Last Days of Pompeii* (1834) and *Rienzi* (1835), and the utopian *The Coming Race* (1871).

Bumblebee, insect belonging to the family Apidae, subfamily Bombinae, having a hairy coat, typically black with orange or yellow stripes, and a sting. Bumble bees range in length from 0.6 to 1 in (1.5 to 2.5 cm). They are social insects, living in colonies consisting of a queen, workers (females), and drones (males). In spring the queen comes out of hibernation and finds a nesting place. She begins laying eggs that develop into worker bees. All summer the workers gather pollen and care for the hive. At the end of summer unfertilized eggs, produced by either the queen or the workers, develop into drones; the colony also rears new queens. Once mature, these queens leave the nest, mate, and find a place to hibernate, while the old colony dies out.

Bunchberry, common name for a low-growing woody perennial (*Cornus canadensis*) related to dogwood. Its clusters of yellowish flowers, surrounded by white bracts, develop into red berries. Bunchberry is found in North America, Greenland, and Asia.

Bunche, Ralph Johnson (1904-71), U.S. diplomat. He entered the UN in 1946, and was undersecretary for political affairs 1958-71. Having supervised the 1959 Arab-Israeli armistice, he became the first African American to win the Nobel Peace Prize (1950).

Bunin, Ivan Alekseyevich (1870-1953), Russian novelist, short-story writer, and poet. He is best known for such short stories as *The Gentleman from San Francisco* (1916). He emigrated to France in 1919, and won the Nobel Prize in literature in 1933.

Bunker Hill, Battle of, one of the first engagements in the American Revolutionary War (June 17, 1775), involving some 2,300 British troops under generals Thomas Gage and Sir William Howe, and some 1,500 inexperienced American volunteers under Colonel William Prescott, Major-General Israel Putman, and General J. Warren. The British had planned to occupy Bunker Hill (near Charlestown, Mass.) as a good site for the defense of Boston. However, the rebels dug themselves into neighboring Breed's Hill under cover of night. Colonial troops opened fire on the arriving British troops, causing heavy casualties. Although the British eventually took Breed's Hill, the Americans, who had lost only about 450 men and proved their skills against seasoned troops, gained greatly in morale.
See also: Revolutionary War in America.

Bunsen, Robert Wilhelm Eberhard (1811-99), German chemist who conducted important work on organo-arsenic compounds and, with G.R. Kirchhoff, pioneered chemical spectroscopy, discovering the elements cesium (1860) and rubidium (1861). He also helped to popularize the gas burner known by his name.

Bunsen burner, gas burner consisting of a metal tube with a gas inlet and adjustable openings for air near the lower end. The air and the gas mix before ignition, producing an extremely hot and smokeless flame. Developed by the German chemist Robert Wilhelm Bunsen (1811-99), the Bunsen burner is used in scientific laboratories.
See also: Bunsen, Robert Wilhelm Eberhard.

Bunting, finchlike bird (especially, genus *Passerina*), with a conical seed-cracking bill. Buntings feed on seeds and live near the ground in woods or grasslands. They range from hot, humid forests of the tropics to polar regions. The snow bunting nests in northern Greenland, farther north than any other land bird.

Buñuel, Luis (1900-83), Spanish-Mexican director of films marked by fierce realism, social criticism, and wry humor. Surrealist fantasy is evident in his work ever since his first film, *Un Chien andalou* (made with Salvador Dali in 1929).

Bunyan, John (1628-88), English author. A tinker by trade, he became a Baptist preacher in 1657. While imprisoned for unlicensed preaching (1660-72; 1675) he wrote his most famous work, *The Pilgrim's Progress* (1678), an allegory in simple prose describing Christian's journey to the Celestial City.

Buonarroti, Michelangelo *See:* Michelangelo.

Burbank (pop. 93,643), city in southern California, 12 mi (19 km) north of Los Angeles in the San Fernando Valley. Incorporated as a town in 1911 and as a city in 1927, Burbank is famous today for its motion picture and television studios.
See also: California.

Burbank, Luther (1849-1926), U.S. horticulturalist who developed more than 800 varieties of plants, including the Burbank potato.
See also: Horticulture.

Burchfield, Charles Ephraim (1893-1967), U.S. watercolorist known for his midwestern landscapes and small-town scenes. A leader of the realistic movement in American painting, he often depicted architectural relics of the late 1800s and was sensitive to lighting and atmospheric effects.

Burdock, any of a genus (*Arctium*) of plants with hairy stems, heart-shaped leaves, and burrs. A North American biennial, also called beggar's-button, burr-bur, cockle button, and stickbutton, it grows to heights of 4 to 9 ft (1 to 3 m).

Burger, Warren Earl (1907-), chief justice of the United States Supreme Court 1969-86. Appointed by President Richard M. Nixon, Justice Burger moved the court in a conservative direction. Before his Supreme Court appointment, he served as judge on the United States Court of Appeals (1955-69) and as an Assistant United States Attorney General (1953-5). Throughout his career, he tended to limit the number of appeals and trials for each court case, to give state courts more authority, and to loosen rules of admission for introducing confessions of the defendants as evidence in trials.
See also: Supreme Court of the United States.

Burgess, Anthony (1917-), English writer, best known for *A Clockwork Orange* (1962), a bitter satire about a violent gang leader in a corrupt, violent society of the near future. His other works include *Inside Mr. Enderby* (1961), *Earthly Powers* (1980), *The Kingdom of the Wicked* (1985), and the critical study *Re Joyce* (1965).

Burghley, Lord (1520-98), English statesman. He was chief advisor to Queen Elizabeth I (1558-98) and her spokesman in Parliament. A supporter of the Anglican Church, he repressed Catholic revolts and advocated the execution of Elizabeth's Catholic sister, Mary Queen of Scots.

Burgoyne, John (1722-92), British general in the American Revolutionary War. He fought in the Seven Years War (1756-63), and became a playwright, socialite, and member of Parliament. Posted to America, he attempted to put into effect his plan to split off the New England colonies, but was forced to surrender by Gen. Horatio Gates at Saratoga (1777).
See also: Revolutionary War in America.

Burgundy (French: *Bourgogne*), historic region of eastern France, occupying what are now the departments of Côte-d'Or, Saône-et-Loire, Nièvre, and Yonne. It was named for the Burgundians, a Germanic tribe. A rich agricultural region, Burgundy is famous for its wines.
See also: France.

Burke, Edmund (1729-97), Irish-born British statesman, political philosopher, and orator. He entered parliament in 1765, and advocated more just policies toward the American colonies, opposing the Stamp Act and (in 1775) arguing for conciliation. Concerned for justice in India, he promoted the impeachment of Warren Hastings (1786-87). His famous *Reflections on the Revolution in France* (1790) presented his rational case against violent change.

Burke, Martha Jane *See:* Calamity Jane.

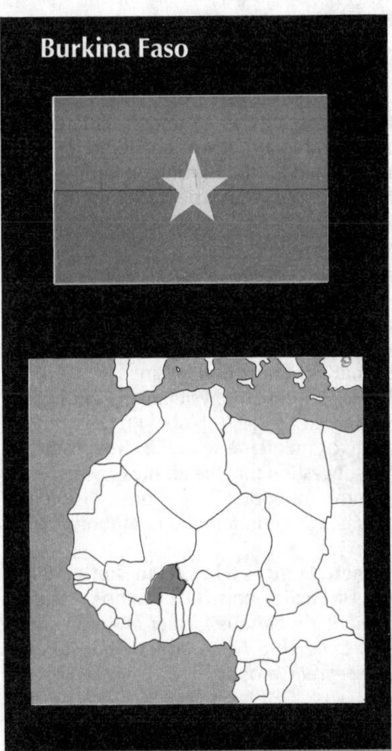

Capital:	Ouagadougou
Area:	105,869 sq mi (274,200 sq km)
Population:	8,714,000
Government:	military regime
Independent:	1960
GNP:	U.S.$1,960,000,000
Per capita:	U.S.$230

Burkina Faso, land-locked country in West Africa known as Upper Volta until 1984. It is bounded on the west and north by Mali, on the east by Niger and Benin, and on the south by Togo, Ghana, and the Ivory Coast. Burkina Faso is a broad expanse too dry to support much vegetation. Water is scarce. Temperatures range from 68°F to 95°F (20°C-35°C). The largest ethnic group in Burkina Faso is the Mossi tribe, but well over half a million nomadic Fulanis and others live in the north. Traditional African religions predominate, but there are also about a million Muslims and a quarter of a million Roman Catholics. The capital is Ouagadougou. French is the official language. Burkina Faso is one of the poorest countries of Africa, and the majority of its work force is engaged in subsistence farming. The country exports cotton, animals, meat, oil seeds, and karité nuts. There are deposits of manganese, limestone, and bauxite, but they have not been fully exploited.
What is now Burkina Faso was once the heart of the great Mossi kingdoms, which dated back to the 1100s and lasted some 500 years. The French made the area a protectorate in 1896 and a colony in 1919. Upper Volta became independent in 1960. The country had a series of civilian and military regimes. A new constitution was introduced in 1978, but the military continued to dominate the country's politics.

Burleigh, Lord *See:* Burghley, Lord.

Burlington (pop. 131,439), city in northwest Vermont; seat of Chittenden County. The largest city in Vermont, situated on Lake Champlain, it was chartered in 1773 and named for the Burlington family, who were pioneer landowners. A summer and winter resort, Burlington is also the state's manufacturing center.
See also: Vermont.

Burma *See:* Myanmar.

Burnet, Sir Frank Macfarlane (1899-1985), Australian physician and virologist. He shared the 1970 Nobel Prize in physiology or medicine with P.B. Medawar for the suggestion that the ability of organisms to form antibodies in response to foreign tissues was acquired and not inborn.

Burnett, Frances (Eliza) Hodgson (1849-1924), English-born U.S. author. She is particularly famous for her children's stories, *Little Lord Fauntleroy* (1885-86) and *The Secret Garden* (1910).

Burney, Fanny (Frances Burney; 1752-1840), English novelist and diarist. Her first novel, *Evelina* (1778), won her the respect of Samuel Johnson. She was a member of Queen Charlotte's household 1786-91. Her *Early Diary: 1768-78* and *Diary and Letters: 1778-1840* provide interesting background to the period.

Burnham, Daniel Hudson (1846-1912), U.S. architect, a pioneer of city planning. He built some of America's early skyscrapers, including the Masonic Temple Building, Chicago (1892), and the Flatiron Building, New York City (1902). He also designed the plan for the Columbian Exposition in Chicago (1893). Much of his improvement plan for Chicago (1907-9) was subsequently put into effect.

Burns, Arthur Frank (1904-87), Austrian-born U.S. economist. An expert on the business cycle, he served as presidential adviser on economics 1953-56 and on labor management 1961-66. Among his many books, the most influential was *Measuring Business Cycles* (1946), written with Wesley Clair Mitchell.

Robert Burns

Burns, Robert (1759-96), Scottish poet. The son of a poor farmer, he himself farmed for a living and later worked as a customs official. In 1786 he published *Poems, Chiefly in the Scottish Dialect* (enlarged 1787). His poetry, in Scots-English idiom, deals with rural life. He also wrote satirical poems such as "The Twa Dogs" and "The Jolly Beggars." Influenced by Scottish folk tradition, he was a master at writing songs to traditional airs ("Auld Lang Syne"). At first taken up by fashionable society, he died neglected and in debt. Other poems are "Tam O'Shanter," "To a Mouse," and "The Cotter's Saturday Night."

Burnside, Ambrose Everett (1824-81), Union general in the U.S. Civil War. Succeeding George McClellan as general of the Army of the Potomac, he resigned after the Union defeat at Fredericksburg in 1862. He was later governor of Rhode Island (1866-69) and U.S. senator (1875-81).
See also: Civil War.

Burr, Aaron (1756-1836), U.S. lawyer and politician, vice president under Thomas Jefferson 1801-5, also known for having killed Alexander Hamilton in a duel (1804). Burr was admitted to the New York bar in 1782 and was attorney general (1789-91) and U.S. senator (1781-97). After his term as vice president he was involved in efforts to expand settlements in the West. He was accused of treason for allegedly trying to establish a private empire. Though acquitted of the charge, in 1812, he retired from public life and returned to practice law in New York.

Burroughs, Edgar Rice (1875-1950), U.S. writer of adventure novels. He is most famous for *Tarzan of the Apes* (1914), whose characters have passed into comic strips, films, and television.

Burroughs, John (1837-1921), U.S. naturalist and author, known for his philosophical nature essays. His *Notes on Walt Whitman* (1867) was the first biographical study of the poet, who was his friend.

Burroughs, William (1855-98), U.S. inventor, best known for his practical and commercially successful adding machine (1898). His firm, the American Arithmometer Company (1886), was later renamed Burroughs Adding Machine Company.

Bursitis, inflammation of a bursa (fibrous sac containing synovial fluid that reduces friction where tendons move over bones), commonly caused by excessive wear and tear or by rheumatoid arthritis, gout, or bacteria. It causes pain and stiffness, and may require cortisone injections and, if infected, surgical drainage.

Burton, Sir Richard Francis (1821-90), English explorer, writer, and linguist. His interest in Muslim culture led him to secretly visit shrines in the holy city of Mecca (1853). In the 1880s, he translated the *Arabian Nights* into English. He was the first European to see Lake Tanganyika in central Africa (1858), and he also explored Santos, Brazil (1865). The motion picture *Mountains of the Moon* is based on his adventures.

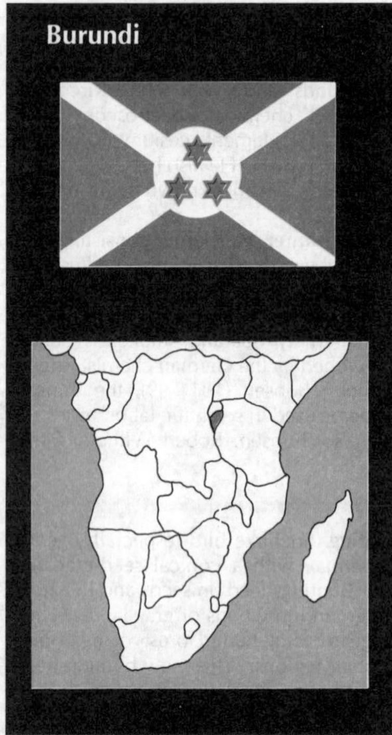

Capital:	Bujumbura
Area:	10,747 sq mi (27,834 sq km)
Population:	5,287,000
Government:	military regime
Independent:	1962
GNP:	U.S.$1,200,000,000
Per capita:	U.S.$230

Kwegura tea plantation in northwest Burundi

Burundi, one of Africa's smallest states, bordered on the east by Tanzania, on the west by Zaïre, on the north by Rwanda, and on the southwest by Lake Tanganyika. The capital, situated alongside the lake, is Bujumbura. The climate is tropical, with a rainy season from Oct. to April and a dry season in June, July, and Aug.
The Hutu and Tutsi are the country's main ethnic groups. There is a small minority of Twa, a pygmy people. The Tutsi dominate the government. The official language is French; the chief African language is Kurundi; Swahili is also widely spoken. About half the people adhere to traditional beliefs, the rest being Christian, principally Roman Catholic. The economy is mainly agricultural. Principal exports are arabica coffee and cotton.
The earliest inhabitants seem to have been the Twa, who were succeeded by the Hutu, who came from the Congo Basin. The Hutu were later subjugated by the Tutsi, who may have originated in northeast Africa. In 1899 Germany claimed Burundi as part of German East Africa. After World War I, Belgium was granted control of the area. In 1962, following a referendum, Burundi be-

monarchy was overthrown and replaced by a republic in 1966. Since independence Burundi has been the scene of recurrent fighting between the Tutsi minority (who dominated the government for a long time) and the Hutu majority (*e.g.* in 1972, 1987 and 1993).

Burying beetle, insect of the carrion beetle family (Silphidae). Averaging 1/2 in (12 mm) in length, the burying beetle digs around and beneath dead insects or animals, effectively burying them. Eggs are laid there, and the hatched larvae feed off the carrion until they reach maturity.

Bush, George Herbert Walker (1924-), 41st president of the United States. Bush's 2 terms as vice president to a popular president and his promise of "No new taxes" helped sweep him into the White House. Almost from the beginning of his time in office, Bush faced a series of crises both foreign and domestic, yet maintained a high level of popularity until well into his third year as president.

Early life. Bush was born in Milton, Mass., in 1924. Soon afterward, his family moved to Connecticut. Bush's father was a successful businessman and, later, a U.S. senator. Young Bush attended private schools, graduating from Phillips Academy in 1942. He then enlisted in the Navy. A fighter pilot, he flew hazardous missions in the Pacific during World War II, earning the Distinguished Flying Cross and three air medals. Returning home from the war in 1945, he entered Yale, from which he graduated in 1948.

Also in 1945, he married Barbara Pierce. The Bushes had 6 children, 1 of whom died of leukemia.

Entering politics. After college, Bush moved to Texas and entered the oil business, at which he was very successful. He became interested in politics and was active in the Republican Party. In 1964, he ran for a U.S. Senate seat in Texas, but lost. Two years later, he won election to the U.S. House of Representatives and was reelected in 1968. In 1970, he again ran for Senate and lost. He then served as U.S. ambassador to the United Nations (1971-73), U.S. envoy to China (1974-75), and director of the Central Intelligence Agency (1976-77).

In 1980, Bush ran for the Republicans' presidential nomination. Ronald Reagan, who won the nomination, chose Bush as his running mate. The Reagan-Bush team defeated the Democratic incumbents, President Jimmy Carter and Vice President Walter Mondale.

Vice presidency. Bush served two terms as vice president to Reagan, working closely with him. Bush filled in briefly for the president in 1981, when Reagan was wounded in an assassination attempt, and again in 1985, when Reagan had minor surgery. In 1988, Bush ran for the presidency, promising "no new taxes," a war on drugs, to protect the environment, and to be "the education president." He and his running mate, Dan Quayle, defeated Democrats Michael S. Dukakis and Lloyd Bentsen by a landslide.

Presidency. Bush faced serious problems: a huge and growing federal budget deficit, foreign-trade deficits, and a financial crisis in which hundreds of failing savings-and-loan institutions required federal aid. Cleanup after the environmentally disastrous wreck of an oil tanker off the Alaska coast also required federal aid.

Overseas, the loosening of communist control in the Soviet Union and Eastern Europe eased long-held tensions between East and West. In 1989, Bush presented an arms-control plan to reduce U.S. military presence in Europe. He sent U.S. troops to Panama in 1989 to arrest strongman Manuel Noriega on drug-trafficking charges.

In response to the Iraqi invasion of Kuwait in August of 1990, Bush initiated operation Desert Shield, which sent thousands of U.S. and allied troops to Saudi Arabia to deter further Iraqi aggression. After 6 months of economic sanctions and diplomacy failed to persuade Iraq to leave Kuwait, Bush and the allies initiated operation Desert Storm in January of 1991. After weeks of relentless air attacks and a ground assault, the Iraqis were forced out of Kuwait in March of 1991.

In the aftermath of the war, Bush has set out to bring peace to the Middle East and to create his "New World Order." On the home front, Bush had problems between the executive and legislative branches in reaching a federal budget that would reduce the deficit without compromising a campaign promise for no new taxes.

See also: Persian Gulf War.

George Herbert Walker Bush

41st U.S. President	
Born:	Milton, Mass.; June 12, 1924
Term:	Jan. 1989-Jan. 1993
Vice President:	Dan Quayle
Political Party:	Republican
Spouse:	Barbara Pierce Bush
Children:	6

Bush, Vannevar (1890-1974), U.S. electrical engineer, director of the Office of Scientific Research and Development in World War II. In the 1930s he developed the differential analyzer—in effect the first analog computer.

See also: Analog computer.

Bushmaster, large tropical American pit viper (*Lachesis muta*), which may grow up to 12 ft (4 m) long and feeds mainly on small mammals. It is light brown and has dark patterns on its back. Its long fangs and large venom glands make it dangerous to humans.

Business cycle, periodic fluctuation in the economy of an industrialized nation, between prosperity and recession or depression, with marked variations in growth rate and employment levels. Recession may be caused by overproduction, declining demand, changes in money supply, and general loss of confidence. Government interventions to moderate the cycle have become common in recent years.

See also: Economics.

Business law *See:* Law.

Bustard, any of Otididae family of large-bodied, strong-legged birds of the Old World and Australia, usually with drab

President Bush and family, 1989

plumage but sometimes with ornamental plumes on the head and neck. They feed on seeds, leaves, and small animals and prefer to run rather than fly. The great bustard is the size of a turkey. Bustards are scarce in many places, as they have been killed for food.

Butane and propane, odorless, colorless, flammable gases. These hydrocarbons (compounds of hydrogen and carbon) are found in natural gas and crude petroleum, and can be produced by cracking, a chemical process by which gasoline is derived from heavy oil. In their liquid form (referred to as LPG, or liquified petroleum gas), they are used as fuels for industry and for isolated homes.

Butler, Benjamin Franklin (1818-93), U.S. politician and Union general in the Civil War. His autocratic rule as military governor of New Orleans (1862) earned him the appellation "Beast," and he was recalled by President Abraham Lincoln. As U.S. representative (1867-75, 1877-79), he supported Reconstruction and voted for the impeachment of President Andrew Johnson. As Populist party candidate, he was elected governor of Massachusetts in 1882 and ran unsuccessfully for president in 1884.

Butler, Nicholas Murray (1862-1947), U.S. educator. President of Columbia College (1902-45), he expanded it into Columbia University. He was president of the Carnegie Endowment for International Peace (1925-45) and, in 1931, shared the Nobel Peace Prize with Jane Addams. He also served as president of the American Academy of Arts and Letters (1928-41).

Butler, Samuel (1835-1902), English novelist. He considered Darwinism too mechanistic and satirized it in *Erewhon* (1872), his version of utopia. His major work is *The Way of All Flesh* (1903), an autobiographical novel satirizing Victorian morality.

Butler, Samuel (1612-80), English poet, author of *Hudibras* (1663-78), a mock-heroic, anti-Puritan satire. He attacked the hypocrisy and pedantry of the Puritans of the Commonwealth.

Butte (pop. 33,336), city in southwestern Montana; seat of Silver Bow County, situated on Silver Bow Creek on a plateau in the Rocky Mountains. The fourth largest city in the state, Butte was founded in 1864. It was first a gold mining camp and then a silver center, and copper was discovered there in 1880. Butte is an important mining center for zinc, silver, gold, copper, arsenic, and lead.

Butter, dairy product made by churning milk or cream, containing fat, protein, and water. Made in some countries from the milk of goats, sheep, or yaks, it is most often made from cow's milk. Continuous mechanized production has been general since the 1940s. After skimming, the cream is ripened with a bacterial culture, pasteurized, cooled to 40°F (4°C), and then churned, causing the butterfat to separate from the liquid residue, buttermilk. The butter is then washed, worked, colored, and salted.

Buttercup, any of 300 species of flower (genus *Ranunculus*), native to temperate North America; especially the familiar gold flower of meadows and pastures. Buttercups have five-petaled flowers and deeply notched leaves that give them the alternative name of crow foot. The common buttercup has an acrid taste and can be poisonous to cattle.

Butterfish, any of several fish of the family Stromateidae. They have mucous-coated slippery skins and live in temperate seas around the world. The most common U.S. butterfish, found along the Atlantic Coast, is also known as the dollarfish (*Poronotus triacanthus*).

Butterfly, flying insect of the order Lepidoptera (which also includes moths), characterized by wide, brightly colored wings. The butterfly undergoes metamorphosis (change in form) several times during its life. The egg grows into a larva called a caterpillar, which feeds on vegetation. During the next stage, the pupa, it does not feed, but is protected by a shell or cocoon while develping into the adult butterfly. Most species of butterflies are members of one of the main family groups: (1) skippers, (2) blues, coppers, and hairstreaks, (3) brush-foots, (4) sulphurs and whites, (5) metalmarks, (6) satyrs and wood nymphs, (7) swallowtail, (8) milkweed butterflies, and (9) snout butterflies. Although butterflies are found worldwide in a variety of climates, the greatest number of species are native to the tropical rainforests. Migratory butterflies such as the monarch may travel thousands of miles to reach warm winter habitats.

Butternut, or white walnut, tree (*Juglans cinerea*) of the walnut family. This deciduous tree with pale gray bark and ridged leaves grows in the eastern and southern United States. Its light brown wood produces fine furniture.
See also: Walnut.

Butterwort, insect-eating plant (genus *Pinguicula*) that grows in damp places in Eurasia and the Americas. The yellow or violet flower grows on a 2 in (5 cm) stalk surrounded by a rosette of light green fleshy leaves that lie flat against the ground. At the slightest pressure, such as the weight of an insect, glands on the upper surfaces of the leaves secrete a sticky fluid and the insect becomes trapped. The fluid also contains a digestive juice that breaks down the insect's body and allows nitrogenous products to be absorbed.
See also: Carnivorous plant.

Buttress *See:* Architecture.

Buxtehude, Dietrich (1637? -1707), German composer and organist, possibly born in Denmark. His cantatas, organ toccatas, and chorale preludes influenced J.S. Bach.

Buzzard, any of a group of medium-sized hawks of the family Accipitridae, identifiable by their soaring flight, widespread wings, and broad tail. They prey on small mammals by swooping from the air or from a perch. In North America they are called hawks, "buzzard" being applied to vultures.

Capital:	Minsk
Area:	80,153 sq mi (207,600 sq km)
Population:	10,346,000
Government:	republic
Independent:	1991
GNP:	U.S. $30,127,000,000
Per capita:	U.S. $2,910

Byelorussia, or Belarus, republic, also known as White Russia. Independent country in eastern Europe, bordered by Russia, Ukraine, Poland, Latvia and Lithuania. Though mainly a plain, Byelorussia has hilly regions and extensive marshes, particularly in the southwest. The climate is mild. There are extensive waterways, in which the Dnieper, Pripet, Berezina, and Western Dvina rivers are linked by canals. About a quarter of the country is forestland. Natural resources include peat, rock salt, phosphorite, limestone, and iron ore. The people are dependent on both agriculture and industry. Products include agricultural machinery, trucks, timber, wood products, and textiles. Minsk, the capital, produces heavy vehicles and tractors. Other cities and industrial centers include Vitebsk, Gomel, and Mogilev. Byelorussia was originally inhabited by Slavic tribes, became

part of Lithuania in the 14th century, and was made part of Poland in the 16th century. When Poland was partitioned in the late 18th century, Byelorussia became part of the Russian Empire. By the Treaty of Riga in 1921, the western part of Byelorussia was ceded to Poland. When the USSR was formed in 1922, Byelorussia became one of the 4 original constituent republics. The region was the scene of bitter fighting during World War II. The collapse of communism in the USSR resulted in the republic's independence in 1991.
See also: Union of Soviet Socialist Republics.

Byrd, Richard Evelyn (1888-1957), U.S. aviator and pioneer of exploration and research in Antarctica. He led the air unit with D. B. MacMillan's 1925 Arctic expedition and, with Floyd Bennett, overflew the North Pole (1926). In 1929 he flew over the South Pole. Beginning as a Navy flier, he rose to the rank of Rear Admiral in 1930. He made 5 important expeditions to Antarctica (1928-1956), established the Antarctic base camp Little America, and spent the entire winter of 1933-34 alone at an advance camp. He was in charge of the U.S. Antarctic program from 1955.
See also: Antarctica.

Byrd, Robert Carlyle (1917-), U.S. legislator. He belonged to the Ku Klux Klan for a year and a half during the 1940s. He ran successfully for the West Virginiaa. State Senate in 1950. After service in the U.S. House of Representative (1953-59), he entered the Senate, 1959. He served as majority whip for the Democrats (1971-77) and then as majority leader (1977-80; 1987-88) and minority leader (1981- 87).

Byrd, William (1652-1704) and **William II** (1674-1744), colonial Virginian father and son. The father attained wealth and influence after developing farmlands at Westover, now Richmond, Virginia. The son, like his father, joined the House of Burgesses (1692) and became a member of the Council of State (1709). William II amassed an impressive library and produced diaries and journals that give a detailed picture of aristocratic life in colonial Virginia.

Byrd, William (1543-1623), English composer. His choral music includes the Great Service for the Anglican Church, Roman Catholic mass settings, and *Cantiones Sacrae* (1589; 1591). He also wrote keyboard music and madrigals. He was closely associated with Thomas Tallis, and in 1575 they were granted a joint monopoly for the printing and sale of music.

Byrne, Jane (1934-), U.S. politician, mayor of Chicago (1979-83). In her first bid for elected office she defeated the remnants of the Democratic machine of her former patron Mayor Richard Daley, becoming the first female mayor in Chicago's history.

Byrnes, James Francis (1879-1972), U.S. statesman. Democratic representative (1911-25) and senator (1931-41) from South Carolina, he served on the U.S. Supreme Court (1941-42), and was director of World War II mobilization (1943-45). As secretary of state (1945-47), he worked to lessen tensions with the USSR. As governor of South Carolina (1951-55), he opposed racial integration.

Byron, George Gordon Byron, 6th Baron (1788-1824), English poet, a leading figure of European Romanticism. Lameness and an unhappy childhood bred morbidity, a scorn for authority, and hatred for oppression. A disastrous marriage and the strictures of English society drove him into exile in Italy (1816). He later joined the Greek revolt against the Turks and died of fever at Missolonghi, Greece. *English Bards and Scotch Reviewers* (1809), a savage riposte to his critics, brought overnight fame, and the first two cantos of *Childe Harold's Pilgrimage* (1812) established his European reputation. The "Byronic" hero of the poetic drama, *Manfred* (1817) became a great Romantic theme. Major works include the incomplete satiric epic *Don Juan* (1819-24) and *The Vision of Judgement* (1812), satirizing the poet laureate Robert Southey and King George III.
See also: Romanticism.

Byssinosis *See:* Brown lung.

Byzantine art and architecture, aesthetic style that arose in the city of Byzantium (Constantinople) after it became the capital of the Roman Empire (330 A.D.), under Constantine the Great. The term also may be applied to art and architecture heavily influenced by Byzantine forms, which spread to Italy, Greece, Russia, and much of the Middle East. The greatest monument of the early phase is the cathedral of Hagia Sophia (Santa Sophia), built 532-537 in Constantinople. Mosaics, the principal form of decoration in Byzantine churches, were highly developed during this period. The minor arts, including ivory carving, silverwork, illuminated manuscripts, and textiles, became very sophisticated. Stylized naturalistic motifs and lavish decorative color were used.
The period after 1204 saw a second great flowering of Byzantine art, known as the Second Golden Age. In church building the favored type, initiated by Basil I, was a plan based on a circle inscribed in a square, a three-aisled plan with five domes, the largest one in the middle. The most famous example of this type is Saint Mark's Venice (11th-13th century). Manuscript illumination also flourished, the most famous example being the Paris Psalter.
Constantinople was sacked by the Crusaders in 1204, and during the next 2 centuries Byzantine art underwent profound changes. Fresco became the most important form of decoration; by the late 14th century mosaics had virtually disappeared. Work in the minor arts was generally of a lower quality. During this late period it was in the outlying areas of the former empire—Russia, Sicily, and the Balkans—that Byzantine art flourished. In 1453 Constantinople was conquered by the Turks, marking the end of the Byzantine state. The style of art and architecture, however, continued to flourish in Russia, Greece, and Bulgaria for several centuries.
See also: Byzantine Empire.

Byzantine Empire, historical term for the successor state to the Roman Empire in the East. Its capital was Constantinople (now Istanbul), founded by Constantine I in 330 at the site of the ancient Greek Byzantium. The heartlands of the empire were Asia Minor and the Balkans, but at its height it ruled southern Spain, Italy, Sicily, northern Africa, Egypt, Syria, Palestine, the Crimean coast, Cyprus, and the Aegean islands. Its religion was Eastern Orthodox Christianity.

Portions of a Byzantine mosaic in the church of S. Vitale in Ravenna, Italy (6th century)

Byzantine missionaries carried Christianity to Russia, and Byzantine theologians were among the chief Church Fathers.
The Roman Empire was divided after the death of Theodosius I in 395. By about 500 the Western Empire had fallen, Germanic invaders occupying Italy, Spain, and northern Africa. In the East, however, Roman institutions continued. However, after about 600, Roman institutions were replaced by typically Byzantine (Greek) ones. From the late seventh century onward, the Byzantine Empire was in frequent conflict both with the West and with the rising Muslim civilization in the East. Much of the empire's territory was lost, first to the Arabs, later to the Turks. The empire finally collapsed in 1453, when the Ottoman Turks captured Constantinople.

Byzantium *See:* Byzantine Empire; Istanbul.

George G. Byron

C

C, third letter of the alphabet, derived from the letter *gimel* of the ancient Semitic alphabet and a rounded form of the Greek *gamma.* The Romans used *C* as an abbreviation for *Gaius,* and *Cn* for *Gnaeus* but also gave the letter a *k*-sound, which survives in modern English (*case, concrete,* etc.) *C* also has the "soft" sound of *s,* as in *face* and *city.* When *C* is combined with the letter *H,* 2 further sounds may be represented (*church, loch*); the combination can also have the *K* sound (*ache, anchor, chronicle*). *C* can also be a superfluous letter, as in *thick.* In musical notation, *C* is a note of the scale. In chemistry, it is the symbol of the element *carbon,* in roman numbers, *C* = 100.

Cabal, secret group or organization engaged in intrigues; also applied to the intrigues themselves. The term was already used in the 17th century for a secret council of the king. The conduct of English king Charles II's ministers Clifford, Arlington, Buckingham, Ashley, and Lauderdale (whose initials spelled "cabal") gave the word a sinister sense.

Cabala, or Kabbalah (Hebrew, "tradition"), body of esoteric Jewish mystical doctrines dealing with the manifestations of and revelation of God. The Cabala attaches mystical significance to every detail in the Torah, the first 5 books of the Bible. Its chief books are the *Sefer Yezirah* (Book of Creation; 3rd-6th centuries) and the *Sefer HaZohar* (Book of Splendor; 13th century). The Cabala arose in France and Spain in the Middle Ages and was later a major influence on Hasidism.
See also: Hasidism.

Cabbage (*Brassica olearacea*), biennial vegetable from which other brassicas, such as kale, cauliflower, and broccoli, have been developed. The cabbage originated many centuries ago from the European wild cabbage. It has a characteristic tight "head" of leaves. Cabbages can be boiled or pickled, or fermented in salt to give sauerkraut; also used as animal feed.

Cabbage palm, name used for various palm trees with edible leaf buds, especially, the palmetto (*Sabal palmetto*), a common fan palm ranging from North Carolina through Central America. It can grow up to 80 ft (24 m) and thrives in swampy country such as Florida everglades. The terminal buds and fruit are edible, the trunks can be used for fences and posts.
See also: Palm; Palmetto.

Cabell, (James) Branch (1879-1958), U.S. novelist, who combined an ironic, often antiromantic style with a strong element of fantasy in plots and settings. His best-known novel is *Jurgen* (1919).

Caber, trunk of a young tree, tossed in the Scottish sport of tossing the caber.

Cabeza de Vaca, Alvar Núñez (1490?-1557?), Spanish explorer. Shipwrecked off the coast of Texas and imprisoned by the Native Americans in 1528, he escaped and made his way to Mexico City (1530-36). His account of southwestern United States, including descriptions of "Seven Cities of Cíbola," supposedly laden with riches, stirred Spanish interest in the area. He was made governor of Paraguay (1542-44), but after a rebellion against him, he was recalled to Spain.

Cabinda (pop. 110,000), city and district in Angola. This coastal district, separated from the rest of Angola by the Congo River and Zaire, produces large quantities of oil. The city is an important seaport. When Angola fought for independence from Portugal (1961-75), Cabinda fought unsuccessfully for its independence from Angola.
See also: Angola.

Cabinet, top-level advisory council to the head of state, usually composed of the heads of the major executive departments. Though not mentioned in the Constitution, the U.S. cabinet has been a consultative body to the executive since George Washington. Normally the cabinet meets weekly with the president, though procedure varies. Members of the cabinet are individually appointed by and responsible to the president. They are not members of either house of Congress and may not address them, though they are often called to testify before committees.

Cable, electric, insulated conductor used to carry electric power or electric signals. A cable consists of a core conducting metal, usually of several wires twisted or stranded together, surrounded by insulating material. The conducting metal is usually copper, aluminum, or steel. The insulation is most often made of plastic or rubber. Multicore cables contain many cores, each insulated from the others, all contained inside a tube of plastic, rubber, copper, aluminum, or lead, which also serve to keep out moisture and heat. Telephone cables contain several thousand cores. Such cables run along the sea bed between the continents; however, satellite communications are replacing such long cables.
Electric power is distributed by power cables. Inside the home they carry electricity at low power (usually 110 volts). Electricity at high power is carried between cities by overhead cables slung from pylons. The cables do not need insulation around the cores as they are kept far enough apart for the air to act as an insulator and prevent sparking between them, but special glass or ceramic insulators are used to attach them to the pylons. Super-voltage power cables carrying currents at up to about 500,000 volts are usually buried underground and filled with oil or gas, such as nitrogen, to remove heat and increase insulation.
Radio, television, telephone, and other electronic equipment uses low-power signals with high frequencies, requiring a coaxial cable, which has a central core of wire surrounded by insulation, then a sheath of wire braid, and finally an insulating outer covering.

Cable, George Washington (1844-1925), U.S. author noted for his depiction of New Orleans and Creole life in works like *Old Creole Days* (1879) and *The Grandissimes* (1880).

Cable car, vehicle to carry passengers up steep gradients. The cable cars in San Francisco travel on rails like street cars, but they are pulled along by means of a continuous underground cable, to which the engineer can hook the car by pulling on a lever. Alpine cable cars are suspended from cables and usually operate on a funicular system, in which one car goes up a slope while another goes down, balancing each other, which demands much less power to operate.

Cable car

Cable television, or CATV (community antenna television), broadcasting by means of coaxial cables rather than airwaves, used originally in areas where mountains or tall buildings made television reception poor or impossible, but now expanding throughout the United States because of the multiplicity of channels and programs it makes available.
See also: Television.

Cabot, John (Giovanni Caboto; c.1450-c.1499), Italian navigator and explorer, probably the first European to reach the North American mainland. In 1497, after receiving permission from Henry VII to sail for England, Cabot sailed in search of a western route to Asia and reached the coasts of Nova Scotia and Newfoundland, where he planted the English and Venetian flags. On a second voyage (1498) Cabot may have reached America again, or may have been lost at sea.

Cabot, Sebastian (1476-1557), explorer and navigator, son of John Cabot. Appointed pilot-major of Spain in 1518, he led an expedition to the Rio de la Plata region of South America in 1526. Its failure led to his banishment from Spain. Though eventually reinstated, he went to England in 1548, and later became governor of the Merchant Adventurers Company.

Cabral, Pedro Alvares (1467-1520), Portuguese navigator. Commanding a fleet that was meant to sail from Lisbon to India, in 1500, Cabral went too far southwest and sighted Monte Pascoal on the east coast of Brazil. After exploring the coast and claiming Brazil for Portugal, Cabral sailed on to India, where he founded a small factory at the port of Calicut. Very little is known of his life after his return to Portugal in 1501.

Cabrillo, Juan Rodríguez (João Rodrigues Cabrilho; d. c.1543), Portuguese explorer in the service of Spain, best known for his discovery of California. In 1542 he explored the coastline from lower California northwards to San Diego Bay.

Cabrini, Saint Frances Xavier (1850-1917), Italian-American nun, first U.S. citizen to be canonized (1946). She founded the Missionary Sisters of the Sacred Heart in 1880, and established 67 houses of the order throughout the world. In 1889 she immigrated to New York from Italy. Her feast day is Dec. 22.

Cacao (*Theobroma cacao*), tropical tree that produces cacao or cocoa beans. The raw material for chocolate is prepared by roasting, grinding, and pressing the dried seeds (or beans) from the woody cacao fruits. Pressing squeezes out cocoa butter and leaves a solid mass that is reground to make cocoa powder. The cacao tree has been cultivated since the time of the Aztecs, who used it for beverages and currency. Christopher Columbus introduced cocoa beans into Europe in 1502.
See also: Chocolate.

Cactus, name for over 1,500 kinds of succulent prickly plant of the Cactaceae family nearly all native to America. Cacti are well adapted for desert life. They have no leaves, allowing them to conserve water. Photosynthesis takes place in the swollen stem, which may be 98% water and can swell to store the water collected by the long roots during rare desert showers. The spines that cover the stem may have 2 functions, protecting the cacti from being eaten and, where the spines form a dense mat, helping to retain moisture. The cacti produce flowers that may last for only a few hours, in some cases opening only at night. The flowers are pollinated by bees, moths, hummingbirds, and bats. Some cacti are edible. Cacti are grown for ornamental purposes and to form hedges. The peyote cactus is the natural source of the hallucinogenic drug mescaline.

Cadence, in musical harmony, successive chores that usually bring a passage of music to a close. One of the most common cadences consists of the chords traditionally sung to the word "Amen" at the end of a hymn or psalm.

Cadillac, Antoine de la Mothe (1658-1730), French colonial governor and founder of Detroit (1701). Governor of Mackinac in 1694, he felt the site of Detroit would be a better strategic position. He was appointed governor of Louisiana (1713) but recalled in 1716.
See also: Detroit.

Cádiz (pop. 154,100), ancient city and port in southwest Spain, on the Atlantic coast northwest of Gibraltar. Founded by the Phoenicians in 1130 B.C. as Gadir, the city came under the rule of Carthage c.550 B.C. and became prosperous under Roman rule after 205 B.C. After the discovery of America it became important as the headquarters of the Spanish fleets. It is now a commercial port noted for sherry exports.
See also: Spain.

Cadmium, chemical element, symbol Cd; for physical constants see Periodic Table. Cadmium was discovered by Friedrich Stromeyer in 1817. It is a soft, bluish-white metal, used in low melting alloys and solders. Compounds of cadmium are used in television tubes. Cadmium sulfide is used as a yellow pigment. Cadmium and its compounds are toxic and should be handled with care.

Cadmus, in Greek mythology, son of Agenor and founder of Thebes. With the help of the goddess Athena, he killed a dragon and sowed its teeth. Where the teeth were sown, soldiers sprang up and helped Cadmus build the city of Thebes.
See also: Mythology; Thebes.

Caecilian, wormlike amphibian that lives in underground burrows. Caecilians are found in America, from Mexico southward, as well as Africa and Asia. The largest species grows to 4 ft (1.4 m).

Caedmon (7th century), illiterate herdsman, English poet who reputedly became a poet overnight after a stranger commanded him in a dream to "sing of the beginning of created things." Author of the Caedmon Hymn, he spent the rest of his life rendering Bible history into verse.

Caesar, (Gaius) Julius (c.100-44 B.C.), Roman general, politician, and writer. Although a member of the ancient patrician Julian clan, he supported the antisenatorial party. His early career through various public offices won him popularity, and in 60 B.C. he formed the First Triumvirate with Pompey, who supplied the army, and Marcus Licinius Crassus, who provided the money. With Caesar as consul they succeeded in controlling Roman politics. Caesar's successful Gallic Wars (58-51 B.C.) gained him great esteem and a loyal and well- trained army. After the death of Crassus, Pompey tried to force Caesar to lay down his command, but in 49 B.C. Caesar crossed the Rubicon River (the boundary between Caesar's Gaúl and Rome), and civil war began. Pompey was finally defeated at Pharsalus in 48 B.C., and by 45 B.C. Caesar had secured the defeat of all the Pompeian forces. In 44 B.C. he was made dictator for life, but on the Ides of March (March 15) he was murdered.
See also: Rome, Ancient.

Cactus plants are found mostly in desert regions but can grow elsewhere. They bear fruit in the form of berries, some of which are edible.

Caffeine, slightly bitter alkaloid used as a stimulant and diuretic and found in coffee, tea, cocoa, and other plants; poisonous when taken in large doses.

Cage, John (1912-), U.S. experimental composer and musical theoretician. He composed for "prepared piano," attaching objects to strings to alter tone and pitch and get percussive effects. Later work included prolonged silences, improvisation, aleatoric (chance) music, and electronic music.
See also: Aleatory music.

Bust of Julius Caesar

Cagney, James (1904-86), U.S. film actor who played cocky, aggressive tough guys in such classic gangster movies as *The Public Enemy* (1931) and *The Roaring Twenties* (1939). He won an Academy Award for his portrayal of George M. Cohan in *Yankee Doodle Dandy* (1942).

Cahokia Mounds, group of prehistoric mounds, mostly in the form of truncated pyramids, near East St. Louis, Ill. The largest of these, Monks Mound, is about 1,200 ft (360 m) by 650 ft (200 m) at base and 100 ft (30 m) high, and is the largest mound in the United States. More than 300 of the mounds have in recent years been bulldozed to make way for agricultural and municipal expansion, but the 18 largest remain.

John Cage

Cahow (*Pterodroma cahow*), bird in the petrel family (Procellariidae). This seabird, often referred to as the Bermuda petrel, was believed extinct for hundreds of years until its rediscovery in 1906. Cahows, of which there are only 100 or so alive today, are approximately 15 in (38 cm) long with dark tops and white undersides. They nest only in the Bermuda Islands.

Cain, in the Old Testament, eldest son of Adam and Eve (Gen. 4:1), a tiller of the ground. Because the offering of his brother Abel was accepted by God, and his own rejected, he murdered Abel, and was doomed to be a wandering fugitive. But God gave him a protective sign and promised sevenfold vengeance if he were slain. He built a city and named it Enoch for his son (Gen. 4:17).
See also: Old Testament.

Cain, James Mallahan (1892-1977), U.S. writer of crime novels admired for their accuracy of dialogue and characterization. His best-known works are *The Postman Always Rings Twice* (1934), *Serenade* (1937), *Mildred Pierce* (1941), and *Double Indemnity* (1943), which have been made into films.

Cairn terrier, breed of dog that originated in Scotland. Its name comes from its ability to dig under cairns (piles of stone) in order to hunt animals. It weighs 13-14 lb (5.9-6.4 kg). Its wiry topcoat is of various colors, but never white.

Cairo, or Al-Qhirah (pop. 6,205,000), capital of Egypt. It lies at the head of the Nile delta and is the largest African city. It was founded in A.D. 969 by the Fatimid dynasty. The founding of al-Azhar University (970-78) made it the intellectual center of the Islamic world. An allied base during World War II and site of the Cairo Conference, it became capital of Egypt (1952), and remains a major Arab political, economic, and nationalist center. The 1977 Egyptian-Israeli talks were held in Cairo. The nearby pyramids, sphinx, and Memphis ruins make it a tourist center.
See also: Egypt.

Cairo's public transportation system consists of buses, trains, and thousands of taxis. For Nile crossings there is a fleet of water-taxis.

Caisson, concrete or steel box, open at both ends, used in civil engineering when excavation or construction must be carried out underwater, particularly in sinking foundations for bridges. Caissons are sunk in the required position and built up to keep the top above water. As the soil is dredged from the bottom, the caisson sinks. It is eventually filled with concrete and acts as part of the foundation of the bridge. Sometimes a pressurized, watertight chamber is built at the bottom of the caisson for workers.

Caisson disease *See:* Bends.

Cajuns (from "Acadian"), descendants of expatriate French-Canadians, living in Louisiana. Cajuns were deported from Acadia (Nova Scotia) by the British in 1755. They have a distinctive patois: a combination of archaic French forms with English, Spanish, German, Native American, and African American idioms.
See also: Acadia.

Calabash (*Crescentia cujete*), tree of tropical America, the woody shell of whose gourdlike fruit is used as a waterproof container. The flowers of calabash trees grow close to the trunk and main limbs, not on the tips of the branches among the leaves. They are pollinated by nectar-drinking bats and develop into 12 in (30 cm) pulpy fruit.

Caladium, genus of tropical American plant in the Arum family (*Aracaea*). Its large, arrow-shaped leaves have vividly colored markings. Caladiums are grown commercially as houseplants.

Calais (pop. 76,500), French seaport on the Pas de Calais (Strait of Dover), 170 mi (274 km) from Paris and 21 mi (34 km) from Dover. Calais is an important port, and the center of heavy passenger traffic between England and continental Europe. The city has fishing industries and textile and paper manufacturing.
See also: France.

Calamity Jane (Martha Jane Canary Burk; 1852-1903), frontier-town prostitute and campfollower who roamed the West in male garb. Famous in Deadwood, S.D., during the 1870s gold boom, she claimed she had been an army scout, a pony express rider, Custer's aide, and Wild Bill Hickok's mistress.

Calcination, process of heating used in chemistry and industry to convert salts containing oxides and to remove volatile constituents from substances. In making quicklime, for example, calcium carbonate is changed into calcium oxide by calcination. Calcination is also used to covert bones into phosphates for use in fertilizer.
See also: Chemistry.

Calcite, soft mineral, consisting of calcium carbonate ($CaCO_3$), found mainly in limestone. Most stalagmites and stalactites are made of calcite. Calcite is usually white, but impurities may give it other colors. Very pure calcite, such as Iceland spar, is often transparent and causes double refraction, so that objects seen through it appear double, making it useful in some optical instruments. Other forms of calcite include marble and Oriental alabaster. Calcite is used to make lime, cement, and fertilizers.
See also: Calcium carbonate; Lime.

Calcium, chemical element, symbol Ca; for physical constants see Periodic Table. It was first isolated in 1808 by Sir Humphry Davy. A member of the alkaline earth group, calcium is the fifth most abundant element in the earth's crust, occurring in numerous compounds. It is an essential constituent of plants and animals, neccessary for building bones and teeth.

Calcium carbide, crystalline compound (CaC_2) made from calcium and carbon. Produced by heating lime and coke, it is used in the manufacture of fertilizers and acetylene, a gas used to cut or weld metals.
See also: Acetylene.

Calcium carbonate, mineral ($CaCO_3$) abundant in nature. Limestone, marble, coral, calcite, and chalk have calcium carbonate as a main ingredient. Calcium carbonate is used in toothpaste, tooth powder, and stomach medicine. Stalactites and stalagmites that form in caves are made from water that deposited this white, crystalline mineral.
See also: Calcite; Chalk.

Calculator, mechanical or electronic machine for performing numerical calculations. Calculators have number keys (0 through 9) and additional keys for computing mathematical equations or functions, which are then displayed on a small screen. Calculators, first made available in the early 1960s, were miniaturized and marketed for consumers during the 1970s.

Calculus, branch of mathematics dealing with calculating rates of change (differential calculus) and determining functions from information about their rate of change (integral calculus).
Differential calculus is used to calculate accelerations, velocities, slopes of curves, and maximum and minimum values, based on experimental or theoretical relationships expressed as continuous equations. If a relationship can be expressed as $y = f(x)$, where the response y is a continuous function of x, then the average rate of change can be found by determining the change in $y (\Delta y = y_2 - y_1 = f(x_2) - f(x_1))$ and dividing it by the change in x ($\Delta x = x_2 - x_1$). The average speed traveling in a car, 55 mph (88.5 kmph), or the average fuel efficiency during a trip, 30 mi/gal (12.8 km/l), are examples. If we take the limit of the expression $\Delta y / \Delta x$ as $\Delta x = x_2 - x_1$ gets smaller and smaller, we arrive at the instantaneous rate of change, which is the derivative of the function $y = f(x)$ expressed as $f'(x) = dy/dx$:

$$f'(x) = \frac{dy}{dx} = \lim_{x_1 \to x_2} \frac{y_2 - y_1}{x_2 - x_1} = \lim_{\Delta x \to 0} \frac{\Delta y}{\Delta x}$$

"the derivative of the function $y = f(x)$ with respect to x." The symbol dy and dx are referred to as the differential of y and the differential of x respectively. In the automobile example above, although the average speed was 55 mph (88.5 kmph) over the length of a trip, each moment the traveler glanced at the speedometer different instantaneous speeds (rates) were observed.
When the derivative of a function $f'(x)$ is known, the function itself can be determined. This process of finding the *antiderivative* is done with integral calculus. Just as differential calculus is concerned with changes and differences, integral calculus is concerned with summations.
Rearranging the expression above, $dy = f'(x)dx$. Summing each side of this equation over a range gives the expression:

$$y = \int_a^b f'(x)\, dx$$

read "y is the integral of f prime of x with respect to x." The elongated s stands for "sum" and is the symbol for integration. The range of summation indicated is from $x = a$ to $x = b$ and takes place over tiny intervals of x, dx. Integration is used to find lengths of curves, areas bounded by curves, volumes enclosed by surfaces, and centers of gravity of attracting bodies.
Many 17th-century mathematicians, astronomers, and physicists contributed to the development of calculus, predominant developers were Isaac Newton and Gottfried Wilhelm Leibniz .
See also: Leibniz, Gottfried Wilhelm; Newton, Sir Isaac.

Calcutta (pop. 3,305,000), capital of West Bengal state, the leading transportation, industrial, financial, and commercial center of eastern India, and the largest city in India, situated on the Houghly River, in the Ganges delta, 80 mi (130 km) north of the Bay of Bengal. Calcutta is accessible to oceangoing vessels and has road and rail links with the whole of northern India, and an international airport.
Calcutta was founded as a permanent settlement by the British East India Company in 1690. In 1756 the British were driven out by the nawab of Bengal, at the time of the infamous Black Hole of Calcutta incident. Robert Clive recaptured the town in 1757, and the British became virtual rulers of Bengal. In 1834 Calcutta became the capital of the British India empire. By 1900 it was the center of a strong nationalist movement, and the developing unrest continued. The capital of India was transferred to Delhi in 1912, but Calcutta's commercial importance continued to grow.
With the partition of India in 1947, Calcutta lost most of its jute-producing hinterland to Pakistan, and was faced with an influx of thousands of Hindu refugees. The city has often been the scene of religious and political strife. In spite of the overcrowding and poverty, Calcutta has continued its development as a commercial city and a vitally important port. Among the principal exports are tea, jute, iron, manganese, and mica. Calcutta's factories produce iron and steel, textiles, shoes, rubber, leather, glass, and cement.
See also: India.

Caldecott, Randolph (1846-86), British painter and illustrator, particularly of children's books. Among his best-known illustrations are those for Washington Irving's *Old Christmas* (1876) and William Cowper's *The Diverting History of John Gilpin* (1878). In 1938 the Caldecott Medal was established as an annual award for the best U.S. children's picture book.

Calder, Alexander (1898-1976), U.S. abstract sculptor and creator of the mobile. His mobiles consist of flat metal shapes connected by rods, wire, or string, which are hung or balanced and moved by motors or by air currents.

Calderón de la Barca, Pedro (1600-81), Spanish playwright and poet. He and Lope de Vega were the leading dramatists of Spain's Golden Age. He wrote over 200 plays, distinguished by their heightened style and poetic symbolism, many on religious themes. Among his most famous works are *The Constant Prince* (1629), *Life Is a Dream* (1635), and *The Surgeon of His Honor* (1635).

Calderone, Mary Steichen (1904-) U.S. physician, health official, and leader in sex education. As a founder (1964) and executive director of Sex Information and Education Council of the United States and earlier as director of Planned Parenthood and a physician in a New York public school system, her aim was to encourage sex education and health counseling.
See also: Sex education.

Sculpture by Alexander Calder

Caldwell, Erskine Preston (1903-87), U.S. author noted for his portrayal of poor Southern whites in short stories and novels such as *Tobacco Road* (1932), *God's Little Acre* (1933), and *Trouble in July* (1940).

Caldwell, Sarah (1924-), U.S. conductor and opera producer. She was director of the Boston University Opera Workshop (1953-57) and founded the Opera Company in Boston (1957). As its artistic director she staged more than 50 productions noted for their originality. She was the first woman to conduct at the N.Y. Metropolitan Opera, 1976.
See also: Opera.

Caledonia, ancient Roman name for what is now Scotland. The area was invaded by Agricola, a Roman general, in A.D. 83. Roman artifacts have been found in present-day Scotland. Caledonia is still used as a poetic name for Scotland.
See also: Scotland.

Pedro Calderón de la Barca

Calendar, method of reckoning days and months of the year. The earliest calendars were based upon the phases of the moon. The first day of each month was the day of the new moon. When the moon had gone through its cycle of phases 12 times, a year was said to have passed. Unfortunately, the moon takes about 29 days to go through its phases, and consequently 12 lunar months (354 days, 8 hrs, 48 min) are 11 days short of a full year. Only by adding an extra month every 3 years or so could the calendar be kept roughly in line with the seasons. The Jewish and Muslim calendars are lunar calendars. The ancient Egyptians used a solar calendar with 12 months of 30 days each and added 5 feast days at the end of the year, making it one of the most accurate early calendars. But the length of the solar year is about 365 days, so that the

A 15th-century saints calendar. The calendar shows half of the month of August. The Roman numerals at left refer to the calculation of the phases of the moon. The ciphers in the next column refer to the Sundays of that year. The third column refers to the Roman calendar.

Egyptian calendar got 1 day out of step with the seasons every 4 years. The Roman calendar, originally contained only 10 months and began with March. Later January and February were added to the end of the year, and the months received their odd numbers of days in an attempt to fit every day of the year into months of roughly equal length. In 46 B.C. Julius Caesar reformed the calendar, making January the first month and adding a leap year day to February in every fourth year to prevent the calendar from getting out of step. This system, the Julian calendar, continued to be used in Europe for over 1,500 years. Because a year is not exactly 365 days long, but slightly shorter (365 days, 5 hrs, 48 min, 46 sec), adding an extra day every 4 years proved too much. By the 16th century the calendar was 10 days out of step with the seasons. Pope Gregory VIII decided that Thursday, Oct. 4, 1582, would be followed by Friday, Oct. 15, thus wiping out the error. To prevent a recurrence, he ruled that a century year could be a leap year only if divisible by 400. The Gregorian, or New Style, calendar, though not perfect, is adequate for most practical purposes and is the calendar in widest use today.

Calendula, or pot marigold (*Calendula officinalis*), annual plant. Infusions of the leaves and yellow flowers are used medicinally for gastrointestinal problems, fever, abscesses, and vomiting.

Calgary (pop. 636,100), city in southern Alberta, Canada, at the junction of the Bow and Elbow rivers, at a height of 3,438 ft (1,048 m). Its name is Gaelic for "clear running water." Founded as a Northwest Mounted Police fort in 1875, it is a center of grain and livestock marketing, located in a good farming and ranch region. Related industries are milling and meatpacking. Nearby coal, oil, and gas have resulted in a rapid expansion of the city. The city is famous for the annual Calgary Stampede, a 10-day rodeo that attracts cowboys from all over North America.
See also: Alberta.

Calhoun, John Caldwell (1782-1850), U.S. congressman, secretary of war, senator, and vice-president known for his lifelong defense of southern interests. Born in South Carolina, he was elected in 1811 to the U.S. House of Representatives, where he ardently supported the War of 1812. In 1817 he was appointed secretary of war by President James Monroe, and in 1824 was elected vice-president under President John Quincy Adams. Calhoun wrote a defense of the states' rights philosophy, which declared that when a state found a federal law in violation of the Constitution, the state had the right to consider the law void. Calhoun served a second term as vice-president under Andrew Jackson but resigned in 1832. He was soon elected to the Senate, where he became the South's leading spokesman. He argued passionately in favor of slavery and the secession of the Southern states.
See also: Secession.

California

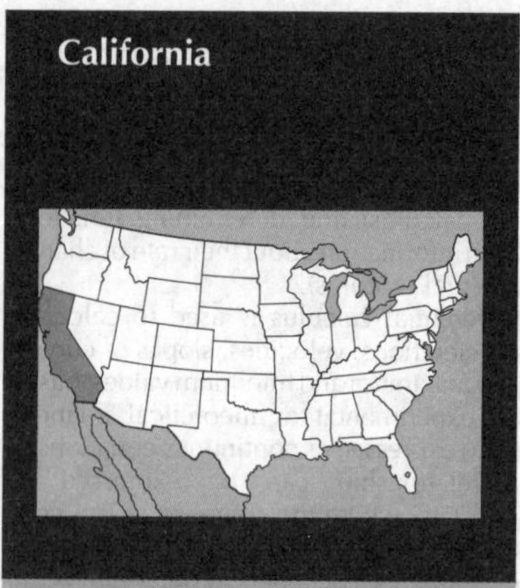

Capital:	Sacramento.
Statehood:	Sept. 9, 1850 (31st state).
Familiar name:	Golden State
Area:	158,706 sq mi (411,049 sq km; ranks 3rd)
Population:	29,839,250 (1990; ranks 1st)
Elevation:	Highest—14,495 ft (4,418 m), Mt. Whitney. Lowest—282 ft (86 m) below sea level near Badwater in Death Valley
Motto:	Eureka ("I have found it")
State flower:	Golden poppy
State bird:	California valley quail
State tree:	California redwood
State song:	"I Love You, California"

California, state in the southwest corner of the United States; bordered by Oregon in the north, Nevada and Arizona in the east, Mexico in the south, and the Pacific Ocean in the west.

Land and climate. Redwood forests and the San Andreas fault, origin of periodic earth tremors and occasional earthquakes, are important features of the Coast Ranges along the Pacific. The Sierra Nevada range to the east is the location of several national parks, including Yosemite and Sequoia, and of Mt. Whitney. Between these 2 mountain chains in the central part of the state is the Great Valley, whose fertile acres are drained by the San Joaquin and Sacramento rivers. To the north, Lassen Peak, an active volcano, and Mt. Shasta are found in the Cascade Mountains. East of the Sierra Nevada is the Basin and Range Region, which is largely desert. It includes Death Valley, with the lowest point in North America. Generally speaking, the state experiences hot, dry summers and warm, relatively wet winters. Principal cities are Los Angeles, San Diego, San Francisco, and Sacramento.

Economy. California is first among the states in manufacturing and agriculture and ranks among the leading states in fishing and mining. Major manufactures include electronic, electrical, and transportation equipment and processed foods, and some of the world's finest wines. California ranks second among the states in the production of milk, cotton, and oranges. It leads the nation in the production of many fruits, including grapes, avocados, and lemons. Tourism is also a large industry, and Disneyland is a primary attraction. California is the nation's film and television production center.

Government. The constitution of 1879 provides for a governor serving a 4-year term. The state legislature consists of 40 senators, elected for 4-year terms, and 80 members of the Assembly, elected for 2-

View of the California coast, from Highway 1

year terms. California sends 2 senators and 52 representatives to the U.S. Congress.

History. The Spanish explorer Juan Rodriguez Cabrillo is usually credited with California's discovery in 1542. The first California mission was established by a Franciscan missionary in 1769. In 1822 California became a province of Mexico. After Mexico's defeat in the Mexican War (1846-48), the area was ceded to the United States. The 1849 gold rush increased the population from 15,000 to over 100,000. The Central Pacific Railroad, completed in 1869, linked California with the East. California became the nation's aircraft center during World War II (1939-45). The postwar population expansion boosted the state's economy, but also created problems that exist today, such as smog and scarcity of water resources.

California is home to the Sequoia National Park. The giant sequoia tree, commonly called redwood, is the world's tallest tree. The sequoia can reach a height of almost 400 ft (120 m) and can live as long as 3000 years.

California, University of, large U.S. state university system, founded 1868. It is housed on 9 campuses (Berkeley, Davis, Irvine, Los Angeles, San Francisco, Riverside, San Diego, Santa Barbara, Santa Cruz). It comprises a library with more than 10 million items, the Lawrence Radiation Laboratory, the Scripps Institute of Oceanography at La Jolla, and the Lick Observatory at Mt. Hamilton.
See also: California.

Californium, chemical element, symbol Cf; for physical constants see Periodic Table. Californium is a radioactive element that does not occur naturally. It was produced in 1950 by Glenn Seaborg and others, by bombarding curium-242 with helium ions in a cyclotron. Californium is metallic, a member of the actinide series. It is produced in nuclear reactors and is a source of neutrons.

Caligula (Gaius Caesar; A.D. 12-41), nickname (meaning "little boots") of cruel and despotic Roman emperor (37-41). He believed he was a god. His demands that his statue be erected in Jerusalem's temple almost precipitated a revolt in Palestine.
See also: Rome, Ancient.

Calla, plant of genus *Calla* or *Zantedeschia* of the arum family *(Araceae)*. Genus *Calla* includes water plants such as the arum lily of North America(*C. palustris*). Plants of genus *Zantedeschia* have showy white, yellow, or pink funnel-shaped leaves (spathes) that look like flowers. The white calla lily (*Z. aethiopica*), golden calla lily (*Z. elliottiana*), and red calla lily (*Z. rehmannii*) are found in South Africa.
See also: Arum.

Callaghan, (Leonard) James (1912-), prime minister of the United Kingdom 1976-79. He was elected Labour party leader on the resignation of Harold Wilson and became prime minister immediately. Labour lost the 1979 general election to Margaret Thatcher's Conservatives.
See also: United Kingdom.

Callaghan, Morley Edward (1903-90), Canadian novelist and short story writer influenced by the style of Ernest Hemingway. His books include the novel *They Shall Inherit the Earth* (1935) and a memoir, *That Summer in Paris* (1963).

Callao (pop. 313,300), Peruvian seaport located 8 mi (13 km) west of the capital city of Lima. As Peru's chief seaport, most of this nation's imports and exports pass through its harbor. The city, which is part of Peru's largest metropolitan area, has survived major earthquakes, tidal waves, and foreign attacks since its founding by Spaniards (1537).
See also: Peru.

Callas, Maria (Maria Kalogeropoulos; 1923-77), leading Greek-American operatic soprano. She was famous for her expressive phrasing and acting ability in a wide variety of roles.
See also: Opera.

Calligraphy, art of penmanship. Combining beauty with legibility, it developed in the Far East, where it was a recognized art form as early as 250 B.C. In early medieval Europe calligraphy was practiced in monastic communities, which developed the Carolingian and Insular scripts. A high point was reached with the Book of Kells and the Lindisfarne gospels. The Italian Renaissance manuscripts provided models for the first printed books and for roman and italic types. Edward Johnston (1872-1944) and his pupil Graily Hewitt (1864-1952) began the modern revival of calligraphy in the early 1900s.

Calliope, keyboard instrument dating from 1855 and much used in circuses and amusement parks. The original version was operated by steam forced through whistles controlled by a keyboard, but later models have used compressed air.

Calms, Regions of, areas characterized by little or no wind. They include *horse latitudes, subpolar regions*, and the equatorial *doldrums. Horse latitudes* lie between 30 degrees north latitude and 30 degrees south. The calms of Cancer and of Capricorn both fall within the horse latitudes. Calms in the subpolar regions are caused by the sinking of the cold air over the North and South poles, which forms high-pressure centers. In the equatorial doldrums, air masses are forced upwards after being heated in the tropics, causing a belt of low pressure to form.
See also: Doldrums; Horse latitudes.

Calorie, amount of heat required to raise the temperature of one gram of water one centigrade degree (more precisely, from 14.5C to 15.5C). One kilocalorie is the amount of heat required to raise 1 kg of water through 1 centigrade degree and is therefore equal to 1,000 calories. The calorific value of foods is actually a measure of the number of kilocalories that can be obtained by the body, in the form of energy, when the foods are broken down.
See also: British Thermal Unit.

Calvary, or Golgotha, Jerusalem hill site of the crucifixion of Jesus. It is traditionally accepted to be the hill on which Constantine founded the church of the Holy Sepulcher in the 4th century.

Calvert, English family that founded and owned colonial Maryland. **George, 1st Baron Baltimore** (c.1580-1632), founded Ferryland, Newfoundland (1621). He petitioned for a grant in northern Virginia (present-day Maryland), granted to his son Cecil in 1632. **Cecil** (or Cecilius), **2nd Baron Baltimore** (c.1605-75), left Maryland's administration to his younger brother **Leonard Calvert** (1606-47). **Charles, 3rd Baron Baltimore** (1637-1715), son of Cecil, governor of Maryland from 1661, and governed the colony in person, 1679-84. In 1689 his Roman Catholic Maryland Administration was overthrown by a Protestant rebellion, and in 1691 the Crown withdrew his authority to govern.
See also: Maryland.

Maria Callas

Calvin, John (1509-64), French theologian. After a "sudden conversion" in 1533, Calvin became a leader of the Protestant Reformation, eventually systematizing his ideas with those of other reformers. His *Institutes of the Christian Religion* (1536) is one of the most important religious works ever written. Calvin's theology, which rejected the authority of the pope, focused on the faith of the individual and study of the Bible. Calvin also believed in predestination, the idea that God preordains some souls for salvation and others for damnation. His church organization became the model for Presbyterianism and the Reformed Churches. Calvin was active in politics, in 1541 establishing in Geneva a

government based on his theology. The academy that he founded in 1559 later became the University of Geneva.
See also: Calvinism; Reformation.

Calvin, Melvin, (1911-), U.S. biochemist who won the 1961 Nobel Prize for chemistry, having led the team that unraveled the details of the chemistry of photosynthesis.
See also: Calvin, John; Chemistry.

Calvinism, Protestant doctrine formulated by John Calvin and stated chiefly in his *Institutes of the Christian Religion* (1536). Its basic tenets are that God is omnipotent; His will is supreme and governs all actions; each person's life is predestined, the salvation or damnation of each soul determined by God before creation; God's elect will be saved and given eternal life, and those He has damned can find no release (justification) from the consequences of their sins except by dedicating themselves to His service. The strict Calvinist maintains that God sees humankind as loathsome and corrupt, with feeble delusions of virtue and worth. Calvinism preaches that the Bible is the only source of God's laws and refers more often to the Old Testament than the New, emphasizing the judgment of sinners more than the love and compassion of God.

Calvino, Italo (1923-85), Italian writer notable for his use of fantasy. Calvino has written in several genres, including science fiction and historical allegory, but he received his greatest acclaim for *Italian Folktales* (1956) and the experimental *If on a Winter's Night a Traveler* (1979; trans. 1981).

Calypso, West Indies musical style notable for its lyrics, which are usually improvised and often humorous or ironic. The music is typically played on steel drums, which carry the tune as well as provide the beat.

Cambodia *See:* Kampuchea.

Cambrian, earliest period of the Paleozoic Era, dated roughly 570-500 million years ago, immediately preceding the Ordovician period. Cambrian rocks contain the oldest fossils that can be used for dating.
See also: Paleozoic.

Cambridge (pop. 98,700), English market town, 51 mi (32 km) from London, and home of the Cambridge University. The town grew up in the 9th century at a ford on the Cam River, near what had been a Roman camp. The first university college, Peterhouse, was founded in 1284. Since then the growth of city and university have been closely linked.
See also: England.

Cambridge (pop. 95,802), city in Massachusetts on the Charles River opposite Boston; seat of Middlesex County. Since the establishment of Harvard University in 1636, the city has been an important educational center. In 1639 the first printing press in the American colonies was established there. In 1879, Radcliffe College for Women was opened, followed by the Episcopal Theological Seminary (1867) and the Massachusetts Institute of Technology (relocated from Boston in 1916). Principal industries include printing and publishing, baking, and the manufacture of light machinery.
See also: Massachusetts.

Cambridge University, one of the world's leading universities, at Cambridge, England. Its history dates from 1209, and its first college, Peterhouse, was established in 1284. Today the coeducational university has about 9,000 students and 29 colleges and approved societies.

Camcorder *See:* Video camera.

Camden (pop. 87,492), city in New Jersey on the Delaware River opposite Philadelphia. Formally laid out as a town in 1773 and chartered as a city in 1828, it is an important manufacturing and shipbuilding city.
See also: New Jersey.

Camel, 2 species of haired, cud-chewing animals with humped backs, long necks, and hooves. The 1-humped Arabian camel or dromedary (*Camelus dromedarius*) of Africa and the Middle East is a widely kept domestic animal. The 2-humped Bactrian camel (*C. bactrianus*) is found from Asia Minor to Manchuria, and a few still live wild in the Gobi Desert. Domesticated in Babylonia about 1100 B.C., camels are invaluable in the desert. They can carry enormous loads and are able to withstand the loss of about one third of their body fluid without danger. Their humps are fatty tissue, not water storage vessels. Their use as bearers has been greatly reduced by the use of motor vehicles.

Camellia, any of a genus *(Camellia)* of evergreen trees and shrubs of Asia that have large fragrant red, pink, or white flowers. The most important of the many cultivated varieties is the tea plant (*Co sinensis*).

Camelot, in Arthurian legend, court of King Arthur and the Knights of the Round Table. It has been identified variously with Caerleon (Wales), Camelford (Cornwall), and South Cadbury (Somerset).
See also: Arthur, King.

Camera, device for forming an optical image of a subject and recording it on a photographic film or plate or (in television cameras) on a photoelectric mosaic.
See also: Photography.

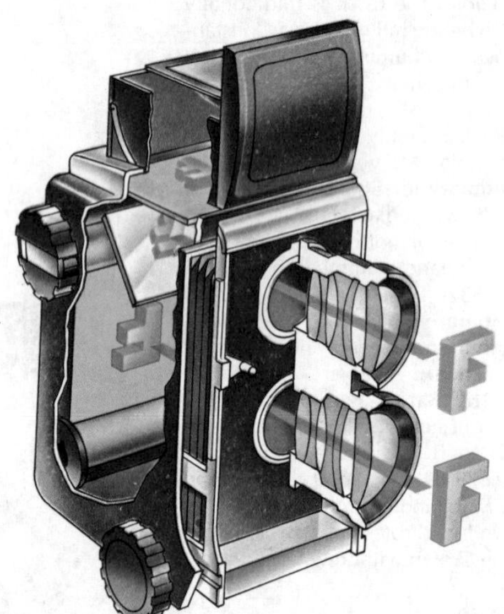

The twin-lens reflex is really two cameras, one for focusing and view-finding and the other for photography.

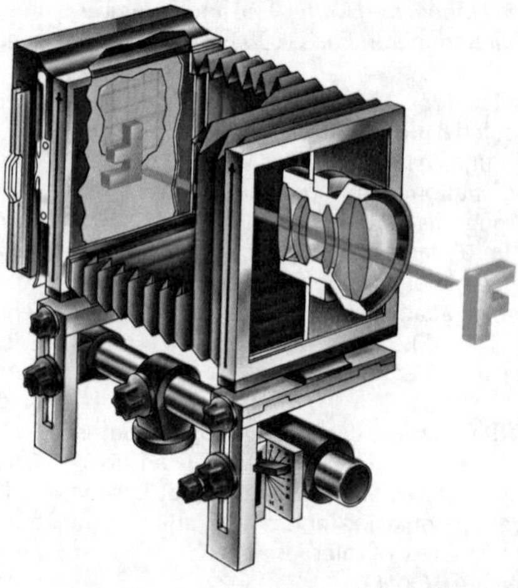

A technical camera is sturdily built, as it does not need to be portable. Focusing is done on a screen in the plane of the film which is replaced by the film when the exposure is to be made.

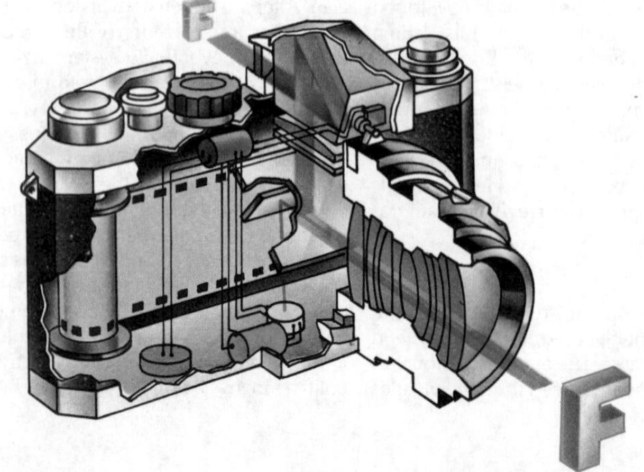

The advantage of a single-lens reflex camera is that it allows the photographer to see exactly what the camera will photograph and eliminates problems of focusing and parallax.

A portrait study by Julia Margaret Cameron.

Cameron, Julia Margaret (1815-79), Indian-born British pioneer photographer, best known for her portraits of such Victorians as Alfred, Lord Tennyson and Ellen Terry. Believing that a photograph should capture the spirit of its subject, Cameron put less emphasis on technique, and the blurred quality of some of her photographs is a distinction of her style. A revised edition of her book *Victorian Photographers of Famous Men and Women* appeared in 1973.

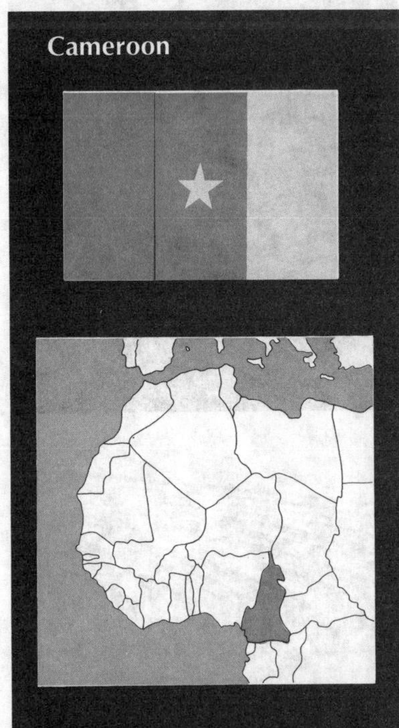

Capital:	Yaoundé
Area:	183,570 sq mi (475,442 sq km)
Population:	11,407,000
Government:	republic
Independent:	1960
GNP:	U.S. $11,270,000,000
Per capita:	U.S. $1,010

Cameroon, federal republic in West Africa. Cameroon is bordered by the Gulf of Guinea (west and southwest), Nigeria (northwest), Chad (northeast), the Central African Republic (east), and the Congo, Gabon, and Equatorial Guinea (south).

Land and climate. The narrow coastal plain of swamps and dense jungle rises to a plateau of savanna and forest some 2,000 ft (610 m) above sea level. The country's highest peak is the volcanic Great Cameroon (13,354 ft/4,070 m). The interior plateau covers about two-thirds of the country. The coast is tropical, the north, near Lake Chad, is semiarid. The central region receives about 30-40 in (76-102 cm) of rainfall annually. The country's capital is Yaoundé.

People. Cameroon's population consists of some 150 different tribes and ethnic groups. The official languages are English and French. Most of the people follow traditional African beliefs but sizable minorities are Christian (in the south) and Muslim (in the north).

Economy. The economy is based mainly on agriculture and forestry. Cameroon is self-sufficient in food and exports coffee, cocoa, and timber as well as bananas, rubber, and aluminum. Aluminum smelting is Cameroon's largest industry.

History. The Sao people, who produced a distinctive kind of art and cast objects in bronze, settled near Lake Chad about 900 A.D. The Portuguese came in 1472 and established the slave trade. In 1884, Germany established a protectorate in the Cameroon area.

British and French troops occupied the area in World War I and afterwards the League of Nations mandated the larger part (Cameroun) to France and the remainder (Southern and Northern Cameroons) to the British. In 1946 they became UN trust territories. In 1960, Cameroun became an independent republic after several years of guerrilla warfare.

After plebiscites in 1961, the Northern Cameroons joined Nigeria, and the Southern Camerouns joined Cameroun to form the Federal Republic of Cameroon. In 1972, the federal system was replaced by a unified republic. In 1980, Ahmadou Ahidjo, president since independence, was reelected. President Paul Biya was elected unopposed in 1984 for his first full 5- year term.

Camomile, also spelled chamomile, any of a genus (*Anthemis*) of various strong-scented herbs with daisylike flowers. The bitter-tasting flowers and leaves have had uses in folk medicine ranging from malaria cure to mouthwash.

Camorra, Italian secret society started in the Kingdom of Naples (1830). Although it specialized in extortion, smuggling, robbery, and assassination, it was often used by the authorities, and it became very powerful. After Italian unification in 1861, attempts were made to suppress the society, but it survived until 1911.

Camp, Walter Chauncey (1859-1925), father of American football. As a player and coach at Yale and Stanford universities, he helped initiate, implement, and develop changes (such as the first down system and the line of scrimmage) that turned European rugby into the American game. Camp authored numerous books on athletics and physical fitness.

Campanella, Roy (1921-), one of the most popular and successful catchers in baseball history. He signed with the Negro leagues in 1936, joining the Brooklyn Dodgers in 1948. Campanella's 10-year major league career was cut short by an automobile accident in 1958 that left him paralyzed. He won the National League's Most Valuable Player award 3 times (1951, 1953, and 1955) playing for the Dodgers.

Campanile, bell tower, usually adjacent to a church. The first campaniles appeared in Italy about the 7th century. As in the round campanile of Sant' Apollinare Nuovo in Ravenna, Italy, the earliest examples probably contained not bells, but semantra, planks of wood or metal that sounded when struck. In the following century, the square campanile became the standard. The campanile has been revived as an element of modern church architecture.

Campanula, plant genus of the family Campanulaceae containing some 700 species of mostly herbaceous (nonwoody) plants. Campanula is often called bellflower, and many of the species have showy, bell-like flowers.

Cameroon contains 5 major geographical regions. The northwestern region is the site of the Mandara Mountains. The basis of the economy is subsistance farming.

Donald Campbell

Campbell, Donald Malcolm (1921-67), English speedboat racer. The first man to break the 200 mph (320 kmph) barrier and survive, Campbell's run, on Ullswater Lake, Cumberland, England in 1955, established a watercraft speed record of 202.32 mph (325.602 kmph). Campbell died in an accident in 1967, while exceeding 300 mph (480 kmph) in his jet-propelled boat.

Campbell, Mrs. Patrick (1865-1940), English actress. Popular on stage for over 40 years, she created many classic roles, including Eliza Doolittle in George Bernard Shaw's *Pygmalion* (1914), a part written for her.

Campbell-Bannerman, Sir Henry (1836-1908), British prime minister 1905-08 and leader of the Liberal party from 1899. A member of the House of Commons from 1868 until his death, he championed progressive causes.
See also: United Kingdom.

Camp David, woodland camp in the Catoctin Mountains in Maryland near Washington, D.C., that has been used by U.S. presidents since Franklin D. Roosevelt as a retreat, workplace, and environment to receive foreign dignitaries.
See also: Maryland.

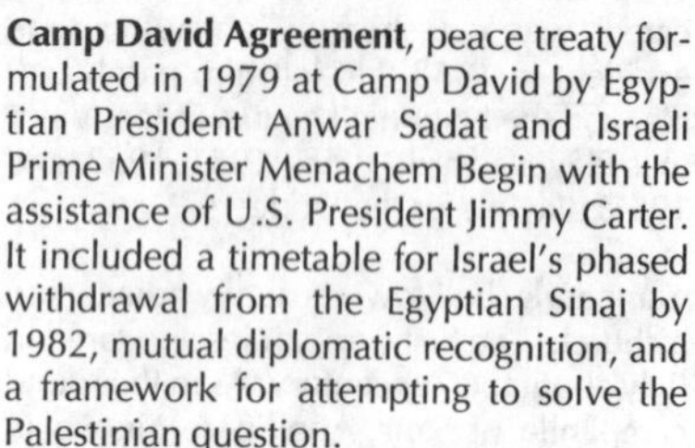

Albert Camus

Camp David Agreement, peace treaty formulated in 1979 at Camp David by Egyptian President Anwar Sadat and Israeli Prime Minister Menachem Begin with the assistance of U.S. President Jimmy Carter. It included a timetable for Israel's phased withdrawal from the Egyptian Sinai by 1982, mutual diplomatic recognition, and a framework for attempting to solve the Palestinian question.

Campeche, state in southeastern Mexico, on the Yucatán Peninsula. Although forest products yield a significant portion of the state's income, commercial fishing is also important. About a third of the inhabitants of Campeche are descended from the Mayas.
See also: Mexico.

Camp Fire, organization for children in the United States. Originally founded for girls in 1910 by Luther and Charlotte Gulick, Camp Fire began admitting boys in 1975. The organization has programs for kindergartners through high-school students. It stresses self reliance through safety courses, camping, and service activities.
See also: Gulick, Luther Halsey.

Camphor, white, crystalline compound ($C_{10}H_{16}O$) distilled from the wood of a species of laurel tree (*Cinnamonum camphora*). It has a strong odor that repels insects and is used medicinally—internally as a pain-killer and antispasmodic, and externally in linaments.

Campin, Robert (1375?-1444), Flemish painter best known for his religious works. His art reflects the influence of manuscript illumination, though with a keener sense of plasticity in rendering the forms. One of his major works is the triptych of the Annunciation (c.1428) known as the *Mérode Altarpiece.* Depicting in realistic detail the daily life of the rising bourgeoisie, Campin became a founder of the Netherlandish School, influencing Jan Van Eyck and Rogier Van Der Weyden, among others.

Campion, plant of genera *Lychnis* or *Silene* grown for showy flowers. Many have escaped from gardens and grow wild. Descriptive names include ragged robin, Maltese cross, and mullein pink.

Camus, Albert (1913-60), French writer and philosopher. He communicated a vision of humanity in an absurd universe and felt that the only possibility for freedom and dignity lay in the awareness of this absurdity. His works include the essay "The Myth of Sisyphus" (1942), which elucidated the philosophical basis of his novel *The Stranger* (1942); the novels *The Plague* (1947) and *The Fall* (1956); the essay "The Rebel" (1951); and the play *Caligula* (1945). He won the Nobel Prize in literature in 1957.
See also: Philosophy.

Canaan, early name for Palestine. The region was inhabited from the 2nd millennium B.C. by Semitic peoples, mainly Amorites, whose script provides the earliest known alphabet. During the 13th century B.C. Canaan was occupied by the Israelites. In the next century its coasts were taken by the Philistines but later, King David (1000-961 B.C.) extended Israelite rule over all Canaan.
See also: Palestine.

Canaanites, people who settled Canaan, the biblical name for Palestine, c.3000 B.C. The chief inhabitants of this land until the Israelites defeated them c.1200 B.C., the Canaanites spoke a Semitic language whose writing system influenced the development of the ancient Hebrew alphabet.
See also: Canaan; Semites.

Canada, independent nation in North America, encompassing a land mass of 3,851,809 sq mi (9,976,185 sq km), making it the largest country in the Western Hemisphere and the second largest country in the world after the USSR. Canada is an autonomous federation with 10 provinces and 2 federally administered territories. It is formally a constitutional monarchy under the British Crown and a member of the Commonwealth of Nations. French and English are the official languages. The federal capital is Ottawa.
Land and climate. Canada is divided into 7 regions. (1) The Appalachian region (New Brunswick, Nova Scotia, Prince Ed-

The Canadian province of Alberta is the home of Banff National Park. Shown is Lake Louise.

Canada is the sixth largest producer of wheat in the world. Most Canadian farms are large and adapted to mechanized tillage and combine harvesting.

Canada

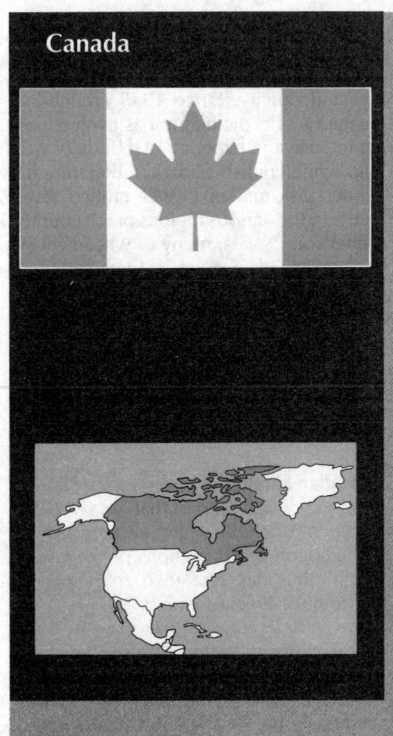

General information	
Capital:	Ottawa
Area:	3,849,675 sq mi (9,970,610 sq km)
Population:	26,189,000
Official languages:	English, French
Monetary unit:	1 Canadian dollar = 100 cents
Main cities:	Toronto, Montreal, Vancouver, Ottawa-Hull, Winnipeg, Edmonton, Calgary, Quebec
Government	
Form:	Federal parliamentary democracy
Independent:	1931
Head of state:	British monarch
Head of government:	Prime minister
Legislature:	two legislative houses (Senate and House of Commons)
Executive:	Cabinet of Federal Ministry
Judiciary:	highest court is the Supreme Court of Canada
Political division:	10 provinces, 2 territories
National economy	
Gross national product:	U.S. $437,471,000,000
Per capita income:	U.S. $16,760
Agriculture:	wheat, barley, corn, rapeseed, oats, hay
Livestock:	pigs, milk cows, other cattle
Fisheries:	1,571,500 metric tons
Mining:	iron ore, zinc, copper, lead, nickel, uranium, gold, silver
Industries:	motor vehicles and parts, crude materials; fabricated materials, food and livestock
Main exports:	wood pulp, crude steel, cement, newsprint, pig iron
Transportation:	58,125 mi (93,544 km) of railroads; 174,140 mi (280,251 km) of roads: 9 international airports
Trading partners:	United States, Japan, Germany, United Kingdom, France, Italy
People	
Urban:	76%
Ethnic composition:	British 45%, French 29%, other European 24.5%, Native American and Eskimo 1.5%
Birth rate:	14.4 per 1,000 population
Death rate:	7.2 per 1,000 population
Infant mortality:	7.3 per 1,000 live births
Life expectancy:	male 73 years, female 80 years

ward Island, and Newfoundland and the Gaspé peninsula) is a geological extension of the Appalachian mountain chain that runs along the eastern United States. The region is a source of varied farm products, timber, coal, and iron ore, and with numerous natural harbors, a major commercial fishing center. (2) The St. Lawrence lowlands, adjacent to the desolate Canadian Shield in the north and bordering on the Great Lakes and the St. Lawrence River in the south, is one of its most productive agricultural belts, containing about half of the total population. The Hudson Bay lowlands, embracing the southwest shore of Hudson Bay and James Bay, are situated in an Arctic zone, the region's swampy subsoil, consisting mostly of clay and sand, frozen the year round. Most of the region's inhabitants are fur trappers and fishers. (3) The Canadian Shield, almost 50% of the country, is a horseshoe-shaped region encircling Hudson Bay and including large portions of the provinces of Quebec, Ontario, Manitoba, and Saskatchewan, the northeastern corner of Alberta, the Labrador portion of Newfoundland, and much of the Northwest territories. The area is characterized by rocky hills and ridges, numerous lakes, and muskeg (a type of bog). Though unsuitable for agriculture, the region is rich in natural resources; forests, mineral deposits, and water power. (4) The Interior Plains reach from the Rocky Mountains to the Canadian Shield and include southern Manitoba and Saskatchewan, almost all of Alberta, and part of British Columbia and the Northwest Territories. The northern half of the Interior Plains is heavily forested, and there is some muskeg and tundra. The southern half includes fertile prairies and also contains rich deposits of natural gas, oil, and coal. (5) The Cordilleran region, between the Pacific Ocean and the Interior Plains of western Canada, is a 500-mi- (800- km-) wide strip of mountainous terrain that includes most of British Columbia, the Yukon territory, and part of western Alberta. Second to the Canadian Shield in wealth of mineral deposits, the region has extensive forests, water resources for hydroelectric plants, fertile soils particularly suited to fruit production, and important commer-

The Canadian capital of Ottawa

cial fishing areas along the Pacific coast. (6) With very limited animal life and vegetation, the Inuitian region in the Arctic Archipelago includes the 800-mi-(1,300-km-) long and 300-mi- (480-km) wide mountainous region extending from northernmost Ellesmere Island south and west to Melville Island. The Arctic lowlands and plateaus include most of Banks Island, southern Ellesmere Island, and eastern Baffin Island. (7) Though rugged and virtually uninhabitable, the Arctic Archipelago possesses rich deposits of coal, salt, gypsum, oil, and natural gas. About 70% of Canadian soil is useless for agriculture, but most of the nonarable soils support vast expanses of forests, and some are suitable for cattle raising. Covering about 40% of the country from coast to coast, the northern forests form Canada's largest belt of natural vegetation. The tundra extending across northern Canada can support only moss, lichens, and grass and flowers during the summer, when the surface layer is frost-free. Ever-frozen subsoil, or permafrost, prevents greater vegetation.

The government has created several game reserves; the land set aside for national parks totals about 29,500 sq mi (76,405 sq km). The largest of the national parks are Jasper, Wood Buffalo, Prince Albert, and Riding Mountain. Each province has also established its own provincial parks.

People. Canada's population is predominantly of British or French stock, though it includes many of German, Italian, Ukrainian, Dutch, and other origins. Native Americans number about 320,000 and Inuit (Eskimos) about 23,000. Population is concentrated in the southern part of the country, the most populous provinces being Ontario, Quebec, and British Columbia. About 76% of Canadians are urban.

Government. Canada has a parliamentary system of government, with executive power vested in a prime minister and cabinet. The federal legislature comprises a Senate of 104 appointed members and a House of Commons whose 282 members are elected for a 5-year term. Each of the 10 provinces has its own premier and elected legislature. The Yukon and Northwest Territories are governed by federally appointed commissioners and elected councils, and each sends 1 representative to the federal parliament.

Economy. Agriculture ranks first in terms of employment and provides about 11% of Canada's total exports. One of the world's chief wheat producers, Canada grows other grains, oilseeds, fruit (especially apples), vegetables, and tobacco. Beef and dairy cattle, hogs, sheep, and poultry are reared. Forestry and fisheries are major industries, and Canada remains a leading source of furs, both farmed and trapped. Mineral resources include petroleum and natural gas, molybdenum, platinum, copper, nickel, iron ore, zinc, lead, silver, gold, asbestos, elemental sulfur, and coal. Two-thirds of all manufacturing plants are located in Ontario and Quebec. Manufacturing accounts for about 20% of all employment. Products include nonferrous metals, machinery, chemicals, plastics, electrical equipment, and textiles.

History. Visited by 11th-century Vikings, Canada was later penetrated by explorers such as John Cabot, Jacques Cartier, and Samuel de Champlain. The French founded Quebec in 1608 and made Canada the royal colony of New France (1663). Anglo-French rivalry culminated in the cession of New France to Britain (Treaty of Paris, 1763). French rights were guaranteed by the Quebec Act (1774). Only 1 serious revolt against British rule took place (1837-38), consisting of separate uprisings led by W.L. Mackenzie in Upper (English-speaking) Canada and Louis Papineau in Lower (French-speaking) Canada. The British North America Act (1867) established Canada as a dominion, the 4 founding provinces being Quebec, Ontario, Nova Scotia, and New Brunswick. The others entered later: Manitoba (1870), British Columbia (1871), Prince Edward Island (1873), Saskatchewan (1905), Alberta (1905), and Newfoundland (1949). The Northwest Territories, formerly administered by the Hudson's Bay Company, became a federal territory in 1870, and the Yukon was made a separate territory in 1898. Separatist tensions, particularly in French-speaking Quebec, developed during the 1960s and have continued. Efforts begun in 1978 to amend the British North America Act in order to "patriate" the Canadian constitution resulted in the Constitution Act (1982).

Canada goose

Canada goose (*Branta canadensis*), large migratory bird common to North America, Greenland, and parts of Asia. It has a long black head and neck and distinctive white cheek bars, and flies in group formations.

Canada thistle (*Cirsium arvense*), weed native to Europe and Asja and now widespread in the northern United States and southern Canada. The weed is difficult to control because new thistle can grow from bits of the old roots.

Canadian literature, body of literary works reflecting the English and French heritage of Canada, often focusing on national identity and duality. Since 1945 French-language Quebecois fiction has evolved into an intense and experimental body of writing, while English-Canadian literature has tended to be marked by well-crafted novels of life in the various regions of the country. Robertson Davies, many of whose widely praised novels are set in Ontario towns, and Margaret Atwood, a poet and novelist whose work often has a strong feminist component, are two of the leading figures of contemporary Canadian literature.

Canadian Mounted Police *See:* Royal Canadian Mounted Police.

Canadian Shield, or Laurentian Plateau, geologic designation of that area of North America (including the eastern half of Canada and small portions of the United States) that has remained more or less stable since Precambrian times.

Canal, artificial waterway used for transportation, drainage, and irrigation. In 521 B.C. a precursor of the Suez Canal joined the Nile to the Red Sea. In China, the Ling Ch'u canal was completed during the 3rd century B.C. and the Grand Canal, joining the Paiho, Yellow, and Yangtze rivers, had sections in use by the 7th century A.D. The Romans built many canals to supply their cities with water and canalized a number of European rivers to create an empire-wide transportation system. In the 15th century the lock, a device for raising boats from one land level to another, was invented. Although one of the great engineering projects of the 19th century, the Suez Canal to the Red Sea, was built entirely without locks, the other great international waterway, the Panama Canal, would not have been possible without them. In North America the canal system included the Erie Canal (1825), linking the Hudson River to Lake Erie and providing an opening to the Middle West. The Welland Canal (1828), between Lake Erie and Lake Ontario, was the next step in an inland waterway transportation network, completed by the opening of the St. Lawrence Seaway (1959). The longest canalized system is the Volga-Baltic Canal (1965), which runs 1,850 mi (2,977 km), from Astrakhan up the Volga, via Kuybyshev, Gorkiy and Lake Ladoga, to Leningrad, USSR.

Canal Zone *See:* Panama Canal Zone.

Canary, name of several small song birds, particularly a finch native to the Canary Islands (*Serinus canarius*). The wild canary is usually gray or green in color, but tame birds have been bred to produce the characteristic "canary yellow." Canaries have been bred in Europe since the 16th century and are valued for their song.

Canary, Martha Jane *See:* Calamity Jane.

Canary Islands, group of islands in the Atlantic Ocean off the northwest coast of

Africa that make up 2 Spanish provinces. The main islands are Tenerife, Palma, Gomera, Hierro, Grand Canary, Fuerteventura, and Lanzarote; their land area is nearly 3,000 sq mi (7,770 sq km).

Canberra (pop. 247,200), capital city of the Commonwealth of Australia and the country's largest inland city. The Australian parliament first met there in 1927. The economy rests mainly on the public service and governmental departments.
See also: Australia.

Cancer, group of diseases in which some body cells change their nature, start to divide uncontrollably, and may revert to an undifferentiated type. They form a malignant tumor that enlarges and may spread to adjacent tissues or through blood and lymph systems to other parts of the body. The American Cancer Society has listed 7 warning signals: (1) change in bowel or bladder habits, (2) a sore that does not heal, (3) unusual bleeding or discharge, (4) thickening or lump in a breast or elsewhere, (5) indigestion or difficulty in swallowing, (6) obvious change in a wart or mole, and (7) nagging cough or hoarseness. Every diagnosis of cancer made by a doctor is subject to confirmation by a biopsy, in which a small piece of tissue is cut into very thin slices, stained with special dyes, and examined under a microscope. Routine periodic physical examinations are important, since the most successfully treated cancers are those that have not progressed to the stage of producing symptoms. The doctor feels, or palpates, parts of the body for unusual lumps or thickenings. A cervical smear is taken from adult women. The rectum and large intestine can be examined by means of a lighted tube, called a proctosigmoidoscope. Periodic self-examination of the skin, mouth, and genital organs is also important. Women should examine their breasts once a month after their menstrual cycles, and men should examine their testicles.

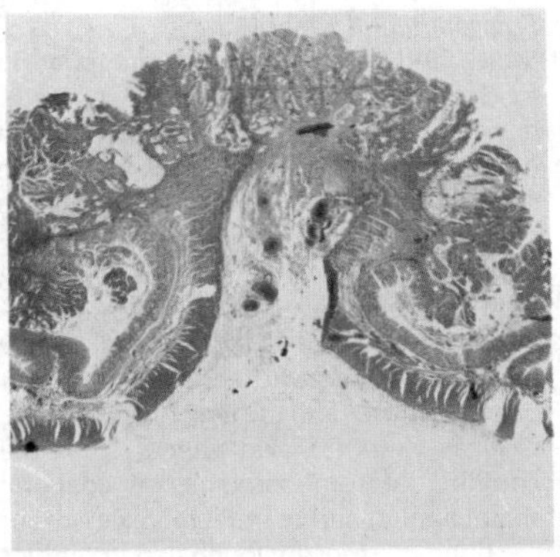

Cancerous tumor of the mucous membrane of the large intestine. The tumor is penetrating the intestinal cavity.

Successful treatment of cancer requires complete removal or destruction of the tumor by surgery, radiation, or drugs (chemotherapy). Some tumors cannot be destroyed by safe amounts of radiation, and some cannot be entirely removed surgically without destroying a vital organ, so surgery, radiation, and drugs may be combined.
Cancer is tenacious, sometimes subsiding but reappearing years after the patient has presumably been cured. For some cancers, even 5 years is not a long enough period; an indefinite length of time with frequent examinations is recommended. Physicians are increasingly reluctant to speak of "5-year cures," preferring more the realistic expression of "5-year survival without clinical evidence of disease."

Known causes of cancer

Agent or circumstance	Site of cancer
Aflatoxin	Liver
Alcoholic drinks	Mouth, pharynx, larynx, esophagus, liver
Alkylating agents:	
Cyclophosphamide	Bladder
Melphalan	Bone marrow
Aromatic amines:	
4-Aminodiphenyl	Bladder
Benzidine	Bladder
2-Naphtylamine	Bladder
Arsenic (certain compounds only)	Skin, lung
Asbestos	Lung, pleura, peritoneum
Benzene	Bone marrow
Bis (chloromethyl) ether	Lung
Busulfan	Bone marrow
Cadmium (certain compounds only)	Prostate
Chewing (betel, tobacco, lime)	Mouth
Chromium (certain compounds only)	Lung
Chlornaphazine	Bladder
Chlorophenol/phenoxy acids	Connective tissue, lymphoid tissue
Furniture manufacture (hardwoods)	Nasal sinuses
Immunosuppressive drugs	Reticuloendothelial system
Ionizing radiations	Bone marrow and probably all other sites
Isopropyl alcohol manufacture	Nasal sinuses
Leather goods manufacture	Nasal sinuses
Mustard gas	Larynx, lung
Nickel (certain compounds only)	Nasal sinuses, lung
Estrogens:	
Unopposed	Endometrium
Transplacental (DES)	Vagina
Overnutrition (causing obesity)	Endometrium, gall bladder
Phenacetin	Kidney (pelvis)
Polycyclic hydrocarbons	Skin, scrotum, lung
Reproductive history:	
Late age at first pregnancy	Breast
Zero or low number of pregnancies	Ovary
Parasites:	
Schistosoma haematobium	Bladder
Chlonorchis sinensis	Liver (cholangioma)
Sexual partners (multiple)	Uterine cervix
Steroids:	
Anabolic (oxymetholone)	Liver
Contraceptives	Liver (hamartoma)
Tobacco smoking	Mouth, pharynx, larynx, lung, esophagus, bladder
Ultraviolet light	Skin, lip
Vinyl chloride	Liver (angiosarcoma)
Virus (hepatitis B)	Liver (hepatoma)

Causes of cancer.

Chemical compounds.

Chemists have manufactured several hundred pure chemicals that produce cancer in animals. In humans, however, research has not found a relationship between chemical structure and cancer-producing activity. Some chemical carcinogens produce cancers at the site of contact, others at distant sites. Some are incomplete or weak in their action and need the action of other chemicals in order to induce tumors. The simultaneous injection of a chemical carcinogen and a closely related inactive compound (anticarcinogen) can prevent or retard the action of the carcinogen. This line of investigation may eventually uncover chemicals to prevent the development of cancer in individuals who are unavoidably exposed to certain cancer-producing hazards.

Environmental hazards.
Molds and bacteria growing naturally on food products may represent a source of environmental carcinogens. The human cancers due to industrial exposure include the following: (1) bladder cancer in aniline dye workers who handle betanaphtylamine, (2) bone cancer due to swallowing radium, (3) lung cancer caused by inhalation of chromium compounds, radioactive ores, asbestos, arsenic, and iron, (4) cancer of nasal sinuses and the lung in nickel mine workers, and (5) skin cancer from the handling of some products of coal, oil shale, lignite, and petroleum. Excessive or continuous exposure to inhaled impurities brings about changes in the bronchial linings and the lungs that may eventually result in disability and illness. If the impurities contain cancer-producing substances, prolonged exposure can lead to cancer.
During the past 40 years, cancer of the lung in the United States has shown the greatest increase of any cancer type. At least 80% of the total increase can be attributed to cigarette smoking. An additional important factor is air pollution caused by industrial wastes, car exhausts, and household sources.
Radiation.
The cancer-producing effects of the ultraviolet rays of sunlight appear to be limited to the skin. Related to the cancer-causing effects of sunlight are those of ionizing radiation from radium and X-rays. Ionizing radiation can cause several forms of cancer in humans and animals. Radiologists and others exposed to increased doses of radiation are more likely to develop leukemia than are people who are not exposed. Radium salts, which are deposited in bone, give rise to cancers of the bone.
Cancer-causing viruses.
Cancer-causing viruses penetrate the cells of victims and become part of the structure of the chromosomes. The presence of the virus in the genetic mechanism of the cell may make the cell behave immediately as a cancer, or the virus can remain dormant until activated by another stimulus. Scientists have identified several dozen types of cancer that are caused by viruses, in many species of animals, including cats, monkeys, chickens, and rodents. It is inevitable that some human cancers will be found to be caused by viruses and that such discoveries may lead to the development of protective vaccines.
Hormones.
Large doses of the female hormone estrogen given over long periods will lead to the development of leukemia and tumors of the testes, uterus, and pituitary in some strains of mice. The increasing use of hormones as treatment for various human conditions does not seem to have led to an increase in the incidence of any specific type of cancer in women or men. However, some girls born of mothers who took large doses of a synthetic estrogen, diethylstilbestrol (DES), during their pregnancy have developed cancer of the vagina. Widespread use of "the pill" (the collective term for a variety of oral contraceptives containing progestogen, often estrogen, and sometimes other hormones) has increased the number of younger women receiving additional hormones. Carefully controlled, long-term observations of "pill" users are necessary to assess increased risks for cancer of the breast, uterus, or ovary.
Established tumors in both humans and laboratory animals have shown varying degrees of hormone dependency. For example, removal of the ovaries in some women with advanced breast cancer or removal of the testes in men with prostate cancer often leads to temporary regression of the tumors.
Nutrition.
There is no diet known to prevent cancer in humans. There is some evidence, that vitamin deficiency in humans plays a role in the occurrence of cancers of the mouth and the esophagus. However, such a deficiency is probably only 1 of a number of factors. The consumption of dietary fiber has been associated with reduced risk of colon cancer.
Heredity.
The limited data available suggest increased familial risk of developing cancer of the same site for cancers of the breast (female), stomach, large intestine, endometrium (lining of the uterus), prostate, lung, and possibly ovary. However, it is not known to what extent the tumors that have been observed to run in some families are due to genetic characteristics or to environmental factors such as diet or occupation that may remain the same from one generation to the next. Brain tumors and sarcomas seem to occur more frequently than expected in brothers and sisters of children with these tumors. When an identical twin has childhood leukemia, the probability that the other twin will develop the disease within 1 or 2 years of the date of diagnosis of the first twin is about 1 in 5. In addition, retinoblastoma, a rare form of cancer of the eye, is known to be due to inherited mutation.

Cancer, Tropic of *See:* Tropic of Cancer.

Cancer Society of America, voluntary organization founded in 1913 to provide a program of services for cancer patients and their families. The Cancer Society also directs public education programs and supports research through grants to individuals and institutions.
See also: Cancer.

Candela, or new candle (symbol: cd), basic unit of measurement of luminous intensity, or candle power. It is defined as equal to one sixtieth of the light reflected by one sq cm of a blackbody (a theoretically perfect absorber and emitter of radiation) at the freezing temperature of platinum (1,769° C) and at standard atmospheric pressure.

Candlepower *See:* Candela.

Candy, any of a great variety of sweet confections. Candy can provide quick energy because the body digests sugar, usually its main ingredient, more rapidly than any other food. Chocolate candies are the best selling among all the different types.

Candytuft, any of several species of a genus (*Iberis*) of low-growing, Old World plants of the mustard family. Often cultivated as a rock garden or border plant, candytuft has variously colored blossoms.

Canetti, Elias (1905-), Bulgarian-born author of prose and plays in the German language. Major works include the novel *Auto da Fé* (1935) and the political study *Crowds and Power* (1960). He received the 1981 Nobel Prize for literature.

Canine *See:* Teeth.

Canis Major, constellation of stars visible in the Southern Hemisphere. It contains the brightest star in the sky, Sirius, (the Dog Star). Canis Major is visible on winter evenings.
See also: Constellation; Sirius.

Canis Minor, constellation appearing north of Canis Major in the Southern Hemisphere. Procyon in Canis Minor is one of the brightest stars in the sky.
See also: Constellation.

Cankerworm, or measuring worm, any of various larvae of insects, especially moths. Cankerworms feed on foliage and can seriously damage fruit and shade trees.

Canna, any of a genus (*Canna*) of tropical plants of the family Cannaceae. Widely cultivated in the United States, canna is bred in hybrid varieties.

Cannabis, tops and leaves of the female plant of Indian hemp (*Cannabis sativa*), from which marijuana, a mood-altering substance, is obtained.
See also: Marijuana.

Cannae, ancient town in southern Italy, site of Hannibal's decisive defeat of the Romans (216 B.C.). The encircling technique he perfected, regarded as a masterpiece of tactics, won him the battle and 10,000 prisoners.
See also: Hannibal; Italy; Punic Wars.

Cannes (pop. 72,300), French resort and seaport on the Mediterranean coast. Its superb climate makes it a center for tourism and festivals, notably the annual International Film Festival.
See also: France.

Cannibalism, consumption by humans of human flesh, common throughout the world at various times in the past and still occasionally practiced, though now generally taboo. Among primitive peoples, the motive appears to have been the belief that eating an enemy or a respected elder transferred that person's strength to the eater.

Canning, process of preserving foods in sealed metal containers, developed by the

Cannes, France, on the French Riviera, attracts world attention every year during the Cannes Film Festival.

French chef Nicolas Appert in 1809 and first patented in the United States by Ezra Daggett in 1815. The fragile glass jars originally used were replaced by tin-coated iron cans after 1810. Today a production line process is used.

Cannizzaro, Stanislao (1826-1910), Italian chemist, teacher, and activist in Garibaldi's movement for Italian unification. Cannizzaro found that benzaldehyde treated with a concentrated alcoholic hydroxide produced equal amounts of benzyl alcohol and the salt of benzoic acid. This became known as the Cannizzaro reaction. In 1858 he differentiated between atomic and molecular weights, a discovery that won him the Copley medal from the Royal Society of London.
See also: Chemistry.

Cannon, large firearm with a barrel, breech, and firing mechanism. First used in warfare around the middle of the 14th century, early cannons were cast of bronze and wrought iron. The term gradually came to refer to any gun that was fired from a carriage or fixed mount and had a bore greater than 1 inch in diameter.

Cannon-ball tree, South American tree (*Couroupita guianensis*) noted for its spherical woody fruit, which resembles a rusty cannon ball. Related to the Brazil-nut tree, the cannon-ball tree sheds its leaves more than once a year.
See also: Brazil nut.

Cano, Juan Sebastián del (1476-1526), Basque sailor who succeeded Ferdinand Magellan as commander of the expedition that completed the first circumnavigation of the globe (1522).
See also: Magellan, Ferdinand.

Canoe, long, narrow, lightweight boat used primarily for fishing and recreational activities on lakes and rivers. Originally canoes were made by hollowing out logs and were used for combat as well as transport. Now they are made from canvas, thin wood, and aluminum. In contrast to kayaks, canoes have an uncovered top.

Canon, form or procedure of contrapuntal musical composition in which one voice or instrument starts to sing or play a theme and other voices or instruments follow at a specified interval of time, all singing or playing the same theme according to the same rule (canon). The composer might specify that later voices enter at different pitches, or even execute the theme upside down or backwards (*cancrizans*, crabwise). In the best-known form of canon, the round, the theme is sung (played) identically by all voices, which enter at regular intervals. This very old musical form originated in the church music of the Middle Ages.

Canonization, process by which a Christian church declares a deceased person to be a saint. In the Roman Catholic Church the process involves a long and careful investigation of the individual's life for sanctity, heroic virtue, and orthodoxy.
See also: Saint.

Canopus, second brightest star in the sky. It lies in the constellation of Carina, the Keel, visible in the Southern Hemisphere. Canopus is used as a guide star for navigating spacecraft.
See also: Carina.

Canova, Antonio (1757-1822), Italian sculptor, a leading exponent of neoclassicism. His works include *Cupid and Psyche* (1787-92), several statues of his patron Napoleon, and a famous statue of Pauline Bonaparte Borghese as the reclining *Venus Victrix* (1808).

Cantaloupe *See:* Muskmelon.

Cannon: the Armstrong Field Gun

Cantata (from: Italian *cantare*, "to sing"), musical composition for solo voice or choir, usually with an instrumental accompaniment. One of the earliest composers of cantatas was Giacomo Carissimi, who wrote such works both for entertainment and for the church. Another important composer in this field was Alessandro Scarlatti, some of whose cantatas were almost as elaborate as opera. J.S. Bach wrote hundreds of cantatas as part of his normal duties as a church choirmaster.
See also: Bach, Johann Sebastian.

Canterbury (pop. 34,400), city and county borough of Kent, on the Stour River 55 mi (89 km) southeast of London. It has been England's ecclesiastical capital since A.D. 597. The archbishop of Canterbury is primate of all England.
See also: England.

Canterbury bell, any of several biennial flowering plants with bell-shaped flowers, in particular the *Campanula medium*. Found wild in woods and stony places, the canterbury bell does not flower until the second (and final) summer of its life. The plant may grow to 3 ft (91 cm) and has hairy, oval leaves.

A 15th-century manuscript of the Canterbury Tales *depicting pilgrims on the way to Canterbury.*

Canterbury Tales, best-known work of English poet Geoffrey Chaucer, written between 1387 and his death in 1400. In 17,000 lines (mostly heroic couplets) it describes a party of 30 pilgrims going to the shrine of St. Thomas à Becket, and their plan to tell 4 tales each on the journey. Only 24 tales were written, 4 of them unfinished, but the work presents a vivid cross section of medieval society and the tales cover most medieval literary genres.
See also: Chaucer, Geoffrey.

Canticle, piece of religious music, similar in character to a psalm, but using a passage from the Bible other than the psalms themselves. Some canticles actually date from biblical times and are therefore very ancient. More recently the word has come to be used for shorter choral works with any kind of religious or semi-religious basis.

Canticles *See:* Song of Solomon.

Canton (pop. 394,106), city in northeastern Ohio, about 60 mi (97 km) south-

east of Cleveland; seat of Stark County. An important industrial center, Canton manufactures rubber goods, steel, bearings, electrical appliances, paints, motors, and bricks. Settled in 1805, Canton was the home of President William McKinley, who is commemorated there by the National McKinley Memorial.
See also: Ohio.

Canton, China *See:* Guangzhou.

Canute (995?-1035), king of England, Norway, and Denmark. The younger son of Sweyn of Denmark, Canute invaded England with his father in 1013. He withdrew in 1014, when Sweyn died, but invaded again in 1015 and became king in 1016 on the death of Edmund II. In 1019 he succeeded his brother as king of Denmark, and in 1028 he conquered Norway, ousting Olaf II. Canute is noted in English history for having brought peace and codifying English law. Anglo-Saxon rule was reestablished in England in 1042, when Edward the Confessor became king.

Canvasback (*Aythya valisneria*), diving duck found in coastal and inland waters of North America. About 2 ft (0.6 m) long and 3 lb (1.4 kg) in weight, it feeds on aquatic plants, shrimps, and small fish.

Canyonlands National Park, in eastern Utah, established in 1964. It covers an area of 337,258 acres (136,488 hectares) and contains red rock canyons, stone needles, arches, rapids, and rock carvings.
See also: National Parks.

Canzoniere *See:* Petrarch.

Capacitance, ability of a system to store an electric charge, measured by the charge that must be communicated to a body to raise its potential 1 unit. Electrostatic unit capacitance is that which requires 1 electrostatic unit of charge to raise the potential 1 electrostatic unit. The farad = $9x10^{11}$ electrostatic units. A capacitance of 1 farad requires 1 coulomb of electricity to raise its potential 1 volt. A conductor charged with a quantity Q to a potential V has a capacitance $C = Q/V$. The capacitance of a spherical conductor of radius r is $C = Kr$. The capacitance of 2 concentric spheres of radii r and r' is $C = K[rr'/(r-r')$. The capacitance of a parallel plate condenser, the area of whose plates is A and the distance between them d, is $C = KA/4\pi d$. Capacitances are given in electrostatic units if the dimensions of condensers are substituted in cm. K is the dielectric constant of the medium.

Capacitor, or condenser, electrical component used to store electric charge and to provide reactance in alternating current circuits. In essence, a capacitor consists of 2 conducting plates separated by a thin layer of insulator. When the plates are connected to the terminals of a battery, a current flows until the capacitor is "charged," with 1 plate positive and the other negative. The ability of a capacitor to hold charge, its capacitance C, is the ratio of the quantity of electricity on its plates, Q, to the potential difference between the plates, V. The electric energy stored in a capacitor is given by CV^2. The capacitance of a capacitor depends on the area of its plates, their separation, and the dielectric constant of the insulator. Small fixed capacitors are commonly made with metal-foil plates and paraffin-paper insulation; to save space, the plates and paper are rolled up into a tight cylinder. Some small capacitors have a mica dielectric. Variable capacitors used in radio tuners consist of intermeshing metal vanes separated by an air gap. In electrolytic capacitors, the dielectric is an oxide film formed on the plates by the action of a solid electrolyte.

Cape Breton Island, island in northeast Nova Scotia, 110 mi (177 km) long, up to 75 mi (121 km) wide, separated from the Canadian mainland by the Strait of Canso (since 1955 joined by a causeway).
See also: Nova Scotia.

Cape Canaveral, promontory on the eastern coast of Florida, site of the John F. Kennedy Space Center called Cape Kennedy 1963-73. It became famous with the launching of the first U.S. satellite, *Explorer 1*, in 1958, and the first manned lunar exploration in 1969. The cape was established as a national seashore in 1975.
See also: Florida; National Aeronautics Space

Cape Cod, peninsula in Barnstable County, southeast Massachusetts, surrounded by the Atlantic Ocean and Cape Cod Bay. It is 65 mi (105 km) long and up to 20 mi (32 km) in width. Site of the first Pilgrim landing in 1620, shipping, whaling, fishing, and salt production were early industries. Today the cape is famous for its cranberries, and its summer resorts such as Provincetown and Hyannis.
See also: Massachusetts.

Cape Cod Canal, sea-level channel cutting through the Cape Cod (Massachusetts) peninsula. The canal was a private commercial project built between 1909 and 1914. In 1928 it was purchased by the U.S. government and since has operated as one of the most heavily used toll-free waterways in the world. The canal, which is 17.5 miles (28 km) long, shortens the shipping route between New York and Boston by more than 75 mi (121 km).
See also: Cape Cod.

Cape Hatteras, promontory lying 30 mi (48 km) off the North Carolina coast and long known as "the graveyard of the Atlantic" because of its rocky shoals.
See also: North Carolina.

Cape Horn, southernmost tip of South America, known for its cold, stormy climate. Part of Chile, the cape's bare headland lies well south of the Strait of Magellan on Horn Island.
See also: Chile.

Cape Kennedy *See:* Cape Canaveral.

Cape May, oldest beach resort in the United States, on Cape May Peninsula, N.J.
See also: New Jersey.

Cape of Good Hope, rocky promontory near the southern tip of Africa, 30 mi (48 km) south of Cape Town, chief navigational hazard in rounding Africa. It was discovered by Bartholomeu Dias in 1488, who named it Cape of Storms. Vasco da Gama first sailed around it in 1497 into the Indian Ocean.
See also: South Africa.

Cape Province, province of South Africa, 278,465 sq mi (721,224 sq km) in area. The capital and chief city is Cape Town. A Dutch colony from 1652, the cape became British in 1806. Many Dutch settlers (Boers) migrated north and west to found independent states. Self-governing after 1872, Cape Colony joined the Union of South Africa in 1910.
See also: South Africa.

Capek, Karel (1890-1938), Czech writer whose works, known for their humor and antiauthoritarian stand, include the plays *R.U.R. (Rossum's Universal Robots,* 1920) and *The Insect Play* (1921) and the novel *The War with the Newts* (1936).

Cape Town (pop. 911,500), legislative capital of South Africa and capital of Cape of Good Hope province. Founded by the

Cape Town, South Africa lies in the shadow of Table Mountain. Cape Town is the oldest city in the country, founded in 1652.

Dutch East India Company in 1652, it has a pleasant climate, excellent beaches, attractive scenery, and the country's largest harbor. Among its major exports are gold, diamonds, fruits, wines, skins, wool, mohair, and corn.
See also: South Africa.

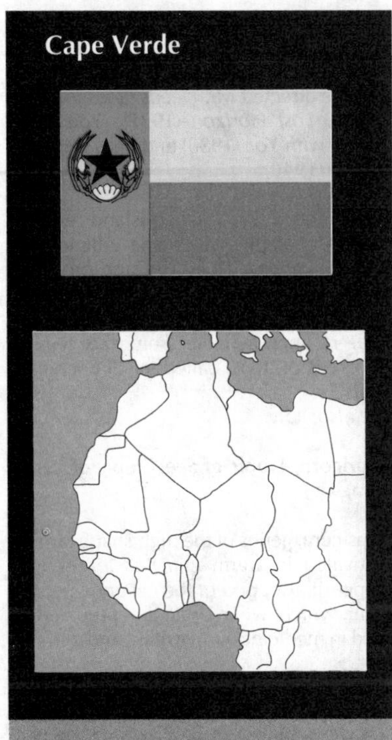

Capital:	Praia
Area:	1,557 sq mi (4,033 sq km)
Population:	337,000
Government:	republic
Independent:	1975
GNP:	U.S. $170,000,000
Per capita:	U.S. $500

Cape Verde, Republic of, independent nation in Africa, lying in the Atlantic Ocean some 400 mi (644 km) west of Senegal. The area is about 1,550 sq mi (4,015 sq km). Cape Verde consists of 10 islands and 5 islets, forming a horseshoe. The islands are volcanic—only about 20% of the land is cultivable. The climate is tropical, with a rainy season, although recently there has been cyclical drought. Over half of the population is of Portuguese and African extraction. Living standards and the rate of literacy are low. Despite a paucity of fertile land, the country is primarily agricultural. However, most food must be imported. The fishing industry provides the major source of exports. Canned fish, salt, bananas, and frozen fish are the primary exports, most going to Portugal. The Portuguese discovered the island in the 15th century. Cape Verde became a supply station for ships and a transit point during the Atlantic slave trade. Blacks from Guinea were taken to the islands to work on Portuguese plantations. Portugal ruled the islands until 1975, when they became independent.

Cape York, point of land on the northwest coast of Greenland. Well north of the Arctic Circle and extending into Baffin Bay, it was used as a base by Admiral Robert E. Peary in his North Pole explorations.
See also: Greenland.

Capella, brightest star of the constellation Auriga, the charioteer. It is a yellow star, about 10 times the diameter of our sun. In midnorthern latitudes Capella appears overhead in winter.
See also: Constellation.

Caper (genus *Capparis*), prickly Mediterranean shrub cultivated for its tender aromatic buds, which are pickled for use in sauces such as tartare sauce.

Capet, Hugh *See:* Hugh Capet.

Capetians, ruling house of France (987-1328) that laid the basis for the French state by consolidating and extending its power. Hugh Capet, founder of the dynasty, was elected king in 987. Though his rule and territory were limited, his successors gradually increased their land and control. Under the Capetian dynasty many basic administration characteristics of the French monarchy were established, including the parliaments (courts) and the States-General (national assembly).
See also: Hugh Capet; Louis (IX); Philip (II; IV of France).

Cap-Haitien (pop. 70,500), seaport on the north coast of Haiti and the country's second largest city. Under French rule it was the capital of the colony ("the Paris of the Antilles"). Today it has less than 10% of the population of Port-au-Prince, the capital.
See also: Haiti.

The port of Mindelo on the island of São Vicente, Cape Verde

Capillarity, or capillary action, rise or fall of a liquid within a narrow tube (less than 0.02 m/0.5 mm in diameter) when one end is placed beneath the surface of a liquid, caused by its surface tension, which is due to the forces of attraction between the molecules of the liquid. Where, in the case of adhesion, these forces are weaker than the attraction of the molecules for the walls of the tube (as with water surrounded by a glass tube), a concave meniscus is formed (that is, the water level is higher wherever the water touches the tube). Surface tension pulls the rest of the surface upwards, and the level rises until the weight of the column balances the surface tension. In the case of cohesion, with a liquid like mercury, where the molecules of the liquid are more strongly attracted to each other than to the walls of the vessel, the reverse takes place and the level falls. Plants obtain food and water from the soil by capillary action, and it also helps the flow of sap up the stem. Blotting paper, towels, and sponges soak up moisture by capillarity.

Capillary, minute blood vessel that connects the arteries and veins. In general, the capillaries comprise fine tubes, approximately 0.004 in (0.1 mm) in diameter, the same order of size as the red blood corpuscles. The capillary walls are one cell thick and arranged in a network throughout every tissue of the body. Here, the primary functions of the circulation—the exchange of gases, nutrients, metabolites, and heat—take place.
See also: Circulatory system.

Capital, in economics, those goods that are used in production, such as plant and equipment (fixed capital) and raw materials, components, and semifinished goods (circulating capital), as opposed to goods intended for immediate consumption. To classical economists, 3 main factors of production were capital, labor, and land. Modern economists add management skill and human capital (education and training). The decision to invest in capital is determined by the cost and availability of labor and natural resources and the cost of capital (e.g., interest on the money used to buy equipment). Modern industrial countries are highly capitalized, but among the less developed countries the lack of capital is often acute.

Capitalism, economic system in which goods and services are provided by the efforts of private individuals and groups (firms) who own and control the means of production, compete with one another, and aim to make a profit. The concept has several overlapping senses, but the idea of private ownership of the means of production and their employment in the search of profit are common to all of them. Capitalism is usually regarded as having

U.S. Capitol

developed through a number of stages, beginning with *commercial capitalism,* under which large merchants came to dominate trade. This was succeeded by *industrial capitalism,* dominated by the owners of factories and mines, and then by *finance capitalism,* in which control passed into the hands of bankers and financiers, who exerted indirect control over industries they did not manage in person. Reference is sometimes made to a fourth form—*state capitalism*—defined by Lenin as a system under which the State owns and uses the means of production in the interests of the class that controls the State. A fifth term, *welfare capitalism,* is used to describe capitalist economies in which there is an increased element of state intervention, either by welfare programs or by taking responsibility for maintaining full employment.
Socialists criticize the system on the grounds that in practice it produces luxuries for the rich rather than necessities for all. Capitalism is defended by the argument that an economic system based on private ownership and investment, if left to operate with a minimum of state interference, will be the most efficient method of raising production, distributing scarce resources rationally, and balancing supply with demand.

Truman Capote

Capital punishment (from Latin *caput,* "head"), originally, death by decapitation; now, execution in general. Historically, there has been a wide variety of death penalties, but in the United States electrocution is the most common, followed by lethal gas and hanging. It has long been debated whether capital punishment deters serious crime or is only a form of revenge. Its use has been declining recently as belief in rehabilitation has grown. In most civilized countries, capital punishment has been discontinued. But those who believe that capital punishment is necessary as a deterrent see their argument supported by recent statistics showing that violent crime has been increasing. In the U.S. it is the state government that determines the use of capital punishment.

Capitol, U.S., building in Washington, D.C. that houses the Congress of the United States. The U.S. Senate occupies the north wing of the Capitol, and the U.S. House of Representatives the south.
The Capitol is a brilliant white structure in the classical style. It occupies about 3 1/2 acres of high ground known as Capitol Hill (a term also used for Congress) in the center of Washington. The most striking feature of the building is its great white-painted iron dome, 288 ft (88 m) high and 135 1/2 ft (41 m) in diameter, with a statue representing freedom on the top. William Thornton designed the Capitol in 1792 and construction began in 1793 when President George Washington laid the cornerstone. Disagreements and war repeatedly delayed completion until 1906, when the wings were finished. In the late 1950s, the central portico of the east façade was extended, adding 2 more acres of floor space.
See also: Congress of the United States.

Capitol Hill *See:* Washington, D.C.

Capone, Al (1899-1947), U.S. gangster. He became head of a lucrative Chicago crime syndicate in the 1920s, and was involved in many gang murders, including the St. Valentine's Day Massacre. Because of the difficulty in securing evidence against him, he was eventually convicted only of income-tax evasion (1931).
See also: Saint Valentine's Day Massacre.

Capote, Truman (1924-1984), U.S. writer. His best-known works are *Breakfast at Tiffany's* (1958) and *In Cold Blood* (1965). His earlier works include *Other Voices, Other Rooms* (1948) and *The Grass Harp* (1951). He was also coauthor of the motion picture *Beat the Devil,* cowrote the screenplay for *The Innocents,* and adapted some of his stories for television.

Capp, Al (1909-79), U.S. cartoonist, creator of the comic strip "Li'l Abner." The *New York Mirror* first published this famous comic about the residents of "Dogpatch U.S.A." in 1934. The characters entertained readers and allowed Capp to develop social commentary on the current events and celebrities of his time.

Capra, Frank (1897-), U.S. film director and 3-time Academy Award winner. With a gift for gentle satire and comic improvisation, he directed *Mr. Deeds Goes to Town* (1936), *Lost Horizon* (1937), *You Can't Take It with You* (1938) and *It's a Wonderful Life* (1946).

Capri (pop. 7,500), Italian island resort in the Bay of Naples, site of the Villa Iovis of Roman Emperor Tiberius. Capri produces olive oil and wine, but its main industry is tourism. Anacapri, at the island's western end, is approachable from the sea by hundreds of steps, called the "Phoenician Stairs."
See also: Italy.

Capricorn, Tropic of *See:* Tropic of Capricorn.

Capsicum, genus of the nightshade family, cultivated in warm climates for its fruit (pepper); also, pod of the cayenne pepper plant, which, when dried and prepared, is used in medicine as an irritant and a stimulant.

Captain Kidd *See:* Kidd, William.

Capuchin (*Cebus capucinus*), small tree-dwelling monkey with a long, prehensile tail. Native to South America, capuchins are popular as pets in North America and Europe because of their great intelligence. They are the traditional organ-grinder's monkey. Capuchins live in troops and feed on fruit, shoots, and small animals.

Capuchins, Roman Catholic order of friars and an independent branch of the Franciscans. Founded (1525) by Matteo di Basico, a Franciscan who sought a return to the simplicity of St. Francis's life, the order is distinguished by the pointed hood, or *capuccino.*
See also: Franciscans.

Capybara (*Hydrochoerus capybara*), world's largest rodent. It looks like a large guinea pig, weighing up to 120 lb (54 kg) and standing 21 in (53 cm) at the shoulder.

Capybara

The fur is coarse and grey-brown. Capybaras are found in wet areas of northern South America where they live a largely aquatic life, swimming with only their high-set nose, eyes, and ears showing.

Car *See:* Automobile; Railroad.

Caracal, or desert lynx (*Felis caracal*), medium-sized cat of Africa and southern Asia that is distinguished by a fawn coat, long legs, and long black ear tufts. It lives in grassland, bush, or rocky country and feeds on small animals.

Caracara, any of a variety of long-legged South American hawks with long narrow wings, related to the falcon. The patch of bare skin at the base of the bill, a characteristic shared with vultures, is an adaptation for carrion-eating, but caracaras also hunt for live prey and will eat fruit. They rob other birds of their food, and the red-throated caracara raids wasps' nests. The Guadeloupe caracara was exterminated before 1911.

Caracas (pop. 3,248,000), Venezuelan capital, near the Caribbean Sea at an altitude of 3,020 ft (920 m). Founded in 1567 by Diego de Losada, it was the birthplace of Simón Bolívar (1783). Independence from Spain was achieved in 1821, as part of the Republic of Gran Colombia. In 1829 Caracas became the capital of independent Venezuela. After World War II and the discovery of oil in Maracaibo, Caracas greatly expanded. Industries include textiles, cement, steel products, paper, leatherwork, and furniture.
See also: Venezuela.

Caramanlis, Constantine (1907-), Greek premier (1955-63, 1974-80) and president (1980-85). Following a dispute with then King Paul, he resigned as premier and went into exile in Paris (1963). He returned 11 years later when the military junta ruling Greece fell because of the Cyprus crisis. He helped restore constitutional government and his party, New Democracy, won a big victory in 1975. The republican form of government he advocated was also approved, and in 1980 he was elected president.
See also: Greece.

Carat, measure of the weight of gems and pearls or of the purity of precious metals. The name comes from the dried seeds of the carob tree, which were used to weigh gold in Africa and diamonds in India. The value of the carat varied from 190 mg to almost 210 mg until 1913, when a standard carat of 200 mg was adopted. As a measure of purity, 1 carat represents 1 part in 24 of the precious metal. Thus 22-carat gold contains 22 parts of gold and 2 of other metal.

Caravaggio, Michelangelo Merisi da (1573-1610), Italian Baroque painter who achieved startling and dramatic effects with a technique of shadow and light called *chiaroscuro.* Among his finest works are the *Death of the Virgin*, the *Fortune Teller*, and *Supper at Emmaus.*
See also: Baroque.

Caraway (*Carum carvi*), biennial or perennial plant of the carrot family, the seed of which is used for flavoring medicinal purposes. The hollow, furrowed, angular, branched stem grows in the second year from a white, carrot-shaped root. The leaves are deeply incised, the small white or yellow flowers form a flat, round cluster, and the fruit is dark brown, oblong, flattened, and 2-seeded.

Caraway, Hattie Ophelia Wyatt (1878-1950), first woman elected to the U.S. Senate. Although Caraway was appointed by the governor of Arkansas to take her husband's place in the Senate when he died in 1931, she won a special election in 1932. She served 14 years in the Senate and was the first woman to head a Senate committee and to preside over a Senate session.

Carbide, any chemical compound of carbon and a metal. Calcium carbide is one of the important ones, a source of acetylene, while carbides of silicon, tungsten, and other elements are known for being hard, strong, and resistant to high temperatures.
See also: Calcium carbide.

Carbine, short, lightweight rifle most useful to soldiers fighting from tanks and other cramped spaces. It fires ammunition heavier than a pistol's but lighter than the larger assault rifles.

Carbohydrate, any of a group of chemical compounds—including sugars, starches, and cellulose—containing carbon, hydrogen, and oxygen only, with the ratio of hydrogen to oxygen atoms usually 2:1. Carbohydrates provide the chief source of energy in most diets; about 50% of the total calories in the diet of a prosperous industrial community come from carbohydrates. In a poor agricultural community, living largely on cereals, the proportion is higher and may be as much as 85%. The chief dietary carbohydrate is starch, which is present in all cereal grains, roots, and tubers.

Carbolic acid, or phenol (C_6H_5OH), first chemical to be used as an antiseptic. Though poisonous and corrosive to the skin, in dilute form it is lethal to microorganisms, without many undesirable side effects on the patient.
See also: Antiseptic.

Carbon, chemical element, symbol C; for physical constants see Periodic Table. Carbon is nonmetallic and was discovered in ancient times. It occurs in 3 allotropic forms: amorphous (as in coal or charcoal), graphite, and diamond. All living things contain carbon, which forms more compounds than any other element. Organic chemistry, the study of carbon compounds, is therefore a major field in biology and medicine.

Caracara

Carbon 14 *See:* Radiocarbon.

Carbonate, salt of carbonic acid that contains the carbonate ion CO_3=. They are produced by reacting a base, such as metal oxide or hydroxide, with carbonic acid, which is formed by dissolving carbon dioxide in water. Calcium carbonate is very abundant in nature, occurring as limestone, chalk, and marble. The mineral dolomite is a mixture of calcium and magnesium carbonates. Commercially, the most important carbonate is sodium carbonate, also called soda ash and washing soda. Carbonates are decomposed by acids, carbon dioxide being given off. Heating carbonates also drives off carbon dioxide, leaving the metal oxide.

Carbon bisulfide *See:* Carbon disulfide.

Carbon black *See:* Carbon.

Carbon dating *See:* Radiocarbon.

Carbon dioxide (CO_2), colorless, odorless, incombustible gas, consisting of 1 carbon atom and 2 oxygen atoms. Carbon dioxide is formed during respiration (as a waste product of the body), combustion, and organic decomposition. The air we breathe is 0.03% carbon dioxide. It is used by plants during photosynthesis.
See also: Photosynthesis.

Carbon disulfide (CS_2), clear, inflammable liquid chemical compound, composed of 1 carbon atom and 2 sulfur atoms, used in the manufacture of viscose rayon and cellophane, as a solvent for fats, rubber, resins, waxes, and sulfur, and in matches, fumigants, and pesticides. It is a typical toxic industrial chemical. The principal route of exposure in humans is by inhalation; skin contact is much less significant, and other routes are of negligible importance. Carbon disulfide is distributed in an organism through the bloodstream. Readily soluble in fats and lipids and bind-

ing to amino acids and proteins, it disappears rapidly from the bloodstream and has a high affinity for all tissues and organs. Hyperactive poisoning caused by massive short-term exposure to high concentrations of carbon disulfide is characterized by sudden coma and eventual death. Cases of poisoning due to relatively short exposures to concentrations of 3,000-5,000 mg per cubic meter are predominantly associated with psychiatric and neurological symptoms: (1) extreme irritability, (2) uncontrolled anger, (3) rapid mood changes, (4) hallucinations, (5) paranoia and suicidal tendencies, and (6) manic delirium. Other symptoms include: (1) memory defects, (2) severe insomnia, (3) nightmares, (4) fatigue, (5) loss of appetite, and (6) gastrointestinal problems. Exposure over many years may produce chronic damage to the brain at first associated with psychological and behavioral changes, later with neurological changes, both in the brain and peripheral nerves. Changes in the blood vessels due to exposure are similar to those of atherosclerosis and mainly affect the arteries supplying the brain and heart muscle. Incidence of coronary heart disease is disproportionately high in exposed workers.
See also: Sulfide.

Carboniferous, collective term used mainly in Europe for the combined Mississippian and Pennsylvanian periods of the geological time scale, 345-280 million years ago.

Carbon monoxide (CO), colorless, odorless, very poisonous gas that burns with a pale blue flame and is a component of coal gas, exhaust fumes, and most smoke (including cigarette smoke). Inhalation of carbon monoxide causes dizziness, headache, and convulsions, and can lead to brain damage, paralysis, and death.

Carbon tetrachloride (CCl_4), colorless liquid with a distinctive smell, used mainly as a solvent. It dissolves fats and oils, and can be used as a dry-cleaning fluid. Widely used in industry to dissolve resins, rubber, and many other organic chemicals, it must be handled carefully. It is not inflammable, but forms highly poisonous substances when heated in a flame. Breathing the fumes over a long period can itself cause kidney and liver damage, so carbon tetrachloride should be used only in well-ventilated places. Carbon tetrachloride is manufactured by passing chlorine gas over red-hot coke.

Carborundum, commercial name for silicon carbide (SiC), widely used abrasive and one of the hardest substances known. Carborundum has a very high melting point (about 4,892F/2,700C) and is used in the manufacture of heat-resistant materials. It conducts electricity and is used in electronic equipment. Carborundum is found in a variety of colors, ranging from blue-black to green, all with a lustrous sheen. A very pure colorless form also exists. Carborundum is widely found over the earth's surface and has also been found in meteorites that have landed on earth. It was first synthesized in 1891 by the American chemist Edward Acheson, who heated coke and clay in a furnace at very high temperatures.

Carbuncle, infection under the full thickness of the skin caused by the pus-forming germ *Staphylococcus.* It produces a large infected area from which the pus escapes by making numerous openings for itself through the skin, producing a sieve-like appearance.

Carburetor, device that mixes air and gasoline in the correct proportion for efficient combustion (about 15:1 by weight) in internal combustion engines (as in automobiles). In its simplest form a carburetor is a tube that is constructed at one point into a narrow throat or venturi. As air flows through the venturi, it speeds up and its pressure decreases. Gasoline from a reservoir (the float chamber) is piped to the venturi and sucked into the airstream. The fuel mixture then passes through a "butterfly" throttle valve into the engine cylinders. The throttle valve controls the rate at which the fuel mixture enters the engine and therefore the engine speed. A butterfly choke valve is fitted in the air intake to the carburetor to cut off the air supply when the engine is started from cold.
See also: Gasoline engine.

Carcassonne (pop. 41,200), city in southern France, southeast of Toulouse. Carcassonne is divided by the Aude River into the old town (Cité) and the newer Ville Basse. The old town is a medieval walled city whose architecture has made Carcassonne a tourist attraction.
See also: France.

Carcinogen *See:* Cancer.

Carcinoma, malignant tumor or new growth (neoplasm) derived from epithelial and glandular tissues, a form of cancer.
See also: Cancer.

Cardamom (*Elettaria cardamomum*), perennial plant the seed of which is used as a spice and for medicinal purposes. The simple erect stem of the plant grows to a height of 6-10 ft (1.8-3 m) from a thumb-thick, creeping rootstock. The leaves are lanceolate (spear-shaped) and dark green. The small, yellowish flowers grow in loose groups on prostrate flower stems. The fruit is a 3-celled capsule holding up to 18 seeds. These are useful in controlling flatulence, but they are usually used to increase the efficacy of other remedies.

Cárdenas, Lázaro (1895-1970), Mexican soldier and politician. He joined the Mexican revolutionary forces in 1913, rising to the rank of general. President from 1934 to 1940, he initiated many radical reforms, including the expropriation of land and nationalization of foreign-owned oil companies.
See also: Mexico.

Card games, games played with rectangular cards marked with number (rank) and symbol (suit). Playing cards probably developed from small stones, scratched with various symbols, used in early cultures for religious ceremonies and magical purposes. These pebbles were eventually used for competitive games, often involving gambling. Cards were used in China in the 10th century A.D. By about the 13th century they had been introduced in Europe by travelers and gypsies from the East. Early cards varied greatly in design. The 14th century Italian tarocchi or tarot deck had 78 cards that included 22 picture cards bearing mainly religious illustrations, and 4 suits each of 14 plain cards. Today, many different decks exist, but the most popular contains 52 cards divided into 4 suits. First used in 14th-century Europe, this 52-deck was introduced to Britain, modified, and eventually popularized by the invention of games requiring such a deck. As games became more sophisticated, it became desirable to have written rules. The English writer Edmond Hoyle (1672-1769) produced a rule book giving details of many games.

Cardiac *See:* Heart.

Cardiff (pop. 269,500), city and seaport near the mouth of the Taff River in southern Wales. The town was established in the 11th century around a Norman castle. Development was gradual until the discovery of coal in the valleys to the north made Cardiff a natural outlet for the export of coal, iron, and steel. Shipping of coal, coke, and steel is still the major industry; there are massive iron and steel works, and copper and tin are also produced. Flour milling and manufacture of chemicals and paper are valuable secondary industries. The city is the administrative center for Wales, and has important educational and cultural institutions including the National Museum of Wales.
See also: Wales.

Cardigan Welsh corgi, breed of dog first raised in Wales. The name derives from the Welsh words for "dwarf dog". The Cardigan Welsh corgi stands about 12 in (30 cm) high. Used for centuries to herd sheep, the corgi makes an affectionate and spirited pet.

Cardinal, or redbird (*Cardinalis cardinalis*), familiar songbird of the finch family, found in North America. It is about 9 in (23 cm) long, with a pointed crest and red beak. The male is scarlet with a black bib and face; the female is a dull brown.
See also: Roman Catholic Church.

Cardinal, hierarchically high-ranking official of the Roman Catholic Church, whose principal duties include the election of the pope, counseling the papacy, and administrating Church government. Cardinals are chosen by the pope and have the title of Eminence. Their insignia consists of scarlet cassock, sash, biretta (skullcap) and hat, and ring. There are three orders: cardinal bishops of the sees near Rome; cardinal priests (cardinal archbishops) with responsibilities outside the district of Rome; and cardinal deacons, who have been titular bishops since 1962. Cardinal bishops and cardinal deacons are members of the Curia, the central administrative body of the Church. They head the tribunals, or the courts of the Church. Together, the cardinals form the Sacred College, which elects the pope. The cardinalate originated in early 6th-century Rome.

Cardinal

Cardinal flower, tall plant (*Lobelia cardinalis*) native to North and Central America. Cardinal flowers thrive in wet soil. Their leafy stems grow up to 5 ft (1.5 m) and bear spikes of bright red flowers.

Cardiology, science of the heart, including the study of its diseases and functions.
See also: Heart.

Cardiopulmonary resuscitation (CPR), restoration of hearbeat and breathing by external cardiac massage and mouth-to-mouth breathing.
See also: First Aid.

Cardozo, Benjamin Nathan (1870-1938), U.S. jurist and Supreme Court justice (1932-38) after an impressive career at the bar and in the New York courts. His many significant decisions reflect his view that the courts should not merely interpret the law but help create it, particularly in adapting it to changing social conditions.
See also: Supreme Court of the United

Cards *See:* Card games.

Carducci, Glosuè (1835-1907), Italian scholar and patriotic poet. His *Hymn to Satan* (1863) is an anticlerical political satire; the *Barbarian Odes* (1877-89) are perhaps his best work. He won the 1906 Nobel Prize for literature.

CARE (Cooperative for American Relief to Everywhere, Inc.), charity founded in 1945, initially for aid to Europe but now operating worldwide. MEDICO (Medical International Cooperation Organization), a medical relief agency, became part of CARE in 1962.

Caribbean Sea, warm oceanic basin off Central America, partly enclosed by islands. The waters of the Caribbean flow into the Gulf of Mexico and thence into the Atlantic Ocean through the narrow strait of Florida. They create the warm current known as the Gulf Stream, which reaches Europe. The lands bordering the Caribbean have a warm and humid climate, with almost continuously high temperatures. The Caribbean was the route taken by the Spanish treasure ships, and became known as the "Spanish Main." It was an area overrun with buccaneers and fiercely disputed by France, England, Spain, and later the United States. At the end of the 19th century U.S. control over the Caribbean area was officially recognized. The building of the Panama Canal increased the importance of this "Mediterranean of the West."

Caribou (*Rangifer tarandus*), the only member of the deer family (Cervidae) in which both sexes bear antlers. They were at one time essential food animals for Native Americans of Canada. They live wild in Canada and Siberia, while the semi-domesticated reindeer, a subspecies, live in Greenland and Scandinavia. They can travel over boggy or snow-covered ground and live on lichen, dry grass, and twigs.

Caribs, Native American tribe encountered by the Spanish conquerors of America in the 16th century. They inhabited the islands of the Lesser Antilles in the Caribbean (which was named after them) and parts of the South American mainland, notably the Guianas. The Caribs grew a variety of crops and hunted with clubs, spears, bows, and blowguns. They were strongly independent and formed no political bonds between their own groups. Their raids on other tribes—including the more peaceful Arawaks—whom they dispossessed of their land, were made in large dugout canoes, and their conquests were celebrated by killing and eating the male captives. After Spanish settlement of the Antilles in 1527, most Caribs were exterminated except for some on the island of Aruba.

Caricature, sketch exaggerating or distorting characteristics of its subject for satirical purposes. It became an established form by the 18th century, in the hands of Francisco de Goya in Spain and William Hogarth in England, followed by Thomas Rowlandson, the Cruikshanks, and John Tenniel, and the savagely witty Honoré Daumier in France. Today, artists such as David Levine and Albert Hirschfeld continue the tradition in the United States.

Carillon, musical instrument, usually permanently set in a bell-tower, consisting of a series of bells on which melodies and simple harmonies are played from a keyboard and pedal console much like that of an organ. Some carillons are played automatically by a pegged rotating drum that operates the bell clappers or hammers. Modern instruments are electrically operated, and some do not have cast bells, but are completely electronic. Carillons

The island of Martinique in the Caribbean Sea

originated in the Low Countries, and the old cities of Belgium and Holland have many notable examples, the oldest being the 24-bell carillon (1554) at the Rijksmuseum, Amsterdam.

Carleton, Sir Guy, 1st Baron Dorchester (1724-1808), English soldier and governor. He was responsible for the Quebec Act of 1774, which guaranteed the French the right to speak French and to practice Roman Catholicism. During the American Revolution, he led the defense of Quebec (1775) against Benedict Arnold and later captured Crown Point, N.Y. (1776). In 1782-83 he was commander-in-chief of the British army in North America; he was governor of Quebec (1786-91, 1793-96) and governor-general of Canada (1793).
See also: Quebec Act.

Carl Gustaf (1946-), king of Sweden (Charles XV Gustavus) from 1973. Carl Gustaf's father died when his son was less than a year old, and Carl Gustaf therefore succeeded his grandfather, Gustavus VI (Gustaf Adolf).
See also: Sweden.

Carlos, Juan *See:* Juan Carlos I.

Carlota, Empress *See:* Maximilian.

Caribou

Carlsbad Caverns National Park, national park in southeastern New Mexico. Its major site is a series of limestone caves about 60 million years old, among the largest caverns in the world. The caverns have spectacular stalagmite formations. The Big Room is a single chamber 1,800 ft (550 m) long, 1,100 ft (335 m) wide, and 225 ft (78 m) at its highest point. Several million bats still inhabit the caverns, which were designated a national park in 1930.
See also: National Parks

Carlyle, Thomas (1795-1881), Scottish essayist and historian. His writings greatly influenced literature and political and religious thought in mid-19th-century Britain. Carlyle was much influenced by Johann Wolfgang von Goethe, whose *Wilhelm Meister* he translated (1824). In 1826 he married Jane Welsh, who greatly helped his literary career. At her farm near Dumfries he wrote *Sartor Resartus* (The Tailor Retailored, 1833-34). Moving to London (1834), he wrote his famous *French Revolution* (1837), which won him immediate recognition. Carlyle believed that progress was due to "heroes" in history. He scorned the idea of democratic equality, exaggerated the importance of individual great men (*On Heroes, Hero-Worship and the Heroic in History*, 1841), and failed to realize the dangers inherent in hero-worship. His capacity for throwing new light on familiar subjects was shown by *Cromwell's Letters and Speeches* (1845), which many regard as his historical masterpiece, and *Frederick the Great* (1858-65), his largest work.

Carman, (William) Bliss (1861-1929), Canadian poet and essayist. His work includes *Low Tide on Grand Pré* (1893) and *Songs from Vagabondia* (1894, 1896, 1901), volumes of love and nature poems.
See also: Transcendentalism.

Carmel-by-the-Sea, or Carmel (pop. 4,239), town in California situated on Carmel Bay south of Monterey. Long an art and literature center that has attempted to maintain its quiet charm free from modern encroachments, Carmel is especially well known as the home of such artists as Henry Miller, James D. Nash, and Joan Baez.
See also: California.

Andrew Carnegie

Carmelites, friars of Our Lady of Mount Carmel, a religious order of the Roman Catholic Church. It is named for Mount Carmel, in Israel, where it originated about 1150. The Carmelites' strict rule was based on silence and solitude, but it was slightly relaxed by the English prior, Saint Simon Stock. The order's typical clothing consists of a brown habit and scapular, with a white mantle and black hood.
See also: Roman Catholic Church.

Carmichael, Hoagy (Hoagland Howard Carmichael; 1899-1981), U.S. songwriter. His 1929 ballad "Star Dust" became a popular classic. Other compositions include "Georgia on My Mind" (1930), "Lazybones" (1933), and "The Nearness of You" (1940). He appeared as a pianist in several films including *To Have and Have Not* (1944), and his song "In the Cool, Cool, Cool of the Evening" won an Academy Award in 1951.

Carmichael, Stokely (1941-), U.S. Black Power leader. Prominent in the civil rights movement in the 1960s, he then advocated violent revolution and spent some time in exile in Algeria. He later argued for the use of political and economic power to attain African American demands.

Carnap, Rudolf (1891-1970), German-U.S. logician and philosopher of science, a leading figure in the Vienna Circle and founder of logical positivism, who later turned to studying problems of linguistic philosophy and the role of probability in inductive reasoning.
See also: Positivism.

Carnarvon, George Edward Stanhope Molyneux Herbert, 5th Earl of (1866-1923), English Egyptologist. His excavations with Howard Carter in the Valley of Kings area revealed tombs of the 12th and 18th dynasties and, in Nov. 1922, the tomb of Tutankhamen.
See also: Tutankhamen.

Carnation, flower popular for buttonholes and in horticulture, subspecies of pink (*Dianthus caryophyllus*). Each carnation has a cluster of flowers, which are pink in the wild state. They have been cultivated since the time of ancient Greece, and their cultivation has become such a popular pastime that the American Carnation Society was established in 1891.

Carneades (213?-129? B.C.), Greek philosopher who rejected the notion of an absolute standard of truth. He founded and led the New Academy at Athens, and although he left no writings, his teachings were preserved by the philosopher Cleitomachus.
See also: Philosophy.

Carnegie, Andrew (1835-1919), U.S. steel magnate and philanthropist. A Scottish emigrant, Carnegie rose from bobbin-boy in a cotton factory to railroad manager and then steel producer at a time of great demand. He believed that the duty of the rich is to distribute their surplus wealth, and in 1900 he began to set up a vast number of charitable foundations and educational institutions.

Carnegie, Dale (1888-1955), U.S. author and lecturer whose *How to Win Friends and Influence People* (1936) became the best-selling nonfiction work of modern times, second only to the Bible. He offered courses in effective speaking and human relations in more than 750 U.S. cities and 15 foreign countries.

Carnegie Foundations, philanthropic organizations established by Andrew Carnegie to advance education, research, and world peace. The Carnegie Institution of Washington, D.C., supports research in physical and biological sciences. The Carnegie Foundation for the Advancement of Teaching works to improve higher education, and the Carnegie Corporation of New York endows projects in preschool education and education for the disadvantaged. The Carnegie Endowment for International Peace promotes peace through studies of international law and diplomacy. These and other organizations set a pattern for other major institutions, such as the Ford and Rockefeller foundations.
See also: Carnegie, Andrew.

Carnelian, or cornelian, one of the chalcedony group of crystalline quartz forms. Carnelian is typically red, but is sometimes yellow or brown, the latter kind being the most precious and known as sard. Used in jewelry, the stones are often artificially colored by heating and dyeing with iron compounds.
See also: Chalcedony.

Carnival, term for any festive season with processions and masquerades, and particularly for the period preceding Lent. Historically, carnival can be traced back at least to the Dionysian festivals of Athens in the 6th century B.C., when a float dedicated to the god was escorted through the city, and to the Saturnalia of ancient Rome. The word *carnival* may have been derived from the Latin *carnem levare* (to put meat aside), a reference to Lenten abstinence. The Christian Church, unable to suppress the traditional pagan festivals, had to adapt and recognize them. Italy, Rome, Venice, and Florence have long been famed for their carnivals. Rio de Janeiro in Brazil, Nice in France, and Cologne in Germany are still noted carnival centers. The festivities traditionally reach their climax on the last night, Mardi Gras (Shrove Tuesday).

Carnivore, order of flesh-eating mammals with daggerlike canine teeth, cutting cheek teeth, and sharp claws. Bears, dogs, cats, hyenas, foxes, and racoons are land carnivores; seals, sea lions, and walruses are fin-footed aquatic carnivores.

Carnivorous plant, or insectivorous plant, term used for plants that have mechanisms for trapping and digesting insects. Over 500 known species of these plants are divided into 6 unrelated families. The diverse group ranges in size from microscopic fungi to the large Pitcher Fungi.

Carnot, Lazare Nicolas Marguerite (1753-1823), French soldier and politician, "Organizer of Victory" for the Revolutionary armies. He later served as minister of war under Napoleon I, resigning in 1800.

Carnot, Nicolas Léonard Sadi (1796-1832), French physicist. Seeking to improve the efficiency of the steam engine, he devised the Carnot cycle (1824), on the basis of which Lord Kelvin and R. J. E. Clausius formulated the second law of thermodynamics. The Carnot cycle demon-

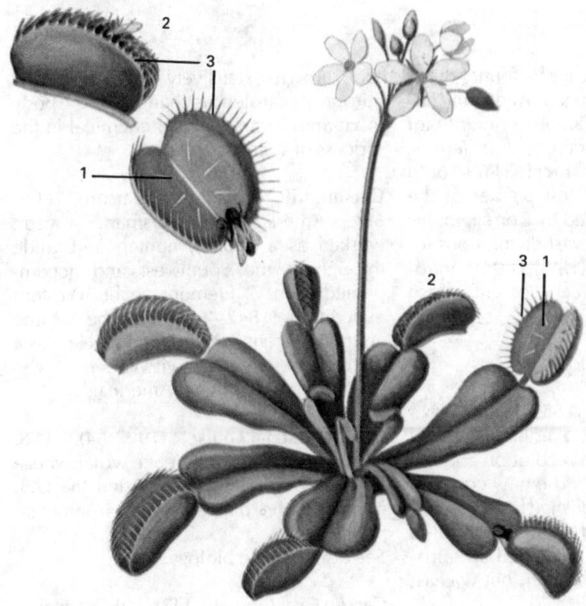

Venus's flytrap is a carnivorous plant which has special leaves for trapping insects. Flies are attracted by a sweet-smelling fluid and land on the leaf (1). This triggers one of the sensitive bristles (3), causing the leaf to close within seconds (2).

strates that the efficiency of a heat engine working at maximum thermal efficiency does not depend on its mode of operation, but only on the temperatures at which it accepts and discards heat energy.
See also: Physics.

Carnotite, yellow mineral found in sandstone and limestone deposits in the Colorado Plateau. Carnotite is a valuable source of radium, uranium, and vanadium.

Caro, Joseph ben Ephraim (1488-1575), Jewish Talmudist and philosopher whose codification of Jewish law, the *Shulhan Arukh* (1565), became the standard authority. Caro's family were Spanish Jews who settled in Constantinople; in later life he became a leader of the Jewish community in Palestine.
See also: Philosophy; Talmud.

Carob, evergreen tree (*Ceratonia siliqua*) native to the Mediterranean but also cultivated elsewhere. The carob, a member of the pea family, has pods that contain a sticky pulp that tastes similar to chocolate. Roasted and ground, it can be used as a chocolate substitute. Untreated carob pods are used as feed for cattle and horses.

Carol, name of 2 kings of Romania. **Carol I** (1839-1914), Romania's first king, brought economic development but no solution to political problems. **Carol II** (1893-1953) became king in 1930. He established a royal dictatorship to counter the growing Fascist movement, but after losing territory to the Axis powers in World War II, he abdicated in 1940 and went into exile.
See also: Romania.

Carol, cheerful song sung at Christmas, but once also performed (as a dance song) at other festive seasons. Some carols have pagan origins, and some of the older carols such as "The Holly and the Ivy" (c.1710) have a folklore element. Certain 19th-century Christmas hymns now rank as carols. Among the oldest is the "Boar's Head Carol," in the collection printed by Wynkyn de Worde (1521). The German *Weihnachtslieder* (Christmas Eve Songs) and French *Noëls* have also provided carols.

Caroline Islands, volcanic islands in the Pacific Ocean, administered as a trust territory by the United States. The 900 islands are inhabited mainly by Malays, with some Japanese, Chinese, and Americans. The Spanish claimed the islands in 1696 and in 1899 sold them to Germany. After World War I they became a Japanese mandate and were invaded by U.S. troops in World War II.

Carolingian, Frankish dynasty founded in the 7th century by Pepin of Landen, whose successors ruled as mayors under the Merovingians until A.D. 751, when Pepin III made himself king. His son Charlemagne, crowned emperor in 800, reigned in the golden age of the Carolingians. His son Louis (814-840) and the Treaty of Verdun (843) partitioned the empire.
See also: Charlemagne; Pepin the Short.

Carolingian art, style created in France and western Germany in the late 8th and 9th centuries. The style, named for Charlemagne, who was crowned emperor of the restored Holy Roman Empire in 800, was an attempt to revive the arts of antiquity. Instead of the abstract geometric patterns and mythical animals used by artists of this region in the preceding centuries, Carolingian artists reintroduced the human figure in natural settings. Carolingian church architecture adopted the basilican plan of the early Christian era, adding towers, chapels, and crypts. Abbots built monasteries in which the church and living and working quarters were joined by covered walks. Artists also worked in metal, manuscript illumination, and ivory carving, combining the ornamental motifs of Anglo-Saxon and Irish art with figures from antiquity. Among the era's most important works still in existence are Charlemagne's chapel in Aachen, West Germany, built in 805, and the Utrecht Psalter, a religious manuscript written in France about 830.
See also: Charlemagne.

Carp (*Cyprinus carpio*), freshwater, bottom-feeding fish native to Asia but now found in Europe and America. It grows up to 3 1/3 ft (1 m) and 60 lb (27 kg) in weight and has a long dorsal fin and 4 barbels (whiskers) around the mouth.

Carpaccio, Vittore (c.1460-1526), Venetian Renaissance narrative painter, influenced by Gentile Bellini. A major work is the cycle of 9 paintings of the *Legend of St. Ursula* (1490-95), typical in its atmospheric use of color and meticulous detail to create fantasy settings.
See also: Renaissance.

Carpal tunnel syndrome, sensation of pins-and-needles or numbness in the thumb and first two fingers, plus pain in the wrist, in the palm, or in the forearm. The carpal tunnel is the part of the wrist that encloses all the wrist tendons and the median nerve, one of the main nerves supplying the hand. This syndrome results from the compression of the median nerve when the fibrous tunnel becomes swollen. This may occur during pregnancy when the tissues are more likely to swell. The syndrome is relatively common, and is seen more often in women. A mild condition that usually responds rapidly to treatment, it can become chronic, and then surgery to remove swollen or damaged tissue may have to be considered. The condition is common among typists and keyboarders.

Carpathian Mountains, European mountain range, about 900 mi (1,448 km) long, an extension of the Alps running from Czechoslovakia through Poland, the USSR, and Rumania. Gerlachovka (8,737 ft/2,663 m) is the highest point.
See also: Alps.

Carpenter, M. Scott (1925-), second U.S. astronaut to circle the earth in a spacecraft. Carpenter served in the Navy in both World War II (1930-45) and the Korean War (1950-53), becoming a test pilot in 1954 and completing Naval Air Intelligence School in 1958. In 1959, he was

Carolingian silver relief from the altar of S. Ambrogio, Milan.

selected as one of 7 men for the National Aeronautics and Space Administration's (NASA) Project Mercury. He made a 3-orbit flight in the Aurora 7 on May 24, 1962. In 1965, he became an aquanaut and directed the Navy's Sealab II experiment, living and working 205 ft (62 m) under the Pacific Ocean, to improve submarine rescue efforts. He returned to NASA in 1966 as branch chief for advanced programs. A year later he resigned from NASA to continue deep-sea research for the Navy, helping to develop Sealab III. In 1969, he retired from the Navy.
See also: Astronaut.

Carpentry, craft of laying floors, building stairways, and erecting ceiling joists and roof rafters of wood using traditional tools such as the hammer, chisel, pincers, plane, square, plumb line, and tape measure. Modern building techniques have created new applications for carpentry, most notably, the development of wooden molds for casting concrete.
See also: Woodworking.

Carpetbagger, Northerner who moved into the South during the Reconstruction after the Civil War. Although many such Northerners legitimately ran businesses and were elected to office on the Republican ticket (with the help of newly enfranchised African Americans), the term is generally used to apply to those corrupt opportunists who sought to make their fortunes and seize political power out of postwar chaos,earning a reputation for graft and wasteful spending.
See also: Reconstruction.

Carpet beetle (*Anthrenus scrophulariae*), destructive household insect whose larvae feed on carpets, rugs, furniture, fur, and clothing. The tiny (under 0.2 in/5 mm long), wormlike larvae, which do more damage than the adult, are the only beetle larvae covered with hair. Adult carpet beetles, which are brownish-black or marked with red or yellowish-white spots, are discovered in infested houses during spring, and are usually found on windowsills attempting to get out to feed on pollen.

Carracci, family of Bolognese painters. **Lodovico Carracci** (1555-1619), a painter of the Mannerist school, founded an academy of art in Bologna. **Agostino Carracci** (1557-1602) is famous primarily for his prints and *Communion of St. Jerome* (c.1590). **Annibale Carracci** (1560-1609) is considered the greatest painter of the family. Much influenced by Correggio, his work, particularly the vast decorations for the Farnese palace (1597-1604), introduced a strong classical element into a basically Mannerist style.

Lewis Carroll's handwritten manuscript of Alice in Wonderland

Carrageen *See:* Irish moss.

Carranza, Venustiano (1859-1920), Mexican political leader. He overthrew General Huerta in the Mexican revolution and became president (1914). The new constitution he supported established basic reforms in land ownership and national control of natural resources. Carranza fled an uprising led by General Obrégon, but was assassinated.
See also: Mexico.

Carrel, Alexis (1873-1944), U.S. surgeon and biologist who received the 1912 Nobel Prize in physiology and medicine for his work in suturing blood vessels, in transfusion, and in organ transplantation. During World War I he developed a treatment for wounds (the Carrel-Dakin method) that reduced the necessity for amputations.
See also: Biology.

Carrier pigeon, breed of show pigeon derived from the rock pigeon. Although this breed is not used for message carrying, the name is also used for the message-carrying homing pigeon.
See also: Pigeon.

Carroll, Charles (1737-1832), U.S. revolutionary leader, member of the Continental Congress, signer of the Declaration of Independence. A Federalist party member, Carroll was elected to Maryland's first state senate (1777), where he served until his retirement in 1801.

Carroll, Daniel (1730-96), U.S. revolutionary politician, signer of the Articles of Confederation and the U.S. Constitution. In 1789 he was elected to the first U.S. House of Representatives.

Carroll, John (1735-1815), first U.S. Roman Catholic bishop, elected by U.S. priests in 1789 and consecrated Bishop of Baltimore in 1790. A friend of Benjamin Franklin and supporter of the American revolution, Bishop Carroll founded Georgetown University and fought against anti-Catholic prejudice in the early United States. He became an archbishop in 1808.

Carroll, Lewis (Charles Lutwidge Dodgson; 1832-98), English mathematician best known for his children's books, *Alice in Wonderland* (1865) and *Alice Through the Looking Glass* (1872), built on mathematical illogic and paradox.

Carrot (*Daucus carota*), biennial vegetable of the parsley family with a swollen, edible root, grown extensively in America and Europe. Its carotene is changed by the body to vitamin A, an essential chemical in the process of vision.

Carson, Kit (Christopher Carson; 1809-68), American frontiersman. Carson worked as a trapper, hunter, and guide throughout the Southwest and accompanied John C. Fremont on his Western expeditions (1842-46). In 1854 he became an Indian agent in New Mexico. He was a Union general in the Civil War.
See also: Pioneer life in America.

Carson, Rachel Louise (1907-64), U.S. marine biologist and science writer whose *Silent Spring* (1962) first alerted the U.S. public to the dangers of environmental pollution.
See also: Marine biology.

Carson City (pop. 40,443), state capital of Nevada, south of Reno. Established as a trading post on the trail from Utah to California, Carson City became important with the discovery of the Comstock Lode in 1859, and as the location of a United States mint from 1870 to 1893.
See also: Nevada.

Cartagena (pop. 168,800), city and seaport on the Mediterranean coast in southeastern Spain. The Carthaginians, attracted by the gold and silver ores there, founded the city about 225 B.C. During the Civil War of 1936-39, Cartagena was a naval base for General Franco.
See also: Spain.

Cartel, formal organization of producers in a particular industry, designed to set prices, control levels of production, and divide markets. Cartels normally attempt to gain sufficient control over supply, demand, and price to produce higher profits for their members. Cartels are illegal in the United States, though U.S. firms are permitted to join international associations. The best known international cartel of the 1970s and 1980s was the Organization of Petroleum Exporting Countries (OPEC).

Carter, Don (1926-), U.S. bowler. Voted the best bowler in history in a 1970 poll of bowling writers, he achieved the sport's first grand slam by winning the 4 major competitions of his day—the World Invitational All-Star, Professional Bowlers Association (PBA) National, and American Bowling Conference (ABC) Masters. He continued to win bowling championships throughout the 1950s and early 1960s. He was named to the ABC Hall of Fame in 1970 and to the PBA Hall of Fame in 1975. He was a founder and first president of the PBA.

Carter, Elliott Cook (1908-), U.S. composer, Pulitzer Prize winner (1960, 1973). Marked by unusual instrumentation and structure, his work is complex and highly contrapuntal, sometimes employing *metric modulation*, a technique he developed for creating subtle shifts in tempo. Among his best-known works are a ballet *The Minotaur* (1947), the *Double Concerto* (1961), and *Concerto for Piano and Orchestra* (1965).

Carter, Howard (1873-1939), English Egyptologist, famous for excavations in the Valley of the Kings at Luxor, Egypt, with Lord Carnarvon that discovered the tomb of Tutankhamen in 1922.
See also: Tutankhamen.

Carter, Jimmy (James Earl Carter, Jr.; 1924-), 39th president of the United States.
Early life. Carter grew up on a Georgia farm and graduated from the U.S. Naval Academy in 1946. In the navy he studied nuclear physics and worked on the atomic submarine program. In 1953 he returned to Georgia, built the family's farm into a prosperous peanut business, and entered politics as a Democrat.
Politics. As governor of Georgia (1971-75) he encouraged electoral and social reforms. Carter rose from relative obscurity to win the Democratic nomination in 1976 after a 2-year campaign in which he cast himself as a political outsider. He defeated Republican incumbent Gerald R. Ford.
President. Carter's relations with Congress were strained. His revision of the Social Security system was passed, but his comprehensive energy program was not. The economic growth rate fell in the last years of his administration, and both inflation and interest rates were high. His anti-inflation program, emphasizing cooperation among government, business, and labour had little success.
In 1977 Carter won congressional approval of a treaty to cede control of the Panama Canal to Panama at the end of 1999. In 1979 the United States established full diplomatic relations with China. But Carter's most significant foreign policy achievement was his brokering of a peace treaty between Egypt and Israel, signed in 1979. In Nov. 1979, Muslim militants in Iran seized the U.S. embassy in Tehran, taking some 60 Americans hostage. Carter's failure to win their release was an important factor in his defeat by Ronald Reagan in the 1980 election.
Retirement. After leaving office, Carter returned home to Plains, Ga. He wrote several books, established an institute at Georgia's Emory University for discussion of international political and social issues, and took part in various international fact-finding and diplomatic missions.

Carteret, Sir George (c.1610-80), English politician, admiral, and lieutenant-governor of East Jersey from 1643. A staunch Royalist, he was rewarded after the Restoration with proprietorships in New Jersey and Carolina.

Cartesian philosophy *See:* Descartes, René.

Carthage, ancient North African city established in 814 B.C. by the Phoenicians, traders of the Mediterranean. Carthage colonized new lands and became the prominent center of the Phoenician world.
See also: Hannibal; Punic Wars.

Carthusians, contemplative and austere Roman Catholic monastic order founded in France in 1084 by St. Bruno. Each monk spends most of his life in solitude in his private cell and garden. Lay brothers prepare the Chartreuse liqueur for which the order is known.
See also: Roman Catholic Church.

Cartier, Sir George Étienne (1814-73), Canadian statesman and leading French-Canadian advocate of confederation. Elected to the Canadian parliament in 1848, he was joint prime minister (1857-62) with Sir John Macdonald, under whom he later served as minister of defense in the first dominion government.
See also: Canada.

Cartier, Jacques (1491-1557), French explorer who discovered the St. Lawrence River while in search of a Northwest Passage in Canada. Between 1534 and 1542 he made 3 voyages, discovering the Magdalene Islands and Prince Edward Island.
See also: Saint Lawrence River.

Cartier-Bresson, Henri (1908-), international French documentary photographer who rose to fame with his coverage of the Spanish Civil War. He has published many photographic books, including *The Decisive Moment* (1952), *China in Transition* (1956), and *Henri Cartier-Bresson, Photographer* (1979), and has also made films.

Cartilage, tough, flexible connective tissue found in all vertebrates, consisting of cartilage cells in a matrix of collagen fibers and a firm protein gel. The skeleton of the vertebrate embryo is formed wholly of cartilage; in most species much of this is replaced by bone during growth. There are 3 main types of cartilage: (1) hyaline, which is translucent and glossy and found in the joints, nose, trachea, and bronchi; (2) elastic, which is found in the external ear, Eustachian tube, and larynx; and (3) fibrocartilage, which attaches tendons to bone and forms the disks between the vertebrae.
See also: Bone.

Cartoon, originally, preparatory sketch in the fine arts; since the mid-19th century, humorous or satirical drawing. Today the term also includes the comic strip, the political cartoon, and cartoon animation. Prominent U.S. cartoonists include Charles Addams, Al Capp, Charles Schulz, Garry Trudeau, and Herblock.

Cartwright, Edmund (1743-1823), English inventor of a mechanical loom (1785) that was the ancestor of the modern power loom. He also invented a woolcombing machine (1789).

Cartwright, Peter (1785-1872), U.S. Methodist preacher, frontier circuit rider (the "Kentucky Boy") and Illinois politician. The life of circuit riders is vividly described in his *Autobiography* (1856).

James Earl (Jimmy) Carter, Jr.

39th U.S. President	
Born:	Plains, Ga.; Oct. 1, 1924
Term:	Jan. 1977-Jan. 1981
Vice President:	Walter F. Mondale
Political Party:	Democratic
Spouse:	Rosalynn Smith Carter
Children:	4

Caruso, Enrico (1873-1921), Italian operatic tenor famous for his voice and his artistry. Caruso sang over 50 roles in Europe, the United States, and Latin America, excelling in works by Puccini and Verdi. His recordings brought him worldwide fame.
See also: Opera.

Carver, George Washington (1860-1943), U.S. chemist, botanist, and educator, born of slave parents in Missouri. As director of agricultural research at Tuskegee Institute, Alabama (1896-1943), he fostered soil improvement by crop rotation, and developed hundreds of industrial uses for peanuts and sweet potatoes.
See also: Botany.

Carver, John (1576-1621), first governor of Plymouth Colony (1620-21). As leader of the Pilgrims, he was largely responsible (1617-20) for getting a charter and financial aid, and for chartering the *Mayflower*.
See also: Plymouth Colony.

Cary, Joyce (1888-1957), English novelist most famous for 2 trilogies: the first on art—*Herself Surprised* (1941), *To Be a Pilgrim* (1942), and *The Horse's Mouth* (1944), and the second on politics—*Prisoner of Grace* (1952), *Except the Lord* (1953), and *Not Honour More* (1955).

Cary, Mary Ann Shadd (1823-1893), U.S. teacher and journalist, first North American black woman to establish and edit a weekly newspaper. Born to free parents, she taught in and established schools for blacks in Delaware, Pennsylvania, and New York (1839-51). After the U.S. Congress passed the Fugitive Slave Act of 1850, allowing for the return of slaves who had escaped into another state, she began actively working to help slaves who had escaped to Canada. In 1851 she moved to Windsor, Ont., where she helped found the *Provincial Freeman*, a weekly newspaper for blacks in Canada. She moved to Washington, D.C. (1869), where she taught school and received a law degree from Howard University. She was active in the suffrage movement.

Casaba (*Cucumis melo*), type of muskmelon, also called winter melon because it ripens in fall and is available in winter. The casaba is round or oval, with a pointed stem, and weighs 2-9 lbs (1-4 kg). Its hard outer skin, which ripens from green to yellow, is smooth but wrinkled. Rich in vitamin C and potassium, its flesh is sweet and juicy and ranges in color from green to white. The casaba, which originated in Iran and the Transcaucasia, is named for the town in southwest Turkey (Kasaba) from which it was introduced in the United States in 1871. It is now grown in California and the Southwest. It is a member of the gourd family and grows on vines.

Pablo Casals

Casablanca (pop. 2,139,000), largest city in Morocco and the country's leading port. Casablanca handles most of Morocco's foreign trade, exporting grain and phosphates. In 1907 the French occupied the port, and remained in control until 1956.
See also: Morocco.

Casals, Pablo (1876-1973), virtuoso Spanish cellist and conductor, brilliant interpreter of the music of J.S. Bach. In 1919 he founded an orchestra in Barcelona to bring music to the working classes. An outspoken antifascist, he left Spain after the Spanish Civil War to settle in Prades, France, and then (1956) in Puerto Rico, organizing music festivals in both places.

Casanova (De Seingalt), Giovanni Giacomo (1725-98), Venetian author and adventurer whose name became a synonym for seducer. His memoirs, both sensual and sensitive, show him as a freethinking libertine; they also give an excellent picture of his times.

Cascade Range, mountain range extending 700 mi (1,127 km) from northern California to British Columbia. Its highest peak is Mt. Rainier (14,410 ft/4,392 m). There are 4 dormant volcanos and the recently active (1980) Mt. Saint Helens.

Cascade Tunnel, longest railroad tunnel in North America, cutting across 7.79 mi (12.5 km) of the Cascade range in the central part of Washington. The tunnel was completed in 1929 at a cost of 25 million dollars.
See also: Cascade Range.

Cascara sagrada, small buckthorn tree of the Western United States whose bark is used in making a laxative. It is also known as coffeeberry, as its berries were used by the pioneers to make a substitute coffee.

Casehardening, treatment of mild steel to give it an extremely hard surface. The steel is heated for several hours in carbon-containing material, such as powdered charcoal. During this process carbon is slowly absorbed to a shallow depth, converting this part to high-carbon steel. On quenching with cold water this "case" becomes hard. An even harder case is produced by "nitriding," in which the steel is heated in gaseous ammonia, from which the surface absorbs nitrogen. Casehardening is commonly used on gears, roller bearings, and crankshafts to produce a wear-resistant surface.
See also: Steel.

Casein, important protein that accounts for 80% of the protein content of milk. It occurs as calcium caseinate. It coagulates to form curds when acted upon by certain acids and by the enzyme rennet. The curds are used to make cheese. Casein also has many industrial uses, especially as paper coatings, adhesives, paints, plastics, and synthetic fibers.

Case method, system of teaching law by the study of actual cases. Introduced in 1870 by Christopher C. Langdell, a Harvard Law School professor, by the early 1900s the case method was adopted by most law schools.
See also: Law.

Cashew (*Anacardium occidentale*), tropical American tree of the sumac family cultivated in Africa and India. It grows up to 40 ft (12 m) high and bears a kidney-shaped nut in a hard covering underneath a fleshy edible "pear," which can be made into "cajee" wine. The nuts are roasted, and the oil surrounding each nut can be used in cooking.

Cashmere, very fine natural fiber, the soft underhair of the Kashmir goat, bred in India, Iran, China, and Mongolia. Cashmere is finer than the best wools, although the name may be applied to some soft wool fabrics.

Caslon, William (1692-1766), English typefounder, inventor of Caslon type, for many years the standard typeface in the 18th century. Although superseded by the "newstyle" faces of John Baskerville and others, versions of it are much in use today.

Casper (pop. 61,226), second largest city in Wyoming, on the North Platte River, at an altitude of 5,140 ft (1,566 m). First a cavalry post, the city became a trading center for sheep and cattle ranchers. Over 400 oil companies are now represented in Casper; coal and uranium ore are mined as well.

Caspian Sea, world's largest inland sea (143,000 sq mi/370,370 sq km), in the southwestern part of the USSR and Iran. Tideless, it is 92 ft (28 m) below sea level and fed mainly by the Volga River. Astrakhan and Baku are the main ports. The northern part of the sea produces caviar.

Cass, Lewis (1782-1866), U.S. soldier and political leader. He rose to the rank of brigadier general in the War of 1812, was governor of Michigan Territory (1813-31), and became secretary of war under Andrew Jackson. He ran as the Democratic presidential candidate in 1848 but lost to Zachary Taylor, due largely to the defection of the Barnburners (radical New York State Democrats) to the Free Soil Party. Twice serving in the Senate (1845-48, 1849-57), he also served as secretary of state (1857-60).

Cassandra, in Greek mythology, prophetess of doom whose warnings were never heeded. The daughter of Trojan King Priam, she was taken prisoner by Agamemnon after the Trojan War and later murdered with him by his wife, Clytemnestra.
See also: Mythology; Troy.

Cassatt, Mary (1845-1926), U.S.-born impressionist painter who lived mainly in Paris. Strongly influenced by her friend Edgar Degas, she painted domestic scenes, especially mother-and-child studies: "The Cup of Tea" (1879), "The Bath" (1891), "The Boating Party" (1893).
See also: Impressionism.

Mary Cassatt's painting At the Opera

Cassava or manioc (genus *Manihot*), potato-like tuber plant, staple in its native Central and South America and in West Africa and southeastern Asia. After being peeled to remove most of the poisonous prussic acid, the tubers are soaked. Lumps of cooked tuber form tapioca, which can be ground to make a flour.

Cassette *See:* Tape recorder; Videotape recorder.

Cassia, genus of tropical plants. Sennas, best known as medicinal plants, are a common species.

Cassino (pop. 26,300), Italian town about 75 miles southeast of Rome, site of Monte Cassino, a Benedictine monastery founded in A.D. 529. During World War II, Cassino was strategically important to the German defense of Rome, and the town and abbey were nearly destroyed in heavy fighting. Both have since been rebuilt.
See also: Italy.

Cassiopeia, w-shaped constellation of the northern hemisphere, which appears between the North Star and the Big Dipper, directly north of the constellation Andromeda. An exploding star (supernova) was observed in Cassiopeia in 1572 by the Danish astronomer Tycho Brahe.
See also: Constellation.

Cassirer, Ernst (1874-1945), German-born philosopher. His work, based on the ideas of Immanuel Kant, examines the ways in which a person's symbols and concepts structure his or her world. He fled Nazi Germany in 1933 and taught at Oxford, in Sweden, and, from 1941, in the United States.
See also: Philosophy.

Cassiterite, or tinstone, principal ore of tin. The brown-to-black-colored mineral is found in veins, along with granite and quartz, and in riverbeds as pebbles. It is mined commercially in Malaysia, China, Bolivia, Indonesia, Thailand, the Congo, and Nigeria.
See also: Tin.

Cassius Longinus, Gaius (d. 42 B.C.), Roman general, conspirator to assassinate Julius Caesar in 44 B.C. He fled to Syria and joined Brutus to fight Octavian and Mark Antony at Philippi. Despairing of victory, he committed suicide.
See also: Rome, Ancient.

Cassowary, large, flightless bird of northern Australia and New Guinea. The largest species is nearly 5 ft (1.5 m) tall. The plumage is coarse. The head and neck are naked and brightly colored with wattles and a bony helmet. The legs are strong, and cassowaries can run at 30 mph (48 km per hour), but they are shy and hide in thick cover. Cassowaries have large, sharp claws on their 3 toes that can be formidable weapons. The eggs are incubated by the male, who also cares for the chicks. They feed on insects and fruit.

Castagno, Andrea del (1423-57), Florentine painter of church frescoes, portraits, and murals. Best known for his *Last Supper* (1445-50) and *Crucifixion* (1499-50), he stressed perspective and a stark, dramatic illumination. He is notable for the vigor and strength of his figure rendering.

Castanets, small percussion instrument consisting of 2 shell-shaped halves, usually made of wood or ivory. They are held in the palm of the hand and tapped by the fingers to produce a clicking sound. Castanets have been used for hundreds of years in Spanish flamenco dancing. More recently some composers have included a part for castanets in their music, especially to suggest a Spanish flavor.

Caste system, division of society into closed groups, primarily by birth, but usually also involving religion and occupation. The most caste-bound society today is that of Hindu India; its caste system, dating from 3000 B.C., was not discouraged until recently.

Castiglione, Comte Baldassare (1478-1529), Italian courtier, diplomat, and author. His *Il Cortegiano* (The Courier) (1528), a portrait of the ideal courtier and his relationship with the prince he serves, greatly influenced Renaissance mores and inspired writers like Edmund Spenser, Sir Philip Sidney, and Miguel Cervantes.
See also: Renaissance.

Castile and Aragón, 2 kingdoms of Spain, united in 1479 by Isabella of Castile and her husband, Ferdinand V. Aragón is in the northeast of Spain, bordering France; Castile, in central and northern Spain, surrounds the city of Madrid. The union of Castile and Aragón formed the core of the modern Spanish state and served as Ferdinand and Isabella's base in their struggle, eventually successful, to drive the Moors from southern Spain (Andalusia).
See also: Spain.

Castilla, Ramón (1797?-1867), president of Peru, 1845-51 and 1855-62. He joined the Peruvian independence movement in 1821 and fought the Spaniards alongside José de San Martín and Simón Bolívar. When he assumed the presidency, he ended a period of anarchy and is credited with bringing peace, stability, and economic improvements. Slavery and the taxation of Indians were abolished under his administration.
See also: Peru.

Casting, production of a desired form by pouring the raw material (alloys, fiberglass, plastics, steel) in liquid form into a suitably shaped mold. In *die casting,* molten metal is forced under pressure into a die; in *centrifugal casting,* used primarily for pipes, molten material is poured into a rapidly rotating mold; in *continuous casting,* material is poured into water-cooled, open-ended molds; in *sand casting* fine sand is packed tightly around each half of a permanent pattern, which is removed, after which the 2 halves of the mold are placed together.

The use of cast iron made possible the construction of the Grand Palais at the World's Fair in Paris in 1900.

Castle, Vernon (1887-1918), and **Irene** (1893-1969), couple who revolutionized ballroom dancing. They introduced the one-step and the Castle walk and popularized the hesitation waltz and tango during a meteoric career that began in 1912 and ended with Vernon's death in an air crash.

Castle, fortified dwelling, built to dominate and guard a region. The term derives from the Roman *castellum* (fort or frontier stronghold). In Western Europe, most of the extant castles were built between 1000 and 1500, often on an artificial mound, with a palisaded courtyard. Later, the stockade was replaced by masonry keeps, or dungeons; defensive outer walls; and frequently a moat and drawbridge. With the decline of feudalism, the castle evolved into the Renaissance château, with its emphasis on splendor rather than on fortification.
See illustrations on following page.

Castlereagh, Robert Stewart, 2d Viscount (1769-1822), Irish born British statesman, creator of the Quadruple Alliance that defeated Napoleon. As secretary for Ireland, he suppressed the 1798 rebellion and forced the Act of Union through the Irish Parliament (1800). He was war minister (1805-6, 1807-9), and as foreign secretary (1812-22), played a major role in the organization of Europe at the Congress of Vienna (1814). Much maligned in his time, he committed suicide.
See also: Vienna, Congress of.

Castor and Pollux, in Greek mythology, twin heroes, called the Dioscuri. Castor the horseman was the son of Leda and Tyndareus; Pollux the boxer was the son of Leda and Zeus.
See also: Mythology.

Castor oil, thick oil obtained from the castor bean, used as a purgative and a lubricant.

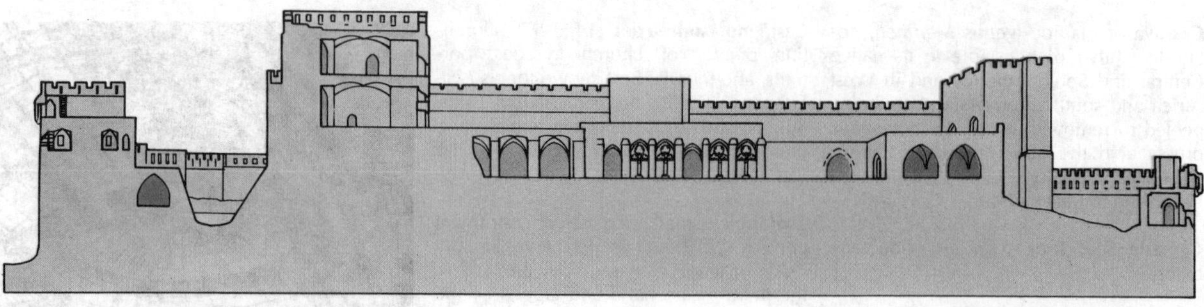

Schematic plan of a concentric castle built in Syria in the 13th century. The diagram at right shows the castle without its outer wall and defensive moat. (The moat doubles as a reservoir.) The inner courtyard, terraced and extensively vaulted, contains a romanesque chapel and the great hall and cloister.

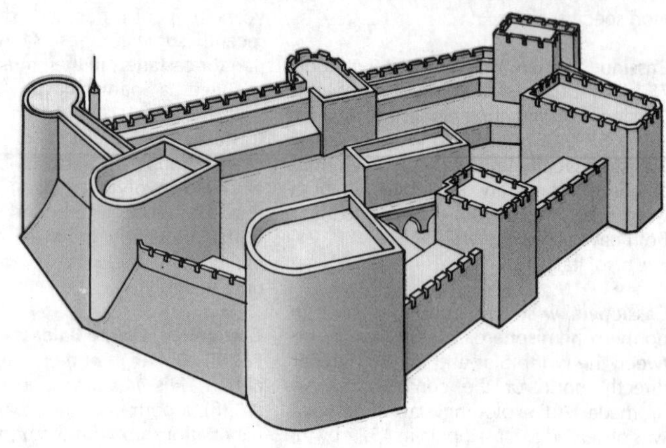

This fortress near Aleppo ,Syria, was built by the knights of the Cross during the Crusades.

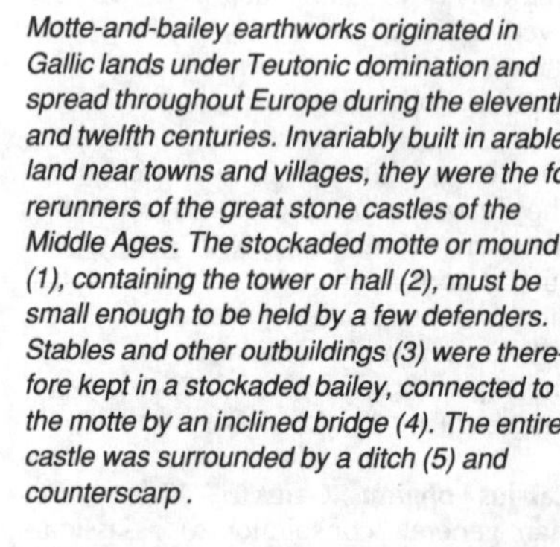

Motte-and-bailey earthworks originated in Gallic lands under Teutonic domination and spread throughout Europe during the eleventh and twelfth centuries. Invariably built in arable land near towns and villages, they were the forerunners of the great stone castles of the Middle Ages. The stockaded motte or mound (1), containing the tower or hall (2), must be small enough to be held by a few defenders. Stables and other outbuildings (3) were therefore kept in a stockaded bailey, connected to the motte by an inclined bridge (4). The entire castle was surrounded by a ditch (5) and counterscarp .

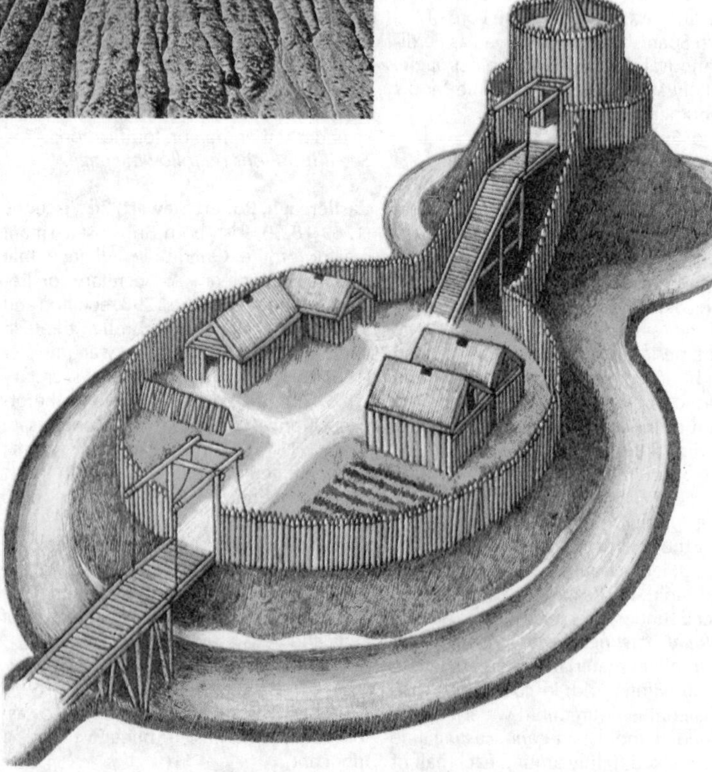

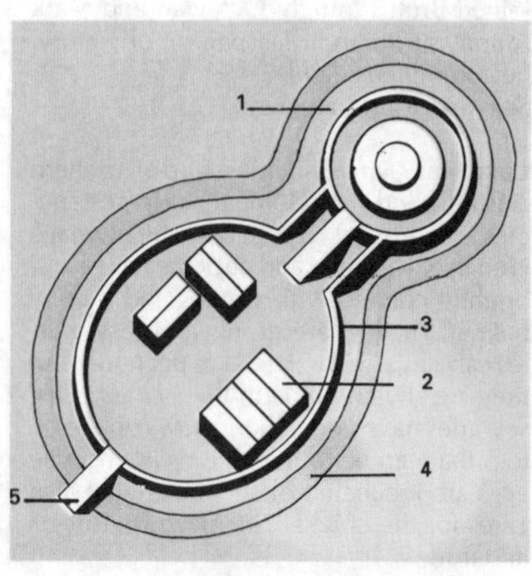

Doornenburg Castle (c. 1500) near Nijmegen, Netherlands, with a keep that expanded into a main castle with a moat and outworks (lower foreground) as extra protection.

Marksburg Castle, on the Rhine River, Germany

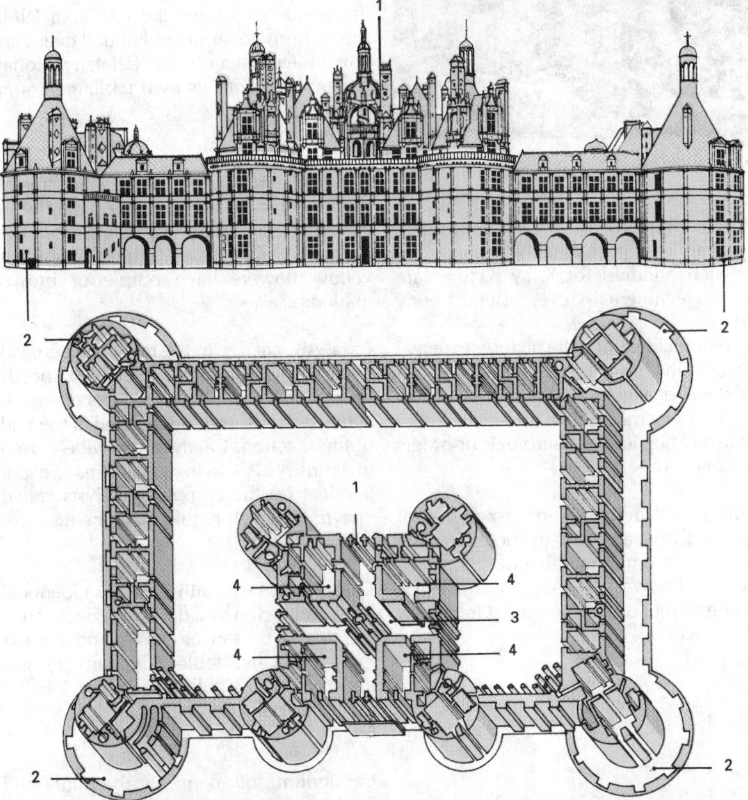

Illustration of the Château de Chambord (1519-47) is ascribed to Italian architect Domenico da Cortona. Its plan remains essentially that of a medieval concentric castle: a dungeon (1), surrounded on three sides by a courtine with massive conical towers (2), its facade (3) aligned with that of the courtine. The arms of the dungeon form a Greek cross and lead from the entrances to a double spiral staircase (4) connecting all floors. Corner suites of rooms—an Italian innovation—form appartements, *the earliest French instance of what became the regular French domestic arrangement for two centuries. The vertical and ornate outline is basically French, clad in Italian decorative detail.*

Photograph of the Château de Chambord in the Loire valley, France

Castries (pop. 49,000), capital and largest city of the Caribbean island nation of St. Lucia. Bordered by a deep-water harbor on the island's northwest coast, Castries is the chief port, exporting bananas, sugarcane, molasses, cacao, and other tropical products. Colonized by France in 1651, St. Lucia was fought over by the French and British until 1814, when Great Britain took control. Britain ruled St. Lucia until 1979, when it became an independent nation.
See also: Saint Lucia.

Fidel Castro

Castro, Fidel (1926-) Cuban premier (1959-) and revolutionary. He led an abortive revolution in 1953 against dictator Fulgencio Batista, and was imprisoned and exiled. In 1956 he invaded Cuba with 81 men and overthrew the regime, establishing himself as premier in 1959. He nationalized industry and collectivized agriculture, becoming increasingly dependent on the USSR for financial support. The U.S. has attempted to isolate Cuba both economically and politically but has not achieved success.
See also: Cuba.

Castro, Raul Hector (1916-), governor of Arizona (1975-77). Born in Mexico, Castro moved to Arizona in 1926 and became a U.S. citizen in 1939. He earned a law degree from the University of Arizona in 1949. He was U.S. ambassador to El Salvador 1964-1968, and to Bolivia 1968-1969. In 1977 he was named U.S. ambassador to Argentina.

Cat, hunting carnivore of the family Felidae, varying in size from the small domestic cat and the small wild cats (lynx and ocelot) to the great cats (lion, tiger, leopard, and cheetah). Cats have short snouts, large eyes, sensitive whiskers, and sharp claws and teeth.
*See also:*Lion; Tiger.

Wild cat

CAT (computerized axial tomography) scan, painless, quick diagnostic procedure in which hundreds of X-ray pictures are taken as a camera revolves around a body part.
A computer integrates the pictures to reveal structures within the body. The CAT scan has created a new era in the history of diagnostic medicine. It is especially effective in the diagnosis of neurologic disorders and cancers.

Catacombs, underground cemeteries of the early Christians, who did not follow the Greek and Roman practice of cremation. The best known and most extensive are outside Rome, built from the 1st to the 5th century A.D.

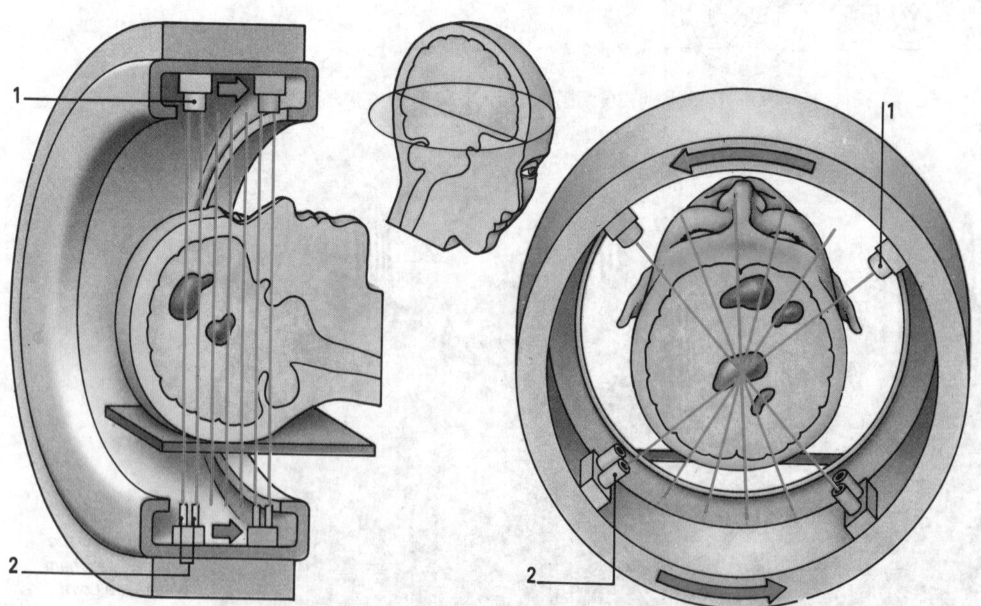

A computerized tomograph consists of an X-ray tube (1) and two moving detectors (2). After a first shooting the tube and the detectors turn to another parallel level. The computer makes up a map of areas with deviant permiability such as tumors.

Catalepsy, condition of loss of voluntary motion in which the arms and legs remain in any position they are placed in. Causes may be organic or psychological. Catalepsy is often associated with severe cases of schizophrenia.
See also: Schizophrenia.

Catalonia, region in northeastern Spain, comprising the provinces of Lérida, Gerona, Barcelona, and Tarragona. It was occupied by the Romans and Goths, who called it Gothalonia. It maintained its own customs and language after its union with Aragon in 1137. There is also a rich body of Catalan literature. It is now the chief industrial area of Spain, and is dependent on the interior for grain and protected markets. It experienced a brief period of independence during the 1930s. In 1980 the Spanish government handed over certain limited functions to a Catalan regional government with its own parliament and premier.
See also: Spain.

Catalpa, genus of ornamental shade tree of the bignonia family, growing naturally in eastern Asia, the West Indies, and the southern United States. Its tubular white or yellow flowers have purple or brown markings.

Catalysis, change in the rate of a chemical reaction by an additive (a catalyst speeds up reactions; an inhibitor slows down reactions) that is itself unchanged at the end of the reaction. Catalysts are widely used in industry. All living organisms are dependent on the complex catalysts called enzymes, which regulate biochemical reactions.

Catamaran, boat with 2 narrow, identical hulls connected by a flat bridge deck. They are driven by sail or power and are extremely fast and stable. Trimarans are similar, but have 3 hulls, the center 1 being longer than the outer 2.

Catamount, folk name for the puma and the lynx. The word is a shortened form of *catamountain*, a form of *cat of the mountain.*

Cataplexy, condition of abrupt and temporary loss of voluntary muscle control brought on by some extreme emotional stimulus, especially fear, anger, or mirth. An attack may last from a few seconds to several minutes, and symptoms may range in severity from a mild weakening to paralysis of most of the muscles of the body.

Catapult, ancient military weapon used for hurling missiles. Some catapults were large crossbows, with a lethal range of over 400 yd (366 m), while others (*ballistas*) used giant levers to hurl boulders. In the Middle Ages catapults were an important part of siege artillery, but they were made obsolete by the cannon. A modern steam-powered version of the catapult launches jets from aircraft carriers.

Cataract, opacity of the lens of the eye, causing a progressive loss of vision. Aging is the most common cause, but cataracts may be hereditary or due to disease, such as diabetes. Cataracts are treated by lens extraction, followed by wearing corrective lenses or having a plastic lens implant.
See also: Blindness.

Catarrh, mild inflammation of a mucous membrane, associated with a copious secretion of mucus. Medically speaking, this refers to any mucous membrane in the body, but popularly it refers to nasal or bronchial catarrh.
See also: Cold, Common; Sinus.

Catbird (*Dumetella carolinensis*), songbird of the thrush family, named for the mewing notes in its imitative song. Catbirds, which are gray with a black cap, live in the United States and in Canada, migrating in winter to Central America or to the West Indies.

Catbird

Catechism, manual of religious instruction arranged in question-and- answer form. First appearing in the 8th and 9th centuries, catechisms were widely used during the Middle Ages. The Anglican catechism is included in the Book of Common Prayer, and the Baltimore Catechism (1885) is used by Roman Catholics.
See also: Book of Common Prayer.

Catechu, strong, astringent substance prepared from the wood of various tropical Asiatic plants and used in medicine with prepared chalk to treat diarrhea.

Caterpillar, larva of a moth or a butterfly, with 13 segments, 3 pairs of true legs, and up to 5 pairs of soft false legs.
See also: Butterfly.

Catfish, freshwater, bottom-feeding fish (suborder Nematognathi) with barbels, or whiskers, around the mouth, tough scaleless skin, and sharp spines. Catfish are an important food source.

Catharsis, in psychoanalysis, bringing into the open of a previously repressed memory or emotion, in the hope of releasing and eliminating stress.

Cathay, name by which China was known in medieval Europe. The word derives from the Khitai, a seminomadic people of southern Manchuria whose rule extended to northern China in the 10th century A.D.
See also: China.

Cathedral, principal church of a diocese, in which the bishop has his *cathedra,* his official seat or throne. A cathedral need not be particularly large or imposing, though its importance as a major center led to the magnificent structures of the Gothic and Renaissance periods. By its prominent position and size, a cathedral often dominated a city and served as the focus of its life. In Europe, most of the older cathedral cities were already important centers in Roman and early Christian times.
See also: Architecture.

Cather, Willa Sibert (1876-1947), U.S. novelist noted for her psychologically astute portrayals of the people of Nebraska and the Southwest. Her works include *O Pioneers!* (1913), *My Antonia* (1918), and *Death Comes for the Archbishop* (1927). She was also a brilliant writer of short stories, the most famous being "Paul's Case."

Catherine, name of 2 Russian empresses. **Catherine I** (1684-1727), wife of Peter I, succeeded him to the throne on his death in 1725. **Catherine II, the Great** (1729-96) married the future Peter III in 1745. After his deposition and murder in 1762, she became empress. Her liberalism was quenched by Pugachev's peasant uprising (1773 - 74) and the French Revolution. She greatly extended Russian territory, annexing the Crimea (1783) and partitioning Poland (1772-95).

Catherine de' Medici (1519-89), daughter of Lorenzo de' Medici, Duke of Urbino; wife of King Henry II of France; and mother of 3 kings of France. After the death of her eldest son, King Francis II (r.1559-60), she acted as regent of France (until 1563) and was adviser to her son, King Charles IX, (r.1560-74) until his death. She helped Charles IX plan the St. Bartholomew's Day Massacre against the Protestants in 1572. Her third son, Henry III, ruled from 1574 to 1589.
See also: Saint Batholomew's Day, Massacre of.

Catherine of Aragon (1485-1536), first wife of Henry VIII of England. The daughter of Ferdinand and Isabella of Spain, she married Prince Arthur (1501) and, after his death, his brother, Henry VIII (1509). Henry's annulment of the marriage (1533) without papal consent led to the English Reformation. She was the mother of Mary I of England.
See also: Henry (Kings of England).

Catherine of Braganza (1638-1705), Portuguese wife of King Charles II of England. The marriage (1662) was intended to promote the Anglo-Portuguese alliance, but she produced no heir. After Charles's death, she returned to Portugal (1692), serving as regent (1704-5).

Catherine of Siena, Saint (1347-80), Italian religious and mystic known for her visions, charity, and diplomatic skill. Her influence over Pope Gregory XI (1331-78) led him to leave Avignon in 1377 and return the papacy to Rome, thus ending the "Babylonian captivity" of the papacy. Her feast day is Apr. 30.

Catherine the Great *See:* Catherine II.

Cathode ray, stream of electrons that flows from a cathode (negative electrode) to an anode (positive electrode) in a vacuum tube when a potential of 4,000-10,000 volts is applied across them. Cathode rays were first detected when a glowing light was seen to emanate from a cathode; this is a secondary effect the rays produce only when traces of certain gases are present.
See also: Electrolysis; Electronics; Vacuum tube.

Catholic Church, Roman *See:* Roman Catholic Church.

Catholic Emancipation Act, British law enacted on Apr. 13, 1829, removing most of the civil disabilities imposed on British Roman Catholics from the time of Henry VIII. A controversial measure, it was introduced by Sir Robert Peel after considerable pressure from Irish campaigners headed by Daniel O'Connell.

Catiline (c.108-62 B.C.), Roman aristocrat who tried to seize power in 63 B.C. He was trapped and killed in battle at Pistoria. Cicero attacked him in a series of 4 celebrated orations.

Catkin, reproductive organ of many common trees. Each catkin bears a cluster of primitive flowers that lack petals and sepals. Instead, the stamens and pistils are protected by small leaves called bracts. 1 Catkin bears either male or female flowers. Plants bearing catkins include beech, birch, walnut, and willow families.

Catlin, George (1796-1872), U.S. artist, noted for his paintings of U.S. Native American life based on his trips to the American West. His books include *Notes on the Manners, Customs, and Conditions of the North American Indians* (1841). A large portion of his work is in the Catlin Gallery of the National Gallery of Art in Washington, D.C.

Catnip, or catmint (*Nepeta cataria*), Eurasian mint naturalized in North America. It is grown for its aromatic leaves, which are stimulating to cats.

Cato, name of 2 Roman statesman. **Marcos Porcius Cato the Elder** (234-149 B.C.), was an orator and prose writer. He became consul in 195 B.C. and censor in 184 B.C. His only surviving work is a treatise on agriculture. **Marcus Porcius Cato the Younger**, (95-46 B.C.), great-grandson of Cato the Elder, was a model stoic and defender of Roman republicanism. He supported Pompey against Gaius Julius Caesar

in the Civil War, but after the final defeat of the republican army at Thapsus (46 B.C.), he killed himself at Utica.
See also: Rome, Ancient.

Cat's eye, any of several gemstones that, when cut to form a convex surface, resemble the eye of a cat. Common cat's eye is chalcedony, a form of quartz. The most kind is a variety of chrysoberyl.

Catskill Mountains, group of mountains west of the Hudson River in the southeastern region of New York, part of the Appalachian system. Geologically unique, with flat- topped plateaus divided by narrow valleys, they are a popular recreational area.
See also: Appalachian Mountains.

Catt, Carrie Lane Chapman (1859-1947), U.S. feminist, suffragist, and founder of the League of Women Voters. She was also an active advocate of international disarmament.
See also: Woman suffrage.

Cattail, wild plant (genus *Typha*) that grows in marshes and other wetland areas. Also called clubrushes and, on the Pacific Coast, tule-reeds, cattails have long, slender leaves and a single tall stem. The female flowers form long brown spikes. The roots, which contain starch, are edible. The soft down produced by cattails is sometimes used for furniture upholstery.

Cattle, large ruminant mammal of the family Bovidae, most of which have been domesticated, including bison, buffalo, yak, zebu, and European cattle. By 2500 B.C. the Egyptians had several breed of cattle, which may have been used as draft animals and for leather . Their dung served as fuel and manure. Today, beef cattle (like Aberdeen Angus or Hereford) are square and heavily built commonly kept on poor grazing land, whereas dairy breeds (like Holstein or Guernsey) have good grazing. Recent breeds are mixed beef and dairy animals. A dairy cow can give as much as 14,000 lb (6,350 kg) of milk in 1 year.

Cattle tick, brown parasitic insect (*Boophilus annulatus*) that lives on cattle. It carries an infectious cattle disease known as Texas fever, which in the mid-1800s threatened cattle throughout the U.S. Southwest. Control measures have all but eliminated cattle ticks in the United States, but they are still common in Mexico.

Catton, Bruce (1899-1978), U.S. journalist and Civil War historian. He is best known for his trilogy on the Army of the Potomac: *Mr. Lincoln's Army* (1951), *Glory Road* (1952), and *A Stillness at Appomattox* (1953). He won the Pulitzer Prize in 1954.
See also: Civil War, U.S

Catullus, Gaius Valerius (c.84-54 B.C.), Roman lyric poet influenced by Hellenistic Greek poetry. He wrote passionate lyrics, epigrams, elegies, idylls, and vicious satires, of which only 116 survive. He influenced the later Roman poets Horace and Martial.

Caucasia, oil-rich region that straddles the Caucasus Mountains in the southwest of the USSR. After the Russian Revolution the southern part, called Transcaucasia, was organized as the republics of Georgia, Armenia, and Azerbaijan. In 1922, they became the Transcaucasian Soviet Federated Socialist Republic, but in 1936 they were again reorganized as 3 distinct republics of the Soviet Union.
See also: Union of Soviet Socialist Republics.

Caucasus, mountain range in the USSR between the Caspian and Black seas, 700 mi (1,127 km) long and up to 120 mi (193 km) wide, including the highest mountain in Europe, Mt. Elbrus (18,481 ft/ 5,633 m). Its northern parts belong to Europe, but its southern regions, bordering on Turkey and Iran, are part of Asia.
See also: Union of Soviet Socialist Republics.

Caucus, closed party meetings to decide on policy or select candidates for public office. The term, possibly derived from the Algonquian *Kaw-Kaw-was* (to talk), originated as the name of a political club in 18th-century Boston. From 1800 until 1824 presidential candidates were nominated by the 2-party caucuses in Congress. Although the national convention system replaced the Congressional nominating caucus, party caucuses are important forums for deciding legislative policy, and they fill party posts such as floor leader and whip. A special form of caucus is the meeting of local party members to nominate candidates for office or elect delegates to party conventions. In the late 19th century political "bosses" and their followers came to dominate these meetings, and primary elections were introduced in order to avoid such abuses in the nominating system.

Cauliflower *(Brassica oleracea)*, variety of cabbage similar to broccoli, in which the edible portion consists of a large mass of unopened flowers.

Caustic, general name for chemicals that burn or corrode other materials such as metal, plastics, and organic substances. Caustic soda, also known as lye, is used in household drain cleaners and in making soap, paper, and textiles. Caustic potash is used in the manufacture of soaps that dissolve easily in water.
See also: Lye.

Cavalry, military force that fights on horseback. It played a key role in warfare from about the 6th century B.C. to the end of the 19th century, when the development of rapid-fire rifles began to reduce its effectiveness.

Cavazos, Lauro Fred (1927-), named secretary of education in 1988, first Mexican American to hold a cabinet post. He was president of Texas Tech University from 1980 to 1988, when he was named secretary of education by President Ronald Reagan; he remained in the post under President George Bush.

Cave, natural hollow or cavern found in rock. The most spectacularl caves are found in limestone rocks beneath the earth's surface. These caves were formed thousands of years ago by water erosion.
See also: Speleology.

Cavefish, common name of several varieties of small, blind, cave-dwelling fish of the family Amblyopsidae. Also known as blindfish, they navigate with the help of rows of small projections on their skin.

Cavell, Edith Louise (1865-1915), British nurse who became a World War I heroine. She was responsible for updating nurses' training in Belgium and eventually was executed by the Germans for helping some 200 Allied soldiers escape.

Cavendish, Henry (1731-1810), English chemist and physicist who showed hydrogen to be a distinct gas, water to be a compound—not an elementary substance, and the composition of the atmosphere to be constant. He also used a torsion balance to measure the density of the earth (1798).
See also: Chemistry; Hydrogen.

Cavour, Count Camillo Benso of (1810-61), Italian statesman largely responsible for the unification of Italy. Cavour, under Victor Emmanuel II, became premier of Piedmont in 1852 and sought to unite the country by making piecemeal additions to Piedmont. A subtle diplomat, he secured the central Italian states. The unification, except for Venice and the province of Rome, was completed in 1861, only a few months before Cavour's death.
See also: Italy.

Cavy, any of a number of related South American rodents (family Caviidae), of which the guinea pig is the best known. Cavies typically have short hair and legs and thick bodies. They are social animals, vegetarians, and generally nocturnal.

Caxton, William (c.1422-91), English printer, trained in Cologne. He produced *The Recuyell of the Historyes of Troye* (Bruges, c.1475), the first book printed in English, and *Dictes and Sayenges of the Phylosophers* (1477), the first dated book printed in English.

Cayenne (pop. 40,000), capital of French Guiana, situated on an island in the Cayenne River. It was founded by the French in 1643 and from the late 17th century until 1946 was a notorious French penal colony. Gold, hides, rum, cocoa, and cayenne pepper pass through the port.
See also: French Guiana.

Cayley, Sir George (1773-1857), British inventor who pioneered the science of aerodynamics. He built the first man-carry-

ing glider (1853) and formulated the design principles later used in airplane construction.
See also: Aerodynamics.

Cayman, crocodilian of South America, notably of the Amazon basin. The dwarf cayman is up to 4 ft (1 m) long but the black cayman may grow to 15 ft (4-1/2 m). Similar to alligators, caymans can be distinguished by bony plates on the underside.
See also: Alligators; Crocodile.

Cayman Islands, British dependency in the Caribbean Sea, about 200 mi (320 km) northwest of Jamaica, consisting of 3 islands: Grand Cayman, Little Cayman, and Cayman Brac. Georgetown, on Grand Cayman, is the capital and largest city. Tourism is the main industry, but low taxes and banking secrecy laws have attracted a variety of companies.

Cayuga, Native American tribe, member of the Iroquois League. They inhabited the area of Cayuga Lake, N.Y., until the American Revolution. Favoring the British, many then moved to Canada, while others dispersed.

CB radio *See:* Citizens band radio.

CD *See:* Compact disc.

Ceausescu, Nicolae (1918-89), president of Romania from 1967 until 1989, when he was overthrown and executed. First elected member of the Romanian Communist Party Central Committee in 1948, he became head of the committee in 1965. As president, he instigated a policy of independence within the Soviet bloc.
See also: Romania.

Cebu, densely populated Philippine island with a narrow coastal plain and interior mountains. The city of Cebu is the main port and commercial center for the surrounding islands. It was the first permanent Spanish settlement in the Philippines (1565).
See also: Philippines.

Cecilia, Saint, early martyr of the Christian church, in 2nd or 3rd century Rome. According to legend, she converted St. Valerian and his brother Tiburtius. The Roman prefect Almachius ordered her burned to death for distributing goods to the poor. Tradition says that she was beheaded when her body would not burn. Though her authenticity is doubted, she continues to be popular and is represented on the church calendar (Nov. 22). She is considered the patron saint of music.
See also: Christianity.

Cedar (genus *Cedrus*), evergreen, cone-bearing tree with fragrant wood. The timber trade calls several unrelated trees "cedar" but the true cedars are species found in the mountains of North Africa and Asia. They are distinguished by being the only evergreen conifers with needles in tufts along the branches.

Cedar Rapids (pop. 168,767), city in east central Iowa, seat of Linn County. Cedar Rapids is situated on the Cedar River in an agricultural area. It produces radio and electronic equipment, corn products, cereal, and meat products.
See also: Iowa.

Celandine (*Chelidonium majus*), low-growing biennial of the poppy family with yellow flowers that are open for most of the spring and summer.

Celery, biennial vegetable (*Apium graveolens*) related to parsley and carrots, eaten either raw or cooked. The seeds are used for seasoning. Celery grows best in cool weather and consists of long stalks topped with feathery leaves. It was first cultivated in France in the early 1600s.

Celery cabbage *See:* Chinese cabbage.

Celesta, keyboard musical instrument that looks like a miniature upright piano. The hammers strike metal bars, producing a delicate, bell-like sound. Introduced during the late 19th century as an improvement on the glockenspiel, the celesta is often used in orchestral compositions.

Celibacy, voluntary abstinence from marriage and sexual intercourse. Celibacy of Roman Catholic church clergy was instituted by Pope Siricius (386), but abandoned by Protestants during the Reformation. In the Eastern Church, married men can be ordained as priests, though bishops must be celibates or widowers.

Céline, Louis-Ferdinand (Louis-Ferdinand Destouches, 1849-1961), French novelist. His first novels, *Journey to the End of Night* (1932) and *Death on the Installment Plan* (1936), made his vivid, hallucinatory style notable.

Cell, in biology, smallest unit that possesses all the essential properties of a living organism: metabolism, reproduction, differentiation, regeneration, and excitability (response to stimulus). A living cell can also be described as having a flow of matter: Chemicals come into the cell; they are broken down or transformed into other chemicals that then leave the cell. There is also a flow of energy: Energy comes into a living system either as chemical energy or as radiant energy from the sun. However, a third element is crucial: information. A living system is a directed and responsive system in which there is control and regulation of chemical reactions. The cell contains a specific information system: the nucleic acids and the proteins, DNA (deoxyribonucleic acid) and RNA (ribonucleic acid). These molecules contain and transmit the genetic information of the cell. All cells have an outer membrane, or cell boundary, cytoplasm (the contents of the cell excluding the nucleus), a cell nucleus, more or less spherical, containing specific molecules, a nucleolus, and organelles (cytoplasmic structures) to which the diverse functions are attributed.
See also: Biology.

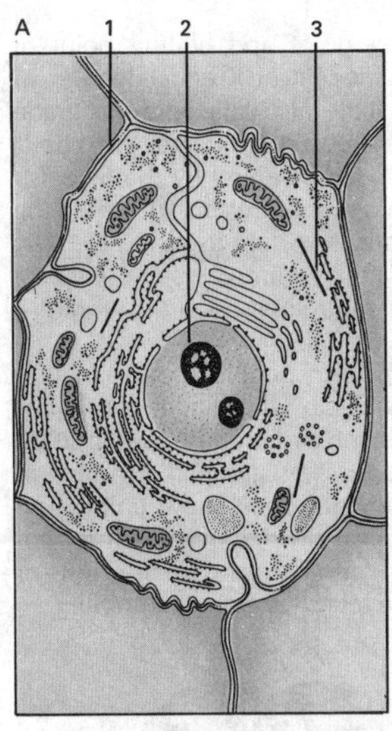

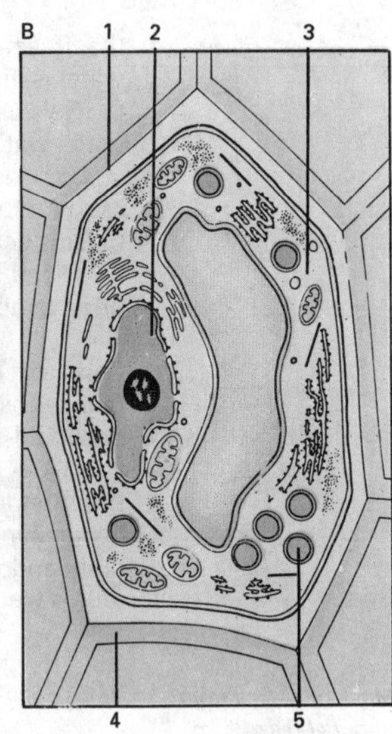

Typical animal (A) and plant (B) cells.
1. cell membrane
2. nucleus
3. cytoplasm
4. cell wall
5. chloroplasts

Cellini, Benvenuto (1500-71), Italian metalsmith, sculptor, and writer. Of his work in precious metals little survives except the gold and enamel saltcellar made for Francis I of France in 1543. His most famous sculpture is *Perseus with the Head of Medusa* (1545-54). His celebrated *Autobiography* (1558-62) is colorful and vigorous, though somewhat exaggerated.

Cello, or violoncello, second largest instrument of the violin family, with 4 strings and a range starting 2 octaves below middle C. Dating from the 16th century, it is the deepest-toned instrument in the string quartet.
See also: Violin.

Cellophane, transparent, nonpenetrable film of cellulose used in packaging, first developed by J. E. Brandenburger (1911). Wood pulp is soaked in sodium hydroxide, shredded, aged, and mixed with carbon sulfide to form a solution of viscose. After an acid bath, the cellulose is regenerated as a film, dried and waterproofed.
See also: Cellulose.

Celluloid, first commercial synthetic plastic, developed by J. W. Hyatt (1869), made by treating nitrocellulose with camphor and alcohol. It is tough, strong, and resistant to water and oils. Used in dental plates, combs, billiard balls, lacquers, and spectacle frames, celluloid is highly inflammable and has been largely replaced by newer plastics.
See also: Plastic.

Cellulose, main constituent of the cell walls of plants. Cellulose is a complex carbohydrate with a structure similar to that of starch. Processed cellulose is used in the manufacture of many goods, among them, paper, explosives, fibers, plastics, and adhesives.

Louis-Ferdinand Celine

Celsius scale, system for measuring temperature in which the interval between the freezing point and boiling point of water is divided into 100 equal degrees. In the Celsius scale, also called the centigrade scale, water freezes at 0 degrees and boils at 100 degrees. Invented by the Swedish astronomer Anders Celsius in 1742, the Celsius scale is widely used in scientific work and is the common system of measuring temperature in most of the world.

Celts, prehistoric people speaking Indo-European dialects, whose numerous tribes occupied much of Europe between 2000 and 100 B.C. They grouped together in small settlements. Their social unit, based on kinship, was divided into a warrior nobility and a farming class. Their priests or druids were recruited from the nobility.

Mask of a Celt from about 400 B.C.

Cement, most important modern construction material, notably as a constituent of concrete. Cement generally is composed mostly of limestone, clays, gypsum, and crushed rock.

Cenozoic Era, third and current geologic era. Beginning about 65 million years ago, the Cenozoic is characterized by mammals and flowering plants.

Censorship, supervision or control exercised by authority over public communication, conduct, or morals. Early censorship in the Greek city-states curbed conduct considered insulting to the gods or dangerous to public order. In Rome the censor dictated public morality. Censorship of books was not widespread (although some books were publicly burned) until the invention of printing in the 15th century. The first *Index of Prohibited Books* was drawn up by the Roman Catholic Church in 1559 in an effort to stop the spread of subversive literature. Similar tactics were employed by Protestants and secular authorities. In the United States, freedom of the press is protected from federal interference by the First Amendment to the Constitution.
See also: Bill of Rights.

Census, enumeration of persons, property, and other items within a community, state, or country. A population census has been conducted in the United States every 10 years since 1790. In addition to population, the United States conducts a census on agricultural production every 5 years on the years ending in 4 and 9. Manufacturing, mining, and business censuses are also performed every 5 years on the years that end in 2 and 7.
See also: Population.

Centaur, in Greek mythology, a creature with the torso, arms, and head of a man and the body of a horse. Most centaurs were considered savages, but a few, such as Chiron, a son of Cronus, the titan, were wise teachers of humans.
See also: Mythology.

Centennial Exposition, International, world's fair held in Philadelphia from May to Nov. 1876, celebrating the 100th anniversary of the Declaration of Independence. Exhibits from the arts and sciences were displayed by 49 nations. The United States exhibited its new mass production techniques. The fair attracted almost 10 million visitors.

Centipede, long-bodied member of the class Chilopoda, phylum Arthropoda with 2 legs to each of their 15 to 100 segments. They are usually 1-2 in (2.5-5 cm) long, though in the tropics some reach 1 ft (30 cm). Normally insectivorous they paralyze their food by injecting poison through a pair of pincers located near the head. Centipedes live in moist places under stones or in soil.

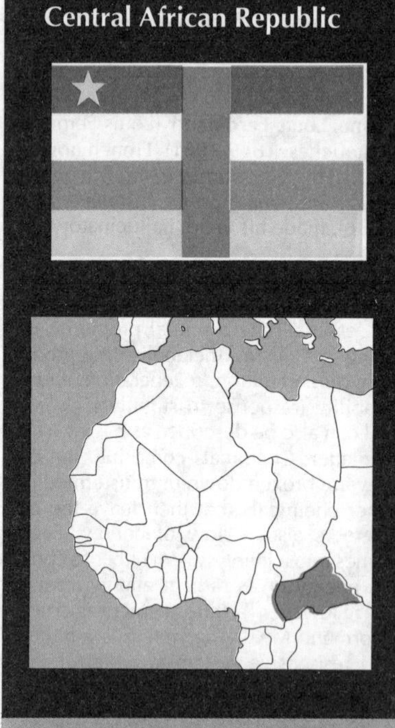

Capital:	Bangui
Area:	240,535 sq mi (622,984 sq km)
Population:	2,813,000
Form:	republic, under military rule
Independent:	1960
GNP:	U.S.$1,080,000,000
Per capita:	U.S.$390

Central African Republic, landlocked country in equatorial Africa, bordered by the Republic of Chad to the north and Sudan to the west.

Land and climate. The republic lies north of the equator and is a rolling plateau at about 2,500 ft (763 m). In the east the Fertit Hills rise to 4,200 ft (1,280 m), and in the northeast the Ouanda-Djale Hills reach 3,750 ft (1,143 m). A dense tropical rainforest covers the southern part of the country; the rest is grassland, becoming drier and treeless toward the northern border. Jungle wildlife is abundant. Rain is abundant in the south, but mainly confined to the season from June to October in both central and northern areas. The chief rivers are the Ubangi and the Shari.

People. The Central African Republic has a population density of less than 5 persons per sq mi (2 per sq km). Ethnic groups include the Zandé, the Banda, and the Mbaka. The small European group is mainly French. French is the official language, but Sango is the language most commonly spoken. Religion is mainly animism, but a growing number of Muslims live near the Chad border. Illiteracy is high, but school attendance is rising. There are technical schools, but no university.

Economy. The country's poor economy is based on farm crops for home consumption and cotton and diamonds for export. The tsetse fly prevents significant expansion of the cattle industry. There are plans to exploit the deposits of iron, limestone, silver, and uranium. The one large industrial complex is the textile plant at Bouali, which uses hydroelectric power. The country's economy suffers from the lack of a seaport and the absence of railways. The capital, Bangui, is a river port, located on the Ubangi, a tributary of the Congo River.

History. The first French outposts were established in 1886. In 1894 the area was called the territory of Ubangi-Shari. In 1910 it was incorporated into French Equatorial Africa. After World War II demands for independence were led by M. Barthélemy Boganda, resulting in the inclusion of Ubangi-Shari in the French Community in 1958. Two years later, on August 13, the country became an independent nation as the Central African Republic. In 1959 David Dacko became the independent nation's first president. He was overthrown in 1966 by a military coup, led by Colonel Jean-Bedel Bokassa, who assumed the presidency and had the nation's sole political party appoint him president for life in 1972. In 1979 Dacko regained control with support from the French, and Bokassa went into exile. Dacko, elected to a 6-year term in 1981, was ousted in a military coup later that year. Bokassa returned in 1986, but was sentenced to life in prison the following year for embezzlement and complicity in several murders.

Central America, North America southeast of Mexico, land bridge to South America, separating the Pacific Ocean from the Caribbean Sea. Its north and south land boundaries, about 1,100 mi (1,770 km) apart, are the Isthmus of Tehuantepec in Mexico and the valley of the Atrato in Colombia. Within this area are the republics of Guatemala, Honduras, El Salvador, Nicaragua, Costa Rica, Belize, and Panama. Most of the people are of Spanish or Native American ancestry, living as farmers in the mountain valleys or working in the forests or mines. The dominant feature of the region is a string of mountain ranges characterized by great volcanic activity and earthquakes. They are part of the same mountain system as the islands of the Greater and Lesser Antilles. Most of the mountains are no more than 6,000 ft (1,829 m), though some volcanoes are higher than 10,000 ft (3,048 m), with Mt. Tajumulco in Guatemala rising to 13,845 ft (4,220 m). The volcanic deposits in the northwest have produced very fertile highlands. Relatively level tracts of land occur on the Yucatán Peninsula and along the coast. These limestone plains of the peninsula are the most extensive in Central America, and support dense tropical forests. The rolling coastal lowlands appear insignificant by comparison, broadening to a width of only 90 mi (145 km) along the Mosquito Coast (on the Caribbean) and never exceeding 30 mi (48 km) along the Pacific coast. A trough, the Nicaraguan Depression, divides the northern part of the isthmus from the narrower southern part and encloses lakes Nicaragua (3,000 sq mi/7,770 sq km) and Managua (386 sq mi/1,000 sq km), the largest in Central America. The climate is basically tropical, but is drier on the Pacific side. The considerable variations in temperature and rainfall are due mainly to differences in elevation. The 2 early civilizations of the region were the Mayan and the Toltec. The Maya reached their highest cultural state between A.D. 300 and 900. They were familiar with mathematics, astronomy, and agricultural techniques; they built cities of stone, erected fine monuments, and developed intricate handicrafts. The Toltec of central and southern Mexico spread their influence to the Yucatán Peninsula and into Guatemala. The Spanish conquerors arrived in the early 1500s to destroy what were already dying civilizations. Hernando Cortes completed the conquest of the whole area by 1525, and it remained a Spanish colony for nearly 300 years. Foreign rule ended in 1821, when a sympathetic Spanish governor was elected the first head of the independent United Provinces of Central America. The union was dissolved in 1838, and the 5 states (Costa Rica, El Salvador, Guatemala, Honduras, and Nicaragua) became independent. Subsequent attempts to reestablish the confederation have failed. A looser form of cooperation was begun with the creation of the Organization of Central American States in the 1950s. Costa Rica is politically the most stable country; the others have suffered from external conflicts, dictatorships, and revolutions.

Central Intelligence Agency (CIA), U.S. government agency established in 1947 by the National Security Act to coordinate, evaluate, and disseminate intelligence from other U.S. agencies and to advise the president and the National Security Council on security matters. The CIA has done much to further the interests of the United States and its allies, but such fiascos as the Bay of Pigs invasion of Cuba, as well as concern over possible misuse of its considerable independence in the wake of "Watergate," led to a major investigation and internal reorganization in 1975.
See also: Intelligence service.

Central Park *See:* New York City.

Central Powers *See:* World War I.

Centrifugal and Centripetal Forces, forces acting on a body as it moves along a curved path. If a stone is whirled in a circular path on a piece of string, it is acted on by a force pulling it toward the center of the circle (centripetal force). The stone also appears to be acted upon by an equal and opposite force pulling it outward (centrifugal force). An example of centripetal force is the force of gravity exerted on the moon by the earth to keep it in orbit. The value of the centripetal force (F) is given by the equation $F=mv^2/r$ where m equals the mass of the body, v is its velocity, and r is the radius of curvature of its path.
See also: Inertia; Newton, Sir Isaac.

Centrifuge, machine for separating mixtures of different densities by rotating them in a container at high speed. The centrifugal force experienced in a rotating frame causes the heavier elements to sink. Centrifuges are used in drying clothes, in separating milk from cream, in chemical analysis, and in atomic isotope separation.

Century of Progress Exposition, international exhibition celebrating Chicago's centenary, held on the shores of Lake Michigan, 1933-34. Primarily concerned with science and technology, it also stimulated design and architecture.

Century plant, any of several desert plants (genus *Agave*) native to warm climates in the Americas. The name arose from the misconception that the plant bloomed only once every 100 years. The century plant, also known as the American aloe, has thick fleshy leaves and produces a yellow flower spike. In Mexico, the sap of some agaves is used to make beverages, and the long tough fiber is formed into cord and rope.

Cephalopoda, class of predatory mollusks including the cuttlefish, octopus, and squid. They swim by forcing a jet of water through a narrow funnel near the mouth. Cephalopods have sucker-bearing arms and a horny beak. The shell, typical of most mollusks, is absent or reduced.

Cephalosporins, group of broad-spectrum antibiotics, most of which are derived from the penicillinlike cephalosporin C that was discovered in sewage in Sardinia. They act against the same bacteria as natural penicillin and can produce allergic reactions.
See also: Antibiotic.

Cepheid variables, yellow giant stars whose brightness varies regularly with a period of 1 to 50 days. The length of their cycle is directly proportional to their brightness, making them useful mileposts for computing large astronomical distances.

Ceram *See:* Indonesia.

Ceramics, materials produced by treating nonmetallic, inorganic substances (originally clay) at high temperatures. Modern ceramics include such diverse products as porcelain and china, furnace bricks, electric insulators, ferrite magnets, rocket nosecones, and abrasives. In general, ceramics are hard, are chemically inert under most conditions, and can withstand high temperatures in industrial applications. Primitive ceramics in the form of pottery date from the 5th millennium B.C.
See also: Pottery and porcelain.

Cerberus, in Greek mythology, huge multiheaded dog, with a mane and tail of snakes, that guarded the entrance to Hades.
See also: Hades.

Cereal, generic name for annual plants of the grass family, including wheat, rice, corn, barley, sorghum, millet, oats, and rye. Cereal is richer in carbohydrates than any other food, and also contains protein and vitamins. About 1,757 million acres of the world's arable land are sown with cereal crops each year.

Cerebellum *See:* Brain.

Cerebral hemorrhage, bleeding from a broken blood vessel in the brain, with damage to or destruction of surrounding tissues. The interruption of circulation also causes damage to tissue elsewhere in the brain. Cerebral hemorrhages are often fatal, and can leave victims suffering from various disabilities, including loss of speech and loss or impairment of muscle control.
See also: Stroke.

Cerebral palsy, diverse group of conditions caused by brain damage around the time of birth and resulting in a variable degree of nonprogressive physical and mental handicap. The condition is often accompanied by abnormalities of muscle control, loss of sensation, and some degree of deafness. Speech and intellectual development can also be impaired but may be entirely normal.

Cerebrospinal fluid, serum-like fluid produced in the lateral ventricles of the brain; it bathes the brain and spinal cord.
Lumbar puncture (spinal tap) between the third and fourth lumbar vertebrae is performed to obtain a specimen of cerebrospinal fluid for diagnostic study of brain and spinal cord disease.
See also: Human body.

Cerebrum *See:* Brain.

Ceres, in Roman mythology, goddess of grain, agriculture, and the harvest. A daughter of Saturn, she was the counterpart of the Greek Demeter. She was honored annually with a festival called Cerealia. The word "cereal" is derived from her name.
See also: Mythology.

Ceres, largest and first discovered (1801) of thousands of asteroids, or minor planets, that orbit the sun between Jupiter and Mars. It is named after the Roman goddess of grain.

Cerium, chemical element, symbol Ce; for physical constants see Periodic Table. A malleable metal, cerium is the most abundant of the rare-earth metals. Cerium was discovered in 1803 by Jons Berzelius and Wilhelm van Hisinger. It is found in various minerals monazite, being the most important source. Cerium and its compounds are used for decolorizing and polishing glass, in incandescent gas mantles, in carbon-arc lighting, and as catalysts.

Cermet, or ceramal, composite material made from mixed metals and ceramics. Cermets combine the hardness and strength of metals with a high resistance to corrosion, wear, and heat, qualities that make it invaluable in jet engines, cutting tools, brake linings, and nuclear reactors.

Cervantes Saavedra, Miguel de (1547-1616), Spanish novelist, poet, and playwright, a major figure of Spanish literature. In 1585 he wrote *La Galatea*, a pastoral novel in verse and prose. In 1605 he published the first part of *Don Quixote de la Mancha*, his masterpiece. A debunking of pseudo-chivalric romance and a rich tragicomic novel, it was an immediate success. He also wrote about 30 plays, of which 16 survive, a volume of short stories, and the second part of *Don Quixote* (1615). His last work was the prose epic *Persilas and Sigismunda* (1617).
See also: Don Quixote.

Statues of Cervantes' greatest creations, Don Quixote and Sancho Panza, located in Madrid, Spain

The Tuareg city of Bardai on the northern flank of the Tibesti Mountains in northern Chad.

Cesarean section, surgical incision through the abdominal wall and uterus, performed to deliver a baby. Usually done when a vaginal delivery is considered dangerous because the woman's pelvis is too narrow or the baby is in an abnormal position.
See also: Birth.

Cesium, chemical element, symbol Cs; for physical constants see Periodic Table. Cesium was discovered spectroscopically by Robert Bunsen and Gustav Kirchhoff in 1860. It is a metal belonging to the alkaline group. Elemental cesium is silvery-white, soft, and ductile; it is one of the three metallic elements that is liquid at room temperature. Cesium is used in ion propulsion systems and in atomic clocks, as well as in optical instruments and in glass and ceramic production.

CETA (Comprehensive Training and Employment Act of 1973), federally funded system for training unemployed people and providing them with jobs and job-related services. The Neighborhood Youth Corps, the Job Corps, and the Young Adult Conservation Corps are CETA programs. In 1981 severe cutbacks in Federal funding eliminated many programs.

Cetacean, any of the mammalian order (Cetacea) comprised of whales, porpoises, and dolphins. Cetaceans have fishlike bodies with virtually no hair and thick layers of blubber to keep them warm. They bear their young alive and live entirely in water.

Cetewayo, or Cetshwayo (1826-84), fourth and last Zulu king (1873-79). In 1879 he declared war on British and Boer settlers in the Transvaal, but was captured and deposed.
See also: Zulu.

Ceylon *See:* Sri Lanka.

Cézanne, Paul (1839-1906), French painter. His early work is impressionist in style, but he later abandoned that mode to develop an approach of his own, lyrical and vibrantly colorful, as in the *Grandes Baigneuses* (1905). Cézanne sought to suggest depth through the use of color and to give his paintings structural strength and formal integrity. He became a prime innovator of modern art, anticipating Cubism and other movements.

Chabrier, Alexis Emmanuel (1841-94), French composer best remembered for orchestral works such as *España* (1883) and various piano pieces. His work influenced Claude Debussy, Maurice Ravel, and Erik Satie.

Chad

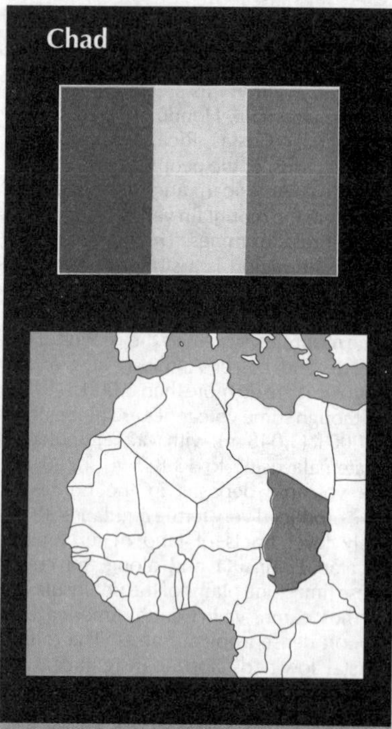

Capital:	N'Djamena
Area:	495,755 sq mi (1,284,000 sq km)
Population:	5,538,000
Form:	republic
Independent:	1960
GNP:	U.S. $850,000,000
Per capita:	U.S. $160

Chad, Republic of, landlocked state in north-central Africa bordered by 6 states, including Libya to the north and the Central African Republic to the south. N'Djamena is the capital.
Land and Climate. Its northern part extends into the Sahara desert, where the Tibesti highlands rise to 11,000 ft (3,353 m). The southern part consists largely of semiarid steppe with wooded grasslands (savannas) near Lake Chad, watered by the Shari and Logone rivers.
People. Northern and central Chad are inhabited chiefly by nomadic Arab-influenced tribes, who are predominantly Muslim; many speak Arabic as well as their tribal language. In the savanna regions the black population speaks tribal languages and includes chiefly animists, although small groups have adopted Islam. Fewer than 5,000 Europeans, mainly French, live in Chad. French is the official language.
Economy. Chad's economy is very poorly developed. The great majority of the population is engaged in subsistence farming. The chief export crop is cotton; some rice, peanuts, meat, hides, and smoked fish are also exported. A major obstacle to economic development is the lack of adequate roads, along with the absence of railroads. Chad depends on air and river transport, but the Shari River is navigable only 4 months of the year from Fort Lamy to Fort Archambault, and other rivers are even less reliable in the dry season.
History. Chad was penetrated by Arab traders and Berbers from the Sahara in the 7th century. The black kingdoms of Wadai and Baguirmi suffered from these incursions, but later became powerful sultanates. The Muslim empire of Kanem controlled most of the area around Lake Chad in the 16th century. The Chad area,

lying in the heart of Africa, was not affected by the slave trade. Lake Chad was reached by British explorers in 1823. In 1850 the first German explorer mapped the area between Lake Chad and the Nile. By 1890 the French were arriving in considerable numbers, and by 1900 the French conquest of the whole area was completed. When French Equatorial Africa was formed in 1910, Chad was part of Ubangi-Shari-Chad and, 10 years later became the separate territory of Chad. In Aug. 1960 Chad became an independent republic within the French Community, with François Tombalbaye as the first president. Tombalbaye was killed in a coup in 1975. A new coalition government took power in 1979, but civil war soon broke out between rebels backed by Libya's Muammar Qadhaffi and government forces supported by France. The conflict has continued, in various forms.

Chadwick, Sir James (1891-1974), English physicist who was awarded the 1935 Nobel Prize in 1932 for his discovery of the neutron.
See also: Physics.

Chagall, Marc (1887-1985), Russian painter. His style is characterized by dreamlike, lyrical fantasy and bright but never harsh colors. His subjects are often derived from the traditions of folklore and Jewish life in Russia before World War I. Chagall also illustrated a number of books and created memorable works in stained glass. Two large murals (1966) are in the Metropolitan Opera House, New York City.

Chagres, river in eastern Panama that was dammed during construction of the Panama Canal, thus forming Gatun Lake.

Chaikovsky, Peter Ilich *See:* Tchaikovsky, Peter Ilich.

Chain, Sir Ernst Boris (1906-79), German-born English biochemist who helped develop penicillin for clinical use. He shared with Howard W. Florey and Alexander Fleming the 1945 Nobel Prize for physiology or medicine.
See also: Biochemistry; Penicillin.

Chain reaction *See:* Nuclear energy.

Chair, everyday piece of furniture that in early civilizations was reserved for persons in high authority. This historical significance is reflected in the term "chairman." A skilled craft became an art in the hands of English makers Thomas Chippendale (1718-79) and George Hepplewhite (d.1786); and U.S. cabinetmakers William Savery (1721-87) and Duncan Phyfe (c.1786-1854). Wood remains a favorite material, but steel and plastics are also now used. Modern chairs are designed on ergonomic principles; to conform to the structure of the body, thus providing support at anatomically correct points.

Chalcedony, mineral consisting of microcrystalline silica (silicon dioxide) with a glassy or waxy luster, sometimes translucent. Chalcedony occurs in a wide range of colors, some forms valued as gems and ornamental stones. Bloodstone (heliotrope), a dark green variety with red spots, was often used in the Middle Ages in sculptures showing martyrdom. Other chalcedonies are jasper, carnelian, agate, and onyx.

Chalcocite, sulfide mineral (Cu_2S) that is an important ore of copper. Shiny gray in color, chalcocite is formed at fairly low temperatures.
See also: Copper.

Chalcopyrite, most important copper ore. It contains iron and sulfur as well as copper, and has the formula $CuFeS_2$. Chalcopyrite has a yellowish coloration with a metallic luster, though it easily tarnishes to produce iridescent colors. It is found worldwide.
See also: Copper.

Chaldea, name for southern Babylonia after its occupation by the Chaldeans in the 10th century B.C. The Chaldeans were accomplished astronomers and astrologers, and ancient writers often used their name as a synonym for "magician." In 626 B.C. Nabopolassar founded the Chaldean Neo-Babylonian Empire, which held sway over the area until it was captured by the Persians in 539 B.C.

Chaliapin, Feodor Ivanovich (1873-1938), Russian operatic bass. Famous for his acting as well as for his voice, he settled in France after the Russian Revolution. His main successes were as Mussorgsky's *Boris Godunov* and Boito's *Mefistofele.*
See also: Opera.

Chalk, soft, white rock composed of calcium carbonate, $CaCO_3$, a type of fine-grained, porous limestone containing the shells of minute marine animals. Widely used in lime and cement manufacture and as a fertilizer, chalk is also used in cosmetics, plastics, crayons, and oil paints.
See also: Calcite; Calcium carbonate.

Challenger, one of the 4 space shuttles of the NASA space program. On Feb. 3, 1984, it began a spectacular flight (its fourth mission) during which 2 astronauts became the first human beings to fly freely in space. On Jan. 28, 1986, Challenger exploded shortly after lift-off with a crew of 7 aboard.

Chamberlain, family name of 3 prominent British statesmen, **Joseph Chamberlain** (1836-1914) entered Parliament in 1876 as a Liberal. He fought for integration of the Empire through preferential tariffs. His son, **Sir Joseph Austen Chamberlain** (1863-1937), entered Parliament as a Conservative in 1892, and held various government offices from 1902. As foreign secretary (1924-29), he helped secure the Locarno Pact, which encouraged stability and good will in Europe following World War I, and shared the 1925 Nobel Peace Prize. Austen's half-brother, **Arthur Neville Chamberlain** (1869-1940), was a Conservative member of Parliament from 1918. He became prime minister in 1937. In his efforts to avert war with Germany, he followed a policy of appeasement and signed the Munich Pact (1938), which surrendered part of Czechoslovakia to Hitler.

Marc Chagall's I and My Village *(1911; Museum of Modern Art, New York)*

Chamberlain, Wilt (1936-), U.S. basketball player. The 7-ft 1-in (216-cm) center, is regarded as one of the most dominant players of all time. Chamberlain holds National Basketball Association (NBA) records for most points in a season (4,029), in a game (100), and most rebounds per season (2,149), and is second on the all-time regular season scoring list (31,419 points). He played for the Philadelphia (now Golden State) Warriors, Philadelphia 76ers, and Los Angeles Lakers of the NBA (1959-72). He was inducted into the Basketball Hall of Fame in 1978.

Chamber music, musical composition intended for a small ensemble. Originally the term meant domestic music, written by a house composer for a patron. It became established as a special genre during the 17th and 18th centuries. The instrumental combinations are varied, usually with not more than 15 instruments. Chamber music is characterized by an intimacy of communication between the performers. The principal form of composition is the string quartet (2 violins, viola, and cello), which was developed by Franz Joseph Haydn and Wolfgang Amadeus Mozart, and expanded to new dimensions by Ludwig van Beethoven.

Chamber of Commerce, association of businesspeople set up to improve business conditions and practices, and to protect business interests. The first in the United States was the New York Chamber of Commerce (1768); now most sizeable cities have one. Activities are coordinated through the U.S. Chamber of Commerce, founded in 1912.

Chambers, Whittaker (1901-61), U.S. journalist and main witness in perjury trial of State Department official Alger Hiss. Chambers joined the Communist Party in 1924, became a Soviet agent during the 1930s, and in August 1948, testified that Alger Hiss passed him U.S. military secrets. Chambers' autobiography, *Witness,* was published in 1952.

Chameleon, lizard of the family Chamaeleonidae, found in Africa and Madagascar, that is well adapted to living in trees. Its tail is prehensile, and its eyes can turn independently in all directions. It feeds on insects that it catches with its long, sticky tongue, and the color of its skin alters swiftly in response to changes of emotion or temperature. There are over 80 species, ranging in length from 2 in to 2 ft (5 cm to 0.6 m).

Most chameleons have a tongue almost as long as their body. The tongue can capture prey in less than one second.

Chamois (*Rupicapra rupicapra*), goatlike mammal of the family Bovidae found in the mountain forests of Europe and Asia Minor. Famous for their agility, chamois are capable of leaps of over 20 ft (6 m). They have thick brown coats and stand about 3 ft at the shoulder. Their hides were used for making the original chamois leather.

Chamomile *See:* Camomile.

Champagne, historic province in northwestern France, famous for the effervescent sparkling white wines from vineyards between Reims and Epernay. The ruling counts of Champagne were especially powerful during the 12th and 13th centuries, and the region had a central role in French history.
See also: France.

Champlain, Samuel de (1567-1635), French explorer, first governor of French Canada. He explored the St. Lawrence Gulf and River (1603) as far as the Lachine Rapids. He explored much of what is now Nova Scotia, founded Quebec in 1608, discovered Lake Champlain in 1609, and was named commandant of New France in 1612. When Quebec surrendered to the English in 1629, Champlain was imprisoned in England; on his release in 1633 he returned to Canada as governor.
See also: Lake Champlain; Quebec.

Champollion, Jean François (1790-1832), French linguist and historian. Professor of history at Grenoble University (1809-16), he was the first to effectively decipher Egyptian hieroglyphics, a result of his research on the Rosetta stone.
See also: Rosetta stone.

Champs Élysées *See:* Paris (city).

Chancellorsville, Battle of, U.S. Civil War battle, May 1-5, 1863. Gen. Joseph Hooker's Union forces crossed the Rappahannock River to Chancellorsville, west of Fredericksburg, Va., in a bid to encircle Gen. Robert E. Lee's Confederate forces protecting Fredericksburg. The ploy failed; Lee's counteroffensive led to a Confederate victory in a battle that claimed 30,000 lives, including that of Gen. Stonewall Jackson.
See also: Civil War, U.S.

Chandler, Raymond Thornton (1888-1959), U.S. detective novelist whose works combine wit and pace with strong characterization, particularly of their hero, Philip Marlowe, a tough but honest private detective. Among Chandler's best- known works are *The Big Sleep* (1939) and *The Long Goodbye* (1953).

Chandler, Zachariah (1813-79), U.S. politician, a founder of the Republican Party. Elected to the Senate in 1857, he firmly opposed slavery and the Confederate cause. He was secretary of the interior, 1875-77.
See also: Republican Party.

Chandragupta, Maurya (4th century B.C.), Indian emperor c.321-297 B.C., founder of the Maurya dynasty. He rose to power after Alexander the Great's withdrawal from India, extending his realm into Afghanistan. His grandson was the emperor Asoka.
See also: Maurya Empire.

Changamire Empire *See:* Zimbabwe.

Channel bass *See:* Redfish.

Channel Islands, archipelago totaling 75 sq mi (194 sq km) in area, in the English Channel off northwestern France. Dependencies of the British crown since 1066, they are administered according to their own local constitutions. The main islands are Jersey, Guernsey, Sark, and Alderney.

Channel Islands National Park (est. 1980), 8 islands off South California, extending over 150 mi (241 k) in the Pacific Ocean. The islands include Santa Barbara, Anacapa, San Miguel, Santa Rosa, and Santa Cruz, known for sea mammals, including the California sea lion, and rich fossil beds.
See also: National Parks.

Channing, William Ellery (1780-1842), U.S. theologian, writer, and philanthropist, leader of the Unitarian movement in New England. Active in antislavery, temperance, and pacifist causes, he believed that moral improvement was humanity's prime concern. He influenced Emerson, Holmes, and Bryant.
See also: Unitarianism.

Chansons de Geste, medieval French epic poems written from the 11th through the 13th centuries. Most deal with the legendary exploits of the Emperor Charlemagne and his knights. The best known is the *Chanson de Roland,* composed c.1098-1100.
See also: Charlemagne.

Chanukah *See:* Hanukkah.

Chaos, in Greek mythology, first being to be created, represented as a living creature made up of all the world's components. It was believed that all other beings emanated from Chaos.
See also: Mythology.

Chaparral, area of plant growth dominated by shrubs, evergreen oaks (including the mountain mahogany and scrub oak), and the chamiso scrub. North American chaparrals exist in southern California, some slopes of the Rocky Mountains, the Sierra Nevada, and Baja California, in Mexico.

Chapel, place of Christian worship, usually located in a chamber within a church. Chapels originated after the early Middle Ages because the increase of relics and altars devoted to certain saints required them. The Sistine Chapel in the Vatican is probably the best known.

Chaplin, Charlie (Sir Charles Spencer Chaplin; 1889-1977), English film actor and director, great comedian of the silent cinema. A vaudeville player, he rose to

Charlie Chaplin

fame in Hollywood, 1913-19 in a series of short comedies, in which he established his Little Tramp character. After 1918 he produced his own feature-length films, including *The Gold Rush* (1925) and, with sound, *Modern Times* (1936) and *the Great Dictator* (1940).

Chapman, George, (1559?-1634), English poet and dramatist. His translations of Homer (1598- 1616), although imprecise and full of his own interjections, long remained standard, and they are still recognized as masterpieces. His plays include *Bussy d'Ambois* (1607).

Chapman, John *See:* Appleseed, Johnny.

Chapultepec, historic hill near Mexico City, site of an Aztec royal residence and religious center in the 14th century. American forces stormed the Spanish- built fort in the Mexican War of 1847. It is now a museum and state residence.
See also: Aztecs; Mexico.

Char, or brook trout, North American member of the trout family, (genus *Salvelinus*) prized for its flesh.

Charcoal, form of amorphous carbon produced when wood, peat, bones, cellulose, or other carbonaceous substances are heated with little or no air present. A highly porous residue of microcrystalline graphite remains. Charcoal as a fuel was used in blast furnaces until the advent of coke. A highly porous form, activated charcoal, is used for adsorption in refining processes and in gas masks.
See also: Carbon.

Charcot, Jean Martin (1825-93), French neurologist whose researches advanced knowledge of hysteria, multiple sclerosis, locomotor ataxia, asthma, and aging. Freud was one of his many pupils.
See also: Neurology.

Chard *See:* Swiss chard.

Chardin, Jean-Baptiste-Simeon (1699-1779), French painter. He is best known for his still-lifes and for his middle-period genre paintings, affectionate depictions of the everyday life of the bourgeoisie (*The Kiss, The Grace*). His work is characterized by a straightforward realism, with atmospheric use of light and color.

Still life by Chardin. Chardin chose simple household items as his subjects: a copper pot, a wooden mortar and pestle, a mound of cheese, and a few eggs.

Chardonnet, Hilaire (1839-1924), French chemist, industrialist, and physiologist who did pioneering work on synthetic fiber, developing what later became known as rayon, first shown to the public at the Paris Exposition of 1889.
See also: Chemistry; Rayon.

Charles, name of 7 rulers of the Holy Roman Empire, starting with Charlemagne.

Charlemagne (Charles the Great; 742?-814), King of the Franks, founder of the Holy Roman Empire. He waged war against the Saxons for 32 years, eventually compelling them to adopt Christianity. Crowned Emperor in Rome by Pope Leo III (800), Charlemagne ruled over a kingdom that included most of the lands that are now France, West Germany, Austria, Switzerland, the Netherlands, Belgium, and Luxembourg. It also included about half of Italy. The establishment of his reign sealed the break between the remnants of the Roman Empire and Byzantium, and thus the split between Roman Catholicism and the Greek Orthodox church. Charlemagne fostered a rich culture that inaugurated the Carolingian Renaissance.
See also: Holy Roman Empire.

Charles, name of 10 kings of France. **Charles I** was Charlemagne. **Charles II** (the Bald; 823-77) reigned as king of the West Franks from 843 and as emperor of the West from 875. Numerous revolts and invasions troubled his reign, culturally the last flowering of the Carolingian renaissance. **Charles III** (the Simple; 879-929), grandson of Charles II, reigned (893-923). **Charles IV** (the Fair; 1294-1328) reigned from 1322. **Charles V** (the Wise; 1337-80) reigned as regent 1356-60 and as king from 1364. In poor health, he nevertheless put down a peasant uprising and various plots by his nobles. He declared war upon England in 1369 and before his death had regained most French territory occupied by the English. **Charles VI** (the Mad; 1368-1422) reigned from 1380. Corrupt advisers often ruled in his stead. England overran most of northern France, and Charles was forced to name Henry V of England his heir. **Charles VII** (1403-61) reigned from 1422. Early in his reign he was unwilling to challenge the English occupation of France, and he allowed Joan of Arc to be burned as a heretic. Later Charles introduced tax reforms, rebuilt his army, and regained all occupied territory except Calais. **Charles VIII** (1470-98) reigned from 1483. **Charles IX** (1550-74), who reigned 1560-98, was dominated by his mother, Catherine de Médici. **Charles X** (1757-1836) reigned 1824-30. He returned to France from exile after the restoration of the monarchy, becoming king on the death of his brother Louis XVIII. He was exiled again after the 1830 revolution.

Charles, Stuart kings of England, Scotland, and Ireland. **Charles I** (1600-49), a Catholic, came to the throne in 1625. His reign is most notable for his continual conflicts with the mainly Puritan Parliament. From 1629 to 1640 he ruled without a parliament, having dissolved it. Civil and religious liberties were eroded, leading to widespread emigration to America and finally, in the 1640s, to a civil war. In 1646-48 the king's supporters were defeated. Charles I was executed. His son, **Charles II** (1630-85) took refuge in France in 1646. In 1651 he returned to Scotland and was crowned king. He attempted to retake England, but was defeated by Oliver Cromwell and fled to France again. In 1660, 2 years after the death of Cromwell, Charles II took the throne again in the Stuart Restoration. Despite his dissolution of Parliament in 1681, that institution's power increased during his reign. Political parties were born, and colonization flourished.

Charles I (1887-1922), last emperor of Austria and King of Hungary (1916-18). When coming to the throne, during World War I, he made peace overtures to the Allies, which provoked opposition in Germany. He abdicated after Austria's defeat in the war, going into exile in Switzerland. Three years later he unsuccessfully tried to regain the throne of Hungary.

Charles Martel (A.D. 688-741), Frankish ruler who, as mayor of the palace (chief minister) from 714, ruled in place of the weak Merovingian kings. The son of Pepin II, he received his surname Martel (the Hammer) after his victory against Muslim invaders in 732. His policies assured Frankish preeminence in northern Europe, which culminated in his grandson Charlemagne's coronation as emperor (800).
See also: Merovingian.

Charles the Great *See:* Charlemagne.

Prince Charles

Charles Philip Arthur George (1948-), Prince of Wales and Duke of Cornwall, heir apparent to the British throne. The first child of Queen Elizabeth II and Prince Philip, he was educated at Cheam, Gordonstoun, and Cambridge. In 1981 he married Lady Diana Spencer; they divorced in 1996.

Ray Charles

Charles, Ray (Ray Charles Robinson; 1930-), U.S. singer, composer, and pianist, credited with synthesizing aspects of gospel, blues and country, and jazz to create a new form of music known as soul. He lost his eyesight at age 6 to untreated glaucoma. Charles's first popular successes were "Baby Let Me Hold Your Hand" (1951) and "I've Got a Woman" (1955). His albums include *Ray Charles* (1957), *Modern Sounds in Country and Western Music* (1962), and *Wish You Were Here Tonight* (1983).

Charleston (pop. 506,875), city in South Carolina and major regional port. The oldest and largest city in the state, Charleston is a tourist center famous for its 18th-century buildings and monuments. It is also a producer of chemicals and steel. In 1861 it was the scene of the first military incident of the Civil War, the firing on Fort Sumter.
See also: South Carolina.

Charlotte (pop. 1,162,093), largest city in North Carolina, seat of Mecklenburg County. A flourishing commercial, industrial, and railroad center, it produces textiles, manufactures chemicals and cottonseed oil, and is the central market for the region's agricultural products. Johnson C. Smith University, Queens College, and a campus of the University of North Carolina are located there.
See also: North Carolina.

Geoffrey Chaucer

Charlotte Amalie (pop. 11,800), capital of the U.S. Virgin Islands, located on St. Thomas. Founded by Danish colonists in 1673, it was purchased by the United States in 1917.
See also: Virgin Islands.

Charlottestown (pop. 15,800), capital of Prince Edward Island, Canada, on an estuary of the Hillsborough River. When the city was founded in 1720 by French colonists, it was known as Port de la Joie, but it was renamed in 1763 for the wife of King George III. Incorporated in 1875, it is now a fishing and shipbuilding center.
See also: Prince Edward Island.

Charlottesville (pop. 131,107), city in Virginia situated in the foothills of the Blue Ridge Mountains; seat of Albemarle County. Founded in 1762, it was named after the wife of King George III. Charlottesville is the site of the University of Virginia, founded in 1819 by Thomas Jefferson, whose home, Monticello (now a national monument), stands on a hill overlooking the city. The area's industries involve agricultural products, textiles, lumbering, and precision instruments.
See also: Virginia.

Charon, in Greek mythology, son of Erebus (the belt of darkness between Earth and Hades) and Nyx (night). His task was to ferry dead souls across the rivers Acheron and Styx to Hades, the underworld.
See also: Mythology.

Charter Oak, celebrated oak tree in which the Connecticut colonial charter was hidden in 1687 to prevent its surrender to the royal governor of New England. The tree was uprooted in a storm in 1856, at an estimated age of 1,000 years.

Chartism, radical and unsuccessful attempt by voteless British laborers to gain economic and social equality, 1838-48. It was one of the first working-class political movements in Britain. William Lovett of the London Workingmen's Association drafted the "People's Charter."

Chartres (pop. 37,100), historic city in northwestern France, capital of Eure-et-Loire department and commercial center of the Beauce region. It is famous for its Gothic Cathedral of Notre Dame, built in the 12th and 13th centuries.
See also: France.

Chartres Cathedral *See:* Chartres.

Charybdis *See:* Scylla.

Chase, Salmon Portland (1808-73), U.S. senator (1849-55, 1860-61), governor of Ohio (1855-59), secretary of the treasury (1861-64), and chief justice of the U.S. Supreme Court (1864-73). An abolitionist, he instituted a national banking system under the Lincoln administration and presided over the impeachment trial of President Andrew Jackson.
See also: Supreme Court of the United States.

Chase, Samuel (1741-1811), U.S. Supreme Court justice (1796-1811). A signer of the Declaration of Independence, he was also a member of the Maryland legislature and the Continental Congress. In 1804 an unsuccessful attempt to impeach him was made by President Jefferson, who believed Chase to be a partisan pro-Federalist.
See also: Supreme Court of the United States.

Chase, William Merritt, (1849-1916), U.S. painter and art teacher known for his portraits and still lifes. Chase taught in New York City and on Long Island. Among his students were Sheeler, Hopper, and O'Keeffe.

Chat, any of several singing birds. The yellow-breasted chat (*Icteria virens*) is the largest wood warbler and is common in thickets over much of the United States.

Château, French term for castle, often applied to any stately mansion; originally a well-fortified medieval castle with a moat, used for defense rather than residence. The 16th century château contained outbuildings and were of a more residential nature. Elegant châteaus in the Loire valley in France are Chenonceaux and Chinon.
See also: Castle.

Chateaubriand, François René, Vicomte de (1768-1848), French writer and diplomat, a founder of the Romantic movement in 19th-century French literature. His works include the North American romance *Atala* (1801), *René* (1802), and *Mémoires d'outre-tombe* (1849-50).
See also: French language.

Chatham, Earl of *See:* Pitt.

Chattanooga (pop. 162,000), city in southern Tennessee, on the Tennessee River near the Georgia border. Chattanooga's strategic position as a railroad junction made it an important Northern stronghold in the Civil War. It later grew into a major transportation and industrial center for textiles and metals.
See also: Tennessee.

Chattanooga, Battle of *See:* Civil War, U.S.

Chatteron, Thomas (1752-70), English poet who at the age of 12 wrote poems in pseudomedieval English that he presented as the work of a 15th-century monk, Thomas Rowley. Despite the success of a burlesque opera, *The Revenge* (1770), he remained destitute and poisoned himself at age 17.

Chaucer, Geoffrey (c.1340-1400), English poet. His early writing, including an incomplete translation of *Le Roman de la Rose*, shows strong French influence. In the 1370s, growing familiarity with Boccaccio and Dante influenced *The Parliament of Fowls* and *Troilus and Criseyde*, a powerful love poem. His masterpiece was *The Canterbury Tales*, a 17,000-line poem, in which pilgrims on their way to the shrine of St. Thomas à Becket pass the time by telling stories ranging from the serious to the comedic and ribald. Apart from creating vivid characters, the tales portray contemporary attitudes toward religion, love, and sex. The language of *The Canterbury Tales* is Middle English, sufficiently different from modern English to require translation to be understood. Changes in the language, particularly the emergence of Early Modern English less than a century after Chaucer's death, vastly reduced the popularity of his work, but since the 18th century, he has come to be regarded as one of the masters of world literature.
See also: Canterbury Tales.

Chauncy, Charles (1705-87), influential American Congregationalist minister, a critic of the Great Awakening religious revivalists. He supported the American Revolution in his sermons.

Chautauqua Movement, U.S. adult education movement that began at Lake Chautauqua, N.Y., in 1874, as a course for Sunday school teachers. The founders, John H. Vincent, a Methodist minister, and

Lewis Miller, a businessperson, organized lectures, concerts, and recreation activities attended by thousands each year until c.1924.

Chavez, Carlos (1899-1978), Mexican composer who founded the Symphony Orchestra of Mexico (1928), which he conducted until 1949. His compositions include the ballet *El fuego nuevo* (1921), the ballet-symphony *H. P.* (1926-27), and *Invention*, for string trio (1965).

Chavez, Cesar Estrada (1927-), Chicano (Mexican-American) labor leader, founder of the United Farm Workers (UFW), an affiliate of the AFL-CIO. The early history of the UFW was marked by bitter strikes and violent clashes with both growers and the Teamsters. In the 1960s and 1970s, Chavez was instrumental in organizing national boycotts of table grapes and lettuce in solidarity with the struggle of the farm workers.

Chayote, climbing vine of the gourd family cultivated chiefly for its pear-shaped, round fruit, which is used in puddings, pies, and salads. The plant is also used as livestock feed.

Checkers, or draughts, game played by two people on a board of 64 alternating light and dark squares. Each player begins with 12 red or black checkers placed on the 12 dark squares nearest him or her. Taking turns, players advance their checkers diagonally in a forward direction. Once the last row of the board is reached, checkers are crowned, becoming kings, which may move forward or backward and can jump backwards over their opponents. The game became popular in Europe in the 16th century, but its origins go back to ancient times.

Checks and balances, term that describes the powers of the 3 branches of government: the legislature, which makes laws; the executive, which enforces them; and the judiciary, which interprets them. Each branch acts independently and participates in the realms of the other 2, thus limiting potential abuse of power.
See also: Government.

Cheese, food made from the milk of cows, sheep, or goats, with a high content of protein, calcium, and vitamins. Hard cheeses include Cheddar and Parmesan, soft cheeses may be unripened (cottage cheese) or ripened (Brie, Camembert) to develop flavor.

Cheetah, tawny-coated, black-spotted cat (*Acinonyx jubatus*), native to Africa and southwest Asia, the fastest land animal, capable of running at speeds of up to 70 mi (113 k) per hr. The average adult weighs 100 lb (45 kg). Hunting has greatly reduced their numbers.

Cheever, John (1912-82), U.S. author. Noted for his irony and poetic style in portraying the lives of the upper middle classes in suburbia, he was awarded the Pulitzer Prize for fiction (1978) for *The Stories of John Cheever*. His novels are *The Wapshot Chronicle* (1957), *The Wapshot Scandal* (1964), *Bullet Park* (1969), *Falconer* (1979), and *Oh What a Paradise It Seems* (1982).

Cheka, Russian abbreviation of "Extraordinary Commission for Combatting Counter-Revolution, Speculation, Sabotage, and Misuse of Authority," the secret police set up by the Bolsheviks in 1917 to eliminate their opponents. Reorganized by Lenin in 1922 and renamed the GPU (State Political Directorate), it was the ancestor of the modern KGB.
See also: KGB.

Chekhov, Anton Pavlovich (1860-1904), Russian dramatist and short story writer. The Moscow Art Theatre produced his 4 major plays, depictions of Russian rural upper- and middle-class life: *The Seagull* (1898), *Uncle Vanya* (1899), *The Three Sisters* (1901), and *The Cherry Orchard* (1904). Chekhov's works emphasize mood and character development more than plot. He was also a physician, and ran a free clinic for peasants in Melikhovo, where he lived.

Chemical and biological warfare, military use of chemical poisons or disease-causing agents against enemy troops, civilians, animals, and plants. In World War I chlorine, mustard gas (causing skin blistering), and phosgene (causing fatal lung irritation), killed 100,000. Newer, deadly nerve gases are weapons of mass destruction. In the war in Vietnam U.S. forces used riot-control gases and chemical defoliants with carcinogenic effects. The Iraqi regime of Saddam Hussein used poison gas against the Kurdish population in Iraq and against Iranian troops during the Iran-Iraq War (1980-88).

Chemical bond *See:* Chemistry; Mineral.

Chemical element *See:* Element, chemical.

Chemical engineering *See:* Engineering.

Chemical reaction, process whereby 1 substance is changed chemically into another through the formation or destruction of bonds between atoms. Chemical equations, consisting of formulas and symbols representing elements and compounds, express the events of chemical reactions.
See also: Chemistry.

Chemical warfare *See:* Chemical and biological warfare.

Chemistry, science dealing with the composition of substances and the changes that occur when they react with one another. All chemical changes take place by the linking-up of atoms into molecules, a molecule being the smallest particle of a chemical compound that has that compound's characteristic properties. Chemical reactions may involve elements themselves, elements and compounds, or compounds and other compounds. Atoms themselves remain fundamentally unchanged in chemical reactions. It is the grouping of the atoms into molecules that is altered. Some chemical changes are relatively simple, while others, such as those that occur during the chemical processes of living matter, are highly complex, involving molecules that may consist of thousands of atoms. Organic chemistry deals with the chemistry of compounds of carbon (the chemical processes of life take place between substances in which carbon plays a major role). Inorganic chemistry is concerned with all the remaining elements. Apart from that broad division, there are other specialized fields. Physical chemistry deals with the physical properties and behavior of chemicals. Analytical

Anton Chekhov and his wife, Olga Knipper

The cheetah is the fastest of all animals and can achieve a speed of 60 mph (95 km).

chemistry develops laboratory methods of determining the chemical structure of materials. Chemotherapy is the treatment of diseases with chemical drugs; biochemistry is concerned with living processes; chemurgy deals with agricultural products; electrochemistry studies the electrical effects of chemical change.

Chemotherapy, use of nonantibiotic chemical substances to treat disease, most often cancer. The drug destroys rapidly spreading cancer cells without significantly affecting normal cells in the body.
See also: Cancer.

Chénier, André Marie de (1762-94), French poet. His work forms a bridge between classicism and romanticism: *Le Jeune Captive* (1795), *Elégies* and *Bucoliques* (1819). He was guillotined during the French Revolution for writing pamphlets against the Reign of Terror.

Chennault, Claire Lee (1890-1958), U.S. pilot. In 1937 he went to China to organize Chiang Kai-shek's air force in the war against Japan. In 1941 he organized in China the American Volunteer Group, the Flying Tigers. From 1942 to 1945 he served as commander of the U.S. air forces in China.
See also: Flying Tigers.

Cheops *See:* Khufu.

Cherbourg (pop. 28,400), seaport and naval station in France, on the English Channel. The harbor is a base for French fishing fleets and a port of call for ocean-going vessels.
See also: France.

Cherimoya (*Annona cherimola*), tropical tree native to Peru and Ecuador. It grows to about 25 ft (7.5 m), bearing oval, deciduous alternate leaves about 10 in (25 cm) long. Its round or conical edible fruit is pale green, 5 in (13 cm) long and weighing 1 lb (.45 kg), with an inner white pulp tasting of pineapple and banana. The cherimoya is cultivated in California and Florida.

Chernenko, Konstantin Ustinovich (1911-85), leader of the Communist Party of the Soviet Union (1984-85). He joined the Communist Party in 1931 and became a protege of Leonid Brezhnev, thus rising in the hierarchy of the party. In 1978, Chernenko was elected a full member of the Politburo, the policymaking body of the Communist Party. He became general secretary of the Communist Party in Feb. of 1984. As its leader, Chernenko renewed arms control talks with the United States. He was succeeded by Mikhail Gorbachev.
See also: Union of Soviet Socialist Republics

Chesapeake Bay Bridge

Cherokees, once the largest Native American tribe in the southeast United States. The Iroquis-speaking Cherokees were decimated by smallpox and by conflicts with European settlers in the 18th century. They were deprived of their lands, and thousands of them died on a march west in 1838, an event known in Cherokee history as the "trail of tears." Today nearly 45,000 Cherokees live in Oklahoma. Several thousand remain in N. Carolina.

Cherry, any of several trees (genus *Prunus*) best known for their red, fleshy fruits with hard pits. Varieties of sweet and sour cherries are grown widely in the United States. Cherry blossom trees are also grown as ornaments and for their fine-grained timber.

Cherry laurel (family Rosaceae, genus *Prunus*), any of various evergreen shrubs native to southeastern Europe and the Orient. The cherry laurel is grown for ornamental use in the United States. Reaching to 18 ft (5.4 m), the shrub bears small, glossy, poisonous leaves, fragrant clusters of small white flowers, and dark purple, foul-tasting friut.

Cherubini, Maria Luigi (1760-1842), Italian composer who spent most of his life in France. He wrote operas: *Medea* (1797) and *Les Deux journées* (1800), which influenced Beethoven, and sacred works, such as the *Requiem in D minor* (1836).
See also: Opera.

Chesapeake and Ohio Canal, waterway along the Potomac River between Washington, D.C., and Cumberland, Md. Planned as a route to the Midwest, it went bankrupt because of competition from the railroads. The canal became a historical park in 1961.

Chesapeake Bay, large inlet of the Atlantic Ocean on the east coast of the United States, an important trade route for ocean-going vessels. About 200 mi (320 km) long and 30 mi (48 km) wide, the bay separates the Delmarva Peninsula from sections of Maryland and Virginia.
See also: Atlantic Ocean.

Chesapeake Bay retriever, medium-sized breed of water-loving hunting dogs of the sporting group. The dog stands 21-26 in (53-66 cm) at the shoulder and weighs 55-75 lbs (25-34 kg), and possesses yellowish eyes. Its short, thick, oily coat ranges from dark brown to light tan in color, resists cold, and easily sheds water. The breed was developed in the United States when two English-stock puppies were found shipwrecked off the Maryland coast (1807) and were bred with local retrievers.

Chesnutt, Charles Waddell (1858-1932), African-American educator, lawyer, and fiction author. *The Conjure Woman* (1899), a group of short stories, related incidents of slavery in a dialectic, folktale style and was his first and best-known book. Chesnutt was the recipient of the Spingarn Medal (1928) for his literary depictions of the struggles faced by blacks in America. He ceased writing in 1905 but continued to practice law until his death. Other works include *The Wife of His Youth and Other Stories of the Color Line* (1899), *The House Behind the Cedars* (1900), and *The Marrow of Tradition* (1901).

Chess, sophisticated board game for 2 players probably invented in India in ancient times. It was introduced into Persia in the 6th century A.D. and was brought to Europeans by the Arabs, probably at the time of the Crusades. By the 13th century, the game was widespread in Europe, and the rules of the modern version were definitively stabilized in the 16th century. The first modern world championship was held in 1851, and world champions have been recognized continuously since then. The game board has 64 squares in 8 rows of 8, and each player has 16 pieces. Each piece moves in specific ways, and the players alternate moves. The object of the game is to capture the opponent's king. If neither player is able to do this, the game is drawn. At the highest levels of international play, draws are common.

Chesterfield, Philip Dormer Stanhope, 4th Earl of (1694-1773), English politician and author chiefly remembered for his posthumously published *Letters to His Son* (1774), which offer vivid, amusing insights into the morality of the age.

Chesterton, G(ilbert) K(eith) (1874-1936), English author and critic, noted for his lyrical style and delight in paradox. He wrote poetry, stories (the Father Brown detective stories, 1911-35), novels (*The Napoleon of Notting Hill*, 1904), literary criticism (on Browning, 1903, and Dickens, 1906); and essays, collected in *Tremendous Trifles* (1909).

Chestnut, any of various deciduous trees (genus *Castanea*) of the beech family, with edible nuts. The American chestnut is rare, having been nearly wiped out by a fungus, "chestnut blight," introduced from Asia in 1904 and spread by woodpeckers. The related chinquapin of the southeastern states appears to be immune. Chestnuts are highly valued for their timber, nuts, and bark.

Chevalier, Maurice (1888-1972), French singer and film star. He gained international fame in the 1920s and 1930s as the embodiment of French charm and light-heartedness. His films include *The Love Parade* (1930), *Gigi* (1958), and *Can-Can* (1959).

Chevrolet, Louis (1879-1941), Swiss-born U.S. automobile racer and designer; in 1911 he designed and built (with William C. Durant) the first Chevrolet, a 6-cylinder car produced to compete with the Ford. He later designed the racers that won the 1920 and 1921 Indianapolis 500-mile race.
See also: Automobile.

Chewing gum, confection made from chicle, other resins and waxes, sugar, and corn syrup. For centuries Native American tribes chewed chicle (gum from the juice of the sapodilla tree) or spruce resin. Early European settlers adopted the habit, and chewing gum has been made commercially in the United States since the 1860s.

Cheyenne (pop. 73,142), capital of Wyoming and center of its agriculture. Founded in 1867 by U.S. Army officers and Union Pacific Railroad engineers, the town became an outfitting station for prospectors going West and a haven for outlaws until vigilantes gained control. Its annual Frontier Days attract thousands of tourists.
See also: Wyoming.

Cheyenne, North American tribe speaking an Algonquian language. By the mid 19th century the Cheyenne had become nomadic hunters on the Great Plains, and after 1860 their fierce battles against encroaching whites culminated in the defeat of General Custer in 1876 by an alliance of Sioux and northern Cheyenne forces. Eventually the Cheyenne were resettled in Oklahoma and Montana.

Chiang, Kai-shek (1887-1975), Chinese Nationalist leader. After Sun Yat-sen's Revolution (1911), Chiang joined the Kuomintang, the governing party, organized the nationalist army, and rose rapidly to power. After Sun's death (1925), Chiang made an alliance with the Communists, but in 1927 he reversed course, initiating a 22-year-long civil war against them. Chiang became president of the Nationalist government in 1928, and he commanded Chinese and later (1942) Allied forces in the war against Japan. In 1949, with the victory of the Communists in the civil war, Chiang withdrew from the mainland to Taiwan, where he became president of Nationalist China (1950).
See also: China.

Chiang Ching-kuo (1910-88), leader of the Nationalist Chinese government on Taiwan (1975- 88). The son of Chiang Kai-shek and his first wife, he was born in Zhejiang province. He attended Chinese schools before going to the Soviet Union to study in 1925, where he graduated from the military-political institute in Leningrad. In 1937 Chiang returned to China, where he advanced rapidly in the Nationalist government, becoming defense minister in 1965, prime minister in 1972, and president in 1978. Chiang was popular for his efforts in eliminating corruption in government.
See also: Taiwan.

Chibcha, inhabitants of the plateau of Bogota in central Colombia. Their highly developed society was based on farming and the worship of the Sun God. The Spaniards destroyed their culture in the 16th century. Over a million descendants survive in the area today.

Chicago (pop. 6,069,974), third-largest city in the United States, on Lake Michigan in Illinois, hub of the U.S. road, rail, and air systems. Industry is diverse, including the famous meatpacking plants, grain elevators, and chemical, metal, and printing industries. Chicago grew as a French trading post in the 1700s, but it was not until after the Black Hawk War (1832) that the city began to grow rapidly. Even the Great Fire of 1871, which destroyed 2,000 acres of property, could not end Chicago's vitality. Downtown Chicago has some of the world's tallest buildings. The North Side, along the lake, is residential. The West Side is a largely white mixture of various ethnic groups, while the South Side is home to most of the city's African-Americans, who constitute nearly 40% of the population.
See also: Illinois.

Chicago, University of, private, nondenominational, coeducational institution in Chicago, Ill, incorporated in 1890. It has about 7,500 students and over 1,000 faculty members. The Pritzker School of Medicine, the Enrico Fermi Institute for Nuclear Studies, and the department of education are among its best-known facilities.

Chicano, person of Mexican-American descent. Chicanos first came to the United States as seasonal field workers. Over 8 million Chicanos now live in mainly southern U.S. cities. A Chicano labor leader, Cesar Chavez, organized the United Farm Workers (1962) and achieved bargaining power for Chicano field workers after years of bitter struggle.

Chichén Itzá, archeological remains of a Maya city in Yucatan, Mexico. Founded c.514 by the Itzá, abandoned (692), reoccupied (c.928), and finally abandoned in 1194, the city connected two great periods of Maya civilization. Its astronomical observatory and temples show Toltec influence.
See also: Yucatán Peninsula.

Chickadee, any of various common small songbirds of the family Paridae (genus *Penthestes* or *Parus*), with dark caps and bibs and white faces. They are noted for their tameness and agility.

Chickamauga, Battle of, bloodiest single battle of the U.S. Civil War, fought in northern Georgia, Sept. 19-20, 1863. The Union forces lost about 16,000 troops, the Confederates some 18,000.
See also: Civil War, U.S.

Section of the business district of Chicago

Chickasaw, Native American tribe speaking a Muskogean language of the Hokan-Sioux grouping. The Chickasaw were moved from northern Mississippi to Oklahoma in 1834.

Chiang Kai-shek

Chicken, domesticated bird raised for its meat and eggs, originating in northern Asia from the jungle fowl. The Leghorn, leading egg breed in the U.S., lays over 300 eggs a year. Chickens raised for meat are marketed as broilers and fryers when under three months old (weighing 2-4 lb/1-2 kg) and as roasters when 4-8 months old (weighing up to about 7 lb/3 kg).

Chickenpox, or varicella, contagious disease caused by a virus and affecting mainly children, usually in epidemics. Its characteristic blister-like, itching rash appears two to three weeks after infection.

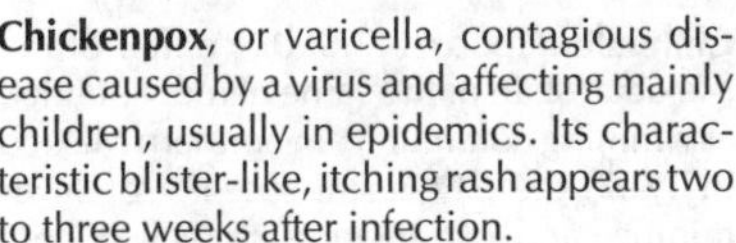

Chickpea, or garbanzo bean (*Cicer arietinum*), bushy annual legume cultivated from antiquity in southern Europe, India,

Some popular breeds of chickens

New Hampshire

Leghorn

Rhode Island Red

and the Middle East, and grown for its edible seeds. The chickpea plant grows to 1-2 ft (30-60 cm) and bears rectangular pods containing 1 or 2 3/8 in (9.5 mm), seeds, which may be white, light yellow, red, brown, or near-black. The chickpea is a good source of protein and carbohydrates.

Chicle, latex of the sapodilla tree, a tropical American evergreen, and the raw material of chewing gum. Obtained by cutting grooves in the bark, the latex is boiled to remove excess water, then molded into blocks.

Chicory, blue-flowered perennial herb (*Cichorium intybus*) of the Composite family, native to the Mediterranean and now grown in the United States. Its leaves are used in salads, and its roasted roots are sometimes added to coffee. Endive is a type of chicory used in salads.

Chigger, larva of the harvest mite, a small arachnid. Chiggers burrow beneath the skin of mammals and can produce troublesome ulcers.
See also: Mite.

Chihuahua, small terrierlike dog. It stands about 5 in (13 cm) high at the shoulder and weighs about 1-6 lbs (0.5-2.7 kg), and possesses a smooth or a long coat of any color or markings. The chihuahua has a friendly and loyal temperament. Native to Mexico, it is named for the Mexican state of Chihuahua, and is called the "royal dog of the Americas."

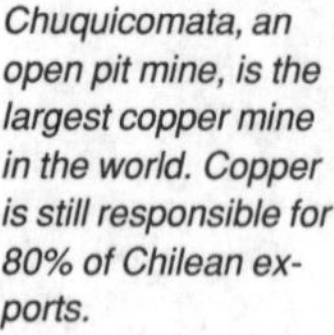

Chihuahua (pop. 447,000), capital of the Mexican state of the same name. Founded as a mining community in northern Mexico in 1707, the city is still a center of silver mining, and of ranching as well. Father Miguel Hidalgo y Costilla, a hero of the Mexican independence struggle, was executed in Chihuahua in 1811. The city was later headquarters for Pancho Villa during the Mexican revolution of 1910- 15.
See also: Chihuahua.

Chihuahua, geographically largest state 95,376 sq mi (247,086 sq km) in Mexico, bordering both Texas and New Mexico. With extensive forests, deep canyons, mineral deposits, and rich grasslands, Chihuahua is the leading cattle-raising and mining state in Mexico.
See also: Mexico.

Chilblain, reaction to cold with pain and itching that can lead to the formation of blisters and ulcers. The blue-red lesions are particularly common on fingers, toes, shins, nose, and ears.

Child abuse, physical, emotional, or sexual injury caused to a child under age 16 by an adult. It is often manifested in cuts, abrasions, bruises, and burns. Incidents of abuse are often detected by an inconsistency between an injury and the explanation of how it occurred. Emotional manifestations of abuse are less easily discovered. Small children who have been abused may be distrustful, passive, and overly concerned with pleasing adults. The emotional impact on children usually becomes obvious at school age, when difficulties in forming relationships with teachers and other children arise.

Child labor, employment of children in industrial or agricultural work, a practice common in the United States in the 19th century. The Fair Labor Standards Act of 1938 forbade the employment of children under 16 in heavy industry, transport, or commerce, and under 18 in occupations detrimental to health.

Children's home, or orphanage, place where foundlings and homeless children live. Children may live in one of these institutions because both parents are deceased or because one or both parents are unable to care for them properly.

Children's literature *See:* Literature for children.

Child welfare, any of various programs, services and, institutions designed to administer to the well-being of children. In the United States such agencies are paid for in part by federal and state taxes. They strive to ensure that children who are suffering from poverty, from the inability of parents to care properly for them, or from neglect or abuse, are provided with food, shelter, medical care, education, and other social services. Some services and organizations that deal with the welfare of children are Aid to Families with Dependent Children (AFDC), Head Start, Medicaid, Department of Health and Human Services, and the Children's Defense Fund.

Chile, country on the Pacific coast of South America, stretching 2,650 mi (1,643 km) from its northern borders with Peru and Bolivia to Cape Horn at the tip of the continent. Chile is narrow, sandwiched between the Pacific Ocean to the west and Argentina to the east; the average distance across the country is only 110 mi (68 km). The Andes Mountains run along the eastern length of the country, and Cerro Ojos del Salado, in the north, is the second-highest peak in the western hemisphere. Most Chileans live in the central part of the country, nearly a third of them in Santiago, the capital and chief industrial city. About 90% of Chileans are Roman Catholics. The national language is Spanish. Chile is a major mining and manufacturing nation (a leading exporter of copper). Colonized by Spain in the 16th century, the country won its independence in 1818. In the 20th century Chile was one of Latin America's most stable democracies. In 1970, the election of Salvador Allende, a Marxist, led to a period of political polarization and economic and civil conflict. It ended in 1973, with a bloody military coup that established a right-wing dictatorship. Civilian rule was restored only in 1990.

Chuquicomata, an open pit mine, is the largest copper mine in the world. Copper is still responsible for 80% of Chilean exports.

Chile

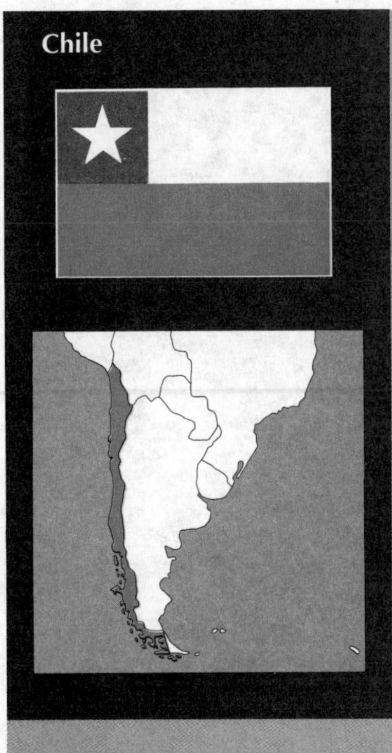

General information	
Capital:	Santiago
Area:	292,135 sq mi (756,626 sq km)
Population:	12,961,000
Official language:	Spanish
Monetary unit:	1 peso = 100 centavos
Main cities:	Santiago, Vina del Mar
Government	
Form:	republic
Independent:	1818
Head of state:	President
Head of government:	President
Legislature:	two legislative houses (Senate and House of Deputies)
Executive:	President and Cabinet
Judiciary:	highest court is the Supreme Court
Political division:	13 regions
National economy	
Gross national product:	U.S. $19,220,000,000
Per capita income:	U.S. $1,510
Agriculture:	sugar beets, wheat, grapes, potatoes, corn, apples
Livestock:	sheep, cattle, pigs
Fisheries:	4,814,000 metric tons
Mining:	copper, molybdenum, manganese, natural gas, petroleum
Industries:	cement, cellulose, fish meal, iron and steel plates, newsprint
Main exports:	copper, industrial products, fruit and vegetables, paper and paper products
Transportation:	5,037 mi (8,107 km) of railroads; 49,227 mi (79,223 km) of roads; 5 international airports
Trading partners:	United States, Germany, Brazil, Japan, United Kingdom
People	
Urban:	81%
Ethnic composition:	mestizo 66%, Spanish 25%, Indian 7%
Birth rate:	22.1 per 1,000 population
Death rate:	5.9 per 1,000 population
Infant mortality rate:	19.1 per 1,000 live births
Life expectancy:	male 68 years, female 75 years

Chillicothe (pop. 21,923), industrial city and agricultural trade center in south central Ohio on the Scioto River and Paint Creek, seat of Ross County. Paper, shoes, and aluminum products are manufactured here. The city, founded in 1796 and incorporated in 1802, was capital of the Northwest Territory 1800-03 and of Ohio 1803-10 and 1812-16.
See also: Ohio.

Chimborazo, inactive volcanic mountain in the Cordillera Occidental of the Andes, located in Chimborazo province in central Ecuador about 120 mi (193 km) from the Pacific Coast. The peak is 20,561 ft (6,267 m) above sea level and Ecuador's highest mountain.

Chimera, in Greek mythology, fire-breathing female monster with a lion's head, goat's body, and serpent's tail. By extension, the word is applied to any imaginary being of incongruous parts, or to any unrealizable plan or scheme. In biology, the term is used for any individual or organ that is composed of tissue of varying genetic origin (e.g. from transplantation).
See also: Mythology.

Chimpanzee, black-haired ape (genus *Pan*) native to central and west Africa. Adult chimpanzees stand up to 5 ft (1.5 m) tall and may weigh 150 lb (68 k). They are the primates most closely related to humans genetically and are considered the most intelligent apes. They eat mainly fruit, leaves, nuts, and termites.

Chimu, ancient Indian culture of coastal northern Peru, developed c.1200. Its capital was the great city of Chan Chan. The Chimu built many cities and had efficient military and social systems, but were overcome by the Inca (c.1400- 60).

China, officially the People's Republic of China, world's most populous country and the third-largest in area. Located in the heart of Asia, China is bordered by the USSR and Mongolia to the north; by North Korea and the Pacific Ocean (East China Sea and South China Sea) to the east; by Vietnam, Laos, Burma, Nepal, and the Indian subcontinent to the south; and by Afghanistan and the USSR to the west.
Land and climate. The country is made up of 3 large geographic regions. Western China is dominated by the high Tibetan Plateau, the mountain ranges that radiate from it, and a great belt of steppe and desert. North China contains lowland areas, dusty highlands, and part of the Gobi Desert. South China is a maze of hills and valleys. The chief rivers are the Yangtze in central China and the Huang He (Yellow) in the north. The capital is Beijing (formerly spelled Peking). The largest city is Shanghai, with a population of more than 8 million. Other cities with more than a million inhabitants are Tianjin (Tientsin), Harbin, Shenyang, Lüda (Lüta), Xi'an (Sian), Qingdao (Tsingtao), Taiyuan, Wuhan, Canton, Chongqing (Chungking), Chengdu (Chengtu), and Nanjing (Nanking).
People. The Han ethnic Chinese constitute nearly 95% of the population, but there are 56 officially recognized minority groups. The national language Putonghua, previously called Mandarin, is based on the spoken form of the Chinese language prevalent in the north, principally Beijing. Different spoken dialects persist in the south, including Cantonese, Wu, and Hakka. The written language, however, is the same everywhere. Traditional Chinese religions were Taoism, and Confucianism. There are substantial minorities of Catholics and Protestants.
History. China has one of the world's oldest civilizations, dating back some 3,500 years. Though ravaged by floods, famines, and wars, it remained politically intact through the centuries, often enjoying levels of civilization unparalleled in the world. The first historic dynasty that ruled the country, the Shang (or Yin) dynasty, arose about 1500 B.C. and lasted for some 500 years. It was under this dynasty that the Chinese writing system developed. The next dynasty, the Chou (c.1027-256 B.C.), saw the rise of classical Chinese philoso-

China

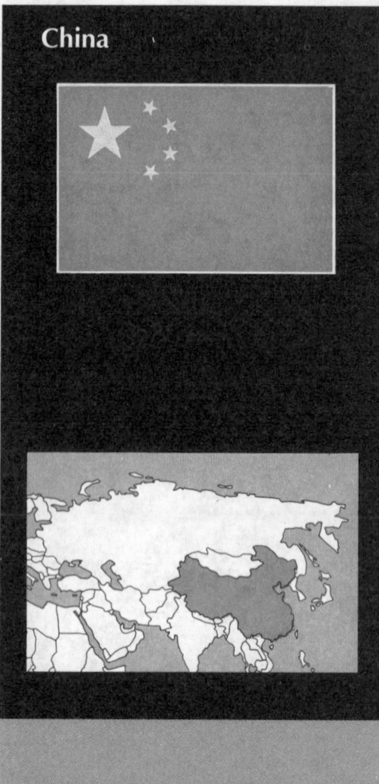

General information	
Capital:	Beijing
Area:	3,695,500 sq mi (9,571,300 sq km)
Population:	1,104,275,000
Official language:	Putonghua (Mandarin)
Monetary unit:	yuan
Main cities:	Shanghai, Beijing, Tianjin, Canton, Shenyang, Wuhan, Chengdu
Government	
Form:	people's republic (communist)
Independent:	1949 (people's republic)
Head of state:	President (elected every 5 years)
Head of government:	Premier
Legislature:	one legislative house (National People's Congress)
Executive:	President and State Council
Judiciary:	highest court is the Supreme People's Court
Political division:	22 provinces, 5 autonomous regions, 3 cities
National economy	
Gross national product:	US $356,490,000,000
Per capita income:	US $330
Agriculture:	rice, vegetables and melons, wheat, corn, sugar cane,tea
Livestock:	pigs, sheep, cattle and buffaloes
Fisheries:	9,346,200 metric tons
Mining:	iron ore, hard and brown coal, tungsten, molybdenum antimony, tin, lead
Industries:	cement, steel, chemical fertilizer, paper and paperboard, sulfuric acid
Main exports:	textiles, rubber and metal products, light industrial products, food and live animals, fuels
Transport:	40,364 mi (64,960 km) of railroads; 610,336 mi (982,243 km) of roads; 7 international airports
Trading partners:	Japan, Hong Kong, United States, Germany, Canada
People	
Urban:	46.5%
Ethnic composition:	Han Chinese 94%, Chuang 1.33%, Hui 0.72%, Uighur 0.59%, Yi 0.54%, Miao 0.50%
Birth rate:	21 per 1,000 population
Death rate:	6.6 per 1,000 population
Infant mortality rate:	32 per 1,000 live births
Life expectancy:	male 68 years, female 71 years

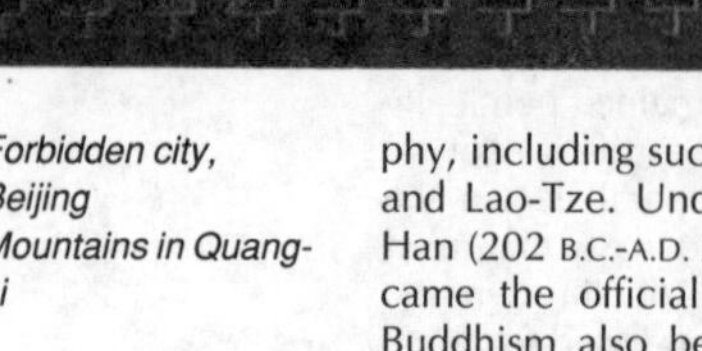

Forbidden city, Beijing
Mountains in Quang-si

phy, including such thinkers as Confucius and Lao-Tze. Under a later dynasty, the Han (202 B.C.-A.D. 220) Confucianism became the official state philosophy, but Buddhism also began to be introduced, and Taoism also grew in influence.

Other major dynasties include the T'ang (618-906), an age of great achievements in poetry and painting; the Sung (960-1279), during which gunpowder was first used for military purposes; and the Yüan (1260-1368), the Mongol dynasty founded by Kublai Khan, the grandson of Jenghiz Khan. It was during the Yüan dynasty that Marco Polo visited China, beginning a period of contact with the West.

The last Chinese monarchy was the Manchu (or Ch'ing) dynasty (1644-1912), founded by the Manchus, a non-Chinese people from Manchuria. It was in the later years of this dynasty that Chinese power gradually weakened, the country losing much of its territory to European, especially British, encroachments.

The monarchy was overthrown in 1912, and a republic was established under Sun Yat-sen. After his death in 1916, China was fragmented among various warlords. In 1927, Chiang Kai-shek (leader of the Nationalist Party) gained control of the government and launched a civil war against the Chinese Communist Party, led by Mao Zedong. The Communists and Nationalists briefly cooperated to resist the Japanese invasion during World War II, but in 1945 civil war broke out again, leading to the victory of the Communists in 1949. The Communist Party established the People's Republic of China, which is now the country's official name. From 1966 to 1969 Mao Zedong, supported by paramilitary groups known as the Red Guard, led the Cultural Revolution, which was an effort to purge the society and government of counterrevolutionary and bourgeois tendencies. During this period many government officials were removed from office, violent demonstrations took place in many cities, and all universities were closed. The late 1980s saw the rise of popular unrest, millions of citizens demanding democratic reforms in the political system.

Great Chinese wall

China Sea, western part of the Pacific Ocean, bordering the east coast of China. Taiwan divides it into the East China Sea to the north, 485,300 sq mi (1,256,927 sq k), maximum depth 9,126 ft (351 m), and the South China Sea to the south, 895,400 sq mi (2,319,086 sq k), maximum depth 15,000 ft (4,572 m). Major seaports are Canton and Hong Kong.

Chinch bug (*Blissus leucopterus*), small insect found in the United States, Canada, Central America, and the West Indies. The adult, about one-fifth in (5 mm) long, is black with red legs and white wings. In spring adults lay eggs on roots and stems in grain fields.

Chinchilla, rodent (genus *Chinchilla*) noted for its soft gray fur. Wild chinchillas were once common in the Andes from Peru to Argentina, but extensive hunting has made them rare. Now reared on fur farms, 100 chinchillas provide the pelts for a single coat.

Chinese, major language of the Sino-Tibetan family, with more native speakers (over 800 million) than any other language in the world. Most Chinese speak Mandarin, a form based on the speech of the educated classes of northern China, particularly the city of Beijing (Peking). Since the early 1950s, this has been called the national language. Other dialects include Cantonese, Hakka, Wu, Fukienese, and Amoy-Swatow. In written form, all these dialects are the same, but the pronunciation may be mutually incomprehensible. Chinese is a tonal, monosyllabic language. The writing system uses an individual character for each syllable, every character representing a word or idea rather than a sound. The characters range from one stroke to as many as 32, but the average is about 11. The earliest witten records in Chinese date back to about 1400 B.C., making Chinese one of the world's oldest, continuously written languages.

Chinese cabbage, common generic name for *pak-choi, pe-tsiao,* and *wong bok,* cabbagelike vegetables of the mustard family with wide, thick leaves on a celerylike stalk used raw in salads and cooked in casseroles and Chinese-style dishes. It is an annual or biennial crop grown in many cool areas of eastern Asia and northern United States.

Chinese Exclusion Acts, legislation limiting immigration of Orientals to the United States. Anti-Chinese prejudice and competition for jobs led to riots preceding the first act (1882), banning Chinese immigration for 10 years. Congress continued these 10-year exclusions until the 1924 law excluded all Asians. In 1943 an immigration quota of 105 Chinese annually was established; the quota was abolished in 1965.

Chinese-Japanese Wars, 2 wars between China and Japan (1894-95 and 1937-45). The first war began after both countries sent troops to quell a rebellion in Korea and ended April 17, 1895 with the Treaty of Shimonoseki granting Korea independence, but giving Japan Taiwan and the Liadong Peninsula. Weakened, China became vulnerable to increased foreign imperialism. Japan seized territory from China (1931-35) resulting in an undeclared war (1937-41). After China declared war on Japan, German, and Italy, and Japan attacked the United States and Great Britain in 1941, the war became part of World War II. When Japan surrendered to the Allies in 1945 the second war ended.
See also: World War II.

Chinese literature, among the world's oldest and greatest, Chinese literary works can be traced back almost 3,000 years. Literature was not considered a separate art form and all cultured people were expected to write with style. As a result, literary topics include history, politics, philosophy, religion, and science.
Historically, government service was the most prestigious vocation in China and most government appointments were made on the basis of an examination which tested the ability to compose both poetry and prose.
Much of Chinese literature deals with moral lessons or the expression of political philosophy. Two early works were *The Book of Songs*, a collection of poems, and *The Book of Documents*, a prose work. Together with *Spring and Autumn Annals*, the *Book of Changes* and the *Book of Rites*, they form the Five Classics as the basis for Confucianism and the ideals of duty, moderation, proper conduct and public service. Taoism, founded by the Laozi during the 300's B.C., was partly a reaction to Confucianism. In contrast to the Confucians, Taoists avoided social obligations and lived simple lives close to nature. *The Classics of the Way and the Virtue* and *The Zhuangzi* are the two literary masterpieces of Taoist thought.
The T'ang dynasty (A.D. 618-907) was the era of four great masters of poetry: Wang Wei, Li Bo, Du Fu and Bo Juyi. Wang Wei's four line poems describe nature. Li Bo wrote of his dreams, fantasies and his love of wine. Du Fu surpassed all others in his range of writing styles and subject matter. Some of his earliest works deal with his disappointment over failing a government service examination. Bo Juyi used satire to protest against numerous government policies.
Both drama and fiction evolved as important forms of Chinese literature in the 1200s. Two famous plays, *The Western Chamber*, by Wang Shifu, and *Injustice to Tou O*, by Guan Hanqing, were written in this period. Tang Xianzu, one of the greatest Chinese playwrights, wrote *Peony Pavillion*, his most notable work, around 1600. Luo Guanzhong wrote in a style resembling the novels of Western writers. In *Romance of the Three Kingdoms*, he describes a power struggle among 3 rival states in the A.D. 100 and 200s. In *The Journey to the West*, also called *Monkey*, Wu Cheng'en uses allegory to relate the adventures of a Buddhist monk on a pilgrimage to India. *Dream of the Red Chamber*, written by Cao Xueqin in the 1700, describes the decline of an aristocratic family. It is perhaps the greatest Chinese novel.

By the 1800, the Chinese had been exposed to Western culture and this influence was evident in the works of Chinese authors in the 1900. With the coming to power of the Communists in 1949 under the leadership of Mao Zedong, literature changed and was directed towards peasants, soldiers and workers. Today, the poems and sayings of Mao Zedong are the most widely read writings in China.

Chinook, Native American tribe of the Pacific Northwest. The Chinook lived along the mouth of the Columbia River, trading, fishing, and gathering berries, nuts, and roots. Religion centered on a ritual welcoming the annual salmon run. Epidemics and contact with European American civilization destroyed Chinook culture in the 1800s. Modern Chinook live in Washington and Oregon making a living by ranching and fishing.

Chinook, warm, dry, westerly wind occurring in winter and spring on the Rocky Mountain eastern slopes. Pacific air condensing moisture on the mountains' western slopes result in air that increases in temperature 1°F for every 180 ft (1°C for every 99 m) as it descends the eastern slope. Chinooks, called snow eaters, rapidly melt and evaporate ground snow. The wind was named by settlers who thought it came from the direction of the Chinook Indian camp along the Columbia River. Similar winds blowing elsewhere are called *foehns*.

Chipmunk, any of various small, striped ground-living rodents (genera *Tamias* and *Eutamias*) of the squirrel family. There are 16 species in North America and 1 in Asia. They feed on fruits and nuts, which they carry in their cheek pouches. Though they do not hibernate, they sleep for long periods in winter.

Chipmunk

Chippendale, Thomas (1718-79), English cabinetmaker whose elegant, individual style blended aspects of Gothic, Rococo, and Chinoiserie. Much 18th-century English furniture is given his name.

Chippewa, or Ojibwa, one of the largest Algonquian-speaking tribes of Native Americans, traditionally living in woodland areas around Lakes Superior and Huron, and to the west. They fought frequently with the Sioux. Longfellow's *The Song of Hiawatha* was based on Chippewa mythology. Today Chippewa live in both the United States and Canada.

Chirac, Jacques (1932-), French political leader, president of the republic since 1995. A Gaullist, he was in the cabinets of 4 premiers before serving as premier (1974-76). He resigned over differences with President Giscard d'Estaing, formed his own party, was elected mayor of Paris (1977-86). Premier from 1986-88 under president Mitterand.

Chirico, Giorgio de (1888-1978), Greek-born Italian painter who founded "metaphysical painting" and influenced surrealism. His works depict desolate, harshly hued scenes and solitary figures that might be seen in a nightmare: *The Soothsayer's Recompense* (1913), *Melancholy and Mystery of a Street* (1914), and *The Poet and His Muse* (c.1925).

Chiron, in Greek mythology, wisest centaur, famous for his knowledge of healing. He taught many Greek heroes, including Achilles. Wounded by Hercules' arrow, he gave up his immortality to Prometheus and was placed in the heavens as the constellation Sagittarius.
See also: Mythology.

Chiropractic, medical therapy based on the theory that disease results from misalignment of the vertebrae, which causes nerve malfunction. Manipulation of the spinal column, massage, and dietary adjustments are the principal methods used.

Chisholm, Shirley (1924-), first black woman to serve in the U.S. Congress, Democratic Representative from 1969-83. She criticized the Vietnam War, and the seniority system in Congress, and advocated for the inner-city poor. From 1964-69 she served in the New York Assembly and campaigned for the 1972 Democratic presidential nomination.

Chisholm Trail, 19th-century route (c.1866-86) for cattle drives between Texas and Kansas, named after the scout and trader Jesse Chisholm. It was superseded by the spread of the railroads.

Chiton, any of an order (Polyplacophora) of primitive mollusks with shells of light overlapping plates and a muscular foot that clings to rocks. Found on shores worldwide, chitons feed on algae scraped from the rocks. They range in length from 1/2 in (1.2 cm) to 1 ft (28.8 cm).

Chivalry, knightly code of conduct in medieval Europe combining Christian and military ideals of bravery, piety, honor, loyalty, and sacrifice, virtues valued by the Crusaders. Chivalry flourished in the 12th to 14th century and declined in the 15th century although it continues to be the basis for gentlemanly behavior. Examples of chivalric literature are the Arthurian legends and the Chansons de Geste.
See also: Knights and Knighthood.

Chive, perennial plant (*Allium schoenoprasum*) of the lily family, of the same genus as the onion. Found wild in Italy and Greece, its leaves are used in salads.

Chlamydia, infectious sexually transmitted disease, caused by various strains of bacteria. Symptoms may include inflamed eyes (conjunctivitis) and pelvic inflammation disease in women. Babies born to mothers with untreated chlamydia may develop pneumonia or the infection itself. One of the most widespread sexually transmitted diseases in the United States, chlamydia is treated with antibiotics.
See also: Venereal disease.

Chloride, chemical compound of chlorine with another element or radical.
See also: Salt, Chemical; Salt.

Chlorine, chemical element, symbol Cl; for physical constants see Periodic Table. Chlorine was discovered by Karl Scheele in 1774. It is a highly reactive, greenish-yellow poisonous gas that combines directly with nearly all elements. It is one of the top 5 industrial chemicals and is used throughout the world to make drinking water safe. It is also used in manufacturing products for sanitizing, bleaching, and disinfecting. Chlorine is a severe respiratory irritant; has been used as a weapon in war.

Chloroform , or trichloromethane, dense, colorless, volatile liquid ($CHCl_3$) produced by chlorination of ethanol or acetone. One of the first anesthetics to be used in surgery, it has since been replaced by less toxic anesthetics, such as ether. It is used in cough medicines and as an organic solvent.

Chlorophyll, green pigment of plants that gives them their color and traps and stores the energy of sunlight required for photosynthesis. The energy is used to convert water and carbon dioxide into sugars.
See also: Photosynthesis.

Chocolate, confection made from cacao beans, used to make candy and beverages. Fermented beans are roasted and ground, then mixed with cacao butter, sugar, and milk solids. The process for making chocolate was perfected in Switzerland around 1876.

Choctaw, Native American tribe traditionally living in what is now southeast Mississippi, speaking a Muskogean language of the Hokan-Siouan family. Under the Removal Act of 1830, they were driven off their lands and transferred to what is now Oklahoma.

Cholera, acute infectious disease involving the small intestine, characterized by diarrhea, vomiting, muscular cramps, and severe loss of body fluid. The disease is caused by a toxin produced by the bacillus *Vibrio cholerae* and is spread by ingestion of water and of foods contaminated by the excrement of infected persons. Cholera can be fatal if untreated. Outbreaks still occur in regions of Africa and Asia where sanitation is poor.

Cholesterol, basic component of fats or lipids, a steroid found in nearly all tissues. Cholesterol is present in large quantity in the nervous system, where it is a compound of myelin, the greasy substance that acts as a sheath around nerve fibers. It is a precursor of bile salts and of adrenal and sex hormones. Large amounts are synthesized in the liver, intestines, and skin. Since abnormal depositing of cholesterol in the arteries is associated with aterio-arteriosclerosis, some doctors advise avoiding high-cholesterol foods and substituting unsaturated for saturated fats. Cholesterol is also a major constituent of gallstones.
See also: Arteriosclerosis.

Chomsky, Noam (1928-), U.S. linguist that revolutionized the study of language structure with his theory of generative grammar, first outlined in *Syntactic Structures* (1957). He was also an influential critic of U.S. foreign policy both during and after the Vietnam War.

Chongqing (pop. 2,730,000), Chungking, or Ch'ung-ch'ing, city in Sichuan province, southwest China, on the Jialing and Yangtze rivers. It is a densely populated political and industrial center, producing steel, medicine, and silk. It became part of China in 220 B.C., served as a treaty port (1891-1943), and was capital of the Nationalist government (1937-46) under Chiang Kai-shek.
See also: China.

Chopin, Frédéric François (1810-49), Polish composer and pianist. In 1831 he moved from Poland to Paris. His chief works are for the piano and include piano concertos in E minor (1833) and F minor (1836), 24 preludes (1838-39), and many waltzes, mazurkas, and polonaises that were inspired by his Polish nationalism. In 1837 he began his friendship with the novelist George Sand. Their relationship ended unhappily in 1847. Chopin died 2 years later of tuberculosis.

Chorale, type of hymn tune developed in Germany during the Reformation. Chorales formed the basis of the new Protestant church music. J.S. Bach harmonized many of these chorale tunes for the Lutheran Church, and used them as a basis for many organ and choral compositions.
See also: Reformation.

Choral music, unaccompanied choral music sung in monasteries during the early Christian era, known as plainsong. Choral music without accompaniment continued through the 16th century. The development of instrumental accompaniment in the 17th and 18th centuries culminated in J. S. Bach's orchestrated cantatas and passions and the oratorios of Handel. Beethoven's inclusion of a choir in the finale of his *Ninth Symphony* (1817-23) marks a turning point in the history of music. Notable among 20th-century choral works are Elgar's *Dream of Gerontius* (1900) and Stravinsky's *Symphony of Psalms* (1930).

Chordate, animal possessing a primitive backbone-like structure (notochord) at some stage in its development. Grouped in the phylum Chordata, chordates include all vertebrates and many small aquatic invertebrates such as the tunicates.

Chorea, disease of the central nervous system causing abnormal, involuntary movements of the limbs, body, and face. Sydenham's chorea (St. Vitus' dance) is a childhood illness associated with rheumatic fever; Huntington's chorea is a rare, fatal hereditary disease of adulthood associated with progressive dementia.
See also: Nervous system.

Chorus, in ancient classical Greek drama, group of actors who commented upon the action. The origin of the chorus is probably the dithyramb, a hymn to the god Dionysus. By the 6th century B.C. the formal dramatic chorus was an integral part of the performance. Gradually the size and role of the chorus was reduced as the actor's role grew. It disappeared by the 2nd century B.C.

Chou En-lai (1898-1976), first prime minister of the People's Republic of China, 1949-76. A founder of the Chinese Communist Party, in 1926 he organized the Shanghai Strike for Chiang Kai-shek and escaped when Chiang betrayed the communists. Director of military affairs for Mao Tse-tung's guerrilla forces, he commanded the first stage of the Long March (1934-35). He won support for China in the Third World and was a major force in taking China into the United Nations (1971) and reestablishing contact with the West in the 1970s.
See also: China.

Chouteau, family of fur traders who helped to open up the Middle West. **(René) Auguste Chouteau** (1749-1829) cofounded with Pierre Laclède the trading past that became St. Louis (1764). Auguste's brother, **(Jean) Pierre Chouteau** (1758-1849), an Indian agent for tribes west of the Mississippi River, co-founded the St. Louis Missouri Fur Company (1809). His son, **Auguste Pierre Chouteau** (1786-1838), was an Indian treaty commissioner and made many expeditions into the West. Auguste Pierre's brother, **Pierre Chouteau** (1789-1865), headed the American Fur Company from 1834. By pioneering the use of steamboats he monopolized trade on the Missouri River.

Chow chow, breed of nonsporting dog believed to have come from China, with a thick, soft coat, and a unique blue-black tongue. The chow chow stands 18-20 in (46-51 cm) at the shoulder and weighs 50-60 lb (23-27 kg).

Chrétien de Troyes (1135-83), French poet who wrote romances rooted in Arthurian legend. His work, including *Erec et Enide, Cligès,* and *Perceval,* influenced French and English literature through the next 2 centuries.

Christ, Jesus *See:* Jesus Christ.

Christchurch (pop. 299,400), New Zealand's third largest city, located on South Island near the east coast. A tourist and commercial center, it produces clothing, electrical goods, and fertilizers, and is served by an international airport, railroads, and tunnels linking the city with Lyttelton, the chief port. An Anglican church group settled Christchurch in 1850 and established the University of Canterbury there in 1873.

Christian *See:* Christianity.

Christian IV (1577-1648), king of Denmark and Norway 1588-1648, longest reigning Danish monarch. He involved Denmark in wars with Sweden (1611-13, 1643-45), and helped Protestants fight Roman Catholics in Germany (1625-29) during the Thirty Years' War. These wars left Denmark bankrupt.

Portrait of the Polish composer and pianist Frédéric Chopin

Christian IX (1818-1906), king of Denmark 1863-1906. During his reign, Denmark acquired the territory of Schleswig in 1863, but in 1864 Prussia and Austria invaded, gaining control of Schleswig and Holstein. Although against democracy, in 1901 he recognized a democratic parliament.

Christian X (1870-1947), king of Denmark (1912-47), king of Iceland (1912-44), symbol of Danish resistance to German occupation during World War II. In 1915, he granted a new constitution ending privileges of upper classes and admitting to women's rights. After the German invasion of Denmark in 1940 he continued to occupy the throne, but was under house arrest 1943-45 for refusing to cooperate with the Germans.

Christian, Charlie (1919-42), influential jazz guitarist who pioneered the use of electrically amplified instruments. While playing in the Benny Goodman orchestra (1939-41), Christian joined with Dizzy Gillespie and Thelonious Monk to create bebop, a modern style of jazz. Christian's career ended when he contracted tuberculosis in 1941.
See also: Jazz.

Christianity, religion founded on the life and teachings of Jesus, acknowledged by all Christians to be the Son of God. Christianity had its beginnings when a small band of Jews recognized Jesus of Nazareth, who died about A.D. 33, as the Messiah, or

Christ. Immediately after the crucifixion of Jesus, Christianity counted only a few hundred members, among them the Apostles, who followed Christ's teachings and preached his Gospel, particularly as it concerned the life, sufferings, death, resurrection, and divine nature of Jesus. The Christian community had its center in Jerusalem but soon spread into Asia Minor, Syria, Macedonia, and Greece. While St. Peter was the leader of the Jewish Christian community, Saul of Tarsus (later known as Paul the Apostle) was preeminent in the task of converting the Gentiles and establishing churches in the Greco-Roman world. As the faith spread, an ecclesiastical structure evolved. Bishops replaced the Apostles as celebrants of the ritual of the Eucharist. They were assisted by presbyters, or elders, who were given the right to perform the sacred duties connected with the Eucharist, while the bishops retained the right of consecrating the presbyters and of confirming the faithful. Various regions were organized into dioceses and provinces. Within 3 centuries, despite persecutions, the Christian religion had become firmly established; in A.D. 324 the emperor Constantine established Christianity as the official religion. In order to settle doctrinal disputes and establish basic tenets, Constantine called the first ecumenical council at Nicaea in 325. The Nicene Creed, adopted at this council, stated the basic truths of the Christian Church; departures from this statement of faith were thereafter regarded as heresy. From earliest times the preeminence of the bishop of Rome was recognized by the entire Western Church. However, the Eastern Church, headed by the patriarch of Constantinople, had traditionally retained jurisdiction over organizational and doctrinal matters in its own sphere. The question of papal authority led to the Great Schism (1054), when the Eastern Church broke its ties with the West. The popes emerged as influential rulers in western Europe during the Middle Ages, contending with the Holy Roman emperors for temporal power as well as spiritual authority. Disputes arose concerning papal succession, and popes and antipopes, supported by rival kings and princes, fought for the right to rule with the authority of the Holy See.
The entire structure of the Church was shaken by this dissension, and abuses such as simony and the sale of indulgences also cried out for reform. In the 14th century reform was advocated by John Wycliffe in England and Jan Hus in Czechoslovakia. The Reformation of the 16th century was led by Martin Luther, who denied the supreme authority of the pope and rejected all but 2 of the 7 sacraments, Baptism and the Eucharist. He affirmed the supreme authority of the Bible in all matters of faith. The Catholic Church responded to the Reformation with the Counter-Reformation, during which abuses were corrected, several new religious orders were formed, and a spirit of Christian mission was fostered among the faithful. It was a highly active era for proselytizing the faith and a period of great creativity in religious art. Since the 16th century there have existed 2 main currents of western Christianity: Protestantism and Roman Catholicism. In Switzerland the Reformation was led by Huldreich Zwingli in Zürich and John Calvin in Geneva. Calvinism, which teaches the predestination of the elect and was adopted by the French Huguenots, forms the basis of modern Presbyterianism and the Reformed churches. During the 18th century John Wesley, who turned from Calvinism to a more traditional Christian view, founded the Methodist church in England.
After the pope refused to annul his first marriage, King Henry VIII declared the Church of England to be free of papal jurisdiction. Under Edward VI and Elizabeth I, the Anglican church became truly Protestant; its tenets were set forth in the Thirty-nine Articles of 1576. The Puritans considered these doctrinal reforms inadequate, however, and sought a form of worship based strictly on the Scriptures. Puritan sects later gave rise to the Baptist and Congregational churches and to the Religious Society of Friends, or Quakers. The settlements founded throughout the American colonies by dissenting members of Protestant churches gave impetus to the development of independent American church bodies, such as the Protestant Episcopal Church, an offshoot of the Church of England. Some distinctly American churches sprang up, among these the Church of Jesus Christ of Latter-Day Saints (Mormons), founded in 1830, and the Church of Christ Scientist (Christian Science), founded in 1882. In all there are more than 200 branches of the Christian Church in the United States.
One of the most significant developments in the continued growth of the Christian church in the 20th century is the ecumenical movement. Although still in an early phase, with its progress often slowed by organizational and doctrinal difficulties, ecumenicism has caught the imagination of a majority of the clergy and the faithful, who envision a future in which the Christian Church will again be one universal body, as it was established by Christ.
See also: Jesus Christ.

Christian Science, religion based on belief in the power of Christian faith to heal sickness. It was founded by Mary Baker Eddy, who organized the first Church of Christ, Scientist at Boston, Mass., in 1879.

Christie, Dame Agatha (1891-1976), British writer of popular detective novels and plays. Her works, which include *The Murder of Roger Ackroyd* (1926), *The Mousetrap* (1952), and *The Pale Horse* (1962) feature her 2 central characters, the egotistical Hercule Poirot and the elderly Miss Jane Marple.

Christmas (Christ's Mass), annual Christian festival observed on Dec. 25 to commemorate the birth of Jesus Christ. The exact date of Christ's birth is unknown. The origin of the Christmas story is based on the Gospels of Luke and Matthew in the New Testament. The first reference to the celebration of Christmas occurred in a Roman calendar of A.D. 336. By the Middle Ages, Christmas had become the most significant religious holiday in Europe, with Saint Nicholas as a symbol of giving. In the 19th century Christmas trees and Christmas cards became customs of the holiday. In the United States, Santa Claus replaced Saint Nicholas as the great gift giver.
See also: Christianity; Jesus Christ; Santa Claus.

Christmas Island *See:* Kiritimati Atoll.

Christmas Tree *See:* Christmas.

Christ of the Andes, statue of Christ created by Mateo Alonzo, in Uspallata Pass on the Argentine-Chile border in the Andes Mountains. It was dedicated on March 13, 1904 to commemorate treaties for perpetual peace between Argentina and Chile.

Christopher, Saint (3rd century A.D.), Christian martyr and patron of travelers. According to legend, he carried the Christ child across a river. The Roman Catholic Church removed his feast day (July 25) from its liturgical calendar for lack of historical evidence as to his existence.

Christophe, Henri (1767-1820), king of North Haiti. A freed black slave, he became president of Haiti in 1806, after plotting the assassination of Dessalines. After 1811 he ruled North Haiti, as King Henri I. Faced with a revolt, he shot himself.

Christus, Petrus (fl. c.1442-73), Flemish painter, early Netherlandish school. His work, strongly influenced by Jan van Eyck, was important in the 15th-century development of realistic perspective: *Madonna with S. S. Francis and Jerome*, *Lamentation*, and *Nativity*.

Christy, Edwin P. (1815-62), U.S. actor who organized the successful Christy Minstrels troupe at Buffalo, N. Y., in 1842. He established the basic format of the minstrel show, popular in the 19th century.

Chrome *See:* Chromium.

Chromic acid, common name for chromium trioxide (H_2CrO_4), an industrial compound used in chromium plating and the manufacture of fire resistant chemicals. Poisonous and caustic, most chromic acid takes the form of bright red crystals.

Chromium, chemical element, symbol Cr; for physical constants see Periodic Table. Chromium was discovered by L.N. Vauquelin in 1797. It is a steel-gray, lustrous, hard metal. Elemental chromium is prepared by reduction of its oxide with aluminum. It is used in the production of stainless steel, in plating, and in the production of other metal alloys. Many compounds of chromium are used to color glass, as pigments, and as mordants in the textile industry.

Chromosome, threadlike body in the cell nucleus, composed of genes, which carry genetic information responsible for the inherited characteristic of all organisms. Chromosomes consist of deoxyribonucleic acid (DNA), a sequence of nucleotides composed of 4 different bases, allowing over 500 million alternatives. The basic proteins are found in a complex with DNA in the cells of human organs and tissues; in general, these are called histones.
The microscope shows that the chromosome is a coiled structure. This coiling should not be confused with the structure of the DNA molecule—a double helix—because there is a difference of several orders of magnitude in the scale. Mitosis is the normal process by which a cell divides, each new cell ending up with the same number of chromosomes as the original cell. Mitotic division occurs in somatic cells (i.e., not sex cells) during periods of growth, when the total number of cells is increasing, or during repair processes, when lost or damaged cells are being replaced. In the resting cell (interphase of mitosis) the chromosomes cannot be detected inside the nucleus as discrete structures. As a cell approaches mitosis, the chromosomes become visible as threads within the nucleus (prophase of mitosis). At the same time, cytoplasmic bodies, the centrioles, divide, and the 2 new centrioles move to opposite poles of the cell. The protein fibers that control the separation of the chromosomes radiate from these bodies. The chromosomes line up in the equatorial plane of the cell (metaphase of mitosis) and separate to form the chromosomes of the 2 new nuclei (anaphase of mitosis). A cleavage furrow begins to divide the cytoplasm of the cell, the chromosomes elongate, and a nuclear membrane re-forms around them. This stage (telophase of mitosis) results in the reconstruction of 2 nuclei that are genetically identical with the parent nucleus.
See also: Deoxyribonucleic acid; Genetics; Heredity.

Chronicles, 2 Old Testament books summarizing Jewish history from Adam through the Babylonian Captivity.
See also: Old Testament.

Chronometer, extremely accurate clock, used especially in navigation. The chronometer invented by John Harrison (1759) allowed navigation to determine longitude accurately for the first time. The mechanical chronometer is spring- driven, like a watch, but its parts are larger and devices in the spring minimize effects of temperature changes and the ship's rolling movements.

Chrysalis, pupa of certain insects, especially butterflies and moths at the state between caterpillar or larva and fully developed imago (winged adult).

Chrysanthemum, genus of popular flowering annual or perennial herbaceous plants of the daisy family (Compositae). The national flower of Japan, chrysanthemums are usually white, yellow, pink, or red and are native to temperate and subtropical areas.

Chrysler, Walter Percy (1875-1940), U.S. industrialist who produced the first Chrysler car (1924) and established the Chrysler Corporation (1925), which became a major auto producer in the United States.

Chrysostom, Saint John (c.347-407 A.D.), Greek Father and Doctor of the Church. He was called Chrysostom ("golden mouthed") for his powers of oratory. He was patriarch of Constantinople (398-404) and became its patron saint.

Chub, any of several small, freshwater carp (family Cyprinidae) found in flowing waters, common to Europe and North America. The chub, 4-12 in (10-31 cm) long, has a large head and wide mouth and is usually a gray-brown or blue and silver color. Being a generally coarse and bony fish, it is not much valued as food, but is popularly used for bait and is caught for sport.

Chuckwalla (*Sauromalus obesus*), lizard of the North American desert. Stoutly built and 1 ft (30 cm) long, it ranges from Arizona and Utah to northern Mexico, feeding on the flowers and leaves of desert plants. During the summer it lives below ground, and when alarmed it retreats into crevices, wedging itself by blowing up its body.

Chuckwalla

Church, Frederick Edwin (1826-1900), U.S. landscape painter noted for his portrayal of light on large canvases. He was a student of Thomas Cole and the most famous member of the Hudson River School. Among his best known works are *Niagara* and *Heart of the Andes*.
See also: Hudson River School.

Church and state, phrase that refers to the relations between organized religion and organized government. This question, which for centuries has been a source of controversy, is whether the religious and political powers in a society should be kept clearly separate from one another. In the United States, due to various legislative acts, neither a state nor the federal government can openly or secretly participate in the affairs of a religious organization, and vice versa. This has led directly to the barring of prayer in U.S. public schools.

Churches of Christ, evangelical Protestant Christian body that teaches strict adherence to principles and practices set forth in the New Testament. Formerly one with the Church of the Disciples of Christ, believed to have been founded at Pentecost and refounded by Thomas Campbell (1763-1854), this conservative church is one of the largest denominations in the United States.
See also: Protestantism.

Churches of God, group of U.S. Pentecostal religious sects. Most of the churches of the group originated as Holiness, Pentecostal, or Adventist churches, which are evolved from Methodism. The Churches of God teach a doctrine of sanctification obtained by "second blessing" or forgiveness, and stress literal interpretation of the Bible.
See also: Adventists; Pentecostal churches.

Churchill, Jennie Jerome *See:* Churchill, Sir Winston Leonard Spencer.

Churchill, John *See:* Marlborough, Duke of.

Churchill, Sir Winston Leonard Spencer (1874-1965), British statesman, soldier, and writer. The son of Lord Randolph Churchill and his U.S. wife, Jennie Jerome, he was educated at Harrow and Sandhurst. He fought in India (1897), the Sudan (1898), and South Africa. A Conservative member of Parliament (1900), he changed to the Liberal party in 1905 and became first lord of the admiralty by 1911, in which office he was held accountable for the failure of the Dardanelles campaign during World War I. Churchill left government and saw active service in France until he was recalled by Lloyd George to serve in several cabinet positions (1917-22). In 1924 he regained a seat in Parliament and was chancellor of the exchequer in Stanley Baldwin's Conservative government (1924-29). Out of favor with his own party, he held no office for the next 10 years, during which time he voiced strong warnings regarding Hitler's activity in Germany. When World War II broke out (1939), Chamberlain appointed him first lord of the admiralty. Upon Hitler's invasion of the

Sir Winston Churchill

Low Countries, Churchill was made prime minister (1940) and minister of national defense. His persuasive oratory and unswerving confidence were instrumental assets in Allied resistance, as were his contributions to military strategy. He was coauthor, with President F.D. Roosevelt, of the Atlantic Charter, and played a key role in the diplomatic conferences that were to shape postwar Europe (e.g., Yalta Conference). In 1951 Churchill returned to power as prime minister for the second time, serving until his retirement from politics (1955). His extensive writings, for which he received the Nobel Prize (1953), include an autobiography, *My Early Life* (1930), *The Second World War* (6 vols., 1948-53), and *A History of the English-Speaking Peoples* (4 vols., 1956-58).
See also: World War II.

Churchill Downs *See:* Kentucky; Kentucky Derby; Louisville.

Churchill River, formerly Hamilton River, river rising in Ashuanipi Lake in southwestern Labrador and flowing about 600 mi (970 km) through Newfoundland in eastern Canada to Lake Melville on the Atlantic Ocean. A large hydroelectric power plant, with a capacity of more than 5 million kilowatts of electricity, was completed in 1974 on the river at Churchill Falls.

Church of Christ *See:* Churches of Christ.

Church of Christ, Scientist *See:* Christian Science.

Church of England, national church of England and parent church of the Anglican Communion. Its doctrine is basically Protestant and its hierarchy and ceremony are rooted in Catholic tradition. The church broke with Rome in 1534 when Henry VIII assumed the title of the head of the church. In the 16th and 17th centuries the church was troubled by Puritan agitation and later by nonconformity. But it remains the established state church and its 26 senior bishops (lords spiritual) sit in the House of Lords, led by the archbishop of Canterbury.
See also: Anglicans.

Church of God in Christ, large Pentecostal denomination. Founded in the United States in 1895 by Bishop Charles H. Mason as a Holiness church, the church now has over 3 million members. It bases its generally fundamentalist faith on personal experience, morality, and the experiences of the Apostles on Pentecost.

Male cicadas produce a loud sound similar to that of a scissor-grinder. In forests of warmer regions the sound produced by cicadas is sometimes deafening.

larva

full-grown

Church of Jesus Christ of Latter-Day Saints *See:* Mormons.

Church of the Nazarene, Protestant evangelical denomination. It was created in Texas in 1908 when 3 Holiness church groups merged.

Churriguera, José Benito (1665-1725), Spanish architect and sculptor who gave his name to the Spanish Baroque style featuring extravagant design, Churrigueresque (1650-1740). Churriguera designed grandiose theatrical altars and the entire urban complex of Nuevo Baztán in Madrid. He was also the architect for the cathedral of Salamanca. His style influenced the Spanish missions of colonial North America.

Chu Teh (1886-1976), Chinese Communist leader. He helped form the Chinese Red Army and joined Mao Tse-tung (1927). As commander in chief, he led the Long March (1934-35) and defeated the Nationalists (1949). He held various high posts in the Communist government including chairman of the National People's Congress in 1959.
See also: China.

CIA *See:* Central Intelligence Agency.

Ciardi, John (1916-86), U.S. poet, translator, and teacher. His poetry volumes include *Homeward to America* (1940) and *For Instance* (1979), and notable translations include Dante's *Inferno* (1954), *Purgatorio* (1960), and *Paradiso* (1970).

Cibber, Colley (1671-1757), English actor-manager and dramatist who introduced sentimental comedy to the theater. He wrote over 30 plays including *Love's Last Shift* (1696) and *Apology* (1740) which offers a vivid depiction of the contemporary theater. He was made poet laureate in 1730.

Cibola, Seven Cities of, golden cities reported in the North American Southwest in the 16th century. The legend attracted Spanish exploration, notably by Francisco Coronado and his 300 Spanish cavalry and 1,000 Native American allies (1540).

Cicada, large insect (order Homoptera) known for its monotonous whining song produced by the rapidly vibrating, drumlike membranes on the male's abdomen (the female is mute). The larvae develop in the soil, feeding on roots; the periodical cicada (genus *Magicicada*) spends 17 years underground and live for 1 week above it.

Cicero, Marcus Tullius (106-43 B.C.), Roman orator, statesman, and philosopher. As consul (63 B.C.) he crushed the Catiline conspiracy. His refusal to submit to the First Triumvirate resulted in banishment in 58 B.C., but he was recalled the next year by Pompey, with whom he sided in the civil war. Cicero's tacit approval of Caesar's murder and his defense of the Republic against Mark Antony in his first and second *Philippics* led to his execution after Octavian took Rome. A master of Latin prose, his great works include personal letters and orations (57 extant).
See also: Rome, Ancient.

Cid, El (Rodrigo Díaz de Bivar; 1040?-99), Spanish soldier and hero. His name comes from the Arabic *El Sayyid,* which means "the Lord." El Cid led the forces of Sancho II of Castile and Alfonso VI of Leon until banishment by Alfonso (c.1081). He then fought for the Arab kings of Saragossa, capturing Valencia (1094), where he remained as ruler until his death. His romanticized exploits appear in literature, notably *The Song of the Cid* (c.1140) and Corneille's *Le Cid* (1636).

Cilia, hairlike projections, often part of a fringe, that provide locomotion for 1-celled organisms, and move fluid within higher forms of life. Cilia protruding from the lining of the upper respiratory tract move to pass on dust, germs, and mucus.
See also: Protozoan.

Ciliate *See:* Protozoan.

Cimabue, Giovanni (Cenni di Pepo or Peppi; c.1240-c.1302), Italian painter. His work shows the transition from the formal Byzantine style of painting to the more lyrical Florentine school of the 14th century. His best known work, *Madonna and Child Enthroned with Angels and Prophets,* is now at the Uffizi Gallery in Florence, Italy.

Cimarosa, Domenico (1749-1801), prolific Italian composer famous for his comic operas, notably *Il Matrimonio Segreto* ("The Secret Marriage"; 1792). He was court composer to Catherine the Great of Russia, 1787-91.

Cimmerians, ancient nomads of the Crimea and Asia Minor. First mentioned in Homer's *Odyssey,* they lived from about 1200 B.C. to 700 B.C., in an area of the Caucasus Mountains, near the Black Sea in what is now the southern USSR. The Cimmerians were warriors who rode horses and used bows and arrows. According to the Greek historian Herodotus, they were driven into Asia Minor by the Scythians. About 700 B.C. the Cimmerians battled the Assyrians, and plundered and destroyed the Phrygian dynasty.

Cimon (c.507-c.449 B.C.), Athenian statesman and military leader in the Greco-Persian Wars. He became the leader of the aristocrats, those opposing the democrat Pericles and his reform-minded followers. He was exiled by Pericles, but returned to Athens in 451 B.C., and eventually effected a reconciliation between Sparta and Athens.
See also: Athens; Greece, Ancient.

Cinchona , or chinchona, genus of evergreen tree of South and Central America, cultivated for its bark, which yields quinine and other antimalarial alkaloids.

Cincinnati (pop. 1,452,645), city in southwest Ohio, on a height overlooking the Ohio River. First settled in 1788, the city grew rapidly after the War of 1812. Manufacturing industries today include chemicals, automobile parts and bodies, soap, machine tools, and engines. Publishing and printing industries also contribute to the economy. The city is a major river and rail transportation center and inland port. Cincinnati's cultural life offers museums (including the Taft Museum; Cincinnati was the birthplace of William Howard Taft and Robert A. Taft), its symphony orchestra, opera, and conservatory.
See also: Ohio.

Cincinnatus, Lucius Quinctius (c.519-c.439 B.C.), statesman and Roman patriotic hero. Cincinnatus was named dictator by the Senate in 458 B.C. When Rome was threatened by the Aequians, he left his farm, defeated the enemy, resigned, and returned to his farm all within 16 days of taking office.
See also: Rome, Ancient.

Cinema *See:* Motion pictures.

Cinnabar, bright-red mercuric sulfide mineral (HgS), an important source of mercury and used in the pigment vermillion. Large deposits are found in Spain, Yugoslavia, Italy, China, and southern California.
See also: Mercury.

Cinnamon (genus *Cinnamomum*), tree or shrub of the laurel family. The inner bark of the Ceylon cinnamon (*C. zeylanicum*) is used as a spice; in medicine, *C. camphora* serves as a digestion stimulant and to treat dyspepsia.

Cinquefoil, low-growing plant (genus *Potentilla*) of the rose family, named for its 5-fingered leaves. The bright yellow and white flowers are widespread over North America and the Pacific coast.

CIO *See:* Congress of Industrial Organizations.

Circadian rhythm *See:* Biological clock.

Circe, in Greek mythology, daughter of Helios (the Sun), enchantress who transformed Odysseus' men into swine; Odysseus himself escaped her spell. Later legends say she had 3 sons by Odysseus, including Telegonus, doomed to slay his father.
See also: Mythology.

Circle, closed plane curve every point of which is at equal distance from a fixed point (center). A line segment between the center and the curve is called a *radius* (r); the word is also used for the length of that segment. A line segment whose 2 ends lie in the curve is a *chord*, and a chord passing through the center point is called the *diameter* (d). The distance around the edge is known as the *circumference* (C); $C = \pi d$. The area of a circle (A) is given by $A = \pi r^2$. The circle has been used to symbolize eternity, the universe, or heaven.

Circuit, electric *See:* Electric circuit.

Circuit breaker, electric device, like a fuse, that will automatically interrupt an electrical circuit (by separating the contacts) when the current exceeds a desired value. Circuit breakers may be reset by hand or automatically, whereas a fuse has to be replaced.
See also: Electricity.

Circuit rider, itinerant preacher of the Methodist church who visited scattered communities to conduct services. John Wesley originated the practice in England in the 18th century, and Francis Asbury adapted it in America. The term also refers to judges in the early days of the United States who were appointed to ride the circuit to hear cases.
See also: Methodists.

Circulation *See:* Circulatory system.

Circulatory system, system of organs that carries blood throughout the body. It consists chiefly of a pump (the heart) and a network of blood vessels (arteries, veins, and capillaries). The circulatory system provides the body with essential food and oxygen while eliminating carbon dioxide and other wastes. In addition, as blood circulates, white blood cells help protect the body from disease by engulfing harmful invaders, and body temperature is regulated by absorbing heat from the cells' production of energy.
Disease or injury may damage the circulatory system, possibly affecting blood flow. Arterioscleroisis, an accumulation of fatty deposits in the arteries, is one such condition. This disease may be associated with high blood pressure, which results from the heart's need to work harder, and may lead to complications such as heart attack, a stroke, or kidney failure.

Circumcision, removal of the foreskin covering the glans of the penis, as a religious requirement (among Jews and Muslims) or as a surgical measure for sanitary reasons. In ancient Egypt circumcision was regarded as an initiation into puberty. For Jews it symbolizes a male's induction into the covenant between God and Abraham, usually 8 days after birth. In some tribes of Africa and South America, and in Islam, female circumcision, involving removal of all or part of the clitoris, is practiced.

Circumference *See:* Circle.

Circumstantial evidence *See:* Evidence.

Circus, form of entertainment featuring trained animals and performances by acrobats, trapeze artists, horseback riders, and clowns, presented within a circular enclosure. Historically, "circus" (the Latin for "ring") referred to chariot races, gladiatorial fighting, and animal events in ancient Rome. U.S. circuses date from colonial times, but the modern circus became popular in the 19th century.

Cirrhosis, chronic disease of the liver marked by progressive destruction and regeneration of liver cells and increased connective tissue (scar) formation. Cirrhosis ultimately results in blockage of portal circulation, raised blood pressure in the portal vein, liver failure, and death. Causes include alcohol consumption (Laennec's cirrhosis, the most prevalent), hepatitis and other infections, and severe malnutrition in children of tropical countries (a condition known as kwashiorkor). Results include jaundice, gastrointestinal problems, and edema. Though irreparable, treatment includes vitamin intake, controlled diet, and diuretics.
See also: Liver.

Cirrus *See:* Cloud.

Cisneros, Henry Gabriel (1947-), first Hispanic mayor of a major U.S. city. Cisneros, a Democrat, was elected to 4 terms as mayor of San Antonio. Tex., (1981-89). Born in San Antonio, Cisneros earned degrees from Texas A&M, Harvard, an George Washington University. As mayor, he was credited with advancing economic development and lessening ethnic polarization. He is now employed in the private sector.

Cistercians, Roman Catholic monastic order. Monks and nuns of this order are often referred to as Trappists, after a 17th-century order of Cistercians in La Trappe, France.
Their order is based on principles of prayer, manual work, and study. Its followers often lead secluded lives.
See also: Trappists.

Citadel, fortress protecting or dominating a town.

Cities of refuge, 6 cities of ancient Palestine. People accused of murders, committed by accident or in self-defense remained safe in these cities until they were tried. If found innocent, they continued to live in the cities of refuge. If found guilty, they were returned to the place of the crime for punishment.
See also: Palestine.

Citizens band radio (CB), radio with a short range. These radios operate on frequencies reserved for private use and transmit signals from 5 mi (8 km) in the city to 20 mi (32 km) in rural areas. Frequencies used for CB radios also operate remote controlled devices, such as garage doors and model airplanes.
See also: Radio.

Citizenship, legal relationship between an individual and the country of nationality, usually acquired by birth or naturalization. Though laws regarding citizenship by birth vary from country to country, such citizenship is generally based on place of birth or the nationality of one or both parents. Some countries grant citizenship by marriage, adoption, long residence, land purchase, entrance into public service, or annexation of territory. It is possible for an individual to be a citizen of more than 1 country or to possess no citizenship at all. Citizenship implies both rights (to a passport, to the protection of the government when appropriate, to constitutional rights) and duties (to pay taxes, to serve in the armed forces) between the citizen and the country.

Citizenship Day, day that honors citizens of voting age and naturalized foreign-born citizens of the United States, Sept. 17 (anniversary of the signing of the U.S. Constitution). Congress passed this act to replace the earlier May celebration called I Am an American Day.

Citrange, hybrid orange produced by crossing the sweet orange and the trifoliate orange. It is stronger and hardier than the sweet orange plant. Citrange is used for cooking and flavoring beverages.

Citric acid, tricarboxylic acid ($C_6H_8O_7$) derived from lemons and similar fruits or obtained by fermentation of carbohydrates; used as a flavoring and to condition water.

Citrin, one of a group of chemicals known as flavinoids. Also referred to as vitamin P and used in medicine, citrin helps control bleeding within capillary (tiny blood vessels) walls. Citrin is often formulated from a mixture of lemon peel and paprika.

Citron *(Citrus medica)*, fruit tree in the citrus family (Rutaceae); also its fruit. The citron is a large yellowish fruit with a thick white rind and a small pulpy though acidic center. It was the first of the citrus fruits to be introduced into Europe from India and Asia. The rind is crystallized as candy, while the juice flavors syrups and beverages.

Citrus, genus of tropical trees of the rue family, providing such edible fruits as the orange, lemon, citron, grapefruit, lime, tangerine, and shaddock, all of which are rich in vitamin C, sugars, and citric acid.

City, large center of population, often distinguished from a town or village by the diversity of its economic and cultural activities; also, a center officially designated as a city for purposes of local government.

City government, government that manages affairs for cities and various other communities. Most cities are incorporated municipalities, that is, corporations defined and empowered by the state through charters. An elected council or commission forms the legislature. The executive branch may be headed by an elected mayor, an appointed city manager, or elected commissioners. Larger cities also have their own court system. The branches of government, its related agencies, and the individual city workers (civil servants) make up a bureaucracy governed by city laws, also known as municipal ordinances. These ordinances cover day-to-day needs of city residents. Property taxes and state or federal grants-in-aid generate most of the money on which cities run.
See also: City.

City planning, planning for the growth of a city or town, taking into consideration the economic, physical, social, and aesthetic needs of its populace and government. Examples of such planning range from the grid-iron organization of ancient Roman cities to the grandiose planning of the Renaissance, usually intended to glorify a ruler or to strengthen his military position; to the piecemeal development of the Industrial Revolution, chaotic due to the enormous population movement; to Pierre L'Enfant's design for Washington, D.C. (1791) and Frederick L. Olmsted's city park designs. In the United States civic reform movements, already active before the Civil War, instigated legislation to enforce slum clearance and to provide better educational and recreational facilities. Today's city planners, many dealing with housing projects and city-center renewal projects, take into account such factors as existing roads and traffic patterns; availability of sanitation service, police and fire protection, employment; zoning regulations; location of schools, hospitals, and recreational facilities.

City-state, independent political community (particularly in ancient Greece) made up of a city and its surrounding countryside, from which it draws food and labor. The Greek city-state, or *polis*, which emerged around 700 B.C., ranged in size from Athens (1,000 sq mi/2,590 sq km) to minute states less than one-hundredth of its size, and ranged in government from monarchies to democracies. The Greeks colonized much of the Mediterranean, spreading the city-state form of organization until Rome became the nucleus of an empire that turned all the city-states into subunits of its administration. City-states have flourished during 3 major periods of Western civilization: the ancient civilizations of the Middle East, the classical period of Greece, and in Europe from the 11th to the 16th centuries.

Ciudad Bolívar (pop. 249,600), commercial center and port of eastern Venezuela, located on the Orinoco River. It was originally founded by Spaniards and called Angostura (1764). Here Simon Bolívar, known as the liberator of South America, claimed independence for Colombia and Venezuela (1819). It was subsequently named after him (Spanish: *ciudad*, city). Exports such as latex, animal skins, and lumber are shipped through Ciudad Bolivar.
See also: Venezuela.

Civet, weasel-like carnivorous mammal of the family Viverridae, found in Africa and South Asia. The African civet, (*Civettictis civetta*), is reared for the musky-smelling oily substance, used as a base for perfumes, that is produced by glands under its tail.

Civics, study of the rights and duties of citizenship. Civics became part of the school curriculum in the United States in the 19th century, after the influx of immigration. Courses cover national and international events, community affairs, political and economic problems, elections, and government.

Civil Air Patrol (CAP), voluntary civilian auxiliary of the United States Air Force. CAP organizes and runs state or district groups (wings) with teenaged cadets as well as adult members. CAP operates an extensive radio network and an educational program, and participates in an international exchange program. Most search and rescue missions in the United States are directed by CAP. Originated in 1941 to organize civilian air participation for wartime tasks, this group is now a nonprofit private organization.

Civil code *See:* Code Napoléon.

Civil defense, nonmilitary measures taken to protect a nation's civilian population and its resources in case of enemy attack. Organized civil defense programs began shortly before World War II, when it was realized that powerful air forces greatly increased the wartime danger to civilians. In the United States, civil defense efforts, including warning systems, the construction and stocking of shelters, and survival planning, are directed and coordinated at the national level by the Office of Civil Defense.

Civil disobedience, form of political action involving intentional violation of the law in order to force concessions from a government or to draw attention to alleged injustices. Henry David Thoreau, in his 19th-century essay *On Civil Disobedience*, expounded on these methods, which were essential in Mohandas Gandhi's 20th-century struggle for India's independence and which have been employed by the suffragettes, the civil rights movement, and Vietnam War protesters. Martin Luther King, Jr. was an advocate of civil disobedience and used it successfully during his career.
See also: Gandhi, Mohandas; Thoreau, Henry David.

Civilian Conservation Corps (CCC), agency founded in 1933 by the U.S. Congress as part of the New Deal. The agency trained and hired unemployed men to develop and conserve natural resources through tree planting, firefighting, and dam construction. Congress abolished the corps in 1942.

Civilization (Latin *civis*, "citizen of a city"), stage of societal development in which complex economic, social, and governmental systems arise. Civilizations first arose as farming on permanent sites replaced the nomadic life of hunters and gatherers. In these new, permanent groups, inventions such as metal tools led to advances in the lives of people, and complex economic, social, and political structures evolved. The Tigris-Euphrates River valleys of the Middle East, the Nile River Valley of Egypt, the Indus River Valley in India, and the Huang He River Valley of China are sites of early civilizations.

Civil law, body of law based on Roman law, dealing with private rights claims between individuals, as opposed to criminal law (offenses against the state). After the fall of the Roman Empire, the customs of the ruling tribes developed into customary law throughout most of continental Europe, including England. Roman law was rediscovered in the 12th century, and European jurists began to codify the existing legal systems with Roman additions. The *Corpus Juris Civilis* of Justinian I (6th century) was of special importance for these evolving legal systems. The development of civil law was further enhanced by the Code Napoleon (1804), which gave France a unified national code. Other countries, mainly in continental Europe and Latin America, followed the French lead. Codes of civil law countries state general legal principles that courts must interpret in the light of particular cases. In common law countries such as Great Britain, Canada, and the United States (excluding Louisiana), the courts are bound by previous decisions (the rule of precedent). Trial by jury and the law of evidence are key features of legal practice in common law countries; they have no counterpart in civil law.

Civil liberties *See:* Civil rights.

Civil rights, rights and privileges enjoyed by citizens. A distinction is sometimes made between civil rights and civil liberties: Civil rights must be granted by the government (for example, the right to vote), while civil liberties are inalienable individual freedoms the government may be prohibited from restraining. In the United States "civil rights" also includes the rights of individuals, particularly members of minority groups, to nondiscriminatory treatment. The concept of civil rights arose in the Roman Empire, whose courts protected the rights of Roman citizens against arbitrary acts by the government. In the Middle Ages nobles issued charters to their followers to protect against other nobles and the king. The rise of absolute monarchs in France, Spain, and other European nations ended many of the civil rights of their subjects. In England, however, the nobles, and later the House of Commons and the common law courts, defended and extended the rights of the people against the crown. The Magna Carta of 1215, under which the king granted specific rights to his lords in return for their support, and the Bill of Rights in 1689 established a basis in common law for the inviolable liberties of individual citizens. Many U.S. and Canadian concepts of civil rights and individual liberty derive from the English example. The so-called natural law theorists of the 17th and 18th centuries, such as Jean-Jacques Rousseau and John Locke, taught that the natural law, reflecting divine law, confers certain rights upon the individual that cannot be legitimately taken away by governments. These ideas are enshrined in the famous words of the Declaration of Independence: "that all men are created equal, that they are endowed by their Creator with certain inalienable Rights..."

With some exceptions, civil rights in American colonial times were often restricted, particularly in matters of religion. The Declaration of Rights and Liberties, passed in 1774 by the Continental Congress, was an important part of the agitation against the British government preceding the American Revolution. The Northwest Ordinance of 1787, which provided for settlement and organization of new territories, established certain liberties for settlers in the new area, including the right of *habeas corpus*, trial by jury, and religious freedom. The basis for the civil rights of all Americans is the Constitution, whose first 10 amendments, known as the Bill of Rights, provide for fundamental liberties: freedom of speech, assembly, the press, and religion; protection against unreasonable searches and seizures; prohibition of double jeopardy and self-incrimination; and the right to a speedy and public trial. The 13th amendment (1865) abolished slavery, and the 14th (1868) established the standards of due process of law and equal protection of the laws of all citizens. The 15th amendment (1870) states that no male citizen could be denied the right to vote because of his race.

The rights of women lagged behind those of former slaves: Women did not receive the right to vote in federal elections until 1920 (the 19th amendment).

The massive civil rights legislation of the Reconstruction era was followed by a prolonged legislative silence on racial discrimination. Moreover, the constitutional amendments and civil rights measures enacted by Congress after the Civil War were largely negated by 2 Supreme Court decisions—the first holding that only the states were prohibited from discriminating, while individuals were not (1883), the second establishing the criterion of "separate but equal" facilities as fulfilling legal requirements (1896). In 1954 the Supreme Court declared "separate but equal" facilities a violation of civil rights and ordered public schools to be integrated "with all deliberate speed." In 1957, after years of effort by civil rights activists, Congress set up the Civil Rights Commission to investigate discrimination, established a Civil Rights Division in the Department of Justice to investigate and prosecute violations of federal law, and empowered the attorney general to bring suit against any person or civic body that denied another's voting rights. The Civil Rights Act of 1960 outlawed infringements of voting rights and ordered all the armed forces desegregated.

A solidaritystrike after the murder of the civil rights leader Martin Luther King (Apr. 4, 1968).

The 24th amendment (1964) outlawed poll taxes; literacy tests as a means of racial discrimination were brought under control in 1965 legislation. The Civil Rights Act of 1964 prohibited discrimination in public accommodations and by employers or labor unions. It also created the Equal Employment Opportunity Commission to ensure that persons were not barred from employment on the grounds of race, religion, or sex. Many women have since successfully sued for their rights under this act. The Civil Rights Act of 1968 outlawed discrimination in the sale or rental of housing and established the protection of the law for those exercising their civil rights or urging others to do so. In 1970 the 1965 Voting Rights Act was renewed and extended, lowering the voting age from 21 to 18.

During this same period major strides were being made to ensure and extend individual civil liberties. The most far-reaching and controversial decisions were in the field of criminal procedure. The *Miranda* case (1966) resulted in a ruling that a citizen placed under arrest must be made aware of his or her constitutional rights and be free to exercise them; a confession obtained in violation of this rule is excluded from evidence in a court of law. The Court further established that a citizen placed under arrest must be made aware of his or her constitutional rights and be able to exercise them.

The international movement to secure civil rights for all people has been strengthened by the work of many agencies, including UNESCO, the International Labor Organization, the European Commission on Human Rights, the Inter-American Commission on Human Rights, the International Commission of Jurists, and the International League for the Rights of Man. The Universal Declaration of Human Rights, endorsed by the General Assembly of the United Nations (1948), includes a list of basic civil rights that should be available to all persons. In December 1965 the

General Assembly approved the convention on the elimination of all forms of racial discrimination.

Civil Rights Act of 1866 *See:* Reconstruction.

Civil Rights, Commission on, independent U.S. government agency whose role is to advance the cause of equal opportunity, established 1957. Public hearings are conducted to assure legal protection of citizens of all races, religions, gender, and national origins. Issues for which the commission seeks equality are voting rights and opportunities in education, housing, and employment. Through investigations initiated by charges of civil rights denials and independent studies, the commission makes recommendations to the President and Congress.

Civil service, body of civilian (non-military) employees of a government, excluding elected officials. Civil service dates from ancient China, where officials were chosen through competitive exams. It was also found in ancient Rome, and in France after Napoleon I. In the United States the civil service suffered from the spoils system (gifts of government jobs as political rewards), firmly established from 1828 under President Andrew Jackson. Attempts to establish a merit system (appointment and promotion based on merit, to secure efficiency and freedom from political influence) failed until the Pendleton Act (1883), which set up the Civil Service Commission to administer federal employment. The Hatch Acts (1939, 1940) forbade federal employees to play any active part in politics beyond voting.

Civil War, U.S. (1861-65), conflict between 11 Southern states (Confederate States of America) and the U.S. federal government (Union). Because the 11 states had attempted to secede from the Union, in the North the conflict was officially called the War of the Rebellion. Since the war was a sectional struggle, North against South, it is sometimes also known as the War Between the States.

Origins. The economy of the South was based on the plantation system of agriculture, which absolutely depended on slave labor. Great staple crops— cotton, tobacco, sugar, and rice—were grown largely for export. The North had no need for slavery; its agriculture, which produced corn and wheat largely for subsistence and internal consumption, was based on small family farms; its industry and towns were expanding rapidly, and it welcomed European immigrants in large numbers to supply its growing labor needs. Political differences came to a head over the question of whether slavery would be permitted in the newly settled western territories, soon to become states. The Missouri Compromise (1820) was the first attempt to ease North-South tensions by admitting Missouri as a slave state and Maine as a free state and forbidding slavery in the Louisiana Territory north of latitude 30°30′. As a long-term solution it failed because expansion continued westward, raising the issue again and more acutely, and also because of the growth of abolitionism in the North. The admission to the Union of the huge slave state of Texas (1845) and the resultant Mexican War renewed the fears of Southern political dominance and the possible extension of slave territory. The Compromise of 1850 seemed to solve the problem, but it was nullified by the Kansas-Nebraska Act of 1854, which gave the residents of those territories the right to vote on whether or not slavery would be permitted. This opened the way for opponents and supporters of slavery to begin a virtual civil war in "Bleeding Kansas." The Dred Scott Decision (1857) further inflamed the problem as the Supreme Court's decision had the effect of declaring the Missouri Compromise unconstitutional. The presidential election of 1860 raised the fears of the South as Abraham Lincoln, the candidate of the newly formed Republican party, was known to be opposed to the further extension of slavery. Lincoln declared: "My paramount object is to save the Union, and not either to save or destroy slavery," but South Carolina voted to secede from the Union (Dec. 20, 1860) and was followed by 6 more states by Feb. 1861. Representatives met at Montgomery, Ala., to draw up a constitution for these Confederate states and elected Jefferson Davis provisional president. When Lincoln announced he was sending supplies to the federal garrison of Fort Sumter, in Charleston harbor, Confederate guns opened fire on the fort (Apr. 12), which surrendered 2 days later. The outbreak of hostilities drove 4 more slave states (North Carolina, Virginia, Arkansas, and Tennessee) into the Confederacy.

First phase of the war—Union defeats. The capture of the Confederate capital seemed the natural objective, and the first rallying cry of the North was "On to Richmond." This simple aim of frontal attack led to the first major encounter, at Bull Run (July 21, 1861), and the Federals were routed. In the meantime the North blockaded the South, but chances of capturing a Southern blockade runner were rated at 1 in 10 and 800 vessels got through in the first year. The blockade, however, became increasingly effective. In Apr. the Union fleet under David Farragut took New Orleans, the first of many essential ports to fall to the North. Northern General George McClellan's Peninsular Campaign (1862) nearly reached Richmond but ended in defeat in the Battles of the Seven Days, and Southern General Robert E. Lee was again victorious at the second Battle of Bull Run. This opened the way for a Confederate invasion of Maryland that was thwarted by a Union victory at Antietam, and Lincoln seized the political initiative by issuing the preliminary Emancipation Proclamation (Sept. 1862) promising freedom to slaves held in the Confederacy. The year closed with a shattering defeat for the Union at Fredericksburg, Va.

Second phase—the Confederacy crushed. The first Union victories had come in the West in 1862, when General Ulysses S. Grant took forts Henry and Donelson, opening the Tennessee River. After the bloody battle of Shiloh, the Federals commanded nearly the entire length of the Mississippi. In 1863 Lee defeated the North at Chancellorsville, but General Stonewall Jackson, one of the ablest Confederate generals, was mortally wounded. Lee struck north into Pennsylvania, but Union forces won the decisive battle of the war after 3 days of costly fighting at Gettysburg (July 1863). On the following day Grant took Vicksburg, which finally gave the Union forces control of the Mississippi, cutting the Confederacy in two and opening the way for the invasion of Tennessee. Grant's attempt to capture Richmond in 1864 was halted in the Wilderness Campaign, but soon after he began the 9-month siege of Petersburg. Sherman meanwhile moved east from Chattanooga to take Atlanta in September 1864. His army marched through Georgia to the sea, leaving behind it a trail of devastation. The capture of Petersburg and Richmond on Apr. 2, 1865, led to Lee's surrender to Grant at Appomattox Court House a week later. Although Confederate forces in the South and West fought on for several weeks, the war was effectively over.

See illustrations on following pages.

Civitan International, service organization of business and professional men and women, striving to promote good citizenship, locally, nationally, and internationally. Founded in 1920, Civitan consists of approximately 50,000 people in about 1,500 clubs. Projects include special olympics and other activities for the physically and mentally handicapped, scholarships, and awards for good citizenship and service.

Claiborne's Rebellion, outbreak of conflict in colonial United States caused by the refusal of William Claiborne, a Virginia fur trader, to accept the authority of Leonard Calvert, governor of Maryland. Kent Island in the Chesapeake Bay area, where Claiborne had established his fur trade, lay within the boundaries of Maryland, according to a charter issued to the Calvert family in 1632. Claiborne, however, had obtained a trading license in England in 1631. Claiborne drove Calvert's forces off the island, but Calvert restored his rule there in 1657.

Clair, René (René Chomette; 1898-1981), French film director, producer, and writer, especially of screen comedies. Born in Paris, he worked on both silent and sound films, including *Sous les Toits de Paris* (1929).

Clam, name given to many edible marine bivalve mollusks that live in sand or mud, including the jacknife clam, the quahog or cherrystone clam, and the pismo clam; also refers to some freshwater bivalves. The giant clams of Indian Ocean and Pacific Ocean coral reefs may reach a diameter of 4 ft (2.4 m) and weigh one-quarter ton (0.27 metric tons).

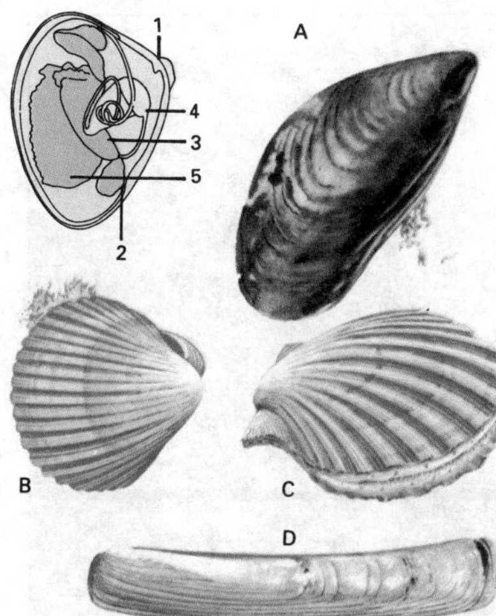

Mollusk anatomy
1. Calcareous shell
2. Muscle for opening and closing
3. Intestine to receive food
4. Internal gills for intake of air and food
5. Muscular foot for movement

A. Mussel
B. Cockle
C. Scallop
D. Razor shell

Clan, social group claiming descent from a common ancestor. Clans have existed all over the world, from primitive societies to the famous Highland clans of Scotland (said to have originated in the 11th century). Some clans have expressed their unity in the symbol of the totem (an object, animal, or plant revered as the ancestor of the group). Most, but not all clans, are exogamous, requiring marriage outside of the clan (marriage within being regarded as incest). Several clans may organize into a larger social structure known as phratry.

Clarendon, Edward Hyde, 1st earl of (1609-74), English statesman and historian. He originally opposed King Charles I, but supported him in 1642 when civil war started. Although Clarendon favored religious toleration, Parliament made him enforce the Clarendon Code, which strengthened the position of the Church of England. In 1667 Charles II made him a scapegoat for failures in the second Dutch War. He was forced into exile, from which he wrote the 10-volume *History of the Rebellion*, defending Royalist activities during the civil war.

Clarinet, single-reed woodwind instrument comprising a cylindrical tube (usually wooden) with a flared bell and tapered mouthpiece, played vertically. Tones are produced by opening and closing holes (some covered by keys) in the tube while blowing air through the mouthpiece. The clarinet, developed in Germany from the chalumeau by Johann Christoph Denner early in the 18th century, features in dance bands, military bands, woodwind groups, symphony orchestras, and as a solo instrument.

Clark, (Charles) Joseph (1939-), Canadian prime minister (1979-80). After election to the House of Commons in 1972, he was elected leader of the Progressive Conservative party in 1976, and prime minister in 1979, replacing Pierre Trudeau and marking the beginning of western Canada's political importance.
See also: Canada.

Clark, Abraham (1726-94), political leader during the American Revolutionary War, member of the 1776 Continental Congress, and a New Jersey signer of the Declaration of Independence. After the Revolution, he called for a bill of rights to be included in the projected U.S. Constitution and earned his nickname, the "Poor Man's Counselor," by defending poor farmers in land cases.

Clark, George Rogers (1752-1818), U.S. frontiersman and Revolutionary War general who led the campaign against the British in the Northwest Territory. With about 175 volunteers, he succeeded in capturing key British forts north of the Ohio River, principally Kaskaskia (1778) and Vincennes (1779). His brother was William Clark, the explorer.
See also: Revolutionary War in America.

Clark, Kenneth Bancroft (1914-), U.S. psychologist whose 1950 report on school segregation was cited in the Supreme Court's 1954 ruling against segregated public schools. A professor at City College of New York (1942-75), he was active in many civil rights and educational organizations and was the first black member of the New York State Board of Regents (1966). His books include *Prejudice and Your Child* (1955), *Dark Ghetto* (1965), and *The Pathos of Power* (1974).
See also: Psychology; Segregation.

Clark, Mark Wayne (1896-1984), U.S. general, commander of Allied ground forces in North Africa and Italy in World War II and commander of UN operations in the Korean War (1952-53). He led the invasion of Italy in 1943.
See also: World War II.

Clark, Ramsey (1927-), U.S. lawyer and politician. He served in the Department of Justice (1961-66) as assistant attorney general and deputy attorney general, becoming U.S. Attorney General in 1966, under President Lyndon B. Johnson. Clark was a strong proponent of civil rights and of the Vietnam War.

Clark, Tom Campbell (1899-1977), U.S. jurist and lawyer, Attorney General under President Harry S. Truman (1945), and associate justice of the U.S. Supreme Court, 1949-67. Generally a conservative supporter of the government's "antisubversion" actions after World War II, Clark was often at odds with the Warren Court. However, he joined the other justices in voting to outlaw school segregation in *Brown* v. *Board of Education*, 1954. He retired in 1967 when his son, Ramsey Clark, became attorney general.
See also: Supreme Court of the United States.

Clark, William (1770-1838), U.S. explorer, a leader of the Lewis and Clark Expedition, 1804-6, and brother of George Rogers Clark. He was superintendent of Indian affairs and governor of Missouri Territory, 1813-21.
See also: Lewis and Clark expedition.

Clarke, Arthur C(harles) (1917-), British science fiction and science writer. Clarke is best known as co-author of the screenplay for the film *2001: A Space Odyssey* (1968) and for his detailed design for communications satellites in 1945. His novels include *Childhood's End* (1953) and *The Fountains of Paradise* (1979).

Class, level of social stratification (e.g., upper, middle, and lower class). Classes lack the rigid boundaries characterizing caste, so that mobility between classes is possible.

Class action, lawsuit in which 1 or more persons represents a group (class) of persons having similar claims. U.S. citizens first used class action suits to recover money in bankruptcy cases. In the 1950s and 1960s civil rights groups used class action to fight school segregation, housing or voting restrictions, and job discrimination. Since then, class actions have expanded to cases involving price fixing, environmental issues, and other social problems.

Classical music, or art music, music composed by individuals and written for instruments, for voices, or for combinations of voices and instruments. Classical music is more complex than *popular music* (country, folk, rock, jazz). Christianity helped spread Western classical music, which began in ancient times. Instrumental music includes solo, chamber, and orchestral music. Perhaps the most popular chamber group is the string quartet, consisting of 2 violins, a viola, and cello. Opera combines a large orchestra with soloists and chorus, and tells a story. Nonwestern classical music includes the music of the highly developed cultures of India, China, and Japan.

Classicism, in painting, sculpture, architecture, literature, and music, the emulation of classical antiquity, emphasizing harmony, order, and clarity of form, rather than subjectivity, heightened emotion, and the uncanny. The aims of the artists in the Italian Renaissance (literally, the "rebirth" of classical culture) were rejected in the 16th and 17th centuries by the mannerist and baroque artists. Classicism was revived in the 18th-century movement known as neoclassicism (also called the Enlightenment). Important artistic figures include Samuel Johnson and Alexander Pope (English literature), Pierre Corneille and Jean Racine (French literature), and Franz Joseph Haydn and Wolfgang Amadeus Mozart (music). The 19th-century romantic movement in art was partly a reaction to perceived overreliance on reason and order in neoclassicism.

Classification, in biology, systematic arrangement of the world's organisms into categories based on their characteristics. This science, sometimes called taxonomy, is often aimed at establishing evolutionary relationships. The system of classification comprises 7 major categories. These are,

The 18 Union states and 11 Confederate states were well matched in land area. The 3 border states were critical in the balance of strength.

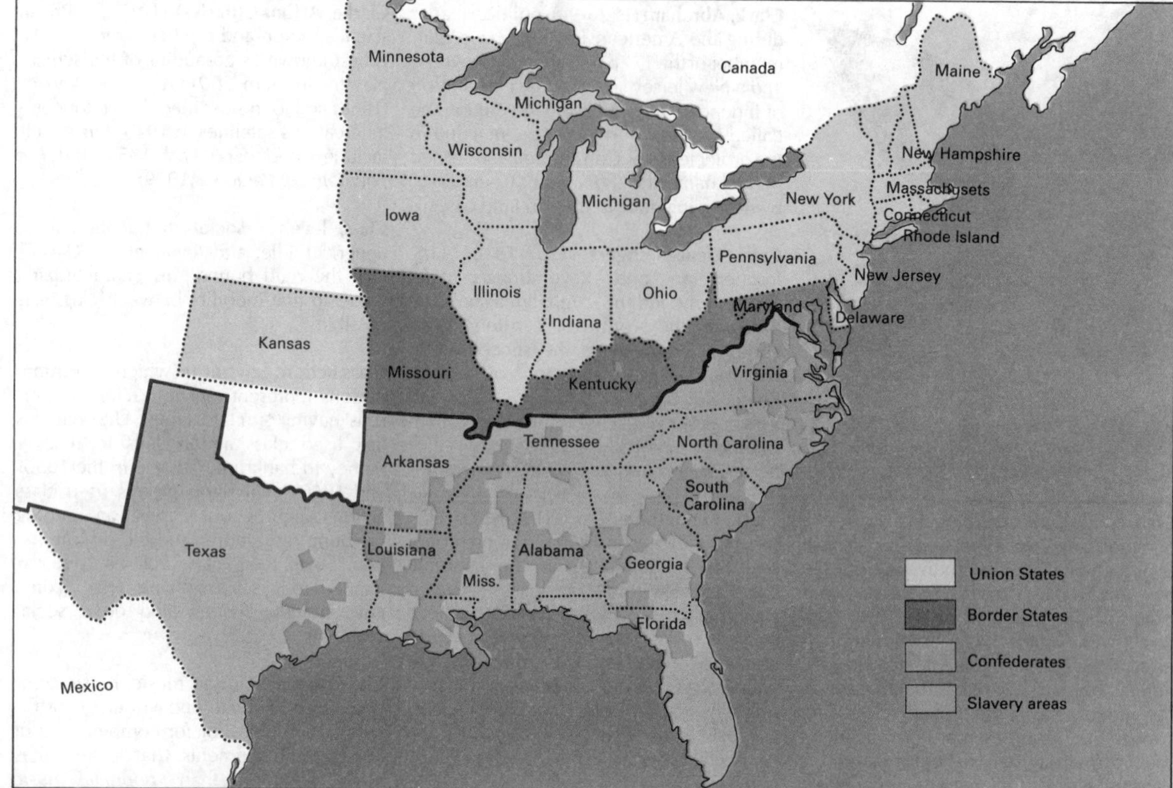

The victory of the Union fleet on the Mississippi River, Apr. 24, 1862, under Admiral David Glasgow Farragut (Currier & Ives, Museum of the City of New York

President Abraham Lincoln paid regular visits to the Union troops at the front.

The artillery of General McClellan in Yorktown, ready for transport

A selection of the weapons in use at the Battle of Gettysburg (1863):
1. *Springfield rifle musket*
2. *Bayonet*
3. *Sharps carbine*
4. *Spencer carbine*
5. *Cavalry sabre*
6. *Colt third model Dragoon*
7. *Remington new model revolver*
8. *Whitney revolver*
9. *Lefaucheux pin-fire revolver*
10. *3-inch rifled " Ordnance Gun"*
11. *Napoleon smooth-bore gun-howitzer*

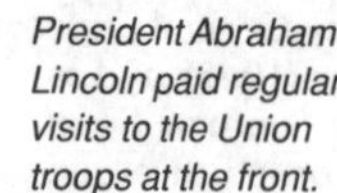

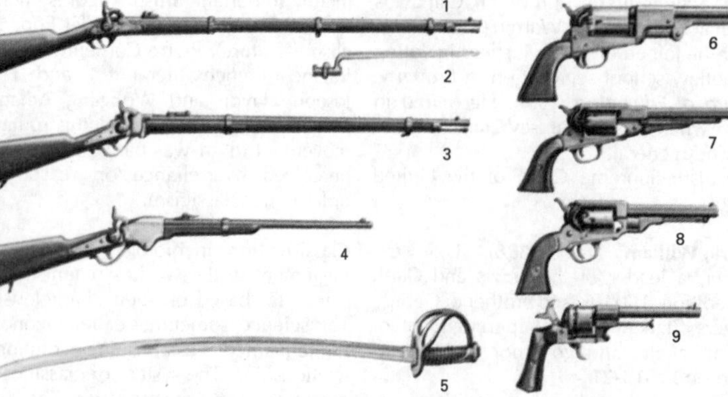

Far left: Ulysses S. Grant

Left: A Southern and a Northern ship engaged in battle (1862).

Below: Robert E. Lee

Top: General W. Sherman, General U.S. Grant, President A. Lincoln, and Admiral D.G. Farragut, in George Healy's The Peace-Makers, painted in 1894

Bottom: The Battle of Antietam (or Battle of Sharpsburg; 1862) was the bloodiest battle of the war. Approximately 5,000 soldiers died and 19,000 were wounded. It was considered a victory for the Union forces.

Left: Union General William Sherman, portrait by George Healy

from most to least inclusive: kingdom; phylum (called division in botany); class; order; family; genus; species. Traditionally, there were only 2 kingdoms, plants and animals. Today, however, most biologists would recognize 3 others: the Protista (1-celled organisms and some forms of algae), the Monera (bacteria and blue-green algae), and the Fungi (mushrooms and molds). The species is the basic unit of classification. As a rule of thumb, 2 animals belong to the same species if they are capable of mating to produce fertile offspring.
See also: Biology.

Eldridge Cleaver

Claudel, Paul (1868-1955), French dramatist, poet, and diplomat. Influenced by Arthur Rimbaud and intensely religious, he drew inspiration for his sensuous, lyrical verse from nature and Oriental thought.

Claude Lorrain (Claude Gelée; 1600-82), a founder of French romantic landscape painting who lived and worked mostly in Rome. His canvases usually show a biblical or classical scene dominated by an idyllically lit landscape (*The Expulsion of Hagar,* 1668; *The Trojan Women Setting Fire to the Greek Fleet; Seaport at Sunset*). His later works are almost visionary in their intensity and inspired such painters as Poussin and Turner.

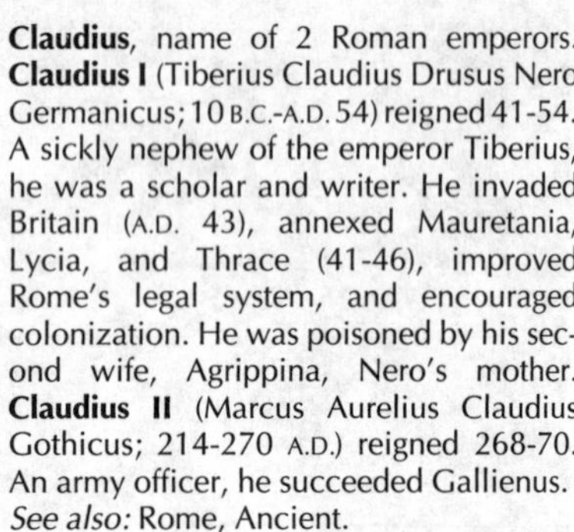

Claudius, name of 2 Roman emperors. **Claudius I** (Tiberius Claudius Drusus Nero Germanicus; 10 B.C.-A.D. 54) reigned 41-54. A sickly nephew of the emperor Tiberius, he was a scholar and writer. He invaded Britain (A.D. 43), annexed Mauretania, Lycia, and Thrace (41-46), improved Rome's legal system, and encouraged colonization. He was poisoned by his second wife, Agrippina, Nero's mother. **Claudius II** (Marcus Aurelius Claudius Gothicus; 214-270 A.D.) reigned 268-70. An army officer, he succeeded Gallienus.
See also: Rome, Ancient.

Clausewitz, Karl von (1780-1831), Prussian general, strategist, and military historian. His book *On War* (1833) revolutionized military thinking after his death. Defining war as an extension of diplomacy, he urged the destruction of enemy forces, morale, and resources, and has thus been called the prophet of total war, although he favored defensive fighting.

Clausius, Rudolf Julius Emmanuel (1822-88), German theoretical physicist. He was first to state the second law of thermodynamics (1850), that heat never flows from a colder to a hotter body without work, and proposed the term *entropy* (1865). He also contributed to kinetic theory and the theory of electrolysis.
See also: Entropy; Thermodynamics.

Clavichord, keyboard musical instrument popular in the 16th to 18th centuries. The strings were struck with metal wedges (a piano uses felt hammers), and the sound was quiet and delicate.

Clay, 1 of 3 main types of earth, found in layers under the earth's crust and often at river mouths. Most clays consist of very small particles of hydrated aluminum silicates (kaolinites) that are usually produced by the weathering of rocks. Clay is easily malleable when wet and retains its shape when dried. If it is fired (baked) in a high-temperature oven or kiln it becomes extremely hard and, if first coated with a glaze, nonporous. Electrical insulators, sewage pipes, cement, kitchen tiles, chinaware, bricks, and paper manufacture all require clay. Clay is essential to the soil, holding moisture and preventing organic material from being washed away.

Clay, Cassius *See:* Ali, Muhammad.

Clay, Cassius Marcellus (1810-1903), U.S. abolitionist, politician, and statesman. Clay founded the antislavery journal *True American,* in Lexington, Ky., 1845. He was a founder of the Republican Party (1854), and U.S. ambassador to Russia (1861-62 and 1863-69).
See also: Abolitionism.

Clay, Henry (1777-1852), U.S. statesman. Clay helped to create the Compromise of 1850, an attempt to reconcile North and South in the pre-Civil War period. He served as secretary of state under President John Quincy Adams (1825-29), ran unsuccessfully as the Whig party candidate for president in 1832 and 1844, and was a U.S. senator, 1849-52.
See also: Civil War, U.S.

Clay, Lucius DuBignon (1897-1978), U.S. general assigned to govern the U.S. zone of West Germany (1947-49). He supervised the Berlin Airlift.

Clayton, John Middleton (1796-1856), politician who served 3 terms as U.S. senator from Delaware. His greatest achievement was the Clayton-Bulwer Treaty of 1850.

Clayton-Bulwer Treaty, agreement signed by the United States and Great Britain in 1850, giving the 2 countries an equal role in protecting a canal to be built through Central America, the 2 countries agreeing to maintain the neutrality of the canal and the land on either side of it. John Clayton, U.S. secretary of state, and Sir Henry Bulwer (1801-72), British minister to the United States, negotiated the treaty, which was replaced in 1901 by the Hay-Pauncefote Treaty, giving the United States the exclusive right to build and manage the canal.
See also: Hay-Pauncefote Treaty.

Clearinghouse, institution or system for exchanging checks among banks for the purpose of collection. The clearinghouse allows the banks in each city to settle their accounts among themselves on a daily basis. When the banks are in different cities, the clearinghouse function is performed by the Federal Reserve Bank of the district.

Cleary, Beverly (1916-), U.S. author of humorous and realistic children's books. The character Henry Huggins was introduced in Cleary's first book (1950). Ramona Quimby first appeared as a major character in *Beezus and Ramona* (1955). These popular youngsters, who live in a middle-class suburb of Portland, Ore., appeared in many books. In 1975, Cleary received the Laura Ingalls Wilder Award for her contributions to children's literature. *Dear Mr. Henshaw* (1883) won the 1984 Newbery Medal. *A Girl from Yamhill* (1988) is her autobiography.

Cleaver, (Leroy) Eldridge (1935-), U.S. black militant, a leader of the Black Panther party. His autobiographical *Soul on Ice* (1968) deals with his own experience of racial hatred and of the U.S. penal system.
See also: Black Panther Party; Black Power.

Cleft palate, congenital malformation in which the tissues that form the palate do not unite in the fetus, leaving a longitudinal gap in the upper jaw. It is often an accompaniment of harelip. The deformity needs surgical repair.

Cleisthenes (6th century B.C.), statesman of ancient Athens who instituted democratic reforms. The noble clan, Alcmaeonid, which Cleisthenes led, had a prophet persuade Cleomenes, king of Sparta, to overthrow Hippias, who had held complete power until 510 B.C. As a result, Cleisthenes was able to set up a democratic form of government, ending the political control of the noble clans.
See also: Athens; Greece, Ancient.

Clematis, genus of vines and free-standing plants whose flowers bear 4 sepals but no petals. They are best known as garden plants, but wild species include the *virgin's bower* of eastern states, whose seeds are buried in a fluffy ball called old-man's beard.

Clemenceau, Georges (1841-1929), French statesman and journalist. Known as "the Tiger," he was founder of the Third Republic and twice French premier (1906-9, 1917-20). He worked with Léon Gambetta (1870) for the overthrow of the Second Empire, supported the writer Emile Zola in the Dreyfus Affair, and headed the French delegation to the Paris Peace Conference at Versailles after World War I.
See also: World War I.

Clemens, Samuel Langhorne *See:* Twain, Mark.

Clemente, Roberto (Walker) (1934-72), Puerto Rican-born U.S. baseball player. A star outfielder for the Pittsburgh Pirates (1954-72), he amassed 3,000 hits with 240 home runs, compiled a .317 lifetime batting average, and was a 5-time National League batting champion. He was elected to the Baseball Hall of Fame in 1973, soon after his death in an airplane crash while helping Nicaraguan earthquake victims.

Clementi, Muzio (1752-1832), Italian composer and pianist, known as "the father of the piano." His compositions include more than 100 sonatas, as well as symphonies and his studies for the piano, *Gradus ad Parnassum* (1817). He enjoyed a successful concert career thoughout Europe. In London he became a partner in one of the first firms to manufacture pianos (1799).

Clement I, Saint, or Clement of Rome (d. c.101 A.D.), citizen of Rome, elected pope c.29 A.D. Third in succession to Saint Peter as bishop of Rome, he is most famous for a letter to the church in Corinth c.96 A.D., condemning pride and arrogance in the church. The letter, which, except for the scriptures, is the oldest surviving Christian text, clarified the order of succession from bishop to presbyter (elder) to deacon (assistant). His feast day is Nov. 23.

Clement VII (1478?-1534), pope (1523-34), reigning ineffectively during a difficult time in European political and religious affairs. Clement was born in Florence, Italy, into the powerful Medici family. When the Holy Roman Empire and France struggled for dominance in Italy, Clement formed an alliance with France. Troops of the Holy Roman emperor Charles V sacked Rome in 1527 and captured Clement. In 1529 Clement accepted peace and recognized Charles as emperor. Because of these preoccupations, Clement vacillated in responding to the Protestant Reformation, which spread in Germany and Scandinavia. The Reformation took hold in England partly because of Clement's unwillingness to grant King Henry VIII of England an annulment of his marriage to Catherine of Aragón.

Clement VII (1342-94), one of the so-called antipopes. In 1309 Pope Clement V moved the seat of the papacy from Rome to Avignon, France, where it was subject to French control. In 1378 Pope Gregory XI returned the papacy to Rome, but died soon after the move. Urban VI was elected his successor, but he alienated the cardinals, who elected Robert of Geneva (Clement VII) pope in his stead. Clement acted as pope in Avignon, while Urban VI was pope in Rome. This period is known in Catholic history as the Great Schism. For 40 years (1378-1418) there were 2 rival lines of popes, until the Council of Constance settled the matter in favor of Rome. Since then, the Church has regarded the line of Avignon popes begun with Clement VII as illegitimate.

Clement VIII (1536-1605), pope (1592-1605). Clement fasted extensively, practiced devotions, and traveled on foot to Rome's pilgrimage churches. Reversing a papal policy, he allied himself with France instead of Spain and recognized Henry of Navarre, a Protestant convert who reverted to Catholicism, as King Henry IV of France.

Clement of Alexandria (c.150-215), Titus Flavius Clemens, Greek theologian of the early Christian Church. His most important work is the trilogy *Exhortation of the Greeks*, the *Tutor*, and *Miscellanies*. In his work he attempted to merge Platonic and Christian ideas.

Cleopatra (69-30 B.C.), queen of Egypt, daughter of Ptolemy XI. When her father died (51 B.C.) she was supposed to share the throne with her young brother-husband, Ptolemy XII, but his advisers drove her out of Egypt (49 B.C.). She won the support of Julius Caesar (48 B.C.), who had come to Alexandria in pursuit of Pompey. She became his mistress, bearing him a son, Caesarion (later Ptolemy XIV). With Caesar's help she recovered her throne. The accidental death of Ptolemy XII was followed by her marriage to a younger brother, Ptolemy XIII, whom she later had murdered (44 B.C.). After the battle of Philippi, Mark Antony summoned her to Tarsus, where she made him her lover. They were married in 37 B.C., but the marriage was not legal in Rome, where she was feared and hated. Antony helped restore Ptolemaic power in Syria, and war with Octavian (later Emperor Augustus) became inevitable. In the sea and land battle at Actium (31 B.C.) the forces of Antony and Cleopatra were routed. Antony killed himself, and Cleopatra, fearing humiliation in Octavian's triumph in Rome, also committed suicide.
See also: Antony, Marc; Caesar, (Gaius) Julius.

Cleopatra's needles, 2 large stone pillars called obelisks, originally erected in 1460 B.C. by Thutmose III before a sun temple at Heliopolis. Sent by Ismail Pasha as gifts (1878, 1880), one currently stands in Central Park, New York City, and the other on the Thames Embankment in London.

Clermont, first steamboat designed by U.S. engineer Robert Fulton. Fulton sailed the wood-burning boat up the Hudson River from New York City to Albany in 1807. Driven by a paddle-wheel, the ship averaged about 5 mi (8 km) per hour. It measured 142 ft (43 m) long and 14 ft (4.3 m) wide.
See also: Fulton, Robert.

Cleveland (pop. 1,831,122), Ohio's largest city, situated on Lake Erie at the mouth of the Cuyahoga River. It is a major port and railway center and an important manufacturer of steel, automobile parts, chemicals, paints, plastics, precision machinery, petroleum products, trucks and tractors, machine tools, and electrical products. When the Ohio and Erie Canal was completed in 1832 with Cleveland as its terminus, the settlement began to grow rapidly. In 1851 the first railroad reached the city, which was established as a major shipping point. Cleveland was a center of the abolitionist movement, aiding escaping slaves on their way to Canada on the underground railway. During the Civil War the city's iron and petroleum industries mushroomed, and the organization of the Standard Oil Company by John D. Rockefeller (1870) made Cleveland the nation's leading oil center. The post-Civil War boom continued until the Great Depression of the 1930s, which saw the collapse of several financial empires. However, because of its industrial diversification, the city survived the depression decade relatively well. In 1967 Cleveland became the first major U.S. city to elect a black mayor, Carl B. Stokes. Surrounded by 15,000 acres (6,000 hectares) of scenic woodland, the central city contains over 2,500 acres (1,000 hectares) of park and recreation area, including Rockefeller Park, which contains the Cleveland Cultural Gardens, and Brookside Park, the site of the Cleveland Zoo. The Cleveland Natural History Museum has a renowned collection, as does the Cleveland Museum of Arts. There is also a unique health museum. Cleveland's universities and colleges include Case Western Reserve University, Cleveland-Marshall Law School, and Cleveland State University. The Cleveland Orchestra enjoys a national reputation for excellence. The city is also the home of the Cleveland Browns football team and the Cleveland Indians baseball team.
See also: Ohio.

Grover Cleveland

22nd and 24th U.S. President

Born:	Caldwell, N.J.; Mar. 18, 1837
Terms:	Mar. 1885-Mar. 1889; Mar. 1893-Mar. 1897
Vice Presidents:	1st term, Thomas Andrews Hendricks; 2nd term, Adlai Ewing Stevenson
Political Party:	Democratic
Spouse:	Frances Folsom Cleveland
Children:	5
Died:	Princeton, N.J.; June 24, 1908

Cleveland, (Stephen) Grover (1837-1908), 22nd and 24th president of the United States (1885-89; 1893-97), the only president to have served 2 non-consecutive terms. Cleveland was first Democratic chief executive after 24 years of Republicans.
Early life. In 1855, Cleveland moved to Buffalo, N.Y., where he worked in a local law office, gaining admittance to the bar in 1859. In 1881, after years in local politics, he was elected mayor of Buffalo on a reform ticket and won a reputation for honesty and hard work. He was elected governor of New York in 1882, and in 1884, after an extremely close race, he defeated Republican candidate James G. Blaine in the presidential election.
First term. As president, Cleveland worked to reform the civil service system and regulated public land sales, leases of Native American land, and railroad grants. In 1887 he began campaigning for lower tariffs. This was a major issue in the 1888 election, which Cleveland lost to Republican Benjamin Harrison, although Cleveland actually won more votes. In the election of 1892, Cleveland defeated Harrison by a comfortable margin.
Second term. Shortly after Cleveland's second inauguration, a severe economic depression broke out (the "panic of 1893"). By the summer, numerous railroad companies had failed, along with thousands of businesses and banks. Unemployment reached 4 million.
In 1894 Cleveland used federal troops to break a strike at the Pullman works in Illinois. In 1896, with Cleveland's popularity at its lowest ebb, the Democratic party nominated William Jennings Bryan for the presidency. Cleveland retired to Princeton, where he became a university trustee and occasional lecturer. In the remaining years of his life, he came to be regarded with respect as an honest president in an era when honest politicians were rare. But despite his attempts to root out corruption, he had failed to deal with the social problems of those years: unemployment and general labor and farmer discontent.

Cliburn, Van (Harvey Lavan Cliburn, Jr; 1934-), U.S. concert pianist. He became world famous after winning the International Tchaikovsky Piano Competition in Moscow in 1958. An international event of the same kind is now held annually in his name in the United States.

Click beetle, long-bodied, short-legged beetle (family Elateridae) that can throw itself over with a "click" if placed on its back. On the underside of the first segment of its thorax is a spine that rests in a groove in the second segment. When upside down, the beetle bends its head back, pulling the spine out of the groove. This is then thrust sharply back, making an audible click and throwing the beetle into the air. The larvae of click beetles are wireworms, serious agricultural pests.

Cliff, steep face of rock. Cliffs are formed by many processes of erosion. Waves cut imposing and scenic cliffs along coastlines. Rivers create deep canyons with steep sides. Glaciers grind away the rock along valley walls and produce cliffs that appear after the glacier melts. Glaciers also pluck rock fragments away from high mountain slopes where snow collects to form walls around amphitheaterlike bassins.

Cliff dwellers, prehistoric Native American people who built elaborate houses, some with hundreds of rooms, sheltered beneath overhanging cliffs in the southwestern United States. The earliest of these multistoried dwellings dates from about A.D. 1000. They were a peaceful agricultural people whose inaccessible communities protected them from roving tribes such as the Apaches. In the 16th century the Spanish found the settlements mysteriously abandoned. Archeologists classify the cliff dwellers as members of the pueblo culture, ancestors of the tribes that built the large pueblo villages on the plains. The ruins of the cliff dwellings, well preserved in the dry desert climate, are found in Mesa Verde National Park, Colo., and in national monuments in Arizona, New Mexico, and Utah.

Clifford, Clark McAdams (1906-), U.S. lawyer who served as a special adviser to presidents Harry S. Truman and John F. Kennedy and was secretary of defense in the cabinet of President Lyndon B. Johnson (1968-69).

Climate, sum of weather conditions, or the characteristic weather, of any area. Weather conditions include temperature, rainfall, sunshine, wind, humidity, and cloudiness. One method of studying climate is to use average figures, but these often conceal wide variations; for example, mean temperatures are of little value in regions of extreme cold or heat. Climatology was developed by the ancient Greeks. Around 500 B.C. Greek philosopher Parmenides suggested that 5 climatic zones encircle the earth: a tropical zone on either side of the equator, 2 temperate zones in the middle latitudes, and 2 cold zones around the poles. This classification was based on latitude, the most important factor affecting climate.
Long after the ancient Greeks, climatologists recognized that many factors besides latitude influence climate, for example, elevation, ocean currents, and variations in atmospheric pressure. In the early 1900s a German meteorologist, Vladimir Köppen, classified the world's climatic zones, combining temperature and rainfall boundaries with vegetation boundaries. He suggested 5 basic regions: tropical rainy climates with no cool season, dry climates, middle latitude rainy climates, northern forest climates, and polar climates with no warm season. Many other classifications exist, and each has its uses, but none takes into account all the features of climate. Paleoclimatologists, who study past climates through the record of rocks and fossils, have shown that climates have changed considerably during the earth's history. For example, coal seams in northern Canada show that swampy tropical forests once grew there. Several theories have been advanced to explain climatic change over time. The theory of continental drift suggests that the continents have moved in relation to the poles. Other theories include sunspots, variations in solar radiation, and changes in the earth's orbit or tilt. Climatologists have observed small changes in climate in the past 100 years. Their findings have raised speculation about our ability to influence climatic change.
See also: Weather.

Clingman's Dome, highest point in Tennessee, located in Great Smoky Mountains National Park. It rises 6,643 ft (2,025 m) on the Tennessee-North Carolina boundary about 35 mi (56 km) southeast of Knoxville. The peak was named for Thomas L. Clingman, U.S. senator from North Carolina, who helped develop the area, a popular resort region.
See also: Great Smoky Mountains.

Clinical psychology, scientific and applied branch of psychology concerned with the study, diagnosis, and treatment of individuals with emotional or behavioral disorders. The disorders which may be brief and minor or more prolonged and serious in nature, such as neuroses and psychoses, are diagnosed through testing and treated through psycho therapy. Research serves as a means of discovering or improving on the various methods of diagnosis and treatment.
See also: Psychology.

Clinton, De Witt (1769-1828), U.S. politician who promoted the building of the Erie Canal and the Champlain-Hudson Canal. As mayor of New York City (most of 1803-15) and governor of New York state (1817-21 and 1825-28), he set up important civic and political reforms and social relief programs for Roman Catholics, slaves, and the poor.
See also: New York..

Clinton, George (1739-1812), U.S. statesman and soldier, vice president (1805-12) under Thomas Jefferson and James Madison. Elected in 1777 as New York's first governor, Clinton was reelected for a record 6 consecutive terms. Originally, he opposed New York's ratification of the U.S. Constitution because he believed in states' rights. His nephew DeWitt Clinton also later served as governor of New York.
See also: New York.

Clinton, Sir Henry (1738-95), British general. He was appointed (1778) commander-in-chief of British forces during the American Revolution after distinguishing himself at Bunker Hill. He captured Charleston in 1780 but resigned in 1781. He was blamed for the British surrender at Yorktown in that year.
See also: Revolutionary War in America.

Clinton, William Jefferson (Bill) (1946-), 42nd president of the United States. A moderate Democrat and longtime Arkansas governor, Clinton was the first U.S. president born after World War II, the third-youngest president, and the first to take office post-Cold War. He was also the first Democratic president in 12 years, defeating Republican incumbent President George Bush and Ross Perot, an independent candidate and Texas businessman.

Early life. Clinton was born William Jefferson Blythe IV on Aug. 19, 1946, in Hope, Arkansas. He was named after his father, who had recently died in a car accident. When Bill was 4, his mother Virginia married Roger Clinton, a car dealer, and shortly thereafter the family moved to Hot Springs, Arkansas. There Virginia and Roger had another son, Roger Jr., and Bill adopted his stepfathers surname.As a young man, Bill earned frequent academic honors. He expressed an early interest in a political career, inspired particularly by a 1963 meeting with President John F. Kennedy. Clinton was 17 at the time, visiting Washington as a delegate to the American Legion Boys Nation.

In 1964 Clinton entered Georgetown University in Washington, D.C., where he majored in international affairs and worked as an intern for Sen. J.W. Fulbright of Arkansas. Upon receipt of his degree, he spent two years as a Rhode Scholar at Oxford University before entering Yale Law School in 1970. Throughout his schooling, Clinton remained politically active, most notably helping to manage 1972 presidential candidate George McGoverns Texas campaign. While at Yale he also met fellow law student/future wife Hillary Rodham. They were married in 1975 and five years later had a daughter, Chelsea.

Entering politics. Law degree in hand, Clinton returned to Arkansas to teach and plan his political career. In 1974 he made a bid for a seat in the U.S. House but was narrowly defeated. He won his first statewide election in 1976, when he became Arkansass attorney general. Two years later he was elected, at age 32, the youngest governor in Arkansas history.

He adopted a liberal, activist agenda, increasing motor vehicle licensing fees to pay for a road-improvement project, and restricting powerful timber and utilities interests. Upset voters failed to reelect him to a second term in 1980. Clinton soon rebounded, however, to win the next four gubernatorial elections in Arkansas on more moderate platforms (1982, 1984, 1986, and 1990). Beginning in 1983, Clinton decided to concentrate on two main problems, education and the economy, rather than a wide range of issues. Under his leadership Arkansas increased teachers salaries, required teacher competency exams, and established a high school entrance test for students. In addition, he expanded health-care services for the poor, introduced welfare reform, and promoted economic growth through favorable tax policies. In 1991 Clinton was rated the most effective governor in the nation in a poll of his colleagues. In addition to his duties as governor, Clinton served as vice chairman of the National Governors Association in 1985, and as chairman of the NGA in 1986 and 87. In 1990 and 91, he headed the Democratic Leadership Council, an organization of moderate Democrats.

Presidential campaign. Clinton campaigned for and won the Democratic presidential nomination in 1992, weathering charges of marital infidelity, draft evasion, and marijuana use. At his request, Senator Al Gore of Tennessee, another moderate Democrat, was selected as his running mate against incumbents President Bush and Vice President Mondale. The two then took the campaign directly to the people, targeting middle-class and young voters, touring the country by bus, and answering questions on television talk shows.

Clintons platform focused primarily on domestic issues, with an emphasis on the economy and the high unemployment rate. He proposed higher taxes for the wealthy, tax cuts for the middle class, job-training programs, and reductions in defense spending. Moreover, he pledged to cut the immense federal budget deficit in half in four years. On social issues Clinton supported freedom of choice on abortion, welfare payments limited to those who cannot find work, and universal health care. His strategy proved successful, and in November his ticket won 43% of the popular vote in addition to an electoral landslide.

Presidency. With one-party control of both the House and the Senate, Clinton had hoped to act on his agenda quickly, and did appoint more women and minorities to his Cabinet than had any previous president. However, his first months in office saw a number of political setbacks: Clintons proposal to end the ban on homosexuals in the military met with with widespread opposition and had to be altered substantially. In addition, the president appeared indecisive in dealing with foreign crises in Bosnia, Somalia, and Haiti. His popularity fell, then plummeted when he failed to cut middle-class taxes. In October of 1993 he sent to Congress a plan for sweeping reform of the health-care industry, but Congress chose not to act on it. On other matters, Clintons 1993 and 1994 budgets did help to reduce the federal budget deficit, and the unemployment rate declined after Clinton took office. The president won a major victory in November 1993, when Congress approved the North American Free Trade Agreement, NAFTA (designed to eliminate trade barriers between the U.S., Canada, and Mexico), and again in August of 1994, when Congress passed an anticrime bill he supported. Additionally, he fulfilled several campaign promises by signing into law the Family and Medical Leave Act, initiating handgun reform, raising taxes on the wealthy, and reducing them for the working poor.

Decisive initiatives to check an Iraqi threat to Kuwait, to halt the development of nuclear arms in North Korea, to oust the military dictatorship in Haiti, and further the peace process in the Middle East briefly lifted Clintons poll popularity late in the year. Nonetheless, in November of 1994, the Democrats lost control of both the legislative and executive branches.

Presidential highlights in 1995 included Clintons trip to Russia in May to hold discussions with Russian President Boris Yeltsin. Also in May, Clinton successfully threatened Japan with tariff increases on their luxury automobiles if they did not loosen restrictions on auto imports. Japanese car companies agreed to work toward this demand.

On December 3, 1995 Clinton formally authorized the first deployment of U.S. troops to Bosnia to perform NATOs peacekeeping duties for one year.

Clinton was re-elected in 1996.

William Jefferson Clinton

42nd U.S. President	
Born:	Hope, Arkansas; Aug. 19, 1946
Term:	Jan. 1993-
Vice President:	Al Gore
Political Party:	Democratic
Spouse:	Hillary Rodham Clinton
Children:	1

Clipper ship, 19th-century sailing ship, the fastest ever built. Clippers evolved from the Baltimore clippers. They were built in the United States and later in Britain. They had a very large area of sail, relied on a good crew, and traded with China and Australia, where speed paid off. Two famous ships were Donald McKay's *Lightning* and the British *Cutty Sark* (now at Greenwich, England).

Clive, Robert, Baron Clive of Plassey (1725-74), British soldier and administrator, twice governor of Bengal, who established British power in India. He defeated both the French at Arcot (1751) and the Bengal nawab, Siraj-ud-Daula, at Plassey (1757), thus securing all of Bengal for the East India Company. He reformed administrative corruption in Bengal. Investigated by Parliament on the charge of dishonesty when in office, he was acquitted, but afterward committed suicide.

Clock, device to indicate or record the passage of time. Generally a clock relies on a source of regular oscillation, such as a swinging pendulum or an electric current. Christiaan Huygens invented what was probably the first pendulum clock in the mid-17th century. The electric clock, commonly found in the home, was invented in the 19th century, and the quartz clock, utilizing the vibrations of a quartz crystal, in the early 20th. The atomic clock, invented in 1948, is accurate to within 1 second in 3 million years. The most common way to display time has been the analogue, with clock hands sweeping over a face, in imitation of the sundial. The most recent type of display is the digital clock, which uses integrated circuits to show the time in changing figures.

Cloisonné, artistic process by which metal objects are decorated with enamel. Metal strips are soldered edgewise onto the surface of the object, creating compartments (*cloisons*) to be filled with colored enamel. When the object is heated, the enamel fuses with the surface. Originally a Persian technique, cloisonné was perfected by the Chinese, Japanese, and French.

Cloister, courtyard surrounded by vaulted and arcaded passageways supported by columns. Usually adjoining an abbey or church, the cloister served as a sheltered access to the surrounding buildings and was mainly used for recreation and exercise. An essential feature of Romanesque and Gothic churches and monasteries since the 11th century, cloisters are found throughout Europe.

Clone, cell or organism genetically identical to the cell or organism from which it has been derived. Clones are produced by asexual reproduction, for example through cell division in bacteria, cell budding in yeasts, or vegetative duplication. Monoclonal systems (systems derived from a single cell) are used for the production of diagnostics and medicines.
See also: Genetic engineering.

Closed shop, establishment where the employer accepts only members of a specified union as employees and continues to employ them only if they remain union members. The Taft-Hartley Act of 1947 forbids closed shops in industries involved in or affecting interstate commerce.

Clothing, one of humanity's most important needs, including the various garments, accessories, and ornaments people throughout the world wear for decoration and protection. People probably began to wear clothing more than 100,000 years ago. By the end of the Old Stone Age (25,000 years ago) the needle had been invented, enabling people to sew skins into clothes. They learned to make yarn from plants and animal fur and to weave yarn into cloth. The advent of sewing machines and other machinery about 200 years ago ushered in the clothing industry, now a major business in many countries.

Cloture, or closure, in parliamentary procedure, closing of debate to ensure an immediate vote on a measure before the legislative body. In most parliamentary bodies, members cannot debate a cloture motion, but the motion must receive more than a majority vote. The main purpose of cloture is to check the *filibuster*, endless debate by a minority of the members to keep a motion from being voted upon. In the U.S. Senate a 60% majority is needed to invoke cloture.

Cloud, visible collection of water droplets suspended in the atmosphere. Clouds whose lower surfaces touch the ground are usually called fog. The water droplets are very small, indeed of colloidal size; they must coagulate or grow before falling as rain or snow. There are 3 main cloud types. Cumulus (heap) clouds, formed by convection, and often mountain- or cauliflower-shaped, are found from about 2,000 ft (610 m) up as far as the tropopause, even temporarily into the stratosphere. Cirrus (hair) clouds are composed almost entirely of ice crystals. They appear feathery, and are found at altitudes above about 20,000 ft (6,100 m). Stratus (layer) clouds are low-lying, found between ground level and about 5,000 ft (1,524 m). Other types of cloud include cirrostratus, cirrocumulus, altocumulus, altostratus, cumulonimbus, stratocumulus, and nimbostratus.
See also: Weather.

Cloud chamber, Wilson *See:* Wilson cloud chamber.

Cloud seeding *See:* Rainmaking.

Clove (*Syzygium aromaticum* or *Eugenia caryophyllata*), tropical evergreen tree of the myrtle family; also, its dried, unopened flower. Originally grown in the Moluccas (Spice Islands), the Philippines, and islands nearby, cloves were first appreciated by the Chinese for perfuming the breath. They are now grown in the West Indies and Mauritius. Their main use nowadays is as flavoring and in medicine.

Clover, familiar small plant (genus *Trifolium*) that grows wild in lawns and pastures and along paths and roads. Some U.S. clovers are natives, others have been introduced from Europe. The red clover, a native of Europe, is the state plant of Vermont. Clover leaves are normally divided into 3 parts, although more divisions are known; 4-leafed clovers are said to bring good luck. Clover is grown as forage and for hay. It is particularly valuable because, like other members of the pea family, its root contains nitrogen-fixing bacteria, so it enriches the soil if plowed back in.

Clovis I (A.D. 466-511), Frankish king (481-511), founder of the Merovingian monarchy. He amassed a huge kingdom from the Rhine River to the Mediterranean, defeating the Romans at Soissons (486) and the Visigoths under Alaric II of Spain at Vouillé (507). He became a Christian c.498 and compiled the code of Salic law.
See also: Merovingian.

Clown, comedy figure of the pantomime and circus. Modern clowns possibly derived from the vice figures of medieval miracle plays and jesters in medieval courts. They later figured as harlequins in the commedia dell'arte; but their grotesque makeup, baggy clothes, and slapstick developed fully only in the 1800s. The best-known 20th-century American circus clown was Emmett Kelly.

Clubfoot, deformity in which there is an abnormal relationship of the foot to the ankle; most commonly the foot is turned inward and down.

Club moss, or ground pine, primitive plant of the order Lycopodiales with small moss-like leaves, related to ferns. Many club mosses have creeping or climbing stems covered with leaves. Their distribution is mainly tropical, but some live in the United States, where they are used for Christmas decorations. Some are used in the manufacture of medicines and of fireworks.

Clumber spaniel, short, heavy hunting dog originally bred in France but developed in England in the 1800s. The Clumber has long, straight, white hair, stands 16-18 in (41-46 cm) high, and weighs 55-70 lb (25-31.5 kg). Uncommon in the United States, the Clumber is a small game hunter and family dog.

Clyde, most important river of Scotland and one of Britain's major commercial waterways. It rises on the Lanarkshire-Dumfriesshire border in southwest Scotland and flows some 106 mi (171 km) to its estuary, the Firth of Clyde. Its upper valley, Clydesdale, is noted for its fruit and market garden crops. Near Lanark, at the Falls of Clyde, the river is harnessed for hydroelectricity. From Lanark on, its valley is occupied by heavy industry. At the head of navigation is the city-seaport of Glasgow, Scotland's chief commercial center. To the west, on the northern bank, is Clydebank, with large engineering interests and shipyards.
See also: Scotland.

Clymer, George (1739-1813), American revolutionary patriot and statesman. One of the first colonists to advocate separation from England, Clymer was one of the signers of the Declaration of Independence and a delegate to the Second Continental Con-

gress. He served in the first House of Representatives 1789-91.
See also: Revolutionary War in America.

Clytemnestra, in Greek mythology, daughter of Leda and Tyndareus, twin sister of Helen of Troy, wife of Agamemnon, and mother of 3 daughters and a son, Orestes. Clytemnestra, along with her lover, killed her husband after he had sacrificed one of their daughters to the gods. She and her lover were both then killed by her son to avenge the death of his father.
See also: Agamemnon; Mythology; Trojan War.

Cnut *See:* Canute.

Coagulant, any substance that causes or stimulates a liquid to change to a thickened curdlike or solidified state.

Coahuila, state in northern Mexico. Industries include livestock, agriculture, mining, and manufacturing. One of the original Mexican states, Coahuila included Texas until 1836.
See also: Mexico.

Coal, hard, black mineral, predominantly carbon, the compressed remains of tropical and subtropical plants, especially those of the carboniferous and Permian geological periods, burned as a fuel. With its by-products coke and coal tar, it is vital to many modern industries. Coal formation began when plant debris accumulated in swamps, partially decomposing and forming peat layers. A rise in sea level or land subsidence buried these layers below marine sediments, whose weight compressed the peat, transforming it under high-temperature conditions to coal; the greater the pressure, the harder the coal. Coals are classified according to their fixed-carbon content, which increases progressively as they are formed. Lignite, or brown coal, which weathers quickly, may ignite spontaneously, and has a low calorific value. Subbituminous coal is mainly used in generating stations; bituminous coal is the commonest type, used in generating stations and the home, and often converted into coke; anthracite is a lustrous coal that burns slowly and well and is the preferred domestic fuel.
Coal was burned in Glamorgen, Wales, in the 2nd millennium B.C. and was known in China and the Roman Empire around the time of Jesus. Coal mining was practiced throughout Europe and known to Native Americans by the 13th century. The first commercial coal mine in the United States was at Richmond, Va. (opened 1745), and anthracite was mined in Pennsylvania by 1790. The Industrial Revolution created a huge and increasing demand for coal. This slackened in the 20th century as coal faced competition from abundant oil and gas, but production is again increasing. Annual world output is about 3 billion tons, 500 million tons from the United States. World coal reserves are estimated conservatively at about 7 trillion tons, enough to meet demand for centuries at present consumption rates.
See also: Diamond.

Coalition, combination or alliance of political groups having mutual interests. In countries with parliamentary systems, governments may be composed of coalitions when no single party has a majority.

Coal oil *See:* Kerosene.

Coal tar, heavy, black, viscous liquid liberated during the distillation of coal, the source of a number of valuable chemicals. Light oil, phenol (or medium oil), heavy oil, and anthracene oil (asphalt) are used as fuels, solvents, preservatives, lubricants, and disinfectants. The chemical products that can be extracted include benzene, toluene, xylene, phenol, pyridene, naphthalene, and anthracene, on which are based several important chemical industries, particularly pharmaceuticals, dyes, and explosives. Coal tar itself is commonly used for street-paving; coal-tar creosote is an important wood preservative.
See also: Coal.

Coanda, Henri Marie (1885-1972), Romanian-born French aeronautics engineer and inventor, who designed an aircraft based on the jet-propulsion system. It crashed in 1912. Coanda also developed a dish-shaped aircraft and invented a device able to convert salt water to fresh water using solar energy.

Coast Guard Academy, United States *S ee:* U.S. Coast Guard Academy.

Coast Guard, U.S., branch of the armed services supervised in peacetime by the Department of Transportation, in war by the navy. It helps to maintain law and safety wherever the United States has jurisdiction on the high seas and navigable inland waters. Formed in 1915 by a union of the Life Saving Service and the Revenue Cutter Service, it is charged with search and rescue operations, maintaining weather ships and navigational aids, including the Loran radio network, collecting meteorological and oceanographic data, ice-breaking in inland waters and patrolling the North Atlantic for icebergs, enforcing navigation and shipping laws and marine safety regulations for sailors and the construction and equipment of ships, and operating against smugglers. In wartime the coast guard assumes the regular duties of the navy.

Coast Ranges, string of mountain ranges along the Pacific coast of North America, running from Kodiak Island in Alaska to southern California. These include the Los Angeles Ranges and the California Coast Range (in southern California); the Klamath Mountains (northern California and southern Oregon); the Oregon Coast Ranges and the Olympic Mountains (Oregon and Washington); the Vancouver Range and the Queen Charlotte Islands (British Columbia); and the Kodiak, Kenai, Chugach, and St. Elias ranges and the Alexander Archipelago (Alaska). These mountains are of widely varying geological origin and composition, the highest peak being Canada's Mt. Logan (19,850 ft/6,050 m).

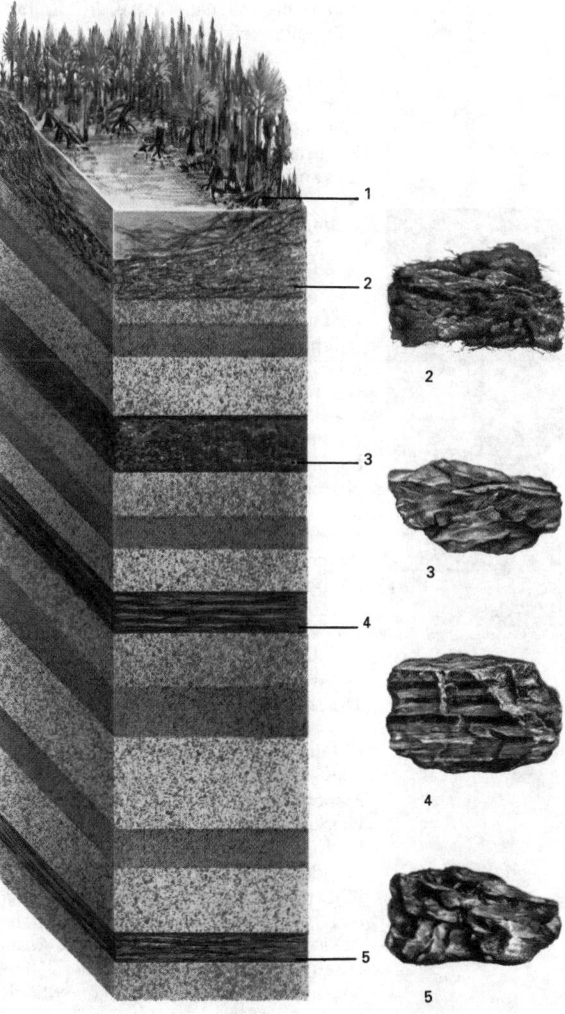

Schematic picture of the process of coal formation.
During this process the volatile components disappear until finally what remains is almost exclusively carbon.

1. marsh vegetation
2. layer of peat
3. lignite
4. bituminous coal
5. anthracite

Coati (*Nasua nasua*), small, carnivorous mammal related to the raccoon. Its long tail is held vertically above its back. It ranges from Arizona to South America. Coatis live in small bands made up of females and young, the males being solitary except in the breeding seasons. They roam through the forest, feeding on small animals and fruit and climbing trees.

Coatsworth, Elizabeth (1893-1986), U.S. author best known for her children's books. She won the 1931 Newbery Medal for *The Cat Who Went to Heaven* (1930).

Coaxial cable, cable consisting of 2 conductors, one within the other, separated by an insulator. The inner is usually a small copper wire; the outer, usually copper braid. Coaxial cables are used in the transmission of TV, telephone, and telegraph signals.

Cobalt, chemical element, symbol Co; for physical constants see Periodic Table. Cobalt was discovered by Georg Brandt in 1735. Cobalt is a gray-white, lustrous, hard and brittle magnetic metal. It is alloyed with other elements to make powerful magnets and high speed cutting tools. Compounds of cobalt have been used for centuries to give a blue color to ceramic materials. Radioactive cobalt-60, an artificial isotope, is a powerful source of gamma rays and is used in the treatment of cancer.

Ty Cobb

Cobb, Ty(rus Raymond) (1886-1961), U.S. baseball player. Nicknamed "Georgia Peach," Cobb is considered one of the greatest players of all time. His lifetime average is the highest in major league baseball history (.367), he is second on the all time hit list (4,191), and third in career stolen bases (892). From 1905-1928 Cobb played outfield for the Detroit Tigers and the Philadelphia Athletics. He was among the first group of players inducted into the National Baseball Hall of Fame (1936).

Cobbett, William (1763-1835), British radical writer and reformer, best known for his book *Rural Rides* (1830), which portrayed the misery of rural workers. His *Weekly Political Register* (founded 1802) was the major reform newspaper of its day. He was elected to Parliament after the 1832 Reform Act.

Cobden, Richard (1804-65), British politician and reformer, leader of the Manchester School. A textile merchant, he was known as "the Apostle of Free Trade." With John Bright and Robert Peel, he founded the Anti-Corn-Law League (1838-39), and was its chief spokesman in Parliament (1841-46). In 2 pamphlets, *England, Ireland, and America* (1835) and *Russia* (1836), he surveyed international relations and argued against British interventionist policies.

Cobra, venomous snake (family Elapidae) that rears up and spreads the ribs of the neck to form a "hood" when alarmed. Cobras are found in Africa and southern Asia. The ringhals, or spitting cobra, of Africa defends itself by spitting venom over a distance of 10-12 ft (3-3.7 m). If venom enters the eye it can cause blindness. The king cobra (*Ophiophagus hannah*) is the longest of all poisonous snakes, reaching a length of 18 ft (5.5 m). The Egyptian (*Naja haja*) and Indian (*Naja naja*) cobras are the traditional snakes of the snake charmer. Like all snakes, they are deaf to airborne sounds and are reacting to the snake charmer's swaying movement, not to the music.

A black and white cobra in the characteristic cobra defensive pose, in which the neck is flattened by expanding the elongated neck ribs

Coca (*Erythroxylon coca*), shrub whose leaves contain various alkaloids. Native to the Andes, it is cultivated in Sri Lanka, Java, and Taiwan. South American Indians chew the leaves mixed with lime, which releases the drug cocaine. Cocaine-free coca extracts are used in making cola drinks.
See also: Cocaine.

Cocaine, colorless or white crystalline alkaloid, member of a broad group of plant substances that includes nicotine, caffeine, and morphine. In nature, cocaine is found in significant quantities in the leaves of 2 species of the coca shrub that grow throughout the eastern highlands of the Andes in Ecuador, Peru, and Bolivia and along the Caribbean coast of South America. In medicine it is used as a local anesthetic. Cocaine is used as a "recreational" drug to produce euphoria and a feeling of energy. Such use is illegal in the United States although cocaine was legal for a long time (it was an ingredient in the early years of the Coca-Cola soft drink). The drug-induced euphoria is most pronounced shortly before the blood concentration has begun to fall, and it disappears several hours before the blood concentration returns to zero. Technically, cocaine is not addictive, as repeated use does not result in tolerance for it (i.e., repeating the same dose causing a diminishing response). There are withdrawal signs (particularly depression, which may be severe), but they are milder than withdrawal syndromes associated with opiates (e.g., heroin), barbiturates, or alcohol. On the other hand, cocaine is severely habit-forming. Chronic use of the drug can cause nervous system disorders and delusions, weight loss, and lessening of physical well-being. U.S. law classifies cocaine as a narcotic. During the 1980s and 1990s a cocaine-derivative, called crack, has become the drug of choice in many urban areas.
See also: Drug abuse; Narcotic.

Cochise (1815-74), chief of the Chiricahua Apache tribe. Aroused by the unjust execution of relatives by soldiers, he began a violent campaign against European Americans in Arizona in 1861 and effectively drove them from the area. In 1862 he was driven back by troops to the Dragon Mountains, which he held until his capture by Gen. George Crook in 1871. He escaped but gave himself up when the Chiricahua Reservation was formed in 1872. After his death, his people were removed from the reservation.

Cochran, Jacqueline (1912-80), U.S. pilot. She obtained her pilot's license in 1932 after only 3 weeks' flying. First woman to fly in a Bendix transcontinental race (1934), she won it in 1938. She organized and headed the Women's Airforce Service Pilots (WASP) in World War II, was the first civilian woman to win the Distinguished Service Cross, and was the first woman to fly faster than sound.

Cockatiel, gray bird (*Nymphicus hollandicus*) found in Australia. It is about 12.5 in (32 cm) long, has a crown of feathers, a long tail, and a heavy beak.

Cockatoo, parrot with erectile crest (especially, genus *Kakatoe*). Its plumage is usually white, sometimes black, pink, or yellow. Cockatoos live in Australia and neighboring parts. They are good talkers.

Cockcroft, Sir John Douglas (1897-1967), English physicist who first "split the atom." With E.T.S. Walton, he built a particle accelerator and in 1932 initiated the first artificial nuclear reaction by bombarding lithium atoms with protons, producing alpha particles. For this work Cockcroft and Walton received the 1951 Nobel Prize for physics.
See also: Atom; Walton, Ernest Thomas Sinton.

Cocker spaniel, popular breed of dog in the United States, bred from the English spaniel. They weigh 22-28 lb (10-13 kg) and stand 15 in (38 cm) at the shoulder.

Cockle, bivalve mollusk (order Eulamel libranchia) with cupped shell ornamented with radiating grooves. Cockles live buried in mud or sand, in shallow water, and dig themselves in by means of a muscular foot that can be protruded between the shells. There are numerous species along the coasts of North America ranging in size from the 4-in (10.2-cm) giant Pacific egg cockle to 1/4-in (0.6-cm) cockles. The common cockle of Europe is edible.

Cocklebur, any of several weeds (genus *Xanthium*) of the composite family. This plant grows throughout Europe and parts of the United States. It has spiny burs that usually contain 2 seeds, 1 of which germinates a season before the other. The seedlings are poisonous to grazing animals.

Cock-of-the-rock, bird of genus *Rupicola*, of the cotingas family, native to South American forests. Cocks-of-the-rock have ornate orange or red plumage and helmet-like crests.

Cockroach, or roach, flat-bodied insect of the family Blattidae with long antennae and hardened forewings that protect the hindwings, as in the beetle. Cockroaches feed on fungi and on plant and animal remains but also come indoors to eat exposed food, book bindings, and even wood. Sizes range from 0.5 in (0.6 cm) to 3 in (7.6 cm). There are about 70 species in the United States. Some species can fly.

Cockscomb, tropical Asiatic flower (*Celosia argentea*) of the amaranth family. The cockscomb grows in tropical America, Asia, the East Indies, and the United States. The rooster's-comb-shaped flowers have been developed into varying shapes and colors.

Coconut palm (*Cocos nuerfera*), tropical tree. Its origin is obscure because coconuts can survive prolonged immersion in the sea, and they have been spread around the world by ocean currents. The height of the coconut palm ranges from 60 to 100 ft (18 to 30 m). The trunk, which often tilts over, bears a cluster of long fronds at the top. A single palm can produce over 400 nuts in the course of a year. The husk surrounding the "nut" (seed) is used for mats and ropes. The nut is at first filled with a jelly. This liquefies when the nut is about 7 months old to become "coconut milk." Over the next 2 to 3 months the liquid solidifies to a white flesh used to make desiccated coconut. Finally, when a year old, the fruit falls of its own accord. The nuts are then cut out and split in two, and the flesh is allowed to dry. Then called copra, it yields an oil used in margarine, synthetic rubber, soap, and other items. Coconut palm fronds are used for thatching, and the copra, without its oil, is used as cattle feed. The tree is also a source of wood.

Cocoon, protective covering enclosing the larvae or pupae of insects. The larva prepares the cocoon as a shelter. While inside the cocoon, the larva becomes a pupa, which in turn develops into an adult insect.

Cocteau, Jean (1889-1963), French author, artist, and film director. He first rose to fame with poetry, ballets such as *Parade* (1917), and the novel *Thomas l'Imposteur* (Thomas the Imposter; 1923). After overcoming opium addiction, he produced some of his most brilliant work, such as the play *Orphée* (1926) and *La Machine Infernale* (The Infernal Machine; 1934). Prolific in many fields, he also made several films, including *Le Sang d'un Poete* (The Blood of a Poet; 1932), *Beauty and the Beast* (1945), *Orpheus* (1949), and *Les Enfants Terribles* (1950).

Cockroach

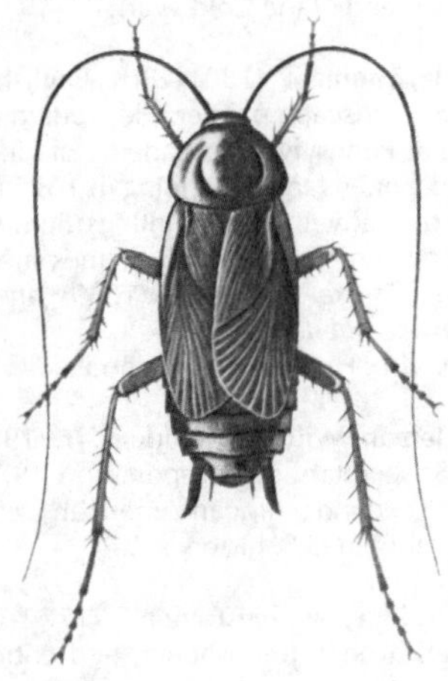

Cod, bottom-feeding fish (family Gadidae) of the northern Atlantic and the Pacific. The record weight is 211 lb (95.7 kg) for an Atlantic cod (*Gadus morrhua*), but the usual range is 2 to 25 lb (0.9 to 11.3 kg). Females lay up to 6 million eggs at a time. Cod fishing has been important in Europe since the 16th century, and Europeans soon discovered the New England and Newfoundland "cod banks," which played an important part in the colonization of the new continent. The cod were salted, their livers yielding an important vitamin-rich oil (cod liver oil), and the swimbladder was used for isinglass, a very pure form of gelatin.

Code, set of laws or rules arranged systematically and put in writing. Legal codes have existed for perhaps as long as writing. One of the earliest known codes is that of Hammurabi, the king of Babylonia, 18th century B.C. Roman law was codified in the form of the Twelve Tables around 450 B.C. By A.D. 534 its principles had been refined into the Code of Justinian, which had an enormous influence on later European law. The code Napoléon, formulated in 1804, served as the basis for the legal system of France and its colonies, including Quebec and Louisiana. In communications, code is a set of symbols made to yield information via specified operations. An example is the Morse code in telegraphy, a system of short and long signals in combinations that indicate letters of the alphabet. Codes whose rules are not revealed are often used for secret messages. Decoding these messages is called cryptography.

Code Civil *See:* Code Napoléon.

Codeine, mild but addictive narcotic alkaloid, analgesic, and cough suppressant derived from opium. It also reduces bowel activity, causing constipation, and is used to cure diarrhea.
See also: Narcotic.

Code Napoléon, French legal code, officially the *Code Civil*. Napoleon I, as first consul, appointed a commission to devise a replacement for the confused and corrupt local systems formerly in force. The code, made up of 2,281 articles arranged in 3 books, was enacted in 1804 and, although much altered, is still in force today.

Codes and ciphers, set of characters or signals, with prearranged meanings as letters or numbers, used for secrecy and brevity in transmitting messages, especially in wartime.

Codling moth, or codlin moth, small, nocturnal moth (*Laspeyresia pomonella*) whose caterpillars live in apples and pears. Infestations of codling moths can cause the destruction of entire orchards.

Cod-liver oil, pale yellow substance obtained from the liver of cod and related fish. Cod-liver oil is rich in vitamins A and D, and was formerly used by people with deficiencies of these vitamins.

Cody, John Patrick Cardinal (1907-82), archbishop of Chicago 1965-82. Cody served on the Vatican staff in the 1930s. He was appointed archbishop of New Orleans in 1964, and became a cardinal in 1967.

Cody, William Frederick *See:* Buffalo Bill.

Coeducation, education of both sexes in the same schools and classes. While coeducation in the primary grades became common in Protestant Europe after the Reformation, it was not introduced at higher educational levels until much later. In 18th- and 19th-century America, any tendency toward a double system of secondary schooling was offset by prohibitive cost. Now the majority of accredited colleges and universities in the United States are coeducational.

Coelacanth, lunged, bony fish of the family Coelacanthidae. Known as predecessors of the amphibians, coelacanths were thought to be extinct until 1938, when one species (*Latimeria chalumne*) was discovered live off the South African coast. They are about 5 ft (150 cm) long, with circular overlapping scales.

Coelenterate, phylum of primitive, invertebrate animals, now renamed the *Cnidaria* (the *C* is silent). It includes anemones, corals, jellyfish, the freshwater hydra, and many others. The basic body form is a two-layered sac, with a mouth at one end surrounded by a ring of tentacles. Food is captured and poisoned by means of *nematocysts*, or "stinging cells," in the tentacles. Coelenterates exist in two forms. Anemones, corals, and hydra are *polyps*, which are anchored and tubular. Jellyfishes are *medusae*, or free-swimming.

Coelom, major body cavity in vertebrates and higher invertebrates. In vertebrates, the coelom is partitioned into the pericardial, pleural, and abdominal cavities, which house the stomach, liver, digestive tract, and other body organs.

Coercive Acts *See:* Intolerable Acts.

Coffee, evergreen shrub or tree (genus *Coffea*) from whose seeds the drink of the same name is made. The plant was first discovered in Ethiopia, where its fruit was used for wine and food before A.D. 1000 The hot drink made of ground and roasted coffee beans was first made in the Arabian peninsula in the 15th century. It reached Europe in the 17th century and then spread, with European settlers, to the Americas. The shrub is now grown in many hot, humid areas of Asia, the Americas, and Africa. The highest quality coffees are varieties of Arabian (*Coffea arabica*). Coffee of Liberian (*C. liberica*) and Congolese (*C. robusta*) origin are also commercially significant. Brazil is the world's largest coffee producer. Other major producing countries are Costa Rica, El Salvador, Guatemala, Honduras, Mexico, Colombia, Ecuador, Cameroon, Ethiopia, Ivory Coast, Uganda, India, and Indonesia.

The red, cherry-like berries of the coffee plant generally contain 2 seeds per berry. These seeds are harvested, cleaned, and roasted. It is the heat of the roasting process that creates the flavor and aroma. The roasting also causes the formation of caffeine, a stimulant that may be harmful in large doses.

Coffee house, variety of commercial establishment that arose in London in the mid-17th century. Coffee houses became centers of business, cultural, political, and religious information exchange. The first English newspapers arose as broadsheets distributed in coffee houses. The institution died away in London in the 19th century, but cafes remain widespread in most European, Mediterranean, and Latin American countries.

Cohan, George M(ichael) (1878-1942), U.S. songwriter, actor, composer and producer of popular, patriotic musicals. He is best remembered for hits like "Give My Regards to Broadway," "You're a Grand Old Flag," "Yankee Doodle Dandy," and the popular World War I song "Over There."

Cohesion, attractive force holding the atoms or molecules of a single substance together. Cohesion is generally contrasted to adhesion, the attractive force between different substances.

Cohn, Ferdinand Julius (1828-98), German botanist, one of the founders of bacteriology. He also contributed to the understanding of heat production by plants.
See also: Botany.

Coin, piece of stamped metal, of a fixed value and weight, issued to serve as money. Until banknotes came into use, coins were the only form of money. The principal metals used in coinage are gold, silver, and copper. They were originally used in their pure state, but were later alloyed (combined) with other substances to make the coins cheaper and more resistant to wear. Coins have presented a constant temptation to engage in monetary trickery. From the time of the Romans, when rulers had large debts, they reduced the amount of precious metals in coins and passed them off on their creditors at the old value; this process is called debasement.
The first known coins were struck in Lydia, Asia Minor, in the 8th century B.C. These coins, called *staters* (a unit of weight), were made of a natural combination of gold and silver and ornamented with crude animal likenesses. The Greek island of Aegina issued better-made silver *staters* about 700 B.C., and the use of coins soon spread throughout the Mediterranean world. The Athenian silver *tetradrachma* was the main coin from the 6th to the 4th centuries B.C., when the coinage of Alexander the Great replaced it. The Chinese independently developed coins about the same time as the Greeks. The first Roman coins, made of bronze (an alloy of copper and tin), date from the 4th century B.C.; during later Roman times, silver and gold coins were used. During the early Middle Ages, only silver coins were struck in western Europe. The breakup of the Roman Empire decreased the volume of trade, and the use of money diminished. In the 12th and 13th centuries, Genoa and Venice led the commercial revival, and their gold coins became a leading international medium of exchange. In modern times, gold replaced silver throughout most of the world. All monies were defined in terms of gold and bore a definite and fixed relationship to the value of gold. World War I and the Great Depression caused this system to break down, and most nations now no longer use gold coins. In the United States, the early colonists used the Native Americans' *wampum*, shell beads formed into belts, as money. Many different European coins circulated in the American colonies, but their value fluctuated widely from place to place. The Massachusetts Bay Colony produced the first American coins in 1652. The first U.S. Mint was established at Philadelphia in 1792, and its first coins date from the following year. U.S. coins have existed in their present metallic state longer than any other coins used today. Many different types of coins have been struck in the course of the history of the United States, and they are still legal tender (though their value to collectors naturally exceeds their face value). Gold coins were used until 1933, when the government discontinued their use in domestic and foreign commerce.

Coin collecting, or numismatics, popular hobby throughout the world. Collecting involves the acquisition of coins of any particular grouping. Coins may be considered desirable for various reasons, including origin, history, rarity, and value. They are commonly graded according to quality. Categories of quality include: poor (features are mostly obliterated); good (worn, but with features mostly visible); very good (evenly worn, but with clear details); very fine or uncirculated (in newly minted condition); proof (specially struck from a highly polished die).

Coke, form of amorphous carbon that is left when bituminous coal is burned in special furnaces to remove volatile constituents. In the United States coke is used primarily as a fuel in metallurgy, especially in blast furnaces to extract metal from ores.
See also: Carbon.

Coke oven gas, hydrogen and methane mixture produced when coal is heated to about 2000°F (1100°C) in an airtight chamber. Coke oven gas is burned as an industrial fuel and for home heating.

Colbert, Jean Baptiste (1619-83), French diplomat and finance superintendent. He became chief finance minister to King Louis XIV in 1661 and held that post for 22 years, supporting French industry and commerce and building a powerful navy.
See also: Louis (kings of France).

Colchicum, poisonous flowering plant (*Colchicum autumnale*) of the lily family, also known as autumn crocus or meadow saffron. Found on the British Isles and in mid- to southern Europe, these plants have crocus-like flowers, whose autumnal blooms range from purple to white. From the underground stems a substance (colcherine) is extracted that is used in the treatment of rheumatism and gout.

Cold, common, viral infection of the mucous membrane of the nose and throat, marked by discharge of mucus, sneezing, and watering of the eyes. More than 100 specific viruses have been identified as causes of the common cold. There is no known cure, but symptoms can be treated. Drinking fluids prevents dehydration. Pain relievers can lower fever. Decongestants may shrink mucous membranes.

Cold-blooded animal, or poikilotherm, animal that cannot maintain a constant internal body temperature and therefore attains a temperature close to that of its environment, making it dangerously subject to climatic changes. Cold-blooded animals include fish, amphibians, and reptiles.

Cold sore, skin lesion, generally of the lips or nose, caused by the Herpes simplex virus. Often characterized by blisters filled with a clear liquid, cold sores may be triggered by infections such as the common cold or pneumonia. The virus frequently becomes dormant, persisting in the skin between attacks.
See also: Herpes.

Cold War, expression used to characterize the conflict after World War II between the Western powers led by the United States and the Communist bloc led by the USSR. The term arose to describe conditions of hostility and military build-up short of actual armed conflict. The 2 largest wars during the Cold War era were in Korea in the 1950s and in Indochina in the 1960s and early 1970s. The period was also characterized by the division of Europe into antagonistic military blocs: the North Atlantic Treaty Organization (NATO) in the West, the Warsaw Pact in the East. Most analysts would argue that the upheavals in Eastern Europe and the USSR in 1989 led to the end of the Cold War.

Cole, Thomas (1801-48), English-born U.S. landscape painter. He studied painting at Pennsylvania Academy of Fine Arts and gained fame beginning in 1825 for his Hudson River Valley paintings. Some of his works which had moral themes included *The Course of Empire* (1839) and *The Voyage of Life* (1840).
See also: Hudson River School.

Coleman, William Thaddeus, Jr. (1920-), U.S. secretary of transportation 1975-77, the second African-American cabinet member in U.S. history.

Coleridge, Samuel Taylor (1772-1834), English poet, philosopher, and critic. His works include the poems "Kubla Khan," "Christabel," and "The Rime of the Ancient Mariner," all 3 of which were included in the volume *Lyrical Ballads* (1798), a collection Coleridge produced with William Wordsworth. The book is one of the major works of English Romanticism.

Colette (Sidonie Gabrielle Colette; 1873-1954), French author noted primarily for her sensual style and her themes of women, love and jealousy. Among her many novels are *Cheri* (1920), *The Ripening* (1923), *The Cat* (1933), and *Gigi* (1945).

Coleus, tropical plant (genus *Coleus)* of the mint family. Native to the African and Indian tropics, the coleus plant grows to a height of 3 ft (91 cm) and is cultivated as a houseplant.

Colfax, Schuyler (1823-85), vice president of the United States during the first term of President Ulysses S. Grant (1869-73). Colfax served 22 years in Congress, the last 6 of which as Speaker of the House.

Colic, acute pain focused in an internal organ, frequently the colon or other component of the digestive tract.

Coliseum *See:* Colosseum.

Colitis, disease characterized by inflammation of the colon (large intestine). Symptoms include abdominal pain, cramps, and diarrhea. If ulcers develop in the walls of the intestine, the condition can become chronic, with fever and complications. Colitis sometimes follows attacks of dysentery, but causative microorganisms have not been traced. There is probably a psychosomatic component, anxiety bringing on attacks of the disease. In severe cases a section of the colon may have to be removed by surgery.
See also: Colon.

Collage, 20th-century art form in which various objects and materials are glued onto a canvas or board, sometimes covered with paint. The term comes from the French word for pasting. The earliest experiments with collage were done by Pablo Picasso and Georges Braque in 1910-11. The technique was further developed by Henri Matisse and by the Dadaists, particularly Kurt Schwitters, who made entire compositions consisting of ticket stubs and other evocative remnants of paper. Later artists, like Jasper Johns, created more elaborate collages of wood, metal, and fabric.

Collagen, major component of connective tissue, constituting 70% of its dry weight. Collagen is an insoluble protein, whose fibers form a mesh. Collagen is also present in bones.

Collarbone, or clavicle, horizontal bone that connects with the breastbone (*sternum*) and the shoulder blade (*scapula*) to support the shoulder and to hold the arm in proper position. It is present in upright-walking mammals and in bats.
See also: Bone.

Collard (*Brassica oreracea)*, headless cabbage of the mustard family commonly grown in the southern United States. Both a summer and winter crop, the collard plant reaches 2-4 ft (60-120 cm), and is a dietary source of vitamins A and C.

Collective bargaining *See:* Labor movement; National Labor Relations Act.

Collective behavior, sociological term for human behavior in crowds and other large, unorganized, temporary groups. Instances of collective behavior include riots, panics, fashions, cults, and revolutionary movements. U.S. sociologists Robert E. Park and Ernest W. Burgess introduced the concept in their book *Introduction to the Science of Sociology* (1921).
See also: Group dynamics.

Collective farm, agricultural enterprise operated cooperatively. The farm's land and equipment may be owned by members of the cooperative group or by the government, which controls production. Stalin introduced collectivization to the USSR in 1929, and it has been widely used in Communist countries and in Israel.

Collectivism, political doctrine that places control of economic activity in the hands of the community or the government, as opposed to individuals, as in the case under capitalism. The term may cover a wide variety of economic systems and structures, but will typically exclude private ownership of major means of production and distribution.
See also: Communal society; Socialism.

College entrance examination, series of tests administered in the United States by 2 agencies, the College Entrance Examination Board (CEEB) and the American College Testing Program (ACT), to determine eligibility for college or university admission. The CEEB gives the Scholastic Aptitude Test (SAT) in 3 sections of multiple-choice questions: verbal, mathematical, and written English; and the Achievement Tests, 14 1-hour tests measuring knowledge in specific areas such as foreign language and science. The ACT examination has 2 parts: an academic test of English, mathematics, natural science, and social studies; and a Student Profile, information about personal goals and interests. Each university or college sets its own standards for score interpretation.

Collie, 2 types of sheepdog, rough-coated and smooth-coated, originating in Scotland in the 1600s and brought to the United States by British colonists a century later. The collie stands 2 ft (60 cm) at the shoulder and may be sable and white, blue, tan, or all white, though early breeds were black. There is also a miniature variety.

Collins, (William) Wilkie (1824-89), English novelist, often considered the originator of the detective novel in English. His works include *The Woman in White* (1860) and *The Moonstone* (1868).

Collie

Collins, Michael, (1930-), U.S. astronaut. A member of the astronaut program 1963-70, he was pilot of the *Columbia* command module on the Apollo 11 mission that landed Neil Armstrong and Edwin Aldrin, Jr. on the moon (1969). In 1971 Collins became director of the National Air and Space Museum in Washington, D.C.

Collodi, Carlo (Carlo Lorenzini; 1826-90), Italian journalist and author of humorous adult fiction and moral children's stories, of which the best known is *The Adventures of Pinocchio* (1883).

Colloid, mixture in which particles of one substance are dispersed in another. Colloids are similar to solutions and suspensions. What determines the difference is the size of the particles of the substance that is distributed. In a solution, the particles are molecules. In a suspension, they are much larger, visible either with the naked eye or a microscope. A colloid has particles larger than molecules but too small to be seen with a normal microscope. Colloids can be categorized according to whether the substances mixed together are solids, liquids, or gases. For instance, a gas may be dispersed in a liquid to form foam. A liquid dispersed in another liquid forms an emulsion. A liquid dispersed in a solid is a gel.

Colobus, or guerza, genus of thumbless, long-tailed, African monkey of the family Cercopithecidae. The colobus is vegetarian, diurnal (active in the daytime), and lives in trees, though it may travel on the ground. Colobus species are divided by color and may be black and white, red, or olive. Young are white at birth. Colobus live in groups of 3 to 80. Some species are aggressively territorial.

Cologne (pop. 916,200), river port and industrial city in western Germany, on the Rhine River. Its products range from heavy machinery to toilet water (eau de cologne). The prosperity of Cologne (Köln in German) dates from its membership in the Hanseatic League in the 15th century.
See also: Germany.

Colombia

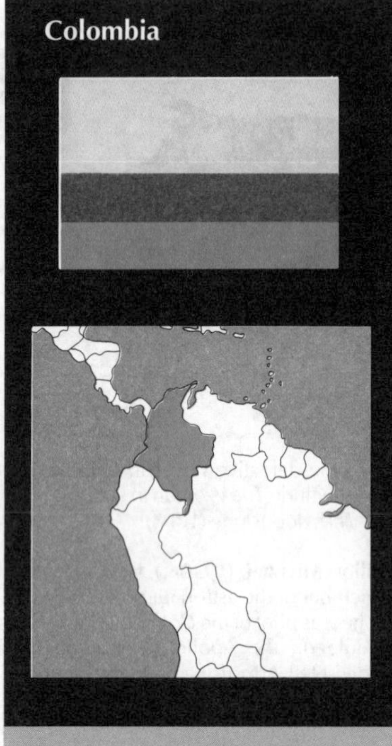

General information	
Capital:	Bogotá
Area:	440,831 sq mi (1,141,748 sq km)
Population:	32,317,000
Official language:	Spanish
Monetary unit:	1 peso = 100 centavos
Main cities:	Bogotá, Medellín, Cali, Barranquilla
Government	
Form:	republic
Independent:	1819
Head of state:	President (elected every 4 years)
Head of government:	President
Legislature:	two legislative houses (Senate and House of Representatives)
Executive:	President and Cabinet
Judiciary:	highest court is the Supreme Court of Justice
Political division:	23 departments, 9 national territories, 1 Special District
National economy	
Gross national product:	US $37,210,000,000
Per capita income:	US $1,240
Agriculture:	coffee, bananas, potatoes, rice, cassava, sugar cane, corn
Livestock:	chickens, cattle, sheep
Mining:	crude petroleum, gold, salt, iron ore, emeralds
Industries:	processed food, beverages, textiles, chemical products, machinery and electrical apparatus
Main exports:	raw coffee, petroleum and petroleum products, fruits, flowers, cotton
Transportation:	2011 mi (3,236 km) of railroads; 66,000 mi (106,218 km) of roads; 11 international airports
Trading partners:	U.S., Germany, Venezuela, France, The Netherlands
People	
Urban:	67%
Ethnic composition:	mestizo 58%, European 20%, mulatto 14%, mixed African-Indian 3%, Native American 1%
Birth rate:	27.9 per 1,000 population
Death rate:	7.4 per 1,000 population
Infant mortality rate:	46 per 1,000 live births
Life expectancy:	male 63 years, female 67 years

Aerial photograph of Bogotá, Colombia, one of the large westernized cities in South America.

Colombia, Republic of, fourth largest country in South America. It extends over 439,737 sq mi (1,138,920 sq km) of the extreme northwest of South America, bounded on the northwest by Panama, on the northeast by Venezuela, on the southeast by Brazil, and on the south by Peru and Ecuador. It is the only South American country that has both an Atlantic and a Pacific coastline.

Land and climate. Nearly half of the country is mountainous; more than half is comparatively uninhabited lowland plain. There are 4 major regions. By far the most important is the Andean region, where 3 great ranges branch out northward from the Pasto knot near the Ecuadorian border: the western, central, and eastern Cordilleras. Some 80% of the population lives in the narrow mountain valleys and basins of this region. Between the central and eastern Cordilleras, the Magdalena (Colombia's chief river) flows for 1,000 mi (1,609 km) to the Caribbean at the port of Barranquilla. A third of the population lives in the eastern cordillera (mountain chain), where the seat of government has been located since Chibcha times. Bogotá, the capital and largest city of Colombia, stands on a plateau at an altitude of 8,661 ft (2,640 km). The Caribbean coastal lowlands are the home of about 17% of the population; the chief centers are the ports of Barranquilla, Cartagena, and Santa Marta. The rivers draining the Caribbean lowlands—the Magdalena, Cauca, San Jorge, and César—form a maze of swamps and lagoons. The Pacific lowlands are a rainy, marshy littoral. Buenaventura and Tumaco are Colombia's chief Pacific ports. The Pacific lowlands and the eastern plains beyond the eastern Cordillera account for only 5% of the population. The northern section of the eastern region is part of the *llanos* (tropical grasslands) of northern South America; the southern section is almost impenetrable jungle. Although most of Colombia lies in the north tropical zone, the climate varies with topography. An excessively high rainfall prevails in the Pacific lowlands. Altitude modifies the climate of the highlands: The semitropical *tierra caliente* (hot land) extends to about 3,000 ft (914 m), where it is succeeded by the *tierra templada* (temperate land) coffee belt (to about 6,500 ft/2,000 m), the *tierra fria* (cold land) (6,500-10,000 ft/2,000-3,000 m) where grain and potatoes are grown, and the almost polar *páramos* (grazing lands) below the snowline. The vast eastern plains are subject to successive wet and dry seasons, while in the Caribbean lowlands a hot, dry climate predominates.

People. More than half of Colombians are mestizos (of mixed European and Native American ancestry); there are about 20% whites, with minorities of mulattoes, blacks, and Native Americans.

Economy. Colombia is a major world coffee producer. It also grows cotton, bananas, sugar, tobacco, cocoa, rice, sorghum, corn, wheat, and barley. The country has the largest coal reserve in Latin America and substantial reserves of uranium. Other resources include oil, gas, and precious metals. Transportation is hindered by mountain ranges, but cities are joined by road, rail, or river and an advanced air network. Tourism is becoming an important source of foreign exchange.

History. Chibcha Native Americans of the eastern cordilleras had a highly developed culture when the Spanish arrived in the early 16th century. Spain ruled the area until independence, which followed Simón Bolívar's Boyacá victory over Spanish colonial forces (1819). At the end of the 19th century thousands died in fighting between liberals and conservatives, Colombia's 2 main political parties. Another civil war between liberals and conservatives, with about 200,000 casualties, lasted from 1948 until 1958, when a democratic government was reestablished. In the mid-1980s the government began battling the large and well-organized drug cartels that traffic in cocaine, which is processed from coca grown in Peru. In 1989 the United States supplied military personnel to help combat the increasing related violence.

The Silvia region of Colombia, one of the drainage areas of the Cauca, which flows northward between the Cordillera Central and the Cordillera Occidental. The rivers in the Andes region follow the north-south directions of the valleys through which they flow.

Colombo (pop. 683,000), capital, chief port, and largest city of Sri Lanka (Ceylon), located on the southwest coast of the island, in the Indian Ocean. The city's harbor, built in 1875 and modernized in the 1950s, is one of the world's largest. Tea, cinnamon, rubber, and coconut products are the chief exports.
See also: Sri Lanka.

Colombo Plan, cooperative program for economic development in South and Southeast Asia, inaugurated in 1951 at Colombo, Ceylon (now Sri Lanka). The first participants were members of the British Commonwealth, joined by the United States, Japan, and several Southeast Asian countries.

Colón (pop. 59,800), third largest city of Panama, established in 1850 at what is now the Atlantic terminus of the Panama Canal. Originally named Aspinwall, the city was renamed to honor Christopher Columbus in 1890. As a duty-free trade zone, Colón is an important commercial port and tourist center.
See also: Panama.

Colon, large intestine from the cecum (the pouch into which the small intestine empties) to the rectum, about 60 in (1.5 m) long. The colon is divided into 4 segments: the ascending, transverse, descending, and the sigmoid, or pelvic.
See also: Intestine.

Colonialism, political and economic subordination of an area by a geographically removed parent country. The ruling country is more technologically advanced than the colony. Often the rulers and the colonial subjects are of different races. Colonialism dates to the Phoenicians; Rome was the largest ancient colonizer. As a vehicle for European expansion, modern colonialism dates from c.1500. Colonialism may be both beneficial and detrimental: Developing areas may receive technological and economic advances, but may have a foreign culture forced upon them or have their resources exploited by the occupying state.

Colonial period, American, nearly 170 formative years of settlement and adventure before U.S. independence. The first colonies were established by chartered trading companies, groups of commercial speculators who shared the profits of the colony in return for putting up the capital necessary for its establishment. The first permanent English settlement in America, at Jamestown (1607), was the project of the London Company, which failed to exploit its new colony of Virginia and surrendered its charter to the crown in 1624. The Pilgrim settlement at Plymouth (1620) merged with the later Puritan settlement at Boston, and the 2 were governed by the charter of the Massachusetts Bay Company until 1691, when it, too, became a royal province under an appointed governor. Connecticut (1662) and Rhode Island (1663) were established by settlers from Massachusetts. New York, originally New Amsterdam, was founded by the Dutch West India Company in 1625 and captured by the English in 1664. Delaware, founded by a Swedish company in 1638, later fell under the control of the Penn family. Under the system of proprietorship, the crown also granted huge tracts of land to individuals or groups. Of the 13 colonies, 7 were founded as proprietorships: Maryland, New Hampshire, New Jersey, the Carolinas, Pennsylvania, and Georgia. All except Pennsylvania and Maryland became royal provinces before 1776.

Economic life. Despite rocky soil and a short growing season, many crops were raised on the small farms of New England. Fishing employed 10,000 people by 1765, and some 300 vessels were engaged in whaling. Shipbuilding was the main industry, though woolen textiles, leather goods, and iron tools and utensils were also produced. In the 18th century the distillation of rum from West Indian molasses became the second most important industry. The Middle Atlantic colonies—New York, New Jersey, and Pennsylvania—supplied New England and Europe with food and raw materials. Manufactures consisted of textiles, paper, glass, and iron. In the 17th century an important fur trade was carried on through the Iroquois country from Albany. In the Plantation Provinces, from Maryland south to Georgia, production became increasingly concentrated on great staple crops—tobacco, rice, and indigo. By the 1770s tobacco exports were around 50 million pounds a year, rice half a million. The forests of the Carolina uplands also furnished lumber for shipbuilding and "naval stores" (pitch, tar, and turpentine), which were vital for the British navy.
Scarcity of labor was a problem common to all the colonies, for the ease with which land could be acquired meant that industrious colonists quickly became landlords in their own right. One solution was the employment of "indentured" servants who were obliged to serve for a fixed period of years, in return for payment of their passage across the Atlantic or sometimes as a punishment for political or religious offenses or crimes. From Virginia southward, African slaves were employed. The first shipload arrived as early as 1619; by 1760 there were 400,000 blacks in the English colonies.

Social and cultural life. The major colonial cities were ports whose main connection with each other was by sea, since roads were very poor. For more prosperous city dwellers life differed little from what they had left behind in England. On the frontier, however, life was crude and hazardous. Hostility from Native Americans encouraged communal settlement, and stockades surrounded the early villages. Food was obtained by hunting and fishing, clothing was made from animal skins, and the log cabin was the standard dwelling. In the cities class distinctions were evident; however, on the frontier a rough democracy prevailed. There were many sects and religions, but toleration was achieved only gradually. The early colonists took an active interest in providing schooling, particularly in New England, where each town maintained a school. In the Middle Colonies schools were run by religious organizations, while in the South private tutors were employed. For the poor, apprenticeship took the place of schooling. Nine colleges were founded in the colonial period. Established primarily for the training of ministers, the colleges at first taught theology and the classics; in the 18th century science, medicine, and modern languages were introduced. Over 50 newspapers were established in the colonial period. The first printing press went into operation in Massachusetts in 1639. Private and public subscription libraries were founded in the 18th century, and the American Philosophical Society (1743), led by Benjamin Franklin, strove to unite scientists and philosophic thinkers. In painting the 18th century produced artists whose reputation reached as far as Europe: John Singleton Copley, Benjamin West, Charles Wilson Peale, and Gilbert Stuart. Singing societies and chamber concerts were popular outside the Puritan areas, and the Moravians were noted for their performances of German church music.

Migration from countries other than England brought new cultural influences to the colonies. King Louis XIV's revocation of the Edict of Nantes (1685) compelled many French Protestants to flee to America, where they became prominent in trade and industry and brought French styles of dress, furnishing, and architecture to Boston, New York, and particularly Charleston. Germans, mostly peasant farmers, settled in Pennsylvania, the Shenandoah Valley, and the Piedmont region of Virginia and North Carolina. Scotch-Irish from Ulster also settled in Pennsylvania and the colonies to its south. By 1775 there were probably 200,000 Germans and 300,000 Scotch-Irish in America as well as Swiss, Welsh, and Dutch. Nevertheless, the English inheritance was predominant: English was the main language and also the basis of a shared literature, legal system, and political outlook. In the free and vigorous atmosphere of colonial America the British tradition of personal liberty was to culminate in revolution and independence.

Colony, area and people controlled by a foreign power. Types of colony defined by social or economic characteristics include settlement, trade, missionary, penal, and protectorate. Since World War II, the trend toward reorganization of empire has allowed many colonies to obtain independence or to be placed under the supervision of the United Nations' General Assembly or Trusteeship System.

The pre-Columbian cliff dwelling in Mesa Verde National Park, southwestern Colorado

Color, visual effect caused by the eye's ability to react differently to different wavelengths of light. Color is a sensation rather than a property of a thing. An object that reflects light of a certain wavelength will appear to be a certain color. The 3 primary colors—red, blue, and yellow—can be combined to form all other colors. Two colors whose light, when combined, produces white, are called complementary. In white light, an object that reflects all wavelengths will appear white, while one that absorbs all wavelengths will appear black.

Colorado

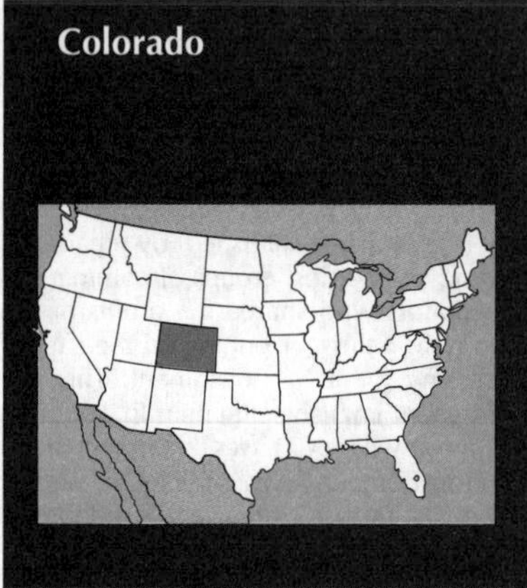

Capital:	Denver.
Statehood:	Aug. 1, 1876 (38th state)
Familiar name:	Centennial State
Area:	104,091 sq mi (269,595 sq km); ranks 8th
Population:	3,307,912 (1990; ranks 26th)
Elevation:	Highest—14,433 ft (4,399 m), Mt. Elbert. Lowest—3,350 ft (1,021 m), Arkansas River
Motto:	Nil sine Numine (Nothing without Providence)
State flower:	Rocky Mountain columbine
State bird:	Lark bunting
State tree:	Colorado blue spruce
State song:	"Where the Columbines Grow"

Colorado, state in the Rocky Mountain region of the United States; bordered by Wyoming in the north, Nebraska in the north and east, Kansas in the east, Oklahoma and New Mexico in the south, and Utah in the west.

Land and climate. Colorado has the highest mean elevation (c. 6,800 ft/2,100 m) of any state. The high plains of the east, part of the Great Plains, cover two-fifths of the state. The land here is extremely flat, but rises in the west to meet the edge of the Rocky Mountains, which cover the middle two-fifths of Colorado. The Continental Divide, the line of elevated land that separates westward-flowing and eastward-flowing waters, runs through the Colorado Rockies. The several ranges that make up the Rockies in Colorado are the tallest in the entire chain: over 50 peaks reach 14,000 ft (4,270 m) or more. These ranges include the Sawatch Range, which contains Mt. Elbert. The Colorado Plateau in the west covers about one-fifth of the state. It is an area of lower mountains, plateaus, and mesas.

The most famous of the state's many important rivers is the Colorado, which drains one-twelfth of the United States. Despite the important rivers, the uneven distribution of water within Colorado is a problem. The mountains are considerably cooler than the plains and plateaus, which are dry and sunny. Principal cities are Denver, Colorado Springs, and Pueblo.

Denver, Colorado

Economy. Major manufactured products are scientific instruments, processed foods, machinery, and printed materials. Livestock and livestock products dominate agriculture. The chief crops, grown mostly on irrigated land, are hay, wheat, and corn. Colorado has vast deposits of petroleum, coal, and natural gas.

Tourism is also important, with spectacular mountain scenery and skiing the major attractions. More than a third of Colorado's land is owned by the U.S. government.

Government. Colorado is governed by the constitution of 1876. The state government is headed by a governor elected for a 4-year term. The state legislature consists of a senate, whose 35 members are elected for 4-year terms, and a house of representatives, whose 65 members serve 2-year terms. It is represented by 2 senators and 6 representatives in the U.S. Congress.

History. Traces of ancient Native American culture in Colorado are evident in the Mesa Verde and other cliff dwellings. In the 1600s Spanish explorers were the first Europeans to enter the region, which was claimed by Spain in 1706. After the Louisiana Purchase (1803), explorers like Zebulon Pike began to open up the territory. The trader William Bent built Bent's Fort, the first permanent European American settlement, in 1833. In the Mexican War (1846-48) the United States conquered further Colorado territory. The discovery of gold near Denver in 1858-59 brought a rush of prospectors. Congress created the Colorado Territory in 1861. In the 1880s, the discovery of rich silver ore in the Leadville area started a boom, but the rapid drop of silver prices in 1893 resulted in unemployment and labor problems. In 1906, the U.S. Mint in Denver began producing coins. During World War II the state prospered as military bases and a flourishing defense industry were established. The subsequent population growth increased Colorado's need for irrigation and water storage, which led to the development of several water projects, the most recent completed in 1985. Colorado's coal and petroleum industries expanded during the energy crisis of the 1970s, but since the end of the boom in the 1980s, the state has faced a sagging economy.

Colorado Desert, arid basin of Southeast California and northwest Mexico, 2,000 sq mi (5,180 sq km). Part of the Sonoran Desert, it is bounded by the Pacific Coastal Ranges, the Colorado River, and the Eagle and San Bernardino Mountains. Much of the Colorado Desert, including the Salton Sea and the Imperial Valley, is below sea level.

Colorado River, major U.S. river, rising in the Rocky Mountains of northern Colorado and flowing 1,450 mi (2,333 km) in a generally southwesternly direction to enter the Gulf of California. The river has formed many canyons, including the Grand Canyon, one of the world's largest.
See also: Hoover Dam.

Colorado Springs (pop. 397,014), city in central Colorado, second-largest in the state and seat of El Paso County. Situated at the base of Pikes Peak, Colorado Springs is a popular resort, as well as an industrial center manufacturing chemicals, tools, airplane parts, and plastics. The United States Air Force Academy is 7 mi (11.3 km) to the north.
See also: Colorado.

Color blindness, inability to tell certain colors apart. An inherited trait, color blindness is caused by a disorder of the cones in the retina of the eye. The commonest form is a difficulty in distinguishing red from green. It is usually found in males. Total color blindness, which is rare, causes a person to see only black, white, and various shades of gray.
See also: Spectrum.

Colosseum, or Coliseum, oval amphitheater in Rome, built c.75-80 A.D., with seats for about 45,000 spectators on 4 tiers. Begun by the Flavian Emperor Vespasian and completed by his son Titus, the Colosseum was used for gladiatorial combat and other events up to the 5th century. Though damaged by earthquakes, much of it still stands.

Colossians, Epistle to the, book of the New Testament written by St. Paul to the Christians of Colossae in southwest Asia Minor. Like Ephesians, it deals with the doctrine of the body of Christ.
See also: Bible; New Testament.

Colossus of Rhodes, one of the Seven Wonders of the World, statue of Helios, the sun god, erected c.290-280 B.C. by the sculptor Chares of Lindos in the harbor of Rhodes. The statue, made of bronze and 100 ft (30 m) high, commemorated the island's successful defense against an invasion in 304 B.C. There is no truth to the medieval legend that the statue straddled the harbor. The Colossus broke off at the knee in an earthquake in 224 B.C. and lay in ruins until A.D. 672, when Arab raiders broke it up and sold it for scrap.
See also: Seven Wonders of the Ancient World.

Colt, Samuel (1814-62), U.S. inventor and industrialist who devised the revolver, a single-barreled pistol with a revolving multiple bullet chamber, in the early 1830s. His factories pioneered mass-production techniques and the use of interchangeable parts.
See also: Revolver.

Colter, John (1775-1813), U.S. trapper and guide, best known for his explorations of what is now Yellowstone National Park. He guided the 1803 Lewis and Clark Expedition and other treks up the Missouri River.

Coltrane, John (1926-67), U.S. musician and composer. A saxophonist, he was one of the leading artists of African-American jazz in the 1950s and 1960s, performing with such gifted players as Dizzy Gillespie, Miles Davis, and Thelonious Monk. In the early 1960s he formed his own group, which soon became the most innovative in U.S. music. As a saxophonist, Coltrane was known for his distinctive tone and superlative technique. As a composer, he introduced the "sheets of sound" style and explored the possibilities of modal compositions, based on unusual scales. In his later years, he was also famous for his encouragement of younger musicians.
See also: Jazz.

Coltsfoot *(Tussilago farfara)*, wild plant of the daisy family Compositae native to Europe and Asia. Dandelion-like yellow blossoms appear in spring before leaves. Coltsfoot grows to 6-18 in (15-45 cm).

Colum, Padraic (1881-1972), Irish poet and dramatist associated with the Celtic renaissance and the Irish National Theater; cofounder of the *Irish Review* (1911) and writer of several plays for Dublin's Abbey Theater including *The Fiddler's House* (1907) and *Thomas Muskerry* (1910). Colum moved to the United States in 1914 and was president of the Poetry Society of America. Other works are *Orpheus* (1929), *The Frenzied Prince* (1943), *Collected Poems* (1953), and *The Poet's Circuits* (1960).

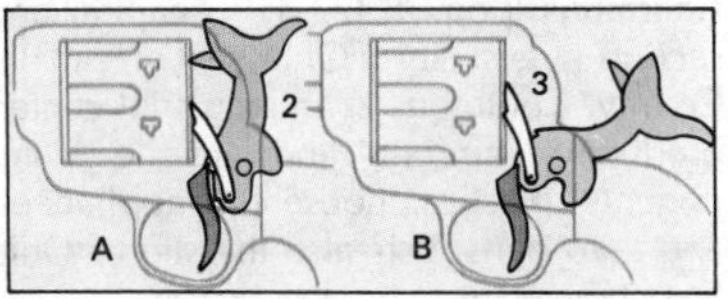

This pistol, the "Colt" of the North American cowboy, was first supplied to the U.S. Army in 1873 in 45 calibre. The single action shown, uncocked (A), needs to be manually cocked (B) before each shot. Almost identical revolvers are still being made a century later.
1. butt
2. hammer
3. trigger
4. chamber/cylinder
5. barrel
6. ejector

Columbia (pop. 95,802), city in central Missouri, seat of Boone County. Settled in 1821 as a stopping point on Boone's Lick Trail, Columbia has become an important medical center. In addition to the Ellis Fischel State Cancer Hospital and the Boone County Hospital, it is the home of the University of Missouri.
See also: Missouri.

Columbia (pop. 453,331), capital and largest city of South Carolina; seat of Richland County. Columbia was purchased in 1786 by the South Carolina legislature as the site for the state capital, established there four years later. An industrial and agricultural center, Columbia produces textiles, lumber, corn, and cotton. The University of South Carolina and five other colleges are located in the city.
See also: South Carolina.

Columbia River, large river arising in the Canadian Rockies in southeast British Columbia, and flowing south into the northwest United States, where it turns west and forms the border between Oregon and Washington and empties into the Pacific Ocean. It is 1,150 m (1,850 km) long, and its volume is the largest of any North American river except the Mississippi.
See also: British Columbia.

Columbia University, one of the major private U.S. universities. Founded as King's College in 1754, it was renamed Columbia College in 1784 and became a university in 1896. Its schools and facilities, mostly in New York City, include important research institutes for international relations and schools of journalism, business, medicine, law, and social work.

Columbine, plant (genus *Aquilegia*) related to the buttercup, with tall, slender stems, lobed leaves, and intricate flowers.

Columbite, dense oxide mineral composed of manganese, niobium, and iron, general chemical formula $(Fe,Mn)Nb_2O_6$. The element tantalum sometimes wholly or

partially replaces niobium. When the mineral contains more tantalum than niobium, it is called tantalite. Both are black, often iridescent, and are found in granite rocks called pegmatites.
See also: Niobium; Tantalum.

Columbium *See:* Niobium.

Columbus (pop. 1,377,419), capital and second-largest city of Ohio, seat of Franklin County. Columbus is an industrial center, producing aircraft and missile components, plastics, household appliances, and auto parts. It is also the site of Ohio State University.
See also: Ohio.

Columbus (pop. 243,072), second-largest city in Georgia, seat of Muscogee County. Situated on the Chattahoochee River in the western part of the state, Columbus is a cotton and textile center and an important industrial city.

Columbus, Christopher (Cristoforo Colombo; 1451-1506), commonly credited as the discoverer of America. Born in Genoa, Italy, he was the son of a wool weaver. An experienced sailor and student of navigation, Columbus was convinced that he could pioneer a new route to the treasures of the Far East by sailing West across the Atlantic. In 1484 he tried to win financial support for his plans from King John II of Portugal, but the king's advisers estimated the distance (surprisingly accurately) at 10,000 nautical miles, which would require a sailing time of 4 months, considered impossible. Columbus presented his plan to Queen Isabella and King Ferdinand of Spain, who, after years of negotiations, agreed to finance his voyage. Three small ships, the *Niña*, the *Pinta*, and the *Santa María*, were equipped with provisions for 1 year. With a crew of 120 men they set sail from Palos on Aug. 2, 1492. On Oct. 12, 1492, when the crew was on the verge of mutiny, Columbus landed on the east coast of one of the Bahama Islands, now called Watling Island. He spent the next 3 months sailing from one Caribbean island to another in search of the eastern Grand Khan, to whom he had a letter of introduction. He left 39 men in Hispaniola (now the Dominican Republic) to establish a colony. On March 15, 1493, he returned to Spain and was welcomed with honors. In Sept. 1493 Columbus left again for the Caribbean with a fleet of 17 ships, this time intending to set up trading posts and colonies, still believing he had discovered India. He discovered Puerto Rico. The men he had left in Hispaniola had been wiped out, so he established a colony further east, named it Isabela, left his brother Bartholomew in charge, and set off in search of the mainland of India. He discovered Jamaica and a number of the Lesser Antilles and explored the coast of Cuba, which he thought was an extension of the mainland. He wanted to take 500 natives back to Spain as slaves, but 200 died during the voyage. In 1498 he embarked on a third voyage. He sailed farther south this time, discovered Trinidad and reached the South American mainland at the mouth of the Orinoco River, mistaking it for a new continent south of India. When he reached Santo Domingo, he found that there had been bloody uprisings because the colonists had divided much of the best land (and the Native Americans on it) among themselves, and he was forced to make compromises in order to prevent a full-scale rebellion. The disorders continued, however, and Francisco de Bobadilla was sent by Spain to take over the government of the colony. He deposed the Columbus brothers, put them in chains, and shipped them back to Spain, where they were immediately released but remained in disgrace. In 1502, after promising King Ferdinand not to enslave the natives, Columbus set out on his fourth voyage. He sailed to Central America, discovered Honduras, and coasted along Nicaragua and Costa Rica to Panama. His ships were worm-eaten and in such poor condition that he had to stop at Jamaica, where he and his crew were stranded for more than a year. Finally, he chartered a ship to bring him back to Spain, where he arrived a few days before the death of Queen Isabella in 1504. King Ferdinand refused to grant him the reinstatement and financial rights he claimed. After 2 years of poverty and neglect, Columbus died on May 20, 1506.

The Columbus family coat of arms. Note the anchors in the lower right and the ocean islands in the lower left. By this time in his career, Columbus already possessed the title of Admiral of the Ocean Sea.

Column, in architecture, vertical structural support, usually cylindrical, consisting of a base, shaft, and capital. Columns support the entablature on which the roof rests. Apart from their utilitarian functions, columns are also decorative, the various types forming the classical orders of architecture.
See also: Architecture.

Coma, state of unconsciousness from which a person cannot be roused by sensory stimulation. Body functions continue but may be impaired, depending on the cause of the coma. Poisoning, head injury, diabetes, and brain dysfunctions (including strokes) are the most common causes.

Comanche, native North Americans of the Southwest, closely related to the Shoshone. Brilliant horsemen and fierce warriors, they were dominant among the southern Great Plains peoples, ranging into Mexico and stubbornly defending the buffalo hunting grounds against white incursions until the 1870s. Some 3,000 Comanche still live in western Oklahoma.

Combine harvester, farm machine that cuts, threshes, and cleans grain. The latest, self- propelled models cut a swath 20 ft wide. Practically all kinds of grain, including rice, can be harvested by the combine, as can soybeans and other legumes. Combines were first developed in Michigan as long ago as the 1830s, but they came into widespread use only in the 1920s.

Combustion, rapid oxidation (or burning) of fuel in which heat and usually light are produced. In slow combustion (for instance, a glowing charcoal fire) the solid fuel may react directly with atmospheric oxygen; more commonly the fuel is first volatilized, and combustion occurs in the gas phase.

Comedy, literary work that aims primarily to amuse, often through ridicule, exaggeration, or satire of human nature and institutions, usually ending happily. Comedy was considered one of the two main dramatic categories in ancient Greece, the other being tragedy.

Comenius, John Amos (Jan Amos Komensk; 1592-1670), Czech educational reformer and Protestant theologian, last bishop of the old Moravian church (from 1632). *The Great Didactic* (1628-32) was his best-known work. He advocated teaching in the vernacular instead of in Latin and favored a universal system open to women as well as men. His *Visible World* (1658) was probably the first children's picture book.

Comet, astronomical body consisting of a small mass, mostly gas and dust, spread over a large volume, orbiting the sun in a highly elliptical path that may take it as much as 150,000 times as far from the sun as the earth is. The head of a comet is bright, probably composed of ice and frozen gases. As it nears the sun, particles and gases are cast off into a tail that may be as long as 100 million mi (160 million km). The tail always points away from the sun. Some comets are visible from the earth at regular intervals. The most famous of these is Halley's comet, which reappears about every 76 years. Its most recent appearance was in 1986. In the past, comets were superstitiously considered omens of

doom. The appearance of Halley's comet in 1066 is recorded on the Bayeux tapestry. De Chéseaux's comet of 1744 showed six separate tails. In 1846 Biela's comet broke in two as it passed the sun. In 1910, shortly before the return of Halley's comet, another comet appeared that was so bright it was visible in daylight. The comet with the shortest periodicity is Encke, which orbits the sun every 3.3 years.
See also: Astronomy.

Comics, also known as comic strips, series of drawings, usually accompanied by captions or dialogue, telling a continuous story. The text, if any, is often conveyed by means of speech "balloons." The first comics were explicitly humorous, but the term is now applied to anything presented in the comic-strip style. Although comics may actually have originated with the English social satirists Thomas Rowlandson and George Cruikshank, they grew in popularity in the late 19th and early 20th century. At first devoted purely to farce and slapstick, the comics soon moved into the adventure market and then into science fiction, illustrated classics, social satire, and serious social criticism. Comics have added words to the American language and influenced dress habits. In 1954 the industry responded to criticism of the violence and horror by issuing a code for conduct.

Cominform (Communist Information Bureau), international organization set up in 1947 to coordinate among Communist parties in the Soviet Union, eastern Europe, and some capitalist countries. Essentially an agency of the Soviet government, it was disbanded by Nikita Khrushchev in 1956.
See also: Communism.

Comintern (Communist International), organization founded by the Russian Communist Party and composed of national Communist parties from all parts of the world. The Russian revolutionary leader V.I. Lenin called for the formation of a world revolutionary organization after the outbreak of World War I in 1914, but the first meeting of the Comintern was held only in 1919. Also known as the Third International (to distinguish it from the Second, or Socialist, International, a world organization of Social Democratic parties), the Comintern attempted during the 1920s to foster workers' revolution on a world scale. During the 1930s, however, it became essentially an organ of the Soviet government. Stalin dissolved it in 1943 as a gesture to his Western Allies during World War II.
See also: Communism.

Comitia, in ancient Rome, assemblies of people summoned in groups to vote on proposals presented by magistrates. Dating from c.500 B.C., comitia performed different functions during various periods of Roman history. The earliest such institution, the Comitia Curiata, confirmed the selection of Roman kings. Later comitia, such as the Comitia Centuriata (organized according to wealth) and Comitia Tributa (organized by tribe) voted on laws, established titles of authority, and judged criminals. By 100 A.D. the comitias' legislative and judicial powers had been abrogated.

Commager, Henry Steele (1902-), U.S. historian and educator, who taught American history at New York University, Columbia University, and Amherst College. His works include *Majority Rule and Minority Rights* (1943), *The American Mind* (1950), and *Freedom, Loyalty, Dissent* (1954). He was a major interpreter of U.S. history and an exponent of liberal democracy.

Commando, military unit trained for swift, guerrilla-like raids into enemy territory. The British army adopted the word and the practice after the Boer War (1899-1902), and battalion-strength units were organized during World War II. The U.S. army Special Forces and Ranger units are modeled after the British commandos.
See also: Guerilla warfare.

Commedia dell'arte, form of Italian comedy that flourished in the 16th-18th centuries. Traveling professional actors (often wearing masks) improvised action and dialogue around outline plots with stock characters. The commedia had a lasting influence on the theater throughout Europe.

Commerce, U.S. Department of, executive department of the U.S. government responsible for commercial policies and programs, formed in 1913, when the former Department of Commerce and Labor (established 1903) was divided in 2. It is headed by the secretary of commerce, a member of the cabinet appointed by the president and confirmed by the Senate. The secretary is the president's chief adviser on federal policies affecting commerce and industry. Principal divisions of the department are: Office of Business Economics, Bureau of Foreign Commerce, Bureau of the Census, Business and Defense Services Administration, Coast and Geodetic Survey, and National Bureau of Standards.

Commercial art, general term for any of the visual arts used in business, especially advertising, such as designing, drawing, and lettering for illustrations and advertisements, design and preparation of posters, billboards, display cards, packages, etc. The commercial arts are often distinguished from the fine arts in that their basic aim is to sell a product or service. But a more significant difference is that the products of commercial art have to be able to be reproduced by such techniques as zinc, steel, and halftone engraving; rotogravure; lithography; etching; electrotyping; and photography.

Commercial paper, generic term for various business documents involving the payment of money. Such documents include drafts, promissory notes, and bills of exchange. In a strict sense, the term denotes a short-term promissory note issued by a corporation. The note is redeemable for its full value, plus interest, on a given date.

Commission, military, written order and oath of service granting an individual the rank and authority of an officer in the armed services. A commission is accepted voluntarily and need not be renewed, though it may be resigned if allowed by law.

Committee for State Security *See:* KGB.

Committee of the whole, committee including the entire membership of an organization. It is convened to discuss matters whose disposition is not delegated to a smaller group.

Committees of correspondence, locally organized groups that formed a communication and information network in the 13 American colonies before and during the Revolutionary War. Initially appointed by legislatures to correspond with colonial agents in England, they later played a major role in unifying the colonial independence struggle. It was the Committees of Correspondence that summoned the First Continental Congress in September 1774.
See also: Revolutionary War in America.

Committees of safety, organizations set up at the urging of the Second Continental Congress to aid in the American transition to self-rule. They arose during the period between the overthrow of colonial governments and the establishment of new state governments.

Commodity Credit Corporation (CCC), government-owned corporation within the U.S. Department of Agriculture. Its purpose is to stabilize, support, and protect farm prices and income, to maintain balanced agricultural supplies, and to assist in the orderly distribution of farm commodities.
See also: Agriculture, U.S. department of

The Italian commedia dell'arte was the origin of the classic pantomime character known as Harlequin.

Commodity exchange, formal market in which participants buy and sell contracts providing for the delivery of certain products at future dates. The world's major commodity exchanges are in New York, Chicago, and London. Prices set in these markets largely determine prices in other parts of the world. Commodities (metals, crops, livestock, etc.) tend to fluctuate in value depending on availability. Since contracts calling for future delivery set the price in advance, commodity exchanges allow for speculation in a rising market and hedging in a falling market.

Common carrier, person or company that transports people, goods, or messages for the public at large. Examples of common carriers are bus lines, railroads, airlines, express companies, telephone and telegraph companies, and pipelines.

Common Cause, national citizens' lobby, organized in 1970 by John W. Gardner, former secretary of Health, Education, and Welfare. Its purpose was to reform campaign financing to end political corruption, to improve the internal workings of the federal and state governments, and to protect the environment. With some 280,000 members, it monitors the work of Congress, recommends legislative reforms to its members, files lawsuits, and engages in lobbying at the federal, state, and local levels.

Commoner, Barry (1917-), U.S. biologist, ecologist, and environmentalist who warned against the environmental threats of technology and nuclear energy in such books as *The Closing Circle* (1971), *The Poverty of Power* (1976), and *The Politics of Energy* (1979).
A democratic socialist, he has spoken out against the concentration of corporate power in the United States and in 1980 ran for the U.S. presidency as the candidate of the Citizens' party.
See also: Environmental pollution.

Common law, body of laws based on court decisions and customs. It is usually contrasted to statute law, which is made by legislatures. Common law grew out of English custom and became established mainly by the adherence of judges to precedents, or previous decisions—a principle known as *stare decisis* (stand on things as decided). The decisions of earlier judges became the law of later ones. As new conditions arose, the body of the common law was expanded, and outdated principles fell into disuse, even if never actually abolished. Thus experience, rather than theorizing, furnished the basis for the development of common law. The body and concept of common law passed from England to the United States (except the state of Louisiana, which made the Code Napoléon the basis of its law), Canada (except Quebec), and other areas of the world that have been ruled or influenced by England. No organized body of law existed in England prior to the Norman conquest in 1066, but the Normans brought many new principles and greatly expanded legal institutions. The term *common law* itself came into general use during the reign of Edward I (1272-1307), who was responsible for a great deal of new legislation. Since by its very nature common law is relatively inflexible and not subject to change or adaptation to suit the needs of a particular case, the system of equity developed to permit judges to resort to the general principles of justice when existing law was inadequate to resolve a case fairly. Eventually, equity was merged with the common law. During the Middle Ages, Italian jurists pioneered the rediscovery of the principles of Roman law. These doctrines were accepted by many European countries, in which they then displaced the customary or common law. But the English legal system withstood the attempts of advocates of Roman law to establish their doctrine. The fight to maintain the authority of the common law, led by great lawyers such as Edward Coke, became part of the constitutional struggle of the 17th century between Parliament and the kings. When the English colonies in North America framed their legal systems after declaring their independence of the mother country, they either kept the English common law as a guide to judges or formally adopted its principles in their statutes and constitutions. There is no federal common law, though precedents in federal cases are very important in later decisions.

Common Market, European, officially the European Economic Community (EEC), an economic union of West European nations. After World War II, West European nations sought new forms of cooperation in order to revive their damaged economies. The first step was the foundation of the European Coal and Steel Community (ECSC), set up in 1952 by the six future members of the EEC. The Treaty of Rome, creating the EEC, was signed in 1957 by West Germany, France, Italy, Belgium, the Netherlands, and Luxembourg. In 1973 "The Six" were joined by Great Britain, Ireland, and Denmark, and in 1981 by Greece. Spain and Portugal joined in January 1986. In 1967, the EEC was absorbed under the larger administration of the European Community (EC). Both the EEC and the EC are often referred to as the European Common Market. The main mechanism in the EEC is the customs union: the abolition of tariffs on trade among member nations and the creation of a common external tariff against non-member countries. The EEC has governed itself with an organizational structure carried over from the ECSC and continued in the EC, including a Council of Ministers, an Executive Commission, a European Assembly, and a Court of Justice.
See also: European Community.

Commons, House of *See:* House of Commons.

Commonwealth, from the phrase "common weal" (public good), form of government based on the power and consent of the people. In the United States, the states of Massachusetts, Pennsylvania, Virginia, and Kentucky were historically known as commonwealths, as is Puerto Rico. The federated states of Australia are known as the Commonwealth of Australia, and various other nations are associated with Britain in the Commonwealth of Nations. In English history, the Commonwealth is the period of republican government (1649-60) that followed the execution of Charles I.

Commonwealth Games, sports competition among amateur athletes from British Commonwealth countries, first held in Hamilton, Ontario, in 1930 under the name of British Empire Games. The games are held in a different Commonwealth city every four years. They include track and field events, badminton, swimming and diving, boxing, wrestling, and weightlifting.

Commonwealth of Nations, association of Britain and over 40 former colonies, now independent states, and their dependencies. Although not governed by a constitution or specific treaty, member states are linked by economic and cultural interests. The British monarch is recognized as the symbolic head of the commonwealth. Commonwealth prime ministers and other officials meet at periodic conferences and exchange views on international, economic, and political affairs of mutual interest. Member states range in size from Canada, Australia, and India to Tonga and Fiji. Ireland, South Africa, and Pakistan have withdrawn from the commonwealth.

Communal society, cooperative group formed on the basis of shared interests (e.g., religious or political) and emphasizing the needs of the community above those of the individual. Communal societies usually forbid private possession of land and often restrict members' contact with the rest of society. Examples of communal societies are collective farms (kibbutzim) in Israel and Hutterite groups in Montana, South Dakota, and Canada.

Commune, term for small, locally governed territorial districts in France and some other countries. The commune's government structure resembles that of a township in the United States and includes a mayor and a council. The term was originally used to designate towns in medieval western Europe that had gained self-government through rebellion, treaty, or charter.

Communication, flow of information from one point (the source) to another (the receiver). The term is also used to describe the act of transmitting or making known.

Communications satellite, artificial earth-orbiting object used to relay radio signals between points on earth. The orbits of most such satellites are above the equator at a height of 22,300 mi (35,900 km). At that altitude a satellite orbits the earth at the same rate as the earth turns; it thus remains over a fixed point on the surface. The satellite carries a number of transponders that receive radio beams from the earth and retransmit them. The satellite is powered by solar cells. Communications satellites carry television programs, telephone calls, and business data.

Communications Satellite Corporation (COMSAT), private corporation established by act of Congress in 1962, to develop satellite systems for relaying telephone, telegraph, and television transmissions. Comsat is the U.S. member and general manager of the International Telecommunications Satellite Consortium (Intelsat), formed in 1964 under the auspices of the United Nations. Comsat's first satellite, Early Bird, also known as Intelsat I, was launched in 1965.

Communion, in Christian churches, name for the sacrament of the Lord's Supper.

The modern communist state was created by V.I. Lenin during the Russian Revolution. This painting depicts Lenin stirring the masses to victory.

Communion, from the Latin word for "participation," is a ritual repetition of the Last Supper before Christ's crucifixion, when he told his disciples, "Take, eat. This is my body... This is my blood... This do in remembrance of me." In most Christian churches, the rite of communion involves the eating of a wafer of unleavened bread and the drinking of wine.
See also: Christianity.

Communism, ideal economic order in which property and the means of production are held in common in a classless society. Elements of communism are as old as the Golden Age described by Greek poets and philosophers as a time long ago when people shared all things equally and lived simply. Primitive forms of communism are also discernible in the communities of early Christians and in the teachings and practices of certain groups considered heretical in the Middle Ages. The *Utopia* of Thomas More (1478-1535) also exerted a powerful influence on Western culture and politics, adding to that body of writings which inspired attempts to create a more perfect society. But modern communism, as developed by Karl Marx and Friedrich Engels through their writings in the mid to late 19th century, is radically different from its predecessors.
As set forth in their seminal work, the *Communist Manifesto* (1848), the economic progress that accompanied the rise of modern capitalism divided society into 2 hostile camps, the bourgeoisie, who controlled capital and the means of production, and the proletariat or working class, who must sell their labor in order to live. This division was not seen as static but rather as dynamic. It was, in fact, a conflict central to understanding historical events, the development of cultures and civilizations, and the evolution of society. Marx and Engels repeatedly pointed out in their writings that their argument was based upon a study and analysis of actual political and economic developments, especially contemporary events, and was not filtered through or distorted by metaphysical abstraction. They argued that their analyses and conclusions rested on a scientific basis and, according to their analyses, the destruction of the bourgeois social and economic order and the rise and spread of a communist order throughout the world was historically inevitable. These ideas were more fully developed in the succeeding decades culminating in Marx's major work, *Das Kapital.*
Marx and Engels were careful to distinguish communism from socialism. As Engels explained in the preface to the English edition of the *Manifesto* (1888), they could not have called their work a *Socialist Manifesto* because the socialists were either followers of Utopian visionaries like Robert Owen or Charles Fourier, or mere "social quacks" trying to remedy specific working class grievances rather than undertake full-scale revolution.
Communist parties were founded to advance the practical and effective cause of the proletariat and achieve communism through political action based upon strict party discipline. V. I. Lenin's Bolshevik party originally split from its fellow communists by espousing the violent overthrow of established regimes. In 1917, it adopted the title of Communist Party, and, thanks to the success of the Russian Revolution, enjoyed nearly unchallenged authority over international communism until 1948, when Yugoslavia rejected Soviet influence. In the 1960s, China under Mao Tse Tung would create a deeper and much more serious rift among communists. In the more than 70 years since the Russian Revolution, communist regimes have proliferated, particularly in the Third World. Politically, they have been characterized by one-party rule, corrupt and inefficient bureaucracies, brutal and repressive secret police organizations, forced labor camps, strict censorship and thought control, the systematic murder of political opponents and entire groups of people considered dangerous to the state or the party and numbering in the millions. Economically, even the larger powers, the Soviet Union and the People's Republic of China, though they have succeeded in creating huge military establishments, have failed to provide for basic needs for their people, including food. Beginning in 1987, major communist regimes, led by the Soviet Union, openly admitted the failures of communism and have been looking to capitalist and pluralist systems in restructuring their governments, economies, and societies.

Communist Manifesto *See:* Communism; Marx, Karl.

Communist Party *See:* Communism.

Community, term used in the social sciences to designate a group of people within a larger society sharing similar customs, interests, characteristics or beliefs. Biologists define communities as ecological entities consisting of interdependent populations of flora (plants) and fauna (animals).

Community property, legal system of property ownership by husband and wife existing in several states in the United States. Under the system, any property acquired by either spouse after marriage, except by gift or inheritance, is considered as being owned by both. Generally, each spouse may dispose by will of only a part of his or her half of the community property and is powerless to affect the other's half. In case of divorce the property is divided.

Comoros

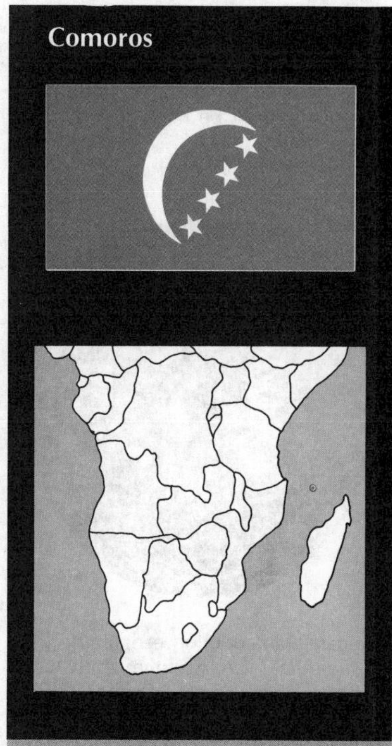

Capital:	Moroni
Area:	719 sq mi (1,862 sq km)
Population:	448,000
Government:	federal Islamic republic
Independent:	1975
GNP:	US $200,000,000
Per capita:	US $440

Comoros, island-state in the Indian Ocean off the east coast of Africa, between Mozambique and Madagascar. Its area is 719 sq mi (1,862 sq km). A former French colony, Comoros declared independence in 1975 and was declared a Federal and Islamic republic in 1978.

Compact disc (CD), small plastic disc used for storage of recorded sound or other data. The disc has a transparent coating that protects the stored information and allows it to be read by a laser beam. In the music recording industry the compact disc has virtually replaced the long-playing record.

Comparative psychology, branch of psychology concerned with the study of animal (including human) behavior at different stages of development to discern similarities and differences in species. A single activity (for example, mating) performed by different species may be investigated, or the behavioral pattern of 2 or more related species may be studied, either in their natural environment or in controlled surroundings. The principal behavioral patterns studied by comparative psychologists include communication, learning, migration, orientation, reproductive behavior, and social behavior.
See also: Psychology.

Compass, instrument used to indicate direction. Navigators on ships and aircraft use a compass to determine the direction in which they are heading. There are 2 main kinds of compasses: magnetic compasses and gyrocompasses. Magnetic compasses point to the magnetic north pole; adjustments must be made to determine the true north.
See also: Navigation.

A liquid compass from the 18th century. The principle behind this compass is that liquid always remains horizontal.

Compass plant, or pilotweed, prairie plant (*Silphium laciniatum*) of the family Compositae. Its name comes from the tendency of its lower leaves to line up in a north-south direction. The compass plant has a tall stalk, up to 12 ft (3.5 m), covered with short, rough hairs and large solitary flowers.

Competency-based education, teaching programs requiring students to attain specified levels of achievement in designated courses or skills. Some programs focus on the fundamental skills of reading, writing, and mathematics, while others include such disciplines as science and social studies.

Compositae, largest family of flowering plants, including more than 20,000 species. Their characteristic feature is that what appears to be a single flower is actually a flower head made up of a large number of florets. Those in the center, closely packed and resembling the pile of a rug, are simple tubular flowers having both stamens (the male part) and pistils (the female part). Surrounding them is a ring of ray flowers, often mistaken for petals, which have flattened corollas and are sterile or bear only pistils.

Compound, in chemistry, any substance composed of atoms of more than one element chemically bonded to form a fixed structure with distinctive properties. Compounds may be separated into two groups: organic (containing carbon atoms) and inorganic (all other compounds). Any compound may be described by a chemical formula that indicates the composition of one of its molecules, the molecule being the smallest unit of that compound to have the characteristics of that compound. The chemical formula for water, for example, is H_2O, which indicates that a molecule of water is made up of two atoms of hydrogen and one atom of oxygen.
See also: Chemistry.

Compound eye, organ of vision consisting of many tiny, closely packed lenses. The number of lenses varies from fewer than 100 to more than 20,000, depending on species. Compound eyes differ from the camera-type eye of only one lens. They apparently produce "mosaics" of light and color rather than clear images. Members of the phylum Arthropoda (spiders, insects, crustaceans, etc.) have compound eyes.
See also: Insect.

Comprehensive Employment and Training Act *See:* CETA.

Compromise of 1850, attempt by the U.S. Congress to resolve North-South conflicts over whether slavery would be extended to new territories, in particular Texas and other lands taken from Mexico in the 1846-48 wars. The compromise included a package of measures sponsored by Stephen Douglas and Henry Clay. They failed to resolve the dispute.
See also: Clay, Henry; Slavery.

Compton, Arthur Holly (1892-1962), U.S. physicist, Nobel Prize winner for physics (1927), for his discovery of the *Compton effect* (x-rays increase in wavelengths when they collide with electrons). At the University of Chicago Compton also contributed to the development of the atomic bomb during World War II.
See also: Physics.

Compton-Burnett, Ivy (1892-1969), English novelist. Her many novels, including *Pastors and Masters* (1925), *Parents and Children* (1941), and *Mother and Son* (1955), often feature crime and violence in English upper middle-class society at the turn of the century.

Computer, automatic device capable of carrying out calculations according to a predetermined set of instructions. First developed in the 1940s, their technological development has been rapid. Computers have taken over routine commercial calculations and are used in scientific research and technology design. Computers are usually classified according to their mode of operation: analog, digital, or a combination of the 2.
Analog computers use some measurable quantity to represent physically the calculation being carried out. They can perform simulations, such as the outcome of a missile launch or the effects of wind and rain on the flight of an aircraft.
Digital computers (such as the personal computer) contain 4 basic units: an input/output device, an arithmetical unit to perform basic math operations, a memory, and a control unit to interpret instructions and supervise operations. The applications of digital computers include forecasting, management, and preparation. Computers in the 1990s are becoming faster, smaller, and more powerful. Engineers are working to make computers more sophisticated, user-friendly, and accessible to all aspects of life.

Computer graphics, use of a computer for drawing lines, graphs, designs, and pictures. With the proper programs, computers are capable of displaying shapes as they would look from any angle. This has revolutionized the process of drafting and has also given rise to new art forms.
See also: Computer.

Computerized axial tomography *See:* CAT scan.

COMSAT *See:* Communications Satellite Corporation.

Comstock Law, U.S. legislation, passed in 1873 and named for anti-vice crusader Anthony Comstock. The law prohibited the mailing of obscene materials, defined at one time to include information on birth control and abortion. Comstock personally was responsible for the destruction of tons of literature and pictures that he considered objectionable.
See also: Obscenity and pornography.

Comstock Lode, enormously rich vein of gold and silver discovered near what became Virginia City in Nevada during the late 1850s. The lode, which eventually earned over $500 million, was named after one of its many claimants, Henry Comstock. The Virginia City mines brought settlers to Nevada, establishing a boom town and overnight fortunes. The lode was abandoned by the turn of the century.

Comte, Auguste (1798-1857), French philosopher and sociologist. His best-

known work is *The Course of Positive Philosophy* (1830-42), which introduced the philosophy that later came to be called positivism. Comte believed that human society had 3 phases of development, which he called theological, metaphysical, and positive. Society is ruled by rational science only when it reaches the last stage. Comte invented the term "sociology" and influenced such thinkers as John Stuart Mill and Herbert Spencer.
See also: Positivism.

Conakry (pop. 800,000), capital and largest city of Guinea in West Africa. Located on Tombo Island on the Atlantic coast, Conakry is a modern port and a commercial center.
See also: Guinea.

Conant, James Bryant (1893-1978), U.S. educator. As president of Harvard University (1933-53), he introduced national scholarships to attract students from all over the United States. Conant was chairman of the National Defense Research Committee (1941-46), American high commissioner for Germany (1953), and ambassador to West Germany (1955-57).

Concentration camp, prison for the detention of political or military suspects, frequently found in totalitarian countries and sometimes in democratic nations during time of war. Concentration camps differ sharply from other prisons in the absence of regular judicial proceedings and the fact that prisoners may be held indefinitely. Camps have often served to confine large segments of the population felt to be dangerous to the government. During World War II the United States placed several thousands of its Japanese-American citizens in camps until the end of the war. The most notorious concentration camps were those maintained by the Nazi regime in Germany before and during World War II. Jews and a minority of nationals from occupied countries performed hard manual labor in a semistarved state. Those unwanted or unfit to work were sent to extermination centers to be gassed and afterward burned in incinerators. Sadism and torture were practiced in these camps. More than 6 million men, women, and children died in the German concentration camps, of which the largest were at Auschwitz, Dachau, Buchenwald, and Belsen.
See also: Auschwitz; Belsen; Buchenwald; Dachau; Holocaust.

Concentration camps were established under Nazi rule during World War II to imprison millions of Jewish, Polish, and Russian people.

Concerto, musical composition in which unequal musical forces play in opposition to each other, usually 1 solo instrument against a large orchestra. The 3-movement orchestral form was elaborated by J.S. Bach out of the *concerto da camera*, a type of chamber music. George Frideric Handel added the *cadenza* (improvised or written out musical interlude for the soloist) as a regular feature. Wolfgang Amadeus Mozart set the style for the modern concerto: The orchestra announces an opening subject with a *tutti* (a passage for full orchestra), then takes a subordinate position when the solo instrument enters, thus establishing the pattern of interchanges.

Conch, name once applied to all mollusks—hence the term "conchology"—but now restricted to certain marine gastropod mollusks with large spiral shells. The shells have been used by primitive people throughout the world as trumpets. Conches are also prized as ornaments and for their meat. They live in warm waters.

Concord (pop. 17,076), town in eastern Massachusetts situated on the Concord River 20 mi (32 km) northwest of Boston. Founded in 1635, Concord was the home of the minutemen and site of the Battle of Concord during the Revolutionary War. Ralph Waldo Emerson, Louisa May Alcott, and Nathaniel Hawthorne all lived there, and Henry Thoreau's Walden Pond is nearby.
See also: Massachusetts.

Concord (pop. 36,006), capital of and third largest city in New Hampshire; seat of Merrimack County. Dating back to 1659, when it was a plantation, and incorporated under its present name in 1765, the historic city is situated on the Merrimack River 75 mi (121 km) northwest of Boston. The city is the financial and political hub of New Hampshire.
See also: New Hampshire.

Concord, Battle of, second engagement in the American Revolutionary War after the Battle of Lexington. Both were fought on April 19, 1775. The British, 700 strong, marched on Concord, Mass., to destroy military stores. The Americans retreated but returned on seeing smoke from burning supplies. Under Major John Buttrick, they met the British at North Bridge and routed them.
See also: Revolutionary War in America.

Concordat, treaty concluded between the pope and the secular government of a state to regulate religious affairs within the state and deal with such questions as the appointment of bishops and the status of church property. The most notable concordat was the Concordat of 1801 between Napoleon and Pope Pius VII which reestablished the Roman Catholic Church in France. The best-known recent concordat (1929) is the Lateran Treaty, arranged between Pius XI and Victor Emmanuel III of Italy which established Vatican City as a sovereign state.

Concrete, versatile structural building material made by mixing broken stone or gravel with sand, cement, and water. Initially moldable, the cement hardens into a solid mass. Concrete is often reinforced by enbedding steel bars in it to bear the tension. It is used for all building elements and for bridges, dams, canals, and highways, often as precast units.
See also: Cement.

Concussion, temporary malfunction of brain activity, often including unconsciousness, due to a blow to the head causing the brain to jolt against the inner skull, injuring the brain's outer surface. Treatment usually consists of rest and close observation.

Condé, Louis II de Bourbon, Prince de (1621-86), also called the Great Condé, an outstanding French general of the Thirty Years' War, related to the Bourbon royal family. He turned against Mazarin, led troops in the Fronde rebellion, and served with Spain; but was pardoned and fought for Louis XIV in the Dutch Wars.

Condensation, in physics, change of a substance from the gaseous (vapor) to the liquid state. Condensation occurs when warm air meets cold surfaces or mixes with cold air. Dew, fog, and clouds are the result of condensation of water vapor in the atmosphere.
See also: Physics.

Condensed-matter physics *See:* Solid-state physics.

Condominium, in real estate, individual ownership in property, such as an apartment, that is part of a larger complex owned in common. In the 1960s and 1970s, a sharp increase in condominiums occurred in the United States. A cooperative building differs from a condominium in that tenants do not actually own their apartments; they hold shares in a corporation entitling them to a long-term "proprietary" lease.
See also: Real estate.

Condor, one of two species of vultures and the largest flying birds in existence. They have broad wings with a span of 10 ft (3 m)

Condor

and weigh up to 25 lb (11 kg). The Andean condor (*Vultur gryphus*), the larger of the two, is still fairly common in the Andes, but the numbers of the California condor (*Gymnogyps californianus*) have been greatly reduced.

Condorcet, Marie Jean Antoine Nicolas de Caritat, marquis de (1743-94), French mathematician and philosopher. A brilliant thinker, he wrote biographies of Voltaire and Turgot, important essays on integral calculus and the theory of probability, and works in political science. He is best known for his *Sketch for a Historical Picture of the Progress of the Human Mind* (1795), which sets forth his belief in the perfectibility of mankind.

Cone, three-dimensional geometric figure whose base is a closed curve, such as a circle or an ellipse, and whose dimensional sides meet at a single point called the vertex.
See also: Geometry.

Conestoga wagon, large covered wagon used by North American pioneers. Originating about 1725 in Pennsylvania, it became the chief means of transporting settlers and freight across the Alleghenies until about 1850. It had big, broad-rimmed wheels and a canvas roof supported by wooden hoops, and was pulled by 4-6 horses.
See also: Pioneer life in America.

Confederate States of America, government formed by the Southern states that seceded from the United States of America between Dec. 1860 and May 1861. South Carolina was the first, followed by Mississippi, Florida, Alabama, Georgia, and Louisiana by the end of Jan. Texas joined them in Feb. and was followed in the spring by Virginia, Arkansas, North Carolina, and Tennessee. Rebels from Missouri and Kentucky (both of which remained in the Union) set up their own governments in exile under the Southern banner and brought the number of Confederate states equal to the original 13. The original 6 seceding states (later joined by Texas) called a constitutional convention for Feb. 4, 1861, at Montgomery, Ala., choosing Jefferson Davis and Alexander Stephens president and vice-president respectively. By Mar. 11 the convention had produced a permanent constitution modeled on that of the United States, but with several exceptions. Congress was forbidden to enact protective tariffs, to limit the spread of slavery, or to appropriate funds for "internal improvements" (except for navigation). Davis was inaugurated under the provisional constitution on Feb. 18, 1861. On Apr. 13, the expected war began with the bombardment of Fort Sumter. In Nov. Davis was elected president. His second inauguration took place at the new capital in Richmond, Va., on Feb. 22, 1862. He was the leader of approximately 9 million people—of whom about 3.5 million were slaves—at war with the nearly 23 million citizens of the Union. The strong states' rights orientation of the South conflicted with traditional wartime executive prerogatives, and the Confederate Congress and president were at odds from the start. However, in common with the president, the main business of the Confederate Congress was the conduct of the war, and most of its legislation was designed to keep a wartime society functioning. The constitution had provisions for a Supreme Court, but these were never carried out. Throughout the war the Confederacy tried to gain diplomatic recognition, aid, and alliances in Europe, but it was difficult to gain recognition for a state based on slavery. The economic factors that had driven the North and South apart were also perhaps the most significant in determining the war's outcome. The South was primarily an agricultural economy; the North, an industrial one. The South lacked the heavy industry to equip an army and the transportation network to supply it. Further, one of its major markets had become the enemy, and its other main buyer and source of money and equipment, Great Britain, was often cut off by the remarkably effective blockade by the Union Navy. Munitions, guns, and domestic supplies grew desperately short as the war drew on. Many soldiers had to supply their own rifles. A relief program for soldiers' families was difficult to administer, and it was increasingly difficult to find the food to distribute. Medicine was particularly scarce. Currency inflation also became disastrous. The South's emphasis on states' rights and its long congressional battles with Northern states over appropriations had made the central government reluctant to levy taxes for what many at first believed would be a very short conflict. The government therefore began printing ruinous amounts of currency and "war bonds." Although realistic taxes were levied by 1863, inflation had gone too far, and the actual resources of the South were too badly depleted for the government ever to regain a reasonable financial position. Despite initial Confederate battlefield victories, the Union's superior numbers and resources eventually overwhelmed the South. That the war lasted as long as it did—some 4 years—is testimony to the South's strong military leadership. After the fall of Richmond, General Robert E. Lee, commander of the Confederate forces, surrendered on Apr. 9, 1865, at Appomattox Court House.
See also: Civil War.

Confederation of Canada, union of British colonies established by the British Parliament in the British North America Act of 1867. This act provided for the formation of the Dominion of Canada and served as its constitution. It defined a self-governing community within the British Empire, not an independent country, with 2 levels of government, provincial and national. The dominion, which initially consisted of New Brunswick, Nova Scotia, Ontario, and Quebec, eventually developed into the Canada of today.

Confession, in Christianity, admission of sin, an aspect of repentance. General confession may be made in a congregation; private confession may be made to God or to a priest. The latter form, a sacrament of the Roman Catholic and Eastern churches, is also observed in some Lutheran and Episcopalian churches.

Confirmation, rite of certain Christian churches, usually administered in adolescence. The candidates confirm the promises made at their baptism, and the bishop lays his hands on them, invoking the Holy Spirit upon them. In the Roman Catholic and Eastern churches confirmation is a sacrament.
See also: Christianity.

Conflict of interest, situation in which an employee, part owner, officer or director of an organization has a financial or other interest in another organization that could cause him or her to favor one at the expense of the other.

Confucianism, philosophy based on the thinking of Confucius, the great Chinese philosopher and moralist. Confucianism teaches a moral and social philosophy and code of behavior based on certain abstract qualities and strengths, such as love, peace, harmony, order, humanity, wisdom, courage, and fidelity, without appealing to any ultimate higher authority or God. Heaven is the highest state one can attain, although no actual God-personality exists. One arrives at this perfect state by cultivating virtues such as curiosity, knowledge, patience, and sincerity, and by developing a personality based on the harmony of emotions and the harmony between the self and the universe. Thus people take their place in the universal pattern of creation, and immortality is won by those whose good name lives after them. Confucianism also has a strong social and political message. It teaches that individuals must not only cultivate themselves but must also enrich other people's lives.
See also: Confucius.

Confucius (551-479 B.C.), Chinese philosopher and sage, founder of Confucianism, the great moral and religious system of China. He began teaching at age 20, gathering about him a group of disciples. During the next 30 years he evolved the code of "right living" that was the basis of his philosophy. The ruling prince of the state of Lu appointed him magistrate of the city of Chang-tu, where Confucius put his principles into effect with great success. But he fell out of favor with the succeeding prince and for 13 years wandered with his followers, vainly seeking a patron and someone he could train as his "model ruler." Confucius's sayings and the most reliable information about his life are preserved in the *Confucian Analects*, compiled by his disciples shortly after his death. Although Confucius takes his place beside Gautama Buddha, Jesus, and Mohammed as founder of one of the world's great religions, he differs from them in being a rationalist who takes no account of mysticism or spirituality. His philosophy of human relationships, based on the golden rule "What you do not wish done to yourself, do not do to others," is essentially an appeal to reason and humanity.

Congenital defect *See:* Birth defect.

Conglomerate, corporation that has expanded into the production and sale of products quite different from those with which it was initially involved. Thus, a company identified with the extraction of metals may become conglomerate by moving into retail food, automobile accessories, and motion pictures.

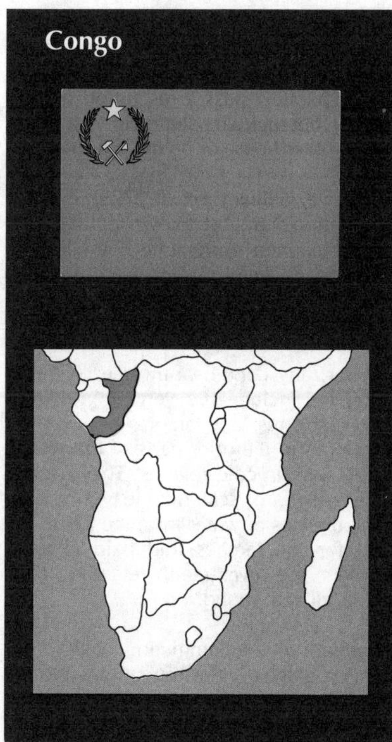

Capital:	Brazzaville
Area:	132,047 sq mi (342,000 sq km)
Population:	2,428,000
Government:	republic
Independent:	1960
GNP:	US $2,502,000,000
Per capita:	US $1,030

Congo (Brazzaville), Republic of the Congo, formerly part of French Equatorial Africa. It lies on the equator, with Gabon and the Atlantic Ocean to the west and Congo (Zaire) to the east.

Land. A low, treeless plain extends from the coast inland for about 40 mi (64 km). The land then rises to the mountainous area of the Mayombé Escarpment, with its series of sharp ridges, a region of dense tropical rain forest. To the north is a plateau covered with grassland. The Congo River basin in the northeast is an area of numerous rivers and dense, tropical forests. The Congo and its tributary, the Ubangi River, form most of the border with Congo (Zaire).

People. Some 60% of the population is rural, but there has been a major drift to the towns. Most people are Bantu speakers. French is the official language. The government has placed an emphasis on education, but the rate of illiteracy is still high.

Economy. Although the Congo has rich oil resources, a varied manufacturing sector, and ports providing it and its neighbors with vital outlets to the world market, it has had serious economic setbacks, mainly due to political instability and poor economic planning and management. The agricultural sector is underdeveloped.

History. The Congo was originally part of the Kingdom of the Kongo, a region first explored by the Portuguese in the 15th century and later broken up into smaller states and exploited by European slave traders. It became a French colony in 1891, an overseas territory of France in 1946, and an independent republic in 1960. Periodic civil strife from 1963 onward led to an army takeover in 1968. Following a presidential assassination in 1977 and subsequent martial law, the Congolese Labor Party, the sole legal party since 1970, confirmed a military head of state, Col. Denis Sassou-Nguesso, in 1979. Democratization in the early 1990s was accompanied by trouble and violence which eased off after a while.

Congo (Kinshasa) *See:* Zaire.

Congo River, or Zaire River, second-longest river in Africa. It flows north and west 2,700 mi (4,345 km) from its source in the Chambezi River, Zambia, to the Atlantic Ocean in western Zaire. In volume of water, it is second only to the Amazon. The Congo River was renamed the Zaire by Zaire's President Mobutu in 1971.

Congregational Church, Protestant church that holds that each local congregation should have complete autonomy, though congregations may form loose associations. In the 16th century Robert Browne first stated Congregational doctrine. In the 17th century Congregationalists established churches in the New England colonies and founded Harvard and Yale universities. Most U.S. Congregationalists merged (1931) with the Christian Church and then with the Evangelical and Reformed Church (1957) to form the United Church of Christ.
See also: Protestantism.

Congressional Budget Office (CBO), agency of the U.S. Congress that provides information on the nation's economy, the federal budget, and federal programs to members of Congress. It prepares optional plans and studies their potential impact on the budget. It also prepares 5-year forecasts based upon existing federal policies of taxation and spending.

Congressional Record, printed daily account of the proceedings in the U.S. Congress. Initiated in 1873, the Congressional Record replaced other records of congressional activity dating from 1789. Because members of Congress may change their speeches before they appear in the Record, and because material other than speeches before Congress is printed there, the Congressional Record is not accurate as a transcript.

Congress of Industrial Organizations (CIO), association of industrial unions. Active from 1938 to 1955, it organized all workers in a plant into an industrial union (as opposed to a craft union, which focuses on one craft). The CIO organized both skilled and unskilled workers in steel, automotive, rubber, and other major industries. The CIO united with the American Federation of Labor (AFL) in 1955.
See also: American Federation of Labor and Congress of Industrial Organizations.

Congress of Racial Equality (CORE), U.S. interracial organization founded in 1942 by James Farmer to promote African American civil rights and liberties through nonviolent direct action projects. Its voter registration drives and "freedom rides" in the South led to civil rights legislation in the 1960s. In the 1970s CORE became more militant. By the 1980s it had virtually ceased to exist.

Congress of the Confederation, political body that operated the government of the United States from Mar. 1781 to Mar. 1789. It was established by the Articles of Confederation and replaced the Continental Congress. Upon adoption of the present constitution, the Congress of the U.S. replaced the Congress of the Confederation.
See also: Articles of Confederation.

Congress of the United States, legislative branch of the U.S. federal government. Congress consists of 2 houses: the Senate, composed of 2 members from each state, and the House of Representatives, in which seats are appointed to the states on the basis of population. House membership, which was 65 in 1789, has grown with the nation's population but is now permanently fixed at 435. Membership is in proportion to state population as determined every 10 years by the census, but every state has at least 1 representative. Each member of the House now represents about 470,000 people. The state legislatures have responsibility for drawing the boundaries of congressional districts, but in 1964 the Supreme Court intervened to order that congressional districts within each state be "substantially equal" in population. The whole House is elected every 2 years. The Constitution grants the House special powers in 3 areas: impeaching federal officials (who are then tried by the Senate), originating all revenue bills, and electing the president if no candidate receives a majority in the Electoral College. The House is not a continuing body; it must organize itself anew when it meets for the first time in January following the election. The clerk of the House conducts the election of the speaker, who then takes office, swears in the other House members, and conducts the election of the other officers. The House adopts the rules of the new session, makes committee assignments, and begins work on a new round of legislation. The speaker is one of the most powerful figures in government, exercising an important influence over the course of legislation.

The U.S. Senate is composed of 100 members, 2 from each state. Since the Senate was created to represent the interests of the states, senators were elected by the state legislatures, rather than by popular vote, until 1913. The Senate is a continuing body; its members serve 6-year terms and only one- third of them are elected every 2 years. If a senator dies in office, the governor of the state names a replacement to serve until the next election. The Senate's advice and consent is necessary for appointments of all important government officials, including ambassadors and federal judges. The Senate also approves treaties, and the Foreign Relations Committee has become one of the most active in Congress, playing an important part in the conduct of foreign affairs. Since senators also represent much larger constituencies than do representatives, national and international issues generally play a larger role in Senate elections than in House contests. The Constitution provides that the vice-president shall preside over the Senate (he often delegates this duty to a senator), but the majority leader is usually the most powerful individual in the Senate. The Senate, being a smaller body than the House, allows much freer and more extensive debate, and many senators can attain considerable national stature.

For a bill (a proposed piece of legislation) to become law, the House and Senate must separately approve an identical text, which the president then must sign. If the latter vetoes (disapproves) a bill, Congress may repass it by two-thirds majority in each house. If the Senate and House versions of a bill differ, a committee is created to resolve the differences through compromise, and both houses vote on the new bill. Occasionally the House and Senate cannot agree, and the bill dies. Debate in the House is severely restricted because of the size of the body, but in the Senate, members may talk indefinitely and thus kill a bill unless cloture (closure of debate) is invoked by a two-thirds vote. Either house may separately pass a resolution on any subject, but such a resolution is not binding on the other house or on the president.

Congreve, William (1670-1729), English Restoration dramatist, known for his comedies of manners. Among his comedies are *The Old Bachelor* (1693), *Love for Love* (1695), and his masterpiece, *The Way of the World* (1700).

Conifer, any cone-bearing tree or shrub. Examples include the yews, pines, redwood, cypress, and araucarias. Conifers are found in the drier parts of the world, particularly in cold regions. They usually have needle- or scale-like leaves that reduce the loss of water from the plant. Except for the larches and bald cypress, conifers are evergreen, retaining their leaves all year round.

Conjunctivitis, inflammation of the conjunctiva of the eye (the mucous membrane that lines the inner surface of the eyelids); also called pink-eye. Viruses and allergies are the most common causes of this condition. Mixed or unidentifiable disease-causing microorganisms may be present, and irritation of the conjunctiva by wind, dust, smoke, and other types of air pollution is often responsible. Conjunctivitis may also accompany the common cold, infections involving skin rashes (especially measles), and irritation of the eye's cornea resulting from intense electric light, sunlamps, and reflections from snow.

Connally, John Bowden (1917-), U.S. secretary of the Navy (1961-63), governor of Texas (1963-69), U.S. secretary of the treasury (1971-72). Connally was seriously wounded while riding in John F. Kennedy's car when the president was assassinated in 1963. A Democrat throughout much of his career, Connally switched to the Republican party in 1973.

Connaught and Strathearn, Duke of (Arthur William Patrick Albert; 1850-1942), governor general of Canada (1911-16), son of Queen Victoria and Prince Albert of Great Britain. In 1874 he was made Duke of Connaught and Strathearn. He served as commander in chief of the British forces of the Mediterranean, 1907-09. As governor general of Canada he helped to inspire patriotism during the early years of World War I, and he reestablished the Canadian Patriotic Fund to help dependents of people serving in the Canadian armed forces.
See also: Canada.

Connecticut

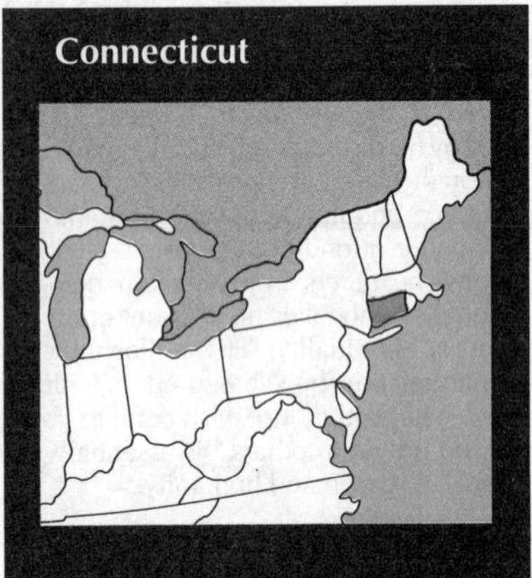

Capital:	Hartford
Statehood:	Jan. 9, 1788 (5th state)
Familiar names:	Constitution State, Nutmeg State
Area:	5,018 sq mi (12,997 sq km; ranks 48th)
Population:	3,295,669 (1990; ranks 27th)
Elevation:	Highest—2,380 ft (725 m), Mt. Frissell. Lowest—sea level
Motto:	Qui transtulit sustinet (He who transplanted still sustains)
State flower:	Mountain laurel
State bird:	American robin
State tree:	White oak
State song:	"Yankee Doodle"

Mystic Seaport, Connecticut

Connecticut, state in the New England region of the United States; bordered by Massachusetts in the north, Rhode Island in the east, Long Island Sound in the south, and New York in the west.

Land and climate. The state is divided by the Connecticut River Valley into the western and eastern New England Uplands. The Taconic Mountains in the extreme northwest include Mt. Frissell. From these peaks the land slopes through rolling hills down to the coastal plain along Long Island Sound. The Connecticut River is the longest in New England. Connecticut's weather is moderate. Principal cities are Bridgeport, Hartford, New Haven, Waterbury, and Stamford.

Economy. Most of the state's prosperity comes from industry: Connecticut produces fabricated metal goods, electrical equipment, machinery, and, most importantly, transportation equipment. Groton is a national center for submarine production. Hartford is an important insurance center in the United States. Yale, founded in 1701, was the nation's third university.

Government. Under the constitution of 1965, the governor is elected for a 4-year term. The general assembly, elected every 2 years, consists of a senate of 36 members and a house of representatives of 177 members. Connecticut has no system of county government; the towns and cities are the units of local government in the state. Connecticut is represented by 2 senators and 6 representatives in the U.S. Congress.

History. In 1614 Adriaen Block, a Dutch explorer, discovered the Connecticut River. English colonists from Massachusetts established Connecticut's first permanent European settlement, Windsor, in 1633. In 1636 Hartford, Windsor, and Wethersfield formed an independent commonwealth, the Connecticut Colony. The colony adopted the Fundamental Orders, regarded by some as the first written constitution, in 1639. As one of the 13 original colonies, Connecticut took an active part in the American Revolution (1775-83). The state was a staunch supporter of the Union during the Civil War (1861-65), supplying 60,000 troops. Connecticut was an important industrial state by the late 19th century, thanks in part to the inventors who worked there, including Eli Whitney, who helped develop the system of mass production in the early 1800s. Except during the Great Depression of the 1930s, Connecticut has prospered throughout the 20th century, and it ranks among the top states in *per capita* income.

Connecticut River, longest river in New England. Rising in northern New Hampshire, the Connecticut flows south 407 mi (655 km) through Massachusetts and Connecticut before emptying into Long Island Sound. Discovered by Dutch explorers in 1614, the river is of great historical, agricultural, and industrial significance to the northeastern United States.

Connective tissue, basic tissue that constitutes the connective and supporting element of the body. Forms of connective tissue include fibrous bands, fat, blood, and bone. All forms of connective tissue consist of cells separated by a medium that has differentiated into matrix (amorphous elements) and fibers (formed elements). The matrix is a jellylike mass containing a variable number of fibers. Young cartilage is composed of a large number of cells surrounded by a firm matrix that contains a small number of fibers. Blood comprises a liquid matrix containing cells and fibers in a soluble form. The development of supporting tissue, such as cartilage and bone, results in cells being enclosed in a matrix that has a firm or hard composition.

Connelly, Marc(us Cook) (1890-1980), U.S. playwright, best known for his Pulitzer Prize-winning play *The Green Pastures* (1930). He collaborated with George S. Kaufman on several plays, including *Beggar on Horseback* (1924).

Connors, Jimmy (1952-), U.S. tennis player. He was the top-ranked player in the world through most of the 1970s. Known for his left-handed, two-fisted backhand, he won the U.S. Open (1974, 1976, 1978, 1982, 1983) and Wimbledon (1974, 1982).

Conquistadors, 16th-century military adventurers who founded Spain's empire in the Americas. Most famous among them were Hernán Cortes and Francisco Pizarro.

Conrad, Charles, Jr. (1930-), U.S. astronaut. In 1965 Conrad made an 8-day spaceflight in *Gemini 5* intended to prove that humans could endure weightlessness long enough to reach the moon and return. In 1970 Conrad was commander of the *Apollo 12* flight, which was the second moon landing.
See also: Astronaut.

Conrad, Joseph (1857-1924), English novelist of Polish birth. His years at sea, during which he acquired a remarkable command of the English language, provided backgrounds for many of his novels. His lasting concern was the individual in isolation, struggling against adversity, moral degradation, and the forces of nature. His early novels include *Almayer's Folly* (1895) and its powerful sequel *An Outcast of the Islands* (1896), both set in Borneo. *The Nigger of the "Narcissus"* (1897), *Lord Jim* (1900), and *Typhoon* (1903) are examples of his skill in creating atmosphere and character. The novella *Heart of Darkness* (1902) takes place on the Congo River, and the book Conrad considered his masterpiece, *Nostromo* (1904), is a story of revolution and corruption in South America.

Conrail, official nickname for Consolidated Rail Corp., a quasi-governmental U.S. organization created to take over 7 bankrupt railroads in the northeastern and northwestern regions, including the Penn Central, Erie & Lackawanna, Lehigh Valley, and Reading. Conrail began operations on April 1, 1976.

Conscientious objector, person opposed to war in any form or in the specific form it is then taking, who by reason of conscience and conviction refuses to bear arms in wartime. The United States requires either noncombat duty within the armed forces or alternative service in a socially useful category for those who, as conscientious objectors, refuse regular services. Many other countries recognize this status—including Great Britain, the Commonwealth Nations, the USSR, and many others in Europe and Latin America. Most require alternative noncombat service.
See also: Pacifism.

Conscription *See:* Draft, Military.

Conservation, management and protection of the earth's natural resources to assure adequate supplies for future generations. Conservation aims to provide an environment free from pollution of air, water, and land, and to protect the welfare of plants, animals, and humans.

Conservatism, term for social and political philosophies or attitudes that stress traditional values and continuity of social institutions and that reject sudden radical change,while maintaining ideals of progress. It was first used in the early 19th century to describe the policies of the British Tory party. Modern conservative political parties include the British Conservative and Unionist Party, the Canadian Progressive-Conservative Party, and, in the United States, the Republican Party.

Conservative Party, one of the two major political parties in Great Britain. The second major political party is the Labor Party. The Conservative Party succeeded the Tory Party that appeared in the late 1600s. Benjamin Disraeli, a founder of the Conservative Party, strongly supported imperialism and advocated rights for the working class. In recent history, the Conservative Party has been in control of the British government since 1979. As head of the Conservative Party 1979-90, Margaret Thatcher became the first woman prime minister in British history. She was succeeded by Conservative John Major.
See also: Disraeli, Benjamin.

Considérant, Victor Prosper (1808-93), French socialist. He promoted the doctrines of Charles Fourier, edited *La Phalange*, and published *Social Destiny* (1834-38) and *Principles of Socialism* (1847). He tried unsuccessfully to establish a communistic community in Texas (1855-57).

Conspiracy, in U.S. law, agreement between two or more people to commit an unlawful act. The act of conspiracy is in itself a crime; the unlawful act does not have to be committed. Conspiracy is punishable by fines or imprisonment.

Constable, John (1776-1837), English painter. He and J.M.W. Turner were England's 2 greatest landscapists. Believing

John Constable's landscapes greatly influenced 19th-century landscape painters. Shown is his painting of Brighton Beach, an English seaside resort. (Victoria and Albert Museum, London)

that painting should be pursued scientifically, he explored techniques of rendering landscape from direct observation of nature under different effects of light and weather.

Constance Missal, one of the earliest books printed in Europe. Believed to be printed by the inventor of movable type, Johannes Gutenberg c.1450, Constance Missal was a book of masses for the German diocese of Constance.

Constanta (pop. 327,700), Romanian Black Sea seaport city. An industrial center with a modern harbor, Constanta exports petroleum and grain and is Romania's primary Air and naval base Founded by the Greeks (7th century B.C.), Constanta became part of Romania in 1878.

Constantine (pop. 448,600), trading center in Algeria about 50 mi (80 km) from the Mediterranean Sea. A natural fortress, the city is on a plateau nearly surrounded by a steep gorge. Named for its patron, the Roman emperor Constantine the Great, it was built in A.D. 313 on the site of Cirta, a city destroyed by war.

Constantine, 2 kings of Greece. **Constantine I** (1868-1923) reigned 1913-17 and 1920-22. During World War I he opposed the Allies and was forced to abdicate the throne to his second son, Alexander. Brought back into power after Alexander's death, he abdicated again after the Greeks were defeated in a war with the Ottoman Empire. **Constantine II** (1940-) was king of Greece 1964-74. As a result of his unsuccessful attempt to overthrow the military junta ruling Greece at the time, Constantine II was forced into exile in Italy. In 1974 the Greek people voted to replace the monarchy with a republican form of government.
See also: Greece.

Constantine I, The Great (c.280-337), first Emperor of Rome to convert to Christianity. After his father, Constantius, died in 306, there was a struggle for the succession. In 312 on the eve of the decisive Battle of Milvian Bridge, near Rome, Constantine, who was already sympathetic to Christianity, is said to have seen a vision of a flaming cross in the sky. He won the battle and became emperor in the West, while his brother-in-law, Licinius, was emperor in the East. In 324 war broke out between them, and in 325 Licinius was killed. Constantine thus became the sole ruler of the Roman world. In 325 he convened the Council of Nicaea, which settled various disputes in church doctrine. He made Christianity the official religion of the empire and moved the capital to the city of Constantinople, named for him and dedicated to the Virgin Mary. Constantine reigned as an absolute ruler until his death.
See also: Christianity; Rome, Ancient.

Constantinople *See:* Istanbul.

Constellation, first U.S. Navy ship to capture a foreign warship. On Feb. 9, 1799, the *Constellation* captured the French frigate *L'Insurgente* during the 1798-1800 undeclared war between France and the United States.

Constellation, group of stars that appear to lie in the same area of the sky. Constellations figure prominently in the mythology and folklore of ancient civilizations. The Greeks, for instance, saw the shape of Orion the hunter, who, with a shield and club, is facing Taurus the bull. Many of the characters in adjoining constellations are related. Cepheus was the husband of Cassiopeia, whose daughter Andromeda was rescued from the sea monster Cetus by Perseus. Many of the star divisions and names were originated by the Greeks.

Constipation, decrease in the frequency of bowel actions from the norm for an individual; also increased hardness of stool. Often precipitated by inactivity or changed diet or environment, it is sometimes due to gastrointestinal tract disease.

Constitution, system of fundamental principles or rules for the government of a nation, society, labor union, or other group that establishes basic guidelines and a framework of orderly procedure. While most Western countries have written constitutions, it is important to distinguish between written and unwritten constitutions. The written constitution of the United States specifically catalogs the powers of the federal government and the rights of the citizens and states. Great Britain has an unwritten constitution in which common law and tradition play a greater part in the framework of the country's political and legal system than any single written document.
There are also "hard" and "soft" constitutions. A "hard" constitution is difficult to alter, thus rendering it unresponsive to short-term political change. With a "soft" constitution alteration can be achieved relatively easily, for example, by a simple vote of the legislature. The constitution of the United States is a fairly "hard" document, since constitutional amendments require lengthy and involved procedures.

Constitution of the United States, supreme law of the nation. Written in Philadelphia in the summer of 1787, the Constitution was approved by the 55 delegates representing the 13 original states and went into effect on March 4, 1789, after ratification by the required 9 states. The actions of the virtually autonomous states and the failure of the country's first constitution, the Articles of Confederation, convinced the delegates that a strong executive and a powerful federal government were needed if the United States were to survive as a cohesive entity. The conflicting desires of large and small states resulted in a bicameral legislature, one house based on population size, the other house with an equal number of seats for each state. Most important was the eventual recognition by all stats that a strong central government would be needed if the United States was to be more than just a loose confederation. The states allayed their fears by constructing a separation of powers to limit governmental power. In 1791 a Bill of Rights to guarantee personal freedoms was added as the first 10 amendments to the Constitution. Only 16 amendments have been added since 1791.

Constitutional law, U.S., section of the law that interprets and enforces the provisions of the U.S. Constitution. Although the Constitution, with its 7,000 words, launched the fledgling Union as a sovereign, democratic nation, it refrained from specifying too precisely the limits of governmental power or the roles of its institutions. A closer definition of these was left to history and experience. Constitutional law studies this historical development and pronounces on the contemporary status of its many concepts, concentrating on 3 topics: judicial review, the separation of powers, and the federal system. Judicial review deals with the powers of the U.S. courts—ultimately the Supreme Court—to pass judgment on the constitutionality of laws or specific acts of government. The U.S. Constitution did not provide for judicial review, but the Supreme Court has claimed, and exercised, the right to decide on constitutionality ever since Chief Justice John Marshall's famous decision in *Marbury* v. *Madison* (1803). His reasoning was simple: The Constitution is the supreme law of the land and it is the function of the courts to uphold the law; consequently, the courts are duty-bound to declare invalid any government law or action in conflict with the basic provisions of the Constitution. The Supreme Court exercises its power of review with restraint, and the burden of proof rests on the party challenging the law's constitutionality, not on the legislation. The Court assumes that the legislation does not enact measures intended to violate the Constitution.

The doctrine of separation of powers maintains that despotism is best prevented by dividing the powers of government among several branches that "check and balance" one another. The Constitution confers the legislative power upon Congress, the judicial authority upon the courts, and executive power upon the president. The federal system divides the powers of government between the national, or federal, government and the state administrators. The powers of the national government are enumerated in the Constitution, all other powers being reserved to the state governments. However, provisions like the clause that gives Congress the power to make all laws "necessary and proper" to carry out its Constitutional function and the right to regulate interstate commerce have greatly increased federal power.

See also: Constitution of the United Staes.

Constitutional Union Party, U.S. political party formed from remnants of the Whig and American parties, active 1859-60. Its platform upheld the Constitution and the Union, while ignoring the slavery issue. As a result, the vote in 1860 was split and Lincoln was elected by the electoral college, the first President without a popular majority.

Constitution, USS, American frigate carrying 44 guns, known as "Old Ironsides." Launched in Boston in 1797, it served in the war with Tripoli and the War of 1812. In 1828 a plan to dismantle the warship provoked Oliver Wendell Holmes's poem "Old Ironsides." The *Constitution* was rebuilt, berthed in Boston, and opened to the public in 1934.

Constructivism, artistic movement developed in Russia 1913-20 by Vladimir Tatlin, Naum (Pevsner) Gabo, and Antoine Pevsner. Partly influenced by cubism and futurism, it was related to technology and industrial materials. Gabo and Pevsner went into exile in 1921 when Soviet authorities moved against all modern art movements.

Consul, official appointed by one country to look after its commercial and cultural interests in another country. Not to be confused with ambassadors, whose primary purpose is to further political understandings with the country to which they are appointed, consuls attend primarily to business and cultural matters. The term *consul* was originally given to the highest magistrates of ancient Rome. At the beginning of the 19th century, the consular system developed universally. Consuls are ranked in importance as consul general, consul, vice or honorary consul.

Consumer Affairs, United States Office of, U.S. government agency that handles government activity related to consumer protection. Although this agency does not have the power to enforce laws or to resolve complaints, it conducts investigations acting on consumer complaints and disseminates product information. The U.S. Office of Consumer Affairs was created by President Richard Nixon (1971).

Consumer Federation of America (CFA), largest consumer protection agency in the United States. Made up of 220 organizations, the CFA influences public policy as represented by Congress, regulatory agencies, and the courts. Established in 1969 and located in Washington, D.C., the CFA also runs a foundation that conducts research and educates the public on consumer concerns.

Consumer Price Index (CPI), statistical measurement of goods and services bought by most people in the United States. Prepared by the U.S. government's Bureau of Labor Statistics, the CPI compares current costs of goods and services with past costs. Separate CPIs are published in order to represent a selection of metropolitan areas, groups of cities, and regions of the United States. The CPI is a measure of inflation and cost of living and is used as a yardstick for revising salaries, wages, social benefits, and other payments that need to keep pace with changing prices.

Consumer Product Safety Commission, independent U.S. government agency that sets national safety standards. The agency promotes the development of voluntary safety standards by manufacturers; establishes and enforces safety standards for product development, manufacture, and performance; investigates product-related injuries; and in some cases recalls or forbids the sale of unsafe products. Established in 1972, the Consumer Product Safety Commission consists of 5 members appointed by the president for a 7-year term.

Consumer protection, state, federal, and local laws that set standards for goods and services sold in the United States and the regulatory agencies that maintain these standards, as well as the efforts of consumers themselves to organize against misleading or unfair marketing practices. Scientific and technological advances have led to increasingly sophisticated goods, but modern sales methods, advertising, prepackaging, and self-service make it increasingly difficult for the consumer to know from personal experience the quality and value of the goods offered. The consumer may also need protection from artificial price-fixing by monopolies and from deliberate fraud. There are more than 1,000 separate federal consumer protection programs under the control of over 400 separate federal agencies and divisions. The federal government sets standards covering definition of weights and measures, packaging, the composition and purity of food and drugs, and descriptions of products in advertisements and brochures. The best-known federal arbiters, inspectors, and enforcers of these standards are the Food and Drug Administration of the Department of Health and Human Services and the Department of Agriculture. But the Departments of Transportation, Justice, Commerce, and House and Urban Development are also heavily involved in consumer protection, as are the Federal Power Commission, the Federal Trade Commission, the Federal Communications Commission, and the Interstate Commerce Commission.

The first important consumer group in the United States, the National Consumer's League (formed in 1899), awarded its own label to manufacturers whose goods passed its inspection, and this label became widely regarded as a guarantee of quality. Its work inspired numerous articles and books, one of which, *The Great American Fraud*, by Samuel Hopkins Adams, contributed largely to the passing of the 1906 Pure Food and Drug Act and the founding, in 1908, of the American Home Economics Association. Consumer protection became a leading feature of this era of "progressive" politics. More dramatically, Upton Sinclair's best-seller *The Jungle* (1906) exposed conditions in the Chicago meatpacking industry and led to the formation of Clean Food clubs. *Your Money's Worth* (1924) compared a wide range of products by brand name. One of its authors, E. J. Schlink, went on to found a Consumer's Club, incorporated in 1929 as Consumers Research, Inc., the first independent testing agency to publish its findings (*Consumer Reports*). Its efforts and the appearance of more books exposing manufacturers' frauds and malpractices led to the passage of the Food, Drug and Cosmetic Act in 1938. During World War II consumer protection was greatly extended by the activities of the Office of Price Administration.

The consumer movement gained new life and impetus in the 1960s, mainly through the efforts of Ralph Nader, who published *Unsafe at Any Speed* (1965), a muckraking look at the auto industry. Nader used the money from his writing to finance further investigations of a broad variety of products. With his volunteer helpers, "Nader's Raiders," he roused the indignation of consumers throughout the country. The word *consumerism* was first used in an uncomplimentary sense, but the movement's broad popularity soon provoked a more responsive attitude from both government and industry. On a federal level the Food and Drug Administration began to make more stringent tests of all the products it passed, as did other government regulatory agencies in all fields. Congress introduced a record number of new bills on the subject, including the Nader-inspired Auto Safety Act (1965) and the "truth in lending" bill (Consumer Credit Protection Act, 1969), and conducted investigations into truth in advertising and packaging.

Consumer protection laws, laws as they relate to consumer protection. Some landmarks of legislation in the field include The Pure Food and Drug Act (1906), prohibiting mislabeling of the contents of food, liquor, and medicine; the Agricultural Meat Inspection Act (1907), providing for federal inspection of meat-packing plants engaged in interstate shipment of meat; the Food, Drug, and Cosmetic Act (1938), strengthening food labeling requirements and extending controls over advertising and labeling; the Child Protection Act (1966), followed by the Toy Safety Act, assuring that toys are not poisonous, flammable, or potentially hazardous in other ways; the Consumer Credit Protection Act (1968), requiring lenders to disclose the true annual interest rate on loans and prohibiting businesses from sending credit cards to persons who do not order them; and the Consumer Product Safety Commission (1972), protecting consumers from dangerous, faulty, or misleading products, and requiring companies to inform and educate consumers about the safe use of products. All states and many cities and counties have agencies that deal with consumer complaints.

Consumers Union, independent, nonprofit organization that tests and rates products and services for the consumer. The monthly magazine, *Consumer Reports*, issued by the Consumers Union, both rates products and keeps readers up to date on consumer issues. To maintain its perspective of fairness, Consumers Union does not accept advertising in any of its publications.

Consumption, in economics, use of goods and services. Wearing clothes, eating food, and washing with soap are examples of consumption. Patterns of consumption are related to size of income. Higher income families tend to spend larger portions of their earnings on nonessentials such as education and entertainment, while lower income families spend the greater part of their income on essentials such as food and housing. Two-thirds of all goods and services in the United States are used by consumers, while the remaining one-third is used or invested by the government.

Contact lens, small lens worn directly on the cornea of the eye under the eyelid to correct defects of vision. Generally made of transparent plastic, contact lenses sometimes give better results than glasses and are less noticeable.

Containerization, method of shipping freight in large containers usually made of aluminum, steel, fiberglass, or plywood. Developed in the mid-1950s, containerization helps prevent damage to freight. It is widely used by the air, shipping, railroad, and trucking industries.

Contempt of court, action that detracts from the dignity or authority of a court or that tends to obstruct the administration of justice. Such actions may be punished by fine or imprisonment, or both, but can generally be appealed. Contempt can be classified as civil or criminal. Civil contempt is failure to obey a court order issued for the benefit of a third party; an example would be failure to produce books for creditors to look at. Criminal contempt is a direct offense to the dignity or authority of a court, such as the use of vulgar language, refusal to obey instructions, or bribery of a juror.

Continent, any of the largest land masses of the earth's surface. The number of continents is popularly reckoned to be 7: the 3 "Old World" continents (Europe, Africa, and Asia), those of the "New World" (North America and South America), and the island continents (Australia and Antarctica). The division between Europe and Asia is purely arbitrary; they are therefore sometimes regarded as one continent, Eurasia.

Continental Association, agreement adopted by the First Continental Congress of the American colonies. The purpose of the Continental Association was to defend American rights by greatly reducing imports, halting participation in the slave trade, stopping consumption of British and Irish goods and some foreign and West Indian goods, and stopping exports to Britain, Ireland, and the West Indies. The agreement was adopted on Oct. 20, 1774.

Continental Congress, legislative body that represented the 13 colonies shortly before and during the American Revolution. The First Continental Congress assembled at Carpenter's Hall, Philadelphia, on Sept. 5, 1774. Its purpose was to secure redress from England for its repressive political and commercial measures. Although endowed with no formal authority, 55 delegates were present, representing all the colonies except Georgia. Initially the congress showed little sentiment for independence; however, on Oct. 14, 1774, a Declaration of Rights was adopted enumerating the colonists' demands and their rights as British citizens. A bold "Plan of Association" was also drafted pledging the colonies to boycott any form of trade with England until these demands were met. The Congress adjourned on Oct. 26, 1774, with the understanding that it would reconvene on May 10, 1775, if its petitions were not honored. Britain failed to respond and the Second Continental Congress was summoned, shortly after the military clashes at Lexington and Concord. The Congress organized an army under the command of George Washington, then adopted the Declaration of Independence on July 4, 1776. The congress also approved the Articles of Confederation, creating a union of the states, on Nov. 15, 1777. However, the articles were not ratified by the newly formed states for another 4 years. In the meantime the Continental Congress assumed the nominal powers of a federal government: maintaining an army, issuing federal currency, and negotiating foreign aid and treaties.

Continental divide, imaginary line that divides a continent at the point where its rivers start flowing in opposite directions and empty into different oceans. In North America it follows the Rocky Mountains, in South America the Andes.

Continental drift, theory that the continents change position over time, moving very slowly. The theory was first suggested in 1912 by Alfred Wegener, a German meteorologist, who believed that the earth's land masses had once been joined in one supercontinent, Pangaea, which broke apart about 200 million years ago, forming the earth's continents. The theory was controversial for a long time, and it has since been revised by the modern concept of plate tectonics, which also incorporates continental drift.

See also: Geology.

Continental shelf, submarine rim around most of the earth's continents, extending on average about 50 mi (80 km) beyond the shoreline before dropping steeply to the ocean floor. They are relatively flat and shallow, between 300 ft (90 m) and 600 ft (180 m) below the ocean surface, although some are cut by deep submarine canyons. They are covered with layers of fine sediment. The shallower portions of the continental shelf were at one time dry land, since the sea level has risen about 300 ft (90 m) from the time of the Ice Ages.

Continental System, attempted economic blockade of England instituted in 1807 by Napoleon I. A counterblockade of the continent by England's superior seapower nullified it. The British blockade, because it interfered with American trade with the continent, was a major cause of the War of 1812.
See also: Napoleon I.

Contraband, trade forbidden by law. The term usually refers to goods that may not be shipped to an enemy during wartime, because those goods may serve a military purpose. In 1908-9, 10 naval powers met in London to create a code to classify contraband and define terms for its seizure. The Declaration of London classified goods in terms of absolute contraband (military equipment), conditional contraband (other goods when being shipped to an enemy), and free goods.

Contraception *See:* Birth control.

Contract, promise or agreement enforceable by law. Contracts are usually written, but they may be merely understood or oral. Some types of contracts, particularly for the sale of real estate or covering a long period of time, must be in writing. Even written contracts, however, often give rise to misunderstandings or disagreements that become the subject of lawsuits. A contract is a bargain between two or more persons, firms, or other organizations, in which there is an offer and an acceptance. Once the offer has been made and accepted, the law enforces the terms agreed to. A *breach of contract* occurs when either party to a contract fails to fulfill promises. The court will then award damages to the other party, usually in the form of a sum of money, sometimes equivalent to what the party has actually lost, or else according to terms specified in the contract.

Contract bridge *See:* Bridge.

Contrail, line of cloud that forms behind aircraft flying at high altitudes. Contrails form when water vapor from the exhaust or in the air condenses into droplets or freezes into ice crystals. Ice crystals from contrails may precipitate rain or snow.

Convent, monastic community of monks, friars, or nuns. Today the term usually applies to the residences of nuns, or, in the case of "convent schools," to girls' schools that are closely associated with convents.
See also: Nun; Religion.

Convertibility, in economics, financial arrangement under which currencies of different countries can be exchanged for each other. Under complete convertibility, all currencies can be exchanged for all others. Under partial convertibility, only certain currencies can be exchanged for certain others. The rate of exchange can be either fixed or floating (changing from day to day). After World War II, the lack of foreign exchange caused many European countries to restrict convertibility, but at the present time all major currencies are freely convertible with each other.

Convertiplane *See:* V/STOL.

Conveyor belt, device that mechanically conveys material. Principally used in factories and on large farms, the conveyor belt is looped over two pulleys, one of which is the drive pulley and is powered by an electric motor. The belt travels over a series of rollers. In factories, materials move along a conveyor belt to be worked on by workers standing along the line. In this way, the conveyor belt plays a major role in such mass-produced goods as automobiles. Other uses for conveyor belts include carrying material into mines and carrying cargo to and from ships, trucks, and railway cars.

Convoy, fleet of merchant or other unarmed vessels sailing under the protective escort of a warship. Since the 17th century, international law has attempted to issue a "right of convoy" mandate to protect neutral shipping from search and seizure on the high seas during time of war.

Convulsion, involuntary contraction of the muscles of the body. Such contractions may be tonic or clonic, according to whether they are continuous or spasmodic, and of either cerebral or spinal origin. Convulsions may be caused by lack of oxygen (e.g., convulsions during some bouts of fainting), toxic conditions (e.g., convulsions due to the poison strychnine), psychological factors (e.g., hysterical convulsions), or epilepsy. The term "convulsion" now usually refers to discontinuous muscular contractions, either brief contractions repeated at short intervals or longer ones interrupted by intervals of muscular relaxation.
See also: Epilepsy.

Cony *See:* Hyrax.

Iraqi contraband: supergun disguised as material for a petrochemical project.

Cook, Frederick Albert (1865-1940), U.S. explorer who claimed to have climbed Mt. McKinley in 1906 and to have discovered the North Pole in 1908, before Peary. Neither claim was widely believed.

Cook, James (1728-79), English navigator and explorer. He led 3 celebrated expeditions to the Pacific Ocean (1768-71, 1772-75, 1776-80), during which he charted the coast of New Zealand (1770), showed that if there were a great southern continent it could not be as large as was commonly supposed, and discovered the Sandwich Islands (1776). He died in an attack by native Hawaiians.
See also: New Zealand.

Cooke, Jay (1821-1905), U.S. financier who helped the federal government finance the Civil War. He formed the banking firm Jay Cooke & Co. in 1861, and sold over $1 billion in war bonds. His firm later underwrote the construction of the North-

The death of Captain James Cook in Hawaii, painted by John Cleveley

ern Pacific Railway but failed in the financial crisis in 1873. Cooke made a second fortune in silver mining (1878-79).
See also: Civil War, U.S.

Cooke, Terence James Cardinal (1921-1983), U.S. Roman Catholic clergyman. He was consecrated bishop in 1965, archbishop of New York in 1968, and cardinal in 1969. At age 48, Cook was the youngest American ever to become a cardinal.

Cooking, preparation of food for consumption, by heating. It is believed that cooking began with primitive peoples who ate meat burned in forest fires. Later the cooking fire was moved indoors, cooking utensils were invented, and the art of preparing foods arose.

Cook Islands, two groups of coral islands in the South Pacific Ocean, discovered by British captain James Cook in 1773. They were made a British protectorate in 1888, and are now self-governing but linked to New Zealand. The islanders are Polynesians, related to the Maoris of New Zealand. Their chief exports are citrus fruits, jewelry, copra, pearl shell, and tomatoes.

Cooley's anemia *See:* Thalassemia.

Calvin Coolidge

30th U.S. President	
Born:	Plymouth, Vermont; July 4, 1872
Terms:	Aug. 1923-Mar. 1929
Vice President:	Charles Gates Dawes
Political Party:	Republican
Spouse:	Grace Anna Goodhue Coolidge
Children:	2
Died:	Northampton, Mass.; Jan. 5, 1933

Coolidge, (John) Calvin (1872-1933), 30th president of the United States. From a farming community in Vermont, Coolidge was taciturn, cautious, and conservative—qualities that made him popular in the aftermath of U.S. involvement in World War I.

Early life. Coolidge graduated from Amherst College, studied law in Northampton, Mass., and was admitted to the bar in 1897. In 1905 he married Grace Goodhue. They had two sons, John and Calvin.

State senator and governor. Active in local Republican politics, Coolidge's rise was rapid. He was a representative in the Massachusetts legislature in 1908, mayor of Northampton in 1910, a state senator in 1911, president of the state senate in 1914, lieutenant governor in 1915, and governor of Massachusetts in 1918. He achieved national prominence in his first year as governor when he used the state militia to break a strike by Boston police. At the 1920 Republican national convention, he was named vice president on the ticket headed by Warren G. Harding.

Presidency. President Harding died in office in 1923, and Coolidge assumed the presidency, carrying on Harding's policies of free-market capitalism and tax cuts. In 1924 he easily won reelection over Democrat John W. Davis and Progressive candidate Robert M. La Follette. Following his dictum that "the business of America is business," Coolidge reduced the national budget and debt, and maintained high tariffs to protect U.S. industry. His public positions tended to fuel the stock-market speculation that finally led to the crash of 1929. But privately, Coolidge was apparently worried about the unchained speculation, which may have accounted for his decision not to run for reelection in 1928. He retired in 1929, a few months before the beginning of the Great Depression. He died in Northampton in 1933.

Cooper, Gary (1901-61), U.S. film actor. He portrayed laconic, romantic heroes in such films as *A Farewell to Arms* (1933) and *For Whom the Bell Tolls* (1943), and won Academy Awards for roles in *Sergeant York* (1941) and *High Noon* (1952).

Cooper, James Fenimore (1789-1851), one of the first important U.S. novelists, who created a number of colorful and enduring characters of the early American frontier. His famous series of *Leatherstocking Tales*, which include *The Pioneers* (1823), *The Last of the Mohicans* (1826), *The Prairie* (1827), *The Pathfinder* (1840), and *The Deerslayer* (1841), centered around the adventures of an intrepid woodsman called Natty Bumppo. Cooper achieved popularity in Europe, where he wrote for several years. Cooper also wrote several works of social criticism.

Cooper, Leroy Gordon, Jr. (1927-), first U.S. astronaut to make two orbital space flights. At the end of his 1963 Mercury space flight, the automatic control system broke down, and Cooper succeeded in manually piloting the *Faith 7* spacecraft back to earth. In August 1965 Cooper served as command pilot of *Gemini 5*, which orbited the earth 120 times.
See also: Astronaut.

Cooper, Peter (1791-1883), U.S. inventor, manufacturer, politician, and philanthropist. He rose from an apprentice carriage builder to become one of the nation's most powerful industrial magnates. Cooper launched a number of successful commercial enterprises, including the Canton Iron Works in Baltimore, which produced the first commercially operated American steam locomotive, the *Tom Thumb* (1830). A strong advocate of free public education, Cooper also founded the Cooper Union in New York City in 1854, to provide free instruction in the arts and sciences. In 1876 he was the unsuccessful Greenback Party candidate for president.

Cooperative, association of producers and consumers for the purpose of sharing among the members profits that would otherwise go to intermediate businesses and individuals. The organized cooperative movement dates from the first half of the 19th century. Social reformers such as Claude Saint-Simon, Louis Blanc, Robert Owen, and Charles Fourier protested the exploitation of the workers associated with the Industrial Revolution and urged collective self-help. The first successful consumer cooperative was the Rochdale Society of Equitable Pioneers, founded in England in 1844. The Rochdale principles, still basic to many cooperatives, call for open membership, democratic control, education of members, and service at cost.
The founding of the National Grange in the United States in 1867 stimulated small-scale efforts to form cooperatives, and it promoted the adoption of the Rochdale principles throughout the country.

Cooperative education, method of combining classroom and practical work experience. The professor Herman Schneider first initiated cooperative education in the United States by developing a program for engineers at the University of Cincinnati in 1906. Typically, formal written agreements between schools and employers allow students to hold jobs, usually for pay, related to their field of study.

Cooperative Extension System, U.S. nationwide educational network. Funded by the government at federal, state, and county levels and by private contributions, the cooperative extension system provides information to community members about farming, natural resources, child care, the development of community resources, and nutrition. Most major U.S. counties and cities have at least one county extension office. The 4-H program for young people falls under the auspices of the Cooperative Extension System.

Cooperstown (pop. 2180), village in central New York State; the seat of Otsego County. Cooperstown is the site of the National Baseball Museum and Hall of

Fame and the legendary hometown of baseball where General Abner Doubleday is said to have laid out a diamond in 1839.
See also: New York.

Coot (genus *Fulica*), common member of the rail family of water birds. The American coot ranges from southern Canada to northern South America and is found on stretches of fresh water, where it is distinguished by its contrasting black plumage and white bill and tail. It paddles with its lobed feet and often skitters over the surface of the water. Other coots found around the world include the giant coot and horned coot of the Andes. The nest of a coot usually floats on the water, and the chicks have surprisingly bright colors.

Copenhagen (pop. 472,700), seaport capital of Denmark, on Sjaelland and Amager islands. It handles most of Denmark's trade, exporting ham, bacon, porcelain, silverware, and furniture. Its main industries are shipping, shipbuilding, brewing, and light manufacturing. Landmarks include Christianborg Palace, Rosenborg Palace, Tivoli amusement park, the National Museum, and several art museums. The city was occupied by the Germans from 1940 to 1945.
See also: Denmark.

Copepod, small crustacean of subclass Copepoda. Of great ecological importance, copepods serve as food for many species of fish. Although there are freshwater copepods, most of the 7,500 known species are marine forms. They are found both at the surface and at great depths of the sea. While most copepods reproduce sexually, some do so by parthenogenesis (the female's eggs produce new copepods without being fertilized).
See also: Plankton.

Copernicus, Nicolaus (1473-1543), Polish astronomer who put forward the theory that the earth and other planets orbit the sun. Until the time of Copernicus, Ptolemy's theory that the earth was the center of the universe and that heavenly bodies, with the exception of the "fixed" stars, rotated around it, was generally accepted.
Copernicus studied mathematics and astronomy at the University of Krakow, and completed his education in Italy, He returned to Poland to become a canon in Frauenberg cathedral.
Many of the astronomers of Copernicus's day were dissatisfied with Ptolemy's theory, which was becoming more and more complex in order to take account of new discoveries about the universe. Copernicus tried to account for the observed motions of the planets by assuming that the earth and planets orbited the sun. He found that his system was much simpler than Ptolemy's complex picture of the universe. Afraid of a hostile reaction to his ideas, Copernicus began to circulate his theory anonymously until a pupil, Georg Joachim Rheticus, published a popular version of it in 1540. This version was enthusiastically received and Copernicus finally published his book *On the Revolutions of the Celestial Spheres.*
See also: Astronomy.

Copland, Aaron (1900-90), U.S. composer. His lyrical and exuberant music incorporates jazz and folk tunes in a distinctively American idiom. His works include the ballet scores *Billy the Kid* (1938) and *Appalachian Spring* (1944), the song cycle *Twelve Poems of Emily Dickinson* (1950), the opera *The Tender Land* (1954), symphonies, piano and chamber works, and film scores. His many awards include the 1945 Pulitzer Prize and Presidential Medal of Freedom in 1964.

Copley, John Singleton (1783-1815), portrait painter of colonial Massachusetts. Although he settled in London, where he painted historical subjects, Copley's modern reputation rests largely on his American portraits, including those of Paul Revere, Samuel Adams (Museum of Fine Arts, Boston), and Daniel Hubbard (Art Institute, Chicago).

Copper, chemical element, symbol Cu; for physical constants see Periodic Table. Copper was discovered in prehistoric times. It is a metallic element occasionally occurring in pure form. The most important ore is chalcopyrite. Copper is a reddish metal, malleable and ductile, a good conductor of heat and electricity. Brass, bronze, monel metal, and gun metal are all important alloys of copper. Most copper is used in the electrical industry. Some copper compounds are used as pesticides.

Copperhead (*Agkistrodon contortrix*), pit viper of hilly country in the eastern United States. It ranges from 2 to 4 ft (0.6 to 1 m) in length and is distinguished by its characteristic copper-colored head and coppertoned markings on a chestnut background. The copperhead strikes without warning, and its bite can cause considerable discomfort, although it is seldom fatal to healthy adults. It feeds mainly on small, warm-blooded animals but will eat frogs and insects when driven by hunger.

Nicolaus Copernicus

Copperheads, Northern Democrats who advocated peace with the Confederacy during the Civil War and who opposed President Lincoln's war policy. The epithet originated in an article in the *New York Tribune* in July 1861 that depicted the antiwar Northerners as venomous copperhead snakes that strike without warning. Most of these "Peace Democrats" confined themselves to agitating for a negotiated end to the war, but several secret Copperhead societies (Knights of the Golden Circle, Order of American Knights, Sons of Liberty) resorted to harassing Northern sympathizers, assisting deserters, and sabotaging Union supplies.

Copra, dried kernel (endosperm) of the coconut fruit, from which oil is extracted. Copra is prepared by drying the exposed coconut meat and then pressing the coconut oil out. Copra yields 50-60% of its weight in oil.

Coptic Church, Christian church that derives from the church of Alexandria in pre-Muslim Egypt. The Copts were de-

Christmas ritual on the walls surrounding the Church of the Holy Maria in Lalibela, nothern Ethiopia. Approximately 20% of the male Christians in Ethiopia are priests.

scended from ancient Egyptians, and spoke their own, now "dead," language. Early in the history of the church doctrinal disputes arose between the Roman Church and Coptic-speaking Christians. Following the Council of Chalcedon in A.D. 451, which condemned the view held by the Copts about the nature of Christ, the Copts broke away from Rome. After the Arab conquest of Egypt in A.D. 640, many Copts became Muslims. The religious head of the church is the Coptic Patriarch of Alexandria, who lives in Cairo. The liturgy of the church is derived from the ancient Greek liturgy and church services are celebrated in Coptic and Arabic. The Coptic church is important in Ethiopia.

Copyright, exclusive right of an author or other creator to publish or sell his or her works. When a work has been copyrighted, other firms and individuals must have permission from the holder of the copyright in order to reproduce the work. If they do so without permission, the holder of the copyright may sue for damages and for an order to stop publication or distribution. Most published books are copyrighted. Other types of works that may be copyrighted include plays, musical compositions, periodicals (including newspapers), motion pictures, photographs, prints, reproductions, works of art, speeches and lectures, and maps and charts. A notice of copyright will usually appear on such published material. In 1978 many U.S. copyright laws were rewritten. At present, a U.S. copyright grants exclusive rights to a work in the United States for the life of the author and 50 years after the author's death.
The Universal Copyright Convention, which is adhered to by many nations including the United States, does not specify the minimum of copyright protection, so long as there is no favoritism.
See also: Patent.

Coral, small, sedentary marine invertebrate of the class Anthozoa. Most corals join together in colonies and secrete external limestone skeletons that form coral reefs and islands in warm seas.

Red coral has been used throughout history to make jewelry. It was first used in Europe in the 15th century.

Coral Sea, part of the southwestern Pacific Ocean, between the northeast coast of Australia and the Solomon Islands. The sea floor is dominated by coral atolls and reefs, among them the Coral Sea Plateau, Osprey and Swain reefs, the Coral Sea Basin, and the Great Barrier Reef, which extends 1,200 mi (1,930 km) along the northeast Australian coast.
See also: Pacific Ocean.

Coral snake, slender poisonous snake (genus *Micrurus*) of the Western Hemisphere. Rings of black, yellow, or white and red cover its body. Two species are found in the southern U.S. states. Coral snakes feed on small reptiles and insects. In many parts of the world there are false coral snakes that have patterns of color similar to coral snakes but are harmless.

Corbett, James John (1866-1933), U.S. boxer. Known as "Gentleman Jim", he became the first man to hold the world heavyweight title under Marquess of Queensberry Rules, beating John L. Sullivan (1892). Corbett reigned for 5 years, until Bob Fitzsimmons knocked him out in 14 rounds in Carson City, Nev. After his retirement from the ring in 1903, Corbett made a successful career on the stage and in motion pictures.

Corbin, Margaret Cochran (1751-1800), American Revolutionary War hero. Replacing her husband at his cannon when he was killed in battle at Fort Washington (now in New York City), Corbin fought until she was seriously wounded. Left disabled, Corbin became one of the first women to receive a military pension from the Continental Congress.
See also: Revolutionary War in America.

Corbusier *See:* Le Corbusier.

Corcoran Gallery of Art, art museum in Washington, D.C. Founded by the banker William Wilson Corcoran (1869) and chartered by the U.S. Congress (1870), the museum exhibits paintings, sculptures, and drawings that span U.S. history from colonial to modern times. The museum also presents changing exhibitions and offers educational courses.

The city of Córdoba. Shown is an ancient Roman bridge leading to the city.

Corday, Charlotte (1768-93), French assassin of the French revolutionary Jean Paul Marat. Objecting to Marat's persecution of the Girondins, she stabbed him to death in his bath on July 13, 1793. She was guillotined by order of the revolutionary tribunal.
See also: French Revolution.

Cordillera (Spanish "chain"), geographical description applied to extended mountain systems in western North America, from Alaska to Nicaragua, including the Rocky Mountains and the Andes.

Cordite, smokeless gunpowder. Composed of 30% nitroglycerin, 65% nitrocellulose, and 5% petrolatum, cordite burns with a great deal of heat. Its name refers to the cordlike lengths in which it is made.
See also: Gunpowder.

Cordoba, monetary unit of Nicaragua, equal to 100 centavos. It is named after the Spanish explores Francisco Fernandez de Cordoba.

Córdoba (pop. 304,800), or Córdova, ancient Moorish city in Andalusia, southern Spain. The capital of Cordoba province, it is located 86 mi (146 km) northeast of Seville. Córdoba was a famous center of Moorish art and culture that reached its peak in the 10th century A.D. A great mosque was built as a Muslim house of worship in the 700s. Made into a Roman Catholic cathedral in 1238, Córdoba's chief landmark is supported by over 1,000 pillars of granite, onyx, marble, and jasper. Today, Córdoba's industries include brewing and metallurgy.
See also: Spain.

Córdoba (pop. 968,700), second-largest city in Argentina, Located on the Rio Primero in north central Argentina. Founded in 1573, Córdoba is an industrial center and home to Argentina's oldest uni-

versity, the National University of Córdoba.
See also: Argentina.

CORE *See:* Congress of Racial Equality.

Corelli, Arcangelo (1653-1713), Italian composer. During Corelli's lifetime the violin, together with the viola and cello, gradually replaced the older stringed instruments called viols. He did much to encourage this change by his own brilliance as a violinist and by his many compositions for the new stringed instruments. He was also a key figure in the development of the concerto grosso as an important new form of orchestral music.

Coreopsis, genus of summer-blooming plant also known as tickseed. This genus is a member of the family Asteraceae, which include about 100 species of herb native to North America. Coreopsis plants can grow to a height of 4 ft (120 cm). They bear yellow, red, or maroon flowers that resemble daisies.

Corgi *See:* Cardigan Welsh corgi; Pembroke Welsh corgi.

Coriander (*Coriandrum sativum*), small annual plant of the carrot family, the seeds of which are used as a spice and for medicinal purposes. Coriander leaves, also called cilantro or chinese parsley, are used to flavor food.

Corinth (pop. 22,500), ancient city of Greece situated on the isthmus between the mainland and Peloponnesus. The old city is dominated by the Acrocorinthus, a rock that rises to 1,886 ft (575 m).
Corinth was conquered by the Dorians c.1100 B.C. By the 6th century B.C. it was the leading mercantile city of Greece, a center of culture, commerce, and entertainment. It fought against Athens during the Peloponnesian War and emerged a weaker power. Later it was controlled by Macedonia. Corinth was destroyed by Rome in 146 B.C., but was rebuilt under Julius Caesar in 44 B.C. and became the capital of the Roman province of Achaea. St. Paul founded a Christian community there, to which he wrote his Epistles to the Corinthians. New Corinth was built 3.5 mi (5.6 km) from its ancient site, after the Hellenic city was destroyed by an earthquake. The modern town exports currants, olive oil, and silk.
See also: Greece.

Corinthians, Epistles to the, two letters written by St. Paul to the Christians of Corinth and forming the 7th and 8th books of the New Testament. The First Epistle, believed to have been written at Ephesus (c. A.D.55), is the longer, and is important for the light it throws on the problems, discipline, and organization of the early Church. The letter was prompted not only by questions raised by the Corinthians, but by Paul's awareness of divisions among them. The Second Epistle, according to modern scholars, may be a combination of two letters written at different times. It is an impassioned defense of Paul's work and authority as an apostle.
See also: Bible; New Testament.

Coriolanus, Gaius Marcius (fl.5th century B.C.), Roman general. Capturing the town of Corioli from the Volscians, Roman enemies, Coriolanus won both a reputation for bravery and his last name. During a famine in 491 B.C., Coriolanus proposed that grain be given to the poor only if they surrendered their right to elect representatives. To express their indignity, the people exiled Coriolanus, who responded by joining the Volscians. According to legend, he led their army to the gates of Rome, where he was stopped from seizing the city only by the pleading of his wife and mother. The betrayed Volscians then killed Coriolanus. The story is told in Shakespeare's tragedy *Coriolanus.*
See also: Rome, Ancient.

Coriolis force, apparent curvature of the path of a moving object due to the rotation of the earth. Because the earth rotates from west to east, any object moving in a straight line in any direction other than due east or due west appears to follow a curved path in relation to the earth's surface: to the right in the Northern Hemisphere and to the left in the Southern Hemisphere. This effect, named for the French physicist Gaspard Gustave de Coriolis (1792-1843), is most apparent in the movement of the winds and the sea. Allowances for this effect must also be made in ballistics in order to be able to calculate where a missile will land.

Cork (pop. 133,300), second largest city in Ireland (after Dublin) situated at the mouth of the Lee River, in the southwest of the republic. Through its fine harbor at Cobh, Cork exports dairy products, leather, iron, and glass. The city has large distilleries and breweries.
See also: Ireland.

Cork, spongy tissue in the bark of trees that acts as an insulation and protection to the delicate growing tissues. It also forms a seal over the wound where a leaf has been shed.
Commercial cork, used for insulation, bottle stoppers, engine gaskets, and floor linings, comes from the cork oak (*Quercus suber*) of southern Europe and North Africa. The cork oak has a layer of cork several inches thick that can be stripped every 10 years. The operation has to be carefully performed so that the delicate underlying tissues are not harmed.

Corliss, George Henry (1817-88), U.S. engineer who contributed to the perfection of the steam engine. Corliss developed an improved governor (feedback device) to cut off engine steam in response to changes in workload. For display at the 1876 Philadelphia Exposition, Corliss designed an engine that was larger than any built before.
See also: Steam engine.

Corm, thick underground stem used by certain plants (e.g., crocus, gladiolus) to store food over the winter to get them ready for flowering in the spring. Corms are very similar to bulbs, but the food is stored in the thickened stem and not in fleshy underground leaves.

Cormorant, any of a number of long-necked seabirds (family *Phalacrocoracidae*). Cormorants feed on fish, diving from the surface of the water. Their nests are built in colonies on rocks or in trees and they can often be seen perching with wings outstretched to dry. Northern cormorants have black plumage, but many of those of the Southern Hemisphere have white underparts; all have patches of naked colored skin on the head. Cormorants have been trained to catch fish for people in Britain, China, and Japan. A ring is usually placed around the neck to prevent fish from being swallowed.

Corn, or maize (*Zea mays*), grain crop cultivated in the Americas long before the arrival of Europeans and now grown extensively throughout the world. About 60% of world production is in the United States, mainly in the Corn Belt of the Midwest where the annual rainfall is more than 20 in (51 cm). It is the most important U.S. crop. Almost 90% is used for feeding livestock and the remainder for human consumption and for various industrial applications. Outside the United States, most of the crop is produced for human consumption.

Corn borer, caterpillars of a moth, especially the Old World maize moth, that feeds on a variety of plants, including beet, beans, and corn. It attacked the Indian corn that was introduced to Europe, and was transported to North America about 1907 to become a serious pest in the Corn Belt and elsewhere. The use of pesticides is effective, but complicated by the need to keep the crop free from contamination. The corn borer still destroys several million bushels of corn every year.

Cornea *See:* Eye.

Corneal transplant *See:* Eye bank.

Corn earworm, larval stage of moth (*Heliothis zea*) in the owlet moth family (Noctuidae). The corn earworm breeds on and attacks corn, tomatoes, alfalfa, and beans; it is called a bollworm when it attacks cotton. Insecticides such as carbaryl are used on some crops to protect them from the corn earworm.

Corneille, Pierre (1606-84), French dramatist, creator of French classical verse tragedy. His masterpiece, *Le Cid* (1637), though controversial in its time, was a great popular success. His many other plays include *Horace* (1640), *China* (1640), and *Polyeucte* (1643). His popularity faded with the rise of his younger rival, Jean Racine.
See also: Cid, The.

Cornell, Ezra (1807-74), U.S. businessman, pioneer in telegraphy. With Samuel Morse he created the United States' first telegraph line (1844), which went from Baltimore to Washington. He was also founder and director of the Western Union Telegraph Company (1855). His gifts helped create Cornell University, Ithaca, N.Y. (1865).
See also: Telegraph.

Cornell, Katharine (1898-1974), U.S. stage actress, noted for her major roles in serious dramas, often directed by her husband, Guthrie McClintic. Her most famous part was Elizabeth Barrett Browning in *The Barretts of Wimpole Street* (1931).

Cornell University, nonsectarian, coeducational university founded in 1865 and located in Ithaca, N.Y. Named for its founder, businessman and philanthropist Ezra Cornell, the university is financed both by its endowment and by public support. The university consists of 15 colleges and schools, including the medical and nursing schools in New York City, and 4 specialized colleges, supported by legislative appropriation, that are part of the State University of New York: the Veterinary College, the College of Agriculture, the College of Human Ecology, and the School of Industrial and Labor relations.

Corner Brook (pop. 22,800), town in Newfoundland, Canada, on the Bay of Islands, near the mouth of the Humber River. Corner Brook is a lumbering and fish-processing center and has one of the world's largest paper mills.
See also: Newfoundland.

Cornering the market, investment term for a speculator conspiracy to drive up stock prices. An investor or group of investors will buy all or most of the available shares in a company, forcing other buyers to pay higher prices for their shares and thus reaping maximum profits. The practice is now outlawed by the U.S. Securities and Exchange Commission.

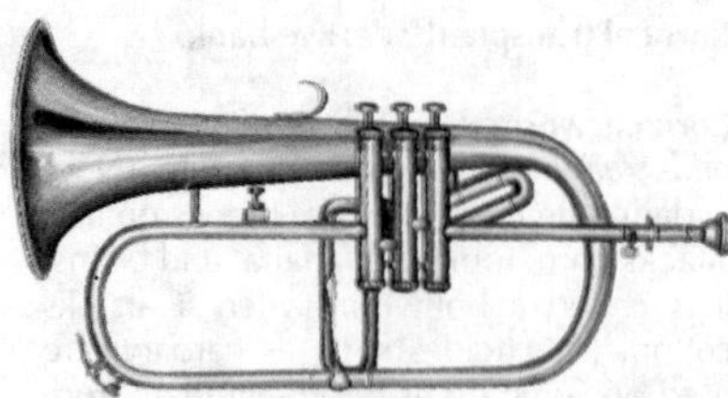
The cornet is a brass wind instrument with a cup-shaped mouthpiece.

Cornet, trumpetlike valved brass wind instrument. It has a mellow tone controlled by lip vibration at the cupped mouthpiece and a two-and-a-half octave range. It is usually tuned to B flat. Cornets have traditionally been used in brass bands but rarely in symphony orchestras. They have, however, found an important place in jazz.

Cornflower (*Centaurea cyanus*), annual herb whose flowers are used for medicinal purposes. The large, blue flowers (white or rose-colored in some varieties) appear from June to August and are popular in U.S. gardens.

Corning (pop. 11,936), city in southwestern New York State, situated on the Chemung River. Corning is the home of the Corning Glass Works, the hub of industrial activity in the city, where the 200-in (508-cm) mirror for the Mt. Palomar observatory was manufactured. It is also a dairy center.
See also: New York.

Corn laws, various laws regulating English import and export of grain from the 14th century to 1849. After the Napoleonic Wars the corn price was raised to offset agricultural depression. But protests from the poor and from manufacturers objecting to agricultural subsidy helped Cobden and Bright, leaders of the Anti-Corn Law League (1839-46), persuade Prime Minister Sir Robert Peel to repeal the Corn Laws (1846 and 1849).

Corn oil, vegetable oil derived from the kernel of the corn plant. In processing, machines separate the germ (or embryo) from the rest of the corn kernel. Then the oil is extracted from the rest of the kernel. Corn oil is made up of about 55% polyunsaturated fat, which many nutritionists consider an essential element in a healthy diet. It is used in cooking and as a salad oil, as well as in margarine and potato chips.

Cornplanter (c.1740-1836), Seneca chief who aided the British during the American Revolution. After the war he helped arrange treaties between U.S. settlers and Native American tribes in western Pennsylvania. In exchange for his signing the Treaty of Fort Stanwix (1784), the Pennsylvania legislature voted him a land grant along the upper Allegheny River.

Cornstalk (1720?-77), Shawnee chief who led his tribe in wars against colonial settlers in the Ohio Territory. He and his warriors were defeated by a regiment of Virginians at the Battle of Point Pleasant (1774). Three years later, while visiting Point Pleasant, Cornstalk and 4 other Shawnees were killed by a mob of townspeople seeking vengeance for the murder of a white settler by members of another tribe. His murder led to other wars between the Shawnees and settlers.

Cornstarch, fine white flour extracted from corn. Ground and refined after the seed-bearing portion (germ) has been removed from the kernels, cornstarch is formed after a wet milling and drying process. It is a key ingredient in baking powder and is used in the manufacture of explosives, paints, and textiles.

Corn syrup, syrup prepared from cornstarch and containing glucose combined with dextrin and maltose. Corn syrup adds a smooth texture to creams such as those used in candies. It is used to sweeten baked goods, candies, canned fruit, ice cream, and soft drinks, and is sometimes added as a flavoring to peanut butter, catsup, salad dressings, processed meats, and other foods.

Cornucopia, or horn of plenty, curved goat's horn symbolizing nature's abundance. Fruit and grain overflow from the mouth of the cornucopia. It is often used as a decorative motif. Legend presents the cornucopia as the horn of the Greek nymph Amalthea that could always be filled with its possessor's desires.

Cornwallis, Charles Cornwallis, 1st Marquis of (1738-1805), British general whose surrender to Washington at Yorktown (Oct. 19, 1781) ended the Revolutionary War. Earlier, he had defeated Nathanael Greene in the Carolinas. He later gave important service as governor-general of India (1786-93 and 1805), and as viceroy of Ireland (1798-1801).
See also: Revolutionary War in America.

Corona, outer atmosphere of the sun or other stars. The term is used also for the halo seen around a celestial body due to diffraction of its light by water droplets in thin clouds of the earth's atmosphere, and for a part appended to and within the corolla of some flowers. Around high-voltage terminals there appears a faint glow due to the ionization of the local air. The result of this ionization is an electrical discharge known as corona discharge, the glow being called a corona.
See also: Star.

Coronado, Francisco Vásquez de (1510-54), Spanish explorer. Coronado was the first European to explore the southwestern United States. Searching for the legendary, gold-laden Seven Cities of Cibola in 1540, he set out from Mexico, traveling through areas that are now Kansas, Oklahoma, Texas, New Mexico, and Arizona. Though Coronado found no riches, he introduced the Spanish to the Pueblo and pioneered colonization in the southwestern United States.
See also: Cibola, Seven Cities of.

Coronary thrombosis, myocardial infarction, or heart attack, one of the commonest causes of serious illness and death in Western countries. The coronary arteries, which supply the heart with oxygen and nutrients, may become diseased with atherosclerosis that reduces blood flow. Significant narrowing may lead to the clotting of blood (thrombosis) in the artery, which can cause sudden, complete obstruction and resulting damage to a substantial area of heart tissue. This may end in sudden death, usually due to abnormal heart rhythm that prevents effective pumping. Characteristic changes may be seen in the electrocardiograph following myocardial (heart muscle) damage, and enzymes appear in blood from the damaged heart muscle.
See also: Heart.

Coronation, ceremony of crowning a sovereign, usually consisting of a solemn ritual of religious as well as secular significance. It generally includes the anointing of the sovereign, investiture with special garments and symbols of royalty such as a crown, pronouncement of the coronation oath, enthronement, and, in Christian countries, taking of Communion. The actual authority of the new sovereign usually commences with the death of the predecessor. The kings and queens of England have been crowned in Westminster Abbey since 1066.

Coroner, public official who investigates sudden, suspicious, or violent death, sometimes with the aid of a jury. Coroners are also responsible for protecting the property of the deceased person until it is relinquished to the person(s) legally entitled to inherit it. A coroner may order an inquest if the death is considered suspicious. In some communities in the United States, medical examiners, who must be physicians, are appointed to serve as coroner, although public prosecutors are assigned to the legal aspects of the investigation. In some states, laymen are permitted to serve as coroner, but they must hire a physician to perform any necessary autopsies.

Corot, Jean Baptiste Camille (1796-1875), French landscape painter. He is best known for the subtly atmospheric paintings that made him popular in the 1850s. While studying in Rome, he broke from the classical tradition and began to achieve sensitive effects of light by painting directly from nature. After his return to France he began to develop the soft, gray-green landscapes that made his reputation. His influence on his fellow artists of the Barbizon School was considerable, and the impressionists learned a great deal from him, though he never shared their views. Most of the world's major art galleries have examples of Corot's work.

Corporation, group of persons regarded as a legal entity apart from the individuals owning or managing it. As a legal person, a corporation can hold property and sue and be sued. Corporations may be either private or public.
The corporate form of business organization has at least 4 advantages. (1) It safeguards its owners, relieving them of legal responsibility as individuals when they act as agents of the business. (2) The owner of shares of stock has limited liability, that is, cannot lose more money than invested and has no personal responsibility for the debts of that "person," the corporation. (3) Corporate stock is transferable. The corporation is not damaged by the death or lack of interest of a particular person. (4) The corporation can raise large amounts of capital by selling stock. The corporate form of organization has some disadvantages for the investor or manager. As a separate legal entity, the corporation must pay taxes. When the business passes along profits in the form of dividends, the individual owners are taxed again on these dividends. Managers are subject to more government regulation than are individual proprietors or partnerships. And ownership becomes separated from management; some managers may be tempted to act more in their own interests than those of the stockholders. There are 5 primary methods used by corporations to raise new capital. (1) Sale of common stock: Investors who buy common stock own shares in the corporation but receive no dividends until interest payments are made on outstanding bonds. If the company's financial health is good and its assets sufficient, it can create capital by issuing additional shares of common stock. As the shares are sold, the funds received can be used for expansion. (2) Issuing preferred stock: If profits are limited, the owner of preferred stock will be paid dividends before those with common stock. (3) Issuing bonds: A bond is a promissory note, usually issued for a specified amount. It is sold on the bond market with the promise to pay interest every 6 months or every year. When the bond reaches "maturity," the company promises to pay back the principal at its face value. Ordinarily, the company agrees to pay interest on its bonds whether or not a profit is made. For this reason a smaller corporation can seldom raise much capital by issuing bonds. (4) Borrowing: Companies can also raise capital by borrowing from lending institutions, primarily banks and savings-and-loan establishments. The borrower must pay the lender interest on the loan, at a rate determined by competitive market forces. (5) Using profits: Some corporations pay out most of their profits in the form of dividends to their stockholders. Investors buy into these companies because they want a high income on a regular basis. Other corporations reinvest most of their profits in expansion. Persons who own such stocks are content to accept a smaller dividend or none at all, if by rapid growth the shares increase in value.

Corporation for Public Broadcasting (CPB), U.S. non-profit organization formed to promote public television and radio. The CPB is funded by the federal government and contributes financially to the nearly 500 public television and radio stations in the United States that broadcast its programs uninterrupted by commercials. CPB is most noted for its research, testing, financing, production, and distribution of educational and cultural programs. CPB was created by Congress in 1967.
See also: Television.

Corps, unit of a military force, usually a tactical division consisting of 2 or more subdivisions. Corps are commanded by lieutenant generals and are usually organized for a specialized function. The term "corps" is often used to identify the U.S. Marine Corps and divisions of the U.S. army.
See also: Army, U.S.

Corpus Christi (pop. 349,894), city in southeastern Texas situated on the Corpus Christi Bay of the Texas Gulf Coast, seat of Nueces County. Corpus Christi was founded in 1839 and played an active role in the Mexican War and the Civil War. The city is the second largest port in Texas, and one of the centers of the vast Texas oil and gas industry. Corpus Christi also refines aluminum and manufactures fertilizers, cotton and corn products, cement, and chemical products.
See also: Texas.

Corpus Christi Naval Air Station, headquarters of the U.S. Naval Air Advanced Training Command in Corpus Christi, Tex. The station was organized in 1941, and became a primary training ground for thousands of naval aviators during World War II. It is now used for advanced training for naval pilots.

Corpuscle, in biology, isolated cell, usually one that can move freely in fluid and is not fixed in tissue. The term corpuscle is often used to refer to red and white blood cells, and to the nerve endings in the skin.
See also: Biology; Blood.

Correggio (Antonio Allegri; 1494-1534), Italian Renaissance painter who influenced the Baroque style. His works (including most of his Parma frescoes) are primarily devotional, and are noted for softness and use of chiaroscuro (dramatic light and shadow).
See also: Baroque; Renaissance.

The baroque painter Correggio's decoration of the cupola of the church of S. Giovanni Evangelista in Parma, Italy. Depicted is the ascension of Jesus.

Corregidor, fortified island near the entrance to Manila Bay and the Philippines. During World War II, Corregidor, was occupied by United States and Filipino troops who defended the island but eventually surrendered in 1942 to Japanese troops after extensive bombing. U.S. military

Bill Cosby

forces reclaimed the island in 1945 and later dedicated the historic fortress as a national shrine to the World War II troops who died there.
See also: World War II.

Corrosion, gradual destruction of a substance, usually a metal, by chemical action. Oxidation is the most common form of corrosion. Rusting of structures made of iron is a familiar example. Corrosion can dangerously weaken structures. The simplest precaution consists of coating the metal with protective layers of paint. Sometimes iron is coated with another metal, notably zinc, to produce *galvanized* iron. Plastic coatings have recently been developed to prevent corrosion. In jet engines and nuclear devices corrosion is a particularly difficult problem, since the metals used are subjected to high temperatures and stresses in circumstances where mechanical failure through corrosion could be disastrous. Radiation may also increase susceptibility to corrosion and also change the mechanical properties of the metal. Special alloys have been developed to overcome these difficulties.
See also: Oxidation; Reduction.

Corsica, Mediterranean island and French department north of Sardinia, off the coast of western Italy, occupying 3,352 sq mi (8,682 sq km). It is largely mountainous, with Mediterranean scrub and forest. Its products include olive oil, wine, and citrus fruits. Its rulers have included Carthaginians, Romans, Vandals, Goths, Saracens, and (1347-1768) the Genoese, who sold it to France. There is strong nationalist feeling on the island. Napoleon Bonaparte was born here.

Cortés, Hernando (1485-1547), Spanish explorer, conqueror of Mexico. In 1504 he settled in Hispaniola (Santa Domingo) and in 1511 joined the conquest of Cuba, becoming mayor of Santiago. Sent to explore the Yucatan, in 1519 he marched on the Aztecs' capital Tenochtitlán, where Montezuma greeted him as the white god Quetzalcoatl. Cortez took Montezuma prisoner, and the latter was killed in an uprising against the Spaniards. Cortez retreated, but returned in 1521 and conquered the capital, ending the Aztec Empire. He later explored Honduras and lower California.

Cortex, cerebral *See:* Brain.

Corticosteroid *See:* Cortisone.

Cortina, Juan Nepomuceno (1824-94), civil rights leader who fought for fair treatment of Mexican Americans. Cortina earned a reputation as the "Robin Hood of South Texas" because he opposed the unfair treatment of Mexican Americans in Texas after the Mexican War (1846-48). Cortina led raids throughout Texas to demand that Spanish-speaking Americans receive the same treatment as their English-speaking counterparts. Cortina was eventually chased by U.S. troops into Mexico, where he became a military leader and governor of the state of Tamaulipas.

Cortisone, one of the group of hormones secreted by the cortex of the adrenal glands. Cortisone was first isolated in 1935 and synthesized in 1944. It proved to be of immense value in treating diseases caused by malfunctioning of the adrenal cortex, such as Addison's disease, and in the treatment of arthritis, some forms of allergy, leukemia, and many other diseases. However, cortisone and the closely related hydrocortisone have undesirable side effects. As a result the drug is used with caution or replaced by a synthetic substitute. The secretion of cortisone is controlled by ACTH (adrenocorticotropic hormone), which is itself secreted by the anterior lobe of the pituitary gland.
See also: Hormone.

Corundum, mineral consisting of alumina (aluminum oxide, Al_2O_3) and second in hardness only to diamond. It forms precious stones, such as rubies, sapphires, topaz, amethyst, and emerald; the "jewels" in watches and instrument bearings are often made of corundum. Because of its hardness, corundum is widely used in emery and other abrasives. Corundum is found in many countries, often in association with quartz.

The mountain town of Sartene, Corsica

Cosby, Bill (William Henry Cosby, Jr.; 1937-), U.S. entertainer. Known mainly as a comedian, he is also an actor, producer, and author. He was the first African-American actor to star in a televison series ("I Spy," 1965-8). He produces and stars in the award-winning television series "Cosby Show" (first aired in 1984). *Uptown Saturday Night* (1974) is one of his movie credits. He is the author of a number of books, including *Fatherhood* (1986), *a collection of witty essays.*

Cosimo de' Medici *See:* Medici.

Cosmetics, preparations applied to the human body to beautify or alter appearance. Cosmetics are used primarily to cleanse, color, condition, or protect the skin, hair, lips, nails, eyes, and teeth. Though cosmetics have been used since ancient times for religious and ornamental rituals, since the early 1900s they have grown into what is now a billion dollar industry. The Food and Drug Administration (FDA), an arm of the U.S. government, regulates production, labeling, and use of cosmetics. Examples of commonly used cosmetics are lipsticks, eye shadows, blushes, deodorants, perfumes, lotions, shampoos, nail polishes, and some toothpastes.

Cosmic rays, highly penetrating radiation that strikes the earth, assumed to originate in interstellar space. They are classed as primary, coming from the assumed source, and secondary, induced in upper atmospheric nuclei by collisions with primary cosmic rays.
See also: Radiation.

Cosmology, study of how the universe originated and how it has evolved. There are 2 main theories. The first, known as the *evolutionary theory*, pictures the universe as having been born, and as evolving and eventually dying. The popular name for this theory is the "big bang" theory, because it assumes that all the material in the universe was at one time packed tightly together and was then flung outward by an enormous explosion. This theory was first put forward in the 1920s by the Belgian astrophysicist and priest Georges Lemaître. It rested on the discovery by Edwin Hubble that the universe seemed to be expanding, like a balloon being blown up. Hubble showed that the galaxies are receding from each other with velocities increasing to nearly half the speed of light as they get farther away. After World War II, Hermann Bondi and Thomas Gold put forward the opposing *steady state* theory, which says that new material is continuously created to fill the space between the galaxies. Although the universe is expanding, the matter in it was never concentrated. New galaxies and old galaxies would exist side by side, and the universe would always look the same. The theory was later developed by the English astronomer Fred Hoyle. Observational tests for these theories rest on the fact that radiation takes time to cross very long distances. By looking deep into space, one looks backward in time, because the radiation now recorded may have left the object long ago. The farthest visible objects are so far away that their radiation has taken billions of years to reach earth.

As one looks back in time, the character of the universe seems to alter. Instead of galaxies one sees quasars, which may be galaxies in the process of formation. At distances past 8 billion light-years, the number of objects seems to decrease, indicating a time when the universe was just forming, which seems to support the evolutionary theory.

Another piece of evidence against the steady state theory is that radio astronomers record a faint radiation from all over the universe. This so-called "background" radiation, discovered in 1965 by Arno Penzias and Robert Wilson, may be the heat left over from a "big bang" explosion. Though it still has adherents, the steady state theory has now largely been abandoned.

See also: Astronomy.

Cosmonaut *See:* Astronaut.

Cosmos, term for the universe and all its components. The ancient Greeks used the term to describe a total universe characterized not by chaos but by systematic harmony. Cosmos is an all-inclusive description of existence consisting of everything from tiny atoms to huge planets and galaxies.

See also: Universe.

Cosmos, genus of tropical fall-blooming flowers of the Compositae family. Cosmos, native to U.S. and Mexican tropics, are tall, brightly-colored annuals and may have either single-stemmed flowers or clustered blooms. Cosmos grow well in full sunlight and moderate soil.

Cossacks, Slavic warrior peasants living on the Ukrainian steppe and famed for horsemanship. Self-governing under leaders like Bohdan Chmielnicki (1595-1657), they resisted outside authority, but served the czars as irregular cavalry, pioneered in Siberia, and fought the Bolsheviks from 1918 to 1921. Collectivization broke up their communities in the 1930s, but Cossack cavalry served in World War II.

Costa Rica, Republic of, republic in the southern part of Central America, between Nicaragua and Panama. Costa Rica is the second smallest of the Central American republics, measuring between 75 and 175 mi (121 and 282 km) from the Caribbean to the Pacific coasts. San José is the capital.

Land and climate. Costa Rica consists of tropical coastal plains, chains of mountain ranges running in a northwest-southeast direction through the interior, and a central plateau. The mountains begin near the Nicaraguan border, split into 2 major ranges curving around the plateau, and continue into Panama. The highest peaks are in the south (Chirripó Grande, 12,533 ft/ 3,820 m) and in central Costa Rica, where 4 volcanic cones reach altitudes from 9,000 to 12,000 ft (2,743 to 3,658 m) above sea

Costa Rican coffee plantation

Costa Rica

General information	
Capital:	San José
Area:	19,730 sq mi (51,100 sq km)
Population:	2,941,000
Official language:	Spanish
Monetary unit:	1 Costa Rican colón = 100 céntimos
Main cities:	San José, Limón, Alajuela
Government	
Form:	republic
Independent:	1838
Head of state:	President (elected every 4 years)
Head of government:	President
Legislature:	one legislative house (Legislative Assembly)
Executive:	President and Cabinet
Judiciary:	highest court is the Supreme Court of Justice
Political division:	7 provinces
National economy	
Gross national product:	US $4,690,000,000
Per capita income:	US $1,760
Agriculture:	sugar cane, bananas, rice, coffee, corn, palm oil
Livestock:	cattle, pigs, horses
Fisheries:	20,000 metric tons
Mining:	gold
Industries:	food products, non-alcoholic beverages, petroleum products, wearing apparel, drugs and medicine
Main exports:	coffee, bananas, cattle and meat
Transportation:	435 mi (700 km) of railroads; 21,970 mi (35,357 km) of roads; 1 international airport
Trading partners:	U.S., Germany, Guatemala, Venezuela, United Kingdom
People	
Urban:	50%
Ethnic composition:	European 87%, mestizo 7%, African/mulatto 3%, East Asian (mostly Chinese) 2%, Native American 1%
Birth rate:	28.9 per 1,000 population
Death rate:	3.8 per 1,000 population
Infant mortality rate:	17.4 per 1,000 live births
Life expectancy:	male 72.5 years, female 77 years

level. The central plateau is the most densely populated section of Costa Rica and the center of coffee cultivation. It lies at an elevation of 3,000-4,000 ft (914-1,219 m) in the climatic zone known as *tierra templada* (temperate land). In the lowlying coastal areas the annual temperature averages close to 80° F (26.6° C). At elevations of more than 5,900 ft (1,800 m), year-round averages drop below 62° F (16.6° C). Rainfall is heaviest along the Caribbean coast, feeding the several short rivers that rise in the mountains. Broadleaf evergreens cover more than half the land, cleared in places for banana plantations. Grasslands cover the Meseta Central.

People. Unlike the peoples of the other Central American countries, most Costa Ricans are of direct Spanish descent, though most also claim to have some Native American blood. A large part of the population is made up of mestizos, people of mixed Spanish and Native American ancestry. About two-thirds of the people live in rural areas, frequently on small farms that they own and work. With the exception of a few Native American tribes, all inhabitants speak Spanish. Costa Rica has the lowest rate of illiteracy in Central America. School attendance is free and compulsory for children between the ages of 7 and 14. The University of Costa Rica is located at San José.

Economy. Though some gold and silver is mined in western Costa Rica, the country's volcanic soil is its most important natural resource. The principal cash crop and export product is high-grade coffee, which is in constant demand on world markets. Bananas, which rival coffee in importance as an export product, are raised on the humid plantations along the Pacific coast, where rubber trees also thrive. Local industry is mainly confined to sugar refining, food processing, and the manufacture of a limited range of consumer products. The discovery of large sulfur deposits has led to the construction of several processing plants. Despite the modest resources and the almost total lack of fuel, Costa Rica is being industrialized at a fairly rapid pace.

History. Columbus discovered Costa Rica in 1502, but because of its lack of resources the region escaped the ravages of the conquistadors. Since few Native Americans survived, the white farmers worked their own land, establishing a significant middle class and avoiding the semifeudal peonage system so destructive in other Latin American countries. In 1821 Costa Rica declared independence from Spain, joining first the Mexican Empire and then the Central American Federation, which dissolved into anarchy in 1838. Despite internal strife in 1919 and 1948, the country's history has been peaceful and its politics democratic. Its welfare system, dating from 1924, is one of the most advanced in the hemisphere. The country has had traditionally good relations with the United States.

Cost-benefit analysis, comparison study of costs versus benefits. Used often for planning, budgeting, or altering societal programs, a cost-benefit analysis measures the relationship between actual prices paid and benefits received. If an analysis identifies that the benefits outweigh the costs, the program is deemed cost-effective. The drawbacks to this economic study lie in the difficulty of determining future costs and placing monetary value on intangible benefits.

Costello, John Aloysius (1891-1976), Irish prime minister (1948-51, 1954-57). Costello's first term was marked by the withdrawal of Ireland from the Commonwealth of Nations (Republic of Ireland Act) and his second term was punctuated by terrorist acts of the Irish Republic Army (IRA).
See also: Ireland.

Cost-of-living index, number or device showing how the cost of living compares at a certain time with the cost at a given time in the past, called the *base period.* Many governments, including the U.S. government, compute such a monthly or quarterly index in order to detect and measure inflationary influences in the economy. Many wage contracts have features that automatically raise or lower wages by a given amount as the cost of living changes. The base period is usually recent enough to make the types of goods bought roughly comparable with those offered for sale at the present time. Economists then compute what the basic collection of goods and services chosen for the base period would cost at the time of the survey. If the cost of these goods and services is set at 100 in the base period, and if the same things now cost 10.2% more, then the cost of living is now 110.2.
See also: Consumer Price Index.

Côte d'Azur, resort area along the eastern Mediterranean coast of France. Part of the French Riviera, the Côte D'Azur includes the coastal villages and cities of Nice, Cannes, Antibes, and Monte Carlo, Monaco. Named for its characteristically deep blue seas and skies and possessing a mild Mediterranean climate, the Côte d'Azur attracts tourists from all over the world.

Cotopaxi, highest active volcano in the world. It is located in the Andes Mountains of Ecuador, 40 mi (64 km) from Quito. The volcano towers 19,344 ft (5,896 m) above sea level and its crater is 2,600 ft (792 m) across. The last recorded eruption was in 1942.

Cottage industry, term used to describe the structure of industry, particularly the spinning and weaving industry in Britain, before the Industrial Revolution. Typically, a trader distributed supplies of wool, and later, cotton, among a series of peasant homes, where spinning and weaving provided a part-time occupation for the women and children of the household. Although the earlier technical advances of the 18th century—James Hargreaves's spinning jenny, for example—were not incompatible with this cottage industry, the introduction of Richard Arkwright's spinning frame (patented in 1769) encouraged mass production and the transfer of spinning to factories. Weaving remained largely a cottage industry until the 1820s, when the factories began to take over in this area as well.

Cotton, subtropical plant (genus *Gossypium*) grown for the soft white fibers attached to its seed, which can be woven into fabric, also called cotton. Examples of woven cotton cloth dating to 3000 B.C. have been found at Mohenjo-Daro, in what is now Pakistan. Samples of prehistoric cotton have also been found in Pueblo ruins in Arizona, and some cotton fabric made before the Inca civilization still is in existence. Despite competition from synthetic fibers, cotton is one of the world's most important crops.
Although the proportion grown in the United States has declined sharply, the United States has more than 11 million acres (4.5 million hectares) planted with cotton, producing about 10 million bales per year. Cotton requires about 200 days of warm, sunny weather and 25-30 in (63.5-76 cm) of rain. It is generally cultivated as an annual plant. When the pods, or bolls, burst to reveal the white fibers (lint) within them, the cotton is ready for harvesting. Since the bolls burst at different times, a field may have to be picked several times during the season.
Each cotton fiber is an elongated plant cell made up of 90% cellulose. Unlike other natural fibers, the cotton fiber has 200-400 twists per inch (500-1,000 twists per cm) along its length. These give it excellent spinning characteristics. The quality of cotton is measured in terms of the length and fineness of the lint. Egyptian-type cotton, grown mainly in Egypt, the Sudan, and Aden, is the finest, producing long fibers (more than 1 1/8 in/2.9 cm) that are strong and silky. It commands the highest prices, but constitutes only about 5% of world production. About 95% of U.S. cotton yields fibers between 7/8 in and 1 1/8 in (2.2 cm and 2.9 cm) long, and perhaps 73% of the world crop produces this fiber length. Cotton is prone to many pests and diseases that cause enormous damage to the crop (averaging nearly $300 million in the United States every year). The main insect pests are the boll weevil in the United States and the pink boll worm in India and Egypt. Destructive fungus diseases that attack the plant include fusarium and verticillium wilt and Texas root rot.

Cotton, John (1584-1652), powerful Puritan minister of Boston, Mass., noted for his didactic writings. Born in England, Cotton fled to the colonies in 1632 to avoid religious persecution. He was later to become involved in the banishment of Anne Hutchinson and Roger Williams for their heretical views.
See also: Puritans.

Cotton gin, machine that separates cotton fibers from the seeds, leaves, and other unwanted matter. Invention of the cotton

gin in 1793, attributed to Eli Whitney, revolutionized the cotton industry in the South. Within 50 years cotton production had increased a thousand-fold. The original machines were of very simple design. A rotating drum with fine wire spikes, turned by hand, drew the fibers through narrow slots in a wire grid. The grid allowed the cotton fibers through, but not the seeds. A set of revolving brushes removed the fibers from the drum to prevent matting and clogging. The basic design of cotton gins has changed little since the 18th century. Modern mechanized versions use blasts of air to remove the fibers and are capable of producing a 500-lb (227-kg) bale of compressed cotton in little more than 10 min.
See also: Whitney, Eli.

Cottonmouth *See:* Water moccasin.

Cottonseed oil, edible oil extracted from cottonseeds. Used chiefly as a salad and cooking oil, cottonseed oil can also be hydrogenated to make shortening and margarine. The hull (outer seed covering), is removed and the seeds are soaked in a solution to extract the oil. Further refining, purifying, and bleaching is necessary to make the oil palatable.

Cottontail *See:* Rabbit.

Cottonwood, tree (genus *Populus*) of the willow family with windblown seeds surrounded by tufts of cottonlike hairs. There are nearly 40 species around the Northern Hemisphere, most of which are called aspens and poplars.

Cotyledon, first leaf developed by a seed plant's embryo. Cotyledons are formed in seeds and function primarily to absorb stored food. Plants with single cotyledon embryos are called monocots; dicots are embryos with 2 cotyledons; and gymnosperms have more than 2 cotyledons.

Cougar *See:* Mountain lion.

Coughlin, Charles Edward (1891-1969), U.S. Roman Catholic priest famous for his vitriolic sermons broadcast by radio from his Shrine of the Little Flower Church in Royal Oak, Mich. He upheld isolationism, attacked President Franklin D. Roosevelt, and preached anti-Semitism. He also disseminated his reactionary views through his magazine, *Social Justice*.

Coulee Dam *See:* Grand Coulee Dam.

Coulomb (coul or C), unit of electricity, the quantity of electricity that must pass through a circuit to deposit .0000394 oz (0.0011180 g) of silver from a solution of silver nitrate. It is named for French physicist Charles Augustin de Coulomb. An ampere is 1 coulomb per second. A coulomb is also the quantity of electricity on the positive plate of a condenser of 1-farad capacity when the electromotive force is 1 volt.
See also: Ampere.

Coulomb, Charles Augustin de (1736-1806), French physicist noted for his researches into friction, torsion, electricity, and magnetism. Using a torsion balance, he established Coulomb's Law of electrostatic forces.
See also: Physics.

Counterpoint, in music, art of combining 2 or more different melodic lines simultaneously in a composition.

Counter-Reformation, reform movement in the Roman Catholic Church during the 16th and 17th centuries. It arose in part as a reaction against the Reformation, which attacked the Church and in the end offered as an alternative the independent Protestant churches founded by Luther and Calvin. The Counter-Reformation, on the other hand, proposed to reform the Church from within. One of the first moves toward religious reform was the founding of the Oratory of Divine Love in 1516, an assembly of pious churchmen intent upon official and authoritative action toward reform. The movement gained impetus with the founding of several new religious orders that emphasized simplicity and austerity. The most important new order was the Society of Jesus (Jesuits), founded by Ignatius Loyola in 1540. The spirit and methods of the Counter-Reformation were enunciated by the Council of Trent (1545-47, 1551-52, 1562-63), which reaffirmed the doctrines of the faith, reorganized ecclesiastical administration, set educational requirements and moral standards for the clergy, and condemned simony (the buying and selling of church offices). In moves to combat heresy, Pope Paul III revived the medieval institution of the inquisition in Italy and Spain and Pope Paul IV authorized the *Index of Forbidden Books*. The spiritual revival was particularly intense in Spain, where Teresa of Ávila and John of the Cross combined a profound mysticism that renewed the spiritual life of the Church with active contributions toward reform of the religious orders.
See also: Reformation; Roman Catholic Church; Trent, Council of.

Country, political nation with geographic boundaries. Independent countries often have distinguishable topographical or cultural features and can vary drastically in size. Countries may be as small as several hundred acres or as large as 1 million sq mi (2.6 million sq km or more).

Country and western music, broad category of popular music that has its roots in rural American music of the 18th and 19th centuries, particularly in the South where black music, religious music, and British folk music fused into a unique American musical genre. Most songs are deeply personal and deal with themes of love, loneliness, and separation, but maintain a strong sense of faith in the human spirit. Songs can be quite festive and funny. Musical instruments often include guitar, banjo, fiddle, horns, drums, pianos, and electric instruments. With the advent of radio broadcasts of this music in the 1920s and 1930s, the genre gained nationwide recognition. The "Grand Ole Opry," the national center of country and western music located in Nashville, Tenn., began radio broadcasts in 1925. The stars of the 1930s and 1940s included Tex Ritter, Jimmy Rodgers, Ernest Tubb, and Gene Autry. In the 1950s, Hank Williams achieved fame with "Your Cheatin' Heart" and "Cold, Cold Heart." The sound of the 1960s and 1970s combined elements of pop music and thus added to the popularity of the music. By the 1980s, country and western performers had achieved superstar status and became active in television and film. Some of the notable performers are Johnny Cash, Loretta Lynn, Dolly Parton, Willie Nelson, the Judds, Reba McEntire, and Randy Travis.

One of the legends of country music — Johnny Cash

County, territorial division of local government. In the United States, the county is the largest division for local government within a state. County functions differ from state to state, but counties generally administer judicial, educational, and political functions and make physical improvements. County boundaries are determined by each state's legislature and funds are raised by real estate and property taxes. Most counties are governed by an elected board of commissioners who serve from 2 to 4 years. The county system is also used in England, Scotland, Ireland, New Zealand, and Canada.

County agricultural extension agent, U.S. government official who advises farmers about agricultural issues. Agricultural extension agents help with farming, financial, and family problems. Agents are coordinated and governed by the Cooperative Educational System, administered jointly by federal, state, and local governments.

County extension home economist, U.S. government official who advises families about consumer education and nutrition.

Agents help with issues of improved diet, family relationships, health, and financial management. Extension home economists are coordinated and governed by the Cooperative Educational System, administered jointly by federal, state, and county governments.

Coup d'état (French, "stroke of state"), sudden and unlawful takeover of a government, usually the result of a country's unsteady and unbalanced politics. Notorious coups in the past include those effected by the Bolsheviks in Russia in 1917 and by the Communists in Czechoslovakia in 1948.

Couperin, François Le Grand (1668-1733), French composer, organist, and harpsichordist, of a family of musicians that included Louis Couperin (1626-61), his uncle. He acted as teacher to King Louis XIV's children, and often exhibited his skill on the harpsichord before the royal court at Versailles. His compositions include 27 suites for harpsichord that make up the *Pieces de clavecin*, as well as church and chamber works. Students of the harpsichord still employ his instruction manual, *L'art de toucher le clavecin.*

Courbet, Gustave (1819-77), 19th-century French painter, an early realist. *The Funeral at Ornans* and *The Stone Breakers* are 2 of his sympathetic depictions of ordinary life.

Coureurs de bois, French-Canadian adventurers, who in the late 1600s and early 1700s, traded furs with the Native Americans. Through their extensive trading contracts with the Native Americans they were able to assist the French in forming strong military pacts against the English in the French and Indian wars.

Courser, any of a genus (*Pluvianus*) of long-legged, short-winged, desert birds, particular to Australia, India, and Africa. They are primarily known for their quick running. The courser rarely flies unless it is bothered or disquieted, and even then, it is only for brief spaces. There are 9 different species, most of which share a distinctive brown and white marking.

Court, judicial portion of government, responsible for the administration of justice. The term also refers to the building in which courts sit and to the proceedings themselves. A typical U.S. court consists of 1 or more judges, a jury when required, attorneys for both parties to the dispute, a bailiff or marshal who carries out court orders and preserves order, and a clerk who records the proceedings.

As a formal institution with definite rules of procedure, the court emerged during the late Roman Empire. Christians, however, were not allowed to participate in courts "of this world," so bishops and ecclesiastical courts ruled on cases involving Christians and developed a body of canon law. After the Norman Conquest (1066), England pioneered in the development of a complex national court system, and the royal courts were soon administering justice to all the king's subjects. Justices of the peace acted as inferior (lower) courts to deal with minor offenses. These courts gradually established a system based not on the power of the king but upon the power of the law. In their decisions, the British courts were in effect creating law by setting judicial precedents that were followed by succeeding courts. As Parliament (originally established as a court to reach decisions in the name of the king) grew in power and the legal precedents set up in earlier courts expanded and became accepted, the courts judged cases according to their merits under this body of common law.

The United States has 2 distinct but related court systems. The state system, which includes county and city courts, hears actions between citizens of that state and cases involving violations of state and local laws. Although all criminal jury trials proceed on lines provided by the Constitution, the composition of municipal courts varies according to local custom. The states generally maintain a system of appellate courts to review lower-court decisions, as well as a state supreme court or its equivalent. The federal judicial hierarchy consists of a 9-member Supreme Court, intermediate courts of appeals, and a large number of district courts, as well as various special courts, such as the Tax Court, Court of Claims, and the Court of Customs and Patent Appeals. In general, the jurisdiction of federal courts is limited to cases arising under the Constitution, federal laws, and treaties; cases affecting ambassadors and consuls; disputes among states or between a state and citizens of another state; controversies to which the U.S. government is a party; maritime cases; and disputes with international aspects. The Supreme Court has original (as opposed to appellate) jurisdiction only in cases to which a state is a party or that involve ambassadors, public ministers, and consuls. For the other types of federal questions, it is only authorized to hear appeals. The Supreme Court's most significant decisions are rulings on such appeals, establishing precedents in constitutional law.

International disputes brought about a movement in the latter part of the 19th century to establish courts to rule on such issues. The First Hague Conference (1899) established the Permanent Court of Arbitration. The League of Nations included a Permanent Court of International Justice. At present, the International Court of Justice functions as an organ of the United Nations. These courts, however, have exercised only marginal influence on international law, for they do not have the power to compel nations and individuals to submit to their jurisdiction.

Court-martial, court for the trial of offenses against military rules and regulations. In the United States there are three types of court-martial: *summary* (which hears charges on minor offenses and can pass sentences of up to 1 month); *special* (which considers more serious offenses and can give sentences of up to 6 months); and *general* (which hears the most serious charges and can pass the death sentence). Courts-martial have no jury, and cases are decided by a simple majority of those on the court. There is an automatic review in all cases, and an appeal can be made to the Court of Military Appeals in serious cases.
See also: Uniform Code of Military Justice.

Court reporter, stenographer who records the proceedings in a court of law. Court reporters use shorthand or a stenography machine to note all testimony word for word (except what the judge or the attorneys deem "off the record"), and later converts it into a typewritten official transcript.

Cousteau, Jacques-Yves (1910-97), French oceanographer who pioneered underwater exploration. In 1943 he co-invented the scuba (self-contained underwater breathing apparatus); later he developed an underwater television system. His popular films and television programs made him world famous.

Cousy, Bob (Robert Joseph Cousy; 1928-), U.S. basketball player. Known for his dribbling and passing, he is considered one of the greatest playmakers of all time. As a guard for the Boston Celtics (1950-63) of the National Basketball Association (NBA), Cousy led the league in assists eight consecutive seasons (1952-60) and helped his team win the NBA championship 6 times. After leaving the Celtics, he coached both college and professional teams for 10 years. Cousy was inducted into the National Basketball Hall of Fame in 1970.

Covenanters, 16th- and 17th-century Scottish Presbyterians pledged by covenants to defend their religion against Anglican influences. They were suppressed both by Oliver Cromwell and by the Stuart kings. Their savage persecution after the Restoration was known as the "killing time."
See also: Presbyterianism.

Coventry (pop. 312,200), cathedral city in England, southeast of Birmingham. Coventry was formerly a small market town but is now an important center for the British automobile industry. It was founded in 1043, and by the 14th century was the fourth largest commercial town in England, famous for its wool and hides. In late 1940, Coventry was the first British town to suffer "saturation" bombing. After 1945 the city was rebuilt in modern style. New buildings include the Belgrade Theater (1958) and the very modern Cathedral of St. Michael (1962).
See also: England.

Covered wagon *See:* Conestoga wagon.

Covington (pop. 43,264), city in northern Kentucky, situated on the Ohio River across from Cincinnati, Ohio. The city was founded in 1815 and named after General Leonard Covington, a cavalry officer from Maryland who fought and died in the War of 1812. Covington is a major distribution

center for Kentucky's products, which include machinery, tobacco, lumber, canned goods, and X-ray and electrical equipment.
See also: Kentucky.

Coward, Sir Noel Pierce (1899-1973), English actor, playwright, and composer. He is famous for his witty comedies of manners, such as *Private Lives* (1930) and *Blithe Spirit* (1941), revues, musicals, and serious plays such as *The Vortex* (1924). Their prevailing cynicism is offset by patriotic works such as the film *In Which We Serve* (1942).

Cowbird, bird of the blackbird family (Icteridae), so named because it follows cattle and feeds on the insects they stir up. Two species live in the United States, but most are South American. Most lay eggs in the nests of other birds, which hatch and raise the cowbird young.

Cowbird

Cowboy, person who handles cattle on horseback. The U.S. cowboy has become a legendary folk hero, celebrated in innumerable films and novels. In the early 1800s in areas such as Texas (then part of Mexico), settlers took over the Spanish practice of using the plains for grazing cattle. At the same time they borrowed from the Spanish the typical equipment and methods of the cattle herder: broad-brimmed sombrero hat, bandanna worn around the neck, high-heeled boots that went with heavy "western" saddle and covered stirrups, leather chaps to protect the legs, and lariat with which to rope cattle. To this was added the "six-shooter" revolver. The cowboy was really created by the "long drive." As the frontier moved westward after the Civil War and the Plains Indians were driven off the open lands into reservations, large herds of cattle, tended by cowboys, were driven every year from the southern plains to the new railheads in the north-central plains. By the 1880s and 1890s the settlement of the central plains and their enclosure with barbed wire put an end to the long drive, but the cowboy continued to be employed in ranch work and even today is known for his riding and roping skills in rodeos.

Cowell, Henry Dixon (1897-1965), U.S. composer. Like John Cage, he sought to explore new sonorities in his music, as with "tone clusters," produced on the piano by striking groups of keys with the forearm.

Cowley, Abraham (1618-67), English poet and essayist of the metaphysical and neoclassical periods. His *Miscellanies* (1656) and *The Mistress* (1647) reflect the themes and motifs of the metaphysical poets. *Davideis* (1656), an unfinished epic in couplets, and the *Pindarique Odes* (1656) are neoclassical in their restraint, and his *Essays in Verse and Prose* (1668) reflect the influence of Montaigne's essays. Cowley sided with the Royalist cause during the English Civil War. Later he studied medicine at Oxford, and helped found the Royal Society, dedicated to the promotion of the physical sciences.
See also: Metaphysical poets.

Cow parsnip (*Heracleum maximum*), large perennial plant of the carrot family. Generally considered a weed, it can serve as a fodder. It thrives in damp soil. Cow parsnip can reach a height of 13 ft (4 m); it bears a white flowers that grow in clusters up to 20 in (50 cm) in diameter.

Cowpea, or black-eyed pea (*Vigna sinensis*), member of the pea family, cultivated widely in warmer climates for its edible beans. One variety is native to India and another, with very long pods, is native to China. In the United States, the cowpea is grown extensively in the South, where it is valued both for its beans and for the plant itself, which is used as manure and hay.

Cowper, William (1731-1800), 18th-century English poet. He wrote about nature and rural life in the English countryside. A strict Calvinist, he wrote the *Olney Hymns* (1779), which contained "Oh! for a Closer Walk with God" and "God Moves in a Mysterious Way." Other works of Cowper's include "The Diverting History of John Gilpin" (1782), *The Task* (1785), and "Yardley Oak" (1791).

Cowpox *See:* Jenner, Edward.

Cowrie, any of a variety of mollusks (family *Cyprocidae*) with shells that have spirals like those of snails but that are obscured by the final dome- shaped twist. Unlike other mollusk shells, these are covered by a layer of flesh and are shiny. Most cowries are found in warm seas. Their shells have been used as money and as ornaments since the earliest times.

Cowslip, or marsh marigold (*Caltha palustris*), marsh plant with large yellow flowers, related to the buttercup. Virginia cowslip, also found in wet places, has blue flowers and grows in the eastern United States. The original cowslip is a yellow-flowered primula of Europe and Asia.

Cox, James Middleton (1870-1957), U.S. politician and journalist who championed liberal reform. He became nationally known as a newspaper publisher, Democratic congressman (1903-13), and governor of Ohio (1913-15; 1917-21). In 1920 he ran for president on the Democratic ticket but lost heavily to Warren G. Harding.

Coyote, or prairie wolf (*Canis latrans*), wild dog of North America. It is well known for its characteristic howl. Once confined to the plains of western North America, the coyote has spread to the Atlantic coast. It feeds mainly on rabbits and small rodents but has become more of a scavenger. Coyotes sometimes interbreed with dogs.

Sir Noel Coward

Coysevox, Antoine (1640-1720), French sculptor. In 1679 he was commissioned by Louis XIV to work on the Palace of Versailles, where he carved the equestrian marble relief of the king, in addition to 2 ornate sculptures for the gardens— "Renown" and "Mercury." He also carved sculptures for the Cathedral of Notre Dame, as well as the tombs of finance minister Jean Baptiste Colbert and Cardinal Mazarin in Paris.

Cozzens, James Gould (1903-78), U.S. novelist. His books, such as *By Love Possessed* (1957) and *Ask Me Tomorrow* (1940), deal with moral conflicts of the professional classes, seen by Cozzens as the custodians of social stability. *Guard of Honor* (1948) won him a Pulitzer Prize.

CPR *See:* Cardiopulmonary resuscitation.

Crab, crustacean with 10 pairs of legs, the first pair usually modified as pincers. Crabs start life as small, swimming larvae that look more like lobsters. After molting several times the larva settles on the bottom and becomes an adult crab, with the typical rounded shell protecting the body. Most crabs are marine or live in brackish water, feeding on small animals and carrion that are torn up with the pincers. The smallest is the pea crab, which lives in the shells of bivalve mollusks. The giant crab of the Pacific is a spider crab with a shell measuring over 1 ft (.03 m) across; like all spider crabs, it has very long legs, the record being a 12-ft (4-m) span. Some crabs spend a considerable amount of time out of water. The fiddler crab, with one large, colored claw, lives in holes on mudflats. Robber crabs climb trees but, contrary to belief, do not appear to be able to open coconuts. Hermit crabs, which shelter in the disused shells of mollusks, are a separate group of crustaceans.

Crab apple (genus *Malus*, family Roseceae), tree that bears small tart-tasting apples, and has fragrant white or pink flowers. It grows in northern Asia and in North America, where the fruit is used for making pies, jellies, and condiments. The tree is usually about 20 ft (6 m) tall.

Craft *See:* Handicraft.

Craft union *See:* Labor movement.

Cramp, painful contraction of muscle—often in the legs. The cause is usually unknown. It may be brought on by exercise or lack of salt. It also occurs in muscles with inadequate blood supply.

Lucas Cranach's painting of a woman with her children

Cranach, Lucas, The Elder (1472-1553), German painter and engraver. As court painter to the electors of Saxony (1505-53), he lived and worked most of his life in Wittenberg. A supporter of the Reformation, he was a close friend of Martin Luther, for whom he did a number of woodcuts. Among his many portraits are those of *Luther* (1553) and *Henry the Pious of Saxony* (1514). Influenced by Albrecht Dürer, his mature style is characterized by highly finished and emotionally expressive figures set in a dreamy and luxuriant landscape.

Cranberry, berry-bearing shrub (genus *Oxycoccus*) found in wet bogs or heaths or in flooded areas known as cranberry bogs. The small cranberry grows in arctic and subarctic regions of Europe and America, while the large American cranberry is native to the northern United States and Canada. The red or bluish-black berries are edible, though somewhat acid in flavor, and are used in sauces, jellies, pies, preserves, and in making cranberry juice.

The dance of the crowned crane (Balearica pavonina), which lives in the steppes and savannahs of Africa. Numerous artists have been inspired by this dance, and the ritual dances of the local people show elements clearly derived from the cranes.

Crandall, Prudence (1803-90), U.S. educator. She opened a school for African-American girls in Canterbury, Conn., despite community opposition and state laws prohibiting it (1833). She was arrested, tried, and found guilty, but her conviction was overturned in 1834. Later that year an angry mob attacked the school, forcing her to close it.

Crane, long-necked, long-legged bird of the family Gruidae. Its plumage is generally white or gray; some species have patches of colored skin around the head. The windpipe is even longer than the neck because it is coiled up in the breast. This long windpipe is responsible for the crane's remarkable trumpeting calls. There are 14 species spread around the world, most of them now rare. Their courtship includes graceful dances in which the birds leap into the air and drift down on outstretched wings. The two cranes of North America are the sandhill crane, common in the prairies, and the whooping crane, which, in 1967, numbered only 48 birds in one flock. Although strictly protected, the whooping cranes have a long, vulnerable migration route from Canada to Texas.

Crane, machine designed to lift loads and move them horizontally. Despite their great variety, all cranes have certain features in common: a winding mechanism, or *winch*, to operate a rope (usually of steel wire), attached to a *pulley block* on which there is a *hook* to pick up the load. In some cranes the rope is looped over a pulley at the top of a boom or *jib*; in others it is suspended from a horizontal beam or girder.

Crane, Hart (Harold Crane; 1899-1932), U.S.poet. One of the earliest "modern" poets, Crane is best known for his long poem, "The Bridge" (1930). The poem was inspired by the Brooklyn Bridge as a symbol of the direction and aspirations of American life, much in the way that an earlier midwestern poet, Walt Whitman, saw America through the flat, plowed prairie in *Leaves of Grass*. It is a difficult, mystical, and heavily symbolic work that was to exert an important influence on later poets such as Ezra Pound and Wallace Stevens.

Crane, Stephen (1871-1900), U.S. author. He wrote one of the earliest of naturalist novels, *Maggie: A Girl of the Streets* (1893), the story of a prostitute driven to despair. Although Crane's short poems anticipated the modern style and he wrote some fine short stories, like "The Open Boat" (1898), he is best known for his fiction, and particularly for *The Red Badge of Courage* (1895), a sensitive study of a soldier during the Civil War that conveys the confusion and fear of battle and the vastness of the conflict. Crane himself had never seen war, but he went on to work as a journalist in New York and then actually became a war correspondent before dying of tuberculosis at the age of 28.

Crane, Walter (1845-1915), English artist and book illustrator. He is best known for illustrating popular nursery rhymes and fairy tales such as *Sing a Song of Sixpence* (1866), *Beauty and the Beast* (1874), *Little Red Riding Hood* (1875), and *Aladdin* (1875). Other children's works include *The Baby's Opera* (1877) and *The Baby's Bouquet* (1878). Crane also illustrated Edmund Spenser's *The Faerie Queene* (1895-97).

Cranmer, Thomas (1489-1556), first Protestant archbishop of Canterbury and English martyr. He was an outstanding scholar and one of the leaders of the English Reformation. He obtained the favor of Henry VIII by proposing to refer the question of the annulment of the king's marriage to Catherine of Aragon to the European universities rather than to the pope. He became the king's chaplain and in 1530 was sent on a mission to the pope to discuss the divorce. In 1533 he was appointed archbishop of Canterbury. In conformity with his belief in the ascendancy of the state over the church, he annulled Henry's marriages to Catherine (1533) and Anne Boleyn (1536). As counselor to Edward VI Cranmer became increasingly Protestant, and compiled the Book of Common Prayer (1549), his most enduring achievement, but suffered impeachment and imprisonment under the Catholic queen, Mary Tudor. After several recantations he stood by his beliefs and met death at the stake at Oxford with great courage.
See also: Book of Common Prayer.

Cranston, Alan Macgregor (1914-), U.S. senator. Elected to the Senate as a Democrat from California in 1969, Cranston has served as assistant majority leader (whip) and chairman of the Senate Veteran's Affairs Committee. In 1984 he made an unsuccessful bid for the Democratic presidential nomination. He was cited by the Senate Ethics Committee for improperly using his influence in behalf of a savings and loan association (1990).

Crappie, any of a genus (*Pomoxis*) of freshwater sunfishes that have been spread across the United States from the east because of their popularity with anglers. The black crappie prefers clear water, the white crappie turbid water.

Crassus, Marcus Licinius (112-53 B.C.), Roman general and political leader. He and Pompey crushed the slave revolt of Spartacus in 71 B.C. Eleven years later, Crassus, Pompey, and Julius Caesar formed the First Triumvirate, an alliance that governed Rome. In 53 B.C., Crassus went to war against the central Asian empire of Parthia and was killed in battle.
See also: Rome, Ancient.

Crater, depression on the surface of the earth or other celestial body. Craters are caused by volcanic activity or the impact of heavy objects from space (meteorites). Most craters on earth are volcanic. Craters are numerous on the moon, which lacks an atmosphere capable of burning out meteorites before they crash into the surface.

Crater Lake National Park, national park in the Cascade Mountains of southwest Oregon. The major feature is the crater lake, which is volcanic and covers 20 sq mi (52 sq km), reaching a depth of 1,932 ft (589 m).
See also: National Parks.

Crawfish *See:* Crayfish.

Crawford, Joan (1908-77), U.S. film actress noted for her roles as self-made, tough-minded women. Her best-known movies were *Rain* (1932), *A Woman's Face* (1941), and *Mildred Pierce* (1945), for which she won an Academy Award.

Crayfish, or crawfish, edible freshwater crustacean found in ponds and streams in most parts of the world except Africa.

Crazy Horse (c.1849-77), Native American leader, chief of the Oglala Sioux. He spent his life defending his tribe's territory in South Dakota and Wyoming. In 1876, he allied with Sitting Bull and annihilated General George Custer's cavalry at the Little Bighorn River, but a year later he was starved into surrender. He was stabbed to death while attempting to escape.

Creationism, also known as Creation Science, theory held by fundamentalist Christians that the Earth and living things were created as described in Genesis rather than through a process of evolution. Creationists have survived numerous setbacks, including the Scopes trial in 1925, the push in the 1960s to improve science education, and a 1980 Arkansas court decision declaring teaching of creationism to be unconstitutional because it is religious.

Crécy, Battle of, key battle in the Hundred Years War between England and France, fought in 1346. The English army under King Edward III was heavily outnumbered by a French force under King Philip VI at the village of Crécy in Normandy. After suffering serious losses from English archery attacks, the French retreated. The battle made an English national hero of the king's son, Edward, the "Black Prince."
See also: Hundred Years War.

Credit, delivery of goods, services, or money with a promise of payment in the future, usually with an interest charge.

Crédit Mobilier of America, construction company instrumental in building the Union Pacific railroad in the 1860s. It became the subject of a financial scandal in 1872, when the founder, Congressman Oakes Ames, awarded himself and other shareholders contracts that produced profits of up to $23 million.

Credit Union, cooperative bank formed by the members of a company, church, labor union, or other organization. Members buy shares with their savings and may borrow money at low interest rates. Any profits are distributed to members periodically in the form of dividends. Credit unions, like other banks, are closely supervised by the government.

Cree, Native American tribe originating in Manitoba. One group of Cree later moved southwest, becoming Plains Cree. Another, the Woodlands Cree, remained in Canada, where they had a deer-based (as opposed to bison-based) culture. Both Cree tribes were ravaged by serious epidemics during the 18th and 19th centuries. The survivors now live on reservations in Canada.

Creek, Native American confederation of tribes and settlements in Alabama and Georgia. The Creek had a stable, agricultural society centered on rivers and creeks. In 1813-14 they lost most of their land in a war led by U.S. general Andrew Jackson. By 1840 the entire tribe had been transported to Oklahoma, where most of their descendants now live.

Creeley, Robert (1926-), U.S. poet and author. Along with Robert Duncan and Charles Olson, Creeley was one of the leading Black Mountain poets. While teaching at Black Mountain College in North Carolina, he was the editor of the *Black Mountain Review*, a literary magazine that pioneered modern forms of poetry and short prose. Creeley's best-known works are compiled in *Collected Poems: 1945-1975* (1983) and *The Collected Prose of Robert Creeley* (1984).

Creeper, any of several small brown birds of the treecreeper family, found in most parts of the world. Creepers use their pointed bills to probe for insects in bark. They get their name from their "creeping" up a tree in a quick, hopping movement.

Creole, term used to describe the descendants of Spanish, Portuguese, and French settlers in the West Indies, Latin America, and parts of the United States. French- and Spanish-based patois are known as Creole languages.

Creosote, thick, oily liquid made by distilling coal or wood tar. Almost colorless, it has a powerful, smoky smell and can be used to protect wood from rot, insects, and marine organisms.
See also: Tar.

Creosote bush (*Larrea divaricata*), evergreen shrub that grows in the deserts of Mexico and southwestern United States. Growing to a height of 5-8 ft (1.5-2.5 m), the creosote bush produces a resin and tiny yellow flowers. Its berries are round and white and have a feltlike texture. Creosote bushes often grow in circles, and botanists believe that some of these colonies are thousands of years old.

Cresol, or hydroxytoluene, group of organic chemical compounds. Cresols are a major component of creosote oil, which is applied as a preservative to railroad ties, fence posts, and other wooden outdoor structures. Obtained from coal tar or a petroleum base, cresols are also used in antiseptic soaps and disinfectants.

Cress, any of various plants of the mustard family. They include watercress, bitter cress, rock cress, and penny cress.

Cretaceous period, geological period from about 140 to 65 million years ago. It is one of the 3 periods of the mesozoic era, the age of reptiles. The separation of Africa and South America occurred during the Cretaceous period, as did the disappearance of the dinosaurs and emergence of snakes and lizards.

Crete, mountainous island in the eastern Mediterranean Sea, about 3,235 sq mi (8,380 sq km). Part of Greece, Crete relies on agriculture and tourism. The island was the home of the ancient Minoan civilization (c.1600 B.C.), with its capital of Cnossus.
See also: Greece.

The village of Sfakion on the southeastern coast of Crete. In the background are the Lefka Mountains.

Cretinism, type of dwarfism characterized by mental retardation. It is caused by a failure of thyroid gland function during fetal development.
See also: Thyroid gland.

Creutzfeldt-Jakob disease, rare, degenerative disease of the nervous system caused by a slow virus that may incubate in the body for months or years before symptoms appear. The disease generally afflicts individuals during middle age. Earliest symptoms are memory loss or peculiar behavior, followed by visual disturbances and loss of muscular coordination. Death usually occurs within a year. There is no treatment or cure for this disease. Creutzfeldt-Jakob disease was first described in separate accounts in the early 1920s by 2 German neuropsychiatrists, Hans G. Creutzfeldt and Alfons M. Jakob.

Crèvecoeur, Michel-Guillaume Jean de (1735-1813), 18th-century French essayist. He chronicled rural life in early America under the pen name J. Hector St. John. The 12 essays that make up his *Letters from an American Farmer* (1782) were influential in persuading many Europeans to settle in America. He sided with the British during the American Revolution, and his *Sketches of Eighteenth Century America* (published posthumously in 1925) was critical of the rebellious colonists. He was French consul to the United States 1783-90.

Crewel, type of woolen yarn as well as a form of embroidery crafted from the yarn. The yarn consists of twin threads twisted together. Most crewelwork is done from patterns stitched on a plain cloth background. As an art form, crewel dates back to the ancient Hebrews and was popular during the Middle Ages.

Cribbage, card game played with standard deck of cards and a special board with pegs for marking the score.

Crib death *See:* Sudden infant death syndrome.

Crick, Francis Harry Compton (1916-), English biologist who shared the 1962 Nobel Prize in physiology or medicine with Maurice Wilkins and James Watson, for establishing the function and structure of DNA, the key substance in transmitting hereditary traits.
See also: Biology; Deoxyribonucleic acid.

Cricket, bat and ball game played extensively in Great Britain and the Commonwealth countries. The opposing teams have 11 players on a side. The rules are complex, and a match may take 3 days to complete.

Cricket, chirping, hopping insect of the Gryllidae family. Its familiar song is produced by the male, rubbing special parts of its front wings together.

Crime, violation of rules of behavior as laid down in a code of law. *Violent crimes* are directed against people; they include murder, assault, rape, and robbery. *Property crimes* include burglary, theft, and other violations of ownership laws.

Crimea, peninsula, 10,425 sq mi (25,900 sq km), on the northern side of the Black Sea, part of the Ukrainian Republic, USSR. Its population today is about 70% Russian and 20% Ukrainian. It was the scene of the Crimean War (1853-56) and was also a battleground during World War I and World War II.
See also: Union of Soviet Socialist Republics.

Crimean War, (1853-56), war between Russia and an alliance of England, France, Turkey, and Sardinia. A chief cause was conflict over Russia's attempt to gain access to Mediterranean warm-water ports. The war ended when the city of Sevastopol, headquarters of the Russian fleet, was captured after a long, destructive siege.

Crime laboratory, law enforcement investigative facility that examines evidence gathered at a crime scene for clues. Numbering about 250 in the United States today, crime labs utilize state-of-the-art technological and scientific methods of analyzing evidence. Forensic pathologists use crime labs to conduct autopsies on the bodies of crime victims, and ballistics experts use them to draw conclusions on weapons used in crimes. Crime labs are also used to isolate fingerprints, determine causes of suspicious fires, and test for substance abuse.

Criminal law, that part of the law that defines criminal offenses, establishes procedures for trying accused persons, and fixes penalties for those convicted of criminal offenses. Many offenses once punished as crimes now come under the civil law. These offenses, which usually grow out of carelessness or accidents, are called *torts.* The penalty is likely to be the payment of damages to the party that has been injured. Generally, crimes are willful acts considered dangerous to society. The modern criminal law of England, the United States, and Canada originated in the English common law of crimes, which grew over hundreds of years from judicial decisions applied throughout the realm and therefore "common." Legislation has supplemented these decisions, particularly in the past two centuries, when types of crime such as embezzlement that were almost unknown to the common law began to occur with frequency. When it achieved independence, the United States incorporated English common law into its legal systems but made it subject to the state and federal constitutions. Many states repealed the common law of crimes. In other states, offenders can be charged under both common law and statutory law.
The common law system has established some general principles of criminal law. One of these is that nothing can be treated as a crime unless there is a law against the conduct in question (in Latin, *nulla crimen sine lege*). A corollary of this is that no punishment can be imposed unless it is provided for by law (*nulla poena sine lege*). Another essential principle is that the crime must be accompanied by *mens rea*, a guilty mind. The criminal had to know what he or she was doing wrong. This principle has led to the difficult question of responsibility for criminal acts. Persons suffering from mental instability or disorder are not responsible for acts that, committed by others, would be crimes. But the legal criterion of mental responsibility, or competence, has long been a matter of controversy. In general, the British and U.S. courts have followed the so-called McNaghten (M'Naghten) Rule: Insanity is a valid defense if the accused was, at the time of the action, suffering from mental disease such that he or she did not know the nature of the act that he or she was committing, or did not know that it was wrong. Other grounds for diminished criminal responsibility include extreme youth and intoxication. There are also complicated questions of procedure involving arrests, confessions, searches, the right to have a lawyer, the right to confront witnesses, the right not to incriminate oneself, and other means of protecting the individual. Criminal law is not only a means of punishing wrongdoers; it is also a method of dealing with conflict, and as such reflects the weaknesses as well as the ideals of a society.
See also: Crime.

Criminology, scientific study of the causes of criminal behavior, its development, and its treatment. Belgian statistician Adolphe Quételet (1796-1874) introduced the correlation of crime and social or environmental conditions, and Italian scholars continued what was known as the positivist study of crime in the late 19th and early 20th centuries. Cesare Lombroso (1836-1909) advanced a now-discredited theory representing criminals as reversions to a more primitive stage of human development. His work was followed by that of Enrico Ferri (1856-1929) and Raffaele Garofalo, both of whom stressed social factors.

Critical mass, minimum mass of material necessary to maintain a spontaneous fission chain reaction. For pure U^{235} it is computed to be about 20 lb (9.1 kg).

Criticism, act of analyzing and evaluating any object or activity, often unfavorably. The term is applied most often to the examination and evaluation of works of art and literature. Critical writings may take the form of prose verse, essays, reviews, or long books. In philosophy, criticism may be defined as an approach to problems in which the thinker weighs the evidence in the manner of a judge. The term *critical philosophy* is used to describe the theories of Immanuel Kant, whose *critiques* offer critical examinations of various ideas.

Crittenden Compromise, proposal sponsored by moderate Southern unionists in 1860 to avert the U.S. Civil War. Senator John Crittenden of Kentucky submitted the package that proposed prohibition of slavery north of lat. 36°30′N and protection of it south of that line; a modified slave act; an end to the slave trade; and confirmation of the existing balance of free and slave states. Most of the measures were defeated.
See also: Civil War, U.S.

Croaker, any of a family (Sciaenidae) of medium-sized fish found in shallow tropical and temperate seas. They are renowned for their calls, a drumming, croaking chorus produced by special muscles that make the swim bladder vibrate.

Croatia, independent country on the east coast of the Adriatic Sea, bordered by Slovenia, Hungary, Federal Republic of Yugoslavia, and Bosnia. Croatia has a diverse landscape, with flat plains, low mountains, a coastline, and several offshore islands. The eastern plain is fertile, and crops like sugar beets, maize, and wheat are produced there. Croatia is a major supplier of coal, petroleum, bauxite, and timber, and industry is reasonably developed. The majority of the population is Croatian, a Slavic people who speak a Serbo-Croatian language. Serbs form an important minority. Roman Catholicism is the predominant religion. United with Hungary in 1102, ruled by the Turks (16th-18th centuries) and then by the Habsburgs (until 1918), Croatia became part of Yugoslavia after World War I. In World War II the Germans ruled it as an Axis satellite. In 1946 Yugoslavia adopted a federal constitution, and Croatia became one of its 6 constituent republics. Beginning in the 1970s, Croatia agitated for greater autonomy; however, by the end of the 1980s demands for autonomy changed to demands for independence, which was attained in 1991. The Serbian minority opposed the independence, and a civil war followed. Despite several cease-fires and the presence of UN-troops, the war in Croatia and neighbouring states continued, disrupting social, political, and economic life in Croatia.

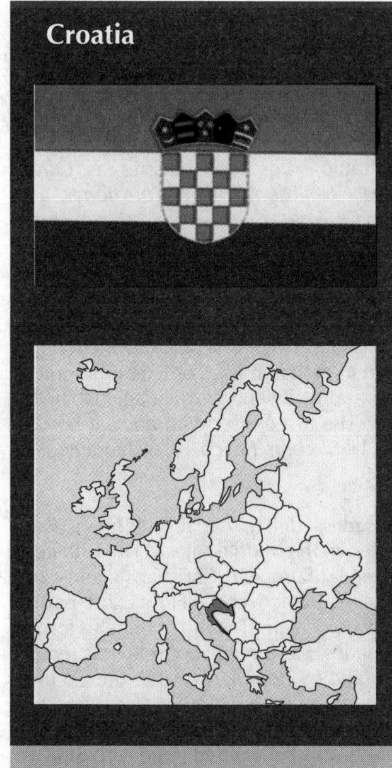

Capital:	Zagreb
Area:	21,829 sq mi (56,538 sq km)
Population:	4,789,000
Government:	republic
Independent:	1991
GNP per capita:	U.S. $1,900

Croce, Benedetto (1866-1952), Italian philosopher and writer. A leading exponent of the modern Idealist school, Croce was the founder and editor of *La Critica*, a scholarly journal devoted to literature, history, and philosophy. Between 1902 and 1917, he produced his best-known work, *Philosophy of the Spirit*. Espousing liberal and intellectual causes, he opposed Mussolini and his Fascist government.

Crochet (from French *croche*, "hook"), method of making fabrics, garments, lace, and even rugs, from threads or yarn, using a hook (made of steel, ivory, bone, or wood). The crochet stitch links each loop of thread to another to produce a foundation *chain*, into which additional rows of stitches are added. Single and double crochet are the basic forms from which all other stitches and patterns have developed.

Crockett, Davy (David Crockett; 1786-1836), U.S. frontiersman, representative from Tennessee (1827-31, 1833-35), and folk hero. Known for his amusing stories and sharpshooting, Crockett failed in his final bid for reelection in 1835, joined the Texan forces in the war of independence from Mexico, and died in the defense of the Alamo.
See also: Alamo.

Crocodile, carnivorous reptile (order Crocodilia) found in both fresh and salt water in tropical and subtropical regions. Crocodiles range in size from 3 ft 9 in (1.14 m; the dwarf crocodile), to 8 ft (2.4 m; the Nile), to 12 ft (3.7 m; the American), to 20 ft (6.1 m; the Orinoco), and are distinguished from the alligator by a narrower snout, greater aggressiveness, and a long protruding fourth tooth.

Crocodile bird (*Pluvianus aegyptius*), African plover that enters the mouth of a crocodile to feed on leeches and scraps of food. The crocodiles, which normally prey on birds, tolerate this behavior.

Crocus, genus of perennial herb of the iris family, originally from Asia and the Mediterranean, usually bearing a solitary blue, yellow, or white flower. The yellow dye, saffron, is produced from the dried flowers of one species. The wild crocus is a member of the buttercup family.

Croesus (d. c.547 B.C.), last king of Lydia (r.560-546 B.C.), and last of the Mermnadae dynasty. Known for his wealth and generosity, he ruled a large part of Asia Minor until he was overthrown by Cyrus the Great of Persia. Legend suggests he became an honored courtier of Cyrus.
See also: Lydia.

Cro-Magnon, race of primitive humans (*Homo sapiens*), indistinguishable biologically from modern human beings. Remains dating from the upper Paleolithic era (40,000-35,000 years ago) were first found in southern France. Cro-Magnon people, like the Neanderthals who preceded them, had high foreheads, developed chins and large brains, and stood erect (males about 6 ft/180 cm). Their advanced culture produced ivory jewelry, bone and flint tools, and sophisticated cave art (especially rock carvings and paintings).

Crompton, Samuel (1753-1827), English inventor. He devised a weaving machine that produced superior cotton fibers for commercial use. By combining the best features of the 2 existing weaving machines, Crompton created the "mule" in 1779. By the early 1800s, more than 4.5 million mules were in use in England, making it the world's leading textile producer of that time.

Cromwell, Oliver (1599-1658), lord protector of England. As a Puritan and member of Parliament (from 1628) Cromwell joined the Puritan opposition to Charles I. During the first civil war he showed a remarkable ability for military strategy and leadership, and organized the Parliamentary forces in the eastern counties. His famous Ironsides regiment (cavalry) was instrumental in the victory of Marston Moor (1644), and in 1645, under Fairfax, he led the New Model Army to rout Charles's forces at Naseby. In the second part of the civil war, after Charles's flight, Cromwell defeated the Scottish royalists at Preston (1648). His political power was increased by the eviction of the Presbyterians from Parliament (Pride's Purge, 1648), and he was highly influential in bringing Charles I to trial and execution. Following the establishment of the Commonwealth, he ruthlessly punished Ireland (1649), routed the Royalist Scots at Dunbar (1650), and quelched the forces of Charles II at Worcester (1651). He replaced the Rump Parliament with the short-lived Barebones Parliament, but this too accomplished very little. Finally, the army officers drew up the instrument of government that made Cromwell lord protector (1653). Although he ruled largely without Parliament, he refused the crown when it was offered (1657). His peace with the Dutch (1654) and treaties with Sweden and Denmark fostered trade, necessary to prevent the return of the Stuarts to power. Although he dreamed of a great Protestant League in Europe, he pragmatically formed an alliance with Catholic France against Spain (1655-59), which he fought over trade rights. The Protectorate did not long survive his death.
See also: Puritans.

Cromwell, Richard (1626-1712), son of Oliver Cromwell. He served as lord protector of England (1658-59) until he was deposed by military coup. He lived in France as John Clarke for the next 20 years, and then in England, still under an assumed name.

Cromwell, Thomas, Earl of Essex (1485?-1540), English statesman under Henry VIII.

A ruthless administrator and the main agent for destroying papal power in England, he supervised the king's break with Rome under the Act of Supremacy (1534) and the dissolution of the monasteries (1536-39), many of whose properties he was eventually rewarded. He arranged the king's marriage with Anne of Cleves, and on its failure was executed without trial on charges of heresy and treason trumped up by his many enemies. He died in the Catholic faith.

Bing Crosby

Cronin, A.J. (1896-1981), British novelist. After quitting the practice of medicine because of ill health, he began to write novels, many of which were turned into films, including *Hatter's Castle* (1931), *The Citadel* (1937), and *The Keys of the Kingdom* (1941). Cronin also wrote an autobiography based on his years of medical practice, entitled *Adventures in Two Worlds* (1952).

Cronkite, Walter Leland, Jr. (1916-), U.S. broadcast journalist. He was anchorperson for the Columbia Broadcasting System (CBS) nightly evening television news (1962-81).

Cronus, in Greek mythology, king of the Titans and ruler of earth. He deposed his father, Uranus, with the help of his mother, Gaea. Cronus married his sister, Rhea, and their children were Zeus, Poseidon, Demeter, Hera, Hades, and Hestia. He was overthrown by Zeus, who succeeded him as king of the gods. Cronus's Roman counterpart was Saturn.
See also: Mythology.

Crookes, Sir William (1832-1919), British scientist and inventor. He is credited with the discovery of the element thallium and experimented with an electronic vacuum tube. The Crookes tube, developed in the 1870s, was the forerunner of the modern cathode ray picture tube used in television sets. He also founded and edited *Chemical News* (1859), a scientific journal.
See also: Thallium.

Crookes tube, tube developed by English scientist Sir William Crookes to demonstrate the properties of cathode rays. A current, passed between metal electrodes in the tube, produces a glowing discharge, which disappears as the pressure is lowered. Cathode rays (beams of electrons) are then produced, striking the walls of the tube and causing it to glow. Experimenting with such a tube, Wilhelm Roentgen discovered X-rays.
See also: Cathode ray; Crookes, Sir William.

Cropping system, any of a number of methods of replenishing soil after crops have been harvested. This can be done with fertilizers or insecticides or by rotation, a system of planting crops that replenish nutrients in the soil the previous crop removed. Chemical analysis of the soil often determines which crops might best replace lost nutrients.

Croquet, lawn game of French origin (17th century) in which players hit wooden balls with wooden mallets through a series of iron hoops (wickets) stuck in the ground. To win, a player must hit the posts at both ends of the field. Croquet is popular in the United States and Britain.

Crosby, Bing (Harry Lillis Crosby; 1904-77), U.S. singer and film actor. A big-band singer known for crooning, he performed on radio, records (his rendition of "White Christmas" is an all-time bestseller), and in films, including the *Road* series with Bob Hope and Dorothy Lamour. He won an Academy Award for his performance in *Going My Way* (1944).

Cross, cultural symbol, often consisting of an upright and a crosspiece. The cross appeared in cultures of Egypt, ancient India, and North America. Used by ancient Romans for execution by crucifixion, it became the principal symbol of the Christian religion. There are 4 basic forms of the Christian cross: the Latin cross, the most common, in which the upright is longer than the transom that crosses it near the top; the Greek cross, an upright crossed at right angles at its center by a beam of the same length; the tau, or St. Anthony's cross, in the form of a T; and St. Andrew's cross in the form of an X. The other forms, such as the papal cross, an upright crossed by 3 bars, are mainly inventions for ecclesiastical or hierarchical purposes.

Crossbill, finch (genus *Loxia*) whose mandibles are so strongly curved that they cross each other. This specialized bill is used for splitting open seeds from the cones of pines and other conifers. Crossbills are found in the Northern Hemisphere.

Crossbow, medieval weapon consisting of a small, powerful bow fixed transversely on a stock, which is grooved to take the missile. Its bowstring is latched onto a trigger mechanism, often by a lever or winch, and fires a shaft (a bolt or quarrel, about 19 in/48 cm long). It has less range and accuracy than the longbow and is slower to load.

Cross-country, long-distance running sport. Cross-country is not confined to a track, but instead uses a mapped-out course over a variety of terrains. High school and collegiate courses may range from 1.5 to 7 mi (2.4 to 11 km), and teams generally consist of 6 to 9 members. Points are assigned to the place runners finish in the race, and the team with the lowest point total is the winner.

Cross-eye *See:* Strabismus.

Croton, shrub (genus *Codiaeum*) of the spurge family. Native to Southeast Asia, it is often used in parks in warm U.S. cities, and its multicolored leaves make it an attractive potted plant. One species, the purging croton, is a source of croton oil, a useful resin.

Croup, condition, common in children 6 mos. to 3 years old, due to allergy or virus infection of the larynx and trachea, causing difficulty in breathing and a hoarse cough due to spasm of the larynx.
See also: Diphtheria.

Crow, glossy black bird (family Corvidae), one of the most intelligent of birds, related to ravens, magpies, and jays. The crow has a harsh, croaking call and can imitate sounds, even the human voice. The American, or common, crow (19 in/49 cm long) feeds and nests in small colonies, killing small animals and grubbing for insects in the soil. It thus destroys farm pests, but is itself a pest, eating grain crops.

Crow, Native American tribe of the Siouan linguistic group, from the North American plains of Montana and Wyoming. Originally they broke away from the Hidatsa tribe into 2 groups, the Mountain Crow and the River Crow. They hunted bison, cultivated tobacco, and had a highly developed social system. Most Crows now live in southern Montana, supported by income from mineral leases, ranching, and tourism.

Crowfoot (1830-90), Canadian Blackfoot chief who discouraged tribal warfare and advocated peace. Though known for his bravery, Crowfoot refused to join the Northwest Rebellion against the Canadian government in 1885.

Crude oil *See:* Petroleum.

Cruikshank, George (1792-1878), English artist and illustrator famous for his caricatures. Among his best-known works were illustrations for such classics as *Oliver Twist, Robinson Crusoe, Tom Jones,* and *Don Quixote.*

Cruiser, warship designed for speed and long-range attack, in size between the destroyer and aircraft carrier. Used as a small battleship in World War II, its function has been to maintain lines of sea communication and to defend carriers against air attack. The first cruiser with nuclear power, the USS *Long Beach*, was launched in 1959.

Crusades, under papal authority, wars waged in the Middle Ages (11th-13th centuries) by European Christians against the Muslims to recover the Holy Land, particularly Jerusalem. The initial impetus for the Crusades was a revival of religious fervor, as urged by Pope Urban II at the Council of Clermont (1095); however, conquest of territory, the attraction of riches, and the possibility of expanded trade with the East were also vital elements. At the end of the **First Crusade** (1095-99) Jerusalem was retaken and the Latin kingdom of Jerusalem was established, as were the orders of the Knights Templars and the Knights Hospitalers. The **Second Crusade** (1147-49), a response to the loss of Edessa (1144) to the Turks, ended in failure. The **Third Crusade** was an attempt to recapture Jerusalem, lost to Saladin in 1187. Holy Roman Emperor Frederick I, Richard I of England, and Philip II of France led this crusade, but were only able to achieve a 3-year truce that gave Christians access to the holy city. During the **Fourth Crusade** (1202-4) the Crusaders seized Constantinople. In 1212 the tragic **Children's Crusade** was waged. Thousands of children died of hunger or disease or were sold into slavery as they headed toward the Holy Land. The goal of the **Fifth Crusade**, another failure, was Egypt. There was a **Sixth Crusade** (1228-29) in which another short-lived truce was arranged with the Muslims, and then 3 additional crusades, but Muslim gains held steady. The last Christian stronghold, Akko (Acre), fell in 1291.

The Seventh Crusade (1248-54), organized by Louis the Pious of France

Crustacean, invertebrate animal (phylum Arthropoda) with a bilaterally symmetrical segmented body, including crabs, shrimps, lobsters, and barnacles. A few live on land and are parasitic, but most are aquatic, breathing by gills or through the skin, their heads covered with a protective shell and bearing paired series of antennae, 3 paired sets of biting mouth parts, and 2 lateral eyes (plus 1 medial). Periodically they shed their exoskeleton (external skeleton).

Cryobiology, the study of the effects of extremely low temperatures on living organisms, generally for the purpose of preserving living material for future use. Cryobiologists use liquid nitrogen to achieve temperatures far below normal freezing temperature, allowing cells to cease working but to remain alive and unchanged for long periods; once thawed, the cells resume their normal work almost instantly. Frozen tissues, including skin, eye corneas, and blood, are stored in banks, allowing ready access to physicians in need of performing a skin graft, for example.

Cryogenics, or low-temperature physics, science that studies the production, maintenance, and effects of very low temperatures. A substance's temperature can be lowered by cooling with liquefied gases, removing energy from it, or successively magnetizing and demagnetizing it. The study of superconductivity and superfluidity, conditions which prevail at very low temperatures, are part of cryogenics.
See also: Absolute Zero; Cryobiology.

Cryotron, miniature switch used in computers, consisting of a short wire around which is wound a fine control coil, kept at the temperature of liquid helium so that the wire and coil are superconducting. A signal in the coil produces a magnetic field that causes the wire to lose its superconductivity and become resistant to electric current. This action stores or produces a "bit" of information. Cryotron computers may contain 100 billion components to the cubic inch, and can obtain a required bit of information from a store of 300,000 in less than a 10-millionth of a second.
See also: Superconductivity.

Crystal, solid substance in which the individual molecules, atoms, or ions are arranged in a geometrical form. Almost all pure substances (chemical elements, compounds, mixtures) can form solid crystals. Substances that do not crystallize are called amorphous. Crystals may be formed from solutions, as salt crystals form when a pool of sea water evaporates in the sun; when liquids solidify, as when water freezes to ice or when molten rocks have solidified and have formed crystals; or when vapors solidify (iodine crystals can easily be made by heating some solid iodine in a closed container). Crystals form into definite shapes because the atoms in the substance always arrange themselves in a specific array called a *lattice*. The lattice consists of rows of atoms at various angles. The shapes of the crystals depend on the angles of the rows. The kind of lattice a crystal possesses can be found by passing X rays through the crystal. The lattice affects the X rays so that they emerge from the crystal with a pattern that can be recorded on photographic film, indicating the kind of crystal being studied. The study of crystals is called crystallography. Since crystals often form with corners missing from the basic shape, crystal systems are best described in terms of their axes, rather than their faces. The axes are imaginary lines across the crystals that join opposite faces. Cubic crystals have 3 equal axes at right angles. Salt and alum are cubic crystals, but whereas a salt crystal looks like a cube, an alum crystal has corners missing and is an 8-sided pyramid, or octahedron. Cubic crystals are also called isometric crystals. Tetragonal crystals also have 3 axes at right angles, but 1 axis is longer than the other 2, so the side faces are rectangular. Tin forms tetragonal crystals. In orthorhombic crystals, the 3 axes are at right angles but of different lengths. Sulfur forms orthorhombic crystals. Monoclinic crystals have 3 unequal axes, only 2 of which meet at right angles. Gypsum forms monoclinic crystals. Triclinic crystals have 3 unequal axes that do not meet at right angles. Copper sulfate forms triclinic crystals. Hexagonal crystals have 4 axes, 3 in one plane, equal in length and at 60° to each other, the fourth longer or shorter and at right angles to the others. Beryl forms hexagonal crystals. Trigonal crystals also have 4 axes, but only 3 basic side faces instead of 6. Quartz is a trigonal crystal. Several electrical effects occur in crystals. Piezoelectric crystals produce an electric signal when they are twisted out of shape and return to their original shape. Rochelle salt crystals can produce electric signals with the frequency range of sound waves and so are used in phonograph pickups, microphones, and hearing aids. Quartz crystals produce signals at only one frequency and so can be used in oscillators, electronic filters, and radio tuners. The electronic properties of a transistor depend on the arrangement of atoms in the lattice of the crystal. The crystals have to be very pure and are made with extreme care by a crystallization process called zone refining. Crystals also have interesting optical properties. Certain types can be used, for example, to produce polarized light.

Ctenophore, or comb jelly, marine invertebrate (phylum Ctenophora) having 8 radially arranged combs of ciliated plates (ctenes) on its body used for swimming. Ctenophores are bioluminescent, carnivorous, usually transparent, and resemble jellyfish.

Cuauhtémoc (c.1495-1525), last Aztec emperor of Mexico, nephew and son-in-law of Montezuma. Cuauhtémoc defended the Aztec capital, Tenochtitlán, in a 4-month siege led by the Spanish conqueror Hernando Cortez. The subsequent capture of the city, in 1521, led to its destruction and massive Aztec casualties. Cuauhtémoc was captured and tortured to get him to reveal the location of supposed Aztec treasure. He refused to speak, and several years later he was hanged on the order of Cortez. Many modern Mexicans honor Cuauhtémoc as a national hero.

Cuba

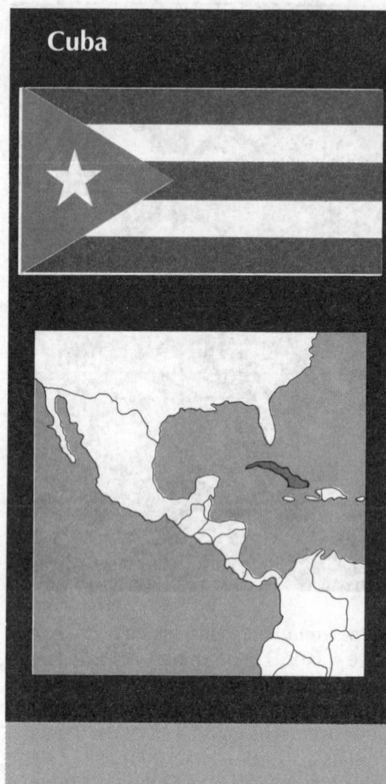

General information	
Capital:	Havana
Area:	42,804 sq mi (110,860 sq km)
Population:	10,540,000
Official language:	Spanish
Monetary unit:	1 Cuban peso = 100 centavos
Main cities:	Havana, Santiago de Cuba, Camagüey
Government	
Form:	socialist republic
Independent:	1902
Head of state:	President (elected every 5 years)
Head of government:	President
Legislature:	one legislative house (National Assembly of People's Power)
Executive:	President and Council of Ministers
Judiciary:	highest court is the People's Supreme Court
Political division:	14 provinces, 169 municipal assemblies
National economy	
Gross national product:	US $26,920,000,000
Per capita income:	US $2,690
Agriculture:	sugar cane, rice, oranges, potatoes, tomatoes, grapefruit
Livestock:	poultry, cattle, pigs
Mining:	nickel, cobalt, chromite, copper, gold
Industries:	processed food, refined sugar, nonelectrical machinery, fuels, beverages and tobacco products
Main exports:	sugar and sugar products, minerals and concentrates, agricultural products
Transportation:	3,140 mi (5,053 km) of railroads; 21,100 mi (34,000 km) of roads; 4 international airports
Trading partners:	U.S.S.R., Germany, Bulgaria, Czechoslovakia, Romania
People	
Urban:	72%
Ethnic composition:	European 66%, mulatto 22%, African 12%
Birth rate:	17.9 per 1,000 population
Death rate:	6.5 per 1,000 population
Infant mortality rate:	12 per 1,000 live births
Life expectancy:	male 73 years, female 76 years

Plaza Vieja, Havana

Cuba, Republic of, tropical island republic in the Caribbean Sea, west of Haiti, east of the Gulf of Mexico, north of Jamaica, and 90 mi (145 km) south of Key West, Fla. Cuba is the largest island in the West Indies, occupying 44,218 sq mi (114,525 sq km), including the Isle of Pines and other offshore islands. The capital is Havana.

Land and climate. Cuba has 3 main mountain ranges: the Sierra de los Organos in the west, the Sierra de Trinidad in the center, and the Sierra Maestra in the southeast. Cuba's upland areas generally go from east to west, cover only about 25% of the island, and are so spaced as to break up its surface into a series of clay and limestone plains, separated by gently rolling slopes. Over half of Cuba is flat or slightly undulating. Because Cuba is narrow, it has few big rivers; the longest is the 155-mi (249-km) Cauto, which rises in the Sierra Maestra and flows west across the lowlands of Oriente Province. It has deep bays on the coast that serve as fine natural harbors. Lying just south of the Tropic of Cancer, Cuba has a warm climate with temperatures between 71° and 82° F (22° and 28° C), though frosts occur in winter on some mountains. Rainfall is generally plentiful, and Cuba is prone to severe hurricanes. Forests of pine, cedar, oak, ebony, and mahogany still clothe much of the mountains, though only scattered royal palms and silk-cotton trees remain in the lowlands, now largely cleared for farming. Grasses and shrubs grow in sub-soil savanna areas, covering about a quarter of the island, and mangrove forests fringe some of the coast.

People. Around three-quarters of the population is of European, chiefly Spanish, descent. About one-seventh of the population is mulatto, and one-eighth black, a legacy of the West African slave trade. The aboriginal Native Americans are extinct. The distinction between blacks and Cubans of European extraction remains a divisive force in society despite the government's proclaimed policy of equality of opportunity of all. The Cuban blend of racial and ethnic elements has produced a rich national culture renowned for the rhythmic vitality of such dances as the conga, habanera, mambo, and rumba.

Economy. Cuba is dependent upon one crop, sugar; tobacco is the second most important export. The island's agriculture has been further diversified by the produc-

Cuban cigars are known throughout the world for their high quality.

tion of coffee, citrus fruit, and rice crops. The fisheries are a growing industry. The largest mineral resource is iron ore, and there are also deposits of nickel, cobalt, copper, and manganese. Before 1959 industrialization was limited; after a period of rapid development (1959-63) it has progressed slowly. Neglected for almost 20 years, tourism began to grow in the late 1970s. All trade, commerce, and industrial production is nationalized, and most of the cultivated land has been reorganized as state cooperatives. Cuba benefits from an extensive transport network.

History. Christopher Columbus discovered Cuba in 1492, and it became important as the base for Spanish exploration of America and as a harbor for Spanish treasure ships. The Native Americans, decimated by ill treatment and disease, were replaced as a work force by West African black slaves, particularly in the 18th century, when the sugar plantations developed rapidly. In the 19th century Spain's colonial policy led to a series of nationalist uprisings, and after the Spanish-American War (1898) Cuba became an independent republic, though under U.S. military occupation (1899-1902, 1906-9). Between 1924 and 1959 Cuba was under virtually continuous dictatorship. Fulgencio Batista, who had come to power in 1940, was overthrown by Fidel Castro, aided by Ernesto "Che" Guevara in 1959. Castro, as premier, established a socialist state and instituted sweeping land, industrial, and educational reforms. After U.S. firms had been nationalized, the United States supported the abortive Bay of Pigs invasion and enforced an economic blockade. Thereafter, the USSR and the communist bloc replaced U.S. trade and provided great economic support. In 1962 Cuba's acceptance of Soviet nuclear missiles led to a major confrontation between the United States and USSR until the missiles were withdrawn. The Organization of American States (OAS) expelled Cuba in 1962 but lifted its sanctions in 1975. Despite many setbacks, the social policies have in general benefited the island. Castro became president in 1976. In the late 1970s a certain rapprochement between Cuba and the United States took place, and reestablishment of diplomatic ties seemed close. Cuban involvement in Africa and in Latin American revolutionary movements, however, strained the relations in the 1980s.

Cube and cube root, terms in geometry. A cube is a closed solid figure with 6 equal square faces; adjoining faces are at right angles to each other. If the edge of a cube is of length a, then its volume is a^3. Conversely, if we start with a cube a^3, then a is called its *cube root.*

See also: Geometry.

Cubeb, dried, berrylike fruit of a climbing plant (*Piper cubeba*) of the pepper family. Cubeb is used as a spice and in many pharmaceutical preparations.

Cubism, art movement that began c.1907, Paris, as an intellectual response to the emotional and sensual art of previous times, primarily as represented in painting. In the analytic period (1907-12) fragmented 3-dimensional subjects were explored from varying points of view simultaneously, art that came to be called conceptual realism because it portrayed its object as perceived by the mind, not the eye. In the synthetic phase (1913 through the 1920s) the cubists used brighter colors and fewer forms, and added the texture and construction of collage (for a *trompe l'oeil* effect) in their creations. Important figures in the analytic period were Pablo Picasso and Georges Braque. Other major cubists include Juan Gris, Fernand Léger, and Jean Metzinger.

Cub Scouts *See:* Boy Scouts.

Cuchulainn, great hero of the Ulster cycle of Irish epic mythological literature. Son of the Celtic god Lugh, Cuchulainn was known for his large size and great strength. He had 7 fingers on each hand, 7 toes on each foot, and was capable of superhuman exploits comparable to those of Achilles, the Greek hero. *The Cattle Raid of Cooley* records his single-handed defense of Ulster against the forces of Queen Mave of Connaught.
See also: Mythology.

Cuckoo, bird of the family Cuculidae, found in the tropics and in temperate regions. The common cuckoo of Europe, Asia, and Africa, a slender bird with long tail and dull-colored plumage, lays its eggs in other species' nests, where they are reared by their foster parents. The North American species, the black-billed and the yellow-billed (*Coccyzus americanus*), raise their own broods. The roadrunner (*Geococcyx californianus*), also of the Cuculidae, is found in the deserts of the Southwest and can run up to 15 mph (24.1 kmph).

Cuckoo-shrike, any of several species (genus *Coracina*) of songbirds of the family Campephagidae. Indigenous to Africa, Asia, Australia and the Pacific Islands, most species have long wings and tails and white and black or gray feathers. Most live in tropical woodlands and eat insects and fruit.

Cucumber, common garden vegetable (*Cucumis sativus*) of the gourd family. The creeping vines and triangular leaves produce yellow or white flowers and bear cylindrical fruit 1 to 36 in (2.5 to 91 cm) long. Cucumbers grow rapidly in warm weather and are easily killed by frost. The fruits are popular eaten raw or pickled.

Cuenca (pop. 152,400), city in the Andes Mountains of south central Ecuador. Founded in 1557 by Spanish colonists, Cuenca is a commercial center for agricultural products, animal hides, and gold.

Cuernavaca (pop. 358,000), capital of the state of Morelos in south central Mexico. Founded in 1521 by Hernando Cortez, the city is an agricultural and industrial center. Local crops include corn, beans, and wheat. Bottling plants and flour and textile mills are among its industries. The semitropical climate and beautiful scenery have made the city a popular resort.
See also: Mexico.

Cuffe, Paul (1759-1817), U.S. merchant and sea captain, part African American, part Native American, who encouraged the resettlement of freed slaves in Sierra Leone, Africa. He also supported rights for African Americans in the United States and was instrumental in passing the 1783 law that gave blacks the right to vote in Massachusetts.

Cuisenaire method, teaching system by which students are introduced to mathematical concepts by manipulating 10 rods of different colors that vary proportionately in length. They can be used to teach addition, subtraction, multiplication, division, factoring, and fractions.

Cullen, Countee (1903-46), African-American poet and member of the Harlem Renaissance of the 1920s. Among his works are *Color* (1925) and *Copper Sun* (1927), both poetry, and a novel, *One Way to Heaven* (1931).
See: Harlem Renaissance.

Cult, religious worship of a supernatural object or of a representation of it. Although any religion may be called a cult, the term is used today primarily to refer to minority groups whose practices set them off from the rest of society in obvious ways. Sun Myung Moon's Unification Church would be an example. There are approximately 3,000 such cults claiming a membership of about 3 million in the world today.

Cultural lag, term developed in the 1920s by U.S. sociologist William F. Ogburn to refer to the unequal rate of development in various facets of culture. Technological change, for example, may produce unemployment and social problems that cause a cultural lag as workers adjust and acquire new skills.

Cultural Revolution *See:* China.

Culture, in biology, a colony of living microorganisms, such as bacteria or fungi, grown in a prepared medium (a watery solution of chemicals that supplies the microorganisms with nutrients). Pure cultures are obtained by introducing the organism into a sterile medium and permitting it to reproduce. Bacterial cultures are used commercially in the preparation of food products such as cheese, yogurt, sour cream, and vinegar. Cultures are also useful in the production of antibiotics, vaccines, and other medical compounds, and in the identification of disease-producing bacteria.
See also: Biology.

Culture, term for the general way of life of a human society, including ways of thinking, beliefs, customs, language, technology, art, music, literature, and traditions.

Pierre and Marie Curie

Cumberland (pop. 101,643), U.S. city in western Maryland, located at Cumberland Narrows. Cumberland is an industrial center whose diversified products include tires, baked goods, paper, plastics, macaroni, microscopic drills, and electronics.
See also: Maryland.

Cumberland Gap, mountain pass through the Cumberland Mountains of the Appalachians near the border of Kentucky and Tennessee. Daniel Boone's Wilderness Road to the West ran through the gap, and it was a strategic military objective of both sides in the Civil War. The pass has been a national historical park since 1940.
See also: Wilderness Road.

Cumberland Mountains, or Cumberland Plateau, part of the Appalachian Mountain Range. It extends 450 mi (725 km), forming the boundary between Virginia and Kentucky. The plateau contains hardwood trees, rich deposits of limestone, coal fields, and fine-grained sandstones used in construction.
See also: Appalachian Mountains.

Cumberland River, major tributary of the Ohio River, originating in the Cumberland Plateau and flowing 687 mi (1,106 km) before joining it. Flooding is frequent in winter and spring, whereas in late summer the river shrinks to become a mountain stream. Nashville and Clarksville, Tenn., are the major cities along the river.

Cummings, e.e. (Edward Estlin Cummings; 1894-1962), U.S. poet whose verse is known for its deliberate violation of grammatical rules, unusual words, and idiosyncratic punctuation and typography. One of the most individualistic writers of his time, cummings produced 12 volumes of verse, collected after his death into his *Complete Poems* (1968).

Cumulus *See:* Cloud.

Cunard, Sir Samuel (1787-1865), British shipowner, founder of the Cunard line. He introduced iron steamers and pioneered regular transatlantic crossings (as of 1840) after winning a contract to carry the mail between England and North America.

Cuneiform, system of writing developed in the ancient Middle East during the 4th millennium B.C. The characters were wedge-shaped strokes that represented words and syllables rather than letters, as in an alphabet. Cuneiform originated with the Sumerian people of the Tigris and Euphrates valley, but was later used to write other languages, including Babylonian and Assyrian.

Cunningham, Merce (1919-), U.S. dancer and choreographer noted for his abstract dances incorporating pure, isolated movements without emotional overtones. As a soloist with Martha Graham's company (1939-45), he created several important roles. He began his choreographic career in 1942, creating dances for the music of modern composers. He formed his own company in 1953.

Cuomo, Mario Matthew (1932-), U.S. politician. He was admitted to the New York bar in 1956; a Democrat, he served as New York's secretary of state (1975-79) and as lieutenant governor (1979-83) before being elected governor of New York in 1982. He is the first Italian-American to hold this office. He is considered a serious presidential candidate for the 1990s.

Cupid, or Amor, in Roman mythology, the god of love, the son and companion of Venus, identified with the Greek god, Eros, son of Aphrodite and Ares. He is usually depicted as a small boy, winged, naked, and armed with bow and arrow, capable of causing those wounded by his arrows to fall in love.
See also: Mythology.

Cuquenán Falls, also called Kukenaam, one of the world's highest waterfalls, on the Cuquenán River along the Guyana-Venezuelan border. The falls drop 2,000 ft (610 m).

Curaçao, island (178 sq mi/461 sq km) in the West Indies, an autonomous part of the Netherlands. Willemstad is the capital. Curaçao is the largest of the islands that make up the Netherlands Antilles. Its income derives largely from tourism and oil refining, the refineries being supplied with crude oil from nearby Venezuela. Settled by Spain in 1527, the island was conquered by Holland in 1634. Today's population is mainly descended from the African slaves imported in the early years of rule.
See also: Netherlands Antilles.

Curare, any of a number of alkaloid plant extracts originally used by South American tribes to make poison arrow tips. Curare paralyzes by blocking the transmission of nerve impulses in skeletal muscle. It is used medically as a relaxant before the administering of anesthesia, enabling the dose of anesthetic to be as low as possible.

Curassow, large forest-dwelling bird (especially genus *Crax*) with dark plumage and a crest of curved feathers. The curassow ranges from Texas to Argentina. Currasow are pheasantlike, with strong legs and heavy tails, and spend their time running along branches and fluttering clumsily from tree to tree. Curassow feed on fruit, leaves, and small animals and are hunted as gamebirds.

Curia Regis, in England, the King's Council, also called King's Court, a medieval council of nobles and church officials who met to advise the king on state issues such as legislation and taxation. The Curia Regis was the forerunner of the House of Lords, one of the branches of Parliament.

Curie, in physics, unit that measures radioactivity. One curie equals precisely 3.7 x 10^{10} nuclear disintegrations per second. The unit is named after the French-Polish physicist Pierre Curie.
See also: Physics.

Curie, Marie Sklodowska (1867-1934), Polish-born French physicist and two-time winner of the Nobel Prize (in physics, 1903, and chemistry, 1911). An early investigator of radioactive elements, including uranium, Curie and her husband, Pierre, discovered the elements polonium and radium in 1898, also determining their atomic weights. The Curies shared the 1903 prize with Antoine Becquerel, for their work on radioactivity. In 1911 Marie Curie became the first person to win a second Nobel Prize, for her study of the chemical properties of radium. She died of leukemia, probably radiation-related.
See also: Radioactivity.

Curie, Pierre (1859-1906), French physicist, professor at the Sorbonne, and winner, with his wife, Marie, and A. H. Becquerel, of the 1903 Nobel Prize for physics. Curie's early work concerned the electrical and magnetic properties of crystals and metals.
See also: Physics.

Curium, chemical element, symbol Cm; for physical constants see Periodic Table.

Curium is a synthetic, radioactive element, discovered in 1945 by Glenn Seaborg and his co-workers. They produced it by bombarding plutonium-239 with alpha particles. Curium is a silvery, hard, brittle, reactive, metal. It is toxic, accumulating in bones, where it injures red blood cells.

Curlew, migratory wading bird of pastures and marshes (especially genus *Numenius*), characterized by a long, down-curving bill. Curlews have become rare as their habitat is turned over to agriculture and building. The Eskimo curlew was once shot in vast numbers as it migrated from Labrador to Argentina. It was thought to have become extinct, but one was seen in Texas in 1959. The first nest of the bristlethighed curlew was found in 1948 near the Yukon River.

Curling, game introduced from Scotland and played in the United States and Canada for over 150 years. Granite stones of up to 3 ft (0.9 m) in circumference are propelled along "rinks" of ice 138 ft (42 m) long, with the object of hitting, or getting nearest to, a tee or target stone at the other end. World championships were introduced in 1959, with Canada and the United States winning all but 1 of the first 11. Curling is also popular in Scandinavia, Switzerland (which has several curling "schools,"), and, of course, Scotland, where a curling stone dated 1551 has been preserved.

Curly coated retriever, hunting dog with a black or liver-colored coat of tight curls, which enables it to endure thorny bushes, challenging terrain, and cold-water temperatures when retrieving shot game.

Curly coated retriever

Currant, bushy plant (genus *Ribes*) of temperate regions; also, the fruit of the plant. Some varieties, such as the golden currant of the West, are native to North America. The fruits of European currants, such as the black and red currants, are cooked or used in jellies. They are very rich in vitamin C. Britain is the chief grower of currants, but both cultivated and wild currants are discouraged in parts of the United States where they are alternate hosts for white pine blister rust.

Currency *See:* Money.

Currier & Ives, establishment of U.S. lithographers who produced over 4,000 popular color prints depicting sports, historic events, and scenes of daily life. The business was founded (1834) in New York City by Nathaniel Currier (1813-88), who was joined (1857) by James Merritt Ives (1824-95). It closed in 1907.
See also: Lithography.

Curry, Jabez Lamar Monroe (1825-1903), U.S. educator who promoted the education of both black and white children in the South. He represented the Peabody Fund for public education and the Slater Fund for the establishment of black schools after 1890. He served in the U.S. House of Representatives (1857-1861) and was president of Howard College (1865-1868).

Curry, John Steuart (1897-1946), U.S. painter best known for his striking portrayals of rural Midwestern life. His works include *Baptism in Kansas* (1928) and *Tornado Over Kansas* (1929).

Curtis, Charles (1860-1936), vice president of the United States under Herbert Hoover (1929-33). Curtis's mother was part Kaw, and he fought for Native American rights, in addition to supporting farm and veteran benefits. He served as U.S. senator (1907-13, 1915-29) before becoming vice president.

Curtis, Cyrus Hermann Kotzschmar (1850-1933), U.S. founder of a publishing empire. From the age of 12 he started or bought magazines and newspapers including *The Saturday Evening Post, The Ladies' Home Journal*, and the *New York Evening Post*.

Curtiss, Glenn Hammond (1873-1930), U.S. pioneer in aviation, who made the first public flight in the United States (1908), opened the first pilots' school (1909), built engines for the first U.S. dirigibles, and built the first planes for the U.S. Navy (1911). He also invented ailerons, movable flaps on wings for better control. His 2 hr 51 min flight from Albany, N.Y., to New York City in 1910 made a spectacular impact.
See also: Aviation.

Curzon Line, boundary between Poland and the Soviet Union, proposed by the Allies in 1919, after World War I. It was named after British diplomat Lord George Curzon. The Curzon Line lost significance after the Russo-Polish War of 1920, but at the Yalta conference (1945) it was officially recognized as the Soviet- Polish border.

Cusco, or Cuzco (pop. 120,100), city in the Andes Mountains of southern Peru. Once the capital of the Inca empire, the city was captured in 1533 by the Spanish colonist Francisco Pizarro, who destroyed many of its palaces and temples. Parts of the old walls remain, however, and there are ruins of an Inca fortress. A cathedral, completed in 1654 on the site of the Inca palace, along with other significant colonial buildings, draws tourists to the city today.
See also: Peru.

Color print produced by Currier & Ives which shows Benjamin Franklin, who was one of the first to study atmospheric processes

Cush *See:* Kush.

Cushing, Harvey Williams (1869-1939), U.S. surgeon. He pioneered many modern neurosurgical techniques and investigated the functions of the pituitary gland.
See also: Pituitary gland.

Cuspid *See:* Teeth.

Custer, George Armstrong (1839-76), controversial U.S. cavalry officer. Custer proved himself an outstanding Union cavalry leader during the Civil War. Appointed as a lieutenant colonel in 1866, he joined General Hancock's successful expedition against the Cheyenne. He was killed in the famous battle of Little Bighorn.

Custis, Martha *See:* Washington, Martha Custis.

Custom, accepted practice or manner of doing things, established by tradition. Customs are handed down from one generation to another and often remain unchanged, especially in isolated communities. Customs vary from group to group, and interaction with other cultures causes changes.

George Armstrong Custer

Customs Service, United States, branch of the Department of Treasury responsible for levying and collecting taxes on imported goods. In the early 1900s most government income was received from the Customs

Service. The revenue it raises is now exceeded only by that brought in by the Internal Revenue Service.

Customs union, agreement between two or more countries aimed at reducing tariffs to encourage trade.

Cutlassfish, long, silver-colored saltwater fish (*Trichiurus lepturus*) found in the western Pacific Ocean and the Caribbean Sea. It has a large mouth and doglike teeth. Adults reach 5 ft (1.5 m) in length and are caught for food in some areas.

Cuttlefish, small cephalopod (family Sepiidae) of Old World coastal waters. Its head is attached to 8 short arms and a pair of long tentacles for catching prey. Inside the body there is a flat, chalky cuttlebone that is used as a support and a buoyancy mechanism. The cuttlefish is a good swimmer. When alarmed, it protects itself by shooting out a jet of inky fluid and jerking violently backwards.

Cutworm, any of more than 20,000 species of caterpillars of the owlet moth or miller family, with the capacity to destroy field crops and fruit trees. Crops such as corn, wheat, beans, tomatoes, cotton, and tobacco are killed or damaged when the cutworm severs the roots and stems near the ground.

Cuvier, Baron (Georges Léopold Chrétien Frédéric Dagobert Cuvier; 1769-1832), French scientist known for his pioneer work in comparative anatomy. He deduced the structures of the soft tissues of fossils from their skeletal remains. His book *The Animal Kingdom* was an important authoritative reference in zoology. He was also the originator of the theory of catastrophism, which claimed that living things were eliminated by volcanic eruptions and other natural catastrophes and then supplanted by completely different species. This theory was later abandoned by scientists in favor of the theory of evolution.
See also: Anatomy.

Cyanides, group of compounds containing the cyanide radical, CN (a carbon atom linked to a nitrogen atom). Organic cyanides, which occur in nature, as in some poisonous plants, are called nitriles. Though extremely poisonous, cyanides have great commercial importance in recovery of gold and silver from their ores, in case-hardening iron and steel, in fumigation and pest control, and in electroplating. The cyanides of potassium, sodium, barium, and calcium must be handled with extreme care because they liberate prussic acid (HCN), a weak acid that prevents the body cells from reacting with oxygen and quickly causes death.

Cyanosis, bluish discoloration of skin and mucous membranes. Central cyanosis results from a lack of oxygen in the blood flowing in the arteries from the lungs. Peripheral cyanosis occurs when there is insufficient oxygen in the haemoglobin of the venous blood, as a result of extensive oxygen extraction at the level of the capillaries.

Cybernetics, branch of learning that deals with control mechanisms and the transmission of information. Cybernetics seeks to integrate the theories and studies of communication and control in machines and living organisms.
See also: Wiener, Norbert.

Cycad, tropical plant of the cycas family, one of the most primitive living seed-bearing plants. They grow in warm climates. Many are cultivated for their ornamental foliage. The leaves grow from the top of a stem that may be underground, giving a palmlike appearance, and some cycads have been incorrectly called palms. The leaves of cycads are poisonous and fatal to livestock. The sago palm is a cycad whose stem provides the sago that is used in puddings. In South Africa the seeds of the bread palm are used to make a meal.

Cyclamen, genus of cultivated plant of the primrose family native to the Mediterranean. After pollination the flower stalk coils down to bring the fruit near the ground.

Cyclone, closed system of winds revolving around a low-pressure area. The air rotates counterclockwise in the Northern Hemisphere and clockwise in the Southern Hemisphere. In the tropics, particularly in the Indian Ocean (where they are sometimes known as *typhoons*), cyclones bring severe tropical storms with winds of 200-300 mph (320-480 kmph). In temperate regions, where they are more common, they are often known as lows, or depressions, and generally bring rain, snow, or strong winds. A cyclone develops when a mass of warmer and lighter tropical air meets a mass of colder and heavier polar air (a polar front). The two masses flow in opposite directions and roughly parallel to each other, but under certain conditions the disturbance of the front may develop into a more serious turbulence. The rotating masses of cold and warm air mutually reinforce their circular movements, giving rise to winds of 30-40 mph (48-64 kmph) toward the center, and producing widespread clouds and rainfall.
See also: Hurricane; Tornado.

Cyclops (plural Cyclopes), in Greek mythology, shaggy giant with a single large eye in the center of his forehead. Homer's Cyclopes were lawless Sicilian herdsmen, one of whom, Polyphemus, was met by Odysseus. Other mythological Cyclopes include 3 blacksmith sons who were imprisoned in Tartarus by their father, Uranus, and who, in return for their freedom, helped Hephaestus make Zeus's thunderbolts in his forge under Mt. Etna; and the Cyclopes who built the great walls of Tiryns and Mycenae.
See also: Mythology.

Cyclosporine, drug used to prevent rejection of tissues and organs in transplant patients. It is produced from cultures of the fungus *Tolypocladium inflatum*. Cyclosporine suppresses the functioning of the immune system, most likely by inhibiting the production of a type of white blood cell—the T- helper cell—that is responsible for attacking foreign substances. Cyclosporine is also showing promise in the treatment of certain immunologic diseases. It is a potent compound with the potential for side effects, the most serious of which include hypertension, reduced kidney function, liver damage, and abnormal growth of hair.

Cyclotron, magnetic resonance particle accelerator. It is used to impart very great velocities to heavier nuclear particles without the use of excessive voltages.
See also: Particle accelerator.

Cygnus, the Swan, large constellation visible in the Northern Hemisphere sky. Because of its shape, it is sometimes called the Northern Cross. It is high in the sky during summer.
See also: Constellation.

Cylinder, 3-dimensional figure consisting of a curved lateral surface and equal parallel ends, or *bases*. The bases may be either circles or ovals. A right circular cylinder is a common shape used for tin cans and automobile cylinders.

Cymbal, percussion instrument of very ancient origin. When 2 of these shallow concave metal discs are clashed together, swept by each other, or hit with a drumstick they produce a variety of sound effects. Today cymbals are made in many different sizes to produce sounds of varying pitch and intensity. The cymbal is a basic instrument in the military band, and is frequently used in modern orchestral music. Cymbals used in jazz or dance bands, mounted in pairs and operated by a foot pedal, are called choke cymbals.

Cynic philosophy, ancient Greek school of philosophy characterized by the unconventional way of life of its adherents. Its founder, Antisthenes, a 4th century B.C. follower of Socrates, held ordinary social conventions in contempt and argued that virtue was the only good and that it could be attained only through independent and austere living conditions.
See also: Philosophy.

Cypress, family of cone-bearing trees, including arborvitae, juniper, and cedar. They have fragrant wood and small, scale-like leaves. Cypresses grow in North America, Europe, and Asia. Red cedar is used for pencils, chests, and closets and white cedar for fencing, shingles, and boats. The bald cypress, which is not a true cypress but kin of the sequoia, often grows in water.

Cyprus, Republic of, island republic situated in the northeastern Mediterranean Sea, about 40 mi (60 km) south of Turkey and 60 mi (97 km) west of Syria. Cyprus, 3,578 sq mi (9,267 sq km) in area, is the

Cyprus, Republic of

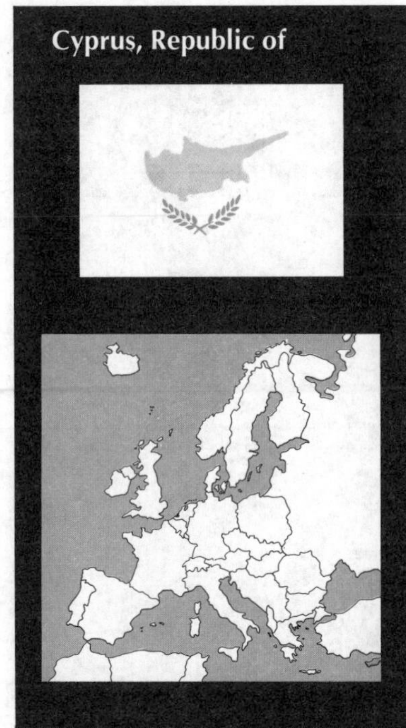

Capital:	Nicosia
Area:	3,572 sq mi (9,251 sq km)
Population:	725,000
Government:	republic
Independent:	1960
GNP:	US $7,070,000,000
Per capita:	US $9,820

Rural church in Cyprus built in Byzantine style

Mediterranean's third largest island. The capital is Nicosia.

Land and climate. Two main mountain ranges dominate the island: the Kyrenia ridge in northern-central Cyprus and the Troödos Mountains in the southwest, including Mt. Olympus (6,403 ft/1,952 km). Between these rugged ranges lies the fertile Mesaöia plain. The island's climate is predominantly dry, with mild winters and hot, sunny summers. The remains of ancient forests of evergreen oak, Aleppo pine, and cypress cling to the rocky mountain slopes, but centuries of timber cutting have almost stripped Cyprus of its native forest cover, which has been largely replaced by poor pasture.

People. About 80% of Cypriots are of Greek extraction; the rest are predominantly Turkish in origin. Each group clings to its own cultural traditions; there are 2 official languages (Greek and Turkish), 2 main faiths (the Orthodox Church of Cyprus and Islam), and even separate schools for Greek and Turkish Cypriots.

History. Neolithic farmers lived on the island as early as 6000 B.C. Around 1200 B.C. Greek-speaking traders arrived, followed by the Phoenicians. Both peoples set up city-states, and Cyprus developed a cosmopolitan Eurasian culture. In 709 B.C., however, Cyprus submitted to Assyria, and from then on was largely dominated by foreign states. The Ottoman Turks (1570-1878) established their own Muslim culture alongside the Christian one that had flourished since A.D. 45. After Britain gained Cyprus in 1878 (making it a crown colony in 1925), conflict between Turkish and Greek Cypriots became a major issue, especially in the 1950s, when Archbishop Makarios led a powerful movement for *enosis*, political union with Greece. Also in the 1950s, Col. Giorgios Grivas headed EOKA, a guerrilla movement aimed at forcibly freeing Cyprus from Britain. In 1960 Britain granted Cyprus its independence. The new republic tried solving its Greco-Turkish problem by constitutional compromise, which failed. Fierce intercommunal fighting and the threat of intervention from both Greece and Turkey led to the arrival of a UN peacekeeping force in 1965. Subsequent talks between President Makarios and Turkish leaders were frequent but fruitless. In 1974 a military group organized by Greek army officers ousted Makarios, whereupon Turkey invaded the island, setting up a "Turkish Federated State of Cyprus" under Turkish occupation in the northeastern third of the island. Although the island remains divided, it is regarded as a Greek nation by the UN.

Cyrano de Bergerac, Savinien de (1619-55), French author. He gave up a military career to write plays and prose. A freethinker, influenced by Pierre Gassendi (1592-1655), he satirized contemporary society in ingenious fantasies about voyages to the sun and moon. Edmond Rostand, in his play *Cyrano de Bergerac*, made him into a flamboyant romantic hero, handicapped in love because of an unusually large nose.

Cyril of Alexandria, Saint (378?-444), Christian theologist and bishop, known primarily for his campaign against Nestorius, the bishop of Constantinople, who denied that the Virgin Mary was the mother of God. When Cyril succeeded his uncle, Archbishop Theophilus, he attacked Christian heretics, pagans, and Jews. He was instrumental in expelling Jews from Alexandria. In 1882 the Roman Catholic church declared Cyril a doctor of the church, a special title granted to saints whose theological writings have particular authority. His feast day is Feb. 9.
See also: Christianity.

Cyrus the Great (c.590-529 B.C.), founder of the Persian empire. He conquered Media (c.559), Lydia (c.547), and Babylonia (c.539), building an empire whose territory extended from the Black and Caspian seas to the Arabian Desert and Persian Gulf. He allowed the Jews to return from Babylonia to Palestine and did not suppress the religions of the various parts of the empire.
See also: Persia, Ancient.

Cyst, abnormal, sac-like growth in the body. Often surrounding a foreign body, oil gland, or hair follicle, cysts are formed by cells within the sac walls.

Cystic fibrosis, CF, or mucoviscidosis, hereditary disease, usually appearing in early childhood, characterized by an abnormality of the exocrine or mucus-secreting glands. An excess of thick, sticky mucus accumulates particularly in the lungs and the pancreas, seriously affecting breathing and the digestion of food. CF patients may be identified by large amounts of salt in their perspiration. As the disease progresses the mucus-secreting glands are replaced by fibroid tissue and cysts. Individuals who are carriers of the CF trait are not afflicted with the disease, although the offspring of 2 carriers may inherit the disease. The control of pulmonary infection is critical to survival in CF patients; antibiotics are routinely used to prevent or treat respiratory infections, and physical therapy and the use of certain inhalants are encouraged to help remove the accumulation of mucus in the lungs.

Czech Republic

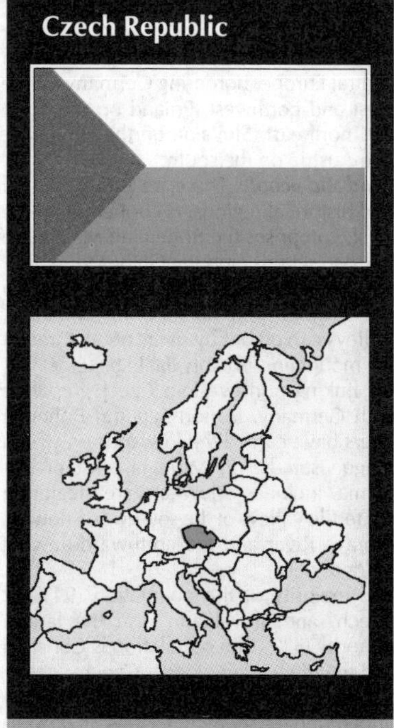

Capital:	Prague
Area:	30,450 sq mi (78,864 sq km)
Population:	10,383,000
Government:	republic

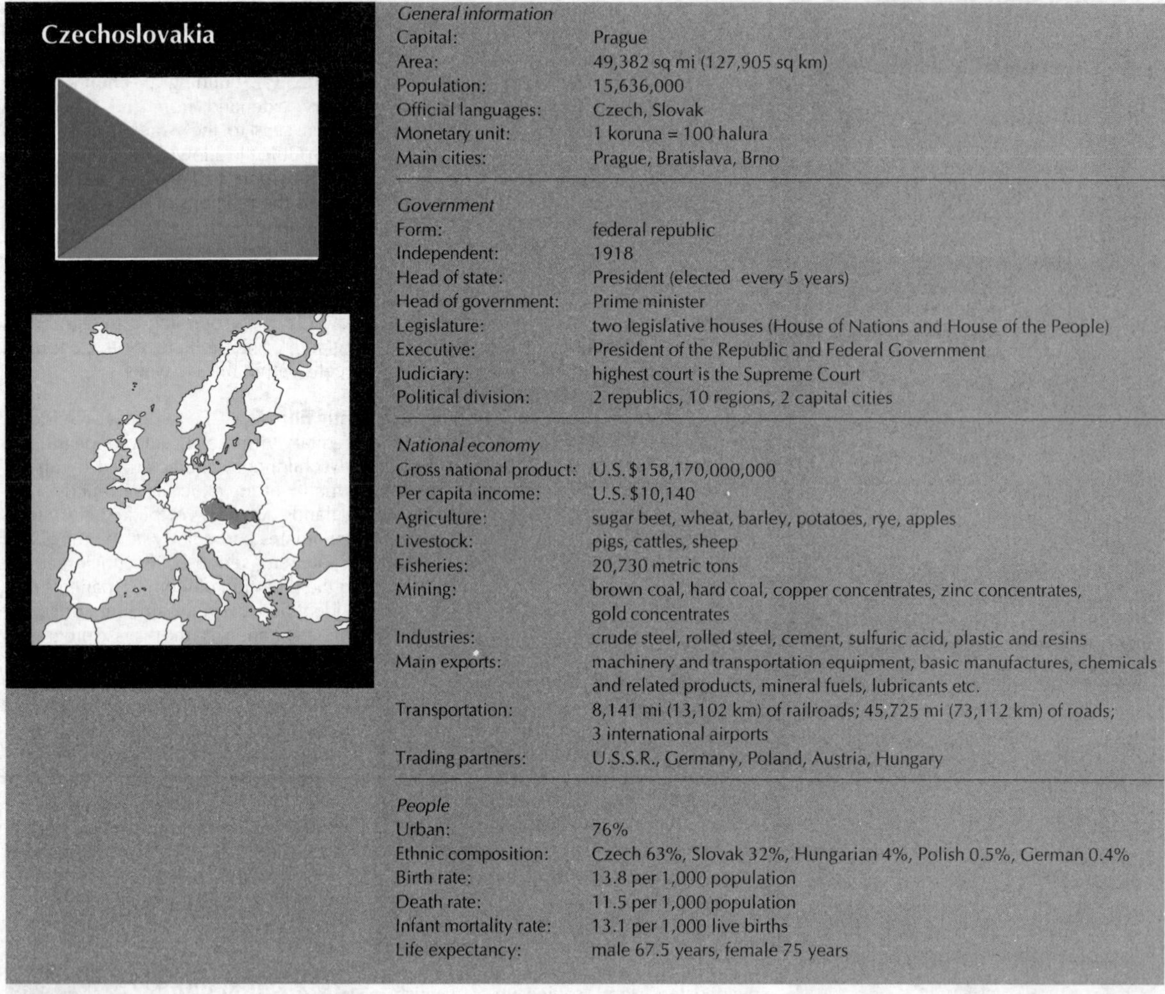

Czechoslovakia

General information	
Capital:	Prague
Area:	49,382 sq mi (127,905 sq km)
Population:	15,636,000
Official languages:	Czech, Slovak
Monetary unit:	1 koruna = 100 halura
Main cities:	Prague, Bratislava, Brno
Government	
Form:	federal republic
Independent:	1918
Head of state:	President (elected every 5 years)
Head of government:	Prime minister
Legislature:	two legislative houses (House of Nations and House of the People)
Executive:	President of the Republic and Federal Government
Judiciary:	highest court is the Supreme Court
Political division:	2 republics, 10 regions, 2 capital cities
National economy	
Gross national product:	U.S. $158,170,000,000
Per capita income:	U.S. $10,140
Agriculture:	sugar beet, wheat, barley, potatoes, rye, apples
Livestock:	pigs, cattles, sheep
Fisheries:	20,730 metric tons
Mining:	brown coal, hard coal, copper concentrates, zinc concentrates, gold concentrates
Industries:	crude steel, rolled steel, cement, sulfuric acid, plastic and resins
Main exports:	machinery and transportation equipment, basic manufactures, chemicals and related products, mineral fuels, lubricants etc.
Transportation:	8,141 mi (13,102 km) of railroads; 45,725 mi (73,112 km) of roads; 3 international airports
Trading partners:	U.S.S.R., Germany, Poland, Austria, Hungary
People	
Urban:	76%
Ethnic composition:	Czech 63%, Slovak 32%, Hungarian 4%, Polish 0.5%, German 0.4%
Birth rate:	13.8 per 1,000 population
Death rate:	11.5 per 1,000 population
Infant mortality rate:	13.1 per 1,000 live births
Life expectancy:	male 67.5 years, female 75 years

Czech Republic, independent country in central Europe, bordering Germany on the west and northwest, Poland on the north and northeast, Slovakia on the southeast, and Austria on the south.

Land and people. There are 2 main natural and historical regions. (1) Bohemia, in the west, comprises the Bohemian Massif, the Ore Mountains, and the Giant Mountains, which serve as natural boundaries between the republic and neighboring countries. Valleys carved out by rivers break through the mountains, notably the Labe (Elbe) valley linking northwestern Czech Republic with Germany. In north-central Bohemia rivers have carved the lowlands on which Prague stands. (2) Moravia, east of Bohemia, includes a lowland area featuring the fertile valleys of the southward-flowing Morava River and the northward-flowing Odra (Oder).

The majority of the population (94%) is Czech, and Slovakians form the largest minority (3%). The population is Christian and the official language is Czech.

Economy. The Czech government continued the economic reforms that were started by the government of Czechoslovakia. After the fall of communism tourism became a major source of trade and employment. Other important economic activities are manufactruing (metallurgy), trade, and services. Important agricultural products include wheat, barley, sugar beets, and hops.

History. Bohemia and Moravia formed a separate entity until 1918. It was successively ruled by the Premysl dynasty, Austria, the Hussites, and the Habsburg dynasty. With the collapse of the Habsburg dynasty during World War I, Bohemia, Moravia, and Slovakia formed the new republic Czechoslovakia. The Czech and Slovakian republics formed a federation in 1968. Slovakia left the federation in 1993. The political and economic liberalization that started after the collapse of communism was pursued by the independent Czech government.

See also: Czechoslovakia.

Czechoslovakia, former nation in central Europe, consisting of the present Czech Republic and Slovakia. With the disintegration of Austria-Hungary at the end of World War I, the Czechs and Slovaks proclaimed the independent republic of Czechoslovakia (1918), which developed as a Western-style democracy. Seized by Nazi Germany (1938-39), Czechoslovakia came under Russian domination after World War II, and a communist regime took power. In 1968-69 an attempt by the Communist Party leader Alexander Dubcek to liberalize the country was crushed by invading Soviet and other Warsaw Pact troops. Dubcek and other moderates were purged and the staunchly pro-Soviet Gustáv Husák put in control. In 1989 the pro-Soviet regime collapsed during the widespread upheavals in Eastern Europe. In the first free elections since 1948, the former dissident playwright Vaclav Havel became president. The new government embarked on a program of democratization and the introduction of a free-market economy. Under pressure of Slovak political leaders, the Czech and Slovak federation was dissolved, and the republics became independent in 1993.

Czechs, Slavic people who settled in Bohemia and Moravia in central Europe in the early Middle Ages and accounted for about two-thirds of Czechoslovakia's population. The city of Prague, center of Czech culture, became one of the great political and artistic capitals of Europe between the 14th and 17th centuries.

Czerny, Karl (1791-1857), Austrian musician and teacher. He studied with Ludwig van Beethoven (1800-3) and became the mentor of Hungarian pianist and composer Franz Liszt. Czerny is well known for his études, compositions for the piano which embody some point of technique but are intended for performance.

D

D, fourth letter of the English alphabet. It is derived from the Phoenician *daleth* and Greek *delta*. It occupied the same position in those alphabets. Thought to originate from a pictorial representation of a door, it may have some connection with the Egyptian hieroglyph for door. In Roman numerals, D represents the number 500.

D.A.V. *see:* Disabled American Veterans.

Dacca *see:* Dhaka.

Dachau, concentration camp in Germany where many thousands, mostly Poles and Jews, were murdered by the Nazis. The camp operated from 1933 until its liberation by U.S. soldiers in 1945.
See also: Concentration camp; Holocaust.

Dachshund, small (5-9 in/13-25 cm), short-legged dog with a long body, long ears, and a smooth, bronze (or black and bronze) coat.

Dada, artistic movement born in Zurich and later spreading to New York, Berlin, and Paris, 1915-22. The poet Tristan Tzara (*Vingtcinque Poèmes*, 1918), the artists Jean Arp (*Two Heads*, 1929) and Marcel Duchamp (*Why Not Sneeze, Rose Sélavy?*, 1921), and the writers Hugo Ball and Richard Huelsenbeck were deliberately provocative Dadaists, aiming at the destruction of aesthetic preconceptions. Favorite techniques of Dada included nonsense poetry, collage, anarchic typography, and outrageous theater events.

Daddy longlegs, or harvestman, relative of the spider with a small rounded body and 8 extremely long and delicate legs. Daddy longlegs are nocturnal, eating plant juices and insects and other small invertebrates.
See also: Arachnid.

Daedalus, in Greek mythology, architect and sculptor. He built a labyrinth for King Minos of Crete. When the king attempted to keep him on the island against his will, he tried to escape by fashioning wax wings for himself and his son Icarus. Daedalus reached Sicily, but Icarus flew too close to the sun; the wings melted, and he fell into the sea.
See also: Mythology.

Daffodil, any of several bulbous, perennial plants (genus *Narcissus*) of the amaryllis family, having yellow trumpet-shaped flowers. Native to Europe and North Africa, daffodils are now grown worldwide as ornamental flowers.

Da Gama, Vasco (1469?-1524), sea captain from Portugal, the first to open sea routes for trade between Europe and Asia. Upon request from King Manuel I of Portugal, da Gama set out to establish trade with India by sailing east around southern Africa. He began his journey July 8, 1497, and reached Calicut, India, May 20, 1498. Muslim merchants resented da Gama's attempts to establish trade, and India's ruler found his gifts unacceptable. His return to Portugal included only limited Indian goods, but King Manuel was satisfied with this initial voyage. He sailed again in 1500, better prepared to conquer the Muslim control and increase trade. He succeeded and the Portuguese became a major trading power in the Indian Ocean.

Dagger, short, knifelike weapon for stabbing, with a sharp-edged, pointed blade.

Daghestan, autonomous republic in southeast Russia, in the USSR, bounded by the Caspian Sea on the east, inhabited by Russians, Azerbaijanis, and various tribes of the Caucasus Mountain region.
See also: Union of Soviet Socialist Republics.

Daguerreotype, early photographic process in which a light-sensitive silver-coated copperplate was treated with iodine vapor. The method was perfected in the 1830s by the French physicist Louis J.M. Daguerre (1789-1851).
See also: Photography.

Dahlia, any of several perennial plants (genus *Dahlia*) of the composite family, having tuberous roots and red, purple, yellow, or white flowers. Over 7,000 varieties have been developed from the original Mexican stock; the largest now have blooms 1 ft (30 cm) across.

Dahomey *see:* Benin.

Daimler, Gottlieb Wilhelm (1834-1900), German engineer who devised an internal combustion engine (1885) and used it in building one of the first automobiles, about 1886.

Dairy farming, all the processes producing milk and milk products. Dairy farming includes the breeding, selection, and management of cattle (and sometimes goats and domesticated buffaloes) to ensure a regular output of good milk. Processing into butter and cheese is generally undertaken in factories. Fresh milk is the single most nutritionally complete food; nearly 20% of all foodstuffs eaten annually in the United States are dairy products.

Daisy, any of various common wild plants of the composite family. The English daisy (*Bellis perennis*), with white, pink, or red flowers, is widely cultivated in the United States. Other species include the oxeye daisy and the yellow daisy, or black-eyed Susan.

Dakar (pop. 979,000), capital and largest city of Senegal, on the far western tip of Africa. The modern city originated in a fort built by French colonists in 1857. Dakar is a cultural center and one of West Africa's main commercial hubs. Its port is the most heavily trafficked in the region.
See also: Senegal.

Dakota *see:* North Dakota; South Dakota.

Dakota *see:* Sioux.

A well-preserved daguerreotype

Daladier, Édouard (1884-1970), French premier (1933-34, 1938-40) who, with British Prime Minister Neville Chamberlain, signed the 1938 Munich Agreement abandoning Czechoslovakia to Hitler. Ousted after failing to aid Finland against the USSR, he was imprisoned by the Vichy government after the fall of France. After the war, he served as a member of the National Assembly (1946-58), as a representative of the Radical Party.
See also: Munich Agreement.

Dalai Lama

Dalai Lama, title of the head of the Tibetan Buddhists. When a Dalai Lama dies, his successor is chosen from among young boys born within two years of his death. Each Dalai Lama is considered by Tibetan Buddhists to be an incarnation of the Bodhisattva Avalokiteshvara, the founder of this branch of Buddhism. The present Dalai Lama, the fourteenth, born Tenzin Cryatso in 1935, took refuge in India in 1959, when the Chinese government put down a rebellion in Tibet against Chinese rule. Since then he has traveled widely throughout the world.
See also: Buddhism; Tibet.

Poster for a Dada party in Germany in 1922

Salvador Dali's surrealist painting Metamorphosis of Narcissus

Dale, Sir Henry Hallet (1875-1968), British biologist who discovered and described the properties of acetylcholine, an agent in the chemical transmission of nerve impulses. In 1936 he shared the Nobel Prize in physiology or medicine with Otto Loewi.
See also: Biology.

Daley, Richard Joseph (1902-76), U.S. politician, state senator from Illinois (1939-46), mayor of Chicago (1955-76). As mayor he was one of the last old-style urban bosses. His handling of antiwar demonstrators at the 1968 Democratic Convention was widely condemnated.

Dali, Salvador (1904-89), Spanish painter, one of the masters of surrealism. Dali sought to portray the life of the unconscious by juxtaposing incongruous elements and emphasizing rich fantasy, combined with a refined draftsmanship. Among his major paintings are *The Persistence of Memory* (1931), *Agnostic Symbol* (1932), *Geopoliticus* (1943).

Dallapiccola, Luigi (1904-75), Italian composer of vocal works and operas who adapted the 12-tone technique to his own emotionally expressive and melodic style.

Dallas (pop. 2,553,362), second-largest city in Texas, founded in 1841 on the Trinity River. In the 1870s the railroads made Dallas a cotton center. By the 1930s, it had become a major oil center. It is now the banking and insurance capital of the Southwest, as well as a manufacturing city and convention center.
See also: Texas.

Dallas, George Mifflin (1792-1864), U.S. vice president (1845-49) under James Polk. He served as U.S. senator from Pennsylvania (1833-35), minister to Russia (1837-39), and minister to Great Britain (1856-61).

Dalles (singular: dell; from French *dalle*, "slab of stone"), deep natural gorges worn into rock by rapidly moving water. Well-known dalles include the Wisconsin Dells on the Wisconsin River, the Saint Louis River Dalles near Duluth, Minn., and the Dalles on the Columbia River, Washington and Oregon.

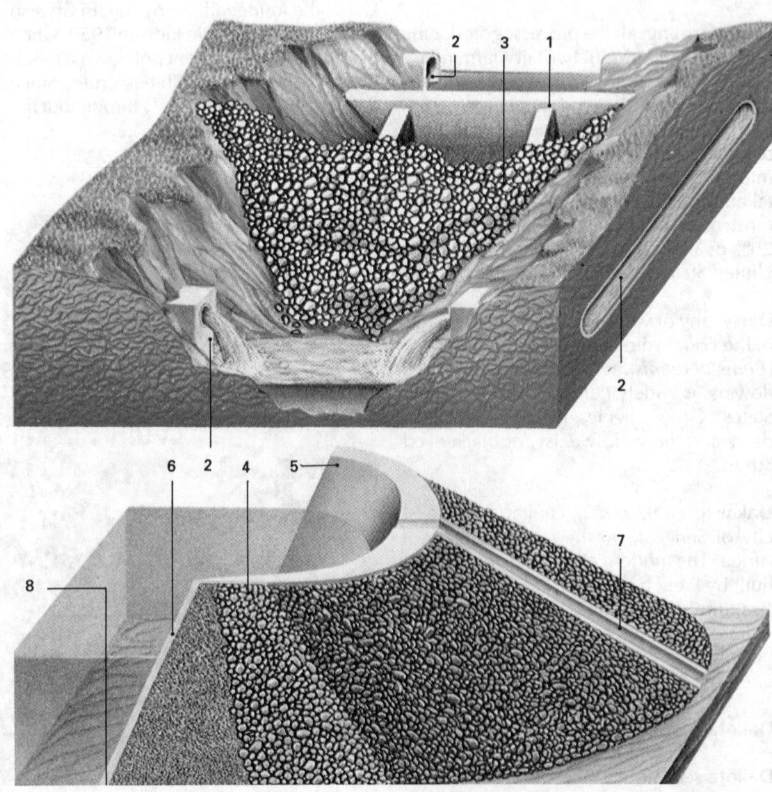

In building a dam, a temporary, or coffer, dam is constructed (1). The river is diverted around the dam site through tunnels (2) in the riverbank. The area behind the coffer dam is then filled with an inclined layer of compacted rocks (3). Carefully graded crushed rock (4) is then spread over the steep concave upstream face (5), and then, with a layer of impervious material (6), a spillway is added to the downstream slope (7). Material is grouted into the bedrock to prevent seepage under the dam (8).

Dalmatia, mountainous region of western Yugoslavia, a province of Croatia, bordering the Adriatic Sea and including about 300 islands. Historically, the area has been dominated by the Romans (1st century B.C.-5th century A.D.), Venetians (1420-1797), and Austrians (1815-1918). Parts have also been dominated by Hungary and Turkey. The present population lives on tourism, fishing, and farming, producing wine, olive oil, and cotton. There is also shipbuilding, bauxite mining, and limestone quarrying.
See also: Yugoslavia.

Dalmatian, sturdy, medium-sized dog thought to have originated in Dalmatia (on the Adriatic Sea) many centuries ago. The dalmatian is born white and develops black or brown spots when just a few weeks old. It is used as a watchdog, for hunting, and is traditionally depicted as a companion on fire engines and coaches.

Dalton, John (1766-1844), English scientist who originated the modern chemical atomic theory. In 1801 Dalton discovered his *Law of Partial Pressures,* which states that the pressure exerted by a mixture of gases equals the sum of the partial pressures of the components. (The partial pressure of a gas is the pressure it would exert if it alone filled the volume.) In 1803 he published the first table of comparative atomic weights, which inaugurated the new quantitative atomic theory. Dalton also gave the first scientific description of color blindness. The red-green type from which he suffered is still known as Daltonism.
See also: Atom.

Dam, barrier built across a river to hold back the water. Dams are built to control flooding, to store water for drinking and irrigation, to improve navigation, or to produce hydroelectric power. The artificial lakes or reservoirs formed behind the dams provide a refuge for wild life and are often used for recreation.

Damascus (pop. 1,200,000), capital and largest city of Syria, founded c.2,000 B.C. and possibly the oldest continuously inhabited city in the world. From its origin until A.D. 635 it was ruled by a succession of all the major powers of the Middle East, including the Egyptians, Israelites, Greeks, Romans, and Byzantines. In 635 it was taken by the armies of the new Muslim state expanding out of the Arabian peninsula. It has been Islamic ever since. During the Umayyad dynasty (661-750), Damascus was the capital of an Arab empire extending from Spain to Persia. After 750 it was held by many rulers, mostly Arab and Turkish. Its major architectural landmark is its Great Mosque.
See also: Syria.

D'Amboise, Jacques (1934-), U.S. dancer and choreographer. He became a soloist with the New York City Ballet and was recognized for his outstanding performance in the ballet *Apollo* by George Balanchine. He is known for his roles in *Western Symphony* (1954), the film *Carousel* (1956), and his own ballet, *Irish Fantasy* (1964). D'Amboise is also known for his work with young people and dance.

Damien, Father (Joseph de Veuster; 1840-89), Belgian Roman Catholic missionary who worked in the leper colony of Molokai Island, Hawaii, which he turned from a mere refuge into a thriving community. He died of leprosy himself.

Damon and Pythias, 2 youths from Greek legend whose commitment, friendship, and faithfulness to each other was demonstrated when Dionysius, leader of the city of Syracuse, condemned Pythias to death. Pythias was permitted to leave Syracuse briefly to put his affairs in order while Damon offered to die in his place if his friend did not return. Pythias returned in time to save Damon, and Dionysius chose to pardon Pythias upon seeing the youths' demonstration of loyalty and friendship.
See also: Mythology.

Damp, in mining, name given to various dangerous gases. *Firedamp* is methane, a colorless compound of hydrogen and carbon that forms a highly explosive mixture with air. *Afterdamp* (mainly carbon dioxide and nitrogen), and *chokedamp* and *blackdamp* (mainly carbon dioxide) are other noxious mine gases.
See also: Methane.

Dampier, William (1652-1715), English explorer. After sailing the Atlantic and Pacific as a buccaneer, he was commissioned by the British Admiralty to explore the southwest Pacific.
The first Englishman to reach Australia, he wrote *A New Voyage Round the World* (1697) and other books.

Damping-off, disease of new plants caused by fungi in the soil. There are 2 types: pre-emergence, causing seeds to sprout and rot in the soil, and post- emergence, in which newly developed seedlings suddenly die. Seeds can be treated with fungicides before planting, or can be planted in fungus-free soil.

Damrosch, name of a father and 2 sons, German-born musicians active in U.S. music education. **Léopold Damrosch** (1832-85), violinist and conductor, established the New York Symphony Society and was the orchestra's conductor until he died. **Frank Damrosch** (1859-1937) was a choral conductor and founder of the Institute of Musical Art (later a part of the Juilliard School of Music). **Walter Johannes Damrosch** (1862-1950), conductor and composer, conducted the New York Symphony during its first radio broadcast (1925) and was the music advisor for the "Music Appreciation Hour" on NBC radio. He composed operas and incidental music for theater, and published an autobiography.

Dana, Charles Anderson (1819-97), U.S. journalist who spent 1841-46 in the Utopian Brook Farm community and later joined the New York *Tribune*, becoming its managing editor in 1849. He resigned from the *Tribune* in 1862 and in 1864-65 served as assistant secretary of war under Lincoln. In 1868 he became part owner of the New York *Sun*, making it a newspaper of national importance.

Dana, Richard Henry, Jr. (1815-82), U.S. lawyer, social reformer, and author of *Two Years Before the Mast* (1840). Written after he had sailed from the east coast to California, around Cape Horn, it exposed the harsh treatment of sailors and started a reform campaign.

Danaë *see:* Perseus.

Da Nang, or Tourane (pop.490,000) large port city in southern Vietnam on the South China Sea. Its accessible harbor and its location near North Vietnam made it a key city during the Vietnam War. After 1965, the United States built a major air base there. The city has a modern textile mill and also produces soap.

Dance, art of moving the body rhythmically, usually to music. Among primitive peoples a belief in the magical potency of dance found expression in fertility and rain dances, in dances of exorcism and resurrection, and in dances preparatory to hunting or fighting. Communal dance as a powerful symbol of group cooperation and mutual regard underlies enduring traditions in folk dancing. Classical ballet had its origins in the court dances in 15th and 16th-century Italy and France. The 19th century saw the development of the waltz, in which social dancing reached the height of popularity. Twentieth-century dance styles, promoted by the syncopated rhythms of popular music, have become vehicles of individual self-expression.

Dandelion, perennial herb (genus *Taraxacum*) of the composite family. Dandelions are common weeds producing a rosette of toothy, edible leaves and a yellow flower with a round head of white down.

Dandie Dinmont terrier, short-legged dog originating in Scotland and England, weighing 18 to 24 lb (8 to 11 kg) and standing 8 to 11 in (20 to 28 cm) tall at the shoulders. It has large eyes, a curved body, and a silky tuft of hair on top of its head. It was named after a character in Sir Walter Scott's novel, *Guy Mannering* (1815).

Dandruff, thin, dry scales of skin that flake off the scalp. Severe dandruff— seborrhea, caused by overly secretive oil glands— must be treated by a dermatologist.

Daniel, Book of, Old Testament book, relating events in the life of the prophet Daniel, who was brought to Nebuchadnezzar's court during the Babylonian Captivity of the Jews, during the 6th century B.C. Daniel is most widely known for his reading of the writing on the wall and his miraculous escape from the lion's den. There is a different version of the book in the Apocrypha.
See also: Bible; Old Testament.

Danilova, Alexandra (1904-), Russian-born U.S. ballerina. She studied in Leningrad and rose to fame in Paris in Sergei Diaghilev's *Ballets Russes*.

D'Annunzio, Gabriele (1863-1938), Italian writer and adventurer, initially famous for his poetry, whose sensuous imagery reflected his own life-style. His many novels include *The Flame of Life* (1900), an account of his affair with the Italian stage actress Eleonora Duse. His nationalist speeches helped bring Italy into World War I on the Allies' side. Later his armed supporters occupied the Dalmatian port of Fiume, where D'Annunzio ruled as dictator until 1921. He was a supporter of Mussolini's fascists from the early days of the movement.

Dante Alighieri (1265-1321), Italian poet, regarded as among the greatest Italian writers in history. A descendant of an old Florentine family, he mastered the art of lyric poetry at an early age. His first major work, *The New Life* (c.1292), describes his love for his lifelong inspiration, Beatrice

Dante Alighieri being led through Hell by Vergil in an illustration of The Divine Comedy

Portinari, who died in 1290. His masterpiece, *The Divine Comedy* (probably written between 1308 and 1320), consists of more than 14,000 lines, divided into three books: *The Inferno* (Hell), *Purgatory*, and *Paradise*. It criticizes the corruption Dante saw in the world around him and codifies the Catholic view of the world. It was also responsible for standardizing what became the modern Italian language.

Danton, Georges Jacques (1759-94), French revolutionary political leader. A Parisian lawyer and member of the Cordeliers, a club that supported the French Revolution, Danton struggled to reconcile the opposing radical revolutionary factions, the Girondins and Jacobins. After the execution of Louis XVI in 1793, he emerged as the head of the Committee of Public Safety, but failed to take positive steps against the growing threat of civil war. Losing power to the militant Robespierre, Danton was unable to stop the Reign of Terror. He was accused of treason and executed by Robespierre's Jacobins.
See also: French Revolution; Marat, Jean Paul; Robespierre.

Danube River, second longest river of Europe. From southwest Germany it flows 1,750 mi (2,816 km) east through Austria, Czechoslovakia, Hungary, Yugoslavia, Romania, Bulgaria, and the Soviet Union before emptying into the Black Sea. With its more than 300 tributaries, the Danube drains almost one-tenth of Europe and provides a major highway for European trade.

Danzig *see:* Gdansk.

Daoism *see:* Taoism.

Daphne, in Greek mythology, nymph who wished to remain chaste but was pursued by Apollo. She was changed into a laurel bush to escape from him. After that the laurel was sacred to Apollo, who wore the leaves for his crown.
See also: Mythology.

DAR *see:* Daughters of the American Revolution.

Dardanelles, narrow strait 40 mi (60 km) long in northwestern Turkey, separating Asia Minor from Europe, called the Hellespont in ancient times. It links the Sea of Marmara with the Aegean Sea and is part of the waterway leading from the Black Sea to the Mediterranean. Together with the Bosporus, the Dardanelles control the access of Soviet vessels to the Mediterranean.
See also: Hellespont.

Dare, Virginia (b. 1587), first child born in America of English parents. Her mother was among a group of settlers of Roanoke Island, Virginia. The colonists vanished without trace, for reasons unknown.

Dar es Salaam (pop. 870,000), capital and largest city of Tanzania, in east Africa. Located on a natural harbor of the Indian Ocean, it is also Tanzania's main port and economic center. Founded by the Sultan of Zanzibar in 1866, Dar-es-Salaam, which means "House of Peace" in Arabic and Swahili, became the capital of German East Africa in 1891 and of the British Colony of Tanganyika after World War I. Tanganyika won independence in 1961, and merged with newly independent Zanzibar in 1964 to form the new state of Tanzania.
See also: Tanzania.

Darío, Rubén (Félix Rubén García Sarmiento; 1867-1916), Nicaraguan poet. He introduced *modernismo*, which revolutionized Spanish and Spanish- American literature. His best-known works are *Profane Hymns* (1896) and *Songs of Life and Hope* (1905).

Darius, Persian kings of the Achaemenid dynasty. **Darius I** (r. 521-486 B.C.), the Great, is regarded as one of the greatest rulers of the ancient Middle East. In 512 he subjugated Thrace and Macedonia and temporarily expelled the Scythians from the Danube region. He then led a series of punitive expeditions into Greece, ultimately leading to the Persian defeat at Marathon in 490. **Darius II** (r. 423?-404 B.C.), seized the throne from his half-brother, beginning a reign marked by corruption and revolts. **Darius III** (r. 336-330 B.C.) was the last ruler of an independent Persian empire, which fell to Alexander the Great.
See also: Persia, Ancient.

Darjeeling (pop. 57,600), city on the lower slopes of the Himalayas, summer capital of West Bengal state, India. Its altitude is 7,100 ft (2,160 m), and the well-known Darjeeling tea thrives in the cool climate on large tea plantations near the city. There are teakwood forests, parks, gardens, museums, hospitals, a zoo, a race course, and colleges, including a medical school. Copper, iron ore, dolomite, and limestone are mined, and major crops include rice, corn, cardamon, and wheat. Mountain ranges and low valleys define 2 distinct regions in the Darjeeling district with a total area of 1,160 sq mi (3,005 sq km).
See also: India.

Dark Ages, popular term for the period in European history from the 5th to the 15th centuries. Beginning with the fall of Rome, the Dark Ages saw the establishment of Feudalism and the spread of Christianity through most of Europe. The term "Dark Ages" refers to the relative stagnation of science and culture, now thought to be exaggerated. The period ended with the Renaissance and the transition to the modern world.
See also: Middle Ages; Renaissance.

Dark matter, most of the invisible material existing in galaxies and clusters of galaxies. Dark matter does not produce, cast, or absorb light, and is 10 times more prevalent than visible matter. Astronomers have determined the amount of dark matter in a galaxy by finding the orbital speed of gas clouds and stars. They conclude that amounts of dark matter were always greater than amounts of visible matter in both galaxies and clusters of galaxies.
See also: Galaxy.

Darling, Ding (Jay N. Darling; 1867-1962), U.S. editorial cartoonist and conservationist. Darling won the Pulitzer Prize for cartooning in 1924 and again in 1943. In 1934 and 1935 he served as chief of the U.S. Biological Survey.

Darling, Grace Horsley (1815-42), English heroine, daughter of a lighthouse keeper. In 1838 she and her father rowed a small boat a mile through storm-tossed seas to rescue five survivors of a shipwreck.

Darling River, Australia's longest river. Originating in the Great Dividing Range in Queensland, it flows across the state of New South Wales and into the Murray River, which empties into the Indian Ocean. In winter the Darling is dry along most of its course, but in summer it is an important source of water for the Murray River.

Darnley, Henry Stuart, Lord (1545-67), second husband of Mary Queen of Scots. Their son became James VI of Scotland and James I of England.

Darrow, Clarence Seward (1857-1938), U.S. lawyer, defense attorney, renowned for his opposition to capital punishment and his championing of underdogs. He left a prosperous corporate practice in 1894 to defend the Socialist leader Eugene Debs and won acclaim in 1925 for his defense of John Scopes, indicted for teaching Darwin's theory of evolution in a Tennessee public school.
See also: Creationism; Scopes trial.

Darter *see:* Anhinga.

Dartmouth (pop. 65,200), city in Nova Scotia, Canada, on Halifax Harbor, linked with Halifax on the western shore by a mile-long bridge. Dartmouth's industries include oil refining, shipbuilding, and aircraft-component manufacture.
See also: Nova Scotia.

Dartmouth College Case, U.S. Supreme Court decision of 1819 that denied the New Hampshire legislature the right to make Dartmouth College public without the consent of the college trustees. Such action was voided as impairing the obligation of contracts.

Darts, game of skill in which small wooden and metal feathered darts are thrown at a bull's-eye target. Singles, doubles, and team games can be played.

Darwin (pop. 73,000), largest city, administrative center, and chief port of the Northern Territory of Australia, on the Timor Sea. Originally called Palmerston, the city was renamed Darwin in 1911.
See also: Australia.

Darwin, Charles Robert (1809-82), English naturalist who formulated and elaborated the theory of evolution by natural selection. Darwin sailed around the world on the H.M.S. *Beagle* (1831-36), collecting data on the variability of species. In 1858 Darwin and Alfred Russel Wallace, working independently, published outlines of their concepts of natural selection. His greatest books were *The Origin of Species* (1859) and *The Descent of Man* (1871), which advanced overwhelming evidence for his theories.
See also: Natural selection; Social Darwinism.

Darwin, Erasmus (1731-1802), English biologist and poet, grandfather of Charles Darwin. His *Zoonomia* (1794-96) presented an early view of the doctrine of evolution.

Date Line, International *see:* International Date Line.

Date palm, date-producing tree (*Phoenix dactylifera*) of hot, dry climates. The many products of the date palm include: food and beverages, timber, materials for baskets and other artifacts, rope, fuel, animal feed, and packing material. In some areas the date palm is also grown as an ornamental tree, and it plays a role in religious ceremonies of Muslims, Christians, and Jews.

Datura, genus of plants of the nightshade family, having large, funnel-shaped flowers and yielding the strong narcotics atropine and hyoscyamine.

Daudet, Alphonse (1840-97), French writer noted for his stories of his native Provence, in southern France. He wrote with humor and compassion about the poor and is best remembered for *Letters from My Mill* (1866) and *Le Petit Chose* (1868).

Daughters of the American Revolution (DAR), patriotic, conservative women's organization founded in 1890 and made up of direct descendants of participants in the American Revolution. The DAR also preserves historical buildings and collects early U.S. records and objects.

Daughters of the Confederacy, United, U.S. organization founded 1894, whose members are descendants of veterans of the Confederate army and navy. The organization preserves Confederate history and provides aid for descendants of Confederates.
See also: Confederate States of America

D'Aulaire, husband and wife team who wrote and illustrated children's books. **Edgar Parin d'Aulaire** (1898-) and **Ingri Mortenson d'Aulaire** (1904-80) were awarded the Caldecott Medal for their 1940 biography *Abraham Lincoln*. In 1970 they won the Regina Medal. Their books include *Ola, Children of the North Lights,* and *George Washington*.

Daumier, Honoré (1808-79), French caricaturist, painter, and sculptor. In some 4,000 lithographs, he satirized the bourgeoisie and contemporary politicians, especially in the series *Parliamentary Idylls* and *The Representatives Represented* (1830-70). In 1832, his cartoon of King Louis-Philippe earned him six months in jail.

Davenport (pop. 350,861), city in east central Iowa, on the Mississippi River. It became a commercial center in 1856, when a railroad bridge was built across the river. Its main products include aluminum, cement, industrial and farm equipment, and processed meats. Davenport and the Illinois cities of Rock Island, Moline, and East Moline make up the metropolitan area referred to as the Quad Cities.
See also: Iowa.

David (c.1012-c.972 B.C.), king of ancient Israel, successor of Saul, and reputed author of many psalms. David is known as the killer of the Philistine giant Goliath. Chosen king of Judah on Saul's death, he seized Jerusalem, making it the religious and political capital of Israel. He was also known for his close friendship with Saul's son Jonathan and for his adultery with Bathsheba, wife of Uriah the Hittite. His reign lasted about 40 years.
See also: Israel.

David, name of 2 kings of Scotland. **David I** (1084-1153), who ruled 1124- 53, unsuccessfully fought England in support of his niece Matilda's claim to the English crown. But he was successful in obtaining Northumberland for his son. **David II** (David Bruce; 1324-71) became king in 1329, but fled to France when England invaded Scotland in 1332. In 1346 he invaded England with French allies. The English captured and held him for 11 years, after which he was ransomed and returned to Scotland.

David, Gerard (1460-1523), last master of the Bruges school of painting. He is noted for his emotional power and accomplished technique, as in the altarpieces *Rest on the Flight into Egypt* and *Madonna with Angels and Saints*.

David, Jacques Louis (1748-1825), French painter and leader of the neoclassical movement. His style, combining formal perfection with romantic feeling and didactic purpose, is exemplified in his *Oath of the Horatii* (1784), *Death of Socrates* (1787), and *Death of Marat* (1793). He was Napoleon's official painter.

David, Saint (c.520-600), patron saint of Wales. He founded many monasteries and churches in the 6th century. His feast day is March 1.

Davidson, Jo (1883-1952), U.S. sculptor who lived in Paris. Among famous sitters for his portrait busts were Gertrude Stein, Will Rogers, Franklin Roosevelt, and Mahatma Gandhi.

Davies, Arthur Bowen (1862-1928), U.S. painter in the romantic-idealist tradition. A leader of the American modern movement and a member of the Ashcan School as well as chief organizer of the 1913 Armory Show, Davis is noted for the lyrical and abstract *Unicorns and Dreams* (1908).

Charles Darwin

Da Vinci, Leonardo (1452-1519), Florentine artist and scientist, whose creative and intellectual talents made him the supreme genius of the Italian Renaissance. One of the greatest painters of the period, he was also an architect, engineer, astronomer, anatomist, botanist, inventor, poet, and musician. Few completed works survive; scholars attribute this to Leonardo's restless movement from one project to another, his dissatisfaction with many of them, which were then left unfinished or were destroyed, and his habit of experimenting with new materials, some of which eventually decayed.

Portrait of Ginevra Benci *by Leonardo Da Vinci (c. 1480)*

Leonardo studied art under Andrea del Verrocchio. His mature style is first glimpsed in the unfinished *Adoration of the Magi* (1481), with its subtle tones of light and shade and its dynamic figures, and comes to full development in *The Madonna of the Rocks* (c.1482), painted when Leonardo was already in the service of the duke of Milan. He worked for the duke for 16 years, designing statuary and fortifications and sketching plans for new towns and cathedrals. He also completed *The Last Supper*, in the monastery of Santa Maria delle Grazie in Milan (c.1498), now badly decayed due to his inexperience with fresco techniques. Leonardo's drawings, which constitute most of his surviving work, display fine shading and delicacy. He used various media—colored chalk, pen, and metal points—and his subject range was enormous, reflecting his interest in nature and including comparative studies of youth and old age and a series on the cataclysmic movements of water. Leonardo returned to Florence in 1500 and painted "Mona Lisa," or *La Gioconda*, a landmark in portraiture. While still in the service of the duke of Milan, Leonardo designed a canal system with locks that is still in operation. For Cesare Borgia he planned fortifications (1502-3), drew excellent maps, and designed a tanklike armored vehicle and a breech-loading cannon. He may have join-

Bette Davis

ed (c.1513) Donato Bramante, Raphael, and Michelangelo in Rome to work on the Vatican and, possibly, plans for the new St. Peter's. Leonardo's notebooks, filled with ideas and sketches on anatomy, hydraulics, aeronautics, and machinery, are the best evidence of his genius; many of his inventions were centuries ahead of their time.

Davis, Benjamin Oliver (1877-1970), first African-American general in the U.S. Army (1940). He later supervised the desegregation of troop units. His son, Benjamin Oliver, Jr. (1912-), became the first African-American general in the Air Force.

Davis, Bette (1908-90), U.S. film actress who won Academy Awards for her roles in *Dangerous* (1935) and *Jezebel* (1938). In the 1960s she won new fame in psychological thrillers. Other major films of hers include *Dark Victory* (1939), *The Little Foxes* (1941), and *All About Eve* (1950).

Davis, David (1815-86), U.S. politician and Supreme Court justice 1862-77. He managed Lincoln's campaign for the presidential nomination at the 1860 Republican convention.
See also: Supreme Court of the United States.

Davis, Henry Gassaway (1823-1916), U.S. politician; U.S. senator from West Virginia 1871-83. In 1904 he was the Democratic candidate for vice president on the Alton B. Parker ticket, which lost to Theodore Roosevelt and Charles W. Fairbanks.

Davis, Jefferson (1808-89), president of the Confederate States of America during the Civil War. U.S. Senator from Mississippi (1847-51, 1857-61) and secretary of War (1853-57), Davis resigned from the Senate after Mississippi's secession from the Union in 1861. In 1862 Davis was inaugurated president of the Confederacy. His war measures weakened states' rights and distanced him from his Congress. Davis served 2 years in federal prison after the surrender of the South in 1865, but was released without being prosecuted.
See also: Civil War, U.S.; Confederate States of America.

Miles Davis

Davis, John (c.1550-1605), English navigator and early Arctic explorer. He discovered the Davis Strait between Greenland and Baffin Island (1587) as well as the Falkland Islands (1592).
See also: Falkland Islands.

Davis, John William (1873-1955), U.S. politician and Democratic presidential candidate in 1924, losing to Calvin Coolidge. After his unsuccessful bid for the presidency, he returned to private law practice. A distinguished constitutional lawyer, he argued 140 cases before the U.S. Supreme Court.

Davis, Miles Dewey (1926-), U.S. jazz musician, one of the pioneers of "bebop" in the 1940s and of "cool" jazz, with its restrained, clear sounds, in the 1950s. A renowned trumpeter, Davis played with many outstanding musicians, including Charlie Parker and John Coltrane. In the late 1960s he produced a new sound, based on a fusion of jazz and rock, and after a period of retirement, he reemerged in the 1980s as one of the major innovators in U.S. music.
See also: Jazz.

Davis, Paulina Wright (1813-76), U.S. social reformer who worked for women's rights, campaigning in the 1840s against property laws that made a man the owner of his wife's possessions. Her efforts helped pass a New York law (1848) allowing women to own property. Anatomy lectures she gave from 1845 to 1849 inspired some women to become doctors. She helped organize the first and second national woman's rights conventions, held in 1850 and 1851. She published *Una*, a woman's rights magazine, from 1853 to 1855.
See also: Women's movements.

Davis, Richard Harding (1864-1916), U.S. writer, journalist, and war correspondent. He also wrote novels, short stories, and plays.

Davis, Samuel (1842-63), Confederate spy, hanged by Union troops for refusing to reveal the source of his information. His birthplace in Tennessee is kept as a shrine.
See also: Civil War, U.S.

Davis, Stuart (1894-1964), U.S. abstract painter, illustrator, and lithographer. His style is characterized by brilliant colors, the use of printed words, and interlocking shapes.

Davis Cup, international men's tennis trophy, first contested in 1900. Sixteen qualifying nations are divided into 4 zones, and their teams compete for the annual award.

Davis Strait *see:* Northwest Passage.

Davy, Sir Humphry (1778-1829), English chemist who pioneered the study of electrochemistry. Electrolytic methods allowed him to isolate the elements sodium, potassium, magnesium, calcium, boron, and barium (1807-8). He recognized the elemental nature of and named chlorine (1810). His early work on nitrous oxide was done at Bristol under Thomas Beddoes, but his later career centered on the Royal Institution, where he was assisted by Michael Faraday. He also invented a miner's safety lamp, known as the Davy lamp.
See also: Electrochemistry.

Dawes, Charles Gates (1865-1951), U.S. politician who shared the 1925 Nobel Peace Prize for the plan named after him. Vice president under Calvin Coolidge (1925-29), he was later ambassador to Great Britain (1929-32).
See also: Dawes Plan.

Dawes Act *see:* Native Americans.

Dawes Plan, program presented by Charles Gates Dawes in 1924 to enable Germany to pay off World War I reparations by means of an international loan and mortgages on German industry and railways.
See also: War debt.

Day, 24-hour period during which the earth completes one rotation on its axis as it rotates around the sun. The day is divided into 2 equal parts: from midnight (the beginning of the new day) to noon is designated as a.m. and from noon to midnight is p.m. The term day commonly refers to the time that the sun actually shines during the 24-hour period (the term night refers to the time it doesn't shine). The amount of daylight varies greatly in different parts of the world.

Day, Clarence (1874-1935), U.S. writer of essays, sketches, reviews, and stories. His best-known works are *Life with Father* (1935) and *Life with Mother* (published posthumously in 1937), which poked affectionate fun at upper-class family life in New York City c.1900.

Day, Dorothy (1897-1980), U.S. social activist. A reporter for left-wing papers, she was active in the Socialist movement before joining the Roman Catholic Church in 1927. She publicized the Catholic Church's social programs in the newspaper *Catholic Worker*, opened a house in New York for the hungry and homeless, and supported numerous liberal causes.

Dayaks *see:* Dyaks.

Dayan, Moshe (1915-81), Israeli military and political leader. Active in Israel's War of Independence (1948), he commanded

the Israeli forces during the 1956 Sinai Campaign. He was minister of defense during the Six Day War of June, 1967 and from 1969 to 1974, when he resigned after being blamed for Israel's unpreparedness in the Yom Kippur War of October 1973. He was foreign minister 1977-79.
See also: Israel.

Dayfly *see:* Mayfly.

Day-Lewis, Cecil (1904-72), English author. *The Magnetic Mountain* (1933) is his best-known volume of verse from the 1930s, but his style matured fully after 1945. He wrote novels under his own name and detective novels as Nicholas Blake. He was poet laureate (1968-72).

Daylight saving time, method of making better use of daylight by setting clocks 1 hour ahead of standard time. Daylight saving time came into use in the United States and other countries during World War I, in an effort to conserve electricity by having business hours correspond more closely to the hours of natural daylight. It was again put into effect on a national scale during World War II, after which the matter was left to the discretion of local authorities. Daylight saving time in the United States now extends from the second Sunday in April to the last Sunday in October.

Day lily, any of several plants (genus *Hemerocallis*) of the lily family, growing 3-5 ft (91-150 cm) high. The day lily has sword-shaped leaves and yellow or orange, funnel-shaped flowers, which live only from sunrise to sunset.

Day of Atonement *see:* Yom Kippur.

Dayton (pop. 951,270), city in southwestern Ohio, seat of Montgomery County. The birthplace of the Wright brothers, who established an aviation research plant there after their historic first flight, Dayton became an industrial research center and producer of precision products.
See also: Ohio.

Dayton, Jonathan (1760-1824), U.S. soldier and politician, youngest signer of the Constitution (1787). He was a congressional representative (1791-99), Speaker of the House (1795-99), and U.S. senator from New Jersey (1799-1805). An associate of Vice President Aaron Burr, Dayton was charged with treason in 1807 but was never brought to trial.

Daytona Beach (pop. 370,712), city in northeastern Florida, 90 mi (145 km) southeast of Jacksonville. Founded in 1870, it is made up of the former communities of Daytona, Daytona Beach, and Seabreeze, which were consolidated and incorporated as Daytona Beach in 1926. Tourism is the area's principal industry. Its hard, flat 23-mi (37-km) long beach has been used for automobile speed trials since 1903.
See also: Florida.

DC *see:* Electric current.

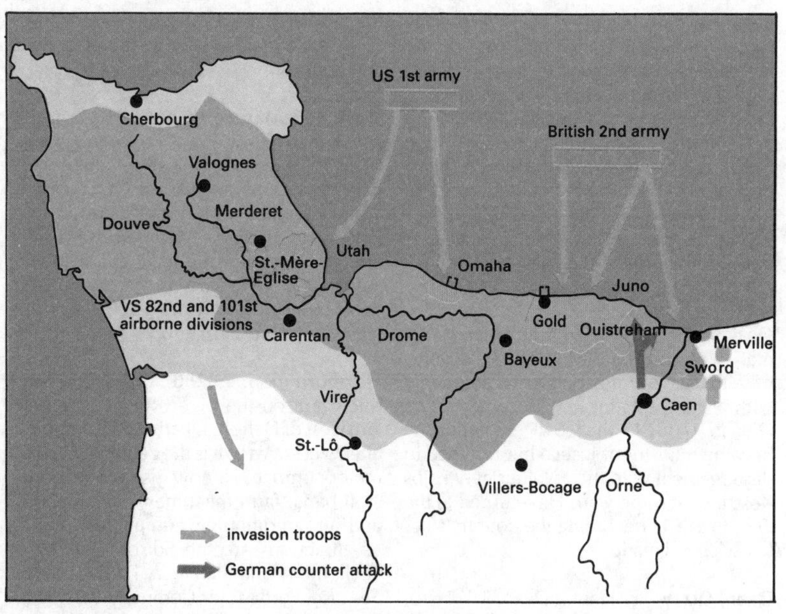

D-Day invasion in Normandy. Eisenhower was in supreme command of the invasion army, the U.S. First Army under Bradley and the Second Army under Dempsey. The landings took place on the beaches codenamed Utah, Omaha, Gold, Juno, and Sword. The colored zones indicate the conquered territory on June 6, June 22, and July 18.

D-Day, in World War II, June 6, 1944, the day Allied troops landed in Normandy, France, thus launching the last major campaign in Western Europe, under the command of General Eisenhower. Over 5,000 ships were used, delivering some 90,000 troops, primarily British, U.S., and Canadian. Some 20,000 more were delivered by parachute and glider. By June 11 the forces had linked up in a solid front. The invasion, code-named Overlord, was one of the most complex feats of organization and supply in military history.
See also: World War II.

DDT (dichloro-diphenyl-trichloroethane), powerful insecticide. Because of concern about the persistence of its toxic residues, DDT is no longer marketed for commercial use in the United States.
See also: Insecticide.

DEA *see:* Drug Enforcement Administration.

Deacon (Greek *diakonos*, "servant"), assistant to the clergy in a Christian church. Deacons form a minor holy order in the Roman Catholic church and an important class of clergy in the Orthodox church. In Protestant churches deacons are usually laymen given special church responsibilities. Some Protestants maintain the office of deaconess, women who undergo religious training and devote themselves to serving the church.
See also: Christianity.

Deadly nightshade *see:* Belladonna.

Dead Sea, salt lake in the Great Rift Valley, on the Israel-Jordan border. About 390 sq mi (1,010 sq km) in area, the Dead Sea extends some 50 mi (80 km) south from the mouth of the Jordan River and is up to 11 mi (17.7 km) wide. Much of it is more than 1,000 ft (305 m) deep; at surface 1,292 ft (394 m) below sea level, it is the lowest point on earth. Its high salt content (over 20%) results from the rapid evaporation in the area's hot climate and prevents any aquatic life from surviving.

Dead Sea Scrolls, group of Hebrew and Aramaic manuscripts discovered in caves near the northwestern coast of the Dead Sea in 1947 and later. The scrolls, preserved in clay jars, were written between the 1st century B.C. and about A.D. 50. Many of the scrolls are books of the Old Testament, the most important of these being 2 complete texts of the Book of Isaiah, at least a thousand years older than any known copy. Among the non-biblical texts is one describing the "war of the sons of light against the sons of darkness," believed to be an allegory on political events of the time.
Another important work is the *Manual of Discipline*, of a group of Jewish ascetics usually identified with the Essenes. Because many of their beliefs were similar to those of the early Christians, it has been suggested that they had some connection with or influence on early Christianity.
See also: Bible.

Deadwood (pop. 1,830), city in the Black Hills of South Dakota; the seat of Lawrence County. A gold rush in 1876 brought a huge influx of prospectors to the area, many of whom settled in Deadwood Gulch, the site of present-day Deadwood. Colorful figures from the town's early days include Wild Bill Hickok, Calamity Jane, and Deadwood Dick.
See also: South Dakota.

Deafness, partial or total impairment of the sense of hearing. Hearing loss is of 2 basic types. In *conductive* deafness, the eardrum cannot make the bones of the inner ear vibrate. The nerve endings deep inside the ear are not stimulated, and the brain receives no message. This may be caused by blockage of the ear canal by wax or a foreign body; infections and perforation of the eardrum are other causes. This form of

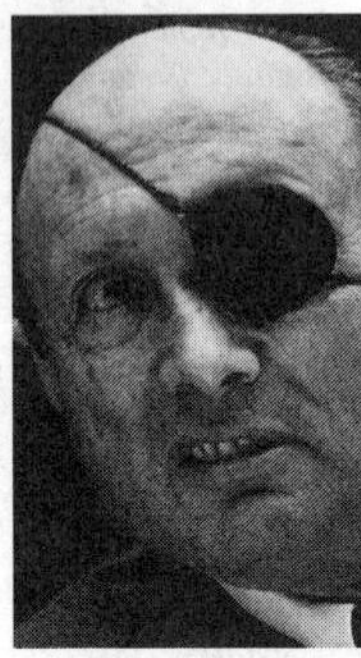
Moshe Dayan

James Dean

deafness can usually be corrected by surgery, antibiotics, hearing aids, or other techniques. *Nerve* (perceptive) deafness, on the other hand, stems from damage to the hearing nerve itself, which prevents the nerve from transmitting to the brain the message it receives from the vibrating eardrum and bones. The most common cause is atherosclerosis of the blood vessels supplying the nerve or injury due to excessive noise. This form of deafness is often permanent.

Deák, Ferenc (1803-76), Hungarian statesman who negotiated the 1867 Compromise that gave Hungary internal autonomy within Austria-Hungary. He entered the Diet in 1833. In the 1848 revolution he became minister of justice but resigned in disagreement with the revolutionary Lajos Kossuth the same year. He returned to the Diet in 1861, becoming the country's acknowledged leader.

Dean, Dizzy (Jay Hanna Dean; 1911-74), U.S. baseball pitcher. He played for the St. Louis Cardinals (1930-37), Chicago Cubs (1938-41), and pitched one game for the St. Louis Browns (1947). Dean's achievements include winning the Most Valuable Player award (1934), and in the same season leading the St. Louis Cardinals to a World Series victory by winning 30 games in the regular season, and 2 in the World Series. Dean was inducted into the National Baseball Hall of Fame in 1953.

Dean, James (1931-55), U.S. actor. Elia Kazan recognized his talent in the New York stage play *The Immoralist* (1954) and cast him in the film *East of Eden* (1955). His next film, *Rebel Without a Cause* (1955), established him as the romantic, rebellious antihero of a generation, but his career ended tragically when he was killed in a car crash.

Deane, Silas (1737-89), U.S. diplomat and first envoy to Europe. Sent to France in 1776, he was successful in recruiting officers and obtaining arms. Unpopular in the United States for urging reconciliation with England (1781), he went into exile in that country.

De Angeli, Marguerite Lofft (1889-), U.S. author and illustrator of children's books. Many of her stories feature children of minority groups, such as the Quaker girl in *Thee Hannah* (1940), the Pennsylvania Dutch boy in *Yonie Wondernose* (1944), and the African-American girl in *Bright April* (1946). *The Door in the Wall* (1949), about English life in the 1300s, won the Newbery Award in 1950.

Dearborn (pop. 89,286), city in southeast Michigan, on the River Rouge 10 mi (16 km) west of Detroit. Dearborn grew rapidly after World War I. It is the center of the Ford motor company. It now also produces aircraft parts, farm machinery, metal goods, and air-conditioning equipment. Among its attractions are the Edison Institute of Technology and the Henry Ford Museum. *See also:* Ford Motor Company; Michigan.

Dearborn, Henry (1751-1829), U.S. soldier and politician. A captain of militia during the Revolution, he was secretary of war under Thomas Jefferson (1801-09). During the War of 1812, he commanded the Northern frontier but incurred heavy losses and was relieved of his command. He also served as a U.S. representative (1793-77) and minister to Portugal (1822-24). Chicago's Fort Dearborn was named for him.

Death, complete and irreversible cessation of life in an organism or part of an organism. The moment of death is conventionally accepted as the time when the heart ceases to beat, there is no breathing, and the brain shows no evidence of function. Since it is possible to resuscitate and maintain heart function and to take over breathing mechanically, the brain may suffer irreversible death while "life" is maintained artificially. In "brain death," reversible causes have been eliminated, and there is no spontaneous breathing, no movement, and no specific reflexes seen on 2 occasions; artificial life support systems can then be reasonably discontinued. After death, enzymes begin the process of *autolysis* (decomposition), which later involves bacteria. In the hours following death, changes occur in muscle that cause rigidity (*rigor mortis*). Death of part of an organism (*necrosis*), such as occurs following lack of blood supply, consists of loss of cell organization, autolysis, and gangrene. The part may separate or be absorbed, but infection is liable to spread to living tissue. Cells may also die as part of the normal turnover of a structure (for example, skin or blood cells), because of compression (for example, by a tumor), or as part of a degenerative disease.

Criteria of death. The entire body does not die at the same rate; breathing and heart action may stop, but other functions may continue. In humans, for example, the kidneys, skin, bone, liver, pancreas, cornea, and heart have been transplanted into needy recipients and may continue to function for a long period. When on an artificial respirator, an individual may maintain a heartbeat. But is that person truly alive? If the respirator were turned off, how long would the person remain alive? What happens to the brain of a person maintained on a respirator? These questions have serious ethical, religious, and legal implications. The sequence of events toward the cessation of life suggests 4 stages: (1) a time of impending death, (2) a period of reversibility, with or without residual change, (3) a period of irreversibility, (4) absolute death, as set forth in the current legal definition, and (5) murder.

Causes of death. Natural death is often assumed to be due to coronary thrombosis ("heart attack"); the most common cause is ischemic (blood-starved) heart disease, though not necessarily the result of thrombosis. Other common causes of death are acute hypersensitive heart failure (that is, due to very high blood pressure), pulmonary embolism (a clot that has traveled to the lung), and subarachnoid or cerebral hemorrhage (stroke).

The principal causes of unnatural deaths are (1) mechanical violence, including traffic accidents, industrial mishaps or disasters, sexual and other forms of assault, and homicide, (2) physical agencies, such as heat, cold, electricity, or radiation, (3) deprivation involving the complete or partial lack of basic essentials, such as water, food, or warmth, and (4) poisoning (chemicals and drugs, anesthetics, intravenous infusions, and blood transfusions).

Death penalty *see:* Capital punishment.

Death's-head moth, large moth (*Acherontia atropos*) of the family Sphingidae. Found in Africa and Europe, it has a thick, hairy body with relatively small wings and feeds on flowers and honey.

Death Valley, arid valley in southeast California and southern Nevada. The United States' highest recorded air temperature—134°F (56°C)—was recorded here in 1913.

Death Valley

Death Valley is 140 mi (225 km) long and up to 15 mi (24 km) wide. The lowest point in the Western Hemisphere, Badwater (282 ft/86 m below sea level), is at the heart of the valley. In 1933 it was made the Death Valley National Monument.

Deathwatch, any of several beetles belonging to the family Anobiidae. They bore through wood and furniture by knocking their heads against it, making a clicking sound. An old superstition held that the sound foretold death.

DeBakey, Michael Ellis (1908-), U.S. heart surgeon who developed the pump for the heart-lung machine (1932), devised a new surgical procedure to treat aneurysm, and successfully implanted a mechanical device to help restore a diseased heart (1967).

Debate, formal and regulated discussion of a given proposition. Platform debates, popular at many high schools and colleges, have precise rules and procedures. Legislative debates are more flexible.

Deborah, prophet and judge in the Old Testament. A member of the tribe of Ephraim, she enlisted the Israelite leader in the fight against the Canaanites, led by Sisera. After the battle at Mt. Tabor, in which the Canaanites were routed, she sang a song of victory (Judges 5), "The Song of Deborah," dedicated to the God of Israel.
See also: Bible; Old Testament.

Debrecen (pop. 211,800), city in Hungary, 120 m (193 km) east of Budapest. A market for surrounding farms since the Middle Ages, it is also a religious, political, cultural, and educational center. In the 1500s it was a stronghold of Protestantism.
See also: Hungary.

De Broglie, Prince Louis Victor (1892-1987), French physicist who received the 1929 Nobel Prize in physics for his discovery that the behavior of electrons, like that of light, could be explained in terms of wave motion. De Broglie's theory led to the development of wave mechanics, an important part of quantum mechanics.
See also: Quantum mechanics.

Debs, Eugene Victor (1855-1926), U.S. labor organizer and socialist political leader. A national leader of the Brotherhood of Locomotive Firemen, he founded the American Railway Union in 1893. Debs was jailed in 1895 for defying a federal court injunction during the Pullman railroad strike. Five times the Socialist party's candidate for the presidency, he waged his last and most successful campaign in 1920, while still imprisoned under the Espionage Act (1917) for his political opposition to World War I. He was released in 1921.

Debt, something owed, whether money, services, or goods. The debtor usually pays interest to the creditor (to whom the debt is owed). If the debtor fails to pay the debt, the creditor can take court action to try to acquire some of the debtor's property. Laws determine what may be seized.

Debussy, Claude Achille (1862-1918), French composer. Although influenced by Wagner in his early years, he later developed a highly original style of musical impressionism, based on his own revolutionary thinking about harmony and his studies of Asian music. *Prelude to the Afternoon of a Faun* (1894), the three *Nocturnes* (1899), and *La Mer* (1905) are among Debussy's most imaginatively scored orchestral works. *Pelléas et Mélisande* (1902) is a landmark in operatic history. His pieces for piano include *Reflets dans l'eau, Jardins sous la pluie, Poissons d'or,* 2 sets of preludes, and 12 études.

Debye, Peter Joseph William (1884-1966), Dutch physical chemist chiefly known for the Debye-Hückel theory of ionic solution (1923). He was awarded the 1936 Nobel Prize in chemistry and was head of the chemistry department of Cornell University (1940-50).
See also: Chemistry.

Decalogue *see:* Ten Commandments.

Decameron, The, collection of 100 stories (written 1348-53) by the Italian author Giovanni Boccaccio. Amusing and often bawdy, the tales are considered among the masterpieces of Italian and world literature. They also provide a shrewd commentary on 14th-century Italian life.
See also: Boccaccio, Giovanni.

Decathlon, 10-event track-and-field contest consisting of the 100-meter dash; the 400-meter and 1,500-meter flat races; the 110-meter hurdle race; pole vaulting; discus throwing; shot putting; javelin throwing; and the broad and high jumps. The decathlon has been an Olympic event since 1912.
See also: Track and field.

Decatur (pop. 117,206), city in central Illinois located on the Sangamon River and named after the U.S. naval officer Stephen Decatur. A principal railroad junction, Decatur is the trading center for the region's farm products and livestock. It was the city where the young Abraham Lincoln made his first home in Illinois.
See also: Illinois.

Decatur, Stephen (1779-1820), U.S. naval hero. He was responsible for many victories in the Barbary Wars (1804) and later in the War of 1812, when he commanded the *United States*. He served as a U.S. navy commissioner until his death in a duel. He is famous for saying: "Our country, right or wrong."

Decembrist revolt, unsuccessful uprising against the tsarist government in Russia organized by army officers in December 1825. The sudden death of Alexander I led to uncertainty and turmoil, and the Decembrists — many of whom had absorbed liberal ideals while serving in West Europe during the Napoleonic Wars — took the opportunity to rise up against Alexander's successor, Tsar Nicholas I. The rebellion was crushed, and 5 of the leaders were hanged. Many others were exiled to Siberia.

Decemvirs *see:* Twelve Tables, Laws of the.

Decibel (dB), measurement of sound intensity; one-tenth of a bel. The human ear can distinguish sounds at a level of 10 dBs and can tolerate sounds up to 120 decibels.

Deciduous tree, any of those trees that shed their leaves each year, usually in the fall. The tree reabsorbs food material from the leaves before they fall, and their loss greatly reduces the amount of water that evaporates from the tree, thus helping survival in bad weather. Trees that retain their leaves all year are called evergreens.

Decimal system, system of computation based on the number 10 (Latin *decem*). Almost all countries use the decimal system. The system uses 10 numerals — 0, 1, 2, 3, 4, 5, 6, 7, 8 and 9 — to represent any number as the sum of powers of 10. The *units* place indicates multiples of 10^0 (defined as 1), the *tens* place indicates multiples of 10^1, the *hundreds* place indicates multiples of 10^2, and so forth. Thus the number 4,256 means $(4x10^3) + (2x10^2) + (5x10^1) + (6x10^0)$. The system is also used to represent numbers between 0 and 1. Thus 1.345 means $(1x10^0) + (3x10^{-1}) + (4x10^{-2}) + (5x10^{-3})$. A decimal point is used to separate the part between 0 and 1 from the rest of the number; 4,256.345.
The decimal system was invented by the Hindus c.600 A.D. They introduced the concept of *zero* or 0. The system was spread throughout North Africa and Europe by the Arabs in the next few centuries.

A portrait of the author of the Decameron, Giovanni Boccaccio

Declaration of Independence, document in which representatives of the 13 American colonies set forth the reasons for their break with Britain. July 4, the day in 1776 on which the Continental Congress adopted the Declaration of Independence, is observed as Independence Day, a U.S. national holiday. A royal proclamation of Aug. 1775 held the colonies to be in a state of rebellion, and in Nov. the British instituted a naval blockade. Prolonged hostilities seemed inevitable, and formal independence was advocated to help the colonies gain assistance from France and Spain. The case for independence was strongly reinforced by the publication of Thomas Paine's *Common Sense* (Jan. 1776). Acting on instructions from the Virginia legislature, Richard Henry Lee introduced a resolution to the Continental Congress on June 7, 1776, stating that "these United Colonies are, and of right ought to be, free and independent States." Congress appointed a committee to draw up a formal declaration of independence for consideration. Thomas Jefferson was assigned to draft the document. On July 2,

12 of the 13 colonies approved Lee's resolution, with New York temporarily abstaining. Debate on the Declaration began on July 3, and after a few alterations, it was adopted the following day. Southern sensitivities over slavery caused the most important change: A clause censuring the king for aiding and abetting the slave trade was struck out. Another section that had placed blame on the people of England as well as the king was also eliminated. Only John Hancock, the president of the Congress, and Charles Thompson, the secretary, signed the document on July 4. On Aug. 2, 50 members signed, with another 6 putting their signatures to it later.

Declaration of the Rights of Man and the Citizen, key philosophical document of the French Revolution, adopted by the National Assembly on August 26, 1789. It reflects the French Enlightenment's rejection of the rule of absolute monarchy in favor of natural rights. These included equality, popular sovereignty (i.e. rule of the people), and individual rights to liberty, property, and freedom from arbitrary government abuse. It was made the preamble to the 1791 Constitution.
See also: French Revolution

Declaratory Act *see:* Revolutionary War in America.

Declination, in astronomy, one of two coordinates used to specify the position of an object in the sky under the equatorial coordinate system. Declination in the sky is roughly equivalent to latitude on earth. An object north of the celestial equator (an extension of the earth's equator) is said to have a positive declination, written with a plus sign. An object south of the celestial equator has a negative, or minus, declination.
See also: Astronomy.

Decode, in information science, the translation or determination of the meaning of a coded set of data. A *decoder* is a matrix of switching elements that selects one or more output channels according to the combination of input signals present.

Decomposition, chemical, reduction of a compound to simpler substances, or to its elemental components. The materials obtained after the chemical breakdown differ in their properties both from each other and from the original substances. Heat is the simplest agent of decomposition. Reducing metallic ores to separate out the pure metal uses heat along with other chemicals. Water can be decomposed into hydrogen and oxygen by electrolysis. The decomposition of organic matter is known as putrefaction.
See also: Compound.

Decompression sickness *see:* Bends.

Decoration Day *see:* Memorial Day.

Decorations, medals, and orders, awards acknowledging exceptional civil or military service, acts of bravery, and notable achievements in the arts and sciences. In the United States the highest civil decoration is the *Presidential Medal of Freedom*; the *Medal for Merit* is also a civil decoration for outstanding services. The highest military decoration "for conspicuous gallantry at the risk of life" is the *Congressional Medal of Honor*. The *Purple Heart* (once George Washington's *Badge of Military Merit* and revived in 1932) is awarded to service people wounded by enemy action. Britain's highest military decoration is the *Victoria Cross*, which, like other British decorations, may also be awarded to nationals of Commonwealth countries such as Canada. France awards the *Médaille Militaire* and the *Croix de Guerre*, and also recognizes outstanding civil or military service by membership (in various grades) in the *Legion of Honor*. There were also different grades of Germany's most famous decoration, the *Iron Cross*, which was awarded up through World War II. The highest award of the German Federal Republic is now the *Order of Merit*. The Soviet Union has many orders, but its highest honor is the *Heroes of the Soviet Union* medal. China has such honors as *Hero of the Army of the People's Liberation*. Japan has the *Order of the Chrysanthemum*.

Decorative arts, term covering a variety of artistic activities (including woodworking, glass handicrafts, textiles, and metalworking) not traditionally included in the fine arts, which include painting, sculpture, and architecture. The aim of the decorative arts is to beautify surroundings. Decorative artisans create furniture, porcelain, jewelry, and fabrics, as well as embellishments of buildings, such as gilding and molded plasterwork.

Decoupage (from French *découper*, "to cut out"), decorative art form in which paper shapes are glued onto other items and covered with coats of varnish. Used first in 17th-century France to embellish furniture, giving it the appearance and texture of enamel, decoupage became popular throughout Europe. A resurgence of interest occurred in the U.S. in the 1960s.

Deductive method, the process of reasoning by which conclusions are drawn by logical inference from given premises. The Aristotelian syllogism is an example of deductive logic. Conclusions reached by deductive reasoning are called valid rather than true to distinguish that which follows logically from that which is the case.

Dee, John (1527-1628), English philosopher and mathematician accused of sorcery against Queen Mary. He was tried and acquitted by the Star Chamber (1555). Dee created special reports for Queen Elizabeth detailing the geographical and aquatic characteristics of newly discovered regions. He also wrote several treatises on alchemy, navigation, and mathematics.

Deed, legal document transferring the ownership of property.

Deep, ocean area with a depth in excess of 18,000 ft (5,490 m). More than 100 deeps have been identified in ocean floors. Mariana Trench, located 200 mi (320 km) southwest of Guam, is the deepest ocean deep with an ocean floor at 36,498 ft (11,033 m) below the surface. The Milwaukee Deep, north of Puerto Rico, has the greatest depth in the Atlantic Ocean at 28,374 ft. (8,648 m).

Deer, any of about 40 species of cloven-hoofed mammals of the family Cervidae, found in Europe, Asia, and the Americas. Their most remarkable characteristic is the antlers of the males. Only the musk deer and the Chinese water deer lack antlers, while both sexes of the caribou and the reindeer are antlered. The smallest deer is the South American pudu, 13 in (33 cm) at the shoulder; the largest is the North American moose, up to 7 ft (2.1 m) and over 1000 lb (454 km) in weight. Though many

Two male deer (bucks) fighting for the attention of the female during mating season

species are abundant, some, such as the axis deer of India and Sri Lanka, are fast becoming rare. The Chinese Pere David's deer survives mainly in zoos but is gradually being re-introduced to the wild in preserves.

Deere, John (1804-86), U.S. inventor who developed and marketed the first steel plows.

Deer fly, insect belonging to the horsefly family, found throughout North America. They bite both large animals and people and sometimes carry disease-causing germs.

Deerhound, Scottish breed of dog skilled at hunting deer by sight. Deerhounds have coarse, wiry coats of gray or tan. They measure 28 to 32 in (71-81 cm) and weigh 75 to 110 lb (34-50 kg).

De facto segregation *see:* Segregation.

De Falla, Manuel *see:* Falla, Manuel de.

Defenestration of Prague *see:* Thirty Years' War.

Defense, Department of, executive department of the U.S. government responsible for the recruitment, training, organization, and operation of the armed forces. The National Security Act of 1947 superseded the War Department and brought the previously separate departments of the Army, Navy, and Air Force into the National Military Establishment, which was renamed the Department of Defense in 1949. The secretary of defense, a civilian, heads the department. The civilian staff also includes a deputy secretary and 7 assistant secretaries. Within the military itself, the chiefs of staff of the Army and Air Force, the chief of naval operations, and the commandant of the Marine Corps constitute the Joint Chiefs of Staff (JCS), which has one additional member: the chairman. The JCS advise the secretary of defense, the national security council, and the president on military questions. They are aided by the Joint Staff, composed of some 500 officers from the three services. The department of defense employs over 5 million people.

Defense mechanism, term in psychoanalysis referring to involuntary or unconscious measures adopted by individuals to protect themselves against painful emotions associated with some disagreeable physical or mental situation of frequent occurrence. Defense mechanisms include repression, which prevents painful ideas from entering the conscious mind; displacement, in which impulses are released through disguised actions; and sublimation, the redirection of impulses into socially acceptable channels.
See also: Psychoanalysis.

Defoe, Daniel (1660?-1731), English author, one of the originators of the English novel. Originally a merchant, he later took to writing essays and pamphlets, including *The Shortest Way with Dissenters* (1702), a satire parodying the leaders of the Anglican High Church (for which he was fined and pilloried). He was nearly 60 when he began writing the realistic novels for which he is best known, including *Robinson Crusoe* (1719), *Moll Flanders* (1722), and *A Journal of the Plague Year* (1722).

De Forest, Lee (1873-1961), U.S. inventor of the triode (1906), an electron tube with three electrodes that could operate as a signal amplifier as well as a rectifier. The triode was crucial to the development of radio and intercontinental telephony.
See also: Vacuum tube.

Degas, (Hilaire Germain) Edgar (1834-1917), French painter and sculptor associated with impressionism. His favorite subjects were ballet dancers and racetrack scenes. From the 1880s, Degas worked regularly in pastel and produced small bronze sculptures of dancers and horses. Among his best-known paintings are *The Bellelli Family* (1859), *The Rehearsal* (1882), and *The Millinery Shop* (c.1885).
See also: Impressionism.

De Gasperi, Alcide (1881-1954), Italian statesman. Active in political life from 1911, he was twice imprisoned for his opposition to the fascist regime. He clandestinely organized the Christian Democratic Party during World War II and, as its leader, became the first premier (1945-53) of the new Italian Republic.
See also: Italy.

De Gaulle, Charles (1890-1970), French soldier and political leader, president 1945-46 and 1958-69. When France fell to Germany in 1940, De Gaulle launched the Free French movement in England. In 1944, his provisional government took power in liberated France. After resigning in 1946, he returned the following year leading a new party, but met with little success and retired in 1953. On June 1, 1958, at the height of the Algerian crisis, he was named premier and assumed new and wider powers, effectively ending the fourth republic. In 1959 a new constitution was adopted, inaugurating the fifth republic, with De Gaulle as president. He was nearly overthrown by worker-student struggles in 1968 and resigned in 1969 upon the defeat of a referendum designed to give him further powers for constitutional reforms.
See also: France.

Charles de Gaulle

Degree, academic, title conferred by a university as a recognition of academic competence. Degrees were originally awarded after the candidate had successfully passed a vigorous oral examination, but abuse of this system (particularly in the 18th century at Oxford and Cambridge) led to the gradual adoption of the written examination, at least for the lower (bachelor) degrees. *Master's* and *doctor's* degrees are usually awarded for research work undertaken after passing a first degree examination. *Honorary degrees* are now awarded to distinguished diplomats or artists, without regard to their academic standing. In the United States special achievement in the bachelor's degree is recognized by the Latin terms (in ascending order of excellence) *cum laude, magna cum laude,* and *summa cum laude.*
The most commonly awarded degrees are B.A. (Bachelor of Arts), B.S. (Bachelor of Science), M.A. (Master of Arts), M.S. (Master of Science), Ph.D. (Doctor of Philosophy), LL.B. (Bachelor of Laws), LL.M. (Master of Laws), LL.D. (Doctor of Laws) or J.D. (Doctor of Jurisprudence), M.D. (Doctor of Medicine), and B.D. (Bachelor of Divinity).

De Groot, Huig *see:* Grotius, Hugo.

Edgar Degas's painting The Tub *(1886)*

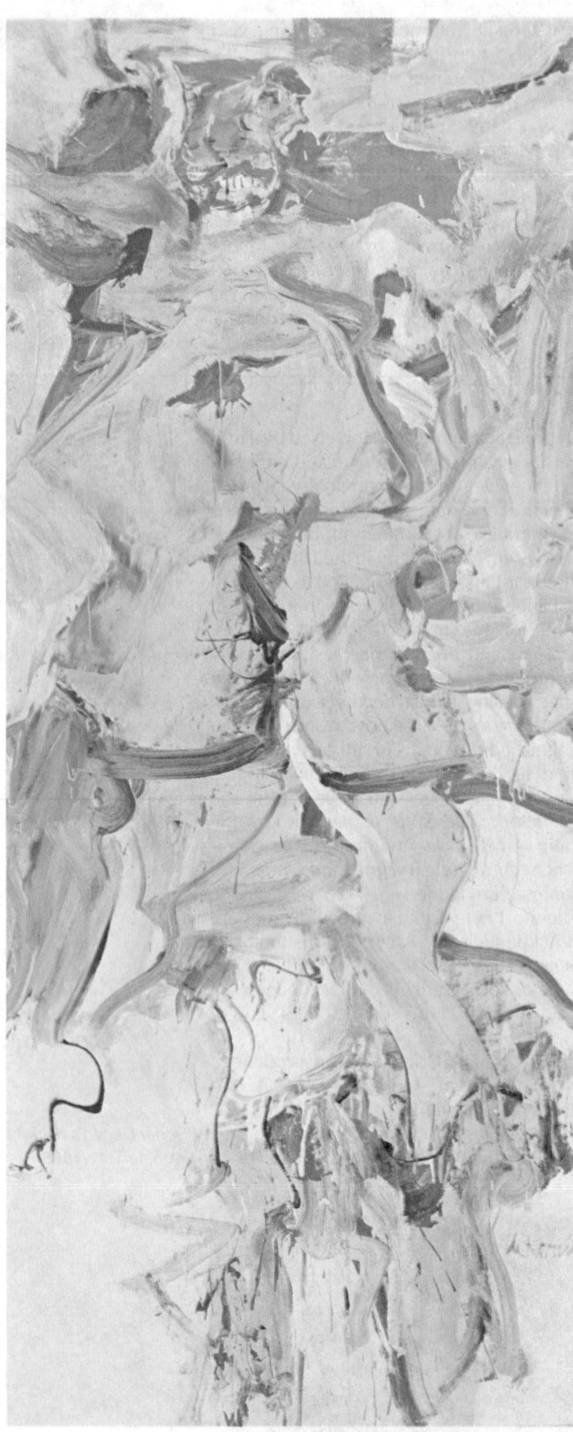

Willem de Kooning's painting Woman *(1964)*

Dehydrated food, food that has been preserved by drying. More than 90% of the water is removed in drying, making dehydrated food light in weight and compact. Food selected for drying must be fresh, clean and at the proper stage of ripeness.

Dehydration, removal of water from substances, usually as part of an industrial process or in the preservation of food. Water may be removed in drying chambers through which hot air or gases are passed. A vacuum may be used instead of hot air or gas to evaporate the water at lower temperatures. In chemical processes, gases are dried by passing them through tubes containing drying agents such as calcium chloride. Substances can be dried and kept away from moisture by placing them in a *desiccator*—an airtight chamber containing a drying agent such as silica gel. Dehydration is an important method of food preservation. Since most food spoilage is caused by bacteria, which can only function in the presence of moisture, dehydration inhibits their activity. Freeze drying, in which foods are frozen and ice removed by sublimation in a vacuum, is increasingly used as it does less damage to the texture and flavor of the food. *Dehydration* also refers to a serious physiological condition in which the body's tissues lose too much water. It is caused by repeated vomiting, diarrhea, bleeding, or exposure to a hot environment without an adequate water supply.

Deism, religious system developed in the 17th and 18th centuries and championed by such thinkers as Voltaire and Jean Jacques Rousseau. Deists held that the rational nature of the universe was evidence of the existence of a Creator God, but they opposed organized religion and rejected supernatural explanations and religious revelation. Some of the leaders of the American Revolution were deists, among them Thomas Jefferson and Benjamin Franklin.
See also: Atheism; Theism.

De jure segregation *see:* Segregation.

Dekker, Thomas (c. 1570-c.1632), English dramatist and pamphleteer. On many plays he collaborated with Philip Massinger, Thomas Middleton, John Ford, and John Webster. His most famous work is the comedy *The Shoemaker's Holiday* (1600), though he is also known for *Old Fortunatus* (1600) and *Satirot* (1602).

De Kooning, Willem (1904-), Dutch-born U.S. painter, among the founders of abstract expressionism. Influenced by Arshile Gorky, Joan Miró, and Pablo Picasso, he painted abstract, highly colored pictures with thickly applied pigment. His series entitled *Woman*—including, for instance, *Woman I* (1952)—contains some of his most famous works.
See also: Abstract expressionism.

Delacroix, Ferdinand - Victor - Eugène (1798-1863), French painter whose themes are typical of Romanticism. Such early works as *The Massacre of Chios* (1824) were influenced by Gericault, but his mastery of rich color schemes and handling of paint were largely learned from Rubens, as shown by *Death of Sardanapalus* (1827), *The Justice of Trajan* (1840), and the many official decorative schemes he undertook. His frescoes for Saint-Sulpice, Paris, influenced impressionism.

De la Madrid Hurtado, Miguel (1934-), Mexican political leader. He was budget minister (1976-82) under President José López Portillo, whom de la Madrid succeeded as president in 1982. His technocratic administration, which held power until 1988, faced grave economic problems, including a huge foreign debt. He was a leader in Latin American efforts to end the strife in neighboring Central American countries.
See also: Mexico.

De La Mare, Walter John (1873-1956), English poet and novelist. His work, much of which was intended for children, is characterized by its evocation of the atmosphere of dreams and the supernatural. His best-known works are the novels *Henry Brocken* (1904) and *Memoirs of a Midget* (1921), and the children's poetry collection *Peacock Pie* (1913).

Delany, Martin Robinson (1812-85), African-American journalist, physician, and army officer. A newspaper publisher until 1849, he received a medical degree from Harvard in 1852. He wrote and worked for abolitionist causes. During the Civil War he became an army surgeon and was the first African-American to reach the rank of major. He later joined the Freedmen's Bureau and became a trial judge in Charleston, S.C.

De la Roche, Mazo (1879-1961), Canadian writer best known for a series of 16 novels that chronicle the Whiteoak family from 1852 to 1954. The first novel, *Jalna,* was published in 1927, the last, *Morning at Jalna,* in 1960. De la Roche wrote plays, short stories, children's stories, travel books, and an autobiography, *Ringing the Changes* (1957).

Delaunay, Robert (1885-1941), French abstract painter. With his wife, Sonia, he founded the Orphist movement in 1910. His pictures comprise forms of brilliantly contrasting color.

Delaware, Native American tribe of the Algonquian linguistic group that lived in the Delaware River basin area until driven into Ohio in the 18th century by the incursions of colonists and the violence of the French and Indian Wars. An agricultural tribe, the Delaware had a sophisticated culture. Today their descendants are scattered through reservations in Oklahoma and Ontario, Canada.

Delaware, one of the mid-Atlantic states of the United States; bordered by Maryland in the west and south, Pennsylvania in the north, and the Delaware Bay in the east.
Land and climate. Delaware is located on the Delmarva Peninsula, along with parts of Maryland and Virginia. Almost all of the state is part of the Atlantic Coastal Plain, which stretches from New Jersey to southern Florida. Delaware's mean elevation above sea level is the lowest of all the 50 states. The land rises gradually to the rolling hills of the Piedmont Plateau, which crosses the northern tip of the state. The most important river is the Delaware. Delaware's climate is temperate but humid. Wilmington is the only major city.

Delaware

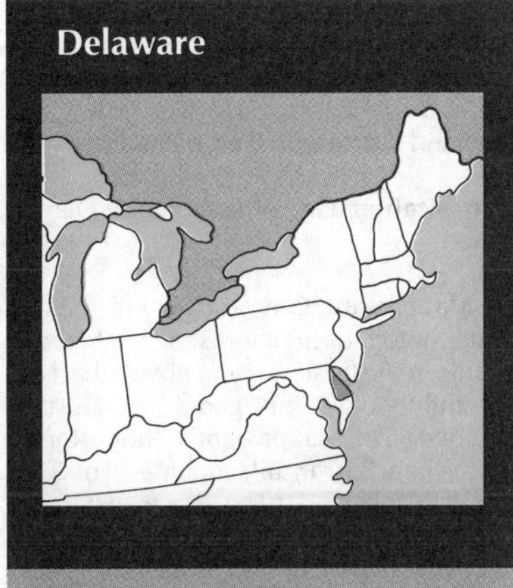

Capital:	Dover
Statehood:	Dec. 7, 1787 (1st state)
Familiar names:	First State, Diamond State
Area:	2,044 sq mi (5,295 sq km); ranks 49th
Population:	668,696 (1990); ranks 46th
Elevation:	Highest—442 ft (135 m), New Castle County Lowest—sea level
Motto:	Liberty and Independence
State flower:	Peach blossom
State bird:	Blue hen chicken
State tree:	American holly
State song:	"Our Delaware"

Economy. The most important economic activity in Delaware is manufacturing. Chemical production is the major industry. Wilmington is the headquarters of one of the largest chemical companies in the world, E. J. DuPont de Nemours & Company. Since corporation taxes are unusually low in Delaware, about 200,000 companies—including many whose business is done elsewhere—have incorporated in the state. Broiler chickens account for more than half of the state's farm income. Soybeans and corn are the 2 leading cash crops.

Government. The state constitution was adopted in 1897. The governor is elected for a 4-year term. The state legislature, also called the general assembly, consists of a senate of 21 members, elected for 4-year terms, and a house of representatives, whose 41 members serve for 2 years. Delaware is the only state in which the legislature can amend the state constitution without voter approval. Delaware sends 2 senators and 1 representative to the U.S. Congress.

History. Henry Hudson, an Englishman in the service of the Dutch, explored Delaware Bay in 1609. Swedish settlers founded New Sweden, the first permanent white settlement in the region, in 1638. After years of dispute, England took possession of the area in 1674. Delaware was ruled as a part of the colony of Pennsylvania from 1682 until the American Revolution (1775-83), although it was granted its own legislature in 1704. Delaware was 1 of the 13 colonies to sign the Declaration of Independence in 1776. In 1802 E. I. DuPont established his gunpowder mills on the Brandywine Creek near Wilmington, laying the foundations of the state's great chemical industry. Until the Civil War (1861-65) Delaware was a slave state, although anti-slavery sentiment was widespread in the industrial north. Large numbers of soldiers fought with the North to preserve the Union, but not to free the slaves. The state prospered during both world wars. In the 1970s Delaware's rapid economic growth slowed, but the economy improved after 1980 with the adoption of a constitutional limit on the state government's spending.

Headquarters for DuPont in Wilmington, Delaware

Delhi, the Red Fort

Delaware Bay, inlet of the Atlantic Ocean, bounded by New Jersey on the north and Delaware on the south and west. It is approximately 50 mi (80 km) long and varies in width from about 4 mi (6 km) to 30 mi (48 km); it ranges from 30 to 60 ft (9 to 18 m) in depth. The ocean entrance into the bay is formed by a channel 12 mi (19 km) wide, bordered by Cape May and Cape Henlopen, leading to the Delaware River. Its major port, Lewes, is located on Cape Henlopen. The inlet also forms the inland waterway to Wilmington and Philadelphia.
See also: Atlantic Ocean.

Delaware River, major waterway (about 410 mi/660 km long) in the eastern United States. Originating in the Catskill Mountains of New York, the river flows southeast, forming part of the Pennsylvania-New York border, then southward through the Delaware Water Gap, forming the boundary between New Jersey and Pennsylvania. It empties into Delaware Bay. It is connected to Chesapeake Bay on the west by the Chesapeake and Delaware Canal.

Delbrück, Max (1906-61), German-born U.S. biologist whose discovery of a method for detecting and measuring the rate of mutations in bacteria opened up the study of bacterial genetics. Along with Alfred Hershey and Salvador Luria, he won the 1969 Nobel Prize for physiology and medicine for work with bacteriophages (viruses that attack bacteria).
See also: Biology.

Del Cano, Juan Sebastián *see:* Magellan, Ferdinand.

De León, Juan Ponce *see:* Ponce de León, Juan.

De Lesseps, Ferdinand Marie (1805-94), French engineer and diplomat, builder of the Suez Canal. He first conceived of the project while serving as a diplomat in Egypt. He supervised its construction (1859-69) and later headed a French company formed to construct the Panama Canal. When this failed through lack of capital (1888), he was ruined mentally and financially.
See also: Suez Canal.

Delgado, José Matías (1767-1832), Salvadoran priest and patriot. He led El Salvador's fight for independence from Spain (1811) and its resistance movement to annexation by Mexico (1822).
See also: El Salvador.

Delhi (pop. 4,884,000), city in northern India, on a plain that has always been strategically important for control of the whole Indian subcontinent. In 1638 it became the capital of the Mogul Empire, and it had previously been the center of the Delhi Sultanate (1192-1398). The city fell

to the British in 1803. In 1912 the administrative center of New Delhi was built immediately adjacent to it, and was designated the capital of British India. The old city, however, has a larger population.
See also: India.

Delhi sultanate, first Muslim empire in India (1192-1398). Established by Qutb ud-Din, a general serving Muhammad of Ghor, the ruler of Afghanistan, the sultanate reached its height in the early 1300s, when it dominated the subcontinent. The sultans constantly battled rival Hindu and Buddhist kings and successfully shielded India from Mongol invasion until 1398, when Delhi was sacked by Tamerlane. That ended the empire, although a sultan continued to rule in Delhi until 1526, when Babur, a descendant of Tamerlane, ousted the sultan and founded the Mogul Empire.

Delian League, confederacy of Greek states formed by Athens in 478 B.C. to follow up the Hellenic League's victories against Persia. It was nominally governed by a council in which each member state had one vote but was in fact dominated by Athens. After success against Persia, Athens began to turn the league into an empire, subjugating reluctant states such as Naxos. The league endured until 404 B.C., when Athens was defeated by Sparta in the Peloponnesian War. A second Delian League was founded in 378 B.C. It was crushed by Philip II of Macedon in 338 B.C.
See also: Athens; Greece, Ancient.

Delibes, (Clément Philibert) Léo (1836-91), French composer. Initially known for his lighter works and operettas, some written in collaboration with Offenbach, he set new standards for ballet music with *Coppélia* (1870) and *Sylvia* (1876), and wrote the grand opera *Lakmé* (1883).

Delilah, Samson's Philistine mistress in the Old Testament. When Samson, an Israelite judge, told her that his long hair was the secret of his strength, she cut his hair, delivering him to the Philistines, who blinded him. When his strength returned, he tore down the Philistine temple, killing himself along with his enemies.
See also: Bible; Old Testament.

Delinquency, juvenile *see:* Juvenile delinquency.

Delphi was one of the most important places in ancient Greece. It was the location of the Delphic Oracle. Shown are the remains of a temple.

Delirium tremens, specific condition of confusion, violent shaking, fever, and hallucinations caused by alcohol withdrawal.
See also: Alcoholism.

Delius, Frederick (1862-1934), English composer. He studied in Leipzig, where he met and was influenced by Edward Grieg. He is best known for orchestral pieces such as *Florida* (1886-87) and *Brigg Fair* (1907), and for tone poems such as *Summer Night on the River* (1911) and *Sea Drift* (1903). His best-known opera is *A Village Romeo and Juliet* (1907). In old age he became blind and paralyzed, but continued to compose by dictation.

Della Francesca, Piero *see:* Piero Della Francesca.

Della Robbia, Luca (1399?-1482), Italian Renaissance sculptor and ceramicist known for his glazed terra cottas. His works include the *Cantoria* (1431-38), 10 panels in relief sculpture depicting children with musical instruments; and *Madonna and Child.* His nephew Andrea and Andrea's sons Luca II, Giovanni, and Girolama continued Della Robbia's work.
See also: Renaissance.

Dells *see:* Dalles.

Deloria, Vine, Jr. (1933-), Native American leader. A Sioux, he advocates the practice of Native American religion and ways of thought. A director of the National Congress of American Indians (1964-67) and co-founder of the Institute for the Development of Indian Law (1971), he has championed Native American economic and legislative causes. His several books include *Custer Died for Your Sins* (1969), *God Is Red* (1973), and *Behind the Trail of Broken Treaties* (1974).

Delphi , Greek town located on the lower slopes of Mt. Parnassus. In ancient times, it was the site of the most important oracle in Greece. The oracle was in a temple to Apollo built in the 6th century B.C. The messages were delivered by a priestess, usually in cryptic form, and were interpreted by a priest.
See also: Greece.

Delphinium *see:* Flower; Larkspur.

Delta, alluvial plain at the mouth of a river, often projecting into a sea or lake and crossed by many water channels. Deltas are generally formed of fertile mud dumped by a slow-flowing river. Often the river divides into two or more streams that thread their way through the delta to reach the sea or lake in different places, producing a tree-shaped pattern when seen from the air. The best-known deltas include the Mississippi Delta, the Nile Delta, and the Ganges-Brahmaputra Delta.

Deluge, in biblical tradition, great flood sent by God to punish humanity, described in Genesis 6-8. Noah, on divine instruction, built the Ark to save human and animal life from the flood.
See also: Bible; Noah.

Demand *see:* Supply and demand.

Demarcation, Line of *see:* Line of Demarcation.

De Maupassant, Guy (1850-93), French writer noted for his short stories. He wrote simple, realistic stories and novels that bear the influence of his godfather, Gustave Flaubert. De Maupassant's short stories, more than 250 in all, include "The Diamond Necklace," "The Piece of String," and "Ball-of-Fat." Among his novels are *A Woman's Life* (1883) and *Bel-Ami* (1885). He stopped writing in 1891, when he was committed to a mental asylum, where he died.

Demeter, in Greek mythology, the goddess of grain, agriculture, harvest, and fertility. She is credited with teaching humans how to farm. The Greeks honored her and her daughter Persephone in the rituals of the Eleusinian Mysteries. The ancient Romans identified Demeter with Ceres.
See also: Mythology.

De Mille, Agnes George (1909?-), U.S. dancer and choreographer; niece of Cecil B. De Mille. She pioneered the combination of ballet and folk music. Her ballets include *Rodeo* (1942) and *Fall River Legend* (1948). Her choreography for the Rodgers and Hammerstein musical *Oklahoma!* (1943) revolutionized dance in musical comedy by using ballet as an integral part of the plot.

De Mille, Cecil Blount (1881-1959), U.S. motion picture producer and director, noted for his use of spectacle; uncle of Agnes George De Mille. He directed such epics as *The Ten Commandments* (1923 and 1956), *The Sign of the Cross* (1932), *Samson and Delilah* (1949), and *The Greatest Show on Earth* (1952).

Democracy, system of government under which all members of society have a say in making political decisions, either directly or indirectly. Direct democracy, in which political decisions are made by citizens meeting together, has generally been superceded by representative democracy, under which the population elects members of a decision-making body. Historically, the portion of the population permitted to participate in the voting process has expanded over time, racial, religious, and sexual restrictions being removed. Many political theorists argue that other rights (besides voting) are equally essential if a system is to be democratic. These include freedom of speech and the press, freedom of assembly, freedom to organize politically, and so on. The concepts of natural rights and political equality expressed by such philosophers as John Locke in the 17th century, Voltaire and Jean Jacques Rousseau in the 18th century, and Jeremy Bentham and J.S. Mill in the 19th century are vital to the theory of representative democracy.

Democratic Party, one of the 2 major political parties in the United States. Democrats trace their history back to the Democratic Republican Party (1792) of Thomas Jefferson, who favored popular control of the government. Following the presidential inauguration of Andrew Jackson in 1828, the Democratic Party's base was broadened, with representation from the new West as well as the East. Jackson's administration marked the beginning of a period of dominance for the Democrats that only ended with election in 1860 of Abraham Lincoln, the first successful candidate of the new Republican Party. The slavery controversy and the Civil War split the Democratic Party into northern and southern sections and, apart from the success of Woodrow Wilson just before World War I, it was not until the election of Franklin D. Roosevelt in 1932 that the party reemerged with its old vigor. Roosevelt's New Deal transformed the party's traditional policies, introducing broad governmental intervention in the economy and social welfare. This approach was continued on Roosevelt's death in 1945 by Democrat Harry S. Truman, whose Fair Deal measures were, however, largely thwarted by a coalition of Republicans and Southern Democrats. In the 1950s, under Dwight D. Eisenhower's Republican administration, the Democratic Party was led by Adlai E. Stevenson. Although it controlled both houses of Congress, the solidity of the South's adherence to the party began to fracture with the drive for black civil rights. The election of Democrat John F. Kennedy in 1960 led to important legislation in this sphere, but also contributed further to the breakup of the traditional alliance between urbanized North, with its many minorities, and the rural, disadvantaged South, which had benefitted from the New Deal policies. On Kennedy's assassination in 1963, Vice President Lyndon B. Johnson came to power. By 1968 the party was riven with dissent, particularly over policy in Vietnam. In 1968 Democrat Hubert H. Humphrey lost the presidential election to Republican Richard M. Nixon, and in 1972 Humphrey was replaced as leader of the party by George S. McGovern. In 1976 Democrat Jimmy Carter was elected president, but he lost his bid for a second term to Republican Ronald Reagan in 1980. Reagan defeated Democrat Walter F. Mondale, Carter's vice president, in the 1984 presidential election. In 1986 the Democrats regained control of the Senate, which they had lost to the Republicans in 1980. Democrat Michael S. Dukakis lost the 1988 election to Reagan's vice president, George Bush. Bush was defeated by the Democrate Bill Clinton in 1993. Clinton, re-elected in 1996, had to face a Republican majority in the Congres and the Senate from 1994.

Democratic-Farmer-Labor Party *see:* Farmer-Labor Party.

Democratic-Republican Party, one of the two political parties founded during the first decades of the United States. It emerged in the 1790s in opposition to the dominant Federalist Party. Initially called the Republican Party and later the Democratic-Republic Party, in about 1830 the name became the Democratic Party. It was formed in the wake of the resignation of Thomas Jefferson as secretary of state in President George Washington's cabinet, in 1793. Jefferson opposed federalist policies favoring the commerce and industry of New England and the Middle Atlantic area. The party came to power in 1800 when Jefferson was elected president, and held the presidency through the administrations of Jefferson, James Madison, and James Monroe. With the emergence of Andrew Jackson, new alignments came into being, and the party evolved into the forerunner of the current Democratic Party.

Democritus (460?-370? B.C.), Greek philosopher who theorized that reality is separated into atoms and the void. According to his theory, atoms make up all existing things and after a period of time, these atoms break apart and are drawn into the void. Democritus also believed true knowledge is derived not from sensory input but from the native intellect.
See also: Philosophy.

Demography, study of the distribution, composition, and changes of human populations. Its prime concerns are birth and death rates, emigration and immigration patterns, and marital patterns.
See also: Census; Population.

De Molay, Order of, international organization of boys and young men between the ages of 13 and 21. Each local chapter is affiliated with a group of Masons. The membership is dedicated to upholding seven virtues: filial love, reverence for God, courtesy, friendship, fidelity, cleanliness, and patriotism. Founded in 1919, the Order is named for Jacques de Molay (1243-1314), the last Grand Master of the Knights Templars, a group of French Crusaders.

Demosthenes (384-322 B.C.), Athenian orator and speech writer, best known for his attempts to rouse Athens to resist the encroachment of Philip of Macedon, the father of Alexander the Great. Demosthenes' series of speeches against Philip were called the *Philippics* (351-341 B.C.). In the same cause he delivered a set of speeches known as the *Olynthiacs* (349 B.C.). In the end, however, Philip conquered Greece, and in 324 B.C. Demosthenes was exiled. He returned after the death of Alexander in 323 B.C., but failed to free Greece from Macedonian rule. He fled, was pursued, and took poison to avoid capture by the Macedonian general Antipater.
See also: Greece, Ancient; Phillip II (Macedonia).

Jack Dempsey

Dempsey, Jack (William Harrison Dempsey; 1895-1983), U.S. boxer. He won the world heavyweight championship from Jess Willard in 1919 and held it until 1926, when he lost a decision to Gene Tunney. Dempsey's loss to Tunney in the 1927 rematch was known for the "long count" in the 7th round. Dempsey knocked Tunney down but refused to go to a neutral corner, thus delaying the start of the referee's count. Tunney, actually down for more than the normal 10 count, got up at the count of 9 and went on to win by decision.

Dempster, Arthur Jeffrey (1886-1950), U.S. physicist, developer of the first mass spectrometer (1918), an instrument that measures the mass of atomic nuclei, thereby providing a way to analyze chemical compositions and to distinguish isotopes. Dempster discovered uranium 235, which is used in atomic bombs and nuclear reactors.
See also: U-235.

Demuth, Charles (1883-1935), U.S. watercolorist and illustrator. Influenced by both cubism and expressionism, Demuth worked in a number of styles, but is best known for his precise and delicate studies of flowers and his stark, simple shapes inspired by the machine age. He is also noted for his illustrations of works by Edgar Allan Poe, Emile Zola, and Henry James.

Dendrochronology, dating of past events by the study of tree rings. A hollow tube is inserted into the tree trunk and a section from bark to center removed. The annual rings are counted and compared with rings from dead trees so that the chronology may be extended further back in time.

Deneb, or Alpha Cygni, blue-white star, brightest star in the constellation Cygnus and one of the brightest in the sky.
See also: Cygnus; Star.

Dengue, or breakbone fever, infectious disease characterized by sudden onset of headache, fever, prostration, severe joint and muscle pain, and swollen glands. A rash appears with a second temperature rise following a period without fever. The disease is caused by a virus transmitted by the mosquito *Aedes aegypti*.

Deng Xiaoping

Deng Xiaoping (1904-97), Chinese Communist leader. A strategist during the civil war, he became vice premier of the People's Republic of China in 1952 and a member of the Communist Party Politburo in 1955. Purged during the Cultural Revolution in 1967, he was rehabilitated in 1973, then purged again in 1976 and rehabilitated in 1977, after the death of Mao Zedong. He then became the central figure in the Chinese government, directing both foreign and domestic policy, often from behind the scenes, until the early 90s.
See also: China.

Denmark, country in northwest Europe consisting of the Jutland Peninsula and 483 islands, of which about 100 are inhabited. The Faeroe Islands, north of Scotland, form a self-governing community within the Kingdom of Denmark; Greenland, the largest island in the world, is a former Danish county that received Home Rule on May 1, 1979. The Jutland Peninsula contains the country's only land frontier, the 42-mi (68-km) long boundary with Germany. The capital of Denmark is Copenhagen.
Land and climate. Denmark is a low-lying country. The average elevation is 100 ft (31 m) above sea level; the highest point, Yding Skovhj (Forest Mountain), in Jutland, is 568 ft (173 m) above sea level. The prevailing climate is maritime, with cool summers and mild to cold winters.
People. The modern Danes are believed to be descended from early migrant hunters and farmers of northern Europe. The Danish language belongs to the Scandinavian group of Germanic languages, with many direct loan words from German and English. Since the late 19th century, English has been the most important secondary language in the country. Over 90% of the people are members of the Evangelical Lutheran Church, which is supported by grants from the state.
Economy. Agriculture was the mainstay of the economy until World War II, but manufacturing now accounts for more than 60% of Denmark's total exports. Among the major products are foodstuffs (particularly dairy products), furniture, glass, silverware, leather goods, and clothing. There are important shipbuilding and agricultural engineering industries, and fishing and tourism also contribute to the economy.
History. Denmark was a center of Viking expansion from the 9th to the 11th centuries. Under the Kalmar Union (1397-1523), with Norway and Sweden, it was the dominant partner. Norway remained under Danish rule until it was taken by Sweden in 1814. Prussia and Austria wrested Schleswig-Holstein from Denmark in 1864, but North Schleswig was restored to Denmark after a plebiscite in 1920. Denmark was occupied by Germany during World War II. The country is governed as a constitutional monarchy. Queen Margaret II ascended the throne in 1972.

Denmark

Capital:	Copenhagen
Area:	16,638 sq mi (43,092 sq km)
Population:	5,181,000
Form:	constitutional monarchy
Independent:	1849 (constitutional monarchy)
GNP:	U.S.$133,941,000,000
Per capita:	U.S.$26,000

Denominator *see:* Fraction.

Density, ratio of mass of a substance to its volume. By extension, the term is also applied to properties other than mass, e.g., charge density refers to the ratio of electric charge to volume.

Dental hygiene, study and practice of techniques designed to maintain good oral health. These techniques include cleaning and polishing teeth, flossing, the application of fluoride or protective sealants to prevent gum disease and cavities, and more complicated procedures involving surgery.

Dentistry, profession that deals with the diagnosis, prevention, and treatment of malformations and diseases affecting the teeth and their related structures, such as gums and oral bones.

Denver (pop. 513,500), capital and largest city of Colorado, situated in the Rocky Mountains foothills, a mile above sea level. Its location has made it the commercial center for the Rocky Mountain region. The Denver Union stockyards include the largest sheep market in the country and one of the largest cattle markets. Other industries include aerospace, food processing, printing and publishing, electronics, textiles and metal and mineral processing. The city maintains the world's largest municipal park and recreation system.
See also: Colorado.

Deoxyribonucleic Acid (DNA) *see:* DNA.

Department of... Departments of the U.S. government are listed under the key word; for example: Education, U.S. Department of.

Depreciation, loss in the value of an asset brought about by age, use, or both. Over the economic life of an asset, depreciation can be considered equal to the difference between the price of the asset when new and its scrap value. In accountancy, the amount needed to compensate for depreciation can be estimated through the course of the asset's economic life. A depreciation reserve can then be built up. Depreciation is allowed for in calculating corporate taxes for items such as equipment, furniture, real estate, and cars.

Depressant, any of various drugs that slow physical, mental, or emotional activity.
See also: Sedative; Tranquilizer.

Depression, in economics, major decline in business activity involving sharp reductions in industrial production, a rise in bankruptcies, increased unemployment, and a general loss of business confidence. Although less serious downturns, called

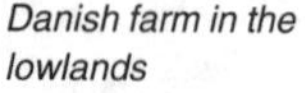

Danish farm in the lowlands

recessions, occur regularly in industrial nations, the most serious and widespread depression was the Great Depression that began in 1929 and lasted worldwide through most of the 1930s.
See also: Business cycle.

Depression, emotional state characterized by sadness, despondency, apathy, and sometimes a deep sense of loss; in psychiatry, clinical depressive illness is more intense and lasts longer than common depressed feelings. Seriously depressed people feel isolated and hopeless and often reproach or blame themselves for exaggerated faults and shortcomings. Fatigue and disturbed sleep are common, while some depressed people sleep more than usual. Crying spells, whether or not there is something to cry about, are also characteristic. Some depressive illness masks itself in physical discomfort or by contributing to alcoholism or drug addiction. Chronic fatigue and boredom, as well as habitual underachievement, may be unrecognized forms of depression. The hyperkinetic (overly active) child, conversely, may be compensating for an underlying depression; drugs that relieve depression in adults seem to help hyperactive children. Not all those suffering from depressive illness attempt suicide, nor are all those who attempt suicide necessarily suffering from depressive illness, but the relationship is striking. It is estimated that as many as 75% of those who attempt suicide are seriously depressed, and other studies indicate that people hospitalized for depression at some time in their lives are about 36 times more likely to commit suicide than are nondepressed people, with the greatest risk being during or immediately following hospitalization. After the age of 40, the possibility of suicide increases in severely depressed persons. Almost twice as many women as men suffer from depressive illness and almost twice as many women attempt suicide, but 3 times more men than women succeed.
Psychogenic (or *reactive*) depression, the most common form of depressive illness, is brought on by a stressful situation. Even in this milder form of depressive illness, suicide is a serious possibility. Often the person can be helped by the comforting of family or friends. Many who suffer the illness, however, require professional assistance. *Endogenous* depression is far more serious. *Unipolar* depression may show itself in severely withdrawn and uncommunicative behavior or agitated activity, such as pacing the floor, wringing the hands, and a rapid stream of talk about feelings and fear. *Bipolar* (or *manic-depressive*) illness shows itself in up-down swings. The manic-depressive is the victim of a cycle of moods, with a phase lasting from several days up to several years. Unlike the psychogenic depressive, these more severely afflicted persons have delusions about being unworthy, condemned, and criticized and often think they are physically altered. The very real danger of suicidal outcome makes hospitalization a usual requirement in treatment.
Involutional depression describes a category of mental illness found in persons in their middle years, due to disturbances of metabolism, growth, nutrition, or endocrine (hormone) function. Recent evidence, however, has cast strong doubts as to whether a special kind of depression actually affects this age group. There is wide agreement that both heredity and environmental factors play an important part in depressive illness. Depression is more likely to occur in a person with a family history of depressive illness. Some investigators have found that nearly 25% of patients had mentally ill mothers and more than 15% had depressed fathers.

Depth charge, explosive weapon used against submarines and other submerged targets. The charge detonates when it is subjected to a predetermined water pressure, and the resulting shock waves destroy the target.

De Quincey, Thomas (1785-1859), English essayist and critic, author of *Confessions of an English Opium Eater* (1822), which established his literary reputation. His output, affected by lifelong opium addiction, was erratic, but included penetrating essays and powerful descriptions of drug-inspired dreams.

Derain, André (1880-1954), French painter, one of the original fauves. He was also attracted to cubism for a time. Later, rejecting nonrepresentational extremes, he returned to a more traditional style.

Derby, annual horse race begun at Epsom, England, in 1780 by the 12th earl of Derby.

Derby, Kentucky *see:* Kentucky Derby.

Dermaptera *see:* Earwig.

Dermatitis, inflammation of the skin, accompanied by moderate to severe itching, with redness, swelling, and sometimes blisters. The causes are not known for sure, but many cases are provoked by chemical irritants.
See also: Eczema.

Dermatology, subspeciality of medicine concerned with the diagnosis and treatment of skin diseases: a largely visual speciality, but aided by skin biopsy in certain instances.

Dermis, or corium, the inner layer of skin beneath the epidermis. It comprises a layer of connective tissue 1 to 4 millimeters thick, that is thicker on the back than on the front of the body. The cells are most numerous just beneath the epidermis, the tissue being more fibrous in its deeper part. The boundary between dermis and epidermis is undulating, the waves being most pronounced where the skin is thick. The dermis contains many nerves, blood vessels, and seat glands. The raised parts of the dermis are called *papillae* and at some sites, such as the fingertips, these are arranged linearly and produce characteristic patterns responsible for individual fingerprints.

Dervish, Muslim mystic, member of a Sufi brotherhood. Members serve a period of initiation under a teacher, and each order has its own ritual for inducing a mystic state that stresses dependence on the unseen world. The best known are the "whirling" and "howling" dervishes, who use forms of dancing and singing.

DES (diethylstilbestrol), synthetic hormone having the properties of estrogen, the main female sex hormone. It was formerly administered to pregnant women to prevent miscarriages, but in the 1970s it was linked to vaginal cancer in women whose mothers had taken the hormone. A movement against the drug during the 1970s raised awareness about this problem and was influential in getting the U.S. Food and Drug Administration (FDA) to rescind its approval of the use of the drug during pregnancy. It is still used as a growth accelerator in beef cattle, but such use is controversial because of the possible carcinogenic effects of DES.
See also: Hormone.

Desai, Morarji (1896-), Indian political leader. A disciple of Mahatma Gandhi and a devout Hindu, he held cabinet posts under Jawaharlal Nehru and was deputy prime minister for Indira Gandhi (1967-69) before breaking with her. He served as prime minister (1977-79).
See also: India.

Desalination *see:* Water.

Descartes, René (1596-1650), French mathematician, scientist, and philosopher, often referred to as "the father of modern philosophy." A dualist who believed the world was composed of 2 basic substances (matter and spirit), he ignored accepted scholastic philosophy and stated a person should doubt all sense experiences; but if a person can think and doubt, he or she therefore exists. Descartes stated this belief in his famous phrase, *cogito, ergo sum* ("I think, therefore I am.") This skeptical philosophy is called Cartesianism and is detailed in Descartes's *Meditations on First Philosophy* (1641). His other major works include the *Discourse on Method* (1637) and *Principles of Philosophy* (1644). Descartes also attempted to explain the universe in terms of matter and motion and invented analytic geometry.
See also: Philosophy.

Deschutes River *see:* Oregon.

Desegregation *see:* Segregation.

Desert, dry region where life has extreme difficulty surviving. There are 2 types. In cold deserts, which cover about one-sixth of the earth's land area, water is unavailable during most of the year because it is trapped in the form of ice. Cold deserts include the Antarctic polar icecap and the barren wastes of Greenland. Warm deserts, which cover about one-fifth of the earth's surface, typically lie between latitudes 20° and 30° north and south, although they exist also farther from the equator in the centers of continental landmasses. They can be described as areas with annual rainfalls of 10 in (25 cm) or less. Plants may survive by being able to store water, like the cacti; by having tiny leaves to reduce evaporation loss, like the paloverde; or by having extensive root systems to capture maximum moisture, like the mesquite. Animals may be nomadic or spend the daylight hours underground. The best-known and largest warm desert is the Sahara.

Desertion, in military law, the abandonment by a soldier of his or her post without the intention of returning. Under the code of military justice, this is a much more serious offense than merely failing to return on time or being absent without leave (AWOL). In civil law, desertion is the act committed by a husband or wife who leaves the other and stays away for a certain statutory period, which in the United States varies from 6 months to 5 years. Desertion is grounds for divorce in many jurisdictions.

Desert Shield, Operation *see:* Persian Gulf War.

Desert Storm, Operation *see:* Persian Gulf War.

De Sica, Vittorio (1901-74), Italian film director. His earlier films, such as *Shoeshine* (1946) and *The Bicycle Thief* (1948), are noted for their compassionate treatment of social problems in the neorealist style. Later films, made in more commercially viable style, include *Marriage, Italian Style* (1964) and *The Garden of the Finzi Continis* (1971).

Design, purposeful arrangement of the elements in a creative work or process. Design is evident in the fine arts, industrial arts, engineering, and architecture, and in systems and processes. Broadly speaking, the aim of design is to unify function and aesthetics in a harmonious whole. Design in the fine arts refers to composition: how color, shape, and line create pattern and visual rhythm. In the applied arts, design also encompasses the product's function, the physical capabilities of the material, and the method of manufacture. Design of a process or system refers to the overall plan: how materials are utilized and coordinated with movement to achieve a purpose. Here criteria are efficiency, economy, and simplicity.

De Sitter, Willem (1872-1934), Dutch astronomer and cosmologist who examined the age, size, and structure of the universe. His greatest achievement was his recognition that distant galaxies are receding at greater speeds than nearer ones, which showed that the universe is expanding.
See also: Astronomy; Cosmology.

De Smet, Pierre Jean (1801-73), Jesuit missionary to the North American Indians. His work among several tribes won their friendship, and he often acted as a peacemaker for the government.
See also: Jesuits.

Des Moines (pop. 392,928), capital and largest city of Iowa. Located in a fertile agricultural region in south-central Iowa, it is an important commercial and industrial center of the Midwest. Des Moines produces airplane parts, farm machinery and tools, and cattle feed. It is also an important hub of communications, served by the nation's major railroads and airlines, and is the home of many insurance companies.
See also: Iowa.

De Soto, Hernando (1500?-42), Spanish explorer, discoverer of the Mississippi River. He served as second in command in Pizarro's conquests in Peru (1531-35), and supported the Inca emperor Atahualpa. He returned to Spain with a fortune and set out again to explore the Florida region. He landed in 1539 at Charlotte Harbor and spent 2 years exploring what is now the southeastern United States. He reached the Mississippi River in May 1541. Turning back in 1542, he died of illness.
See also: Mississippi River.

Despotism, absolute government by one person who rules without any constitutional controls. A despot need not necessarily be a tyrant. Indeed, in the 18th century, the concept of "benevolent" or "enlightened" despotism came into fashion. The theory was that people were not capable of governing themselves and needed a ruler who would look after their interests. Frederick the Great of Prussia considered himself an enlightened despot.

Desprez, Josquin (1440?-1521), Flemish composer who wrote both secular and sacred music for voice. He excelled at the canon, a composition in which a single melody is sung by several voices starting at different times, and the motet, an unaccompanied choral piece in which several voices sing different pitches to produce chords.

Dessalines, Jean Jacques (1758-1806), first black ruler of Haiti. Brought to Haiti as a slave, he took part in the rebellion against the French in the 1790s. After the final expulsion of the French in 1803 he became governor-general. In 1804 he proclaimed an independent country and took the title of Emperor Jacques I. His rule, characterized by extreme hostility to whites, ended when he was killed in a mulatto revolt.
See also: Haiti.

Destouches, Henri-Louis *see:* Céline, Louis-Ferdinand.

Destroyer, small, fast naval warship that evolved in the 1890s out of British torpedo boats. In the 2 world wars destroyers were used principally as escorts for convoys and for attacking submarines. Some of the modern destroyers are nuclear-powered and many carry guided missiles. Some carry 1 or 2 helicopters. A new class of destroyer, the *Spruance* class, displacing 7,800 tons, is replacing some of the World War II destroyers still in service with the U.S. Navy.

De Sucre, Antonio José *see:* Sucre, Antonio José de.

Detective story, popular form of fiction in which a detective solves a crime, usually a murder, by discovering and interpreting clues. The detective is often an amateur and may appear in a series of mysteries. Sherlock Holmes, introduced in 1884 by Arthur Conan Doyle, is a prime example. The detective story and its conventions originated with Edgar Allan Poe's short story "Murders in the Rue Morgue" (1841). Wilke Collins' *Moonstone* (1868) is one of the first important detective novels. In the 1920s, the hard-boiled detective story emerged. This style features a tough detective, snappy dialogue, and quick action. Its leading practitioners were Dashiell Hammet, Raymond Chandler, and Ross Macdonald. Other masters of the detective story include Agatha Christie, P. D. James, Ellery Queen, Georges Simenon, and Rex Stout.

Détente (French, "relaxation"), name given to the policy of easing tensions between the United States and the USSR that occurred in the late 1960s and 1970s. It was particularly associated with President Richard Nixon (and his adviser Henry Kissinger) during whose presidency the Strategic Arms Limitation Treaty (SALT) I was signed (1972). It was continued by President Ford, who signed the Helsinki Accords (1975). In the last years of the 1970s, however, tensions between the United States and the USSR rose again, and SALT II and détente were temporarily abandoned with the Soviet invasion of Afghanistan in 1979.
See also: Cold War.

Detergent, synthetic chemical that has the same cleaning action as soap but does not form a scum when used in hard water. Most stains are caused by oily films holding dirt particles. Detergent molecules surround a particle of dirt and carry it into suspension in the water. Detergents are made with chemicals obtained from petroleum. Biological or enzyme detergents contain enzymes that digest organic matter and are very good at removing marks such as coffee stains, but they have been known to cause skin problems. Detergents are mostly used in water, but they may also be dissolved in other liquids. Hydrocarbons containing detergents are used in dry cleaning, and automobile engine lubricants use detergents to reduce buildup of carbon deposits.

Determinism, philosophical theory that all events are determined (inescapably caused) by preexisting events that, when

considered in the context of inviolable physical laws, completely account for the subsequent events. The case for determinism has been variously argued from the inviolability of the laws of nature and from the omniscience and omnipotence of God. Determinism is often taken to be opposed to the principles of free will and indeterminacy.
See also: Philosophy.

De Tocqueville, Alexis *see:* Tocqueville, Alexis de.

Detonator, device used to set off a high-explosive charge. A high explosive such as dynamite is not sensitive to small shocks and can therefore be handled safely. The detonator sets off a minor explosion to produce a shock large enough to initiate the main explosion. Alfred Nobel, the inventor of dynamite, also produced the first effective detonator.
See also: Explosive.

Detroit (pop. 4,382,299), Michigan, fifth-largest city in the United States, often called the "Motor City" because it produces over a quarter of all the nation's cars and trucks. Detroit fronts on the Detroit River, which connects Lake Erie with Lake St. Clair. A bridge and 2 tunnels link Detroit with Windsor, Ontario. Almost since its founding (1701) Detroit has been a major lake port, and with the construction of the St. Lawrence Seaway (opened 1959) it has become an intercontinental port of considerable importance. The city sprawls over 140 sq mi (363 sq km), with the principal streets radiating from Grand Circus Park near the riverfront. The rapidly growing suburbs to the north and west contain many of the automobile factories that have made the city's fortune, as well as some of the most handsome residential areas in the country.
See also: Michigan.

Detroit River, river flowing about 30 mi (48 km) from Lake St. Clair to Lake Erie, separating southeastern Michigan from southern Ontario, and thus forming part of the international boundary between the United States and Canada. It is a busy commercial waterway. Road and railroad tunnels under the river connect Detroit, Mich., with Windsor, Ont.

Deucalion, in Greek mythology, son of the Titan Prometheus. Deucalion and his wife, Pyrrha, were the sole survivors of a flood visited on humanity by Zeus. After the flood, Deucalion and Pyrrha cast stones that turned into men and women who repopulated the earth. Deucalion and Pyrrha's own son, Hellen, is regarded as the ancestor of the Greeks.
See also: Mythology.

Deuterium, or heavy hydrogen (D or H_2), isotope of hydrogen in which the atomic nucleus contains a neutron as well as a proton, giving it an atomic weight of approximately 2. Deuterium was discovered by H.C. Urey in 1932 and is used as a tracer in biological research, in experiments for particle accelerators, and in the hydrogen bomb.
See also: Hydrogen.

Deuteron *see:* Deuterium.

Deuteronomy, fifth book of the Old Testament and last book of the Pentateuch. Supposedly a testament left by Moses to the Israelites about to enter Canaan, it is primarily a recapitulation of moral laws and laws relating to the settlement of Canaan. Much of it was written long after Moses, parts being added during the reforms under King Josiah (621 B.C.). It may have been the "Book of the Law" discovered by Hilkiah in the Temple in Jerusalem at that time.
See also: Bible; Old Testament.

Deutschland über Alles, or "Germany Above All Else," the German national anthem from 1922 until the division of Germany after World War II. In 1952 the Federal Republic of Germany adopted the song's third stanza as its anthem. "Deutschland über Alles" was composed by Hoffmann von Fallersleben in 1841.

Deutzia, genus of shrubs having clusters of white, pink, or purple, 5-petalled flowers and serated, fuzzy leaves. Native to Asia, deutzias are grown widely in gardens.

De Valera, Eamon (1882-1975), Irish statesman; prime minister 1932-48, 1951-54, and 1957- 58; and president of Ireland 1959-73. Born in New York City, he was raised in Ireland, and became an ardent republican. Only his U.S. citizenship saved him from execution after the 1916 Easter Rebellion. He was imprisoned by the Irish Free State for refusing to recognize the Anglo-Irish treaty of 1922; in 1924 he organized the Fianna Fáil Party, which won power in 1932. As prime minister he declared Ireland independent of Britain (1937), and preserved Irish neutrality during World War II.
See also: Ireland; Sinn Féin.

De Valois, Dame Ninette (Edris Stanus; 1898-), Irish dancer and choreographer. She founded the ballet company at Sadler's Wells, which in 1956 became the Royal Ballet, and was its director (1931-63).
See also: Ballet.

Devaluation, reduction of the official value of a currency, the opposite of revaluation. Aimed at reducing imports and stimulating exports that have become uncompetitive as a result of internal inflation, it has been used by many countries when their monetary reserves are threatened by a balance-of- payments crisis.

Developing country, term used for any nation with a weak industrial base, a low per capita income, and low gross national product.

Developmental psychology, study of behavioral changes that occur during the years from birth to early childhood. In particular, developmental psychologists will examine the process by which a child acquires skills of language, reasoning, and interaction with others.
See also: Psychology.

Detroit, Michigan

Devil, in Western religions and sects, chief spirit of evil and commander of lesser evil spirits or demons. Dualistic systems—notably Zoroastrianism, gnosticism, and Manichaeism—have regarded the devil as the uncreated equal of God, engaged in an eternal war for evil against good. Such beliefs have appeared sporadically in connection with the occult and devil worship. In Judaism, Christianity, and Islam, the devil, Satan, is a fallen angel, powerful but subordinate to God, who opposes God and tempts humanity, but is to be utterly defeated and bound at the Last Judgment.

Eamon De Valera

Devil's Island, small island off the coast of French Guiana, the site of a French penal colony (1852-1951) for political prisoners, among them Alfred Dreyfus.

Devil's paintbrush, plant with orange-red flowers on a leafless stem up to 28 in (71 cm) long, with oblong leaves growing from the base. The row of bristles on the seed lends the plant its name. Devil's paintbrush is found in Europe and eastern North America.

Devil's Triangle *see:* Bermuda Triangle.

Devil worship, worship of Satan, demons, or evil spirits. Its rituals may take the form of a mockery of the Christian mass and include elements of witchcraft and black magic.

Devolution, War of (1667-68), conflict between Spain and France over the right of succession to the Spanish Netherlands. Louis XIV of France claimed that by an old law the territory should have reverted to France. Although his military campaign was successful, he was forced to withdraw in the face of the Triple Alliance of England, the United Provinces, and Sweden.

Devonian Period, fourth period of the Paleozoic Era, beginning about 400 million years ago and lasting 55 million years. During this period the oceans covered

much of what is now dry land, and fish were the dominant life form.
See also: Paleozoic.

De Voto, Bernard Augustine (1897-1955), U.S. journalist and author. He won national fame as a contributor to *Harper's magazine.* His books include *Mark Twain's America* (1932), the Pulitzer Prize-winning *Across the Wide Missouri* (1947), and the novel *The Crooked Mile* (1924).

De Vries, Hugo (1848-1935), Dutch botanist who developed the theory of mutation, suggesting that new plant and animal species are the result of sudden transformations that occur spontaneously and are continued for generations. His findings stimulated advances in the study of heredity, and he was one of the first to introduce the experimental method in the investigation of the mechanisms of evolution.
See also: Botany.

Dew, layer of water droplets that forms at night on or near the ground. Dew may form in two ways: First, water vapor may rise out of the ground by capillary action and form droplets on reaching cooler surfaces (leaves, rocks) near ground level. Second, and more commonly, moisture from the air may condense in contact with relatively cool objects. In arid and semiarid areas, dew is an important source of moisture for plants.

Dewberry, trailing bramble (genus *Rubus*) with blackberry-like fruit, the only U.S. member of the blackberry group that is cultivated. Loganberries arose from a chance crossing of dewberry and raspberry.

Dewey, George (1837-1917), U.S. naval hero promoted to admiral of the navy (the highest rank) for his victory at the Battle of Manila Bay and the capture of the Philippines from Spain. On May 1, 1898, during the Spanish-American War, Dewey led the Asiatic squadron into Manila Bay and, without losing a man, destroyed the Spanish eastern fleet. In Aug., aided by Filipino rebels and U.S. army forces, he received the surrender of Manila; the Philippines then fell to the United States. Dewey later served as president of the general board of the Navy Department.
See also: Spanish-American War.

Dewey, John (1859-1952), U.S. philosopher and educator. Dewey founded the philosophical school known as instrumentalism (or experimentalism) and was the leading promoter of educational reform in the early years of the 20th century. Profoundly influenced by the pragmatism of William James, Dewey developed a philosophy in which ideas and concepts were validated by their practicality. He taught that "learning by doing" should form the basis of educational practice, though in later life he came to criticize the "progressive" movement in education, which,

John Dewey

in abandoning formal tuition altogether, he felt had misused his educational theory.
See also: Pragmatism.

Dewey, Melvil (1851-1931), U.S. librarian, inventor of the scheme for organizing library collections known as the Dewey decimal classification system. The system uses the numbers 000 to 999 to cover broad subjects, while more specific knowledge is classified using decimals. In 1876 Dewey helped found the American Library Association and the *Library Journal.* As chief librarian at Columbia College, he founded the School of Library Economy (1887), the first professional school for teaching librarians. From 1889 to 1906 he was director of the New York State Library.
See also: Dewey Decimal System.

Dewey, Thomas Edmund (1902-71), U.S. lawyer and politician. As Republican presidential candidate he was defeated in 1944 by Franklin D. Roosevelt and in 1948 by Harry S. Truman, although his election had been thought a foregone conclusion. In the 1930s, as U.S. attorney for the southern district of New York state and then as special prosecutor in New York City, Dewey gained a national reputation for successful campaigning against organized crime. He was governor of New York from 1943 to 1955. He declined the post of chief justice under Richard M. Nixon (1968).

Dewey decimal system, devised by Melvil Dewey (1851-1931) for classification of books in libraries, based on the decimal system of numbers. Dewey divided knowledge into 10 main areas, each of these into 10 subdivisions, and so on. Thus a book could fall into one of a thousand categories, from 000 to 999. Extensions of this system added further classificatory numbers after the decimal point.
See also: Dewey, Melvil.

De Witt, Jan (1625-72), Dutch statesman. He was grand pensionary (ruler) of Holland (1653-72) and republican opponent of the House of Orange. In 1667 he made peace with England, and in 1668 he negotiated the Triple Alliance with England and Sweden against Louis XIV of France to end the War of Devolution.
See also: Devolution, War of.

Dew line, acronym for Distant Early Warning line, consisting of 31 radar tracking stations between Alaska and Greenland designed to watch for Soviet air attacks. It was maintained by the United States and Canada until 1985 when Canada assumed full responsibility. It is now called the North Warning System.
See also: Radar.

Dew point, air temperature at which water vapor turns to liquid. Through a process called condensation, moisture (dew) forms on plants and outdoor surfaces when the relative humidity in the air is 100% and a cooling process occurs around the exposed surfaces. Excessive condensation attained at dew point results in the formation of fog. Water formed at dew points below freezing temperature (32°F, 0°C) yields frost.

Dextrin, chemical substance formed when starch is broken down by the body during digestion. Dextrin can also be produced artificially for commercial or industrial use. It is used in manufacturing the glue for postage stamps and to stiffen paper and textiles.
See also: Starch.

Dextrose, chemical name for pure glucose sugar. It is produced commercially by subjecting starch to a pressurized heating process that converts it into a solid form of glucose. The final product usually takes the form of fine white granules. Dextrose is used to bake candy and pastries and as a base in high-fructose corn syrup, a soft-drink sweetener.
See also: Glucose.

Dhaka (formerly Dacca; pop. 2,366,000), capital of the independent state of Bangladesh (formerly East Pakistan). Located on the Burhi Ganga River in the Ganges-Brahmaputra Delta, the city is a marketing and processing center for the products (mainly jute) of the surrounding agricultural region. Since the 18th century it has been noted for is delicate hand-woven muslins. The city became an important commercial, political, and cultural center under India's Mogul emperors, and has many fine examples of Mogul art and architecture. Under British rule it was the capital of a province from 1905 to 1911. In 1971 Dacca was involved in the fighting betweeen West Pakistan forces and the Indian and guerrilla forces that led to the creation of the independent state of Bangladesh.
See also: Bangladesh.

Dharma, concept of the eternal truth or law in Hinduism, Buddhism, and Jainism. To Hindus, it denotes the universal law ordaining religous and social institutions, the rights and duties of individuals, or, simply,

virtuous conduct. Buddhists consider it the universal truth proclaimed to all people by Buddha. In Jainism, it also represents an eternal substance.
See also: Buddhism; Hinduism.

Diabetes , or diabetes mellitus, disease characterized by the absence or inadequate secretion of insulin. Normally, sugars and starches (carbohydrates) in food are processed by digestive juices into a form of sugar called glucose, or blood sugar, which is the fuel used by the body. Insulin, a hormone produced by the pancreas, is a major regulator of this process. In the diabetic individual, either the body does not produce enough insulin, or the available insulin is somehow blocked or inactivated by other substances and is prevented from performing its primary function. Because of this impairment, excessive amounts of glucose accumulate in the blood and tissues and overflow into the urine. In juvenile-onset diabetes, there is a total or substantial lack of insulin, and daily injections of the hormone are necessary for survival. Juvenile-onset diabetes usually begins in the early years, from infancy to young adulthood. In adult-onset diabetes, which accounts for 85-90% of all cases, most individuals do not require insulin treatment and can maintain their blood sugar at relatively normal levels by controlling their weight and adhering to a prescribed diet. In general, women are more susceptible to this type than men, and the disease tends to occur most frequently in certain "high-risk" groups: close relatives of individuals who have diabetes, people who are overweight or over 40, and women who have given birth to large infants.
The early symptoms of diabetes stem from the increased amount of sugar in the blood and urine. Since the kidneys excrete excessive amounts of water along with the excess sugar, uncontrolled diabetics are likely to urinate frequently and to be constantly thirsty. Because the sugar in the blood is not being converted to energy, they will be weak, tired, and hungry. Because of the calories lost in the urine, they will lose weight, no matter how much they eat. Treatment may include diet, exercise, and insulin. Diabetics must generally cut down on sugar and sugar-rich foods, and on fats found in fatty meats, most cheese, butter, margarine, and nuts. Regular exercise increases the ability of the body to use food. All juvenile-onset and a few adult-onset diabetics must take insulin in order to use blood sugar in a comparatively normal manner.
"Hypo" attacks, due to *hypoglycemia* (too little sugar in the blood), may result when the diet-exercise-insulin balance is disrupted. Symptoms include tremor, hunger, sweating, headache, nausea, blurred vision, and eventually, if not promptly treated, loss of consciousness (diabetic coma). Prompt relief can usually be obtained by taking sugar in water.
Hyperglycemia (too much sugar in the blood) can occur when a diabetic fails to take sufficient insulin or to follow a meal plan; other contributory causes can be infection and illness. In this condition, fat is burned to supply energy, producing an increasingly acid condition of the blood and other body fluids (*acidosis*) due to the accumulation of so-called ketone substances, including acetone. Usual symptoms are nausea, drowsiness, extreme thirst, headache, blurred vision, abdominal pains, and rapid breathing. Acetone and high blood sugar levels can be detected in routine urine tests. As diabetics are more susceptible to infections than other individuals, even minor wounds should receive careful attention. Serious infections are frequently a precipitating factor in acidosis and diabetic coma. Despite satisfactory control of blood sugar levels through diet and the administration of insulin, in many cases long-term complications of diabetes develop, primarily those affecting blood vessels, nerves, kidneys, and eyes. In general, the juvenile diabetics are more severely affected.

Diaghilev, Sergei Pavlovich (1872-1929), Russian impresario and founder (Paris, 1909) of the Ballets Russes, which inaugurated modern ballet. His magazine *World of Art* (1899-1904) led a movement for Russian involvement in Western European arts. He moved to Paris in 1906. The Ballets Russes broke with the formalism of classical choreography and aimed to unify music, dance, and stage design. Its productions included the dancers and choreographers Michel Fokine, Anna Pavlova, Vaslav Nijinsky, and Léonide Massine, the composers Igor Stravinsky and Sergei Prokofiev, and the designers Aleksandr Benois and Léon Bakst. Matisse, Picasso, Debussy, Ravel, and many others also worked for Diaghilev.
See also: Ballet.

Dialectic *see:* Hegel, G. W. F.

Dialectical materialism *see:* Materialism; Philosophy.

Dialysis machine *see:* Kidney.

Diamond, mineral allotrope (molecular form) of carbon forming colorless cubic crystals (the other forms being graphite and the recently discovered fullerene). Diamond is the hardest known substance, with a Mohs hardness of 10, which varies slightly with the orientation of the crystal. Thus diamonds can be cut only by other diamonds. They do not conduct electricity, but conduct heat extremely well. Diamonds occur naturally in the mineral kimberlite, notably in South Africa (Orange Free State and Transvaal), Tanzania, and in the United States at Murfreesboro, Ark. They are also mined from secondary (alluvial) deposits, especially in Brazil, Zaire, Sierra Leone, and India. The diamonds are separated by mechanical panning, and those of gem quality are cleaved (or sawn), cut, and polished. Inferior, or industrial, diamonds are used for cutting, drilling, and grinding. Synthetic industrial diamonds are made by subjecting graphite to very high temperatures and pressures, sometimes with fused metals as solvents.
See also: Carbon.

Sergei Diaghilev, drawn by Pablo Picasso

Diana, in Roman mythology, goddess of the moon and the hunt, later identified with the Greek goddess Artemis. The sister of Apollo, she was the protectress of slaves and the lower classes and a special goddess of women and childbirth. The most famous Greek temple for the worship of Diana (Artemis) was at Ephesus in Asia Minor. There were also temples of Diana at Aricia on the shores of Lake Nemi, Italy, and on the Aventine Hill in Rome. Diana is usually represented as a huntress, carrying a quiver and accompanied by a hound or a deer.
See also: Mythology.

Diaphragm, in anatomy, dome-shaped, muscular partition separating the chest cavity from the abdominal cavity in humans and mammals. It plays an important role in respiration. By contracting when a person inhales, the diaphragm helps to pull air into the lungs. When a person exhales, the muscle relaxes, forcing air out of the lungs.
See also: Respiration.

Diarrhea, abnormally frequent evacuation of watery stools. *Choleraic diarrhea* refers to acute diarrhea with watery stools, resembling the major symptoms of cholera. A specific type of diarrhea runs in certain families; called *familial chloride diarrhea,* it is characterized by severe watery diarrhea with an excess of chloride in the stools, beginning in early infancy, and marked by a distended abdomen, lethargy, and retarded growth and mental development. *Parenteral diarrhea* is due to infections outside the gastrointestinal tract. "Summer diarrhea" is an acute form that was formerly found in children during the intense heat of summer but now tends to occur at other times of the year as well; it may be caused by the *E. coli* microbe. *Traveller's diarrhea* occurs particularly in those visiting tropical or subtropical areas where sanitation is not optimal; it too may be due to infection with *E. coli.*

Diary, book containing a daily record of events and personal observations. Diaries are often of great value to historians and biographers, especially those written for private personal gratification rather than for later publication. The Romans kept daily records of various kinds, and there are fascinating Japanese diaries of the 10th and 11th centuries. The earliest known English diaries were written by the astrologer John Dee (1527-1608) and Edward VI. The 17th century produced famous literary diarists such as John Evelyn and Samuel Pepys. In the 18th century John Wesley kept a journal for 66 years. Fanny Burney (Madame D'Arblay) recorded her meetings with George III, Samuel Johnson, and other notables. Queen Victoria's monumental diary spans her entire life from the age of 13.

Dias or **Diaz, Bartholemeu** (d. 1500), Portuguese navigator and explorer who, in 1488, discovered the sea route around Africa past the Cape of Good Hope to India. He explored much of the west coast of Africa. In 1500 he took part in Pedro Cabral's expedition, which discovered Brazil. He died at sea.

Diaspora *see:* Jews.

Diathermy, therapeutic use of high-frequency electric current to induce heat within deep tissues of the body that cannot be reached by surface heat. Deep heat can promote rapid healing by increasing the circulation of the blood, and it alleviates the pain of rheumatic conditions, joint dislocations, and sprains and fractures.

Diatom, single-celled alga plant (class Bacillariophyceae) of fresh and salt water. Their delicately sculptured cell walls contain silica, and the two halves fit together like the halves of a pill box. Diatoms are important as food for many small animals, and when they die their siliceous skeletons sink to the bottom. In some parts of the world deposits many feet thick have formed over a period of millions of years. These deposits (there is one over 1,000 ft/305 m thick in California) are excavated as *fuller's* or *diatomaceous earth.* The fine silica grains are used in metal polishes and toothpaste, as they scour but do not scratch. Diatoms are also connected with the formation of petroleum deposits.

Adolf Hitler, dictator of Germany from 1933 to 1945

Díaz, Porfirio (1830-1915), Mexican general and president. Renowned for his part in the war against the French (1861-67), he came to oppose Benito Juárez and gained power in 1877. President until 1880 and again from 1884, he was politically ruthless. His policies and foreign investment brought stability and prosperity, while peasant conditions were wretched. He was overthrown in 1911 and died in exile in Paris.
See also: Mexico.

Dice (singular: die), two 6-sided cubes with sides numbered from 1 to 6. They are used in gambling games and in many board games. Dice in games of chance go back at least 5,000 years, the earliest such cubes found in the Sumerian royal tombs of Ur, date to the third millennium B.C.

Dick, Philip Kendrid (1928-82), U.S. science fiction author whose works illustrate his philosophical ideas and concentrate on the characters instead of action or technology. Dick's most popular novel is *The Man in the High Castle* (1962); other works include *Do Androids Dream of Electric Sheep?* (1968), the basis for the movie *Bladerunner* (1982); and *Dr. Bloodmoney* (1965).

Dickcissel (*Spiza americana*), small bird of the prairies of the central United States, named for its song. A finch, it resembles a colorful sparrow. It feeds on insects and migrates to South America in the winter.

Dickcissel

Dickens, Charles (1812-70), English novelist. His brief childhood experience in a debtor's prison and work in a blacking factory shaped his future imagery and sympathies. Trained as a stenographer and lawyer's clerk, he began his literary career in London as a magazine contributor, under the pseudonym "Boz," publishing *Sketches by "Boz"* in 1836. His comic work *The Pickwick Papers* (1837) made him famous. His chief concern was the effect of moral evil, crime, and corruption on society. He created some memorable comic characters, as in *David Copperfield* (1850), which was based on his own experiences. His works include *Oliver Twist* (1838), *Bleak House* (1853), *Little Dorrit* (1857), *Great Expectations* (1861), and *Our Mutual Friend* (1865). Dickens's novels were dramatized, and he made successful reading tours of England and the United States.

Charles Dickens's work was made popular by the extraordinary illustrations of George Cruikshank and Hablot Knight Browne (Phiz). Depicted is the title page of The Pickwick Papers *drawn by Phiz.*

Dickey, James Lafayette (1923-), U.S. poet, novelist, and critic. Dickey is best known for his novel *Deliverance* (1970), which was made into a movie in 1972. His collection of poems *Buckdancer's Choice* (1965), which, like his novel, explores themes of violence, won a National Book Award in 1966. Another poetry volume was *The Zodiac* (1976).

Dickinson, Anna Elizabeth (1842-1932), U.S. abolitionist and orator who spoke out for the rights of women and African-Americans. Between 1860 and the end of the Civil War she made many speeches denouncing slavery and also became one of the leading feminists of her time.
See also: Abolitionism; Women's movements.

Dickinson, Emily (1830-86), U.S. poet. She spent most of her life secluded in her father's home in Amherst, Mass. Her concise lyrics, witty and aphoristic in style, simple in expression, and notable for metrical variations, are chiefly concerned with immortality and nature. Of 1,775 poems, only 7 were published during her lifetime.

Dickinson, John (1732-1808), U.S. statesman. Opposed to British colonial policy but against separation from Britain, he wrote *Letters from a Farmer in Pennsylvania* (1767-8) and, while a member of the Continental Congress (1774-6), probably drew up the *Declaration... Setting Forth the Causes and Necessity of Their Taking Up Arms* (1775). He wrote the first draft of the Articles of Confederation.
See also: Articles of Confederation.

Dictatorship, form of government in which one person holds absolute power and is not subject to the consent of the governed. The term derives from the Roman dictator who was a magistrate appointed to govern for a 6-month period, following a state emergency. Both Lucius Sulla and Julius Caesar, however, abolished the constitutional limits to their dictatorial power. In the 20th century, Adolf Hitler and Josef Stalin assumed dictatorial powers and committed hideous atrocities; there have also been dictatorships in Portugal, Spain, and Greece, and in many South American and African countries. Current dictators include Col. Muammar Qadhaffi of Lybia and Saddam Hussein of Iraq.

Dictionary, listing of the words of a language, usually in alphabetical order, with the meaning of each word, as well as information on pronunciation and etymology and examples of usage, with synonyms and antonyms. Foreign language dictionaries generally list only the translations of words without their definitions. Specialized or technical dictionaries define terms used in a particular field. The term "dictionary" is sometimes applied to reference works arranged alphabetically, such as a dictionary of biography or *Grove's Dictionary of Music and Musicians.* The term "dictionary" (Latin: *dictionarium,* from *dicere,* "to say") first appeared c.1225 as the title of a book by the Englishman John Garland, a manuscript of Latin words to be learned by heart, arranged by subject rather than in alphabetical order. Some scholars consider Richard Huloet's *Abcedarium Anglico-Latinum pro Tyrunculis* (English-Latin Lexicon for Young Beginners; 1552) the first English dictionary, since it defined each English word in English before giving the Latin equivalent. Others give the honor to Robert Cawdrey's *The Table Alphabeticall of Hard Words* (1604), which contained about 2,500 words defined in "plaine English [for] Ladies, Gentlewomen, or any other unskilfull persons." Nathaniel Bailey's dictionary (1721) gave the etymology of each entry and was among the first works to indicate pronunciation. Samuel Johnson's *A Dictionary of the English Language* (1755) was the outstanding lexicon of its century and remained the authority until well into the 19th century. Noah Webster's *An American Dictionary of the English Language* (1828) quickly became the most authoritative U.S. dictionary. Although Webster died in 1843, many modern dictionaries still bear his name. The first (1890) and second (1934) editions of *Webster's International Dictionary* were considered authoritative. The third edition (1961) was attacked by some for its "permissive" policy of description, rather than prescription, of usage.

The most comprehensive English-language dictionary project was probably the *New English Dictionary on Historical Principles,* later known as the *Oxford English Dictionary* (OED). Hundreds of scholars from Great Britain and the United States worked on this great lexicon, begun in 1858; the last section appeared in 1928 (a supplement appeared in 1933). The OED lists and defines every English word that has appeared from the 7th century to the 20th, with all known variants, as well as etymologies, quotations, usages, and pronunciation.

Diderot, Denis (1713-84), French encyclopedist, philosopher, and writer. His versatility as a novelist, playwright, and art critic made him prominent in the Enlightenment. His fame rests on the *Encyclopédie* (1751-71), which he edited with Jean d'Alembert. The *Encyclopédie,* attempting a comprehensive presentation of human thought and knowledge, presented the scientific discoveries and more advanced thought of the time. As a result, the French government tried to suppress it in 1759. Diderot's works include the play *Le Père de Famille* (1761) and the novel *Jacques le Fataliste* (1796).

Didion, Joan (1934-), U.S. writer concerned with the "atomization" of post-World War II society. Her work includes the essay collections *Slouching Towards Bethlehem* (1968) and *The White Album* (1979) and the novels *Play It As It Lays* (1970) and *A Book of Common Prayer* (1977).

Didrikson, Babe *see:* Zaharias, Babe Didrikson.

Diefenbaker, John George (1895-1979), Canadian prime minister, 1957-63. Becoming leader of the Progressive Conservative Party in 1956, he headed a minority government in 1957, after 22 years of Liberal rule. The 1958 election produced a record government majority. He instituted agricultural reforms, but the economic recession, the Cuban missile crisis, and the nuclear arms debate, which aggravated relations with the United States under President John F. Kennedy, brought on his defeated in 1966 by Lester Pearson and the Liberals. He served in the Commons until his death.
See also: Canada.

Diego Garcia, island in the Indian Ocean southwest of Sri Lanka. It is the site of a strategic communications center for U.S. and British naval troops and a refueling stop for military ships and aircraft. Diego Garcia is administered as a dependency of the British Indian Ocean Territory.

Diem, Ngo Dinh *see:* Ngo Dinh Diem.

Diemaking *see:* Dies and diemaking.

Dien Bien Phu, military outpost in North Vietnam where in 1954 France was finally defeated in the Indochina War. During the 56-day siege the French army lost 15,000 men in its bid to resist the onslaught of Gen. Vo Nguyen Giap's Vietminh forces. France formally withdrew from Indochina at the Geneva Conference (1954).
See also: Vietnam.

Dies and diemaking, tools and procedures for casting molds to shape metal in industrial processes. Raw materials—usually metals or plastics—are cast into uniform shapes and sizes by dies that may be used many times for the same purpose. The dies are made from rubber, metal, or plastic and require constant maintenance.

Denis Diderot

Diesel, Rudolf (1858-1913), German engineer and developer of the oil-fueled internal-combustion engine that is named after him. After working as a mechanic, parts designer, and thermal engineer, Diesel began work on his design in 1885, patented it in 1892, and had a working model by 1897.
See also: Diesel engine.

Diesel engine, internal combustion engine patented in 1892 by the German engineer Rudolf Diesel (1858-1913). Unlike the gasoline engines used in most modern automobiles, the diesel engine does not ignite the fuel with an outside source of heat such as a spark plug, but uses the heat generated by compression to ignite the fuel-air mixture in its cylinder. To achieve the necessary high temperatures diesel engines must have a high compression ratio. Compression ratios of 16:1 are most commonly used. At this ratio, the temperature within the cylinder reaches 940°F (504°C) and the

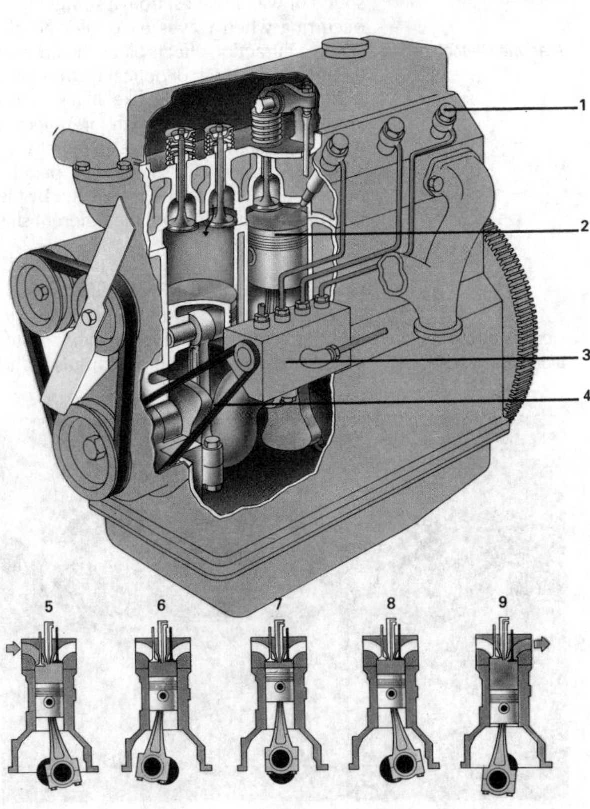

Diesel engines work on the principle of fuel injection, unlike most conventional internal combustion engines. Diesel fuel is sprayed under high pressure from an injector into the combustion chamber. The increased temperature caused by the compression of air in the chamber is sufficient to ignite the fuel. The accelerator controls the amount of fuel delivered by the pump and hence the power of the engine.

Key:
1. Injector
2. Piston in combustion chamber
3. Fuel pump
4. Chain drive from crank-shaft to pump
5. Inlet valve opens and air is drawn into chamber
6. Both valves are closed and piston compresses air
7. Just before maximum compression fuel is injected into chamber where it vaporizes
8. Fuel ignites spontaneously and drives piston down to turn engine
9. Exhaust valve opens and piston clears the chamber

pressure equals 546 lb (248 kg) per sq inch. (Ordinary gasoline engines have compression ratios between 4:1 and 10:1.)
See also: Diesel, Rudolf.

Diet, customary or specified kind of food and drink taken daily. Doctors, nurses, and dieticians must be skilled in dietetics (the science of diet and nutrition) so that they can advise on the selection, preparation, and presentation of food for patients. A balanced diet includes proteins, fats and carbohydrates, minerals, and vitamins. Special diets for weight loss or gain are designed according to the intake of calories, which measure energy yielded by food. Other diets may involve restriction of salt (for heart disease) or sugar (for diabetes).

Dietitian, one who applies the principles of nutrition to the feeding of an individual or a group of individuals.
See also: Nutrition.

Marlene Dietrich

Dietrich, Marlene (Maria Magdalene von Losch; 1904-), German-born U.S. actress and cabaret artist. Early in her career she studied acting with Max Reinhardt and acted on the Berlin stage. Her "femme fatale" image originated with her first major film role, the dance-hall girl in *The Blue Angel* (1930). Her other well-known films include *Morocco* (1930) and *Shanghai Express* (1932). She became a U.S. citizen in 1937.

Dietrich of Bern *see:* Theodoric.

Diffraction, deviation and spreading of waves (such as electromagnetic radiation, sound or water waves) from a straight line, occurring when waves encounter an obstacle. Diffraction effects place the limit on the resolving power of optical instruments, radio telescopes, and the like. In a spectrograph, light passed through or reflected from a diffraction grating, a series of very accurately ruled slits or narrow parallel mirrors, produces a series of spectra by the interference of light from the different slits or mirrors.

Diffusion, gradual mixing of different substances placed in mutual contact, due to the random thermal motion of their constituent particles. Most rapid with gases and liquids, it also occurs with solids. Diffusion rates increase with increasing temperature; the rates at which gases diffuse through a porous membrane vary as the inverse of the square root of their molecular weight (gases of low molecular weight diffuse more quickly than those of high molecular weight). Gaseous diffusion is used to separate fissile uranium-235 from nonfissile uranium-238, the gas used being uranium hexafluoride (UF_6).

Houses on a dike along the river Rhine

Digestive system, organs in the body that play a major role in the digestion of food, including the mouth, esophagus, stomach, and bowels. The pancreas and liver secrete juices that assist in the digestive processes. The muscular activity of the digestive tract disturbs the daily existence of humans. Hunger and the desire to defecate may arise from awareness of the movement of a part of the tract. Hunger contractions are a stimulus for food intake and arise when the stomach is empty. A few minutes after a meal, food, broken down by enzymes (digestive juices) into chyme, begins to leave the stomach, which is usually empty within 3 hours. On leaving the stomach, the food passes fairly rapidly through the small intestine, where it is further broken down, and within 3-4 hours the unabsorbed remnants begin to reach the colon, the residues of the various meals taken every day lying in the descending colon until expulsion. Defecation usually takes place once a day, but it is not abnormal for it to occur 3 times daily or to be withheld for up to 3 days. The muscle of the digestive tract regulates the passage of the contents to allow adequate time for digestion and absorption. Mastication (chewing) is a voluntary movement, and swallowing can be initiated voluntarily, so the muscles of the mouth and pharynx are all striated, and the esophagus contains both striated and smooth (involuntary) muscle. From the stomach to the anus there is only smooth muscle, except for the external anal sphincter, which is again striated.

Digital computer *see:* Computer.

Digitalis, drug prepared from leaves of the foxglove plant (genus *Digitalis*). Its main effect is cardiotonic, causing the heart muscle to pump more forcefully and effectively, thereby improving the circulation of the blood and promoting the normal elimination of excess fluid. Digitalis is often used to treat heart failure because it can relieve one of the early effects of the condition—buildup of fluid in the body tissues. Digitalis and its derivates (digitoxin and digoxin) are the most frequently used cardiotonic drugs; other examples are ouabain and strophanthus.

Dik-dik, small African antelope (genus *Madoqua*), standing only 14 in (36 cm) high at the shoulder. The male has short, spiky horns.

Dike, artificial embankment for controlling water flow. Made of rock, clay, or cement, dikes are shaped in the form of a mound high enough to prevent an overflow of water. Often they are equipped with gates in order to permit irrigation of farmland. Dikes are a common feature in the Dutch landscape, since most of the Netherlands is below sea level. The term originally referred to a trench dug into the earth as a defensive measure. As water naturally collects in such trenches, *dike* also came to mean a natural or artificial water channel.

Dill (*Anethum graveolens*), annual or biennial of the carrot family cultivated for its leaves and seeds, which are used as flavorings. Dill originated around the Mediterranean.

Dillinger, John (1903-34), U.S. gangster who terrorized the Midwest in 1933 after escaping from jail. Responsible for 16 killings, he was the FBI's Public Enemy Number 1. FBI agents killed him in Chicago in 1934.

Dilthey, Wilhelm (1833-1911), German philosopher. He sought to achieve for the human sciences (law, religion, history, psychology, and the arts) a methodology free of the influence of the natural sciences.
See also: Philosophy.

DiMaggio, Joseph Paul (1914-), U.S. baseball player. Nicknamed "the Yankee Clipper," DiMaggio is considered one of the greatest outfielders of all time, and set a major league record by hitting safely in 56 consecutive games (1941). He won the American League's most valuable player award 3 times (1939, 1941, and 1947), and in 1948 he led the league in home runs (39) and runs batted in (155). DiMaggio, who played for the New York Yankees (1936-51) and led them to 10 World Series appearances, played in 11 All-Star games and was inducted into the National Baseball Hall of Fame (1955).

Joe DiMaggio

Dimethyl sulfoxide *see:* DMSO.

D'Indy, (Paul Marie Théodore) Vincent (1851-1931), French composer. A pupil of César Franck and cofounder (1894) of the

Schola Cantorum academy in Paris, he admired the German classics and Renaissance polyphony and urged a renovated French style derived from folk idioms. His works include *Symphony on a French Mountain Air* (1886).

Dine, Jim (James Dine; 1935-), U.S. artist. His work makes use of "found" objects, such as old shoes or tools, which he attaches to his canvases.

Dinesen, Isak (Baroness Karen Blixen; 1885-1962), Danish author of romantic tales of mystery, such as *Seven Gothic Tales* (1934) and *Winter's Tales* (1942). Dinesen wrote in both English and Danish. The autobiographical *Out of Africa* (1937) was based on her 20 years in East Africa.

Dinka, plains tribe of southern Sudan, in Africa. The Dinka are primarily farmers and cattle herders who supplement their diet with fish. Their religion centers around a single god and many spirits.

Dinkins, David (1927-), first African-American mayor of New York City, elected 1990. Prior to his election Dinkins served as Manhattan borough president (1985-89). A graduate of Howard University (1950) and Brooklyn Law School (1956), Dinkins was a New York State assemblyman (1966) and New York City clerk (1975-85).

Dinoflagellate, single-celled organism that occurs in vast numbers in fresh and salt water. Each one is covered by a layer of cellulose that is a distinctive, and often elaborate, shape. Some contain chlorophyll while others do not, so they may be classed as animals or plants. Dinoflagellates are important as food for many animals, but some are poisonous. Swarms of one form, the "red tide" of tropical waters, kill fish and damage beaches. Certain dinoflagellates create the phosphorescence of the sea.

Dinosaur (Greek, "terrible lizard"), extinct reptile that flourished between about 220 and 63 million years ago and then suddenly disappeared. Dinosaurs dominated the land life during most of this period and occurred in a wide variety of forms, some no bigger than a chicken and others weighing many tons. The dinosaurs arose in the Triassic Period (early Mesozoic Era) from a group of small reptiles called *thecodonts.* They evolved into 2 great groups, or orders, the Saurischia, or "lizard-hipped," and the Ornithischia, or "bird-hipped." Saurischian dinosaurs include 2-legged carnivores-the theropods and 4-legged herbivores-the sauropods. The sauropods were the giant dinosaurs, including such types as the apatosaurus (brontosaurus) and the diplodocus, with tiny heads, very long necks and tails, and pillar-like legs. The theropods ranged from the fast-running coelurosaurs, which fed on insects and perhaps on eggs, to the carnosaurs like the Tyrannosaurus and allosaurus, which had enormous skulls and dagger-like teeth and could grow to a height of 20 ft (6m). Ornithischians diversified into many types, some producing strange body armor. All were herbivorous. Four-legged forms include the stegosaurs, which had triangular bony plates along the back, the armadillo-like ankylosaurs, and the ceratopsians, such as the triceratops, which carried 3 horns and a bony frill on the skull. The 2-legged ornithischians included the duck-billed dinosaurs. At the end of the Cretaceous Period (about 65 million years ago) dinosaurs disappeared. The reason for their extinction is unknown. It has been suggested that disease killed them off or that mammals preyed excessively on their eggs. Climactic and other changes caused by the impact of a huge asteroid have also been proposed.
See illustrations on following page.

Dinwiddie, Robert (1693-1770), lieutenant governor of colonial Virginia (1751-58), who made alliances with Native American tribes to prevent French encroachment into western Pennsylvania and the Ohio Valley. In 1753 forces recruited by Dinwiddie attacked the French stronghold at Fort Duquesne (present-day Pittsburgh). After quarreling with the Virginia Colonial Assembly over the appropriation of war funds, Dinwiddie gave up his post and returned to England.

Diocletian (Gaius Aurelius Valerius Diocletianus; A.D. 245-313), Roman emperor A.D. 284-305. He reformed the army and administration, dividing the empire into 4 regions (293), ruled by 2 emperors and 2 caesars. Much of his great palace at Split, Yugoslavia, survives. In 303 he initiated the last universal persecution of the Christians. He abdicated in 305.
See also: Rome, Ancient.

Diode *see:* Electronics.

Diogenes (412?-323 B.C.), Greek philosopher. Contemptuous of his contemporaries and their values, he was nicknamed "the Dog" and his followers the *cynics* (Greek: *kynikos,* "doglike"). He abandoned all his possessions, begged his living, and reputedly lived in a tub. Supposedly, when Alexander the Great asked what he could do for him, Diogenes answered, "Just step out of my light."
See also: Cynic philosophy.

Dionaea *see:* Venus's-flytrap.

Dionysius the Elder (430?-367 B.C.), Greek soldier who distinguished himself in battle against Carthage and thus got himself elected sovereign general of Syracuse (in 405 B.C.). He converted the office into a tyranny, raising a large army of mercenaries.
See also: Greece, Ancient.

Dionysus, in Greek mythology, god of wine and fertility, generally thought of as a son of Zeus. He founded the art of vine cultivation. In early times his devotees, notably the Maenads, practiced an orgiastic cult of divine possession. Greek drama developed from the celebrations in honor of Dionysus. The Romans identified their wine god Bacchus with Dionysus.
See also: Mythology.

Diogenes meets Alexander the Great

Diopside, mineral of the silicate family. Rich in calcium and magnesium, it is occasionally used as a gemstone. It has a glassy surface and can range in color from white to light green. Diopside is a metamorphic rock formed by intense heat and pressure on limestone-based dolomite. It can also be formed when molten rock (magma) crystalizes.

Dior, Christian (1905-57), French fashion designer. Dior helped reestablish Paris as the leader in fashion after World War II. His salon, opened in 1946, branched out into subsidiary companies to manufacture perfume and clothing accessories. Known worldwide, Dior was the undisputed leader of fashion until his death.

Dioxin, toxic chemical produced in some chemical-manufacturing processes, contaminating various herbicides. The effects on human health of long-term exposure to dioxin are disputed, although it is generally accepted that dioxin causes chloracne. U.S. chemical workers have filed suits

Dionysus meets Ariadne (detail from an ancient Greek beaker)

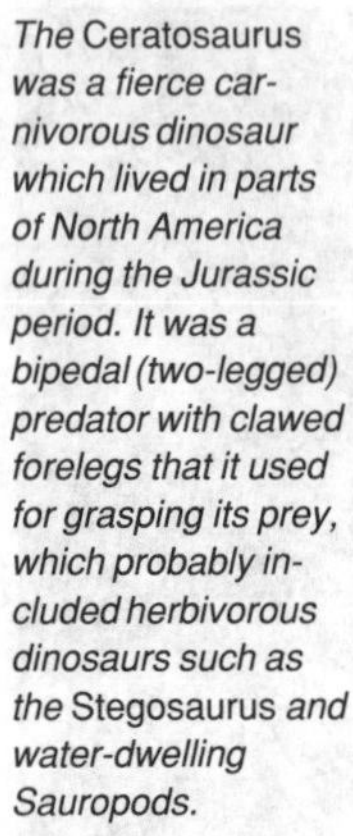

The Ceratosaurus *was a fierce carnivorous dinosaur which lived in parts of North America during the Jurassic period. It was a bipedal (two-legged) predator with clawed forelegs that it used for grasping its prey, which probably included herbivorous dinosaurs such as the* Stegosaurus *and water-dwelling* Sauropods.

The Tarbosaurus *was a large theropod dinosaur over 45 ft (14 m) long. It was an asian relative of the North American* Tyrannosaurus.

The Oviraptor *(egg-stealer), one of the ostrich-like dinosaurs of the Cretaceous period, is thought to have fed on the eggs of other reptiles. It was bipedal, and able to run fast.*

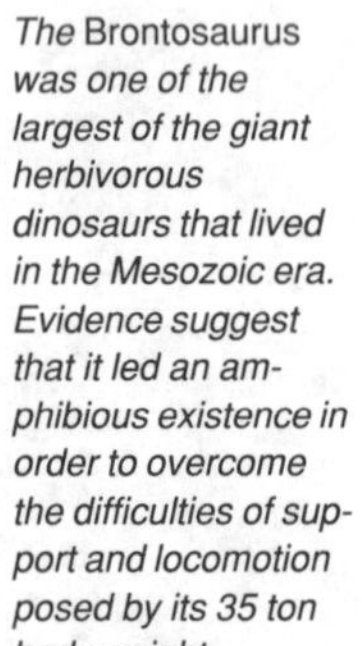

The Brontosaurus *was one of the largest of the giant herbivorous dinosaurs that lived in the Mesozoic era. Evidence suggest that it led an amphibious existence in order to overcome the difficulties of support and locomotion posed by its 35 ton body weight.*

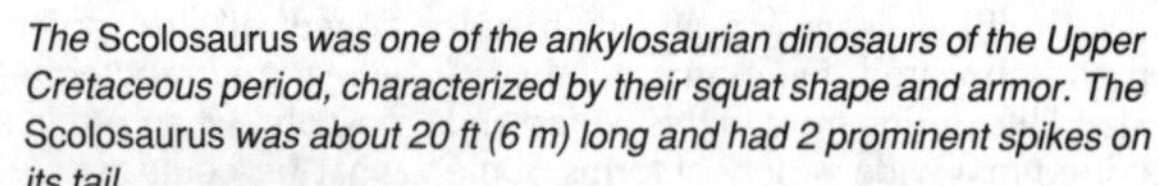

The Scolosaurus *was one of the ankylosaurian dinosaurs of the Upper Cretaceous period, characterized by their squat shape and armor. The* Scolosaurus *was about 20 ft (6 m) long and had 2 prominent spikes on its tail.*

against employers for serious health problems, and Vietnam veterans also claimed damages for exposure to Agent Orange, a defoliant contaminated by dioxin. There were cleanups in the 1980s of dioxin deposits on sites in Missouri and New Jersey.
See also: Agent Orange.

Diphtheria, acute contagious disease caused by *Corynebacterium diphtheriae*, characterized by the formation of a soft crust (pseudomembrane) that forms in the inflamed throat, and by tissue damage in the heart and nervous system, a result of poisons produced by the bacteria. An effective vaccine prevents diphtheria.

Diplodocus *see:* Dinosaur.

Diplomacy, conduct of negotiations and maintenance of relations in time of peace between sovereign states. A diplomatic mission is generally headed by an ambassador, supported by attachés, chargés d'affaires, and other officials specializing in economic, political, cultural, administrative, and military matters. An embassy building is considered to have extraterritoriality (to be outside the jurisdiction of the receiving state). Accredited diplomats are immune from prosecution and customs regulations. Abuse of this privileged diplomatic immunity can lead to a diplomat being asked to quit the host country as *persona non grata*. The most common abuse is espionage. The whole body of diplomats in a capital is known as the diplomatic corps, and its spokesperson is the longest-serving ambassador. The first permanent residential missions were established by the Italian city-states c.1400. Diplomatic protocol and the forms of accreditation owed much to the practice of papal missions from the Vatican. Latin was the official language of diplomacy until the 17th century, when it was superseded by French, later joined by English. The Congress of Vienna (1815) further clarified diplomatic procedure. The traditional formulas of diplomatic exchange allow sharp expressions of protest without ruptures in international dealing. Improved communications have strengthened direct links between governments, and diplomacy is now often conducted at summit conferences between heads of state.

Dipper, small wrenlike bird (genus *Cinclus*) that dives under water. The American dipper (*C. mexicanus*) is slate-gray and lives along mountain streams in the western United States. It has a thick underplumage and large oil glands to keep the plumage waterproof.

Dirac, Paul Adrien Maurice (1902-84), English theoretical physicist. He shared the 1933 Nobel Prize in physics with E. Schrödinger for their contributions to wave mechanics. Dirac's theory (1928) took account of relativity and implied the existence of the positive electron, or positron, later discovered by C.D. Anderson. Dirac was also the codeveloper of Fermi-Dirac statistics.
See also: Quantum mechanics.

Direct current *see:* Electric current.

Director *see:* Motion pictures; Theater.

Direct Selling Association, U.S. organization of some 150 companies that sell goods or services directly to the public. Founded in 1910, the group monitors federal legislation and maintains a lobby on Capitol Hill. Products marketed by DSA members include clothing, housewares, jewelry, cosmetics, and reference books.

Dirigible *see:* Airship.

Dirksen, Everett McKinley (1896-1969), U.S. legislator. Illinois Republican representative (1933-48) and senator (1950-69), Dirksen was Senate minority leader from 1959 until his death. He delivered conservative Republican support of major bipartisan legislation, most notably in the case of the landmark Civil Rights Act of 1964.

Disabled American Veterans, organization aimed at helping wounded war veterans, founded in 1920 by Judge Robert S. Marx of Cincinnati. It has more than 1 million members in 2,500 chapters.

Disarmament, procedure for abolishing, limiting, regulating, or reducing a nation's military forces or weapons arsenal. Widespread or universal disarmament has been a long-sought goal of many. After World War II, the existence of nuclear weapons and the split of the world into 2 hostile camps lent a new urgency to curbing the destructive power of nations. Several treaties (Nuclear Test Ban Treaty, 1963; Nuclear Non-Proliferation Treaty, 1968, a non-binding treaty under UN auspices) were negotiated in the 1950s and 1960s. The Strategic Arms Limitation Talks (SALT) were unsuccessful in the 1970s, but the Strategic Arms Reduction Talks (START) between the United States and the USSR went on throughout the 1980s. With the end of the cold war in Europe in 1989-90 and the dismantling of the Warsaw Pact Alliance, major reductions in military personnel and materiel throughout Europe and Russia became feasible, and are currently being planned and executed.

Dipper

Disarmament in action: Russian troops withdraw from East Germany

Disaster relief *see:* Civil defense; Coast Guard, U.S.; National Guard; Red Cross; Salvation Army.

Disciple *see:* Apostles.

Disciples of Christ (The Christian Church), now the International Convention of Christian Churches, U.S. religious body founded (1832) by followers of Alexander Campbell. It has no formal ministry or creed, teaching personal faith in the Bible and the gospel of Christ. It has missions all over the world.

Discrimination, in science, perception of difference or of differential response, or ability to perceive slight differences. A discrimination experiment tests the presence of the ability to discriminate under certain conditions. A discrimination reaction is a variation between 2 or more stimuli before reacting; the time that is needed is the discrimination time.

Discus, disk thrown in athletic competition. The wooden disk has a smooth metal rim and brass plates set flush within its sides. Discus throwing was popular in classical times as a form of exercise and for athletic contests. The discus, then made of stone or metal, was thrown for distance, with a combination of strength, skill, and grace. The discus thrown by men in modern competition weighs not less than 4 lb 6.5 oz (2 kg). The women's discus weighs 2 lb 3 oz (1 kg).

Disease, disturbance of normal body function in an organism. Disease is usually brought to a person's attention by symp-

toms of an abnormality of, or change in, body function: pain, headache, fever, cough, shortness of breath, dyspepsia, constipation, diarrhea, loss of blood, lumps, paralysis, or numbness, or loss of consciousness. Diagnosis is made on the basis of symptoms and from signs on discovered physical examination and from laboratory and X-ray investigations.
Trauma (injury) may cause skin lacerations and bone fractures as well as disorders specific to the organ involved. Congenital diseases include hereditary conditions and diseases beginning in the fetus, such as those due to drugs or maternal infection during pregnancy. Infectious diseases caused by viruses, bacteria, and parasites are usually communicable; insects, animals, and human carriers may be important in their spread, and epidemics may occur. Inflammation is often the result of infection, but inflammatory disease can also result from disordered immunity and other causes. In vascular diseases, organs become diseased as a result of disease in their blood supply; examples are atherosclerosis, aneurysms, thrombosis, and embolism. In tumors, including benign growths, cancer, and lymphoma, abnormal growth of a structure occurs and leads to a lump, causing pressure or spreading to other organs. In degenerative disease, death or premature aging of parts of an organ or a system lead to a gradual impairment of function. Deficiency diseases result from inadequate intake of nutrients; resulting disorders, including hormonal disorders, can lead to metabolic disease. An increasingly recognized side- effect of industrialization is occupational disease caused by chemicals, dust, or molds encountered at work. An iatrogenic disease is one produced by medical intervention in an attempt to treat or prevent another disease. Finally, psychiatric disease, including psychoses (schizophrenia and severe depression) and neuroses, are functional disturbances of the brain; they may represent disturbances of brain metabolism.
The characteristics of acute disease may be exemplified by acute infections. The onset of the condition is frequently sudden, and there may be almost total prostration, but there is the prospect of a limited period in this state. Most acute diseases, because of their finite duration, pose a minimal threat to the subject. The onset of chronic disease, on the other hand, is usually slow; there may be a progression of symptoms, or more permanent problems may develop as the sequel to a number of acute episodes.

Benjamin Disraeli

Disinfectant, chemical substance or other agent, such as ultraviolet light, used to disinfect inanimate objects, with the aim of destroying or inhibiting the activity of disease-producing microorganisms.

Dislocation, movement of an organ, bone, or other body part away from its normal position, in particular the displacement of the bones of a joint. Dislocations are said to be simple (bearing no external wound) or complex (involving a wound that breaks the skin).

Dismal Swamp, coastal region straddling the boundary of Virginia and North Carolina. It occupies some 750 sq mi (2,000 sq km). The swamp contains a dense growth of juniper, cypress, white cedar, and black gum trees, though much of it is now drained and used for commercial lumbering and agriculture. It is crossed by Dismal Swamp Canal, a part of the Intracoastal Waterway. Near the center is Lake Drummond (6 sq mi/15.5 sq km), a popular fishing area.

Disney, Walt (Walter Elias Disney; 1901-66), U.S. pioneer of animated film cartoons. Starting in the 1920s, the Disney studios in Hollywood created the cartoon characters Mickey Mouse, Pluto, Donald Duck, and Goofy. Disney produced the first full-length cartoon feature, *Snow White and the Seven Dwarfs* (1938), which was followed by *Pinocchio* (1940), *Fantasia* (1940), and *Bambi* (1942), among others. The company he founded continues to make movies in his tradition, such as *The Fox and the Hound* (1981), *The Little Mermaid* (1989), and *Beauty and the Beast* (1991). Disney also produced many popular nature films. He opened the first of his theme parks, Disneyland, in Anaheim, Calif., in 1955. The park now includes over 160 acres of elaborate mechanized amusements and re-creations based on Disney movie features. Built on a permanent World's Fair scale, the park is one of the major tourist attractions in the United States. A similar, far larger park opened in 1971 on a 27,400-acre site near Orlando, Fla.; it was joined by the futuristic Epcot Center in 1982. The Tokyo Disney World also opened in 1982 and a European Disney World is scheduled to open in 1991. *See also:* Cartoon.

Walt Disney designing one of his figures

Dispersion, optical phenomenon whereby a beam of white light is broken up into its component colors when it passes through a triangular glass prism. Each color has a different index of refraction; that is, it bends at a characteristic angle when passing from one medium to another (air to glass, for instance). Since white light is made up of all the colors of the spectrum, the colors separate when they pass through glass prisms. Rainbows are formed by the refraction and dispersion of sunlight through raindrops.

Displaced person *see:* Refugee.

Disraeli, Benjamin, 1st earl of Beaconsfield (1804-81), British Conservative statesman, prime minister 1868 and 1874-80. Baptized a Christian, Disraeli was the first British prime minister of Jewish ancestry. A member of Parliament from 1837, he was chancellor of the exchequer 1852, 1858-59, and 1866-68. His influence was crucial in the passing of the 1867 Reform Bill, which enfranchised some 2 million working-class voters. His brief first ministry ended when the Liberals under William Gladstone won the 1868 elections. His second period of office included domestic reforms: slum clearance, public-health reform, and improvement of working conditions. Abroad, Disraeli fought imperial wars, bought control of the Suez Canal (1875), had Queen Victoria proclaimed Empress of India (1876), and annexed the Transvaal (1877). In the confrontation between Russia and Turkey (1877-78), he forced concessions on Russia in the Congress of Berlin. A prolific writer, he published many books, notably the novels *Coningsby* (1844) and *Sybil* (1845), both on social and political themes.

Dissection *see:* Anatomy.

Distant Early Warning line *see:* DEW line.

Distemper, term applied to several animal diseases, but particularly referring to a specific viral disease of dogs. It commonly occurs in puppies, with fever, poor appetite, and discharge from mucous membranes; bronchopneumonia and encephalitis may be complications. Vaccination is protective.

Distillation, method of separating the parts of mixtures of liquids or of separating liquids from solids. The mixture or solution is heated so that the liquid vaporizes. The vapor is then condensed to form a liquid, called the distillate. The distillate is a purified form of the original solution, since the less volatile components are left behind as residue. Distillation is used in industry to separate and purify petroleum products, alcohols, and benzene hydrocarbons. It is also used in making alcoholic drinks. Distillation is carried out in a *still* consisting of a boiler, where the liquid is heated; a condenser, where the vapors are condensed; and a receiver to collect the distillate. Distillation can be carried out under high pressure or under reduced pressure or a vacuum to raise or lower the boiling points of the liquids involved.

Distilling, production of strong alcoholic drinks by distillation of the weak alcoholic liquors obtained in the fermentation of sugary substances with yeast. Brandies, whiskeys, gins, rum, vodka, tequila, and liqueurs are produced by distilling. Spirits have been made in the United States since the 17th century and remain very popular. The strength of an alcoholic drink is usually expressed by comparing it with "proof spirit," which in the United States is taken to be a mixture of equal volumes of alcohol and water. Thus 50% alcohol corresponds to 100° proof, and a drink containing 40% alcohol would be labeled 80° proof. Millions of gallons of distilled liquor are consumed in the United States every year at a cost of over $4 billion. The production of distilled alcohol is strictly controlled by law. Several thousand illegal stills are seized every year.

District attorney, state or municipal official in charge of prosecuting criminal cases. The district attorney may be either elected or appointed. After the police make an arrest, the district attorney decides whether there are sufficient grounds to prosecute. To proceed, he or she normally must first obtain an indictment from a grand jury, although some states have abolished the grand jury and allow the district attorney to issue an indictment on his or her own initiative. He or she then gathers evidence and prepares the case against the defendant.

District court, federal court of original jurisdiction in the U.S. judicial system. It hears both criminal and civil cases that primarily involve federal laws and, in the case of diversity jurisdiction, state laws. Each district court is headed by a judge who is appointed (for life) by the President and confirmed by the Senate. Cases decided by the district courts may be appealed to the Courts of Appeal, the next level in the federal court system.
See also: Apellate court.

District of Columbia (D.C.) *see:* Washington, D.C.

Disulfiram, sulphur-based drug used to treat alcoholism. Discovered in 1948 by two Danish physicians, Jens Hald and Erik Jacobsen, disulfiram makes alcohol unpalatable to the user. Mixing alcohol with the drug causes dizziness, nausea, and possible vomiting.
See also: Alcoholism.

Dittersdorf, Karl Ditters von (1739-99), Austrian composer and violinist. He composed light operas, establishing the singspiel form. Among his works are the operas *Doktor und Apotheker* (1786), *Hieronymus Knicker* (1789), and *Das Rote Käppchen* (1790).
See also: Opera.

Diuretic, drug that increases urine production by the kidneys, removing excess sodium and water from the body. Alcohol and caffeine are mild diuretics. Thiazides and other diuretics are commonly used in treatment of heart failure, edema, high blood pressure, and liver and kidney diseases.

Diverticulitis, disease of the intestine involving inflamation of diverticula, pouches or sacs that sometimes appear in the surface of the colon, causing it to bulge out in weak points. The appearance of these abnormal diverticula is called diverticulosis, which affects 5 to 10% of people over 40. About one-fifth of the people with diverticulosis will also get diverticulitis. Symptoms include fever, spasms, and cramplike pain in the lower left part of the abdomen. Treatment may range from bed rest to drug therapy to combat infection.
See also: Intestine.

Divide, line of high ground, such as a mountain ridge or chain of hills, that determines the direction of flow of streams and rivers. It is sometimes called a watershed. A divide may extend the length of a continent, as does the Continental Divide formed by the Rocky Mountains in North America. Rivers east of this divide flow into the Gulf of Mexico or the Atlantic Ocean, and rivers west of it flow into the Pacific Ocean.

Divination, any of various methods of foretelling the future by means of oracles, omens, or signs. These methods include dream interpretation, astrology, investigation of parts of the body (e.g., palmistry, phrenology), study of the animal entrails, and interpretation of the cries of birds and animals (augury). Divination is one of the most ancient of practices, and has been found in almost all societies.

Divine, Father (George Baker; 1880?-1965), African-American religious leader. He was the founder of the Peace Mission Movement, a nonsectarian, interracial church that worked to promote racial justice, peace, and an end to poverty. The movement began in Harlem and won the support of many people throughout the United States. Deified by his devotees, Father Divine was harshly criticized by others for his lavish life-style.

Diving *see:* Swimming and diving.

Diving, deep-sea, descent by divers to the seabed, usually for extended periods, for purposes of exploration, recreation, or salvage. In 1715 John Lethbridge devised the forerunner of the armored suits used today in deepest waters. In 1802 William Forder devised a suit into which air is supplied by a pump. The diving suit today has a metal or fiberglass helmet with viewports and inhalation and exhalation valves, joined by an airtight seal to a metal chestpiece, itself joined to a flexible watertight covering of rubber and canvas; weights, especially weighted boots, provide stability and prevent the diver from shooting toward the surface. Air or, more often, an oxygen/helium mixture is conveyed to the diver via a thick rubber tube. Nowadays, self- contained underwater breathing apparatus (scuba diving), where the diver has no suit but carries gas cylinders and an aqualung, permits great mobility. In all diving great care must be taken for proper decompression to avoid the bends, a dangerous condition in which gas bubbles enter the blood and tissue during overly rapid ascent to the surface.

Divining rod, forked stick used by diviners, or dowsers, to find buried objects or water. Diviners believe that if they hold the forked end of the rod and pass over an area where water is located, the pointed end will be attracted to the water and pull downward. Diviners often officially refer to their skill as rhabdomancy. Although dowsers have claimed remarkable success on many occasions, tests and experiments have not been able to demonstrate more than a chance relationship to results.

Division, major combat unit of the U.S. armed forces. Army divisions consist of from 6 to 15 battalions and function as self-contained units that include all the services and equipment needed to conduct military campaigns. Marine divisions are made up of 3 regiments, while Air Force divisions are composed of 2 or more *wings.*
See also: Army, U.S.

Divorce, legal dissolution of a valid marriage, as distinguished from separation, in which the partners remain married but live apart, and annulment, in which the marriage is deemed to be invalid. In most cases, divorce leaves the partners free to remarry, sometimes after a set period. Divorce has existed in most cultures, but its availability and the grounds for it have varied widely. Christianity regards marriage as a sacrament that may not lightly be set aside, and this view has affected the Western concept of divorce. The Roman Catholic Church still does not allow divorce, but most other churches do. In the United States each state makes its own divorce laws. Adultery is the most widely accepted ground for divorce; others include cruelty, alcoholism, insanity, desertion, and conviction of a serious crime. A modern trend is to make irreparable breakdown of the marriage another ground, without involving the misconduct of either party; the first states to introduce this were California and Iowa. Divorce is a major social problem in the United States; it has been estimated that 1 in every 2 marriages ends in divorce.
See also: Marriage.

Deep-sea divers sometimes use special submarine vessels to explore the continental shelves.

Dix, Dorothea Lynde (1802-87), U.S. social reformer and crusader for the humane and scientific treatment of mental illness. Shocked to see mentally sick people in jail, in 1841 she launched a successful campaign to establish mental hospitals in the United States, Canada, and Europe.

Dix, Otto (1891-1969), German painter and leader of the "new objectivity" school of social realism. His most famous work is the cycle of 50 etchings entitled *The War* (1924) that depicts the horrors of World War II. He was jailed (1939-45) by the Nazi government. In later years his work reflected religious mysticism.

Dixie, popular term for the southern states of the United States, particularly those that formed the Confederacy. There are a number of explanations of the origin of the term. One is that "Dixie" derives from the pre-Civil War issue of 10-dollar notes by the Citizens Bank of New Orleans. The notes carried the French word *dix* ("ten") on the reverse side for the benefit of the area's many French-speaking people, so Louisiana and later the whole South became known as the land of "Dixies." Other stories connect the name with a slaveowner named Dixie or with the Mason-Dixon line. "Dixie" is also the name of a popular song written in 1859, often regarded as the national anthem of the Confederacy.
See also: Confederate States of America.

Dixiecrat Party, southern faction of the U.S. Democratic Party that opposed the 1948 party platform on civil rights. They ran their own candidates, Governor Strom Thurmond of South Carolina for president and Governor Fielding Wright of Mississippi for vice-president, against the incumbent president, Harry S. Truman, and received 1,169,000 national and 39 electoral votes.
See also: Democratic Party.

Dizziness, sensations of whirling, giddiness, and vertigo caused by abnormal stimulation of receptors of balance or by rapid movements of the visual field, sometimes accompanied by nausea and nystagmus (rapid, jerky eye movements). It can also be caused by psychological disorders.

Djakarta *see:* Jakarta.

The presidential palace, Djibouti

Djibouti (pop. 220,000), capital of the Republic of Djibouti. A port city located on the Gulf of Aden, it is the country's only economic center. Founded by the French in 1888 and developed as a colonial capital, the city has since grown rapidly and is now plagued by poverty and inadequate housing.
See also: Djibouti.

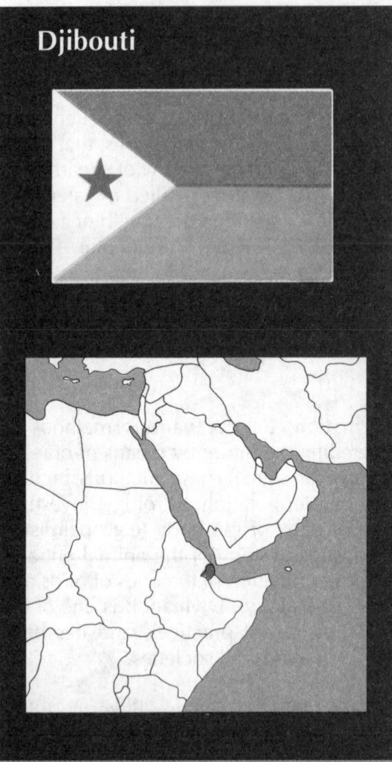

Capital:	Djibouti
Area:	8,950 sq mi (23,200 sq km)
Population:	512,000
Government:	republic
Independent:	1977
GNP:	U.S. $301,540,000
Per capita:	U.S. $740

Djibouti (official name, Republic of Djibouti), formerly French Somaliland, republic in northeastern Africa, situated where the coast of Africa approaches the Arabian peninsula, bounded by Ethiopia and Somalia. Its area is about 8,950 sq mi (23,200 km). The languages are Arabic and French. The official religion is Muslim.
Land and economy. Most of the country is stony desert. The climate is hot. Rainfall is usually scant, but in some years torrential rainfall causes flooding. Agricultural activity is limited. There are no known mineral resources, and industry is negligible. Hides and skins and live animals are the main exports.
People. The population is almost evenly divided into 2 ethnic groups: the Afars (from Ethiopia) and the Issas (from Somalia). The Issas are more urbanized than the Afars. The nation's government is carefully balanced between the two groups, but historical rivalries persist. The capital, also called Djibouti, is the economic and political hub of the country, with a port and a railway terminus.
History. In 1896 France signed treaties with Britain, Italy, and Ethiopia to define the boundaries of French Somaliland. In 1967 the colony voted to remain a French possession and became the French Territory of the Afars and Issas. It became independent in 1977. Djibouti has remained neutral during strife between its neighbors, Somalia and Ethiopia, despite close ethnic ties. Thousand of refugees have streamed into Djibouti, creating serious economic problems. Djibouti was among the African countries severely affected by drought in 1984-85.

Djilas, Milovan (1911-), Yugoslav communist leader and writer. He was a leading World War II partisan alongside Marshal Tito, and became a vice-president after the war. But because of his outspoken criticisms of the regime and his general indictment of communism as a form of government, he was imprisoned 1956-66. Among his works are *The New Class* (1957), *Conversations with Stalin* (1962), and *Tito* (1980).
See also: Yugoslavia.

Dmitri (d. 1606), tsar of Russia. The real Dmitri, son of Ivan the Terrible, is thought to have been murdered in childhood. The false Dmitri enlisted the aid of the Polish and Lithuanian nobility and invaded Russia, defeating Boris Godunov. On Boris's death in 1605, he was crowned tsar. Although he had the support of the peasantry, the boyars (nobles) opposed his Western ideas and had him murdered.
See also: Tsar.

DMSO, drug (dimethyl sulfoxide) proposed as an effective analgesic and anti-inflammatory agent in treating arthritis and bursitis. The U.S. Food and Drug Administration has banned external use of the drug because of eye damage it has caused in experimental animals. DMSO has been approved for internal use only, in the treatment of interstitial cystitis, a bladder condition.

DNA (deoxyribonucleic acid), informational molecules contained in the nucleus of every living cell that, along with ribonucleic acid (RNA), transmit all genetic information. The instructions of the nucleic acids are finally expressed by proteins, which form many of the structural and mechanical components of living systems and act as catalysts in the chemical activity of cells. The DNA molecule is an extremely long chemical thread made up of 2 strands that are held as a pair forming a spiral, or double helix. Each strand consists of a long chain of the sugar deoxyribose and phosphate residues. Two purines—adenine (A) and guanine (G)—and 2 pyrimidines—thymine (T) and cytosine (C)—are also commonly found in DNA. In the DNA thread the purine and pyrimidine bases lie opposite one another in the structure, and the pattern is always one in which

a T on one strand is faced by an A, and a G by a C. There is always one molecule of A to every molecule of T and one G for every C. The base pairs are stacked on top of one another like a pile of pennies. One millimeter of DNA contains about 5 million base pairs. The DNA of a human cell is about 16 in (41 cm) long.
See also: Genetics.

Dnepropetrovsk (pop. 1,140,000), city in the Ukrainian Republic of the USSR, on the Dnepr River. It is a major center of rail and water-transport and a leading producer of iron, steel, and chemicals. Founded in 1787 as Ekaterinoslav, the city took its present name in 1926.
See also: Union of Soviet Socialist Republics.

Dnepr River, or Dnieper River, second-longest river in the European USSR, about 1,400 mi (2,253 km) long, navigable for nearly its whole length. Rising in the Valdai Hills, it flows in a southwestern direction to empty in the Black Sea east of Odessa. Leading tributaries are the Desna, Pripyat, Berezina, and Sozh. It is a major water transport route and also has many hydroelectric plants.

Dniester River, river in the Soviet Union, about 875 mi (1,408 km) long. Rising in the Carpathian Mountains, in the western Ukraine, it flows southeast through the Ukraine and Moldavia, and empties into the Black Sea southwest of Odessa.

Doberman pinscher, breed of dog originating in Germany. Developed by Louis Dobermann in the late 1800s, it is prevalent in guard and police work because of its alertness, intelligence, loyalty, and excellent sense of smell. Dobermans average 24-28 in (61-71 cm) shoulder height and are generally black with rust-colored markings.

Dobson fly *see:* Hellgrammite.

Dobzhansky, Theodosius (1900-75), U.S. biologist, famed for his study of the fruit fly, *Drosophila.* His work demonstrated that a wide genetic range can exist even in a well-defined species and that the greater the "gentetic load" of unusual genes in a species, the better equipped it is to survive in changed circumstances.
See also: Biology; Fruit fly.

Dock, large-leafed plant (genus *Rumex*), of the buckwheat family with clusters of small green flowers. There are many species throughout the world, some of which are weeds, although the spinach dock is eaten. Sorrel is a dock but appears distinct from the others at first sight.

Doctor *see:* Degree, Academic; Medicine.

Doctorow, E(dgar) L(aurence) (1931-), U.S. novelist. His books include *The Book of Daniel* (1971), a historical novel about Julius and Ethel Rosenberg and their children; *Ragtime* (1975), which interweaves fictional portraits of Sigmund Freud, C.J. Jung, Harry Houdini, and Henry Ford, among others; *Loon Lake* (1980), set during the Great Depression; and *Billy Bathgate* (1989).

Dodder, parasitic plant (genus *Cuscuta*), that bears no leaves and gains all its nourishment from the host plant. There are nearly 200 species around the world. As each dodder plant develops, it reaches out for a host plant into which it sends suckers that penetrate the living tissues. Eventually the host plant becomes smothered in straggling stems of the dodder.

Dodecanese, group of about 20 Greek islands in the southeastern Aegean Sea off Turkey. Except for Rhodes and Kos, the 12 main islands are largely rocky and infertile. In 1912 Italy seized the group from the Turks, but after World War II they were ceded to Greece.
See also: Greece.

Dodge, family name of two early developers of the automobile. Both **John Francis Dodge** (1864-1920) and **Horace Elgin Dodge** (1868-1920) were born in Michigan and began working with cars in Detroit in 1901. At first they built car parts in their machine shop for the Ford and Olds motor companies, but later they began developing their own automobile. In 1914 they produced a car with an all-steel body. They founded the Dodge Company, which merged with the Chrysler Corporation in 1928.
See also: Automobile.

Dodge, Mary Elizabeth Mapes (1831-1905), U.S. children's author who founded and edited the magazine *St. Nicholas* (1873). She is best known for *Hans Brinker, or The Silver Skates* (1885), a classic of children's literature.

Dodge City (pop. 21,129), city in southwest Kansas, on the Arkansas River, seat of Ford County. In the late 1800s it was a cattle center on the Santa Fe Trail, at the head of the Santa Fe Railroad, and it became notorious for its wild frontier life and its cemetery, Boot Hill. Today Dodge City is an important commercial center.
See also: Kansas.

Dodgson, Charles Lutwidge *see:* Carroll, Lewis.

Dodo (*Raphus cucullatus*), extinct turkey-sized flightless bird with strong legs and a big bill, formerly found on the island of Mauritius. The last dodo died around 1681, but a few stuffed birds and skeletons can be seen in museums.

Dodoma (pop. 45,700), city in central Tanzania. It is a marketing and transportation center whose industries include brick manufacturing and clay processing. In 1973 it was selected to replace Dar es Salaam as the capital city, but that move has not yet been effected.
See also: Tanzania.

Doenitz, Karl (1891-1980), German admiral, head of the World War II U-boat service and later commander in chief of the German navy (1943-5). On Hitler's death in 1945 he became head of state and subsequently surrendered to the Allies. He was tried for war crimes at Nuremberg and served 10 years in prison.
See also: World War II.

Doesburg, Theo van (1883-1931), Dutch painter and author. A leader of the de Stijl group, he turned to abstract art in 1916, influenced at first by Piet Mondrian. He taught at the Bauhaus (1921-3).

Dog, carnivorous mammal of the family Canidae. The wild dog, usually with long legs, long muzzle, and bushy tail, lives by chasing its prey. Many live in packs. Wild dogs include the raccoon dog of Asia and several South American forms, such as the bush dog and the maned wolf. Domestic dogs are members of the species *Canis familiaris.* There are more than 200 known breeds of highly variable appearance, classified as sporting dogs, nonsporting dogs, working dogs, toy dogs, hounds, and terriers. The dog may have been the first domesticated animal.

The dog is an invaluable servant to humans—it can hunt, lead the blind, and transport.

Dogbane, plant (genus *Apocynum*), with clusters of small pinkish-white flowers and poisonous leaves and stems. Plants related to dogbane are used in the manufacture of poison for arrows.

Dogfish, any of various small sharks of the family Squalidac. Dogfish rarely reach 5 ft (1.5 m). They have the ugly heads and rough skins of the typical sharks and feed on the bottom of the sea, catching worms, shrimps, fish, and mollusks. The eggs are laid in horny cases. Dogfish are sold as grayfish for human consumption, and their flesh is used as a fertilizer. At one time an oil was extracted from them. They are now best known as subjects for dissection classes.

Dog racing, spectator sport in which people gamble on dogs chasing a mechanical hare (or other lure) around a track which is generally .25 mi (.4 km) in diameter. Greyhounds, the most common racing dog, can reach speeds of over 40 mph (64 kph). Each year over $3 billion is bet on dog-racing.

Dog Star *see:* Sirius.

Dogtooth violet (*Erythronium dens-canis*), also known as adder's tongue or trout lily, wildflower of eastern North America belonging to the lily family. Unrelated to true violets, its flowers are bell-shaped and bear no resemblance to a dog's tooth.

Dogwood, or cornel, name for any tree or shrub of the genus *Cornus*. The bunchberry (*C. canadensis*) is a herbaceous wildflower, and the flowering dogwood (*C. florida*) is a small tree. Some dogwoods are grown as ornamental plants.

Doha (pop. 217,000), or Ad Dawhah, capital of the Middle Eastern state of Qatar. Once a small fishing village, it developed into a major port of the Persian Gulf and important commercial center when Qatar's oil production began in the 1950s. Doha contains the majority of the country's people.
See also: Qatar.

The Dolomites

Dohnanyi, Ernst von (1877-1960), Hungarian composer and pianist, conductor of the Budapest Philharmonic Orchestra (1919-44). His music, influenced by Brahms, includes the lighthearted *Variations on a Nursery Song* (1913) and *Ruralia Hungarica* (1924), both for piano and orchestra.

Doldrums, narrow belt of light, variable winds located between the trade winds near the equator. Calm weather predominates in this low-pressure area; sailing ships can be stranded here for days without wind.
See also: Calms, Regions of.

Dole, Elizabeth Hanford (1936-), U.S. politician; wife of politician Robert Dole. She served as secretary of labor in President George Bush's administration until her resignation in 1990. She held administrative positions under presidents Lyndon B. Johnson, Richard M. Nixon, Gerald R. Ford, Jimmy Carter, and Ronald Reagan. In 1990 she became executive director of the American Red Cross.

Dole, Robert J. (1923-), U.S. politician; husband of politician Elizabeth Dole. He was the unsuccessful Republican vice-presidential candidate in 1976 as running mate of Gerald Ford. Twice decorated in World War II, he was Republican national chairman (1971-73) and has been senator from Kansas since 1969.

Dole, Sanford Ballard (1844-1926), U.S. judge and leader of the Republic of Hawaii. In 1893, he led the movement that overthrew Queen Liliuokalani and resulted in the establishment of the Hawaiian republic, of which Dole became president (1894-1900). After the United States annexed Hawaii (1898), he served as territorial governor (1900-3).
See also: Hawaii.

Dolin, Sir Anton (1904-83), English choreographer and dancer. He worked closely with dancer Alicia Markova, as her partner, choreographer, and cofounder of several companies. Among the ballet companies he founded were the Royal Ballet and the American Ballet Theater. Among the works he choreographed was *Le Pas de Quatre*. Dolin also wrote several books on the dance.
See also: ballet.

Doll, miniature representation of the human form, used as a toy or, in some societies, a sacred object. The practice of making dolls is an ancient one. Some of the earliest examples, made from a wide range of substances including wood, bone, ivory, and clay, have been found in Pakistan at Mohenjo-Daro (3000 B.C.), and on Babylonian, Egyptian, and Aztec sites. In ancient societies dolls were often entombed with the dead. In America, they are still used in Hopi and Zuni rites. The modern doll has its origin in medieval doll nativity scenes and in the 14th-century fashion dolls of France and England. During the 16th century, Germany became a major center of doll making, noted particularly for its figures carved from wood. Papier-mâché and wax were used in the 19th century as materials for fashioning dolls' heads. Present-day dolls are made from a variety of synthetic materials, their designs incorporating such sales gimmicks as "voices," working limbs, and moving eyelids.

Dollar, monetary unit originating in the 16th century as the German thaler, named after the Joachimsthal silver mines in Bohemia. It was used widely in the West Indies and the American mainland in the colonial period because of its standard weight and purity. Divided into 100 cents, it now is the basis of currency of many countries worldwide. Since World War II, the U.S. dollar has become the basic currency unit of the international monetary and economic system. During the 1980s and 1990s the economic success of Germany and Japan has lifted the value of their currency — the German Mark and Japanese yen — to a level that rivals the dollar in international importance.
See also: Money.

Dollar Decade *see:* Roaring Twenties.

Dollar diplomacy, U.S. foreign policy that attempts to protect the nation's political and financial interests through diplomacy. First in use during the presidency of William Howard Taft (1909-13) in such areas as the Caribbean, it has since been practiced by many U.S. administrations.
See also: Taft, William Howard.

Dollarfish *see:* Butterfish.

Dollinger, Johann Joseph Ignaz von (1799-1890), German Roman Catholic historian and theologian, excommunicated (1871) for rejecting the doctrine of papal infallibility. A professor of ecclesiastical history and law at Munich University (1826-71), his books include *The Pope and the Council* (1869), which criticizes papal authoritarianism. He was an early leader of the Old Catholics.
See also: Roman Catholic Church.

Dolomite, calcium magnesium carbonate mineral; chemical formula $CaMg(CO_3)_2$. There are large deposits of dolomite in the Alps, England, and the United States. It is similar to limestone and is used chiefly as a building material.

Dolomites, mountain range in the eastern Alps, northeastern Italy. The mountains are composed mainly of vividly colored dolomitic limestone. The highest peak is Marmolada (10,965 ft/3,342 m). The Dolomites are a popular tourist and climbing resort. The region's main center is Cortina d'Ampezzo.
See also: Italy.

Dolphin, Pacific spout fish (genus *Coryphaena*), of the family Coryphaenidae. It has a blunt head and forked tail and can swim at great speed. It is a popular food fish in Hawaii, where it is called dorado, or mahi mahi.

Dolphin, any of a family (Delphinidae) of small-toothed whales living in schools and feeding mainly on fish. The largest, the killer whale (*Orcinus orcat*), also feeds on seals. The best-known is the bottle-nosed dolphin (genus *Tursiops*), a highly intelligent mammal with an amazingly developed system of echolocation for finding food and avoiding obstacles. A second family of dolphins (Platanistidae) lives in fresh water, and includes the Chinese lake dolphin and the blind susu, or Ganges dolphin. The dolphin has been threatened by reckless tuna fishers whose nets entangle the fish.

Domagk, Gerhard (1895-1964), German pharmacologist who discovered the antibacterial action of the dye prontosil red, which led to the discovery of other sulfa drugs. In recognition of this, Domagk was offered the 1939 Nobel Prize for physiology or medicine, but the Nazi government did not allow him to accept it at the time. He received the Nobel Prize medal in 1947.
See also: Pharmacology; Sulfa drug.

Dome, in architecture, oval or hemispherical vault, used to roof a large space without interior supports. The first domes were built around 1000 B.C. by the Persians and Assyrians, but these were small, and the dome did not become architecturally significant until the time of the Romans. The Pantheon in Rome (2nd century A.D.), in which the dome rests on a drum-shaped building, is an outstanding example of the large-scale dome. The Byzantine architects of Hagia Sophia (A.D. 532-537) in Constantinople developed the *pendentive*, a device enabling the construction of a great dome over a square central area. Brunelleschi's dome on the cathedral in Florence has an inner and an outer shell; Sir Christopher Wren's dome for St. Paul's, London, has 3 shells. Modern techniques and lightweight materials permit the spanning of vast areas, as in the case of the Houston Astrodome.
See also: Architecture.

Domenichino (Domenico Zampieri; 1581-1641), Italian Baroque painter noted for the landscape settings of his pictures. He painted large frescoes, notably *The Life of St. Cecilia* (1613-14), in palaces and churches in Rome.
See also: Baroque.

Dome of the Rock *see:* Jerusalem.

Domesday Book, inventory of most of the land and property in England compiled by order of William the Conqueror (completed in 1086), giving the Norman overlords of the newly conquered country a basis for local control and taxation. Today it is an important source for historians interested in the period before and after the Norman Conquest. The book records not only the value of the land, but also the number of livestock and serfs in each locality.
See also: Norman Conquest; William (kings of England).

Domingo, Placido (1941-), Spanish operatic tenor. In 1961 he made his Mexican debut as Alfredo in *La Traviata* and his U.S. debut with the Dallas Civic Opera. He sang in Israel (1963-65) and with the N.Y. City Opera (1965-67) before joining the Metropolitan Opera (1968).
See also: Opera.

Dominic, Saint (1170?-1221), Spanish-born founder of the Dominican order. Sent by Pope Innocent III in 1205 to Languedoc (southern France) to convert the Albigensian heretics, Dominic and his band of priests were successful, and in 1216 he was given papal support for the new order he had established. His feast day is Aug. 4.
See also: Dominican Order.

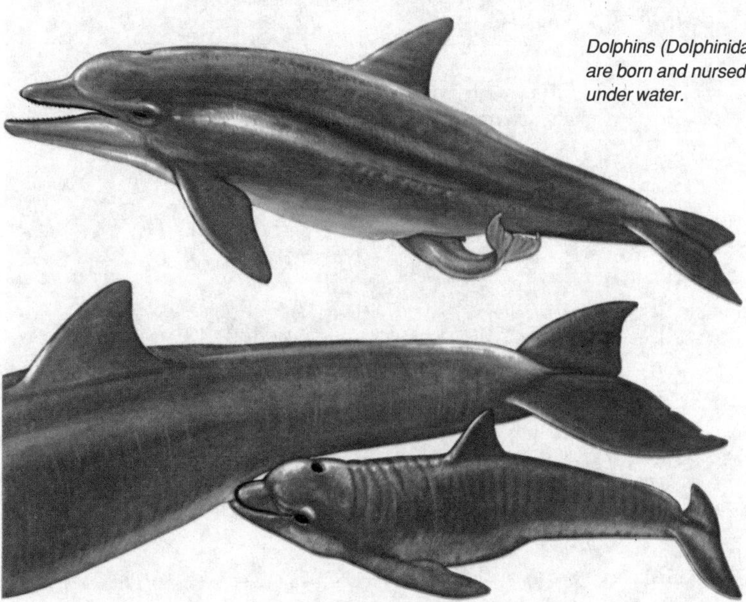

Dolphins (Dolphinidae) are born and nursed under water.

Dominica

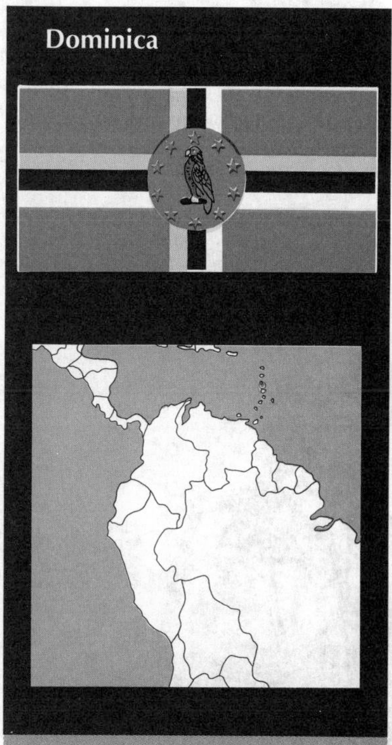

Capital:	Roseau
Area:	290 sq mi (751 sq km)
Population:	82,800
Government:	republic
Independent:	1978
GNP:	U.S.$130,000,000
Per capita:	U.S.$1,650

Dominica (official name, Commonwealth of Dominica), independent state, the largest island in the Windward Islands of the Lesser Antilles group, between Guadeloupe and Martinique. Its area is 290 sq mi (751 sq km). The population is largely descended from slaves brought to the island from Africa in the 18th century. The rich volcanic soil produces bananas, coconuts, citrus fruits, and cinnamon. Dominica also exports pumice. Discovered by Columbus in 1493, Dominica was colonized by France in the early 17th century, acquired by Britain in 1805, and became internally self-governing in 1967. In 1978 the island achieved full independence within the British Commonwealth. The capital city is Roseau.

Dominican Order, Roman Catholic religious order founded by Saint Dominic and confirmed by Pope Honorius III in 1216. Officially known as the Order of Preachers (O.P.) and sometimes unofficially as the Black Friars, for the black cloak they wear when preaching, the Dominicans grew from a band of priests sent to combat the Albigensian heresy. Priests make up the first order of Dominicans, cloistered nuns the second order, and regular nuns and laymen and women the third order. Throughout their history the Dominicans have been noted for their scholarship and intellectual activity. Thomas Aquinas, Albert the Great, Vincent Ferrer, Catherine of Siena, and Rose of Lima were Domini-

cans, as were Savonarola and Fra Angelico. As guardians of scholastic theology, Dominicans took part in the Inquisition; in recent centuries they have been in the vanguard of theological and biblical studies.
See also: Dominic, Saint.

Dominican Republic, country in the Caribbean Sea, occupying the eastern two-thirds of the island of Hispaniola. (The western third is Haiti.)

The Dominican Republic is a lush and beautiful country with many natural resources such as cocoa, coffee, and bananas. Tourism is a major industry.

Land and climate. Parallel mountain chains cross the country from northwest to southeast. Between them are the Cibao and Vega Real lowlands, the country's main agricultural areas. The climate is subtropical, with lowland temperatures averaging 70°F (21°C). Annual rainfall averages over 50 in (127 cm), with hurricanes common between Aug. and Nov. Apart from the capital, Santo Domingo, the greatest concentration of people is in and around the rich agricultural valleys. Other major cities include Santiagi and Puerto Plata.
People. The official language of the country is Spanish, and most of the population professes the state-supported religion, Roman Catholicism.
Economy. The economy of the Dominican Republic is agricultural, with sugar the major export. Tourism is also a major source of foreign currency. In addition, the country produces coffee, cocoa, tobacco, and bananas. Industry is concentrated around the capital and, apart from agricultural processing, includes cement, plastic, and textile manufacturing. There is some mining of bauxite and nickel, and tourism is also important.
History. After centuries of turmoil, including conflict between the local population and Spain and Haiti, the independent Dominican Republic emerged in 1844. The new country was long troubled by political strife and economic instability. From 1916 to 1924, it was occupied by U.S. Marines. In 1930, an army revolt brought the dictator General Rafael Trujillo Molina to power. Free elections follwed Trujillo's assassination in 1961, but the newly elected left-wing government of Juan Bosch was overthrown by a military coup in 1963. An attempt to reinstate Bosch led to armed intervention by the U.S. in 1965. Joaquín Balaguer served as president from 1966 to 1978; he and his successors focused on improving the economy.

Dominoes, game for 2 to 4 people, played with flat rectangular blocks usually made from wood, ivory, or bone. The game, introduced to Europe, probably from China, in the middle of the 18th century, is normally played with a set of 28 pieces. The face of each piece is divided into 2 sections, each of which either is blank or has up to 6 dots. The set of dominoes contains every possible combination of numbers from 0-0 (double blank) to 6-6 (double six). During play, each player in turn must attempt to match a number on one of the dominoes or "bones" in his or her hand with one of the two exposed ends on the table. Failing to do so, the player must draw a further piece from the central pool, or boneyard. Play stops when a player has disposed of all his or her dom-

Dominican Republic

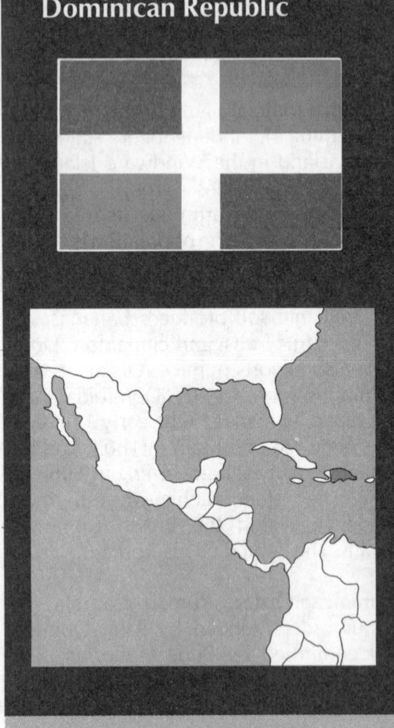

General information	
Capital:	Santo Domingo
Area:	18,704 sq mi (48,443 sq km)
Population:	7,012,000
Official language:	Spanish
Monetary unit:	1 Dominican peso = 100 centavos
Main cities:	Santo Domingo, La Romana, Santiago de los Caballeros
Government	
Form:	republic
Independent:	1844
Head of state:	President (elected every 4 years)
Head of government:	President
Legislature:	two legislative houses (Senate and Chamber of Deputies)
Executive:	President and Cabinet
Judiciary:	highest court is the Supreme Court of Justice
Political division:	30 provinces
National economy	
Gross national product:	U.S. $4,690,000,000
Per capita income:	U.S. $680
Agriculture:	sugar cane, plantains, bananas, rice, mangoes, tomatoes, avocados, cacao, coffee, tabacco
Livestock:	pigs, cattle, goats
Fisheries:	21,000 metric tons
Mining:	silver, gold, ferro-nickel
Industries:	food products, alcoholic beverages, refined petroleum, cigarettes, cement
Main exports:	sugar, alloy of gold and silver, ferro-nickel, coffee, cocoa beans
Transportation:	1,028 mi (1,654 km) of railroads; 7,084 mi (11,400 km) of roads; 3 international airports
Trading partners:	United States, Venezuela, Mexico, The Netherlands, Puerto Rico
People	
Urban:	56%
Ethnic composition:	mulatto 73%, European 16%, African 11%
Birth rate:	31.3 per 1,000 population
Death rate:	6.8 per 1,000 population
Infant mortality:	70 per 1,000 live births
Life expectancy:	male 64 years, female 68 years

inoes. A number of variations on the game have been developed, and the number of pieces may also vary.

Domitian (A.D. 51-96), Roman emperor (81-96), son of Vespasian and brother of Titus, whom he succeeded. He governed efficiently but harshly, his last years amounting to a reign of terror. He was assassinated at the instigation of his wife.
See also: Rome, Ancient.

Domus Aurea *see:* Rome.

Donatello (Donatello di Niccolo di Betto Bandi; c.1386-1466), Florentine sculptor, a major figure of the Italian Renaissance. He trained as a metalworker with Lorenzo Ghiberti and as a marble sculptor. His many commissions for the cathedral of Florence include the famous *putti* for the singing gallery. Other major works are *St. George Slaying the Dragon* (1415-17), the bronze *David* (1432) in the Bargello, Florence, and the equestrian statue known as the Gattamelata Monument (1447-53) in Padua.
See also: Renaissance.

Donetsk (pop. 1,064,000), large city in the Ukraine. Located in the Donets River basin, it is one of the most important industrial cities in the USSR. The rich coal deposits of the region are used in the production of iron, steel, machinery, and food products. Founded in the 1870s, it became Stalino in 1935, but its name was changed back to Donetsk in 1961.
See also: Ukraine.

Donizetti, Gaetano (1797-1848), Italian opera composer. Influenced by Gioacchino Rossini, he developed the traditions of serious and comic opera. His operas include *The Elixir of Love* (1832), *Lucia di Lammermoor* (1835), and *Don Pasquale* (1843). He was an important influence on Giuseppe Verdi.
See also: Opera.

Donjon *see:* Castle.

Don Juan, legendary libertine of Spain, often the subject of dramatic and literary works in which, after a dissolute life, he is led off to hell. The earliest- known dramatization is Tirso de Molina's *The Rake of Seville* (1630). Other versions are by Molière, W.A. Mozart (*Don Giovanni*), Byron, and G.B. Shaw (*Man and Superman*).

Donkey, herbivorous (plant-eating), hoofed mammal (*Equus asinus*), domesticated form of the wild ass. The donkey is related to the horse, but it is smaller and has long ears, a large head and short mane, a tuft of hair at the end of the tail, and no callosities (hardened skin) on the hindlegs. A dark band usually runs along the back and another over the shoulder. Several species of wild asses are found in Africa (*E. asinus*) and Asia (*E. hemonius*), particularly in northeastern India, where large herds wander about the desert regions. The donkey is descended from the African wild ass of Ethiopia. It is much used as a pack animal, and shows tremendous powers of endurance. It is surefooted and intelligent, well adapted to heavy loads over rough terrain. Crossbreeding with a horse produces the mule or the hinny, which are sterile.

Donleavy, J(ames) P(atrick) (1926-), U.S. novelist and playwright. He is known for his black humor vision of life in such works as *The Ginger Man* (1955), *A Singular Man* (1963), and *Shultz* (1979).

Donne, John (1572-1631), English metaphysical poet and clergyman. His love poems and religious verse and prose are characterized by sophisticated argument, complex metaphors, and a passionate and direct tone. His imagery relies upon both scholastic philosophy and 17th-century scientific thought. After a long period of exclusion from court life, he took religious orders in 1615 and became dean of St. Paul's, London, where he gave many sermons. His most famous writings are the love-lyrics *Songs and Sonnets*, and the religious works *Holy Sonnets*, *Sermons*, and *Devotions*.
See also: Metaphysical poets.

Donnelly, Ignatius (1831-1901), U.S. politician and writer. A Republican congressman for Minnesota 1863-9, he later led the Greenback Party and the Populist Party. He wrote the Populist platform and was that party's nominee for vice president in 1900. He wrote several speculative works, including the utopian novel *Caesar's Column* (1891).
See also: Greenback Party; Populism.

Donner Pass, pass in the Sierra Nevada mountains of California, where a group of pioneers were trapped by snow during the winter of 1846-47. They were forced to camp at Truckee Lake (now Lonner Lake) 7,135 ft (2,175 m) above sea level. Of the 82 men, women, and children, only 47 survived, avoiding starvation by eating the flesh of those who had died. The pass is now the site of the Donner State Historic Monument.

Don Quixote, classic novel by Spanish author Miguel de Cervantes. Published in two parts (1605 and 1615), its titular character is a bored landowner whose fantasies of knighthood lead him to perform deeds he sees as courageous but are merely comic. Accompanied by his attendant, Sancho Panza, the two characters represent the practical and the ideal in life.
See also: Cervantes Saavedra, Miguel de.

Don River, river in the Soviet Union, about 1,220 mi (1,930 km) long. Rising in the central Russian upland, about 100 mi (160 km) south of Moscow, it flows generally southward, passes through the 100-mi-(160-km-)long Tsimlyansk Reservoir and empties into the Sea of Azov. A canal, built in 1952, connects the Don with the Volga River. Most of the Don is navigable by barges, except in winter, and it can accommodate oceangoing vessels as far upstream as Rostov, at the head of the river's delta outlet. Leading tributaries are the Donets, Khoper, and Voronezh rivers.

Doodlebug *see:* Ant lion.

Dooley, Thomas Anthony (1927-61), U.S. physician, author, and a founder (1957) of Medico, an international medical aid organization for underdeveloped countries. In *Deliver Us from Evil* (1956), he tells how he supervised care for 600,000 Vietnamese refugees in Haiphong in 1954-5.

Doolittle, Hilda (1886-1961), U.S. poet who lived in Europe after 1911. She wrote under the pseudonym H.D. H.D. was one of the first imagists in the United States, and she continued to develop the imagist style in her poetry. Works include *Sea Garden* (1916), *The Walls Do Not Fall* (1944), and a novel *Bid Me to Live* (1960).

Doolittle, James Harold (1896-), U.S. pilot and World War II air hero. Famous as a racing pilot in the 1920s and early 1930s, he led the first air raid on Tokyo on April 18, 1942, thereby slowing the Japanese offensive. After the war he was an executive in the aerospace industry.
See also: World War II.

Doomsday Book *see:* Domesday Book.

Doppler effect, apparent change in frequency of waves of light or sound due to the motion of an observer relative to the source. If either source or observer is approaching the other, the waves are bunched together, like the folds of a squeezed accordion. The observer encounters more waves in a given period of time than would be the case if both observer and source were stationary, so the observed frequency of the waves increases. Waves of high frequency have a shorter wavelength than waves of low frequency. In the case of light, a shortening of the wavelength makes the object seem bluer than normal, because blue light has the shortest wavelength. In the case of sound, the pitch, as of the whistle of an approaching train, will seem higher. When the source and the observer are moving apart, the waves are stretched out, like the folds of an extended accordion. Because the speed of the whole wave train is constant—the speed of light or the speed of sound—the waves pass less frequently. The distance between waves (the wavelength) seems to increase. If the waves are of light, the object appears redder than normal. If the waves are of sound, the note changes to a lower pitch. Named after its discoverer, the Austrian physicist Christian Johann Doppler (1803-53), the effect has proved of particular use to astronomers in analyzing the light of distant objects in space. The light of these objects is reddened by the Doppler effect, from which it follows that the universe is expanding.

Dorado *see:* Dolphin.

The statue of Saint George by Donatello

Doré, Gustave (1832-83), French engraver, illustrator, and painter. He created dreamlike, grandiose scenes in a fantastic, bizarre style and is known especially for line engravings of unusual power in editions of Balzac's *Contes Drolatiques* (1855), Dante's *Inferno* (1861), Cervantes's *Don Quixote* (1863), and the Bible (1866).

Dorians, people of ancient Greece. Originating from the lower Balkans, they probably defeated the Achaeans and conquered the Peloponnese between 1100 and 950 B.C., subsequently extending their influence to the Aegean Islands, Crete, Sicily, and parts of Asia Minor, Africa, and Italy.
See also: Achaeans; Peleponnesus.

Dorion, Marie (1790?-1850), Native American of the Iowa tribe, known for her bravery in the Astor Overland Expedition. She was the only woman in the 11-month expedition, which began in St. Louis (1811) and ended in Oregon (1812). During the 3,500-mi (5,630-km) trip, which she traveled mostly on foot with her husband and 2 sons, she gave birth but caught up to the group the following day. After her husband and the other men were killed in Oregon (1814), she survived with her children by building shelter in the snow.

Dormancy *see:* Germination.

Dormouse, squirrel-like, nocturnal rodent of the family Gliridae that feeds on seeds, shoots, and small animals. There are several species scattered over Europe, Asia, and Africa. All hibernate. The common dormouse (*Muscardinus avellanarius*) of Europe and western Asia grows as large as 4 in (10 cm) long. The Romans fattened dormice for eating.

Fyodor Dostoevsky

Dorr Rebellion, armed rebellion led by lawyer Thomas W. Dorr against the government of Rhode Island in 1842. The uprising resulted from opposition to a colonial charter that denied landless people the right to vote. While the rebellion failed, it did help to bring about a new, more democratic constitution in 1845.

Dos Passos, John (Roderigo) (1896-1970), U.S. novelist and writer of social history. His trilogy, *U.S.A.* (1937), depicts 20th-century life up to 1929, making use of innovative, collage-like reportage techniques. Other works include *Manhattan Transfer* (1925), *District of Columbia* (a trilogy; 1952), and *Midcentury* (1961).

Dostoevsky, Fyodor Mikhaylovich (1821-81), Russian novelist. He spent several years in the army but resigned his commission in 1844 to devote himself to writing. His first novel, *Poor Folk* (1846), was well received. Arrested in 1849 as a member of a socialist circle, Dostoyevsky was condemned to be shot; however, the sentence was commuted in the execution yard to 4 years' hard labor in Siberia. *The House of the Dead* (1862) tells of his experiences there. During the 1860s he founded two journals and traveled in Europe after his consumptive wife and his brother had died, and after he had incurred large gambling debts, returning to Russia in 1871. In 1876 he edited his own monthly *The Writer's Diary*. Suffering from epilepsy for most of his life, he died after an epileptic attack. Dostoyevsky's major novels, *Crime and Punishment* (1866), *The Idiot* (1868), *The Devils* (1871-72), and *The Brothers Karamazov* (1879-80), reveal his deep understanding of psychology and the problems of sin and suffering.

Dou, Gerard (1613-75), Dutch painter. A pupil of Rembrandt (1628-31), Dou developed the tradition of small, minutely finished pictures with enamel-like surfaces, painting portraits, still lifes, landscapes, and scenes from everyday life.

Douala (pop. 1,000,000), largest city and major port of Cameroon, west central Africa, on the Wuori River, near the Gulf of Guinea. A commercial and transportation center, its chief economic activities are shipping and related businesses. Developed as a center of slave trade after the Portuguese arrived in 1472, it was later ruled by the Germans and then by the French.
See also: Cameroon.

Doubleday, Abner (1819-93), U.S. Union general. Credited with the invention of baseball in 1839 at Cooperstown, N.Y., although a game much like baseball, however, had been played long before Doubleday's time. He fired the first Union gun in defense of Fort Sumter and was a hero of the Battle of Gettysburg.
See also: Baseball; Civil War, U.S.

Double jeopardy, prosecution of an individual twice for the same crime. The 5th Amendment of the U.S. Constitution protects a person against being tried twice on the same charge. The U.S. Supreme Court, in *Benton* v. *Maryland* (1969), held that this principle was applicable to the states through the "due process" clause of the 14th Amendment. Neither federal nor state officers can appeal a verdict of acquittal, but the accused may appeal a verdict of guilty.

Double star *see:* Binary star.

Doughnut, small cake made of sweetened and flavored leavened dough, shaped as a "nut," or ring, deep-fried in fat, and sprinkled lightly with sugar. Friedcake and cruller, despite traditional differences, are alternative names.

Doughty, Charles Montagu (1843-1926), English traveler and author. *Travels in Arabia Deserta* (1888), written in Elizabethan style, describes his experiences living and traveling with the Bedouins in the 1870s.

Douglas *see:* Man, Isle of.

Douglas, Lloyd Cassel (1868-1951), Protestant minister and novelist. The author of works such as *Magnificent Obsession* (1929) and *The Robe* (1942), he was mainly interested in inspiring religious feeling; his fiction, however, achieved wide popular appeal.

Douglas, Stephen Arnold (1813-61), U.S. politician, Democratic representative (1843-47) and senator (1847-61) from Illinois, affectionately known as the "Little Giant." He is remembered for his debates with Abraham Lincoln in the Illinois senatorial campaign of 1858, which brought Lincoln to national attention. Involved in the issue of allowing slavery in the new states, he helped draft the Compromise of 1850, based on Squatter Sovereignty, and the Kansas-Nebraska Act (1854). In 1860 he was the unsuccessful Democratic presidential candidate, but he later supported Lincoln and the Union.

Douglas, William Orville (1898-1960), justice of the U.S. Supreme Court 1939-75, the longest tenure to date. An expert on business law, he had been chairman of the Securities and Exchange Commission. As a justice he favored a broad exercise of court powers and was an ardent defender of civil rights and free speech. He wrote some 30 books, many defending nature and wilderness.
See also: Supreme Court of the U.S.

Douglas fir (*Pseudotsuga menziesii*), a cone-bearing pine tree valued for its lumber. Found in North America, it supplies more lumber to the continent than any other species. The trees, which may grow to 250 ft (76 m) and live as long as 800 years, provide a home for rare plants and animals. Disagreement exists about how Douglas fir forests should be used.

Douglas-Home, Alexander Frederick *see:* Home, Lord.

Douglass, Frederick (Frederick Augustus Washington Bailey; 1817?-95), U.S. abolitionist, orator, and political activist who dedicated his life to the eradication of slavery and support for black rights. Born into slavery in Tuckahoe, Md., he was sent to work in Baltimore (1826), were he educated himself with the assistance of a slave master's wife. At the age of 20, he escaped and assumed the name of Douglass to avoid being identified. In 1841 Douglass

began lecturing for the Massachusetts Antislavery Society and throughout the 1840s protested against segregation. He spoke on trains and in churches, and, in some cases, had to be physically removed from passenger trains. His autobiography, *Narrative of the Life of Frederick Douglass* was published in 1845 (he later revised this work in two addional publcations — *My Bondage and My Freedom* (1855) and *Life and Times of Frederick Douglass* (1881). Fearing reprisal for the publication, Douglass moved to England where he continued his struggle against prejudice. In 1847 he returned to the United States and established the anti-slavery newspaper, North Star, in Rochester, N.Y. His home in Rochester became a stop on the Underground Railroad, among the network of homes and hiding places that aided slaves in their escape to freedom. During the Civil War (1861-65), he encouraged blacks to join the Union Army. He also had several meetings with President Abraham Lincoln to discuss the issue of slavery. He later served as a U.S. minister to Haiti (1889-91).
See also: Abolitionism.

Doukhobors, pacifist religious sect of Russian origin. They derive their name from the Russian word meaning "spirit wrestlers." Nonconformist peasants formed the first Doukhobor communities in Russia in the 18th century; they held that all men are equal and should be treated as brothers. Therefore they refused to fight or kill. The sect was repeatedly persecuted by the Russian government and the Orthodox clergy. Under Nicholas II the Doukhobors were driven from their farms. They went first to Cyprus in 1898 and then in 1899 to Canada, where about 7,500 immigrants settled.

Doum palm, or doom palm, fruit-bearing tree of the palm family found in the Middle East and northern and central Africa. The tree has an oval fruit about the size of an apple. The Ancient Egyptians often put large quantities of the fruit in the tombs of their pharoahs.

Dove, name sometimes given to a small member of the pigeon family, for example, the rock dove (*Columba livia*). There is no real difference between pigeons and doves, and species are labeled arbitrarily.

Dove, Arthur Garfield (1880-1946), U.S. abstract painter. Recognized as an early proponent of abstract expressionism, he painted fluid, poetic compositions based on natural forms and created constructions similar to collages. Never a popular success, he was supported by photographer and art dealer Alfred Stieglitz.
See also: Abstract expressionism.

Dover (pop. 32,800), seaport in Kent, England. It is situated on the Strait of Dover, the narrowest part of the English Channel. The first settlement on the site was the Roman town of Dubris. The Saxons built fortifications on the cliffs above the town, later replaced by the Norman castle that stands on the chalk cliffs. In the Middle Ages, Dover became one of the privileged Cinque Ports, a group of channel ports given seafaring power in return for their contribution to England's sea defense. The main center for the evacuation from Dunkirk during World War II, it was heavily damaged by bombardment.
See also: England.

Dover (pop. 27,630), city, capital of Delaware and seat of Kent County, situated in central Delaware on the St. Jones River, 40 mi (64.4 km) south of Wilmington. Surrounded by a rich farming area, Dover serves as a marketing, shipping, and processing center. Among its industries are hosiery, rubber goods, and plumbing supplies. William Penn, the founder of Pennsylvania, planned the town in 1683, and it was laid out in 1717. In 1777 Dover replaced New Castle as the state capital. Dover is the site of Wesley Junior College and the Delaware State College.
See also: Delaware.

Dover, Strait of, narrow passage separating southeastern England from northern France, connecting the English Channel with the North Sea. It is about 19 mi (30 km) across at its narrowest point. The chief ports are Dover and Folkestone in England, Calais and Boulogne in France. Of great strategic importance, the strait was the scene of the first repulse by the English of the Spanish Armada (1588), the Dover (antisubmarine) Patrol of World War I, and the evacuation from Dunkirk (1940). The strait is frequently crossed by long-distance swimmers.

Dow, Herbert Henry (1866-1930), pioneer in the U.S. chemistry industry. In 1897 Dow founded the Dow Chemical Company in Midland, Mich. At first Dow focused on deriving the maximum value from brines (concentrated solutions of salt and water), developing insecticides and pharmaceuticals. The first important producer of iodine, Dow was eventually granted more than 100 patents and became one of the world's largest chemical companies.
See also: Chemistry.

Dow Jones Industrial Average, most frequently cited gauge of U.S. stock market performance. Compiled since 1884, the Dow Jones Average is a composite of the prices of 30 leading industrial stocks. In addition, Dow Jones compiles a Transportation Average (20 stocks), a Utility Average (15 stocks), and a Combined Average (all 65). Other key market indicators are Standard and Poor's 500 and the New York Stock Exchange Price index (all stocks traded on the exchange). On April 17, 1991 the Down Jones Industrial Average broke the 3000 mark with a record 3004.06.
See also: Stock exchange.

Dowland, John (1563-1626), English composer and lutenist, best known for his songs and the collection of lute pieces *Lachrimae* (1604). He traveled to France, Italy, Germany, and Denmark in the service of various kings and princes. From 1612 he served in the court of James I.

Down's syndrome, formerly called mongolism, chromosomal aberration resulting in mental retardation and physical abnormalities. In about 95% of cases of Down's syndrome, there is an extra chromosome 21, making 3 in all, hence its technical name trisomy 21. The overall incidence is about 1 in every 700 live births, but there is a marked variability depending on maternal age: In the early childbearing years, the incidence is about 1 in every 2,000 live births; for mothers over age 50, it rises to about 1 in every 45 live births. The cause of this genetic disorder is unknown. Infants tend to be placid, rarely cry, and have flabby muscles. Physical and mental development are both retarded and the mean IQ is about 50. Down's syndrome children have smaller than average heads and moon-shaped faces. Their eyes are slanted, usually with epicanthal folds above the eyelids. The bridges of their noses are flattened, and their mouths are often held open because of their large, protruding, furrowed tongues. Their hands are short and broad, with a single crease across the palm, and short fingers. Their feet have wide gaps between the first and second toes, and there is a furrow on each sole. The life expectancy of these children is decreased by heart disease and by susceptibility to acute leukemia. Most of those without a major defect survive to adulthood, but the aging process seems accelerated, with death occurring in their 40s and 50s.

Dowser *see:* Divination.

Dowson, Ernest Christopher (1867-1900), English poet, one of the Decadents of the 1890s. From a life of misery and squalor he produced a delicate, lyrical poetry on themes of love and lost childhood.

Doyle, Sir Arthur Conan (1859-1930), British writer, creator of the detective Sherlock Holmes, featured in many short stories and 4 novels. A doctor, soldier, and campaigner for law reform, he also wrote historical novels like *Micah Clarke* (1889) and science fiction like *The Lost World* (1912). In later life he became an adherent of spiritualism.

Sir Arthur Conan Doyle's greatest creation—Sherlock Holmes

D'Oyly Carte, Richard (1844-1901), English impresario. He produced Gilbert and Sullivan's first operetta, *Trial by Jury*, in 1875. He founded the D'Oyly Carte Opera Company (1878) and built the Savoy Theatre, London, as a stage for works by Gilbert and Sullivan (1881).
See also: Gilbert and Sullivan.

Draco (fl. c.621 B.C.), lawgiver in Athens. His code made serious and trivial crimes alike punishable by death—hence the term "draconian" to describe any harsh legal measure. Solon later repealed all the laws except those dealing with homicide.
See also: Greece, Ancient.

Dracula, novel (1897) by English writer Bram Stoker about a Transylvanian vampire count. Dracula became the subject of many horror films. The name, meaning "dragon," was applied to Vlad IV the Impaler, the cruel 15th-century Walachian prince upon whom Stoker based the character.

Draft, military, or conscription, system of raising armed forces by compulsory recruitment. The modern practice is more aptly described as selective service. Obligatory military service dates back to ancient times, but modern conscription began in the late 18th century when Napoleon I imposed universal conscription of able- bodied males. Peacetime conscription became standard practice in Europe in the 19th century, except in Britain, where it was not imposed until just prior to World War II (wartime conscription was practiced in both Britain and the United States during World War I). During the Civil War both North and South used conscription. In the United States peacetime conscription was first introduced in 1940 and, though dropped briefly in 1947, continued through to 1973 to meet the demands of the Korean and Vietnamese commitments. Conscription has frequently given rise to civil protest. During Lyndon Johnson's presidency (1963-69), antidraft demonstrations became a popular form of protest against military involvement in Vietnam. In June 1980 President Jimmy Carter reinstated the Selective Service System, which had been in a "standby" position since the start of the All Volunteer Force in 1973. U.S. males born in 1960 or later and at least 18, including citizens, resident aliens, and conditional entrants to the country, are required to register with the service through the post office. In Israel the draft is applied to unmarried women as well as to men.

Francis Drake

Dragon (Greek: *drakon*, "serpent"), legendary monster, usually represented as a fire-breathing, winged serpent or lizard with crested head and large claws. Apart from the wingless Chinese and Japanese dragons, which are considered beneficent, dragons have usually been regarded as symbols of evil, and dragon-slayers, for example Saint George, as saints and heroes.

Dragonfly, insect of the order Odonata, indentifiable by its long, slender, abdomen, 2 pairs of transparent wings, each covered in a network of veins, and large compound eyes, which may contain 30,000 separate facets. Dragonflies are superb fliers, some being credited with speeds of 60 mph (97 kmph), and can dart forward, hover, then shoot forward again. Each dragonfly patrols an area, usually near water, where it feeds on insects. The eggs are laid in water, and the nymphs (larvae) live underwater for a year or more. They have gills inside the intestine and can shoot water out of the rectum in a form of jet propulsion. The largest living dragonfly, from Borneo, has a 7-in (18-cm) wingspan, but fossilized remains have been found of a crow-sized dragonfly with a 27-in (68.6-cm) wingspan.

Drainage, removal of surplus water from land. Withot drainage, successful crop production and retention of soil fertility would be impossible. Wet lands are difficult to work with modern machinery, and most crops suffer from root injury if grown on water-logged ground. Undrained soils are structureless, with tightly packed subsoils full of stagnant water. Buildings and houses benefit from drainage, which is essential for sanitation and good health. Roads are not passable in wet weather unless provided with drains. Undrained swamps afford breeding grounds for malaria-carrying mosquitoes, and accumulated sewage becomes a source of disease epidemics. Early drainage consisted mainly of open ditches, often using natural watercourses. During the 18th century farmers began to employ patterns of underground channels covering whole fields, which collected and discharged surplus water into several outfalls. The invention and mass production of U-shaped clay or concrete drain tiles in England in the mid-19th century opened the way for the wide adoption of tile draining. On clay land, *mole draining* is effective: A mole plow moves over the surface of the ground, drawing a cylindrical mole through the subsoil, making a channel about 3-4 in (7.5-10 cm) wide, some 2 ft (60 cm) below the surface. This method, with the variations, comes under the heading of surface drainage. Excess water can also be pumped off land.

Draisine *see:* Bicycle.

Drake, Edwin Laurentine *see:* Petroleum.

Drake, Sir Francis (1543-96), English admiral, the first English explorer to sail around the world (1577-80). During his circumnavigation aboard the Golden Hind, Drake seized a fortune in booty from Spanish settlements along the South American Pacific coast. He was knighted on his return by Queen Elizabeth I. In 1587 he destroyed a large part of the Spanish fleet at anchor in Cadiz harbor. The following year he was joint commander of the English fleet that, with the help of a storm, dispersed and destroyed the Spanish Armada (1588).

Dram *see:* Apothecaries' weight.

Drama *see:* Theater.

Dramamine, brand name of the drug dimenhydrinate, used to prevent motion sickness and to control the nausea and vomiting associated with certain illnesses. An antihistamine, Dramamine may act as a mild sedative; it can cause drowsiness.

Draughts *see:* Checkers.

Dravidian, member of a subgroup of the Hindu race, including some 100 million people of (mainly) southern India. They are fairly dark-skinned, stocky, broad-nosed, and commonly dolichocephalic (long-headed). The **Dravidian languages** are a family of some 22 languages, perhaps the most important from a philological point of view being Tamil, texts which date back to at least the 1st century B.C.

Drawbridge *see:* Bridge; Castle.

Drawing, pictorial representation by means of line on any surface. An artistic expression, drawing has developed in 3 main directions: as the independent, preparatory sketch for work in another medium; as the preliminary sketch eventually incorporated into another medium (for example, as the basic outline for a painting, fresco, or mural); and as an independently conceived and executed work. Little is known of the early history of drawing in European cultures. With the advent of the Renaissance and the emphasis on perspective and detailed rendering, drawing became the object of serious study. The availability of good-quality paper by the end of the 15th century also influenced the development of drawing. Drawing was the subject of several treatises by Renaissance theoreticians, and around the end of the 16th century the collection of drawings became a hobby of the rich. In the 18th century drawing became a prerequisite for the study of painting and sculpture in the academies. In England the art of caricature and political cartooning was brought to a high level in the satirical drawings of William Hogarth and Thomas Rowlandson, as it was in France by Honoré Daumier and in Spain by Francisco de Goya. The 19th-century neoclassicist Jean Ingres, the romanticist Théodore Géricault, and the early-modern masters Paul Cézanne, Vincent van Gogh, Henri Toulouse-Lautrec, Auguste Renoir, Edgar Degas, and Georges Seurat were eminent. Great draftsmen of the 20th century include Pablo Picasso, Joan Miró, Paul Klee, and Vasili Kandinsky. Drawing plays a great part in commercial art, illustrating advertisements, textbooks, brochures, and articles in magazines and periodicals. The availability of high-grade materials and the development of media have widened the modern graphic artist's choice of technique.

Dreadnought, British battleship (built 1906) whose design became the model for warships of the first half of the 20th century. Weighing 18,000 tons and capable of traveling at 21 knots (24 mph/38 kmph), the *Dreadnought* carried ten 12-in (30.5-cm) guns. At the time of its completion there was nothing afloat to match its speed and firepower. By the outbreak of World War I 9 *Dreadnought*-class ships and 12 other big-gun battleships were in service in the British navy.
See also: Battleship.

Dream, mental activity that occurs during sleep. Dreaming occurs during the REM (rapid-eye movement) period of sleep. Dreams are often quite vivid, though research indicates that most people forget the majority of their dreams. The interpretation of dreams has played an important part in pre-modern cultures, and major theories of dreams and their significance have been put forward by Sigmund Freud, Carl Jung, and others. In the latter 20th century, scientific thinking about dreams has focused on research into the physiological characteristics and mechanisms of sleep and the activity of the brain while in the sleeping state.

Dredging, removal of silt, mud, and sand from harbors and navigation channels to keep them open for shipping. Of the 3 kinds of dredging vessels, the *bucket dredger* is the most widely used: A continuous moving chain of buckets extends down beneath the keel into the mud to be dredged. The *grab dredger* is a floating crane that drops a heavy scoop, or grab, into the mud and then hauls it to the surface. A more modern type is the *suction*, or *hydraulic dredger* which sucks up the mud through a pipe that is lowered to the seabed. The biggest hydraulic dredgers can dredge and discharge 20,000 tons or more in an hour. Dredgers may discharge their "spoil" into their own holds; into hopper barges moored alongside; or by means of a floating pipeline, directly onto the land. Dredgers are also used for mining deposits of heavy minerals that occur in alluvial gravels (deposited by running water). Tin, gold, platinum, and diamonds are often mined in this way.

Dred Scott case, suit brought by Dred Scott, a slave from Missouri, on the grounds that temporary residence in a territory in which slavery was banned under the Missouri Compromise had made him free. The majority opinion of the U.S. Supreme Court in 1857, read by Chief Justice Roger Taney, held that Scott could never be a citizen of any state and therefore could not sue his owner in federal court. Taney also declared the Missouri Compromise was unconstitutional. This decision inflamed and divided the nation, making the Civil War all but inevitable.
See also: Slavery; Civil War, U.S.

Dreiser, Theodore (1871-1945), U.S. novelist whose naturalistic fiction is concerned with the dispossessed and criminal. He wrote about the impersonal social and economic forces that compel behavior, and generally with grimmer realities of U.S. life. His novels include *Sister Carrie* (1900) and *An American Tragedy* (1925).

Dresden (pop. 519,900), historic German city on the Elbe River, administrative center of the district of Dresden, in southeastern Germany. Products include porcelain, chemicals, various light-engineering products, and beet sugar. Its river location and site on a network of railroads link Dresden with other major eastern German cities. It is also famous as a cultural center and contains world-famous art museums. Dresden originated as a Slav fishing village. The town developed during the 13th century and became the residence of the Saxon sovereigns in 1485. In the late 17th and early 18th centuries many rococo and baroque buildings were constructed. It survived the Battle of Dresden (1813), Napoleon's last great victory, but many historic buildings were destroyed in a devastating air raid in World War II which claimed thousands of lives and razed the city. The city has since been largely restored.
See also: Germany.

A dreadnought-*class ship*, USS Wisconsin

Dresden china, or Meissen ware (after the town near Dresden where china has been made since 1710), Europe's first true porcelain. The process of its manufacture was discovered by Johann Friedrich Böttger in 1707.

Drew, Charles Richard (1904-50), African American physician, surgeon, and medical researcher who founded the American Red Cross blood bank.

Dreyfus, Alfred (1859-1935), Jewish French army official who became the center of a bitter political quarrel known as the Dreyfus affair.
See also: Dreyfus Affair.

Dreyfus Affair, French political scandal of the Third Republic. In 1894, Alfred Dreyfus (1859-1935), a Jewish army captain, was convicted of betraying French secrets to the Germans. Further evidence pointed to a Major Ferdinand Walsin Esterhazy as the traitor, but when tried (Jan. 1898), Esterhazy was acquitted on secret, forged evidence. Dreyfus's conviction had aroused anti-Semitism, and although evidence against him had been forged, the army was relunctant to admit the error. As public interest in the case was aroused, it became known that the Roman Catholic Church supported the conviction. After Esterhazy's acquittal, the French novelist Émile Zola published an attack on the army's integrity, *J'accuse* ("I accuse"), which roused intellectual and liberal opinion to a furor. With the suicide of an army officer who had acknowledged the forgeries and with Esterhazy's flight from France, a new court-martial began, but Dreyfus was found "guilty with extenuating circumstances" (Aug. 1899). Public opinion was outraged, and in Sept. the government gave him a pardon. He served in World War I and retired a lieutenant-colonel. The scandal had thrown government, army, and church into disrepute. Legislation followed that led to separation of church and state (1905). The original verdict against Dreyfus was quashed in 1906.
See also: Dreyfus, Alfred.

Drill, tool for cutting or enlarging holes in hard materials. *Rotary drills* are commonly used in the home for wood, plastic, masonry, and sometimes metal. In mettallurgy the mechanical drilling machine, or drill press, operates one or several drills at a time. Most metallurgical drills are of high-speed steel. Dentists' drills rotate at extremely high speeds, powered by an electric motor or by compressed air; their tips (of tungsten carbide or diamond) are water-cooled. Rotary drills are also used for deeper oil well drilling: A cutting bit is rotated at the end of a long, hollow drill pipe, new sections of pipe being added as drilling proceeds. The *percussive drills* are used for rock-boring, for concrete and masonry, and for shallower oil well drilling. Rock drills are generally powered by compressed air, the tool rotating after each blow to increase cutting speed. The pneumatic drill familiar in city streets is also operated by compressed air. Ultrasonic drills are used for brittle materials; a rod attached to a transducer is placed against the surface, and to it are fed abrasive particles suspended in a cooling fluid. It is these particles that actually perform the cutting.

Rotary drills used in oil exploration

Drill, planting implement consisting of 4 parts: a hoe or opener that digs a row, a hopper that holds the seed, a seed meter that ensures even spacing of seeds in the furrows, and a chain or press wheel that covers the seed with soil.

Drive-in U.S. marketing and service innovation designed to allow people to use the services provided without leaving their cars. At various times, the concept has been applied to restaurants, banks, movies, and churches.
See also: Restaurant.

Drought, excessively dry climatic conditions, generally due to absence of rainfall. Permanent drought conditions prevail over approximately one-third of the world's land surface, the sand deserts alone covering a total area more than twice as large as the United States. A region is classed as arid or drought-stricken when the annual precipitation is below 10 in (25.4 cm). Under such conditions, farming becomes extremely difficult. Recently, however, progress has been made in dry land reclamation by means of new irrigation schemes. Experiments for inducing artificial rainfall through cloud-seeding techniques have also been promising.
See also: Climate.

Drowning, death caused by suffocation due to immersion in water or any other liquid. In most cases of drowning, the heart continues to beat for several minutes after loss of consciousness. This means that mouth-to-mouth resuscitation can save the victim's life by renewing the flow of oxygen.

Drug, substance affecting the body and that may be used to treat illness or alleviate symptoms. Antibiotics, antitoxins, sulfa drugs, insulin, narcotics, contraceptives, stimulants, depressants, the special drugs used in chemotherapy to treat cancers are just a few of the many drugs that have transformed medical practice.
Drugs may be derived from organic substances, they may be manufactured through chemical modifications of natural products, or they may be synthetic. Some can be purchased over the counter, while others require a doctor's prescription. Drug research and the manufacture of new drugs has become a highly complex, technologically sophisticated, and highly capitalized industry. In the U.S. newly developed drugs are closely monitored by the Food and Drug Administration, which has authority over their testing and marketing. The modern pharmacopeia is so large that specialists must keep abreast of new developments through constantly revised standard references like the United States Pharmacopeia—National Formulary and the Physician's Desk Reference.
Side by side with scientific progress in the development of new drugs and their applications to medicine, there has been an increase in the manufacture, trade, and use of various narcotics. As a result, social, political, and religious institutions have tried to formulate responses to substances that, in one form or another, raise far-reaching ethical, moral, and legal questions.

Drug abuse, non-medical use of certain chemical substances that can induce unusual states of consciousness, relieve pain, increase endurance, or heighten sensation. The use of such substances very likely predates the historical record, and cultures and civilizations have taken varying attitudes to prohibition or legalization of various substances. In modern times, drug abuse refers to dependence upon any of a range of narcotics (marijuana, hashish, morphine, opium, and their derivatives), stimulants (cocaine and amphetamines), depressants (alcohol, barbituates, and sedatives), and many hallucinogenic agents.
See also: Drug.

Drug addiction, physical rather than psychological dependence upon an intoxicating substance, such that deprivation causes the addict to experience withdrawal. Common drugs that can produce addictions include alcohol, nicotine (in tobacco), caffeine, barbiturates, and opiates (opium, morphine, heroin). Not all who take dependence-producing drugs become dependent on them. Withdrawal from addictive drugs such as alcohol can itself be dangerous, and detoxification is often medically supervised.

See also: Drug; Narcotic.

Drug Enforcement Administration (DEA), U.S. government agency that enforces federal laws against narcotics. Through 19 divisional offices in the U.S., the DEA also governs the manufacture and distribution of controlled substances. Established in 1973 as part of the U.S. Department of Justice, the DEA cooperates with the Federal Bureau of Investigation to prevent drug trafficking, and with state and local law enforcers and the agencies of other nations to combat illegal drug abuse and trade.
See also: Drug; Narcotic.

Druids, ancient Celtic priestly order in Gaul (France), Britain, and Ireland, respected for their learning in astronomy, law, and medicine, for their gift of prophecy, and as lawgivers and leaders. Little is known of their religious rites, though human sacrifice may have been involved. Because of their power, they were banned by the Romans.

Drum, musical instrument of the percussion family, common to most cultures. It consists of a shell, cylindrical or conical, with a membrane, or skin, stretched over one or both ends. The skin is struck with the hand or with sticks. The principal drum in the symphony orchestra is the kettledrum, or tympanum, whose pitch can be adjusted by the tightening or loosening of the membrane. Other orchestral drums include the tenor, snare, and bass drums and the tamborine. Snares are important in popular maintaining rhythm in popular marching music.

Drum, any of about 200 species of fishes of the family Sciaenidae. Some species produce a deep sound by means of an air bladder in the abdomen.

Drumlin *see:* Glacier.

Druses, or Druzes, Islamic sect living in Lebanon, Syria, Israel, and the United States. They form a closed community, and most of their doctrines are kept secret. They have their own scriptures, and profess monotheism and the divinity of al-Hakim, sixth caliph (996-1021) of the Egyptian Fatimid dynasty.

Dry cleaning, use of liquids other than water to clean fabrics. In the United States, perchlorethylene is used in addition to petroleum solvents. Trichlorethylene is favored in other countries. The garments are placed in a washer along with the solvent, which removes grease and oil. Dust, dirt, lint, and other insoluble particles are removed by agitation and are carried away in the cleaning fluid, which is filtered and recycled. Solvent is removed in a centrifuge, and the fabric is dried. Spots and stains are removed by a specially trained "spotter," who uses chemicals appropriate for the type of fabric and stain. Finally, the garments are pressed with a steam press.

Dryden, John (1631-1700), English poet, dramatist, and literary critic. Dryden's career began around the time of the Restoration (1660). He became poet laureate in 1668 and historiographer royal in 1670. His plays include *Marriage à la Mode* (1672) and *All for Love* (1677). *Essay of Dramatick Poesie* (1668) did much to establish the primacy of Shakespeare and to promote English dramatic approach in place of the academicism of the Continent. Among his many great poems are *Absalom and Achitophel* (1681) and *Mac Flecknoe* (1682) brilliant satires, and *Religio Laici*, setting forth his religious credo. After the ascension of William of Orange, Dryden no longer the English laureate, worked on translations, notably of Vergil (1697).

Dry farming, type of agriculture without irrigation used in areas where less than 20 in (50 cm) rainfall per year prevents the use

of traditional methods of farming. After harvest the land is tilled and kept free of weeds to reduce loss of moisture. Where crops are sown in spring, stubble of the previous year's crop is often allowed to stand over winter to trap snow. In very dry areas ground is left fallow in alternate years, allowing it to store up moisture. Fields are contoured and clods of dead vegetable matter are kept in the fields to prevent water runoff and make possible more efficient use of rainfall. Dry farming is frequently practiced in the U.S. and Canadian West, the Great Plains, the Mediterranean basin, the Soviet Union, and interior areas of Australia and Asia. Among the crops appropriate for dry farming are corn, sorghum, and wheat. Crops grown this way are usually small in size and are quicker to mature than those grown in more moist areas.
See also: Agriculture.

Dry ice, common name (originally a trade name) for solid carbon dioxide (CO_2). Since it does not melt, but sublimates (turns directly into a gas), dry ice is a more efficient coolant than ordinary ice and does not corrode containers. It is much used in long-distance transportation of perishable products such as ice cream and meat. Because dry ice is usually at a temperature of —110°F (—43.3°C) or lower, it damages the skin on contact
See also: Carbon dioxide.

Dry rot, wood decay caused by a fungus that feeds on wood, making it lighter, weaker, and more brittle. It is sometimes found in houses. Dry rot does not attack living trees. Despite its name, dry rot cannot live in dry wood, and a good way of avoiding it is to use well-seasoned timber and ensure that there is good ventilation around the structure.

Dry Tortugas, group of 7 coral islands about 50 mi (80 km) west of Key West, Fla. They were discovered in 1513 by Juan Ponce de León, who gave them the Spanish name for the turtles with which the islands abound. The largest of the group, Loggerhead Key, is approximately 1 mi (1.6 km) in length.

DT's *see:* Delirium tremens.

Dualism, any religious or philosophical system characterized by a fundamental opposition of two independent or complementary principles. Among religious dualisms are the unending conflict of good and evil spirits envisaged in Zoroastrianism and the opposition of light and darkness in Gnosticism and Manichaeism. The Chinese complementary principles of *yin* and *yang* exemplify a cosmological dualism, while the mind-body dualism of René Descartes is the best-known philosophical type. Dualism is often opposed to monism and pluralism.

Duarte, José Napoleón (1925-90), president of El Salvador 1980-82 (appointed) and 1984-88 (elected). His nation suffered from a civil war and attendant economic crises throughout his public life. A Christian Democrat, he promoted democracy and reconciliation as his nation's only hopes, but his efforts were in vain. Terminally ill, he declined to run again for office in 1989.
See also: El Salvador.

Du Barry, Marie Jeanne Bécu, Countess (1743-93), last mistress of Louis XV of France. Her years as mistress (1769-74) were marked by her generosity and good nature but little political influence. She was executed in Paris for aiding royalist émigrés during the French Revolution.

Dubcek, Alexander *see:* Czechoslovakia.

Dubinsky, David (1892-1982), U.S. labor leader; president of the International Ladies Garment Workers Union (1932-66). Known for combating Communist and underworld infiltration of the union, he negotiated increased benefits for its members. He was a founder of New York's Liberal Party (1944) and a vice president of the AFL-CIO (1955-66).
See also: Labor movement.

Dublin (Baile Atha Cliath; 502,700), city capital of the Republic of Ireland (Eire) and of County Dublin. Located at the mouth of the Liffey River and Dublin Bay on the Irish Sea, Dublin is the political and cultural center of Ireland. Its fine buildings include Four Courts, the Custom House, Trinity College, the National Library, Museum and Gallery, and the Royal Irish Academy. There is also a famous medical center and zoological gardens dating from 1830, as well as the Abbey Theatre and University College. English rule, which severely restricted Dublin's commercial development, was finally removed after the Easter Rebellion (1916) and the establishment of the Irish Free State (1921). Dublin is an industrial seaport, and the city manufactures stout, whiskey, and textiles. There is a direct rail and steamer link to London.
See also: Ireland.

Trinity college, Dublin

Dubois, Eugène (1858-1941), Dutch anatomist and physical anthropologist who in 1891-92, in Java, discovered the fossilized bones of a human-like creature who walked erect. Dubois named his discovery *Pithecanthropus erectus*. It led to the theory that there was a single "missing link" in the chain of evolution joining apes and human beings. It is now generally believed that there were various intermediary forms in human evolution, of which *Pithecanthropus erectus* was one.
See also: Anthropology; Prehistoric people.

Du Bois, W(illiam) E(dward) B(urghardt) (1868-1963), African American educator and author. He was a proponent of equality for blacks, and later for Pan-Africanism, a movement to coordinate the struggle for equal rights of all people of African descent around the world. Professor of economics and history at Atlanta University (1897-1910), and head of its sociology department (1934-44), his many works include *The Philadelphia Negro* (1899), *The Souls of Black Folk* (1903), and *Black Reconstruction* (1935). He also edited *The Crisis*, the magazine of the NAACP until 1932. Increasingly alienated from the United States, he joined the Communist Party in 1961 and moved to Ghana, where he died in self-imposed exile.
See also: African Americans.

Dubos, René Jules (1901-82), French-born U.S. microbiologist who developed tyrothricin (1939), the first antibiotic to be used clinically. He wrote more than 30 books, including *So Human an Animal* (Pulitzer Prize, 1969), and founded the René Dubos Center for Human Environments.
See also: Antibiotic; Microbiology.

Dubuffet, Jean (1901-85), French artist influenced by spontaneous primitive amateur art, known as *art brut* (raw art). He used gravel, tar, and other unusual materials to produce fantastic impasto paintings that constitute fierce protests against conventional aesthetic criteria.

Dubuque (pop. 86,403), city in eastern Iowa, seat of Dubuque County. Dubuque is a Mississippi River outlet for a large agricultural area and a thriving industrial center, producing farm machinery, furniture, and meat products. The city is named for Julien Dubuque, a French Canadian who began mining lead locally about 1788. Dubuque received its charter in 1841. Its educational institutions include Dubuque University, known for its agricultural school.
See also: Iowa.

Duccio di Buoninsegna (1255?-1319?), Italian painter, first great master of the Siennese school. Combining Byzantine austerity with French Gothic grace, Duccio's work strongly influenced the development of Renaissance painting. The altarpiece *Maestà* is regarded as his masterpiece.

Marcel Duchamp's The Chess Players *(1911)*

Duchamp, Marcel (1887-1968), French artist, a pioneer of dadaism, cubism, and futurism, initially influenced by Paul Cézanne. Duchamp often used common objects as art. This is the so-called "ready-made" art, which includes the well-known controversial *Fountain*—nothing more than an ordinary toilet. The motive behind such displays was to propel the viewer into examining his or her criteria for art. His *Nude Descending a Staircase, No. 2* (1912), made up of superimposed images to suggest movement rather than to represent a figure, shocked the U.S. public. Having settled in New York in 1915, he became a U.S. citizen in 1955.
See also: Dada; Surrealism.

Duck, aquatic bird, any of the smaller members of the family Anatidae, which also contains the geese and swans. The word is properly used to describe the females of many members of the Anatidae, the term for the male being *drake*. Ducks are, broadly, of 3 types: surface-feeding (dabbling), diving, and fish-eating. The most familiar are the dabblers such as the mallard, which is found throughout the Northern Hemisphere and is the ancestor of the domestic duck. Many ducks are killed for sport and food. Their down (soft layer of feathers), particularly that of the eider duck, is of commercial importance.

A flight of ducks

Duckbill *see:* Platypus.

Duck hawk, name used in the United States for the peregrine falcon, a bird that can fly at speeds of more than 200 mi (320 km) per hour. Peregrines range from 13 to 19 in (33 to 48 cm) long. They fly high and dive at tremendous speeds, killing their prey (ducks and shorebirds) upon impact. The peregrine falcon was the first animal in the United States declared an endangered species.

Duckweed, aquatic plant (genus *Lemna*) with small round leaves, no stem, and a few rootlets, and simple flowers. Duckweeds float on the surface of still water, forming an almost continuous layer, and sink in winter.

Ductility, plastic property of certain substances, notably metals, which allows them to be drawn into the form of wires or extruded through an aperture without rupturing or returning to their original shape. Gold is the most ductile of all metals, but silver, platinum, copper, aluminum, and iron also exhibit a high degree of ductility. Hot glass can be drawn into very fine threads, though it is very brittle at ordinary temperatures.

Duel, prearranged armed combat between 2 persons, usually in the presence of witnesses, for the purpose of deciding a quarrel, avenging an insult, or vindicating the honor of one of the combatants or a third party. While the purpose in modern times was seldom to kill the opponent, deaths did occur, and public ourtrage resulted in the banning of duels in most modern nations. The earliest form of duel was trial by battle, which probably originated among the Germanic tribes and became established in Europe in the early Middle Ages. The accuser threw down a gauntlet (glove) in the presence of a judge, and the opponent picked it up as a sign of acceptance of the duel. The belief was that God defended the right cause. Judicial duels died out in France in the 16th century but took place in England as late as 1818. Private duels or duels of honor were particularly common in France, and participants were often killed. Henry IV's edict of 1602 declared persons fighting unauthorized duels guilty of treason, but dueling remained popular, and duels for political reasons were frequent during the 19th century. The most famous duels in the United States took place in 1804, when Aaron Burr killed Alexander Hamilton, and in 1820, when James Barron killed Stephen Decatur. By the time of the Civil War the practice had ended.

Due process, constitutional guarantee of fairness in the administration of justice. The concept can be traced back to the Magna Carta and is embodied in the 5th Amendment to the U.S. Constitution: "No person shall be deprived of life, liberty or property without due process of law." The 14th Amendment extended this limitation on the federal government to include the states. Due process has 2 aspects: *Procedural* due process guarantees fair trial in the courts, and *substantive* due process places limitations on the content of the law. It is under the latter heading that the Supreme Court has struck down many state laws restricting civil liberties as infringements of the Bill of Rights.
See also: Habeas Corpus.

Dufay, Guillaume (1400?-74), French composer. Attached to Cambrai Cathedral from 1445, he was an early master of counterpoint and wrote church music and songs, developing the mass in a graceful, expressive style.

Dufy, Raoul (1877-1953), French painter. He was influenced by fauvism, cubism, and the works of Cézanne. He is best known for lively sporting scenes in brilliant colors.

Dugong, or sea cow, (*Dugong dugong*) seal-like aquatic mammal found around the coasts of the Indian Ocean from Madagascar to Australia. Dugongs live in family groups, feeding on the leaves and roots of sea plants, which they root up with their thick, bristly lips. Hunted for their hide, meat, and oil, their numbers have been greatly reduced.

Duisburg (pop. 518,300), trading and manufacturing city in western Germany. The largest inland port in Western Europe, Duisburg is located where the Ruhr and Rhine rivers meet. It is a major producer of iron and steel.
See also: Germany.

Dukakis, Michael Stanley (1933-), U.S. politician, unsuccessful Democratic candidate for president in the 1988 election. He served in the Massachusetts House of Representatives (1963-70) and was elected governor of Massachusetts in 1974. After losing his bid for reelection in 1978, he regained the post in the election of 1982. He declined to run for reelection in 1990.

Dukas, Paul Abraham (1865-1935), French composer and critic. Best known for *The Sorcerer's Apprentice,* written in 1897 in the lively symphonic form known as *scherzo,* Dukas also composed the opera *Ariadne and Bluebeard* (1907) and the ballet *The Peri* (1912).

Dukenfield, William Claude *see:* Fields, W. C.

Dulcimer, musical instrument consisting of a set of strings stretched across a thin, flat soundbox and struck with mallets. Of ancient origin, it is still used in the folk music of central Europe, where it is called the cimbalom. The Kentucky dulcimer, a U.S. folk instrument, is plucked.

Dulles, name of 2 prominent U.S. lawyers and statesmen. **John Foster Dulles** (1888-1956) was U.S. secretary of state under President Dwight D. Eisenhower (1953-59), employing a strong foreign policy to block Communist cold war expansion. He was legal counsel at the World War I peace conference, worked on the UN charter during World War II, and negotiated the Japanese peace treaty (1951). His brother, **Allen Welsh Dulles** (1893-1969), an intelligence official, negotiated the Nazi surrender in Italy in World War II. He directed the Central Intelligence Agency 1953-61, considerably influencing foreign policy, as in the U.S.-backed Bay of Pigs invasion of Cuba.

Duluth (pop. 239,971), city in northeastern Minnesota at the western end of Lake Superior. It is Minnesota's third largest city and one of the largest U.S. ports, serving as a western terminal of the St. Lawrence Seaway. Duluth ships out iron ore and grain and imports coal, except when icebound in winter. It also produces iron, steel, machinery, and canned meat and serves as a vacation center. Its educational institutions include a branch of the University of Minnesota and the Benedictine College of St. Scholastica. The city was named for the French trader, Daniel Greysolon, Sieur Duluth, who visited the area in 1679. The American Fur Company opened a trading post in the vicinity in 1817. Settlement developed in the 1850s.
See also: Minnesota.

Duma, name for several elected assemblies is tsarist Russia in 1906. The first 2 dumas (1906 and 1907), instituted by Nicholas II, were radical and were swiftly dissolved by Nicholas. The third and fourth (1907-12 and 1912-17), though restricted, introduced some reforms. Revolution in 1917 did away with the institution.

Dumas, name of two 19th-century French authors, a father and his illegitimate son. **Alexandre Dumas père** (1802-70) wrote the famous historical novels *The Three Musketeers* (1844) and *The Count of Monte Cristo* (1845). **Alexandre Dumas fils** (1824-95), his son, won fame with his tragic play *La Dame aux Camélias* (*Camille*; 1812), which formed the basis of Verdi's opera *La Traviata.* He also wrote moralizing plays aimed at the reform of social evils.

Du Maurier, name of 2 English novelists. **George Louis Palmella Busson du Maurier** (1834-96), caricaturist, illustrator, and novelist, is best known for his novels *Peter Ibbetson* (1891) and *Trilby* (1894). **Daphne Du Maurier** (1907-89), his granddaughter, wrote romantic novels. Her most famous work is *Rebecca* (1938).

Dumbarton Oaks Conference, meeting of diplomats of the "Big Four" (China, United States, USSR, and England), held Aug. 24-Oct. 7, 1944, at the Dumbarton Oaks estate in Washington, D.C. Its discussions were the first major step toward establishing a postwar international security.
See also: United Nations.

Dunbar, Paul Laurence (1872-1906), African American poet and novelist. His poems about black rural life were influenced by the sentimental dialect poems of James Whitcomb. His works include *Lyrics of Lowly Life* (1896) and the novel *The Sport of the Gods* (1902).

Dunbar, William (c.1460-1520), Scottish poet. He became a priest and was employed by James IV on court business. His poems show great satiric power, originality, versatility, and wit.

Duncan, Isadora (1878-1927), U.S. pioneer of modern dance. Encouraging a spontaneous personal style, she danced in a loose tunic, barefoot, to symphonic music. After European concert successes, she founded schools of dancing in Germany, the USSR, and the United States. She was strangled by a scarf caught in a car wheel.

Dundee (pop. 177,700), major industrial center and seaport on the east coast of Scotland. An important trading center since the Middle Ages, Dundee developed the world's largest jute industry during the 1800's. When the jute industry declined, workers turned to light engineering industries.
See also: Scotland.

Dung beetle *see:* Scarab.

Dunham, Katherine (1910-), U.S. choreographer, dancer, and anthropologist known for her interpretations of Afro-Caribbean dance forms. She toured extensively with her own company and also worked as choreographer on Broadway musicals and motion pictures. She is the author of *Katherine Dunham's Journey to Accompong* (1946) and also wrote an autobiography and numerous articles.

Duniway, Abigail Jane Scott (1834-1915), suffragette whose efforts helped win voting rights for women in Idaho (1896), Washington (1910), and Oregon (1912). She published *The New Northwest,* a weekly newspaper devoted to demanding equal rights for women.
See also: Women's movements.

Dunkerque , or Dunkirk (pop. 73,100), seaport in northern France, on the English Channel, 10 mi (16 km) from Belgium. It is a shipbuilding, oil-refining, and food-processing center and railway terminus. In World War II some 1,000 vessels evacuated 337,000 trapped British and Allied troops from the town (May 27-June 4, 1940).
See also: France; World War II.

Dún Laoghaire, seaport town on the east coast of Ireland, 7 mi (11 km) southeast of Dublin. Dun Laoghaire was named in 1920 after an Irish king who lived in the 400s. Once a fishing village, it grew into a large residential town serving Dublin after the construction of a harbor was begun in 1817.
See also: Ireland.

Dunlap, William (1766-1839), U.S. dramatist. Dunlap wrote the first U.S. play based on native material, *Andre* (1798). He also adapted plays from French and German. His *History of the American Theatre* (1832) is the earliest historical record of the American stage. Also a painter, Dunlap was a founder of the National Academy of Design, a New York art institution.

John Foster Dulles

Dunmore, John Murray, 4th Earl of (1732-1809), British governor of New York (1770-1), Virginia (1771-6), and the Bahamas (1787-96). He launched Lord Dunmore's War (1774) against the Indians. Opposing the rebels, he 3 times dissolved the Virginia assembly (1772-4), but in 1776 an uprising forced him out of Virginia.

Dunning, John Ray (1907-75), U.S. physicist whose research on the discharge of neutrons from uranium fission contributed to the development of the atomic bomb. Using a *cyclotron,* Dunning produced high energy particles for changing one kind of atom into another.
See also: Physics.

Dunsany, Lord (1878-1957), Irish author and dramatist who created a credible fantasy world in such plays as *The Gods of the Mountain* (1911) and *A Night at an Inn* (1916). His more than 50 books include verse plays, novels, and memoirs.

Duns Scotus, John (1265?-1308?), Scottish philosopher and theologian. He joined the Franciscans in 1280, was ordained in 1291, and taught at Cambridge, Oxford, Paris, and Cologne. His system of thought, embodied chiefly in his commentary on Peter Lombard's *Sentences,* was adopted by the Franciscans and was highly influential. Typical of his scholasticism, and contrary to the thought of St. Thomas Aquinas, he asserted the primacy of love and the will

over reason. He was the first in the West to defend the Immaculate Conception.
See also: Scholasticism.

Duodenum, first part of the small intestine, extending from the pylorus valve of the stomach to the jejunum. The human duodenum is horseshoe-shaped and about 10 in (25 cm) long.
See also: Intestine.

Duplicator, any of various machines that make copies of two-dimensional materials from a master copy. Three of the most common duplicating machines are the spirit, the stencil, and the offset duplicator. As distinct from a photocopier, all three require the preparation of a master copy, a special form from which the copies are made.

Du Pont, U.S. industrial family of French origin. **Pierre Samuel du Pont de Nemours** (1739-1817), French economist and statesman, publicized the Physiocrats' doctrines. He was a reformist member of the Estates General (1789) and secretary general of the provisional government (1814). He fled to the United States in 1799 and, having returned to France in 1802, fled again in 1815. His son **Éleuthère Irénée du Pont** (1771-1834) established a gunpowder factory near Wilmington, Del., in 1802. The company expanded enormously during the Mexican, Crimean, and Civil wars under Éleuthère's son **Henry du Pont** (1812-89), who in 1872 organized the "Gunpowder Trust" that soon controlled 90% of explosives output. **Alfred Irénée du Pont** (1864-1935), **Thomas Coleman du Pont** (1863-1930), and **Pierre Samuel du Pont** (1870-1954) reorganized the firm in 1902, and after World War II it exploited the valuable dye-trust patents confiscated from Germany. Under Pierre's brothers **Irénée du Pont** (1876-1963) and **Lamont du Pont** (1880-1952) the firm built up an immensely powerful synthetic chemicals industry, developing rayon, cellophane, neoprene, nylon, and other materials.

Watercolor by Albrecht Dürer

Du Pont Company, one of the world's largest manufacturers and marketers of chemicals and chemical products. Founded in 1802 by Eleuthère Irénée du Pont, the company began by producing gunpowder; in 1880 it began to produce high explosives, and later expanded into applications of cellulose in lacquers, adhesives, and plastics. Since the early 20th century, Du Pont has expanded its list of products, of which there are now over 40,000. Du Pont manufactured plutonium during World War II, and since 1950 it has operated a plant in South Carolina for the Atomic Energy Commission. The company pioneered the development of such widely used synthetic fibers as Orlon acrylic and Dacron polyester, as well as Teflon, a utensil coating that prevents sticking.

Duralumin, any of a group of aluminum-copper alloys. Typically made of 95% aluminum, 4% copper, 0.5% magnesium, and 0.5% manganese, duralumin is widely used in the aircraft industry because of its lightness and hardness.
See also: Alloy.

Durand, Asher Brown (1796-1886), U.S. painter and engraver, a founder of the Hudson River School. He made his reputation by engraving John Trumbull's painting *The Signing of the Declaration of Independence.* He painted realistic landscapes and portraits, and also designed banknotes.
See also: Hudson River School.

Durant, William Crapo (1861-1947), U.S. automobile executive. He founded the General Motors Corporation in 1916 with the aid of Louis Chevrolet (1879-1941), but lost control of General Motors in 1920.

Durant, Will(iam James) (1885-1981), U.S. educator and popular historian. He wrote the lively bestseller *The Story of Philosophy* (1926) and, with his wife **Ariel** (1898-1981), the 11-volume *Story of Civilization* (1935-75).

Duras, Marguerite (1914-96), French writer, associated with the New Wave in France during the 1950s and 1960s. Her works include the novels *The Sea Wall* (1950) and *Moderato Cantabile* (1958), and the film scripts *Hiroshima Mon Amour* (1959) and *The Lover* (1984).

Durban (pop. 982,100), city in the Republic of South Africa, province of Natal. It is the third-largest city in southern Africa and South Africa's biggest seaport, providing a major outlet to the Indian Ocean, equipped with ship-repair yards and floating docks. Exports include coal, mineral ores, and agricultural products; imports include petroleum, grain, and timber. Durban's manufactures include fertilizers, textiles, and metalware, along with sugar and petroleum refining. Durban's beaches and parks and African and Indian markets have made it one of the country's leading tourist resorts, and it is also a cultural center.
See also: South Africa.

Dürer, Albrecht (1471-1528), German painter and engraver. He introduced the Italian Renaissance outlook and style to Germany, tempering it with the Gothic tradition. Dürer visited Venice (1494-95 and 1505-07) and was influenced by Jacopo Bellini, Andrea Mantegna, and Leonardo da Vinci. He became court painter to the emperors Maximilian I (1512) and Charles V (1520). Dürer produced a huge output of masterly, vividly detailed drawings, engravings, woodcuts, and paintings. His themes include religious subjects, plant and animal studies, and evocative landscapes in watercolor. His woodcuts include the 16 subjects of *The Apocalypse*; among his well-known engravings are *Death and the Devil* and *St. Jerome in His Cell*; his paintings include *Adam and Eve* and *Four Apostles.*
See also: Gothic art and architecture.

Durham (pop. 26,500), fortress town in northern England. A natural defensive site, Durham is located on a peninsula formed by an incised meander of the River Wear. The site was chosen by William I the Conqueror (r. 1066-87) as a bulwark against the Scots to the north. The peninsula was fortified by a wall early in the 12th century, and most of the wall has been preserved. Durham Cathedral was built (in the 11th and 12th centuries) on the site of a shrine to the 7th-century ecclesiastic St. Cuthbert. Many tourists visit Durham Cathedral and the Norman castle that houses the University of Durham.
See also: England.

Durham (pop. 136,611), city in north central North Carolina. By 1900 Durham was a major manufacturing center for the tobacco industry. The Duke family of Durham played a central role in the development of the tobacco industry. Durham became an educational center after James Buchanan Duke founded Duke University in 1924.
See also: North Carolina.

Durham, John George Lambton, 1st Earl of (1792-1840), British statesman. He authored Durham's Report, which laid down the basic principles of British colonial administration. A radical Whig, he was lord privy seal (1830-3) and helped draft the Reform Bill of 1832. Governor general of Canada (1838), he was criticized for his leniency toward rebels and resigned.

Durkheim, Émile (1858-1917), pioneer French sociologist. He advocated the synthesis of empirical research and abstract

theory in the social sciences and developed the concepts of "collective consciousness" and the "division of labor." His works include *The Rules of Sociological Method* (1895) and *Elementary Forms of Religious Life* (1912).
See also: Sociology.

Durocher, Leo (1905-), U.S. baseball player and manager. He began his major league career in 1925. A brilliant defensive shortstop, he played for the New York Yankees, St. Louis Cardinals, Cincinnati Reds, and Brooklyn Dodgers. He went on to manage the Brooklyn Dodgers and New York Giants, winning the world championship with those teams in 1941, 1951, and 1954, and became manager of the Chicago Cubs in 1966. Also known as "Leo the Lip," Durocher is famous for his colorful, argumentative personality and fiercely driving team spirit. He shocked the sports world with his motto, "Nice guys finish last."

Durrell, Lawrence George (1912-90), English novelist and poet, known for the lyricism and vitality of his style. His works include *The Alexandria Quartet—Justine* (1957), *Balthazar* (1958), *Mountolive* (1958), and *Clea* (1960)—and several volumes of poetry and travel literature.

Dürrenmatt, Friedrich (1921-90), Swiss playwright and novelist. His often bizarre tragicomedies, which employ biting satire, include *The Visit* (1956) and *The Physicists* (1962). He also wrote crime novels.

Duse, Eleonora (1859-1924), Italian dramatic actress, rivaling Sarah Bernhardt as the greatest actress of her period, notably in plays by Henrik Ibsen and by Duse's lover, Gabriele D'Annunzio.

Dushanbe (pop. 539,000), capital and largest city of the Tajik Soviet Socialist Republic in central Asia, USSR. Established in 1926 when 3 small villages merged, Dushanbe is an important transport junction and accounts for a third of the Tajik Republic's industrial output, which includes textiles, automatic looms, electric cable, and refrigerators.
See also: Tajikistan.

Düsseldorf (pop. 561,700), city in western Germany, 25 mi (40 km) northwest of Cologne. It is the capital of the state of North Rhine-Westphalia. Düsseldorf is an important Rhine River port, a road and railroad junction for the industrial Ruhr region, a West European air terminal, and a leading manufacturing and financial center. Iron and steel, chemicals, textiles, and machinery are among its main products. The city has study centers for medicine, metallurgy, and art.

Dust Bowl, area of some 50 million acres (20 million hectares) in the southern Great Plains region of the United States that, during the 1930s, suffered violent dust storms owing to accelerated soil erosion. Grassland had been plowed up in the 1920s and 1930s to plant wheat. A severe drought then bared the fields, and high winds blew the topsoil into huge dunes.

Dust storm, heavy winds carrying fine particles of earthy materials such as clay and silt for long distances. In the United States, a dust storm is declared when blowing dust reduces visibility below 5/8 mi (1 km). One of the factors causing soil erosion, dust storms occur where the ground has little vegetation to protect it.

Dutch, western Germanic language spoken in the Netherlands and (as Flemish) in North Belgium, as well as in Suriname and the Dutch Antilles. Afrikaans, spoken in South Africa, is derived from Dutch. Dutch evolved largely from the speech of the Franks, who settled in the Low Countries in the 4th-5th centuries. About 20 million people speak Dutch.

Dutch Antilles *see:* Netherlands Antilles.

Dutch East India Company, trading company chartered by the Netherlands States General in 1602 and given a monopoly on all Dutch trade east of the Cape of Good Hope and west of the Strait of Magellan. The company functioned almost as an independent state, conquering territory and competing with other colonial countries. It was dissolved in 1798, its possessions coming directly under the authority of the Dutch state.

Dutch East Indies *see:* Indonesia.

Dutch elm disease, severe fungal disease of the elm tree. First identified in Holland in 1919, it was observed in America in 1930, in an area close to New York City. It now afflicts trees nationwide. The fungus, carried by certain beetles, can kill a tree within four weeks. Cutting and burning affected trees is one way to control the spread of the disease; another is the use of fungicides. But there is no safe cure for dutch elm disease.

Dutch Guiana *see:* Suriname.

Dutchman's-breeches, perennial plant (*Dicentra cucullaria*) of the Fumariaceae family. Native to eastern and midwestern North America, it is most often found in woodland areas. The yellow-tipped white flowers, resembling pantaloons hanging upside down, inspired the plant's name.

Dutch West India Company, trading and colonizing company chartered by the Netherlands States General in 1621 to compete with Portuguese and Spanish colonies in North America and Africa. The company founded posts in the West Indies, Guiana, and parts of Brazil, as well as establishing the cities of Fort Orange (now Albany) and New Amsterdam (New York) in what is now New York State. The charter was dissolved in 1674.

Dutch West Indies *see:* Netherlands Antilles.

Duvalier, François (1907-71), president of Haiti (1957-71), nicknamed "Papa Doc." A physician turned politician, he was elected to power as a reformer but ruled as dictator, helped by a political police force, the Tonton Macoutes. He made himself president for life in 1964. After his death his son, Jean-Claude Duvalier ("Baby Doc"), succeeded him as dictator.
See also: Haiti.

Duvoisin, Roger Antoine (1904-80), Swiss-born U.S. author and illustrator of children's books. Duvoisin won the 1948 Caldecott Medal, a major U.S. award for children's book illustration for *White Snow, Bright Snow*, written by Alvin Tresselt. He wrote and illustrated the popular *Petunia* and *Veronica* series, and illustrated the series *Happy Lion*, written by his wife, Louise Fatio.

Dvina River, name of 2 rivers in the USSR. The Western Dvina or Daugava rises west of Moscow and flows 633 mi (1,019 km) east, to the Gulf of Riga in Latvia. The Northern Dvina flows 455 mi (732 km) northwest to the port of Archangel on the White Sea.

Dvorák, Antonín (1841-1904), Czech composer and violist. With composer Bedrich Smetana, he developed a Czech national style. His lyrical music began to win him acclaim in the 1870s. He spent 1892-95 in the United States, as director of the National Conservatory of Music, New York City. His works include 9 symphonies (including *From the New World*), 10 operas, concertos, the Slavonic dances and other orchestral compositions, choral works, and chamber music.

Dwarf, person with an underdeveloped skeleton caused by cartilage cells that fail to grow and divide properly. Chondrodystrophic dwarfism exists when certain cartilage cells are defective. Chromosome-related dwarfism occurs when all of the cells are defective. Hormonal dwarfism occurs when a hormone deficiency interferes with the growth of normal cartilage cells. Nonhormonal dwarfism results when disease or severely impaired nourishment blunts the normal growth of cartilage cells.

Dwarf star *see:* Star.

Dyak or Dayak, indigenous people of Sarawak, largest state in Malaysia on the island of Borneo. Living by fishing and hunting, the Dyak have been little affected by modern civilization. There are two groups: Iban, who live along the seacoast and rivers, and Land Dyak, who live inland and call themselves by the name of their village or locality. The Dyak live in longhouses and grow crops communally. They practice the religious cults of shamanism and animism.

Dye, chemical compound used to color material or food. Natural dye comes from plants, animals, and minerals. Since the

E

19th century, manufacturers have brought synthetic dyes into wide use. There are several kinds of synthetic dyes, as well as methods to get them to bond to fibers and materials.

Dylan, Bob (Robert Allen Zimmerman; 1941-), U.S. folksinger and composer. His distinctive blues style and lyrics were influenced by Woody Guthrie. His songs, at times sharply protesting social injustice, at times densely surreal and elusive, had a strong influence on popular music in the 1960s. He later turned to country and ballad music.
See also: Guthrie, Woody.

Bob Dylan in concert

Dynamite, high explosive invented by Alfred Nobel (1866), consisting of nitroglycerin absorbed in an inert material such as kieselguhr (a chalky earth) or wood pulp. Unlike nitroglycerin itself, it can be handled safely, and does not explode without a detonator. In modern dynamite sodium nitrate replaces about half the nitroglycerin. Gelatin dynamite, or gelignite, also contains some nitrocellulose.
See also: Explosive; Nobel, Alfred Bernhard; TNT.

Dysentery, group of diseases characterized by inflammation of the colon resulting in pain, spasm of the rectum, intense diarrhea, and the frequent passage of small amounts of mucus and blood, with symptoms of generalized poisoning of the body. Amoebic dysentery is caused by amoebas and treated with amoebicides. Bacillary dysentery is caused by bacteria and is treated with antibiotics.

Dyslexia, difficulty in learning to read when intelligence, vision, and available education are not limiting factors. The ophthalmologist W.P. Morgan described dyslexia in 1896 as "word blindness."
See also: Learning disabilities

Dyspepsia, or indigestion, abnormal visceral sensation in the upper abdomen or lower chest, often of a burning quality. Heartburn from esophagitis and pain of peptic (gastric or duodenal) ulcers are usual causes. Antacids and milk are used for relief.

Dysprosium, chemical element, symbol Dy; for physical constants see Periodic Table. Dysprosium, a metallic element, was discovered by Lecoq de Boisbaudran in 1886. The most important natural source of the element is the mineral monazite. It is a member of the lanthanide series of elements and is prepared by the reduction of the trifluoride with calcium metal. Ion-exchange and solvent extraction techniques have led to much easier isolation of the so-called "rare-earth" elements. Dysprosium and its compounds are used in nuclear control rods, laser materials, and as a source of infrared radiation, as well as special glasses and enamels.

Dystrophy, muscular *see:* Muscular dystrophy.

Verreaux's eagle soars over rocky areas in its East African habitat, searching for its prey. When a prey animal is located the eagle swoops down and grasps it between two powerful talons. Key:
A. Hunting range, consisting of isolated hyrax colonies.
B. Eagle swoops on its hyrax prey.
C. Toes 1 and 2 kill the prey with a powerful grip, while toes 3 and 4 provide balance.

E, fifth letter in the English alphabet. While it is the same letter as in the Greek and Latin alphabets, the ancient Phoenician letter from which it is derived was a smooth *h* sound, which it has retained in the Semitic alphabets. It is thought that the letter was originally a pictorial representation of a window or a fence. Pronounced variously in English, the most common uses are a short vowel as in *met*, a long vowel as in *feet*, or a silent *e* at the end as in *bite*. In musical terms, *E* represents the sound of *mi* in the scale of C.

$E=mc^2$, formula that relates mass (matter) and energy. Albert Einstein announced the formula in 1905, and it laid the basis for the application of nuclear energy. *E* stands for energy, *m* stands for mass, and *c* is a constant factor equal to the velocity of light. The formula states that large quantities of energy can result from tiny amounts of mass, if that mass is completely transformed into energy. In the 1930s scientists found a way to split the atoms of certain heavy elements into atoms of lighter elements. Reasoning that the lost mass turned into energy, they were able to use $E=mc^2$ to calculate the amount of mass changed into energy.
See also: Einstein, Albert.

Eagle, large bird of prey of the hawk family. Eagles have large eyes with extremely keen eyesight, hooked beaks for tearing their prey, and strong feet and talons (claws) for grabbing, killing, and carrying prey. Their size and noble attitude have led to their use in national and other emblems. The bald eagle (*Haliaetus teucocephalus*), named for its white head and neck, is the emblem of the United States of America, and the golden eagle was the emblem of the Roman legions. The largest eagles are the harpy eagle of South America and the Philippine eagle, whose wingspans reach 8 ft

(2.4 m). Eagles spend much of their time perching on trees or rocky crags or soaring at great heights. Eagles generally feed on small mammals and birds, usually caught by pouncing from a height. The golden and bald eagles also eat carrion, although the latter is mainly a fish eater. Sea eagles and African fish eagles are fish eaters, the snake and harrier eagles eat mainly reptiles, and the black eagles rob other birds of their eggs.

Eakins, Thomas (1844-1916), U.S. realist painter. Eakins studied in Philadelphia and abroad, and went on to teach at the Philadelphia Academy. His teaching influenced the painters William Glackens, Robert Henri, and John Sloan. Considered a master portraitist, his most famous portraits include *Walt Whitman, The Thinker,* and the group portraits *The Clinic of Dr. Gross* and *The Clinic of Dr. Agnew.* Eakins placed great emphasis on the study of anatomy and perspective. Among his most famous paintings of sporting events are *Max Schmitt in a Single Hull* and *Between Rounds.* Eakins, who was also a sculptor, helped develop photographic techniques for studying the human body in motion.

Eames, Charles (1907-78), U.S. designer who influenced contemporary furniture design. He created plywood and fiberglass form-fitting chairs and the upholstered "Eames chair."

Ear, organ of hearing and of balance. The ears convert the vibrations of air produced by sound into minute electrical impulses that can be sensed by the brain. They also contain a delicate and vital mechanism that enables the body to maintain its balance. In humans and many other higher animals, the visible part of the ear, or *auricle,* acts as a funnel for sound waves, directing them into the *auditory canal.* The auricle and the auditory canal together constitute the outer ear. The vibrations caused by sound waves first strike the eardrum, or *tympanum,* a membrane across the auditory canal that separates the outer ear from the middle ear. From the eardrum the vibrations are then transmitted to the 3 bones, or auditory ossicles, of the middle ear—the hammer (*malleus*), the anvil (*incus*), and the stirrup (*stapes*). These bones hinge on each other and act like a system of levers, transforming the relatively large but feeble vibrations of the eardrum into finer but much stronger vibrations of the same frequency. These enter the spiral-shaped *cochlea* of the inner ear via a small opening called the oval window. Within the fluid-filled cochlea the vibrations are converted into nerve signals and transmitted to the brain. Also within the inner ear are 3 semicircular canals and 2 saclike organs at the base where they meet. The canals are at right angles to each other. Two are vertical, one is horizontal, and they are filled with fluid. These organs send signals to the brain indicating the position and movement of the head. The signals are essential for keeping balance.

Earhart, Amelia (1898-1937), U.S. pioneer aviator. She was the first transatlantic woman passenger (1928) and the first solo transatlantic woman pilot (1932), and made the first solo flight from Hawaii to the U.S. mainland (1935). She disappeared over the Pacific Ocean during an around-the-world flight in 1937.
See also: Aviation.

Earl, Ralph (1751-1801), American portrait and landscape painter. His distinctively rugged portraits were influenced by John Singleton Copley. He is noted for his Revolutionary War battle scenes.

Early, Jubal Anderson (1816-94), Confederate general. In his famous advance on Washington, D.C. (1864), he cleared the Shenandoah Valley of Union forces. His army was subsequently forced to retreat and was defeated by Union troops under Philip Sheridan.
See also: Civil War, U.S,

Early human being *see:* Prehistoric people.

Earp, Wyatt Berry Stapp (1848-1929), U.S. frontier lawman and folk hero. He was deputy sheriff and U.S. marshal in several Kansas and Arizona "cow towns." He is most famous for taking part in the gunfight at O.K. Corral in Tombstone, Ariz. (1881).
See also: Western frontier life.

Ear shell *see:* Abalone.

Earth, only planet in the solar system on which the presence of living things is definitely known. It is the third planet outward from the sun, the fifth largest in the solar system. Together with its single moon, it travels around the sun at an average distance of 92,960,000 mi (149,600,100 km). The earth also spins on an axis that is tilted at 23.5° from a line perpendicular to its path around the sun. This spinning motion makes the sun appear to travel across the sky from east to west, and it also causes day and night. The tilt of the earth's axis and its movement around the sun causes the change of seasons. The moon affects the earth's path around the sun and, together with the sun, causes tides. According to the most recent estimate, the earth is 4.55 billion years old. The first signs of life on the planet are some fossilized bacteria found in rocks estimated to be 3.3 billion years old.
The earth consists of 3 main zones: the atmosphere; the hydrosphere, including all the bodies of water and ice on earth; and the lithosphere, the rocks that form the earth's crust, mantle, and core. The atmosphere provides the air for breathing, shields plants and animals from excess heat from the sun, and filters out the lethal shorter ultraviolet rays that would otherwise destroy life. The hydrosphere is also essential for life. Water and ice cover more than 70% of the earth's surface, making possible the hydrologic cycle by which water is evaporated from the oceans and precipitated as rain or snow, moistening the land and then returning to the oceans. Finally, the lithosphere makes up the land masses or continents, sea beds, and the inner mass of the planet. The earth's crust varies in thickness from between an average of 20 mi (32 km) under the continents to 5 mi (8 km) under the oceans. Beneath the crust, the distinct zone called the mantle is some 1,800 mi (2,900 km) thick. Within the mantle lies the earth's core, with a diameter of about 4,300 mi (6,900 km). Seismic data suggest that the core may consist of a solid center surrounded by a liquid outer core.
See also: Solar system.

Earthquake, vibration or series of vibrations in the earth's crust. Earthquakes are the result of sudden vertical or horizontal movements along faults, or fractures, in the earth's crust. Some faults, such as the 600-mi (966-km) San Andreas fault in California, can be seen on the earth's surface, but most of the faults associated with earthquakes are underground. Scientists have recently suggested that the origin of many earthquakes is linked with continental drift. Many earthquakes also occur under the oceans. Underwater earthquakes or earthquakes that occur near coastlines may cause destructive waves called *tsunamis,* which may travel vast distances at speeds approaching 500 mph (805 kmph).
Seismologists have studied earthquakes by recording the seismic waves that travel through the earth. Information from several seismographic stations makes it possible to locate the point of origin, or focus, of an earthquake, and also the epicenter, the point on the earth's surface directly above the focus. The most common and most destructive earthquakes are shallow-focus, that is, their focus lies within about 30 mi (48 km) beneath the epicenter. Intermediate and deep-focus earthquakes, which may occur as deep as 400 mi (644 km) below the surface, are less destructive. The magnitude of an earthquake is a measure of the strength of the seismic wave it generates. It is usually measured on the Richter scale, devised by U.S. seismologist C.F. Richter in 1935. The scale ranges from 0 to 8.4, with higher numbers signifying greater magnitude. The intensity of an earthquake is a measure of its effect in a particular area and varies with the distance from the epicenter. The Modified Mescalli scale, which ranges from 1 (not felt) to 12 (nearly total damage), is normally used. Although scientific knowledge about earthquakes has greatly increased, there is still no effective way of forecasting them.
See also: Seismology.

Earth science, study of the origin, development, and makeup of the planet earth. A broad field that includes geology, meteorology, oceanography, and physical geography, earth science focuses on the forces that have formed and altered the earth's surface.

Earthworm, name of a large number of common worms of the Lumbricidae family with simple tubular bodies made up of a series of rings. The body tapers toward the head end, where there is a mouth. Earth-

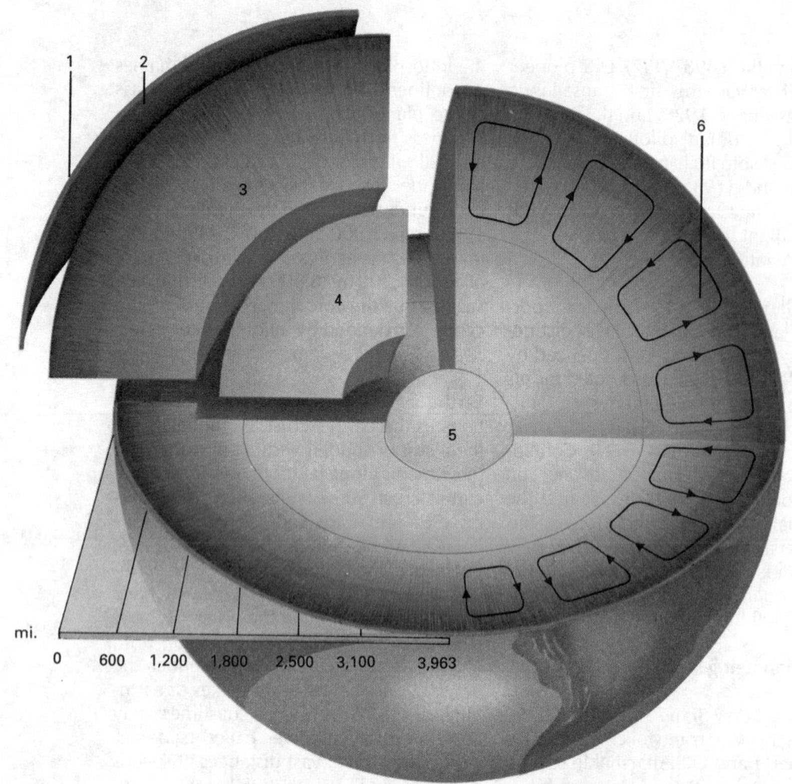

The Earth is composed of several distinct layers. The crust (1) is the top layer and ranges in thickness from 3 miles (5 km) to 25 miles (40 km). Under the crust is the Mohorovicic (Moho) discontinuity (2), which forms the base of the crust and occurs at an average depth of 20 miles (35 km). The Moho separates the crust from the mantle (3), which achieves a thickness of 1,800 miles (2,900 km) and dominates the composition of the Earth. The liquid outer core (4) is 1,400 miles thick (2,200 km) and the solid inner core (5) is 1,600 miles (2,500 km). Convection currents (6), perhaps created by the heat emanating from the liquid core, are responsible for the shifting sections, or plates, which in turn cause earthquakes, and the creation of new mountains.

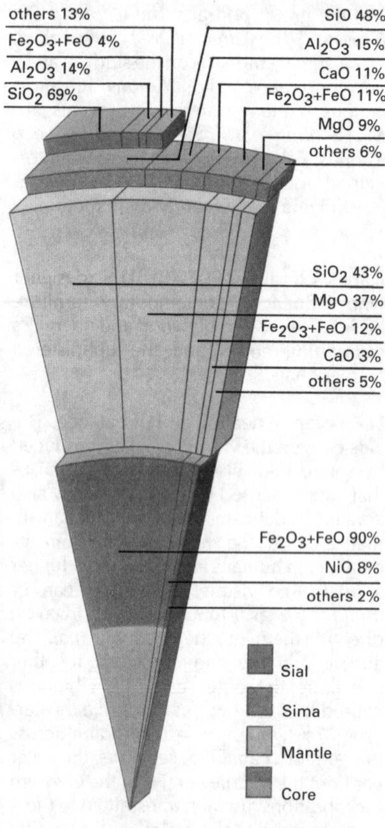

The chemical composition of the Earth changes from layer to layer. The continental crust is mostly granite, filled with silicon (Si) and aluminium (Al), while the oceanic crust is composed of silicon (Si) and magnesium (Mg). The mantle is mostly magnesium and iron silicates, while both cores are iron and nickel oxides.

The Earth as seen from outer space.

worms move by extending and contracting these rings, anchoring them by means of short bristles. They feed on plant material in the soil. Some species eject the indigestible remains on the surface as worm casts, thereby improving the soil. The population of earthworms in the soil varies widely, but in some grazing lands it may reach 5 million per acre. A few species climb trees and are found under bark. Each earthworm is both male and female but mates with another earthworm before laying eggs. These are deposited in a cocoon which is secreted by the *clitellum*, the broad band near the front of the worm. Size varies, with some species as small as 1/25 in (1 mm) long, and one Australian species growing to 11 ft (3 m).

Earwig, insect of the order Dermaptera distinguished by the pair of pincers at the tip of the abdomen. The short forewings act as covers for the membranous hindwings. Earwigs are nocturnal, hiding by day in crevices. They eat plant material, and the introduced European earwig is a pest in greenhouses in the United States. The female guards and cleans the eggs. The insect is named from the mistaken belief that it crawls into the ears of sleeping persons.

Easement, right of a property owner to use the adjacent property of another for a specified purpose. For instance, 2 homeowners may use a common driveway, half of which belongs to each. Each would then have an easement on the other's property "of necessity" in the law. The right of easement may be established through necessity, contract, or custom.

East *see:* Cold War.

East Berlin *see:* Berlin.

East China Sea *see:* China Sea.

Easter, chief festival of the Christian church year, celebrating the Resurrection of Jesus Christ, associated with spring and subsuming the Jewish Passover. Easter has been observed by the Western Church since the Council of Nicaea (325), on the Sunday after the first full moon following the vernal equinox. Easter is celebrated at a later date by the Eastern churches.

Easter Island, easternmost island of Polynesia in the South Pacific, about 2,000 mi (3,200 km) west of Chile, which annexed the island in 1888. This small, grassy, volcanic island features hundreds of colossal stone statues up to 40 ft (12 m) high, carved and raised on burial platforms, which have been the subject of much speculation by the explorer Thor Heyerdahl and others. Easter Island was discovered on Easter Sunday, 1722, by the Dutch admiral Jacob Roggeveen.

Easter lily, tall plant of the lily family bearing large, white, fragrant, trumpet-shaped flowers (especially *Lilium longiflorum*). Grown and cultivated throughout the world, the Easter lily has become a symbol of Easter.

Eastern Hemisphere *see:* Hemisphere.

Eastern Orthodox Church, one of the 2 major branches of the Christian Church. From the apostolic age a natural distinction arose between the Greek-speaking church of the eastern Roman empire and the Latin-speaking church of the west. The Eastern Church developed its own liturgical traditions. It became a family of orthodox churches, finally breaking with Rome in the Great Schism of 1054.
See also: Christianity.

Eastern question, international political problems raised in the 19th century by the decline of the Ottoman Empire. The ambitions of Russia, Austria-Hungary, Britain, and France in the East Mediterranean led to the Crimean War (1854-56) and Balkan Wars (1912-13) and were partly responsible for the outbreak of World War I.

Eastern Star, organization associated with the men's fraternal society of the Masons. With 3 million members (chiefly women) throughout the world, Eastern Star supports charitable projects and sponsors social activities. There are several groups of Eastern Star, among which the General Grand Chapter is the largest, comprising 56 grand chapters in the United States. The title of the woman who is the executive officer of the General Grand Chapter is Most Worthy Grand Matron.
See also: Masonry.

Easter Rebellion, rebellion in Dublin, Ireland, in April 1916, in an attempt to secure Irish independence from Britain. Led by Patrick Pearse of the Irish Republican Brotherhood and James Connolly of the Sinn Fein nationalist movement, the rebellion began on Easter Monday. It grew out of a long opposition to British rule in Ireland. The rebels, who called themselves the Irish Republican Army (IRA), were about 1,000 strong. They seized the Dublin General Post Office and other public buildings. There was serious street fighting and loss of life; British forces quickly suppressed the rebellion, and Pearse and Connolly were executed, along with a number of other leaders. With nationalist feelings strengthened by this episode, the rebels continued to carry on guerrilla warfare throughout the 20th century, including the assassination of General Montgomery.
See also: Irish Republican Army; Sinn Fein.

East Germany *see:* Germany.

East India Company, name of several private trading companies chartered by 17th-century European governments to develop trade in the Eastern Hemisphere, after the discovery of a sea route to India. They competed for commercial supremacy and eventually aided European colonial expansion.

East Indies, formerly Dutch East Indies, now Indonesia. Modern usage confines the term to the Malay Archipelago. It is the largest island group in the world.
See also: Indonesia.

Eastland, James Oliver (1904-86), Democratic U.S. senator who served from 1943 to 1979. Eastland served in the Mississippi House of Representatives from 1928 to 1932. As chairman of the Senate's powerful Judiciary Committee from 1956 to 1979, Eastland supported internal security measures and opposed civil rights bills. Against his opposition, Congress passed a series of civil rights bills promoting racial integration in the 1960s.

Eastman, George (1854-1932), U.S. inventor. Eastman invented the dry-plate photographic process in 1880 and shortly thereafter established one of the first factories for the production of photographic supplies. In 1884 he perfected a flexible paperbacked roll film, and 4 years later he brought out the small Kodak camera. In 1892 he founded the Eastman Kodak Co., a pioneer in mass production. He amassed an enormous fortune, most of which he gave away. He committed suicide in 1932.
See also: Photography.

Eastman, Max Forrester (1883-1969), U.S. poet and influential critic. His *Enjoyment of Poetry* (1913) proved a popular intro-

Easter Island was named by the Dutch seafarer Jacob Roggeveen (1722). It is famous for its gigantic stone figures.

George Eastman

duction to the subject. A Marxist, Eastman edited the left-wing journals *The Masses* (1911) and *The Liberator* (1918), but later rejected communism. His collected verse appeared in *Poems of Five Decades* (1954).

East Pakistan *see:* Bangladesh.

East River, strait connecting Long Island Sound and Upper New York Bay. The East River is joined with the Hudson River by the Harlem River and Spuyten Duyvil Creek. The 16-mi (26-km) East River separates the boroughs of Brooklyn and Queens from Manhattan and also separates Queens from the Bronx. Seven bridges cross over the East River, and 11 tunnels pass under it.

East Roman Empire *see:* Byzantine Empire; Rome, Ancient.

Eaton, Theophilus (1590-1658), founder of New Haven colony. As one of the original patentees of Massachusetts Bay Company, the Puritan Eaton led 250 colonists from England to Boston in 1637. Seeking to escape the controversy over Anne Hutchinson and also looking for a good harbor, Eaton and his friends settled in New Haven in 1638. They purchased land from the Native Americans, and created a church and court. Eaton served as governor of New Haven from 1639 until his death.
See also: Puritans.

EBCDIC, in computer technology, acronym for Extended Binary Coded Decimal Interchange Code. The 8-bit code is used to encode specific character sets. Based on the original punched card code, it encodes essentially the same characters as ASCII, but in a different numerical order.

Eberhart, Richard (1904-), U.S. poet and founder of the Poet's Theatre, Cambridge, Mass. Eberhart published his first book of poems, *A Bravery of Earth*, in 1930. His poetry makes use of the surprise effects of mixed abstractions and outcry, rough meters, inverted word orders, and sudden, striking lyricism. Eberhart served as Poetry Consultant and Honorary Consultant in American Letters to the Library of Congress. He won the Bollingen Prize in poetry in 1962, the Pulitzer Prize in 1966 for his *Selected Poems (1930-1965)*, and the National Book Award in 1977 for *Collected Poems, 1930-1976*.

Ebony, hard, heavy heartwood of several trees (family Ebonaceae, genus *Diospuros*) native to equatorial Africa, southern Asia, and North and South America. Ebony can be highly polished and is used for small statues, cabinet work, golf clubs, and the black keys of pianos. The genus also includes persimmon trees.

EB virus *see:* Epstein-Barr (EB) virus.

Ecclesiastes, 21st book of the Old Testament. It consists of about 40 aphorisms, including the famous phrase, "vanity of vanities, all is vanity." Pessimistic in tone, Ecclesiastes opposes the view that virtue is always rewarded and sin punished. Nevertheless, it exhorts people to fear God and keep his commandments, even without hope of reward in this or future life. It has traditionally been attributed to the Hebrew King Solomon, but was probably written as late as the 2nd or 3rd century B.C.
See also: Bible; Old Testament.

ECG *see:* Electrocardiogram.

Echeverria, Luis (1922-), Mexican political leader. After holding several political and academic posts, he was president of Mexico (1970-75). Rapid population growth in cities, inflation, and unemployment burdened his administration.

Echidna, or spiny anteater (*Tachyglossus aculeatus*), nocturnal hedgehog-like animal of Australia, Tasmania, and New Guinea. Like the platypus, it is an egg-laying mammal, or *monotreme*. It has fur as well as spines and uses its beaklike snout to root out termites, which it licks up with a long tongue. A single egg is laid into a pouch, in which the young echidna hatches and is fed on milk from "milk patches" that open into the pouch from the mother's body. The young echidna is later placed in a burrow, where it is visited by its mother for feeding.

Echinoderm, member of a large group, or *phylum*, of marine invertebrates with an external skeleton of plates just under the skin. Some live fixed on the ocean floor; others move slowly by means of arrays of tube-feet. Many classes of echinoderms are extinct, but 5 are still in existence and are very abundant: Crinoidea (sea lilies and feather stars), Asteroidea (starfishes), Ophiuroidea (brittle stars), Echinoidea (sea urchins and sand dollars), and Holothuroidea (sea cucumbers).

Echo, in Greek mythology, mountain nymph who helped Zeus carry on his affairs by distracting Hera with her endless chatter. She was punished by being able to speak only when spoken to. Later she fell in love with Narcissus, and when her love was not returned, she faded away to a mere voice.

Echo, sound reflected or reverberated from a distant surface, with at least a 0.1-sec time lag, allowing the reflection to be distinct from the original sound; or, in computer technology, a character received from the keyboard and fed back to the printer or cathode ray tube for display.

Eck, Johann (1486-1543), German scholar and theologian. Though advocating church reform, he was a bitter opponent of Martin Luther and the Reformation. He openly disputed with Luther at Liepzig in 1519, influenced the 1520 papal bull against Luther, and presented the Roman Catholic case at the Diet of Augsburg (1530).
See also: Luther, Martin; Reformation.

Eckhart, Meister (Johannes Eckhart; 1260?-1328?), German theologian and preacher. He taught that to unite with God, one must conquer basic human nature and withdraw from sin. Then, a divine spark within one's soul can form a mystical bond with God. In 1329 Pope John XXII condemned many of Eckhart's ideas as heresy.
See also: Theology.

Eclampsia *see:* Toxemia of pregnancy.

Eclipse, blocking off of light from the Sun from one celestial body by another. An eclipse of the Moon (lunar eclipse) occurs when the Moon enters the shadow of the Earth. An eclipse of the Sun (solar eclipse) occurs when the Earth enters the shadow of the Moon. Other planets can also eclipse their own moons, and in the case of a double star, one star can eclipse the other. There are usually 2 or 3 lunar eclipses each year. Shadows have a central dark part

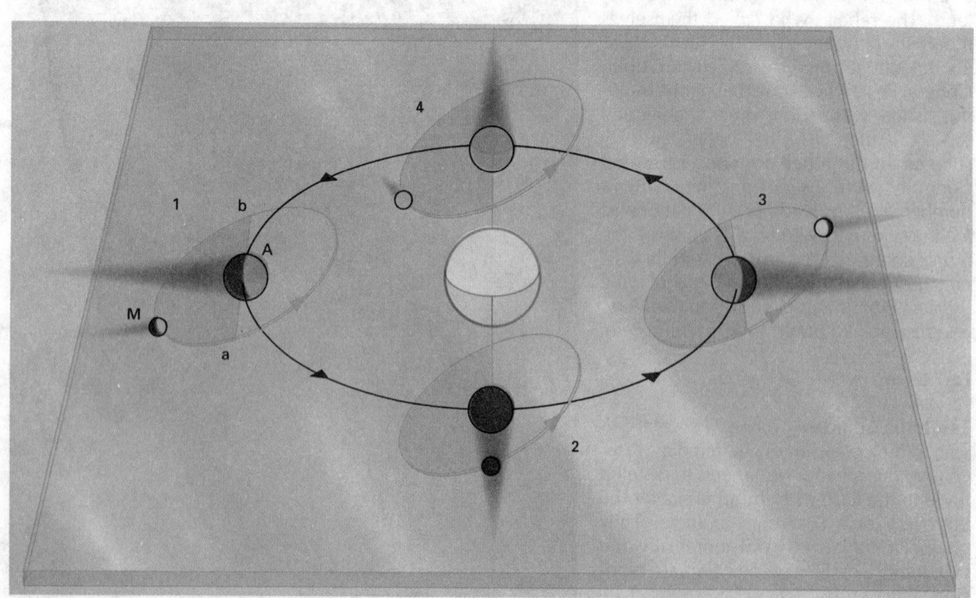

An eclipse can only occur when there is full Moon. That is when the Earth (A) is standing opposite the Sun. If the orbit of the Moon (M) would lie on the same level as the orbit of the Earth, there would be an eclipse every full Moon. But the orbit of the Moon is titled 5° up (1) or under (3) the orbit of the Earth. Only when the Moon is exactly on the intersection-curve (a-b) of both orbit levels, an eclipse occurs (2). At that moment, the intersection curve is pointing to the Sun. Six months later that is also the case (4), but there is no full Moon then. About 3 times every 2 years, both conditions make the occurence of an eclipse possible.

called the *umbra,* and a less dark outer region called the *penumbra.* In the penumbra of the Earth's shadow, part of the light from the Sun is cut off from the Moon. In the umbra, all the Sun's light is cut off. Since the Earth's umbra is much wider than the diameter of the Moon, a total lunar eclipse can last up to 1 3/4 hours from the time the Moon first enters the umbra at one side to the time it moves out again at the opposite edge of the shadow. More often, the Moon moves through only part of the Earth's umbra, and the eclipse is somewhat shorter. The umbra of the Moon's shadow on the Earth is never wider than 170 mi (274 km), and the maximum diameter of the penumbra is 4,000 mi (6,437 km). Inside the umbra there is a total eclipse of the Sun, which can never last longer than 7 min and is usually less than half this duration. In the penumbra a partial eclipse is visible. Because of the Moon's motion, the track of a solar eclipse sweeps across the surface of the Earth at over 1,000 mph (1,600 kmph). An *annular* or ring eclipse occurs when the Moon is at its farthest from Earth. At this distance it is not big enough in appearance to completely obscure the Sun, and a ring of light remains surrounding the shadow. Eclipses of the Sun, particularly total eclipses, have provided a lot of information about the outer layers of the Sun (the *corona* and the *chromosphere*), and about the Earth's upper atmosphere.

Ecliptic, in astronomy, the plane, passing through the center of the sun, that contains the orbit of the earth. All the planets orbit the sun in approximately the same plane, so that they are always seen near the ecliptic.
See also: Astronomy.

École des Beaux-Arts (École Nationale Supérieure Des Beaux-Arts), school of design and architecture established in Paris in 1648. In the early 1900s it influenced architecture in the United States and elsewhere by promoting ancient Greek and Roman models. The school today offers courses in architecture, drawing, engraving, lithography, mosaics, and sculpture to students entering after a highly competitive enrollment procedure.

Ecology, study of the relationships between living organisms and their environment. The earth is covered from pole to pole with a thin, intricate web of interdependent living organisms called the *biosphere.* Within the biosphere there are many clearly defined subunits, or *ecosystems.* Ecosystems (for example, ponds, forests, fields of grass, deserts, or oceans) vary greatly in size, but in each case the animals and plants within them have a pattern of feeding relationships called a food chain or web. The ultimate foundation of the food chain is plant life and the process of photosynthesis, by which energy from the sun is converted to organic material. Within an ecosystem, every species occupies a distinct ecological niche. The nature of the niche is determined by the space required by the species to survive, and the nature and availability of its food. Over a period of time, the numbers and types of animals and plants in the system change. This change is actually a process of succession and is accompanied by continually increasing complexity. The process begins with an elementary ecosystem and culminates in what is called a climax community, an ecosystem capable of supporting an enormous number of species. Climax communities, such as tundra, forests, or deserts, are stable until humans or natural geological upheaval destroys them, thereby starting an entirely different ecosystem. The growth and stability of ecosystems depend entirely on the cycles that expand and renew the chemicals that are essential to life. Among the most common of these are the carbon and nitrogen cycles and photosynthesis. Any serious or prolonged disturbance of these vital cycles threatens the existence of an ecosystem and of the species it contains. The environment, left to itself, can continue to support life for millions of years. The single most unstable and potentially disruptive element in the scheme is the human species. Human beings with modern technology have the capacity to bring about, intentionally or unintentionally, far-reaching and irreversible change. In addition to studying nature, ecology also considers the effects upon the environment and particular ecosystems of various human activities. The body of knowledge and insights unique to ecology are not only significant in their own right, but are also important in the development of environmentalism.

Econometrics, branch of economics that uses statistical methods to describe economic phenomena and thus discover how they affect each other. Econometrics came into use during the 1930s when many governments wanted to obtain empirical information to solve the problems of the Depression. Econometricians are concerned primarily with the construction of mathematical models of the economy in order to test them against reality. Such a model is basically a system of national accounts that record, from empirical data, the flow of goods and services among the various sectors of the economy.

Economic determinism, theory, first fully developed by Karl Marx in the mid-1800s, that a society's basis is determined by its economic structure. Fundamental changes in a society are produced not by educational or religious theories, but by alterations in that society's ability to manufacture and distribute goods. The ruling class of a society is that which controls material production. Only by changing its influence on the economic system is a class able to gain strength in the political system of a society.
See also: Marx, Karl.

Economics, study of how goods and services are produced and how they are distributed. Resources are scarce or limited and not all needs can be met. Economics is concerned with how to distribute scarce resources in the most efficient, equitable way. Macroeconomics is the study of an entire economic system. Microeconomics deals with economic activity in the individual case.

Ecosystem *see:* Ecology.

Ectoplasm, in biology, outer portion of the cytoplasm of a cell; in spiritualism, glowing substance that resembles the face or hand of a dead person, through which communication with the dead is possible.
See also: Biology.

Ecuador, republic in northwestern South America. It lies south of Colombia, west and north of Peru, and east of the Pacific Ocean. Its territory includes the Galapagos Islands, 650 mi (1,046 km) off the Ecuadorian coast. The country takes its name from the equator (Spanish, *ecuador*), which runs through the north. The capital is Quito and the country's largest city and main trading center is Guayaquil.
Land and climate. Ecuador is dominated by 2 chains of the Andes traversing the center of the country from north to south. These ranges contain some of the highest peaks in South America and many volcanoes. The area is also subject to disastrous earthquakes. Between the 2 Andean chains lies a string of 10 high plateaus or basins some 7,000-9,000 ft (2,100-2,700 m) above sea level. The area is the most densely populated in the country. Ecuador's ports are situated on the coastal lowlands to the west. Lowlands in the east are covered with equatorial forests and are sparsely populated. The climate of both the

Ecuador's coarse grasslands on the Sierra support flocks of sheep, tended by herdsmen. Livestock on the Sierra totals about a million sheep and a similar number of cattle, which provide much of the meat for the people living in the towns of the region.

Ecuador

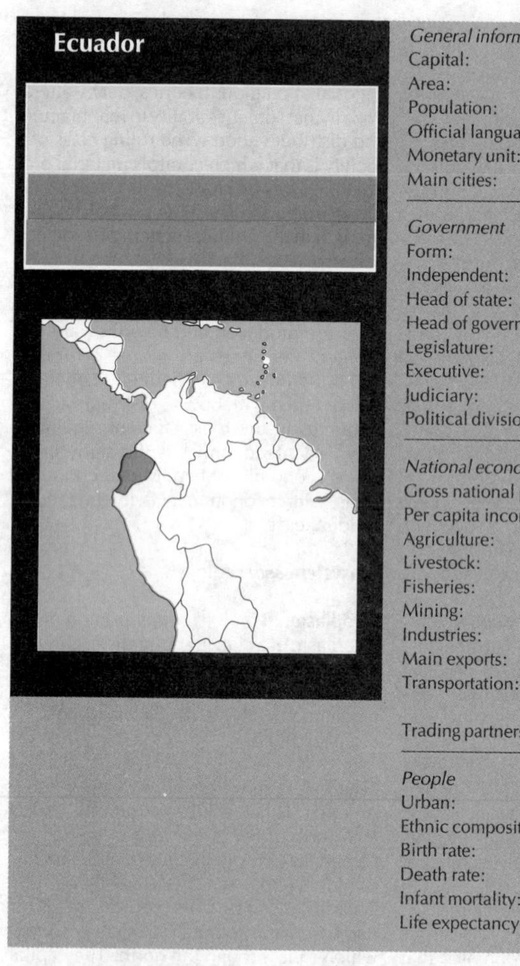

General information	
Capital:	Quito
Area:	104,506 sq mi (270,670 sq km)
Population:	10,490,000
Official language:	Spanish
Monetary unit:	1 Sucre = 100 centavos
Main cities:	Guayaquil, Quito, Cuenca
Government	
Form:	republic
Independent:	1830
Head of state:	President (elected every 4 years)
Head of government:	President
Legislature:	one legislative house (National Congress)
Executive:	President and Cabinet
Judiciary:	highest court is the Supreme Court
Political division:	19 provinces, 1 island territory, 3 regions
National economy	
Gross national product:	U.S. $10,920,000,000
Per capita income:	U.S. $1,080
Agriculture:	sugarcane, bananas, plantains, rice, corn, potatoes, cacao, coffee
Livestock:	cattle, sheep, pigs
Fisheries:	679,000 metric tons
Mining:	petroleum, zinc, copper, silver, gold
Industries:	petroleum products, food products, textiles and clothing, cement
Main exports:	petroleum, bananas, coffee, seafood
Transportation:	600 mi (965 km) of railroads; 22,487 mi (36,187 km) of roads; 2 international airports
Trading partners:	United States, Japan, Germany, Venezuela, Brazil
People	
Urban:	54%
Ethnic composition:	Quechua 50%, mestizo 40%, European 8.5%
Birth rate:	35.4 per 1,000 population
Death rate:	7.6 per 1,000 population
Infant mortality:	63 per 1,000 live births
Life expectancy:	male 60 years, female 63.5 years

eastern and western lowlands is equatorial, with heavy rainfalls in the east. The Andean areas have a more temperate climate that varies with the altitude.

People. Though the official language is Spanish, Quechua or Jarvo and other Native American dialects are also spoken. The majority of the people are Roman Catholic.

Economy. Agriculture was the basis of Ecuador's economy until 1972, when exploitation of petroleum began. Ecuador is now a leading producer of oil in Latin America. Exports also include bananas, coffee, cocoa, and fish products. Economic growth in the 1980s led to industrial development in textiles, food processing, cement, and pharmaceuticals.

History. Following the conquest of the Incas by Pizarro in 1533, Ecuador became part of the Spanish Empire. Liberated from Spain in 1822, it has been an independent republic since 1830, but has always suffered from political instability marked by conflict among the conservative landed bourgeoisie of the Andean region and the Roman Catholic Church, the liberal mercantile interests centered in Guayaquil, and, more recently, the urban working classes. Military coups have been endemic—the most recent successful one in January 1976. A civilian government was installed in 1979 under a new constitution providing for an elected executive and legislature and, to date, has proven to be stable.

Ecumenical council, general council of the leaders of the entire Christian Church. The first was at Nicaea (325) and there have been 20 since; the most recent being the Second Vatican Council (1962-65). Roman Catholics recognize all 21 councils; the Orthodox Church recognizes only the first 7 councils.
See also: Christianity.

Ecumenical movement, modern movement among the Christian churches to encourage greater cooperation and eventual unity. Organizations such as the International Missionary Council and the Life and Work and the Faith and Order conferences studied the churches' doctrinal differences. But substantial progress was not made until 1948, when representatives of 147 world churches agreed to form the World Council of Churches. Most Protestant Orthodox churches have since joined the council, and the Roman Catholic Church, though not a member, participates in some joint studies.
See also: Christianity.

Eczema, collective term for many inflammatory noncontagious conditions of the skin. The term *dermatitis,* often used incorrectly as a synonym for eczema, means any inflammation of the skin. Eczema causes one or more of the following physical changes to the skin: erythema (blood congestion), infiltration of plasma into the tissues, vesicles (blisters), and papules (pimples). Secondary changes include erosion of tissue, exudation of fluid onto the skin, crusts, lichenification (thickened areas of itchy skin), and scaling.

Edda, name for 2 Icelandic collections about the exploits of heroes and gods: *Saemund's Edda,* or the *Poetic Edda,* and *Snorri's Edda,* or the *Prose Edda.* The Prose Edda was compiled by Snorri Sturluson (1179-1241) as a handbook for the numerous allusions to mythology in poetry. The Poetic Edda, named by the Icelandic Bishop Brynjólf Sveinsson, who discovered the 13th-century manuscript in 1643, is a heterogeneous collection of poems celebrating the old heroes and gods, probably dating in part from the 9th century. Eddic poetry is generally written in short, rhythmical lines.

Eddington, Sir Arthur Stanley (1882-1944), English astronomer and physicist. He conducted significant research on the interiors of stars—how they transmit light and heat and how the mass of a star is related to its luminosity. Eddington supported the theory of relativity early on when he found that light rays are bent in a gravitational field. He wrote *The Internal Constitution of the Stars* (1926) and *The Expanding Universe* (1933).
See also: Astronomy; Star.

Eddy, Mary Baker (1821-1910), U.S. founder of Christian Science. As a young woman she suffered from ill health and unhappiness and came to believe that the cure for her condition must be spiritual. In 1866, having been seriously injured in a fall, she made a sudden and unexpected recovery that she attributed to the illumination given her by the Bible. In the next few years she developed her discovery, and in 1875 she published *Science and Health with Key to the Scriptures.* In 1877 she married Dr. Asa Gilbert Eddy, one of her earliest followers, and 2 years later she organized the First Church of Christ, Scientist, in Boston. She also founded the newspaper *The Christian Science Monitor.*
See also: Churches of Christ.

Edelweiss, small flowering herb (genus *Leontopodium*) that grows high in the mountains of the European Alps, Asia, and South America. It is the national flower of Switzerland. The name means "noble white," referring to the plant's clusters of white flowers, a symbol of purity.

Edema, or dropsy, swelling of bodily tissues due to the accumulation of fluid. It most commonly affects the lower parts of the body, such as the ankles and lower part of the abdomen. Edema is generally the sign of a serious disease. A failing heart may cause edema because it cannot pump blood fast enough to carry away body fluids efficiently. Edema may be a sign of liver or kidney disease or of preeclampsia (toxemia that may occur late in pregnancy). The potbellies of starving children are also cases of edema. The basic cause of the edema must be removed to cure it, but the physician may also prescribe diuretic drugs to rid the body of excess water.

Eden, Garden of, in the Old Testament (Genesis), the first habitation of humans. Eden was created for Adam and Eve. It is described as being watered by the Euphrates, the Tigris, and 2 lesser-known streams, the Gihon and the Pishon, thus its location was probably in ancient Mesopotamia (modern Iraq). However, it is more important as a symbol of a natural state of perfection before sin. Its name is often synonymous with paradise.
See also: Bible; Old Testament.

Eden, Robert Anthony, Earl of Avon (1897-1977), British diplomat and prime minister. Eden became foreign secretary in 1935 but resigned in 1938 in protest against Prime Minister Neville Chamberlain's appeasement of the Axis dictators Adolf Hitler and Benito Mussolini. He served again in the foreign office 1940-45 and 1951-55. As prime minister (1955-57) he promoted an ill-advised invasion of Egypt (1956) to restore Anglo-French control of the Suez Canal after the Egyptians had nationalized it. He resigned the next year because of ill health.

Edentate, member of an order of mammals (*Edentata*) that have no teeth or only primitive, rootless teeth without enamel. Sloths, anteaters, and armadillos are the only members of the group. They are found mainly in tropical and subtropical climates.

Ederle, Gertrude Caroline (1906-), U.S. swimmer, the first woman to swim the English Channel. She broke all previous records, crossing the 35 mi (56.3 km) from France to England on Aug. 6, 1926, in 14 hr 39 min.

Edgerton, Harold Eugene (1903-1990), U.S. electrical engineer. He revolutionized photography with the invention of the electronic or stroboscopic flash. This light flashes at a fraction of a second's duration, enabling photographs to be taken of an object moving at high speed. Night aerial and oceanographic depth photography were made possible by Edgerton's invention.
See also: Photography.

Edgeworth, Maria (1767-1849), Anglo-Irish novelist. Her gifts for social observation and colorful, realistic portrayal of Irish domestic life and youth influenced later novelists including Sir Walter Scott. Among her works are *Tales of Fashionable Life* (1809-12).

Edinburgh (pop. 439,700), capital of Scotland since 1437 and the nation's second-largest city. The city is in southeastern Scotland south of the Firth of Forth and north of the Pentland Hills. Edinburgh Castle, crowning Castle Hill (the neck of an extinct volcano), dominates the city and separates the so-called Old Town (dating from the 11th century) to the east from the New Town (planned in 1767) to the north. The wide thoroughfare of Princess Street in the New Town is one of Europe's best-known streets. Other landmarks include the nearby extinct volcano called Arthur's Seat and many fine parks and gardens. Edinburgh has long been famous as a center of Scottish culture. Its university dates from 1583, and famous figures including James Boswell and Sir Walter Scott had links with the city. Edinburgh is known for public art galleries and, since 1947, its annual international arts festival. The city is also a leading government, banking, and insurance center. Its industries include brewing, distilling, printing, publishing, and electrical and chemical engineering.

Edirne (pop. 86,900), formerly Adrianople, ancient city in northwest Turkey near the Greek and Bulgarian borders where the Maritsa, Arda, and Tunca rivers converge. It is a regional trade and agricultural center producing *peynir* (white cheese), cotton, and grains. The architect Sinan built its Selimiye Mosque in the 1500s. Originally called Uskudama, it was renamed Hadrianopolis (C.A.D. 125) by the Roman emperor Hadrian, became the Ottoman Empire capital (1413-58), and was occupied by Russians, Bulgarians, and Greeks before being restored to Turkey (1922).
See also: Turkey.

The first incandescent commercial lamp, provided with a wooden base and two clamps to fasten the electric wires.

Edison, Thomas Alva (1847-1931), U.S. inventor, the "Wizard of Menlo Park." The *New York Times* calculated when he died that the total value of commercial enterprises derived from his inventions was $25,683,544,343, thus crediting his brain with the highest cash value of all time. Edison had only 3 months of formal schooling; his teacher said he was "addled." He received the rest of his education from his mother. From 16 to 21 he roamed the United States and Canada as an itinerant telegraph operator. Arriving in New York penniless, he borrowed a dollar, found work with a company controlling stock-ticker apparatus, invented an improved ticker system, and sold it for $40,000. He opened a small factory to produce the device and continued inventing. In 1876 Edison moved to Menlo Park, N.J., where he set up the world's first industrial research laboratory. There he developed a carbon transmitter for the new but impractical Bell telephone, and sold it for $100,000. Further experimentation produced the phonograph (1877). Edison then turned to the problem of electric lighting, creating the filament and vacuum bulb that enabled an incandescent light to be steadily maintained (Dec. 31, 1879). His company, the Edison Machine Works, a forerunner of the giant modern utilities, was moved in 1886 to Schenectady, N.Y., which then became a major technological and manufacturing center. Edison moved his laboratories the following year to West Orange, N.J. His

Thomas Alva Edison

next great invention was the kinetoscope, or motion picture viewer. He also experimented with the concept of talking pictures. Among his many productions were a kiln for Portland cement, a synthetic substitute for carbolic acid, and a high-efficiency automobile battery. He also established the first electric power station at Pearl Street in New York City. His best-known remark was that genius is "1 percent inspiration and 99 percent perspiration."

Edmonds, Sarah Emma Evelyn (1841-98), Civil War soldier who used the name Frank Thompson and a male disguise to serve as nurse, messenger, and spy for the Union Army, 1861-63. In 1865 she authored *Nurse and Spy in the Union Army,* a fictionalized account of her experiences. After petitioning Congress she was granted a veteran's pension (1884), and became the only woman member of the Grand Army of the Republic (1897), a Union Army veterans' organization.
See also: Civil War, U.S.

Edmonds, Walter Dumaux (1903-), U.S. writer of historical fiction. His novels, which focus on the area of upstate New York, include *Drums Along the Mohawk* (1936) and *Chad Hanna* (1940). For his book *Bert Green's Barn* (1975), he won the 1976 National Book Award for children's literature.

Edmonton (pop. 574,000), capital of the Canadian province of Alberta, situated on the North Saskatchewan River. Edmonton was founded in 1795 by the Hudson's Bay Company on the traditional boundary between Cree and Blackfoot territories. A railroad link with Calgary, completed in 1891, helped the town to develop as a supply center and starting point for the Klondike gold rush (1898) and as a market town for farmers settling the rich surrounding agricultural region. The city is the leading transportation and marketing center for northern Alberta and is served by transcontinental railroads, the Alaska Highway, and a major airport. It is a leading oil-refining center, using the by-products in chemicals and plastics, and also produces building materials and agricultural products. Edmonton is also a cultural center, with the University of Alberta (founded 1906), a symphony orchestra, and 2 museums. Elk Island National Park lies east of the city. Industrialization has been rapid since the local discovery of oil in 1947.
See also: Alberta.

Learning the Koran means learning to read, and often, to write as well. Traditionally this education is available only for boys.

Edom, ancient kingdom in what is now southern Jordan, between the Dead Sea and Gulf of Aqaba. Edomites, who were, according to the Old Testament, descendants of Esau, occupied the area around the 13th century B.C. and had frequent conflicts with Hebrews. Between 1200 and 700 B.C. Edom prospered because of its strategic trade route location and copper industry. Between 500 and 400 B.C. Edom was invaded by the Nabateans, an Arab people, and Edomites migrated to southern Judaea, where they established the territory of Idumea.

EDP, in computer technology, acronym for Electronic Data Processing, data processing performed largely by electronic digital computers.

Education, the process of establishing habits of critical and independent appraisal of information for the purpose of intellectually developing the whole person. Socrates held that the beginning of real learning was the realization that we do not know. Education can take place formally in schools with teachers, students, courses, books and activities. It can also take place informally in homes, streets, or meeting places when ideas and information are exchanged.

Education, U.S. Department of, cabinet-level department established Sept. 27, 1979 as part of President Jimmy Carter's plan to reorganize the federal government. With an initial budget of $14.1 billion and some 17,400 employees, it was created when the Department of Health, Education and Welfare was split into the Department of Health and Human Services and the Department of Education.

Education, vocational *see:* Vocational education.

Education Association, National *see:* National Educational Association of the United States.

Educational measurement *see:* Testing.

Educational psychology, application of psychology to education, especially to problems of teaching and learning. By ascertaining typical student behavior at various stages, teaching methods for different age groups can be refined and developed. The German philosopher Johann Friedrich Herbart (1776-1841) is considered the pioneer of the application of psychology to the art of teaching. Since then many others have contributed, notably William James, (often considered the first theorist of American educational psychology), and John Dewey, founder of the liberal philosophy known as instrumentalism.
See also: Herbart, Johann Friedrich.

Edward, 11 kings of England. There were 3 Saxon kings: Edward the Elder (A.D. 870-924), Edward the Martyr (963-978), and Edward the Confessor (1002-1066). Since the Norman Conquest in 1066, there have been 8 English kings named Edward. **Edward I** (1239-1307) reigned 1272-1307. He subjugated Wales and, inconclusively, Scotland, centralized the national administration, and reduced baronial and clerical power. He also summoned the Model Parliament (1295). **Edward II** (Edward of Caernarvon; 1284-1327), first heir apparent to be created prince of Wales (1301), reigned 1307-27. He spent his reign resisting his barons. His poorly directed Scottish campaigns were highlighted by his defeat at Bannockburn (1314) by Robert Bruce. In 1326 he was unseated in a revolt led by his wife, Queen Isabella, and her paramour Roger de Mortimer. Edward was imprisoned and forced to abdicate in favor of his son, and was probably murdered. **Edward III** (1312-77) reigned 1327-77. Edward's claim to part of Guienne in France was one of the causes of the Hundred Years War. Despite decisive victories at Crécy (1346) and Poitiers (1356), he had lost most French territory by the end of his reign. In 1348-49 the Black Death decimated the population, resulting in major economic and social upheavals. **Edward IV** (1442-83) reigned 1461-70 and 1471-83 during the Wars of the Roses. A Yorkist, Edward deposed the Lancastrian Henry VI in 1461 and again in 1471 after the latter had been restored in 1470 by the Earl of Warwick. Edward reestablished the power of the monarchy, improved administration and law enforcement, and increased England's trade and prosperity. **Edward V** (1470-83?), who reigned April-June 1483, was one of the "princes in the tower." He is believed to have been murdered at the order of his uncle and protector, Richard Duke of Gloucester, who became Richard III. **Edward VI** (1537-53), Henry VIII's only son, reigned 1547-53. A sickly child who was to die of consumption, he succeeded to the throne as a minor. Struggles over the succession and between Protestants and Roman Catholics soon engulfed him. His reign saw the introduction, under Archbishop Cranmer, of the first *Book of Common Prayer* (1549). **Edward VII** (1841-1910), king of Great Britain and Ireland 1901-10, had a reputation as a *bon vivant.* He was concerned with Britain's role in Europe and helped to promote ententes with France and Russia and to defuse the rivalry with Germany. **Edward VIII** (1894-1972), king of Great Britain and Ireland Jan. 20-Dec. 11, 1936, had enjoyed great popularity as prince of Wales and heir, but his association with U.S. divorcée Wallis Warfield Simpson was treated as a scandal by the press and met stern opposition from government and Church. To avoid a constitutional crisis, Edward abdicated, becoming duke of Windsor. He married Mrs. Simpson in 1937 and thereafter lived mainly in France.

Edward the Black Prince (1330-76), prince of Wales and eldest son of Edward III of England. When only 16 he fought bravely at the Battle of Crécy (1346), his father's great victory, supposedly wearing black armor, which gave rise to his name. In 1356, at the Battle of Poitiers during the Hundred Years War, he defeated and captured King John II of France. In 1361 he married his cousin Joan, "the fair maid of Kent," and the following year was put in charge of the English possessions of France. After further fighting in Castile and in France, he gave up his military career but continued to play an important part in the political struggles of England. He died before his father and thus never became king. He was considered a model of medieval chivalry.
See also: Crécy, Battle of; Hunderd Years' War.

Edwardian era, in English history, period from the accession of Edward VII to the outbreak of World War I, 1901-14. Apart from general peacefulness, opulence, and elegance, it was characterized by a growing awareness of social problems, questioning of established authority, and disregard for traditions. In politics the era was dominated by the Liberal Party (led by Herbert Asquith), the rise of the Labour Party, and the agitation for women's suffrage. Representative literature included the novels of Arnold Bennett and H.G. Wells, the plays of George Bernard Shaw, and the poetry of Rupert Brooke. Major figures in the visual arts were Walter Sickert, P. Wilson Steer, and Wyndham Lewis, and in music, Edward Elgar.

Edwards, Jonathan (1703-58), New England theologian and philosopher. A Calvinist in the Puritan tradition, he furthered the Great Awakening by his preaching. He was dismissed by his church in 1749 for his opposition to the taking of the sacrament of the Lord's Supper by those who had not experienced conversion. In 1757 he became president of the College of New Jersey. Influenced by John Locke, he wrote many works of philosophical theology, most notably *Religious Affections* (1746) and *The Freedom of the Will* (1754).
See also: Calvinism; Great Awakening.

Edwards Air Force Base, site of U.S. Air Force Flight Test Center, Ames-Dryden Flight Research Center of the National Aeronautics and Space Administration (NASA), and landing site for U.S. space shuttles. Established in the Mojave Desert northeast of Los Angeles, Calif. in 1933 as a bombing and gunnery range, it became Muroc Army Air Field (1940). There Captain Charles E. Yeager became the first person to break the sound barrier (1947). It was renamed in memory of Captain Glen Walter Edwards, a test pilot (1949).

Edward the Confessor, Saint (1002?-66), king of the English 1042-66. Brought up in Normandy, he was respected for his piety. During most of his reign the government was dominated by the powerful Earl Godwin. Edward alienated the country by attempting to exile Godwin and introduce Normans into the government. He had named William of Normandy as his heir, but on his deathbed chose Harold, Godwin's son, precipitating the Norman Conquest. His feast day is Oct. 13.

Elvers of the European eel (Anguilla anguilla). *During the metamorphosis from young lancet-shaped larva to narrow, round elvers, the animals travel within 2 to 3 years to fresh water. There chromatophores are formed in the skin of the transparent elver, giving it its final color. From that moment on it is called an eel.*

Eel, long slender fish of the order Anguilliformes, without pelvic fins and with dorsal and ventral fins joining the tail fin. The order includes the conger, moray, snake, snipe, and freshwater eel families. Some eels are covered in slime, and some have tiny scales on the skin. Moray eels live in warm water and are a danger to divers because of their bite. American and European freshwater eels spawn in the Sargasso Sea. The leaf-like larvae cross the ocean and enter rivers as young eels, or elvers. When adult, they swim back to the Sargasso Sea to spawn and die.

Eelgrass (*Zostera marina*), grasslike plant of brackish estuaries and lagoons. It bears 3-ft (1-cm) narrow leaves that float in the water. In very salty water eelgrass reproduces by budding, but in fairly fresh water it produces flowers. Eelgrass is an important food for geese, manatees, and marine turtles.

Eelworm, any of the minute nematode worms, the largest being less than 1/50 in (0.5 mm) long. They are found in vast numbers in soil, in fresh water, and on the seashore. Many attack plants and insects and some are serious pests. The *stem and bulb eelworm*, for instance, stunts or kills a wide variety of crops, such as cereals, bulbs, and strawberries. They may be transmitted by plant-sucking bugs and themselves transmit diseases such as tobacco mosaic.

Efficiency, ratio of the useful work derived from a machine to the energy put into it. The mechanical efficiency of a machine is always less than 100%, some energy being lost as heat in friction. A typical gasoline engine may have a thermal efficiency of only 25%, a steam engine, 10%.
See also: Energy.

Effigy mounds, prehistoric Native American burial mounds in northeastern Iowa. Located west of the Mississippi River, the mounds were probably constructed about A.D. 1000. There were probably about

100,000 mounds, many in the form of birds or animals, but many have been destroyed by farming.
See also: National Parks.

Efflorescence, in chemistry, loss of water from crystals. If the pressure of the water vapor produced by the crystals is greater than the pressure of water vapor in the atmosphere, the crystals will lose water and develop a crumbly appearance. The opposite of efflorescence, absorbtion of moisture from the atmosphere, is called *deliquescence*.

Eft *see:* Newt.

EFTA *see:* European Free Trade Association.

Egbert (A.D. 775?-839), king of Wessex in England (802-39). After being driven into exile by the king of Mercia, he gained the West Saxon throne. He conquered Cornwall, Kent, Surrey, and Sussex, also dominating Mercia, East Anglia, and Northumbria, thus expanding Wessex and making it the dominant kingdom of England.

Egg, or ovum, in biology, female gamete or germ cell, found in all animals and in most plants. Popularly, the term is used to describe those animal eggs that are deposited by the female either before or after fertilization and develop outside the body, such as the eggs of reptiles and birds. The egg is a single cell that develops into the embryo after fertilization by a single sperm cell, or male gamete. In animals, it is formed in a primary sex organ, or gonad, called the ovary. In fishes, reptiles, and birds there is a food store of yolk enclosed within its outer membrane. In plants called angiosperms, the female reproductive organs form part of the flower. The egg cell is found within the ovules, which upon fertilization develop into the embryo and seed.
See also: Reproduction.

Eggplant (*Solanum melongena*), plant of the nightshade family, native to India but now grown around the world. It has lobed leaves and grows egg-shaped fruit up to 12 in (30.5 cm) long. These are eaten boiled, baked, stewed, or fried.

Eglantine, or sweetbrier, fragrant, branching rose originating in England, especially *Rosa eleganteria*. It grows wild in the eastern United States, and is used in landscaping. The shrub has curved stems with sharp thorns, small, dark green leaves, pink flowers, and bright red or orange fruit.

Eglevsky, André (1917-77), Russian-born U.S. virtuoso ballet dancer and teacher. He was a member of the Ballet Russe de Monte Carlo (1939-42) and the New York City Ballet (1951-58).
See also: Ballet.

Ego (Latin: "I"), psychological concept, first proposed by Sigmund Freud, referring to a part of the human personality that mediates between the *id*, or instinct, and the *superego*, or conscience. The ego represents what may be called reason and common sense.
See also: Psychoanalysis.

Egret, name of a group of small herons (family Ardeidae), wading birds with long necks, long legs, and pointed bills, with lacy, usually white, plumage, found around the world. The great, or common, egret (*Casmerodius albus*) ranges from Europe to New Zealand and throughout the Americas. Other American species include the snowy egret (*Egretta thula*) and reddish egret (*E. rufescens*). The cattle egret (*Bubulcus ibis*) feeds on insects, often following cattle to catch insects which they flush from the grass. At one time the plumes of the egret were highly valued as items of ceremonial or fashionable dress, and the birds were nearly hunted to extinction. They are now protected by law and numbers are increasing once again.

Egypt, Arab nation in northeast Africa, bounded on the north by the Mediterranean Sea, on the east by Israel and the Red Sea, on the south by the Sudan, and on the west by Libya.
Land and climate. The Sinai peninsula, which is the northwest corner of Egypt, is divided from the rest of the country by the Suez Canal, linking the Mediterranean and the Red Sea. Most of the country's territory is in the western desert, which is the edge of the Sahara. Nearly all the population, however, lives in a narrow band around the Nile, the world's largest river, which runs north from Africa for more than 4,000 mi (6,500 km) and empties into the Mediterranean. The vast, triangular Nile delta, a rich plain of river mud about 150 mi (241 km) across, is known as lower Egypt, and is the major population center. Cairo, Africa's largest city and the capital of Egypt, stands at the head of the Nile delta. Alexandria, a Mediterranean port at the western edge of the delta, is Egypt's second-largest city. Although there has been considerable industrialization since World War II, the country is still predominantly agricultural, dependent on the highly fertile land along the river. The climate is generally dry, hot, and sunny. Only the Mediterranean coast and parts of southern Sinai receive more than 2 in (5 cm) of rain a year.
People. Arabic is the national language. Most Egyptians are Sunni Muslims, but there is a minority (5-10%) of Christians called Copts, who use a form of the ancient Egyptian language in their religious ritual.
Economy. Agriculture is based mainly on upon irrigation. The amount of available farmland was increased appreciably by the Aswan Dam. The principal export crop is cotton, but Egypt also raises wheat, corn, millet, and rice. Mineral resources include iron ore, salt, natural gas, petroleum, and phosphates. The production of textiles and processed foods dominate the industrial sector. Tourism and the Suez Canal are important sources of foreign currency.
History. Egypt's history goes back thousands of years, but the modern roots of the country begin with the Arab invasion of A.D. 641, when the majority of the people embracced Islam and were integrated into Arab civilization. For about 500 years the country was ruled by caliphs based in Damascus, Baghdad, and other cities. In 1250 power was taken by a Turkish dynasty, the Mamelukes, and in 1517 it became part of the Ottoman Empire. The modern Egyptian state was formed in 1805 by Muhammad Ali, a soldier of Turkish origin. In the late 19th century Egypt fell under British influence, and during World War I London proclaimed the country a British protectorate. In 1937 a formally independent state was created, with King Farouk as monarch. He was overthrown in 1952 by a group of army officers who proclaimed a republic with Gamal Abdel Nasser as president. During Nasser's reign, Egypt was the center of Arab nationalism. There were two wars with Israel, in 1956 and 1967, during which Egypt lost much territory, including the entire Sinai peninsula.

The magnificent rock-carved Sphinx (Aby-al-Hul) stands near the Great Pyramid of Cheops (Khufu) at Giza. The Sphinx has a human head and the body of a lion, symbolizing kingship and power.

Egypt

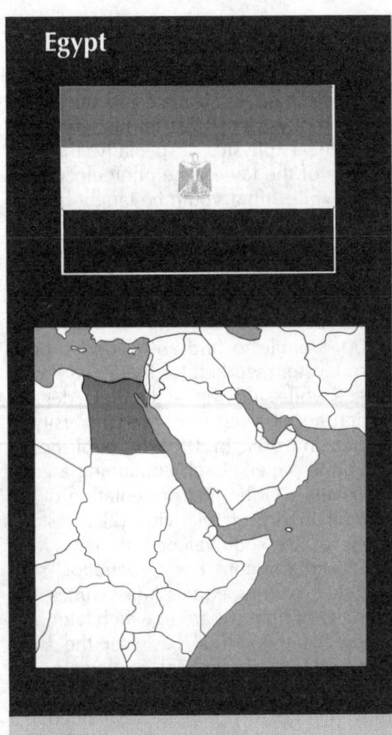

General information	
Capital:	Cairo
Area:	385,229 sq mi (997,739 sq km)
Population:	51,748,000
Official language:	Arabic
Monetary unit:	1 Egyptian pound = 100 piastres
Main cities:	Cairo, Alexandria, al-Jizah
Government	
Form:	Republic
Independent:	1922
Head of state:	President (elected every 6 years)
Head of government:	Prime Minister
Legislature:	one legislative house (People's Assembly)
Executive:	President and Council of Ministers
Judiciary:	highest court is the Supreme Constitutional Court
Political division:	26 governorates, 4 regions
National economy	
Gross national product:	U.S. $33,250,000,000
Per capita income:	U.S. $650
Agriculture:	sugarcane, tomatoes, corn, wheat, rice, cotton, oranges, potatoes
Livestock:	cattle, goats, buffaloes
Fisheries:	250,000 metric tons
Mining:	crude petroleum, natural gas, iron ore, phosphate rock, salt
Industries:	cement, nitrate fertilizers, petroleum products, phosphate fertilizers, sugar, steel
Main exports:	petroleum and petroleum products, textile fibres and products, vegetable products
Transportation:	3,327 mi (5,355 km) of railroads; 20,034 mi (32,241 km) of roads; 2 international airports
Trading partners:	Italy, United States, France, Germany, Japan
People	
Urban:	45%
Ethnic composition:	Egyptian 99.5%, other 0.5%
Birth rate:	39.3 per 1,000 population
Death rate:	8.7 per 1,000 population
Infant mortality:	70 per 1,000 live births
Life expectancy:	male 59 years, female 62 years

On Nasser's death in 1970, Anwar al-Sadat became president. He joined Syria and Iraq in the War against Israel in October 1973. Shortly after that, Sadat broke Nasser's alliance with the USSR and sought closer ties with the United States. In 1979 Sadat and Menachem Begin of Israel signed a peace treaty and Israel began a phased withdrawal from the Sinai. In 1981 Sadat was assassinated by Muslim fundamentalists. He was succeeded by his vice president, Hosni Mubarak, who has continued Sadat's general policies, both foreign and domestic.

Egypt, Ancient, great civilization that arose along the banks of the Nile River more than 5,000 years ago.

Egypt became a single nation c.3100 B.C., when the kingdoms of Upper (southern) and Lower (northern) Egypt were unified by Menes, who founded a capital at Memphis, about 12 mi (18 km) from what is now Cairo. The state inaugurated by Menes, called the Old Kingdom, lasted until c.2200 B.C. It was during this period that the great pyramids of Giza were built. The largest was constructed under the reign of the pharaoh Cheops, dates from about 2500 B.C. It was during the Old Kingdom that writing and paper were developed, and Egyptian commerce flourished.

The fall of the Old Kingdom resulted in two

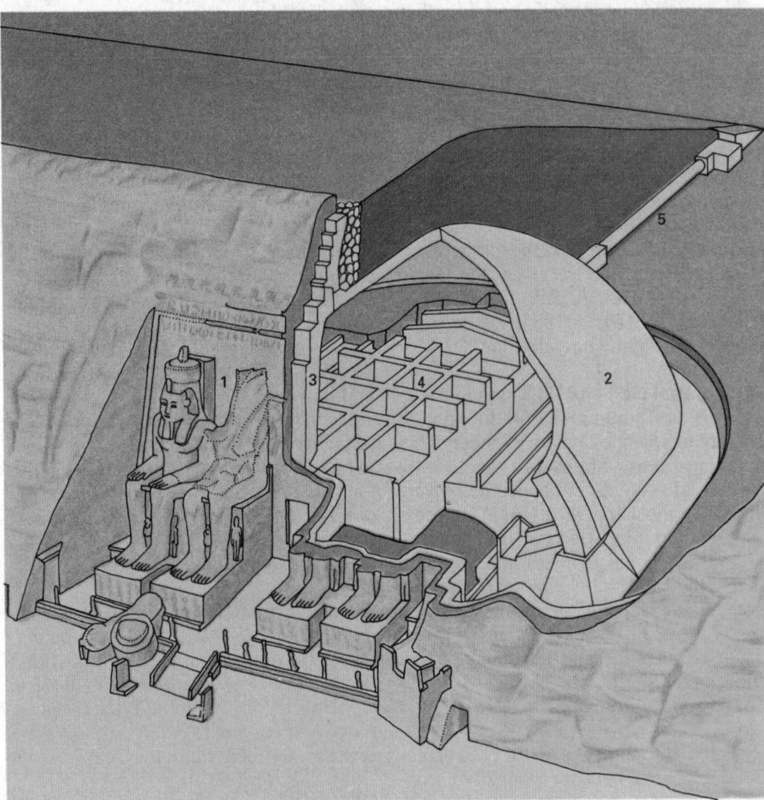

The Great Temple at Abu Simbel (c. 1301 B.C.), one of two temples built here by Ramses II. In front of its facade (1), are four colossi of Ramses. In 1964, UNESCO sponsored a reconstruction to save the Abu Simbel complex from Nile water rising behind the Aswan dam. The temples were reassembled 266 ft (81 m) higher. Beneath an artificial mountain an immense concrete dome (2) protects the Great Temple from tons of rocks piled up in imitation of Abu Simbel's original setting. Stepped walling (3) reinforces the colossi. A grid-like structure (4) supports the ceiling blocks of the inner chambers. A rear pipe (5) draws fresh air into the shrine.

centuries of chaos, ending c.2100 B.C. with the establishment of the Middle Kingdom, whose capital was at Thebes, in southern (Upper) Egypt. The Middle Kingdom flourished until the 18th century B.C. when the country fell before the Hyksos, Asiatic nomads. The rule of the Hyksos marked the second intermediate period (1786- c.1570 B.C.). A native uprising under the princes of Thebes led to the gradual reconquest of Egypt from the Hyksos, and the foundation of the New Kingdom in about 1570. It was during the XVIII dynasty (1570-c.1352 B.C.) that Egyptian civilization reached its height. Thebes and Memphis became the world's greatest centers of commerce and culture, and Egyptian rule extended from the Sudan to the Euphrates River.

Adolf Eichman in his bullet-proof defendant's booth during the reading of the verdict on Dec. 11, 1961. The trial against him took eight months.

Egyptian power began to decline after the war with the Hittites in Syria (1296-1279 B.C.). Ramses III (d. 1167 B.C.) was the last great ruler of the New Kingdom. Following his reign, Egyptian politics were dominated by divisive intrigue, civil war, and weak and ineffective leadership. In 525 B.C. Persia conquered and annexed Egypt, and when Alexander the Great overthrew Darius III of Persia (333 B.C.), he was welcomed into Egypt, which became part of his empire. Upon the death of Alexander, Ptolemy, one of his generals, established a new dynasty in Egypt. The first Ptolemy (r.305-285 B.C.) built the great museum and library at Alexandria. The Ptolemy dynasty lasted until 30 B.C., when Cleopatra died and Egypt was annexed by Rome.

Christianity was introduced in Egypt in the 2nd, 3rd, and 4th centuries, and around A.D. 390 the country became part of the Byzantine Empire. With the Arab invasion of A.D. 640, the population was Arabized culturally and linguistically, and since then Egypt has been part of the Muslim world.

Egyptology *see:* Egypt, Ancient.

Ehrenburg, Ilya Grigoryevich (1891-1967), Russian writer. He lived in Western Europe (1909-17 and 1921-41), as a journalist and novelist: *The Love of Jeanne Ney* (1924) and *Out of Chaos* (1933). He returned to Russia in 1941, becoming a war correspondent. He received the Stalin Prize for the novel *The Fall of Paris* (1942). His novel *The Thaw* (1954) was a major work of post-Stalin liberalization.

Eiffel Tower

Ehrlich, Paul (1854-1915), German bacteriologist and immunologist, founder of chemotherapy and an early pioneer of hematology. His discoveries include a method of staining and hence identifying the tuberculosis bacillus (1882); the reasons for immunity in terms of the chemistry of antibodies and antigens, for which he shared the 1908 Nobel Prize for physiology or medicine with Élie Metchnikoff; and the use of the drug salvarsan to cure syphilis, the first drug to be used in treating the root cause of a disease (1911).
See also: Bacteriology.

Ehrlich, Paul Ralph (1932-), U.S. ecologist. Ehrlich first became aware of the consequences of overpopulation on a visit to India. In 1967 he forecast massive worldwide famines within the next 2 decades. He has suggested that all U.S. aid to foreign countries be made conditional upon stringent birth control and that the United States itself should discourage population growth by taxation. He wrote *The Population Bomb* in 1968.

Eichmann, Adolf (1906-62), German lieutenant-colonel in the Nazi Gestapo, head of the Jewish Division from 1939. He was responsible for the deportation, maltreatment, and murder of European Jews in World War II. He escaped to Argentina but was abducted, tried, and executed in Israel.
See also: Holocaust.

Eider, name of several species of diving ducks of northern latitudes. The common eider is famed for the soft, insulating down of its breast, which it plucks to line its nest. Of commercial value, the down is collected to fill eiderdowns (comforters). In Iceland and Norway, eiders are encouraged to nest on "eider farms" for this purpose.

Eielson, Carl Ben (1897-1929), U.S. explorer and aviator. He and Australian Hubert Wilkins flew the first airplane across the Arctic Ocean from Point Barrow, Alaska to Spitsbergen, an Arctic Ocean island (April 1928), made the first air explorations of Antarctica (Dec. 1928), and charted unknown islands near the Antarctic Peninsula. Eielson became a pilot in the U.S. Army Air Service (1918), founded an Alaskan commercial air service (1923), and established the first Alaskan airmail route (1924).
See also: Antarctica.

Eiffel, Alexandre Gustave (1832-1923), French engineer best known for his design and construction of the Eiffel Tower, Paris (1887-89), from which he carried out experiments in aerodynamics. In 1912 he founded the first aerodynamics laboratory.

Eiffel Tower, famous tower dominating the skyline of Paris, designed by Alexandre Gustave Eiffel as the focal point of the Universal Exposition of 1889. From masonry piers, 4 iron columns, connected by delicate arches, sweep gracefully inward and upward. At 620 ft (189 m) they converge to form one column and continue to a height of 984 ft (289 m; now 1,056 ft/321 m including the television antenna). Elevators and staircases give visitors access to 3 observation platforms.

Eighteenth Amendment *see:* Volstead Act.

Eijkman, Christiaan (1858-1930), Dutch pathologist. He discovered that beriberi results from a thiamine (vitamin B_1) deficiency. He was awarded (with Sir F.G. Hopkins) the 1929 Nobel Prize for physiology or medicine.
See also: Beriberi; Pathology.

Eilat *see:* Elat.

Einstein, Albert (1879-1955), German-born U.S. physicist, one of the greatest scientific figures. He received the Nobel Prize in physics in 1921 for his services to theoretical physics, especially the discovery of the law of the photoelectric effect. While still a youth he taught himself calculus and science. In 1896 he entered the Swiss Federal Polytechnic School in Zurich, where he trained as a teacher of physics and mathematics. He became a Swiss citizen on receiving his diploma in 1900. Unable to find an academic position, Einstein worked for the Swiss Patent Office while studying for the Ph.D. degree, which he received from the University of Zurich in 1905. In 1905 he published 4 scientific papers, each containing a great discovery: (1) the first presentation of the special theory of relativity; (2) the statement of the equivalence of mass and energy (the famous $E=mc^2$ equation, stating that energy equals mass times the velocity of light squared), which later provided the theoretical basis for the atom bomb; (3) a theoretical explanation of Brownian motion, the incessant erratic movement of tiny particles suspended in a fluid; and (4) his application of Planck's quantum hypothesis to the investigation of the nature of light, in which he showed that light behaved as if it were composed of independent quanta (tiny units) of energy called photons, and not simply of waves. In 1914 he became professor at the University of Berlin and director of the Kaiser

Albert Einstein

Wilhelm Physical Institute, resuming his German citizenship. In 1916 he published his general theory of relativity. Much of the rest of his life was spent in an unsuccessful effort to produce a *unified field theory*, that is, to show that both gravitational and electromagnetic phenomena derive from the geometrical properties of space-time. The task has still not been completed. With the rise of the Nazis, Einstein, a Jew, found his position in Germany impossible, and in 1932 he resigned from his post at Berlin. In 1933 he moved to the Institute for Advanced Study at Princeton, N.J. He became a U.S. citizen in 1940. Just before World War II, Einstein wrote a letter to President Franklin D. Roosevelt, pointing out the

theoretical possibility of a nuclear bomb and warning of the danger that Germany might develop the bomb first. This resulted in the establishment of the Manhattan Project. He retired from the institute in 1945 but continued to work there until his death in 1955.
See also: $E=mc^2$; Relativity.

Einsteinium, chemical element, symbol Es; for physical constants see Periodic Table. Einsteinium was discovered in 1952 in the debris of the first thermonuclear explosion by Albert Ghiorso and co-workers at Berkeley, Calif. A special magnetic-type balance was used to weigh the amount of einsteinium-253 obtained, about 0.01 g. The element is prepared by irradiation of plutonium isotopes in a high flux reactor. It is a metallic element and a member of the actinide series. All of its 14 known isotopes are radioactive.

Einstein theory *see:* Relativity.

Einthoven, Willem (1860-1927), Dutch physiologist, awarded the 1924 Nobel Prize for physiology or medicine for his invention of, and investigation of heart action with, the electrocardiograph. In 1903 he devised the string galvanometer, a single fine wire placed under tension in a magnetic field. Current passed through the wire causes a deflection that can be measured, for greater accuracy, by a microscope. This galvanometer was sensitive enough for him to use it to record the electrical activity of the heart.

Éire *see:* Ireland.

Eisenhower, Dwight David (1890-1969), 34th president of the United States, nicknamed "Ike". Eisenhower's two terms in office are remembered as peaceful years, because one of his first official acts was to move for an end to the unpopular Korean War. They were also, however, tense years of Cold War with the communist bloc.
Early life. A year after graduating from high school in 1909, Eisenhower won admission to the U.S. military academy at West Point, from which he graduated in 1915. In 1916 he met and married Mary "Mamie" Geneva Doud. They had two sons, one of whom died in infancy.
Military commander. During World War I, Eisenhower remained in the United States as an instructor. He became an aide to General Douglas MacArthur in 1933 and, in 1935, accompanied MacArthur on a mission to reorganize defenses in the Philippines. In 1939 World War II began in Europe, but the United States did not become involved until Japan bombed Pearl Harbor in Dec. 1941. The following year, Eisenhower became commander of an Allied attack in North Africa. By 1943 he was a full general and, later that year, was made supreme commander of Allied forces in Europe. He planned and oversaw the Allied attack that began June 6, 1944 (D-Day); its success aided an Allied push that led to Germany's surrender.
In 1948 Eisenhower retired from active duty with the rank of five-star general to become president of Columbia University. In 1950 he was appointed supreme commander of the North Atlantic Treaty Organization (NATO).
President. In 1952 Eisenhower resigned from the army and was nominated as the Republican candidate for president. He and his running mate, Richard M. Nixon, won by a landslide, defeating the Democratic ticket of Adlai E. Stevenson and John J. Sparkman.
Eisenhower had pledged to bring the Korean War to "an early and honorable end" and, six months after he took office, a truce was signed. However, other objectives of his administration were hampered by conflicts between moderate and conservative Republicans and by a Democratic majority in both houses of Congress after 1954. Despite Eisenhower's health problems (a heart attack in 1955 and emergency surgery in 1956), his popularity with voters remained high. In 1956 he was reelected by an overwhelming margin.
In foreign affairs, the Eisenhower administration's policies were devoted to "containing" communism and building a strong defense. In 1958 Eisenhower sent U.S. troops to the Middle East to restore peace in Lebanon and to protect U.S. oil interests. On the domestic front, he ordered federal troops to Little Rock, Ark., in 1957 to safeguard the attempt of nine black children to integrate all-white schools. He also signed the Civil Rights Acts of 1957 and 1960—the first such bills passed by Congress since Reconstruction.
Retirement. Eisenhower left office at age 70 and retired to his farm at Gettysburg, Pa. Succeeding presidents consulted him until he died of heart failure in Washington, D.C., in 1969.

Dwight David Eisenhower

34th U.S. President

Born:	Denison, Tex.; Oct. 14, 1890
Terms:	Jan. 1953-Jan. 1961
Vice president:	Richard Milhous Nixon
Political party:	Republican
Spouse:	Mary (Mamie) Geneva Doud Eisenhower
Children:	2
Died:	Washington, D.C.; Mar. 28, 1969

Eisenstaedt, Alfred (1898-), pioneering U.S. photojournalist. He worked for *Life* magazine for over 30 years. From the early 1930s he helped to develop news and candid photography from mere reportage into an art form.
See also: Photography.

Eisenstein, Sergei Mikhailovich (1898-1948), Soviet film director. A major influence on the development of the cinema, he extended editing techniques, especially the use of montage. His films, notably *The Battleship Potemkin* (1925), *Ten Days That Shook the World* (1927), *Alexander Nevsky* (1938), and *Ivan the Terrible* (1944-46), are undisputed classics.

EKG *see:* Electrocardiogram.

El Aaiun, also Aiun (pop. 25,000), Laayoune, or Ayun, city in Western Sahara (territory in northwest Africa occupied by Morocco), about 10 mi (16 km) from the Atlantic Ocean. It is an important shipping center for phosphates. The area was controlled from the early 1900s by Spain, who founded the city in 1940. El Aaiun was capital of the province of Spanish Sahara until Spain withdrew in 1976, at which time it was incorporated by Morocco.

El Alamein, Egyptian city 65 mi (105 km) east of Alexandria. The city is linked by coastal railroad to Alexandria, and an oil field is in operation nearby. During World War II Britain defeated Germany in 2 decisive battles at El Alamein (1942), preventing the conquest of Egypt. The battles at El Alamein are noted for the brilliant commanders facing each other—Montgomery for the British defeated Rommel of Germany.
See also: World War II.

Eland, largest antelope (6 ft/180 cm), belonging to the family Bovidae, with spiral horns and a short mane. Found in central and southern Africa, elands live in herds of up to 100. Attempts have been made to domesticate elands, because they can survive in very dry conditions and give excellent milk and meat.

Elat, or Eilat (pop. 19,600), town at the southern tip of Israel on the Gulf of Aqaba. It is Israel's only port, with direct access to East Africa and South Asia via the Red Sea. Established in 1948, it began to grow after 1956 when the Egyptian blockade on the Gulf of Aqaba was lifted. The blockade's resumption in 1967 precipitated the Six-

Day Arab-Israeli War. Exports include textiles, citrus fruit, and manufactured goods; lumber and crude petroleum are among the major imports. Its warm, dry climate has made Elat a winter resort with the additional attraction of the nearby Red Sea and its tropical fish and corals.

Elba, Italian island in the Mediterranean, 6 mi (9.7 km) off the west coast of central Italy. At various times under the rule of Pisa, Spain, and Naples, it was the site of Napoleon I's exile, 1814-15. The island is about 20 mi (32 km) long and less than 10 mi (16 km) wide and is very mountainous. Industries include iron mining, marble quarrying, fishing, and agriculture.
See also: Italy.

Elbe River, major river in central Europe. It rises in northwestern Czechoslovakia and flows 725 mi (1,167 km) north through Germany into the North Sea beyond Hamburg. The river is navigable for some 525 mi (845 km) and is connected by a canal system to the Oder River. Important cities on the Elbe include Hamburg, Dresden, and Magdeburg.

Elder, or elderberry, tree or shrub (genus *Sambucus*) of the honeysuckle family, native to temperate and subtropical regions. The plant bears white flowers that mature to juicy purple or red berries, used in pies and wines.

Elderberry *see:* Elder.

El Dorado (Spanish, "the gilded one"), legendary South American king who was reputed to cover himself with gold dust at festivals and then, as a sacrifice, wash it off in a lake into which his subjects also threw gold; also, legendary kingdom on the Amazon River, sought for its reputed wealth by Spanish explorers of the 16th century.

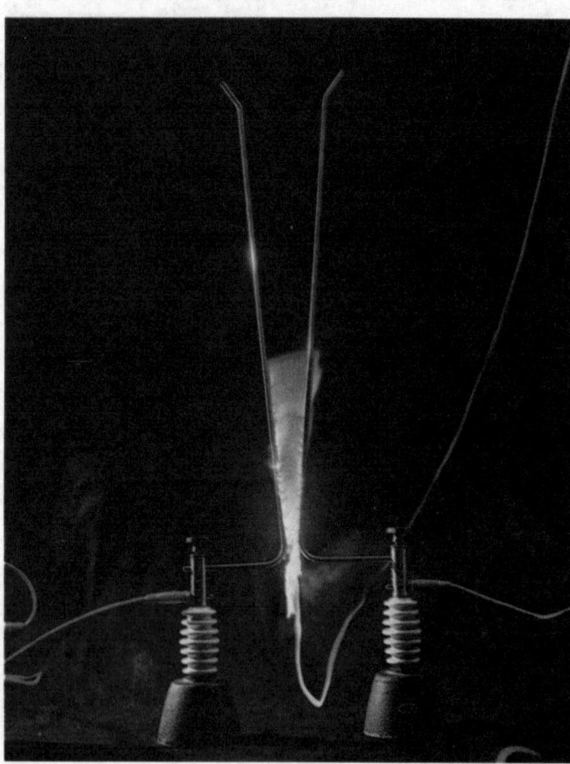

Electric arc (method of obtaining ionized gas, permitting electric discharges).

Eleanor of Aquitaine (1122-1204), daughter and heir of William X, duke of Aquitaine; queen consort first to Louis VII of France (marriage annulled 1152) and then to Henry II of England. Her marriage to Henry in 1152 brought almost all of western France under English domination. In 1173 she supported her sons (later kings Richard I and John) in unsuccessful rebellion against their adulterous father and was afterward kept in captivity until Henry's death in 1185. She was subsequently active in politics in support of her sons.

Elecampane (*Inula helenium*), large coarse herb with yellow flowers, native to Europe and Asia as far east as the Himalayas. It was introduced to North America, where it now grows wild. The thick, fleshy roots are used medicinally.

Election, selection of public officeholders by vote. Elections may be direct or indirect. In direct elections the voters themselves choose among the candidates for office or proposals in a referendum. In indirect elections voters choose delegates who cast the final and decisive votes. A well-known example of this process is the American electoral college, the body of delegates that, theoretically, elects the president and vice-president of the United States. Elections may be based on the plurality system or on proportional representation. Under the former system, which is used in the United States and in most English-speaking countries, the candidate who receives the largest number of votes in a district, not necessarily a majority, is the winner. The legislature is then composed of the winners of the individual contests. Under proportional representation, each party nominates a slate of candidates in each district, usually equal in number to the total number of seats to which that district is entitled. The parties are then allocated seats based on the percentage of the total vote they win in the district, with some minimum, such as 5%, required for any representation at all. The idea that representative democracy requires the participation of all adults developed only slowly in the 19th century. Religious and property qualifications disappeared gradually. By 1920, when the 19th Amendment to the U.S. Constitution was ratified, giving women the vote, most Western nations had adopted universal suffrage. The 26th Amendment, passed in 1971, lowered the voting age in the United States to 18.

Election campaign, period before an election when candidates and political parties carry out actions to win votes. A campaign organization plans strategies to announce the candidacy, develop support, win the nomination, and get out the vote. Modern campaigning makes great use of broadcast media, targeting potential voters with demographic surveys and canvassing. U.S. campaigns are run for the presidency, Congress, state office, and to win voter approval for proposals through referendums. Federal and state legislation now regulate some aspects of campaign financing and spending.
See also: Election.

Electoral college, body elected by popular vote that in turn elects the president and vice president of the United States. The college was conceived as a compromise between direct popular elections and rule by appointment or inheritance. The voters of each state choose electors (whose names often do not appear on the ballot) by indicating their choice for president and vice president. The winning party's electors then cast the state's votes for the candidates chosen. Each state has as many votes in the college as the total number of its senators and representatives. If no candidate receives a majority of electoral votes, the House of Representatives elects the president from among the top 3 candidates. This happened twice in U.S. history, in the elections of Thomas Jefferson (1800) and John Quincy Adams (1824). The winning candidate in each state receives all that state's electoral votes, regardless of the proportion of popular votes won. Thus it is possible for the losing presidential candidate to receive more popular votes than the winning candidate. This happened when John Quincy Adams defeated Andrew Jackson (1824); when Rutherford B. Hayes defeated Samuel Tilden (1876); and when Benjamin Harrison defeated Grover Cleveland (1888). Despite dissatisfaction with this shortcoming, the institution survives.
See also: Election.

Electoral Commission, group of 15 members (5 senators, 5 representatives, 5 Supreme Court justices) created by Congress in 1877 to determine the winner of the presidential election of 1876. Discrepancies in electoral votes resulted in Democrats and Republicans both claiming victory. Congress carefully selected 7 members from each party, but the 2 Democratic and 2 Republican justices, who had power to choose the fifth justice, were forced to select a Republican after the only independent chosen decided to run for office instead of serving on the commission. The Republican majority of 8 to 7 resulted in a strict party vote electing Republican Rutherford B. Hayes over Democrat Samuel J. Tilden.

Electra, in Greek mythology, daughter of Agamemnon and Clytemnestra, and the older sister of Orestes. To avenge the murder of Agamemnon, she helped Orestes slay the murderers, Clytemnestra and her lover, Aegisthus. This theme was the subject of tragedies by Aeschylus, Sophocles, and Euripides, as well as by Eugene O'Neill in his trilogy *Mourning Becomes Electra* (1931), and by composer Richard Strauss in his opera *Elektra* (1909).
See also: Mythology.

Electra complex, in psychoanalysis, the attraction of a daughter to her father, named for Electra, daughter of Agamemnon in Greek mythology.
See also: Psychoanalysis.

Electrical engineering *see:* Engineering.

Electric arc, area of intense light and heat produced by the passage of electricity across a small gap between 2 electrodes. Electricity is able to span the gap because it ionizes the surrounding air, which then serves as a conductor. The arc light, which uses carbon electrodes, is commonly used as a spotlight in the theater and as a floodlight. The heat produced by an arc is used in welding to melt metal rods, which solidify to provide a strong joint between 2 metal surfaces.

Electric battery *see:* Battery.

Electric car, automobile powered by electricity. Electric cars were in use in the United States in the 1870s and remained in production until 1930, when they were displaced by the gasoline engine. Recently the electric car has been under reexamination because it is quiet, cheap to run, requires no oil or water, and emits no pollutants. A rechargeable battery or bank of batteries drives an electric motor that turns the wheels. The range of electric cars on single charge is still very limited, up to about 40 mi (64.4 km). Higher capacity silver/zinc and sodium/sulfur storage batteries under development promise a longer range. Fuel cells similar to those used to power spacecraft systems have also been applied to electric car propulsion, giving a theoretical range of about 150 mi (242 km). But many serious problems remain to be solved before family-sized electric cars become practical.

Electric circuit, path followed by an electric current. It consists of 3 basic parts: an energy source (e.g., battery or generator) that converts nonelectric energy into electric energy, an output device (e.g., motor or lamp) that uses electric energy to do work, and a connection (e.g., wire or cable) that allows electric current to flow between the source and output device. Circuits can be switched on and off. An open circuit has gaps, preventing the current from completing its path, while a closed circuit has no gaps.
See also: Electricity.

Electric current, flow of electric charges. Protons, part of every atom's nucleus, have a positive charge; electrons surrounding the nucleus have a negative charge. Substances that freely give up electrons, such as aluminum, copper, and silver, are good *conductors*, allowing electric current to flow freely. Poor conductors, such as lead and tin, are more resistant to electric current. Substances that do not conduct electricity, such as glass and rubber, are insulators. Direct current (DC), used to power automobiles, always flows in 1 direction, while alternating current (AC), used in homes and for many electronic devices, reverses direction periodically.
See also: Alternating current; Direct current.

Electric eel (*Electrophorus electricus*), eel-like species of fish of the family Electrophoridae that can produce an electric discharge, found in northern South America. Electricity, generated by electric organs composed of modified muscle cells or electroplaques, is used to detect and stun prey, repel enemies, and communicate with other electric eels. These long, narrow fish can grow to 8 ft (2.4 m), are colored olive brown, and can produce 350-650 volts of electricity.

Electric eye, or photoelectric cell, electronic device either producing current or allowing current to flow when light shines on it, used for controlling such devices as lights and burglar alarms, and for measuring light for photographic and video equipment. They react rapidly to light changes and respond to visible as well as invisible (infrared and ultraviolet) light waves. Phototubes, solar cells, and photoconductive cells are types of electric eyes.
See also: Electronics.

Electric field, field that surrounds an electric charge and exerts force on any nearby electric charges. The concept of field considers one charge as central. The force is an attractive force between unlike charges and repellent between like charges. In empty space, unit charges 1 cm apart produce a force of 1 dyne. The force is reduced when a medium, or dielectric, separates the charges.
See also: Electricity.

Electric fish, any of various fishes having the ability to generate electric currents for stunning prey or enemies or for locating nearby objects. The electric currents are generated in specialized muscles. Fish that stun their prey or their adversaries include the Mediterranean electric ray, which delivers a charge of 200 volts, the marine stargazers, the electric catfish of Africa, and the electric eel of the Amazon. The last is not a true eel; its body organs are squeezed into the head end, and most of the eellike body is given over to an electric organ that discharges 500 volts. The electric eel also discharges a very weak current in the form of continuous pulses, forming an electromagnetic field, allowing the fish to detect disturbances in this field. The elephant-snout fish and the knifefish of Africa also have this faculty.

Electric furnace, furnace powered by electricity and used for melting, alloying, and heat-treating steel alloys and for manufacturing high-speed tools. The chamber, salt bath, arc, and induction furnaces produce temperatures up to 1500°C and can melt 100 tons of steel.
See also: Furnace.

Electric fuse *see:* Fuse.

Electric generator, or dynamo, machine producing electricity most often by converting mechanical energy into electrical energy. They are used for factory machines, lighting, and home appliances. They can be either direct current (DC), producing electric current flowing in one direction, or alternating current (AC), producing electric current that reverses direction periodically. Some scientific instruments use midget generators while larger generators can supply electricity for entire cities.
See also: Electricity.

Electric heating *see:* Heating.

Electric induction *see:* Induction, electric.

Electricity, phenomenon of charged subatomic particles at rest or in motion. Electricity provides a highly versatile form of energy. *Electric charge* is an inherent property of matter. Electrons carry a negative charge and protons carry a positive charge. For each electron in the atom, there is normally 1 proton. When this balance is disturbed, a net charge is left on an object; the study of such isolated charges is called *electrostatics*. Like charges repel and unlike charges attract each other with a force proportional to the 2 charges and inversely proportional to the square of the distance between them (the inverse-square law). This force is normally interpreted in terms of an *electric field* produced by one charge with which the other interacts. Pairs of equal but opposite charges separated by a small distance are called *dipoles*; the product of charge and separation is called the *dipole moment*. The amount of work done in moving a unit charge from one point to another against the electric field is called the electric *potential difference*, or voltage, between the points; it is measured in volts. The ratio of a charge added to a body to the voltage produced is called the *capacitance* of the body. The presence of an electric field in a conductor produces a steady flow of charge in the direction of the field; such a flow constitutes an *electric current*, measured in amperes. Electric sources such as batteries and generators convert chemical, mechanical, or other energy into electrical energy and pump charge through conductors much as a water pump circulates water in a radiator heating system. Batteries create a constant voltage, producing a steady, or direct, current (DC). Many generators, on the other hand, provide a voltage that changes in direction many times a second and so produces an alternating current (AC), in which the charges move to and fro instead of continuously in one direction. The latter system has advantages in generation, transmission, and application and is now used almost universally for domestic and industrial purposes. Static electricity was known to the ancient Greeks. The 18th century saw the initiation of many experiments with conduction and other aspects of electricity. The inverse square law was hinted at by J. Priestley in 1767 and later confirmed by H. Cavendish and C.A. Coulomb. G.S. Ohm formulated his law of conduction in 1826, although its essentials were known before then. The common nature of all the "types" of electricity then known was demonstrated in 1826 by M. Faraday, who also originated the concept of electric field lines.

Electric light, device using electric energy to produce visible light. Incandescent lamps have 3 basic parts: the filament, a wire through which electricity flows; the bulb, which protects the filament; and the base, which holds the lamp connecting it to an electric circuit. Gaseous-discharge lamps (fluorescent, neon, metal halide lamps) use pressurized gases instead of filaments. Light-emitting diodes (LEDs), used in computers and digital watches, and electroluminescent panels, used as night lights and on instrument panels, produce dim light directly from electric energy, and do not require a bulb, electric discharge, or filament. Thomas Edison developed the first incandescent light (1879).
See also: Edison, Thomas Alva.

Electric measurement, measurable, observable effects (heat, force, magnetism) of electric current. Electric current is measured in *amperes* (1 ampere is roughly 6 billion electrons per sec). The quantity of electricity carried by current is measured in *coulombs* (quantity transmitted by 1 ampere in 1 sec). Units of electric force are measured in *volts* (difference in potential energy between 2 points on a wire carrying 1 ampere, producing 1 watt). A *kilowatt-hour* is the power produced by 1,000 watts in 1 hr. Resistance (opposition of material to electric current) is measured in *ohms* (resistance of a conductor carrying 1 ampere when the potential difference across the conductor is 1 volt).
See also: Ampere; Coulomb.

Electric meter, instrument for measuring the consumption of electricity. Domestic electric meters register the quantity of electricity used in the home in kilowatt-hours (KwH). The meter contains a metal disk that rotates in a magnetic field produced by an electromagnet inside the meter. The greater the rate at which power is consumed, the faster the disk rotates. The disk is connected to the dials of the meter through a train of wheels. The amount consumed is periodically read by an official of the electricity company. Other electric meters used to measure the various factors of an electric current, such as ammeters, voltmeters, wattmeters, and ohmmeters, depend mostly on electromagnetism. Some electric meters combine all these instruments in one large instrument that can be switched from one kind of measuring operation to another.

Electric motor, machine for converting electric energy into mechanical energy. Appliances such as refrigerators and dishwashers, and power tools such as electric drills all use electric motors. Alternating current (AC) motors are ordinarily used in household appliances. The direct current (DC) motors are commonly used by machinery in factories.
See also: Alternating current; Direct current.

Electric power, electric energy used for work, measured in units called watts. Electric power plants create mechanical energy that is converted via a generator into electricity. Fossil-fueled steam electric power plants produce electricity by burning fossil fuels (coal, oil, natural gas), and hydroelectric power plants use the energy of falling water. Nuclear power plants use heat produced by nuclear fission (splitting nuclei of atoms of uranium or other heavy elements in a nuclear reactor). While fission is a highly efficient form of power, it yields dangerous radioactive wastes. Other sources of power valued for being nonpolluting and for not depleting natural resources include geothermal power, using heat from the earth, and plants using wind and solar energy. Electricity is distributed to consumers using a system of transmission lines to carry current and transformers to change voltage. Electric utilities are the organizations generating, transmitting, or distributing electric power.
See also: Electricity.

Electric railroad, fast, quiet, non-polluting, electrically powered, high-speed railway system including passenger and freight trains, subways, and elevated systems. Electricity is received by the train through an overhead wire (catenary) or electrified third rail. A framework (pantograph) atop the train conducts electricity from the catenary to a propulsion system moving the train, or a metal device (shoe) slides along an electrified third rail conducting electricity to the propulsion system. Only 1% of U.S. track is electrified, but electric railroads are common in Europe and Japan.
See also: Railroad.

Electric ray *see:* Torpedo.

Electric shock *see:* Shock treatment.

Electric switch, device used to open and close an electric circuit. The most common type is the snap-action toggle switch. A circuit is completed when the switch is turned on, and broken when it is turned off.

Electric train *see:* Electric railroad.

Electric wiring, system of wires that carries electric current through a building. The United States' National Electric Code specifies safe installation and selection of electric wires, an important function, since faulty wiring is a common cause of fire. Most homes use 120-volt circuits of 15 amperes, although large appliances and machinery use 240-volt circuits with greater amperage.

Electrocardiogram (ECG or EKG), measurements of the wave patterns produced by the electrical currents generated by the contractions of the heart muscles. The electrocardiogram is the main diagnostic technique of electrocardiography, which is the science of measuring and interpreting the electrical activity of the heart. During an EKG electrodes are attached to the hands, feet, and chest, and the electrical currents are recorded on light-sensitive film. Deviations from the normal shape of the electrical waves point to various disorders of the heart.
See also: Heart.

Electrochemistry, branch of physical chemistry dealing with the effect of electricity on chemical charge and the interconversion of electrical and chemical energy. To produce electrochemical reactions, 2 *electrodes* or conductors are placed in liquid medium or *electrolyte*, producing an environment allowing the free flow of electrons.
See also: Chemistry; Electricity.

Electrocution, usually fatal effect of passing a high-energy electrical current through a body. Electricity passing through the body fluid, which acts as a resistor, causes burns at sites of connection and along the electrical pathway. Convulsions

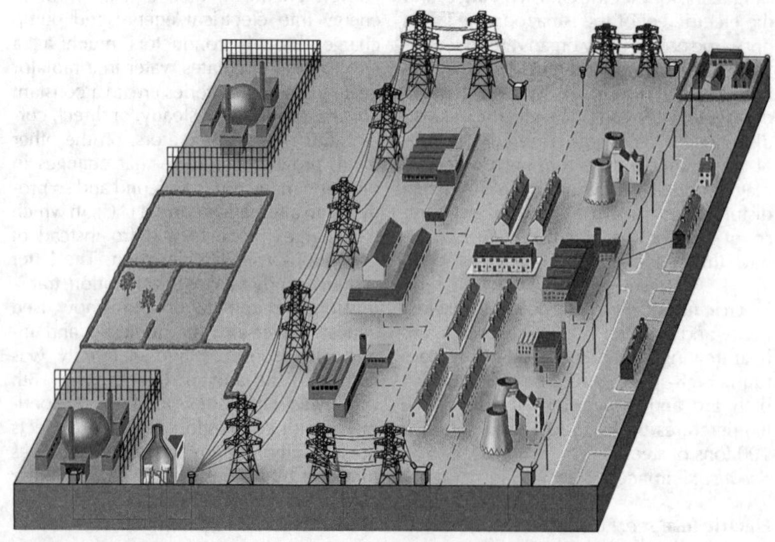

Electricity is transmitted from the generating station to the consumer by a network of overhead lines or underground cables. The loss of energy in such cables is related to the current flowing, and to achieve a minimum loss the voltage must be as high as possible. A typical system is shown. The voltages used at each stage depend on whether the transmission is overhead or underground and on the type of consumer.

and rhythm disturbances in the heart are usual; the latter are the cause of immediate death. Artificial respiration with cardiac massage must be started immediately if resuscitation is to be successful.

Electrode, electric conductor that supplies current. Electrodes are used in electrolytic cells, and electric furnaces contain electrodes between which an electric arc forms for heating. Electronic tubes and discharge tubes contain electrodes for the transmission of an electric current through gas at low pressures. The anode is the electrode carrying a positive charge, and the cathode has a negative charge.

Electroencephalograph, instrument for recording the brain's electrical activity using several small electrodes on the scalp. Its results are produced in the form of an electroencephalogram (EEG). The EEG is a convenient method for the investigation of brain disturbances and disease (benign and malignant tumors, disturbances in blood vessels, epilepsy, inflammation, metabolic changes). The German psychiatrist Hans Berger began to record electrical activity in human brains in 1929. There are certain normal patterns for "brain waves" in the alert and the sleeping individual. In a normal person, several varieties of rhythmic activity appear in different circumstances. The most prominent rhythm, noticeable when a healthy subject closes his or her eyes, shows a period of 8-13 cycles per sec that is chiefly present at the occipital pole of the cerebral hemispheres. This is the *alpha rhythm.* Sleep removes this rhythm and may substitute others in its place. *Theta rhythm,* with a frequency of 4-7 cycles per sec, occurs typically in the parietal and temporal regions of the brain and is associated with childhood and with emotional stress in some adults. *Beta rhythm,* with frequencies higher than 15 cycles per sec, is generally associated with activation and tension.
See also: Brain.

Electrolysis, process of changing the chemical composition of a conducting material (electrolyte) by sending an electric current through it.

Electrolyte, electrical conductor in which the current is in the form of ions—atoms with an electric charge—rather than free electrons, as is the case with a wire. Electrolytes are usually liquids, usually water solutions of acids, bases, or salts.

Electromagnet, device that produces a temporary magnetic field when an electric current flows through it. It contains a core, usually of iron, around which a coil of wire is wound. Electromagnets are used to produce strong magnetic fields in generators and motors, electric relays, and bells. They are also used to lift heavy metal loads.
See also: Henry, Joseph.
See also: Magnetism.

Electromagnetic force *see:* Grand Unified Theories.

Electromagnetic waves, patterns of electric and magnetic force. Gamma rays, X-rays, ultraviolet light, visible light, infrared rays, microwaves, and radio waves are different kinds of electromagnetic radiation, all of which behave as waves. In 1865 the Scottish scientist James Clerk Maxwell published his equations describing the behavior of electromagnetic waves. These equations have proven to be one of the most successful theories of modern science.
See also: Magnetism.

Electromagnetism, in physics, relation between electricity and magnetism based on the facts that electric currents produce magnetic fields and magnetic fields produce electric fields. These discoveries were made in the 1820s by physicists Hans Oersted (Denmark) and André Marie Ampère (France), working independently. Their work led to the development of the electromagnet, the basis of the electric motor, the telephone, and the loudspeaker, among other devices. *Electromagnetic induction* is the production of an electric current as a conductor moves in a magnetic field, or is situated in a magnetic field that is changing in strength. This effect was discovered by physicists Michael Faraday (England) and Joseph Henry (U.S.) in 1831, again independently. It is the basis of the electric generator and the transformer.

Electromotive force (emf), loosely, voltage produced by a battery generator or other source of electricity; more precisely, unit of measure of electrical energy per unit of electricity from a generator.

Electromotive series, or electromechanical series, ranking of metals according to their tendency to lose electrons in chemical reactions. Metals that lose electrons more easily will generally react more easily with other elements.

Electron, elementary particle circling the nucleus of an atom. By convention, an electron is one negative charge. The flow of electrons is an electrical current. Joseph John Thomson demonstrated the existence of the electron in 1897.
See also: Atom.

Electron gun, device that produces and aims a beam of electrons to produce a visual pattern on a phosphorescent screen. Electron guns are used in televisions, X- ray machines, and electron microscopes.

Electronic game, game generally featuring lights and sounds on a screen, controlled by microprocessors or tiny computers. Themes for the games vary enormously, and players can compete against the computer itself or against one another.

Electronic music, music composed of sounds and manipulated, created solely on electronic equipment. Concrete music uses recordings of natural sounds as the basis for composition, and works mixing both approaches are called "tape music." Experiments with electronic composition began as early as the 1890s, but widespread production began only after World War II, as universities and broadcasting authorities in many countries began setting up studios to encourage this use of modern technology. Edgard Varèse, John Cage, and Karlheinz Stockhausen have produced important works in this field.

Electronics, applied science dealing with the development and behavior of devices in which the motion of electrons is controlled. It covers the behavior of electrons in gases, vacuums, conductors, and semiconductors. Its theoretical basis lies in the principles of electromagnetism and solid-state physics discovered in the late 19th and early 20th centuries. Electronics began to grow in the 1920s with the development of radio. During World War II, the United States and Britain concentrated resources on the invention of radar and pulse transmission methods, and by 1945 they had enormous industrial capacity for producing electronic equipment. The invention of the transistor in 1948 as a small, cheap replacement for vacuum tubes led to rapid development in such areas as computers, radio and TV receivers, and sound production and reproduction. Now, with the widespread use of integrated circuits, electronics plays a vital role in communications and industry. All electronic circuits contain both active and passive components and transducers (e.g., microphones), which change energy from one form to another. *Passive components* are normally conductors and are characterized by their properties of resistance, capacitance, and inductance. *Active components* are electron tubes or semiconductors; they contain a source of power and control electron flow. Semiconductor diodes and transistors, which are basically sandwiches made of 2 different types of semiconductor, now usually perform the general functions once done by tubes, being smaller, more robust, and generating less heat. Demands for increased cheapness and reliability of circuits have led to the development of microelectronics. In printed circuits, printed connections replace individual wiring on a flat board to which about 2 components per cu cm are soldered. Integrated circuits assemble tens of thousands of components in a single structure, formed directly by evaporation or other techniques as films about 0.03 mm thick on a substrate.

Electron microscope, microscope that uses beams of electrons to produce extremely high magnifications. The optical microscope cannot produce images of objects smaller than the wavelength of the light used. But when the French physicist Victor De Broglie discovered in 1924 that electrons could behave like waves, it became apparent that streams of electrons could be manipulated to produce magnified images. A wavelength 100,000 times shorter than that of green light could be produced, making enormous magnifications possible. In 1935 an instrument was produced that exceeded the resolution of the optical microscope. An electron gun, consisting of a hot tungsten filament and electrodes carrying up to 100,000 volts, generates a stream of high-velocity electrons. This electron beam is controlled by a system of magnetic fields generated by circular coils that are analogous to the lenses in ordinary microscopes. The beam has to travel in a high vacuum (about 1/10,000,000 atm) to avoid scattering the electrons and blurring the image. The object to be examined must be extremely thin to allow the passage of the electrons. On passing through the specimen, the electrons are scattered to varying extent by the different atoms in it. The scattered electrons produce contrast in an image either on a photographic plate or on a fluorescent screen. Further magnification can be obtained by enlarging the photograph. Instrumental magnifications up to 200,000 are common, and with photographic enlargements, magnifications exceeding 2 million can be made. On May 20, 1970, Albert V. Crewe of the University of Chicago succeeded in taking pictures of individual uranium and thorium atoms in organic compounds. He has also taken remarkably fine pictures of DNA, the complex helical molecule that carries genetic information in almost all living organisms.

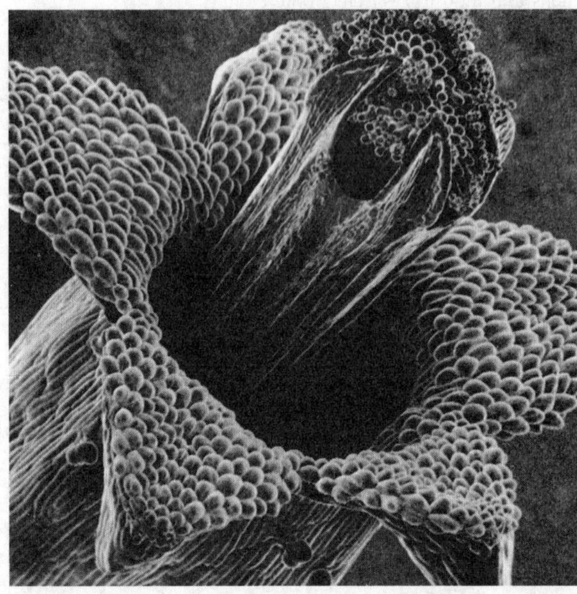

Ductal flower of a composite (daisy) magnified 80 times by means of a screen electron microscope. The large depth of focus gives the image a much more natural appearance than is possible with the simple microscope.

Electron tube, device used for amplifying electrical signals or currents. It consists of electrodes sealed in a glass tube that may contain a vacuum, but usually includes traces of gas. Once widely used in radio, television, and computers, electron tubes have been largely replaced by the transistor.

Electrophoresis, process by which components of large biological molecules are separated by being subjected to electric fields. An electric current causes positively and negatively charged molecules to move in opposite directions, thus separating them.

Electroplating, process by which a metal coating is produced by the action of an electric current. The object to be plated is placed in a solution of the metal it is to be coated with. The metal's atoms are ions—that is, electrically charged. The immersed object is negatively charged by an applied electric current, and the ions of the metal are attracted, affixing themselves to the object. A variety of metals, from gold to cadmium or nickel, are used in electroplating. Most coatings are quite thin, from 0.001 to 0.002 in (0.03 to 0.05 mm).

Electroscope, instrument for detecting electrostatic charge. It works on the principle that 2 bodies having the same charge will repel each other. In the *gold leaf electroscope* the 2 bodies are a rod and a piece of gold leaf, or two pieces of gold leaf. If the electroscope can be used to measure the charge, it is also known as an *electrometer.* The *quadrant electrometer* consists of a hollow circular box divided into 4 quadrants. A hollow plate inside the box is deflected by the quadrants when a charge is applied, and the amount of deflection gives the quantity of electrostatic charge. Other kinds of electrometers include instruments that depend on the deflection of a quartz fiber in an electrostatic field and modern instruments containing electronic amplifiers. Electroscopes can detect and measure the intensity of ionizing radiations such as X-rays.

Electrostatic precipitator, device that removes smoke and other particles from industrial fumes. The fumes pass through a chamber that is hung with steel tubes or plates, within or between which are suspended thin rods. A high-voltage current is fed to the rods, producing a negative charge on the particles in the fumes. The particles are then attracted by electric forces to the plates and precipitated from the fumes. The plates are shaken or knocked to dislodge the resulting deposits, which fall into a hopper and are removed. Up to 97% of particles in fumes can be captured in a precipitator. Frederick G. Cottrell built the first practical precipitator in 1904.

Electrotyping, method of creating reproductions of type, engravings, or etchings. The process was initially publicized in St. Petersburg by M.H. von Jacobi in 1838. Electrotyping was widely used until the 1960s, when more advanced techniques became available.

Elegy, in classical poetry, lyric poem of alternate 2-line stanzas written in a distinctive meter. In English, an elegy is a poem expressing sorrow, particularly about death, such as John Milton's "Lycidas" (1637), Thomas Gray's "Elegy Written in a Country Churchyard" (1750), and Percy Bysshe Shelley's "Adonais" (1821).

Element, in chemistry, substance that cannot be broken down into simpler substances by normal chemical processes. Elements are generally mixtures of different isotopes. The elements are classified by physical properties as metals, metalloids, and nonmetals, and by chemical properties and atomic structure according to the periodic table. Most elements exhibit allotropy (more than one elemental form), and many are molecular. The elements have all been built up in stars from hydrogen by complex sequences of nuclear reactions.

Robert Boyle (1627-91) was the first to distinguish between elements and compounds. The first scientific list of elements was prepared by Antoine Lavoisier in 1789. He listed 33 substances, mistakenly including heat and light. By the mid-1800s it became apparent that certain elements had similar properties and could be grouped together. The first periodic tables were produced and stimulated the search for the undiscovered elements that would fill the gaps in the table. By 1925 all the naturally occurring elements had been discovered. Now, 109 elements are known, although elements 104 through 109, created within the past 30 years, have not been officially recognized by the International Union of Pure and Applied Chemistry. Sixteen of these have been produced artificially.

See also: Boyle, Robert; Chemistry.

Element 104 (unnilquadium), chemical element, symbol (Unq); for physical constants see Periodic Table. The name of this element is temporary, proposed by the International Union of Pure and Applied Physics. In 1964, Soviet workers at the Joint Institute for Nuclear Research at Dubna (USSR) produced what they claimed was isotope ^{260}104, by bombarding plutonium-242 with neon-22 ions. In 1969, scientists working under Albert Ghiorso at the University of California at Berkeley reported that they were unable to reproduce the work of the Dubna group but had produced isotopes of element 104, with mass numbers 257 and 259104 among them, by bombarding californium-249 with carbon-12 and carbon-13 ions. The names kurchatovium and rutherfordium have been proposed.

Element 105, chemical element; for physical constants see Periodic Table. In 1967, Georgii N. Flerov and his associates at the Joint Institute for Nuclear Research at Dubna (USSR) reported producing element 105 with mass numbers 260 and 261 by bombarding americium-243 with neon-22. In Oct. 1971, element 105 with mass number 261 was reported to have been synthesized by Albert Ghiorso and his co-workers by bombarding californium-250 with nitrogen-15, and by bombarding berkelium-249 with oxygen-16. Element 105 with mass number 262 was produced by bombarding berkelium-249 with oxygen-18.

Element 106, chemical element; for physical constants see Periodic Table. In June 1974, workers at the Joint Institute for Nuclear Research at Dubna (USSR) reported producing element 106 by bombarding lead-206, 207, and 208 with chromium-

54. In Sept. 1974, Albert Ghiorso and co-workers bombarded californium-249 with oxygen-18 to produce element 106 with mass number 263. In 1984, Peter J. Armbruster and his co-workers in West Germany at the Heavy Ion Research Laboratory (GSI) at Darmstadt produced element 106 with mass number 261. It was seen to be a decay product of element 108 at this time.

Element 107, chemical element; for physical constants see Periodic Table. In 1976, Soviet scientists at the Joint Institute for Nuclear Research at Dubna (USSR) produced what they claimed was element 107 with mass number 261, by bombarding bismuth-204 with chromium-54. In 1981, Peter J. Armbruster and his co-workers in West Germany at the Heavy Ion Research Laboratory (GSI) at Darmstadt produced element 107 with mass number 262 by bombarding bismuth-209 with chromium-54 nuclei as well. The recoiling product atom was separated by a newly developed velocity filter. The new element decayed by three consecutive alpha-particle emissions to element 105 in 165 ms to lawrencium in 1.2 sec. and to mendelevium in 18.1 sec. It then became fermium by electron capture and emitted an alpha-particle to become californium.

Element 108, chemical element; for physical constants see Periodic Table. Peter J. Armbruster and his co-workers in West Germany at the Heavy Ion Research Laboratory (GSI) at Darmstadt produced element 108 with mass number 265 by bombarding lead-208 with iron-58 nuclei. The recoiling product atom was separated by a newly developed velocity filter. The new element decayed by three consecutive alpha-particle emissions to element 106 in 2.4 ms and then to element 104 in 360 ms, and finally to nobelium in 9.8 seconds.

Element 109, chemical element; for physical constants see Periodic Table. Peter J. Armbruster and his co-workers in West Germany at the Heavy Ion Research Laboratory (GSI) at Darmstadt produced element 109 and confirmed its existence by four independent measurements on Aug. 29, 1982. It was produced by bombarding bismuth-209 with iron-58 nuclei. The recoiling product atom was separated by a newly developed velocity filter. The new element decayed by consecutive alpha-particle emissions to element 107 in 5 ms and then to element 105 in 22 ms. element 105 became element 104 by electron capture and this decayed by spontaneous fission.

Element 110, chemical element; for physical constants see Periodic Table. Yuri T. Oganessian and co-workers in Dubna in the USSR claimed discovery of element 110. It is a spontaneous fissioning nuclide with a mass of 272 and a half-life of 10 ms.

Elementary school, also known as grade school or grammar school, first school in the normal sequence of public education, consisting of the first 6 to 8 grades. Many school systems designate the 7th and 8th grades as a separate junior high school. The first effort to legislate for education in America was in Massachusetts in the 1640s, when parents and masters of apprentices were directed to take care for "the ability to read and understand the principles of religion and the capital laws of the country." Education, in other words, was to ensure the citizen's obedience to God and the state. Public education in the first instance was particularly for the poor. The rich were educated either at home by a tutor or in private schools dependent upon bequests and tuition fees. When state money was available for education it was more likely to be spent on colleges and universities than on "common schools." The workingmen's societies that appeared in the urban North in the 1830s helped lead eventually to both the labor union movement and universal public education. The latter became a principle of Jacksonian democracy and came from a faith in common education as a means of erasing social differences. Whatever their political beliefs, U.S. citizens have tended to share a common faith in education as the most effective means of achieving a free and democratic society. Since the influence of John Dewey at the beginning of the 20th century, there has been a growing belief in elementary education as a means to develop the whole person rather than to produce a conditioned response through rote learning. The liberal view received a temporary setback in the 1950s, when the USSR's apparent victory in the space race led to the demand for a vigorous revival of the "three Rs" (reading, writing, and arithmetic). Elementary education has also come under attack for its lack of success in teaching some children to read effectively. Many schools located in urban centers have been increasingly unable to deal with overcrowded classrooms, and the wide range of the students' cultural background which makes traditional teaching difficult.
See also: Education.

Elephant, largest living land animal, of which there are 2 species, the African (*Loxodonta africana*) and the Indian (*Elephas maxima*). The African elephant is the larger of the 2, standing up to 11 1/2 ft (3.5 m) and weighing 6 tons (5,400 kg). It has larger ears and tusks, a sloping forehead and 2 "lips" at the end of the trunk, compared with the Indian elephant's 1 "lip." The trunk is a long, flexible snout with nostrils at the tip, and the sense of smell is very acute. The trunk is also used for carrying food and water to the mouth and for spraying water during bathing. The African elephant is found over most parts of Africa south of the Sahara, usually in open country. It uses its large ears as radiators to keep cool. The Indian elephant lives from India to Sumatra and stays mainly in dense cover. The habits of the 2 species are similar. They live in herds that are led by an elderly cow, the old bulls being solitary. They feed on grass, foliage, and twigs and in some places destroy woodland by pushing over trees and bushes. The Indian elephant is used as a beast of burden. African elephants were once trained for use in warfare. Elephants are the major source of commercial ivory, and uncontrolled hunting considerably reduced their number, particularly in Africa. Since the 1970s international wildlife organizations have worked to prohibit sale of tusks and ivory products.

Tamed Indian elephants in Indo-China are still used as pack and draught animals in forestry.

Elephant bird, extinct, flightless bird (genus *Aepyornis*) of Madagascar. Elephant birds were like massive ostriches, up to 10 ft (3 m) tall, with eggs over 1 ft (0.3 m) long. They may have been the origin of the legend of the giant roc bird.

Elephantiasis, chronic disease characterized by gross thickening of the skin or swelling of the lower limbs and external genital organs. The most common form is a tropical disease due to filariae (parasitic worms) entering the lymph channels and causing obstruction.
See also: Filaria.

Elephant's ear, plant of the arum family, especially *Colocasia antiquorum*, grown for its large ornamental leaves, which spring from a rhizome (underground stem). Two species, *dasheen* and *taro*, are grown in Southeast Asia for their edible rhizomes.

Eleusinian mysteries, secret religious rites in ancient Greece. They were originally performed in honor of Demeter, goddess of agriculture, at Eleusis, near Athens, dramatizing the descent of her daughter Persephone into the underworld and her inevitable return from the land of the dead, symbolizing the endless seasonal cycles. Later the rites were performed in Athens.
See also: Greece, Ancient.

Elevator, device that transports people or goods from one floor to another in a building. Elisha Otis's invention of an elevator

with an automatic safety device (1840s) permitted the construction of tall buildings and skyscrapers. Most elevators use an electric traction system that lifts the elevator car with steel cables. Geared traction elevators can travel up to 450 ft (137 m) per min, while gearless ones can travel up to 2,000 ft (600 m) per min.
See also: Otis, Elisha Graves.

Eleventh Amendment *see:* Constitution of the United States.

Elgar, Sir Edward William (1857-1934), English composer. Elgar followed the German orchestral and choral traditions of the 19th century, but his *Enigma Variations* (1899) and *Pomp and Circumstance* marches (1901-30) reflect a distinct English style. Other important works include the oratorio *The Dream of Gerontius* (1900), 2 symphonies, violin and cello concertos, and the concert overture *Cockaigne* (1901).

Elgin Marbles, ancient sculpture (mostly from the Acropolis) that Thomas Bruce, 7th Earl of Elgin and British envoy at Constantinople (1799-1802) shipped from Athens, Greece (then a Turkish possession), to London. They were bought by the government (1816) for half the cost of their transportation and are preserved in the British Museum, London. They include a frieze from the Parthenon by Phidias and parts of the temple known as the Erechtheum.

El Greco *see:* Greco, El.

Elhuyar, Fausto and Juan José de *see:* Tungsten.

The English novelist, George Eliot, painted at the age of 23 by Charles Bray

Elijah, or **Elias** (9th century B.C.), Hebrew prophet who, according to the Book of Kings of the Old Testament, resisted pagan idol worship during the reign of Israel's King Ahab. An outspoken enemy of Queen Jezebel, he was instrumental in thwarting her attempts to introduce the worship of Baal into Israel. During his own lifetime a number of supernatural events were ascribed to him, including restoring a dead child to life. The Bible recounts that he ascended to heaven in a fiery chariot.
See also: Bible; Old Testament.

Elijah Muhammad *see:* Muhammad, Elijah.

Eliot, Charles William (1834-1926), U.S. educator, president of Harvard University from 1869-1909 and editor of the original *Harvard Classics* series. Eliot profoundly influenced American education by developing Harvard into a great university.

Eliot, George (Mary Ann Evans; 1819-80), English novelist. Her writing was distinguished by a subtle style and compassionate understanding of character. Through her work for the *Westminster Review* she met writer George Henry Lewes, who recognized her talent and encouraged her to write. They lived together from 1854 till his death in 1878. From 1858 to 1866 she published *Scenes of Clerical Life, Adam Bede, The Mill on the Floss, Silas Marner, Romola,* and *Felix Holt the Radical. Middlemarch* (1871-72) is generally considered her finest work.

Eliot, John (1604-90), Puritan clergyman. Born in England, he emigrated to Massachusetts in 1631 and devoted himself to the conversion of local Native Americans. He translated the Bible into an Algonquian language (1661-63) and wrote *Indian Primer* (1669).
See also: Puritans.

Eliot, T(homas) S(tearns) (1888-1965), U.S.-born poet, dramatist, and critic. His learned, ironic, witty (and sometimes obscure) poetry and criticism influenced the literature of an entire generation. His first important poem, "The Love Song of J. Alfred Prufrock," appeared in 1915, and *The Waste Land* appeared in 1922. These early poems, critical of the shallowness and squalidness of modern life, are in marked contrast to the later religiously colored poetry, such as *Ash Wednesday* (1930), and *Four Quartets* (1943). In 1927 he became a British citizen, declaring himself an "Anglo-Catholic in religion, royalist in politics, and classicist in literature." Reviving verse drama, he wrote *Murder in the Cathedral* (1935), *The Family Reunion* (1939), *The Cocktail Party* (1950), and *The Confidential Clerk* (1953). He was awarded the Nobel Prize for literature in 1948.

Elisha (9th century B.C.), Hebrew prophet, disciple of and successor to Elijah, whose life is described in II Kings of the Old Testament. Like Elijah, he acted as the conscience of the Hebrew king. He engineered the downfall of the dynasty of Omri and the rise of the house of Jehu. He was reputedly gifted as a soothsayer and healer.
See also: Old Testament.

Elixir, liquor sought by alchemists of the Middle Ages for turning metals into gold or prolonging life. In medical practice of today, the term is used to describe a tincture composed of various aromatic substances held in solution by alcohol in some form.

Elizabeth, name of 2 queens of England. **Elizabeth I** (1533-1603) was queen of England and Ireland (1558-1603) and the last Tudor monarch. A daughter of Henry VIII, who had broken with the Catholic Church to marry Anne Boleyn, her mother, her initial task as queen was to reestablish her supremacy over the English Church after the reign of her Catholic sister, Mary I. The defeat by her navy of the Spanish Armada (1588) established England as a major European power. At home, industry, agriculture, and the arts (especially literature) throve under conditions of relative peace and financial stability, and colonization of the New World was encouraged. The reign was plagued by the question of the Protestant succession as Elizabeth was unmarried and childless. After the execution of her Catholic cousin, Mary Queen of Scots, a possible heir, Elizabeth finally acknowledged the succession of James VI of Scotland, Mary's son, thus securing the peaceful union of England and Scotland. **Elizabeth II** (1926-) is queen of the United Kingdom of Great Britain and Northern Ireland (from 1952) and head of the Commonwealth of Nations. One of the world's few remaining monarchs, she is extremely popular at home and abroad and has traveled extensively as her country's representative. She married Philip Mountbatten, Duke of Edinburgh, in 1947 and has 4 children: Prince Charles, Princess Anne, Prince Andrew, and Prince Edward.

Elizabeth (1709-62), empress of Russia (1741-62), daughter of Peter the Great. She staged a coup against her cousin, Ivan VI, to gain the throne. She rid the court of German influence, founded Moscow University, and pursued the Seven Years War against Prussia.

Elizabeth (pop. 106,201), city in northeastern New Jersey, seat of Union County. An important port, it stands on Newark Bay, 12 mi (19.3 km) southwest of New York City. Products include sewing machines, toys, and chemicals. New Jersey's oldest English settlement, Elizabeth originated in 1664 and still has some colonial buildings. In 1746 Elizabeth became the first site of the College of New Jersey (later Princeton University). Its industrial development began in earnest in 1873, when the Singer Sewing Machine Company made its headquarters there. Other large industrial plants soon followed.
See also: New Jersey.

Elizabeth, Queen Mother of England *see:* George VI.

Elizabeth, Saint, mother of St. John the Baptist and kinswoman of Mary. According to Luke I, the angel Gabriel predicted the birth of John to Elizabeth and her husband Zechariah. Nov. 5 is the feast day for St. Elizabeth.
See also: Bible; New Testament.

Elizabethan Age *see:* Elizabeth I.

Elk, large member of the deer family. It inhabits some of the forest areas of northern Europe and Asia and is closely related to the larger American moose (*Cervus candensis*). The American elk (*Alces americana*) is also called the wapiti.

Ellery, William (1727-1820), U.S. political leader. He was a signer of the Declaration of Independence and a Rhode Island delegate to both the Continental Congress (1776-81) and the Congress of Confederation (1783-5).

Ellesmere Island, Canadian Arctic island off northwest Greenland, occupying about 80,000 sq mi (207,200 sq km) and consisting of ice-capped plateaus and mountains flanked by a coastline pierced by

deep fjords. Cape Columbia is North America's northernmost point.
See also: Baffin, William; Peary, Robert Edwin.

Ellice Islands *see:* Tuvalu.

Ellington, Duke (Edward Kennedy Ellington; 1899-1974), U.S. composer, pianist, and orchestra leader, one of the giants of jazz music. After a formal musical education, Ellington formed his first band in 1918 and by the 1930s enjoyed an international following. His superbly disciplined orchestra remained the envy of the jazz world for several decades, playing music composed by its leader for its well-known instrumental soloists. Ellington wrote such hit songs as "Mood Indigo," "Sophisticated Lady," and "Satin Doll," suites such as *Black, Brown and Beige* (1943), and late in life, considerable sacred music. He was awarded the Presidential Medal of Freedom in 1969.
See also: Jazz.

Ellipse, geometrical figure shaped like a circle viewed at an angle. There are 2 focal points in an ellipse, and the sum of the radii from them to any point on the curve is constant. It follows that an ellipse can be drawn with the help of 2 thumbtacks stuck in a piece of paper at the 2 foci with a loop of string attached to them. If the string is kept taut by a pencil, an ellipse will be generated as the pencil is moved along the string. The orbits of planets and their satellites are elliptical.

Ellis, (Henry) Havelock (1859-1939), British writer known for his studies of human sexual behavior and psychology. His major work was *Studies in the Psychology of Sex* (1897-1928).
See also: Psychoanalysis.

Ellis Island, island of about 27 acres (10.9 hectares) in upper New York Bay, within the boundaries of New York City. Bought by the government in 1808, it was the site of a fort and later an arsenal. From 1892 to 1954 it was an immigration station through which some 20 million immigrants entered the United States. It is now a national monument.
See also: Immigration.

Ellis Island, New York

Ellison, Ralph Waldo (1914-), African-American writer. His novel *Invisible Man* (1952), a story of black alienation in a hostile white society, won a National Book Award. *Shadow and Act* (1964) and *Going to the Territory* (1986) are collections of his essays and speeches.

Ellsworth, Lincoln (1880-1951), U.S. explorer and scientist. In 1925 he made the transpolar flight with the Amundsen expedition. The following year he flew from the Spitsbergen archipelago in the dirigible *Norge* across the North Pole to Alaska. In 1936 Ellsworth made the first flight across Antarctica, traveling 2,300 mi (3,700 km) in a single-engine airplane.
See also: Antarctica.

Ellsworth, Oliver (1745-1807), chief justice of the U.S. Supreme Court (1796-1800). At the Constitutional Convention of 1787 he proposed the Connecticut Compromise, which balanced the legislative representation of the large and small states by establishing the 2 Houses of Congress. As U.S. senator he was responsible for establishing the federal court system.
See also: Supreme Court of the United States.

Elm, deciduous tree (genus *Ulmus*) common to North America, Europe, and parts of Asia. It has toothed leaves and the seeds are carried on the wind by a wing. Elms, which grow to 160 ft (50 m) have tough wood, used in furniture and barrels. They are often grown as shade trees. The American, or white, elm (*U. americana*) is rapidly being killed off by Dutch elm disease, a fungus disease that is carried by the elm bark beetle. The disease, first identified in the Netherlands, appeared in the United States in the 1930s, spreading rapidly from New England. Other less valuable elms are immune to the disease.

Elman, Mischa (1891-1967), Russian-born U.S. violinist. He made his international debut in Berlin (1904), and first performed in the United States in 1908. He became a U.S. citizen in 1923.

El Misti, 19,101-ft (5,822-m) dormant volcano located in the Western Cordillera mountain range in Peru. El Misti had religious significance for the Incas and has inspired many Peruvian legends and poems.

El Niño, current that travels south along the Pacific coasts of Peru and Ecuador approximately every 4 years, warming the normally cold waters. The unusual warmth kills many fish and birds, and a particularly strong El Niño can cause severe storms and floods as far away as California.

Elodea, any of several underwater plants of the genus *Elodea*, some living in salt water, others in fresh water. They are sometimes used to help maintain the oxygen balance in aquariums.

Elohim, most common name for God used in the Old Testament. Although it is a plural form in Hebrew, the Canaanite root is singular. The Hebrews believed that the name of God should not be spoken, and therefore used substitutes such as Elohim and Adonai ("my Lord").

Duke Ellington

El Paso (pop. 591,610), city in western Texas and the seat of El Paso County. It is the largest city on the U.S.-Mexico border, situated on the Rio Grande, opposite Ciudad Juárez in Mexico. Copper smelting and refining are the major industries. Tourism, oil refining, lead smelting, meat packing, cement manufacture, brewing, and cotton processing also figure in its economy. El Paso is a regional headquarters for numerous federal agencies, and is also the site of Texas Western College. Nearby is Fort Bliss, a U.S. Army post and experimental station for guided missiles. Prior to the Texan declaration of independence (1836), which preceded the territory's annexation, the area was part of Mexico. The present site, settled in 1827, was named El Paso in 1859; it was incorporated in 1873.

El Salvador, republic in Central America, bordered by Guatemala to the west, Honduras to the north and east, and the Pacific Ocean to the south.
Land and climate. El Salvador is the only country in Central America with no Caribbean coastline. Two parallel mountain ridges cross the country from east to west enclosing generally fertile plateaus and valleys. The Lempa River (200 mi/322 km), Central America's largest, cuts across western and central El Salvador.
Economy. El Salvador has a high population density and a weak economy. Agriculture is the principal means of livelihood, and coffee is the major export. The land also yields food crops such as corn, rice, and beans, but El Salvador must import food to meet its needs. About 9% of the labor force is involved in the processing of food products and the production of a limited range of consumer goods.
History. El Salvador was colonized by Spain in 1524. After unsuccessful uprisings in 1811 and 1814, independence was won in 1821. The country was briefly part of a Mexican Empire (1821-23), and joined the United Provinces of Central America in 1825. Following the breakup of the federa-

El Salvador

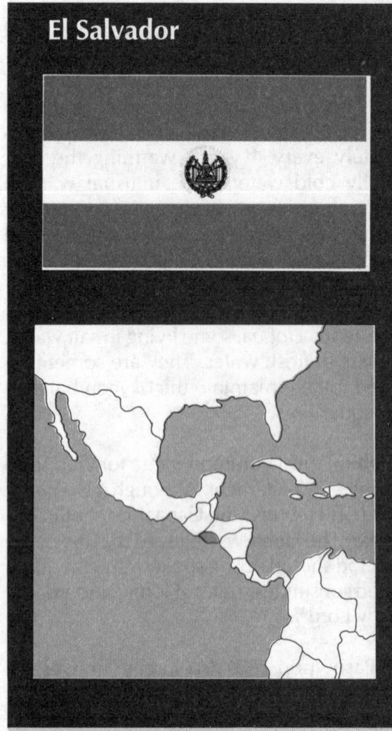

General information	
Capital:	San Salvador
Area:	8,260 sq mi (21,393 sq km)
Population:	5,138,000
Official language:	Spanish
Monetary unit:	1 Colón = 100 centavos
Main cities:	San Salvador, Santa Ana, Mejicanos
Government	
Form:	republic
Independent:	1841
Head of state:	President (elected every 5 years)
Head of government:	President
Legislature:	one legislative house (Legislative Assembly)
Executive:	President and Council of Ministers
Judiciary:	highest court is the Supreme Court of Justice
Political division:	14 departments
National economy	
Gross national product:	U.S. $4,780,000,000
Per capita income:	U.S. $950
Agriculture:	corn, coffee, sugarcane, rice, cotton, beans
Livestock:	cattle, pigs, horses
Fisheries:	120 metric tons
Mining:	very limited amounts of gold, silver, limestone
Industries:	food products, beverages, petroleum products, textiles, chemical products
Main exports:	coffee, footwear, clothing
Transportation:	374 mi (602 km) of railroads; 7,558 mi (12,164 km) of roads; 2 international airports
Trading partners:	United States, Guatemala, Germany, Japan, Mexico
People	
Urban:	47%
Ethnic composition:	mestizo 80%, Indian 15%, European 5%
Birth rate:	37 per 1,000 population
Death rate:	10 per 1,000 population
Infant mortality:	88 per 1,000 live births
Life expectancy:	male 56 years, female 61 years

El Salvador's Lempa River with moutain landscape

tion, El Salvador became an independent republic in 1839. During much of the 19th century the neighboring states of Guatemala and Nicaragua largely dominated the country's leadership. The development of the coffee crop led to the concentration of land ownership and wealth, and social and economic inequality generated deep divisions in society. The failure of land reforms led to armed violence between leftists and rightists throughout the 1970s and 1980s, with the United States backing various right-wing regimes, while Cuba and Nicaragua under the Sandinistas gave some help to the left-wing guerrillas. Between 1980 and 1986 some 56,000 people, most of them noncombatants, died in the bitter civil war, which continued into the 1990s.

Elzevir, family of Dutch printers and publishers. **Louis Elzevir** (1540?-1617) founded a bookselling business in Leiden (1583). **Bonaventure** (1583-1652), a son, and **Abraham** (1592-1652), a grandson, became printers to the university. The business later expanded to other Dutch cities, and the Elzevir printers were widely admired for their design and typography. In the early 18th century, the Elzevir company was the largest publishing company in the world.

Emancipation Proclamation, decree issued by President Abraham Lincoln on Jan. 1, 1863, abolishing slavery in the rebelling Confederate states. A shrewd military and political maneuver designed principally to deprive the Confederacy of its economic base, slavery, the proclamation also boosted the abolitionist cause, and 3 years later the 13th Amendment brought slavery in the U.S. to an end.
See also: Lincoln, Abraham.

Embalming, artificial process by which a corpse is prevented, at least temporarily, from decomposing. Embalming first appeared in ancient Egypt. Modern embalming began after William Harvey's discovery of the blood circulation in 1628. Embalming fluid is injected into an artery (arterial fluid) while blood is drained from a vein; then a stronger fluid (cavity fluid) is injected into the body's orifices and hollow organs. The most commonly used embalming fluid is formaldehyde.

Embargo, government detention of ships to prevent their departure from a port. A civil embargo applies to the ships and goods of the state issuing the order, while a hostile or political embargo is one imposed on ships and goods of another state, frequently involving war materials.

Embargo act, in U.S. history, statute prohibiting trade with other nations, usually for diplomatic reasons. The term refers to seagoing trade and technically means a refusal to let ships leave or enter port. The most controversial embargo was passed in 1807 by President Thomas Jefferson to prevent the warring nations of France and Britain from interfering with U.S. ships in order to enforce their blockades of each other's ports. Not only did the act fail in this regard, it also caused great economic loss to U.S. merchants and shippers. The measure's enormous unpopularity led to its replacement by the weaker Noninter-

course Act of 1809, and the entire dispute finally led the United States into the War of 1812.
See also: Jefferson, Thomas; War of 1812.

Embezzlement, crime involving someone legally entrusted with property belonging to another who takes it for personal use. Complicated bookkeeping and accounting procedures make detecting embezzlement difficult.

Embolism, presence of substances other than liquid blood in the blood circulation, causing obstruction in arteries or interfering with the pumping of the heart. The common causes of embolism are the breaking-away of fatty material from the wall of an artery, and thrombosis (blood clot formation) in a blood vessel or on the heart walls, where a fragment of clot breaks away. Fat globules from bone marrow may form emboli after major bone fractures. Emboli may also consist of bacteria, air bubbles, or amniotic fluid. Stroke (transient cerebral episodes), pulmonary embolism (in the lung), coronary thrombosis, and obstruction of the blood supply to a limb or organ with consequent cell death are common results, some of them fatal. Some emboli may be removed surgically, but prevention is preferable.
See also: Stroke.

Embossing, mechanical reproduction, by pressure, of designs and patterns in relief on various materials, such as metal, leather, fabrics, cardboard, and paper. The process involves passing the material between suitable dies or plates that impress the design from the back. Fabrics are embossed by passing them between copper cylinders, one engraved with the design, the other covered with felt and acting as the countercylinder, providing enough pressure to force the fabric into the hollows of the die-cylinder.

Embroidery, decorations on fabric produced by stitching with a needle and colored thread. A variety of threads and backing material are used. The basic stitches are flat, knotted, chained, or looped. This form of ornamentation has been used to decorate household items, peasant clothing, and the apparel of royalty for thousands of years, in many cultures around the globe.

Embryo, name for the young of plants or animals at the earliest stage of development, after fertilization. In seed-bearing plants, the term applies to the stage before the plant emerges from its seed. In egg-laying animals, it refers to the period before hatching. In mammals, the embryonic stage lasts until the creature's basic body shape and organs are formed, at which point it is called a fetus. Animal embryos have their origin in a zygote, an ovum (egg) that has been fertilized by a sperm. By the process of cell division, the ovum forms a small solid cluster called the morula. In the next stage, a hollow cavity one-cell thick called a blastula develops. A second layer of cells develops, forming a 2-layered gastrula. In higher animals there is a third cell layer. The outermost layer, the ectoderm, develops into skin, feathers, or scales, and the nervous system. The innermost layer, the endoderm, gives rise to the lining of the alimentary canal and certain internal organs. The middle layer, the mesoderm, becomes the skeleton, muscular system, heart and circulatory system, kidneys, and reproductive organs. Exactly how a set of virtually identical cells develops into a great variety of specialized tissues remains one of biology's mysteries.
See also: Birth.

Embryology, study of the development of embryos of animals and humans, based on anatomical specimens of embryos at different periods of gestation, obtained from animals or from human abortion. Embryology aids in the study of anatomy and of the development of organ systems and the origins of congenital defects. It may reveal the basis for the separate development of identical cells and for control of growth.
See also: Embryo.

Emerald, valuable green gemstone, a variety of the mineral beryl. Its beautiful color is attributed to the presence of a small amount of chromium. The best emeralds are mined in Muzo, Colombia. Good quality emeralds are also found in the Ural Mountains of the USSR. Since 1946 synthetic emeralds have been made in the United States. They fluoresce deep red in ultraviolet light, whereas natural emeralds do not fluoresce.

Emerald Isle, poetic name for Ireland, probably based on the predominant green color of the Irish landscape. The term was coined in the poem "Erin" (1795) by William Drennan (1754-1820).

Emerson, Ralph Waldo (1803-82), U.S. philosophical essayist, poet, and lecturer. He resigned a Unitarian pastorate (1831) and, after traveling in Europe, settled in Concord, Mass. His *Nature* (1836) was the strongest motivating statement of U.S. transcendentalism. After 1837 he became nationally renowned as a public speaker, and after 1842 as editor of the transcendentalist journal, *The Dial*. He later adjusted his idealistic view of the individual, expressed in essays and addresses like "The American Scholar" and "Self-Reliance," to accommodate the U.S. experience of humanity's historical and political limitations, especially over the issue of slavery.
See also: Transcendentalism.

Emery, naturally occurring impure form of corundum containing iron oxides and other minerals. It has long been used as an abrasive. A layer of finely ground emery is coated onto grinding wheels, paper, or cloth. Though synthetic abrasives have replaced it in many applications, it is still used to polish precious stones and in the manufacture of lenses, prisms, and optical equipment. The major source of emery is the island of Naxos in the Aegean Sea.

Emetic, substance used to induce vomiting. Emetics are of 2 main types. *Centrally acting emetics* stimulate the nerve center that controls vomiting. Apomorphine and picrotoxin are the best examples. *Reflex-action emetics*, including copper sulfate, mustard, ipecac, and solutions of common salt, irritate the mucous membrane of the stomach. Emetics are used primarily as emergency measures in cases of serious poisoning and acute indigestion.

Eminent domain, in the United States, government's inherent right to take private property for public use without the owner's consent. This right is often invoked to acquire land for highways, utilities, and harbors. Municipalities may also "condemn" property to build schools and hospitals, clear slums, or create parks. The 5th Amendment to the U.S. Constitution guarantees "just compensation" to the private owner.

Emin Pasha (Eduard Schnitzer; 1840-92), physician and explorer. Emin Pasha became a surgeon in the Turkish and Sudan armies. He was appointed governor of a Sudan province in 1873, and in 1887 he was created a pasha by Egypt. He was rescued from a Mahdi uprising in 1889 but was murdered by Arab slave traders while engaging in explorations for the German East Africa Company.

Emmet, Daniel Decatur (1815-1904), U.S. songwriter and minstrel show entertainer. His song "Dixie" (1859), originally written as a conclusion to a minstrel show, became the anthem of the Confederate Army during the Civil War.

Emotion, state of both body and mind consisting of a subjective feeling that is either pleasant or unpleasant but never neutral, accompanied by expressive behavior or posture and by physiological changes.

Empedocles (c.495-c.435 B.C.), Greek philosopher who lived in Sicily. He invented the theory that the universe was composed of 4 fundamental elements: earth, air, fire, and water. In medicine he taught that good health consisted of a balance of the 4 bodily "humors," corresponding to the 4 elements.

Emphysema, disease marked by the enlargement of the air sacs in the lungs, which interferes with breathing. Emphysema is probably caused by chronic bronchitis, genetic factors, smoking, air pollution, or various combinations of these factors. Lung infections are common side effects. The disease is generally chronic.

Empire State Building, office building in New York City. Rising 1,250 ft (381 m), it is one of the highest buildings in the world. It is one of the most popular tourist attractions in New York, and on a clear day there is a 50-mile (80.5-km) view from the top of its 102 stories. It was built in 1930-31 and designed by the architectural firm Shreve, Lamb and Harmon.

Empire style furniture and ornament originating in France 1800-1825 - was basically a revival of classical Greek, Roman, and ancient Egyptian forms. Classical fauna such as the winged lion (and lion's paw foot) on chair arm (1), and swan (2) appeared on all categories of Empire furniture as did the term (6) and other human based forms. Classically inspired motifs were used on pierced chair back, the "palmettes" back (3) being an important example. The lyre-shape was used in this way and as a table support (5). Applied gilded bronze ornaments drawn from the classical repertoire are an integral part of Empire style; (4) shows a detail of such ornament while (7) shows a couch side enhanced by gilded ornament.

Empire style, French neoclassical style in architecture, interior decoration, and furniture design that peaked during the Napoleonic empire (1804-14). In architecture, Roman grandeur was imitated; mahogany and gilt were favored materials for furniture; and costume design was inspired by classical drapery.

Empiricism, philosophical theory that regards experience, mental or physical, as the only source of knowledge. With its emphasis on experimentation and its opposition to the concept of innate ideas, empiricism arose parallel to the development of experimental science during the 17th and 18th centuries, especially in England. Its major originators were John Locke (1632-1704) and David Hume (1711-76).

Employee benefits *see:* Pension; Profit sharing.

Employee Stock Ownership Plan (ESOP), program allowing workers to own part of the stock in a company. Each worker's share is usually proportionate to his or her salary. The company also contributes to the ESOP on a regular basis. Employees either cash in their shares upon retirement or collect yearly dividends.

Employment agencies, privately or publicly owned organizations that help workers find employment and employers to find workers. Private employment agencies receive a fee for their services usually based on the salary to be paid. In the U.S. there is an extensive network of public employment offices, whose services are free. The U.S. Employment Service in the Department of Labor coordinates the efforts of state agencies.

Employment Service, United States, agency of the U.S. Department of Labor. As part of the Employment and Training Administration, this agency helps match employees with employers and visa versa. Also known as USES, it sets national policies for public employment services, provides a network of computerized job banks, and dispenses funds for state employment services, of which there are about 2,200 offices.

Emu, flightless, ostrichlike bird (*Dromiceius novaehollandiae*) of Australia, having long, coarse feathers that hide its wings. Emus are large (up to 6 ft/1.8 m tall) and are fast runners. The male incubates the eggs and guards the chicks.

Emulsion, preparation of minute drops of one liquid dispersed evenly throughout another liquid. Each liquid is called a *phase*. One phase is usually water or an aqueous solution, and the other phase is usually an oil or other immiscible liquid. An emulsion consisting of oil droplets dispersed in water, called an *oil-in-water* emulsion, has properties like those of water, although an oil-in-water emulsion may contain so much oil that it is a semisolid paste in consistency. If water droplets are dispersed in oil, the emulsion is a *water-in-oil* emulsion and has the properties of an oil. An emulsion is made by shaking or stirring the 2 liquids together, or beating them in a homogenizer. Unless the emulsion is very dilute, it requires an emulsifying agent such as a soap to prevent the dispersed droplets from coagulating together. Milk, butter, and mayonnaise are all emulsions. Emulsions are used in pharmaceutical preparations, cosmetics, paints, asphalt, and lubricants. The word *emulsion* is also used to describe the light-sensitive coating on a photographic film.

Enabling act, legislation giving special powers to individuals or groups. It was by an enabling act in 1933 that the German National Socialists (Nazis), with Nationalist and Catholic Center support, obtained dictatorial powers. Enabling acts have been used in the United States to set up governments in the territories before they were joined to the Union as states.

Enamel, vitreous (glasslike) glaze fused on metal for decoration and protection. Silica, potassium carbonate, borax, and trilead tetroxide are fused to form a glass (called flux) which is colored by metal oxides; tin oxide makes it opaque. The enamel is powdered and spread over the cleaned metal object, which is then fired in a furnace until the enamel melts.

Encephalitis, inflammation of the brain and spinal cord. It may be a specific disease due to an insect-borne virus, or it may occur as a result of influenza, measles, German measles, chicken pox, or other diseases. Symptoms include headache, listlessness, and convulsions. A large number of organisms may invade the nervous system or its coverings (meninges), thus causing many forms of encephalitis or meningitis or a combination of both. When the disorder is described as meningitis, damage to the brain or spinal cord is secondary to the inflammation of the coverings. In encephalitis, if the coverings or meninges suffer at all, they do so secondarily to the inflammation of the brain and spinal cord.

Encephalograph *see:* Electroencephalograph.

Encomienda, labor system imposed by the Spanish in South America in the 16th century. Native Americans were required to pay tribute for their lands in return for Spanish protection. The system destroyed much of Indian culture.

Encounter group *see:* Sensitivity training.

Encyclical, letter from the Pope to the bishops of the Roman Catholic Church. Papal encyclicals set out guidelines for the application of theological and social Church teachings. Among the best-known encyclicals are *Rerum Novarum* (1891), on the condition of the working classes, by Leo XIII; *Pacem in Terris* (1963), on relationships between the Church and state, by John XXIII; and the controversial *Humanae Vitae* (1968), on birth control, by Paul VI.

Encyclopedia, reference work that summarizes all knowledge or a particular branch of knowledge in a series of articles arranged alphabetically or by subject. The original aim of the encyclopedia was to provide a general education. The word *encyclopedia* is of Greek origin, meaning instruction in the complete circle (*en kykloi*) of learning (*paideia*). While fragments of earlier works are known, the earliest extant encyclopedia is that of Pliny the Elder (1st century A.D.). Its 37 volumes concentrate on the natural sciences and are arranged by subject (rather than alphabetically). In the early Middle Ages, Isidore of Seville (6th-7th centuries) wrote ency-

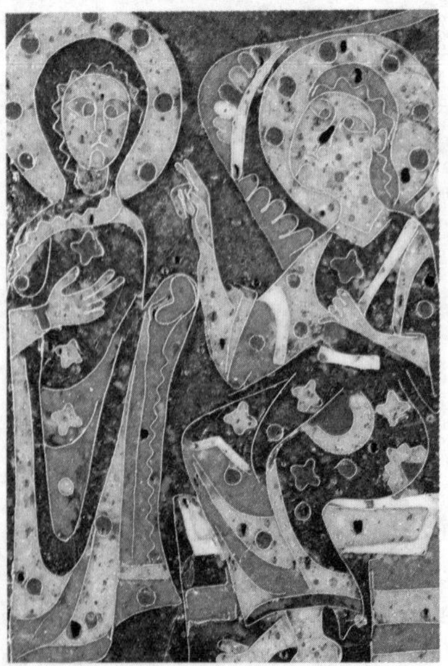

Enamel ornament, "Mary Magdalene with Angel at the Grave of Christ," on the Evangelarium of Aribert

clopedias based on 4 organizational principles: history, biography, arts, and words or subjects. His *Etymologiae* (also called *Origines*) in 20 books was an attempt to cover all knowledge, including the liberal arts, law, medicine, God, the Church, society, humanity, geography, food and drink, and tools. The most famous medieval encyclopedia was the *Speculum Majus* (Great Mirror) of Vincent of Beauvais (13th century), whose goal was to reflect "all things of all times." One of the earliest encyclopedias in English was the *Mirror of the World*, a translation of Beauvais, issued in 1481 by William Caxton. The 18th century inaugurated the great age of encyclopedias. The first English alphabetical encyclopedia, John Harris's *Lexicon Technicum* (1704), which emphasized the sciences, was soon superseded by Ephraim Chambers's *Cyclopaedia* (1728), which was among the first works to use articles written by specialists and to employ cross-references. The most important of the several German encyclopedias issued in this period was J.H. Zedler's *Great Complete Universal Lexicon*, issued in 64 volumes, 1732-50. The French *Encyclopédie*, the most famous and perhaps the most influential encyclopedia of all time, was edited by the philosopher Denis Diderot and Jean d'Alembert, 1751. The work promoted rationalism and scientific truth in the name of enlightenment. The *Encyclopaedia Britannica* began with a modest 3 volumes (1768-71) published by a "Society of Gentlemen in Scotland." Though it covered a great many subjects, it was mainly the work of a few men. Modern encyclopedias employ hundreds of specialists and large editorial staffs.

Endangered species *see:* Wildlife conservation.

Endecott, John (c.1589-1665), governor of the Massachusetts Bay Colony. He led the first group of Puritan colonists from England in 1628 and established a colony at Salem, Mass. In 1636 he conducted an expedition against the Pequot Indians and in 1644 became governor of the colony, serving for several terms. A zealous Puritan, he was intolerant of other religions.
See also: Massachusetts Bay Company; Puritans.

Enderby Land, western region of Antarctica extending from Ice Bay to Edward VIII Bay. It was first explored by John Biscoe (1831), an English navigator employed by the Enderby Brothers whaling company. Today it is the site of a Soviet research base.

Enders, John Franklin (1897-1985), U.S. microbiologist who shared the 1954 Nobel Prize for physiology or medicine with F.C. Robbins and T.H. Weller for their cultivation of the poliomyelitis virus in non-nerve tissues, an achievement that prepared the way for the development of polio vaccines.
See also: Microbiology.

Endive, leafy plant (*Cichorium endivia*) of the composite family, of the same genus as chicory. Used as a salad green or cooking vegetable, endive comes in curly-leaf and narrow-leaf varieties.

Endocrine gland *see:* Gland; Hormone.

Endocrine system, ductless glands that secrete chemicals called hormones, which regulate body functions. These organs and their general location are: pituitary gland in the brain, thyroid gland in the neck, parathyroid glands in the neck, adrenal glands in the abdomen, pancreas in the abdomen, ovaries in the abdomen (in females), and testes in the scrotum (in males). The hormones produced by the endocrine glands are extremely potent chemical substances that are effective in very minute quantities. They are secreted directly into the bloodstream and transported throughout the body.
See also: Hormone.

Endometriosis, condition in which tissue resembling the mucous membrane of the uterus—the endometrium—is present abnormally in various locations in the pelvic cavity. The endometrium normally builds up and flushes out periodically, but in endometriosis endometrial cells break off into cysts that move freely through the abdomen, attaching themselves to the ovaries and other organs and irritating surrounding tissue. The disease can cause infertility.

Endorphins, proteins produced by the pituitary gland (at the base of the brain) inhibiting certain brain cells from transmitting impulses and thereby blocking or reducing the sensation of pain. Endorphins were discovered in the 1970s, after it was realized that morphine and other opium-derived drugs inhibited pain by attaching to particular receptor sites in the brain. Endorphins are chemically similar to the opiates and function as natural painkillers.
See also: Pituitary gland.

Endymion, in Greek mythology, youthful lover of the goddess Selene. Various myths explain the eternal sleep and youth of the immortal Endymion. In one, Selene herself casts the spell; in another, Zeus offers eternal sleep and youth as an alternative to death. A poem named after Endymion was written by the English poet John Keats (1818).
See also: Mythology.

Energy, in physics, the capacity to do work. There are various forms of energy. Kinetic energy is the energy of motion, and is equal to one-half the mass of the moving body multiplied by the square of its velocity ($^1/_2mv^3$). Potential energy is the energy a body possesses by virtue of its position. A body raised to a certain height, *h*, for example, has a potential energy equal to its mass multiplied by *h* multiplied by the force of gravity. If the body were dropped, it would fall, and its potential energy would become kinetic. Other forms of energy include heat energy (the vibration of the molecules or atoms that make up substance), electrical energy (the motion of electrons), chemical energy (released by chemical reactions). Nuclear energy is produced when the nuclei of atoms disintegrate or combine, producing both heat and atomic and subatomic particles. One of the consequences of Einstein's theory of relativity is that mass and energy are mutually convertible. The relation between the 2 is described by the formula $E=mc^2$, where E is energy, m is mass, and c is the velocity of light. Since c^2 is a very large number, the transformation of even a small amount of matter (mass) into energy yields great quantities of energy. This is what happens in the explosion of a hydrogen bomb. Although matter can be transformed into energy and vice versa, and one form of energy can be transformed into another, neither mass nor energy can be created or destroyed. This is known as the law of conservation of mass-energy.
See also: Nuclear energy; Physics.

Energy, U.S. Department of, cabinet-level agency created Aug. 1977 to centralize national energy planning. The new department consolidated activities previously conducted by the Department of the Interior, the Energy Research and Development Administration, the Federal Energy Administration, and the Federal Power Commission.

Energy supply, total amount of energy available, from all sources, including fossil fuels (coal, oil, natural gas), water power, nuclear energy, solar energy, wind power, etc. Currently, fossil fuels supply the great majority of energy used in industry. The pollution caused by these fuels has stimulated the search for alternate sources of energy that would be clean, practical, and renewable.

Enewetak, or Eniwetok, atoll in the central Pacific Ocean, at the northwestern end of the Marshall Islands, a U.S. Trust Territory. It was used as a test site for nuclear weapons in the late 1940s and early 1950s.

Engels, Friedrich (1820-95), German socialist, philosopher, and associate of Karl Marx, with whom he founded modern communism. Born into a wealthy family, he went to England in 1842 to work in his father's textile mill. There he wrote his first major work, *The Condition of the Working Class in England* in 1844 (published 1845). Engels became a socialist as a result of his exposure to the negative effects of capitalism, and in 1844 he and Marx began a collaboration that lasted until Marx's death. In 1848 they published *The Communist Manifesto*, setting forth the principles of communism. After being active in revolutionary groups in France, Belgium, and Germany during the unsuccessful revolutions of 1848, Engels returned to England in 1850. He supported Marx financially while Marx worked on writing his greatest work, *Das Kapital*, and after Marx's death, he completed the second and third volumes of that work. Among his other works are *The Origins of the Family, Private Property, and the State* (1844) and

Friedrich Engels

Anti-Dühring (1878), a philosophical polemic that laid the basis for Marxism's claim to be a "scientific," as opposed to utopian, socialism.
See also: Communism; Marx, Karl.

Engine, machine that transforms energy into useful mechanical work. The most familiar engines are heat engines, which transform heat energy, obtained by burning fuel, into a force that turns wheels, propellers, turbines, and so on. Other types of engines include hydroelectric plants, which use the energy of falling water to spin rotors that generate electricity, and windmills, which harness the energy of the wind. Engines may be classified by the fuel they use (gasoline engine), by the way they burn their fuel (internal or external combustion), and by the way they produce motion (reciprocating, rotary, or reaction). In internal combustion engines combustion takes place inside the engine cylinders. The gaseous products of combustion press against pistons in the cylinders to produce reciprocating, or back-and-forth, motion. Jet and rocket engines work on the principle of reaction. They burn fuel in a combustion chamber to produce hot gases that leave the engine at high velocity through a nozzle. Reaction to the backward stream of gases thrusts the engine forward. Jet engines take in oxygen from the atmosphere to burn their fuel; rockets carry their own oxygen supply as well as their fuel and are thus independent of the atmosphere. The industrial equivalent of the jet engine is the gas turbine in which a turbine drives a shaft. Gas turbines are used mainly to drive generators, but they also power locomotives, ships, and even some experimental automobiles. Steam engines and steam turbines are external combustion engines, since they burn their fuel in a furnace outside the engine itself. The heat is used to produce steam in a boiler, and the steam drives a piston back and forth or spins the blades of a turbine. Steam turbines, which are highly efficient, are the major propulsion units in ships and the most widely used engines in the world's electricity-generating stations.
See also: Combustion; Steam engine; Turbine.

Windsor Castle, England

Chalk cliffs on the southern coast of England

Signpost of an English pub

Yorkshire moors, England

Engine analyzer, instrument that analyzes the performance of an automobile engine. Specific information about the engine's condition is obtained with oscilloscopes (instruments that measure electric current for the ignition system), tachometers (instruments that measure idling speed), and other devices that form part of the engine analyzer.

Engineering, applied science devoted to the design and construction of machinery and transportation and communications networks. Engineering is divided into many specialties (aeronautical, civil, chemical, electrical, mechanical, and so on), though the branches naturally overlap. The Engineers' Council for Professional Development, formed in 1932, recognizes 25 different branches. Until the 19th century, the term *engineer* signified a military engineer, responsible for fortifications, tunnels, and explosives, or a civil engineer, responsible for designing and building such structures as dams and bridges. The industrial revolution, however, opened up the fields of mechanical, chemical, and electrical engineering. The entry to engineering may be a 3-year or longer course at a university, engineering school, or technical institute, followed by practical experience in working on actual projects.

Engineers, Army Corps of, technical and combatant corps of the U.S. army, performing tasks of civil as well as military construction and projects such as harbors, waterways, airfields, and missile bases.

England, largest of the four countries that make up the United Kingdom of Great Britain. The others are Northern Ireland, Scotland, and Wales. England is governed by a constitutional monarchy. Queen Elizabeth II is the head of state but a cabinet of government ministers rule the country. England (pop. 48 mil.) is an urban country, with 95% of its citizens living in cities. London (pop. 7 mil.) is the capital and largest city. The major industries are manufacturing, mining, agriculture, and fishing. The official church is the Church of England (Anglican Church).
See also: Northern Ireland; Scotland; United Kingdom; Wales.

English Channel, arm of the Atlantic Ocean separating Great Britain and France. About 300 mi (483 km) long, it varies in width from about 112 mi (180 km) to about 21 mi (34 km) at the Strait of Dover.

English cocker spaniel, breed of sporting dog, most popular as a pet. The average English cocker spaniel stands 16 in (41 cm) tall at the shoulder, weighs from 26 to 34 lb (12 to 15 kg), and comes in a variety of colors.

English foxhound, breed of hound dog with a short, glossy coat, bred to follow the scent left by a fox. They are white with black or tan patches, stand 23 in (58 cm), on average, at the shoulder, and weigh 60 to 75 lb (27 to 34 kg).

English horn, musical instrument, in the oboe family, somewhat larger than a standard oboe. Its "bell" is pear-shaped , and its mouthpiece is a double reed.

English language, native language of more than 400 million people in the United States, the British Isles, Canada, Australia, New Zealand, and South Africa. English belongs to the Germanic branch of the Indo-European family of languages and is most closely related to Dutch, Flemish, and German. Old English originated when the languages of the Angle and Saxon tribes replaced those of the native Britons in invasions from the 6th to the 8th century. Only about one-fifth of modern English vocabulary comes from Old English, but this includes many words in frequent use, such as, *eat, drink, child,* and *house.* Scandinavian invasions from the 8th to the 11th centuries contributed Norse elements to the language. Old English evolved into Middle English largely as a result of the Norman invasion of 1066. The old inflectional endings of words began to disappear, and many thousands of French words were introduced. Early modern English began to emerge in about 1500, with major shifts in the pronunciation of vowels and drastic changes in the verb system. Greek and Latin words were absorbed into the language, partly as a result of the influence of the Renaissance, and spelling began to be made uniform. By the early 17th century, the language had attained something like its present form. American English evolved from the language of the early settlers, which varied according to their origin and social status. In some cases English words took on a new meaning; in others, Americans continued to use words no longer in use in England. Mostly because of its varied origins and international influences, the English language today has the largest vocabulary of any language. It has the second-highest number of native speakers (after Chinese), and the widest geographical influence.

English literature, poetry, prose, and drama written by authors from the British Isles, primarily England, Scotland, and Wales, and, to a certain extent, Ireland. English literature mirrors the development of the English language and is inextricably bound up with the country's history, politics, and social developments.

Old English literature (500-1100). Old English (OE) is the form of English spoken by the tribes of Angles, Saxons, and Jutes who settled in the British Isles in the 400s and 500s. The epic poem *Beowulf* is the first significant piece of English literature; its author is unknown. OE poetry is characterized by the use of alliteration (the repetitive use of words beginning with the same sound) and by its use of elaborate metaphoric phrases called kennings. The sea, for instance, may be referred to as "the whale-road." Caedmon (fl. 670) is the first known English poet, and the only work ascribed to him (by the Venerable Bede in 731) is a nine-line "Hymn of Caedmon." Prose works of that time comprised mostly histories and religious writings, Bede's *Ecclesiastical History of the English Nation* being the first and most important.

Middle English literature (1100-1485). The mixture of Latin (from the Catholic Church) and French (from the Norman invaders), overlaid on the earlier OE and local dialects, created Middle English (ME). ME literature developed the romances (primarily adventure stories told mostly in verse). The cycle of legends about King Arthur and the Knights of the Round Table is a major example of this genre. The most complete version (*Le Morte d'Arthur,* or *The Death of Arthur*) was written in the late 1400s by Sir Thomas Malory. The most important English author of ME literature was the poet Geoffrey Chaucer (c. 1340-1400). His *Canterbury Tales* (late 1300s) employed end rhymes and a five-beat line (iambic pentameter) that is still a mainstay of English poetry.

Development of modern English. During the 1400s, changes in the language brought about modern English; for example, by the late 1500s, people were writing and speaking in a language we can recognize today. During the reign of Queen Elizabeth I (1558-1603), England experienced a golden age of poetry and drama. William Shakespeare (1564-1616) is the greatest figure of English drama, but contemporaries included Ben Jonson (*Volpone, Bartholomew Fayre*) and Christopher Marlowe (*Tamburlaine the Great, The Tragical History of Doctor Faustus*).

In poetry, longer narrative verse was written by William Shakespeare (*Venus and Adonis*) and Edmund Spenser (*The Faerie Queene*). Both also wrote sonnet sequences (a series of sonnets on a single topic or person) which were a popular verse form of the time.

The Later Renaissance and the Commonwealth (1600-60). James I, a Stuart, ascended the throne after Elizabeth I. In 1648 the Puritans under Cromwell overthrew the monarchy and established a Commonwealth. The theater continued under James, but it took on a darker tone. Known as Jacobean drama, these plays often concentrated on action, violence, and the theme of revenge. John Webster's *Duchess of Malfi* (c. 1612-14) is a prime example of Jacobean tragedy. Other playwrights included Francis Beaumont and John Fletcher (*The Maid's Tragedy*), and John Ford (*The Witch of Edmonton*). The Puritans closed the theaters in 1648. John Donne was the leading *metaphysical* poet (a school of poetry that used vivid, common speech together with complex metaphorical allusions called *conceits*). Others in the group included Henry Vaughan and George Herbert. The Cavalier poets, on the other hand, concentrated on lighter verse. They are typified by the works of Robert Herrick and Richard Lovelace. The greatest poet of the era was John Milton, whose epic *Paradise Lost* (1667) was based on the Bible story of Adam and Eve. Perhaps the most enduring, influential prose work of the era was the King James version of the Bible (translated in 1611).

The Restoration (1660-1700). After the monarchy was restored in 1660, drama returned principally in the form of Restoration comedy, a comedy of manners that concentrated on the amorous pursuits of the upper class. Chief among the Restoration playwrights was William Congreve, whose *The Way of the World* (1700) is still a repertory staple. Others included William Wycherley, and Colley Cibber. Prose works of the era included John Bunyan's *Pilgrim's Progress* (1678). Serious drama and poetry were served by the outstanding poet John Dryden, as exemplified in his play *All for love* (1678) and his satire *MacFlecknoe* (1682).

The Augustinians (1700-50). The early 18th century saw a revival of classical, mainly Roman, aesthetics with an emphasis on reason, proportion, and elegance. This was especially manifest in the poetic satires of Alexander Pope, most notably in *The Rape of the Lock* (1712), and in the prose writings of the powerful satirist Jonathan Swift, author of *Gulliver's Travels* (1726). The novel came into its own in this period, with such writers as Henry Fielding, Tobias Smollett, Samuel Richardson, and Daniel Defoe. From mid-century to about 1785, criticism reached new heights with the works of Samuel Johnson and his circle, which included James Boswell, biographer, and Edward Gibbon, historian, and the playwright/poet Oliver Goldsmith.

Romantic literature (1785-1837). Pre-romantics, principally the poet William Blake, began the shift in emphasis from reason to feeling and emotion, as exemplified in his *Songs of Innocence* (1789) and *Songs of Experience* (1794). Other pre-romantic poets of the era included Thomas Gray, William Cowper, and the great Scottish poet Robert Burns.

The great romantic poets of the early 19th century were William Wordsworth and Samuel Taylor Coleridge. Their joint effort *Lyrical Ballads* (1798) heralded a change to elemental human emotions and a deep, personal tone. Later, the extraordinary group of Lord Byron, Percy Bysshe Shelley, and John Keats brought romantic poetry to its heights. The novel was also well-served by Jane Austen, *Pride and Prejudice* (1813), and Sir Walter Scott, *Ivanhoe* (1819). The Gothic novel (horror story) was created by Horace Walpole with the *Castle of Otranto* (1754) and was taken up by Mary Shelley, *Frankenstein* (1818).

The Victorian Age in literature (1837-1901). In 1837, Victoria was crowned Queen and inaugurated the longest reign in England (till 1901) and one of its most illustrious literary eras. The novel is the jewel in the crown of Victorian literature. Charles Dickens created worlds of vivid, memorable characters in works like *The Pickwick Papers* (1836-37) and *Oliver Twist* (1837-39) and, later, the grimmer side of Victorian life in *Bleak House* (1852-53) and *Hard Times* (1854). Major novelists of this period also included: William Makepeace Thackeray (*Vanity Fair*, 1847-48), Emily Brontë (*Wuthering Heights*, 1847), and Charlotte Brontë (*Jane Eyre*, 1847). Later Victorian novelists include such important figures as George Eliot (pen name of Mary Ann Evans), Thomas Hardy, and George Meredith.Late 19th-century poets often assumed a darker, more problematic tone, as in Lord Alfred Tennyson (*In Memoriam*, 1850), Matthew Arnold ("Dover Beach," 1867), and Robert Browning (*The Ring and the Book*, 1868-69). Drama came back after something of a hiatus for most of the century. By 1900, Oscar Wilde (*The Importance of Being Earnest*, 1895), and George Bernard Shaw (*Man and Superman*, 1901-03; *Major Barbara*, 1905) were producing witty comedies and socially trenchant dramas.

Twentieth-Century literature. Joseph Conrad (*Heart of Darkness*, 1902) wrote penetrating psychological novels while John Galsworthy (*The Forsyte Saga*, 1906-21, a series of three works) wrote realistic novels and plays. Virginia Woolf, largely forsaking normal plot and character development, wrote novels to describe inner reality using a technique called "stream of consciousness," as in *To the Lighthouse*, 1927. The Irish novelist James Joyce broke new ground in writing highly stylized, literary works that utilized interior monologues and random associations in ways not tried before, as in *Ulysses* (1922). The American-born T.S. Eliot (*The Waste Land*, 1922) wrote poetry in a distinctly modern idiom. Through both World Wars and up to today, literature in the British Isles has made major contributions to world culture. Among the significant novelists are D.H. Lawrence, Aldous Huxley, George Orwell, Graham Greene, and Evelyn Waugh. More recent novelists include C.P. Snow, Doris Lessing, and John LeCarré. Poets include W.H. Auden, Stephen Spender, Dylan Thomas, Philip Larkin, and Ted Hughes. Playwrights include: Christopher Fry, John Osborne, Tom Stoppard, and David Hare.

English setter, breed of sporting dog, with silky coats and long hairs (feathers) on their legs and tails. Setters stand, on average, 25 in (64 cm) at the shoulder and weigh from 50 to 70 lb (23 to 32 kg). Their strong sense of smell enables them to discover game for hunters.

English sparrow, or house sparrow, bird (*Passer domesticus*) of the weaverbird family. English sparrows were introduced into the United States from Europe in 1852 and have since become abundant both in cities and the countryside. About 6 in (15 cm) long, with reddish-brown streaked feathers, they are omnivorous.

English springer spaniel, breed of sporting dog, the original hunting spaniel, popular with Renaissance hunters. Springer spaniels stand, on the average, 18 to 21 in (46 to 53 cm) at the shoulder and weigh 37 to 55 lb (17 to 25 kg). They have long, thick, protective coats.

English toy spaniel, small dog, originally bred in Asia, which became popular with the English aristocracy in the 17th century. On the average, toy spaniels stand 10 in (25 cm) at the shoulder and weigh from 9 to 12 lb (4.1 to 5.4 kg). The King Charles is black and tan; the Prince Charles is black, tan, and white; the Blenheim is red and white; and the Ruby is red.

Engraving, art of cutting lines in wood, metal, or some other material to produce writing, ornamental designs, or illustrations. Most often, engraving means incising designs or illustrations onto a block or plate for reproduction by printing. The prints obtained by this process are also called engravings. In relief engraving, the background is cut away, leaving a raised design as the printing surface, while the more common intaglio process involves cutting the design into the block or plate, leaving concave traces that hold the ink. Various metals have been used as plates. Because of its durability, steel was fashionable in the 19th century. Copper, although subject to rapid wear, gives higher-quality results. The design may be cut into the metal with a sharp tool or with acid.

Enid (pop. 56,735), town in northwestern Oklahoma, originally a stopping place on the Chisholm Trail in the 1800s, now the fourth largest wheat storage space in the world.

Eniwetok *see:* Enewetak.

Enlightenment *see:* Age of Reason.

Ennius, Quintus (239-169 B.C.), classical Roman poet. His most important work was the epic *Annales*, a literary history of Rome beginning with the fall of Troy. It was the national poem of Rome until Vergil's *Aeneid*.

Ensor, James Sydney, Baron (1860-1949), Belgian painter whose bizarre, sometimes macabre canvases were influenced by Hieronymus Bosch and Pieter Bruegel and anticipated surrealism. Among his best-known works are *Entry of Christ into Brussels* (1888) and *The Temptation of St. Anthony* (c. 1888).

Entente, Triple *see:* Triple Entente.

Entomology, study of insects, of which there are more species than of any other animal. Entomology is important not only as an academic discipline, but also because insects are among the most important pests and transmitters of disease.
See also: Insect.

Entropy, in thermodynamics, the amount of disorder in a system. The second law of thermodynamics states that as any process goes on, the entropy of the system concerned either remains the same or rises. Disorder, in this sense, is mathematically defined as randomness. In everyday language, this means, roughly, that any physical system, left to itself, will tend to become increasingly chaotic.
See also: Thermodynamics.

Environment, total of affecting or influencing circumstances surrounding an organism's growth and development. Temperature, other people, and food supply are some of the components of a person's environment. A flower's environment includes soil, animals that feed on it, and sunlight.

Environmental impact statement, report on the possible environmental effects of a proposed construction project. Federal, state, local, and private projects for major construction on dams, highways, power plants, etc., in the United States must submit such a statement, which is required by the National Environmental Policy Act (1970). Results of this statement may become the basis for altering the project if its impact on the environment would be too seriously negative.

Environmental pollution, contamination of the air, land and water caused by human products. The sources of pollution include chemicals released by industrial processes, exhaust from gasoline-powered vehicles like automobiles, refuse and gases emitted by factories, sewage and garbage disposed of by cities, and pesticides used in agriculture. Greater awareness of health and environmental hazards has created pressure for laws that control the amount of released pollutants. Conservation efforts, such as recycling, also help to reduce pollution, and new technologies allow industry to release fewer pollutants into the environment. The long-term effects of pollution are not yet precisely known, but it is widely believed by scientists that global warming—the heating of the earth's atmosphere as a result of the greenhouse effect—is a threat to most forms of life on the planet.

Environmental Protection Agency (EPA), independent agency of the U.S. government established in Dec. 1970 to centralize government programs related to control of environmental pollution. The EPA employs more than 12,000 people, and through its Washington, D.C., headquarters and regional offices offers incentives to encourage cleanup efforts and enforces laws to curb pollution. The agency conducts research, provides technical assistance to states and cities, determines legal limits to pollution, and establishes timetables to bring polluters into line with standards.

Enzyme, any of the more than 1,000 proteins that act as catalysts in chemical reactions in life processes. Generally, enzymes speed up chemical reactions in cells that otherwise would occur too slowly to sustain life. The enzyme itself is not changed

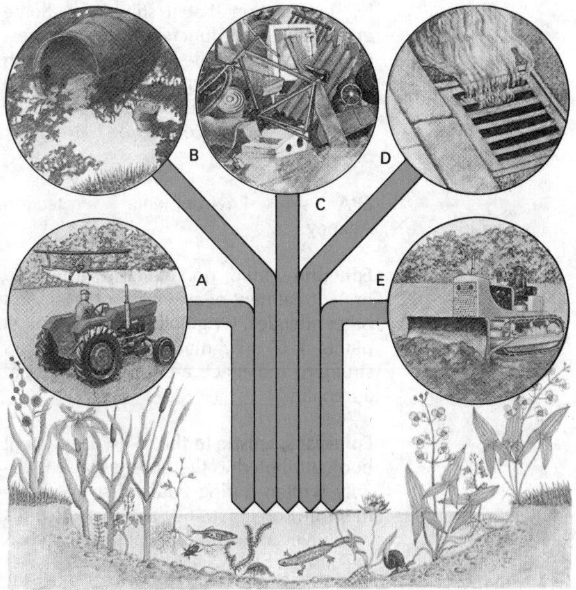

Ponds are now in the process of being destroyed. The following conditions are responsible: (A.) excess fertilizer, pesticides, and herbicides in the form of run-off or spray drift from farms; (B.) residue from rusty metal containers; (C.) rubbish; (D) run-off from drains containing oil deposits; (E.) land fill.

Some main sources of pollution: nuclear power plants (radiation), industrial pollution (sulfur dioxide, nitrogen dioxide), automobiles (carbon monoxide), and illegal dumping (pesticides, herbicides).

by the reaction that it stimulates. Some enzymes cannot function without accessory substances, called coenzymes, which are supplied by food. Many minerals and vitamins act as coenzymes, which is why their absence in a diet may be harmful.
See also: Protein.

EPA *see:* Environmental Protection Agency.

Ephedrine, mild, nonaddictive drug used in the treatment of asthma, hay fever, and other allergies. Originally obtained from a plant, it is now made synthetically. Its structure and effects are similar to those of adrenalin.

Ephesians, Epistle to the, New Testament book attributed to the apostle Paul. Probably written during Paul's first imprisonment in Rome, A.D. 60, its main theme is the universality and unity of the Church.
See also: Bible; New Testament.

Ephesus, ancient Greek city in Asia Minor, in what is now Turkey. The temple of Artemis, built in Ephesus in the 6th century B.C. and excavated by archaeologists in 1869, was one of the seven wonders of the ancient world. A major Greek seaport, Ephesus was later the Asian capital of the Roman Empire, before becoming a Christian center. It was destroyed in the early 15th century.
See also: Seven Wonders of the Ancient World.

Epic, long narrative poem concerned with heroism. *Gilgamesh*, the earliest known epic, dates from 2000 B.C. Many epics, such as the *Odyssey*, the *Iliad*, and *Beowulf*, existed as oral tradition before being written down. Literary epics, such as Vergil's *Aeneid*, Edmund Spenser's *Faerie Queene*, and John Milton's *Paradise Lost*, depict the eras of their heroes.

Epictetus (c.A.D. 55-135), Greek Stoic philosopher. An educated Roman slave, he held that virtue lies within oneself regardless of external conditions. His teachings were recorded by his pupil Arrian in the *Discourses* and the *Encheiridion*.

Epic theater, form of revolutionary theater developed in the late 1920s by Erwin Piscator and Bertolt Brecht, emphasizing the narrative and political aspects of staged events. Brecht's theories stressed the arousal of a critical response by alienating the spectator from the staged action: *Man is Man* (1926), *The Threepenny Opera* (1928), and *Mother Courage and Her Children* (1941).

Epicurus (341-270 B.C.), Greek philosopher, founder of epicureanism, which is named after him. Reviving the atomism of Democritus, he preached a materialist philosophy that argued that happiness was the goal of life. He saw happiness not as the pure indulgence of pleasure, but as the attainment of honesty and social justice.
See also: Philosophy.

Epidaurus, ancient Greek city about 40 mi (54 km) southwest of Athens. The 4th-century B.C. temple of Asclepius, the Greek god of healing, and the 3rd-century B.C. outdoor theater are 2 of the major ruins found in Epidaurus today.

Epidemic, outbreak of a disease in a given area affecting a large number of people.

Epidemiology, study of epidemics, diseases that affect large numbers of people. Epidemiology uses statistical and other methods to discover the cause of a disease, determine the elements affecting rate of incidence and degree of severity, and establish the means of control. AIDS is one of the most devastating epidemies in the 1980s and 1990s.

Epigram, short, pithy saying in verse or prose, often with a satirical turn. Originating in ancient Greece as a monument inscription, the English epigram is associated with Ben Jonson, John Dryden, Jonathan Swift, and the most famous of all, Alexander Pope. Modern epigrammatists include Oscar Wilde, W.B. Yeats, and Hilaire Belloc.

Epilepsy, brain disorder characterized by susceptibility to seizures and convulsions that can cause loss of consciousness and muscle control. The causes of epilepsy are not well understood. Among children it may be a result of brain injuries during birth or of abnormalities in fetal development. In adults it can be caused by head injuries and tumors. It is normally treated with drugs that prevent or inhibit seizures.

Epinephrine, or adrenalin, hormone secreted by the adrenal glands. The release of epinephrine causes a rise in blood pressure, an increase in the heart rate, and a rise in muscle strength. Emotions like fear and anger, typically associated with "fight or flight" situations, trigger the release of this hormone.
See also: Hormone.

Epiphany (from Greek *epiphania*, "manifestation"), Christian feast held annually on Jan. 6 to celebrate Jesus's baptism, the visit of the 3 wise men to the manger in Bethlehem, and the transformation of water into wine at Cana. The night before Epiphany, 12 days after Christmas, is called the Twelfth Night.
See also: Christmas.

Epiphyte, or airplant, plant that grows on another but that does not obtain food from it. Various lichens, mosses, ferns, and orchids are epiphytes, usually living on trees. Epiphytes thrive in warm, wet climates.

Episcopal Church, Protestant, U.S. Christian denomination formed of the remnants of the colonial Church of England after the American Revolution. Its first general convention was held in Philadelphia in 1789. The church now has 100 dioceses and a membership of some 2.5 million. It is governed by the triennial General Convention, composed of a House of Bishops and a House of Clerical and Lay Deputies. The Episcopal Church is part of the Anglican Communion, and in recent years has been prominent in the ecumenical movement.
See also: Protestantism.

Epistemology (from Greek *episteme*, "knowledge"), branch of philosophy that inquires about the sources of human knowledge, its possible limits, and to what extent it can be certain or only probable. Epistemology is connected with psychology and logic.
See also: Philosophy.

Epistle, special, formal letter in the New Testament of the Bible. There are 21 epistles—14 are attributed to Paul, 2 to Peter, 3 to John, 1 to James, and 2 to Jude. Those ascribed to Paul are known as Pauline epistles, while the others are called Catholic, or general, epistles.
See also: New Testament.

Epithelioma, tumor of the epithelium. Although epithelioma can be benign or malignant and can occur in any part of the body, the term most often refers to basal cell carcinoma, a common form of skin cancer that rarely metastasizes (spreads through the blood or lymph system) and is treatable by surgery. Basal cell tumors can result from prolonged exposure to the sun, X-rays, or carcinogens like tar.
See also: Epithelium.

Epithelium, tissue covering external surfaces of the body, such as the skin, and lining various bodily tubes and cavities. It consists of one or more layers of cells variously modified to provide protection or aid in excretion of waste products and the assimilation of nutrients. The epithelium that covers the surface of the skin consists of one or more layers of adjoining cells. Often strands of cells grow from the epithelium into deeper-lying layers and differentiate to form glands. Some sensory organs are specialized forms of epithelium.

E pluribus unum ("out of many, one"), Latin motto referring to the unification of the original 13 American colonies. Chosen for the Continental Congress by John Adams, Benjamin Franklin, and Thomas Jefferson, it is now inscribed on the Great Seal of the United States and on many U.S. coins.
See also: Great Seal of the United States.

Epsom salts, common name for magnesium sulfate, so called because it was first found at Epsom, England. The bitter-tasting substance has long been used as a laxative.

Epstein, Sir Jacob (1880-1959), U.S. sculptor, living in London, whose controversial early work was influenced by African sculpture, Constantin Brancusi, and Auguste Rodin. After 1915 he turned to religious subjects and portraiture. His works include the Oscar Wilde Memorial (1911), *Rock Drill* (1913), and *Ecce Homo* (1935).

Epstein-Barr (EB) virus, herpes virus that causes several diseases in humans. The virus, identified in 1964 by British scientists Michael A. Epstein and Y. M. Barr, is associated with infectious mononucleosis (common in the United States), Burkitt's lymphoma (a skin cancer in Africa), and a nasopharyngeal (nose-throat) cancer (in China). The EB virus, which can remain dormant in the body for long periods, infects certain white blood cells and reproduces in mucous membranes.

Equal Rights Amendment (ERA), proposed Constitutional amendment prohibiting discrimination on grounds of sex. Introduced in Congress in various years beginning in 1923, it finally passed in 1972. In 1978 the deadline for ratification by 38 states was extended to June 30, 1982, but that deadline passed without the necessary approval by state legislature.
See also: Women's movements.

Equation, statement of equality. Mathematical equations are often expressed in algebraic notation, where known and unknown quantities can be represented by symbols. Notations of branches of mathematics such as differential calculus or logic can also be used to represent relationships of equality. Other disciplines have created shorthand notations representing equalities, as in chemistry, where chemical equations represent chemical reactions. One of the most familiar forms of equations in mathematics is the *n degree polynomial equation* (of order *n*):
$ax^n+bx^{n-1}+cx^{n-2}+... z=0$
Here *x* is a variable denoting an unknown quantity and *a, b, c ... z* represent known values.
If $n=2$, the generalized form reduces to a *quadratic equation*: $ax^2+bx+c=0$. Such equations have 2 solutions or *roots*:

$$x=\frac{-b+\sqrt{b^2-4ac}}{2a} \text{ and}$$
$$x=\frac{-b-\sqrt{b^2-4ac}}{2a}$$

Because these examples have only one unknown variable, solutions can be found. Equations can have more than one unknown. In such cases there must be as many equations as there are variables in order to solve for the unknowns. Consider the equation: $2x+xy+3=0$. Without additional information it is impossible to determine either *x* or *y* explicitly. However, with the additional information of another equation such as: $x+2xy=0$, finding values for both variables *x* and *y* that simultaneously satisfy each equation of the system is possible. By mathematical manipulation the solution to the system made up of the 2 equations is: $x=-2$ and $y=-{}^1/_2$. the formulation and solving of systems of equations are used extensively in operations analysis, economics, psychology, and the sciences.

Equator, imaginary great-circle line around the earth equidistant from the North and South poles. The equator divides the globe into the northern and southern hemispheres and forms the zero axis of latitude.

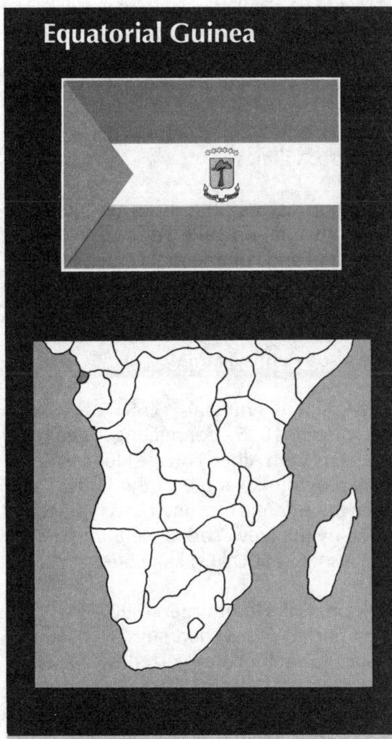

Capital:	Malabo
Area:	10,831 sq mi (28,051 sq km)
Population:	401,000
Government:	republic
Independent:	1968
GNP:	U.S. $140,000,000
Per capita:	U.S. $350

Equatorial Guinea, republic in west-central Africa, formerly a Spanish colony, independent since 1973. The country consists of the mainland province of Río Muni, bounded on the north by Cameroon and on the east and south by Gabon, and several islands off the Atlantic coast. Bata (on the mainland) is the largest city, Malabo (on the island of Bioko) the capital. Main products include cocoa, coffee, bananas, palm oil, and timber. The main ethnic groups are the Fang in Río Muni and the Bubi in Bioko. Spanish is the official language.

Equatorial Islands *see:* Line Islands.

Equilibrium, chemical, condition in which a chemical reaction and its reverse reaction are taking place at equal velocities, so that the overall concentrations of reacting substances remain constant.

Equinox, (1) either of the 2 times each year when day and night are of equal length. The spring, or vernal equinox occurs in Mar., the autumnal equinox in Sept., (2) either of the 2 intersections of the ecliptic and equator on the celestial sphere. In other words, the equinoxes are the points at which the Sun crosses the celestial equator.

Equity, in law, group of rules and principles arising in the English Chancery Court to compensate for the rigidity of common law. Equity generally referred to that which was considered morally right as opposed to that which is stated in the laws and statutes. Courts of equity originated in the 17th century, but soon developed their own body of rules.

ERA *see:* Equal Rights Amendment.

Erasistratus (3rd century B.C.), Greek physician of the Alexandrian School of Medicine, credited with the foundation of physiology as a separate discipline. He studied brain convolutions, named the trachea, and distinguished between motor and sensory nerves.

Erasmus, Desiderius (1466?-1536), Dutch Roman Catholic humanist and advocate of church and social reform. One of the lead-

Portrait of Erasmus by his friend Hans Holbein the Younger

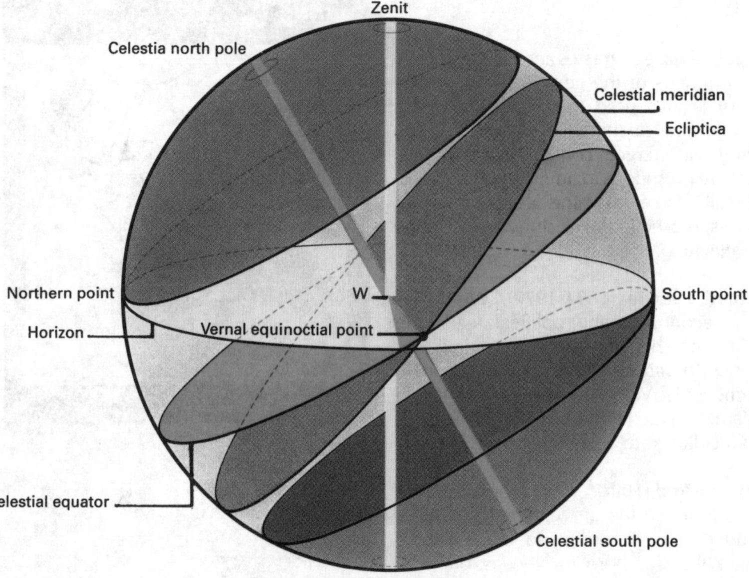

The most important circles on the stationary and the moving celestial globe with respect to observer W on Earth. An observer at the North Pole or the South Pole sees the celestial pole straight above his head, at the zenith. On the equator the northern and the southern celestial poles coincide with the north point and the south point, respectively, on the horizon.

ing scholars of the Renaissance, he did the first Latin translation of the New Testament from the original Greek and edited the works of the Church fathers. His works include *The Christian Soldier's Handbook* (1503) and *In Praise of Folly* (1509), a witty satire on Church corruption. Although he advocated church reform, he opposed the Protestant Reformation. He had a bitter debate with Martin Luther on the issue of predestination and free will.
See also: Humanism.

Erastus, Thomas (1524-83), Swiss theologian. Erastianism, his doctrine, held that the state should have complete control over the affairs of the Church. An adherent of Zwingli, he clashed with the Calvinists, particularly over the practice of excommunication, which he opposed in his *Explicatio gravissimae quaestionis* (1589).

Eratosthenes (c.275-c.195 B.C.), Greek mathematician and astronomer. Postulating that the earth was round and that the sun's rays were parallel, he measured the lengths of shadows in different locations and used geometrical reasoning to estimate the circumference of the earth with remarkable accuracy. He also determined the size and distance of the sun and moon. The sieve of Eratosthene is a practical method for identifying prime numbers.

Erbium, chemical element, symbol Er; for physical constants see Periodic Table. Erbium was discovered in 1843 by Carl G. Mosander. It occurs in the minerals *xenotime, gadolinite, euxenite, fergusonite*, and is obtained commercially from *monazite*. It is prepared by reducing anhydrous chloride with calcium metal. Erbium is a silvery, soft, reactive metal, belonging to the series of elements known as the rare-earth metals. Ion-exchange and solvent extraction techniques have led to much easier isolation of the rare-earth elements. Erbium and its compounds are used in carbon-arc lighting applications, special glasses and enamels, and refractory materials.

Ergot, disease of grasses and cereals caused by a fungus of the genus *Claviceps*. The word is also used to apply to the dark purple spots on the heads of rye caused by the disease. Ergots contain toxic alkaloids that are poisonous to animals and humans. The alkaloid ergotamine, also contained in ergots, is used in the treatment of migraine headaches.

Erhard, Ludwig (1897-1977), West German economist and political leader. In 1949 he became economics minister under Konrad Adenauer; he was the prime architect of West Germany's post World War II revival. He succeeded Adenauer as chancellor from 1963-66.

Eric the Red, 10th-century Norse explorer who founded the first colonies in Greenland c.985. According to the Icelandic sagas, he was born in Norway but emigrated to Iceland. Arrested for manslaughter, he sailed westward in quest of a strange land sighted in 876 by the Norse searover Gunnbjorn Ulfsson; Eric named the place Greenland. His son, Leif Ericson, was also an adventurer. It is beleived that he landed in North America in 1000.
See also: Vikings.

Erie (pop. 275,572), city in northwestern Pennsylvania, on Lake Erie. An important industrial and commercial center, Erie produces processed foods, electric locomotives, turbines, and paper. It is also a Great Lakes port.
See also: Pennsylvania.

Erie Canal, artificial U.S. waterway completed 1825, connecting Buffalo on Lake Erie with Albany on the Hudson River, thus providing a route to the Great Lakes from the Atlantic Ocean. It was replaced in 1918 by the New York State Barge Canal.
See also: Great Lakes; Lake Erie.

Erikson, Erik Homburger (1902-), German-born U.S. psychoanalyst who defined 8 stages, each characterized by a specific psychological conflict, in the development of the ego from infancy to old age (*Childhood and Society*, 1950). He also introduced the concept of the identity crisis.
See also: Psychoanalysis.

Erin *see:* Ireland.

Eritrea

Capital:	Asmara
Area:	46,774 sq mi (121,144 sq km)
Population:	3,200,000
Government:	republic
Independent:	1993

Eritrea, independent state in East Africa, bounded by the Red Sea, Sudan, Ethiopia and Djibouti. A hot, dry, mountainous region, Eritrea is populated partly by nomadic herders, but there are also areas of agriculture and several cities, including Asmara, the capital. After several hundred years under the Ottoman Empire, Eritrea became an Italian colony in 1890. In 1962 it was annexed by Ethiopia. The Eritreans fought a war of independence since the 1960s. Two years after the installation of a more autonomous Eritrean government, the republic became independent in 1993.
See also: Ethiopia.

Ermine, term for any weasel that turns white in winter. In the Middle Ages ermine fur was used only by royalty; later it was associated with high court judges.

Ernst, Max (1891-1976), German-born artist, leader of the dada and surrealism movements in Paris. He developed the expressive techniques of *collage* and *frottage* (rubbing on paper placed over textured surfaces). He also painted in oil and produced graphics and sculpture. Two well-known paintings are *Woman, Old Man, and Flower* (1923-24) and *The Eye of Silence* (1943-44).
See also: Dada; Surrealism.

Eros, in Greek mythology, the god of sexual love. The Romans identified him with Cupid, son of Venus and Mars. The name was used by psychiatrist Sigmund Freud to personify the life-force and the sexual instincts.

Erosion, gradual wearing away of the land by natural forces. The main agents of erosion are weathering, running water, ice, winds, waves, and ocean currents. Natural erosion is an extremely slow process. For example, an average of 1 ft (0.3 m) of land is worn away from the surface of the United States every 900 years. But this rate is accelerated if the natural vegetation that covers and protects the surface is stripped away. Natural erosion is a continuous process, beginning as new land masses are uplifted and continuing until they are worn down.

Ervin, Samuel James, Jr. (1896-1985), U.S. senator from North Carolina (1954-74). He served in the U.S. House and on the superior and supreme courts of North Carolina. A constitutional expert, he headed the committee investigating the Watergate affair (1973-74), fighting President Nixon's use of executive privilege to withhold evidence and testimony, and enlivening the hearings with humor and biblical quotations.
See also: Watergate.

Erving, Julius (1950-), U.S. basketball player. Erving, nicknamed "Dr. J.," stood 6'6" (198 cm) and played forward and guard. Known for his leaping ability and high-flying style of play, Erving ushered in the age of dunking and "playing above the rim." After attending the University of Massachusetts (1968-71), he played for the Virginia Squires (ABA, 1971-73), the New York Nets (ABA, 1973-76), and the Philadelphia 76ers (NBA, 1976-87). He retired in 1987, having been named Most Valuable Player by the ABA (1974, 1975) and NBA (1981).

Erysipelas, contagious skin infection caused by streptococci bacteria, which generally enter through a small wound. The area affected becomes red and slightly swollen; the patient often has a fever and feels tired. If not treated, erysipelas can spread to deeper tissues, causing serious complications. Treated with antibiotics.

Erythema, redness of the skin resulting from dilation of the capillaries of the skin to allow extra blood to flow. It has many causes, from blushing and sunburn to infection.

Erythromycin, antibiotic synthesized by the soil bacterium *Streptomyces erythreus*. Discovered in 1952, erythromycin is used to treat staphylococcus and streptococcus infections, meningitis, scarlet fever, and Legionnaires' disease. It is also helpful in treating patients who are allergic to penicillin.

Esau, or Edom, in the Bible (book of Genesis), son of Isaac and Rebecca, elder twin brother of Jacob. Esau was tricked by Jacob into selling his birthright. Esau's descendants, the Edomites, were consistently hostile to the Israelites, descendants of Jacob.

Escalator, moving stairway used in public buildings to transport passengers from one level to another. The steps move on a continuous belt and fold flat at the top and bottom to allow passengers to step on and off easily. An average-size escalator can carry over 5,000 passengers an hour.

Escape velocity, speed an object must reach in order to break free from the gravitational pull of a massive body, such as the earth, moon, or sun. The escape velocity depends upon the mass of the body and the distance of the moving object from it. The escape velocity from the earth's surface is about 7 mi/sec (11.3 km/sec).
See also: Astrophysics.

Escobedo v. Illinois, 1964 U.S. Supreme Court decision ruling that police must inform arrested suspects of their right to counsel and to remain silent, and must allow them access to counsel. Statements made by suspects interrogated without being informed of these rights are inadmissible in court. The Escobedo Rule, based on the 6th Amendment of the Constitution, was elaborated in the 1966 Supreme Court decision in *Miranda* v. *Arizona*.
See also: Miranda v. Arizona.

Escorial, monastery and palace in central Spain, 26 mi (42 km) northwest of Madrid. One of the most imposing buildings in Europe, it was built (1563-84) by Philip II and houses a church, palace, college, and mausoleum in which many Spanish kings are buried. Its art collection contains works by Velásquez, El Greco, and Tintoretto, among others.

Esdraelon, or plain of Jezreel or of Megiddo, plain in northern Israel, about 200 sq mi (520 sq km), stretching along the coast near Mt. Carmel and the Jordan River valley. This plain, referred to in the Book of Revelation as Armegeddon, was often the site of battle. Though Esdraelon was formerly a low ground filled with water, sponge, and fungus, it has since been drained, and has grown to become one of Israel's most populous and fruitful lands.

Esfahan *see:* Isfahan.

Eshkol, Levi (1895-1969), Israeli political leader, one of the founders of the state, prime minister, 1963-69. Born in the Ukraine, he moved to Palestine in 1914. He helped create the Mapai (Jewish Labor Party) and served as minister of agriculture and minister of finance under David Ben-Gurion. He was prime minister during the June 1967 war with Egypt, Jordan, and Syria.
See also: Israel.

Eskimo, European name for the Inuit people, indigenous inhabitants of the Arctic regions of northeast Asia, North America, and Greenland. Probably of Asian origin, the Eskimos speak languages of the Aleut group. Anthropologists believe that the Eskimos came to North America by crossing the Bering Strait land-bridge from Asia c.2000 B.C. Their traditional way of life was strongly influenced by the severity of the Arctic climate. Since the ground is seldom frost-free, agriculture is undeveloped, and vegetation is limited to small plants. The only wood available is driftwood. The Eskimos depend mainly on seals, fish, walrus, and shales for food, fuel, and clothing. Their main weapon is the harpoon. The *kayak*, a one-person canoe covered with skin, and the *umlak*, a larger skin boat, are used for fishing and hunting. Most Eskimo property is traditionally communal, and the people tended to live in relatively small groups. In recent years growing numbers of Eskimos have left their traditional way of life to take jobs and settle in the less remote areas of Alaska and Canada.

Eskimo dog, large, wolflike Arctic dog, used in teams to draw sleds and for hunting. The name is often used to include the Alaskan malamute and Siberian husky breeds. The Eskimo dog generally weighs 50-85 lbs (23-39 kg) and stands 16-18 in (40-45 cm). Its long, coarse coat and oily undercoat protect it from cold and dampness.

Esophagus, thin muscular tube leading from the pharynx to the stomach. Food passes down it by means of gravity and peristalsis.
See also: Alimentary canal; Digestive system.

ESP *see:* Extrasensory perception.

Esperanto, artificial language designed by Dr. Ludwig Lazarus Zamenhof (1859-1917) of Warsaw, Poland, and first proposed to the public in 1887. Based upon the main European languages, Esperanto is simple and easily learned. Pronunciation is phonetic, and its rules of grammar have no

Precipitation in mountainous regions collects in a number of small valleys known as rills and gullies. They collect water from the catchment area. Where these small valleys meet a main valley they deposit debris as an alluvial fan or cone.

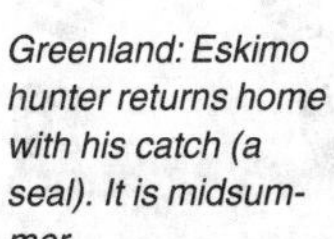

Greenland: Eskimo hunter returns home with his catch (a seal). It is midsummer.

exceptions. Esperanto is one of various artificial languages meant to facilitate international communication. It is the most widely used.

Espionage, systematic secret gathering of information about the plans and activities of foreign governments or competing businesses. Espionage is as old as war itself, but modern military intelligence gathering developed under Frederick the Great of Prussia in the 18th century. Extensive espionage networks were developed during World War II, and since then intelligence agencies have become significant components of the state apparatus in many countries.

Espionage expert Mata Hari, a Dutch spy (1876-1917)

Esposito, Phil (1942-), Canadian hockey player. He is fourth on the all time regular season scoring list (1,590 points) and is among the top goal scorers in National Hockey League (NHL) history (with 717 goals). Esposito led the league in scoring for five seasons (1969, 1971-74) and won the Hart Memorial Trophy as most valuable player in 1969. Esposito played center for the Chicago Black Hawks (1963-67) and the Boston Bruins (1967-75), where he led the Bruins to 2 Stanley Cup championships (1970, 72). He finished his career with the New York Rangers (1975-81) and was inducted into the Hockey Hall of Fame in 1984.

Phil Esposito

Essay, literary composition in which the writer deals with a single topic or attempts to convert the reader to a point of view. The informal essay, often humorous, was mastered by Mark Twain. The formal essay, as written by Matthew Arnold, is opinionated and informative.

Essen (pop. 626,100), city in western Germany, on the Ruhr River. Established in the 9th century around a convent, it became an industrial center in the 19th century. The Krupp steelworks company, located in Essen, was a major arms manufacturer during both world wars, and much of Essen was destroyed by Allied bombings during World War II.
See also: Germany.

Essene, member of an ascetic Jewish sect that flourished in Palestine around the time of the birth of Jesus. Living in their own communities, the Essenes generally withdrew from public life, appearing only occasionally to warn others that the end of the world was at hand. Some scholars believe that the Dead Sea Scrolls belonged to an Essene group.
See also: Dead Sea Scrolls.

Essex, Robert Devereux, 2nd Earl of (1567-1601), English courtier, a favorite of Queen Elizabeth I. He acquired fame in European military campaigns, was knighted in 1589, and made lord lieutenant of Ireland in 1599, a post he lost by failing to crush the Earl of Tyrone's rebellion..

Established Church *see:* Church of England.

Estates-General, or States-General, French national assembly (first summoned in 1302) composed of representatives from the 3 "estates" or social classes: clergy, nobility, and commoners. During most of its existence it was an advisory body with little legislative power, and in fact it did not meet between 1614, when it was dismissed by King Louis XIII, and 1789, when it was called into session by King Louis XVI on the eve of the French Revolution. Traditionally each estate met and voted as a separate house, but in 1789 the 3rd estate declared itself a national assembly, each member having one vote. It was this decision that inaugurated the revolution.
See also: French Revolution.

Estéban *see:* Estevanico.

Esters, organic compounds formed by condensation of an acid (organic or inorganic) and an alcohol, water being eliminated. This reaction, esterification, is the reverse of hydrolysis. Esters of low molecular weight have fruity odors and are used in flavorings and perfumes and as solvents; those of higher molecular weight are fats and waxes.

Estevanico, or Estéban (1500?-39), explorer in colonial America. A Moroccan slave who came to North America as the servant of an explorer in 1528, he later became an interpreter and guide for the advance party of Francisco Coronado, which explored the Southwest (1539), searching for the Seven Cities of Cibola, cities of gold Estevanico had been told about by Native Americans. He was killed at Cibola by members of the Zuñi tribe.
See also: Cibola, Seven Cities of.

Esther, book of the Old Testament. It tells of Esther (also called Hadassah), a Jewish queen of the Persian king Ahasuerus, who prevented the king's favorite, Haman, from massacring Persian Jews. The story is the origin of the feast of Purim.
See also: Bible; Old Testament.

Estivation, dormant state entered into by some animals in hot, dry climates, to conserve moisture during the summer. The slowing of body processes permits survival. Animals that estivate include many reptiles, amphibians, insects, snails, and fish.
See also: Hibernation.

Estonia, independent country on the east coast of the Baltic Sea, bordered by Russia in the west, and Latvia in the south. The largest cities are Tallinn, the capital; Tartu; and Pärnu. A third of the land, which consists of plains and low plateaus, is forested. The climate is temperate. Estonians are ethnically and linguistically related to the Finns. More than half the population is urban, although agriculture, especially dairy farming, is the chief industry. Estonia became an independent state in 1918, but was annexed by the USSR in 1940 (along with Latvia and Lithuania) under the terms of a secret agreement between the Soviet Union and Nazi Germany. The country

Capital:	Tallinn
Area:	17,462 sq mi (45,227 sq km)
Population:	1,526,000
Government:	republic
Independent:	1991
GNP:	U.S. $4,297,000,000
Per capita:	U.S. $2,750

was occupied by Germany during World War II and again taken over by the USSR in 1945. An independence movement gained massive support in the late 1980s, and independence was attained in 1991.

Estrogen, any of a group of female sex hormones that regulate the menstrual cycle and control the development of secondary sex characteristics. After the menopause, production of estrogen decreases.
See also: Hormone.

Estrous cycle, in most female mammals, periodic readiness for mating, regulated by environmental signals and the release of hormones. The length of the cycle and of estrus (the period of fertility and receptivity to mating) varies among species. The female is sexually receptive during estrus, and most female mammals will not mate at any other time.
See also: Reproduction.

Etching, method of engraving in which acid is used to carve the lines into a metal plate; also, the print obtained from such a plate. Modern plates are usually copper or zinc. The plate is covered with an "etching ground," an acid-resistant film of mixed waxes and resins, on which the etcher draws. The plate is then submerged in an acid bath until the faintest lines have been bitten. It is then removed, and these lines are "stopped out" (protected) with varnish. The process is successively repeated until the darkest lines (those exposed longest to the acid) have been bitten.

Ethane, hydrocarbon (C_2H_6) of the paraffin series of chemical compounds. Ethane is a colorless, odorless, flammable gas that boils at –127°F (–89°C). A constituent of natural gas, it has a high fuel value.
See also: Hydrocarbon.

Ether, or aether, in physics, hypothetical substance that was once believed essential for transmission of light waves through space. Scientists assumed that waves re-

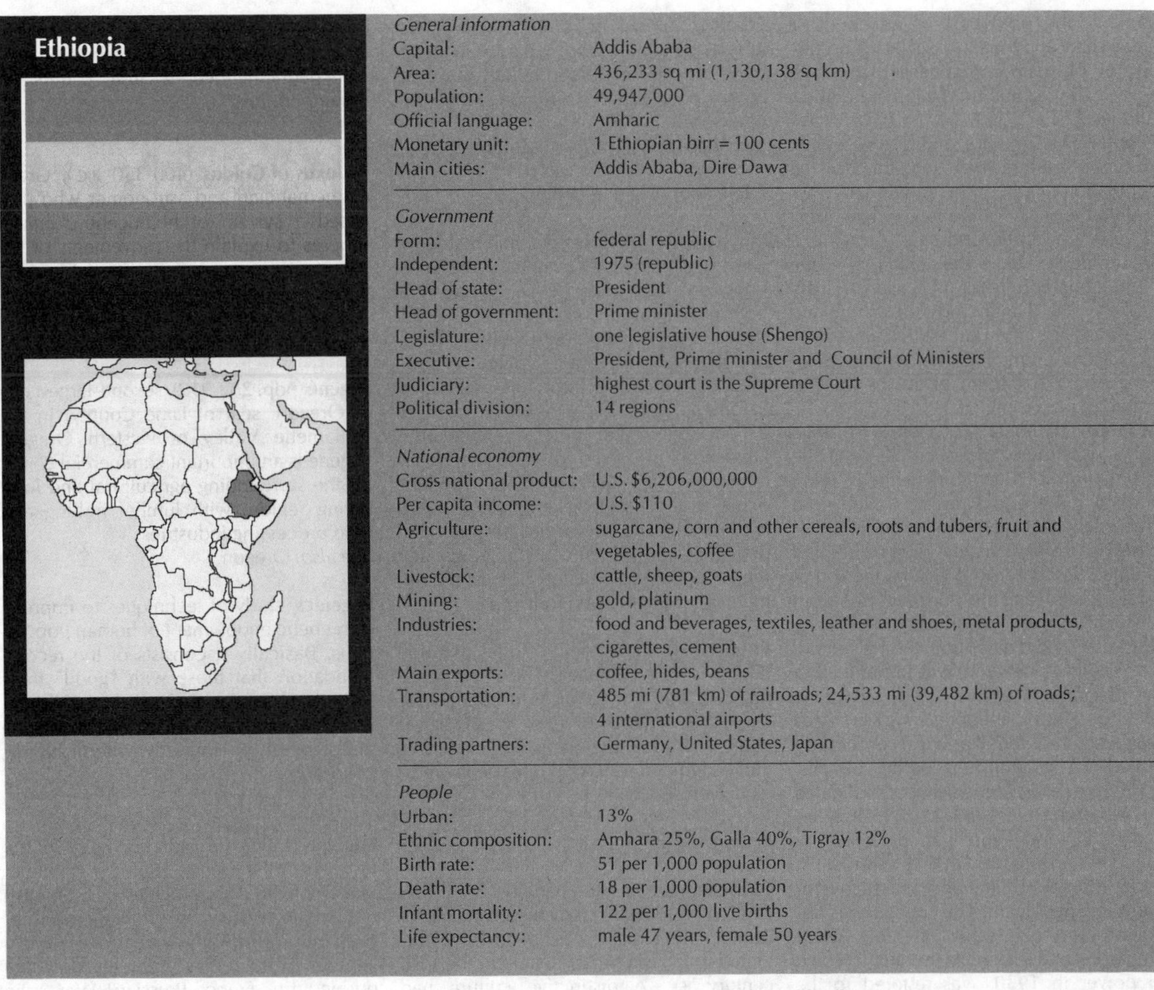

Ethiopia

General information	
Capital:	Addis Ababa
Area:	436,233 sq mi (1,130,138 sq km)
Population:	49,947,000
Official language:	Amharic
Monetary unit:	1 Ethiopian birr = 100 cents
Main cities:	Addis Ababa, Dire Dawa
Government	
Form:	federal republic
Independent:	1975 (republic)
Head of state:	President
Head of government:	Prime minister
Legislature:	one legislative house (Shengo)
Executive:	President, Prime minister and Council of Ministers
Judiciary:	highest court is the Supreme Court
Political division:	14 regions
National economy	
Gross national product:	U.S. $6,206,000,000
Per capita income:	U.S. $110
Agriculture:	sugarcane, corn and other cereals, roots and tubers, fruit and vegetables, coffee
Livestock:	cattle, sheep, goats
Mining:	gold, platinum
Industries:	food and beverages, textiles, leather and shoes, metal products, cigarettes, cement
Main exports:	coffee, hides, beans
Transportation:	485 mi (781 km) of railroads; 24,533 mi (39,482 km) of roads; 4 international airports
Trading partners:	Germany, United States, Japan
People	
Urban:	13%
Ethnic composition:	Amhara 25%, Galla 40%, Tigray 12%
Birth rate:	51 per 1,000 population
Death rate:	18 per 1,000 population
Infant mortality:	122 per 1,000 live births
Life expectancy:	male 47 years, female 50 years

quired some medium. Observations of stars had suggested that the ether must be stationary in space, and that the earth therefore moved through it. In 1887 the U.S. scientists Albert A. Michelson and Edward W. Morley tried to measure the effect of the "ether wind," but found no sign of it. The theory of ether was finally abandoned when Albert Einstein's theory of relativity showed that electromagnetic radiation is not a mechanical distortion of a medium, but a type of energy that travels through a vacuum.

Ether, $(C_2H_5)_2O$, flammable liquid that causes unconsciousness when inhaled. It was widely used as an anesthetic during the 19th and early 20th centuries. But its uncomfortable side effects and flammability led to its being replaced by other anesthetics.
See also: Anesthesia

Etherege, Sir George (c.1634-91), English dramatist, writer of restoration comedy, who influenced both William Congreve and William Wycherley. His three plays are *The Comical Revenge* (1664), *She Wou'd If She Cou'd* (1668), and *The Man of Mode* (1676).

Ethics, branch of philosophy devoted to the consideration of the moral principles of human behavior and social organization. Over the centuries, various theories have been put forward to explain how it is that people develop awareness of and opinions about what is right and wrong. Some have argued that these values are absolute and/or innate, others that they are dependent on individual expertise or historical circumstances. Historically, ethics has been closely tied to religion, but in Europe and America, in the 19th and 20th centuries, there have been philosophical currents that have argued ethical positions from a non-religious standpoint.

Ethiopia, formerly Abyssinia, country on the eastern edge of Africa, bordered by Eritrea on the north, the Sudan on the west, Kenya and Somalia on the south, and Somalia and Djibouti on the east.
Land. Geographically, Ethiopia consists of two great plateaus, separated by part of the Great Rift Valley. The Ethiopian plateau, to the west of the Great Rift Valley, is the most fertile and most densely populated part of the country. East of the Great Rift Valley is the Somali Plateau, which slopes eastward to the Ogaden Plateau and reaches over 14,000 ft (4,267 m) in the Urgoma Mountains. The Great Rift Valley separating the plateaus is a long, narrow cleft dotted with lakes and broadening in the north to form the Danakil Depression, a desert. Lake

Falls in the Awash River near Koka Dam, south of Addis Ababa, Ethiopia

Huts with woven roofs at Sidamo (South Ethiopia)

Tana in the northwest is the country's largest lake and the source of the Blue Nile, one of the main components of the Nile River. The capital of Ethiopia is Addis Ababa.

People. The Amhara and Tigray ethnic groups constitute about one-third of the population and have traditionally accounted for most of the ruling class. Most of them are Coptic Christians. Amharic, a Semitic language, is the official language of the country, although English is widely spoken. The Galla, most of whom are Muslims, are the largest single ethnic group, accounting for 40% of the population. About one-tenth of the population practices tribal religions.

Economy. Ethiopia's economy is based upon agriculture and about 75% of the population is directly dependent upon farming and livestock raising. Coffee is the chief cash crop and principal export.

History. Traditionally, the kings of Ethiopia claimed descent from Menelik, the son of King Solomon and the Queen of Sheba, but the first Ethiopian kingdom to have left any historical record dates from the 1st century A.D. Coptic Christianity was introduced in the 4th century A.D. Throughout most of the Middle Ages Ethiopian power was weakened by internal political conflict and armed clashes with neighboring Somalis. In modern times, Menelik II reconsolidated the old empire in 1889. In 1895 Italy invaded Ethiopia but was defeated by Menelik's troops in 1896 at Aduwa. In 1936 Mussolini's Italian Fascist government invaded again. The country was liberated from occupation in 1941 when Emperor Haile Selassie, who had first come to power in 1930, was restored to the throne. His rule lasted until 1973, when army officers ousted him and inaugurated a one-party state that nationalized most of the economy. The military government has continued a war against the forces struggling for the independence of Eritrea, a territory annexed by Ethiopia in 1962, and there have been repeated armed clashes with Somalia over a territorial dispute. Compounding the country's troubles, reduced rainfall in the early 1970s led to serious drought and famine. The civil war with the Eritreans ended in 1991 and Eritrea became independent in 1993.

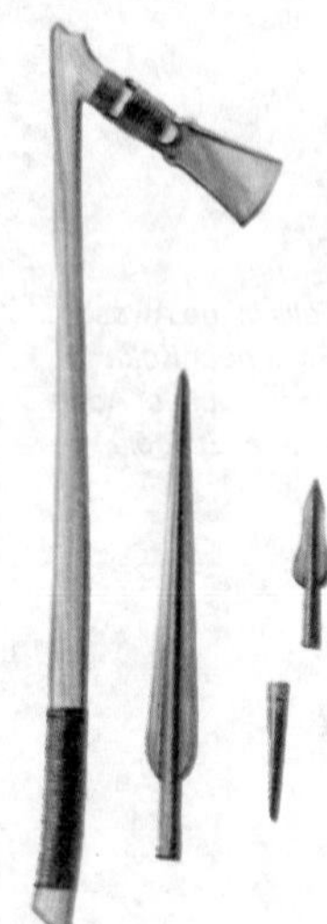

Etruscan armaments

Ethnic group, collection of individuals united by ties of culture and/or heredity who are conscious of forming a subgroup within society. Major U.S. ethnic groups include Irish, Italian, Polish, Jewish, Chinese, Japanese, and Hispanic Americans.

Ethnocentrism, belief that the characteristics of one's own culture or race are superior to those of other groups or races. The differences in other cultures are seen as deviations from the correct approach taken by one's own culture.

Ethnography, branch of anthropology concerned with the investigation of contemporary culture, particularly treating ethnic groups one by one.

Ethology, branch of zoology dealing with animal behavior. Ethologists try to determine the reasons behind such things as mating rituals, social structures, and care of offspring in various animals.
See also: Frisch, Karl von; Zoology.

Ethyl alcohol *see:* Alcohol.

Ethylene (C_2H_4), colorless, flammable organic gas. Ethylene is one of the most important industrial chemicals. Found in both petroleum and natural gas, it is obtained in large quantities by heating ethane and propane with steam. Ethylene is polymerized (combined into large molecules) to form polyethylene, a plastic widely used in packaging and other manufactures. Ethylene is also used to make styrene for other plastics. Converted to ethylene oxide, it is used to make ethylene glycol (antifreeze), and in various solvents and detergents. Ethylene occurs in plants, acting as a growth regulator; it is used commercially to help ripen fruit.

Etiquette, formal system of rules to guide human social behavior. The word originated in the 17th century to refer to the elaborate ceremonial rules of the royal court in France. By extension, it refers to the recognized ways of proper behavior in any given setting.

Etruria *see:* Etruscan.

Etruscan, name for the people whose civilization flourished in Italy before the rise of Rome. The Etruscans seem to have migrated from Asia Minor to Italy in the 12th century B.C. A distinctive culture had emerged by the 8th century, reaching its peak in the 6th. The early governments were monarchical and changed subsequently to republican states that were controlled by oligarchies. The Etruscans carried on extensive maritime trade with the Greeks and Phoenicians and had colonies in Sicily, Corsica, Sardinia, the Balearic Islands, and Spain. After the 5th century B.C. the Etruscan cities were absorbed by the expanding Roman state.
See also: Rome, Ancient.

Etymology, study of the origin and evolution of words. The history of language was first seriously studied in the 19th century. This led to the comparative analysis of languages that turned out to be related. Etymologists began to concentrate on the evolution of words within families of languages, especially examining changes in meaning according to context.
See also: Linguistics.

Eucalyptus, any of a genus (*Eucalyptus*) of tall evergreen trees of the myrtle family, indigenous to Australia. The leaves of some species are used for medicinal purposes. The blue gum (*E. globulus*) is the best-known eucalyptus grown in the U.S.

Euclid (c.300 B.C.), Greek mathematician of Alexandria whose major work, the *Elements*, still constitutes a basis of many courses in geometry. Euclid was most notable for introducing the method of logically deducing theorems from axioms and other theorems.
See also: Geometry.

Eudoxus of Cnidus (400-350 B.C.), Greek mathematician and astronomer who proposed a system of homocentric crystal spheres to explain the movements of the planets; this system was adopted in Aristotle's cosmology. He was probably responsible for discovering parts of geometry detailed in Euclid's *Elements.*

Eugene (pop. 282,912), second-largest city of Oregon, seat of Lane County, in the Willamette Valley of western Oregon. Eugene is an important commercial center for the surrounding agricultural and lumbering region, with lumber milling and food processing industries.
See also: Oregon.

Eugenics, study of techniques to improve the genetic endowment of human populations. Basically it consists of the recommendation that those with "good" traits should be encouraged to have children, while those with "bad" traits should be discouraged or forbidden from having children.
See also: Genetics.

Eugénie (Marie de Montijo; 1826-1920), empress of the French 1853-70 as wife of Napoleon III. The daughter of a Spanish noble, she was a major influence on her husband and on three occasions was regent in his absence. After his downfall during the Franco-Prussian War, she escaped to England.
See also: Napoleon III.

Eugenius III (d. 1153), pope 1145-53, promoter of the Second Crusade. In 1146 Rome revolted against papal rule, and Eugenius was driven from the city. He lived in France and Germany and returned to Rome only in 1153.

Eugenius IV (1383-1447), pope (1431-47). He fought with the Council of Basel (1431-49) to affirm the pope's supreme authority over church councils. He also succeeded in obtaining a temporary reunification with the Greek Orthodox and other Eastern churches (1438). He reigned from Florence 1434-43 because of civil disturbances in Rome.

Euglena, any of several microscopic, one-celled organisms found mainly in stagnant water. Euglenas show both plant and animal characteristics. Like plants, they can manufacture their own food and are capable of photosynthesis; like animals, they can move about freely, propelled by their whiplike flagella. They possess a red-pigmented "eyespot" that is sensitive to light.

Eulachon, saltwater fish (*Thaleichthys pacificus*) of the smelt family, native to the North Pacific. The 8-in (20-cm) fish are harvested with nets when they swim up rivers to spawn. West Coast Native Americans dried the fish to use as candles.

Eulenspiegel, Till, Brunswick trickster hero of a group of German tales originally published 1515. His pranks demonstrated peasant cunning triumphing over establishment figures of his day. He was the subject of a tone poem by Richard Strauss in 1895.

Euler, Leonhard (1707-83), Swiss mathematician who worked in St. Petersburg, Russia, and Berlin. He contributed to nearly all fields of mathematics, making major contributions to algebra and calculus in particular.
See also: Algebra; Calculus.

Euphrates River, Western Asia's longest river, over 2,200 mi (3,540 km). It rises in northeastern Turkey, crosses that country, then flows southeastward over the Syrian plateau and through Iraq, where it flows together with the Tigris River to form the 120-mi (193-km) long Shatt al Arab, which empties into the head of the Persian Gulf. The Euphrates has had great historical significance above all for its lifegiving waters, which irrigated the crops supporting great civilizations in Mesopotamia from pre-Babylonian times. It is still an important source of irrigation for Iraq and Syria.
See also: Tigris River.

Euripides (c.480-406 B.C.), ancient Greek playwright, writer of tragedies. He is thought to have written 92 plays, of which 19 have survived. The best known include *Medea, The Trojan Women, Electra, Orestes,* and *The Bacchae.*

Europa, in Greek mythology, daughter of King Agenor of Phoenicia. Zeus fell in love with her and came to her in the form of a gentle white bull, enticing her to climb onto his back. He then carried her away to Crete, where she bore him three sons, Minos, Rhadamanthus, and Sarpedon.
See also: Mythology.

Spanish village on Menorca

Europe, world's second smallest continent in area, second largest in population (after Asia). Geographically, Europe is a peninsula of the Asian landmass. Traditionally, the division between Europe and Asia is considered to be the Ural Mountains, which run north-south through Russia, and the Ural River, which flows into the Caspian Sea. On the south, Europe is divided from Asia by the Caucasus Mountains and the Black Sea, including the Bosporus and the Dardanelles straits. By that reckoning, Europe has an area of about 4,000,000 sq mi (10,360,000 sq km), somewhat larger than the United States. It is separated from Africa by the Mediterranean Sea and the Strait of Gibraltar. Parts of Europe's irregular coast form major peninsulas themselves, notably the Scandinavian and Jutland peninsulas in the north, and the Iberian, Italian, and Balkan peninsulas in the south.
Europe's geological structure is marked by the relatively recent rise of the great Alpine mountain system, which cuts across the continent from west to east and includes the Pyrénées, Alps, Apennines, Carpathi-

Charlemagne

Queen Elizabeth II

One of the most famous fortified cities in Europe; Naarden.

Country house in Belgium

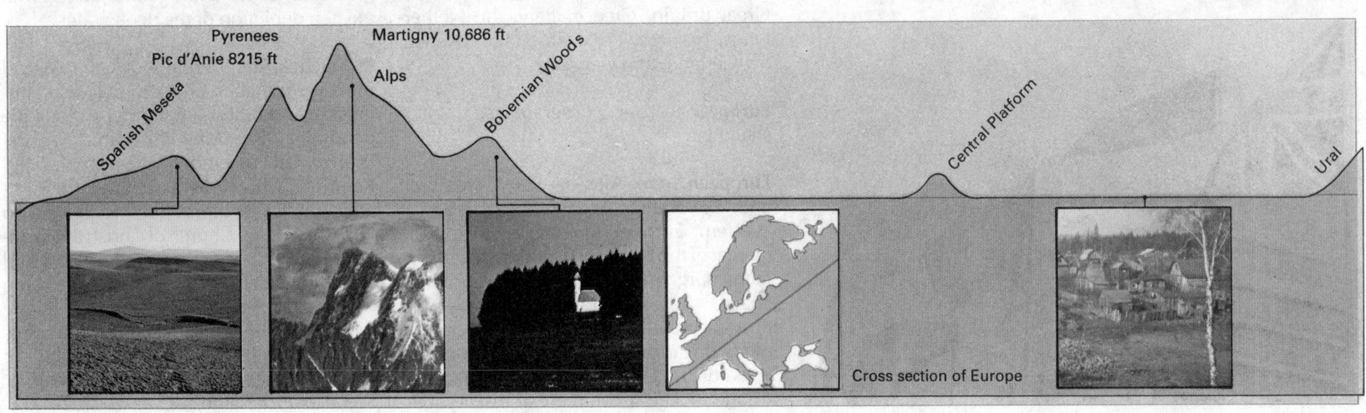

Cross section of Europe

ans, Balkans, and Caucasus. The highest peak in Caucasus is Mt. Elbrus (18,480 ft/5,633 m), the highest in the Alps is Mont Blanc (15,781 ft/4,810 m). The continent also has a complex network of rivers, the largest of which are the Volga, in Russia, and the Danube, which flows through (or forms borders between) Germany, Austria, Slovakia, Hungary, Croatia, Federal Republic of Yugoslavia, Romania, Bulgaria, and Ukraine. Much of Europe consists of a fertile plain extending from the shores of the Atlantic to the Urals. Except for the polar areas of Scandinavia and Russia, the climate is generally mild. These two factors, combined with rich offshore fisheries, many inland rivers, and abundant natural resources, have made the continent a major food producer, able historically to feed its large population, which now numbers around 700 million.

Europe has great linguistic diversity: as many as 5 dozen languages are spoken, almost all of the Indo-European group. The largest religious grouping is Christianity, including Roman Catholicism, Protestantism, and the Eastern Orthodox church. Muslims and Jews account for the two largest religious minorities. The independent states of Europe are, in alphabetical order, Albania, Andorra, Austria, Belgium, Bosnia Hercegovina, Bulgaria, Byelorussia, Croatia, Czech Republic, Denmark, Estonia, Finland, France, Germany, Greece, Hungary, Iceland, Ireland, Italy, Latvia, Lithuania, Liechtenstein, Luxembourg, Macedonia, Malta, Moldavia, Monaco, the Netherlands, Norway, Poland, Portugal, Romania, the European part of the Russian Federation, San Marino, Slovakia, Slovenia, Spain, Sweden, Switzerland, the European part of Turkey, Ukraine, the United Kingdom (of Great Britain and Northern Ireland), Vatican City, and the Federal Republic of Yugoslavia. There are at least 30 cities with populations greater than 1 million.

European Common Market *see:* European Community.

European Community, organization of Western European nations formed to regulate trade, agriculture, labor, transportation, and industrial standards. The European Community was formed in 1967 by consolidating the European Coal and Steel Community, the European Economic Community (the Common Market), and the European Atomic Energy Community (Euratom). Membership includes Austria, Belgium, Denmark, Finland, France, Germany, Great Britain, Greece, Ireland, Italy, Luxembourg, the Netherlands, Portugal, Spain and Sweden. Tariffs on trade between members have been abolished. Legislation is proposed by the 17-member Commission to the Council of Ministers for approval. The European Parliament, whose 518 members have been elected directly by voters since 1979, advises both the Commission and the Council. The Court of Justice hears appeals from individuals as well as countries, making binding decisions regarding compliance with European Community rules.

The "glass palace" in Brussels, which is the seat of the European Economic Community.

European Economic Community *see:* Common Market, European.

European Free Trade Association (EFTA), customs union and trading group formed in 1960 by Austria, Great Britain, Denmark, Norway, Portugal, Sweden, and Switzerland to promote free trade between members, other countries followed. Denmark, Great Britain, and Portugal later left to join the Common Market (European Community). In the 1990s Iceland, Liechtenstein, Norway and Switzerland became members.

European Monetary System (EMS), Western European organization established (1979) to link currencies of its members for the purpose of stabilizing exchange rates and offsetting inflation. Organization has 8 full members (Belgium, Denmark, France, Ireland, Italy, Luxembourg, the Netherlands, Germany) and 2 members who are not full participants (Great Britain, Greece); all are members of the European Community.

European Organization for Nuclear Research, or CERN (Conseil Européen pour la Recherche Nucléaire), research center for particle physics (the study of subatomic particles), funded by 14 European members and located near Geneva, Switzerland. Established 1954, it has a staff of more than 3,500, and its facilities, including large particle accelerators, are available to researchers from any country. Its members are Austria, Belgium, Denmark, France, Great Britain, Greece, Italy, the Netherlands, Norway, Portugal, Spain, Sweden, Switzerland, and Germany.

European Recovery Program *see:* Marshall Plan.

European Space Agency (ESA), research and exploration agency for nations of Western Europe, formed 1975 by the merger of the European Launcher Development Organization and the European Space Research Organization. ESA develops satellites and instruments for exploration, designs experiments, and collects data. The agency developed the Ariane rocket, a commercial research vehicle that has put many satellites into orbit under the auspices of Arianespace, a private organization formed by ESA. The agency also developed Spacelab, first carried into orbit by the space shuttle *Columbia* (1983), and sent the *Giotto* probe to fly by Halley's comet (1985). The members contribute funds to the agency according to their support of various projects.

Europium, chemical element, symbol Eu; for physical constants see Periodic Table. Europium was discovered in 1901 by Eugène Demarcay. The element occurs in the minerals monazite and bastnasite, the two principal sources of the rare-earth elements. It is prepared by heating the oxide with excess lanthanum metal under high vacuum in a tantalum crucible. Europium is a silvery-white, soft metal, and the most reactive member of the elements known as the rare-earth metals. Ion-exchange and solvent extraction techniques have led to much easier isolation of the rare-earth elements. Europium and its compounds are used in laser materials, as neutron absorbers in nuclear reactors, and in color phosphors for TV tubes.

Eurydice, in Greek mythology, nymph who married the musician Orpheus but died on her wedding day. Orpheus descended to the underworld in search of her. Hades and Persephone, rulers of the underworld, agreed to release Eurydice to follow Orpheus if he promised not to look back at her. But he was unable to resist, and Eurydice was taken back to the underworld forever.

Eustachian tubes, narrow tubes running from the middle ear to the back of the throat. They are vital in regulating pressure within the ears.
See also: Ear.

Euthanasia, practice of hastening or causing the death of a person suffering from an incurable disease. Its moral and legal implications are highly controversial in most cultures, and it is illegal in the majority of countries.

Eutrophication, increasing concentration of plant nutrients and fertilizers in lakes and estuaries, partly by natural drainage and partly by pollution. It leads to excessive growth of algae and aquatic plants, with oxygen depletion of the deep water.

Evangelicalism, Protestant theological movement that emphasizes personal conversion and biblical authority. Among the denominations using the name are the Evangelical Lutherans; the Evangelical and Reformed Church, which joined the Congregational Christian Churches in 1961 to form the United Church of Christ; the Evangelical Covenant Church of America; and the Evangelical United Brethren. The name was also applied to the movement led by John Wesley in the 18th century that eventually separated from the Church of England to become the Methodist Church.
See also: Protestantism.

Evangelical Lutheran Church in America, U.S. religious denomination formed in 1988 by the merger of the Lutheran Church in America, the American Lutheran Church, and the Association of Evangelical Lutheran Churches. Based in Chicago, it is the largest Lutheran denomination and the fourth largest Protestant church in the United States, with 65 synods (regional units), mostly in the East and Midwest, each headed by a bishop, and a total membership of about 5.3 million. The church supports minority participation and ordains women. Like its precursors, it maintains extensive national and international missions and education programs.
See also: Lutherans.

Evangeline (1847), long narrative poem by U.S. poet Henry Wadsworth Longfellow. The poem tells of the ill-fated love affair of 2 French citizens expelled by the British from their home in Acadia (now eastern Canada) during the French and Indian Wars. The form of the poem is modeled on such classical epics as Homer's *Odyssey*.

Evans, Mary Ann *see:* Eliot, George.

Evans, Sir Arthur John (1851-1941), English archeologist famous for his discovery of the Minoan civilization from excavations at Knossos in Crete. He was curator of the Ashmolean Museum, Oxford (1884-1908) and professor of prehistoric archeology at Oxford from 1909.
See also: Archaeology.

Evans, Walker (1903-75), U.S. photographer best known for documenting the effects of the Depression in the southern United States. His photographs were an important part of *Let Us Now Praise Famous Men* (1941), written by James Agee. His work also appeared in *Fortune* magazine, of which he was an editor.
See also: Photography.

Evaporation, escape of molecules from the surface of a liquid such that they attain a gaseous state. Only those molecules with sufficient kinetic energy (i.e., heat) are able to overcome the cohesive forces holding the liquid together and escape from the surface. This leaves the remaining molecules with a lower average kinetic energy and hence a lower temperature. In an unenclosed space, the entire body of the liquid can eventually evaporate, which means that the matter will have changed from a liquid to a gas.

Eve *see:* Adam and Eve.

Evelyn, John (1620-1706), English writer and humanist whose *Diary* (1818) is one of the most important historical sources for English life in the 17th century.

Evening primrose, any of various wildflowers of family Onagraceae, native to North America. These annual, biennial, or perennial plants are 1-6 ft (30-180 cm) high, with hairy leaves and saucer-shaped white, yellow, or pink flowers. The name refers especially to *Oenothera biennis*, a biennial 3-5 ft (90-150 cm) tall, with yellow flowers 1-2 in. (3-5 cm) in diameter that open in the evening.

Evening star, general term for a bright planet (most often Venus) that appears in the western sky at sunset or in the early evening. Planets do not give off their own light, but the light they reflect from the sun makes them appear bright, and they were thought at one time to be wandering stars.
See also: Planet.

Everett, Edward (1794-1865), U.S. statesman and orator. A Unitarian clergyman, he became professor of Greek at Harvard in 1815, was a congressman (1825-35) and governor (1836-39) of Massachusetts, minister to England (1841-45), president of Harvard (1846-49), secretary of state (1852-53), senator (1853-54), and in 1860 the Constitutional Union Party's vice-presidential candidate.

Everglades, swampy region of southern Florida covering an area of about 5,000 sq mi (12,950 sq km), extending from Lake Okeechobee in the north to the southern tip of the Florida peninsula. In 1947 the Everglades National Park was established.

Evergreen, plant that retains its leaves the year round; the leaves are continually shed and replaced. The term is usually applied to coniferous, or cone-bearing, trees.

Evers, name of 2 African-American civil rights leaders. In 1969 **(James) Charles Evers** (1922-) became the first black mayor of Fayette, Miss., and in 1971 and 1983 he ran unsuccessfully for governor of Mississippi. **Medgar Wiley Evers** (1925-63), his brother, was the state's first African-American field secretary of the National Association for the Advancement of Colored People (NAACP). He was an active organizer of voter-registration drives until he was murdered by a sniper.

Evert, Chris(tine) (1954-), U.S. tennis player. Known for her strong two-handed backhand, she set a record by winning 4 consecutive U.S. Opens (1975-1978); she won again in 1980 and 1982. Evert also captured 3 Wimbledon titles (1974, 1976, 1981) and 2 Australian Opens (1982, 84).

Evidence, in law, that which is advanced by parties to a legal dispute to prove, or contribute to the proof of, their case. To be admissible in court evidence must conform to various rules designed to ensure its clear and fair presentation to the judge and jury. Evidence may consist of the oral testimony of witnesses summoned by either side or of documents or physical objects. Evidence may be direct, supporting the facts of the case, or circumstantial: information from which facts may reasonably be deduced. An eyewitness account of an auto accident is direct evidence; unaccountable damage to the defendant's auto may be circumstantial evidence. In a criminal case, the burden of proof rests with the prosecution, whose evidence must demonstrate the guilt of the defendant. In a civil suit, both sides must present evidence to support their claims.
See also: Crime laboratory.

Evolution, process by which organisms have changed and species have arisen and disappeared since the origin of life. The formulation of the theory of evolution in its modern form is credited to Charles Darwin and Alfred Russel Wallace, 19th-century British scientists who proposed that the central mechanism of evolution was natural selection. In essence, this theory states that life forms with certain characteristics tend to reproduce in larger numbers and survive environmental changes better than other, similar life forms that lack these characteristics. These forms then tend to become dominant within the population, and the characteristics are inherited by subsequent generations. Integral to the theory is the notion that all species of life on earth are interrelated, ultimately having common ancestry.
Today, the evidence for evolution is overwhelming and comes from many branches of science, including biology, anatomy, embryology, paleontology, biochemistry, genetics, and other fields. The discovery of the phenomenon of genetic mutation and the increased understanding of the structure of genes has helped to answer many of the questions about the mechanisms of the changes that life forms undergo. The field of ecology has given new insight into how different species of plants and animals interrelate with and affect one another. Although the theory of evolution has undergone various important changes since the 19th century, it still rests basically on the foundations laid down by Darwin and Wallace and has been one of the most successful and influential theories in the history of science.
See also: Darwin, Charles Robert.

Ewe *see:* Sheep.

Examinations *see:* College entrance examination; Testing.

Excalibur, in Arthurian legend, the name of King Arthur's sword. In Thomas Malory's 15th-century version, Arthur came into possession of the sword as a boy, when he alone was able to remove it from the stone in which it was lodged. In another version of the legend, the sword was given to Arthur by the Lady of the Lake.
See also: Arthur, King.

Excess-profits tax, tax levied on profits above a legislated level, generally enacted during wars to raise state revenue at a time when some businesses make "windfall profits." U.S. and British corporations were subject to such taxes during and after World War I (1917-21), and during World War II (1940-45). U.S. excess- profits taxes were imposed during the Korean War (1950-53). Some countries maintain an excess-profits tax in peacetime. The U.S. "windfall profits" tax on oil companies in

1980 was technically an excise tax, imposed on a specific product rather than on profits.
See also: Taxation.

Exchange rate, rate at which one country's currency is valued in terms of another's. For instance, at a given time a British pound may be worth $1.50. If the exchange rate were to become $1.60, British imports in the United States would become more expensive. Floating exchange rates, which prevail today, allow the relative values of currencies to fluctuate on the free market, although governments intervene to prevent extreme rises and falls. In the late 19th and early 20th centuries, most currencies did not float but were valued in gold under the international gold standard. After World War II, most currencies were valued in terms of the U.S. dollar, which was convertible for gold. In the 1970s, however, President Nixon ended this system, thus inaugurating floating rates.

Excommunication, expulsion of a person from a religious group. This practice exists in most Christian churches, most notably Catholicism. In the Roman Catholic Church an excommunicate may not attend mass or receive the sacraments and is denied a Christian burial. Excommunication was important in the Middle Ages as a punishment meted out by ecclesiastical courts. It was sometimes used to force temporal rulers to submit to papal authority.

Excretion, or elimination, removal of waste material from the body, including the undigested residue of food and the waste products of metabolism. The main organs responsible for elimination in humans are the kidneys and large intestine, which process liquid and solid wastes respectively. Wastes such as water and salt are also eliminated through the skin in the form of sweat, and through the lungs, which expel water vapor and carbon dioxide.

Executive, the part of government that implements laws; also, the head of that part. In the United States the executive shares power with the legislative and the judiciary branches. It is headed by the president, who appoints all executive officers, usually subject to Senate approval. The cabinet, federal departments such as the defense department, foreign ambassadors, and hundreds of boards and commissions come under the jurisdiction of the executive. The term is also used generally for that part of a private organization or company that manages and controls its business.
See also: President of the United States.

Executor, person appointed to administer the estate of a deceased person. The testator (one who makes a will) has the right to make his or her own choice of executors. If a person fails to name executors, the court may appoint administrators. Executors' duties involve the paying of debts and distribution of the property in the estate according to the terms of the will. The executors' position is therefore one of trust, and they may be sued if they fail in their duties.
See also: Will.

Exeter (pop. 102,000), port city on the Exe River and capital of Devonshire, England. The center of transportation and trade for southwestern England, it is an area of much historic interest, containing ancient Roman ruins as well as the Norman Cathedral, built in the 12th century. Parts of the city were restored after severe damage during World War II.
See also: England.

Exile, expulsion or voluntary prolonged absence from one's homeland. In ancient Palestine, Greece, and Rome, exile was commonly used as a form of criminal punishment. During the 18th century, Great Britain exiled prisoners to provide labor in Australian and North American colonies. In the 20th century, the Soviet Union has exiled citizens to work camps in Siberia. The only form of exile now permitted in the United States is the deportation of noncitizens to their country of origin.

Eximbank *see:* Export-Import Bank of the United States.

Existentialism, 20th-century philosophical current that stresses personal responsibility and the relation of the individual to the universe or to God. In general, existentialists emphasize the fear and despair that isolated individuals feel. An important precursor of existentialism was Søren Kierkegaard, who held that one's sense of dread and despair arose from one's responsibility for one's own decisions and for one's relationship with God. Theologians influenced by Kierkegaard include Karl Barth, Martin Buber, Karl Jaspers, Reinhold Niebuhr, and Paul Tillich. Edmund Husserl and Martin Heidegger are often considered existentialists, but the only major philosopher to accept that designation was Jean-Paul Sartre, who argued that there was no God and that human nature was infinitely variable: humans were free to make their own destiny and therefore responsible for their own lives.

Exobiology, or xenobiology, study of possible life forms elsewhere than on earth. Drawing on many other sciences (e.g., biochemistry and physics), exobiology deals in hypotheses, since no extraterrestrial life has yet been found.

Exocrine gland *see:* Gland.

Exodus, second book of the Old Testament and of the Torah (Pentateuch). It describes the liberation of the Israelites from slavery in Egypt and the covenant made at Mt. Sinai between God and Moses. The Ten Commandments are given in Exodus.
See also: Bible; Old Testament.

Exorcism, ritual expulsion or casting out of malignant spirits and demons by incantations, prayer, and ceremonies.

Expansion, in physics, increase in the volume of a substance due to a rise in temperature. Virtually all substances expand when heated, whether in a gaseous, liquid, or solid state. Conversely, they contract when cooled. Water, an exception, expands on cooling below 4°C (39°F), which is why ice floats on water. Expansion occurs because molecules move further apart as they vibrate more violently under the influence of heat. The increase in the length of a solid when it is heated by 1°C is called the *coefficient of expansion.* A bimetallic strip made of 2 metals with different coefficients of expansion is used in the thermostat. The expansion of mercury or alcohol is used to measure temperature in thermometers. Engineers must allow space for expansion when they build bridges, highways, buildings, railways, and any other structure subject to temperature changes.
See also: Physics.

Ex Parte Milligan, U.S. Supreme Court ruling (1866) that civilians may not be tried in military courts except in the immediate area of a theater of war. The ruling overturned the 1864 conviction of Lambdin P. Milligan by an Indiana military court on charges of aiding the Confederacy. The Supreme Court generalized the ruling to protect civilians from military power, stating that the president and Congress do not have the authority to set up military courts for civilian trials where civilian courts are still functioning, thus setting an important civil liberties precedent.

Exploration, discovery and surveying of unknown parts of the world and the universe. Among the purposes of exploration are settlement, commerce, conquest, and increase of scientific knowledge. The earliest records of exploration in the Western world go back to about 3000 B.C. Many early explorations were undertaken in search of trade routes, as in the case of the Phoenician and Greek seamen who explored the Black Sea and the Mediterranean, and even ventured into the Atlantic.

Explosive, substance that decomposes suddenly, but controllably, forming gas and releasing heat in the process. The resultant shock wave has many applications, including mining, demolition, missile propulsion, and warfare (bombs). Most explosives contain nitrogen, hydrogen, carbon, and oxygen in an unstable molecular configuration which, as the result of a spark, blow, or other small explosion, react extremely rapidly to produce carbon dioxide, steam, and nitrogen, with some carbon monoxide and hydrogen. Explosives may be solid, liquid, or gas. They are generally classified as low explosives, primary explosives (also called initiators or primers), and high explosives.

Export-Import Bank of the United States (Eximbank), U.S. government agency set up in 1934 to assist foreign exports. It makes loans to foreign borrowers who wish to buy U.S. goods and services. Eximbank helped develop trade with Latin America and the Allied countries after World War II. It is now active in supporting U.S. exports to developing countries.

Exports and imports, goods shipped out of or into a country. A country exports products it can produce cheaply or plentifully; it imports products it cannot produce or can produce only at high cost. Imports may compete with domestically produced goods, and a country may protect its own producers by levying import tariffs (taxes) on specific foreign products, or by limiting imports. Governments encourage exports by providing subsidies making it profitable for producers to export, or by granting tax exemptions to export industries. Governments may also control exports and imports by manipulating currency exchange rates. The ratio of the value of a country's imports and exports is called the balance of trade.
See also: Trade.

Ex post facto, in law, retroactive legislation, most commonly to make illegal actions that were legal when committed. The expression comes from the Latin phrase meaning "after the fact." The U.S. Constitution prohibits *ex post facto* criminal laws. In English law they are permitted but rare.

Expressionism, early 20th-century movement in art and literature that held that art should be the expression of subjective feelings and emotions. Expressionist painters preferred intense coloring and primitive simplified forms, in that these seemed to convey emotions directly. Vincent Van Gogh and Edvard Munch influenced the movement, which developed in both France and Germany after 1905. In France the style was represented by the fauvists Henri Matisse and Georges Rouault, and in Germany by Die Brücke and the Blaue Reiter artists like Wassily Kandinsky, Ludwig Kirchner, and Franz Marc. Expressionist writers include August Strindberg, Frank Wedekind, and Franz Kafka.

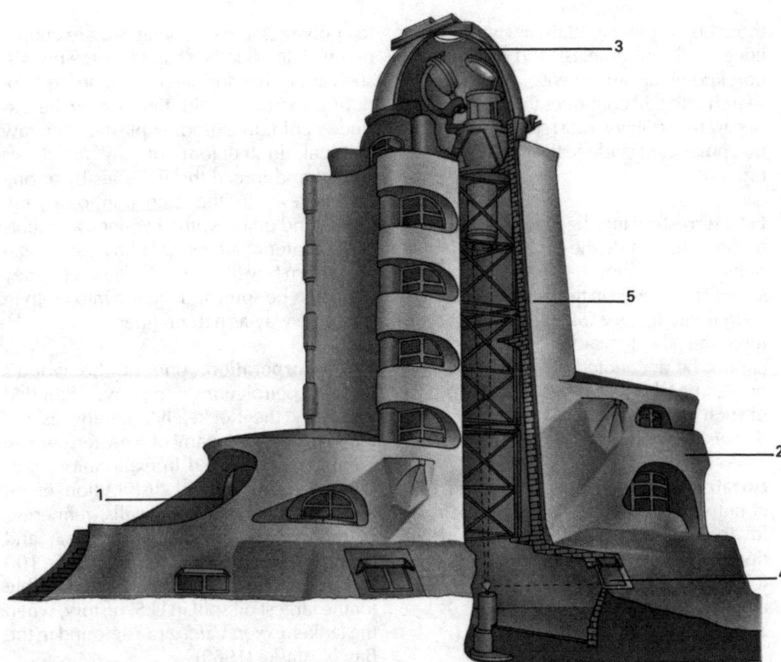

Expressionism in architecture: the design for the Einstein Tower.
1. Entrance
2. Living quarters
3. Cupola
4. Basement laboratory
5. Cement rendering on top of brick construction

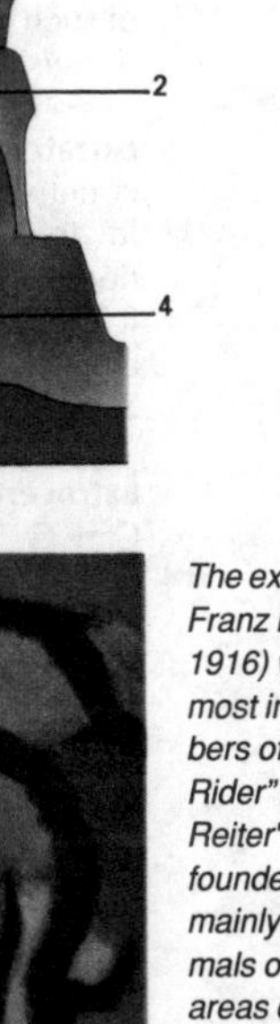

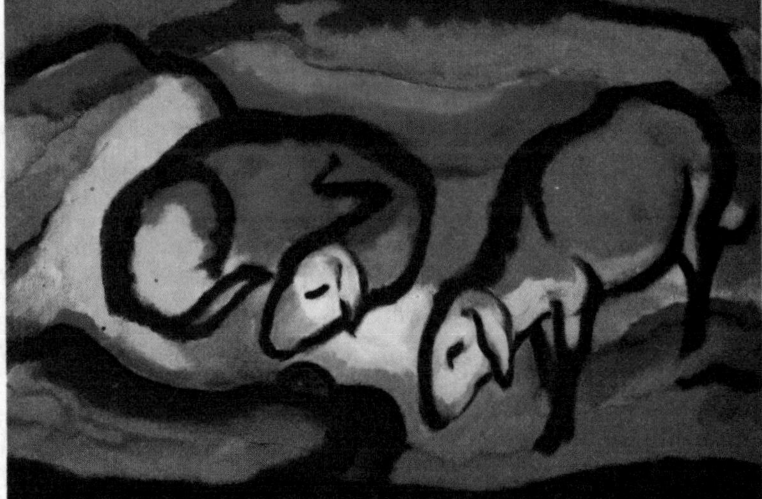

The expressionist Franz Marc (1880-1916) was one of the most important members of "The Blue Rider" ("Der Blaue Reiter") group, founded in 1911. He mainly painted animals over broad areas of color, using heavy contours. This painting, Sheep, *is at Saarbrücken at the Saarlandmuseum.*

Extension program, usually a non-degree educational program offered by a college or university, generally off campus. Extension students may take courses to advance their careers or for personal enjoyment or development. Some extension courses are now offered for college credit and can be counted toward degree requirements. Early extension programs were developed by Cambridge University in England (1873) and the University of Chicago (1892). Programs are now common in the U.S.

Extinct species, in biology, species of which no living individuals remain. Extinction is most often the result of changes in food supply, habitat, or climate. Massive environmental changes may result in the mass extinction of many species at once. Rapid changes in environment caused by humans since industrialization have resulted in the extinction of many species of plants and animals.

Extract, concentrated essence of plant or animal material, used as food flavoring, in drugs, and in cosmetics. Food extracts may be produced by a combination of crushing and cooking to extract oil and other flavorings. Some extracts, like vanilla, are prepared in a solution of alcohol; others may use glycerol or propylene glycol. Morphine is an extract of the opium poppy. Common cosmetic extracts include musk and balsam.

Extraction, selective removal of a substance or substances from a mixture by use of carefully selected solvents. The solvent is chosen so that the desired material dissolves more readily than the rest of the mixture. When the mixture is composed of solids, the process is known as leaching. Salt can be removed from a mixture of sand and salt by leaching with water, and metals can be separated from their ores by leaching with other solvents. Extraction can also be used to separate liquid and gaseous mixtures. The technique is widely used in the petroleum and chemical industries and in metallurgy. It is also used to obtain oil from oil seeds and sugar from sugar beet.

Extradition, surrendering of a person wanted for trial of a criminal offense by 1 state or country to another. International extradition only operates where a treaty has been signed by both countries involved. A country may refuse the extradition if the offender is to be tried for a political offense. Although the U.S. Constitution provides for the extradition of a criminal from 1 state to another, the governors are not bound to comply with an extradition order.

Extrasensory perception (ESP), communication or perception without use of sight, hearing, taste, touch, or smell. ESP includes telepathy (perception of the thoughts of others), clairvoyance (knowledge of distant objects), and precognition (foreknowledge of events). Although research into ESP continues through the field of parapsychology, most scientists feel that no convincing evidence of it has ever been offered.

Extraterrestrial intelligence, intelligent life originating outside the earth and its atmosphere. While none has been discovered, scientists engaged in the search for extraterrestrial intelligence (SETI) have been scanning the sky for radio frequencies that cannot be accounted for by natural phenomena and might indicate the existence of such life.
See also: Exobiology.

Extraterritoriality, privilege granted by a country to resident foreign nationals, allowing them to remain under the jurisdiction of the laws of their own country only. It is generally extended only to diplomatic agents.
See also: Diplomacy.

Extrovert, term used by Swiss psychiatrist Carl G. Jung to describe a person who prefers being surrounded by other people and much activity, as opposed to an introvert, who is happier with solitude and contemplation. While most people combine tendencies of both, Jung believed that one tendency or the other is generally predominant.
See also: Jung, Carl Gustav.

Extrusion, process for shaping materials—especially metals, but also such nonmetals as rubber, plastic, and glass—by forcing them through a small orifice or die. Hydraulic or mechanical rams are employed to apply pressure to a billet (square chunk) of the material to be shaped. Some metals, such as copper and steel, must be kept hot during extrusion, aluminum may be extruded cold. In extruding plastics, the raw material, in the form of tiny pellets, is heated and forced through dies by a long feed screw. In the extrusion of nylon, rayon, and other synthetic fibers, filaments of the material are extruded by centrifugal force from tiny dies called *spinnerets.* They may then be spun and woven into cloth in the same way as natural fibers.

Exxon Corporation, one of the world's largest petroleum company, founded 1882, by the Rockefeller family, as the Standard Oil Company of New Jersey. The company is involved in exploration, production, refining, and distribution of oil and natural gas. It owns wells, refineries, petrochemical plants, pipelines, and tanker fleets, and operates in nearly 100 countries. The company was responsible for the largest oil spill in U.S. history, when the tanker *Exxon Valdez* ran aground in the Bay of Alaska (1989).

Eyck, Jan Van *see:* Van Eyck, Jan.

Eye, organ of vision possessed by all vertebrate and most invertebrate animals. Eyes vary widely in complexity. Many invertebrates have simple cup-shaped eyes containing light-sensitive cells that merely perceive the intensity of light. Insects and crustaceans have compound eyes comprising many hundreds of units that build up a picture composed of minute light and dark spots like a newspaper photograph. Vertebrates and a few invertebrates (such as the squid) have eyes with lenses that focus images onto a light-sensitive surface. The human eye is roughly spherical and is moved in its socket by 6 muscles. The wall of the eyeball has 3 main layers. The outermost layer is the tough and fibrous *sclera,* which merges at the front into the *cornea,* a hard transparent layer. Beneath the sclera is the *choroid,* which contains a dark pigment to prevent scattering of light within the eye. Toward the front, the choroid forms the *ciliary body,* whose muscles control the lens. The ciliary body merges with the *iris,* the colored part of the eye, whose muscles respond to varying light intensity by widening and closing the *pupil,* the opening in the iris through which lights enters. The innermost layer of the eye is the *retina,* which contains light-sensitive nerve endings that send signals to the brain through the *optic nerve.* Since the nerve itself is not sensitive to light, there is a blind spot where it leaves the eye. The blood vessels supplying the retina enter the eye through the center of the optic nerve and spread out over the retina.
Light entering the eye first passes through a thin transparent layer of skin, the *conjunctiva,* which is lubricated by the tears, secreted by a gland above the eye. The *lens* lies behind the pupil and focuses an image on the retina. Spread over the surface of the retina are some 130 million minute light-sensitive nerve endings. About 7 million of these, shorter than the others, are called *cones.* The other nerve endings, called *rods,* are spaced out much more evenly. The cones are responsible for color vision, but function well only in fairly bright light. The rods operate at much lower levels of lighting, but their image is only in shades of gray. The optic nerve carries the signals via the *optic chiasma,* a major nerve junction, to the visual part of the brain, the *occipital lobe,* where the information from the two eyes is combined to give a stereoscopic image.

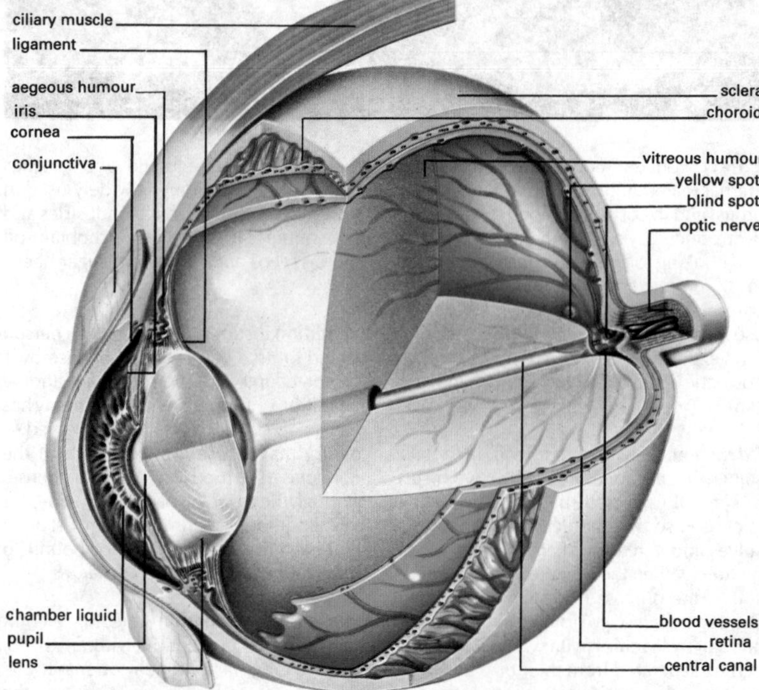

Cross-section of the eye. The eyeball is composed of three layers: the fibrous layer, the vascular layer, and the retina. The retina contains the cells that are sensitive to light and is provided with blood via the uveal layer. At the front of the eye are the lens and the cornea. Light reaches the eye via the pupil, an opening in the iris. Muscles turn the eyeball, dilate and narrow the pupil depending on the amount of light available and alter the shape of the lens to focus the eye. The eyeball is filled with a jelly-like substance, the vitreous humour.

Eye bank, place where corneas removed from newly dead persons are stored until needed for transplantation to restore the sight of those with corneal defects.

Eyeglasses *see:* Glasses.

Ezekiel, Book of, book of the Old Testament of the Bible, named after the early 6th-century B.C. Hebrew priest and prophet. The book prophesizes disastrous consequences for the people of Jerusalem because of their sinful lives. Ezekiel, Jeremiah, and Isaiah are considered the major interpreters of the Babylonian Exile, the era following the Babylonian conquest of Palestine (587- 586 B.C.).
See also: Bible; Old Testament.

Ezra, Book of, book of the Old Testament of the Bible, named for the 5th-century B.C. Babylonian Jewish priest and religious leader. Ezra advocated an exclusive and legalistic doctrine prohibiting marriages between Jews and gentiles. In Jewish editions of the Bible, the books of Ezra and Nehemiah are combined in Writings.
See also: Bible; Old Testament.

F, sixth letter in the English alphabet. It occupies the same place in the Latin alphabet and in the early Greek alphabet, although it is omitted in the classical Greek alphabet. F is derived from the Phoenician *vav* or *waw*, which was the symbol for a hook or peg. In Latin, the *v* sound was represented by *u* and thus *f* acquired its present sound. In musical terminology, it represents *fa* in the scale of C. It is also the sign for Fahrenheit in measurement of temperature.

Faber, Eberhard (1822-79), founder of the first large-scale pencil factory in the United States. The family business began when Eberhard's great-grandfather, Kasper Faber, began making pencils in Bavaria, now Germany, in 1761. Eberhard's brother, Lothar von Faber, established branches of the business in Europe and the United States. When Eberhard moved to New York City in 1848 he opened a branch of the family's business, selling pencils he imported from Bavaria. In 1861, partly to avoid an import tariff, Eberhard Faber established a pencil factory in New York City. He later expanded the business to include other stationery products. The international business remains under family control.

Fabergé, Peter Carl (1846-1920), Russian goldsmith famous for the jewelry he made for the Russian tsars and other royalty, especially the jeweled and enameled Easter eggs. He went into exile in Switzerland in 1917.

Fabian Society, English society for the propagation of socialism. Established 1883-84, it took its name from the Roman general Fabius Cunctator, who delayed fighting Hannibal in order to avoid defeat. Fabians rejected violent revolution, seeking to change society gradually. They helped form the Labour Representation Committee, which became the Labour Party in 1906. Leading Fabians were Sidney and Beatrice Webb and George Bernard Shaw.
See also: Labour Party; Socialism.

Fable, short story that usually teaches a moral. The characters are generally animals with human characteristics; they illustrate human follies humorously. The earliest collection is the *Fables of Aesop* 4th century B.C. As a literary form the fable flourished in France, particularly in the 17th century with Jean de la Fontaine.
See also: Aesop; Allegory; Folklore; La Fontaine, Jean de.

Fabre, Jean Henri Casimir (1823-1915), French entomologist who used direct observations of insects in their natural environments in his pioneering researches into insect instinct and behavior.
See also: Entomology.

Face fly (*Musca autumnalis*), insect that feeds on the body fluids of livestock. It is speculated that the first face flies, discovered in Nova Scotia in 1952, came from Europe. The face fly can transmit diseases to horses, donkeys, and cattle. Resembling the common house fly, the face fly is different in that the larvae (maggots) develop faster than house fly maggots and are yellowish instead of white.

Facsimile, precise reproduction of an original document; in modern usage, a reproduction transmitted over telephone lines. The image is scanned at the transmitter ("fax" machine), reconstructed at the receiving station, and duplicated on paper.

Factor, in mathematics, whole number (integer) that may be divided into another number a whole number of times without remainder. Thus the factors of 12 are 1, 2, 3, 4, and 6.

Faeroe Islands

Capital:	Thorshavn
Area:	540 sq mi (1,399 sq km)
Population:	47,800
Government:	self-governing region of the Danish realm
GNP:	U.S. $686,000,000
Per capita:	U.S. $14,600

Faeroe Islands, group of 18 Danish islands (540 sq mi/1,399 km) in the North Atlantic, northwest of the Shetland Islands and southeast of Iceland. The largest of these volcanic islands are Strömö and Österö. The main economic activities are fishing and sheep raising. The islands have been under Danish control since the 14th century but were granted a large degree of self-government in 1948.

Fahd ibn Abdul Aziz (1922-), king of Saudi Arabia (1982-). Fahd, a son of Ibn Saud, was interior minister from 1962 to 1975, when his half-brother, King Khalid, named him crown prince. He succeeded upon the death of Khalid, whose cautious policies he generally followed. He was deeply involved in discussions and decisions which led to the presence of allied forces on Saudi Arabian soil during operation Desert Shield, which would later become operation Desert Storm.
See also: Persian Gulf War; Saudi Arabia.

Fahrenheit, Gabriel Daniel (1686-1736), German-born Dutch physicist and instrument maker. He introduced the mercury-in-glass thermometer and discovered the variation of boiling points with atmospheric pressure, but is best remembered for his Fahrenheit temperature scale. This has 179 divisions (degrees) between the freezing point of water (32°F) and the boiling point (212°F). Although still commonly used in the United States, elsewhere the Fahrenheit scale has been superseded by the Celsius scale.

Fairbanks (pop. 30,843), second largest city in Alaska, located in central Alaska in the Yukon Valley. The city was settled in 1902 during the gold rush days and was incorporated in 1906. It serves as an agricultural market and mining center for the surrounding area and is the northern terminus of the Alcan highway. Concrete blocks, lumber, and mining equipment are processed there. Three mi (5 km) from the city are the University of Alaska and the Fairbanks branch of the University Agricultural Experiment Stations.
See also: Alaska.

Fairbanks, Douglas, Sr. (1883-1939), U.S. film actor famous for his romantic and swashbuckling roles in films such as *Robin Hood* (1922) and *The Black Pirate* (1926). In 1919 he founded United Artists Studio with his wife Mary Pickford, Charlie Chaplin, and D.W. Griffith.

Fairbanks, Douglas, Jr. (1909-), U.S. movie actor and the son of the silent film star Douglas Fairbanks. Fairbanks, Jr., made his film debut in 1923. His best-known movies include *The Prisoner of Zenda* (1937), *Gunga Din* (1939), and *Sinbad the Sailor* (1947). The autobiographical book *The Salad Days* (1988) covers his early years.

Fahd ibn Abdul Aziz

Fairchild, David Grandison (1869-1954), U.S. botanist who introduced many useful plants into the United States. One of the founders of the U.S. Department of Agriculture's section of Foreign Seed and Plant Introduction, Fairchild served it as agricultural explorer, administrator, and, after retirement, collaborator. His books include *Exploring for Plants* (1930) and the autobiographical *The World Was My Garden* (1938).

Fairbanks, Douglas, Jr.

Fairchild, Sherman Mills (1896-1971), U.S. inventor of aerial mapping photography. Already the inventor of several cameras, he developed his Fairchild Flight Analyzer Camera in 1953. The first camera capable of taking distortion-free aerial pic-

tures in a continuous sequence of action, it has been used to track guided missiles and to study takeoffs and landings of missiles and planes.
See also: Camera; Photography.

Fair Deal, domestic program proposed by President Truman (1945-48), covering civil rights, education, health services, agriculture, and employment. Congress rejected many of the proposals as being too expensive, but the 1946 Employment Act and other measures resulted.
See also: Truman, Harry S.

Fair housing laws *see:* Open housing.

Fair Labor Standards Act, U.S. law passed in 1938 under the Roosevelt administration's New Deal to guarantee most workers a minimum wage and a 44-hr maximum working week. The act was subsequently extended and improved.
See also: Wages and hours.

Fair-trade laws, laws developed for the purpose of preventing a particular business from selling goods at extremely low prices in an attempt to abolish competition. Adopted in 1931, the first law was intended to prevent the large chains of stores from cutting prices to hurt the business of independent retailers. By 1950, 45 states had such laws, but opponents of fair-trade laws insisted that they resulted in increased spending for consumers, and many states repealed them. In 1975, the U.S. Congress abolished remaining fair-trade laws by repealing the Miller-Tydings and MaGuire acts, which had protected them.

Fairy tale, tale involving fantastic events and characters, not necessarily fairies. Many originate in myth and folklore, but an equal number have been written for adults, among them those by Charles Perrault, the brothers Grimm, Johann Wolfgang von Goethe, and Hans Christian Andersen. Modern writers J.R.R. Tolkien and C.S. Lewis incorporated fairy-tale elements in their works.
See also: Folklore.

Falcon

Falkland Islands: bay of New Island

Faisal, or **Feisal**, name of 2 kings of Iraq. **Faisal I** (1885-1933) took part in the Arab revolt against the Ottoman Turks in 1915 and was king 1921-33. **Faisal II** (1935-58) reigned 1939-58. His uncle, Abdul Ilah, ruled Iraq as regent till 1953. In 1958 they were both murdered in a revolution.
See also: Iraq.

Faisal, or **Feisal** (Faisal ibn Abdul Aziz al Faisal al Saud; 1905-75), king of Saudi Arabia from 1964, when his brother, King Saud, was forced to abdicate. A pious, moderate, and able ruler, Faisal instituted a far-ranging program of social reform. Friendly to the West, he nevertheless joined the campaign against Israel and supported the Arab oil cartel. He was assassinated by a nephew in Mar. 1975.
See also: Saudi Arabia.

Faith *see:* Religion.

Falange Española, recognized as the only legal political party in Spain under dictator Francisco Franco. Founded by José Antonio Primo de Rivera in 1933, the fascist Falange joined the Nationalist forces of Franco during the Spanish Civil War (1936-39). Franco assumed control of the party in 1937, and in 1945 the Falange became known as the National Movement. It was outlawed by the democratic government of Spain in 1977, after Franco's death, but is still active.

Falcon, name generally applied to about 60 species of hawk, though the true falcons of the family Falconidae number about 35 species. They are birds of prey, feeding mainly on other birds, which they kill in the air. They inhabit most parts of the world, making their nests on rocky ledges or tree forks. Falcons in the United States include the prairie falcon and the sparrow hawk.

Falkland Islands, or Islas Malvinas, self-governing British colony, also claimed by Argentina, consisting of 200 islands totaling 4,700 sq mi (12,200 sq km) in the South Atlantic about 480 mi (770 km) northeast of Cape Horn. The capital is Stanley. In 1982 Argentina seized them, but British forces retook them. The inhabitants are mostly of British descent. The economy is largely dependent on sheep raising.

Falla, Manuel de (1876-1946), Spanish composer. He studied in Madrid and Paris, and his work was heavily influenced by Maurice Ravel and by native Andalusian folk music. His works include the ballets *El Amor Brujo* (1915) and *The Three-Cornered Hat* (1917), the opera *La Vida Breve* (1905), and *Nights in the Gardens of Spain* (1916), for piano and orchestra.

Falling bodies, Law of, group of rules that tell what an object does when it falls freely to the ground. The force of gravity acts on all bodies in the same way, regardless of their shape, size, or density. Distance, velocity, and acceleration are the 3 factors to be considered when studying the laws of falling bodies. The velocity of a falling body is determined by how much the air resists it, which may in turn be determined by its shape. Acceleration is the rate at which a body's speed increases as it falls. The 16th-century scientist Galilei was instrumental in proving the laws of falling bodies.
See also: Galileo Galilei; Physics.

Fallout, radioactive debris produced by the explosion of nuclear weapons. Local fallout rains down over an area up to about 50 mi (80 km) downwind of the explosion for several hours afterwards. The radiation produced by the fallout causes severe radiation sickness and possibly death to any people living within this area. More fallout rises into the lower atmosphere (the *troposphere*) and is washed down with rain over a wider area over the next few months. Still more rises even higher, into the *stratosphere*, where it may be blown around the globe for months or years before it descends to the ground. Some isotopes in fallout keep producing radiation for a long time and become absorbed by plants, animals, and human beings.
See also: Nuclear weapon; Radiation.

Fallout shelter, building or underground structure whose purpose is to protect people from the effects of fallout, or radiation. In 1961 the U.S. government began to designate certain buildings as public fallout shelters. Buildings with thick layers of brick, concrete, or stone may serve as fallout shelters, and well-protected underground areas might also serve. Home fallout shelters, which need to be supplied with basic provisions, are usually underground buildings with thick walls.
See also: Civil defense; Fallout.

Fall River (pop. 157,272), city in southeastern Massachusetts, situated on Mount Hope Bay, at the mouth of the Taunton River. Settled in 1656 and incorporated in 1834, Fall River has been a cotton textile center since 1811. It is home to a maritime museum and to the battleship USS *Massachusetts.*
See also: Massachusetts

Family planning *see:* Birth control; Planned Parenthood Federation of America.

Famine, acute food shortage resulting in widespread starvation. It is usually caused by natural disasters such as drought, floods, or plant diseases causing crop failure. Famines have often dramatically influenced the course of history. In the Irish famine (1846-47), caused by potato blight, millions died and around 1.5 million emigrated, mostly to the U.S. Recently there have been crippling famines in Bangladesh and Africa.

Fan, instrument that excites a current of air by the agitation of a broad surface, vanes, or disks. In computer terminology the term *fan-in* is used to denote an electrical load presented to an output by an input. A *fan-out* is an electrical load that an output is capable of driving, usually expressed as the number of inputs that can be driven from a given output signal.

Faneuil, Peter (1700-43), wealthy Boston merchant. In 1742 Faneuil built a public market and meeting place which he named after himself. Faneuil Hall became known as the Cradle of Liberty because of the historic meetings that took place there during the Revolutionary and Civil wars. Today Faneuil Hall houses a library and a military museum.

Fannie Mae *see:* Federal National Mortgage Association.

Fanon, Frantz Omar (1925-61), French black psychoanalyst and social philosopher. He condemned racism in his book *Black Skin, White Masks* (1952). In *The Wretched of the Earth* (1961) he advocated extreme violence against whites as a cathartic expression for black people.
See also: Psychoanalysis.

Fantin-Latour, Ignace Henri Jean Théodore (1836-1904), French painter known for his flower paintings, his illustrations of the works of Robert Wagner and Louis-Hector Berlioz, and his group portraits of artists, such as *Homage to Delacroix* (1864) and *A Studio at Batignolles* (1870).

FAO *see:* Food and Agriculture Organization.

Farad (F), unit of electrical capacitance. A 1-volt-per-sec change in voltage across a 1-farad capacitor will require 1 ampere of current flow. The farad is named for English physicist Michael Faraday.
See also: Electric current.

Faraday, Michael (1791-1867), English chemist and physicist, pupil and successor of H. Davy at the Royal Institution. He discovered benzene (1825), first demonstrated electromagnetic induction and invented the dynamo (1831), and, with his concept of magnetic lines of force, laid the foundations of classical field theory later built upon by J. Clerk Maxwell. He discovered the laws of electrolysis that bear his name and demonstrated a connection between light and magnetism. The *Faraday effect* is the rotation of the plane of polarization produced when plane-polarized light is passed through a substance in a magnetic field, the light traveling in a direction parallel to the lines of force. For a given substance, the rotation is proportional to the thickness traversed by the light and to the magnetic field strength. Faradays' laws state that in the process of electrolytic changes, equal quantities of electricity charge or discharge equivalent quantities of ions at each electrode.
See also: Electrolysis; Electromagnetism.

Farce, comedy based on exaggeration and broad visual humor. Its traditional ingredients are improbable situations and characters developed to their limits. Farcical elements are present in the plays of Aristophanes, Plautus, Shakespeare, Molière, and many others; such 19th-century writers as Georges Feydeau and W.S. Gilbert helped establish farce as a respected theatrical form.

Far East, term often used for eastern Asia, comprising China, Japan, Korea, Taiwan, and eastern Siberia in the Soviet Union. Sometimes the term extends to include the nations of Southeast Asia: Brunei, Myunmar (Burma), Indonesia, Cambodia (Kampuchea), Laos, Malaysia, the Philippines, Singapore, Thailand, and Vietnam. The term Far East was originated by the Europeans to describe an area of Asia far to the east of them.

Fargo (pop. 153,295), largest city in North Dakota and seat of Cass County. The city lies on the Red River, whose fertile valley forms an important farming region. Iron and steel, glass, canvas, and concrete products are manufactured there. It is a transportation center and the site of North Dakota State University of Agriculture and Applied Science. Founded in 1871 by the Northern Pacific Railway, the city was named for William George Fargo of the famous stagecoach company.
See also: North Dakota.

Fantin Latour's painting Flowers and Fruits *(1865; Louvre, Paris)*

Fargo, William George (1818-81), cofounder of Wells and Company (later Wells-Fargo), the pioneer express service, in 1844. In 1850 it merged with other companies to become the American Express Company, of which he was president until his death.

Farm and farming, setting and activity of the cultivation of crops and the raising of livestock. Since the 1800s scientific advances have made farms increasingly productive. In the United States farms are either specialized or mixed. About 95% of U.S. farms are specialized; they raise the best single crop or livestock for their environment. About 5% of U.S. farms are mixed, producing a variety of crops and livestock. Scientific techniques have been developed to help crop farmers nourish their soil, irrigate dry areas, control pests (such as insects), and plant and cultivate their crops. Livestock farmers must feed, shelter, and provide grazing land and health care for their animals, as well as breed and finish (or fatten) them. Farm management includes everything a farmer does to make farming profitable.

Farm Credit System, network of cooperatively owned banks regulated by the Farm Credit Administration (FCA). Originally established with capital from the government (1923), this system enables farm and fishing cooperatives to obtain loans from borrower-owned banks and credit associations. There are 12 U.S. Farm Credit districts each with a Federal Land Bank, Federal Intermediate Credit Bank, and a Bank for Cooperatives. A participating cooperative can obtain monies through various financial transactions that take place within the system. The Farm Credit System Capital Corporation administers the system, of which 3 members are selected by district banks, 2 are appointed by the FCA, 1 is elected by the corporation members, and 1 is selected by the secretary of agriculture if federal funds are added to the system.

Farmer *see:* Farm and farming.

Farmer, James Leonard (1920-), U.S. civil rights leader. He founded the Congress of Racial Equality (CORE), serving as head 1942-66, utilizing nonviolent techniques of protest. He was assistant Secretary of Health, Education, and Welfare 1969- 70. *See also:* Congress of Racial Equality.

Farmer-Labor Party, minor U.S. political party founded 1919 to promote the interests of small farmers and city workers. The party soon foundered nationally, but the separate Minnesota Farmer-Labor Party elected its candidate, F.B. Olsen, governor in 1930, 1932, and 1934. The party merged with the Minnesota Democratic Party in 1944.

Farmers Home Administration, U.S. Department of Agriculture agency that promotes nationwide rural development by providing credit for those who may not be able to obtain reasonable credit elsewhere. Established in 1946, the Farmers Home Administration extends credit to improve the income of the small farmer, and also helps to finance business and industrial development, community facilities, and housing in rural areas.

Farming *see:* Agriculture; Farm and farming.

Farnsworth, Philo Taylor (1906-71), U.S. radio research engineer who pioneered television technology. As a teenager, Farnsworth developed an electronic television system superior to the mechanical discs in limited use at the time. In 1927 Farnsworth publicly demonstrated his electronic television tube, an image dissector that created an image by producing an electronic signal that matched the brightness of the object being televised. By 1939 the Radio Corporation of America (RCA) obtained a license from Farnsworth to use his technology along with their own.
See also: Television.

Faroe Islands *see:* Faeroe Islands.

Farouk I *see:* Faruk I.

Benito Mussolini, the fascist leader of Italy, was very popular during the 1920's and 1930's.

Farquhar, George (1678-1707), English dramatist. His most successful plays, *The Recruiting Officer* (1706) and *The Beaux' Strategem* (1707), are characterized by vigorous language and pungent satire, and more realism than was then fashionable.

Farragut, David Glasgow (1801-70), U.S. admiral and Civil War hero. He captured New Orleans, a Confederate supply center, in 1862 and gained control of the Mississippi River in 1863. In a daring attack on Mobile, Ala., in 1864 he gave the now proverbial command "Damn the torpedoes! Full speed ahead!"
See also: Civil War, U.S.

Farrell, James Thomas (1904-79), U.S. writer. He is known for his social novels, particularly the *Studs Lonigan* trilogy (1932-35), which depicts the often harsh life of the Irish on Chicago's South Side.

Farsightedness, or hyperopia, defect of vision in which light entering the eye from nearby objects comes to a focus behind the retina instead of on it. Near objects are blurred; far objects are seen clearly. The condition may be corrected by wearing eyeglasses with convex lenses.

Faruk I, or **Farouk I** (1920-65), king of Egypt (1936-52). He was considered weak and incompetent, and his rule was marked by corruption, alienation of the military, and many internal rivalries. This led to a military coup by Gamal Abdal Nasser, which forced Faruk's abdication.
See also: Egypt.

Fascism, originally, political system of Italy under Benito Mussolini (1922-45); more broadly, authoritarian and antidemocratic political philosophy placing the state above the individual, and stressing absolute obedience to a glorified leader. Adolf Hitler's Nazi Party is generally considered fascist. Under facism, industry is privately owned but under government control. Nationalism, racism, and militarism are logical products of facism.
See also: Mussolini, Benito.

Fashion, prevailing style of dress, particularly new designs representing changes from previous seasons. Fashion in both dress and interior design is believed to have originated in 14th-century Europe and was set by monarchs and other prominent persons, with descriptions conveyed by travelers, in letters, and by exchange of the fashion doll. The first fashion magazine is thought to have originated in late 16th-century Germany. In the U.S., *Godey's Ladies' Book* was established in 1830. For many decades it was the leading U.S. source of fashion news, bringing to women the latest creations from Paris, the leading arbiter of fashion since the Renaissance. By the mid-19th century, designer-dressmakers became prominent in the fashion world for the first time. Other important fashion centers have been London, New York, and Rome.

Fat, compound of carbon, hydrogen, and oxygen found in certain parts of the body, an important constituent of diet. Fat is the most concentrated source of food energy, supplying 9 calories per gram; protein and carbohydrate, the other 2 sources of food energy, supply only 4 calories per gram. Fats are the chief sources of essential fatty acids (EFAs), as well as carriers of vitamins A, D, E, and K. Three molecules of fatty acid combined with one molecule of glycerol constitute 1 molecule of fat, the chemical name of which is a triglyceride. A fatty acid is *saturated* if its chain of carbon atoms contains all the hydrogen it can hold, or if there are no double bonds between carbon atoms. Saturated fats are usually solid at room temperature; they occur in both animal and vegetable fats, but chiefly in the former. A fatty acid is *unsaturated* if its chain of carbon atoms has 1 or more double bonds where hydrogen could be added. The process of adding hydrogen to a double bond in an unsaturated fatty acid to make it more saturated is called *hydrogenation. Monounsaturated* fatty acids have only 1 double bond where hydrogen could be added. *Polyunsaturated* fatty acids have 2 or more double bonds where hydrogen could be added. Polyunsaturated fats are usually oils and are most abundant in plant and fish oils. Nearly all fats from plant sources are unsaturated; the only major exception is palm (or coconut) oil, which is highly saturated. The utilization of fat in humans is affected diet and state of nutrition, the endocrine system, degree of activity, age, heredity, and diseases that may interfere with the absorption and metabolism of fat. Diets high in fat can lead to above-normal amounts of lipids (triglycerides, fatty acids, cholesterol, and other fat-like substances) in the blood, associated with atherosclerosis. Changes in dietary habits to reduce the risk of coronary heart disease in later life include adjusting caloric intake to maintain an optimum weight, reducing fat intake so that fat supplies less than 35% of the total number of calories (of which less than 10% should be from saturated fats and up to 90% from polyunsaturated fats, with the remainder supplied by monounsaturated fats) and limiting the daily intake of cholesterol to fewer than 10.6 oz (300 mg).

Fates, in Greek and Roman mythology, goddesses of destiny, called *Moirai* by the Greeks and *Parcae* by the Romans. Three Fates rule human lives: Clotho, who spins the web of life; Lachesis, who measures its length; and Atropos, the inevitable, who cuts it.
See also: Mythology.

Father Divine *see:* Divine, Father.

Father of Medicine *see:* Hippocrates.

Father of the Constitution *see:* Madison, James.

Fathometer, underwater device used on ships to measure the depth of water. As the speed of sound in water is known, the

fathometer works by sending a sound down through the water, to be returned by echo. The fathometer dispatches sound through a submarine oscillator and receives it through a hydrophone echo receiver. First manufactured in 1927, the fathometer is the trade name for a refined sonic depth finder. The first sonic depth finder was developed in 1919 by the U.S. Navy.
See also: Sonar.

Fatimids, Muslim dynasty that ruled a North African empire from its conquest of Egypt in A.D. 969 until 1171. The first rulers claimed descent from Fatima, Muhammad's youngest daughter. In 969 al-Mu'izz established his capital at Cairo, bringing a religious and cultural renaissance to the city. At one time all of North Africa, Sicily, and Syria were under Fatimid rule, but the dynasty was overthrown in 1171 by Saladin.

Faulkner, William (1897-1962), U.S. writer, known for his vivid characterization and complex, convoluted style in novels and short stories set in fictional Yoknapatawpha County, based on the area of his hometown, Oxford, Miss. His works include the novels *The Sound and the Fury* (1929) and *Light in August* (1932) and the short story "A Rose for Emily." He painted a vivid picture of the decadent and dying South, seeing in it a microcosm of human destiny. He explored stream-of-consciousness techniques in his writing. He was awarded the Nobel Prize for literature in 1949 and won 2 Pulitzer prizes (1955 and 1963). He also worked as a Hollywood scriptwriter.

Fault, fracture in the earth's crust along which there has been relative movement and displacement of the rocks on each side. *Dip-slip faults* involve movement up or down an inclined fault plane. *Reverse* or *thrust faults* involves relative displacement upward of the overlying rocks and results from compressive stress. *Strike-slip faults* such as the San Andreas Fault in California, involve horizontal displacement and result from shearing stress.

Faun, in Roman mythology, woodland spirit, usually portrayed as having a human upper body and goat legs. Faunas, god of nature and fertility, was the Roman equivalent of the Greek god Pan.

Fauré, Gabriel Urbain (1845-1924), French composer. He was director of the Paris Conservatory (1905-20), where his pupils included Maurice Ravel. His works include the *Requiem* (1887), the orchestral suite *Pelléas et Melisande* (1898), and the song cycle *La bonne chanson* (1894).

Faust, legendary German enchanter, based on a 16th-century charlatan, who sold his soul to the devil Mephistopheles for knowledge and pleasure. Christopher Marlowe made the tale a tragedy of human presumption *Dr. Faustus* c.1590, while Johann Wolfgang von Goethe (*Faust*, 1808, 1832) made Faust a Romantic idealist whose sins are forgiven because of his continual striving after good.
See also: Goethe, Johann Wolfgang von; Marlowe, Christopher.

Fauves (French, "wild beasts"), group of French painters whose style emphasized intense color, often applied directly from the paint tubes, and vigorous brush strokes. Although the term was originally used derisively, the artists adopted it and their movement became known as fauvism. Led by Henri Matisse, fauvism flourished from 1903 to 1907, and its members included Raoul Dufy and Georges Rouault. Although the painters evolved other styles after 1907, fauvism influenced other movements, particularly German expressionism.

Fawkes, Guy (1570-1606), Roman Catholic Englishman, hired by the Gunpowder Plot conspirators as an explosives expert while he was serving in the Spanish army. Arrested while setting explosives beneath the House of Lords, he was tortured and hanged. In England he is burnt in effigy on Guy Fawkes Day, Nov. 5.

Feather, covering of a bird's body, made up of a central *shaft*, with the hollow *quill* at the tip, and the vane on each side, consisting of rows of fine threads called *barbs*, which are held together by hooked *barbules* to form a web. Feathers keep birds warm and enable them to fly.

Feather star *see:* Sea lily.

Febold Feboldson, Swedish-American folk hero, popular in tall tales of the Great Plains. Personifying the pioneer spirit, Feboldson used his amazing strength and ingenuity to solve problems and accomplish great feats. Possibly based on an actual Swedish-American pioneer, the folk character was created in the 1920s by Don Holmes and Wayne T. Carroll.

Federal Aviation Administration (FAA), agency of the U.S. Department of Transportation created in 1958 to regulate air transportation. The agency's main responsibility is the operation and maintenance of the national air traffic control system in the interests of efficiency and safety. It also took over most of the functions of the Civil Aeronautics Board, in preparation for the CAB's end in 1985. In 1981 the FAA terminated the services of some 12,000 air controllers who went on strike in violation of federal law.

Federal Bureau of Investigation (FBI), investigative branch of the U.S. Department of Justice. Established in 1908, the FBI is responsible for the investigation of possible violations of all federal laws except those for which enforcement is specifically assigned to another agency. The bureau is also concerned with internal security, counterespionage, organized crime, and corruption. FBI history was dominated by J. Edgar Hoover, director 1924-72, a conservative figure who held the post until his death. Its first permanent director after Hoover was Clarence M. Kelley, who served 1973-78 and modernized the bureau's procedures. William H. Webster, ex-federal judge and FBI director (1978-87), restructured the bureau in the light of revelations that its agents had committed illegal acts during Hoover's tenure. His tenure was followed by appointment in 1987 of William Sessions.

William Faulkner

Federal Communications Commission (FCC), independent U.S. agency that regulates communication by radio, television, wire and cable. Created in 1934, its most important functions are the licensing of commercial radio and television stations and the assignment of broadcasting frequencies.

Federal court *see:* Court; United States, Government of the.

Federal Crop Insurance Corporation (FCIC), U.S. Department of Agriculture agency that offers insurance to farmers. Created in 1938, the FCIC provides insurance against loss of crops from natural hazards. Through 17 regional offices, the FCIC provides insurance, at varying rates, to over half the nation's agricultural counties.

Federal Deposit Insurance Corporation (FDIC), U.S. agency that insures bank deposits in all federal reserve system banks Federal Reserve System. Created (1933) to promote confidence in banks, it also acts as a watchdog over banking practices.

Federal Election Commission, independent U.S. government agency that enforces the Federal Election Campaign Act, which governs campaign spending for election to federal offices. The act mandates disclosures of campaign spending and expenses, and restricts the size of campaign contributions from groups or individuals. Corporation and labor union contributions are prohibited under the Federal Election Campaign Act. Established in

1974 and with members appointed by the president and approved by the Senate, the Federal Election Commission has the power to investigate and audit campaign funds.

Federal government *see:* Federalism.

Federal Hall, building in Lower Manhattan, New York City, that served as first capitol of the United States under the Constitution. An earlier structure on the site, the city hall, served as U.S. capitol under the Articles of Confederation (1781-89). The building was reconstructed by Charles L'Enfant, and it was here, on April 30, 1789, that George Washington was inaugurated as first president of the United States. Philadelphia became the U.S. capitol in 1790. The present structure was built in 1842 and became a national memorial in 1955.

Federal Highway Administration (FHWA), U.S. Department of Transportation agency that supervises federal aid for construction, operation, and improvement of highways. Established by Congress in 1966, the FHWA oversees about 835,000 mi (1,344,000 km) of U.S. highways. The federal government pays 90% of the cost of construction and improvement of interstate highways, while the states pay the remaining 10%. For state or local highways, the federal government pays 75% and the states pay 25%.

Federal Home Loan Bank Board, independent U.S. federal agency, made up of 3 presidential appointees, that supervised and regulated savings and loans associations between 1932 and 1990. The board was the country's major private source of funds to pay for building and buying homes. It operated the Federal Savings and Loan Insurance Corporation (FSLIC) to protect the savings of those who had money in accounts with FSLIC-insured associations. In the late 1980s it was discovered that FSLIC funds were not actually sufficient to cover its responsibilities. A scandal ensued, with many indictments for fraud, and the result that the federal government will have to bail out the FSLIC for what will probably be hundreds of billions of dollars.

Federal Housing Administration (FHA), U.S. government agency created to bolster lender confidence in mortgage loans and increase housing demand and construction. Established in 1934, the FHA became part of the Department of Housing and Urban Development in 1965. The functions of the FHA include insuring mortgages, determining minimum property standards for housing, and analyzing local housing markets.

Federalism, system of government in which states form a union by granting a central government supreme power in common or national affairs, while retaining their independent existence and control over local affairs. Federations today include the United States, Canada and Australia. In the United States, the federal government is supreme in defense, foreign affairs, the postal and monetary systems, and interstate and foreign commerce. All levels of government may levy taxes and spend money, but the federal government accounts for the vast majority of public spending.

Federalist Party, early U.S. political party, in power from 1797 to 1801. The Federalists, under the leadership of President George Washington's secretary of the treasury, Alexander Hamilton, advocated a strong central government, one whose power could be increased through liberal interpretations of the Constitution. The Democratic-Republicans, led by Thomas Jefferson, supported strict interpretations of the Constitution and greater powers for states and citizens. The Federalists fell out of power when Jefferson was elected president in 1801.

Federalist, The, series of papers on the proposed new U.S. Constitution that originally appeared in New York newspapers in 1787-88. Written by Alexander Hamilton, James Madison, and John Jay, the papers had a major influence on ratification of the Constitution. Later published in book form, the papers both argued logically and appealed to prejudice by emphasizing the weakness in the Articles of the Confederation, the dangers in British sea power and Spanish intrigue, and the need for a strong central government. *The Federalist* is considered a comprehensive analysis of the means by which the ideals of justice, general welfare, and individual rights could be realized.

Federal Land Bank *see:* Farm Credit System.

Federal Maritime Commission, independent U.S. government agency, composed of 5 presidential appointees, that regulates the nation's shipping laws. Overseeing both foreign and domestic offshore commerce, the commission regulates the rates, services, and agreements of U.S. shipping companies. Established in 1969, the commission guards against unauthorized monopoly in the waterborne commerce of the United States. Among other responsibilities, the commission ensures that ship owners and charterers are financially able to pay any claims involving accidental injuries or death aboard their vessels.

Federal Mediation and Conciliation Service (FMCS), independent U.S. government agency whose function is to protect the public interest by mediating those labor-management disputes that affect interstate commerce. Either management or union are required by law to notify the FMCS if they have not been able to successfully renew a labor contract 30 days before it is due to expire or to be changed. Although it does not serve as a law enforcement agency, the FMCS can intervene in a labor-management dispute without being requested, depending upon persuasion to settle disputes. It has 76 regional offices in principal U.S. industrial areas.

Federal National Mortgage Association (FNMA), or "Fannie Mae," government-chartered corporation that acts as a secondary mortgage market for banks. It was created as a government-owned corporation in 1938 to make mortgage funds widely available in the post-World War II housing surge. It was jointly held by the government and private stockholders from 1954, and became a privately owned corporation in 1970.

Federal Reserve Bank *see:* Federal Reserve System.

Federal Reserve System, central U.S. banking authority. In 1913 Congress passed the Federal Reserve Act, dividing the country into 12 districts, each with a Federal Reserve Bank. A 7-member Board of Governors (Federal Reserve Board) in Washington, D.C., coordinates these banks, which constitute a central banking system, handling the government's transactions, coordinating and controlling commercial banks, and helping to regulate the nation's money supply. The Federal Reserve System, or Fed, is responsible directly to Congress. Its main purpose is to control the supply of money and credit through monetary policy. When business worsens, it expands the amount of money and credit, but if prices start rising too rapidly, the Fed will do all it can to reduce the supply of money and credit. The first step is to require the nation's banks to keep a larger amount of their deposits on reserve. With less money to lend, credit becomes "tight," increasing the rate of interest. Businesses expand less rapidly, families cannot afford large purchases like houses or cars, and other forms of buying slow down. When the economy slows, the Fed reverses the process and makes more money available. The Fed possesses 2 other weapons against inflation and depression. First, it can go into the market and "buy" money, in what are called "open market operations." Usually this money is in the form of short-term government bonds bought from insurance companies, banks, and big business firms, which are then free to invest the money they receive in exchange for the bonds. More money becomes available for loans, lowering interest rates and down payments. With a 20% reserve requirement, $1,000 million spent in the marketplace would add up to $5,000 million of new money. Second, the Fed lends money to member banks, loans called *discounts.* By regulating the discount rate (the interest banks pay to borrow from the Fed), the Fed encourages or discourages borrowing. Discount rates are usually tied to interest rates on the open market.

Federal system *see:* Federalism.

Federal Trade Commission (FTC), U.S. agency established (1914) to prevent unfair business practices, particularly monopolies, and to maintain a competitive economy. The FTC studies the effects of business mergers and price agreements, issuing cease and desist orders when necessary; it also attempts to prevent misleading advertising and to protect public health. Its 5 commissions are appointed by the president for 7-year terms.

Feininger, Lyonel (1871-1956), U.S. artist. Influenced by cubism, his style is based on planes of color that create geometric designs. He lived in Germany (1887-1936), teaching at the Bauhaus (1919-32). Also a caricaturist, he produced a comics page for the *Chicago Tribune* (1906-07).
See also: Bauhaus; Cubism.

Feisal *see:* Faisal.

Feke, Robert (1707?-52?), New York-born painter. Although Feke traveled frequently in search of commissions, he painted portraits in Boston, Philadelphia, and in his home at Newport, R.I. Among the portraits for which he is known are *Portrait of Isaac Royall and his Family* (1741) and *Samuel Waldo* (c.1742).

Feldspar, abundant mineral consisting of potassium-, sodium-, and calcium-aluminum silicates. Feldspars make up 60% of the earth's crust. They form a leading raw material for porcelain and ceramic glazes; some, such as moonstone, are used as gems.

Feller, Bob (Robert William Andrew Feller; 1919-), U.S. baseball star, pitcher with the Cleveland Indians (1936-56). In 1946 he set a season record of 348 strikeouts (a record broken in 1973 by Nolan Ryan). He was elected to the Baseball Hall of Fame in 1962.

Fellini, Federico (1920-), Italian film director. His first major success was *La Strada* (1954), a film starring Anthony Quinn and Fellini's wife, Giulietta Masina. His early films, such as *La Dolce Vita* (1960), portray human disillusionment in a corrupt society. Later films such as *8 1/2* (1963) and *Satyricon* (1970) are often dreamlike and fantastic.

Felony, criminal offense more serious than a misdemeanor; the distinction between the two is generally the severity of the prescribed penalty. In U.S. law homicide, robbery, burglary, theft, and rape are the main felonies, punishable by imprisonment for more than one year or, under special circumstances that vary from state to state, by death.
See also: Crime.

Feminism, 19th- and 20th-century movement for women's political, economic, and social equality with men. Early feminists fought for women's rights to own property and enter the professions. U.S. women obtained the right to vote in 1920; in Great Britain women were enfranchised in 1928. Feminism had a major resurgence in the 1960s; current issues in the movement are equal pay and employment opportunities, abortion rights, and freedom from sexual harassment.
See also: Women's movements.

Fencing, sport of combat using a blunted sword (foil, epee, or saber), descended from the duel. In fencing the object is to touch, not wound, one's opponent. Fencers wear protective clothing and masks. Only the tip of the flexible foil and the stiffer epee may be used to score hits.

Fénelon, François de Salignac de la Mothe (1652-1715), French theologian, archbishop of Cambrai from 1695. His reform writings, especially those on education, were in advance of their day. For the duke of Burgundy, heir of Louis XIV, he wrote *Fables: Dialogues of the Dead* (1690) and the novel *Telemachus* (1699).
See also: Theology.

Fenian movement, movement for Irish independence from Great Britain in the mid- to late 1800s. Named after warriors from Irish mythology, the Fenians organized both in the United States and England. Also known as the Irish Republican Brotherhood, they directed raids in Ireland, England, and Canada. Later Irish republican movements advanced the goal of independence for Ireland and, after years of skirmishes and guerilla warfare, independence was won for southern Ireland (1921), northern Ireland remaining under British control.

Fennec (*Fennecus zerda*), small desert fox with long ears. A nocturnal hunter, it lives in the deserts of North Africa and Arabia and can go for long periods without water.

Fennel (*Foeniculum vulgare*), perennial herb of the parsley family native to southern Europe and cultivated widely for its licorice-flavored foliage and seeds.

Ferber, Edna (1887-1968), U.S. author, noted for her novels about 19th-century life, including *So Big* (1924), for which she won a 1925 Pulitzer Prize, *Show Boat* (1926), *Cimarron* (1930), and *Giant* (1952). Ferber also coauthored plays with George S. Kaufman, including *Dinner at Eight* (1932).

Fer-de-lance (*Bothrops atrox*), large, poisonous snake of the viper family, found on the eastern coast of South America and on some West Indian islands.

Ferdinand, name of 3 Holy Roman Emperors. **Ferdinand I** (1503-64), emperor 1558-64, was king of Bohemia and Hungary from 1526. The Peace of Augsburg ended religious conflict in Germany and his capable administration stabilized the unwieldy empire. **Ferdinand II** (1578-1637) reigned as emperor 1619-37. His attempts to enforce Catholicism in Protestant Bohemia led to a revolt in 1619, which began the Thirty Years' War. **Ferdinand III** (1608-57) succeeded his father Ferdinand II as emperor in 1637. A capable ruler, he compromised with Protestant powers in the Peace of Westphalia (1648).
See also: Holy Roman Empire.

Ferdinand, Spanish kings. **Ferdinand V** (1452-1516), also known as Ferdinand II of Aragon and Ferdinand III of Naples, married Isabella I of Castile in 1469, thus unifying Aragon and Castile. In 1492 he conquered Granada, becoming king of

Federico Fellini

Scene from Satyricon, *directed by Fellini (1969)*

Spain. A supporter of the Spanish Inquisition, he expelled the Jews from Spain. **Ferdinand VI** (1713-59) became king in 1746. A capable ruler and patron of the arts, he carried out administrative reforms and kept Spain neutral during the Seven Years' War. **Ferdinand VII** (1784-1833) acceded in 1808 but was deposed by Napoleon 2 months later and imprisoned until his restoration in 1814. A cruel and repressive absolutist, he revoked the new, liberal constitution twice; in 1823 he was backed by the French military. He was unable to prevent the complete loss of Spain's American possessions.
See also: Spain.

Ferdinand, Archduke *see:* World War I.

Ferlinghetti, Lawrence (1919-), U.S. poet who was at the center of the "beat generation" writers of the 1950s. Ferlinghetti's work reflects the movement's condemnation of commercialism and middle-class values. His poetry is written in a colloquial free-verse style, and he is most known for the satiric criticism of U.S. culture in *A Coney Island of the Mind* (1958). More recent publications include the fiction work, *Love in the Days of Rage* (1988). Ferlinghetti is also the publisher and founder of City Lights, an avant-garde publisher and bookstore in San Francisco.

Fermat, Pierre de (1601-65), French mathematician, founder of modern number and probability theories. Fermat's Last Theorem, which has never been proven, states that there is no whole number solution of $x^n+y^n=z^n$, where x, y, and z are nonzero integers and n is an integer greater than 2. Fermat's Principle states that light (or other waves) will follow the path with the shortest travel time between 2 points.
See also: Mathematics.

Enrico Fermi

Fermentation, chemical reaction that involves degradation of a carbohydrate (organic) material without the presence of oxygen. Agents of fermentation include bacteria, molds, and yeasts. Products of fermentation include alcohols, acids such as lactic acid, and gases such as carbon dioxide. Fermentation has been used in making bread, alcoholic beverages, and cheese for thousands of years.

Fermi, Enrico (1901-54), Italian atomic physicist who won the 1938 Nobel Prize for physics for his experiments with radioactivity. He showed that neutron bombardment of most elements produced their radioisotopes. Fermi emigrated to the United States to escape the fascists, becoming professor at Columbia University (1939) and at University of Chicago (1942), where he built the world's first nuclear reactor (1942).
See also: Atom.

Fermium, chemical element, symbol Fm; for physical constants see Periodic Table. Fermium was discovered by Albert Ghiorso and co-workers in 1952 from the debris of a thermonuclear bomb exploded in the Pacific. It is a metallic element and a member of the actinide series. It has been produced by intense irradiation of plutonium and other lower elements with neutrons as well as by bombarding uranium-238 with oxygen-16 ions in a cyclotron. All of its 16 known isotopes are radioactive. The chemical identification of fermium-250 as a decay product is confirmation of nobelium-254.

Fern, green, nonflowering plant of the class Filicineae having creeping or erect rhizomes (rootstocks) or an erect aerial stem and large conspicuous leaves. Ferns may have appeared on earth more than 350 million years ago. The fern as it is commonly recognized is in its asexual *sporophyte* stage. Spores are produced on the underside of the leaf and germinate to form the sexual *gametophyte* stage of the life cycle. Ferns are widely distributed throughout the world and range in height from 1 in (2.5 cm) to 65 ft (20 m).

Ferraro, Geraldine Anne (1935-), U.S. politician. She served 3 terms (1979-84) as Democratic congressional representative of New York's 9th district in Queens. In 1984 she became the first woman nominated for the vice presidency by a major U.S. political party (as Walter Mondale's running mate).

Ferret, small mammal of the weasel family. One species, the domesticated polecat of Europe and Asia (*Mustela putorious*), is kept to catch rabbits, mice, and rats. The black-footed ferret (*M. nigripes*) is an endangered species native to North America.

Ferrous sulfate ($FeSO_4$), iron salt of sulfuric acid consisting of light-green crystals that turn dark when exposed to air. In industry, ferrous sulfate is used to purify water, make ink, dye fabric, and preserve wood.

Ferry, Jules François Camille (1832-93), French statesman. As minister of education (1879-80, 1882) he organized the modern French educational system. He sought to exclude the clergy from education. As premier (1880-81, 1883-85), he directed the acquisition of many colonies.

Fertile Crescent, historic area in the Middle East, birthplace of the Sumerian, Phoenician, and Hebrew civilizations. It extends in an arc, or crescent, from the north coast of the Persian Gulf to the east coast of the Mediterranean Sea, with the Nile river to the west and the Tigris and Euphrates rivers to the east. Natural irrigation made this semi-arid land fertile.

Fertilization, in biology, union of 2 unlike gametes (sex cells: female egg and male sperm) in the sexual reproductive process, involving fusion of the 2 nuclei that combines hereditary traits of both parents to produce new individuals. The sperm may swim to the egg through fluid in the female or through an external medium, as in certain lower plants and animals, or pollination may facilitate contact, as in some higher plants. In humans and many other animals, fertilization takes place inside the female's body (internal fertilizaton) following copulation.

Fertilizer, material added to soil to provide essential plant nutrients. Fertilizers increase crop yields and, when used properly, add to the efficiency of farming and gardening. They include both organic materials, such as farmyard manure, compost, and activated sewage sludge, and inorganic chemical salts, known as artificial fertilizers, which contain phosphorus, nitrogen, and potassium as needed in a particular crop. Fertilizers may be used to change the mineral, vitamin, and protein contents of the produce. There is evidence that prolonged and overintensive use of fertilizers may damage the fertility of the soil by disrupting the communities of microorganisms in the soil, and that fertilizers that enter rivers and lakes contribute to the process of *eutrophication* (deficiency of dissolved oxygen and overabundance of dissolved nutrients, e.g., phosphates) that has polluted many bodies of water.

Fès *see:* Fez.

Fescue, tufted perennial grass (genus *Festuca*) common in meadows of temperate zones, used for pasture and hay crops.

Festival of Lights *see:* Hanukkah.

Fetish, inanimate object, such as a stone or a tree, worshipped for its magical powers. A fetish is often thought to be inhabited by a spirit. In psychiatry, a sexual fetish is not in itself erotic but it may be stimulating to certain people—a foot or a shoe, for example.

Fetus, unborn or unhatched vertebrate whose basis structural plan is in place; in humans, the period from 3 months' gestation to birth. The fetus lives in a sac of amniotic fluid that protects it and allows it to move about. Blood circulation takes place via the *placenta* and the *umbilical cord*—the sources of oxygen and nutrients and the means for waste excretion. During fetal life, organ development is consolidated so that function may be sufficiently mature at birth.
See also: Reproduction.

Feudalism, system of social, economic, and political relationships that shaped society in medieval Europe. It originated in the 9th century and flourished from the 10th to the 13th centuries. The system rested on the obedience and service of a vassal to his lord in return for protection, maintenance, and, most particularly, a tenancy of land (a *fief*). The duty owed by a vassal included military service, counsel and attendance at court, and contribution towards the lord's extraordinary expenditures, such as ransoms or dowries. At the apex of the social pyramid was the king, vassal only to God. His vassals were his great nobles, holding land or some other

source of income in fief from him. They in turn invested, or *enfeoffed,* their own vassals, the lords of the manor (*seigneurs* or *suzerains*). At the base of the pyramid were the serfs, or villeins, permanently tied to the land. They worked both for the lord and for themselves, unpaid. Serfdom offered a degree of security in that, if a serf could not leave the land, neither could it be taken from him. In effect feudalism tended to allow vassal lords unrestricted freedom, at least in their own holdings. With the tendency towards centralized government this liberty was curbed. The system assumed a subsistence economy; the growth of trade and of economically powerful towns attacked. By the 15th century the system was dying out, although many feudal institutions persisted into the 19th century.
See also: Middle Ages.

Feuerbach, Ludwig Andreas (1804-72), German philosopher. A student of G.W.F. Hegel's, he eventually rejected idealism for a naturalistic materialism (which greatly influenced Karl Marx's development of dialectical materialism). Feuerbach attacked orthodox religion, analyzing the Christian concept of God as an illusory outward projection of human inward nature.

Fever, rise of body temperature above normal (98.6°/37°C), but varying from 97° to 99°F (36° to 37.2°C). Fever arises due to infection or to allergic or toxic reaction, and moderate fever is actually helpful in that it speeds up the body's chemical processes and mobilizes its immunological defenses against infectious organisms.

Feverfew (*Chrysanthemum parthenium*), small hardy plant with daisylike flowers, once thought to cure fever.

Feynman, Richard Phillips (1918-88), U.S. physicist. He shared the 1965 Nobel Prize for physics for work on quantum electrodynamics. He worked on the development of the atomic bomb, developed a system of notation (the Feynman diagram) for recording and calculating subatomic reactions, and, with Murray Gell-Mann, explained the interactions of weak nuclear force.
See also: Quantum electrodynamics.

Fez, traditional Turkish headgear first made in Fez, Morocco. A tall, red, brimless cap with a colored tassel, the fez was once colored only by a dye made from the juice of red berries found in Morocco.

FHA *see:* Federal Housing Administration.

Fiber, thin thread that may be spun into yarn. Natural fibers may be of vegetable, animal, or mineral origin. Artificial fibers combine compounds to make synthetics, such as nylon and rayon. Fibers are used for textiles.

Fiberglass, flexible fibers made of glass. Molten glass is forced through a platinum-plate "sieve," producing durable, chemical- and temperature-resistant fibers that can be wound onto a spindle before being used to make glass wool, yarns, textiles, insulation, and automobile and boat bodies.
See also: Glass.

Fiber optics, branch of physics based on the transmission of light pulses along hair-thin glass fibers. Fiber optics is used in telecommunications; information is coded as a series of light pulses and thus can be transmitted over distances of up to 100 mi (160 km). There are 2 types of optical fibers: single-mode and multi-mode. Single-mode fibers are used for long-distance transmissions and require the use of a laser as a light source, while multi-mode fibers can use more types of light sources but cannot be used over long distances. Fiber optics is also used in instruments like the gastroscope, allowing physicians to view internal body parts without performing surgery, and aiding in surgery.
See also: Optics; Physics.

Fibonacci, Leonardo (Leonardo Pisano; 1189?-1250), Italian mathematician whose *Liber Abaci* (1202) was the first European account of Indian and Arabian mathematics. He created the Fibonacci sequence, used in higher mathematics, in which each term is the sum of the 2 preceding terms (0, 1, 2, 3, 5, 8, 13, 21, ...).
See also: Mathematics.

Fibrin, insoluble fibrous protein that enables the blood to clot. *Fibrinogen,* a protein synthesized in the liver, dissolves in the blood and circulates in the body. If the body is wounded, the fibrinogen is converted by the action of the enzyme thrombin into fibrin, which builds up a spongy, fibrous network joining the edges of the wound by trapping red blood cells that form a clot to prevent further bleeding.
See also: Protein.

Fichte, Johann Gottlieb (1762-1814), German philosopher and metaphysician. At first a disciple of Kant, he became an early exponent of ethical idealism and set forth a science connecting practical reason with pure reason and the individual ego with an absolute ego (moral will of the universe). His work, including *The Vocation of Man* (1800), influenced G.W.F. Hegel, Arthur Schopenhauer, and Freidrich Schelling, among others. His political theories, including his concept of the nation as a manifestation of divine order and as expressed in his *Address to the German People* (1808), stimulated German nationalism and won him great respect among the revolutionaries of 1848.
See also: Metaphysics; Philosophy.

Fiction, division of literature consisting of narrative prose works with invented characters and incidents.
See also: Novel; Short story.

Fiddler crab, small tropical crab (genus *Uca*) that burrows in mud. The males have one oversized colored claw, which they wave to warn off other males and to attract females.Fiedler, Leslie A(aron) (1917-), U.S. social historian and literary critic, noted for *An End to Innocence: Essays on Culture and Politics* (1955), *The Jew in the American Novel* (1959), *Being Busted* (1969), and *Collected Essays* (1971). He has also written stories, novels, and poetry.

Field, U.S. family prominent in merchandising, publishing, and philanthropy. **Marshall Field I** (1834-1906) established the highly successful Marshall Field & Co., a department store in Chicago. His grandson, **Marshall Field III** (1893-1956), founded the Chicago *Sun,* and later merged it with the *Daily Times* to create the Chicago *Sun-Times,* which operates today. Field III also published *The World Book Encyclopedia* and *Childcraft.* His son, **Marshall Field IV** (1916-65), was editor and publisher of the Chicago *Sun-Times* and in 1959 bought the Chicago *Daily News.* **Marshall Field V** (1941-) was publisher of the *Sun-Times* (1969-80) and of the *Daily News* from 1969 until it went out of business in 1978. His new Field Company remains active in paper manufacturing and publishing.

Field, U.S. family prominent in law and industry in the 19th century. Three sons of Congregational minister and historian **David Dudley Field** (1781- 1867) distinguished themselves. **Cyrus West Field** (1819-92) was an industrialist and promoter of the first transatlantic telegraph cable in 1858, financed by English and U.S. companies. Though it failed 3 weeks later, he raised new funds for a new, successful cable (1866). **David Dudley Field, Jr.** (1805-94), jurist, was appointed by the state of New York in 1857 to draw up civil, political, and penal codes. In 1973 he became the president of the International Law Association. **Stephen Johnson Field** (1816-99) became chief justice of California and a U.S. Supreme Court justice in 1863.

Field glasses *see:* Binoculars.

Field hockey, team game played with a stick and a leather ball. Two teams of 11 players each play on a field measuring 90-100 yds (82-91 m) long by 50-60 yds (46-55 m) wide. Players advance the ball by hitting it with a stick toward their goalpost at the end of the field. Only the goalkeeper may kick the ball.
See also: Hockey.

Fielding, Henry (1707-54), English novelist and dramatist. His satirical comedies and farces, especially *Tom Thumb* (1730), a burlesque on the popular playwrights of the day, angered the government of Robert Walpole, provoking the enactment of a law to censor the stage. Fielding abandoned writing for the stage and turned to novels. *Joseph Andrews* (1742) and his masterpiece, *Tom Jones* (1749), are boisterous, picaresque works with strong, moral content.

Field-ion microscope *see:* Ion microscope.

Field Museum of Natural History, Chicago museum housing one of the largest and best-known natural history collections in the world. Founded by the merchant and philanthropist Marshall Field I in 1893, the museum currently has more than 13 million objects in the fields of anthropology, botany, geology, and zoology.

W.C. Fields in the film Poppy *(1936)*

Fields, W.C. (William Claude Dukenfield; 1880-1946), U.S. comedian and actor who often played a cantankerous, drunken, witty misogynist and child-hater. His movies include *It's a Gift* (1934), *My Little Chickadee* (1940), and the classic farce, *The Bank Dick* (1940), which he wrote.

Fifth Column, term describing agents working within a country for the overthrow of the government, through their activities of spying, sabotage, and distributing propaganda.

Fifty-Four Forty or Fight, slogan used by U.S. extremists in the controversy with Great Britain over the Oregon country. Through an 1818 treaty, both the United States and England had rights to occupy the Oregon country set between 42° and 54°40′ north latitude. The slogan was used by James Polk in his 1844 presidential campaign to convey his ambition to acquire the whole area. In 1846 the boundary was set at 49°, giving the United States land south of the line and Britain land to the north.

Fiji: view of Nausori Highlands, Viti Levu

Fig, any of over 600 species of shrubs, trees, and vines (genus *Ficus*) of the mulberry family, particularly the common fig (*F. carica*) native to the Mediterranean. The edible fruits, which, when dried, can be used medicinally as laxatives and poultices, are in fact a mass of female flowers enclosed in a fleshy receptacle. The rubber tree (*F. elastica*) and the weeping fig (*F. benjamina*) are popular house plants.

Fightingfish, small, brilliantly colored, long-finned freshwater fish (genus *Betta*) of southeastern Asia. The Siamese fightingfish, in confinement with another male, will battle to the death. Bets are often placed on the outcome.

Figure skating *see:* Ice skating.

Figwort family, or *Scrophulariaceae*, group of about 3,000 species of plants growing mainly in temperate regions. Members of the family have bell-shaped flowers and thin stems, and the leaves often grow in pairs. The wild mullein and the cultivated snapdragon are figworts. Some figworts are used in medicine, including a species of foxglove from which the heart medication digitalis is produced.

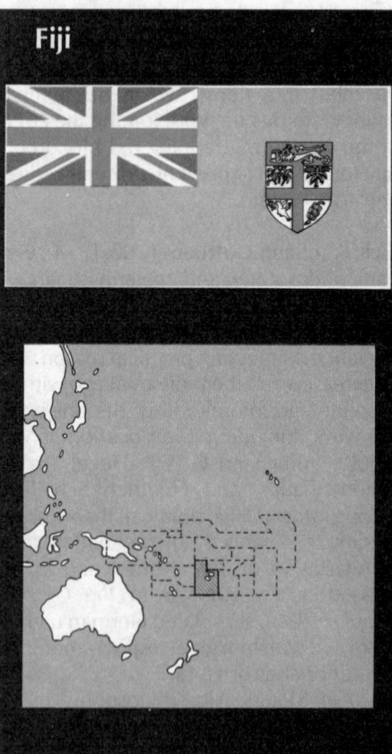

Capital:	Suva
Area:	7,095 sq mi (18,376 sq km)
Population:	734,000
Government:	republic
Independent:	1970
GNP:	U.S.$1,130,000,000
Per capita:	U.S.$1,540

Fiji, or Viti, independent republic in the southwest Pacific Ocean, comprising about 320 islands (about 105 inhabited) and about 7,095 sq mi (18,376 sq km). Viti Levu (capital city Suva) and Vanua Levu are the 2 largest islands, volcanic in origin. Discovered by Dutch navigator Abel Tasman (1643), the islands were visited by Capt. James Cook (1774) and settled by Europeans in 1804. Britain annexed Fiji in 1874, and over the course of time, brought many indentured servants from India; they eventually came to outnumber the native population (Melanesian and Polynesian in origin). Fiji gained Commonwealth status in 1970 and became a republic in 1987. Chief crops include sugarcane, ginger, and copra; exports include fish and gold; tourism is another major source of income.

Filaria, parasitic roundworm (class Nematoda) that can live in the bodies of human beings or animals. The larvae (young worms) are born alive, and can be seen in the blood near the skin of their host (animal or human in which they live). When an insect bites the host, it takes the filaria with it, then releases the filaria into whatever host it bites next. In this way, the filaria continues to infect new hosts. Commonly found in tropical and subtropical countries, the filaria can cause inflammation and disease in the animal and human tissues in which it settles.

Filbert, any of various trees and shrubs of (genus *Corylus*) belonging to the birch family. The plant may grow 60 ft (18 m) tall. Native to the north temperate zone, filberts thrive in the U.S. Pacific Northwest and in southern Europe. Filberts (particularly *C. avellana*) are cultivated for their edible nuts (called filberts, hazelnuts, or cobnuts).

Filibuster, practice of prolonging debate to prevent the adoption of a measure or procedure, especially in the U.S. Senate. Opponents of a measure can organize a continuous succession of long speeches; however, two-thirds of the senators present can vote to end the filibuster.

Filipinos *see:* Philippines.

Fillmore, Millard (1800-74), 13th president of the United States. Fillmore served only 2 years in office, stepping into the executive post from the vice presidency after the death of President Zachary Taylor. As president, Fillmore preferred to take the role of moderator in the fierce debates raging throughout the country and the Congress in the turbulent pre-Civil War years.

Early life. At age 15 Fillmore was apprenticed to a clothmaker. Two years before the apprenticeship term was to end, he bought his freedom and took up the study of law, supporting himself by teaching school. In 1823 he was admitted to the bar and opened a law office. In 1826 he married Abigail Powers.

Legislator. Fillmore, a political moderate, was elected to the New York House of Representatives in 1828 with the support of Albany publisher Thurlow Weed, who helped found the Whig Party. In 1832 Fillmore was elected to The U.S. House of Representatives, where he served 1833-35 and 1837-43. As a member of Congress he opposed the annexation of Texas as a slave territory, approved protective tariffs, and advocated the right to petition against slavery. In 1844 he ran unsuccessfully as the Whig candidate for governor of New York. He served briefly as chancellor of the University of Buffalo (N.Y.) but returned to public service 3 years later, when he became state controller. He was nominated for vice president on the 1848 Whig ticket and elected to office under President Zachary Taylor.

President. When Taylor died on July 9, 1850, Fillmore became president. One of his first, and most important, acts in office was to approve the Compromise of 1850, a complicated legislative package concerning slavery that probably held the Union together for another decade but included provisions odious to both North and South. It included the Fugitive Slave Law, providing for stiff penalties for anyone who aided an escaped slave. In signing this law, designed to placate the South in exchange for concessions to the North that excluded some territories from slavery, Fillmore performed the most unpopular act of his career. It severely harmed his reelection campaign. In foreign affairs, the Fillmore administration's main accomplishment was to send Admiral Matthew C. Perry to Japan. Perry's successful mission to open trade with that country was a major diplomatic step in U.S. relations with the East.

Retirement. In 1852 Fillmore ran for renomination by the Whigs and lost. In 1856 the short-lived Know-Nothing Party nominated him for president. He came in third, winning electoral votes from Maryland only. Fillmore took no further part in public life. His wife had died less than a month after he left office; in 1858 he remarried. He retired at Buffalo and died there in 1874.

Film *see:* Motion pictures; Photography.

Finance *see:* Banking; Budget; Economics; Money.

Finch, songbird of the family Frangillidae, typified by stout, conical bills adapted for opening seeds. Found year round and worldwide, except Australia, these highly developed birds are classified as triangular-billed (sparrow, canary, bullfinch, goldfinch); cross-mandibled (crossbill); or round-billed (cardinal).

Fine arts, art, such as painting, sculpture, architecture, music, literature, and theater, created with an esthetic goal rather than with functional application.

Fine Arts, Commission of, independent U.S. agency that makes recommendations to the federal government and the District of Columbia on questions of architecture, art, and design. Composed of 7 members appointed by the president, the commission reviews proposals for public buildings and spaces that will affect the appearance of Washington, D.C., recommends designs for coins, medals, and insignia, and examines building permit applications for private construction in historic Washington, D.C. areas such as Georgetown.

Finger Lakes, 11 narrow, glacially formed lakes in west central New York. The largest are Seneca, Cayuga, and Canandaigua.

Fingerprint, impression of the underside tip of the finger or thumb, which has patterns of ridges unique to each person, used as a means of identification since ancient times. The first police system employing dactyloscopy (fingerprinting) was developed (1888) by Jean Vucetich in Argentina. English scientist Sir Francis Galton and others in the late 19th century developed the methods upon which current systems are based, systems extensively employed in the armed services, criminal investigations, government employment, and banking. The U.S. Federal Bureau of Investigation maintains a national fingerprint file.

Fink, Mike (1770?-1823), U.S. frontiersman and folk hero. A Mississippi keelboatman and famous sharp-shooter renowned for his drinking, brawling, and bragging, he was murdered by the friend of a man he had killed in a drunken game.

Finland, Republic of (Finnish: *Suomi*), independent republic of northern Europe, east of the Scandinavian peninsula. This "land of thousands of lakes" is bounded by 2 arms of the Baltic Sea in the southwest and south, the Soviet Union in the east, and Norway and Sweden in the north and northwest. About one-fourth of Finland lies inside the Arctic Circle, and about one-tenth consists of inland waters. Cessions to the Soviet Union cost the Finns about one-tenth of their pre-World War II area. The principal cities are the capital, Helsinki; Tampere, a major industrial city on the southwestern rim of the lake district; and Turku, a leading port on the southwest coast and Finnish capital until 1812. Finland has one important natural resource: timber. Forestry and allied industries in wood products are successful.

Land and climate. Finland has tens of thousands of lakes, linked in many cases by rivers and canals. Around the lakes are extensive areas of swamps and forests. Most of the rivers are short and swift, and rapids render navigation difficult. The longest river is the Kemi (340 mi/547 km). The coastal plain extends to about 80 mi (130 km) in width and includes most of the larger cities and the bulk of the farming land. The plateau region is heavily forested and ranges from 300 to 600 ft (90 to 180 m) above sea level. In the third region (Lapland), the uplands in the north rise to 1,500 ft (450 m) and contain the highest point in Finland, Mount Haltia (4,343 ft/1,324 m) on the Norwegian border. Wildlife includes large numbers of seabirds and waterfowl. The reindeer is disappearing from the northern forests, but bears, wolves, lemmings, and lynxes can be found. Salmon, trout, and whitefish are plentiful in the rivers, and seals and herring are caught off the coasts. The Gulf Stream helps keep the climate relatively mild in the south and central areas, with short, warm summers and long, cold winters. The north has a subarctic climate, with long, severe winters and the famous "midnight sun" from May to the end of July.

People. The Finns are related directly to the Estonians and, more distantly, to Hungarians and Russians. Most live on farms or in small villages; only 3 cities have a population over 100,000. There is a Swedish minority of and a Lapp minority (largely nomads). The Swedes, who controlled Finland from the 13th century to the beginning of the 19th, have had a marked cultural influence on the nation. Both Finnish and Swedish are official languages. Finnish is not a Scandinavian language, but is a member of the Finno-Urgic group, which includes Hungarian and Estonian.

Economy. About 35.5% of the work force is in agriculture, 31.5% in industry, and 33% in other sectors. The government exercises considerable control over economic activities, operating the rail system and communications. It also monopo-

Millard Fillmore

13th U.S. President

Born:	Locke (now Summerhill), N.Y.; Jan. 7, 1800
Term:	July 1850-Mar. 1853
Vice president:	None
Political party:	Whig
Spouses:	Abigail Powers Fillmore; Carolyn Carmichael McIntosh Fillmore
Children:	2
Died:	Buffalo, N.Y.; Mar. 9, 1874

Finland

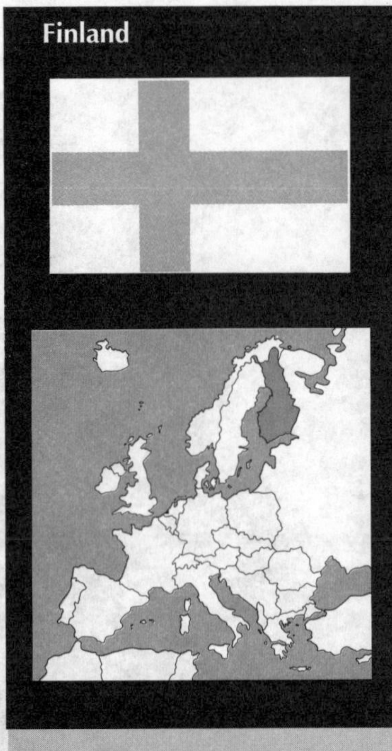

General information	
Capital:	Helsinki
Area:	130,559 sq mi (338,145 sq km)
Population:	4,960,000
Official languages:	Finnish and Swedish
Monetary unit:	1 Markka = 100 pennia
Main cities:	Helsinki, Turku, Tampere, Espoo
Government	
Form:	republic
Independent:	1917
Head of state:	President (elected every 6 years)
Head of government:	Prime Minister
Legislature:	1 legislative house (Parliament)
Executive:	President and Council of State
Judiciary:	highest court is the Supreme Court
Political division:	12 provinces
National economy	
Gross national product:	U.S. $92,015,000,000
Per capita income:	U.S. $18,610
Agriculture:	barley, oats, potatoes, sugar beets, wheat, rapeseed
Livestock:	chickens/other poultry, cattle, pigs
Fisheries:	159,000 metric tons
Mining:	zinc ore, silver, copper ore, lead ore, gold, iron ore
Industries:	paper and paper products, beverages and tobacco, nonelectrical machinery, chemicals, rubber and plastic products, graphic arts
Main exports:	wood and wood products, pulp, iron and steel, clothing
Transportation:	5,553 mi (8,936 km) of railroads; 47,453 mi (76,369 km) of roads; 1 international airport
Trading partners:	Sweden, Germany, USSR, United Kingdom, United States
People	
Urban:	62%
Ethnic composition:	Finnish 93.5%, Swedish 6%, other 0.5%
Birth rate:	12.8 per 1,000 population
Death rate:	9.9 per 1,000 population
Infant mortality:	6 per 1,000 live births
Life expectancy:	male 70.5 years, female 78.5 years

Reindeer herd in the Lapland region of northern Finland

lizes trade with the USSR. Paper, pulp, and wood-working products account for over half of total exports. Other exports include dairy products, copper, and furs and hides.

History. Finland was colonized from the south and by the 9th century formed 3 tribal states, Karelia, Tavastenland, and Suomi. Sweden progessively colonized the area, and after the 14th century Finland became a Swedish grand duchy. In 1809 Sweden was forced to cede it to Russia. Tsar Alexander I maintained the country as a grand duchy but allowed it considerable autonomy under a governor-general. This period saw the rise of nationalism: The Swedish language was replaced by Finnish, particularly after the publication of the national folk-epic, the *Kalevala* (1835). Under Alexander III a policy of "Russification" was adopted and generally bitterly resisted until World War I. In 1917 the parliament declared independence from the new regime in Russia, and Bolshevik forces were defeated in a brief civil war. In 1919 a republic was declared. In 1939, in breach of a nonaggression pact, the USSR invaded Finland, but was stalled by fierce resistance. For the German aid Finland received during World War II, it was made to pay massive postwar reparations to the USSR and lost southern Karelia. During the postwar period the Finnish government sought a peaceful rapprochement with the USSR, despite much Soviet interference in Finnish affairs.

Finlay, Carlos Juan (1833-1915), Cuban physician who first proposed (1881) that yellow fever is transmitted by the mosquito. Experiments by Walter Reed in 1900 proved his theory.
See also: Yellow fever.

Finnish, most important of the Finno-Urgic languages, spoken by around 5 million people in Finland. It has a written tradition dating from the 16th century but achieved official status only in the 19th century.

Finns *see:* Finland.

Fiord, or fjord, coastal inlet characterized by sheer parallel walls. Deep bays and inlets along the mountainous coastline of Norway, fiords were probably formed by rivers and deepened by glaciers millions of years ago. Norway's fiords are noted for their size: Sognafiord is 4,000 ft (1,220 m) deep and over 100 mi (160 km) long. The terms *sea loch* and *firth* are used for similar inlets in Britain.

Fir, common name for various evergreen members of the pine family, including 9 true firs (genus *Abies*) native to the United States. The fragrant balsam fir (*A. balsainea*) is a popular Christmas tree. The *Douglas fir* (*Pseudotsuga menziesii*), valued for its timber, is not a true fir.

Firbank, (Arthur Annesley) Ronald (1886-1926), English novelist known for his eccentric, innovative style and his verbal wit. Among his best-known works are *Vainglory* (1915), *Inclinations* (1916), and *Valmouth* (1919), which influenced Evelyn Waugh and Aldous Huxley.

Firdausi (Abul Qasim Mansur; 940?-1020?), Persian epic poet, author of the *Shah Namah* (*Book of Kings*), Persia's first great literary work. The poem, 60,000 verses long, recounts the story of Persia, legendary and historical, until the Muslim conquest (A.D. 641).
See also: Persia, Ancient.

Fire *see:* Combustion.

Fire ant, omnivorous ant (genus *Solenopsis*), primarily of the tropics, that inflicts an extremely painful sting. Two species, one introduced from Argentina, are found in the southern United States and are pests in fruit plantations.

Firearm, weapon from which a missile, as a bullet, is projected by firing explosive charges. Firearms, are classified as either artillery (heavy firearms) or small arms.
See also: Gun.

Firecracker flower (*Dichelostemma idamaia*), perennial plant belonging to the amaryllis family and native to California. It is named for its bright red tubular blossoms, which grow on a slender stalk up to 3 ft (91 cm) high.

Firedamp *see:* Damp.

Fire extinguisher, portable appliance for putting out small fires. Extinguishers work either by cooling or by depriving the fire of oxygen (as typified by the simplest, a bucket of water or sand), and most do both. The *soda-acid extinguisher* contains a sodium bicarbonate solution and a small, stopped bottle of sulfuric acid. Depression of a plunger shatters the bottle, mixing the chemicals so that carbon dioxide (CO_2) gas is generated, forcing the water out of a nozzle. *Foam extinguishers* employ a foaming agent (usually animal protein or detergent) and an aerating agent. They are effective against oil fires, as they float on the surface. *Carbon dioxide extinguishers* provide a smothering blanket of CO_2. *Dry chemical extinguishers* provide a powder consisting mainly of sodium bicarbonate, from which the fire's heat generates CO_2.

Firefly, any of various soft-bodied, carnivorous, nocturnal beetles of the family Lampyridae that produce an intermittent greenish light in their abdominal organs. The light is created by the oxidation of luciferin under the influence of an enzyme, luciferase. In some species females are without wings and are known as *glowworms.* The lights serve to attract mates.

Firestone, Harvey Samuel (1868-1938), U.S. industrialist, founder of one of the largest rubber companies in the world, the Firestone Tire & Rubber Company. His million-acre rubber plantation in Liberia played a large role in that country's economic development starting in 1926.
See also: Rubber.

Fireweed, or willow herb (*Epilobium angustifolium*), tall perennial plant of temperate regions of the Northern Hemisphere. The fireweed, so named because it springs up quickly after a forest fire, grows 3 to 6 ft (0.9 to 1.8 m) high and bears rose-purple flowers.

Fireworks, combustible or explosive preparations used for entertainment, probably first devised in ancient China to frighten off devils. Their initial European use was as weaponry, and not until after about 1500 were they employed for entertainment. Compounds of carbon, potassium, and sulfur are the prime constituents in fireworks, colors being produced by metallic salts (e.g., blue, copper; yellow, sodium; red, lithium or strontium; green, barium), and sparks and crackles by powdered iron, carbon, or aluminum, or by certain lead salts.
See also: Explosive.

First aid, treatment that can be given by minimally trained people for accident, injury, and sudden illness, until more skilled persons arrive or the patient is transferred to a hospital. Recognition of the injury or the nature of the illness and its gravity are crucial first measures, along with prevention of further injury to the patient or helpers. Clues such as medical bracelets or cards, evidence of food, drink, or drugs, and evidence of external injury should be sought and appropriate action taken. Cessation of breathing should be treated as a priority by clearing the airway of dentures, gum, vomit, and other foreign material and by the use of artificial respiration. Cardiac massage may be needed to restore blood circulation if major pulse cannot be felt. In traumatic injury, fractures must be recognized and splinted to reduce pain; the possibility of injury to the spine must be considered before moving the patient, to avoid unnecessary damage to the spinal cord. External hemorrhage should be arrested, usually by direct pressure on the bleeding point; tourniquets are rarely needed and may be dangerous. Internal hemorrhage may be suspected if shock (depression of vital signs) develops soon after collapse or trauma without obvious bleeding. Burns and scalds should be treated by immediately cooling the burned surface to reduce the continuing injury to skin due to retained heat. The use and, if necessary, improvisation of simple dressings, bandages, splints, and stretchers should be known; simple methods of moving the injured, should this be necessary, must also be understood. Accessory functions such as contacting ambulances or medical help, direction of traffic, and different aspects of resuscitation should be delegated by the most experienced person present. The inquisitive should be kept away and a calm atmosphere maintained. Prevention as a part of first aid includes due care in the home: avoiding highly polished floors and unfixed carpets, obstacles on or near stairs, loose cords, overhanging saucepan handles, and unlabeled bottles of poison; drug cupboards accessible to children also present significant dangers. Effective first aid depends on prevention, recognition, organization, and, in any positive action, adherence to the principle of "do no harm."

First Continental Congress *see:* Continental Congress.

Firth, arm of the sea or the opening of a river into the sea. Firths are similar to fiords but distinguished from them by lower walls. The term is used for such inlets in Scotland, including those of the rivers Forth, Clyde, and Tay.
See also: Fiord.

Firth of Clyde, bay-like mouth of the River Clyde in southwest Scotland 50 mi (80 km) long and 30 mi (50 km) wide. The term *firth,* used largely in Scotland, denotes an arm of the sea or an estuary (a river mouth that empties into the sea).

Firth of Forth, broad mouth of the River Forth on Scotland's east coast. It is spanned by one of the world's longest suspension bridges—8,244 ft (2,514 m), with a 3,300-ft (1,006-m) center span.

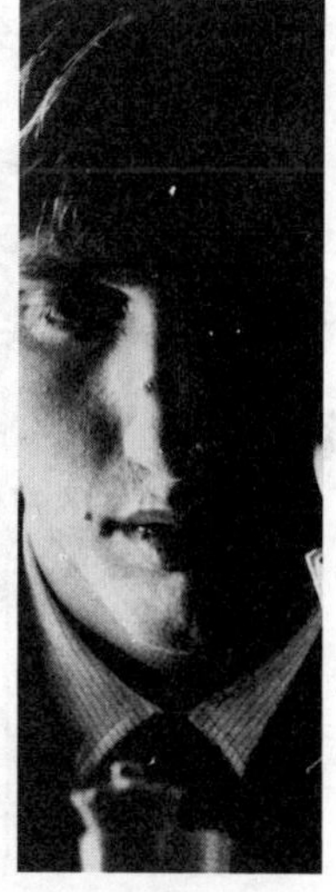
Bobby Fischer

Fischer, Bobby (Robert James Fisher; 1943-), U.S. chess player, In 1958, he became the youngest player to attain the rank of international grand master. In 1972 in Iceland, he became the first American to win the world championship, defeating the Russian Boris Spassky in a widely publicized tournament. He subsequently refused to defend his title, which was awarded to Anatoly Karpov in 1975.

Fischer-Dieskau, Dietrich (1925-), German baritone. He achieved international fame in the 1950s as an opera singer and an interpreter of German lieder, notably those of Brahms, Schubert, and Wolf.
See also: Opera.

Fish, cold-blooded aquatic vertebrate that breathes by means of gills. Typically, a fish's body is streamlined and covered by a layer of scales. Fish swim by means of fins, especially a vertical tail fin. All fish possess a 2-chambered heart. Fish are found wherever there is natural water, unless it is poisoned. Some fish, such as the African lungfish, spend some time out of water, breathing by means of a lunglike air bladder. Modern fish can be divided into 2 main groups: the cartilaginous fish (sharks, skates, and rays) and the bony fish. There are over 20,000 species of bony fish, ranging in size from the 1/2-in (1.3-cm) freshwater goby of the Philippines to the 20-ft (6-m) sturgeon of the USSR. The largest of all fish, the 50-ft (15-m) whaleshark, is a cartilaginous fish. Most fish reproduce by shedding eggs into the water at the same time as the sperm and allowing fertilization to take place in the water. Perhaps 1 or 2 eggs in 10,000 grow to maturity. The female mouthbreeder, however, keeps the eggs and later the young in her mouth, and the discus, after carefully tending the eggs, secretes a special mucus in its skin to feed the young. These fishes do not need to lay thousands of eggs, as chances of survival

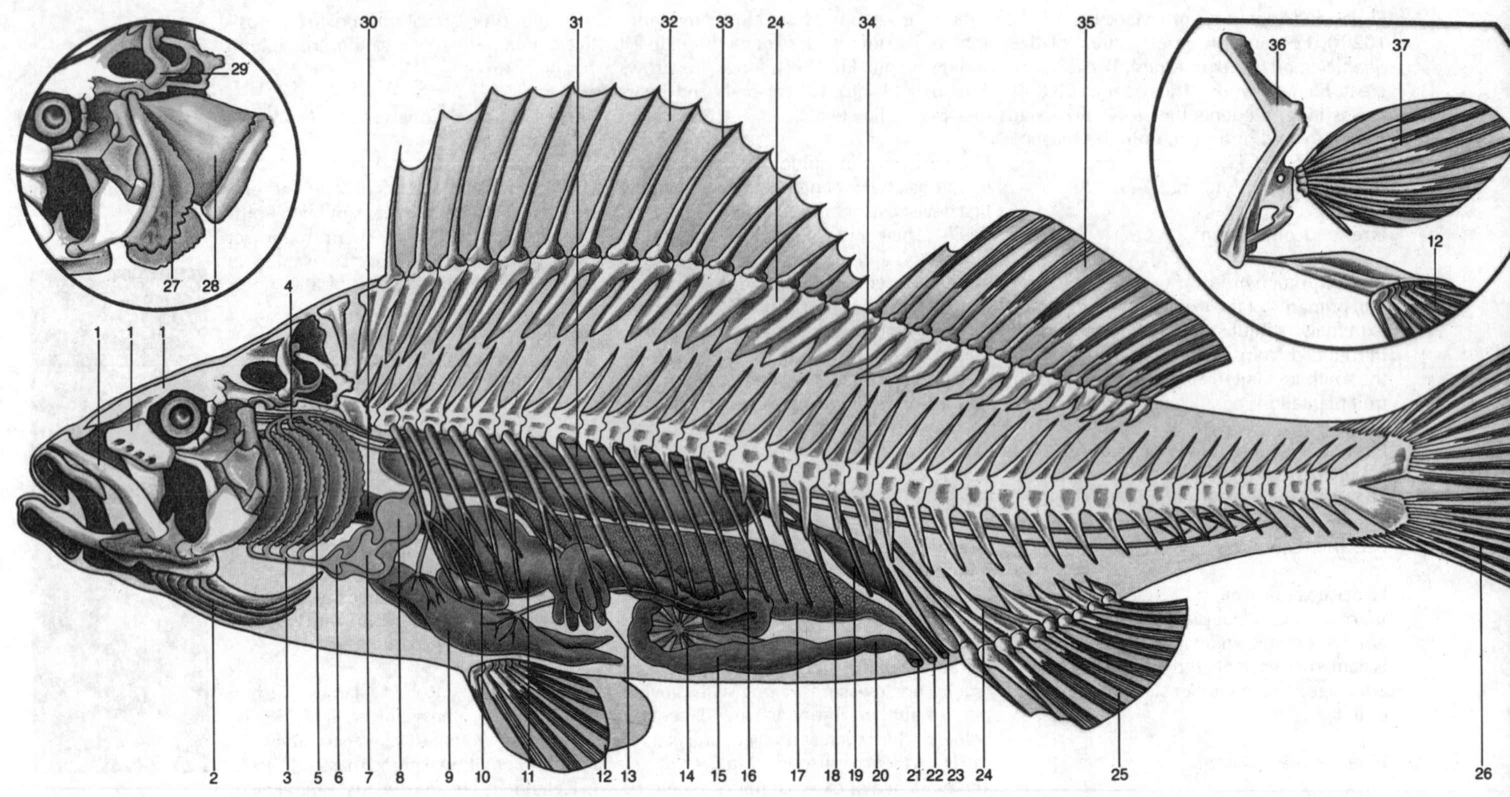

Anatomy of a fish (perch); 1. headskeleton; 2. bottom of the mouth with branchiostegal beams; 3. ventral aorta; 4. dorsal aorta; 5. gillblades; 6.7.8. heart with bulbous arteriosus, ventricle, and chest respectively; 9. liver; 10. gallbladder; 11. stomach; 12. pelvic fin; 13. blind pockets; 14. mesenterium; 15. intestine; 16. swimming bladder; 17. ovarium; 18. rib; 19. bladder; 20. rectum; 21.anus; 22. gender marking suffix; 23. urethra; 24. supportbones of the finbeams; 25. pelvic fin; 26. tail fin; 27. & 28. fillcover bones; 29. auditory organ; 30. esophagus; 31. kidney; 32. dorsal fin; 33. fin beam; 34. spine; 35. second dorsal fin (like the pelvic-, pectoral-, and tailfin with soft beams, as opposed to the first dorsal fin, which has stiff beams); 36. shouldergirdle; 37. pectoral fin.

improve with care. There must be, overall, a delicate balance between the number of eggs laid and the amount of care taken. Fish's eyes are adapted to underwater vision. Some, like the archer fish, which catches flying insects, can see well in air. The four-eyed fish can see out of the water and under water at the same time as it cruises just under the surface. The upper part of the eye focuses light in air and the lower half focuses in water. The sense of smell is developed variously, and some fish can taste as well as feel with barbels or other fleshy protuberances that trail in the water or along the bottom to detect food. Fish's ears are poorly developed, but a special sense organ, the lateral line system, enables fish to detect and identify many kinds of vibrations in the water. Some fish survive if blinded, but have great difficulty both in catching food and in escaping enemies without their lateral line system. Fish have bodies denser than water and would have to swim constantly to keep from sinking if it were not for the swimbladder, a sac that contains air or some gas secreted by the fish. The fish regulates the amount of gas by secreting more or by expelling some of it and thus keeps itself at its preferred depth. A few species of fish are able to generate electricity. Specially developed muscles build up a charge of electricity that is emitted to repel possible enemies. The South American electric eel is the most powerful, emitting up to 550 volts, enough to kill fish and even possibly a human.

Fish, Hamilton (1808-93), U.S. statesman. A Whig representative (1843-45) and senator from New York (1851-57), Fish was President Ulysses S. Grant's secretary of state (1869-77). He helped bring about the 1871 Treaty of Washington, which settled the Alabama Claims with Britain.

Fish and Wildlife Service, U.S. federal agency within the Department of the Interior, created in 1956, concerned with conservation and development of fish and wildlife resources, wilderness areas, and river basins. It maintains waterfowl refuges and fish hatcheries, prepares federal hunting regulations, performs research for the fishing industry, protects threatened wildlife, manages the fur seal herds of Alaska, and administers international agreements.

Fisher *see:* Marten.

Fisher, Saint John (1469-1535), English cardinal. As bishop of Rochester (1504-34), he refused to recognize the divorce of Henry VIII from Catharine of Aragon, was imprisoned in the Tower, and later beheaded. Canonized in 1935, his feast day is June 22.

Fishes, Age of *see:* Devonian Period.

Fish hawk *see:* Osprey.

Fishing, form of recreation that is probably the world's most popular participant sport; it is also one of the oldest. People fished for food in prehistoric times, probably first by using the "tickling" method of catching fish by hand, which is still very popular in the Rocky Mountain regions of the United States. Today there are millions of people who fish for pleasure or in competition; they are called anglers. There are more than 20 million fishing licenses issued annually. Competitively, the modes of fishing are almost as numerous and varied as the types of fish to be caught in fresh or salt water. World records by weight, length, and girth exist for every type of fish from albacore to yellowtail. The bait itself is subject to strict rules and regulations for competitive fishing, and skill in accuracy and length of casting is the subject of national and world championships.

History of the sport. References to fishing as a sport go back at least as early as Roman times, when Ovid, Martial, and Ausonius all remarked upon it in their writings. Even the specialized branch of flycasting was the subject of a work by Aelian in the 2nd century A.D. However, the best research on the subject came in 3 books published in England within the space of 40 years in the 17th century: John Denny's *Secrets of Angling* (1613), Thomas Barker's *Art of Angling* (1651), and Izaak Walton's *Compleat Angler* (1653). The first fishing club in North America, formed in 1732, was called the Schuylkill Fishing Company of Philadelphia, and one of its earliest guests was George Washington. However, national organizations for the sport did not exist until the formation of the American Rod and Reel Association early in the 19th century, and even then real impetus to competitive fishing was left to the Chicago Fly-Casting Club, formed in 1893, which played a leading part in organizing the first recognized national championships. This preceded the formation of the governing body, the National Association of Scientific Angling Clubs, in 1906.

Modes of angling. The 3 main types of modern angling are pan angling, game angling, and sea angling. Pan anglers stick mainly to angling for fish in slow and deep rivers or canals; game anglers go for trout, salmon, and other fish that populate fast-running streams or mountain rivers and can only be caught by accurate casting of the appropriate lure; and sea anglers generally fish for the larger catches, such as shark, tuna, tarpon, and barracuda. In the modern era, sea angling has been the fastest of all in developing and has opened up wide areas of fishing off the coasts of Florida, Hawaii, California, the Carribbean, Australia, New Zealand, and England.

Fishing industry, worldwide economic activity that includes the production, marketing, and conservation of fish, shellfish, and related products, such as seaweeds. Fish are an important source of protein, and two-thirds of the world's catch is used for human consumption; one-third is used in making animal feed and industrial products. Oceans supply most of the world's catch; rivers and lakes supply a small percentage, and fish farms—enclosed areas on land or in the natural bodies of water—supply a still smaller portion. Ocean fish include herring, sardines, and tuna, which are caught near the surface, and flounder, cod, and pollack, which are found near the ocean floor. Freshwater fish, which are found in lakes and rivers, include carp and catfish. To control overfishing and enforce conservation laws, in the 1970s most countries that border the sea established fishery conservation zones that extend 200 mi (320 km) from a country's coast.

Fisk, James (1834-72), U.S. financial speculator, notorious for stock manipulation. With Jay Gould he engaged in a brutal stock market struggle for control of the Erie Railroad. Their attempt to corner the gold market in 1869 led to the Black Friday scandal. He was shot by a business associate and rival for the affections of an actress.
See also: Black Friday.

Fiske, Minnie Maddern (Marie Augusta Davey; 1865-1932), U.S. actress known for her performances of the modern realistic dramas of the Norwegian playwright Henrik Ibsen. She made her stage debut at age 3, performing children's roles for several years and making her first appearance in an adult role in 1882. She married the playwright and theatrical manager Harrison Grey Fiske in 1890. She achieved her first major success in the 1897 dramatization of Thomas Hardy's novel *Tess of the D'Urbervilles.*

Fission, nuclear reaction in which the atom is split into 2 approximately equal masses. Fission is accompanied by the emission of extremely high quantities of energy, since the sum of the masses of the 2 new atoms is less than the mass of the parent heavy atom. The energy released is expressed by Einstein's equation $E=mc^2$.
See also: Atom; Nuclear energy; Uranium.

Fitch, (William) Clyde (1865-1909), U.S. playwright known for his social satires and character studies. After graduating from Amherst College in 1886, he moved to New York City and began writing short stories for magazines. During his career he wrote and produced 30 plays and 22 adaptations of novels, including *Beau Brummel* (1890), *Captain Jinks of the Horse Marines* (1901), *The Girl With the Green Eyes* (1902), and *The City* (1909).

Fitch, John (1743-98), U.S. inventor and engineer. Fitch built the first practical steamboat (1787), larger vessels being launched in 1788 and 1790. All were paddle-powered; his later attempt to introduce the screw propeller was a commercial failure.
See also: Steamboat.

FitzGerald, Edward (1809-83), English poet and scholar, translator of Omar Khayyam's *Rubaiyat.* FitzGerald's version of this Persian poet's quatrains (4-line rhymes) is not a literal and exact translation, but instead captures the spirit of the original to create a masterpiece of English poetry. The *Rubaiyat,* FitzGerald's only significant work, first appeared in 1859, and its tone of gentle melancholy had an important influence on later English poets.

Fitzgerald, Ella (1918-96), U.S. jazz singer. She began her career in New York in 1935, singing in Chick Webb's orchestra. Since then she toured widely abroad and was internationally known as one of the most original interpreters of jazz.

Fitzgerald, F(rancis) Scott (Key) (1896-1940), U.S. novelist and short-story writer. The "spokesman" of the Jazz Age in the 1920s, he wrote about the frenetic life-style of the post-World War I generation and the spiritual bankruptcy of the so-called American Dream. His celebrated novel *The Great Gatsby* (1925) explores the ruthless society of the 1920s. *Tender Is the Night* (1934) draws upon the experience of American expatriates in Paris and upon the schizophrenic gaiety and breakdown of his wife, Zelda. *The Last Tycoon* (1941) is an unfinished work concerning Fitzgerald's final years, which were spent as a Hollywood scriptwriter.

Five Books of Moses *see:* Pentateuch.

Five Civilized Tribes, alliance of 5 Native American tribes—the Cherokee, Chickasaw, Chocktaw, Creek, and Seminole—forced to leave their lands east of the Mississippi and resettle in the Indian Territory (Oklahoma) under the Removal Act of 1830. There the tribes established their own government, schools, and flourishing agricultural communities. Each tribe was organized as a "nation," with a constitution and laws based on those of the U.S. government. The tribes lost their independence after 1893, when the government once again confiscated their lands.

Fjord *see:* Fiord.

Flag, piece of cloth or other material, usually rectangular, bearing a distinctive design and displayed as a symbol or signal. The U.S. flag, officially adopted by Congress on June 14, 1777, now consists of 13 alternate red and white stripes representing the original colonies, and 50 white stars on a dark blue background representing the present states.

Flagstad, Kirsten (1895-1962), Norwegian singer, one of the greatest Wagnerian sopranos. She made her New York debut as Sieglinde in *Die Walküre* in 1935 and retired from public singing in 1953, though she continued making records.

Ella Fitzgerald

Flagstaff (pop. 34,743), city in northern Arizona near the San Francisco Mountains. Although the city's chief industry is lumbering, tourism has become increasingly important. Flagstaff is noted for its proximity to Native American ruins, the Grand Canyon National Park, and skiing facilities. It is also the site of the Lowell Observatory, from which the planet Pluto was first observed.
See also: Arizona.

Flaherty, Robert Joseph (1884-1951), U.S. pioneer documentary filmmaker. He is chiefly famous for *Nanook of the North* (1922), a study of Eskimo life, and *Man of Aran* (1934), about life on the Aran Islands of Ireland.

Flamenco, folk music of Andalusia in southern Spain. Like most folk music traditions, flamenco combines singing and dancing. The influence of Moorish music has helped to create one of the most distinctive, colorful, and exciting of all folk music styles. True flamenco singing and dancing requires a considerable amount of training and skill, and professional flamenco groups are admired throughout the world.

Flamenco dancers

Flamingo, several species of colorful water birds of the family Phoenicopteridae, related to herons. Flamingos have long spindly legs and necks, and large bills with bristles that they use to sift their food from the water. Their plumage is white, pink, and black. They live in large flocks on alkaline lakes in America, Africa, and southern Eurasia.

Flanagan, Edward Joseph (1886-1948), Irish-born U.S. Roman Catholic priest who founded Boys Town, a self-governing community of homeless boys, near Omaha, Nebr., in 1917. After World War II he helped organize youth facilities abroad for the U.S. government.
See also: Boys Town.

Flanders, medieval county on the coast of northwestern Europe, largely corresponding to northern Belgium, with smaller portions in the Netherlands and France. In the 14th and 15th centuries, wealth from trade and textile manufacture enriched the chief towns (Antwerp, Ypres, Bruges, and Ghent) and made Flanders a major cultural center.

Its famous artists included the Bruegel family, Peter Paul Rubens, and Anthony Van Dyck.

Flanders Fields, U.S. military cemetery in Belgium. Many soldiers who died in World War I (1914-18) are buried there. A famous World War I poem, "In Flanders Fields," was written under fire by the Canadian physician and poet John McCrae.
See also: World War I.

Flatboat, bargelike craft used in the westward movement of the United States in the 1800s. Flat, with square ends, flatboats carried pioneers and their belongings, floating them to new settlements. They moved on river currents and by long oars, which were also used for steering. The keelboat, a long, narrow craft pointed at one or both ends, is sometimes called a flatboat; it was also used for transporting people and goods during the 1800s.

Flatfish, any of an order (Hetero somata) of plate-shaped fish with both eyes on one side of the head. A flatfish starts life as a normal-looking fish, but after a few days, one eye starts moving around the head, the dorsal fin grows along the head, and the mouth becomes twisted. The fish then lies on its side on the bottom. The underside stays pale, and the top becomes pigmented and can change color to match the background. Some of the 500 species are important food fishes, including flounder, halibut, sole, and turbot.

Flatheads, Native American tribe of the Salish linguistic family inhabiting western Montana. Neighboring tribes, who shaped the front of their heads to a point, called them "Flatheads." The Flatheads were early converts to Christianity, and most now live in Flathead Lake, Montana.

Flatworm, major group of simple animals that includes the parasitic flukes and tapeworms and the free-living flatworms. Flatworms have long, unsegmented, extremely thin bodies. The largest free-living species grow 1 ft (30 cm) long, though parasitic species may attain 40 ft (12 m). They are found under bark, in fresh water, and in the sea. Freshwater planarian flatworms are often used in biological research.

Gustave Flaubert

Flaubert, Gustave (1821-80), French novelist. He was a scrupulous observer and stylist whose work influenced much subsequent French writing. His first work, *Madame Bovary* (1856-57), brought him immediate fame. The vividly naturalistic tragedy of a provincial wife who attempts to live out her fantasies, it was unsuccessfully prosecuted as an offense against public morality in 1857. The exotic Carthaginian setting of *Salammbô* (1862) showed an equal mastery of romantic style. His *Three Tales* (1877), set in modern, medieval, and ancient times, combined both romanticism and realism.

Flax (genus *Linum*, especially *L. usitatissimum*), plant of temperate and subtropical areas grown for its fiber, which is spun into linen, and for linseed oil. Flax was first cultivated in the Mediterranean basin, and has been an important crop for thousands of years.

Flea, wingless insect (order Siphonaptera) with legs developed for jumping and a laterally compressed body. It sucks the blood of host animals, and can carry such diseases as typhus and the bubonic plague. The flea survives its early stages in unsanitary conditions; when newly emerged, adults leap onto passing hosts.

Fleabane, any of 200 species of an aster-like flowering plant (genus *Erigeron*) that grows in temperate climates around the world. So named because it was thought to repel or kill fleas, fleabane is often planted in rock gardens; some varieties grow as common weeds. A Canadian variety known as horseweed or bloodstanch yields a drug called erigeron, or fleabane, which is used to treat diarrhea and control bleeding. Mosquito repellents often contain oil of fleabane.

Fleet Prison, historic London jail in use from the 1100s, when it was the king's jail, until the 1800s, when it was torn down. Named for the nearby Fleet stream, the prison in turn gave its name to secret marriages called "Fleet marriages," which were performed in the jail by the clergy during the 1600s and 1700s.

Fleming, resident of Flanders (northern Belgium). Flemings, who make up about 55% of Belgium's population, are descended from the Franks and speak Dutch. The French-speaking Walloons, who live in Wallonia (southern Belgium), are descended from the area's original inhabitants, the Celts. When the Franks invaded what is now Belgium during the 3rd and 4th centuries, they pushed the Celts southward to the present north-south division between the 2 regions. When the newly independent country declared French its official language in 1830, the Flemings protested. Dutch was given official recognition in the late 1800s, but frictions have continued. In 1980 the government granted limited independence to Flanders and Wallonia. The Flemings dominated European commerce in the Middle Ages, and today are primarily involved in the manufacture of textiles. From the 1400s to the 1600s Flanders produced some of the world's most famous painters, including Pieter Brueghel the Elder and Jan van Eyck.
See also: Flanders.

Fleming, Ian Lancaster (1908-64), British author and creator of the James Bond series of spy thrillers. His novels, which won international fame, include *Casino Royale* (1953) and *Goldfinger* (1959). In the late 1920s and early 1930s Fleming worked as a journalist in Moscow. During World War II he did espionage work for British Naval Intelligence.

Fleming, Sir Alexander (1881-1955), British bacteriologist, discoverer of lysozyme (1922) and penicillin (1928). Lysozyme is an enzyme present in many body tissues and lethal to certain bacteria; its discovery prepared the way for that of antibiotics. His discovery of penicillin was largely accidental, and penicillin was developed as a therapeutic drug later, by Howard Florey and Ernst Chain. All 3 scientists received the 1945 Nobel Prize for physiology or medicine for their work.
See also: Bacteriology; Penicillin.

Fleming, Sir Sandford (1827-1915), Canadian civil engineer and builder of that country's Intercolonial Railway. In 1867 he was named chief engineer for the dominion government. Under his tenure the Intercolonial Railway was built and surveys were made and construction begun for the Canadian Pacific Railway (now CP Rail). After his retirement in 1880, he designed a telegraph communication system for the British Empire. The first link of this system was the Pacific cable between Canada and Australia. He was knighted in 1897.
See also: Standard time.

Flemish, form of Dutch traditionally spoken in North Belgium. Given official equality with French in 1898, it became the official language of North Belgium in 1934. Approximately 5 million people in Belgium and another 200,000 in France speak Flemish.

Flesh-eating animal *see:* Carnivore.

Fletcher, John (1579-1625), English author of plays. Primarily known for his collaborations with the playwright Francis Beaumont (1584?-1616), Fletcher wrote many of his own dramas before and after the active period of their partnership. Popular along with other great playwrights in his time, he also collaborated with Shakespeare on *Henry VIII* and *The Two Noble Kinsmen*.
See also: Beaumont, Francis.

Fletcher v. Peck, 1810 Supreme Court case that established the supremacy of the U.S. Constitution over state laws. After members of the Georgia legislature had taken bribes in 1795 to grant land to several companies, the next legislature revoked the grants, even though some of the land had already been sold by the companies. The new landowners sued, arguing that the state had interfered with a legal contract. The Supreme Court agreed, ruling that the violation of a contract by a state is prohibited by the Constitution.

Flicker (*Colaptes auratus*), woodpecker of North America, known for its colorful plumage and loud calls. Its main food is ants.

Flickertail state *see:* North Dakota.

Flint, or chert, sedimentary rock composed of microcrystalline quartz and chalcedony. Found as nodules in limestone and chalk and as layered beds, it is mainly formed from marine sediments, and preserves many fossil outlines. A hard rock, flint may be chipped to form a sharp cutting edge, and it was used by Stone Age people for their characteristic tools.

Flood, flow of water from a river, lake, or ocean over normally dry land. Most floods are destructive to homes and other property, and can leave the land barren by carrying off topsoil. Some can be helpful: the annual floods of the Nile River in Egypt made the desert land of the Nile Valley fertile by depositing rich soil carried from far upstream. River floods, which are the most common type, are usually caused by heavy rains and sudden melting of ice and snow. Ocean floods are most often caused by hurricanes or other strong storms that raise the height of waves and push water far inland. Floods also occur when wave heights are raised by earthquakes or volcanoes. Abnormally high tides can also occasionally cause flooding. Lakeshore flooding is also usually caused by strong storms.

Flora, term used to refer to the plant life of a region or a particular time. *Fauna* is the corresponding term for animal life. The word *flora* comes from the Roman goddess of flowering plants.

Florence (Italian: *Firenze*; pop. 453,300), historic city of central Italy, capital of Firenze province, on the Arno River at the foot of the Apennines. A town on the Cassian Way during Roman times, it grew to become a powerful medieval republic, dominating Tuscany. Florence was a major commercial and artistic center during the Renaissance. It retains many architectural and other art treasures which, together with the proximity of the Apennines, serve to make the city an important tourist center. The great art museums of Florence include the Uffizi Gallery, the Pitti Palace, and the Accademia. Famous figures associated with Florence include Brunelleschi, Dante, Giotto, Machiavelli, Masaccio, Michelangelo, and Savonarola. Glass and leatherware, pottery, furniture, and precision instruments are among its products. In 1966 floods seriously damaged many of Florence's art treasures.
See also: Italy.

Flores Island, westernmost island of the Portuguese Azores, in the North Atlantic. Named for its lush flora, the 55 sq mi (143 sq km) island is volcanic in origin and has many crater lakes that offer good fishing. Santa Cruz is the chief town, and cattle raising and dairy farming are the island's main industries.

Florey, Howard Walter (1898-1968), Baron Florey of Adelaide, Australian-born British pathologist. He worked with E.B. Chain and others to extract penicillin from *Penicillium notatum* mold for use as a therapeutic drug (1934-44). He shared with Chain and Alexander Fleming the 1945 Nobel Prize for physiology or medicine.
See also: Pathology; Penicillin.

Floriculture, cultivation of flowers and ornamental plants for commercial business. Scientific research has provided floriculturists with techniques for controlling the blooming of flowers, so that, for example, poinsettias bloom with red leaves at Christmas. Research has also produced such new varieties as thornless roses and the double snapdragon. Floriculturists work in public and private gardens, nurseries, seed companies, and landscape design companies.

Florida, southeasternmost state of the United States, on a peninsula that separates the Gulf Of Mexico from the Atlantic Ocean, bordered to the north by Georgia and Alabama.

Florence: view of the Duomo, Campanile, and Palazzo Vecchio

Florida

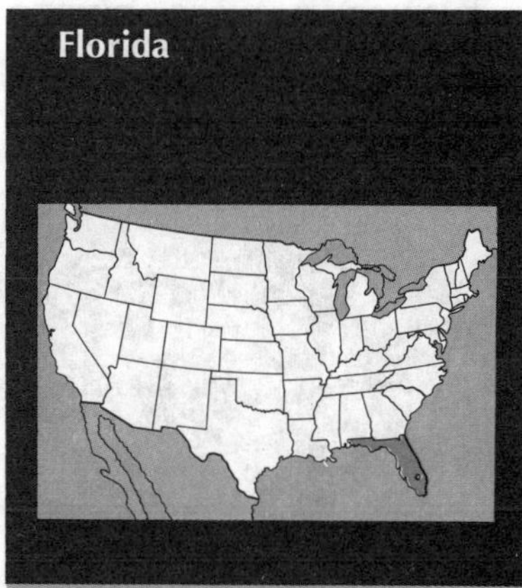

Capital:	Tallahassee
Statehood:	Mar. 3, 1845 (27th state)
Familiar name:	Sunshine State
Area:	58,664 sq mi (151,939 sq km); ranks 22nd
Population:	13,003,362 (1990); ranks 4th
Elevation:	Highest—345 ft (105 m), Walton County Lowest—sea level
Motto:	In God We Trust
State flower:	Orange blossom
State bird:	Mockingbird
State tree:	Palmetto or sabal palm
State song:	"Old Folks at Home" ("Swanee River")

Florida: view of Miami Beach

Land and climate. The Florida panhandle extends to the west along the northern shore of the Gulf of Mexico. The Florida uplands run down from the northwest into the center of the state. They are characterized in the south by rolling hills studded with thousands of lakes, including Lake Okeechobee, the second-largest natural body of fresh water entirely within the United States. The low, level plains along the eastern coast are protected from the Atlantic by a strip of sandbars and islands. Big Cypress Swamp and the Everglades cover much of southern Florida. The small islands called the Florida Keys curve southwestward for 150 mi (241 km) from the tip

Florida, Mangrove trees

of the peninsula. Florida's shoreline is 1,350 mi (2,173 km) long, longer than that of any state except Alaska. The average climate is warm and rainy. The extreme south of Florida and Hawaii are the only places in the United States to have a wet and dry tropical climate. Principal cities are Miami, Jacksonville, Tampa, Saint Petersburg, and Fort Lauderdale.

Economy. An unrivaled climate, hundreds of miles of sandy beaches, and such attractions as Walt Disney World have made tourism Florida's largest industry. Florida is a major agricultural state, producing winter vegetables, greenhouse and nursery products, and fruits, including two-thirds of the nation's oranges. Major manufactures are electrical equipment and food products. Florida processes nearly all of the orange juice produced in the United States. The state ranks as a leader in commercial fishing. Shrimp, lobster, and scallops are the leading catches. Florida is the most important source of phosphate in the country.

Government. Florida's constitution, ratified in 1969, provides for a governor elected to a 4-year term. The state legislature comprises 40 senators elected for 4-year terms and 120 representatives elected for 2-year terms. Florida is represented by 2 senators and 23 representatives in the U.S. Congress.

History. Juan Ponce de León discovered and named Florida in 1513 and claimed the territory for Spain. In 1565 Spain founded Saint Augustine, which survives as the oldest city in the United States. In 1819 Spain ceded Florida to the United States. The territory of Florida was established in 1822. Resistance to white settlement by the Seminoles culminated in the second Seminole War (1835-42). Florida seceded from the Union in 1861 and was readmitted in 1868. Major economic growth began late in the 19th century when an expanding railroad system brought on a real estate boom, followed by a second boom in the 1920s. In the 1950s Cape Canaveral became a space and rocket center. Economic expansion has been great since World War II, but the growing population— including more than 100,000 Cuban and Haitian refugees since 1980—has put increasing strains upon social services, public utilities, transportation, and the dwindling tracts of subtropical wilderness.

Florida, Strait of, or Florida Strait, channel between the Florida Keys and the northern coast of Cuba. About 110 mi (177 km) wide, it links the Gulf of Mexico with the Atlantic Ocean and is the channel by which the Gulf Stream flows into the Atlantic.

Florida Keys, chain of about 20 small coral islands off southern Florida. Their arc curves southwest from Biscayne Bay south of Miami to Key West. Causeways bearing some 160 mi (257 km) of highway link most of the islands, which support fishing and farming and attract vacationers.

Florin, solid-gold coin introduced in Florence, Italy, in 1252 and made until the early 1500s. Florins have a lily, symbol of Florence, on one side and an image of Saint John the Baptist, patron saint of Florence, on the other. Britain, one of many countries to produce versions of the coin, first introduced a silver florin in 1849.

Flotation, industrial process used to separate valuable mineral compounds from low-grade ores. The ore is pulverized into minute particles and mixed with water. Then special chemicals, called flotation reagents, are added to prevent the water from wetting those substances to be extracted. When air is sprayed into the mixture a foam develops and carries to the surface the dry particles, which are then easily removed. The waste materials sink to the bottom of the mixture.

Flotsam, jetsam, and lagan, terms in maritime law relating to goods lost at sea. Goods thrown overboard (to lighten a ship) and that float are *flotsam*; those that sink are *jetsam*, but if they sink and are flagged to indicate ownership, they are *lagan*. These goods are subject to the law of salvage whereby the finder is entitled to reward.
See also: Salvage.

Flounder, any of a group of edible saltwater flatfish (families Pleuronectidae and Bothidae) of the Pacific and Atlantic. The halibut and turbot belong to the group.
See also: Flatfish.

Flour, fine powder ground from the grains or starchy portions of wheat, rye, corn, rice, potatoes, bananas, or beans. Plain white flour is produced from wheat; soft wheat produces flour used for cakes, and hard wheat, with a higher gluten content, makes flour used for bread. Flour is made from the endosperm, which constitutes about 84% of the grain; the remainder comprises the bran, which is the outer layers of the grain, and the germ, which is the embryo.

Flour beetle (*Tribolium confusum*), small (1/7 in/4 mm long), dark-red beetle that feeds on dried foods, flour, and other grain products. Found throughout the world, flour beetles are more common in warm, dry climates. Remains of flour beetles were discovered in a grain jar in an Egyptian tomb dating to about 2500 B.C.

Flower, part of a plant that is concerned with reproduction. Each flower is borne on a stalk or *pedicel*, the tip of which is expanded to form a receptacle that bears the floral organs. The *sepals* are the first of these organs and are normally green and leaflike. Above the sepals there is a ring of *petals*, which are normally colored and vary greatly in shape. The ring of sepals is termed the *calyx*, and the ring of petals, the *corolla*. Collectively the calyx and corolla are called the *perianth*. Above the perianth are the reproductive organs comprising the male organs, the *stamens* (collectively known as the *androecium*) and the female organs, the *carpels* (the *gynoecium*). Each stamen consists of a slender stalk, or filament, that is capped by the pollen- producing *anther*. Each carpel has a swollen base, the *ovary*, that contains the *ovules* that later form the seed. Each carpel is connected by a *style* to an expanded structure called the *stigma*. Together, the style and the stigma are sometimes termed the *pistil*. There are 3 main variations of flower structure. In hypogynous flowers (e.g., the buttercup) the perianth segments and stamens are attached below a superior ovary, while in perigynous flowers (e.g., the rose) the receptacle is cuplike, enclosing a superior ovary, with the perianth segments and stamens attached to a rim around the receptacle. In epigynous flowers (e.g., the dandelion) the inferior ovary is enclosed by the receptacle and the other floral parts are attached to the ovary. In many plants, the flowers are grouped together to form an *inflorescence* (flower cluster). Pollen produced by the stamens is transferred either by insects or the wind to the stigma, where pollination takes place. Many of the immense number of variations of flower form are adaptations that aid either insect or wind pollination.

Flowering maple, or Chinese bell flower, name for a number of trees and shrubs of the mallow family, and not, in fact, maples. Flowering maples come from southern Asia and South America. Some are now naturalized in North America. One, the velvetleaf, is cultivated for its fibers, called "China jute," used in rugmaking.

Flowering tobacco, any of several species of plants (genus *Nicotiana*) in the nightshade family that grow wild or are cultivated for their sweet-smelling flowers. Flowering tobacco plants are native to the South American tropics. They have hairy, sticky leaves and tube-shaped red, white, yellow, or purple flowers. One species, *N. tabacum*, is the source of tobacco.

Floyd, William (1734-1821), leader in the U.S. fight for independence and a N.Y. signer of the Declaration of Independence. He was a member of the Continental Congress from 1774 to 1777 and from 1778 to 1783. He served as a member of the U.S. House of Representatives from 1789 to 1791.

Flu *see:* Influenza.

Fluke, name for various parasitic flatworms, some of which are important disease carriers. The sheep liver fluke lives in the bile duct of mammals. Its eggs pass out of the intestine into water, where the larvae infect water snails, then wait on vegetation to be eaten by mammals. The blood fluke (bilharzia) is responsible for the disease schistosomiasis, which is thought to affect 250 million people throughout the world.

Fluorescence, property of emitting visible radiation as the result of absorption of radiation from some other source. The emitted radiation persists only as long as the fluorescent material is subjected to radiation, which may be either electrified particles or waves. The fluorescent radiation generally has a longer wavelength than does the absorbed radiation. If the fluorescent radiation includes waves of the same length as that of the absorbed radiation, it is termed *resonance* radiation.
See also: Radiation.

Fluorescent lamp, tube-shaped electric light from which light is emitted by the process of fluorescence. Fluorescent lamps produce about one-fifth the heat of light bulbs (incandescent lamps), use one-fifth the electricity, and lasts far longer. Fluorescent lamps, first introduced at the N.Y. World's Fair in 1938-39, are used largely in offices, schools, and factories. Inside a fluorescent lamp's glass tube is a small amount of mercury and a chemically inactive gas such as argon. The surface of the inside of the tube is coated with chemicals called phosphors. On each end of the tube is an electrode, which is a coated coil of tungsten wire. A *ballast* provides voltage to start the lamp and also regulates the flow of current. When a fluorescent lamp is turned on, electricity flows through the electrodes, heating it so that it gives off electrons. Some of these electrons hit the argon atoms and *ionize* them, giving them a positive or negative charge. Once ionized, the argon can conduct electricity. A current flowing through the gas from electrode to electrode forms a stream of electrons, exciting the electrons in the mercury. As the electrons in the mercury return to their normal state, they emit ultraviolet rays, which in turn cause the phosphors to glow (fluoresce).
See also: Fluorescence.

Fluoridation, addition of small quantities of fluorides to public water supplies, bringing the concentration to 1 part per million, as in some natural water. It greatly reduces the incidence of tooth decay by strengthening the teeth. Despite some opposition, many authorities now fluoridate water.

Fluoride, chemical compound of the element fluorine, and an important trace constituent of the human body. The bones and teeth contain most of the body's fluoride. Sea fish and tea are rich sources, but intake is mainly from drinking water. Fluoridation of water that contains the ideal level of 1 part per million (ppm) significantly reduces the incidence of dental decay (caries). Excess accumulation of fluoride (called fluorosis) occurs in teeth and bone in proportion to the level and duration of intake, and communities in which the level in drinking water exceeds 10 ppm are commonly affected.

Fluorine, chemical element, symbol F; for physical constants see Periodic Table. Fluorine was discovered in 1886 by Henri Moisson. It occurs chiefly in the form of the minerals fluorspar (calcium fluoride) and cryolite (sodium aluminum fluoride). It is obtained by electrolyzing a solution of potassium hydrogen fluoride in anhydrous hydrogen fluoride. Compounds of fluorine were used for years before the element was finally isolated. Fluorine is a member of the halogen family of elements. Fluorine is a pale yellow, corrosive, and poisonous gas and is the most electronegative and reactive of all elements. Commercial production of the element began only after World War II for preparing uranium hexafluoride. Fluorine and its compounds are used for glass etching, production of fluorocarbons, and in drinking water to prevent dental cavities. Fluorine and the fluoride ion are highly toxic.

Fluorite, or fluorspar, common mineral composed mainly of calcium fluoride. Fluorite is mined in many parts of the world and is important as a flux in the iron and steel industries. It is sometimes used in making optical lenses and as a catalyst in the manufacture of high-octane fuels. Fluorite is found in a wide range of colors, including light green, yellow, blue-green, purple, and, rarely, pink and red.

Fluorocarbon, organic compound in which hydrogen atoms are replaced by fluorine atoms. Fluorocarbons are often similar to hydrocarbons, but because of the stability of the carbon-fluorine bond, they are unreactive and do not break down with heating. Fluorocarbons are used as lubricants in conditions where hydrocarbon lubricants would be attacked by chemicals or by heat. They are also used in the chemical industry as a corrosion-resistant and insulating coating. Polytetrafluoroethylene (*Teflon*) is a solid fluorocarbon that is used to make artificial joints and plates for surgical implantation. Its lack of reactivity makes it safe to use in the body. It is also the basis of the coatings on nonstick frying pans and the heatshields of spacecraft. Liquid fluorocarbons such as **freon** are used as refrigerants.

Fluoroscope, device used in medical diagnosis and engineering quality control that allows the direct observation of an X-ray beam that is being passed through an object under examination. It contains a fluorescent screen, which converts the X-ray image into visible light, and, often, an image intensifier.
See also: X rays.

Flute, musical instrument belonging to the woodwind group, although most modern orchestral flutes are made of metal. The flute differs from most other woodwind instruments in that it is played in a sideways position. For this reason it was once often called the transverse flute, to distinguish it from similar instruments like the recorder. It is also distinguished in that the sound is produced by blowing directly across the mouthpiece instead of into it as in the bassoon, oboe, and clarinet.
Flutes, often made of clay, existed in ancient Sumer, Egypt, and Israel, as well as the Americas. In Europe technical improvements made the wooden flute an important solo instrument from the 17th century. Throughout the 18th century, from Bach to Mozart, the flute was very popular, both in orchestral and chamber music, and it remains an important member of the orchestra today. A much smaller version of the flute is the *piccolo* (Italian, "little"), which has a correspondingly higher range of notes and a shriller tone. It came into orchestral use during Beethoven's lifetime and is regularly included in military bands.

Fly, insect of the order Diptera, characterized by the presence of only 1 pair of wings. Well-known species include the common house fly, mosquitoes, and gnats. Many flies are known to transmit diseases such as malaria and dysentery, while others are beneficial as pollinators and as laboratory specimens in genetic studies. Approximately 100,000 varieties are found worldwide, ranging in size from 1/20 in (1.3 mm) to 3 in (7.6 cm).

Flycatcher, or tyrant flycatcher, family of birds found throughout the Americas, including kingbirds, phoebes, and pewees. They have broad bills with stiff bristles around the base. Their food usually consists of insects that they catch by flying out from a perch. Larger species, such as Kittlitz's ground tyrant, feed on lizards, mice, and small birds. The flycatchers of the Old World belong to a different family but have similar feeding habits.

Flycatcher

Flying buttress, arch of brick or stone on the exterior of a building, spanning the roof of an aisle of a church or cathedral, or a half-arch issuing from the upper part of a wall. The flying buttress helped make possible the tall, light churches of Gothic architecture.

Flying dragon, tree-dwelling lizard (genus *Draco*) of southeastern Asia and the East Indies. The flying dragon's body is about 8 in (20 cm) long and has thin folds of skin along each side. By spreading these "wings," the lizard can glide from tree to tree.

Flying dragon

Flying fish, tropical food fish of the family Exocoetidae, that propels itself out of the sea by an elongated lobe of the tail. It can glide on its fins, but the flights are usually 180 ft (55 m) or less. The flight allows the fish to escape predatory fish.

Flying fox, or fruit bat, large bat of the family Pteropidae, found in tropical regions, especially Australia and the Philippines. The largest has a 5-ft (1.5-m) wingspan. Flying foxes roost in large groups in trees and fly out in the evening to feed on flowers and fruit of trees.

Flying lemur, or colugo, nocturnal mammal (genus *Cynocephalus*) of the East Indies and Philippines, similar in appearance but unrelated to the lemurs. It has flaps of skin running between fore- and hindlimbs that enable it to glide 150 yd (137 m) from one tree to another. Its food consists of leaves, buds, and flowers.

Flying saucer *see:* Unidentified flying object.

Flying squirrel, omnivorous, nocturnal squirrel that glides on a web of skin between its legs. Flying squirrels use their tails for balance and as a rudder. They are found in Asia, Europe, and North America. The 2 North American species are genus *Glaucamys.*

Flying Tigers, nickname for the American Volunteer Group, a civilian force of World War II pilots. The U.S. aviators were recruited by Col. Claire L. Chennault to fight for China against Japan (1941-42).
See also: Chennault, Claire Lee; World War II.

The E-III monoplane, designed by Anthony Fokker, was used by the Germans in World War I.

Flynn, Elizabeth Gurley (1890-1964), labor leader, political activist, and first woman leader of the Communist Party in the United States. Flynn attended Socialist meetings with her family as a child, and at the age of 16 joined the Industrial Workers of the World. She helped form the American Civil Liberties Union (ACLU) in 1920 and joined the Communist Party in 1937, becoming chairperson in 1961. Flynn was imprisioned from 1955 to 1957 under the Smith Act, which made it a crime to advocate or belong to a group that advocated overthrow of the U.S. government.

FM *see:* Frequency modulation.

Foch, Ferdinand (1851-1929), French army marshal. His courageous stand against the Germans at the Marne in 1914 led to further commands, and he became chief of the French general staff in 1917. He commanded the Allied armies in France from Apr. to Nov. 1918, launching the Aisne-Marne offensive that ended World War I.
See also: World War I.

Fog, cloud near the earth's surface. It is generally formed when the air has cooled so much that it cannot hold all its water vapor, and the excess is precipitated in the form of water droplets. Fog may also form from the addition of water vapor to already saturated air. Fog is most common near large inland bodies of water and along the coasts in temperate zones.
See also: Cloud.

Fokine, Michel (1880-1942), Russian-born U.S. dancer and choreographer, a founder of modern ballet. Influenced by the work of Isadora Duncan, he stressed the total effect of expressive dancing, costume, music, and scenery. He worked in Paris as chief choreographer of Sergei Diaghilev's Ballets Russes (1909-14), and from 1925 directed his own company in the United States.
See also: Ballet.

Fokker, Anthony Herman Gerard (1880-1939), Dutch pilot and pioneer in aircraft design. In World War I he designed pursuit planes for Germany, developing a synchronizer mechanism by which guns could be fired from directly behind a plane's propeller blades. In 1922 Fokker emigrated to the United States, where he designed for the Army Air Corps and build transport planes like the Fokker T-2, which in 1923 made the first nonstop flight across the United States.
See also: Aircraft, Military.

Folger Shakespeare Library, institution in Washington, D.C. possessing the world's largest collection of Shakespeariana, including 79 first folios, and a host of material on the Tudor and Stuart periods. Opened in 1932, the collection was assembled initially by U.S. philanthropist Henry Clay Folger (1857-1930) and his wife, Emily Jordan Folger (1858-1936).

Folk art, paintings, sculptures, or crafts created by individuals according to local needs, tastes and traditions. Folk art is most often functional and representative of everyday life. In the United States folk artists have designed shop signs, weather vanes, and decoys. Craftworkers have made kitchen utensils, dishes, quilts, and furniture according to the needs of the community. The portrayal of everyday life in the objects of folk art makes it a valuable source of history.

Folk dancing, traditional popular dancing of a nation or region. Folk dances derive variously from ancient magic and religious rituals and also from the sequences of movement involved in certain forms of communal labor. Famous national dances include the Irish jig, the Italian tarantella, and the Hungarian czardas. The American Folk Dancing Society popularizes American folk dances, notably the square dance, in which an expert "caller" gives rhyming instructions. Many U.S. dances have European origins, but the barn dance setting is authentically American.

Folk literature *see:* Folklore; Literature for children.

Folklore, traditional beliefs, customs, and superstitions of a culture, handed down informally in fables, myths, legends, proverbs, riddles, songs, and ballads. Folklore studies were developed in the 1800s, largely through collection and collation of material by the Grimm brothers in Germany, and folklore societies were set up in Europe and the United States. The American Folklore Society was founded in 1888. Folktale themes are echoed and paralleled among distinct and isolated cultures. One of the major studies of this phenomenon is Sir James Frazer's *Golden Bough* (1890).

Folk music, traditional popular music of a regional or ethnic group. Compositions are usually anonymous and, being in the main orally transmitted, often occur in several different versions. Folk music of the United States includes the English ballads of Kentucky, Mexican music of the Southwest, and African American music of the South. Among classical composers influenced by folk music are Béla Bartók, Zoltán Kodaly, Aaron Copland, and Ralph Vaughan Williams.

Fonda, family of U.S. actors. **Henry Fonda** (1905-82), appeared in over 80 films, notably *The Grapes of Wrath* (1940), *The Ox-Bow Incident* (1943), and *Twelve Angry Men* (1957). He won an Academy Award for his performance in *On Golden Pond* (1981), in which his daughter, **Jane Fonda** (1937-), also appeared. She won Academy Awards for her performances in *Klute* (1971) and *Coming Home* (1978). She is also known for her political activism. Her brother, **Peter Fonda** (1939-), coproduced and starred in *Easy Rider* (1969), a film that made him a popular antihero of a generation.

Henry Fonda in his last film On Golden Pond *(1981)*

Fontainebleau (pop. 14,700), town in the department Seine-et-Marne, France, 27 mi (60 km) southeast of Paris. The town did not develop until the 19th century. Fontainebleau is primarily a recreation and tourist town. The magnificent palace of the French kings, built in the 16th century on the site of a royal hunting lodge, stands just outside the town. It was the scene of Napoleon's farewell to his army after his abdication in 1814. Fontainebleau forest, once a royal hunting ground, was a favorite subject for the 19th-century landscape painters known as the Barbizon school.
See also: France.

Fontane, Theodor (1819-98), German author known for his novels about Prussian society. Most of Fontane's stories involve Berlin's upper class in the 1800s, their social lives, morals, and personal conflicts. Fontane's works include *Trials and Tribulations* (1888), *Jenny Treibel* (1892), and his masterpiece, *Effi Briest* (1895).

Fontanne, Lynn (1887-1983), English-born U.S. actress, famous for many lead roles. Married to actor Alfred Lunt (1922), she costarred with him in such plays as *The Guardsman* (1924), *Design for Living* (1933), and *The Great Sebastians* (1956).

Fonteyn, Dame Margot (1919-91), English prima ballerina of the Royal Ballet. Before World War II she had danced leads in *Giselle, Swan Lake*, and *The Sleeping Beauty*, and Frederick Ashton had begun choreographing works for her. She retired from the Royal Ballet in 1959 but continued to appear as a guest star, and in 1962 she formed a dance partnership with Rudolf Nureyev that won new international fame for both of them.

Food, frozen, food that is kept at a constant temperature of 0°F (-18°C). A widely used method of food preservation, freezing inhibits the growth of organisms that cause spoilage. Foods can be frozen slowly in home freezer compartments or quickly in commercial processing. Clarence Birdseye developed a quick-freezing method in 1925 to produce frozen foods commercially. Today foods are quick-frozen using blasts of cold air, refrigerant-cooled plates, and freezing with nitrogen, dry ice, or liquid freon. These methods cause little structural change in food, therefore resulting in a higher quality product.
See also: Birdseye, Clarence.

Food and Agriculture Organization (FAO), agency of the UN, established in 1945, with headquarters in Rome. It provides member nations with information on food and agricultural problems and with technical and financial aid.
See also: United Nations.

Food and Drug Administration, U.S. (FDA), federal agency in the Department of Health and Human Services, set up to enforce the laws maintaining standards in the sale of food and drugs. Originally concerned largely with preventing adulteration and poor food hygiene, the FDA is now also involved in testing the safety, reliability, and usefulness of drugs and chemicals, and assessing the effects on health of "accidental additives" such as pesticides.
See also: Pure food and drug laws.

Food for Peace, federal program (Public Law 480), established 1954, regulating the donation and distribution of food to developing or underdeveloped countries.

Food poisoning, disease resulting from ingestion of unwholesome food, usually resulting in colic, vomiting, diarrhea, and general malaise. While a number of viruses, contaminants, and irritant and allergic factors may play a part, 3 specific microorganisms are commonly responsible: *Staphylococcus, Clostridium*, and *Salmonella* bacteria. Inadequate cooking, allowing cooked food to stand for long periods in warm conditions, and contamination of cooked and uncooked food by bacteria from humans are usual causes. Staphylococci may be introduced from a boil or from the nose of a food handler; they produce a toxin if allowed to grow in cooked food. Sudden vomiting and abdominal pain occur 2 to 6 hours after eating. Clostridium poisoning causes colic and diarrhea 10 to 12 hours after ingestion of contaminated meat. Salmonella enteritis causes colic, diarrhea, vomiting, and often fever, starting 12 to 24 hours after eating; poultry and human carriers are the usual sources. Botulism, caused by a toxin produced by Clostridium bacteria, is an often fatal form of food poisoning. In general, food poisoning is mild and of limited duration, and only the treatment of symptoms is needed; antibiotics rarely help.

Food preservation, techniques used to delay the spoilage of food. The most common forms of preservation are heating, sealing, refrigeration, and freezing. Heating destroys enzymes that over-ripen food and bacteria that are responsible for decay. Sealing in sterile cans or bottles isolates food from air-borne bacteria. Refrigeration and freezing slow the enzyme action and the reproduction of the bacteria, and freezing preserves flavor better. Dehydration, irradiation, and preservatives are also used. Traditional means of preservation include smoking, salting, and pickling.

Food Stamps, locally administered, federally funded U.S. program, established 1964, that enables poverty-level families to buy a greater variety and quantity of food. Stamps are received in proportion to total net income and the number of people in the household. The program helps feed about 22 million people.
See also: Welfare.

Fool's gold *see:* Pyrite.

Foot, anatomical structure, part of the lower extremity, bearing weight and providing locomotion. The bones that make up the foot and their arrangement are designed to form a stable structure, somewhat limited in range of movement.

Foot, Michael (1913-), British political leader. A member of Parliament for 30 years, Foot served as secretary of state for employment (1974-75), Speaker of the House of Commons (1976-79), and leader of the Labour Party (1980-83).

Foot-and-mouth disease, or hoof-and-mouth disease, highly contagious viral disease affecting cattle, hogs, sheep, and other animals with cloven (split) hoofs. The disease is spread directly from animal to animal or indirectly by contaminated food, soil, or water. Symptoms include blisters in the mouth and in the split in the hoof, fever, and loss of appetite. Epidemics cause severe losses, and although vaccines are available, they provide only short-term protection and are expensive.

Football, in the United States and Canada, team sport in which the object is to deliver a ball over a goal line and to prevent the opposing team from reaching its own goal line at the opposite end of a demarcated field. Teams include 11 men. The field is 100 yd (91.4 m) long by 53 1/3 yd (48.7 m) wide. Lines are marked across the field at 5-yd (4.6-m) intervals. Behind each goal line is an area 10 yd (9.1 m) deep called the end zone, at the end of which is the goal post. A touchdown—running or passing the ball (to a receiver) over the goal line—is worth 6 points. The field goal, or place-kick over the crossbar and between the goalpost uprights, is worth 3 points. A safety, where a man in posession of the ball is downed in back of his own goal line, is 2 points. A conversion kick, allowed after each touchdown, is worth 1 point; an alternative in college play is the 2-point conversion, which allows the ball to be run or passed over the goal line. Officials may penalize a team by moving the ball closer to its goal line when it violates a rule. Minor

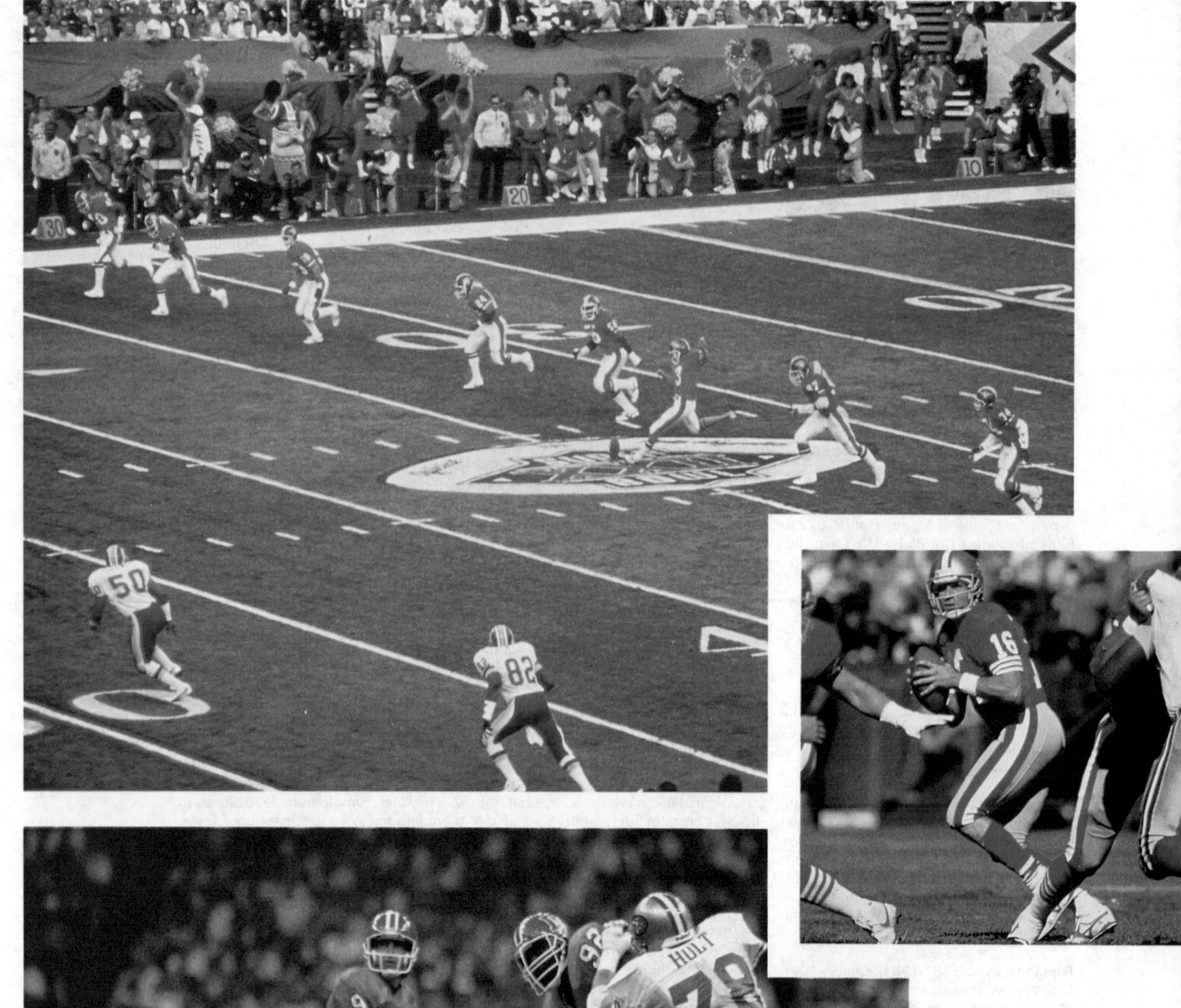

Three moments in a game: the kickoff, run and tackle, and the pass

fouls cost 5 yd (4.6 m). Major fouls are penalized 15 yd (13.7 m).

Early games, dating back to about 1820 in the eastern United States, were informal, soccerlike affairs. In 1880, along with a new method of putting the ball into play (by the holder snapping it back with his foot to the quarterback), came the "block game." Teams took the kickoff and retained the ball with no effort to advance it, resulting in dull, scoreless ties. Yale University coach Walter Camp solved this problem by the system of *downs* that became a rule in 1882. The team in possession was given 3 plays, or downs, to advance the ball 5 yd (4.6 m). If successful, it retained possession and started another series of 3 downs; it if failed it had to turn the ball over to the opponent. This rule—changed to 10 yd (9.1 m) in 4 downs in 1912—has remained the heart of American football. It led to the use of strategy, to the disuse of kicking as the predominant offense, and to the development of the running attack by short, hard rushes. A rule in 1894 decreed that the ball had to travel at least 10 yd (9.1 m) on the kickoff. This put a stop to the dangerous "V trick" and later flying wedge, whereby the "kicker" merely touched his toe to the ball, picked it up, tucked himself within a wedge formed by his teammates, and ran to a huge gain against his foes. Nevertheless, with players left largely unprotected by primitive helmets and pads, the concentrated power plays were causing many injuries, even deaths. President Theodore Roosevelt, himself a fan, demanded that football be made safer, and in 1906 mass formations, hurdling, and other dangerous strategems were banned. The game was reduced from 70 to 60 min, and the forward pass was legalized.

In college football, the new open game spawned the breakaway halfbacks, players with speed and agility in carrying the ball, like Jim Thorpe of the Carlisle Indian School and, in the early 1920s, Harold "Red" Grange of the University of Illinois. Free substitution was permitted in 1941, but the rule was not exploited until 1945, when Fritz Crisler of Michigan divided his team into offense and defense platoons. Soon all teams were using the 2-platoon system, costs soared, and in 1953 free substitution was outlawed by the Football Rules Committee. It was restored during the early 1960s, largely to compete with the flourishing pro leagues, which had adopted it. Ex-collegians who worked in the small industrial towns of western Pennsylvania and formed pickup teams during the 1890s were the first professionals; they received $10 a game, when paid. In 1920 at Canton, Ohio, 11 teams formed the United States Professional Football Association, with Jim Thorpe as its president and star player. Franchises, today worth millions, cost $100 each. The league changed its name to the National Football League (NFL) in 1921 but did not begin to gain recognition until the signing in 1925 of Illinois star Red Grange; other college stars followed as the league prospered. In 1933 the league reorganized into 10 teams, mostly in major cities and evenly divided between 2 divisions. The annual college draft was initiated in 1935, giving weaker clubs the first chance to select college stars and thus maintaining a talent balance. By 1946 interest in pro football had grown to a point where a second league, the All America Conference (AAC), was started. It lasted only 4 seasons. During the 1960s attendance records climbed due to the wide-open style of play and the spectacle of violence created by agile, 260-lb linemen crunching into each other and sometimes into the game's lighter specialists. In 1960 the American Football League (AFL) started play. Green Bay, coached by Vince Lombardi, beat the AFL's Kansas City team in 1967 in the first Super Bowl, which pitted the NFL champion against the AFL champion. In 1970 the NFL's 16 teams combined with the AFL's 10 to form the National Football League, which is divided into National and American conferences (with 3 divisions within each conference) that correspond roughly to the old NFL-AFL alignments. The Canadian Football League has a total of 8 teams in its 2 divisions.

Foote, Andrew Hull (1806-63), Union naval officer during the U.S. Civil War. His fleet of gunboats joined with the army to break Confederate defenses along the Mississippi River in northern Tennessee (1862). Foote was active in disbanding slave trade off the African coast (1849-51) and was instrumental in abolishing liquor on U.S. warships (1862).
See also: Civil War, U.S.

Forbes, Esther (1891-1967), U.S. author of historical novels. In 1943 she won the Pulitzer Prize in American history for her biography *Paul Revere and the World He Lived In.* In 1944 she won the Newbery Medal for her young adult novel *Johnny Tremain,* about a young apprentice during the time of the American Revolution.

Forbidden City, walled enclosure in Beijing (Peking), China, containing the imperial palace, its grounds, reception halls, and state offices. In imperial times, the Forbidden City was closed to the public.
See also: Beijing.

Force, in mechanics, physical quantity that, when acting on a body, either causes it to change its state of motion (i.e., imparts to it an acceleration), or tends to deform it (i.e., induces in it an elastic strain). Dynamical forces are governed by Newton's laws of motion, from the second of which it follows that a given force acting on a body produces in it an acceleration proportional to the force, inversely proportional to the body's mass, and occurring in the direction of the force. Forces are thus *vector* quantities with direction as well as magnitude. Four naturally occurring forces are gravity, electromagnetism, and the strong and weak nuclear forces within atoms.
See also: Mechanics.

Ford, Ford Madox (Ford Madox Hueffer; 1873-1939), English author. His novels *The Good Soldier* (1915) and the tetralogy *Parade's End* (1924-28), describe the decline of the English upper classes before World War I. As first editor of *The English Review* (1908-11), he encouraged such writers as Joseph Conrad (with whom he also collaborated), Ezra Pound, Robert Frost, and D.H. Lawrence.

Ford, Gerald Rudolph, Jr. (1913-), 38th president of the United States. Ford succeeded Richard M. Nixon as president after one of the gravest traumas in U.S. political history forced Nixon to resign.

Early life. Ford was christened Leslie King, Jr. When his parents were divorced, his mother's second husband, Gerald Rudolph Ford, adopted and renamed the boy. Ford grew up in Grand Rapids, Mich., and attended the University of Michigan. After graduating in 1935, Ford worked his way through Yale University Law School and received his law degree in 1941. Soon after, he began almost 4 years' service in the U.S. Navy during World War II. He finished as a lieutenant commander and resumed his law practice.

U.S. Representative. In 1948, at the urging of Senator Arthur H. Vandenberg, Ford ran for Congress. He unseated the Republican incumbent and arrived in Washington, D.C., newly married to Elizabeth (Betty)

Gerald Rudolph Ford, Jr.

38th U.S. President	
Born:	Omaha, Neb.; July 14, 1913
Term:	Aug. 1974-Jan. 1977
Vice president:	Nelson Aldrich Rockefeller
Political party:	Republican
Spouse:	Elizabeth (Betty) Bloomer Warren Ford
Children:	4

Bloomer. Ford became known as a hard-working member of Congress and of his party. In 1953 he was named to the House Appropriations Committee and, in 1963, to the Warren Commission (set up to investigate the assassination of President John F. Kennedy). He became House minority leader in 1965.

Vice President. Mentioned as a possible vice presidential nominee, Ford preferred to remain in the House. However, in Oct. 1973 Spiro T. Agnew resigned as vice president and President Nixon nominated Ford to replace him. The Senate approved the nomination, making Ford the first appointed vice president in U.S. history. After Nixon's involvement in the Watergate scandal led to his own resignation in Aug. 1974, Ford was thrust into the presidency.

President. "Our long national nightmare is over," Ford announced. In world affairs, he continued the widely endorsed policies of his predecessor. He reaffirmed U.S. commitment to traditional allies and announced plans to visit China and the Soviet Union. Ford made the nation's serious economic problems a top priority. He worked to establish a broad-ranging program that would generate more economic activity and reduce unemployment, continue efforts against inflation, and help reduce U.S. dependence on foreign sources of energy. Pushing for a reduction in government spending, Ford engaged in a running battle with what he referred to as "the spendthrift Democratic Congress." By Nov. 1976, when the next presidential election was held, Ford could argue that the economy was in better shape than it had been when he took office. Perhaps angered by Ford's decision to pardon former President Nixon, voters elected the Democratic nominee, Jimmy Carter, to the presidency.

Retirement. After leaving office, Ford toured the nation, speaking before organizations and lecturing at colleges and universities. He also served on the boards of directors of various companies, worked on several projects for President Ronald Reagan, and published his autobiography.

Ford, Henry (1863-1947), U.S. automobile production pioneer. He produced his first automobile in 1896 and established the Ford Motor Company in Dearborn, Mich., in 1903. By adopting mass-assembly methods, and introducing the moving assembly line in 1913, Ford revolutionized automobile production. Ford saw that mass-produced cars could sell at a price within reach of the average U.S. family. Between 1908 and 1926 he sold 15 million Model T's. Ford was a paradoxical and often controversial character. Although a proud anti-intellectual, he set up several museums and the famous Ford Foundation. A violent antiunionist, he reduced the average working week, and introduced profit sharing and the highest minimum daily wage of his time. In 1938 he accepted a Nazi decoration and became a leading isolationist. At the outbreak of war, however, he built the world's largest assembly plant, to produce B-24 bombers.

Henry Ford in his first automobile

Some of the Model T Fords produced by the Ford Motor Company were fitted with racing bodies.

Ford, John (1586-1640), English dramatist. Three tragedies, *'Tis Pity She's a Whore* (c.1627), *The Broken Heart* (c.1629), and *Love's Sacrifice* (1630), are his best-known works. Considered decadent by earlier critics because of his lack of moral comment, in the 20th century Ford is admired for his insight into human passion.

Ford, John (1895-1973), U.S. motion picture director. One of the great masters of his craft, he began directing the first of his more than 125 films in 1917. He won Academy awards for *The Informer* (1935), *The Grapes of Wrath* (1940), *How Green Was My Valley* (1942), and *The Quiet Man* (1952). In later years, his principal output consisted of Westerns, a form he had pioneered with such early films as *The Iron Horse* (1924) and *Stagecoach* (1939).

Ford Foundation, philanthropic corporation founded by Henry Ford in 1936. With assets of over $3 billion, it is the world's largest philanthropic trust. The foundation uses its funds for educational, cultural, scientific, and charitable purposes in the United States and abroad.

Ford Motor Company, one of the U.S. automotive industry giants, established in 1903 by Henry Ford. The Ford Motor Company has about 75 assembly and manufacturing plants in the United States, the largest of which is near Detroit, Mich. Manufacturing subsidiaries are Canada, Mexico, South America, Europe, and Australia. Ford is also a joint owner with companies in Asia, South Africa, and Turkey. Production of the Model N began in 1906, followed by the Model T in 1908 and the Model A in 1928. The company now builds Ford, Mercury, and Lincoln automobiles, trucks, tractors, and other farm and industrial machinery.

Ford's Theatre *see:* Lincoln, Abraham.

Foreign Aid Programs, financial, military, and technical assistance given by one country to another. The Lend-Lease program provided over $40 billion to U.S. allies after World War II. The Marshall Plan strengthened the weakened economies of Western Europe (1948-51). In 1949 the Point Four Program initiated U.S. aid to underdeveloped countries, particularly in Asia. Credit facilities were set for these nations in 1957 with the creation of the Development Loan Fund. A diversification of U.S. aid programs (in Asia, Africa, and Latin America), and establishment of the Peace Corps and the Alliance for Progress began in the 1960s.

Foreign Legion, mercenary army created in 1831 by the French to save manpower in Algeria. The legion fought mainly outside France, in Morocco, Madagascar, Spain, Mexico, the Crimea, and Indochina, until Algerian independence (1962).

Foreign Service, diplomatic and consular employees of the U.S. Department of State. They staff embassies and consulates, promote friendly relations between the United States and countries in which they serve, advise on political and economic matters, protect and aid U.S. citizens abroad, and deal with aliens seeking entry to the U.S.

Foreman, George Edward (1948-), U.S. boxer, world heavyweight champion from Jan. 1973 to Oct. 1974. He won the gold medal in the heavyweight competition in the 1968 Olympic Games in Mexico and turned professional in 1969. He had won 40 consecutive bouts when defeated by Muhammad Ali in 1974. Foreman retired in 1977, but returned to boxing 10 years later. In April of 1991, he once again fought for the championship against Evander Holyfield but lost a 12-round decision.

Forensic science *see:* Crime laboratory.

Forest, area of land covered by trees. Forests are important for their economic, environmental, and recreational uses, and as habitats for plants, insects, birds, and other animals. As ecosystems, forests are classified as tropical rain forests, tropical seasonal forests, temperate deciduous forests, temperate evergreen forests, boreal forests, and savannas. They may also be classified by dominant tree type, such as needleleaf, coniferous, or deciduous. Before the 1600s most of the land between the Atlantic Ocean and the Mississippi River was covered by forests. Today, the United States has about 753 million acres (322 million hectares) of forest area.

Forest fire *see:* Forestry.

Forest products, products derived from trees that since prehistoric times have provided food, shelter, clothing, and fuel. Most forest products are classified as wood, fiber, chemical, or fuel. From these, such things as lumber, paper, acetate, and charcoal are produced. About 1.5 million people are employed in the forest products industry in the United States. They produce about $120 billion worth of forest products annually.

Forestry, management of forests for productive purposes. In the United States, a forestry program emerged in the 1890s because of fears of a "timber famine" and following exploitation of the Great Lakes pine forests. Congress authorized the first forest reserves in 1891; creation of the Forest Service in 1905 put forestry on a scientific basis. The most important aspect of forestry is the production of lumber. Because of worldwide depletion of timber stocks, it has become necessary to view forests as renewable productive resources, and because of the time scale and area involved in the growth of a forest, trees need more careful planning than any other crop. Forestry work plans for a continuity of timber production by balancing planting and felling. Foresters also work to prevent and extinguish forest fires, which destroy about 3 million acres (1.2 million hectares) of timber each year. Other important functions are disease, pest, and flood control. The forester must control the density and proportions of the various trees in a forest and ensure that people do not radically disturb a forest's ecological balance. The science of forestry is well advanced in the United States, which is the world's largest timber producer and has more than 25 forestry schools across the country. However, only 20% of the world's forests are being renewed, and timber resources are declining.

Forest Service, U.S., Department of Agriculture agency, created in 1905 to manage and protect the national forests. Nearly 190 million acres (77 million hectares) of national forests and grasslands, as well as 480 million acres (194 million hectares) of forests and watersheds belonging to state and local governments and private owners, benefit from the service's conservation, research, development, and advisory programs.

Forgery, in law, the making or altering of a written document with intent to defraud. Imitations of works of art, literature, and signatures are common forgeries. Counterfeit refers to forgery of objects, such as bills, coins, and gems.

Forget-me-not, any of various annual or perennial wild and garden flowers (genus *Myosotis*), native to North America, Europe, and Asia. Most have pink flower buds that become blue as the flower opens. It has long been a symbol of constancy. Yellow forget-me-not is a plant of western deserts.

Forging, shaping metal by hammering or pressing, usually when the workpiece is red hot (about 400°-700°C) but sometimes when it is cold. Unlike casting, forging does not alter the granular structure of the metal, and hence greater strength is possible in forged than in cast metals. The most basic method of forging is that of the blacksmith, who heats the metal in an open fire (forge) and hammers it into shape against an anvil. Today, metals are forged between two dies, usually impressed with the desired shape. Techniques include *drop forging*, where the workpiece is held on the lower, stationary die, the other being held by a massive ram that is allowed to fall; *press forging*, where the dies are pressed together; and *impact forging*, where the dies are rammed horizontally together, the workpiece between.

Formaldehyde (HCHO), colorless, acrid, toxic gas; the simplest and most reactive aldehyde. Formaldehyde was discovered by A.W. von Hofmann in 1867. It is made by catalytic air oxidation of methanol vapor or of natural gas. Formaldehyde gas is unstable, and is usually stored as an aqueous solution, formalin, used as a disinfectant and preservative for biological specimens. Formaldehyde is used in the manufacture of pharmaceuticals, dyes, and plastics. Formaldehyde gas causes severe symptoms of the respiratory tract, and may be a carcinogen.
See also: Aldehyde.

Formalin *see:* Formaldehyde.

Formic acid (CH_2O_2), industrial chemical used to process textiles, leather, rubber, and other products. Produced from carbon monoxide and sodium hydroxide, formic acid is a strong-smelling, corrosive, colorless liquid.

Formosa *see:* Taiwan.

Forrest, Edwin (1806-72), prominent U.S. tragedian, the first U.S. actor actively to encourage native playwrights. His feud with English actor William Macready led to a notorious riot at New York's Astor Place Opera House on May 8, 1849.

Forrest, Nathan Bedford (1821-77), Confederate cavalry general. He was esteemed for his bravery and leadership. His several victories over Union forces included capturing Fort Pillow, Tenn. (1864), during which many African-American defenders were killed. Later that year he commanded all cavalry under J.B. Hood in the Tennessee campaign.
See also: Civil War, U.S.

Forrestal, James Vincent (1892-1949), U.S. secretary of defense, first head of the newly formed defense department (1947). He had previously served as secretary of the navy. Emotional and physical stress caused his resignation in 1949, and he committed suicide shortly thereafter.
See also: Defense, Department of.

Forster, E(ward) M(organ) (1879-1970), English writer and critic, whose works reflected his sharp wit and graceful style. His most famous novels are *Howards End* (1910) and *A Passage to India* (1924), which illustrate Forster's interest in personal relationships and the racial and psychological impediments to these relationships. His other works include *Where Angels Fear to Tread* (1905), *The Longest Journey* (1907), *A Room with a View* (1908), and *Maurice* (1913-14).

Forsythia, or golden bell, shrub (genus *Forsythia*) native to eastern Europe and Asia as far east as Japan. It is widely grown in the United States for ornamental purposes. It has slender, arching branches and yellow flowers that open in spring before the leaves.

Forsythia

Fort Benning, U.S. Army Infantry Center near Columbus, Ga. Established in 1918 and named after Brigadier General Henry L. Benning of the Confederate Army, Fort Benning covers 182,000 acres (73,650 hectares) of land.

Fort Bragg, center for U.S. Army airborne units and the Special Warfare Center, near Fayetteville, N.C. Established in 1918 and named after Confederate General Braxton Bragg, this fort covers 149,000 acres (60,000 hectares). During World War II, the U.S. Army's first 2 airborne divisions (82nd and 101st) were trained at Fort Bragg.

Fort Lauderdale, Florida

Fort Dix, U.S. Army base located in southern New Jersey. Covering an area of 31,000 acres (13,000 hectares), it is the site of basic training, discharges, and recruitment for overseas duty. By 1995 many of its operations will be moved to other facilities.

Fort Duquesne, fort built by the French in 1754 near the present-day site of Pittsburgh, Pa. The area was the site of the Battle of the Great Meadows (1754) and other battles of the French and Indian Wars. The fort was burned down by the retreating French in 1758.
See also: French and Indian Wars.

Forten, James (1766-1842), black U.S. entrepreneur and abolitionist during the early 1800s. Born in Philadelphia, at age 15 Forten was captured by the British while serving as a sailor during the Revolutionary War and spent 7 months on a prison ship. He became foreman in a sailmaking shop in Philadelphia, and subsequently, its owner. Forten recruited black patriots to help defend Philadelphia from British invasion during the War of 1812. An active supporter of abolitionist William Lloyd Garrison, he also helped runaway slaves seeking freedom.
See also: Abolitionism.

Fort Eustis, home of the U.S. Army Transportation Center and the Aviation Logistics School, near Williamsburg, Va. Established in 1918 and named after Brigadier General Abraham Eustis, artillery officer of the early 1800s, Fort Eustis covers 8,200 acres (3,300 hectares).

Fort George G. Meade, headquarters for the First U.S. Army and the National Security Agency, located in Maryland about 15 mi (24 km) northeast of Washington, D.C. Established in 1917, it was named after Union general Meade. This fort currently covers 13,000 acres (5,300 hectares).

Fort Knox, U.S. military reservation in Hardin County, north central Kentucky. Established in 1917 as a training camp, it was named for Major General Henry Knox, first secretary of war. It is now the site of the U.S. Army Armor Center, which includes the U.S. Gold Bullion Depository, and covers 110,000 acres (44,500 hectares).

Fort Lauderdale (pop. 1,255,488), city in southeastern Florida. Located 25 mi (40 km) north of Miami, it is a popular winter resort and tourist area. Although it is the site of a fort established in 1838, its development dates to 1906, when the draining of the mangrove swamps began. Crossed by a large number of waterways and canals, it is sometimes called the Venice of America. Port Everglades, the deepest harbor south of Norfolk and east of New Orleans, is located there.
See also: Florida.

Fort Leavenworth, in Missouri, site of the Combined Arms Center of the U.S. Army and the army's chief tactical training center. It also houses a military prison. It is located on 5,600 acres (2,300 hectares) on the Missouri River near Kansas City.

Fort Leonard Wood, in Missouri, site of the Engineer Center and School of the U.S. Army. Located on 65,000 acres (26,000 hectares) in the Mark Twain National Forest, it has facilities for basic and advanced training.

Fort McClellan, in Alabama, site of the U.S. Army Chemical School, Military Police School, and Department of Defense Polygraph Institute. It also provides basic training. Located on 47,000 acres (19,000 hectares), it was named after Civil War general George B. McClellan.

Fort McHenry, fort in Baltimore Harbor, Md. During the War of 1812, it withstood overnight bombardment by a British fleet, inspiring Francis Scott Key, a spectator, to write the words to *The Star-Spangled Banner,* which became the U.S. national anthem.
See also: Star-Spangled Banner.

Fort McPherson, headquarters for the U.S. Army Forces Command, located in Atlanta, Ga. Established in 1889 and named after Union General James B. McPherson, this fort covers 480 acres (190 hectares).

Fort Monmouth, in New Jersey, site of Communications-Electronics Command of the U.S. Army. Located on 1,550 acres (630 hectares) about 40 mi (65 km) from New York City, the fort contains a school for military chaplains, a military academy, and facilities for electronics research.

Fort Monroe, U.S. Army Training and Doctrine Command headquarters near Norfolk, Va. Used as a fortification since 1609, the fort was named after President Monroe in 1832 when it was rebuilt by Robert E. Lee. Edgar Allan Poe, the poet, served at Fort Monroe before going to West Point, and Jefferson Davis, president of the Confederacy, was imprisoned at this fort after the Civil War.

Fort Moultrie, historic fort on Sullivan's Island in Charleston Harbor, S.C. First called Fort Sullivan, it was renamed after Revolutionary War commander Colonel William Moultrie. Fort Moultrie was occupied by both American and British troops during the Revolution, and by both Union and Confederate forces during the Civil War, U.S.

Fort Necessity, historic fort built by George Washington in 1754, located in southwestern Pennsylvania. It was surrendered to the French in 1754. The fort became a national battlefield in 1961.

Fort Niagara, fort on the eastern shore of the Niagara River (now on the New York-Ontario border) built by the French in 1726 to guard the river entrance to the fur country. Captured by the British during the French and Indian Wars, it was given to the United States in a 1796 treaty, temporarily taken back, then finally returned to U.S. hands in 1815.

Fort Riley, home to the U.S. Army's 1st Infantry Division, near Kansas City, Kans. It was built in 1853 and named after Major General Bennett Riley, who served during the Mexican War. Several cavalry regiments, including Custer's 7th Cavalry, were organized at Fort Riley.

Fort Rucker, home of the U.S. Army Aviation Center, northwest of Dothan, Ala. Established in 1942 and named after Confederate officer Colonel Edmond W. Rucker, this fort also houses the Army Aeromedical Center, the Army Safety Center, and the Aviation Development Test Activity. Fort Rucker covers 64,000 acres (26,000 hectares), and is the training center for pilots and maintenance personnel for small airplanes and helicopters.

Fort Sam Houston, fort in San Antonio, Tex., built in 1876. It was named after Samuel Houston, first president of the Republic of Texas. It covers 3,160 acres (1,280 hectares) inside the city limits and is the headquarters of the 5th U.S. Army. It also has one of the world's largest medical training centers, the Academy of Health Science.

Fort Sill, U.S. Army Field Artillery Center, located near Lawton, Okla. Built in 1869 and named after Union Brigadier General Joshua W. Sill, it covers 94,220 acres (38,000 hectares). Apache leader Geronimo is buried at Fort Sill.

Fort Smith (pop. 175,911), city in Arkansas, originally established as a U.S. Army installation (1817). A manufacturing and transportation center, the Fort Smith area is also important for natural gas and coal deposits, farming, and timber. The courtroom of frontier "hanging judge" Isaac C. Parker is located in downtown Fort Smith.

Fort Sumter, fort in Charleston Harbor, S.C., where the first shots in the Civil War were fired on Apr. 12, 1861. When South Carolina seceded from the Union (1860), U.S. Major Robert Anderson received a rebel summons to surrender his garrison. He refused, Sumter was fired upon, and the war began. The fort was retaken when Confederates evacuated Charleston in Feb. 1865.

Fort Ticonderoga, Revolutionary War post located at Lake Champlain, N.Y. Used alternately by the British and U.S. soldiers, this fort was rebuilt in 1908 as a museum for Revolutionary War artifacts.
See also: Revolutionary War in America.

Fort Wayne (pop. 363,811), city in northeastern Indiana, the site of a settlement of the Miami tribe visited by French explorer La Salle in 1670. Named for General Anthony Wayne, who built a fort there in 1794 and incorporated it as a city in 1840, Fort Wayne is the principal industrial and commercial center of northeastern Indiana and a wholesale outlet for the surrounding agricultural area.
See also: Indiana.

Fort Worth (pop. 1,332,053), city in northern Texas, seat of Tarrant County. Located on the Trinity River about 30 mi (48 km) west of Dallas, Fort Worth was founded in 1849 as an outpost against Native American attacks. The city became a major trading center during the cattle drives of the 1870s and was known as the place "Where the West Begins." It was incorporated in 1873 and has a council-manager government. Fort Worth is one of the major grain-storage and flour-milling centers in the southwest. It lies in the heart of one of the most important oil-producing regions of Texas and is the headquarters of numerous oil companies. One of the biggest aircraft factories in the country, and the largest stockyards and meat-processing plants in the South, are also major elements in Fort Worth's economy. The city is the home of Southwestern Baptist Theological Seminary, Texas Christian University, and Texas Wesleyan College. Its symphony orchestra and opera association are known throughout the nation.
See also: Texas.

Forty-Niners, name given to those who flooded into California following the gold strike of 1848. News of the gold discovery by James Marshall at Sutter's Mill started a migration from all over the world. By the end of 1849 California's population had swelled from 20,000 to over 107,000.
See also: Gold rush.

Forum, public meeting or meeting place used for open discussion of current topics of general interest. In modern usage a forum may be a radio or TV program in which such current matters are discussed by leading personalities and authorities. The forum was the principal public square or marketplace in any ancient Roman city, where citizens gathered to discuss important issues, and where judicial and other public business was transacted. The forum contained colonnades, shops, temples, and other important buildings. The city of Rome had several forums, the oldest and best known being the Roman Forum below the Capitoline Hill.

Foscolo, Ugo (1778-1827), Italian author. His books include the novel, *The Last Letters of Jacopo Ortis* (1802) and the ode *The Sepulchers* (1806-07). He left Italy in 1815 and spent the rest of his life in England, writing essays and teaching Italian.

Fosdick, Harry Emerson (1878-1969), U.S. Protestant preacher. Fosdick opposed fundamentalists, preaching that science had its place in the world along with religion. He was professor at the Union Theological Seminary in New York and author of such books as *The Meaning of Prayer* and *The Modern Use of the Bible.*

Foss, Lukas (Lukas Fuchs; 1922-), German-born U.S. composer who developed a method of simultaneous improvisation and experimented with electronic effects, the use of prerecorded tape, and avant-garde composition, as in *Echoi* (1961-63), *Cello Concerto* (1966), and *Fanfare* (1973). He conducted the Buffalo Philharmonic (1963-71) and was appointed music director of the Brooklyn Philharmonia in 1971.

Fossey, Dian (1932-85), U.S. zoologist. A graduate of San Jose State College, Fossey went to Africa in 1963 to study the wild mountain gorilla. In 1966 she was selected by British anthropologist Louis Leakey to conduct a long-term study of the gorilla. Fossey studied the animals daily, learning their habits. When some of the gorillas were killed, she directed her work toward the protection of the animals from poachers and the preservation of their habitat. She founded the Karisoke Research Center in Rwanda, where she lived for 18 years. She was murdered in 1985. Her book *Gorillas in the Mist* (1983) and the movie with the same title (1988) tell her story.
See also: Zoology.

Fossil, evidence of ancient plant or animal life preserved in sediment or rock. Preservation of an organism in its entirety (i.e., unaltered hard and soft parts together) is exceptional. Entire mammoths have been preserved in Siberian permafrost. Unaltered hard parts are common in post-Mesozoic sediments but become increasingly scarce further back in geologic time. *Petrification* describes 2 ways in which the shape of hard parts of the organism may be preserved. In *permineralization* the pore spaces of the hard parts are filled by certain minerals (e.g., silica, pyrite, calcite) that infiltrate from the local groundwater. The resulting fossil is thus a mixture of mineral and organic matter. In many other cases substitution or replacement occurs, in which the hard parts are dissolved away but the form is retained by newly deposited minerals. Where this has happened very gradually, even microscopic detail may be preserved, but generally only the outward form remains. Often the skeletal materials are dissolved entirely, leaving either internal or external *molds.* The filling of a complete mold may also occur, forming a *cast.* The complete filling of a hollow shell interior may form a *core* or *steinkern* such as the corkscrewlike filling of a coiled snail shell. In the process of *carbonization* the tissues decompose, leaving only a thin residual carbon film that shows the outline of the organism's flattened form.

Fossil fuel *see:* Energy supply.

Foster, Stephen Collins (1826-64), U.S. composer of over 200 songs and instrumental pieces. His "Oh! Susannah," "My Old Kentucky Home," and "Old Black Joe" and other Southern dialect songs are essentially so simple and so popular that they are often mistakenly considered folk music.

Foucault, Jean Bernard Leon (1819-68), French physicist. He is best known for showing the rotation of the earth with the Foucault pendulum, for inventing the gyroscope, and for accurately determining the velocity of light.
See also: Gyroscope; Pendulum.

Founding Fathers, statesmen of the American Revolution, in particular writers of the Constitution of the United States. They included George Washington, Benjamin Franklin, Alexander Hamilton, and James Madison.
See also: Constitution of the United States.

Foundry, metal casting plant. Founding is a process of pouring metals such as iron, aluminum, or lead into molds made with clay and sand. From this process, objects ranging from toy soldiers to automobile engine blocks are created.
See also: Casting; Forging.

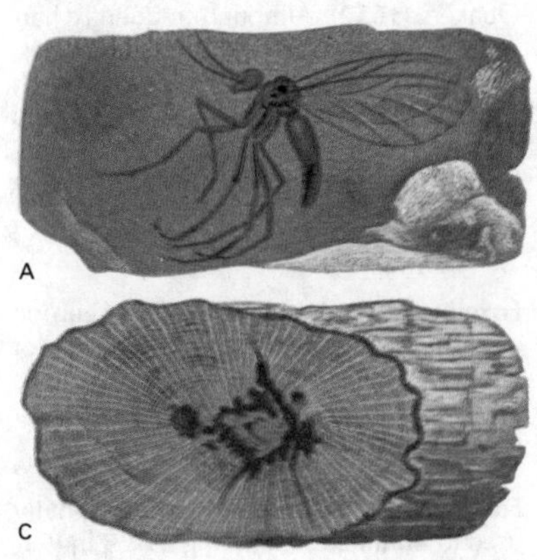

Fossils of:
A. an insect
B. a leaf
C. part of a tree
D. a shell

Fouquet, Jean (c.1420-80), French painter who helped bring the Italian Renaissance style to France. His miniatures, panels, portraits, and manuscript illuminations are realistic and precisely detailed. Among his finest works are the *Melun Diptych* (c.1450), and an illuminated Book of Hours for Étienne Chevalier.
See also: Renaissance.

Four freedoms, freedom of speech and worship and freedom from want and fear. First presented by President Roosevelt in 1941 as a basis for world peace, after World War II the freedoms became enshrined in the UN Charter.

Four Horsemen of the Apocalypse, allegorical biblical figures (Revelation 6:1-8). The red horse's rider represents war; the black's, famine; and the pale horse's, death. The rider on the white horse is usually taken to represent Christ.

Fourier, François Marie Charles (1772-1837), French Utopian socialist. Rejecting capitalism, he devised a social system based on cooperative, primarily farming communes of about 400 families. Fourierism gained considerable following in France and the United States, but attempts to put his theories into practice, as at Brook Farm, Mass., were short-lived.
See also: Socialism.

Fourier, Jean Baptiste Joseph, Baron (1768-1830), French mathematician best known for his equations of heat transmission and for showing that all periodic vibrations can be reduced to a series of simple, regular wave motions.

Fourteen Points, war objectives for the United States, proposed by President Woodrow Wilson in Jan. 1918, incorporated in the armistice of Nov. 1918. The points were that there should be open covenants of peace, freedom of the seas, abolition of trade barriers, general disarmament, settlement of colonial claims, evacuation of conquered Russian territories, evacuation and restoration of Belgium, return of Alsace-Lorraine to France, readjustment of Italian frontiers, autonomy for the subject peoples of Austria and Hungary, guarantees for the integrity of Serbia, Montenegro, and Romania, autonomy for the subject peoples of the Ottoman Empire, an independent Poland, and a general association of nations. These points formed the basis of the Treaty of Versailles and the League of Nations.
See also: Wilson, Woodrow; World War I.

Fourth of July *see:* Independence Day.

Fowl *see:* Chicken; Poultry farming.

Fowler, Henry Watson (1858-1933), English lexicographer, best known for his *A Dictionary of Modern English Usage* (1926). Fowler collaborated with his brother, Francis G. Fowler, on several reference works, including *The Concise Oxford Dictionary of Current English* (1911).

Fowles, John Robert (1926-), English novelist. His works include *The Magus* (1966; rev. version, 1978), *The French Lieutenant's Woman* (1969), and *Daniel Martin* (1977).

Fox, any of various small, bushy-tailed members of the dog family. Foxes feed mainly on small mammals and live alone or in pairs. The common red fox (*Vulpus fulva*) of the Northern Hemisphere is the quarry of British fox hunts; American foxes include the gray fox (*Urocyon cinereoargenteus*) and the desert kit fox (*Vulpus velox*). The Arctic fox (*Alopex lagopus*) lives in northern tundras and has a white winter coat. The insect-eating, bat-eared fox (*Otocyon megalotis*) is native to Africa.

Fox, Charles James (1749-1806), English statesman and orator, champion of political and religious freedom, and fierce opponent of George III and the power of the crown. Originally a Tory but later a Whig, he was elected to Parliament in 1768. He championed the colonists in the Revolutionary War (1775-83) and supported the French Revolution (1790s).

Young fox

Fox, George (1624-91), English religious leader, founder of the Society of Friends or Quakers (1652). Although frequently harassed and imprisoned by the authorities, Fox traveled widely in Europe and North America preaching his doctrine—derived from his conversion experience (1646)—that truth comes through the inner light of Christ in the soul.
See also: Quakers.

Foxglove, plant (genus *Digitalis*) of Europe and Central Asia grown for its tall stem of hanging tubular flowers. The drug digitalis is extracted from its leaves and is used as a heart stimulant.

Foxhound, medium-sized hound originally used to hunt foxes. Standing 21-25 in (53-64 cm) at the shoulder and weighing 60-70 lb (27-32 kg), the foxhound, which has short, glossy black, white, or tan hair, is recognized as a breed by the American Kennel Club.

Fox terrier, breed of small dog developed in England in the mid-1800s to flush out foxes during hunts. It measures about 15 in (38 cm) at the shoulder and weighs about 18 lb (8 kg). Two separate breeds have been developed: the wire fox terrier, with a rough, wiry white coat, often with black and brown patches, and the smooth fox terrier, with similar coloring but a smooth coat.

Foxx, James Emory (1907-67), U.S. baseball player. In a 21-season career with the Philadelphia Athletics (1925-35), the Boston Red Sox (1936-42), the Chicago Cubs (1942-44), and the Philadelphia Phillies (1945), Jimmy Foxx hit 534 home runs. His usual position was first base. He was elected to the Baseball Hall of Fame in 1951.

Fra Angelico (Guido di Pietro; 1400-55), Italian painter and Dominican friar. His church frescoes (Convent of San Marco, Florence) and altarpieces combined traditionally bright, clear colors with the new use of perspective settings. His Tuscan backgrounds are among the great Renaissance landscapes.

Fraction, in mathematics, expression representing the ratio of 2 numbers. In the fraction $^3/_4$, 4, the number after or below the bar (the *denominator*) may be thought of as the total number of equal parts into which the unit has been divided, and 3, the number before or above the bar (the *numerator*) how many parts are being considered. In decimal fractions, the division of the numerator by the denominator is computed: $^3/_4=0.75$.
See also: Mathematics.

Fracture, break of a a bone. Diagnosis is made by X ray, which shows the breakline in a bone, and the identification of swelling and localized tenderness to pressure or percussion (tapping). Depending on the size and type of the fracture, strapping, an elastic bandage, a plaster cast, or metal fixation may be necessary for healing. In *simple* fractures the bone is completely broken but there is no wound through the skin. In *compound* fractures one end of the broken bone has penetrated and torn the skin. (This type is particularly dangerous, as it allows microorganisms to enter the wound.) In *comminuted* fractures the bone has broken into several smaller pieces. In *greenstick* fractures, common in the pliable bones of the young, the break only runs part of the way across the bone. The *stress* fracture is a gradually developing fault in bone caused by repetitions of a force. This common condition has been found in practically every bone in the body and often occurs in people who take unaccustomed prolonged exercise.
See also: Bone.

Fragonard, Jean-Honoré (1732-1806), French painter. An artist who worked in the rococo style, he was a noted portraitist. His work is characterized by a lightness of touch and a use of radiant color. Among his masterpieces are *The Swing* (1766) and *Fête at St Cloud* (1775), which convey the atmosphere of erotic playfulness and gaiety cultivated at the court of Louis XV.

France (official name République Française), republic of Western Europe, the third largest country of Europe (in area) after Germany and the USSR. The capital is Paris.

Land and climate. Roughly square, France extends for about 600 mi (966 km) from Flanders to the Spanish border, and for about the same distance west to east. It borders the sea in 3 directions and has a coastline of almost 1,900 mi (3,058 km). Beyond the mainland the French Republic includes the Mediterranean island of Corsica and the overseas departments of Réunion, Guiana, Martinique, and Guadeloupe. In general, the western and northern parts of France are composed of low-lying plains and plateaus, while the eastern and southern sections are characterized by hilly or mountainous terrain. The 3 major mountain ranges are the Pyrénées, the Alps, and the *Massif Central.* There are 4 major river systems. The Rhône rises in the Swiss Alps and flows swiftly south through Provence to empty into the Mediterranean, west of Marseilles. The Garonne rises in the Pyrenees and flows through the Aquitaine Basin to empty into the Bay of Biscay through a long estuary known as the Gironde. The Seine drains most of the large Paris Basin, flowing through Paris, then goes on to Rouen and finally joins the English Channel at Le Havre. It is the most navigable of French rivers. The Loire, the longest river of France, flows from the southeastern portion of the *Massif Central* north to Orléans, then west to the Atlantic at St. Nazaire. Except for the Mediterranean coast, the climate is mild. The north and west have warm summers, mild winters, and a moderate rainfall. The Mediterranean coast has mild winters and hot summers; some areas have fewer than 50 days of rain a year.

In the northern and central regions there are forests of oak and beech, with smaller numbers of poplars and pines. The high hills south of the Loire grow heather and gorse. The roads in much of France are often planted with long lines of poplars and other trees. Oak and chestnut are common in the west and alluvial valleys. In the Massif Central area are forests of beech and chestnut. In the south the vegetation is mainly evergreen.Among forest animals are deer, martens, and badgers. The many field animals include foxes, hedgehogs, mice, rats, rabbits, and moles. Mountain species include the chamois, marmot, and ibex. Birdlife is also plentiful. The rivers and mountain streams contain many kinds of fish. Lobsters and crayfish are among the products of the Mediterranean, Biscay, and the English Channel.Among the main mineral resources of France are coal, iron ore, and bauxite (for aluminum); the bauxite reserves of central France are among the richest in the world.

People. The accessibility of France brought many invasions and a broad mingling of racial and national types including Celtic, Roman, Germanic, Scandinavian, and Basque. After about the 9th century A.D., large-scale migrations ceased, and the many peoples gradually combined to become one nation with a single language. Among the many dialects, that of the le de France (in which Paris is located) came to dominate, and became the official language in the 16th century. There are minority groups speaking other languages, including Breton in Brittany, Basque and Catalan in the southwest, Italian in Corsica and the Nice area, German in Alsace and Lorraine, and Flemish in the Dunkirk region. A great number of castles, churches,

France

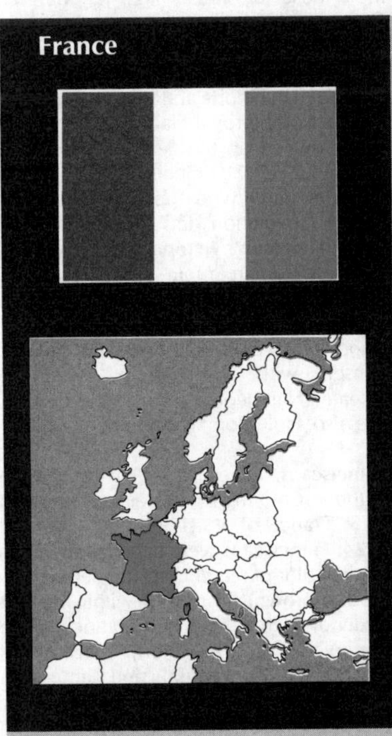

General information	
Capital:	Paris
Area:	210,026 sq mi (543,965 sq km)
Population:	56,107,000
Official language:	French
Monetary unit:	1 Franc = 100 centimes
Main cities:	Paris, Marseille, Lyon, Toulouse, Nice, Nantes, Strasbourg, Bordeaux

Government	
Form:	republic
Independent:	1871 (republic)
Head of state:	President (elected every 7 years)
Head of government:	Prime Minister
Legislature:	2 legislative houses (Senate and National Assembly)
Executive:	President and Council of Ministers
Judiciary:	highest court is the Court de Cassation
Political division:	22 regions, containing 96 departments

National economy	
Gross national product:	U.S. $898,671,000,000
Per capita income:	U.S. $16,080
Agriculture:	wheat, sugar beets, corn, barley, grapes, potatoes, apples
Livestock:	cattle, pigs, sheep, chickens
Fisheries:	844,000 metric tons
Mining:	hard coal, iron ore, salt, natural gas, zinc concentrates
Industries:	automobiles, cement, crude steel, pig iron, sulfuric acid, rubber products
Main exports:	machinery and transportation equipment, basic manufacturing, chemicals and related products, food and livestock
Transportation:	21,528 mi (34,647 km) of railroads; 500,165 mi (804,940 km) of roads; 10 international airports
Trading partners:	Germany, Italy, Belgium-Luxembourg, United Kingdom, United States, Spain

People	
Urban:	73%
Ethnic composition:	French 93%, recent immigrants (largely Mediterranean) 7%
Birth rate:	13.8 per 1,000 population
Death rate:	9.4 per 1,000 population
Infant mortality:	8 per 1,000 live births
Life expectancy:	male 71.5 years, female 79.5 years

One of the famous castles near the Loire River: Azay-le-Rideau

France: the Seine valley near La Roche Guyon

Grape cultivation for wine in France

cathedrals, parks, libraries, museums, and other cultural attractions are scattered throughout France. The nation is highly conscious of its cultural heritage, and national laws protect the more important monuments of the past. Among the best known of such institutions are the Louvre Museum and the Bibliothèque Nationale (National Library) in Paris. The theater flourishes, and many of the principal ones are subsidized by the state—for example, the Comédie Française, the Opéra Nationale, and the Opéra Comique.

Economy. France is a major agricultural and industrial country. Leading crops include wheat, oats, rye, corn, sugar beets, rice, and all kinds of fruits. Millions of beef and dairy cattle, sheep, and hogs are reared. France is an important silk producer, and it leads in the production of high-quality wines. About 30% of the land is forested. Industry includes iron and steel production, oil refining and petrochemicals, aircraft, automobiles, and textiles. Paris is the chief manufacturing center. Tourism is important, and so is the production of high- fashion clothing, gloves, perfume, jewelry, and watches.

History. Greeks founded Marseilles about 600 B.C. The country was progressively settled and unified under the Gauls, Romans, and Franks. On Charlemagne's death (A.D. 814) the Frankish Empire disintegrated and feudal rulers became powerful. Their territories were increasingly welded together under the Capetians (987-1328), and the Hundred Years War (1338-1453) saw the eviction of the English. Under Louis XI (1461-83) and later monarchs, royal power was strengthened, reaching its zenith with Louis XIV (1643-1715). Continuing royal extravagance culminated in the French Revolution (1789), the execution of Louis XVI, and the establishment of the First Republic. The Bourbon restoration following the downfall of Napoleon (1815) was short-lived, and Louis Philippe was put on the throne (July Revolution, 1830). After his deposition, Louis Napoleon headed the Second Republic (1848), then made himself Emperor Napoleon III (1852). Defeat in the Franco-Prussian War (1870) led to his downfall and to the Third Republic. World War I left France victorious but devastated, and in World War II the country was occupied by Germany (1940). The Fourth Republic (1946) proved unstable and Gen. Charles de Gaulle was recalled to head the Fifth Republic (1958). He established a strong presidential government and gave independence to most French possessions (notably Algeria, 1962). He pursued conservative policies at home and stressed greater independence from the United States in foreign policy. After de Gaulle resigned over a constitutional issue (1969), his conservative policies were maintained by his successors Georges Pompidou and Valéry Giscard d'Estaing. In 1981 François Mitterand, a Socialist, was elected president and instituted substantial changes in French domestic policy. In 1986 Conservatives won control of the Parliament, putting Jacques Chirac in office as prime minister, but Mitterand regained control in the 1988 elections. Chirac became president in 1995

France, Anatole (Jacques Anatole François Thibault; 1844-1924), French novelist and critic. Though he believed in and worked for social justice, his work is deeply pessimistic. Among his best-known books are *Penguin Island* (1908) and *The Revolt of the Angels* (1914). He won the 1921 Nobel Prize in literature.

Francesca, Piero della *see:* Piero della Francesca.

Francis, 2 kings of France. **Francis I** (1494-1547), king from 1515, strengthened royal power at the expense of the nobility. Failing in his candidacy for Holy roman emperor (1519), he conducted costly wars against the Habsburg emperor Charles V, including abortive Italian campaigns. Although he suppressed Protestantism, he fostered Renaissance ideals and was a great patron of arts and letters. He was also a great builder of palaces. **Francis II** (1544-60), king from 1559 and first husband of Mary Queen of Scots, was dominated by the House of Guise and his mother, Catherine de Medicis.

Francis II (1768-1835), last emperor of the Holy Roman Empire and ruler of Austria. A member of the royal Habsburg family, he was crowned on the death of his father, Leopold II (1792). Francis II was a conservative monarch who opposed ideas of the French Revolution and political reform. Upon Napoleon's victory in Austria (1806), the Holy Roman Empire came to an end. For political reasons, Francis II allowed his daughter, Marie-Louise, to marry Napoleon (1810), although he aligned himself with those who eventually defeated Napoleon.
See also: Holy Roman Empire.

Franciscans, largest order in the Roman Catholic Church. The order was founded by St. Francis of Assisi between 1209 and 1224. Franciscans were called Gray Friars for the color of their habits (modern habits are dark brown). Dissension within the First Order divided it into 3 main branches, the Observants (Friars Minor), Conventuals (Friars Minor Conventual), and Capuchins. The Second Order are nuns, known as Poor Clares for their foundress St. Clare. The Third Order is mainly a lay fraternity, though some members live in community under vows.

Francis de Sales, Saint (1567-1622), French nobleman, Roman Catholic bishop of Geneva-Annecy from 1603. Author of popular works such as *Introduction to the Devout Life* (1608), he was respected even by the Calvinists for his good nature and humility. He helped found the Order of the Visitation (1610). He was canonized in 1665. His feast day is Jan. 29.

Francis Ferdinand (1863-1914), Austrian archduke and heir apparent of the Austro-Hungarian throne. The assassination of the archduke and his wife, Sophie, in Sarajevo, Yugoslovia by the Serbian Gavrilo Princip precipitated the outbreak of World War I.
See also: World War I.

Francis Joseph I, or Franz Josef I (1830-1916), emperor of Austria-Hungary (1848-1916) and king of Hungary from 1867. A member of the Habsburg family. He came to the throne in a year of revolutions and was at first highly absolutist. He suppressed a Hungarian revolt in 1849, but in 1867 further unrest forced him to create the dual (Austro-Hungarian) monarchy, giving Hungary internal autonomy. Alliance with Germany (1879) and Italy (1882) created the Triple Alliance. His harsh policies against Serbia were among the causes of World War I. He was a conservative autocrat and a patron of arts and learning. His only son, Rudolph, committed suicide in 1889, and his wife Elizabeth and grand nephew and heir apparent, Francis Ferdinand, were both assassinated (1898 and 1914 respectively).
See also: Austria-Hungary; Habsburg, House of.

Francis of Assisi, Saint (1182?-1226), Italian Roman Catholic mystic, founder of the Franciscans. In 1205 he turned away from his extravagant life and wealthy merchant family and entered a religious life of utter poverty. He was given oral sanction by Pope Innocent III to form an order of friars in 1209. With his many followers Francis preached and ministered to the poor in Italy and abroad, stressing piety, simplicity, and the love of all living things. Eventually the order expanded beyond the control of its founder; Francis relinquished the leadership in 1221. His feast day is Oct. 4.
See also: Franciscans.

Francis Xavier *see:* Xavier, Saint Francis.

Saint Francis of Assisi by Giotto (13th century)

Francium, chemical element, symbol Fr; for physical constants see Periodic Table. Francium was discovered by Marguerite Perey in 1939. It is found in uranium minerals and is formed by the decay of actinium. Francium can also be produced by bombarding thorium with protons. It is the heaviest member of the alkali metal series and the most unstable of the first 101 elements. The longest lived isotope, francium-223, has a half-life of 22 minutes.

Franck, César Auguste (1822-90), Belgian-French composer. Organist of St. Clothilde, Paris, from 1858, he became a professor at the Paris Conservatory in 1872. Though at first little appreciated, his compositions greatly influenced French Romantic music. Among his famous works are the tone poem *The Accursed Hunter* (1882) and the *Symphony in D minor* (1888).

Franco, Francisco (1892-1975), Spanish general, dictator of Spain from 1939. Franco commanded Spanish troops in Spanish Morocco 1912-27, helping to suppress rebellion against colonial domination. In 1934 he helped put down a leftist revolt in Spain. After leftists won national elections in 1935, the military plotted to overthrow the government. Civil war broke out in 1936, and Franco became commander in chief and dictator of the right-wing Nationalists, supported by the fascist governments of Italy and Germany. In the post-World War II period his rule became less totalitarian, but he retained power. In the late 1960s increasing unrest caused him to harden the regime once more; he remained in control until shortly before his death, when he named Prince Juan Carlos to rule as king and successor.
See also: Spain.

Franco-Prussian War (July 1870-May 1871), war arising from Prussian premier Otto von Bismarck's desire to unify the German states against a common enemy and Napoleon III's fear of an alliance against him if a Prussian prince succeeded to the Spanish throne. Provoked by the "Ems dispatch" (Bismarck's version of French demands concerning the Spanish question), France declared war; the more efficient Prussians trapped a large French army at Metz, and in Sept. 1870 captured the main French army and Napoleon himself at Sedan. The Second Empire fell, and Paris was besieged; despite vigorous resistance led by Léon Gambetta, the city capitulated in Jan. 1871. William I of Prussia was declared German emperor at Versailles, and Germany was thus unified. In the treaty, France lost Alsace-Lorraine and incurred crushing indemnities.
See also: Bismarck, Prince Otto von; Germany.

Frank *see:* Franks.

Frank, Anne (1929-45), German born Dutch Jew who with her family lived in hiding from the Nazis in Amsterdam (1942-44). Betrayed and sent to a concentration camp, she died there of typhus. Her diary, published in 1947, provided the material for a popular play and film.
See also: Holocaust.

Frankenstein, novel by Mary Shelley (1818). In an attempt to recreate life, its title character makes a hideous, suffering creature who seeks to torment its creator. The name has become attached to the creature, particularly as portrayed in film versions more or less loosely related to the novel.
See also: Shelley, Mary Wollstonecraft.

Frankenthaler, Helen (1928-), U.S. painter whose work is considered transitional between abstract expressionism and color-field painting. She often uses stains and diluted paints to achieve her effects.

Frankfort (pop. 25,968), capital of Kentucky and seat of Franklin County, located in the bluegrass region on the Kentucky River. The city's main industry is bourbon distilling. It is also a trade center for the surrounding area, which produces grain, tobacco, and thoroughbred racehorses. The state capitol building, completed in 1910, was modeled on the U.S. Capitol in Washington, D.C. The Old Capitol (1827-30) now houses the Kentucky Historical Society. Liberty Hall (1796), designed by Thomas Jefferson, and Daniel Boone's grave are of historical interest. Incorporated in 1786 and designated state capital in 1792 when Kentucky was admitted to the Union, the city has a council-manager government.
See also: Kentucky.

Frankfurt (pop. 595,300), city in central Germany, on the Main River. A major transportation center, it is one of the busiest European inland ports, with a large airport and a sophisticated network of highways and railroads. It was the original home of the Rothschild family and remains a banking and commerce center. A Roman fort, it became a Frankish settlement in A.D. 500, and flourished under the Holy Roman Empire. It was rebuilt after being heavily bombed by Allied forces in World War II. The birthplace of Goethe, it is a center of cultural and intellectual activity.
See also: Germany.

Frankfurter, Felix (1882-1965), U.S. Supreme Court justice (1939-62), legal adviser to presidents Woodrow Wilson and Franklin D. Roosevelt. He advocated the doctrine of judicial restraint, minimizing the judiciary's role in the process of government; he was equally opposed to attempts to obstruct "progressive" legislation and to attempts to further it by undue interpretation.
See also: Supreme Court of the United States.

Franklin, Benjamin (1706-90), U.S. printer, publisher, writer, politician, economist, scientist, statesman, and diplomat. At the start of his career he made his fortune as a publisher and printer and derived substantial revenue from writing his famous Poor Richard's almanacs (pub-

César Franck

Francisco Franco as a young general at the beginning of the Spanish Civil War (1936-39)

Benjamin Franklin

lished annually between 1732 and 1757). As a writer, however, he is best revealed in his personal letters, journals, and autobiography, where he appears the most pragmatic of idealists, the most haphazard of scientists, and, most particularly, a witty and cynical observer of society. As a scientist, Franklin had practical ingenuity and produced bifocals and the Franklin stove. His main contributions to pure science were experiments with electricity. His famous experiment with the key and kite during an electrical storm, which confirmed that lightning was actually electricity, is typical of his genius. While realizing the tremendous implications of his discovery, he left most of the unraveling of his theories to others, while he himself produced the eminently practical lightning rod. In 1736 Franklin became the clerk of the Pennsylvania State Assembly and began gradually to give up the management of his business concerns to devote his full time to public service, writing, and scientific inquiry. In 1753 he was made deputy postmaster general of the colonies. In 1754 he gave his support to the British colonial effort against the French in the French and Indian Wars, organizing a volunteer army and supervising the construction of a fort in frontier Pennsylvania. In July 1757 he was sent to England to represent the colony of Pennsylvania. There he made a spectacular showing before the House of Commons, successfully arguing for repeal of the hated Stamp Act. Impressed by his achievements, the colonies of Georgia, New Jersey, and Massachusetts also decided to retain him as their agent. He continued to represent colonial causes in England until after the battles of Lexington and Concord, when he saw that there was no hope of reconciliation between England and America and returned home. There he joined the second Continental Congress, serving on the committee that drafted the Declaration of Independence. He was sent to France in 1776 to plead for support, and was instrumental in winning the military support of Lafayette and others. He was appointed minister to France in 1778. Returning to Philadelphia in 1787, he was an influential figure in the drafting of the Constitution.

Franklin, John Hope (1915-), black U.S. historian, educator, and author of books on African American history, including *From Slavery to Freedom* (1947), *The Emancipation Proclamation* (1963), and *Racial Equality in America* (1976).

Franklin, Rosalind Elsie (1920-58), British chemist and biologist. Her contributions, including information leading to the construction of a deoxyribonucleic acid (DNA) model (1953), made use of X-ray diffraction technique.
See also: Biology; Deoxyribonucleic acid.

Franklin, Sir John (1786-1847), British rear admiral and Arctic explorer. In expeditions during 1819-22 and 1825-27 he charted territory from Hudson Bay North to the Arctic. He set out in 1845 with 2 ships to find the Northwest Passage; trapped in the ice, the entire expedition perished and was not traced until 1859.
See also: Northwest Passage.

Franklin, State of, area between Tennessee and North Carolina, organized between 1784 and 1788, but never admitted as a state. Controlled by North Carolina in 1788, Franklin became part of Tennessee in 1789, and John Sevier, who had governed Franklin, became Tennessee's first governor.
See also: Sevier, John.

Franklin's gull (*Larus pipixcan*), insect-eating land-based bird. It spends summers on the prairies of North America and winters in Louisiana and South America. The Franklin's gull is about 14 in (36 cm) long and is white and gray.

Franks, Germanic tribes, originally living east of the Rhine. In the 3rd-5th centuries A.D. they repeatedly invaded Gaul and finally overran it (486). Clovis I united the disparate tribes under his rule, founding the Christian Merovingian dynasty; this was weakened by internal conflict, and finally deposed by the Carolingians in the 8th century. Under the rule of Charlemagne the Franks reached the height of their power. France and Franconia in Germany are named for them.

Franz Josef Land, group of 85 islands in the Arctic Ocean. Northernmost land in the Eastern Hemisphere, these islands, which were discovered in 1873, were claimed by the Soviet Union in 1926. They cover about 8,000 sq mi (21,000 sq km), and are uninhabited. Temperatures range from an average of 10°F (–12°C) or more in the summer to an average of –22°F (–30°C) in the winter.

Fraser, Douglas Andrew (1916-), U.S. labor leader. Born in Glasgow, Scotland, Fraser became an auto worker in Detroit at age 18. He was president of the United Automobile Workers union from 1977 until 1983. In 1980 he was elected to the board of directors of Chrysler, the first union leader to be elected to the board of a U.S. firm.

Fraser, John Malcolm (1930-), Australian prime minister (1975-83). First elected to Parliament in 1955, he served in various posts in Liberal Party governments, 1966-71. In 1975 he became Liberal leader and later prime minister. His party easily won reelection in 1977. He pursued a policy of cutbacks in public expenditures in order to halve the inflation rate; however, a high unemployment rate continued in the country.

Fraser River, river in British Columbia, 850 mi (1,370 km) long, named for Simon Fraser, who explored it in 1808. It is famous for its salmon fisheries, and is an important shipping route. The Fraser rises in the Rocky Mountains, flows between the Rocky and Caribou ranges, then turns south and west to empty into the Georgia Strait south of Vancouver. It is navigable for about 90 mi (145 km) from its mouth.

Fraud, in law, any willful action intended to cheat another person by false pretenses or misrepresentation. The remedy granted to someone who can prove fraud is either compensatory damages or cancellation of the fraudulent contract.

Fraunces Tavern, historic building in New York City located at the corner of Broad and Pearl streets. The former De Lancey mansion, it was purchased in 1762 by Samuel Fraunces, a West Indian, and became the Queen's Head Tavern. Before the American Revolution it was a meeting place for patriotic groups, including the Sons of Liberty. George Washington said farewell to his officers here in 1783.

Frazer, Sir James George (1854-1941), British social anthropologist. In *The Golden Bough: A Study in Magic and Religion* (1890; enlarged 1907-15) he proposed a parallel evolution of thought in all peoples, from magic through religion to science, each mode of thought with its distinct notion of cause and effect.
See also: Anthropology.

Frazier, Edward Franklin (1894-1962), black U.S. sociologist and writer. Frazier received his Ph.D. from the University of Chicago. He headed the sociology department of Howard University for 25 years. His books include *The Free Negro Family* (1932), *The Negro Family in the United States* (1939), and *Black Bourgeoisie* (1957).

Freckle, small area of skin pigmentation, usually occurring on the face, arms, and hands. Freckles are most frequently found in fair-skinned blonds and redheads because the pigment cells in their skin respond only slightly and irregularly to sunlight. The tendency to form freckles is often inherited.

Frederick, name of 3 Holy Roman Emperors. **Frederick I Barbarossa** (1123?-90) was elected king of Germany in 1152. Having pacified Germany, where he promoted learning, primary and secondary ed-

ucational systems, and economic growth, he occupied Lombardy and was crowned king of Italy in 1154 and Holy Roman emperor in 1155. He was drowned while leading the Third Crusade, and passed into legend as Germany's savior. **Frederick II** (1194-1250) became king of Sicily in 1198 and of Germany in 1211. He was crowned Holy Roman emperor in 1220. Made titular king of Jerusalem in 1227, he acquired territory in the Holy Land and was crowned in 1229. He was continually at odds with the papacy and was excommunicated 3 times. A capable administrator, scholar, and patron of the arts, he went into a decline after a serious defeat at Parma in 1248. **Frederick III** (1415-93) was chosen king of Germany in 1440 and obtained election as Holy Roman emperor in 1452 by making concessions to the papacy, weakening the empire.
See also: Holy Roman Empire.

Frederick, name of 3 kings of Prussia. **Frederick I** (1657-1713), elector of Brandenburg from 1688, sought the title of king from the Emperor Leopold I. In 1700 he obtained it in exchange for military assistance and in 1701 he crowned himself king of Prussia, which was the major part of his domain. **Frederick II (the Great)** (1712-86) was one of the most influential 18th-century monarchs. As a boy his inclinations were artistic rather than military. He succeeded his father Frederick William I, in 1740. He almost immediately used his father's strong army to win Silesia from Austria, thus precipitating the War of the Austrian Succession. There followed a period of peace, which he used to strengthen Prussia, encouraging both arts and commerce. Fearing attack by an alliance of Austria, Russia, and France, he made a preemptive attack on Saxony in 1756, beginning the Seven Years War, from which Prussia emerged unscathed but exhausted. Frederick rebuilt the economy at considerable personal expense. Through the partition of Poland and the War of the Bavarian Succession he made further territorial gains for Prussia. By the end of his reign he had doubled the country's area and left it rich, powerful, more humanely governed, and dominant in Germany. **Frederick III** (1831-88), son of Emperor William I, was cultivated and liberal. A distinguished army commander, he was a determined opponent of Bismarck's imperial policies. He died of cancer only 3 months after his coronation.
See also: Prussia.

Frederick the Great *see:* Frederick II of Prussia.

Frederick William (1620-88), elector of Brandenburg from 1640, known as the Great Elector. By skillful shifting of alliances in an attempt to establish a balance of power, he was able to shield his country from the worst of the Thirty Years War and add Prussia to Brandenburg (1660). This and the modern army he created laid the foundations for the country's future predominance in Germany.

Frederick William I (1688-1740), king of Prussia from 1713. He centralized and radically reformed his administration. He spent freely on building up a powerful army but was otherwise frugal to the point of miserliness.
See also: Prussia.

Fredericton (pop. 44,400), capital of New Brunswick province in eastern Canada, on the St. John River. Founded by the British in 1762 and named after Prince Frederick, son of King George III, Fredericton became the provincial capital in 1785.
See also: New Brunswick.

Frederik, or **Frederick**, name of Danish kings, including 2 of the House of Schleswig-Holstein-Sonderburg-Glücksburg. **Frederik VIII** (1843-1912) was born in Copenhagen and ruled from the time of his father's death in 1906 until his own death. His sister was Queen Alexandra of England and his brother was King George I of Greece. **Frederik IX** (1899-1972) was married to Princess Ingrid of Sweden, spent 35 years as a crown prince, then ruled as king of Denmark from 1947 until his death.

Freedmen's Bureau, U.S. Bureau of Refugees, Freedmen, and Abandoned Lands (1865-72), established during Reconstruction to act as a welfare agency for freed slaves in the South. It was headed by Major O.O. Howard. Handicapped by inadequate funding and personnel, the bureau nevertheless built hospitals, schools, and colleges for African Americans. It had little success in improving civil rights, due to judicial and congressional hostility; its influence had declined by the time it was dissolved.
See also: Reconstruction.

Freedom of Information Act (FOIA), act giving the public right of access to governmental records. Enacted in 1966 and strengthened in 1974, FOIA provides that agencies must respond to requests for information within 10 working days; appeals are supposed to be settled in another 20. Most requests under the act come from businesses seeking information in governmental files about their competitors. Some records are exempted from the act, including confidential files of law enforcement and intelligence agencies and information gained by the Federal Trade Commission through subpoenas. In 1981 the Reagan administration proposed that such exemptions be broadened.
See also: Sunshine laws.

Free enterprise system *see:* Capitalism.

Freemasonry *see:* Masonry.

Free Methodist Church, U.S. denomination founded in 1860 by members excluded from the Methodist Episcopal Church for trying to restore Wesleyan principles. This church follows the teachings of John Wesley.

Free-piston engine, engine that produces hot gas, which is used to run turbines. It was invented in the 1920s by the Spanish engineer, Pateras Pescara. Able to burn almost any liquid fuel, this engine has facing pairs of pistons that move back and forth from the fuel ignition and resulting air compression.

Freesia, sweet-scented flowering plant (genus *Freesia*) of the iris family, originating in South Africa. The flowers, which are most often white, yellow, or purple, grow in clusters on long stalks.

Freesia

Free silver, 19th-century U.S. political movement attempting to boost the price of silver, which had been hit by world prices and demonetization in 1873. People believed that having more money in circulation would lessen their debts with cheaper dollars. After the 1893 depression (which it helped precipitate) free silver became the major issue of the 1896 and 1900 presidential campaigns of William Jennings Bryan.
See also: Bryan, William Jennings; Populism.

Frederick II (the Great)

Free Soil Party, short-lived U.S. coalition party formed in New York in 1848 to oppose the extension of slavery into the territories gained after the Mexican-American War. It attracted many famous men, including President Martin Van Buren, who was its first presidential candidate, but polled few votes in the 1848 and 1852 elections, and the party merged with the Republican Party in 1854.

Freethinker, person who does not accept religious dogma. The English philosopher Anthony Collins used the word in *Discourse of Freethinking* (1713), an argument against the authority of the church. Freethinking movements were active in 18th-century England, Germany, and France. The necessity for such movements diminished with the establishment of freedom of religion.

Free trade, international commerce, free from tariffs, quotas, or other legal restrictions, except nonrestrictive tariffs levied for revenue only. The opposite of free trade is protectionism. Among early advocates of free trade were the physiocrats, Adam Smith, David Ricardo, and J.S. Mill. Modern economists generally accept free trade but advocate varying degrees of protection to safeguard employment and developing industries, as in the theories of J.M. Keynes. The United States had traditionally been protectionist but after World War II became committed to free trade.

Free verse (from French *vers libre*), verse without conventional rhythm or meter, relying instead upon the cadences of the spoken language. It was first developed in 19th-century France as a reaction to the extreme formality of accepted styles. Among its exponents in English are Walt Whitman, D.H. Lawrence, Ezra Pound, and T.S. Eliot.

Freeze-drying, or lyophilization, process that removes water from foods, drugs, and other substances, preserving the items for later use. Unlike other food-drying processes, the costly freeze-drying method freezes the items, then changes any frozen moisture into water vapor in refrigerated vacuum chambers. Freeze-dried substances retain most of their original characteristics, do not shrink, and are easily dissolvable.

Frege, Gottlob (1848-1925), German logician, father of mathematical logic. Inspired by the earlier work of Leibniz, he tried to show that all mathematical truths could be derived logically from a few simple axioms. After criticism that his system contradicted itself, he wrote little more. However, his work did influence later philosophers such as Bertrand Russell and Ludwig Wittgenstein.
See also: Logic.

Frémont, John Charles (1813-90), U.S. explorer, general, politician, and popular hero. He mapped much of the territory between the Mississippi valley and the Pacific during the early 1840s. He was caught up in the struggle with Mexico over California, being appointed military governor but later convicted of mutiny (1847-48), a sentence commuted by President James Polk. Frémont stood as the Republican Party's first presidential candidate (1856) but was defeated by James Buchanan. He had to resign as commander of the Department of the West during the Civil War for exceeding his office by declaring martial law. He was governor of Arizona territory 1878-83.

French *see:* French language.

French, Daniel Chester (1850-1931), U.S. sculptor. He is best known for his monumental statuary, such as his first work, *The Minute Man* (1875), in Concord, Mass., and the seated *Lincoln* (1922) in the Lincoln Memorial, Washington, D.C.

French, John Denton Pinkstone, 1st Earl of Ypres (1852-1925), British field marshal, commander of the British Expeditionary Force at the beginning of World War I. He was relieved of his command after the costly retreat from Mons and the battles of Ypres and Loos (1914-15).

French Academy *see:* Académie Française.

French and Indian wars, conflict over control of North America that erupted into a series of wars involving England and its North American colonies against France and the colony of New France: King William's War (1689-97), Queen Anne's War (1702-13), King George's War (1744-48), and the French and Indian War (1754-63). In Europe these wars are known, respectively, as the War of the League of Augsburg, the War of the Spanish Succession, the War of the Austrian Succession, and the Seven Years War, but Americans generally use these names only for the European phase of each war. All of these wars combined the struggle for specific North American territories between France and Britain with their battle for world power. In each struggle the French lost some territory, and in the last war they were forced entirely out of the North American mainland.
The dispute that erupted in 1754 concerned rival French and English claims to the upper Ohio Valley. Both French and English fur trading was expanding, and territories were not clearly marked, so disputes became increasingly frequent. In 1748 the Ohio Company, formed by English colonists from Virginia and Maryland, claimed the Ohio region, which was occupied by the French. The French reacted by harassment of English traders and by constructing forts along the Allegheny. In 1753 George Washington was sent to warn the French that they were trespassing and to bring about their withdrawal. His mission was ineffective, and the Ohio Company began to build a fort on the present site of Pittsburgh. The French arrived before the fort was completed, and Washington withdrew to Fort Necessity. In 1754 he was forced to surrender this position. England's George II finally ordered General Edward Braddock to help the colonies. In July 1755 Braddock was ambushed and defeated near Fort Duquesne. After repeated French victories, William Pitt began the reorganization of the British forces in America. He strengthened the navy and recruited men like Lord Jeffrey Amherst and James Wolfe. In 1758 Louisbourg fell to Amherst, and forts Frontenac and Duquesne were forced to surrender. In 1759 forts Niagara and Ticonderoga and Crown Point fell. Finally on Sept. 13, 1759, General Wolfe, at the cost of his life, defeated the French near Quebec City, which surrendered on Sept. 17. Montreal surrendered in Sept. 1760. After the fall of Spanish Havana to the British forces in 1762, the Treaty of Paris was negotiated and signed in Feb. 1763. France gave up Canada and the lands east of the Mississippi to England. New Orleans and the French territory of Louisiana west of the Mississippi were transferred by Britain to Spain, in exchange for British possession of Spanish Florida.

French Canada *see:* Canada; Quebec.

French Canadians *see:* Canada; Canadian literature; Quebec.

French Equatorial Africa, 4 territories in Central Africa that were colonized by France in 1839 and became the independent countries of Gabon, Chad, Congo, and Central African Republic in 1960. Covering an area of about 969,000 sq mi (2.5 million sq km), these countries are rich in timber, minerals, farming, and livestock.

French Foreign Legion *see:* Foreign Legion.

French Guiana, French overseas department on the northeast coast of South America. It is bounded by Surinam on the west and Brazil on the east and south, and consists of a strip of lowland along the 200-mi (322-km) Atlantic coastline and a hilly interior stretching about 225 mi (363 km) inland. Its economy rests on the timber trade from its massive forests and on shrimp fishing. It was made an overseas department in 1947. The chief city is Cayenne.

French Guinea *see:* Guinea; French West Africa.

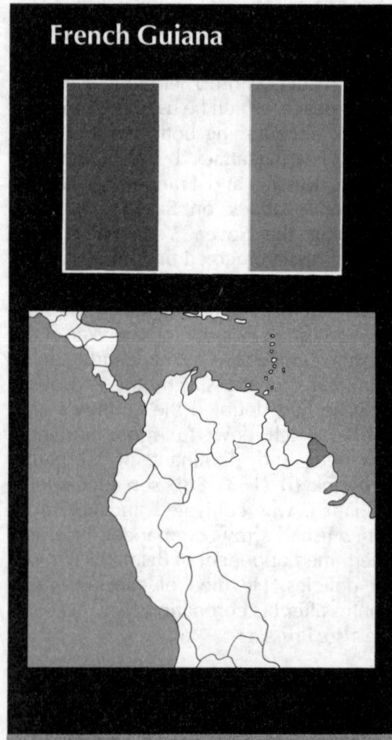

Capital:	Cayenne
Area:	33,399 sq mi (86,504 sq km)
Population:	95,000
Government:	overseas department (administrative district) of France
GNP:	U.S. $176,000,000
Per capita:	U.S. $2,130

French horn, musical horn instrument. Its circular shape, created by coiled brass, opens into a bell. Musical notes are created as the musician blows into the mouth piece, presses one or more of the three valves with one hand while the other hand creates sound effects by its placement in the bell. This horn was introduced into orchestras shortly after its invention in the mid-17th century. The original, valveless version of this horn was used for hunting.

French language, Romance language spoken in France and parts of Belgium, Switzerland, Canada, and former French and Belgian colonies; it is the official language of 21 countries. It developed from Latin during and after the Roman occupation of Gaul and also from Celtic and Germanic elements. By the 11th century 2 dialects had developed: in the south the *langue d'oc*, in the north the *lange d'öil*. From the latter came *francien*, the Paris dialect that became modern French, spoken and written since the 17th century.

French literature, poetry, prose, and drama written by authors of France in standard modern French, as well as works in the medieval French dialects, in Breton, and in Provençal. French literature has exerted a strong influence on the writers of many nations, right up to the present.
Medieval French literature. Provençal, the language of the south of France, seems to be the first vernacular language used in French commerce and literature. It drew on elements of Latin and Arabic and flourished during the 11th and 12th centuries, when troubadours (musicians/poets) composed love songs. The form traveled to northern France, where it was imitated by the *trouvères*. In addition, *jongleurs* (itinerant poets and entertainers) popularized such songs throughout France and Norman England. François Villon (b.1431?) was the most remarkable medieval lyric poet.
The *jongleurs* and *trouvères* also developed epics and romances. The *chansons de geste* were epics that concentrated on a particular hero, the best known being the *Song of Roland* (c.1100). Romances were based on classical themes (e.g., the Trojan War) or on the Celtic legends of Breton (the Arthurian cycle). Chrétien de Troye's *Lancelot* (late 12th century) is a prime example. The allegorical romance, a symbolic story, also developed about this time. The greatest of these is the *Romance of the Rose* (c.mid-12th century). Prose was confined to historical chronicles, while drama developed in the mystery plays (depicting scenes from Scripture), miracle plays (about the saints and the Virgin Mary), and morality plays (meant to educate).
Renaissance French literature. The outstanding writer of the French Renaissance was François Rabelais (c.1490-1553). His 2 great prose narratives, *Gargantua* and *Pantagruel* (1532-52), are large, sprawling, often ribald works that satirize and comment on serious questions pertaining to education, politics, religion, and certain social institutions of the day. *La Pléiade* (c.1553) were a group of 7 poets, led by Pierre de Ronsard, who encouraged writing poetry in French rather than Latin and sought to create a French literature equal to other literatures. Michel Montaigne (1533-92) was the last of the major French renaissance writers. He wrote several books of essays on a wide range of subjects. They are written in an informal, conversational style, but they reveal a sophisticated, skeptical, urbane mind. They have been widely read since their publication (late 16th century), and they greatly influenced English literature.
Classical French literature. During the 17th century, French literature enjoyed a golden age. French classicism was manifest in the 3 great dramatists, Pierre Corneille (*Polyeucte*, 1642), Jean Racine (*Andromaque*, 1667), and Molière (*Tartuffe*, 1664-69). The works of these playwrights still hold the stage today in France and in many other countries as well.
The philosophers René Descartes (*Discourse on Method*, 1637) and Blaise Pascal (*Pensées*, 1670) wrote clear, elegant prose that typified classical thought. Descartes was influential in furthering rationalist thinking while Pascal examined closely his deep commitment to the Christian religion, especially as embodied in the Jansenist sect. Pascal was also a mathematician and scientist (Pascal's Law on the properties of liquids). Madame de La Fayette's *The Princess of Cleves* (1678) was one of the first French novels; it is still read for its psychological analysis and its fine style.
Classical French poetry began with the poet/critic François de Malherbe. His critical works, especially, influenced French literature, as he was a consistent advocate of precise language, objectivity, and serious intent in all literary endeavor, all of which became the hallmarks of French classicism. Other writers of this period include the historian Jacques Boussuet, La Rochefoucauld, La Fontaine, Madame de Sévigné, and La Bruyère. In addition, during this period Richelieu founded the Académie Français (1634).
French literature and the Age of Reason. The Age of Reason (18th century) saw some of its most influential political and philosophical writing come from France. The rationalist satires of Voltaire (*Candide*, 1759) and the enormous *Encyclopédie* (1751-72), compiled under Denis Diderot, are prime examples of the period's sense that truth could be obtained mainly through reason. Other notable writers of the time included Charles Montesquieu, whose social commentaries affected the makers of the American Revolution; the playwrights Pierre Beaumarchais and Pierre Marivaux; and the novelists Alain René Lasage and the Abbé Prévost.
French literature and romanticism. Tow ards the end of the 18th century, a new sensibility took hold, due in part to the upheavals of the French Revolution. Jean Jacques Rousseau (*Confessions*, 1764-70) was a precursor of the movement in that he emphasized the primacy of feeling over reason and valued spontaneity over self-discipline. François René de Chateaubriand and Madame de Staël also heralded the romantic emphasis on feeling and self by the end of the century. The great figures of 19th-century French romantic literature were Victor Hugo (*Les Misérables*, 1862), a poet, dramatist, and novelist, and the poet Alphonse de Lamartine (*Poetic Meditations*, 1820). Other major romantic writers included Alfred de Vigny, Alfred de Musset, and Alexandre Dumas *père* (*The Three Musketeers*, 1844) and Dumas *fils* (*Camille*, 1852).
Some writers of the period mixed romantic sensibility with a more realistic depiction of the human condition. Among them were Honoré de Balzac (*The Human Comedy*, 1842-48, a collection of almost 100 novels and stories); George Sand, (*The Haunted Pool*, 1846); and Stendhal (*The Red and the Black*, 1831).
French literature and realism/naturalism. By the mid-19th century, the movement toward depicting life realistically, honestly, and objectively had begun to supplant the romantic sensibility. The novels of Gustave Flaubert (*Madame Bovary*, 1857), Émile Zola, and the brothers Goncourt are major examples. Other writers included Guy de Maupassant, Prosper Mérimée, and Alphonse Daudet; playwrights Eugène Scribe and Henri Becque; and critics Charles Sainte-Beuve and Hippolyte Taine.
French literature and symbolism. Late in the 19th century, a group of poets turned against both romanticism and realism/naturalism to write prose whose aim was to suggest meaning through impressions and intuition rather than by objective description. Known as *symbolists*, these poets included Charles Baudelaire (*Flowers of Evil*, 1857), Stéphane Mallarmé (*Afternoon of a Faun*, 1876), Paul Verlaine (*Songs Without Words*, 1874), and Arthur Rimbaud (*A Season in Hell*, 1873).
French literature in the 20th century. Early-20th-century French literature was dominated by 4 figures: André Gide, Paul Claudel, Marcel Proust, and Paul Valéry. Also important at this time was the devel-

French Guiana: St-Laurent du Maroni

opment of surrealism, an ill-defined movement that placed emphasis on randomness and unconscious thought processes. Surrealism was manifest notably in the poetry of Guillaume Apollinaire and, later, in that of René Char and Louis Aragon.
During World War II a school of philosophy called *existentialism* became a rallying point for French writers, especially Jean-Paul Sartre (*No Exit,* 1944). Allied with him were several writers who also emphasized involvement with the moral and social problems of the day. These included Albert Camus (*The Stranger,* 1942), Simone de Beauvoir (*The Mandarins,* 1955), and, to a certain extent, Jean Genet, who wrote plays (*The Maids,* 1948) and autobiographical prose works. Both Sartre and Camus wrote plays as well as novels. Other significant playwrights of the mid-20th century included Jean Anouilh, Jean Giraudoux, and Jean Cocteau. Later in the century came Theater of the Absurd, primarily evidenced in the works of Samuel Beckett and Eugène Ionesco, neither of whom were French-born but wrote in the language. The New Novel (*nouveau roman*) turned away from traditional concerns of the novel with plot and character to depictions of the characters' internal reactions to the outside world. Writeıs of these experimental novels included Alain Robbe-Grillet, Nathalie Sarraute, Michel Butor, and Claude Simon. Recent feminist writers include Marguerite Duras and Hélène Cixous.

French Morocco *see:* Morocco.

French Polynesia, French territory in the South Pacific that includes Tahiti, one of the Society Islands. The island groups in the territory include the Austral, Gambier, Marquesas, Society, and the Tuamotu. The capital city in the territory is Papeete, Tahiti. The peoples of these islands, which lie 2,800 mi (4,500 k) south of Hawaii, are mainly Polynesian. The economy of the islands is based on farming, fishing, and tourism. The official language is French.

French Quarter *see:* New Orleans.

French Revolution, first European revolution in modern times, (1789-99). Through its wars, the revolution spread the explosive ideas of the sovereignty of the people, liberty of the individual, and equality before the law. By 1788 in a time of the rise of the middle classes, the country was still ruled by the privileged nobility and clergy, the 2 upper Estates of the States-General. The tax burden fell on the Third Estate, made up of the middle classes and the landowning peasantry; it was further increased by the corruption of the fiscal system. When the nobility thwarted attempts by the royal ministers such as the popular director of finances, Jacques Necker, to reform government finance, the king was forced to summon the Estates-General; when the Third Estate, which outnumbered the other 2 chambers, was not given a majority, it declared itself the National Assembly (June 20, 1789). When Louis XVI

In October 1789, when the people organized a march to Versailles, the heads of some of the officers of the Royal Guard were triumphantly carried by the demonstrators.

accepted the National Assembly but dismissed Necker, crowds stormed the Bastille prison on July 14 and pillaged the nobility's country estates. The royal family fled in June, hoping to join their sympathizers, who had fled abroad, but they were arrested at Varennes and returned to Paris. On Aug. 4 the Assembly abolished the feudal system and approved the Declaration of the Rights of Man; the royal family was threatened by mobs; the Church, disestablished and largely suppressed. In Oct. 1791 the Legislative Assembly convened under a new constitution and became increasingly radical. Threat of attack from abroad by émigrés and their foreign supporters precipitated the French Revolutionary Wars. In the face of this crisis the mob again threatened the king, forcing him to replace the Assembly with the radical National Convention, elected in Sept. 1792, during mob massacres of jailed royalists. The First Republic was established, and the king was tried for treason and executed in Jan. 1793. In the face of royalist insurrection and foreign hostility the Jacobins seized power from the more moderate Girondins, transferring power from the Convention to arbitrary bodies such as the Committees for Public Safety and General Security. Dominated by Georges-Jacques Danton and Maximilien Robespierre, these brought about the Reign of Terror, during which France became a police state and all were threatened with execution for the mere suspicion of disloyalty. This ended with Robespierre's execution by the Convention in July 1794. The Convention then introduced a new constitution, setting up the Directory, which proved ineffectual and corrupt. In 1799 it was overthrown by the army, led by the popular general Napoleon Bonaparte. He established the Consulate, effectively ending the revolutionary period.

French Somaliland *see:* Djibouti.

French Southern and Antarctic Territories, island possessions of France in the Indian Ocean and along a coastal portion of Antarctica. Covering an area of 3,300 sq mi (7,770 sq km), the territories include the Kerguelen and Crozet archipelagos, the islands of Saint Paul and Amsterdam, and the Adélie Coast of Antarctica. The area is inhabited by penguins, seals, and whales. Scientists live in the region to conduct research.

French West Africa, federation of 8 French overseas territories, 1895-1959. Its members were Dahomey (now Benin), French Guinea (now Guinea), Ivory Coast, Mauritania, Niger, Senegal, Sudan (now Mali), and Upper Volta (now Burkina Faso), now independent countries.

French West Indies, Caribbean islands of Martinique and Guadeloupe, French colonies until 1946.

Freneau, Philip (1752-1832), U.S. journalist and poet. His poem "The British Prison Ship" (1781) was inspired by his experiences after being captured while running the British blockade. Other poems included "The Wild Honeysuckle" (1786) and "The Indian Burying Ground" (1788). Freneau was also the editor (1791-93) of the *National Gazette,* an anti-Federalist Party newspaper.

Freon *see:* Fluorocarbon.

Frequency band, or waveband, radio frequency range assigned to a broadcasting station by the Federal Communications Commission. TV and AM and FM radio stations, as well as those for commercial or government (e.g., police, amateur, and airplane radio), are given specific numerical frequency ranges in *kilohertz* (1,000 cycles per second) to prevent stations from interfering in each other's broadcasts.
See also: Radio.

Frequency modulation, one of two chief methods of sending sound signals on radio waves. More commonly referred to as FM, the frequency of a radio wave is adjusted higher or lower to match sound vibrations. This kind of signal may also be transmitted along two paths, or channels, to provide stereo broadcasting to a listener who has the appropriate radio receiver. Invented by Edwin H. Armstrong in 1933, FM is also used in television and long-distance telephone systems.
See also: Radio.

Fresco, painting dry earth pigments mixed with water on fresh, wet lime plaster. Fresco painting began with the Etruscans and Romans and was used extensively in Europe during the Middle Ages and the Renaissance. Michelangelo's fresco decoration of the Sistine Chapel is a famous example of the technique. Among modern masters it has been used in Mexico by José Orozco and Diego Rivera.

Freud, Anna (1895-1982), Austrian-born British pioneer of child psychoanalysis. Her book *The Ego and Mechanisms of Defense* (1936) is a major contribution to the field. After escaping with her father, Sigmund Freud, from Nazi-occupied Austria (1938), she established an influential child therapy clinic in London.
See also: Psychoanalysis.

Freud, Sigmund (1856-1939), Austrian neurologist, author, psychiatrist, and founder of almost all the basic concepts of psychoanalysis. He graduated with an M.D. from the University of Vienna in 1881, and for some months in 1885 he studied under J.M. Charcot, whose work in hysteria converted Freud to the cause of psychiatry. Dissatisfied with hypnosis and electrotherapy as treatment techniques, he evolved the psychoanalytic method, founded on dream analysis and free association. Because of his belief that sexual impulses lay at the heart of neuroses, he was reviled professionally for a decade, but by 1906 disciples like Alfred Adler and Carl Gustav Jung were gathering around him (both were later to break away from the International Psychoanalytic Association, dissenting with Freud's views on infantile sexuality). For some 30 years he worked to establish the truth of his theories, and these years were especially fruitful. Fleeing Nazi anti-Semitism, he left Vienna for London in 1938 and there spent the last year of his life.
See also: Psychoanalysis.

Sigmund Freud and his wife-to-be, Martha Bernays (1885)

Frey, in Scandinavian mythology, god of fertility, sunshine, and rain. Like his sister Freya, the goddess of love, he was associated with the return of spring. Particularly venerated by the Swedes, his chief temple was at Uppsala.
See also: Mythology.

Friars Minor *see:* Franciscans.

Frick, Henry Clay (1849-1919), U.S. industrialist and art collector. He started a business in coke (coal byproduct used in metal refining) in 1868, and in 1882 he became an associate of Andrew Carnegie, managing his steel company 1889-99. He bequeathed his extensive art collection, housed in his New York mansion, to the public as a museum.

Friction, resistance to motion arising at the boundary between two touching surfaces. As the force applied increases, equal force of static friction opposes it, reaching a maximum limiting friction just before sliding begins. Lubrication is used to overcome friction in machine bearings.

Friedan, Betty (1921-), U.S. feminist leader and author. Her book *The Feminine Mystique* (1963) challenged attitudes that had led women to become housewives and mothers at the expense of more ambitious careers. She was founding president of the National Organization for Women (1966-70) and helped organize the National Women's Political Caucus (1971). *It Changed My Life* (1976) concerns her participation in the women's movement; *The Second Stage* (1981) charts the movement's course.
See also: National Organization for Women.

Friedman, Milton (1912-), U.S. economist, proponent of the monetarist theory, which regards the money supply as the central controlling factor in economic development. A professor at the University of Chicago from 1946, he has written *A Monetary History of the U.S.: 1867-1960* (1963) and *Free to Choose* (1980; with Rose Friedman), a defense of free market capitalism. He was awarded the 1976 Nobel Prize in economic science.

Friends, Society of *see:* Quakers.

Frigatebird, any of a family (Fregatidae) of large seabirds with long pointed wings, forked tails, and weak legs. They are superb fliers and spend most of their lives in the air, feeding by snatching fish from the water, picking up baby turtles from the beach, and stealing the food of other birds. They breed in tropical seas. During the mating season, the male has a red throat pouch that may be inflated, for display, to the size of a human head.

Friml, (Charles) Rudolf (1879-1972), Czech-born U.S. composer of operettas and film scores. His best-known works include *The Firefly* (1912), *Rose Marie* (1924), and *The Vagabond King* (1925).

Fringe tree, tree of the olive family named for its fringe-shaped, white flower petals. This tree, which reaches a height of 35 ft (11 m), grows wild from the east coast of the United States to Missouri, and in China.

Frisch, Karl von (1886-1984), Austrian zoologist best known for his studies of bee behavior, perception, and communication, discovering the "dance of the bees." With Nikolaas Tinbergen and Konrad Lorenz, he was awarded the 1973 Nobel Prize for physiology or medicine for his work.
See also: Zoology.

Frigatebird

Frisch, Max (1911-91), Swiss architect, journalist, and playwright best known for his play *The Firebugs* (1958) and the novels *I'm Not Stiller* (1954), *Homo faber* (1957), and *Man in the Holocene* (1980). His dominant theme is the destructive effect of modern society upon individuals.

Frisch, Ragnar (1895-1973), Norwegian economist. He and Jan Tinbergen of the Netherlands were the first winners of the Nobel Prize in economics (1969). Frisch won the prize for his pioneering work in *econometrics,* the statistical analysis of economic problems. He was professor of economics at Oslo University and a founder of the Econometric Society (1930).
See also: Econometrics.

Fritillary, genus of herbs of the family Liliaceae that includes about 80 species of hardy perennials native to the north temperate zone. Fritillaries have bell-shaped flowers and are spring blooming.

Frobisher, Sir Martin (1539-94), English navigator and explorer. In search of a northwest passage to the Pacific, he led 3 expeditions to northern Canada (1576-78), landing at Labrador and Frobisher Bay and at Greenland, mistaking them for Cathay.

Froebel, Friedrich Wilhelm August (1782-1852), German educator noted as the founder of the kindergarten system. He believed in play as a basic form of self-expression and in the importance of spiritual development.
See also: Kindergarten.

Frog, jumping, tailless amphibian. Strictly, the name applies only to true frogs, members of the family Ranidae, but other members of the order Anura (which also includes the toads) are sometimes called frogs. True frogs are characterized by shoulder girdles that are fused down the midline. They are found throughout the world except in the southern parts of South America and Australia.

The golden treefrog of Australia

Froissart, Jean (1337?-1410?), French poet and chronicler. He traveled widely in search of material for his *Chronicles of France, England, Scotland and Spain*, which present a colorful, if not scrupulously accurate or objective, picture of events between 1325 and 1400. His poetry ranges from light verse to the romance *Meliador.*

Fromm, Erich (1900-80), German-born U.S. psychoanalyst. He combined the ideas of Sigmund Freud and Karl Marx for the analysis of human relationships and development in the context of social structures and for proposed solutions to the problems of the modern industrial world, such as alienation. His books include *Escape from Freedom* (1941), *The Art of Loving* (1956), and *The Anatomy of Human Destructiveness* (1973).
See also: Psychoanalysis.

Fronde, series of uprisings against the French crown, 1648-53. At first largely popular uprisings against heavy taxation, they were later fomented by the *parlements* and discontented members of the aristocracy, such as Louis II, prince de Condé, against the autocratic chief minister, Cardinal Mazarin, whose decisive intervention in 1652 finally crushed the Fronde.

Front, in meteorology, boundary between air masses. A cold front occurs when a cold air mass pushes a warm air mass ahead of it. A warm front occurs when a warm air mass pushes a cold air front. An occluded front occurs when a warm and a cold front meet; the warm air in between then rises.
See also: Meteorology.

Frontenac, Louis de Baude, Comte de Palluau et de (1620-98), French soldier and governor of New France (1672-82 and 1689-98). Recalled to France in 1682 after his controversial handling of relations with Native Americans, he returned in 1689. In the first French and Indian War he successfully held Quebec against the English. He maintained the French position in New France up to the Treaty of Ryswick (1697).

Frontier, in U.S. history, boundary between the settled and unsettled areas of the country. It was constantly changing as the descendants of the original settlers of the 13 colonies spread out north, south, and especially, west. In the early days expansion was slow, consisting largely of migrations into the Appalachian area and into what is now Pennsylvania. By the time of Independence, Kentucky had been settled and the frontier was in Tennessee. The new government provided for surveying, settlement, and administration of new areas. The frontier moved steadily westward, and new states were formed in quick succession until, by 1848, Mexico was forced to cede the Southwest, and settlement began on the west coast. Native Americans suffered badly under the government's policy of moving them to make way for settlers and struggled to resist it. After the Civil War, wars with Native Americans broke out again, but by the 1870s and 1880s the growth of cities and the enclosure of much of the land meant that the settlers were firmly established. In 1890 the Bureau of the Census officially declared the frontier closed; its way of life and the peculiar mythology it created have had a great influence on U.S. culture.

Frost, frozen atmospheric moisture formed on objects whose surface temperature is below 32°F (0°C), the freezing point of water. Hoarfrost forms in roughly the same way as dew, but owing to the low temperature, the water vapor sublimes from gaseous to solid state to form ice crystals on the surface. The delicate patterns often seen on windows are hoarfrost. Glazed frost usually forms when rain falls on an object below freezing; it can be seen, for example, on telegraph wires. Rime occurs when supercooled water droplets contact a surface that is also below 32°F; it may result from fog or drizzle. The first frost of the year signifies the end of the growing season.

Frost, Robert Lee (1874-1963), U.S. poet. For most of his life he supported himself by farming and part-time academic work. His first volumes of poetry, *A Boy's Will* (1913) and *North of Boston* (1914) were published during a stay in England. His reputation grew in the United States, and he won many honors, including 4 Pulitzer prizes. Outwardly colloquial and concerned with commonsense rural wisdom, his poetry is also richly symbolic. Frost's complete poems were published in 1967.

Frostbite, damage occurring in skin and adjacent tissues caused by freezing. Extreme cold causes blood vessels in the hands, feet, ears, or nose to constrict, depriving tissues of nutrients. Warming and measures to maximize blood flow may reduce tissue loss.

Frozen food *see:* Food, frozen.

FRS *see:* Federal Reserve System.

Fructose ($C_6H_{12}O_6$), sugar found in honey and fruits, used as a fluid and nutrient replenisher.

Fruit, ripe ovary of a flowering plant containing the seed or seeds. The fruit begins to develop after fertilization; its main functions are to protect the developing seeds and to help to scatter them when they are ripe. The majority of fruits are formed only from the carpel or carpels of the flower; they are known as true fruits. Some fruits include other parts of the flower, especially the receptacle; these are called false, or accessory, fruits. True fruits include dry fruits and juicy fruits. The dry fruits include those that split open and release their seeds (dehiscent) and those that do not split open (indehiscent). Juicy fruits also fall into 2 main groups. The drupes are the stone fruits: The inner layer, which is hard and woody, is the stone; the single seed is inside it. Berries are juicy fruits with many seeds in them, but without stones around the seeds.

Fruit bat *see:* Flying fox.

Fruit fly, small winged insects of the families Tephritidae and Drosophilidae that feed on decaying vegetation and ripe fruit, sometimes causing great damage to crops. Some species, such as the vinegar fly (*Drosophila melanogaster*), are used for genetics experiments because they breed rapidly.

Fry, Christopher (1907-), English verse dramatist and film writer. His plays, often in ancient settings, deal with contemporary themes. His best-known play, *The Lady's Not for Burning* (1949), is a dry comedy centering on witchcraft hysteria. His screenplays include *Ben Hur* (1959, Academy Award) and *The Bible* (1966).

Fry, Elizabeth Gurney (1780-1845), British Quaker philanthropist whose inspections of prisons throughout Britain and Europe led to great advances in the treatment of the imprisoned and the insane. Her proposed reforms of London's notorious Newgate prison, including segregation of the sexes and the provision of employment and religious instruction, were largely accepted.
See also: Quakers.

Fu-chou *see:* Fuzhou.

Fuchs, Klaus (1911-88), German-born physicist and convicted spy. During World War II, Fuchs—a British citizen and Soviet agent—worked on the top-secret, atomic bomb project in the United States (1943-45). He supplied the Russians with designs for the uranium and plutonium bombs. Released from a British prison in 1959, he returned to East Germany, where he directed the Institute for Nuclear Physics (1959-79).
See also: Espionage; Manhattan Project.

Fuchsia, tropical plant (genus *Fuschia*) of South America and New Zealand, named for the German botanist Leonhard Fuchs. From a few species, over 2,000 varieties have been produced, some of which can be grown out of doors. The hanging flowers have a tubular calyx that flares out into wings, and from this dangle 4 petals and a group of stamens. The word also names the reddish purple hue associated with the flowers.

Fuel cell, device that produces electricity through the chemical reaction between 2 substances. The most common type is powered by the reaction between hydrogen and oxygen. Two porous electrodes are immersed into an electrolyte (usually an alkali). Through oxidation, hydrogen is supplied to the anode, and oxygen is allowed to diffuse through the cathode. At the anode, hydrogen gives up electrons to form hydrogen (H^+) ions, which react with hydroxyl (OH^-) ions in the solution to give water. The electrons pass around the external circuit to the cathode, where they react with oxygen and water to form more hydroxyl ions. The overall reaction is therefore the combination of hydrogen and oxygen to form water. The electric potential created is up to 1 volt. An ordinary battery is a type of fuel cell, but its electrodes are eaten away during use, whereas true fuel cells have an extremely long life and provide more power relative to their weight than other sources of electricity. Though fuel cells are theoretically more efficient than other generators, they are still very expensive and are only used for special purposes. The Apollo spacecraft use fuel cells to supply electricity. Scientists are working to produce fuel cells that can used low-cost fuels, such as gasoline or diesel fuel, which would make them practicable for domestic use.

Fuel-injection system, method of supplying fuel to internal combustion engines. It has always been used in diesel engines, where fuel is sprayed into the cylinder; when the inlet valve or port closes, the high pressure developed as the piston moves up the cylinder ignites the fuel. In gasoline engines there is a separate fuel injection line for each cylinder. Fuel is injected into a port, not into the cylinder. Electronic or mechanical devices ensure that each cylinder receives the correct mixture of fuel and air for efficient combustion. A fuel-injection system thus replaces the carburetor in gasoline engines. First used on aircraft and racing car engines, since 1957 it has been used on some automobiles.
See also: Engine.

Fuentes, Carlos (1928-), Mexican author of novels, essays, and short fiction. His works emphasize the elusive nature of time, historical truth, and personal identity, and tend to be unconventionally structured. Among his best known novels are *Terra Nostra* (1975) and *The Hydra's Head* (1977). Fuentes served as ambassador to France 1975-77.

Fugard, Athol (1932-), South African playwright of Dutch descent known for his political dramas. A passionate opponent of apartheid, his plays reflect the ways in which blacks, coloreds, and disenfranchised whites are damaged by South Africa's racist policies. Among his best known works are *The Blood Knot* (1961) and *Master Harold ... and the Boys* (1981).

Fugitive slave laws, laws passed by U.S. Congress in 1793 and 1850 to deter slaves from fleeing to nonslave states. The 1793 act denied runaway slaves the benefit of jury trial. However, some states in the North passed personal-liberty laws providing the right to trial for fugitives. The Compromise of 1850, an attempt to preserve the Union, which was threatened by tensions between the South and the North over the spread of slavery to the western territories, imposed severe fines and imprisonment on U.S. marshals and citizens who helped or failed to apprehend runaway slaves. The laws only hardened opposition and were defied by abolitionists, further fueling the Southern desire for secession. The laws were repealed in 1864.
See also: Slavery.

Fugue (Italian, "flight'), musical form in which 2 or more parts (voices) enter successively in imitation and combine in developing a theme. The classic fugue begins with the *exposition* of the theme or *subject* in successive voices. This is followed by variations on the subject, with *episodes* linking full statements. The subject may undergo various contrapuntal transformations, such as the *stretto*, in which it is stated in rapid, overlapping entrances. The fugue dates from the 16th-century canon and round. The greatest achievements in the fugue are by J.S. Bach (1685-1750).
See also: Counterpoint.

Fuji, Mount *see:* Mount Fuji.

Fujiyama *see:* Mount Fuji.

Fulani, people of West Africa living throughout a wide area from Senegal to Cameroon. They include nomadic pastoralists as well as settled communities. The Fulani have a deep-rooted culture based on Islam and have strong ties with the Hausa.

Fulbright, James William (1905-), U.S. political leader and lawyer, initiator of the Fulbright Act (1946), providing for international exchange of students and teachers. Fulbright was elected to the House of Representatives in 1942, and served in the Senate (1944-75). He was chairman of the Senate Foreign Relations Committee (1959-74), becoming an outspoken critic of U.S. policy in Vietnam.

Fulcrum *see:* Lever.

Fuller, Margaret (1810-50), U.S. critic and advocate of female emancipation. A friend of Ralph W. Emerson, she edited the transcendentalist magazine *The Dial*, 1840-42. She became literary critic for the *New York Tribune* in 1844 and in the following year published *Woman in the Nineteenth Century*. In 1848-49, with her husband, the Marchese Ossoli, she served the revolutionary cause in Italy under Mazzini.

Fuller, Melville Weston (1833-1910), U.S. jurist. He was a member of the Illinois constitutional convention, Illinois state legislator (1862), arbitrator in the Great Britain-Venezuela boundary dispute (1897-99), and peace commissioner at the Hague (1900-10). As chief justice of the U.S. Supreme Court (1880-1910), Fuller wrote 2 important opinions (1895): *Pollock* v. *Farmer's Loan and Trust Co.*, in which he invalidated the national income tax and *United States* v. *E.C. Knight Co.*, in which he so narrowly defined the Sherman Anti-Trust Act that it applied only to transportation.
See also: Supreme Court of the United States.

Fuller, R(ichard) Buckminster (1895-1983), U.S. inventor, philosopher, author, and mathematician. He was a prolific source of original ideas for maximizing efficiency in numerous technologies (he called it the Dymaxion principle). He is best known for his concept "Spaceship Earth" and for designing the geodesic dome.

Fulton, Robert (1765-1815), U.S. inventor who improved both the submarine and the steamboat. His submarine *Nautilus* was launched at Rouen, France (1800), with the aim of using it against British warships: in fact, the British repeatedly escaped, and the French lost interest. His first steamship was launched on the Seine River (1803). After this success he returned to the United States, launching the first commercially successful steamboat, the *Clermont*, from New York (1807). He built several other steamboats and the *Demologus*, the first steam warship (launched 1815).
See also: Steamboat.

Fundamentalism, U.S. conservative Protestant movement, upholding evangelicalism against modernism. The movement has flourished, particularly in the South, since the early 20th century. Its chief doctrines, set out in a series of pamphlets, *The Fundamentals* (1910-12), are Christ's virgin birth, physical resurrection, and second coming, the substitutionary theory of the atonement, and the absolute infallibility of the bible. The last led to a denial of biblical criticism and the theory of evolution. Leading advocates of the movement include W.J. Bryan and the theologian John Gresham Machen. Modern fundamentalism is mostly dispensationalist, pietist, and revivalist.
See also: Protestantism.

Fungi, subdivision (phylum Eumycota or Eumycophyta) of the plant kingdom that comprises simple plants that reproduce mostly by means of spores and that lack chlorophyll. Fungi are now often considered a separate kingdom, not part of the plant kingdon. The majority of true fungi produce microscopic filaments (hyphae) that group together in an interwoven weft, called the *mycelium*. Reproduction is sometimes by budding (yeasts) but more normally by the production of asexual and sexual spores. Some fungi produce large fruit bodies; these are the structures commonly associated with fungi. Eumycota includes the myxomycetes, or slime molds. The true fungi are classified as the chytridomycetes, which produce motile gametes, or zoospores, with a single flagellum; the oomycetes, which have biflagellate zoospores and produce dissimilar male and female reproductive organs and gametes; zygomycetes, which do not produce motile zoospores and reproduce sexually by fusion of identical gametes; the ascomycetes, including yeasts, which reproduce asexually by budding or by the production of spores (conidia) and sexually by the formation of ascospores within saclike structures (asci) that are often enclosed in a fruiting body, or ascocarp; the basidiomycetes, in which sexual spores are produced or there are enlarged cells (basidia) that often occur on large fruiting bodies; and the deuteromycetes, or imperfect fungi, which are known to reproduce asexually, although sexual forms are often classified as ascomycetes and basidiomycetes.

Fungicide, substance used to kill fungi and so to control fungal diseases in humans and plants. In medicine some antibiotics, sulfur, carboxylic acids, and potassium iodide are used. In agriculture a wide variety of fungicides are used, both inorganic (e.g., Bordeaux mixture and sulfur) and organic (generally containing sulfur or nitrogen). They are applied to the soil before planting or around seedlings, or they are sprayed or dusted onto foliage.

Funj Sultanate, Muslim empire that ruled the Sudan of east Africa from c.1500 to 1821. Under 'Amarah Dunqas, who founded the capital at Sennar (1504-5), and throughout the 16th century, the Funj people, a group of uncertain origin, extended their dominion northward and over most of the area between the White Nile and the Blue Nile. They established supremacy by 1608 and reached the summit of their power c.1650 under Badi II Abu Daqn. By 1744 they had subdued the Kordofan region and Ethiopia. The Funj dynasty declined following the reign of Badi II, chiefly because of internal conflict between the ruler and the Funj aristocracy. In 1821 the Turkish government of Egypt invaded and conquered the Funj state.
See also: Muslims.

Funny bone, point at the bend of the elbow where the ulnar nerve passes over the ulna (1 of the 2 long bones of the forearm), and if struck, causes pain or tingling in the arm and fingers.

Fur, dense hair covering the skin of many mammals. Fur is an excellent heat insulator and protects against cold. It consists of a soft undercoat, generally interspersed with longer and stiffer guard hairs that form a protective outer coat and prevent matting. Fur clothing has long been valued for its beauty and warmth, and was an aristocratic luxury until the discovery of America, in whose exploration and economic development trapping and fur trading played a major role. Demand is still high, threatening some fur-bearing species with extinction; this has led to fur-farming of suitable animals such as mink and to the development of artificial furs made of synthetic fibers. The anti-fur consumer movement and groups for the humane treatment of animals have led to the banning of certain cruel forms of trapping and seal hunting in some countries.

Furfural ($C_5H_4O_2$), organic chemical belonging to the aldehyde family, used commonly in industry. A colorless liquid with irritating fumes, it is used in the manufacture of synthetics such as plastics, rubber, and nylon; as an insecticide and germicide; and in the refining of petroleum.

Furies, in Roman mythology, goddesses of vengeance. Known as Erinyes in Greek mythology, they were often depicted as 3 old women with snakes in their hair. In his tragedy *The Eumenides,* Aeschylus tells of how they punished Orestes for killing his mother by driving him insane.

Furnace, insulated structure in which high temperatures can be produced and controlled. In most furnaces the heat is produced by burning a fuel such as coal, oil, or gas, though some use the heating effect of electricity. In the so-called atomic furnaces (nuclear reactors), the heat comes from the splitting or fission of atoms and is used to generate electricity. In solar furnaces the heat is produced by concentrating the rays of the sun. Simple furnaces are used in the home to heat water for the heating system. Much larger ones are used in industry to heat, melt, and vaporize all kinds of materials. Metallurgical furnaces, massive structures that produce temperatures of thousands of degrees, are lined with refractory (heat-resistant) bricks that may also be water-cooled. In blast furnaces, used for reducing iron from its ore, fuel (coke) is burned in a blast of hot air inside a vertical cylindrical furnace. In the open hearth, or reverberatory furnace, the heating flame passes over the charge to be melted, and heat reflected from the low roof melts the charge; since there is no contact with the fuel, the charge does not receive any impurities. In the converter type of furnace, such as the Bessemer converter, which is used for refining pig iron, air or oxygen is blown through molten metal to burn out impurities; no fuel is necessary since the "blow" itself generates heat. The electric furnace heats the charge externally and so does not contaminate the product.

Furniture, movable objects and accessories that add to the comfort, beauty, usefulness, and storage capacity of a dwelling. The development of furniture and increasing sophistication is closely allied to that of architecture. Furniture may be classified as *supporting* pieces (for example, chairs, tables, beds) and *storage* pieces (for example, chests, cupboards, and other boxlike containers). Accessories like rugs, drapes, and mirrors may also be considered furniture.

Furze, whin, or gorse (*Ulex europaeus*), thorny shrub of the pea family native to Europe and Africa. Furze has yellow flowers on dark green stems. It is valuable for holding soil in place and is sometimes cultivated as winter fodder.

Fuse, safety device placed in an electric circuit to prevent overloading. It usually comprises a wire of low-melting-point metal mounted in or on an insulated frame. Current passing through the wire heats it, and excessive current heats the wire to the point that it melts, breaking the circuit. In most domestic plugs, the fuse consists of a cylinder of glass capped at each end by metal, with a wire running between the metal caps. Similar, but larger, cartridge fuses are used in industry.

Fusion, in physics, collision of 2 highly accelerated atomic nuclei to form the single nucleus of a heavier element. Fusion reactions (also called thermonuclear reactions) require extreme heat and release large amounts of energy. They occur naturally in space but are human-made phenomena on earth. Hydrogen bombs use the fusion process.
See also: Atom; Nuclear energy.

Fusion bomb *see:* Nuclear weapon.

Futures *see:* Commodity exchange.

Futurism, Italian 20th-century art movement. It was based on the "Manifesto of the Futurist Painters" (1910) issued by the Italian publicist and poet F.T. Marinetti with a group of like-minded Italian artists, emphasizing speed and the dynamic forces of a mechanical age. The manifesto declared that "a roaring motor car is more beautiful than the *Winged Victory of Samothrace.*" It glorified war and violence and called for the destruction of all museums, libraries, and ancient monuments. This first general manifesto was followed by 2 further manifestos on futurist painting, also obsessed with the idea of universal dynamism. A typical futurist painting shows, for example, a dog with many legs to give the impression of movement. Futurist sculpture emphasizes sharp angles and jagged profiles. Futurism also exerted some influence on architecture and decorative art, particularly in the field of theatrical design. As a literary movement, futurism was never a major force.

Fuzhou, also Foo-chow or Fu-chou (pop. 1,129,300), port on the Min River, capital of Fujian province, southeastern China. Occupying both an ancient walled town and a modern city, Fuzhou is an industrial center known for electronics, chemicals, lacquerware, and food processing. It was a "treaty port" following the Opium War (1839-42) and was occupied by the Japanese in World War II.
See also: China.

G

G, seventh letter of the English alphabet. Like the *c*, it developed from the Semitic *ghimel* and Greek *gamma*. The Romans, who used the same letter for the *k* sound and the hard *g* sound (as in go), added a small line to the *c*. English has a soft *g* sound (gelatin) in front of the vowels *e*, *i*, and *j* in words of French, Latin, or Greek origin.

G (gravitational constant), symbol that stands for the force of gravity. Newton's law of gravitation states that the gravitational attraction between any 2 bodies is directly proportional to the product of their masses and inversely proportional to the square of the distance between them. In other words, the greater the mass of 2 bodies, the greater the force of attraction between them; the further apart 2 bodies are, the less the force of attraction between them is. The gravitational constant, G, is the constant of proportionality in these equations.
See also: Gravitation.

G.A. *see:* Gamblers Anonymous.

G.I. Bill of Rights, Serviceman's Readjustment Act of 1944, which provided government aid for demobilized members of the U.S. armed services after World War II. Designed to prevent a repetition of the social problems that had followed World War I, it provided financial aid for the purchase of houses, farms, and businesses, and funds for veterans' hospitals, unemployment benefits, and vocational training. Most significant was the educational aid, which paid for 4 years of college education, including basic living expenses. Veterans of the Korean and Vietnam wars also received benefits.

G.O.P. *see:* Republican Party.

Gaberones *see:* Gaborone.

Gable, Clark (1901-60), U.S. film star. Gable won a 1934 Academy Award for a comedy role in *It Happened One Night.* His most famous role was Rhett Butler in *Gone with the Wind* (1939). Called "the King," he was a leading box-office draw for more than 2 decades.

Gabo, Naum (Naum Pevsner; 1890-1977), Russian sculptor, pioneer of constructivism. With his brother, Antoine Pevsner, he issued the *Realist Manifesto* (1920). After he left Russia, he taught at the Bauhaus in Germany (1922-32). In 1946 he emigrated to the United States. He is noted for his kinetic sculptures and geometrical constructions in metal, plastic, and nylon.

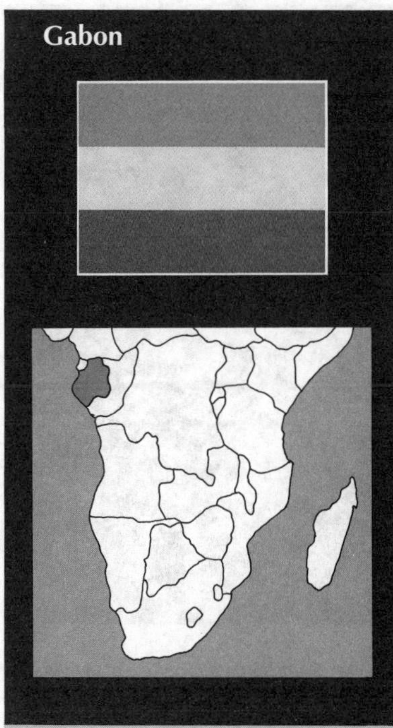

Capital:	Libreville
Area:	103,347 sq mi (267,667 sq km)
Population:	1,245,000
Government:	republic
Independent:	1960
GNP:	U.S. $3,200,000,000
Per capita:	U.S. $2,970

Gabon (officially Gabonese Republic), independent state in West Africa straddling the equator. It is bordered by the Atlantic Ocean on the west, Equatorial Guinea and Cameroon on the north, and the Republic of the Congo on the east and south.
Land and climate. The Atlantic coastline is backed by a narrow coastal plain that rises to rolling hills, leading to plateaus and mountains cut by the Ogooué River and its tributaries. The climate is tropical, with heavy, daily rainfall.
People. The largest ethnic group is the Fang; other groups include the Batoka, the Eshira, and Omiéné. The official language is French, though tribal languages are also spoken. The largest city and capital is Libreville. Port Gentil is the other major center. Lambaréné, in the interior, is renowned as the site of a hospital established in 1913 by Dr. Albert Schweitzer and run by him until his death in 1965.
Economy. Gabon is rich in timber and oil. The latter accounts for two-thirds of export earnings, but other minerals, including manganese and gold, are also exported. Cocoa is also an important cash crop. Gabon is an associate member of the European Economic Community.
History. Gabon was a center of the slave trade from the arrival of the first Portuguese navigators in the late 15th century until the 1880s. Libreville was established in 1849 by slaves freed from a slaving ship. By the end of the century, the French had taken over most of the territory that is now Gabon. In 1910 the area officially became a French colony. Following World War II, Gabon became an overseas territory, and in 1958 it became a self-governing member of the French Community. Two years later Gabon proclaimed its independence and became a member of the United Nations. Close relations have been maintained with France, while rising living standards have contributed to relative political stability.

Gabor, Dennis (1900-79), Hungarian-born British physicist who invented holography, for which he was awarded the 1971 Nobel Prize for physics. He had developed the basic technique in the late 1940s, but practical applications had to wait for the invention of the laser (1960) by C.H. Townes.
See also: Holography.

Gaborone (pop. 96,000), capital of Botswana, an independent state in southern Africa. Gaborone is a governmental, cultural, and educational center and is served by an international airport and railroad.
See also: Botswana.

Gabriel, archangel in the Bible and the Koran. In St. Luke's gospel, Gabriel, meaning man of God in Hebrew, appeared to Zacharias, to Daniel, and then announced to Mary that she had conceived Jesus. In the Koran, Gabriel is the medium of revelation to Muhammad.

Gadhafi, Muammar Muhammad al- *see:* Quadhafi, Muammar Muhammad al-.

Gadolinium, chemical element, symbol Gd; for physical constants see Periodic Table. Gadolinium, a rare-earth metal, was discovered by J.C.G. de Marignac in 1880. It occurs in bastnasite and monazite, which are the principal sources of the element. The metal is prepared by reducing the anhydrous fluoride with calcium. Gadolinium is silvery-white, soft, malleable, and ductile. It has the highest neutron capture cross-section of any element. Gadolinium is strongly magnetic but loses this property on heating. Gadolinium and its compounds are used in microwave applications and as color TV phosphors.

Gadsden, family name of two distinguished South Carolinians. **Christopher Gadsden** (1724-1805) became known as the *Flame of Liberty* for his participation in the Revolutionary War as an officer in the Continental Army, and as lieutenant governor of South Carolina. **James Gadsden** (1788-1858), Christopher's grandson, was an army officer, diplomat, and railroad executive. As U.S. minister to Mexico, he arranged for the purchase of the land that now makes up much of Arizona and New Mexico.

Gadsden Purchase, Mexican territory bought by the United States in 1853, to add to lands acquired in the war of 1848. The extra land, some 30,000 sq mi (77,700 sq km) cost $10 million. It provided a rail route through the conquered land to the Pacific. The purchase was negotiated by James Gadsden, U.S. minister to Mexico.

Gadwall, grayish-brown duck (*Anas strepera*), of the family Anatidae. Gadwalls are about 20 in (51 cm) long and weigh about 2 lbs (0.9 kg). They have white spots on their wings.

Clark Gable in a scene from Gone with the Wind *(1939)*

Gaea, or Ge, Mother Earth personified as a goddess. According to Greek myth, Gaea emerged out of Chaos and produced the sky, sea, and mountains. By her union with Uranus (heaven), she brought forth the Titans, Cyclopes, and Giants.
See also: Mythology.

Gaelic, group of Celtic languages, a subfamily of the Indo-European languages, native to Ireland (Irish Gaelic), the Isle of Man (Manx), and the Scottish Highlands (Scottish Gaelic).

Gaelic literature, writings in the Gaelic language. Irish Gaelic has 3 periods: Old Irish (up to 10th century), Middle Irish (up to mid-15th century), and Modern Irish. The early literature consists chiefly of lyric verse and sagas, of which the *Ulster Cycle* is a famous example. Scottish Gaelic diverged from the Irish tradition in 1300 and developed particularly in the area of poetry.

Gaels, or Goidels, Gaelic-speaking Celtic peoples of Ireland, Scotland, and the Isle of Man, as opposed to the Celtic peoples of Wales, Cornwall, or Brittany, who speak Brythonic.

Yuri Gagarin

Gagarin, Yuri Alekseyevich (1934-68), Soviet cosmonaut, first human in space. His capsule, *Vostok 1*, was launched on Apr. 12, 1961, and orbited the earth once. A deputy to the Supreme Soviet from 1962, he died in a plane crash.
See also: Astronaut.

Gage, Thomas (1721-87), British general, from 1763 commander-in-chief of British forces in North America and governor of Massachusetts (1774-75). His attempt to take an arms depot at Concord resulted in the first battles of the Revolutionary War. He resigned after the disaster at Bunker Hill.
See also: Revolutionary War in America.

Gag rules, resolutions passed in the U.S. House of Representatives, 1836-40, to prevent discussion in the House of petitions for the abolition of slavery. The rules, which infringed upon the right of petition, were repealed in 1844 as the result of a campaign led by John Quincy Adams and Joshua Giddings.

Gaillardia, any of several species of flowers (genus *Gaillardia*) of the composite family. Native to the central and western U.S., they are also called blanketflowers and fire wheels. They resemble daisies, with tubular disk flowers surrounded by ray flowers. Depending on the species, gaillardias have purple or crimson disk flowers and yellow, red, orange, or white ray flowers.

Gainsborough, Thomas (1727-88), English portraitist and landscape painter. He painted numerous society portraits, and in 1780 he was commissioned to portray George III and Queen Charlotte. The landscapes in which many of his portraits are set were his primary interest. His work influenced John Constable and English landscape painting in the 19th century. Perhaps his most famous painting is *The Blue Boy.*

Thomas Gainsborough's portrait of Madame Vacoeli

Galago, any of several species of small mammals (genus *Galago*) of the loris family, native to African forests. They can leap great distances between trees by using their long hind legs. Galagos range in size between large squirrels and chipmunks. They have soft, woolly fur, and large eyes and ears. Active at night, they feed on insects as well as small birds, eggs, lizards, and fruit.

Galahad, Sir, in British medieval legends, one of King Arthur's knights. He was the son of Sir Lancelot, one of the bravest of Arthur's knights, and of Elaine of Astolat, daughter of King Pelses. Noble and pure, he led other knights in a search for the Holy Grail. Galahad's story is told in *Le Morte d'Arthur* (1470), by Sir Thomas Malory, and in a poem by Alfred Lord Tennyson.
See also: Arthur, King.

Galapagos Islands, or Archipiélago de Colón, group of volcanic islands in the Pacific, on the equator west of Ecuador and belonging to that country. They were named for the giant tortoises found there in 1535 by the Spaniard Thomas de Berlanga. The islands have unique vegetation and wildlife. In 1835 Charles Darwin studied this wildlife, finding in it confirmation for his theory of evolution. There are large marine and land iguanas, scarlet crabs, penguins, a flightless cormorant, unique finches, and the giant tortoises, which are now rare. The main islands in the archipelago are Isabella, Santa Cruz, Fernandina, San Salvador, and San Cristobal; they are now a national park and wildlife sanctuary.
See also: Ecuador.

Galatia, ancient territory of central Asia Minor overrun by Gauls in the 3rd century B.C. Subjugated by Rome in 189 B.C., it became part of the Roman province of Galatia (which extended south) in 25 B.C.; by A.D. 200 it had merged with Anatolia.

Galatians, Epistle to the, 9th book of the New Testament, a letter written by St. Paul to the Christians in Galatia (now central Turkey) to counter the influence of those who taught that Christians must observe Jewish law. It sets forth the basis of Christian freedom, the union with Christ through faith.
See also: Bible; New Testament.

Galaxy, aggregation of stars, dust, and gas. The earth's galaxy is average sized: It contains approximately 100 billion stars, a beam of light would take approximately 100,000 years to cross from 1 side to the other, and it is shaped like a disk, with arms spiraling out from the bright nucleus. At the edge of the galaxy is the bright band of stars called the Milky Way. The sun, a star, lies about two-thirds of the way to the edge of the galaxy and takes about 250 million years to circle the galaxy once. The galaxy, often referred to simply as the Milky Way, has 2 small companion galaxies, called the Magellanic Clouds after the explorer Ferdinand Magellan. Other galaxies may be round or elliptical in shape, with no arms. Others are S-shaped. The nearest large galaxy, the Andromeda Nebula, is named after the constellation of Andromeda, inside whose borders it appears. The term *nebula* describes its cloudlike appearance. When the Andromeda Nebula was named, it was thought to be a cloud of gas in the earth's galaxy. In 1923 the astronomer Edwin Hubble found that it was a separate galaxy over a million light years away. Later studies showed that the 2 galaxies are near-twins, both in size and appearance. Galaxies tend to congregate in groups, linked by gravity, suggesting a common origin; they may have condensed out of 1 giant cloud of gas. The Milky Way is in a group including the Andromeda Nebula and about 20 other galaxies. Perhaps a billion galaxies are visible in the telescopes operating today.
Galaxies emit radio waves. The strongest emitters, known as radio galaxies, seem to have suffered internal explosions. There are often radio-emitting areas on either side of a galaxy. Quasars, star-like objects that emit strong radio waves, may be galaxies in the making. A quasar quiets down as it gets older, becoming a radio galaxy. Seyfert galaxies, discovered by Carl Seyfert, are galaxies with quasar-like characteristics and may be another stage of a galaxy's growth.

Galbraith, John Kenneth (1908-), Canadian-born U.S. economist and author, ambassador to India 1961-63. A Harvard professor (1949-75) and an activist in the liberal wing of the Democratic Party. Galbraith has been a consistent advocate of Keynesian economics, supporting active state intervention into the economy and urging government efforts to fight poverty and unemployment. His major books include *The New Industrial State* (1967; rev. ed. 1978), *Money* (1975), and *The Age of Uncertainty* (1977), and *Affluent Society* (1958; rev. ed. 1985).

Galen (A.D. 129-c.200), Greek physician at the court of the Roman emperor Marcus Aurelius. His writings drew together the best of classical medicine and provided the form in which the science was transmitted in the West through the Middle Ages and Renaissance. He himself contributed many original observations in anatomy and physiology, employing dissections of mammals to establish the field of comparative anatomy.
See also: Anatomy; Physiology.

Galicia, historic region in east-central Europe, now part of Poland and Russia's Western Ukraine. It is rich in minerals and agriculture. Part of Poland since the 14th century, it was annexed by Austria in the 18th century, but was again Polish after World War I. After World War II its eastern portion passed to the USSR.

Galilee, in ancient Roman times, hilly region of northern Palestine between the Sea of Galilee and the Jordan River (now part of Israel). It was the homeland of Jesus, who was sometimes referred to as the Galilean, and a center for Jewish learning after the Roman destruction of the temple in Jerusalem in A.D. 70.

Galilee, Sea of, lake in northern Israel, also called Lake Tiberias. Fed and drained by the Jordan river, it contains many fish, and its water is used for irrigation. Many Bible stories, such as Jesus's transformation of water into wine, are set along this sea. Ruins of ancient cities lie along its northern shores.

Galileo Galilei (1564-1642), Italian mathematician and physicist who discovered the laws of falling bodies and the parabolic motion of projectiles. The first to turn the newly invented telescope to the heavens (1609), he was among the earliest observers of sunspots and the phases of Venus. A talented publicist, he helped to popularize the pursuit of science. However, his quarrelsome nature led him into an unfortunate controversy with the Roman Church. His most significant contribution to science was his provision of an alternative to Aristotelian dynamics, expressed in his *Dialogue Concerning the Two Chief World Systems* (1632). The motion of the earth thus became a conceptual possibility, and scientists at last had a genuine criterion for choosing between the Copernican and Tychonic hypotheses in astronomy. In 1633, the Vatican condemned Galileo as a heretic for claiming that the earth revolved around the sun. He was forced to recant the Copernican theory. Pope John Paul II started the move toward a reconciliation when he conceded in a 1979 speech that the astronomer had suffered at the hands of the Church.

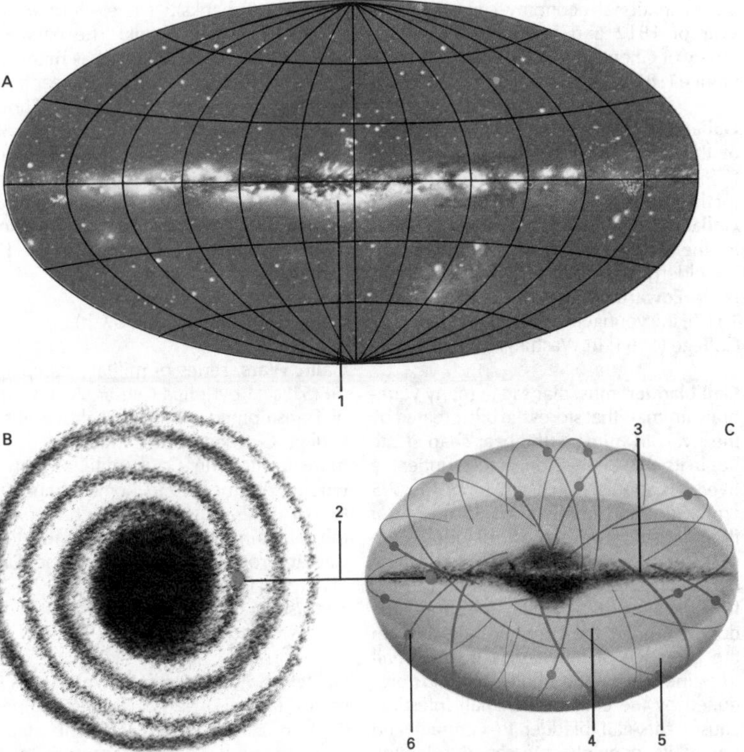

Galaxy. The Sun is one of a 100 thousand million stars which comprise our own galaxy (A). To us the galaxy appears as a band of light across the sky which contains dust as well as stars. In fact, the center of the galaxy (1) in Sagittarius is obscured by dust (B). The overall shape is of a two-armed spiral with the Sun (2) on one arm about half way between rim and center. Viewed sideways it appears as a hubbed disc (3) surrounded by two regions: the spherical halo (4) containing globular clusters (5) and high velocity stars and the intermediate system (6) containing e.g. planetary nebulae.

Gall (c. 1840-94), Sioux chief who aided Sitting Bull in defeating General Custer at the Battle of the Little Bighorn (1876). After a subsequent battle in 1881, he surrendered and settled in a reservation in the Dakota Territory, where he worked to improve relations between Native Americans and white settlers.

Gall, abnormal growth on trees caused by parasites such as fungi and insects. Fungal galls are usually irregular in shape, whereas insects produce galls that are often spherical, like the oak apple. The adult insect lays its eggs in the plant's tissue, and the larvae cause the growth of the gall. They then feed on the deformed tissues and eventually bore their way out as adults. Gall insects include certain small flies and many small wasps. It is often possible to identify the insect by the shape of its gall. Galls are often a serious nuisance and destroy many acres of valuable crops. Some, however, are useful. The oak apple, for example, is a source of tannin, which is used in tanning leather.

Gallatin, (Abraham Alfonse) Albert (1761-1849), Swiss-born U.S. statesman. As representative (1795-1801) he defended U.S. relations with France. As secretary of the treasury (1801-14), he objected to the drain

In August 1609 Galileo demonstrated his first telescope to the Doge of Venice, which aroused great admiration and for which he received a significant increase in allowance.

on the national economy caused by the War of 1812 and helped negotiate the Treaty of Ghent (1814). He was minister to France (1816-23) and Britain (1826-27).

Gallaudet, family name of U.S. educators of the deaf. **Thomas Hopkins Gallaudet** (1787-1851) founded the Hartford School for the Deaf in 1817. His older son, **Thomas Gallaudet** (1822-1902), founded a church for the deaf in New York City and a home for elderly deaf mutes in Poughkeepsie, N.Y. **Edward Miner Gallaudet** (1837-1917), the younger son, founded Gallaudet College (1864) in Washington, D.C.

Gall bladder, muscular sac in many vertebrate animals that stores the bile created by the liver. In humans the pear-shaped sac lies in its own depression, or foss, under the liver. It is about 3.5 in (9 cm) long, 1 in (2.5 cm) wide, and holds about 35 cu cm of fluid. Arising from the gall bladder is the cystic duct, which is connected to the liver by the common hepatic duct, and to the first part of the small intestine, the duodenum, by the common bile duct. In the presence of fatty foods in the small intestine, a hormone, cholecystokinin, produced by the cells of the small intestine, causes the gall bladder to contract and empty its contents into the duodenum. Cholecystitis (inflammation of the gall bladder resulting from infection by bacteria) can be acute or chronic. In most instances, acute cholecystitis is caused by a gallstone blocking the cystic duct. Chemical irritation and the digestive activities of certain enzymes can also play a contributing role. A sharp pain in the right upper part of the abdomen is a prominent symptom. The condition may require surgical removal of the gall bladder. The chronic condition is sometimes associated with cancer of the gall bladder.

Gallegos, Rómulo (1884-1968), Venezuelan novelist and statesman. Elected president of Venezuela in 1947, he was almost immediately overthrown by a military coup. His short stories and novels, of which the best known is *Doña Bárbara* (1929), are primarily didactic and ideological works concerned with social reform.
See also: Venezuela.

Galleon, sailing vessel with 3 or 4 masts and 2 to 4 decks. Most ships of this type were clumsily built, with projecting forecastles and square sterns. Used in the 16th and 17th centuries as warships and for carrying cargo, galleons were capable of relatively fast speeds. But they had to be handled with care, as their heavy superstructure made them subject to capsizing. Galleons varied greatly in size, the largest having displacements of about 1,200 tons (1,100 metric tons).

Galley, early seagoing warship, propelled by oars, sometimes with auxiliary sails. The galleys that made up the ancient Greek and Roman navies were classified according to the number of banks of oars on each side: *uniremes* (1 bank), *biremes* (2 banks), and *triremes* (3 banks). There were usually about 25 oars per bank. The oars were 40-50 ft (12-15 m) long and as many as 7 slaves were required to work each oar. Galleys were long and narrow. Though fast, they were difficult to handle in rough seas. They were equipped with catapults and carried archers and soldiers who would board an enemy ship that had been rammed. Galleys were used in the Mediterranean and other seas until the late 17th century.

Gallfly *see:* Gall (plant growth).

Gallic Wars, series of military campaigns (58-51 B.C.) by Julius Caesar. As governor of Transalpine Gaul, Caesar drove out invading German tribes while occupying more territory in Gaul, until almost the whole country was in Roman hands (55 B.C.). In 53-52 B.C. he put down revolts by the chieftains Ambiorix and Vercingetorix. Caesar wrote *Commentaries on the Gallic War* (c.50 B.C.).
See also: Gaul; Rome, Ancient.

Gallienus, Publius Licinius Valerianus Egnatius (A.D. 218?-268), Roman emperor (253-268). He ruled with his father, Valerian, until Valerian's capture by the Persians in 260. Under pressure from German, Persian, and Gothic invasions and provincial revolutions, Gallienus reorganized the army and reduced the power of the Senate. He also ended official persecution of the Christians. Gallienus was assassinated in Milan while quelling a revolt.

Gallinule, any of several species of water birds (genus *Gallinula*) of the rail family. About 12 to 18 in (30 to 45 cm) long, gallinules have brightly colored feathers and long, thin toes. They are poor fliers but excellent swimmers.

Gallipoli Peninsula, 50-mi (80-km) strip of land in European Turkey between the Aegean Sea and the Dardanelles. A strategic point of defense for Istanbul, it was fought over during the Crimean War and World War I. In 1915 an Allied expedition of British, Australian, French, and New Zealand forces failed to dislodge Turkish troops in an effort to gain control of the Dardanelles.

Gallium, chemical element, symbol Ga; for physical constants see Periodic Table. Gallium was discovered spectroscopically by P.E. Lecoq de Boisbaudran in 1875. The element occurs in the minerals diaspore, sphalerite, germanite, bauxite, and coal. It can be produced by electrolysis of a solution of the hydroxide in KOH. Gallium is a silvery, amphoteric metal that can be liquid near room temperature. It wets glass and has a long liquid range and low vapor pressure even at high temperatures. Gallium and its compounds are used in phosphors, semiconductors, solid-state devices, and low-melting alloys.

Gallstone *see:* Gall bladder.

Gallup (pop. 18,200), city in New Mexico. With Navajo, Zuñi, and Hopi reservations nearby, it is the central trading center of the Southwest tribes and headquarters of the Bureau of Indian Affairs in that area. Native American ceremonial events are held there each Aug. Industries include Native American arts and crafts, tourism, cattle shipping, wool, and forest products.
See also: New Mexico.

Gallup, George Horace (1901-84), U.S. pollster. In 1935 he established the American Institute of Public Opinion, which undertakes the Gallup polls, periodic samplings of public opinion on current issues. His several books include *The Pulse of Democracy* (1940) and *The Gallup Poll: Public Opinion, 1935-71* (1972).

Gallup Poll *see:* Gallup, George Horace; Public opinion poll.

Galsworthy, John (1867-1933), English novelist and playwright. His novels of the Forsyte family, grouped in trilogies—*The Forsyte Saga* (1922), *A Modern Comedy* (1928), and *End of the Chapter* (1934)—depict the life and attitudes of the English upper-middle classes, typical of the "man of property" Soames Forsyte. Galsworthy was awarded the Nobel Prize for literature in 1932.

Galton, Sir Francis (1822-1911), British scientist, author of *Hereditary Genius* (1869). The founder of eugenics (talent is inherited) and biostatistics (the application of statistical methods to animal populations), Galton developed one of the first systems for identifying fingerprints.

Galvani, Luigi (1737-98), Italian anatomist who discovered "animal electricity" (c.1786). This discovery resulted from the observation of the twitching of a frog's leg when touched by 2 metals in a moist environment. A controversy with Alessandro Volta over the nature of animal electricity stimulated research in electrotherapy.
See also: Anatomy.

Galvanizing, industrial process for coating iron or steel with a thin layer of zinc to prevent rusting. It was discovered in 1742 but only named in 1830 after Luigi Galvani (1737-98), who demonstrated that 2 unlike metals in contact produce an electric current, though he did not know why. There are several stages in galvanizing. The metal is thoroughly cleaned with solvents and acid, and a zinc ammonium flux is applied. The article is dipped into a bath of molten zinc kept at about 842°F (450°C), and a coating of layers of iron-zinc alloys or pure zinc forms. Finally, the article may be quenched in cold water to remove the flux and freeze the coating. Small items like nails are galvanized in wire baskets; sheet and wire are treated continuously in an automatic process. The sheet is widely used in building, automobile manufacture, and outdoor structures. In an alternative process, electrogalvanizing, a flow of elec-

tricity through a zinc sulfate solution causes a layer of zinc to adhere to steel.
See also: Electroplating.

Galvanometer, instrument used for measuring minute electrical currents. The modern instrument consists of a coil of wire delicately suspended by a thin conducting filament between the poles of a permanent magnet. The galvanometer is connected to a circuit, and when an electrical current flows, the coil is deflected at an angle directly proportional to the strength of the current. A small mirror attached to the coil reflects a spot of light onto a scale that indicates the current's strength.
See also: Electric current.

Galveston (pop. 217,399), city in southeastern Texas and seat of Galveston County. Located on the Gulf of Mexico, the city is an important seaport, commercial fishing center, and the world's largest cotton-shipping port. Meat packing, shipbuilding, oil refining, and the manufacture of wire, nails, textiles, and chemicals are important industries. Michel Menard, a Canadian civil engineer, laid out the town in 1836. That same year the city became the temporary capital of the Republic of Texas. During the Civil War it was a major supply port for the Confederacy, although it was occupied by the Union troops for several months. It has operated with a council and city manager since 1961.
See also: Texas.

Galway (pop. 47,100), port city and commercial center in western Ireland. Industries include clothing, foods, electrical equipment, and furniture. Many other Irish products, such as wool, marble, china, and metals are exported from Galway.
See also: Ireland.

Gama, Vasco Da *see:* Da Gama, Vasco.

Gambia (officially Republic of The Gambia), independent country in West Africa.
Land and climate. Gambia is a narrow strip of land 7-20 mi (11-32 km) wide, stretching inland from the Atlantic Ocean, for about 200 mi (322 km) along the Gambia River. It is surrounded on three sides by Senegal. At the mouth of the Gambia River, on St. Mary's Island, is Banjul, the capital city and port.
People. The Mandingo ethnic group accounts for about 40% of the population. Other groups include the Fulani, Wolof, Jola, and Serahuli. More than 90% of the people are Muslim, the rest being animist or Christian. English is the official language, but tribal languages are also spoken.
Economy. The economy is largely agricultural, peanuts being the main cash crop. Millet, corn, and rice are grown for domestic consumption.
History. Portuguese navigators explored the mouth of the Gambia River in the 15th century, trading in gold and slaves. In 1588 the British obtained control of the trade on the Gambia River. During the following centuries the slave trade flourished, even after its official abolition by Britain in 1807.

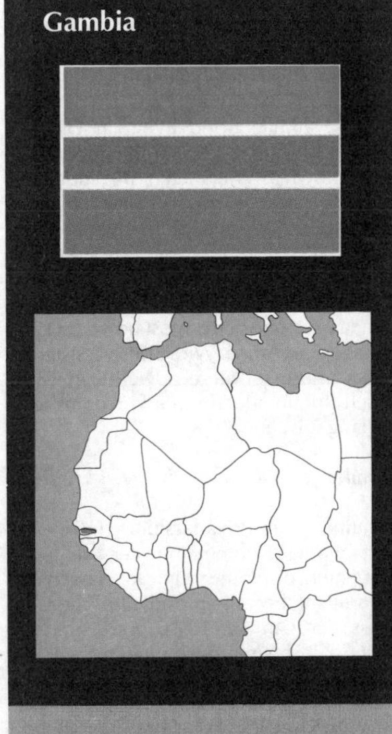

Capital:	Banjul
Area:	4,361 sq mi (11,295 sq km)
Population:	735,000
Government:	republic
Independent:	1965
GNP:	U.S. $180,000,000
Per capita:	U.S. $220

In 1843 the area around St. Mary's Island was made a British colony, and the interior settlements along the river were declared a British protectorate in 1894. In 1963 Gambia became self-governing, and in 1965 it became an independent member of the British Commonwealth. Relations with Senegal were close, and in 1981 a confederation called Senegambia was declared, linking the two economies while maintaining formal separate sovereignty.

Gamblers Anonymous (G.A.), international organization designed to help people with an uncontrollable urge to gamble. G.A. consists of people who have quit or want to quit gambling. Regular meetings are held at which members support one another's efforts to quit gambling by discussing and sharing their experiences.
See also: Gambling.

Gambling, betting money or valuables on the outcome of some future event that is more or less unpredictable. Gambling is at least as old as recorded history. Dice games were popular in ancient Rome, and loaded dice found among the ruins of Pompeii indicate that some, at least, were rigged. The Roman historian Tacitus tells of Romans and Germans gambling themselves into social disgrace, financial ruin, and slavery. At the height of the West African slave raids in the 18th century, there were instances of Africans gambling away their families and even themselves. In China, there are reasonably authenticated cases of people staking their limbs and hacking them off when they lost.
Today, U.S. legislation relating to gambling deals mainly with the penalties for illegal betting and the provision of revenue by means of taxation on legal betting. It has been estimated that about $50 billion is staked by gamblers in the United States each year. With this huge turnover and because of the high rate of taxation on most forms of gambling, illegal gambling is widespread. The criminal underworld is closely connected with most forms of gambling, and bribery and corruption of officials is common. In most courts, games of skill are distinguished from games of chance, the latter being illegal when played for money. This kind of legislation eliminates organized gambling clubs but permits friends to play games of skill for money. Unfortunately, it is not easy to determine the relative effects of chance and skill in most games. Betting on horses may be a skillful exercise for some, although most people talk of good or bad "luck." In California, draw poker is considered a legal game of skill, whereas stud poker is regarded as an illegal game of chance.
Horse racing is one of the most popular sports with gamblers. In many parts of the United States, the bettor can place bets with the parimutuel, a computer-operated pooling system. A proportion of the total money staked is retained, and the rest paid out to winning bettors. The payout on any horse depends on the total amount in the pool and the number of winning bettors. Bookmaking and off-track betting are illegal in the United States, except in Nevada and New York, although illegal facilities can be found in most states.

Game, contest or sport played by rules. Games may test mental and/or physical skills, and may be played by one or more persons. They range from crossword puzzles, card, and board games to organized sporting events played by competing teams. Some rely on skill and practice, others involve luck.

Gamete, male or female reproductive cell, whether in animals, humans, or plants. In human beings, the female ovum and the male sperm are the gametes.
See also: Reproduction.

The message from this 19th-century woodcut is clear: whoever has dealings with gambling falls into still bigger crime.

Roulette wheel

Game theory, branch of mathematics concerned with a mathematical process of selecting an optimum strategy in the face of an opponent's strategy. The term was initially used to describe the strategy of winning at poker. It has applications in such areas of competition as military and economic planning.
See also: Von Neumann, John.

Gamma globulin, portion of blood protein containing antibodies. Several types of gamma globulin are recognized. Although they share basic structural features, they differ in size, site, behavior, and response to different antigens. Absence of all or some gamma globulins causes disorders of immunity, increasing susceptibility to infection, while the excessive formation of one type is the basis for myeloma, a disease characterized by bone pain, pathological fractures, and liability to infection. Gamma globulin is available for replacement therapy, and a type from highly immune subjects is sometimes used to protect against certain diseases (e.g., serum hepatitis, tetanus).
See also: Immunity; Plasma.

Mohandas Karamchand Gandhi

Gamma rays, electromagnetic wave energy similar to, but of much higher energy than, ordinary X rays. The energy of a quantum is equal to hv ergs, where h is Planck's constant (6.6254×10^{-27} erg sec) and v is the frequency of the radiation. Gamma rays are emitted by the nuclei of uranium and other radioactive elements. They are highly penetrating, an appreciable fraction being able to traverse several cm of lead. In large amounts they can be harmful to body tissue, but small quantities are used in radiation treatments for cancer.
See also: Radioactivity; X rays.

Gamow, George (1904-68), Russian-born U.S. physicist and science writer, best known for his work relating to the evolution of stars and for his support of the "big bang" theory of cosmology. In genetics, he did significant research on cell structure.
See also: Cosmology; Genetics.

Ganda, ethnic group living in Uganda, constituting about 30% of the population. Also known as Waganda or Baganda, they speak a Bantu language called Luganda. The Ganda have adopted many aspects of modern Western culture and are successful in farming, business, and government. In the early 1800s their territory, called Buganda, was one of the most powerful kingdoms of East Africa. With British assistance, it became even more powerful in 1896, when Britain added more kingdoms to it, making it Uganda.

Gander *see:* Goose.

Gandhi, Indira Priyadarshini (1917-84), first woman prime minister of India. Daughter of Prime Minister Jawaharlal Nehru, she became president of the Congress Party in 1959. As prime minister (1966-77) she improved relations with the USSR and helped India to become the dominant power in the region. In 1975 she was found guilty of electoral malpractice. During the ensuing constitutional crisis she declared a state of emergency and jailed nearly 700 political opponents. The Indian Supreme Court overruled the verdict against her and upheld her electoral and constitutional changes; however, she was briefly turned out of office (1977). She regained the premiership in 1980. She was assassinated by her Sikh bodyguards in 1984.
See also: India.

Gandhi, Mohandas Karamchand (1869-1948), nationalist leader of India. He was called the *Mahatma* ("Great Soul"). After studying law in London, he went to South Africa, where he lived until 1914, becoming a driving force in the Indian community's fight for civil rights. During this campaign he developed the principle of *satyagraha*, nonviolent civil disobedience to achieve economic, political, and social change, and held to it despite persecution and imprisonment. When he returned to India, he had achieved substantial improvements in civil rights and labor laws. In India he became leader of the Congress Party, initiating the campaign that led to the independence of India after World War II. He was assassinated by a Hindu fanatic who disapproved of his tolerance of Muslims. Gandhiwrote an autobiography, *My Experiment With Truth*, and edited the newspaper *Indian Opinion*.
See also: India.

Masses of Hindu pilgrims annually visit the holy cities along the Ganges (of which Varanasi is one of the most important) in order to undergo a ritual cleansing.

Gandhi, Rajiv (1944-91), prime minister of India (1984-87). He studied engineering at Cambridge University and returned to India to work as a commercial pilot. Elected to Parliament in 1981, he was appointed secretary of the Congress Party by his mother, Indira Gandhi, in 1983, and became prime minister after she was assassinated. During the election campaign of 1991 he was assassinated.

Gang, group of people who come together for social purposes, often criminal. A gang may be tightly organized, with a definite leadership, or it may be a loose grouping. Some juvenile gangs have been known to be involved in delinquent behavior. In the 1920s and 1930s, crime organizations in the United States, such as the one led by Al Capone, were known as gangs.

Ganges River, in India, the most sacred Hindu river, believed to be the reincarnation of the goddess Ganga. It rises in the Himalayas and flows through northern and northeastern India, following a southeastern course across the plain of India. It joins the Brahmaputra River in Bangladesh, then continues through the vast Ganges delta to empty through several mouths (Meghna, Tetulia, Hooghly) into the Bay of Bengal. The river waters irrigate a populous agricultural area. Many cities line the river's banks, including the holy Indian cities Varanasi (Benares), Allahabad, and Calcutta, and the Bangladesh city of Dacca.

Gang of Four, group of supporters of China's Mao Tse-tung who, after Mao's death, were tried and convicted for the excesses of the Cultural Revolution of the late 1960s. Principal charges included planning a coup. Mao's widow, Jiang Qing, was identified as the group's leader; the others were Wang Hongwen, Yao Wenyuan, and Zhang Qunqiao. Imprisoned in 1976, their sentences (1981) ranged from death to 20 years in prison.
See also: China; Mao Zedong.

Gangrene, death of tissue following loss of blood supply, often after obstruction of arteries by injury, thrombosis (clot formation on a damaged artery wall), or embolism (blockage by an air bubble, clot, or other debris). Dry gangrene is seen when arterial blockage is followed by slow drying, blackening, and finally separation of dead tissue from healthy. Its treatment includes improvement of the blood flow to the healthy tissue and prevention of infection and further obstruction. Wet gangrene occurs when the dead tissue is infected with bacteria. Gas gangrene involves infection with gas-forming organisms (e.g., *Clostridium welchii*), and its spread is particularly rapid. Antibiotics, hyperbaric chambers (in which oxygen is kept at high pressure), and early amputation are often required.

Gannet (*Morus bassanus*), large, white seabird of the North Atlantic. It nests on isolated islands, as in the Gulf of St. Lawrence and the British Isles, and feeds on fish that it catches by spectacular vertical dives into the sea. Related species are found off South Africa, Australia, and New Zealand.

Ganymede, in Greek mythology, a young Trojan prince. Zeus, the ruler of the Gods, was fascinated by the prince's beauty and brought Ganymede to Mt. Olmypus to be his cupbearer.

Gar, freshwater fish of the family Lepisosteidae with long, thin bodies, long jaws, and an armor of diamond-shaped scales. Gars are usually found in shallow, weedy water from Canada to Costa Rica, but the alligator gar (*Lepisosetus spatula*), which can reach 10 ft (3 m) in length, may be found in saltwater.

Garamond, Claude (1480-1561), French type designer and publisher. He created typefaces that helped establish Roman type in place of Gothic or black letter as standard type. His royal Greek and italic types were also influential.

Garand rifle, single-shot, semiautomatic weapon. Also known as the M1, this .30-caliber gas-operated rifle was the standard rifle of the U.S. Army from 1936 to 1960. *See also:* Rifle.

Garbage, generally, refuse consisting of organic (animal or vegetable) or other matter. In computer science, the term describes inaccurate or useless data from a computer program, usually resulting from equipment malfunction, a mistake in a computer program, or unwanted or meaningless data carried in storage.

Garbo, Greta (Greta Lovisa Gustafsson; 1905-90), Swedish-born U.S. film actress. She was a talented actress known for her aura of glamor and her passion for privacy; her 24 films include *Anna Christie* (1930), *Camille* (1937), and *Ninotchka* (1939). She retired in 1941.

García Lorca, Federico (1898-1936), Spanish poet and dramatist. Inspired by his native Andalusia and by gypsy folklore, he made his reputation with *Gypsy Ballads* (1928) and the surrealism-influenced *Poet in New York* (published 1940). He returned to folk themes in the plays *Blood Wedding* (1933), *Yerma* (1935), and *The House of Bernarda Alba* (1936). He was also a musician and theater director. He was murdered by Franco's Nationalists in the Spanish Civil War.

García Márquez, Gabriel (1928-), Colombian novelist. Winner of the 1982 Nobel Prize in literature, he first achieved world prominence in 1967 with *One Hundred Years of Solitude.* Set in the imaginary jungle town of Macondo, this novel tells of the decline of the town and the Buendía family. It perpetuates and brings to its fullest literary expression a literary style known as magical realism. Macondo was also the setting for two earlier works, *Leaf Storm* (1955) and *No One Writes to the Colonel* (1968). Later novels include *The Autumn of the Patriarch* (1975), a portrait of an aged and isolated dictator; *Chronicle of a Death Foretold,* a story of love, jealousy, and murder; and *Love in the Time of Cholera* (1988), a love story. *The General in his Labyrinth* (1989), a novel about the South American 19th-century revolutionary Simón Bolívar, generated great controversy.

Gardenia (genus *Gardenia*), evergreen flowering shrub native to subtropical Asia and Africa that bears waxy, fragrant white flowers and has dark green, glossy leaves. It grows outdoors in the southern United States and blooms from May to September. In colder climates it is grown in greenhouses.

Gardening, process of cultivating plants, often as a hobby to beautify homes, sometimes to produce herbs, vegetables, and fruits for consumption.

Garden of Eden *see:* Eden.

Gardner, Erle Stanley (1889-1970), U.S. mystery writer, creator of lawyer-detective Perry Mason. Gardner wrote over 140 novels under his name and the pseudonym A. A. Fair.

Garfield, James Abram (1831-81), 20th president of the United States. Fatally wounded by an assassin less than four months after his inauguration, Garfield served only 199 days in office.

Early life. Garfield, grew up on a frontier farm near Orange, Ohio, working as a canal bargeman, farmer, and carpenter. He graduated from Williams College, Mass., and returned to Ohio to teach. A supporter of the newly founded antislavery and antisecessionist Republican party, Garfield was elected to the Ohio state senate in 1859.

War and politics. When the Civil War began, Garfield helped organize the volunteer 42nd Ohio Infantry and fought in some of the war's bloodiest battles. In 1862 he was elected to the House of Representatives. On Reconstruction, a critical postwar issue, he sided with the radical Republicans, voting for the impeachment of President Andrew Johnson and favoring the continued presence of federal troops in the former Confederacy. After the 1876 presidential election, Garfield served on the commission created to decide the disputed returns. He voted along party lines to give the office to Republican Rutherford B. Hayes.

President. After 18 years in the House, Garfield was elected to the Senate in 1880. Later that year the Republican presidential convention was deadlocked between two frontrunners, James G. Blaine and former president Grant. Blaine's supporters eventually voted for Garfield as a compromise candidate. Support for Garfield grew, and he won the nomination. In the Nov. election, Garfield defeated Democrat Winfield Scott Hancock by only 7,023 votes.

Garfield's presidency was so brief that it was notable only for constant quarreling over political appointments. On July 1, 1881, Charles J. Guiteau, a disappointed office-seeker, shot Garfield at the Washington, D.C., train station. The assassination caused Congress to begin reforms to abolish the "spoils system" of distribution of federal jobs and set up competitive examinations in the civil service to ensure fairer political appointments.

Garfish *see:* Gar.

James Abram Garfield

20th U.S. President

Born:	Orange, Ohio; Nov. 19, 1831
Term:	Mar. 1881-Sept. 1881
Vice president:	Chester Alan Arthur
Political party:	Republican
Spouse:	Lucretia Rudolph Garfield
Children:	7
Died:	Elberon, N.J.; Sept. 19, 1881

Greta Garbo

Gargoyle

Gargoyle, decorative waterspout on a building, used to throw rainwater clear of the walls. Though sometimes of plain geometric form, in medieval buildings of the 13th-16th centuries gargoyles were fanciful or grotesque images of demons or animals, with the water pouring out of the open mouths. Although gargoyles are to be found on many ancient buildings, including the Parthenon in Athens, they are mostly associated with medieval structures such as the cathedrals of Milan, Italy, and Notre Dame in Paris.

Garibaldi, Giuseppe (1807-82), Italian patriot and general. After fighting in a republican uprising in Genoa in 1834, he fled to South America, leading guerrilla revolutions in Brazil and Uruguay. In 1848 he returned to Italy to fight against Austrian, French, and Neapolitan armies in support of Mazzini's short-lived Roman Republic. On its collapse, Garibaldi fled to the United States. Returning to Italy in 1854, he led guerrilla campaigns (1859-62) against Austria and captured Sicily and Naples with a volunteer army, his famous "Red Shirts," in the most decisive campaign of the Risorgimento. He surrendered the territories to King Victor Emmanuel, effectively unifying Italy. In 1862 and 1867 Garibaldi unsuccessfully tried to capture Rome from the pope. Subsequently he fought for the French against Prussia (1870). In 1874 he was elected to the Italian parliament.

Garland, (Hannibal) Hamlin (1860-1940), U.S. writer. His fiction portrays pioneering midwestern farm life with bitterness and realism. Among his work is the story collection *Main-Travelled Roads* (1891) and his autobiographical "Middle Boarder" stories (4 vols., 1917-28). He won the 1921 Pulitzer Prize for biography for *A Daughter of the Middle Border*, about his wife and her family.

Garland, Judy (Frances Gumm; 1922-69), U.S. singer and movie actress. Garland was the daughter of vaudeville performers. She costarred with Mickey Rooney in 9 films, and starred in *The Wizard of Oz* (1939), *Meet Me in St. Louis* (1944), and *A Star Is Born* (1954).

Garibaldi enters Naples, Sept. 7, 1860

Garlic (*Allium sativum*), perennial plant of the lily family; also, its edible bulb. Garlic is rich in calcium, potassium, phosphorus, and other nutrients. It is claimed to have a beneficial effect on the digestive system and the mucous membranes and to be helpful in treating high blood pressure, respiratory diseases, and other disorders.

Garlic

Garment Worker's Union, International Ladies, labor union with branches in the United States and Canada, comprising workers who produce women's and children's clothing. The union was founded in 1900 with a charter from the American Federation of Labor (AFL) and was instrumental in forming the Committee for Industrial Organization (now the Congress of Industrial Organization, or CIO) in 1935.

Garner, John Nance (1868-1967), U.S. vice president (1933-41) under Franklin D. Roosevelt. A Democratic member of the U.S. House of Representatives (1903-33) and its speaker (1931-33), he was a skillful behind-the-scenes politician. He ran unsuccessfully for the Democratic presidential nomination in 1940.

Garnet, group of common silicate minerals, including some gemstones and some varieties used as abrasives. They are transparent to translucent, red, brown, green, yellow, and white, and have a glassy luster. The most highly valued garnet gem is *demantoid*, an emerald green variety found in the USSR and Italy. Perhaps the most popular is a ruby red *pyrope* found in South Africa, Bohemia, Arizona, and New Mexico. Crushed garnet is used as an abrasive for sand-blasting, dental wheels, lens grinding, and sandpaper.
See also: Gem.

Garrett, Pat (1850-1908), U.S. frontier sheriff. He arrested Billy the Kid in 1880. After "the Kid's" escape from jail in New Mexico, Garrett pursued and shot him in 1881.
See also: Billy the Kid.

Garrick, David (1717-79), English actor, manager, and dramatist. He introduced a more natural acting style to the English stage in roles such as Hamlet and partially restored the original versions of Shakespeare's plays. He managed the Drury Lane Theatre, 1747-76.

Garrison, William Lloyd (1805-79), leader of the U.S. abolitionist movement. From 1831-65 he published *The Liberator*, an influential crusading journal that opposed slavery, war, and capital punishment and supported temperance and women's rights. He was president of the American Anti-Slavery Society (1843-65), which he helped found in 1833.
See also: Abolitionism.

Garter, Order of the, highest order of British knighthood, established in 1348 by King Edward III. It consists of the sovereign, the Prince of Wales, 25 knights, and such foreign rulers and others as the monarch may name. Its patron is St. George.
See also: Knighthood, Orders of.

Garter snake, any of the harmless snakes of the genus *Thamnophis*. Garter snakes are the most common snakes of North America, growing to a length of 20-30 in (50-70 cm) and feeding on frogs or salamanders. Some are aquatic or semi-aquatic and kept as pets.

Garvey, Marcus Moziah (1887-1940), U.S. black nationalist leader, born in the British West Indies. In 1914 he founded the Universal Negro Improvement Association in Jamaica and in 1916 introduced it to the United States, where it gained a widespread following. It emphasized the kinship of blacks and a "back to Africa" movement. He promoted the Black Star Line, a shipping company for trade with Africa, but in 1925 was convicted of mail fraud in connection with its funds. His sentence commuted by President Calvin Coolidge (1927), he was deported to Jamaica.

Gary (pop. 116,600), city in northwest Indiana, on Lake Michigan. It was founded 1906 by the U.S. Steel Corporation as the site for a steel plant, and subsequently become one of the major steel producing areas in the world.

Gary, Elbert Henry (1846-1927), U.S. lawyer and industrialist, founder of Gary, Ind. He organized the U.S. Steel Corporation and was its chairperson, 1901-27. He promoted good working conditions but opposed unions.

Gas, form of matter having no fixed shape or volume, as distinct from a solid, which has a distinct shape and volume, or a liquid, with distinct volume. Boyle's law, Charles' law, and Avogadro's law describe the relationship between the pressure, temperature, volume, and number of particles of gas in a given container.

Gas, gaseous fuel, not to be confused with gasoline, which is a liquid fuel often referred to as gas. An important energy source for homes, institutions, and industries, gas is used to heat and cool buildings, cook, heat water, and create steam. Chemicals in gas are used to produce plastics, drugs, and cleansers. Gas is used to create many products, such as metals, paper, fabrics, glass, and cement. Two kinds of gas exist: *natural* and *manufactured.* Natural gas is found by drilling into a gas deposit in the earth; manufactured gas is created by processing coal or petroleum. The U.S. is a leading natural gas producing country and has nearly 2 million miles (3,200,000 km) of gas pipeline through which gas is transmitted and distributed. Because the use of gas does not create much air pollution, scientists are trying to develop ways in which it can be used as a transportation fuel to power cars, trucks, and ships.

Gas meter, device that measures the volume of gas delivered to a consumer. Meters usually have several measuring chambers. As one chamber is being emptied, the other is being filled. This provides a steady flow of gas to the consumer. The total volume of gas used is determined by counting the number of times each chamber is filled and emptied.

Gasohol, fuel made by mixing 90% unleaded gasoline with 10% alcohol made by fermenting farm crops such as potatoes and grains. Used in automobile and truck engines, gasohol produces less air pollution than gasoline.

Gas oil, one of several liquids obtained by distilling petroleum. Heavier than gasoline, it has a very high boiling point. It is used as diesel fuel for train, truck, and bus engines, and is the source from which heating fuel and lubricating oils are produced.

Gasoline, liquid fuel, a mixture of hydrocarbons produced by refining petroleum. It is known as petrol in Britain and various other countries. Used to power engines in cars, trucks, airplanes, and motorboats, it is an important transportation fuel. It is also used as a cooking fuel.

Gasoline engine, engine that uses gasoline as fuel. Gasoline engines are internal-combustion engines because the fuel, mixed with air, is burned inside the engine itself to produce hot gases that cause parts of the engine to move. These movements in turn cause other mechanical parts of the vehicle to operate. Gasoline engines power most transportation vehicles, such as cars, trucks, airplanes, and motorcycles, as well as lawn mowers, snowmobiles, and small tractors.
See also: Gasoline.

Gaspé Peninsula, peninsula, about 150 mi (240 km) long, in the southeastern region of Quebec, Canada, projecting into the Gulf of St. Lawrence. Scenic and popular with tourists, it has a forested interior, with lakes and rivers, providing excellent hunting and fishing.
See also: Quebec.

Gas poisoning *see:* Chemical and biological warfare; First aid.

Gastritis, inflammation of the stomach lining, which can be either acute or chronic. Symptoms include sensation of dullness in the upper abdomen, loss of appetite, fever (in acute gastritis), nausea and vomiting (in acute gastritis), diarrhea, general aches and pains, intolerance to certain foods (in chronic gastritis), and anemia (in chronic gastritis). The acute condition may be caused by dietary indiscretion, specific food intolerances, chemical irritants (such as alcohol and aspirin), or food poisoning or many types of inflammation caused by bacteria or other microorganisms. Chronic gastritis, less common, can be associated with gastric ulcer, cancer of the stomach wall, and pernicious anemia. Diagnosis is established with the chemical and histological analysis of gastric secretions, gastroscopy, and X rays. For acute gastritis, treatment usually consists of removal of irritants and resting of the stomach.
See also: Stomach.

Gastropod *see:* Mollusk.

Gastroscope, tubelike instrument for visual examination of the inside of the stomach. The instrument employs fiber optics to light the stomach wall and transmit the image back to a lens. The gastroscope's flexible tube reaches the stomach via the mouth and esophagus.
See also: Stomach.

Gas turbine *see:* Turbine.

Gates, Horatio (1727-1806), American Revolutionary War general. As a commander of the Northern army he defeated General Burgoyne at the battle of Saratoga in 1777. After an unsuccessful attempt to replace Washington as commander-in-chief, Gates took command in the South in 1780 and was badly defeated at Camden.
See also: Revolutionary War in America.

Gatling, Richard Jordan (1818-1903), U.S. inventor. After improving upon numerous agricultural techniques and inventing such equipment as the wheat planting machine in the early 1850's, Gatling patented his most famous invention, the Gatling gun, in 1862. A crank operated, multibarrel machine gun, the Gatling gun fired 600 rounds per minute. It was used in the Spanish-American War.

Gatun Lake, artificial lake in Panama Canal Zone created in 1912 by the damming of the Chagres River. Its water makes up part of the Canal route and is used to operate the canal's locks.
See also: Panama Canal Zone.

Gaucher's disease, rare, sometimes hereditary, disorder of lipid metabolism resulting in an abnormal accumulation of fats and fatlike substances (lipids) in the liver and spleen, greatly enlarging those organs, as well as jaundice, skeletal lesions, and anemia. The disease is the result of the body's inability to produce enzymes to break down fats. It is incurable, although surgical removal of the spleen can relieve some of the symptoms.

Gaucho, cowboy of the South American pampas (prairies). Gauchos flourished in the 18th and 19th centuries; they were skilled riders, usually employed to herd cattle. Their function ceased with the fencing of the pampas and reorganization of the cattle industry, but like the U.S. cowboys they survived as local folk heroes.

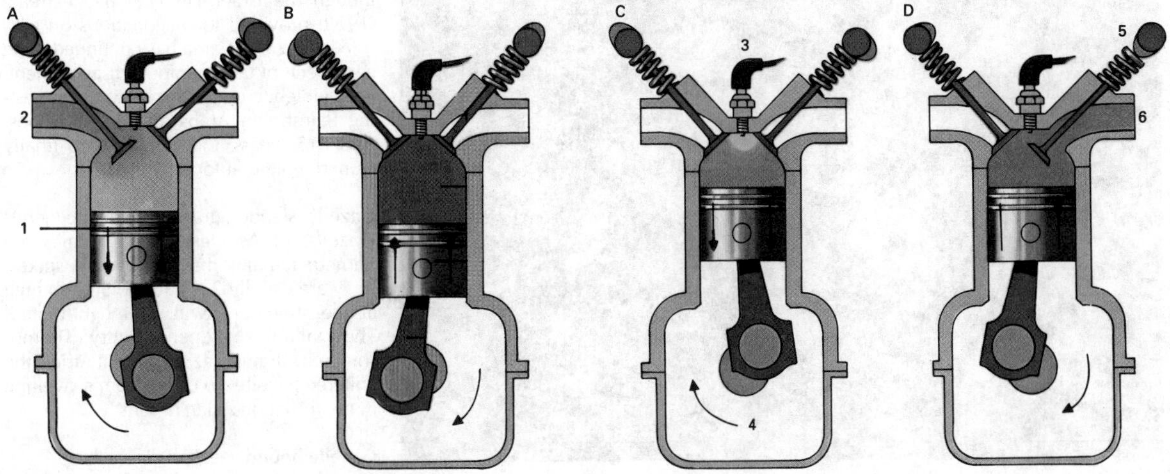

Gasoline engine. On the induction stroke (A) the descending piston (1) draws in a fuel/air mixture through the inlet valve (2). On the compression stroke (B) both valves are shut and the mixture is compressed. When the piston is close to the top (C), the spark plug (3) ignites the mixture which drives the piston and turns the crankshaft (4). The exhaust valve (5) opens on the exhaust stroke (D) and the hot gas escapes, clearing the cylinder (6) for the next induction stroke.

Gaudí, Antonio (Antoni Gaudí i Cornet; 1852-1926), Spanish architect. His fluid, intricate, and bizarre designs express Art Nouveau. He used glazed tiles to color his sculpted architecture. He worked mostly in Barcelona, creating the Casa Milá, the Park Güell, and his masterpiece, the Church of the Holy Family (1882-1930).
See also: Art nouveau.

Gauguin, Paul Eugène-Henri (1848-1903), French postimpressionist painter noted for his pictures of Polynesian life. After painting in a symbolist style at Pont-Aven, Brittany, and working with Vincent van Gogh, he went to Tahiti (1891-93; 1895-1901) and the Marquesas (1901-3) in the South Pacific. He painted scenes in brilliant colors and flattened, simplified forms. His concept of primitivism in art influenced expressionism.

Gaul, name given by the ancient Romans to the 2 regions inhabited by the Celts: Gallia Cisalpina, or northern Italy, and Gallia Transalpina, the area roughly equivalent to modern France, including parts of modern Belgium, Germany, Switzerland, and the Netherlands. Northern Italy was conquered by Celtic invaders in the 5th century B.C.; they in turn were subjugated by the Romans in the 3rd century B.C. Julius Caesar gave Roman citizenship to the Cisalpine Celts, and in 42 B.C. Augustus Caesar incorporated Cisalpine Gaul into Italy. Transalpine Gaul came under Celtic control in the 5th century B.C., and from about 400 B.C. Rome and the Greek colony of Massilia (Marseilles) were allied. In the late 2nd century B.C. the Romans took more decisive control of this region. At the same time Germanic tribes were crossing the Rhine River and pushing southward into Gaul. The Romans fully occupied southern Gaul around 121 B.C., and during the Gallic Wars (58-51 B.C.) Julius Caesar repulsed the Germanic tribes and conquered the whole of Gaul. Under Roman rule, Gaul was divided into a number of provinces that adopted Roman laws and customs. Cities were founded, roads built, and the area prospered. It remained under Roman rule until the 5th century A.D., when it was overrun by various Germanic tribes.

Paul Gauguin depicted the landscape and people of Tahiti in a great number of paintings, such as Et l'or de leur corps *(1901)*

Gauley River *see:* Kanawha River.

Gaulle, Charles André Joseph Marie de *see:* De Gaulle, Charles.

Gauntlet, protective glove worn by medieval knights. Early ones were made of very small chain links. Later ones were of leather covered with hinged steel plates.

Gauss, Johann Friedrich Carl (1777-1855), German mathematician who discovered the method of least squares (for reducing experimental errors), made many contributions to the theory of numbers, and discovered a non-Euclidean geometry. He directed the astronomical observatory at Göttingen (1807-55). In 1833 he invented, with Wilhelm Weber, the electric telegraph.
See also: Geometry, Telegraph.

Gautama *see:* Buddha, Gautama.

Gautier, Théophile (1811-72), French poet, novelist, and critic. He was a supporter of the aesthetic movement calling for "art for art's sake," which he explained in the preface to his novel *Mademoiselle de Maupin* (1835-36). He wrote art, drama, and ballet criticism. His volumes of verse include *Enamels and Cameos* (1852).

Gavial (*Gavialis gangeticus*), harmless, slender-nosed relative of alligators and crocodiles. It is found in Indian rivers, where it grows to a maximum of 20 ft (6 m) on a diet of fish. The false gharial is a crocodile of southeastern Asia.

Gawaine, Sir *see:* Round Table.

Gay, John (1685-1732), English poet and dramatist, author of *The Beggar's Opera* (1728). Using English ballads, he satirized Italian operatic forms and contemporary politics in this comedy of highwaymen, thieves, and prostitutes, on which Brecht based his *Threepenny Opera*.

Gay Rights *see:* Homosexuality.

Gay-Lussac, Joseph Louis (1778-1850), French chemist and physicist. He is best known for Gay-Lussac's law (1808), which states that when gases combine to give a gaseous product, the ratio of the volumes of the reacting gases to that of the product is a simple, integral one. He also showed that all gases increase in volume by the same fraction for the same increase in temperature, 1/273.2 for 33.8°F (1°C), and made 2 balloon ascents to investigate atmospheric composition and the intensity of the earth's magnetic field at altitude. His many important contributions to inorganic chemistry include the identification of cyanogen gas (1815).

Gay Nineties, common name for the 1890s in U.S. history. Although the early years of the decade were marked by economic expansion, there was a serious depression from 1893 to 1897, millions of industrial workers lost their jobs. Farmers suffered too. Many had gone into debt to purchase machinery that would increase their production, and falling prices left the farmers with too little money to repay their debts. The depression ended only with the Spanish-American War, which marked the emergence of the United States as a world power. The term "Gay Nineties" came into use in the 1930s, when the worldwide economic crisis made people nostalgic for what they chose to remember about the 1890s: the victorious war, the prosperity experienced by some, and the simpler charm of life.

Gaza Strip, narrow piece of land in the former southwestern Palestine, about 26 mi (42 km) long, 4-6 mi (6.4-8 km) wide. After the Arab-Israeli war of 1948, it was granted to Egypt, and many Arab refugees fled there. Israel occupied the area as a result of the 1967 Arab-Israeli war. Although the Israeli-Egyptian peace treaty (1979) provided for negotiations on self-rule in Gaza, the area has continued to be a subject of acrimonious disagreement, with violence occurring between protesting Palestinian Arabs and Israeli troops. After 15 years the Palestinians finally gained limited autonomy in 1994.

Gazelle, slender, graceful antelope (genus *Gazella*) of Asia and Africa. Males are horned; females may have short spikes. They are usually 2-3 ft (60 to 90 cm) high at the shoulder, swift, and light-footed. They inhabit dry open country. Thompson's and Grant's gazelles live in Africa; the goitered gazelle, so called from a swelling in the throat, in Asian deserts.

Gazelle hound *see:* Saluki.

Gdansk (pop. 468,600; formerly Danzig), large Polish industrial city and port on the Baltic Sea, with some of the world's largest shipyards. Its economy rests on mechanical engineering and chemical industries. Once a major city in the Hanseatic League, since 1772 Gdansk has alternately been a free city and a city under German or Polish control. The German invasion of Poland in 1939, on the pretext of reestablishing the city as German territory, precipitated World War II. The city became a center of the workers' rights movement led by Lech Walesa during the 1970s and 1980s.
See also: Poland.

Gê, group of Native American tribes in east central Brazil. The Gê traditionally had a sophisticated social structure with intricate rituals and ceremonies. For food, the men hunted animals and the women gathered wild plants and raised potatoes and yams. Although modern times have changed their lives, several Gê tribes still practice some of their traditions.

Gear, toothed wheel forming part of a system by which motion is transmitted between rotating shafts. By selecting gear wheels with different numbers of teeth, the shafts can be made to rotate at different speeds from each other, as in an automobile gearbox.

Gehrig, Lou (Henry Louis Gehrig; 1903-41), U.S. baseball player. As first baseman for the New York Yankees (1923-39) he set a record by playing 2,130 consecutive games. He had a .361 batting average in 7 world series, a lifetime average of .341, and 493 home runs. He died of a rare muscle-wasting disease, amyotrophic lateral sclerosis, called Lou Gehrig's disease. Gehrig was inducted into the National Baseball Hall of Fame in 1939.

Geiger counter, or Geiger-Müller tube, instrument for detecting the presence of and measuring radiation, such as alpha particles, and beta, gamma, and X rays. It can count individual particles at rates up to about 10,000/sec and is used widely in medicine, in industries that use radioactive materials, and in prospecting for radioactive ores. A fine wire anode runs along the axis of a metal cylinder that has sealed insulating ends, contains a mixture of argon or neon and methane at low pressure, and acts as the cathode, the potential between them being about 1 kV. Particles entering through a thin window cause ionization in the gas; electrons build up around the anode, and there is a momentary drop in the interelectrode potential, which appears as a voltage pulse in an associated counting circuit.
See also: Radiation.

Lou Gehrig

Geisel, Theodor *see:* Seuss, Dr.

Geissler tube, tube lamp invented by Heinrich Geissler in 1858. It consists of a glass tube containing gas and air under low pressure, with metal electrodes at each end. When electricity is applied to the electrodes, a current passes through the tube and causes the gas within to glow.

Gelasius, Saint (?-496), Roman Catholic pope elected 492, noted for his 494 letter to Byzantine emperor Anastasius I setting forth the relationship between spiritual authority and secular power. He contended that the power of the popes stood above that of secular leaders.

Gelatin, colorless protein substance obtained from heating collagen, which is extracted from the skin, connective tissue, and bones of cattle and hogs, in boiling water or acid. Gelatin is used as an ingredient in jellies and baked goods, to form capsules around pills, and to coat photographic film.

Geldof, Bob (1954-), rock musician who launched a musical mobilization to aid starving people in Africa. In 1984 a single record by a group of British rock stars ("Band Aid") organized by Geldof raised $11 million. The Live Aid concert, held in London and Philadelphia in July 1985 and broadcast around the world, brought in an additional $72 million.

Gell-Mann, Murray (1929-), U.S. physicist. He was awarded the 1969 Nobel Prize for physics for his work on the classification of subatomic particles (notably K-mesons and hyperons) and their interactions. He (and independently George Zweig) proposed the quark as a basic component of most subatomic particles.
See also: Particle physics.

Gelsemium, any of various climbing shrubs belonging to the family Loganieaceae, with sword-shaped, glossy leaves, clusters of flowers, and fruit containing winged seeds. The flowers, roots and leaves are poisonous.

Gem, mineral or stone prized for its beauty and rarity and durable enough to be used in jewelry and for ornaments. Most types of gem are found in igneous rocks. The chief ones have a hardness of 8 or more on the Mohs' scale and are relatively resistant to cleavage and fracture, though some are fragile. They are identified and characterized by their specific gravity and optical properties, especially the refractive index. Gems of high refractive index show great brilliancy and prismatic dispersion ("fire"). Other attractive optical effects include chatoyancy (changeable color or luster), dichroism (different color in different light), opalescence (reflection or iridescence), and asterism (a star-shaped gleam caused by regular intrusions in the crystal lattice). Since earliest times gems have been engraved. Somewhat later cutting and polishing were developed, the cabochon (rounded) cut generally being used. In the late Middle Ages faceting, now the commonest cutting style, arose. The most valuable gems are diamonds, rubies, sapphires, and emeralds. Other materials—such as aquamarine, garnet, jade, opal, turquoise—are considered semiprecious stones. Amber, coral, and pearls are gems of organic origin.

Gazelle

Gemayel, Amin (1942-), president of Lebanon (1982-88), elected after the assassination of his brother, president-elect Bashir Gemayel. He worked to suppress factional strife between his Christian Phalange party and Druze, Palestinian, and Lebanese Muslims and to secure the withdrawal of Syrian and Israeli forces from the country.

Gemini missions, series of American orbital space flights using the 2-person Gemini capsule. Gemini 3 was launched by the 2-stage Titan 2 rocket on Mar. 23, 1965. The Gemini 4 mission in June 1965 lasted 97 hrs and 56 mins, carrying astronauts James A. McDivitt and Edward H. White II; White walked in space for over 20 min. The last mission, Gemini 12, was in Nov. 1966.
See also: Space exploration.

Gender, in grammar, the designation of nouns and nounlike words as belonging to distinct categories. (The word comes from *genus*, the Latin word for "kind.") Many languages divide nouns into the 2 genders of animate and inanimate, but more common are the classifications masculine, feminine, and neuter. These three genders exist in Russian and German, there are remnants of them in English ("he", "she", and "it".). Other languages—such as French, Spanish, Italian, and Portuguese—have only 2 genders, masculine and feminine. Nouns that refer to males and females are often assigned their "natural gender" (French, *le fils*, "son", is masculine), but the gender of most nouns is independent of sexual class (French, *une proposition*, "suggestion", is feminine; German, *das Mädchen*, "girl", is neuter). Usually, gender depends on the spelling or derivation of the word. The spelling of a word's ending often indicates the gender. Many but not all languages classify words by gender.

Gene, smallest particle of hereditary information that is passed from parent to offspring. Genes consist of chainlike molecules of nucleic acids: DNA in most organisms and RNA in some viruses. The genes are normally located on the chromosomes found in the nucleus of each cell. The genetic information is coded by the sequences of the 4 bases present in nucleic acids, with a differing 3-base code for each amino acid, such that each gene contains the information for the synthesis of 1 protein chain.
See also: Heredity; Deoxyribonucleic acid; Genetic engineering.

Genealogy, study of family origins and history involving the compilation of lists of ancestors showing the line of descent. Apart from its value to the general historian, genealogy represents both a highly skilled professional activity and a widespread amateur preoccupation. In modern times, the main purposes of genealogy are to gain historical information to settle legal questions, such as inheritance, and to gain membership in certain patriotic and hereditary organizations, such as the Daughters of the American Revolution. Although genealogies existed in ancient times among the Babylonians and the Hebrews, they were passed on by oral tradition and cannot be historically verified. In medieval Europe, family names were used only by the upper classes, and genealogical records for the other classes are nonexistent. In England, parish records were instituted for the general public in the 16th century. In the United States the earliest census record was 1790.

Gene mapping, delineation of the genes on a cell's chromosomes, implying the identification of the complete sequence of the DNA, the material that makes up a gene. One current method of gene mapping is to isolate the DNA by cleaving the chromosome. Cleavage is achieved by the introduction of a restriction enzyme, which digests DNA at a specific recognition site. The recognition site also serves as a location marker, and by using a series of restriction enzymes, researchers can investigate a small segment of a chromosome. Other mapping techniques involve the use of radioactive DNA or RNA, which isolates a specific sequence in the gene, and molecular cloning, which allows the artificial generation of genes with a known composition. The genes of some simple organisms (like viruses) have been completely mapped. A vast project to map the human genome is now underway.
See also: Gene.

General Accounting Office (GAO), independent agency of the U.S. Congress, created in 1921 for auditing government spending. Headed by the U.S. Comptroller General, it sets up accounting and management standards, settles claims for or against the government, collects debts, and assesses the public expenditures for most government agencies.

General Assembly, branch of the United Nations (UN) where all member nations are represented and have a vote. The Assembly convenes annually or in special sessions and has some elements of control over all the other organs of the UN. Its functions are financial, supervisory, and deliberative and include control of the UN budget, admitting new members, advising the Security Council, and selecting the UN secretary general.
See also: United Nations.

General Electric Company (GE), large U.S. corporation, manufacturing household and industrial electrical devices. The company was founded in 1892, with the merger of the Thomas-Houston Electric Company and the Edison General Electric Company. In 1986 it merged with the RCA Corporation.

General Motors Corporation, major U.S. manufacturer of motor vehicles and auto parts. Founded in 1908 to consolidate companies producing the Buick, Oldsmobile, Cadillac, and other cars, it also became producer of the Pontiac, the Chevrolet, and GMC trucks. General Motors now has factories and distribution facilities throughout the world.
See also: Automobile.

General Radio Service *see:* Citizens band radio.

General Services Administration (GSA), independent U.S. federal agency established in 1949 to maintain government property and records. Its 5 branches deal with quality-controlled supplies for government use, emergency stockpiles of strategic materials, erection and management of public buildings, transportation and telecommunications, and the preserving of historical records and archives.

Generator *see:* Electric generator.

Genesis, first book of the Old Testament and first of the Five Books of Moses (the Pentateuch), the oldest part of the Old Testament. Its name comes from the Greek for "birth" or "beginning," a translation of the first word in the original Hebrew text. The Book of Genesis begins with the creation of the world, and includes the stories of Adam and Eve, Cain and Abel, and Noah. Chapters 12-36 deal with the origins of the Hebrew people and the accounts of the patriarchs, Abraham, Isaac, and Jacob. Genesis ends with the story of Joseph and the arrival of Jacob and his sons in Egypt (Chapters 36-50).

Genêt, Edmond Charles Édouard (1763-1834), French diplomat, also known as Citizen Genêt, minister to the United States (1793-94). He tried to bring the United States into the war against Britain during the French Revolution, but his demands were opposed by President Washington, and Genêt was replaced.

Genet, Jean (1910-86), French playwright and novelist. Pardoned from life imprisonment for repeated burglary convictions in 1948, Genet wrote of the homosexual underworld of France and the borderline between acceptable and unacceptable social behavior. His works include *Our Lady of the Flowers* (1943), *The Thief's Journal* (1948), and the plays *The Balcony* (1956) and *The Blacks* (1958).

Genetic code *see:* Cell.

Genetic counseling, advice sought by couples concerned about the possibilities of passing inherited defects to children. Counselors can calculate the probabilities of a child being born with the hereditary defect.

Genetic engineering, scientific discipline of altering or combining the genes in a living organism, first developed in the 1970s. This is accomplished through the manipulation of DNA, which is the primary component of the heredity-controlling chromosomes. In order to genetically alter an organism, a particular gene must be isolated through a process known as gene splicing, which permits the transference of a gene from one species to another. The scientific objective of genetic engineering is its enormous potential application in the fields of medicine, agriculture, and business. In medicine, the use of gene therapy may be an important new development in the treatment of diseases. Genetic engineering offers the possibility for the elimination of genetic defects. In industry, genetic engineering may be used to eliminate environmental hazards because certain genes can detoxify dangerous elements. In agriculture, healthier and stronger animals can be produced. Genetic engineering does, however, have a controversial side. Environmentalists fear that some accident or misapplication might produce devastating consequences. The moral implications of how human reproduction might be affected is a very important issue in the field. To this end, the National Institute of Health has issued guidelines (1976, 1985) that control many procedures.
See also: Biotechnology; Gene.

Genetics, study of the inheritance of biological characteristics from parent to offspring. The smallest unit of inheritance is the gene, which is contained within the gametes, or germ cells, that unite at fertilization. Genetics as a science arose at the end of the 19th century when Gregor Mendel's theories of certain basic laws determining some inherited characteristics were rediscovered. It has developed rapidly in the 20th century, spurred on by the growth of physics, chemistry, statistics, and biochemistry. The greatest advance was the discovery (1953) of the chemical nature of the genetic material, deoxyribonucleic acid (DNA), which carries the information necessary for the growth and development of the new individual.
See also: Gene; Heredity.

Geneva (pop. 159,900), city and capital of Geneva canton, Switzerland, on Lake Geneva at the Rhône River outlet. It is the headquarters of the World Health Organization, the International Labor Organization, and the International Red Cross. It is an important cultural, scientific, theological, industrial, and banking city and the center of the Swiss watchmaking industry. The College de Genève was founded (1559) by John Calvin.
See also: Switzerland.

Geneva accords, agreements reached during a series of conferences held in Geneva, Switzerland, Apr.-July 1954, to settle the conflict in Indochina, which was then a French colony. The negotiations were attended by delegates from the United States, the Soviet Union, Great Britain, France, China, and several of the contending forces in Indochina, especially Vietnam. The pacts provided for cease-fires in Laos and Cambodia and the temporary division of Vietnam along the 17th parallel. Control of northern Vietnam was ceded to the revolutionary forces led by Ho Chi Minh; southern Vietnam was controlled by the government of the Emperor Bao Dai, supported by France. Nationwide elections were supposed to be held by July 20, 1956 to unify the country. Bao Dai's government refused to hold the elections, the division of North and South Vietnam become frozen, and the stage was set for the next Vietnam war; which began in 1960.

Geneva Conventions, 4 international agreements signed by a large majority of sovereign nations for the protection of soldiers and civilians from the effects of war. Convention I derived from a conference in 1864, in which the work of Jean Dunant, founder of the Red Cross, led to an agreement to improve conditions for sick and wounded soldiers in the field. Convention II (1906) dealt with armed forces at sea, Convention III (1929) with treatment of prisoners of war, and Convention IV (1949) with protection of civilians.
See also: Prisoners of war; Red Cross.

Genghis Khan (Temujin; 1167?-1227), Mongol ruler of one of the largest empires in world history. After 20 years of tribal warfare he was acknowledged Genghis Khan ("universal ruler") in 1206. He campaigned against the Chin empire in North China (1213-15), and in 1218-25 he conquered Turkestan, Persia, Afghanistan, and South Russia. His empire stretched from the Caucasus Mountains to the Indus River and from the Caspian Sea to Peking (now Beijing). Genghis Khan was not only a fearsome warrior but also a skilled political leader.
See also: Mongol Empire.

Genie, or Jinni, good or evil supernatural spirit in Muslim and Arab folklore; an invisible body made from smokeless flame and possessing the power to assume human or animal form. In the *Arabian Nights* the spirit of Aladdin's lamp is a genie.

Genoa (pop. 760,300), capital of Genoa province and of the region of Liguria, northwestern Italy, 71 mi (114 km) southwest of Milan. Italy's largest port, it is second only to Marseilles on the Mediterranean. In ancient times it was the headquarters of the Roman fleet. In the 12th and 13th centuries it was an independent republic with its own fleet and possessions on the eastern Mediterranean. The city's principal industries include shipbuilding, iron and steel making, and oil and sugar refining.
See also: Italy.

Genocide, deliberate extermination by a government of a national, ethnic, or religious group. The term originated in 1944 with references to the German Nazi systematic killing of Jews. In 1948 the UN drew up a convention defining, ratified by the United States in 1986, the crime of genocide.

Gent *see:* Ghent.

Gentian, any of the herbs of the family Gentianacea (genera *Gentiana* and *Dasystephana*), with intense blue or yellow flowers, common in the Northern Hemisphere and often a feature of high mountain slopes.

Gentile, word used in the Bible to refer to people who are not Jewish. In modern times the term is often used, incorrectly, to mean "Christian." Muslims and members of the Church of Jesus Christ of Latter Day Saints also refer to nonmembers of their faith as gentiles.

Gentlemen's agreement, informal pact between Japan and the United States in 1907. The United States promised to end discrimination against the Japanese, and the Japanese agreed to stop unrestricted emigration to America. It lapsed in 1924 when Congress restricted Japanese immigration.

Genus *see:* Classification.

Geochemistry, study of the chemistry of the earth (and other planets). Chemical characterization of the earth as a whole relates to theories of planetary formation. Classical geochemistry analyzes rocks and minerals.
See also: Chemistry.

Miniature from a 15th century manuscript showing Gengis Khan entering a mosque.

Geode, hollow mineral formation that is found in limestone areas, usually having an outer layer of chalcedony and an interior lining of crystals, usually quartz. Geodes are generally between 1 in (2.5 cm) and 12 in (30 cm) in diameter.

Geodesic dome *see:* Fuller, R(ichard) Buckminster.

Geodesy, in geophysics, specialty that seeks to determine the precise size and shape of the earth. The ancient Greeks attempted to measure the earth, and Eratosthenes (3rd century B.C.) obtained a very accurate figure for the circumference. Geodesy began, however, in the 18th century, when surveyors found that they needed accurate reference points. Geodetic work consists of refining previous estimates of the shape of the earth. The earth is approximately an *oblate spheroid*—that is, it bulges somewhat at the equator because of its rotation and is correspondingly somewhat flattened at the poles (by about 13 mi/ 21 km). But topographical irregularities cause the curvature of the earth to vary from point to point. Such bulgings and flattenings are noted by geodesists carrying out surveys over great arcs of the globe. Since 1957 satellites have provided information about the earth's shape.
See also: Geophysics; Surveying.

Geodetic center of North America, point located in Osborne County, Kans., and chosen in 1901 by the Coast and Geodetic Survey, a U.S. agency, as the origin of all U.S. mapping. In 1913 it was recognized as the geodetic center of North America by Mexico and Canada.

Geoduck (*Panope generosa*), edible clam of the Pacific coast that may weigh over 5 lb (2.3 kg).

Geoffrey of Monmouth (1100?-54?), British bishop and chronicler whose *History of the Kings of Britain* (c.1135), a romantic and fictional account of early Britain, introduced the Arthurian legends to the continent.
See also: Arthur, King.

Geographic center of the United States, point in Butte County, S. Dak., about 17 mi (27 km) west of Castle Rock. With the admission of Alaska to the union (1959), the geographic center of the United States changed from Smith County, Kans., to Butte County, S. Dak. Later that year, when Hawaii became a state, the point moved 6 mi (10 km) to the west-southwest.

Geographic center of North America, point in Pierce County, N. Dak., on which North America would balance if it were a level plane.

Geography, study of all phenomena associated with the earth's surface, including the forces that act upon it. Geography also includes the study of the interaction between the earth and plant, animal, and human life. Some of the matters geographers deal with are the measurement of the earth, navigation, surveying, photogrammetry (mapping from aerial photographs), and cartography (including the study of map projections). Physical geography includes the study of landforms, the relationship between landforms and rocks in the earth's crust, the evolution of landforms, climatology, meteorology, oceanography, and the origin and distribution of soils. Human geography studies human responses to and effects upon an environment, including the location, development, and use of natural resources.

Geology, scientific study of the physical history and structure of earth. Branches of geology include geomorphology (the study of how natural forces shape and alter land forms), petrology (the study of rocks), and mineralogy (the study of minerals). Geochemistry bridges geology and chemistry, investigating the chemical composition of the earth and the origin and distribution of the elements within it. Structural geology studies mountain-building processes and the folding, jointing, and fracturing of rocks. Geophysics bridges geology and physics, applying the law of physics to the study of the earth's interior, atmosphere, and oceans; it includes the study of earthquakes (seismology), volcanoes (volcanology), radioactivity, geomagnetism, and geoelectricity. One of the newest branches of geology is the investigation of plate tectonics, which accounts for the shifting of great land masses that used to be called continental drifts.

Geomagnetic North Pole *see:* North Pole.

Geomagnetic South Pole *see:* South Pole.

Geometry, branch of mathematics concerned with spatial figures, their relationships, and deductive reasoning concerning these figures and relationships. Different geometric systems exist, each based on its own rules (axioms or postulates), components (objects), and self-consistent conclusions (theorems). *Euclidean* geometry, the most familiar type of geometry, was developed by the Greek mathematician Euclid in 300 B.C. It was the first formalized deductive mathematical system, serving as a model for later systems. The axioms it is based on describe points, lines, and circles in a flat surface (plane). They also describe relationships among these objects. According to Euclidean geometry, a straight line may be drawn between any 2 points; a circle may be drawn with a point as its center and any given radius; and through any point outside a line 1 and only 1 parallel line can be formed. *Non-Euclidean* geometries are based on axioms and objects that differ in part or completely from those of Euclidean geometry. Euclidean geometry was the predominant geometric description for centuries. It was not until the 19th century that Nikolai Lobachevski, Janos Bolyai, and G.F.B. Riemann verified the existence of self-consistent systems based on all of Euclid's axioms except the one concerning parallel lines. Through deductive logic, Lobachevski proved the existence of geometric systems where more than one parallel line can be drawn. Riemann's non-Euclidean geometry is a system where no parallel lines exist. Navigation, based on a geometrical system concerned with relationships on the surface of a sphere rather than in a plane, is an example of Riemannian geometry. In it a straight line is defined as a "great circle" (a circle with its center and radius being the same as that of the sphere), and no 2 great circles are parallel. Other geometries exist. *Analytic* geometry, established in 1637 by René Descartes, significantly enhanced the development of geometry by generalizing it through the application of algebra. As a result, figures can be specified relative to coordinate systems by sets of numbers or equations and problems can be solved using algebraic and geometric methods. *Projective* geometry, developed around 1820 by Jean-Victor Poncelet, was a modification of Euclidean space by including points at infinity. Perspective drawing uses these concepts. *Topology,* the most recent branch of geometry (dating from 1911 with the work of Dutch mathematician L.E.J. Brouwer), deals with geometric objects that remain unchanged upon deformation.

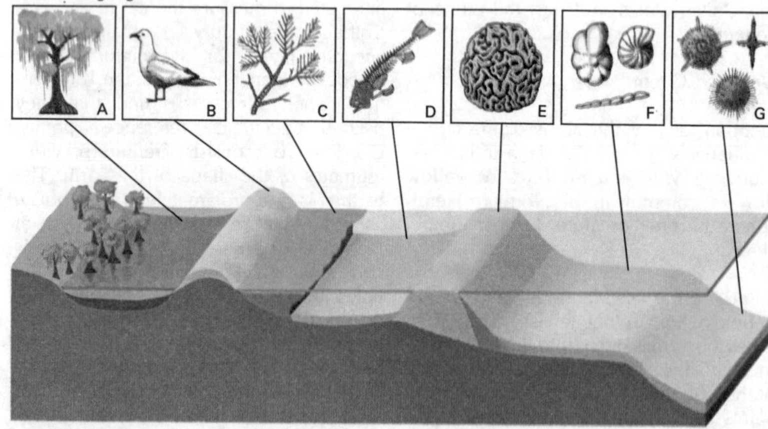

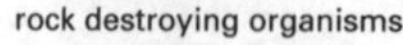

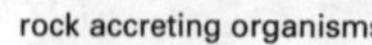

Geology. Living organisms may form rocks by the deposition of their own remains or by the collection and deposition of other material. They may also destroy rocks by their life processes. Key:
A. Peat, lignite or coal making vegetation
B.Guano producring sea-bird
C. Calcareous algae
D. Fish
E. Coral
F. Globigerina
G. Radiolaria
H. Rock splitting roots
I. Pholas (rock-boring mollisc)
J. Mangrove
K. Grass growing on sand

Geomorphology, study of the shape of the earth's surface and the way that landforms are produced.
See also: Tectonics.

Geophysics, physics of the planet earth, including studies of the lithosphere (seismology, geomagnetism, gravitation, radioactivity, electric properties, and heat flow) and studies of the atmosphere and hydrosphere. Geophysical techniques are used extensively in the search for mineral deposits, an area known as exploration geophysics, or geophysical prospecting.

Geopolitics, study of politics in relation to geography and demography. The term was originally applied to the theories of the biologist and geographer Friedrich Ratzel

(1844-1904), who sought to apply evolutionary theory to the rise and fall of nations. In the 1900s the British geographer Sir Halford Mackinder extended these, seeing the international struggle for survival as hanging on control of the heartlands, or interior lands, of the world's great landmasses, particularly the "world island" of Eurasia. The German geographer Karl Haushofer combined these theories to preach the eventual regeneration of Germany through its inevitable demand for *Lebensraum* (German: "living space," space for expansion), which would require sacrifice by the seaboard countries to the more dynamic countries of the heartland. Haushofer's theory was seized upon by Adolf Hitler and became a cornerstone of Nazi doctrine.

George, 6 kings of Great Britain and Ireland. **George I** (1660-1727; r. 1714-27), great-grandson of James I. Of German origin, he was the first king of the House of Hanover (1698). Unable to speak English, he was unpopular and isolated. **George II** (1683-1760; r. 1727-60), son of George I, was preoccupied with military adventures and relied heavily on the advice of Queen Caroline and his ministers. **George III** (1738-1820; r. 1760-1820) was the grandson and successor of George II. His reign saw the American revolution, the expansion of the British Empire in Asia, and the beginning of the industrial revolution. **George IV** (1762-1830; r. 1820-30), son of George III, was despised for his personal extravagances. **George V** (1865-1936; r. 1910-36), son of Edward VII, changed the name of the royal house to Windsor during World War I. **George VI** (1895-1952; r. 1936-52), younger son of George V, came to the throne upon the abdication of his brother Edward VIII. **Queen Elizabeth II** is the older daughter of George VI.

George, 2 kings of Greece. **George I** (1845-1913; r. 1863-1913), a Danish prince, was elected king of Greece after Otto I was deposed in 1862. During George I's reign, which ended with his assassination, Greece increased its territory and adopted a democratic constitution (1864). **George II** (1890-1947; r. 1922-23, 1935-47) went into exile (1923) when the country became a republic. He was restored to the throne in 1935 and instituted a dictatorship run by General John Metaxas. Upon the German invasion of Greece (1941), George fled, spending the war in exile. He returned in 1946, during the civil war, and in 1947 was succeeded by his brother Paul.

George, David Lloyd *see:* Lloyd George, David.

George, Saint, patron saint of England. Possibly a Christian convert martyred in 303, George became connected with many medieval legends, including his rescue of a maiden from a dragon. His feast day is Apr. 23.

George, Stefan (1868-1933), German poet. His symbolist and formally rigorous poems appeared in such volumes as *Algabal* (1892), *The Soul's Year* (1897), and *The New Kingdom* (1928). He was leader of a circle of intellectuals who shared his belief that art should shun the everyday and his devotion to German language and culture.

Georgetown (pop. 72,000), capital and largest city of Guyana, on the north (Atlantic) coast of South America, at the mouth of the Demarara River. The Dutch settled the city in the 1600s and named it Stabroek; in 1812 it came under British control and acquired its current name.
See also: Guyana.

George Washington Bridge, suspension bridge across the Hudson River linking New York City and Fort Lee, N.J. Designed by Othmar Ammann, it was completed in 1931. It has a main span 3,500 ft (1,067 m) in length.

Georgia, independent country in the Caucasus region, bordered by Russia, Azerbaijan, Turkey, Armenia, and the Black Sea. The Caucasus Mountains run across the north of the republic. The capital is Tbilisi. Georgia has a subtropical climate, and the lowland areas near the Black Sea produce tea, fruit, wine, tobacco, and cereals. There is much heavy industry, iron, steel, textiles, and chemicals constituting the main products. Georgians form the majority of the population (70%), and with the remainder comprised of Armenians, Russians, Azerbaijani, Ossetians, Greeks, and Abkhazians. The ancient kingdom of Georgia, dating from the 4th century B.C., reached its height in the 12th and 13th centuries but was partitioned by Turkey and Persia in 1555. Georgia fell under Russian influence in the late 18th century and was annexed in 1801. An attempt to regain independence after the Revolution of 1917 was crushed in 1921. Independence was attained in 1991.
See also: Union of Soviet Socialist Republics.

Georgia

Capital:	Tbilisi
Area:	26,911 sq mi (69,700 sq km)
Population:	5,493,000
Government:	republic
Independent:	1991
GNP:	U.S. $4,659,000,000
Per capita:	U.S. $850

Georgia

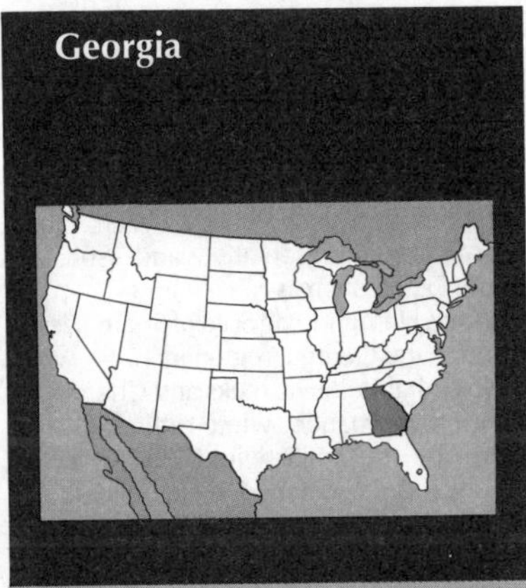

Capital:	Atlanta
Statehood:	Jan. 2, 1788 (4th state)
Familiar name:	Peach State, Empire State of the South
Area:	58,910 sq mi (152,576 sq km) (ranks 21st)
Population:	6,917,000 (1993) (ranks 11th)
Elevation:	Highest—4,784 ft (1,458 m), Brasstown Bald Mountain; Lowest—sea level
Motto:	Wisdom, Justice and Moderation
State flower:	Cherokee rose
State bird:	Brown thrasher
State tree:	Live Oak
State song:	"Georgia on my mind"

Georgia, state in the southeast United States; bordered by the Atlantic Ocean and South Carolina in the east, Florida in the south, Alabama in the west, and Tennessee and North Carolina in the north.
Land and climate. The southern half of Georgia is a low-lying coastal plain that extends along the Atlantic and Gulf coasts. The land slopes gradually upward, becoming more hilly near the point at which the plain meets the Piedmont, which consists of fertile, gently rolling hills. The territory north of the Piedmont is divided into the Appalachian Plateau in the extreme northwest, the Appalachian Ridge and Valley region in the far north, and a portion of the Blue Ridge Mountains in the extreme northeast. Major rivers are the Savannah

and the Chattahoochee. About 70% of the state is covered by forests. Georgia shares one of the largest natural bird refuges in the United States, the Okefenokee Swamp, with Florida. Georgia has a mild, moist climate. Principal cities are Atlanta, one of the nation's leading commercial and finance centers, Columbus, Macon, and Savannah.

Economy. Georgia is one of the most important manufacturing states in the South. Major products include textiles, transportation equipment, processed foods, and paper. The state is a leading producer of eggs and broiler chickens, and it ranks 1st in the nation in peanut production. Other important crops are tobacco and peaches. Georgia's most valuable mineral products are clays, including kaolin. The state is also an important producer of lumber and other forest products.

Government. The state constitution was adopted in 1983. The governor is elected for a 4-year term. The general assembly, Georgia's legislature, consists of a 56-member senate and a 180-member house of representatives serving for 2 years. Georgia sends 10 representatives and 2 senators to the U.S. Congress.

History. Hernando de Soto of Spain passed through the Georgia region in 1540, when it was inhabited by Creeks and Cherokees. The first permanent white settlement was made by the English in 1733. Much of Georgia, the last of the 13 original colonies to be founded, was captured during the American Revolution (1776-83). The state, which depended on slave labor to support its cotton-based economy, seceded from the Union in 1861. Many battles of the Civil War (1861-65) were fought in Georgia, which suffered considerable damage, including the burning of Atlanta by General William T. Sherman in 1864. The state was readmitted to the Union in 1870. Industry began to expand that year. By mid-20th century, more Georgians worked in manufacturing than in agriculture. Although Georgia passed laws against compulsory segregation in 1960, school integration is still a concern, and industrial and population growth have caused urban problems.

Georgian architecture, 18th-century architectural style in Britain and the British North American colonies. In Britain it refers to the classically formal and elegant style, influenced by the Italian Renaissance architect Andrea Palladio and the English Palladian Inigo Jones, popular during the reigns of the first 3 Georges. In the United States it refers to the style prevailing between 1700 and the Revolution, deriving more from Christopher Wren and the Baroque; Palladian influences entered later. Fine examples are Independence Hall, Philadelphia (1745), and King's Chapel in Boston (1754).

Geothermal power *see:* Energy supply; Volcano.

Geranium, any of the cosmopolitan, hardy perennial herbs of the family Geraniaceae, some of which are cultivated in gardens and as house plants, especially the popular pot and bedding plants of the genus *Pelargonium.* Common, or zonal, geraniums have white, salmon, pink, or red flowers, single or semidouble, some with bronze or maroon zones on the leaves. Another decorative-leafed variety is the ivy-leaf geranium (*P. peltatum*).

Geranium

Gerbil, or sand rat, small rodent of the family Cricetidae found in desert or semidesert regions of Africa and Asia. It has fine, dense fur and a long tail and can move fast by hopping. Gerbils live in burrows and eat seeds, flowers, and roots. As they are easy to keep, needing little water and simple food, they are popular as laboratory animals and as pets.

Geriatrics, branch of medicine specializing in the care of the elderly. Although concerned with the same diseases as the rest of medicine, the different susceptibility of the aged and a tendency for these people to have a number of disorders at the same time make its scope different. In addition, the psychological problems of old age differ markedly from those encountered in the rest of the population and require special management.

Géricault, (Jean Louis André) Théodore (1791-1824), French painter. His style combined a massive, dynamic romanticism with a minutely detailed realism. In his studies of lunatics, his horse paintings, and the *Raft of the Medusa* (1818-1819), Géricault's revolutionary approach helped eclipse the classical school in French art.

Germ *see:* Bacteria; Disease; Virus.

German Democratic Republic *see:* Germany.

Germanium, chemical element, symbol Ge; for physical constants see Periodic Table. Germanium was discovered in 1886 by Clemens Winkler. It occurs in the mineral germanite, in zinc ores, and in coal. It is produced by reducing its dioxide with hydrogen. Germanium is a crystalline, brittle metalloid. It is used extensively in semiconductors. Germanium and its compounds are used in transistors, alloys, and phosphors and as catalysts.

German, official language of Germany and Austria and an official language of Switzerland and Luxembourg, native tongue of more than 100 million people. Modern German is descended from 2 main forms. Low German, spoken mainly in the north, is the ancestor of both Dutch and Flemish. High German, spoken in central and southern Germany is, historically, the classical German. A large part of medieval German literature, such as the 12th and 13th century epics, is in Middle High German. Today the written language is standardized, but there are still great differences between spoken northern and southern German. Modern German is a highly inflected language with 3 genders and 4 cases, and requires agreement in number, gender, and case, as in Latin. Many words are formed by compounding.

German literature, literature of the German-speaking peoples in Europe, primarily the Germans, Austrians, and Swiss. The German language, like its literature, has strong regional characteristics. The language of southern and central Germany is considered High German, while the language of the northern regions is called Low German. Almost without exception, the great works of German literature have been written in High German.

Early German literature. The earliest works in German literature date from the 9th Century A.D. and were inspired by the growth of monasteries. The monks disseminated Christian thought through literature. As a result, poems and stories based on biblical sources were popularized. The first known German author of this period was a monk, Otfried von Weissenberg, who wrote *The Book of Gospels* in rhyme. In addition, the monks chronicled some of the more ancient heroic sagas and invented new ones. One of the classics of this era is the story *Lay of Hildebrand,* whose author is anonymous.

The golden ages of German literature. The first great, or golden, age of German literature occurred in the 12th century and was inspired by the Crusades and chivalry. Many of the great works were epics written by knights, who through the literature expressed love, courage, and a belief in God. Wandering minstrels, or minnesingers, composed poems of love and adventure. Perhaps the most famous minnesinger was Walther von der Vogelweide. One of the great works of this era is the epic poem *Song of the Nibelungs.* Another major influence on the German literature of this period is the legend of King Arthur, which came to Germany from France. The German poet Hartmann von Aue, inspired by these Arthurian tales, composed an important work of this period in Germany: *Poor Henry.* The greatest work of the German Middle Ages, however, was a poem about a knight's search for God written by Wolfram von Eschenbach: *Parzival.* Another major work of this golden age is *Tristan and Isolde* (early 13th century), written by Gottfried von Strassburg.

The highest literary expression during the Renaissance (16th century) was influenced by the events of the Reformation and the development of humanism. It is, however, in the 18th century that the second golden age began and the greatest cultural achievement was accomplished in Germany. During this era the works of Johann Wolfgang von Goethe in drama (*The Sorrows of Young Werther, Faust*); Friedrich Schiller in drama, poetry, and history (*The Robbers, Wallenstein, William Tell*); Immanuel Kant in metaphysics (*Critique of Pure Reason, Critique of Practical Reason*); and the brothers Grimm in folk literature (*Fairy Tales*) were all created.

German literature of the late 19th and early 20th centuries. The late 19th and early 20th centuries were characterized by a literature of naturalism characterized by social concern exemplified in the works of Karl Marx (*Communist Manifesto, Capital*) and Friedrich Nietzche (*Thus Spake Zarathustra*). Also from this era are the works of more impressionistic writers whose focus was more idealistic, including Thomas Mann (*Buddenbrooks, The Magic Mountain*), Herman Hesse (*Demian, Steppenwolf, Siddartha*), and Arthur Schnitzler (*The Reckoning, Anatol*). In poetry, the works of Rainer Maria Rilke and Stefan George are most notable. The literature after World War I is often referred to as expressionistic, but shares with the naturalistic literature an emphasis on social concerns. Its unique characteristic, however, is the often terrifying and horrific dimension of the works. Its most important author is Frank Kafka (*The Trial, The Castle, Amerika*). Two of his short stories deserve particular distinction because they have become classics of world literature: "The Metamorphosis" and "A Country Doctor."

German literature after 1945. The literature immediately following World War II dealt mostly with the war and its impact on German spirit and civilization. Most notable are the works of Heinrich Böll (*Group Portrait with Lady*), Günter Grass (*The Tin Drum*), and Siegfried Lenz, whose works continued into the 1970s and 1980s.

German measles, or rubella, infectious viral disease causing rash and fever. Although physical symptoms are usually mild, it is dangerous if contracted by a woman during the first 3 months of pregnancy, since it can then seriously harm the fetus, causing birth defects.

There is a vaccine, which is usually given to children and to women of childbearing age who have not had the disease. Those who have already had it are immune to getting it again.

See also: Measles.

German shepherd dog, breed of dog developed in Germany in the early 1900s to be a herder. Also called a German police dog, it is now used in police and military work and as a guide dog. German shepherds are muscular, with large, pointed ears, long snouts, and dense black, gray, or tan coats. They stand about 24 in (61 cm) and weigh 60-85 lb (27-39 kg).

German short-haired pointer, dog used by hunters for pointing, following game, and guarding. It stands 24 to 25 in (62 to 64 cm) tall, weighs 55 to 70 lbs (25 to 32 kg), and has a keen sense of smell.

German wirehaired pointer, hunting dog and retriever, first bred in Germany in the mid-1800s by crossing the German short-haired pointer and the poodle-pointer. The German wirehaired pointer stands 24 to 26 in (61 to 66 cm) at the shoulder and weighs 55 to 65 lb (25 to 29 kg). Its coat may be brown or brown and white with liver-colored spots.

Germany, country of central Europe that was divided into 2 nations after World War II. In 1990 the Federal Republic of Germany (West Germany) joined with the German Democratic Republic (East Germany) to form a single German state. Germany is

Germany

General information	
Capital:	Bonn (Germany: Berlin; Bonn seat of government)
Area:	137,854 sq mi (357,042 sq km)
Population:	77,744,000
Official language:	German
Monetary unit:	1 Deutsche Mark = 100 Pfennige
Main cities:	Berlin (aggl. more than 3,000,000 inh.), Hamburg, Munich, Cologne
Government	
Form:	Federal republic
Independent:	divided after Word War II; united in 1990
Head of state:	President (elected every 5 years)
Head of government:	Chancellor
Legislature:	two legislative houses (Federal Council and Federal Diet)
Executive:	President and Federal Government
Judiciary:	Highest court is the Federal Constitutional Court
Political division:	16 states
National economy	
Gross national product:	U.S.$1,138,913,000,000
Per capita income:	about U.S. $15,000
Agriculture:	sugar beet, wheat, barley, potatoes, oats, maize
Livestock:	pigs, cattle, sheep
Fisheries:	335,800 metric tons
Mining:	brown and hard coal, natural gas, iron and copper ore, potash salts
Industries:	metal products and machinery, food, beverages and tobacco, chemicals and chemical products, iron and steel, paper
Main exports:	machinery and transport equipment (automobiles), basic manufactures, chemicals and related products, miscellaneous manufactured articles)
Transport:	railway since 1835, 50,226 mi (80,829 km) of railroads, 382,020 mi (614,700 km) of roads, 8 international airports
Trading partners:	France, The Netherlands, United Kingdom, United States, Eastern Europe
People	
Urban:	83.5%
Ethnic composition:	German 94%, Turkish 2%, others 4%
Birth rate:	11.2 per 1,000 population
Death rate:	11.6 per 1,000 population
Infant mortality:	9 per 1,000 live births
Life expectancy:	male 71 years, female 76.5 years

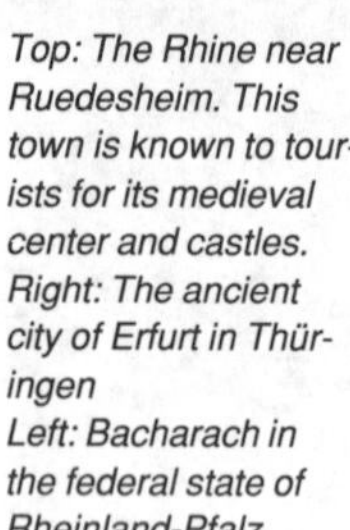

Top: The Rhine near Ruedesheim. This town is known to tourists for its medieval center and castles.
Right: The ancient city of Erfurt in Thüringen
Left: Bacharach in the federal state of Rheinland-Pfalz.

bordered by Austria and Switzerland in the south; France, Luxembourg, Belgium, and the Netherlands in the west; the North and Baltic seas and Denmark in the north; and Czechoslovakia and Poland in the east.

Land and climate. The northern part of Germany is a lowland area, while the south and central parts contain highlands. The western section has the Black and Bohemian forests. The eastern part is mostly flat, but it contains the Thuringian, the Bohemian, and the Oberfalz forests. Germany's climate is temperate with mild summers and cool winters and moderate precipitation in all seasons. A maritime climate prevails in the western section, whereas more extreme continental influences are felt in the east.

People. Essentially, the Germans are of 2 distinct types: the Nordic people, usually tall, fair-skinned, and blue-eyed, and the stockier Alpine type of the south, who are often dark-haired and brown-eyed. More than 80 percent of the German people live in urban areas; the area around the Rhine and Ruhr rivers is one of the most heavily populated sections of Europe. The language is German, divided into 2 distinct forms: High German, spoken in the north, and Low German, spoken in the south. In addition, there are numerous dialects confined to certain regions and cities.

The dismantling of Checkpoint Charlie, Berlin, June 22, 1990, in presence of the ministers of foreign affairs of the Allies of World War II and those of the two Germanies.

Economy. Germany (at least the former western part) has one of the strongest economies in Europe. It is a world leader in manufacturing and heavy industry, due mainly to its large coal deposits, which provide the necessary energy for these enterprises. It is also a major producer of chemicals, for industrial use and for use in medicines, plastics, fertilizers, and synthetic fabrics. Its optics and electronics industries are world leaders in these technologies, and their products are noted for their quality and dependability. Its financial and banking network is one of the most powerful in the world. The smaller part that formerly made up East Germany suffered from 40 years of mismanagement under its communist government, and its economy lags far behind the highly developed west both in quantity and quality of its output. The new German government has made it clear it will raise the backward economy of the east to the level of the rest of the country.

History. The Romans succeeded in conquering the west bank of the Rhine (1st century B.C.-1st century A.D.) but they could not bring the Teutonic tribes of the area into the empire. It was the Romans who named the tribes' land *Germania.* In A.D. 768, Charlemagne, the great Frankish ruler, came to power and united most of the territory of modern France and Germany into the Frankish empire. In 843, the empire was divided among Charlemagne's 3 grandsons, with the area east of the Rhine going to Louis the German. Louis's kingdom subsequently was divided into independent duchies, and efforts to create a single state remained unsuccessful until the 19th century. The modern state of Germany was first created in the late 19th century by Otto von Bismarck. In a successful series of wars, he brought much of Germany under Prussian domination, and in 1871 he saw King Wilhelm I of Prussia crowned kaiser (emperor) and hereditary monarch of the empire. In 1890, Kaiser Wilhelm II (grandson of Wilhelm I) dismissed Bismarck as chancellor and embarked on a policy of nationalistic expansionism that brought Germany repeated conflict with other European states. In 1914 the strains proved too much, and Europe plunged into World War I. Germany was defeated, and in 1919 it gave up both empire and king and became the Weimar Republic. Throughout the 1920s and 1930s the republic suffered severe economic crises and social unrest, partly due to the harsh treatment of the Treaty of Versailles that ended World War I. As a result, in 1933 Adolf Hitler became chancellor of Germany and set about establishing a dictatorship (the Third Reich) that fostered extreme military aggression, nationalism, and racial violence. Hitler's expansionism (reoccupation of the Rhineland in 1936, annexation of Austria in 1938, and the takeover of Czechoslovakia in 1939) alarmed other European powers. Finally, Germany's invasion of Poland in Sept. 1939 triggered World War II. In 1945, the Allies defeated the Third Reich, ending World War II in Europe. Germany was occupied by the 4 victorious powers (United States, Soviet Union, France, and England) and in 1949 was divided into 2 sectors: East Germany (which became a communist state under Soviet influence) and West Germany (which became a republic allied with the western democracies and the United States). West Germany flourished economically while East Germany stagnated. In 1990, following the collapse of the Soviet-led alliance of eastern European nations, Germany was reunified, this time as a republic firmly rooted in the democratic, free-enterprise European Economic Community. It is now the largest and most prosperous country in the community and a worldwide economic and industrial power. It is expected to play a major role in helping to shape the new political and economic relationships of post cold-war Europe.

Germicide *see:* Antiseptic; Disinfectant.

Germination, resumption of growth of a plant embryo contained in the seed after a period of reduced metabolic activity or dormancy. Conditions required for germination include an adequate water supply, sufficient oxygen, and a favorable temperature. Rapid uptake of water followed by increased rate of respiration are often the first signs of germination. During germination, stored food reserves are rapidly used up to provide the energy and raw materials required for the new growth. The embryonic root and shoot that break through the seed coat are termed the radicle and plumule, respectively. In hypogeal germination the seed leaves, or cotyledons, remain below the ground. In epigeal germination they grow above the ground and become the first photosynthetic organs.

Germ theory *see:* Medicine.

Germ warfare *see:* Chemical and biological warfare.

Geronimo (1829-1909), greatest war leader of the Apache tribe of Arizona. When his tribe was forcibly removed to a barren reservation, he led an increasingly large band of hit-and-run raiders (1876-86). Twice induced to surrender by Lt. Col. George Crook, he was driven to escape again by maltreatment. Persuaded to surrender a third time by Gen. Nelson Miles, he was summarily exiled to Florida and resettled in Oklahoma, where he became a successful farmer.

Gerontology *see:* Old age.

Gerry, Elbridge (1744-1814), U.S. politician for whom the gerrymander (arrangement of election districts virtually to ensure the success of a candidate) was named. He signed the Declaration of Independence and attended the Constitutional Convention (1787), was a member of Congress (1789-93), governor of Massachusetts (1810-12), and vice president under James Madison (1813-14).

Gerrymander, political practice, usually employed by the party in power as a means of staying in power, involving the division of the electoral boundaries of a city, state, or county to favor a particular party or candidate. The term came into use in 1812 when Elbridge Gerry was governor of Massachusetts.

Gershwin, George (1898-1937), U.S. composer. From an immigrant background, he rose to fame first as a songwriter and then with musical shows like *Lady, Be Good!* (1924), his first Broadway success, and the Pulitzer Prize-winning satire *Of Thee I Sing* (1931), among many others. He also wrote highly regarded orchestral pieces, *Rhapsody in Blue* (1924), *Piano Concerto* (1925), and *An American in Paris* (1928), and an opera, *Porgy and Bess* (1935), noted for its lyricism and emotional power. Many of his songs, as well as *Porgy and Bess*, were written in collaboration with his lyricist brother, **Ira Gershwin** (1896-1983). His work shows the influence of Maurice Ravel, Igor Stravinsky, and, especially, U.S. jazz.

Gessler *see:* Tell, William.

Gestalt psychology, school of psychology concerned with the tendency of the human (and even primate) mind to organize perceptions into "wholes"—for example, to hear a symphony rather than a large number of separate notes of different tones—due to the mind's ability to complete patterns from the available stimuli. Its main proponents were Max Wertheimer, Kurt Koffka, and Wolfgang Köhler. Focusing on the patterns formed by a subject in order to deal with experience, the school provides an alternate to the structuralist approach.
See also: Koffka, Kurt; Köhler, Wolfgang; Psychology; Wertheimer, Max.

Gestapo, abbreviated form of *Geheime Staatspolizei* (secret state police), the executive arm of the Nazi police force, 1936-45, possessing almost unlimited authority. Under the control of Heinrich Himmler, it

Geronimo, chief of the Appaches, famous for their fierce struggle against the whites.

shared responsibility for internal security and administered the concentration camps. The Gestapo arrested and sent to the camps thousands of Jews, intellectuals, clergy, homosexuals, and other "undesirables." It was declared a criminal organization at the Nuremburg Trials (1945-46).
See also: Himmler, Heinrich; Nazism.

Gethsemane (Hebrew: *gat semanim,* "oil press"), the garden across the Kidron valley, on the Mount of Olives, east of the old city of Jerusalem, where Jesus prayed on the eve of his crucifixion and was betrayed. Gethsemane was probably an olive grove; its precise location is disputed.

Getty, J(ean) Paul (1892-1976), U.S. business executive and one of the richest men in the world. He inherited his father's oil company, vastly expanded its wealth, and became an important art collector, founding and endowing the J. Paul Getty Museum in Malibu, Calif. (1954). From the early 1950s Getty lived in England. At his death, he left the museum $750 million.

Gettysburg (pop. 7,025), town in Pennsylvania and seat of Adams County, situated near the Maryland border, about 36 mi (58 km) southwest of Harrisburg. Gettysburg is a noted tourist attraction as the site of the Civil War Battle of Gettysburg and of President Abraham Lincoln's famous Gettysburg Address. The Gettysburg National Military Park contains many Civil War monuments. President Dwight D. Eisenhower made his home at Gettysburg.
See also: Pennsylvania.

Gettysburg, Battle of, central conflict of the U.S. Civil War, fought July 1-3, 1863. In a daring maneuver, Confederate general Robert E. Lee struck deep into Union territory, reaching Pennsylvania in June 1863. He and the Union Army of the Potomac, under Gen. George G. Meade, converged upon Gettysburg, Pa. On July 1 and 2 there were many inconclusive attacks and

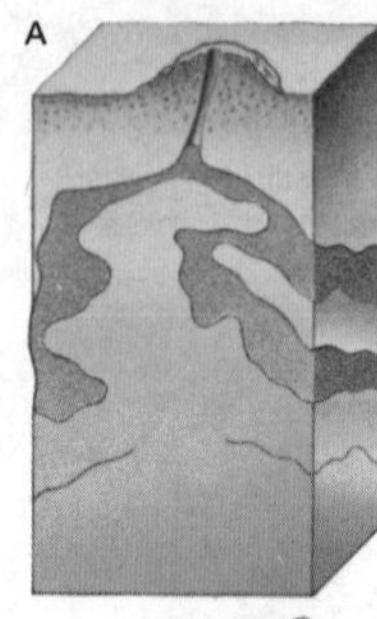

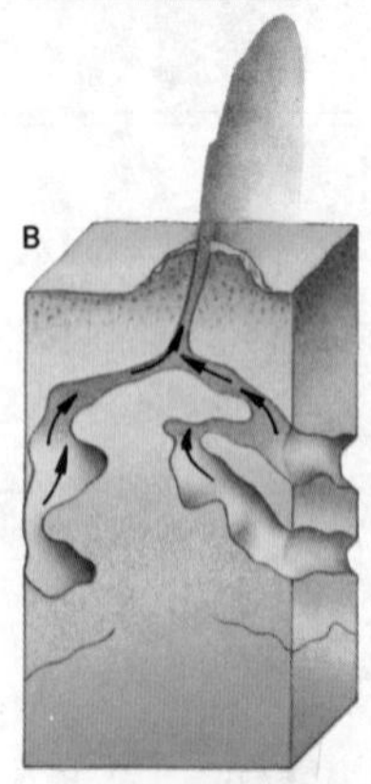

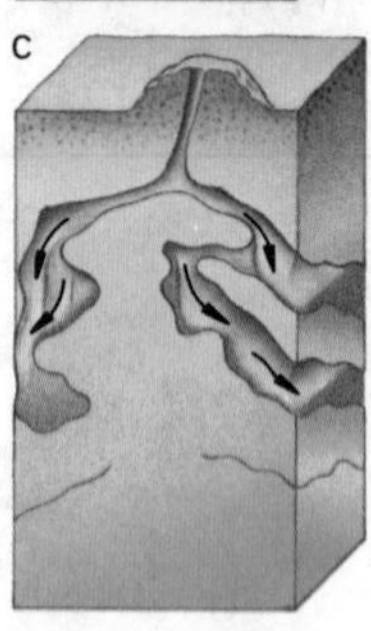

Geyser.
A. Interconnecting series of underground chambers filled with water and heated from below.
B. Expansion of steam at the bottom forces water out of the top, reducing pressure and producing more steam.
C. The system refills with ground water and the cycle starts again.

counterattacks. Union reinforcements arrived on July 2. On July 3 suicidal Confederate attacks broke the Union line on Cemetery Ridge but were driven back in disorder. On July 4, after a day of stalemate, Lee retreated under cover of night and rain. Union losses were over 23,000, around 25%; Confederate losses were around 25,000, a similar percentage. The costly battle marked a reversal in the fortunes of the Confederacy, paving the way for the eventual Union victory.
See also: Civil War, U.S.

Gettysburg Address, speech delivered by President Abraham Lincoln at the dedication of the national cemetery at Gettysburg, Pa., on Nov. 19, 1863. A brief masterpiece of oratory, it combined the themes of grief for the dead with the need for maintenance of the principles they had died to uphold.

Getz, Stan(ley) (1927-), U.S. jazz musician. He played the saxophone under bandleaders Stan Kenton, Benny Goodman, and Woody Herman, before forming his own smaller groups. Influenced by jazz saxophonists Lester Young and Charlie Parker, during the 1950s Getz evolved his distinctive, intimate and reflective, "cool" jazz style.
See also: Jazz.

Geyser, hot spring, found in currently or recently volcanic regions, that intermittently jets steam and superheated water into the air. It consists essentially of a system of underground tubelike fractures leading down to a heat source. Groundwater accumulates in the tube, that near the bottom being kept from boiling by the pressure of the cooler layers above. When the critical temperature is reached, bubbles rise, heating the upper layers, which expand and well out of the orifice. This reduces the pressure enough for substantial steam formation below, with subsequent eruption. The process then recommences. The famous Old Faithful in Yellowstone National Park used to erupt every 66.5 min, but has recently become less reliable.

Ghana, in West Africa, independent country bordered by the Atlantic Ocean (Gulf of Guinea) on the south, by the Ivory Coast on the west, by Togo on the east, and by Burkina Faso on the north. Accra, on the coast, is the capital and largest city.
Land and climate. Ghana is generally a low-lying country. Beyond the narrow coastal plain, the Kwahu Plateau extends inland, giving way to rolling savanna in the north. A belt of tropical rainforest covers much of the plateau. The Volta River system with its tributaries, the Black and White Voltas and the Oti, covers much of the country and forms a delta with lagoons and swamps at its mouth, east of Accra. With the completion of Akosombo Dam in 1965, about 70 mi (113 km) from the sea, the Volta formed a lake of over 3,000 sq mi (7,770 sq km) for hydroelectric power and irrigation.
People. Ghana has many ethnic groups, the most numerous being the Akan family, which includes the Fanti and Ashanti tribes. Other large groups are the Ga, the Ewe, and the Mole-Dagbani. The official language is English, though tribal languages are also used. About 40% of the people are Christian and about 10% are Muslim. The rest practice traditional African religions. The education system is highly developed. Institutions of higher learning include the University of Ghana, the University of Science and Technology at Kumasi, the University College of Cape Coast, and many technical schools. Though most of the population still depend directly on agriculture, urbanization is developing rapidly.
Economy. Cocoa is Ghana's biggest export, but coffee and tobacco are also grown, and there are mineral exports of gold, industrial diamonds, manganese, and bauxite. Local industries include aluminum, timber, and food processing.

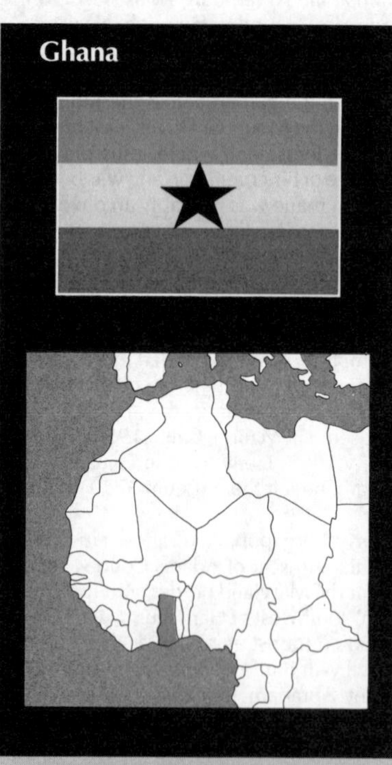

General information	
Capital:	Accra
Area:	92,098 sq mi (238,533 sq km)
Population:	14,566,000
Official language:	English
Monetary unit:	1 Cedi = 100 pesewas
Main cities:	Accra, Kumasi, Tamale
Government	
Form:	republic
Independent:	1957
Head of state:	Chairman of the Provisional National Defence Council
Head of government:	Chairman of the Defense Council
Legislature:	no legislative body
Executive:	Chairman of the Provisional National Defence Council and Committee of Secretaries
Judiciary:	highest court is the Supreme Court
Political division:	10 regions
National economy	
Gross national product:	U.S. $5,610,000,000
Per capita income:	U.S. $400
Agriculture:	cassava, yams, plantains, cocoa beans, tomatoes
Livestock:	goats, sheep, cattle
Fisheries:	372,000 metric tons
Mining:	manganese ore, bauxite, diamonds, gold ore
Industries:	kerosine, gasoline and diesel fuel, cement, wheat flour, soap, cocoa products
Main exports:	cocoa, gold, sawn timber, logs
Transportation:	592 mi (953 km) of railroads; 17,600 mi (28,300 km) of roads; 1 international airport
Trading partners:	United Kingdom, Nigeria, Germany, Japan, United States
People	
Urban:	32%
Ethnic composition:	Akan 52.5%, Mossi 16%, Ewe 12%, Ga-Adangme 8%
Birth rate:	44.3 per 1,000 population
Death rate:	13.1 per 1,000 population
Infant mortality:	90 per 1,000 live births
Life expectancy:	male 52 years, female 56 years

Ghana. The ruler of one of the ethnic groups and his court.

History. Before colonialism, Ghana had a number of independent kingdoms, mainly the Ashanti Federation and Fanti states along the coast. The first European colonizers were the Portuguese, who arrived in 1482. The French, Danes, Dutch, and British all competed in the slave and gold trade, and in the 19th century the Ashanti organized a resistance. They were defeated by the British in 1874, and in 1901 Ghana formally became a British colony, called the Gold Coast. Ghana was a center of African nationalism, and it was one of the first African countries to win independence, in 1957. Kwame Nkrumah became premier. In 1960 he declared the country a republic, with himself as president for life. While he made reforms in education, transportation, and other social services, during his rule many political opponents were jailed, and government became increasingly inefficient and corrupt. In 1966 Nkrumah was deposed. After political instability throughout the 1970s, civilian rule was restored in 1979. But economic conditions did not improve, and at the end of 1981 the military, under Jerry Rawlings, again took control.

Ghana, Ancient Empire of, former empire in West Africa, centered between the Niger and the Senegal rivers. At the height of its power, the empire stretched from the Atlantic Ocean nearly as far as Timbuktu. Probably founded about the 4th century A.D., it reached its height in the 10th century. In the 11th century the invasions of the Muslim Almoravids of North Africa greatly weakened the empire. The empire regained its independence but never recovered its power. It was eclipsed by the rise of the Mali Empire in the 13th century and became part of that empire. Ghana carried on a flourishing trade with Morocco and was a highly organized state, with a powerful military force. *Ghana* was the title of the ruler and also the name of some of the various capitals. The name has been taken by the modern African state of Ghana.

Ghent (pop. 236,500), historic city in western Belgium, at the junction of the Lys (Leie) and Scheldt rivers. Former capital of Flanders, it was the textile center of medieval Europe. Its textile industry is still important, along with paper, chemical, and metal production. It also has a major port. In the 16th and 17th centuries it was a center of Flemish art.
See also: Belgium.

Ghent, Treaty of, treaty concluded on Dec. 24, 1814, in Ghent, Belgium, formally ending the War of 1812 between Britain and the United States. Because the war had developed into a military stalemate, the treaty was essentially a return to prewar status. No concession was made over the impressment of former British citizens from U.S. ships, a major U.S. grievance, but the resulting British withdrawal from interference in the affairs of the American Northwest opened the frontier to westward expansion.
See also: War of 1812.

Ghetto, in European history, street or section of a city once set aside for the compulsory residence of Jews. The word itself is probably derived from the name of the area of Venice to which the Jews of that city were confined in 1516. Ghettos spread throughout Italy during the Counter-Reformation (the late 16th century) and had already been in existence in northern Europe for hundreds of years. The ghetto was surrounded by walls, and it was illegal for a Jew to remain outside its gates after the curfew hour. The French Revolution and reform movements of the 19th century removed legal discrimination against Jews in Western Europe and the ghettos were abolished. However, the practice was revived by fascist governments in World War II. Today the term refers to slum areas of inner cities in which minority groups are compelled to live, not by law, but by the forces of discrimination and poverty.

Ghibellines *see:* Guelphs and Ghibellines.

Ghiberti, Lorenzo (1378-1455), Italian sculptor. A Florentine, he was a leading figure of the early Renaissance, famous for his second pair of bronze doors, *Gates of Paradise* (1425-52), for the Florence baptistery.

Ghirlandajo, or **Ghirlandaio, Domenico** (Domenico di Tommaso Bigordi; 1449-94), Florentine Renaissance painter said to have taught Michelangelo. His frescoes include *St. Jerome* (1480) and the *Last Supper* (1480), both in the Church of the Ognissanti, Florence. He also helped decorate parts of the Sistine Chapel, and is noted for his portraits, among them *Grandfather and Grandson*.

Ghost dance, ceremonial ritual of a religion originated by the Paiute Indians in Nevada c.1870. It was led by the mystic prophet Wovoka, who prophesied the rebirth of the dead and the restoration of the Indians to their lands. The ritual took place over several days and was characterized by hypnotic trances. The Sioux performed the ritual prior to their massacre at Wounded Knee in 1890 in the belief that they would be protected from the bullets.

Giacometti, Alberto (1901-66), Swiss-born sculptor and painter who lived in Paris. He is best known for his elongated and skeletal human figures, which convey a sense of extreme spiritual isolation—*Man Pointing* and *Man Walking* (1947). His early work was influenced by primitive art and surrealism (*The Palace at 4 A.M.*, 1932).

Giant, in myths, human creature of great size and strength; survivor of races that lived before humanity. The Greek giants, the Titans, warred against the gods of Olympus. Other giants, such as the biblical

Ghent, the Gravensteen

Goliath, are probably exaggerated memories of large, fierce men.
See also: Mythology.

Giant panda *see:* Panda.

Giant schnauzer, largest dog of the schnauzer breed, standing about 25 in (65 cm) and weighing about 76 lb (35 kg). The giant schnauzer was developed in southern Germany in the 1700s by crossbreeding standard schnauzers with German sheepdogs. It is highly regarded as a watchdog.

Giant sequoia *see:* Sequoia.

Gibberellin, any of a group of chemical compounds that stimulate plant growth. Some gibberellins are plant hormones. Gibberellins cause dwarf varieties of peas, beans, corn, and coffee to grow as high as tall varieties, induce dormant seeds to germinate, and make sugarcane longer, thus increasing its yield of sugar. They may also be useful for stimulating growth of pastures and lawns during winter. The gibberellins were first noticed by a Japanese plant pathologist, E. Kurosawa, in 1926, during his investigations of a fungus disease of rice that caused elongation of the plant.

Gibbon, smallest of the apes, distinguishable by its very long arms. It is the only ape to walk upright with ease. Six species live in Southeast Asia. They can leap over 30 ft (9 m) and swing nimbly through the trees.

Gibbon, Edward (1737-94), English historian, author of *The History of the Decline and Fall of the Roman Empire* (6 vols., 1776-88), the greatest historical work of the 18th century and a literary masterpiece. Gibbon served somewhat unsuccessfully as a member of Parliament (1774-83).

André Gide

Gibbons v. Ogden, U.S. Supreme Court decision of Mar. 2, 1824, important in defining the power of Congress. Aaron Ogden, a steamship operator, held a license from a company given a monopoly of steamship traffic on the Hudson River by the New York legislature. He sought to prevent Thomas Gibbons, who held a license from the federal government, from competing with him. Chief Justice John Marshall's decision upholding Gibbons was widely praised because it affirmed Congress's power over interstate commerce and broke up a powerful monopoly of steamboat travel.

Gibbs, Josiah Willard (1839-1903), U.S. physicist best known for his pioneering work in chemical thermodynamics and his contributions to statistical mechanics. In *On the Equilibrium of Heterogeneous Substances* (1876, 1878) he states Gibbs's Phase Rule for chemical systems. In the course of his research on the electromagnetic theory of light, he made fundamental contributions to the art of vector analysis.
See also: Thermodynamics.

Gibraltar, self-governing British colony, 2.3 sq mi (6 sq km) in area, on the rock of Gibraltar at the southern tip of the Iberian peninsula. The population is mixed; natives are of English, Genoese, Portuguese, and Maltese descent. The economy rests on light industry, shipping, and tourism, and on the important British naval and airbases. Gibraltar was captured from Spain in 1704. A 1967 referendum showed overwhelming opposition to a return to Spanish rule.

Gibraltar, Strait of, narrow body of water between Spain and North Africa, connecting the Mediterranean Sea with the Atlantic Ocean. It is the only natural waterway between the Mediterranean and any ocean. Through this narrow strait (only about 8.5 mi/13.7 km wide) a strong current flows into the Atlantic. The strait gives access from Northern Europe and North America not only to the Mediterranean basin, but also to the Black Sea and, via the Suez Canal, to East Africa, the Persian Gulf, and south Asia.

Gibran, Kahlil (1883-1931), Lebanese essayist and philosopher-poet who blended elements of Eastern and Western mysticism. Influenced by Blake and Nietzsche, he published *The Prophet*, his best-known work, in 1923; *The Garden of the Prophet* appeared in 1934.
See also: Philosophy.

Gibson, Althea (1927-), U.S. golf and tennis player, the first black to enter the United States women's tennis championship singles. She won that tournament in 1957-58, along with the Wimbledon women's singles championship. She then turned professional and began competing in golf tournaments.

Gibson, Charles Dana (1867-1944), U.S. artist, a fashion illustrator who created the "Gibson Girl." Based on his wife, she was an elegant and high-spirited figure who typified the ideal American woman in the early 20th century.

Gide, André (1869-1951), French writer. His relentless examination of his own standards and assumptions and the resulting inner conflicts made him one of the foremost figures in French literature in the first half of the 20th century. In 1947 he was awarded the Nobel Prize for literature. Among his best-known works are the novels *The Immoralist* (1902) and *The Counterfeiters* (1926), and 4 volumes of *Journals* (1889-1949).

Gideon, in the Bible (Judges), leader and judge of Israel who, by his exploits in repelling the desert raiders, the Midianites, became a national hero. Having put the invaders to flight with a small force of 300 of his clan, Gideon was offered the crown. Though he declined it, his son Abimelech briefly asserted the authority his father had earned and became king.
See also: Bible.

Gideon v. Wainwright, case involving the right of a defendant in a criminal case to legal counsel. In 1963 the U.S. Supreme Court ruled that Clarence Gideon, an indigent convicted of burglary by a Florida court, had been wrongfully imprisoned because, not being able to afford a lawyer, he had defended himself. The Supreme Court held that all defendants in criminal cases are entitled to counsel and that attorneys must be provided for defendants who are indigent. This ruling overturned that in *Betts* v. *Brady* (1942), which had established that the right to a lawyer was not essential.

Gielgud, Sir (Arthur) John (1904-), British actor, producer, and director, noted early in his career for his Shakespearean roles, especially Hamlet and Richard III. Highly versatile, he created many modern roles in his maturity in numerous stage, film, and television performances.

Gierek, Edward (1913-), first secretary of the Polish Communist Party (1970-80). He was appointed to improve the standard of living following food riots in late 1970. A failing economy and labor unrest led to his fall from power in 1980.
See also: Poland.

Gila monster (*Heloderma suspectum*), stout-bodied lizard, up to 2 ft (61 cm) long. It and the related beaded lizard (*H. horridum*) are the only poisonous lizards. Both live in the deserts of the southwestern states and in Mexico. The gila monster is so rare that it is protected by law.

Gila River, river in Arizona and New Mexico, flowing westward and joining the Colorado River near Yuma, Calif. Over 600 mi (960 km) long, the river provides irrigation water for the surrounding farmland. Coolidge Dam is situated on the Gila River.

Gilbert, Sir Humphrey (1539?-83), English soldier and explorer. Granted a royal charter to colonize unclaimed lands in North America (1578), he founded England's first North American colony, at St. John's, Newfoundland (1583). He went down with his ship at sea near the Azores.

Gilbert, William (1544-1603), English scientist. Regarding the earth as a giant magnet, he investigated its field in noted studies of magnetism and electricity.
See also: Magnetism.

Gilbert and Sullivan, English theater collaborators who wrote lighthearted musical satires of Victorian England and the British Empire. Sir William Schwenck Gilbert (1836-1911) wrote the words and Sir Arthur Seymour Sullivan (1842-1900) the music. Their major operettas include *H.M.S. Pinafore* (1878), *The Pirates of Penzance* (1879), *Patience* (1881), *Iolanthe* (1882), *Princess Ida* (1884), *The Mikado* (1885), *Ruddigore* (1887), and *The Gondoliers* (1889). Both enjoyed independent success as well, Gilbert as a journalist and playwright and Sullivan as a composer.

Gild *see:* Guild.

Gilded Age, sardonic name for the post-Civil War period up to around 1880 in the United States, a time of rampant corruption in politics and commerce. The term derives from the title of a novel by Mark Twain and C.D. Warner.

Gilgamesh, Epic of, earliest known epic poem, written in the Akkadian language and originating in Mesopotamia in the 3rd millennium B.C. The fullest surviving text, preserved on clay tablets, was found in 1872 in a library at Nineveh from the 7th century B.C. The poem tells of the semi-divine Gilgamesh (a historical 3rd-millennium king of Uruk), who seeks the secret of eternal life after the death of his friend Enkidu. At the end of his quest he hears the story of an ancient worldwide flood that closely parallels the story of Noah.
See also: Epic.

Epic of Gilgamesh. This relief shows the hero as a tamer of wild animals.

Gill, thin-walled, external respiratory organ of many aquatic animals. They take in oxygen from the water, and give off waste carbon dioxide. Usually either thin flat plates or finely divided feathery filaments, gills may take on the transport of food and the excretion of excess salt.

Gillespie, Dizzy (John Birks Gillespie; 1917-), U.S. jazz musician. With Charlie Parker he led the jazz movement of bop in the 1940s, playing the trumpet.
See also: Jazz.

Gillyflower *see:* Wallflower.

Gilman, Charlotte Perkins (1860-1935), U.S. writer and women's rights activist. Opposed to traditional marriage, Gilman urged women to gain economic independence by working outside the home. She promoted her ideas through her books, *The Yellow Wallpaper* (1890), *Women and Economics* (1898), *Concerning Children* (1900), and *The Home* (1903), and through her monthly magazine, *Forerunner* (1909-16).
See also: Women's movements.

Gilman, Nicholas (1755-1814), New Hampshire politician. A signer of the Constitution of the United States, Gilman's main contribution was securing its ratification in New Hampshire. He served 4 terms (1789-97) in the House of Representatives and was a United States Senator (1805-14).

Gilmore, Patrick Sarsfield (1829-92), foremost U.S. bandmaster of the 1800s and creator of Gilmore's Band, considered the first great U.S. band. He altered the instrumentation of the band to include more reeds, particularly clarinets, creating the standards for modern concert bands. Under the pseudonym Louis Lambert, he wrote "When Johnny Comes Marching Home" (1863).

Gin, cotton *see:* Cotton gin.

Ginger, herb of the family Zingiberaceae, grown in Japan, the West Indies, South America, and West Africa; also, the spice derived from the root, or rhizome, of the plant. The 4 principal varieties of the species are preserved, dried, black, and white. Ginger is used to season baked goods, meats, vegetables, and beverages.

Gingivitis, inflammation of the gums. Symptoms include swelling, redness, and tenderness of the gums, which may bleed with chewing and toothbrushing. Daily use of dental floss and prompt care by a dentist to clean the plaque from the teeth is the best treatment, before increasing inflammation leads to loosening of the teeth and periodontitis.

Ginkgo, or maidenhair tree (*Ginkgo biloba*), tree with fan-shaped leaves that is often grown in cities because of its tolerance for smoke, low temperatures, and mineral water. A "living fossil," the ginkgo is the remnant of a group of trees that flourished over 100 million years ago.

Ginsberg, Allen (1926-97), U.S. poet of the beat generation. He was active in protesting U.S. conformity and politics. His writings show the influence of his studies of religions of the East and West. His works include the poem "Howl" (1956) and "Kaddish" (1961) and *The Yage Letters* (1963).

Ginseng (genus *Panax*), small perennial plant that grows in damp woodlands in Korea and in the United States. The Chinese esteem ginseng root for its medicinal value.

Giorgione (1478?-1510), Renaissance Venetian painter, student of Giovanni Bellini. Subordinating line to light and color, he achieved a unity of human figures with landscape that influenced Titian. Among his works are *The Tempest* (1501), *Madonna and Child Enthroned* (1504), and *The Three Philosophers* (1510).
See also: Renaissance.

Giotto (Giotto di Bondone; c.1266-c.1337), Florentine painter and architect. Profoundly influential for many generations, he painted monumental figures dramatically and emotionally, giving the vast fresco scenes a sense of movement and spatial depth. Among his famous works are frescoes in Padua (*Life of the Virgin*, 1303-06), and Florence (*St. John the Baptist*, and *Life of St. Francis*, c.1320).

Giotto's fresco of The Judas Kiss *in the Arena Chapel at Padua*

Giovanni, Nikki (Yolande Cornelia Giovanni, Jr.; 1943-), African American poet. Her collections include *Black Feeling, Black Talk* (1968), *My House* (1972), and *Cotton Candy on a Rainy Day* (1978).

Gipsie *see:* Gypsy.

Giraffe (*Giraffa camelopardalis*), tallest mammal, native to Africa, reaching 18 ft (5.5 m), with extremely long neck (up to 7 ft/2.1 m) and legs. Its buff-colored coat is spotted with red-brown patches. A short, bristly mane runs along its spine from head to tail. Giraffes live by grazing on trees. They are speedy runners.

Giraudoux, (Hippolyte) Jean (1882-1944), French playwright. Known for his imaginative, satirical dramas, his major works include *Tiger at the Gates* (1935) and *Electra* (1937), both based on Greek mythology, and *The Madwoman of Chaillot* (1945).

Dizzy Gillespie

Girls Clubs of America, association of U.S. clubs designed to assist girls in their physical, emotional, and educational growth. Additional goals reflect community and member needs. Staff for each Girls Club includes 1 professional, along with paid workers and volunteers. Funds are received from United Way, foundations, corporations, and individuals.

Girl Scouts and Girl Guides, association promoting fitness, citizenship, outdoor living, and community service among girls. The movement was founded in England in 1909 by Lord Baden-Powell, who also founded the Boy Scouts. In 1912, Juliette Gordon Low began the first U.S. troop of Girl Scouts in Savannah, Ga. There are now about 14 million Girl Scouts in over 80 countries.
See also: Baden-Powell, Robert Stephenson Smyth.

Girondists, group of middle-class republicans in the French Revolution. The Girondists came into power under the 1791 Constitution but lost ground to the Jacobins. In June 1793, 29 Girondists were expelled from the National Convention; many were guillotined in the Reign of Terror.
See also: French Revolution.

Girty, Simon (1741-1818), American frontiersman called the Great Renegade. He was captured by the Seneca Indians at age 15. During the Revolutionary War, he deserted the Colonists to serve the British as a scout and interpreter and led numerous raiding parties against the colonies.

Giscard d'Estaing, Valéry (1926-), president of France 1974-81. A member of the national assembly from 1955, he was minister of finance under Presidents de Gaulle (1962-66) and Pompidou (1969-74). As president his austerity program failed to solve problems related to inflation, unemployment, and the balance of payments. He was defeated in his bid for reelection by Socialist candidate François Mitterand.
See also: France.

Gish sisters, U.S. actresses best known for silent films, especially in the pioneering epics of D. W. Griffith. In *The Birth of a Nation* (1915), **Lillian Diana** (1896-) won world fame; with **Dorothy** (1898-1968), she starred in *Orphans of the Storm* (1921). Lillian later appeared in plays, including *All the Way Home* (1960) and *Uncle Vanya* (1973).

Gissing, George Robert (1857-1903), English novelist. His most famous novel, *New Grub Street* (1891), depicts much of the hardship he himself experienced as an aspiring writer. Influenced by Dickens, he is noted for his starkly realistic studies of late Victorian lower- and middle-class life, as in *The Private Papers of Henry Ryecroft* (1903).

Giza (pop. 1,870,500), or Al Jizah, Egypt's third largest city, a suburb of Cairo, and the site of the 3 largest pyramids and the Great Sphinx. Its luxurious houses and apartments are homes to many wealthy Egyptians, diplomats, and business people. Unskilled workers arrive in Giza daily looking for factory work and hoping to settle there. Factory products include bricks, chemicals, cigarettes, and machine tools. Dozens of motion picture films are made in Giza each year.

Gizzard, thick-walled, muscular part of the stomach of birds that uses gravel to help digest grains and other partly digested food.

Glaciation *see:* Ice Age.

Glacier, mass of ice that flows outward from ice caps or down from above the snow line. Glaciers cover about one-tenth of the earth's land area. They are classified as continental glaciers or ice caps, valley glaciers, and piedmont glaciers. The largest ice caps occur in Antarctica and Greenland. Almost all of Antarctica and about 85% of Greenland are buried by ice. Smaller ice caps occur in the islands of northern Canada and in Iceland and Norway. Valley glaciers occur in mountain ranges on every continent. Piedmont glaciers form when glaciers flow out from their valleys to form an ice sheet at the foot of a mountain range. Glaciers originate in areas above the permanent snow line, that is, above the level where snow does not melt completely during the summer. In Antarctica the permanent snow line is at sea level, but around the equator it is about 17,000-18,000 ft (5,200-5,500 m) above sea level. Snow that accumulates on gentle slopes forms snowfields, in which the snow is compacted into a white, spongelike substance called firn or névé. Under pressure, the névé is gradually transformed into hard, clear, blue ice, which consists of interlocking crystals. Pressure causes molecules of water to be released in the ice, lubricating the crystals, allowing them to glide over each other. Most valley glaciers move a few feet a day. They may produce rounded hollows called cirques, or turn the valleys into U-shaped troughs with steep sides. Glaciers cease to flow at a point where melting, evaporation, or the breaking away of icebergs balances the rate of accumulation of ice at the source. The surfaces of glaciers are pitted with crevasses. Lines of rock fragment called moraines are also trapped within the ice, and some rocks are torn from the ground by the ice and frozen into the base and sides of the glacier. As the ice moves, this debris acts like sandpaper and wears away the bedrock over which it passes. It produces smooth land surfaces and may turn valleys into U-shaped troughs with steep sides. A moraine is deposited at the snout of the glacier as the ice melts. Sometimes streams form and transport eroded debris beyond the end of the glacier and deposit it over a wide area. Such deposits are called glacial drift. Among the types of glacial drift are drumlins, which are oval-shaped hills, and eskers, which are long ridges of sand and gravel.

The Colombia glacier in Banff National Park, Canada, has incised a broad, U-shaped valley.

Glacier Bay National Park, located in southeastern Alaska, covering 3,878,269 acres (1,569,481 hectares), and visited by over 100,000 people every year. Although covered with glacial ice 200 years ago, the park now includes vast forests and a variety of wildlife, including Alaskan brown bears, mountain goats, wolves, and many types of birds. Made a national monument in 1925, Glacier Bay was designated a national park area in 1980.

Glacier National Park, created 1910 in the Rocky Mountains in northwest Montana. The park covers 1,013,595 acres (410,188 hectares) on the Continental Divide and borders on Canada's Waterton Lakes National Park. Along with immense glaciers and mountain peaks, Glacier has many beautiful lakes. It provides a protected home for a variety of wildlife.

Glackens, William James (1870-1938), U.S. illustrator and painter, member of The Eight (the Ashcan School) in New York City. Influenced by Renoir, he painted everyday subjects and landscapes. Among his works are *Hammerstein's Roof Garden*

(1901), *Chez Mouqin* (1905), and *Nude with Apple* (1910).
See also: Ashcan School.

Gladiator (Latin: *gladius,* "short sword"), warrior-entertainer of ancient Rome. Gladiators fought each other and wild beasts in public arenas with a variety of weapons, including swords, for the favor of the crowds. They were recruited from prisoners of war, slaves, criminals, and sometimes freemen. The tradition survived into the 5th century A.D.

Gladiolus, genus of tall erect plants of the iris family with sword-shaped leaves and large flowers, native to South Africa and the Mediterranean area, popular in American and European gardens.

Gladstone, William Ewart (1809-98), British statesman, Liberal Party; 4 times prime minister (1868-74; 1880-85; 1886; 1892-94). A powerful orator, dedicated social reformer, and deeply religious man, he introduced the secret ballot, the extension of the franchise, the abolition of sales of army concessions, the first Education Act, the Irish Land Act, and the disestablishment of the Anglican Church in Ireland.
See also: Liberal Party.

Gland, in animals, organ that secretes essential substances. *Endocrine glands* (thyroid, adrenals, and pituitary) secrete hormones into the bloodstream. *Exocrine glands* secrete substances (perspiration, tears, mucus, saliva) via ducts into internal organs or onto body surfaces.
See also: Hormone.

Glanders, fatal contagious, bacterial disease of horses, donkeys, and mules that can be transmitted to humans. The nasal membranes, the lungs, and the skin are infected with lumps that release germ-spreading pus. Animals with glanders must be destroyed.

Glandular fever *see:* Mononucleosis.

Glasgow (pop. 733,800), Scotland's largest city and principal port, on the River Clyde. It is a major commercial and industrial center for shipbuilding, metal working, and manufacturing. A cultural center, it is home to the Scottish Opera, the Scottish National Orchestra, the Citizens Theatre, and 2 important museums: the Burrell Collection and the Kelvingrove Museum. The University of Glasgow, Scotland's second oldest university, was founded in 1451. Glasgow was founded in the 6th century. It became an important port with the unification of Scotland and England (1707) and by the late 18th century was the second-largest city in the British Empire (after London).
See also: Scotland.

Glass, hard, brittle, transparent substance composed mainly of silicates. A natural black glass called obsidian occurs when the molten rock from an erupting volcano cools rapidly, and rock crystals, made of quartz, are another type of naturally occurring glass. The ancient Egyptians and Romans manufactured glass, and stained glass became important in medieval art and architecture in Europe. The mass production of glass is carried out in long "tank" furnaces that may hold over 100 tons. The raw materials are melted and fused at high temperatures, then poured into molds or drawn into shape. For glassware of the highest quality, handblowing is still practiced. The glassblower dips a long blowpipe into the furnace and withdraws a "gob" of molten glass that is blown down the pipe and inflated like a balloon. By deft manipulation of the pipe, shapes are formed. Bottles are blown mechanically. Ordinary window glass, or sheet glass, is made by drawing a wide ribbon of glass upwards from the furnace and through tall cooling towers, at the top of which it is cut into sheets. After glass has been shaped, it usually has to be reheated and cooled at a carefully controlled rate in a special oven called a leer. This process, called annealing, reduces the stress produced in the glass by uneven cooling.

Glass, Philip (1937-), U.S. composer. He was strongly influenced by rock, African and, through his studies with Ravi Shankar, Indian music. He composed music in a style called minimalism and he played combinations of classical Western, rock, and African and Indian music on his electronic keyboards. His best known operas are *Einstein on the Beach* (1976) and *Satyagraha* (1980).

Glasses, or spectacles, lenses mounted in a frame and worn in front of the eyes to correct defects of vision. Converging lenses have been worn to correct farsightedness (hyperopia) since the late 13th century and diverging lenses for nearsightedness (myopia) since the 16th. Glasses with cylindrical lenses are used to correct astigmatism, and those having bifocal lenses (2 different powers in the upper and lower areas of each lens) or even trifocals (3 powers) may be worn for presbyopia (loss of elasticity of the eye's lens).
See also: Lens.

Glass lizard, or glass snake (genus *Ophisaurus*), legless, snakelike lizard. Unlike snakes, it has moveable eyelids, ear openings, a breakable tail, and nonexpandable jaws. It lives in loose soil or under roots and rocks. It reaches about 2 ft (61 cm) in length.

Glassware *see:* Glass.

Glasswort (*Salicornia*), plant belonging to the goosefoot family. It grows 4 to 20 in (10 to 51 cm) tall and has jointed bright green stems with small flowers growing at the joints.

Glastonbury (pop. 93,000), town in Somerset County, England. Archeologists have discovered artifacts from prehistoric Iron Age dwellings just north of Glastonbury and have found numerous types of pottery there dating from 60 B.C. According to legend, England's first Christian church was established in Glastonbury by St. Joseph of Arimathea, who was thought to have brought the chalice from the Last Supper to this site. It was also reputed to contain the graves of King Arthur and Queen Guinevere of the Arthurian legends. The town's economy is now supported by tourism and light industry.
See also: Arthur, King; England.

Glauber's salt, trade name of a drug containing sodium sulphate, used as a laxative.
See also: Salt, Chemical.

Glaucoma, eye disease characterized by an increased pressure on the retina within the eyeball, caused by an excess of watery fluid. Symptoms range from blurred vision to loss of peripheral vision and even blindness.
See also: Eye.

Glauconite, or greensand, greenish iron-silicate mineral that resembles tiny flake-like particles or little lumps of clay. Large deposits have been found in Colorado, New Jersey, and Wisconsin. Glauconite is used as a water softener. Its natural content of silicate of potassium and iron makes it invaluable to geologists in dating rocks and fossils.

Glendale (pop. 180,038), city in California, suburb of Los Angeles. An industrial center where electronic equipment, pharmaceuticals, cameras, automobile and aircraft parts are manufactured, Glendale is the site of Forest Lawn Cemetery.
See also: California.

Glenn, John Herschel, Jr. (1921-), U.S. astronaut and senator. On Feb. 20, 1962, in the space capsule *Friendship 7,* he orbited the earth 3 times. Active in Ohio politics after retiring from the U.S. Marines as a colonel, he was first elected a Democratic senator in 1974. He was an unsuccessful candidate for the 1984 presidential nomination.
See also: Astronaut.

Glider, nonpowered airplane launched by air or ground towing and kept aloft by its light, aerodynamic design and the skill of the pilot in exploiting rising air currents. Gliding is a popular sport throughout the world.
See also: Airplane.

Glinka, Mikhail Ivanovich (1804-57), Russian composer. His 2 operas, *A Life for the Tsar* (1836) and *Russlan and Ludmilla* (1842), started a nationalistic Russian school of music.
See also: Opera.

Globe Theatre, London open-air public theater where most of Shakespeare's plays were first performed. Built on the Thames River in 1598, it was destroyed in 1644 by the Puritans.
See also: Shakespeare, William.

The Globe Theatre was built mainly of wood. The playhouse was circular in shape and partially open to the elements.

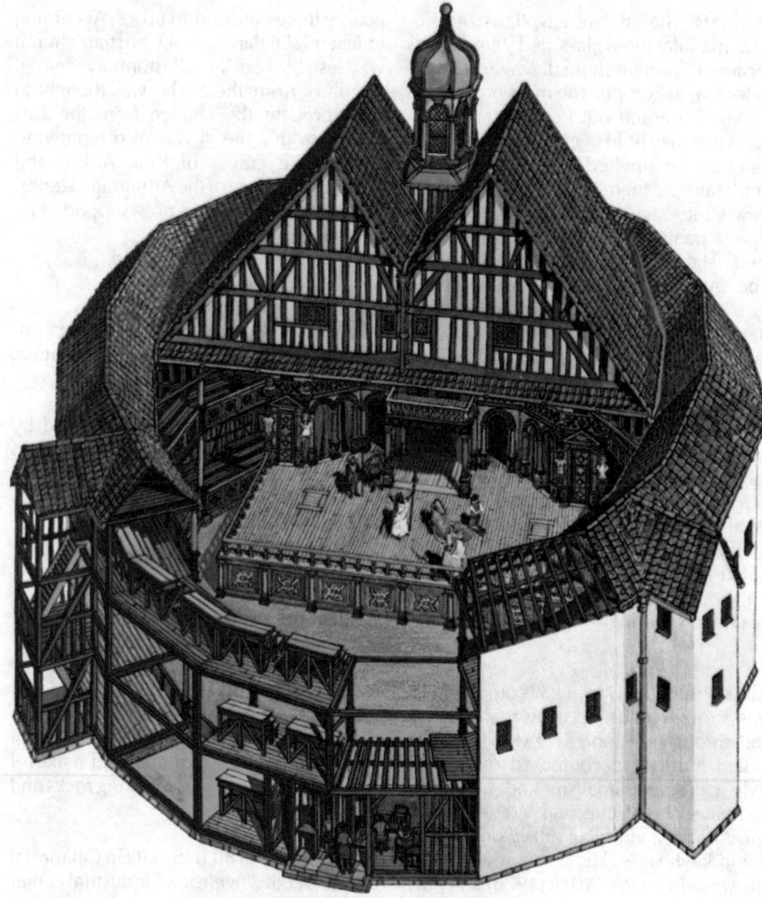

Globulin, large family of proteins distributed in plants and animals, insoluble in water but soluble in dilute saline solutions. In humans, blood globulins resist disease.

Glockenspiel, or bells, pitched percussion instrument, originally a set of graduated bells, but now 2 rows of tuned steel bars on a frame. The bars are hit with hard mallets made of rubber, brass, or steel. The instrument originated in the Netherlands between 1650 and 1700. It became part of the orchestra during the 18th century.

Glomerulonephritis *see:* Nephritis.

Glorious Revolution, events of 1688-89 that led to the deposition of King James II of England. When the birth of James's son threatened to turn England into a Catholic monarchy, the Whigs and Tories united and invited the Dutch prince William III and his wife Mary (James's daughter) to rule. In 1689, Parliament restricted royal powers in the Bill of Rights.

Gloucester (pop. 27,768), coastal city in northeastern Massachusetts, about 30 mi (48 km) northeast of Boston. Its excellent harbor has been used for fishing for over 300 years. Fish processing and manufacture of fish products are the main industries today. Gloucester was settled in 1623 and became a city in 1873. It is now a summer resort and artists' colony.
See also: Massachusetts.

Glowworm *see:* Firefly.

Gloxinia (*Sinningia speciosa*), Brazilian plant prized for its colorful, velvety leaves and bell-shaped flowers. A new plant can be grown from a single leaf stuck in the soil.

Gluck, Christoph Willibald von (1714-87), German operatic composer. In *Orpheus and Euridice* (1762) he introduced a new kind of opera combining drama, music, and emotion. His *Alceste* (1767) considerably influenced Mozart. His greatest work is *Iphigenia in Tauris* (1779).

Glucose ($C_6H_{12}O_6$), simple sugar found in certain foods, especially fruits. The chief source of energy for living organisms, it is absorbed directly into the bloodstream. Excess glucose is converted into glycogen and stored in the liver and muscles; beyond that, it is converted to fat. Glucose in urine may be a symptom of diabetes.

Glue, adhesive material produced from vegetable (starch, gum, soybeans) or animal (bones, hides, oil) substances. Glues dry to a strong film that bonds paper, wood, leather, and similar porous materials.

Gluon, elementary subatomic particle that holds the parts of protons and neutrons together. Gluons have no mass, move at the speed of light, and multiply themselves so rapidly that they intensify their force. The theory of gluons, first presented by U.S. physicists H. David Politzer, David J. Gross, and Frank A. Wilczek in 1974, is called quantum chromodynamics (QCD).
See also: Physics.

Gluten, mixture of 2 proteins, gliadin and glutenin, found in wheat, rye, and other cereal flours. When bread rises, gluten forms an elastic network that traps carbon dioxide. The high gluten content of hard wheat is right for bread and pasta, while soft wheat (low gluten) is used for biscuits and cakes.

Glutton *see:* Wolverine.

Glycerin *see:* Glycerol.

Glycerol, or glycerin, colorless, sticky, sweet-tasting liquid alcohol. Its fatty-acid esters constitute natural fats and oils, from which soap is made. It is used to reduce inflammation, as a mouthwash, and as a sweetener.

Glycogen, animal starch made up of glucose molecules, stored in the liver and muscles, and used to replenish the glucose levels burned for energy in the body.

Glycol, group of alcohols, all of which have 2 hydroxy (OH) groups. The simplest is ethylene glycol (CH_2OH, CH_2OH), widely used as an antifreeze. Glycols are used as plasticizers and solvents.

Gnat, small biting fly such as a mosquito, belonging to the order Diptera.

Gnatcatcher, genus (*Polioptila*) of small, insect-eating birds of the Western Hemisphere, from the Old World warbler family, Sylviidae. Two species, the blue-gray and the black-tailed, are found in the United States. Others are found in Central and South America.

Gneiss, crystalline metamorphic rock, made up of quartz, feldspar, and mica combined in different proportions to produce distinct layers. Blocks of gneiss are sometimes used to pave streets.

Gnosticism, dualistic religious system of early Christians. Gnosticism held that matter is evil and spirit good, and that salvation comes from secret knowledge (gnosis) granted to initiates. Gnosticism declined after the 2nd century A.D.

Gnotobiotics, laboratory organism that is either free of all known contaminating organisms (bacteria, fungi, yeasts) or specifically contaminated with a known organism. Gnotobiotic animals are used in medical research.

Gnu, or wildebeest, antelope (genus *Connochaetes*) with a large buffalo-like head and shoulders, curved horns, and a horse-like body and tail. The brindled gnu (*C. taurinus*) lives in herds in South and East African grasslands. It weighs 500 lb (225 kg) and is 4 ft (135 cm) tall.

Goanna *see:* Monitor.

Goat, member (genus *Capra*) of the cattle family and closely related to sheep. Goats have hollow horns, coarse hair, and "beards." They live in herds in mountainous areas, grazing on bushes and grass. They are valuable for their milk and their hair (mohair) and wool (cashmere).

Two different breeds of goats: the Angora goat (left) and the British alpine (right)

Goatsucker, or nightjar, mostly night-flying bird of the family Caprimulgidae, which includes the nighthawk and whippoorwill. Goatsuckers are found in temperate and tropical regions. They are primarily brown and gray in color and fly with their mouths gaping open in order to catch insects.

Gobi, vast desert in central Asia, which extends to North China. It covers about 500,000 sq mi (1,295,000 sq km) in the Mongolian plateau and is between 3,000 to 5,000 ft (910 to 1,520 m) high, with fierce wind and sand storms. Its steppeland fringes are inhabited by Mongol herdsmen. There are valuable coal and oil deposits in the Gobi.

God, in religion, term for the "supreme being." In polytheistic systems, one god is generally regarded as the ruler of the others. The Hindu pantheon reflects this hierarchy by regarding Brahman as the supreme being, although other gods are worshiped as aspects of his being. True monotheism emerged in the religion of the Hebrews, whose one God, Yahweh, is a personal being with whom the Hebrews established a covenant. The Christian concept of God is based on the Hebrew tradition, expanded to include the doctrines of the divine nature of Jesus Christ and the Trinity of 3 persons in 1 God. Another monotheistic religion, Islam, worships Allah. The major religions of the Far East—Buddhism, Shintoism, Taoism, and Confucianism—are philosophical, moral, and contemplative, but they are not essentially monotheistic. The principal arguments developed in the West to prove the existence of God are the ontological, put forth by Anselm of Canterbury, that the idea of a perfect being necessitates the existence of that being; the cosmological, best stated by Thomas Aquinas, arguing there must be a First Cause; the teleological, that the order of the universe indicates an orderer; and the moral, enunciated by Immanuel Kant, based on humanity's inherently moral nature. Another school of thought holds that God is revealed directly through mystical experience. Philosophers have often conceived of God as a transcendent and impersonal being that shows itself in the world and the universe but creates no personal relationship with people. The pantheists believe that God is the sum of the universe and that all things, including humanity, are part of God. Deists see God expressed in the rational pattern of the universe but withdrawn from the events of the world. Both the industrial and scientific revolutions have had far-reaching effects on the nature of belief in God. For many people, materialism and skepticism have replaced the earlier certainty of religion. Considerable numbers of people are agnostic (neither believing nor disbelieving in the existence of God), with a smaller group professing to be atheist. The old opposition of science and faith has lessened, as science has uncovered more mystery in the universe and religion has shown itself less dogmatic about the nature of the objective world.

Godard, Jean-Luc (1930-), French film director, a pioneer of the "new wave" school with his film *Breathless* (1959). Godard's imagery and innovative camera techniques in films such as *My Life to Live* (1962) and *Weekend* (1967) influenced a whole generation of filmmakers.

Goddard, colonial American family who worked as editors, printers, and publishers. **Sarah Updike Goddard** (1700?-70), her daughter **Mary Katherine** (1736-1816), and her son **William** (1760-1817) financed, printed, and published 3 colonial newspapers (in Rhode Island, Pennsylvania, and Maryland) from 1762 until 1774. William relinquished his interest in the newspaper in 1774 to develop a mail-carrying system. The system, adopted by the Continental Congress in 1775, became the U.S. Post Office. In 1777 Mary Katherine Goddard became the first to publish the Declaration of Independence with the signers' names included.

Goddard, Robert Hutchings (1882-1945), U.S. physicist, pioneer of rocketry. In 1926 he launched the first liquid-fuel rocket. He developed many of the basic ideas of modern rocketry; among over 200 patents was one for a multistage rocket.
See also: Physics; Rocket.

Godden, (Margaret) Rumer (1907-), British author whose novels, poems, and children's books are distinguished by their warm characterization and lyric style. Her novels include *Black Narcissus* (1939), *The River* (1946), *In This House of Brede* (1969), and *The Dark Horse* (1982).

Goddess *see:* Mythology.

Godetia, genus of flowering annuals named after the Swiss botanist Charles H. Godet. There are about 25 different kinds of godetias grown in North America. They belong to the family Onagraceae, characterized by flowers with 4 sepals, 4 petals, and 4 or 8 stamens. The farewell-to-spring (*G. Amoena*) grows 12 to 30 in (30 to 76 km) high and produces white, pink, or red flowers.

Godiva, Lady (c.1040-80) noted for her legendary ride through Coventry, England, to persuade her husband Leofric, earl of Mercia, to reduce heavy taxes. She rode naked on a white horse.

Gods *see:* Mythology; Polytheism; Religion.

Godthåb (pop. 11,200; Greenlandic: *Nuuk*), capital city of Greenland, located on the southwestern shore of the island, on Davis Strait. The harbor is icefree in winter and fishing, canning, smoking, and drying fish are the main industries. Europeans first settled near Godthåb in the 11th century.
See also: Greenland.

Godwin, William (1756-1836), English political theorist and novelist. In his *Enquiry Concerning Political Justice* (1793) and in his novels *The Adventures of Caleb Williams* (1794), and *Fleetwood* (1805), Godwin rejected government as corrupting; he believed that humans are rational beings able to live without laws and institutions. Godwin influenced his son-in-law, poet P. B. Shelley.

Godwit, large wading bird with long, slightly upcurved bill, belonging to the snipe and sandpiper family. It is found worldwide on grassy plains, wet meadows, and prairie marshes. Many of its breeding places on the Canadian prairies have been plowed up.

Goebbels, (Paul) Joseph (1897-1945), Nazi propagandist. Appointed minister of propaganda by Hitler in 1933, Goebbels skillfully organized political campaigns and used the mass media (cinema, radio, newspapers) to promote Nazism throughout Germany until the end of World War II. He committed suicide with his family in Berlin in 1945.
See also: Nazism; World War II.

Goeduck *see:* Geoduck.

Goering, Hermann Wilhelm (1893-1946), German political leader and Hitler's deputy, 1939-45. He organized the Gestapo (secret police) and, as commander of the German Air Force, prepared for the aerial *blitzkrieg* campaigns of World War

II. By 1936 Goering was economic dictator of Germany, but his power dwindled when he failed to stop Allied air attacks. Convicted of war crimes at the Nuremburg trials in 1946, he poisoned himself in prison.
See also: World War II.

Goes, Hugo Van der *see:* Van der Goes, Hugo.

Goethals, George Washington (1858-1928), U.S. army engineer who completed construction of the Panama Canal, 1907-14. Goethals overcame difficulties caused by the climate, disease, and the labor force. He served as governor of the Canal Zone, 1914-16.
See also: Panama Canal.

Goethe, Johann Wolfgang von (1749-1832), German poet, novelist, and playwright. His monumental work ranges from correspondence and poems to 14 volumes of scientific studies and is crowned by *Faust* (part I, 1808; part II, 1833), written in stages during 60 years, in which he synthesized his life and art in a poetic and philosophical statement of the search for complete experience and knowledge. Among his best-known novels are *The Sorrows of Young Werther* (1774) and *The Apprenticeship of Wilhelm Meister* (1795-96).

Gogh, Vincent Van *see:* Van Gogh, Vincent.

Gogol, Nikolai Vasilyevich (1809-52), Russian short story writer, novelist, and dramatist. His comic stories of Ukrainian peasant life and later bizarre tales set in St. Petersburg, such as "The Overcoat" (1872), put him among the most original of Russian authors. Adverse reaction in Russia to his satirical drama *The Inspector-General* (1836) drove Gogol abroad, where he wrote his greatest work, the picaresque novel *Dead Souls* (1842).

Goiter, medical condition causing the front of the neck to swell, due to an enlargement of the thyroid gland. Goiters occur because the thyroid gland is too active (hyperthyroidism) or not active enough (hypothyroidism). When hyperthyroidism occurs, the thyroid gland produces too much thyroxine and the gland enlarges. Symptoms of this type of goiter include weight loss and nervousness. When hypothyroidism takes place, the pituitary gland secretes too much thyroid-stimulating hormone, causing swelling. Symptoms include physical and mental slowness and weight gain.

Golan *see:* Cities of refuge.

Golan Heights, strategic area, formerly part of Syria, between southern Lebanon and southwestern Syria. Israel occupied the Golan Heights after the Arab-Israeli war of 1967, officially claiming it in 1981. Syria does not accept Israel's claim. The Golan Heights is 454 sq mi (1,176 sq km), overlooking the Sea of Galilee and the Jordan River.

Gold, chemical element, symbol Au; for physical constants see Periodic Table. Gold has been known and highly valued from earliest times. It is found free in nature and in combination with tellurium. It is recovered from its ores by cyaniding, amalgamating, and smelting. Gold is a soft, yellow, unreactive metal not attacked by common acids. It is the most malleable and ductile of all metals and is a good conductor of heat and electricity. Gold is used in coinage and is a standard for monetary systems in many countries. Gold and its compounds are used for jewelry, decoration, dental work, and plating.

Goldberg, Arthur Joseph (1908-90), U.S. labor lawyer and public servant. He served as secretary of labor (1961-62), associate justice of the Supreme Court (1962-65), and U.S. representative to the United Nations (1965-68). Goldberg was instrumental in the 1955 merger of the American Federation of Labor and the Congress of Industrial Organizations (AFL-CIO).

Gold Coast *see:* Ghana

Golden Age, in Greek and Roman mythology, era of perfect happiness, prosperity, and innocence that preceded recorded history. As described by the Latin poet Ovid, it knew no wars and laws were unnecessary; the earth bore fruits spontaneously and harmony prevailed.
See also: Mythology.

Golden Fleece, in Greek mythology, golden wool of a sacred winged ram. King Pelias sent his nephew Jason to retrieve the fleece from its guarded grove to determine whether Jason was worthy of the throne. Before succeeding, Jason had to sow the teeth of a dragon and fight the fierce men who grew from these seeds.
See also: Mythology.

Golden Gate Bridge, bridge spanning the entrance to San Francisco Bay, Calif., built in 1933-37. Its 4,200-ft (1,280-m) central span, between 2,746-ft (227-m) towers, is the second longest in the world and carries 6 traffic lanes.

Golden Hind *see:* Drake, Sir Francis.

Golden retriever, gold-colored, thick-coated hunting dog, originally bred in Scotland around 1870. The good-natured, intelligent animal has been used as a guide dog for the blind and as a family companion. Heights average 23 in (58 cm) at the shoulder and weights range from 55 to 75 lb (25 to 34 kg).

Golden robin *see:* Baltimore oriole.

Goldenrod, tall plant (genus *Solidago*) with masses of yellow or white flowers that bloom in the autumn. Growing wild in the eastern United States, goldenrod is the state flower of Kentucky and Nebraska.

Golden rule, precept stated by Jesus in the Sermon on the Mount: "Treat others as you would like them to treat you" (Matt. 7.12). The rule existed earlier among Greeks and Jews in a negative form (that one should not treat others in a manner in which one would not wish to be treated oneself), and was also stated by the Chinese philosopher Confucius.

Goldenseal, or orange root, perennial herb (*Hydrastis canadensis*) of the buttercup family, found in the eastern United States and in Japan. Its yellow, knotted roots were once used medicinally.

Golden State *see:* California.

Goldfield, village in southwestern Nevada, seat of Esmeralda County. Goldfield flourished as a center of a gold-mining region after the discovery of gold nearby in 1903. Over $11 million worth of gold and other metals had been mined by 1910, but by 1918 extensive mining had almost exhausted gold deposits, and the population began to decline.
See also: Nevada.

Goldfinch, small, short-tailed bird (genus *Carduelis*) of the finch family, also called wild canary because of its musical song and the male's bright yellow color. North American goldfinches include the lesser goldfinch, Lawrence's goldfinch, and the American goldfinch. The European goldfinch was introduced to North America in the 1800s but is found only in Europe today. The American goldfinch is approximately 5 in (13 cm) long.

Goldfish (*Carassius auratus*), freshwater fish of the carp family. The goldfish is native to China and was domesticated more than 2,000 years ago. In its wild form it is olive in color and grows up to 16 in (40 cm) long; the domesticated goldfish may be as small as 1-4 in (2.5-10 cm) long and is often red, although some are bred for mottled colorings as well as elaborate fins.

Golding, William Gerald (1911-), English novelist. His powerful allegorical works explore the nature of humanity, and include *Lord of the Flies* (1954), *The Spire* (1964), and *Darkness Visible* (1979). He received Britain's Booker McConnell Prize in 1980 and the Nobel Prize for literature in 1983.

Goldman, Emma (1869-1940), Russian-born U.S. anarchist, she emigrated to the United States in 1886 and was imprisoned many times for her activities against militarism, for labor rights, and for advocating birth control. In 1919 she was deported to Russia along with Alexander Berkman, her copublisher of the paper *Mother Earth*. She opposed the repressive policies of the Bolshevik government and left Russia in 1921, for England and later Canada. Among her writings are *Anarchism and Other Essays* (1910) and her autobiography *Living My Life* (1931).
See also: Anarchism.

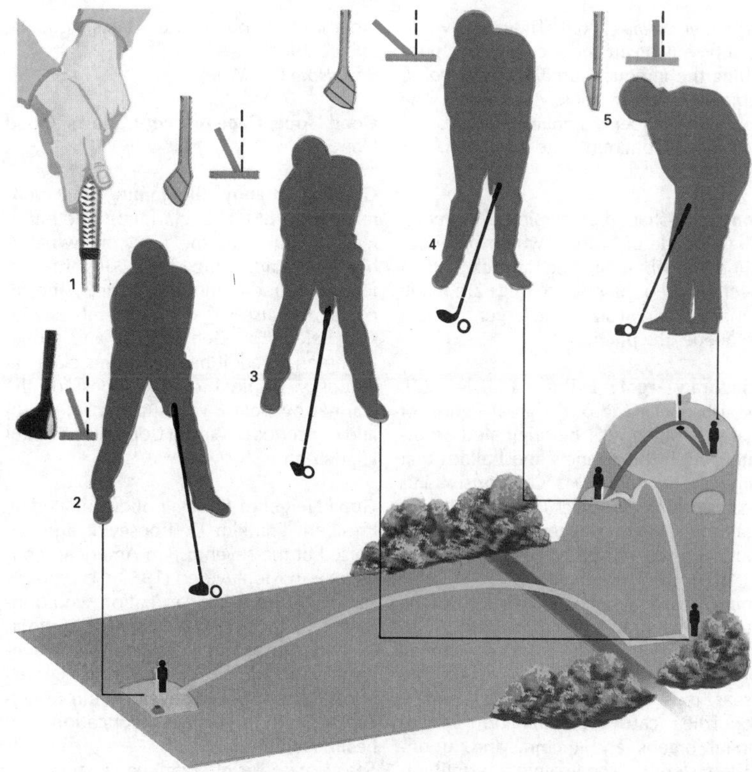

A hypothetical par-4 hole is illustrated, showing the use of various clubs, their angle of loft, and the orthodox stance from which to execute the appropriate shot. Using the correct grip for the driver (1), the players drives off from the tee (2), straight down the fairway, clearing the natural hazard of the road. Some 120 yards from the hole he plays a 5- iron approach shot (3); landing in a bunker, he is forced to use a sand wedge (4) to blast out. The loft on this club means there will be almost no run when the ball lands on the green and he can putt (5) into the hole.

Goldoni, Carlo (1707-93), Italian dramatist. His classical character comedy led to the decline in popularity of the rival commedia dell'arte. Goldoni directed the Comédie Italienne in Paris, 1762-64. Among his 150 comic plays are *The Mistress of the Inn* (1753), *The Accomplished Maid* (1756), and *The Fan* (1763).

Gold Rush, influx of prospectors following the discovery of a new gold field. From 1848-1915, in the Americas, Australia, and South Africa, there were numerous gold rushes attracting thousands of prospectors: in California (1849), Australia (1851-3), Canada and the Klondike (1897).

Goldsmith, Oliver (1730?-74), Anglo-Irish author. His best-known works include the novel *The Vicar of Wakefield* (1766), the comedies *The Goodnatured Man* (1768) and *She Stoops to Conquer* (1773), and the pastoral poem *The Deserted Village* (1770). A member of the literary circle around Samuel Johnson, he achieved considerable literary fame and widespread popularity in his day. His works attacked pedantry and sentimentalism and stressed simple virtues.

Gold standard, monetary system in which a standard currency unit equals a fixed weight of gold. Since World War II most countries no longer have an internal gold standard, but do use a limited international standard to convert their currencies into gold or U.S. dollars for international payments. In 1976 the International Monetary Fund created a system of controlled floating rates that diminished the importance of gold in international transactions. The U.S. went on the gold standard in 1900, but the Gold Reserve Act of 1934 prohibited the redemption of dollars into gold. And in 1970 the U.S. Treasury ended its requirement that Federal Reserve notes be backed 25% by gold deposits, in effect taking the U.S. completely off the gold standard.
See also: Money.

Goldwater, Barry Morris (1909-), U.S. conservative senator from Arizona (1953-65, 1969-87), and unsuccessful Republican presidential candidate against Lyndon B. Johnson in 1964. His writings include *The Conscience of a Conservative* (1960) and *Why Not Victory?* (1962).

Goldwyn, Samuel (Samuel Goldfish; 1882-1974), Polish-born U.S. film pioneer. He formed Goldwyn Pictures Corp. (1917), which later merged with L.B. Mayer's company (1924) to form Metro-Goldwyn-Mayer. The producer of more than 70 films, he won an Academy Award for *The Best Years of Our Lives* (1946).

Golf, game in which players hit a small, hard ball with special clubs on an outdoor course (links), attempting to use as few strokes as possible to deposit the ball into a cup (hole). Playing a hole, of which there are 18 on a standard course, involves driving the ball from a raised peg (tee) across the fairway, which is flanked by obstacles to be avoided, such as sand traps and water, toward the green (a smooth area around the hole at a distance of 100-600 yd/91-541 m from the tee). Golf clubs include 3 or 4 woods, 9 or 1U irons, and a putter (used on the green). Written records of golf date from the 15th century in Scotland, and though the game may have been introduced to the United States in the 17th century, the first permanent U.S. golf club did not come into being until 1888. In 1916 the Professional Golfers' Association (PGA) championship began and to this day has been dominated by U.S. golfers such as Bobby Jones, Arnold Palmer, and Jack Nicklaus.

Golgotha *see:* Calvary.

Goliath, in the Bible, a Philistine giant, and a warrior who challenged the Israelites. He was killed by the young David, who struck him with a single stone from his sling (1 Sam.17.)
See also: Bible.

Gomorrah *see:* Sodom and Gomorrah.

Gompers, Samuel (1850-1924), English born U.S. labor leader. A member of the cigar makers' union, he helped found and became first president (1886-1924, except 1895) of the American Federation of Labor (AFL). Gompers fought for higher wages, shorter working hours, and more freedom. He opposed militant political unionism, and advocated organizing skilled workers on the basis of their trades, as opposed to industrial unionism, in which workers, skilled and unskilled, are organized by industry.
See also: American Federation of Labor and Congress of Industry.

The golfer's basic requirements are spiked shoes, a glove for the top hand, a golf bag (1), containing woods (2), irons (3), putter (4), tees (5) and balls (6). There are two sizes of ball in general use; the traditional British ball (minimum diameter 1.6 inches) and the larger American ball (minimum diameter 1.7 inches).

Gomulka, Wladyslaw (1905-82), Polish communist leader. As first secretary of the Polish Communist Party (1956-70), he encouraged social and economic freedoms for Poles while maintaining close ties with the USSR. He resigned following food price riots.

Goncourt brothers, **Edmond Louis Antoine Huot de Goncourt** (1822-96) and **Jules Alfred Huot de Goncourt** (1830-70), French authors who pioneered the naturalist school of fiction. Their novels explore aspects of French society, notably *Germinie Lacerteux* (1864), a study of working-class life, *Renée Mauperin* (1864), and

Benny Goodman

Mme Gervaisais (1869). They also wrote perceptively on art and social history, publishing the famous *Journal des Goncourt,* depicting Parisian society, 1851-95. The Goncourt Academy annually awards the prestigious Goncourt Prize for fiction.

Gong, disk-shaped percussion instrument, usually made of bronze, which produces sound by vibrating when struck with a special kind of hammer. Gongs are made in many different sizes; the larger the size, the deeper the pitch.

Góngora y Argote, Luis de (1561-1627), Spanish poet. One of the great figures of Spain's Golden age, he originated an ornate style in his sonnets and ballads that came to be known as Gongorism. His greatest work, *Solitudes* (1613), is exemplary in its use of exaggerated metaphors, allusion, and Latin-based vocabulary.

Gonorrhea, acute infectious disease of the mucous membranes lining the urethra, cervix of the uterus, and rectum, which may spread bacteria in the bloodstream. The disease is usually spread by sexual contact. Gonorrhea causes inflammation of the genital organs and urethra and, if untreated, sterility. The treatment is antibiotics, especially penicillin.
See also: Venereal disease.

Mikhail Gorbachev

Gonzales, Pancho (Richard Alonzo Gonzales; 1928-), U.S. tennis player. He began to play tennis at the age of 12, becoming the top-ranking amateur in the United States by 1948. He won 2 U.S. amateur singles titles and helped the U.S. team defeat Australia in the 1949 competition. He became a professional player in 1949.

González Márquez, Felipe (1942-), prime minister of Spain (1982-) and head of Spain's first leftist government since the 1936 Civil War. González Márquez also holds the position of first secretary of Spain's Socialist party and is a lawyer. Under his leadership, Spain joined the European Common Market in 1986.
See also: Spain.

Goober *see:* Peanut.

Goodall, Jane (1934-), English zoologist who gained recognition through her years of study and work with chimpanzees. She learned that chimpanzees' use of tools is second only to humans'. She also discovered that they eat pigs, small monkeys, and other medium-sized game, and that groups may actually war on each other. Her books include *My Friends, the Wild Chimpanzees* (1967), *In the Shadow of Man* (1971), *The Innocent Killers* (1971), and *The Chimpanzees of Gombe* (1986).
See also: Zoology.

Good Friday, in Holy Week, the Friday before Easter, the anniversary of the Crucifixion of Jesus Christ, observed in most Christian churches as a day of fasting and mourning. Its observance dates from the 2nd century.
See also: Holy Week.

Good Hope, Cape of *see:* Cape of Good Hope.

Goodman, Benny (Benjamin D. Goodman; 1909-86), U.S. clarinetist and bandleader, known as the King of Swing. A big-band leader since the 1930s, he performed for radio, motion pictures, and records, and also led small ensembles with such talents as Gene Krupa and Lionel Hampton. In addition to jazz, his classical virtuosity inspired compositions for the clarinet by Béla Bartók (*Contrasts*, 1938) and concertos by Aaron Copland and Paul Hindemith.

Good Neighbor Policy, policy initiated by President Franklin D. Roosevelt and endorsed at the seventh Pan-American conference in Montevideo (1933). The policy stated that no American nation would interfere in the internal affairs of another. Exchange programs were set up for teachers and technical experts, and the United States agreed to help develop Latin American agriculture, business, education, and health facilities.
See also: Roosevelt, Franklin Delano.

Goodyear, Charles (1800-60), U.S. inventor (in 1839) of vulcanized rubber (patented 1844). In his search to find a way to keep rubber from melting and sticking in hot weather, he bought the patents of N.M. Hayward, who had had some success treating rubber with sulfur. Vulcanization gives rubber its elasticity and strength.
See also: Rubber.

Goose, swimming bird (family Anatidae) related to the swan and duck. Technically, "goose" refers to the female of the species, "gander" to the males. Geese migrate in flocks (known as skeins) reportedly flying as high as 29,000 ft (8,838 m). The Canada, or wild, goose (*Branta canadensis*) is the best known in North America, and the domestic Toulouse, or gray, goose is a descendant of the European graylag. In medieval times the Barnacle goose of Europe was thought to arise from barnacles, and, as such, was counted as fish and could be eaten on Fridays.

Gooseberry, shrub (genus *Ribes*) bearing purple berries, originally found growing wild in southern Europe and North Africa. First cultivated in the 17th century, the berries are eaten fresh or used in pies, sauces, or preserves. Cultivation of the shrubs are banned by law in some states because they are host to blister rust disease.

Gopher, or pocket gopher, burrowing rodent of the family Geomyidae, native to North and Central America. The gopher is a solitary animal, from 5 to 12 in (13 to 30 cm) in length, with large claws and very long teeth. It has fur-lined outside cheek pouches for carrying food and nesting material.

Gorbachev, Mikhail Sergeyevich (1931-), Soviet political leader who succeeded Konstantin Chernenko as general secretary of the Communist party of the Soviet Union in 1984 and became President of the USSR in 1990. Gorbachev had worked his way up through the ranks of the Communist party in the Russian city of Stavropol in the 1950s and 1960s. In 1970 he was elected to the Supreme Soviet. In 1971 he was added to the Communist party's Central Committee. He moved to Moscow in 1978 and in 1980 became a full member of the party's Politburo, then the country's chief policy-making body. Soon after he became general secretary, Gorbachev launched a series of reforms in both domestic and international policy. His program of *perestroika* (restructuring) was aimed at altering the economic and social systems, loosening central state control. The reforms of *glasnost* (openness) eased the system of censorship, allowing considerable freedom of speech and of the press. The Communist party's formal monopoly on political activity was lifted, and a new political system, involving some free elections, was introduced. Internationally, Gorbachev withdrew Soviet troops from Afghanistan and proclaimed a policy of non-interference when Communist rule collapsed in Eastern Europe in 1989 and 1990. Gorbachev's cooperation was instrumental in the reunification of Germany, and for this and other aspects of his international policy, he was awarded the Nobel Peace Prize in 1990.
Major problems faced by Gorbachev include the continued crisis of the Soviet economy, the rise of ethnic conflicts and of demands for independence by various republics of the USSR, and the continuing power of the old Communist party bureaucracy, especially in the army and police.

Gordian knot, in Greek mythology, an intricate knot by which King Gordius of Phrygia joined the yoke and pole of an oxcart. A prophecy holding that anyone undoing the knot would rule all Asia came true when Alexander the Great severed the knot with his sword.
See also: Mythology.

Gordon, Charles George (1833-85), British soldier, known as "Chinese Gordon." He helped suppress the Taiping Rebellion (1863-64) in China, and governed the Egyptian Sudan (1877-80), where he established law, improved communications, and attempted to suppress the slave trade. In 1885 he was killed while defending Khartoum against the Mahdi's forces.

Gordon setter, breed of hunting dog dating from 17th-century Scotland. Its superior sense of smell and retrieving ability make it an excellent hunting companion. The Gordon setter adapts well to families and has a natural guarding instinct. It weighs 55 to 75 lb (24 to 33 kg) and reaches 23 to 25 in (59 to 64 cm) at the shoulder. Its long coat is black and tan.

Gorgon, in Greek mythology, term for 3 hideous winged and snake-haired sisters—Stheno, Euryale, and Medusa—who turned anyone who looked at them to stone. Medusa, the youngest Gorgon and the only mortal one, was killed by Perseus.
See also: Mythology.

Gorilla, largest of the primates (*Gorilla gorilla*), native to equatorial western Africa. A quadruped that rises to 2 legs only when displaying, the male ranges from 5 to 6 ft (150 to 190 cm) in height and weighs c.450 lb (200 kg); his brow ridge is prominent and his canine teeth enormous. Females are about half the size of males. Gorillas are generally shaggy, brown or black in color. They are highly intelligent, mostly vegetarian, and usually shy and gentle, despite their great strength. The mountain gorilla of central Africa is an endangered subspecies.

Gorilla

Gorki, or Gorky (pop. 1,392,000), city in the eastern European port of the Soviet Union, situated at the confluence of the Oka and Volga rivers, about 260 mi (318 km) east of Moscow. Its diverse industries include automobiles, ships, airplanes, locomotives, machinery, and chemicals, as well as the refining of petroleum and natural gas. Formerly Nizhny Novgorod, it was renamed in 1932 in honor of the writer Maxim Gorki, who was born there.

Gorki, Maxim (Alexey Maximovich Pyeshkov; 1868-1936), Russian author. His pen name is the Russian word for *bitter.* Gorki's works, noted for their stark naturalism, include the play *The Lower Depths* (1902), the novel *Mother* (1906), and the autobiographical trilogy *Childhood* (1913), *In the World* (1916), and *My Universities* (1923). Gorki was exiled to the United States after the failure of the Russian Revolution of 1905. He returned to Russia in 1914. A personal friend of Lenin, he became head of the state publishing house after the 1917 revolution, until 1921, when he went abroad again. He returned in 1928 and became a supporter of the Stalin regime. Many consider him the founder of the literary style called socialist realism.

Gorky, Arshile (1904-48), Armenian-born U.S. painter, pioneer of abstract expressionism. Influenced by surrealism, he began to create abstractions of organic forms (c.1940). He influenced the work of Jackson Pollock and Willem de Kooning.
See also: Abstract expressionism.

Goshawk *see:* Hawk.

Gospel, one of the 4 New Testament books—Matthew, Mark, Luke, and John—that tell the story of the life of Jesus, written to spread the gospel ("good news") of Christian salvation. The first 3, called the Synoptic Gospels, agree on the order of events.
See also: Bible; New Testament.

Göteborg (pop. 424,100), second largest city in Sweden and its most important coastal port. Its harbor is ice-free throughout the year. It has fisheries and shipyards, and is the largest shipbuilding site in Scandinavia. It was founded by Charles IX in 1604.
See also: Sweden.

Gothenburg *see:* Göteborg.

Gothic art and architecture, the Gothic style of art and architecture flourished in Europe, particularly in France, from the mid-12th century to the end of the 15th century. The style was first referred to as "Gothic" (after the Goths, who invaded the Roman Empire in the A.D. 200s) by Renaissance artists and writers who sought to condemn it as barbaric. Gothic architecture developed from the style called Romanesque, combining the latter's barrel vault and the stone rib to produce its most characteristic feature, the rib vault. This was first perfected at the Abbey Church of St. Denis near Paris (1140). The rib vault made possible a lighter, almost skeletal building. The flying buttress, also characteristic, was first used at Notre Dame in Paris. During the 13th century, the style known as High Gothic was perfected, and cathedrals with higher vaults and more slender columns and walls were constructed, as at Chartres and Reims in France, Salisbury in England, and Cologne in Germany. In the 14th and 15th centuries Gothic works became more elaborate and ornate. Sculptural decoration was an essential part of Gothic architecture, as were stained glass windows, the most notable examples of which are at Chartres. The period is also noted for its manuscript illumination in missals, books of hours, Bibles, and psalters.

Gothic novel, genre of fiction whose terror-laden stories are usually set against a menacing, medieval background. Early examples are Horace Walpole's *Castle of Otranto* (1765) and Ann Radcliffe's *The Mysteries of Udolpho* (1794). Modern Gothic novels are often formulaic historical romances.

Goths, ancient Germanic peoples, split into Ostrogoths (East Goths) and Visigoths (West Goths) in the 3rd century. The Ostrogoths, subjects of the Huns until A.D. 453, went on to settle in Pannonia (modern Hungary) as allies of the Byzantine Empire, and then (after 493) in Italy, claiming lands when their ruler, Theodoric the Great, defeated the barbarian ruler Odoacer. Defeated in turn by Justinian I, their kingdom was crushed after an Ostrogothic revolt in 552. The Visigoths moved (376) into Roman territory, sacking Rome (410) and heading north to the Loire valley; they made Toulouse their capital before taking Vandal lands in Spain. At the peak of their power they were led by King Euric (r. 466-c.484). After losing lands north of the Pyrénées to the Franks, they were restricted to Spain, became Christians, and merged with the Spanish population. Defeat by the Moors in 711 ended the Visigothic kingdom.

An essential part of Gothic architecture were stained glass windows, like these lancet and rose windows in the cathedral at Reims.

Gottfried von Strassburg, medieval German poet (late 12th-early 13th century), famous for his unfinished Middle High German masterpiece *Tristan* (c.1210), an epic based on Celtic legend. It became the basis of Richard Wagner's opera *Tristan und Isolde* (1859).

Gottlieb, Adolph (1903-74), U.S. artist, known for his oversized abstract expressionist landscapes, which feature bursts of color. He derived his early style from pictographs, arranging abstract symbols in grids.

Gottschalk, Louis Moreau (1829-69), U.S. composer and pianist, internationally celebrated as a virtuoso. Influenced by the Creole and black rhythms of his native New Orleans, his compositions include *Tremolo Étude, Bamboula,* and *The Last Hope.*

Gould, Glenn (1932-82), Canadian virtuoso pianist, famous for his performances of Bach, Beethoven, and Brahms. From the late 1960s he abandoned live performances, making records and documentary films.

Gould, Jay (1836-92), U.S. railroad speculator. He denied Cornelius Vanderbilt control of the Erie Railroad by selling stock illegally. With James Fisk he tried cornering the gold market (1869) and triggered the Black Friday panic. From 1872 he built up the Gould railroad system in the Southwest, which included the Union Pacific.

Gounod, Charles François (1818-93), French composer, best known for the operas *Faust* (1859) and *Romeo and Juliet* (1867), and the song "Ave Maria," based on Bach's first prelude. Additional works include 10 other operas, oratorios, masses, and cantatas.

Gourd, any of a variety of plants, chiefly vines, of the family Cucurbitaceae, producing fruit known as gourds that are used as food and utensils. The *Cucumis* genus includes melons (except watermelons), cucumbers, and gherkins (*C. anguria*); the *Cucurbita* genus represents winter squash (*C. maxima*) and summer squash and pumpkins (varieties of *C. pepo*). Durable-shelled gourds have been used as water carriers, ornaments, resonators of musical instruments, and utensils (ladles, dippers, bowls). The fruit of the loofah (*Luffa cylindrica*), fibrous in texture, is dried for use as a sponge.

Gout, recurrent acute arthritis of peripheral joints caused by excess uric acid in the blood and tissue fluids. It may be precipitated by minor injury, overindulgence in food or alcohol, surgery, fatigue, emotional stress, infection, or administration of penicillin, insulin, or mercuric diuretics. The symptoms and signs include severe pain in a single joint, swelling of overlying skin, and inflammation. Treatment medicines help to speed elimination of uric acid by the kidneys.
See also: Arthritis.

Government, system of control and regulation of social activities by the state, also referring to the agency that exercises such control. Governments have the power of coercion to enforce law. They define crimes and administer punishment. To defend its existence and the integrity of its territory against both internal and external enemies, most governments maintain armed forces. In modern industrialized countries the economic and social functions of governments include providing public services (such as building roads, and supplying water and sanitation facilities), and supervising education. The issuance of currency is a government monopoly. In recent times, governments have become involved in the direct management of the economy, regulating commerce, labor relations, and international trade and credit. Governments have also undertaken responsibility for social security, unemployment insurance, old age pensions, and aid to dependent children.

Grackle

Government regulation, government supervision of industry to protect the interests of individuals and society as a whole. Federal, state, and local agencies regulate, oversee, and control prices, health and safety measures, and quality of service. U.S. regulation of the railroads began in 1887 with the establishment of the Interstate Commerce Commission (ICC). Under President Roosevelt's economic recovery plan of the 1930s, the federal government established such regulatory agencies of the Federal Communications Commission (FCC) and the Securities and Exchange Commission (SEC). In the 1970s the Environmental Protection Agency (EPA) and the Occupational Safety and Health Administration (OSHA) were established with a much narrower regulatory focus.

Governor, in the United States, the executive head of each of the 50 states, whose duties and authority usually include responsibilities for the administrative affairs of state, appointment of nonelective government officials and judges, preparation of the budget, and command of the state police force. They may also be given the power to veto legislative measures and to pardon or commute the prison sentences of convicted criminals.

Goya, Francisco (1746-1828), Spanish painter and graphic artist. Master of satire, his keen sense of observation and ability to depict reality graphically and with almost savage detail served him from his early works, designing cartoons for tapestries (1775-79), to his later appointment (1799) as court painter to Charles III and Charles IV. However, illness, which left him deaf in 1793, marked a turning point in his work. A world that had previously been depicted with brilliant colors, suggesting charm and delight, became grim and grotesque. His disillusionment became apparent in works from this period, including the paintings *Maja Nude* and *Maja Clothed*; the frescoes for Madrid's Church of San Antonio de la Florida, and the etchings *Disasters of War*, suggested by Napoleon's invasions of Spain. Near the end of his life, Goya surrounded himself with his "Black Paintings," including *Witches' Sabbath* and *Satan Devouring His Children*. Goya's work was a major influence on Edouard Manet and the French impressionists.

Francisco Goya, selfportrait

Gracchus, family name of 2 Roman brothers, social reformers and political leaders, known together as the Gracchi. **Tiberius Sempronius Gracchus** (163?-133 B.C.), was elected to the popular tribune in 133. He proposed what became called the Sempronian Law to redistribute public land to landless citizens in order to restore the ruined middle class of small independent farmers. At the next election he renominated himself, and when the Senate ordered the election postponed, there was a riot in which Tiberius was killed. **Caius Sempronius Gracchus** (153?-121 B.C.), was elected a tribune in 123 and took over leadership of the reform movement, suggesting democratic government to replace aristocracy and proposing citizenship for all Latins. When the Senate moved to revoke his bills, fighting broke out and Caius was killed.

Grace, in Christian theology, favor shown by God toward sinful and needy people. Grace is at the heart of salvation and is necessary for faith and good works. The means of grace include holy scripture, the sacraments, prayer, and Christian fellowship.

Graces, in Greek mythology, goddesses of fertility, personifying charm and beauty. Also known as the Charites, they were daughters of Zeus and the nymph Eurynome. Their names were Aglaia (radiance), Euphrosyne (joyfulness), and Thalia (bloom). The Romans called them the Gratiae.

Grackle, songbird of the family Icteridae, including blackbirds, orioles, and bobolinks. The grackle, generally black-hued, feeds on a wide variety of foods, including grain, bananas, and nuts; it is also known to destroy the eggs and young of other birds.

Grade school *see:* Elementary school.

Graduate school *see:* Universities and colleges.

Grady, Henry Woodfin (1850-89), U.S. editor and orator. As editor of *The Atlanta Constitution* (from 1879), he encouraged reconciliation after the Civil War.

Graf, Steffi (1969-), German tennis player, known for her powerful forehand. Ranked number one in the world (1987-90), in 1988 Graf won the grand slam (consisting of the Australian Open, the French Open, Wimbledon, and the United States Open) and Olympic gold medal in women's singles. In 1989 Graf captured 3 out of the 4 grand slam events, losing only in the finals of the French Open.

Grafting, in horticulture, uniting of 2 closely related varieties of plants so that they grow as one. The stem or bud of the plant to be grafted (the scion) is attached to the stem or roots of the other (the stock or rootstock). The result is known as a hybrid. Grafting is used to increase productivity, to create seedless fruits, to breed disease- and pest-resistant stock, and to grow plants in unfamiliar environments by using stock compatible to that environment.

Graham, Billy (William Franklin Graham; 1918-), U.S. evangelist. Ordained a Southern Baptist minister (1939), he gained national prominence on the revivalist circuit (c.1949) and went on to establish an international reputation as a leader of mass religious rallies and an adviser and confidante of U.S. presidents.

Billy Graham

Graham, Katharine Meyer (1917-), publisher of *The Washington Post* (1968-79) and head of its parent company, which also controlled *Newsweek* magazine and several television stations.

Graham, Martha (1894-91), U.S. dancer, choreographer, and teacher. A pupil of Ruth St. Denis, she made her debut in the Denishawn companies (1920) and formed her own troupe in 1929. A major influence and pioneer in modern dance, she choreographed such works as *Appalachian Spring* (1944), *Clytemnestra* (1958), and *The Archaic Hours* (1969). In 1976 she was awarded the U.S. Medal of Freedom.
See also: Ballet.

Grahame, Kenneth (1859-1931), British writer of children's stories *The Golden Age* (1895), *Dream Days* (1898), and the classic *The Wind in the Willows* (1908), featuring animals with appealingly human characteristics.

Grail, Holy *see:* Holy Grail.

Grain, in agriculture, the dry seedlike fruit of a cereal grass; also, the plant that bears these fruits, including wheat, rice, oats, millet, maize, and rye. The main dietary staple of both humans and domesticated animals, grain, whole and ground, is primarily a source of carbohydrates, though some protein, vitamins, and other nutrients are present. Half of the world's cropland grows grain (corn, wheat, and rice).

Grainger, Percy Aldridge (1882-1961), Australian-born composer and pianist, a naturalized American from 1914. Influenced by his friend Grieg, he collected and edited English folk music, basing short orchestral pieces upon it.

Grain sorghum (*Sorghum vulgare*), plant of the grass family (Gramineae) producing clusters of small starchy seeds. It is used widely for livestock feed; in Asia and Africa, it is ground into flour for making bread and cereal. The plant is native to Africa, but is grown widely in the United States today. It grows about 2 to 6 ft (61 to 183 cm) tall.

Grain weevil, or snout beetle, small destructive beetle of the weevil family that attacks and damages stored grain. The female bores into healthy grain seeds with her snout and lays eggs. Hatched grubs consume the inside of the seed and mature in about a month. This worldwide pest is controlled by spraying silos and grain bins before a new harvest.

Grammar, structures of a language and of its constituents; also, the science concerned with the study of those structures. The grammarian concentrates on *syntax*, the ways that words are put together to form sentences; *accidence*, or *morphology*, the ways that words are inflected (altered) to convey different senses, such as past or present tense or singular and plural; and *phonology*, the ways that sounds are used to convey meaning. Since sentences of widely different outward form may have the same meaning, many grammarians hold that there is a deep structure of language that can be resolved into a few basic elements whose combinations can be used to produce an infinite number of sentences. As a consequence, grammatical studies are probing at the very roots of the human psyche.
See also: Language.

Grammar school *see:* Elementary school.

Granada, name of a province of southeastern Spain and of the capital (pop. 280,600) of that province. The Moorish sovereignty of that name was overtaken by Ferdinand and Isabella's armies in 1492. In the 1800s it was divided into the 3 provinces of Granada, Málaga, and Almería. The province of Granada is 4,838 sq mi (12,530 sq km). It is rich in minerals and has fertile soil. The Alhambra, a Moorish fortress and palace, and the palace of Charles V, a Holy Roman emperor, are the city's major tourist attractions.

Granada (pop. 58,100), oldest city in Nicaragua, located on Lake Nicaragua. The city, founded in 1523, was raided by pirates throughout the 1600s. It was burned in 1856 by U.S. adventurer William Walker, and rebuilt shortly thereafter. The city has many ornate Spanish-style churches and fine mansions.

Granada, Kingdom of, medieval Arab Islamic kingdom in southern Spain. Founded 1238 by the Nasrid dynasty, with its capital in Granada, the kingdom was the center of Moorish culture, a leading world center of art, science, and literature, with an extremely tolerant policy toward non-Muslims. In the 15th century internal dissensions furthered the kingdom's ultimate conquest by the Spanish monarchs Ferdinand and Isabella, who took over in 1492 and drove the Muslims and Jews out of Spain.

Gran Chaco, lowland plain in Paraguay, Argentina, and Bolivia. Occupying c.250,000 sq mi (647,500 sq km), this extremely hot, sparsely populated region is prone to droughts and flooding. Among its resources are oil and quebracho (a source of tannin).

Grand Alliance, or League of Augsburg, name of 3 separate European alliances created to control the invasions of King Louis XIV of France. The first (1673-79) included the Holy Roman Empire, Prussia, and several German states. The second alliance (1689-97), between the Netherlands, England, Spain, and the Holy Roman Empire, fought against France in the War of the League of Augsburg. The third alliance (1701-14), made up of some German states, Prussia, Austria, England, and the Netherlands, fought France in the War of the Spanish Succession.
See also: Succession wars.

Grand Army of the Republic (GAR), society of Union Civil War veterans. Founded in 1866, it assisted veterans and their families by founding veterans' homes and by lobbying for government pensions. Over 400,000 veterans were members in 1890; the order was discontinued in 1956.
See also: Civil War, U.S.

Grand Banks, underwater plateau off southeast Newfoundland, Canada, where the Labrador Current and Gulf Stream meet. Its shallow waters abound in cod, haddock, and halibut, making it one of the world's richest fishing grounds.

Grand Canyon, spectacular gorge cut by the Colorado River in northwest Arizona. It is more than 200 mi (320 km) long, 4-18 mi (6-29 km) wide, up to 1 mi (1.6 km) deep, and flanked by a plateau 5,000-9,000 ft (1,524-2,743 m) above sea level. The main canyon contains many smaller canyons, peaks, and mesas, and is walled by colorful layers of rock dating back more than 2 million years. Grand Canyon National Park attracts about 2 million visitors each year.

Grand Canyon, Arizona

Grand Canyon National Park, U.S. park covering 1,218,375 acres (493,059 hectares) in Arizona, established in 1919 and expanded in 1975. The park receives about 2 million visitors annually. Some 300 species of birds and 120 other kinds of animals inhabit it. Some 300 Havasupai Native Americans live on a reservation just outside the park.

Grand Coulee Dam, 550 ft (168 m) high and 4,173 ft (1,272 m) long dam on the Columbia River in the state of Washington. Built 1933-42, it is part of one of the world's largest hydroelectric generating plants.
See also: Columbia River.

Grandfather clause, legal device in Southern states to deny blacks the right to vote by giving it to males with high literacy and property qualifications or to those whose fathers and grandfathers had been qualified to vote on Jan. 1, 1867 (before the 15th Amendment). First used in South Carolina in 1895, it was declared unconstitutional in 1915.

Grand jury, group of citizens who decide whether there is enough evidence to charge an individual with a crime. A grand jury never tries a case; its job is only to inquire and accuse. Originally, during the time of Henry III of England (1216-72), the grand jury not only inquired and accused, but also tried cases. In the United States the grand jury usually consists of 16 to 23 people, all legally adults and citizens.

Grandma Moses *see:* Moses, Grandma.

Grand National, world's most prestigious steeplechase race held annually since 1839 at the Aintree race course in England. The difficult and dangerous 4.5 mi (7.2 km) course includes 30 jumps, mostly over thorn hedges. Horses must be at least 6 years old to enter.

Grand Old Party *see:* Republican Party.

Grand Ole Opry *see:* Country and Western music.

Grand Portage National Monument, memorial erected in Grand Portage, Minn., on Lake Superior near the Canadian border. Here the Native Americans, European pioneers, and fur traders carried their boats and supplies overland 9 mi (14 km) to avoid rapids and the treacherous 70-ft (20-m) Pigeon Falls on the Pigeon River. In 1803, when the British North West Company left and the United States took over the territory, use of the portage declined. Summer tours are now given between Grand Portage and nearby Isle Royale National Park.

Grand Pré, historic town in Nova Scotia, Canada, founded by French colonists in 1680. The French settled in Acadia, now Nova Scotia, in 1604 and developed Grand Pré into an enterprising farming community, doing business with neighboring towns. When the colonists refused to pledge allegiance to England, the British burned the town, forcing its settlers into exile. The event is immortalized in Henry Wadsworth Longfellow's poem, *Evangeline.*
See also: Nova Scotia.

Grand Prix *see:* Automobile racing.

Grand Rapids (pop. 688,399), city (inc. 1850), in western Michigan, on the Grand River; seat of Kent County. Famous for its furniture manufacturing, begun by Dutch settlers in the early 1800s, the city today supports many industries and is the market for the area's truck farming industry. Other products include gypsum and gravel. It is also the home of several colleges, and is a gateway to Michigan's recreation area.
See also: Michigan.

Grand Teton National Park, created 1929 in the Rocky Mountains in northwestern Wyoming. The spectacular area, occupying about 500 sq mi (1,395 sq km), comprises major peaks of the Teton Range and the valley of Jackson Hole.

Grand unified theories (GUT's), theories that attempt to explain the physical universe by a unified concept of 3 of the 4 fundamental forces: the weak nuclear force, which controls radioactive decay of atomic nuclei; electromagnetism, which secures the electrons to the nucleus; and the strong nuclear force, which ties the nucleus together. The fourth fundamental force, gravitation, has not yet been included in GUT's. It is not known if it is indeed possible to explain all events and phenomena of the universe in such a unified manner.

Grange, National, U.S. agrarian organization, officially the National Grange of the Patrons of Husbandry. Founded as a fraternal order for social and educational purposes in 1867, it led the Granger movement of the 1870s to protect farmers against economic abuse (high prices imposed on farmers by railroads and grain-storage facilities). The constitutional principle of public regulation of privately owned services was established in the Granger cases, including the landmark Supreme Court decision *Munn* v. *Illinois* (1876).

Grange, Red (1930-91), U.S. football player. He was known as the Galloping Ghost after scoring 5 touchdowns for the University of Illinois in a game against the University of Michigan in 1924. Grange became a professional player in 1925 and joined the Chicago Bears. He retired in 1935 after scoring 1,058 points and in 1963 was inducted into the Pro Football Hall of Fame.

Red Grange

Granger cases, 5 Supreme Court cases in 1877 that established a state's right, "Granger laws," to regulate privately owned services affecting the public interest. The cases arose from the Granger movement, which aimed at curbing high prices imposed on farmers by railroads and grain processors. The first and most important Granger case was *Munn* v. *Illinois*, a landmark in U.S. law.

Granite, coarse-grained rock, composed chiefly of feldspar (orthoclase and microcline) and quartz. Generally believed to have solidified from a molten form (igneous), some granite is also believed to have been metamorphic (rock transformed by heat, pressure, or chemically active fluids). A hard, weather-resistant rock, usually pink or gray, granite is often used in building, paving, and monuments.

Grant, Cary (Archibald Leach; 1904-86), English born U.S. actor. Honored in 1970 with an Academy Award for general excellence, his films include *Bringing Up Baby* (1938), *The Philadelphia Story* (1940), *To Catch a Thief* (1955), and *North By Northwest* (1959).

Grant, (Hiram) Ulysses Simpson (1822-85), 18th president of the United States. Grant led the Union forces to victory in the Civil War, but the qualities that made him a military hero did not make him a great president. Although Grant was a man of outstanding personal integrity, his administration was riddled with corruption and mismanagement.

Early life. In 1838 Grant entered the U.S. military academy at West Point. After graduating in 1843, he served in the Mexican War. Following the Mexican surrender, Grant married his fiancée, Julia Dent, but found little to do as a peacetime solider. He began to drink heavily and wandered from job to job, including farming, selling real estate, and working as a clerk in his father's store.

Military leader. The outbreak of the Civil War in 1861 reprieved Grant from failure. His originality in military strategy helped him win the first important Union victories and earned him the nickname Unconditional Surrender Grant. He moved onto greater victories at Shiloh, Vicksburg, and Chattanooga. In 1864 President Abraham Lincoln gave Grant command of the entire Union army. After a series of bloody battles, Grant received the surrender of Confederate General Robert E. Lee at Appomattox Court House on Apr. 9, 1865. In 1866 Grant was made a full general, the first such appointment since George Washington's. Grant was now a national hero, which made him attractive to the Republican Party. He was nominated as its presidential candidate in 1868 and defeated his Democratic opponent, Horatio Seymour, by a narrow popular majority. Among Grant's supporters were blacks of the South, who were voting for the first time.

President. Grant's first term was marked by quarrels with Congress and setbacks for his policies. His executive appointments were not politically astute, and he filled many posts with personal friends. While Grant's relative leniency to the South helped heal the wounds of war, his administration marked the beginning of a decline in the rights of blacks. In 1872 Grant defeated publisher Horace Greeley to win a second term. Grant's White House soon became enmeshed in scandal. The Crédit Mobilier fraud involved numerous politicians. Some of Grant's close associates were tarnished in a scheme to defraud the collection of internal revenue. His secretary of war resigned to avoid impeachment over corruption. Grant's honesty and ability were unquestioned, but his strong sense of loyalty to his friends only compounded the problems.

Retirement. After leaving office in 1877, Grant settled in New York. In 1884 he was rendered penniless in the collapse of a firm in which he had invested heavily. He grew seriously ill with throat cancer.

Grant wrote his memoirs with the help of Mark Twain, who published them. Grant died shortly after completing the manuscript, but royalties from the book restored his family's security. He was buried with great public mourning in Riverside Park, New York City, where an elaborate mausoleum was dedicated in 1897.

Grape, shrub and its fruit, of the family Vitaceae, native to tropical, subtropical, and temperate regions. One of the oldest of all cultivated fruits, grapes are eaten fresh or dried (raisins), and are used in wine making. There are 2 main types of grapes: European, from the wine grape of Europe and Asia, and American, native to North America or developed from crossbreeding with the European variety.

Grapefruit, evergreen tree (*Citrus paradisi*) of the rue family, and its citrus fruit, which weigh from 1-5 lb (0.45-2.27 kg). First discovered in the West Indies, the grapefruit is believed to be a mutation of the Asian pomelo (*C. maxima*).

Graph, diagram showing the relations between quantities.

Graphic arts, techniques of drawing and engraving words and pictures, including block printing, etching, lithography, silkscreening, and engraving. The capacity to reproduce identical books quickly came about in 1440 when Johannes Gutenberg invented movable print. Block printing and engraving were mastered in Europe at the end of the Middle Ages, and graphic arts were used for original artwork as well as to create reproductions. Graphic artists include Albrecht Dürer of Germany, and Francisco Goya and Pablo Picasso of Spain.

Graphite, also known as carbon plumbago or black lead, mineral that is the crystalline form of carbon. Graphite is a good conductor of electricity and is used to make electrodes. Its inertness makes it valuable for the construction of metallurgical crucibles. It is also used as a lubricant, a moderator in nuclear reactors, and, mixed with clay, becomes the "lead" of pencils.

Graphology, the study of handwriting, particularly for information about the character of the writer.

Grass, any plant of the family Gramineae. This group of mostly annual and perennial herbs has great economic importance: as a food source (cereal grass: wheat, rice, corn, rye, barley, and oats; hay and pasture plants, e.g., bluegrass and sorghum; sugarcane); in construction and thatching (bamboo and reed species); as raw material for paper and liquors. Grass-family plants, with their hollow or pithy jointed stems, are also instrumental in preventing erosion.

Grass, Günter Wilhelm (1927-), German novelist and playwright. His works, deeply affected by the post-World War II sense of national guilt, are usually centered around grotesque motifs and have strong moral content. His best-known works include the novels *The Tin Drum* (1959), *Local Anaesthetic* (1969), and *The Flounder* (1977), and the controversial play *The Plebeians Rehearse the Uprising* (1965).

Grasse, François Joseph Paul, Comte de (1722-88), French naval commander whose fleet made possible Washington's decisive victory over the British at the siege of Yorktown (1781). Grasse landed 3,000 troops to aid the siege, and also blockaded General Cornwallis's British fleet.

Grasshopper, plant-eating, winged insect of the order Orthoptera, with powerful hind legs for jumping and springing to flight. Divided into 2 families, long-horned (e.g., katydid) and short-horned (e.g., locust), grasshoppers range from 0.5-4 in (1-10 cm) in length. The males sing by rubbing their hind legs against folded wings.

Grassland, land whose predominant vegetation consists of grasses and forage plants; excellent for cultivation. Savanna, or tropical grassland found in Africa and South America, has coarse grasses, occasional clumps of trees, and some shrubs; prairie has tall, deep-rooted grasses and is

Ulysses Simpson Grant

18th U.S. President

Born:	Point Pleasant, Ohio; Apr. 27, 1822
Terms:	Mar. 1869-Mar. 1877
Vice presidents:	Schuyler Colfax; Henry Wilson
Political party:	Republican
Spouse:	Julia Dent Grant
Children:	4
Died:	Mt. McGregor, N.Y.; July 23, 1885

found in Middle and North America, Argentina, the Ukraine, South Africa, and Australia; steppes have short grasses and are found mainly in Central Asia.

Grasso, Ella Tambussi (1919-81), first U.S. woman governor (Connecticut, 1975-81) elected in her own right, not in succession to a husband. Previously Connecticut secretary of state (1959-70) and a member of the U.S. House of Representatives (1971-75), she cut spending to revive the state's economy. She resigned because of ill health.

Grave Creek Mound *see:* Mound builders.

Graves, Morris Cole (1910-), U.S. painter. His interest in Eastern art and Native American mythology is seen in his delicate images of blind birds, pine trees, and waves.

Graves, Robert Ranke (1895-1985), English poet and novelist, best known for his novels set in imperial Rome: *I, Claudius* and *Claudius the God* (both, 1934). *Goodbye to All That* (1929) described his experiences in World War I, and *The Long Week-End*, the interwar period.

Gravitation, one of the fundamental forces of nature, the force of attraction existing between all matter. It is much weaker than nuclear or electromagnetic forces and plays no part in the internal structure of matter. It plays a vital role in the behavior of the universe: The gravitational attraction of the sun keeps the planets in their orbits, and gravitation holds the matter in a star together.

Gravity, Center of, in physics, point within an object where gravitational forces appear to act, and where the mass can be considered concentrated. This point is the same as the object's center of mass. The movement of an object is determined by where force is exerted in relation to the center of gravity.
See also: Gravity, Specific; Physics.

The New York Stock Exchange in Wall Street experienced a turbulent period in 1929.

Gray, Asa (1810-88), U.S. botanist. Being a prominent Protestant layman, his advocacy of the Darwinian thesis carried special force. However, he never accepted the materialist interpretation of the evolutionary mechanism, and taught that natural selection was indeed consistent with a divine teleology.

Gray, Elisha (1835-1901), U.S. inventor. He patented several electrical appliances, mostly related to the telegraph. While experimenting with transmitting musical notes, he tried transmitting the human voice. In 1876, he filed for a patent for the telephone device but Alexander Graham Bell's final patent had been registered a few hours earlier.
See also: Telegraph.

Gray, Robert (1755-1806), first American sea captain to circumnavigate the world, 1787-90. In 1782 he discovered the Columbia River and established the American claim to the Oregon territory.
See also: Columbia River.

Gray, Thomas (1716-71), English poet. His "Elegy Written in a Country Churchyard" (1751) is one of the most popular English poems; among his other main works are the odes "The Progress of Poesy" and "The Bard" (both 1757).

Gray fox *see:* Fox.

Grayling, freshwater game fish (genus Thymallus) whose flesh is regarded as a delicacy. It is related to the trout but has a smaller mouth and a larger dorsal fin. The largest grayling weigh about 4 lb (2 kg). Graylings are found in only a few parts of the northern United States, but are abundant in the colder waters of Canada and northern Eurasia.

Gray Panthers, national group organized in 1970 to fight discriminatory practices against senior citizens. The organization protests mandatory retirement, age segregation in housing, and negative representation of the elderly by the media.

Graz (pop. 243,500), second largest city in Austria, capital of the province of Styria, located on the Mur River. The city was founded around the 12th century. Local industry produces iron and steel products, leather, paper, and textiles. Graz has a 15th-century cathedral, the Johanneum museum, and the Schlossberg castle.
See also: Austria.

Greasewood, any of various spiny shrubs of the alkaline soils of southwestern deserts and semideserts, especially *Sarcobatus vermiculatus.* One shrub, *Larrea divaricata*, is also known as the creosote bush for the tarry odor of its leaves.

Great Awakening, intense and widespread religious revival in 18th-century North America, forming part of the international evangelical revival. Starting in New Jersey (1726), the movement quickly spread across New England. In reaction to the prevailing rationalism and formalism, its leaders—notably Jonathan Edwards and George Whitefield—preached evangelical Calvinism and discouraged excessive emotionalism. The 1740s saw the zenith of the Awakening, which led to the rapid growth of the Presbyterian, Baptist, and Methodist churches, continuing to the end of the century. A similar revival beginning in the 1790s is known as the Second Great Awakening.
See also: Revivalism.

Great Barrier Reef, series of massive coral reefs off the northeast coast of Australia, extending for about 1,250 mi (2,000 km). The reef, which is the world's largest coral formation, can be safely crossed only at certain passages, the chief of which is Rains Inlet.

Great Basin, desert region in the western region of the United States between the Wasatch and Sierra Nevada mountains, in Nevada, Utah, and parts of adjacent states. A subdivision of the Basin and Range physiographic province, the Great Basin of Nevada contains Death Valley, Reno, Las Vegas, and Salt Lake City. Mineral mining and agriculture are the main industries.

Great Bear Lake, largest lake in Canada and fourth largest in North America. It has an area of 12,275 sq mi (31,792 sq km) and an elevation of 390 ft (119 m) above sea level. Its deepest point is 1,350 ft (411 m). It is located about 250 mi (402 km) east of the Rocky Mountains, and lies partly within the Arctic Circle. Pitchblende ore, which contains radium and uranium, is mined on the southeast shore of the lake.

Great Britain *see:* United Kingdom.

Great-circle route, route on the earth's surface based on the *great circle*, any circle that divides a sphere into equal halves. The great-circle route is always the shortest route between 2 points. It appears on a *gnomonic projection* map as a straight line; on flat maps it often appears as a longer curve. By the 1800s ship navigators set their compasses to follow lines called *rhumb* lines, which join selected points along the great-circle route. Airplanes follow the great-circle route by using a method called *inertial guidance.*

Great Dane, large, strong dog developed in Germany in the 1500s and originally used as a boarhound and a guard dog. It weighs from 120 to 175 lb (54 to 79 kg) and is from 30 to 34 in (76 to 86 cm) high at the shoulder. Great Danes have short, thick coats that may be tan, brown with black stripes, black, or blue to white with black patches.

Great Depression, period of U.S. and world economic depression during the 1930s that was immediately precipitated by the disastrous stockmarket collapse on Wall Street on Black Friday, Oct. 29, 1929. This heralded a period of high unemploy-

ment, failing businesses and banks, and falling agricultural prices. Millions of workers were unemployed during the period (some 16 million in the United States alone in 1933). There were many causes of the depression: Easy credit had led to widespread stock speculation; the world had not completely recovered from World War I; U.S. economic policies under President Herbert Hoover had created domestic overproduction and less foreign trade. Franklin D. Roosevelt, elected president in 1932, brought in the New Deal measures, but full recovery of the economy occurred only with the beginnings of defense spending immediately prior to World War II.
See also: United States of America.

Great Divide, or Continental Divide, mountain points in North America that separate the waters ultimately flowing into the Atlantic Ocean from those flowing ultimately into the Pacific. In the United States and Canada, the Great Divide runs through the Rocky Mountains.

Great Falls (pop. 77,691), largest city in Montana and seat of Cascade County. Situated on the Missouri River, to the east of the Rocky Mountains and in the north central part of the state, it is an important commercial and industrial center. The city lies in a major mining region, near deposits of lead, coal, copper, zinc, and iron, on which much of its refining and manufacturing industry is based. Cattle, sheep, and wheat from the surrounding area are also marketed and processed here. Settled in 1883, Great Falls was incorporated in 1888.
See also: Montana.

Great Lakes, chain of 5 large freshwater lakes in North America, forming the largest lake group in the world and covering an area of 95,170 sq mi (246,490 sq km). From east to west the lakes are Ontario, Erie, Huron, Michigan, and Superior. They are connected by several channels. Once important for fur trade, the lake system is used for the transportation of iron ore, steel, petroleum, coal, grain, and heavy manufactured goods. Import Great Lakes cities include Milwaukee, Chicago, Detroit, Cleveland, Buffalo, and Toronto. In recent years, the lakes, particularly Lake Erie, have suffered from serious pollution.

Great Lakes-Saint Lawrence Seaway *see:* Saint Lawrence Seaway and Great Lakes Waterway.

Great laurel *see:* Rhododendron.

Great Plains, large plateau in the western region of central North America, extending for over 1,500 mi (2,400 km) from the Saskatchewan River in northwest Canada to the Rio Grande in Mexico and the Gulf coastal plain in the southern part of the United States. The plateau slopes gently downward from the Rockies in the west, extending about 400 mi (640 km) east. The natural vegetation is buffalo grass, and the area generally has hot summers and cold winters with an average annual rainfall of 20 in (50 cm). The plains are the "granary of the world" owing to their vast wheat production; livestock is also important.

Great Purge *see:* Union of Soviet Socialist Republics.

Great Pyrenees, breed of sheepdog originating in the Pyrenees Mountains. The dog, 27 to 32 in (69 to 81 cm) in height and weighing 90 to 125 lb (41 to 57 kg), is strong and muscular with a bearlike head. Its thick coat is white, sometimes with tan or gray markings. Obedient, hardworking, and easily trained, the Great Pyrenees is used as a guard dog, guide dog, and rescuer of avalanche victims.

Great Rift Valley, large geological depression extending more than 3,000 mi (4,800 km) from southeast Africa to northern Syria. In Africa its west course is partly occupied by lakes Malawi (Nyassa), Tanganyika, Kivu, Edward, and Albert; its east course by Lake Turkana.

Great Salt Lake, shallow saline inland sea in the northwestern region of Utah, about 5 mi (8 km) northwest of Salt Lake City. Its size and depth vary yearly, but on average the lake is 72 mi (116 km) long and 30 mi (48 km) across at its widest point, with a maximum depth of 270 ft (82 m). It is the largest brine lake in North America. Industrial plants along the shore extract some 300,000 tons of salt from the lake every year, and plans are under way for tapping other mineral resources.

Great Salt Lake Desert, part of a flat low area in northwest Utah, about 140 mi (225 km) by 80 mi (130 km), bordering Great Salt Lake to the northeast. The explorer John Frémont discovered it in 1845. The Bonneville Salt Flats occupy its west central area, and are famous for auto speed testing.

Great Schism, 2 divisions in the Christian Church. The first was the breach between the Eastern and Western churches. Longstanding divergences in tradition, combined with political and theological disputes, came to a head in 1054 when Pope Leo IX sent legates to refuse the title of Ecumenical Patriarch to the patriarch of Constantinople and to demand acceptance of the *filioque* ("and from the Son") clause in the Nicene Creed. The patriarch refused and rejected the claim of papal supremacy. Reciprocal excommunications and anathemas followed. Later councils were unsuccessful in healing the breach. The second Great Schism was the division within the Roman Catholic Church (1378-1417) when there were 2 or 3 rival popes and antipopes, each with his nationalistic following. The Council of Constance ended the schism by electing Martin V sole pope.

Great Seal of the United States, symbol of the sovereignty of the nation, adopted by the government in 1782. The design on the seal's face—an American eagle with a shield on its breast, an olive branch in its right talon, and 13 arrows in its left talon—is used to authenticate important documents. Reverse side of the seal is displayed on the back of the one-dollar bill, but is not used as a seal.
See also: E pluribus unum.

Great Salt Lake

Great Slave Lake, located in Canada's Northwest Territories, 250 mi (400 km) east of the Rocky Mountains. Fed mainly by the Slave River and marking the beginning of the Mackenzie River, the lake is one of America's largest and the deepest in North America—2,015 ft (615 m). It covers an area of 10,980 sq mi (28,438 sq km). The name was derived form the tribe called the Slave, who originally inhabited the area. Small settlements around the lake are supported by fishing, lumbering, and the mining and smelting of lead, zinc, and gold ores.

Great Smoky Mountains, range of the Appalachian Mountains forming the border between North Carolina and Tennessee. The "Great Smokies" are almost entirely within the 800 sq mi (2,080 sq km) Great Smoky Mountains National Park. The mountain valleys are often filled with a smoky-blue haze, from which the name of the range derives.
See also: Appalachian Mountains.

Great Smoky Mountains National Park, park situated in the Great Smoky Mountains, on the Tennessee-North Carolina boundary, established in 1930. The highest of its 16 peaks is Clingmans Dome, 6,642 ft (2,024 m) high. The park's lush forests, shrubs, and plants include several varieties of orchid. The Cherokee were the original settlers of the region.

Great Society *see:* Johnson, Lyndon Baines.

Great Victoria Desert, large area of shifting sand dunes in southwestern Australia, south of Gibson Desert and north of the Nullarbor Plain. The desert, 250,000 sq mi (647,000 sq km) in area, was named by explorer Ernest Giles in 1875. An aboriginal reserve occupies much of the desert's eastern end. The area is tracked for the recovery of missiles from the weapons-testing range at Womera.

El Greco painted The Burial of the Count of Orgaz *at the church of Santo Tomi in Toledo*

Great Wall of China, world's longest wall fortification, in northern China. It extends over 1,500 mi (2,400 km), roughly following the southern border of the Mongolian plain. Construction was begun in the Ch'in dynasty (third century B.C.) to defend China against invasion from the north and mostly completed during the Ming dynasty (1368-1644). Its average height is 25 ft (7.6 m); it is wide enough (about 12 ft/3.6 m) for people on horseback to ride along it.
See also: China.

Grebe, group of highly specialized aquatic birds of the family Podicipedidae, of which 6 species are found in North America. They are diving birds of lakes or coastal waters. The feet are not webbed but "lobed" with flaps along the toes. Many of the grebes are brightly colored and bear tufts or crests. Courtship displays are often complex and spectacular. All grebes eat quantities of their own feathers, which collect around fishbones in the gut, allowing these indigestible remains to be formed into a pellet and evacuated.

Greco, El (Domenikos Theotokopoulos; 1541-1614), Greek-born Spanish painter. First in Venice, where he was influenced by Tintoretto, and later in Toledo, Spain, he developed his distinctive style of painting characterized by dramatically elongated figures and contrasting colors. Among his most famous works are *The Burial of the Count of Orgaz* (1586), *The Portrait of Cardinal Niño de Guevara* (1600), and *View of Toledo* (1608).

Greco, José (1918-), world renowned dancer. In 1942, he joined with the dancer Argentinita to form a nightclub act. In 1949, Greco created his own company.

Greece, independent country in southeast Europe, occupying the southern part of the

Greece

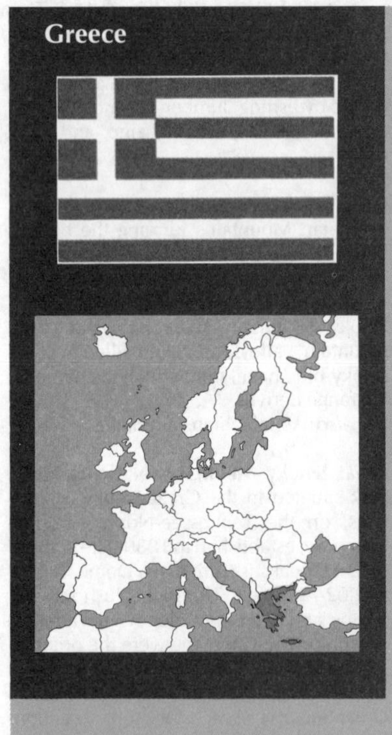

General information

Capital:	Athens
Area:	50,949 sq mi (131,957 sq km)
Population:	10,096,000
Official language:	Greek
Monetary unit:	1 Drachma = 100 lepta
Main cities:	Athens, Thessaloniki, Piraeus

Government

Form:	republic
Independent:	1830
Head of state:	President (elected every 5 years)
Head of government:	Prime Minister
Legislature:	one legislative house
Executive:	President and Cabinet
Judiciary:	highest court is the Special Supreme Tribunal
Political division:	52 departments

National economy

Gross national product:	U.S. $48,040,000,000
Per capita income:	U.S. $4,790
Agriculture:	wheat, corn, sugar beets, tomatoes, grapes, olives, cotton, lemons, tobacco
Livestock:	chickens, sheep, goats
Fisheries:	135,000 metric tons
Mining:	lignite, bauxite, crude petroleum, magnesite, marble
Industries:	food, beverages and tobacco, textiles, chemicals, clothing and footwear, paper and printing
Main exports:	basic manufacturing, food and livestock, miscellaneous manufactured articles, mineral fuels and lubricants, etc.
Transportation:	1,540 mi (2,479 km) of railroads; 64,191 mi (103,306 km) of roads; 9 international airports
Trading partners:	Germany, United States, Italy, France, United Kingdom

People

Urban:	58%
Ethnic composition:	Greek 95.5%, Macedonian 1.5%, Turkish 1%
Birth rate:	10.6 per 1,000 population
Death rate:	9.5 per 1,000 population
Infant mortality:	13 per 1,000 live births
Life expectancy:	male 72 years, female 76.5 years

Apostle bay (left)
The olive tree is certainly the most characteristic form of cultured vegetation in Greece (right)

Balkan peninsula and many surrounding islands in the Ionian, Mediterranean, and Aegean seas. Greece is bordered by Albania, Yugoslavia, and Bulgaria on the north, by Turkey and the Aegean Sea on the east, by the Ionian Sea on the west, and by the Mediterranean Sea on the south. The capital and largest city is Athens.

Land and climate. Almost 20% of its land area is accounted for by its islands, of which the largest is Crete. More than 160 other islands are inhabited, including Corfu, Lesbos, Milos, Rhodes, and Samos. The mainland is mountainous. The climate of Greece is typically Mediterranean along the coasts, which have hot, dry summers and mild winters. Most rain falls in the winter months and is concentrated along the western shores.

Economy. The leading farm products are fruits and vegetables, wheat, cotton, tobacco, wine, and olive oil. Both sheep and goats are raised in large numbers. Recently, industry has outdistanced agriculture as the major source of income. Products include textiles, chemicals, and ships, with most manufacturing in or near Athens. Greece has traditionally had a prosperous shipping industry; in 1983 its merchant fleet ranked third in the world. In the past several decades tourism has become increasingly important to Greece's economy. In 1981 the country joined the European Economic Community.

History. In the 15th century, with the fall of the Byzantine Empire, Greece was conquered by Turkey and was part of the Ottoman Empire until the successful War of Independence (1821-29). A constitutional monarchy was then established, but the country was marked by continual political instability and conflict between monarchists and republicans. During World War II Greece was occupied by German forces (1941-44). A major civil war between 1944 and 1949 between monarchists and a left-wing coalition led by communists left nearly a million dead. U.S. intervention was a major factor in ensuring the victory of the monarchists. Continuing political instability during the 1950s and 1960s led to a military coup and the establishment of a dictatorship in Apr. 1967. The monarchy was abolished in July 1973, and a revolt Nov. of that year overthrew the dictatorship. In 1974 the Greek people voted for a constitutional republic rather than a restoration of the monarchy, and a new constitution was adopted in June 1975. Since then Greece has lived under democratic rule.

Greece, Ancient, independent cities and states of classical times occupying the Balkan peninsula and the surrounding islands. The earliest major civilization in this area was the Minoan culture centered on the island of Crete (c.2200-1500 B.C.). In the next few centuries the Mycenaean civilization (named after the city of Mycenae on

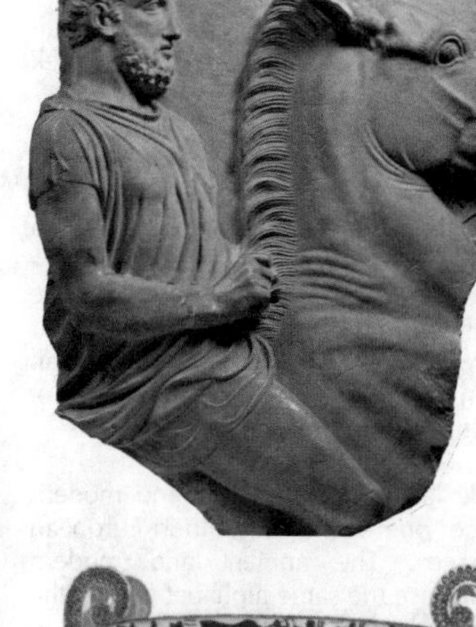

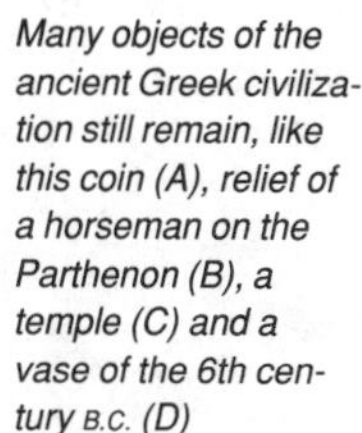

Many objects of the ancient Greek civilization still remain, like this coin (A), relief of a horseman on the Parthenon (B), a temple (C) and a vase of the 6th century B.C. (D)

the mainland) flourished (1600-1200 B.C.). The period between 1200 and 750 B.C. is known as the Dark Ages of Greek history. Dorian invaders overwhelmed the culture of Mycenae, but the Greek iron age was introduced. In the 8th and 7th centuries B.C. the first Greek city-states emerged, along with a culture based on the Greek language. Homer's epics date from this time. Trade with Egypt, Syria, and Phoenicia grew, and the city-states formed colonies throughout the Mediterranean area. From the 6th century, Athens and Sparta became the most powerful city-states. The 5th century B.C. began with a thwarted Persian invasion. The Persians were defeated on land at the Battles of Marathon (490 B.C.) and Plataea (479 B.C.) and at sea near Salamis. Athens emerged as the undisputed leader of Greece and led a number of Ionian cities in the formation of the Delian League, whose purpose was to protect commerce and resist further Persian invasions.

The latter half of the 5th century B.C., especially the reign of Pericles, was the Golden Age of Athens, a period of unparalleled cultural activity ranging from the building of the Parthenon to the ideas of Socrates. But resentment against Athenian power led eventually to Athens' defeat by Sparta in the Peloponnesian War (431-404 B.C.).

In the 4th century B.C. Athens' artistic and intellectual achievements continued to flourish. This was the century of Plato, Aristotle, the sculptor Praxiteles, and many others. In 338 B.C. Philip of Macedon became the ruler of Greece. Philip's son, Alexander the Great (356-323 B.C.), expanded Greek power into an empire that extended eastward to the Iudus River, and south to Egypt. In the period that followed his death, called the Hellenistic Age, Greek culture and civilization spread throughout the western world.

Rome first became involved in Greek affairs in 220 B.C. and in 197 B.C. Greek opponents of Macedonia helped the Romans defeat the Hellenistic rulers. From 146 B.C., Greece fell under Roman domination and in 27 B.C. it became the Roman province of Achaea. From A.D. 395, when the Roman Empire was divided into a Western and an Eastern Empire, Greece was incorporated into the Byzantine Empire, which lasted until 1453. After the fall of Constantinople (1453), it became part of the Ottoman Empire.

Greek, language of ancient and modern Greece, one of the oldest Indo-European languages. The ancient and modern tongues use the same alphabet (which the Greeks adopted from the Phoenicians in the 8th century B.C.), but differ greatly in grammar, vocabulary, and pronunciation. The earliest known records of ancient Greek date from around 1400 B.C. and use a form of writing known as Minoan linear script. Classical Greek is based on Athenian dialects spoken from the 6th to the 4th centuries B.C. During Hellenistic times a simplified Greek known as Koine became the common language of the civilized world. There are 2 forms of modern Greek: Koine for everyday use and an official state language that incorporates classical forms and words.

Greek Church *see:* Eastern Orthodox Church; Greece.

Greek fire, liquid mixture of unknown composition that took fire when wet, invented by a Syrian refugee in Constantinople in the 7th century A.D. and used by the Byzantine Empire and others for the next 800 years. Thrown in grenades or discharged from syringes, it wrought havoc in naval warfare until superseded by gunpowder. It appears to have been a petroleum-based mixture.

Greek games *see:* Olympic Games.

Greek gods *see:* Mythology.

Greek literature, earliest and most important literature known to the Western world. It is completely original and natural in that there were no earlier literary models that the Greeks could look to for guidance. The distinguishing characteristic of classical Greek literature is that it was oral, meant to be delivered by mouth and heard by the ears.

Early literature. Epic poetry, long narratives depicting heroic deeds of both gods and mortals, was the first important form of Greek literature. Homer, the greatest Greek poet, composed 2 epics, the *Iliad* and the *Odyssey*, in the 8th century B.C. The *Iliad* tells the story of the Trojan War. The *Odyssey* records the adventures of the Greek hero, Odysseus, upon his return home after the fall of Troy. Both emphasize the importance of honor and bravery. Hesiod, the first major poet to follow Homer, flourished during the 7th century B.C. Hesiod founded the didactic epic, which celebrated the hard work, thrift, and good judgment of the Greek peasant.

Lyric poetry, sung to the music of the lyre, evolved about 650 B.C. and dealt with human emotions. Sappho, a poet of the 6th century B.C., composed a special type of lyric poem called the melic poem, which was sung, not recited. The melic poems are characterized by highly emotional, nondidactic text. Sappho's love poetry is without parallel in Greek literature and is noted for its expression of passion and tragedy. Choral lyrics, sung by groups accompanied by music and dancing, were another form of lyric poetry. The victory odes of Pindar are choral masterpieces.

Elegiac poetry, which is related to lyric poetry, consisted of couplets that alternated a line of hexameter (6 feet) with a line of pentameter (5 feet).

The Golden Age. For a period of about 200 years, beginning in the late 500s B.C., Athens was the center of Greek culture. The height of this period, from 461 B.C. to 431 B.C., is often called the Golden Age. During this period, largely as a result of the emergence of democracy, literature flourished. Drama in the form of tragedy became the most important literary form. Aeschylus, Sophocles, and Euripides are the 3 greatest tragic playwrights. Aeschylus's plays are noted for seriousness, majestic language, and complexity of thought. Those of Sophocles are noted for characterization, graceful language, and sense of proportion. Euripides, the "philosopher of the stage," explored human emotions and passions.

Comedy was also prominent in the 400s B.C. The plays of Aristophanes, a writer of bawdy and satiric comedy, reflected the sense of freedom, vitality, and spirit that pervaded Athens at the time.

Herodotus, called the "father of history," traveled throughout the civilized world in the mid-400s B.C., recording the manners and customs of nations and peoples. He and the other historians wrote in prose. Thucydides, in his account of the Peloponnesian War, attempted to explain the effects of politics on history.

Philosophical literature evolved about 450 B.C. with a group of philosophers called sophists. Scholars and teachers of theories of knowledge, they invented rhetoric, the art of persuasive speaking. Literature was essentially oral and spoken in prose.The ideas of Socrates are preserved in the writing of his student, Plato.

The Hellenistic Age. During the reign of Alexander the Great in the 300s B.C., Greek ideas and culture spread throughout the civilized world to the East. The period following his death in 323 B.C. is called the Hellenistic Age. During this time, Athens gave way to Alexandria, Egypt, as the center of Greek civilization. Theocritus, an important poet of this period, introduced pastoral poetry, which expressed an appreciation for nature. Callimachus and others produced short, witty poems called epigrams. Apollonius of Rhodes continued to write the traditional long epic poetry.

The Greco-Roman Age. The period of the Roman conquest of Greece in 146 B.C. saw prose as the prominent literary form. Plutarch wrote biographies contrasting Greek and Roman leaders. Lucian of Samosata satirized the philosophers of his day. Epictetus founded the stoic school of philosophy, which stressed acceptance and endurance. Pausanias wrote an important history of ancient Greece in the A.D. 100s. Galen's medical writings appeared in this period. Ptolemy, an astronomer, mathematician, and geographer, produced scientific writings. Longus wrote *Daphnis and Chloë*, the forerunner of the novel, in this period. Plotinus founded the Neoplatonic school, the last great creation of ancient philosophy.

Medieval literature. From 395 until 1453 Greece was a part of the Byzantine Empire. Constantinople (Istanbul) was the center of Greek culture and literature. Christian religious poetry became the dominant form. Romanos the Melode, who composed long metrical hymns called *kontakia*, was the greatest Greek poet of the medieval period.

Modern Greek literature. In the 1800s Dionysios Solomos wrote his poems in demotic Greek, the language of the common people. Prior to World War I Greek prose was limited to short stories depicting provincial life. The period after the war saw the rise of the psychological and sociological novel. Greek poets achieved renown in this period. In 1963 George Seferis, a lyric poet, became the first Greek to win the Nobel Prize for literature. Odysseus Elytis, also a poet, was awarded the Nobel Prize for literature in 1979.

Greek mythology *see:* Mythology.

Greek Orthodox Church *see:* Eastern Orthodox Church.

Greeley, Horace (1811-72), U.S. journalist and reformer, founder and editor of the New York *Tribune* (1841). One of the most influential figures of the pre-Civil War period, he endorsed abolitionism, helped found the Republican Party, and was instrumental in the candidature and election of Lincoln. However, his popularity was diminished during and after the Civil War by his confused attitude toward the South, and by his pleas for total amnesty for the Confederacy. He was defeated for the presidency in 1872.

Green, William (1873-1952), U.S. labor leader. A union official from his youth, he served as president of the American Federation of Labor (1924-52). He wrote *Labor and Democracy* (1939).
See also: Labor movement.

Green almond *see:* Pistachio nut.

Greenaway, Kate (1846-1901), English children's book illustrator. She designed Christmas and Valentine's Day cards and drew magazine sketches. Her best-known works are *Under the Window* (1878), *The Language of Flowers* (1884), and *Marigold Garden* (1885).

Greenback Party, U.S. political group active between 1876 and 1884. Founded largely by farmers, its main aim was to expand the circulation of greenback currency to bring about inflation, and thus end the depressed agricultural prices and make debts easier to pay. In 1878 the party elected 14 congressional representatives, but it rapidly declined in the 1880s. Many of the party's supporters and leaders turned to populism in the 1890s.

Green Bay (pop. 194,594), city in northeastern Wisconsin and seat of Brown County. Situated at the head of Green Bay on Lake Michigan, it is an important industrial and commercial center and a lake port. Industries include cheese processing, meat packing, and the manufacture of paper, machinery, and auto parts. The city is the home of the Green Bay Packers professional football team.

Green Berets, elite Unit of Special Forces in the U.S. Army trained in guerilla warfare tactics. The unit derives its name from the hat worn by its members.

Greenbrier, horse brier, or catbrier, any of a genus (*Smilax*) of common thorny vines of the lily family. Found primarily in the eastern United States, greenbriers spread rapidly and are considered weeds. They produce yellowish-green flowers and black or red berries.

Greene, Graham (1904-91), British novelist, best known for *The Ministry of Fear* (1943), *Our Man in Havana* (1958), and the screenplay for *The Third Man* (1950). His more serious work is influenced by Roman Catholicism, expressing the need for faith and the possibility of personal salvation, as in *Brighton Rock* (1938), *The Power and the Glory* (1940), and *The Heart of the Matter* (1948).

Graham Greene

Greene, Nathanael (1742-86), American military commander in the Revolutionary War. Washington's second-in-command, he became general of the Southern army in 1780. His strategy at the battles of Guilford Court House, Hobkirks Hill, and Eutaw Springs in 1781 did not bring outright victory, but wore out the British forces.
See also: Revolutionary War in America.

Greenfield Village, group of about 100 historic buildings in Dearborn, Mich. The 200-acre site includes the birthplaces of W.H. McGuffey, Noah Webster, Luther Burbank, and the Wright Brothers, in addition to 2 of Thomas Edison's workshops. Many of the buildings were collected and restored by Henry Ford.

Greenhouse, structure, built mainly of glass, for the cultivation and protection of young or delicate plants. It enables plants to be grown where the climate would normally be unsuitable, makes it possible to "force" plants so they blossom or fruit out of season, and provides suitable conditions for the raising of young plants. Not all greenhouses are heated, but even unheated houses help protect plants from frost. Proper ventilation is vital to prevent the greenhouse from becoming too hot in summer and to reduce the risk of fungus diseases that flourish in such damp atmospheres. Shading may also be necessary to keep the temperature down.

Greenhouse effect, phenomenon whereby the earth's surface becomes hotter. Sunlight radiated at visible and near-ultraviolet wavelengths provides most of the earth's incoming energy. Some of it is absorbed, some reradiated. Although the atmosphere is transparent to incoming solar radiation, reradiated heat from the earth's surface is absorbed by atmospheric water vapor and carbon dioxide and again reradiated toward the surface. Over time, the process causes the surface temperature of the earth to rise. A relatively small increase in the amount of carbon dioxide in the atmosphere might have the effect of causing a long-term warming of the earth that could threaten life.

Greenland (officially Kalâtdlit Nunât), world's largest island that is not considered a continent, located mainly north of the Arctic circle, in the North Atlantic. Greenland is a province of Denmark with its own 16-member legislature.
Land. An ice cap covers four-fifths of the island and reaches a thickness of about 3 mi (4.8 km). Along the coasts mountain peaks penetrate the ice. At the edge of the ice cap wide glaciers sometimes move toward the coast at speeds of up to 20 yd (18 m) per day and have carved deep fjords in the coast. When these glaciers reach the sea, large pieces break off to form icebergs. The island is about 1,670 mi (2,688 km) long and 800 mi (1,287) across its widest part, but only two narrow coastal strips are habitable. Vegetation along the coasts is sparse and small but highly varied; there are about 400 species of flowering plants and several hundred types of mosses and lichens. Animals include muskoxen, reindeer, arctic hares, lemmings, blue and white arctic foxes, the white arctic wolf (almost extinct), and the polar bear. Birds include geese, gulls, sea eagles, owls, ptarmigan, buntings, and falcons. There are freshwater fish but not reptiles or amphibians.
Economy. Hunting and fishing are the two most important occupations. The world's main deposit of cryolite (used in making aluminum) is at Ivigtut. Iron, graphite, and lead are mined. The Royal Greenland Trading company handles all the island's import and export trade, with about 75% of

Icebergs on the western coast of Greenland, near the fiord of Umanak

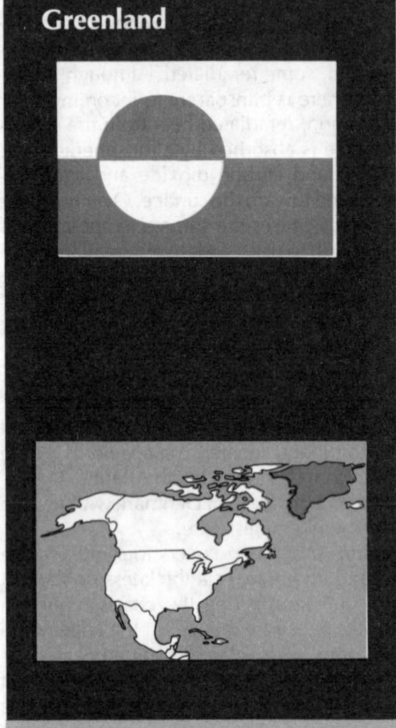

Capital:	Nuuk (Godthåb)
Area:	840,000 sq mi (2,175,600 sq km)
Population:	55,400
Government:	Integral part of the Danish realm
Independent:	dependent
GNP:	U.S. $139,000,000
Per capita:	U.S. $8,780

exports going to Denmark. There is almost invariably an annual trade deficit, made up by the Danish government. When Denmark joined the Common Market in 1973, Greenland also became a member, but the island independently withdrew from the organization in 1982.

History. It is uncertain when Eskimo tribes first crossed to Greenland from northern Canada. The Vikings, led by Eric the Red, reached the island in 981. Eric the Red returned in 985 with a fleet of 14 ships to settle the Greenland shores. In about 1000 Lief Ericsson, his son, began to convert the population to Christianity, and Greenland was given its own bishop. The colonies were a republic until 1261, when they placed themselves under Norwegian sovereignty. In 1380 both Greenland and Norway fell under Danish rule. In 1953 Greenland gained control over its local affairs.

Green Mountain Boys, group of armed fighters from Vermont who fought in the American Revolution. Formed by Ethan Allen before the Revolution, they raided settlements in upper New York to protest New York's claims to Vermont. During the war they won key victories at Fort Ticonderoga (1775) and Bennington (1777). In 1791 their efforts led to Vermont's admission to the Union as the 14th state.
See also: Revolutionary War in America.

Green Mountains, mountain range covering most of Vermont, extending about 160 mi (260 km) northward into Canada and southward into Massachusetts and Connecticut. The range is part of the Appalachian system. Low and rounded from erosion, the Green Mountains are a valuable source of marble, slate, and granite. The land in the lower river valleys is used for grazing, while the higher regions are heavily forested. The highest points of the range are Mt. Mansfield (4,393 ft/1,339 m) and Killington Peak (4,241 ft/1,293 m). The Green Mountains are the site of many ski resorts, including Stowe, Killington, and Mount Snow.
See also: Appalachian Mountains.

Green Mountain State *see:* Vermont.

Greenough, Horatio (1805-52), U.S. neoclassical sculptor and art critic who spent most of his working life in Italy. His best-known work is the large statue of George Washington in the Smithsonian Institution (1841).

Greenpeace, international organization of environmental activists, particularly protesting against nuclear and atomic testing and waste. The organization, founded by Canadians in 1969, uses nonviolent means to protest and block activities it considers environmentally harmful. On its way to the French testing grounds in Oceania in 1985, the Greenpeace ship *Rainbow Warrior* was attacked and sunk and one person killed. The French government admitted responsibility.

Green Revolution, recent agricultural trend that has greatly increased crop production in India, Pakistan, and Turkey. Based on new varieties of crops and dependent on pesticides and fertilizers, the Green Revolution's goals of feeding the world's increasing population have been thwarted by high prices and ecological problems.

Greensboro (pop. 942,091), second largest city in North Carolina, seat of Guilford County. Located in the Piedmont region, about 78 mi (126 km) northwest of Raleigh, it is a major industrial center. Noted for its textile manufacturing, it also has terra-cotta works, machine shops, and cigarette plants. In addition, it is an insurance center and trading center for tobacco grown in the surrounding region. Among its many educational institutions are Greensboro College, the North Carolina Agricultural and Technical College, Bennett College, Guilford College, and the University of North Carolina at Greensboro. Settled in 1749, it was chartered in 1808. The city is named

Greenpeace uses many non-violent means: e.g. each year when the sealing season starts, members of Greenpeace set out to mark the younger and sometimes the older animals with paint. This serves to make their pelts worthless for the fur trade and the animals are in this manner protected against massive slaughter.

for the Revolutionary War general Nathanael Greene, who commanded one of the last battles of the war, fought in the vicinity.

Greenspan, Alan (1926-), U.S. economist. Greenspan served as chairman of the Council of Economic Advisers from 1974 to 1978, under Presidents Richard Nixon and Gerald Ford. He was appointed chairman of the Board of Governors of the Federal Reserve System (FRS) by President Ronald Reagan in 1987. Greenspan is credited with helping banks remain solvent during the New York Stock Exchange crash on Oct. 19, 1987.

Greenwich Meridian, also called the prime meridian, the longitude line passing through the London country of Greenwich, labelled 0° longitude. Designated by an international conference in 1884 as the prime meridian, all other meridians of longitude are numbered east or west of it. The Greenwich Meridian is also the beginning of the earth's 24 time zones, each of which covers an area of 15° longitude. *See also:* Longitude.

Greer, Germaine (1939-), Australian-born feminist author. In *The Female Eunuch* (1970), she charged that society tried to force women into passive, insipid feminine roles that they should reject. Greer received a doctorate from Cambridge University and taught at the University of Warwick (1967-73).

Gregorian calendar, system of measuring years used by most of the world today. Developed by Pope Gregory XIII in 1582, it replaced the Julian calendar established by Julius Caesar in 46 B.C. The Julian calendar year, which was about 11 minutes longer than the solar year, had become 10 days ahead by A.D. 1580. Gregory dropped 10 days from October 1582 to bring the calendar year into conformity with the solar year. He also established leap year.

Gregory, name of 16 popes. **Saint Gregory I** (540-604), called Gregory the Great, was pope from 590 to 604. His papacy laid the foundation for the political and moral authority of the medieval papacy. He reorganized the vast papal estates scattered all over Italy, providing an economic foundation for the Church's power. In 596 he sent St. Augustine to Britain, beginning its conversion to Christianity. **Saint Gregory II** (669-731), pope from 715 to 731, held office at a time of increasing conflict between Rome and Byzantium, and eventually excommunicated Patriarch Anastasius of Byzantium. **Saint Gregory III** (d. 741), pope from 731 to 741, continued to be involved in conflicts with Byzantium, excommunicating Byzantine Emperor Leo III. **Saint Gregory VII** (Hildebrand; c.1025-85), was pope from 1073 to 1085. One of the great medieval reform popes, he attacked corruption in the Church, and insisted on the celibacy of the clergy and on the sole right of the Church to appoint bishops and abbots. These reforms threatened the power of the German monarchy, leading to disputes and war with Henry IV of Germany. In 1084 Henry seized Rome, forcing Gregory to flee. **Gregory IX** (Ugolino; c.1170-1241) was pope from 1227 to 1241. His papacy was marked by conflict with Holy Roman Emperor Frederick II, leading eventually to war in Italy between imperial and papal factions. **Gregory X** (Tedaldo Visconti; 1210-76) pope from 1271 to 1276, instituted policies that regulated papal elections and prevented vacancies of long duration. **Gregory XI** (1329-78) was pope from 1370 to 1378. Elected pope in Avignon, he managed to return the papal court to Rome in 1377. **Gregory XIII** (Ugo Buoncompagni; 1502-85), pope from 1572 to 1585, promoted the Counter-Reformation through his pledge to execute the decrees of the Council of Trent. A patron of the Jesuits, he is remembered for the calendar reform he sponsored and for his lavish building program, which emptied the papal treasury. He celebrated the massacre of the Huguenots on St. Bartholomew's Day, 1572, with a *Te Deum.* **Gregory XVI** (1765-1846), pope from 1831 to 1846, strengthened the papacy, aligning it with Austria under Metternich, with whose help he suppressed a revolt in the Papal States.

Gregory, Lady (1859-1932), Irish dramatist and director, responsible for the production of Yeats's and Synge's plays at the famous Abbey Theatre in Dublin. Her plays include *Spreading the News* (1904), *The Rising of the Moon* (1907), and *The White Cockade* (1908). She wrote *Our Irish Theatre* (1913), on the Irish renaissance.

Grenada, island country in the West Indies, one of the smallest independent countries in the Western Hemisphere. Its area is 133 sq mi (344 sq km).

Land and climate. The island of Grenada is the southernmost of the Windward Islands, 90 mi (145 km) north of Trinidad. The state consists of the main island, which is mountainous, and the southern group of the Grenadine islands. The climate is semitropical.

People and economy. The population is descended from African slaves and European settlers. Exports include nutmeg, cocoa, mace, sugar, cotton, coffee, lime oil, and bananas. Tourism is becoming an important source of income, but Grenada is still a very poor country.

History. Discovered by Christopher Columbus in 1498, Grenada was first colonized by the French but became British in 1762. It achieved internal self-government in 1967 and became fully independent within the Commonwealth in 1974. After a bloodless coup in 1979 a left-wing government was installed. In the course of an army-supported coup in 1983, Prime Minister Maurice Bishop and several other leaders were slain. The United States then sent troops, aided by units from other Caribbean nations, to protect about 1,000 U.S. citizens on the island and to restore constitutional government.

Grenada

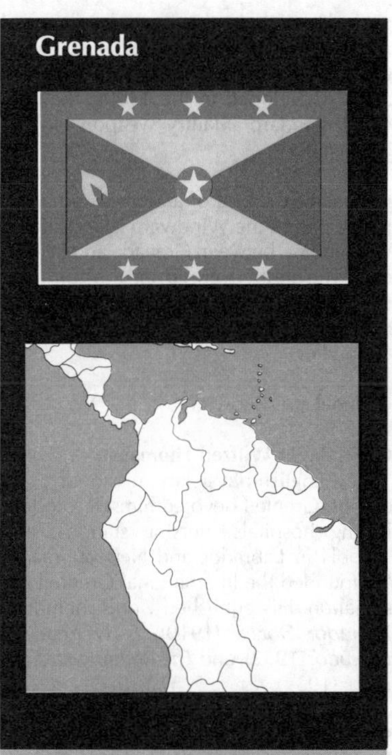

Capital:	Saint George's
Area:	133 sq mi (345 sq km)
Population:	96,600
Government:	constitutional monarchy
Independent:	1974
GNP:	U.S. $139,000,000
Per capita:	U.S. $1,370

Grenade, small explosive device used in warfare. It is activated by pulling a pin and throwing it toward a specific target. When

This familiar type of hand grenade was used by the US Army for 50 years. The thrower crooks his left forefinger through ring (1), holding the grenade in his right hand. Pulling the right hand to the right, withdrawing the pin, the thrower then hurls in an over-arm action. Lever (2) flies off, sprung striker (3) detonates percussion cap (4), and the powder train (5) fires the detonator (6) after a typical delay of 4 seconds. This detonates main charge (7), sending lethal fragments of cast-iron case (8) in all directions

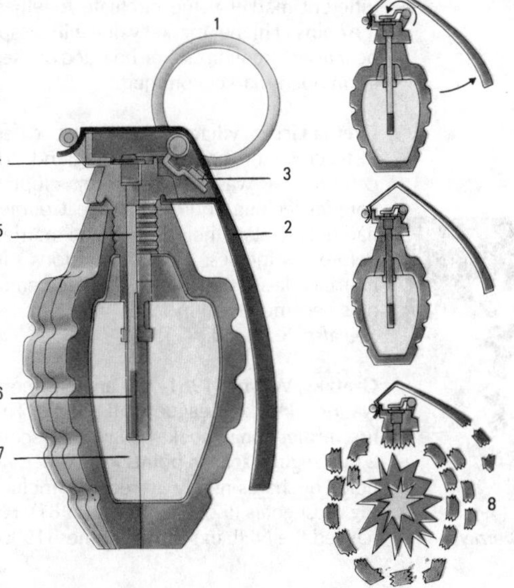

grenades explode, they send deadly metal fragments flying or release lethal gas. Some grenades are used to illuminate darkened areas. Developed in the 1400s, they became standard infantry weapons in the 20th century.

Grenadines, group of about 600 small islands, part of the Windward Islands in the West Indies, between Grenada and St. Vincent. The northern group and the north part of Carriacou (the largest island) belong to St. Vincent. The southern group belongs to Grenada.

Grendel *see:* Beowulf.

Grenfell, Sir Wilfred Thomason (1865-1940), English physician, missionary, and author. Grenfell devoted himself to establishing hospitals, nursing stations, and schools in Labrador and Newfoundland. He founded the International Grenfell Association. His published works include *A Labrador Doctor* (1919), *Forty Years of Labrador* (1932), and *The Romance of Labrador* (1934).

Grenoble (pop. 156,600), city in eastern France, located in a valley of the French Alps. A winter sports center, Grenoble hosted the 1968 Winter Olympics. The city is also a center for manufacturing and scientific research and is home to the University of Grenoble, founded in 1339. Grenoble was established by the Gauls c.400 B.C.
See also: France.

Grenville, Sir Richard (1542-91), English naval hero. He commanded Raleigh's first expedition (1585) to colonize Roanoke Island, N.C. In a British attempt (1591) to intercept Spanish treasure ships off the Azores in his ship, *Revenge*, Grenville held an entire Spanish fleet in combat for 15 hours before he was mortally wounded and captured.

Gresham's Law, economic principle (attributed to Sir Thomas Gresham) that "bad money drives out good." This means that when coins of the same face value but of different market value circulate together, the coins of higher market value will disappear from circulation to be hoarded or used as an open-market commodity.

Gretna Green, village in Scotland. Located just across the border from England, for centuries it was a mecca for eloping couples seeking a quick marriage. Couples had only to state their desire to be married before witnesses. With revisions in marriage laws, the Gretna Green ceremonies became illegal in 1939.
See also: Scotland.

Wayne Gretzky

Gretzky, Wayne (1961-), Canadian-born National Hockey League (NHL) center. The first professional hockey player to score 2,000 regular season points in a career, he holds or shares nearly 50 records, including most goals (92) in a season (1981). He has led the NHL in scoring 9 times (1980-87, 88), won 9 Most Valuable Player awards (1980-87, 89), and while playing for the Edmonton Oilers led the team to 4 Stanley Cup championships (1984, 85, 87, 88). In 1988 he was traded to the Los Angeles Kings.

Grew, Joseph Clark (1880-1965), U.S. diplomat. The last ambassador to Japan before World War II, he predicted the Japanese attack on Pearl Harbor, but his warnings to the State Department went unheeded.

Grey, Charles, 2nd Earl Grey (1764-1835), English prime minister (1830-34) responsible for the passage of the Reform Bill (1832), which extended the vote to the middle classes. As Whig leader of the House of Commons, he helped abolish the slave trade (1807).
See also: England.

Grey, Lady Jane (1537-54), queen of England for 9 days in 1553. The Duke of Northumberland, her father-in-law and powerful advisor to the dying Edward VI, persuaded the king to name Jane heir to the throne. She reluctantly accepted the crown, but Mary Tudor, Edward's half sister, had the country's support, and was proclaimed queen by the lord mayor of London. Lady Jane and her husband were beheaded for treason.

Grey, Zane (1875-1939), U.S. author of sagas about the American West. His 54 novels, of which *Riders of the Purple Sage* (1912) is the most popular, have sold over 15 million copies.

Grey Cup, trophy awarded to the playoff winner in the Canadian Football League (CFL). Named after Earl Grey, a Canadian governor general, it was first presented to the nation's amateur rugby champion in 1909. Since 1954 it has been given to professional football teams. Edmonton has won the most Grey Cups (10), followed by Winnipeg and Hamilton (6).

Greyhound, breed of dog used widely in racing. First raised in Egypt 5,000 years ago, greyhounds were used for hunting in England and North America before being adapted for racing. Greyhounds weigh 60-70 lb (27-30 kg) and have long, slender bodies, powerful legs, and short coats.

Grieg, Edvard Hagerup (1843-1907), Norwegian composer who based much of his work on traditional national folk music. He wrote many songs and piano pieces. His best-known orchestral works are the *Piano Concerto* (1869), the *Peer Gynt* suites (1876), and the *Holberg Suite* (1885).

Griffin, mythological animal having the head and wings of an eagle and the body and hindquarters of a lion. The legend of the griffin probably originated with the ancient Hittites and was a popular subject for Assyrian and ancient Greek sculpture. In heraldry the griffin appears as a symbol of vigilance.

Griffith, Arthur (1872-1922), Irish nationalist who founded Sinn Féin, a major force in Ireland's struggle for independence from England. He led the Irish delegation in negotiating the treaty (1921) that established the Irish Free State. He was the first vice president of the Dáil Eireann, an assembly that declared Irish independence, and briefly succeeded de Valera as its president (1922).
See also: Sinn Féin.

Griffith, D(avid) W(ark) (1875-1948), U.S. silent-film director and producer, often considered the father of modern cinema. His immensely popular *Birth of a Nation* (1915), later much criticized for its racist views, introduced major principles of film technique. Griffith also pioneered the film "spectacular." Among his other films are *Intolerance* (1916), *Way Down East* (1920), and *Orphans of the Storm* (1922).

Scene from Griffith's The Musketeers of Pig Alley *(1912)*

Grimké, Angelina Emily (1805-79) and **Sarah Moore** (1792-1873), sisters, U.S. abolitionists and women's rights crusaders. Angelina's *An Appeal to the Christian Women of the South* and Sarah's *An Epistle to the Clergy of the Southern States* (both 1836) urged opposition to slavery.
See also: Abolitionism.

Grimm brothers, **Jakob Ludwig** (1785-1863) and **Wilhelm Karl** (1786-1859), German folklorists and philologists who compiled a collection of popular fairy tales. They began the project in 1812 and wrote the final volume of 210 stories in 1857. Some of the best-known tales are "Hansel and Gretel," "Snow White," "Sleeping Beauty," "Cinderella," and "Little Red Riding Hood." Jakob also wrote *German Grammar* (1819-37), and the brothers collaborated on the *German Dictionary* which began in 1854 and was completed by others in 1960.
See also: Grimm's fairy tales.

Grimmelshausen, Hans Jakob Christoffel von (1625?-76), German novelist. His picaresque romance *Simplicissimus* (1669), set during the Thirty Years' War, ranks as the most important 17th-century German novel.

Grimm's fairy tales, stories by two brothers, Jakob (1785-1863) and Wilhelm (1786-1859) Grimm, who collected folk tales from friends and acquaintances in and around Kassel, 1807-14. They saw the tales as an expression of the romantic spirit of the German people. They include "Hansel and Gretel," "Little Red Riding Hood," "Snow White," "Rumpelstiltskin," "Sleeping Beauty," "Cinderella," and "Rapunzel."
See also: Grimm brothers; Fairy tale.

Grinding and polishing, finishing of metal and other surfaces by the use of abrasive materials. In grinding, hard abrasives are used to wear down the metal surface appreciably. In polishing, much softer abrasives are used to smooth the surface, removing a negligible amount of metal.

Gris, Juan (José Victoriano González; 1887-1927), Spanish cubist painter. A follower of Picasso, he developed the style known as synthetic cubism, which he applied to still lifes in increasingly free compositions.

Grison, weasel-like animal (genus *Galictis*), also known as huron. There are 2 types of grisons—the greater grison, which has gray/brown fur and may reach a length of 27.5 in (70 cm), and the little grison, which has yellow/brown fur and is considerably smaller. All grisons have a white strip of fur across their forehead and down the sides of their neck and their diet includes snakes, mice, birds, and insects. Found in Central and South America, grisons are diurnal creatures who live in both forests and open country and make their dens under tree roots, rocks, or logs.

Grissom, Gus (1926-67), U.S. astronaut. He was the second American to be launched into space (July 21, 1961) and the first American to make 2 space flights. In Mar. 1965 Grissom and John W. Young piloted the first 2-man orbital flight. He was scheduled to head the first 3-man flight, but a fire broke out during a launch pad test at Cape Canaveral on Jan. 27, 1967, killing Grissom and astronauts Edward White and Roger Chaffee.
See also: Astronaut.

Grizzly bear (*Ursus arctos horribilis*), one of the largest of the North American brown bears. The name refers to the grizzled coat rather than to the beast's temper, but despite this the grizzly population has been killed off and the species is considered threatened in the United States. Though classed with the carnivore, the grizzly is largely vegetarian and rarely eats fish. An imposing, even terrifying animal, the grizzly plays a major role in the legends of the North American pioneers.

Grofé, Ferde (1892-1972), U.S. composer and pianist. His best-known works are the *Mississippi Suite* (1924), the *Grand Canyon Suite* (1931), and the orchestration of George Gershwin's *Rhapsody in Blue* (1924).

Gromyko, Andrei Andreyevich (1909-89), Soviet politician and diplomat. In a rapid rise after Stalin's purges, he became ambassador to the United States in World War II and UN representative of the USSR after the war. Named foreign minister in 1957, he held that post until 1985, during periods of cold war, disarmament talks, détente, and incidents of Soviet military interventions in several countries. He was a member of the Politburo, the governing body of the Communist party. He became president of the USSR in 1985.
See also: Union of Soviet Socialist Republics

Gropius, Walter (1883-1969), German architect and teacher. He was founder of the Bauhaus school and originated the profoundly influential style, characterized by a marriage of form and function and the use of modern materials (especially glass). He fled Germany when the Nazis came to power, settling in the United States in 1937. His designs include the Bauhaus in Dessau (1926) and (in collaboration) the Pan Am Building in New York (1958).
See also: Bauhaus.

Grosbeak, name of various finches having a strong conical bill for cracking seeds. The male of the blue grosbeak of the southern United States (*Guiraca caerulea*) is dark blue all over and can be mistaken for the indigo bunting. The pine grosbeak (*Pinicola enucleator*), native to Canada, is mainly pink. The females are drab.

Gross national product (GNP), total value of goods and services produced by a national economy before any deduction has been made for depreciation (net national product). The annual growth of the GNP is often taken as an indicator of the state of a country's economy. *Real GNP*, which is adjusted for inflation, is of greatest significance.

Gros Ventre (French: "big belly"), 2 Native American tribes, the Atsina and the Hidatsa, of the northern Great Plains. The Gros Ventre were named for their sign language, which consisted of hand signals in front of their stomachs. The Atsina, a branch of the Arapaho, live on Montana's Fort Belknap Reservation; the Hidatsa, relatives of the Crow, live on Fort Berthold Reservation in North Dakota.

Grosz, George (1893-1959), German-American satirical artist, a Dadaist. His powerful caricatures, especially those attacking corruption and militarism in post-World War I Germany, include *Fit for Active Service* (1918) and *The Face of the Ruling Class* (1919); *The Stickman* (c.1947) is American influenced.
See also: Dada.

Grotius, Hugo (1583-1645), Dutch jurist, considered the founder of international law. In 1619 he was condemned to life imprisonment for his political activity, but he escaped to Paris. There he wrote *On the Law of War and Peace* (1625), a study of all the laws of humanity with an emphasis on rules of conduct applying to states, nations, and individuals.
See also: International law.

Walter Gropius

Ground effect machine *see:* Air cushion vehicle.

Ground hog *see:* Woodchuck.

Groundnut *see:* Peanut.

Ground pine *see:* Club moss.

Ground sloth (genus *Megatherium*), prehistoric member of the sloth family, about the size of an elephant. They originated in South America and migrated to North America during the Ice Age. Ground sloths were herbivores (plant eaters). They probably used their powerful hind legs and tails to stand and feed on high branches and leaves.

Ground squirrel, any of various small burrowing rodents (genus *Citellus*) of the squirrel family. North American species include the 13-striped ground squirrel, or spermophile, of the prairies, the rock squirrel

Grizzly brown bear and black bear in spring and in summer. The geographical ranges of these animals overlap, but they are ecologically separated by habitat and diet preferences

of canyons and rocky slopes in the West, and the golden-mantled squirrel of woodlands. Chipmunks, prairie dogs, and woodchucks may also be considered ground squirrels.

Ground water, water accumulated beneath the earth's surface in the pores of rocks, spaces, cracks, etc. Most underground water originates as precipitation that sinks into soil and rocks. Permeable, water-bearing rocks are *aquifers*; rocks with pores small enough to inhibit the flow of water through them are *aquicludes*. Buildup of groundwater pressure beneath an aquiclude makes possible construction of an artesian well. The uppermost level of groundwater saturation is the water table.

Group dynamics, in sociology, study of the behavior and interactions of people as members of groups. It includes setting up specially constructed experimental groups, as well as the study of existing groups such as committees and military units. Some of the simpler studies have been carried out to try to determine the chain of command within a group and its influence on the group's performance.

Grouper, sea fish of the sea bass family with large mouth and sharp teeth, mainly of tropical seas. Groupers are as small as 1 in (2.5 cm) long; the Queensland grouper of the Great Barrier Reef grows up to 7 ft (2 m) and can be a danger to skindivers. The Nassau grouper of the coasts of the southeastern states is noted for its ability to change color.

Grouper

Group of Seven, group of seven 20th-century Canadian painters known primarily for their colorful landscapes. The original members were Franklin Carmichael, Lawren Harris, Alexander Y. Jackson, Franz Johnston, Arthur Lismer, J.E.H. MacDonald, and Fred Varley. An eight member, Tom Thompson, died in 1917, 3 years before the group's first show. The group later grew to include new members and changed its name to the Canadian Group of Painters (1933).

Group therapy *see:* Psychotherapy.

Grouse, family (Tetraonidae) of chicken-like game birds usually brown, gray, or black in plumage, native to cool regions of the Northern Hemisphere. They are ground birds living on open moorland or heath, and are well camouflaged. Three species moult into a white or particolored winter plumage for camouflage in snow. Grouse feed largely on plant material—shoots, buds, and fruits—but will also eat insects. In many species males perform elaborate courtship displays at established display grounds, or "leks." Common North American species include the ruffed grouse (*Bonasa umbrellus*) and the spruce grouse (*Dendragapus canadensis*).

Growth, increase in the size of an organism, reflecting an increase in the number of its cells, an increase in its protoplasmic material, or both. Cell number and protoplasmic content do not always increase together. Cell division can occur without any increase in protoplasm, thus giving a larger number of smaller cells. Alternatively, protoplasm can be synthesized with no cell division so that the cells become larger. Any increase in the protoplasm requires the synthesis of cell components (such as nuclei, mitochondria, thousands of enzymes) and cell membrane. These, in turn, require the synthesis of macromolecules such as proteins, nucleic acids, and polysaccharides from amino acids, sugars, and fatty acids. These subunits must be synthesized from still simpler substances.
One of the major differences between plants and animals is that the final shape and size of an animal can be predicted within fine limits, whereas it is much more difficult to say just how tall a plant will be or how many branches it will have. Growth in plants is, however, better understood than animal growth.

Grub, wormlike larva of insects. The body is fat and soft and there are no legs. Since the grub is surrounded by food, in the case of certain flies and beetles, or is fed by adults, as with bees and wasps, there is no necessity for it to be able to move.

Grumman, Leroy (1895-1982), U.S. businessman and manufacturer who founded the Grumman Aircraft Corporation (now Grumman Corporation) in 1929 and served as its chairman of the board. The Grumman Corporation pioneered the use of retractable landing gear on fighter planes and today produces both military (e.g. F-16) and civilian aircraft, as well as boats, trucks, and other forms of transportation.
See also: Airplane.

Grünewald, Matthias (c.1475-1528), German painter who, with his contemporary Albrecht Dürer, is considered one of the 2 great masters of the German Renaissance. His most characteristic theme is the crucifixion, a subject in which he combined beauty and delicacy of style with a savage and harrowing realism. His masterpiece is the altarpiece of St. Anthony's monastery at Isenheim, with subjects such as the *Resurrection* and the *Temptation of St. Anthony* (1513-15).
See also: Renaissance.

Grunion (*Leuresthes tenuis*), small fish whose breeding habits have become a tourist attraction in California. For 3 or 4 nights in succession, when the tide is at its highest, the grunions leap from the waves onto the beach in thousands. Each female is accompanied by a male who fertilizes her eggs as she lays them in the sand. After spawning, the fish go back into the water. Two weeks later, when the tides are at their peak again, young grunions pop out of the eggs and are washed back into the sea.

Grunt, colorful marine fish (family Pomadasidae) found in warm waters. The pigfish (*Orthopristis chrysopterus*) is a grunt found along the Atlantic and Gulf coasts of the United States. Grunts are named for the sounds they make by grinding their teeth, which are in the throat. Many species are important food fish.

Guacharo *see:* Oilbird.

Guadalajara (pop. 1,725,000), second-largest city in Mexico and capital of the state of Jalisco. Located on a high plain in west-central Mexico, Guadalajara is an important manufacturing center known for glassware and pottery, textiles, soft drinks, beer, bottled water, construction materials, animal feed, and fertilizer.
See also: Mexico.

Guadalcanal, largest of the Solomon Islands, in the South Pacific. Volcanic and mountainous, it supports extensive coconut plantations that are the economic mainstay; copra and timber are the main exports. The island was the scene of a decisive battle of World War II in 1943, when it was recaptured by Allied troops from the Japanese.
See also: Solomon Islands.

Guadalupe Hidalgo, Treaty of, peace treaty signed by the United States and Mexico in 1848 to end the Mexican War. Mexico agreed to cede what are now Texas, California, Utah, Nevada, and parts of New Mexico, Arizona, Colorado, and Wyoming to the United States in return for $15 million and the settling of over $3 million in claims of U.S. citizens against Mexico.
See also: Mexican War.

Guadalupe Mountains National Park, established 1966, covers 129 sq mi (334 sq km) of Texas east of El Paso. An area of geological interest, particularly for its limestone formations and fossil reefs, it contains prehistoric Indian ruins and varied wildlife.
See also: National Parks.

Guadeloupe, overseas department of France in the eastern part of the Caribbean Sea, composed of Grande-Terre, Basse-Terre, and some smaller islands, covering a total area of 687 sq mi (1,779 sq km). Discovered by Columbus (1493) and a French settlement since 1635, it was captured by the British in the Seven Years' War and confirmed as French in 1815. The population, of mixed African and European ancestry, speaks a French patois. Bananas, coffee, cacao, and vanilla are produced.

Guam, largest and southernmost of the Mariana Islands, in the Pacific Ocean 6,000 mi (9,656 km) west of San Francisco. A U.S. territory since 1898 and an important U.S. naval and air base, Guam was captured by the Japanese in 1941, and was recaptured by the United States in 1944.
See also: Mariana Islands.

Guan, tropical Central and South American game bird of the family Cracidae, resembling small or medium-sized turkeys. Guans have dark feathers and eat mostly fruit.

Guanaco, wool-bearing member of the camel family, found on the mountains or plains of South America. Guanacos have long, thick, reddish brown hair above and white hair below, with a grayish head. They feed on grass and small plants and grow 3 1/2 to 4 ft (107-122 cm) high at the shoulder.

Guangzhou (pop. 3,220,000), called Canton by Westerners, largest city in southern China and one of China's most important ports. Located at the head of the Pearl River, the city is linked to the interior by a network of railroads, and its economy has been based on trade for centuries. Locally produced products include paper, sewing machines, cement, and textiles. Shipbuilding and sugar refining are other important industries, as are handicrafts. China's largest trade fair is held annually in Guangzhou, which is also known for being the birthplace of the Chinese Nationalist leader Sun Yat-sen and a center of the revolution of 1911.
See also: China.

Guantánamo (pop. 167,400), city in southeast Cuba, about 20 mi (30 km) inland from Guantánamo Bay, the location of a U.S. naval base established in 1903. Since the revolution of 1959, Cuba has refused to cash the $2,000 per year rental check the United States has sent and has pressed for the base's return to Cuba. Guantánamo is a sugar-refining center and also serves as a hub for processing cacao, coffee, and corn.
See also: Cuba, Republic of.

Guar, tough legume (*Cyamopsis tetragonoloba*) of the pea family, often grown to enrich worn-out soil. The seeds and pods are used as fodder. Guar was brought to the United States from India in the early 1900s.

Guaraní, group of South American tribes, linked by language, who once lived in an area now included in Paraguay, Brazil, and Argentina. Conquered by Spain in the 16th century, their numbers have been reduced by disease. Their language, however, is now the second language of Paraguay.

Guarneri, family of violin makers of Cremona, Italy. **Andrea Guarneri** (1626-98), with Antonio Stradivari, an apprentice of Nicolò Amati, founded the dynasty. His sons **Pietro Giovanni Guarneri** (1655-1720?) and **Giuseppe Guarneri** (1666-1739?), and grandson **Pietro Guarneri** (1695-1762) continued the trade. The most renowned member of the family was the eccentric and experimental **Giuseppe Bartolomeo Guarneri** (1687-1745), known as "Giuseppe del Jesu," nephew of Andrea.

Guatemala , republic of, northernmost republic of Central America, bordered by Mexico on the north and west, Belize and the Caribbean Sea on the east, Honduras and El Salvador on the southeast, and the Pacific Ocean on the southwest. The capital is Guatemala City.
Land and climate. Guatemala is a mountainous country composed largely of volcanic highland. The eastern and western highlands are not very fertile. To the north is the Petén, a rain forest plateau with areas

Guatemala

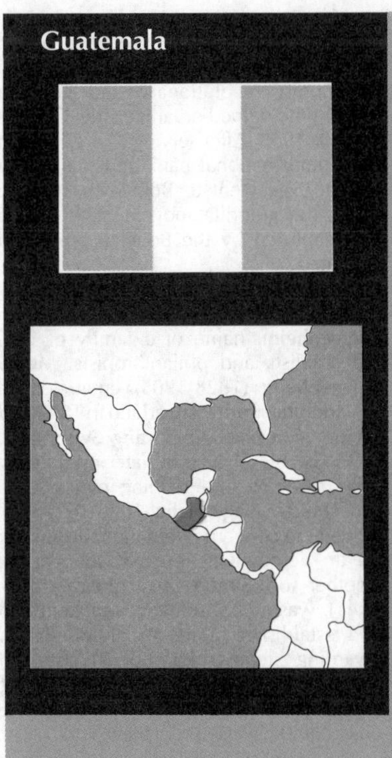

General information

Capital:	Guatemala City
Area:	42,042 sq mi (108,889 sq km)
Population:	8,935,000
Official language:	Spanish
Monetary unit:	1 Guatemalan quetzal = 100 centavos
Main cities:	Guatemala City, Quetzaltenango, Escuintla

Government

Form:	republic
Independent:	1839
Head of state:	President (elected every 5 years)
Head of government:	President
Legislature:	one legislative house (Congress of the Republic)
Executive:	President and Cabinet
Judiciary:	highest court is the Supreme Court of Justice
Political division:	22 departments

National economy

Gross national product:	U.S. $7,620,000,000
Per capita income:	U.S. $880
Agriculture:	bananas, sugarcane, cardamon, coffee, dry beans, wheat, corn, cotton
Livestock:	cattle, pigs, sheep
Fisheries:	2,000 metric tons
Mining:	petroleum, iron ore, antimony ore
Industries:	sugar, drugs and medicines, beverages, textiles, rubber products
Main exports:	coffee, cotton, bananas, chemical products
Transportation:	561 mi (903 km) of railroads; 10,700 mi (17,300 km) of roads; 1 international airport
Trading partners:	United States, Germany, El Salvador, Japan, Mexico

People

Urban:	41%
Ethnic composition:	Maya 55%, Mestizos 42%, European or African 3%
Birth rate:	36.5 per 1,000 population
Death rate:	9.5 per 1,000 population
Infant mortality:	66 per 1,000 live births
Life expectancy:	male 58 years, female 62 years

Guatemala City (below) and Lake Atitlan with the Toliman volcano (above)

of savanna, covering a third of the country. The climate varies from the tropical Petén and coastal areas to the subtropical and temperate highlands.

People. The Native Americans (Mayans) account for a little more than half the population; most of the rest are a mixture of Spanish and Mayan. The official language is Spanish, but many Native American languages are also spoken. The main religion is Roman Catholicism.

Che Guevara

Economy. Coffee accounts for almost half the nation's revenues. Cotton is also an important product, having superseded banana cultivation since the 1930s. Other exports are tobacco, vegetables, fruit, and beef. Manufacturing industries are mainly devoted to the processing of local produce. Although Guatemala joined the Central American Common Market in 1961, the United States remains its principal trading partner.

History. The Mayas ruled the area from about A.D. 300, but they were unable to offer much resistance to the invading Spaniards in 1524. Guatemala became independent in 1821 and subsequently was a member of the Central American Federation (1824-39). The post-World War II governments, especially under Jacobo Arbenz Guzmán, had socialist tendencies. After a U.S.-supported military coup in 1954, Guatemala was plagued by political violence and coups. In 1985 Marco Vinicio Cerezo Arévalo became the first civilian to be elected president of Guatemala in 15 years.

Guatemala City (pop. 754,000), capital and largest city of Guatemala, in Central America. The city's population nearly doubled in the 1980s. The hub of the country's social, cultural, and political life, Guatemala City is also the chief manufacturing center, producing textiles, beverages, and processed foods. It was almost completely destroyed by an earthquake in 1917, and another earthquake killed thousands in 1976.
See also: Guatemala.

Guava, small tree (genus *Psidium*, especially *P. guajava*) with thick leaves and white flowers, cultivated for its red or yellow fruit. Native to Mexico, South America, and the West Indies, and now grown in Florida and California. The fruit, up to 4 in (10 cm) in diameter, is slightly acid and musky. It is used in jellies, pies, and drinks and is eaten raw.

Guayaquil pop. 1,199,300), Ecuador's largest city, main port, and industrial center, located 40 mi (64 km) from the Pacific Ocean on the Guayas River. Founded by Spaniards in 1535, the city was liberated from Spain in 1821. Guayaquil manufactures textiles and has flour mills, sawmills, breweries, ironworks, and a cement plant.
See also: Ecuador.

Guayule, desert shrub (*Parthenium argentatum*) of the composite family containing rubber that can be accessed only by crushing the top of the plant. Guayule is native to the Chihuahuan desert of Mexico and southwestern Texas. It grows to about 2 ft (60 cm) and has silver, spear-shaped leaves.

Guelphs and Ghibellines, opposing political and warring factions in 13th to 15th-century Italy. The Guelphs supported the pope, the Ghibellines the Holy Roman emperor. Both originated in 12th-century Germany, in opposition over territories of the Holy Roman Empire.
See also: Holy Roman Empire.

Guenon, any of approximately twenty species of monkeys of the family Cercopithecidae living in Africa south of the Sahara Desert. All have long tails and weigh from 3 to 15 lb (1.4 to 7 km). Almost all guenons live in trees in tropical rain forests, wooded plains, or swamps. Humans, leopards, and eagles are the guenon's chief enemies.

Guernsey *see:* Cattle (dairy).

Guernsey, second-largest of the Channel Islands at the west end of the English Channel, 30 mi (48 km) west of Normandy, France. The triangular-shaped island is approximately 24 sq mi (63 sq km) in area. The Guernsey cattle for which it is famous are found mostly in the south. Greenhouses in the north produce tomatoes, flowers, and grapes. Guernsey was home to French author Victor Hugo from 1855 to 1870; his house is now a museum. St. Peter Port is the capital and main town.

Guerrilla warfare, warfare waged by irregular forces in generally small-scale operations, often in enemy-held territory. The term (Spanish: "little war") originally applied to the tactics of Spanish-Portuguese irregulars in the Napoleonic Wars. Traditionally, guerrilla warfare has been waged against larger and better-equipped conventional forces, as in the Viet Cong forces opposing the United States in Vietnam. It is often part of a wider strategy, as for example the activities of the resistance movements in Nazi-occupied Europe, which were part of overall Allied strategy. Guerrilla fighters must avoid open battle as much as possible, exploiting the mobility gained from lack of equipment and supply lines, and making use of popular support. They must rely on hit-and-run tactics, ambush, sabotage, and the psychological effects of unpredictable attack.
Recent years have seen the development of the "urban guerrilla," whose desire is not to expel an invader by a general insurrection but to so disorganize the fabric of society that a faction can seize power without relying on popular support. To this end, ambush, hijacking, and bombing, directed both at specific targets and at the populace at large, have become increasingly common. With the advent of the nuclear age, guerrilla warfare is perceived to have distinct advantages. It avoids large-scale confrontations that might lead to escalation, is less expensive for aggressors than all-out war, and can be easier to disclaim.

Guevara, Ché (Ernesto Guevara de la Serna; 1928-67), Argentinean-born Cuban communist revolutionary and guerrilla leader who helped organize Fidel Castro's coup in 1959. After serving as president of the Cuban national bank and minister of industry, he went to Bolivia in 1966 to direct the guerrilla movement there. He was captured by the Bolivian army and executed.

Guggenheim, name of a family of U.S. industrialists and philanthropists. **Meyer Guggenheim** (1828-1905) emigrated to Philadelphia from Switzerland in 1847 and set up a business importing Swiss lace. Aided by his 7 sons, he later established large smelting and refining plants. One son, **Daniel Guggenheim** (1856-1930), extended the concern internationally and set up an aeronautics research foundation. Another son, **Simon Guggenheim** (1867-1941), was a U.S. senator from Colorado and established a memorial foundation awarding fellowships to artists and scholars. The sixth son, **Solomon Robert Guggenheim** (1861-1949), founded the Guggenheim Museum in New York.

Guggenheim Museum, major gallery of modern art, noted above all for its building, designed by Frank Lloyd Wright and completed in 1959, Wright's final work and his only one in New York City. The circular glass-domed structure houses major sculptures and paintings of the 19th and 20th centuries. The Solomon R. Guggenheim Foundation promotes art education and maintains the museum, established in 1939.

Guiana, region in northern South America that includes the states of French Guiana, Suriname, and Guyana. Guyana (formerly British Guiana) became independent in 1966; Suriname (Dutch Guiana) became independent in 1975; French Guiana remains still an overseas territory of France.

Guided missile, flying weapon that can alter its course during flight toward a target. It usually consists of a rocketlike body containing a rocket or jet engine and an explosive warhead. The length of a guided missile may range from 4 ft (1.2 m) to 60 ft (18 m). Its course may be controlled by instruments in the missile itself or by a crew operating ground controls. Guided missiles are commonly classified as surface-to-surface, surface-to-air, air-to-air, and air-to-surface. They can be fired from permanent or mobile launchers, from ships and submarines, and from airplanes. Though unguided rockets were first developed by the Chinese in the 13th century and used by the British in war during the 19th century, the first guided missiles used in combat were developed by Germany during World War II. Since then, the United States and the USSR have been leading developers of guided missiles.

Guild, economic and social association of merchants or craftspeople in the same trade or craft to protect the interests of its members. Guilds flourished in Europe in the Middle Ages. Merchant guilds were often very powerful, controlling trade in a geographic area; the Hanseatic League controlled trade in much of northern Europe. The craft guilds (as of goldsmiths, weavers, or shoemakers) regulated wages, quality of production, and working conditions for apprentices. Wealthy guilds built extensive headquarters for themselves, some of which still stand. The guild system declined from the 16th century because of changing trade and work conditions.

Guillemot, seabird of the auk family (genera *Uria* and *Cepphus*). The black guillemot (*C. grylle*) is found on Atlantic coasts and the pigeon guillemot (*C. columba*) on Pacific coasts. Both are black with large white patches on the wings. In winter both become mainly white. Like other auks, guillemots swim underwater with their wings instead of paddling with their feet. They spend most of their time at sea, feeding on fish, and come to land only to breed. They nest on cliffs, usually laying a single egg in rocky clefts.

Guinea, (officially People's Revolutionary Republic of Guinea), independent country in West Africa, bordered by Guinea-Bissau and Mali on the north, Mali and the Ivory Coast on the east, Liberia and Sierra Leone on the south, and the Atlantic Ocean on the west. The capital is Conakry, located on Tombo Island.

Guinea

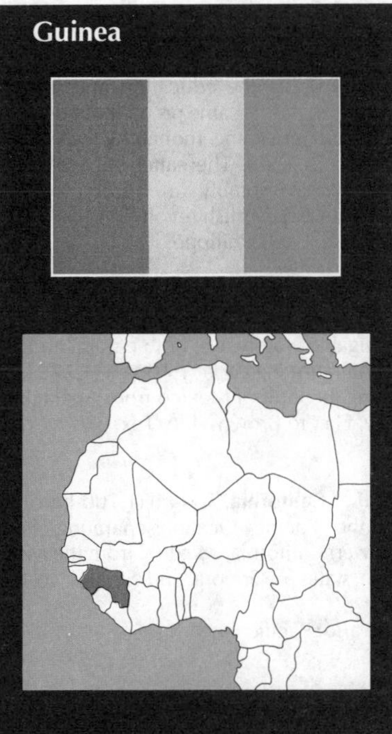

Capital:	Conakry
Area:	94,926 sq mi (245,857 sq km)
Population:	6,705,000
Government:	republic
Independent:	1958
GNP:	U.S. $2,300,000,000
Per capita:	U.S. $350

Guinea. This elegant if precarious foot bridge is made of the woody, twining stems of climbing plants called lianas, characteristic of tropical rain forests.

Land and climate. Guinea is tropical and humid, with cooler conditions and greater temperature ranges in the inland highlands. The rainy season is Apr. through Nov., and rainfall is exceptionally heavy along the coast. Vegetation includes the oil-palm of the coastal plain; the lianas, bamboos, and gum-producing trees of the forests; and the rare grasses and sedges of the Fouta Djallon, a mountainous region. Wildlife includes the lion, leopard, antelope, hippopotamus, buffalo, chimpanzee, and crocodile. Guinea also has parrots, egrets, pelicans, and many other varieties of birds.

People and economy. Agriculture is central to the country's economy. Major exports are palm kernels, coffee, pineapple, bananas, aluminum, bauxite, iron ore, and diamonds. Islam is the main religion, and French is the official language.

History. Portuguese exploration in the 15th century led to a slave trade in which the British and French were major participants. France made most of the country a protectorate in 1849, and in 1895 Guinea became part of French West Africa. In 1958 Guinea, led by the nationalist revolutionary Sékou Touré, rejected membership in the French community and opted for full independence. Sékou Touré established a one-party state, which lasted until his death in 1984. Power was then seized by military officers.

Guinea region with indistinct boundaries on Africa's west coast. Guinea is also part of the name of three separate countries in the area—Equatorial Guinea, Guinea-Bissau, and the Republic of Guinea. Equatorial Guinea was once a Spanish colony, Guinea-Bissau belonged to Portugal, and the Republic of Guinea was a French colony.

Guinea-Bissau

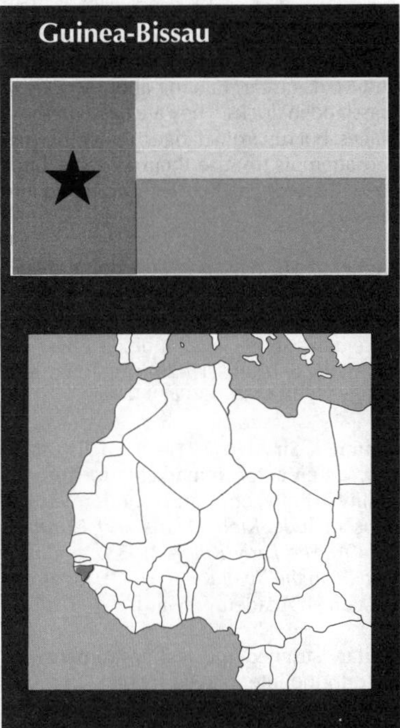

Capital:	Bissau
Area:	13,948 sq mi (36,125 sq km)
Population:	953,000
Government:	republic
Independent:	1974
GNP:	U.S. $145,000,000
Per capita:	U.S. $160

Guinea Bissau is intersected by many rivers and sea inlets, which makes water transport important.

Guinea-Bissau (formerly Portuguese Guinea), republic in West Africa between Senegal to the north and the Republic of Guinea to the east and west, with various coastal islands and an offshore archipelago in the Atlantic. The mainland consists of coastal swamps, a heavily forested central plain, and savanna grazing land in the east. The climate is hot and humid, with heavy rains from May to Oct. Africans form 98% of the population; most are engaged in agriculture, on which the economy is based. Seafood is an increasingly important export. Industry is limited but expanding. The largest town and main port is Bissau, the capital.

Guinea fowl (*Numida meleagris*), bird that resembles a turkey and has been domesticated since Roman times. It is distinguished by a naked head and dark gray, spotted plumage. Wild guinea fowl live in Africa and Madagascar, moving about woods or grassland in flocks. They are eaten in some places, but run from danger, rather than fly, and attempts to raise them as game birds have, therefore, failed. They do fly up into trees to roost.

Guinea pig (*Cavia porcellus*), domestic pet related to the cavies, South American rodents. It has a plump body, no tail, and extremely short legs. Guinea pigs are generally 6-10 in (15-25 cm) long, and weigh 1-2 lb (450-900 g).

Guinness, Sir Alec (1914-), English stage and screen actor, remarkable for his versatility in both comic and serious roles. His films include *Kind Hearts and Coronets* (1949), *The Lady Killers* (1955), and *The Bridge on the River Kwai* (1957), for which he won an Academy Award.

Guitar, stringed musical instrument, related to the lute, played by plucking. Unlike the lute, it has a flat back and curve-waisted sides. The guitar evolved in Spain during the Middle Ages, apparently from Arabic instruments introduced by the Moors. The 5-string Spanish guitar evolved in the 1500s, becoming the Spanish national musical instrument. The modern guitar has 6 strings, generally made of metal or nylon. The guitar has become an important instrument in blues, jazz, and rock music.

Guizot, François Pierre Guillaume (1787-1874), French statesman and historian. Under Louis Philippe he held various offices, notably the education and foreign ministries. He became premier in 1847 but resigned when the monarchy was overthrown in 1848. Thereafter he wrote history, most notably a history of the 17th-century English revolution.
See also: Louis Philippe.

Gulf Intracoastal Waterway, system of navigable waterways, both natural and artificial, running about 1,100 mi (1,770 km) along the Gulf of Mexico from Apalachee Bay, Fla., to Brownsville, Tex.

Gulf of California, 700-mi (1,100-km) arm of the Pacific Ocean separating Baja (Lower) California, Mexico, from the Mexican states of Sonora and Sinaloa to the east.
See also: Pacific Ocean.

Gulf of Genoa *see:* Map of Italy.

Gulf of Guinea *see:* Map of Africa.

Gulf of Mexico, arm of the Atlantic Ocean bounded by the southeastern United States, Mexico, and Cuba. It is linked to the Atlantic by the Strait of Florida and to the Caribbean by the Strait of Yucatan. Extensive petroleum deposits are worked offshore.
See also: Atlantic Ocean.

Gulf of Oman *see:* Map of Persian Gulf.

Gulf of Saint Lawrence, almost landlocked body of water, opening into the Atlantic Ocean in eastern Canada. Newfoundland borders the gulf on the east, Nova Scotia and New Brunswick on the south, and Quebec on the west. As the outlet for the Great Lakes and St. Lawrence River, the gulf is the gateway to trade for the interior of North America.

Gulf of Tonkin Resolution, resolution put before the U.S. Congress on Aug. 4, 1964, by President Lyndon B. Johnson, following attacks by North Vietnamese vessels on U.S. destroyers. The resolution gave the president power to take measures necessary to repel other attacks and prevent aggression. The resolution was later seen as the beginning of full-scale U.S. involvement in the Vietnam War and was attacked for giving excessive power to the president. In July 1970 the Senate voted to revoke its authorizations.
See also: Vietnam War.

Gulf Stream, warm ocean current flowing north, then northeast, off the east coast of the United States. Its weaker, more diffuse continuation is the east-flowing North Atlantic Drift, which is responsible for warming the climates of western Europe. The current, often taken to include the Caribbean Current, is fed by the North Equatorial Current, and can be viewed as the western part of the great clockwise water circulation pattern of the North Atlantic.

Gulick, Luther Halsey (1865-1918), U.S. physical education teacher and physician who spent much of his life promoting physical fitness. Gulick lectured and wrote books on good hygiene and the importance of physical activity. From 1886 to 1903 he was director of the physical training course at the Young Men's Christian Association Training School in Springfield, Mass. Gulick and his wife, Charlotte Vetter Gulick, also founded the Camp Fire Girls (now Camp Fire) in 1910.
See also: Camp Fire.

Gull, strong seabird forming the subfamily Larinae. The plumage is basically white with darker wings and back. Some species develop a dark hood in the breeding plumage. There are altogether some 40 species of gulls, and the group is widespread. Gulls are a very successful and adaptable group and many species have now become common inland as scavengers on refuse or on plowed land.

Gulliver's Travels, satire published in London in 1726 as *Travels into Several Remote Nations of the World*, under the name of Lemuel Gulliver, supposedly a ship's surgeon. The actual author was Jonathan Swift, who was satirizing both England and human foibles more generally.
See also: Swift, Jonathan.

Pewit gulls

Gum, sticky substance from plants that hardens when dry. *Gum arabic* is obtained from certain African acacia trees. It is used as an adhesive on envelopes and postage stamps. *Gum guaiacum*, from the lignum vitae tree, is used for treating gout and for detecting bloodstains, which cause it to change color. Chewing gum comes from the sap of the sapodilla tree.

Gum resin, vegetable substance obtained by making an incision in a plant and allowing the juice that flows out to solidify. Gum resins are often used in medicines and perfumes.

Gum tree, popular name for the eucalyptus tree.

Gun, weapon of destruction able to project a missile at a distant target. Heavy guns, such as cannons, mortars, and howitzers, are usually regarded as artillery, whereas lighter, portable guns such as pistols, rifles, revolvers, and machine guns are regarded as firearms.
See also: Revolver; Rifle.

Gun control, laws aimed at governing ownership of firearms. Many states, as well as the federal government, have passed laws restricting guns, but these vary widely and have been difficult to enforce. Advocates of tighter gun control argue that stricter laws would reduce violent crime. Opponents deny that claim, and say that the U.S. Constitution guarantees the right of citizens to own guns.
See also: Gun.

Guncotton, form of cellulose nitrate resembling cotton, used in explosives and propellants. Guncotton is prepared by first treating cotton or wood fibers with a mixture of strong nitric and sulfuric acids. After this nitration process, the fibers are washed, ground, pressed, and dried. Extreme care is necessary in the handling and storing of guncotton, as it can be ignited by impact, friction, or excessive heat.

Gunpowder, or black powder, low explosive, the only one known in the West from the 13th century until the mid-19th century. It consists of about 75% potassium (or sodium) nitrate, 10% sulfur, and 15% charcoal; it is readily ignited and burns very rapidly. Gunpowder was used in fireworks in 10th-century China, as a propellant for firearms from the 14th century in Europe, and for blasting since the late 17th century. It is now used mainly as an igniter, in fuses and in fireworks.
See also: Explosive.

Gunpowder Plot, conspiracy of a group of English Roman Catholics to blow up King James I, his family, and Parliament on Nov. 5, 1605. Guy Fawkes was arrested while setting charges under the Houses of Parliament; the conspirators were executed. In England Guy Fawkes Day, Nov. 5, is celebrated with bonfires, fireworks, and the burning of effigies.
See also: Fawkes, Guy.

Guppy (*Poecilia reticulata*), small fish of northern South America and the Caribbean named for the Reverend Thomas Guppy, who discovered it in Trinidad in 1866. It is also called the rainbow fish, a more appropriate name, because the male is brilliantly colored. The females are usually drab and grow up to 2 in (5 cm) long—twice as big as the males. Guppies are popular aquarium fish. The young are born alive and have to take a gulp of air before they can swim properly. Guppies feed on algae and insect larvae. For this reason they have been released into ponds in many parts of the world to control mosquitoes.

Gupta dynasty, North Indian dynasty that ruled from A.D. 320 to 550, a period that produced some of the finest Indian art and literature. From a small area in the Ganges valley their power spread out to most of India, and under Chandragupta II (385-414) scholarship, law, and art reached new heights. The White Hun invasion (450) reduced the Gupta empire to a portion of Bengal.

Gurnard, common name for tropical fish of the family Dactylopteridae. The gurnard has large pectoral fins with lower fin rays that move separately like fingers. Gurnards seem best suited for life on sea bottoms.

Gustavus, name of 6 kings of Sweden. **Gustavus I Vasa** (1496?-1560) was founder of the modern Swedish nation. A Swedish noble, he led the successful revolt against the Danes (1520-23) and was elected king. Instrumental in the establishment of Lutheranism and the growth of the economy, he took firm control of the country and established an hereditary monarchy. **Gustavus II Adolphus** (1594-1632) reigned from 1611. One of the great generals of modern times, he made Sweden a European power. When he came to the throne, Sweden was at war with Denmark, Russia, and Poland. He ended the Danish war (1613) and the Russian war (1617) victoriously. With his chancellor Count Oxenstierna he introduced wide internal reforms. He joined the Thirty Years' War in 1631, scoring the first Protestant victory at Breitenfeld (1631). He was killed in his victory at Lützen in 1632. **Gustavus III** (1746-92) became king in 1771, at a time of factionalism and unrest. He regained much of the monarchy's lost power in 1772, and ruled well, introducing many liberal reforms. He was assassinated by a conspiracy of discontented nobles. **Gustavus IV** (1778-1837) reigned from 1792 to 1809. In 1805 he joined a coalition against Napoleon and lost Swedish Pomerania and territory in Germany; despite English help he lost Finland to Russia in 1808. He was then deposed and exiled. **Gustavus V** (1858-1950), a popular sovereign, reigned from 1906. **Gustavus VI Adolphus** (1882-1973) reigned from 1950. He was an able and popular monarch; in 1971 the monarchy was stripped of its powers, but this was deferred during his reign and did not take effect until 1975. He was also a noted archeologist.

Gutenberg, Johannes (c.1400-68), German printer, usually considered the inventor of printing from separately cast metal types, used for movable type. By 1450 he had a press in Mainz, financed by Johann Fust (1400-c.1466). In 1455 he handed the press (and his invention) over to Fust in repayment of debts; by which time the Gutenberg (or Mazarin) Bible was at least well under way.

Guthrie, Woody (Woodrow Wilson Guthrie; 1912-67), U.S. folksinger whose compositions and guitar style have shaped modern folk music. As a migrant worker in the 1930s, he developed the characteristic social and political themes of his protest songs, which influenced younger performers like Bob Dylan. His son, **Arlo Guthrie** (1947-) has followed in his father's path as a performer and songwriter.

Gutiérrez, José Angel (1944-), proponent of Mexican-American civil rights and founder of *La Raza Unida*, a political party that ran Mexican-American candidates for public office. In 1970, the year he founded the organization, Gutiérrez was elected president of the school board of Crystal City, Tex. Gutiérrez was elected a county judge in Texas in 1974.

GUT's *see:* Grand unified theories.

Guyana

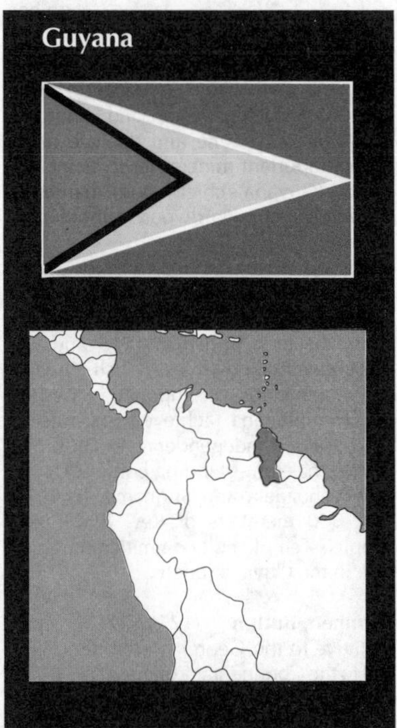

Capital:	Georgetown
Area:	83,000 sq mi (215,000 sq km)
Population:	790,000
Government:	republic
Independent:	1966
GNP:	U.S. $327,000,000
Per capita:	U.S. $410

Traditional village in Guyana

Guyana, Cooperative Republic of, independent country on the northern coast of South America, largest of the three countries of the Guiana region. Guyana is bordered by the Atlantic Ocean on the north, Suriname on the east, Brazil on the south, and Venezuela and Brazil on the west. The capital is Georgetown. Most of the population lives along the coastal plain. The interior is hilly and heavily forested.
People. The main ethnic groups are East Indians (descendants of imported labor) and blacks; there are also about 30,000 Native Americans. Many of the professional classes are European or Chinese. English is the official language. The religions are Islam, Christian, and Hinduism.
Economy. Sugarcane and rice are major crops. Important mineral reserves include bauxite (Guyana's chief export), diamonds, and manganese. Hardwood is another important resource.
History. Guyana was colonized by the Dutch in the 1600s. Slaves were important to work sugar and tobacco plantations. The region became British in 1815 and was subsequently known as British Guiana. East Indian labor was imported in the 19th century. Guyana achieved self-rule in 1961 and full independence in 1966. The country has long-standing border disputes with Venezuela and Suriname. In 1979, over 900 members of Rev. Jim Jones's People's Temple cult committed mass suicide in the Guyana jungle.

Gwinnett, Button (1735?-77), representative to the Georgia Assembly (1769) and to the Continental Congress (1776-77); signer of the Declaration of Independence. A merchant and plantation owner, he was killed in a duel with Continental general Lachlan McIntosh.

Gymnastics, sport and system of exercise designed to maintain and improve the physique. In ancient Greece, gymnastics—including track and field athletics and training for boxing and wrestling—were important in education. Competitive gymnastics are a series of exercises on set pieces of apparatus: parallel bars, horizontal bar, side and vaulting horses, beam, and asymmetric bars. The U.S. system, derived from the German, is designed to assist physical growth; the Swedish system aims at rectifying posture and weak muscles; and the Danish system seeks general fitness and endurance.

Gymnosperm, smaller of the 2 main classes of seed-bearing plants, the other being the angiosperm. Gymnosperms are characterized by having naked seeds usually formed on open scales produced in cones. All are perennial plants and most are evergreen. There are several orders, the main ones being the Cycadales, the cycads or sago palms; the Coniferales, including pine, larch, fir, and redwood; the Ginkgoales, the ginkgo; and the Gnetales, tropical shrubs and woody vines.

Gynecology, branch of medicine and surgery specializing in disorders of the female reproductive tract; often linked with obstetrics, which specializes in pregnancy and childbirth. Gynecology deals with contraception, abortion, sterilization, infertility, abnormalities of menstruation, and diseases of reproductive organs.
See also: Reproduction.

Gyroscope

Györ (pop. 129,100; German: *Raab*), capital city of Györ-Sopron county, northwest Hungary. The city is a commercial and manufacturing center, producing machines and textiles. Györ was the site of a Stone Age settlement, a Celtic town, and a Roman camp. Lying on the trade route between Vienna and Budapest, it flourished in the Middle Ages. Industrialization began in the mid-19th century, and growth has been very rapid since the end of World War II.
See also: Hungary.

Gypsum, common soft white mineral, a hydrate of calcium sulfate ($CaSO_42H_2O$), used to make plaster. Alabaster, a variety of gypsum, is carved to make ornamental objects. Gypsum has been used as a fertilizer because of its calcium content. Hard well and spring water often contain gypsum.

Gypsy, member of a nomadic people of Europe, Asia, and North America. Gypsies are believed to have originated in India; their language, Romany, is related to Sanskrit and Prakrit. They probably began their westward migration about A.D. 1000. By the 15th century they had penetrated the Balkans, Egypt, and North Africa. In the 16th century they were to be found throughout Europe. In World War II a half-million European gypsies were executed by the Nazis. There is a strong gypsy tradition of folklore, legend, and song, and this, combined with the independence of their lives, has inspired the romantic imagination of many musicians, artists, and writers.

Gypsy moth (*Porthetria dispar*), winged insect originating in Europe and later introduced to North America. In the New World, in the absence of natural enemies, it has become a serious pest; the caterpillars feed on the leaves of the deciduous trees, particularly fruit trees, and their occasional mass outbreaks can lead to complete defoliation.

Gyropilot, or automatic pilot, automatic device for keeping a ship or airplane on a given course using signals from a gyroscopic reference. The marine version operates a ship's rudder by displacement signals from the gyrocompass. In an airplane, the gyropilot consists of sensors that detect deviations in direction, pitch, and roll and pass signals via a computer to alter the controls as necessary.

Gyroscope, heavy spinning disk mounted so that its axis is free to adopt any orientation. The fact that a spinning top will stay upright as long as it is spinning fast enough demonstrates the property of gyroscopic inertia: the direction of the spin axis resists change. This means that a gyroscope mounted universally, in double gimbals, will maintain the same orientation in space however its support is turned, a property applied in many navigational devices.

H

H, eighth letter of the English alphabet, derived from the Semitic letter *cheth*, which represents a similar but more guttural sound. In Greek the *h* was dropped and remained only as a symbol for the long *e* vowel. It is silent in many of the Roman languages and in English has a sound close to that of breathing. In many words that have a French origin, the *h* is silent (as in *honor*). This sound creates problems for foreigners learning English and for many native speakers.

Haakon VII (1872-1957), king of Norway from 1905. A Danish prince, he was elected constitutional monarch when Norway became independent of Sweden. During the German occupation of Norway (1940-45), he led a government-in-exile in London. He was succeeded by his son, Olaf V.

Habakkuk, Book of, book of the Old Testament, eighth of the Minor Prophets. Though nothing is known of Habakkuk himself, the book probably dates from the late 7th century B.C. It consists of poems about God's using the Chaldaeans to punish Judah and includes promises of divine justice.
See also: Bible; Old Testament.

Habana, La *see:* Havana.

Habeas corpus, in common law, a writ ordering that a person held in custody or under arrest be brought before a court to determine whether the dentention is lawful. Habeas corpus (from the Latin "you should have the body") originated in medieval England and became a major civil right with the 1679 Habeas Corpus Act. It was designed to make sure that arrested individuals received due process of law. Embodied in the U.S. Constitution, habeas corpus may not be suspended except in cases of rebellion or invasion. (President Lincoln suspended it in 1861 at the onset of the Civil War.)

Haber-Bosch process *see:* Haber process.

Haber process, main commercial method of manufacturing ammonia. The process was invented by Fritz Haber (1868-1934), a German chemist who received the Nobel Prize in chemistry for the discovery in 1918. It was developed on an industrial scale by Karl Bosch in 1913 and is also known as the Haber-Bosch process. The procedure involves the mixing of hydrogen and nitrogen at high temperatures and pressures.
See also: Ammonia.

Habit, learned stimulus-response sequence. The term is also used to apply to an automatic response to a specific situation, normally acquired through repetition.

Habitat, environment of an animal or plant. All living organisms can tolerate a certain amount of variation in their environment. Within the major divisions of habitat (sea water, fresh water, desert, swamp, etc.) there are minor factors, such as temperature, acidity, rainfall, and the presence of other organisms.
See also: Ecologie.

Habsburg, House of , European family from which came rulers of Austria (1282-1918), the Holy Roman Empire (1438-1806), Spain (1516-1700), Germany, Hungary, Bohemia, and other countries. Count Rudolf IV, who was crowned King Rudolf I of Germany in 1273, founded the imperial line. Thereafter Habsburg (also spelled Hapsburg) power and hereditary lands grew until, under Charles V, they included most of Europe (excepting France, Scandinavia, Portugal, and England). After Charles, the Habsburgs were divided into Spanish and imperial lines. When the Spanish line died out, Charles V's granddaughter, Maria Theresa, gained the Austrian title. Her husband, Francis I (Duke of Lorraine), became Holy Roman Emperor (1745), and the Habsburg-Lorraine line ruled the Holy Roman Empire until its demise. The last Habsburg ruler, Charles I, emperor of Austria and king of Hungary, abdicated in 1918, after World War I.
See also: Austria-Hungary; Holy Roman Empire.

Hackberry, any of various trees (genus *Celtis*) of the elm family. The small, round fruit of many species are edible, and the wood is used for furniture; some varieties are grown ornamentally. The trees have smooth gray bark and pointed leaves that grow in two rows.

Hackmatack *see:* Larch.

Hadassah, U.S. Zionist organization of Jewish women, supporting social services, education, and land reclamation in Israel. The name is Hebrew for Queen Esther, Old Testament heroine of the Persian Jews.
See also: Szold, Henrietta; Zionism.

Haddock, North Atlantic fish (*Melanogrammus aeglefinus*) resembling a cod, distinguished by its 3 dorsal fins and the dark patch just behind the gills, known as St. Peter's thumbmark, which the cod lacks. Haddock live in shoals and feed on worms, shellfish, and other bottom-living animals. They are caught in trawls along with cod, and are important commercially, being marketed salted or as smoked Finnan haddock.

Hades, in Greek mythology, the realm of the dead. The name originally referred to the god of the underworld, Pluto, but it later came to refer to the underworld itself. It was pictured as guarded by Cerberus, a many-headed dog with a tail of snakes, and was separated from the land of the living by rivers. The most well-known river was the Styx, across which the dead were transported. The dead were met by 3 judges, who sent heroes to the Elysian fields, while the evil were sent to Tartarus.

Hadj *see:* Hajj.

Hadrian (Publius Aelius Hadrianus; 76-138 B.C.), Roman emperor from 117 to his death, successor of Trajan. He traveled the empire, reforming and restoring imperial rule. An effective administrator and soldier, he was a talented poet and an admirer of Greek civilization. He was responsible for the construction (c.122-126) of Hadrian's Wall in Britain. His plan to build a new city at Jerusalem sparked a Jewish revolt (132-135), which he repressed.
See also: Rome, Ancient.

Remains of Hadrian's Wall in Northumberland and Cumberland, Great Britain

Hadrian's Wall, ancient Roman fortification built by the emperor Hadrian (c.122-126) and lengthened about a hundred years later by the emperor Severus. It ran 74 mi (119 km) across the northern part of England and had a series of forts along its length. It represented the northern limit of the empire.

Hadron, name for two of the four basic classes of subatomic particles. These four classes, from lightest to heaviest, are: bosons, leptons, mesons, and baryons. Me-

Punishment in Hades depicted on an ancient Greek vase. (Left) Sisyphus carries a rock up a mountain slope for eternity because the rock always rolls to the bottom as he approaches the summit. (Right) Prometheus bound is attacked by an eagle who eats his liver.

sons and baryons are considered hadrons. Mesons are the particles that hold atomic nuclei together. Baryons are the largest class of particles; both protons and neutrons, which are the main particles of nuclei, are baryons. The reason that mesons and baryons are sometimes considered together as hadrons is that both are subject to the strong nuclear force (one of the four basic forces of nature; the others being gravitations, electromagnetisms, and the weak nuclear force). The other two classes of particles—bosons and leptons—are not subject to the strong nuclear force. Current theory assumes that all hadrons are composed of more basic particles, called quarks.
See also: Baryon; Meson; Quark.

Haeckel, Ernst von (1834-1919), German biologist best remembered for his vociferous support of Darwin's theory of evolution and for his own theory that ontogeny (the development of an individual organism) recapitulates phylogeny (its evolutionary stages), a theory now discredited.
See also: Biology; Darwin, Charles Robert.

Alexander M. Haig

Hafiz (Shams ad-din Mohammed; c.1325-c.90 B.C.), Persian lyric poet and courtier at Shiraz, considered one of the greatest medieval Islamic poets. He used the traditional verse form ghazal (rhyming couplets), using it to express a sensuality and gaiety sharpened by the philosophical mysticism of sufism.

Hafnium, chemical element, symbol Hf; for physical constants see Periodic Table. Hafnium was discovered in 1923, by Dirk Coster and Georg von Hevesey, identified by means of X-ray spectroscopic analysis of zircon. It is found in most zirconium minerals. Zirconium and hafnium are 2 of the most difficult elements to separate. The element is prepared by reducing the tetrachloride with magnesium. Hafnium is a brilliant silver, ductile, corrosion- resistant metal. It is used in nuclear reactor control rods. The metal is pyrophoric in finely divided form and absorbs hydrogen at elevated temperatures. Hafnium carbide is the most refractory binary composition known, and hafnium nitride is the most refractory metal nitride. Hafnium is used in alloys and as a getter in gas-filled and incandescent lamps.

Hagar *see:* Ishmael.

Hagfish, any of a family (Myxinidae) of predatory marine fishes related to the lamprey. They resemble eels and have circular mouths ringed by tentacles. Their tongues have sharp teeth, and they feed on worms, crustaceans, and fish located by smell. Hagfish grow to just over 2 ft (61 cm) long and are found in seas around the world on soft mud in fairly deep water. If a hagfish is roughly handled, it secretes a large quantity of shiny mucus, for which it is sometimes called the slime eel.

Haggai, Book of, book of the Old Testament, 10th of the Old Testament Minor Prophets, dated 520-519 B.C. It consists of 4 oracles urging the Jews to rebuild the temple at Jerusalem and prophesying the glories of the messianic age.

Haggard, Sir Henry Rider (1856-1925), English author of romantic adventure novels with authentic African backgrounds. He is best known for *King Solomon's Mines* (1885) and *She* (1887).

Hagia Sophia, or Santa Sophia, massive cathedral raised in Constantinople (now Istanbul) by the Byzantine emperor Justinian I; completed in A.D. 537. Its name means "Holy Wisdom" in Greek, and it was the greatest achievement of Byzantine architecture. Turned into a mosque after the Turkish conquest (1453), it is now a museum.

Hague, Frank (1876-1956), U.S. politician, mayor of Jersey City, N.J., for 30 years, and controller of one of the United State's most powerful political machines. Following accusations of financial irregularities in city financial affairs, his power began to decline. He was voted out of office by a reform movement.

Hague, The (Dutch: *Gravenhage* or *Den Haag*; pop. 449,300), seat of government of the Netherlands, capital of South Holland province, and headquarters of the International Court of Justice. Its Binnenhof palace houses the Dutch legislature. The city was the site of the Hague Conferences (1899, 1907) which were international meetings to discuss rules of war. The Hague has gained a reputation as the city for peace conferences. It is also an educational and cultural center.
See also: Netherlands.

Hague Peace Conferences, 2 conferences (1899, 1907) held at The Hague, the Netherlands, at Russia's request, to discuss belligerency rules and war conventions. The first conference established the International Permanent Court of Arbitration (the Hague Tribunal).
See also: Hague Tribunal; World War I.

Hague Tribunal, or International Permanent Court of Arbitration, court established by the first Hague Peace Conference (1899). It is now supported by 76 nations. The court supplies arbitrators to decide international disputes submitted to them. After World War I it was supplemented by the World Court and, later, the International Court of Justice.
See also: World War I.

Hahn, Otto (1879-1968), German chemist awarded the 1944 Nobel Prize for chemistry for his splitting of the uranium atom in 1939 and his discovery of the possibility of chain reactions.

Hahnemann, (Christian Friedrich) Samuel (1755-1843), German physician and founder of homeopathic medicine. He believed that diseases should be treated with small doses of drugs that produced symptoms in healthy persons similar to those caused by the disease to be treated.
See also: Homeopathy.

Haida, tribe of Native Americans of the Pacific northwest, living primarily on islands off the coast of British Columbia and Alaska. The Haida are known for their large oceangoing canoes and wooden totem poles. They mark important occasions with *potlatches*, ceremonies of excessive gift-giving.

Haifa (pop. 266,100), port city in northern Israel, an important manufacturing and transportation center. The ancient city, dating from the 3rd century, was destroyed (1191) during the Third Crusade. Later rebuilt, it became a major port in the late 19th century. It is the world headquarters of the Baha'i religion.
See also: Israel.

Haig, Alexander Meigs, Jr. (1924-), U.S. general and secretary of state (1981-82). Deputy to Henry Kissinger on the National Security Council in 1969, he was named President Nixon's White House chief of staff during the Watergate affair. Later (1974-79) he was supreme commander of North Atlantic Treaty Organization (NATO) forces in Europe. He was appointed secretary of state by President Ronald Reagan in 1981 and resigned in 1982. In 1988 he ran unsuccessfully for the Republican presidential nomination.

Haig, Douglas, 1st Earl (1861-1928), British commander in World War I, blamed for the misconduct of the Somme and Ypres campaigns (1916-17). Hampered by the hostility of British premier Lloyd George, Haig was denied effective command until 1918, when he displayed far greater generalship.

Haiku, traditional unrhymed Japanese poem of 3 lines of 5, 7, and 5 syllables. It evolved in the 17th century from a 31-syllable form. Haikus use images from nature to create a mood or feeling.

Hail, ice pellets that sometimes fall during thunderstorms. Hailstones usually consist of kernels of ice surrounded by distinct layers formed as moisture freezes around the kernel. As they are carried higher by winds, they collect further layers of ice. When they become too heavy to be supported, they fall. They are usually less than .5 in (1.3 cm) in diameter, but can reach diameters over an inch (2.5 cm) and can severely damage crops and buildings.

Haile Selassie (1891-1975), reigning name of Ras Tafari, emperor of Ethiopia (1930-74). He led Ethiopia's resistance to the Italian Fascist invasion of the country in 1935-36 and lived in exile until British forces restored him to his throne in 1941. His autocratic rule provoked opposition in later years, and he was deposed by his army in 1974 in the midst of a nationwide famine. He died in captivity.
See also: Ethiopia.

Haile Selassie

Haiphong (pop. 1,191,000), city in northeast Vietnam, on the Red River delta near the Gulf of Tonkin. A major southeast Asian port, in the 19th century, Haiphong was the site of the main French naval base in Indochina. During the Vietnam War the city was heavily bombed by the United States (1965-68, 1972). It has since been rebuilt as an industrial and shipping center.
See also: Vietnam; Vietnam War.

Hair, outgrowth of the skin in mammals, sometimes thickening to form wool or fur. Each hair consists of a shaft, most of which extends above the surface of the skin, and a root located in a tubular follicle below the skin surface. The lower end of the root is enlarged to form the bulb, the lower part of which surrounds a cone-shaped projection of connective tissue, the papilla. The blood supply to the hair follicle comes through capillary networks that enter the papilla. The root of the hair forms a matrix of growing and dividing cells. As new cells are formed, the older cells are pushed upward and the hair "grows." The hairshaft in the upper part of the follicle and the exposed part of the shaft above the skin consists of dead, cornified cells. Cutting the exposed part of the shaft has no effect on the growth of the hair. Associated with the hair follicles are the sebaceous glands, which secrete an oily substance that lubricates the shaft of the hair.

Hairdressing, care and arranging of hair, including cutting, setting, styling, tinting, bleaching, straightening, waving, and other procedures. Professional salons usually offer manicuring, facial massage, make-up, eyebrow-shaping, and the making, cleaning, and styling of wigs and hairpieces. The styling and adornment of hair has often indicated social status, e.g. the Chinese braid, the elaborate Greek knot, and the fantastic creations of French aristocrats in the 18th century. Hair styles sometimes have religious significance, too, as shown by the shaved heads of Catholic nuns, monks, and Orthodox Jewish married women, or the long hair of Sikhs and Rastafarians. Earlier civilizations indicated mourning by unkempt hair strewn with ashes, and joy by annointing the hair with perfumes or unguents, as well as feathers, jewels, flowers, ribbons, or combs.
See also: Cosmetics.

Hair snake *see:* Horsehair worm.

Hairworm *see:* Horsehair worm.

Haise, Fred Wallace, Jr. (1933-), U.S. astronaut (1966-79), pilot of the lunar module of the Apollo 13 mission (1970), during which an explosion disabled the command module and prevented the lunar landing. The 3 astronauts—Haise, James A. Lovell, Jr., and John L. Swigert, Jr.— survived the return to earth in the lunar module.
See also: Astronaut.

Haiti, Republic of, independent country occupying the western third of the island of Hispaniola in the Caribbean Sea. The Dominican Republic occupies the rest of the island. The capital is Port-au-Prince.
Land and Climate. Haiti is mountainous, dominated by two peninsulas extending westward into the Windward Passage, which separates Hispaniola from Cuba. Between the peninsulas is the Gulf of Gonaïves, with Gonâve Island in the center. The coastline consists of beaches, coral reefs, mangrove swamps, and steep cliffs. Vegetation includes cedar, pine, and mahogany, as well as scrub forests.
People. The great majority of Haitians are descendants of African slaves. The official language is French, but most Haitians speak Creole, a mixture of French and African languages, with some English and Spanish words. The official religion is Roman Catholicism, but large numbers practice voodoo, a religion that mixes African beliefs with some elements of Catholicism.
Economy. Haiti is very densely populated and has the lowest per capita income in the Western Hemisphere. About 90% of the population is engaged in raising corn, rice, fruit, yams, and vegetables, or in fishing. The chief cash crop is coffee. Sisal fiber, sugarcane, cotton, and cocoa are also exported.
History. Officially a Spanish colony from the early 1500s, Hispaniola was settled by the French during the 1600s. Sugar plantations were created; and slaves were imported to work them. In 1697 Spain ceded Haiti to France. During the French Revolution, the ideas of liberty and equality spread to the colony and stimulated slave revolts. Under the leadership of Toussaint L'Ouverture, a freed slave, the slaves obtained their freedom in 1793. Proclaiming independence in 1801, Toussaint became governor-general of Hispaniola but was defeated and captured by Napoleon. In 1803, a black army drove the French out, and independence was declared on January 1, 1804, making Haiti the second country of the Western Hemisphere to win its independence from a European colonizer. But stable rule was not established; and Haitian history has been marked by poverty and dictatorship. From 1915 to 1934 the country was occupied by U.S. marines.
In 1957 François ("Papa Doc") Duvalier

Haiti

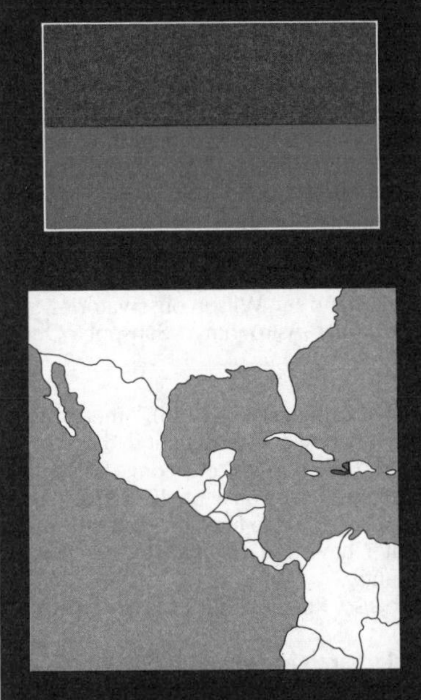

Capital:	Port-au-Prince
Area:	10,714 sq mi (27,750 sq km)
Population:	5,520,000
Government:	republic (military)
Independent:	1804
GNP:	U.S. $2,240,000,000
Per capita:	U.S. $360

Haiti: landscape around the Citadel Laferriere

One of the many Haitian Victorian villas

became president and soon established an extremely repressive dictatorship, supported by a personal police force known as the *tontons macoutes*. In 1971 Duvalier died and was succeeded by his son, Jean-Claude ("Baby Doc."), who fled the country during a mass rebellion in 1986. In 1991 Father Aristide, was elected president in the first free election. Aristide was ousted by a military coup in 1991, but returned to Haiti in 1994 through the agency of the US.

Hajj or **Hadj**, pilgrimage to the Muslim world's holiest city, Mecca, in what is now Saudi Arabia. The goal of a hajj is the mosque whose court encloses the Kaaba, a cube-shaped building containing the sacred Black Stone. Muslims are required to make the pilgrimage to Mecca at least once in their lifetime, if at all possible.
See also: Mecca; Muslims.

Goal of a hajj, the Great Mosque, Mecca

Hake, any of various fish of the family Merlucciidae, related to the cod but with a different arrangement of fins. Hake live in deep water and have large mouths set with sharp teeth for catching other fish, such as herring. The teeth can hinge backward to allow large pieces of food to slip in easily. There are several kinds of hake, including the silver hake of the American Atlantic coast and the stockfish of South Africa. In some parts of the world, hake are extensively fished for food.

Hakluyt, Richard (1552?-1616), English geographer and promoter of exploration and colonization. He published many early accounts of the Americas and a major account of English voyaging and discoveries.

Halas, George Stanley (1895-1983), founder, owner, and coach of the Chicago Bears (originally called the Decatur Staleys), one of the founding teams of the National Football League (NFL). After serving in the U.S. Navy and playing a season of professional baseball with the New York Yankees, Halas founded and played end for the Bears (1920-29). As coach (1933-42, 1946-55, 1958-68) he helped develop modern football strategy and led the team to 6 NFL championships. He was inducted to the NFL Hall of Fame in 1963.

Halcyon days, period of tranquility. The phrase comes from the legend of the kingfisher, or halcyon, said to have incubated her eggs for 14 days on the ocean's surface, during which time the waves were perpetually calm.

Haldeman, H.R. *see:* Watergate.

Haldimand, Sir Frederick (1718-91), Swiss-born British general and governor of Quebec (1778-86). A former mercenary, he commanded the British North American Army (1773-74).

Hale, Edward Everett (1822-1909), U.S. author, editor, and Unitarian minister, best known for his short novel *The Man Without a Country* (1863). He also wrote *A New England Boyhood* (1893) and the novel *In His Name* (1873), and edited the magazine *Old and New*. An advocate of social reforms, Hale was chaplain of the U.S. Senate (1903-09).

Hale, George Ellery (1868-1938), U.S. astronomer who discovered the magnetic fields of sunspots and invented (c.1890) the spectroheliograph. His name is commemorated by the Hale Observatories in California. He also founded the Palomar Observatory and founded and directed the Yerkes and Mt. Wilson observatories.
See also: Astronomy; Sunspot; Observatory.

Hale, Nathan (1755-1776), American revolutionary who was caught in disguise behind British lines on Long Island and hanged as a spy on Sept. 22, 1776. His last words are said to have been: "I only regret that I have but one life to lose for my country."
See also: Revolutionary War in America.

Hale, Sarah Josepha (1788-1879), U.S. feminist journalist, editor of *Ladies' Magazine* (1828-37) and *Godey's Lady's Book* (from 1837). She championed higher education for women and was the author of the nursery rhyme "Mary Had a Little Lamb" (1830).
See also: Feminism.

Haleakala National Park, park on the island of Maui, in Hawaii, encompassing the dormant volcano Mt. Haleakala, which last erupted in 1790, and surrounding rain forests and coastal cliffs. It became a separate national park in 1961, having been part of Hawaii National Park since 1916. It is over 28,000 acres (11,000 hectares) in area.
See also: National Parks.

Hale Observatories *see:* Mount Wilson Observatory; Palomar Observatory.

Halevi, Judah (1085?-1141?), Jewish rabbi, philosopher, and poet who lived and worked in Muslim Spain. His *Sefer ha-Kuzari* was his most important philosophical work.
See also: Philosophy.

Haley, Alex Palmer (1921-92), U.S. author. His book *Roots* (1976) tells the story of his family, beginning in the mid-18th century with the capture of one of his African ancestors, who was taken to America as a slave. The book, which combines fiction with extensive research, was dramatized on U.S. television (1977) and earned Haley the Spingarn Medal and a citation from the Pulitzer Prize board. Haley's writing career began while he was serving in the U.S. Coast Guard (1939-59). He later became a journalist and collaborated with Malcolm X in the writing of *The Autobiography of Malcolm X* (1965).

Half-life *see:* Radioactivity.

Halibut, any of various fish of the family Hippoglossidae. Halibuts are flatfish, living in cold water and having both eyes on one side of its body. The largest Atlantic halibuts (Hippoglossus hippoglossus) can reach lengths of 12 ft (3.6 m) and can weigh as much as 700 lb (317.5 kg), living as long as 40 years. They are important commercial fishes and are caught in North Atlantic and North Pacific waters by trawling or on long lines. Halibut liver oil was once an important source of vitamin A.

Halifax (320,500), capital of Nova Scotia and eastern Canada's chief winter (ice free) port. The industrial, cultural, and commercial center of the province, it stands on a rocky peninsula jutting into a harbor large enough to accommodate the world's biggest ships. The city was built as a British fortress in 1749, and repeated fortifications in succeeding years made it one of the best-defended cities outside Europe. It was a British army base until 1906, when it was handed over to the Canadian government. During World Wars I and II Halifax served as an important Allied naval base. The city is a manufacturing center for food products, candy, furniture, and electronic equipment. Exports are mainly fish and fish products, lumber, and foodstuffs.
See also: Nova Scotia.

Halite *see:* Salt.

Hall, Granville Stanley (1844-1924), U.S. psychologist and educator best known for founding the *American Journal of Psychology* (1887), the first U.S. psychological journal. He was the first president of the

American Psychological Institute (1894), and the first president of Clark University.
See also: Psychology.

Hall, James N. *see:* Nordhoff and Hall.

Hall, Lyman (1724-90), American Revolutionary leader. Educated at Yale College, he became a doctor and settled in Georgia. He served as a delegate to the Continental Congress (1775-80) and signed the Declaration of Independence. In 1783 he was elected governor of Georgia.

Hall, Prince (1748-1807), founder of the African Lodge, the first all-black Masonic lodge in America (chartered by the English Masons 1787). A self-educated man, Hall was born in the West Indies, moved to Boston in 1765, and became a Methodist minister.

Halleck, Henry Wager (1815-72), U.S. Civil War general and military theorist, whose *Elements of Military Art and Science* (1846) was a training manual in the war. At the war's onset he was appointed major-general in command of the Western theater and in 1862 general-in-chief. In 1864 he was relieved. He served as chief-of-staff until 1865.
See also: Civil War, U.S.

Hall effect, electrical effect produced when current flows through a magnetic field. Voltage occurs at right angles to the current. Its level is proportional to the intensity of the current and of the magnetic force.
See also: Electric current; Magnetism.

Haller, Albrecht von (1708-77), Swiss biologist. Best known for his work on human anatomy and physiology, he is credited with being the founder of experimental anatomy. In physiology he investigated respiration, the blood circulation, the nervous system, and the irritability and sensibility of different types of body tissues.
See also: Anatomy; Physiology.

Halley, Edmund (1656-1742), English astronomer. In 1677 he made the first full observation of a transit of Mercury and in 1676-79 prepared a major catalog of southern hemisphere stars. He encouraged Isaac Newton to write the *Principia*, whose publication he financed. In 1720 he succeeded John Flamsteed as astronomer royal. He is best known for his prediction that the comet of 1682 would return in 1758, based on Newton's calculations of the comet's elliptical orbit around the sun. When the prediction was born out, the comet was named after him.
See also: Astronomy.

Halley's Comet, first periodic comet to be identified (by Edmund Halley) and the brightest of all recurring comets. It has a period of about 76 years. Records exist for every appearance of the comet since 240 B.C., except that of 163 B.C. The comet's most recent reappearance was in 1986.
See also: Comet; Halley, Edmund.

Halliburton, Richard (1900-39), U.S. explorer and writer. His travels, which he recounted in *The Glorious Adventure* (1927), *The Flying Carpet* (1932), and other books, retraced the steps of such historical figures as Hannibal (Carthage to Italy) and Hernán Cortés (Mexico). Halliburton and his crew were lost at sea in a storm while trying to sail a Chinese junk from Hong Kong to San Francisco.

Hall of Fame (formerly The Hall of Fame for Great Americans), memorial to Americans who have achieved great fame in various fields. It was founded in 1900 in a colonnade designed by Stanford White and has niches for about 150 busts. Elections of new members were suspended in 1977, but the monument is still open. It is on the campus of Bronx Community College, in New York City.

Halloween, festival held on Oct. 31, the eve of All Saints' Day, a holiday of the Roman Catholic and Anglican churches held to honor all the saints. The name comes from the medieval English "All Hallows' Eve." Originally a Celtic festival to mark the new year, welcome the spirits of the dead, and appease supernatural powers, Halloween was introduced to the United States by Scottish and Irish immigrants and is now a children's festival famous for "trick-or-treat."

Hallucinogenic drug, consciousness-altering drug that causes hallucinations or illusions, usually visual, together with personality and behavior changes. LSD (lysergic acid diethylamide), mescaline (peyote), and psilocin and psilocybin (derived from certain mushrooms) are common hallucinogenic drugs. The type of hallucination is not predictable, and may be unpleasant. They have been used for centuries in many cultures in connection with religious rituals. Although they are not physically addictive, a high degree of tolerance to LSD and psilocybin develops rapidly, such that higher and higher doses are required to produce an effect. The long-term biological and psychological consequences are unknown.
See also: Drug; Drug abuse.

Halo, in meteorology, luminous ring sometimes observed around the sun or the moon, caused by refraction and reflection of light by ice crystals in the atmosphere of the earth. Such crystals are frequently contained in high clouds. The French philosopher and scientist René Descartes was the first to offer the correct explanation of the formation of a halo. In art, the circle of light often depicted around the head of a saint is also called a halo.
See also: Meteorology.

Halogen, any of the group of 5 elements consisting of fluorine, chlorine, bromine, iodine and astatine. These make up group VIIa of the Periodic Table and are highly reactive nonmetals. Apart from astatine, which is radioactive, the halogens are common elements and form many compounds with one another and with other elements. In their pure form, the halogens form molecules composed of 2 atoms.
See also: Element.

Halothane, chemical compound ($C_2HBrClF_3$) used as a general anesthetic. The clear, colorless liquid is inhaled as a vapor. Valued for being nonflammable and neither nauseating nor irritating, it has been in use since 1951.
See also: Anesthesia.

Hals, Frans (c.1580-1666), Dutch portrait painter. Many of his greatest works, such as the *Lady Governors of the Old Men's Home at Haarlem* (1664), are civic portraits. His later works have a somber serenity, but many portraits and genre scenes,

Halley's comet depicted in Bayeux tapestry (11th century)

Halley's comet on its return in 1910, photographed on May 12 and May 15. The comet has been observed during all its appearances since 87 B.C.

Frans Hals, Portrait of a gypsy woman

such as *Banquet of the Officers of the St. George Militia* (1616) and the *Laughing Cavalier* (1642), are infused with a rich joviality. Five of his sons were also painters.

Halsey, William Frederick "Bull," Jr. (1882-1959), U.S. admiral during World War II. After commanding a Pacific carrier division 1940-42, he took command of the Pacific theater. As commander of the 3rd Fleet he helped destroy the Japanese fleet at Leyte Gulf in 1944. He resigned as fleet admiral in 1947.
See also: World War II.

Dag Hammarskjöld

Ham, cured thigh, buttock, or leg of a hog. The meat is usually cured with salt, and sometimes molasses or sugar. Some hams are impregnated with brine, either by injection or by soaking. The ham is then dried and smoked to prevent it from spoiling.

Hamadryas *see:* Baboon.

Hamburg (1,580,000), historic seaport, capital city of Hamburg state; largest city in western Germany, near the mouth of the Elbe River. Probably founded by Charlemagne, it was a dominant member of the Hanseatic League and has always been a flourishing commercial center. Hamburg was devastated in World War II, but has been rebuilt and now has shipyards and a wide range of industries. It is a transport hub and a center of the country's fishing industry.
See also: Germany.

Oscar Hammerstein II and Richard Rodgers

Hamilcar Barca (d. c.228 B.C.), Carthaginian general, father of Hannibal. He became commander of Sicily in 247 B.C., during the First Punic war. In 241 he returned to Carthage, quelled a mercenary revolt, and became a dictator. In 237 he led a successful occupation of Spain, but was later killed there.
See also: Carthage; Hannibal.

Hamilton (pop. 2,000), capital and principal port of Bermuda, situated on Main Island.

Hamilton (pop. 304,000), city in the province of Ontario, Canada, built on the plain between a landlocked harbor on Lake Ontario and the 250-ft (76-m) Niagara escarpment. Hamilton is heavily industrialized, being Canada's largest iron and steel producer. It is also a major Great Lakes port.
See also: Ontario.

Hamilton (pop. 62,368), industrial town in southwest Ohio on the Great Miami River, seat of Butler County. Local products include coated paper, safes, presses, parts for automobiles and aircraft, textiles, and machinery and machine tools. The town was founded in 1794 as Fairfield, and later renamed after U.S. political leader Alexander Hamilton.
See also: Ohio.

Hamilton, Alexander (1775-1804), U.S. political leader, a founder of the country. He was George Washington's secretary during the American Revolution, later serving as a delegate to the Continental Congress (1782-83). A delegate (from New York) to the Constitutional Convention of 1787, he was a strong supporter of the Constitution and was instrumental in getting it adopted. A founder of the Federalist Party, he advocated strong, centralized government and was co-author, with John Jay and James Madison of the *Federalist Papers* (1787-88), considered classics of political theory. His advocacy of close ties with Britain and his opposition to the French Revolution brought him into conflict with Thomas Jefferson and the Democratic Republicans. In 1789 Hamilton became the first secretary of the treasury and in 1791 he created the Bank of the United States. Though he left the cabinet in 1795, he continued to influence policy until the victory of Jefferson in the presidential election of 1800. Hamilton was killed in a duel with Aaron Burr, Jefferson's vice president, whose presidential ambitions Hamilton had been instrumental in blocking.

Hamilton, Alice (1869-1970), U.S. physician and social reformer. She was the first woman on the faculty of the Harvard Medical School (1919-35) and the first researcher to study industrial diseases and industrial hygiene in the United States. Her work was instrumental in the passage of worker's compensation laws.
See also: Worker's compensation.

Hamilton, Emma, Lady (1765-1815), celebrated English beauty who became the mistress of Lord Nelson and the subject of many portraits by leading artists. She was the wife of Sir William Hamilton, British envoy in Naples.

Hamilton, Virginia (1936-), U.S. author of children's books. Her novel *M.C. Higgins* won the Newbery Medal and the National Book Award (1975). In addition to her fiction books concerned with the African-American experience and her collections of black folk tales, Hamilton wrote biographies of notable African Americans for children, including *W. E. B. Du Bois* (1972) and *Paul Robeson* (1974).

Hamites, peoples inhabiting eastern Africa, especially Somalia and Ethiopia, and northern Africa, where they are known as Berbers. Strictly speaking, Hamitic is a linguistic classification rather than an ethnic one. Many believe that the Hamitic-speaking peoples originated on the Arabian peninsula, but this is not at all certain.

Hamlin, Hannibal (1809-91), U.S. vice president under Abraham Lincoln, 1861-65. Originally a Democrat, he joined the Republicans in 1856 because of his antislavery views. He was a senator from Maine, 1848-56 and 1869-81, and an ardent Reconstructionist.

Hammarskjöld, Dag (1905-61), Swedish politician, UN secretary general 1953-61. He was instrumental in negotiations to bring about a truce in the Korean War and a settlement of the Suez crisis of 1956. In 1960 he directed the UN intervention in the Congo (now Zaire). His actions were condemned by the USSR, but he refused to resign. He was killed in an airplane crash in the Congo and was posthumously awarded the 1961 Nobel Peace Prize.
See also: United Nations.

Hammerstein, name of 2 U.S. theatrical producers. **Oscar Hammerstein** (1846-1919) a German-born tobacco magnate who emigrated to the United States and became an opera impresario, opening theaters in New York, London, and Philadelphia. **Oscar Hammerstein II** (1895-1960), his grandson, became famous as a lyricist and producer of musical comedies in partnership with composers Richard Rodgers, Jerome Kern, and others. Among his successes were *Oklahoma!* (1943), *Carousel* (1945), *South Pacific* (1949), *The King and I* (1951) and *The Sound of Music* (1959).

Hammer throw, Olympic sports event in which the athlete throws a 16-lb (7.26-kg) "hammer" (actually a metal sphere with a handle), spinning in place to gain momentum before releasing it. The sport, which originated in the British Isles centuries ago, was standardized as a track and field event in 1875 and became part of the Olympic Games in 1900.

Hammett, (Samuel) Dashiell (1894-1961), U.S. writer and left-wing political activist. He was known for his hard-boiled detective novels, and his character Sam Spade became one of the prototypes of the fictional U.S. detective. Hammett's best-known works are *The Maltese Falcon* (1930) and *The Thin Man* (1932).

Hammond (pop. 93,700), industrial city in northwest Indiana, in the Calumet region, near Lake Michigan. Together with Gary and East Chicago, it forms a metropolitan area that borders Illinois. The city was founded in 1869, when G. H. Hammond opened a meat-packing plant there. It is now home to light industry, including a large bookbindery.
See also: Indiana.

Hammurabi, or Hammurapi, sixth king of the first dynasty of Babylonia (r. 1792-50 B.C.). He conquered and united Mesopotamia, establishing an empire that did not long survive him. He was responsible for the Code of Hammurabi, the fullest known collection of Babylonian laws. The best source of the code is a black stone column found at Susa, Iran, in 1901.
See also: Babylonia and Assyria.

Hampton, Lionel (1913-), U.S. jazz vibraphonist and bandleader. Originally a drummer with Louis Armstrong in 1928, he first recorded on vibraphone in 1930. He was a member of Benny Goodman's quartet 1936-40 and later became leader of his own band. He was known for his showmanship as well as his virtuoso technique.
See also: Jazz.

Hampton, Wade (1818-1902), U.S. politician and soldier. Although opposed to secession, he joined the Confederate army and became General Lee's cavalry commander. He was later governor of South Carolina (1877-79) and U.S. senator (1879-91).
See also: Civil War, U.S.

Hampton Court Conference, meeting held at Hampton Court Palace, England, in 1604 to consider Puritan demands for reform in the Church of England, especially of the episcopal system of Church government and the *Book of Common Prayer.* James I rejected most of these, but the conference endorsed the King James translation of the Bible.

Hampton Roads, natural harbor and port in southeast Virginia formed by the confluence of 3 rivers—the James, Nansemond, and Elizabeth—that flow into Chesapeake Bay. The Virginia cities of Newport News and Hampton face the channel on the north shore, Norfolk and Portsmouth on the south. The area is the headquarters of armed forces installations that make up the world's largest naval complex. Hampton was one of the earliest English settlements in the country, founded in 1610. During the Civil War Hampton Roads was the scene of the naval battle between the *Monitor* and the *Merrimack,* the first ironclad warships.

Hampton Roads, Battle of *see:* Monitor and Merrimack.

Hampton Roads Conference, meeting held on Feb. 3, 1865 aboard the *River Queen,* anchored in Chesapeake Bay, in an attempt to end the Civil War. President Lincoln and Secretary of State William H. Seward represented the North; Confederate Vice President Alexander H. Stevens, Sen. Robert M. Hunter, and Assistant Secretary of War John A. Campbell represented the South. Lincoln insisted on the emancipation of the slaves and restoration of the Union, and no agreement was reached.
See also: Civil War, U.S.

Hampton University, private college in Hampton, Va., founded 1868 to educate freed slaves and later funded for the education of Native Americans. Originally the Hampton Normal and Agricultural Institute, it adopted a college curriculum in 1923 and subsequently became Hampton Institute (1930) and Hampton University (1984). Its library includes the noted George Foster Peabody Collection of materials on black history.

Hamster, any of various short-tailed rodents of Europe and Asia. Hamsters feed chiefly on cereals, but also on fruits, roots, and leaves. They carry food back to their nests in large cheek pouches. The most familiar species, the golden hamster (*Mesocricetus auratus*), makes an attractive pet. Both it and the common hamster (*Cricetus cricetus*) are nocturnal.

Hamsun, Knut (1859-1952), Norwegian novelist. In his youth he led a wandering life, which became the theme of many of his novels, such as *Hunger* (1890) and his masterpiece, *The Growth of the Soil* (1917). He was awarded the Nobel Prize for literature in 1920. His popularity declined as a result of his Nazi sympathies during World War II.

Hancock, John (1737-93), U.S. revolutionary leader, president of the Continental Congress (1775-77) and first signer of the Declaration of Independence. Hancock was also governor of Massachusetts (1780-85 and 1787-93).

Hancock, Winfield Scott (1824-86), U.S. general and politician. He distinguished himself as a Union general in the Civil War. As Democratic nominee for the presidency in 1880, he was narrowly defeated by James A. Garfield. *See also:* Civil War, U.S.

Hand, Learned (1872-1961), U.S. jurist noted for his profoundly reasoned rulings in almost 3,000 cases. He served as a federal judge in New York from 1909 to 1951. Although never a Supreme Court justice, he was highly influential, known especially as a supporter of free speech. He was often referred to as "the 10th justice of the Supreme Court."

Handball, court game played by 2 to 4 people. There are 2 versions of the game: 1-wall handball and 4-wall handball. Players attempt to hit a hard rubber ball against 1 or more of the walls in such a fashion as to prevent opponents from returning it before it bounces twice on the floor. Handball may be one of the world's oldest games, dating back to ancient Egypt. The modern version was probably invented in the Basque country of northern Spain.

Handel, George Frideric (1685-1759), German-born composer who settled in England in 1712, one of the greatest composers of the baroque period. After establishing himself as an opera composer in Germany and Italy, he turned to oratorio to suit British tastes. His most famous works in this genre are *Saul* (1739), *Israel in Egypt* (1739), *The Messiah* (1742), and *Belshazzar* (1745). The rest of his vast output includes 46 operas, almost 100 cantatas, many orchestral works, and 28 additional oratorios.

Handicap, physical or mental disability, congenital or acquired, that inhibits a person from participating in normal life. In recent years technology and changes in attitudes have greatly improved the lives of the disabled. Sophisticated rehabilitation techniques and other tools, often using computers, have allowed a wide range of vocational and recreational activity. The U.S. Rehabilitation Act of 1973 requires federally funded businesses to provide equal treatment—particularly, equal employment opportunity and equal access—to the handicapped. The 1975 Handicapped Children Act requires states to provide free education for those with special needs.

Handicraft, name given to the process of making objects by hand; also refers to the products of that process. Traditional hand-

A mother hamster, busy keeping watch for possible dangers.

icrafts include basket-weaving, carpentry, carving, ceramics, embroidery, knitting, sewing, and leatherwork. The teaching of handicrafts has been widely included in school curricula and is also used in occupational therapy.

Handwriting on the wall, incident in the Old Testament (Book of Daniel). The Aramaic words *mene, mene, tekel* mysteriously appeared written on the wall and only the Babylonian ruler Belshazzar could see them. The Hebrew prophet Daniel interpreted them to mean that God intended to destroy Belshazzar and his kingdom, which fell to Cyrus of Persia that night. The phrase is now used to refer to any sign heralding disaster.

Handy, W(illiam) C(hristopher) (1873-1958), U.S. songwriter, bandleader, and jazz composer. He conducted his own band 1903-21. In 1912 he published one of the first popular blues songs, "Memphis Blues," and in 1914 wrote "St. Louis Blues." He became a music publisher in the late 1920s.

Han dynasty, dynasty that ruled China 202 B.C.-220 A.D. It was founded by Liu Bang after a period of oppressive centralized rule under the Ch'in dynasty. At the height of its expansion, the Han dynasty held power from Korea and Vietnam to Uzbekistan. It was during this period that Confucianism became the official ideology of the state and Buddhism was introduced in China.
See also: Liu Bang.

Hanging Gardens of Babylon *see:* Seven Wonders of the Ancient World.

Hangzhou, or Hangchow (pop. 1,192,000), city of eastern China, capital of Zhejiang province. The city is a tourist center and manufactures chemical and electronic products, iron, steel, and motor vehicles. Historically it was a center of silk and tea production. The city was rebuilt after its destruction during the Taiping Rebellion (1850-64). It was occupied by Japan (1937-45).
See also: China.

Han Kao-tsu *see:* Liu Bang.

Hankou *see:* Wuhan.

Hanna, Mark (1837-1904), U.S. Republican politician and industrialist whose financial backing helped bring about William McKinley's victory over William Jennings Bryan in the 1896 presidential elections. Hanna was appointed and subsequently elected U.S. Senator from Ohio (1897-1904) and remained a close presidential adviser.

Grecian bust of Hannibal

Hannibal (247-183? B.C.), Carthaginian general who almost defeated Rome in the Second Punic War (218-201 B.C.). Son of Hamilcar Barca, he commanded Carthaginian forces in Spain. When the second war between Rome and Carthage broke out, he crossed the Pyranees with a seasoned force whose supplies were carried by elephants. In an extraordinary feat of organization, he took his forces through the Alps in winter and invaded the Po River valley, defeating Roman forces under Scipio and winning great victories at Lake Trasimene in central Italy (217 B.C.) and at Cannae (216 B.C.). Rome detained him with harassing tactics while Roman armies reduced Carthaginian possessions in Spain, and Hannibal was recalled to defend Carthage itself. He was ultimately defeated at Zama (202 B.C.) by a Roman army commanded by Scipio Africanus Major. Driven into exile c.195 B.C., he joined Syrian operations against Rome. When the defeated Syrians promised to surrender him to Rome, he poisoned himself.
See also: Carthage; Punic Wars.

Hannibal (pop. 18,046), town in Marion county, northeastern Missouri, on the Mississippi River. It was the boyhood home of Samuel Clemens (Mark Twain) and the setting for his *Adventures of Tom Sawyer.* Founded in 1819, Hannibal is located in a rich farming area, and is a trade center for agricultural products. Its light industry includes machinery and tools, building materials, and shoes.
See also: Missouri.

Hanoi (pop. 1,444,000), capital of North Vietnam (1954-76) and of united Vietnam since 1976. Founded in the 7th century, it is an important shipping, industrial, and transport center on the Red River. The city suffered heavily from U.S. bombings during the Vietnam War.
See also: Vietnam War.

Hanover, or Hannover, region of northwest Germany. As Brunswick-Lüneburg it became an electorate of the Holy Roman Empire in 1692 (its elector, or ruler, helped elect the emperor). It began a period of association with England (1714-1837) when its elector became King George I of England. During this association Hanover was invaded twice: during the Seven Years War (1756-63) and the French Revolutionary and Napoleonic Wars. Disputed by the French and Prussians, it was annexed by Prussia after the Seven Weeks' War (1866), remaining a part of Prussia until 1946, when it became part of the state of Lower Saxony, West Germany. Major cities of Hanover include Hanover and Göttingen.

Hanover (pop. 508,300), or Hannover, city on the Leine River in northwest Germany, capital of the state of Lower Saxony. A railway and manufacturing center, Hanover produces iron, steel, and machinery, and is known for its annual industrial fair. The city was chartered in 1241, and was the capital of the electorate of Hanover from 1692 and of the kingdom of Hanover 1815-66. It has been rebuilt since its bombing during World War II.
See also: Germany.

Hanover, House of, reigning family of Hanover, in Germany, and of Great Britain (1714-1901). In 1658 the 1st Elector of Hanover married Sophia, granddaughter of James I, heir to the British throne by the Act of Settlement (1701). Her son became George I of Britain. By Salic law, his descendant, Victoria, could not become queen of Hanover, and from 1837, when she assumed the British crown, the thrones separated. On Edward VII's accession (1901) the family name became Saxe-Coburg (after Prince Albert), and in 1917 was changed to Windsor.

Hansberry, Lorraine (1930-65), African American playwright and civil rights activist. She was the youngest American to win the New York Drama Critics Circle Award for her play *A Raisin in the Sun* (1959), about a black family living in Chicago. The first play by a black woman to run on Broadway, it was made into a film (1961), for which it won a Cannes Film Festival award. *The Sign in Sidney Brustein's Window* (1964), a play completed during her final illness, portrays conflicts in the life of a Jewish liberal. Other selected writings were collected in *To Be Young, Gifted, and Black* (1969).

Hanseatic League, medieval confederation of North German towns and merchants organized to protect their trading interests in the Baltic Sea and throughout Europe. The league was created by the Hansas, companies having trading interests outside Germany. It arose informally in the late 12th century, and by the middle of the 14th century, more than 70 German cities had entered into mutual alliance treaties. In 1358 the league was formally declared. Its capital was Lübeck on Germany's northern coast. Assemblies were held there to decide on monopolies, trading rights, and other policy matters. Members of the league established commercial centers in many foreign towns, including Bergen (Norway), London, and Novgorod (Russia). The league's strength declined with the rise of nationalism in Europe, and it disappeared in the 17th century.

Hansen's disease *see:* Leprosy.

Hanson, Howard (1896-1981), U.S. conductor, teacher, and composer in the Romantic tradition. He won a Prix de Rome (1921) and was director of the Eastman School of Music, Rochester, N.Y. (1924-64). Hanson's *Fourth Symphony* won a Pulitzer Prize in 1944.

Hanson, John (1721-83), U.S. political leader, first president of the Congress of Confederation, under the Articles of Confederation (1781). He served in the Maryland Assembly (1757-1779) and was a leader in both civil and military resistance to the British during the Revolutionary War.

Hanukkah, Jewish holiday commemorating the rededication of the Temple of Jerusalem in 164 B.C. after Judas Maccabeus's victory over the Hellenic king Antiochus IV. Known as the Festival of Lights, it is celebrated by the lighting of

candles in an 8-branched candle holder called a menorah. The holiday lasts for 8 days, beginning on the 25th of Kislev the third month of the Jewish calendar (approximately Dec.).
See also: Judaism.

Hanyang *see:* Wuhan.

Hapsburg, House of *see:* Habsburg, House of.

Hara-kiri, or *seppuku*, ancient Japanese act of ceremonial suicide, in which a short sword was used to slash the abdomen from left to right, then upward. Used by warriors to escape capture by the enemy, obligatory hara-kiri was abolished in 1868.
See also: Samurai.

Harappa *see:* Indus Valley civilization.

Harare (formerly Salisbury; pop. 656,000), capital and largest city of the Republic of Zimbabwe. It was founded as Fort Salisbury in 1890 by the British South Africa Company and became the capital of the colony of Southern Rhodesia in 1923. It remained capital during the period of the colonial Federation of Rhodesia and Nyasaland (1953-63), and under the white minority rule of the Ian Smith government (1964-79). It became the capital of the independent country of Zimbabwe in 1980, changing its name to Harare in 1982. Harare is Zimbabwe's financial, commercial, and manufacturing center. Its industries include steel, chemicals, and textiles.
See also: Zimbabwe.

Harbin (pop. 2,590,000), city in northeast China on the Sungari River, capital of Heilongjiang province. Established by Russia as a railroad administration center (1895), Harbin once had a large European population. It was controlled by China and Japan jointly after the Russo-Japanese War (1904-5) and was occupied by Japan 1932-45. Still a major railway center, it is also an important port and a center for the Manchurian machinery, chemical, oil, and coal industries.
See also: China.

Hardening of the arteries *see:* Arteriosclerosis.

Harding, Warren Gamaliel (1865-1923), 29th president of the United States. Harding's administration was marred by scandals, and his imprudent political appointments and lack of personal decisiveness have made historians rank him as one of the weakest presidents in U.S. history.
Early life. Harding studied law, sold insurance, and taught school before finding his vocation—journalism—while working for the *Marion Democratic Mirror.* In 1884, Harding and a friend bought a newspaper, the *Marion Star*, and built it into a flourishing enterprise. In 1891, he married Florence Kling DeWolfe, a wealthy divorcée.
Politics. Harding's impressive appearance and speaking ability made it natural for him to enter politics. In 1898, he won a seat in the Ohio Senate. He was reelected in 1900 and, in 1903, was elected lieutenant governor. In 1910, he was defeated as the Republican candidate for governor. Two years later, he was chosen to nominate William Howard Taft, a fellow Ohioan, for a second term as president.
At the urging of Mrs. Harding and Harry M. Daugherty, a close friend and active lobbyist, Harding entered and won the 1914 race for U.S. Senate. Popular among senators, Harding gained national notice as keynote speaker and permanent chairman of the 1916 Republican national convention. He was persuaded, again by his wife and Daugherty, to seek the presidency in 1920. When the party convention in Chicago was deadlocked between chief contenders Leonard Wood and Frank Lowden, powerful Republican senators and party bosses met at Chicago's Blackstone Hotel in what Daugherty called the "smoke-filled room." They agreed on Harding as a compromise candidate and he was nominated the next day.
Harding's promise of a return to "normalcy" struck a resonant chord in war-weary voters. He and his running mate, Calvin Coolidge, easily defeated Democratic candidates James M. Cox and Franklin D. Roosevelt.
Presidency. As president, Harding largely acquiesced to Cabinet officers, Congress, and pressure groups. He refused to enter the League of Nations but his secretary of state, Charles Evans Hughes, called the Washington Disarmament Conference of 1921 and 1922. Harding's administration cut public debt and cut or abolished high wartime taxes.
Harding gave important government posts to many of his friends, "the Ohio gang," among whom corruption and dishonesty slowly emerged. In the Teapot Dome scandal, Harding's secretary of the interior, Albert B. Fall, was convicted of accepting a bribe for leasing government-owned oil reserves to influential oilmen. Scandal also enveloped Secretary of State Harry Daugherty when an aide's suicide revealed corruption at the Department of Justice, the Treasury, and the Veterans' Bureau. In June 1923, working to restore his administration's crumbling popularity, Harding embarked on a speaking tour through the West. While in Alaska, he received upsetting news of the Senate investigation of the Teapot Dome scandal. His friends' betrayal broke Harding's spirit, and he fell ill. He died on August 2. News of the scandals had scarcely broken; the unknowing public deeply mourned his passing. Vice President Calvin Coolidge completed his term.

Warren Gamaliel Harding

29th U.S. President

Born:	Corsica (now Blooming Grove), Ohio; Nov. 2, 1865
Term:	Mar. 1921-Aug. 1923
Vice president:	Calvin Coolidge
Political party:	Republican
Spouse:	Florence Kling DeWolfe Harding
Children:	None
Died:	San Francisco, Calif., Aug. 2, 1923

Hardness, measure of the resistance of a substance to being scratched by another substance. Resistance to scratching is measured on a scale named for Friedrich Mohs (1773-1839), who chose 10 minerals as reference points, ranging from talc (hardness 1) to diamond (10). A modified Mohs scale is now usually used, with 5 additional reference points. Resistance to indentation is also measured by other scales as well, such as the Brinell, Rockwell, and Vickers scales.

Hardy, Oliver *see:* Laurel and Hardy.

Hardy, Thomas (1840-1928), English novelist and poet. His first successful novel was *Far from the Madding Crowd* (1874). Nine others, including *The Return of the Native* (1878) and *Tess of the d'Urbervilles* (1891), appeared over the next 20 years. *Jude the Obscure* (1895), partially autobiographical, so offended Victorian morality that Hardy abandoned novels but continued writing poetry. His epic verse drama *The Dynasts* (1903-08) and his later lyric poetry are highly regarded. The "last of the great Victorians," Hardy influenced 20th-century English literature. His view of life was essentially tragic, his characters often seeming to be victims of malignant fate.

Hare, any of various species (genus *Lepus*) of herbivorous mammals of the rabbit family, including the jackrabbit. Adapted for swift jumping and characterized by long ears, powerful hindlegs and feet, and short tails, hares live entirely above ground

Hare

in grasslands in Eurasia, Africa, and North America. Unlike rabbits, they move by jumping instead of running. Some species molt into a white coat in winter.

Harebell *see:* Bluebell.

Hare Krishnas, popular name for members of a Hindu sect (the International Society for Krishna Consciousness), known for their orange robes, shaved heads, and public chanting of "Hare Krishna" in praise of the Hindu god Krishna. The movement was founded in 1965 in New York City by A.C. Bhaktivedanta Swami Prabhupada and teaches devotion to Krishna as a way to enlightenment.
See also: Hinduism.

Harelip *see:* Cleft palate.

Hargreaves, James (1720?-78), British inventor of the spinning jenny (1764), a machine for spinning several threads at once. Public uproar over loss of jobs forced him to flee his native Blackburn for Nottingham (1768), where he patented the jenny (1770).

Hari-kari *see:* Hara-kiri.

Harkins, William Draper (1873-1951), U.S. chemist who predicted the existence of the neutron (1927) and theorized the possibility of nuclear fusion: the combination of 4 hydrogen atoms to become 1 helium atom with a minute extra mass converted into energy. He was the first to propose that this fusion process fueled stars.
See also: Fusion; Neutron.

Harlan, 2 associate justices of the U.S. Supreme Court, grandfather and grandson. **John Marshall Harlan** (1833-1911) served as a Supreme Court justice from 1877 to 1911. An independent, he is best known for his 1896 dissenting opinion that Jim Crow laws, which established the principle of "separate but equal" racial segregation, in fact deprived black citizens of equal protection of the law. **John Marshall Harlan** (1899-1971) was appointed to the Supreme Court by President Dwight D. Eisenhower in 1955 and served until 1971. He had served as assistant U.S. attorney, chief counsel to the N.Y. State Crime Commission, and member of the U.S. Court of Appeals.
See also: Supreme Court of the United States.

Harlem, neighborhood in the northern part of the borough of Manhattan, New York City. Founded in 1658 as the Dutch settlement of Nieuw Haarlem, 10 mi (16 km) north of New Amsterdam, Harlem remained a rural village until the mid-19th century, when it became a middle class residential section of the city. An influx of African Americans beginning just before World War I turned it into the most vibrant black community in the United States. In the 1920s it was the center of the explosion of African-American culture known as the Harlem Renaissance. Economic conditions deteriorated after World War II, but the neighborhood has retained its cultural and political importance.

Harlem Renaissance, period of cultural development among U.S. blacks, centered on Harlem, New York City, in the 1920s. In this period African-American literature changed from imitative works to penetrating analyses of black culture and novels of protest, displaying racial pride. Notable writers included Countee Cullen, Langston Hughes, Jean Toomer, and Zora Neale Hurston.

Harlequin snake *see:* Coral snake.

Harlow, Harry Frederick (1905-81), U.S. psychologist who studied the effects in monkeys of deprivation of maternal love and other social contact. Harlow's conclusions were that social contact in childhood is necessary for adult sociability and that maternal attention in infancy is necessary for the development of adult maternal instincts.
See also: Psychology.

Harlow, Jean (1911-37), platinum-blonde U.S. film actress who began her career as a sex symbol and developed into a gifted comedienne. Her films include *Hell's Angels* (1930), *Platinum Blonde* (1932), and *Dinner at Eight* (1933).

Harmonica, or mouth organ, musical instrument that contains a number of small metal reeds of graduated size enclosed in slots in a short narrow box. This is held to the lips and moved from side to side to obtain notes.

Harmonic motion, vibrating or oscillating motion that repeats itself in equal time intervals, as in the motion of a swinging pendulum. This is known as simple harmonic motion (SHM). The central point about which oscillation takes place is called the *equilibrium point*, and the distance of the object from this point at a given time is called its *displacement*. Harmonic motion occurs only within certain limits. If either the pendulum or the spring is displaced too far, the motion will become irregular.

Harmonics, basic compounds of a musical tone, consisting of the various vibrations of sound that produce what sounds like a single tone. The string of a guitar, for instance, will vibrate along its whole length, but also in partial segments, making a blend of tones that gives the instrument its characteristic sound.
See also: Sound; Tone.

Harmonium, small reed organ with pedals for pumping air past the reeds. It was popular in the late 19th century as a family instrument, but has mostly been used in chapels as a substitute for a standard organ.

Harmony, in music, the simultaneous sounding of 2 or more tones or parts; also the relation and progression of chords and the rules governing their relationship. Traditional harmony is based on a 3-tone musical structure, with notes named for their position on the musical scale: the lowest tone is called the root, the middle tone is called the third (because it is the third tone above the root), and the next is called the fifth (5 tones above the root). Chords can be erected on any note of the traditional 8-note scale.

Harness racing, form of horse racing in which each horse draws a lightweight, two-wheeled cart (called a sulky) driven by a driver. Most harness races are run by pacers, horses who move two legs on the same side at the same time, producing a fast, rocking gait. Other races are for trotters, who move opposing pairs of legs together. Harness racing is generally run by standardbred horses on an oval dirt and clay track 1/2-1 mi (0.8-1.6 km) long. The major annual event in U.S. harness racing is the Hambletonian. Harness racing originated in Asia Minor in ancient times and became popular in the United States and Europe in the 19th century.

Harnett, William Michael (1848-92), Irish-born U.S. painter. Such still lifes as *After the Hunt* show his extremely realistic *trompe-l'oeil* (eye-deceiving) style.

Harold, name of two kings of England. **Harold I** (d. 1040), called Harefoot, ruled England 1035-40. He was the illegitimate son of King Canute, Danish king and ruler of England, whose legitimate son Hardecanute succeeded Harold. Harold's reign was characterized by violent struggles with other royal claimants. **Harold II** (1022?-66), last Anglo-Saxon king of England ruled in 1066. As Earl of Wessex (1053), he was one of the most powerful men in England. When King Edward the Confessor died in 1066, both Harold and Duke William of Normandy claimed the throne. The English nobility supported Harold's claim, and William invaded England. Harold was killed fighting William's forces in the Battle of Hastings.
See also: England.

Harold, kings of Norway. **Harold I** or **Harold Fairhair** (c.860-c.940) was the first king of Norway. He succeeded his father,

Halfdam the Black, as king of Vestfold (in southeast Norway) and then unified Norway by defeating contending local rulers. **Harold III** or **Harold Hardrada** (1015-66), ruled jointly with his nephew Magnus I (1046-47), and singly after the death of Magnus (1047-66). He founded the city of Oslo. He tried to extend his rule to Denmark and England, but was killed by the forces of Harold II of England during an invasion of England.
See also: Norway.

Harp, musical instrument consisting of a number of strings of different lengths stretched across a frame. The modern harp is over 5 ft (1.5 m) tall and rests on the ground, with the player seated next to it. It has 7 pedals to adjust the strings and alter the pitch of the notes and a range of nearly 7 octaves.

Harper, Frances Ellen Watkins (1825-1911), African-American writer and lecturer. Her collected *Poems* (1871), and other books (later published in such collections as *Poems on Miscellaneous Subjects* [1954]), deal with antislavery and other racial themes. She also wrote a novel, *Iola Leroy* (1893). Born in Baltimore of free parents, she began writing poetry in her teens, and in 1854 began delivering antislavery lectures in the United States and Canada. Later she spoke in support of women's suffrage and was active in the Woman's Christian Temperance Union.

Harpers Ferry (pop. 400), town in eastern West Virginia, site of a federal armory established by George Washington. The Potomac and Shenandoah rivers meet at Harpers Ferry, forming the borders of Maryland, Virginia, and West Virginia. John Brown's dramatic raid on the arsenal there in 1859 was one of the events leading to the Civil War. Because of its strategic location, the town was the scene of many battles during the war. General Thomas J. "Stonewall" Jackson captured it from Union forces in 1862, taking 12,000 prisoners, the largest number captured in a single battle during the war. Union forces later retook it. Today it is a small residential town, the site of a national park in which the Civil War battle sites are preserved.
See also: Brown, John; Civil War, U.S.

Harpsichord, keyboard instrument in which the strings are plucked by quills rather than hit by felt hammers as in a piano. The harpsichord was very popular from the 14th to the 16th century, and much great music was written for it, notably by J.S. Bach, François Couperin, and Domenico Scarlatti. Its popularity declined with the development of the piano.

Harpy, in Greek mythology, birdlike monster with the head of a woman. Harpies were agents of divine punishment.
See also: Mythology.

Harpy eagle, large bird of prey (*Harpia harpyja*) of the hawk family, native to tropical forests of the Western Hemisphere. This large eagle weighs over 10 lbs (4.5 kg) and may have a wingspan of 7 ft (2 m). It has a black-crested gray head, black back, and white underside. It preys on monkeys, sloths, opossums, and porcupines. The harpy eagle is named for a flying predatory creature of Greek mythology.

Harrier, breed of dog developed for fox and hare hunting, possibly as long ago as A.D. 1,000 Harriers stand about 21 in. (50 cm) tall and weigh 35 to 55 lbs (16 to 25 kg). Compact and sturdy, with a keen sense of smell, they have been used in the U.S. for rabbit hunting since colonial times.

Harriman, family name of a father and son prominent in U.S. commerce and government. **Edward Henry Harriman** (1848-1909) was a railroad tycoon and stockbroker who, after financial struggles with J.J. Hill, joined with Hill and J.P. Morgan to create a holding company designed to prevent competition on the railroads. It was dissolved by the Supreme Court in 1904. His son, **W(illiam) Averell Harriman** (1891-1986), was board chairman of Union Pacific 1933-46, served under Franklin D. Roosevelt in the National Recovery Administration, and carried on lend-lease negotiations in Britain (1941-42). Named U.S. ambassador to Moscow in 1943, he took part in all the major wartime conferences. He was the ambassador to London in 1946, became secretary of commerce in 1946-48, and was governor of New York 1955-59. He was under-secretary of state 1963-65 and ambassador-at-large 1963-65. In 1968 he was the head U.S. negotiator at the Paris peace talks on the Vietnam war.

Harrington, James (1611-77), English philosopher best known for his *Commonwealth of Oceana* (1656), a treatise on the ideal state ruler. His ideas prefigured doctrines of the American and French revolutions.

Harris, Benjamin (1673-1716), English-American bookseller and writer, publisher of the first newspaper in America (1690). An Anabaptist and Whig, he left England in 1686 to escape punishment for his written attacks on Roman Catholics and Quakers. In Boston he ran a bookstore and coffeehouse and tried to publish *Publick Occurrences, Both Foreign and Domestick,* which Boston authorities suppressed after just one issue. He later published *The New-England Primer*, a speller based on his politically inflammatory textbook, *The Protestant Tutor* (1679). He returned to London in 1695 and published the *London Post* 1699-1706.

Harris, Frank (1856-1931), British author best known for his biographies of Shakespeare, Oscar Wilde, and G. B. Shaw. (1915-27) and his 3-volume autobiography, *My Life and Loves* (1923-27).

Harris, Joel Chandler (1848-1908), U.S. southern journalist and regional author. His tales of plantation life, many featuring the former slave and folk philosopher Uncle Remus, were based on African-American folklore and written largely in dialect. Some of his most well-known works are *The Tar Baby* (1904) and *Uncle Remus and Br'er Rabbit* (1906).

Primitive arched harps were played 5,000 years ago in ancient Egypt (right). By the 8th century the frame harp, with forepillar, had developed (left). Key:
1. neck
2. metal plate
3. tuning pegs
4. bridge pins
5. rotating discs
6. strings
7. forepillar containing seven pedal rods
8. sound board
9. eyelets
10. pedals
11. feet.

Harris, Patricia Roberts (1924-85), U.S. public official, first African-American woman to be a U.S. ambassador, to hold a cabinet post, and to serve as a director of a U.S. corporation. Active in the Democratic Party and the civil rights movement, she was appointed ambassador to Luxembourg by President Lyndon B. Johnson in 1965. She was dean of Howard University School of Law 1969-70 and was later a director of International Business Machines Corporation (IBM). Under President Jimmy Carter she was secretary of housing and urban development (1977-79) and secretary of health, education, and welfare (1979-81).

Harris, Roy (1898-1979), U.S. composer. He studied in Paris with Nadia Boulanger and later won fame as a teacher. The *Third Symphony* (1937) is perhaps his best-known work. His work is characterized by its energy and melodious tones.

Harrisburg (pop. 587,986), state capital of Pennsylvania and seat of Dauphin County. Located in the southeastern part of the state on the Susquehanna River, Harrisburg was first settled in 1718. The construction of the Erie Canal and the Pennsylvania Railroad helped maintain its prominence as a trading center. It is now known for its steel plants. Other industries include meatpacking, printing, airplane parts, and machinery.
See also: Pennsylvania.

Harrison, Benjamin (1726-91), American Revolutionary leader. He was a Virginia delegate to the Continental Congress (1774-78) and a signer of the Declaration of Independence. He also served as governor of Virginia (1781-84) and member of the Virginia legislature (1749-75, 1784-91). Both his son and his great-grandson, William Henry Harrison and Benjamin Harrison, became U.S. presidents.

Harrison, Benjamin (1833-1901), 23rd president of the United States. Harrison, the grandson of President William Henry Harrison, gained the presidency at a time when labor unrest, agricultural depression, and fiscal controversies were beginning to shake the Republican party's hold over national affairs.

Early life. After graduating from Miami University of Ohio in 1852, Harrison studied law in Cincinnati; the following year, he married Caroline Lavinia Scott. In 1854, Harrison was admitted to the bar and set up practice in Indianapolis, where he became active in the newly formed Republican party. During the Civil War, Harrison helped recruit the 70th Indiana Volunteers and fought in General William Tecumseh Sherman's Atlanta campaign. After the war, Harrison resumed his Indianapolis practice, becoming a well-known corporation attorney.

Politics. Harrison lost Indiana's 1876 gubernatorial race but, in 1881, was elected to the U.S. Senate by the Indiana legislature. As a senator, Harrison supported high tariffs, civil-service reforms, generous veterans' pensions, and the admission of new states to the Union. In 1887, he missed reelection by a single vote. As Indiana's favorite-son candidate at the 1888 Republican convention, Harrison won the presidential nomination. He won by a majority of electoral votes, although Grover Cleveland, the incumbent president, had more popular votes.

President. Under Harrison, U.S. expansionism took important strides forward. U.S. claims to Samoa were established, the first Pan-American Conference was held in Washington, and a long-standing dispute with Britain over fur-seal hunting in the Bering Sea was arbitrated. During Harrison's first 2 years in office, the Republicans held a majority in both houses of Congress. However, Harrison could exercise little executive leadership because the party was controlled by political leaders and bosses over whom he lacked influence. He signed an act that nearly doubled the pensions of incapacitated Civil War veterans. He also signed the McKinley Tariff Act, which imposed the highest duties on imported goods the nation had ever experienced. The cost of living shot up, causing widespread discontent.

A growing agricultural depression and drought in the Great Plains caused farmers to organize into Farmers' Alliances that evolved into the People's, or Populist, party. To help raise farm prices, Harrison signed the Sherman Silver Purchase Act. He also aided passage of the Sherman Antitrust Act, which declared illegal all trusts or monopolies that restrained trade. But farmers' discontent continued to grow and, in 1890, the Democrats won control of the House of Representatives. The second 2 years of Harrison's term were largely barren of results.

Growing Populist unrest and such bitter labor disputes as the Homestead Strike probably cost Harrison the 1892 election. Grover Cleveland won a solid victory, while James Weaver, the Populist candidate, received more than a million votes.

Retirement. Harrison returned to his Indianapolis law practice. His first wife had died 2 weeks before his electoral defeat; in 1896, he married her widowed niece, Mary Dimmick. Harrison, who continued to gain distinction as a lawyer, died at his home in Indianapolis in 1901.

Benjamin Harrison

23rd U.S President

Born:	North Bend, Ohio; Aug. 20, 1833
Term:	Mar. 1889-Mar. 1893
Vice president:	Levi P. Morton
Political party:	Republican
Spouses:	Caroline Lavinia Scott Harrison; Mary Scott Lord Dimmick Harrison
Children:	3
Died:	Indianapolis, Ind.; Mar. 13, 1901

Harrison, George *see:* Beatles, The.

Harrison, William Henry (1773-1841), 9th president of the United States. Harrison, a military hero and the first successful candidate of the Whig party, died 1 month after taking office—the briefest term of any U.S. chief executive.

Early life. Harrison's father was a prominent figure in Virginia politics and a signer of the Declaration of Independence. The young Harrison attended Hampden-Sydney College, then studied medicine in Philadelphia. After his father's death in 1791, he entered the army and fought Indians in the Northwest Territory. He rose rapidly in rank and was given command of Fort Washington (now Cincinnati, Ohio) in 1795. He married Anna Symmes the same year.

In 1798, Harrison resigned from the army and settled at North Bend, Ohio. He was elected territorial delegate to Congress in 1799 and was appointed governor of Indiana Territory in 1800. By a series of treaties with the Indians (1802-09), Harrison opened 33 million acres of Ohio and Indiana to large-scale white settlement. But the Indians, led by Shawnee chief Tecumseh, formed a confederation with British support and threatened war if U.S. settlers occupied the Wabash Valley. Harrison, leading the territorial militia, invaded the Wabash Valley in 1811. He repulsed an Indian attack at the mouth of Tippecanoe Creek, which made him a national hero—"Old Tippecanoe." During the War of 1812, Harrison, who commanded all U.S. troops in the Northwest, defeated the British and Native Americans at the Battle of the Thames in Ontario.

Politics. In 1814, Harrison left the military and entered politics. He served in the U.S. House of Representatives (1816-19), Ohio Senate (1819-21), and U.S. Senate (1825-28). After a brief stint as U.S. minister to Colombia, he retired to North Bend, where he served as county recorder and clerk of the county court.

In 1836, Harrison was one of the disunited Whig Party's 3 presidential candidates. He garnered the most votes of any Whig, but Democrat Martin Van Buren won the presidency. At the Whigs' first national convention in 1839, they nominated Harrison for the presidency and John Tyler for the vice presidency.

The 1840 campaign was the most colorful the United States had ever experienced. The slogan "Tippecanoe and Tyler Too" glossed over the Whigs' lack of any positive program or political position. When the Democrats sneered at Harrison as the "log cabin and hard cider" candidate, Whigs built campaign log cabins and freely dispensed hard cider. Harrison supporters represented the well-born candidate as a humble son of the people to contrast him with Van Buren, "the aristocrat." In the largest turnout the nation had ever seen, the popular balloting was close but Harrison won by an overwhelming majority of electoral votes.

President. The inauguration was held March 4, 1841, in a cold drizzle. Harrison, who delivered his inaugural address without hat or overcoat, caught a cold that developed into pneumonia. He died on April 4, precisely one month after taking office.

Harsha, or Harshavardhana (A.D. 590?-647), king of northern India (606-47), patron of the arts, and writer. Harsha added conquered territory to the kingdoms he inherited, establishing a unified monarchy after the anarchy that had followed the Hun invasions of the 5th and 6th centuries. His writings included poetry and 3 well-known Sanskrit plays, *Nagananda, Ratnavali,* and *Priyadarsika.*

Hart *see:* Red deer.

Hart, Gary Warren (1936-), U.S. politician. A lawyer for the U.S. Department of Justice (1964) and special assistant to the U.S. secretary of the interior (1966), he served as U.S. Senator from Colorado (1974-88). Hart gained nationwide attention in his 1984 campaign for the Democratic presidential nomination and also pursued the 1988 nomination, but withdrew from the campaign after newspaper accounts of his personal life suggested marital infidelity.

Hart, John (1711?-79), American Revolutionary leader. He served in the New Jersey Assembly (1761-71) and as speaker of the N.J. General Assembly (1776). He was a delegate to the Continental Congress (1776) and a signer of the Declaration of Independence.

Hart, Lorenz Milton (1895-1943), U.S. lyricist who collaborated with Richard Rodgers on 29 musical comedies. The most famous are *A Connecticut Yankee* (1927), *The Boys from Syracuse* (1938), and *Pal Joey* (1940).

Hart, Moss (1904-61), U.S. dramatist and director. With George S. Kaufman he wrote *You Can't Take It with You* (1936) and *The Man Who Came to Dinner* (1939). He directed the Broadway hits *My Fair Lady* (1956) and *Camelot* (1960).

Harte, Bret (Francis Brett Harte; 1836-1902), U.S. writer whose short stories of frontier life helped create the mythology of the West. Among the stories that brought him worldwide fame are "The Luck of Roaring Camp" (1868) and "The Outcasts of Poker Flat" (1869). He was U.S. consul in Germany and Scotland (1878-85), and when his popularity in the United States declined, he settled in Britain, where he spent his last years.

Hartebeest, large antelope (genus *Alcelaphus*) with a long and narrow head and lyre-shaped horns. Hartebeest used to live all over Africa and are still common in many places. Related to the gnu, they are very fast runners, perhaps second in speed only to the cheetah.

Hartford (pop. 767,841), capital and largest city of Connecticut, situated near the center of the state on the Connecticut River. Hartford is called the insurance capital of the world, and more policies are underwritten there than anywhere else in the Western Hemisphere. The headquarters of more than 30 insurance companies are located in and around the city, which was an important commercial and intellectual center in the early years of the United States. Today the city produces a wide range of manufactured goods, including electrical equipment, precision tools, office machines, and airplane parts.
See also: Connecticut.

Hartford, George Huntington (1833-1917), U.S. merchant, cofounder of the Great Atlantic and Pacific Tea Company (A&P). Started as a tea trading company (1859), the corporation was expanded to a mail order house, and then to a chain of retail stores (1869). The stores were the forerunners of the modern supermarket (the first A&P supermarkets opened in 1936).

Hartford Convention, assembly of Federalist delegates from Massachusetts, Connecticut, Rhode Island, and Vermont, held secretly in Hartford, Conn., Dec. 1814, to Jan. 1815. Its purpose was to discuss New England's grievances against the federal government resulting largely from federal neglect during the War of 1812. The possibility of secession was raised, but with the end of the war the convention's recommendations were undercut, and the prestige of the Federalist party was ruined.

Hartley, Marsden (1877-1943), U.S. artist who experimented with cubism and abstraction and later returned to impressionistic but realistic depictions of natural scenes. He was best known for paintings of his native Maine.

Harun al-Rashid (ar-Rashid; 766-809), fifth Abbasid caliph of Baghdad (r. 786-809) whose empire extended from northern Africa to the Indus River in India. His rule marked the acme of Arab civilization and culture, with an unparalleled flourishing of science and the arts. He appears as a character in many of the stories of the *Arabian Nights.*

William Henry Harrison

9th U.S. President	
Born:	Charles City County, Va.; Feb. 9, 1773
Term:	Mar. 1841-Apr. 1841
Vice president:	John Tyler
Political party:	Whig
Spouse:	Anna Symmes Harrison
Children:	10
Died:	Washington, D.C.; Apr. 4, 1841

Harunobu (Suzuki Harunobu; 1725-70), Japanese artist who perfected multicolored printmaking. At a time when the

A print by Harunobu

Japanese were limited to black-ink prints with no more than 2 other colors, Harunobu refined a process of using wood blocks to print with as many as 10 colors. His subjects typically captured the calmness and intimacy of ordinary life.

Harvard, John (1607-38), U.S. cleric, first benefactor of Harvard College. Born in London, he emigrated to Massachusetts in 1637 to become Charlestown's minister. In 1638 he bequeathed half his estate and his library to the college, which was named for him in 1639.

Harvard University, oldest university in the United States, founded by the General Court of Massachusetts in 1636. Originally an educational institution for Puritan ministers, it evolved into a general university. Under the presidency of C.W. Eliot (1869-1910) Harvard developed into one of the world's great universities, with many graduate schools affiliated to it. It now has nearly 200 allied institutions, including libraries, laboratories, museums, and observatories. Harvard University derives its name from John Harvard, the first benefactor of the institution.

Harvestman *see:* Daddy longlegs.

Harvest mite *see:* Chigger.

Harvest moon, popularly, the full moon that occurs nearest to the time of the autumnal equinox (around Sept. 23). The moon rises at about the same time for several nights and may be bright enough to help farmers in harvesting their crops. The effect is most pronounced in high latitudes, such as in Canada. In the southern hemisphere the harvest moon occurs around the time of the vernal equinox (around Mar. 21).

Harvey, William (1578-1657), British physician who pioneered modern medicine, discovering the circulation of blood. In *On the Movement of the Heart and Blood in Animals* (1628) he argued that the heart acts as a pump and that the blood circulates endlessly about the body; that there are valves in the heart and veins that cause blood to flow in one direction only; and that the necessary pressure comes from the lower left-hand side of the heart. His theories were not fully confirmed until the early 19th century. He also made important studies of the development of the embryo.
See also: Circulatory system; Heart.

Hashemite Dynasty, Arab royal family claiming descent from the grandfather of the prophet Muhammad, hereditary sharifs of Mecca from the 11th century until 1919. After World War I the Hashemites Faisal I and Abdullah Ibn Hussein became kings of Iraq and Jordan respectively; Abdullah's grandson Hussein is the present king of Jordan.

Hashish, drug produced from a resin obtained from the top and the flowers of the hemp plant (*Cannabis sativa*). It is a physically nonaddictive drug whose effects range from a feeling of euphoria to distortion of perception. Hashish comes from the same plant as marijuana (which is made from the dried leaves and stalks), but contains from 5 to 8 times as much Tetrahydrocannabinol (THC), the chemical responsible for the mind-altering effects. Hashish is mainly produced in the Middle East and India and has been in use for many centuries, although it is still illegal in many countries.
See also: Drug; Drug abuse.

Hasidism, Jewish pietistic movement, that can be divided into 3 distinct historical eras. During the 2nd and 3rd centuries B.C. the first Hasidim (Hasideans or Assideans) were devout members of the Jewish faith who resisted Greek influence. In Germany during the Middle Ages there developed a messianic Hasidim known as Hasidei Ashkenaz. In 18th-century Poland, Israel ben Eliezer (Ba'al Shem Tov), reacting against the studious formalism of rabbinical traditions established a movement grouped around *tzadikkim*, holy men, whose followers are *hasidism* ("pious ones"). Hasidism still flourishes in Israel and the United States.
See also: Ba'al Shem Tov.

Haskalah (Hebrew, "enlightenment"), cultural movement that attempted to reform traditional Jewish customs. It was initiated during the late 18th century by some Jews who had experienced European lifestyle and wanted to modernize Jewish customs to fit more easily into mainstream society, after centuries of Jewish discrimination. Haskalah incorporated such ideas as having Jews wear a more contemporary dress instead of the traditional Jewish clothing and having Jews adopt the local language instead of speaking Yiddish. The movement also encouraged Jews to add nonreligious curriculum to schools and to begin careers in t' ◦ liberal arts.

Hassam, Childe (1859-1935), U.S. painter and graphic artist. He studied in Paris and was one of the first U.S. artists to adopt the techniques of impressionism, painting many New York and New England landscapes.

Hassan II (1929-), king of Morocco since 1961. He initiated a partial democratization in 1962, but has retained nearly absolute power, despite an attempted coup in 1971. A protracted war (beginning in 1976) to gain control of Western Sahara, a former Spanish Sahara colony, has strained the Moroccan economy.
See also: Morocco.

Hastie, William Henry (1904-76), first black judge appointed to the U.S. Court of Appeals and first black governor of the Virgin Islands (1946-49). Hastie served on the bench from 1950 until he retired in 1971. Earlier, he was on the board of directors of the National Association for the Advancement of Colored People (NAACP).

Hastings, Battle of, first decisive military encounter of the Norman conquest of England, fought between the troops of King Harold of England and Duke William of Normandy on Oct. 14, 1066. William crossed the English Channel while Harold was in northern England defeating a Norwegian invasion. Forced marches brought Harold south with an exhausted and depleted force. Harold's axmen were swept from a strong hilltop position, and Harold himself was killed in the battle. By 1070 most Anglo-Saxon nobles were dead or expropriated, and a new, French-speaking ruling class was imposed on England.
See also: Norman Conquest.

Hastings, Warren (1732-1818), first governor-general of British India (1774-84). Starting as a clerk in 1750, he rose high in the British East India Company. Criticized in England as an aggressive and sometimes arbitrary governor, he was impeached (1787) on charges of extortion despite his earlier resignation. He was acquitted after a very long trial (1788-95).

Hat, head covering, usually with a brim all around it, as distinct from a brimless cap or hood. In various countries and cultures hats symbolize social status or function, as well as being fashion items.

Hatch Act, U.S. law sponsored by Sen. Carl Hatch in 1939, amended in 1940. It prohibits most federal employees from actively participating in political campaigns and outlaws offering employment or other compensation in exchange for political support in election campaigns. Parts of the Hatch Act barring state employees from political activities were repealed in 1974.

Hatcher, Richard Gordon (1933-), U.S. politician. When elected mayor of Gary, Ind., in 1967, Hatcher, a Democrat, became one of the first blacks to govern a major U.S. city. He rallied for civil rights issues and was popular among both black and white constituents. He won 4 reelections, serving 20 years until he was defeated in 1987.

Hathor, or Athyr, in ancient Egyptian religion, goddess of the sky. She has been associated with both Horus, a sky god, and Re, the sun god. Her son, Ihy, was a god of music. Hathor was often pictured as a woman with a 2-horned headpiece that held a sun.
See also: Mythology.

Hatshepsut (d. 1481 B.C.), queen of Egypt, 18th dynasty. She ruled with her husband and half-brother Thutmose II (r. 1512-1504 B.C.), becoming regent to his son and then assuming the powers and titles of pharaoh. She presided over a period of prosperity, and built the great temple of Der el-Bahri near Thebes.
See also: Egypt, Ancient.

Hauptmann, Gerhart (1862-1946), German author and playwright who pioneered naturalism in the German theater. His first play, *Before Dawn* (1889), dealing with social problems, won him overnight fame. It was followed by *The Weavers* (1892), a drama of working-class life, and many other works, both novels and poetry. He was awarded the 1912 Nobel Prize for literature.

Hausa, people of northwest Nigeria and neighboring Niger, numbering about 9 million, predominantly Muslim since the 14th century. Their language, also called Hausa, is widely spoken in West Africa, and they play a major role in Nigerian politics.

Havana (pop. 1,925,000), capital and largest city of Cuba, on the Gulf of Mexico. One of the largest cities in the West Indies, it was founded by the Spanish in 1515. It has an excellent harbor and is an industrial center. Oil and sugar refining, tobacco products, and rum distilleries are the main economic activities. The U.S. battleship *Maine* was sunk in Havana harbor and was the incident that ignited the Spanish-American War in 1898. The Cuban Revolution of 1959 deprived Havana of millions of dollars from U.S. tourists. In the early 1990s the government of Fidel Castro made some attempts to revive the previously important tourist industry.
See also: Cuba. Republic of.

Havel, Václav (1936-), Czech playwright and political leader, elected president of Czechoslovakia in 1989. A resistence leader under the Communist regime from the mid-1960s until 1989, he was repeatedly jailed, and his works (such as the play *The Memorandum*, 1965) were banned.

Haversian canals, minute passages in the outer bone layers. The canals carry blood to the inner bone tissue through combined efforts of blood and lymph vessels, nerves, and connective tissues. The canals are surrounded by bone tissue; together they make up a compact bone structure called the *Haversian system*, or *osteon*. The structure is named for the English physician Clopton Havers, who first noted the canals in the 17th century.

Haw *see:* Hawthorne.

Hawaii, fiftieth state of the United States, a chain of 8 major and more than 100 minor islands in the central Pacific Ocean, about 2,100 mi (3,380 km) from the U.S. mainland.

Hawaii

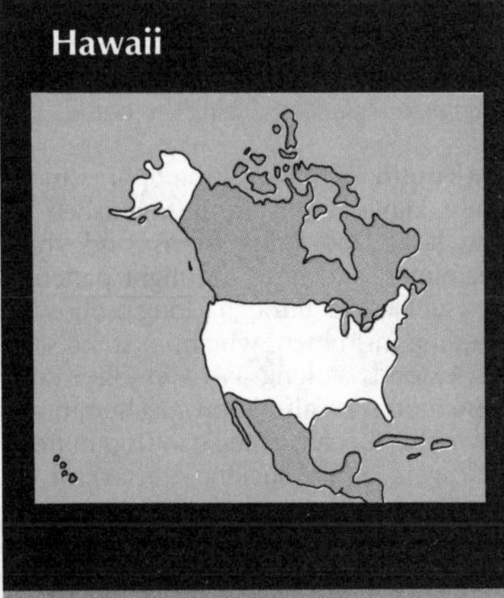

Capital:	Honolulu
Statehood:	August 21, 1959
Familiar name:	The Aloha State
Area:	6,471 sq mi (16,759 sq km) (ranks 47th)
Population:	1,115,274 (1990) (ranks 40th)
Elevation:	Highest—13,796 ft (4,205 m), Mauna Kea. Lowest—sea level
Motto:	*Ua mau ke ea o ka aina i ka pono* (The Life of the Land Is Perpetuated in Righteousness)
State flower:	Yellow Hibiscus
State bird:	Nene (Hawaiian goose)
State tree:	Kukui (Candlenut)
State song:	"Hawaii Ponoi" ("Hawaii's Own").

Oahu, one of the Hawaiian islands

Land and climate. Hawaii's islands are of volcanic origin, although all but the 8 major islands at the southeastern end of the chain have been reduced to coral atolls and small rock outcroppings. The largest island, Hawaii, which has given its name to the entire chain, has 5 volcanoes, including the extinct Mauna Kea (13,796 ft/4,025 m) and the active Mauna Loa (13,677 ft/4,169 m). Haleakala (10,023 ft/3,055 m), one of the world's largest extinct volcanic craters, is located on Maui. Oahu is home to 80% of the state's population and is the site of Honolulu. One of the largest natural harbors in the world, Pearl Harbor, is located on the south coast of Oahu. Located on Kauai, the garden island, is Mt. Waialeale (5,080 ft/1,548 m), one of the rainiest spots on earth, with an average yearly rainfall of 460 in (1,170 cm).
Kahoolawe, Molokai, Lanai, and Nihau are the other principal islands. The Hawaiian islands are in the path of cooling trade winds that give the subtropical state a mild climate throughout the year.
Economy. Tourism and military spending are the mainstays of the economy. Industry is largely devoted to food processing, the most important products being refined sugar and canned pineapple. Sugar cane is Hawaii's most important crop, and the state is one of the world's leading producers of pineapples.
Government. Hawaii's constitution, adopted in 1950, calls for a governor serving a 4-year term. The state legislature comprises 25 senators serving 4-year terms and 51 representatives serving 2-year terms. Hawaii sends 2 representatives and 2 senators to the U.S. Congress.
History. Polynesians settled the islands over 2,000 years ago. An Englishman, Capt. James Cook, was the first European to discover the islands, in 1778. In 1795, King Kamchamcha I united the islands

Hawaii's traditional hula dance

under his rule. The arrival of U.S. missionaries in 1820 began the process of westernization, and the first permanent sugar plantation in Hawaii was started by a U.S. company in 1835. As many as 300,000 native Hawaiians were living on the islands when the Europeans first arrived, but by 1853 the population was reduced to less than 75,000, due mainly to diseases brought by traders throughout the 1800s. Hawaii's monarchy fell in 1893, and the islands became a U.S. territory in 1900. The Japanese attack on Pearl Harbor, a U.S. naval base, on Dec. 7, 1941, brought the country into World War II (1939-45). Since the end of the war and statehood, Hawaii has continued to grow.

Hawaiian goose *see:* Nene.

Hawaiian honeycreeper, any of a family (Drepanididae) of small songbirds exclusive to Hawaii. There are 22 species. Honeycreepers have 3 types of bills, each suited to a different method of feeding. Honeycreepers with long, curved bills suck nectar from flowers, those with heavy bills crush seeds and insects, and those with strong, straight bills chisel tree bark. Many of the species are now extinct or endangered.

Hawaii Volcanos National Park, on Hawaii Island, established 1916, has among the largest and most active volcanos in the world. Mauna Loa (13,680 ft/4,170 m) has the Mokuaweoweo crater at its summit. Kilauea, 4,090 ft (1,247 m)

high and over 4 sq mi (10.4 sq km) in area, has a fiery floor called Halemaumau. The park has an area of 317 sq mi (821 sq km).
See also: National Parks Table.

Hawk, any of various fast-flying hunting birds of the Accipitridae family. Hawks have rounded wings and live mainly in woodlands and forests. Some catch their prey by fast flight while others soar in circles overhead and then drop to catch their prey in their talons. Most hawks feed on rodents or small birds.

Hawk

Hawke, Robert James Lee (1929-), prime minister of Australia 1983-90. He was the leader of the landslide election victory for the Australian Labor Party in March 1983. He was elected to three successive terms in office and was instrumental in the effort to refocus the economy from the export of raw material to the export of manufactured items.
See also: Australia.

Nathaniel Hawthorne

Hawking, Stephen William (1942-), British theoretical physicist and cosmologist who has applied general relativity and quantum mechanics to the theory of black holes in novel ways and produced results of great originality. His book *A Brief History of Time* (1988) helped popularize current thinking on the development of the universe. He holds the post of Lucasian professor of mathematics, once held by Sir Isaac Newton. He has done all of this while suffering from Amyotrophic lateral sclerosis (Lou Gehrig's disease).
See also: Black hole.

Franz Joseph Haydn

Hawkins, Coleman (1904-69), U.S. tenor saxophonist. Hawkins's musical style, punctuated by full, energetic tones, forced people to recognize the tenor saxophone as an integral jazz instrument. His improvisational style was well liked internationally and influenced many musicians of the 1930s and 1940s.

Hawkins, Sir John (1532-95), British admiral. He was a slave trader and ship captain who became treasurer of the navy and sponsored reforms in ship design and gunnery that contributed to victory over the Spanish Armada (1588), also commanding an English squadron during the battle.

Hawk moth, member of the Sphinx moth family. Hawk moths are distinguished by their large, powerful forms and their streamlined and hovering flight patterns. They suck nectar through a long proboscis, a feeding instrument which, in some species, extends as long as 13 in (32.5 cm). These moths are also known as hummingbird moths (because they can stop in front of flowers while sucking nectar) or as sphinx moths (because their resting position and profile resembles the Egyptian sphinx).

Hawks, Howard (1896-1977), U.S. film director who specialized in sharp dialogue and visual clarity. Hawks helped to create the film genre known as screwball comedy, in which the eccentric lifestyles of the rich were ridiculed. His movies include *Dawn Patrol* (1930), *Scarface* (1932), *20th Century* (1934), *The Big Sleep* (1946), and *Red River* (1948).

Hawthorn, any of several hundred species of shrubs and small trees (genus *Crataegus*) of the rose family. In the spring they are covered with fine white or pink blossoms that later turn red or develop into dark blue fruits (haws) resembling tiny apples. In Europe the hawthorn was the subject of many legends. Sprigs of hawthorn were thought to protect people against thunder or witches.

Hawthorne, Nathaniel (1804-64), major U.S. novelist and short story writer whose novels *The Scarlet Letter* (1850) and *The House of the Seven Gables* (1851) are considered masterpieces of psychological portraiture, capturing the dark atmosphere of Puritan New England. His short stories—collected in *Twice-Told Tales* (1837, 1842) and *Mosses from an Old Manse* (1846)—did much to establish the genre in the United States. He also authored works for young people, *A Wonder Book* (1852) and *Tanglewood Tales* (1853).

Hay, John Milton (1838-1905), U.S. politician and author, secretary to President Lincoln (1860-65). As secretary of state under Presidents William McKinley and Theodore Roosevelt (1898-1905), he established U.S. sovereignty over Hawaii and the Philippines, and negotiated the Hay-Pauncefote Treaties (1899, 1901) and the Hay-Bunau-Varilla Treaty (1903), which together ensured U.S. control of the Panama Canal. He was also an architect of the so-called Open Door policy toward China. His writings include *Pike County Ballads* (1871) and (with J.G. Nicolay) *Abraham Lincoln: A History* (10 vols., 1890).
See also: Hay-Pauncefote Treaties; Open-Door Policy.

Hayakawa, S(amuel) I(chiyé) (1906-), Canadian-born U.S. language expert, specializing in the study of semantics. He was also a U.S. senator. Hayakawa became president of San Francisco State College (now San Francisco State University) in 1969 amid numerous student protests and became famous for his firm stand against them. After retiring in 1973, Hayakawa, a Republican, represented California in the U.S. Senate from 1977 to 1983. His books include *Language in Thoughts and Action* (1941) and *Symbol, Status and Personality* (1963).
See also: Semantics.

Hayden, Melissa (Mildred Herman; 1923-), Canadian-born U.S. ballet dancer, teacher, and director. Hayden was internationally renowned for her performances as a principal ballerina with the New York City Ballet from 1950 until 1973, during artistic director George Balanchine's regime.

Haydn, Franz Joseph (1732-1809), Austrian composer who established the accepted classical forms of the symphony, string quartet, and piano sonata. He was court musician to the Esterházy family from 1761 to 1790 and was a close friend of Mozart. His huge output includes 107 symphonies, hundreds of chamber works and violin and piano concertos, some 25 operatic works, several great masses (notably the *Nelson* mass), and various religious works, including two oratorios *The Creation* (1798) and *The Seasons* (1801).

Hayes, Helen (Helen Hayes Brown; 1900-), U.S. actress. Beginning her career at age 5, she became one of America's most versatile and admired performers, winning numerous awards for stage, screen, radio, and television performances. Some of her most notable starring roles were in *Dear Brutus* (1918), *Victoria Regina* (1936), and *A Touch of the Poet* (1958). A New York theater was named for her.

Hayes, Rutherford Birchard (1822-93), 19th president of the United States. Hayes, who won office in a bitterly contested election, began his term during a period of sectional and economic crisis. By the time he left office, economic prosperity had been restored and Reconstruction in the South brought to a close. These accomplishments carried a high price, however: For Southern blacks, the end of Reconstruction meant the loss of protection for newly won civil rights.

Law, war and politics. Hayes graduated from Kenyon College in 1842, went on to study at Harvard Law School, and then returned to Ohio to practice law.

In 1858 Hayes was elected city solicitor of Cincinnati. During the Civil War, he fought on the Union side with distinction, winning promotions rapidly. Between 1865 and 1877, Hayes served in the U.S. House of Representatives (1865-67) and as Ohio's governor (1969-72 and 1876-77). In 1876, the Republican Party nominated him for president.

The contested election. Early returns in the 1876 election seemed to indicate a

Democratic victory. Samuel J. Tilden, Hayes's Democratic opponent, had won 250,000 more popular votes than Hayes. However, the totals from 4 states—Florida, South Carolina, Louisiana, and Oregon—were in dispute. The 20 electoral votes of these states, if awarded to Hayes, would give the victory to him. To resolve the dispute, Congress appointed a special 15-member Electoral Commission. The Commission, dominated by Republicans, awarded the 20 electoral votes, and the presidency, to Hayes.

President. Southern Democrats were not easily persuaded to accept the Electoral Commission's decision. In return for their support, Republican leaders promised to end Reconstruction and withdraw the remaining federal troops from the South. Republicans also pledged that federal jobs and congressional spending would be more evenly distributed between North and South. President Hayes kept his side of the agreement. Within 2 months of his inauguration, the last federal troops departed the South. Hayes also appointed an ex-Confederate, David M. Kay, to his cabinet. The Compromise of 1877 averted a crisis that had threatened to erupt into war. But it also resulted in the virtual extinction of the Republican Party in the South and the end of protection for Southern blacks' civil rights. Hayes began early in his term to grapple with the problem of civil service reform. He made executive appointments on the basis of merit rather than party loyalty. In doing so, he alienated powerful leaders within his own party.

During the first years of Hayes's administration, the nation was in an economic depression. Wage reductions caused large-scale strikes, including a 10-state railroad stoppage in 1877. Hayes ordered federal troops to the scenes of the trouble, and the strike collapsed. Agriculture was also hard hit by the depression. Farmers demanded "easy money": more paper currency and the coinage of more silver. Hayes, who believed in "sound money," opposed these measures. His administration successfully accumulated a gold reserve to back all paper money, which helped to restore business confidence. By the end of Hayes's presidency, the nation had emerged from the depression. In 1880, Hayes's friend and fellow Ohioan James A. Garfield was elected president. Hayes saw this as a gesture of support for his own policies, and he left office feeling relief and satisfaction.

Hay fever, common allergy to the pollen of grasses and trees. Symptoms include rhinitis (runny nose) and conjunctivitis (itching eyes). Susceptibility is often associated with asthma, eczema, and aspirin sensitivity. Possible treatment includes avoiding the things to which the person is allergic, desensitizing injections, antihistamines (drugs that can reduce the severity of attacks), or steroid sprays in difficult cases.

Hay-Herrán Treaty, agreement (1903) between the United States and Colombia that would have given the United States rights to the Panama Canal Zone. When the Colombian congress refused to ratify, U.S. President Theodore Roosevelt gave aid to a revolutionary force, which declared Panama independent.

Haymarket Square Riot, violent confrontation between labor organizers and police in Chicago's Haymarket Square on May 4, 1886. After several workers were killed and others injured in a May 3 demonstration for the 8-hr work day, an outdoor meeting was held the following day. During the meeting a bomb was thrown at the police, who were attempting to disband the crowd of some 1500 people. In the ensuing riot, 4 workers and 7 police officers died. Afterward 8 anarchists were convicted of inciting violence, although no evidence was ever found linking them to the bomb. Four of them were hanged, 1 committed suicide, and 3 were pardoned by Governor John Atgeld in 1893.

Hayne, Robert Young (1791-1839), U.S. politician. He championed states' rights and supported state nullification of federal laws in a famous Senate debate with Daniel Webster (1830).

Hay-Pauncefote Treaties, agreements between the United States and Great Britain negotiated in 1899 and 1901, giving the United States the sole right to construct and control the proposed Panama Canal. The treaty derives its name from the two men who negotiated—U.S. Secretary of State John Hay and the British ambassador to the U.S. Lord Pauncefote. The first treaty was amended by Congress (1900) and then rejected by Britain. The second treaty gave the U.S. the right to control the canal and build fortifications.
See also: Panama Canal.

Haywood, William Dudley (1869-1928), U.S. labor leader and principal organizer of the Industrial Workers of the World (1905). He was expelled from the Socialist party due to his excessive militancy. In World War I he was convicted of sedition but escaped to Russia in 1921.
See also: Labor movement.

Hazardous wastes, chemicals and their by-products that are dangerous to humans or pollute the environment. The Resource Conservation and Recovery Act of 1976 deems a material hazardous if it is poisonous, radioactive, or toxic; corrodes another material; explodes or ignites easily; reacts with water; or is unstable to heat. Industries, factories, laboratories, and hospitals are the biggest producers of hazardous wastes. The harmful effects include polluted groundwater, rivers, and lakes which could severely limit a city's drinking water and food supply. The Superfund Act, also known as the Comprehensive Environmental Response, Compensation, and Liability Act of 1980, helps fund ways to fix unsafe hazardous waste dumps.

Hazel, shrub or small tree (genus *Corylus*) that produces catkins early in the spring. The male catkins are yellow, dangling clusters, like "lambs' tails." Pollen from these fertilizes the small red-tipped female flowers, which then produce nuts with a thick green husk. Hazelnuts are edible and are particularly liked by squirrels. A related European tree, the filbert (*C. avellena*), is cultivated for its larger nuts.

Rutherford Birchard Hayes

19th U.S. President	
Born:	Delaware, Ohio; Oct. 4, 1822
Term of office:	March 1877-March 1881
Vice president:	William A. Wheeler
Political party:	Republican
Spouse:	Lucy Webb Hayes
Children:	Eight
Died:	Spiegel Grove, Ohio; Jan. 17, 1893

Hazlitt, William (1778-1830), English literary critic and essayist. His observations of culture, politics, and English manners appeared in *Characters of Shakespeare's Plays* (1817) and *Lectures on the English Comic Writers* (1819). His wit and versatility are reflected in the miscellaneous essays of *Table Talk* (1821-22) and *The Spirit of the Age* (1825).

H-bomb *see:* Nuclear Weapon.

Headache, common ailment and manifestation of many diseases and disorders involving the brain, eyes, nose, throat, teeth, and ears. Most headaches seem to arise from pressure upon or displacement of the blood vessels of the brain. The major covering of the brain (the dura mater) also registers pain. Other headaches derive from the vessels outside the skull, such as the scalp and neck muscles. Infrequent headaches can usually be related to acute causes, such as fatigue, fever, or the drinking of alcohol. The cause of chronic or recurrent headache is often difficult to diagnose.

Headhunter, one who cuts off the head of a defeated enemy to preserve it as a trophy or for religious reasons or in the belief that it strengthens one's own tribe while weakening the enemy. Many primitive tribes of Malaysia, Borneo, parts of Africa, Melanesia, and South America practiced headhunting.

Headphones, device that allows a person to hear sound reproductions in private. Headphones typically have 2 earphones connected by a band that fits over the head. They are often used when surrounding noise is overpowering or when the user needs freedom of hand movement. Headphones operate much like miniature speakers by transmitting electric sound waves from a central source to a private earphone.

Head Start, U.S. government program established in 1964 by the Economic Opportunity Act to prepare disadvantaged children for school and to involve parents and local communities in the effort. The Head Start program was so successful that Follow-up programs for children in kindergarten were added in 1967. It has been one of the most widely hailed government programs ever.

Health, according to the World Health Organization, "a state of complete physical, mental and social well-being and not merely the absence of disease or infirmity." The practices that help a person to maintain health —including proper nutrition, exercise, and cleanliness— are called hygiene.

The heart

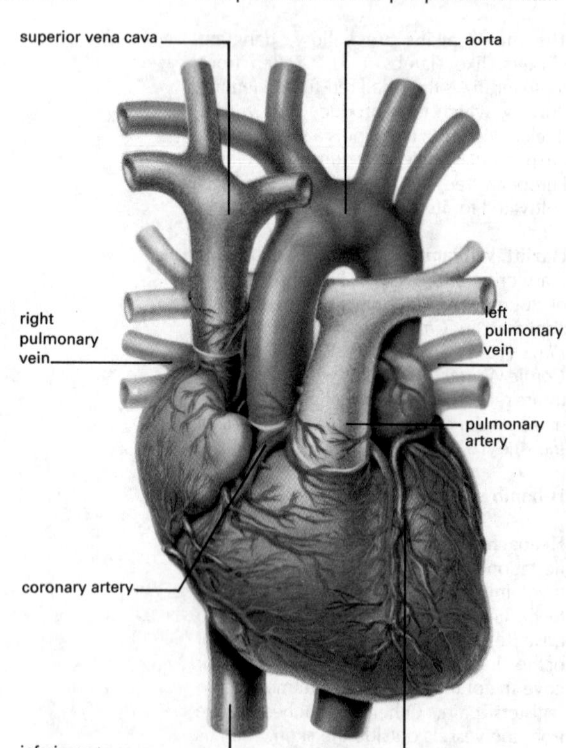

Health, Education, and Welfare, Department of *see:* Health and Human Services, U.S. Department of.

Health, National Institutes of *see:* National Institutes of Health.

Health, public *see:* Public health.

Health and Human Services, U.S. Department of, (HHS), federal executive department created in 1979 as the successor to the Department of Health, Education, and Welfare. The second-largest federal department (after the Department of Defense), the HHS is responsible for over 300 federal health and human service programs. It includes the Offices of Human Developmental Services, the Public Health Service, the Social Security Administration, the Office of Child Support Enforcement, and the Health Care Financing Administration, which is in charge of Medicare and Medicaid.

Health Insurance, National (NHI), program that provides health care for a country's citizens. Also known as socialized medicine, NHI began in Germany in the late 1800s and is found in all industrialized countries in the world except the United States. Many U.S. citizens favor the idea of national health care, but have not agreed on a uniformly structured and administered program. The American Medical Association (AMA) is opposed to NHI, arguing that such a program would provide lower quality of medical services.

Healy, James Augustine (1830-1900), first U.S. black bishop and priest of the Roman Catholic Church. Appointed by Pope Pius IX in 1875, Healy served as Bishop of Portland, Me., a primarily white diocese.

Hearing *see:* Ear.

Hearing aid, device to improve hearing by amplifying sound waves. The first hearing aid was a tube called the ear trumpet, a flared tube held up to the ear. The early electronic hearing aid consisted of a small battery-powered amplifier, housed with a microphone in a small case. Signals picked up by the microphone were amplified, then fed via a flexible cord to a small earphone fitting over the ear. Transistors made it possible to reduce the size of hearing aids and to increase efficiency. Modern devices employ advanced microcircuitry and are small enough to be built into spectacle frames or hair slides. Some fit behind the ear and transmit sounds through the bones of the skull, while others are small enough to fit inside the ear.
See also: Ear.

Hearing loss *see:* Deafness.

Hearn, Lafcadio (1850-1904), U.S. writer of Irish-Greek origin. His move to Japan and naturalization as a Japanese citizen brought about his best work: *In Ghostly Japan* (1899), *Shadowings* (1900), *Kwaidan* (1904), and *Japan: An Attempt at Interpretation* (1904).

Hearne, Samuel (1745-92), English explorer and fur trader. In 1770 he led an expedition that traced the Coppermine River to the Arctic Ocean. Subsequently he discovered that a short Northwest passage did not exist.

Hearst, Phoebe Apperson (1842-1919), U.S. philanthropist; mother of William Randolph Hearst. A former teacher, Hearst strongly supported education and cofounded the National Congress of Mothers, which later became the National Congress of Parents and Teachers and sprouted local parent-teacher associations (PTAs). She funded one of the first kindergarten associations in California.
See also: National Congress of Parents and Teachers.

Hearst, William Randolph (1863-1951), U.S. newspaper and magazine publisher. Hearst's business acumen emerged early in his career, and he quickly built a huge, powerful newspaper empire. Spending big sums to attract readers, he competed with other publishers by employing sensationalistic journalism, printing splashy headlines, and pioneering color comics. By 1937, Hearst owned 25 daily newspapers and such magazines as *Cosmopolitan, Good Housekeeping, House Beautiful*, and *Harper's Bazaar.*
Politically ambitious, he represented New York in the U.S. House of Representatives (1903-07). He ran unsuccessfully for governor of New York and mayor of New York City and failed in his attempt to become the Democrats' nominee for president (1904). His lavish castle residence, San Simeon, near San Francisco, is now a state museum. In 1974, the kidnapping of one of his granddaughters, Patricia Hearst, initiated one of the biggest, most-publicized searches in U.S. history.

Heart, muscular organ whose purpose is to pump blood through the body. The human heart is about the size of the closed fist, shaped like a blunt cone and is located in the chest cavity, slightly left of center. The heart is divided into right and left halves by a muscular partition. Each half is subdivided into two cavities, the upper (atrium) and the lower (ventricle). Blood from the veins of the body flows to the right atrium. From there it goes to the right ventricle, which pumps it to the lungs. From the lungs, the blood, now rich in oxygen, is carried back to the left atrium. It then flows into the left ventricle, from where it is pumped throughout the body. A series of valves between the right and left atria and ventricles and at the entrances to the main blood vessels prevent blood from backing up as it circulates. Diseases of the heart and blood vessels, whiche cause about half of all deaths in the United States, are called cardiovascular diseases. Three major kinds

of heart disease are hypertension, arteriosclerosis, and rheumatic fever.
See also: Circulatory system.

Heart Association, American (AHA), U.S. health organization that structures programs to fight heart disease. The AHA conducts research and public services and provides information about diseases affecting the heart and blood vessels. Supporting about about 105,000 members, the AHA is funded by contributions.

Heart murmur, abnormal sound heard on listening with a stethoscope to the chest over the heart. Normally there are 2 major heart sounds due to valve closure, separated by silence. Murmurs can arise in heart valve disease, with narrowing (stenosis) or leakage (incompetence). Holes between the heart's chambers, valve roughening, and high flow of blood also cause murmurs. Most murmurs are completely harmless.
See also: Heart.

Heat, internal energy of a body resulting from the motion of its atoms and molecules. The kinetic energy of these atoms and molecules is expressed as temperature. The quantity of heat energy may be measured in calories or BTUs (British Thermal Units).
See also: British thermal unit.

Heat capacity, quantity of heat required to increase the temperature of a system or substance 1° of temperature. It is expressed in calories per gram per degree Celsius or British thermal units per pound per degree Fahrenheit.
See also: Heat.

Heath, low woody plants (family Ericaceae) found on poor, acidic soil in parts of Asia and Europe and naturalized in North America. They may cover large areas of country, which are often called heaths. Other names for these plants are *ling* and *heather*. Scottish people have used the tough plants for bedding, thatching, and brooms. Sheep graze the fresh shoots and grouse eat the seeds, and a particularly fine honey is obtained from the bell-shaped flowers. Heaths are often grown in gardens, and white heath, or *bruyère*, of the Mediterranean is used to make briar pipes, manufactured from the roots.

Heath, Edward Richard George (1916-), British prime minister, 1970-74. He was elected to parliament in 1950, and after holding Conservative Party positions, he became party leader in 1965. As prime minister, he brought Britain into the Common Market (now the European Community). He employed austerity measures to fight inflation and resorted to a 3-day work week to save fuel during a miners' strike. In 1975, a year after being turned out of office, he resigned as party leader.
See also: United Kingdom.

Heath hen *see:* Prairie chicken.

Heating, process of providing heat and controlling the temperature in a particular environment. Human beings are warm-blood animals, most comfortable in an atmosphere between 70° F (21° C) and 78° (26° C). Heating provides a way for people to function in very cold climates. Central heating systems provide consistent and monitored heat for a building or home and are regulated by a thermostat, a device that automatically measures and adjusts an area's temperature. These systems are powered by electricity, gas, or oil and are common in the United States. Other countries often use fireplaces, room heaters, or wood-burning stoves.
See also: Heat.

Heat pipe, device that moves heat while keeping the temperature relatively constant. A heat pipe consists of a sealed metal tube with a porous lining that holds a boiling liquid. To transfer heat, one end is immersed in the heat source, and the liquid's temperature is gradually brought to boiling, which forces the vapor to move to the colder end of the pipe. The vapor then condenses and releases the heat. Heat pipes are extremely efficient because they can transfer large amounts of heat over long distances and keep the temperature constant without using an external power supply.

Heat pump, device that simultaneously transports heat and increases its temperature. To heat an area, the heat pump absorbs outside heat and brings it inside the area. A fluid called a *refrigerant* circulates through the heat pump, absorbs the outside heat, and travels first into a compressor that increases its temperature, and then into a heat exchanger to release its heat to room air. The refrigerant is then filtered through a valve that lowers its temperature and allows the process to begin again. The process can also be reversed to cool an area by absorbing inside heat and discharging it outside the area, as with a refrigerator.
See also: Air conditioning.

Heat rash *see:* Prickly heat.

Heatstroke *see:* Sunstroke.

Heaven, in many religions and cultures, the abode of God, gods or spirits, and the righteous after death. In the Old Testament God, who dwells in heaven, also transcends it. Not until late Judaism was heaven generally regarded as the abode of the righteous. In Christian thought heaven is the eternal home of true believers or the state of living in full union with Christ, which the perfected soul enters after death. In Islam heaven is viewed as a garden where faithful Muslims may see the face of God. In the Eastern religions of Buddhism and Hinduism heaven consists of many levels that must be achieved over many lifetimes until a soul attains the eternal state of nirvana.

Heaves, or broken wind, lung disease of horses, resulting in difficult expiration and a chronic cough. It can be caused by an allergic reaction to poor quality feed, inflammation of the lung airways by dust and mold, and viral or bacterial infections.

Heavy hydrogen *see:* Deuterium.

Heavy water, or deuterium oxide (D_2O), chemical compound that occurs as 0.014% of ordinary water, which it closely resembles. It is used as a moderator in nuclear reactors and as a source of deuterium and its compounds. It is toxic in high concentrations. Heavy water freezes at 38.8°F (3.8°C) and boils at 214.5°F (101.4°C). Water containing tritium or heavy isotopes of oxygen (^{17}O and ^{18}O) is also called heavy water.
See also: Deuterium.

Hebe, daughter of Zeus and Hera and in Greek mythology goddess of youth. She served youth-giving nectar to the gods and goddesses of Mount Olympus and was wife of Hercules.
See also: Mythology.

Hébert, Jacques René (1757-94), French revolutionary. Through his newspaper *La Père Duchesne* he roused the extremist *sansculottes*. Falsely charged with conspiracy, he was executed in Mar. 1794.

Hebrew, Semitic language in which the Old Testament was written, and official language of the modern nation of Israel. The earliest extant Hebrew writings date from at least the 11th century B.C. Now a sacred tongue and a common written language for religious Jews, Hebrew died out as a spoken language by the 3rd century B.C. but was revived as the language of the modern Jewish nation, largely owing to Eliezer Ben Jehudah, who compiled a Hebrew dictionary in the 19th century. Hebrew is written from right to left.

Hebrews, Epistle to the, New Testament book of unknown authorship, traditionally ascribed to St. Paul. Addressed to Jewish converts to Christianity who were in danger of apostasy, it explains the fulfillment in Christ of the Old Testament.
See also: Bible; New Testament.

Hebrides, group of about 500 islands off the northwest coast of Scotland, fewer than 100 of them inhabited. The Outer Hebrides (Western Islands) include Harris, Lewis, North and South Uist, Benbecula, and Barra; Skye, Mull, and Iona lie among the Inner Hebrides. Apart from tourism, industries include fishing, farming, sheep-raising, distilling, and tweed-making.

Hebron (pop. 50,000), city in Jordan, located near Jerusalem on the West Bank, one of the oldest cities in the world. Part of Palestine until 1950, the city has religious significance for Jews, Muslims, and Christians alike. Hebron is a center of marketing, industry, and administration for the West Bank region. Israel occupied the city following the 1967 Arab-Israeli War.
See also: Jordan.

Hecate, in Greek mythology, goddess of ghosts and black magic. Originally represented as a beneficial goddess with the power to grant good fortune, she was later associated with evil and the underworld. According to myth, she haunted graveyards and crossroads, attended by hellhounds.
See also: Mythology.

Hecht, Ben (1894-1964), U.S. dramatist, screenwriter, and novelist. He collaborated with Charles MacArthur on the highly successful plays *The Front Page* (1928) and *Twentieth Century* (1932). He also worked on the screenplays for *Gunga Din* (1938), *Wuthering Heights* (1939), and *Notorious* (1946). His autobiography is *A Child of the Century* (1954).

Georg Wilhelm Friedrich Hegel

Hecker, Isaac Thomas (1819-88), U.S. Roman Catholic priest, founder in 1858 of the Paulist Fathers, an order dedicated to the conversion of U.S. non-Catholics. Hecker also established the magazine *Catholic World* and the Catholic Publication Society.

Heckler, Margaret Mary (1931-), U.S. Secretary of Health and Human Services 1983-1985, named U.S. ambassador to Ireland in 1985. Prior to these appointments, Heckler served as a Republican member of the House of representatives for 16 years, where she was a strong supporter of women's rights, the Equal Rights Amendment, and Medicare reform.

Heinrich Heine

Hector, in Greek mythology, hero prince of Troy, eldest son of the Trojan King Priam and Queen Hecuba and the husband of Andromache. In Homer's Iliad, Hector is the champion of the Trojans, killed in battle by the wrathful Achilles, who drags his body 3 times around the walls of Troy before Priam finally persuades him to give up the body to the Trojans. Hector is sometimes described as the son of Apollo.
See also: Mythology; Trojan War.

Hecuba, in Greek mythology, second wife of Priam, king of Troy and mother to Hector, Paris, and Polydorus. She was taken as a slave by Odysseus after the Trojan War. Upon discovering that King Polymestor of Thrace had murdered Polydorus, Hecuba blinded him and killed his two sons.
See also: Mythology.

Hedgehog

Hedge apple *see:* Osage orange.

Hedgehog, small insectivore (genus *Erinaceus*) of Asia, Africa, and Europe covered with spines. Each spine is a modified hair about 1 in (2.5 cm) long. The Eurasian species is the common hedgehog, *E. europaeus.* Nocturnal mammals, they wander about searching the ground for worms, beetles, and slugs. Hedgehogs are able to roll up for protection against predators and become entirely enclosed by the spiny part of the skin.

Hedonism, philosophical doctrine that regards pleasure as the ultimate good. The view of the Cyrenaics and Aristippus (c.435-360 B.C.) was that the sentient pleasure of the moment was the only good, whereas Epicurus thought one's aim should be a life of lasting pleasure best attained by the guidance of reason. In the 19th century, utilitarianism, seeking "the greatest good of the greatest number," was a revival of hedonism. Hedonism has often been attacked, for instance by 18th-century English theologian Joseph Butler, who saw pleasure as a bonus when a desire is fulfilled, rather than as an end in itself.
See also: Philosophy.

Hegel, Georg Wilhelm Friedrich (1770-1831), German philosopher of idealism. During his life he was famous for his professorial lectures at the University of Berlin, and he wrote on logic, ethics, history, religion and aesthetics. The main feature of Hegel's philosophy was the dialectical method by which an idea (*thesis*) was challenged by its opposite (*antithesis*), the two ultimately reconciled in a third idea (*synthesis*) that subsumed both. Hegel found this method both in the workings of the mind, as a logical procedure, and in the workings of the history of the world, which to Hegel was the process of the development and realization of the world spirit (*Weltgeist*). His chief works were *Phenomenology of the Mind* (1807) and *Philosophy of Right* (1821). Hegel had an immense influence on 19th- and 20th-century thought and history. Among his many important followers, Karl Marx developed the concept of dialectical materialism, explaining history without resorting to the fundamental idealism of Hegel.
See also: Idealism.

Hegira, also spelled hijra or hejira, flight of Muhammad from Mecca to Medina in A.D. 622, which is the year from which Muslims date their calendar.
See also: Muhammad; Muslims.

Heidegger, Martin (1889-1976), German philosopher. Influenced by Soren Kierkegaard and Edmund Husserl, he was concerned with the problem of how one's awareness of oneself is dependent on a sense of time and one's impending death. Heidegger rejected traditional metaphysics and criticized many aspects of modern technological and mass culture as a "forgetfulness of being." His major work, *Being and Time* (1927), has been fundamental in the development of existentialism, although Heidegger denied he was an existentialist.
See also: Philosophy.

Heidelberg (pop. 134,700), historic city in western Germany, in Baden-Wüttemberg on the Neckar River. Overlooking the city is the ruined castle of the former electors of the Palatinate. Heidelberg has the oldest German university (established 1386). The city is the European headquarters of the U.S. Army.
See also: Germany.

Heidelberg, University of, oldest university in Germany, established in 1386. Modeled on the University of Paris, Heidelberg became a center of Protestant education in the 1500s. Its focus shifted to the study of medievel literature and folklore in 1803. Today its faculties include theology, law, medicine, and philosophy.

Heidelberg man, prehistoric human thought to have lived over 300,000 years ago. Evidenced only by the discovery of a huge jaw found in 1907 near Heidelberg, Germany, Heidelberg man is a European example of *Homo erectus.* Scientists believe Heidelberg man lived by hunting and probably fashioned tools out of stone.
See also: Heidelberg; Prehistoric people.

Heifetz, Jascha (1901-87), Russian-born U.S. violinist. He was a child prodigy, giving concerts by 1911, and making his U.S. debut at Carnegie Hall in 1917. His virtuosity and technique were compared to those of Niccolò Paganini. He retired from the concert stage in 1972, but continued to teach at the University of Southern California in Los Angeles until shortly before his death.

Heimlich maneuver, emergency first-aid technique for choking victims whose breathing is blocked by food or a foreign element lodged in the airway. The person applying the technique places his or her arms around the standing victim and puts a fist above the navel; the person then grabs the fist with the other hand and presses in and up with short thrusts.

Heine, Heinrich (1797-1856), German romantic lyric poet and essayist. His best-known work, *Book of Songs* (1827), was influenced by German folk songs. His prose writings, such as *Travel Pictures* (1827-31), although poignant, are often satirical. His poems have been set to music by composers including Robert Schumann, Franz Schubert, and Mendelssohn.

Heinlein, Robert Anson (1907-88), U.S. author who specialized in science fiction for both adults and children. He attended the United States Naval Academy and served 5 years in the Navy. This provided Heinlein with a scientific/technological background which, combined with his interests in economics and history, give his novels unusual depth and complexity. Heinlein's *Stranger in a Strange Land* (1961) examines unconventional notions about religion, sex, and morality. His other works include *Tunnel in the Sky* (1955), *Starship Troopers* (1959), *The Moon Is a Harsh Mistress* (1966), and *I Will Fear No Evil* (1970).

Heisenberg, Werner Karl (1901-76), German mathematical physicist generally regarded as the founder of quantum mechanics. His uncertainty principle (1927) overturned traditional physics. He received the Nobel Prize in physics in 1932.
See also: Quantum mechanics.

Heisman Trophy (John W. Heisman Memorial Trophy), annual award since 1935 given to the best college football player. It is most often bestowed on a running back. The award is named after John W. Heisman, a football coach (1892-1927) who modernized the strategy and rules of football.

Hejira *see:* Hegira.

Hel, in Scandanavian and early German mythology, cruel, greedy goddess of the dead, ruler of the underworld (Niflheim), and daughter of the evil Loki. The underworld itself became known as Hel and, eventually, as a place of punishment like the hell of Christian belief.
See also: Mythology.

Held, John, Jr. (1889-1958), U.S. cartoonist and illustrator. He captured the mood of the 1920s with his famous line drawings of bobbed-haired flappers and their raccoon-coated escorts. His work appeared frequently in *The New Yorker, Smart Set,* and *Vanity Fair.*

Helena (pop. 24,569), state capital of Montana and seat of Lewis and Clark County. Located in the fertile Prickly Pear Valley, Helena lies in the mountainous west-central part of the state at an altitude of 4,155 ft (1,263 m). In 1864 gold was discovered in Last Chance Gulch, and Helena became a boom town. Gold and silver mining still provide a large revenue, along with agricultural produce and manufactured items like paint, machine parts, cement, and fire engines. Lead and zinc ores are refined in East Helena. The State Historical Museum and Library, containing an important collection of Western art, and Carroll College (established 1909) are located here.
See also: Montana.

Helen of Troy, in Greek mythology, most beautiful of all women. Daughter of Zeus and Leda, she was wife of Menelaus, king of Sparta, from whom the Trojan prince Paris abducted her. The Greeks, seeking to return her to Menelaus, united in a 10-year siege of Troy, finally destroying the city. With the Greeks victorious, she returned to Sparta with Menelaus.
See also: Mythology; Trojan War.

Helgoland, or Heligoland, island in the North Sea. Strategically important to Germany during both world wars, it was the target of extensive Allied bombing during World War II. After the war, the British evacuated the population and destroyed the remaining military installations by setting off high explosives that altered the features of much of the island. Returned to West Germany in 1952, the island has been developed as a resort area.

Helicopter, exceptionally maneuverable aircraft able to take off and land vertically, hover, and fly in any horizontal direction without necessarily changing the alignment of the aircraft. Lift is provided by 1 or more rotors mounted above the craft and rotating horizontally about a vertical axis. Change in the speed of rotation or in the pitch (angle of attack) of all the blades at once alters the amount of lift; cyclic change in the pitch of each blade during its rotation alters the direction of thrust. Most helicopters have only a single lift rotor and thus have a tailmounted vertical rotor to prevent the craft from spinning around; change in the speed of this rotor is used to change the craft's heading. Helicopter toys were known to the Chinese and in medieval Europe, but because of problems with stability, it was not until 1939, following the success of the autogiro (1923), that the first fully successful helicopter flight was achieved by Russian-born U.S. engineer Igor Ivanovich Sikorsky. Used in combat in Vietnam, the helicopter has become increasingly important in military use. It has given ground forces entree to areas hitherto inaccessible. Its firepower and maneuverability permit close air support of ground forces. Its extreme mobility allows evasive action and the potential to surprise the enemy. Its capacity to hover makes it a relatively stable weapons platform.
In civilian use, helicopters have proved valuable for city-to-airport and city-to-suburb transportation and for monitoring traffic, spotting forest fires, patrolling pipelines, and performing rescue work.

Heliopolis (Greek, "city of the sun"), ancient Egyptian city located at the apex of the Nile Delta, 6 mi (10 km) from Cairo. It was the center of worship of the sun god Ra until c.2100 B.C.
See also: Egypt, Ancient.

Helios, in Greek mythology, god of the sun and son of the Titans Hyperion and Theia. Helios is often represented driving a 4-horse chariot that rises from the ocean in the east in the morning and descends into the western sea at night. In Hellenistic times he became identified with Apollo.
See also: Mythology.

Helicopter. Key: The cyclic pitch lever (1) tilts the lower fixed swashplate (2) by means of the jacks (3). The upper rotating swash plate (4) also tilts, which changes the pitch of the rotor blades as they pass round the rotor disc. In forward flight the pitch is at a maximum in the rear of the disc which effectively tilts the disc and therefore the helicopter forwards. The collective-pitch lever (5) raises or lowers the swashplate without tilting it, causing a change in the overall lift. The rudder pedals (6) alter the tail-rotor pitch by a similar mechanism to change the heading.

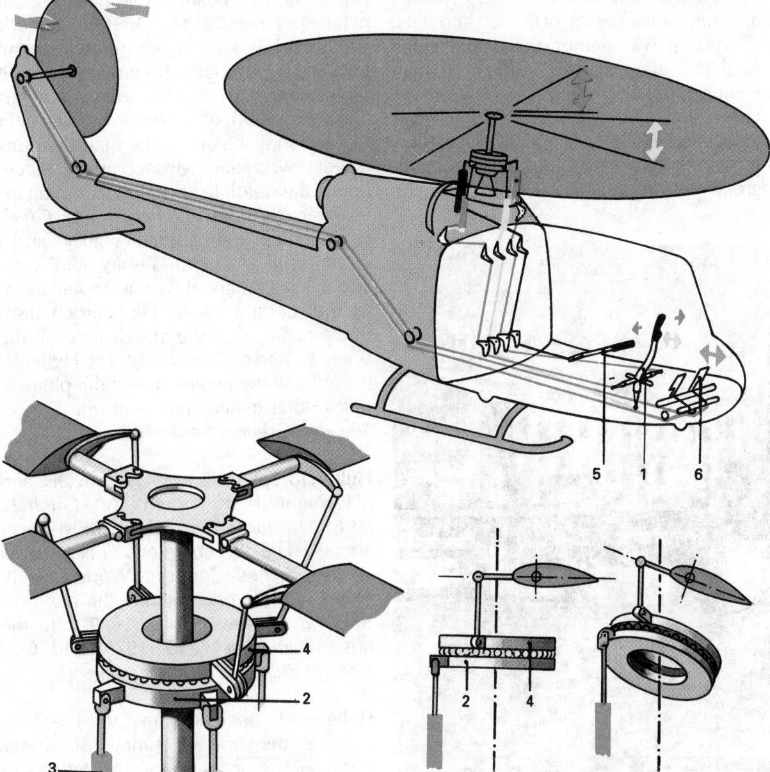

Many products of the Hellenistic Age remain, like this statuette of mother and child.

Heliotrope, fragrant plant (genus *Heliotropium*) once popular in gardens. Its name, made up of the Greek words for *sun* and *turn*, points to the fact that it always turns its flowers and leaves to face the sun. The cultivated heliotropes come mainly from Peru and Ecuador, but there are a few North American species.

Helium, chemical element, symbol He; for physical constants see Periodic Table. Helium was discovered by Pierre J. Janssen during the solar eclipse of 1868, when he detected a new line in the spectrum of the sun's chromosphere. After hydrogen, it is the second most abundant element in the universe. It is important in the proton-proton reaction and the carbon cycle, which account for the energy of the sun and stars. In 1907 it was demonstrated that alpha particles are charged helium nuclei. Helium is obtained commercially from certain natural gas deposits with which it is associated. Helium is a monatomic, colorless, inert, lighter-than-air gas. It belongs to group VIIIA of the chemical elements, the inert gases. As a liquid it exists in 2 forms, He I and, below about 2.2 °K, He II. He II is a superconductor. Helium is used in airships and balloons, in synthetic breathing mixtures, for pressurizing liquid fuel rockets, and in lasers. Liquid helium is used in the production of low temperatures.

Port of Helsinki in winter

Hell, in several religions, abode of evil spirits and of the wicked after death, usually thought of as an underworld or abyss. In Christian theology, those damned by God are sent to hell for eternity. The New Testament describes hell as a place of corruption and unquenchable fire and brimstone. Muslims have a similar hell. Buddhists and Hindus may descend into one of many hells because of evil karma, but their souls may leave hell when the effects of the karma are removed.

Hellebore, any of a genus *(Helleborus)* of perennial plants of the crowfoot family, found mainly in Europe and Asia. It has very thick roots and large flowers. The Christmas rose, or black hellebore (*H. niger)*, blooms from late fall to early spring and has white and purple flowers, which contain a strong poison. The American white hellebore, or Indian poke (*Veratrum viride*), is a false hellebore, unrelated to the true hellebores. It can be found from Canada to Georgia and grows from 2 to 8 ft (0.6 to 2.4 m) high, with green flowers. Its roots are used as an insecticide.

Hellenistic Age, period in which Greco-Macedonian culture spread through the lands conquered by Alexander the Great. It is generally accepted to run from Alexander's death (323 B.C.) to the annexation of the last Hellenistic state, Egypt, by Rome (31 B.C.) and the death of Cleopatra VII, last of the Ptolemies (30 B.C.). After Alexander's death, and despite the temporary restraint imposed by Antipater, his empire was split by constant warring between rival generals eager for a share of the territory. Even after the accomplishment of the final divisions (Egypt, Syria and Mesopotamia, Macedonia, the Aetolian and Archaean Leagues in Greece, Rhodes, and Pergamum), Greek remained the international language and a commercial and cultural unity held sway. The age was marked by cosmopolitanism (sharply contrasting with the parochialism of the earlier Greek era), advances in the sciences, and naturalistic art. The Hellenistic age saw the emergence of the philosophies Stoicism and Epicureanism.
See also: Greece, Ancient.

Heller, Joseph (1923-), U.S. novelist and playwright best known for *Catch-22* (1961), a grotesquely humorous novel about a U.S. bombardier's "deep-seated survival anxieties" during World War II. Other satiric works include the play *We Bombed in New Haven* (1967) and the novels *Good as Gold* (1979) and *God Knows* (1984).

Hellespont, ancient name for the Dardanelles, the strait separating Asia Minor from Europe, named for the legendary Helle, who drowned here while fleeing to Colchis with her brother Phrixus.
See also: Dardanelles.

Hell Gate, channel in the East River in New York City. Probably named by early Dutch settlers for its turbulent current and dangerous rock formations, it was reconstructed in the late 1800s and used for travel. It is spanned by the Hell Gate Bridge, the Triborough Bridge, and a railroad bridge.

Hellgrammite (*Corydalus cronutus*), large, brown, aquatic larva of the 4-winged dobsonfly. Hellgrammites live beneath rocks in North American streams and feed upon small water animals. When fully mature, they leave the water, cocoon for a 2-week period, and emerge as dobsonflies. Hellgrammites are widely used as fishing bait.

Hellman, Lillian (1905-84), U.S. playwright, screenwriter, and autobiographer. A mordant social critic, she wrote plays, such as *The Children's Hour* (1934), *The Little Foxes* (1939), and *Watch on the Rhine* (1941), that studied the evil effects of ruthless ambition and exploitation in personal, social, and political situations. Her books of reminiscences, such as *An Unfinished Woman* (1969), for which she won a National Book Award, 1970) and *Scoundrel Time* (1976), are fascinating for their portraits of famous people and events.

Helmholtz, Hermann Ludwig Ferdinand von (1821-94), German physiologist and physicist. In the course of his physiological studies he formulated the law of conservation of energy (1847). He was the first to measure the speed of nerve impulses, and he invented the ophthalmoscope (both 1850). He also made important contributions to the study of electricity, non-euclidean geometry, and musical acoustics.
See also: Ophthalmoscope.

Helmont, Jan Baptista van (1580-1644), Flemish chemist and physician, regarded as the father of biochemistry. He discovered that there were airlike substances distinct from air and first used the name "gas" for them.
See also: Biochemistry.

Helms, Jesse Alexander, (1921-) U.S. senator from North Carolina. Elected in 1973, he is known for his controversial bill denying a woman's right to seek an abortion during any time in her pregnancy. Other bills he has sponsored include those which support prayer in the public schools and prohibit school busing to achieve racial balance. In 1989-90 he promoted a stipulation to appropriation bills for the National Endowment for the Arts prohibiting funding of "obscene" art.

Héloïse *see:* Abelard, Peter.

Helsinki (Swedish: *Helsingfors*; pop. 490,000), capital of Finland, situated on a rocky peninsula of southern Finland, in the Gulf of Finland. Called "white city of the north" because much of it is built of local white granite, it is Finland's chief industrial center and seaport. Its main industries are shipbuilding, foundries, textiles,and paper and machinery manufacture. Chief exports are timber, pulp, and metal goods. It was founded by Swedish king Gustavus Vasa in 1550 and established as the nation's capital in 1812.

Helsinki Accords, final act of the Conference on Security and Cooperation in Europe, which began in 1972, on Aug. 1, 1975, by the United States, Canada, the USSR and 35 European countries. Though nonbinding, it outlines a broad basis for peaceful relations in Europe, particularly between Western and Eastern (Soviet bloc) European nations, including the promise of 21 days notice of military maneuvers by more than 25,000 troops, respect for human rights, and recognition of existing European frontiers. Each side later accused the other of violating these accords. In Sept. 1983, nonetheless, 35 foreign ministers met in Madrid to mark the end of 3 years of negotiations on a document to augment the 1975 accords.

Helvetia *see:* Switzerland.

Helvetians, tribe that lived just east of the Roman province of Gaul, now northwestern Switzerland. When Switzerland was conquered by the Roman emperor Augustus, who ruled from 27 B.C. to A.D. 14, the Helvetians were forced to adopt the language and customs of Rome. The area as still sometimes called *Helvetia* by its residents.
See also: Rome, Ancient; Switzerland.

Hemangioma *see:* Birthmark.

Hematite, common mineral consisting largely of iron oxide. An important iron ore, it is also used for making paints and polishes. Hematite occurs as a gray-black to red-brown mineral in both sedimentary and metamorphic rocks. Hematite may form spectacular shapes. In Brazil it occurs as large flat plates 6 in (15 cm) or more across. In the Alps it is found in masses called iron roses, and in Cumberland, England, it occurs as kidney-shaped red-clack stones. In North America large deposits of hematite are found around Lake Superior and in the Appalachians.

Hemingway, Ernest (1899-1961), U.S. novelist and short-story writer. His terse prose style was widely emulated. His first major novel, *The Sun Also Rises* (1926), chronicled the postwar experiences of what his friend Gertrude Stein called the lost generation of World War I. *A Farewell to Arms* (1929) and *For Whom the Bell Tolls* (1940) were based on his own experiences in World War I and the Spanish Civil War, respectively, and added greatly to his reputation as a writer. *The Old Man and the Sea* (1952) won a 1953 Pulitzer Prize, and he won the Nobel Prize for literature the next year. Increasingly depressed and ill in later years, he committed suicide.

Hemisphere (from the Greek *hemisphairion*, "half a sphere"), term referring to any half of the earth. The globe can be divided into 3 sets of hemispheres. The northern and southern hemispheres make up one set: everything north of the equator is in the northern hemisphere and everything south of the equator is part of the southern hemisphere. The eastern and western hemispheres form another set: the eastern hemisphere comprises Europe, Asia, Africa, and Australia, and the western hemisphere is made up of North and South America. The generally accepted boundary lines are 20′ west and 160′ east longitudes. The earth may also be separated into the land hemisphere (the half with the most land, centered close to London, England) and the sea hemisphere (the half made up mostly of water, centered near New Zealand).

Hemlock, or poison hemlock (*Conium macalatum*), poisonous herb of the parsley family found in Europe, Asia, and Africa. Hemlock was used in ancient Greece to put condemned prisoners, including Socrates, to death.

Hemlock, any of a genus (*Tsuga*) of evergreen trees belonging to the pine family. Found in the forests of North America and Asia, hemlock is used both ornamentally and for its lumber, bark, and pulp. Varieties of hemlock include Eastern hemlock (*T. canadensis*), Carolina hemlock (*T. caroliniana*), and Western hemlock (*T. heterophylla*). Poison hemlock is an herb unrelated to the pine family.

Hemoglobin (Hb), oxygen-carrying pigment found in the red blood cells of all vertebrates and some invertabrates. Produced in the bone marrow, hemoglobin carries oxygen from the lungs to the rest of the body.
See also: Blood.

Hemophilia, hereditary disease in which the blood clots very slowly, such that a minor cut or bruise can cause prolonged bleeding, and there is a tendency to bleed internally without any obvious cause. It affects only males, but is transmitted in the genes of females. The genetic defect is the inability to synthesize a protein—factor VIII—needed for normal clotting of the blood. The severity of the disease depends on how much factor VIII is produced by the body; in severe cases, where no factor VIII is made, internal bleeding can lead to massive hemorrhages and can erode the joints of the arms and legs. The disease can now be controlled by giving the hemophiliac transfusions or intravenous injections of factor VIII that has been collected from donated blood. A small percentage of hemophiliacs lack clotting factor IX; this type of hemophilia is known as Christmas disease.
See also: Blood.

Hemorrhoid, commonly called pile, varicose veins of the rectum or anus that may either be internal and bleed frequently, thus producing anemia, or become large and protrude from the anus, causing pain and discomfort. There is no known cause, although they are more common in pregnant women and in those with cirrhosis of the liver. The pain and discomfort can be relieved by the application of suppositories, and they can be treated by the injection of an irritant fluid that will cause scarring around the hemorrhoid and so obstruct it. Surgery can also be employed to close hemorrhoids off. All hemorrhoids should be treated by a doctor. They mimic the early signs of cancer of the rectum and colon, making a proper diagnosis vital.

Hemp (*Cannabis sativa*), tall herbaceous plant of the mulberry family native to Asia but now widely cultivated for fiber, oil, and a narcotic drug called cannabis, hashish, or marijuana. The fibers are used in the manufacture of rope. They are separated from the rest of the plant by a process called retting (soaking), during which bacteria and fungi rot away all but the fibers, which are then combed out. Hemp oil obtained from the seed is used in the manufacture of paints, varnishes, and soaps.

Ernest Hemingway

Henderson, Fletcher (1898-1952), jazz musician who first introduced the "big band" sound. His band, which used written arrangements as well as improvised material, helped pave the way for the more formalized dance orchestras of the 1930s. Although never achieving the popular success critics felt he deserved, he played a part in bringing to public attention such famous musicians as Louis Armstrong, Benny Goodman, and Coleman Hawkins.

Hendricks, Thomas Andrews (1819-1885), U.S. Vice President under Grover Cleveland. After serving in the U.S. House of Representatives, the Senate, and as Governor of Indiana, he was elected Vice President in 1884. He died in office eight months later.

Hendrix, Jimi (1942-70), U.S. rock music performer. An unconventional musician, he experimented with the electronic guitar, creating new sounds and expanding the guitar's capabilities. Hendrix's music was frequently loud and characterized by long, emotional solos and a powerful beat. After playing with various rhythm and blues musicians, he went to England in 1966 and formed a band called the Jimi Hendrix Experience, which enjoyed worldwide success with numerous world tours and concert performances. Hendrix died in London of a drug overdose.

Jimi Hendrix

Henequen, fiber made from the henequen plant. The leaves of the henequen, a plant that grows on the Yucatan peninsula in Mexico, consist of tough yellow fibers that are separated by machine and then dried to make twine and rope. Mexico is the only important producer of this fiber.

Henna (*Lawsonia inermis*), small shrub from whose leaves an orange dye is extracted. The plant grows in Africa, southern

Asia, and Australia. Its leaves are dried, then pounded and mixed with water to make a gumlike substance. This is applied to fabrics or to the skin and hair to dye it rust red. The use of henna as a cosmetic dates back to ancient Egypt, and its use is widespread in Asia and northern Africa, where many women paint intricate patterns on hands and feet, while men dye only the palms of the hands and the beard.

Hennepin, Louis (1640-1701?), Belgian Franciscan missionary and explorer. He went to Quebec (c.1675) as chaplain to La Salle and joined his 1679 expedition. Captured but well treated by Sioux, he was rescued in 1680. His exaggerated accounts of his travels were very popular.

Henri, Robert (Robert Henry Cozad; 1865-1929), U.S. painter and art teacher, founder of the Ashcan School of realistic painters. He studied and traveled in Europe, 1888-1900, then taught in New York, where he organized the 1908 exhibition of The Eight. His philosophy is expressed in his widely read book *The Art Spirit* (1923).
See also: Ashcan School.

Henry, name of 8 kings of England. **Henry I** (1068-1135), reigned 1100-35. The son of William I, he seized the English throne on the death of his brother William II, while his other brother, Robert, was on a Crusade. **Henry II** (1133-89), reigned 1154-89, was the grandson of Henry I. He founded the Plantagent line. In 1152 he married Eleanor, Duchess of Aquitaine, thus acquiring vast lands in France. His policy of strengthening royal authority in England led to conflict with Thomas à Becket, the archbishop of Canterbury, who was murdered in 1170. **Henry III** (1207-72), reigned 1216-72, was a grandson of Henry II. His unpopular rule was marked by administrative and diplomatic incompetence and by the revolts of nobles who forced him to yield much power to them. **Henry IV** (1367-1413), was the first ruler of the House of Lancaster. He usurped the throne after forcing Richard II to abdicate. His reign was marked by struggles with Owen Glendower and Sir Henry Percy. **Henry V** (1387-1422), reigned 1413-22, was the son of Henry IV. He defeated the French at Agincourt in 1415, married Catherine of Valois, and became successor to the French throne. **Henry VI** (1421-71), reigned 1422-61 and 1470-71, became king as an infant. The country was ruled by 2 of his uncles, who led the English forces that were defeated by the French under Joan of Arc. Henry VI's rule was marked by factional struggles that led to the dynastic Wars of the Roses. He was deposed for 9 years and eventually murdered. **Henry VII** (1457-1509), reigned 1485-1509, was the first of the Tudor rulers, uniting the houses of York and Lancaster. He killed Richard III in the last battle of the Wars of the Roses. He restored order to England and Wales and promoted efficient administration. **Henry VIII** (1491-1547), reigned 1509-47, was the son of Henry VII, and was one of the most powerful and formative rulers in British history. His religious policies and matrimonial problems led to clashes with the Pope and the Act of Supremacy (1534), in which Parliament renounced papal authority and established the Church of England with the king as supreme head. He replaced feudal authority with a central system of government and created the navy that later became the basis of British world power. His matrimonial problems, which led to the conflict with the Catholic Church, arose from his search for a male heir. He was first married to Catherine of Aragon, whom he divorced for Anne Boleyn (mother of Elizabeth I). He had her beheaded, then married Jane Seymour (mother of Edward VI), who died in childbirth. His next wives were Anne of Cleves (divorced within a year), Catherine Howard (beheaded), and Catherine Parr, who survived him.
See also: England.

Henry IV of France

Henry, name of 4 kings of France. **Henry I** (c.1008-60) reigned 1031-60. His rule was disturbed by feudal conflicts organized by his mother and brother. One of his chief enemies was the future William I of England. **Henry II** (1519-59) reigned 1547-59. In 1533 he married Catherine de Medícis, but he was dominated by his mistress, Diane de Poitiers, and his military commander, Anne de Montmorency. A fanatic Catholic, he persecuted the Huguenots and continued the war against the Holy Roman Emperor and Spain. **Henry III** (1551-89) reigned 1574-89. He collaborated with his mother Catherine de Medícis in the Saint Bartholomew's Day massacre (1572). He was dominated by the Guise family, and his reign was unstable. He was assassinated by a Jacobin friar. **Henry IV** (1553-1610), who reigned 1589-1610, was king of Navarre 1572-1610, and the first French Bourbon king. A protestant leader of the Huguenots, he converted to Roman Catholicism in 1593, granting religious freedom with the Edict of Nantes (1598). He brought unity and economic stability to France but was assassinated by a Catholic extremist.
See also: France.

Henry, name of 7 kings of Germany, 6 of whom were also Holy Roman emperors. **Henry I**, or Henry the Fowler (c.876-936), reigned 919-36. He established Germany as a new kingdom. **Henry II** (973-1024) reigned 1002-24 and was emperor from 1014. By political astuteness he ensured secular and clerical support. He was canonized in 1146; his feast day is July 15th. **Henry III** (1017-56) reigned 1039-56 and was emperor 1046-56. During his reign the Holy Roman Empire was probably at its greatest power and unity. He carried out important papal reforms. **Henry IV** (1050-1106) reigned 1056-1105 and was emperor 1084-1105. He deposed Pope Gregory VII, but Gregory excommunicated him, and Henry yielded to papal authority at Canossa in Italy in 1077. Gregory then supported a rival king of Germany, and Henry replaced him with the antipope Clement III. He captured Rome in 1084 and was crowned emperor. After 2 sons rebelled against him, he was forced to abdicate in favor of his son Henry V. **Henry V** (1081-1125) reigned 1105-25, as emperor 1111-25. He unified Germany and continued Henry IV's struggle against the papacy. **Henry VI** (1165-1197) reigned 1190-97, as emperor from 1191. He was made king of Sicily in 1194. He died before being able to implement plans to invade the Holy Land. **Henry VII** (c.1275-1313) reigned 1308-13, as emperor from 1312. He invaded Italy in 1310 in an abortive attempt to make it the base of imperial power.

Henry, John, African American folk hero. The subject of many stories and songs, he was a railroad worker in West Virginia in the 1870s who staged a one-man race against a experimental steam drill. Although he won the race, he was reportedly crushed by a falling rock. In the popular folk ballad, John Henry died from exhaustion. The legend of John Henry symbolizes the worker's struggle against replacement by machines.

Henry, Joseph (1797-1878), U.S. physicist best known for his electromagnetic studies. His discoveries include induction and self-induction, though in both cases Michael Faraday published findings first. He also devised a much improved electromagnet by insulating the wire rather than the core, invented one of the first electric motors, helped Robert Morse and Sir Charles Wheatstone devise their telegraphs, and found sunspots to be cooler than the surrounding photosphere.
See also: Electromagnetism.

Henry, O. (William Sidney Porter; 1862-1910), U.S. short-story writer noted for the "surprise ending." He began writing stories while imprisoned in Ohio for embezzlement, and was already popular when released. He moved to New York City in 1902 and wrote over 300 stories, collected in *The Four Million* (1906), *The Voice of the City* (1908), and many other books. His last years were marred by an unhappy marriage and financial difficulties.

Henry, Patrick (1736-99), statesman, orator, and prominent figure of the American Revolution. Elected to the Virginia legislature in 1765, he persuaded it to reject the Stamp Act, then joined the first Continental Congress in 1774. In a speech at Virginia's second revolutionary convention in 1775, advocating war rather than negotiations, he coined the famous phrase, "Give me liberty, or give me death!" He served as governor of Virginia 1776-9 and 1784-6. He furiously opposed the ratification of the U.S. Constitution in 1788, because he felt it gave too much power to the federal government over states and individuals. Once the Constitution was adopted, he promoted the Bill of Rights.

Henry of Navarre *see:* Henry (IV, of France).

Henry the Navigator (1394-1460), Portuguese prince, third son of King John I of Portugal, whose active interest inaugurated Portuguese maritime exploration and expansion overseas. He sponsored the exploration and mapping of the west coast of Africa, and his expeditions discovered the Madeira and the Azore islands and rounded Cape Verde.
See also: Exploration.

Henson, Jim *see:* Muppets.

Henson, Matthew Alexander (1866-1955), African-American Arctic explorer who, with Robert Peary, discovered the North Pole in 1909. He had already accompanied Peary to the Arctic 7 times. He served as clerk in the U.S. Customs House in New York City, 1913-36.
See also: Peary, Robert Edwin.

Henze, Hans Werner (1926-), German composer. He is known for his symphonies, concertos, and operas, which include *Elegy for Young Lovers* (1961), for which W.H. Auden and Chester Kallman wrote the libretto.

Hepatica, or liverwort, plant (genus *Hepatica*) of the buttercup family with 3-lobed leaves that derives its Latin and English names from its resemblance to the human liver. Medieval doctors used it as a cure for liver diseases. It is an almost stemless plant about 3 in (7.6 cm) high that grows in woodlands and produces brightly colored flowers in the spring. After the flowers have died, new leaves sprout and displace the old foliage that has persisted over the winter.

Hepatitis, inflammation of the liver, caused by a virus. The symptoms include fever, nausea, loss of appetite, and jaundice. At least two distinct forms of the disease are recognized. Hepatitis A (formerly called infectious, or epidemic, hepatitis) is spread by contaminated drinking water or food. In young children, the infections tend to be mild, but the clinical severity increases with the age of the patient. Hepatitis B (formerly called serum hepatitis) is usually transmitted by transfusions of infected blood or blood products. It is particularly common among intravenous drug users, who may use contaminated needles. The Hepatitis B virus has been detected in a variety of body secretions, including saliva, sperm, and vaginal fluid, and may be transmitted by some forms of sexual contact. Exposure to hepatitis B usually results in an acute self-limiting infection with mild symptoms. In adults, 5-15% of infections fail to resolve, and the affected individuals become persistent carriers of the virus, which is responsible for many cases of liver cancer. There is a vaccination against hepatitis B, which was approved for use in the United States in 1982. In recent years, a third form of the disease, sometimes called hepatitus C, has been detected. Its cause is not known.
See also: Liver.

Hepburn, Katharine (1909-), U.S. stage and film actress. She has won 4 Academy Awards for best actress, for *Morning Glory* (1933), *Guess Who's Coming to Dinner* (1967), *The Lion in Winter* (1968), and *On Golden Pond* (1981).

Hephaestus, or Hephaistos, Greek god of fire. Blacksmith to the gods and the patron of metalworkers, he was responsible for such works as Achilles' armor and Zeus's throne. A powerful god, he was also lame. His marriage to Aphrodite represented the union of Art and Beauty.
See also: Mythology.

Hepplewhite, George (d. 1786), English furniture maker and designer, influenced by Robert Adam. His furniture is characterized by elegant, fine carved forms and painted or inlaid wood.

Heptarchy (from the Greek for "rule of seven"), the 7 kingdoms of Anglo-Saxon Britain before the 9th-century Danish conquests. The kingdoms, founded by the Angles, Saxons, and Jutes, were Kent, Sussex, Wessex, Essex, Northumbria, East Anglia, and Mercia.

Hepworth, Dame Barbara (1903-75), English sculptor. Her abstract work in stone and bronze, like that of Henry Moore, is concerned with surface textures and the contrast of space and mass.

Hera, in Greek mythology, queen of the Olympian gods and sister and wife of Zeus; the goddess of marriage and birth. A jealous and quarrelsome wife, she often persecuted those who rivaled her for Zeus's affections. She was the patroness of the cities of Argos, Sparta, and Mycenae and the island of Samos. Her sacred symbols were the cow and the peacock. Hera is often represented as a regal figure wearing a bridal dress, carrying a scepter or with a wreath on her brow. The Romans identified her with the goddess Juno. A supporter of the Greeks against the Trojans in Homer's *Iliad*, she was also the protector of heroes.
See also: Mythology.

Heracles *see:* Hercules.

Heraclitus (c.540-c.480 B.C.), Greek philosopher. His main theory was of universal impermanence ("You cannot step twice into the same river") and the interrelation of all things, especially opposites. He held that fire was the fundamental element of the universe.
See also: Philosophy.

Heraldry, system of devising designs or insignia displayed on shields or coats of arms to identify individuals, families, towns, universities, military regiments, or nations. Heralds of the Middle Ages announced tournaments and became expert in identifying the armorial bearings of the participants. The origins of heraldry is uncertain but may have begun in 12th century Germany. Heraldry proliferated throughout Europe due to the popularity of tournaments which attracted Knights from many regions of Europe.

Herb, name applied to any plant with soft stems and leaves that die at the end of the growing season; more specifically, those plants of which leaves or other parts are used medicinally and as spices to flavor food.

Herbart, Johann Friedrich (1776-1841), German philosopher and educator best remembered for his pedagogical system, which stressed the interrelated importance of ethics (to give social direction) and psychology (to understand the mind of the pupil). One of his most important works is *Application of Psychology to the Science of Education.*
See also: Philosophy.

Herbert, George (1593-1633), English poet and clergyman. His metaphysical poetry was published posthumously in a collection entitled *The Temple* (1633).

Herbert, Victor (1859-1924), Irish-born U.S. operetta composer and conductor. The conductor of the Pittsburgh Symphony Orchestra (1878-1904), he was famous for *Babes in Toyland* (1903), *Naughty Marietta* (1910), and *Eileen* (1917). He also wrote two grand operas and a cello concerto.

Herbicide, chemical compound used to kill plants. Selective herbicides kill only weeds. Nonselective ones are used to clear land of plant life. Many of these chemicals are dangerous to human and animal life and must be used with great care. One of

Katharine Hepburn

Heraldic tinctures are divided into metals, colors and furs. The tinctures with their heraldic name are given.

Key:
1. Red/Gules
2. Gold/Or
3. Black on white/Ermine
4. Blue/Azure
5. Silver/Argent
6. Vair pattern/Vair and Cour
7. Black/Sable
8. Green/Vert
9. Purple/Purpure

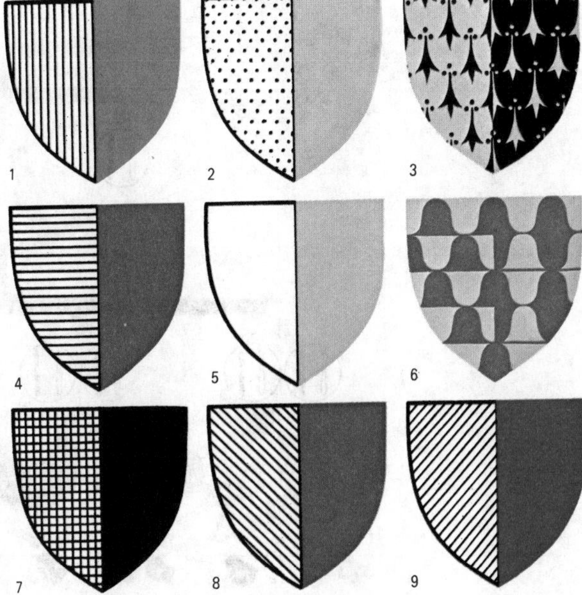

the more deadly herbicides in recent history was Agent Orange, a defoliant used by the U.S. during the Vietnam War. It is responsible for serious illnesses among veterans and their offspring.

Herbivores, dietary classification of the animal kingdom including all animals that feed exclusively on plant materials. Preyed on by many carnivorous animals, they form the lower links of food chains.

Herblock *see:* Block, Herbert Lawrence.

Hercegovina *see:* Bosnia and Hercegovina.

Herculaneum, ancient city at the foot of Mt. Vesuvius in Italy. Along with Pompeii, it was destroyed in A.D. 79 by the eruption of Vesuvius, which engulfed it in preservative volcanic mud. Rediscovered in 1709, it is still being excavated.
See also: Vesuvius, Mount.

Hercules, or Heracles, in Greek mythology, hero famed for his strength and courage. The son of Zeus and Alcmene, he was hated by Zeus's wife Hera, who caused him to go mad. While insane, he killed his own wife and children. He then tried to purify himself by performing 12 labors set for him by King Eurystheus. After his death he rose to Mount Olympus, the dwelling place of the gods and made his peace with Hera.
See also: Mythology.

Hercules, constellation located in the Northern Hemisphere. In the southernmost part of the constellation, a huge red star marks the head of Hercules. The northwest side of the constellation, 30,000 light-years away from earth, is barely visible without a telescope.
See also: Constellation.

Hercules beetle, any of a genus (*Dynastes*) of large beetles belonging to the scarab family and found in North America. Males of the species have pincer-like horns that curve out from the head and upper body. Some male Hercules beetles may grow to 5 or 6 inches (13 to 15 centimeters) in length.

Herder, Johann Gottfried von (1744-1803), German writer, critic, philosopher, and clergyman. A leader of the *Sturm und Drang (Storm and Stress)* movement in German literature, his ideas about poetry, art, language, religion, and history influenced many prominent theorists and writers. Opposed to German imitations of classic works, he translated folk songs as well as the plays of Shakespeare. These translations helped inspire the work of the German Romanticists who followed him, particularly Goethe.

Heredity, process by which characteristics are passed on to offspring. Inherited characteristics are passed on in units called genes. Genes are normally located on the chromosomes in the nuclei of cells. Each chromosome carries many genes that may be transmitted together and are said to be "in coupling." The genetic composition, or genome, of an individual is established at conception; thereafter, a complex interaction of genes and environment (both internal and external) shapes his or her development.
See also: Genetics.

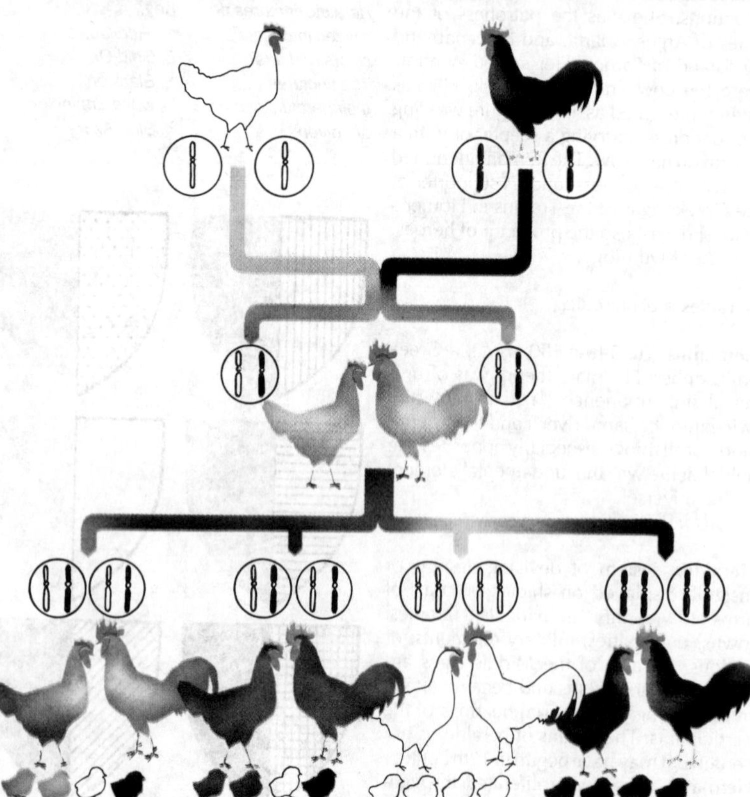

Heredity: All offspring produced by crossing a black with a white fowl carry one factor of each type and are mixed in color because both factors contribute to the appearance of the individual. When two of these cross-bred birds are mated, a quarter of the offspring will be black, and all their chicks will be black. Another quarter will be white and will have white chicks. The remaining half will be splashed white as they receive both factors.

Herman, Woody (Woodrow Charles Herman; 1913-87), U.S. musician and bandleader. He flourished during the 1930s and 1940s, but remained popular beyond the big band era because of his ability to adapt to changing styles in jazz. Herman played the clarinet and alto saxophone. His best known song was "Woodchopper's Ball" (1939).
See also: Jazz.

Hermaphrodite, organism with both male and female reproduction organs. Usually, an individual functions in only 1 sexual role at a time, but in a few species, e.g., earthworms, each of a pair of partners fertilizes the other during copulation. Hermaphrodite plants are usually referred to as being bisexual.

Hermes, in Greek mythology, one of the 12 Olympian gods, son of Zeus, messenger of the gods, guard of roads and highways, and guide of souls to Hades. He was usually depicted wearing a hat with wings. The Romans identified him with Mercury.
See also: Mythology.

Hermes of Praxiteles, statue of Hermes, messenger of the gods in Greek mythology, created by the Athenian sculptor Praxiteles in 330 B.C. It portrays Hermes holding his infant brother Dionysus and offering him grapes. The original statue was lost, but a copy was made by the Greek sculptor Pasiteles c.100 B.C.

Hermitage, Soviet art museum in Leningrad. Its famed collections, begun by Empress Catherine II in the 18th century, contain art treasures obtained worldwide, including masterpieces by Rembrandt, Picasso, and Matisse.

Hermit crab, crustacean with soft body that occupies the empty shells of sea snails. The hermit crab has a spiral-coiled abdomen, well-developed pincers, and two pairs of walking legs. It withdraws into the borrowed shell if attacked.

Herndon, William Henry (1818-91), U.S lawyer and biographer (1889) of Abraham Lincoln, his friend and law partner from 1843. His portrayal of Lincoln is considered a valuable record of the president's life.

Hernia, protrusion of an internal organ through an opening in the wall surrounding it. Hernias may be congenital or caused by muscle weakness in the lower abdomen (inguinal hernia), diaphragm (hiatus hernia), or navel. Corrective surgery is sometimes necessary.

Hero and Leander, tragic lovers in Greek folklore. Hero was a virgin priestess of Aphrodite. Every night Leander would swim across the Hellespont, or Dardanelles, to meet her, guided by a light from her tower. One night a storm blew out her lamp and Leander, unable to see his way across, drowned. The next morning, when Hero saw his body floating in the water, she drowned herself in sorrow.
See also: Mythology.

Herod, dynasty ruling in Palestine for nearly 150 years around the time of Jesus. The family fortune was founded in c.65 B.C., but its best-known leader was **Herod the Great** (73-4 B.C.), who ruled Judaea from 37 B.C. His allies, who helped preserve his powers, included Marc Antony and Augustus. Although he was a skilled ruler, he was hated for his ruthlessness, ordering the massacre of the Innocents. His son **Herod Antipas** (21 B.C.-A.D. 39) ruled Galilee at the time of the crucifixion of Jesus and had John the Baptist executed.

Herodotus (484?-425? B.C.), Greek historian, often called "the Father of History" for his writings about the causes of the Persian Wars fought between Greece and Persia (499-479 B.C.). Although his accuracy is often questioned, he was the first to treat human history in a narrative form. His work is characterized by warmth and a great diversity of information.

Heroin, highly addictive narcotic derivative of morphine. The symptoms of withdrawal may appear as early as 4 to 6 hours after the last dose of the drug; they generally peak within 36 to 72 hours.
See also: Drug; Drug abuse.

Heron, long-billed, long-legged wading bird of the family Ardeidae. Herons are predators, with sharp bills that can kill frogs, fish, eels, and watervoles. The egret is in the same family.

Herpes, virus with various forms, causing painful blisters usually on the lips or genitals. The best known of several related herpes viruses is herpes simplex. It is the cause of the common cold sore (fever blister) that frequently appears on the lips. The herpes simplex infection is usually acquired before the age of 5. The virus then becomes dormant but causes recurrent blisters throughout the life of the infected person. In most instances, the sores heal within a week or two and are not serious. Herpes simplex II causes sores in, on, and around the genital organs and urinary passageways. Genital herpes can cause miscarriage, especially in the early months of pregnancy, and can also damage the central nervous system of the fetus. A third strain of the virus is called herpes zoster, or varicella-zoster virus, the cause of chicken pox and shingles. While chicken pox is commonly a childhood disease, herpes zoster generally occurs in late-middle and old age.

Herrera, Tomás (1804-54), Panamanian political leader. He led the 1840 movement to make Panama a free state, separate from Colombia. He served as president of Panama during its single year of independence. Herrera later became a high-ranking Colombian official and put down a rebellion in 1854.
See also: Panama.

Herrick, Robert (1591-1674), English lyric poet. Writing in the classical tradition of the Latin lyricists, he was also greatly influenced by the dramatist Ben Jonson. His poems are concerned with nature, youth, and love. His best-known line: "Gather ye rosebuds while ye may." Most of his work appeared in *Hesperides* (1648).

Herring, narrow-bodied blue and silver fish of the family Clupidae, common in the North Atlantic and the Pacific. Herring schools often contain millions of fish and are food for many other animals. They feed on plankton, minute sea organisms. Most of the herring eaten by people is preserved by salting or smoking.

Herriot, Edouard (1872-1957), French politician. As leader of the Radical Socialists Herriot was elected premier of France 3 times (1924-25 and 1932). In 1942 he was imprisoned by the Germans for opposition to the Vichy government. He later became president of the National Assembly (1947-54).
See also: France.

Herschel, family of British astronomers of German origin. **Sir Frederick William Herschel** (1738-1822) built reflecting telescopes, discovered Uranis (1781), showed the sun's motion on space (1783), discovered the relative orbital motion of double stars (1793), and studied nebulae. His sister, **Caroline Lucretia Herschel** (1750-1848), discovered eight comets. His son **Sir John Frederick William Herschel** (1792-1871) published a catalog of nebulae and clusters, first used sodium thiosulfate as a photographic fixer, and studied polarized light.
See also: Astronomy.

Hersey, John Richard (1914-), U.S. author, Pulitzer Prize winner with his first novel, *A Bell for Adano* (1944). His experiences as a war correspondent gave him material for his books, which include *Hiroshima* (1946) and *The Wall* (1950).

Herskovits, Melville Jean (1895-1963), U.S. anthropologist, particularly interested in culture change and African ethnology. In 1927 at Northwestern University, he founded the first U.S. college course in African studies.
See also: Anthropology.

Hertz, Gustav Ludwig (1887-1975), German physicist who shared with J. Franck the 1925 Nobel Prize for physics for their experiments showing the internal structure of the atom to be quantized. He developed a way to isolate isotopes (1932) that is in use today in uranium separation plants.
See also: Atom; Bohr, Niels Henrik David.

Hertz, Heinrich Rudolph (1857-94), German physicist who first broadcast and received radio waves (1886). He showed that they could be reflected and refracted like light, and that they traveled at the same velocity. The hertz, a unit of frequency, is named after him.
See also: Physics; Radio.

Hertzog, James Barry Munnik (1866-1942), South African prime minister (1924-39). Founder of the Nationalist party (1914), he worked for separate development of Afrikaner culture and an independent republic of South Africa.

Statue of Herod the Great

Herzen, Aleksander Ivanovich (1812-70), Russian writer and early advocate of socialism. He was banished to the countryside in 1834 for subversive activities and left Russia for England permanently in 1847. His weekly journal *Kolokol* (1857-62) was smuggled into Russia and influenced the revolutionary movement there. One of his more notable books is *My Past and Thoughts* (1855).

Herzl, Theodor (1860-1904), Austrian writer and founder of the political Zionist movement. Convinced by the anti-Semitism surrounding the Dreyfus Affair that Jewish assimilation was impossible, he proposed the establishment of a Jewish state and in 1897 organized the first Zionist World Congress.
See also: Zionism.

Hesiod (8th century B.C.), Greek epic poet. His major works are the didactic *Theogeny*, describing the gods and heroes of Greek mythology, and *Works and Days*, dealing with the everyday life of a farmer.

Hesperides, in Greek mythology, nymphs who guarded the golden apples, which were a wedding gift from Gaea, goddess of earth, to her children, Zeus and Hera, Hercules stole the apples as one of his 12 labors.

Hesperornis, any of a genus (*Hesperornis*) of extinct birds that lived in North America during the Cretaceous Period, 60 to 125 million years ago. One species, *H. regalis*, was nearly 6 ft (1.8 m) long. The hesperornis could not fly with its undeveloped wings, but was a good diver.

Sir Frederick William Herschel

Hess, Dame Myra (1890-1965), English pianist noted for her interpretations of Bach, Mozart, and Scarlatti. During World War II, when London's concert halls were closed, Hess established a series of morale-boosting lunchtime concerts in the National Gallery for which she was named Dame Commander in the Order of the British Empire by King George VI.

Hess, Rudolf (1894-1987), German Nazi leader, Hitler's deputy (1933-39). In May 1941 he flew secretly to England in an

Rudolf Hess

attempt to convince Britain to withdraw from World War II. He was arrested and interned in Britain for the rest of the war. In 1946, at the Nuremberg Trials, he was condemned to life imprisonment for war crimes.
See also: Nazism.

Hesse, state in western Germany, located along the Rhine River in an important agricultural and mining region. Covering an area of 8,152 sq mi (21,113 sq km), the present boundaries of Hesse were formed after World War II from a combination of several other states and former Prussian provinces. The capital is Wiesbaden; other principal cities are Darmstadt, Frankfurt, and Kassel.
See also: Germany.

Hesse, Hermann (1877-1962), German-born Swiss poet and novelist. The solitude, especially of artists, is a recurrent theme in his work. His novels include *Demian* (1919), *Siddhartha* (1922), *Steppenwolf* (1927), and *The Glass Bead Game* (1943). In 1946 he won the Nobel Prize in Literature.

Hessian fly, small, biting insect (*Mayetiola destructor*) so named because it was brought to North America from Europe in straw used for the horses of Hessian soldiers employed by the British during the American Revolution. The larvae of the Hessian fly burrow into wheat stems and destroy them.

Hessians, German mercenaries, mostly from Hesse-Kassel, sold into British military service by their government to fight against the colonials in the American Revolutionary War. After the war many settled in the United States and Canada.
See also: Revolutionary War in America.

Hestia, in Greek mythology, goddess of the hearth. She was also worshiped as protector of the home and the nation, as well as the guardian of fire. The oldest child of Cronus and Rhea, she helped her brother, Zeus, overthrow Cronus's rule over earth and was rewarded by Zeus with the largest portion of the people's material sacrifices. Her Roman counterpart was Vesta.
See also: Mythology.

Heterotropia *see:* Strabismus.

Thor Heyerdahl reached the Caribbean island of Barbados from Morocco in the papyrus boat Ra II in 57 days.

Hevesey, George Charles de (1885-1966), Hungarian chemist, awarded the 1943 Nobel Prize for chemistry for his work on radioactive tracers. He was also the codiscoverer of the element hafnium.
See also: Hafnium.
See also: Chemistry.

Hewes, Joseph (1730-79), American patriot. He represented North Carolina as a delegate to the Continental Congresses of 1774-77 and 1779 and was a signer of the Declaration of Independence. As the first head of the U.S. Navy, his most famous act was the appointment of John Paul Jones as an officer.

Heydrich, Reinhard (1904-42), German Nazi leader, head of the security police, chief deputy to Himmler, head of the SS and organizer of the extermination of European Jews. Known as "the Hangman," he was assassinated in 1942 by Czech resistance forces. In retaliation, the Nazis destroyed the town of Lidice, Czechoslovakia.
See also: Nazism.

Heyerdahl, Thor (1914-), Norwegian ethnologist and author best known for his expeditions to prove the feasibility of his theories of cultural diffusion. In 1947 he and his crew sailed the Pacific on rafts to demonstrate the possibility that the Polynesians may have originated in South America. His book *Kon-Tiki* was an account of the voyage. He also sailed across the Atlantic in rafts (*The Ra Expeditions*, 1969 and 1970) and did the same in the Persian Gulf, trying to show that the Sumerians could have reached Africa by sea (*Tigris*, 1977-78).
See also: Ethnography.

Heyse, Paul Johann Ludwig von (1830-1914), German writer. Center of the traditionalist Munich circle, he was noted for his romantic short stories. He won the Nobel Prize for literature in 1910.

Heyward, DuBose (1885-1940), U.S. author, best known for his novel *Porgy* (1925), about the plight of Southern blacks, on which George Gershwin based his opera *Porgy and Bess*.

Heyward, Thomas, Jr. (1746-1809), American patriot. A Revolutionary War soldier from South Carolina, Heyward also represented his state in the Continental Congresses of 1776-78 and was a signer of the Declaration of Independence.

Heywood, Thomas (1574?-1651), English dramatist and actor. He wrote over 200 dramas, but only about 20 have survived. His best-known play is *A Woman Killed with Kindness* (1603).

Hezekiah, (d. c.686 B.C.), Judean king (c.715-c.686 B.C.). He defied the Assyrian army under Sennacherib, which besieged Jerusalem (701 B.C.). With the prophets Micah and Isaiah as his advisers, Hezekiah removed idols from the Holy Temple and restored the temple's status as the focal point for Jewish religious worship.

Hibbing (pop. 18,046), city located in the heart of Minnesota's Mesabi Range. Named after Frank Hibbing, a prominent lumber dealer, the city is often called the "Iron Ore Capital of the World" for the rich deposits lying nearby, discovered in the early 1900s. It has the world's largest open-pit iron mine, a popular tourist attraction.
See also: Minnesota.

Hibernation, protective mechanism whereby certain animals reduce their bodies' activity and sleep through winter. Animals prepare by storing extra fat several weeks before the onset of hibernation. When temperatures drop, the animal's pulse rate and breathing drop to a minimum.

Hibiscus, any of various herbs, shrubs, and trees (genus *Hibiscus*) of the mallow family, having large showy flowers. A single bloom can be over 6 in (15 cm) wide.

Hibiscus

Hickok, Wild Bill (James Butler Hickok; 1837-76), legendary U.S. frontier law officer. During the Civil War he was a Union scout and spy. As U.S. marshal at the lawless frontier towns of Hays and Abilene, Kans. (1869-71), he won a reputation for marksmanship. He was murdered in South Dakota by Jack McCall.
See also: Western frontier life.

Hickory, tree (genus *Carya*) of the walnut family. Commonly found in the eastern United States, the hickory produces edible nuts and strong wood used in industrial tool handles and golf clubs and is used to make top-grade charcoal for smoking meats. The tallest of the hickories, the pecan tree, produces America's second most popular edible nut.

Hicks, Edward (1780-1849), U.S. painter. A Quaker preacher, he is best known for over 50 versions of *The Peaceable Kingdom*, based on Isaiah's prophecy of peace among all creatures.

Hidalgo y Costilla, Miguel (1753-1811), Mexican revolutionary priest, known as "the father of Mexican independence." He organized a rebellion against Spanish rule in 1810 and won initial victories with an army made up mainly of Indian peasants. The revolt was defeated in 1811, and Hidalgo was executed.

Hidatsa *see:* Gros Ventre.

Hideyoshi (Toyotomi Hideyoshi; 1536-98), Japanese military leader and dictator (1585-98). He served as a general in the army under the dictator Nobunga. As ruler of Japan, Hideyoshi brought order to the country following a civil war and formed alliances that enabled him to defeat all opposition to his rule. His attempts to conquer Korea were unsuccessful. He beautified his capital, Osaka, and made it a cultural center.

Hieroglyphics, writing system used in ancient Egypt and several other civilizations. It is based on pictures that represent objects, ideas, or sounds. Egyptian hieroglyphics were used from 3000 B.C. until about 500 B.C. They consisted of 604 symbols that could stand for words, sounds, or classifications. The French Egyptologist Jean François Champollion (1790-1832) was the first person in modern times to make real progress in deciphering hieroglyphics.

Hi-fi *see:* High fidelity.

Higginson, Thomas Wentworth (1823-1911), U.S. pastor, abolitionist, and author. His liberal ideas cost him his first Unitarian church post. In the Civil War he was colonel of the first black regiment. He edited Emily Dickinson's *Poems* (1890-91) with M.L. Todd.
See also: Abolitionism; Civil War, U.S.

High blood pressure *see:* Hypertension.

High Desert, or Great Basin, sparsely populated region of south-central Oregon, lying east of the Cascades and south of the Blue Mountains. The High Desert averages 4,000-5,000 ft (1,200-1,500 m) high in elevation. With a low annual rainfall, lakes and rivers there are intermittent. Sections of the landscape are marked by cinder cones and volcanic craters. Cattle, sheep, and wild antelope graze on the short grass.

High fidelity, reproduction of an electronic signal or sound with a minimum of distortion, especially by phonographic equipment. High fidelity systems are sometimes called hi-fi systems.

High jump, track and field event. It requires jumping over a bar 6-8 ft (1.83-2.44 m) high and 12 ft (3.66 m) long. From a running start, jumpers must clear the bar and land in a cushioned pit on the other side. Two styles are used in high jumping, the "straddle" (forward) and the "Fosbury flop" (backward). Athletes are scored on their best jumps, but those who knock the bar down 3 consecutive times are disqualified.

Highlands *see:* Scotland.

High priest, in Jewish history, head of the Israelite priesthood, whose duties included supervising worship in the temple of Jerusalem and conducting services on the Day of Atonement. The office existed until the destruction of the temple by the Romans in A.D. 70.

High seas, in maritime law, the sea beyond territorial waters, usually 200 nautical mi (370 km) from the coasts of nations that border the oceans. Since the 19th century freedom of the seas has been recognized as a rule of international law, but recently the discovery of minerals under the sea and the importance of the airspace above it have made the concept crucial. Attempts by any state to extend its jurisdiction should be ratified by international agreement. The Law of the Sea Treaty (1982) received majority approval in the UN, largely because of Third World support, but the United States voted against it.

Hijacking, mid-air takeover of aircraft. Since the first American plane was forced to fly to Cuba in 1961, thousands of travelers from 88 countries have been involved in hijacking attempts.

Hijra *see:* Hegira.

Hiking, exercise in the form of endurance walking. It can range in duration from a few hours to a few days or weeks and can be done on woodland trails, riverbanks, lakeshores, mountains, or city streets. Hikes of more than 1 day involve camping out, and these hikers usually carry tents, sleeping bags, and backpacks with food supplies and changes of clothing.

Hill, James Jerome (1838-1916), U.S. railroad magnate. After purchasing the St. Paul and Pacific Railroad, he extended it to the Pacific at Seattle (1893). Later, working with J.P. Morgan, he consolidated his holdings in the Great Northern Railway Company.
See also: Railroad.

Hill, Joe (Joseph Hillstrom; 1879-1915), legendary Swedish-born U.S. labor organizer for the Industrial Workers of the World. He immigrated to the United States in 1902 and was the author of many songs of the early socialist labor movement. He was convicted of murdering a man in Utah in 1915 and sentenced to death, though many people believed that he was innocent. His funeral was attended by about 30,000 people.
See also: Labor movement.

Hill, Octavia (1838-1912), English social reformer. She was instrumental in improving housing conditions for London's poor and in establishing and preserving the city's parks and playgrounds. Hill also served on the board of several charitable organizations, and her concern for the preservation of natural beauty and historic structures led to the formation of the National Trust.

Hieroglyphic script in a fragment of the Egyptian Book of the Dead

Hillary, Sir Edmund Percival (1919-), New Zealand explorer and mountaineer. In 1953 he and Tenzing Norkay, a Sherpa from Nepal, were the first to reach the summit of Mt. Everest, the world's highest mountain.
See also: Mount Everest.

Hillel (c.70 B.C.-10 A.D.), Jewish scholar born in Babylonia, one of the founders of rabbinic Judaism, and ethical leader of his generation. He was opposed by Shammai, another teacher. His "Seven Rules" of exegesis laid the groundwork for a liberal interpretation of scriptural law.
See also: Judaism.

Hilliard, Nicholas (1537-1619), English miniature painter. As court artist to Elizabeth I, his style was characterized by exquisite jewellike detailing and fine drawing.

Hillman, Sidney (1887-1946), U.S. labor leader. A Lithuanian immigrant, who came to the United States in 1907, Hillman became the first president of the Amalgamated Clothing Workers (1914), a post he held until his death. He supported industrial unions, helped to found the Congress of Industrial Organizations (CIO), and advised government on labor relations.
See also: Labor movement.

Hills, Carla Anderson (1934-), U.S. government official. As Secretary of Housing and Urban Development (1975-77) under President Gerald R. Ford, she was the third woman Cabinet member in U.S. history. In 1989 President George Bush appointed her as a special trade representative.

High jump innovator and champion, Dick Fosbury, executing the Fosbury flop.

Hilo (pop. 35,400), city on the eastern shore of Hawaii Island. The state's second-largest city and Hawaii County's seat of government, it is also the southernmost large city in the United States. Ancient Polynesian sailors settled Hilo, and a U.S. mission was opened c.1820. It is a leading exporter of sugar cane and coffee and a hub for tourists visiting the nearby volcanic region.
See also: Hawaii.

Hilton, Conrad Nicholson (1887-1979), U.S. hotel chain founder. Beginning with his first hotels in New Mexico and Texas, Hilton expanded his holdings to most major U.S. and foreign cities and resort areas. By 1967 Hilton hotels were in 37 nations, and the international operation of the company became a subsidiary of Trans World Airlines (TWA).

Hilton, James (1900-54), English novelist. His books include *Lost Horizon* (1933), *Good-bye, Mr. Chips* (1934), and *Random Harvest* (1941), which were made into films.

Himalayas, highest mountain system in the world, over 1,500 mi (2,410 km) long, extending from Pakistan through India, Tibet, Nepal, Sikkim, and Bhutan. The northern range is called the Trans-Himalayas. The southern range has three parallel zones: the Great Himalayas, including the 29,028-ft (8,848-m) Mt. Everest, the Lesser Himalayas, and the southernmost Outer Himalayas.

Himmler, Heinrich (1900-45), German Nazi leader. A founder of the Nazi party, head of the SS from 1929 and of the Gestapo from 1936, he was responsible for the murder of millions in concentration camps. Named interior minister in 1943, he became the main leader of Germany's internal affairs. He was captured by the British army in 1945 and committed suicide.
See also: Holocaust; Nazism.

Hindemith, Paul (1895-1963), German-born U.S. composer and teacher. Denounced as a modernist because of his dissonant harmonies and counterpoint, he was banned by the Nazis in Germany and immigrated to the United States in 1937. He later returned to more tonal, neoclassical forms. Among his major works are the symphony (1934) and opera (1938) *Mathis the Painter, Symphonic Metamorphoses on Themes of Carl Maria von Weber* (1943), and *The Four Temperaments* (1944).

Hindenburg *see:* Airship.

Hindenburg, Paul von (1847-1934), German general, president of Germany (1925-34). Together with Ludendorff he directed German military strategies in World War I. As president he was chiefly a figurehead. In 1933 he appointed Hitler chancellor.
See also: World War I.

Hindenburg Line *see:* Siegfried Line.

Hindi, official language of India, a written form of Hindustani. It is written in Devanagari script, reading from left to right. Hindi belongs to the Indic group of the Indo-European family of languages.

Hinduism, chief religion of India, embracing many different sects and trends. In terms of numbers of adherents, it is the third largest of the world's religions, after Christianity and Islam. Hinduism is based on the Veda, sacred writings dating back some 3,000 years. The Veda comprised four types of writing: the Samhita, which in turn consists of 4 books of hymns, chants, and prayers—the Rig-Veda, the Sama-Veda, the Yajur-Veda, and the Atharva-Veda; the Brahmanas, which are prose; the Aranyakas, containing instructions for meditation; and the Upanishads, mystical works stating the Veda's doctrine of the soul. Between 800 B.C. and 500 B.C. Hinduism began to change under the impact of two new, rival religions: Buddhism and Jainism. It absorbed many village and tribal gods into a pantheon dominated by Brahma (the creator), Vishnu (the preserver), and Shiva (the destroyer). In this period important social and philosophical

Himalayas seen from the hills of southern Nepal.

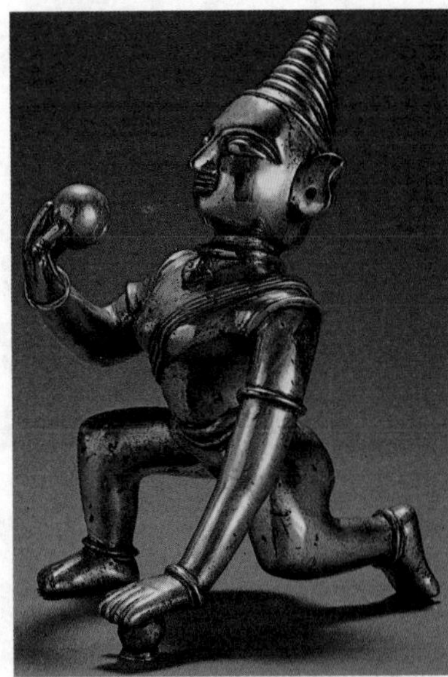

Top: the Hindu god, Vishnu, who protects the universe and (bottom) Shiva temple in India.

changes occured: the caste system was established, and the learned Brahman, often a priest, became the supreme figure in society. The doctrine of reincarnation and the transmigration of the soul also became part of the creed. A further addition was the concept of *karma*, the idea that every individual is punished for wrongdoing and rewarded for righteousness, if not in the present life, then in a reincarnation. The aim of every Hindu should be to rise, through just living, higher and higher in the scale of existence with each reincarnation, finally attaining absorption into the personality of Brahma. Hinduism has various subcults, of which those of Shiva, Vishnu, Krishna, Shakti, and the Matris are the most important.

Hindu Kush, mountain range in Asia, stretching about 500 m (800 km) from northeast Afghanistan to north Pakistan. High-altitude passes cross the range. The highest peak is Tirich Mir (25,260 ft/ 7,699 m).

Hines, Earl "Fatha" (1905-83), U.S. jazz musician, pianist and composer. A member of Louis Armstrong's group, the Hot Five (late 1920s), he later formed a band of his own, featuring Charlie Parker and Dizzy Gillespie, which introduced bebop. Hines's powerful percussive style greatly influenced modern piano techniques.
See also: Jazz.

Hinton, S(usan) E(loise) (1948-), U.S. author of books for teenagers. Her novels are set in Tulsa, Okla., where Hinton was born and raised. Her characters, often teenagers themselves, reject authority and must cope with the problems of poverty, drug abuse, and violence on their own. Hinton's first and most widely recognized novel, *The Outsiders* (1967), written when she was 16, is noted for its action and harshly realistic characters. Her other works include *That Was Then, This Is Now* (1971), *Rumble Fish* (1975), and *Tex* (1979).

Hip, freely movable ball-and-socket joint formed by the cup-shaped hollow of the pelvic bone and the smooth, rounded head of the thighbone. The adult hipbone combines three bones that are separate in youth: the ilium, ischium, and pubis.

Hipparchus (c.180 B.C.-125 B.C.), Greek scientist, pioneer of systematic astronomy. He compiled the first star catalog and ascribed magnitudes to stars. He also estimated the size of the moon and its distance from the earth, and was probably the first to discover the precession of the equinox.
See also: Equinox.

Hipparchus (6th century B.C.), Greek political figure. Son of Pisistratus, ruler of Athens in the mid-500s, Hipparchus shared power with his brother, Hippias, when their father died in 527. A patron of the arts, Hipparchus brought the poets Anacreon and Simonides to Athens. He got involved in a plot to overthrow his brother and was killed when the revolt was suppressed.
See also: Greece, Ancient.

Hippies, anti-establishment subculture in the U.S. in the 1960s, principally people under 25 who rejected conservative values and traditional authority. Opposed to the Vietnam War and known for loose sexual conventions, use of drugs, and long hair, hippies gravitated to the East Village in New York City and the Haight-Ashbury district in San Francisco.

Hippocampus *see:* Seahorse.

Hippocrates (c.460-c.377 B.C.), Greek physician often called the father of medicine. He was probably the author of the *Hippocratic Collection*, some 70 books on all aspects of ancient medicine. The Hippocratic Oath, a statement of medical ethics and good practice, is still sworn to by graduates of many medical schools.
See also: Medicine.

Hippodrome, any open or closed structure for circuses or similar spectacles. Originally a Greek outdoor course for horse and chariot races, it was adopted by the Romans, who built numerous hippodromes. Shaped like the letter U, with tiers of open seats on 3 sides and closed across the fourth by an area for distinguished guests, such a stadium was frequently up to 400 ft (120 m) wide and 700 ft (210 m) long. The most famous hippodrome was the Circus Maximus at Rome, which could hold over 300,000 spectators.

Hippopotamus, one of the largest living terrestrial mammals (*Hippopotamus amphibius*), distantly related to the pig, widespread in Africa. Hippopotamuses generally are about 5 ft (1.6 m) tall and weigh about 5 tons (4,500 kg). They have massive bodies set on short legs, each with four toes with hoof-like nails. Their noses, eyes, and ears are on top of their heads, which allows them to spend most of the day submerged in rivers. At night they come on land to graze.

Hippopotamus

Hirohito (1901-89), emperor of Japan from 1926 until his death. After World War II the recognition of the emperor as a god was rescinded, and Hirohito became a "symbol of the state and unity of the people," without political or sovereign power. He was instrumental in persuading the government to accept unconditional surrender in World War II.
See also: Japan.

Emperor Hirohito

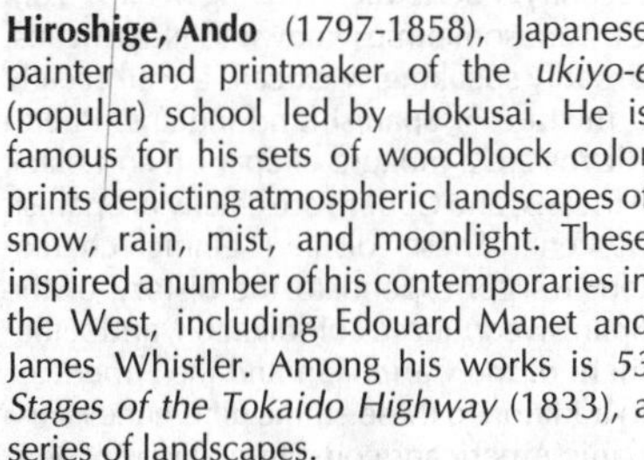

Hiroshige, Ando (1797-1858), Japanese painter and printmaker of the *ukiyo-e* (popular) school led by Hokusai. He is famous for his sets of woodblock color prints depicting atmospheric landscapes of snow, rain, mist, and moonlight. These inspired a number of his contemporaries in the West, including Edouard Manet and James Whistler. Among his works is *53 Stages of the Tokaido Highway* (1833), a series of landscapes.

Hiroshima (pop. 1,044,000), industrial city on Honshu Island, Japan, located on a bay in the Inland Sea, capital of Hiroshima Prefecture. A thriving industrial and commercial center, it was chosen as the target for the U.S. atomic bomb attack of Aug. 6, 1945. There were at least 80,000 people killed, many more injured or made ill by radiation, and nine-tenths of the city was

Hiroshima's bombing melted in time.

destroyed. It has been largely rebuilt since 1950 and is again an important industrial marketing center.

See also: Japan; Nuclear bomb; World War II.

Hiroshima: the aftermath of an atomic bomb

Hispanic Americans, in the United States, those who have come from Spanish countries or their descendants. There are approximately 20 million Hispanic Americans, making up some 8% of the U.S. population, the second-largest minority in the country after African Americans. Thanks to both a high birth rate and continued immigration, Hispanic Americans are expected to become the largest minority in the United States in the 21st century. Hispanic Americans are unified in certain important respects, principally the Spanish language and the Roman Catholic religion. Their diversity stems from differences of history and culture among their various countries of origin as well as the causes and circumstances leading to immigration to the United States.

The majority of Hispanic Americans, some 63%, are of Mexican descent. Puerto Ricans comprise 12% and Cubans 5% of the total. The remaining 20% come from Spain and countries of South and Central America, including Colombia, the Dominican Republic, Ecuador, Guatemala, El Salvador, and Nicaragua. Consequently, Hispanic Americans are referred to broadly as Latinos. More specifically, Mexican Americans are known as Chicanos and, more recently, Puerto Ricans living in New York City are sometimes known as Nuyoricans. Broadly speaking, Mexicans are ethnically a mixture of Spanish and Indians; Puerto Ricans are a mixture of Spanish and black Africans; and Cubans are chiefly of Spanish descent. These distinct ethnic characteristics correspond to the history of the Spanish conquest, colonization, and settlement of the Caribbean and the Americas. In addition to these ethnic differences, Hispanic Americans come from different periods of immigration at different points in the history of the United States as well as in the histories of their respective countries of origin.

Though the Spanish were a significant presence in Florida as early as the 16th century, Spanish influence in North America proved to be strongest in California and the Southwest. In the aftermath of the Mexican American War (1846-48), there were some 80,000 Mexican Americans living in Colorado, Nevada, Utah, New Mexico, Arizona, Wyoming, and California. From the early 20th century, immigration from Mexico grew. By 1930 about 680,000 Mexicans had come to the United States, and, since World War II, from the 1950s to the 1980s, immigration has continued. Puerto Rico has been a U.S. possession since 1898 and its people U.S. citizens since 1917, but the major wave of immigration took place between 1940 and 1960, when some 545,000 Puerto Ricans came to the United States, principally to New York City. Cubans emigrated to the United States in large numbers as the result of Fidel Castro's successful revolution. From 1959 to 1980, about 625,000 Cubans emigrated to the United States. In addition, the 1970s saw large numbers of Central Americans, especially from El Salvador and Nicaragua, fleeing civil war, political persecution, or economic hardship.

Throughout the 20th century, the U.S. government has adopted various policies aimed at limiting or reversing Hispanic immigration, including, at one time, a program of repatriation. More recently, the U.S. government has adjusted its immigration policy to correspond to its foreign policy. As a result, Central Americans fleeing war and political unrest in their countries throughout the 1980s were refused political asylum in most cases. More recently, the U.S. government, in an attempt to deal with large numbers of illegal aliens, extended a limited amnesty to those who registered with the immigration authorities by a certain date.

The history of official U.S. resistance to Hispanic immigration has gone hand in hand with discrimination. Ironically, it has been in response to discrimination and to problems of education and economic opportunity that Hispanic Americans, in all of their diversity, have forged a common ground and have come to participate more directly and effectively in U.S. life. Through their own efforts, Hispanic Americans have improved working conditions for many immigrants, won widespread acceptance of bilingual education, and have broken down many of the barriers of discrimination. As a result, many Hispanic Americans have become prominent in U.S. life. Celia Cruz, Cesar Chavez, and Roberto Clemente are readily recognized. Joseph Montoya served as senator from New Mexico, Bob Martinez was governor of Florida, and, under President George Bush, Lauro Cavazos was secretary of education and Manuel Lujan is secretary of the interior.

Hispaniola, second largest island in the West Indies, located west of Puerto Rico and east of Cuba. The island is shared between the Republic of Haiti (west) and the Dominican Republic (east).

Hiss, Alger (1904-), U.S. public official accused of spying for the USSR. Hiss was an adviser to the U.S. State Department on economic and political affairs. In 1948 he was brought before the House Committee on Un-American Activities (HUAC), and in 1950 he was convicted of perjury. He served 4 years in prison. Maintaining his innocence, Hiss has devoted the rest of his life to clearing his name. Legal scholars are sharply divided on his guilt.

Histamine *see:* Allergy; Antihistamine.

Histology, scientific study of the structure of the tissues that make up organisms.

Histoplasmosis, infectious disease that is endemic in parts of Africa, South America, and the United States, caused by the fungus *Histoplasma capsulatum.* It is characterized by damage to the lungs and occasional anemia, with ulcerations of the mouth and the gastrointestinal tract, enlargement of the liver and spleen, disorder of the lymph glands, and necrosis (tissue death) of the adrenal glands. If not treated early with an antifungal agent, a severe attack can be fatal. It is particularly common in infants and older men.

History, study of the past through documents, reports, and other artifacts. The past can be inferred through many sources—chronicles, myths, buildings, monuments, business documents, newspapers, works of art, archeological objects. Earlier times for which no such sources exist are known as *prehistory.* History as a branch of knowledge is generally confined to the written records of human activities, which limits its scope to the invention of writing, about 5,000 years ago.

The oldest historical writings stem from China, where archeologists found historical records written before 1,000 B.C. In the older civilizations of Egypt and Mesopotamia historical records also appear soon after the introduction of writing. The conscious writing of history is generally considered to have begun in Greece about the 5th century B.C. with Herodotus's description of the wars between Greece and Persia. What made his work history was his conscious attempt to record events of importance and to set forth the motivations of the people involved. This causal approach to events of the past earned Herodotus the title "Father of History," although, unlike modern historians, he did not try to verify all his facts and mixed tradition, oral remembrances, and fable along with actual occurrences and customs. A more analytical method of writing about the past was developed by his successor, Thucydides, whose *History of the Peloponnesian War* is a grave, authentic account of the 27-year war between Athens and Sparta. A third great Greek historian, Xenophon, concentrated more on the purely narrative aspects of history. These types of historical writing, the compendious, the analytical, and the narrative, are still in evidence today. Roman historians include Livy (*History from the Founding of the City*), Tacitus (*Annals* and *Histories*), and Julius Caesar (*Commentaries*), although Caesar's work tends more towards reportage than pure history. During medieval times, Christian monks developed the idea of a *universal history,* which attempted to unite Christian history with the Greek and Roman records. Eusebius's *Ecclesiastical History* is an example, as is Saint Augustine's *City of God,* which presented, in addition, a philosophy of history. At the same time, annals of events called *chronicles* were compiled, mainly by members of the clergy. Bede's *Ecclesiastical History of the English Nation* was the great historical work of the Middle Ages. In more modern times, history developed into a serious discipline pursued by scholars. Edward Gibbon's *History of the Decline and Fall of the Roman Empire* (1776-88) is an early example of dedicated and thorough scholarship. In the 1800s critical, objective history developed into an academic discipline, as exemplified by the works of the German historian Leopold von Ranke and his followers. This German school established canons of criticism and methods of historical analysis that are still in evidence today. The 20th century saw a broadening of the scope of history to include more than the concentration on political events that characterized history up until the 19th century. Today, events of the past are analyzed using tools from many disciplines, including economics, psychology, sociology, and anthropology. Our technological society also fostered an interest in the history of science and in the effect technology has on society. Today, all aspects of the life of peoples and societies form the proper concern of historians.

Hitchcock, Lambert (1795-1852), U.S. cabinetmaker who, in 1818, established a furniture factory at Barkhamsted, Conn. Hitchcock chairs, black with stenciled designs, combined simplicity with elegance. They are now collector's pieces.

Hitchcock, Sir Alfred Joseph (1899-1980), British film director known for his skillful suspense and macabre humor. He made over 50 films, among the best of which were *The Thirty-Nine Steps* (1935), *The Lady Vanishes* (1938), and, in Hollywood, *Rebecca* (1940), *Spellbound* (1945), *Notorious* (1946), *Rear Window* (1954), and *Psycho* (1960).

Hitler, Adolf (1889-1945), Austrian-born dictator of Germany, founder of the Nazi party. Drafted in World War I, he was wounded and awarded the Iron Cross. He blamed the German defeat in the war on Jews and Communists, and in 1920 helped to found the National Socialist (Nazi) Workers Party. In 1923, after an abortive coup against the Bavarian government (the "beer hall putsch"), he served 9 months in prison. There he wrote *Mein Kampf* (My Struggle), an anti-Semitic, anti-Communist diatribe outlining his strategy for remaking Germany and becoming a conquering power throughout Europe. The Nazi party grew rapidly after the outbreak of economic depression in 1929, becoming the largest single party in the country. Although the Nazis never won a national election, their paramilitary street violence made them a powerful force. In 1933 Hitler was named chancellor, and in 1934 he secured his position by liquidating potential opponents within the party. The opposition was crushed, all other parties were outlawed, concentration camps were established, trade unions were eliminated or placed under state control, and anti-Semitism became state policy, enacted into law. In the meantime, a war economy was established. Hitler had the main responsibility for German war strategy, and despite a failed military coup against him in 1944, he remained in complete control of the German armed forces and insisted on fighting on in the face of defeat. He committed suicide in Apr. 1945 in his bunker in Berlin, as Soviet troops entered the city.
See also: Holocaust; Nazism; World War II.

Hittites, Indo-European people of the Middle East in the 2nd millennium B.C. Of unknown origin, they appear to have first settled in southern Turkey (c.1900 B.C.); they conquered central Turkey and became a dominant power. The downfall of the Hittite empire came about 1200 B.C. when it was overrun and fragmented by a vast migration of uncertain origin, called by the Egyptians "peoples of the sea."

Hives, or urticaria, itchy skin condition characterized by the formation of welts with surrounding erythema (reddening) due to histamine release in the body's tissues. It is usually provoked by allergy to food, pollens, fungi, drugs, or parasites, but it may be symptomatic of infection, systemic disease, or emotional disorder. *Dermographism* is a condition in which slight skin pressure produces marked hives, like linear marks that appear after writing on the skin.

Hoatzin (*Opisthocomos hoatzin*), bird that lives in the flooded forests bordering the rivers of northern South America. The adult, which is slightly larger than a pigeon, has a long crest and blue cheeks. It can barely fly, its flight muscles being small to make way for a large crop in which it stores its meals of leaves and fruit. The chicks have 2 movable claws on each wing that help them clamber through foliage. When alarmed, they jump into the water, swimming and even diving easily, then clamber back up the tree when danger has passed.

Hoban, James (1762-1831), Irish-born U.S. architect. He designed and built the White House (1792-1801) and supervised construction of the Capitol and other buildings in Washington, D.C.

Hobart (pop. 127,100), capital of the island of Tasmania, south of the eastern tip of the Australian mainland. This port city, founded in 1804, was originally involved in Antarctic whaling. It took on its present name in 1881. Its industries include textiles, metal products, chemicals, and glass.
See also: Tasmania.

Hobart, Garret Augustus (1844-99), U.S. vice president (1897-79) in the McKinley administration. He was speaker of the New Jersey State Assembly (1873-74) and president of the state senate (1880-82). Upon his death, Theodore Roosevelt was appointed to complete his term.

Adolf Hitler (left) with his cohorts after the failed Beer Hall Putsch (1923), Rudolf Hess is second from right.

Hobbema, Meindert (1638-1709), Dutch landscape painter, taught by Jacob van Ruisdael. His atmospheric river scenes and his later forest and road landscapes, such as *The Avenue at Middelharnis* (1689), foreshadowed John Constable and others.

Hobbes, Thomas (1588-1679), English political philosopher who sought to apply rational principles to the study of human nature. In Hobbes's view, humans are materialistic and pessimistic, their actions motivated solely by self-interest, thus a state's stability can only be guaranteed by a sovereign authority, to which citizens relinquish their rights. *Leviathan* (1651), his most celebrated work, expresses these views. Hobbes saw matter in motion as the only reality; even consciousness and thought were but the outworkings of the motion of atoms in the brain. During and after his lifetime, Hobbes was known as a materialist and suspected of atheism, but in the 20th century his reputation as an able thinker has overshadowed his former notoriety.

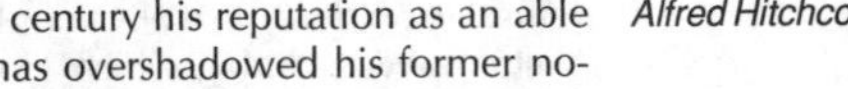

See also: Philosophy.

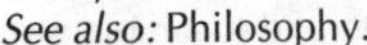

Alfred Hitchcock

Thomas Hobbes

Hobby, Oveta Culp (1905-), U.S. publisher and public servant. Director of the Women's Army Corps (1942-45), she became the first secretary of the Department of Health, Education, and Welfare under President Dwight D. Eisenhower (1953-55). She became chairperson of the board of the Houston *Post* in 1965.

Hobson, Laura Zametkin (1900-86), U.S. author born in New York City, the setting for most of her novels. Her most famous work, *Gentleman's Agreement* (1947), deals with prejudice and religious intolerance. In *The Tenth Month* (1971) and *Consenting Adults* (1975), Hobson addressed the controversial issues of unwed motherhood and homosexuality, respectively. Her other works include *The Celebrity* (1951), *First Papers* (1964), and *Over and Above* (1979).

Hochhuth, Rolf (1931-), German playwright whose first controversial play, *The Deputy* (1963), attacked Pope Pius XII for his stand on the Jews in World War II, and whose second, *Soldiers* (1967), portrayed Winston Churchill as a murderer.

Ho Chi Minh

Ho Chi Minh (Nguyen Van Thanh; 1890-1969), president of North Vietnam (1954-69). From 1911 to 1941 he lived in England, France, the USSR, and China. He helped found the French Communist Party and, later, founded the Vietnamese Communist Party. In 1941 he returned to Vietnam and organized an independence movement, the Viet Minh, that fought against the Japanese in World War II and then against the restored French colonial government. After the decisive Viet Minh victory over the French at Dien Bien Phu in 1954, Vietnam was temporarily divided at the 17th parallel, and Ho became president of North Vietnam. South Vietnam's refusal to hold national elections led to the Vietnam War, during which Ho and his military commander, Gen. Vo Nguyen Giap, proved resolute and tenacious war leaders. In failing health, Ho lived to see the Tet offensive of 1968 and the start of peace negotiations that led ultimately to North Vietnamese victory.
See also: Vietnam War.

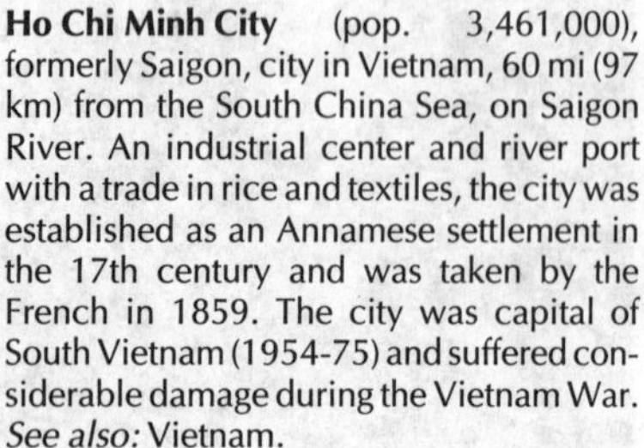

Ho Chi Minh City (pop. 3,461,000), formerly Saigon, city in Vietnam, 60 mi (97 km) from the South China Sea, on Saigon River. An industrial center and river port with a trade in rice and textiles, the city was established as an Annamese settlement in the 17th century and was taken by the French in 1859. The city was capital of South Vietnam (1954-75) and suffered considerable damage during the Vietnam War.
See also: Vietnam.

Höchstädt, Battle of *see:* Blenheim, Battle of.

Hockey, game played on ice in which 2 opposing teams of skaters, using curved sticks, try to shoot a flat, rubber disk called a puck, into the opposing goal, which is 4 ft (1.2 m) high and 6 ft (1.8 m) wide. Each goal scored is 1 point and the team with the most goals at the end of the game is the winner. The ice surface, or rink, is usually 200 ft (61 m) long and 98 ft (30 m) wide and is divided into three zones: offensive, defensive, and neutral. Each team has 6 players on the ice at once: 1 center, 2 wings, 2 defensemen, and 1 goaltender. Together, the center and wings are called forwards and they try to score goals for their team, while the defensemen work to prevent the opposing team from getting chances to score. The goaltender, or goalie, is the last line of defense and always plays directly in front of his team's goal, in an area called the crease. The goalie's only job is to prevent shots by the opposing team from entering the goal. Penalties of varying length are handed out by the referee to a player who breaks the rules, and the team must play with one less skater for the duration of their player's penalty. The most popular league is the National Hockey League (NHL) which consists of 21 teams from the United States and Canada. Hockey is played worldwide, with the Soviet Union historically dominating most Olympic and international competition.
Field hockey, a variation of ice hockey, is played outdoors and on foot. The 2 teams try to shoot a small ball into a slightly larger goal: 7 ft (2.13 m) high and 12 ft (3.66 m) wide. The field is 100 yards (91 m) long and 60 yards (55 m) wide and each team plays 11 players at once: 5 forwards, 3 halfbacks, 2 fullbacks, and a goaltender. Field hockey is an international sport and women's field hockey became an Olympic sport at the 1980 Summer Games.

Hockney, David (1937-), English artist whose emphases are on figurative work and brilliant color. His characteristic painting *A Bigger Splash* (1967) was also the title of a semi-autobiographical documentary film (1974).

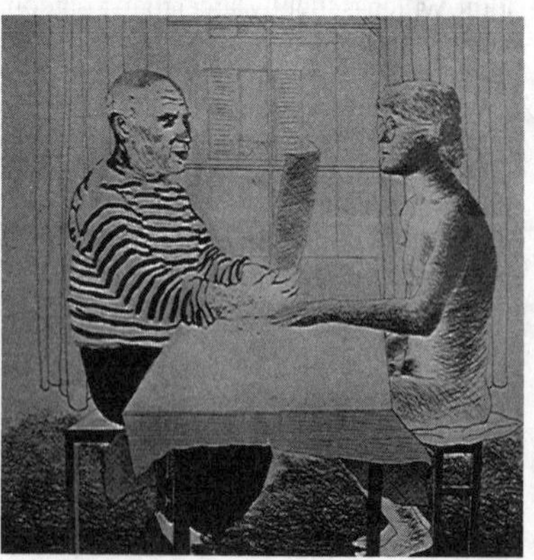

David Hockney's The Painter and His Model

Hodgkin, Alan Lloyd (1914-), English physiologist awarded (with A. F. Huxley and J. Eccles) the 1963 Nobel Prize for physiology or medicine for his work on the chemical basis of nerve impulse transmission.
See also: Physiology.

Hodgkin, Dorothy Mary Crowfoot (1910-), British chemist awarded the 1964 Nobel Prize for chemistry for determining the structure of vitamin B_{12}.
See also: Chemistry

Hodgkin's disease, or lymphadenoma, form of cancer affecting the lymphatic system. It was named for Thomas Hodgkin, the English physician who first described the disease in 1832. It usually causes swelling of lymph glands in the neck, armpits, or the groin. The lymph glands manufacture lymphocytes, a type of white blood cell that fights the spread of infection. In Hodgkin's disease, these cells proliferate in a variety of abnormal forms, leaving the body with fewer normal lymphocytes to fight infection. As the disease progresses, the body becomes less able to combat infections, and damage to vital organs occurs.
See also: Lymphatic system.

Hoffa, James Riddle (1913-75?), U.S. labor leader, president of the International Brotherhood of Teamsters from 1957. After an investigation (led by U.S. attorney general Robert F. Kennedy) into his underworld links, Hoffa was convicted in 1964 of tampering with a jury over a bribery charge and jailed from 1968 to 1971, when Richard M. Nixon commuted his sentence. In 1975 he disappeared mysteriously and is thought to have been murdered.
See also: Labor movement.

Hoffer, Eric (1902-1983), self-educated U.S. author and philosopher. A migratory worker and longshoreman until 1967, he won immediate acclaim with his first book, *The True Believer* (1951), a study of mass movements. *The Passionate State of Mind* (1955), a volume of maxims, followed.

Hoffman, Dustin (1937-), U.S. actor, known for his versatility in portraying different character types. Hoffman made his film debut in *The Tiger Makes Out* (1967) and became famous with his performance in *The Graduate* (1967). He was awarded the Academy Award for best actor for *Kramer vs. Kramer* (1979) and *Rain Man* (1988). His other films include *Midnight Cowboy* (1969), *All the President's Men* (1976), and *Tootsie* (1982).

Hoffmann, E(rnst) T(heodor) A(madeus) (1776-1822), German romantic author, composer, and critic. He is best remembered today for his fantastic short stories,which inspired E.A. Poe and others, and the opera *Tales of Hoffmann*, composed by J.L. Offenbach and based on 3 of his stories.

Hofman, Josef (1876-1957), Polish-born U.S. pianist who made a spectacular debut in New York City at the age of 11. He was noted for his authoritative interpretations of the works of Chopin and Liszt.

Hofmann, Hans (1880-1966), German-born U.S. artist and teacher, prominent in the abstract expressionism movement. His vigorous and colorful style, inspired by Wassily Kandinsky, is exemplified by *The Gate* (1959). In 1934 he opened the influential Hans Hofmann School of Fine Arts in New York City.

Hofmannsthal, Hugo von (1874-1929), Austrian neoromantic poet and dramatist. His early style was influenced by the German poet Stefan George (1868-1933) and the Pre-Raphaelites. His adaptation of Sophocles' *Elektra* (1903) was made into an opera by Richard Strauss in 1909, beginning a long collaboration, including *Der Rosenkavalier* (1911), *Ariadne auf Naxos* (1912), and *Die Frau ohne Schatten* (1919). His poems, plays such as *Jedermann* (Everyman, 1911), and opera librettos make him a major figure of Austrian literature.

Hog, pig, or swine, domestic animal (family Suidae) bred for its flesh and fat. Hogs are descended from the wild boars (*Sus scrofa*)of Europe and Asia, which live in small herds in woodland. The weight of the male, or *boar*, can be up to 400 lb (181 kg), while the female, or *sow*, only weighs 300 lb (136 kg). The boar has tusks up to 1 ft (30 cm) long and can be dangerous. Hogs were probably among the earliest domesticated animals. They were allowed to run free in the woods, feeding on seeds such as acorns. Domestic hogs have retained the varied diet of their ancestors and will eat roots, fallen fruit, and even meat. A sow produces litters of up to 12 piglets.

Hogan, Ben (1912-), U.S. professional golfer. His achievements include winning the PGA Championship (1946, 48), U.S. Open (1948, 50, 51, 53), Masters (1951, 53) and British Open (1953).

Hogarth, William (1697-1764), British painter and engraver. He is best known for his 3 series of moralistic and satirical engravings, *The Harlot's Progress* (1732), *The Rake's Progress* (1735), and *Marriage à la Mode* (1745). His first success was as a portraitist, and some of his finest works, such as *Captain Thomas Coram* (1740) and *The Shrimp Girl* (1760), are in this field.

Hogg, Helen Sawyer (1905-), U.S.-born Canadian astronomer noted for her *Catalogue of Variable Stars in Globular Clusters* (1939). Her work involved measurement of the period of variable stars, which helps to determine their distance from earth.

Hognose *see:* Adder.

Hogweed *see:* Ragweed.

Hohenstaufen, medieval German dynasty of Swabian origin whose members ruled Germany and the Holy Roman Empire. The great Hohenstaufen emperors were Conrad III, Frederick I Barbarossa, Henry VI, Frederick II, and Conrad IV. Their concept of a strongly centralized empire brought them into continual conflict with the papacy and with the 2 powerful opposing groups, Guelphs and Ghibellines.

Hohenzollern, German ruling dynasty that first rose to prominence in the 12th century. In 1192 Frederick III of Zollern became the ruler of Nuremburg, and his descendants founded the Swabian and Franconian lines. From the latter were descended the electors of Brandenburg and the dukes and kings of Prussia, who ruled as emperors of Germany, 1871-1918.
See also: Germany.

Hohokam *see:* Pima.

Hokusai, Katsushika (1760-1849), Japanese painter, printmaker, and book illustrator, greatest master of the Japanese *ukiyo-e* (popular) school. Interested in every aspect of life, Hokusai worked under a number of different names in a variety of styles, producing over 30,000 drawings of great imagination, compositional mastery, and technical excellence. The most famous collections are *36 Views of Fuji* (1823-29) and *Mangwa, or Ten Thousand Sketches* (1814-18), many of which were admired in Paris and London as well as in the Far East.

Holbein, name of 2 German painters, **Hans Holbein the Elder** (c.1465-1524) was a German Gothic painter of great distinction, best known for his many altarpieces and other church decorations, such as the Kaisheim altar (1502). His middle and later work may have been influenced by Grünewald. His son, **Hans Holbein the Younger** (1497?-1543), a religious painter and portraitist, lived in many European countries and later entered the service of Henry VIII of England, whose most famous portraits are by him.

Holberg, Ludvig (1864-1754), Norwegian-born Danish playwright and educator. A professor at the University of Copenhagen, he was a philosopher and historian as well as an author. His plays were mainly comedies influenced by earlier Roman works. The comedy *Erasmus Montaus* (1731), the satirical poem *Pedar Paars* (1719-20), and *History of the Danish Kingdoms* (1732-35) are among his best-known works.

Hölderlin, Johann Christian Friedrich (1770-1843), German lyric poet, noted for the grandeur of his images, derived from classical Greek themes. Among his best-known poems are *Bread and Wine*, *The Rhine*, and *The Death of Empedocles*. *Hyperion* is a semi-autobiographical prose novel.

Hans Holbein the Younger's painting of John More (father of Saint Thomas More)

Holding company, in finance, company that holds a majority or substantial minority of the stock in another company or companies in order to control policies. The constituent corporations of a holding company are called *subsidiaries*. By *pyramiding* such companies, that is, by creating additional companies to control the stock of holding companies lower in the pyramid, the firm at the apex can control assets many times greater than its own.
See also: Corporation.

William Hogarth

Holiday, originally *holyday*, day commemorating an event, person, or religious occasion on which people set aside their

Hokusai painting of one of the 36 views of Fuji Yama

normal work to rest, celebrate, or pray. Seasonal days of pagan origin are still celebrated at the summer solstice, the harvest, and the end of winter.

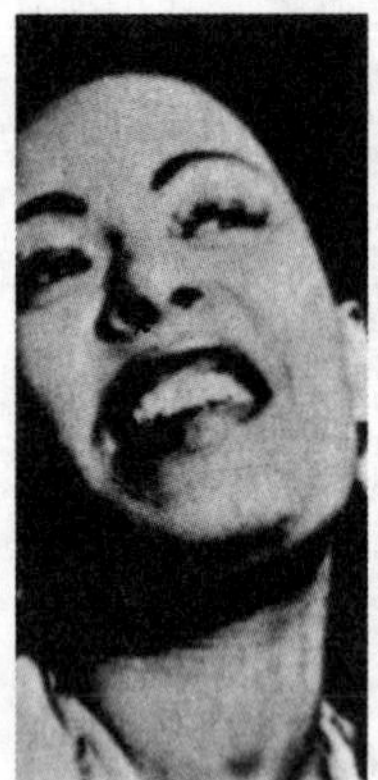

Billie Holiday

Holiday, Billie (Eleanora Fagan; 1915-59), U.S. jazz singer. She started her career at 16, singing in Harlem cafés and night spots. Her highly individual style was soon recognized, and she sang with many famous bands and small groups in the 1930s and 1940s. In later years she suffered from heroin addiction.
See also: Jazz.

Holinshed's Chronicles, or *Chronicles of England, Scotland, and Ireland,* purported histories of the 3 countries, largely edited by Raphael Holinshed (d. c.1580). Colorful, imaginative, and inaccurate, they provided plots for many Elizabethan dramatists, including William Shakespeare.

Holistic medicine, approach to health and medical care based on the principle that the "whole" person must be treated comprehensively, taking physical, psychological, and environmental factors into account. Treatments include herbs, acupuncture, relaxation therapy, yoga, meditation, vitamin therapy, and biofeedback (body self-monitoring technique). Traditional medicines and surgery are generally avoided.

Holland *see:* Netherlands.

Holland, John Philip (1840-1914), Irish-born U.S. inventor who built the first fully successful submarine, the *Holland,* launched in 1898 and bought by the U.S. Navy in 1900.
See also: Submarine.

Holland Tunnel *see:* Hudson River tunnels.

Holly, any of various species of evergreen trees and shrubs (genus *Ilex*) with glossy, spiny leaves and red or black fruits, usually called berries. The European holly (*I. acquifolium*), used at Christmas and in early pagan ritual, is very similar to the common American holly (*I. opaca*), but there are some species in the Americas that are not evergreen and not spiny. Yaupon (*I. vomitoria*), a holly of the southeastern states, has leaves containing large amounts of caffeine and was used by Native Americans to induce vomiting. The leaves of South American maté (*I. paraguayensis*) are dried and used to make maté tea.

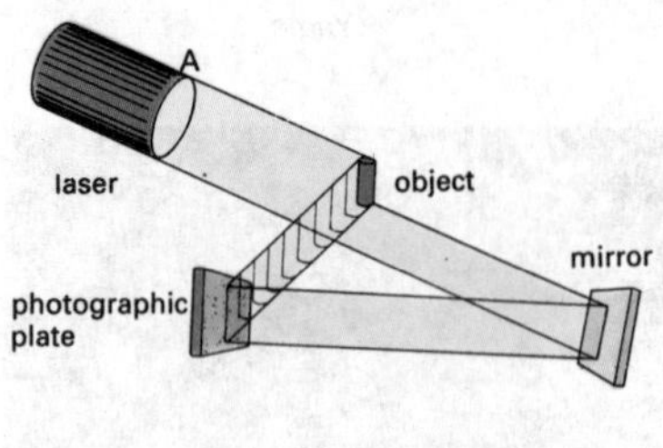

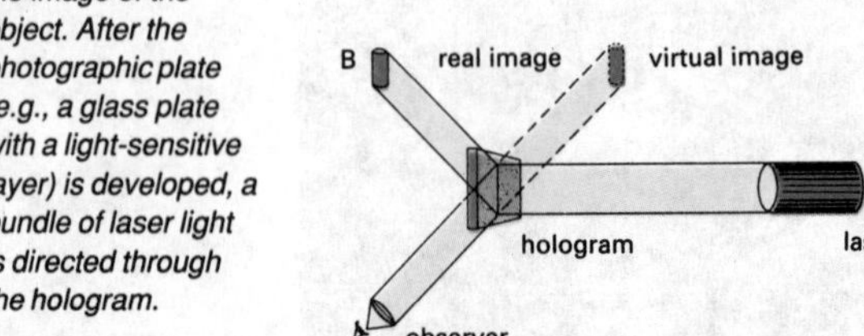

A. Making a hologram. Part of the laser light beam falls onto the plate via a mirror. The object beam interferes with this beam.
B. Reconstructing the image of the object. After the photographic plate (e.g., a glass plate with a light-sensitive layer) is developed, a bundle of laser light is directed through the hologram.

Holly, Buddy (Charles Hardin Holly; 1936-59), U.S. singer, guitarist, and composer, one of rock music's first major performers. Holly's style combined several components of country music with a powerful background rhythm. In 1957 his band, the Crickets, recorded the hit song, "That'll Be the Day." In the same year, Holly released a solo hit, "Peggy Sue." His career was cut short when he was killed in a plane crash outside of Mason City, Iowa.

Hollyhock (*Althaea rosea*), one of the tallest garden flowers. Its flowers grow on short stems along the tall, upright main stalk and open in succession from the bottom of the stem upwards. Cultivated from earliest times because it was thought to have healing properties, it has spread from its native China to the United States via Europe.

Hollywood (pop. 210,000), district of Los Angeles, Calif. Its name became synonymous with the U.S. film industry in the 1920s. Few films are made there, but it now produces a large percentage of U.S. television material.
See also: California.

Holmes, Oliver Wendell (1809-94), U.S. author and physician. The father of jurist Oliver Wendell Holmes, Jr., he is best known for his light essays and poems, which appeared in the *Atlantic Monthly* from 1857, and in book form as *The Autocrat of the Breakfast-Table* (1858) and 3 sequels. He taught at Harvard, 1847-82; his paper *The Contagiousness of Puerperal Fever* (1843) is considered the first major contribution to medicine by an American.

Holmes, Oliver Wendell, Jr. (1841-1935), U.S. jurist, Supreme Court justice (1902-32). He is often called the Great Dissenter, but this reflects the significance rather than the number of his dissenting judgments. In *Lochner* v. *New York* (1905) and *Hammer* v. *Dagenhart* (1918) he reinforced arguments for legislative checks on the economy. His dissent in *Abrams* v. *United States* (1919) was a powerful defense of free speech.
See also: Supreme Court of the United States.

Holmes, Sherlock, fictional detective created by the English author Sir Arthur Conan Doyle. Holmes solves difficult crimes through observation and deduction. A complex character, he has knowledge of chemistry, literature, and the arts, and is an accomplished violinist. He is assisted by his close friend and partner, Dr. John Watson. Holmes first appeared in the novel *A Study in Scarlet* (1887).
See also: Doyle, Sir Arthur Conan.

Holmium, chemical element, symbol Ho; for physical constants see Periodic Table. Holmium was discovered spectroscopically in 1878 by M. Delafontaine and J.L. Soret. It occurs in gadolinite and other rare-earth minerals and is commercially obtained from monazite. Elemental holmium is prepared by reducing its anhydrous chloride with calcium metal. Holmium is a silvery, soft, reactive metal. It has interesting magnetic properties. Holmium belongs to the series of elements known as the rare-earth metals. Ion-exchange and solvent extraction techniques have led to much easier isolation of these elements. Holmium and its compounds are used in carbon-arc lighting applications, special types of glass, enamels, and refractory materials.

Holocaust, term applied to the systematic execution of 6 million European Jews by the German Nazi regime, 1933-45. Adolf Hitler had exploited anti-Semitic feelings in his rise to power and later called for a "final solution to the Jewish question." Most Jews in countries overrun by the Nazis who did not emigrate in time were victims of the Holocaust, which effectively obliterated the Jewish secular and religious life that had flourished in Europe for centuries.
See also: Nazism; World War II.

Holography, technique for recording and reproducing 3-dimensional images by means of laser beams. The picture taken by the technique, the *hologram,* is a piece of photographic film that records not the scene itself but the unfocused pattern of light waves coming from the scene. A hologram is made by illuminating both the scene and the film with laser light, which has the important property of containing light of only 1 color (or wavelength). Light reflected from objects in the scene interferes with light from the direct, or *reference,* beam, producing a light-and-dark pattern of interference fringes. When light from a laser is passed through the developed hologram, the original pattern of light from the scene viewed is recreated in every respect. Thus the original scene will be visible in 3 dimensions, and the person viewing can look "behind" it by moving his or her head sideways. The method was invented in the 1940s by D. Gabor, who received the Nobel Prize in physics in 1971 for his work.

Holst, Gustav Theodore (1874-1934), English composer. He is best known for *The Planets* (1914-16), a massive symphonic suite, each piece representing a planet characterized in myth and astrology. Its popularity has overshadowed his other works, such as the opera *Savitri* (1908).

Holy Alliance, collective security agreement created at the Congress of Vienna in 1815 by Russia, Austria, and Prussia and later joined by most other European powers (excluding Britain, Turkey, and the Vatican). Its avowed aim was to promote

mutual relations according to Christian principles. It had little importance in itself, except as a symbol of reaction; revolts in Spain and Naples in the 1820s were suppressed in its name.
See also: Vienna, Congress of.

Holy Bible *see:* Bible.

Holy Grail, legendary talisman, given various forms in various legends. In his *Conte del Graal* (c.1180) Chrétien de Troyes made it the chalice from which Christ drank at the Last Supper and that was used to catch his blood on the Cross. The knight Perceval, as in the poem by Wolfram von Eschenbach *Parzival* (1210), seeks the Grail to redeem himself and others. *Queste del Saint Graal* (1200) linked the Grail with the Arthurian legends and was the source of Thomas Malory's *Morte d'Arthur* (1470). The Grail legends have inspired such modern writers as T.H. White, T.S. Eliot, and Alfred Lord Tennyson, and also Richard Wagner's operas *Lohengrin* (1848) and *Parsifal* (1882).

Holy Land *see:* Palestine.

Holy Roman Empire, European empire centered in Germany that endured from medieval times until 1806. It was effectively established in A.D. 962 when the pope crowned Otto I, king of Germany, emperor of Rome. It derived its political claim to the Roman Empire based on Charlemagne's belief that his empire was the legitimate successor to ancient Rome. In theory, the Holy Roman emperor was God's temporal ruler of all christians. In reality, the political control was somewhat different. At its height, it included all the German principalities, Austria, Bohemia, Moravia, Switzerland, the Low Countries, eastern France, and northern and central Italy. Up until 1562 the emperor was crowned by the pope, thereafter the coronation was performed in Frankfurt. The Holy Roman Empire was in constant conflict with the pope and the Italian states over temporal and religious issues. It was seriously weakened by the Reformation which challenged the allegiance of German Protestant princes to the emperor. The Thirty Years War (1618-1648) almost totally destroyed the German people and the Holy Roman Empire. In fact, it never recovered from this conflict. France emerged as a central power from the war and its continued military successes, from the time of Louis XIV to Napoleon I, eradicated the political reality of the Holy Roman emperor. The official end came in l806 when Francis II renounced the title, proclaiming himself Francis I, emperor of Austria.

Holy wars *see:* Crusades.

Holy Week, in the Christian church year, week preceding Easter, observed in most churches as a time of solemn devotion to the passion of Christ. From the 4th century the events of the week of the crucifixion have been liturgically reenacted, now especially on Palm Sunday, Maundy Thursday, Good Friday, Holy Saturday, and Easter Sunday.
See also: Christianity.

Home, Lord (1903-), British politician, prime minister (1963-64). Early in his career he served as a Conservative party member in the House of Commons (1931-45). He was also foreign secretary (1960-63, 1970-74).
See also: United Kingdom.

Home economics, in education, all the disciplines necessary to home maintenance: cooking, nutrition, sewing, the nature and use of textiles, household equipment, and budgeting. Originally it was not considered a scholastic subject, but today it is a common high school elective, and colleges offer degree courses in it. In the United Kingdom it is called domestic science.

Homelessness, term coined in the 1980s to describe the growing condition of mostly city-dwelling people who have no permanent place to live. In the United States, causes of homelessness range from untreated mental illness to joblessness among the poor and lack of low-income housing. The total number of homeless people in the U.S. is thought to be in the millions.

Homeopathy, system of treating disease by administering small doses of a drug that would cause a healthy person to have the symptoms of the disease under treatment. Homeopathy takes a holistic approach, claiming to treat the physical, emotional, and mental states of the patient at once. Homeopathy was introduced in the West by the German doctor Samuel Hahnemann (1755-1843), author of the controversial *Organon of the Art of Healing.*
See also: Hahnemann, (Christian Friedrich) Samuel.

Homeostasis, self-regulating mechanisms through which biological systems maintain a stable internal condition in the face of changes in the external environment. The French physiologist Claude Bernard (1813-78) was the first to show that the internal environment of any living organism is maintained within certain limits. Homeostasis is generally achieved through on-off control and feedback control. Hormones often play a vital role in it.
See also: Bernard, Claude.

Homer (8th century B.C.?), Greek epic poet to whom are ascribed the *Iliad* and *Odyssey*, universally regarded as among the greatest works of western literature. Both poems deal with events related to the Trojan War. The *Iliad* is about a single episode of the war—the anger of the Greek warrior, Achilles, and its tragic results. The *Odyssey* tells of the adventures and quests of another Greek warrior, Odysseus, after the war. Historically, there has been much debate about whether the poems were really written by one author, but most scholars now believe that they were.
See also: Iliad; Odyssey.

Homer, Winslow (1836-1910), U.S. painter who often worked in watercolor, best known for his landscapes and sea studies of New England and Florida, such as *Gulf Stream* (1899). Originally an illustrator, he recorded the Civil War for *Harper's Weekly.* His quasi-impressionist paintings revolutionized the style of U.S. painting in the 1880s and 1890s.

Winslow Homer's Breezing Up *(National Gallery of Art, Washington, D.C.)*

Home Rule, U.S. system of self-government under which some states grant cities and counties the right to adapt their own charters and laws, provided these do not conflict with the state and federal constitutions. The system, which arose in the 19th century, led to the rise of autonomous city and county government.

Homestead Act, act of the U.S. Congress (1862) granting 165 acres (65 hectares) of unoccupied land for small sums of money, to any citizen who lived on the land for 5 years. The act helped to encourage westward movement.
See also: Westward movement.

Homestead Strike, bitter labor dispute (1892) between steel workers and the Carnegie Steel Company, in Homestead, Pa., a landmark in the history of the U.S. labor

Bust of Homer (Museo Nazionale, Naples)

movement. A clash between strikers and the company's 300 Pinkerton private guards left 10 dead. The national guard was sent in, and the strike was broken, but at a high cost to the reputations of Carnegie and President Benjamin Harrison.
See also: Labor movement.

Homicide, killing of a human being by another. Criminal homicide is classified as either murder or manslaughter. Some homicides are determined to be excusable or justifiable, based on such circumstances as self-defense. Sentencing for homocide varies between U.S. states, some of which consider it a capital offense.
See also: Crime.

Homing pigeon, bird of the family Columbidae able to return to its loft from vast distances, selectively crossbred to combine speed and stamina. The racing of homing pigeons has been a popular sport since the 19th century. A well-trained bird may travel over 1,000 mi (1,600 km); the record flight is over 2,300 mi (3,700 km).

Homo erectus, early species of human being, having larger teeth and smaller brains than modern humans (*Homo sapiens*). They lived from about a million and a half years ago to 300,000 years ago. *Homo erectus* probably originated in Africa and later moved into Asia and Europe. Fossils of *Homo erectus* have been found in Indonesia (Java), China, and Kenya. *Homo erectus* made stone tools and used fire.
See also: Heidelberg man; Java man; Peking man.

Homogenization, process to delay the separation of fat in milk, an unstable emulsion containing fat globules that tend to coalesce. In homogenization the milk is heated to about 140°F (60°C) and passed at pressure through small openings. The fatty clusters are broken up by shearing as they pass through the holes, by the action of pressure, and by impact with components of the homogenizer.

Homo habilis, oldest species of human being yet discovered, believed to have lived in Africa about 2 million years ago, probably the first known human to make stone tools. The brain of *Homo habilus* seems to have been about half the size of the modern human brain. Fossil discoveries in Kenya suggest that *Homo habilis,* like apes, spent a great deal of time in trees.
See also: Australopithecus; Homo erectus.

Remains of a Mayan temple in Copán, Honduras

Homologue, in biology, structure or organ with the same evolutionary origin as an apparently different structure in another species. For example, there is little apparent similarity between a horse's leg and the flipper of a whale, but they have similar embryonic histories and are therefore homologues.
See also: Biology.

Homo sapiens, species of humans approximately 450,000 years old, with the oldest known fossil remains dating back about 375,000 years. Neanderthal man is the most well known example of *Homo sapiens* and lived in Africa, Asia, and Europe from 100,000 to 35,000 years ago. Modern human beings are classified as a subspecies of *Homo sapiens, Homo sapiens sapiens.*

Homosexuality, sexual attraction to persons of one's own sex. Female homosexuality is called lesbianism. Although many theories have tried to account for homosexuality as a deviation from the norm, in 1975 the American Psychiatric Association removed homosexuality from its list of mental disorders. Homosexuality was widely accepted in ancient Greece, and there have been prominent homosexuals throughout history. However, legal persecution and public censure have forced homosexuals to live restricted and secret lives. In the United States hostility towards and discrimination against homosexuals remains widespread. Since the 1960s the gay rights movement has fought vocally for housing, employment, and other rights. In the 1980s the AIDS epidemic provided an excuse for a new rise in anti-homosexual attitudes. Homosexual acts between consenting adult and conducted in private remain illegal in many states, although they are rarely prosecuted.

Honduras, Republic of, country in Central America bordered by the Caribbean Sea on the north, Nicaragua on the east and south, El Salvador and the Pacific Ocean on the south and west, and Guatemala on the west. The capital is Tegucigalpa.
Land and people. Most of Honduras is mountainous, but there are swamps and forests in the east, along the Mosquito Coast. Enclosed within the mountain ranges are several basins that have become the major population centers. The official language is Spanish, and Roman Catholicism is the dominant religion.
Economy. U.S.-owned banana and coffee plantations dominate the economy, and the bulk of the population works on the land. Coffee replaced bananas as the main export in 1975; other exports are timber, meat, cotton, and tobacco. There is little industry, and transport facilities are poor.
History. From the 4th to the 7th centuries the ancient city of Copán was a center of the civilization of the Mayas, but when Columbus reached the Honduran coast on his 1502 voyage, the country was inhabited only by seminomadic tribes. A Spanish colony for almost 300 years, Honduras was generally governed from Guatemala. In 1821 it won independence from Spain and became part of the Mexican empire, along with 4 other Central American States. Subsequently the 5 states formed the United Provinces of Central America, of which the Honduran patriot Francisco Morazán was president until its dissolution in 1838. Since that time, Honduras has been an independent republic. Its history has been marked by conflicts, revolutions, and military rule. The 1980s saw occasional border clashes with neighboring Nicaragua, and rightist military officers generally dominated politics.

Honduras

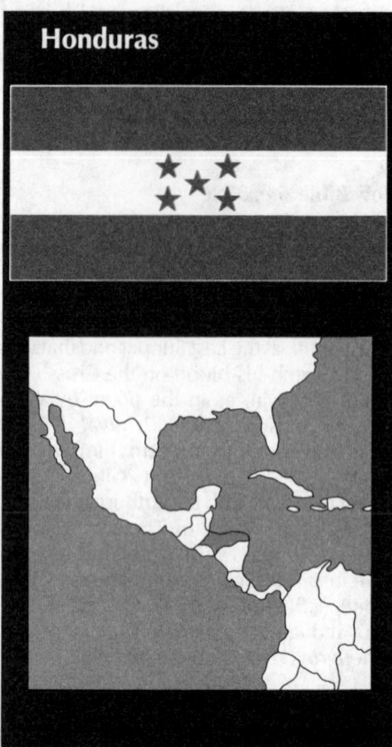

Capital:	Tegucigalpa
Area:	43,277 sq mi (112,088 sq km)
Population:	5,106,000
Government:	republic
Independent:	1838
GNP:	U.S. $4,110,000,000
Per capita:	U.S. $850

Honecker, Erich (1912-), leader of East Germany (1971-89). He joined the Communist Party (1929) as a youth and was imprisoned by the Nazis (1935-45). After World War II, he rose to the top of the political ranks in East German and Communist Party politics. He resigned in 1989, not long before the beginning of the process of German reunification.

Honegger, Arthur (1892-1955), Swiss-French composer, member of the French Les Six group, best known for his popular *Pacific 231* (1923) and his oratorio *King David* (1921-23).

Honey, sweet substance made through enzyme action by bees from the nectar of flowers. As a sweetener, there is very little difference between honey and sucrose (table sugar), although the former does contain minimal quantities of vitamins, minerals, and amino acids. Honey is available in comb or syrup form. There are different types depending on what flowers the bees have fed on; some popular varieties are sage, clover, and wildflower.

Honey badger *see:* Ratel.

Honey bear *see:* Sloth bear.

Honey bee *see:* Bee.

Honeyeater, any of several birds of the family Maliphagidea, native to Australia, New Zealand, and the Pacific Islands. They feed on nectar and insects and some are pests in orchards because they eat flowers and fruit. Some species are very rare or extinct because they have been hunted and their forest homes cut down. The moho, which ranged as far as Hawaii, was prized for its yellow and black feathers, used by the Hawaiians for ceremonial cloaks. It is now extinct.

Honey locust, any of several trees (genus *Gleditsia*) of the pea family. Often used for its shade and ornamentation, the honey locust is commonly found in the eastern United States. It has large flat pods whose pulp cattle eat. Its wood is often used for railroad ties, fence posts, or fuel.

Honeysuckle, common name for shrubs and vines of the family Caprifoliaceae, found in the Northern Hemisphere. Their flowers contain a large amount of nectar, which makes them a favorite of insects, such as hawk moths. Many of them produce an attractive scent. The berries are popular with birds.

Hong Kong, Special Administrative Region in China, on the coast of southeast China, about 90 mi (145 km) from Canton, consisting of mainland territories and numerous offshore islands. Hong Kong island was ceded to the British after the Opium War in 1842. Mainland Hong Kong includes Kowloon, acquired in 1860, and the New Territories, leased to Britain for 99 years in 1898. In 1985 an agreement was reached between the United Kingdom and the People's Republic of China regarding turnover of Hong Kong to Chinese sovereignty on July 1, 1997. The Chinese guaranteed the preservation of Hong Kong's social and economic rights for at least 50 years. Of the rocky land surface, 75% is unsuitable for building, and a mere 14% is urbanized, accommodating 90% of the population. Since the early 1900s refugees from China's political upheavals have swelled the colony's population. During Japanese wartime occupation (1941-45) the trend was briefly reversed, but since then the population has increased rapidly. Hong Kong is a free trade area and one of the world's principal ports. It has much light industry, particularly textiles and electrical goods. The region depends on China for most of its food and water.

Hong Kong

Capital:	Victoria
Area:	403 sq mi (1,045 sq km)
Population:	6,060,000
Government:	Special Administrative Region in China
GNP:	U.S.$89,274,000,000
Per capita:	U.S.$15,380

Honiara (pop. 35,300), capital of the Solomon Islands, an independent state (and member of the British Commonwealth) in the southwest Pacific Ocean. Honiara is located on the island of Guadalcanal. It was the site of a World War II U.S. military base and earlier of a Japanese military base.
See also: Solomon Islands.

Honolulu (pop. 371,300), capital and chief seaport of Hawaii, seat of Honolulu County, located on the southeast coast of Oahu Island. Honolulu grew from a fishing village in 1820 to the capital of independent Hawaii (1845) and then the territorial capital when Hawaii was annexed by the U.S. (1898). It is important as a shipping center, for sugar and pineapple processing, and as the tourist hub of Hawaii.
See also: Hawaii.

Honorius I (d. 638), pope of the Roman Catholic Church, elected 625. An aristocrat from southern Italy, he oversaw missionary activities in Britain and negotiated a peace settlement with the German Lombard tribe. He apparently supported monotheletism, a theological trend that argued that Christ had a dual nature but a single will. This idea was declared heretical at the third Council of Constantinople (680).

Honeyeater

Honorius III (d. 1227), pope of the Roman Catholic Church, elected 1216. He inaugurated campaigns for new Crusades in Spain and France and sanctioned new religious orders (the Dominicans, the Franciscans, and the Carmelites).

Hood, John Bell (1831-79), Confederate general in the U.S. Civil War, a commander in the second Battle of Bull Run,

Hong Kong sampans serve as home and freight vessels for thousands of inhabitants

the battle of Gettysburg, and in the resistance to General William Sherman's drive on Atlanta (1864). Disastrously defeated at the battle of Nashville (Dec. 1864), he was relieved of his command at his own request.
See also: Civil War, U.S.

Hood, Thomas (1799-1845), English humorist and editor, known for his *Comic Annuals* (1830-39, 1842). He is also regarded as a poet of protest against industrial conditions, e.g. "Song of the Shirt" (1843).

Hoof, enlarged, heavy toenail developed by many herbivorous animals. Since speed is a large herbivore's best defense against a predator, it is an advantage to be able to run on the tips of the toes, as this adds length to the stride. Hooves give stability to this tiptoe stance. Animals with hooves include horses, rhinoceroses, antelopes, goats, sheep, hogs, hippopotamuses, camels, and cattle.

Hoof-and-mouth disease *see:* Foot-and-mouth disease.

Herbert Clark Hoover

31st U.S. President	
Born:	West Branch, Iowa; Aug. 10, 1874
Term of office:	March 1929-March 1933
Vice president:	Charles Curtis
Party:	Republican
Spouse:	Lou Henry Hoover
Children:	Two
Died:	New York, N.Y.; Oct. 20, 1964

Hooke, Robert (1635-1703), English experimental scientist and one of the greatest inventors of his age. Hooke entered his most creative period in 1662, when he became the Royal Society of London's first curator of experiments. He invented the compound microscope, the universal joint, the spiral spring for watches, and a type of telescope. His microscopic researches were published in the beautifully illustrated *Micrographia* (1665), a work that also introduced the term *cell* to biology. He is best remembered for Hooke's law (1678) that the deformation occurring in an elastic body under stress is proportional to the applied stress. He also theorized a precursor to Newton's law of universal gravitation.
See also: Microscope.

Hooker, Joseph (1814-79), U.S. general during the Civil War. Appointed commander of the Army of the Potomac (1863), he was defeated by General Robert E. Lee at Chancellorsville and relieved as army commander.
See also: Civil War, U.S.

Hooker, Richard (1554-1600), English theologian whose 8-volume work *Of the Laws of Ecclesiastical Polity*, a landmark of Anglican theology, defended the Elizabethan religious settlement against both Roman Catholics and Puritans.
See also: Theology.

Hooker, Thomas (1586-1647), early American Puritan clergyman. A religious exile from England, he came to Massachusetts via Holland (1633) and became minister at the New Town (now Cambridge) settlement. Conflicts with the Massachusetts leaders drove him and his congregation to Connecticut (1635-36), and he and his followers founded Hartford.
See also: Puritans.

Hooks, Benjamin Lawson (1925-), U.S. lawyer, minister, and leader of the African-American community. President Nixon appointed him to the Federal Communications Commission in 1972. In 1977 Hooks succeeded Roy Wilkins as executive director of the National Association for the Advancement of Colored People.

Hookworm, any of various intestinal parasites (order Strongiloidae) of humans and domesticated animal. The life cycle involves a free-living larval stage followed by direct infection of the host, with no intermediate host. The parasitic adults are blood feeders and attach themselves to vessels in the wall of the intestine. Each worm may cause the loss of up to 0.25 ml of blood a day.

Hooper, William (1742-90), colonial lawyer and politician from North Carolina. He was a representative in the provincial congresses of North Carolina and in the Continental Congress (1774-77) and was a signer of the Declaration of Independence (1776).

Hoopoe (*Upupa epops*), large bird of Europe, Asia, and Africa, named for its call. Since recorded time hoopoes have been prized for their pink plumage, black and white barred wings, and large crest.

Hoosac tunnel, rock tunnel in western Massachusetts, in the Berkshire Hills. Completed in 1876, it was the first tunnel to be blasted out with nitroglycerin and drilled through with a power tool powered by compressed air. A total of 136 lives were lost during the construction of the 4 mi (6 km) tunnel.

Hoosier Poet *see:* Riley, James Whitcomb.

Hoosier State *see:* Indiana.

Hooton, Earnest Albert (1887-1954), U.S. physical anthropologist known for his attempts to relate behavior to physical or racial type. His books include *Up From the Ape* (1931) and *The American Criminal* (1939).
See also: Anthropology.

Hoover, Herbert Clark (1874-1964), 31st president of the United States, who held office during the onset of the Great Depression of the 1930s. Hoover's measures against the Depression were widely criticized as being too little and too late. He did, however, to a limited degree, try to use the powers of the government to restore prosperity.
Early life. Hoover entered Stanford University in 1891 and received his A.B. in 1895, after specializing in geology and engineering. For the next two decades he traveled throughout the world as a mining engineer and executive. By 1914, when World War I broke out in Europe, he had become a millionaire.
Relief work. Hoover, who was living in London when the war started, helped organize the return of 120,000 Americans then in Europe. He also became active in relief efforts, heading an organization that sent food, clothing, and medical supplies to people in German-occupied Belgium and northern France. Returning home in 1917, he was appointed head of the U.S. Food Administration.
Political career. By 1920, Hoover was an internationally known figure. In 1921, President Harding appointed him as secretary of commerce, and he continued to serve under President Coolidge. In 1928, the Republican party nominated him to run for president. He won the election easily, defeating Democrat Alfred E. Smith by a huge margin.
President. After a good-will tour of Latin America, Hoover took office on March 4, 1929. He embarked on a program of economic reform, encouraging Congress to pass laws providing financial support to farmers and higher tariffs. Hoover was optimistic about the nation's economic future; however, in October 1929, barely eight months into his term, the stock market crashed and the Great Depression began. Stocks dropped some 40% in value overnight. Millions of people became unem-

ployed. Families lost their life savings and thousands of businesses failed.
Hoover hoped to remedy the crisis by restoring business confidence, paring back government expenditures, and balancing the budget. But the Depression continued to worsen.
The president was reluctant to involve the federal government in direct relief measures. He felt that states and localities should initiate public works and relief programs. However, he did ask Congress to create the Reconstruction Finance Corporation (RFC), which lent money to banks, railways and other businesses. Eventually, it lent money to the states to help jobless workers. Hoover also supported a number of federal flood control and navigation projects, which helped to create jobs.
In June 1932, an "army" of 15,000 unemployed World War I veterans came to Washington. They were hoping Congress would agree to immediate payment of bonuses due them in 1945. Hoover had the army eject the veterans by force, which had a damaging effect on his reputation.
Although Hoover won the Republican nomination again in 1932, no one expected him to win the election. He was defeated by Democrat Franklin Delano Roosevelt, who would eventually lead the nation out of the Depression and through the years of World War II.
Hoover lived for more than 30 years after leaving the presidency. After a long illness, he died in his sleep in New York City on Oct. 24, 1964.

Hoover, J(ohn) Edgar (1895-1972), director of the Federal Bureau of Investigation (FBI) from 1924 until his death. Hoover made the FBI an efficient apparatus to fight organized crime. After World War II, at Hoover's direction, the FBI began a crusade against "subversives," targeting leftist activists. By the 1960s and 1970s Hoover's conservative political views and the FBI's violation of the civil rights of its opponents made him the center of controversy. He published a number of books, including *Masters of Deceit* (1958) and *J. Edgar Hoover on Communism* (1969).
See also: Federal Bureau of Investigation.

Hoover Commission, common name for Commission on Organization of the Executive Branch of the Government, an advisory commission to prepare improvements in the efficiency of the executive branch of government. The first such commission (1947-49) submitted 273 proposals and was responsible for the establishment of the Department of Health, Education and Welfare. A second commission (1953-55) made 314 recommendations, more than half of which were adopted.

Hoover Dam, formerly Boulder Dam (1933-47), on the Colorado River between Nevada and Arizona. It is 736 ft (244 m) high and 1,244 ft (379 m) long. The dam impounds Lake Mead and has a hydroelectric capacity of 1.3 Mw. Built in 1931-35, it began operating in 1936.

Hop, tall prickly perennial vine (*Homulus lupulus*) of the mulberry family whose dried female flowers, called hops, contain *lupullin*, a substance that gives beer its bitter flavor and is used as a preservative. Hops were first grown by the Greeks, who ate the young shoots. They were first used for flavoring beer by the Germans in the 8th century.

Hope, Bob (Leslie Townes Hope; 1903-), English-born U.S. comedian, born in Eltham, England. He emigrated to the United States as a child and began his career in vaudeville, becoming famous in the 1930s through radio and motion pictures, notably in the "Road" series of movies with Bing Crosby. Since World War II he has made regular overseas tours to entertain U.S. troops and has specialized in topical political humor.

Hope, John (1868-1936), U.S. educator and civil rights leader. Son of a black mother and white father, he advocated advanced education at a time when Booker T. Washington was inclined to restrict black education to the purely technological. The first African American president of Morehouse College in Atlanta, Ga., in 1906, he became first president of Atlanta University in 1929.
See also: Civil rights.

HOPE Project, or Health Opportunity for People Everywhere, independent, nonprofit organization established in 1958 by Washington, D.C., physician William B. Walsh to promote the teaching of new techniques to medical personnel in developing nations. In 1960 Project HOPE sent medical educators aboard the world's first peacetime hospital ship, the S.S. HOPE. Today Project HOPE has training programs in over 15 countries.

Hopewell *see:* Mound Builders.

Hopi, Pueblo Native American tribe of northeast Arizona. The Hopi have a complex society based on clans organized around matrilineal extended households. Since the 1820s there have been territorial conflicts between the Hopi and Navajo. In 1975 the federal government redrew territorial boundaries, making several thousand Navajo move. The Hopi are known for their elaborate religious ceremonies, which feature dancing and the kachina figure.

Hopkins, Gerard Manley (1844-1889), English poet and Jesuit priest. Hopkins's work was experimental, using natural speech and "sprung rhythm" rather than syllable counts. Unappreciated in his lifetime, his poetry has had great influence in the 20th century. "The Windhover" and "God's Grandeur" are two of his major poems. His work was published posthumously in 1918.

Hopkins, Harry Lloyd (1890-1946), U.S. politician. He was administrator of the Federal Emergency Relief Administration (1933), director of the Works Project Administration (1935), secretary of commerce (1938), and U.S. Lend Lease administrator (1941). As President Franklin D. Roosevelt's aide throughout World War II, he carried out important negotiations with Russia for both Roosevelt and President Harry S. Truman.

Hopkins, Johns (1795-1873), U.S. financier and philanthropist. A Quaker, he made his fortune as a wholesale grocer. He bequeathed $7 million to endow Johns Hopkins University and Johns Hopkins Hospital in Baltimore.

Hopkins, Stephen (1707-85), cultural and political leader in colonial Rhode Island. A signer of the Declaration of Independence, he was a delegate to the Continental Congress (1774-80).

Hopkinson, Francis (1737-91), American composer, delegate to the Continental Congress, and signer of the Declaration of Independence. His 1788 song collection was dedicated to George Washington. His son **Joseph Hopkinson** (1770-1842) wrote the words to "Hail Columbia."

Hopper, Edward (1882-1967), U.S. painter and engraver. First recognized for his etchings, he returned to painting late in

Hopi painting, The Little War God

Edward Hopper's View from the Williamsburg Bridge *(1920, Metropolitan Museum of Art, New York).*

life and became known for large, quiet urban studies of subtle composition, often reflecting loneliness and alienation.

Hopper, Grace Murray, (1906-), U.S. computer scientist whose belief that computer languages should be more like everyday language led, in the 1950s, to the invention of COBOL (Common Business Oriented Language), a widely used computer language. After graduating from Vassar in 1928, Hopper went on to earn a Ph.D in mathematics from Yale. In 1943 Hopper joined the Navy, where she attained the rank of rear admiral.

Hoppner, John (1758-1810), English portraitist to the Prince of Wales (1789), elected to the Royal Academy (1795). His portraits include studies of Nelson, Wellington, and Sir Walter Scott.

Horace (Quintus Horatius Flaccus; 65-8 B.C.), Roman lyric poet and satirist. At first supported by a rich patron, Maecenas, he later became the favored poet of the emperor Augustus. Horace's surviving works include four books of *Odes*, two of *Satires*, two of *Epistles*, and his *Episodes*, These and the *Art of Poetry* have had deep influence on European literature.
See also: Rome, Ancient.

Horatius (Publius Horatius Cocles), legendary Roman hero. He and two companions are said to have held off an invading Etruscan army at the Sublician Bridge across the Tiber River. The Romans cut the bridge behind him, blocking the Etruscan advance, and Horatius escaped by swimming across the river.
See also: Rome, Ancient.

Horehound (*Marrubium vulgare*), aromatic plant in the mint family, with wrinkled leaves and clusters of small flowers found growing in waste places. It was once popular as a flavoring in candies and cough medicines.

Horizon, apparent line where the sky meets the land or sea. At sea, its distance varies in proportion to the square root of the height of the observer's eyes above sea level. The celestial horizon is the great circle on the celestial sphere at 90° from the zenith (the point immediately above the observer).

Hormone, chemical substance produced in living organisms by the endocrine system. Hormones act to regulate many biological processes, including growth, metabolism, digestion and reproduction. They are "messengers," usually acting at a distance from their site of origin. Hormones are carried from ductless glands through the bloodstream to their point of action.
See also: Endocrine system.

Hormuz, Strait of, 30-50 mi (48-80km) wide waterway leading out of the Persian Gulf to the Gulf of Oman and the Indian Ocean. Most Middle East oil tankers pass through the strait, which is commanded by Qishm Island (Iran) and three other islands—Greater Tunb, Lesser Tunb, and Abu Musa—currently held by Iran but claimed by the United Arab Emirates.

Horn, in music, brass wind instrument. Horns are derived from the animal horns used by primitive societies. Metal was found to produce a better tone, and horns became increasingly sophisticated and complex. Horns were introduced into orchestral music in the early 18th centrury. Valved horns (such as the trumpet) were developed in the 19th century.

Horn, bony extension, usually elongated and pointed, growing from the heads of some mammals, including cattle, sheep, and goats. The antlers of deer are not true horns. Both males and females may grow horns, which consist of a central core of bone-like material encased by a layer of the skin protein keratin. Animals use their horns for protection, either by fighting with them or by displaying them in a threatening manner.

Hornbill, any of various birds of the family Bucerotidae noted for their huge bills, which in some species bear an additional growth called a casque. Hornbills are found in most of Africa and southern Asia as far east as the Philippines. Most live in forests, but the large ground hornbill lives in open country. They feed mainly on fruit, but some hornbills eat insects or lizards. Their nesting habits are unusual. The eggs are laid in a hole in a tree trunk, and the female walls herself in with mud; while incubating the eggs, she is fed by the male through a slit in the mud wall.

Hornblende, dark green or black mineral of varied composition, usually including silicates of aluminum and other abundant elements. It forms vitreous glassy rocks. Often found in igneous and metamorphic rock, hornblende is a major constituent of the amphibole group of minerals.

Hornbook, children's primer used before printed books became cheap and widely available. Hornbooks consisted of printed sheets showing the alphabet and numerals; the sheets were pasted to a wooden, short-handled tablet and covered with a thin, transparent layer of horn for protection.

Horne, Lena (1917-), U.S. actress and blues singer. Horne began her career as a 16-year-old chorus dancer in New York City's Cotton Club and made her movie debut in *The Duke Is Tops* (1938). Horne gained widespread recognition for her singing in the movie *Stormy Weather* (1943) and went on to be a popular night-club singer in Europe and the United States.

Horne, Marilyn (1934-), U.S. mezzo-soprano. A pupil of Lotte Lehmann, she is known for her mastery of bel canto roles in Bellini and Rossini operas. She made her Metropolitan Opera debut in 1970 as Adalgisa in Bellini's *Norma*.

Horned lizard, name for several species of lizards (genus *Phrynosoma*) native to North America, from Canada to Mexico. Because of their shape, they are often called horned toads. The body is covered with spiny scales that are particularly long on the head. Horned lizards live in dry regions, where they can bury themselves in the sand by rapid sidewise movements. They feed on insects, especially ants.

Hornet, any of several kinds of large social wasps (family Vespidae), that, unlike the more common yellow jackets, build their nests in trees or in human dwellings. The nest, enclosed in a paperlike shell, consists of a series of horizontal combs. Hornets make the papery material by chewing woody plant matters. Female hornets can inflict an extremely painful sting.

Horney, Karen (1885-1952), German-born U.S. psychoanalyst, founder of the American Institute of Psychoanalysis

(1941). She stressed the importance of environmental and cultural factors in character development, rejecting many of the basic principles of Freud's psychoanalytic theory, especially his stress on the libido as the root of personality and behavior. Her best known work is *Neurosis and Human Growth* (1950).

Hornsby, Rogers (1896-1963), U.S. baseball player and manager. Hornsby, a second baseman, is considered one of the greatest right-handed batters in the game's history. His achievements include 7 National League batting titles (consecutively from 1920-25, 1928), hitting .424—the single season record (1924), and a lifetime batting average of .358, second only to Ty Cobb's .367. Hornsby played for the St. Louis Cardinals (1915-26, and 1933), New York Giants (1927), Boston Braves (1928), Chicago Cubs (1929-32), and the St. Louis Browns (1933-37). He went on to manage after his 1937 season and was inducted into the National Baseball Hall of Fame (1942).

Hornwort, any one of a group of plants related to liverworts and mosses and growing world-wide, but most commonly in warm, moist regions. A hornwort reproduces in a cycle known as the *alternation of generations.* It forms a gametophyte in the first stage of its life and a sporophyte in the second stage. The gametophyte is a small plant body called a *thallus.* The sporophyte is from 3/16-4 3/4 in (0.5-12 cm) high and resembles the horns of a cow.

Horowitz, Vladimir (1904-89), Russian-born U.S. virtuoso pianist. After a brilliant debut in Kiev (1922), he toured the USSR and Europe (1924) and the United States (1928). He became a U.S. citizen in 1944.

Horse, hoofed, herbivorous mammal (genus *Equus*). This is the only living genus of the family Equidae; the donkey and the zebra are different species of the same genus. Wild horses occurred in prehistoric times over most of Eurasia. Today, the only surviving true wild horse is the Przewalski horse of Siberia, Mongolia, and western China. Domestic horses (*E. caballus*) can be grouped as ponies, heavy draft horses, lightweight draft, and riding horses; they originated from North African stock. Thoroughbreds are descended from Arabian stock. The fossil record of the horse family provides a classic example of evolution in action. The earliest animal that can be placed in the family was Eohippus, which was the size of a fox terrier and had 3 toes of equal size on each hindfoot and 4 toes on each forefoot. The development of the single-toed foot of modern horses was an adaptation to running on hard dry grassland. The changes in tooth pattern allowed the animal to eat abrasive grasses. The increase in size may be followed through a continuous series of intermediate stages to the present day. The various species of the genus *Equus* can often interbreed (e.g., horses and donkeys), but the offspring (e.g., mules) are generally sterile.

Horse brier *see:* Greenbrier.

Horse chestnut, popular name for various trees and shrubs (genus *Aesculus*) of the family Hippcastanaceae. In winter the twigs bear sticky buds that develop into conspicuous leaves and big flowers. In the fall large, shiny seeds similar to chestnuts are released from fleshy coats. The Ohio buckeye (*A. glabra*) is the state tree. Horse chestnut wood is light and strong and is used for boxes and coffins.

Horsefly, any of various two-winged flies (family Tabanidae), so called because they bite horses, as well as other mammals. Only the females bite, piercing the skin with specialized mouthparts and sucking blood. Female horseflies require a blood-meal before laying eggs. They transmit a few diseases, but their main significance as pests is in the sting of their bite.

Przewalski horse

Horsehair worm, hair snake, or hairworm, any of about 200 types of long, thin worms making up the phylum Nematomorpha. They may grow to 28 in (70 cm). The young are hatched from eggs and form cysts, which may be eaten by insects. The larva then leave the cysts and live in the insects as parasites. The worms leave the insects' bodies when they reach adulthood.

Horse latitudes, regions of calm, quiet winds situated on either side of the equator, between 30°N and S latitudes. In early colonial days, ships bound for the Americas were often becalmed in these latitudes. The horses died from lack of fresh water and were cast overboard. This gave the regions their name.
See also: Calms, Regions of.

Horse nettle *see:* Solanum.

Horsepower, unit of power used to indicate the rate at which work is done. In the 18th century inventor James Watt experimentally determined that a strong horse can lift up to 33,000 foot-pounds 1 foot per minute. This has become the definition of 1 horsepower. In electrical units 1 horsepower is equivalent to 746 watts; the heat equivalent is 2, 545 BTU (British thermal units) per hour.

Vladimir Horowitz

Horse Racing, sport involving trials of speed between horses, watched by millions of people in many countries. Its interest as a spectator sport is largely based on the practice of on-and off-track betting. The oldest stake race is the English St. Leger, first run in 1776. In the United States, the most famous race is the Kentucky Derby, first run in 1875. Besides flat racing, there are steeplechasing and harness racing.

Horseradish, common name for a perennial herb (*Armoracia rusticana*), of the mustard family. Native to Eurasia, it is widely cultivated for its white, edible, pungent roots, which grow to a length of 12 in (30 cm) and are used to make a popular relish with a sharp flavor.

Horseshoe crab, or king crab, any of several marine arthropods of the order Xiphosura, "living fossils" whose almost identical ancestors have been found in rocks 175 million years old. King crabs are not true crabs but are more closely related to spiders. If the dome-shaped shell is turned over it shows a horseshoe outline and a series of jointed legs. King crabs live near sheltered shores on the Atlantic coast of the United States and around the coast of Asia. In some places king crabs are fished for pig and chicken feed, and fertilizer. They are pests in clam beds.

Horseshoe Falls *see:* Niagara Falls.

Horseshoe pitching, game played on a court by 2 or more people, in which players attempt to throw horseshoes to encircle an iron stake. The court, usually out-of-doors, is 50 ft (15.2 m) long and 10 ft (3m) wide. The iron stakes, set at either end of the court, are 1 ft (0.3m) high. Scoring is based on a system of point values placed on how close a horseshoe is to a stake. Encircling the stake, called a *ringer*, is the highest point-scoring throw, with a value of 3. A horseshoe that is only touching the stake is called a *leaner* and has a value of 2. The game originated in Roman army camps c.100 A.D.

Horsetail, primitive plant (genus *Equisetum*) related to the fern that once dominated the plant world and was important in the formation of coal. One fossil horsetail was 100 ft (30 m) high, but living species are rarely more than 2 to 3 feet (0.6 to 0.9 m) high. Each horsetail plant lasts several years. It has an underground stem that sends up hollow vertical stems each year. Each vertical stem is jointed and at each joint there is a ring of small leaves. The plant is coated with gritty silica, thus it has been called scouring rush and has been used for cleaning pans. Some horsetails have 2 kinds of stems. The first bears a spore-producing organ at the tip. The spores are released and drift away to produce small sexual plants as in ferns. These stems then die down and are replaced by taller green stems that last all season.

Horthy de Nagybanya, Miklós (1868-1957), Hungarian admiral and politician who led the counter-revolutionary army that overthrew the Communist and socialist coalition under Béla Kun (1919). From 1920 he acted as regent. He joined the Axis powers in World War II, but after trying to make peace with the USSR in 1944, he was imprisoned in Germany. Freed by U.S. forces, he settled in Portugal (1949).
See also: Hungary.

Horticultural grafting, technique of propagating plants by attaching the stem or bud of one plant (the scion) to the stem or roots of another (the stock, or rootstock). Only closely related species can be grafted. Roses and fruit trees are often grafted so that good flowering or fruiting varieties have the benefit of strong roots.

Hostages displayed on T.V. by Saddam Hussein.

Horticulture, branch of agriculture concerned with producing fruits, flowers, and vegetables. It can be divided into *pomology* (growing fruit), *olericulture* (growing vegetables), and *floriculture* (growing shrubs and ornamental plants). About 3% of U.S. cropland is devoted to horticulture. It was originally practiced on a small scale, but crops such as the potato and tomato are now often grown in vast fields.

Horus, ancient Egyptian god. Originally a sky god, depicted as a falcon or as falcon-headed, he became thought of as the son of Isis and Osiris. He avenged his father's murder by defeating Set, the spirit of evil, and succeeded Osiris as king.
See also: Mythology.

Hosea, Book of, first of the Old Testament Minor Prophets. Its material originated in the prophecies of Hosea, delivered in Israel in the 8th century B.C. It compares God's abiding love for idolatrous Israel to Hosea's love for his prostitute wife, whom he divorced but remarried.
See also: Bible; Old Testament.

Hospice, facility for the care of terminally ill patients. Its professional staff seeks to provide alleviation of pain (rather than life-prolonging medical services), supportive psychological and spiritual counseling, and easy access for family and friends in a dignified and noninstitutional environment. The first hospice was opened in England in 1967 by Dr. Cecily Saunders. In the United States the cost of hospice care is now reimbursable under both Medicaid and Medicare.

Hospital, institution for the care of the sick or injured. Simple hospitals were first set up in Babylonian, Egyptian, Greek, and Roman communities, and in India hospitals had been established before A.D. 400. The early Christians did much to help the sick, and established the first charity hospitals, but medical knowledge was far from adequate, and death rates in hospitals were very high. Little had changed by the year 1123, when St. Bartholomew's Hospital was established in London. The majority of people admitted were either homeless or had little hope of recovery. Most physicians, apothecaries, and surgeons rendered their services at home or in an office rather than at a hospital. The first general hospital built in the United States was the Pennsylvania Hospital in Philadelphia, established in 1751. Others were built soon afterward, and medical technology improved rapidly during this period. but it was only when men like Joseph Lister obtained an understanding of the nature of infection and the importance of aseptic surgery that hospitals became safe places for treatment. Until then, a patient admitted to a hospital was more likely to die than one who remained at home. Today there are more than 9,500 hospitals in the United States, with over 2,100,000 beds, admitting over 35,000,000 patients each year. The average duration of a stay is just over 1 week.

Hostage, traditionally, a person delivered as a token of good faith; now hostages are more often kidnapped and tortured by political dissidents demanding concessions. Iran's taking of U.S. hostages (1979), with demands for the return of their deposed Shah, resulted in a major crisis for President Jimmy Carter's administration. A UN treaty outlawing the taking of hostages went into effect in 1983.

Hostel *see:* Youth hostel.

Hotel, a building that provides the public with overnight lodging. Although the basic purpose is to provide rooms for travelers to sleep in, many hotels also provide meals, entertainment, and other personal services. There are 4 major types of hotel: commercial hotels, residential hotels, resort hotels, and motor hotels (motels). Hotels date from ancient times, and can be found in almost any country in the world.

Hot Line, direct White House-Kremlin emergency communications link, established in 1963. It aims to reduce the risk of war occurring by mistake or misunderstanding. Telegraphic and radio circuits run via London, Copenhagen, Stockholm, and Helsinki.

Hot rod, automobile with improved engine or body design, giving greater acceleration and speed. Following World War II a cult of street racing developed in the United States, consisting of acceleration races between traffic lights. In the 1950s "drag racing" on special tracks was encouraged by police departments to try to prevent this. The term "hot rod" now includes recognized "stock" sedans and specially designed "dragsters."

Hot Springs (pop. 32,462), city in central-western Arkansas, 47 mi (76 km) west and southwest of Little Rock. The city was founded in 1807 by Manuel Prudhomme, a trapper. It is the site of Hot Springs National Park (designated in 1921), which encompasses almost the entire city.
See also: Arkansas.

Hot springs, or thermal springs, natural discharges of heated water from within the earth. Most hot springs originate when water passes close to or through hot, igneous rock. They can form as streams, calm pools, geysers, fumaroles, or mudpots. Modern energy concerns have aroused interest in the possible uses of geothermal energy to generate electrical power.

Hot Springs National Park, park in the Ouachita Mts., Arkansas. It is a popular tourist and health resort noted for its 47 thermal springs. The park, created in 1921, comprises 5,826 acres (2,358 hectares).
See also: National Parks.

Hottentot *see:* Khoikhoi.

Houdini, Harry (Erich Weiss; 1874-1926), U.S. magician and escapologist. He was world famous for his escapes from seemingly impossible situations, as from a sealed chest underwater. He also pursued a campaign of exposing fake mediums and spiritualists.

Houdon, Jean-Antoine (1741-1828), French sculptor famous for his portraits. His sitters included Catherine the Great (1773), Voltaire (1781), and Benjamin Franklin (1791). The best known of his mythological works is *Diana* (1777).

Hound, group of dogs that hunt by sight or by following scent. Sight hounds chase quarry, overtake it, then kill or capture it. They include the greyhound, Afghan hound, Saluki, and Irish wolfhound. Scent hounds, or tailing hounds, follow the scent of their quarry and flush it out. They include the beagle, bloodhound, bassett hound, and dachshund. In general, hounds are strong, alert, and loyal dogs.

Houphouët-Boigny, Félix (1905-), president of the Ivory Coast since it gained independence (1960). He was elected to a new term in 1980. In 1946 he helped found the Rassemblement Democratique Africain (RDA), which paved the way for independence of the French West African colonies. He was a French minister of state from 1956 to 1957.
See also: Ivory Coast.

Hour, one twenty-fourth of a day. In one hour the earth rotates through 15°. Therefore an event such as sunrise occurs one hour later for every 15° west on the earth's surface. Each hour contains 60 minutes and 3,600 seconds. In astronomy, degrees of longitude are not used for measuring star positions. Astronomers instead talk of *hours of right ascension*. Each hour of right ascension corresponds to 15° on the celestial sphere. The hour as a unit of timekeeping has been in use only since the invention of clocks.

Hourglass, ancient instrument to measure the passage of time. A quantity of fine, dry sand is contained in a bulb constricted at its center to a narrow neck. The device is turned so that all the sand is in the upper chamber. The time taken for the sand to trickle into the lower chamber depends on the amount of sand and on the diameter of the neck. Small hourglasses are used in the home as egg timers.
See also: Time.

Housatonic River, river rising in the Berkshire Hills of western Massachusetts. An important source of hydroelectric power in the New England area, the Housatonic River is about 148 mi (238 km) long. It flows southward from Pittsfield, Mass., through Connecticut, and enters Long Island Sound just outside of Bridgeport.

House, building in which one or a few families live. It may be built of wood, brick, or stone. It usually consists of several rooms, which are heated by a furnace and wired for electricity. Most modern houses also contain plumbing to supply water and carry away waste. They may vary in design, size, and in their number of rooms. The housing industry actually consists of a number of related professions and involves banks, real estate and insurance companies, architects, carpenters, plumbers, and electricians.

House, Edward Mandell (1858-1938), U.S. diplomat and adviser to President Woodrow Wilson. During World War I he acted for Wilson in Europe and was responsible for arranging the peace conference and acceptance of Wilson's Fourteen Points. In 1919 his conciliatory approach during the Treaty of Versailles negotiations led to a rift with Wilson.
See also: World War I.

House Committee on Un-American Activities *see:* Un-American Activities Committee.

House of Burgesses, the first representative legislative body in colonial America, formed at Jamestown on July 30, 1619. Two burgesses represented each of the 11 boroughs of Virginia. The House of Burgesses, which was neither approved nor disapproved of by England, conformed to English law and managed all affairs of the colony. The House was dissolved in 1774, and many of the delegates were then elected to the First Continental Congress.

House of Commons, lower house of the British parliament. It consists of 635 members elected by simple majority in single-member constituencies. It is the assembly to which the government is ultimately responsible; it legitimizes legislation, votes money, and acts as a body in which complaints can be raised. Proceedings are regulated by the speaker, and a majority of members must assent before a bill becomes law.
See also: Parliament.

House of Lords, upper house of the British parliament. Members consist of the Lords Temporal: hereditary peers, life peers, and ex-officio law lords; and Lords Spiritual: the 2 archbishops and 24 most senior bishops.
See also: Parliament.

House of Representatives, one of 2 chambers of the U.S. Congress, the legislative branch of the federal government. It consists of 435 members apportioned from each state according to population. Representatives serve 2-year terms. To be elected, they must be at least 25 years of age, a U.S. citizen for at least 7 years, and a resident of the state from which he or she is chosen. The House is presided over by the Speaker of the House, who is elected by consensus of the majority party. He or she appoints joint committees and gives representatives permission to debate. Representatives serve on 4 committees: standing (permanent), select, conference, and joint. The committee system has the power to control proposed bills.
See also: Congress of the United States.

Housing, any building, or group of buildings, that provide shelter for people. In the United States people live in more than 80 million housing units, which may include single-family homes, condominiums, apartments, hotels, motels, motor homes (trailers), and shelters for the homeless. The production of housing has grown in complexity with the enlarging population and with the advent of city planning, transportation needs, commuter demands, community services, and the desire for safe dwellings.

Housing and Urban Development, U.S. Department of (**HUD**), executive department of the federal government established 1965 to coordinate programs relating to housing problems. It took over the Housing and Home Finance Agency (HHFA). The department supervises the federal aid programs.

Housman, A(lfred) E(dward) (1859-1936), English poet and classical scholar. His poetry, at its best intensely felt and always well crafted, is collected in *A Shropshire Lad* (1896), *Last Poems* (1922), and *More Poems* (1936).

Houston (pop. 3,301,937), city and seat of Harris County in southeastern Texas and a major U.S. seaport. It is situated about 25 mi (40 km) southwest of Galveston Bay on the Houston Ship Channel. Founded in 1836 and named for Sam Houston, it remained relatively unimportant until 1901 when oil was discovered in the area. It is now a prosperous industrial, manufacturing, and wholesale distribution center.
See also: Texas.

Houston, Sam(uel) (1793-1863), U.S. frontiersman and politician, leader in the struggle against Mexico to create an independent Texas. He commanded a force of fewer than 800 settlers in a decisive battle

Houston skyline

at San Jacinto (1836) and went on to become the first president of the Republic of Texas (1836-38). During a second term as president (1841-44) he worked to bring Texas into the Union (1845). Houston served as U.S. senator (1846-59) and was governor of Texas (1859-61). He was deposed after refusing to support the Confederacy.
See also: Texas.

Hovercraft *see:* Air cushion vehicle.

Hovhaness, Alan (1911-), U.S. composer of Armenian descent, noted for his innovative use of Eastern musical materials. Among his best-known works are *Mysterious Mountain* (1955) and *Magnificat* (1957).

Howard, John (1726-90), English public official and noted reformer. Serving as high sheriff of Bedfordshire, Howard had access to Bedford jail, where the conditions in which prisoners were kept appalled him. His subsequent efforts led to an act of Parliament (1774) to improve sanitation in prisons and abolish the systems of discharge fees. He visited prisons throughout Britain and Europe and published *The State of Prisons in England and Wales* (1777), a study that inspired further reform.

Howard, Sidney (1891-1939), U.S. playwright whose work is noted for its realism. He won the 1925 Pulitzer Prize with *They Knew What They Wanted* (1924). Other well-known plays include *Lucky Sam McCarver* (1925) and *The Silver Cord* (1926).

Howard University, private, coeducational institution in Washington, D.C., established in 1867 to educate newly freed slaves. The university includes 17 schools and colleges and 12 research centers and institutes and maintains the most extensive library collection of materials on African American life in the United States. Howard admits all students, but has a special responsibility, dating to its founding, to educate black students.

Hubble Space Telescope

Howe, name of 2 brothers who were British commanders in the American Revolutionary War. **Richard, Earl Howe** (1726-99) commanded the British fleet in America (1776-8) but is best known for his victory over the French off Ushant (1794) as commander of the Channel Fleet. **William, 5th Viscount Howe** (1729-1814) was a commander in the British army (1775-8). He won 2 major victories in 1777 at Brandywine and Germantown.
See also: Revolutionary War in America.

Howe, name of a U.S. husband and wife who were prominent social reformers. The physician and teacher **Samuel Gridley Howe** (1801-76) ran a school for the blind in Boston (later the Perkins School for the Blind), where he achieved outstanding successes, most notably in teaching the deaf-blind child Laura Bridgman. He was also an active abolitionist and published the antislavery journal *Commonwealth.* **Julia Ward Howe** (1819-1910), an author, is best known for her words to the "Battle Hymn of the Republic" (1862). She was coeditor of *Commonwealth* and a campaigner for women's rights.

Howe, Elias (1819-1867), U.S. inventor of the first viable sewing machine (patented 1846). His early machines were sold in Britain, as in the United States there was at first no interest. Later Howe fought a protracted legal battle (1849-54) to protect his patent rights from infringement in the United States.
See also: Sewing machine.

Howe, Gordie (1928-), record-setting U.S. ice hockey player. He played 26 seasons in the National Hockey League (NHL) with the Detroit Red Wings (1946-71) and Hartford Whalers (1979-80) and was named the league's most valuable player 6 times (1952, 53, 57, 58, 60, 63). Howe holds career records for most games played (1,767), most goals scored (801) and was selected as an all-star 22 times. He played for the Houston Aeros (1973-77) of the World Hockey Association (WHA) and was named its most valuable player (1974). Howe was inducted into the Hockey Hall of Fame in 1972.

Howells, William Dean (1837-1920), U.S. author, critic, and chief editor of the *Atlantic Monthly* (1871-81). He was a pioneer of U.S. social fiction. His finest and most famous novel is *The Rise of Silas Lapham* (1855). Among those influenced by his work were Stephen Crane and Theodore Dreiser.

Howler , monkey (genus *Alouatta*) named for its low, carrying call. Troops of howler monkeys set up a chorus of howls when they spot another troop near their territory. To produce this call they have a large bony box in the throat, which is a resonating chamber. Howlers are found in forests from southern Mexico to northern Argentina.

Hoxha, Enver (1908-85), Albanian leader. He helped found the Albanian Communist party in 1941 and was the first premier of the new communist government (1944-54). Continuing as party secretary after 1954, he remained a Stalinist and fell out with the USSR during the latter's de-Stalinization phase. Hoxha became allied with Communist China in the early 1960s. Later this friendship cooled when China moved toward closer ties with the West.
See also: Albania.

Hoyle, Edmond (1672-1769), English authority on card and board games, especially whist. He wrote *A Short Treatise on the Game of Whist* (1742), as well as treatises on other games, including chess and backgammon. The expression "according to Hoyle," meaning according to the rules, derives from his name.

Hrdlicka, Ales (1869-1943), Bohemian-born U.S. physical anthropologist. He expounded the generally accepted theory that the Amerinds (Native Americans or Eskimos) are of Asiatic origin. Among his works are *Old Americans* (1925) and *Alaska Diary 1926-1931* (1943).
See also: Anthropology.

Hsi Chiang *see:* Xi Jiang.

Hsun-tzu *see:* Xunzi.

Hua Kuo-Feng (Hua Guofeng; 1920-), Chinese political leader. Achieving swift promotion during the Cultural Revolution, he was made premier following Chou En-Lai's death and then succeeded Mao Tse-Tung as Communist party chairman in 1976. As China turned toward more pragmatic policies, Hua's close identification with Mao proved a handicap, and he fell from power in 1981.
See also: China

Huang He, or Huang Ho, river in north-central and eastern China. The Huang He rises in Amne Machin Shan, Qinghai Province, and flows through Inner Mongolia, emptying into the Yellow Sea. At 2,903 mi (4,673 km), it is China's second longest river, but it is unused by ships due to its alternately swift and shallow composition. Due to years of flooding, the river is also called "China's Sorrow."

Huang Ho *see:* Huang He.

Hubble, Edwin Powell (1889-1953), U.S. astronomer who first showed (1923) that certain nebulae are in fact galaxies outside the Milky Way. By examining the red shifts in their spectra, he showed that they are receding at rates proportional to their distances.
See also: Astronomy.

Hubble Space Telescope, orbiting reflecting telescope built to send data from space to astronomers on earth via radio waves. It

was released into space on April 25, 1990 from the space shuttle *Discovery.* It orbits about 360 mi (580 km) above the earth's surface. With information sent to earth from the Hubble Telescope, astronomers hope to learn more about the cosmos, particularly "dark matter," areas in space that emit little or no light. Unfortunately, the telescope malfunctioned in space due to manufacturing flaws. Its ultimate usefulness is now questionable.
See also: Hubble, Edwin Powell; Telescope.

Huckleberry, shrub (genus *Gaylussacia*) related to the blueberry and cranberry that produces dark berry fruits. There are several species growing in the eastern United States, including the blue huckleberry (*G. frondosa*). The fruits are used to make jams and preserves.

Hudson, Henry (d. 1611), English navigator and explorer who gave his name to the Hudson River, Hudson Strait, and Hudson Bay. After voyages for the English Muscovy Company to find a northeast passage to China (1607 and 1608), Hudson turned to the west where, with Dutch and then once more English backing (1609 and 1610), he made his most successful voyages. He reached the river known as the Hudson in 1609 and the following year entered Hudson Strait and Hudson Bay, establishing an English claim to the area. After the bitter winter, he was set adrift by a mutinous crew and left to die.
See also: Exploration.

Hudson, William Henry (1841-1922), English author and naturalist, born in Argentina of American parents. *Green Mansions* (1904), his best-known novel, is set in the South American pampas. He also wrote studies of bird life and books on the English countryside, such as *A Shepherd's Life* (1910).

Hudson Bay, shallow, epicontinental sea in the northern part of Canada, named for Henry Hudson. Up to about 850 mi (1,370 km) long and 600 mi (970 km) wide, it is linked to the Atlantic Ocean by Foxe Channel. James Bay, the largest inlet, extends southward between Ontario and Quebec provinces. Hudson Bay shipping is restricted because the bay freezes over in winter.
See also: Hudson, Henry.

Hudson River, U.S. river rising in the Adirondacks, flowing generally south for 315 mi (507 km) through New York, and emptying into the Atlantic at New York City. It was discovered in 1524, but only explored fully by Henry Hudson in 1609. It is an important commercial waterway, being navigable by ocean ships as far upstream as Albany. A canal system links it to the Great Lakes. A major program was begun in 1975 to prevent further pollution and make the river safe for fishing and swimming.
See also: Hudson, Henry.

Hudson River School, group of 19th-century U.S. landscape painters. The founders were Thomas Cole, Thomas Doughty, and Asher Durand, who were especially interested in the Hudson River Valley and New England. The school later included artists who took their inspiration from other parts of the United States.

Hudson River tunnels, 7 underwater commuter tunnels extending under the Hudson River and linking New York City's Manhattan Island and New Jersey. The Port Authority Trans-Hudson Corporation (PATH) operates 4 rapid transit tunnels, all over 5,000 ft (1,500 m) long. Passenger trains pass through Amtrak's Hudson River Tunnel, and motor vehicles travel via the Holland or Lincoln tunnels. Before 1900, when the first tunnels were built, people traveling between Manhattan and New Jersey were required to ferry across the Hudson River.

Hudson's Bay Company, mercantile corporation established by the British in 1670 for trading in the Hudson Bay region. The original intention was also to colonize the area and seek a northwest passage, but the company's major activity was fur trading with the Native Americans. It played an important part during the next 2 centuries in opening up Canada. Although its vast lands were sold to the Dominion in 1870, it is still a major fur-trading company and one of Canada's chief business firms, with holdings in metal ores, oil, gas, and timber.

Hue (pop. 209,000), third largest city in Vietnam, located in central Vietnam, near the eastern coast. Founded in the 3rd century, Hue was capital of Vietnam during the rule of the Nguyen dynasty, beginning in the 16th century. The city was occupied by the French in 1883. It became a part of South Vietnam in 1954. Much of the city was destroyed during the Tet offensive in the Vietnam War, but it is under reconstruction.
See also: Vietnam.

Huerta, Victoriano (1854-1916), Mexican general and dictator (1913-14). After first supporting President Porifiro Diaz and then Francisco Madero, he rebelled, proclaiming himself president in February 1913, and had Madero and his vice-president murdered. Revolution at home and U.S. hostility combined to force him into exile.
See also: Mexico.

Hufstedler, Shirley Mount, (1925-), U.S. jurist and first secretary of education (1979-81), appointed by President Jimmy Carter. Hufstedler was a county and state judge in California (1961-68) and was appointed a federal judge in the U.S. Court of Appeals in San Francisco (1968-79) by President Lyndon B. Johnson, at which time she became the nation's highest ranking female judge.

Hugh Capet (c.938-996 A.D.), king of France (987-996), founder of the Capetian dynasty. The son of Hugh the Great, the duke of the Franks, he was elected king in the place of the legitimate Carolingian heir, Charles of Lower Lorraine.
See also: Capetians.

Sunset, 1860, *by Frederick E. Church of the Hudson River School*

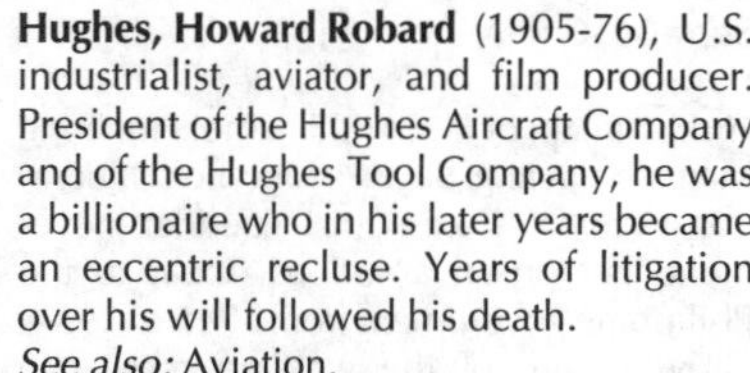

Hughes, (James) Langston (1902-67), African-American poet and writer. He is best known for adapting the rhythms of African-American music to his poetry. His works include the poetry collections *The Weary Blues* (1926), and *One-Way Ticket* (1949), and the prose *Not Without Laughter* (1930).

Hughes, Charles Evans (1862-1948), U.S. jurist and statesman. He was Republican governor of New York (1906-10) and narrowly missed in his run for the U.S. presidency in 1916 when Woodrow Wilson was elected. He served as secretary of state (1921-25) and as chief justice (1930-41) during the New Deal.
See also: Dawes Plan.

Henry Hudson

Hughes, Howard Robard (1905-76), U.S. industrialist, aviator, and film producer. President of the Hughes Aircraft Company and of the Hughes Tool Company, he was a billionaire who in his later years became an eccentric recluse. Years of litigation over his will followed his death.
See also: Aviation.

Hughes, Ted (1930-), English poet whose work is noted for its brutal, often violent animal imagery. Among his many collections are *The Hawk in the Rain* (1957), *Lupercal* (1960), *Crow* (1970), *Selected Poems: 1957-1967* (1972), and *Moortown* (1980). He was married to the poet Sylvia Plath.

Hughes, Thomas (1822-96), English jurist, reformer, and author of *Tom Brown's School Days* (1857) which, through its emphasis on Christian virtues and athletic ability, helped shape the popular image of the English public school.

Hugo, Victor Marle (1802-85), French novelist, playwright, and poet. He is best known for his historical novel *The Hunchback of Notre Dame* (1831). Among his several important collections of verse are *Les Feuilles d'Automne* (1831) and *Les Châtiments* (1853). Hugo went into exile when Napoleon III became emperor

The young Victor Hugo

(1851), and during this period produced his famous, socially committed novel *Les Misérables* (1862). He spent his last years in France, recognized as one of his country's greatest writers and republicans.

Huguenots, French Protestants, followers of John Calvin's teaching. The Huguenot movement originated in the 16th century as part of the Reformation and found support among all segments of French society, despite constant and severe persecution. Some respite was provided by Henry IV's Edict of Nantes (1598), but this was revoked in 1685, and many thousands of Huguenots were forced into exile in America and elsewhere. Full civil and religious liberty was not granted to Huguenots until 1789.
See also: Calvin, John.

Huizinga, Johan (1872-1945), Dutch historian and writer, noted for his writings about the cultural history of the Middle Ages, which portrayed the spirit of the entire age. Huizinga's works include *The Waning of the Middle Ages* (1919), *In the Shadow of Tomorrow* (1935), and *Homo Ludens* (1938). During World War II, he was imprisoned by the Nazis and died shortly after his release.

Huizong, or Hui Tsung (1082-1135), last Chinese emperor of the northern Sung dynasty (r. 1101-25). He founded the first imperial Chinese academy of painting. An accomplished painter himself, Huizong urged other artists to be "true to color and form," as his realistic paintings of birds and flowers show. He spent his final decade in captivity and died in exile in Manchuria, after being overthrown by the Tartars.
See also: China.

Hukbalahap, or Huks (full name: Hukbong Magpapalayang Bayan, "People's Liberation Army"), Communist guerilla movement that posed a serious threat to the Philippine government from 1945 to 1954. Growing out of the wartime resistance movement against Japanese occupation, the Huks were chiefly disaffected peasants. Eventually the Huks were largely won over by a program of land reforms and settlement schemes. Much of the credit for the rehabilitation of the Huks goes to Ramón Magsaysay, who, mainly on the strength of the achievement, was elected president of the Philippines in 1953.
See also: Philippines.

Hull, Bobby (Robert Marvin Hull; 1939-), Canadian ice hockey player. Thought to be the greatest left wing in the history of the sport, he ranks as the fifth highest goal scorer (610) in National Hockey League (NHL) history and was selected as an all-star 9 times. Hull was nicknamed the "Golden Jet" because of his blond hair, his speed, and the power of his shots, which at times traveled at 110 mph (177 kph). In 1974-75 Hull set a World Hockey Association (WHA) single season record by scoring 77 goals while playing for the Winnipeg Jets (1972-78). He starred for the Chicago Black Hawks (1957-72) and Hartford Whalers (1980) of the NHL. Hull retired in 1981, and in 1983 was inducted into the Hockey Hall of Fame.

Hull, Clark Leonard, (1884-1952), U.S. psychologist whose research on the learning process and mathematical approach to theories strengthened the scientific character of the field of psychology. Hull studied human behavior in a scientific manner. He is best known for his mathematical theory of learning, based on the relationship between habit (learning) and drive (motivation).
See also: Psychology.

Hull, Cordell (1871-1955), U.S. statesman, secretary of state (1933-44) under F.D. Roosevelt. He was a congressman (1907-21 and 1923-30) and senator (1931-33). As secretary of state he developed the "Good Neighbor" policy in relations with South American states and helped maintain relations with the USSR in World War II. After the war he was a major force behind U.S. acceptance of the UN, for which he was awarded the 1945 Nobel Peace Prize.

Hull, Isaac (1773-1843), U.S. naval officer. He was commander, during the War of 1812, of the frigate *Constitution* ("Old Ironsides"), which defeated the British frigate *Guerrière.* He later commanded the Pacific Squadron (1824-27) and the Mediterranean Squadron (1838-41).
See also: War of 1812.

Hull, William, (1753-1825), army officer in the American Revolutionary War and the War of 1812. On Aug. 16, 1812, Hull surrendered Detroit, without resistance, to the British. He was prosecuted for treason by Martin Van Buren. Hull was court-martialed and condemned to death, but was reprieved by President James Madison.
See also: Revolutionary War in America; War of 1812.

Hull House, one of the first U.S. social settlement houses. Founded in Chicago in 1889 by Jane Addams and Ellen Gates Starr, it provided community services and recreational facilities to a poor community.
See also: Addams, Jane.

Human being (*Homo sapiens*), extremely adaptable mammal with highly-developed brain and nervous system, and ability to speak. Related to monkeys and apes, human beings differ from them physically by having the ability to stand and walk upright and by having a larger and more fully developed brain. Humans also use language, a trait that significantly distinguishes them from every other animal. Most scientists believe that the first recognizably human-like beings appeared in what is now Africa some 2 million years ago. This prehistoric human, referred to as *Homo habilis,* later developed into *Homo erectus,* who lived throughout Africa, Asia, and Europe and probably learned how to make and use fire. *Homo erectus* also hunted and used tools. The physical form humans have today began to appear about 40,000 years ago. Generally, humans seem to have begun as hunters and gatherers of food and to have gradually developed agricultural and industrial societies.

Human body, complex organism consisting of some 50 trillion cells, organized into tissues, organs, and structures. The body can best be studied as a complex of systems.
(1) The skeletal system, the body's framework, consists of more than 200 bones tied together with strong yet elastic ligaments. It accounts for about 18% of the body's weight.
(2) The muscular system consists of more than 650 distinct muscles that, by pulling on bones and bending joints, cause the body to move. Also part of this system are the visceral muscles, which cause movement in internal organs. The muscular system accounts for about 40% of body weight.
(3) The skin covers the whole body, allowing the maintenance of a constant internal environment. The sweat glands play an important part in excretion. Nerve endings in the skin provide the sense of touch and warn the body of external danger. The skin serves as a barrier against destructive organisms and foreign bodies.
(4) The circulatory system, consisting of the heart and thousands of miles of blood vessels and lymphatics, carries blood to all parts of the body, supplying every cell with oxygen and food and carrying from it carbon dioxide, water, and other wastes. The blood also carries hormones (the body's chemical messengers), which attack invading microorganisms, and help repair wounds by clotting.
(5) The respiratory system-including the lungs and the respiratory passages-allows the interchange of oxygen and carbon dioxide with the blood.
(6) The digestive system takes in food and breaks it down into a usable form that can be absorbed into the bloodstream. Basically, it consists of a tube extending from mouth to anus, with various organs, such as the stomach and accessory glands (including liver and pancreas) attached.
(7) The main organs of the urinary system are the kidneys, which remove waste from the blood, and the bladder, which stores and then expels that waste in the form of urine. (8) The reproductive system ensures the continuation of the species and the passing along of traits that may be necessary for survival.
(9) The nervous system consists of the central nervous system (CNS), comprising the brain and spinal cord, and the peripheral nervous system, the nerves that carry messages to and from the CNS.
(10) The endocrine system, consisting of the hormone-producing glands, responds to nervous commands or to other hormones and along with the nervous system, coordinates the activities of other organs and adjusts their functioning in relation to the external and internal environment.
(11) The body possesses a number of

specialized senses, including sight, hearing, balance, and the visceral sensations such as hunger.

Human Development Services, Office of, section of the U.S. Department of Health and Human Services, established in 1973 to govern various government social and rehabilitation programs. The Office of Human Development Services supports and funds groups with special needs, such as Native Americans, children, the elderly, the developmentally disabled, and low-income families. The agency has 4 main divisions: the Administration on Aging, the Administration for Native Americans, the Administration on Developmental Disabilities, and the Administration for Children, Youth and Families.

Humane society, organization whose purpose is to protect children and animals from mistreatment. Local humane societies in the United States fused in 1877 to become the American Humane Association.

Humanism, originally, Renaissance revival of the study of classical (Latin, Greek, and Hebrew) literature following the scholasticism of the Middle Ages, more broadly, philosophy centered on humankind and human values, exalting human free will and superiority to the rest of nature. Renaissance thinkers such as Petrarch began a trend toward humanism that embraced such diverse figures as Boccaccio, Machiavelli, Thomas More, and Erasmus and that led to much subsequent secular thought and literature, as well as to the Reforma-

Placing of the organs:
1. thyroid gland
2. collarbone
3. first rib
4. second rib
5. left lung
6. liver
7. stomach
8. spleen
9. transverse colon
10. descending colon
11. small intestine
12. urethra
13. bladder
14. pubis
15. prostate gland
16. ischium
17. atlas
18. cervical vertebral column
19. esophagus
20. shoulder blade
21. lumbar vertebral column
22. ilium
23. sacrum
24. rectum
25. coccyx
26. ureter

Digestive system:
1. tongue
2. mouth
3. sublingual and submaxillary salivary glands
4. parotid gland
5. throat
6. esophagus
7. stomach
8. pylorus
9. liver
10. gall bladder
11. bile duct
12. pancreas
13. duodenum
14. small intestine
15. ileum
16. colon
17. cecum
18. vermiform appendix
19. rectum
20. anus

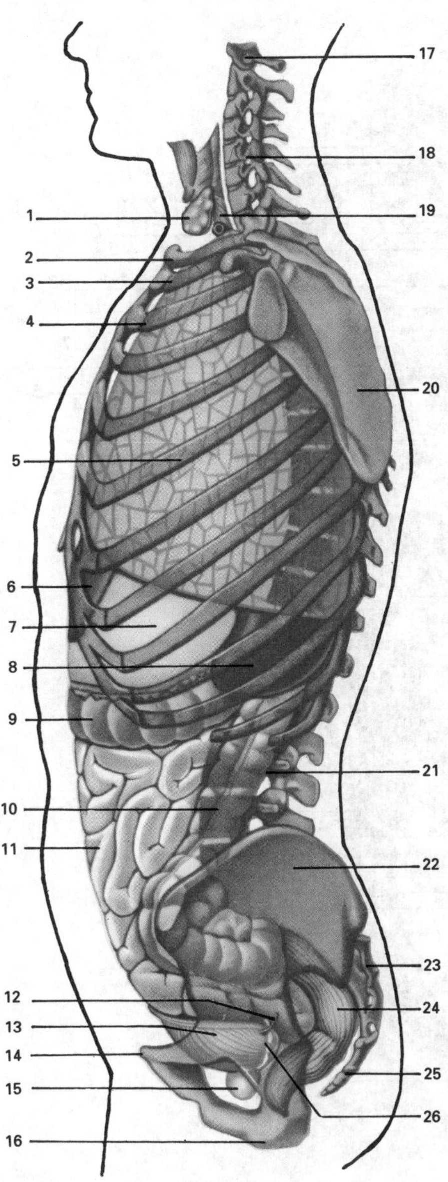

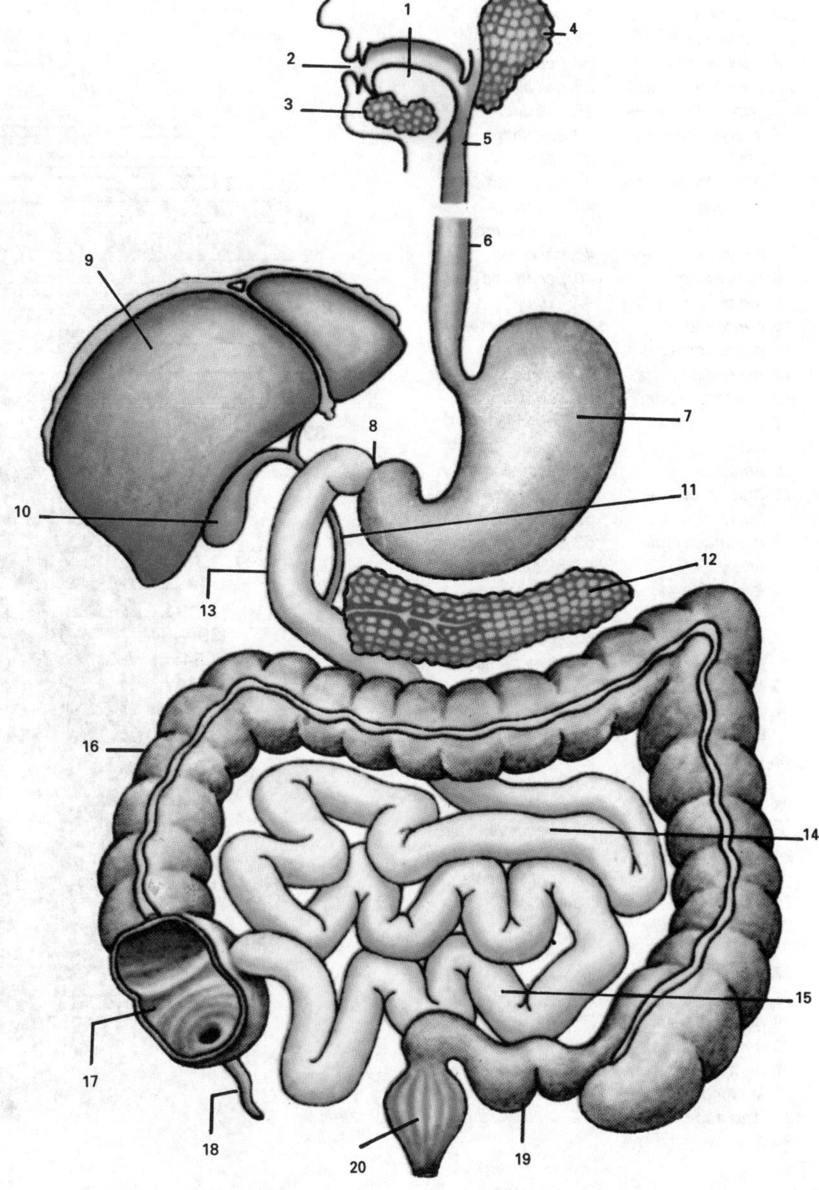

Baron van Humboldt

tion. Modern humanism tends to be non-theistic, emphasizing the need for people to work out their own solutions to life's problems, but has a strong ethic similar to that of Christianity. Both Roman Catholic and Protestant theologians have sought to show that Christian beliefs embody true humanism.
See also: Renaissance.

Human relations, study of group behavior and how the individual, as an inherently social being with personal needs, may achieve desired goals without losing, or causing others in the general population to lose, the basic rights of dignity, respect, and self-determination. Experts in the field of human relations must understand conflict, human needs, human nature, and how individuals and groups respond to one another.

Human Rights, Declaration of, United Nations document outlining the civil, economic, political, and social rights and freedoms for all the people of the world. Adopted by the General Assembly on Dec. 10, 1948, it declares all people to be free and to have equal rights and dignity.
See also: United Nations.

Humber, River, river in Humberside county, England, flowing eastward into the North Sea. The river's length is about 40 mi (64 km); its width is 1-7 mi (1.6-11 km). Two important tributaries are the Ouse and Trent rivers. The cities of Hull and Grimsby lie on the Humber's banks. The Humber Bridge has the longest main span (4,626 ft/1,410 m) of any suspension bridge in the world.

Humboldt, Friedrich Heinrich Alexander, Baron von (1769-1859), German naturalist. With the botanist Aimé Jacques Alexandre Bonpland he traveled for 5 years through much of South America (1799-1804), collecting plant, animal, and rock specimens and making geomagnetic and meteorologic observations. Humboldt published their data in 30 volumes over the next 23 years. In his most important work, *Kosmos* (1845-62), he sought to show a fundamental unity of all natural phenomena.

Humboldt Current *see:* Peru Current.

Hume, David (1711-76), Scottish Enlightenment philosopher, economist, and historian. His *Treatise of Human Nature* (1739-40) is one of the key works in the tradition of British empiricism, but it was his shorter *Enquiry Concerning Human Understanding* (1748) that prompted Immanuel Kant to his most radical labors. His influential *Dialogues Concerning Natural Religion* were published posthumously in 1779, long after their composition. In epistemology Hume argued that people had no logical reason to associate distinct impressions as cause and effect; if they did so, it was only on the basis of custom or psychological habit. His skepticism in this respect has always been controversial. In

Inner organs:
1. left ventricle
2. right ventricle
3. apex of the heart
4. papillary muscles
5. interventricular septum
6. right atrioventricular valve
7. left atrioventricular valve
8. right atrium
9. left atrium
10. pericardium
11. pulmonary vein
12. ascending aorta
13. pulmonary artery
14. superior vena cava
15. aortic arch
16. brachio-cephalic trunk
17. common carotid artery
18. left subclavian artery
19. right carotid artery
20. left carotid artery
21. right subclavian artery
22. internal jugular vein
23. right subclavian vein
24. left subclavian vein
25. trachea
26. external jugular vein
27. larynx
28. collarbone
29. pulmonary apex
30. right bronchus
31. right lung
32. left lung
33. diaphragm
34. liver
35. hepatic vein
36. portal vein
37. hepatic artery
38. gall bladder
39. bile duct
40. stomach
41. spleen
42. splenic artery
43. splenic vein
44. duodenum
45. pancreas
46. pancreatic duct
47. kidney
48. greater omentum
49. ileum
50. cacum
51. vermiform appendix
52. mesocolon
53. ascending colon
54. transverse colon
55. descending colon
56. sigmoid flexure
57. rectum
58. urethra
59. bladder
60. abdominal aorta
61. lower peritoneal artery
62. testicular artery
63. common iliac artery
64. external iliac artery
65. inferior vena cava
66. common iliac vein
67. right testicular vein

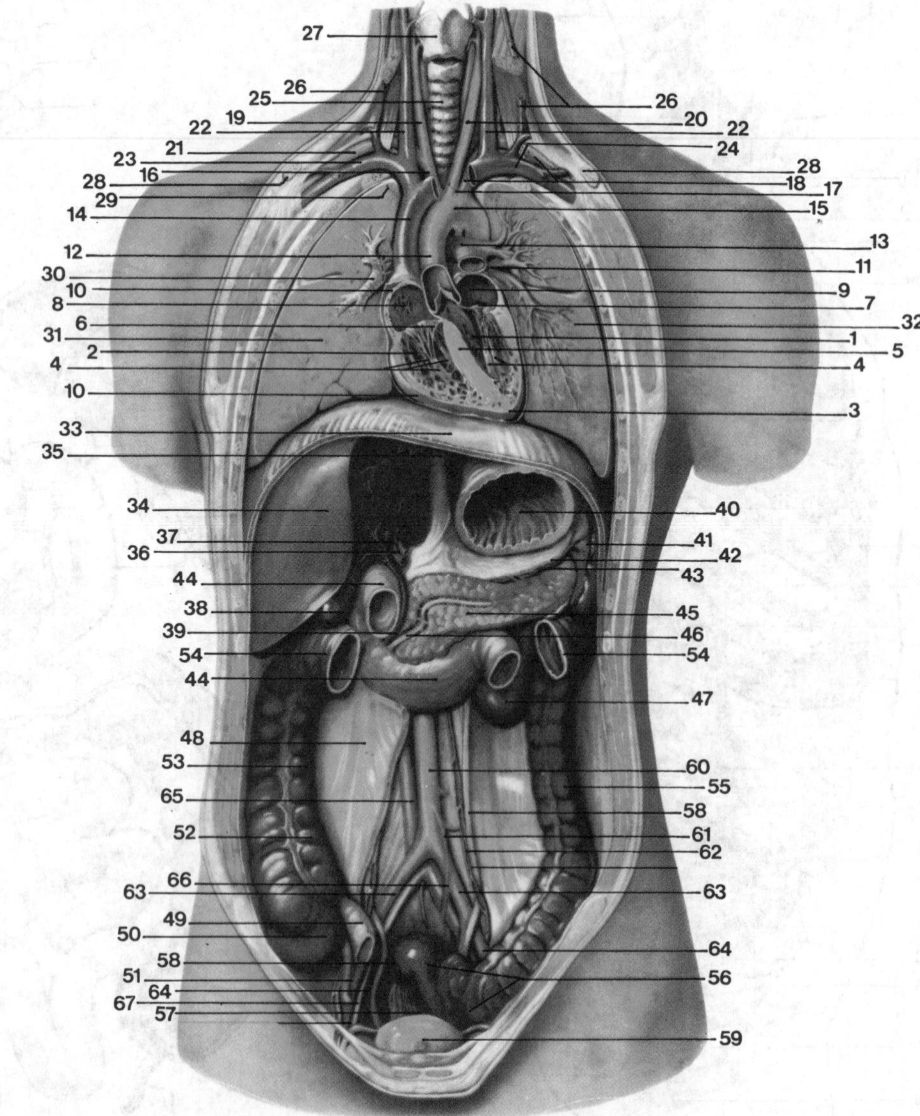

his own day, Hume's most popular work was his *History of England* (1754-63).
See also: Philosophy.

Humidity, amount of water vapor in the air. *Absolute humidity* measures mass of water per unit volume of air. Saturation of the air, or *dew point*, occurs when the water vapor pressure reaches the vapor pressure of liquid water at the temperature concerned; this rises rapidly with temperature. *Relative humidity*, expressed as a percentage, is the amount of water in the air at any given time compared with the amount the air could hold at that temperature before becoming saturated. The physiologically tolerable humidity level falls rapidly as temperature rises, since humidity inhibits body cooling by impeding the evaporation of sweat.

Hummingbird, tiny nectar-feeding bird of the family Trochilidae. It takes its name from the noise of its rapid wingbeats—up to 70 a second in smaller species—as it hovers at flowers to feed. Hummingbirds are colorful, with a body size in most species 2 in (5 cm) or less. With their small size and fierce activity, hummingbirds must feed about once every 10-15 min. Highly adapted to flight, hummingbirds have short legs and little feet, used only for perching. They can hover in one place and are the only birds capable of flying backward.

Hummingbird

Hummingbird moth *see:* Hawk moth.

Humor, according to the ancients, any of the 4 bodily elements: phlegm, blood, choler, and black bile, corresponding to the 4 natural elements: earth, air, fire, and water. In the well-adjusted person, the 4 humors are in balance. If one preponderates, the person is of unequal temper: If phlegm preponderates then the person is phlegmatic; if blood, the person is sanguine; if choler, the person is choleric; if black bile, the person is melancholic. The person not in "good humor" behaves eccentrically, and is thus an object of ridicule. The word "humor" thus came to mean mocking laughter.

Humperdinck, Engelbert (1854-1921), German composer. He was much influenced by Richard Wagner, whom he assisted at the Bayreuth Festival. He wrote several operas; only *Hansel and Gretel* (1893) is widely performed today, although *The Royal Children* (1910) is revived from time to time.

Humphrey, Doris (1895-1958), U.S. modern dancer and choreographer. Influenced by Ruth St. Denis and Ted Shawn, she set up a school and company with Charles Weidman (1928) to develop her own expressive style, based upon her innovative theories of movement. Humphrey founded (with Martha Graham) the U.S. modern-dance form.

Humphrey, Hubert Horatio (1911-78), U.S. political leader, vice president from 1965 to 1969. A Democrat, he was mayor of Minneapolis, then was elected senator from Minnesota in 1948. Identified with many liberal causes, as vice president under Lyndon Johnson he nonetheless supported U.S. Vietnam policy. Unsuccessful as the Democratic candidate for president (1968), he returned to the Senate (1970).

Humus, organic substance formed in soil when microorganisms, bacteria, and fungi decompose plant and animal material. Humus is soft, spongy, and dark brown. It affects the soil's structure, water retention, nutritional value to plants, and erosion resistance.

Hun, nomadic, probably Mongolian, race that invaded southeastern Europe during the 4th and 5th centuries. They crossed the Volga River in c.372 A.D. and attacked the Germanic Goth tribes. By 432 they had invaded the Eastern Empire. Under their great leader Attila, they threatened the Roman Empire, unsuccessfully invading Gaul in 451. In 452 their Italian invasion was halted at Lake Garda. After Attila's death in 453, the Hun empire gradually disintegrated.
See also: Attila.

Hunchback, or kyphosis, deformity of the spine causing bent posture with or without twisting (scoliosis) and abnormal bony prominences. Tuberculosis of the spine may cause sharp angulation, while congenital diseases, ankylosing spondylitis, vertebral collapse, and spinal tumors cause smooth kyphosis.

Hundred Days, in French history, period between Napoleon's return to Paris from exile on Elba and the second Bourbon restoration (Mar. 20-June 28, 1815). During this time Napoleon attempted to reinstate himself as ruler of France on a more liberal basis. He was defeated at Waterloo, and Louis XVIII was restored to the French Throne.
See also: Napoleon.

Hundred Years War, sporadic series of wars fought mainly between England and France from 1337 to 1453. They originated

The Hundred Years War was the cause of internal conflict in France between nobility and farmers. Depicted is one of the many conflicts.

in disputes over English possessions in France, and the claims of Edward III of England to the throne of France. In 1337 he invaded Gascony and won the battles of Sluis (1340), Crécy (1346), and Poitiers (1356), and seized Calais, gaining important concessions at the Treaty of Brétigny (1360). The French under Charles V retained much of their lost territory (1369-75) and attacked the English coast. Henry V of England destroyed the resulting uneasy truce when he invaded France in 1415, in pursuit of a dream of establishing himself as monarch of Britain and France; he captured Harfleur and defeated a superior French force at Agincourt. At the Treaty of Troyes (1420) Henry V was recognized as heir to the French throne, and from 1422 his infant son, Henry VI, ruled the dual monarchy, with John, Duke of Bedford, as French regent. His able rule won French support, and only the resurgence led by Joan of Arc in 1429 halted English gains. Although the dauphin (French heir to the throne, son of Charles VI) was crowned Charles VII at Reims in 1429, the English position was not assailed until 1435, when Philip the Good of Burgundy recognized Charles VII as king of France. After 1444 the English were driven back until they held only Calais (until 1448) and the Channel Islands.

Hubert H. Humphrey

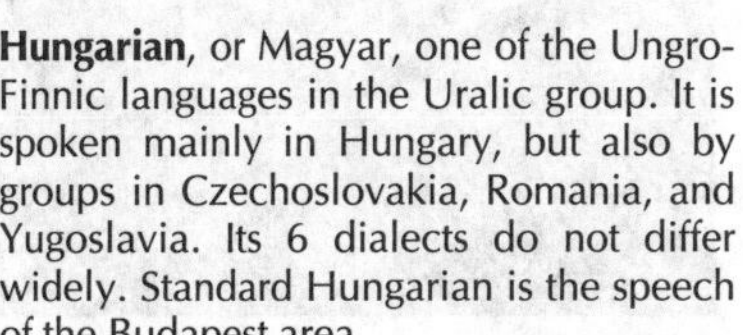

Hungarian, or Magyar, one of the Ungro-Finnic languages in the Uralic group. It is spoken mainly in Hungary, but also by groups in Czechoslovakia, Romania, and Yugoslavia. Its 6 dialects do not differ widely. Standard Hungarian is the speech of the Budapest area.

Hungarian pointer *see:* Vizsla.

Hungary, country in east-central Europe, bordered by Czechoslovakia on the north, the USSR and Romania on the east, Yugoslavia on the south, and Austria on the west. The capital is Budapest, where nearly 20% of the population lives.
Land. Hungary is basically a fertile plain, drained by the Danube River, which forms part of the border with Czechoslovakia and then turns south through the country. The Dráva, which forms part of Hungary's border with Yugoslavia, is the only other important river. Most of the country has black, very fertile soil. Lake Balaton, the

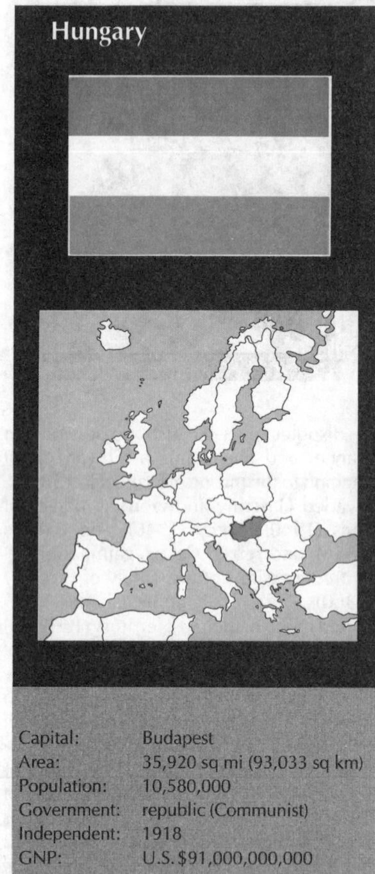

Capital:	Budapest
Area:	35,920 sq mi (93,033 sq km)
Population:	10,580,000
Government:	republic (Communist)
Independent:	1918
GNP:	U.S.$91,000,000,000
Per capita:	U.S.$8,500

Budapest, Hungary

Rural homestead near Bupac, Hungary

largest lake in Europe (48 mi/77 km long), begins southwest of Budapest and extends southwest toward the Yugoslav border. The country is rich in game, including deer, fox, wild boar, and hare.

People. The official language is Hungarian. About two-thirds of the population is Roman Catholic, and one-third Calvinist.

Economy. Hungary was traditionally agricultural, but there has been significant industrialization since World War II. There are important electrical, chemical, food-processing and textile plants. Leading crops include corn, wheat, oats, rye, potatoes, sunflowers, and sugar beets. Apricots, grapes, paprika, and tobacco are also grown, and hogs, sheep, and cattle are raised.

History. The area that is now Hungary was conquered by the Magyars c.896 and Christianized in the 900s. A feudal system flourished until the Ottoman Turkish invasion defeated King Lewis II at Mohács (1526). Most of the country was divided between the Ottoman Empire and Austria, the west and north coming under Habsburg rule in 1687. A bid for independence led by Lajos Kossuth (1848) failed but led to the establishment of the Dual Monarchy (1867): the Austrian Emperor Francis Joseph I was crowned King of Hungary, and the Austro-Hungarian empire was born. That empire was destroyed in World War I, and an independent Hungarian state was proclaimed in 1918. A Communist revolution in 1919 was put down by Romanian intervention, and in 1920 Admiral Nicholas Horthy de Nagybanya, a right-wing dictator, came to power. Hungary was an ally of Nazi Germany during World War II. Occupied by the USSR (1945), it became a "people's republic" in 1949. An uprising against the repressive regime was crushed by Soviet intervention (1956), and a puppet government under János Kádar was set up. Kádar introduced cultural and economic reforms in the 1960s that temporarily improved Hungarians' living standards, but his refusal to introduce further reforms during the economic decline of the 1970s led to his replacement in 1988.The Communist regime collapsed in 1989 during the general upheaval that swept Eastern Europe.

Hunger, appetite (impulse, drive) for food, often referring also to the mass of uneasy sensations from the gut and particularly from hunger contractions in the stomach, which accompany the appetite; also used to describe sexual appetite.

Hunt, (James Henry) Leigh (1784-1859), English critic, journalist, and poet. He was editor of the liberal *Examiner* (1808-22) and other journals. Hunt was a friend of the leading literary figures of his day, notably Keats and Shelley, whose poetic careers he furthered; Lamb; Hazlitt; Byron; and eventually Carlyle. His most highly regarded works are *Lord Byron and Some of His Contemporaries* (1828), *Autobiography* (1850), and the short lyric poems "Abou Ben Adhem" (1834) and "Jenny Kissed Me" (1844).

Hunt, H(aroldson) L(afayette) (1889-1974), U.S. oil magnate. In the 1920s he invested in Arkansas oil fields. The Hunt Oil Company, founded in 1936, became one of the largest independent U.S. oil and natural gas corporations.

Hunt, Richard Morris (1828-95), U.S. architect. He trained and worked in Europe (1843-54), and his style in the United States was historically eclectic. He built the Statue of Liberty base and the 1893 Chicago Exposition administrative building. *See also:* Architecture.

Hunt, William Holman (1827-1910), English painter who helped found the Pre-Raphaelite movement. His work is noted for its brilliant color and accurate details. *The Light of the World* (1853) is his best-known painting.

Hunting dog rouses game birds from the field

Hunting, pursuit and killing of wild animals for subsistence, profit, or sport. In Western Europe hunting means the pursuit and capture of a wild animal with the aid of hounds. In the United States and elsewhere the term means the field sport of shooting large and small game.

Hunting was an important source of food, clothing, and sometimes shelter for primitive people. Cave paintings in France and Spain indicate that these people hunted wild horses, prehistoric cattle, reindeer, and mammoths, often with the bow and arrow. Hunting as a sport was practiced by the earliest known civilizations, such as those in Babylonia and Egypt. Hunts full of pageantry and splendor were popular with kings and princes, who often gained status according to the number of animals they had killed.

With the exception of the Native Americans of the Southwest, the Southeast, and adjoining regions, the North American tribes lived almost exclusively by hunting. With the arrival of European colonists, hunting became important for the fur trade. As white settlers occupied increasing amounts of land, however, the wild game gradually disappeared; thus, in most areas of the present-day United States, game animals, especially the larger ones, exist in relatively small numbers and sometimes are even brought into a region to provide quarry for hunters. Game is also limited in variety, with rabbits and deer probably the most plentiful overall.
Western and northern Canada and Alaska are exceptions to this general scarcity; wildlife of many sorts still abounds there. Regulatory measures and the vigilant efforts of conservationists help to save game animals threatened with extinction through indiscriminate hunting. Certain African countries, mostly in East and South Africa, have also made ambitious efforts to save their often unique wildlife by establishing and patrolling enormous animal sanctuaries where the camera is the only "weapon" permitted.

Huntington (pop. 312,529), largest city in West Virginia, located on the Ohio River. It was founded in 1871 as the western terminus for the Chesapeake and Ohio Railroad and was named for Collis P. Huntington, the president of that railroad. Numerous and varied industries produce such important commercial goods as nickel and nickel alloys, furniture, railroad equipment, shoes, and glass. Huntington suffered many serious floods before the construction of an 11-mi long (18-km) flood wall that now protects the city. Marshall University is located there.
See also: West Virginia.

Huntington, Collis Potter (1821-1900), U.S. railroad tycoon. He was the chief promoter of the West's first railroad company, the Central Pacific (1861), and he established the Southern Pacific (1884). He left most of his fortune to his nephew, Henry E. Huntington.
See also: Railroad.

Huntington, Henry Edwards (1850-1927), U.S. financier; nephew and heir of Collis P. Huntington. He formed and endowed a world-class art collection and research library at San Marino, Calif., that specializes in Anglo-American legal documents, Western Americana, and English 18th-century art and literature.

Huntington, Samuel (1731-96), Connecticut political figure who signed the Declaration of Independence. He served as a governor's council member (1755-83) and Continental Congress representative (1776-81) before becoming a Connecticut delegate to the Confederation Congress (1781-84). After being appointed chief justice of the Connecticut Supreme Court (1784), he served as lieutenant governor (1785) and governor (1786-96).

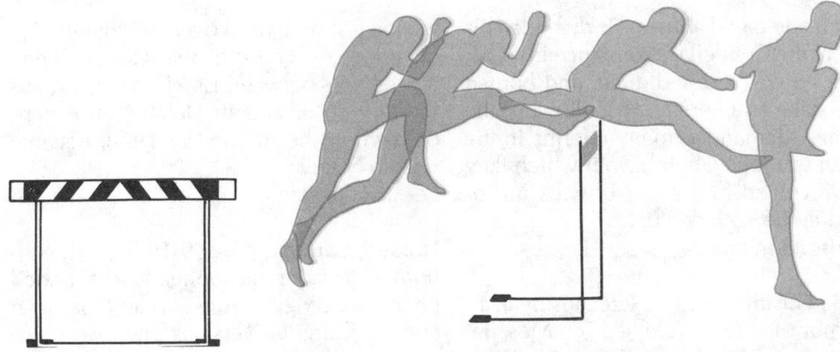

Hurdling techniques

Huntington's disease (Huntington's chorea), disease marked by progressive degeneration of the central nervous system. An inherited, ultimately fatal disease that breaks out in adulthood, its symptoms are involuntary, jerky body movements and mental disturbances. It was first identified in 1871 by the American neurologist Dr. George Huntington.

Huntsman's-cup *see:* Pitcher plant.

Huntsville (pop. 238,912), city in northeastern Alabama. Founded in 1805, Huntsville was the site of the state constitutional convention in 1819, which resulted in statehood for Alabama. In the 1950s, with the establishment of the U.S. Redstone Arsenal as a research base, the city became an important center for the aerospace industry and is now known as "Rocket City, USA."
See also: Alabama.

Hunza, district in northern Kashmir controlled by Pakistan. The largest city is Karimabad. Woolen cloth and handicrafts are leading industries. Burushaski is the spoken language, but there is no written language. Most of the people are Muslims.
See also: Pakistan.

Hurdling, track and field sport in which runners jump over obstacles called hurdles, which stand at specific heights and are set equal distances apart on the track. Runners adjust their stride and bring one leg over the hurdle at a time to clear hurdles without breaking stride. Hurdles may be knocked down, but disqualification occurs if done so by runner's hand.

Huron, league of 4 Native North American tribes, approximately 20,000 strong, who lived in South Ontario in the 1600s. Members of the Iroquoian language group, they were an agrarian society who were attacked and nearly destroyed by the Iroquois (1650). Small numbers of Hurons remain in Quebec and in Oklahoma.

Hurricane, tropical cyclone of great intensity. High-speed winds spiral in toward a low-pressure core of warm, calm air (the eye). Winds of over 185 mph (298 kmph) have been measured. The direction of spiral is clockwise in the southern hemisphere and counterclockwise in the northern hemisphere. Hurricanes form over water when there is an existing convergence of air near sea level. The air ascends, losing moisture as precipitation as it does so. If this happens rapidly enough, the upper air is warmed by the water's latent heat of vaporization. This reduces the surface pressure and thus accelerates air convergence. Since they require large quantities of moist warm air, hurricanes rarely penetrate far inland. Hurricanes of the North Pacific are often called typhoons.

Hurston, Zora Neale (1901-60), U.S. author known for her literary interpretations of African-American folklore of the southern United States and the Caribbean. Her novels were *Jonah's Gourd Vine* (1934) and *Their Eyes Were Watching God* (1937). *Mules and Men* (1935) and *Tell My Horse* (1938) are collections of retold folktales.

Hus, Jan (1370-1415), Bohemian religious reformer and Czech national hero. Influenced by John Wycliffe, Hus attacked

Hurricane Gladys (1986) photographed over the Caribbean by Apollo 7.

Church and papal abuses. He defended his ideas at the Council of Constance in 1414, where he was arrested, tried, and burned at the stake as a heretic. His followers, the Hussites, demanded many reforms in the Roman Catholic Church, with which they were involved in a series of wars in Bohemia in the 15th century.
See also: Bohemia.

Husák, Gustav (1913-), Czechoslovakian Communist leader. Taking a pro-Moscow line after 1968, he replaced Secretary Dubek as leader of the Communist Party in 1969 He served as president of Czechoslovakia from 1975 to 1987.
See also: Czechoslovakia.

Husein Ibn Ali (1854-1931), sharif of Mecca (1908-16) and king of Hejaz (1916-24). In 1916 he led the World War I Arab revolt against the Turks and proclaimed himself king of all Arabia. Assisted by T. E. Lawrence, he drove the Turks from Syria, northern Arabia, and Transjordan. In 1924 Ibn Saud forced him to abdicate, and he died in exile.

Husky *see:* Siberian husky.

Hussar, European soldier who was a member of light cavalry units used for scouting. The Hussar uniform included a high, cloth cap (busby), a loose cape (dolman), and a heavily braided jacket. Napoleon perfected the efficiency of these soldiers, who became known for their fighting abilities. Hussars were no longer used after World War I.

Saddam Hussein

Hussein, Saddam (1937-), Arab nationalist leader, president and dictator of Iraq from 1979. As chair of the Revolutionary Command Council of the Arab Ba'ath Socialist Party, a pan-Arab organization that controls all facets of Iraqi society, he established a regime marked by widespread repression, imprisonment, and fear. At the same time, the government made significant progress in industrialization. The Ba'ath took power in Iraq in 1963. Hussein, though formally second in command, was the de facto ruler as early as 1969. In 1980 he launched an attack on Iran that led to the 8-year-long Iran-Iraq war. On Aug. 2, 1990 the Iraq army invaded Kuwait. The pretext for the invasions was Iraq's territorial claim to Kuwait. Shortly after the invasion, the United States and a combined allied military force established a military presence in Saudi Arabia. After 6 months of United Nations' diplomatic efforts at peace failed, the allied forces declared war on Iraq. On Jan. 16, 1991 hostilities commenced and a ceasefire was announced on Feb. 21, 1991.
See also: Iraq; Persian Gulf War.

Christiaan Huygens

Hussein I (1935-), king of Jordan since 1953. His policies are generally pro-Western, and he is a spokesperson for moderation in the conflict between the Arab nations and Israel. Jordan's loss of the West Bank in the 1967 Arab-Israeli war led to civil war in 1970, when King Hussein gained firmer control over the country. He declined to endorse the Camp David agreements between Israel and Egypt. His fourth wife, Elizabeth Halaby, an American, whom he married in 1978, became Queen Noor.
See also: Jordan.

Husserl, Edmund (1859-1938), Czech-born German philosopher who founded phenomenology. Professor at Göttingen and Freiburg universities, he was concerned with what constitutes acts of consciousness and how they relate to experience. He held that consciousness is "intentional" in that it is always "conscious of" an object. Husserl's investigations influenced Heidegger, Sartre, and other thinkers of 20th-century existentialism.
See also: Phenomenology.

Huston, name of 3 film personalities. **Walter Huston** (1884-1950), Canadian-born U.S. actor, is best known for his roles in the play *Dodsworth* (1936), the musical comedy *Knickerbocker Holiday* (1938), and the film *The Treasure of Sierra Madre* (1947) directed by his son **John Huston** (1906-87), Hollywood writer, then director, whose other films include *The Maltese Falcon* (1941), *The Asphalt Jungle* (1950), *The African Queen* (1951), *Moby Dick* (1956), and *The Dead* (1987). John Huston's daughter **Anjelica Huston** (1951-) won the Academy Award for best supporting actress in *Prizzi's Honor* (1985).

Hutchins, Robert Maynard (1899-1977), U.S. educator, president (1929-45) and chancellor (1945-51) of the University of Chicago. He advocated the integration and synthesis of academic disciplines. In 1959 he founded the Center for the Study of Democratic Institutions as an ideal "Community of Scholars." His books include *The Higher Learning in America* (1936) and *University of Utopia* (1953).

Hutchinson, Anne Marbury (1591-1643), English Puritan religious leader, one of the founders of Rhode Island. She emigrated to Massachusetts in 1634, where she preached that faith alone could achieve salvation. She opposed obedience to the strict laws of the Puritan community. In 1638 she and her followers were banished, and they established a settlement on Aquidneck Island (now Rhode Island). She later moved to New York, where she was killed by Native Americans.
See also: Puritans.

Hutchinson, Thomas (1711-80), American colonial governor of Massachusetts, 1770-74. A political enemy of Samuel Adams, he opposed American independence, and enforced the Stamp Act (1765) although considering the act unwise. In 1773 he insisted that duty be paid on tea cargoes in Boston, which led to the Boston Tea Party. In 1774 he went to England, where he served George III as an adviser.

Hutterites, or Hutterlan Brethren, Protestant sect found primarily in South Dakota, and Canada. Like the Mennonites, they believe in common ownership of goods and are pacifists. The sect originated in 1533 as a branch of the Anabaptists and takes its name from Jacob Hutter, martyred in 1536.
See also: Anabaptism.

Hutton, James (1726-97), Scottish geologist who proposed, in *Theory of the Earth* (1795), that the earth's natural features result from continual processes, occurring now at the same rate as they have in the past. These views were little regarded until Charles Lyell's work some decades later.

Huxley, British family of writers and scientists. **Thomas Henry Huxley** (1825-95), biologist, is best known for his support of Darwin's theory of evolution, without which acceptance of the theory might have been long delayed. Most of his own contributions to paleontology and zoology (especially taxonomy), botany, geology, and anthropology were related to this. He also coined the word "agnostic." His son **Leonard Huxley** (1860-1933), writer, wrote *The Life and Letters of Thomas Henry Huxley* (1900). Of his children, 3 earned fame. **Sir Julian Sorell Huxley** (1887-1975) is best known as a biologist and ecologist. His early interests were in development and growth, genetics, and embryology. Later he made important studies of bird behavior, studied evolution, and wrote many popular scientific books. **Aldous Leonard Huxley** (1894-1963) was one of the 20th century's foremost novelists. Important works include *Crome Yellow* (1921), *Antic Hay* (1923), and *Point Counter Point* (1928), characterized by their wit and attitude toward lofty pretensions, and the famous *Brave New World* (1932) and *Eyeless in Gaza* (1936). After experimenting with hallucinogenic drugs he became interested in mysticism. Later works include *The Devils of London* (1952), *the Doors of Perception* (1954), and *Island* (1962). **Andrew Field Huxley** (1917-) shared the 1963 Nobel Prize for physiology or medicine with A.L. Hodgkin and Sir J. Eccles for his work with Hodgkin on the chemical basis of nerve impulse transmission.

Hu Yaobang (1915-89), general secretary of the Chinese Communist Party (1981-87). A friend and associate of Deng Xioping, he was removed as chairman of the party in January 1987 in the face of student demonstrations for freedom of expression.
See also: China

Huygens, Christiaan (1629-95), Dutch scientist. He formulated a wave theory of light, first applied the pendulum to the regulation of clocks, and discovered the surface markings of Mars and the rings of Saturn. In his optical studies he stated Huygens's Principle, that all points on a wave front may at any instant be considered sources of secondary waves that, taken together, represent the wave front at any later instant. Huygens' theory of light states that light is a disturbance traveling through

some medium, such as the ether. Thus light is due to wave motion in ether.
See also: Optics; Physics.

Hyacinth, plant (genus *Hyacinthus*, especially *H. orientalis*) of the lily family grown from a bulb that produces a head of beautifully colored and perfumed flowers. It originated in the Mediterranean region. Water hyacinths (*Eichhornia crassipes*) are unrelated plants. They float on water and have been introduced to many places where they become a nuisance by blocking waterways.

Hyacinth

Hyaline membrane disease, or respiratory distress syndrome, lung condition that is a common cause of death in premature babies. The disease is characterized by underdeveloped lungs that lack pulmonary surfactant, a substance that prevents the collapse of air sacs after breathing has begun. Immature lungs produce a glassy membrane that covers open bronchioles. Breathing becomes strained and death frequently occcurs from lack of oxygen.

Hybrid, crossbred animal or plant; an offspring of 2 different breeds, genera, or varieties. A hybrid computer system is a system that uses both analog and digital equipment. Hybrids in data communications are circuits fabricated by interconnecting smaller circuits of different technologies mounted on a single substrate.

Hyderabad (pop. 751,500), third largest city in Pakistan, located on the Indus River in Sind province. It is an important transportation and trade center, with various chemical, engineering, and milling industries.
See also: Pakistan.

Hyderabad (pop. 2,187,000), capital of the Indian state of Andhra Pradesh and historically of the region also called Hyderabad. The metropolitan area is a trade and manufacturing center producing textiles, guns, and glass products.
See also: India.

Hyderabad, region on the Deccan plateau that was once a state of south central India. Historically, Hyderabad was the site of a Hindu civilization taken over by the Muslim Mogul Empire in the 17th century. It became part of India in 1948, after a plebescite rejected independence. In 1950 it was divided among the states of Andhra Pradesh, Maharashtra, and Karnataka. Crops include cotton, rice, and grain. Mineral deposits are also present in the area.
See also: India.

Hydra, in Greek mythology, serpent with many heads, also known as Lernaean Hydra or Hydra of Lerna. Whenever a head was cut off, 2 new ones replaced it. Hercules killed the Hydra, burning the necks after decapitating it.
See also: Mythology.

Hydra, genus of freshwater animal of the phylum Coelenterata, perhaps the most familiar of the class Hydrozoa. The hydra is found in ponds, lakes, and streams throughout the world. The body is an elongated 2-in (2.5-cm) column with a mouth at one end surrounded by tentacles. Normally attached by the other end to the substrate, hydras can move by "looping" across a plane surface or by free-swimming. Hydras reproduce by asexual budding when food is abundant. When food is scarce, ovaries and testes develop on the column, and sexual reproduction gives rise to resistant, dormant embryos.

Hydrangea, genus of ornamental shrub of the saxifrage family originally from China and Japan, widely grown in pots and gardens. Its heads of small, flat-petaled flowers range from pale blue to pink, changing color in response to soil acidity.

Hydrate, any of various chemical compounds composed of water and some other substance. Common hydrates include blue vitriol ($CuSO_45H_2O$) and Glauber's salt ($Na_2CO_310H_2O$). As water evaporates, most hydrates change structure. Water that is retained by the hydrate is known as water of crystallization or hydration. Hydrates that have lost all water are called anhydrous.

Hydraulic brake *see:* Brake.

Hydraulic engine, or fluidic engine, machine that uses the motion or pressure of fluids (like oil, silicone, gas, and sometimes water) to produce power. These engines are used in jacks, hoists, hydraulic elevators, and some turbine generators.
See also: Hydraulics.

Hydraulics, branch of science concerned with the application of the properties of liquids (particularly water), at rest and in motion, to engineering problems. Since any machine or structure that uses, controls, or conserves a liquid makes use of the principles of hydraulics, the scope of this subject is very wide. It includes methods of water supply for consumption, irrigation, or navigation and the design of associated dams, canals, and pipes; hydroelectricity, the conversion of water power to electric energy using hydraulic turbines; the design and construction of ditches, culverts, and hydraulic jumps (a means of slowing down the flow of a stream by suddenly increasing its depth) for controlling and discharging flood water; and the treatment and disposal of industrial and human waste. Hydraulics applies the principles of hydrostatics and is hence a branch of fluid mechanics.

Hyderabad, India is the home of the Char Minar mosque which is distinguished by its four minarets.

Hydrazine chemical compound (H_2NNH_2), used in jet and rocket fuels, explosives, and corrosion inhibitors. Also known as hydronitrogen, it is a colorless liquid that absorbs water and alcohol. It has an acrid smell, burns in air, and is corrosive.

Hydriodic acid *see:* Hydrogen iodide.

Hydrobromic acid *see:* Hydrogen bromide.

Hydrocarbon, any organic compound of hydrogen and carbon. They are divided into two classes: *aliphatics*, in which the carbon atoms are arranged in chains, and *aromatics*, in which they are arranged in rings. The aliphatics are divided into various sub-groups according to the way the carbon atoms are bonded together. Hydrocarbons occur in petroleum and natural gas. Commercial products include gasoline, kerosene, airplane fuel, lubricating oils, and paraffin.

Hydrochloric acid, chemical compound (HCL) with many industrial uses. A colorless, extremely corrosive liquid that fumes when exposed to air, it is used in metallurgy and food processing. It is produced naturally in the human stomach as a digestive aid, but stomach ulcers can form if it is present in excess.

Hydroelectric power *see:* Electric power; Water power.

Hydrofluoric acid, inorganic chemical compound (HF), also called hydrogen fluoride, formed when hydrofluoric gas is dissolved in water. It is used industrially in manufacturing aluminum, in etching glass, and as a catalyst for chemical reactions.

Hydrofoil, structure that, when moved rapidly through water, generates lift in exactly the same way and for the same reasons as does the airfoil. It is usually mounted beneath a vessel (also called a

Hydrofoil

hydrofoil). Much of a conventional boat's power is spent in overcoming the drag (resistance) of the water; as a hydrofoil vessel builds up speed, it lifts out of the water until only a small portion of it (struts, hydrofoils, and propeller) is in contact with the water. Thus drag is reduced to a minimum. Hydrofoils can exceed 75 mph (121 kmph) as compared with conventional craft, whose maximum speeds rarely approach 50 mph (80 kmph).

Hydrogen, chemical element, symbol H; for physical constants see Periodic Table. Hydrogen was prepared for many years before it was recognized as a distinct substance by Henry Cavendish in 1766. It is the most abundant element in the universe, making up about three quarters of the mass of the universe. On earth hydrogen occurs chiefly in combination with oxygen in water. Hydrogen is prepared commercially by the action of steam on heated carbon or iron. Hydrogen is a diatomic, colorless, explosively reactive gas, the lightest of all gases. Production of hydrogen in the United States alone amounts to hundreds of millions of cubic feet per day. Hydrogen gas is a mixture of 2 kinds of molecules, known as *ortho-* and *para-*hydrogen, which differ from one another by the spins of their electrons and nuclei. Hydrogen is used in nitrogen fixation, as rocket fuel, in reducing metallic ores, for welding, as heavy water in nuclear reactors, and as a neutron moderator. Liquid hydrogen is used in cryogenics.

Hydrogenation, chemical process that adds hydrogen to some other substance. The resulting reaction is used to change liquid oils into solid fats, powdered coal into crude oil, and nitrogen into ammonia.

Hydrogen bomb, or thermonuclear bomb, very powerful bomb whose explosive energy is produced by nuclear fusion of hydrogen isotopes, as of 2 deuterium atoms or of a deuterium and a tritium atom. The extremely high temperatures required to start the fusion reaction are produced by an atomic bomb. Lithium-6 deuteride (^{6}LiD) is the explosive; neutrons produced by deuterium fusion react with the ^{6}Li to produce tritium. The end products are the isotopes of helium, ^{3}He and ^{4}He. In warfare hydrogen bombs have the advantage of being far more powerful than atomic bombs, their power being measured in megatons (millions of tons) of TNT, capable of destroying a large city. In defensive and peaceful uses they can be modified so that the radioactivity produced is reduced. Hydrogen bombs were first developed in the United States (1949-52) by Edward Teller and others, and have been tested by the USSR, Great Britain, China, and France.
See also: Fallout; Nuclear weapon.

Hydrogen bromide, chemical compound (HBr) that is a colorless, corrosive gas. If exposed to humid air it will fume; when combined with water it forms hydrobromic acid. The gas is used in various chemical reactions to make organic bromides and compounds, as a reducing agent, and as a catalyst.

Hydrogen fluoride *see:* Hydrofluoric acid.

Hydrogen iodide, chemical compound (HI) that is a colorless gas with a sharp odor. It fumes when exposed to humid air and combines easily with water to form hydriodic acid. It is used to make iodine salts, as a reducing agent, and for medical purposes in a diluted form.

Hydrogen peroxide (H_2O_2), unstable chemical compound that acts as an oxidizing agent that may cause poisoning. Hydrogen peroxide is marketed as an aqueous solution ranging from the common concentration of 3% as a topical antiseptic, 6% in hair preparations (bleaches, neutralizers, and so forth), to 30% for industrial and laboratory use and 90% for use in rocket propulsion. Decomposition of hydrogen peroxide may release large volumes of oxygen (10 times the volume for a 3% solution). Dropping a 3% solution on the eye, 3-5 times a day has been reported to be innocuous, but high-concentration hydrogen peroxide is generally feared as a cause of severe corneal damage. Ingestion of the commonly available household products (3-6%) should cause no problem other than possible mucous membrane and gastrointestinal irritation, while higher concentrations (such as 30%) are considered corrosive.
See also: Antiseptic.

Hydrogen bomb test in the Pacific Ocean

Hydrogen sulfide, colorless, poisonous, flammable gas (H_2S) with an odor of rotting eggs. When combined with water it forms hydrosulfuric acid. The gas can be found around cesspools and in mines as a by-product of the decomposition of substances containing sulfur. The gas is also produced in laboratories for use as an analytical reagent.

Hydrology, branch of geophysics concerned with the hydrosphere (all the waters of the earth), with particular reference to water on and within the land. The science was born in the 17th century with the work of Pierre Perrault and Edmé Mariotte.
See also: Geophysics.

Hydrolysis, in chemistry, double decomposition effected by water, according to the general equation $XY + H_2O \rightarrow XOH + YH$. If XY is a salt of a weak acid or a weak base, the hydrolysis is reversible, and affects the pH of the solution. Reactive organic compounds such as acid chlorides and acid anhydrides are rapidly hydrolyzed by water alone, but other compounds require acids, bases, or enzymes as catalysts. Industrial hydrolysis processes include the alkaline saponification of oils and fats to glycerol and soap, and the acid hydrolysis of starch to glucose.

Hydrometer, device that measures the specific gravity of a liquid (its density relative to that of water). It is based on Archimedes' principle that states that a floating object is buoyed up by a force equal to the weight of the fluid it displaces. The instrument is a long thin glass bulb held upright by a weight at one end, allowed to float in the test liquid. The denser the liquid, the less the hydrometer sinks. The tube is calibrated in such a way that the specific gravity can be read off by comparing the level to which the bulb sinks with a scale along the side of the hydrometer. A form of hydrometer called an acidimeter is used in testing storage batteries by measuring the specific gravity, and therefore the strength, of the acid they contain.
See also: Density.

Hydrophobia *see:* Rabies.

Hydroplane, speedboat designed so that the hull rides above the surface of the water. When the boat accelerates rapidly and maintains speed, water pressure allows the flat or slightly curved bottom of the boat to skim the water.

Hydroponics, or soil-less culture, technique by which plants are grown without soil. All the minerals required for plant growth are provided by nutrient solutions in which the roots are immersed. The technique has been highly developed as a tool in botanical research, but commercial exploitation is limited primarily because of the difficulty of aerating the water and providing support for the plants. Gravel culture has overcome these problems to some extent and is used to grow some horticulture crops.

Hydrosphere, all the waters of the earth, in whatever form: solid, liquid, gaseous. It thus includes the water of the atmosphere, water on the earth's surface (e.g., oceans, rivers, ice sheets), and groundwater.

Hydrotherapy, external application of water for therapeutic purposes. The body or any of its parts may be immersed in water or water may be applied to the surface with or without the intermediary of absorbent materials. In partial baths, water may be applied by immersion, pouring, or compress to a small area of the body. For an eye wash, a hemispherical container filled to the brim with water is applied to the open eye, and as the head is tilted, the water bathes the corneal surface. The ear may be washed with a stream of water applied with a rubber bulb or syringe, usually to dislodge ear wax from the canal. The nasal passages may be bathed by sniffing water from the cupped hands, and the mouth may be washed by rinsing or irrigation.

Hydroxide, chemical compound containing the negatively charged hydroxyl ion (OH^-), used in the manufacture of detergents and medicines. Most hydroxide compounds are water soluble and can be caustic to varying degrees. Household ammonia is a familiar example of a basic hydroxide. Hydroxides are inorganic compounds; organic compounds containing the hydroxyl ion are called alcohols.

Hyena, 3 species of carnivorous mammals, family Hyaenidae, native to Asia and Africa. They are distinctive in having the shoulders considerably higher than the hindquarters and having an unusual gait, moving both limbs on one side of the body together. All 3 species have massive heads with powerful jaws. Though reviled as scavengers and carrion feeders, hyenas are active and skillful predators in their own right, hunting in packs of up to 20.

Hygiene *see:* Health.

Hygrometer, device to measure humidity (the amount of water vapor the air holds). Usually, hygrometers measure relative humidity, the amount of moisture as a percentage of the saturation level at that temperature. In the hair hygrometer, which is of limited accuracy, the length of a hair (usually human) increases with increase in relative humidity. This length change is amplified by a lever and registered by a needle on a dial. The wet- and dry-bulb hygrometer (psychrometer) has 2 thermometers mounted side by side, the bulb of one covered by a damp cloth. Air is moved across the apparatus (e.g., by a fan) and evaporation of water from the cloth draws latent heat from the bulb. Comparison of the 2 temperatures, and the use of tables, gives the relative humidity. In the dewpoint hygrometer, a polished container is cooled until the dew point is reached, giving a measure of relative humidity. The electric hygrometer measures changes in the electrical resistance of a hygroscopic (water-absorbing) strip.
See also: Humidity.

Hyksos, Asian group who invaded Egypt in the 18th century B.C. and formed the 15th and 16th dynasties of Egypt. They introduced the Asian light horse and chariot, bronze weapons, and the compound bow.

Hymn, sacred song in praise of gods or heroes, found in almost all cultures, ancient and modern. Jewish psalms, sung in the temple worship, were adopted by the early Christian Church and supplemented by distinctively Christian hymns such as the canticles. There is a continuous English hymn, tradition from the 7th century that includes 16th-century carols such as "Hark, the Herald Angels Sing." Modern hymns were developed by Isaac Watts, John Wesley, and many others in the 1700s. There are over 400,000 hymns, ranging from Gregorian chants (plainsongs) to rousing gospel music.

Hyperactive child, excessively active child who cannot concentrate on any one task for more than a few minutes. Hyperacitivity is called hyperkinesis by physicians. Symptoms exhibited by a hyperactive child range from persistent yelling and moving about to disobedience and an inability to socialize. Once thought to be mentally deficient, hyperactive children are now known to be generally of average to above-average intelligence. New teaching methods and family counseling have become part of the treatment of the condition. Stimulants and tranquilizers may also be prescribed, though drug therapy has become less popular in recent years, because its long-term effects are unknown.

Hyena mother carries newborn to safety. Newborn hyenas are born black and with no spots.

Hyperbola, in geometry, curve consisting of 2 separate branches opening out in opposite directions. The hyperbola is one of the conic sections, formed when a right circular cone is intersected by a plane. It may be expressed in analytic geometry by the equation $y = 1/x$.
See also: Geometry.

Hyperkinesis *see:* Hyperactive child.

Hyperopia *see:* Farsightedness.

Hypertension, abnormally high blood pressure. Blood pressure is the pressure that the heart and arteries apply in order to squeeze the blood around the body. In a normal person, when sitting or lying quietly, the blood pressure stays at a steady, or resting, level. In moments of exercise, excitement, anger, or anxiety, the level of blood pressure is raised by te release of adrenaline and other hormones to increase the blood flow to the brain and muscles. In the hypertensive individual, blood pressure remains high; although there may be no immediate symptoms, long-term effects can be serious or fatal, and may include damage to the heart and brain. Causes include diet, kidney disorders, stress, and hereditary factors. Hypertension is treated with diet and medication.
See also: Blood pressure.

Hyperventilation, abnormal, deep and rapid breathing, frequently caused by anxiety. The level of carbon dioxide in the blood decreases, which restricts arteries, lowers blood pressure, and may result in dizziness or fainting.

Hypnos, in Greek mythology, the god of sleep. His mother was the goddess of the night, and his twin brother was Thantos, or Death. Among his sons was Morpheus, the Greek god of dreams.
See also: Mythology.

Hypnosis, artificially induced mental state characterized by an individual's loss of critical powers and consequent openness to suggestion. It may be induced by an external agency or self-induced (autohypnosis). Hypnotism has been widely used in medicine (usually to induce analgesia) and especially in psychiatry and psychotherapy. Here, the particular value of hypnosis is that while in trance, the individual may be encouraged to recall deeply repressed memories that may be at the heart of an emotional conflict; once such causes have been elucidated, therapy may proceed. Hypnosis seems to be as old as human society. However, the first definite information comes from the late 18th century with the work of Franz Mesmer, who held

I

that disease was the result of imbalance in a patient's "animal magnetism," and hence attempted to cure this by the use of magnets. Some of his patients were cured, presumably by suggestion; the term mesmerism is still used for hypnotism.

Hypochlorous acid, weak inorganic acid (HOCl) used in bleaches and disinfectants. It is formed when chlorine is combined with water. Used to disinfect public drinking water and swimming pools, hypochlorous acid is also a strong oxidant.

Hypochondria, or hypochondriasis, mental condition involving undue anxiety about real or supposed ailments, usually in the belief that these are incurable. The source of hypochondria was once thought to be the hypochondrium, that part of the abdomen containing the spleen and liver.
See also: Neurosis.

Hypoglycemia, abnormally low level of glucose in the blood. Symptoms are tremulousness, sweating, irritability and restlessness, feeling of extreme hunger, headache and nausea, chronic fatigue and weakness. With severe hypoglycemia, the person may lose consciousness. Another form of hypoglycemia occurs in people who have had a large amount of alcohol to drink, either without eating or along with very high quantities of sugar-containing mixes.

Hypothalamus, central part of the base of the brain, closely related to the pituitary gland. It contains vital centers for controlling the autonomic nervous system, body temperature, and water and food intake, and is the center for primitive physical and emotional behavior. It also produces hormones for regulating pituitary secretion and systemic hormones including vasopressin and oxytocin.
See also: Brain.

Hypothermia, subnormal temperature of the body. Initial symptoms are weakness, slurred speech, confusion, shivering, and clumsiness. If the condition progresses, the weakness is replaced by stiff muscles, the person feels unable to move, and drowsiness and sleepiness occur. The body is no longer able to conserve heat, and the body temperature falls rapidly. Eventually, if nothing is done to return the temperature to normal, breathing will cease and the heart will stop. Activities that involve a high risk of hypothermia are swimming or other water activities; mountain climbing, skiing, and other activities that couple cold, wetness, and wind with exertion and sweating; and being out in the cold weather without proper clothing to provide warmth and protection from wetness. Special precautions must be taken with the very young and the elderly, who are the principal victims of hypothermia.
Drunkenness, exhaustion, hunger, disease, and illness all put people at greater risk of hypothermia. It is critical to stop the process immediately. Remove all wet clothing (it retains the cold and wetness); if possible, rewarm the body with whatever is available (dry clothing, towels, blankets, jackets, sweaters, even paper), and in an emergency, use the warmth (body heat) of others; a warm (not hot) bath is helpful. The person should be seen by a doctor as soon as possible.

Hyrax, or cony, rabbit-sized mammal of Africa and South Asia, of the order Hyracoidea, closely related to the elephant. The hyrax resembles the guinea pig, with short legs, ears, and tail. Some species are tree-dwelling and others, called dassies, live among rocks. They feed on plants and fruits.

Hyssop, herb (*Hyssopus officinalis*) of the mint family. Once used as a household remedy for sore throat, hyssop is now used primarily as a seasoning for meats and vegetables. The oil from its evergreen leaves has been used in the manufacture of perfumes. Grown throughout southern Europe and in parts of the United States, the hyssop plant may reach 2 ft (61 cm) in height.

Hysterectomy, surgical removal of the womb, with or without the ovaries and fallopian tubes. It may be performed via either the abdomen or the vagina and is most often used for fibroid tumors (benign tumors of womb muscle), cancer of the cervix or body of the womb, endometriosis, or other diseases causing heavy menstruation. If the ovaries are preserved, hormone secretion remains intact, though menstrual periods cease and infertility is inevitable. Recent controversy has questioned the overuse of the procedure because of the negative effects on general health.

Hysteria, or conversion disorder, medical diagnostic term for illness characterized by physical complaints without physical cause. The word "hysteria" derives from the ancient Greeks, who applied the term solely to diseases of women, which were explained as being due to malfunctioning of the uterus (hystera).

I, ninth letter of the English alphabet. It originated in the ancient Semitic alphabet, where it may have derived from an early symbol for "hand." It later passed into the Greek alphabet and was called *iota.* The original letter was probably a consonant representing our *y* sound, but in most Greek and Latin, as well as in many modern European languages, its sound is that of the vowel in *meet.* In English it may be short, as in *fit,* or long, as in *fine,* or it may combine with other letters for a great variety of sounds. The dot over the lowercase *i* first appeared in the 11th century. In chemistry, *I* is the symbol for iodine.

I.Q. *see:* Intelligence quotient.

Iacocca, Lee (1924-), U.S. businessman and automobile executive; chairman and chief executive of the Chrysler Corporation. Originally an engineer and salesman with the Ford Motor Company, he rose to vice president and helped develop the Ford Mustang, a popular sports car. Beginning in 1970, he served as Ford's president, until a disagreement with Henry Ford II caused Iacocca to join the Chrysler Corporation in 1978. In 1980 he secured a U.S. government guarantee for $1.5 billion in private loans, a move that saved Chrysler from bankruptcy. The loans were repaid in 1983.

Ibadan (pop. 885,300), second largest city in Nigeria. Founded in the 1830s, Ibadan is located in the rich agricultural region of southwest Nigeria, and is a major commercial and industrial center. Ibadan's industries and products include brewing, producing canned goods, paint, plastics, furniture, and soap. Ibadan came under British protection in 1893. It is the capital of Nigeria's Oyo state.
See also: Nigeria.

Ibáñez, Vicente Blasco *see:* Blasco Ibáñez, Vicente.

Iberian Peninsula, landmass in southwestern Europe, occupied by Spain and Portugal. It is mostly surrounded by the waters of the Mediterranean Sea (east) and the Atlantic Ocean (west) and separated from North Africa by the Strait of Gibraltar. The Pyrenees Mountains to the north form a natural barrier between the peninsula and the rest of Europe.

Ibert, Jacques (1890-1962), French composer of piano pieces, orchestral works, symphonic poems, and operas. Among his well-known works are a cantata, *Le Poète et la Fée* (1919), a ballet based on Oscar Wilde's *Ballad of Reading Gaol* (1922), the orchestral suites *Escales* (1922) and *Divertissement* (1930), and the light opera for radio *Barbe-bleue* (1943).

Iberville, Sieur d' (1661-1706), French-Canadian fur trader and explorer, founder of Louisiana. In 1699 he began exploring the mouths of the Mississippi River; he built a fort on Biloxi Bay and established a post at the site of Mobile, Ala.
See also: Louisiana.

Ibex, 7 species of wild goats (genus *Capra*) of the Eastern Hemisphere that differ from true goats in their flattened foreheads and

The ibex lives above the tree line, and only at the beginning of winter does it move to lower regions.

usually broad-fronted horns. Always found in mountainous areas, ibex live for most of the year in separate-sex herds, with the males forming harems only during the 7- to 10-day rut.

Ibis, heronlike wading bird (family Threskiornithidae) of moderate size, characterized by a long, thin, downward-curving bill. Ibises have a worldwide distribution in tropical, subtropical, and temperate regions, and are usually found near fresh water, feeding on small aquatic animals. Ibises are gregarious and frequently raucous. Species include the sacred ibis (*Threskiornis aethiopica*), honored in ancient Egypt, and the Eastern glossy ibis (*Plegadis Falcinellus falcinellus*), common in the United States.

Ibizan hound, rare dog breed from Ibiza, an island off the eastern coast of Spain. A modern relative of an ancient Egyptian hunting dog, it is similar to the greyhound, with a slender build, a long snout, upright ears, and a long neck. It has amber eyes and a pink nose, and its coat may be long or short and red, white, brown, or a mixture of colors. It stands up to 27 in (69 cm) high and weighs up to 50 lb (23 kg).

Ibn Batuta (1304?-78?), greatest Arab traveler of the Middle Ages. He spent about 25 years traveling in Africa, Asia, and Europe. His notes (the *Rihlah*, or *Travels*) provide a priceless account of life before the rise of Europe.

Ibn Khaldun (1332-1406), Arab historian and sociologist. *Muqaddama*, the first volume of Ibn Khaldun's *Universal History*, contains the first attempt to interpret the patterns of history in the purely secular terms of geography, sociology, and allied subjects.
See also: Sociology.

Ibn Saud (1880-1953), creator of the kingdom of Saudi Arabia. Inheriting the leadership of the orthodox Wahabi movement, in 1900 he and a small band of followers captured the city of Riyadh, from which his family had been exiled, and by 1912 had conquered the Nejd from Turkey. During World War I the British favored his rival, King Husein ibn-Ali of Hejaz, in their campaign against the Turks, but in 1924-25 ibn-Saud defeated Husein, combining Hejaz and the Nejd to form the kingdom of Saudi Arabia. He imposed order and religious orthodoxy. In the 1930s he awarded oil concessions to U.S. companies from which his family began to derive enormous wealth. Neutral in World War II, ibn-Saud took little part in the Arab-Israeli war of 1948.
See also: Saudi Arabia.

Ibn-Sina *see:* Avicenna.

Ibo *see:* Igbo.

Ibsen, Henrik (1828-1906), Norwegian playwright and poet. The pioneer of modern drama, his work developed from national Romanticism (*The Vikings at Helgoland*, 1858) to the realistic and effective presentation of contemporary social problems and moral dilemmas in such plays as *A Doll's House* (1879), *Ghosts* (1881), *The Wild Duck* (1884), and *Hedda Gabler* (1890). Very different, but as important to his philosophy, are his verse-dramas *Brand* (1866) and *Peer Gynt* (1867).

Ibuprofen, drug used for the relief of headaches, muscle aches, pain, and for the reduction of fever. Familiar trade names for ibuprofen include Advil, Motrin, and Nuprin. An anti-inflammatory agent and pain reliever, ibuprofen is also used to treat arthritis. Of a group of drugs called *propionic acid derivatives* developed in the 1960s and early 70s, ibuprofen is today the most widely used. Since 1984, ibuprofen has been available for sale without a prescription.
See also: Drug.

Icarus, in Greek mythology, son of Daedalus, with whom he was imprisoned in the labyrinth by King Minos of Crete. To escape Minos's wrath, they attached feathered wings to their shoulders with wax and flew away. Icarus, however, flew too high; the sun melted the wax, and he plunged into the sea and was drowned.
See also: Mythology.

ICBM *see:* Guided missile.

Ice, frozen water; colorless crystalline solid in which the strong, directional hydrogen bonding produces a structure with much space between the molecules. Thus ice is less dense than water and floats on it. The expansion of water on freezing may crack pipes and automobile radiators. Seawater freezes at about 28°F (–2°C). Ice has a very low coefficient of friction, and some fast-moving sports (ice hockey and ice skating) are played on it; slippery, icy roads are dangerous. Ice deposited on airplane wings reduces lift. Ice is used as a refrigerant and to cool some beverages.
See also: Water.

Ice age, any of several periods in geologic time when thick ice caps and glaciers covered large areas of the earth that now have temperate or warm climates. In 1837 Louis Agassiz, a Swiss-U.S. naturalist, was one of the first to argue that a great ice age in the past explained land features associated with glaciation hundreds of miles from permanent ice. Geologists later established that there have been several ice ages. Ice ages occurred in Australia, Canada,

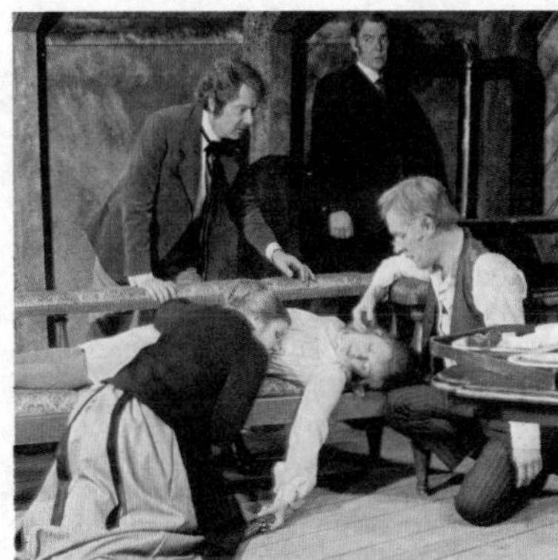

A scene from Ibsen's The Wild Duck *performed at the Globe Theatre.*

Henrik Ibsen

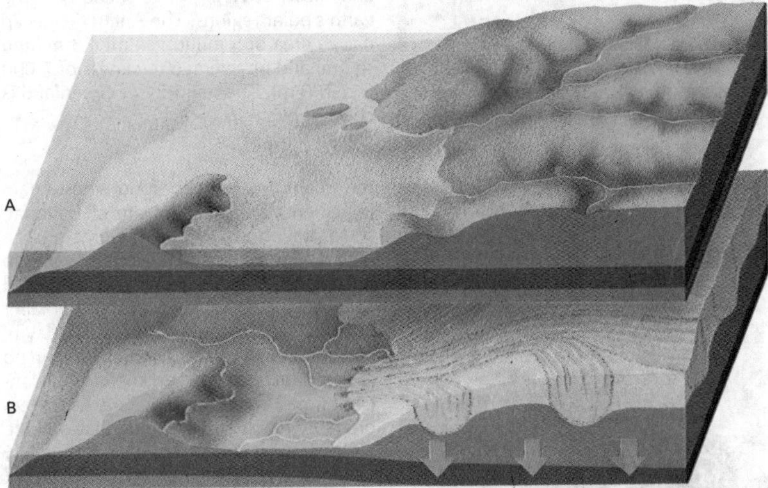

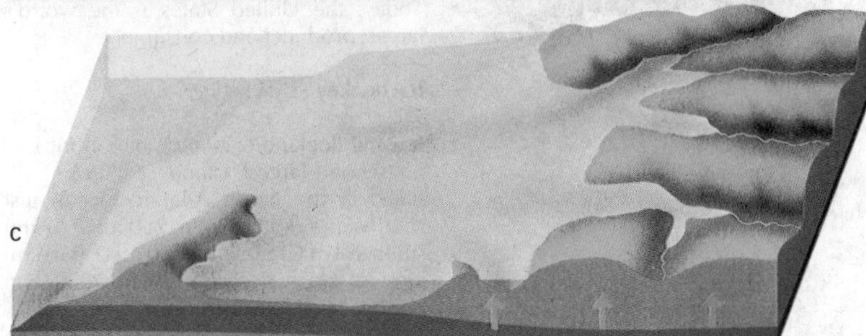

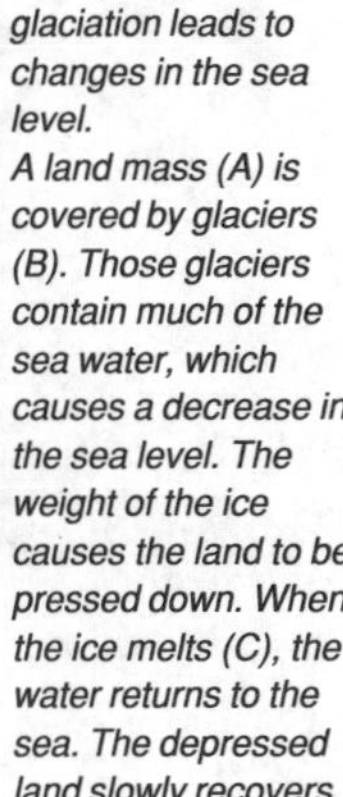

During an ice age, glaciation leads to changes in the sea level. A land mass (A) is covered by glaciers (B). Those glaciers contain much of the sea water, which causes a decrease in the sea level. The weight of the ice causes the land to be pressed down. When the ice melts (C), the water returns to the sea. The depressed land slowly recovers.

China, India, South Africa, and other places more than 700 million years ago, but little is known about them. Another great ice age affected the Southern Hemisphere during the early Permian period, which began c.275 million years ago. The ice ages about which most is known occurred in the Northern Hemisphere during the Pleistocene epoch in the past million years. There were 4 main glacial ages when the ice advanced: the Nebraskan (which began c.600,000 years ago), the Kansan (which began 476,000 years ago), the Illinoian (which began 230,000 years ago), and the Wisconsin (which began 115,000 years ago and ended c.10,000 years ago). The European names for these glacial ages are the Günz, Mindel, Riss, and Würm. These were separated by 3 interglacial ages during which the weather became warmer and the ice retreated. In North America the interglacials are named the Aftonian, the Yarmouth, and the Sangamon. Geologists do not know whether the close of the Wisconsin glacial age marked the end of the recent ice ages, or whether the present time is the fourth interglacial, preceding a fifth glacial age.

Iceberg, large floating mass of ice. In the Southern Hemisphere, the Antarctic ice sheet overflows its land support to form shelves of ice on the sea; huge pieces, as much as 150 mi (240 km) across, break off to form icebergs. In the Northern Hemisphere, icebergs are generally not over 175 yds (160 m) across. Most are "calved" from some 20 glaciers on Greenland's west coast. Small icebergs (*growlers*) may calve from larger ones. Some 75% of the height and over 85% of the mass of an iceberg lies below water. Northern icebergs usually float for some months to the Grand Banks, off Newfoundland, there melting in a few days. They endanger shipping, the most famous tragedy being the sinking of the *Titanic* (1912). The International Ice Patrol now keeps a constant watch on the area.
See also: Ice.

Russian icebreaker

Icebreaker, vessel designed to break channels through ice for other ships, chiefly in harbors and rivers. They are of special importance in Canada, the USSR, and Scandinavia. An icebreaker has a very strong reinforced hull and is equipped with high-powered engines that transmit power to the rugged propeller by electrical means. This enables the vessel to develop maximum power from a standing start. When breaking thin ice, the ship rams its way forward, sometimes assisted by turbulence created by a propeller at the bow. For breaking thick ice the vessel moves fast enough to ride up onto the ice, which then breaks under its weight. The shape of the hull makes icebreakers roll heavily in open water, but this also helps to break the ice. Special canting tanks containing water can also induce rolling and prevent the ship from getting trapped. The U.S. Coast Guard has a number of these vessels, with their distinctive, sharp, upward-slanting bows. The world's first atomic-powered icebreaker, the 16,000-ton (7,258 kg) *Lenin*, was launched by the USSR in 1957.

Icecap, extensive perennial cover of ice and snow, covering huge sections of the earth's polar regions. The Antarctic icecap has an area of 5 million sq mi (13 million sq km) and an average thickness of 7,000 ft (2,100 m). The majority of Greenland is covered by an icecap.
See also: Ice.

Ice cream, frozen dairy food whose main ingredients are sugar, cream or butterfat, water, flavorings, and air. Ice cream has a high caloric value and a very high vitamin A content, as well as being protein- and calcium-rich. It is also a source of smaller quantitites of iron, phosphorus, riboflavin, and thiamin. Water ices, which contain no milk products, have been known since ancient times in Europe and Asia. Ice cream probably reached the United States in the 17th century, and was first commercially manufactured by Jacob Fussel (1851). Today, the United States is the world's largest producer and consumer.

Ice hockey *see:* Hockey.

Iceland (Icelandic: *Island*), nation located on second-largest island of Europe, situated in the North Atlantic Ocean just south of the Arctic Circle, 200 mi (320 km) southeast of Greenland, 650 mi (1,050 km) west of Norway, and 500 mi (800 km) northwest of Scotland.
Land and climate. Iceland has more than 100 volcanic peaks with varying degrees of activity. Enormous ice explosions sometimes take place due to eruptions of volcanoes beneath ice fields, flooding large areas. Iceland's numerous hot springs and geysers are also of volcanic origin. Water from the springs is widely used for heating purposes. Lava fields account for more than a tenth of Iceland's surface. There are also enormous glaciers. The coastline is highly irregular, indented with numerous fjords and navigable bays, including the large Faxa Bay on the southwest coast, where Reykjavík, the nation's capital,

Iceland

Capital:	Reykjavík
Area:	39,769 sq mi (103,000 sq km)
Population:	252,000
Government:	republic
Independent:	1944
GNP:	U.S. $5,019,000,000
Per capita:	U.S. $10,500

Icelandic scenery

stands. A plateau at an altitude of 2,000 ft (610 m) covers a large portion of the interior of the country. There are numerous rivers, but none is navigable. There are also many lakes. Iceland's marine climate is modified by the warm North Atlantic Drift. The average winter temperature in Reykjavík, in the south, is 30°F (–1°C) and the average summer temperature is 52°F (11°C), but the north is much colder. Only about a quarter of Iceland's surface bears natural vegetation, often a thick moss carpet found in areas not covered with snow. Only in areas protected by a winter snow cover is vegetation more dense. The lowlands have large areas of grass and, in sheltered regions, even some trees, the most common being dwarf willows, birches, and mountain ash. Native animals include the Arctic fox and various birds, of which the eider duck is valued for its down. The reindeer and mink were imported to the island.

People. Except for some blending of Irish blood, most of the people of Iceland are directly descended from the Vikings or other Scandinavians. In the second half of the 19th century, due to the country's poor economic situation, about 25,000 emigrated, mainly to Canada. Today Iceland has one of the world's highest birthrates, an extremely low infant mortality rate, and a low deathrate. Three-quarters of the population is centered in urban areas along the coast, over one-third of the population living in Reykjavík, the cultural center, with its own university (founded 1911). The Icelandic language is of the Scandinavian group. It has undergone very few changes since the 12th and 13th centuries, an era in which the famous Icelandic sagas and prose narratives were written, so that this literature is still understandable to modern readers. Iceland was almost entirely free of illiteracy by the beginning of the 19th century. Education is compulsory and free from ages 7 to 15. Christianity was established in Iceland about a thousand years ago. By far the most prominent church today is the Evangelical Lutheran Church.

Economy. Fishing (especially cod, haddock, and herring) and fish-processing are the mainstay industries and provide two-thirds of Iceland's exports. A long dispute with Great Britain over fishing rights in the waters off Iceland led to a series of "cod wars." In 1975 Iceland extended its "economic" sea limits to 200 mi (322 km) and the next year broke diplomatic relations with Britain for 4 months. There is some small-scale agriculture and manufacturing. Iceland's vast resources of natural energy in its rivers, hot streams, and geysers, as well as its important volcanic mineral potential, are only beginning to be exploited for industrial and commercial purposes.

History. Discovered by the Norse C.A.D. 870, Iceland was under Norwegian rule from 1262 and then under the Danes from 1380. The tradition of democratic government dates from A.D. 930, when the Althing, the world's oldest parliament, was established. Iceland has been entirely self-governing since 1918, and it became a fully independent republic on June 17, 1944.

The capital of Iceland, Reykjavík

Ice skating, winter sport in the United States, Canada, and the countries of northern Europe. Originally confined to natural settings and conditions, such as frozen lakes and rivers, the sport has been widely popularized by the introduction of artificial rinks. Competitive skating, which requires many years of intensive practice, consists of figure skating and speed skating. Figure skating is a highly technical and demanding form of body control. The skater must master a large number of school figures (including turns, brackets, rockers, and loops) based on a figure eight, and must develop striking routines of individual free skating (including jumps, spins, spirals, and free movements performed to music). In competition, school figures account for 60% of the skater's score and free skating for 40%. Speed skating takes place over distances from as little as 50 yd (46 m) to as much as 5 mi (8 km). In the United States, skaters generally race against each other directly whereas in European and Olympic events they race against the clock, 2 at a time. Good speed skaters can average 20 mph (32 kmph) or more. Ice skating dates back at least as far as the 8th century and attained its first national popularity in the Netherlands in the 15th century. Metal blades first appeared in the 16th century. The first U.S. skating club was formed in Philadelphia in 1849, but it is only in the present century that skating has become a major North American sport.

Ice skating champion Eric Heyden

I Ching, or Book of Changes, ancient Chinese philosophical and literary classic dating to c.12th century B.C. Its set of symbols and texts are used for divination. The *I Ching* was a major influence on Confucianism and Taoism. There has been a revival of interest in the *I Ching* in recent years.
See also: Confucianism; Taoism.

Ichneumon wasp, parasitic wasp (family Ichneumonidae) equipped with a long egg-laying organ, the *ovipositor*, like a hypodermic needle. It lays its eggs in the larvae of other insects and when its own larvae hatch they feed on the tissues of host or hosts. The host, such as a caterpillar, continues to live with the ichneumon larva inside it until pupation. Then the parasite kills its host and pupates itself. Some species of ichneumon wasps can penetrate 2 in (5 cm) of wood with their ovipositors to lay eggs on the larvae of horntails (large sawflies that are pests in timber plantations). These ichneumon wasps have been specially introduced into plantations to keep down the numbers of horntails.

Ickes, Harold Le Claire (1874-1952), U.S. government official. Ickes was secretary of the interior (1933-46) under Presidents Franklin D. Roosevelt and Harry S. Truman, and he also served as head of the Public Works Administration (1933-39). An able and responsible administrator, Ickes was a central figure in Roosevelt's New Deal.

Icon (Greek, "image"), religious image in the Eastern and Russian Orthodox churches. Icons play an important part in liturgy. The Virgin Mary and Jesus were traditional icon figures; by the 7th century icon worship was an officially encouraged cult in the Byzantine Christian Church.
See also: Eastern Orthodox Church.

Sixteenth-century Russian icon with the face of Christ

Iconoclast (Greek *eikon*, "image" + *klastes*, "breaker"), person who practices iconoclasm, opposition to the religious use of images. Although religious pictures and statues have long been an important part of Christian worship, iconoclasts claim they lead to idolatry. Historically, the use of images in religious worship has been in dispute. In A.D. 843 the Eastern Church reached a settlement that permitted pictures but not complete images or statues.

Id *see:* Psychoanalysis.

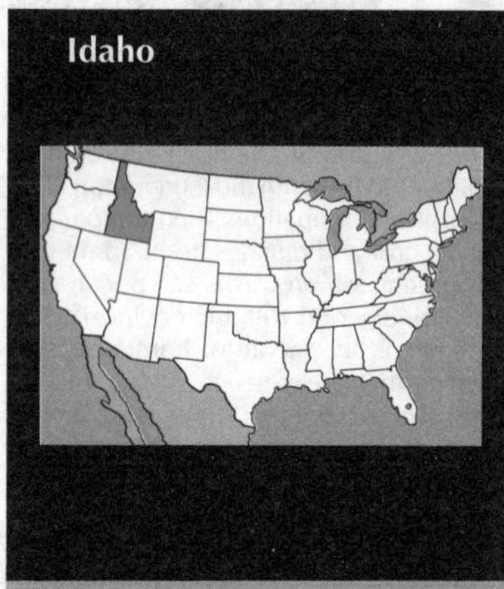

Capital:	Boise
Statehood:	July 3, 1890 (43rd state)
Familiar name:	Gem State
Area:	83,564 sq mi (216,432 sq km; ranks 13th)
Population:	1,011,986 (1990; ranks 42nd)
Elevation:	Highest—12,662 ft (3,859 m), Borah Peak Lowest—710 ft (216 m), Snake River at Lewiston
Motto:	Esto Perpetua (It Is Perpetual)
State flower:	Syringa (mock orange)
State bird:	Mountain bluebird
State tree:	Western white pine
State song:	"Here We Have Idaho"

Idaho cornfields

Idaho, state in the Rocky Mountain region of the United States; bordered on the east by Montana and Wyoming, on the south by Utah and Nevada, on the west by Oregon and Washington, and on the north by British Columbia.

Land and climate. Idaho is dominated by the Rockies, including the Bitterroot, Salmon River, and Sawtooth ranges. About 50 of the state's peaks are over 10,000 ft (3,000 m) high. The Snake River (1,038 mi/1,671 km) flows across southern Idaho and curves north to form part of the western boundary of the state. The irrigated Snake River Plain is Idaho's major agricultural region. The high mountains have cool summers and severe winters, while the summers are hot on the Snake River Plain. Principal cities are Boise, Pocatello, and Idaho Falls.

Economy. Unlike many of the other western states, Idaho has vast water resources, and its dams provide hydroelectric power and water for irrigation. Idaho's chief agricultural products are cattle and dairy goods, and it is the leading producer of potatoes in the United States. Lumber and wood products are major manufactures of the heavily forested state, as are processed foods. The Sunshine Mine is the largest silver-producing mine in the country. Tourism is also important.

Government. Idaho's constitution, adopted in 1889, provides for a governor, serving a 4-year term. The legislature consists of a 42-member senate and an 84-member house elected to 2-year terms. The state sends 2 senators and 2 representatives to the U.S. Congress.

History. The area was inhabited by Native Americans more than 10,000 years ago. The first European Americans to explore the Idaho region were Meriwether Lewis and William Clark in 1805. At that time local tribes included the Nez Percé, Shoshone, Coeur d'Alene, and others. David Thompson, a British fur trader, set up Idaho's first trading post in 1809, and Mormons founded Franklin, Idaho's first permanent settlement, in 1860. That same year, gold was discovered, attracting scores of settlers. In 1863, the Idaho Territory was established. The U.S. Army defeated the Nez Percé Indians in 1877. Agriculture expanded during the early 20th century with the development of irrigation projects. Increasing demands for hydroelectric power led to the construction of a series of dams on the Snake River in the 1950s and 1960s. Agriculture remains an important sector of Idaho's economy, although other industries, including tourism, continue to grow.

Idaho Falls (pop. 39,734), third largest city in Idaho, located in the southeastern portion of the state, on the Snake River. Population growth in Idaho Falls flourished during the early 1900s when flour mills and sugar factories sprung up. In 1949 the U.S. Atomic Energy Commission constructed a nuclear reactor testing station 30 mi (48 km) west of Idaho Falls. Today, Idaho Falls serves as a commercial and processing center for the farm, livestock, and dairy area of upper Snake Valley.
See also: Idaho.

Idealism, any one of a variety of systems of philosophical thought that would make the ultimate reality of the universe expressible or intelligible only in terms of ideas rather than in terms of matter or space.
See also: Berkeley, George; Hegel, Georg Wilhelm Friedrich; Kant, Immanuel.

Ideology, set of beliefs based on related political, social, and economic assumptions. People who hold to a particular ideology often rely on its system of thought in forming decisions about the way they live or work. Ideologies may be religious, such as Catholicism, or artistic, such as Impressionism. Communism, socialism, democracy, fascism, and totalitarianism are different kinds of political ideologies. For example, until 1989 the government of West Germany adhered to a form of democracy, whereas the government of East Germany adhered to a form of communism: both democracy and communism are political ideologies.

Ideology celebrated. The 50th anniversary of the October Revolution celebrated in Moscow in 1967.

Ides, 15th day of Mar. in the ancient Roman calendar and the day in 44 B.C. on which Julius Caesar was assassinated in the Roman senate. In the Roman calendar, the 15th of Mar., May, July, and Oct. and the 13th of the other months were called the ides.

Idolatry, in religion, worship of an image or statue representing a god or spirit. Overt forms of idolatry consist of explicit acts of reverence addressed to a person or object, such as dancing to the sun. Idols are generally found in animal or human form, and may be cared for as if they were alive. Christians, Jews, and Muslims consider the worship of images a sin, and the use of lifelike images has been prohibited in Islamic and Jewish art since ancient times.
See also: Icon.

Idyl (Greek, "little picture"), short poem that deals with rural scenery, beauty, and tranquility. Idyl is often used as a synonym for pastoral. The 10 famous idyls by the Greek Theocritus became the models for idyls written in later centuries. Selections from the Bible, such as the Song of Songs, are considered idyls. Many British poets of the 16th and 17th centuries wrote pastoral poems; John Milton's *Lycidas* is an example of one of the finest idyls from this time period.

Ife, town in the Oyo province in southwestern Nigeria. Ife is the oldest town of the Yoruba tribe. Beginning about A.D. 1000, Ife was an important center of black African culture. The Yoruba people created sculptures of terra cotta and bronze. Never having achieved great political or military power, Ife declined in the early 1800s. The current city of Ife is a major collecting point for cacao and cotton, palm oil and kernels, yams, cassava, maize, pumpkins, and kola nuts. Most of its inhabitants are town-dwelling farmers.
See also: Nigeria.

Igbo, or Ibo, large ethnic group in Nigeria. Although the origin of the Igbo people is not precisely known, recent archeological evidence suggests that the Igbo's artistic culture was supported by both agriculture and flourishing trade. Located near the Nigerian coast, the early Igbo civilization participated in the slave trade, which lasted from the 1400s to the 1800s. During the 1800s and 1900s Nigeria fell under British rule, and in 1967 the Igbo homeland, along with the entire Eastern Region of Nigeria, proclaimed itself the independent republic of Biafra. Today, many Igbo occupy villages of dispersed homesteads in rain-forest country and are subsistence farmers.

Igloo, shelter or hunting ground dwelling for the Canadian Eskimos. Traditionally made of snow, sod, or stone, the best-known igloo was made of hard-packed snow cut into blocks from 2 to 3 ft (61 to 91 cm) long and 1 to 2 ft (30 to 61 cm) wide. After a first row of these blocks were laid down in a circle, the top surfaces of the blocks were shaved off in a sloping angle to form the first rung of a spiral. Additional blocks were added to draw it inward in a dome shape. One hole was left in the top for ventilation, and the igloo was kept warm mainly by a sealskin flap fit over the main entrance and seal oil lamps. Prefabricated houses have replaced igloos.
See also: Eskimo.

Ignatius Loyola, Saint *see:* Loyola, Saint Ignatius.

Ignatius of Antioch, Saint (d. C.A.D. 100), Christian bishop of Antioch, condemned to death in Trajan's reign. Ignatius wrote 7 letters (now precious early church documents) in which "Catholic Church" was first used to denote Christians everywhere, and in which he tried to prove that Docetism, a doctrine that held that Jesus' bodily sufferings were only "appearance," was heresy.
See also: Christianity.

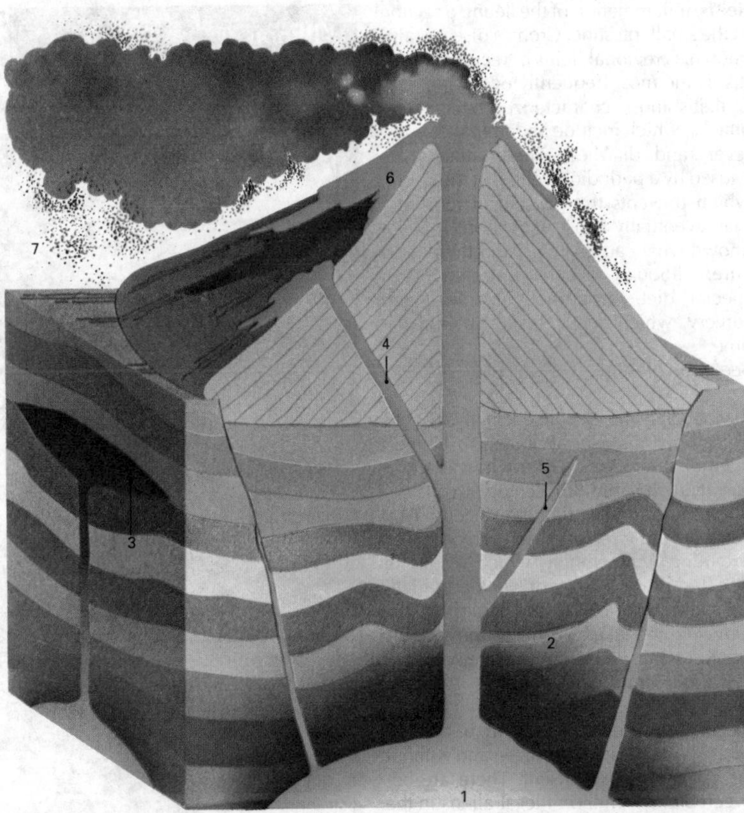

Igneous rocks can have several forms, like the pluton (1), sill (2), laccoliths (3), neck (4), dike (5), lava (6) and volcanic ashes (7).

Igneous rock, one of the 3 main classes of rocks, that whose origin is the solidification of molten material, or detrital volcanic material. It crystallizes from lava at the earth's surface (extrusion) or from magma beneath (intrusion). There are 2 main classes: *Volcanic* rocks are extruded, typical examples being lava and pyroclastic rocks. *Plutonic* rocks are intruded into the rocks of the earth's crust at depth, a typical example being granite; those forming near to the surface are sometimes called hypabyssal rocks. Types of intrusions include batholiths, dikes, sills, and laccoliths. As plutonic rocks cool more slowly than volcanic, they have a coarser texture, more time being allowed for crystal formation.
See also: Basalt; Granite.

Ignition, system used to start an engine. In an internal combustion engine the ignition system sets fire to a mixture of fuel and air to generate power. Most automobiles use spark ignition systems, in which spark plugs create electric sparks to set fire to fuel. When a spark ignition system is turned on, an electric current flows from a battery to the ignition coil, where it is increased in voltage and then sent to a distributor. In the distributor, a rotor directs the current to the automobile's set of spark plugs. At this point, the spark plugs produce the electric sparks that ignite the fuel and air mixture to start the engine.
See also: Engine.

Iguana, family of lizards, the largest and most elaborately marked lizards of the New World. It includes insectivorous, carnivorous, and herbivorous species. Many species are territorial. Iguanas characteristically show ornamental scales and a dorsal fringe, and bear tubercles on the head and body. Some species have an erectile throat fan. There are 2 major groups: ground iguanas and green iguanas; there is also 1 species of marine iguana. All species are hunted for food, although this is greatly depleting their numbers.

Ikhnaton *see:* Akhenaton.

Iguana

Ileitis, inflammation of the ileum, a section of the small intestine. Crohn's disease, also known as regional ileitis or regional enteritis, is the most frequently occurring form of ileitis and is characterized by sporadic attacks, which include abdominal cramps, fever, and diarrhea. These attacks are caused by a periodic swelling of the ileum, which prevents the passage of food and may eventually cause starvation. It is not known what causes ileitis, and there is no cure, although it can be treated with special diet, intravenous feeding, and surgery, which is successful 50% of the time.
See also: Intestine.

Iliad, ancient Greek epic poem of 24 books in hexameter verse, attributed to Homer; internal references suggest it was composed in the mid-8th century B.C. It describes a quarrel during the siege of Troy between the Greek warrior-hero Achilles and King Agamemnon, which results in Achilles' brutal slaying of Hector, the Trojan warrior-prince. A companion to the *Odyssey*, the *Iliad* is one of the world's greatest tragic works of literature.
See also: Homer.

Illegal alien, person living in a country where he or she is not a citizen and without the government's consent. There are between 3 and 6 million illegal aliens in the United States, half of whom are assumed to be from Mexico. Most illegal aliens have jobs; about half work in the manufacturing or service fields. They are called undocumented workers because they have no immigration papers and therefore cannot legally be employed. In 1986, the Immigration Reform and Control Act was passed in Congress. It set a ceiling on the number of undocumented workers allowed to come to the United States and set severe penalties for employers who hired illegal aliens. The act also granted amnesty to approximately 2 million illegal immigrants.

Illicium, sole genus of plant belonging to the family Illiciales, of the illiciales order. Comprised of 42 species, illicium is a group of trees and shrubs with evergreen leaves and bisexual flowers. The inner petals of the illicium flowers grade into stamens, or male, structures, while the female portion of the flower is usually located at its base and consists of 7 to 15 carpels (ovule-bearing structures). The name *illicium* means *allurement* in Latin, and probably alludes to the pleasant aroma of the illicium flower.

Illinois, state in the north central United States; bordered by Lake Michigan in the northeast, Indiana in the east, Kentucky in the southeast, Missouri in the southwest, Iowa in the northwest, and Wisconsin in the north.

Illinois

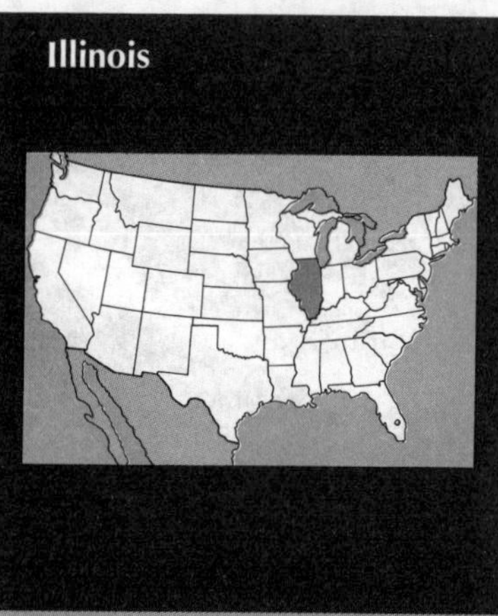

Capital:	Springfield
Statehood:	Dec. 3, 1818 (21st state)
Familiar names:	Land of Lincoln, the Prairie State
Area:	56,345 sq mi (145,934 sq km); ranks 24th
Population:	11,466,682 (1990); ranks 6th
Elevation:	Highest—1,235 ft (376 m), Charles Mound Lowest—269 ft (82 m), Mississippi River
Motto:	State Sovereignty, National Union
State flower:	Native violet
State bird:	Cardinal
State tree:	Oak
State song:	"Illinois"

Capitol building, Springfield, Illinois

Land and climate. Illinois consists almost entirely of a rolling plain that slopes gradually from north to south. Much of the north and central portions of the state are covered by dark prairie soils and loams, which are especially rich and productive. The Shawnee Hills cross the southern part of the state in a band varying from 5 to 40 mi (8 to 64 km) wide. Illinois possesses an extensive river system. The Mississippi River, which forms the state's western border, is linked with Lake Michigan by the Illinois Waterway, which includes the Chicago, Des Plaines, and Illinois rivers. The Illinois (273 mi/439 km), the largest river lying wholly within Illinois, drains about half the state. Illinois has a continental climate, with cold winters and hot summers. Chicago is the state's and region's leading city and is the third largest city in the nation. Other major cities include Springfield, Peoria, and Rockford.

Economy. A leading agricultural state, Illinois produces corn, hogs, cattle, and soybeans. Industry includes the manufacture of machinery, electrical and electronic equipment, processed foods, metal products, and chemicals. Illinois is a leading coal producer and also has significant oil resources.

Government. The state's government is based on the constitution of 1970. The governor serves a 4-year term. The General Assembly consists of 59 senators serving 2- and 4-year terms and 177 representatives serving 2-year terms. Illinois sends 22 representatives and 2 senators to the U.S. Congress.

History. A prehistoric Native American people, the mound builders, were the first known inhabitants of what is now Illinois. By the 17th century, the principal inhabitants of the region were the Illinois, a confederation of Algonquian-speaking tribes. The first Europeans known to have visited the region were Louis Jolliet and Jacques Marquette, in 1673. In 1763, at the end of the French and Indian War, Illinois was ceded to the British. After the American Revolution the region became part of the Northwest Territory of the United States. It was made a separate territory in 1809. With the defeat of the Sauk and Fox in the Black Hawk War of 1832, the last barrier to European American settlement of the state was removed. The debates between Abraham Lincoln and Stephen A. Douglas in the senatorial race of 1858 brought Lincoln to national attention. After the Civil War, industry made great progress as immigrants poured in on the newly completed railroads. Decades of labor unrest reached their climax in the Haymarket Riot of 1886 in Chicago. Agriculture suffered a serious depression through the 1920s, to be joined by the rest of the economy during the Great Depression of the 1930s. Today Illinois continues to attract hundreds of new factories, and space age industries and atomic research facilities are thriving.

Illinois, tribal confederation of Native Americans belonging to the Algonquian linguistic group and related to Ojibwas and Miamis. Their territory originally included Illinois and parts of Iowa, Wisconsin, and Missouri. After tribal wars with the Iroquois and other northern tribes, the few survivors moved to Kansas (1832) and later to an Oklahoma reservation (1867).

Illinois River, major waterway linking the Mississippi River with Lake Michigan. Formed by the confluence of the Des Plaines and Kankakee rivers, about 45 mi (72 km) southwest of Chicago, the Illinois River flows west and southwest for about 275 mi (443 km). It joins the Mississippi about 16 mi (26 km) above Alton, Ill.

Illiteracy, inability to read and write at least simple messages. Illiteracy is therefore the absence of such ability. As civilization grows more complex, mathematical literacy also becomes an important factor, mathematics also being a kind of language.

Illumination, the decoration of a handwritten text with ornamental design, letters, and paintings, often using silver and gold leaf. Illumination flourished between the 5th and 16th centuries A.D. The art was highly developed in the Middle East, the Orient, and in Christian Europe, where monks and others skilled in calligraphy and painting often devoted their lifetimes to embellishing manuscripts of all kinds, particularly religious. Among the most celebrated manuscripts are the Irish *Book of Kells*, the Carolingian *Utrecht Psalter*, and the *Très riches heures* commissioned by Jean, duc de Berry, from the Limbourg brothers.

Illusion *see:* Optical illusion.

Illyria, ancient country in the northwestern part of the Balkan peninsula. It was settled in the 10th century B.C. by Illyrians, an Indo-European-speaking people who extended their influence from the Danube River to the Adriatic Sea in modern-day Yugoslavia and Albania. It became the Roman province of Illyricum (168 B.C.).

Ilmenite, heavy black metallic oxide mineral that is a source of titanium. Formed at high temperatures and containing 36.8% iron and 31.6% titanium, ilmenite is not widely used as iron ore because of difficulties in *smelting*, or separating the metallic constituents. The chemical formula for ilmenite is $FeTiO_3$.

Iloilo (pop. 244,800), major port of the Philippines located on the island of Panay, one of the Visayan Islands. It is also the main cultural location for the region.
See also: Philippines.

Imagists, group of poets writing in the early 20th century in the United States and England who rebelled against the artificiality and sentimentality of much 19th-century poetry. Free, idiomatic verse, unusual rhythms, and sharp, clear imagery were characteristics of their work, which was influenced by French symbolism. The movement embraced Ezra Pound, Hilda Doolittle (H.D.), Amy Lowell, D.H. Lawrence, and James Joyce.

Imago, psychoanalytic term for the unconscious, idealized representation of oneself or of an important figure from childhood, often a parent.
See also: Psychoanalysis.

Imam (Arabic, "leader") term used in Islam to denote a religious leader. In the Sunnite branch of Islam any devout Muslim may perform the services of imam in leading public worship. In the Shi'te branch the imam is a caliph, or ruler, and must be appointed by God in the line of descent from Muhammad. The term is also applied by some Muslims to any religious teacher or scholar.
See also: Islam.

Imhotep (fl.c.2980-2950 B.C.), Egyptian architect of the Step Pyramid at Saqqara. Chief minister, priest, and scribe to Pharaoh Zoser, Imhotep's fame spread and after his death he became a god of medicine. He is considered the first doctor known to history by name.
See also: Egypt, Ancient.

Immaculate Conception, Roman Catholic dogma, officially defined in 1854, that the Virgin Mary was conceived free from original sin, owing to a special act of redemptive grace. The feast of the Immaculate Conception is celebrated Dec. 8.
See also: Roman Catholic Church.

Immigration, movement of people into a country to establish a new permanent residence. People become immigrants primarily for economic, political, or religious reasons. The United States is a nation of immigrants. It has received more immigrants from more places than any other country—about 38 million from the 1820s to the 1930s—and is thus known as a "melting pot" of the world's nations. Its growth and prosperity were stimulated by great waves of immigrants in the 19th and 20th centuries. Immigration accelerated economic development by providing an abundant labor supply, while for the newcomers America offered hope of a freer and more prosperous life. Until World War I the United States maintained, more or less, an open-door policy toward immigrants, but social and economic conflicts between various ethnic groups and between the older and newer immigrants led to a major policy reversal. Restrictions had been placed on Asians (Chinese and Japanese) and other so-called undesirables even before World War I. In 1917 a literacy test was made compulsory for all immigrants. In 1921 and 1924 quotas were fixed, favoring immigration from northern Europe, especially the United Kingdom, but imposing an overall limit of 150,000 European immigrants a year. In 1952 the McCarran-Walter Act banned communists and other subversives, removed racial exclusions, and strengthened the quota system's ethnic and national system. A 1965 act abolished the quotas discriminating among nationalities, substituting professional qualifications and skills and kinship with U.S. citizens or resident aliens as criteria. Provision also was made for political refugees. The collapse of U.S-supported regimes in Southeast Asia brought in new waves of immigrants in the 1970s. In the same decade, Mexicans, seeking relief from poverty, arrived in large numbers. South America received large numbers of immigrants before the 1930s. Since World War II an entirely new phase of immigration has taken place within Europe itself. West Indians, Asian Indians, and Pakistanis have settled in the United Kingdom, claiming their rights as members of the Commonwealth. Since 1962, the British government has introduced new laws reducing this trend. Western and northern Europe have admitted large numbers of immigrants from the less-developed parts of southern Europe. The European Community requires all its member countries to allow free movement of labor across their borders.

Illuminated French manuscript, 15th century

Immortelle (*Xeranthemum annuun*), any of several species of flower belonging to the composite family and related to the asters. The largest of what is known as everlasting flowers, the immortelle has flower heads composed of many small flowers, called florets. The yellow immortelle is characterized as an everlasting flower because it retains its natural form and color even after it has been dried.

Immunity, system of defense in animals protecting against foreign materials, specifically, infectious microorganisms, parasites, and their products. For many diseases, *humoral immunity*, exposure to the causative organism in disease itself or by vaccination, provides acquired resistance to that organism, making further infection with it unlikely or less severe. The antigen (foreign microorganism or other substance) provokes the formation of an antibody specific to that antigen. The antibody tends to neutralize viruses or to bind to antigens, encouraging destruction of bacteria by white blood cells. A number of diseases are due to the systemic effects of immune complexes (antibodies linked to antigens) that arise in the appropriate response to an infection or in serum sickness, and these especially affect the kidneys, skin, and joints. In *autoimmunity* antibodies are produced to antigens of the body's own tissues, for reasons that are not always clear; secondary tissue destruction may occur. The second major type of immunity, *cell-mediated immunity*, only occurs with certain types of infection (tuberculosis, histoplasmosis, and fungal diseases) and in certain probable autoimmune diseases. It is also important in the immunity of transplants. Lymphocytes, primed by infection or by the autoimmune or graft reaction, produce substances that affect both lymphocytes and the source of infection and result in a type of inflammation with much tissue damage. Investigation of the role of immunity and its disorders in the causation and manifestations of many diseases has led to the development of immunosuppressive drugs and other agents that are able to interfere with abnormal or destructive immune responses. Immune deficiency dis-

eases have provided models for the separate parts of the immune system, and have led to methods of replacement of absent components of immunity. The epidemic of acquired immune deficiency syndrome (AIDS) has added some urgency to research. Passive immunity, the transfer of antibody-rich substances from an immune subject to a non-immune subject who is susceptible to disease, is important in infancy, where maternal antibodies protect the child until its own immune responses have matured. In certain diseases, such as tetanus and rabies, immune serum gives valuable immediate passive protection in non-immune subjects.

Immunization, process of becoming, or rendering a body, resistant to a particular disease. Immunization occurs naturally when disease antibodies develop through exposure or are passed from mother to fetus or nursing child, but the term generally refers to the medical procedure of administering vaccines or serums. *Vaccines* activate the production of antibodies by introduction into the bloodstream of germs, toxins, etc. (*active immunization*). *Serums* contain antibodies produced by another body (*passive immunization*) and provide only temporary immunity. The first method of immunization was Edward Jenner's smallpox vaccine (1796). Immunization should be performed in children for at least 5 dangerous diseases: whooping cough (pertussis), diphtheria, tetanus, poliomyelitis, and measles. Due to immunization, many serious diseases are now rare.
See also: Immunity.

Impeachment proceedings in the Watergate affair forced President Richard Nixon to resign on August 9, 1974.

Impala (*Aepyceros melampus*), one of the most abundant African antelopes. Impala are about 40 in (102 cm) high and red-brown in color. Males have long, black, lyre-shaped horns. Animals of the woodland edge, impala live in big herds in the dry season, breaking up into single-male harems in the wetter months for breeding. Impala herds of 10 associate with baboons for protection against predators.

Impeachment, formal accusation of a crime or other serious misconduct brought against a public official by a legislature. The term sometimes includes the trial by the legislature that follows. Impeachment began in England as a way of putting officials on trial who were derelict in their duties. Under U.S. constitutional procedure the House of Representatives has the power to impeach; the Senate tries the impeached officials. Grounds for impeachment are: "Treason, Bribery or other High Crimes and Misdemeanors," generally interpreted as being limited to demonstrably criminal acts in the United States. Conviction requires a two-thirds vote of all senators present and voting, providing there is a quorum, and entails automatic removal from office. The chief justice of the United States presides. In U.S. history Congress has impeached 11 officials and convicted 4. President Andrew Johnson was impeached but later acquitted in the Senate by one vote. In 1974, after the House Judiciary Committee recommended his impeachment, Richard M. Nixon resigned as president of the United States.

Imperialism, policy of one country or people, usually "developed," to extend its control or influence over other territories or peoples, usually "underdeveloped." There are many different kinds of imperialism—political, financial, economic, military, and cultural. The justification for imperialism has been that backward countries are advanced technologically, economically, and culturally by the influence of more developed nations. However, imperialist policies have also restricted individual and national freedoms and have often exploited undeveloped natural resources and native populations.

Impressionistic painting by Claude Monet, Impression: Soleil levant.

Imperial Valley, agricultural area in the low-lying Colorado Desert of southeastern California, extending into Mexico, called the "Winter Garden" of America. Since the construction of the 80-mi (129-km) All-American Canal irrigation and soil reclamation projects in the 1940s and 1950s, the valley has become a highly fertile farm region producing alfalfa, melons, tomatoes, lettuce, and sugar beets. Even the January temperature averages 53°F (12°C).

Impetigo, superficial skin infection, usually of the face, caused by streptococcus or staphylococcus. It starts with small vesicles that burst and leave a characteristic yellow crust. It is easily spread by fingers from a single vesicle to affect several large areas and may be transmitted to other people. It is common in children and requires antibiotic cream or sometimes systemic penicillin.

Import *see:* Exports and imports.

Impressionism, dominant artistic movement in France from the mid-1860s to 1890, characterized by the use of brushstrokes of contrasting colors to convey the impression of objects by the light they reflect. The impressionist painters, who include Edouard Manet, Claude Monet, Camille Pissarro, and others, painted landscapes and scenes of leisure in contemporary Paris. They usually worked outdoors, recording the scenes before them spontaneously and directly. The term "impressionist" was first used as a criticism of Monet's *Impression: Soleil levant* (1874). The artists organized 8 independent exhibitions for their pictures. The U.S. painters Mary Cassatt and Childe Hassam were influenced by the impressionists. The term "impressionism" is also applied to other art forms, notably literature that uses symbolic imagery and music that expresses mood and feeling.

Inca, Native American empire in the western region of South America which, at the time of the Spanish conquest, occupied what is now Peru, parts of Ecuador, Chile, Bolivia, and Argentina. It extended some 3,000 mi (4,800 km) from north to south, stretching back between 150 and 250 mi (240 and 400 km) from the narrow Pacific coastal plain into the high Andes. The name "Inca" refers to the people of the empire and is also the title of the ruler. Communications were maintained along brilliantly engineered and extensive roads, carried over the sheer Andean gorges by fiber cable suspension bridges. Trained relay runners carried messages 150 mi (240 km) a day and the army had quick access to trouble spots. Restive subject tribes were resettled near Cuzco, the capital. Detailed surveys of new conquests were recorded by *quipu*, a mnemonic device using knotted cords. Writing, like draft animals and wheeled transport, was unknown; so too was monetary currency. Taxation and tribute were levied in the form of labor services. In other respects the culture was highly advanced. At sites such as Machu

Picchu, Inca architects raised some of the world's finest stone structures; precious metals from government-controlled mines were worked by skilled goldsmiths; bronze was also used; ceramic and textile design was outstanding. Agriculture was based on elaborate irrigation and hillside terracing. The Spanish domination of the Incas began with the arrival (1532) of Francisco Pizarro, who executed the Incan emperor and conquered their cities.

Incandescent lamp *see:* Electric light.

Inchon (pop. 1,387,500), Yellow River port city located in the northwestern part of South Korea. In ancient times Inchon relied mainly upon fishing, but after foreign nations forced Korea to open up to international trade in the 1880s, it developed into a major port. In 1950, during the Korean war, the U.S. made a surprise landing at Inchon, turning back the invading North Koreans. Located about 20 mi (32 km) from the capital city of Seoul, Inchon has been a major industrial center since the late 1960s. It produces chemicals, iron, steel, and textiles, in addition to thriving in the areas of fishing and shipping.
See also: Korea; Korean War.

Inchworm *see:* Measuring worm.

Incisor *see:* Teeth.

Income, payment, whether money (pecuniary, cash, or monetary income) or as goods and services (real income), received in return for goods and services. For most people cash income takes the form of a wage or salary, usually expressed as so much per week or month. Cash income is also derived from stock dividends and from rent paid for the use of property. Many people in developing countries depend largely on noncash incomes. Even in industrialized countries some people get at least a part of their income in the form of goods rather than cash, for example, farmers who use some of their own produce. Income is distinguished from assets. For example, say that a person spends $8,000 in the course of a year but earns only $6,000, drawing the remaining $2,000 from savings. That person's income is only $6,000. The remaining $2,000 has been spent by consuming assets. Equally, if a person borrows money or receives a gift of cash, such sums are not rated as part of income, since they do not stem from productive work or investment. People regularly spend more than their income, borrowing cash and buying on credit. Businesses, too, regularly look to borrowed funds to pay for their expansion. This presupposes that borrowed money can be repaid from future income.

Income tax, the major source of government revenue. As opposed to excise taxes levied on goods, it is a tax on the incomes of individuals, proportionate to their incomes, or on corporations. At first imposed only to meet extraordinary expenditures such as war financing, income tax became permanent in Britain in 1874. In the United States it was levied during the Civil War, but an attempt to make it a permanent federal tax was ruled unconstitutional. The 16th Amendment (1913) authorized the federal government to levy the tax, and since 1919 most states have also adopted this mode of revenue raising. It is assessed on net income after allowances have been deducted for family dependents, contributions to charities, and certain other expenditures. Incomes below a certain level are entirely tax exempt; above this level the rate rises progressively to about one-third of a person's earnings.
See also: Internal Revenue Service; Taxation.

Incubation, method of keeping microorganisms such as bacteria or viruses warm and in an appropriate medium to promote their growth (e.g., in identification of the organisms causing disease); also, period during which an organism is present in the body before causing disease. Infectious disease is contracted from a source of infective microorganisms. Once these have entered the body they divide and spread to different parts, and it may be some time before they cause symptoms due to local or systemic effects. This incubation period may be helpful in diagnosis and in determining length of quarantine periods.

Incubation
Incubation periods (in days)

Chicken pox	11-21
Common cold	1-2
Diphtheria	2-5
Dysentery (amebic)	2-28
(bacillary)	2-7
Encephalitis	4-21
German measles (rubella)	12-21
Glandular fever	5-15
Gonorrhea	1-8
Influenza	1-3
Malaria	7-14
Measles	10-15
Meningitis	2-10
Mumps	14-28
Paratyphoid fever	2-10
Poliomyelitis	3-21
Rabies	14-40
Scarlet fever	2-7
Smallpox	7-16
Syphilis	About 21
Tetanus	4-21
Tuberculosis	28-42
Typhoid fever	6-21
Typhus fever	About 12
Undulant fever	7-35
Whooping cough (pertussis)	7-21
Yellow fever	3-7

Indentured servant, person bound to labor for a stated period, usually 5 to 7 years. In the 17th and 18th centuries, people often agreed to indenture in return for passage to the American colonies. Others were enticed or kidnapped into indentured service. Convicts were sometimes sentenced and deported to indentured labor. With the use of slave labor, the practice of indenture disappeared.

The Inca fortress city of Machu Picchu was discovered in 1911.

Incan ritual knife found in Cuzco

Fragment of cloth with Inca symbols

Independence (pop. 111,806), city in Missouri, seat of Jackson County. Located about 10 mi (16 km) east of Kansas City, Independence is largely a residential suburb. Its industries include oil refining and the manufacture of cement, plastics, and farm machinery. Founded in 1827, it was the site of a Mormon colony from 1831 to 1834, and is now the headquarters of the Reorganized Church of Jesus Christ of Latter-Day Saints. The home of former President Harry S. Truman, it is the site of the Harry S. Truman Library.
See also: Missouri.

Independence, Declaration of *see:* Declaration of Independence.

Independence, War for *see:* Revolutionary War in America.

Independence Day, or Fourth of July, the principal nonreligious holiday in the United States. It commemorates the signing of the Declaration of Independence (July 4, 1776).
See also: Declaration of Independence.

Independence Hall, old state house of Philadelphia, Pa., where the Declaration of Independence was proclaimed and the

Constitutional Convention of 1787 met. It now houses the Liberty Bell and a small museum.
See also: Declaration of Independence.

Index, reference list of the topics, subjects, or names in a printed work and where they may be found. There are 2 types of indexes: alphabetical, in which the entries are listed from A to Z, and analytical, in which subtopics are listed under major subject headings.

Indian government palace in New Delhi

Index of Forbidden Books (*Index Librorum Prohibitorum*), official list of books banned by the Roman Catholic Church as being in doctrinal or moral error. A book could be removed from the index by expurgation of offending passages, and special permission could be given to read prohibited books. The index ceased publication in 1966.

India, union of 22 states and 9 territories, the world's seventh-largest country, occupying most of the Indian subcontinent, the land mass of south central Asia that tapers southward from the Himalayan mountain system to Cape Comorin and Sri Lanka. India shares the subcontinent with Pakistan, Bangladesh, and the Himalayan states of Sikkim, Nepal, and Bhutan, with Sri Lanka off its coast. Only the People's Republic of China has a greater population than India.
Land and climate. The chief geographical regions of North India are the Thar Desert along the Pakistan border, the mountain valleys of Kashmir (disputed with Pakistan), the fertile plains of the Ganges and Brahmaputra rivers, and the Himalaya Mountains, which shield India from the cold winter winds of central Asia. The Deccan plateau, bordered by the western and eastern Ghats mountain ranges, occupies most of South India. The rich volcanic soil is used mainly for cotton growing, though there are also important mineral deposits. Most of the country has a tropical monsoon climate, temperatures reaching 120°F (48.8°C) in the hot season on the northern plains and, in the cool seasons, falling below freezing in the mountains. The monsoon rains are especially heavy on the western Ghats and in northeast India; some places average more than 426 in (1,082 cm) of rain a year.
People. About 80% of the population lives in small villages, though the towns are growing fast. The chief cities are the seaports of Bombay, Calcutta, and Madras and the capital, New Delhi. The dominant religion is Hinduism, which, through its caste system, profoundly affects the nation's social structures. Islam, Christianity, Buddhism, Sikhism, and Jainism are also found. Education is free for ages 6-14.
Economy. Two-thirds of the labor force is engaged in agriculture. Rice, beans, peas, tea, sugarcane, jute, pepper, and timber are the main agricultural products. Output remains relatively low overall. Improvements are being sought by irrigation, land reclamation projects, and the introduction of improved strains of crops and fertilizers.

India

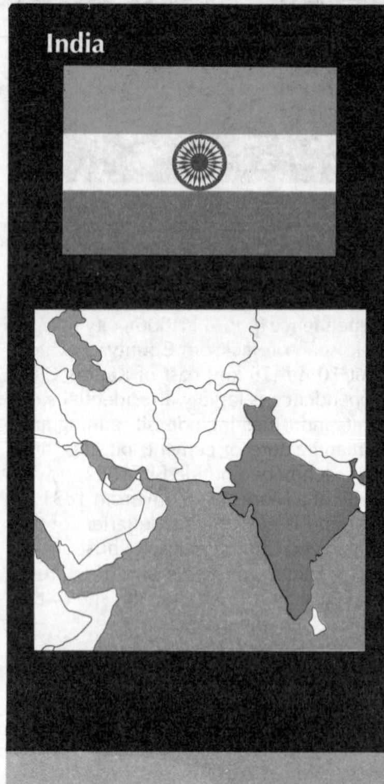

General information	
Capital:	New Delhi
Area:	1,269,219 sq mi (3,287,263 sq km)
Population:	835,812,000
Official languages:	English, Hindi, 14 regional languages
Monetary unit:	1 Indian rupee = 100 paisa
Main cities:	Bombay, New Delhi, Calcutta, Madras, Bangalore
Government	
Form:	federal republic
Independent:	1947
Head of state:	President (elected every 5 years)
Head of government:	Prime Minister
Legislature:	two legislative houses (Council of States and House of the People)
Executive:	President and Council of Ministers
Judiciary:	highest court is the Supreme Court
Political division:	25 states, 7 union territories
National economy	
Gross national product:	U.S. $271,440,000,000
Per capita income:	U.S. $330
Agriculture:	sugar cane, rice, wheat, potatoes, sorghum, cotton, jute, tea, spices, cashew nuts
Livestock:	cattle, goats, buffaloes
Fisheries:	2,893,000 metric tons
Mining:	coal, limestone, iron ore, crude petroleum, copper, bauxite, manganese, lead, zinc
Industries:	clothing, cement, steel ingots, pig iron, finished steel, refined sugar, machinery
Main exports:	machinery and transportation equipment, chemicals products, iron ore, mineral fuels, lubricants, coffee, cashew nuts
Transportation:	38,500 mi (62,000 km) of railroads; 1,101,000 mi (1,772,000 km) of roads; 4 international airports
Trading partners:	U.S., Japan, USSR, Germany, United Kingdom
People	
Urban:	27%
Ethnic composition:	Hindi 28%, Telugu 8%, Bengali 8%, Marathi 7.5%, Tamil 7%
Birth rate:	31.9 per 1,000 population
Death rate:	11.2 per 1,000 population
Infant mortality:	98 per 1,000 live births
Life expectancy:	male 58 years, female 58 years

About 45% of the industrial labor force works in the jute, cotton, and other textile mills. Mineral resources include oil, iron ore, coal, natural gas, copper, bauxite, manganese, and mica but are poorly exploited.

History. The Indus Valley civilization, in modern Pakistan, was the first great culture on the subcontinent. It succumbed in 1500 B.C. to Aryan peoples invading through the northwestern mountain passes; they brought the Sanskrit language and Hinduism to India. The Maurya Empire and Gupta dynasties represented high points of Buddhist and Hindu rule, but India was never united, and from the 10th century Muslim invaders added to the conflicts. In the 14th century the Delhi Muslim sultanate and the Hindu kingdom of Vijayanagar in the south were dominant. In the 1520s the Muslim empire of the Moguls was founded. Europeans also began to exert influence in the Indian subcontinent. In 1510 the Portuguese took Goa, and soon the Dutch, British, and French were vying for Indian trade. In the 18th century English and French interests contested for control of the moribund empire. Victory went to the British East India Company. After the Sepoy Rebellion (1857-58), the British government took over rule of much of the country, and the remaining independent princes, both Muslim and Hindu, recognized British primacy. In 1885 the Indian National Congress Party was set up; under Mohandas Gandhi and Jawaharlal Nehru it led the movement for independence. Muhammad Ali Jinnah led the Muslim League, urging partition into India and Pakistan on religious grounds. Many thousands died in fierce communal riots following partition in 1947.

India achieved sovereign status in 1948. The constitution (1949) provided for a bicameral, democratically elected parliament and a cabinet government, with a prime minister and a president. Domestic politics has been concerned with the problem of food supply, the drive toward industrialization, the mitigation of the worst injustices of the caste system, and, since the late 1960s, tension between the central and provincial governments. The dispute with Pakistan over Kashmir flared into war in 1965. A frontier war in 1962 also emphasized the strained relations between India and China. Sikkim became an Indian state in 1975, the same year Indira Gandhi, Nehru's daughter and successor as prime minister, was convicted of election irregularities. She declared a state of emergency, jailed her opponents, and began to rule by decree. Her party was defeated in the general election in 1977. The new government dismantled the state of emergency, but the coalition that had defeated Mrs. Gandhi began to disintegrate, and in 1980 she again became prime minister. In 1984, after she had ordered attacks on Sikh separatists that left more than 1,000 Sikhs dead, she was assassinated by Sikhs in her bodyguard. Her son, Rajiv Gandhi, became her successor and prime minister (1984-89). In 1991, he was murdered while campaigning for his re-election.

India. Periyar wildlife reserve

Indian, American *see:* Native Americans.

Indian art and architecture, classical tradition dates from the fall of the Indus Valley civilization (1500 B.C.) and the establishment of the Indo-Aryan culture based on Hinduism. The naturalistic Aryan pantheon assimilated local deities and concepts to produce a complex system, celebrated in the sacred Hindu texts, the Vedas. Statues, paintings, and ornate temples symbolize and embody the gods and their attributes or powers. With the spread of Buddhism under Asoka (d.232 B.C.), the stupa, a round brick- or stone-faced earth mound, containing a relic or tomb and surrounded by a square stone railing, was the favored religious architectural form. Painting and sculpture, notably in the Ajanta caves and the art of Gandhara, portray episodes in the physical and spiritual life of the Buddha. The golden age of Indian culture came during the Gupta dynasty (A.D. 320-500). Resurgent Hinduism soon adapted the Buddhist styles in the classic porch, pillared hall, and cella of the Hindu temple, often surmounted by massive conical spires. In the 13th century southern India perfected the Dravidian pyramidal temple and produced superb bronze sculptures, such as the famous dancing Siva. Indian Muslim art reached its peak under the Moguls.

Indiana, state of the north-central United States; bordered by Michigan and Lake Michigan (north), Ohio (east), Kentucky (south), and Illinois (west).

Land and climate. Indiana's Great Lakes Plains are characterized by rich, black soils and many small lakes, the result of Ice Age glaciers. Along the state's Lake Michigan shorelines lie great sand dunes. The Till Plains of central Indiana are a part of the Midwestern Corn Belt. The southern third of the state, not reached by the glaciers, is marked by gorges and steep hills called knobs. The Wabash River and its many tributaries drain about two-thirds of the state. Indiana has a humid, continental climate, with warm summers and cold winters. Principal cities are Indianapolis, Fort Wayne, and Gary.

Indiana

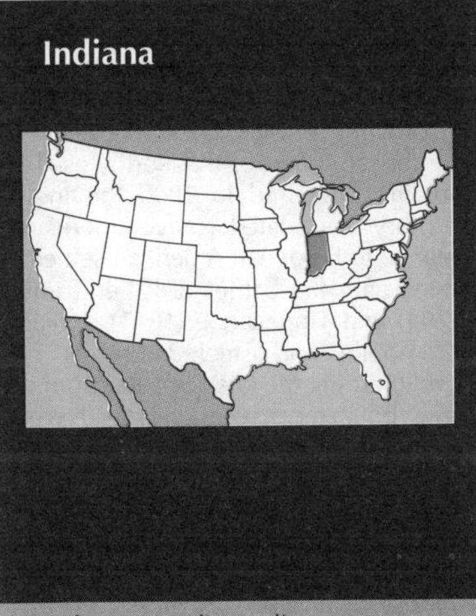

Capital:	Indianapolis
Statehood:	Dec. 11, 1816 (19th state)
Familiar name:	Hoosier State
Area:	36,185 sq mi (93,720 sq km; ranks 38th)
Population:	5,564,228 (1990; ranks 14th)
Elevation:	Highest—1,257 ft (383 m), WayneCounty Lowest—320 ft (98 m), Ohio River
Motto:	The Crossroads of America
State flower:	Peony
State bird:	Cardinal
State tree:	Tulip (poplar)
State song:	"On the Banks of the Wabash, Far Away"

Indiana farmland

Economy. Steel and other metal production are Indiana's principal industries. Other industries produce transportation and electrical equipment and chemicals. About three-quarters of Indiana is covered by farmland. The state is a leading producer of corn, soybeans, and hogs. Bituminous coal is the state's most important mineral, and about two-thirds of the nation's limestone comes from Indiana.

Government. Indiana is governed by the constitution of 1851. The governor serves a 4-year term. The General Assembly is composed of 50 senators serving 4-year terms and 100 representatives serving 2-year terms. Indiana sends 10 representatives and 2 senators to the U.S. Congress.

History. Indiana's earliest known inhabitants were the prehistoric Mound Builders. The area was occupied mainly by the Miami tribe when French fur traders explored it in the 17th century. After the French and Indian Wars, the area passed to the British (1763) and, after the American Revolution, to the United States. The region became part of the Northwest Territory in 1787, and in 1800 the Indiana Territory was created. Native American resistance to European American settlement ended after the battles of Fallen Timbers (1794) and Tippecanoe (1811). Indiana's automobile and steel industries grew rapidly during the late 19th and 20th centuries, but in recent years the state has been hard hit by the general decline in industry in the Midwest.

Indian Affairs, Bureau of, U.S. federal agency, part of the Department of the Interior, set up in 1824 to safeguard the welfare of Native Americans. It acts as trustee for tribal lands and funds, supervises the reservations, and provides welfare and educational facilities.

Indianapolis (pop. 1,249,822), capital and largest city of Indiana, located near the center of the state. The city is one of the largest in the world not situated on a navigable waterway. This deficiency made its growth slow from around 1819, when the first settlers arrived, until 1847, when the first railroad reached the town. Additional railroads and roads made it a leading transport terminus. Modern Indianapolis contains the state's main airport (Weir Cook), and is a vital highway center, actually chosen to be the junction of more interstate highways than any other U.S. city. The capital is the marketing and distribution center for much of Indiana's agriculture and industry. Its major industries include transportation equipment, chemicals, and electrical machinery. Others are livestock sales, printing and publishing, and telephones and hardware. Just outside the city is the famous Indianapolis Speedway, site of the yearly Memorial Day 500-mi (800-km) race.
See also: Indiana.

Indianapolis 500 *see:* Automobile racing.

Indian bean *see:* Catalpa.

Indian Desert *see:* Thar Desert.

Indian fig *see:* Prickly pear.

Indian hemp *see:* Dogbane.

Indian mallow (*Abutilon theophrastii*), weed of the mallow family, a group of dicotyledonous flowering plants. The Indian mallow grows from under 1 ft (30 cm) to over 6 ft (1.8 m) tall, and has orange-yellow flowers. The Indian mallow was given its common name because it originally grew in India, but has also been called *velvet leaf* and *stump weed*, the latter because it was once used to stamp designs onto butter.

Indian Mutiny *see:* Sepoy Rebellion.

Indian Ocean, world's third largest ocean (28,350,000 sq mi/73,426,500 sq km), bounded by Antarctica to the south, Africa to the west, and Australia and Indonesia to the east. The Indian subcontinent divides the northern part of the ocean into 2 great arms, the Arabian Sea to the west and the Bay of Bengal to the east. Largest of its many islands are Madagascar and Sri Lanka.

Indian paintbrush, any of about 200 species (genus *Castilleja*) of wildflower in the figwort or snapdragon family of flowering plants. Also called *painted cup*, the Indian paintbrush gives forth tiny flowers that are mostly green, while its leaves are brightly colored—commonly red, pink, yellow, or lavender. A species (*C. linariaefolia*) of Indian paintbrush is the state flower of Wyoming.

Indian pipe (*Monotropa uniflora*), low, flowering plant of the family Ericaceae. Often mistaken for fungus, which actually serves as food for it, the indian pipe grows in moist woods in eastern Asia and North America. Its scaly stem grows 6 to 10 in (15 to 25 cm) tall. The Indian pipe got its name because it resembles a group of clay pipes.

Indian reservation, land set aside by the U.S. government for use by Native Americans. The first Indian reservation was established for a Delaware Indian tribe in the New Jersey colony in 1758. During the early and middle 19th century, as white settlers claimed more Indian land in the eastern U.S., the government established Indian reservations west of the Mississippi River. In 1823 the Bureau of Indian Affairs, an agency of the Department of the Interior, was formed to oversee affairs on these reservations. Since 1970, when President Nixon called for a new era of Indian self-determination, the tribes have had increased authority over all aspects of their welfare. There are now approximately 285 federal and state Indian reservations, covering 50 million acres in about 30 states.
See also: Native Americans.

Indian root *see:* Spikenard.

Indians *see:* Native Americans.

Indian Territory, region west of Arkansas, into which the Cherokee, Creek, Seminole, Choctaw, and Chickasaw tribes were forcibly moved under the 1830 Indian Removal Act. In 1866 they were penalized for supporting the South in the Civil War by having other tribes resettled in the western part of this territory. Massive white settlement of other portions after 1889 led to disorder and the collapse of tribal government; by 1906 white settlers outnumbered Native Americans six to one, and the territory was incorporated into the state of Oklahoma.

Indian tobacco *see:* Lobelia.

Indian turnip *see:* Jack-in-the-pulpit.

Cross-section of Indian Ocean from Madagascar to Sumatra. The Java Trench is the deepest point in the ocean.

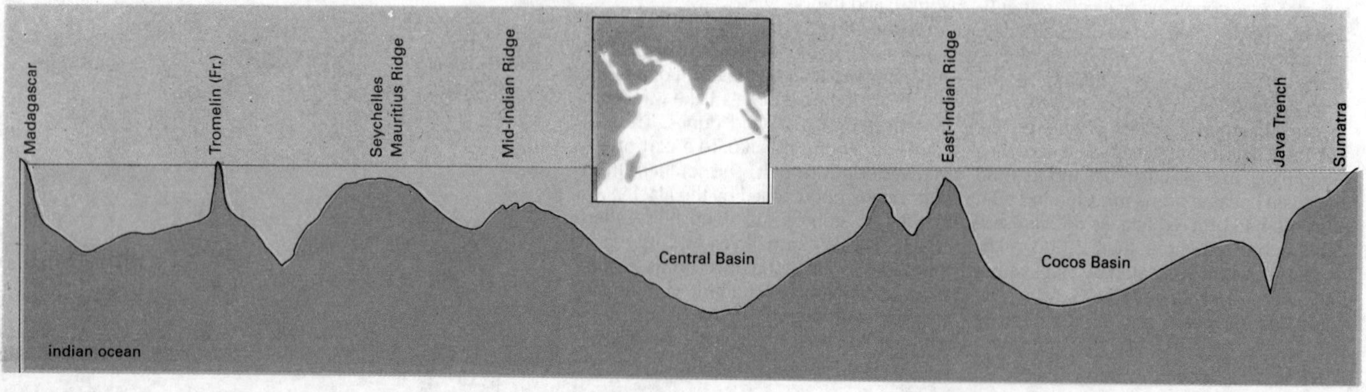

Indian wars, struggle in North America between the Native Americans and European colonizers from the earliest colonial times to the late 19th century. Despite peaceful trade under Powhatan, hostilities between Native Americans and the English settlers of Jamestown, Va., began in 1622, and by 1644 the native tribes had been crushed. In New England, war with the Pequot tribe (1636) resulted in their massacre. With the end of King Philip's War in 1678, Native American resistance in New England was broken. During the Revolutionary War trade regulations were introduced to protect Native Americans from exploitation. Trade and land companies continued to cheat them, however, provoking uprisings. In 1811 an alliance of southern and western tribes under the Shawnee chieftain Tecumseh was defeated at the Tippecanoe River; Tecumseh's death in 1813 ended tribal resistance in this area. The Seminole in Florida, however, continued hostilities until 1816. In 1830 the Indian Removal Act, passed by President Andrew Jackson, authorized the transfer of southeastern tribes to land west of the Mississippi. Native American resistance was met by illegal force; Jackson even ignored a Supreme Court order upholding the land rights of the Cherokees. In 1855 the defeated Nez Percé tribes were given land in the northwestern states, but when gold was found in the area they were again forced to move. Chief Joseph led an unsuccessful revolt against this in 1877. The second half of the 19th century saw the final suppression of the Native Americans. The Navaho, holding the land between the Rio Grande and California, were defeated by Kit Carson in 1863 and transferred to northwestern Arizona. After the Civil War attempts were made to restrict the Apaches, though Cochise and others resisted; their last war chief, Geronimo, surrendered in 1886. In 1871 the government ceased to recognize tribes as independent nations. The Great Plains, home of the Sioux, Apache, and Cheyenne, were subdued in 1870-90 by a combination of military force and the depletion of buffalo herds. The Native American victory at the battle of Little Bighorn only hastened their defeat. Crazy Horse surrendered in 1877, and there was a final massacre at Wounded Knee, S. Dak., in 1890.

Indies *see:* East Indies; West Indies.

Indigo bunting (*Passerina cyanea*), North American songbird of the family Emberizidae, which includes the bunting, finches, grosbeaks, and sparrows. The male bunting of this species has a deep indigo blue head and blackish wings and tail, while the female is brown with darker wings and lighter underparts. Helping farmers by feeding on insects and weed seeds, the indigo bunting ranges from Ontario and New Brunswick to as far south as the Gulf states.

Indium, chemical element, symbol In; for physical constants see Periodic Table. Indium was discovered spectroscopically by Ferdinand Reich and H.T. Richter (1863). The element is most frequently associated with zinc minerals, but is also found in iron, lead, and copper ores. It is prepared as a byproduct in the smelting of zinc. Indium is a silvery-white, soft, low-melting metal. Indium and its compounds are used in making dental alloys, bearing alloys, transistors, solar batteries, and other semiconductor devices.

Indochina, political term for peninsular Southeast Asia between China and India. It was formerly French Indochina, and is now divided into Vietnam, Laos, and Kampuchea (Cambodia). The area contains two densely peopled, rice-rich deltas (Red River in the North, Mekong River in the south), separated by the Annamite mountain chain. Thais, Laos, and Annamese (Vietnamese) settled Indochina from the north. From the second century A.D., many states and cultures affected by India and China rose and fell there, including Funan, the Khmer Empire, Champa, and Annam. European penetration began in the 16th century. France concluded a treaty with Annam in 1787, annexed Cochin China in 1862, and by 1900 had welded separate states into the single political unit of French Indochina. World War II and militant nationalism destroyed France's authority and in 1949 Cambodia and Laos gained independence. The communist Vietminh drove the French out of Vietnam; the United States continued France's anticommunist role in the long Vietnam War, but by 1976 Indochina was effectively under communist control.

Indo-European languages, large family of language spoken throughout most of Europe and much of Asia, and descended from a hypothetical common ancestor, Proto-Indo-European, extant more than 5,000 years ago. There are 2 main branches: the Eastern, with 6 main groups, and Western, with 4. The Eastern branch includes the extinct Anatolian and Tocharian groups, as well as Albanian, Armenian, Balto-Slavic, and Indo-Iranian (with its important sub-group, the Indo-Aryan languages). The Western branch includes Celtic, Greek, Romance or Italic (Latin and the languages derived from it), and Teutonic or Germanic (one of which is English). Until the beginning of the 20th century it was thought that Sanskrit inscriptions represented the oldest written form of any of the family; however, both ancient Hittite and Linear B, which have since been deciphered, are older.

Indonesia, republic of southeast Asia occupying most of the Malay archipelago, the world's largest archipelago, consisting of more than 13,000 islands and islets strung out along the equator from Sumatra facing the Indian Ocean in the west to New Guinea in the east. These were the Indies sought by Christopher Columbus and other explorers. The Moluccas, part of Indonesia, were the Spice Islands of the merchant venturers.

Land and climate. Extending for more than 3,000 mi (4,828 km) from west to east, Indonesia's islands range in size from small deserted reefs to large islands like Sumatra (182,860 sq mi/473,607 sq km), the world's sixth-largest island. About half of New Guinea, the world's second-largest island, and about three-quarters of Borneo, third-largest island, belong to Indonesia. More than 6,000 of Indonesia's islands are inhabited. Many of the islands have luxuriant tropical rain forests containing valuable hardwoods. Although some have areas of low-lying plain or swamp, most are mountainous. Java, Sumatra, and the Little Sunda group have a great line of volcanic peaks. The eruption in 1883 of Krakatoa, in the strait between Java and Sumatra, resulted in the loss of 30,000 lives. There are few large rivers. Rivers flowing into the comparatively shallow South China, Java, and Arafura seas build up deltas, often at a remarkably rapid rate. Coastal scenery ranges from coral reefs, sandy beaches, and mangrove forests to cliffs. Vegetation and wildlife are varied. Some islands, like Java and Borneo, have distinctly Asiatic types, while New Guinea has Australian types, both types being blended in the islands in between. The rain forests contain teak, ebony, and other hardwoods, giant creepers, and shade-loving plants. Along the coasts there are casuarina trees, coconut, and other palms and, where it is muddy, extensive mangrove forests. Wildlife includes elephants, tigers, rhinoceros, orangutans, and, in the eastern islands, pouched animals like the opossum, wallaby, and cuscus. There are many beautiful and brightly colored birds. Snakes and crocodiles abound, but Indonesia's most famous reptile is the Komodo dragon, the giant lizard of the small island of Komodo east of Sumatra. The main islands fall into 3 groups: (1) the Greater Sunda Islands: Java, Sumatra, In-

The island of Bali forms part of the Indonesian archipelago.

Indonesia

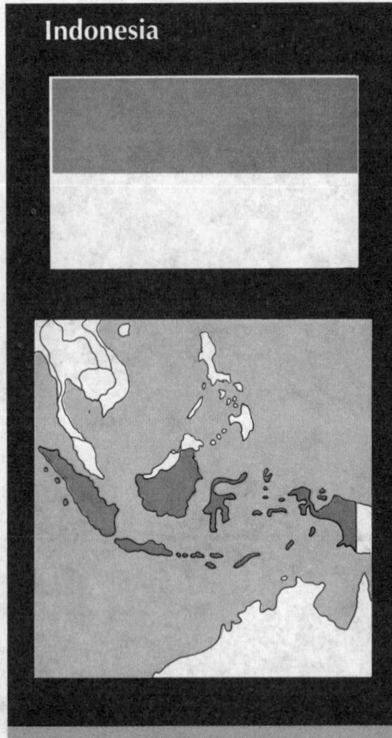

General information	
Capital:	Jakarta
Area:	741,101 sq mi (1,919,443 sq km)
Population:	177,046,000
Official language:	Bahasa Indonesia
Monetary unit:	1 Indonesian rupiah = 100 sen
Main cities:	Jakarta, Surabaya, Medan, Bandung
Government	
Form:	republic
Independent:	1949
Head of state:	President (elected every 5 years)
Head of government:	President
Legislature:	two legislative houses (House of People's Representatives and People's Consultative Assembly)
Executive:	President and Cabinet
Judiciary:	highest court is the Supreme Court
Political division:	24 provinces, 2 special autonomous districts, 1 metropolitan district
National economy	
Gross national product:	U.S. $75,960,000,000
Per capita income:	U.S. $430
Agriculture:	sugar cane, rice, cassava, coconuts, fruit, vegetables, rubber, coffee, bananas
Livestock:	goats, cattle, pigs, poultry
Fisheries:	2,670,000 metric tons
Mining:	coal, nickel ore, natural gas, bauxite, crude petroleum, copper, tin
Industries:	petroleum products, cement, fertilizer, paper, cotton yarn, beer, radio and television receivers
Main exports:	mineral fuels, lubricants, basic manufacturing, crude materials, food and livestock
Transportation:	4,091 mi (6,583) of railroads; 136,578 mi (219,791 km) of roads; 8 international airports
Trading partners:	Japan, U.S., Singapore
People	
Urban:	26%
Ethnic composition:	Javanese 40%, Sundanese 15.5%, Malay 12%, Madurese 4.5%
Birth rate:	27.2 per 1,000 population
Death rate:	11.1 per 1,000 population
Infant mortality:	83 per 1,000 live births
Life expectancy:	male 55 years, female 57.5 years

Borobudur Temple (9th century) in Indonesia reflects the Buddhist influence of its early history.

donesian Borneo (Kalimantan), and Celebes (Sulawesi); (2) the Lesser Sunda Islands, including Bali, Flores, Lombok, Sumba, Sumbawa, and Indonesian Timor; (3) the Moluccas (Maluku), including Ambon, Aru Islands, Banda Islands, Buru, Ceram, Halmahera, and the Tanimbor Islands. Including West Irian (formerly Netherlands New Guinea), Indonesia has a total area of more than 735,200 sq mi (1,904,168 sq km). Its most important islands, in terms of population density and economic and cultural activity, are Java, Bali, and Sumatra. Indonesia has a hot, rainy, equatorial climate that is modified by monsoonal winds. From mid-June to Oct. the southeast monsoon brings dry air from Australia. From Nov. to Mar. a north or northeast monsoon blows from mainland Asia across the South China Sea, where it collects much moisture and brings heavy rains. Violent tropical thunderstorms occur almost daily.

People. Two-thirds of the population lives on Java, site of the capital and chief port, Jakarta. The population can be broadly divided into Malays and Papuans, with Chinese, Arabs, and others. Bahasa Indonesia is the official language, but over 250 other languages are spoken. Education is compulsory, and most Indonesians are literate. There are more than 50 universities and technological institutes.

Economy. Some 70% of the population is in farming, producing rice, coconuts, cassava, corn, peanuts, sweet potatoes, spices, and coffee, and raising cattle, goats, hogs, and chickens. The economy rests largely on agriculture, forestry, and fisheries, but mineral resources are being increasingly exploited. Coal, bauxite, copper, manganese, nickel, and precious metals are mined. Indonesia's most important products are oil, its chief export, and tin, of which it is one of the world's major producers. There is some light manufacturing, mostly centered on Java.

History. Hominids lived on Java 1 million years ago. Civilization grew under Indian influence after the 4th century A.D.; several kingdoms flourished from the 12th to 14th centuries. Islam spread swiftly in the 15th century. European impact began in 1511, when the Portuguese captured Malacca. But Portugal eventually kept only East Timor, losing control to the English and Dutch. The Dutch East India Company founded Batavia (Jakarta) in 1619 and dominated the so-called Dutch East Indies until the Netherlands assumed control in 1798. Britain occupied the islands (1811-16) during the Napoleonic Wars, then returned them to the Dutch, who greatly expanded cash-crop exports during the 19th century. Nationalist movements emerged in the early 1900s, and after Indonesia's occupation by Japanese forces in World War II, Sukarno proclaimed Indonesia an independent republic. The Dutch were forced to grant independence in 1949. President Sukarno's dictatorial, anti-

Western regime and extravagant spending damaged the economy. General Suharto deposed Sukarno in 1968. He suppressed left-wing groups, severed links with Communist China, and restored relations with the West, seeking to stabilize the economy. In 1975, after Portugal withdrew from East Timor, Indonesian troops invaded, and in 1976 the region was proclaimed a province of Indonesia, a move not recognized by the UN.

Induction, electric, name of the phenomenon whereby an electrically charged object charges another object without touching it. As distinct from electromagnetic induction, which is the force produced on an electrically charged particle by a changing magnetic field, electric induction is caused by the attraction that opposite electrical charges have for each other (electrostatic attraction). In electric induction if a body is positively charged electrons in the uncharged body will be attracted to it; if the opposite end of the body is then grounded, electrons will flow into it to replace those drawn to the other end. Therefore, the body acquires a negative charge after the ground connection is broken. The Van de Graaff generator, used in nuclear physics experiments, utilizes electric induction.
See also: Van de Graaff generator.

Inductive method, logical process which starts from the particular and goes to the general. For example, a person may experience several rainy days while staying in a particular area and generalize that the area has a rainy climate; it is a method that leads to probabilities, not certainties. Francis Bacon proposed induction as the logic of scientific discovery, but the empirical sciences use both induction and deduction, which involves drawing particular conclusions by reasoning from general premises.
See also: Deductive method.

Indulgence, in the Roman Catholic Church, remission of the temporal punishment (on earth or in purgatory) that remains due for sin even after confession, absolution, and doing penance. In consideration of prayers and good works, the Church may grant plenary (full) or partial indulgences by administering the merits of Jesus and the saints. Sale of indulgences was denounced by the Protestant reformers, and the abuse was abolished by the Council of Trent.
See also: Trent, Council of.

Indus River, river rising in the Himalayas of western Tibet and flowing 1,800 mi (2,900 km) through Kashmir and Pakistan to its 75-mi-(121-km-)long delta on the North Arabian Sea. Cradle of the ancient Indus Valley civilization, it is now an important source of hydroelectric power and irrigation.

Industrial arts, area of general education that includes automobile mechanics, electronics, graphic arts, industrial crafts, industrial drawing, metalworking, plastics, photography, and woodworking. Also known as *technology education*, industrial arts began as a curriculum area in the U.S. during the late 1800s. Until the 1970s most industrial arts programs enrolled only boys, but today most programs are coeducational. Industrial arts courses may focus on one skill in depth, or several skills in a broader way. Among the goals of industrial arts programs are to teach the use of tools and machines and to encourage creativity.

Industrial design, expression of the special relationship between the artist, the consumer, and the manufacturer in a developed, industrialized society. Its origins lie in the Industrial Revolution of the late 18th century, which began to link mass production with a powerful new form of distribution, the steam train, and with a growing consumer-oriented community. Its full expression is everywhere present—from the mass-produced automobile to the mass-produced ready-to-wear suit. Slowly but certainly, the craftsperson, whose products were based on an individual relationship with the consumer, has all but disappeared.

Industrialism *see:* Industrial Revolution.

Industrial pollution *see:* Environmental pollution.

Industrial relations, conduct of relations between organized labor and management and the relations between individual workers and their supervisors. Wage rates, work conditions, and productivity are among potential sources of conflict between the 2 sides. Unresolved conflicts can result in strikes and lockouts that cut output and profits and thus harm employees and employer alike. In the United States the federal government helps to settle major industrial disputes, the National Labor Relations Board serving as adjudicator. U.S. industrial relations are largely governed by the Wagner Act of 1935 and the Taft-Hartley Act of 1947.

Industrial Revolution, period of rapid transition from an agrarian to an industrial society; specifically, the prototype of such periods, the late 18th and early 19th centuries in the United Kingdom. This period saw Britain transformed from a predominantly agricultural society into the world's first industrial nation. In the 18th century, British imperialism, technology, economic development, and natural resources combined to provide unique opportunities for building business fortunes. The growth of capitalism developed the factory system to harness new inventions that cheaply mass-produced textiles to exploit the expanding world market for British cloth. Key inventions in textile production included John Kay's flying shuttle (c.1733), James Hargreaves's spinning jenny (c.1764), Richard Arkwright's water frame (1769), and Edmund Cartwright's powered loom (1785). In 1709 Abraham Darby had learned to smelt iron with coke; in 1781, James Watt patented a steam engine producing rotary motion. Soon many factories were using steam-powered iron machinery. Canals and, from the 1830s, railroads and steamships provided a transportation network linking new industrial cities with sources of supply and markets. The urban masses were supported by increasingly efficient agriculture, due to scientific advances and the stimulus to self-sufficiency of the Napoleonic Wars. Largely through improvements in food supply, sanitation, and medicine Britain's population rose from under 7 million in 1750 to over 20 million in 1850, creating an increased labor force while escalating consumer demand. Factory workers endured appalling work-

The Industrial Revolution was possible due to the uses of steam power. Illustrated is James Nasmyth's steam hammer invented in 1842. (Below) In Europe the blast furnace helped the development of industrialization.

ing and living conditions before legislation brought improvements. The wealth they had created, however, made possible a more general prosperity.

Industrial Workers of the World (IWW), U.S. labor organization, founded in 1905 by revolutionary socialists to radicalize the labor movement. It reached its greatest influence 1912-17, and at its peak it had almost 100,000 members. Unlike the American Federation of Labor (AFL), it aimed not at improving labor conditions but at revolution. It lost support by attempting to exploit World War I; its strikes were considered treasonable. IWW leaders were imprisoned and the movement almost wholly suppressed.
See also: Labor movement.

Indus Valley civilization, centered around the Indus River in India and Pakistan, the earliest known urban culture of the Indian subcontinent. Superimposed on earlier stone- and bronze-using cultures dating from 4000 B.C., the Indus Valley civilization, with its main cities Harappa and Mohenjo-Daro, lasted from 2500 to 1750 B.C. About 100 of its towns and villages, some with citadels, have been identified.
See also: Indus River.

Inert gas *see:* Noble gas.

Inertia, in physics, tendency of a body to persist in its state of rest or motion. The term is sometimes used in psychology to describe latency or resistance to change.
See also: Motion; Newton, Sir Isaac.

Inertial guidance, method by which a vehicle is guided without contact with a ground base. Used primarily to guide missiles, airplanes, and submarines, inertial guidance provides navigation information through use of an *inertial navigator.* This device consists of a *gyroscope,* which indicates direction, and an *accelerometer,* which measures changes in speed and direction. Then a computer processes this information to calculate the vehicle's position and guide it. The inertial guidance system is based upon the ancient navigational technique by which speed and direction were used to calculate a vehicle's direction.
See also: Navigation.

Infant *see:* Baby.

Infantry, body of soldiers who fight on foot using light weaponry, such as rifles, machine guns, bazookas, mortars, and grenades. Despite the mechanization of warfare, infantry units still form the largest combat branch of most armies. In the U.S. army an infantry division consists of about 15,000 infantry members and normally includes 8 armored battalions equipped with tanks and heavy weapons.
See also: Army.

Infection, state or condition in which the body or a part of it is invaded by a pathogenic (disease-causing) microorganism or virus that, under favorable conditions, multiplies and produces effects that are injurious. Localized infection is usually accompanied by inflammation, but inflammation may occur without infection.
The 5 classical symptoms of infection listed by early medical writers are: (1) *dolor*—pain; (2) *calor*—heat; (3) *rubor*—redness; (4) *tumor*—swelling; (5) *functio laesa*—disordered function.
Pain is especially prominent when the infection is confined within closed cavities and is in proportion to the virulence and extent of the infection. Redness and swelling are not evident when infection is within some rigid tissue or deep within some cavity; they are more apparent when superficial structures are involved. In fact, "discoloration" would be a better term than "redness," for the color is more blue, or purple in advanced infections, while tuberculosis infections have long been called "white swellings." Heat may be evident on the surface, but there may be considerable elevation of body temperature even with small infections. "Disordered function" depends upon the part affected as well as upon the virulence. With almost all acute infections, there is either an absolute or relative increase of polymorphonuclear leukocytes in the blood.

Infertility, inability or diminished ability to produce offspring. Infertility affects about 15% of couples in the United States and the United Kingdom. Male fertility depends on adequate production of sperm by the testicles, unobstructed transit of sperm through the seminal tract, and satisfactory depositing of it within the vagina. Causes of impaired spermatogenesis include certain environmental poisons, undescended testicles, injury- or infection-related testicular atrophy, drug effects, prolonged fever, and endocrine disorders. Obstruction of the seminal tract may result from congenital defects and from inflammation of the testicles, epididymis, vas deferens, and prostate gland, and seminal surgical division of both vasa deferens (vasectomy). Defective delivery of sperm into the vagina may result from surgery of the bladder neck, removal of the prostate gland, hypospadias, premature ejaculation, functional or organic impotence, or structural abnormalities of the female genital tract.
Female infertility first of all depends on the ability to develop ova (eggs) in the ovaries. These eggs must be able to leave the ovaries and travel into and down the fallopian tubes. For sperm to be able to reach them, the structure of the vagina, cervix, and the main body of the uterus must not impair them, and the mucus surrounding the cervix must be abundant, clear, and elastic. The fallopian tubes must be clear, from the uterus up to the place where the sperm meet the eggs. In addition, after conception has occurred, the lining (endometrium) of the uterus must be able to take the implantation of the fertilized egg; otherwise, there will be an early miscarriage. Infertility in women can result from disease, disturbance, or deformity of any of these structures or functions. The most common reason for infertility is hormonal imbalance that affects the woman's ability to produce viable eggs or the type of cervical mucus that she produces. The fallopian tubes can become blocked by scars due to inflammation. There also may be some abnormality of the vulva, cervix, or uterus.
See also: Reproduction.

Infinity (∞), quantity greater than any finite quantity. In modern mathematics infinity is viewed in 2 ways. In one, the word has a definite meaning; and with transfinite cardinal numbers, for example, it may have a plurality of meanings. In the other, infinity is seen as a limit: to say that parallel lines intersect at infinity, for example, means merely that the point of intersection of 2 lines may be made to recede indefinitely by making the lines more and more nearly parallel. Similarly, in $f(x)=1/x$ it is meaningful to say that $f(x)$ tends to infinity as x tends to zero; again, the sequence $1,2,3,....n$ tends to infinity because, however large n is chosen, there is an $(n+1)$ greater than it. In advanced set theory an infinite set is defined as one whose elements can be put in a one-to-one correspondence with those of a proper subset of the set (i.e., a subset that is not the whole set).
See also: Set theory.

Inflation, in economics, decline in the value of money, which implies a general increase in the prices of commodities and services. Deflation means the opposite—generally falling prices, usually accompanied by lower profits and fewer jobs. Times of mild inflation are usually characterized by high employment, with factories producing near their capacities to capture the increased amount of currency available. Once full employment has been reached and factories begin operating at or near capacity, however, additional increases in national spending drive prices higher at a rapidly increasing rate. The reason for this is that a relatively static amount of goods and services is being "chased" by an increased number of dollars. Further increases in spending or shortages in goods and services lead to rapid inflation. Industries raise prices because their costs are going up. In turn, labor asks for higher wages to offset the increase in the cost of living. Extreme inflation can lead to major disruption in the social order. People buy property, stock, or commodities, expecting a rapid increase in value. Prices can rise out of proportion to real value. In the United States, inflation averaged less than 1% yearly during the 1950s and about 3% in the 1960s. Since then, inflation has been considerably greater, averaging over 6% for 1970-77, with periods of double-digit (10% or greater) inflation at the end of the decade and into the 1980s. Government attempts to limit the impact of runaway inflation through monetary and fiscal policies, as well as "jawboning," that is, making public speeches to apply political pressure to corporations and labor unions to act in the public interest. Similar tactics, as well as

the limited power of the presidential veto, can be used against congressional spending proposals that are deemed inflationary.
See also: Economics.

Inflection, in grammar, changes in form that words undergo with each change in grammatical function. For example, the English verb *write* becomes *writes* in the third person singular of the present tense. *Write* has 3 additional forms: *wrote, written,* and *writing.* This set of inflections for a verb is called *conjugation.* The set of inflections for a noun or pronoun is called *declension.* For example, the English noun *dog* has 4 forms: *dog, dogs, dog's,* and *dogs'.*
See also: Grammar.

Inflorescence, arrangement of flowers on the stem of a plant. Tulips and anemones, among other plants, carry single flowers at the tops of their stems. Most plants, however, carry their flowers in clusters called *inflorescences.* This is especially true of those species whose individual flowers are small. The inflorescence is thought to be more attractive to pollinating insects than a single flower would be. The commonest type of inflorescence is the *raceme,* in which numerous flowers are borne on one or more sides of the main stem. The oldest flowers are always at the bottom. The individual flowers normally have short stalks. If they are stalkless the inflorescence is often called a *spike.* The foxglove is a typical raceme. In the *corymb* the individual flower stalks on the lower part of the stem are longer than those higher up. The result is that all the flowers are brought to more or less the same level and make a conspicuous display. In the *umbel,* which looks similar to the corymb, the main stem stops growing after a while and all the flower stalks come from one point. The oldest flowers are on the outside. Umbels are characteristic of the carrot family. The *cyme* is an inflorescence in which the main stem produces only 1 or 2 side shoots before ending in a flower. Each of the side shoots then does the same. Where 2 branches are formed each time, there is a continued forking of the stem, with a flower in the center of each fork. There are several other kinds of inflorescence. The dandelion or daisy head, for example, is a very condensed inflorescence called a *capitulum.* Very often the flowering shoot will produce several branches, and each branch may then form a raceme, a corymb, or an umbel. Branched inflorescences of this kind are called *panicles.*

Influenza, specific acute respiratory disease caused by viruses and characterized by fever, head cold, cough, headache, malaise, and inflamed mucous membranes of the respiratory tract. It usually occurs as an epidemic in the winter. Hemorrhage, bronchitis, pneumonia, and sometimes death occur in severe cases. Acute epidemics occur about every 3 years. Persons at high risk of developing severe diseases are those with chronic lung disease, heart valve disease, or congestive heart failure; pregnant women in the third trimester; and elderly persons who are confined to bed. The antiviral drug amantadine has a beneficial effect on fever and respiratory symptoms if given early in uncomplicated influenza. It is of no benefit when the illness is complicated with pneumonia, but might improve recovery from a lung infection. The basic treatment otherwise is the relief of symptoms. Aspirin, paracetamol, and other drugs to lower the temperature and relieve pain are helpful. Vaccines that include the prevalent strains of influenza viruses have a 60% chance of reducing the incidence of infection for 1 to 2 years after vaccination. The immunity is less when the virus changes appreciably (antigenic drift) and when a major viral mutation occurs (antigenic shift). No significant protection is afforded unless the new strain is incorporated into the vaccine. Vaccination is especially important for the aged and for those with heart, lung, or other chronic diseases.

Information Agency, U.S. (USIA), independent, U.S. government agency that conducts international communication, education, cultural, and exchange programs to foster understanding between the citizens of the United States and those of other nations. It performs a variety of communication activities, using academic and cultural exhibits, newspapers, and films. Founded in 1953 and headquartered in Washington, D.C., the USIA brings worldwide leaders in politics, social welfare, and other fields to meet with their colleagues in the United States.

Information theory, or communication theory, mathematical discipline that aims to maximize the information that can be conveyed by communications systems and minimize the errors that arise in the course of transmission. The information content of a message is conventionally quantified in terms of bits (binary digits). Each bit represents a simple alternative: in terms of a message, a yes or no; in terms of the components in an electrical circuit, that a switch is open or closed. Mathematically the bit is usually represented as 0 or 1. Complex messages can be represented as a series of bit alternatives. Five bits of information only are needed to specify any letter of the alphabet, given an appropriate code. Thus able to quantify information, the theory employs statistical methods to analyze practical communications problems. The errors that arise in the transmission of signals, often termed *noise,* can be minimized by the incorporation of redundancy, wherein more bits of information than are strictly necessary to encode a message are transmitted so that if some are altered in transmission there is still enough information to allow the signal to be correctly interpreted. The handling of redundant information costs something in reduced speed of or capacity for transmission, but the reduction in message errors compensates for this loss. Information theoreticians often point to an analogy between the thermodynamic concept of entropy and the degree of misinformation in a signal.
See also: Mathematics.

Infrared rays, rays resembling light rays, but undetectable by the human eye. Also called *heat rays,* infrared rays are given off by objects in relation to their temperature. Emission of infrared rays increases as an object gets hotter. The British astronomer Sir William Herschel discovered infrared rays in 1800 by observing the effect of the heat they produced. The *sniperscope* is an instrument that perceives infrared rays from objects that are warmer than their surroundings. The military utilizes infrared radiation and the sniperscope in missile detection, guidance systems, and night-vision apparatus.
See also: Electromagnetic waves.

Inge, William (1913-73), U.S. playwright. He was noted for psychological studies of life in small Midwestern towns, in such plays as *Come Back, Little Sheba* (1950), *Picnic* (1953), which won a Pulitzer Prize, *Bus Stop* (1955), and *A Loss of Roses* (1959).

Ingres, Jean Auguste Dominique (1780-1867), French neoclassical painter. He is known for his mastery of line and superb draftsmanship. *The Vow of Louis XII* (1824) won him acclaim as the foremost classicist of his time, but today he is better known for portraits and nude studies such as the *Odalisque* (1814). A disciple of Raphael, he was a determined opponent of the romantic movement and an inspiration to many later artists, including Edgar Degas, Pierre-Auguste Renoir, and Pablo Picasso.

The Turkish Bath, *painted by Ingres in 1863 (Louvre, Paris).*

Inheritance tax, assessment on property bequeathed by a deceased person to a specific legatee. It thus differs from an estate tax, levied on a deceased person's estate as a whole. In the United States most states levy both estate and inheritance taxes; since 1916 the federal government has levied only an estate tax.
See also: Taxation.

Initiative, referendum, and recall, methods by which voters may directly intervene to influence government policy between elections. Initiative, provided for in most U.S. states, is a procedure whereby a new law is proposed in a petition, then submitted to a vote by the legislature or electorate or both. Laws so passed are generally not subject to veto. Referendum allows citizens a direct vote on proposed laws and policies. A referendum may be demanded by petition, but in most U.S. states it is mandatory for measures such as constitutional amendments and bond issues. Recall, adopted by many cities and some states, provides for the removal of an elected official by calling a special election. Such an election must usually be demanded in a petition whose signers number at least 25% of the votes originally received by the official. Recall has rarely succeeded at state level.

Injunction, formal written court order commanding or prohibiting any act. An injunction may be temporary, pending the outcome of a court action, or permanent, if the court's decision confirms the injunction's validity. Such writs are widely applied to prevent, for example, the misuse of property; the wrongful denial of, or cancellation of membership in, a union or other organization; the infringement of copyrights or patents; violent action in labor-management disputes; or the removal of a child from the care of a parent. Violation of an injunction is punishable as contempt of court. In Topeka, Kans., in 1954, an injunction forbade the exclusion of a black student from a segregated school.

Ink, liquid or paste used for writing or printing. Writing inks were used as early as c.2500 B.C. by Egyptians and Chinese, who created ink from natural materials such as berries, bark, linseed oil, and soot. Today, there are thousands of kinds of inks, used both in the printing industry and in ballpoint and fountain pens for writing. Most printing inks contain pigments, as opposed to dyes. Vehicles, which carry the pigment and help bind it to the paper, vary greatly in printing. Thick, sticky inks are used in the printing of books and magazines, and many contain *driers* to speed up the chemical reaction of oxidation and help the ink dry faster. Most writing ink consists of dyes and resins dissolved in a solvent, such as water and *glycol*, an alcohol.

Inness, George (1825-94), U.S. landscape painter. His best-known works, such as *The Lackawanna Valley* (1855), show the influence of Jean-Baptiste Camille Corot and the Barbizon school. Another principal work is *June* (1882). His later work, such as *The Home of the Heron* (1893), is less realistic and more atmospheric.

Innocence *see:* Bluet.

Innocent, name of 13 popes. **Saint Innocent I** (d.417) was pope from 401. He championed papal supremacy, but failed to prevent the sack of Rome by Alaric in 410. **Innocent II** (Gregorio Papareschi; d.1143) was pope from 1130. He convened the Second Lateral Council (1139). **Innocent III** (Giovanni Lotario de'Conti; 1161-1216) was pope from 1198. Under him the medieval papacy reached the summit of its power and influence. In an assertion of temporal power he forced King John of England to become his vassal and had Holy Roman Emperor Otto deposed in favor of Frederick II. He initiated the Fourth Crusade (1202) and supported the crusade against the Albigenses (1208). He presided over the Fourth Lateran Council (1215), the culmination of the entire medieval papacy. **Innocent IV** (Sinibaldo de'Fieschi; c.1190-1254), pope from 1243, clashed with Emperor Frederick II over the temporal power of the papacy, and was forced to flee to Lyons, France, until Frederick's death. He worked for the unification of the Christian churches. **Innocent VIII** (Giovanni Battista Cibo; 1432-92), pope from 1484, was worldly and unscrupulous. He fomented the witchcraft hysteria and meddled in Italian politics. For a fee he kept the brother and rival of Sultan Bayazid II imprisoned. **Innocent XI** (Benedetto Odescalchi; 1611-89) was pope from 1676. An opponent of quietism, he favored toleration of Protestantism, and over this and the issue of papal power clashed with Louis XIV of France. **Innocent XII** (Antonio Pignatelli; 1615-1700) was pope from 1691. A stern reformer, he abolished nepotism and was renowned for his piety and charity. **Innocent XIII** (Michelangelo Conti; 1655-1724) was pope from 1721. He bestowed Naples and Sicily on their de facto possessor, the Emperor Charles VI, and recognized the claims of James, the Old Pretender, to the British throne in the hope of a Catholic revival.

Innsbruck (pop. 116,100), capital of the Austrian Tyrol province, located on the Inn River, at an altitude of 1,880 ft (573 m) between steep Alpine ranges. Innsbruck became a prosperous town mainly because of its position near the Brenner Pass. Modern manufactures include textiles, chemicals, metal goods, and mosaics. There are many notable medieval castles in the city, including the 15th-century castle Fürstenburg. Innsbruck University was founded in the 17th century. The city is noted for the scenic beauty of its surroundings and is a popular tourist center in both winter and summer.
See also: Austria.

Inoculation, introduction of a germ, a poison produced by a germ, or serum into the body to set up the production of antibodies that will subsequently protect the individual from an attack of the disease, rendering the individual immune.
See also: Immunization.

Inouye, Daniel Ken (1924-), U.S. senator from Hawaii (1962-). A member of the Watergate committee (1972-74), Inouye was chairman of the 1987 congressional committee that investigated the Iran-Contra Affair.

Input-output analysis, method of studying the relationship between various parts of the economy, developed by U.S. economist Wassily Leontif. It relies upon the use of complex numerical tables.
See also: Economics.

Inquest, formal legal inquiry to ascertain a fact. It is most commonly used to investigate death under circumstances where violence is suspected. The coroner, or in some cases a medical examiner, invites the jury to view the body. Then, depending on the evidence presented, the jury decides whether to order a post-mortem examination. It may recommend that a suspect be detained for trial. Inquests are also held to determine damages in cases where the defendant has not appeared in court. The institution is rooted in early English law.

Inquisition, medieval agency of the Roman Catholic Church to combat heresy, first made official in 1231 when Pope Gregory IX appointed a commission of Dominicans to investigate heresy among the Albigensians of southern France. It aimed to save the heretic's soul, but a refusal to recant was punished by fines, penance, or imprisonment, and often by confiscation of land by the secular authorities. Later the penalty was death by burning. Torture, condemned by the former popes, was permitted in heresy trials by Innocent IV (d. 1254). The accused were not told the name of their accusers but could name their known enemies so that hostile testimony might be discounted. Often the Inquisition was subject to political manipulation. In 1524 it was reconstituted to counter Protestantism in Italy; its modern descendant is the Congregation of the Doctrine of the Faith.
The Spanish Inquisition, founded in 1478 by Ferdinand and Isabella, was a branch of government and was distinct from the papal institution. Its first commission was to investigate Jews and Muslims who had publicly embraced Christianity but secretly held to Judaism or Islam. Under the grand inquisitor Torquemada, it became an agency of official terror—even St. Ignatius Loyola was investigated. It was extended to Portugal and South America and not dissolved until 1820.
See also: Torquemada, Tomás de.

Insect, member of the class Insecta, phylum Arthropoda, or invertebrate animals with jointed legs. There are about 750,000 known species of insects, and more are being discovered every year.
Anatomy. The body of an insect, like that of other arthropods, is covered by a hard, waterproof "shell" that forms an external skeleton to which the muscles are attached. The head bears jaws and other structures for dealing with food. It also carries several sense organs, including the compound eyes made up of clusters of separate units. The antennae, or feelers, are organs of touch, smell, and occasionally of hearing. Sense organs are also found on other parts of the body: Grasshoppers and crickets have ears on the legs or thorax, and houseflies have tastebuds on their feet. The middle section, or thorax, bears the limbs. It consists of 3 parts, each of which carries a pair of jointed legs ending in hooks that

allow the insect to hang on walls or ceilings. Two pairs of wings sprout from the back of the thorax. Some insects have no wings, and the flies have turned one pair into balancing organs. The abdomen is the largest section of the body and has no visible external organs except those concerned with reproduction and occasionally a pair of short sense organs, such as antennae called cerci (for example, in earwigs). Insects do not have a closed system of blood vessels. The heart simply pumps blood through the arteries to the extremities, where it washes around the organs and slowly drains back to the heart. Nor do insects have lungs. Air is carried into the body down minute tubes, called tracheae, which run from openings in the skin into each organ.

Life cycles. Most insects lay eggs, but some give birth to live young. The mother usually abandons her eggs, but the social insects, including bees and wasps, have elaborate systems of caring for their young. The eggs hatch into larvae, such as the maggots of flies, the caterpillars of butterflies and moths, and the nymphs of dragonflies. The development into an adult insect is accomplished in one of two ways. (1) *Incomplete metamorphosis*: In dragonflies, grasshoppers, and others, the newly hatched larva looks rather like the adult. It molts several times, shedding its skin each time and growing a little larger. Adult features such as wings become more apparent at each molt until, at the final molt, the adult insect crawls out of the old skin. (2) *Complete metamorphosis*: The larva is very different from the adult. After growing for some time, it changes into the adult in one drastic step. To do this it forms a pupa or chrysalis in which it can reorganize its structure. In this way a sausage-shaped caterpillar turns into a butterfly. A single insect is able to exploit 2 very different ways of life. Thus a caterpillar feeds on leaves and a butterfly drinks nectar.

Habitat. Insects vary in size from almost microscopic wasps to the huge extinct dragonflies with wingspans of over 2 ft (61

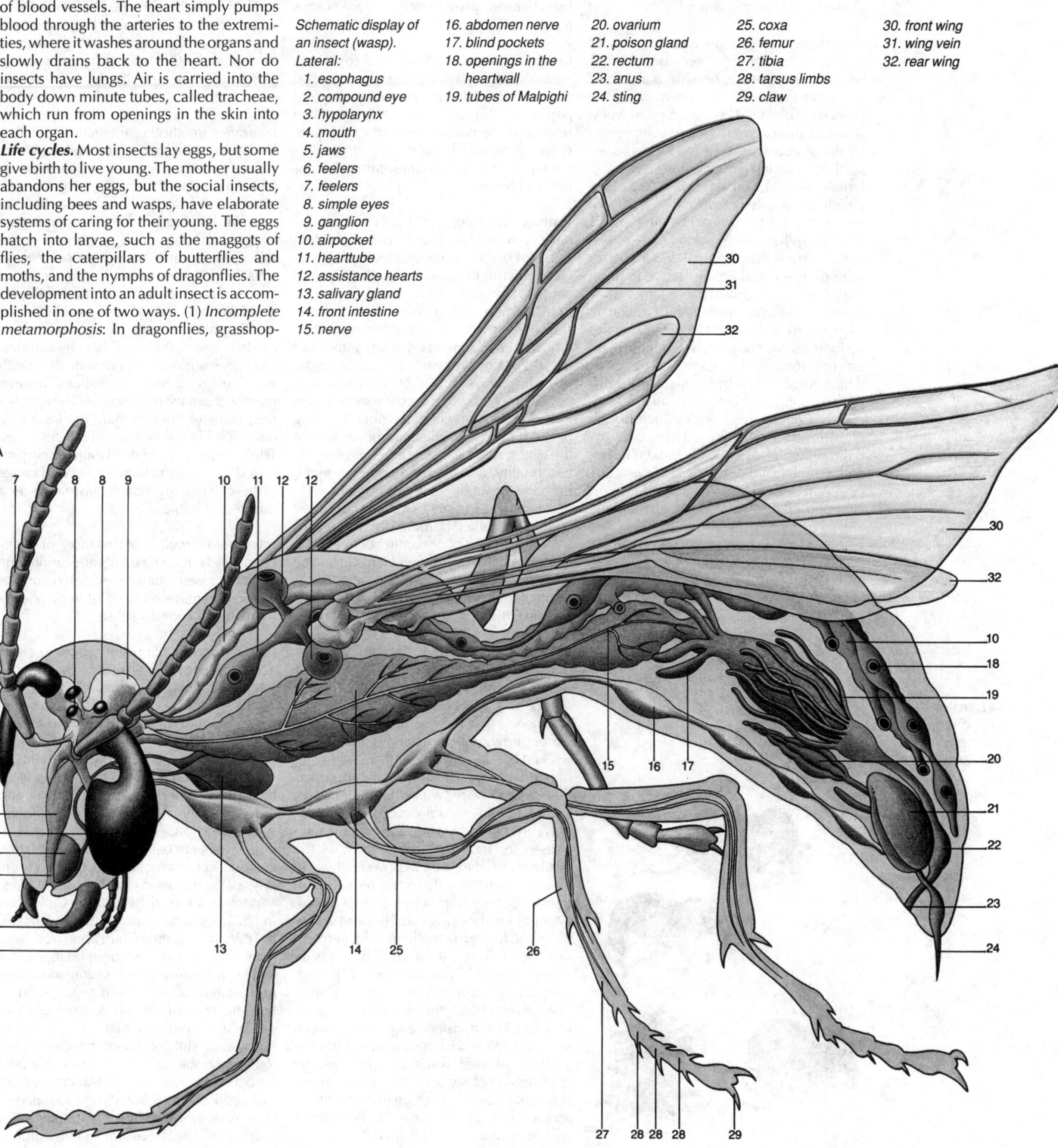

Schematic display of an insect (wasp). Lateral:
1. esophagus
2. compound eye
3. hypolarynx
4. mouth
5. jaws
6. feelers
7. feelers
8. simple eyes
9. ganglion
10. airpocket
11. hearttube
12. assistance hearts
13. salivary gland
14. front intestine
15. nerve
16. abdomen nerve
17. blind pockets
18. openings in the heartwall
19. tubes of Malpighi
20. ovarium
21. poison gland
22. rectum
23. anus
24. sting
25. coxa
26. femur
27. tibia
28. tarsus limbs
29. claw
30. front wing
31. wing vein
32. rear wing

cm). They live in many different environments, boring into wood, burrowing underground, living in other animals, and swimming underwater. They are found in the hottest deserts, on the coasts of Antarctica, in hot springs, and in the saltiest lakes (such as Salt Lake, Utah); the petroleum fly lives in pools of crude petroleum oil in California. They may also exist in huge numbers. Locust swarms may contain 1 billion individuals, and springtails form dense carpets on the ground.

Insecticide, any substance toxic to insects and used to control them in situations where they cause economic damage or endanger the health of humans and their domestic animals. There are 3 main types: stomach insecticides, which are ingested by the insects with their food; contact insecticides, which penetrate the cuticle (exterior covering); and fumigant insecticides, which are inhaled. Stomach insecticides are often used to control chewing insects like caterpillars and sucking insects like aphids. They may be applied to a plant prior to attack and remain active in or on the plant for a considerable time. They must be used with considerable caution on food plants or animal forage. Examples include arsenic compounds, which remain on the leaf, and organic compounds, which are absorbed by the plant and transported to all its parts (systemic insecticides). Contact insecticides include the plant products nicotine, derris, and pyrethrum, which are quickly broken down, and synthetic compounds such as DDT (and other chlorinated hydrocarbons), organophosphates (malathion, parathion), and carbamates. Polychlorinated biphenyls (PCBs) are added to some insecticides to increase their effectiveness and persistence. Highly persistent insecticides may be concentrated in food chains and exert harmful effects on other animals such as birds and fish.
See also: Insect.

The common shrew, an insectivore, consumes its own weight in food each day.

Insectivore, order (Insectivora) of small insect-eating mammals, regarded as the most primitive group of placental mammals, having diverged little from the ancestral form. The skull is generally long and narrow, with a primitively large complement of unspecialized teeth in the jaw. Ears and eyes are small and often hidden in fur or skin. The group includes shrews, hedgehogs, and moles.

Insectivorous plant *see:* Carnivorous plant.

Installment plan, system of credit by which merchandise is paid for over a fixed period of time in installments known as deferred payments. Normally, part of the purchase price must be paid at the time of the sale. Goods generally bought using an installment plan are automobiles, farm machinery, and homes.

Instinct, in biology and psychology, behaviors in reaction to external stimuli that have not been consciously learned. It is in fact difficult to separate such inherited genetic behaviors from those stemming from learned and environmental factors, since higher animals placed from birth in artificial environments display some, but not all, instinctive reactions characteristic of their species. It has been further suggested that embryos may have some learning ability—that is, that some learning before birth is possible. Numbered among the instincts are the sex drive, aggression, territoriality, and the food urge, but much debate surrounds such classification. In psychology, "instinct" (sometimes called "drive") is studied particularly with regard to the frustration of or conflict between the existence of two fundamental instincts: the life instinct, akin to the libido, and its opposite, the death instinct.
See also: Biology; Psychology.

Insulation, inhibiting or limiting the conduction of electricity or heat through the use of specific materials. An electric current or voltage is contained by materials (insulators) that offer a high resistance to current flow, will withstand high voltages without breaking down, and will not deteriorate with age. The mechanical properties desired vary with the application: Cables require flexible coatings, such as polyvinyl chloride, while glass or porcelain is used for rigid mountings, such as the insulators used to support power cables. In thermal insulation, there is a reduction of transfer of heat from a hot area to a cold. Thermal insulation is used to keep something hot, to keep something cold, or maintain something at a roughly steady temperature. Heat is transferred through conduction, convection, and radiation. The vacuum bottle thus uses 3 techniques to reduce heat transfers: a vacuum between the walls to combat conduction and convection; silvered walls to minimize the transmission of radiant heat from one wall and maximize its reflection from the other; and supports for the inner bottle made of cork, a poor thermal conductor.

Insulin, protein hormone manufactured in the pancreas by minute areas of tissue called the islets of Langerhans, and then secreted into the blood, where it controls the digestion of carbohydrates. A lack of insulin or a disturbance of its use by the cells is the cause of diabetes.
See also: Diabetes; Hormone.

Insull, Samuel (1859-1938), English-born U.S. financier. Secretary to Thomas Edison in the 1880s, he became head of the Chicago Edison Co. and built a huge conglomerate supplying electricity throughout Illinois and other states. It collapsed in 1932. Later he was tried for fraud and acquitted.

Insurance, method of financial protection by which one party undertakes to indemnify another against certain forms of loss. An insurance company pools the payments for this service and invests them to earn further funds. Each insured person pays a relatively small amount, the premium, for a stated period of coverage. In return the company will, subject to an assessment of a claim, reimburse the insured for loss caused by an event covered in the policy. Forms of insurance have existed since the earliest civilizations. Modern insurance began with the medieval guilds, which sometimes insured members against trade losses. The specialized fields of fire and maritime insurance developed in the 17th and 18th centuries. The development of probability theory allowed the statistical likelihood of damage to be calculated, making insurance as a business possible.

Integrated circuit, combination of interconnected circuit elements and amplifying devices inseparately associated on or within a continuous layer of semiconductor material, called a substrate.

Integration, in U.S. history, right to equal access for people of all races to such facilities as schools, churches, housing, and public accommodations. It became an issue of public importance in the United States after the Civil War and the pasage of the 13th, 14th, and 15th amendments to the Constitution, 1864-70, which declared the African American free and equal, and the Civil Rights Act of 1866. Although slavery was ended as a legal institution, state laws were passed during the reaction against Reconstruction to enforce the physical segregation of blacks and whites. Tennessee adopted the first "Jim Crow" law in 1875, segregating public transportation. In 1896 the Supreme Court approved "separate but equal" accommodations for blacks, following which segregation laws proliferated. In the North segregation in housing created the black slum ghettos; while less common than in the South, segregation still continued in factories, unions, and restaurants. In 1910 the National Association for the Advancement of Colored People (NAACP) was founded in New York, followed by the National Urban League in 1911. Several activist groups were formed in the 1940s, including the Congress of Racial Equality (CORE). The NAACP won its greatest legal victories in 1954 and 1955, when the Supreme Court outlawed segregation in the public schools and ordered that integration be implemented "with all deliberate speed." Among black leaders advocating passive resistance to discriminatory local laws was Martin Luther King, Jr. His Southern Christian Leadership Conference and the more radical Student Non-Violent Coordinating Committee exerted political pressure to enact the Civil Rights Act of 1964 and the Voting Rights Act of 1965. Integration was more generally accepted during the 1970s, although serious unrest occurred over busing practices to end school segregation in many cities.

Intelligence, mental ability, including learning ability, problem-solving ability, and the capacity for abstract thinking. There has been much debate as to whether intelligence is inherited or a product of the environment. The fact is that physical constitution may contain developmental potentialities, but the environment decides to what extent and in what ways these potentialities are realized. Heredity and environment interact to such a degree that a clear distinction between their contributions is often impossible.

Intelligence quotient (IQ), index of intelligence determined through a subject's answers to arbitrarily chosen questions. The IQ is merely a standard score that places an individual in reference to the scores of others within his or her age group. Mental age represents the age level corresponding to the score reached on the test. Thus, if a child 10 years old gives a test score appropriate to that of the average 12-year-old child, his or her mental age would be 12 and his or her IQ is 120. This method works reasonably well for younger children but has grave disadvantages when applied to older children or adults. In psychological literature, the following classification is found:

Above 140	"Near" genius or genius
120-140	Very superior intelligence
110-120	Superior intelligence
90-110	Average intelligence
80-90	Dull normal
70-80	Borderline deficiency
50-70	Educable mentally retarded
30-50	Trainable
20-30	Severely mentally retarded

See also: Binet, Alfred.

Intelligence service, institution of a national government that gathers information; particularly about clandestine activities of other countries or enemies, for the purpose of protecting national security. Such functions were once performed chiefly by foreign ambassadors. Under Elizabeth I, England was among the first Western countries to set up an elaborate intelligence service, privately financed by Sir Francis Walsingham. Joseph Fouché established an equally vital network for Napoleonic France. Britain's intelligence service reached its highest point during World War II, with the brilliant amateurs of MI-5. In the United States, military espionage first assumed great importance during the Civil War, in which it was employed extensively by both sides. During World War I the U.S. intelligence service was organized largely by the Office of Strategic Services (OSS). It was given its present form in 1947 with the creation of the Central Intelligence Agency (CIA). The CIA, which came under investigation and some censure in the late 1970s, coordinates the intelligence functions of all government departments and agencies. All the armed services have their own intelligence branches.

Intelligence test *see:* Intelligence quotient; Testing.

Inter-American conferences *see:* Pan-American conferences.

Intercontinental ballistic missile *see:* Guided missile.

Interest, money paid for the use of money loaned. It is generally expressed as a percentage of the principal (sum loaned) per period (usually per year or per month). In *simple interest*, interest is calculated on the basis of the sum loaned. In *compound interest*, interest is paid on the principal plus the accumulated interest, recalculated periodically. Actual payments for compound interest are thus higher (and more complex to calculate). *Discount interest* is subtracted from the principal before the money is given to the borrower.

Interference, in physics, mutual action of waves of any kind upon each other, by which their vibrations and effects are increased, diminished, or neutralized. In information science the term is used to denote the occurrence of unwanted signals that degrade the quality of wanted signals.
See also: Physics.

Interferometer, any instrument of measurement employing interference effects of waves. Interferometers are used for measuring the wavelengths of light, radio, sound, or other wave phenomena or the refractive index of gases. Some interferometers measure very small distances using radiation of known wavelength. In acoustics and radio astronomy, they are used for determining the direction of an energy source. In most interferometers the beam of incoming radiation is divided in two, led along paths of different but accurately adjustable lengths, and then recombined to give an interference pattern. Perhaps the best-known optical instrument is the Michelson interferometer devised in 1881. More accurate for wavelength measurements is the Fabry-Perot interferometer, in which the radiation is recombined after multiple partial reflections between parallel, lightly silvered glass plates.
See also: Interference.

Interferon, class of small soluble proteins produced and released by cells invaded by a virus, that inhibits viral multiplication. Interferon production may also be induced by certain bacteria and specifically sensitized lymphocytes. There are indications that interferon may be useful in the treatment of certain types of cancer. A nasal spray containing interferon produced in the laboratory prevented between 78% and 84% of colds caused by rhinoviruses in families participating in 2 independent studies published in January 1986 in the *New England Journal of Medicine*.
See also: Cancer.

Interior, Department of the, department of the executive branch of the federal government, headed by the secretary of the interior. Founded in 1849, its original task was to administer the census and Indian affairs and to regulate the exploitation of natural resources. Today it has 5 major areas of responsibility, each in the charge of an assistant secretary: Fish, Wildlife, Parks, and Marine Resources; Mineral Resources; Water and Power Development; Water Quality and Research; and Public Land Management (which includes the Office of the Territories, and the Bureau of Indian Affairs).

Interior decoration, design and arrangement of decorative elements in a home or public building. Until relatively recently, architectural and interior styles were almost inseparable and the names used to characterize each period applied both to the architecture of buildings and their interior decor.

Interior decoration in the French rococo period: oval salon at Hotel Soubise in Paris, decorated 1736-39 by Germain Boffrand.

Interleukin, generic term for a group of proteins, formed in white blood cells known as leucocytes, that activate the body's immune system. There are 3 types of interleukin: IL-1, IL-2, and IL-3. All 3 act in concert to remove or destroy any harmful bacteria or foreign substance that invades the body.
See also: Immunity.

Internal combustion engine, heat engine in which fuel is burned inside the engine itself. It contrasts with an external combustion engine (such as the steam engine), in which fuel is burned in a separate furnace. By far the most common type of internal combustion engine is the gasoline engine, which propels practically all automobiles. Another common type is the diesel engine used in trucks and many locomotives and ships. Both types work in a similar way, burning fuel inside closed cylinders to produce reciprocating (to and fro) motion of pistons. As machines, these engines are very inefficient. The gasoline engine can convert only about 20% of the heat energy released by burning fuel into useful work. The diesel engine is a little more efficient, being able to utilize some 30% of the energy released. Gas turbines and jet and rocket engines can also be classified as internal combustion engines, although they are of a rather different kind. They burn fuel continuously in a combustion chamber, generating hot gases that spin turbines or producing propulsive thrust by reaction.
See also: Engine.

Internal medicine, medical specialty that focuses on disorders of the internal body structures of adults. Through asking questions and administering a thorough physical exam, a practitioner called an *internist* concentrates upon all the organ systems. He or she interprets all the information in order to make an evaluation and determine treatment.
See also: Medicine.

Internal revenue, income a government takes in from its own sources, such as excise, sales, payroll, estate, income, and gift taxes. About 95% of the total U.S. revenue comes from its internal revenue, as opposed to outside revenue such as income from import and export duties. The U.S. government collects about $700 billion a year from the sum of its various types of internal revenue.
See also: Taxation.

Internal Revenue Service (IRS), agency of the U.S. Department of the Treasury created by Congress in 1789 to assess and collect domestic or "internal" taxes. These include federal taxes on goods and services, income taxes, and corporate taxes, as well as gift and estate taxes. The service is headed by a commissioner of internal revenue appointed by the president. Its headquarters are in Washington, D.C., and it has 7 regional and 58 district offices. IRS rules are based on the Internal Revenue Code, a huge compilation of tax laws passed by Congress and interpreted through regulations issued by the IRS. As administered by the agency, the tax system has been called inequitable and inefficient by some critics, who claim that IRS regulations are intricate, confusing, and frequently not fully understood even by the IRS itself. To gain the full benefit of the tax laws, taxpayers must often buy the services of expert tax accountants.
See also: Taxation.

International, The, common name of a number of socialist-communist revolutionary organizations. Three of these have had historical significance. The First International, officially the International Working Men's Association, was formed under the leadership of Karl Marx in London in 1864 with the aim of uniting workers of all nations to realize the ideals of the *Communist Manifesto.* Divisions grew between reformers and violent revolutionaries; these became increasingly bitter, culminating in the expulsion of the faction led by Mikhail Bakunin after a leadership struggle in 1872. The association broke up in 1876. The Second, commonly called the Socialist International, was founded in Paris in 1889 by a group of socialist parties that later made their headquarters in Brussels. The leading social democratic parties, including those of Germany and Russia, were represented. Among the representatives were Jean Jaurés, Ramsay MacDonald, Lenin, and Trotsky. The Second International influenced international labor affairs until World War I, when it broke up. The Third or Communist International, generally known as the Comintern, was founded by Lenin in 1919 in an attempt to win the leadership of world socialism; Zionview was its first president. Soviet-dominated from the outset, it aimed, in the 1920s, to foment world revolution. In the 1930s, under Stalin, it sought contacts with less extreme left-wing groups abroad, to assuage foreign hostility. Stalin dissolved it in 1943 as a wartime conciliatory gesture to the Allies.

International Bank for Reconstruction and Development *see:* World Bank.

International code *see:* Morse code.

International Court of Justice, highest judicial organ of the United Nations, founded in 1946 to provide a peaceful means of settling international disputes according to the principles of international law. Like its predecessor under the League of Nations, the World Court, it sits at The Hague, the Netherlands. In practice its authority is limited by frequent refusals of various states to accept its decisions.
See also: Hague, The; International law; United Nations.

International Criminal Police Organization *see:* Interpol.

International Date Line, imaginary line that runs down the middle of the Pacific Ocean and mostly follows the 180th meridian. Its purpose is to mark the spot on the earth's surface where each new calendar day begins. Clocks are set 1 hour earlier for every 15° ($^1/_{24}$ of the 360° circle) westward around the globe. A full circuit would move back the calendar as well as the clock. It has thus been necessary, particularly with the advent of rapid global communication and travel, to institute an arbitrary date line. When Tuesday is dawning just east of this line, Wednesday is dawning just west. Thus Japan is one of the first countries to reach the new day, while the United States is one of the last.

International language *see:* Universal language.

International law, body of laws assumed to be binding among nations by virtue of their general acceptance. The beginnings of international law lay in attempts to humanize the conduct of war. The seminal work of Hugo Grotius, *On the Law of War and Peace* (1625), was one such; he also formulated several important principles, including a legal basis for the sovereignty of states. The works of Grotius and his successors were widely acclaimed but never officially accepted; however, legal principles were increasingly incorporated into international agreements such as the Congress of Vienna as well as into the constitution of the United Nations. International laws may arise through multilateral or bilateral agreements, as with the Geneva Convention, or simply by long-established custom, as with a large part of maritime law. In some cases, as with the war crimes rulings of the Nuremberg trials, they may be said to arise retrospectively. Because few nations are willing to relinquish any sovereignty, the law lacks a true legislative body and an effective executive to enforce it. The International Court of Justice is the international judicial body, and the UN in the process of compiling an international legal code is the nearest thing to a legislature, but these bodies are limited by the willingness of states to accept their decisions. These difficulties have led some theorists to deny international law true legal status, but this is an extreme view. The need for international rules is widely recognized, as shown by the increasing tendency to anticipate problem areas such as space exploration and exploitation of seabed resources and to attempt to develop international rules to regulate them.

International relations, relationships between nations, through politics, treaties, military confrontation or cooperation, economics, or culture. Peacetime contact is generally maintained through diplomacy; each nation maintains embassies in other countries it recognizes as nations. Even when states do not maintain mutual embassies, however, they may find it desirable to keep contacts open, often through the offices of a third nation. The other primary link is through membership in various international organizations, either for global politics (e.g., United Nations), defense (NATO), or simply mutual convenience (Universal Postal Union). From 1946 on international relations were dominated by the concept of the Cold War, in which the complications of world diplomacy were reduced to an oversimplified model of an ideological contest between 2 global antagonists, the communist and capitalist systems as personified by the Soviet Union and the United States. In the 1960s the rise of the Third World countries negated this simple division, though many of these countries took one or the other side. In the 1970s relations between the United States and the Soviet Union improved, largely through trade and nuclear limitation agreements and also because of the rise of China as a rival superpower. The endurance and value of the resulting détente, however, remained doubtful as the 1980s saw new—and continuing—areas of conflict between the superpowers. In 1990, the Charter of Paris for a New Europe was signed by the United States and the Soviet Union, effectively ending the Cold War.

International System of Units *see:* Metric system.

International trade, or world trade, exchange of goods and services between nations. Since the 18th century it has become a vital element in world prosperity, largely because it is thought more profitable for countries to specialize in producing goods in which such factors as natural resources, climatic conditions, availability of raw materials, and a skilled labor force or low labor costs give them a special advantage. This is known as the international division of labor. Some countries, such as Japan, rely largely on exports; U.S. exports amount to 15% of the world total, but are less vital to the country's economy. In prehistoric times the amber route carried trade between tribes thousands of miles apart. The ancient Greeks, Romans, and Phoenicians were active traders. Chinese merchants penetrated most of Asia, and Arabs operated trade routes on the Indian Ocean and in Africa. Most explorers before the 20th century sought to open trade routes. Early trade was largely in goods yielding high prices on small amounts because of the difficulty of transportation. Only with modern transport did international trade become economically vital. After World War II efforts were made to promote free trade throughout the world. In 1948 the United States and 23 other nations made an agreement within the framework of the United Nations known as the General Agreement on Tariffs and Trade (GATT). In 1962 Congress passed the Trade Expansion Act, enabling President John F. Kennedy to lower or remove tariffs affecting the European Common Market countries. Subsequently, a series of tariff reductions have been negotiated under what is known as the "Kennedy Round." The Common Market had as its main aim free trade among its members, but it also created a system of common external tariffs in agriculture, a source of continual controversy. One of the biggest unsolved problems of international trade is the balance between industrialized countries and the developing countries of the Third World. Since the latter export mainly food and raw materials, which rise only slowly in price, and import manufactured goods, their expansion is much slower than that of rich countries.
See also: Trade.

Interpol, International Criminal Police Organization, a clearinghouse for police information that specializes in the detection of counterfeiting, smuggling, and trafficking in narcotics. Established in 1923, its headquarters are now in Paris.
See also: Police.

Interstate commerce, in the United States, all commercial transactions that concern more than one state and relate to the national interest. The Interstate Commerce Act (1887) marked the beginning of federal government regulation of interstate commerce, specifically the railroads. The Sherman Antitrust Act (1890) was passed by Congress to control monopolies in all industries. The Federal Trade Commission (1914) protects fair and free commercial competition.

Interstate Commerce Commission (ICC), independent U.S. government agency, the first regulatory commission in U.S. history. It was established in 1887 in response to western farmers' protests against the rate-setting practices of the railroads. Eventually its authority was extended over all surface transportation of passengers and freight across state lines. The deregulation movement of recent years has seen the curtailment of ICC power over railroads (1980), trucking (1980), and intercity buses (1982).

Intestine, in animals, alimentary canal extending from the pylorus of the stomach to the anus. The human intestine is approximately 24 ft (7 m) long and is divided into the small intestine and large intestine, or colon. The small intestine has a total length of approximately 10 ft (3 m). It begins with the duodenum, which receives the food mass from the stomach through the pylorus, bile from the liver and gall bladder, and pancreatic juice from the pancreas. It connects with the jejunum, which in turn joins the ileum, which is attached to the large intestine by the ileocecal, or colic, valve, controlling passage of food into the large intestine. The inner surface of the small intestine is folded to give a greater amount of surface—estimated to be 957 sq yd (800 sq m)—and it is entirely lined by minute fingerlike *villi*, through which the products of digestion are absorbed. There are 10-40 villi to each sq mm of intestinal mucous membrane. The large intestine extends from the ileum to the anus, and consists of the cecum, colon, and rectum. The first portion of the colon, the ascending colon, extends from the cecum to the undersurface of the liver, where it becomes the transverse colon, which, in turn, at the splenic flexure, becomes the descending colon. This continues downward on the left side of the abdomen until it reaches the pelvic brim and curves like the letter *S* in front of the sacrum until it becomes the rectum. This S-shaped section is known as the sigmoid colon. The rectum passes downward to terminate in the lower opening of the tract, the anus, or anal opening.
See also: Digestive system.

One of the developers of international law—Hugo Grotius

Intolerable Acts, or Coercive Acts, name given by patriots in the American colonies to 5 acts of the British Parliament passed in 1774 to control political and other activities of the colonists. Four of the acts were intended to penalize dissidents in Massachusetts. The Boston Port Act closed the harbor in default of compensation for the Boston Tea Party. The Massachusetts Bay Regulating Act suspended many of the colony's original rights. The Impartial Administration of Justice Act ordained that British officials accused of crimes within the colonies should be tried in other colonies or in England. The Quartering Act required colonists to shelter and feed British troops. The Quebec Act extended Quebec's boundary south to the Ohio River. These strong measures were widely protested throughout the colonies and led to the calling of the First Continental Congress and hence the Revolutionary War.
See also: Revolutionary War in America.

Intrauterine device *see:* Birth control.

Introvert, nontechnical psychological term referring to someone whose thoughts are generally turned inward. The term originated with the 20th-century Swiss psychiatrist Carl Jung, who also coined the term *extrovert*, meaning someone who tends to direct their thoughts and actions outward, and who is more naturally sociable. An introvert tends more toward shyness and a focus on the inner processes than he or she does toward extroverted behavior. Jung believed that a well-balanced person possesses qualities of both the introvert and extrovert.

Intrusive rock *see:* Igneous rock.

Inuit *see:* Eskimo.

Inverness (pop. 40,000), town in the Highland region of northern Scotland which serves as the region's administrative and commercial center. Archeologists have shown evidence that people lived on the site of Inverness as early as 4000 B.C. It was the site of battle between British and Scottish forces before 1750. Lying on the River Ness in a lowland near Loch Ness and the Moray Firth, Inverness is overlooked by a castle built in the 19th century that now houses law courts and other offices. After World War II light industry was established; today the town's products include Scotch whisky and woolen textiles.
See also: Scotland.

Invertebrate, animal without a backbone. Invertebrates are a miscellaneous collection of groups from single-celled protozoa to highly specialized insects and spiders, although the term usually refers to multicellular organisms. Apart from the universal lack of an internal backbone or vertebrae, many of these groups have little in common.

Investment, in economics, productive employment of resources (capital) or the transformation of savings into active wealth (capital formation); more commonly, use of funds to obtain dividends, for example, from corporate stock or government bonds.
Investment, savings, and the economy. Modern industry's large demands for capital funds are met in large measure by employing the savings of innumerable individuals, scattered over vast areas. The complex structure of available savings and planned investment is achieved through an elaborate system of institutions and intermediaries, including stock markets, investment banks, industrial finance corporations, and commercial banks. Thanks to the work of the economist J.M. Keynes, it is now understood that the relation between investment and saving is a fundamental determinant of the level of national income. Investment is now one of the prime areas of concern for governments seeking to influence or control the progress of their economies. Many economists see capital formation (investment) as being one of the major problems faced by underdeveloped countries seeking to industrialize. U.S. economist W.W. Rostow has suggested that if a nation can reach and maintain a minimum investment rate of 10% of its national product, it will be launched into sustained economic growth.
Foreign investment. Foreign investment can take 2 forms: portfolio investment, which is simply the purchase of the stock of foreign corporations, and direct investment, the establishment or expansion of a corporation in a foreign country, where the corporation is under the investor's control. U.S. foreign investment is mainly of the direct kind, the main areas of activity being Canada, Central and South America, and, increasingly, Europe.
See also: Economics.

Eugene Ionesco

The ions in a solid are arranged regularly in a crystal (1). A solvent can remove ions from the surface (2) and cause them to enter the solution (3,4). The molecules of the solvent orient themselves with their negative sides pointing towards positive ions (3) or with their positive sides pointing towards negative ions (4). A solution of ions is able to pass a current between two electrodes to which a voltage is applied (5). The molecules of the solvent only orientate themselves in the direction of the electric field (6,7).

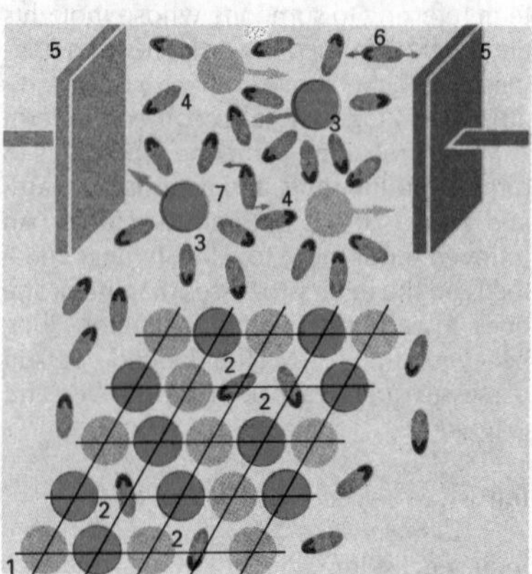

Io, in Greek mythology, princess of Argos and mistress of the god Zeus. One myth maintains that Zeus changed Io into a cow in order to disguise her from his jealous wife, Hera. Another myth holds that Hera herself transformed Io into a heifer. Io was eventually driven to Egypt, and she has been identified with the Egyptian Isis.
See also: Mythology.

Iodine, chemical element, symbol I; for physical constants see Periodic Table. Iodine was discovered 1811 by Bernard Courtois. It occurs as iodides in sea water, in brines, and in brackish waters from oil wells. It is obtained commercially from *caliche*, Chilean nitrate-bearing earth, and from seaweed ash. Iodine is prepared by displacement of an iodine compound with chlorine. It is a shiny, bluish-black solid, which volatilizes at ordinary temperatures into an irritating, blue-violet gas. Iodine is the least reactive of the halogens. Lack of iodine in humans is the cause of goiter. Radioactive iodine has been used in treating the thyroid gland. Iodine and its compounds are used in organic chemistry, medicine, and photography.

Ion, atom or group of atoms that has become electrically charged by gain or loss of negatively charged electrons. In general, ions formed from metals are positive (cations), those from nonmetals negative (anions). Crystals of ionic compounds consist of negative and positive ions arranged alternately in the lattice and held together by electrical attraction. Many compounds undergo ionic dissociation in solution. Ions may be formed in gases by radiation or electrical discharge, and occur in the ionosphere. At very high temperatures gases form plasma, consisting of ions and free electrons.
See also: Atom; Electron.

Ionesco, Eugène (1912-), Romanian-born French playwright, a leading figure in the so-called theater of the absurd. Among his best-known works are *The Bald Soprano* (1950), *Rhinoceros* (1959), and *Exit the King* (1962).

Ionian Islands, group of islands off the southwest mainland of Greece, chief of which are Cephalonia, Cerigo, Corfu, Ithaca, Leukas, Paxos, and Zante. A Byzantine province in the 10th century, the islands passed through periods of Venetian, French, Russian, and British control before becoming part of Greece in 1864. Exports include wine, cotton, olives, and fish.
See also: Mediterranean Sea.

Ionians, ancient Greek people who colonized the west coast of Asia Minor that became known as Ionia (now in Turkey). They are said to have been driven from the mainland by invading Dorians. The Ionians made a major contribution to classical Greek poetry and philosophy.
See also: Greece, Ancient.

Ionian Sea, arm of the Mediterranean Sea, between southeast Italy and western Greece. It is connected to the Adriatic by the Strait of Otranto and to the Tyrrhenian Sea by the Strait of Messina.

Ionization detector *see:* Smoke detector.

Ion microscope, magnifying instrument capable of magnifying up to 2 million times and with enough clarity to make individual atoms visible. Invented by the German physicist Erwin W. Muller, the ion microscope was used in 1951 to take the first picture of the arrangement of atoms on a metal's surface. The microscope works on the principle of electrical attraction and repulsion. Scientists use it, among other purposes, to study the physics and chemistry of surfaces and impurities in metals.
See also: Microscope.

Ionosphere, layer of the atmosphere extending from roughly 50 mi (80 km) to 250 or 300 mi (400 or 480 km) above the earth. It is composed of ions (atoms or molecules carrying an electric charge). The atmosphere is thin at that point, and radiation from the sun is able to ionize most of the particles of gas that are present. While the ionosphere is a permanent phenomenon, its structure varies according to season, latitude, and solar activity. The ionosphere is important in radio transmission. Longer-wave signals entering it from below are reflected back toward the earth, making it possible to receive such transmissions over long distances. Shorter waves, such as TV and FM waves, are not reflected by the ionosphere. The aurora borealis (northern lights) takes place in the ionosphere.
See also: Atmosphere.

Iowa, midwestern state in the north-central United States; bordered by Minnesota in the north, Wisconsin and Illinois in the east, Missouri in the south, and Nebraska and South Dakota in the west.
Land and climate. Iowa is gently rolling plain, sloping toward the southeast. Great glaciers covered Iowa during the Ice Age,

Iowa

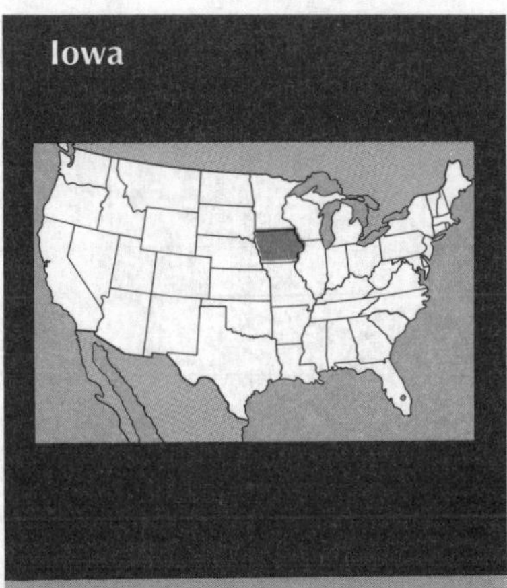

Capital:	Des Moines
Statehood:	Dec. 28, 1846
Familiar name:	Hawkeye State (29th state)
Area:	56,275 sq mi (145,753 km); ranks 25th
Population:	2,787,424 (1990); ranks 30th
Elevation:	Highest—1,670 ft (509 m), Osceola County; Lowest—480 ft (146 m), Mississippi River in Lee County
Motto:	Our Liberties We Prize and Our Rights We Will Maintain
Flower:	Wild rose
Bird:	Eastern goldfinch
Tree:	Oak
Song:	"The Song of Iowa"

leveling hills and filling valleys with rich soil. In the southern portion of the state is a region of rich, wind-deposited soil and low hills and ridges cut by rivers. Northeast Iowa escaped most of the glaciers, and vertical cliffs rise as high as 400 ft from the river banks. Two of the nation's great rivers form part of Iowa's borders—the Mississippi, which forms the state's entire eastern boundary, and the Missouri, comprising most of the western border. All of Iowa's rivers drain into this great river system. The tributaries of the Mississippi—the Des Moines, Skunk, Iowa, Maquoketa, and Sapsipinicon rivers—drain in the eastern two-thirds of the state. The Missouri's principal tributaries include the Big Sioux, Little Sioux, Nishnabotna, Boyer, and Floyd rivers. Iowa has many small lakes and ponds concentrated in the north and northwest. Iowa's soil is probably the richest in the nation—85% to 90% of the state's area is suitable for cultivation, and about one-fourth of all the finest U.S. agricultural land is found in Iowa. The state has a continental climate, marked by cold winters and hot summers. Principal cities are Des Moines, Cedar Rapids, and Davenport.

Economy. Iowa is a leading agricultural state. Corn is Iowa's leading crop; Iowa produces about one-fifth of all corn grown in the United States. Other major crops are soybeans, oats, and hay. Iowans also raise large quantities of alfalfa, clover, sugarbeets, and wheat. Iowa raises more hogs than any other state, and ranks high in beef cattle, dairy cattle, and milk production. In manufacturing, food processing is Iowa's leading industry. Machinery production is second in importance. Iowa's chief mining product is limestone. It also produces gypsum, sand, and gravel.

Government. Iowa's constitution was adopted in 1857. The governor serves a 4-year term. The state legislature, called the General Assembly, consists of 50 senators serving 4-year terms and 100 representatives serving 2-year terms. In the U.S. Congress, Iowa is represented by 2 senators and 6 representatives.

History. In prehistoric times, the area was home to Native Americans called the Mound Builders. When French explorers visited the region in 1673, it was home to Plains and Woodland tribes. By 1682, France had claimed the area. The territory west of the Mississippi was ceded to Spain (1762-1800), but in 1803 France sold it to the United States under the Louisiana Purchase. At first it remained Native American land, but by 1851 it had been opened to white settlers. The Territory of Iowa was created in 1838. In 1857, the state capital was established at Des Moines. World War II brought a growing demand for farm products, boosting Iowa's economy. New industries poured into the state from 1945 through the 1960s, but the 1980s brought hard times to farmers, including declining farm prices and land values. Its population has been dropping as young people leave to seek jobs elsewhere.

Iowa, Siouan-speaking Native American tribe of North America. Farmers and buffalo-hunters, they lived in what is now Iowa. Today they are scattered through Nebraska, Kansas, and Oklahoma.

Iphigenia, in Greek mythology, daughter of Clytemnestra and Agamemnon and sister of Orestes. Iphigenia comes to a different fate in each of two versions of her role during the Trojan War. In one, she dies when her father Agamemnon sacrifices her to the goddess Artemis in exchange for Artemis favoring his fleet on its journey to Troy. In another version of the myth, Iphigenia does not die during the sacrifice, but is spared by Artemis and later becomes a priestess at Taurus. As this version goes, Iphigenia saves her brother, and the two flee to Greece.
See also: Mythology; Trojan War.

Iqbal, Sir Muhammad (1873-1938), Indian Muslim poet, philosopher, and politician. He was president of the Muslim League in 1930 and is considered one of the spiritual founders of Pakistan.
See also: Muslims.

IRA *see:* Pension.

IRA *see:* Irish Republican Army.

Iran, officially the Islamic Republic of Iran, country in southwest Asia, bordered by the Soviet Union and the Caspian Sea in the north, Afghanistan and Pakistan in the east, Turkey and Iraq in the west, and the Persian Gulf and the Gulf of Oman in the south. The capital and largest city is Teheran.

View of Missisippi River in Iowa

Land and climate. Most of the country is a high plateau lying between the Elburz and Zagros mountain ranges. An interior desert contains salt wastes. The climate is marked by hot summers and cold winters. About 11 percent of the land is forested. The country is also subject to numerous severe earthquakes.

People. Persians comprise the largest ethnic group in Iran (about 60% of the total). Other groups include Kurds, Azerbaijanis, Tatars, and Arabs. The official language is Persian (Farsi), an Indo-European language written in the Arabic script. The state religion is Islam. About 98% of the population are Muslims, the majority of them Shi'tes.

Economy. Iran is one of the world's major oil producers, and oil exports provide most of the country's foreign exchange, but nearly three-fourths of the work force is employed in agriculture and forestry. Natural resources other than oil include natural gas, coal, manganese, salt, and copper. Other manufacturing includes textiles, sugar refining, food processing, machine tools, and traditional handicrafts (most notably carpets).

History. Iran is an ancient country. The earliest village settlements of the Iranian plateau date back to c.4000 B.C., and by c.550 B.C. the Persian empire, founded by Cyrus the Great and centered in what is now Iran, was one of the world's major civilizations. In 331 B.C. the empire was overthrown by the Greeks under Alexander the Great, and later, c.250 B.C., Persia was invaded and occupied by armies from the kingdom of Parthia. In 224 A.D. the Persians regained control of their land under Ardashir, who founded the Sassanid dynasty, a state that lasted for about 400 years. In 641 the Sassanids fell to the Arab invasions, and the religion of Islam was introduced. Iran was invaded by the Turks (10th century), and by the forces of Genghis Khan (13th century) and Tamerlane (14th century). Order was restored by the Safavid dynasty (1501-1736). In the 18th

Iran

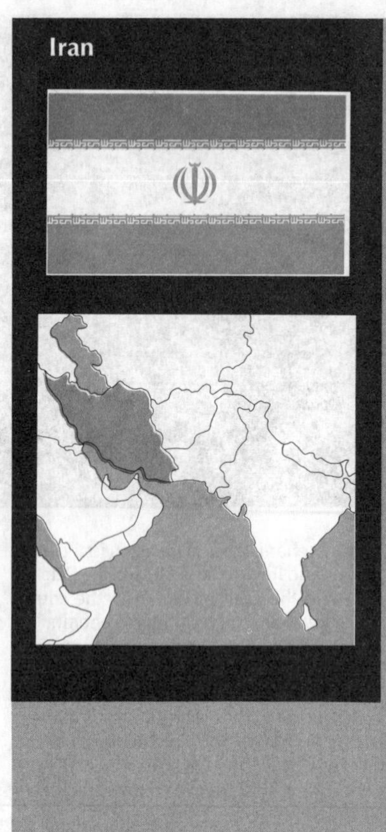

General information	
Capital:	Teheran
Area:	636,372 sq mi (1,648,196 sq km)
Population:	59,791,000
Official language:	Farsi (Persian)
Monetary unit:	1 Rial = 100 dinars
Main cities:	Teheran, Mashhad, Esfahan, Tabriz, Shira
Government	
Form:	Islamic republic
Independent:	1979 (republic)
Head of state:	President (elected every 4 years)
Head of government:	President
Legislature:	one legislative house (Islamic Consultative Assembly)
Executive:	President and Council of Ministers
Judiciary:	highest court is the Supreme Court
Political division:	25 provinces
National economy	
Gross national product:	U.S. $130,910,000,000
Per capita income:	U.S. $2,190
Agriculture:	wheat, sugar beets, barley, sugar cane, potatoes, rice
Livestock:	sheep, goats, cattle
Fisheries:	150,000 metric tons
Mining:	crude petroleum, iron ore, copper, chromium ore, manganese
Industries:	petroleum products, machinery, textiles, clothing and leather, nonmetallic mineral products, food processing, chemicals
Main exports:	petroleum and petroleum products, agricultural goods
Transportation:	2,837 mi (4,567 km) of railroads; 86,599 mi (139,368 km) of roads; 3 international airports
Trading partners:	Germany, Italy, Japan, Turkey, United Kingdom
People	
Urban:	54%
Ethnic composition:	Persian 65%, Azerbaijani 20%, Kurdish 10%
Birth rate:	42.4 per 1,000 population
Death rate:	8 per 1,000 population
Infant mortality:	63 per 1,000 live births
Life expectancy:	male 65 years, female 65.5 years

Iran was the site of the ancient Achaemenid Dynasty in the 6th century B.C. The ruins of Persepolis, one of several ceremonial capitals, is shown.

century a decline began, leading to increased influence by European powers in Iran, although the country was never formally colonized. The discovery of oil in the early 1900s sharpened European interest, and the country was divided into British and Russian spheres of influence from 1907 until after World War I. In 1921, an army officer named Reza Khan seized power in a coup, and in 1925, as Reza Shah Pahlevi, he established the Pahlevi dynasty. In 1941 he abdicated in favor of his son, Mohammad Reza Shah Pahlevi, who became the new shah (king).

In the early 1950s the shah's power was challenged by a new prime minister, Muhammad Mossadegh, who nationalized the oil industry. The shah fled, but recovered his throne in 1953, with support of Iranian military officers and the U.S. Central Intelligence Agency (CIA). The shah's regime became increasingly repressive, and popular support for it evaporated almost completely. In 1979 massive street demonstrations forced the shah to leave the country.

The Ayatollah Ruhollah Khomeini, a revered Islamic leader living in exile, returned to head the newly established Islamic Republic, a highly repressive regime based on the power of the mullahs, Muslim religious leaders who ultimately determine the way the country is run. In retaliation for U.S. support of the shah and an attempt to force the return of the shah toIran, Iranians captured the U.S. embassy in Teheran, holding embassy workers hostage (1979). The shah died in exile (1980) and the hostages were eventually released (1981). The crisis was a major factor in Ronald Reagan's defeat of President Jimmy Carter in the 1980 election. Meanwhile, in Sept. 1980, Iraq invaded Iran, triggering an 8-year war that inflicted massive damage and high casualties on both countries. Khomeini died in 1989, and Ali Khamenei succeeded him as supreme religious leader. Rafsanjani became president; in 1997 he was succeeded by the more liberal Mohamad Khatami.

Iran-Contra affair, secret U.S. government effort in 1986 by the Reagan administration to gain the release of U.S. hostages in the Middle East by selling weapons and munitions to the Iranian government. The money raised from the sale was to be an illegal means of supporting the anti-government rebels (Contras) in Nicaragua. National Security Council members Admiral John Poindexter and Lt. Colonel Oliver North were implicated in the scandal by a Congressional committee in 1988 and were convicted on criminal charges in 1989 and 1990 trials, but North's convictions were set aside by the courts in 1990. *See also:* North, Oliver Laurence.

Iraq, country in southwest Asia, bordered by Turkey in the north, Iran in the east, Kuwait and Saudi Arabia in the south, and Jordan and Syria in the west. The capital is Baghdad. Other large cities are Basra and Mosul.

Land. Iraq is mountainous in the northeast, but much of the country is composed of low-lying grasslands between the Tigris and the Euphrates rivers. The lower plain includes the fertile delta where the 2 rivers meet, forming the Shatt al-Arab waterway, which flows into the Persian Gulf. The southwestern part of the country is desert.

People. Arabs comprise about 80 percent of the Iraqi population. Most of them are Shi'te Muslims. The major non-Arab minority is the Kurds, about 15 percent of the population, who are mostly Sunni Muslims. The Kurds live mainly in the northern part of the country. They speak their own language, Kurdish. The official language of Iraq is Arabic.

Economy. Oil production, begun in 1928, dominates the Iraqi economy. The oil industry was nationalized in the early 1970s, and the income earned from oil was used to finance extensive efforts at industrialization and militarization. Agricultural products include dates, cotton, and grain.

History. Mesopotamia, the territory between the Tigris and Euphrates rivers, was the site of one of the world's first civilizations, dating back to c.3500 B.C. Sumeria, Assyria, and Babylonia were 3 of the ancient states of this region. In 539 B.C. it became part of the Persian empire, in turn

Baghdad, Iraq

Iraq

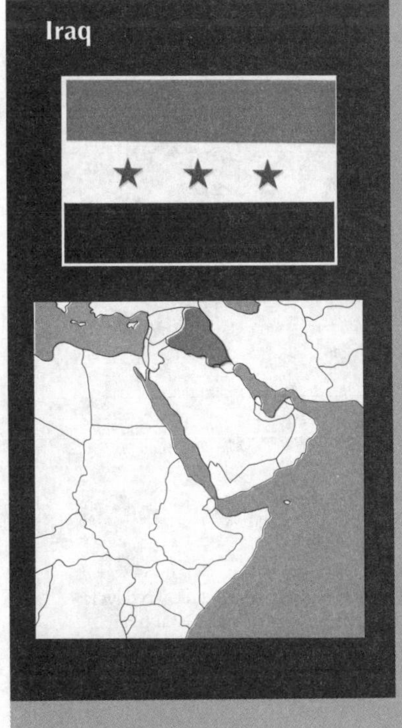

General information	
Capital:	Baghdad
Area:	169,235 sq mi (438,317 sq km)
Population:	17,215,000
Official language:	Arabic
Monetary unit:	1 Iraqi dinar = 1,000 fils
Main cities:	Baghdad, Basra, Mosul
Government	
Form:	republic
Independent:	1932
Head of state:	President
Head of government:	President
Legislature:	one legislative house (National Assembly)
Executive:	President, Revolutionary Command Council, and Council of Ministers
Judiciary:	highest court is the Court of Cassation
Political division:	15 governorates, 3 Kurdish autonomous regions
National economy	
Gross national product:	U.S. $40,700,000,000
Per capita income:	U.S. $2,420
Agriculture:	barley, wheat, tomatoes, grapes, dates, cucumbers
Livestock:	sheep, cattle, goats
Fisheries:	21,000 metric tons
Mining:	crude petroleum, natural gas, sulfur, gypsum
Industries:	petroleum products, industrial chemicals, pottery and glass products, machinery and transportation equipment, food products, textiles
Main exports:	petroleum and petroleum products, food and agricultural raw materials
Transportation:	1,516 mi (2,439 km) of railroads; 20,653 mi (33,238 km) of roads; 2 international airports
Trading partners:	Brazil, Turkey, Italy, France, Japan, Germany
People	
Urban:	66%
Ethnic composition:	Arabs 80%, Kurds 15%, Turks 1.5%
Birth rate:	45.1per 1,000 population
Death rate:	8.6 per 1,000 population
Infant mortality:	63 per 1,000 live births
Life expectancy:	male 61 years, female 64.5 years

conquered by the Greeks (under Alexander the Great) in 331 B.C. Subsequently the region was incorporated into the Roman, and later the Byzantine, empire. In 637 the Arabs swept into Mesopotamia, bringing the Arabic language and the religion of Islam with them. About a century and a half later, Baghdad became the capital of the Abbasid caliphate. As such, it was the center of the Arab world during its golden age (9th century). In 1258, Mongols from central Asia invaded Mesopotamia and sacked Baghdad. The country remained weak and impoverished for a long period. In 1534 Iraq was taken over by the Ottoman Empire, remaining under Turkish rule until the defeat of the Ottomans in World War I.

In 1920 Iraq was made a British mandate by the League of Nations. A kingdom was established in 1921, under British control. In 1932 the League of Nations mandate was officially terminated, winning formal independence, though the British retained great influence. In 1958 the monarchy was overthrown in a military coup led by General Abdul Karim Qassim, a nationalist officer. In 1963 Qassim was overthrown by officers of the Baath Party. The Baathist regime established a repressive government ideologically based on pan-Arab nationalism and supported by an enormous military and police apparatus. The Baath Party took control of virtually all aspects of Iraqi society. The architect of that program was Saddam Hussein, who was the power behind the scenes from 1968 onward and officially became president in 1979. The Saddam Hussein regime has been marked by wars against the Kurdish minority in the north, the 8-year war against Iran, and the Persian Gulf War of 1991.

See also: Persian Gulf War.

Ireland (Gaelic: *Eire*), officially the Republic of Ireland, independent country in northwestern Europe occupying five-sixths of the island of Ireland. The country is bounded on the west and south by the Atlantic Ocean and separated from Great Britain by the Irish Sea. A land boundary separates it from Northern Ireland (Ulster). The capital is Dublin. Ireland is sometimes called *Erin*.

Land and climate. Ireland can be likened to a saucer, with a flat, central limestone plain, averaging 300 ft (90 m) above sea level, rimmed with low mountains along the coasts. On the eastern coast, north of Dublin, the plain stretches to the sea, and the eastern and southern coasts are generally regular. In contrast, the rugged Atlantic coast is broken by countless rocky inlets and islands, including Achill Island and the Aran Islands. The almost treeless central plain is studded with low ridges and innumerable lakes, around which are vast areas of peat bogs. The plain is drained into the Atlantic by the 250-mi (400-km) Shannon River, into the Irish Sea by the Boyne and Blackwater rivers, and into Dublin Bay by the Liffey. The largest lakes are the Ree and Derg on the Shannon, and the Mask, Corrib, and Conn in the northwest, but the most famous are the 3 Lakes of Killarney, in County Kerry. The chief mountain ranges are the Wicklow on the eastern coast south of Dublin, and the mountains of Kerry in the southwest. Ireland's climate is extremely moist. Strong southwest winds from the Atlantic bring heavy rainfall. The currents of the Gulf Stream warm the southwestern portion of the island, and temperatures generally vary only from an average of 40°F (4.4°C) in January to 60°F (15.5°C) in July. This damp, temperate climate produces the bright green grass of the "Emerald Isle" and favors the dairy industry and livestock raising. It also supports the extensive marshlands and peat bogs. Heather and small shrubs cover the higher moorlands of the west. Many varieties of native grasses remain perpetually green. Fauna include a variety of birds and small mammals (hedgehogs, badgers, and foxes). Fishing is the chief occupation of the inhabitants of

Ireland

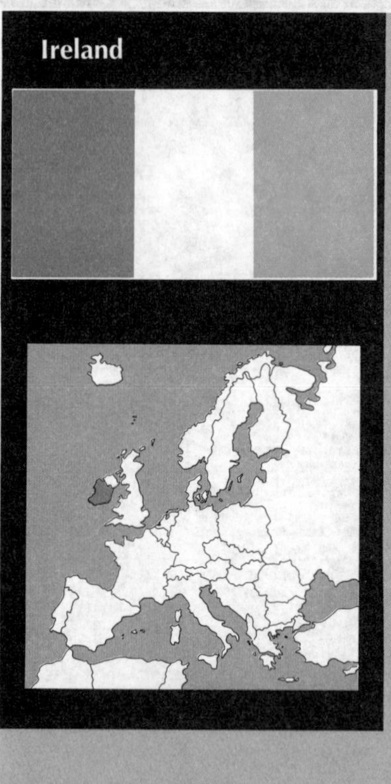

General information	
Capital:	Dublin
Area:	27,137 sq mi (70,285 sq km)
Population:	3,515,000
Official languages:	English, Gaelic
Monetary unit:	1 Irish pound = 100 pence
Main cities:	Dublin, Cork, Limerick
Government	
Form:	republic
Independent:	1937
Head of state:	President (elected every 7 years)
Head of government:	Prime Minister
Legislature:	two legislative houses (Senate and House of Deputies)
Executive:	President and Cabinet
Judiciary:	highest court is the Supreme Court
Political division:	27 counties
National economy	
Gross national product:	U.S. $26,750,000,000
Per capita income:	U.S. $7,480
Agriculture:	sugar beets, barley, potatoes, wheat, oats
Livestock:	cattle, sheep, pigs, poultry
Fisheries:	247,000 metric tons
Mining:	natural gas, peat, zinc, coal, lead
Industries:	metals and engineering goods, food products, chemical products, nonmetallic mineral products, paper, printing and publishing
Main exports:	food and livestock, machinery and transportation equipment, chemicals and related products, basic manufacturing
Transportation:	845 mi (2,953 km) of railroads; 57,357 (92,303 km) of roads; 4 international airports
Trading partners:	United Kingdom, U.S., Germany, France, Japan
People	
Urban:	57%
Ethnic composition:	more than 94% Irish nationality
Birth rate:	15.3 per 1,000 population
Death rate:	8.9 per 1,000 population
Infant mortality:	7 per 1,000 live births
Life expectancy:	male 70 years, female 75.5 years

the western coastal villages and islands, where herring and mackerel are abundant. Ireland has long been famous for its fine horses, trained as racers or hunters.

People. The Mediterranean people who first reached Ireland c.6000 B.C. were assimilated by Celtic tribes that appeared in the 4th century B.C. Lesser immigrations of Scandinavians, Normans, and English were absorbed. About 20% of the population lives in Dublin and surrounding areas. Education is compulsory between ages 6 and 14.

Economy. The economy is based mainly on small mixed farms rearing cattle or engaged in dairying (especially in the south), with barley, wheat, oats, potatoes, turnips, and sugar beets as the chief arable crops. Ireland is relatively poor in minerals, but some coal is mined, along with recently discovered deposits of lead, zinc, copper, and silver. Peat from the bogs is a valuable fuel, used for home heating and electricity generation. Industries include food-processing, distilling, tobacco products, textiles, clothing, and engineering.

History. In the 4th century B.C. the Gaels evolved a Celtic civilization that in its full flowering, after St. Patrick introduced Christianity in the 5th century, produced superb works of art and sent religious and cultural missionaries to the rest of Europe. It was severely damaged by the Vikings in the 9th and 10th centuries. In 1166 the Anglo-Normans invaded Ireland, and thereafter the English tried continually to assert their authority over the native Irish and the settlers, who quickly became assimilated. The Act of Union (1801) ended parliamentary independence from England; nevertheless, despite the potato famine and Fenian violence, a measure of independence by constitutional means was slowly attained through agitation for Catholic Emancipation and the emergence of leaders like Daniel O'Connell and C.S. Parnell. One result was the cultural Celtic Renaissance of the 1890s. The inability of British governments to implement Home Rule led to the bitter Easter Rebellion (1916), and the armed struggle after World War I resulted in Britain's grant of dominion status to the Irish Free State (1921), but the civil war was continued on a terrorist basis by the Irish Republican Army (IRA) until 1923. Eamonn de Valera, in power from 1932, broke with the British Crown and renamed the country Eire (1937). In 1949, as the Republic of Ireland, it left the British Commonwealth.

Ireland, Northern, 6 counties of Ulster in northeastern Ireland, covering 5,452 sq mi (14,121 sq km). Since 1922 it has been a province of the United Kingdom. It has a predominantly Protestant population; its Roman Catholic minority has swelled in recent years to around 30%. The largest towns are the capital, Belfast, and Londonderry. Major manufactures include machinery and shipbuilding, textiles (artificial fibers and linen), and electronics.

History. The Ulster counties chose to remain British after Ireland (Eire) became independent in 1921 and maintained this resolve despite occasional outbreaks of terrorism by the Irish Republican Army (IRA). Discrimination led the growing Catholic minority to form a civil rights movement (1968) that was used to justify renewed IRA terrorism. The resulting violence and civil unrest led the UK government to suspend the Northern Ireland Parliament at Stormont (1972) and assume direct rule of the province. Though a new Northern Ireland Assembly was elected (1975) in an effort to promote power sharing, neither Catholic nor Protestant extremists accepted it; violence by both sides has continued.

Irenaeus, Saint (A.D. 130?-202?), important theologian and leader during the 2nd century A.D. Born in Asia Minor, Irenaeus is thought to have served as a missionary to southern Gaul and as conciliator among the churches of Asia Minor that had been upset by heresy. A strong opponent of Gnosticism, a spiritual movement that took up pagan, Jewish, and Christian forms, Irenaeus attacked the movement in his preeminent work, *Against Heresies*. Irenaeus upheld the validity of the Old Testament, as well as of several writings that were destined to become part of the New Testament. He became the Bishop of Lugdunum, which is now Lyons, France, in about A.D. 177.
See also: Theology.

Iridium, chemical element, symbol Ir; for physical constants see Periodic Table. Iridium was discovered by Smithson Tennant in 1804. It occurs in the presence of platinum and other metals in alluvial deposits. It is obtained as a byproduct of nickel smelting. Iridium is a silvery-white, hard, brittle unreactive metal. It is the most corrosion-resistant metal known. The metal is used in high-melting, hard, and unreactive alloys. Iridium and its compounds are used in crucibles, pen nibs, electrical contacts, and organic catalysts. It has the highest density of all the elements.

Iris, any of a genus (*Iris*) of perennial herbaceous plants with intricate and colorful flowers, found in temperate parts of Europe, Asia, Africa, and North America. The iris is a member of the family Iridaceae, which includes the crocus, freesia, and gladiolus. Irises grow from rhizomes (swollen underground stems) or from bulbs. Many varieties have been cultivated for their 3-part flowers, on which the *fleur-de-lis* (French, "flower of the lily") of heraldry was based. The dried rhizome of certain irises is called *orrisroot*; it smells of violets and is used in cosmetics and medicines.

Iris, colored circular part of the eye made of muscle and fiber and surrounding the black pupil. Responsible for regulating the amount of light entering the eye, it separates the front and back chambers of the eyeball and rests against the front of the crystalline lens. Its color is determined by the location of pigment bodies known as melanophores: if these are at the back of the iris, it appears blue or gray; if in the middle, it appears brown.

County Kerry, Ireland

Northern Ireland. Protestant demonstrators in Belfast.

Irish *see:* Gaelic.

Irish literature, composite of folk tales, lyric and narrative poetry, novels, short stories and drama from ancient to present-day Ireland. Irish literature is notable for having been written in both Gaelic and English. During its Golden Age (c.700-1000), Gaelic lyric poetry and myths flourished. The Irish continued to write good poetry in Gaelic through the mid-1800's. During the 1800s a group of Irish writers, led by playwrights William Butler Yeats and Lady Gregory, created a singularly Irish literature in English, and thereby an Irish literary revival. James Joyce, the author of the revolutionary *Ulysses* (1922), was a key figure in the development of modern Irish literature. Among other important modern authors are the playwright George Bernard Shaw and the fiction writer Frank O'Connor.

Irish moss, or carrageen (*Chondrus crispus* or *Gigartina mamillosa*), small red seaweed. It contains a large amount of gelatin and is used in jellies and puddings and as an ingredient in shampoos, cosmetics, and shoe polishes. Irish moss is harvested in Europe and Japan, and in Massachusetts.

Mural paintings glorifying the Irish Republican Army, Londonderry

Irish Republican Army (IRA), Irish nationalist organization opposed to British rule and committed to the unification of Northern Ireland and the Republic of Ireland. The IRA evolved from militant remnants of the Irish Volunteers, who planned and fought in the Easter Rebellion (1916). Refusing to accept the separation of Northern Ireland, it became a secret terrorist organization, connected with the Sinn Fein party. Loss of popular support because of its violence and pro-German activities in World War II, and strong repressive action by the government, reduced its role until the 1960s. In 1969 the IRA split into the antiterrorist "officials" and the terrorist "provisionals," who rely on Irish-American financial aid. The provisionals then launched a campaign of bombings and assassinations in Northern Ireland and England, intended to maintain pressure on Great Britain. IRA terrorists were responsible for the murder of Lord Mountbatten in 1979. Imprisoned IRA gunmen resorted to hunger strikes, sometimes fatal, to gain attention for their cause in 1981 and 1985.
See also: Ireland; Sinn Féin.

Irish Sea, arm of the Atlantic, separating Ireland from the island of Great Britain. Connected to the Atlantic by the North Channel to the northwest and St. George's Channel to the south, it is about 130 mi (210 km) across.

Irish setter, sporting dog and popular pet. Bred originally in Ireland. The Irish setter has a coat of either solid red or red with white markings. In the U.S. and Canada the red coat is preferred for professional showing. Irish setters are between 25 and 27 in (64 and 69 cm) high at the shoulder, and usually weigh 60 to 70 lb (27 to 32 kg). The Irish setter was developed in the 18th century as a hunting dog.

Irish terrier, dog that resembles a wire-haired fox terrier. About 18 in (46 cm) high and weighing about 27 lb (12.3 kg), the Irish terrier breed is thought to be about 2,000 years old. Once used to bore into the dens of small animals, and to carry messages on battlefields during World War I and World War II, the Irish terrier today is mainly kept as a pet.

Irish water spaniel, dog breed from the early 1800s. Probably created by crossing a poodle and Irish setter, this spaniel has been called the clown of the dog family. A valuable hunting dog both on land and in the water, where it is an excellent duck retriever, the Irish water spaniel is 21 to 24 in (53 to 61 cm) high and weighs from 45 to 65 lb (20 to 29 kg).

Irish wolfhound, hound which is the tallest of all dog breeds. Standing at 32 to 34 in (81 to 86 cm) and weighing between 126 and 145 lbs (57 to 66 kg), the Irish wolfhound has a wiry coat and a gentle temperament. It was used by the ancient Celts to hunt wolves.

Iron, chemical element, symbol Fe; for physical constants see Periodic Table. Iron has been used since prehistoric times. It is the fourth most abundant element on earth. The earth's core is thought to be composed mainly of iron. It is found in nature as the minerals *hematite, magnetite, limonite, siderite*, and *taconite*. It is a major component of some meteorites. Iron is prepared by reduction of its oxides with carbon in a reverberatory furnace. Iron is a silvery-white, soft, malleable, ductile, magnetic metal. The commercial metal appears in three forms: cast iron, wrought iron, and steel. Iron is used to produce many important alloys, particularly steels. Nickel, chromium (stainless), tungsten, molybdenum, manganese, and aluminum steels being the most widely used. Compounds of iron are used in inks, pigments, mordants, water purification, and medicine. It is essential to plant and animal life. Iron is the most important of all metals.

Iron Age, stage of humankind's material cultural development, following the Stone Age and the Bronze Age, during which iron was generally used for weapons and tools. Though used ornamentally as early as 4000 B.C. in Egypt and Mesopotamia, iron's difficulty of working precluded its general use until efficient techniques were developed in Armenia, 1500 B.C. By 500 B.C. the use of iron was dominant throughout the known world, and by 300 B.C. the Chinese were using cast iron. Some cultures, as those in America and Australia, are said not to have had an iron age.

Iron and steel, materials essential to all modern industrialized economies. Iron is a common element throughout nature and is even an important component of our blood. This discussion focuses on iron as a useful metal. The highest natural concentrations of iron are found in meteors. A common element in the earth's crust, iron is combined in varying concentrations with oxygen, carbon, sulfur, and silicon. In its raw state it is iron ore. Steel does not occur in nature; it is man-made and requires refined iron for its manufacture. Steel is made by melting, purifying, and blending iron with other metals.
There are several kinds of iron ore; they are graded according to the percentage of iron they contain. The richest ores, hematite and magnetite, consist of about 70% iron. Other ores include limonite, pyrite, siderite, and taconite. Taconite is about 30% iron. When ore is found close to the earth's surface, it is gathered by open-pit mining. If it is necessary to reach an especially rich but deep seam of ore, shaft mining is used, but it is more expensive and more dangerous than open-pit mining. Though vast quantities of iron ore have been mined, including most of the top-grade ores, supplies are still abundant. The USSR, Brazil, and Australia are major producers of iron ore. In the United States, the Mesabi Range in Minnesota is a major source of ore.
Once it has been mined, the ore must be processed to separate the iron. The particular process used will depend upon the purity of the ore. The raw iron is then shaped into pellets; it is this iron that is further refined in furnaces, where it is mixed with various elements and melted to remove oxygen. The most common method for purifying iron is the blast furnace, so called because of the superheated air forced into the furnace through pipes located in its lower section. The blast of hot air melts the iron and burns off impurities. The purified molten iron is then poured into molds, where it hardens into pig iron. Pig iron can then be melted and combined with other elements to yield cast iron or wrought iron, but most pig iron is used to manufacture steel.
Huge furnaces are also used to make steel, but the processes are more varied and sophisticated. There are basically 4 kinds of steel. Carbon steel is the most common, with a carbon content of less than 1%. Stainless steel, with an admixture of chromium, is more resistant to corrosion. Tool steel is used to make special tools and is extremely hard. Finally, there is a wide variety of alloy steels whose composition may include aluminum, manganese, titanium, nickel, or vanadium.
Steel is made by further purifying or refining pig iron. The principal task in making steel is to reduce the carbon content of the iron to less than 2% and to blend the resultant metal with other metals or alloys to produce a steel of the appropriate hardness, tensile strength, lightness, malleability, or resistance to corrosion. Depending upon the application, the steel used may be fairly commonplace and inexpensive to produce or exotic and manufactured only for special purposes. Steel can be produced in huge open hearths, in electric furnaces, or in furnaces that use an oxygen process in which oxygen is blown into the furnace to purify the metal. Operating an open hearth furnace requires large amounts of fuel oil and causes considerable air pollution. As a result, the open hearth method has been largely replaced by the oxygen process or by cheaper and more efficient electric furnaces.
Molten steel is cast into various forms, one of the more common being ingots. Steel is then shaped or finished by means of rolling, forging, or extruding. Rolling literally presses or squeezes steel into sheets or strips. Forging requires that the steel be reheated and then hammered or pressed

into the desired shape. Extrusion is a process whereby hot steel is forced through an opening that shapes it into forms like I-beams or rails. Rolling, forging, and extruding are done in huge mills equipped with powerful machinery. Other common forms of finished steel include tubing and wire. At this point, the steel may be given its final form or it may be shipped to manufacturers who will use it in their own plants to produce everything from forks and spoons to automobiles, aircraft, machines, or appliances.
Iron, principally from meteorites, was used by our ancestors as early as 4000 B.C., but iron made from ore by means of systematic refinement dates to the Hittites, about 1400 B.C. Over the centuries, various improvements were made in furnaces, but it was not until early modern times, about A.D. 1500, that large amounts of iron could be made for commercial purposes.
Small amounts of steel had been made from as early as 300 B.C., but even as late as 1740 steel could be made only in small quantities. The Englishman Henry Bessemer developed a process that revolutionized the making of steel by forcing hot air into the molten iron to purify it. After Bessemer's breakthrough in the mid-19th century, further developments in steel manufacture rapidly followed, giving birth to the steel industry and providing the material and tools that have made possible the world as we know it.

Ironclad *see:* Monitor and Merrimack.

Iron Curtain, term for self-imposed isolation of the USSR and its Eastern European satellite countries, a policy established after World War II. The term was popularized by Sir Winston Churchill in a speech at Fulton, Mo., on Mar. 5, 1946.
See also: Cold War.

Iron lung, tank covering the entire body except the head, in which air pressure is increased and decreased to provide artificial respiration. First developed in 1928 by Philip Drinker and Louis Shaw at Harvard's School of Public Health in Boston, the iron lung was widely used during the polio epidemics of the 1950s. Other types of respirators are employed today.

Iron ore *see:* Iron and steel.

Iron pyrite *see:* Pyrite.

Ironsides, Old *see:* Constitution, USS.

Ironwood, or hornbeam, name given to several plants with very hard wood, belonging to the birch family. The American hornbeam (*Carpinus caroliniana*), found in the northeastern United States, is an ironwood.

Iroquois, Native American tribes of the Iroquoian linguistic family, members of the Iroquois League. This political union of the Mohawk, Oneida, Onondaga, Cayuga, and Seneca tribes was founded in the 16th century by the Onondaga chief Hiawatha and Dekanawida, formerly a Huron. The Tuscarora joined in 1722. Hunters and farmers, the Iroquois tribes lived in stockaded villages of longhouses. Families were matrilineal, and belonged to an intertribal clan system. During the French and Indian Wars the Iroquois supported the British, but the league split over the Revolutionary War.

Irradiation, exposure to radiation such as ultraviolet rays, X rays, and gamma rays, or to beams of atomic particles such as neutrons. The body requires ultraviolet radiation to manufacture vitamin D. Ultraviolet irradiation is used in the food and pharmaceutical industry. Irradiation by X rays is used as a method of destroying cancerous tissue. Irradiation by gamma rays is used to sterilize insects and prevent them from reproducing and continually infesting grain and other foodstuffs. Gamma-ray irradiation may also kill bacteria in food and preserve it for long periods. Irradiation of elements with beams of particles in a nuclear reactor is a method of making radioisotopes.
See also: Radiation.

Irrawaddy River, main waterway of Burma, formed by the confluence of the Mali and Nmai rivers. It flows south for about 1,350 mi (2,160 km) to empty into the Bay of Bengal. Its delta is one of the world's richest rice-growing areas.

Irrigation, artificial application of water to soil to promote plant growth. Irrigation is vital for agricultural land with inadequate rainfall. The practice dates back at least to the canals and reservoirs of ancient Egypt. There are 3 main irrigation techniques: *surface irrigation*, in which the soil surface is moistened or flooded by water flowing through furrows or tubes; *sprinkler irrigation*, in which water is sprayed on the land from above; and *subirrigation*, in which underground pipes supply water to roots.
See also: Agriculture.

IRS *see:* Internal Revenue Service.

Irving, John (1942-), U.S. author of the best-sellers *The World According to Garp* (1978) and *The Hotel New Hampshire* (1981). His writing stresses the passionate, comic, and grotesque aspects of life.

Irving, Sir Henry (John Henry Brodribb; 1838-1905), greatest English actor-manager of his day. At the Lyceum Theater in London, from 1878 to 1902, he staged spectacular Shakespeare productions, often with Ellen Terry as his leading lady.

Irving, Washington (1783-1859), first U.S. writer to achieve international acclaim. Born in New York, he became a writer and publisher; he went to Europe in 1815 on business and remained there until 1832. His most famous stories, "Rip Van Winkle" and "The Legend of Sleepy Hollow," appeared first in *The Sketch Book of Geoffrey Crayon* (1820). None of his later works approached the success of this collection. He served as U.S. minister to Spain 1842-46, but spent the rest of his life in Tarrytown, N.Y., near the setting of many of his tales.

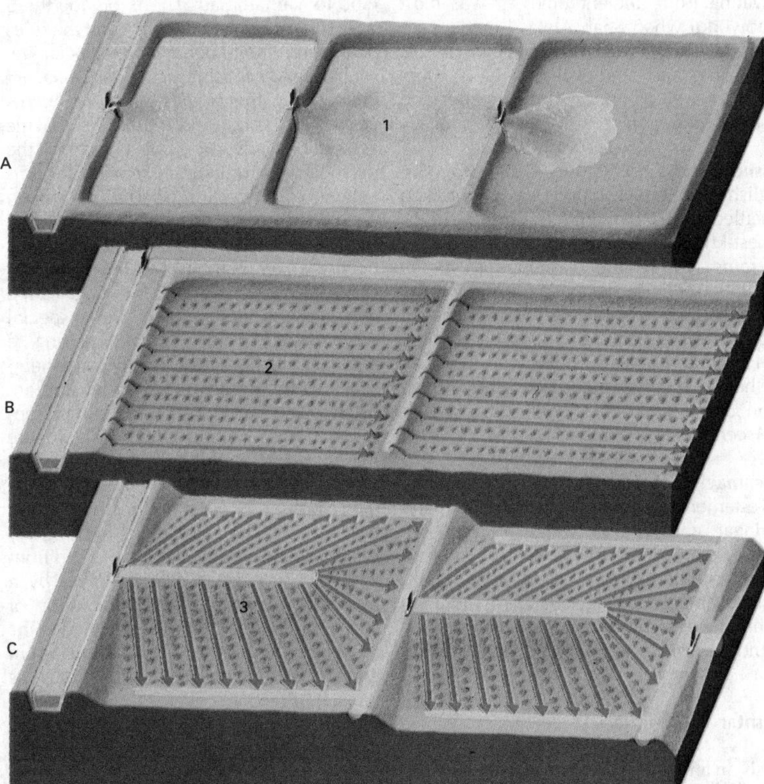

Irrigation: water is distributed over the land in many different ways, depending on the slope of the land, the crop and the amount of water available. The oldest method is flooding the land (A), when a large amount of water is available for fields or basins (1). An other method is building small dikes and channels (B). Certain amounts of water can be brought into these channels (2). An other method (C) is the use of streaming water along a slope. The water flows from the canals into the land (3).

The goddess Isis

Isaac, in the Old Testament (Genesis), second of the Hebrew patriarchs. Son of Abraham and Sarah and half-brother of Ishmael, he was spared at the last moment from being sacrificed as proof of his father's faith. He married Rebecca and fathered Esau and Jacob.

Isabella, name of 2 queens of Spain. **Isabella I** (1451-1504) was queen of Castile from 1474 and of Aragon from 1479. Her marriage to Ferdinand V unified Christian Spain; royal power was strengthened and the Inquisition reestablished, Isabella supporting its call for the expulsion of Spanish Jews. She financed Columbus's expedition in 1492, and helped direct the conquest of Moorish Granada. **Isabella II** (1830-1904) was queen of Spain (1833-68). Her succession was disputed by the Carlists, provoking civil war (1833-39). Her personal rule proved arbitrary and ineffectual. She was deposed in 1868 and abdicated in 1870.

Isaiah, Hebrew prophet of the 8th century B.C. for whom the Old Testament Book of Isaiah was named; probably only the first 36 chapters represent his teachings, the remainder (often known as Deutero- and Trito-Isaiah) being additions by his followers. Isaiah condemned the decadence of the kingdom of Judah, foretelling coming disaster; he warned against trusting in foreign alliances rather than in God, and heralded the Messiah.

Iscariot, Judas *see:* Judas Iscariot.

Isfahan, or Esfahan (pop. 926,600), city in west-central Iran, on the Zayandeh River. Dating from ancient times, it was most powerful when Shah Abbas I made it his capital (1598-1629). It is known for its mosques and medieval Islamic architecture as well as hand-painted textiles and steel production.

Islamic call to prayer from atop a minaret in Istanbul

Isherwood, Christopher (1904-86), English-born novelist and playwright who settled in the United States in 1939. His best-known novels are *Mr. Norris Changes Trains* (1935) and *Goodbye to Berlin* (1939), set in the decaying Germany of the 1930s. These were later adapted into a play, *I Am a Camera* by John Van Druten (1951), and into a film musical, *Cabaret.* Isherwood collaborated with W.H. Auden on 3 plays, the best known being *The Ascent of F.6* (1936).

Ishmael (Hebrew, "outcast"), in the Old Testament (Genesis), son of Abraham and Hagar and half-brother of Isaac, considered an ancestor by Arabs. Abraham, at the insistence of his jealous wife, Sarah, sent Ishmael and Hagar (Sarah's handmaid) into the desert. Ishmael was saved by God and became a great warrior and the father of 12 sons.

Ishtar *see:* Astarte.

Isis, in ancient Egyptian mythology, nature goddess, sister and wife of Osiris, mother of Horus. The worship of Isis was associated with magic and mystery. The cult of Isis spread throughout the Mediterranean.

Islam (Arabic, "submitting oneself to God"), one of the major world religions, the youngest of the 3 monotheistic religions developed in the Middle East. Most of the more than 600 million followers of Islam, or Muslims, live in the Arab countries of southwestern Asia, in northern and eastern Africa, Turkey, Iran, Afghanistan, Pakistan, the Malay Peninsula, and Indonesia. There are also large numbers in the Soviet Union, China, India, and the Philippines. Islam was founded by Muhammad, who was born c.570 A.D. in Mecca In his travels as a merchant he came to know the Christian and Jewish religions. After a period of meditation, during which he said the archangel Gabriel spoke to him, Muhammad began preaching in Mecca. He denounced the worship of idols and proclaimed that there was only one God (*Allah*, in Arabic) and that he was God's messenger to carry the teaching to the pagans. He angered many of the people of Mecca, who forced him to flee to Medina c.622. There, he gathered followers and returned to Mecca in 630 to wage a *jihad* (holy war). Islam was finally accepted by the Meccans, who called Muhammad their prophet. In the 100 years after Muhammad's death (632), Arab armies swept across Asia as far as India and across North Africa and into Spain, building the great Muslim Empire, spreading their religion and culture. The holy book of Islam is the Koran (Qur'an), which sets forth the fundamental beliefs of Islam as revealed by God to Muhammad. These include the 5 basic duties of every Muslim and the rules that govern moral behavior and social life. Muhammad's teachings, called *Sunna*, are collected in the *Hadith* ("traditions"). Together, the Koran and the Sunna provide instructions governing all aspects of the personal and communal life of Muslims. A system of law, the *Shari'a*, has been developed on the basis of the Koran and the Sunna. At various times, the Shari'a has been the law of many Muslim countries. Public worship is held in buildings called mosques. At midday every Friday special services are held. Before entering a mosque, Muslims must ritually wash themselves in the courtyard. The mosques are usually elaborately decorated, but no representations of animal or human figures are permitted because of proscriptions against idolatry. When praying, 5 times during the day, Muslims face in the direction of their holy city, Mecca. Worship is led by a lay religious leader called an *imam.* Traditionally, Muslims are called to prayer by a *muezzin*, who chants from a rooftop or from a *minaret,* a tall tower attached to the mosque. The 2 main sects of Islam, Sunni and Shiah, originated in the 7th century as a result of disputes over the succession of *caliphs* or religious rulers. Sunnites form the majority, while the large Shi'te minority predominates in Iran and has given rise to other smaller sects.

Islamabad (pop. 236,000), city in northeast Pakistan, capital since its construction in the 1960s. This planned city replaced the former capital, Karachi.
See also: Pakistan.

Islamic art, art and architecture that grew out of the Islamic way of life. Because there was no strong tradition of Arab art, it adapted the Byzantine, Sassanian, and

Islamic architecture. The 17th century Mashid-y-Shah mosque in Iran.

Coptic styles of Muslim-dominated lands. Arab influence added a sense of visual rhythm and an interest in astronomy and mathematics. Interpretations of the prophet Muhammad's sayings, however, forbade portrayals of people or animals either in religious art or elsewhere. In general, designs relied on abstract and mathematical forms, as well as the calligraphic rendering of Koranic texts; often every available piece of a building is so decorated. Early examples of Islamic architecture are the Kaaba and the Dome of the Rock in Jerusalem. The dominant style of mosque, with a minaret tower, was introduced under the Umayyad dynasty. A characteristic feature of Islamic buildings is the arch, in horseshoe, trefoil, and zigzag forms. The greatest Muslim mausoleum is the Taj Mahal. The Moorish Alhambra in Granada, Spain, is the most famous palace in the Islamic style. In craftwork there is also a distinctive Islamic tradition; as well as its famous rugs and textiles, the Islamic world developed beautiful pottery, including luster-glazed ceramics and metalwork.
See also: Islam.

Island, land area entirely surrounded by water, but not so large that it ranks as a continent (such as Australia). The world's largest islands are Greenland (840,000 sq mi/2,175,600 sq km) and New Guinea (342,400 sq mi/886,820 sq km). Of the lesser islands, only Borneo, Madagascar, and Sumatra exceed 160,000 sq mi (414,400 sq km). Some islands were once part of the continents they adjoin (British Isles); others are built up by volcanic activity (Hawaii). Many Pacific islands are the work of coral polyps (marine animals).

Isle of Man *see:* Man, Isle of.

Isle of Wight *see:* Wight, Isle of.

Islets of Langerhans *see:* Pancreas.

Isocrates (436-338 B.C.), Greek orator and pupil of Socrates who founded a celebrated school of rhetoric in Athens. His vision of a Greece united to invade Persia influenced Alexander the Great.

Isolationism, national policy of avoiding entanglement in foreign affairs, a recurrent phenomenon in U.S. history. In 1823 the Monroe Doctrine tried to exclude European powers from the Americas. The United States entered World War I reluctantly, stayed out of the League of Nations it helped create, and entered World War II only when attacked. Thereafter it joined the UN and international defense pacts (NATO, SEATO) and played an active role in international affairs. British policy was essentially isolationist in the period between the world wars.

Isomers, chemical compounds having identical chemical composition and molecular formula, but differing in the arrangement of atoms in their molecules, and having different properties. The 2 chief types are stereoisomers, which have the same structural formula, and structural isomers, which have different structural formulas.

Isoptera, order of insects that live in colonies and have a highly developed social organization. Insects in this category are called termites.

Isotope, atom of a chemical element which has the same number of protons in the nucleus, but a different number of neutrons, i.e., having the same atomic number but different mass. Isotopes of an element have identical chemical but varying physical properties. Most elements have several stable isotopes, being found in nature as mixtures. A few elements have natural radioactive isotopes (radioisotopes), which are unstable, and others of these can be made by exposing stable isotopes to radiation in a reactor.
See also: Element.

Israel, republic in southwest Asia, at the eastern end of the Mediterranean Sea. The capital is Jerusalem.

Land. Israel is 7,992 sq mi (20,700 sq km). On the west is a long, straight coastline on the Mediterranean; to the south, a very short coastline gives it access to the Gulf of Aqaba of the Red Sea through the port of Elath. The 3 geographical regions are the mountainous Galilee region of the north, the western coastal plain, and the Negev desert in the south. To the east is an extensive depression, parts of which are the Huleh Valley, the Sea of Galilee, and the Jordan River. In the south the same geographical fault includes the Dead Sea and runs on to the Gulf of Aqaba, forming the southern border with Jordan. A short corridor extends from the coastal plain through the Judean hills to the city of Jerusalem. The narrow coastal plain (4-20 mi/6.4-32 km in width) is the most fertile part of the country. It is here that Israel's extensive orange groves are found. It also contains Tel Aviv-Jaffa, the country's most

Israel

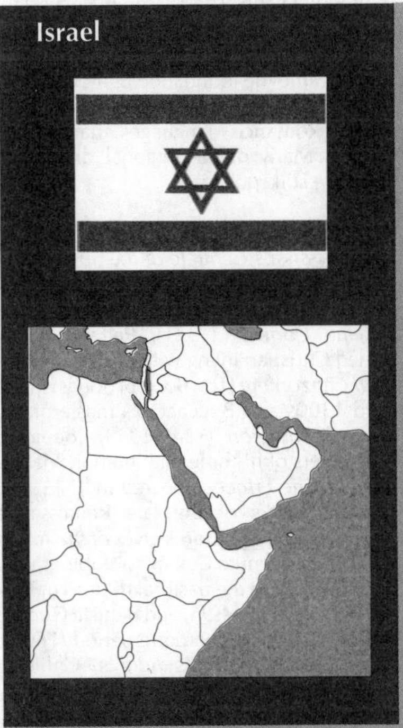

General information	
Capital:	Jerusalem
Area:	7,992 sq mi (20,700 sq km)
Population:	4,563,000
Official languages:	Arabic, Hebrew
Monetary unit:	1 New shekel = 100 agorot
Main cities:	Jerusalem, Tel Aviv-Yafo, Haifa
Government	
Form:	republic
Independent:	1948
Head of state:	President (elected every 5 years)
Head of government:	Prime Minister
Legislature:	one legislative house (Knesset)
Executive:	President and Cabinet
Judiciary:	highest court is the Supreme Court
Political division:	6 districts
National economy	
Gross national product:	U.S. $38,440,000,000
Per capita income:	U.S. $8,650
Agriculture:	citrus fruit, vegetables, wheat, potatoes, melons and pumpkins, avocados, cotton
Livestock:	poultry, cattle, sheep
Fisheries:	29,000 metric tons
Mining:	phosphate rock, potash, natural gas
Industries:	wheat flour, sulfuric acid, polyethylene, cardboard, paper, diamond cutting
Main exports:	machinery, diamonds, metals and metal products, fruit and vegetables
Transportation:	328 mi (528 km) of railroads; 7,968 mi (12,823 km) of roads; 1 international airport
Trading partners:	U.S., Belgium-Luxembourg, Germany, United Kingdom, Switzerland
People	
Urban:	90%
Ethnic composition:	Jewish 83.0%, Arab 17%
Birth rate:	22.6 per 1,000 population
Death rate:	6.6 per 1,000 population
Infant mortality:	10 per 1,000 live births
Life expectancy:	male 73.5 years, female 77 years

Jerusalem, Israel

populous city. The northern Negev has fertile, wind-deposited soil but little rainfall; much of the southern Negev is dry, barren rock. Israel has seen extensive land reclamation and development undertaken by Jewish settlers in the 20th century. The former Huleh Lake in the north was drained to provide farmland. The Dead Sea, however, has remained much the same. Lands occupied by Israeli forces in 1967 during the Six-Day War included portions of Egypt (the entire Sinai Peninsula up to the banks of the Suez Canal, as well as the Gaza Strip, a mandated territory that had been administered by Egypt but was not formally a part of it), Jordan (the entire sector of that country west of the Jordan River), and Syria (the strategic Golan Heights, east of the Sea of Galilee).

People. The majority of Israel's citizens are Jews, and of these the greatest number are immigrants. The largest minority group (over 15% of the population) is of Arabs, for the most part in self-contained rural communities. Other minority groups include Druses, Circassians, and Samaritans. The official language is Hebrew, but because of the high percentage of immigrants, many Israelis remain more literate in languages other than Hebrew. The second most dominant language is Arabic, and many native-born Israeli Jews speak it. English is also widely spoken, along with French, German, and Yiddish. Elementary schooling is free and compulsory, and there are reduced fees and special grants for promising students in secondary schools. A large minority of pupils attend state-supported religious schools. Arab pupils generally attend their own schools. There are also schools run by Christian communities and missionary groups. Universities and institutions of higher learning include the Hebrew University in Jerusalem, Tel Aviv University, Bar Ilan University in Ramat Gan, the Technion in Haifa, and the Weizmann Institute of Science in Rehovot. The majority of Israel's population is urban, but its rural population is highly important. There are over 200 agrarian settlements known as *kibbutzim,* in which the members share all goods and receive no wages; all meals are eaten together, important decisions are made by a general meeting of all the members, and children are raised in special houses, away from their parents. Other agricultural settlements also practice cooperative or communal living to some degree, such as common ownership of land or cooperative purchasing and marketing.

Economy. Land reclamation and irrigation have nearly tripled the cultivated area since 1955. Major crops include citrus fruit, grains, olives, melons, and grapes. Mineral resources include gypsum, natural gas, oil, and phosphates; potash, magnesium, and bromine come from the Dead Sea. Light industry is developing, and manufactures include chemicals, textiles, and paper. Tourism is a major industry. Because of heavy defense spending and reliance on imported oil, Israel suffers from severe payments deficits and one of the world's highest inflation rates—exceeding 100% per year.

History. In 1947 the UN voted to divide Palestine (then under British mandate) into Jewish and Arab states. After the subsequent British withdrawal, Palestine Arabs and Arab troops from neighboring countries immediately tried to eradicate Israel by force, but the Israelis defeated them, capturing almost all of Palestine. Arab refugees, settled in southern Lebanon, the West Bank, and Gaza Strip in UN-administered camps, are a continuing social and political problem. Refugee camps have proved a fruitful recruiting area and cover for Palestinian guerrilla groups. When Egypt nationalized the Suez Canal in 1956 and closed it to Israeli shipping, Israeli troops overran Gaza and Sinai, winning the right of passage from Elath to the Red Sea. In the Six-Day War (1967) Israel acquired large tracts of its neighbors' territories, including the West Bank and East Jerusalem; these it refused to return without a firm peace settlement. It lost some of these in the Yom Kippur War (1973). In 1978 Egypt and Israel reached the so-called Camp David accords, and Israel began returning the Sinai to Egypt. In 1978 and 1981 Israeli troops invaded south Lebanon in retaliation for Palestinian attacks in Israel, and Israeli bombers destroyed an alleged atomic bomb plant in Iraq in 1981. In 1982 Israeli forces invading Lebanon besieged Beirut; in time Palestinian guerrillas left the city and the Israelis partially withdrew from Lebanon. In 1985 Israeli forces left Lebanon except for a small strip of land in the south. Israel's continued occupation of the West Bank and Gaza remained a problem for Arabs and was a factor in making the country a target of Iraqi missiles in the War in the Persian Gulf (1991). In the early 1990s negotiations regarding the occupied territories improved, and Jericho district on the West Bank and the Gaza Strip attained some form of autonomy in 1994. During the peace process prime minister Rabin was killed (Nov. 1995). Under his successor Netanyahu the process stagnated.

See also: Palestine; Palestine Liberation Organization; Zionism.

Israel, Kingdom of, Hebrew kingdom, first as united under Saul, David, and Solomon (1020-922 B.C.), and then the breakaway state in the north founded by Jeroboam I in the territory of the 10 tribes. In 722 B.C. this was overrun by the Assyrians; the tribes were killed, enslaved, or scattered.

Israelites *see:* Jews.

Istanbul (pop. 6,620,200), city in northwest Turkey, lying on the Sea of Marmara and divided by the Bosporus (strait). Until 1930 its official name was Constantinople, of which Istanbul was originally a contraction. Built in A.D. 330 on the site of a former Greek town, Byzantium, it reached its cultural height under Justinian I in the 6th century. After years of decay it was taken by the Ottoman Turks in 1453, and was rebuilt as the Turkish capital, which it remained until 1923 when the capital was moved to Ankara. It is still the economic and cultural heart of Turkey, a port, transport hub, and manufacturing center.

See also: Turkey.

Isthmus, narrow strip of land connecting 2 large land masses. Examples are the Isthmus of Panama, linking North and South America, and the Isthmus of Suez, linking Africa and Asia.

Italian, one of the Romance languages, spoken in Italy and in parts of Switzerland, France, and Yugoslavia. It derives from colloquial Latin. The Tuscan dialect established in the late Middle Ages as a literary language by Dante, Petrarch, and Boccaccio became the foundation of modern Italian. Since the Renaissance, words from other Romance languages have been added. Many of the regional dialects of Italy are still spoken.

Italian literature, literature dated to Francis of Assissi's *Canticle of the Sun* (1226), written not in Latin but the vernacular. The love theme was expressed in Dante's *The Divine Comedy* (1321). Petrarch combined Christian living with classical ethics in *Il Canzoniere* (The Book of Songs) in the mid 1300s and Boccaccio's masterpiece, *The Decameron* (1349-1353), depicted characters of his time with humor. Machiavelli's *The Prince* appeared in 1513. Important works of the late Renaissance include Giorgio Vasari's *Lives of the Artists* (1550), Benvenuto Cellini's autobiography (1558-62), and the pastoral dramas of Torquato Tasso (1544-95) and Battista Guarini (1536-1612). The baroque period (1600s) gave rise to Marino's Adonis, Galileo's scientific prose and Camparella's *The City of the Sun.* The Age of Reason (1700s) was characterized by a less elaborate poetic style. Among the most significant works were the opera libretti (texts) by Pietro Metastasio (1698-1782) and plays of Carlo Goldoni (1707-93), which drew heavily on the tradition of improvised comic theater called *commedia dell'arte.* Romanticism (1800s) celebrated sentiment over reason. A major figure was the poet, novelist, and playwright Alessandro Manzoni (1785-1873). A major movement in Italian literature and theater of the late 19th century was *verismo,* in which the harsh realities of

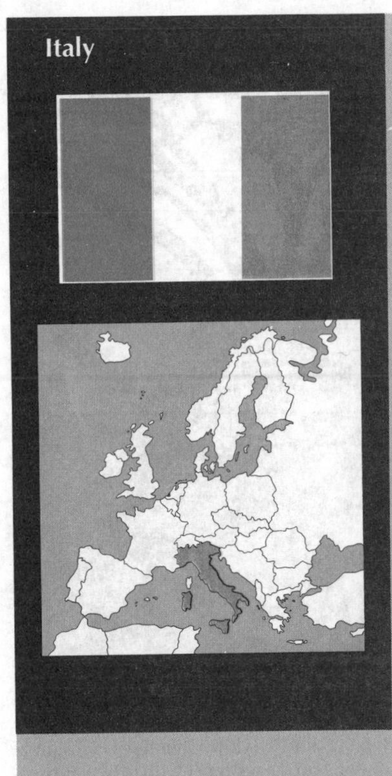

General information	
Capital:	Rome
Area:	116,324 sq mi (301,277 sq km)
Population:	57,436,000
Official language:	Italian
Monetary unit:	1 Lira = 100 centesimi
Main cities:	Rome, Milan, Naples, Turin
Government	
Form:	republic
Independent:	1946 (republic)
Head of state:	President (elected every 7 years)
Head of government:	Prime Minister
Legislature:	two legislative houses (Senate and Chamber of Deputies)
Executive:	President and Council of Ministers
Judiciary:	highest court is the Constitutional Court
Political division:	20 regions, 94 provinces
National economy	
Gross national product:	U.S. $765,282,000,000
Per capita income:	U.S. $13,320
Agriculture:	sugar beets, grapes, wheat, corn, tomatoes, olives, citrus fruits
Livestock:	sheep, pigs, cattle
Fisheries:	554,000 metric tons
Mining:	salt, lignite, pyrites, fluorspar, barytes, asbestos, natural gas, marble, granite
Industries:	cement, crude steel, pig iron, chemical fertilizers, sulfuric acid
Main exports:	machinery and transportation equipment, clothing, shoes, chemicals
Transportation:	12,156 mi (19,563 km) of railroads; 187,391 mi (301,577 km) of roads; 25 international airports
Trading partners:	Germany, France, U.S., United Kingdom, Switzerland, The Netherlands
People	
Urban:	67%
Ethnic composition:	Italian 94%, Sardinian 2.5%, Rhaetian 1.5%
Birth rate:	9.6 per 1,000 population
Death rate:	9.3 per 1,000 population
Infant mortality:	10 per 1,000 live births
Life expectancy:	male 71.5 years, female 78 years

the lives of the poor were portrayed. The futurism movement, typified by the writings of Filippo Tommaso Marinetti (1876-1944), employed language glorifying the violence of the machine age. Luigi Pirandello (1876-1936), who won the 1934 Nobel Prize for literature, wrote novels but was best known for such ironic and philosophical plays as *Six Characters in Search of an Author* (1921).

The post-World War II neorealists include Alberto Moravia (1907-) and Cesare Parese (1908-50). Recently the novelist Italo Calvino (1923-85) and the playwright Dario Fo (1926-) have achieved international fame.

Italian Somaliland *see:* Somalia.

Italo-Ethiopian War (1935-36), Fascist Italy's conquest of Ethiopia, launched from Italian-held Eritrea and Somalia. Refusing to accept the League of Nations proposals for settling border disputes, Benito Mussolini used planes, guns, and poison gas to overwhelm the ill-equipped Ethiopians, and to forge a new empire. Too weak to halt aggression, the League merely voted economic sanctions against Italy, which simply left the League.
See also: Mussolini, Benito.

Italy, republic in southern Europe, mainly a long, narrow, boot-shaped peninsula that extends into the Mediterranean Sea. It is bounded on the north by France, Switzerland, Austria, and Yugoslavia; on the west by the Ligurian and Tyrrhenian seas; on the east by the Adriatic Sea; and to the south by the Ionian Sea. The islands of Sicily and Sardinia and numerous smaller islands are parts of its territory. Within its borders are 2 separate, sovereign states: the Republic of San Marino and the Vatican City. The capital is Rome.

Land and climate. A predominantly mountainous country, Italy is divided by a number of natural barriers into distinct regions. In the north is the great curve of the Alps, along which lie Italy's borders with its northern neighbors. In north-central and northeastern Italy are the lakes of Como, Maggiore, and Garda. The Apennine chain runs the length of the peninsula, extending in an easterly direction from Genoa to central Italy and then in a westerly direction into Calabria, the "toe" of the Italian "boot." There are a number of crater lakes in these regions, and the volcanoes of Vesuvius near Naples, Etna in Sicily, and Stromboli in the Lipari Islands are still active. The mountains of Sicily are a continuation of the Apennines, and Sardinia is also mountainous. Italy's single large plain lies in the Po Valley, which crosses the country from west to east just below the Alps. There are narrow coastal plains on either side of the Apennines, and a low, relatively small plateau lies below the Gargano spur. These alluvial plains constitute Italy's most fertile soil. The mountainous areas are largely unproductive. The Po River is Italy's largest and most important river. The Tiber flows through Rome to the Tyrrhenian Sea, and the Arno passes

The Chianti Hills of Italy produce the famous Chianti wine.

through Florence and Pisa to empty into the Ligurian Sea. Both rivers rise in the Apennines. Most other rivers in Italy are seasonal, and their volume is greatly diminished during the summer. In the Alps, the Po Valley, and the high ranges of the Apennines, winters are cold and summers can be rainy and variable. The rest of the peninsula has a Mediterranean climate: hot, dry summers and mild, rainy winters. Southern Italy and Sicily are especially arid, and irrigation is essential for successful cultivation. Remnants of great forests are found in the Alps, where fir and pine trees grow, and in the remote areas of the Apennines, where there are stands of chestnut, pine, oak, and beech trees. In central and southern Italy olive groves cover much of the land, while the southern regions also produce cacti, citrus trees, and palm trees. With the exception of bears, chamois, deer, and wolves in some remote mountain regions, Italy has few large mammals. Tuna, anchovies, and sardines are plentiful in offshore waters.

Rome contains imposing ruins of its past glory as capital of the western world and is of commercial and cultural importance. The cities of Milan, Turin, and Genoa in the north form the so-called industrial triangle, Milan leading in finance and commerce, Turin in heavy industry, and Genoa in international shipping. Italy's art cities—Venice, Verona, Bologna, Ravenna, Florence, and Siena—bear witness to the significance of Italian culture. Naples, the south's principal city and an international port, is a center for excursions to nearby Sorrento, the islands of Capri and Ischia, and the ruins of Pompeii and Herculaneum. Palermo, the capital of Sicily, has medieval relics of the Norman occupation.

People. Italy is one of the most densely populated countries in the world. The highest concentrations are in the industrial cities of the north, the Po Valley, and the areas around Rome and Naples, almost half the population being urban. Italian, which is derived from Latin, is the official language and is spoken by most citizens, along with a number of regional dialects. Roman Catholicism is the state religion and is taught in the public schools, but freedom of religion is guaranteed.

Economy. Foreign aid and founder membership in the European Common Market boosted postwar economy before the oil crises of the 1970s damaged it. Increased industrial output (steel, chemicals, automobiles, typewriters, machinery, textiles, and shoes) enriched the north, but a faltering agriculture kept the south poor. The main farm products are grapes, citrus fruits, olives, grains, vegetables, and cattle. Mineral resources are limited, but Italy has hydroelectric power, natural gas, and oil. There are also a few nuclear power stations. Tourism helps the trade balance.

History. The Romans, a Latin people of central Italy, held most of the peninsula by 200 B.C., absorbing the Etruscan civilization in the north and Greek colonies (dating from the 8th century B.C.) in the south. In the 5th-6th centuries A.D., barbarian tribes (Visigoths, Ostrogoths, and Lombards) overran Italy, forming Germanic kingdoms. These kingdoms were disputed by the Byzantine Empire, whose lands in Italy became the core of the Papal States. Italy was to remain divided for over 1,000 years, although nominally part of Charlemagne's empire from 774 and part of the Holy Roman Empire from 962. In the Middle Ages the south came under Norman rule. Powerful rival city-states emerged in the center and north, from the late Middle Ages under the Medici and other dynasties. Italy pioneered the Renaissance, but Spain (from the late 1400s) and Austria (from the early 1700s) controlled much of the land until the nationalistic Risorgimento culminated in unity and independence under King Victor Emmanuel II (1861). Italy gained Eritrea, Italian Somaliland, and Libya in Africa, and fought alongside the Allies in World War I. In 1922 the fascist dictator Benito Mussolini seized power, later conquering Ethiopia and siding with Nazi Germany in World War II. Defeated Italy emerged from the war as a republic shorn of its overseas colonies and firmly allied with the West.

Charles Ives

Iturbide, Agustín de (1783-1824), Mexican revolutionary and emperor of Mexico (1822-23). As a royalist officer, he united the revolutionaries with his Plan of Iguala (1821), which proclaimed Mexican independence. Exploiting political divisions, he became emperor of independent Mexico. But opposition to his capricious rule brought abdication, exile, and (on his return) execution.

Ivan, name of 6 Russian rulers. **Ivan I** (c.1304-40) was grand prince of Moscow 1328-40. **Ivan II** (1326-59) was grand prince of Moscow 1353-59. **Ivan III**, Ivan the Great (1440-1505), was grand duke of Moscow 1462-1505. He paved the way for a unified Russia by annexing land, repelling the Tatars, strengthening central authority over the Church and nobility, and revising the law code. **Ivan IV**, Ivan the Terrible (1530-84), was grand prince from 1533 and the first tsar of Russia (1547-84). He annexed Siberia, consolidated control of the Volga River, and established diplomatic and trading relations with Europe. He strengthened the law and administration, but was notoriously cruel. **Ivan V** (1666-96) was co-tsar (with Peter I) 1682-90. **Ivan VI** (1740-64) was tsar 1740-41.

Ivan V *see:* Peter I, the Great.

Ives, Charles Edward (1874-1954), U.S. composer. Ives was a major 20th-century innovator. His music (mostly pre-1915) incorporated popular songs and hymn tunes, and exploited dissonance, polytonality, and polymetric construction. Ignored by his contemporaries, he influenced later composers. His best-known works include *Three Places in New England* (1908-14) and *Piano Sonata No. 2* (*Concord, Mass., 1840-1860*) (1909-15). His *Symphony No. 3* (1904-11) won a 1947 Pulitzer Prize.

Ives, James Merritt *see:* Currier & Ives.

Ivory tusks destroyed to prevent illegal trade

Ivory, hard white dentine substance making up the tusks of elephants, walruses, and other tusked mammals. Ivory has been greatly prized as a material for carving decorative objects for centuries. The poaching of elephants for their tusks threatens their existence in Africa.

Ivory Coast, republic in West Africa. The capital is Abidjan.

Land and climate. The Ivory Coast occupies about 124,500 sq mi (322,450 sq km) on the northern coast of the Gulf of Guinea and is bordered on the east by Ghana, on the west by Liberia and Guinea, and on the north by Mali and Upper Volta. Behind the sand spits, navigable lagoons, and surf beaches of the 315-mi (507-km) coastline, a dense rain forest extends northward over more than a third of the country. Beyond the forest the ground rises to a plateau, with grass and woodland savannas and isolated granitic masses. The northwest is mountainous. The Sassandra, Bandama, Comoé, Cavally, and other rivers flow southward to the Gulf of Guinea, but only short distances are navigable owing to the many rapids. The climate is hot. The rainy season lengthens and the amount of rain increases the farther one goes south. The extreme south has 2 distinct rainy seasons.

People. The population contains many ethnic and tribal groups, the most important being the Baoulé, Agnis-Ashantis, Kroumen, Mandé, Dan-Gouro, and Koua. Nearly a million Africans from Upper Volta, Guinea, and Mali live in the Ivory Coast, and there are some 35,000 French, Lebanese, and others. Less than 20% of the population lives in the towns, the largest of which is Abidjan, capital, chief port, and university center. Over 60% of the population is animist; 25% (mainly in the north) is Muslim, and nearly 13% is Christian. Some 60 tribal languages are spoken, but

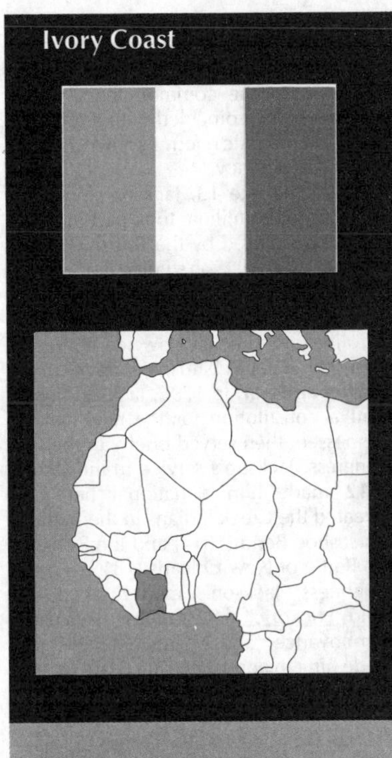

Ivory Coast

General information	
Capital:	Yamoussoukro
Area:	124,503 sq mi (322,462 sq km)
Population:	12,135,000
Official language:	French
Monetary unit:	1 CFA franc = 100 centimes
Main cities:	Abidjan, Bouaké, Yamoussoukro
Government	
Form:	republic
Independent:	1960
Head of state:	President (elected every 5 years)
Head of government:	President
Legislature:	one legislative house (National Assembly)
Executive:	President and Council of Ministers
Judiciary:	highest court is the Supreme Court
Political division:	34 departments
National economy	
Gross national product:	US $8,590,000,000
Per capita income:	US $740
Agriculture:	yams, sugar, cane, cassava, bananas, corn, cocoa, beans, coffee, pineapples
Livestock:	sheep, goats, cattle
Mining:	crude petroleum, diamands, manganese
Industries:	cement, beer, carbonated beverages, synthetic fibers, cotton fiber and textiles
Main exports:	cocoa beans, coffee, fuels, cocoa butter
Transportation:	341 mi (549 km) of railroads; 33,560 mi (54,000 km) of roads, 1 international airport
Trading partners:	France, The Netherlands, Italy, Germany, Nigeria, U.S.
People	
Urban:	47%
Ethnic composition:	Akan 41.5%, Kru 17%, Voltaic 16%, Malinke 15%, Southern Mande 10%
Birth rate:	46 per 1,000 population
Death rate:	13 per 1,000 population
Infant mortality:	102 per 1,000 live births
Life expectancy:	male 51, female 54 years

French is used officially and in commerce and education. The republic devotes 25% of its annual budget to education.

Economy. The Ivory Coast is one of the most prosperous countries in West Africa. Farming, forestry, and fisheries provide most of the gross national product. Major cash crops are cotton, coffee, and cocoa. Palm oil, pineapples, and bananas are also exported, as are hardwoods, including mahogany, iroko, satinwood, and teak. Diamonds and manganese are mined. Trade is chiefly with European Community (EC) countries and the United States. The Ivory Coast is an associated state of the EC.

History. Once a French colony, the Ivory Coast became autonomous within the French Community in 1958, but soon opted for full independence (1960). Close economic, cultural, and defense ties with France were retained. Its attitude has tended to be pro-Western, but so far as East-West relations are concerned its official line is neutrality.

Ivory palm, or ivory nut palm (Phytelephas macrocarpa), slow-growing palm with a short trunk, native to South America. Plants are male or female. Female flowers form a cluster of seeds that ripen and fall to the ground. Hard and white, the seeds are easy to carve and are used for buttons, chess pieces, and small ornaments.

Ivy, hardy, evergreen plant (genus *Hedera*) of the family Araliaceae. The English ivy (*H. helix*) is a popular house plant, coming in a number of dwarf, climbing, and variegated varieties. Several other plants that have ivylike leaves are also called ivy, for example ground ivy (*Glectoma hederacea*) and Boston or grape ivy (*Parthenocissus tricuspidata*).

Iwo Jima, Japanese island in the western Pacific, scene of a fierce battle in World War II. Largest of the Volcano islands (about 8 sq mi/21 sq km), it was annexed by Japan in 1891 and captured by U.S. marines in Feb.-Mar. 1945 at the cost of over 21,000 U.S. casualties. U.S. administration ended in 1968.
See also: World War II.

Ixtacihuatl, or Iztaccihuatl (Aztec, "white woman"), dormant volcano in central Mexico, about 35 mi (56 km) southeast of Mexico City. Its 3 snow-covered peaks resemble the head, breasts, and feet of a sleeping woman.

Izmir (Greek: Smyrna; pop. 1,489,700), port city on the west coast of Turkey, at the head of the Gulf of Izmir, about 45 mi (72 km) from the Aegean Sea. Founded by Ionians in the 11th century B.C., the city came under Roman rule. In the 4th century A.D. it became part of the Byzantine Empire and, in 1424, of the Ottoman Empire. The Greeks occupied the city in 1919. The Treaty of Lausanne (1923) restored Izmir to Turkey, and an exchange of populations was made. The city is rich in antiquities, including the agora, or ancient marketplace, and remains of aqueducts.
See also: Turkey.

Church in Yamoussouko, Ivory Coast, designed to resemble St. Peter's Church in Rome

J

J, tenth letter of the English alphabet. One of the last letters added to the alphabet, *j* is a variant of the letter *i*, from which it became formally distinguished only with the advent of printing. Before that time, *j* was simply an elongated *i*, and the 2 characters were used interchangeably. Thus, in Roman numerals, *j* sometimes replaced *i* to signify 1. It has the sound of *y* in Latin, German, and Scandinavian languages. In Spanish it has the sound of *h*.

Jabbar, Kareem Abdul- *see:* Abdul-Jabbar, Kareem.

Jabiru, any of various large birds of the stork family found from Mexico to Argentina. Jabirus are white with dark blue and red naked skin on the head and neck. Among the largest flying birds in the world, they may reach 55 in (125 cm) in length. They nest in palm trees.

Jaçana, any of several water birds of the jaçana family with long legs and toes that enable it to walk on water lilies and other floating plants. Jaçanas are brightly colored and are found in Africa, southern Asia, Australia, and in the Americas.

Andrew Jackson

7th U.S. President

Born:	Waxhaw settlement, S.C.; Mar. 15, 1767
Term:	Mar. 1829-Mar. 1837
Vice presidents:	John C. Calhoun; Martin Van Buren
Political party:	Democratic
Spouse:	Rachel Donelson Robards Jackson
Children:	None
Died:	Nashville, Tenn.; June 8, 1845

Jacaranda, any of various species of flowering tree (genus *Jacaranda*) native to South America and the West Indies and grown widely in Africa, the southern United States, and other warm places. The foliage is made up of fern-like fronds of small leaves; the blue or violet flowers grow in clusters.

Jackal, carnivorous mammal (genus *Canus*) closely related to dogs and wolves. The four species are distributed throughout Africa and South Asia. Though often considered primarily scavengers, jackals will also hunt and kill birds, hares, mice, and insects. Small packs may form temporarily, but they are usually solitary animals.

Jackdaw, small crow (*Carrus monedula*) of Europe, western Asia, and North Africa. It is renowned for its inquisitive and thievish nature and its ability to imitate speech.

Jack Frost, personification of winter, depicted in many children's stories as a rosy-cheeked imp. During the night he paints the world with frost, tracing delicate patterns on window panes and leaving icicles on trees. He probably originated in Scandinavian mythology.

Jack-in-the-pulpit, any of several plants of the arum family (genus *Arisaema*) that flower in spring before the leaves appear. The flower is really an elaborate, colored tubular structure called a spathe. It surrounds a stem, the spadix, on which many small flowers grow. The flowers are fertilized by flies, and by autumn the spathe falls away to reveal a cluster of bright red berries which are poisonous when eaten raw.

Jack rabbit, common name for hares of the genus *Lepus*. All seven species are found in central and western North America. Jackrabbits have large ears and longer hind legs than rabbits. Found in open, comparatively arid plains, they flourish in drought-stricken, overgrazed areas. They move by jumping rather than running.

Jackson (pop. 395,396), capital and largest city of Mississippi, located on the west bank of the Pearl River. Local industries include processing of cottonseed oil, lumbering, and manufacture of agricultural machinery. There are many oil and gasfields in the region. Founded as a trading post around 1780, Jackson was incorporated in 1821 and named after Andrew Jackson. The city was nearly destroyed during the Civil War.
See also: Mississippi.

Jackson, Alexander Young (1882-1974), an original member of "The Group of Seven" Toronto landscape artists of the 1920s and 1930s. He painted in bold, fresh colors, portraying the beauty of the Canadian wilderness.
See also: Group of Seven.

Jackson, Andrew (1767-1845), 7th president of the United States. Jackson, the first person from west of the Appalachians to be elected president, transformed the presidency with his rugged frontier virtues and devotion to "the common man." His 2 terms in office coincided with a great period of democratic reforms known as "Jacksonian Democracy."

Early life. At age 13, Jackson joined the South Carolina militia, took part in battle, and was captured by the British. He was later released. Jackson studied law and was admitted to the bar in 1787. In 1788, he moved to Nashville—then part of North Carolina—to practice law. In 1791, he married Rachel Robards, a widow.

Politics and war. In 1796, Jackson helped draft a constitution for the new state of Tennessee, then served briefly in the U.S. Congress. Jackson's service in the War of 1812 made him a national hero. He defeated the Creek Indians in the Battle of Horseshoe Bend (1814) and the British in the Battle of New Orleans (1815). For his toughness, Jackson's men dubbed him "Old Hickory." His military successes, flamboyance, and aggressive patriotism made him an appealing candidate for high office. In 1824, he ran for the presidency and won the most votes, but not a majority. The decision went to the House of Representatives, which elected John Quincy Adams. In 1828, Jackson again ran against Adams in a long, bitter, vituperative campaign. Jackson won the presidency; John C. Calhoun became vice president.

President. To eliminate the closed political-caucus system and the rule of wealth and privilege, Jackson introduced a system of "rotation in office." The procedure, meant to shake up the bureaucracy and reward his friends, became known as "the spoils system."

Jackson believed in the slogan "Let the people rule," but also strengthened his power as president. His enemies organized into an opposition party called the Whigs—and the United States once more had a two-party system. Discord within Jackson's administration deepened when Vice President Calhoun opposed the high tariff acts of 1828 and 1832. Calhoun's native state, South Carolina, claimed that states had the right to nullify any federal laws they considered oppressive, and threatened to secede from the Union. To enforce the law and preserve the Union, Jackson ordered troops to Charleston. Calhoun resigned and South Carolina backed down, but this dispute over states' rights remained unsettled until the Civil War.

One of the biggest conflicts of Jackson's presidency was his "Bank War." The Bank of the United States, said Jackson, was an unconstitutional and privileged monopoly that would soon control the government. He turned the 1832 presidential campaign into a vendetta against the Bank and easily defeated opponent Henry Clay.

In Jackson's second term, he supported the Indian Removal Act of 1830, which authorized forced removal of thousands of Indians from traditional homelands, pushed France to pay for damages to U.S. shipping during the Napoleonic Wars, and established diplomatic relations with the new Republic of Texas.

Retirement. Jackson left office in 1837 and spent the last 8 years of his life at the Hermitage, his estate near Nashville.

Jackson, Helen Hunt (1831-85), U.S. author who publicized the mistreatment of Native Americans. *A Century of Dishonor* (1881) condemned governmental malpractice; the novel *Ramona* (1884) described the plight of Native Americans in California's missions.

Jackson, Henry Martin (1912-83), U.S. political leader, Democratic representative (1941-53) and senator from Washington (1953-83). He was chair of the Senate Committee on Energy and Natural Resources, and as ranking Democrat on the Armed Forces Committee he became a major spokesperson on national defense issues. In foreign affairs he was an articulate ally of Israel. In 1972 and 1976 he sought but did not win the democratic presidential nomination.

Jackson, Jesse Louis (1941-), U.S. clergyman and political leader. An associate of Martin Luther King, Jr. during the civil rights movement in the 1960s, Jackson later founded Operation Breadbasket (1966) and People United to Save Humanity (1971). He was the first African American to wage major, though unsuccessful, campaigns for the presidential nomination, running in Democratic primaries in 1984 and 1988. Since the 1988 elections, Jackson has continued his activities as an eloquent and effective speaker on vital national and foreign issues.

Jackson, Mahalia (1911-72), African-American gospel singer whose powerful and expressive contralto voice gained her a worldwide reputation. She was active in the civil rights movement in the 1960s.

Mahalia Jackson

Jackson, Michael (1958-), U.S. rock singer, songwriter, and dancer. His album *Thriller* (1982) sold 40 million copies worldwide, making it the largest-selling record ever. Jackson's career began in 1966, when he was the lead singer of his family's band, The Jackson Five.

Jackson, Robert Houghwout (1892-1954), U.S. Supreme Court justice from 1941 to 1954 and chief U.S. prosecutor at the Nuremberg Trials. A supporter of the New Deal, he served as solicitor general (1938-40) and attorney general (1940-41).
See also: Supreme Court of the United States.

Jackson, Shirley (1919-65), U.S. author. Her best-known works, such as *The Haunting of Hill House* (1959) and the short story "The Lottery" (1948), blend Gothic horror with psychological insight. Autobiographical works, such as *Raising Demons* (1957), are in a contrastingly humorous vein.

Jackson, Stonewall (Thomas Jonathan Jackson; 1824-63), Confederate general in the American Civil War. He earned his nickname for his stand against the Union forces at the first battle of Bull Run (1861). After his bold tactics in the 1862 Shenandoah Valley campaign (May-June 1862), he fought brilliantly at the battles of Richmond, the Seven Days Battles, Cedar Mountain, the second battle of Bull Run, Antietam, and Fredericksburg. At Chancellorsville he was fatally wounded by accidental fire from his own troops.
See also: Civil War, U.S.

Jackson, William Henry (1843-1942), U.S. photographer known for his documentation of the scenery of the West. His photos of Yellowstone for the U.S. Geological Survey led to its being named the first national park. After 1924, he worked as a painter.

Jackson Hole, fertile valley in northwestern Wyoming partially lying in Grand Teton National Park. Part of the Snake River valley, Jackson Hole extends along the Teton Range for about 50 mi (80 km). The valley abounds in wildlife, providing feeding grounds for moose, deer, and elk. Jackson Wildlife Range, within the park, provides an area for naturalist observation and study. The area also attracts many skiers because of its excellent ski conditions.

Jacksonville (pop. 906,727), city in Florida, seat of Duval County. It is located in the northeastern part of the state, on the St. Johns River, about 20 mi (32 km) from the Atlantic Ocean. Jacksonville is a major port and commercial center. Among its industries are the manufacture of paper, wood products, fertilizer, cigars, and machinery. It is also the site of 2 naval air stations. First settled in 1816, Jacksonville was laid out in 1822 and named for Andrew Jackson. It was incorporated in 1832.
See also: Florida.

Jack the Ripper, unknown murderer of at least seven prostitutes in London between Aug. 7 and Nov. 10, 1888. Each victim's throat was cut. Failure to solve the mystery led to the resignation of the head of Scotland Yard.

Jacob, in the Old Testament, son of Isaac and Rebecca, ancestor of the Israelites. He fled after tricking his older twin, Esau, out of his birthright. He settled in Mesopotamia, later returning to Canaan. After wrestling with an angel, he was given the name Israel. He had 2 wives, Leah and her younger sister, Rachel. (Gen. 25-50.)
See also: Bible; Old Testament.

Jacob, François (1920-), French biologist who shared with J.L. Monod and A.M. Lwoff the 1965 Nobel Prize for physiology or medicine for his work with them on regulatory gene action in bacteria.

Jacobean style, term applied to early English Renaissance architecture and furniture that flourished during the reign of James I. Decorative motifs from the late Perpendicular period were combined with crude classical details. In furniture of this period, strapwork, or forms carved in flat relief, was popular, along with Flemish-inspired classical ornament. In furnishings, the style lasted into the late 17th century. Many examples of Jacobean style can be seen in the colleges of Oxford and Cambridge universities.
See also: Renaissance.

Jesse Jackson

Jacobins, powerful political clubs during the French Revolution, named for the former Jacobin (Dominican) convent where the leaders met. Originally middle-class, they became increasingly radical advocates of terrorism. After they seized power in 1793, the extremists, led by Robespierre, instituted the Reign of Terror. In the Thermidor reaction the clubs were suppressed, to revive under the Directory and finally be put down by Napoleon.
See also: French Revolution; Robespierre.

Jacobites, supporters of that branch of the House of Stuart exiled by the Glorious Revolution of 1688; a large number were Highland Scots. Jacobites sought to regain the English throne for James II and his descendants, notably James Edward Stuart (1688-1766), "The Old Pretender," and Charles Edward Stuart (1720-88), "Bonnie Prince Charlie." After rebellions in 1715, 1719, and 1745, they were effectively crushed at the battle of Culloden Moor (1746).
See also: England; Stuart, House of.

Jacobs, Joseph (1854-1916), English scholar and writer of children's fairy tales. His works include *Aesop's Fables* (1889), *Celtic Fairy Tales* (1891), and *More Celtic Fairy Tales* (1894), which include "Jack and the Beanstalk" and "The Three Little Pigs." He was also secretary (1882-1900) of the Russo-Jewish Committee (London), formed to improve the condition of Jews in Russia.

Jade, name for either of 2 tough, hard minerals with a compact interlocking structure, commonly green but sometimes white, mauve, or yellow. Jade is used as a gem stone to make carved jewelry and ornaments. Nephrite, the commoner form of jade, occurs in China, the USSR, New Zealand, and the western United States. Jadeite, rarer and prized for its more intense color and translucence, is found chiefly in Burma, China, and Japan.

Jade statue

Jaeger, any of various large, fast-flying birds (genus *Stercoranius*) of the northern seas. Jaegers nest in the Arctic but migrate south along the coasts of the United States. They can be recognized by their slender, bent wings and their fan-shaped tails, with 2 long feathers in the center.

Jaffa, port on the coast of the Mediterranean Sea, just south of Tel Aviv, Israel, with which it was merged in 1949. Jaffa is one of the oldest cities in the world, dating back to ancient Egypt. Most of its mainly Arab population left in 1948.
See also: Israel.

Jagger, Mick *see:* Rolling Stones.

Jaguar, large cat (*Panthera onca*) found in Mexico and Central and South America. The jaguar's coat bears black spots arranged in rosettes on a background varying from white to yellow. It lives in thick cover in forests or swamps. Though they are accomplished swimmers, jaguars hunt mostly on the ground or in trees. Adult males stand about 2.5 ft (76 cm) tall at the shoulder and weigh about 200 lb (90 kg).

Jaguar

Jaguarundi, long-tailed, short-legged cat (*Felis jaguarondi*) that resembles a large weasel. Its fur is rusty red or gray. The jaguarundi lives in brush and grassland from the southwestern United States to Argentina. It feeds on small animals and fruit.

Jahan, Shah *see:* Shah Jahan.

Jahn, Helmut (1940-), German-born U.S. architect whose work emphasizes steel, glass, and concrete, erected straight lines and overlapping planes, as exemplified in Kemper Arena (1974) and Bartle Convention Center (1976), both in Kansas City, Mo. In 1980 he shifted to a post-modern style combining modern and historical elements.
See also: Architecture.

Jai alai, or pelota, Spanish-Basque game similar to handball, from which it evolved in the 17th century. The ball, or *pelota*, is made of hard rubber covered with goatskin. Each player is equipped with a *cesta*, a narrow, basket-shaped racket of wicker, which is strapped to the player's wrist. The jai alai court, or *cancha*, is enclosed by three walls, the fourth side consisting of a wire screen that protects spectators. The players alternately throw the ball against the front wall, catching it in the cesta either on the fly or after one bounce on the floor. A player is awarded a point if he/she served, and their opponent is unable to return the ball off the front wall. The game is extremely popular in Cuba, Mexico, and Spain. It is usually associated with betting.

Jainism, philosophy and religion with about 2 million adherents, mainly in India. It was founded in about the 6th century B.C. as a protest against the ritualism of Hinduism. The last of its succession of 24 original saints, called Mahavira or Jina, seems to have been a historical figure. He taught the doctrine of *ahimsa*, or non-injury to all living animals. Jains do not believe in a creator God, but see the universe as divided into two independent eternal categories: "life" and "non-life". They maintain that people can reach perfection only through ascetic, charitable, and monastic discipline.

Jakarta (pop. 6,503,000), capital and largest city of Indonesia, in northwestern Java. It is the country's commercial, transport, and industrial center, manufacturing automobiles, textiles, chemicals, and iron products, and processing lumber and food. Much of Indonesia's foreign trade passes through the port. The city grew out of the Dutch East India Company settlement of Batavia (1619). With independence in 1949 it was made the capital and renamed Djakarta, now officially spelled Jakarta.
See also: Indonesia.

Jakes, Milos (1922-), former president of Czechoslovakia (1987-89). A politcally active communist since l945 who studied in Moscow, Jakes was appointed secretary-general of the communist party and president in l987. The weakening of the communist party in l989 and the growth of a reform movement led to his resignation that year.
See also: Czechoslovakia.

Jamaica, third-largest island in the West Indies, situated in the Caribbean Sea, 90 mi (145 km) south of Cuba and 100 mi (161 km) west of Haiti. The name Jamaica is derived from the Arawak Indian name *Xaymaca* (isle of woods and water).

Land and climate. Jamaica's surface is largely a limestone plateau, with a backbone of mountains and volcanic hills running east and west. In the east, Blue Mountain has an elevation of 7,402 ft (2,256 m), the highest point on the island. Sugar, bananas, allspice, coffee, ginger, and citrus fruits are grown on the warm mountain slopes. Rain forests in the north and northeast supply bamboo, mahogany, and ebony. Vegetation is generally richly tropical or subtropical, with over 3,000 species of flowering plants. Jamaica is generally rainy, with the heaviest falls occurring in May and Oct. Kingston, the capital, is fairly dry, with only 30 to 35 in (76 to 89 cm) per year. Hurricanes may occur between Aug. and Nov.

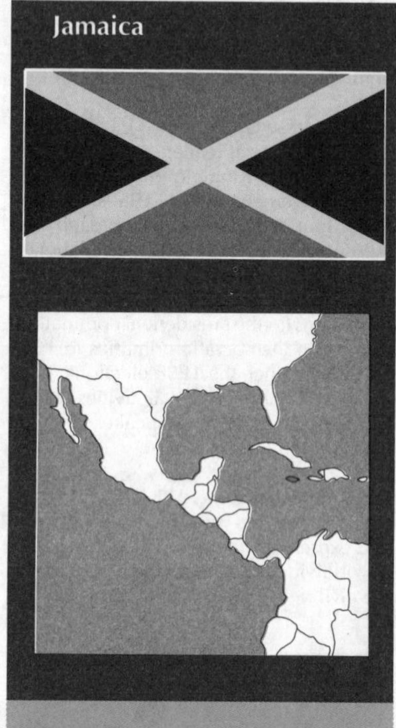

Capital:	Kingston
Area:	4,244 sq mi (10,991 sq km)
Population:	2,376,000
Government:	constitutional monarchy
Independent:	1962
GNP:	U.S. $2,610,000,000
Per capita:	U.S. $1,080

Fishing in Jamaica, using wide nets close to shore, is an important part of the national economy.

People. Most Jamaicans are of African descent. The others are East Indians, Chinese, and Europeans, mainly British. English is spoken throughout the island, and a local patois (a mixture of African and archaic English words) is also used. Most people are Protestants, either Anglican or Baptist. There are over 800 schools on the island, but people in remote rural areas are often illiterate. The principal campuses of the University of the West Indies are located in Jamaica. Over 60% of the people live in rural areas, but in recent years the population of the two major towns, Kingston and Montego Bay, has increased. The birthrate is high, and the density of population (556 persons per sq mi) creates serious problems.
Economy. Jamaica is predominantly agricultural. Sugar refining and the manufacture of molasses and rum are the principal industries. The island also has a thriving tourist industry. In 1942 deposits of bauxite were discovered, and today Jamaica is one of the world's chief suppliers of this aluminum ore. Gypsum is another important export commodity.
History. In 1494, Christopher Columbus discovered Jamaica, which was thinly settled by the Spaniards in 1509 and remained a Spanish colony until it was ceded to the British in 1670. By the 18th century the original inhabitants, the Arawak Indians, had been killed off by disease and the harsh treatment of their colonial rulers. From 1660 African slaves were imported to work in the lucrative sugar industry. Jamaica was particularly prosperous under Sir Henry Morgan, a buccaneer who served as lieutenant-governor from 1674 to 1683. By the 18th century the island was a leading slave trading center.
When slavery was abolished in 1834, the sugar industry declined. Thereafter unemployment, poverty, and overpopulation caused tension, and riots occurred, especially in the 19th and early 20th centuries. To improve conditions, crop diversification was encouraged, including the cultivation of bananas, and substantial governmental changes were made between 1930 and 1940. In 1962, after 3 centuries as a British colony, Jamaica became an independent nation within the Commonwealth of Nations.

James, name of 6 kings of Scotland. **James I** (1394-1437) technically became king in 1406, but he was held prisoner in England 1406-24. After being ransomed by Scottish nobles, he returned to Scotland and suppressed a turbulent aristocracy; he was assassinated during an abortive aristocratic revolt. **James II** (1430-60) reigned 1437-60. His son, **James III** (1451-88), reigned 1460-88. His son, **James IV** (1473-1513), king from 1488 to his death, was the great Renaissance king of Scotland. He reformed law and administration, extended royal authority, built a powerful navy, and was a patron of the arts and sciences. He married Margaret, daughter of Henry VII of England. He was killed at the battle of Flodden Field during an attempted Scottish invasion of England. **James V** (1512-1542), his son, was king from 1513, but actually reigned 1528-42, during the beginnings of the Reformation. He supported Catholicism for financial and political reasons. His daughter was Mary Queen of Scots. He died soon after his army was defeated by the English at Solway Moss. **James VI**, king of Scotland from 1567, became James I of England.
See also: Scotland.

James, name of 2 kings of England, Scotland, and Ireland, both belonging to the House of Stuart. **James I** (1566-1625), became king of Scotland in 1567, when his mother, Mary Queen of Scots, was forced to abdicate. Until 1583, when James turned 17, the country was ruled by regents. James supported Elizabeth I of England and in 1587 accepted the execution of his mother. In 1603 he succeeded Elizabeth, becoming king of England. His early popularity waned as he sought autocratic control over Parliament, bolstered by his belief in the divine right of kings. He sponsored the translation of the Authorized Version of the Bible (1611), also known as the King James Version. His strict anti-Puritan views caused many Puritans to flee to America, where they founded Plymouth Colony (1620). **James II** (1633-1701), reigned 1685-88. He was the second son of Charles I, successor of James I. During the English civil war he fled to France (1648). He returned to England in 1660, at the time of the Restoration. A Roman Catholic, James II acceded to the throne in 1685, after the death of Charles II. His autocratic methods and pro-Catholic appointments made him unpopular, and in 1688 James II was ousted by William of Orange, his Protestant son-in-law, in what became known as the Glorious Revolution. In 1689 James tried to restore his rule from his base, Ireland, but his forces were defeated in the battle of the Boyne (1690).
See also: England.

James, Epistle of, 20th book of the New Testament, traditionally attributed to St. James, the Less. One of the Catholic (general) Epistles, it is primarily a homily on Christian ethics.
See also: Bible; New Testament.

James, Henry (1843-1916), U.S.-born novelist and critic, brother of William James. He settled in London in 1876 and became a British citizen in 1915. A recurring theme in his work is the corruption of innocence, particularly as shown by the contrast between sophisticated, corrupt Europeans and brash, innocent Americans. James's most famous works, distinguished by subtle characterization and a precise, complex prose style, include *The Americans* (1877), *Daisy Miller* (1878), *The Portrait of a Lady* (1891), *The Turn of the Screw* (1898), and *The Golden Bowl* (1904).

James, Jesse (1847-82), U.S. outlaw. A member of William Quantrill's raiders during the Civil War, he and his brother Frank led the James Gang, robbing banks and trains from Arkansas to Colorado and Texas, beginning in 1866. Living as an ordinary citizen in St. Joseph, Mo., he was murdered for a $5,000 reward by gang member Robert Ford.

James, P(hyllis) D(orothy) (1920-), English mystery writer. In her novel *Cover Her Face* (1962), she created the character of Adam Dalgliesh, Scotland Yard commander. He was also the hero of *Death of an Expert Witness* (1977) and *A Taste of Death* (1986). She also introduced Cordelia Gray, a London detective, in *An Unsuitable Job for a Woman* (1972) and *The Skull Beneath the Skin* (1982).

James, Saint, Christian leader of the 1st century A.D., referred to as the brother of Jesus in the Galatian Epistles, though theologians have disputed any blood relationship between them. James is credited as the author of the Epistle of James in the New Testament, but true authorship is uncertain. His feast day is May 3.
See also: Apostles.

James, William (1842-1910), U.S. philosopher and psychologist, considered the originator of the doctrine of pragmatism; brother of novelist Henry James. His first major work was *Principles of Psychology* (1890). Turning his attention to questions of religion, in 1902 he published *The Varieties of Religious Experience*, which has remained his best-known work. James's pragmatism, which he called "radical empiricism," argued that the truth of any proposition rested on its outcome in experience, and not on any eternal principles.
See also: Pragmatism.

James Bay, inlet of the southern part of Hudson Bay, Canada. The bay was named for Captain Thomas James, who made extensive explorations of the area in 1631. Several early Hudson's Bay Company colonies were established there.

James River, river in Virginia, formed by the confluence of the Jackson and Cowpasture rivers and flowing east and southeast past Lynchburg and Richmond to Chesapeake Bay. About 340 mi (547 km) long, it is navigable for about 150 mi (241 km) between Richmond and the bay.

James the Greater, Saint, one of the twelve apostles of Jesus along with his brother, St. John. He was the first apostle to be martyred, and he is venerated widely in Spain, as Santiago.
See also: Apostles.

James the Less, Saint, one of the twelve apostles of Jesus. He is often associated with James the Younger and James, the "brother" of Jesus, but they are probably three different people.
See also: Apostles.

Jamestown, former village in southeastern Virginia, on the James River, first permanent English settlement in North America. Founded in 1607 by colonists from the

London Company, it was named for King James I. Lord De la Warr reinforced it in 1610, and John Rolfe introduced tobacco cultivation in 1612. In 1619 the House of Burgesses, first representative government of the colonies, met there. The village was destroyed during Bacon's rebellion in 1676.
See also: Virginia.

Part of the ever-changing skyline of Tokyo.

Janácek, Leo (1854-1928), Czech composer and collector of Moravian folk music, best known for his operas *Jenufa* (1904), *Katia Kabanova* (1921), and *The Makropulos Case* (1926). First professor of composition at the Prague Conservatory (1919), he wrote many songs, as well as chamber and choral works, in particular the *Glagolitic Mass* (1926).

Janissaries, elite Turkish infantry of the 14th-19th century, conscripted from prisoners of war and Christian children abducted and reared as fanatical Muslims. From 1600 Turks gradually infiltrated the highly privileged corps, which became increasingly corrupt. Unruly and rebellious, it was massacred by order of Sultan Mahmud II in 1826.
See also: Infantry.

Jansen, Cornelius (1585-1638), Dutch Roman Catholic theologian. In 1636 he was appointed bishop of Ypres, Belgium. In *Augustinus* (published posthumously, 1640), Jansen argued for a return on the part of Christians to the positions of St. Augustine on grace, free will, predestination, and salvation. Though counter to church doctrine, these ideas attracted many Catholic followers in France and the Low Countries. Early 18th-century papal bulls discredited Jansenism, but in parts of the Netherlands Jansenists still have churches.
See also: Theology.

Jansky, Karl Guthe (1905-50), U.S. radio engineer. While studying static interference for the Bell Telephone Laboratories (1931), he discovered radio waves from sources outside the earth. This led to the development of radio astronomy.

Janus, in Roman mythology, guardian of gateways and doors and god of beginnings. The first hour of each day and first day of each month was holy to him. January is named for him, and many Roman doorways and arches bear his image: a double-faced head looking in 2 directions.
See also: Mythology.

Japan (Japanese: *Nippon*), country off the east coast of Asia, an archipelago of 4 principal islands (Hokkaido, Honshu, Kyushu, and Shikoku), 500 smaller islands, and 3,000 minor ones. The capital is Tokyo.
Land. The Japanese archipelago extends 1,300 mi (2,092 km) from northeast to southwest. Most of its area of 142,726 sq mi (369,660 sq km) is accounted for by the 4 main islands. More than 4/5 of Japan is

Japan

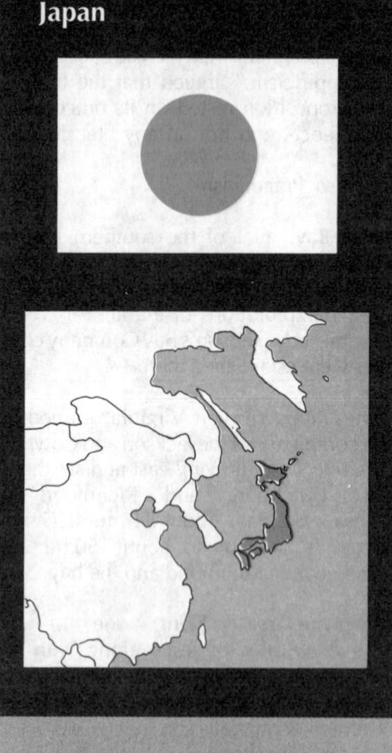

General information	
Capital:	Tokyo
Area:	145,883 sq mi (377,835 sq km)
Population:	123,120,000
Official language:	Japanese
Monetary unit:	1 Yen = 100 sen
Main cities:	Tokyo, Yokohama, Osaka
Government	
Form:	constitutional monarchy
Independent:	1947 (constitutional monarchy)
Head of state:	Emperor
Head of government:	Prime minister
Legislature:	two legislative houses (House of Councillors and House of Representatives)
Executive:	Prime minister and Cabinet
Judiciary:	highest court is the Supreme Court
Political division:	10 regions, 47 prefectures
National economy	
Gross national product:	U.S. $2,576,541,000,000
Per capita income:	U.S. $21,040
Agriculture:	rice, potatoes, sugar beets, sugar cane, tangerines, onions, tea, cabbage
Livestock:	chickens, pigs, cattle
Fisheries:	12,465,000 metric tons
Mining:	limestone, zinc, lead, copper, silica stone, natural gas, coal
Industries:	steel, automobiles, pig iron, cement, paper pulp, plastic products, calculators, computers, optical equipment, TV sets, watches
Main exports:	food and livestock, machinery and transportation equipment, miscellaneous manufactured articles, basic manufactures, chemicals
Transportation:	16,016 mi (25,776 km) of railroads; 682,800 mi (1,090900 km) of roads; 3 international airports
Trading partners:	U.S., Germany, South Korea, Taiwan, China
People	
Urban:	76%
Ethnic composition:	Japanese 99.5%, Korean 0.5%
Birth rate:	11 per 1,000 population
Death rate:	6 per 1,000 population
Infant mortality:	5 per 1,000 live births
Life expectancy:	male 75 years, female 81 years

mountainous; the highest peak is Mount Fuji (12,385 ft/3,775 m). More than 250 Japanese peaks are higher than 6,500 ft (1,981 m); there are about 50 active volcanoes. Most Japanese live in the 1/5 of the country that is relatively flat. There are many streams and rivers; among many inland lakes, Lake Biwa is the largest.

Japan is poor in certain resources, with almost no iron ore and with petroleum that meets less than 1/10 of its requirements. Luxuriant forests cover 2/3 of the country. Large mammals include deer, monkeys, bears, wild boars, and wolves; smaller mammals are badgers, ermines, foxes, hares, mink, otters, and squirrels. About 450 species of birds have been observed.

People. The world's most densely populated nation, Japan has more than 123 million people. Its population density of 844 people per sq mi creates economic, social, and pollution problems.

The Japanese are basically a Mongoloid people; centuries of isolation and inbreeding have produced a homogenous racial stock. Japanese is the universal language, except among the 15,000 Ainus (a primitive people of Caucasian origin) and 700,000 foreigners (mostly Korean) living in the country. English is the main foreign language.

The 2 major religions are Buddhism and Shinto. Many Japanese observe practices of both, with a Shinto family shrine and a Buddhist family altar. Schools are crowded, but the literacy rate is 99%, Asia's highest. The higher education system includes 475 colleges and universities and 610 junior colleges.

Economy. Having moved from feudalism to capitalism in just over a century, Japan is one of the world's leading industrial nations. Products range from ships and automobiles to electronic equipment, cameras, and textiles. Imports include coal, petroleum, and industrial raw materials. Rice is the chief agricultural crop. Japan has extensive fisheries.

History. Artifacts dating from at least 4000 B.C. have been found in Japan. The first Japanese state was ruled by the Yamato clan, from whom the present imperial house is said to descend. Japan has been subject to cultural influences from China by way of Korea. Rice cultivation was introduced from China (c.250 B.C.) and Buddhism from Korea (c.A.D. 538). In the 7th century A.D., Chinese ideographic script was adapted to the Japanese language, and the administrative system of the T'ang Dynasty was adopted. Land became the property of the emperor, who distributed it, and clan chiefs became imperial officials.

In 1192 Minamoto Yoritomo seized power as shogun (military dictator). Successive shoguns ruled absolutely, with the emperors as figureheads. Power was based on a vassal class of warrior knights, or samurai. Feudal warfare (1033-1573) paved the way for powerful lords who were free of shogun rule.

In 1543, the Portuguese visited Japan, followed by other European traders and Christian missionaries. A policy of isolation (sakoku) closed Japan to all foreigners except a few Dutch and Chinese traders until 1853-4, when U.S. Commodore Matthew Perry negotiated a trade treaty. Similar treaties with Britain, France, the Netherlands, and Russia followed. The shogunate collapsed in 1867. Under Emperor Meiji (1867-1912), Tokyo became the capital, and a program of westernization began. Japan's victories in the Russo-Japanese War and Sino-Japanese Wars won her recognition as a world power, as did her support of the Allies in World War I. In the 1930s a militarist regime took power, built a large Asian colonial empire, and formed an alliance with Nazi Germany and Fascist Italy. Japan entered World War II with a surprise attack on Pearl Harbor (1941). The war brought economic ruin and nuclear devastation, and the Japanese surrendered in 1945. Since World War II, Japan has concentrated on economic development.

Tradition and modernity side by side in Japan

Japan, Sea of, arm of the Pacific Ocean between Japan and the eastern coast of Asia. It has an area of about 400,000 sq mi (1 million sq km) and is warmed by the Japan Current. Average depth is 4,500 ft (1,370 m), with some trenches descending to 12,000 ft (3,660 m).
See also: Pacific Ocean.

Japan clover *see:* Lespedeza.

Japan Current, or Kuroshio, warm strong ocean current running northeast along the southeastern Japanese coast. In summer, some of the current splits off, eventually reaching the Sea of Japan; most however, turns east past the Aleutians to form the North Pacific Current.

Japanese, language spoken by more than 100 million people, most of them in Japan. Japanese seems not to be related to any other language, although some linguists believe there may be a connection with Korean. Written Japanese originally used only adapted Chinese characters (*kanji*); in the 8th century phonetic characters (*kana*) were added.

Japanese beetle, metallic green beetle (*Popillia japonica*), related to the june beetle. In the United States, where it was accidentally introduced from Japan in 1917, it is an agricultural pest because none of its natural enemies was established. The larvae live underground and feed on plant roots.

Japanese chin, or Japanese spaniel, dog native to China. A favorite pet among Japanese royalty for centuries, the species was brought to the United States in the mid-1850s after Commodore Perry's expedition. The dogs have a soft white coat with uniform black or red patches around the face. They weigh about 5-9 lb (2-4 kg).

Japanese literature, one of the world's great literatures, consisting of works written in the Japanese language. Around the 6th century, largely through Korean influences, the Japanese came into contact with Chinese culture and civilization and adopted Chinese ideograms. By the early 8th century, the Japanese had begun to produce a native literature. The *Kojiki* (Record of Ancient Matters), the sacred book of Shinto, dates from 712 A.D. A work glorifying the imperial family and its divine descent, the *Kojiki* also recounts early folk tales, legends, myths, and songs. The *Nihonshoki* (The Chronicles of Japan) are the earliest Japanese historical work; they date from 720 A.D. Toward the end of the 8th century, after 771 A.D., came the *Man'yoshu*, a remarkable compendium of 4,500 poems, a wide-ranging record of lyric expression in the native language.

The Heian period (794-1185) marked the end of Japan's absorption of the Chinese influence and the emergence of its own distinct literary character and genius. The Chinese ideograms were too complex for rapidly recording running throught or quick impressions, so the Japanese developed two distinct cursive scripts, the flowing *hiragana* and the angular *katakana*. The greatest work of the Heian period and one of the great works of world literature was composed in the *hiragana* script by a prominent woman of the Heian court, Lady Murasaki Shikibu. Her *Tale of Genji*, written in the early 11th century, is an elaborate tale of the love and intrigues of a certain Prince Genji. The work is not only a skillfully told story but is also rich in its portrayal of character and deeply colored by a Buddhist sensibility.

The Heian court and its aristocracy were replaced by a military government and, from 1185 to 1587, the samurai, or soldier, class became dominant. The change was reflected in literature. *The Tale of the Heike*, Japan's greatest historical fiction, was written in the early 1300s. *Tanka* continued to be composed, but poems called *renga* were also written. *Renga* consisted of chains of poems made by several poets, usually composed as they drank. But it was also during these centuries that two great literary forms were developed. The Noh drama, powerful in its solemnity and restraint, featured a masked actor, dance, chanting, and musical accompaniment. It was perfected by the actor and playwright Zeami Motokiyo. The *kyogen* was slapstick farces which accompanied Noh performances.

The reign of the samurai was marked by frequent instability and bloody warfare. Power was finally consolidated under a single clan which gave its name to an era, the Tokugawa (1603-1867). Under the Tokugawa, the written language was standardized. The kabuki theater developed with its brilliant costumes, melodramatic tales, and energetic acting style. And, in the early 1700s, the puppet theater, or *bunraku*, was brought to a high level of refinement.

Wojciech Jaruzelski

Heian literature was dominated by an aristocratic sensibility; the literature of the Tokugawa era was patronized by the bourgeoisie. In the late 1600s, Ihara Saikaku (1642-93) gave up a career as a poet to pursue a successful career writing fiction. His contemporary, Matsura Basho (1648-94) developed the *haiku*, a poetic form of 17 syllables, which challenged and eventually supplanted the *tanka*. The Tokugawas pursued a policy of strict isolation for Japan. That policy ended with the arrival of Commodore Perry in 1858. In 1867, the samurai were replaced by the Emperor Meiji. Just as early Japan had studied China, Meiji Japan set out to study the West, and the impact of those studies opened new fields for Japan's literary talents. Prominent among the Meiji writers of the 1880s who learned western languages, studied western literature, and took the first decisive steps toward mastering the new forms were Yamada Bimyo, Koyo Ozaki, Rohan Koda, Futabatei Shimei, and Tsubouchi Shoyo. Tsubouchi Shoyo was a Shakespeare scholar and urged Japanese writers to compose European-style novels. In response, Futabatei produced *Drifting Clouds* in 1889.

In a remarkably short time, Japanese writers created outstanding works. Perhaps the greatest Japanese novelist was Natsume Soseki, who began his career with the now-famous *I Am a Cat* in 1905. Ryonosuke Akutagawa wrote brilliant stories and fables, including *Rashomon*. Shiga Naoya wrote *A Dark Night's Passing* in 1937. Japan's outstanding contemporary writers include Jun'ichiro Tanizaki, author of *The Makioka Sisters*; Jiro Osaragi; Osamu Dazai; Kobo Abe; Yasunari Kawabata, author of *Snow Country* and recipient of the Nobel Prize for literature in 1968; Yukio Mishima, author of *Confessions of a Mask*; and Oaka Shohei.

Virtually everyone in Japan can read. As a result, all branches of literature have benefited. Apart from numerous publications and periodicals, it has been observed that more works of the world's literature have been translated into Japanese than into any other single language.

Japanese print, fine art developed in 17th-century Japan. The artist drew a pattern onto a wood block and a carver cut the pattern, leaving only a portion of the surface raised. The design could be reproduced many times by applying ink to its surface and printing it on paper. Printmaking was originally done in black and white, but color techniques were introduced by the mid-1700s.

Japanese spaniel *see:* Japanese chin.

Jarrell, Randall (1914-65), U.S. poet and influential critic. His poetry is emotional and often pervaded with a sense of tragedy and alienation; best-known collections are *Selected Poems* (1955), *The Woman at the Washington Zoo* (1960), and *The Lost World* (1965). *Poetry and the Age* (1953) is the first of three collections of his criticism.

Jaruzelski, Wojciech (1923-), Polish general and politician, appointed both premier and Communist party leader in 1981 to resolve the crisis involving the independent trade union Solidarity. He arrested the Solidarity leaders and imposed martial law, but he was unable to remedy the country's economic difficulties. In 1985 he became president under a new system of government and resigned as premier. In Sept. 1990 he indicated his intention to step down in order that an election might take place.

Jasmine, or jessamine, vine or shrub (genus *Jasminum*) with yellow or white star-shaped flowers, noted for their fine scent. It is found throughout Europe, Asia, and Africa and has become naturalized in the United States. In the south of France, acres of jasmine are grown and their flowers plucked for the oil, which is used in perfumes.

Jason, Greek mythological hero. Jason laid claim to the kingdom of Iolkos, which his uncle, Pelias, had seized from Jason's father, Aeson. Pelias agreed to return the kingdom if Jason brought him the magical Golden Fleece, held by King Aeetes of Colchis. Jason assembled a force, the Argonauts, who set sail in the Argo to seek the fleece. After many adventures, they recovered the fleece, with the aid of Aeetes's daughter, Medea, who fell in love with Jason. She accompanied him back to Greece and became his queen. But when Jason tried to divorce Medea, she destroyed Creusa, his bride-to-be, as well as Creusa's father, and (in some versions of the story) her own children. The gods then caused Jason to wander aimlessly until his death.

See also: Argonauts; Mythology.

Jasper, opaque, compact, fine-grained variety of quartz used in jewelry and interior decoration. Its color varies from red, yellow, brown, and dark green to grayish blue.

Jasper National Park, park in the Canadian Rockies of western Alberta, established 1907. Covering an area of 4,200 sq mi (10,900 sq km), it is a scenic preserve of peaks, glaciers, lakes, rivers, canyons, waterfalls, and hot springs. Many vanishing species are protected, including wolves, bears, and herds of elk.

See also: National Parks.

Jaspers, Karl (1883-1969), German philosopher noted for his steadfast opposition to Nazism and his acute yet controversial analyses of German society. Early work in psychopathology led him into the Heidelberg University philosophical faculty in 1913. He there became one of Germany's foremost exponents of existentialism.

See also: Existentialism.

Jaundice, abnormal yellowing of skin and the whites of the eyes caused by excess bilirubin, normally removed by the liver and excreted as bile, in the blood. Jaundice occurs with liver damage (hepatitis, late stages of cirrhosis) and when the bile ducts leading from the liver to the duodenum are obstructed by gallstones or by cancerous tumors.

Java, island in southeastern Asia, part of the Republic of Indonesia, about 600 mi by 120 mi and bounded on the south and southwest by the Indian Ocean. Java accommodates nearly two-thirds of the population of Indonesia, together with the capital, Djakarta. Other important cities include Bandung, Surabaja, and Medan.

Java is traversed from east to west by a chain of volcanic mountains, the highest of which is Mt. Semeru (12,060 ft/3,676 m). The fertile tropical plain along the northern coast is drained by the Solo and Brantas rivers, and rainfall is heavy, for Java lies just south of the equator.

The Javanese are mainly farmers (many are smallholders), producing rubber, coffee, tea, sugar, cocoa, and cichona bark (from which quinine is derived) for export. Small-scale manufacture of consumer goods was encouraged by the former Dutch administration and has been further developed by the present Indonesian government. For centuries handicrafts have been important to the economy, and Java is noted for its artistic silverwork and batik textiles. By far the most important of Java's mineral resources, oil, is found in the northeastern

part of the island and is well exploited. Other mineral deposits include gold, phosphate, and manganese.
See also: Indonesia.

Java man, early human species. Fossils found on the Indonesian island of Java in 1891 gave scientists evidence to date the species from 500,000 to 1 million years ago. Java man is an instance of *Homo erectus*, a stage of human development when humans began to stand erect. Examination of skulls show large jaws and teeth.
See also: Prehistoric people.

Javelin, spear made from lightweight metal or wood with a sharp pointed tip. Javelin throwing, a track and field competition, is an Olympic sport. After a running start, the competitor throws the javelin over the shoulder, releasing it in a high arc, in an attempt to gain the greatest distance on each throw.

Javelina *see:* Peccary.

Jay, brightly colored, noisy bird of the crow family. Many jays bear crests. They are found in North and South America, Europe, and Asia. The blue jay (*Cyanocitta cristata*) lives in eastern North America, while the scrub jay (*Aphelocoma coerulescens*), Steller's jay (*C. stelleri*), and piñon (*Gymnorhinus cyanocephalus*) are found in the Rocky Mountains.

Jay, John (1745-1829), U.S. lawyer, first chief justice of the Supreme Court. He helped draft the N.Y. state constitution in 1777, and in 1778 he was elected president of the Continental Congress. In 1782, along with Benjamin Franklin and John Adams, he negotiated the Treaty of Paris (1783) which ended the Revolutionary war. As secretary for foreign affairs (1784-89) he supported the new constitution, believing in the need for a strong central government. He was chief justice of the Supreme Court (1789-95). In 1794 he negotiated the unpopular Jay Treaty. A conservative member of the Federalist Party, he served as governor of N.Y. 1795-1801.
See also: Supreme Court of the United States.

Jay Treaty, agreement between the United States and Britain negotiated by John Jay, 1794, to settle conflicts arising out of violations of the 1783 Treaty of Paris and to regulate trade and navigation in the Atlantic. The Jay Treaty provided for British evacuation of northwestern forts, compensation for confiscated U.S. shipping, U.S. repayment to Britain of prewar debts, and limited trading concessions to the United States. No mention was made of the impressment of U.S. seamen or compensation for abducted U.S. slaves. For this reason the treaty was considered a capitulation to the British.

Jazz, unique form of American music. A piece of jazz music begins with a melody and a harmonic scheme, on which the players improvise variations, typically using syncopated rhythms. The word "jazz" may derive from a slang word describing a swaying kind of walk, or it may come from the French word *jaser*, to gossip.

Jazz greats Thelonius Monk (piano) and Charlie Parker (alto-saxophone).

Jazz musicians of great fame: Dizzy Gillespie (left) and John William Coltrane (right)

The origins of jazz are found in the work songs, laments, and spirituals of the slaves of the U.S. South. With the abolition of slavery and the migration of thousands of black workers to southern towns and cities, especially New Orleans, these songs and spirituals were given a new impetus. As they were played by the street bands that accompanied weddings and funerals and by the smaller bands that played in the cafés of the Storyville district of New Orleans, such forms as the blues, ragtime, and the stomp were established.

The original New Orleans style started to change in the 1920s as blacks moved to the cities of the North. New styles emerged, such as the piano boogie woogie, and jazz began to find a wider audience, thanks to the radio and phonograph. In the 1930s and 1940s, big bands, composed mainly of white musicians, played a commercialized type of jazz called swing, which became the most popular dance music on both sides of the Atlantic. In the late 1940s a completely new jazz style, called bebop, appeared on the scene, pioneered by several brilliant black musicians. Bebop was the start of the modern jazz era. "West Coast" and "cool" jazz styles followed in the 1950s and 1960s. The latest jazz developments are almost totally removed in both form and spirit from the original New Orleans style.

One element in jazz that has not changed much is its instrumentation. The old New Orleans bands generally consisted of trumpet or cornet, trombone, clarinet, saxophone, piano, double-bass, and drums. The majority of jazz musicians still play one or another of these instruments.

Many jazz musicians figure in the history of 20th-century music. Joe "King" Oliver, Edward "Kid" Ory, Sidney Bechet, Ferdinand "Jelly Roll" Morton, Louis Armstrong, Thomas "Fats" Waller, and the first great white jazzman, Leon "Bix" Beiderbecke, were among the early masters of jazz. Fletcher Henderson, Edward "Duke" Ellington, and William "Count" Basie led some of the great bands of the 1930s and 1940s, while Glenn Miller, Benny Goodman, and Woodrow "Woody" Herman were among the band leaders of the swing

Redecorated Army jeep popular in the Philippine capital of Manila.

era. Perhaps the most passionate jazz has come from the great blues singers, such as Bessie Smith and Billie Holiday. Modern jazz can be traced through the playing of musicians like Coleman Hawkins, Lester Young, Earl Hines, Charlie Parker, John "Dizzy" Gillespie, Miles Davis, and John Coltrane. In the 1960s a new "free form" jazz was developed by Ornette Coleman, Cecil Taylor, and others.

Jazz Age *see:* Roaring Twenties.

Thomas Jefferson

3rd U.S. President	
Born:	Shadwell, Goochland (now Albemarle) County, Va.; Apr. 13, 1743
Term:	Mar. 1801-Mar. 1809
Vice presidents:	Aaron Burr; George Clinton
Political party:	Democratic-Republican
Spouse:	Martha Wayles Skelton Jefferson
Children:	6
Died:	Charlottesville, Va.; July 4, 1826

Jean Baptiste de la Salle, Saint (1651-1719), French Roman Catholic priest canonized in 1900. He founded the Order of the Christian Brothers, which brought religious instruction to the poor. In the 1680s he established the Institute of Brothers of the Christian School, and other schools were established by his order throughout Western Europe.

Jeanne d'Arc *see:* Joan of Arc, Saint.

Jeanneret-Gris, Charles Édouard *see:* Le Corbusier.

Jeddah *see:* Jidda.

Jeep, 4-wheel-drive vehicle used for navigating rough terrain. Popular with the army, jeeps came into widespread use during World War II. The name evolved from the initials G.P., standing for "general purpose" vehicle. They became the prototypes for civilian vehicles of the same name, which is now a registered trademark of the Chrysler Corporation.

Jeffers, Robinson (1887-1962), U.S. poet. His powerful poetry, its tone disillusioned, laments human fate and glorifies nature. *Tamar and Other Poems* (1924) is his best-known collection, but his chief success was an adaptation of Euripides' *Medea* (1946).

Jefferson, Joseph (1829-1905), U.S. actor best known for his portrayal of Rip van Winkle, a role he created in London in 1865 and played for the rest of his life.

Jefferson, State of, proposed state in the Texas Panhandle, in the northwestern part of Texas. The area was proposed for statehood by the Texas legislature in 1915, but the proposal was never enacted into law. *See also:* Texas.

Jefferson, Thomas (1743-1826), third president of the United States and principal author of the Declaration of Independence. Jefferson was highly accomplished in many fields—politics, diplomacy, science, architecture, education, farming, and music, to name only a few. He was a brilliant writer and a philosopher of democracy—on behalf of the American cause in the Revolution and as the foremost advocate of popular rule in the young republic.

Early life. Jefferson attended William and Mary College, graduated in 1762, then studied law, being admitted to the bar in 1767. In 1770, he began building Monticello, the home near Charlottesville, Va., that he had designed. In 1772, he married Martha Wayles Skelton. Only 2 of their 6 children survived infancy.

The Revolution. In 1769, Jefferson entered the House of Burgesses, Virginia's colonial assembly. As relations with Britain deteriorated, he joined the revolutionaries' cause. A radical democrat, he believed men should be free to govern themselves, and opposed aristocracy of birth or wealth. His writings made him one of the leading political theorists in the colonies. In 1776, as a delegate to the Continental Congress, Jefferson was named to a 5-man committee to prepare a declaration justifying independence; Jefferson wrote most of it. It is considered the most eloquent statement of his views on democracy and government. The Continental Congress adopted the declaration on July 4, 1776. Jefferson returned to Virginia's legislature, then became governor in 1779. In 1783, he was elected to the new U.S. Congress.

Service to the nation. Jefferson served as the U.S. minister to France (1785-89) and as the first U.S. secretary of state (1789-93). Although President George Washington disliked the idea of political parties, 2 parties formed around Jefferson and Alexander Hamilton, secretary of the treasury. Jefferson's followers became known as Democratic-Republicans (or Republicans) and Hamilton's as Federalists. Jefferson believed in the rationality of man and saw the nation's future as an egalitarian, agricultural society of small landholders. He opposed the idea of strong, central government, believing that all governments should be kept from gaining too much power. Hamilton considered the people "a great beast" and wanted the nation to develop into a commercial and industrial one led by a strong national government and a wealthy aristocracy. Washington was unable to settle the dispute between his 2 top advisers; Jefferson resigned in 1793. Three years later, the Democratic-Republicans persuaded him to run against Federalist John Adams for the presidency. Jefferson lost by a narrow margin, thus becoming Adams's vice president. In 1800, Jefferson and running mate Aaron Burr ran against Federalists John Adams and John C. Pinckney. Jefferson and Burr received equal electoral votes, so the House of Representative had to decide who would be president. It chose Jefferson.

President. Jefferson's greatest diplomatic coup was the Louisiana Purchase (1803), which doubled the size of the nation. The following year, he sent Lewis and Clark to explore the new territory. Their expedition led to the settlement and eventual incorporation of the West into the nation. Under Jefferson, the Democratic-Republicans balanced the budget, built a surplus, and reduced the national debt. Jefferson's personal popularity carried him and running mate George Clinton to an overwhelming victory in the 1804 presidential election, but his second term was beset by foreign-affairs problems, particularly a conflict between Britain and France. Hoping to avoid war, Jefferson established an embargo forbidding the export of U.S. products and prohibiting U.S. ships from sailing to foreign ports. The embargo, however, hurt U.S. traders far more than it did Europe. Jefferson's presidency ended under a cloud of unpopularity.

Retirement. Jefferson retired to Monticello. Active to the end, he pursued his many interests and founded the University of Virginia. He died on July 4, 1826—the 50th anniversary of the signing of the Declaration of Independence and the same day as his old friend and rival, John Adams.

Jefferson City (pop. 33,619), capital of Missouri and seat of Cole County. Located on the Missouri River, in the central part of the state, Jefferson City is the commercial center for the surrounding agricultural region. Industries include food processing, printing, and publishing. The city was laid out in 1822 and named for Thomas Jefferson.
See also: Missouri.

Jeffersonian democracy *see:* Jefferson, Thomas.

Jefferson Memorial, monument in Washington, D.C., dedicated in 1943 to the memory of Thomas Jefferson. A white marble structure in classical style, it was designed by John Russell Pope and contains a statute of Jefferson by Rudulph Evans.

Jefferson Territory, area comprising what is now the state of Colorado and parts of Utah, Nebraska, and Kansas. Thousands of settlers came to the area in 1859 after rumors that gold had been discovered there. A provisional government was established, but Congress refused to recognize the Jefferson Territory as a state.

Jeffersonville (pop. 21,220), city in southern Indiana, on the Ohio River across from Louisville, Ky. Built on the site of Fort Steuben, the community was designed by President Thomas Jefferson in 1802. The seat of Clark County, it is a river port and manufacturing center and houses the Southeast Campus of Indiana University.
See also: Indiana.

Jeffries, James Jackson (1875-1953), U.S. heavyweight boxer who won the championship from Bob Fitzsimmons in 1899. He retired undefeated in 1905; returning to the ring in 1910 he was defeated by Jack Johnson.

Jehoiakim, king of Judah (r.c.608-598 B.C.). Son of King Josiah, Jehoiakim was placed on the throne by Necho, the Egyptian pharaoh who defeated Josiah. Jehoiakim later switched his alliance from Necho to the Babylonian king, Nebuchadnezzar II, but then revolted against him. Jehoiakim died under mysterious circumstances during the Babylonian siege of Jerusalem.

Jehoshaphat, king of Judah (r.c.873-849 B.C.). An ally of King Ahab of Israel, Jehoshaphat was the first Judean king to make a treaty with Israel. He reigned during an era of relative peace and solidified his alliance with Israel by having his son, Jehoram, marry the daughter of King Ahab.

Jehovah, variant of the name of God in the Old Testament. The four Hebrew letters YHWH, referring to God, were considered sacred and unpronounceable. In reading the Hebrew Bible, the word *Adonai* (Lord) was substituted. Medieval translators believed YHWH should be read "Yahweh," and the name "Jehovah" was incorrectly derived from that.

Jehovah's Witnesses, international religious movement founded in 1872 by Charles Taze Russell in Pittsburgh, Pa. Their central doctrine is that the Second Coming of Christ is imminent. They avoid participation in secular government, which they see as diabolically inspired. Over a million members proselytize by house-to-house calls and through publications such as *The Watchtower* and *Awake*, issued by the Watchtower Bible and Tract Society.

Jehu, king of Israel (r. c.842-815 B.C.). An officer in the army of King Jehoram, Jehu was anointed king by a disciple of the prophet Elisha after Jehoram began promoting the worship of Baal. Jehu murdered Jehoram, Queen Jezebel (Jehoram's mother), King Ahaziah of Judah, and other members of the royal family. After ordering all the followers of Baal into their temple, Jehu's soldiers slaughtered them. Jehu restored traditional Jewish worship and began a dynasty that ruled for another century.
See also: Israel.

Jellicoe, Sir John (1859-1935), British admiral of the fleet (1919), commander of the British grand fleet at the battle of Jutland (1916). He was governor-general of New Zealand (1920-24).
See also: Jutland, Battle of.

Jellyfish, familiar name for the free-swimming stage of various invertebrate animals of the phylum Cnidaria. They often have a pulsating jellylike bell and trailing tentacles. Many Cnidarian classes display an alternation of generations, where a single species may be represented by a polyp form, usually asexual, and a medusoid, sexually reproductive stage. These medusoid forms are frequently referred to as jellyfish. The true jellyfish all belong to the class Scyphozoa, where the medusa is the dominant phase and the polyp or hydroid is reduced or absent. Jellyfish are radially symmetrical. Rings of muscle around the margin of the bell contract to expel water and propel the jellyfish forward.

Jenghis Khan *see:* Genghis Khan.

Jenkins, Charles Francis (1867-1934), U.S. inventor. His "phantascope" (1895) was a motion picture projector that enlarged narrow film images into life-sized figures. He also patented an airplane braking device, an altimeter, and a mechanical automobile starter.

Jenkins, Roy Harris (1920-), British political leader. Elected to the House of Commons in 1948 as a Labour Party member, he served as minister of aviation, chancellor of the exchequer, and twice held the post of home secretary. He was president of the Commission of the European Community (1977-81). In the early 1980s he helped found the Social Democratic Party, a split from the Labour Party, and in 1982 he was elected to Parliament under the party's banner. He lost his seat in 1987.
See also: Parliament; United Kingdom.

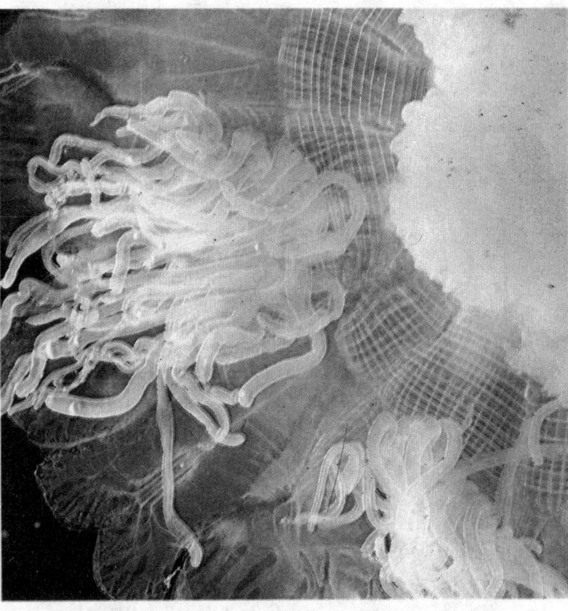

Cornflower jelly fish indigenous to the Atlantic Ocean and the North Sea. The white mass at the top is the mouth.

Jenne, or Djenné, city in southern Mali. Founded c.1300 in a swampy lowland between the Niger and Bani rivers, Jenne became a trade hub between the West African coastal region and the lower Sahara. In 1468 it was conquered by the Songhai Empire, and in the mid-1600s it was a focal point for black Muslim culture and learning.
See also: Mali.

Jenner, Edward (1749-1823), English physician, pioneer of vaccination. He took note of the country saying that dairy-maids who had had cowpox would not contract smallpox, and this led him, in 1796, to inoculate a boy, James Phipps, with cowpox. When the procedure made the boy immune to smallpox, the modern science of immunology was born.
See also: Immunization; Vaccination.

Jenner, Sir William (1815-98), Victorian-era British physician. Best known for his research on typhus and typhoid fever, Jenner was one of the first members of the medical profession to draw a distinction between them and prescribe appropriate treatment. Jenner was also a pioneer in the treatment of diptheria. He served as president of the Royal College of Physicians (1881-88) and was the personal physician of Queen Victoria and other members of the royal family.
See also: Typhoid fever; Typhus.

Jenney, William Le Baron (1832-1907), U.S. architect and designer of the Home Insurance company in Chicago. He used metal columns instead of stone, which reduced the weight of the building and allowed for taller structures.
See also: Architecture.

Jensen, J. Hans (1906-73), German physicist who shared the Nobel Prize for physics (1963) with Maria Goeppert Mayer and Eugene Paul Wigner for research on the shell structure of atomic nuclei.

Jenson, Nicolas (1415?-80), 15th-century French printer who designed several important typefaces still in common use today. He was sent by the king of France to Mainz, Germany, to learn book printing from Johannes Gutenberg. In 1470 Jenson devised a system of roman type that later evolved into other practical fonts.
See also: Printing.

Jerboa, any of various small desert-living rodent (family Dipodidac) with long tails and long hind legs. Jerboas have large eyes and ears, short front legs, and move by hopping. They are common in the deserts of North Africa and Asia, where they live in holes and emerge at night to feed on leaves and seeds.

Jeremiah, book of the Old Testament, 24th in the Authorized Version, second of the Major Prophets. It tells of the prophecies of Jeremiah, who called for moral reform, threatening the population with doom otherwise. He continued prophesying in Egypt after Jerusalem fell to Babylon.
See also: Bible; Old Testament.

Jericho (pop. 5,300), ancient village in Palestine, north of the Dead Sea. Excavations have suggested that Jericho may be the site of the oldest known human permanent settlement in the world. In the Bible, it was captured from the Canaanites by Joshua. It has periodically been destroyed and rebuilt. In 1967 it was occupied by Israel.
See also: Palestine.

Jeroboam, 2 kings of ancient Israel. **Jeroboam I** (r. 922-909 B.C.) led the rebellion of the northern tribes of Judea after King Solomon died, which resulted in Israel and Judah splitting into separate kingdoms. He restored Jewish shrines at Bethel and Dan, thus releasing the people from their obligation to make pilgrimages to the Holy Temple in Jerusalem, the capital of Judah. **Jeroboam II** (r. 785-745 B.C.) ruled during a time when Israel was a political and economic power, despite widespread corruption.
See also: Israel.

Jerome, Jerome Klapka (1859-1927), English humorist and playwright, who wrote the classic comic novel *Three Men in a Boat* (1889), a work cherished for its broad humor and sentimentality.

Jerome, Saint (Sophronius Eusebius Hieronymus; c. 340-420), biblical scholar, one of the first theologians to be called a Doctor of the Church. After being educated in classical studies, he fled to the desert as a hermit to devote himself to prayer. Subsequently papal secretary, he translated the Old Testament into Latin and wrote New Testament commentaries. His feast day is Sept. 30.
See also: Bible.

Jersey, largest and southernmost of the British Channel Islands. Its main industries are tourism and agriculture. It contains numerous remnants of prehistoric life and was known to the Romans as Caesarea.

Jersey City (pop. 553,099), city in northeastern New Jersey, seat of Hudson County. Located across the Hudson River from Manhattan, Jersey City is a major transportation center with extensive port facilities, several major railways, and tunnel and ferry connections with New York City. Its industries include shipping, oil refining, chemicals, and the manufacture of consumer products. The city is also the site of a stockyard. First settled by the Dutch in 1618, it became the town of Jersey in 1804 and was incorporated as a city in 1820.
See also: New Jersey.

Jersey Lily *see:* Langtry, Lillie.

Jerusalem (pop. 469,000), capital (since 1980) and largest city of Israel. It stands on a ridge west of the Dead Sea, 35 mi (56 km) from the Mediterranean. The city may date from the 4th millennium B.C. In c.1000 B.C. King David captured it from the Jebusites and made it his capital. The great Temple was built by David's son Solomon in 970 B.C. David's dynasty was ended in 586 B.C. by the invasion of King Nebuchadnezzar, who sacked the Temple and deported most of the Jews to Babylon. Cyrus II of Persia allowed the Jews to return and the Temple was rebuilt. Jerusalem was subsequently ruled by Syria, the Roman Empire, and the Byzantine Empire. It was taken over by the Muslims in 637 and has been part of the Muslim world ever since, except for a period of rule by the Crusaders (1099-1187). The 1947 UN resolution establishing the state of Israel made it an international city, but in the 1948 Arab-Israeli conflict it was divided, the Old City being under Jordanian administration, the New City under Israeli rule. In the 1967 Arab-Israeli War, Israel took the Old City, and all of Jerusalem was placed under unified administration. There are traditional Armenian, Christian, Jewish, and Muslim quarters in the Old City, which is also the site of three of Jerusalem's holiest places: the Wailing Wall (Jewish); the Church of the Holy Sepulcher (Christian); and the Dome of the Rock (Muslim). Government, tourism, and religious activity dominate life in Jerusalem.
See also: Israel.

Jerusalem artichoke (*Helianthus tuberosus*), North American flowering plant closely related to wild sunflowers. It produces edible tubers that have a taste similar to artichokes, hence the name. They are also a source of fructose and alcohol. The plants can grow to 12 ft (3.7 m) in height. They bear yellow flowers.

Jessamine *see:* Gelsemium.

Jesuits, name given to members of the Society of Jesus, an order of Roman Catholic priests and brothers dedicated to foreign missions, education, and studies in the humanities and sciences. Jesuit life is regulated by the constitutions written by the founder of the Society, St. Ignatius of Loyala. Vows of poverty, chastity, and obedience to the pope are taken, and training may last up to 15 years. After its founding in 1534, the order undertook missions in Asia under St. Francis Xavier and participated in the Counter-Reformation in Europe. Their influence and power led to their expulsion from many countries, and in 1773 Pope Clement XIV dissolved the Society. It was restored, however, in 1814.
See also: Roman Catholic Church.

Jesus Christ (4? B.C.-A.D. 29?), central figure of the Christian religion. Jesus is believed by Christians to be the Son of God and the Lord and Savior of mankind. The name "Jesus" is the Greek rendering of the Hebrew *Joshua* (Savior). The title "Christ" comes from *Christos,* the Greek translation of the Hebrew *Messiah* (Anointed One).
The main source for information about the life and teachings of Jesus are the 4 Gospels—Matthew, Mark, Luke, and John—and the epistles of the New Testament. From the numerous details given there, it is possible to form a vivid picture of Jesus. These details are given with an intention expressly stated by John: "These are written that you may believe that Jesus is the Christ, the Son of God, and that believing you may have life in his name" (John 20:31).
According to the Gospels, Jesus was born of the Virgin Mary, wife of Joseph, in Bethlehem, Judea. Their home was in Nazareth, Galilee. Little is known of his childhood except that, when he was 12, he went to the Temple in Jerusalem with Mary and Joseph. When Jesus was about 30 years old, his cousin John the Baptist began preaching repentance in the wilderness of Judea and baptizing penitents in the Jordan River. As Jesus was being baptized by John, a voice from heaven affirmed that Jesus was the Son of God (Mark 1:11). For some time after that Jesus traveled about the country, teaching and healing, mainly in Galilee but also in other parts of Palestine. He gathered 12 followers, or disciples, who helped spread the new ideas.
Jesus' interpretation of the Jewish law and his messianic claims alarmed the established religious authorities. On his last journey to Jerusalem for the Passover, Jesus entered the city in triumph. The authorities, threatened by his popularity, plotted against him. After the Last Supper, Jesus went to the Garden of Gethsemane to pray. One disciple, Judas Iscariot, betrayed him, and he was taken prisoner. Brought before members of the ecclesiastical court of the Jews, he was found guilty of blaspheming. He was then taken for sentencing to the Roman civil governor, Pontius Pilate, who charged him with treason against Rome and condemned him to death by crucifixion.
The resurrection of Jesus on the third day after his death and burial convinced the disciples that he was indeed the Son of God. They continued to spread Jesus' teachings, and hundreds of Jews and later

Gentiles were converted to the new faith. Although the Christian Church eventually split into many parts, the accuracy of the Gospels and the divinity of Jesus are universally held Christian beliefs.
See also: Bible; Christianity; New Testament.

Jet, form of lignite coal valued for its gemlike properties. In its raw state it is hard and black and has a smooth surface. After polishing, it resembles black glass and is often used to make buttons, costume jewelry, and other decorative items.

Jet airplane *see:* Airplane; Aviation.

Jet engine *see:* Jet propulsion.

Jet lag *see:* Biological clock.

Jet propulsion, propulsion of a vehicle by reaction to the rapid expulsion of a gas backward. The reaction imparts an equal forward momentum to the vehicle. The chief use of jet propulsion is to power airplanes. The first jet engine was designed and built by Sir Frank Whittle (1937), but the first jet-engine aircraft to fly was German (Aug. 1939). Jet engines are internal-combustion engines. The turbojet is the commonest form. Air enters the inlet diffuser and is compressed in the air compressor. It then enters the combustion chamber, where the fuel is injected and ignited, and the hot, expanding exhaust gases pass through a turbine that drives the compressor and engine accessories. The gases are expelled through the jet nozzle to provide the thrust.

Jet Propulsion Laboratory, research facility in Pasadena, Calif. The laboratory, which is operated by the California Institute of Technology under the aegis of the National Aeronautics and Space Administration (NASA), pioneered the development of space probes for the United States. These included the first unmanned crafts to survey the moon and land on its surface in the 1950s and 1960s. Other probes developed there explored the solar system and flew close enough to some of the outer planets to photograph them, thus providing valuable data.
See also: Jet propulsion; National Aeronautics and Space Administration.

Jet stream, narrow bands of fast easterly-flowing winds, stronger in winter than in summer, found at altitudes of 7 to 8 mi (11-13 km). Speeds average about 40 mph (64 kmph) in summer and 80 mph (128 kmph) in winter, though more than 200 mph (320 kmph) has been recorded.

Jetty, man-made pier designed to aid in navigation. They are constructed primarily of wood, stone, concrete, or combinations of these materials. Breakwater jetties reduce the force of waves on a harbor or shoreline, while river jetties expedite the flow of silt through a delta. Jetties at the mouths of rivers such as the Mississippi and the Columbia funnel the water through narrow channels, thus forcing the currents to carry silt further out to sea.

Jewel Cave National Monument, national monument in western South Dakota that preserves an extensive complex of interconnected limestone caverns in the Black Hills and contains one of the longest underground cave systems in the U.S. Jewel Cave was set aside as a national monument in 1908.

Jewelry, ornaments worn by people to enhance their physical appearance, to display wealth, or to follow custom. Bracelets, rings, necklaces, and earrings are the most common types of jewelry. Made from precious metals such as gold and silver, colorful polished stones (gems), or other attractive natural materials, jewelry is an art form that has existed since earliest times. Ancient peoples wore jewelry made from such materials as feathers, shells, and teeth before they wore clothes. Jewelry found at the sites of early civilizations can yield clues to the technological development of ancient cultures.

Jewett, Sarah Orne (1849-1909), U.S. author. She wrote about late 19th century life in her native New England, often using seaports and rural towns of Maine as settings. Her best-known works are *Deephaven* (1877), *A Country Doctor* (1884), and *The Country of the Pointed Firs* (1896). She also wrote poetry and children's stories.

Jewfish (*Epinephelus itajara*), large game fish of the sea bass family. Jewfish and related species inhabit the eastern and western coastal waters of the United States and Latin America. The largest known species grows to 12 ft (3.75 m) and weighs up to 680 lb (310 kg).

Jewish community centers (JCC's), centralized facilities offering social functions for Jews. JCC's serve about 1 million people of all ages in 275 locations throughout North America and are operated by the National Jewish Welfare Board (JWB). JCC's usually feature arts and crafts, drama, recreation and sports, and educational programs.

Jewish feasts *see:* Judaism.

Jews, followers of Judaism, a group held together by a shared religion and a common history and culture more than 3,000 years old.
Jewish history begins with the patriarchs: Abraham, his son Isaac, and his grandson Jacob (also named Israel). Abraham led his family from Mesopotamia to Canaan (Palestine). The children of Israel (Joseph and his brothers, the sons of Jacob) migrated to Egypt, where a pharaoh enslaved the Israelites until Moses led them out in the Exodus.
After 40 years of wandering, the Israelites reentered Canaan (c.1200 B.C.). They united in a monarchy under King Saul. His successor, David, brought prosperity and peace, and conquered Jerusalem. David's son, Solomon, built the Temple at Jerusalem. Under Solomon's son Rehoboam, the kingdom split into Judah and Israel. The monarchies ended with the defeat of Israel by the Assyrians (721 B.C.) and the defeat of Judah and destruction of the Temple by the Babylonians (587 B.C.). Many of the inhabitants of both kingdoms were deported; those from Israel lost their identity, becoming the "Ten Lost Tribes." The term *Diaspora* is used to refer to the settling of scattered colonies of Jews outside Israel.
During the 2nd and 1st centuries B.C., the Maccabees briefly restored Jewish independence before the Romans established domination over the Jews. They rose against the Romans in A.D. 66; when the revolt was put down 4 years later, Jerusalem was destroyed.
The rise of Christianity brought increasing harassment of the Jews. During the Middle Ages in many countries they were confined to ghettos and excluded from trades, professions, and ownership of land. At the time of the Crusades, a new wave of persecution began; one by one Western European nations expelled the Jews, until they were

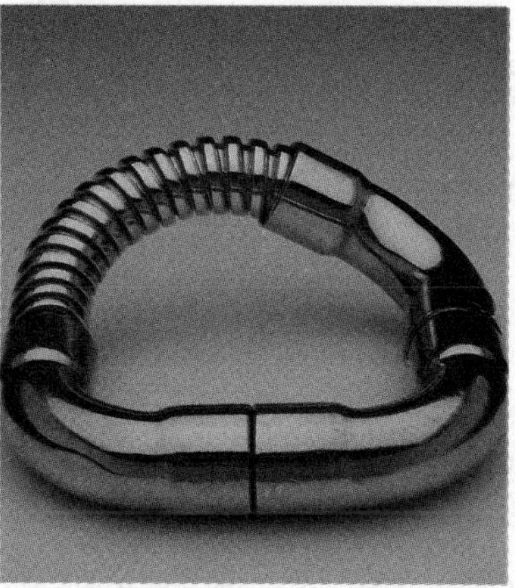

Modern jewelry: shower hose bracelet, designed by Marion Herbst.

Gold cross pendant from the 5th or 6th century, probably from Syria.

The Torah ("Written Laws") contain the sacred laws of the Jewish people. The scrolls are often stored in beautiful cloth covers.

Steven Jobs

allowed to live only in parts of Germany and Italy. The Jews found refuge in the Ottoman Empire, in the New World, and in Eastern Europe, where they became increasingly trapped in a life of poverty and persecution in lands under Russian rule.
The Enlightenment and the advent of capitalism for a time benefitted the Jews economically and socially. Prejudice against them (anti-Semitism) continued, however, and gave rise in the late 19th century to renewed Zionism, the movement for reestablishing a Jewish state in Palestine that dated from the destruction of Jerusalem in A.D. 70.
Meanwhile (1881-1914), one-third of Eastern European Jews (1 million people) emigrated; 90% settled in the United States. In 1917 the Balfour Declaration guaranteed "a national home for the Jewish people" in Palestine, but Jewish settlement there aroused the hostility of the Arab inhabitants.
In the 1930s, all other Jewish problems were overshadowed by the rise of Nazism. With the outbreak of World War II, the Nazis began murdering the Jews of Europe, eventually killing 6 million. Reaction to this catastrophe led to the establishment of the state of Israel in 1948.
Today there are 13 million Jews worldwide. The Jews of Israel number more than 4 million, and some 6 million Jews live in the United States.
See also: Israel; Judaism.

Jew's-harp, or jaw's harp, musical instrument that produces a resonant sound. It is held up to the mouth, and a thin, metal tongue between 2 prongs of a circular frame is plucked, producing vibrations. Notes are formed by the player changing the size or shape of the mouth cavity.

Jiang Qing, or Chiang Ch'ing (1914-), Chinese Communist leader; widow of Mao Zedong. She joined the Communist Party in 1933 and married Mao in 1939. During the 1960s she led the Cultural Revolution and was elected to the Politburo in 1969. Accused by Mao's successors of leading a coup attempt, she and 3 other radicals (the "Gang of Four") were arrested and charged with treason. Jiang was condemned to death, but her sentence was commuted to life imprisonment in 1983.
See also: China; Gang of Four; Mao Zedong.

Jicama, yam bean, or Mexican turnip, vine belonging to the pea family, native to parts of Latin American and Asia. The Jicama plant is cultivated for its edible tubers.

Jidda, or Jiddah (pop. 1,210,000), city in western Saudi Arabia, situated on the Red Sea. Jidda has the country's largest airport and is the port of entry for millions of Muslims making pilgrimages to Mecca and Medina. Founded in the 7th century A.D., Jidda is a banking, oil refining, and manufacturing center.
See also: Saudi Arabia.

Jigger *see:* Chigger.

Jim Crow, name for a system of laws and customs in the southern United States to segregate African Americans from white society. The name comes from a minstrel song. The laws dated from the 1880s and applied to schools, transportation, theaters, and parks. These laws were invalidated by Supreme Court decisions in the 1950s and 1960s and the Civil Rights Acts of 1964 and 1968.
See also: Segregation.

Jiménez, Juan Ramón (1881-1958), Spanish poet. At first influenced by symbolism, in *Diary of a Poet and the Sea* (1917) he developed a free, direct style of his own: *poesía desnuda* (Spanish "naked poetry"). After the Spanish Civil War he moved to Puerto Rico. He received the Nobel Prize for literature in 1956.

Jiménez de Quesada, Gonzalo (1500?-79?), Spanish conquistador who claimed the area around Colombia for Spain as New Granada. He settled there, doing much to improve the colonists' lot, and founded Bogotá (1538). He led a disastrous expedition in search of El Dorado (1569-71).

Jimmu Tenno, mythical Japanese military and political leader. According to legend, he conquered large areas around the Inland Sea and became Japan's first emperor in the 600s B.C., but historians dispute the dates and question his existence. Jimmu Tenno is said to be a descendant of the sun goddess, leading to popular acceptance of the divinity of the Imperial Family, whose lineage is traced to him.
See also: Japan.

Jimsonweed, or thorn apple, low shrubby plant (*Datura stramonium*) with thick leaves and white trumpet-shaped flowers. All parts of the plant are poisonous. It is named for Jamestown, Virginia, where a party of English soldiers died after eating it as a vegetable.

Jinnah, Muhammad Ali (1876-1948), Indian Muslim lawyer and political leader, founder of Pakistan. At first a member of the Indian Congress Party, he resigned in 1921, charging it with Hindu bias. From 1934, as head of the Muslim League, he campaigned for Muslim rights in an independent state. In 1947 he became Pakistan's first head of state.
See also: Pakistan.

Jinrikisha, or ricksha, 2-wheeled passenger vehicle pulled manually. The runner, or *hiki*, runs between 2 long poles extending from the body of the carriage. Used as a public vehicle in China and Japan around the turn of the century, jinrikishas carried 1 or 2 people. Jinrikishas were later considered demeaning to humans and outlawed.

Jiulong *see:* Kowloon.

Jiva *see:* Jainism.

Jívaro, South American tribe inhabiting the lower Andes mountains in eastern Ecuador and Peru. Their principal activities are fishing, hunting, pottery-making, and weaving. A people once famous for ritual head-shrinking, they fiercely resisted Spanish encroachment.

Joan of Arc, Saint (1412?-31), French heroine of the Hundred Years War. A peasant girl from Domremy, Lorraine, she heard "voices" telling her to liberate France from the English. Given command of a small force by the Dauphin (later Charles VII), she inspired it to victory at Orléans in 1429. She stood beside the Dauphin when he was crowned Charles VII that year and joined him in his unsuccessful siege of Paris. Captured at Compiègne (1430), she was tried for heresy by an ecclesiastical court of French clerics who sympathized with the English, and burnt at the stake. The verdict was posthumously reversed in 1456, and she was canonized in 1920.
See also: Hundred Years' War.

Job, Book of, book of the Old Testament, 18th in the Authoized Version. Apparently based on a folk tale in dialogue form, it is about the problem of good and evil. God permits Satan to torment the virtuous Job with the loss of family, wealth, and health. Finding small comfort in wife and friends, Job is bitter, but remains faithful. He is restored to good fortune in old age.
See also: Bible; Old Testament.

Jobs, Steven Paul (1955-), U.S. computer designer and businessman, founder with Stephen Wozniak of Apple Computer, Inc. (1976). The company's success reshaped the personal computer industry. Managerial disputes caused Jobs to leave Apple in 1985. In 1988 he unveiled a computer system aimed at the college and university market, called NeXT.
See also: Computer

Job's Daughters, international order affiliated with the Masons. Open only to girls between 11 and 20 who are related to Master Masons, the organization has about 49,000 members in 1,600 chapters in the United States and abroad. It promotes knowledge, patriotism, parental respect, devotion to Christian principles, and aid to charitable causes.

Jodl, Alfred (1890-1946), German-Nazi officer, chief of operations in World War II. He signed the surrender at Rheims, May 7, 1945. Convicted of war crimes at the Nuremberg Trials, he was executed.
See also: Nazism.

Jodrell Bank Observatory, or Nuffield Radio Astronomy Laboratories, English space tracking station and research facility, located near Manchester. Housing one of the world's largest radio telescopes, Jodrell Bank tracked *Sputnik I*, the first satellite ever launched. It also transmitted the first photographs from a Soviet probe on the moon in 1966.
See also: Astronomy.

Joel, Book of, book of the Old Testament, 29th in the Authorized Version, second of the Minor Prophets. Messianic in nature, it forecasts the Day of the Lord in apocalyptic terms.
See also: Bible; Old Testament.

Joey *see:* Kangaroo.

Joffre, Joseph Jacques Césaire (1852-1931), commander-in-chief of the French army (1914-16). He underestimated German power at the start of World War I, but he shared credit with Gen. J.S. Gallieni for the victory on the Marne. After the mismanagement of Verdun he resigned, but he was immediately made a marshal of France.

Joffrey, Robert (1930-88), U.S. dancer and choreographer. His company, the Robert Joffrey Theater Dancers, was founded in 1954. By 1976, when it became the Joffrey Ballet, it was one of the most highly regarded of U.S. companies. The touring Joffrey II Company was formed in 1970 to develop young dancers.

Jogues, Saint Isaac (1607-46), 17th-century French Jesuit missionary. Sent to Canada and western New York to convert Native Americans and Canadians, Jogues first sighted the strait connecting Lake Superior with Lake Huron, which he named Sault de Sainte Marie. Jogues was held captive and tortured by Iroquois warriors in 1642, but he managed to escape. On Oct. 18, 1646, he was murdered while on a mission among the Mohawks in western New York. He was canonized in 1930.
See also: Jesuits.

Johanan Ben Zakkai (d. c.80), Jewish Pharisee who, after the destruction of the Temple by Rome in A.D. 70, founded the academy at Jabneh (Yibna), thus ensuring the survival of Judaism.
See also: Judaism.

Johannesburg (pop. 704,000), city in northeastern South Africa. It is the hub of a prosperous mining region, with the world's largest gold field, the Witwatersand, nearby. First settled by prospectors in 1886, Johannesburg is South Africa's largest metropolitan area and a thriving cultural, commercial, and industrial center.
See also: South Africa.

Johanson, Donald Carl (1943-), U.S. anthropologist. His discovery of fossilized remains in Africa, estimated to be between 2.5 and 3 million years old, gave scientists evidence of some of the earliest origins of the human species. In 1974 Johanson uncovered the skeleton of what is believed to be the first humanlike creature to walk erect (classified as *Australopithecus afarensis*). In 1986 he found a skull and bones of an individual of the species *Homo habilis*, enabling scientists to piece together a link between humans and their ape-like predecessors.
See also: Anthropology; Prehistoric people.

John, name of 22 popes and 2 antipopes. **Saint John I** (d.526), pope (523-26), was sent to Constantinople by Theodoric, the Ostrogoth king, to win toleration for Arianism from the emperor; Theodoric imprisoned him when he failed. **John VII** (d.882), who reigned from 872 to 882, sought political power for the papacy. He attempted (and failed) to keep the Muslims out of Italy and was forced to pay tribute in order to spare Rome. He momentarily resolved a dispute with the Eastern Church by recognizing Photius as patriarch of Constantinople (879), after the death of his enemy, St. Ignatius. He crowned emperor Charles II (the Bald, in 875) and Charles III (the Fat, in 881). He was assassinated by members of his household. **John XXII** (1249-1334) was the second pope (1316-34) at Avignon; he filled the college with French cardinals. A skillful administrator, he lost popularity when he persecuted the Franciscan Spirituals, observers of strict evangelical poverty. When he contested the election of Louis IV, the king attempted to have him declared a heretic; this prompted John to imprison Nicholas V, the antipope Louis had appointed. The name of **John XXIII** was first taken by Baldassare Cossa (c.1370-1419), a Neapolitan antipope (1410-15). As a cardinal, he supported the Council of Pisa (1409), which tried (unsuccessfully) to end the Great Schism between the popes of Rome and Avignon. Elected pope by the Council, he defended Rome against his rival, Gregory XII, and, pressured by Emperor Sigismund, convened the Council of Constance to attempt reconciliation again. He agreed to abdicate if his rivals would as well, but then reneged. The Council accepted Gregory's resignation and deposed the other two. The name **John XXIII** was next taken by Angelo Giuseppe Roncalli (1881-1963). Of peasant stock, he was elected pope in 1958 after serving as cardinal and patriarch of Venice since 1953. He made major changes in the church, promoting cooperation with other Christian churches and other religions. The encyclical *Mater et Magistra* (1961) advocated social reform in underdeveloped countries. In 1962 he convened the Second Vatican Council.

John (1167-1216), king of England, from 1199 to his death. The youngest son of Henry II, John succeeded his brother Richard I as king. John's refusal to accept a papal nominee as archbishop of Canterbury led to his excommunication in 1209. High military spending during his reign alienated the nobles, and in 1215 they forced John to sign the Magna Carta, confirming their feudal rights. John later repudiated it and waged a war against the barons, who summoned French support. John died while the issue was still in doubt.
See also: England.

John III Sobieski (1624-96), late-17th-century king of Poland. Ascending to the throne in 1674 during a time of frequent wars and civil unrest, Sobieski united the Polish people against the incursions of their warlike neighbors and led a Christian army to victory over Turks outside the gates of Vienna in 1683. Following his victory, Sobieski formed a military alliance with the pope, the Holy Roman emperor, and Venice against the Muslims.

John VI (1769-1826), early-19th-century king of Portugal. He became regent in 1792 when his mother, Maria I, was judged mentally unfit to rule. He fled to Brazil in 1807 when an invasion by Napoleon was feared. In 1816, while still in Brazil, John became Portugal's king, but he didn't return until a revolution in his favor 5 years later. In 1822 his son, Pedro I, declared Brazil independent.

John, Epistles of, three New Testament epistles (23rd-25th) ascribed to St. John the Apostle. First John is a discourse about the 2 aspects of religion, practical and mythical. Second John warns against denials of the reality of Jesus's history. Third John protests an obstinate church leader's failure to receive missionaries.
See also: Bible; New Testament.

John, Gospel of *see:* Gospel.

John, Saint, one of the Twelve Disciples, (called the Evangelist, the Divine, and the Beloved Disciple), son of Zebedee and brother of St. James the Greater, thought to be the author of the fourth Gospel, 3 New Testament epistles and the Revelation.

John Birch Society, U.S. anti-Communist organization. Established in 1958 by Robert Welch and named after a U.S. military officer killed by Chinese Communists in 1945, the society grew to 3,000 chapters by fueling fears of Communist plots in the United States and around the world. Its controversial methods include "smear campaigns" launched against public officials they believe to be Communist sympathizers.

John Bull, personification of the typical Englishman, created by John Arbuthnot (1667-1735) in a series of pamphlets (1712) satirizing Whig policy. The character was usually portrayed as a burly, good-natured farmer or tradesman.

John Chrysostom, Saint *see:* Chrysostom, Saint John.

John Henry *see:* Henry, John.

John of Austria (1547-78), Spanish military commander, illegitimate son of Emperor Charles V. Noted for his skill and gallantry, he commanded the Christian fleet and defeated Turks at Lepanto (1571) and conquered Tunis (1573). Governor general of the Spanish Netherlands (1576-78), he fought the rebellion of William the Silent.

John of Damascus, Saint (c.675-c.749), Orthodox Syrian theological writer and antagonist of iconoclasm. He resigned an inherited post under the Saracen caliph to become a monk.

Pope John XXIII

Pope John Paul I

Pope John Paul II

John of Gaunt (1340-99), duke of Lancaster, fourth son of Edward III of England. Through marriage to his cousin Blanche, he became the duke of Lancaster. (Their eldest son became King Henry IV.) A commander in France under his brother, Edward the Black Prince, during the Hundred Years War, he married again, in 1371. Through his second wife, Constance of Castile, he gained a claim to the kingship of Castile and Léon. He ruled England for his senile father when the Black Prince was taken ill and his nephew, Richard II, was too young to assume leadership. His economic policies made him unpopular in many quarters, as did his unsuccessful campaigns (1386-88) to claim the Castilian throne. He remained influential during Richard II's reign, helping to effect peace between Richard and his barons. In 1396 he married Catherine Swynford, his third wife. They were ancestors of the Tudors. *See also:* England; Tudor, House of.

John of Leiden (c.1509-36), Dutch innkeeper who became leader of the Anabaptists in Münster and in 1534 set up a brutally corrupt theocracy, the Kingdom of Zion, with himself as "king," in which private ownership was abolished. In 1535 the bishop of Münster crushed the revolt; John was tortured and executed.

John of the Cross, Saint (1542-91), Spanish poet and mystic, founder of a reformed Carmelite order. Influenced by St. Theresa of Avila, he is remembered for such treatises as *The Dark Night of the Soul*. Canonized in 1726, he was made a Doctor of the Church in 1926.

John Paul I (Albino Luciani; 1912-78), pope (1978). A moderate traditionalist, patriarch of Venice when elected pope, he died of a heart attack 34 days after his election. His was the shortest papal reign in nearly 400 years.

John Paul II (Karol Wojtyla; 1920-), first non-Italian pope elected in 450 years (1978). A Pole who was archbishop of Krakow before becoming pope, John Paul II has maintained a theologically conservative position on such controversial issues as birth control, abortion, and liberation theology. He has been outspoken on world events, and has spent much of his time traveling to many countries around the world.

John the Baptist, Saint (d. C.A.D. 30), Jewish prophet, son of Zacharias and Elizabeth, who was a relative of Mary. John preached a mission of repentance in the Jordan Valley, predicting the imminent coming of the Messiah. He baptized his followers and also baptized Jesus, whom he considered the son of God.

John the Evangelist, Saint *see:* John, Saint.

Johns, Jasper (1930-), U.S. artist. A leading exponent of pop art, he used common objects in artistic contexts in such works as *Flag* (1958), and *Painted Bronze* (1960). Johns was influenced by Marcel Duchamp.

Johnson, Andrew (1808-75), 17th president of the United States. Johnson was the only U.S. president to be impeached by the House of Representatives. The difficulties of Reconstruction demanded an outstanding president, but Johnson—an accidental chief executive facing a hostile Congress—was temperamentally unsuited for the office.

Early life. Poverty kept Johnson from receiving any formal education. At age 13, he was apprenticed to a tailor, but ran away after 2 years. He later settled in Greeneville, Tenn., and opened a tailor shop. In 1827, he married Eliza McCardle, who taught him writing and arithmetic.

Public career. Johnson became involved in local politics as a Democrat and was elected town alderman before he was 21. He became mayor, then served in the Tennessee House of Representatives, the state Senate, and the U.S. House of Representatives. After 4 years as Tennessee's governor, he was elected to the U.S. Senate in 1857.

Johnson sympathized with the poor and uneducated, and championed mountaineers and small farmers against wealthy plantation owners. A slave owner, he opposed abolition and supported the Fugitive Slave Law of 1850. But he also supported legislation that would help small farmers by opening the West to settlement—even though it meant more free states would be added to the Union.

Republican Abraham Lincoln won the 1860 presidential election, causing most Southern leaders to call for secession. Johnson, however, remained devoted to the Union. In 1864 the Republicans renominated Lincoln and, to win support from "War" Democrats, they made Johnson his running mate. Their ticket won. In April 1865—six weeks after the inauguration—Lincoln was assassinated, thrusting Johnson into the presidency.

President. The Civil War had just ended, and Johnson faced the difficult task of reconstructing the South—and the Union. He issued a controversial proclamation granting amnesty to most Confederates who would swear loyalty to the Constitution. Most Southern states ratified the 13th Amendment abolishing slavery. However, they also passed the first in a series of laws that severely restricted the rights of African Americans.

Johnson maintained that reconstruction was exclusively an executive function; Congress disagreed. It passed the Civil Rights Act of 1866 over Johnson's veto and put forth other measures he opposed. In

Andrew Johnson

Born:	Raleigh, N.C.; Dec. 29, 1808
Term:	Apr. 1865-Mar. 1869
Vice president:	None
Political party:	Democratic (but elected on the "National Union" ticket with Republican Abraham Lincoln)
Spouse:	Eliza McCardle Johnson
Children:	5
Died:	Carter Station, Tenn.; July 31, 1875

Jasper Johns, Three Flags *(1958)*

1867, the Reconstruction Act was passed; thereafter, Congress exercised unprecedented authority over national policy.

Impeachment. Johnson removed an opponent from the Cabinet without consent of Congress, violating its Tenure of Office Act. The House impeached him for this and other reasons and, in March 1868, the Senate held Johnson's trial for "high crimes and misdemeanors." Conviction required a two-thirds majority; Johnson escaped conviction by a single vote. The power of the presidency was saved and balance between the branches of government preserved.

Other than the acquisition of Alaska by Secretary of State William Seward, Johnson's administration had few successes. Johnson was not nominated to the 1868 Democratic ticket, and left the presidency a bitter and disappointed man. He twice ran for Congress, but lost. Finally, in 1874, he won an election. The only former president to become a U.S. Senator, Johnson served only a special brief session in March 1875. He died soon after.

Johnson, Charles Spurgeon (1893-1956), U.S. educator, sociologist, and first black president of Fisk University (1946-56). He also helped reorganize the Japanese educational system after World War II and was U.S. delegate to UNESCO.

Johnson, Earvin *see:* Johnson, Magic.

Johnson, Hiram Warren (1866-1945), U.S. statesman. As a prosecuting attorney in San Francisco he successfully prosecuted corrupt political bosses (1908). He was governor of Cal. (1911-17) and U.S. senator (1917-45). He was a hard-line isolationist, opposing U.S. membership in the League of Nations and any war preparations.

See also: Isolationism.

Johnson, Jack (1878-1946), U.S. boxer, first African American to win the world heavyweight championship (1908). He fled the country (1912), jumping bail after his arrest on charges of violation of the Mann Act (a law prohibiting the transportation of women across state lines for immoral purposes). Johnson's outspokenness and refusal to submit to white supremacy made him highly controversial in the United States. He lost the title to Jess Willard in Havana in 1915, in a fight that he later claimed was fixed.

Johnson, James Weldon (1871-1938), U.S. author and political leader. He was U.S. consul in Venezuela and Nicaragua (1906-12) and a founder and secretary of the National Association for the Advancement of Colored People (1916-30). His books include *The Autobiography of an Ex-Colored Man* (novel, 1912), *God's Trombones* (1927), and *Black Manhattan* (1930).

Johnson, John Harold (1918-), U.S. publisher of black-interest magazines such as *Negro Digest, Ebony,* and *Jet.* He founded the Johnson Publishing Co. in Chicago in 1942. Since 1962 he has also published books directed mainly to black readers.

Johnson, Lyndon Baines (1908-73), 36th president of the United States. Johnson became chief executive upon the assassination of President John F. Kennedy, then was elected to a full term by an unprecedented majority. His 5 years in office were marked by far-reaching liberal legislation, but also by mounting domestic unrest and massive escalation of the U.S. war in Vietnam.

Early life. After graduating from high school in 1924, Johnson worked at various jobs before attending college, from which he graduated in 1930. After teaching high school for 2 years, he went to Washington, D.C., as the secretary to a new member of Congress from Texas. In 1934, Johnson married Claudia Alta "Lady Bird" Taylor. The Johnsons had 2 daughters.

Political career. In 1937, Johnson was elected to the U.S. House of Representatives. He was reelected 5 times. In 1948, he was elected to the Senate; in 1955, he became Senate majority leader. Johnson became one of the most powerful figures on Capitol Hill. One of his most notable achievements was the Senate's 1957 passage of the first major civil-rights bill since Reconstruction.

In 1960, Johnson ran for the Democratic presidential nomination, but John F. Kennedy won it. Johnson accepted the vice-presidential nomination. The Kennedy-Johnson ticket narrowly defeated Republican candidates Richard M. Nixon and Henry Cabot Lodge.

As vice president, Johnson held an office with relatively little power. That changed suddenly on Nov. 22, 1963, when President Kennedy was assassinated in Dallas, Tex. Johnson took the oath of office the same afternoon.

President. Johnson promised to continue the Kennedy program, and Congress soon passed the Civil Rights Act of 1964 and a new tax law, both Kennedy measures. Johnson also proposed a "War on Poverty" and persuaded Congress to appropriate almost $950 million for anti-poverty programs. In 1964, Johnson and running mate Hubert H. Humphrey won a landslide victory over Barry Goldwater and William Miller. Now president in his own right, Johnson formulated a wide-reaching program, called "the Great Society," for improving U.S. life. At first, Johnson enjoyed unrivaled popularity and wielded tremendous influence. From 1963 to 1967, Congress enacted 226 major proposals out of 252 requests—a 92% rate of success for Johnson's administration.

But the overwhelming issue of Johnson's presidency was an unpopular and bloody war. Kennedy had sent the first U.S. troops to Vietnam, but under Johnson their advisory role became a combative one. Johnson gradually committed more troops; by mid-1966, 300,000 U.S. troops were in Vietnam and the fighting showed no signs of nearing an end, despite massive U.S. bombing of North Vietnam and heavy loss of life on both sides.

Lyndon Baines Johnson

36th U.S. President	
Born:	Near Stonewall, Tex.; Aug. 27, 1908
Term:	Nov. 1963-Jan. 1969
Vice president:	Hubert H. Humphrey (Jan. 1965-Jan. 1969)
Political party:	Democratic
Spouse:	Claudia Alta "Lady Bird" Taylor Johnson
Children:	2
Died:	Johnson, Tex.; Jan. 22, 1973

By 1966, the U.S. was deeply divided over the war. Racial unrest—including riots in the overcrowded slums of several large cities—further taxed an already strained administration. On Mar. 31, 1968, Johnson announced that he would not run for reelection.

Retirement. After leaving office in Jan. 1969, Johnson retired to his Texas ranch. He avoided involvement in politics, devoting his time to publishing his memoirs, establishing the Lyndon B. Johnson Library, and running his ranch. He died on Jan. 22, 1973.

Johnson, Magic (Earvin Johnson, Jr.; 1959-), U.S. professional basketball player. Johnson, a 6-ft 9-in (206 cm) guard, has revolutionized the role of a "big-man." His passing, shooting, and ball-handling ability are unparalleled for a player his size. After leading Michigan State University to the National Collegiate Athletic Association (NCAA) basketball championship (1979), he went on to star for the Los Angeles Lakers (1979-) and has helped them win 5 championships (1980, 82, 85, 87, 88). In 1991 Johnson became the all time NBA assist leader (9,921). His other achievements include 7 Most Valuable

Player (MVP) awards—3 regular season (1987, 89, 90), 3 playoff (1980, 82, 87), and 1 All-Star MVP (1990). Only Kareem Abdul-Jabbar has won more MVP awards.

Johnson, Philip Cortelyou (1906-), U.S. architect and historian. Together with Henry-Russell Hitchcock, he wrote *The International Style* and became a major exponent of the new architecture. His glass house (1949) at New Canaan, Conn., won him international recognition. It is clearly influenced by Miës van der Rohe, with whom he designed the Seagram Building, New York City (1958). Johnson's later work includes the New York State Theater at Lincoln Center (1964) and the American Telephone and Telegraph Headquarters Building (1978), in New York City.
See also: Architecture.

Johnson, Richard Mentor (1780-1850), ninth vice president of the United States. He served under President Martin Van Buren from 1837 to 1841, following terms in the Kentucky state legislature, the U.S. House of Representatives, and the U.S. Senate. Johnson was the only vice president in U.S. history ever elected by the Senate, after none of the 4 candidates received a majority of the electoral votes in the 1836 election.

Johnson, Samuel (1709-84), English author, one of the major poets, critics, conversationalists, and lexicographers of his time. He wrote for various London magazines beginning in 1737, publishing the poem *London* (1738), which inaugurated his fame. From 1746 to 1755 he prepared his pioneering *Dictionary of the English Language* (1755). The moral romance *Rassalas* (1759) followed, and then the *Idler* essays (1758-60). In 1763 he met James Boswell, his biographer, who recorded much of Johnson's brilliant conversation. In 1764 he founded his Literary Club (with Joshua Reynolds), an elite circle centered around "Doctor" Johnson, which included Burke, Garrick, Boswell, and Goldsmith. In 1765, he published his edition of Shakespeare, the model for those to follow. *Lives of the Poets* (1779-81), a 10-volume work, was one of his last. Johnson's contributions were central in defining the period of English literature that came to be known as the Augustan Age.

Al Jolson in the film The Jazz Singer *(1927)*

Johnson, Walter (1887-1946), U.S. baseball player. Nicknamed "The Big Train," Johnson was a right-handed pitcher famous for his fastball. His achievements include winning the second most games in major league history (416) and pitching the most career shutouts (110). He played for the Washington Senators (1907-27) and was among the first group of players inducted into the National Baseball Hall of Fame (1936).

Johnson, Sir William (1715-74), British superintendent of Indian affairs in North America (1755-74). His just and honest conduct kept the Iroquois nations, into which he was adopted, on the British side in the French and Indian War. He commanded the victorious forces at the battle of Lake George.
See also: French and Indian Wars.

Johnson Space Center, formerly the Manned Spacecraft Center renamed in 1973 after former President Lyndon Johnson's death. Built in the early 1960s, it became the National Aeronautics and Space Administration (NASA) headquarters for all U.S. manned space missions in 1964. The center also serves as a training base for U.S. astronauts as well as a construction site for spacecraft. The center, located in Houston, Texas, covers an area of 1600 acres.
See also: National Aeronautics and Space Administration.

Johnston, Albert Sydney (1803-62), brilliant Confederate general, secretary of war for the Texas Republic (1838-40). Confederate second-in-command, he was driven back by superior forces on the Mississippi-Allegheny front. His daring strategy almost won the battle of Shiloh, but he was mortally wounded in the first day's fighting.
See also: Civil War, U.S.

Johnston, Joseph Eggleston (1807-91), Confederate general, credited with the victory at Bull Run in 1861. Wounded at Fair Oaks, he was relieved of command in 1864 after a feud with Jefferson Davis; he returned to command in 1865 but had to surrender to Gen. Sherman after 2 months. In 1879-81 he was a member of the U.S. House of Representatives.
See also: Civil War, U.S.

Johnstown (pop. 241,247), city in southwestern Pennsylvania, in the heart of a rich coal belt on the Conemaugh River. Settled in 1770 Johnstown has long been an important iron, steel, and coal center, especially since the Civil War. In 1889, the city suffered a disastrous flood that killed more than 2,200 people when the dam at the South Fork Reservoir broke.
See also: Pennsylvania.

Joint, in anatomy, junction or union between two or more bones, especially one in which bones move. Generally speaking, three kinds of junctions can be distinguished. A fibrous junction consists of connective tissue; almost no movement is possible in this type of joint. A cartilaginous junction is composed of cartilage; here only moderate movement is possible. The synovial junction is the most familiar type of joint. Here the extremities of the facing bones are covered with a thin layer of smooth cartilage, separated from each other by synovial fluid. This kind of joint permits the greatest amount of movement. The type of movement possible depends on the type of joint. Some examples are the hinge (knee and elbow), the pivot (neck and skull connection), and the ball and socket (hip and shoulder).
See also: Bone.

Joint Chiefs of Staff, U.S. agency within the Dept. of Defense, meant to advise the president and secretary of defense on military matters. Set up in 1942, it has five members: a chairman, the Army and Air Force chiefs of staff, the chief of naval operations, and the Marine Corps commandant.
See also: Defense, Department of.

Joint-stock company, forerunner of the modern corporation, a form of business association in which the working capital is obtained by selling shares of stock to individuals who may transfer them without the consent of the group. The shareholders are collectively responsible for the company's debts. The most famous early joint-stock companies were the British East India Company (1600) and the Hudson's Bay Company (1670).
See also: East India Company.

Joint tenancy, ownership of real property by 2 or more persons, each having equal rights to its use during their lifetimes. To qualify, the partners must enter into possession at the same time and hold the title in common. If one tenant dies, the property falls in its entirety to the survivor(s).

Jojoba (*Simmondsia californica* or *S. chinensis*), desert plant of northern Mexico and the U.S. Southwest. Jojoba beans yield a high-quality oil similar to sperm whale oil, which has been banned in the United States since 1971. Processed as a substitute for whale oil, jojoba is used in shampoos, cosmetics, and industrial chemicals.

Joliot-Curie, Irène (1897-1956), French physicist, daughter of Pierre and Marie Curie. She and her husband, **Frédéric Joliot-Curie** (1900-58), shared the 1935 Nobel Prize in chemistry for artificially producing radioactive materials by bombarding elements with alpha particles. In 1940 they turned their attention to the chain reaction in nuclear fission. Both helped organize the French atomic energy commission, but Frédéric was removed as first chairman in 1950 because of his leftist political views. Irène became chairwoman in 1951. Like her mother, Irène died from leukemia probably contracted as a result of prolonged exposure to radioactive materials.
See also: Nuclear energy; Radiation.

Jolliet, or **Joliet**, **Louis** (1645-1700), 17th-century French-Canadian explorer. He traversed and mapped out much of the upper Great Lakes and the Mississippi River. Accompanied by Father Jacques Marquette, he explored the Mississippi by canoe in 1673, beginning from what is now Wisconsin and traveling over 1,000 miles to the mouth of the Arkansas River. In later years, Jolliet explored the Hudson Bay region and the Labrador coast.

Jolson, Al (Asa Yoelson; c.1866-1950), Russian-born U.S. singer and actor. Star of the first full-length sound film, *The Jazz Singer* (1927), Jolson popularized such songs as "Sonny-Boy," "Swanee," and "Mammy."

Jonah, Book of, in the Old Testament, 32nd in the Authorized Version, 5th of the Minor Prophets. Unique in its entirely narrative form, it tells of the Hebrew prophet Jonah, who disobeyed God's command to travel to Nineveh to convert the city. Instead Jonah sailed away, and his crew threw him overboard during a storm brought on by his disobedience. Swallowed by a "great fish," Jonah was cast out of the fish's body three days later. He then returned to Nineveh to fulfill his mission.
See also: Bible; Old Testament.

Inigo Jones designed this building in Greenwich, England for James I's queen, 1616-35. It now houses the National Maritime Museum.

Jones, Absalom (1746-1818), early African-American religious leader. He founded the St. Thomas African Episcopal Church (1794), the first black Episcopal church in the United States, and became the first black Episcopal priest (ordained 1804). Born a slave, Jones bought his freedom in 1784. Three years later, while serving as a lay preacher at a predominantly European-American church in Philadelphia, Jones and Richard Allen founded the Free African Society. They led a walkout by black congregation members, protesting segregated seating policies. The St. Thomas African Episcopal Church was formed when the Free African Society split in two.
See also: Allen, Richard.

Jones, Bobby (Robert Tyre Jones, Jr.; 1902-71), U.S. golfer. Although he was an amateur, he won the U.S. Open four times (1923, 1926, 1929, 1930) and the British Open three times (1926, 1927, 1930). In 1926 he became the only golfer ever to win both those titles in the same year. He won a total of five U.S. Amateur tournaments (1924, 1925, 1927, 1928, 1930). In 1930 he won golf's grand slam, winning the amateur and open championships in both Britain and the United States. After his retirement, he and banker Clifford Roberts founded the Augusta National Golf Club in Georgia, establishing what is now called the Masters tournament.

Jones, Casey (John Luther Jones; 1863-1900), U.S. railroad engineer and folk hero who drove the *Cannon Ball* express from Memphis, Tenn. to Canton, Miss. When it collided with a freight train on Apr. 30, 1900, Jones applied the brakes in time to save the passengers and crew, but he was killed.

Jones, Ernest (1879-1958), British physician and psychologist. A colleague of Sigmund Freud and author of a comprehensive 3-volume book on him, Jones introduced Freudian theories and principles to the United Kingdom, the United States, and Canada. His efforts led to the general acceptance of Freud by the medical and scientific communities. In 1911 Jones was one of the founders of the American Psychoanalytic Association, and 2 years later he helped establish its British counterpart.
See also: Freud, Sigmund; Psychoanalysis.

Jones, Inigo (1573-1652), English architect. After studying the works of Palladio in Italy, he designed sets and costumes for court masques and later became the king's surveyor of works (1615-44). His masterpieces include the Queen's House at Greenwich, the banquet hall at Whitehall, and St. Paul's Cathedral in Covent Garden, London. His departure from the Jacobean style marked the beginning of England's Renaissance and Georgian periods, and he is considered one of the first great architects of England.
See also: Renaissance.

Jones, James (1921-77), U.S. novelist. His first book, *From Here to Eternity* (1951), portrayed the degradation of army life on the eve of World War II. Other works include *Some Came Running* (1957), *The Pistol* (1959), and *The Thin Red Line* (1962).

Jones, James Earl (1931-), U.S. actor who achieved stardom for his portrayal of Jack Johnson in the stage productions of *The Great White Hope* (1968). He is also an acclaimed Shakespearian actor noted for his role in *Othello* (1963, 1982). Jones won a Tony Award for his performance in the Broadway production of *Fences* (1986). His distinctive voice was used as that of DarthVader, in the classic science fiction film series, *Star Wars*.

Jones, John Paul (1747-92), Scottish-born U.S. naval hero of the Revolution. He raided British ships during the war for independence, capturing the *Drake*, a British warship, and the *Serapis* (1779). During the battle with the *Serapis*, Jones was the commander of the *Bon Homme Richard*. When the *Richard* was badly damaged, Jones was asked to surrender, but told the British commander, "Sir, I have not yet begun to fight!"
See also: Revolutionary War in America.

Jones, LeRoi *see:* Baraka, Imamu Amiri.

Jones, Mary Harris (1830-1930), U.S. labor leader known as "Mother Jones." She was one of the organizers of the International Workers of the World (IWW), a radical labor group whose members were often involved in violent incidents around the turn of the century. Jones was jailed on 4 occasions between 1902 and 1914 for inciting miners to go on strike in West Virginia and Colorado.

Jonson, Ben (1572-1637), English dramatist and lyric poet. His play *Every Man in His Humour* (1598) established his reputation. That was followed by *Every Man out of His Humour* (1599) and *The Poetaster* (1601), a satire. His best-known works were biting comic plays: *Volpone* (1606), *Epicoene* (1609), *The Alchemist* (1610), and *Bartholomew Fair* (1614). His poetry includes the collections *The Forrest* (1616), containing the song "Drink to me only with thine eyes," and *Underwoods* (1640).

Joplin, Scott (1868-1917), African-American composer and pianist, the best known practitioner of the style called ragtime. His works include the "Maple Leaf Rag" (1899) and the opera *Treemonisha* (1911).

Jordan, nonnavigable river beginning in north Israel and flowing about 200 mi (320 km) south through the Sea of Galilee and the Ghor Valley into the Dead Sea. The portion of the river between the Sea of Galilee and the Dead Sea forms the border between the Kingdom of Jordan and the West Bank, occupied by Israel since the 1967 war.

Jordan, officially Hashemite Kingdom of Jordan, country in southwest Asia, bordered by Israel to the west, Syria to the north, Iraq to the northeast, and Saudi Arabia to the south and east. The capital is Amman.
Land and climate. The area east of the Jordan River, with 94% of the country's area, is mostly desert. West of this area is the Jordan Rift, which includes the Jordan River, the Dead Sea, and the Araba, a low, dry riverbed extending down to the Gulf of Aqaba. West of the Jordan River is the most fertile part of the country, the West Bank. It was incorporated into Jordan in 1950 but has been occupied by Israel since June 1967. In addition to the Old City of Jerusalem (annexed by Israel in 1967), the West Bank contains the cities of Nablus, Bethlehem, Hebron, Jericho, Jenin, Ramallah, and Tulkarm.
People. The population is mainly Arab, and about half are Palestinians, most of whom live in the urban centers. Almost 95% of the people are Sunni Muslims, the re-

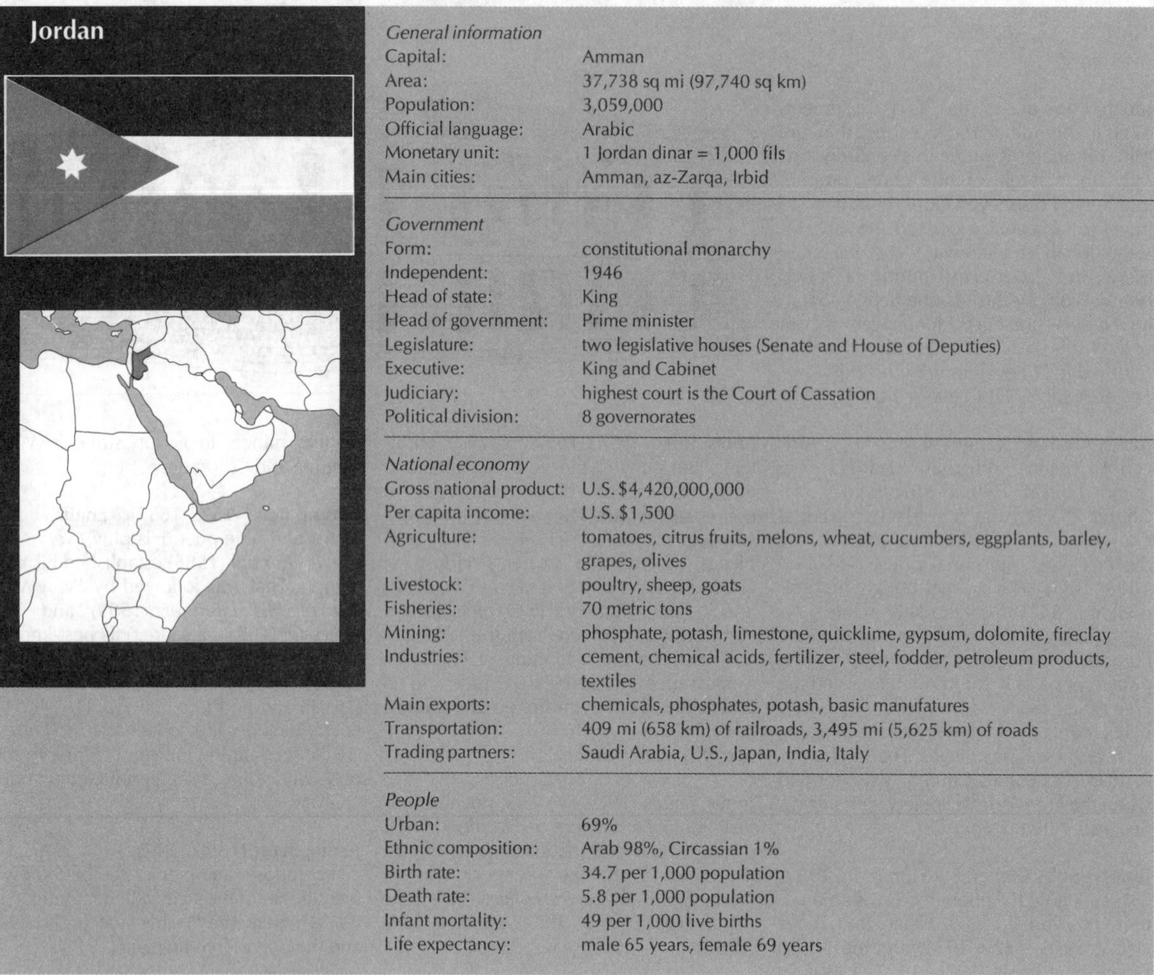

Jordan

General information	
Capital:	Amman
Area:	37,738 sq mi (97,740 sq km)
Population:	3,059,000
Official language:	Arabic
Monetary unit:	1 Jordan dinar = 1,000 fils
Main cities:	Amman, az-Zarqa, Irbid
Government	
Form:	constitutional monarchy
Independent:	1946
Head of state:	King
Head of government:	Prime minister
Legislature:	two legislative houses (Senate and House of Deputies)
Executive:	King and Cabinet
Judiciary:	highest court is the Court of Cassation
Political division:	8 governorates
National economy	
Gross national product:	U.S. $4,420,000,000
Per capita income:	U.S. $1,500
Agriculture:	tomatoes, citrus fruits, melons, wheat, cucumbers, eggplants, barley, grapes, olives
Livestock:	poultry, sheep, goats
Fisheries:	70 metric tons
Mining:	phosphate, potash, limestone, quicklime, gypsum, dolomite, fireclay
Industries:	cement, chemical acids, fertilizer, steel, fodder, petroleum products, textiles
Main exports:	chemicals, phosphates, potash, basic manufatures
Transportation:	409 mi (658 km) of railroads, 3,495 mi (5,625 km) of roads
Trading partners:	Saudi Arabia, U.S., Japan, India, Italy
People	
Urban:	69%
Ethnic composition:	Arab 98%, Circassian 1%
Birth rate:	34.7 per 1,000 population
Death rate:	5.8 per 1,000 population
Infant mortality:	49 per 1,000 live births
Life expectancy:	male 65 years, female 69 years

Jordan's modern capital, Amman

mainder Christians. The official language is Arabic.

Economy. Jordan's economy is largely agricultural, with wheat, barley, and fruits the principal crops. Most industry is limited to food processing and textiles, although there is some oil refining, and cement and fertilizer manufacturing. Phosphate is mined. The economy was greatly disrupted by the loss of the West Bank, and Jordan relies heavily on foreign aid, mostly from Saudi Arabia and the United States.

History. The region that is now Jordan has been ruled by many different empires, including Alexander the Great's, the Roman, and the Byzantine. It was conquered by the Arabs in the 7th century and from then on was part of the various Arab dynasties, including the Umayyads and Abbasids. In 1516 the Ottoman Empire took control, and until the end of World War I Jordan was ruled by the Turks. After the war, it became part of the mandate of Palestine. The Hashemite family, driven out of Arabia by the Saudis, became the local rulers. In 1946 Jordan became an independent state, with the Emir Abdullah as king. In the 1948 war with Israel, the Jordanian army conquered the West Bank. In 1951 Abdullah, who had made a truce with Israel, was assassinated; his grandson, Hussein, was enthroned the following year. Jordan's subsequent involvement in the June 1967 Arab-Israeli War cost it the West Bank, which was occupied by Israel. In 1970 the growing power of the Palestinian guerrillas in Jordan led to a bitter civil war after which the Palestinian fighters were expelled from the country. In 1974, however, Hussein recognized the Palestine Liberation Organization as the sole legitimate representative of the Palestinian people, and in 1988 he renounced Jordan's claim to the West Bank.

Jordan, Barbara Charline (1936-), first African-American woman from a Southern state to serve in the U.S. Congress. A Democrat, Jordan represented Texas in the U.S. House of Representatives for 3 terms (1973-79). In 1974, as a member of the House Judiciary Committee, she became nationally known during the impeachment hearings for President Richard Nixon. Two years later she was the first black keynote speaker at a national Democratic Party convention.

Jordan, Ernst Pascual (1902-), German physicist. He was a pioneer in the field of quantum mechanics, a method of analyzing atomic structures and particle motion. Along with Max Born and Werner Heisenberg, Jordan contributed to the development of the first mathematical formula for quantum mechanics in 1925. *See also:* Quantum mechanics.

Jordan, Michael (1963-), U.S. professional basketball player. A 6-ft 6-in (198 cm) guard and forward for the Chicago Bulls of the National Basketball Association, he is considered one of the best players of all time. His vertical-leap, athleticism, and slam-dunks, have become his trade-marks. After helping North Carolina win the National Collegiate Athletic Association championship (1982) he led the 1984 U.S. Olympic basketball team to a gold medal. Jordan was named NBA Rookie of the Year (1984-85), won the Most Valuable Player (MVP) award (1987-88, 1990-91 seasons), and has led the league in scoring from 1987-1990 (averaging 34.6 points over the 4-year period).

Joseph, in the Bible, favored son of Jacob and Rachel. His brothers, jealous of his dreams and his coat of many colors, sold him into slavery. He was eventually taken to Egypt, where he became an influential member of the house of Potiphar. He was later unjustly imprisoned, on the basis of accusations made by Potiphar's wife. Joseph won his release by interpreting the pharaoh's dreams, and the pharaoh made him governor of Egypt. While holding that post, he rescued his family from famine.

Joseph, Chief (Hinmaton-Yalaktit; c.1840-1904), leader of the Nez Percé, a Native American tribe. He non-violently resisted the forced resettlement of his people under a treaty fraudulently obtained by the United States in 1863. In 1877, when fighting broke out, he led a 1,000-mi (1,609-km) mass flight from Oregon to Canada. The Nez Percé were defeated only 30 mi (48 km) from the border. Joseph lived out his life on Colville Reservation in Washington.

Joseph, Saint, in Christian tradition, husband of the Virgin Mary, a descendant of David. He is honored by Orthodox and Roman Catholics as the foster father of Jesus. His feast day is March 19.

Josephine (Marie Josèphe Rose Tascher de la Pagerie; 1763-1814), first wife of Napoleon Bonaparte; empress of France (1804-9). At 17 she married Vicomte Alexandre de Beauharnais, who was executed by the revolutionary government in 1794. Two years later, she met and married Napoleon. Josephine's inability to bear children who could succeed Napoleon resulted in an amicable divorce in 1809. She remained in love with him for the rest of her life and asked to join him in exile on Elba. He refused, but she died before his refusal reached her.
See also: Napoleon I.

Josephus Flavius (c.A.D. 37-100), Jewish historian and soldier in the Jewish revolt against the Romans (A.D. 66). After the revolt, Josephus won the favor of the Roman general Vespasian. He took Roman citizenship and became governor of Galilee. His writings include *History of the Jewish War*, *Antiquities of the Jews*, and *Against Apion* (a defense of the Jews).

Joshua, book of the Old Testament, sixth in the Authorized Version. Joshua was the successor of Moses as leader of the Israelites. The book of Joshua describes his command of the Israelite armies in their campaign of conquest of Canaan and the division of the land among the Twelve Tribes of Israel. The Battle of Jericho was one of the major victories of the conquest.

Joshua tree *see:* Yucca.

Josiah, king of ancient Judah (r. 639-609 B.C.). His reign was marked by a revival of traditional Jewish worship. Josiah reinstated religious services in the Jerusalem Temple after destroying the idols his father, King Amon, had placed there. During restoration of the Temple, the laws of Moses were found and Josiah read them to the people. Josiah declared independence from the Assyrian Empire and was killed in battle with the Egyptian Pharaoh Necho II at Megiddo.

Jouett, Jack (1754-1822), U.S. patriot. Known as the "Paul Revere of the South," he is credited with preventing the capture of Thomas Jefferson during the American Revolution. After learning of the British plan to kidnap Jefferson and members of the Virginia legislature in 1781, Jouett rode more than 40 mi (64 km) on horseback to alert them

Joule, James Prescott (1818-89), English physicist who determined the relationship between heat energy and mechanical energy and discovered the first law of thermodynamics, a version of the law of conservation of energy. The joule (a unit of work or energy) is named for him.
See also: Thermodynamics.

Journalism, preparation of information for communications media, including newspapers, magazines, radio, and television. Education to formalize journalism began in the late 19th century, and universities and colleges throughout the United States now offer degrees in journalism.

Jove *see:* Jupiter.

Joyce, James (1882-1941), Irish novelist, considered by many the leading 20th-century master of the English language. Though Joyce left his homeland at age 20, returning only infrequently for brief visits, he nevertheless was greatly influenced by his Irish roots. *Dubliners*, short stories written in 1914, was published in London but suppressed in Ireland because of its topical references. During World War I he worked on the autobiographical novel *A Portrait of the Artist as a Young Man* (1916), following his protagonist as he comes to realize the grip Irish society has on him and his need for freedom from it. *Ulysses*, written 1914-21, follows Homer's *Odyssey* in themes and allusions. It recounts a particular day—June 16, 1904—in the life of three characters, the salesman Leopold Bloom, his wife, Molly, and Stephen Dedalus (the young man in *A Portrait*). Publication was delayed due to charges of obscenity, and *Ulysses* did not appear in the United States until 1933. In *Finnegans Wake* (1939) Joyce develops a complex exploration of dream consciousness. The meaning of the work has been vigorously debated since its publication. Other writings include three volumes of poetry—*Chamber Music* (1907), *Pomes Penyeach* (1927), and *Collected Poems* (1937)—and the play *Exiles* (1918).

J particle *see:* Psi particle.

Juana Inés de la Cruz (1651-95), Mexican-Spanish poet and scholar. As a girl she left court to become a nun. Criticized for her "unwomanly" studies, she defended women's education in a vigorous letter to her bishop (1691). Her lyric poems, especially the sonnets, are among the finest in Spanish. She died nursing epidemic victims in Mexico City.

Journalists began using cameras in war coverage during the Crimean War (photograph by Roger Fenton, 1855).

Journalism nowadays can use many modern techniques, like live reports by means of satellites. (Peter Arnett for CNN television from Baghdad, Iraq, during the Persian Gulf War).

Juan Carlos I (1938-), king of Spain since 1975. Groomed as Gen. Francisco Franco's successor, he was so named in 1969. In 1975, when Franco died, he became the first Spanish king since the deposition of his grandfather (1931). He proved to be an unexpectedly strong force for stability and democracy and was instrumental in thwarting an attempted right-wing military coup in 1981.
See also: Spain.

Juan de Fuca, Strait of, waterway between Vancouver Island and the Olympic Peninsula of Washington state. Forming part of the boundary between the United States and Canada, the strait is about 100 mi (160 km) long and 11 to 17 mi (18 to 27 km) wide. It is an important shipping channel for the ports of Seattle, Washington, and Vancouver and Victoria, British Columbia. The passage's name comes from a Greek navigator who sailed for Spain and claimed discovery in 1592, although his claim has been disputed.

James Joyce, in a 1935 painting by Jacques-Emile Blanche

Juan Fernández, 3 small, sparsely populated Chilean islands in the Pacific Ocean. Lying 400 mi (640 km) west of Chile, they were discovered by Spanish explorer Juan Fernandez c.1563. One of the islands, Róbinson Crusoe, is believed to be the site of the self-imposed exile of Alexander Selkirk, the inspiration for Daniel Defoe's *Robinson Crusoe*. The other islands are Alejandro Selkirk and Santa Clara.

Juárez (pop. 597,100), or Ciudad Juarez, city in Mexico, situated on the Rio Grande opposite El Paso, Tex. Juarez serves as a major port of entry from the United States. Founded by Spanish colonial soldiers in 1662, the city's original name was El Paso del Norte ("North Pass"). In 1888 it was renamed in honor of Mexican leader Benito Juarez. Today Juarez is an important cotton-processing center and popular tourist destination.
See also: Mexico.

Juárez, Benito Pablo (1806-72), Mexican political leader and president (1857-65, 1867-72). He enacted major reforms within the military and the church to reduce their power and redistributed large portions of land to poor farmers (*peons*). In the mid-1850s, he overthrew the dictator, Santa Anna, and led the nation's liberal faction in the "War of Reform." Between 1864 and 1867 he fought the French and deposed their puppet emperor, Maximilian.

Judah, biblical figure of ancient Canaan. He was the ancestor of one of the 12 tribes of Israel that bears his name. As the fourth son of Jacob and Leah, Judah is credited with persuading his other brothers not to kill Joseph. During the great famine in Canaan, Judah, his brothers, Jacob, and their families settled in Egypt at Joseph's invitation. Judah's name was later given to the kingdom with Jerusalem as its center.

Silver and wood case for a Jewish Torah, made in Baghdad (1825)

Judah Halevi *see:* Halevi, Judah.

Judah Maccabee (d.160-? B.C.), Jewish leader of the Hasmonean dynasty who, upon his father's death, took leadership of the revolt against the Syrian ruler Antiochus IV, who had initiated religious persecution of the Jews. Judah Maccabee's rededication of the temple of Jerusalem is commemorated by the Hanukkah.

Judaism, religion of the Jewish people, the oldest of the world's monotheistic faiths. The essence of Judaism is the belief in one God. At daily prayers and services Jews repeat the words of Deuteronomy 6:4: "Hear O Israel: The Lord our God, the Lord is One." In Jewish beliefs, Abraham, the Jewish patriarch, made a covenant with God that he and his descendants would carry the message of the one God. This covenant, the burden of special service to God, is Judaism's reason for being, and the relationship between God and the Chosen People is the subject of the Hebrew Bible, the foundation of Judaism. The Torah, the first part of the Bible (known as the Five Books of Moses, or the Pentateuch), contains the Ten Commandments and the ritual laws and ethical precepts that form the structure of the Jewish religion. In the centuries after the Bible was completed, its text was explained and adapted by a set of traditions and interpretations known as the Oral Law. When the Temple of Jerusalem and the hereditary priesthood were destroyed in A.D. 70, the Oral Law was recorded in a work known as the Mishnah, the discussion and interpretation of which forms a commentary called the Gemara. These two works together make up the Talmud, second only to the Bible in its authority. Differences over ritual observance are the chief characteristics of the groups within Judaism today. Reform Judaism began in the 19th century in answer to the challenge of rationalism. Reform Jews believe that each generation has the right to adapt or discard traditions it finds no longer meaningful. Much of the Reform synagogue service in the United States is in English, and the compatibility of Judaism with modern secular values is emphasized. Orthodox Judaism accepts the totality of the Bible and the Oral Law as divine revelation and holds strictly to all dietary laws and codes of conduct. Religious services are conducted solely in Hebrew, men and women sitting in separate parts of the synagogue. The extremes of Reform and Orthodox Judaism have to some extent been bridged in the United States by the Conservative movement, which has attempted to combine the traditions of Orthodox observance with some of the freedom of choice and adaptability found in Reform Judaism.

Judas Iscariot, in the Bible, one of the Twelve Apostles, the one who betrayed Jesus. For 30 pieces of silver he identified Jesus to the soldiers at Gethsemane by a kiss of greeting. According to Matthew, he later repented and hanged himself.
See also: Apostles.

Judas Maccabaeus *see:* Judah Maccabee.

Judas tree *see:* Redbud.

Juddah *see:* Jidda.

Jude, Epistle of, brief letter near the end of the New Testament. It warns against false teachers and the consequences of heresy within the church. Of unknown authorship, the 25-verse epistle is believed to have been written around A.D. 100.
See also: Bible; New Testament.

Jude, Saint, or Saint Judas, one of the Twelve Apostles, also called Lebbaeus or Thaddaeus, possibly the author of the New Testament epistle of Jude, which warns against heresy. Jude is an anglicized form of Judas, to distinguish him from Judas Iscariot. His feast day is Oct. 28.
See also: Apostles.

Judea, ancient name for south Palestine. Originally known as Canaan, it was called Judea after the Hebrews returning from Exodus took possession of it. The name was derived from Judah, ancestral patriarch of one of the 12 tribes of Israel, and the term Jews is a shortened form of Judeans. King David was the first ruler of a united Judea, with Jerusalem as the capital. After the death of his son, King Solomon, Judea split into 2 kingdoms: Israel and Judah.

Judges, Book of, in the Old Testament, 7th of the Authorized Version, the sequel to Joshua. It recounts the Hebrews' successive apostasies from God and their punishment by enemy oppression. The judges were mainly military leaders sent by God to deliver the people. The main judges are Barak, Deborah, Gideon, Abimelech, Jephthah, and Samson.
See also: Old Testament.

Judgment, legal decision made by a court. A judgment is legally binding upon the parties named in it and often involves restitution imposed on a guilty party by a judge or someone acting in a legal capacity. Once a judgment is handed down, it has the force of law behind it, and violations can be punished by the court. Judgments made in criminal cases can usually be appealed to a higher court, which can either overturn or uphold a lower court ruling.

Judicial Conference of the United States, policymaking and review arm of the U.S. judicial system. It consists of 25 members and is presided over by the Chief Justice of the U.S. Supreme Court. Established in 1922, the conference meets once a year to review caseloads in all federal judicial districts and circuits and reviews complaints against federal judges. Recommendations are submitted to Congress and the U.S. Supreme Court and go into effect after 3 months unless Congress rejects them.

Judicial department *see:* Constitution of the United States; Justice, Department of; Supreme Court of the United States.

Judith, book of the Apocrypha of the Authorized Version of the Bible, present in the Old Testament of the Western canon but not in the Hebrew Bible. It tells how a young Jewish widow, Judith, saves her city, Bethulia, by seducing and murdering the Assyrian general Holofernes.
See also: Bible.

Judo, form of unarmed combat, a Japanese sport developed by Jigoro Kano in 1882 using the principles of jujitsu. It combines the use of balance, timing, and force to use one's opponent's own strength against him. Colored belts, ranging from white for beginners to black for experts, denote proficiency grades.

Judson, Adoniram (1788-1850), U.S. missionary. His 30-year work in Burma resulted in the first translation of the Bible into Burmese (1834) and an English-Burmese dictionary (1849). Judson entered the ministry and helped organize a Congregationalist missionary society, which sent him to India in 1812. Disagreements with certain Congregationalist practices led him into the Baptist ministry. He helped the Baptists organize a similar missionary society, and in 1813 he was assigned to Burma.
See also: Baptists

Juggernaut, or Jagannatha (Sanskrit, "lord of the world"), Hindu temple and idol in Puri, India. The shrine was completed in the 12th century. Once a year, during the June-July Rathayatra festival, the huge Juggernaut and its brother and sister idols are placed on wheeled carts and rolled through the streets, requiring the work of hundreds of people to move them. The word *juggernaut* has come to mean a heavy, unstoppable force.

Juggling, art of keeping several objects in motion in the air simultaneously and catching them. Juggling was practiced by the Egyptians, Greeks, and Romans; the French equivalent was a medieval troubadour who juggled, sang, and danced. Juggling came into its own in circuses and music halls in the 19th century. The word juggling has also come to mean dishonest manipulation, especially of money.

Jugoslavia *see:* Yugoslavia.

Jugular vein, any of several veins on each side of the neck that return venous blood from the head. Their proximity to the surface makes them liable to trauma.
See also: Vein.

Juilliard, Augustus (1836-1919), wealthy U.S. patron of the performing arts. After making his fortune in the textile industry, Julliard devoted time and money toward promoting cultural endeavors. He became president of New York's Metropolitan Opera Company in 1892 and served until his death. Large sums of money bequeathed from his estate established the Julliard Musical Foundation, which supports the Julliard School, a prestigious musical education institute.

Jujitsu *see:* Judo.

Julian (A.D. 331-363), 4th-century Roman emperor, known as *The Apostate* (the traitor). He was the last ruler to oppose the spread of Christianity in the Roman Empire. The nephew of Constantine I, Julian rejected his Christian education and tried to promote worship of the Roman gods after becoming emperor in 361. He prevented Christians from teaching in Roman schools, but his death in battle against the Persians 2 years later ended the persecutions.

Julian, Percy Lavon (1899-1975), U.S. chemist and chemical business executive. He developed several important soybean-based products, including a synthetic progesterone used to prevent miscarriages. He also created physostigmine, a drug used to treat glaucoma.
See also: Chemistry.

Juliana (1909-) queen of the Netherlands (1948-80) following the abdication of her mother, Queen Wilhelmina. She abdicated (1980) in favor of her daughter Beatrix.
See also: Netherlands.

Julian calendar, system of time measurement widely used between 46 B.C. and 1582. It was named for Julius Caesar, who devised it. The Julian calendar was based on solar cycles. The year was divided into 12 alternating 30- and 31-day months, with Feb. (29 days) being the exception. The Julian year was 11 min. and 14 sec. longer than the annual solar cycle, resulting in a discrepancy of 10 days by 1582. Pope Gregory XIII corrected the problem, bringing his Gregorian calendar into synchronization with the solar year.
See also: Calendar.

Julius Caesar *see:* Caesar, (Gaius) Julius.

Julius II (1443-1513), pope (1503-13). As Cardinal Giuliano della Rovere he went into exile (1492-1503) when his bitter enemy Borgia became pope Alexander VI. As pope, Julius commanded the armies that reconquered the Papal States; he then led the Holy League against France (1510). The fifth Lateran Council (1512), which he assembled, attacked corruption in the church. A patron of Raphael, Michelangelo, and Bramante, Julius II laid the foundation stone of St. Peter's Cathedral.

July Revolution, popular revolt in France in July 1830 against King Charles X. Middle-class opposition was aroused when the king's ultraroyalist minister, Jules Armand de Polignac, published the July Ordinances, which suspended freedom of the press, dissolved the chamber of deputies, and reduced the electorate by 75%. Rioting broke out, and though Charles repealed the Ordinances, he was forced to abdicate. His cousin the duke of Orleans became King Louis Philippe.
See also: France.

A judo teacher demonstrates a holding grip to students

Jumna River, or Yamuna River, tributary of the Ganges, in Northern India. It begins in the Himalayas and is nearly 900 mi (1,400 km) long. Canals draining water from the Jumna irrigate about 12,000 sq mi (31,100 sq km) in central India. The cities of Delhi and New Delhi lie along the banks of the Jumna, and it flows close to Agra, site of the Taj Mahal. The Jumna joins the Ganges near Allahabad. Their confluence is considered sacred to Hindus.

Jumping *see:* Olympic Games; Track and Field.

Jumping bean, seed of various Mexican shrubs, principally those of the genera *Sebastiania* and *Sapium* of the spurge family. The appearance of jumping is due to movement of the larva of the moth *Carpocapsa saltitans* contained inside.

Junco, any of several species of small North American finches (genus *Junco*), usually ashen in color but with conspicuous white lateral tail feathers. The slate-colored junco nests up to the treeline in Alaska, migrating south in winter. Some have crossed the Atlantic.

Juneau (pop. 19,528), capital of Alaska and port city in the southeast panhandle, situated at the foot of Mt. Juneau, on the Gastineau Channel. Ice free even in winter, Juneau supports fishing (especially salmon), lumbering, sawmilling, and tourism. The surrounding mountains yield asbestos, nickel ore, limestone, and marble, and the rapid mountain streams are a source of

hydroelectric power. Juneau was founded by prospectors in 1880, when gold-bearing quartz was discovered nearby. It has the largest area (3,108 sq mi/8,050 sq km) of any U.S. city.
See also: Alaska.

June bug, or June beetle, any of many large flying beetles (family Melolonthidae) that feed on the leaves of trees. The white larvae live underground, feeding on the roots of grasses and plants, causing considerable damage.

Jung, Carl Gustav (1875-1961), Swiss psychiatrist, founder of analytical psychology. Jung's work on mental complexes brought him into contact with Sigmund Freud in 1907, a relationship that lasted until 1912, when Freud broke with Jung upon the publication of Jung's *Psychology of the Unconscious.* In this book Jung argued that there were two components of the unconscious: repressed or forgotten information of an individual's life and collective information shared by all human beings or by those in particular cultural groups. In 1921 Jung expounded on introversion and extroversion in *Psychological Types.* Jung believed that harmony between the conscious and unconscious was the most important psychological goal for the individual.
See also: Psychoanalysis.

Carl Jung saw traditional "magic circles" like this Tibetan mandala as symbols of the integration of the self.

Jungfrau (German, "maiden"), mountain in the Swiss Alps. The Jungfrau is 13,642 ft (4,158 m) high and presents a formidable challenge for mountain climbers. It is also the site of the highest railroad in Europe, constructed between 1896 and 1912. The railway ends at a level pass, 11,333 ft (3,454 m) high, between the Jungfrau and its neighboring peak.

Jungle fowl, any of several wild birds (genus *Gallus*), from which domestic fowls probably descended. Found in the forests of southeast Asia, the jungle fowl is becoming rarer as its habitat is destroyed.

Junior Achievement, U.S. organization aimed at teaching students about the nation's business system. Founded in 1919, Junior Achievement has about 785,000 student members from the fifth through the 12th grades. They learn how to set up corporations, buy and sell stock, keep records, and handle payrolls. Programs are sponsored by local businesses and industries, and volunteers from those businesses often serve as advisers and teachers.

Juniper, any of several species of evergreen trees or shrub (genus *Juniperus*) of the cypress family, found in northern temperate zones. The cones of the common juniper (*J. communis*) are fleshy, like berries, and are used to flavor gin. Some junipers are used for lumber and oil; those called cedars, e.g., the American eastern red (*J. virginiana*), supply insect-repellant closets and fenceposts. Its oil is used in perfume and medicine.

Junípero Serra *see:* Serra, Junípero.

Junk, any of various Chinese sailing vessels, used in the Far East for thousands of years. Junks are wooden craft, up to 30 by 10 ft (9 by 3 m), with flat-bottoms, high sterns (rears) and square bows (fronts). They have tall, heavy masts, up to 5 in number, with sails made of cotton cloth or straw matting. They have deep rudders and little or no keel. Though some people live on junks, they are now mainly used for transporting goods on rivers and coastal waters.

Juno, in Roman mythology, queen of the gods. She was the sister and wife of Jupiter, king of the gods, and revered by Roman women as the goddess of marriage and childbirth. Representations of Juno adorned some of the most famous temples of the Roman Empire, and she played a prominent part in *The Aeneid*, Vergil's epic poem about the founding of Rome. Juno's Greek counterpart was Hera.

Jupiter, in astronomy, largest planet in the solar system (equatorial diameter of 89,400 mi/143,800 km), fifth planet from the Sun (average distance 483.6 million mi/778.3 million km). Jupiter is larger than all the other planets combined, with a mass 317.9 times that of Earth. Believed to have a solid core of rocky material, it is mostly gaseous with an atmosphere composed mostly of hydrogen and helium but including traces of ammonia and methane. Prominent cloud belts paralleling its equator are occasionally interrupted by stormlike turbulences, particularly the Great Red Spot, an elliptical area at least 300 yrs old and measuring 30,000 by 10,000 mi (48,000 by 16,000 km). Jupiter has 16 known moons, the largest and most distant of which, Callisto and Ganymede, are larger than Mercury. Io, the satellite closest to Jupiter, exhibits volcanism, probably because of tidal action resulting from its close proximity to the planet. Jupiter, also has a ring system, much fainter than that of Saturn and invisible from Earth. In 1973, 1974, and 1979, U.S. space probes (*Pioneers 10* and *11* and *Voyagers 1* and *2*) collected data on the Jovian system. Plans for another probe, the *Galileo,* which will orbit the planet and enter its atmosphere, are being made.
See also: Planet; Solar system.

The planet Jupiter, photographed by U.S. space probe Voyager I *in Feb. 1979*

Jupiter, in Roman mythology, king of the gods and supreme ruler over the entire universe. Patterned after Zeus, king of the Greek gods, Jupiter overthrew his father, Saturn, and married his sister, Juno. Jupiter's other brothers and sisters were Neptune, Pluto, Ceres, and Vesta. His children were Mars, Vulcan, Apollo, Bacchus, Mercury, Diana, Hercules, and the 9 Muses of the arts. Jupiter's temple on the Capitoline Hill in Rome was the focal point of Roman polytheistic worship.
See also: Mythology.

Jura Mountains, forested mountain range in western Europe, crossed by gorges, and fertile valleys, extending from the Rhone River to the Rhine River on the Swiss-German border. The highest peak in the Juras is Cret de la Neige (5,652 ft/1,723 m).

Jurassic, the middle period of the Mesozoic era, lasting from about 195 to 140 million years ago.

Jury, in common law, body of laypeople assembled to study evidence and make judgments in legal proceedings. In England, the jury was probably an extension of the Norman practice of calling character witnesses, people who had personal knowledge of a dispute. Over time, the make-up of the jury changed: disinterested parties were presented with formally produced evidence. This system was adopted from English law into the United States in the 18th century. The sixth and seventh amendments to the U.S. Constitution provide for jury trial in most criminal and civil cases. A grand jury (12-23 people) hears evidence and decides whether a trial is justified; a petit (small) jury of 6 or 12 people sits at the trial proper. Until 1970, verdicts had to be unanimous, but certain exceptions are now permissible. A hung jury (one that is unable to reach a verdict) necessitates a new trial with a new jury.

Justice, Department of, federal executive department created by Congress (1870). Headed by the attorney general, its functions are to enforce federal laws, furnish legal counsel to the federal government and represent it in Supreme Court cases, administer federal prisons, and supervise district attorneys and marshals. Its agencies include the Federal Bureau of Investigation, the Immigration and Naturalization Service, and the Drug Enforcement Administration. Its divisions include Antitrust, Civil, Civil Rights, Criminal, Land and Natural Resources, and Tax.

Justinian Code, collection of early Roman civil laws, known as *Corpus Juris Civilis* (Latin, *Body of Civil Law*). Compiled by legal scholars at the behest of the Byzantine emperor Justinian I (r. A.D. 527-565), the code formed the basis of the legal systems of many Western nations for centuries afterward. Justinian had his scholars determine which Roman laws should remain in force, be modified, or be repealed. The code also proposed new laws. The 4 parts of the code are the *Institutes*, the *Digest*, the *Codex*, and the *Novels*.
See also: Law; Rome, Ancient.

Justinian I (483-565), Byzantine emperor (527-65), nephew of Justin I. His attempts to impose heavy taxation and religious orthodoxy on the diverse peoples and sects of the empire, especially the Monophysites (a Christian minority), led to the Nika riots (532), which were quelled by Empress Theodora, aided by Justinian's generals Belisarius and Narses. Among Justinian's accomplishments are the codification of Roman law (*Digests*) and such great churches as Hagia Sophia and San Vitale.
See also: Byzantine Empire.

Justin the Martyr, Saint (c.100-165), Christian theologian who opened the first school of Christian studies in Rome. He was martyred under Marcus Aurelius. His *Apology* and *Dialogue* defended Christianity against charges of impiety and sedition.

Jute, annual plant (genus *Corchorus*) of the linden family, and its fiber. Cultivated in India and Bangladesh, stems of the *C. capsularis* and *C. olitorius* are cut and laid in water until the long fibers can be separated. The fibers are then dyed and spun and used for making burlap, insulation, and rope.

Jutes, Germanic people who originated in Scandinavia, probably in Jutland, the Danish peninsula. With the Angles and Saxons they invaded England in the 5th century, settling in the south and southeast. Their national identify was soon lost, although some cultural influence seems to have survived in Kent.

Jutland, Battle of, only major naval battle of World War I, fought between the British and German fleets off the coast of Jutland (Denmark) on May 31, 1916. Though greatly outnumbered the Germans performed masterfully and escaped in the fog. The British fleet under Admiral Jellicoe suffered heavy losses leading to controversy about Jellicoe's tactics.

Juvenal (Decimus Junius Juvenalis; A.D. 60?-140?), Roman poet. His 16 satires are scathing attacks on the corruption of social and political life in Rome. Many of his epigrammatic sayings ("A sound mind in a sound body") have passed into everyday use.

Juvenile court, court with special jurisdiction over young offenders (usually up to age 18). In many nations, special provisions are made in legal proceedings involving minors. Rehabilitation, rather than punishment, is normally emphasized, including removal from parental care if the home environment is thought to contribute to delinquency. In the interest of flexibility and informality, certain ordinary courtroom practices may be suspended in juvenile court.

Juvenile delinquency, term applied to violations of the law by those legally considered under the age of majority. The maximum age for juveniles varies from place to place. Most countries deal with young offenders in special juvenile courts. Many sociologists contend that criminal activities are only one expression of a disturbed life pattern, of which transiency, violence, poverty, and the failure of family relationships are also typical. The high rate of illegal activity in adolescence probably reflects the general disturbances common to this age group. Action taken by the juvenile courts is theoretically correctional rather than punitive.

K

K, 11th letter of the English alphabet, is derived from the Semitic *kaph*, representing the palm of the hand, and from the ancient Greek *kappa*. After C was given the K sound, the Romans stopped using K except as an abbreviation. K is sometimes used as an abbreviation for *knight*, as in K.C. (Knights of Columbus); for *kilo*, a prefix meaning 1,000; and in chess, for *king*. In chemistry K is the symbol for potassium.

K2, mountain peak in the Himalayas of northern Kashmir, near the China-India border, second highest in the world. Also known as Mount Godwin-Austen and Dapsang, K2 is 29,064 ft (8,859 m) high. It was first scaled in 1954 by an Italian team under the leadership of Ardito Desio. Henry Haversham Godwin Austen surveyed the mountain in 1856.

Kaaba, or Caaba, most sacred shrine of Islam, the chief goal of pilgrimage, in the courtyard of the Great Mosque at Mecca, Saudi Arabia. Pilgrims must circle this flat-roofed building 7 times, and then kiss the venerated object encased within—the Black Stone, said to have been given to Adam on his fall from paradise. The Kaaba is the center of the Muslim world, and it is in its direction that Muslims face in prayer.

Kaaba

Kabalevsky, Dmitri (1904-87), Russian composer and critic. His works include symphonies, ballet, chamber music, and operas, such as *Colas Breugnon* (1938) and *The Taras Family* (1949).

Kabbalah, or Cabala (from the Hebrew word for "traditional lore"), mystical Jewish interpretation of the Torah and other holy writings. Based largely on doctrines of post-biblical sages, it entails the idea that every word and letter of the holy writings contains hidden meanings whose mystery must be uncovered through constant study. Under the guidance of Isaac Luria in the

late 16th and early 17th century, Kabbalism became more messianic in orientation. Hasidism, a Jewish movement that began in the 18th century, adopted many Kabbalist beliefs.
See also: Judaism.

Kabuki, traditional Japanese popular theater that developed in the 17th century in contrast to the aristocratic Noh theater. A blending of dance, song, and mime, kabuki dramatizes both traditional stories and contemporary events in a stylized but exuberant fashion. It remains popular today and has influenced much Western theatrical thought.

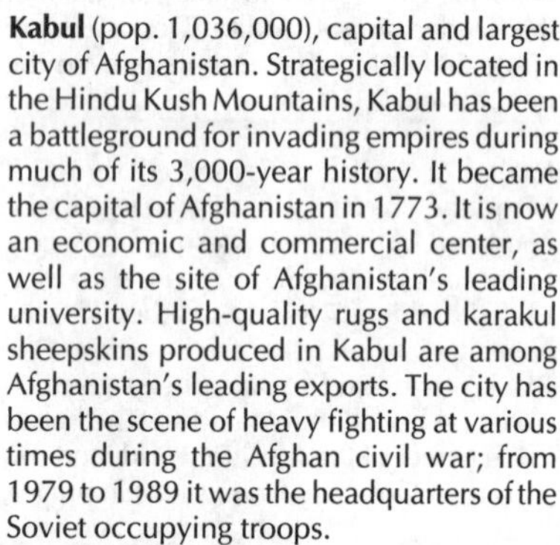

Franz Kafka

Kabul (pop. 1,036,000), capital and largest city of Afghanistan. Strategically located in the Hindu Kush Mountains, Kabul has been a battleground for invading empires during much of its 3,000-year history. It became the capital of Afghanistan in 1773. It is now an economic and commercial center, as well as the site of Afghanistan's leading university. High-quality rugs and karakul sheepskins produced in Kabul are among Afghanistan's leading exports. The city has been the scene of heavy fighting at various times during the Afghan civil war; from 1979 to 1989 it was the headquarters of the Soviet occupying troops.
See also: Afghanistan.

Kabul, with Mount Paghman in the background

Kádár, János (1912-), Hungarian Communist leader. In the 1956 uprising, he left his position in Imre Nagy's cabinet to lead the Soviet-supported counter-government that crushed the revolt. He became premier (1956-58, 1961-65) and first secretary of the party (1956). His leadership brought a liberalization to all facets of Hungarian life.
See also: Hungary.

Kaddafi, Muammar Muhammad al- *see:* Qadhafi, Muammar Muhammad al-.

Kaesong (pop. 345,600), city in North Korea near the South Korean border, about 30 mi (48 km) northwest of Seoul. It is a key agricultural and industrial hub and the site of many historic cultural landmarks. Chosen as the first capital of a united Korean kingdom (Koryo) in the 10th century, Kaesong was the country's leading city until 1392, when the ruling dynasty fell and the capital was moved to Seoul. In 1951 it was the site of the first peace talks aimed at ending the Korean War.

Kafir (*Sorghum vulgare*), type of grain of the grass family. Commonly grown on the North American plains and used as cattle feed, kafir was imported from Africa. The plants resemble cornstalks, attaining heights of 4 to 7 ft (1.2 to 2.1 m). Kafir is closely related to the sorghum grains of Africa and Asia.

Kafka, Franz (1883-1924), German writer. Kafka was born in Prague, of Jewish parents. Kafka created stories of conflicts for isolated, guilt-ridden protagonists—conflicts that could not be resolved or escaped, no matter their personal effort. His executor ignored instructions to destroy all his work, and subsequently published his novels, including *The Trial* (1925), *The Castle* (1926), and *Amerika* (1927), and his short stories, including "The Metamorphosis" (1915), "A Country Doctor" (1919), and "In the Penal Colony" (1920).

Kahn, Louis Isadore (1901-74), U.S. architect, noted for his work on housing projects like Carver Court (1944), Coatesville, Pa., and university buildings. His work also included the planning of the Kimbell Art Museum (Fort Worth, Tex.), and the Yale University Art Gallery. Kahn held a professorship at the University of Pennsylvania from 1957 until his death.
See also: Architecture.

Kaiser, Henry John (1882-1967), U.S. industrialist, founder of the Kaiser-Frazer Corp., automobile manufacturers. He contributed greatly to the Allied war effort during World War II by his development of faster production techniques for ships, aircraft, and military vehicles, especially the famous jeep.

Kala-azar, dumdum fever, or visceral leishmaniasis, severe infectious disease found chiefly in Asia and caused by a protozoa (*Leishmania donovani*) and transmitted by the bite of sand flies. Symptoms include fever, anemia, leukopenia, and enlargement of the spleen and liver.

Kalahari Desert, arid plain in southwest Africa, lying mainly in Botswana but extending into Namibia and South Africa. The region, 100,000 sq mi (260,000 sq km) in area, has low annual rainfall (5-20 in/13-51 cm), seasonal pasture for sheep, and a wide variety of game. It is inhabited principally by the nomadic San (Bushmen) and Khoikhoi.

Kale, edible green vegetable (*Brassica oleracea*) of the mustard family. Valued as a source of vitamins A, B-complex, and C, kale's curled leaves are usually boiled or steamed before eating. Plants may attain heights of 24 to 30 in (61 to 76 cm), while dwarf varieties range from 12 to 15 in (30 to 38 cm).

Kaleidoscope, optical device that produces colorful patterns and designs. It consists of a tube with mirrors and pieces of colored beads and glass that is held to the eye and rotated to form symmetrical color patterns. Patented in 1817, the kaleidoscope is used by designers to formulate carpet and wallpaper patterns.

Kaliningrad (pop. 380,000), port city in western USSR, on the mouth of the Pregolya River, which flows into the Baltic Sea. Formerly called Königsberg, Kaliningrad was founded in 1255 as part of East Prussia. In 1945 it was absorbed by the Soviet Union and renamed Kaliningrad. Today it is a naval base for the Soviet Baltic Fleet. Fishing, machine building, and shipbuilding are the main industries.
See also: Union of Soviet Socialist Republics.

Kalmar Union, treaty whereby Denmark, Norway, and Sweden were united under Margaret of Denmark and her heirs. It was signed at the Swedish port of Kalmar (1397), which became the Union's political center. The Union endured until 1523.

Kalmia *see:* Mountain laurel.

Kamchatka Peninsula, peninsula in northeastern USSR, extending 750 mi (1,210 km) south from the Asian mainland to separate the Sea of Okhotsk from the Bering Sea and Pacific Ocean. It is largely tundra and pine forest, with 2 volcanic ranges. Geographic features include Siberia's highest peak, Kluychevskaya Sopka (15,584 ft/4,750 m), and 22 active volcanoes, along with geysers and hot springs. Main occupations include lumbering, fur-trapping, and fishing. The peninsula's main city is Petropavlovsk-Kamchatski.
See also: Union of Soviet Socialist Republics

Kamehameha I (1738?-1819), Hawaiian king from 1790. This benevolent despot, who conquered and ruled all the Hawaiian islands (1810), encouraged foreign contact and trading.

Kamenev, Lev Borisovich (1883-1936), Russian Bolshevik leader, active in the Russian Revolution and member of the first politburo of the Communist party. After Lenin's death (1924) he joined Stalin and Zinoviev to defeat Trotsky's bid for power. However, Stalin ousted Kamenev and Zinoviev in 1925 and they joined Trotsky's opposition movement. In 1936, Stalin had both Kamenev and Zinoviev arrested and executed for treason.
See also: Bolsheviks; Russian Revolution.

Kamikaze (Japanese, "divine wind"), Japanese force of suicide pilots in World War II. Inspired by the ancient samurai code of patriotic self-sacrifice, they deliberately crashed bomb-bearing planes onto Allied ships and installations. They inflicted particularly heavy damage at Okinawa.
See also: World War II.

Kampala (pop. 458,400), capital and largest city of Uganda, on Lake Victoria in east Africa. When Uganda became self-

governing in 1962, Kampala superseded Entebbe as the capital. The city was originally constructed on six adjacent hills. Uganda's agricultural and commercial markets are concentrated in Kampala.
See also: Uganda.

Kampuchea (officially Cambodia), republic in Southeast Asia, bordered on the north by Thailand and Laos, on the east and southeast by Vietnam, on the southwest by the Gulf of Siam, and on the west and northwest by Thailand. The capital is Phnom Penh.

Land and climate. Mainly a broad plain, Kampuchea occupies 69,898 sq mi (181,035 sq km), and is separated from Thailand by the Dangrek Mountains in the north and the Cardamom Mountains in the west. The Mekong, one of the most important rivers in southern Asia, enters Kampuchea from Laos and crosses the country from north to south. A large, shallow lake, the Tônlé Sap, occupies central Kampuchea. Annual inundations caused by the overflow of the Mekong River create excellent conditions for rice cultivation. The climate is tropical and humid, with a rainy season lasting from May to Oct. Rainfall is plentiful, reaching as high as 250 in (635 cm) per year in the Cardamom Mountains. Temperatures range from 68° to 97°F (20° to 36°C).

Wildlife is abundant, particularly in the forests, and includes elephants, water buffaloes, tigers, leopards, honey bears, crocodiles, and snakes. Elephants are often domesticated. There are abundant freshwater fish. Plant life is also rich. The country produces tropical hardwood trees, as well as rubber, coconut, mango, orange, banana, and kapok trees.

People. About 85% are Khmers. The Chinese and Vietnamese each constitute about 5%, and there are small numbers of Chams, Europeans, Indians, Thai, and primitive tribes. The modern official language is Khmer, spoken by about 60% of the population, and French is used by a sizable minority. Numerous other languages are found among the hill peoples. Theravada Buddhism is practiced, and most Kampuchean males spend at least a short time in Buddhist monasteries, many of which are also educational establishments. There are several technical schools, and the Buddhist University and the former Royal Khmer University are located in Phnom Penh. The literacy rate is about 40%.

Located at the confluence of the Mekong and Tônlé Sap rivers, Phnom Penh is the principal city of the country. Other towns are generally much less than 50,000 in population. The majority of Khmers live in villages in the Mekong and Tônlé Sap basins. Their houses, often of bamboo and thatch, are built on stilts in preparation for the rainy season. Most Kampucheans are skilled in art, music, and dancing, and their many temples are elaborately carved.

Kampuchea: Bullock carts are common in the countryside of Indochina.

Economy. Small and often primitive rice farms on the plains around the Tônlé Sap are the basis of Kampuchea's economy. Food production is sufficient for the population, and rice is the chief export. Rubber is the second most important. In addition, corn, livestock, sugar, pepper, tobacco, cotton, coffee, and soybeans are raised. Deep-sea fishing in the Gulf of Siam is an important commercial activity, while the Tônlé Sap and the Mekong rivers provide the greatest concentration of freshwater fish in southeast Asia. The extensive forests are largely untouched and, because of

Kampuchea (Cambodia)

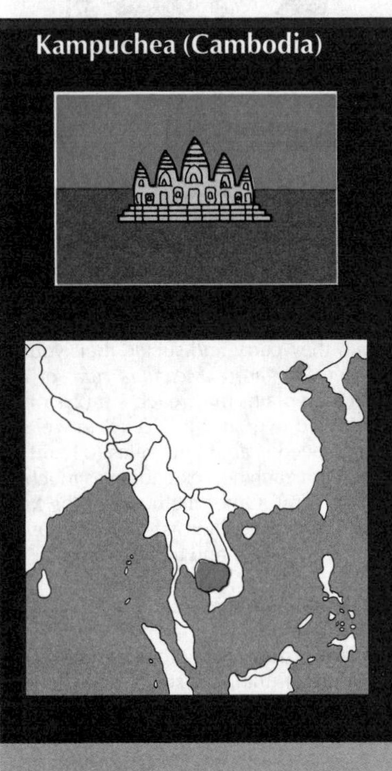

General information	
Capital:	Phnom Penh
Area:	69,898 sq mi (181,035 sq km)
Population:	6,900,000
Official language:	Khmer
Monetary unit:	1 Riel = 100 sen
Main cities:	Phnom Penh, Kâmpóng Cham
Government	
Form:	people's republic
Independent:	1953
Head of state:	President of the Council of State
Head of government:	Chairman Council of Ministers
Legislature:	one legislative house (National Assembly)
Executive:	Council of State and Council of Ministers
Judiciary:	highest court is the Supreme People's Court
Political division:	20 provinces
National economy	
Gross national product:	U.S. $600,000,000
Per capita income:	U.S. $90
Agriculture:	rice, vegetables and melons, sugar cane, bananas, rubber, soybeans
Livestock:	cattle, pigs, buffaloes
Fisheries:	74,000 metric tons
Mining:	salt, iron, copper
Industries:	cement, rubber, footwear, beef and veal, plywood, textiles
Main exports:	rubber, beans, rice, sesame seeds
Transportation:	380 mi (621 km) of railroads, 8,296 mi (13,351 km) of roads; 1 international airport
Trading partners:	USSR, Japan, U.S., France, Australia
People	
Urban:	11%
Ethnic composition:	Khmer 88%, Chinese 4.5%, Vietnamese 4.5%
Birth rate:	40.9 per 1,000 population
Death rate:	16.4 per 1,000 population
Infant mortality:	129 per 1,000 live births
Life expectancy:	male 47.5 years, female 50 years

transport problems, high-grade iron ore deposits in the north are also unexploited.
History. Mythology claims that the country was founded by a Hindu king, Kambu, who gave the country the name Kambuja. In the 1st century A.D., Hindu people established the flourishing kingdom of Funan, which ruled large areas. Toward the end of the 6th century, the territory was split up among rival groups. The most powerful of these, the Khmer, founded the great Angkor Dynasty between 800 and 850. This Khmer kingdom reached its greatest power about 1100 and attained a high level of civilization. Much of Thailand, Laos, and Vietnam were part of the Khmer empire, which began its decline in the late 14th century. By the middle of the 19th century the country was approximately its present size and in 1863, to prevent its complete conquest, King Norodom asked for the protection of the French. In 1887, Cambodia became part of the French Union of Indochina.
In the 1930s, a Cambodian nationalist movement gained strength and by 1940 anti-French feeling was running high. In 1953 Cambodia achieved full independence. Norodom Sihanouk became prime minister after the elections of 1955 and remained so for 5 years. In 1960 Sihanouk was made head of state, without the title of king. A member of the United Nations since 1955, Cambodia proclaimed a policy of neutrality. Aid from both communist and Western countries was used to develop the economy: to build roads, air-transport facilities, and irrigation systems. In 1963, Sihanouk refused further economic and military aid from the United States, and in 1965 diplomatic relations were broken off. The military coup d'etat of 1970, when Sihanouk was deposed in his absence, together with incursions of North Vietnamese troops, precipitated internal crises. General Lon Nol established a military government (the Khmer Republic) in Phnom Penh, but the new and inexperienced Cambodian army proved a poor match for the Vietcong. U.S. and South Vietnamese forces crossed the border to clear out enemy "sanctuaries" in April 1970, but American troops soon withdrew. The Cambodian communists (Khmer Rouge) emerged in 1970 as a powerful political group with a standing army of 3,000 men. In alliance with the Khmer Rouge, Sihanouk formed an exile government in Peking. Civil war raged between Lon Nol's government forces and the Khmer Rouge, who by 1973 numbered 30,000 and were gaining control of the country despite intensive U.S. bombing. In Apr. 1975 Phnom Penh was besieged and surrendered to the Khmer Rouge. "The Royal Government of the National Union of Cambodia (Kampuchea)" returned from exile under Sihanouk. Following the resignation of Sihanouk in 1976, Pol Pot became prime minister of the newly named Democratic Kampuchea. The regime enacted harsh measures, evacuating all cities and suppressing opposition. Hundreds of thousands of people died or were killed. In 1978 Vietnam launched attacks against Kampuchea, and in 1979 Vietnamese troops captured Phnom Penh and proclaimed the People's Republic of Kampuchea. Pol Pot, as commander-in-chief of the Khmer Rouge forces, continued to fight the Vietnamese from unoccupied parts of the country. In 1983, Vietnam launched major offensives against the rebel forces and by Feb. 1985 had overrun all Khmer Rouge bases. In 1989 the Vietnamese forces withdrew.

Kanawha River, chief river of West Virginia, formed by the confluence of the New and Gauley rivers. It flows about 97 mi (156 km) northwest to join the Ohio River at Point Pleasant.

Kandinsky, Wassily (1866-1944), Russian painter and theorist, widely regarded as one of the originators of abstract art. Influenced by fauvism in postimpressionist Paris, his early work aimed at pure aesthetic expression by using bursts of color in nonrepresentational paintings. He was a founder, along with Paul Klee, of the Blaue Reiter art movement in Munich (1911; named for his own painting, *Le cavalier bleu*, "The Blue Rider"). He studied the psychology of color and its effects in *Concerning the Spiritual in Art* (1912) and expressed his viewpoint on art and color in *The Art of Spiritual Harmony* (1914). Geometric compositions came into play in his paintings of the 1920s, at which time he also joined the faculty of the Bauhaus design school in Weimar (1922-33).

Wassily Kandinsky, White Zigzag *(1922)*

Kanem, African empire that lasted from 700 A.D. through the 1800s. It included parts of modern Cameroon, Chad, Libya, Niger, Nigeria, and the Sudan. Kanem declined in the late 1800s when trade routes shifted away from it.

Kangaroo

Kangaroo, herbivorous, marsupial mammal of the family Macropodidae, with large hind feet, strong hind legs, and a tail used for balancing, native to Australia and nearby islands. Like other marsupial females, female kangaroos have a pouch in which they carry and suckle their young. The red kangaroo (*Megaleia rufa*) of the Australian plains may reach 7 ft (2.1 m) in height and over 200 lb (90 kg) in weight. Its top speed is about 40 miles (64 km) an hour, with each hop extending as much as 18 ft (5.5 m). Other members of the kangaroo family, classified as genus *Macropus*, include wallabies and tree kangaroos.

Kangaroo apple *see:* Solanum.

Kangaroo court, unofficial and illegal gathering of unauthorized persons for the purpose of passing sentence upon a wrongdoer. Such sentences have been imposed in many countries by citizens' groups, such as vigilante societies in the United States and the illegal Irish Republican Army. The name was first used c.1853 to refer to the "instant justice" meted out by frontier judges in the United States who "hopped" like kangaroos from place to place on their legal circuits.

Kangaroo rat, pouched, burrowing, nocturnal rodent (genus *Dipodomys*) similar to the gerbil. It has long hind legs, a long tail, and moves by jumping. Kangaroo rats live in arid regions of the southwestern United States.

Kanishka (d.A.D. 160?), greatest king of the Kushan Empire, which included what is now Pakistan, Afghanistan, and northern India. A patron of Buddhism, Kanishka built a monument in his capital, Peshawar, to house relics of Buddha. He established the Gandharan school of art, which blended eastern and western influences in sculpture.
See also: Kushan Empire.

Kanpur (pop. 1,482,000), city in the state of Uttar Pradesh, north central India, on the Ganges River. An industrial center manufacturing silk, cotton, wool, and leather goods, Kanpur first became an economic power in 1801, when it was ceded to the British East India Company. During the Sepoy Rebellion of 1857 the entire British garrison of the city was wiped out.

Kansa, also known as Kaw or Kansas, Native American tribe of eastern Kansas. This agricultural and hunting plains tribe, for whom the state of Kansas was named, lived along the Kansas River until their lands were taken by the U.S. government (1873) and they were moved to a reservation in Oklahoma. Decimated by disease, very few Kansa survive today.

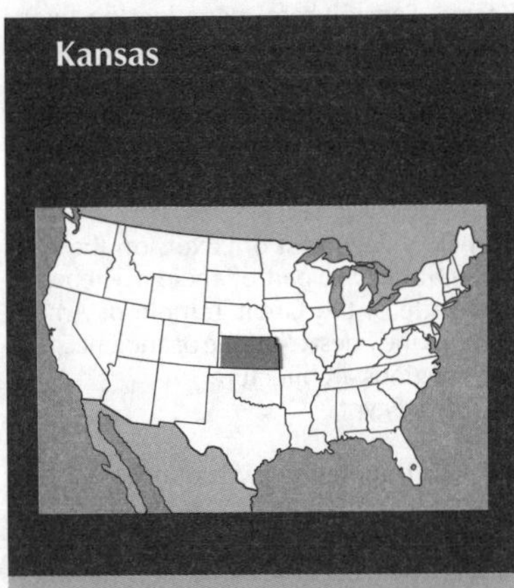

Capital:	Topeka
Statehood:	Jan. 29, 1961 (34th state)
Familiar name:	Sunflower State
Area:	82,277 sq mi (213,098 sq km); ranks 14th
Population:	2,485,600 (1990); ranks 32nd
Elevation:	Highest—4,039 ft (1,231 m), Mt. Sunflower; Lowest—680 ft (207 m), Verdigris River in Montgomery County
Motto:	*Ad Astra per Aspera* (To the Stars Through Difficulties)
Flower:	Sunflower
Bird:	Western meadowlark
Tree:	Cottonwood
Song:	"Home on the Range"

Kansas, state in the central United States; bordered by Nebraska to the north, Missouri to the east, Oklahoma to the south, and Colorado to the west. Nicknamed "Midway, U.S.A." and "Heart of the Nation," Kansas is halfway between the Atlantic and Pacific Oceans.
Land and climate. Kansas lies in the transition area between the prairies and the high plains. It consists of 3 principal land regions: the Great Plains, covering the western two-thirds of the state; the Dissected Till Plains in the northeast corner; and the Southeastern Plains. The Great Plains are slightly rolling, rather dry land, sloping downward from the Colorado border to the east. The Dissected Till Plains region was the only one covered by glaciers during the Ice Ages; as a result, it has deposits of rich soil cut through by rivers to leave high bluffs. The Southeastern Plains are often divided into the Flint Hills in the west and the Osage Plains in the east. Kansas does not have extensive water resources, but more than 100 artificial lakes add to its irrigation and recreation resources. Its major river systems are the Kansas, the Arkansas, and their tributaries. Kansas soils are generally dark, fertile loam suitable for raising a variety of crops. Like most of the U.S. interior, Kansas has cold winters and warm-to-hot summers. Principal cities are Wichita, Kansas City, and Topeka.
Economy. Often called the "Breadbasket of America," Kansas is one of the top agricultural states. It leads the nation in wheat production, and is the leading producer of beef cattle. Other major crops include grain sorghum, hay, corn, and hogs.
Kansas's leading industrial products are transportation equipment, processed foods, and printed materials. Wichita is the nation's largest aviation-production center. Automobiles, trucks, and railroad cars are produced in Atchison, Kansas City, Lawrence, Topeka, and Wichita. One of the world's largest meat-packing plants is in Garden City; large producers of pharmaceuticals and other chemicals operate in the Kansas City area. Service industries account for the largest share of the state's income. Kansas's mineral resources include petroleum, natural gas, helium, limestone, coal, and salt.
Government. The Kansas constitution was adopted in 1859. The governor serves a 4-year term. The state's legislature consists of 40 senators serving 4-year terms and 125 representatives serving 2-year terms. In the U.S. Congress, Kansas is represented by 2 senators and 5 representatives.
History. Native Americans inhabited the region long before the first white settlers arrived. Gold-seeking Spaniards were the first Europeans to enter the area (1541); in the late 1600s, French explorers claimed the land. The U.S. acquired most of Kansas as part of the Louisiana Purchase (1803). In the mid-1800s, the nationwide debate over slavery led to a series of disorders and killings that earned the territory the nickname of "Bleeding Kansas." In 1861 Kansas became the 34th state, supporting the Union cause during the Civil War. After the war, settlement and economic expan-

Grain elevator and church in Danville, Kansas

sion progressed rapidly until the 1930s, when Kansas was hit hard by drought and depression. World War II brought recovery to agriculture, and new cultivation methods restored prosperity. In the decades since, Kansas's small towns have declined in population as its urban centers and industries have grown.

Kansas City (pop. 1,566,280), name of 2 adjacent cities at the junction of the Missouri and Kansas rivers, one in northeast Kansas (inc. 1859) and one in northwest Missouri (inc. 1850). This area, as eastern terminus of the Santa Fe trail (1850), served as the starting point for many Western expeditions and gave rise to several settlements in the early 19th century. The building of the railroads increased the importance of Kansas City. Today the cities serve as an industrial, cultural, transportation, and commercial center, with extensive stockyards, grain elevators, mills, and refineries. Leading products include automobiles, farm machinery, and printed materials. Sights include the Nelson Gallery-Atkins Museum (Missouri), a Shawnee mission (1839), and an agricultural museum (Kansas).
See also: Kansas; Missouri.

Kansas-Nebraska Act, bill passed by the U.S. Congress (1854) to establish the territories of Nebraska and Kansas. Territorial organization of this region had been stalled due to conflict over slavery and the routes of the transcontinental railroad. The proposed Missouri Compromise, which would have organized the area as one territory but would not have allowed slavery in the region, was not supported by the South, and was defeated at every presentation. As a compromise, Sen. Stephen Douglas proposed the creation of 2 territories, each to decide the slavery question for itself. As both North and South flooded the territories with settlers in an attempt to establish control, the conflict escalated, culminating in the Civil War.
See also: Civil War, U.S.; Slavery.

Kant, Immanuel (1724-1804), German philosopher, founder of critical philosophy. Though originally influenced by the rationalism of Leibniz, Kant was awakened from his "dogmatic slumber" by the work

Immanuel Kant (painted in 1931 after a 1791 miniature by G. Doeppler)

of skeptic David Hume and thus led to greatness as a metaphysician. In *Critique of Pure Reason* (1781), Kant proposed that objective reality (the phenomenal world) can be known only because the mind imposes its own structure (time and space) on it. Things beyond experience (noumena) cannot be known, though we may presume to know them. The questions of the existence of God, immortality, freedom—all metaphysical questions—cannot be answered by scientific means, and thus cannot be proved or disproved. But, according to Kant in *Critique of Practical Reason* (1788), their existence must be presumed for the sake of morality. Kant's absolute moral law states, "Act as if the maxim from which you act were to become through your will a universal law." In *Critique of Judgment* (1790), beauty and purpose form the bridge between the sensible and the intelligible worlds that he sharply divided in his first 2 *Critiques*. Kant's influence is extensive, particularly in Germany. G.W.F. Hegel, F.W.J. von Schelling, and J.G. Fichte, influenced by Kant, developed German idealism; Ernst Cassirer of the physical sciences and Heinrich Rickert of the historical and cultural sciences applied neo-Kantian insights to their studies. Kant influenced the theology of F.D.E. Schleiermacher, the pragmatism of U.S. philosophers William James and John Dewey, and Gestalt psychology.
See also: Metaphysics; Philosophy.

Kantor, MacKinlay (1904-77), U.S. screenwriter and author. A newspaper writer (1921-31), Kantor also wrote screenplays and several books, including *Long Remember* (1936), *The Voice of Bugle Ann* (1935), *Arouse and Beware* (1936), *Happy Land* (1943), and *Andersonville* (1955).

Boris Karloff

Kaolin, or china clay, soft, white clay composed chiefly of the mineral kaolinite, mined in England, France, Czechoslovakia, China, and the southern United States. It is used for filling and coating paper, filling rubber and paints, making pottery and porcelain, and in medicine, to treat diarrhea.

Kapitsa, Pyotr (1894-1984), Russian physicist best known for his work in low-temperature physics (cryogenics). During the 1920s and early 1930s he worked at Cavendish Laboratory in Cambridge, England. After returning to the USSR (1934) he directed the Institute for Physical Problems. He was an outspoken advocate of freedom of thought and scientific exchange and was awarded the 1978 Nobel Prize for physics.
See also: Physics.

Kapok (*Ceiba pentandra*), tropical tree; also, the water-repellent fiber of its seeds. Kapok is used as a stuffing for life jackets, mattresses, pillows, and cold-weather clothing, and as insulation against heat and sound. Oil from its seeds is used in the manufacture of soap. Kapok trees are found in India, Indonesia, Africa, and other tropical regions.

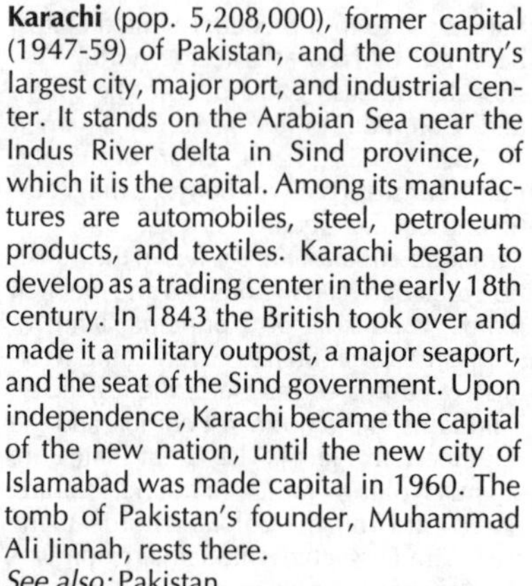

Karachi (pop. 5,208,000), former capital (1947-59) of Pakistan, and the country's largest city, major port, and industrial center. It stands on the Arabian Sea near the Indus River delta in Sind province, of which it is the capital. Among its manufactures are automobiles, steel, petroleum products, and textiles. Karachi began to develop as a trading center in the early 18th century. In 1843 the British took over and made it a military outpost, a major seaport, and the seat of the Sind government. Upon independence, Karachi became the capital of the new nation, until the new city of Islamabad was made capital in 1960. The tomb of Pakistan's founder, Muhammad Ali Jinnah, rests there.
See also: Pakistan.

Karajan, Herbert von (1908-90), Austrian conductor. He directed the Berlin State Opera (1938-45), the Vienna State Opera (1956-64), and the Berlin Philharmonic Orchestra (1955-89).

Karakorum, ancient capital of Genghis Khan's empire. Its ruins, discovered in 1889, stand in what is now the Mongolian People's Republic, on the Orhon River. Established c.1220, it fell into decay by the 16th century. Marco Polo visited Karakorum c.1275.
See also: Genghis Khan.

Karakul, any of several species of sheep of Central Asia, bred primarily for their fur-bearing skin. The pelts of the Karakul are called Persian lamb, broadtail, and caracul. The wool of the lamb is lustrous, smooth, and often black. A mature Karakul's fleece is thick and rough in texture and may have a range of colors including white, brown, gray, and yellow.

Kara Kum, desert region in the Turkmen Republic of the USSR, in central Asia, covering about 135,000 sq mi (330,000 sq km) in area. The Kara Kum canal, extending from the Amu Darya River through two oases to the city of Ashkhabad, enables parts of the desert to be irrigated and used for grazing sheep, goats, and camels.

Karamanlis, Constantine *see:* Caramanlis, Constantine.

Kara Sea, branch of the Arctic Ocean about 300 miles (480 km) long and 200 miles (320 km) wide off the north central coast of Siberia. The sea is bounded on the east by the Yamal Peninsula and on the west by the Novaya Zemlya Islands.
See also: Arctic Ocean.

Karate (Japanese: "empty hand"), unarmed combat and sport, originating in the Orient. Hands, knees, elbows, and feet are all used to deliver blows against vulnerable pressure points on the body of the attacker.

Karelia, self-governing republic in the northwestern USSR. Its capital city is Petrozavodsk. Bordering Finland, it has an area of about 70,000 sq mi (181,000 sq km), with vast pine forests and more than 2,000 lakes. Lumbering, forest industries, iron working, and fishing are the major sources of employment.
See also: Union of Soviet Socialist Republics.

Karl-Marx-Stadt, formerly Chemnitz (pop. 316,400), industrial city in eastern Germany and chief center of the Karl-Marx-Stadt district, situated on the Chemnitz River. Famous since medieval times for its textiles, Karl-Marx-Stadt now also produces machinery, machine tools, chemicals, and optical instruments. The city was chartered in 1143, destroyed during the Thirty Years War, and severely damaged in World War II. It was renamed Karl-Marx-Stadt in 1953. In 1990 the name reverted back to Chemnitz.
See also: Germany.

Karloff, Boris (William Henry Pratt; 1887-1969), English-born U.S. actor renowned for his parts in horror films. His most famous roles were as the monster in *Frankenstein* (1931) and *The Bride of Frankenstein* (1935).

Karlovy Vary (pop. 58,600), resort and spa in western Bohemia, Czechoslovakia, famed for its mineral springs. The most celebrated of its 17 functioning springs is the Vridlo. Glassware, china, and pottery are the main industrial products.
See also: Czechoslovakia.

Karma, Sanskrit term denoting the inevitable effects of a person's physical and mental actions on his or her destiny in successive lives, central to Buddhist and Hindu thought.
See also: Sikhism.

Karnak, village east of Luxor, on the Nile in central Egypt, part of ancient Thebes. It is the site of the Great Temple of Amon, perhaps the finest example of ancient Egyptian religious architecture.
See also: Egypt.

Karnak, Temple of *see:* Thutmose III.

Karpov, Anatoly (1951-), a Russian chess prodigy who became the Soviet champion in his early twenties. He was awarded the world chess championship in 1975, after reigning champion Bobby Fischer of the United States had repeatedly refused to defend his title. In 1981 Karpov defeated his principal challenger, Viktor Korchnoi, for the second time. In 1985 he lost his title to Gary Kasparov in a second match for the world title. Karpov's most recent attempt to regain his championship ended unsuccessfully when he was beaten again by Gary Kasparov in a 24-game match in Dec. 1990.
See also: Chess.

Karsh, Yousuf (1908-), Canadian portrait photographer of Turkish-Armenian birth. In 1935 he was appointed the Canadian government's official photographer.
See also: Photography.

Kart racing, sport that features single-seated, rear-engine racing cars. Referred to as go-karts, these automobiles can reach speeds of 140 mph (225 kmph) In most national competitions, drivers must be 16 years or older, but competitions for children ages 8 and 9 are quite popular. Very popular in Europe, kart racing was invented in 1956 in the United States.

Kasavubu, Joseph (1917?-69), African politician, first president (1960-65) of the Republic of the Congo (now Zaïre). He ousted Premier Patrice Lumumba but was himself supplanted (1965) by Gen. Joseph Mobutu.
See also: Zaire.

Kashmir, disputed territory in southern Asia, administered since 1972 as the Indian state of Jammu and Kashmir (capital: Srinagar; 54,000 sq mi/139,000 sq km) and the Pakistani Azad Kasmir (capital: Muzafarabad; 32,000 sq mi/82,900 sq km), bordering China. This beautiful region, which includes sections of the Himalayan and Karakorum mountain ranges, centers around the Vale of Kashmir, the agricultural area where rice and wheat are grown, fed by the Jhelum River. After years of rule by Hindus and Buddhists, Islam took hold in the late 14th century, and Kashmir became part of the Mogul empire (1586). In the mid-19th century the British restored Hindu rule. Since India's partition (1947) the territory has been the source of a dispute between India and Pakistan, with some interference from China (1959-63). Current boundaries were established in 1972.
See also: India; Pakistan.

Kasparov, Gary (1963-), Russian chess prodigy who at 22 became the sport's youngest world champion by beating Anatoly Karpov (1985). He has successfully defended his title, most recently by beating Anatoly Karpov in a 24-game match that ended on Dec. 31, 1990.

Kassebaum, Nancy Landon (1932-), U.S. Republican senator from Kansas since 1978. Having never held political office before, Kassebaum became the first woman ever elected to the U.S. Senate without having first been appointed to a congressional seat to complete a spouse's term. Her father, Alfred M. Landon, was one-time governor of Kansas and lost the 1936 presidential election to Franklin D. Roosevelt by a wide margin.

Katayev, Valentin Petrovich (1897-1987), Russian novelist, poet, and playwright. Among his best-known works are the novels *The Embezzlers* (1926) and *Lonely White Sail* (1936), and the farce *Squaring the Circle* (1928).

Kathmandu (pop. 393,500), capital of Nepal, 4,500 ft (1,370 m) above sea level in a Himalayan valley in central Nepal. The city lies on an ancient route from India to Tibet and China and is a vital commercial and administrative center. Important sites include temples, the royal palace, and Sanskrit libraries.
See also: Nepal.

Katmai National Park, large wilderness region covering 4,430,125 acres (1,792,810 hectares) in southwestern Alaska. The violent eruption of the Novarupta volcano in 1912 eradicated Mount Katmai and created a broad dish of ash known as The Valley of Ten Thousand Smokes. There are fifteen volcanoes in the area, although none are very active. The Katmai National Park has a rich range of wildlife, including Alaskan brown bears, sea otters, and bald eagles.
See also: National Parks.

Katydid, name for several large, green, winged insects of the long-horned grasshopper family (Tettigoniidae), native to the Western Hemisphere. Katydids, which range in length from 1.25 to 5 in. (3 to 12.5 cm), are tree-dwelling and nocturnal. Males produce a song, which sounds like "Katy did, Katy didn't," by rubbing together specialized parts of their wings.

Katyn forest, site in the USSR of a massacre of some 4,250 Polish officers in World War II. The mass grave was reported in 1943 by the Germans, who accused the Soviets, who in turn accused the Germans. Stalin refused a Red Cross inquiry, and the Polish government-in-exile in London took this as an admission of Soviet guilt. A U.S. congressional investigation in 1952 charged the Soviets with responsibility. In 1990 the Soviet government admitted responsibility for the massacre.
See also: World War II.

Kauffmann, Angelica (1741-1807), Swiss painter. Her works often depict mythological and historical events from ancient Greece and Rome. Initially a portrait painter in Italy, she traveled to England and in 1768 became a founding member of London's Royal Academy of Arts. Kauffmann returned to Italy in 1781. She is known for her wall paintings decorating English residences designed by Robert Adam. Other works include *Religion* and *La Pensierosa.*

Kaufman, George S. (1889-1961), U.S. playwright and stage director. His collaborations (over 40 plays and musicals), often noted for their satire, included *Beggar on Horseback* (1924, with Marc Connelly), *Of Thee I Sing* (1932, with Morrie Ryskind and George Gershwin; Pulitzer Prize), *Dinner at Eight* (1932, with Edna Ferber), and some of his most successful, written with Moss Hart, *You Can't Take It with You* (1936, Pulitzer Prize) and *The Man Who Came to Dinner* (1939).

Kaunas (pop. 400,000), former capital city of Lithuania. Founded in 1030, it is Lithuania's second largest city and produces one-quarter of its manufactured goods, which include machine tools, paper, radio, and textiles. A cultural center as well, Kaunas has several museums and many buildings dating from the 15th century.
See also: Lithuania.

Kathmandu's Pashupatinath Temple, a Hindu holy place

Kenneth David Kaunda

Kaunda, Kenneth David (1924-), African political leader, president of Zambia since 1964. From 1953 he worked for African rule in Northern Rhodesia, which was then a British dependency, suffering exile and imprisonment. Released in 1960, he headed the new United National Independence Party, and became Zambia's first president upon independence (1964).
See also: Zambia.

Kava, shrub (genus *Piper*) native to the Pacific Islands and Australia, closely related to the pepper plant. Kava may reach a height of 5 ft (1.5 m), and has round leaves and yellowish-cream flowers. Juice taken from the root of the shrub is used to produce a nonalcoholic intoxicant called kava or kavakava.

Kaw *see:* Kansa.

Kawabata, Yasunari (1899-1972), Japanese novelist. He is noted for his impressionistic, lyrical style and a preoccupation with loneliness and death. One of his best-known works is *Snow Country* (1947). He was awarded the 1968 Nobel Prize for literature, the first Japanese to win the prize.

Kawasaki disease, disease believed by many doctors to be caused by a virus, affecting children, primarily boys of Asian ancestry from middle- and upper-class backgrounds. Its symptoms include high fever, sore throat, redness of the eyes, and sore, bleeding lips. It can result in inflammation and scarring of the artery walls. Palliative treatment with aspirin and gamma globulin reduces the risk of heart damage.

Kaye, Danny (1913-87), American comedian and entertainer whose films, television shows, and personal appearances made him an international personality. He first gained attention in 1940 in the Broadway musical *Lady in the Dark*. Among his more important films were *The Secret Life of Walter Mitty* (1947), and *The Inspector General* (1949). He was an ambassador-at-large for Unicef.

Kazakhstan

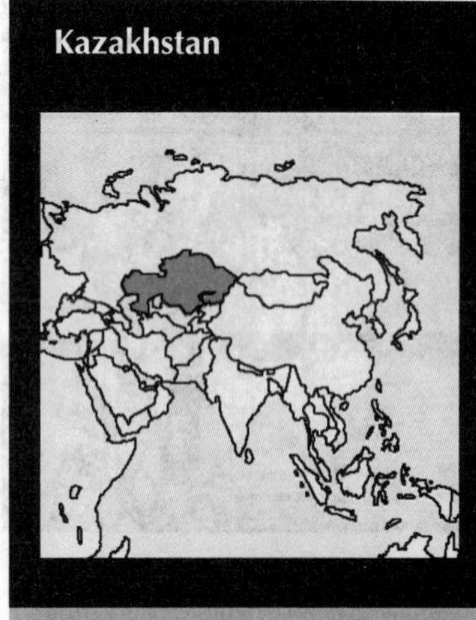

Capital:	Almaty
Area:	1,049,150 sq mi (2,717,300 sq km)
Population:	16,954,000
Government:	republic
Independent:	1991
GNP:	U.S.$28,584,000,000
Per capita:	U.S.$1,680

Buster Keaton

Kazakhstan, independent country in central Asia, bounded by Russia, Mongolia, China, Kirghizstan, Uzbekistan, Turkmenistan, and the Caspian Sea. The population is 40% Russian and Ukrainian, 40% Kazakh. The capital is Alma-Ata. A producer of wheat, cotton, sheep, and cattle, Kazakhstan is also rich in minerals. Formerly one of the 15 constituent republics of the USSR, Kazakhstan became independent in 1991. After independence the differences between the north, where most Russians live, and the south became more pronounced.
See also: Union of Soviet Socialist Republics.

Kazan (pop. 1,103,000), capital of the Tatar Autonomous Republic in eastern European Russia. Founded in 1401, it is the cultural center for the Tatars. It was conquered by Ivan the Terrible in 1552. A major port on the Volga River, it is an industrial center.
See also: Union of Soviet Socialist Republics.

Kazan, Elia (1909-), Turkish-born U.S. film and stage director. He is best known for realistic films on social issues, such as *On the Waterfront* (1954). Other films include *A Streetcar Named Desire* (1951) and *Viva Zapata!* (1952). He also wrote and directed *The Arrangement* (1967) and *The Assassins* (1972).

Kazantzakis, Nikos (1883-1957), Greek writer and statesman. He served as minister of public welfare (1919-27) and minister of state (1945-46). Among his best-known works are the novels *The Greek Passion* (1938) and *Zorba the Greek* (1946) and his epic poem *The Odyssey: A Modern Sequel* (1938).
See also: Greece.

Kea (*Nestor notabilis*), New Zealand parrot with an immensely powerful bill. Keas live in flocks and feed mainly on insects, leaves, buds, nectar, and berries; in winter they occasionally attack living sheep.

Kearny, Stephen Watts (1794-1848), U.S. general. During the Mexican War (1846-48) he conquered New Mexico by diplomacy, persuading the more powerful Mexican force to withdraw peacefully. He subdued California also, despite conflict with fellow officers Robert Stockton and John Frémont. Governor of Veracruz and Mexico City in 1848, he died there of yellow fever.
See also: Mexican War.

Keaton, Buster (Joseph Francis Keaton; 1895-1966), U.S. silent-film comedian and director. In such films as *The Navigator* (1924) and *The General* (1927), masterpieces of comic inventiveness, he created the character of a deadpan innocent in conflict with malevolent machinery. Keaton designed and performed his own elaborate and often dangerous film stunts.

Keats, John (1795-1821), English Romantic poet. He gave up medicine in 1816 to devote himself to poetry. The epic "Hyperion," the ballad "La Belle Dame sans Merci," and "The Eve of St. Agnes" were written about 1817. In May 1819 he wrote 4 great odes—"To a Nightingale," "On a Grecian Urn," "On Melancholy," and "On Indolence." "Lamia" and "To Autumn," effectively his last works, followed that summer. In 1820 he developed tuberculosis and died in Rome at age 25.

Keelboat *see:* Flatboat.

Keeshond, or Dutch barge dog, national dog of the Netherlands, related to the Samoyed and chow chow. The keeshond has a foxlike face with a long, thick, black-tipped gray coat. Fully grown, it stands 17-18 in (43-46 cm) and weighs 35-40 lb (16-18 kg). Keeshonden make excellent guards and companions.

Kefauver, Estes (1903-63), U.S. Democratic senator from Tennessee, known for his investigations into organized crime. He studied law at Yale, supported Franklin D. Roosevelt's New Deal, and entered Congress in 1939, becoming a senator 10 years later. In 1952 Adlai Stevenson defeated Kefauver for the Democratic presidential nomination, but lost the election to Dwight Eisenhower. In 1956 he was Stevenson's running mate for the presidency, but the Democrats again lost to Eisenhower.

Keillor, Garrison Edward (1942-), U.S. writer, creator of the fictional town of Lake Wobegon, Minnesota. Keillor has told stories about the town on his radio program *A Prairie Home Companion* (1974-87, 1989-) and in *New Yorker* magazine articles. His books include *Happy to Be Here* (1982), *Lake Wobegon Days* (1985), *Leaving Home* (1987), and *We Are Still Married* (1989).

Keitel, Wilhelm (1882-1946), German field marshal, head of the armed forces high command during World War II. On May 8, 1945, he ratified Germany's unconditional surrender in Berlin. He was convicted at Nuremberg of violations of international law and executed.
See also: World War II.

Kekkonen, Urho Kaleva (1900-86), president of Finland, 1956-81. Head of the Agrarian Party, he held cabinet posts and was prime minister 1950-56. He resigned the presidency in 1981 because of poor health and was succeeded in 1982 by Mauno Koivisto.
See also: Finland, Republic of.

Kekulé von Stradonitz, Friedrich August (1829-96), German chemist regarded as the father of modern organic chemistry. At the same time as Archibald Scott Couper (1831-82) he recognized the quadrivalency of carbon and its ability to form long chains. With his later inference of the molecular structure of benzene as a ring, structural organic chemistry was born.
See also: Chemistry; Organic chemistry.

Keller, Helen Adams (1880-1968), U.S. author and lecturer. Blind and deaf from age 1 1/2, she was taught by Anne Sullivan from 1887, learned to read, write, and speak, and graduated from Radcliffe College with honors in 1904. Her books include *The Story of My Life* (1902) and *Helen Keller's Journal* (1938).

Kelley, Florence (1859-1932), U.S. social reformer and lawyer. A campaigner for labor legislation to protect women and children and for minimum wage laws, she was director of the National Consumers League from 1899.

Kellogg, Frank Billings (1896-1937), U.S. diplomat, senator (1917-23), ambassador to Great Britain (1924-25), and U.S. secretary of state (1925-29). His most important achievement was the Kellogg-Briand Peace Pact (1928). He was awarded the Nobel Prize for peace and became a judge of the Permanent Court of International Justice (1930-35).
See also: Kellogg-Briand Peace Pact.

Kellogg, Will Keith (1860-1951), U.S. industrialist and philanthropist. He made his fortune through the breakfast cereal industry he established in 1906 at Battle

Creek, Mich., originally to manufacture the cornflakes developed as a health food by his physician-brother.

Kellogg-Briand Peace Pact, or Pact of Paris, agreement signed on Aug. 27, 1928, by 15 nations (eventually ratified by 64) renouncing "war as an instrument of national policy." Conceived by Aristide Briand of France and U.S. Secretary of State F.B. Kellogg, it lacked enforcement powers and proved ineffectual.

Kelly, Gene (1912-96), U.S. actor, dancer, and director, known for his spontaneous, athletic dancing routines. Kelly made his Broadway debut in *Leave It to Me* (1938), gained recognition for his role in *Pal Joey* (1940), and made his first film appearance in *For Me and My Gal* (1942). He helped choreograph many of his musicals, including *Cover Girl* (1944), *Anchors Aweigh* (1945), *On the Town* (1949), and *Singin' in the Rain* (1952).

Kelly, George Edward (1887-1974), U.S. playwright. Kelly achieved success with his satiric renderings in *The Torch Bearers* (1922), *The Show-Off* (1924), and *Craig's Wife* (1925), for which he received the Pulitzer Prize (1926).

Kelly, Grace (1929-82), U.S. motion picture actress and, later, Princess of Monaco. Kelly first appeared in the film *Fourteen Hours* (1951) and her first starring role was opposite Gary Cooper in *High Noon* (1952). She won an Academy Award for her role in *The Country Girl* (1954) and appeared in several other films, including *Dial M for Murder* (1954), *To Catch a Thief* (1955), and *High Society* (1956). Kelly married Prince Rainier III of Monaco in 1956. She died in an automobile crash near Monaco.

Grace Kelly

Keloid, scar tissue raised above the skin surface at the site of a wound. Keloids result from an overproduction of fibrous tissue in the skin. They can be surgically removed but frequently reappear. Keloids are found most frequently in people of African descent.

Kelp, name for various large brown seaweeds of orders Laminariales and Fucales. Edible kelps are rich in iodine, calcium, potassium, and the trace minerals. Dehydrated kelp tablets, powder, and granules are used as a mineral supplement and as a salt substitute.

Kelvin, William Thomson, Lord (1824-1907), British physicist. He formulated the second law of thermodynamics and introduced the Kelvin, or absolute temperature, scale. His work on electromagnetism gave rise to the theory of the electromagnetic field, and his papers influenced J. Clerk Maxwell's work on the electromagnetic theory of light. His work on telegraphic signaling played an essential part in the successful laying of the first Atlantic cable. *See also:* Galvanometer; Thermodynamics.

Kelvin scale *see:* Absolute zero; Kelvin, William Thomson, Lord; Metric system; Temperature.

Kemal Atatürk *see:* Atatürk, Kemal.

Kempis, Thomas à *see:* Thomas à Kempis.

Keneally, Thomas (1935-), Australian writer, known for his powerful and turbulent novels, which often take place in a particular historical period. His works include *The Chant of Jimmie Blacksmith* (1972) and *Schindler's List* (1982).

Kennan, George Frost (1904-), U.S. diplomat, one of the main authors of the U.S. postwar policy of "containment" of Russian expansionism. He served as ambassador to the USSR (1952) and Yugoslavia (1961-63). His books include *Russia Leaves the War* (1956) and *Memoirs, 1925-1950* (1967), both Pulitzer Prize winners.

Kennebec River, river in southern Maine, flowing about 150 mi (240 km) southward from Moosehead Lake to empty into the Atlantic at Popham, Maine's first English settlement (1607). The state capital, Augusta, lies on the Kennebec. The river is an important source of power for Maine's industries.

Kennedy, U.S. family prominent in government, politics, and business. **Joseph Patrick Kennedy** (1888-1969) chaired the Securities and Exchange Commission (1934-35) and the U.S. Maritime Commission (1936-37) and served as U.S. ambassador to Great Britain (1937-40). The oldest son of Joseph Patrick and Rose Kennedy, **Joseph P. Kennedy, Jr.** (1915-44), a U.S. Navy pilot, was killed in World War II. **John Fitzgerald Kennedy** (1917-63) was elected 35th president of the United States in 1960. **Robert Francis Kennedy** (1925-68) was appointed U.S. attorney general in 1961 and elected U.S. senator from New York in 1965. A fourth son, **Edward Moore Kennedy** (1932-), has been a U.S. senator from Massachusetts since 1962. The 5 Kennedy daughters are Rosemary, Kathleen, Eunice, Patricia, and Jean.
See also: Kennedy, Edward Moore; Kennedy, John Fitzgerald; Kennedy, Robert Francis.

Kennedy, Anthony McLeod (1936-), associate justice of the United States Supreme Court (1988-), appointed after Justice Lewis Powell retired. A Stanford University graduate (1958), Kennedy earned a law degree from Harvard University (1961). He practiced law until 1975, when he was appointed to the United States Court of Appeals (Ninth Circuit) by President Gerald Ford. Kennedy taught constitutional law at the McGeorge School of Law (1965-88).

Gene Kelly

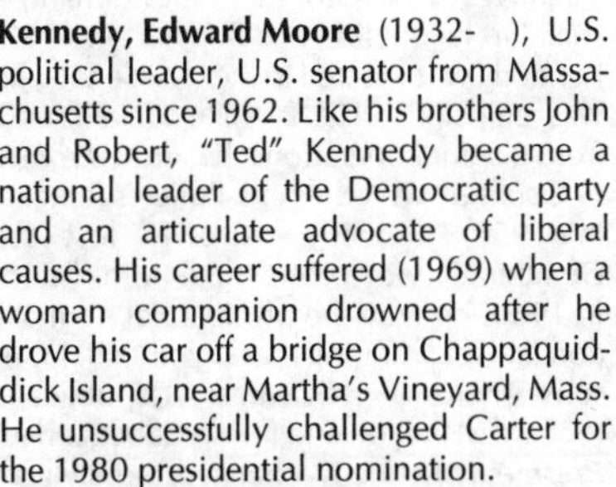

Kennedy, Edward Moore (1932-), U.S. political leader, U.S. senator from Massachusetts since 1962. Like his brothers John and Robert, "Ted" Kennedy became a national leader of the Democratic party and an articulate advocate of liberal causes. His career suffered (1969) when a woman companion drowned after he drove his car off a bridge on Chappaquiddick Island, near Martha's Vineyard, Mass. He unsuccessfully challenged Carter for the 1980 presidential nomination.

Edward M. Kennedy

John Fitzgerald Kennedy

35th U.S. President

Born:	Brookline, Mass.; May 19, 1917
Term:	Jan. 1961-Nov. 1963
Vice president:	Lyndon B. Johnson
Political party:	Democratic
Spouse:	Jacqueline Lee Bouvier Kennedy
Children:	2
Died:	Dallas, Tex.; Nov. 22, 1963

Kennedy, John Fitzgerald (1917-63), 35th president of the United States. Kennedy was the youngest person and the first Roman Catholic ever elected to the post.

Kennedy was shot in Dallas, Tex., after 1,037 days in office. After his death, a legend grew up around his youth, good looks, intelligence, idealism, and vigor that has become inseparable from his more concrete accomplishments.

Early life. Kennedy graduated *cum laude* from Harvard University in 1940. While serving in the Navy (1941-45), he was honored for his heroism.

Entering politics. At age 29, Kennedy was elected to the U.S. House of Representatives (1947-53). In 1953, he married socialite Jacqueline Lee Bouvier. In 1952, Kennedy was elected to the U.S. Senate; he was reelected in 1958. While convalescing from 2 spinal operations, he wrote *Profiles in Courage*, which won a Pulitzer Prize.

In 1956, Kennedy narrowly lost the Democratic vice-presidential nomination. In 1960, he won the presidential nomination. He and running mate Lyndon B. Johnson narrowly defeated Republicans Richard M. Nixon and Henry Cabot Lodge.

Robert F. Kennedy

President. Kennedy changed the style of the presidency. His White House was known for its elegant receptions for artists and intellectuals and for the restoration of the White House supervised by Mrs. Kennedy. For its gracious social atmosphere and Kennedy's outstanding Cabinet appointments and new "brain trust" of political advisers, his administration was dubbed "Camelot."

Kennedy's program was largely unsuccessful in Congress. He failed to win approval of expanded medical care for the elderly, tax reform, the creation of an urban-affairs department, comprehensive federal aid to education, and a new farm program. The major civil-rights bill he drafted passed only after his death. However, he did obtain the first major minimum-wage increase in a generation and passage of an urban-renewal and housing program. He also called for a bold new space program, and, in 1961, pledged that the United States would land a man on the moon within the decade. Kennedy was able to accomplish more through executive action, particularly in civil rights.

Kennedy promoted foreign aid and freer trade, launched a new program of cooperation for economic and social development in Latin America, and created the Peace Corps to aid underdeveloped areas of the world.

In 1961 Kennedy sent military advisers and equipment to Vietnam; allowed a U.S.-backed invasion of Cuba at the Bay of Pigs, which failed; and called up U.S. army reserves after East Germany erected the Berlin Wall. In Oct. 1962 the Cuban Missile Crisis took the United States to the brink of nuclear war with the Soviet Union. Kennedy demanded that the USSR remove its missile bases from Cuba. After a tense stalemate, the missiles were removed. Afterward U.S. and Soviet leaders signed a treaty banning atomic tests in the atmosphere.

Death in Dallas. Kennedy was fatally shot as he rode in an open car through Dallas, Tex., on Nov. 22, 1963. The presumed assassin, Lee Harvey Oswald, was shot to death 2 days later. Despite an investigation by a special commission headed by Chief Justice Earl Warren, the circumstances of the assassination remain a source of controversy.

Kennedy, Joseph P. *see:* Kennedy.

Kennedy, Robert Francis (1925-68), U.S. attorney general (1961-64) and U.S. senator from New York (1965-68). He was chief counsel to the Senate subcommittee investigating labor union racketeering in the late 1950s, and elder brother John's senatorial campaign manager in 1962. As attorney general in President John F. Kennedy's cabinet, Robert Kennedy supervised enforcement of civil rights legislation in the South. After his brother's death he led the liberal wing of the Democratic party. In a controversial move after Eugene McCarthy's strong showing in the New Hampshire primary of 1968, Kennedy entered the race for his party's presidential nomination. On the evening of his victory in the California primary, June 5, 1968, he was shot and killed in Los Angeles by Sirhan Sirhan.

Kennedy, Ted *see:* Kennedy, Edward Moore.

Kennedy Center for the Performing Arts, part of the Smithsonian Institution, Washington, D.C., designed by U.S. architect Edward Durell Stone as a national memorial to the late president. The center, which opened 1971, houses 3 main theaters: the Eisenhower Theater, which seats 1,000 persons and offers dramatic productions; the Opera House, which seats 2,200 and presents opera, ballet, and musical comedies; and the Concert Hall, which seats 2,750 and features concert music. *See also:* Smithsonian Institution.

Kenny, Elizabeth (1886-1952), Australian nurse. She is best known for developing the treatment of infantile paralysis combining hot, moist applications with exercise. She coauthored *the Kenny Concept of Infantile Paralysis and Its Treatment* (1942) and *And They Shall Walk* (1943).

Kensington rune stone, inscribed stone found in 1898 on a farm near Kensington, Minn. The inscription in runes (alphabet used by Germanic and Scandinavian peoples in the Middle Ages) is purportedly an account of Norse exploration of the Great Lakes in 1362. Most scholars now agree that the stone is of much more recent origin, probably a hoax.

Kent, James (1763-1847), U.S. jurist. He was the first professor of law at Columbia College (1793-98; 1823-26) and judge and chief judge (1798-1823) of the New York Supreme Court. As chancellor of the New York Court of Chancery (1814-23) he revived equity law in the United States. He wrote the monumental *Commentaries on American Law* (1826-30).

Kent, Rockwell (1882-1971), U.S. writer and artist. He is best known for his illustrations of popular classics and for his original works, which include the paintings *Toilers of the Sea* and *Winter* and the books *Wilderness* (1921) and *This Is My Own* (1940).

Kenton, Stan (1912-79), U.S. bandleader, pianist, and composer. Kenton experimented with the size and concept of his bands and sometimes combined Afro-Cuban music, modern jazz, and classical music. He introduced a brass instrument called the mellophonium, with a range between the trumpet and the trombone. His compositions include "Artistry in Rhythm" and "Eager Beaver." He helped establish the careers of jazz greats Lee Konitz and Art Pepper on alto saxophone, trumpeter Maynard Ferguson, drummer Shelly Manne, and trombonist Kai Winding.

Kentucky

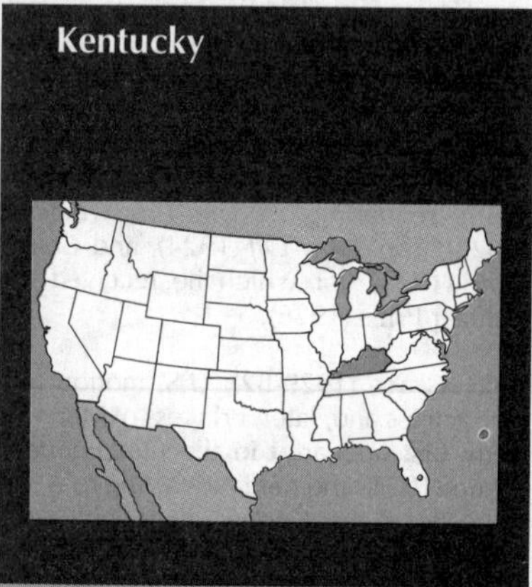

Capital:	Frankfort
Statehood:	June 1, 1792 (15th state)
Familiar name:	Bluegrass State
Area:	40,409 sq mi (104,660 sq km); ranks 37th
Population:	3,698,969 (1990); ranks 23rd
Elevation:	Highest—4,145 ft (1,263 m), Black Mountain; Lowest—257 ft (78 m), Mississippi River in Fulton County
Motto:	United We Stand, Divided We Fall
Flower:	Goldenrod
Bird:	Kentucky cardinal
Tree:	Kentucky coffee tree
Song:	"My Old Kentucky Home"

Kentucky, state in the south central United States; bordered by Illinois, Indiana, and Ohio to the north; West Virginia and Virginia to the east; Tennessee to the south; and Missouri to the west.

Land and climate. Kentucky can be divided into 3 distinct topographical regions: the Gulf Coastal Plain, the Interior Low Plateau, and the Appalachian Plateau. The Gulf Coastal Plain in the extreme west has wide flood plains that are the site of cypress swamps and oxbow lakes. The Interior Low Plateau in central and northern Kentucky consists of the Western Coal Field, with its rich coal reserves and good farmland; the Bluegrass Region (named for

Kentucky Derby, Churchill Downs

the blue blossoms of its grasses), with its gently rolling pastureland and farm areas; and the Pennyroyal Region (named for an herb common in the area), with its flat and rolling farmland in the south, treeless "Barrens" in the center, and rocky ridges and bluffs in the north. The Appalachian Plateau in the east is a mountainous area of narrow valleys and sharp ridges. Kentucky lies in the drainage basin of the Mississippi River and the Ohio, which forms the state's northern boundary. Important rivers include the Tennessee, Cumberland, Green, Kentucky, and Licking rivers. Kentucky's largest lakes were created by dams built by the Tennessee Valley Authority. Kentucky is generally warm and rainy. Principal cities are Louisville and Lexington.

Economy. Service industries account for more than half of Kentucky's gross state product (GSP)—the total value of all the goods and services a state produces in a year. Manufacturing, however, is Kentucky's major economic activity. Leading manufactured products are transportation equipment, chemicals, electrical equipment, and machinery; others include processed foods and beverages, tobacco products, printed materials, and bourbon whiskeys. Kentucky's agricultural income is led by livestock and livestock products, including beef cattle, milk, hogs, eggs, and broilers (chickens). The state is famous for its thoroughbred horses—and the annual Kentucky Derby horse race. Important crop products include tobacco, soybeans, corn, and wheat. Kentucky leads the U.S. in coal production. Other important mining products include natural gas, petroleum, and limestone.

Government. Kentucky's present constitution was adopted in 1891. The governor serves a 4-year term. The state's legislature, called the General Assembly, consists of 38 senators serving 4-year terms and 100 representatives serving 2-year terms. In the U.S. Congress, Kentucky is represented by 2 senators and 7 representatives.

History. Native Americans lived in the area well before the first white settlers arrived in the mid-1700s. In the late 1760s, Daniel Boone opened settlement by blazing the Wilderness Trail through the Appalachians' Cumberland Gap. After the American Revolution, thousands of new settlers poured into the area. Originally part of Virginia, Kentucky gained statehood in 1792, becoming the first state west of the Appalachians. In the Civil War, Kentucky was a border state, drawn to both North and South. It eventually declared allegiance to the Union. World War I prosperity was followed by economic distress in the 1920s and 1930s; World War II brought recovery. Industrial expansion has continued in recent decades, but pockets of poverty still exist, particularly in eastern coal-mining areas, where unemployment is high (due to mechanization of the industry) and adequate health and education services are lacking.

Kentucky and Virginia Resolutions, resolutions in support of states' rights and civil liberties, passed by the legislatures of Kentucky and Virginia in 1798 and 1799, in response to the Alien and Sedition Acts. The Kentucky Resolutions, drafted by Thomas Jefferson, claimed that the states could declare unconstitutional any congressional acts based on powers not specifically delegated to the federal government. The Virginia Resolutions, drafted by James Madison, declared the same theory in milder form.
See also: Alien and Sedition Acts.

Kentucky coffeetree (*Gymnocladus dioica*), state tree of Kentucky. Its natural range is from New York to Oklahoma. In colonial times its seeds were used as a coffee substitute. It grows to 30 m (100 ft) and has a dark gray scaly bark. The Kentucky coffee tree is one of the first trees to lose its leaves in autumn and one of the last to open its buds in spring. Its fruit are dark brown seed pods 6-10 in (15-25 cm) long.

Kentucky Derby, annual thoroughbred horse race for 3-year-olds run over a course of 1 1/4 mi (2 km) at Churchill Downs, Louisville, Ky. The Derby was founded in 1875 by Col. M. Lewis Clark, and is currently attended by more than 120,000 fans each year, and is the most popular horse race in the United States. The Preakness and the Belmont Stakes are the other 2 races which comprise the Triple Crown of horse racing.

Kentucky Lake, one of the world's largest human-made lakes. It covers 247 sq mi (640 sq km) in Kentucky and Tennessee, and was created as a reservoir by the vast Tennessee Valley Authority (TVA) Kentucky Dam, built across the Tennessee River in the 1940s.

Kentucky River, 250 mi (402 km) long, rises in the Cumberland Mountains, flows northwest through Kentucky's bluegrass region, and empties into the Ohio River at Carrollton. Small craft navigate as far upstream as Frankfort.

Kenya, independent republic of East Africa. Since achieving independence from Britain in 1963, Kenya has been one of the most prosperous and politically stable new African states, although economic and social progress has been made more difficult by the rapid growth of population.

Land and climate. Kenya has an area of 224,960 sq mi (582,646 sq km). Its northern neighbors are the Sudan and Ethiopia, with Somalia in the northeast. On the west, Kenya is bordered by Uganda; on the south, by Tanzania. Straddling the equator, the country has a varied landscape, with 4 main regions: the coastal strip bordering the Indian Ocean; the vast, dry plains of the Nyika; the highlands; and the western plateau.

The coastal strip is narrow and fertile, with scattered rain forest, mangrove swamps, and coconut palms. The plains extend from northern Kenya over more than half of the country, and are about 150 mi (240 km) wide in the south, where they are crossed by Kenya's 2 chief rivers, the Tana and the Athi. They are mostly scrubland pasture, but the Tana Valley and the Taita Hills are cultivated.

The highlands, where most Kenyans live, are mainly in the southwest, and are cut from north to south by the Great Rift Valley, of which Lake Rudolf (in the north) is part. They are mostly 5,000-8,000 ft (1,525-2,440 m) above sea level, but volcanic action has raised such lofty cones as Mount Kenya (17,058 ft/5,200 m), Kenya's highest mountain, and Mount Elgon (14,178 ft/4,321 m). With rich volcanic soils, moderate temperatures, and ample rainfall, the highlands provide most of Kenya's farm crops.

Beyond the Great Rift Valley and the highlands, the western plateau (sometimes called the Nyanza Plateau) stretches to Lake Victoria. At an average altitude of

Kenya's characteristic grassland with scattered acacia trees

Kenya

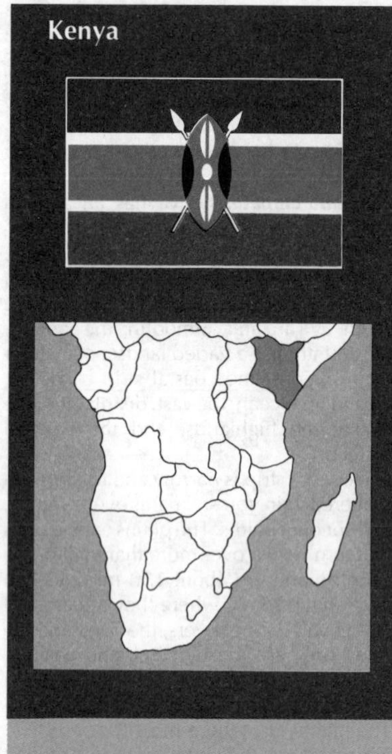

General information	
Capital:	Nairobi
Area:	224,961 sq mi (582,646 sq km)
Population:	23,883,000
Official language:	Swahili
Monetary unit:	1 Kenya shilling = 100 cents
Main cities:	Nairobi, Mombasa, Kisumu
Government	
Form:	Republic
Independent:	1963
Head of state:	President (elected every 5 years)
Head of government:	President
Legislature:	one legislative house (National Assembly)
Executive:	President and Cabinet
Judiciary:	highest court is the Kenya Court of Appeal
Political division:	8 provinces
National economy	
Gross national product:	U.S. $8,310,000,000
Per capita income:	U.S. $360
Agriculture:	sugar cane, coffee, tea, sisal, bananas, cassava, corn, wheat, pineapples
Livestock:	cattle, goats, sheep
Fisheries:	131,000 metric tons
Mining:	soda ash, salt, fluorspar, limestone products, corundum, gold
Industries:	cement, sugar, wheat flour, soap, petroleum products, machinery, textiles
Main exports:	coffee, tea, petroleum products, pineapples
Transportation:	1,649 mi (2,654 km) of railroads, 33,700 mi (54,300 km) of roads; 2 international airports
Trading partners:	United Kingdom, Germany, U.S., The Netherlands, Japan, France
People	
Urban:	20%
Ethnic composition:	Kenyan 99% (Kikuyu 21%, Luhya 14%, Luo 13%, Kamba 11.5%, Kalenjin 11%)
Birth rate:	53.9 per 1,000 population
Death rate:	11.9 per 1,000 population
Infant mortality:	72 per 1,000 live births
Life expectancy:	male 56.5 years, female 60.5 years

Muslim mosque, Kenya

4,000 ft (1,220 m), this well-watered plateau has good farmlands, forests, and grasslands. Kenya is famous for its big game, including elephants, hippos, giraffes, and antelopes. There are many national parks and game reserves, the largest and best known being the Tsavo National Park (8,034 sq mi/20,809 sq km) in southeast Kenya. Every year many visitors come from abroad to go on safari with guns or camera.

People. Nearly 98% of the population is African, comprising more than 40 ethnic groups, chief among which are the Kikuyu. There are also Indian, Arab, and European (primarily British) communities. Most Kenyans live in the southwest, mainly in the highlands where Nairobi, the capital and largest city, is situated.

Economy. Agriculture is the major occupation, with coffee, tea, timber, fruit, and vegetables the main exports. Chief industries center around food processing, textiles, footwear, and clothing. There is also a large livestock industry. Kenya has few natural resources, and its reliance upon imported oil places a strain on the economy. Hydroelectric and geothermal power sources are being developed. Tourism is also important.

History. Until 1887 the coast was under Arab control. The British then opened the interior with imported Indian labor and encouraged European settlement. In 1944 the first African nationalist party was set up, and Jomo Kenyatta became its leader in 1947. Discontent led to the formation of the Mau Mau terrorist organization. Pacified by reforms, Kenya gained independence in 1963, becoming a republic in 1964 under Kenyatta's presidency. In 1978 Kenyatta died. His vice president, Daniel arap Moi, was elected unopposed.

Kenyatta, Jomo (1893?-1978), Kenya's first president (1964-78). His early political career was concerned with rights of his Kikuyu people. In 1953 he was imprisoned by the British on charges of leading the Mau Mau, a terrorist Kikuyu group. His release came in 1961 following pressure from African nationalists; he negotiated Kenya's independence in 1963.
See also: Kenya.

Keogh plan *see:* Pension.

Kepler, Johannes (1571-1630), German mathematician and astronomer. Kepler advanced Copernicus's heliocentric model of the solar system in showing that the planets followed elliptical paths. His 3 laws describing the revolution of the planets around the sun, presented in *Astronomia nova* (1609) and *Harmonice mundi* (1619), guided Isaac Newton to the formulation of his theory of gravitation.
See also: Copernicus, Nicolaus; Newton, Sir Isaac.

Keratin, any of various fibrous proteins concentrated in the outermost layer of the skin of vertebrates and acting as a constituent of hair, nails, claws, and horns.

Kerensky, Alexander Feodorovich (1881-1970), Russian revolutionary, head of the provisional government that followed the Russian Revolution from July to Oct. 1917. Overthrown in the Bolshevik Revolution (Nov. 1917), he fled to Western Europe and in 1940 escaped to the United States. His books include *The Prelude to Bolshevism* (1919), *The Catastrophe* (1927), and *The Kerensky Memoirs* (1966).
See also: Russian Revolution.

Kerguelen Islands *see:* French Southern and Antarctic Territories.

Kern, Jerome (1885-1945), U.S. composer. His most famous musical is *Show Boat* (1927), which includes the song "Ol' Man River." Among his classic songs are "Smoke Gets in Your Eyes" and "The Song Is You."

Kerner Commission, appointed by President Lyndon B. Johnson in 1967 to investigate the causes of the race riots of the mid 1960s. The commission, headed by Gov. Otto Kerner of Ill., put most of the blame on "white racism." It concluded that the United States was moving toward 2 societies, one black and one white—"separate but unequal." It suggested improvements in schools and housing and better police protection for residents of black neighborhoods.

Kerosene, colorless, thin oil, a mixture of hydrocarbons, used mainly as a fuel for jet engines, and also for heating and lighting and as a solvent and paint thinner. Although it can be derived from oil, coal, and tar, most kerosene is produced from distilled petroleum.

Kerouac, Jack (Jean-Louis Lebris de Kerouac; 1922-69), U.S. novelist and poet. His best-known book is *On the Road* (1957), describing his life of freedom from conventional middle-class values. He was a leading figure of the beat generation.

Kerry blue terrier, breed of dog produced by the union of the Irish terrier and the Dandie Dinmont. Named for County Kerry in Ireland, where it was originally bred in the 1700s to herd sheep and cows, the Kerry blue has a thin, elongated body, stands about 18-19 inches tall (46-49 cm), and weighs 33-38 pounds (15-17 kg).

Kesselring, Albert (1885-1960), German field marshal of World War II. He became commander in chief in Italy (1943) and in the West (1945). He was convicted of war crimes (1947) and sentenced to life imprisonment, but he was released in 1952.

Kestrel, name given in the Old World to various small falcons. The European kestrel (*Falco tinnunculus*) is closely related to the American sparrow hawk.

Ketchikan, town in southeastern Alaska, on the southwestern edge of Revillagigedo Island, a port of entry for ships and vessels navigating the Inside Passage. Fishing, logging, and tourism are the major sources of income.

Kettering, Charles Franklin (1876-1958), U.S. inventor of the first electric cash register and the electric self-starter. He made significant contributions to automobile technology.

Kettledrum *see:* Drum.

Kettle hole, depression or cavity in solid rock formed by a block of glacial ice. The size may vary from 15 ft (5 m) to 8 mi (13 km) in diameter with depths of up to 140 ft (45 m).

Key, musical term denoting the arrangement of notes in a certain kind of scale. On the piano keyboard there are 12 notes, black and white, between each octave, each of which can be the starting point for 2 scales, one in the major mode and one in the minor mode. Thus if a piece of music is written for a major scale starting on the note C, then the key of the piece will be C major. If the piece is written for the minor scale starting on the note G, then the key will be G minor. Major scales all have one particular sequence of pitch intervals between the notes, while all the minor scales have a different sequence of pitch intervals. To maintain the same sequence of pitch intervals for all the major and minor scales, adjustments to the pitch of individual notes need to be made from scale to scale. Notes will either need to be raised by half a tone (sharpened) or lowered by half a tone (flattened). The number of sharpened or flattened notes required for any key is called the *key signature* and is always written at the start of a piece. Each major key has a corresponding minor key in terms of a shared key signature. For example, a sharpened F is the key signature for both the key of G major and E minor; a flattened B indicates either the key of F major or D minor; and so on through the 24 major and minor keys.

Key, Francis Scott (1779-1843), U.S. poet and lawyer who wrote the words to the "Star-Spangled Banner" after witnessing the night bombardment of Fort McHenry by the British in Sept. 1814. It became the U.S. national anthem by act of Congress (1931). Key's works include *The Power of Literature and Its Connection with Religion* (1834) and *Poems* (1857).
See also: Star-Spangled Banner.

Keyboard instrument *see:* Celesta; Clavichord; Harpsichord; Organ; Piano.

Keynes, John Maynard (1883-1946), British economist at Cambridge University, a pioneer in the development of modern economics. He resigned in protest as treasury representative at the Versailles Peace Conference after World War I, stating his objections to the possible outcome of the treaty in *The Economic Consequences of the Peace* (1919). His chief work, *The General Theory of Employment, Interest, and Money* (1936), formed the basis of Keynesian economics, showing how government intervention could be used to maintain high levels of economic activity.
See also: Economics.

Key West (pop. 24,382), city on an island at the southwestern tip of the Florida Keys, about 150 mi (240 km) from Miami and 90 mi (145 km) from Cuba. Key West, the southernmost point of the continental United States, is a fishing and vacation center and has long been considered a dwelling for artists.

KGB, Committee for State Security, government organization in the USSR functioning as a secret police force. The KGB is one of the state bodies exercising control over Soviet oppositionists. Its intelligence network keeps track of political and military activities abroad as well. Given its present name in 1953, the KGB is the successor to the earlier state security groups, the Cheka and the NKVD.

Khachaturian, Aram Ilich (1903-78), Soviet-Armenian composer. His music was influenced by the folk music of Armenia and the Orient. He is famous for the *Violin Concerto* (1940), the "Saber Dance" in his ballet *Gayané* (1942), and the orchestral suite *Masquerade* (1944).

Khalid ibn Abd al-Aziz Al Saud (1913-82), king of Saudi Arabia (1975-82). Appointed crown prince in 1965, Khalid acceded to the throne in 1975 on the death of his brother Faisal. His regime showed some restraint on oil prices and otherwise took cautious positions on Middle East issues.

Khamenei, Hojatolislam Ali (1939-), Iranian religious and political leader (1989-). He served in the legislature (1980-81) and as Iran's president (1981-89). A Shi'te Muslim and follower of the Ayatollah Ruhollah Khomeini, he took part in the 1979 revolution which overthrew the shah.

Kharkov (pop. 1,536,000), city in the Ukraine, in the southwestern USSR, at the confluence of the Kharkov, Lopan, and Udy rivers. Founded in the 18th century, Kharkov is now the fifth largest city in the Soviet Union and was the capital of the Ukraine until 1934, when it was superseded by Kiev. An industrialized city, Kharkov produces metals, chemicals, and heavy machinery.
See also: Ukraine

Khartoum (pop. 476,200), capital of Sudan. It is a cotton trading center linked by rail and river to Egypt and Port Sudan, and headquarters for the Bank for African Development, linking North and South Africa economically. The city was founded in 1821 as an Egyptian army camp. British General Gordon was killed here in 1885 defending the city against the Muslim religious leader known as the Mahdi.

Khayyam, Omar *see:* Omar Khayyam.

John Maynard Keynes, in a portrait by Gwen Raverat

Khazars, Turkic people whose empire in southern Russia and the Caucasus controlled trade between the Slavs, Byzantium, and the Far East from 550 until the Byzantines and Russians overwhelmed it (969-1030). The king and nobility adopted Judaism in about 740.

Khmer *see:* Kampuchea.

Khmer empire, ancient Southeast Asian empire dating from the 6th century, occupying much of modern Laos, Thailand, and Vietnam. Its Angkor period (889-1434) produced beautiful architecture and sculpture. After the empire fell to the Thais in 1434, the court moved to Phnom Penh.

Khmer Rouge *see:* Kampuchea.

Khoikhoi, or Hottentot, member of a southern African group similar to the San. Members of the group call themselves "Khoikhoi"; "Hottentot" is now considered an insulting name. Small in stature, they have brown skin, prominent cheekbones, broad noses, and coarse hair. They were nomadic herders and farmers, but this way of life largely disappeared as a result of conflicts with other tribes and the Dutch settlers. Remaining members of the group live in Namibia.

The Ayatollah Khomeini

Khomeini, Ruhollah (Ruhollah Moussavi; 1900?-89), spiritual and political leader of Iran, 1979-89. Khomeini received the title *Ayatollah* (Persian, "reflection" or "sign") for achieving the highest status that can be bestowed upon a Shi'te Muslim. He was forced into exile in 1963 because of his opposition to the rule of the shah (king), Muhammad Reza Pahlevi. In exile in Turkey, Iraq, and France, he emerged as the leader of the anti-shah forces, which overthrew the Pahlevi regime. He returned to Iran in Jan. 1979 to become absolute leader of his new Islamic republic. He held U.S. hostages (1979-81) and waged war with Iraq (1980-88).
See also: Iran.

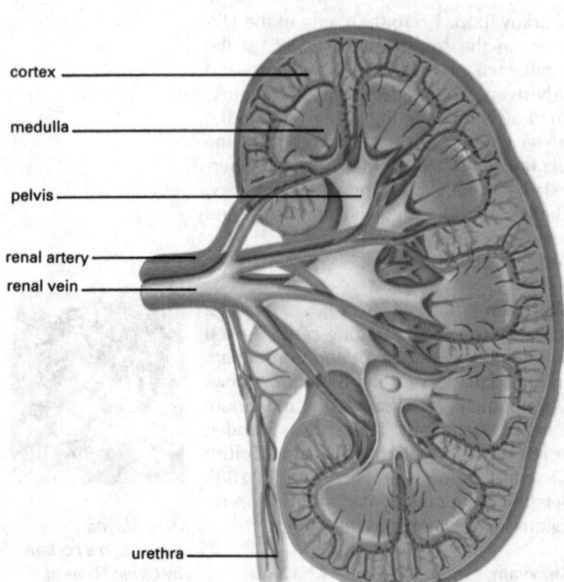

Cross-section of a human kidney

Khrushchev, Nikita Sergeyevich (1894-1971), Soviet premier, 1958-64. As a loyal Stalinist during the great purges of the 1930s he managed the Communist Party in the Ukraine. During World War II he was a political adviser in the army, defending Stalingrad. When Josef Stalin died in Mar. 1953, Khrushchev became a member of the Soviet Union's "collective leadership," taking over as first secretary of the Central Committee. His famous "secret speech" of 1956, attacking Stalin, inaugurated the policy of "de-Stalinization," and by 1958 Khrushchev had made himself both premier and party head. During his rule Khrushchev traveled extensively, addressing the UN General Assembly in New York in 1959 on disarmament, and meeting with President Kennedy in Vienna in 1961. His main setback in foreign policy came in 1962, when the United States forced him to withdraw Soviet missiles secretly installed in Cuba. This crisis, his rift with the People's Republic of China, and repeated crop failures led to his removal from power.
See also: Union of Soviet Socialist Republics.

Nikita Krushchev at the UN General Assembly, Oct. 12, 1960

Khufu, or Cheops (fl. c.2680 B.C.), Egyptian pharaoh of the 4th dynasty. He built the greatest pyramid at Gizeh, near Cairo; it is known as one of the Seven Wonders of the Ancient World.
See also: Egypt, Ancient.

Khyber Pass, mountain pass on the Pakistan-Afghanistan border, about 3,500 ft (1,070 m) high and 28 mi (45 km) long. For centuries it was the main western land entry to India. Now a modern highway and a 34-tunnel railroad are on this site.

Kibbutz, type of collective farm in Israel established in the early 20th century. Land held by the Jewish National Fund is rented to the kibbutz inexpensively. Nearly all property on the kibbutz is collectively owned. All work, economic, and municipal activities are done communally. Kibbutzim provide food, accommodations, nurseries, and elementary education.

Kickapoo, Algonquian-speaking Native American tribe living in the Great Lakes region at the time of the arrival of European settlers. The Kickapoo lived by hunting, fishing, and farming. Opposed to the Europeans' incursion in their lands, they became formidable warriors, fighting against the United States in the American Revolution and the War of 1812. Forced to cede their land to the United States in 1819, most went to Kansas or Missouri, but later some went to Mexico. Today only 800 Kickapoo remain in Oklahoma, Kansas, and along the Texas-Mexico border.

Kidd, William (1645?-1701), British pirate. Employed in 1695 by the British to privateer against French ships in King William's War, he later plundered the British in the Indian Ocean and was hanged in London for murder and piracy.
See also: Pirate.

Kidnapping, the forcible abduction of a human being, whether or not for ransom. A famous early example was the kidnapping of Richard I of England for a huge ransom, on his way home from the crusades in 1192. In the 17th century the term referred to the practice of abducting children for labor on U.S. plantations. The first major U.S. kidnapping case occurred in 1874, but after 1920, with the growth of gangsters kidnappings increased at an alarming rate. The abduction and murder of the infant son of Charles A. Lindbergh in 1932 so aroused the public that legislation making kidnapping a federal crime, in some cases punishable by death, was passed in 1932 and 1934. Thereafter, kidnappings for ransom in the United States declined sharply. In modern times revolutionary groups have kidnapped ambassadors, consuls, businesspersons, and politicians, sometimes for ransom, sometimes to force the release of political detainees.

Kidney, one of a pair of organs of the urinary system, located in the back part of the abdomen, on each side of the vertebral column; the left lies slightly higher than the right. A high concentration of blood vessels gives the kidney a dark, reddish-brown color, and each is bean-shaped and slightly tilted. In adults, the kidney is about 4 in (10 cm) long and 2.5 in (6.5 cm) wide. At least one kidney must function for life to be maintained.
Through the activity of millions of nephrons, filtering units that are the organ's basic functional components, the kidneys perform a number of tasks: the removal from the blood of nitrogenous waste, mostly in the form of urea (a main constituent of the urine that the kidneys form); the maintenance of the body's electrolyte balance; the maintenance of the body's water balance; the regulation of the body's acid-base balance. In addition, the kidneys release a number of chemical substances (acting as hormones) into the blood.
Urine is formed in the kidneys as an aqueous solution (95% water) containing metabolic waste products, foreign sub-

Killer whale

stances, and water-soluble constituents of the body. The quantity of urine produced by the kidneys depends on the balance of water and other essential substances in the body.
Among the most common kidney diseases are pyelonephritis, or kidney infection, and a type of inflammation called glomerulonephritis (formerly Bright's disease). If a person loses or suffers damage to both kidneys, he or she may be kept alive by a dialysis machine. The machine is attached to an artery in the patient's arm; blood flows through one tube into the machine, which removes wastes, and then flows back into the patient through a second tube. The patient must undergo this procedure for several hours, three days a week.

Kidney stone, hard mineral deposit that forms in the kidney as a result of excessive concentrations of mineral salts in the urine. If the stone is not passed through the urine or dissolved by natural or medical means, it can seriously disrupt regular kidney function.

Kidney transplant *see:* Tissue transplant.

Kiel (pop. 245,700), city in northwest Germany, on the Baltic Sea at the eastern end of the Kiel Canal. An important shipping and industrial center, it was Germany's chief naval base, 1871-1945. Kiel was founded in 1242 and joined the Hanseatic League in 1284.
See also: Germany.

Kiel Canal, German canal extending 61 mi (98 km) from the mouth of the Elbe River to Holtenau near Kiel. It opened in 1895 to facilitate movement of the German fleet between the North and Baltic seas. Because of its military and commercial value, it was internationalized after World War I until Hitler denied its status in 1936.

Kierkegaard, Søren Aabye (1813-55), Danish religious philosopher, precursor of existentialism. Opposing G.W.F. Hegel, he emphasized that one has a free will and can pass from the aesthetic (or material) to the ethical point of view and finally, through "a leap of faith," to the religious. Ignored in the 19th century, he has influenced 20th-century Protestant theology and modern literature and psychology. His main works are *Either/Or* (1843), *Fear and Trembling* (1843), and *Philosophical Fragments* (1844).
See also: Existentialism.

Kiev (pop. 2,409,000), third-largest city in the USSR and capital of the Ukraine, on the Dnieper River. Founded before the 9th century, it was the seat of the Russian Orthodox Church from 988. More than 40% of Kiev was destroyed in World War II, but after extensive reconstruction it is now an industrial, communications, and cultural center.
See also: Ukraine.

Kigali (pop. 155,000), capital and largest city of Rwanda, in east-central Africa. Established by German colonists in 1907, Kigali is now an administrative and commercial center.
See also: Rwanda.

Kikuyu, agricultural Bantu-speaking tribe, one of the largest groups (about 2 million) in Kenya, living north of Nairobi. Racial and tribal tensions led to the formation of the Mau Mau, a secret terrorist Kikuyu group involved in a nationalist uprising against European colonists in the late 1940s and 1950s.

Kilauea, world's largest active volcano, located on the southeastern part of Hawaii island. It is about 8 mi (13 km) in circumference and 3,646 ft (1,111 m) deep, with a lake of molten lava 740 ft (230 m) below its rim.

Kilimanjaro, extinct volcano and Africa's highest mountain, in northeastern Tanzania, near the Kenyan border. Its highest, snow-capped peaks are Kibo (19,340 ft/5,895 m) and Mawenzi (17,564 ft/5,354 m).

Killarney (pop. 7,800), town district in southwestern Ireland, County Kerry. Though it has some light industry, Killarney is primarily a tourist center, the main attraction being the surrounding countryside, especially the Lakes of Killarney.
See also: Ireland.

Killdeer (*Charadrius* or *Oxyechus vociferus*), shorebird, named for its noisy call. Marked with bold black and white rings on head and breast, killdeer breed from Canada to Chile, spending the winter in large flocks. They feed on insects and other small animals and kill harmful ticks and boll weevils.

Killer whale (*Orcinus orca*), small, toothed, carnivorous whale of the dolphin family, but lacking a beak. Voracious predators, killer whales eat dolphins, porpoises, seals, and fish. They may hunt in small groups or form packs of 40 or more, driving their prey into shallow water where escape is impossible. Their average length is about 20 ft (6 m), and they are found worldwide.

Kilmer, Joyce (1886-1918), U.S. poet remembered for his sentimental poem "Trees" (1913). He was killed in World War I.

Kiln, oven or furnace usually designed for "firing" earthy materials to make bricks, pottery, or quicklime. Limestone for quicklime is often roasted in a *shaft kiln*, being heated by hot gases flowing upward as it falls through the shaft. Clay and limestone, used to make cement, are usually burned in a *rotary kiln*, a long tube (up to 610 ft/186 m) that rotates slowly. The materials are heated as they shift gradually along it. Bricks and pottery, stacked on small cars, may be fired continuously in a *tunnelkiln*. The clay is prewarmed and hardened as it approaches the center firing zone and gradually cools as it leaves. Clayware is also fired in batches in *periodic kilns*. Ware is stacked, heated, and allowed to cool before repeating the process.
See also: Pottery and porcelain.

Kimberley (pop. 70,920), city in Cape Province, South Africa, about 540 mi (870 km) northeast of Capetown, famed for having some of the world's largest diamond mines. The city was named for the Earl of Kimberly, colonial secretary at the time the area was settled by Britons.

Kim Il Sung (1912-), North Korean political leader, premier 1948-72, president since 1972. Trained in Moscow, he returned to Korea as head of a provisional Soviet-supported government in 1946. His invasion of South Korea precipitated the Korean War, and only Communist Chinese intervention saved his regime. He then launched a vast industrial and military buildup.

Kindergarten, school for children aged 4-6, conceived by German educator F.W.A. Froebel in 1837. The school aims to develop a child's self-expression and sociability through games, play, and creative activities. One of the first American kindergartens was opened in 1860 by Elizabeth Peabody.
See also: Froebel, Friedrich Wilhelm August.

Kinesics, systematic study of nonverbal communication through body motions. Developed by Ray L. Birdwhistell, an American anthropologist, kinesics examines gestures such as winking, or eyebrow raising, as well as involuntary reactions like blushing, in an effort to interpret the feelings and messages being relayed through such gestures.

King, Billie Jean (Billie Jean Moffitt; 1943-), U.S. tennis player. She was a prominent figure in the international game, whose efforts have done much to improve

Billie Jean King

the status of women in tennis. Kings achievements include winning the U.S. Open 4 times (1967, 71, 72, 74), Wimbledon 6 times (1966, 67, 68, 72, 73, 75), and the Australian Open and French Open once (1968, 1972).

King, Coretta Scott (1927-), U.S. civil rights leader, widow of Martin Luther King, Jr. As president of the Martin Luther King, Jr. Center for Social Change, she continues the legacy of her late husband's work. She is the author of *My Life with Martin Luther King, Jr.* (1989).
See also: Civil rights; King, Martin Luther, Jr.

King, Ernest Joseph (1878-1956), U.S. admiral, commander of the U.S. fleet and naval operations chief in World War II. His recognition of the importance of the air war and the superiority of aircraft carriers to battleships led to Japan's naval defeat.
See also: World War II.

King, Karl (1891-1971), U.S. composer and conductor of musical bands, creator of more than 300 musical works, 200 of which were marches. King composed most of his pieces with the circus in mind. His "Barnum and Bailey's Favorite" (1913) became the theme song of the circus of that name.

King, Martin Luther, Jr. (1929-68), black U.S. clergyman and civil rights leader, recipient of the 1964 Nobel Peace Prize for his work for racial equality in the United States. King organized the boycott of the Montgomery, Ala., transit company in 1955 to force desegregation of the buses. Under his leadership in the late 1950s and 1960s, civil disobedience and nonviolent tactics, like the Washington March of 250,000 people in 1963, brought about the Civil Rights Act of 1965. Black militants challenged his methods in 1965, but in 1966 he extended his campaign to slum conditions in the northern cities of the United States, and in 1968 he set up the Poor People's Campaign. He was less successful in this effort because the Vietnam War distracted national attention from civil rights and urban issues. He was assassinated in Memphis, Tenn. In 1983 Congress designated the third Monday in January a national holiday to commemorate his birthday.
See also: Civil rights.

Kingfisher

King, Stephen (1947-), U.S. novelist and short-story writer. His best-selling occult thrillers about families threatened by malevolent supernatural forces include *Carrie* (1974), *The Shining* (1976), *Cujo* (1981), and *Misery* (1987).

King, William Lyon Mackenzie (1874-1950), Canadian statesman, Liberal prime minister (1921-30, 1935-48). He established Canada's right to act independently of Great Britain in international affairs, introduced old age pensions (Canada's first national social security scheme), and directed the Canadian war effort in World War II.
See also: Canada.

King, William Rufus Devane (1786-1853), U.S. politician. King served as U.S. senator from North Carolina and was elected vice president under President Franklin Pierce. He died before being inaugurated.

King Arthur *see:* Arthur, King.

Kingbird, aggressive North American flycatcher (genus *Tyrannus*), usually with gray head and a black stripe through the eye. It feeds on insects and defends its nest vigorously, even attacking humans.

Martin Luther King, Jr.

King crab *see:* Horseshoe crab.

Kingdom, in biology, large group of organisms that share basic characteristics. Biologists recognize 5 kingdoms of organisms: Monera, Protista, Fungi, Plantae, and Animalia.
See also: Classification.

Kingfish, any of several large food and game fishes, including the mackerel and drum, especially of the genus *Menticirrhus*. Kingfish live in the warm waters of the Atlantic and Pacific coasts.

Kingfisher, family (Alcedinidae) of brightly colored, strong-beaked birds of rivers, lakes, and streams worldwide. The bird perches until prey is sighted, then dives arrowlike into the water to take the fish. The belted kingfisher (*Megaceryle alcyon*) is the only species widely found in the United States.

King George VI Falls, collection of waterfalls and rapids descending some 1,600 feet (488 meters), situated in northwestern Cape Province, South Africa. The falls, on the Utishi river, are the major attraction of the Aughrabies National Park.

Kinghead *see:* Ragweed.

King James Version *see:* Bible.

Kinglet, tiny, olive-green songbird (genus *Regulus*) living in the temperate woodlands of the Northern Hemisphere. It feeds on small insects with its thin, pointed bill.

Kingmaker *see:* Warwick, Earl of.

King Peak, one of the highest mountains in North America, rising 17,130 ft (5,221 m) in the St. Elias Mountains of northwestern Canada.

King Philip's War (1675-76), last Native American resistance to the whites in New England. In 1675 the Plymouth Colony executed 3 Native Americans for an alleged murder. Metacom, a Wampanoag chief also called King Philip, led an alliance of tribes in fierce guerrilla raids. The whites replied in kind, and Metacom was killed when his secret refuge was betrayed. The colonists then drove most of the Native Americans from New England.

Kings, Books of, in the Old Testament, called First and Second Kings in the Authorized Version, and Third and Fourth Kings in the Greek versions and the Western canon. They cover Israelite history from the reign of Solomon through the period of the 2 kingdoms of Israel and Judah to the destruction of Judah by the Babylonians.
See also: Old Testament.

Kings Canyon National Park, area of about 460,100 acres (186,200 hectares) in the Sierra Nevada, south central California, established as a national park in 1940. Two immense canyons are formed by the Kings River. The park features snow-covered peaks, rich wildlife, and sequoia trees.
See also: National Parks Table.

Kingsley, Charles (1819-75), English writer and clergyman and an advocate of social reform. His early novel *Alton Locke* (1850) is a sympathetic study of working-class life. He also wrote historical novels, notably *Westward Ho!* (1855) and the children's fantasy *The Water Babies* (1863).

Kingsley, Sidney (1906-), U.S. playwright noted for his treatment of social problems. His first play, *Men in White* (1933), won a Pulitzer Prize.

Kingsnake, nonpoisonous snake (genus *Lampropeltis*) of the central and southern United States. Kingsnakes grow up to 6 ft (2 m) long and are often brightly colored.

They feed on rodents, birds, and snakes, even rattlesnakes, since kingsnakes are immune to venom.

Kingston (pop. 24,481), industrial city of New York, on the west bank of the Hudson River about 92 mi (148 km) north of New York City. Founded by the Dutch (1652), the city was burned by the British a few months after being made the state capital in 1777.
See also: New York.

Kingston (pop. 643,800), capital and largest city of Jamaica, in the Caribbean Sea. Famed for its botanical gardens, Kingston is the economic hub of the island nation. Industries include oil refining, food processing, and tourism. The city was founded in 1693 and superseded Port Royal as capital in 1872.
See also: Jamaica.

Kingstown (pop. 19,000), capital of St. Vincent and the Grenadines, in the Caribbean Sea. Situated on the southwest seashore of St. Vincent's island, Kingstown is the country's chief port. The economy is based largely on import/export activities. Kingstown was ruled by England for nearly 200 years (1783-1979), until its integration with the self-governing body of St. Vincent and the Grenadines.
See also: Grenadines.

King William's War *see:* French and Indian Wars.

Kinkajou (*Potos flavus*), relative of the raccoon that can hang by its tail. It grows up to 3 ft (1 m) long and has short legs and a very long tail covered in soft fur. The kinkajou lives in tropical forests from southern Mexico to Brazil. It moves cautiously through the branches using its tail as an anchor. Although kinkajous are members of the Carnivora (flesh eaters), they eat mainly fruit and a few insects.

Kinnock, Neil Gordon (1942-), British politician, elected youngest Labour Party leader in 1983 at the age of 41. Known for his left-wing views and fervent public speaking skills, Kinnock has strived to promote unity between the party's left-wing and moderate factions in the area of policy.

Kino, Eusebio Francisco (1644?-1711), Italian Jesuit missionary who explored lower California and parts of Arizona. His map (1705) remained the basis of maps of the southwest and northwest Mexico for a century.
See also: Jesuits.

Kinsey, Alfred Charles (1894-1956), U.S. biologist best known for his statistical studies of human sexual behavior, published as *Sexual Behavior in the Human Male* (1948) and *Sexual Behavior in the Human Female* (1953).
See also: Biology; Sex.

Kinshasa (pop. 2,800,000), capital and largest city of Zaïre. It was founded in 1881 by the British explorer Henry M. Stanley, who named it Leopoldville after King Leopold II of Belgium. Its name was changed to Kinshasa in 1966, after Zaïre became independent.
See also: Zaire.

Kiowa, Native American tribe of the North American plains. A nomadic people, they were followers of sun dance and ghost dance cults. A Kiowan uprising was put down by the U.S. army in 1874. They were settled in Oklahoma, and presently number about 2,000.

Kipling, Rudyard (1865-1936), Indian-born English writer. Among his works are short stories about Anglo-Indian life, such as *Plain Tales from the Hills* (1888); poems, including "Mandalay" and "Gunga Din"; and children's books, including *The Jungle Book* (1894), *Kim* (1901). He won the Nobel Prize for literature in 1907.

Kirchhoff, Gustav Robert (1824-87), German physicist best known for his work on electrical conduction, showing that current passes through a conductor at the speed of light, and deriving Kirchhoff's Laws. With Robert Bunsen he discovered the elements cesium and rubidium and pioneered spectrum analysis, which he applied to the solar spectrum, identifying several elements and explaining the Fraunhofer lines.
See also: Physics.

Kirchhoff's Laws, two laws governing electric circuits involving Ohm's law conductors and sources of electromotive force, stated by Kirchhoff. They assert that the sums of outgoing and incoming currents at any junction in the circuit must be equal and that the sum of the current-resistance products around any closed path must equal the total electromotive force in it.
See also: Kirchhoff, Gustav Robert.

Kirchner, Ernst Ludwig (1880-1938), German expressionist graphic artist and painter, cofounder of the Brücke (bridge) movement (1905-13). He is noted for his powerful, savagely expressive woodcuts and, in his painting, for his vigorous, distorted use of color and form. When his work was condemned by the Nazis as degenerate, Kirchner committed suicide.

Kirghizstan, or Kyrgyzstan, republic in central Asia, bordered by Kazakhstan, China, Tajikistan, and Uzbekistan. The country is almost entirely mountainous. Its capital is Bishkek. The wool from its sheep is an important product, and the region also has deposits of coal and natural gas. About 60% of the population are Kirghiz, a Muslim people speaking a Turkic language; other inhabitants include Russians and Uzbeks. Formerly one of the 15 constituent republics of the USSR, the country became independent in 1991. After independence the political and economic policies of the government have been aimed at reforming the old communist structures.
See also: Union of Soviet Socialist Republics.

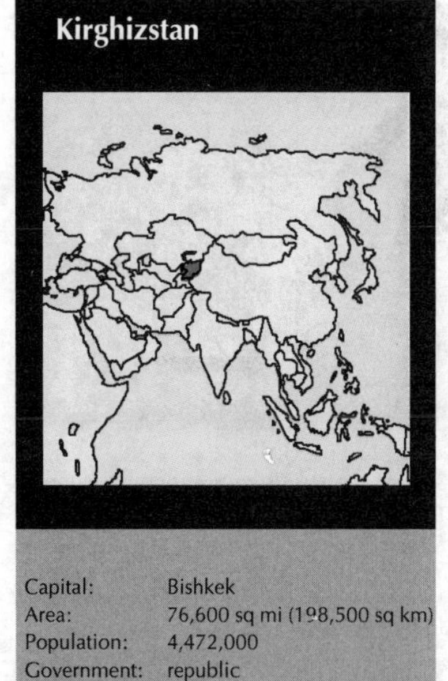

Capital:	Bishkek
Area:	76,600 sq mi (198,500 sq km)
Population:	4,472,000
Government:	republic
Independent:	1991
GNP:	U.S. $3,667,000,000
Per capita:	U.S. $810

Kiribati, independent island republic in the central Pacific, consists of 3 groups of coral atolls and 33 islands astride the equator. The land area is 324 sq mi (811 sq km), spread across 2,400 mi (3,860 km) of ocean. The population of 75,000 is mostly Micronesian. The capital, Bairiki, is on Tarawa, where over 30% of the total population lives. Fishing constitutes the main-

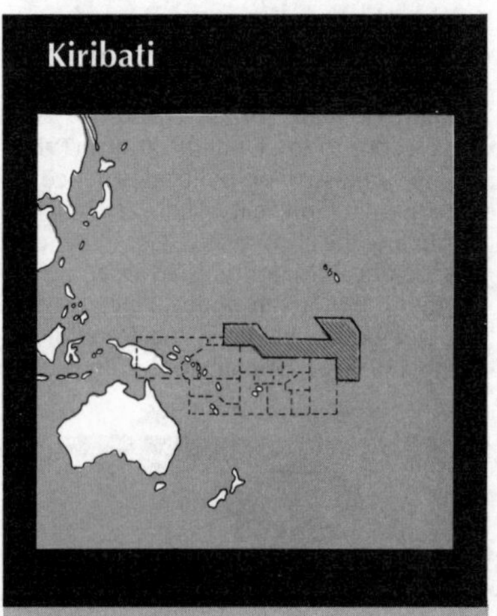

Capital:	Bairiki
Area:	324 sq mi (811 sq km)
Population:	75,000
Government:	republic
Independent:	1979
GNP:	U.S. $52,000,000
Per capita:	U.S. $700

The island of Tarawa, Kiribati

stay of the subsistence economy, supplemented by the cultivation of taro and fruits. Formerly part of the British protectorate called British Gilbert and Ellice Islands (since 1892), Kiribati was granted independence in 1971.

Kiritimati Atoll, or Christmas Island, one of the largest coral islands in the Pacific, covering 140 sq mi (360 sq km) and with a coastline of 80 mi (130 km). It is 1,300 mi (2,100 km) south of Honolulu. On Christmas Day, 1777, British explorer James Cook became the first European to reach the island. It was used for nuclear testing by both Britain and the United States. In 1979 it became part of the nation of Kiribati.

Kirkland, Lane (1922-), U.S. labor leader, president of the American Federation of Labor and Congress of Industrial Organizations (AFL-CIO) since 1979. He was executive assistant to AFL-CIO president George Meany (1961-69) and secretary-treasurer from 1969. Succeeding Meany as president, he became known as a strong supporter of civil rights and national defense.

Kirkpatrick, Jeane Jordan (1926-), U.S. ambassador to the United Nations (1981-85). A professor of political science at Georgetown University, she was a charter member of the conservative Coalition for a Democratic Majority, advocating a tougher U.S. foreign policy. After leaving her UN post she joined the Republican Party and was appointed by President Ronald Reagan to serve on the National Commission on Space and the Foreign Intelligence Advisory Board.

Henry Kissinger

Kirlian photography, or electromagnetic discharge imaging (EDI), technique of recording an image on photographic film by applying a high-frequency electric field to it and recording the resulting pattern of luminescence. The electromagnetic field causes electrons and positive ions in the gas surrounding an object to accelerate and frees them from the object's surface. When the electrons and ions recombine, the objects photographed appear surrounded by light. The process is named after Soviet scientists Semyon and Valentina Kirlian, who systematized it c.1940.
See also: Photography.

Kirstein, Lincoln (1907-96), U.S. ballet promoter who persuaded George Balanchine to come to the United States and helped him organize the School of American Ballet in New York (1934) and the New York City Ballet (1948). Kirstein also wrote several books on ballet.
See also: Ballet.

Kirtland Air Force Base, nuclear research facility in Albuquerque, N.M., established 1941. It is named after Air Force Col. Roy S. Kirtland. The U.S. Air Force Weapons Laboratory and Special Weapons center are located here.
See also: Nuclear energy.

Kissinger, Henry Alfred (1923-), German-born U.S. adviser on foreign affairs. Professor at Harvard when his book *Nuclear Weapons and Foreign Policy* (1957) brought him international recognition, Kissinger served as special assistant for national security affairs (1969-75) and secretary of state (1973-77) under presidents Nixon and Ford. He was instrumental in initiating the Strategic Arms Limitation (SALT) Talks on disarmament (1969), in ending U.S. involvement in Vietnam, and in opening U.S. policies toward China.

Kitasato, Shibasaburo (1852-1931), Japanese bacteriologist. He discovered with Emil von Behring that graded injections of toxins could be used for diphtheria immunization (1890). He also discovered (1894) the infectious agent of bubonic plague (which he described simultaneously with A.E.J. Yersin).
See also: Bacteriology.

Kitchen Cabinet, popular name for an unofficial body of advisers to President Andrew Jackson (1829-31). It included editors F.P. Blair and Amos Kendall, politicians, and government officials.

Kitchener (pop. 356,400), Canadian cultural and industrial city 65 mi (105 km) west of Toronto. Named Berlin in 1830 and populated by German immigrants, it is noted for an Oktoberfest celebration based on the beer festival of Munich, Germany. During World War I the city's residents renamed it after the British war hero Horatio H. Kitchener to demonstrate support for Canada and Great Britain.
See also: Canada.

Kitchener, Horatio Herbert (1850-1916), British field marshal, secretary of state for war in World War I. In the Sudan in 1898, he defeated the Mahdis at Omdurman and retook Khartoum. He was commander in chief in the Boer War, 1900-2, and in India, to 1909. His appeals during World War I raised thousands of army volunteers. He drowned when a ship taking him to Russia hit a mine and sank.
See also: Boer War; World War I.

Kite, any of various predatory birds of the hawk family (Accipitridae) with long, pointed wings and a forked tail. Kites live near water in tropical zones, preying on reptiles, frogs, and insects.

Kite, aircraft consisting of a light frame covered with thin fabric (e.g., paper) and flown in the wind by aerodynamic lift at the end of a long string. Originating in the ancient Far East, kite flying has long been a popular sport, and has been used for meteorological observations.

Kittiwake, small gull (genus *Rissa*) that nests on narrow cliff ledges around the coasts of the North Atlantic, the North Pacific, and on the islands of the Arctic Ocean. Named for its noisy call, the kittiwake feeds on fish, mollusks, and plankton and flies far out to sea.

Kitty Hawk *see:* Wright brothers.

Kiwanis International, community service association for business and professional men, having some 4,500 clubs and 285,000 members in the United States and Canada. Its objectives are to promote higher standards in business, to promulgate the Golden Rule, and to take part in community affairs. Founded in Detroit in 1915, its headquarters are in Chicago.

Kiwi, 3 species of flightless New Zealand birds (genus *Apteryx*), about 18 in (46 cm) high, lacking a tail, with gray-brown, hair-like feathers concealing their wings. The long slender bill probes into soil at night for worms, insects, and berries.

Kiwi fruit, or Chinese gooseberry (*Actinidia chinensis*), fruit originating in China and named for the kiwi bird of New Zealand (where it was first established as a commercial crop). Green-fleshed, with a thin, fuzzy, brown skin, it is similar in size and shape to an egg. It has a pungent flavor and is rich in vitamin C. The fruit is also found in France, the United States, Italy, Spain, and Japan.

Klaipeda, or Memel (pop. 191,000), city in western Lithuania, USSR, on the Baltic Sea. Named Memelburg by Teutonic Knights who conquered a fort here in 1252, it was renamed after the Memel Territory became part of Lithuania in 1923. It is an ice-free seaport and trade center specializing in

fishing, food processing, shipping, shipbuilding, and textile production.
See also: Lithuania.

Klamath, Native American tribe of southeastern Oregon and northern California, neighbors of the Modoc tribe, with whom they share a reservation around Upper Klamath Lake, established in 1864.

Klee, Paul (1879-1940), Swiss painter, graphic artist, and art theorist. From 1906, he exhibited with the German expressionist Blaue Reiter (Blue Rider) group. He taught at the Bauhaus 1920-31, publishing a textbook on painting (*Pedagogical Sketchbooks,* trans. 1944). Sensitive line, color, and texture are combined in Klee's paintings with wit and fantasy: *Landscape with Blue Birds* (1919), *Jorg* (1924), and *Diana* (1931).

Klein, Lawrence Robert (1920-), U.S. economist. A professor at the Wharton School of the University of Pennsylvania from 1958, he was an adviser to President Jimmy Carter (1976-81) and winner of the 1980 Nobel Prize in economic science.
See also: Economics.

Kleist, Heinrich von (1777-1811), German dramatist and writer of novellas, known for his power and psychological insight. His works include the plays *Penthesilea* (1808) and *Prince Friedrich von Homburg* (1821) and the novels *Michael Kohlhaas* (1808) and *The Marquise of O* (1810-11).

Klemperer, Otto (1885-1973), German conductor. As director of the Kroll Opera House, Berlin (1927-33) he introduced many modern works and new interpretations of classics. After a period of crippling illness he revived his career in 1947, notably as an interpreter of Beethoven and Mahler.

Klimt, Gustav (1862-1918), Austrian painter and designer, a leader of the Vienna Secession (1897), noted for his lavishly ornamented, mosaic-patterned style. His interior designs, as for the Palais Stoclet, Brussels, and in Vienna, influenced Jugendstil (German "art nouveau").

Kline, Franz (1910-62), U.S. abstract expressionist painter. His huge, stark, black-and-white compositions influenced the "calligraphic" style of the 1950s New York school. Later, Kline reintroduced color into his works.

Klondike, subarctic region in the west central Yukon Territory, northwest Canada, site of the gold rush of 1896. By 1900 $22 million was being panned annually from a tributary of the Klondike River, but the creeks were mined out in about 10 years.
See also: Yukon Territory.

Knee, front of the leg where the femur (thighbone) and tibia (shinbone) meet, and the joint itself, covered by the patella, or kneecap. Because the bony surfaces do not match exactly, the knee joint is one of the body's weakest joints. Its strength lies in the number, size, and arrangement of the ligaments, and the powerful muscles and fibrous membranes that pass over the joint and enable it to withstand the leverage of the 2 longest bones in the body.
See also: Joint.

Knife, hand-held cutting instrument used as a tool and a weapon since early history. Made from stone, bone, metal, wood, and plastic, knives are broadly categorized as fixed-blade or folding, also known as pocket knives.

Knight, Eric (1897-1943), English-American author best known for his children's novel *Lassie Come Home* (1940). Other works include the novels *The Flying Yorkshireman* (1937), *This Above All* (1941), and the short-story collection *Sam Small Flies Again* (1942). He was killed in an airplane crash while on a World War II mission.

Knighthood, Orders of, religious, honorary, or other fraternal society. Knights of the Middle Ages, vowing loyalty to their king, formed orders to defend his lands. During the crusades religious orders of knights fought the Muslims for the Holy Lands. The most famous of the religious orders were the Knights of St. John, the Knights Templars, and the Teutonic Knights. In Great Britain honorary orders of knights include the Order of the Garter (1349), the Order of the Thistle (1687), the Order of the Bath (1725), the Order of St. Michael and St. George (1818), the Royal Victorian Order (1896), and the Order of the British Empire (1917). Other European orders are the Seraphim of Sweden (1748), the Golden Fleece of Spain and Austria (1429), the Danish Order of the Elephant (1462), St. Andrew of Russia (1698), the Black Eagle of Prussia (1701), the Legion of Honor of France (1802), the Order of St. Olaf in Norway (1847). In the United States, the Knights of Columbus are a fraternal order of Roman Catholic men.

Knights and knighthood, part of the feudal system of the Middle Ages in Europe. Knights were mounted and armed sworn defenders of a feudal superior, generally having previously served as page and squire. Chivalry was the code of honor practiced by knights. They were known by their clothing, armor, and participation in tournaments in which they fought each other. The legend of King Arthur is the most famous literary account of knighthood.
See also: Feudalism.

Knights Grand Cross of the Bath *see:* Bath, Order of the.

Knights Hospitallers *see:* Knights of Saint John.

Knights of Columbus, U.S. fraternal organization for Roman Catholic men, founded at New Haven, Conn., in 1882 and now claiming more than a million

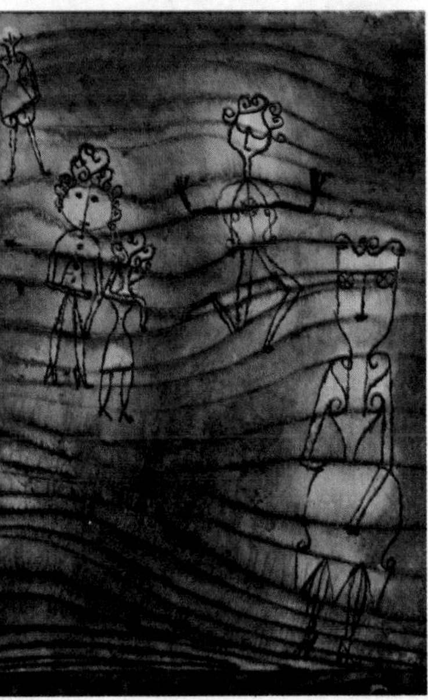

Paul Klee,
Promenade *(1923)*

members. The society sponsors charitable and educational causes and protects the interests of the Roman Catholic Church.
See also: Roman Catholic Church.

Knights of Labor, U.S. labor organization founded in 1869 in Philadelphia. Some of its goals were an 8-hour work day, abolition of child labor, and equal pay for equal work. It led successful strikes in 1884-86, but declined after the Haymarket Square riot in Chicago in 1886.
See also: Labor movement.

Knights of Pythias, U.S. fraternal organization, incorporated by an act of Congress in 1864. Its aims are charity, friendship, and benevolence. It contributes to disaster funds, blood banks, children's camps, and other humanitarian causes.

Knights of Saint John (officially, Order of the Hospital of St. John of Jerusalem; also known as Hospitallers, Knights of Rhodes, or of Malta), religious order founded by papal charter (1113) to tend sick pilgrims in the Holy Land. It became a military order as well in 1140, and after the fall of Jerusalem was based successively on Cyprus (1291), Rhodes (1309), and Malta (1530) to provide a defense against Muslim seapower. Expelled from Malta by

In the story told by Chrétien de Troyes, medieval knight Lancelot undergoes humiliation to prove his devotion to Queen Guinevere

Napoleon in 1798, the Knights have been established at Rome since 1834.
See also: Knighthood, Orders of.

Knights of the Bath *see:* Bath, Order of the.

Knights of the Round Table *see:* Arthur, King; Round Table.

Knights Templars, Christian military order founded in 1118, with its headquarters on the site of Solomon's Temple in Jerusalem, to protect pilgrims. It provided elite troops for the kingdom of Jerusalem. Its immense riches from endowments and banking excited the greed of Philip IV of France, who (1307-14) confiscated its property and forced the pope to suppress the order.

Knitting, production of fabric by using needles to interlock yarn or thread in a series of connected loops, using basic knit and purl stitches. It was practiced in North Africa in the 3rd century B.C. and was taken to Europe by Arab traders. The first knitting machine was invented by William Lee in England in 1589.

Knitting machine, manufacturing device for knitting fabrics ranging from delicate lace to rugs, invented by the Englishman William Lee in 1589. The 2 main types of machines are weft, which produces fabric that stretches elastically, and warp, with lengthwise stitches that produce a flat, less elastic fabric.
See also: Knitting.

Knopf, Alfred A. (1892-1984), U.S. publisher. He founded Alfred A. Knopf, Inc. (1915), a prestigious publishing house with many Nobel Prize-winning authors. Random House acquired the company in 1960, but the imprint remains.

Knossos, ancient city on the north coast of Crete, the center of Minoan civilization. Excavations by Sir Arthur Evans revealed settlements dating from before 3000 B.C.. The great palace of Knossos comprises more than 5 acres (2 hectares) of halls, ceremonial rooms, and staircases, with magnificent fresco decorations, advanced sanitation, and every luxury. Fire destroyed it c.1400 B.C.
See also: Crete.

Knossos

Knotgrass, knotweed, or doorweed (*Polygonum aviculare*), plant of the buckwheat family, found in Canada and the northern United States. It is short and thick with bluish green leaves and pinkish green flowers.

Knots, hitches, and splices, methods to tie or fasten ropes. A knot is a fastening of cord or ropes. A hitch is used to tie a rope to a ring, spar, post, or other object. A splice joins 2 rope ends permanently. Sailors, explorers, mountain climbers, and builders make wide use of knots. The Gordian knot of Greek mythology, which reputedly could not be untied except by a person predestined to do so, is used as a metaphor for any unsolvable problem.

Know-Nothing Party, U.S. political party formed in the 1840s to exclude recently immigrated Roman Catholics from poiitics. The party sought to elect only native-born citizens to office and to require 25 years of residence for citizenship. It won success in the 1854 election as the American Party, but split irremediably in 1856 over the slavery issue. Its name came from its members' habit of saying they "knew nothing" of the movement.

Knox, John (1514?-72), Scottish Protestant Reformation leader. A Catholic priest, Knox converted to Protestantism and fled in 1554 from the Roman Catholic regime of English queen Mary I to Geneva, where he became a follower of John Calvin. He returned to Scotland in 1559 ardently preaching Protestantism. When it became the state religion (1560) Knox gained great political influence, opposing Mary Queen of Scots. His writings include his unfinished *History of the Reformation in Scotland* (pub. 1644), *First Blast of the Trumpet Against the Monstrous Regiment of Women* (1556-58), and the *Book of Common Order*, which regulated Scottish worship.
See also: Reformation.

Knoxville (pop. 604,816), city in eastern Tennessee, at the edge of the Great Smoky Mountains on the Tennessee River. Founded in 1785, Knoxville was occupied by Union troops during the Civil War. In the 1930s the huge dam complex of the Tennessee Valley Authority (TVA) was built nearby.
See also: Tennessee.

Koala, or koala bear (*Phascolarctos cinereus*), pouched tree-dwelling mammal of eastern Australia. Koalas have thick, gray fur, a black nose, and no tail, and are 2-2$^1/_2$ ft (60-75 cm) long. They eat only eucalyptus leaves. Koalas are marsupials, bearing and nursing their young in a pouch, although unlike must marsupials, they do have a true placenta. The koala has been considered an endangered species but is now increasing in numbers again.

Koala

Kobe (pop. 1,411,000), city located on the southern coast of the island of Honshu, Japan. This major seaport is a hub for export and import as well as industry and shipbuilding. It is also considered to be a cultural center, with many places of worship and centers of learning. Modern Kobe is largely the result of rebuilding after the heavy bombings of World War II.
See also: Japan.

Koblenz, or Coblenz (pop. 110,800), city in west-central Germany, located on the Rhine River in the state of Rhineland-Palatinate. It serves as an administrative, industrial, trade, and cultural center for Germany. One of the oldest German settlements, it was founded in 9 B.C. as a Roman fortress. A popular landmark is the Ehrenbreitstein Castle, a fortress built around the 11th century, destroyed by the French in 1801, and restored by 1832.
See also: Germany.

Koch, Edward Irving (1924-), U.S. Democratic representative from New York (1969-77), and mayor of New York City (1977-89). He steered the city through a severe fiscal crisis by cutting city expenditures, while trying to maintain essential services. As a popular, hard-working mayor, Koch won both the Democratic and Republican party nominations for reelection in 1981. Koch's third term in office was marked by political scandal within his administration and racial unrest in the city of New York. These events contributed to Koch's failure to gain his party's candidacy to run for a fourth term of office.

Koch, Robert (1843-1910), German bacteriologist. He was awarded the 1905 Nobel Prize for physiology or medicine for developing a test for tuberculosis. His innovative methods of obtaining pure cultures are still used. He discovered the bacilli responsible for anthrax (1876), tuberculosis (1882), and cholera (1883).
See also: Bacteriology.

Kocher, Emil Theodor (1841-1917), Swiss surgeon. He won the 1909 Nobel Prize for medicine for his research of the physiology, pathology, and surgery of the thyroid gland. In 1878 he performed the first operation for the removal of an enlarged thyroid gland.

Kodály, Zoltán (1882-1967), Hungarian composer and, with Béla Bartók, an ardent researcher of Hungarian folk music. Folk influences are evident in such works as the cantata *Psalmus Hungaricus* (1923), the opera *Háry János* (1926), and the orchestral *"Peacock" Variations* (1938-9).

Koestler, Arthur (1905-83), Hungarian-born British writer. His novel *Darkness at Noon* (1941), based on his own experiences in a Spanish death cell, analyzed the psychology of victims of Stalin's 1930s purges. Many later works on philosophical and scientific subjects include *The Sleepwalkers* (1964), *The Case of the Midwife Toad* (1971), and *The Thirteenth Tribe* (1978).

Koffka, Kurt (1886-1941), German-born U.S. psychologist who, with Wolfgang Köhler and Max Wertheimer, was responsible for the development of Gestalt psychology.
See also: Gestalt psychology; Köhler, Wolfgang; Wertheimer, Max.

Kohl, Helmut (1930-), German politician. Leader of the conservative Christian Democratic party, he succeeded Social Democrat Helmut Schmidt as chancellor of West Germany in 1982 and sanctioned U.S. nuclear missile installations there (1983). Under his leadership West Germany was reunited with East Germany in 1990.

Köhler, Wolfgang (1887-1967), German-born U.S. psychologist, a founder of Gestalt psychology. He studied problem-solving among chimpanzees.
See also: Gestalt psychology; Koffka, Kurt; Wertheimer, Max.
See also: Gestalt psychology.

Kokoschka, Oskar (1886-1980), Austrian expressionist painter and writer. He is known for psychologically acute portraits such as *The Tempest* (1914) and forlyric land- and townscapes including *Jerusalem* and *View of the Thames* (1925-26).

Kola, tropical tree (genus *Cola*, especially *C. nitida*) that yields fruit containing caffeine-producing seeds. In its native West Africa, the seeds are chewed to combat feelings of tiredness and are also exported for use in beverages (colas) and medicine.

Kollwitz, Käthe (1867-1945), German artist known for her lithographs, woodcuts, and sculpture. Opposed to social injustice, she often depicted human misery and tragedy using the theme of mother and child. Among her well-known works are *War* (1923), a series of 7 wood-block prints, and the sculptures *The Mother* and *The Father* (1931-32), a war memorial.

Köln *see:* Cologne.

Komodo dragon (*Varanus komodoensis*), largest of living lizards, reaching a length of 10 ft (3 m). It lives on Komodo and a few other Indonesian islands.

Komondor, all-white Hungarian sheep dog. These dogs weigh approximately 90 lb (40 kg), and are about 31 in (76 cm) tall. Komondors were brought to Hungary in the late 9th century by Magyar invaders.

Kongo, kingdom of central Africa from the 15th to the 18th century, covering an area now in Angola and Zaïre, south of the Congo River. The king or *Mani-Kongo* ruled from the capital of Mbanza over a hierarchy of provincial and village governments, exercising political and religious authority without military force. The Kongolese traded in ivory, copper, and slaves. The Portuguese, who first explored the area in 1482, began converting the Kongolese to Christianity, but soon also became active in enslaving them. Portuguese slave trade seriously weakened the hierarchy of the kingdom, and Portugal took control by invading the Kongo in 1665, killing the king. By the early 18th century the kingdom was destroyed.

Konoye, Prince (Fumimaro Konoye; 1891-1945), Japanese premier (1937-39, 1940-41). A moderate, he appeased the military extremists and so furthered expansionism. His suicide prevented his trial as a war criminal after World War II.
See also: Japan; World War II.

Kon-Tiki *see:* Heyerdahl, Thor.

Kookaburra, or laughing jackass (*Dacelo novaguineae*), crow-sized bird, an Australian kingfisher, named for its gurgling, laughing call.

Koop, Charles Everett (1916-), U.S. surgeon general (1982-89). Known for his vigorous opposition to cigarette smoking and abortion, in 1987 Koop proposed extensive sex education and the use of condoms to halt the spread of AIDS.
See also: Surgeon general of the United States.

Kootenay *see:* Kutenai.

Koppel, Ted (Edward James Koppel; 1940-), U.S. news reporter, host of the popular T.V. news program *Nightline*. A Vietnam war correspondent, Koppel was made chief diplomatic correspondent for ABC News in 1971. He became famous for his coverage of the Iran hostage crisis in 1979 and has won many journalistic awards.

Koran, sacred scripture of the religion of Islam and the supreme authority of the Islamic tradition. To Muslims the book is not only divinely inspired but enshrines the actual words of God, as made known by the angel Gabriel to Muhammad in the 7th century A.D. After his death in 632 these sayings were collected in the Koran, and a standard text was formulated about 652.

Komodo dragon

Basically the Koran is a collection of laws, moral teachings, and stories written in highly charged, poetic Arabic, much of it rhymed. About 80,000 words long, it is made up of 114 *suras*, or chapters, arranged according to length from the longest to the shortest—except for the first, "The Opening," which is a brief prayer, the equivalent of the Lord's Prayer in Christianity.
Just as the word *Islam* means "surrender" to the will of God, so the Koran passionately demands this same spiritual surrender. The Koran, it teaches, is the revelation of God, known in Arabic as *Allah*, who is compassionate and merciful. It was given to Muhammad, last and greatest of the prophets, but Adam, Noah, Abraham, Moses, and Jesus are also counted among the prophets. However, the requirement in the Koran that the faithful should make at least one pilgrimage to Mecca probably reflects earlier Arab religions, and the complete subordination of women in the Koran is also in the Arabic tradition.
The Koran sets forth many rules governing moral behavior and social life. Alcoholic drinks and gambling are forbidden. The Koran is far more than a religious scripture. Because, as the first book written in Arabic, it formed a point of unity for all Arabs and for the diverse peoples they conquered, it is in a sense the foundation of Islamic civilization, as well as the molder and pre-

Pakistani children studying the Koran

Page from the Koran (14th-century manuscript, Granada, Spain)

server of the Arabic language. As it is forbidden to recite the Koran in any language other than Arabic, the language was perpetuated in its purest form, with no corruption from the languages of the many peoples who were converted to Islam. The Koran today is the inspiration and guide for millions of Muslims.
See also: Islam.

Korea, peninsula (600 mi/966 km long) of eastern Asia that separates the Yellow Sea and the Sea of Japan. Korea has been divided since the end of the Korean War in 1953 into 2 countries: the communist Democratic People's Republic (North Korea) and the Republic of Korea (South Korea). This artificial division, and incidents and tensions along the border between the 2 (near the 38th parallel of latitude), give little credibility to the Korean name for the peninsula: *Choson,* Land of the Morning Calm. The Koreans are a remarkable people, the heirs of an ancient civilization. Korean astronomers were studying the heavens one hundred years before the birth of Christ. Koreans were printing from movable metal type in the late 1300s, about 50 years before Johann Gutenberg used this method in Europe. In the late 1500s a Korean engineer built what was probably the world's first suspension bridge.

Land and climate. Korea (85,677 sq mi/221,903 sq km) is mostly mountainous, with the main ranges along the east and in the north. In the extreme northeast, Mt. Kwanmo rises to 8,337 ft (2,541 m). There are large coastal plains in the west, and lesser plains and river valleys among the mountains. The northern boundary with China and the Soviet Union is marked mainly by the Yalu and Tumen rivers. Most Korean rivers flow west and south from the mountains to the Yellow Sea. The southward-flowing Naktong River empties into the Korean Strait, which separates the peninsula from Japan.
Korea has a moderate climate. Winters are mild in the south but cold elsewhere, and summers everywhere are hot. Rainfall, higher in the south than in the north, occurs mainly during summer.
Korea is at present divided into South Korea, with an area of 38,452 sq mi (99,591 sq km) and North Korea, 47,225 sq mi (122,313 sq km). Running along the border between the 2 is a demilitarized zone (487 sq mi/1,261 sq km), in which stands Panmunjom, the scene of North-South negotiations.

People. Although South Korea is smaller, it is much more densely populated than North Korea. Korea's 2 largest cities are the 2 capitals: Seoul (South Korea) and Pyongyang (North Korea). Other important centers in the South are Pusan, the chief port; Inchon, a port on the Yellow Sea; and Taegu and Taeyan. Northern towns include the ports of Chongjin and Hungnam; and Sinuiju, a commercial center. Less than 30 of every 100 Koreans live in the towns. Most Koreans are farmers, and many still live in traditional small houses, which have clay walls, thatched roofs, and doors, windows and interior partitions of oiled paper. Buddhism, Confucianism, and Christianity all have followers, and animism also survives. In the North, as in other Communist countries, all religious beliefs are discouraged.

North Korean rivers and lakes provide fertile land for agriculture.

Korea, North

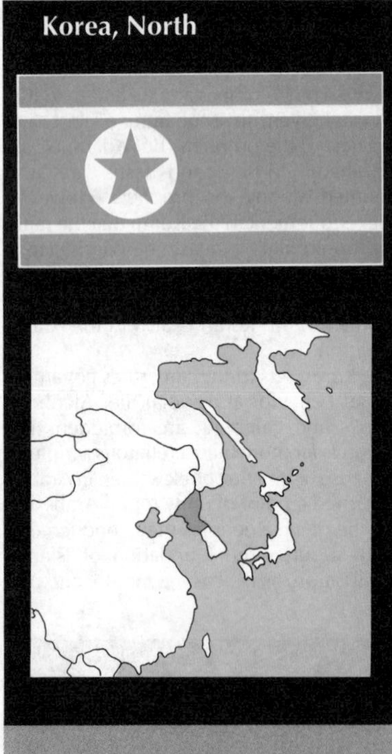

General information

Capital:	Pyongyang
Area:	46,540 sq mi (120,538 sq km)
Population:	22,418,000
Official language:	Korean
Monetary unit:	1 Won = 100 chon
Main cities:	Pyongyang, Hamhung-Hungnam

Government

Form:	people's republic (communist)
Independent:	1948
Head of state:	President (elected every 4 years)
Head of government:	Premier
Legislature:	one legislative house (Supreme People's Assembly)
Executive:	President, Central People's Committee and Administration Council
Judiciary:	highest court is the Central Court
Political division:	9 provinces, 4 municipalities

National economy

Gross national product:	U.S. $20,000,000,000
Per capita income:	U.S. $910
Agriculture:	rice, corn, potatoes, wheat, millet, sweet potatoes, tobacco
Livestock:	pigs, cattle, sheep
Fisheries:	1,800,000 metric tons
Mining:	anthracite, bituminous coal and lignite, gold, iron ore, magnesite, tungsten
Industries:	cement, pig iron, crude steel, chemical fertilizers, steel products
Main exports:	minerals, metallurgical products, cement, agricultural products, manufactured goods
Transportation:	5,280 mi (8,500 km) of railroads, 13,670 mi (22,000 km) of roads; 1 international airport
Trading partners:	USSR, China, Japan, West European countries, Hong Kong

People

Urban:	64%
Ethnic composition:	Korean 99%, Chinese 1%
Birth rate:	28.9 per 1,000 population
Death rate:	5.4 per 1,000 population
Infant mortality:	24 per 1,000 live births
Life expectancy:	male 66 years, female 72.5 years

Korea, South

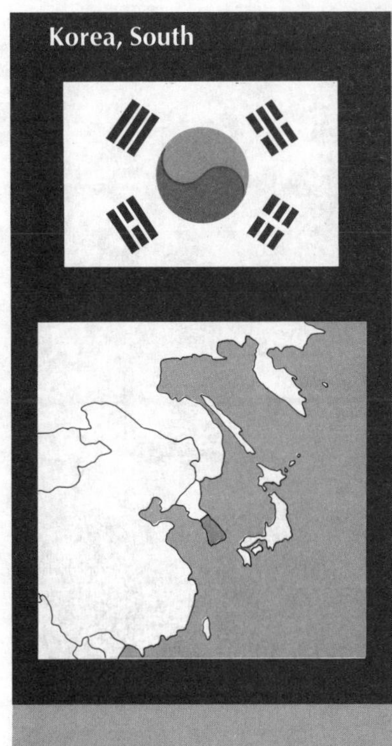

General information	
Capital:	Seoul
Area:	38,316 sq mi (99,237 sq km)
Population:	43,663,000
Official language:	Korean
Monetary unit:	1 Won = 100 chon
Main cities:	Seoul, Pusan, Taegu
Government	
Form:	republic
Independent:	1948
Head of state:	President (elected every 5 years)
Head of government:	Prime minister
Legislature:	one legislative house (National Assembly)
Executive:	President and State Council
Judiciary:	highest court is the Supreme Court
Political division:	9 provinces, 6 special cities
National economy	
Gross national product:	U.S.$296,349,000,000
Per capita income:	U.S. $6,790
Agriculture:	rice, apples, sweet potatoes and yams, onions, melons, barley, cabbage, soybeans
Livestock:	chickens, pigs, cattle
Fisheries:	3,332,000 metric tons
Mining:	zinc ore, lead ore, anthracite, tungsten ore, iron ore, graphite, coal
Industries:	cement, crude steel, pig iron, chemical fertilizers, radio and television receivers, computer equipment, clothing, ships
Main exports:	transport equipment, electrical machinery, footwear, textile fabrics
Transportation:	3,939 mi (6,340 km) of railroads, 33,982 mi (54,689 km) of roads; 3 international airports
Trading partners:	Japan, U.S., Germany, Canada, Saudi Arabia
People	
Urban:	69%
Ethnic composition:	Korean 99.5%, other 0.5%
Birth rate:	18.6 per 1,000 population
Death rate:	6.2 per 1,000 population
Infant mortality:	25 per 1,000 live births
Life expectancy:	male 66.5 years, female 72.5 years

Economy. In both North and South Korea less than half the working population is engaged in agriculture. Rice is the leading crop, followed by barley, wheat, and millet. Other crops include oats, beans, cotton, corn, and potatoes. Most of North Korea's land is farmed by cooperatives and agriculture is highly mechanized. Most of Korea's mineral wealth is in the North, where large amounts of coal, iron ore, lead, zinc, copper, tungsten, nickel, manganese, oil and graphite are mined. The South has some of the world's largest deposits of tungsten (the Sangdong mine) but only small deposits of coal, iron ore, and other minerals.

South Korea's chief industry is cotton textiles, but silk is also important. Other products include cement, paper, chemicals, electrical goods, and steel. The North has many industries, including iron and steel, chemicals, textiles (cotton, wool, silk, and manufactured fibers), cement, and fertilizers. Hydroelectric power production is being expanded.

History. The half-legendary founder of the kingdom of Choson was Kija, who led a group of exiles from China to Korea in 1122 B.C. But there were other kingdoms on the peninsula, and Korea was not united until the 7th century A.D. Most of its early civilization was destroyed by the Mongol invasions (1231-92), but with the establishment of the Yi dynasty (1392) Korea entered a golden age that lasted until 1592, when Japan invaded the peninsula.

Although the invaders were finally driven out, the Koreans never fully recovered from the years of bloody fighting. For 300 years Korea, known as the Hermit Kingdom, cut itself off from the world. In the late 1800s, Japan and the United States began trading with Korea. In 1910 Japan annexed Korea. After 35 years of Japanese exploitation, Korea was liberated in 1945 by Russia in the North and by the United States in the South. Despite United Nations intervention, no agreement was reached on a united Korea. The North became a rigidly controlled Communist state under the former guerrilla leader Kim Il Sung (1912-94). Free elections held in the South, under UN supervision, produced a republic under Syngman Rhee.

On June 25, 1950, the Communists of the North invaded South Korea, thus beginning the Korean War. The heavy fighting was eventually stopped by an armistice between the UN forces and the Communists, and by the establishment of the demilitarized zone (1953). Since then the uneasy peace has often been disturbed.

In South Korea, Syngman Rhee became increasingly autocratic and unpopular, and in 1960, after his opponents charged election-rigging, he left Korea. After a confused period of military rule, democratic government was restored (1963) by General Park Chung Hee, who was elected president and returned to power repeatedly. In July 1979 General Park Chung Hee was assassinated and replaced by General Chun Doo Hwan, who established his own autocratic rule. In 1987 Roh Tae Woo was elected president of South Korea. He was succeeded by the first elected civilian president Kim Young Sam in 1992, who continued the liberalization proces started in 1987. In North Korea Kim Il Sung continued his policy of regimented development until his death in 1994. He was succeeded by his son Kim Young Il.

South Korea: street scene in its capital, Seoul

Korean War (1950-53), conflict between forces of the UN (primarily the United States and South Korea) and forces of North Korea and (later) communist China. In 1945 Korea was divided along latitude 38°N, Russia occupying lands north of this line, and the United States those south of it. The war began when North Korea launched a surprise invasion against South Korea and UN forces were sent to assist South Korea under Gen. Douglas MacArthur. By Nov. 1950 Chinese troops had joined North Korean forces and the fighting was situated over the 38th parallel. MacArthur was replaced in April 1951 by Gen. Matthew B. Ridgway. Two years of negotiations achieved an armistice signed at Panmunjom on July 27, 1953.
See also: Korea; United Nations.

Kornberg, Arthur (1918-), U.S. biochemist awarded with Severo Ochoa the 1959 Nobel Prize for physiology or medicine for discovering an enzyme (DNA polymerase) that could produce from a mixture of nucleotides exact replicas of DNA molecules. He thus extended Ochoa's related work.
See also: Biochemistry; Deoxyribonucleic acid.

Sandy Koufax

Korsakoff's syndrome, amnesic state in which, because of an inability to record new memory traces, a person can carry out complex tasks learned before his or her illness but cannot learn the simplest new skills. The syndrome is often transient and has a good prognosis in head injury. In alcoholism (where the syndrome, sometimes called alcoholic dementia, is caused by a lack of thiamine, a B vitamin that is destroyed by alcohol) and in other conditions where destruction is irreversible, the prognosis is poor and prolonged institutional care may be required.

Korzeniowski, Józef *see:* Conrad, Joseph.

Kosciusko, Thaddeus (1746-1817), Polish soldier and patriot who fought in the American Revolution. In 1794 he led an unsuccessful fight for Poland's unification and independence from Russia and Prussia.
See also: Poland.

Košice (German: *Kaschau*; Hungarian: *Kassa*; pop. 196,200), city in eastern Czechoslovakia, on the Hornad River. Since the end of World War II it has been the chief industrial city of the region of Slovakia, with large steelworks as well as chemical, food-processing, and textile plants. The old center city was established by Hungary in 1241; its St. Elizabeth cathedral was built in the 14th century. The region became part of the newly established Czechoslovakia in 1918. It was controlled by Hungary and Germany during World War II, but returned to Czechoslovak control in 1945.
See also: Czechoslovakia.

Kosinski, Jerzy (1933-91), Polish-born U.S. writer best known for his semi-autobiographical novel *The Painted Bird* (1965). Its vivid, often shockingly brutal imagery deals with "daily life among the violations of the spirit and body of human beings." Among his other works are *Steps* (1968), for which he won a National Book Award, and *Being There* (1971).

Kossuth, Lajos (1802-94), Hungarian patriot and statesman who campaigned against Austrian rule and led the Hungarian revolution of 1848-49. A minister in the government set up in 1848, he engineered Hungary's declaration of independence as a republic the following year and became president. Austria, with the aid of Russian troops, forced a surrender, and Kossuth fled. He was received as a hero in the United States and England, where he lived for many years, and he died in Italy.
See also: Hungary.

Kosygin, Aleksei Nikolaevich (1904-80), Soviet premier, 1964-80. In 1939 he was appointed to the central committee of the Communist party; in 1960 he became first deputy to Nikita Khrushchev, whom he succeeded. Sharing leadership with Leonid Brezhnev, Kosygin concentrated on modernizing industry and agriculture.
See also: Union of Soviet Socialist Republics

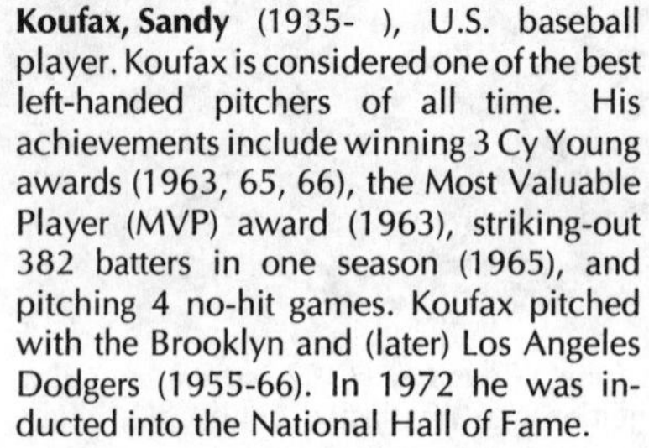

Koufax, Sandy (1935-), U.S. baseball player. Koufax is considered one of the best left-handed pitchers of all time. His achievements include winning 3 Cy Young awards (1963, 65, 66), the Most Valuable Player (MVP) award (1963), striking-out 382 batters in one season (1965), and pitching 4 no-hit games. Koufax pitched with the Brooklyn and (later) Los Angeles Dodgers (1955-66). In 1972 he was inducted into the National Hall of Fame.

Koumiss *see:* Kumiss.

Kouprey, also known as the Indonesian forest ox, rare wild cattle found in southeastern Asia. Six ft (1.8 m) tall at the shoulder, kouprey have small ears and a long tail, with the males (bulls) having large horns and blackish-brown hides. Females (cows) and calves are gray.

Koussevitzky, Serge (1874-1951), Russian-born U.S. conductor. He left the USSR for England in 1920 and settled in the United States, where he became conductor of the Boston Symphony Orchestra (1924-49). In 1940 he established the Berkshire Music Center at Stockbridge, Mass. He is remembered as a champion of contemporary composers.

Kowloon, Juilong, or Chiulung (pop. 799,100), peninsula across Kowloon Bay from the island of Hong Kong, near Guangzhou (Canton), southern China, but part of the British Crown Colony of Hong Kong since 1860. Only 4 sq mi (10 sq km), it is one of the most densely populated areas in the world. It is an important transportation and commercial link between the People's Republic of China and the West.

View of Kowloon

As part of British Hong Kong it is scheduled to revert to Chinese control in 1997.
See also: Hong Kong.

Krakatoa, volcanic island in the Sunda Strait, Indonesia. The eruption of Aug. 1883, one of the most violent ever known, caused a tidal wave killing 36,000 people in neighboring Java and Sumatra, and threw debris as far as Madagascar.

Kraków, or Cracow (pop. 744,000), city in south-central Poland, on the Vistula River. By the 8th century the city was a major trading center on routes between Europe and Asia. It was the capital of Poland from the late Middle Ages until Warsaw was made capital in 1596. Dating from that period are the Jagiellonian University (founded 1364), the 14th-century cathedral and market square, and the 16th-century royal castle. From the 18th century it was at times under Austrian, Prussian, and Russian rule, but it has once again been part of Poland since 1920. It is now a manufacturing center for iron and steel, chemicals, textiles, and other products.
See also: Poland.

Kramer, Jack (John Albert Kramer; 1921-), U.S. tennis player, Wimbledon singles (1947) and doubles (1946-47) champion. He won the U.S. singles (1946-47), doubles (1940-41, 43, 47) and mixed doubles (1941) titles. In 1942, Kramer won 10 straight singles tournaments and in 1946 and 1947 was a member of the United States Davis Cup team that defeated Australia in the finals. An active promoter and organizer of professional tennis tours, Kramer was elected to the National Lawn Tennis Hall of Fame in 1968.

Krebs, Sir Hans Adolf (1900-81), German-born British biochemist awarded (with F.A. Lipmann) the 1953 Nobel Prize for physiology or medicine for his discovery of the citric acid cycle, or Krebs cycle, the principle means by which living organisms produce energy.
See also: Biochemistry.

Kreisler, Fritz (1875-1962), Austrian-U.S. violinist. He was an extremely popular performer, known for his elegance of style. A collector of manuscripts of violin music, he published violin pieces of his own composition which he at first attributed to various baroque and classical composers. He composed the operettas *Apple Blossom* and *Sissy* as well as numerous violin pieces, including *Liebesfreud*, *Liebesleid*, and *Caprice*. His arrangements of compositions by earlier composers became part of the standard repertoire.

Kremlin, fortified portion of medieval Russian cities, originally a place of refuge to nearby inhabitants; especially, the Kremlin in Moscow, now the political and administrative center of the USSR. The greater part of the Moscow Kremlin dates from the 15th and 16th centuries. Peter the Great transferred the capital to St. Petersburg (1712), but in 1918 the Russian regime returned the government to Moscow and the Kremlin.
A leading tourist attraction, the Kremlin contains 3 cathedrals, a bell tower, and the throne and banqueting hall of the czars.
See also: Moscow.

Kreps, Juanita Morris (1921-), U.S. economist, author, public official. Kreps was U.S. secretary of commerce (1977-79), the first woman to hold that office. She has been a teacher of economics at colleges since 1945, and vice president of Duke University since 1979. In 1972 Kreps became one of the 10 public directors on the newly reorganized board of directors of the New York Stock Exchange, the first woman to serve on the NYSE's policy-making board. Her writings include books dealing with the rights of women and the aged: *Lifetime Allocation of Work and Income: Essays in the Economics of Aging* (1971); *Women and the American Economy* (1976).

Krill, small marine animal (genus *Euphausia*) resembling shrimp. There are over 90 species, ranging from 3/8 in (1 cm) to nearly 6 in (15 cm). Krill live in the open sea at depths of more than 6,600 ft (2,000 m). Most species have special organs (photophores) that make them visible in the dark. At night they swim in swarms of thousands to the surface to feed on microorganisms. Krill are an important food source for birds, seals, and whales, especially blue and finback whales. Rich in vitamin A, krill have been considered as a possible human food source.

Krishna *see:* Bhagavad-Gita; Vishnu.

Kris Kringle *see:* Santa Claus.

Kroeber, Alfred Louis (1876-1960), U.S. anthropologist who made contributions to many areas of cultural anthropology and archeology, particularly with reference to Native Americans. His books include *The Nature of Culture* (1952) and *Style and Civilization* (1957).
See also: Anthropology.

Kruger, Paulus (1825-1904), South African Boer leader. He opposed the annexation (1877) of the Transvaal by the British and the Boer rebellion of 1880. He was elected president of the new self-governing Transvaal Republic (1883). During the second Boer War (1899-1902) he went to Europe and sought vainly for support for the Boers.
See also: Boer War.

Krupa, Gene (1909-73), U.S. jazz musician, member of the Benny Goodman Orchestra (1935-38). The first famous drum soloist, Krupa was known for his frenzied performing style and exceptional drum technique. From 1938 to 1951 he played with his own successful band and continued to perform and tour with a quartet throughout the 1950s and 60s.

Krupp, family of German armaments makers. The firm was founded in Essen (1811) by **Friedrich Krupp** (1787-1826) with a small steel casting factory, and under his son, **Alfred Krupp** (1812-87), became the largest cast steel enterprise in the world, playing a key role in the Franco-Prussian War, World War I, and World War II. After World War II, **Alfred Krupp von Bohlen und Halbach** (1907-67), head of the firm from 1943, was imprisoned (1948-51) for war crimes. The company, now a public corporation, concentrates on heavy industrial equipment.

Krupskaya, Nadezhda Konstantinovna (1869-1939), Russian revolutionary and educational theorist. She married Vladimir Ilyich Lenin (1898) while both were exiled in Siberia, thereafter sharing his life in Europe and after his return (1917) to Russia. An opponent of Stalin, she lost her considerable influence in the Communist party after Lenin's death.
See also: Lenin, Vladimir Ilyich; Russian Revolution.

Krypton, gaseous element, symbol Kr; for physical constants see Periodic Table. Krypton was discovered by William Ramsay and M.W. Travers in 1898. It is a colorless, odorless, and chemically inert gas. Krypton is used in certain flash lamps for high-speed photography and some types of electric bulbs.

Kuala Lumpur (pop. 937,900), capital and largest city of Malaysia, on the South Malay Peninsula. It was founded in 1857 as a mining camp. The city owed much of its rapid growth to the local abundance of tin and rubber.
See also: Malaysia.

Kublai Khan (1216-94), Mongol emperor from 1259, founder of the Yüan dynasty of China and grandson of Genghis Khan. He defeated the Chinese Sung dynasty in 1279. Under his rule China flourished both economically and culturally; his new capital Cambuluc, described by Marco Polo, became the nucleus of modern Peking.
See also: Mongol Empire.

Kubrick, Stanley (1928-), U.S. film director and writer noted for the strong social commentary of his work. His most famous films include the controversial *Dr. Strangelove* (1964), which treated the accidental triggering of nuclear war as a bitter joke; *2001: A Space Odyssey* (1968), his own story of humanity's distant past and future, which won an Academy Award for special effects; and *A Clockwork Orange* (1971), a terrifying look at criminal rehabilitation. *Paths of Glory* (1958) was Kubrick's first feature-length film, and *Lolita* (1962) his treatment of Vladimir Nabokov's novel of obsession. More recent movies include *The Shining* (1980) and *Full Metal Jacket* (1987).

Kuching (pop. 120,000), capital of Sarawak, a Malaysian state on the island of Borneo. Archeologists confirm it to have been an ancient trading center. The modern city was founded by the British in 1841. Located on the Sarawak River 18 mi (29 km) inland from the South China Sea, it is a major livestock trading and fishing center. It exports rubber, pepper, and timber. Kuching is home to a modern airport and the Sarawak Museum, which is set in scenic gardens and exhibits collections representing the history and archeology of Borneo.
See also: Sarawak.

Kudu, large antelope (*Tragelaphus strepsiceros*) with long spiral horns. It feeds mainly on leaves. The coat is fawn or gray with white spots and stripes. The greater kudu lives in Africa, south of the Sahara, in scrub or dry bush country. The lesser kudu lives in the northeastern corner of Africa.

Kudzu, long semi-woody vine (*Pueraria thunbergiana*) belonging to the pea family. Kudzu is common to the southeastern United States, where it was introduced in the 1800s from Asia. It can grow to 60 ft (18 m) and has broad leaves. The pealike purple flowers have a yellow patch on the

Krupp factory manufacturing weaponry for Germany, 1944

upper petal and smell like grapes. Kudzu has been used as a decorative porch vine, as food for livestock, and as ground cover to prevent soil erosion, but it grows so quickly out of control that it is most often treated as a weed. A fine white flour can be made from the peeled and washed roots.

Kuhn, Richard (1900-67), Austrian chemist. He was awarded the 1938 Nobel Prize for chemistry, but the Nazi government prevented him from accepting the award until after World War II. Noted for his research into vitamins and carotenoids (yellow to red coloring found in plants and animals), he isolated vitamins B_2 (riboflavin) and B_6.
See also: Chemistry.

Kuibyshev *see:* Kuybyshev.

Kuiper, Gerard Peter (1905-73), Dutch-born U.S. astronomer who discovered carbon dioxide in the atmosphere of Mars (1948) and satellites of Uranus and Neptune (1948-49). He directed the Ranger space program (early 1960s), which provided close-up photographs of the moon essential in the landing site selection for the moon landings (1969).
See also: Astronomy.

Kukenaan Falls *see:* Cuquenán Falls.

Ku Klux Klan, secret organization originally begun (1866) by ex-Confederates in the U.S. South to conduct a campaign of terror against newly enfranchised blacks. Its members disguised themselves in hoods and white sheets and used whippings and lynchings to terrorize their victims. Although the first Klan was officially disbanded in 1869, many members remained active throughout reconstruction and beyond. The second Klan, organized in 1915, extended its hostilities to Jews, Catholics, pacifists, and the foreign born. In the 1920s it had 5 million members and its political power extended to the North. Officially disbanded in 1944, the Klan revived in response to civil rights activism of the 1960s and was involved in violent racial confrontations in the early 1980s.
See also: Racism.

Kukui (*Aleurites moluccana*), tree of the spurge family, Hawaii's state tree. Commonly found on mountain slopes, it has light green leaves and may grow as tall as 60 ft (18 m). Its branches spread out and grow long, making it a popular shade tree. The oil produced from these trees is used for fuel and in the manufacture of varnish.

Kumiss, koumis, kumys, or koumyss, alcoholic milk beverage of Asian origin. Primarily a product of the USSR, it is traditionally made from mare's or camel's milk. This thick, sour, effervescent drink was at one time used for treating tuberculosis in sanitoriums.

Kumquat, dwarf evergreen (genus *Fortunella*) belonging to the rue family, grown for its citrus fruits, which resemble small oranges. The kumquat tree measures from 10 to 15 ft (3 to 5 m); it is grown in China, Japan, and in warm regions of the United States such as Florida and California. The fruits are eaten whole or in preserves.

Kuomintang *see:* Chiang Kai-shek.

Kurchatovium *see:* Element 104.

Kurds, people of Kurdistan in western Asia. Traditionally nomadic, most Kurds today are settled farmers and are Muslims. Kurds have struggled vigorously against various rulers for an independent Kurdistan; in the 1970s Kurds fought Iraqi troops unsuccessfully for self-government. With the defeat of Iraq in the Persian Gulf War (1991), the Kurds once again took up arms against Iraqi authority. The Kurds, lacking adequate military equipment, were supressed, but then were subject to massacres staged by the Iraqi military. Fearing annihilation, the Kurds fled their homes for the borders of Turkey and Iran. This mass migration caused incredible suffering and thousands of deaths and forced the U.S. government to establish refugee camps in the north of Iraq.

Kurdish freedom fighters

Kuril Islands, chain of 56 volcanic islands, stretching from the Kamchatka Peninsula of Siberia to Hokkaido Island, Japan. Sparsely inhabited, the islands are the subject of a territorial dispute, held by the USSR since the Soviet occupation during World War II but claimed by Japan.

Kurosawa, Akira (1910-), Japanese film director. Renowned for cinematography, his films include *Rashomon* (1950), *Seven Samurai* (1954), and *Ran* (1985), an interpretation of *King Lear.* He often adapts foreign classics, blending Eastern and Western styles.

Akira Kurosawa's film Kagemusha *(Shadow Warrior) was made at the age of 70.*

Kuroshio *see:* Japan Current.

Kush, ancient kingdom located along the Nile River in what is now Sudan. Lasting from about 2000 B.C. to A.D. 350, Kush was an important center of trade and learning. Exports included cattle and gold. It was also an important slave trading center. The people of Kush developed their own spoken language, writing system, architectural styles, and religion. Exact details of the kingdom's decline and end remain unknown.

Kushan Empire, dynasty of northern India, Afghanistan, and central Asia, from A.D. 50 to the 3rd century. Emperors of the dynasty opened important trades routes between China and India and between India and Rome. Along these trade routes both goods and ideas were exchanged. The dynasty's greatest ruler and an important proponent of Buddhism, its chief religion, was Kanishka, who lived in the 1st century A.D. During his reign Buddhism probably first reached China, and influential artistic concepts from Greece and Rome were incorporated into Indian religious art.
See also: Kanishka.

Kuskokwim River, second longest river in Alaska. Originating south of the Yukon, it flows southwest for about 600 mi (970 km) and empties into Kuskokwim Bay, an inlet of the Bering Sea.

Kutenai, Native American tribe of the U.S.-Canadian border. Once mountain dwellers, their activities included hunting and fishing. They now live in reservations in Idaho, Montana, and British Columbia.

Kuvasz, breed of powerful, sturdily built dog. Bred in Hungary, it was popular in the Middle Ages as a guard dog of the nobility. Used now as a shepherd and guard dog, the typical kuvasz has a pure white, mostly short-haired coat, stands 26 in (66 cm), and weighs about 70 lbs (32 kg).

Kuwait

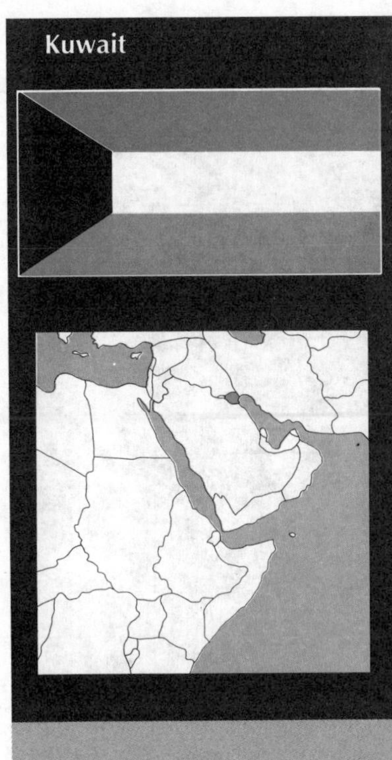

General information	
Capital:	Kuwait
Area:	6,880 sq mi (17,818 sq km)
Population:	2,048,000
Official language:	Arabic
Monetary unit:	1 Kuwaiti dinar = 1,000 fils
Main cities:	as-Salimiyah, Hawalli, Kuwait City
Government	
Form:	constitutional monarchy
Independent:	1961
Head of state:	Emir
Head of government:	Prime minister
Legislature:	single parliamentary house (National Assembly)
Executive:	Prime minister and Council of Ministers
Judiciary:	highest court is the High Court of Appeal
Political division:	4 governorates
National economy	
Gross national product:	U.S. $26,250,000,000
Per capita income:	U.S. $13,680
Agriculture:	tomatoes, onions, melons, dates, cucumbers and gherkins
Livestock:	goats, sheep, cattle
Fisheries:	6,000 metric tons
Mining:	petroleum, sulfur, asphalt
Industries:	petroleum products, flour, salt
Main exports:	mineral fuels, lubricants, petroleum (products)
Transportation:	2,405 mi (3,871 km) of roads; 1 international airport
Trading partners:	Japan, U.S., Italy, Germany, The Netherlands
People	
Urban:	90%
Ethnic composition:	Kuwaiti Arab 40%, non-Kuwaiti Arab 38%, Asian 21%
Birth rate:	26.2 per 1,000 population
Death rate:	2.2 per 1,000 population
Infant mortality:	17 per 1,000 live births
Life expectancy:	male 70.5 years, female 73 years

Kuwait, small independent Arab state on the northwest coast of the Persian Gulf, bordered by Iraq (northwest) and Saudi Arabia (south).

Though mostly desert, it has been a major oil-producing country and possesses more than 10% of the world's estimated oil reserves. Its independence was jeopardized in Aug. 1990, when Iraq, on the pretext of settling a border dispute but also interested in obtaining control of Kuwaiti oil, invaded the country and announced its annexation. The ensuing Persian Gulf War (begun in Jan. 1991) pitted the United States and its allies, with the sanction of UN resolutions calling for the restoration of Kuwait's independent status, in a military action against Iraq to roll back the invasion.

Economy. Kuwait's traditional economy was based on the export of wool and hides and pearl fishing. With the discovery (1946) and exploitation of its huge oil reserves, the enormous wealth generated by the petroleum industry allowed the government to establish a widespread social welfare system that made Kuwait one of the world's wealthiest nations on the basis of per capita income. In the 1960s the government also embarked on an ambitious modernization and diversification program. Until the Iraqi invasion, the capital, also called Kuwait, was a thoroughly modern city. The ruler, called *emir*, appointed the prime minister.

More than half the population was made up of non-Kuwaiti citizens, who held a majority of the jobs, as many native Kuwaitis lacked adequate education and training. The government had put special effort into training Kuwaitis to help them take more control of their economy.

Modern architecture in Kuwait

History. In the early 19th century Arabs settled on the southern shore of Kuwait Bay and elected the head of the Al-Sabah family to be their ruler, establishing a dynasty unbroken to the present.

Even as part of the Ottoman Empire, Kuwait retained its independent government under the Al-Sabahs. It was a British protectorate from 1897 until 1961, when it became independent. In 1967 Kuwait sided with Egypt in its war against Israel, as it did again in 1973. Also in that year, Kuwait, a member of the Organization of Petroleum Exporting Countries (OPEC), joined with other Arab oil-exporting countries in halting oil shipments to countries that supported Israel. In 1976 the emir dissolved the National Assembly. A new assembly was elected in 1981 but dissolved by the emir in 1986.

During the Iran-Iraq War (1980-88) Iran began attacking Kuwaiti oil tankers because Kuwait had sided with Iraq and was aiding that country with financial and other support. In 1987 Kuwait requested help from the Soviet Union and the United States to protect its shipping. The Soviet Union leased some ships to Kuwait that carried the Soviet flag, which prevented Iran from attacking them. The U.S. Navy provided armed escorts for Kuwaiti-flagged

L

ships in the Persian Gulf. Soon after a cease-fire in 1979 ended Iran-Iraq hostilities, Iraq turned on its former ally and demanded settlement of a dispute involving an oil field along their mutual border and some small islands in the Persian Gulf. In Aug. 1990 Iraq sent troops into the lightly defended country and proclaimed it part of Iraq. Saudi Arabia and other Gulf states, fearful that a powerful Iraq might continue its agression against them, asked the United States and the United Nations to condemn the action and restore Kuwait to its independence. A large multinational force, overwhelmingly composed of the U.S. military, rushed to Saudi Arabia to protect it against aggression. In Jan. 1991 this force commenced hostilities against Iraq and its troops in Kuwait with the aim of restoring the pre-invasion status of Kuwait. However, as many Kuwaitis fled the country and as Kuwait itself suffered so much damage from the occupation and the allied efforts to dislodge it, expectations are that restoring Kuwait to its former condition will be a long process.

Kuwait (pop. 168,000), capital and the most important city in the country of Kuwait and founded in the 18th century by a tribal confederation of Arabic people. It is the chief economic center with an excellent harbor on the Persian Gulf. The port was established in the 18th century and was a shipbuilding center. The city is highly modernized because of the wealth generated by the petroleum industry which has developed since the end of World War II. In Aug. of 1990, the military forces of Iraq invaded the nation of Kuwait and occupied the city. This event precipitated the Persian Gulf War.
See also: Persian Gulf War.

Kuybyshev, formerly Samara (pop. 1,250,000), city in the east-central European USSR, located on the Volga River. It is an important port and industrial center, where automobiles, locomotives, and aircraft are manufactured. It is also the site of a hydroelectric power plant. Founded as Samara in 1586, the city was renamed in 1935.
See also: Union of Soviet Socialist Republics.

Kwajalein, world's largest atoll, situated in the Marshall Islands in the west central Pacific. Now in the U.S. Trust Territory of the Pacific Islands, Kwajalein is the site of a U.S. military missile range.

Kwakiutl, Native American tribe of Wakashan linguistic stock, native to Vancouver Island and coastal British Columbia, Canada. Skilled in fishing and crafts, they had a strictly hierarchical society in which the potlatch ceremony played a significant part.

Kwashiorkor, severe condition of protein deficiency common in children of some areas of the Third World. It causes excess body fluid, distended abdomen, skin and hair changes, loss of appetite, apathy, diarrhea, liver disturbance, stunted growth, and sometimes, death. Its name derives from the Ghanaian for "deposed one," from its occurrence in children who are removed from breastfeeding too soon.

Kyanite, or cyanite, blue or white aluminum silicate mineral found in metamorphic rocks, occurring as long crystal blades. Because it is heat resistant, kyanite is used in spark plugs and as lining for ovens used in the manufacture of glass. Some kyanite is used for jewelry. It is found in the United States, India, Italy, and the USSR.

Kyd, Thomas (1558-94), English dramatist whose *The Spanish Tragedy* (c.1586) was a prototype of the Elizabethan and Jacobean revenge tragedy. The work is partly modeled on Seneca but is more lurid and more psychologically acute. Kyd may have written a version of the Hamlet story.

Kyoto (pop. 1,473,000), capital of Kyoto prefecture, Honshu Island, Japan, about 25 mi (40 km) northeast of Osaka. The national capital from its foundation A.D. 794 until supplanted by Tokyo in 1868, Kyoto is rich in architectural relics and art treasures. Still a cultural and religious center, it also has leading educational establishments and large-scale mixed industry with manufactures that include electrical equipment, cameras, chemicals, silk, and porcelain.
See also: Japan.

Kyzyl Kum, or Kizil Kum, sandy desert of Soviet Central Asia, lying southeast of the Aral Sea and covering about 88,000 sq mi (228,000 sq km) of southern Kazakhstan and northern Uzbekistan between the Syr Darya and Amu Darya rivers. Some parts have been irrigated for crop growing (cotton, rice, and wheat), and the area has significant deposits of gold.

Kyoto

L, the 12th letter of the English alphabet. It is derived from the Semitic *lamedh* (perhaps itself based on an Egyptian hieroglyphic), representing an oxgoad, and from the Greek *lambda*. In Roman numerals, L is 50. The British symbol for the pound sterling (£) is another form of the letter, derived from the Latin *libra*, originally a pound in weight.

Labor *see:* Birth.

Labor *see:* Labor movement.

Labor, Department of, federal department, independent since 1913, responsible for U.S. workers' welfare. Headed by the secretary of labor, a cabinet member, it is concerned with the enforcement of federal laws regulating hours, wages, and safety measures, collects and issues industrial statistics, administers job-training programs, and provides information in labor disputes. Its specialized divisions include the Occupational Safety and Health Administration, the Bureau of Labor Statistics, the Employment and Training Administration, the Bureau of International Labor Affairs, and the Labor-Management Services Administration.

Labor Day, official holiday in the United States and Canada since 1894, held on the first Monday in Sept. to honor the workers. In socialist countries, labor is honored on May Day (May 1).

Labor force, that part of a nation's population that is either employed or capable of employment. In the United States, the labor force includes all citizens above the age of 16 who are working, actively looking for work, or in the armed forces. Those who are retired, full-time homemakers, students, or handicapped are excluded.

Labor movement, movement to organize industrial workers and improve their working conditions. The need for organized labor did not occur until the late 19th century when the poorly treated and underpaid unskilled labor force—including children under 16 years old—in urban areas reached 40%. A secret society made up of Philadelphia garment workers, the Knights of Labor (1869), organized both skilled and unskilled laborers. This group declined by the 1880s after an unsuccessful strike against the railroad tycoon Jay Gould (1886).

In 1881 the predecessor of the American Federation of Labor (AFL) had its beginning. It was organized by specific craft unions, not workers as a whole; therefore unskilled workers were not represented. This loose federation consisted of the iron workers, molders, printers, carpenters, glass workers, and cigar makers. Samuel Gompers, its leader from the cigar makers group, proposed a 3-point program: practical benefits of higher wages and better working conditions, federalism allowing each union considerable internal freedom to organize and operate according to its own needs and style, and non-federally involved collective bargaining that also rewarded politicians who held pro-Union opinions and defeated those that did not.

Despite the successful beginning of the AFL, labor organizers faced employers reluctant to recognize and work with unions; *blacklisting* (agreement between companies not to hire pro-union workers or to hire those who signed anti-union documents called *yellow dog contracts*), and court injunctions, which usually resulted in pro-management decisions. It was not until the failure of business in the Great Depression and the New Deal policy of President Franklin Roosevelt that union organization and workers' rights found widespread support.

The Congress of Industrial Organizations (CIO) helped with a favorable attitude in Congress, launched a campaign to organize great industries such as steel, automobiles, oil, and rubber—over the bitter opposition of the managements of these corporations. Federal legislation favored both sides: the *Wagner Act* (1935), which protected the right for unions to organize and participate in *collective bargaining*—negotiations between management and elected union officials—and the *Taft-Hartley Act* (1947), which protected non-union workers and allowed the Attorney General to suspend strikes after 90 days.

In 1955, headed by George Meany (president of the AFL), the AFL and CIO merged to represent an organized labor voice before Congress and a strong united stand against industry. Not all unions became or remained members of this federation—such as the automobile workers headed by former CIO head Walter Reuther—due to political differences. Using AFL-CIO guidelines, unions and collective bargaining have become an essential part of U.S. industry. The groups elected to represent workers follow procedures for negotiations with management on wages, hours, pensions and health insurance, seniority rights of workers, and grievance procedures. When agreement is reached, a contract is signed by both sides—often to cover a 2 to 3 year period. If agreement cannot be reached by both parties, a neutral third party called a *mediator* suggests solutions. If a mediator cannot bring both parties to agreement, a specialist called an *arbitrator* hears both sides and renders a binding decision to which both sides must adhere. Since the 1880s unions have helped to increase hourly wages, to reduce the length of the work week, to increase worker safety, provide insurance and pensions, and to support paid vacation and holiday time for workers. New and important unions have been established since the AFL-CIO merger, such as the United Farm Workers Union (UFW) in the 1960s, led by the Mexican-American labor leader Cesar E. Chavez of California.

Labour Party, English political party founded in 1900 by trade unions and socialist groups—the Independent Labour Party (1893) and the Fabian Society—with James Keir Hardie as its first leader. It gained nationwide support after World War I, first coming to power under Ramsay MacDonald in 1924. His second administration (1929-31) ended in coalition with the Conservatives, division within the party, and electoral defeat. The first effective socialist program was implemented by the Labour government of Clement Attlee (1945-51), instituting the National Health Service and nationalizing the Bank of England and major industries. Attlee was followed as leader by Hugh Gaitskell, who was succeeded at his death (1963) by Harold Wilson. Prime minister in 4 Labour governments (1964-70, 1974-76), he was succeeded by James Callaghan. Callaghan yielded leadership in 1979 to Michael Foot, a member of the party's left wing. As Labour became deeply embroiled in factionalism, several leaders resigned to form the new Social Democratic Party in 1981. After the party's decisive loss in the June 1983 general election, Neil Kinnock replaced Foot. In 1994 Tony Blair became the new leader; Labour won a landslide victory in the 1997 general election.

Labrador, large peninsula in northeast Canada. It is a land of long, severe winters with temperatures falling to –40°F (–40°C), and short, hot summers, during which temperatures rise to 80°F (27°C). Its population is about 97% white and 3% Inuit (Eskimos), Naskapi, and Montagnais. Labrador is rich in iron ore, timber, and cod fish. Its hydroelectric plant, which began operation in 1971 on the Churchill River at Churchill Falls, is one of the largest in the Western Hemisphere, with a capacity of $5^1/_4$ million kilowatts of electricity.
See also: Canada.

Labrador retriever, breed of sporting dog originating in Newfoundland, Canada and further developed in England. A strongly built dog standing 21-24 in (93-100 cm) and weighing 60-75 lb (27-34 km), the

Child labor in the mines, around 1840

Labrador has a stable temperament, a keen sense of smell, and an innate love of water. Distinctive features are its short, thick, water-resistant coat (usually black, but sometimes yellow or dark red-brown) and its thick-based "otter tail." The Labrador is used in hunting to retrieve waterfowl and other small game.

Labrador tea, 6 species of small evergreen shrubs (genus *Ledum*; especially, *L. groenlandicium*) containing in their aromatic leaves tannin and a mild narcotic that is the active ingredient in the tea and beer brewed from the leaves. These plants are found in swampy areas of subarctic North America, Greenland, and northern Europe.

La Brea tar pits, asphalt bog in Hancock Park, Los Angeles, containing skeletons of prehistoric (Pleistocene) animals, including mammoths, saber-toothed cats, and giant sloths, preserved by tar.
See also: Prehistoric animal.

Laburnum, genus of small trees belonging to the pea family (Fabaceae or Leguminosae), characterized by glossy green leaves, yellow blossoms, and fine-grained, hard wood. A poison called cytisine is present in their roots, seeds, and other parts. The common laburnum (*L. anagyroides*) is native to Asia and is also called golden chain, bean tree, and bean trefoil.

Labyrinth, complex of buildings or hedges with many passages and dead ends, designed to baffle strangers trying to find the way in or out; a maze. The most famous

Laburnum

labyrinth of antiquity, according to Greek legend, was built in Crete by Daedalus to house the Minotaur. Other famous labyrinths were in Lemnia and in Italy. The maze at Hampton Court Palace, England, is an example of a garden labyrinth.

Lac, sticky residue secreted by a species of scale insect (*Laccifer lacca*) and used to produce shellac and lac dye. The secretion, called stick lac in its natural state, is harvested by gathering the twigs in which the insect resides.

Lace, fine openwork decorative fabric made by braiding, looping, knotting, or twisting thread, usually linen or cotton, sometimes silver and gold. Before 19th-century mechanization, it was handmade by needlepoint or with bobbins. Lace was developed in 16th-century Italy and Flanders.

Ladybug

La Ceiba (pop. 61,900), city in northern Honduras, located in the Gulf of Honduras at the base of Mt. Bonito. It is an industrial center and a major Caribbean port for the distribution of goods produced locally.
See also: Honduras.

Lacewing, insect of the order Neuroptera, named for its double pair of delicate, lacy wings. The two most common families are the green or golden-eyed lacewings (Hemerobiidae) and the smaller brown lacewings (Chrysopidae). These insects are also called stinkflies because of the strong odor they emit to repel predators. Larvae, often called aphid lions, use their large jaws to suck fluids from aphids and other insects.

Lacewing

Lacquer, solution used as a coating for wood, metal, paper, clothing, or porcelain to provide a lustrous, protective finish. Lacquers can be made from either natural (tree sap, resins, lac, cellulose) or synthetic compounds.

Lacrimal gland *see:* Tears.

Lacroix, Christian (1950-), French designer of *haute-couture* fashion. In 1987 the Council of Fashion Designers of America voted him best foreign designer. He is best known for his "bubble" dress.

La Crosse (pop. 97,904), city in western Wisconsin, seat of La Cross County, located at the junction of the Black, La Crosse, and Mississippi rivers. Founded in 1842, the city was named after the Native American game of lacrosse. Today it is active in manufacturing auto parts, aircraft instruments, and consumer goods.
See also: Wisconsin.

Lacrosse, team game derived by French settlers from the Native American game of baggataway, now the national game of Canada. It is played with a stick called a crosse having a net at one end. The crosse is used to catch, throw, and carry a hard rubber ball, with the aim of sending it into the opposing goal. In men's lacrosse, played in Canada, the United States, and the United Kingdom, each team has 10 members. Women's lacrosse is usually played with 12 to a side.

Lactic acid ($C_3H_6O_3$), organic acid that is the end product of the metabolism of sugar, the formation of which causes milk to sour. Lactic acid is produced in muscles after their cells have broken down glycogen for energy; it is this accumulation of lactic acid that causes muscle fatigue. Blood levels of lactic acid are also elevated in persons with lactic acidosis, diabetes, anemia, leukemia, and other abnormal conditions.
See also: Scheele, Carl Wilhelm.

Ladybug, lady beetle, or ladybird, small, almost round beetle of the family Coccinellidae. Ladybugs are named for their association with the Virgin Mary. Their shiny wing-cases are brightly colored (red, yellow, or black) and usually have patterns of spots (black with a red or yellow case, or red or yellow with a black case). They hibernate in groups under bark or in caves and rock crevices. They emerge in the spring to lay their eggs, and both adults and larvae feed on aphids and scale insects, thus playing an important role in controlling these insect pests. A few species eat plants, and the Mexican bean beetle is a pest of beans, alfalfa, clover, and other crops.

Lady's-slipper, moccasin flower, or squirrel's shoes, any of various species of the orchid family that bear a single flower on each stem. The lower petal is shaped like a slipper, and the sepals look like a bow securing it. Lady's-slippers are found in damp woodlands and bogs in North America, Europe, and Asia. They are fertilized by queen bumblebees, which are heavy enough to force their way in through a slit in the "slipper."

Lady's-thumb *see:* Smartweed.

Laënnec, René Théophile Hyacinthe (1781-1826), French surgeon, physician, and inventor of the stethoscope. Laënnec specialized in heart and lung pathology and is considered the founder of chest medicine. He described his research in *A Treatise on Mediate Auscultation* (1819).
See also: Stethoscope.

Laetrile, alleged anticancer drug (chemical name, amygdalin) created from an extract of apricot pits in 1926 by Ernst Krebs, Sr., and refined by his son, Ernst Krebs, Jr., who patented it in 1949. Though considered worthless by the medical establishment and banned by the U.S. Food and Drug Administration, it was legalized in 14 states by 1978, when a U.S. appeals court ruled that the drug could not be withheld from terminally ill people, since the government's criteria of "safety" and "effectiveness" had no meaning in their case.
See also: Cancer.

La Farge, John (1835-1910), U.S. artist and writer. He was noted for his fine mural painting and stained glass, chiefly executed for churches, such as the mural *Ascension* in the Church of the Ascension, New York City. He also produced fine watercolors and drawings and was a lecturer and writer of art criticism.

Lafayette, Marquis de (1757-1834), French soldier and statesman who fought in the American Revolution and worked for French-American alliance. He came to America in 1777, joined George Washington's staff as major general, and fought in the campaigns of 1777-78 and at Yorktown (1781). On a visit to France (1779) he persuaded Louis XVI to send troops and a fleet to aid the colonists. In the French Revolution he supported the bourgeoisie, helped set up the National Assembly, drafted the Declaration of the Rights of Man, and commanded the National Guard, but he fell from power after ordering his troops (July 1791) to fire on the populace. In 1824 he revisited the United States, hailed as a hero. He was a leader of the July Revolution (1830) in France.
See also: French Revolution; Revolutionary War in America.

La Fayette, Marie Madeleine Pioche de la Vergne (1634-93), French writer. She is epsecially noted for *The Princess of Clèves* (1678), whose sensitivity and psychological realism make it the first great French novel. She also wrote *The Princess of Montponsier* (1622) and *Zayde* (1670).

Laffite, Jean (c.1780-1825?), French pirate and smuggler who attacked Spanish ships south of New Orleans. He and his men received a pardon from President James Madison in return for aiding General Andrew Jackson against the British in 1815, but they later went back to piracy. When Laffite attacked U.S. ships (1820), the navy sailed against him, and he set out in his favorite ship, the *Pride*, never to be seen again.

La Follette, family name of 2 generations of influential U.S. politicians from Wisconsin. **Robert Marion La Follette, Sr.** (1855-1925) was a U.S. statesman and reform legislator. He served in the House of Representatives, 1885-91. As Wisconsin governor (1901-6), he was supported by progressive Republicans, and initiated the "Wisconsin idea" reform program, proposing direct primaries and a state civil service. He served as U.S. senator, 1906-25, during which time he founded the Progressive Party, opposed U.S. entry to World War I and the League of Nations, and ran unsuccessfully for president in 1924. One son, **Robert Marion La Follette, Jr.** (1895-1965), was U.S. senator from Wisconsin (1925-47) and another, **Philip Fox La Follette** (1897-1965), was governor of Wisconsin (1931-33, 1935-39).

La Fontaine, Jean de (1621-95), French writer. He is remembered especially for his *Fables* (1668-94), moral tales drawn from Aesop and Asian sources that he used to comment satirically on contemporary society, and for his humorous, bawdy *Tales and Novels in Verse* (1664-66).
See also: Canada

LaFontaine, Sir Louis Hippolyte (1807-64), Canadian politician and judge. Leader of the French Canadians from 1837 and twice joint prime minister with Robert Baldwin (in 1842-43 and 1848-51, when the "great ministry's" legislation included the Rebellion Losses Bill). He was chief justice of Lower Canada from 1853-64.

Lagerkvist, Pär Fabian (1891-1974), Swedish poet, novelist, and dramatist, winner of the 1951 Nobel Prize for literature. He was much disturbed by World War I and later also protested against fascism. His works, which include the novels *The Hangman* (1933) and *Barabbas* (1950), and the play *Man Without a Soul* (1936), explore the problem of good and evil in humanity.

Lagerlöf, Selma (1858-1940), Swedish novelist, the first woman to win a Nobel Prize for literature (1909). Her works, rooted in legend and the folklore of her native Värmland, include *The Story of Gösta Berling, The Wonderful Adventure of Nils* (1906, a children's classic), and a trilogy, *The Ring of the Lowenskolds* (1931).

Lagos (pop. 1,125,000), capital and chief port of Nigeria, on the Gulf of Guinea (West Africa). The city occupies Lagos, Victoria, and Iddo islands, between the Bight of Benin and Lagos Lagoon, and also part of the mainland, where its main deepwater harbor and the terminal of the Lagos-Kano-Nguru railroad are located at Apapa. Lagos has been a trade center since the 15th century. It now handles most of Nigeria's seaborne exports, mainly palm products, peanuts, cocoa, tin, hides, and skins. Manufactures include textiles, furniture, and metal products. Its university (1962) specializes in law, medicine, and business administration.
See also: Nigeria.

Lagrange, Joseph Louis (1736-1813), French mathematician and astronomer who made important contributions to calculus and differential equations and was influential in adopting the decimal system in metrics. He worked also on celestial mechanics, in particular explaining the moon's libration (swinging movement). His most important work is the *Mécanique analytique.*
See also: Number theory.

La Guardia, Fiorello Henry (1882-1947), U.S. statesman and mayor of New York City. As a Republican member of Congress (1917-19, 1923-33) he supported liberalizing and prolabor measures, including the Norris-La Guardia Act forbidding the use of injunctions in labor disputes. As mayor (1933-45) he instituted major reforms in New York and fought corruption.

Lahore (pop. 2,953,000), city in eastern Pakistan, capital of the province of Punjab, lying on the Ravi River. Lahore is Pakistan's second largest city and is a center for education, steel production, film-making, and textile manufacturing. The city served as a capital for the Mogul and Sikh empires before being taken over by the British in 1849.
See also: Pakistan.

Laissez faire (French, "leave alone"), doctrine that opposes state intervention in economic affairs. First enunciated by the French physiocrats in the 18th century as a reaction against mercantilism, the idea was taken up by Scottish economist Adam Smith and became a cornerstone of classical economics.
See also: Smith, Adam.

Lake Agassiz, ancient North American lake that covered much of what is now the Canadian province of Manitoba and parts of other provinces and the United States. It was formed by melting glaciers during the last ice age. Lake Agassiz was the largest of the glacial lakes, reaching its maximum size (approximately 135,000 sq mi/350,000 sq km) between 7900 and 7500 B.C. The continued runoff from the glaciers caused the lake to drain into the Hudson Bay, except for the deeper areas that became smaller lakes such as Manitoba, Winnipeg, and Winnipegosis.

Portrait of Jean de la Fontaine by Nicolas de Largilliere (1656-1746)

Lake Albano, crater lake inside an extinct volcano in west-central Italy, southeast of Rome in the Albani hills. Lake Albano served as a vacation spot for ancient Romans and is still a site for resorts, including Castel Gandolfo, the papal summer residence.

Lake Albert, or Lake Mobutu Sese Sekolake, lake in east central Africa between Zaire and Uganda, linked to Lake Edward to the south by the Semliki River. It was named (1864) for England's Prince Albert, husband of Queen Victoria. The lake is approximately 100 mi (160 km) in length and 20 mi (32 km) in width, covering about 2,059 sq mi (5,333 sq km). It is a water source for the Nile River.

Lake Baikal, world's deepest lake (maximum depth 5,315 ft/1,620 m), located in southeastern Siberia, USSR. It is about 395 mi (636 km) long and 49 mi (79 km) wide, covering an area of about 12,200 sq mi (31,500 sq km). It contains about 20% of the world's unfrozen fresh water (more than any other lake).

Lake Chad, largest lake in west central Africa, fourth largest on the African continent. Lake Chad lies within the boundaries of 4 African nations: Chad (containing the major portion of the lake), Cameroon, Nigeria, and Niger. Its shallow basin, approximately 22 ft (7 m) at the deepest, allows easy overflow into surrounding areas. The size of the lake fluctuates depending on the season, the volume of water received from inflowing rivers, and the rate of evaporation.

Lagos, Nigeria

Lake Champlain, long, narrow lake forming much of the border between New York State and Vermont, with its northern tip extending into the Canadian province of Quebec. Named after the first European to see it, French explorer Samuel de Champlain, it is 107 mi (172 km) long, 1-14 mi (1.6-22 km) wide, and up to 400 ft (122 m) deep. Lake Champlain was the site of many naval battles during the Revolutionary War and the War of 1812.

Lake Charles (pop. 168,134), inland port city of southwest Louisiana, on the Calcasieu River, linked by a 33-mi (53-km) channel with the Gulf of Mexico. It lies at the center of a rich rice- and cattle-producing region. A commercial and industrial city, it ships chemicals, synthetic rubber, petroleum products, timber, rice, and cotton.

Lake Como (Italian: *Lago di Como*), lake in the northern Italian province of Lombardy, at the foot of the Alps, 25 miles (40 km) north of Milan. Lake Como is a popular tourist attraction, famed for the beauty of its setting and the elegant villas lining its shores.

Lake District, scenic region in northwestern England, about 30 mi (50 km) wide. It contains the highest mountain in England (Scafell Pike, 3,210 ft/978 m) and 15 lakes, including Windermere, Ullswater, and Derwentwater. William Wordsworth, Samuel Coleridge, and Robert Southey are among the writers and artists who lived here in the early 19th century.

Loweswater, in England's Lake District

Lake dwelling, shelter built on stilts or piles in the waters of a lake. Stone Age and Bronze Age lake dwellings can be found in parts of Europe, and in some parts of the world they are still built. Crannogs, strongholds built on artificial islands, were built in Ireland, Scotland, and England from the Late Stone Age until the Middle Ages.

Lake Edward, lake in the Rift valley of East Africa, on the border between Uganda and Zaire. Explorer Henry M. Stanley named it in 1889 for Albert Edward, Prince of Wales (later King Edward VII). Lake Edward, approximately 40 mi (64 km) long, 32 mi (51 km) wide, and 830 sq mi (2,150 sq km) in area, is a water source for the Nile. The Semliki River connects it to Lake Albert to the north.

Lake Maggiore

Lake Erie, one of the 5 Great Lakes, fourth on the border between the United States and Canada. Lake Erie is 240 mi (386 km) long, 38-57 mi (61-92 km) wide, and has an area of about 10,000 sq mi (26,000 sq km). It is the southernmost of the Great Lakes and is a link in the St. Lawrence Seaway.
See also: Great Lakes.

Lake Garda, largest lake in Italy, about 143 sq mi (370 sq km). Its southern end is about 65 mi (105 km) east of Milan. Its scenery has made it a popular resort area.

Lake Geneva, crescent-shaped lake, one of Europe's largest, between southwestern Switzerland and France. With an area of about 224 sq mi (581 sq km), Lake Geneva is known for the clear, blue water of its western end and its lakeshore resorts.

Lake George, long, narrow, deep lake in the Adirondack Mountains of New York state. Now a summer resort, the lake was the scene of several important clashes during the American Revolutionary War.

Lake Huron, one of the 5 Great Lakes, 206 mi (332 km) long and 183 mi (295 km) wide, with an area of about 23,000 sq mi (60,000 sq km). Lake Huron is bordered by the Canadian province of Ontario on the north, east, and southeast, and by Michigan on the west and southwest. It is part of the St. Lawrence Seaway and is heavily used by maritime commercial traffic.
See also: Great Lakes.

Lake Itasca, lake of glacial origin in Minnesota. The chief source of the Mississippi River, Lake Itasca is about 1.8 sq mi (4.7 sq km) in area.

Lake Ladoga, lake in northwest Russia, about 40 mi (64 km) northeast of Leningrad. At 6,835 sq mi (17,703 sq km), Lake Ladoga is the largest in Europe. It forms part of a canal system connecting the Baltic and White Seas.

Lake Lugano, lake on the border between Switzerland and Italy. It is located east of Lake Maggiore at the southern foot of the Alps. It is connected to Lake Maggiore by the Tresa River. It is 20 m (32km) in length and 2 m (3 km) wide.

Lake Maggiore, lake lying mostly in Italy, but extending into the Swiss Alps. Its area is 82 sq mi (212 sq km), making it Italy's largest lake. The western and eastern shores are home to lakeside resorts and small villages.

Lake Manitoba, narrow, shallow lake in south-central Manitoba, Canada. There is an important waterfowl-research station on the lake's southern shore.

Lake Maracaibo, lake in northwestern Venezuela, in the oil-producing region. Connected to the Carrribean Sea by a dredged channel, Lake Maracaibo has an area of 5,217 sq mi (13,512 sq km), making it South America's largest lake. The southern shore produces agricultural products, notably sugarcane, coconuts, cacao, and coffee.

Lake Mead, largest reservoir in the United States, located in northwestern Arizona and southeastern Nevada, built by confining the Colorado River at the Hoover (Boulder) Dam. Lake Mead is located approximately 15 mi (24 km) east of Las Vegas, Nev. It is about 250 sq mi (650 sq km) in area, 115 mi (185 km) long, and 1-10 mi (2-16 km) wide. It was named after Elwood Mead, reclamation commissioner (1924-36).
See also: Hoover Dam.

Lake Michigan, largest freshwater lake lying entirely within the United States, and the third largest of the 5 Great Lakes. It is 307 mi (494 km) long, 118 mi (190 km) at its widest point, and up to 923 ft (281 m) deep. Its borders are Wisconsin and Illinois on the west, Michigan on the east and north, and Indiana on the southeast. It is connected to the Great Lakes St. Lawrence Seaway that goes east to the Atlantic Ocean and south to the Gulf of Mexico via the Mississippi River, serving international commerce.
See also: Great Lakes.

Lake Neagh *see:* Lough Neagh.

Lake of Lucerne (German: *Vierwaldstätter See*), major lake in Switzerland, between the Rigi and Pilatus mountains. It is around 24 mi (39 km) long and up to 2 mi (3 km) wide and has the appearance of an imperfect cross. Adventures of the legendary William Tell took place along Lake Uri's shores.
See also: Tell, William.

Lake of the Woods, lake located mostly in Ontario, Canada along the Minnesota border, with 2 bays reaching into Manitoba. It is 100 mi (160 km) long and 10-50 mi (16-80 km) wide, with an area of 1,485 sq mi (3,846 sq km). Waters from the Rainy River run into the lake from the southeast. The lake is drained in the north by the Winnipeg River, which flows into Lake Winnipeg in Manitoba. At the end of the Revolutionary War it was declared an official boundary. The island-filled lake is now a tourist attraction.

Lake Okeechobee (Seminole, "big water"), largest freshwater lake in the southern part of the United States, located in central Florida just north of the Everglades. The lake is 35 mi (56 km) long, about 680 sq mi (1,760 sq km) in area, and up to 15 ft (4.6 m) deep. In 1937 a 155-mi (249-km) cross-state waterway was completed to control seasonal flooding. Canals were constructed as outlets to the Atlantic

Ocean and Gulf of Mexico, and to supply needed water to communities along Florida's eastern coastline.

Lake Onega, second largest lake in Europe (3,753 sq mi/9,720 sq km), located in the northwestern part of the USSR. It is an important transportation connection between the Baltic and White seas. The lake has productive fisheries along its coast.

Lake Ontario, one of the 5 Great Lakes, located in New York State and Ontario, Canada. It is fed mainly by the Niagara River, and flows into the Atlantic Ocean through the St. Lawrence River, making it an important part in transportation of goods through the St. Lawrence Seaway system. It is about 193 mi (311 km) long and 53 mi (85 km) wide, with depths ranging from 500 to 802 ft (152 to 244 m). Its low elevation above sea level (245 ft/75 m) and great offshore depths keep it from freezing during the winter. It tempers the surrounding climate, producing cool summer days along the eastern shore and allowing fruit crops to produce successfully on the southern shore.
See also: Great Lakes.

Lake Peipus, or Chudskoe, lake in the USSR between the Estonian and Russian republics. It has depths up to 50 ft (15 m) and an area of 1,400 sq mi (3,626 sq km), and is frozen about 6 months out of the year. During World War II, when the Germans surrounded Leningrad and cut off all supply routes, Russian volunteers used small trucks to transport food across the thick ice to feed more than 3 million starving people.

Lake Placid, small lake in the northeastern Adirondack Mountains, New York, about 3 mi (5.6 km) long and 1 mi (2.4 km) wide. Its beauty attracts visitors for boating, swimming, hiking, ice skating, and skiing. It was the site of the 1980 Winter Olympics. Just south of Lake Placid lies the grave of abolitionist John Brown.

Lake Poets, name given to the English poets William Wordsworth, Samuel Taylor Coleridge, and Robert Southey, who lived in the Lake District for a time. The critic Francis Lord Jeffrey was first to characterize them as constituting the "Lake school of poetry," although the 3 friends do not form a group stylistically.
See also: Coleridge, Samuel Taylor; Wordsworth, William.

Lake Pontchartrain, lagoon-like lake in southern Louisiana, connected to the Mississippi River through the Inner Harbor Navigation Canal. Its briny water provides abundant game fish for the numerous small resorts along its shores. It is 40 mi (64 km) long and 25 mi (40 km) wide. It is crossed by the Lake Pontchartrain Causeway, the world's longest bridge (29.2 mi/47 km).

Lake Powell, lake on the Utah-Arizona border, formed by the Glen Canyon Dam and fed by the Colorado River. It is 186 mi (299 km) long and 500 ft (150 m) deep. The dam was built to produce hydroelectric power. Lake Powell is a popular recreation site.

Lakes of Killarney, 3 scenic lakes lying southwest of the town of Killarney in County Kerry, Ireland. The lakes—Lough Leane ("Lower Lake"), Muckross Lake, and Middle Lake—have a combined area of nearly 10 sq mi (17 km). They form part of Killarney National Park, a popular tourist attraction.

Lake Superior, largest freshwater lake in the world, largest of the 5 Great Lakes, located along the United States-Canadian border, with Michigan and Wisconsin on the south, Minnesota on the west, and Ontario on the north. It is 350 mi (563 km) long, 160 mi (257 km) wide, and up to 1,333 ft (406 m) deep. An important waterway for shipping, it connects to the Atlantic Ocean through the St. Lawrence Seaway, and to the Gulf of Mexico through the Great Lakes and the Mississippi River.
See also: Great Lakes.

Lake Tahoe, deep glacial lake on the California-Nevada border. It is 22 mi (35 km) long, 12 mi (19 km) wide, and up to 1,640 ft (500 m) deep. Its waters flow into the Truckee River and on to Pyramid Lake. It is a popular tourist resort offering fishing, boating, waterskiing, and hunting.

Lake Tana, major water source for the Blue Nile River, located in northwestern Ethiopia. Its blue color comes from the lake's silt-free water. It is 47 mi (76 km) long and 44 mi (71 km) wide, and lies 6,000 ft (1,800 m) above sea level.

Lake Tanganyika, longest freshwater lake in the world (420 mi/680 km), located in the Great Rift valley between Tanzania and Zaire in east central Africa. The lake has depths to 4,708 ft (1,435 m).

Lake Texoma, one of the largest artificially created lakes in the United States, formed by the Denison Dam and located along the Texas-Oklahoma border. The dam was built in 1944 to produce hydroelectric power and control flooding. Lake Texoma provides recreational boating, waterskiing, hunting, and fishing.

Lake Tiberias *see:* Galilee, Sea of.

Lake Titicaca, highest lake in South America, located in the Andes Mountains between Peru and Bolivia. Its altitude of 12,507 (3,812 m) makes it the highest lake in the world to provide large boat transportation. It is 110 mi (180 km) long and 45 mi (72 km) wide, with depths up to 900 ft (270 m). There are 41 islands of varying size throughout the lake. Over 25 rivers empty into the lake, but only the Desaguadero River acts as drainage. The shores have been home to Native American settlements for centuries.

Lake trout *see:* Trout.

Lake Victoria, largest freshwater lake in Africa, located in Tanzania, Uganda, and Kenya; major water source for the Nile River. The lake is 210 mi (337 km) long and 150 mi (241 km) at its widest point. The Owen Falls Dam, constructed on the Nile River to generate hydroelectric power (1954), raised the level of the lake about 3 ft (1 m) to a depth of 270 ft (82 m). Numerous islands rise from the lake, Ukerewe being the largest and most populated. There are several million people living within a 50-mi (80-km) radius of Lake Victoria, making it the most heavily populated area in Africa.

Lake Volta, one of the largest human-made reservoirs in the world, in Ghana, West Africa. Created by the construction of the Akosombo Dam across the Volta River (1965), it is 250 mi (400 km) long and covers 3,275 sq mi (8,482 sq km). Water from the lake is used to produce electric power.

Lake Winnebago, lake in east-central Wisconsin. It is connected to the Fox River, which flows into the lake on the west and leaves at the northwest end. It is the largest lake in the state, measuring about 30 m (48 km) in length and 5 to 10 m (8 to 16 km) in width.

Lake Winnipeg, located in Manitoba, Canada, it is one of the largest lakes in Canada. The lake is 258 miles (416 km) long and ranges from 20 to 60 miles (32 to 97 km) in width. The fisheries on the lake are the most important in Manitoba.

Lake Winnipesaukee, lake in east-central New Hampshire. It lies in a depression caused by glacial activity. It measures almost 70 sq m (180 sq km) and contains 365 islands. During the summer, it serves as a popular recreational spot.

Lake Xochimilco, 5 shallow "floating garden" lakes in Mexico City, Mexico, made by building mud dikes in the original lake

An Uru paddling the traditional reed boat on Lake Titicaca

and seeding them with flowers and vegetables. The gardens thus created are a tourist attraction.

Lakeland terrier, dog originally bred in northern England's Lake District to hunt foxes and protect sheep. The average lakeland has a narrow body, stands 14.5 in (37 cm) at the shoulder and weighs 17 lbs (7.7 kg). It has a wiry coat, a bearded chin, and an upright, docked tail.

Lalo, Édouard (1823-92), French composer. Many of his works were influenced by Spanish music, including *Symphonie Espagnole* (1875) for violin and orchestra, first performed by Spanish virtuoso violinist Pablo Sarasate. Other famous works are the ballet *Namouna* (1882) and the opera *Le Roi d'Ys* (1888).

Procession of Tibetan lamas of the Yellow Cap order

Lamaism, popular term for Tibetan Mahayana Buddhism, which evolved from Indian Buddhism starting in the 7th century A.D. This religion combined intellectual discipline with the ritual of tantric yoga and shamanism. The spiritual and political head of the hierarchy of monks or *lamas* is the Dalai Lama (Tibetan, "oceanic teacher"). He is chosen as a young boy and considered to be the reincarnation of previous lamas and of Avalokitesvara, a *bodhisattva* (spiritually enlightened being who remains on earth to help others achieve enlightenment). The intensely religious society remained unchanged until the Communist Chinese invasion of Tibet (1959), which forced the Dalai Lama into exile.
See also: Buddhism.

Lamarck, Jean Baptiste de Monet, chevalier de (1744-1829), French biologist whose pioneering work in taxonomy (especially that of the invertebrates) led him to formulate an early theory of evolution. Where Darwin was to propose natural selection as a mechanism for evolutionary change, Lamarck theorized that organisms could develop new organs in response to their need for them and that these acquired characteristics could be inherited. His theory is known as Lamarckism.
See also: Biology; Evolution.

Lamartine, Alphonse Marie Louis de (1790-1869), French poet and politician, briefly head of government after the 1848 revolution. His collection *Poetic Meditations* (1820) was a landmark of French Romantic literature and contains the famous poem "The Lake"; lyric evocations of love and nature are underlaid by gentle melancholy and religious feeling. *Harmonies* (1830) and *Jocelyn* (1836) were other poetic works.

Lamb, Charles (1775-1834), English essayist and critic who often wrote under the name "Elia." With his sister Mary Ann Lamb he wrote *Tales from Shakespeare* (1807) for children. His *Essays of Elia* (1823, 1833) contain insightful and humorous personal comments on many subjects. He helped revive interest in Elizabethan drama with *Specimens of English Dramatic Poets* (1808).

Lamb's-quarters, pigweed, or goosefoot (*Chenopodium album*), annual herbaceous plant related to spinach, sugar beets, and chard. The plants, native to Europe, Asia, and North America, grow from 1 to 10 ft (30 cm to 3 m) and have diamond-shaped leaves and groups of small greenish flowers.

Lamentations, book of the Old Testament, traditionally ascribed to the prophet Jeremiah, though this is disputed by modern scholars. It consists of a series of 5 poems (the first 4 are acrostics) lamenting the fall of Jerusalem at the hands of the Babylonians (586 B.C.).
See also: Bible.

Lammergeier, bird belonging to the Old World vulture family and native to the mountain regions of Europe, Asia, and Africa. One of the largest of the vultures, it has a wingspread of 9 to 10 ft (2.7 to 3 m). It is recognized by its dark wings with white streaks, its orange neck and breast, and by the black feathers underneath its bill. It subsists on the flesh of dead animals but is also known to kill live ones.

L'Amour, Louis (1908-1988), popular U.S. novelist who wrote stories about the American frontier, many of which have been adapted for film and television. He is noted for his compassionate treatment of Native Americans and Mexicans and for the authenticity of his historical and geographic detail. Much of his material was drawn from his own travels in the West as well as from the stories told to him by his grandfather. His most popular novels include *Hondo* (1953), *The Daybreakers* (1960), and *The Lonesome Gods* (1983).

Lamp, implement that produces light and usually heat using one of 3 methods: combustion of fats or oils, combustion of gases, or electricity. Fat lamps burn fat, oil, paraffin, or grease utilizing a simple wick that pulls the fuel up to the flame. These were the first lamps, dating from prehistoric times, when they were made of hollowed rocks with grass wicks. Gas lamps, dating from 1792, produce light when air mixes with such gases as natural gas, butane, or acetylene. Electric lamps, developed about 1879, utilize electrical energy by directing it through a glass bulb containing inert gas that charges a tungsten filament.

Lamprey, primitive fish of the Petromyzontidae family, one of the 2 remaining groups of jawless fish (Agnatha), found both in freshwater and in the sea. Its body is eellike, and its round, sucking mouth has horny teeth with which it rasps away at its prey. Many species are parasitic when adult, feeding on the flesh of living fishes. The blind, wormlike, filter-feeding larva is totally unlike the adult.

Lanai *see:* Hawaii.

Lancaster, English royal family. **Edmund Crouchback** (1245-96), second son of Henry III, was first earl of Lancaster (1267); his son **Thomas** (d. 1322) led baronial opposition to Edward II. **John of Gaunt** (1340-99) became duke of Lancaster by marriage in 1362, and his son and grandson became Henry IV (1399) and Henry V (1413). The Lancastrians were deposed by the house of York during the Wars of the Roses (1455-85), which began during the reign of Henry VI, but the heir to Lancaster claims, Henry Tudor, reestablished the line (as the house of Tudor) in 1485, becoming Henry VII.
See also: England.

Lancaster (pop. 422,822), city in southeast Pennsylvania, county seat of Lancaster County. It is located 60 mi (96 km) west of Philadelphia, on the Conestoga River. Lancaster, settled in 1709 by the Amish,

Lammergeier

Moravian, and German Mennonites, is an agricultural, manufacturing, and marketing center. Points of interest include President James Buchanan's home, Wheatland; Mill Bridge Village; and nearby Amish and Mennonite farms.
See also: Pennsylvania.

Lancelet *see:* Amphioxus.

Lancelot, Sir, legendary medieval knight. The son of the king of Brittany, he was taken as an infant to the undersea castle of the Lady of the Lake, who brought him to the court of King Arthur after he had attained manhood. As a Knight of the Round Table, he achieved great fame and fortune, however his passionate involvement with King Arthur's wife, Queen Guenevere, led to scandal and Lancelot's ultimate ruin. During his life he involved himself in the search for the Holy Grail, but his moral flaw prevented him from finding it. The Holy Grail was, however, found by Galahad, Lancelot's illegitimate son—the product of Lancelot's youthful affair with a British Princess. Lancelot was the hero of various medieval romances. He was also a central figure in a series of poems by Alfred Lord Tennyson called *Idylls of the King*.
See also: Arthur, King; Round Table.

Sir Lancelot and Queen Guenevere (from a 15th-century French manuscript)

Lan-chou *see:* Lanzhou.

Land, Edwin Herbert (1909-91), U.S. physicist, inventor, and manufacturer. He invented a material called Polaroid, which provided a cheap and adaptable means of polarizing light (1932), and the Polaroid Land Camera (1947). In 1937 he set up the Polaroid Corporation to manufacture scientific instruments and antiglare sunglasses incorporating Polaroid.

Land Bank, Federal *see:* Farm Credit System.

Landes, Bertha Knight (1868-1943), first female mayor (1926-28) of a major U.S. city. Landes, a Republican, was elected mayor of Seattle, Wash., after serving on the city council (1922-26).

Land-grant colleges, U.S. colleges set up by the Morrill Act of 1862. Congress granted the states federal lands to be sold to establish agricultural, engineering, and home economics colleges. There are some 70 land-grant colleges today, including many state universities.

Landon, Alfred Mossman (1887-1984), U.S. politician. He was governor of Kansas (1933-37) and Republican presidential candidate in 1936. His daughter, Nancy Landon Kassebaum, was elected to the Senate in 1978.

Landowska, Wanda (1877-1959), Polish harpsichord virtuoso, largely responsible for the revival of the harpsichord. Living in Paris (1900-40), she founded the Ecole de Musique Ancienne. In the United States after 1940, she was famous as a performer, teacher, and authority on early music.

Land reform, governmental redistribution of land ownership, the purpose of which is to lessen the personal wealth, power, and political influence accorded those with large land holdings. Land reform is usually utilized at times of social or political unrest to more fairly distribute land, particularly farmlands, to those with little or no land of their own. The recipients of land are often given technical training, favorable financing, and low tax rates.

Land's End, England's westernmost point of land, located in Cornwall. Land's End, a turf-covered headland of granite cliffs 60-100 ft (18-30 m) high, juts into the English Channel, near the Atlantic Ocean, and is surrounded by rocky shores and hazardous reefs.

Landsteiner, Karl (1868-1943), Austrian-born U.S. pathologist. He was awarded the 1930 Nobel Prize for physiology or medicine for discovering the major blood groups and developing the ABO system of blood typing. He also contributed to the identification of the Rh factor.
See also: Blood type; Rh factor.

Lanfranc (d. 1089), archbishop of Canterbury (1070-89). He appointed reforming Norman bishops, enforced clerical celibacy, and strengthened the monasteries. As a scholar he helped shape the doctrine of Transubstantiation, writing *Concerning the Body and Blood of the Lord* (c. 1059).
See also: Church of England.

Lang, Andrew (1844-1912), Scottish writer and scholar. He explored folklore in *Custom and Myth* (1884) and *Myth, Literature, and Religion* (1887), and published translations of Homer, fairy tale collections, poetry, and historical works.

Lang, Fritz (1890-1976), Austrian-U.S. film director. He first established himself as a leading director of expressionist silent films, including *Metropolis* (1926), a bleak futuristic drama. In *M* (1931), a sound film about a child murderer, Lang explored the psychology of evil. After emigrating to the United States in 1933, he created such Hollywood films as *Fury* (1936), *Clash by Night* (1952), and *Beyond a Reasonable Doubt* (1956).

Scene from Fritz Lang's *Metropolis*

Lange, David Russell (1942-), New Zealand's prime minister from 1984-89. He received a law degree at the University of Auckland and has been active in politics since 1976.

Lange, Dorothea (1895-1965), U.S. documentary photographer. Her powerful, stark pictures of Depression victims, migrant workers, and the rural poor greatly influenced photo-journalistic technique. In 1939 she published *An American Exodus*.

Langland, William (1332-1400), presumed poet of *The Vision of Piers Plowman*, a religious allegory representing a dream-vision of the Christian life and a satire, one of the finest examples of Middle English alliterative verse.

Langley, Samuel Pierpont (1834-1906), U.S. astronomer, physicist, and meteorologist. He invented the bolometer, which measures radiant energy (1878), and an early heavier-than-air flying machine. His most important work was in the investigation of the sun's role in bringing about meteorological phenomena.
See also: Astronomy, Bolometer.

Langmuir, Irving (1881-1957), U.S. physical chemist awarded the 1932 Nobel Prize for chemistry for his work on thin films on solid and liquid surfaces (particularly oil on water), giving rise to the new science of surface chemistry.

Langton, Stephen (c. 1155-1228), English cardinal and theologian whose appointment as archbishop of Canterbury (1207)

led to a quarrel between Pope Innocent III and King John. Langton led opposition to the king, and his is the first signature on the Magna Carta.
See also: Magna Carta.

Langtry, Lillie (Emily Charlotte Le Breton; 1853-1929), English actress. Known, because of her birthplace (Jersey, Channel Islands), as the Jersey Lily. In 1881 she made a sensation by being the first society woman to go on the stage, making her debut at the Haymarket Theatre, London, in *She Stoops to Conquer.*

Language (from Latin *lingua,* "tongue"), means by which humans express themselves vocally and communicate with others. A language subset is part of a language that can be used independently of the rest of the language. Language translation is the process of changing information from one language to another.

Langur, any of various brightly colored, long-tailed monkeys (family Colobidae) of India and Southeast Asia. Langurs have patches of colored skin, crests of hair on the head, bushy eyebrows, and a chin tuft, and some have long, upturned noses, as in the proboscis monkey. Langurs live in troops in forests, where they eat leaves. The entellus, or Hanuman langur, is sacred in India.

Lanier, Sidney (1842-81), U.S. poet and musician. A Southerner who fought in the Civil War (recalled in his novel *Tiger-Lilies,* 1867), he practiced law, and became a professional flutist, writing a study of the interrelation of music and poetry, *The Science of English Verse* (1880). He also published *Poems* (1877).

Lansing (pop. 432,674), capital of Michigan, in the southern part of the state at the junction of the Grand and Cedar rivers. It is an important automobile-manufacturing and transportation center and the trading center of a rich farming area. Lansing was settled c.1837, succeeding Detroit as state capital in 1847. It was chartered as a city in 1859. Michigan State University is in East Lansing.
See also: Michigan.

Lansing, Robert (1864-1928), U.S. international lawyer and statesman. He founded the *American Journal of International Law* (1907), and as secretary of state (1915-20) he concluded the Lansing-Ishii agreement with Japan (1917), reaffirming the Open Door policy toward China.

Lanternfish, deep-sea fish (family Myctophidae) that has numerous light organs along the sides of its body and on its head. Lanternfish are found in both the Atlantic and Pacific oceans. The particular pattern of light identifies sex and species. Lanternfish come to the surface at night to feed on small animals.

Lanthanide *see:* Rare earth.

Lanthanum, chemical element, symbol La; for physical constants see Periodic Table. Lanthanum was discovered by Carl Mosander in 1839. It occurs in the minerals *cerite, bastnasite,* and *monazite* which is the principal source of the element. The metal is prepared by reducing the anhydrous fluoride with calcium. Lanthanum is silvery-white, malleable, ductile, and soft enough to be cut with a knife. Ion-exchange and solvent extraction techniques have led to much easier isolation of the so-called "rare-earth" elements. Lanthanum and its compounds are used in carbon lighting applications, special glasses, hydrogen sponge alloys, and misch metal.

Lanzhou, or Lanchow (pop. 1,460,000), capital city of Gansu Province in northwestern China, on the Huang He River. An industrial and transportation hub, the city produces chemicals and petroleum products and is the center of China's nuclear energy industry.
See also: China.

Laocoön, in Greek mythology, priest of Apollo who warned the Trojan people not to accept the gift of the wooden horse from the Greeks, with whom they had been at war for 10 years. When Laocoön was killed while worshipping, the Trojans took this as a sign of the gods' displeasure with him and brought the horse into Troy. The horse was filled with Greek soldiers, who seized the city.
See also: Mythology; Trojan War.

Laos, officially Lao People's Democratic Republic, Southeast Asian country formerly part of French Indochina. It is bordered by China to the north, Vietnam to the east, Kampuchea to the south and Thailand and Burma to the west. It is a small country (650 mi/1,046 km-long and in places barely 50 mi/81 km-wide).The administrative capital is Vientiane. The total population is over 4,000,000.

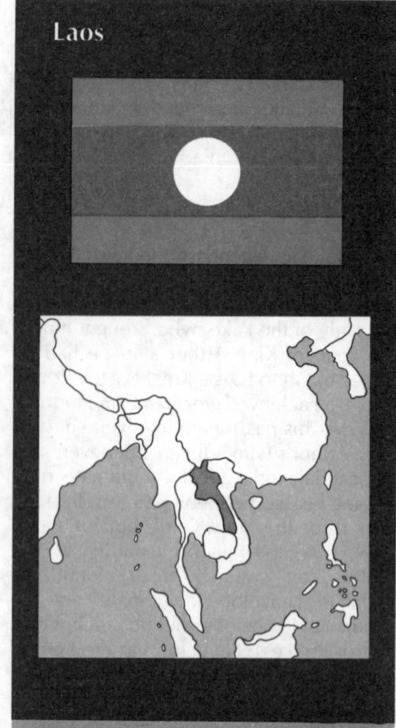

Capital:	Vientiane
Area:	91,400 sq mi (236,800 sq km)
Population:	3,936,000
Form:	people's republic (communist)
Independent:	1953
GNP:	U.S. $710,000,000
Per capita:	U.S. $480

Land and climate. Laos is dominated by mountain chains and plateaus, cut by deep, narrow valleys, covered by forests interspersed with patches of grassland. The Mekong, the river that creates the important Mekong Basin, forms the border with Burma and most of Thailand.

High in the mountains of northern Laos, funeral ceremony for a victim of the Indochinese War

Laos has a tropical monsoon climate, with near-drought from Nov. to Apr. and a wet season from May to Oct.

People. The people of Laos include various ethnic groups, the largest being the Lao, who total over half of the population. Their language, Lao, is the official language. Most practice Hinayana (Theravada) Buddhism. The rest of the population consists of the Kha—original inhabitants of Laos—and mountain tribes, which include the Mons, Thai, Meos and Hos. The education system is poorly developed. There is one university, at Vientiane, the University of Sisavang Vong. Smaller urban areas include Luang Prabang (the royal capital), Pakse and Savannakhet.

Economy. Laos is one of the poorest countries in the world. The people of Laos are mostly primitive farmers who mainly grow rice. Some coffee, corn, hemp, cotton and opium poppies—although illegal—are grown, and the Mekong River and its many tributaries provide fish for local consumption as well as the major means of transportation.

The forests provide good teak and bamboo, charcoal, benzoin (used in perfumes) and stick lac (for shellac). Rich iron ore deposits are known to exist, but only the tin ore is exploited commercially. Industry is on a very limited scale. There are no railways and few reliable roads. There is an international airport at Vientiane.

History. Part of the Khmer empire, the territory was settled from the 10th to 13th centuries by Thai Lao. By the 17th century a powerful Lao kingdom had emerged; but in the early 1700s it split into the principalities of Luang Prabang, Vientiane, and Champasak. In 1893 France made Laos a protectorate. After World War II national insurgency of various factions (including the Communist Pathet Lao with Vietnamese support) won the country independence within the French Union in 1949; it remained in the French Union until 1954. In 1959 renewed civil war between the neutralist premier Souvanna Phouma and right- and left-wing rivals brought intervention from the great powers. A coalition government was formed in 1973. In Dec. 1975 the king abdicated, and the country became a Communist republic under the Pathet Lao, strongly influenced by Vietnam. In 1990 a small guerrilla resistance force took action against the communist government, but the effect was minimal.

Lao Tzu, or Lao Tze (Old Master), legendary Chinese philosopher of the 6th century B.C., said to be the founder of Taoism and the author of *Tao-te-ching.* Tao, or the Way, emphasizes simplicity, naturalness, and spontaneity in life.
See also: Taoism.

La Paz (pop. 881,400), largest city and administrative capital of Bolivia (the legal capital being Sucre). Founded in 1548 by the conquistadors, it is located in the La Paz river valley in western Bolivia. At some 12,000 ft (3,700 m) above sea level, it is the world's highest capital. Local products include cement, glass, textiles, and consumer goods. Lake Titicaca, South America's largest freshwater lake, is a popular tourist attraction of the region.
See also: Bolivia.

Lapland, region in the extreme north of Europe, the homeland of the Lapps (or Finns, as they are called in Norway). Lying primarily within the Arctic Circle, it embraces northern parts of Norway, Sweden, and Finland, and the Kola Peninsula of the USSR, with an area of 150,000 sq mi (388,000 sq km). It has tundra vegetation, with some forest vegetation in the south. Its wildlife, especially the economically important reindeer, were severely hurt by radioactive contamination from the 1986 Chernobyl nuclear disaster.

Lapps *see:* Lapland.

Lapwing, or peewit (*Vanellus vanellus*), shore bird found in Western Europe and the British Isles. The lapwing, named because of its slow, ungainly wingbeat, has an iridescent green-black back, blue-black throat, white belly, and long, wispy, black crest.

Laramie (pop. 24,410), city in southeast Wyoming, county seat of Albany County, and the third largest city in the state. Named after Jacques La Ramie, a French-Canadian trapper, it was settled in 1868 and grew with the onset of railroad, mining, and cattle-producing industries. Laramie is the home of the University of Wyoming.
See also: Wyoming.

Larceny, in law, the unlawful removal of the property of another person without the owner's consent and with intent to steal. Grand larceny, a felony, is generally the theft of valuable property, while petty larceny, usually a misdemeanor, involves less valuable goods. Embezzlement, robbery, and fraud are generally considered larceny.
See also: Crime.

Larch, pine (genus *Larix*) that is unusual in being deciduous rather than evergreen, shedding its needles in winter, becoming completely bare. The several kinds of larch flourish in the Northern Hemisphere as far north as the Arctic Circle. The European larch is a source of turpentine, and several larches, including the tamarack (*L. laricina*), yield a timber that lasts well in water and is used for piers.

Lardner, Ring (1885-1933), U.S. sports journalist and short-story writer. Stories like "You Know Me, Al" (1916), satirize vulgarity and greed in U.S. life. Short-story volumes include *What of It?* (1925) and *Round Up* (1929). With G.S. Kaufman, he wrote the play *June Moon* (1929).

Laredo (pop. 133,239), city in southern Texas, on the Rio Grande River. Laredo, founded in 1755, is a principal port of entry, with one-half the tourists and 60% of the U.S.-Mexico import-export trade passing through its customs stations. Industries include natural gas production, oil refining, clothing manufacture, agriculture, and ranching.
See also: Texas.

Traditional households of Lapland such as this are now rare.

Lares and penates, in Roman mythology, household guardian gods. The lares were godly ancestor figures; the penates were guardians of the storeroom.
See also: Mythology.

Lark, any of a family (*Alaudidae*) of small terrestrial songbirds of Europe, Asia, North America, and Africa. The birds are streaked brown or gray, and feed on insects and seeds, walking or running at great speed along the ground. Larks are known for their beautiful songs, usually delivered on the wing.

Larkspur, any of a genus (*Delphinium*) of flowering plants of the buttercup family, growing mostly in the temperate zones of the Northern Hemisphere. The loosely clustered flowers, which grow on spikes ranging from 1 to 7 ft (30 cm to 2.1 m), have 5 sepals, one of which forms a spur. Larkspurs may be white, blue, or pink.

Lark

La Rochefoucauld, François, Duc de (1613-80), French writer. He is known for his *Memoirs* (1662) of the Fronde, and his *Maxims* (1665), a collection of more than 500 moral reflections and epigrams, generally paradoxical, often pessimistic, usually acute.

La Rochelle (pop. 75,800), French city on the Atlantic coast, capital of the Charente Maritime department. The city, chartered in the 12th century, is a yachting and fishing center. During the persecution of the Huguenots (French Protestants) by the Roman Catholics in the 16th century, La Rochelle was among the 100 communities established by the Edict of Nantes as a haven for Protestants. In 1627 the city was forced to return control to the French government.
See also: France.

LaRouche, Lyndon Hermyle, Jr. (1922-), U.S. political leader and thrice-unsuccessful candidate for the presidency of the United States. In 1948, he began his career with the progressive Socialist Worker's Party, but in the 1970s he began to ally himself with reactionary interests, founding such organizations as the National Caucus of Labor Committees and the National Democratic Policy Committee. In 1989 he was sentenced to 15 years in prison for mail fraud and conspiracy.

Larva, metamorphic stage of development in some animals in which the young are noticeably different in feature and behavior from their parents. Larvae most often occur in the metamorphoses of insects and aquatic animals. The length of the larval phase varies according to species. Examples of larvae are the tadpoles of frogs and toads and the caterpillars of butterflies and moths.

Larynx, specialized organ of the respiratory tract used in voice production. It lies above the trachea in the neck, forming the Adam's apple, and consists of several cartilage components linked by small muscles. Two folds, or vocal cords, lie above the trachea and can be pulled across the airway so as to regulate and intermittently occlude air flow. It is the movement and vibration of these that produce voice.

Laser surgery

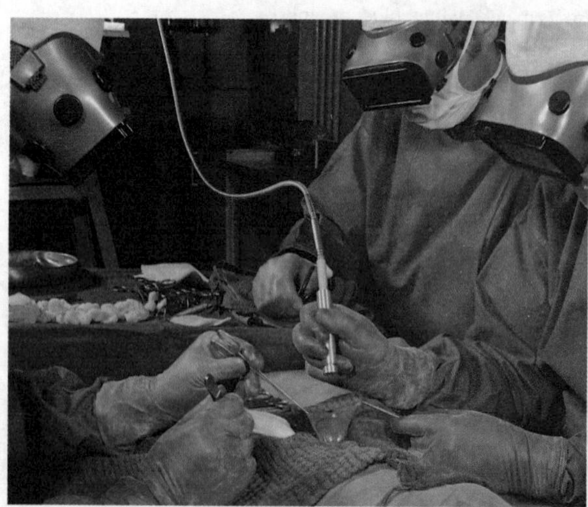

La Salle, Jean *see:* Jean Baptiste de la Salle, Saint.

La Salle, Robert Cavelier, Sieur de (1643-87), French explorer and fur trader in North America who claimed the Louisiana territory for France. In Canada from 1666, he commanded Fort Frontenac, sailed across Lake Michigan (1679), explored the Illinois River, and followed the Mississippi River to its mouth on the Gulf of Mexico. In 1684, sailing to plant a colony there, his fleet was wrecked by storms and Spanish raiders. He was killed by a mutinous crew.

Las Campanas Observatory *see:* Mount Wilson Observatory.

Las Casas, Bartolomé de (1474-1566), Spanish missionary in Central America. He exposed the forced labor of the Indians, persuaded Madrid to enact the New Laws for Indian Welfare (1542), and in his *History of the Indies* recorded data valuable to modern anthropology.

Laser, device that produces an intense beam of light with a precisely defined wavelength. The name is an acronym for "*l*ight *a*mplification by *s*timulated *e*mission of *r*adiation." The light produced by conventional sources travels in all directions. With lasers, the source atoms radiate in step with each other and in the same direction, producing coherent light. Laser beams spread very little as they travel and thus provide high-capacity communication links. They can be focused into small spots and have been used for cutting and welding—notably for refixing detached retinas in the human eye. Lasers also find application in distance measurement by interference methods, in spectroscopy, and in holography.

Laski, Harold Joseph (1893-1950), English political therorist and economist, active in the Fabian Society and the Labour Party. A lecturer at the London School of Economics (1920-50), his books include *Democracy in Crisis* (1933), *Liberty in the Modern State* (1948), and *The American Democracy* (1948).
See also: Fabian Society; Labour Party.

Lassen, Mount, volcano in Lassen Volcanic National Park, northeastern California. The peak rises to an altitude of 10,457 ft (3,187 m). It erupted on May 30, 1914, and again in 1921.

Lasso, Orlando di (1532-94), Flemish Renaissance singer, choirmaster, and composer of a wide range of more than 2,000 sacred and secular works. Orlando di Lasso is the Italian version of his Flemish name, Roland de Lassus.

Last Supper, the final passover meal held by Jesus and his disciples in Jerusalem before his crucifixion. In it he distributed bread and wine to them, instituting the Christian sacrament of Holy Communion. Leonardo da Vinci's well-known fresco of the Last Supper is in Milan.
See also: Jesus Christ; Passover.

Las Vegas (pop. 741,459), city in southwestern Nevada, seat of Clark County. It is renowned for "The Strip," with its casinos (state-legalized gambling), luxury hotels, bars, and nightclubs. The city is also a mining and cattle-farming center. There are artesian springs nearby. It is one of the fastest growing cities in the United States.
See also: Nevada.

Las Vegas

Latakia, or Al-Ladhiqiyah (pop. 234,000), principal seaport city in western Syria, on the Mediterranean Sea, about 110 mi (177 km) north of Beirut. Latakia dates to antiquity, when it was the Phoenician city Ramitha. Exports include tobacco, cotton, bitumen, asphalt, and coffee.
See also: Syria.

Lateran, district of southeastern Rome, given to the church by Emperor Constantine I in 311. The Lateran palace—the papal residence until 1309—was demolished and replaced in the 16th century. The basilica of St. John Lateran is the cathedral church of the pope as bishop of Rome.

Lateran Treaty, concordat between the papacy and the government of Italy, signed 1929 in the Lateran palace and confirmed by the 1948 Italian constitution. It established Roman Catholicism as Italy's state religion and Vatican City as an independent sovereign state.

Latex, milky substance extracted from various plants and trees that serves as the source of natural rubber. Synthetic latex has been used since the 1940s to make paints and coatings. Its properties are hardness, flexibility, toughness, adhesion, color retention, and resistance to chemicals.
See also: Rubber.

Lathrop, Julia Clifford (1858-1932), U.S. social worker, founder of the first U.S. Juvenile Court (1899) and first head of the Children's Bureau of the Department of Labor (1912-21).

Latimer, Hugh (c.1490-1555), English Protestant martyr and Reformation leader. He defended Henry VIII's divorce from Catherine of Aragon, and was made bishop of Worcester in 1535. With Nicholas Ridley, he was burned at the stake as a heretic by order of the Roman Catholic Queen Mary I.

Latin, Indo-European language of the Italic group, language of ancient Rome, and ancestor of the Romance languages. Originating in Latium (about 8th century B.C.), Latin spread with Roman conquests throughout the empire, differentiating into vulgar Latin and classical (literary) Latin. It is a logical and highly inflected language that has furnished scientific and legal terminology and is still used in the Roman Catholic Church. It was the international language of scholarship and diplomacy until the 18th century. About half of all English words are Latin in origin.

Latin America, 33 independent countries and 13 other political entities in Central and South America where Romance languages are spoken: Spanish in most of Latin America; Portuguese in Brazil; and French in Haiti. Sometimes the term includes Guyana, Suriname, and French Guiana in South America, and, less often, also all the Caribbean islands.

People. The population growth of almost 2% per year is one of the highest in the world. The population lives by the Pacific or Atlantic oceans, rivers, or in highland farm areas. The people are of European, African, Indian, and mixed ancestry. After World War II, large numbers of people moved from rural to urban areas in search of employment, and most large cities suffer from overcrowding, pollution, homelessness, inadequate medical services, and high unemployment. The literacy rate varies from less than 50% (Haiti) to more than 90% (Argentina).

Economy. Historically, Latin America economies depended on one export commodity—oil, copper, tin, coffee, bananas, livestock, fish—to earn foreign currency. In several countries there have been efforts at diversification, but economic development is hampered by poor transport, political instability, and burdensome effects of foreign aid. Although about half of the people work on the land, agriculture is mostly primitive and inefficient. Important changes in recent decades include the emergence of Brazil as a leading industrial power, and use of oil revenues in Mexico and Venezuela to finance economic growth. Argentina, Brazil, Mexico and other nations borrowed huge sums from the International Monetary Fund and from private banks, leading to a near-crisis in the 1980s when they were unable to repay their debts.

History. Before the arrival of Columbus in 1492, several highly developed civilizations flourished in the region, most notably the Mayans, Aztecs and Incas. During the conquest the indigenous populations were decimated by war and European diseases. Spanish and Portuguese colonial rule lasted about three hundred years, and by 1825 most of the colonies, inspired by the leadership of Bolivar and San Martin, gained their independence. Power and wealth, however, remained in the hands of tiny minorities, and political life was marked by corruption and instability. In the 20th century, several countries have enjoyed long peaceful periods of constitutional rule while others have experienced military dictatorships, revolution, and violent factional strife.

Latin-American literature, literature of the Spanish-speaking countries of the Western Hemisphere. It also includes Brazil, where the native language is Portuguese, not Spanish. The literary period began with the explorations in the 1400s and lasted some 300 years. The earliest literature was written by soldiers and missionaries describing new lands and civilizations. Hernando Cortés, the conqueror, wrote his *Five Letters* (1519-1526) for King Charles I of Spain, outlining his campaign in great detail. Many works deal with the period of conquest. Bartolomé de las Casas wrote of the brutal treatment of the Indians by the Europeans in *The Devastation of the Indians: A Brief Account* (1552). *La Araucana* (1569-1589) by Alonso de Ercilla y Zúñiga is considered the greatest poem of the time and heralded the bravery of the Chilean Indians in resisting the Spanish invaders.
The ornate baroque style arose in the latter 1600s. The Mexican nun, Sor Juana Ines de la Cruz, wrote plays, satire, philosophical works and poetry in the baroque style.
In the early 1800s, Romanticism, stressing individualism, nationalism and artistic freedom spread to Latin America. Nomadic cowboys called Gauchos became a literary topic. The best example of this is the epic poem *Martin Fierro* (1872-79) by José Hernandez of Argentina. The Romantic period gave rise to the novel. Jorge Issacs of Columbia wrote a sentimental love story *Maria* (1867) that remains popular today. The "noble savage" theme was popular among the romantics who felt that the Indians were superior to the corrupt Europeans. Realist writers, seeking to capture external reality in an objective way, emerged in the 2nd half of the 19th century. The modern period lasted from 1888 to 1910 and Nicaraguan poet Rubén Darió gave it its form. His books of poems *Azul* (1888) marked the beginning of the period. Jose Martí of Cuba was a celebrated journalist, essayist and poet of this period. In the 20th century women poets emerged with work dealing with love and the role of women in society. Gabriela Mistral of Chile won the Nobel Prize for literature (1945). Novels explored social and political problems. The Mexican revolution (1910) inspired Mariano Azuela's novel *The Underdogs* (1916). Poets experimented with form and technique. Vincente Huidobro and Pablo Neruda of Chile, César Vallejo of Peru, Mario de Andrade of Brazil and Jorge Luis Borges of Argentina created poetry with unusual imagery. In the mid 1940s the "new novel," combining authentic subject matter with various themes and experiments, appeared. *The President* (1946) by Miguel Angel Asturias of Guatemala and *The Edge of the Storm* (1947) by Augustín Yáñez of Mexico are well known examples of the new novel. Since the 1950s Latin American novelists have enjoyed international renown. The best known authors of this period are Carlos Fuentes of Mexico; Alejo Carpentier of Cuba, who coined the term "magical realism;" Julio Cortázar of Argentina; Mario Vargas Llosa of Peru; and Gabrial García Márquez of Colombia, who brought the use of realism to its greatest expression in his novel *One Hundred Years of Solitude* (1967), considered by many one of the most important literary works of the 20th century. Márquez was awarded the Nobel Prize for literature in 1982.

Latin literature, all literary works of ancient Romans, written in Latin. Latin literature, beginning as a derivation of Greek literature, and evolving over several literary eras, came to express the nature, politics, and history of the people, and developed into a highly distinctive standard for all written language. Although early Latin literature (240 B.C.) contained translations of the Greek classics, poetry, and drama, much of it has been preserved in the form of comedies. The comedies of Plautus and Terence were based on Greek themes with creative variations. Cato the Elder (f. 160 B.C.) produced the most impressive prose of the early period. He also wrote the first history of Rome in Latin. The early period ended with a new kind of poetry by Gaius Lucilius. The *Satires* of Juvenal are also of this era. The apex, or Golden Age, occurred around the 1st century B.C. Cicero was the most accomplished writer of this period. His literary works are a treasure chest of information about life in Rome. His works on education, philosophy, and oratory have endured throughout the ages as classics. In this period, Julius Caesar wrote his works on the Gallic and Civil Wars. The lyric poetry of Catullus appeared at this time. The reign of the emperor Augustus (27 B.C. to A.D. 14) saw the creation of Vergil's *Aeneid* and *Georgics*. The work of Horace and Ovid also appeared in this era. After the death of Augustus, Roman writers demonstrated new styles. The works of Seneca, Lucan, and Petronius' *Satyricon* are of this era. The *Satyricon* is considered the first Latin novel. Other notable writers are the historian Tacitus and Pliny the Younger. The foundations of Christian Latin literature were laid during the 4th and 5th centuries by church fathers like Augustine, Jerome, and Ambrose.

Latitude, distance from the equator, measured in degrees, of any point on the surface of the earth. The equator is considered 0° latitude; the north pole is 90°N, the south pole 90°S. Lines of latitude run parallel to one another.
See also: Equator; Longitude.

Latium, historic region of Italy, "the cradle of the Roman people," extending from the Tiber River to the Alban Hills. It is now part of the western region of Lazio, and includes the provinces of Rome, Frosinone, Latina, Rieti, and Viterbo.

Latrobe, Benjamin Henry (1764-1820), English-born U.S. architect and engineer. His work includes the southern wing of the Capitol in Washington, D.C., and the Roman Catholic cathedral in Baltimore. A pioneer of the Classical revival, he was the first major professional architect in the United States.

Latter-day Saints, The Church of Jesus Christ of *see:* Mormons.

Latvia

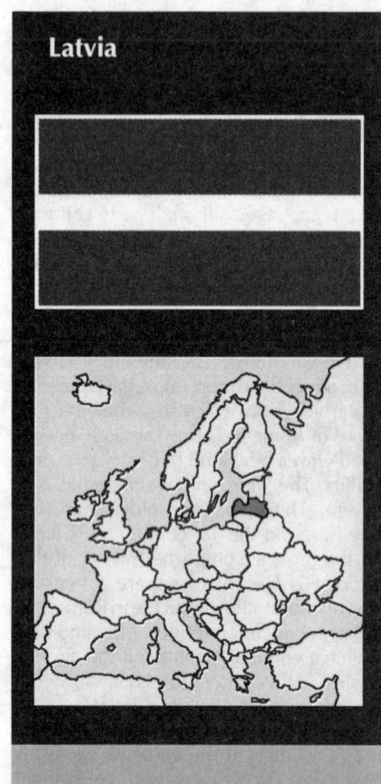

Capital:	Riga
Area:	24,938 sq mi (64,589 sq km)
Population:	2,617,000
Government:	republic
Independent:	1991
GNP:	U.S. $5,080,000,000
Per capita:	U.S. $1,930

Latvia, independent country, bordering on the Baltic Sea, between Estonia, Russia, and Lithuania. Its capital is Riga. It is a lowland country, covering some 24,938 sq mi (64,589 sq km), with a moderate continental climate. Nearly a third of the people are Russians, but the majority are Letts, an ancient Baltic people. Minorities include Byelorussians, Ukrainians, Lithuanians, and Poles. While cattle and dairy farming, fishing, and lumbering are of considerable importance, highly developed industries also exist and include shipbuilding, engineering, and the manufacture of steel, textiles, cement, and fertilizers. Christianized by the German Livonian Knights in the 13th century, Latvia was ruled by Poles, Swedes, and, from the 18th century, Russians. From 1920 to 1940 (when it was reabsorbed into the USSR), it enjoyed a precarious independence. Beginning in the late 1980s, Latvia, together with Lithuania and Estonia, was involved in a sometimes violent struggle for economic self-determination, religious freedom, and autonomy from the central Soviet government. With the collapse of communism in the USSR in 1991 Latvia formally attained independence. After independence Latvia pursued Western political and economic policies, and their relationship with Russia deteriorated.
See also: Union of Soviet Socialist Republics.

Laud, William (1573-1645), archbishop of Canterbury from 1633 and a chief advisor of Charles I. He enforced High Church beliefs and ritual, and his persecution of English Puritans and Scottish Presbyterians provoked parliamentary impeachment (1640). He was executed for treason.
See also: Church of England.

Laudanum *see:* Opium.

Laue, Max Theodor Felix von (1879-1960), German physicist awarded the 1914 Nobel Prize for physics for his discovery of X-ray diffraction in crystals.
See also: Physics; X rays.

Laughing gas *see:* Nitrous oxide.

Laughton, Charles (1899-1962), English-born actor, a U.S. citizen from 1950. Films include the award-winning *The Private Life of Henry VIII* (1933), *The Hunchback of Notre Dame* (1939), and *Advise and Consent* (1962). He directed *Night of the Hunter* (1955).

Laureate *see:* Poet laureate.

Laurel, family (Lauraceae) of evergreen trees and shrubs that grow in the tropics and subtropics. The flowers are inconspicuous and last for only a short time before forming a berry. The classical, or bay, laurel (*Laurus nobilis*), which produces the bay leaf used popularly as a seasoning, is a native of the Mediterranean. It was sacred to Apollo, and its shiny leaves were woven into garlands by the Greeks and Romans. Other laurels include avocado, camphor, cinnamon, and sassafras.

Laurel (pop. 21,897), city in southeast Mississippi, seat of Jones County. Laurel was founded in 1822 to mill and process yellow-pine timber. Other products now include petroleum, canned vegetables, chemicals, electrical parts, and textiles. The Lauren Rogers Museum of Art and the Masonite Corp. are located in Laurel.

Laurel and Hardy, famous comedy team of Hollywood films. The English-born **Stan Laurel** (Arthur Stanley Jefferson; 1890-1965) and the U.S.-born **Oliver Hardy** (1892-1957), thin man and fat man, simpleton and pompous heavy, made over 200 films between 1927 and 1945. Their style, shaped by Laurel, ranged from slapstick to slow-paced comedy of situation and audience anticipation. In the early 1990s several original films were released on videotape.

Laurel and Hardy in Jitterbugs *(1943)*

Laurencin, Marie (1885-1956), French painter and printmaker, designer of textiles, clothing, and stage decorations for the Ballet Russe and the Comédie Française. Her personal style was characterized by simplified images, usually of women, and pastel colors. Works include *The Assembly* (1910) and *In the Park* (1924).

Laurentian Plateau *see:* Canadian Shield.

Laurier, Sir Wilfrid (1841-1919), first French-Canadian prime minister of Canada (1896-1911). Leader of the federal Liberal party (1887-1919), he encouraged provincial autonomy while seeking to unite the country. Many of his attempts to protect the rights of French-Canadians, particularly in education, met with little success.

Lausanne (pop. 117,500), city in western Switzerland, on the north shore of Lake Geneva. An ancient Celtic, then Roman, settlement, it was a bishopric from A.D.590 until 1536, when it was defeated by Bern, which established Protestantism. The Bernese retained power until 1798, and in 1803 Lausanne became the capital of the new Vaud canton. It is a cultural, industrial, and tourist center. The Flon and Louve rivers flow through the city. Historic features include the Cathedral of Notre-Dame (consecrated 1275) and the tower of the former Bishop's Palace, now a history museum.
See also: Switzerland.

Lava, molten rock rising to the earth's surface through volcanoes and other fissures, or the same after solidification. Originating as magma deep below the surface, most lavas are basaltic (subsilicic) and flow freely for considerable distances. Lavas of intermediate silica content are called andesite. Silica-rich lavas, such as rhyolite, are much stiffer.
See also: Volcano.

Laval (pop. 284,200), city in Quebec province, southeastern Canada, part of the Montreal metropolitan area. Covering the island called Ile Jésus, 27 mi (43 km) long and 7 mi (11 km) wide, it is separated from Montreal, to the south, by the Des Prairies River, and from the mainland by the Mille Isles River. An amalgam of 6 former cities and 7 towns, Laval was created in 1965.
See also: Quebec.

Laval, Pierre (1883-1945), French politician who collaborated with the Germans in World War II. A socialist and pacifist, he served as premier (1931-32, 1935-36). Believing that Nazi victory was inevitable, he allowed himself to be installed as a Nazi puppet premier (1942-44). He surrendered to the Allies (1945) and was executed for treason.

Lavender (*Lavandula vera*), shrub of the mint family, cultivated for its aromatic flowers that, along with the leaves, are used for medicinal purposes. Lavender is normally used in the form of an oil derived from the flowers and distilled with water. It is used for flatulence, migraine, headache, fainting, and dizziness. It also has some antiseptic properties and is useful against putrefactive bacteria in the intestines.

Laver, Rod (Rodney George Laver; 1938-), Australian tennis player. He was the first person to win the grand slam (consisting of the Australian Open, the French Open, Wimbledon, and the United States Open) twice (1962, 69). He also played on 4 winning Davis Cup teams and captured 4 Wimbledon titles (1961, 62, 68, 69).

Laveran, Charles Louis Alphonse (1845-1922), French army physician. He won the Nobel Prize in medicine (1907) for his research on protozoa in the generation of tropical diseases. As a surgeon in Algeria (1880), he discovered the malarial parasite and demonstrated its spread by mosquito. He joined the Pasteur Institute in Paris in 1894.
See also: Malaria.

Lavoisier, Antoine Laurent (1743-94), French scientist, foremost in the establishment of modern chemistry. He showed that when substances burned, they combined with a component in the air (1772). In 1779 he named this substance *oxygen* (from Greek *oxys*, "acid"), believing it was a component of all acids. He discredited the phlogiston theory of combustion, proposed a new chemical nomenclature (1787), and published the epoch-making *Elementary Treatise of Chemistry* (1789). In the years before his death on the guillotine, he also investigated the chemistry of respiration, demonstrating its analogy with combustion.
See also: Chemistry.

Law, body of rules governing the relationships between the members of a community and between the individual and the state. In England, the British Commonwealth, and the United States, the law is based upon statute law, or laws enacted by legislative bodies such as Congress, and upon common law, the body of law created by custom and adherence to rules derived from previous judgments. The other main system, civil law, derives from the laws of ancient Rome and relies not on precedent but on a code of rules established and modified only by statute. This is the dominant system in most of Europe and in many other countries of the world.
All major bodies of law break down into 2 divisions, public law and private law. Public law governs matters that concern the state. Private law governs the relationship between individuals (including corporate bodies such as companies).
The first legal system of which we have any detailed knowledge is that of the Babylonian king Hammurabi in 1700 B.C., whose complex code linked crime with punishment and regulated the conduct of everyday affairs. Like the Hebrew Mosaic Law, it treated law as a divine ordinance. The ancient Greeks were probably the first to regard law as made by man for his own benefit. Roman law was based on the Laws of the Twelve Tables, compiled 451-450 B.C. The Romans developed a complex equity system when these principles became outdated; the Byzantine emperor Justinian I produced the last definitive code in an attempt to clear up resulting difficulties. Much medieval law was based on Church law, although an independent system arose quite early in England. This grew into the common law and spread outwards with the growth of the British Empire. Napoleon revised Roman law as the basis for his Code Napoléon, the model for most subsequent civil law codes. U.S. law grew out of the common law, but has been much modified by the federal system.

Law enforcement, method used by the various levels of government to regulate social conduct. Laws, the rules by which society recognizes obedience, are enforced by agencies given public authority to impose penalties or sanctions when they are broken. These agencies are usually a combination of a police force and the courts. In the United States most municipal police forces operate independently of state influence, and city police chiefs are traditionally appointed, while sheriffs, who enforce county laws, are elected to office. The Federal Bureau of Investigation (FBI) maintains an enforcement branch and assists local authorities in federal cases. The International Court of Justice, an agency of the UN with 15 international judges, sits at The Hague, Netherlands, and hears disputes between countries.

Lawn tennis *see:* Tennis.

Law of the land *see:* Due process.

Lawrence, D.H. (David Herbert Lawrence; 1885-1930), English author. He combined a vivid prose style with a solid background of ideas and intense human insight. From a working-class background (reflected in *Sons and Lovers*, 1913), he believed that the Industrial Revolution had resulted in dehumanization. Stressing the supremacy of instinct and emotion over reason in human relationships, he advocated absolute sexual candor; his novel *Lady Chatterley's Lover* (1928) was notorious for this to the exclusion of its other themes. His other novels include *The Rainbow* (1915) and *Women in Love* (1920).

Lawrence, Ernest Orlando (1901-58), U.S. physicist awarded the 1939 Nobel Prize for physics for his invention of the cyclotron and his studies of atomic structure and transmutation.

Lawrence, James (1781-1813), U.S. naval officer. He was captain of the frigate *Chesapeake*, sunk by the British frigate *Shannon* off Boston in 1813. His dying words, "Don't give up the ship!" have become proverbial.

Lawrence, T(homas) E(dward) (1888-1935), called Lawrence of Arabia, English scholar, writer, and soldier, legendary guerrilla fighter with the Arabs against the Turks in World War I. As a British intelligence officer he joined Prince Faisal I in a successful guerrilla campaign against Turkish rail supply lines and was with the Arab forces that captured Damascus in 1918. In *The Seven Pillars of Wisdom* (1918) he described his wartime experiences and his personal philosophy. He joined the Royal Air Force and Royal Tank Corps under assumed names (1923-25, 1925-35).

Lawrence of Arabia *see:* Lawrence, T(homas) E(dward)

Lawrencium, chemical element, symbol Lr; for physical constants see Periodic Table. Lawrencium was discovered by Albert Ghiorso and co-workers in Mar. 1961. It was incorrectly identified as Lawrencium-257, later changed to Lawrencium-258. It was prepared by bombarding a mixed-isotope californium target with boron-10 or boron-11. It has also been prepared by bombarding americium-243 with oxygen-18 ions. It is a metallic element and a member of the actinide series. Lawrencium-261 has a 40 minute half-life. That is the longest of the ten isotopes of the element now known. Lawrencium is the last member of the actinide transition series.

Lawson, Ernest (1873-1939), U.S. impressionist painter. One of the eight members of the Ashcan School, he exhibited at their controversial Armory Show. Seeking a greater degree of naturalism, he specialized in serene landscapes, rendered in glowing colors, such as *Winter* (1914) and *High Bridge* (1939).

Laxative, drug or food taken to promote bowel action and to treat constipation. Laxatives may act as irritants (cascara, senna, phenolphthalein, castor oil), softeners (mineral oil), or bulk agents (bran,

Law courts are often adorned with the personification of Justice as a woman holding a balance scale, as in this 17th-century statue. Usually she is shown blindfolded, to show her impartiality.

T.E. Lawrence

methylcellulose, magnesium sulphate). Laxative abuse may cause gastrointestinal tract disorders, potassium deficiency, and lung disease.

Lazarus, in the New Testament, brother of Mary and Martha of Bethany, who was restored to life by Jesus 4 days after his death (John 11:1-44; 12:1-5); also in the New Testament, beggar at the rich man's gate in a parable (Luke 16:19-25).
See also: New Testament.

Lazarus, Emma (1849-87), U.S. poet best known for the sonnet, "The New Colossus," engraved at the base of the Statue of Liberty. Much of her work is based on Jewish culture, such as the poems *Songs of a Semite* (1882).

Leacock, Stephen Butler (1869-1944), Canadian writer, scholar, and humorist. Although he was a distinguished professor of political science and wrote numerous books on political science, economics, history, and literary criticism, he was perhaps best known for his satiric essays and short stories written in dead-pan style. These humorous works were first published in newspapers and magazines and later appeared in collections. In 1946, his unfinished autobiography, *The Boy I Left Behind Me,* was published posthumously.

Lead, chemical element, symbol Pb; for physical constants see Periodic Table. Lead was known and used by the ancients. It is sometimes found native and occurs in the minerals *anglesite, cerussite, mimetite,* and *pyromorphite.* It is obtained by roasting its most common ore, *galena,* a sulfide, to its oxide and reducing with carbon in a blast furnace. Lead is a silvery, soft, heavy, metal. It is a poor conductor of heat and electricity. The metal has long been used in the lead-chamber process for the production of sulfuric acid. In the decay of uranium, thorium and actinium, a different stable isotope of lead is the end product. Lead and its compounds are used in storage batteries, X-ray shielding, cable sheathing, insecticides, detonators, solders, shot, and type metal.

Lead monoxide *see:* Litharge.

Lead pencil *see:* Graphite.

Leaf insect, Phyllium crunifolium

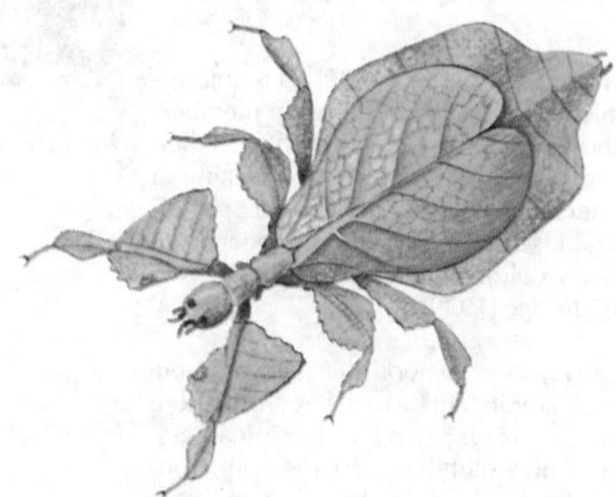

Lead poisoning, cumulative chronic disease caused by excessive lead levels in tissues and blood. Lead may be absorbed in industrial settings, through air pollution due to lead-containing fuels, or, in children, through eating old paint. Brain disturbance, with coma or convulsions, peripheral neuritis, anemia, and abdominal colic are important effects. Chelating agents are used in treatment, but preventive measures are essential.
See also: Lead.

Leadwort *see:* Plumbago.

Leaf, green outgrowth from the stems of higher plants; the main site of photosynthesis. The form of leaves varies from species to species, but the basic features are similar. Each leaf consists of a flat blade or *lamina* attached to the main stem by a leaf stalk or *petiole.* Leaflike stipules may be found at the base of the petiole. The green coloration is produced by chlorophyll, located in the *chloroplasts.* Most leaves are covered by a waterproof covering or *cuticle.* Gaseous exchange takes place through small openings called *stomata,* through which water vapor also passes. The blade of the leaf is strengthened by veins that contain the vascular tissue responsible for conducting water and the substances essential for metabolism through the plant. Leaves may be adapted to catch insects or to reduce water loss. *Bracts,* leaves produced immediately below the flowers, may be highly colored and thus mistaken for flowers (as in the poinsettia).

Leafhopper, about 70 genera and over 700 species of slender, sucking insects of the family Cicadellidae. Leafhoppers may be brilliantly colored, green, or brown, and are 1/20-1/2 in (1.3-12.7 mm) long. They occur worldwide and on almost any type of plant, particularly fruits, grains, sugar beets, and roses. Leafhoppers carry fungus and bacterial diseases and in large numbers may cause severe crop damage.

Leaf insect, any of about 25 species of herbivorous, tropical, usually nocturnal insects of the family Phylliidae, whose green, ribbed, and veined wings and flat shape make them appear leaflike. Leaf insects are 3-4 in (8-10 cm) long and have irregularly shaped bodies.

Leaf miner, name for many species of insect, including flies, moths, wasps, caterpillars, beetles, and weevils, whose larvae infest and feed within leaves. Leaf miners burrow into leaves and other plant parts and leave blotches or tunnels.

Leaf-monkey *see:* Colobus; Langur.

League of Nations, (1920-1946), the first major international association of countries, set up after World War I. The charter, or covenant, was incorporated into the Treaty of Versailles by the War's victors, among them France, Great Britain, Italy, Japan, and the United States. The United States failed to ratify the treaty and join the League. Though the League grew during the 1920s, it was never effective in settling major disputes (e.g., Italy's invasion of Corfu in 1923, Japan's invasion of Manchuria in 1931, Italy's invasion of Ethiopia in 1935). After World War II proved it a failure, the League was dissolved (1946), but its successor, the United Nations, used it as a model.
See also: United Nations; Versailles, Treaty of.

League of Women Voters, nonpartisan organization with about 125,000 members in the United States and Puerto Rico, founded in 1920 by members of the National American Women Suffrage Association. Apart from political education for its members, the league researches and campaigns economic and social issues. It does not sponsor electoral candidates or political parties. Men gained admittance to the organization in the mid-1970s.
See also: Woman suffrage.

Leakey, family name of English archeologists and anthropologists. **Louis Seymour Bazett Leakey** (1903-72) is best known for his findings of hominoid fossils and artifacts, especially in the region of Olduvai Gorge, Tanzania, and for his (sometimes controversial) views on their significance. His wife, **Mary Leakey** (1913-96), collaborated with him. Their son **Richard Leakey** (1944-) continues their work.
See also: Anthropology; Archaeology.

Leander *see:* Hero and Leander.

Leaning Tower of Pisa, white marble bell tower, or campanile, in Pisa, Italy. Building was started in 1174, reputedly by Bonanno Pisano, but the foundations were unsound and the 184.5-ft (56-m) tower had already begun to lean by the time of its completion in the 14th century. It now tilts more than 17 ft (5 m) from the perpendicular.

Leaning Tower of Pisa

Lear, Edward (1812-1888), English artist and writer, best known for his limericks and nonsense rhymes, such as "The Owl and the Pussy-Cat" (1871). His landscapes and illustrated journals are highly regarded.

Learning, the process by which behavior is modified through experience and practice. All animals are capable of learning. Humans far surpass all these in the ability to learn, especially in the ability to acquire a language. Psychologists do not agree about how learning takes place, but certain principles seem clear.

Classical conditioning. The simplest type of learning is the formation of *conditioned reflexes* in this process, an individual learns to associate 2 events, or stimuli, and to respond in the same way to both. During early life, much behavior is learned in this way. A wide range of behavior patterns are conditioned and always occur when the right stimuli are presented.

Instrumental conditioning. Much behavior is learned as a result of random acts that *elicit*, or draw forth, a response. Satisfying *drives*, such as hunger and thirst, are important in this kind of learning. If a particular act reduces the drive, that act will more likely be repeated next time the drive seeks satisfaction. Positive reinforcement—reduction of a drive by a satisfying reward—is usually more effective than negative reinforcement; thus a child who wins approval for performing a task well is more likely to be successful than a child whose "reward" is simply the avoidance of punishment for performing the task badly. Instrumental conditioning is particularly important in the development of acceptable social behavior during the early years of life.

Problem solving and insight learning. There are 2 ways to solve a problem: firstly, by *trial and error* and secondly, by reasoning out a solution, using *insight*. Learning by trial and error is encouraged by presenting the problem a number of times and only rewarding the correct solution. Insight learning involves thinking about the problem and grasping the solution without any trial and error.

Human learning. Many psychologists agree that the upper and lower limits of a person's ability to learn are determined by inherited factors. But related factors such as personality, social background, early childhood experiences and level of motivation make it difficult to predict how well a person will perform. A given amount of time is more effective if distributed over several short sessions. Practice is more efficient if directed toward part of a learning task at a time. Trying to learn 2 similar pieces of information at the same time often leads to confusion between the 2. Actually performing a practical task is better than watching others do it. Activities such as writing down notes will lead to faster learning than just reading about or listening to the facts. Mastering one subject will make it easier to learn a closely related subject. It is easier to remember something if there is a period of inactivity, especially sleep, between learning and attempts to remember.
An especially important aid to learning is knowledge of performances as one is actually progressing with a learning task. This is one advantage of teaching machines, which only move on to a new problem after the student has correctly solved the previous one.

Learning disabilities, conditions or factors that hinder one's comprehension or impairs one's ability to use standard educational tools and methods. An inability to perform in the school environment at the same level as one's peers can be the result of an inherited condition causing mental retardation, a developmental defect, a physical handicap such as impaired hearing or vision or muscle incoordination, an allergy causing hyperactivity, or even a reaction to medications taken to control hyperactivity. Learning problems are first identified through tests that measure reading, writing, and arithmetic performance correlated to age, experience, and family background. One common learning disability is *dyslexia*, the mental reversing of printed letters and inability thus to comprehend the meaning of written text. Its cause can lie in the brain, the eyes, or another part of the body. Writing disabilities frequently come from a lack of coordination between the brain and the muscles. A mathematics disability seems to reflect problems of memory and can exist with or without a reading problem.
See also: Dyslexia; Hyperactive child.

Leather, animal hide or skin preserved by tanning. After the hair, fat, and flesh have been removed from the hides, they are soaked in enzymes for softening, then pickled in acid. The tanned leather is lubricated with oil and resins, and often dyed.

Leathernecks *see:* Marine Corps, U.S.

Leavenworth (pop. 33,656), city in northeastern Kansas, on the Missouri River. The oldest city in the state, it was organized in 1854 by proslavery settlers near Ft. Leavenworth on the Santa Fe Trail. In 1855 it became the first incorporated town in Kansas Territory. Leavenworth is an industrial and marketing center producing wood, meat, and dairy products, structural steel, greeting cards, and mill machinery. It is the site of Leavenworth Prison.
See also: Fort Leavenworth; Kansas.

Lebanon, small republic of about 3 million people in southwest Asia, on the Mediterranean, bordered by Syria on the north and east and Israel on the south. Modern Lebanon is the only Arab State with a large Christian community. The capital is the free port of Beirut. Since the Civil War and subsequent conflicts (beginning in the 1970s), the strong financial and trade industries have weakened as well as other sectors of the Lebanese economy.

Land and climate. Geographically the country can be divided into 4 regions, all more or less parallel to the sea: a flat coastal strip along the Mediterranean, the Lebanon mountain range, the narrow Bekaa (Biqa) Valley, only 10 mi wide and the Anti-Lebanon Mountains of the eastern border. The Bekaa Valley, lying between the 2 major mountain ranges, is the country's most fertile area,though the coastal strip is also entirely fertile. Lebanon is fortunate in having more rainfall and a more moderate climate than most of the neighboring countries. In the past the country was famed for the cedars of Lebanon, which probably covered large tracts of its mountain ranges. Today only a few small cedar groves remain. The capital, Beirut, is a seaport of relatively recent origin. Other important cities are Tripoli (Tarabulus), the ancient Tyre and Sidon along the coast, and Zahle in the interior.

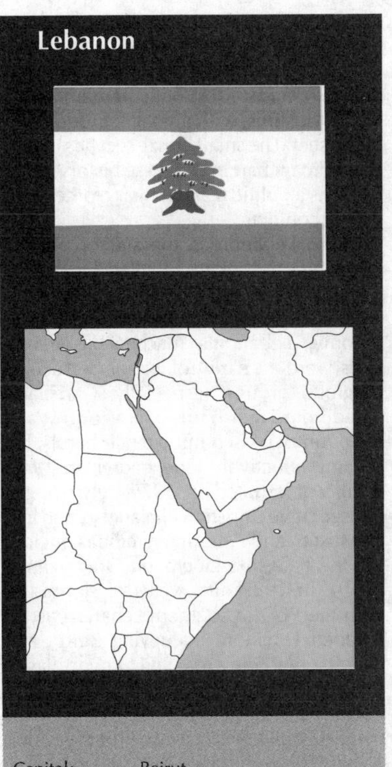

Capital:	Beirut
Area:	4,015 sq mi (10,400 sq km)
Population:	2,897,000
Form:	republic
Independent:	1943
GNP:	U.S. $2,800,000,000
Per capita:	U.S. $1,090

Because Lebanon has limited natural resources, it must exploit its hydro-electric potential. Here, near Tripoli, windmills are used to remove the salt from seawater.

People. The people of Lebanon are of mixed ancestry, but mostly Arab. About 40% are Christians. An Armenian community also exists. Most of the remainder are Sunni Muslims, with a smaller group of the Shi'te sect. The small Druze sect has played a significant part in Lebanese history, especially as a political and military force in the recent conflicts.

History. Lebanon is the site of ancient Phoenicia. Although engulfed by successive invaders—Greek, Roman, Arab and Turkish—it preserved some degree of autonomy. Lebanon's inaccessible mountains were an early refuge for persecuted religious groups, especially Christians. Freed from Turkish rule after World War I, the country passed into French hands, becoming effectively independent in 1943. Civil war erupted in 1975 between the conservative Christian Phalangists and leftist Muslim and Palestinian militias, including the Palestine Liberation Organization (PLO). In 1982 after years of skirmishes with the PLO in southern Lebanon, Israel invaded Lebanon, occupying Beirut and eventually forcing many PLO guerrillas to leave the country. A multinational peacekeeping force, including U.S. marines, arrived (1982) in Beirut, but withdrew within 1 year. The withdrawal was due, in part, to a terrorist attack on U.S. and French compounds which killed over 241 Marines (Oct. 23, 1983). By 1985 Israeli troops also withdrew from all but southern Lebanon. Since 1985 various attempts at ceasefires and political settlements have been made by Syria and other countries involved in the conflict.

Le Carré, John (David John Moore Cornwell; 1931-), English author of novels of international espionage, including *The Spy Who Came in from the Cold* (1963), *Tinker, Tailor, Soldier, Spy* (1974), *The Little Drummer Girl* (1983), and *The Russia House* (1989).

Lecithin *see:* Soybean.

Le Corbusier (Charles-Édouard Jeanneret; 1887-1965), Swiss-born, French-trained architect, a founder of the international style. His austere, rectangular designs of the 1920s and 1930s reflect his view of a house as a "machine to live in." Later influential designs (featuring reinforced concrete) include apartments at Marseilles, a chapel at Ronchamp, and buildings in Chandigarh, India.
See also: Architecture.

Notre-Dame-du-Haut in Ronchamp, a modern cathedral designed by Le Corbusier (1955)

Lederberg, Joshua (1925-), U.S. geneticist awarded (with G.W. Beadle and E.L. Tatum) the 1958 Nobel Prize in physiology or medicine for his work on bacterial genetics. He showed that sexual recombination occurs in bacteria. Later he established that genetic information could be carried by bacterial viruses.
See also: Genetics.

Lederman, Leon Max (1922-), U.S. physicist who was part of a team that won the 1988 Nobel Prize. Together with colleagues Melvin Schwartz and Jack Steinberger, he discovered a new subatomic particle (neutrino) and developed a way of synthesizing neutrinos in the laboratory. Lederman served on the faculty of Columbia University and was an adviser to the Atomic Energy Commission.
See also: Neutrino.

Lee, Charles (1731-82), American major general in the Revolutionary War. He refused orders from George Washington (1776), planned betrayal while in British captivity (1776-78), and retreated at the Battle of Monmouth (1778), robbing Washington of a victory. He was court-martialed and dismissed (1780).
See also: Revolutionary War in America.

Lee, Francis Lightfoot (1734-97), American patriot and revolutionary leader. As a member of the Virginia House of Representatives (1758-76), Continental Congress delegate (1775-79), and a signer of the Declaration of Independence, Lee consistently advocated rebellion against England. He helped draft the Articles of Confederation.
See also: Committees of Correspondence.

Lee, Harper (1926-), U.S. author whose only novel, *To Kill A Mockingbird* (1960), won the Pulitzer Prize for fiction. The novel vividly depicts the racism and prejudice of a small southern town by focusing on the sensitive perceptions of the story's narrator, Finch's young daughter.

Lee, Henry (1756-1818), American cavalry officer in the Revolutionary War (known as "Light Horse Harry") and father of Confederate Civil War general Robert E. Lee. He was governor of Virginia (1791-94) and a representative in Congress (1799-1801).
See also: Revolutionary War in America.

Lee, Richard Henry (1732-94), American Revolutionary statesman. He was a Virginia delegate (1774-79, 1784-87) and president (1784-85) of the Continental Congress. On June 7, 1776, he introduced the motion that led to the Declaration of Independence. He opposed ratification of the U.S. Constitution, fearing its limits on states' rights. As a U.S. senator from Virginia, 1789-92, he helped secure adoption of the Bill of Rights.

Lee, Robert Edward (1807-70), U.S. general and commander of the Confederate Army in the Civil War. His father, Henry "Light-Horse Harry" Lee, was a noted cavalry leader during the Revolutionary War, and 2 other Lees were among the signers of the Declaration of Independence.
During the Mexican War (1846-48), Lee served brilliantly on the headquarters staff. After the war he was appointed superintendent of West Point (1852-55). In 1859 Lee was sent to arrest John Brown and restore order after the raid on Harper's Ferry.
When in 1861 civil war appeared imminent, President Abraham Lincoln offered Lee the post of field commander of the Union forces. Although opposed to slavery and secession, Lee declined out of loyalty to his native state. He accepted a post in the Confederate Army and for a year served as military adviser to Confederate President Jefferson Davis. In May 1861 he was made a full general and in June 1862 was given command of the Army of Northern Virginia.
Lee's first great success was the defense of Richmond in the Battles of the Seven Days (June 26-July 2, 1862), in which he neutralized superior Union numbers and forced retreat. After the Confederate victory at the second Battle of Bull Run, Lee invaded Maryland but was halted at Antietam, one of the bloodiest battles of the war, and withdrew to Virginia. At Chancellorsville (May 1863) Lee overcame a 2-to-1 troop disadvantage by dividing his forces and forcing the Union army to retreat. Lee again invaded the North and met the Union forces at Gettysburg, Pa. (July 1863).
During the Wilderness campaign (May-June 1864) and the siege of Petersburg (July 1864), superior Northern numbers and resources battered the exhausted Confederate Army. On Apr. 9, 1865, Lee surrendered to Grant at Appomattox Court House, Va. Lee's mastery of maneuver, his skills in communication, and his ability to inspire devotion in his men had delayed but could not prevent the Union victory. After the war, Lee became president of Washington College (later renamed Washington and Lee University), a post he held until his death.
See also: Civil War, U.S.

Leech, annelid (segmented) worm (class Hirudinea) with a prominent attachment sucker at the posterior end and another sucker around the mouth. Leeches are hermaphroditic. Freshwater or semiterrestrial animals, they feed by sucking the blood or other body fluids of mammals, small invertebrates, worms, insect larvae, or snails.

Leechee *see:* Litchi.

Leeds (pop. 710,900), city in western Yorkshire, northern England. A weaving town in the Middle Ages, it remains a major center for textiles and clothing, particularly woolens. Other industries include electronics, machinery, chemicals, aircraft, vehicles, and food products. On the River Aire, Leeds has canal links to both coasts,

and the Yorkshire coal fields lie nearby. It is the site of Leeds University as well as the 12th-century Kirstall Abbey ruins and Temple Newsom, once a mansion of the Knights Templar.
See also: England.

Leek (*Allium porrum*), relative of the onion, originating in the Middle East. This biennial plant is now cultivated throughout Europe and is the national plant of Wales.

Lee Kuan Yew (1923-), prime minister of Singapore since 1959. A labor attorney, Lee helped establish the People's Action Party (1954), and during his years in office has helped the country achieve political independence and a strong economy.
See also: Singapore.

Lee Teng-hui (1923-), Taiwanese politician who became interim president of Taiwan in 1988 as a result of the death of President Chiang Kai-shek. He had formerly served as a member of the Joint Committee on Rural Reconstruction (1957-61). He was mayor of Taipei (1978-81), governor of Taiwan province (1981-84), and vice president of Taiwan (1984-88).

See also: Taiwan.

Leeuwenhoek, Anton van (1632-1723), Dutch microscopist who made important observations of capillaries, red blood corpuscles, and sperm. He is best known for being the first to observe bacteria and protozoa (1674-6), which he called "very little animalcules."
See also: Microscope.

Leeward Islands, chain of about 15 islands and many islets in the West Indies, northernmost group of the Lesser Antilles. They include Antigua, Anguilla, Montserrat, and the British Virgin Islands (British colonies); St. Kitts-Nevis (a former British colony, independent since 1983); St. Eustatius, Saba, and St. Martin (Dutch); Guadeloupe and dependencies (French); and the U.S. Virgin Islands.

Léger, Fernand (1881-1955), French painter. A cubist, he used strong colors and geometrical shapes and introduced industrial images like cogwheels and pistons. His preoccupation with the machine age may be seen in paintings like *The City* (1919). He designed a mural for the United Nations General Assembly auditorium in New York City (1952).

Legion, principal unit of the Roman army, having between 3,000 and 6,000 infantry with attached cavalry. By the 1st century B.C. the cohort, composed of 6 companies, was the tactical unit. There were 10 cohorts to a legion. The leader of a legion was a legate or a consul. Soldiers of the Roman Empire were recruited to a legion for a term of 20 to 25 years.

Legion, American *see:* American Legion.

Legion, Foreign *see:* Foreign Legion.

Legionnaires' disease, severe lung infection. Legionnaires' disease appeared in 1976 when 182 delegates attending an annual convention of the American Legion in Philadelphia contracted a severe respiratory infection. Of 147 of those hospitalized, 90% developed pneumonia and 29 died. All had stayed in, or visited, the same hotel during the 4-day convention. Five months later, the organism responsible, a small Gram-negative, non-acid-fast bacillus, was isolated from the lung tissues of 4 fatal cases, and was subsequently named *Legionella pneumophila.* It is now clear that the organism is a significant respiratory pathogen, in both the United States and Western Europe.
After an incubation period of 2 to 10 days, the illness begins with symptoms of malaise, headache, and muscular aches and pains, succeeded in a few hours by high fever and shivering. A dry cough, or a cough producing small amounts of blood-stained sputum, begins on the second or third day, with pleurisy (inflammation of the pleura, the membrane covering the lungs) a common occurrence. Watery diarrhea with abdominal distention, occurring in around 50% of the sufferers, may precede the onset of fever. The antibiotic erythromycin is the most effective treatment for the disease.

Legislature, representative assembly empowered to enact, revise, or repeal the laws or statutes of a community. The earliest modern legislatures were the British Parliament and the French States-General, which were forerunners of the contemporary bicameral system of upper and lower houses. In the United States the 2 chambers are the Senate and the House of Representatives, which together are called the Congress. In most bicameral systems both chambers must approve a bill before it becomes law. Under a parliamentary system, like Britain's or Canada's, the prime minister, who heads the government, remains in power only as long as his or her party retains a majority in the main legislative chamber. Under the U.S. system, the president's stay in office is independent of the majority party in the legislature.

Legume, any of nearly 17,000 species of plant of the pulse or pea family (Leguminosae) including peas, beans, lentils, soybeans, and peanuts, fodder plants such as clover, alfalfa, and cowpeas, and hardwoods such as ebony, locust, mahogany, and rosewood. Legumes are widely distributed and variable in growth. The species are distinguished by their flowers, usually bilaterally symmetrical blooms, and by their fruits, seed pods with 2 splitting sides.

Lehár, Franz (1870-1948), Hungarian composer of Viennese-style light opera. His works include the melodious operetta *The Merry Widow* (1905).

Le Havre (pop. 199,400), French seaport on the English Channel and the Seine River. It is a transatlantic trade center that manufactures and imports ships, automobiles, electronics, petroleum products, steel, chemicals, sugar, flour, and beer. A fishing village before 1516, when Francis I began the harbor construction, Le Havre lost 80% of its buildings in World War II. The city was subsequently rebuilt, and the harbor was renovated and expanded in the 1970s.
See also: France.

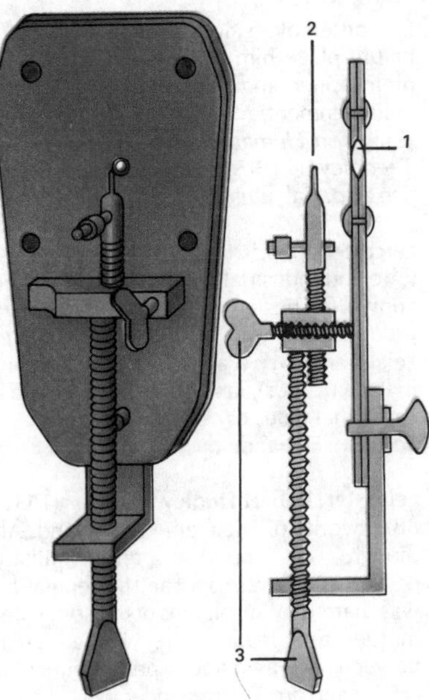

Anton van Leeuwenhoek's microscope. The lens (1) was mounted between 2 plates. The specimen (2) was mounted on the point and brought into focus by 2 screws (3).

Lehmann, Lotte (1888-1976), German-born U.S. soprano. She sang with the Vienna State Opera (1914-38) and in the United States at the Metropolitan (1934-45). Famous for her portrayal of the Marschallin in *Der Rosenkavalier*, she created roles in other Richard Strauss operas and was a skilled interpreter of lieder.

Lehmbruck, Wilhelm (1881-1919), German sculptor noted for his images of pathos and heroism of spirit. Influenced by Rodin, Brancusi, and Maillol, he depicted his human subjects as ascetic, angular figures, such as *Standing Woman* (1910) and *Kneeling Woman* (1911).

Lehn, Jean-Marie (1939-), French chemist and university professor who was part of a team that won the 1987 Nobel Prize for chemistry. Along with Americans Donald James Cram and Charles John Pedersen, Lehn created an artificial molecule that transmits signals to the human brain.
See also: Chemistry.

Leibniz, Gottfried Wilhelm von (1646-1716), German philosopher, historian, jurist, geologist, and mathematician, codiscoverer of the calculus, and author of the theory of monads. His discovery of the calculus was independent of, though later than, that of Sir Isaac Newton; it is the Leibnizian form that predominates today. He devised a calculating machine and a symbolic mathematical logic. His concept of the universe as a "preestablished harmony," his analysis of the problem of evil,

Gottfried Wilhelm Leibniz

his epistemology, logic, and philosophy of nature place him in the foremost rank of philosophers and helped mold the German Enlightenment. His writings include *New Essays on Human Understanding* (1704), *Theodicy* (1710), and *Monadology* (1714).
See also: Calculus.

V.I. Lenin, Moscow, 1919

Leicester (pop. 281,100), important historic and industrial city in central England known for hosiery, shoes and machinery products. It is the site of the University of Leicester, Jewry Wall (built by the Romans in the A.D. 100s), landmark churches and a castle that dates back to the 1100s.
See also: England.

Leicester, Robert Dudley, Earl of (1532-88), favorite of Elizabeth I of England. Although his political and military performances were poor and his reputation was marred by suspicions of treason, wife-murder and bigamy, he wielded great power and was made a privy councillor (1558) and army commander.

Leiden, or Leyden (pop. 103,800), city in western Netherlands, center for science and light industry, particularly printing and textiles. It is the seat of Leiden University (est. 1575), the oldest in the Netherlands and important for Protestant theology and scientific research. Leiden is noted for its museums, laboratories, and botanical gardens. It was Rembrandt's birthplace and home to some of the English Pilgrims from 1609 until they sailed for the New World in 1620.
See also: Netherlands.

Leipzig(pop. 554,600), city in eastern Germany, former capital of Leipzig district. A major cultural, commercial, and manufacturing center, it has fine medieval and renaissance architecture. Composers J.S. Bach, Felix Mendelssohn, and Robert Schumann were active in the city.
See also: Germany.

Le Mans (pop. 147,700), city in northwestern France on the Sarthe and Huisne rivers, dating from pre-Roman times. A diocese from the 3rd century, Le Mans was invaded by the English in the Hundred Years War (1337-1453) and was the site of important battles in the French Revolution (1793). It is a marketing and industrial center, and is best known for its 24-hour annual sports car competition on 8 mi (13 km) of winding road.
See also: France.

Lemming

Lemming, Arctic rodent, about 3-6 in (7-15 cm) in length, closely related to the vole. Genera include *Lemmus* and *Dicrostonyx*. Like many small mammals of simple ecological systems, lemmings show periodic fluctuations in numbers. These 3- to 4-year fluctuations result in spectacular mass migrations in search of food. One species, *L. lemmus*, is particularly noted for migrations that lead many members to accidental drowning in the ocean.

Lemon (*Citrus limon*), small evergreen tree that produces sour yellow fruits that are rich in vitamin C. The fruits also contain an oil that is used in cooking and the manufacture of perfume. The United States and Italy are chief producers of lemon fruit.

Lemur, family of cat-sized primates found only on Madagascar and small islands nearby, related to primitive ancestors of the whole primate group of monkeys and apes. They are nocturnal and strictly arboreal, feeding on insects, fruit, and even small mammals. The family Lemuridae includes 2 subfamilies: the Cheirogaleinae, or mouse lemurs, and the Lemurinae, true lemurs.

Lendl, Ivan (1960-), Czechoslovakian-born U.S. tennis player. Known for his power and consistency, Lendl held the number one ranking from 1985 to 1987. His achievements include victories at the United States Open (1985, 86, 87), the French Open (1984, 86, 87) and the Australian Open (1989, 90).

Lend-lease, program by which the United States sent aid to the Allies in World War II, during and after neutrality. President Franklin D. Roosevelt initiated the program in 1941 to help countries "resisting aggression." Total aid exceeded $50 billion and not only bolstered Allied defense but developed the U.S. war industries and helped mobilize public opinion.
See also: World War II.

L'Enfant, Pierre Charles (1754-1825), French-American engineer and architect who fought in the Revolutionary War and was commissioned (1791) to plan Washington, D.C. Because of opposition his plans were shelved, but in 1901 they became the basis for the development of the capital. L'Enfant also designed Federal Hall in New York City.
See also: Architecture.

Lenin, V.I. (1870-1924), Russian revolutionary, founder of the Bolshevik (later Communist) Party, leader of the Bolshevik Revolution of 1917, and founder of the Soviet state. Born Vladimir Ilyich Ulyanov, Lenin become a revolutionary after his older brother was executed (1887) on charges of plotting to assassinate the tsar. By then a follower of the ideas of Karl Marx, Lenin was arrested and exiled to Siberia in 1895. In 1900 he and his wife, Nadezhda Krupskaya, went into exile in western Europe. In 1902 he published his famous pamphlet *What is to Be Done*? arguing that only a highly disciplined party of revolutionaries could cause the overthrow of the tsar. In 1903 the Russian Social Democratic Workers Party, meeting in London, split over this and related issues. Lenin's supporters became known as the Bolsheviks (from the Russian word for "majority"); his opponents were called Mensheviks (from "minority"). Lenin and his fellow Marxists returned briefly to Russia during the unsuccessful revolution of 1905. In 1907 he went into exile again. When the tsar was overthrown by the Feb. 1917 revolution, in the midst of World War I, Lenin returned to Russia. Reacting against the rush of Socialist parties in Europe to support their own governments in World War I, he issued a call for the formation of a new revolutionary international organization. In Oct. 1917 the Bolshevik Party, under the leadership of Lenin and Leon Trotsky, seized power in Russia at the head of a popular insurrection, and Lenin became the head of the new, Soviet state. The revolutionary organization he had called for came into being as well, as the Communist International.
Lenin led the revolutionary state for its first 6 years, a period that saw the civil war and the nationalization of industry. With the end of the civil war in 1921 he turned to a more liberal economic approach, known as the New Economic Policy. This allowed some development of private enterprises, especially in the countryside. At the same time, however, his government banned all opposition parties. Considerable state resources were devoted to the Communist International and to attempts to foster other revolutions in other countries, especially in Europe. In the late months of 1923 Lenin began warning about the rising bureaucratization of the state and about the growing ambition of Stalin. In Jan. 1924, however, before any of those warnings would be acted on, he died from a series of strokes.
Lenin had a greater influence on communism than anyone else except Karl Marx. In fact, after his death the theory of communism came to be called Marxist-Leninism. His major contribution to the political doctrine was his concept of the revolutionary party, and he was the first to implement that concept successfully. In that sense he was one of history's greatest revolutionaries and one of the most influential political leaders of the 20th century.
See also: Russian Revolution; Union of Soviet Socialist Republics.

Leningrad (pop. 4,295,000), second largest city and chief port of the USSR, on the Gulf of Finland, and former Russian capital (as St. Petersburg, 1712-1914, and Petrograd, 1914-24). It was founded in 1703 by Tsar Peter I (Peter the Great). Linked by its port with western Europe, it rapidly became a

cultural and commercial center. Industrial expansion during the 19th century was followed by a temporary decline during World War I and the Russian Revolution. The city was renamed for V.I. Lenin in 1924. Leningrad endured great destruction and loss of life in the German siege (1941-44) during World War II. Today industries include heavy machinery manufacturing, shipbuilding, chemicals, and textiles. The city is home to the University of Leningrad, one of the USSR's largest universities; the Hermitage, a world-renowned museum, and the Conservatory of Music, whose graduates include the composers Sergei Prokofiev and Peter Ilich Tchaikovsky. Leningrad has figured in the writings of Russian authors Alexander Pushkin and Fyodor Dostoevsky.
See also: Union of Soviet Socialist Republics.

Lennon, John (1940-1980), rock musician, a founding member of the Beatles. Along with Paul McCartney he wrote most of the Beatles' music, including "Help" (1965), "Strawberry fields" (1966) and "A Day in the Life" (1967). As a social critic he wrote "Give Peace a Chance" (1969) and "Imagine" (1971). Lennon married Yoko Ono in 1969 and continued to compose and sing after the Beatles disbanded (1970). He was shot to death on Dec. 8, 1980 by Mark David Chapman.
See also: Beatles, The.

Lenoir, Jean Joseph Étienne (1822-1900), French inventor. He built the first practical internal combustion engine for use in industrial machinery and one of the first gas-powered automobiles (1862). He also invented a railroad brake (1855) and a motorboat (1886).
See also: Internal combustion engine.

Le Nôtre, André (1613-1700), French landscape architect. Under Louis XIV, his strictly geometrical creations, including the gardens of Versailles and the Tuileries, featured splendid vistas and radiating paths.
See also: Architecture.

Lens, transparent substance, usually glass, having 2 opposite surfaces, either both curved or one curved and one straight, used for refraction, (changing the direction of light rays). Lenses are used in eyeglasses to correct errors of vision, in cameras to focus images on film, and in microscopes and telescopes to magnify images. The term is also used for the part of the eye that focuses light rays on the retina.

Lent (from Old English *lencten*, "spring"), period of 40 days dedicated by Christians to penitential prayer and fasting as a preparation for Easter. In the West it begins on Ash Wednesday.
See also: Christianity; Easter.

Lentil (*Lens culinaris*), leguminous plant grown in warm parts of the Old World. It was one of the first cultivated crops. The seeds, which are rich in proteins, are cooked as porridge or soup. The mess of potage for which Esau sold his birthright (Genesis 25-28) was made from lentils.

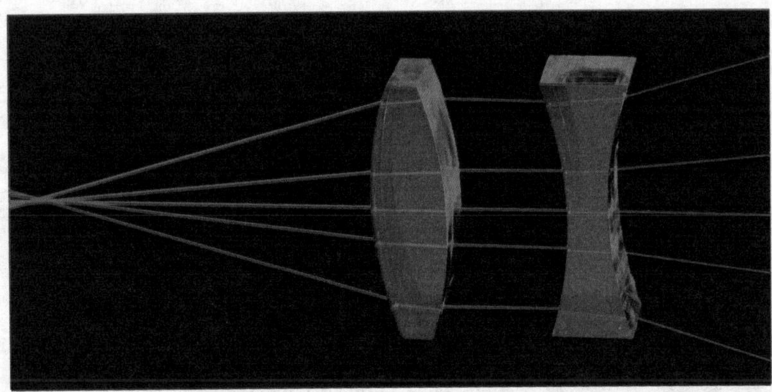

Lenses are used to control laser beams as well as normal light beams. The beams converge when passed through a convex lens (left), diverge when passed through a concave lens (right).

Lenya, Lotte (1900-81), Austrian-born U.S. singer and actress. She performed on the stage in Berlin (1920-33), notably in *The Three-Penny Opera* (1928), composed by her husband, Kurt Weill, in collaboration with Brecht. She sang and acted in several Weill works, including *Mahogonny* and *Cabaret,* in the United States after 1933.

Leo, name of 13 popes. **Saint Leo I** (c. 400-461), an Italian, r. 440-461. Called "the Great," he suppressed heresy and established his authority in both the West and East. He persuaded the barbarian leaders Attila (in 452) and Genseric (in 455) not to destroy Rome. **Saint Leo III** (d. 816), a Roman, r. 795-816. He crowned Charlemagne "Emperor of the Romans" in Rome on Christmas Day, 800, thus allying church and state. **Saint Leo IX** (Bruno of Egisheim; 1002-1054),a German, r. 1049-54. He fought against simony (the selling of church offices) and vigorously enjoined clerical celibacy. The Great Schism between the Western and Eastern churches began in his reign. **Leo X** (Giovanni de Medici; 1475-1521), a Florentine, r. 1513-21. He made Rome a center of the arts and literature and raised money for rebuilding St. Peter's by the sale of indulgences—a practice attacked by Martin Luther at the start of the Reformation. **Leo XIII** (Gioacchino Pecci; 1810-1903), an Italian, r. 1878-1903. He worked to reconcile Roman Catholicism with science and liberalism and generally applied Christian principles to the religious and social questions of his time. His *Rerum Novarum* (1891), an encyclical (letter to the Roman Catholic Church) on the condition of the working classes, strengthened Roman Catholicism's links with the working-class movement and helped counter anticlericalism at home and abroad.

León, medieval kingdom of northwestern Spain, including the provinces of León, Salamanca, and Zamora. Forged in the 10th century by the rulers of Austria, the kingdom spearheaded the Christian reconquest of Spain from the Moors. It was permanently joined to Castile in 1230.

Leonard, Sugar Ray (Ray Charles Leonard; 1956-), U.S. boxer. He was the Olympic gold medalist in the light welterweight class (Summer Games, 1976), and won the World Boxing Council (WBC) welterweight title (1979) and World Boxing Association (WBA) junior middleweight title (1981). After suffering a detached retina Leonard retired (1982) but staged a comeback, capturing the WBC middleweight title (1987) and WBC super middleweight and light heavyweight titles (1988). He retired again in 1991.

Leonardo da Vinci *see:* Da Vinci, Leonardo.

Leoncavallo, Ruggiero (1858-1919), Italian opera composer. *I Pagliacci* (The Clowns, 1892), a classic *verismo* (realistic) opera, is the only one of his works that is still widely known.
See also: Opera.

Leonidas I (d.480 B.C.), king of Sparta. Leonidas, with 300 Spartans and about 1,000 other Greeks, died heroically defending the pass of Thermopylae against the huge invading Persian army of Xerxes.
See also: Sparta; Thermopylae.

Leopard (*Panthera pardus*), big cat similar to the jaguar, with a yellow coat marked with black rosettes, or with black fur (the panther). Found in a variety of habitats across Africa and Asia, it is agile and relies when hunting on its power to spring quickly. The leopard is known for its habit of dragging its kill up into a tree out of the reach of jackals and hyenas. The kill may weigh more than the leopard itself.

Leopard cat *see:* Ocelot.

Leopardi, Giacomo, (1798-1837), Italian poet and philosopher, foremost writer of his time. Acutely unhappy, he expressed himself most fully in his brilliant, supple, lyric poetry: *Songs* (1836). *Moral Essays* (1827) reveals his bleak philosophy.
See also: Philosophy.

Leopold, Aldo (1886-1948), American outdoors enthusiast, naturalist, and conservationist. His writings include *Game Management* and *A Sand County Almanac*. An employee of the U.S. Forest Service (1909-27), he later held a faculty position at the University of Wisconsin.

Léopoldville *see:* Kinshasa.

Lepidoptera *see:* Butterfly; Moth.

Leprosy, or Hansen's disease, chronic infectious disease caused by *Mycobacterium leprae* and chiefly found in tropical zones. It leads to skin nodules with loss of pigmentation, mucous membrane lesions in nose and pharynx, and neuritis with nerve thickening, loss of pain sensation, and patchy weakness, often involving face and hand muscles. The type of disease caused depends on the number of bacteria encountered and basic resistance to the disease. Treatment is with sulfones.

Lepton, one of the 4 classes of elementary particles (the others are bosons, measons, and baryons). Leptons are larger than the massless bosons, but smaller than mesons and baryons. There are a total of 12 particles in the lepton class, of which the electron is probably the most familiar. These 12 come in pairs, one of each pair being positively charged, the other being negatively charged. (The positron is the positively charged mate of the electron, which is negative.)
See also: Particle physics.

Lerner, Alan Jay (1918-86), U.S. lyricist and dramatist. Along with the composer Frederick Loewe, he created such musical comedies as *My Fair Lady*, *Brigadoon*, *Paint Your Wagon*, and *Camelot*. Lerner and Loewe won an Academy Award for the title song in *Gigi*. Lerner himself won Academy Awards for the screenplays of *Gigi* and *An American in Paris*.

Le Sage, Alain René (1668-1747), French novelist and dramatist. His picaresque masterpiece *Gil Blas* (1715-35), a witty satirical account of French society, influenced the development of the realistic novel in France. He also wrote the comedy *Turcaret* (1709).

Lesbos, Greek island in the Aegean Sea, near Turkey. Also known as Mitilini, it spans about 630 square miles (1,630 sq km) and produces olives, wheat, wine, grapes, and tobacco. A cultured center of ancient Greece, Lesbos was the home of Sappho, Aristotle, and Epicurus.
See also: Greece.

Lesotho's barren basalt plateau

Lesch-Nyhan syndrome, hereditary metabolic disorder, affecting the central nervous system. First described in 1964 by William Nyhan and Michael Lesch, it is caused by a defective enzyme hypoxanthine-quinine-phosphoribasyl-transferase, which is normally very active in brain cells. It is characterized by mental retardation, aggressive behavior and a tendency to inflict self injury. The syndrome is transmitted by a recessive sex-linked gene and primarily affects males. There is no cure or effective treatment.

Lesotho

Capital:	Maseru
Area:	11,720 sq mi (30,355 sq km)
Population:	1,715,000
Form:	republic
Independent:	1966
GNP:	U.S. $690,000,000
Per capita:	U.S. $410

Lesotho (formerly Basutoland), landlocked kingdom surrounded by, and economically dependent on, the Republic of South Africa.
Land and climate. Part of the great plateau of South Africa, Lesotho lies mainly between 8,000 ft (2,439 m) and 11,000 ft (3,353 m). In the east and the north is the Drakensberg mountain range. The chief rivers are the Orange River and its tributaries. Annual rainfall averages less than 30 in (76 cm), and temperatures vary seasonally from 93°F (34°C) to 30°F (–1°C). Sparsely forested, Lesotho is mainly dry grassland.
People and economy. The Basuto, who comprise 99% of the population, are chiefly rural. Education is mainly in the hands of missionaries. The literacy rate is about 50%, and around 70% of the people are Christians. An agricultural country, Lesotho is heavily dependent on livestock and food crops such as wheat and maize. Poor farming techniques have resulted in a shortage of good land. Although Lesotho is opposed to apartheid, it depends heavily upon South Africa for trade and employment.
History. The nation was established c.1829 by Chief Moshoeshoe I, who secured British protection from Boer encroachment. As Basutoland, it was under British rule from 1884, gaining independence in 1966.

Lespedeza, any of a genus (*Lespedeza*) of shrublike plants and herbs characterized by 3-parted leaves and smooth edges. The plants are grown in clusters and have pea-shaped flowers; the fruits are single seeded with short pods.

Lesseps, Ferdinand Marie de (1805-95), French diplomat and engineer who conceived the idea for the Suez Canal. Lesseps supervised the building of it (1859-69) himself. His later plans for the Panama Canal ended in bankruptcy (1888) and a conviction for misappropriation of monies.
See also: Suez Canal.

Ferdinand de Lesseps attempted construction of the Panama Canal

Lessing, Doris (1919-), British novelist, raised in Southern Rhodesia (now Zimbabwe), who has dealt perceptively with the struggles of intellectual women for political, sexual, and artistic integrity. Her major works include *The Golden Notebook* (1962), *The Four-Gated City* (1969, part of the *Children of Violence* series), and *The Sirian Experiments* (1981).

Lessing, Gotthold Ephraim (1729-81), German playwright, critic, and philosopher. He rejected French classicism and pioneered German bourgeois tragedy with *Miss Sara Sampson* (1755). He also wrote the influential comedy *Minna von Barnhelm* (1763), the prose tragedy *Emilia Galotti* (1772), and the dramatic poem *Nathan the Wise* (1779). His treatise *Laokoön* (1766) critically contrasted the natures of poetry and painting.

Lethe (Greek, "forgetfulness"), in Greek mythology, river in Hades. When the souls of the dead drank from Lethe, they forgot their lives on earth.

Lettuce, popular garden plant (genus *Lactuca*) of the composite family. Cultivated for salad since ancient times, lettuce is harvested before its flower stem shoots up to bear its small yellow flowers. There are 3 main types: leaf lettuce has a loose crown of leaves; head lettuce has compact leaves; romaine (or Cos), with elongated leaves, is the most resistant to heat.

Leucippus (c.400 B.C.), Greek philosopher who developed the theory of atomism (from Greek *atamos,* "uncuttable"). He was the first to state that matter consists of small, constantly moving particles, or atoms. Although little is known about Leucippus's life, *The Great World System* and *On The Mind* are believed to have been written by him.

Leukemia, common name for any of various cancerous diseases of the blood or bone marrow, characterized by malignant proliferation of white blood cells. It may be divided into acute and chronic forms. In acute forms, progression is rapid, with patients suffering anemia, bruising, and infection. Chronic forms may have milder systemic symptoms, including susceptibility to infection and enlarged lymph nodes. Chemotherapy and antibiotics have greatly improved survival prospects.
See also: Cancer.

Leutze, Emanuel Gottlieb (1816-68), U.S. historical painter. His large-scale, patriotic works include *Westward the Course of Empire Takes Its Way* and *Washington Crossing the Delaware.*

Lever, simplest type of machine, consisting of a rigid beam supported at a stationary point (the fulcrum) so that a force applied to one point of the beam can shift a load at another point. There are 3 classes of lever: those with the fulcrum between the effort and the load; those with the load between the fulcrum and the effort; and those with the effort between the fulcrum and the load.

Levi-Montalcini, Rita (1909-), U.S. scientist, shared the Nobel Prize for physiology or medicine (1986) with Stanley Cohen for their discovery (1952-53) of a natural substance that stimulates the growth of nerve cells.

Levine, James (1943-), U.S. pianist and conductor. In 1964-70 he was an apprentice conductor of the Cleveland Symphony Orchestra under George Szell and then assistant conductor. In 1972 he became principal conductor at the Metropolitan Opera, where he was appointed music director in 1975 and artistic director in 1983.

Lévi-Strauss, Claude (1908-90), Belgian-born French anthropologist, best known as the founder of structuralism, an analytical method whereby different cultural patterns are compared so as to examine the way they order the elements of their environment into systems. His writings include *Structural Anthropology* (1958), *The Savage Mind* (1962), and *The View from Afar* (1985).

Levites, in ancient Israel, tribe descended from Levi, son of Jacob. As priestly auxiliaries, they were assigned responsibility for the care of the Ark and the Sanctuary; in Jerusalem they had hereditary duties at the Temple.

Leviticus, book of the Old Testament, third of the 5 books of the Pentateuch, traditionally ascribed to Moses. It is a collection of liturgical and ceremonial laws.

Lewis, C(live) S(taples) (1898-1963), British author, literary scholar, and defender of Christianity. Of more than 40 books his best-known is *The Screwtape Letters* (1942), a diabolical view of humanity. *The Allegory of Love* (1936), his major critical work, studies love in medieval literature. He also wrote a science-fiction trilogy and the *Narnia* fantasies.

Lewis, Francis (1713-1802), New York delegate to the Continental Congress (1774-79) and a signer of the Declaration of Independence. His son, Morgan Lewis, served as governor of New York (1804-07).

Lewis, John L. (1880-1969), U.S. labor leader, president of the United Mine Workers of America, 1920-60. He was one of the founders of the Congress of Industrial Organizations (CIO) in 1935, advocating the organization of workers on an industrial, rather than a craft, basis. Initially a supporter of President Franklin D. Roosevelt, Lewis turned against Roosevelt and resigned as president of the CIO in 1940, when the CIO backed Roosevelt's bid for reelection. Lewis was a militant advocate of workers' rights, organizing several strikes of coal miners during World War II and refusing to obey a court order to end a long strike in 1948.
See also: Labor movement.

Lewis, Meriwether (1774-1809), American explorer and commander of the Lewis and Clark Expedition, which penetrated to the Northwest Pacific coast 1803-06. In 1808 he became governor of the Louisiana Territory.
See also:; Lewis and Clark expedition.

Lewis, Sinclair (1885-1951), U.S. novelist, best known for 5 novels presenting a devastatingly critical view of life in the Middle West. *Main Street* (1920) was his first major success. *Babbitt* (1922), a portrait of a provincial small businessman, is perhaps his best-known book. He refused a Pulitzer Prize for *Arrowsmith* (1925), a satirical look at the medical profession. *Elmer Gantry* (1927) and *Dodsworth* (1929) followed. In 1930 he became the first American to win the Nobel Prize in literature.

Lewis, Wyndham (1882-1957), controversial English painter, critic, and writer, the founder of the vorticism movement, which simplified forms into machinelike angularity. He is best known for his savage satirical novel, *The Apes of God* (1930).

Wyndham Lewis's The surrender of Barcelona *(1936; Tate Gallery, London)*

Lewis and Clark expedition, first overland expedition to the northwest Pacific coast (1804-06), under the command of Meriwether Lewis (1774-1809) and William Clark (1770-1838), with Sacagawea, the Native American wife of an expedition member, acting as interpreter and guide. Setting out from St. Louis, the expedition explored the Louisiana Purchase and crossed the Rockies, reaching the Pacific Ocean at the mouth of the Columbia River. It caught the popular imagination and played a major part in establishing the view that it was the "Manifest Destiny" of the U.S. to expand to the Pacific Ocean.
See also: Clark, William; Lewis, Meriwether.

Claude Lévi-Strauss

Lewiston (pop. 88,141), second largest city in Maine, first settled in 1770. Lewiston and Auburn, across the Androscoggin River, constitute the leading industrial area of southwestern Maine, producing textiles and footwear and housing metallurgical plants.
See also: Maine.

Lexington (pop. 348,428), second largest city in Kentucky, in the bluegrass region in the north central part of the state. The city is known throughout the United States as the leading center for raising thoroughbred horses and as a major market for tobacco.
See also: Kentucky.

Lexington, Battle of *see:* Revolutionary War in America.

Leyden *see:* Leiden.

Leyden jar, simplest and earliest form of capacitor, a device for storing electric charge, developed at the University of

Leiden, Holland, in the 18th century. It consists of a glass jar coated inside and out with metal foil, and a conducting rod that passes through the jar's insulated stopper to connect with the inner foil. The jar is usually charged from an electrostatic generator. The device is now little used outside the classroom.

Lhasa (pop. 105,900), capital and largest city of the Tibet Autonomous Region of China. Once known as the Forbidden City, Lhasa was the center of Tibetan Buddhism until the Chinese invasion of 1951. The Potala, former palace of the Dalai Lama, head of Tibetan Buddhism and now in exile, is in the city.
See also: Tibet.

Champion of liberalism, English philosopher and jurist Jeremy Bentham (1748-1832)

Lhasa apso, small dog, 10 in (25 cm) high, that originated in Tibet as a watchdog. The Lhasa apso is covered with long hair that falls over its face, and its thick tail curls over its back.

Liana, any climbing vine with roots in the ground, most often found in tropical forests. Lianas wind around trees or other plants for support. Kudzu, grapevines, and ivy are lianas.

Libel, false and malicious statement in permanent form, such as in writing or on film, tending to injure the reputation of a living person, or blacken the memory of the dead. The truth of the statement creates a valid defense in an action for libel.

Liberalism, political philosophy that stresses individual liberty and equality of opportunity. Classical liberalism developed in Europe in the 18th century as part of a rationalist critique of traditional institutions and a distrust of state power. Since the 1930s, modern liberalism has advocated state intervention in the economy but is still concerned with social issues such as civil rights and equality of opportunity.

Liberal Party, British political party, powerful from about 1832 to 1922. Originating in the Whig party, the Liberals were backed by the industrial owners and were associated with such policies as free trade, laissez-faire economics, and religious liberty, while initially opposing most social legislation. The Liberal party enjoyed its golden age under the prime ministers Gladstone, Asquith, and Lloyd George. In the 1920s it was supplanted by the Labour party as the chief opposition to the Conservative party, and by the 1930s it became a relatively small third party attracting about 10% of the vote nationally. In 1981 the party formed an alliance with the new Social Democratic party, but its strength has not substantially increased.

Monrovia, Liberia

Liberal Republican Party, U.S. political party formed in 1872, during the administration of President Ulysses S. Grant to oppose the policies and the corruption of the administration. The Liberal Republicans nominated Horace Greeley for president, but when he was defeated (despite Democratic support), the party effectively broke up.

Liberia

Capital:	Monrovia
Area:	37,743 sq mi (97,754 sq km)
Population:	2,508,000
Form:	republic
Independent:	1847
GNP:	U.S.$1,051,000,000
Per capita:	U.S.$450

Liberia, independent republic on the west coast of Africa, with a land area slightly larger than the state of Ohio. It has a coastline of over 300 mi (483 km) on the Atlantic Ocean. Liberia is the oldest republic in Africa. It originated from the efforts of American philanthropists who in 1822 organized the first settlement of freed American black slaves near the place where the capital, Monrovia, now stands. In 1847 Liberia became an independent republic modeled on the United States.

Land and climate. The terrain varies from a sandy coastal plain cut by lagoons to densely forested mountains in the north. The central part consists mainly of plateau, a rolling plain broken by many hills that are encircled by swamps. Edged in places by steep escarpments above the coastal plain, the plateau ranges in height from 600 ft (183 m) to 1,500 ft (457 m) above sea level. The Nimba Mountains in the northeast rise to 4,528 ft (1,380 m). Several rivers flow from the mountains and plateau into the Atlantic, the most important being the St. Paul, with Monrovia at its mouth.

Liberia is hot and humid, with an average temperature of 80°F (26°C). The rainy season lasts from Apr. to Oct., when the region receives about 150 in (381 cm) of rain, and inland areas about 100 in (254 cm). The *harmattan*, a hot, dry wind from the Sahara, often blows during the dry season. About half the land is covered by dense tropical rain forests. Wildlife includes chimpanzees, monkeys, zebras, antelopes, the rare pygmy hippopotamus, and birds and reptiles. Among Liberia's mineral resources are rich deposits of iron ore, some gold, and diamonds.

People. Over 90% of the people are indigenous Africans belonging to more than 26 tribal groups. The leading citizens are the descendants of freed American slaves, known as Americo-Liberians. There are some Lebanese traders, and Europeans who manage the industries. Most of the tribal peoples are subsistence farmers. The Mandingos practice Islam, but most other tribal groups are animists. The Americo-Liberians, who dominate the government, education, and the professions, are mainly Christians and live in the urban coastal areas.

Although English is the official language, most of the people speak one of many African languages or dialects. The education system includes public, mission, and tribal schools, but about 90% of the population is illiterate. Liberia has one university. There are few urban areas, except along the coast. The capital, largest city, and chief port is Monrovia. Eight smaller ports include Marshall, Robertsport, Buchanan, Greenville, and Harper.

Economy. The Liberian economy is underdeveloped. Its main industries are rubber plantations, established in the 1920s, and the mining of iron ore, dating from the 1950s; both have been run and maintained by U.S. firms. Liberia also exports several crops, including coffee, sugarcane, bananas, and cocoa. Foreign exchange is earned by registering foreign ships under lax rules.

History. The first repatriated slaves arrived from the United States in 1822 under the sponsorship of the American Colonization Society. The settlement was named Monrovia in honor of U.S. President James Monroe. In 1847 the settlers declared their independence. Liberia gradually extended its territory by signing treaties with local chiefs, or by buying or claiming land. Inequities in the wealth and political power have caused antagonisms between Americo-Liberians and Indigenous Africans.

Libertarian Party, U.S. political party that upholds the unfettered right of private property and a laissez-faire, free-market economy, and opposes restrictions on individual rights. Libertarians regard the state as the greatest threat to liberty and oppose government inteference in private lives. Founded in 1971, the party nominated a 1980 presidential candidate, Ed Clark, who was on the ballot in every state. He polled 921,188 votes, or 1.1% of the total cast.

Liberty Bell, historic bell housed near Independence Hall, Philadelphia. It was rung on July 8, 1776, to announce the adoption of the Declaration of Independence. It was thereafter rung on each anniversary of the Declaration's adoption until 1835, when it cracked. Originally called the Old State House Bell, it was renamed Liberty Bell by abolitionists about the mid-19th century.

Liberty Island, in New York Bay, it is the home of the Statue of Liberty. Prior to l956 the island was called Bedloe's Island. The property belongs to the U.S. government.
See also: Statue of Liberty.

Liberty Party, antislavery political party founded in 1839 by James G. Birney and other abolitionists. In 1840 and 1844 Birney made unsuccessful runs for president. In 1848 the party united with other groups to form the Free Soil Party.
See also: Free Soil Party.

Li Bo, Li Po, or Li Bai (A.D. 701-762), considered one of China's foremost poets. He is admired for his descriptions of nature and for his poems on ethics and morality.

Library, collection of books, manuscripts, films, musical recordings, and other materials arranged in convenient order for use but not for sale. The earliest libraries were kept by the ancient peoples of Mesopotamia; inscribed clay tablets have been found going back to about 3500 B.C. The first public library in Greece was established in 330 B.C. The most famous library of the ancient world was begun at Alexandria, in Egypt, by Ptolemy I Soter (305-283 B.C.). The Roman Empire acquired many libraries through their conquests of Greece, Asia Minor, and Syria (1st-2nd century B.C.). During the Middle Ages the Church kept the library tradition alive in Europe. The Renaissance saw the formation of many new libraries, such as the Vatican Library (1447), the oldest public library in Europe. The growth of libraries was further stimulated by the invention of printing in the 15th century. The Bodleian Library, Oxford, England, dates from 1602. It was the 18th century that saw the formation of many of the great national libraries: the British Museum Library (1753), Italy's National Central Library at Florence (1741), and the USSR's Saltykov-Shchedrin Library in Leningrad.
The oldest library in the United States originated in 320 books bequeathed by John Harvard (1638), Harvard University's chief benefactor. The present Library of Congress developed from a purchase (1814-15) of Thomas Jefferson's personal library by Congress. One of the first tax-supported public libraries in the United States was established in New Hampshire in 1833. The American Library Association, a professional association to foster the development of the nation's libraries, was founded in 1876. An important figure in library history is Melvil Dewey, whose decimal classification system has now been adopted in many countries. In the late 19th century the industrialist Andrew Carnegie was an important benefactor of libraries. In the 20th century the public library system has been extended and consolidated and has at its disposal such technological innovations as microfilm, photocopiers, and computer data banks.

Library of Congress, U.S. national library located east of the Capitol in Washington, D.C. Originally established by Congress in 1800, it now contains more than 80 million items—including books, pamphlets, maps, photographs, and the like—making it one of the world's largest research libraries. The library's catalog, the National Union Catalog, lists books in libraries all over the United States and Canada.
See also: Library.

Libya

Capital:	Tripoli
Area:	685,524 sq mi (1,775,500 sq km)
Population:	4,080,000
Form:	people's republic
Independent:	1951
GNP:	U.S. $23,000,000,000
Per capita:	U.S. $5,410

Libya, independent Arab republic in North Africa, consisting of 10 administrative divisions that occupy an area of 679,358 sq mi (1,759,540 sq km). Less than 10% of Libya's land is fertile, most of the remainder being part of the Sahara Desert. The exploitation of oil resources (discovered in the late 1950s) provides the wealth that is transforming Libya from a poor peasant nation into an educated and affluent one.
Land and climate. Most of Libya is covered by the shifting sands of the Sahara,though the fertile strip along the Mediterranean coast, with an average rainfall of 10 in (15 cm) and mild winters, supports some cultivation. Even on the coast the rainfall fails about 2 years in every 10. Inland extreme desert conditions exist, and many areas do not see rain for several years at a time. The range of temperature is very wide, from over 120°F (48°C) in summer, to frost level in winter. Suffocating dry desert winds, the *quibli*, bring quantities of dust that destroy much vegetation in the interior.

Libya's ancient settlements are strategically located on the rugged terrain.

Most of the country's inhabitants live within 75 mi (120 km) of the Mediterranean coast. In this belt enough rain falls to grow citrus fruit, barley, wheat, dates, olives, and almonds. Further inland is a grazing area in which only scrub or tough esparto grasses can grow.
In the central part of the Sahara region, there are massifs as high as 2,000 ft (610 m) but no real mountains exist in the country other than the low Tibesti Mountains on the southern border, with altitudes of 4,000 ft (1,220 m) or more. The highest point in Libya is Bette Peak in the south, at 7,500 ft (2,286 m).
Economy. Though the economy depends on the export of crude oil, which accounts for 99% of export revenue, agriculture employs 50% of the labor force. In the coastal area barley, wheat, millet, oranges, olives, almonds, and groundnuts are grown. Dates are plentiful in the desert oases, and nomads raise livestock. Libya consumes much of its own agricultural produce and is a net importer of foodstuffs. Petrochemicals have been added to the traditional textile and leather industries.
History. Because of Libya's strategic position on the Mediterranean coast, it has been occupied by many foreign powers—

the ancient Greeks, Egyptians, Romans, Arabs, and Ottoman Turks controlled the country successively. In 1912 Italy annexed Libya, although it was not able to end Libyan armed opposition until 1932. In World War II Libya was an Axis military base and the scene of desert fighting between the Axis powers and the British. In 1951 the United Nations declared Libya an independent sovereign state under the rule of King Idris I. He was overthrown in 1969 by a military coup led by Colonel Muammar al-Qaddafi, who proclaimed Libya a republic; it is now in effect an Islamic military dictatorship. In 1973 Qaddafi launched a "cultural revolution," including nationalization of key industries. A prominent follower of pan-Arabism, he has attempted to unite Libya with Egypt (1973), Tunisia (1974), and Syria (1980), and has intervened militarily in Chad (from 1980). Qaddafi is a fervent opponent of Israel. The United States launched an air strike on Tripoli (1986) and shot down 2 Libyan fighter (1989) in retaliation of alleged Libyan backing of terrorist activities.

Lichee *see:* Litchi.

Lichen, name given to plants that consist of algae living in association with fungi. The fungi gets food from the algae and absorbs the water that is used by the algae to make its own food in the process called photosynthesis. This relationship is a form of symbiosis. Lichens generally live on the bark of trees, rotting wood, rocks, or soil.

Lichtenstein, Roy (1923-), U.S. painter prominent in the Pop Art movement of the early 1960s. He depicted comic strip frames and used commercial art techniques, such as Benday dots, in his work.

Roy Lichtenstein, Okay, Hot Shot, Okay *(1963; R. Morone Collection, Turin, Italy)*

Licorice, European herb (*Glycyrrhiza glabra*) with blue flowers and lemon yellow roots that contain a juice used as a flavoring. Licorice has long been used to treat sore throats and is often added to medicines to mask disagreeable tastes. It is also widely used to flavor candy.

Lidice (pop. 500), village in northwestern Czechoslovakia. In 1942 the Nazis completely demolished the village, killing the men and deporting the women and children, in retaliation for the assassination of Reinhard Heydrich, Nazi governor of Bohemia, by the Czech Resistance. A new village has been built near the site, which is now a national monument.
See also: Czechoslovakia; World War II.

Lidocaine, drug used as a local or block anesthetic, which bars pain in specific areas of the body. It can be administered by injection or used topically, directly on the skin.

Lie, Trygve (1896-1968), Norwegian political leader, first secretary-general of the United Nations, 1946-53. He incurred Soviet hostility because of his support of UN action in Korea. After leaving office, he returned to Norway, serving in ministerial posts.

Liechtenstein

Capital:	Vaduz
Area:	62 sq mi (160 sq km)
Population:	28,300
Form:	constitutional monarchy
Independent:	1866
GNP:	U.S. $450,000,000
Per capita:	U.S. $16,500

Liechtenstein, European principality in the Alps, between Switzerland and Austria. Vaduz is the capital. With a total area of 61 sq mi (157 sq km), Liechtenstein is one of the world's smallest countries. Because of low taxes and bank secrecy, it is the nominal headquarters of thousands of international corporations, and Vaduz is a thriving tourist center. Roman Catholicism is the state religion; German is the official language. Liechtenstein was a principality of the Holy Roman Empire from 1719. It was incorporated into the German Confederation in 1815 and became independent in 1866. Until 1919 it was closely associated with Austria, but since then its interests abroad have been represented by Switzerland, and much of its economy is owned by the Swiss.

Liège (pop. 207,500), city and cultural center on the Meuse River in eastern, French-speaking Belgium. Liège is an industrial city noted for its production of glassware and armaments

Life, despite the lack of any generally accepted definition of life, physiologists regard as living any system capable of eating, metabolizing, excreting, breathing, moving, growing, and reproducing, and able to respond to external stimuli. Metabolically, life is a property of any object surrounded by a definite boundary and capable of exchanging materials with its surroundings. Biochemically, life subsists in cellular systems containing both nucleic acids and proteins. For the geneticist, life belongs to systems able to perform complex transformations of organic molecules and to construct from raw materials copies of themselves capable of evolution by natural selection. As to the origin of life, many believe it was created by God. Scientists believe in the formation of organic substances in the atmosphere over 2 billion years ago; they joined water to form a "nutrient broth" that evolved into life.

Life expectancy, number of years a person in a particular population group is expected to live, based on actuarial calculations. A statistical quantity, it is not meant to be a prediction applied to individuals.

Ligament, band of strong fibrous tissue connecting bones at a joint or serving to hold body organs in place.
See also: Human body.

Light, the portion of electromagnetic radiation that the human eye can see. To be seen, light must have a wavelength between 400 and 750 nanometers, a range known as the visible spectrum. The eye recognizes light of different wavelengths as being of different colors, the shorter wavelengths forming the blue end of the visible spectrum, the longer the red. The term *light* is also applied to radiations of wavelengths just outside the visible spectrum: those of energies greater than that of visible light are called ultraviolet light, and those of lower energies are called infrared. For many years the nature of light aroused controversy among physicists. Although Christiaan Huygens had demonstrated that reflection and refraction could be explained in terms of waves (1690), Isaac Newton preferred to think of light as composed of material corpuscles, or particles (1704). Thomas Young's interference experiments reestablished the wave hypothesis (1801) and A. J. Fresnel gave it a rigorous mathematical basis (1814-15). At the beginning of the 20th century, the nature of light was again debated as Max Planck and Albert Einstein proposed explanations of blackbody radiation (1900) and the photo-electric effect (1905) respectively, both of which assumed that light comes in discrete quanta (bundles) of energy.

Light, invisible *see:* Infrared rays; Ultraviolet rays.

Light bulb *see:* Edison, Thomas Alva; Electric light.

Lighthouse, tower with a light at its head, erected on or near a coast or on a rock in the sea, as a warning to ships. One of the earliest lighthouses was on the Pharos peninsula in 3rd-century B.C. Alexandria, considered one of the 7 wonders of the world. In modern lighthouses, the lantern usually consists of a massive electric light with an elaborate optical system producing intense beams.

Light meter, device that measures the intensity of light. Some light meters contain photo cells made up of the chemicals cadmium sulfide or gallium arsenide, while others utilize cells of selenium. Both are used in specialized professions such as astronomy and photography.

Lightning, discharge of atmospheric electricity resulting in a flash of light in the sky. Flashes range from a few miles to about 100 mi (170 km) in length and typically have an energy of about 300 kWh and an electromotive force of 100 MV. Lightning results from a buildup of opposed electric charges, usually in clouds. The electrical nature of lightning was proved in 1752 by Benjamin Franklin.

Lightning bug *see:* Firefly.

Lignum vitae, either of 2 species (*Guaiacum officinale* and *G. sanctum*) of flowering evergreen tree of the West Indies, Mexico, and Florida. Its extremely heavy wood is used for ship construction, furniture, and mallets. The wood also contains a resin used in some drugs.

Ligurian Sea, portion of the Mediterranean Sea enclosed by the Italian regions of Liguria and Tuscany in the north and east and the French island of Corsica in the south.
See also: Mediterranean Sea.

Lilac, shrub or small tree (genus *Syringa*) whose pyramids of small, sweet-scented flowers cap heart-shaped leaves. Lilacs originated in Asia and eastern Europe and are now widely grown as ornamentals.

Liliuokalani, Lydia Kamekeha (1838-1917), last queen of Hawaii, who reigned 1891-93. She succeeded her brother, King Kalakaua. When she tried to assert her royal powers, American sugar planters living in Hawaii fomented a revolt in which she lost her throne. She wrote the well-known farewell song "Aloha Oe."

Lille (pop. 168,400), city in northern France. Best-known for its textile industry, Lille also produces automobiles, electronic equipment, and petrochemicals. Lille was founded c. 1030 by the Flemish, who gave the city to France in 1312.
See also: France.

Lillie, Beatrice (1894-1989), Canadian-born English comedienne internationally famous for her sophisticated wit, displayed in such performances as her monologue "Double Damask Dinner Napkins."

Lilongwe (pop. 175,000), capital, since 1975, of Malawi in southeast Africa. Located on the Lilongwe River, the city is the center of a rich agricultural region. Lilongwe, settled in 1902, became a city in 1966.
See also: Malawi.

Lily, common name for plants of the family Liliaceae, which have prominent flowers and grasslike leaves. True lilies have 3 showy sepals and petals and 6 stamens, and generally grow from bulbs. The best known varieties are the Madonna lily (*Lilium candidum*) and white-trumpet lily (*L. Longiflorum*), which flower in the spring and are seen at Easter. Many wild lilies flower only once in several years.

Rubrum lily

Lily of the valley, any of several species of woodland plants (genus *Convallaria*) widely grown in gardens and indoor pots. It produces white, bell-shaped flowers that hang from a long stalk and show up against a backdrop of 2 broad, overlapping leaves. The flowers are sweet-scented and are used in perfume. They produce large red berries.

Lima (pop. 4,165,000), capital and largest city of Peru, about 8 mi (13 km) inland from the Pacific port of Callao. Founded in 1535, Lima was the chief residence of the Spanish viceroys. Earthquakes in 1687 and 1746 destroyed much of the city, but many old buildings remain. The University of San Marcos dates from 1551. Rapidly expanding, Lima now has many industries, including textiles, chemicals, oil refining, and food processing.
See also: Peru.

Lima bean, any of several highly nutritious beans of the pea family, rich in protein. Native to tropical America, lima beans are now grown in warm climates throughout the world. The beans grow in 2- to 3-in (5- to 7.6-cm)-long pods on a bush, or on a vine that can be trained to grow on trellises or poles.

Lighthouse on Trinity Shoal, in the Gulf of Mexico

Limbourg, Pol de (d.1416), Flemish manuscript illuminator, one of three brothers who after 1404 worked for the Burgundian duke of Berry. Their renowned devotional book of hours, the *Très Riches Heures* (c.1415) shows courtly life and landscape in brilliant detail and dazzling color; it profoundly influenced Flemish painting.

Lime, shrublike citrus tree (*Citrus aurantifolia*) that grows a green fruit smaller and more acidic than the lemon. Limes are

The changing of the guards at the Presidential Palace in Lima

grown around the Mediterranean, in the West Indies, Central America, and India. Rich in vitamin C, they were once important in preventing scurvy among sailors on long sea voyages.

Lime, quicklime, or calcium oxide, a caustic industrial chemical (CaO). It is most often made by heating limestone until carbon dioxide is released. Lime's uses include purifying sugar, neutralizing acidic soil and sewage, and making porcelain and glass.

Limerick, humorous verse form consisting of 5 lines, named for the Irish city of Limerick but of unknown origin. Limericks were popularized by the English poet Edward Lear (1812-88). An example:
There was a young lady named Bright
Whose speed was far faster than light
She went out one day
in a relative way
And returned on the previous night.

Limestone, sedimentary rock consisting mainly of calcium carbonate. Some limestones, such as chalk, are soft, but others are hard enough to be used in building. Limestone may be formed inorganically by the evaporation of seawater or freshwater containing calcium carbonate, or organically from the compressed shells of mollusks or skeletons of coral on sea beds.

Lime tree *see:* Linden.

Limon, José (1908-72), Mexican-U.S. dancer and choreographer. In the 1930s he danced with the Humphrey-Weidman company. He formed his own company in 1946, choreographing *Moor's Pavane* (1949), *The Visitation* (1952), and *A Choreographic Offering* (1963).

Limonite, or brown hematite, mineral formed by the decomposition of other minerals that contain iron, found in France, Cuba, and Canada. It is used as an iron ore and as a source of ocher, a yellow iron ore used as a pigment.

Limpet, mollusk, related to the pond snail, with a conical instead of a spiral shell and a muscular foot that can cling to rocks. Limpets can trap water under their shells to survive even when exposed by the ebbing tide. They can grow as long as 4 in (10 cm), but are usually smaller.

Limpopo River, or Crocodile River, river dividing South Africa from Botswana and Zimbabwe. The Limpopo, which empties into the Indian Ocean, is about 1,000 mi (1,600 km) long.

Lincoln (pop. 213,641), capital and second-largest city of Nebraska, 56 mi (90 km) southwest of Omaha. A trade center for livestock and grain, transportation hub, and industrial and educational center, Lincoln also produces motor scooters, freight cars, rubber tires, and electrical appliances.
See also: Nebraska.

Lincoln, Abraham (1809-65), 16th president of the United States. Lincoln led the North during the Civil War, the nation's greatest crisis. He was determined to restore the Union at any cost—and prevailed. Besides his preservation of the Union and the Emancipation Proclamation, Lincoln is remembered for his eloquent oratory, particularly his Gettysburg Address and inaugural speeches.
Early life. Lincoln was born in a log cabin on the frontier in Kentucky, to a poor carpenter and his wife. Lincoln had less than a year of formal schooling, but taught himself to read. At 22, he left home, working as a storekeeper, rail splitter, farmhand, village postmaster, and surveyor while teaching himself law. In 1837, he was admitted to the bar and moved to Springfield, Ill., to practice law. Soon after moving there, he met Mary Todd, whom he married in 1842. They had 4 children.
Political career. Lincoln, a successful lawyer, was more interested in politics. He lost his first election in 1832, but in 1834 won a seat in the state legislature, where he served 4 2-year terms. He rose quickly within the Whig party, becoming Whig floor leader in the Illinois house by age 28. In 1847, he was elected to the U.S. House of Representatives, where he served only 1 term, because his opposition to the Mexican War made him unpopular with his constituents. He returned to his Springfield law practice in 1849. A national debate over slavery brought Lincoln back into politics—he gave speeches attacking slavery as a "great moral wrong." He lost the 1854 and 1858 elections for the U.S. Senate, but his public debates with his opponent, Stephen A. Douglas, made him a national figure. In 1860, the Republicans nominated him for the presidency. The Democratic Party was split between a Northern candidate and a Southern one, helping Lincoln and his running mate, Hannibal Hamlin, to win the election.
President. Before Lincoln even took office, 7 Southern states had seceded. The great question was no longer slavery or freedom in the territories, but the preservation of the Union itself. Lincoln was inaugurated on Mar. 4, 1861; on Apr. 12, 1861, the Civil War broke out when the South attacked Fort Sumter in Charleston, S.C. Affairs began badly for Lincoln: 5 more states seceded and the North lost the war's earliest battles. The 1862 midterm elections brought sizable Republican losses, and slavery again became a major political issue. Hoping to settle at least that issue, Lincoln issued the Emancipation Proclamation on Sept. 22, 1862. It freed all slaves in states or parts of states in rebellion against the Union as of Jan. 1, 1863.
The tide of the war slowly turned in 1863, with important Northern victories. Lincoln was gloomy about his prospects of reelection in Nov. 1864, but he and running mate Andrew Johnson did win. Soon after Lincoln's second inauguration, the war ended with Gen. Robert E. Lee's surrender on Apr. 9, 1865.
Assassination. Five days later, Lincoln and his wife went to Ford's Theatre for a performance of *Our American Cousin.* During the third act, John Wilkes Booth crept into the presidential box and shot Lincoln. Lincoln died the next morning. Booth, who had fled, was eventually found and shot while trying to escape.
See also: Civil War, U.S.; Emancipation Proclamation.

Lincoln, Mary Todd (1818-1882), wife of U.S. president Abraham Lincoln from 1842 until his death. Her snobbish manner made her an unpopular first lady. In addition, because she was from the South and had relatives serving in the Confederate Army, she was regarded with suspicion during the Civil War.

Lincoln, Robert Todd (1843-1926), only son of Abraham Lincoln to reach adulthood. After serving on General Grant's staff in the Civil War, he became a corporation lawyer and was later U.S. secretary of war (1881-85) and minister to Great Britain (1889-93).

Lincoln Center for the Performing Arts, in New York City, complex of buildings (constructed 1959-72) designed by leading

Abraham Lincoln

16th U.S. President	
Born	Hardin Co. (now Larue Co.), Ky.; Feb. 12, 1809
Term	Mar. 1861-Apr. 1865
Vice presidents	Hannibal Hamlin; Andrew Johnson
Political party	Republican
Spouse	Mary Todd Lincoln
Children	4
Died	Washington, D.C.; Apr. 15, 1865

modern architects including Eero Saarinen and Philip Johnson, to accommodate a number of vital performing arts institutions, which today include the Metropolitan Opera, New York Philharmonic Orchestra, the New York City Opera, and the Chamber Music Society of Lincoln Center. Also at Lincoln Center is a branch of the New York Public Library devoted to the performing arts; a prominent school of music, dance, and theater, the Juilliard School; and other institutions devoted to film and jazz.

Lincoln Memorial, marble monument to Abraham Lincoln in Washington, D.C., dedicated in 1922. Its 36 Doric columns represent the states of the Union when Lincoln was president. The great hall contains a huge statue of Lincoln by Daniel Chester French and 2 murals by Jules Guerin.

Lind, Jenny (1820-87), Swedish soprano who had brilliant success in opera, concert singing, and oratorio. In 1850-52 she toured the United States under the management of the promoter P.T. Barnum.

Lindbergh, Charles Augustus (1902-74), U.S. aviator who made the first solo, nonstop flight across the Atlantic, in 33 1/2 hours, on May 21, 1927, in *The Spirit of St. Louis.* The flight made him a popular hero. The kidnapping and murder of his son in 1932 led to a federal law on kidnapping, popularly known as the Lindbergh Act. Lindbergh and his wife, the writer Anne Spencer Morrow Lindbergh, moved to England in 1936. Criticized for his pro-German, isolationist stance in 1938-41, Lindbergh resigned his commission in the air reserves, but he later flew 50 combat missions in the Pacific during World War II. He won a Pulitzer Prize for his autobiography, *The Spirit of Saint Louis* (1953).

Linden, any of a family (Tiliaceae) of shade trees native to temperate regions. Lindens are also known as lime trees, bee trees, and basswoods. There are 35 species. The most common North American species is the American linden (*Tilia americana*), which can reach 120 ft (37 m).

Lindsay, Vachel (1879-1931), U.S. poet of rhythmic, ballad-like verse designed to be read out loud. Among the best known are "The Congo" (1914) and "Abraham Lincoln Walks at Midnight" (1914). *Collected Poems* was published in 1938.

Linear accelerator, device that produces beams of electrons, protons, and other charged particles and directs them against various atomic targets in order to study the structure of atomic nuclei. Linear accelerators vary in the way in which they speed up particles to produce the beams, which move in straight paths. (Other particle accelerators produce circular paths of particles.) Usually the acceleration is accomplished by means of electromagnetic waves.
See also: Particle accelerator.

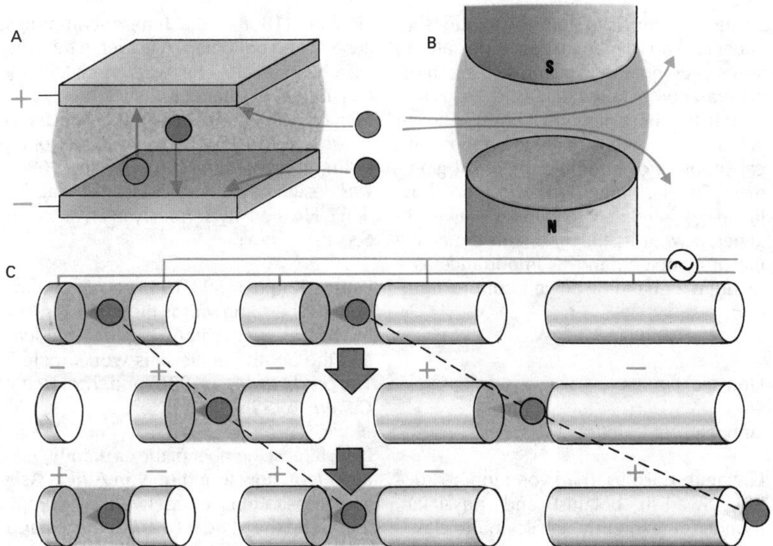

A linear accelerator is a type of particle accelerator that moves particles (electrons, protons, and atomic particles) in a straight line. Particle accelerators work on the concept that an electric field (A) accelerates the parallel movement of positive or negative particles. In a magnetic field (B) the particles move at right angles within the field. In a "drift tube" accelerator (C), which is part of a "standing-wave" linear accelerator, electromagnetic waves (standing waves) move the particles in a straight path.

Linear electric motor, automatic device used to move vehicles without wheels. The motor consists of a row of electromagnets that are turned off and on in succession, producing a wave of magnetism that propels the vehicle. In the linear induction motor the electromagnets are located in the vehicle and face a strip of nonmagnetic metal called a reaction rail. The magnetism induces an electric current in the reaction rail, which in turn produces a second magnetic field that pushes against the first, thereby moving the vehicle. In the *linear synchronous motor* an electromagnet is mounted beneath the vehicle's track. It reacts with magnets on the vehicle itself to propel the vehicle.

Line Islands, string of 11 coral islands in the west and southwest Pacific Ocean. Also known as the Equatorial Islands, they total 222 sq mi (576 sq km) in area and are politically divided. Some of the Northern Line Islands are part of the British crown colony, while others are under U.S. jurisdiction. The Central and Southern Line Islands are part of Gilbert and Ellice Islands, a British crown colony.

Line of Demarcation, line decreed by Pope Alexander VI in 1494 to divide Spanish and Portuguese colonial possessions on a world scale. Running from north to south about 350 mi (563 km) west of the Azores and Cape Verde islands, the Line of Demarcation granted Spanish rights to all land west of the line and Portuguese rights to all land east of it. The line was moved farther west under the 1592 Treaty of Saragossa, thus allowing Portugal to claim what is now eastern Brazil and Spain to claim the Philippine Islands.

Lingonberry, small fruit of an evergreen shrub (*Vaccinium vitisidaea*), related to the cranberry. A member of the heather family, the lingonberry grows wild in northern North America. The berry is shiny and bright red. As the raw berry is bitter, it is usually cooked into jellies and sauces.

Linguistics, scientific study of language in all its aspects. This includes, first, the physical and biological factors that are involved in speech. Secondly, it embraces the study of the structure of language, which includes its range of sounds (phonology), its grammatical structure (morphology and syntax), and the relation of words to what they mean (semantics). In comparative lin-

Charles Lindbergh arrives in Paris, May 21, 1927

Carolus Linnaeus

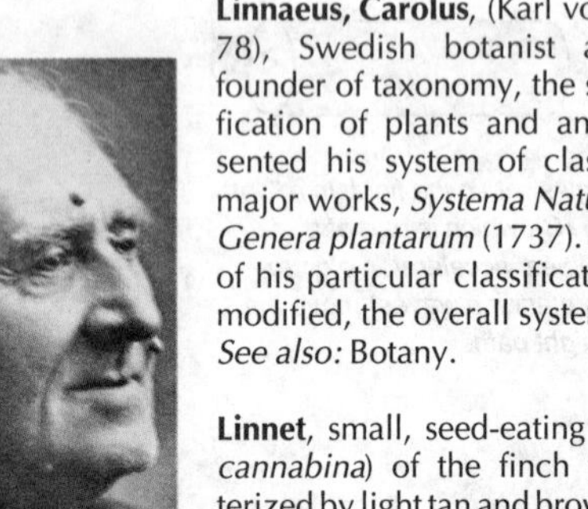

Franz Liszt

guistics, the aim is to study the relationship between various languages, especially in terms of comparative grammar. At its most general, comparative linguistics leads to a search for those features common to all languages, which is really the philosophical problem of finding a universal grammar. Finally, linguistics considers how language is related to human activity in general, what its function is in the active life of a society, and its importance as a medium for handing down a cultural tradition.
See also: Language.

Linn *see:* Linden.

Linnaea *see:* Twinflower.

Linnaeus, Carolus, (Karl von Linné; 1707-78), Swedish botanist and physician, founder of taxonomy, the scientific classification of plants and animals. He presented his system of classification in 2 major works, *Systema Naturae* (1735) and *Genera plantarum* (1737). Although many of his particular classifications have been modified, the overall system is still in use.
See also: Botany.

Linnet, small, seed-eating bird (*Carduelis cannabina*) of the finch family, characterized by light tan and brown feathers with darker patches on the back and shoulders. The crown and breast of the male linnet change to crimson in the spring and summer. In the fall and winter linnets flock together in open country regions, some migrating to warmer areas.

Linotype, mechanical typesetting machine that revolutionized printing and made possible the publication of low-priced books and newspapers. Invented by Ottmar Merganthaler in 1884, the machine, operated by a typewriter keyboard, assembles brass matrices of type into a line and casts the line as a single metal slug. Various photographic and lithographic printing techniques have virtually replaced the linotype machine.
See also: Merganthaler, Ottmar; Printing.

Lin Piao (1908-71), Chinese communist general and politician. A leader in the Long March (1934-35), he was crucial in the final defeat of Chiang Kai-shek by his capture of Manchuria in 1948. Minister of defense from 1959, he was a leader of the Cultural Revolution (1965-69). In 1969 he was designated the successsor of Mao Zedong. He died mysteriously in an air crash.
See also: China.

Linton, Ralph (1893-1953), U.S. anthropologist best known for his studies in cultural anthropology in Africa, the Americas, and the South Pacific. His works include *The Study of Man* (1936) and *The Tree of Culture* (1955).

Lion, largest member of the cat family (*Panthera leo*), now found only in Africa, Asia, and zoos. Lions once lived in Europe, India, and the Middle East, but the expanding human population has eliminated lions from these regions. Lions live in family groups called prides. There may be as many as 30 lions in one pride, and they usually spend their time playing, resting, sleeping (a lion can sleep almost 20 hr a day), eating, and hunting. The pride tends to live together like a family for many years, but males are forced to leave at two or three years of age. A hungry lion may travel as much as 20 miles in one day in search of food. The male lion may reach 9 ft (2.7 m) and weigh as much as 400 lb (180 kg). The female can weigh up to 300 lb (140 kg) and can achieve a length of 8 ft (2.4 m). Because lions do not have exceptional speed, they must rely on the element of surprise for the hunt. They are fond of hunting at night. Most hunting is done by the lioness, and the prey is usually a large animal like a zebra, wildebeest, antelope, or buffalo.

Lipchitz, Jacques (1891-1973), Lithuanian-born French sculptor whose early works consisted of spaces and volumes in a cubist style. Beginning in 1925 he produced a series called "transparents," which, as in the *Harpist* (1928), emphasized contour. His later work was more romantic and metaphorical.

Lion with a common prey

Li Peng (1928-), Chinese premier (1988-). Li Peng has been a member of the Chinese Politburo, the policymaking arm of the government, since 1985. In 1989, when citizens demonstrated for increased democracy, Li Peng advocated the use of force to quell the demonstrations.

Lipid, any of a group of organic compounds found in plants, animals, and micro-organisms that are insoluble in water but dissolve in fat solvents such as ether, chloroform, and alcohol. Lipids are classified into fatty-acids, phospholipids, waxes, steroids, terpenes, and other types, according to their products on hydrolysis.

Li Po *see:* Li Bo.

Lippi, name of 2 Italian Renaissance painters in Florence. **Fra Filippo Lippi** (c.1406-69) was influenced by Masaccio, Donatello, and by Flemish painting. His frescoes in the Cathedral of Prato are his most important works. **Filippino Lippi** (c.1457-1504), his son, influenced by Botticelli, painted the brilliantly detailed *Adoration of the Magi* (1496).

Lippmann, Walter (1889-1974), influential U.S. political columnist and foreign affairs analyst. His column, "Today and Tomorrow," first appeared in the *New York Herald Tribune* (1931-62), then the *Washington Post* (1962-67); it won two Pulitzer prizes (1958, 1962). Books include *Public Opinion* (1922) and *The Good Society* (1937).

Lisbon (pop. 810,000), capital and largest city of Portugal, on the Tagus River estuary near the Atlantic Ocean. Its harbor handles the bulk of the country's foreign trade. A Roman settlement from c.200 B.C., Lisbon was conquered by the Moors in 716. It was reconquered in 1147 and became the capital c.1260. In the 16th century it was the center of Portugal's colonial empire. Much of the city was rebuilt after a disastrous earthquake in 1755. Current industries include steel, petroleum refining, textiles, chemicals, paper, and metal products.
See also: Portugal.

Lister, Sir Joseph (1827-1912), English surgeon who pioneered antiseptic surgery. Pasteur had shown that microscopic organisms (bacteria) are responsible for infection, but his sterilization techniques were unsuitable for surgical use. Through experimentation Lister succeeded in using carbolic acid as a sterilization agent. This greatly reduced post-operative fatalities caused by infection.

Liszt, Franz (1811-86), Hungarian composer and virtuoso pianist who revolutionized keyboard technique. Director of music in Weimar, Germany, 1843-61, he later moved to Rome and took minor holy orders in 1865. His music includes 13 symphonic poems (a form he invented), symphonies such as *Faust* (1854), the Sonata in B Minor for piano (1853), *Transcendental Studies* for piano (1852); and 20

Hungarian rhapsodies. His daughter, Cosima, married Richard Wagner.

Litchfield (pop. 7,605), village in western Connecticut declared a National Historic Landmark in 1978. During the American Revolution it served as a supply point and rest stop for Revolutionary soldiers. Birthplace of the Revolutionary leader Ethan Allen and the author Harriet Beecher Stowe, Litchfield is also noted as the site of the first U.S. law school, Litchfield School of Law, which later became Tapping Reeve Law School.
See also: Connecticut.

Litchi, or lichee, evergreen Chinese tree (*Litchi chinensis*) grown in warm climates, a member of the soapberry family. Prized for its juicy fruit, the litchi has been cultivated in southern China for over 2,000 years. The round fruit ranges from 1/2 to 1 1/2 in (1.3 to 3.8 cm) in diameter and has a rough, brittle skin and white flesh with a single large brown seed inside. Rich in vitamin C, the fruit is eaten fresh or canned in a syrup. When dried, it is called litchi nut.

Literature for children, a special branch of creative writing that is geared to young readers, ranging from the preschool age to the teenage years. The literature consists of almost every genre used in adult literature: novels, plays, biographies, poetry, collections of folk tales, and informative works on the arts, science, and social affairs. These works for children are written expressly at their level, and they are designed and illustrated to capture the imagination of young readers. Some books that were written for adults have taken on the status of children's literature because of their popularity with young people. Among these are the collection of folk tales assembled by the brothers Grimm (*Grimm's Fairy Tales*), Mark Twain's *Tom Sawyer* (and to a lesser extent *Huckleberry Finn*), Daniel Defoe's *Robinson Crusoe*, and Jonathan Swift's *Gulliver's Travels*. Also, many adult works have been adapted for children in different versions, for example, the ever-popular story of King Arthur and his knights, from Thomas Malory's *Morte D'Arthur*. Adults, of course, have told stories to children from time immemorial. It must be remembered that before the invention of printing in Europe (around the mid-1500s), there was little literacy in the general population. The ability to read was confined largely to the clergy and the nobility. Moreover, books were copied out laboriously by hand and were much prized by the few who could afford them or use them. Children's literature, under those circumstances, was, like the literature of the general public, based on an oral tradition, which consisted for the most part of myths, fables, ballads, and poems. Some early books for children were produced, but they were primarily instructional in nature. Saint Aldhelm, Bishop of Sherborne, is thought to have written the first such text for children in English sometime during the A.D. 600s. It was written in catechism style, that is question and answer, and that format for children's instructional and devotional texts remained popular for the next 1,000 years. The first recognized classic of children's literature appeared in France in 1697, a book of eight tales collected by Charles Perrault entitled *Stories and Tales of Times Past with Morals; or, Tales of Mother Goose*. In England, in 1744, John Newbury published *A Little Pretty Pocket-Book*, one of the first children's books designed primarily to amuse rather than to educate. Newbury was also one of the first important publishers of children's books. During the 1800s, publishing and writing for children became a distinct branch of literature. Also at that time, illustration developed as a major feature of books for children, as exemplified by John Tenniel's illustrations for *Alice in Wonderland* and *Through the Looking Glass*. It was the 20th century that saw an explosive growth in children's books. The picture book, a book where illustrations carry the story and interest as much as the text, developed in the 20th century. Beatrix Potter's *The Tale of Peter Rabbit* (1901) is the first of this genre. Books are now available for almost every stage of childhood, covering almost every possible subject. Fantasy and adventure are always popular, but children's books today deal with social problems (race, drugs, sex) as well as with history and biography. Children's books are now available in all formats and price ranges, and they are very much a part of growing up in the modern world.

Litharge, poisonous compound (PbO) of lead and oxygen, also called lead monoxide. Litharge is a yellow or reddish-yellow solid produced by heating lead or lead compounds in air. It is used in storage batteries and in making lead glass, rubber, and pottery glazes.

Lithium, chemical element, symbol Li; for physical constants see Periodic Table. Lithium was discovered by Johann August Arfvedson in 1817. It is found in nearly all igneous rocks. *Spodumene* (lithium aluminum silicate) is an important mineral of lithium. Lithium is recovered commercially from brines. The metal is produced by the electrolysis of its fused chloride. Lithium is a silvery-white, reactive metal, the first of the alkali metal group. It is the lightest of all metals and has the highest specific heat of any solid element. Lithium and its compounds are used in lithium-hardened bearing metals, batteries, heat transfer applications, special glasses and ceramics, and in medicine for manic-depressive illness.

Lithography, form of printing used in both fine art and in commercial printing, invented by Aloys Senefelder in Germany c.1798. The technique consists of making a drawing in reverse on the surface of a stone, usually limestone, with an ink containing grease. When the grease has penetrated the stone, the drawing is washed off with water. The grease resists the water, but will accept ink, which is spread over the moist stone. The stone is then used to print the drawing. In the United States, lithographic artists include A.B. Davies, George Bellows, and Currier & Ives.
See also: Printing; Senefelder, Alois.

Lithuania, independent country bordering on the Baltic Sea, surrounded by Poland, Russia, Byelorussia, and Latvia. Although timber and agricultural products remain important, Lithuania is now mostly urban. As such, shipbuilding, and the manufacture of machinery and building materials have taken over as the most important industries. The chief cities and industrial centers are Vilnius (the capital), Kaunas, and Klaipeda, the main port. Roman Catholicism is the traditional religion. Lithuanian, a member of the Baltic branch of the Indo-European family, is the main language. About 80% of the population is Lithuanian; Russians and Poles are the largest minorities. Fourteenth-century Lithuania, which included Byelorussia and parts of the Ukraine and Russia, was central Europe's most powerful state. In 1386 Lithuania and Poland were united under Grand Duke Jagiello. In 1795 the partition of Poland brought Lithuania under Russian rule. In 1918 independence was declared, and Lithuania, like the other Baltic republics, became a separate state, although Poland occupied Vilnius from 1920 to 1939. In 1940 the Soviet Union invaded Lithuania and the other Baltic republics, and after World War II all 3 were incorporated in the Soviet Union. Nationalist sentiment grew in the late 1980s, and in 1990 the Lithuanian republican government declared independence from the USSR, a declaration not recognized by the Moscow government until 1991.
See also: Union of Soviet Socialist Republics.

Lithuania

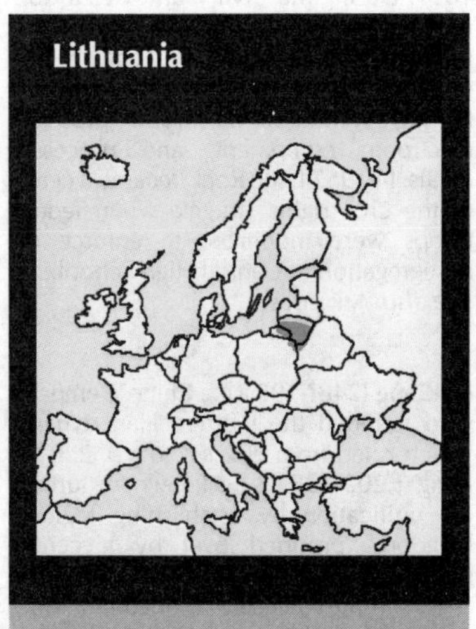

Capital:	Vilnius
Area:	25,212 sq mi (65,300 sq km)
Population:	3,754,000
Government:	republic
Independent:	1991
GNP:	U.S. $4,922,000,000
Per capita:	U.S. $1,310

The human liver

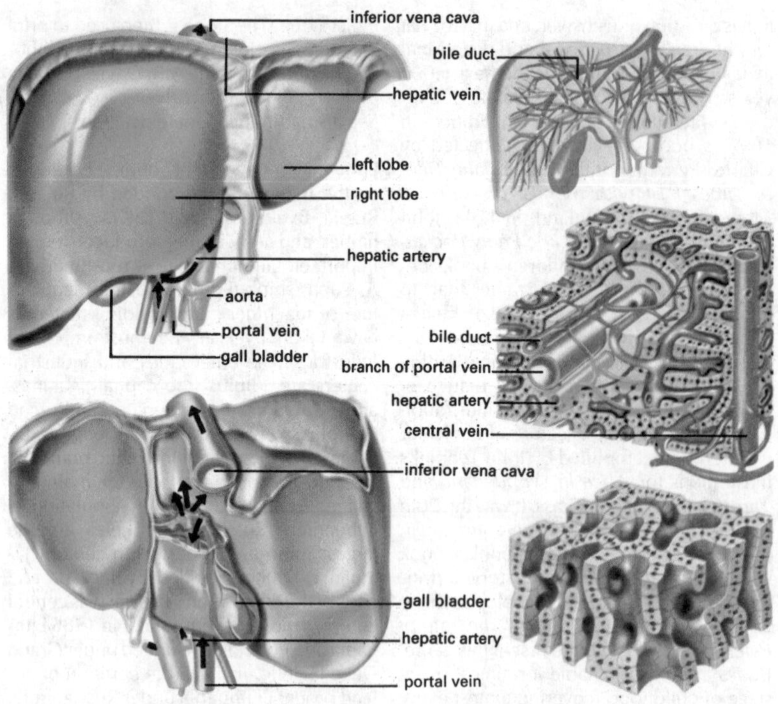

Little Bighorn, Battle of, battle in southeastern Montana, near the Little Bighorn River, June 25-26, 1876, in which Colonel George A. Custer was killed and his troops annihilated by Sioux and Cheyennes led by chiefs Sitting Bull and Crazy Horse.

Little Dipper *see:* Big and Little Dippers.

Little Rock (pop. 513,117), state capital and principal commercial center of Arkansas, on the Arkansas River. Little Rock, originally a river crossing, became the capital of the Arkansas territory in 1821. During the Civil War it was a Confederate stronghold but was captured by the Union forces in 1863. Today it produces metal products, cottonseed, cotton fabrics, furniture, hardwood products, electronic equipment, and processed meats. In 1957 Little Rock became a center of the civil rights struggle when federal troops were mobilized to enforce the desegregation of Central High School.
See also: Arkansas.

Liu Bang (248?-195 B.C.), Chinese emperor who founded the western Han dynasty, which ruled from 202 B.C. to A.D. 220 Liu Bang (r.202-195 B.C.) is known for furthering unification by establishing regional kingdoms presided over by a central government.
Although he defeated Mongolian tribes that invaded China and eliminated certain harsh laws, Liu Bang is historically considered a cruel emperor. He began his career as one of the generals who led revolutionary forces against the Ch'in dynasty in 207-206 B.C.
See also: Han dynasty.

Liu Pang *see:* Liu Bang.

Liu Shao-Ch'i (1893-1969), Chinese communist leader who succeeded Mao Tse-Tung as chair of the Chinese People's Republic (1959-68). In 1968 he was publicly denounced for embracing capitalism and dismissed. In 1980 he was posthumously exonerated by Deng Xiaoping.
See also: China.

Live oak, any of several species of North American evergreen trees (genus *Quercus*) of the beech family. The American oak, *Q. virginiana*, flourishes along the southeastern coast of the United States and is also found in Cuba. It can reach a height of about 50 ft (15 m), and many of its limbs fan out horizontally to form a dense web. Its leaves are dark green and shiny above, whitish and furry below. The live oak is both a timber tree and a popular ornamental tree.

Liver, in anatomy, the largest glandular organ in the human body, lying on the right of the abdomen beneath the diaphragm. It consists of 4 lobes made up of between 50,000 and 100,000 lobules. The metabolic cells of the lobules perform the work of the liver, which includes several functions. The liver aids in digestion by converting nutrients in the blood into a form suitable for storage called glycogen and by producing bile, which breaks down fats. The liver also purifies the blood by converting harmful substances into products that may be excreted in urine or bile. Diseases of the liver include cirrhosis and hepatitis.
See also: Human body.

Liverleaf *see:* Hepatica.

Liverpool (pop. 491,500), industrial city in northwestern England, one of its major ports, on the Mersey River, 3 mi (5 km) from the Irish Sea. The borough was chartered in 1207. In the 18th century it was a major slave-trading port. Food processing and chemicals are now important local industries.
See also: England.

Liverwort, primitive plant that lives in moist places. With the mosses, liverworts bridge the gap between the water-dwelling algae and the land-dwelling ferns and flowering plants.

Livestock, general term for animals raised to be sources of meat, milk, wool, leather, or labor. Cattle, hogs, poultry, sheep, and horses are all considered livestock. In some parts of the world donkeys, goats, mules, and rabbits are also livestock.

Livingston, Philip (1716-78), U.S. political leader, signer of the Declaration of Independence. A delegate to both the Stamp Act Congress (1765) and the Continental Congress (1774-78), Livingston was also an early promoter of King's College, which later became Columbia University in New York City.

Livingston, Robert R. (1746-1813), U.S. politician. A delegate to the Continental Congress, he helped draft the Declaration of Independence and, a year later, the New York state constitution. As chancellor of New York state (1777-1801) he administered the presidential oath of office to George Washington. In 1801 he began the negotiations that led to the Louisiana Purchase.

Livingstone, David *see:* Stanley and Livingstone.

Livy (Titus Livius; c.59 B.C.-A.D. 17), Roman historian. Of his 142-volume *History of Rome*, 35 books survive, with fragments and an outline of the rest. It traces the city from its founding in 753 B.C. to the end of the reign of Nero Drusus in 9 B.C. Although Livy is not always accurate, he is admired for his style and for his effort to view the development of the empire historically.

Li Yuan (A.D. 566-636), first emperor (618-627) and founder of the Tang dynasty (618-907), one of the greatest periods in China's history. His son, Li Shimin, forced him from power.
See also: Tang Dynasty.

Lizard, any of many reptiles of the order Squamata, which also includes snakes. Lizards usually possess well-developed limbs, though these are reduced or absent in some species. Lizards typically eat insects, though some will take eggs or small mammals. Unlike snakes, lizards have ear openings and movable eyelids. The smallest are less than 3 in (7.6 cm); the largest is the Komodo dragon of Indonesia, which can be 10 ft (3 m) long.

Llama, domesticated South American hoofed mammal (*Lama glama*) of the camel family. Resembling a large, long-necked

Llamas

sheep, it has thick fleece that may be used for wool and is the principal beast of burden of Native Americans from Peru to Chile, thriving at altitudes of 7,500-13,000 ft (2,280-4,000 m).

Lloyd, Harold Clayton (1894-1971), U.S. comedian of the silent screen, famous as the disaster-prone naive young man in glasses and straw hat. Among his best-known films are *Safety Last* (1923), *The Kid Brother* (1927), and *Feet First* (1930).

Lloyd, Henry Demarest (1847-1903), U.S. reforming journalist. He distinguished himself as a muckraker, exposing the misconduct of big business monopolies, notably in his contributions to the *Chicago Tribune* (1872-85) and his book *Wealth Against Commonwealth* (1894), a history of the Standard Oil Company. He became an active supporter of the Socialists, and ran for Congress on the National People's Party ticket (1894).

Lloyd George, David, (1863-1945), Welsh political leader, British prime minister 1916-22. Elected a Liberal Member of Parliament in 1890, he served the same Welsh constituency until his death. As chancellor of the exchequer (1908-15) under Prime Minister Herbert Asquith he led in initiating British welfare legislation. In World War I Lloyd George became, successively, minister of munitions, minister of war, and finally prime minister of a coalition government. He was one of the architects of the Treaty of Versailles, which ended the war. His coalition fell in 1922, when the Conservatives withdrew from it. In the 1930s he led the remains of the Liberal Party and opposed policies of appeasement toward Nazi Germany.

Lloyd Webber, Andrew (1948-), popular British composer whose first success was the musical *Jesus Christ Superstar* (1971). His other musicals include *Evita* (1978), a fictional account of the life of Eva Peron; *Cats* (1981), based on the poems of T.S. Eliot; and *The Phantom of the Opera* (1986), based on Gaston Leroux's novel.

Loadstone, hard black mineral (Fe_3O_4) with magnetic properties, also called lodestone and magnetite. It is found in the form of rocks, crystals, and sand in Siberia, South Africa, and parts of Italy and the United States. Loadstone was used as a precursor to the compass, when ancient Europeans discovered that if an oblong piece of it was suspended from a string, it would point north and south.
See also: Magnetism.

Lobbying, attempting to influence legislators' votes by an agent of a particular political pressure group. The word derives from the practice of agents talking with legislators in the lobby of the legislature. The system is controlled by the Federal Regulation of Lobbying Act of 1946.

Lobelia, any of several species of annual or biannual plants (genus *Lobelia*) found in pastures, meadows, and cultivated fields. Its clusters of flowers are used for medicinal purposes because of its antispasmodic, diuretic, emetic, and expectorant properties.

Lobster, large marine crustacean with 5 pairs of jointed legs, the first bearing enormous claws. True lobsters (genus *Homarus*) live in shallow water and feed on carrion, small crabs, and worms. The 2 large claws differ in structure and function, one being adapted for crushing, the other for fine picking or scraping. The dark blue pigment of the living lobster is a complex compound that turns red when exposed to intense heat.

Lobworm, also called lugworm or lugbait, seaworm (class Polychaeta) much used as bait for deep-sea fishing. Lobworms live along the Atlantic coasts of North America and Europe and near the Mediterranean Sea.

Local government, in the United States embraces a wide variety of governmental units, such as cities, counties, townships, and school districts. The average citizen comes into contact with local government quite often because it provides a variety of functions and services important in his daily life. These include garbage collection, police protection, education, firefighting, traffic regulation, street and road lighting, water supply and sewage control, public health and medical services, the recording of births, deaths, and marriages, and many others.
Municipal government includes the established authorities of cities, towns, and villages. The most common form is the *mayor-council*, of which the chief executive officer is a mayor elected on a partisan ballot. He generally has wide powers of administration and appointment, and may veto acts of the city council. The latter, also elected on a partisan ballot, raises funds for the municipality, and passes laws and bylaws. Many smaller cities have a *council-manager* system, in which an elected city council sets the broad outlines of policy and appoints a nonpartisan professional city manager to carry out the day-to-day administrative work. This system removes many government functions from the arena of politics.
County governments administer rural areas. They are usually headed by an elected board and include a number of other elected officials for specific functions such as sheriff, coroner, assessor, and clerk. Normally there is no one principal executive officer such as a mayor.

Locarno Treaties, pacts drawn up in Locarno, Switzerland, in 1925 providing for the demilitarization of the Rhineland and specifying the borders of Belgium, France, Germany, Poland, and Czechoslovakia. The participants included those 5 countries plus Britain and Italy. The "spirit of Locarno," supposedly heralding peace, died in 1936 when Hitler denounced the pacts and moved troops into the Rhineland.

Loch Lomond, largest lake in Scotland, located in the highlands about 20 mi (32 km) north of the city of Glasgow. It is 23 mi (37 km) long and 5 mi (8 km) wide at its widest point. Loch Lomond is the subject of a familiar Scottish folk song, and Scottish clans in ancient times used its shores as a gathering place.

David Lloyd George (right) with Woodrow Wilson

Lock, device that fastens shut and prevents the opening of doors, windows, lids, and other objects. Types of lock include key, combination, chain, and electronic. Most common door locks have a bolt that fits into a metal plate in the door frame. The first key-operated lock, invented in Egypt c.2000 B.C., was a large wooden bolt fastened to the outside of a gate and stabilized by pegs inserted through it; a key raised the pins to free the bolt.

Locke, John (1632-1704), English philosopher, founder of empiricism, whose writings helped initiate the European Enlightenment. His *Essay Concerning Human Understanding* (1690) opposed the

Andrew Lloyd Webber's Cats

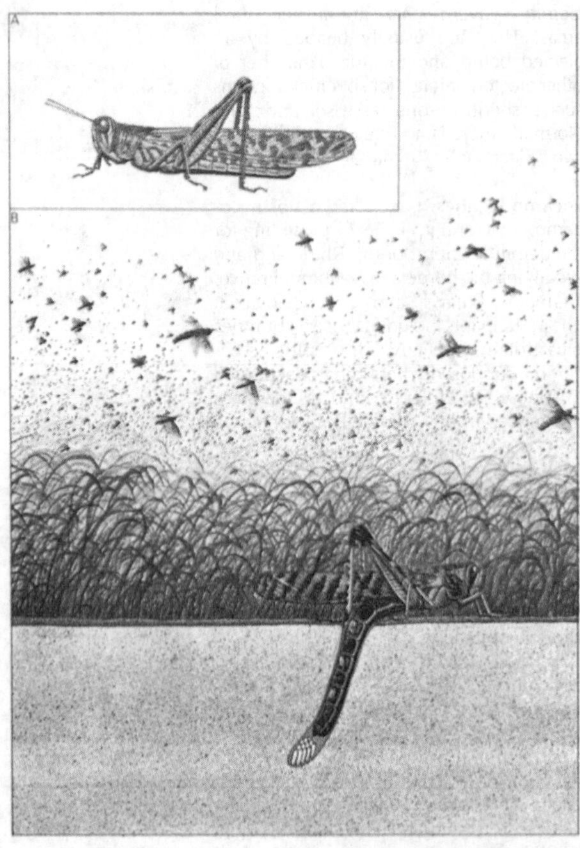

A. Locust
B. Locusts swarming: at the bottom is an ovipositing (egg-laying) female

view that there were innate ideas; he held instead that the human mind was like a blank slate on which knowledge is inscribed by experience. His *Second Treatise of Civil Government* (1690) established him as Britain's leading philosopher of politics. In it he argued that all people had the right to "life, health, liberty, and possessions." He proposed a "social contract" to guarantee these rights. Locke also held that revolution was justified and even necessary in some circumstances, and he upheld both religious toleration and government by checks and balances, as later adopted in the U.S. Constitution. A believer in progress and the scientific method, Locke was one of the most influential thinkers of the modern era.

Lockjaw *see:* Tetanus.

Lockwood, Belva Ann Bennett (1830-1917), attorney, suffragette, and Equal Rights Party nominee for president of the United States in 1884 and 1888. The first woman authorized to argue before the U.S. Supreme Court, Lockwood won equal pay for women working in government. She is also known for her successful defense of the threatened land rights of the North Carolina Cherokee.
See also: Women's movements.

Locomotive, power unit used to haul railroad trains. The earliest railroad locomotives, invented in England in the early 19th century, used steam engines, which remained popular until the mid-20th century. Although electric locomotives have been in service in the United States since 1895, the high capital cost of converting tracks to electric transmission has prevented their widespread adoption. Since the 1950s, most U.S. locomotives have been built with diesel engines. Elsewhere in the world, particularly in Europe, much greater use is made of electric traction, the locomotives usually collecting power from overhead cables via a pantograph. Although some gas-turbine locomotives are in service in the United States, this and other novel power sources have not made much headway.

Locomotor ataxia *see:* Ataxia.

Locoweed, any of several leguminous plants of the genera *Astragalus* and *Oxytropis* native to dry regions of the west and southwestern United States. The plants are poisonous, causing livestock to become stuporous and to stagger, a disease commonly known as locoism.

Locust, in zoology, name for about 50 species of tropical grasshoppers that have a swarming stage in their life cycle. Locusts breed in huge numbers where conditions are suitable, then fly in swarms when they reach maturity. The swarms may contain as many as 100 billion insects and can cause agricultural disaster when they land and devour crops.

Locust, in botany, deciduous tree or shrub (genus *Robinia*) with large thorns. Locusts have flowers like those of sweet peas and compound leaves made up of double rows of leaflets. They grow rapidly, and their roots send up suckers, making them effective for holding shifting ground. The timber does not shrink or swell and is used to make wooden pins and railroad ties.

Lodestone *see:* Loadstone.

Lodge, name of 2 U.S. statesmen from Massachusetts. **Henry Cabot Lodge** (1850-1924), U.S. senator, 1893-1924, was a conservative Republican known for his support of the Spanish-American War and opposition to U.S. membership in the League of Nations. He was also a prominent historian. His grandson, the diplomat **Henry Cabot Lodge, Jr.** (1902-85), was a Republican U.S. senator, 1937-44 and 1947-52. He lost his seat to John F. Kennedy. He served as U.S. ambassador to the UN (1953-60), ambassador to South Vietnam (1963-64 and 1965-67), and ambassador to West Germany (1968-69). He was also chief U.S. negotiator at the Vietnam peace talks in Paris (1969).

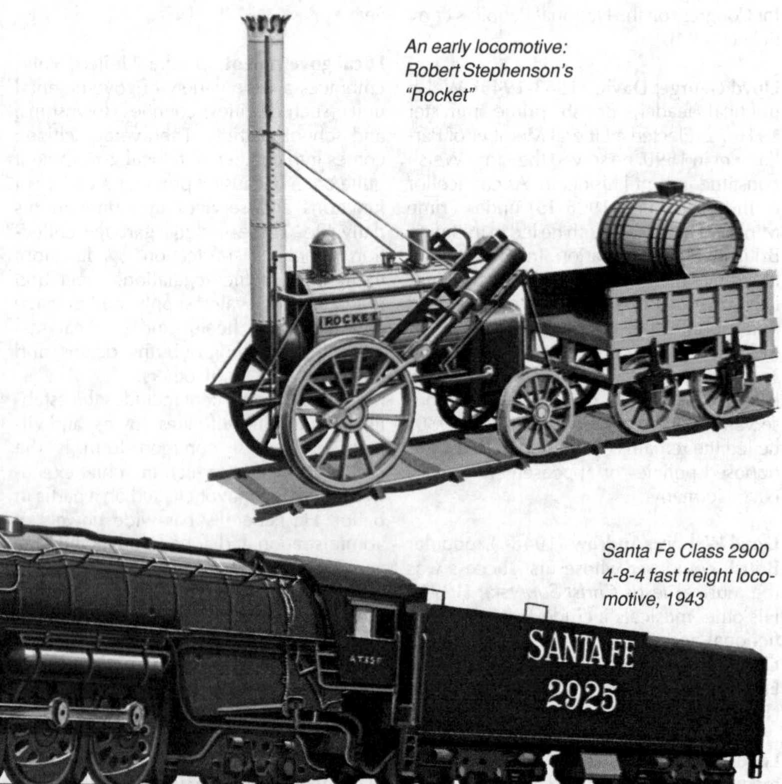

An early locomotive: Robert Stephenson's "Rocket"

Santa Fe Class 2900 4-8-4 fast freight locomotive, 1943

Lódz (pop. 847,900), city in central Poland, the country's second largest. Chartered in 1423, the city was taken over by Prussia in 1793 and by Russia in 1815. Only in 1919 did it revert to Poland. German troops occupied and severely damaged Lódz during World War II; it has since been rebuilt. Today it is Poland's leading textile manufacturing city, as well as the center of its motion picture industry.
See also: Poland.

Loeb, Jacques (1859-1924), German-born U.S. biologist best known for his work on parthenogenesis, especially his induction of artificial parthenogenesis in the eggs of sea urchins and frogs. Parthenogenesis is the process by which an unfertilized egg develops into an embryo.

Loesser, Frank (1910-1969), U.S. composer of music and lyrics. He won the Academy Award for his song "Baby It's Cold Outside"(1949) and shared the Pulitzer Prize with Abe Burrows for the musical comedy *How to Succeed in Business Without Even Trying* (1962).

Löffler, Friedrich (1852-1915), German bacteriologist who co-discovered the diphtheria bacillus in 1884. Loffler found a way to cultivate the bacillus and perfected a staining method by which it could be carefully observed under a microscope. His demonstration that some animals are immune to diphtheria influenced Emil von Behring in the development of a diphtheria antitoxin. Loffler is also credited, along with Paul Frosch, for discovering that foot-and-mouth disease is viral and for developing a serum against it.

Lofting, Hugh (1886-1947), English-born U.S. author and illustrator of the famous *Dr. Dolittle* stories, begun in letters to his children during World War I. *The Voyages of Dr. Dolittle* , the second in the series, won him the Newbery medal in 1923.

Log, in nautical measurement, device used to measure a ship's speed. It consists of a piece of board in the form of a quadrant of a circle, balanced so as to float upright. When thrown from the ship, it drags on the line to which it is attached, causing it to unwind at a rate corresponding to the ship's velocity.

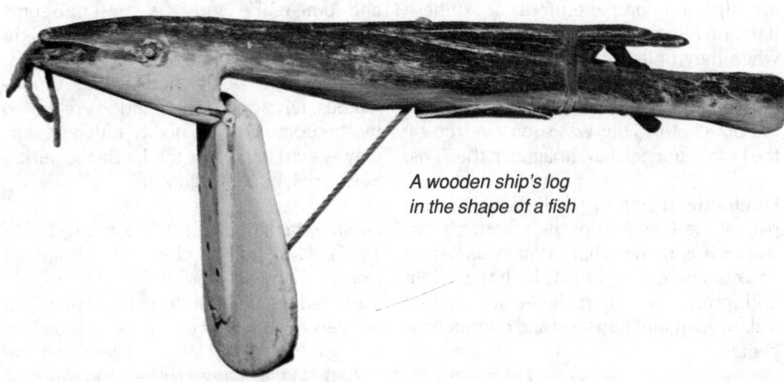

A wooden ship's log in the shape of a fish

Logan (1725?-80?), a leader of the Cayugas during the American colonial period. At first Logan established peaceful relations with white settlers in Pennsylvania and in the Ohio territory, but he led raids on white settlements after members of his family were killed by colonists in 1774. His explanation of his refusal to participate in peace talks was praised by Thomas Jefferson for its eloquence. During the Revolutionary War, Logan aligned himself with the Mohawk auxiliaries of the British forces.

Logan, John Alexander (1826-86), Union general during the Civil War. Logan fought in the Western campaigns under Ulysses S. Grant and served with General William T. Sherman on his march through Georgia. After the capture of Vicksburg, Miss., Logan was made a general in command of volunteers. In a later political career, Logan represented Illinois in the U.S. House of Representatives (1859-62, 1867-71) and in the senate (1871-77, 1879-86). He is also known as the originator of Memorial Day.
See also: Civil War, U.S.; Memorial Day.

Logan, Joshua (1908-1988), U.S. director and dramatist. He shared a Pulitzer Prize with Oscar Hammerstein II and Richard Rogers for *South Pacific* (1950). He coauthored and directed *Mr. Roberts* (1948) and directed the musicals *Knickerbocker Holiday* (1938), *Annie Get Your Gun* (1946), *Fanny* (1954) and the play *Picnic* (1953).

Logan Act, U.S. law enacted in 1799 prohibiting private citizens from entering into negotiations with a foreign government involved in a dispute with the United States. The law was a reaction to the activities of George Logan, who in l798, attempted to negotiate a settlement to a Naval dispute with France.

Loganberry, hybrid bramble produced from the dewberry and the raspberry. It is named for Judge Logan, who developed it in 1881.

Logarithm, power to which a fixed number, called the base, must be raised to produce a given number. The base is usually 10 or *e*. For example: $2^3 = 8$; 3 is the logarithm of 8 to the base 2.
See also: Napier, John.

Logic, the science of dealing with formal principles of reasoning and thought. Aristotelian, or classical, logic is characterized by a concern for the structure and elements of argument based on the belief that thought, language, and reality are interrelated. Classical logic's influence on Western Civilization has been enormous and enduring. In the 19th and 20th centuries symbolic logic has achieved preeminence. It is rooted in mathematical theory (Set Theory) and has been instrumental in the evolution of modern mathematics.

Loire River, longest river in France, rising in the Cévennes Mountains of central France and flowing north and west through the Massif Central about 650 mi (1,050 km) to the Atlantic. The Loire Valley is famous for its opulent chateaux.

Loire valley, chateau Chenonceau

Loki, in Norse mythology, the god who personified trouble and deceit. Although some myths show Loki to be helpful to the gods, he is generally portrayed as evil. He is most infamous for his role in the killing of Balder, the son of the chief god Odin.

Lollards, name given to the 14th-century followers of the English religious reformer John Wycliffe (c.1328-84). Wandering preachers, the Lollards taught that ministers should be poor and that Christians should interpret the Bible themselves. They held that the Bible, and not an organized church, should be the supreme authority. Although repressed during the early 15th century, Lollard beliefs were linked with radical social unrest and remained as underground influences on later movements.

Lombardi, Vince (1913-70), U.S. football coach of the Green Bay Packers of the National Football League (NFL). Under Lombardi's leadership (1959-68) the Packers won 5 NFL titles and two Super Bowls (1967, 68). Known for his intense, uncompromising style of coaching, Lombardi is given credit for coining the phrase "winning isn't everything, its the only thing." He was inducted into the Pro Football Hall of Fame in 1971.

Lombards, Germanic people who moved from northwestern Germany toward Italy in the fourth century. In 568 they crossed the Alps and conquered most of northern Italy, dividing it into dukedoms until 584, when they united into a kingdom against the threat of Frankish invasion. The kingdom reached its height under Liutprand in the 8th century, but was soon overrun by the Franks under Charlemagne in the 770s.

Lombardy, region of northern Italy, once part of the kingdom of the Lombards, for whom it is named. Italy's main industrial and commercial region, it also has efficient and prosperous agriculture. Its capital, Milan, is a major transport and commercial center.

London (pop. 269,100), manufacturing and commercial city on the Thames River in southeast Ontario, Canada. Settled by British colonists on Iroquois land in 1826, London was destroyed by fire in 1845, but soon rebuilt. Today it is the home of more than 300 manufacturing plants, producing goods such as beverages, foods, diesel vehicles, chemical and electrical products, and telephone equipment.
See also: Ontario.

London (pop. 6,770,000), capital of Great Britain. Divided into 33 boroughs, Greater London covers over 650 sq mi (1,684 sq km) along both banks of the Thames River in southeast England. The national center of government, trade, commerce, shipping, finance, and industry, it is also one of the cultural centers of the world.

London, the Tower Bridge

The Port of London handles over 33% of British trade. London is also an important industrial region in its own right, with various manufacturing industries. Many of the most important financial and business institutions, such as the Bank of England, the Stock Exchange, and Lloyd's of London, as well as many banking and shipping concerns, are concentrated in the single square mile (2.6 km) known as the City. The ancient nucleus of London, the City has its own Lord Mayor. To the west of the City are the Law Courts, the Inns of Court, and the governmental area in Westminster centered on the House of Commons and House of Lords.London is a historic city with many beautiful buildings; the Tower of London, Westminster Abbey, and Buckingham Palace are major tourist attractions. Home of universities, colleges, and some of the world's greatest museums and libraries, it also has a flourishing night life. London's art galleries, concert halls, theaters, and opera houses are world-famous. Distant areas of London are linked by the complex and highly efficient subway system known as the Underground.
See also: United Kingdom.

London, Jack (John Griffith London; 1876-1916), U.S. author of novels and short stories, many set during the Yukon Gold Rush and treating the struggles of men and animals to survive. His works include *The Call of the Wild* (1903), *The Sea Wolf* (1904), *White Fang* (1906), and *Burning Daylight* (1910). He also wrote an autobiographical novel *Martin Eden* (1909), and a political novel, *The Iron Heel* (1907), dramatizing his socialist beliefs and predicting the rise of fascism. Alcoholism and financial problems led him to commit suicide at the age of 40.

London Bridge, historical succession of bridges over the Thames River in London, England. The first bridge, dating from the 10th century, was wooden. In 1176-1209 it was replaced by a stone bridge with many buildings along it, including a chapel and defensive towers. Rebuilt many times, it was demolished and replaced in 1831 by a granite bridge, called New London Bridge. That structure was dismantled in 1968 and moved to Lake Havasu City, Ariz., as a tourist attraction. A new concrete bridge over the Thames replaced it.

Londonderry (pop. 95,300), seaport in northwest Northern Ireland, on the Foyle River. It was known as Derry until 1613 and is still called that by Irish nationalists. It has a traditional shirtmaking industry and some light manufacturing industries. Since 1968 it has been a center of violent conflict between Protestants and Roman Catholics.
See also: Ireland.

Lone Star State *see:* Texas.

Long, powerful political family in Louisiana history. **Huey Pierce Long** (1893-1935), known as "Kingfish," was elected both governor (1928-31) and U.S. senator (from 1930). A radical advocate of social reforms who gained national renown for his "Share-the-Wealth" programs and his corrupt and demagogic methods, he was assassinated by a political enemy, Dr. Carl A. Weiss, in Sept. 1935. **Russell Billie Long** (1918-), a son of Huey, served in the U.S. Senate from 1948 to 1987. **Earl Kemp Long** (1895-1960), younger brother of Huey, was governor of Louisiana three times. **George Shannon Long** (1883-1958), older brother of Huey, served in the U.S. House of Representatives from 1953.

Long, Crawford Williamson (1815-78), U.S. physician who first used diethyl ether as an anesthetic during surgery (1842). His discovery followed his observation that students under the influence of ether at a party felt no pain when bruising or otherwise injuring themselves.

Long, Stephen Harriman (1748-1864), U.S. explorer, army engineer, and surveyor. He explored the upper Mississippi River (1817), the Rocky Mts., where Longs Peak is named for him (1819-20), and the Minnesota River (1823). His survey for the Baltimore and Ohio railroad resulted in a railroad manual.

Long Beach (pop. 361,355), seaport, industrial center, and tourist area in southern California, on San Pedro Bay, about 20 mi (32 km) southeast of Los Angeles. After 1921, when oil was tapped in Signal Hill, there was a population boom in the town. Aircraft and electronic manufacturing and oil production are among its leading industries.

Longbow *see:* Archery.

Longfellow, Henry Wadsworth (1807-82), U.S. poet, one of the most popular poets of his generation. A contemporary of Hawthorne at Bowdoin College, he became a professor of modern languages there (1829-35) and at Harvard (1836-54). His principal works were the narrative poems *Evangeline* (1847), *The Song of Hiawatha* (1855), and *The Courtship of Miles Standish* (1858), and *Paul Revere's Ride* (1861). Famous individual poems include "The Wreck of the Hesperus" and "Excelsior."

Longinus (fl. 1st cent. ?A.D.), Greek writer to whom the ancient Greek essay on literary criticism *On the Sublime* has been attributed. The treatise discusses "loftiness of style" in literature. It quotes the Greek orator Demosthenes and the Roman orator Cicero to make comparative points about literary style, and it is the source of the text of Sappho's second ode.

Long Island, island off the southeastern coast of New York, extending east for about 118 mi (190 km) from the mouth of the Hudson River. Its width ranges between 12 mi (19 km) and 20 mi (32 km). The New York City boroughs of Brooklyn and Queens are at the western end. Nassau and Suffolk counties, which take up the bulk of the island, were predominantly agricultural until World War II but now have much residential and light industrial development. The beaches and bays of its southern shore, on the Atlantic Ocean, make Long Island a popular summer resort.

Long Island Sound, arm of the Atlantic Ocean separating the state of Connecticut from Long Island. About 110 mi (177 km) long and 20 mi (32 km) wide at most points, Long Island Sound is part of the Atlantic Intracoastal Waterway.

Longitude, measure of the distance, in angular degrees, of any point on the earth's surface east or west of the prime meridian, which is 0° longitude. The prime meridian is the imaginary great circle line, running from pole to pole, that runs through the city of Greenwich, England. Meridians of longitude and parallels of latitude form a grid

that can be used to locate the position of any point on the earth's surface.
See also: Latitude; Prime Meridian.

Long March, the 6,000-mi (9,656-km) march (1934-35) of the Chinese communists, from Jiangxi in the Southeast to Shaanxi in the extreme Northwest, which saved the movement from extermination by the Nationalist (Kuomintang) forces of Chiang Kai-shek. Led by Mao Zedong, the Red Army of some 100,000 trekked over 18 mountain ranges and 24 rivers under constant air and land attack by Kuomintang troops and local warlords. The march, which lasted for one year, took the lives of almost one-half of its participants.
See also: China; Mao Zedong.

Long Parliament, English legislative assembly that met between 1640 and 1660. Convened by Charles I, it tried to check his power. The conflict between the crown and Parliament culminated in the Civil War (1642-45), during which Parliament remained in session. In 1648 it was "purged" of accused supporters of the king, and in 1649 those who were left, known as the Rump Parliament, had Charles beheaded for treason. In 1653 Parliament was suspended under the Protectorate led by Oliver Cromwell. It was briefly reconvened in 1660 prior to the Restoration.
See also: Parliament.

Longstreet, James (1821-1904), Confederate general in the U.S. Civil War, who fought at Fredericksburg and Antietam. His delay in the attack at Gettysburg (1863), where he was second in command, is generally thought to have been decisive in losing the battle. He also fought in the last defense of Richmond, Va.
See also: Civil War, U.S.

Lon Nol (1913-85), Cambodian general and head of state (1970-75). In 1970 he led a coup to depose Prince Norodom Sihanouk. Although Lon Nol declared Cambodia as a republic he ruled as a dictator, cooperating with the U.S. invasion in the spring of 1970. Overthrown by Khmer Rouge guerillas in 1975 after a bloody civil war, Lon Nol fled to Hawaii, where he settled.
See also: Kampuchea.

Loon, waterbird (family *Gaviidae*) of northern countries, known in England as the diver. These birds have webbed feet set well back on their bodies and are very ungainly on land. They are best known for their eerie, wailing calls. They make their nests on the edges of ponds, and the chicks sometimes ride on their parents' backs. They catch fish by diving, sometimes below 200 ft (61 m).

Loosestrife, popular name of any of several species of primulaceous plants (genus *Lysimachia*) with leafy stems and yellow-white flowers.

López de Santa Anna, Antonio *see:* Santa Anna, Antonio López de.

López Portillo, José (1920-), president of Mexico (1976-82), during a period of rapid economic growth, especially in the energy field. He was notably assertive in his relationship with the United States.
See also: Mexico.

Loquat, subtropical evergreen tree (*Eriobotrya japonica*) of the rose family that bears an egg-shaped orange or yellow fruit. Loquats grow from 18 to 25 ft (5.5 to 7.6 m) tall and have fleshy, tough-skinned, many-seeded fruits borne in loose clusters. Most widely found in Japan, the loquat was introduced to the United States in 1784. Its fruit has a pleasant tart flavor and can be eaten raw, cooked, or in the form of jelly.

Lorca, Federico García *see:* García Lorca, Federico.

Lord's Prayer, or Our Father, chief Christian prayer, taught by Christ to his disciples (Mat. 6.9-13; Luke 11.2-4) and prominent in all Christian worship. Addressed to God the Father, it contains seven petitions, the first three for God's glory, the last four from bodily and spiritual needs. The closing doxology, used by most Protestants ("For thine is the kingdom" etc.), was added to the Roman Catholic version after the Second Vatican Council (1962-65).
See also: Christianity.

Lorentz, Hendrik Antoon (1853-1928), Dutch physicist awarded with Pieter Zeeman the 1902 Nobel Prize for physics for his prediction of the Zeeman effect (the effects of magnetism on light). Lorentz also introduced the idea of "local time," that is, that the rate of time's passage differed from place to place. Incorporating this idea with George Francis Fitzgerald's proposal that a moving body decreases in direction of motion (the Fitzgerald contraction), he derived the Lorentz transformation, a mathematical statement that describes the changes in length, time, and mass of a moving body. His work, with Fitzgerald's, laid the foundations for Albert Einstein's theory of relativity.
See also: Zeeman effect.

Lorenz, Konrad Zacharias (1903-89), Austrian zoologist, founder of ethology, the study of animal behavior. He is best known for his studies of bird behavior and of human and animal aggression. His books include *King Solomon's Ring* (1952) and *On Aggression* (1966). He shared the 1973 Nobel Prize for physiology or medicine with Karl von Frisch and Nikolaas Tinbergen.
See also: Ethology.

Lorenzini, Carlo *see:* Collodi, Carlo.

Lorenzo the Magnificent *see:* Medici.

Loris, any of several species of primates related to the lemurs. They have large eyes, no tail, spindly legs, and hands adapted for grasping twigs. Native to the forests of southern Asia, they move slowly but deliberately along the lower branches of trees and bushes at night in search of fruit, leaves, and small animals such as insects and nesting birds.

Loris

Loon

Lorrain, Claude *see:* Claude.

Lorraine *see:* Alsace-Lorraine.

Los Alamos, town in New Mexico, 25 mi (40 km) northwest of Santa Fe. It was selected as the site for a scientific laboratory where the world's first atomic and hydrogen bombs were developed (1942). Government research continued at this location until 1962. The Univ. of California currently operates The Los Alamos Scientific Laboratory. The laboratory has been designated as a national landmark.
See also: Manhattan Project; New Mexico.

Los Angeles (pop. 8,863,164), city in southern California, second-largest in the United States, a sprawling city of some 464 sq mi (1,201 sq km), the center of a metropolitan area with a population of over 8 million. Los Angeles is the third-largest industrial center in the United States, producing among other things aircraft, electrical equipment, canned fish, and refined oils. It is also a major center of the motion-picture and television industries, and a distribution and commercial center for the nearby mining regions, oilfields, and rich farm areas. Its port, San Pedro, handles more tonnage than any other U.S. Pacific port, and accommodates a large fishing fleet. The city has several museums and 4 universities. The geo-

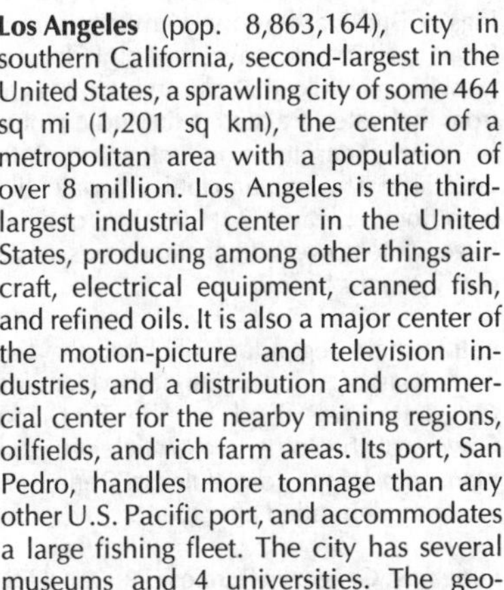

Los Angeles freeways, with central business district in the distance

graphical setting and the large concentration of automobiles and industry have created a serious problem of smog and air pollution, the worst in the United States. Founded by the Spanish in 1781, Los Angeles was taken from Mexico in 1846. It was linked with the transcontinental railroad system in the 1870s and 1880s. Oil was discovered in the region in the 1890s, leading to rapid population growth.
See also: California.

Lost Colony, English settlement on Roanoke Island off the coast of North Carolina that disappeared without trace. It was founded in 1587 by 117 settlers led by John White, sponsored by Sir Walter Raleigh. Supplies ran out and White visited England for help. When he returned in 1591, the colony was gone, possibly having been wiped out by hostile Native Americans.

Lot, in the Old Testament, son of Abraham's brother Haran. He lived in the city of Sodom. Warned that both Sodom and Gomorrah were to be destroyed because of their wickedness, he fled with his wife and 2 daughters. Told not to look back, his wife disobeyed and was turned into a pillar of salt (Gen. 11-14:19).

Portrait of Louis XIV by court painter Hyacinthe Rigaud

Lotus, any of several kinds of water lilies. The sacred lotus of India figures in paintings of Buddha. It grows in marshes from Egypt to China, its leaves and pink flowers growing on stalks that rise about 3 ft (1 m) from the water. Related to the Indian lotus is the American lotus or duck acorn. Both are edible. The Egyptian lotus is a water lily with floating leaves 2 ft (.6 m) across and large white flowers. In ancient times it was cultivated for its fruit.

Lotus-eaters, legendary inhabitants of the north coast of Africa mentioned in Homer's *Odyssey*. They lived on the fruit and flowers of the lotus tree, which drugged them into happy forgetfulness. Tennyson wrote a poem titled after them.

Louganis, Gregory Efhimios (1960-), U.S. diver. He won gold medals in the Olympic Games (1984, 1988) for springboard and platform diving.

Lou Gehrig's disease *see:* Amyotrophic lateral sclerosis.

Lough Neagh, lake in Antrim, Northern Ireland. At about 18 mi (29 km) long and 11 mi (18 km) wide, Lough Neagh is the largest lake in the British Isles. Among the wild fowl found on or near the lake is the rare whooper swan. Plentiful in eel, salmon, and trout, the lake is a popular fishing site.

Louis, name of 18 kings of France. **Louis I** (778-840), Holy Roman Emperor 814-40, known as the Pious. The third son of Charlemagne, he divided the empire among his sons, thereby contributing to its fragmentation but laying the foundations of the state of France. **Louis II** (846-79), reigned 877-79. **Louis III** (c.863-82), reigned 879-82. As king of northern France he defeated Norman invaders. **Louis IV** (c.921-54), reigned 936-54. He was called Transmarinus because of his childhood exile in England. **Louis V** (c.966-87), reigned 986-87. The last Carolingian ruler of France, he was known as the Sluggard. **Louis VI** (1081-1137), reigned 1108-37. He subdued the robber barons around Paris, granted privileges to the towns, and aided the Church. He engaged in war against Henry I of England (1104-13 and 1116-20). **Louis VII** (1120-80), reigned 1137-80. He joined the Second Crusade (1147-49) in defiance of a papal interdict. From 1157 onward, Louis was at war with Henry II of England, who had married Louis' former wife, Eleanor of Aquitaine. **Louis VIII** (1187-1226), reigned 1223-26. Nicknamed the Lion, he was a great soldier and was at first successful in his attempts to aid the barons rebelling against King John of England. **Louis IX, Saint** (1214-70), reigned 1226-70. He repelled an invasion by Henry III of England (1242) and led the Seventh Crusade (1248), but was defeated and captured in Egypt and had to be ransomed. In 1270 he led another crusade, but died of plague after reaching North Africa. A just ruler, he was regarded as an ideal Christian king. **Louis X** (1289-1316), reigned 1314-16, a period in which the nobility reasserted their strength. **Louis XI** (1423-83), reigned 1461-83. A cruel and unscrupulous king, he plotted against his father for the throne but unified most of France. **Louis XII** (1462-1515), reigned 1498-1515. Nicknamed Father of the People, he was a popular ruler who inaugurated reforms in finance and justice and was ambitious for territorial gains. **Louis XIII** (1601-43), reigned 1610-43. A weak king, he was greatly influenced by the chief minister, Cardinal Richelieu. **Louis XIV** (1638-1715), reigned 1643-1715, known as Louis the Great and the Sun King. The archetypal absolute monarch, he built the great palace at Versailles. "The state is myself," he is said to have declared. His able ministers, Mazarin and Colbert, strengthened France with their financial reforms. But Louis squandered money in such escapades as the War of Devolution (1667-68) and the War of the Spanish Succession (1701-14), which broke the military power of France. **Louis XV** (1710-74), reigned 1715-74), nicknamed the "Well-Beloved." He was influenced by Cardinal Fleury until the cardinal's death in 1743. A weak king dependent on mistresses (especially Madame de Pompadour), his involvement in foreign wars created enormous debts. **Louis XVI** (1754-93), reigned 1774-92. Although he accepted the advice of his ministers on the need for social and political reform, Louis was not strong enough to overcome the opposition of his court and his queen, Marie Antoinette. This led to the outbreak of the French Revolution in 1789, with the formation of the National Assembly and the storming of the Bastille. In 1791 Louis attempted to escape but was brought back to Paris and guillotined. **Louis XVII** (1785-95), son of Louis XVI, king in name only. He was imprisoned in 1793 and was reported dead in 1795. **Louis XVIII** (1755-1824), brother of Louis XVI. He escaped from France in 1791 For more than 20 years he remained in exile, but after the final defeat of Napoleon in the Battle of Waterloo (1815), he became firmly established, proclaiming a liberal constitution. On his death the reactionary Ultraroyalists gained control under Charles X.

Louis, Joe (Joseph Louis Barrow; 1914-81), U.S. boxer. Louis won the heavyweight title in 1937, held it longer than anyone in boxing history (1937-49), and fought 25 successful title defenses. He retired in 1949 having lost only once, to Max Schmeling (1936), a defeat he later avenged, knocking Schmeling out in a rematch (1938). In 1950 he tried to return to the ring, but quit after losing to Ezzard Charles and Rocky Marciano.

Louisbourg (pop. 1,400), town in northeastern Nova Scotia, Canada, on the Atlantic. A French fortress founded in 1713, it was captured by American colonials in 1745, restored to France in 1748, and taken by the English in 1758. The remains of the fortress are now part of a National Historic Park, and Louisbourg is a port for coal-shipping and fishing.

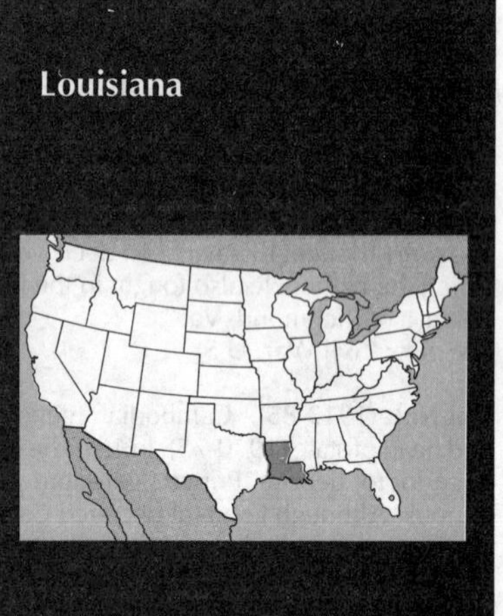

Capital	Baton Rouge
Statehood	Apr. 30, 1812 (18th state)
Familiar name	Pelican State
Area	47,752 sq mi (123,677 sq km); ranks 31st
Population	4,238,216 (1990); ranks 21st
Elevation	Highest—535 ft (163 m), Driskill Mountain; Lowest—5 ft (1.5 m) below sea level, at New Orleans
Motto	Union, Justice, and Confidence
Flower	Magnolia
Bird	Brown pelican
Tree	Bald cypress
Song	"Give Me Louisiana"

Louisiana, state in the south-central United States; bordered by Arkansas to the north, Mississippi to the east, the Gulf of Mexico to the south, and Texas to the west.

Land and climate. Part of the lowland that lies along the entire Gulf coast of the U.S., Louisiana is divided into 3 natural regions: the East and West Gulf Coastal Plains and, between them, the Mississippi Alluvial Plain (often called "the Delta" by Louisianans, although it extends well north of the actual river delta). The Alluvial Plain averages about 40 mi (64 km) in width, but broadens toward the south to form the fertile but low and swampy delta. The Mississippi and other rivers are flanked by a system of levees (earthen walls), both natural and artificial, that prevent high water from flooding the lower backlands away from the river. The East and West Gulf Coastal Plains are composed of low, rolling hills; prairie lands; and steep bluffs toward the north, but along the Gulf are sandy beaches and inland marshes. The Mississippi is Louisiana's most important river. Its rich delta covers about one-third of the state's land area. Other major rivers include the Red, Sabine, Pearl, Ouachita, Atchafalaya, and Calcasieu rivers. The largest of the state's numerous lakes is Lake Pontchartrain, which lies north of New Orleans. Louisiana's climate is semitropical, with long, hot, humid summers and brief, cool winters. Principal cities are New Orleans, Baton Rouge, and Shreveport.

New Orleans, Louisiana

Economy. Service industries account for about two-thirds of the total value of all the goods and services Louisiana produces in a year. A leading producer of petroleum and natural gas, Louisiana is second (after Texas) in mineral production. Soybeans are the leading farm product. Other major crops include rice, sweet potatoes, cotton, sugarcane, and corn. Livestock produced are beef and dairy cattle, chickens, eggs, and hogs.

Government. Louisiana's present constitution was adopted in 1974. The governor serves a 4-year term. The state's Legislature consists of 39 senators and 105 representatives; all serve 4-year terms. In the U.S. Congress, Louisiana is represented by 2 senators and 8 representatives. Louisiana is the only state whose legal system is derived from civil law, based on France's *Code Napoléon,* instead of on English common law and precedent. Louisiana's local government is based on parishes rather than counties.

History. Spanish explorers were the first Europeans in the area—already home to about 12,000 Indians—in the 1500s. The region was claimed by France in 1682; parts were later transferred from France to Spain and back again. The U.S. acquired it in the Louisiana Purchase (1803). Louisiana became the 18th state in 1812. The final engagement of the War of 1812, the Battle of New Orleans, was fought here in 1815. In 1861, Louisiana joined the Confederacy; it was readmitted to the Union in 1868. The discovery of large deposits of oil (1901) and natural gas (1916) attracted many new industries to Louisiana, but farmers suffered hard times in the 1920s and 1930s. World War II revived the state's industries. Rapid growth continued until the mid-1980s, when a drop in oil prices launched an economic decline and Louisiana's unemployment rate became the nation's highest.

Louisiana Purchase, territory purchased by the United States from France in Apr. 1803. It stretched from the Mississippi River on the east into the Rockies on the west, north almost to the Canadian border and south to the Gulf of Mexico, some 828,000 sq mi (2,144,520 sq km) in all. Its acquisition more than doubled the area of what was then the United States. The price was $15 million. In 1800 Napoleon persuaded the Spanish to return what had been the French province of Louisiana. President Thomas Jefferson instructed Robert R. Livingston and James Monroe to purchase New Orleans and other strategic parts of Louisiana from France. To the surprise of the U.S. delegation, Napoleon, who was expecting war with England, offered to sell the entire territory to the United States, and the envoys quickly accepted the offer.
See also: Livingston, Robert R.

Louis Napoleon *see:* Napoleon III.

Louis Philippe (1773-1850), king of France, 1830-48. Exiled from France in 1793, he traveled in Europe and the United States until 1815. He was accepted as a compromise candidate for the crown in 1830. As king he refused to extend the voting franchise, and the revolution of Feb. 1848 led to his abdication. The monarchy was abolished and Louis Philippe fled to England, where he died.

Louisville (pop. 952,662), largest city in Kentucky, on the Ohio River, whose falls provide hydroelectric power for the city. A major river port, transportation hub, and commercial, manufacturing, and cultural center, Louisville produces tobacco products, whiskey, and gin, as well as plumbing equipment, motor vehicles, and baseball bats. Among the several institutions of higher learning is the University of Louisville (1798). Incorporated in 1828, Louisville was named for King Louis XVI of France in recognition of his help during the American Revolutionary War.
See also: Kentucky.

Lourdes (pop. 17,300), town in southwestern France and site of Roman Catholic pilgrimage. The Virgin Mary is said to have appeared to St. Bernadette, then a 14-year-old peasant girl, in Lourdes in 1858. Lourdes is visited by some 3 million pilgrims annually.

Louse, any of several wingless parasitic insects of 2 orders, Mallophaga (bird lice or biting lice) and Anoplura (mammalian or sucking lice). With flattened bodies and broad, clearly segmented abdomens, lice are well adapted to moving between hair or feathers, and are usually host-specific. Bird lice feed by chewing on feather fragments or dead skin, occasionally biting through the skin for blood. Mammalian lice feed purely on blood obtained with needle-like sucking mouthparts. The human lice spread several diseases.

Louvre, historic palace in Paris, mostly built during the reign of Louis XIV, now one of the world's largest and most famous art museums. Its treasures include paintings by Rembrandt, Rubens, Titian, and Leonardo da Vinci, whose *Mona Lisa* is there. Other masterpieces in its collection are the painting *Arrangement in Gray and Black,* known as "Whistler's Mother," and the Greek statues, the *Venus of Milo* and *Victory of Samothrace* ("Winged Victory").

The Louvre, seen from the Tuileries

Lovebird, any of various small gray or green parrots known for their close pair-bond and the frequency with which they preen their mate, particularly genus *Agapornis* of Africa.

Lovelace, Richard (1618-57?), English Royalist soldier and Cavalier poet. His poems, in 2 volumes, were published in 1649 and 1660.

Lovell, James Arthur, Jr. (1928-), U.S. astronaut who commanded Apollo 13, the spacecraft scheduled to land on the moon in Apr. of 1970. The safety of Lovell and fellow astronauts Fred W. Haise, Jr. and John L. Swigert, Jr. was endangered when an oxygen tank aboard Apollo 13 exploded. The others were forced to cancel the mission and pilot the spacecraft to a premature landing in the Pacific Ocean. Lovell's first space flight, with Frank Borman, was the 14-day earth orbit of Gemini 7 in 1965. Gemini 7 joined in space with Gemini 6 to achieve the first successful space rendezvous. Lovell was also on the crew of Gemini 12 and Apollo 8, which was the first manned craft to orbit the moon.
See also: Astronaut.

Saint Ignatius Loyola

Lovell, Sir Bernard (1913-), British radio astronomer. As director of the Jodrell Bank (now Nuffield Radio Astronomy Laboratories) he was instrumental in constructing one of the world's largest steerable radio telescopes (1957).
See also: Astronomy; Jodrell Bank Observatory.

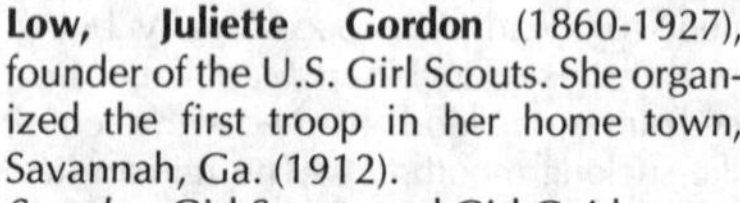

Low, Juliette Gordon (1860-1927), founder of the U.S. Girl Scouts. She organized the first troop in her home town, Savannah, Ga. (1912).
See also: Girl Scouts and Girl Guides.

Lowell, industrial city in northeastern Massachusetts, on the Merrimack and Concord rivers northwest of Boston. Originally settled in 1653, it developed with the building of cotton mills (from 1822) advocated by the pioneer textile manufacturer Francis Cabot Lowell (1775-1817), for whom it was named. Today Lowell makes electronic equipment as well as textiles and other products.
See also: Massachusetts.

Lowell, Amy (1874-1925), U.S. critic and poet of the imagist school. Her collections of verse include *Sword Blades and Poppy Seed* (1914), *Men, Women and Ghosts* (1916), and the Pulitzer Prize-winning *What's o'Clock?* (1925).

Lowell, James Russell (1819-91), U.S. poet, editor, essayist, and diplomat. His poetry includes the didactic *Vision of Sir Launfal* (1848) and the satirical *The Biglow Papers* (1848 and 1867). He was professor of modern languages at Harvard (1855-76) and U.S. minister to England (1877-85); his speeches were published in *Democracy and Other Addresses* (1887).

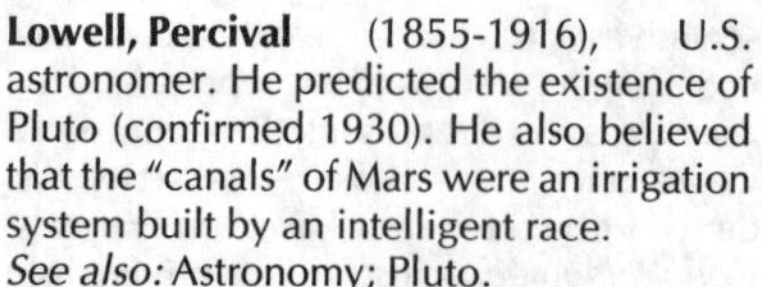

Lowell, Percival (1855-1916), U.S. astronomer. He predicted the existence of Pluto (confirmed 1930). He also believed that the "canals" of Mars were an irrigation system built by an intelligent race.
See also: Astronomy; Pluto.

Lowell, Robert (1917-77), U.S. poet and playwright. His collections include the autobiographical *Life Studies* (1959), and the Pulitzer Prize-winning *Lord Weary's Castle* (1946) and *The Dolphin* (1973). His free adaptations of Greek tragedy and European poets brought him acclaim as a translator.

Lowry, Malcolm (1909-57), English novelist. His greatest work, *Under the Volcano* (1947), was concerned in part with alcoholism, which eventually proved fatal to the author. A reworking of his first novel, *Ultramarine* (1933), and two volumes of short stories were published posthumously.

Loyola, Saint Ignatius (1491-1556), Spanish founder of the Society of Jesus (Jesuits), a Roman Catholic order. A Basque nobleman and soldier, Loyola converted to religious life in 1521. His major work, *Spiritual Exercises*, was begun 1522-23. He later went to Paris with St. Francis Xavier to form the new order (1534). Loyola was its first general (1541-56). His feast day is July 31.
See also: Jesuits.

LPG *see:* Butane and propane.

LSD, or lysergic acid diethylamide, hallucinogenic drug that induces a state of excitation of the central nervous system and overactivity of the autonomic nervous system, manifested as changes in mood (usually euphoric, sometimes depressive) and perception. LSD was invented in 1938 by 2 Swiss chemists, Arthur Stoll and Albert Hofmann. No evidence of physical dependence can be detected when the drug is abruptly withdrawn. A high degree of tolerance develops and disappears rapidly. The chief danger to the individual is the psychological effect and impairment of judgment, which can lead to dangerous decisionmaking or accidents.
Responses to LSD depend on several factors, including the individual's expectations, the setting, and his or her ability to cope with perceptual distortions. Untoward reactions to LSD apparently have become rare, but adverse reactions appear as anxiety attacks, extreme apprehensiveness, or panic states. Most often these reactions quickly subside with appropriate management in a secure setting. However, some individuals remain disturbed and may even show a persistent psychotic state. It is unclear whether the drug use has precipitated or uncovered a pre-existing psychotic potential or whether this can occur in previously stable individuals.
Some persons, especially those who are chronic or repeated users, may experience drug effects after they have discontinued use of the drug. Referred to as "flashbacks," these episodes most commonly consist of visual distortions, but can include distorted perceptions of time, space, or selfimage. Such episodes may be precipitated by the use of marijuana, alcohol, or barbiturates or by stress or fatigue, or they may occur without apparent reason. The mechanisms that produce flashbacks are not known, but they tend to subside over a period of 6 months to 1 year.
See also: Drug; Drug abuse.

Luanda (pop. 600,000), capital and largest city of Angola. Located on the west coast of Africa, Luanda is a manufacturing center and port. Its industries include saw and textile mills, cement, printing, and food processing plants. Luanda was founded in 1576 by Portuguese settlers who built fortresses, churches, and public buildings patterned after European styles of architecture. After Angola gained independence from Portugal in 1975, most of the Portuguese left.

Luba, African ethnic group comprised of Bantu-speaking tribes. Living predominantly in the grasslands of central and southeastern Zaire, the Luba are composed of tribes linked by similar cultures and related languages. The 3 major Luba subdivisions—the Luba-Shankaji of Shaba, the Luba-Bambo of Kasai, and the Luba-Hemba of northern Shaba and southern Kivu—are connected by history, language, and culture to other peoples of the Congo basin. Traditionally, they live in thatched-roof huts along single-street villages. During the twentieth century many Luba-Kasai moved to urban areas.

Lubbock (pop. 222,636), city in northwest Texas known for its production of cottonseed products. Lubbock developed as a cattle-ranching center in the 1880s. It was named after Confederate Lieutenant Colonel Thomas S. Lubbock.
See also: Texas.

Lübeck (pop. 210,300), city in Schleswig-Holstein, northern Germany, on the Trave River near its mouth at the Baltic Sea. Lübeck has been an important trading center since its founding in 1143. Today it is also a center of ship-building and machine manufacturing. It is also known for its candy products, especially the almond and sugar candy known as marzipan.
See also: Germany.

Lubitsch, Ernst (1892-1947), German film director, noted for the sophisticated comedies he made after his emigration to Hollywood in 1923. Among his films are *Forbidden Paradise* (1924), *Ninotchka* (1939), and *Heaven Can Wait* (1943).

Lucan (Marcus Annaeus Lucanus; A.D. 39-65), Roman poet, nephew of Seneca, best known for his *Bellum civile*, an epic literary work on the clash between Julius Caesar and Pompey. A protégé of Nero, he eventually aroused the latter's jealousy. Lucan joined the Pisonian conspiracy against Nero and when this failed, committed suicide.

Luce, Clare Booth (1903-87), U.S. playwright, editor, and politician. Her most successful play, later made into a movie, was *The Women* (1936), which satirized wealthy and idle U.S. women. Luce worked in editorial positions at *Vogue* and *Vanity Fair.* In 1935 she married Henry Luce, the founder of *Time* and *Life* magazines. She served in the U.S. House of Representatives as a Republican from Connecticut (1943-47). She was U.S. ambassador to Italy (1953-56) under the Eisenhower administration.

Luce, Henry Robinson (1898-1967), U.S. editor and publisher. He and Briton Hadden founded the weekly news magazine *Time* in 1923. He also produced *Fortune* (1930), *Life* (1936), and *Sports Illustrated* (1954). He was married to Clare Booth Luce.

Lucerne (pop. 60,600), city in central Switzerland, on the banks of the Reuss River and western shore of Lake Lucerne, capital of Lucerne canton. The city is considered one of the most picturesque in Switzerland, the old town on the bank of the Reuss containing many historic structures, including houses dating back to medieval times. Lucerne is a major European tourist center, with casinos, beaches, horse-racing and jumping competitions, and a traditional pre-Lenten carnival.
See also: Switzerland.

Lucian (A.D. 125-190), Syrian-Greek satirist. Among his best-known works are *Dialogues of the Gods,* a parody of mythology; *Dialogues of the Dead,* a biting satire on human vanities; and *True History,* a lampoon of fantastic travelers' tales, which influenced Rabelais and Jonathan Swift.

Lucifer, the devil. In the Bible, the reference to Lucifer is applied to the King of Babylon, but was misunderstood to mean the fallen angel. Lucifer thus came to be another name for Satan.

Lucknow (pop. 895,900), capital of the state of Uttar Pradesh in northcentral India. Founded as a Muslim fort in the 13th century, Lucknow was incorporated into the British empire in 1856. Indian soldiers seized the city during the Sepoy Rebellion in 1857, but it was reclaimed by Britain the following year. Today Lucknow combines modern offices and industries with an old commercial district of silversmith and handicraft shops.
See also: India.

Lucretius (c.99-c.55 B.C.), Roman poet and philosopher. He was the author of *De rerum natura* ("On the nature of things") and the last classical exponent of atomism, a belief that everything is made up of atoms controlled by the laws of nature. Considered antireligious in his time, many of his theories were later validated.
See also: Philosophy.

Ludendorff, Erich (1865-1937), German general who with von Hindenburg did much to defeat the invading Russian armies in World War I. He was responsible for German military strategy 1917-18 and for the request of an armistice in 1918. After the war he took part in Hitler's abortive coup in Munich in 1923.
See also: World War I.

Ludington, Sybil (1761-83), American Revolutionary War hero. The daughter of Colonel Henry Ludington, Sybil Ludington is known for her heroism in rallying her father's soldiers in Putnam County, N.Y., for a fight against the British. Responding to a messenger's warning that the British were attacking Danbury, she rode nearly 40 mi (64 km) to successfully alert her father's regiment.
See also: Revolutionary War in America.

Luftwaffe, title of the German air force. Formed in 1935 under Hitler, it was commanded by Herman Goering during World War II.

Luge, winter sport competition where one or two persons ride a sled feet first down an ice covered track. The sled is about 4 ft (1.2 m) long, 18 in (46 cm wide and 8 in (20 cm) high and is steered by shifting weight, pulling straps attached to the runners and using the feet.

Luisetti, Hank (1916-), U.S. basketball player. His revolutionary one-handed push shot increased the scoring and tempo of the game. As a Stanford University student, Luisetti broke the national college four-year scoring record, with 1,596 points. In 1938 he became the first player to score 50 points in a single game, against Duquesne University.

Luke, Saint (fl. 1st century A.D.), traditional author of the third Gospel and the Acts of the Apostles. A Gentile and a physician, he was influenced by his friend, St. Paul, whom he accompanied on missionary journeys. His feast day is Oct. 18.
See also: Bible.

Luks, George Benjamin (1867-1933), U.S. realist painter, one of the Eight and the Ashcan School. His bold and vigorous style in such works as *The Wrestlers* (1905) may have owed to his work as a cartoonist.
See also: Ashcan School.

Lully, Jean-Baptiste (1632-87), Italian-born French composer. A favorite with Louis XIV, he conducted the court orchestra and wrote numerous court ballets. He wrote stage music for Molière, and his operas, particularly *Alceste* (1674), *Amadis* (1684), and *Armide* (1686), founded a French operatic tradition.

Lumbee, largest Native American tribe east of the Mississippi River. A popular academic theory holds that the Lumbee are descended from the Hatteras tribe and the English colonists who settled on Roanoke Island in 1587. Other theories cite the Cherokee, Sioux, or Tuscarora as possible ancestors. Today, more than 40,000 Lumbee live in and around Robeson County in southeastern North Carolina. Many are farmers.

Lumber, cut wood, especially when prepared for use. There are two kinds of lumber: hardwood and softwood. Softwood comes from trees called conifers, or evergreens, such as pines and firs. Hardwood comes from deciduous trees such as oak, maple, birch, aspen, and cottonwood. Lumbering, the extraction of timber from the forest, is a major industry in the United States. In world timber production, the USSR is first, then the United States, Japan, and Canada.

Jean-Baptiste Lully

Lumen *see:* Candela.

Lumière brothers, **Auguste** (1862-1954) and **Louis Jean** (1864-1948), French inventors noted for their "Cinématographe," a motion-picture camera/projector. The Lumiere brothers are credited with producing the first movie, whose title in English is *Lunch Break at the Lumiere Factory.* Although the Cinématographe was patented in 1895, the brothers did not regard it as important as some of their improvements in color photography.

Luminescence, nonthermal (heatless) emission (particularly light) caused by electron movement from more energetic states to less energetic states. Including fluorescence and phosphorescence, types of luminescence are named for the mode of excitation. In chemiluminescence the energy source is a chemical reaction, while bioluminescence occurs in biochemical reactions.
See also: Bioluminescence; Fluorescence; Phosphorescence.

Louis and Auguste Lumière

Lumpfish, common name for various fishes of the Cyclopteridae family, that inhabit cold, northern ocean waters. They have short, thick-set bodies with scaleless skin. Lumpfish have strong sucking discs on their underside, which they use to hold themselves to the sea bottom.

Luna, in Roman mythology, goddess of the moon, who drives across the night sky in a chariot. According to the myth, when Luna leaves the sky to visit her lover, the mortal shepherd Endymion, the night is moonless.
See also: Mythology.

Lunar eclipse *see:* Eclipse.

Lunda, indigenous people of Zaire, Angola, and Zambia. The Lunda people, who speak a Bantu language, had a powerful kingdom in the early 1600s, encompassing large parts of present-day Zaire, Angola, and Zambia. Although most Lunda still live in small country villages where they farm and fish for a living, many have migrated to urban areas since the 1960s.

Lundy, Benjamin (1789-1839), U.S. abolitionist. An activist whose efforts paved the way for the national antislavery movement, Lundy organized the Abolitionist Union

Humane Society in Ohio in 1815. As an editor, he published *The Genius of Universal Emancipation* and the *National Enquirer*. Lundy traveled widely in search of places where free blacks could settle. In his effort to prevent slavery from expanding, Lundy worked closely with John Quincy Adams, when Adams was a congressman.
See also: Abolitionism.

Lung, major organs in the respiratory system of mammals, birds, reptiles, and most adult amphibians. These elastic organs pick up oxygen from the air and release carbon dioxide back out. The body requires oxygen to burn food for energy; carbon dioxide is a waste product. In humans, air passes through the *pharynx* and *larynx* to the *airways*, the tubes leading to the lungs. One of these tubes, the *bronchi*, branches off within the lungs, leading to the many *alveolar sacs* that make up the *respiratory units*. The exchange of gases takes place within the *pulmonary capillaries* of this part of the lungs. Lungs help clean the blood of impurities. By exhaling air that makes vocal chords vibrate, they help to effect the sound of speech.
See also: Human body; Respiration.

Lungfish, name for various fishes of Africa, Australia, and South America that can breathe through lungs. The African (family Protopteridae) and South American (family Lepidosirenidae) lungfishes are eellike, with slender fins. They can survive dry conditions by burrowing into mud and forming a cocoon. The Australian lungfish (family Ceratodontidae) has a broad body covered with large scales and cannot survive drying out.

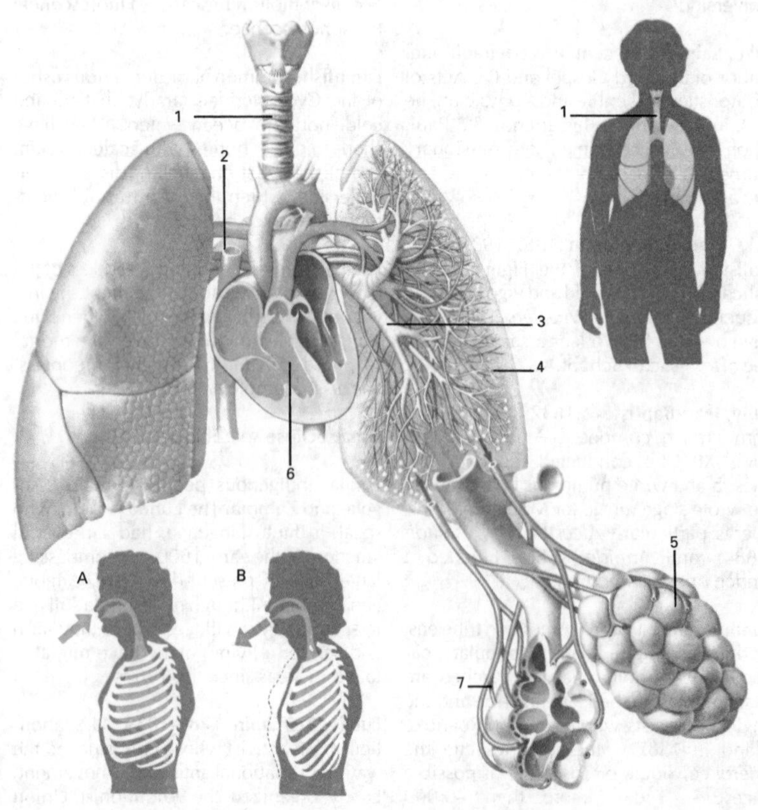

Air enters the lungs through the trachea (1) and bronchii (2). Within the lungs, bronchioles (3) divide into tubules (4), ending in alveoli (5). Blood pumped from the heart (6) receives oxygen in the capillaries (7). (A) and (B) show the movement of the rib cage and diaphragm in breathing.

Lungwort (*Pulmonaria officinalis*), perennial plant that grows in shady areas. Its flowering herb is used medicinally for lung disorders.

Lunt, Alfred (1892-1977), U.S. stage actor generally regarded as one of the outstanding performers of his generation. Married in 1922 to the British actress Lynn Fontanne, Lunt performed in a partnership with her for most of his career. They starred together in 22 productions. Among the most famous were *Design for Living* (1933), *The Taming of the Shrew* (1935), *The Seagull* (1938), and *The Visit* (1958).

Lupercalia, ancient Roman religious festival celebrated on Feb. 15, to enhance fertility for people, animals, and land. The most noted of the activities of the celebration involved naked young men called *luperci* circling the walls of the Palentine Hill in Rome and thrashing women with whips made from the skins of sacrificed animals. It was believed that the women struck by the whips would be rendered fertile.

Lupine, plant (genus *Lupus*) found wild in North America and around the Mediterranean. Lupines range from 2 in (5 cm) to 10 ft (3 m) in height. The flowers are pealike and cluster around a tall stem.

Lupus, disease in which the immune system produces antibodies that attack healthy tissue. In Systemic lupus erythematosus (SLE) patients develop antibodies to their own cell structures, ultimately causing the failure of many organs, especially the heart and the kidneys.

Lusaka (pop. 870,000), capital and largest city of Zambia, in the south-central part of the country. Founded as a European trading post (1905), it was the capital of British-ruled Northern Rhodesia from 1935 until Zambian independence (1964). Intersecting road and railway lines make Lusaka a transportation center, with highways leding to Tanzania, Malawi, and Zimbabwe. The city is also a commercial and government center as well as home to the University of Zambia.
See also: Zambia.

Lusitania, British passenger ship torpedoed and sunk by a German submarine during World War I, on May 7, 1915. A total of 1,198 people were killed, 128 of them U.S. citizens. The Germans claimed that ammunition was being transported on the ship. The incident aroused popular sentiment in the United States for joining the Allied side in the war.
See also: World War I.

Lute, plucked string instrument with a pear-shaped body and a fretted neck, related to the guitar. It was most popular in Europe between 1400 and 1700. Instruments of the lute type date at least from 2000 B.C. in Mesopotamia. The direct ancestor of the European lute of the Renaissance was an Arabian instrument, from which it gets its name (Arabic: *al-oud*, the wood); the Middle Eastern lute is still called an oud.

Lutetium, chemical element, symbol Lu; for physical constants see Periodic Table. Lutetium (formerly spelled "lutecium") was discovered by Georges Urbain in 1907, by separating the ytterbia then known into neoytterbia and lutetia, rare-earth oxides. It occurs in all minerals contaning yttrium, and in *monazite*, which is the source. Lutetium is prepared by reducing the anhydrous chloride or fluoride with an alkali or alkaline earth metal. Lutetium is a silvery-white, soft, reactive metal. It is the second rarest of the rare earth metals. Ion-exchange and solvent extraction techniques have led to much easier isolation of the so-called "rare-earth" elements. Lutetium and its compounds are as catalysts in organic chemistry reactions.

Luther, Martin (1483-1546), German Reformation leader and founder of Lutheranism. Following a religious experience he became an Augustinian friar, was ordained in 1507, and visited Rome (1510), where he was shocked by the worldliness of the papal court. While professor of Scripture at the Univ. of Wittenberg (from 1512), he wrestled with the problem of personal salvation, concluding that it comes from the unmerited grace of God, available through faith alone. When Johann Tetzel toured Saxony (1517) selling papal indulgences, Luther denounced the practice in his historic 95 theses, for which he was fiercely attacked. In 1520 he published *To the Christian Nobility of the German Nation*. It denied the pope's final authority to determine the interpretation of Scripture, declar-

ing instead the priesthood of all believers, and it rejected papal claims to political authority, arguing for national churches governed by secular rulers. Luther denied the special spiritual authority of priests and advocated clerical marriage. In Dec. 1520 he publicly burned a papal bull of condemnation and a copy of the canon law; he was excommunicated in 1521. Summoned by Emperor Charles V to renounce his heresies at the Diet of Worms (1521), he refused. He was outlawed but, protected by Frederick III of Saxony, he retired to the Wartburg castle. There he translated the New Testament into German in 6 months and began work on the Old. His hymns have been translated into many languages, and he wrote 2 catechisms (1529), the basis of Lutheranism.
See also: Protestantism; Reformation.

Lutheran Church in America *see:* Evangelical Lutheran Church in America.

Lutherans, supporters of the Protestant church founded by Martin Luther (1483-1546), German leader of the Reformation. Luther, a scholar and priest, believed that faith rather than Catholic ritual would save people from sin and enable them to receive the grace of God. The largest Protestant sect in the world today, Lutheranism is the state church in the Scandinavian countries and is strong in Germany. In the 18th century German immigrants founded Lutheran churches in the mid-Atlantic American colonies, and the Evangelical Lutheran Church is now the fourth largest Christian sect in the United States.
See also: Christianity; Luther, Martin.

Luthuli, Albert John (1898-1967), Zulu chief and political leader in South Africa. As head of the African National Congress (ANC), he won the 1960 Nobel Peace Prize for his efforts to end apartheid in South Africa through non-violent passive resistance. In that same year, the ANC was banned and Luthuli's activities were severely restricted by the South African government.

Luxembourg, small independent duchy in Europe, bordered by Germany, France, and Belgium, and without access to the sea. Under their hereditary ruler, the Grand Duke, the bilingual Luxembourgers (just over one-third of a million) show a strong sense of national pride. The majority live in compact village communities. Luxembourg is one of the Low Countries and a member of the European Community. The capital is also named Luxembourg.
Land. Only 55 mi (89 km) long and 35 mi (56 km) wide, Luxembourg is divided into several topographical areas. The Oesling, or E'sleck, in the north is part of the rugged highland of the Ardennes, with large forests but poor soil. The Bon Pays, or Gutland (Good Country), in the south is a low, hilly, fertile area of intensive farming; it is also the site of the capital. The southwest region is rich in iron ore. The largest industrial center here is Esch-sur-Alzette. The area to the southeast, where the Moselle River marks the German border, is fertile and widely cultivated.
People. The native dialect, a low German with French and Dutch components, is referred to as Letzeburgesch. French and German are also widely spoken. The prevailing religion is Roman Catholic, and there are small numbers of Protestants and Jews. Education is compulsory between the ages of 6 and 15. There are several technical and professional colleges. The capital is the site of the International University of Comparative Science, founded in 1958.
Economy. The iron and steel industry, centered in the southwest, provides more than four-fifths of Luxembourg's gross income. There is no coal, but fuel for the steel works is imported, and they in turn provide electricity for much of the country. Slate and limestone are the only other mineral resources. Metallurgy may provide most of the nation's income, but agriculture employs the majority of the people. The fertile Gutland provides potatoes, rye, barley, oats, and wheat. Frisian cattle are kept. Near the German border the equally fertile Moselle region produces fruits and white wine.
History. Founded by Count Siegfried of Ardennes in 963, Luxembourg grew in size during the reigns of his successors. It was converted from a county into a duchy by Emperor Charles IV in 1354. After a long period of foreign rule, Luxembourg was granted independence at the London Conference of 1867. The Treaty of London also declared Luxembourg's neutrality and it was demilitarized. In 1945 Luxembourg became a charter member of the United Nations. Three years later it entered into a customs union with Belgium and the Netherlands, referred to as Benelux. Luxembourg was a charter member of the European Community.

Luxembourg

Capital:	Luxembourg
Area:	999 sq mi (2,586 sq km)
Population:	377,000
Form:	constitutional monarchy
Independent:	1867
GNP:	U.S. $8,372,000,000
Per capita:	U.S. $12,600

Martin Luther

Luxembourg (pop. 76,700), capital and largest city of the country of Luxembourg, located on a plateau above the Alzette and Petrusse rivers. It is an international financial center. Luxembourg grew up around a castle built by Siegfried, count of Ardennes, in A.D. 963. A picturesque city, its points of interest include the Grand Ducal Palace (16th century) and the Cathedral of Notre Dame (early 17th century).
See also: Luxembourg.

Clervaux Castle in Luxembourg

Luxemburg, Rosa (1871-1919), Polish-born German Marxist revolutionary. She was cofounder with Karl Liebknecht of the Spartacus Party, Germany's first Communist party, and editor of their journal, *Red Flag.* She was killed by soldiers during an uprising in Berlin.
See also: Marxism.

Luzern *see:* Lucerne.

Lvov (pop. 728,000), city in the USSR, in the western part of the Ukraine, near the Polish border. A major center for industry, culture, and transportation, Lvov was founded c.1256 and became a commercial center on the trade route between Vienna and Kiev, the Ukrainian capital. The region around the city was ruled by Poland, Turkey, and Sweden between the 13th and the 18th century. In 1772 Austria took control of the city and changed its name to Lemberg, making it the capital of the region called Galicia. Poland again ruled the city from the end of World War I until 1939. Lvov is known for its university, founded in 1611.
See also: Ukraine.

Lyceum, gymnasium in ancient Athens where male youth received physical and intellectual training. In 335 B.C. Aristotle established his famous Lyceum outside the walls of the city. The school was named in

honor of the god Apollo Lykeios. In the U.S. during the 19th century there was a lyceum movement which attempted to improve education.
See also: Greece, Ancient.

Lychee *see:* Litchi.

Lycopodium *see:* Club moss.

Lycurgus, ancient Greek political leader, possibly legendary, credited as founder of the legal institutions of the city-state of Sparta. Tradition says that during the 7th century B.C. Lycurgus instituted a new system of military discipline and training. Ancient historians cite him as a member of one of Sparta's royal families.
See also: Sparta.

Lydia, ancient kingdom of western Asia Minor, of legendary wealth. The Lydians invented metal coins in the 7th century B.C. Sardis was the capital and cultural center of this growing empire until the defeat of Croesus (546 B.C.) by Cyrus of Persia.

Sir Charles Lyell

Lye, strong alkali used in soap-making and cleaning. Originally the name was given to potassium carbonate (K_2CO_3), which was obtained by soaking wood ash in water. It now most often refers to sodium hydroxide (NaOH) solution.

Lyell, Sir Charles (1797-1875), British geologist. He promoted James Hutton's theory of uniformitarianism and Charles Darwin's theory of evolution in his *Principles of Geology* (1830-33).
See also: Geology.

Lyly, John (c.1554-1606), English author best known for his *Euphues* (*The Anatomy of Wit*, 1578; *Euphues and His England*, 1580), a two-part prose romance in a highly artificial and suggestive style. Lyly also wrote elegant comedies on classical themes, influencing other Elizabethan playwrights.

Lynx

Lyme disease, infection caused by the bacterium *Borrelia burgdorferi* and transmitted by ticks. It is accompanied by fever and a red, ring-shaped skin rash surrounding the tick bite. The disease is treated with antibiotics. Left untreated, it can lead to nervous disorders and arthritis. The disease derives its name from the town of Lyme, Conn. where a high incidence of the disease occurred in the 1970s.

Lymphatic system, network of vessels and nodes that carry tissue fluid, or lymph, from the tissues to the veins of the circulatory system. Lymph is a transparent fluid that carries oxygen and nutrients to cells and carries away waste products. Ingested fats are digested and absorbed into the bloodstream with the help of lymphatic vessels. The body fights infections through lymphocyte and macrophage cells found in lymph nodes in the armpits, groin, neck, and other parts of the body. Most lymph passes directly into capillaries, but some is carried back to the blood by the lymphatic system; whose main ducts feed into the circulatory system near the collarbone.

Lynch, Thomas, Jr. (1749-79), colonial politician from South Carolina. He signed the Declaration of Independence and served in the first general assembly of South Carolina and in the Second Continental Congress.

Lynx, any of various ferocious cats with a short tail, long legs, and tufted ears, found in northern regions of North America, Europe, and Asia. They are hunted for their fur and because they kill domestic animals. Species include the North American, or Canadian, lynx (*Lynx canadensis*), and the common lynx of Europe and Asia (*L. lynx*).

Lyon (pop. 413,100), city in southeastern France. Capital of the Rhône department in the Rhône-Alpes region, it is the third largest city in France. During Roman times, Christianity was introduced to the Gauls from Lyons. Since the 16th century, Lyons has been known for its textiles, and today it is a leading producer of silks and rayons. It is also known for being the center of the French Resistance during the Nazi occupation (1940-44).
See also: France.

Lyon, Mary (1797-1849), U.S. educator. A pioneer in education for women, she founded (1837) the oldest U.S. institution for women's higher education, Mount Holyoke Seminary of Massachusetts, now known as Mount Holyoke College.

Lyre, musical stringed instrument. In ancient Greece the lyre, with 3 to 12 strings, was a symbol for the God Apollo. The English term *lyric* comes from the Greek use of the lyre to accompany songs and poems. The strings were plucked either with the fingers or with a pick. They were strung vertically from a sound box to a crossbar held in place by 2 outer vertical arms.

Lyrebird, either of 2 species of Australian birds (genus *Menura*) of the family menuridae. The male has very long tail feathers he displays, shaped like a lyre, during courtship. Similar in appearance to chickens, lyrebirds nest on the ground and do not fly.

Lyon, France

Lysander (?-395 B.C.), naval commander of Sparta. During the Peloponnesian War he led the Spartan forces to victory against Athens in the decisive battle of Aegospotami (405 B.C.). He died in battle during the Corinthian war.
See also: Sparta.

Lysergic acid diethylamide *see:* LSD.

Lysias (459?-380 B.C.), ancient Greek orator and speech writer. Although as many as 35 speeches attributed to Lysias have survived, he is best known for a simple though passionate attack on a ruling tyrant of Athens entitled "Against Eratosthenes." A citizen of Athens, he escaped after his arrest by the Thirty Tyrants, Spartan rulers installed at the end of the Peloponnesian War. When democracy was restored in Athens, Lysias returned and again wrote speeches on a professional basis.
See also: Greece, Ancient.

Lysippus (380s?-306 B.C.), sculptor of ancient Greece. Although he is said to have created some 1,500 works, no authenticated originals remain. Influenced by the earlier Greek sculptor Polykleitos, Lysippus developed more slender, active looking figures. He is known mostly for his sculptures of male athletes, cast and often copied in his preferred medium, metal.
See also: Greece, Ancient.

M, 13th letter of the English alphabet, corresponds with the 13th Semitic letter *mem*, represented by a zigzag, wavelike form that scholars relate to the Hebrew *mayim* (water). M is *mu* in the Greek alphabet and the 12th letter of the Roman alphabet. Its present form comes directly from classical Latin. In Roman numerals M represents 1,000. In the French language M. is the abbreviation for *monsieur* (Mr.).

Maazel, Lorin (1930-), U.S. conductor. A musical child prodigy born in France, he first conducted an orchestra in the United States at the World's Fair in New York (1939). He has gone on to become musical director of famous orchestras worldwide, including the Pittsburgh Symphony since 1986, the Cleveland Orchestra (1972-82), and the Vienna State Opera (1982-88).

Macadam, road-building system devised by the Scots engineer John Loudon McAdam (1756-1836). The soil beneath the road, rather than foundations, bears the weight, the road being waterproof and well-drained to keep this soil dry. For modern highways a first layer of larger rocks is laid, then smaller rocks and gravel; the whole is bound with (usually) asphalt or tar.
See also: McAdam, John Loudon.

Macadamia nut, edible seed from the macadamia tree (*Macadamia terrifolia*), a member of the *protea* family. Native to Australia, the nut of this tropical evergreen is an important Hawaiian crop today. Roasted, the round white nuts—also known as bush nuts, among other names—may be eaten by themselves or incorporated into baked or cooked foods.

Macao, or Macau, Portuguese overseas province in southeastern China, on the western side of the Pearl River Estuary, at the head of which is Canton. Lying just within the tropics, Macao is 6 sq mi (16 sq km) in area. The territory came into Portuguese possession in 1557 and was granted broad autonomy in 1976. It will revert to the PRC in 1999. The territory comprises a narrow peninsula projecting from the mainland province of Kwangtung, as well as the adjacent islands of Taipa and Colôane. Macao is a popular gambling center and important commercial port. Fishing and some textile manufacturing are significant economic activities.

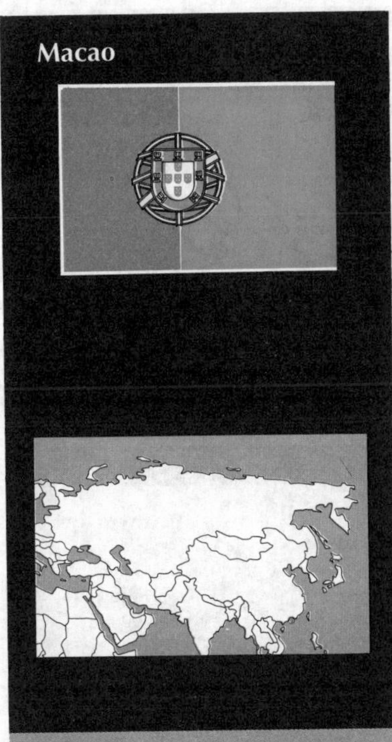

Capital:	Macao
Area:	6.5 sq mi (16.9 sq km)
Population:	466,000
Form:	overseas territory (Portugal)
Dependent:	on Portugal until 1999; thereafter on China
GNP:	U.S.$2,262,000,000
Per capita:	U.S.$5,210

Macaque, several species (genus *Macaca*) of the Old World monkey family. They are found in North Africa, Japan, India, and Malaysia. A reddish face and rump are features seen in all macaques. The Barbary ape is tailless, while the bonnet macaque and toque monkey of southern India and Ceylon have tails longer than their bodies. The Japanese macaque has brown fur but a short tail. The rhesus monkey of India is used in medical research.

MacArthur, Douglas (1880-1964), U.S. general and hero of World War II. He commanded the 42nd (Rainbow) Division in World War I and was superintendent of West Point (1919-22). In 1930 he became chief of staff of the U.S. Army, the youngest man ever to hold the post, and was promoted to general. He retired from the army in 1937, but was recalled in 1941 as commander of U.S. Army forces in the Far East. In 1942 he became Allied commander of the Southwest Pacific Allied forces, and in 1944 general of the army. MacArthur received the Medal of Honor for his defense of the Philippines. Signatory of the Japanese surrender, he led the reconstruction of Japan, as Allied supreme commander from 1945. When the Korean War broke out (1950) he was selected commander of the UN forces sent to aid South Korea. His unwillingness to obey President Harry S. Truman's orders to restrict the war to Korea rather than extend it to China led to his dismissal the following year. Some Republicans tried unsuccessfully to nominate MacArthur for the presidency in 1944, 1948, and 1952. His memoirs, *Reminiscences,* were published in 1964.
See also: Korean War; World War II.

Macau *see:* Macao.

Macaulay, Thomas Babington (1800-59), historian and essayist. Babington was elected to Parliament in 1830, became a brilliant speaker, and served on the Supreme Council governing India before undertaking his *History of England from the Accession of James II* (5 vol, 1849-61). The clarity and readability of this work made it a success. Like the *History,* his *Essays* display great range and brilliance, together with supreme confidence of judgment. While continuing as a leading orator in Parliament and holding several government jobs, Babington also wrote *Lays of Ancient Rome* (1842), a popular collection of poems.

Macaw, any of several colorful, long-tailed parrots of the genus *Ara.* Macaws have powerful beaks, which they use for cracking open nuts, and their faces are bare of feathers. The largest parrots, macaws measure 12-39 in (30-100 cm) long and eat nuts, seeds and fruit. Easily tamed, they live in screeching flocks in forested areas of tropical America and Mexico.

Macbeth (d. 1057), king of Scotland, formerly chief of the province of Moray. Macbeth seized the throne of Scotland after killing King Duncan I in battle (1040). He upheld his wife's royal descent as his basis for claiming the crown. In 1057 Malcolm III, son of Duncan I, killed Macbeth at Lumphanan. Shakespeare's tragedy *Macbeth* is partially based on Holinshed's *Chronicles* of these events.
See also: Scotland; Shakespeare, William.

Maccabee, Judah *see:* Judah Maccabee.

Maccabees, Books of, 2 books of the Old Testament Apocrypha that tell the story of the Maccabees, or Hasmoneans, Jewish rulers of the 2nd and 1st centuries B.C. who fought for the independence of Judea from Syria. First Maccabees, a prime historical source, was written c.100? B.C. Second Maccabees is a devotional work of low historical value, written before A.D. 70. Two other books, Third and Fourth Maccabees, are among the Pseudepigrapha.
See also: Old Testament.

MacDiarmid, Hugh (Christopher Murray Grieve; 1892-1978), Scottish poet. Founder of the Scottish Nationalist Party, he gave fresh impetus to Scottish literature. He is best known for the long rhapsodic poem *A Drunk Man Looks at the Thistle* (1926).

MacDonald, J.E.H. (1873-1932), English-born Canadian landscape painter. As a member of a Canadian school of painters known as the Group of Seven, he often depicted the Ontario wilderness, combining influences from Scandinavian painters and designers from the *art nouveau* movement.

MacDonald, James Ramsay (1866-1937), English statesman who led Britain's first Labour Party government. He was prime minister of the first and second labour governments (1924 and 1929-35). He headed a national coalition government of Labour, Conservative and Liberal Party members (1931-35) that attempted unsuccessfully to deal with England's

depressed economic conditions. He was replaced as prime minister in 1935.
See also: Labour Party.

Macdonald, Sir John Alexander (1815-91), Canadian statesman, first prime minister of the Dominion of Canada. Elected to the Ontario legislature in 1844, he became prime minister in 1857 as head of a Conservative coalition that was joined (1864) by George Brown and others. He led subsequent negotiations that resulted (1867) in the confederation of Canada, for which he was knighted by Queen Victoria. The Pacific Scandal (1873), involving corruption charges in completing the Canadian Pacific Railway, caused his government's resignation. However, Macdonald served as prime minister again from 1878 until his death.
See also: Canada.

Macdonald, John Sandfield (1812-72), Canadian politician. An opponent of confederation, he served as prime minister of Canada (1862-6). When, in 1867, Canada was confederated, he served as the first prime minister for his home province, Ontario (1867-71). Educated and trained in law, he served at various posts in both Liberal and Conservative governments (1840-71).
See also: Canada.

Macdonough, Thomas (1783-1825), U.S. naval officer who defeated the British at the decisive Battle of Plattsburgh (1814) on Lake Champlain, N.Y., during the War of 1812. His victory saved New York and Vermont from invasion.
See also: War of 1812.

MacDowell, Edward Alexander (1861-1908), U.S. composer and pianist. He is remembered for his lyrical piano works, such as the collection *Woodland Sketches* (1896). He headed the newly formed music department at Columbia University in New York City (1896-1904). His widow founded the MacDowell Colony in Peterborough, N.H., a retreat for creative artists.

Macedonia, mountainous ***region*** in southeastern Europe, extending from the northwestern Aegean coast into the central Balkan peninsula. Divided among Greece, Macedonia, and Bulgaria, it covers 25,636 sq mi (66,397 sq km). Ethnically mixed, Macedonia is inhabited mainly by Slavs in the north and Albanians (23%) in the west. The region is primarily agricultural, with tobacco, grains and cotton the chief crops. One of the great powers of the ancient world under Alexander the Great, Macedonia was later ruled by Romans, Byzantines, Bulgars, and Serbs. From 1389 to 1912 it was part of the Ottoman Empire.
Country: With the collapse of Yugoslavia in 1991 Yugoslavian Macedonia became an independent country, named Former Yugoslav Republic of Macedonia.
See also: Alexander the Great; Greece, Ancient; Yugoslavia.

MacGregor, Robert *see:* Rob Roy.

F.Y.R. Macedonia

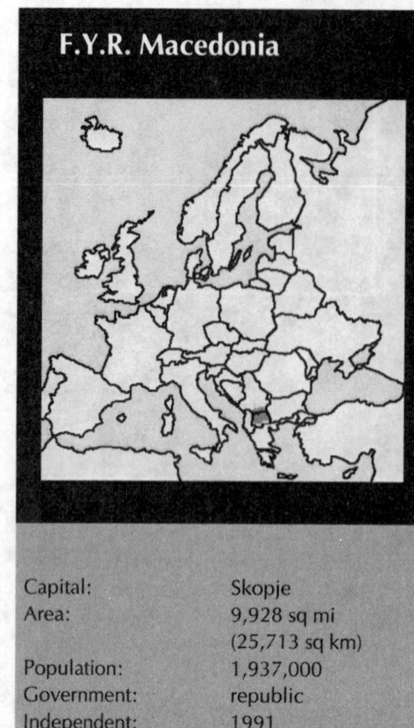

Capital:	Skopje
Area:	9,928 sq mi (25,713 sq km)
Population:	1,937,000
Government:	republic
Independent:	1991
GNP per capita:	U.S. $770

Mach, Ernst (1838-1916), Austrian physicist and philosopher. His name is commemorated in the Mach number, used as a measure of the speed of bodies in terms of the speed of sound. His greatest influence was in philosophy; he rejected from science all concepts that could not be validated by experience. This approach helped inform the logical positivism of the Vienna Circle—a prominent group of intellectuals in Vienna at that time.
See also: Philosophy; Physics.

Machaut, Guillaume de (1300-77), French poet and composer. He was a leading figure in the 14th-century Ars Nova ("new art") school of music, which developed many new forms. His *Mass for Four Voices* was the first complete polyphonic setting by a single composer.

Machiavelli, Niccolò (1469-1527), Florentine politician and political theorist. He served the Republic of Florence, and was its emissary on several occasions. When the Medici family returned to power in 1512, Machiavelli was imprisoned and tortured on suspicion of plotting against Medici rule; on his release less than a year later he devoted himself principally to writing. Despite his belief in political morality and his undoubted love of liberty, as revealed in his *Discourses* (1531), his master-work *The Prince* (1532; written 1513) describes the amoral and unscrupulous political calculation by which an "ideal" prince maintains his power. Machiavelli also wrote *History of Florence* (1532). The expression "Machiavellian" denotes devious political manipulations.

Machine Age *see:* Industrial Revolution.

Machine gun, military small arm capable of rapid fire. After the invention of the percussion cap by Joshua Shaw, the reliability of firing was greatly increased. In 1862, Richard Jordan Gatling invented a single-barreled machine gun with a rotary chamber, it was used in the Civil War. Gatling's multibarreled gun was capable of firing up to 3,000 rounds a minute.
The first fully automatic machine gun was a single-barreled water-cooled weapon patented by Hiram Steven Maxim in 1885. In World War I, the machine gun was responsible for over 80% of all casualties. In 1957, the U.S.Air Force introduced the Vulcan gun, capable of firing up to 7,000 rounds per minute.

Machine tool, nonportable, power-driven tool used industrially for working metal components to tolerances far finer than those obtainable manually. The fundamental processes used are cutting and grinding, individual machines being designed for boring, broaching, drilling, milling, planing, and sawing. Essentially a machine tool consists of a jig to hold both the cutting tool and the workpiece and a mechanism to allow these to be moved relative to each other in a controlled fashion. A typical example is the lathe. Auxiliary functions facilitate the cooling and lubrication of the tool and workpiece while work is in progress using a cutting fluid. The rate at which any piece can be worked depends on the material being worked and the composition of the cutting point. High-speed steel, tungsten carbide, and corundum are favored materials for cutting edges. Modern industry would be inconceivable without machine tools. It was only when these began to be developed in the late 18th century that it became possible to manufacture interchangeable parts and thus initiate mass production.

Mach number *see:* Mach, Ernst.

Machu Picchu, ancient (16th-century) Inca fortress city in Peru, about 50 mi (80 km) northwest of Cusco. An impressive ruin dramatically situated on a high ridge of the Andes, the pre-Columbian city is 5 sq mi (13 sq km) of terraced stonework connected by 3,000 steps. Probably the last Inca stronghold after the Spanish Conquest (begun 1532), it was discovered almost intact in 1911 by the U.S. explorer Bingham.
See also: Peru.

Macintosh, Charles (1766-1843), British chemist and inventor. Trained as a chemist, he developed a method (1823) by which fabrics were treated with chemicals to create a waterproof garment. One raincoat, popularly referred to as a macintosh, is named after him.
See also: Chemistry.

Mack, Connie (Cornelius McGillicuddy; 1862-1956), U.S. baseball manager and owner. Known for his work and dedication to baseball, Mack helped establish the American League. As owner and manager of the Philadelphia Athletics (1901-50), he led his team to victory in 5 World Series. He was inducted into the National Baseball Hall of Fame in 1937.

Mackay, last name of father John William (1831-1902) and son Clarence Hungerford (1874-1938), both U.S. businesspeople. With wealth gained from his interests in the Comstock lode, one of the largest gold and silver mines in Nevada, John William developed the Postal Telegraph Cable Company (1886), breaking Western Union's monopoly. Clarence Hungerford, business partner with his father and subsequent director of Postal Telegraph, developed transoceanic cable communications between the United States and the Far East (1904), Cuba (1907), and both Southern and Northern Europe. The Mackay telegraph and cable companies were combined with Western Union Telegraph Company in 1943.

Mackenzie, Sir Alexander (1764-1820), Canadian fur trader and explorer. Mackenzie was the first non-native to cross the northern part of North America to the Pacific. Born in Scotland, he emigrated to Canada; in 1789 he made an expedition down the Mackenzie River (named for him) to the Arctic Ocean. In 1793 Mackenzie crossed the Rocky Mountains to the Pacific coast, becoming convinced that searching for a Northwest Passage to the Orient would be futile.

Mackenzie, Alexander (1822-92), Canadian politician. Born in Scotland, he emigrated to Canada in 1842. He entered the legislative assembly in 1861, having worked his way up to the editorship of a Liberal paper. From 1873 to 1878 he was Canada's first Liberal prime minister. Serving during a worldwide depression, Mackenzie confronted many national economic difficulties. He promoted democratic government and greater independence from Great Britain.

Mackenzie, Roderick (1760?-1844), Canadian politician and pioneer Commander of Fort Chipewyan (1789-93), he built it with his cousin, Sir Alexander Mackenzie, after they had trailblazed their way west to this northeastern point in Alberta. Later, in eastern Canada, he served as a member of the Legislative Council of Lower Canada.

Mackenzie, William Lyon (1795-1861), Canadian journalist and politician. Publisher of the *Colonial Advocate* (1824-34) and denouncer of the governing clique, the Family Compact, Mackenzie led the Reform Party as the first mayor of Toronto (1834). After subsequent defeat he led them in an unsuccessful revolution (1837). He fled to the United States, but he was imprisoned for violating neutrality laws. He returned to Canada in 1849 after receiving amnesty, and served in Parliament.
See also: Canada.

Mackenzie River, in northwestern Canada, flowing from Great Slave Lake to the Arctic Ocean. The Mackenzie, which drains the northern portion of the Great Plains, is about 1,120 mi (1,800 km) long and is the main channel of the Finlay-Peace-Mackenzie river system (2,600 mi/4,180 km). It is navigable from June to Oct. only.
See also: Mackenzie, Sir Alexander.

Mackerel, commercially important food fish of the family Scombridae. Mackerel have small scales, deeply forked tails, and rows of finlets on the rear part of their streamlined bodies. Known as fast swimmers, the species includes the tuna (the largest, up to .75 ton/680 kg), albacore, and bonito.

Mackinac, Straits of, channel separating the Upper and Lower Peninsulas of northern Michigan. It connects Lakes Huron and Michigan and is spanned by the Mackinac Straits Bridge from Mackinac City to St. Ignace.

Mackinac Island, Northern Michigan island in the Straits of Mackinac. First settled by Native Americans, then French missionaries, this island became an outpost for the British (1780) before its present-day development as a summer resort. Today no automobiles are allowed on the island, and ferry service transports people and goods from the mainland to either Mackinac City or St. Ignace. This island contains an ancient Native American burial ground called *Michilimackinac* ("great turtle").

MacLeish, Archibald (1892-1982), U.S. poet and playwright. His works include *Conquistador* (1932), a long narrative on the conquest of Mexico; the lyrical verse of *Collected Poems 1917-1952* and *J.B.* (1958), a verse drama based on the story of Job, all of which won Pulitzer prizes. Cultural adviser to Franklin D. Roosevelt, he was librarian of Congress (1939-44) and undersecretary of state (1944-45).

Macmillan, Donald Baxter (1874-1970), U.S. arctic explorer. His 1st north-polar expedition with Commander Robert Peary in 1908 was followed by 30 others, including those he led to Labrador, Greenland, and Baffin Island (1913-37). His writings on the region include *Four Years in the White North* (1918), *Etah and Beyond* (1927), and *How Peary Reached the Pole* (1932).

Macmillan, Harold (1894-1986), British politician. Entering Parliament as a Conservative in 1924, he served in ministerial posts throughout World War II and the 1950s. As prime minister (1957-63), he restored Anglo-U.S. ties after the Suez Canal intervention, tried to improve East-West relations, and tried to gain Britain's entry into the Common Market. He served as chairman of Macmillan publishing house (1963-74) and was made an earl in 1984.

Macon (pop. 281,103), city in central Georgia, on the Ocmulgee River; seat of Bibb County. The commercial and shipping center for a cotton, truck-farming, and livestock area, its industries include textiles, chemicals, and lumber. Macon (incorporated 1823) was named for Nathaniel Macon. Near the city are the prehistoric Indian mounds and towns of the Ocmulgee National Monument.
See also: Georgia.

Macramé, art form based on knotting techniques. This art, originally an activity of 13th century Arab sailors before its popularity in Europe, was revived in the 1960s. Garment accessories, wall hangings, and other practical or decorative items are created through arrangements of knots in various patterns.
See also: Knots, hitches and splices.

Harold Macmillan

Madagascar, formerly Malagasy Republic, since 1975 the Democratic Republic of Madagascar, republic in the Indian Ocean comprising the large island of Madagascar and several small islands.
Land and climate. Separated from the southeast African mainland by the Mozambique Channel, Madagascar is the world's fourth largest island. It has rugged central highlands and fertile low-lying coastal plains. The highlands have several extinct volcanoes and mountain groups which rise to over 9,000 ft/2,743 m. In the highlands the climate is pleasantly cool, but it occasionally becomes cold. The coastal plains tend to be hot and humid, with luxuriant vegetation.
People. The people of Madagascar can be broadly divided into two groups. The Merinas, of Indonesian and Polynesian descent, live mainly in the highlands. The majority of people living in the coastal regions are of black African descent. The principal languages are French and Malagasy, an Indonesian language. Over 90% of the people live in rural areas. About 40% of the population is Christian, 5% is Muslim, and the remainder observe various traditional beliefs. The capital is Antananarivo (Tananarive).
Economy. The island is predominantly farming and stock-raising country. Coffee, cloves, and vanilla are principal foreign exchange earners. Meat and prawns are also exported. Chromite, graphite, mica, and phosphates are important minerals. Oil and gas deposits have been discovered. Growing industries include food processing, oil refining, vehicle assembly, and textile manufacture.
History. The first peoples to settle Madagascar were black Africans and Indonesians some 2,000 years ago. Western Europeans did not reach the island until the 16th century. A native kingdom, the Merina kingdom, gained hegemony over the island in alliance with Europeans. At the same time, the Portuguese, English, and French strove with one another for dominance. Finally, the French invaded and annexed the island in 1885, but had to fight until 1905 to overcome a determined Merina kingdom. In 1947, a revolt against French rule was crushed, but in 1958 the island gained self government as the Malagasy Republic and became fully inde-

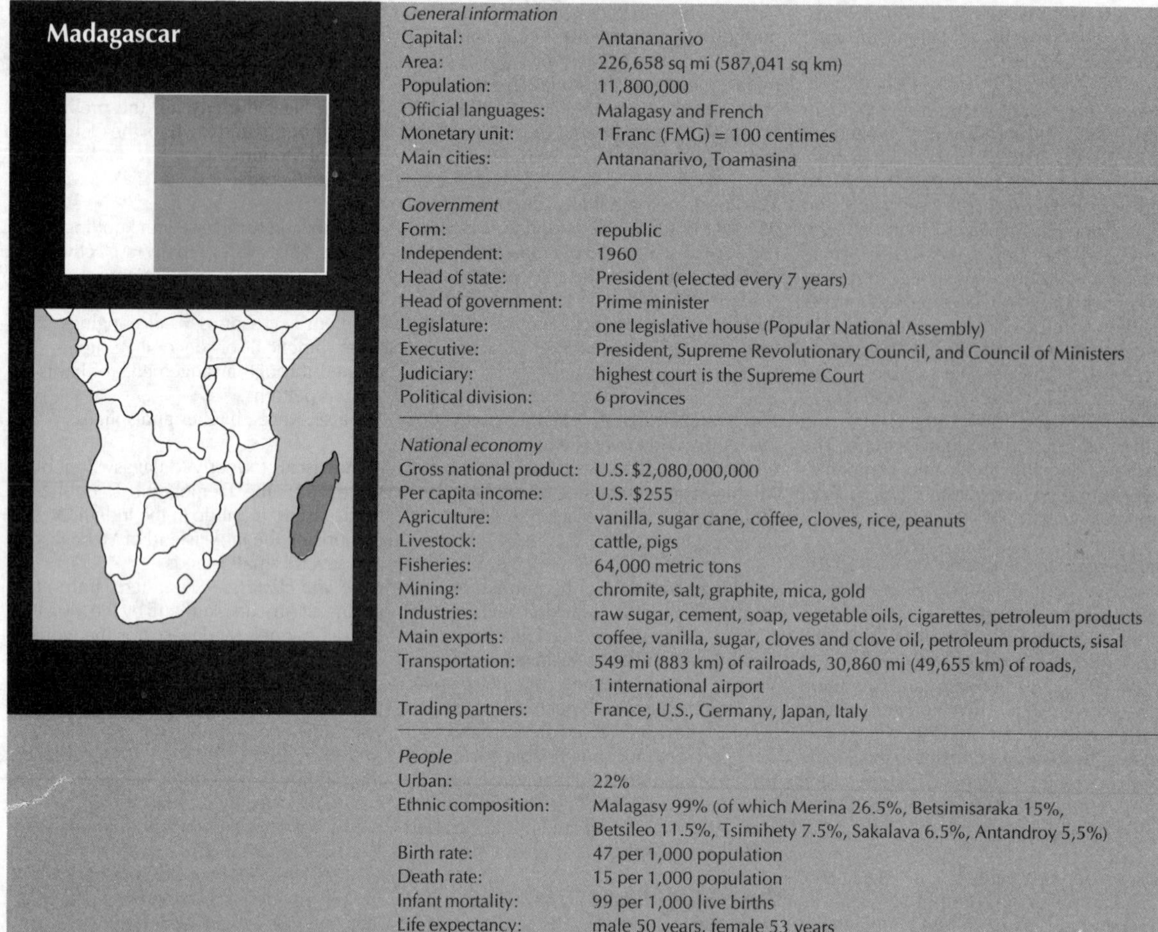

Madagascar

General information	
Capital:	Antananarivo
Area:	226,658 sq mi (587,041 sq km)
Population:	11,800,000
Official languages:	Malagasy and French
Monetary unit:	1 Franc (FMG) = 100 centimes
Main cities:	Antananarivo, Toamasina
Government	
Form:	republic
Independent:	1960
Head of state:	President (elected every 7 years)
Head of government:	Prime minister
Legislature:	one legislative house (Popular National Assembly)
Executive:	President, Supreme Revolutionary Council, and Council of Ministers
Judiciary:	highest court is the Supreme Court
Political division:	6 provinces
National economy	
Gross national product:	U.S.$2,080,000,000
Per capita income:	U.S.$255
Agriculture:	vanilla, sugar cane, coffee, cloves, rice, peanuts
Livestock:	cattle, pigs
Fisheries:	64,000 metric tons
Mining:	chromite, salt, graphite, mica, gold
Industries:	raw sugar, cement, soap, vegetable oils, cigarettes, petroleum products
Main exports:	coffee, vanilla, sugar, cloves and clove oil, petroleum products, sisal
Transportation:	549 mi (883 km) of railroads, 30,860 mi (49,655 km) of roads, 1 international airport
Trading partners:	France, U.S., Germany, Japan, Italy
People	
Urban:	22%
Ethnic composition:	Malagasy 99% (of which Merina 26.5%, Betsimisaraka 15%, Betsileo 11.5%, Tsimihety 7.5%, Sakalava 6.5%, Antandroy 5,5%)
Birth rate:	47 per 1,000 population
Death rate:	15 per 1,000 population
Infant mortality:	99 per 1,000 live births
Life expectancy:	male 50 years, female 53 years

The cultivation of rice in Madagascar

pendent in 1960. 1972 marked the beginning of a period of political and economic unrest and in 1975 a Marxist military took power. In 1977, national elections were held to create a legislature. Didier Ratsiraka, who had ruled as Madagascar's military leader since 1975, won the first presidential election (1982); under his leadership, the government has loosened its restrictions on the economy. The current prime minister is Victor Ramahatra.

Madder, tropical and subtropical trees, shrubs, and herbs of the family Rubiaceae, native to northern South America. The family yields economically important crops, e.g., coffee and quinine, and ornamentals, e.g., the gardenia, madder, and bedstraw (used for mattress filling because of its pleasing odor). Also called turkey red, the true madder (*rubia tinctorum*) of southern Europe was used to create brilliant red dye pigments, now produced artificially.

Madeira Islands, archipelago, 308 sq mi (789 sq km), owned by Portugal, in the Atlantic Ocean about 350 mi (560 km) west of Morocco. Madeira, the largest island and site of the capital, Funchal, is a year-round resort; Porto Santo is also inhabited. The Desertas and Selvagens are uninhabited islands. Known to the Romans and rediscovered under Henry the Navigator in the 15th century, the islands produce sugarcane and Madeira wine.

Madeira River, largest tributary of the Amazon River. Flowing northeastward, this important South American waterway runs along the Brazil-Bolivia border and continues for approximately 2,000 miles (3,200 km)—some of which are still uncharted or explored. The river is navigable by boat for the first 700 miles (1,126 km), then a railroad follows the riverbank for more than 200 miles (320 km) of rapids. The river opens into the Amazon east of the city of Manaus, Brazil.

Madero, Francisco Indalecio (1873-1913), president of Mexico (1911-13). A democratic idealist, he opposed Porfirio Díaz in the 1910 election and was imprisoned. He escaped to Tex. and there declared a revolution; joined by Pancho Villa and Emiliano Zapata, he deposed Díaz in 1911 and was elected president (1911-13). His administration was marred by his ineptitude and division and corruption among his followers. In the face of widespread revolt he was deposed and murdered by Gen. Victoriano Huerta.
See also: Mexico.

Madison (pop. 367,085), state capital of Wisconsin, seat of Dane County, in south-central Wisconsin. The city is home to the main campus of the Univ. of Wisconsin, state government buildings, and facilities for manufacturing, trade, finance, and re-

search. Popular for recreation, 3 lakes are found within the city borders: Mendota, Monona, and Wingra.
See also: Wisconsin.

Madison, Dolley Payne (1768-1849), wife of President James Madison. Known as an accomplished hostess during her husband's administration, she helped the widowed President Jefferson entertain during his presidency (1809-17). During the War of 1812, she fled the capital while it was under attack, rescuing a portrait of George Washington and important government documents.

Madison, James (1751-1836), 4th president of the United States. Madison, called "the father of the Constitution," was a penetrating political thinker who guided the deliberations of the Constitutional Convention. He was not a successful war president, but his last years in office inaugurated an "era of good feelings" and unprecedented economic growth.

Early life. Madison, born into a prominent plantation family of Virginia, graduated from the College of New Jersey (now Princeton University) in 1771. He planned to enter the ministry, but soon became involved in politics. In 1776, he helped draft Virginia's first constitution and its declaration of rights. He was a delegate to the Continental Congress (1780-83).

Political career. Under the Articles of Confederation, the new U.S. government was weak. Madison pushed for a stronger central authority, leaving to states only matters that concerned them individually. He drafted the Virginia Plan (also called the Randolph Plan), which was developed into the Constitution. Madison wrote many of the pro-Constitution papers known as *The Federalist.* During the Constitution's ratification process, many state conventions called for it to be amended to protect individual rights. Madison, elected to the House of Representatives in 1789, helped draft what became the Bill of Rights, the first 10 amendments to the Constitution.

Madison helped to form the new Democratic-Republican Party, largely to oppose the fiscal policies of the Federalist Party's Alexander Hamilton, first secretary of the U.S. treasury. Until Madison left Congress in 1797, he led the new party in the House. His opposition of the Federalists' Alien and Sedition Acts helped unify his party.

As President Jefferson's secretary of state (1801-09), Madison helped the U.S. gain the Louisiana Purchase. His wife, Dolley (whom he had married in 1794), served as White House hostess for Jefferson. In the 1808 presidential election, Madison defeated Charles C. Pinckney, the Federalist candidate.

President. As president, Madison faced the same foreign-relations problem he had as secretary of state: the continuing war between France and Britain. Impressment of U.S. sailors, seizure of goods, and blockades had serious damaged U.S. shipping. Tensions arose until Congress declared war on Britain in June 1812. The War of 1812 went badly for the U.S. Madison's popularity fell; New England Federalists opposed "Mr. Madison's War" and demanded his resignation. However, he won reelection five months after the war began. In August 1814, Madison—and the nation—suffered humiliation when British troops stormed Washington and burned the White House and the Capitol. The Treaty of Ghent, signed Dec. 24, 1814, ended the war in a stalemate.

With peace, however, Madison regained his popularity. His new domestic program appeased the Federalists somewhat and helped launch a "new nationalism."

Retirement. After leaving the presidency in 1817, Madison retired to Montpelier, his Virginia plantation. In 1826, he became rector (president) of the University of Virginia. He died at Montpelier in 1836.

Madonna (Madonna Louise Ciccone; 1960-), U.S. rock and roll performer. Madonna's early training was as a dancer studying ballet, modern, and jazz dancing. In the 1970s she performed with the Pearl Lange and Alvin Ailey dance companies. After joining a series of club bands as an instrumentalist, she set out to become a singer. The success of her singing career began when her songs became dance club favorites. She rose to superstar status with her songs and trend-setting fashions. Some of her well-known hits are "Like a Virgin," "Material Girl," and "Crazy For You."

Madonna

Madonna and Child, among the most important art subjects of Christian religion. The Virgin Mary and child Jesus were first accepted as symbols of Christian faith following the Council of Ephesus in A.D. 431. The earliest Madonna and Child paintings were found in early Christian catacombs; styles developed and transformed through the Byzantine and Renaissance periods. There are 5 general styles of treatment of Madonna paintings: portrait, the Madonna enthroned, in glory (hovering in the sky with halo and attendants), in pastoral scenes, and in a home environment. Raphael's *Sistine Madonna* (1515) hangs in the Dresden Gallery in Germany. Other painters who depicted the Madonna and Child include Luca Della Robbia, Giovanni Bellini, Leonardo da Vinci, Michelangelo, Fra Filippo Lippi, Andrea del Sarto, and Titian.
See also: Christianity.

Madras (pop. 3,277,000), large coastal city in southeastern India. Capital city of the state of Tamil on the Bay of Bengal, Madras once served as a British outpost (17th century) and center for trade. Today it serves as one of India's important ports and commercial centers. Hindu and Christian landmarks as well as the Univ. of Madras and the British Fort St. George may be found alongside modern industry and transportation.
See also: India.

Madrid (pop. 3,124,000), city, capital of Spain and of Madrid province, on the Manzanares River in New Castile. A 10th-century Moorish fortress captured by Castile in

James Madison

4th U.S. President

Born	Port Conway, Va.; Mar. 16, 1751
Term	Mar. 1809-Mar. 1817
Vice Presidents	George Clinton; Elbridge Gerry
Political party	Democratic-Republican
Spouse	Dorothea (Dolley) Payne Todd Madison
Children	None
Died	Orange County, Va.; June 18, 1836

Madrid, Spain

1083, it was made the capital by Philip II (1561) and expanded by the Bourbons in the 16th century. Now Spain's administrative,financial, and transportation center, it has a wide range of industries. A cultural center, its landmarks include the Prado art museum, the royal palace, and the university city.
See also: Spain.

Madrid Hurtado, Miguel de la *see:* De la Madrid Hurtado, Miguel.

Madrigal, poetic part song for 2 or more voices singing separate melodies. Originating in 14th-century Italy, it reached the height of its popularity in the 16th century, through the works of Monteverdi and Gesualdo. *The Triumphes of Oriana* (1601) is a famous collection of English madrigals by 21 composers.

Madroña, shrub or tree (*Arbutus menziesii*) in the heath family. Commonly found on the west coast of the United States and Canada, this species also called laurelwood, grows to about 75 ft (23 m), has cinnamon-colored peeling bark, thick evergreen leaves, tall white flowers, and red berrylike fruit. The tree is used for decorative purposes.

Maecenas, Gaius (70?-8 B.C.), Roman statesman famous as the patron of Horace, Vergil, and Propertius. Friend, adviser, and agent of the emperor Augustus, he was criticized by Seneca for his extravagance. His name came to symbolize patronage.
See also: Rome, Ancient.

Large Maggelanic Cloud (detail)

Maenads, in Greek and Roman mythology, female devotees of Dionysus or Bacchus. Also called *bacchantes,* they were known for their ecstatic frenzies.
See also: Mythology.

Maeterlinck, Maurice (1862-1949), prolific Belgian poet and playwright influenced by French symbolists. His works include the tragedy *Pelléas et Mélisande* (1892), set as an opera by his friend Debussy, *Manna Vanna* (1902), and the dramatic fable *The Blue Bird* (1909). He was awarded the Nobel Prize for literature in 1911.

Maffei, Paolo *see:* Maffei galaxies.

Maffei galaxies, 2 galaxies near the Milky Way, discovered behind cosmic dust clouds through the use of a special infrared-sensitive telescope and photographic system by Italian astronomer Paolo Maffei (1968). Maffei I is an elliptical galaxy of about 100 billion stars, located approximately 3,000,000 light-years away. Maffei II is a spiral galaxy of about 10 billion stars, located approximately 9,000,000 light-years away.
See also: Galaxy.

Mafia, name given in the 19th century to Sicilian secret criminal societies who sought justice outside of the established legal system and dominated the peasantry through terrorism (e.g., the vendetta). Despite repression by successive governments, including Mussolini, in the late 19th and early 20th centuries, the Mafia survived. *Mafiosi* emigrated to the United States organized in "families," and prospered in bootlegging, gambling, narcotics, labor unions, and some legitimate business.

Magdalene *see:* Mary Magdalene.

Magellan, Ferdinand (c.1480-1521), Portuguese navigator who commanded the first expedition to sail around the world. Magellan received Spanish backing (from Charles I) for his proposed voyage in search of a western route to the Spice Islands (East Indies), then believed to be only a few hundred miles beyond America. He set sail with 5 ships in 1519, explored the Río de la Plata, sailed south to Patagonia, discovered the straits now named for him, then sailed northwest across the Pacific. Near starvation, the expedition reached Guam and the Philippines in 1521; Magellan was killed 10 days later in a skirmish with natives. Only one ship, the *Victoria,* returned to Spain.

Magellan, Strait of, north of Cape Horn, separating mainland South America from Tierra del Fuego; about 330 mi (530 km) long and 2.5-15 mi (4-24 km) wide. An important route before the Panama Canal, the straits were discovered by Ferdinand Magellan in 1520.
See also: Cape Horn.

Magellanic Clouds, 2 irregular galaxies nearest the Milky Way, visible in the far southern sky. The Large Magellanic Cloud (Nubecula Major), about 15,000 light-years in diameter, is located mostly in the constellation Dorado; the Small Magellanic Cloud (Nubecula Minor) is about 10,000 light-years across and is almost entirely in the constellation Tucana. Both are about 200,000 light-years from the earth.
See also: Galaxy.

Maggot, the soft-bodied larva of a winged insect, e.g., a fly. It has no legs and lies in its food, which may be plants, meat, or decaying matter.

Magi, hereditary members of the priestly class of the ancient Persian Empire. Revered for their wisdom and their ability to interpret dreams and omens, the Magi were also the acknowledged priests of the ancient Persian religion Zoroastrianism, which advocated worship of a single supreme deity. According to one tradition, the Magi kept watch for a great star that was to signal the arrival of a savior. This helps to explain the connection between the Magi and the three wise men who, according to the New Testament, were led by a star to Bethlehem, where they honored the infant Jesus with gifts.
See also: Persia, Ancient; Zoroastrianism.

Magic, prescientific belief that an individual, by use of a ritual or spoken formula, may achieve superhuman powers. Should the magic fail to work, it is assumed to be due to deviations from the correct formula. In his classic work *The Golden Bow* (1890) Sir James George Frazer classified magic under 2 main heads: imitative and contagious. In *imitative magic* the magician acts upon or produces a likeness of the desired object: Rainmakers may light fires, the smoke of which resembles rain clouds; voodoo practitioners stick pins in wax models of their intended victims. In *contagious magic* it is assumed that 2 objects once close together remain related even after separation: the magician may act upon hair clippings in an attempt to injure the person from whose body they came. Magic is crucial to many primitive societies, most tribes having at least an equivalent to a medicine man, who is believed to be able to provide them with extra defense against hostile tribes or evil spirits.

Maginot Line, massive French fortifications system, built 1930-34 between the Swiss and Belgian borders. Named for war minister (1929-32) André Maginot, it linked underground fortresses and was considered impregnable. However, it was easily flanked by the German mobile advance in World War II.

Magma, molten material formed in the upper mantle, or crust, of the earth, composed of a mixture of various complex silicates in which are dissolved various gaseous materials, including water. On cooling, magma forms igneous rocks, though any gaseous constituents are usually lost during the solidification. Magma extruded to the surface forms lava. The term is loosely applied to other fluid substances in the earth's crust.

Magna Carta, or *Magna Charta* (Latin, "great charter"), major British constitutional charter forced on King John I by a baronial alliance at Runnymede (1215). A reaction to John's heavy taxation and his exclusion of the barons from government, the charter was designed to prevent royal restriction of baronial privilege and feudal rights and to safeguard church and municipal customs. Altered forms of the decree were issued on John's death in 1216 and again in 1217 and 1225. Now generally recognized as a reactionary measure to guarantee feudal rights, it has, in the past, been interpreted to suggest and defend such civil rights as habeas corpus and jury trial. It paved the way for constitutional monarchy by implicitly recognizing that a king may be bound by laws enforceable by his subjects.

Magnesia, chemical compound (MgO), also called magnesium oxide. Used in the manufacture of refined metals, crucibles, and materials for insulation, it also has medicinal purposes. Made from magnesia chloride, magnesia is a white, powdery substance that has no taste.

Magnesium, chemical element, symbol Mg; for physical constants see Periodic Table. Compounds of magnesium have been known and used for hundreds of years. It was discovered by Humphry Davy in 1808. The eighth most abundant element in the earth's crust, it is extracted commercially by the electrolysis of fused magnesium chloride taken from sea water or other brines. Magnesium is a light, silvery-white, hard, reactive, metal. It plays an essential role in both plant and animal life. Magnesium and its compounds are used in light metal alloys, incendiary devices, flash bulbs, flares, and in medicine.

Magnetic compass *see:* Compass.

Magnetic equator, also called the *aclinic line*, imaginary line around the earth where the magnetic pull of the 2 poles is equal. In theory, the earth is a magnet with poles that are magnetized in the north (Bathurst Island, Canada) and south (Wilkes Land, Antarctica). A metal object placed on the magnetic equator, near the geographic equator, will not be inclined north or south.

Magnetic levitation vehicle *see:* Transportation.

Magnetic pole *see:* North Pole; South Pole.

Magnetic resonance imaging (MRI), technique which produces images of tissues inside the body and allows physicians to identify abnormal tissue without surgery. MRI enables physicians to see through bones and organs using a powerful magnet, radio waves, and a computer, and has been used to detect tumors, diseases of the circulatory system, birth defects, and certain injuries. The examination is supervised by a radiologist though no radiation is involved.

Magnetic storm, temporary, violent agitation in the earth's magnetic field caused by the *solar wind*—a stream of positively charged atoms and negatively charged electrons that flow from the sun. Solar winds are caused by the energy created during bursts of solar activity.
See also: Magnetism; Solar wind.

Magnetism, name for a force that occurs naturally in certain substances and can be transferred to or induced in others. The basic properties of magnetism are its complementary forces of attraction and repulsion and its capacity to align itself on a roughly north-south axis. These properties occur naturally in magnetite and, in the form of the lodestone, were observed and exploited to some degree in ancient times. The force of magnetism is dipolar, on a north-south axis, corresponding approximately to the north and south magnetic poles of the earth. In a magnet, unlike poles attract; like poles repel. And if it is divided, the parts of a magnet will also be dipolar. It was early discovered that magnetism not only attracts iron, but can be transferred to iron. Metals which can be readily magnetized are called ferromagnetic and, besides iron and steel, include nickel and cobalt. A magnet, then, is anything that has the properties of magnetism.
Magnetism also exhibits a field. The shape of a magnetic field and its lines of force can be seen by sprinkling iron filings over a sheet of paper placed on top of a magnet. In the 19th century, scientists made discoveries about the relationship between magnetism and electricity. It was found that the forces between magnetic dipoles are identical to those between electrical dipoles and that electric currents generate a magnetic field. Further research revealed that it is possible to generate an electric current in a conductor by changing the magnetic fields around it, a phenomenon known as electromagnetism. This interrelation between electrical charge and magnetic force is present in matter on the atomic level as well. And the earth itself has a magnetic field which scientists hypothesize is generated and maintained by large electric currents caused by movement in the planet's liquid core.

Magneto, small electric generator that produces pulses of electricity. Magnetos are used as an ignition source in airplane piston engines and motorcycle engines, among other things. In mining, magnetos are used to fire explosives. The magneto works on the principle of electromagnetic induction. It consists of a permanent magnet and a soft iron core wound with wire. The core is rotated between the poles of the magnet, generating a low-voltage alternating current in the coil windings. This low voltage may be transformed to a higher voltage by induction in a second set of coil windings.
See also: Electric generator.

Magnetohydrodynamics (MHD), method of generating electricity by passing a high-velocity stream of plasma (gas at very high temperature) across a magnetic field. As the stream moves through the magnetic field, it has an electric current generated in it. The principle is the same as that of the electric generator, except that in magnetohydrodynamics the plasma stream rather than a coil of wire acts as the conductor. If electrodes are inserted into the plasma, a current will flow in an external circuit between them. In this way heat can be almost directly converted into electrical energy. But magnetohydrodynamics is still in the development stage, and a full-scale MHD plant has yet to be built. In practice the plasma would be heated by burning fuel or by a nuclear reactor to a temperature of 2,000°C-3,000°C (3,632°F-5,432°C). At these temperatures the gas is ionized (has electrons stripped from its atoms) and becomes conducting. Strong magnetic fields are required, and these may be provided by superconducting magnets. So far a few kilowatts of power have been generated by MHD for only a few seconds, and improvements in high-temperature technology will be needed before substantial progress can be made.
MHD plants could in theory be smaller than conventional power stations and achieve a much greater efficiency because of the elimination of moving parts.
See also: Electric generator; Magnetism.

Magnetometer, instrument that surveys the strength of a magnetic field and registers its results through electronic voltage. Magnetometers are used by biomedical technicians to measure the magnetic field of certain body organs, such as the brain. They are used in industry, especially by

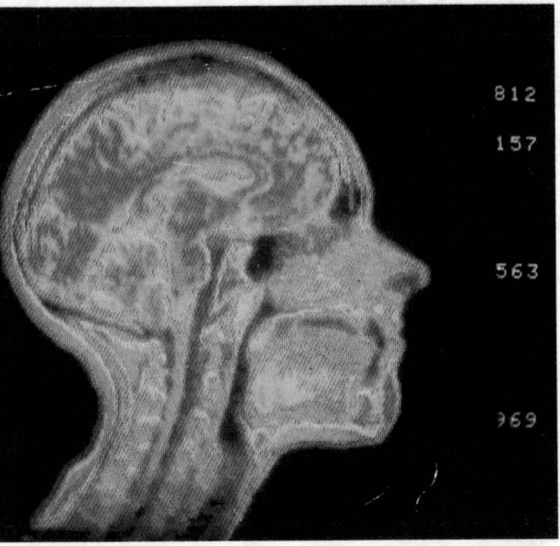

Magnetic resonance imaging (MRI)

those working with superconductors, and by prospectors attempting to detect ore or petroleum beneath the ground.
See also: Magnetism.

Magnitude, measure of a celestial object's brightness. The foundations of the system were laid by Hipparchus (120 B.C.), who divided stars into 6 categories of relative brightness, as seen from the earth (apparent magnitude). On a logarithmic scale, the difference of 1 magnitude of brightness between objects is determined by a factor of 2,512 (the 5th root of 100). The sun's magnitude is 26.8; bright stars, about +1. *Absolute magnitude* (measure of intrinsic brightness) is defined as the apparent magnitude if located at a distance of 10 parsecs.
See also: Astronomy; Hipparchus.

René Magritte's The Human Condition *(1932)*

Magnolia, any of the evergreen or deciduous trees or shrubs (genus *Magnolia*) from the family Magnoliaceae, often with showy flowers, found chiefly in temperate zones. Principally an Asiatic genus, native American magnolia species include the southern magnolia, or the bull bay (*M. grandiflora*), the cucumber tree (*M. acuminata*), the umbrella tree (*M.tripetala*), and the tulip tree, or yellow poplar (*Liriodendron tulipfera*), whose soft, yellowish wood is valued for furniture and cabinetwork.

Magnolia State *see:* Mississippi.

Magpie, long-tailed bird of the crow and jay family (especially genus *Pica*). The North American *black-billed magpie* (*Pica pica*) has black feathers and white wings and abdomen. These scavengers, collectors of bright objects, often learn to imitate words in captivity.

Magritte, René (1898-1967), Belgian surrealist painter. His style, influenced by Chirico, often combined realism with irony, as in fantasy painting such as *The False Mirror* (1928), *The Red Model* (1935), and *The Empire of Lights* (1950).
See also: Surrealism.

Magpie

Maguey, plant in the agave family. The Mexican plant, which grows up to 9 ft (3 m) long and 1 ft (30 cm) wide, has long green stalks with green flowers. The pulque agave (*Agave atrovirens*) is used to make beverages, both pulque and tequila. In Indonesia and the Philippines, the maguey is referred to commonly as cantala, and fibers from the plant, which may grow to 30-60 ft (75-150 cm) long, are used to produce twine.

Magyars, dominant people of Hungary and their language (from the Finno-Ugric language group). A nomadic warrior people, originally from the Urals, they were forced into present-day Romania by the Turkish Pechenegs and then into Hungary in the 9th century. They went on to conquer Moravia, advancing into Germany until stopped by Otto I in 955. They adopted Christianity in the 11th century.

Mahabharata, Sanskrit epic poem ascribed to the sage Vyasa, comprising some 110,000 32-syllable couplets, probably written before 500 B.C. though with many later passages in 18 books. It concerns the lengthy feud between 2 related tribes, the Pandavas and the Kauravas, and has as its central episode the Bhagavad-Gita, the religious classic of Hinduism.
See also: Hinduism.

Mahan, Alfred Thayer (1840-1914), U.S. naval officer and historian. His works on the historical significance of sea power, classics in their field, stimulated worldwide naval expansion. They include *The Influence of Sea Power upon History, 1660-1783* (1890) and *The Influence of Sea Power upon the French Revolution and Empire, 1793-1812* (1892).

Mahathir bin Mohammad, Datuk Seri (1925-), prime minister of Malaysia since 1981. Trained in medicine, he has made his career in politics. Mahathir served as deputy prime minister (1976-81) before succeeding Prime Minister Hussein bin Onn. A Malay nationalist, he was elected president of his party, the United Malays National Organization, in 1981.
See also: Malaysia.

Mahatma *see:* Gandhi, Mohandas Karamchand.

Mahdi (Arabic, "the guided one"), the prophet or savior who Muslims believe will bring peace and justice to the world. A notable claimant was Ubaydullah (r. 909-34), founder of the Egyptian Fatimid dynasty. Another was Muhammad Ahmad (1843?-85), who raised a revolt against Egyptian rule in the Sudan and fought the British (1883-85).
See also: Muslims.

Mahfouz, Naguib, or Mahfuz, Nagib (1911-), Egyptian novelist, playwright, and screenwriter. Among his works, which focus on urban life, are *Midaq Alley* (tr. 1975), *Miramar* (tr. 1978), and the short story collection *God's World* (tr. 1973). He won the 1988 Nobel Prize for literature. His books have been banned in many Arab countries for his expression of support of the 1979 Egypt-Israel peace treaty and other controversial views.

Mahican, Native American group of tribes of the Eastern Woodlands. These Native Americans lived along the Hudson River in longhouses and spoke an Algonquian language. They were active in the 17th-century fur trade along with their rivals, the Mohawks. Today surviving Mahicans live on Stockbridge Reservation in Wisconsin, named after the western Massachusetts town to which they were driven in the 17th century. Both Mahicans and Mohegans, a tribe of the Mahican group, are often referred to as Mohicans, after the fictional tribe in James Fenimore Cooper's *The Last of the Mohicans*.
See also: Mohegan.

Mah-jongg, game of Chinese origin played with a set of 136 standard domino-like tiles and several additional tiles, usually by 4 players. It is a collecting game where tiles are drawn and discarded until 1 player has a winning hand.

Mahler, Gustav (1860-1911), Austrian composer and conductor. He completed 9 symphonies and a number of song cycles, most notably *Songs of a Wayfarer* (1883-85) and *Kindertotenlieder* (*Songs on the Death of Children*; 1901-04). The symphonies are a culmination of 19th-century romanticism, but their startling harmonic and orchestral effects link them with early 20th-century works. Mahler was director of the Imperial Opera in Vienna (1897-1907).

Mahogany, chiefly tropical trees and shrubs, family Meliaceae, whose scented, termite-resistant hardwood is used extensively for furniture. The American genus *Swietenia* and the African genus *Khaya* are the principal sources of mahogany.

Mahomet *see:* Muhammad.

Mahratta, or Maratha, central Indian Hindu warrior people. Their empire was founded by Sivaji in 1674; it dominated India for about 150 years, following the Mogul empire, but the British broke its power in 1818.

Maidenhair tree *see:* Ginkgo.

Maidu, Native Americans who lived mainly in the Sacramento Valley and the Sierra Nevada, Calif. Maidus are part of the Penutian linguistic family. Today they number fewer than 200.

Mail *see:* Postal service, U.S.

Mailer, Norman (1923-), U.S. novelist and journalist. After the great success of his first novel, *The Naked and the Dead* (1948), he became a critic of the American way of life. He combines journalism, fiction, and autobiography, as in his collection *Advertisements for Myself* (1959). He has been awarded 2 Pulitzer Prizes, one for *the Armies of the Night* (1968), an account of the 1967 Washington peace march, and the other for *The Executioner's Song* (1979).

Maillol, Aristide (1861-1944), French sculptor. His chief subject was the female nude, which he sculpted in monumental, static forms that represent a revival of classical ideals.

Maimonides, Moses (Solomon ben Maimon; 1135-1204), medieval rabbi, physician, and Jewish philosopher. Born in Muslim Spain, his family was driven to Egypt under persecution, where Maimonides became renowned as court physician to Saladin. Two of his major works were the *Mishneh Torah* (*Strong Hand*; 1180), a codification of Jewish doctrine, and *Guide to the Perplexed* (1190), in which he attempted to interpret Jewish tradition in Aristotelian terms. His work influenced many Jewish and Christian thinkers.
See also: Philosophy.

Maine, largest New England state in the northeasternmost United States; bordered by Canada to the northwest, north, and east, by the Atlantic Ocean to the south, and by New Hampshire to the southwest.
Land and climate. During the Ice Age, Maine was covered by glaciers that pushed down the coastline, creating offshore islands. The moving ice rounded the mountains and left hundreds of lakes and ponds. Today, forests cover nearly 90% of the state. Maine has 3 distinct land regions. (1) The Coastal Lowlands extend inward from the Atlantic 10-40 mi (16-64 km). The land is gently rolling; along the coast are many rocky bays, inlets, and rugged peninsulas, and more than 1,300 islands. (2) The Eastern New England Upland runs northeast to southwest down the middle of the state. This rolling, heavily forested land contains hundreds of rivers and lakes. The Aroostook Plateau in the northeast is the state's most fertile area. (3) The White Mountains Region covers northwestern Maine and extends into New Hampshire and Vermont. This region includes most of Maine's higher peaks, including Mt. Katahdin. Moosehead Lake is Maine's largest lake. The state has more than 5,000 rivers and streams; major rivers include the Kennebec, Penobscot, St. John, Androscoggin, and Saco. Maine's climate is moist, cooler than most of the United States. Arctic air and coastal winds make Maine colder than many other places in the same latitude. Principal cities are Portland, Lewiston, and Bangor.

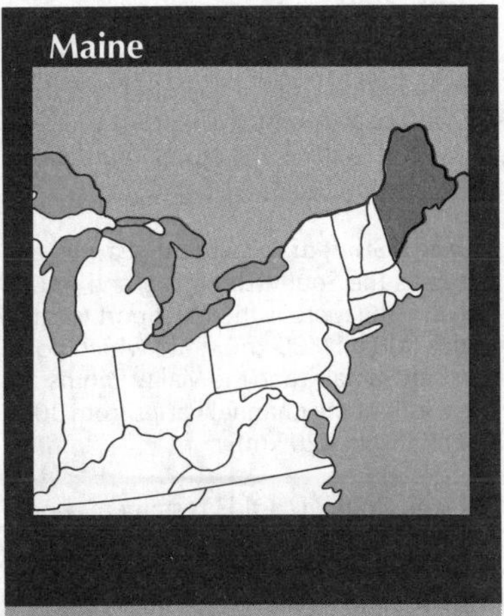

Capital:	Augusta
Statehood:	Mar. 15, 1820 (23rd state)
Familiar name:	Pine Tree State
Area:	33,215 sq mi (86,026 km); ranks 39th
Population:	1,233,223 (1990); ranks 38th
Elevation:	Highest—5,268 ft (1,606 m), Mt. Katahdin Lowest—sea level
Motto:	*Dirigio* (I Direct)
State flower:	White pine cone and tassel
State bird:	Chickadee
State tree:	White pine
State song:	"State of Maine Song."

Economy. Service industries account for approximately 70% of the total value of all goods and services Maine produces in a year, but manufacturing is the main economic activity. Maine's abundant forests provide the raw materials for its paper industry and for such manufactured products as cardboard boxes, paper bags, lumber, and toothpicks. Other leading manufactured products include electrical equipment, processed foods, leather products, and textiles. Tourism, based on the striking Atlantic scenery and plentiful recreation facilities, is another major source of income for the state. Maine produces the nation's third-largest potato crop (after Idaho and Washington). Milk, eggs, and broilers (chickens) are the top livestock products. Mineral products include construction sand and gravel, cement, and crushed stone.
Government. Maine's constitution was adopted in 1819. The governor serves a 4-year term. The state legislature consists of 35 senators and 151 representatives; all serve 2-year terms. In the U.S. Congress, Maine is represented by 2 senators and 2 representatives.
History. Vikings may have been the first Europeans to explore Maine, C.A.D. 1000. Italian sea captain John Cabot probably explored the coast in 1498. The area was home to thousands of Native Americans when the first European-American settlers arrived in the early 1600s. Becoming part of the Massachusetts Bay Colony in the mid-1600s, Maine was a battleground during the French and Indian Wars; Maine soldiers played an active part in the American Revolution. In 1819, the people voted to separate from Massachusetts, and Maine became a state in 1820. During the Civil War, it was a strong antislavery state. After the war, industrial development extended until the 1930s Great Depression and rose again after World War II, when tourism also boomed. Since the early 1970s, however, the state's economic development has been uneven. In the 1940s, Maine's Margaret Chase Smith became the first woman elected to both houses of the U.S. Congress.

Norman Mailer

A typical Maine farm

Maine, U.S. battleship, sent to protect U.S. citizens and property in Cuba. It blew up in Havana harbor on Feb. 15, 1898, with a loss of 260 men. "Remember the Maine" became the war's rally cry. The incident, never satisfactorily explained though 2 inquiries were conducted, helped spark the Spanish-American War.
See also: Spanish-American War.

Mainstreaming *see:* Special education.

Maintenon, Marquise de (1635-1719), second wife of Louis XIV of France. After the death of her first husband (1660), she became governess to the sons of Louis and his mistress, Mme de Montespan. She replaced the latter in Louis' affections and, on the death of the queen, was married to him though she did not share his title and estate.

Mainz (pop. 188,600), city in west-central Germany. As the capital of the state of Rhineland-Palatinate state, it is located on a junction of two German rivers, the Rhine and the Main. Originally a Roman camp (1st century B.C.), it became an important religious and printing center in medieval times and a fortress for the German Empire (1873-1918). The city is known as home to historic buildings, a center for German Rhine wines, and manufacturing (e.g., motor vehicles and chemicals).

Maitland, Frederic William (1850-1906), English jurist and legal historian. He was particularly concerned with early English law and founded the Selden Society (1887). Notable among his works is *The History of English Law before the Time of Edward I* (1895), written with Sir Frederick Pollock.

Maize *see:* Corn.

Major *see:* Rank, military.

Major, John (1943-), British politician of the Conservative Party who succeeded Margaret Thatcher as Prime Minister in 1990. Prior to becoming Prime Minister, Major was a member of Parliament, Foreign Secretary, and Chancellor of the Exchequer. Major left school at the age of 16 and never attended college. He entered the banking industry at the age of 22 before entering politics. He lost the 1997 general election to Tony Blair's Labour Party.
See also: United Kingdom.

Archbishop Makarios

Majorca, or *Mallorca*, largest of the Balearic Islands of Spain, in the west Mediterranean. Majorca is a major tourist center with many resorts, including its capital, Palma.

Majorca

Major leagues *see:* Baseball.

Makarios III (Michael Christodoulos Mouskos; 1913-77), archbishop of the Cypriot Orthodox Church from 1950, and president of independent Cyprus (1960-77). During British rule he led the movement for *enosis* (union with Greece). As president after independence, he worked to reduce conflict between the island's Greek and Turkish population. He survived 4 assassination attempts and fled temporarily during the political disturbances of 1974.

Mako shark *see:* Shark.

Malabo (pop. 33,000), capital city of Equatorial Guinea. Founded by the British (1827) as Clarencetown, it was later named Santa Isabel by the Spanish (1844) until the independence of Equatorial Guinea (1973). Located on the island of Bioko in the Gulf of Guinea, the city is important in import-export trade.

Malacca, Strait of, important sea passage that links the South China Sea and Indian Ocean. Singapore is the chief port located on this 500 mi (800 km) strait, which flows between Sumatra and the Malay Peninsula. The width of the channel varies from 30 to 200 mi (50 to 320 km).

Malachi, Book of, Old Testament book, 39th and last in Authorized Version, 12th of the Minor Prophets. Written anonymously c.5th century B.C., it prophesies judgment for insincerity and negligence at the coming of the Messiah.
See also: Old Testament.

Malachite, $CU_2CO_3(OH)_2$, green, translucent mineral containing crystals of hydrated copper carbonate. It is widely distributed, usually occurring near copper deposits, in the United States, Russia, Chile, Congo, Zimbabwe and Australia. It is used as a source of copper, an ornamental stone, and, when ground, as a pigment.

Malagasy Republic *see:* Madagascar.

Malamud, Bernard (1914-86). U.S. novelist and short story writer. He won a National Book Award for his stories in *The Magic Barrel* (1958) and the Pulitzer Prize for his novel *The Fixer* (1966). Malamud's work deals mainly with Jewish life and traditions in the United States. The heroes of his books are often humble, solitary individuals, though *Dubin's Lives* (1979) marked a departure in subject matter.

Malamute *see:* Alaskan malamute.

Malaria, infectious parasitic disease causing fever, violent chills, enlargement of the spleen, and occasionally jaundice and anemia. Bouts often reoccur and can be acute or chronic. Widespread in tropical and subtropical areas, malaria is due to infection with the *Plasmodium* parasite carried by the *Anopheles* mosquitoes from the blood of infected persons. Derivatives of quinine are used both in prevention and treatment of the disease.

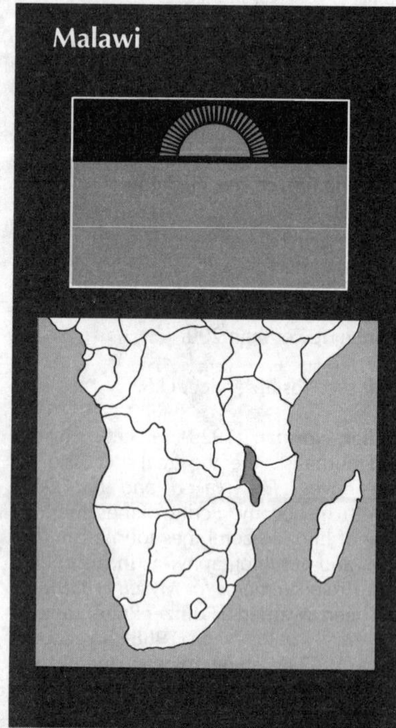

Capital:	Lilongwe
Area:	45,747 sq mi (118,484 sq km)
Population:	9,085,000
Form:	republic
Independent:	1964
GNP:	U.S.$1,896,000,000
Per capita:	U.S.$210

Malawi, republic of east Africa lying west and south of Lake Malawi, and bordered by Tanzania to the north, Mozambique to the east and south, and Zambia to the west.
Land and climate. Malawi has an area of about 45,747 sq mi (118,484 sq km), controls much of lakes Malawi and Chiuta, and includes the lakes Malambe, Chilwa, and several other large lakes. The lakes are part of the great African Rift Valley, which crosses the region from north to south and includes the Shire River valley. Bordering highlands and plateaus average 3,500 ft (1,067 m) in height, and the Shire highlands in the south and southeast rise to 9,843 ft (3,000 m) at Mlanje Peak. The valleys are hot; the highland climate is moderate.

Malawi landscape

People. The people of Malawi are almost entirely Bantu-speaking black Africans. About 75% of the people are Christians with the balance professing Islam or practicing native religions. English and Chichewa are the country's official languages, though other African languages are spoken. The largest city is Blantyre, the capital is Lilongwe. More than 90% of the people live in villages in the countryside.
Economy. Malawi's economy is agricultural. Tea and tobacco are grown in the highlands; cotton in the lowlands. Other crops include peanuts, corn, rice, and sugar. There is some light industry at Blantyre and Lilongwe. The Shire River is harnessed for hydroelectricity at Nkula Falls. The country's mineral resources remain mostly undeveloped.
History. Seat of a powerful black African kingdom between the 15th and 18th centuries, Malawi was later prey to the slave trade. In 1859 the British missionary Dr. David Livingstone visited Malawi. Subsequently, missions were set up and the slave trade suppressed. An attempt by the Portuguese to seize the south was defeated leading to the establishment of a British protectorate in 1890. Shortly thereafter the area became known as Nyasaland. In 1953 the country entered the Federation of Rhodesia and Nyasaland, but the association with white dominated Rhodesia was an uneasy one and lasted only until 1963. In 1964, Nyasaland became the independent state of Malawi. On July 6, 1966 it was proclaimed a republic under the presidency of Dr. Hastings K. Banda. Malawi is a one-party country. Under Dr. Banda Malawi has pursued a controversial foreign policy of openly maintaining relations with South Africa.

Malay Archipelago, (East Indies), the world's largest group of islands, off the coast of southeastern Asia, between the Indian and Pacific Oceans. It includes the 3,000 islands of Indonesia, the 7,000 islands of the Philippines, and New Guinea.

Malayo-Polynesian languages, or Austroenesian languages, family of some 500 languages found throughout the Central and South Pacific, especially in Malaysia and the Indonesian islands. There are 2 main groups: Oceanic to the east and Indonesian to the west.

Malay Peninsula, southernmost peninsula in Asia, comprising western Malaysia and southern Thailand. It is one of the world's richest producers of rubber and tin.

Malaysia, Federation of Malaysia, independent federation in Southeast Asia, comprising West Malaysia on the Malay Peninsula and East Malaysia, formed by Sabah and Sarawak on the island of Borneo.
Land and climate. East Malaysia is separated from the Malay Peninsula for a distance of about 400 mi (644 km) by the South China Sea. West Malaysia is bordered by Thailand to the north, Singapore to the south, the South China Sea to the east, and the Strait of Malacca and the Andaman Sea to the west. East Malaysia is bordered on the south and west by Indonesia, on the north by the South China and Sulu Seas and by Brunei, and on the east by the Celebes Sea. West Malaysia is mainly mountainous with narrow coastal plains and lush equatorial forests. Sarawak and Sabah also have mountainous interiors and large areas of rain forest.
People. The majority of Malaysians live on the peninsula and most are Malays or Chinese with sizable minorities of Indians and Pakistanis. Malay is the official language, but many Malaysians also speak other languages including Chinese, English, and Tamil. Islam is the official religion. The capital is Kuala Lumpur.
Economy. Malaysia is rich in natural re-

Malaysia

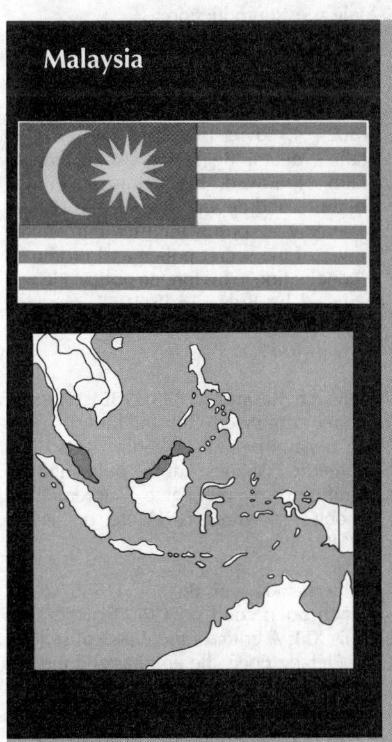

General information	
Capital:	Kuala Lumpur
Area:	127,584 sq mi (330,442 sq km)
Population:	17,421,000
Official language:	Malay (Bahasa Malaysia)
Monetary unit:	1 ringgit = 100 sen
Main cities:	Kuala Lumpur, Ipoh, Pinang
Government	
Form:	federal constitutional monarchy
Independent:	1963
Head of state:	Monarch (elected every 5 years)
Head of government:	Prime minister
Legislature:	two legislative houses (Senate and House of Representatives)
Executive:	Prime minister and Cabinet
Judiciary:	highest court is the Supreme Court
Political division:	13 states, 1 federal territory
National economy	
Gross national product:	U.S. $34,300,000,000
Per capita income:	U.S. $1,870
Agriculture:	rice, coconuts, natural rubber, palm kernels, sugar cane, bananas, copra, pepper
Livestock:	pigs, chickens, cattle
Fisheries:	571,000 metric tons
Mining:	bauxite, iron ore, copper ore, tin, crude petroleum
Industries:	rubber products, cement, processed palm oil, iron and steel products, paints, plywood
Main exports:	machinery and transport equipment, crude materials, mineral fuels, lubricants and related materials, animal and vegetable oils and fats
Transportation:	1,381 mi (2,222 km) of railroads, 24,276 mi (39,069 km) of roads, 5 international airports
Trading partners:	Japan, U.S., Singapore, Germany, South Korea
People	
Urban:	38%
Ethnic composition:	Malay and other indigenous peoples 61%, Chinese 30.5%, Indian 8%
Birth rate:	29.3 per 1,000 population
Death rate:	6 per 1,000 population
Infant mortality:	31 per 1,000 live births
Life expectancy:	male 65 years, female 70 years

Malaysian fishing village

sources, but the economy is still predominantly agricultural. Rice is the chief food crop, but bananas, yams, cocoa, pepper, tea, and tobacco are also grown. In addition, the forests yield valuable timber, palm oil, and coconuts. The relatively small industrial sector produces petroleum, iron ore, bauxite, coal, and gold. The country's principal exports are petroleum, rubber, tin, palm oil, and timber.

Malcolm X

History. In the 9th century Malaysia was the seat of the Buddhist Srivajava Empire. Beginning in the 14th century the population was converted to Islam. The Portuguese took Malacca in 1511, but were ousted by the Dutch in 1641. The British formed a trading base of the East India Company in Penang in 1786, and in 1826 united Penang, Singapore, and Malacca into the Straits Settlement. Between 1888 and 1909 the British established many protectorates in Malaya and Borneo. After the Japanese occupation in World War II (1941-45), Malaya was reorganized as the Federation of Malaya (1948), gaining independence within the British Commonwealth in 1957. In 1963 the union of Malaya with Singapore, Sarawak, and Sabah formed the Federation of Malaysia. Indonesia waged guerilla warfare against the Federation from 1963 to 1965. In 1965, Singapore seceded and became an independent republic. Parliament was suspended for 22 months beginning in 1969 after race riots broke out between Malays and Chinese in West Malaysia. Racial and religious strife again broke out among Malays, Chinese, and Hindus in the late 1970s and early 1980s. Ethnic and religious tensions remain the major threats to the Federation's stability and, in response, government has become more repressive.

The atolls of the Maldives

Malcolm X (Malcolm Little; 1925-65), U.S. black militant leader. He was also known as El-Hajj Malik El-Shabazz. While in prison for burglary (1946-52), he was converted to the Black Muslim faith and upon release became a Muslim minister and leader of the black separatist movement. In 1964 he split with another leader, Elijah Muhammad, to form the Organization of Afro-American Unity, speaking for black nationalism but allowing racial brotherhood. He was assassinated at an OAAU meeting in New York City in 1965, purportedly by Black Muslims. The *Autobiography of Malcolm X* (1964) is a classic concerning the black power movement of the 1960s.
See also: Black Power.

Maldives, officially Republic of Maldives, formerly *Maldive Islands,* republic, a series of coral atolls (115 sq mi/298 sq km) in the northern Indian Ocean, about 420 mi (675 km) southwest of Sri Lanka. They comprise some 2,000 islands, of which about 200 are inhabited. The official religion is Islam and the language, Dhivehi. Malé, the capital, is the largest island. The chief industries are fishing, coconut products, shipping, and tourism. Grains are grown on a limited scale, but most food staples are imported. Originally settled by southern Asians, the introduction of Islam in the 12th century and the arrival of the Portuguese in the 16th century strongly influenced the history of the islands. They became a British protectorate (1887-1965) with internal self-government before finally achieving independence as a sultanate in 1965. When the ad-Din dynasty, which had ruled since the 14th century, ended in 1968, a republic was declared. Britain closed its air force base on Gan in 1976.

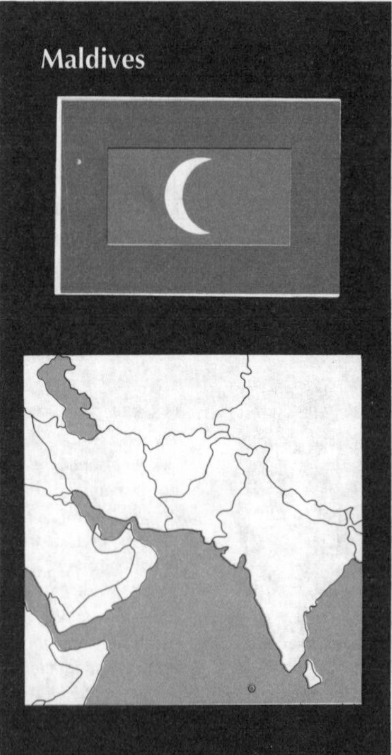

Capital:	Male
Area:	115 sq mi (298 sq km)
Population:	209,000
Form:	republic
Independent:	1965
GNP:	U.S. $80,000,000
Per capita:	U.S. $410

Malé (pop. 46,300), port and capital city of the Republic of Maldives, or Maldive Islands, in the Indian Ocean. Located on the island of the same name in this South Pacific atoll, Malé's main products are fish and tropical fruits and vegetables. Islam is the religion of its people, and Muslim mosques make Malé an important tourist site.

Male *see:* Reproduction.

Malemute *see:* Alaskan Malamute.

Malenkov, Georgi Maximilianovich (1902-), Soviet premier 1953-55, after Stalin's death. Beginning as an aide to Stalin, followed by entrance to the politburo and deputy premiership (1946), Malenkov as prime minister curbed the power of the secret police and promoted reconciliation in his foreign policy. He was replaced by Bulganin in 1955, expelled from the Presidium in 1957, and from the party in 1961.

Malevich, Kasimir (1878-1935), Russian painter, a pioneer of abstract art. In 1913 he began painting works based on geometric shapes and published a manifesto to propagate suprematism. Among his works is *White on White* (1918).

Malherbe, François de (1555-1628), French poet; court poet to Henry IV and Louis XIII. A critic of the classical style of the Pléiade poets, he emphasized the importance of French classic language and of precision in expression. His best-known poem is *Cosolation à Monsieur du Périer* (c.1590).

Mali, officially Republic of Mali, West Africa's largest country (478,764 sq mi/1,240,000 sq km), Mali is bordered by Senegal, Guinea, and Mauritania (west), Niger (east and southeast), Algeria (north), and Burkina Faso and Ivory Coast (south).
Land and economy. The land in the south, fed by the Niger and Senegal rivers, supports the chief cash crops of peanuts and cotton and subsistence crops of rice, millet,

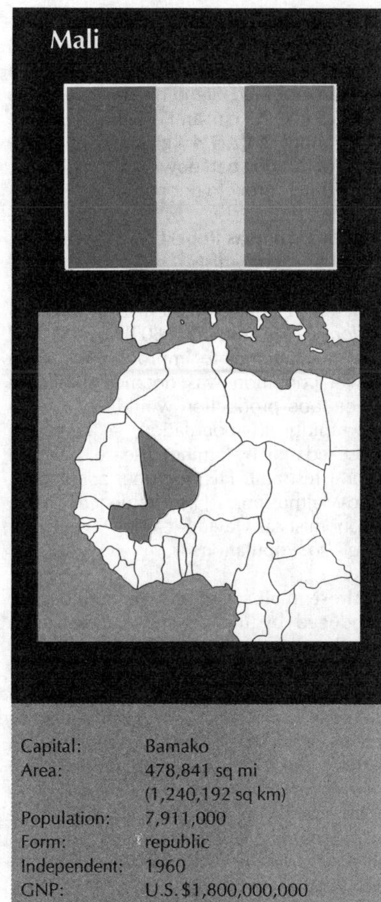

maize, and sorghum. Exports include fish from the Niger and livestock. Extensive mineral resources are largely untapped, though some salt, gold, and phosphates are mined. Industries include textiles, food processing, and cotton ginning. Land in the north, site of the Sahara Desert, is primarily arid, supporting minimum grazing (cattle, goats, sheep).

People. The population basically comprises 6 tribal groups, who speak the official language, French, and several indigenous tongues. About 65% are Muslims; the rest are animists.

History. The early 14th century saw the zenith of the powerful medieval empire of Mali, one of the world's chief gold suppliers. Its cities of Timbuktu and Djenné were major cultural and trade centers. The Songhai empire of Gao was prominent in the late 15th century before a Moroccan army destroyed its power (1590) and the region divided into small states. French conquest of Mali was complete by 1898, though they had faced a resurgence of Islam and were opposed by Muslim emperors. Mali became French Sudan and then part of French West Africa. After World War I, the Sudanese Union, a militant political force of the new nationalist movement, led by Modibo Keita, gained momentum, resulting in the autonomous Sudanese Republic in 1958. The republic joined with Senegal in 1959 to become the Mali Federation, a union that ended in 1960 as the Republic of Mali became fully independent and broke with the French Community. The one-party, socialist state, led by President Keita, left the French bloc (1962) but returned in 1967, due to financial difficulties. Keita was overthrown by the military (1968), displaced by Lt. Moussa Traoré as head of the military regime. In the 1970s a severe drought damaged Mali's agrarian economy and contributed to the deaths of nearly 100,000 people. A new constitution calling for civilian rule was implemented in 1979, reelecting Traoré as president. Nationalist Party leader Eddie Fenech Adami became prime minister in 1987.

Mali Empire, one of the great Sudanese empires of West Africa. Founded in the 13th century, it reached its height under Mansa Musa, who reigned 1312-37. He and his successors were devout Muslims, and the towns of Mali and Timbuktu became centers both of the caravan trade and of Islamic culture. The empire declined in the 15th century, mainly because of expansion of the Songhai empire of Gao.
See also: Mansa Musa.

Malinke *see:* Mandingo.

Malinowski, Bronislaw (1884-1942), Polish-born English anthropologist, founder of social anthropology. In his theory of "functionalism," all the mores, customs, and beliefs of a society perform a vital function that must be taken into account in the study of that culture. His research included the cultures of Trobriand Island, Africa, and the Americas. Writings include *Crime and Custom in Savage Society* (1926), *Sex and Repression in Savage Society* (1926), and *Magic, Science and Religion* (1948).
See also: Anthropology.

Mallard, wild duck of the family Anatidae. The dull brown feathers of the female are in sharp contrast to the iridescent green head and purple chest feathers of the courting male. These ducks, which grow to 28 in (71 cm), migrate from northern marshes in summer to warmer southern wetlands in winter. They are abundant in North America, Europe, and Asia.

Mallarmé, Stéphane (1842-98), French poet, forefather of the symbolists. He held that poetry should suggest or evoke the transcendental, not describe in literal terms. Although the language of his poems is obscure and nontraditional, he had considerable influence on French poetry. His works include *Herodias* (1869), *The Afternoon of a Faun* (1876), which inspired Debussy, and *A Throw of the Dice Will Never Eliminate Chance* (1897).

Mallorca *see:* Majorca.

Mallory, Stephen Russell (1813?-73), both U.S. and Confederate politician. After his resignation as U.S. senator (1850-61) from Florida, Russell was appointed by Jefferson Davis, president of the confederacy, as secretary of the Confederate Navy. Under his leadership, the South developed a powerful force of ironclad ships that overpowered the North's naval forces until near the end of the war. After a year of imprisonment following the war, Russell, along with other Confederates, was pardoned (1867) by President Andrew Johnson.
See also: Civil War, U.S.; Confederate States of America.

Mallow, shrub and herb of the family Malvaceae, usually with showy flowers and disk-shaped fruits. True mallows (genus *Malva*) of the Old World, false mallows (genus *Malvastrum*), and rose, or swamp, mallows (genus *Hibiscus*) of North America comprise the family. The perennial hollyhock (*Althea rosea*), from China, is the most popular ornamental; the pods of the mallow okra, or gumbo, are used as a vegetable; and the most economically important member is cotton. The marsh mallow of Europe is used medicinally and was once used to make marshmallow.

Malnutrition, shortage of vital nutrients. Malnutrition may be partial or total and may be the result of poor eating habits, as often occurs among the aged, or due to the unavailability or lack of food caused by disasters such as famine, drought, or war. Malnutrition may also be symptomatic of a gastrointestinal disorder, a malfunctioning of one of the body's major organs, or it may even be associated with diarrhea. Malnutrition affecting all parts of the diet is called marasmus. In marasmus, the body breaks down its own tissues to meet the needs of metabolism. The result is extreme wasting and, in children, extreme growth retardation. A shortage of the body's essential proteins is a variety of malnutrition known as kwashiorkor and shortages of essential vitamins manifest themselves as pellagra, beriberi, or scurvy.
Malnutrition is especially dangerous in pregnant women and in children. In children it can lead to growth disorders, both physical and mental, and reduce their resistance to disease. Though malnutrition is most readily associated with poor and underdeveloped countries in which its manifestations can be severe and are often fatal, it also occurs in rich and developed countries as the result of poverty or diets lacking in essential nutrients.

Malocclusion *see:* Orthodontics.

Malory, Sir Thomas (?-1471), English author who wrote *La Morte d'Arthur.* With romances (adventure stories) a favorite genre of his time, Sir Thomas Malory was the first to write, in English, the popular and legendary tales of King Arthur and his Knights of the Round Table. Believed to be completed in 1470, a first edition was printed by the first English printer, William Caxton (1485).

Malpighi, Marcello (1628-94), Italian physician and botanist who made significant advances in the understanding of human anatomy. His mastery of the micro-

scope enabled him to perform important research on animal tissues. He discovered that lungs are made up of small air sacs, called alveoli and that the veins connect to the arteries. He was the first person to describe red blood cells. Other significant contributions were made in the study of insect and plant anatomy. Malpighi was also a professor of medicine at the University of Bologna and served as the personal physician to Pope Innocent XII.
See also: Botany; Anatomy.

Malraux, André (1901-76), French author and political activist. His social novels, such as *Man's Fate* (1933) and *Man's Hope* (1937), describe political struggles both factually and poetically. In real life, Malraux became involved in many political struggles, including the Chinese civil war, the Spanish civil war, and the French resistance against the Nazis in World War II. He was France's first secretary of cultural affairs (1958-68), under Charles De Gaulle.

Malt, product made from any cereal grain by steeping it in water, allowing it to germinate, and then drying it. This activates dormant enzymes, such as diastase, that convert the kernel starch to maltose (malt sugar). Malt is used as a source of enzymes and flavoring.

Malta, officially Republic of Malta, republic in the Mediterranean Sea south of Sicily, made up of the islands of Malta, Gozo, Comino, and some uninhabited islets, for a total area of 122 sq mi (316 sq km). The capital and chief port is Valletta.

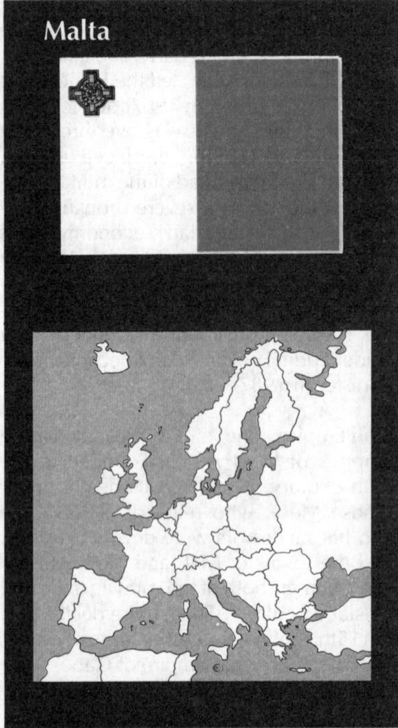

Capital:	Valletta
Area:	122 sq mi (316 sq km)
Population:	349,000
Form:	republic
Independent:	1964
GNP:	U.S. $1,740,000,000
Per capita:	U.S. $5,050

The port of Valletta on the island of Malta

Land. The islands are chiefly layers of limestone, with a thin topsoil, and reach their greatest height (827 ft/252 m) near Dingli, on Malta. Their fertile slopes and valleys are intensively cultivated, usually under irrigation.
People. The state religion is Roman Catholicism, and the official languages are English and Maltese, a Semitic language; Italian is widely spoken.
Economy. Malta has almost no mineral wealth or valuable natural resources and must import most of what it needs.
Agriculture, tourism, shipbuilding, and light industry, as well as traditional handicrafts (lave and ceramic), support the economy.
History. Malta is rich in prehistoric remains, but the first known inhabitants were the Phoenicians, who were succeeded by the Greeks, Carthaginians, Romans, and Saracens. Saint Paul was shipwrecked on Malta about A.D. 60. In 1530, after occupation by the Arabs, Normans, and Spaniards, Malta was granted to the Knights Hospitalers (later Knights of Malta), who defeated the Turks in the Great Siege (1565) and built Valletta. They were ousted by Napoleon I (1798), and 2 years later Malta passed to the British. Malta's courage under siege and intensive Axis bombardment during World War II was recognized by the award of the George Cross to the entire population. The country became independent within the Commonwealth in 1964.

Malta fever *see:* Brucellosis.

Maltese, breed of toy dog. This breed probably descends from lap dogs popular 2,000 years ago with women of Greek and Roman nobility. Standing no taller than about 5 in (12.7 cm) and weighing no more than about 7 lb (1.4 kg), the long white hairs of this dog part down the middle and, sometimes, grow to floor length.

Malthus, Thomas Robert (1766-1834), English economist, sociologist, and pioneer in the study of the population problem. In *An Essay on the Principal of Population* (1798; rev. ed. 1803), he asserted that any attempt to improve the human social condition was doomed to failure since food production would never grow as rapidly as population, a condition checked only by famine, disease, war, and moral restraint. His doctrine, adapted by neo-Malthusians, has influenced such economists as David Ricardo.
See also: Population.

Maltose, malt sugar; a disaccharide sugar produced by the action of diastase on starch and yielding glucose with the enzyme maltase.

Mamba, any of 4 or 5 species of snakes in the cobra family. Found in sub-Saharan Africa, these aggressive, thin, whip-like snakes can inflict a fatal, poisonous bite to man. Hoodless, unlike the familiar image of a cobra, the green mamba grows to about 9 ft (2.7 m) and the black mamba grows to about 14 ft (4.3 m).

Mamelukes, group of ruling warriors in Egypt. First brought to Egypt as slaves (10th century), many members of this warrior caste eventually rose to power (1250-1517). After 1517, when Ottoman rule of Egypt was established, the Mamelukes became influential whenever the ruling Turks' power waned. The Mamelukes headed an unsuccessful attack against Napoleon I in Egypt (1798), and were massacred by the Turks shortly afterwards.

Mamet, David (1947-), U.S. playwright. Among his successful works, which compare the American dream with the corruption of modern society, are *American Buffalo* (1977, New York Drama Critics Circle Award), *Glengarry Glen Ross* (1984, Pulitzer Prize and New York Drama Critics Circle Award), and *Speed-the-Plow* (1988). He also wrote screenplays for such movies as *The Verdict* (1982), *The Postman Always Rings Twice* (1984), and *The Untouchables* (1987).

Mammal, warm-blooded animal best distinguished by the possession of milk glands for feeding its young. Hair is a feature of mammals, although some, like the whales, have little or none. All mammals, except monotremes like the platypus, bear their young alive. Other shared characteristics are a lower jaw formed from 1 bone, 3 small bones in the middle ear, a neck of 7 vertebrae (even in giraffes), a diaphragm that forms a partition under the ribs, and a 4-chambered heart.

Mammals evolved from reptiles, but due to gaps in the fossil record, various stages in their development from reptiles are as yet undetermined. It is probable that the different groups of mammals arose independently from several kinds of intermediate mammal-like reptiles, so that there was no single ancestral mammal. The first mammals are believed to have been small and lived at the same time as the giant dinosaurs.
Mammals have evolved into many forms, and constitute some 3,200 species alive today. Mammals are divided into 3 main groups. The monotremes are the most primitive mammals and include the platypus of Australia. They lay eggs and feed their babies milk secreted from pores in the skin and not from milk glands with nipples. Marsupials are the pouched animals, including the kangaroo, opossum, wallaby, and Tasmanian devil. The young are born in an undeveloped state and complete their development in a pouch. Marsupials are found only in Australia and parts of America. Placental mammals, including humans, are the largest and most successful group. The young are born in varying states of development, from the relatively helpless human offspring to those like horses that are able to run within a few hours after their birth or, in the case of whales and dolphins, are able to swim as soon as they are born.

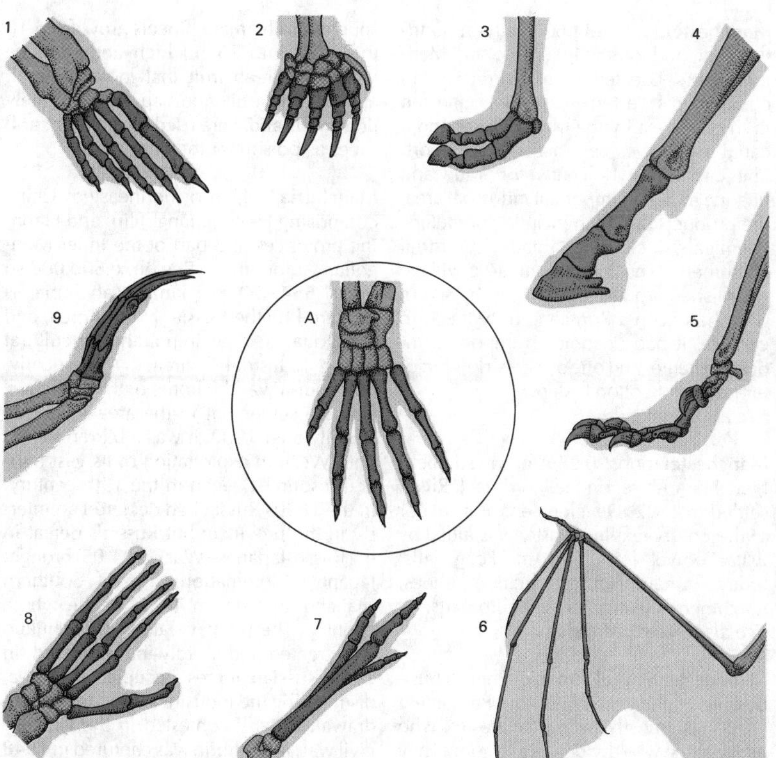

Seals (1) have webbed paddle shaped limbs for swimming. Moles (2) have short, powerful forelimbs for digging. Each of the camel's feet (3) has two toes linked by pads to form a wide shoe for walking on sand. Horses (4) and cheetahs (5) have elongated feet adapted for speed. Bats (6) have elongated fingers on the forelimb to support wing membrane for flight. Kangaroos (7) have elongated digits on the hind feet, which are placed flat on the ground to give leverage for jumping. Apes (8) and sloths (9) have forelimbs adapted for grasping tree branches.

Mammary glands, special glands present in mammals, situated ventrally in pairs, modified in females to produce and secrete milk to nourish offspring. The milk, secreted by cells lining the small compartments, or lobules, that make up each gland, then travels from the lobules along ducts to the nipple, where it is emptied. Mammary glands, which develop in female humans at the onset of adolescence, remain undeveloped in male mammals.

Mammoth, any of several extinct, prehistoric elephants (genus *Mammuthus*) found in North America and Eurasia. Distinguishable from today's elephants by their shaggy coats, long, upward-curving tusks, and complex molar teeth, the species included the imperial mammoth of North America, 13.5 ft (4.1 m) high at the shoulder.

Mammoth Cave, limestone cavern about 85 mi (137 km) southwest of Louisville, Ky., containing a series of vast subterranean chambers. It includes lakes, rivers, stalactites, stalagmites, and formations of gypsum crystals. The mummified body of a pre-Columbian man has been found there. It is part of Mammoth Cave National Park.

Man *see:* Human being.

Man, Isle of, island, 227 sq mi (588 sq km) in the Irish Sea off the northwestern coast of Great Britain; the capital is Douglas. It became the base for Irish missionaries after St. Patrick, and at one time was a Norwegian dependency sold to Scotland (1266). A dependency of the British Crown since 1765, it has its own legislature (Court of Tynwald) and representative assembly (House of Keys). Tourism is the main industry. The Manx language is now virtually extinct.

Management and Budget, Office of (OMB), U.S. government office that helps the president prepare the federal budget and formulate fiscal programs. The OMB was known as The Bureau of the Budget before 1970. At first part of the Treasury Department, it became part of the Executive Office of the President in 1939.

Managua (pop. 682,000), capital city of Nicaragua, located on the southern shore of Lake Managua. Made capital in 1855 to end a feud between León and Granada, it has been rebuilt on numerous occasions after destruction by earthquakes (1931, 1972) and fires (1931, 1936).
See also: Nicaragua.

Manakin, bird in the family Pipridae. Found in Central and South America, these small birds are known for the male courtship rituals. In specially selected dancing grounds called leks, the males create unusual sounds and movements in competitions as the females look on. Both sexes are greenish in color, although the males have splashes of color. These birds grow to no more than 5 in (13 cm) and are believed to live approximately 20 years.

Manama (pop. 677,700), also known as al-Manamah, capital city of Bahrain. Located in the Persian Gulf, this major port for the island nation of Bahrain lies on an important trade and shipping route. Since the discovery of oil (1932), Manama has become a center for finance and commerce, with a new harbor fully equipped to dock and repair large oceangoing vessels.
See also: Bahrain.

Manassas, Battles of *see:* Bull Run, Battles of.

Manatee, large, aquatic, herbivorous mammal of tropical and subtropical Atlantic coasts and large rivers. They and the dugongs are the only living sea cows (order Sirenia). They have powerful, flat, rounded tails that provide propulsion. The forelimbs are small and hindlimbs completely absent. Manatees may be 12 ft (3.6 m) long and weigh 600 lb (270 kg).

Manatees

Manchester (pop. 434,600), city in northwest England, on the Irwell, Irk, and Medlock rivers. Located about 35 mi (56 km) off England's western coast, it is connected to the Irish Sea by the Mersey River and a canal and serves as a major inland port. The city is also a center for trade and finance and is an important industrial area, the products of which include computers, chemicals, clothing, and industrial machinery. The city began as a village established around A.D. 700 on the site of what had been a Roman fort. By the 19th century, it had become an important industrial center and one of the world's major producers of cotton textiles.
See also: England.

Nelson Mandela

Manchester (pop. 90,936), city in southern New Hampshire, on the Merrimack River, settled in 1722. Development of its major 19th-century textile industry was aided by water power from the Amoskeag Falls; today's manufactures include shoes, machinery, electronics, and auto parts.
See also: New Hampshire.

Manchester School, group of English businessmen and members of Parliament (1820-60), mostly from Manchester, who advocated worldwide free trade. They were led by John Bright and Richard Cobden, who formed the Anti-Corn-Law League in 1838 and brought about the repeal of the corn laws in 1846.

Manchester terrier, popular breed of dog. They were bred into existence in the 1800s in Manchester, England, when black and tan terriers were mated with swift whippets to compete in rat-killing matches. They are black with tan markings on their faces and chests and weigh 12-22 lb (5.4-10 kg). A toy variety weighs 5-12 lb (2.3-5.4 kg).

Manchineel, or poison guava tree (*Hippomane mancinella*), native to tropical regions of the United States. A member of the spurge family, manchineels grow from 10 to 50 ft (3 to 15 m) high and produce yellowish green fruit that look like crab apples. The fruit and sap are extremely poisonous and were used by ancient Carib tribes as poison for their arrows.

Mandalay is famous for its temples, statues, and pagodas. Shown is a giant Buddha.

Manchuria, region of northeastern China comprising Heilongjiang, Jilin, and Liaoning provinces and part of the Inner Mongolian Autonomous Region; c.600,000 sq mi (1,554,000 sq km). Manchuria is bordered by the Russia, North Korea, and Mongolia. It is an important agricultural and industrial area. Historically, Manchuria was the home of the Manchus. Chinese settlement in the area increased steadily after 1900. It was a barren steppe until Western exploitation of its vast mineral resources began in the 19th century. In the 1890s Russia had declared an interest in the province; but Russia's defeat in the Russo-Japanese War (1904-05) brought Japanese domination, first of Southern Manchuria, then, in 1932, of the whole country. The puppet state of Manchukuo was created and rapidly industrialized. In 1945 Russian forces occupied the area, dismantling the industries upon their withdrawal. Bitterly contested in the Chinese civil war, Manchuria was captured in 1948 by the communists, who redrew the provincial boundaries.

Manchus, a Manchurian people descended from the Jurchen tribe of the Tungus. Originally a nomadic, pastoral people, they came to China in the 12th century, only to be driven out by the Mongols. They eventually settled in the Sungari Valley and went on to conquer China in 1644, forming the Ch'ing dynasty and reigning until 1912. The Manchus have now been racially and culturally absorbed with the Chinese, and their language is virtually extinct.

Mandalay (pop. 533,000), city in central Myanmar (Burma), on the Irrawaddy River. It is the center of Burmese Buddhism, with numerous monuments, including the Arakan pagoda, and is the country's transportation center. Mandalay was founded in the mid-19th century and served (1860-85) as the last capital of the kingdom of Burma before annexation by the British.

Mandan, Native American Plains tribe of the upper Missouri valley. Of Siouan linguistic stock, they came from the east in the 18th century to inhabit what is now North Dakota. An agricultural people, the tribe was almost wiped out by disease and war in the early 19th century. The surviving Mandans, together with other tribes, live today on reservations in North Dakota.

Mandarin, important civil servant or military official in imperial China. Mandarin Chinese, formerly an upper-class language, is the official language of China.

Mandela, Nelson (1918-), South African political leader and a major figure in the black protest movement against the racial segregation policies (known as apartheid) of the white-dominated South African government. Son of a tribal chief of the Transkei territory, he became a lawyer in 1942 and joined the African National Congress (ANC) in 1944. He gained prominence as a leader of the black protest movement in the 1950s. In 1960 he was arrested and charged with treason but was acquitted. Arrested again in 1962, he was later convicted of sabotage and conspiracy and sentenced to life imprisonment. In jail he became an international symbol of black defiance of the apartheid system.
In February 1990 Mandela was released from prison and assumed leadership of the ANC, pledging to work for a peaceful end to the hated apartheid regime. In early 1991, President F.W. de Klerk of South Africa called for the end of the racial segregation laws that were the underpinning of apartheid, and Mandela's goal of a race-free state seemed possible. Despite the opposition of conservative white South Africans, apartheid was abolished and the transition to a democratic government started. Notwithstanding the growing tensions between the ANC and the Inkatha Freedom Party of Zulu chief Buthelezi, the ANC won the majority in parliament in the first democratic elections held in 1994, and Mandela became South Africa's first black president.
See also: Apartheid; South Africa.

Mandela, Winnie (Winifred Nomzamo Madikileza; 1936?-), anti-apartheid activist in the Republic of South Africa, wife of Nelson Mandela. During her husband's imprisonment (1962-90) she frequently spoke on his behalf. Her popularity has declined since 1988 as a result of her supposed involvement in various crimes, particularly her link with the so-called Mandela United Football Club, blamed for the kidnapping and assault of African youths. In 1991, after a 14-week trial, Mandela was found guilty of kidnapping 4 black youths from a church in 1988, as part of an alleged conspiracy to discredit a white minister. The conviction is being appealed.
See also: Apartheid; Mandela, Nelson.

Mandelstam, Osip Emilievich (1891-1938?), Russian poet. At first a member of the neoclassicist Acmeist school, he was arrested in 1934 and exiled until 1937. Rearrested in 1938, he reportedly died soon afterwards in a Siberian prison. His works include *Stone* (1913) and *Tristia* (1922). After his death his widow, **Nadezhda Mandelstam** (1899-1981), spent many years collecting his verse and smuggling it to the West. Her memoirs, *Hope Against Hope* (1970) and *Hope Abandoned* (1972), were powerful indictments of Stalinism.

Mandeville, Bernard (c.1670-1733), Dutch-born English philosopher and satirist. Best known as the author of a work in verse, *The Fable of the Bees* (1714), he attempted to establish that every virtue is based on self-interest.

Edward Manet's The Flute Player *(1866)*

Mandingo, West African ethnic group, descendants of the founders of the Mali Empire, (fl.1240-1500). Most Mandingos belong to the Malinke group and practice tribal religions and customs in small rural villages. They are chiefly farmers and cattle ranchers and about one-fifth of them have converted to Islam. Their language, which has many different dialects, belongs to the Mande language group.

Mandolin, instrument of the lute family. It has a pear-shaped body, fretted neck, and 4 or 5 pairs of strings that are plucked with a plectrum. Composers who have used the mandolin in their works include Mozart and Beethoven, but it is best known as a popular Neapolitan instrument.

Mandrake, herbaceous perennial plant (*Mandragora officinarum*) of the nightshade family, with purplish or white flowers, a thin stalk, and a forked root resembling the human form. A native of the Himalayas and the Mediterranean, its poisonous root has been used to produce vomiting and bowel movements and as a pain-killer. In North America, the may-apple is called mandrake.

Mandrill, colorful monkey (*Mandrillus sphinx*) of central West Africa. Mandrills are jungle dwellers that move about on the ground and through trees and they feed on fruits and insects. They resemble baboons and may weigh up to 90 lb (40 kg). The males are brightly colored with blue, purple, yellow, and red faces and rumps and can protect groups of up to 150 against predators.

Manet, Edouard (1832-83), French painter. Influenced by Goya and Velázquez, his work, in broad, flat areas of color, introduced a new pictorial language, and was often severely criticized by the art establishment, who considered his subject matter and technique heresy. His paintings *Olympia*, a nude courtesan, and *Luncheon on the Grass*, a nude woman and a partially dressed woman lunching in the woods with 2 clothed men (both 1863 Louvre), were thought scandalously bold. He strongly influenced the impressionists, though he did not employ their techniques and refused to exhibit with them. Another major work is *The Fife Player* (1866).

Manganese, chemical element, symbol Mn; for physical constants see Periodic Table. Manganese was discovered by J.G. Gahn in 1774. It is a steel-gray, hard, brittle, reactive, metal. The element forms many important alloys with steel, as well as with aluminum, ferromagnetic alloys, antimony, and copper. It is an essential trace element in humans and animals. Manganese and its compounds are used in dry cell batteries, paint dryers, as an oxidizing agent, and in medicine.

Mange, disease of the skin that affects domestic and farm animals. Small parasites (mites) burrow into the skin and cause inflammation. The skin is usually covered with sores, and the animal's hair falls out. There are a number of different mites that can cause mange, and the exact symptoms and severity of the disease depend on the species of mite involved. Inadequate nutrition is also an important factor. Mange is treated by pesticides and by ensuring that the animal receives a nutritious diet.

Mango, tropical evergreen tree (*Mangifera indica*) of the sumac family, and its fruit, originally from eastern Asia. The trees, which can grow to 90 ft (27 m), produce a rich yellowish-red juicy fruit with a hard pit, a staple in the tropics.

Mangosteen (*Garcinia mangostana*), tropical tree of the garcinia family, native to Southeast Asia; also, the fruit of that tree. The tree grows about 30 ft (9 m) tall, bearing large, stiff leaves and large white or pink flowers. The fruit, about 2 in (6 cm) in diameter, has a thick red-brown rind and white flesh tasting something like pineapple, peach, and tangerine.

Mangrove, evergreen tree (genus *Rhizophora*) native to tropical and subtropical coasts, estuaries, and swamps. The trunk of the mangrove produces aerial roots, which support the tree and form a mass of tangled vegetation. Its fruit, a cone-shaped berry, contains a single seed that germinates within the fruit and produces a long root that imbeds the seedling within the mud when the fruit falls. The mangrove's bark is rich in tannin.

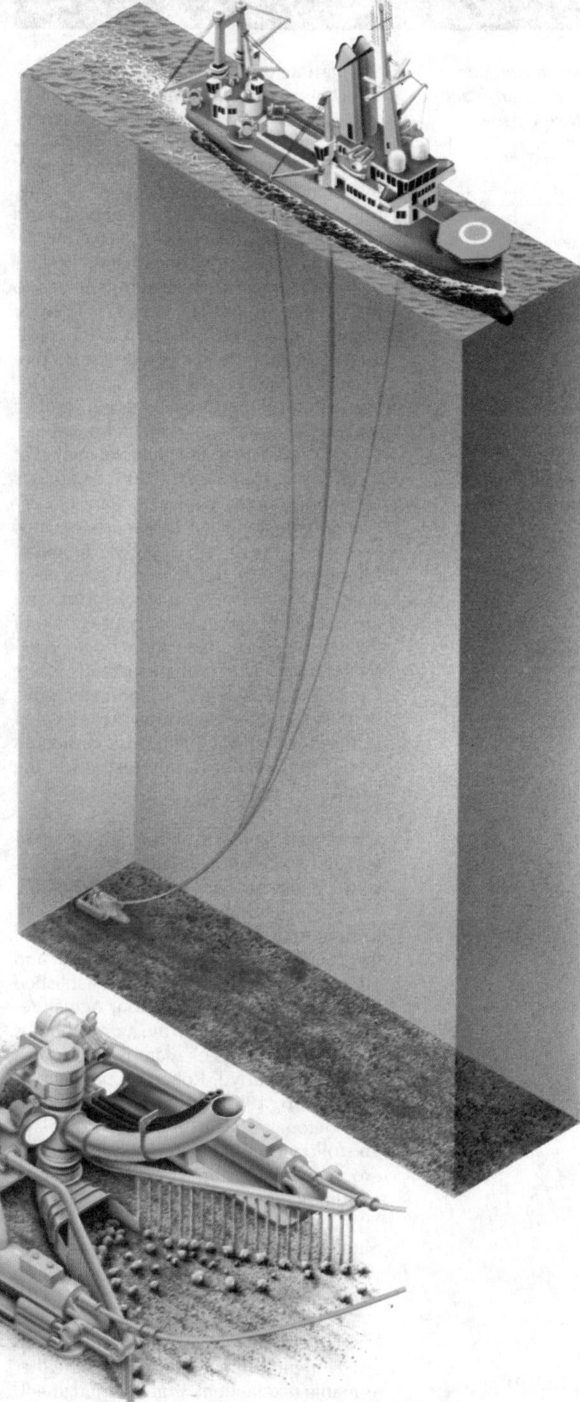
A ship and a "retriever" are used to mine manganese from the ocean, as shown. Also shown is a close up of a retriever on the ocean floor.

Manhattan, seen from Liberty Park, New Jersey

Manhattan, one of the 5 boroughs of New York City, consisting mainly of Manhattan Island, bounded by the East River, the Harlem River, the Hudson River, and New York Bay. Peter Minuit originally bought the island from a Native American tribe, the Manhattan, for $24 worth of beads and cloth in 1626 and called it New Amsterdam. The commercial and financial center of New York City, Manhattan is linked to the other boroughs by numerous bridges, tunnels, and ferries. Its many land marks and tourist attractions include the Empire State Building, World Trade Center, Central Park, Lincoln Center, the United Nations headquarters, and Rockefeller Center. Wall Street, the financial capital of the world for much of the 20th century, is located in downtown Manhattan. Inaddition, Manhattan is a center of the arts. Museums such as the Metropolitan Museum of Art, the Museum of Natural History, the Museum of Modern Art, and the Guggenheim Museum house some of the world's most prized and renowned exhibits. A variety of clubs, especially in the Greenwich Village area, offer many forms of music, and the Broadway area, located in the heart of Manhattan, is considered one of the premier theater districts in the world.

Manhattan Project, wartime project begun in 1942 to develop nuclear weapons. A team headed by Enrico Fermi initiated the 1st self-sustaining nuclear chain reaction. In order to obtain the necessary amounts of the required isotopes, uranium-235 and plutonium-239, centers were established in Tennessee and Washington. Actual design and construction of the atomic bombs was carried out at Los Alamos, N.M., by a group headed by J. Robert Oppenheimer. On July 16, 1945, the first atomic bomb was detonated near Alamogordo, N.M. The following month a uranium bomb was dropped on Hiroshima (Aug. 6) and a plutonium bomb on Nagasaki (Aug. 9).

Mani *see:* Manichaeism.

Mania *see:* Mental illness.

Manic-depressive disorder, or bipolar disorder, mental illness characterized either as mania (excitement, irrational judgment, increase in activity) or depression (lethargy, feelings of worthlessness, guilt), and, in some cases, alternating between mania and depression. Treatment involves the drug lithium, to control mood swings, and anti-depressants.

Manichaeism, or Manichaeanism, religion founded by Mani (C.A.D. 216-76), a Persian sage who claimed to be the Paraclete (intercessor) promised by Christ. Mani borrowed ideas from religions such as Buddhism, Christianity, Gnosticism, and Zoroastrianism; he preached dualism (between good and evil), the continuing life of the soul, and the hope of salvation. The Magians, who opposed him and his teachings, brought about his crucifixion. St. Augustine was a Manichee in his youth. The religion survived until the 6th century in the West and until the 13th century in the East.
See also: Religion.

Manifest Destiny, phrase coined in 1845 that implied divine sanction for the United States "to overspread the continent allotted by Providence for the free development of our multiplying millions." The concept was used to justify most U.S. territorial gains, especially during the Spanish-American War.
See also: Westward movement.

Manila (pop. 7,000,000), city (founded 1571) on Manila Bay, capital of the Philippines (before 1948 and after 1976). It is the commercial, industrial, and cultural center, developed by Spanish missionaries and then taken by the United States (1898) in the Spanish-American War, and chief port of the islands. Manila was occupied by the Japanese (1942-45), nearly destroyed in the Allied attack, and almost completely rebuilt after the war. Buildings of interest include the Church of San Agustin (1606) and the Philippine Cultural Center complex. Industries include textiles, chemicals, and automobiles.

Manila hemp *see:* Abacá.

Manioc *see:* Cassava.

Manitoba, sixth largest province in Canada and easternmost of the Prairie Provinces. Manitoba is bordered by Ontario and Hudson Bay on the east, Saskatchewan on the west, Minnesota and North Dakota to the south, and the Northwest Territories to the north.
Land and climate. The province has an area of 251,000 sq mi/650,090 sq km including 39,225 sq mi/101,593 sq km of inland waterways. There are some 100,000 lakes in the province, most notably Lake Winnipeg, thirteenth largest lake in the world, as well as numerous rivers draining into Hudson Bay. Most of the province is divided by an escarpment into 2 plains regions, one of which, the Saskatchewan Plain, is Manitoba's richest farm region. About 60% of Manitoba is forested. Spruces are the most common tree, but the forests also contain balsam, fir, birches, cedars, poplars, and tamaracks. Wildlife is abundant. Manitoba has pleasant summers, but its winters are long and cold with January temperatures averaging 0°F/–18°C in the south and –20°F/–29°C in the north. About 50 in/127 cm of snow falls every year.
People. The people of Manitoba are mostly descendants of Europeans who settled in provinces, principally Scots, English, and French, but more recently also Russians, Germans, Poles, and Scandinavians. The major religious denominations are Roman Catholic and the United Church of Canada. The capital of the province is Winnipeg and more then half the population is concentrated in the city and its metropolitan area.
Economy. Manufacturing is Manitoba's largest industry, including processed foods and beverages, metal products, clothing, furniture, chemicals, and oil refining. Nickel, zinc, copper, and tantalite are mined and Manitoba's oil wells produce about 4 million barrels of oil a year. Agriculture, formerly the mainstay of the province's economy, is still one of its chief industries. Wheat is the most important crop, followed by oats, barley, flax, and rye. Wheat is also a major export. Beef cattle, dairy farming, and the fur and lumber industries also contribute to the province's economy.
History. The first European settlers to arrive in Manitoba were fur traders of the Hudson's Bay Company in 1670. French and English fur traders competed in the area until their rivalry was settled in the French and Indian War of 1763. As a result, France ceded its Canadian lands to Britain. The first farming settlement was founded by Thomas Douglas, 5th Earl of Selkirk, along the Red River in 1812. Resultant tensions between farmers and fur trappers were not resolved until 1821. The Dominion of Canada acquired the rights to land in Manitoba from the Hudson's Bay Company in 1869 and Manitoba became a province in 1870, but not before a rebellion of fur trappers and their descendants led by Louis Riel was settled. The export of wheat began in 1876. The first railroad reached Winnipeg in 1878 and rapid settlement followed. During the first half of the 20th century, agricultural expansion increased at a tremendous rate and the province's economic growth was further stimulated by the discovery of valuable mineral deposits leading, in turn, to the growth of industry and manufacturing.

Manitoba, Lake *see:* Lake Manitoba.

Manitoba, University of, major educational institution of Manitoba, in western Canada. Located in Fort Garry, a Winnipeg suburb, it was founded in 1877 and is coeducational and government-supported. The university offers undergraduate and graduate programs and degrees and consists of 4 separate colleges. There is also a branch in Winnipeg specializing in the health sciences.

Manitoulin Islands, chain of islands situated northwest of Georgian Bay and separated from the northern shore of Lake Huron by the North Channel. Manitoulin is the largest of the islands as well as being the world's largest inland island, with an area of 1,067 sq mi/2,754 sq km. Popular fishing resorts, the islands are all part of the province of Ontario except for Drummond Island, which belongs to Michigan. Manitoulin contains many lakes and is connected to Ontario by a causeway and ferry service. The Manitoulin derives from Manitou, the great god of the Chippewa.

Mann, Horace (1796-1859), U.S. educator, lawyer, and politician. As secretary of the Massachusetts Board of Education (1837-48), he revolutionized public school organization and teaching, promoting public education for all children, and established the first normal school in the United States. A member of the U.S. House of Representatives (1848-53), he became the first president of Antioch College (1852-59), and was elected to the American Hall of Fame (1900).

Mann, Thomas (1875-1955), German writer, winner of the 1929 Nobel Prize for literature. He left Germany (1933), settled in the United States (1938), and became a U.S. citizen (1944). His works include *Buddenbrooks* (1901), his first novel, which brought him fame; *Death in Venice* (1912), addressing Mann's recurring themes of the relationship between art and neurosis and the challenge to the values of an artist in a bourgeois society; and *The Magic Mountain* (1924), his major work. He denounced fascism in *The Order of the Day* (1942), a political writing. His later works include *Doctor Faustus* (1947) and *Confessions of Felix Krull* (1954).

Manned Spacecraft Center *see:* Johnson Space Center.

Mannerheim, Carl Gustaf Emil von (186 7-1951), Finnish soldier and president (1944-46). He successfully led the Finnish nationalists against the Russo-Finnish communists in 1918. He also led the Finish forces in the Russo-Finnish War (1939-40), holding the *Mannerheim Line* of defense, which he planned, on the Karelian Isthmus until 1940, when the Soviets broke through.
See also: Finland.

Mannerism, artistic and architectural style (c.1520-1600) developed in Bologna, Florence, and Rome as a reaction to the classical principles of the Renaissance. Exaggeration of form, and strained and unbalanced proportions, such as those in the Uffizi Palace and Laurentian Library in Florence (planned by Vasari and Michelangelo respectively) were the trademarks of the Mannerists. Other Mannerist artists were Parmigiano, Pontormo, Tintoretto, and El Greco; sculptors were Cellini, Bologna, and Goujon of France. They confused scale and spatial relationships, used harsh lighting, and depicted bizarre forms. The end of the 16th century the Baroque replaced Mannerism.

Manners and customs *see:* Custom; Etiquette.

Mannheim (pop. 295,000), city in southwestern Germany, one of Europe's major inland ports. Founded in the early 1600s, it is situated near the junction of the Rhine and Neckar rivers in the heart of a major industrial region. It has also been a center for art, music, and drama since the 1700s and is the site of a major university containing striking examples of Baroque architecture. Heavily damaged in World War II, Mannheim was extensively rebuilt. Cultural sights include the National Theatre and several art museums.
See also: Germany.

Man-of-war bird *see:* Frigatebird.

Manometer, instrument for measuring the pressure of gases and vapors, especially those too low to be measured by a pressure gauge. A *sphygmomanometer* is used by doctors to measure blood pressure in the arteries.
See also: Barometer.

Manorialism, socio-economic system of Europe in the early Middle Ages. It was a decentralized form of government that replaced the central authority of the Roman Empire and continued until the revival of commerce in the towns and cities in the later Middle Ages. Centering around a powerful lord who owned a large estate (manor), manorialism depended on peasants to work the land for the lord and themselves in exchange for protection and their homes.
See also: Middle Ages.

Man o' War, U.S. racehorse. Known as "Big Red," he won 20 of 21 races, including the Belmont and Preakness stakes, in 1920 (he was not entered in the Kentucky Derby). His prize money amounted to a then-record $249,465.

Man Ray *see:* Ray, Man.

Mansa Musa (?-1337?), ruler of the Mali Empire (1312-37?). During his reign, Mali was the most powerful empire of West Africa, and the cities of Gao and Timbuktu became centers of learning, justice, trade, and culture. As a Muslim, Mansa Musa made a flamboyant pilgrimage to Mecca in 1324, bringing back scholars to help educate his people and architects to design the mosques of his cities.
See also: Mali Empire.

Mansfield, Katherine (Kathleen Beauchamp; 1888-1923), New Zealand-born English writer. Known foremost as a master of the short story, collections include *Bliss* (1920), *The Garden Party* (1922), and *Something Childish* (1924).

Manship, Paul (1885-1966), U.S. sculptor best known for his interpretations of classical mythological subjects, among which is his statue *Prometheus* (1934) at Rockefeller Center, Nev. York City.

Manslaughter, in U.S. criminal law, unlawful but unpremeditated killing of another human being. In many states 2 kinds of manslaughter are defined: *voluntary*, where injury is intended, as in a killing arising out of a quarrel; and *involuntary*, where there is no such intent, such as death caused by reckless driving. The penalty for manslaughter in the United States ranges from 1 to 14 years in prison.
See also: Crime.

Thomas Mann

Manta ray *see:* Ray.

Mantegna, Andrea (1431-1506), Italian painter and engraver. He was a member of the Paduan school, acclaimed for his mastery of anatomy and illusionistic perspective, and was attracted to the antique, as evidenced in his collection of Greek and Roman works. Among his most famous works are the altarpiece at St. Luke's (Milan), the bridal chamber of the Gonzaga palace (Mantua), where the illusion of sky on the ceiling was widely copied during the Baroque period; and the cartoons of the *Triumph of Caesar* (1495). Also known for his copper-plate engravings and drawings, Mantegna was influential in the development of printing. His initial letters for *Geography*, by Strabo, recaptured the Roman art of inscription.

Mantid, or praying mantis, large predatory insect of the Mantidae family (or order Mantodea). Most species are native to tropical and subtropical climates, although some, including varieties that have been introduced in North America, are found in temperate zones. The nickname "praying mantis" is suggested by the posture of its front legs and by its gentle swaying movement. Mantids measure 2-5 in (5-13 cm) and tend to resemble the green or brown twigs on which they perch, camouflaging them from both predators and insect or other prey. Females are known for their practice of eating males during or after mating. Mantids are harmless to humans and are sometimes useful in consuming insect pests.

Mantle, Mickey (1931-), U.S. baseball player. Primarily an outfielder, he played for the New York Yankees (1951-68), hitting 536 home runs, 18 of them during World Series play. A switch-hitter (both right- and left-handed), he led the American League in 1956 with an average of .353 and 52 home runs and was voted the league's most valuable player 3 times (1956, 57, 62). Mantle was inducted into the National Hall of Fame in 1974.

Mantra, in Hinduism and Buddhism, sacred utterance believed to possess supernatural power. The constant repetition of a mantra is used to concentrate the mind on an object of meditation, e.g., the syllable *om*, said to evoke the entire Veda.

Manu, in Hindu mythology, the lawgiver. Compiled into the *Manu Smriti* (*Code of Manu*) between 200 B.C. and A.D. 200, these laws delineated the classes (castes) in

Hindu society and formed the basis for the life plan of all Hindus in 4 stages. It also set forth the goals they are expected to attain during those 4 stages.

Manuelito (1818?-1893), Navajo tribal leader. In the 1860s he led the Navajos in their fight against white settlers encroaching on their territory in what is now northern Arizona. Manuelito's forces were defeated by the United States Army (led by Kit Carson), which was sent in to help the settlers, and Manuelito surrendered in 1866. Two years later the Navajo Reservation was set aside in parts of Arizona, Utah, and New Mexico, and Manuelito led the tribal police force founded in 1872.

Manuscript, document or work written by hand as distinguished from those typewritten or printed (although the typescript of a book is often called the author's manuscript).
The oldest manuscripts are on papyrus, made from the papyrus plant, the writing material of ancient Egypt and also used in ancient Greece and Rome until superseded by parchment. The earliest surviving papyrus manuscript dates from about 3500 B.C. The Egyptians first wrote with brushes, using ink made from lampblack and water; later they used reed pens. They pasted their papyrus sheets together to make long rolls. Those of the *Book of the Dead*, the earliest known illustrated manuscript, are more than 100 ft (30.5 m) long. Wax tablets were also extensively used for manuscript writing in the ancient world.
Parchment, or vellum—made from the skins of sheep and other animals and more durable than papyrus—was first used in Pergamum in the 2nd century B.C., but did not come into general use in Europe until about A.D. 300. Some types (palimpsests) could be washed or scraped and used again or even a third time (double palimpsests). The illumination (ornamentation and illustration) of manuscripts was developed by the medieval monastic schools of Europe.
In the Far East paper (invented by the Chinese about A.D. 100), silk, bamboo, and palm leaves were used as writing materials. Paper did not reach Europe until the 11th century and did not begin to supplant parchment until the 1400s. Even after the development of printing, parchment was used for legal and other special documents.

Manzanita, ornamental shrub (*Arctostaphylos tomentosa*), of the heath family. Native to the Pacific Coast of the United States and Canada, manzanita is an evergreen that reaches heights of 20 ft (6 m). It produces pink or white bell-shaped flowers and bright red berries and is cultivated for its decorative value.

Manzoni, Alessandro (1785-1873), Italian novelist and poet. He was a leading figure in the romantic movement, and his novel *The Betrothed* (1825-26) influenced Italian prose writers. Among his poems is the well-received *Fifth of May* (1821), on Napoleon's death. His own death inspired Verdi's *Requiem* (1874).

Maori, original inhabitants of New Zealand. Of Polynesian origin, they settled New Zealand between 800 and 1350 and were hunters and farmers. They lived in small villages of communal homes and each village shared a common ancestry. In the 1860s they fought the English colonists and lost most of their lands. Today many still practice the old customs and speak the Maori tongue, a language related to Tahitian and Hawaiian.

Mao Tse-tung *see:* Mao Zedong.

Mao Zedong (1893-1976), founder of the People's Republic of China. Born to an educated peasant in Hunan province, he joined the newly founded Shanghai Communist Party in 1921, and in 1927 led the Autumn Harvest uprising, which was crushed by the local Kuomintang militia, Mao fled to the mountains, where he built up the Red Army and established rural soviets. Surrounded by Kuomintang forces in 1934, the army was forced to embark on the famous Long March from Jiangxi to Yan'an in Shoanxi province. The appalling rigors of the march united the communists behind Mao, and he was elected chairman. In 1937 an uneasy alliance was made with the Kuomintang under Chiang Kai-Shek against the Japanese; after World War II Mao's forces expelled the Kuomintang to Taiwan. Mao then became chairman of the new People's Republic. In 1958 he turned his attentions to industrial growth, with his program the Great Leap Forward. Its failure spurred his replacement as chairman of the party, but he retained party leadership. He later (1966-69) attacked the chairman, Liu Shao-Sh'i, by organizing the Cultural Revolution, which created widespread agitation and led to a consolidation of Mao's power in the 1970s. Mao steered China ideologically away from the USSR and his teachings came to have great influence in the Third World. He appeared to favor a decree of deténte with the West, especially Europe, and in 1972 met with President Nixon, signaling closer relations with the United States.

Mao Zedong meets Henry Kissinger

Map, representation on a flat surface of part or all of the earth's surface, or of another spherical body, showing each point and feature on a predetermined reduced scale and in accordance with a definite projection. Globes provide the most accurate representation of the earth, with regard to area, scale, shape, and direction. Any flat map will create some distortion. The making and study of maps is called cartography.
Of the many different kinds of maps, those for general reference include physical maps (relief and natural features) and political maps (national borders, administrative divisions, cities, and towns). Thematic maps include economic maps, (industrial centers, transportation routes and so on); demographic maps (distribution of the population); geological maps (classifying and dating the surface rocks); meteorological maps (information about climatic zones, rainfall, air pressures, and temperatures); historical maps and the road maps for tourists. There are also celestial and stellar maps showing the planets, stars, and constellations. Maps used for sea and aerial navigation are called charts.

Maple, common name for the deciduous trees and shrubs of the genus *Acer*, found throughout the Northern Hemisphere. Maples, which are characterized by their winged seeds, are noted for the breathtaking colors they produce in the fall. The North American sugar maple (*A. saccharum*) and the black maple (*A. nigrum*) are 2 of the species that provide the close-grained hardwood used for furniture making; they are also tapped to produce maple syrup. Two other members of the genus are the swamp, or red, maple (*A. rubrum*) and the box elder (*A. negundo*) tapped to produce maple syrup.

Maputo (pop. 510,000), capital (1907) and largest city of Mozambique. Founded around 1780 by Portuguese colonists, it was called Lourenço Marques until 1976, the year after Mozambique gained independence. Maputo is located on the Indian Ocean and is a popular beach resort. It also serves as a rail terminal for several of southern Africa's landlocked nations who ship their goods through Maputo's harbor.

Marabou, large stork (*Leptoptilos crumeniferous*) with a heavy bill, naked head and neck, and a pink, fleshy pouch dangling from its neck. Marabous, found in many parts of Africa, are scavengers and feed on refuse and carrion.

Maracaibo (pop. 1,152,000), city in northwestern Venezuela. Located on the shore of Lake Maracaibo, it is the capital of the state of Zulia and the hub of the nation's petroleum industry. Maracaibo was founded by the Spanish in 1571 and experienced a population boom after the discovery of oil in the lake in 1912. It is also a major coffee and seafood exporting port.

Marajó, Brazilian island in the mouth of the Amazon River. With an area of 15,500 sq mi (40,000 sq km), Marajó lies between the Amazon to the north, the Rio Pará to the south, and the Atlantic Ocean to the east. The island is flooded by river overflow 6 months of the year, and cattle and water buffalo graze the grasslands left by the flooding during the dry season.

Marat, Jean Paul (1743-93), French Revolutionary politician. A doctor and journalist, he founded the journal *L'Ami du peuple* at the onset of the Revolution. His vociferous attacks on those in power led to outlaw status and flight to England (1790, 1791). He continued to publish in secret and was elected to the National Convention in 1792, a leader of the radical faction. Chief instigator of the September Massacre (1792) in which over 1,200 died, he was an active supporter of the Jacobins and their Reign of Terror. Marat was murdered in his bath by Charlotte Corday.
See also: French Revolution.

Marathon, village and plain northeast of Athens, Greece, site of an Athenian victory (490 B.C.) over the Persians. The runner Pheidippides carried a report of the victory to Athens, after which he collapsed and died. The modern Olympic Games (1896) standardized the marathon race at 26 mi, 385 yd (42.2 km) in 1908. Boston and New York City each hold annual marathons, attracting thousands of runners.
See also: Greece.

Marble, rock form of limestone consisting of crystals of calcite or dolomite. Marble is formed when limestone is *metamorphosed* (changed by great heat and pressure) so that the rock is recrystallized and hardened. Pure marble, which is snow-white in color, has been prized by sculptors and architects since ancient times. Some of the finest marble comes from the Carrara quarries in Italy, and in the United States, from Vermont. Marble often contains impurities, which affect is color. Exposed to acid fumes and water, marble will corrode.

Marble bones *see:* Osteosclerosis.

Marbury v. Madison, U.S. Supreme Court case decided in 1803. William Marbury sued James Madison, then secretary of state, for failure to deliver a federal appointment promised by the previous administration. Chief Justice Marshall held that the act upon which this case relied was unconstitutional. This was the first decision to invalidate an act of Congress and established the judicial right to review, greatly expanding the power of the judiciary.

Marc, Franz (1880-1916), German expressionist painter, with Wassily Kandinsky a cofounder of the Blaue Reiter group. His work is characterized by vigorous lines and a vivid, symbolic use of color.

Marceau, Marcel (1923-), French mime. Marceau studied drama in Paris and rose to fame with a brief mime role in the film *Les Enfants du Paradis* (1944). His best-known characterization is the white-faced clown Bip. He became world famous with stage appearances in the 1950s.

Marcel, Gabriel (1889-1973), 20th-century French philosopher. A Christian existentialist, Marcel stressed the value of understanding life through human experience. His best-known books include *Metaphysical Journals* (1927), *Being and Having* (1935), *Homo Viator* (1945), *Man Against Society* (1951), and *Presence and Immortality* (1959).
See also: Existentialism.

March, Peyton Conway (1864-1955), U.S. Army general and chief of staff during World War I. Often credited with modernizing and streamlining the army and Department of War, March was responsible for landing 1.2 million U.S. troops in France. A West Point graduate (1888), he fought in the Spanish-American War and was in charge of United States artillery forces in France prior to being named chief of staff.
See also: World War I.

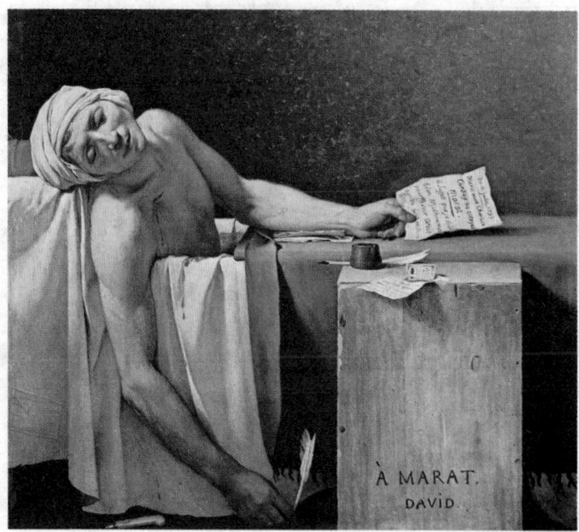

The Death of Marat *(1793), by Jacques Louis David*

Marciano, Rocky (Rocco Marchegiano; 1923-69), U.S. boxer, considered to be one of the most powerful punchers of all time. Marciano won the heavyweight championship by knocking out Jersey Joe Walcott in the 13th round (1952), and successfully defended his title until his retirement in 1956. He is the only major prizefighter to have remained undefeated throughout his professional career, fighting 49 bouts in 9 years, winning 43 by knockout. He was killed in a plane crash.

Marcion (d. A.D. 160), founder of a heretical Christian sect. He joined the church in Rome c.140 but was excommunicated in 144. Influenced by gnosticism, he taught that there were 2 rival Gods: one, the tyrannical creator and lawgiver of the Old Testament; the other, the unknown God of love and mercy who sent Jesus to purchase salvation from the creator God. Marcion rejected almost the complete bible. This forced the orthodox church to fix its canon of Scripture. Marcionism spread widely but by the end of the 3rd century had mostly been absorbed by Manichaeism.
See also: Christianity.

Marconi, Guglielmo (1874-1937), Italian physicist, awarded (with K.F. Braun) the 1909 Nobel Prize in physics for his work in devising a wireless telegraph. By 1895

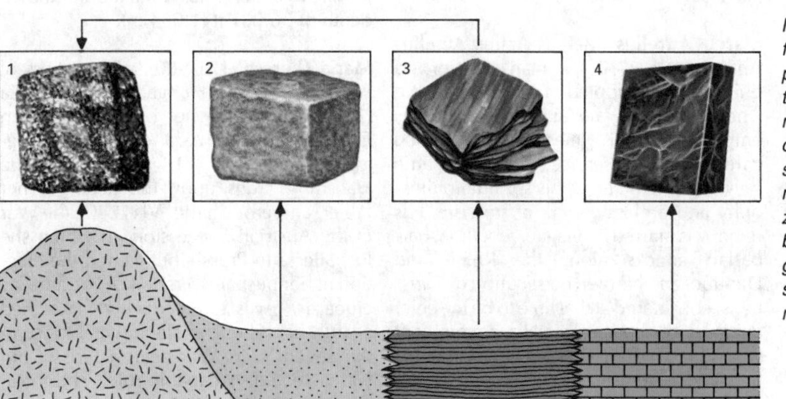

Metamorphic rock is formed by heat or pressure. Under these conditions igneous rock may become gneiss or schist (1), sandstone may become quartzite (2), shale may become slate or gneiss (3), and limestone may become marble (4).

Marconi and his assistant George Kemp, in 1901 with their receiving apparatus at Signal Hill (Newfoundland) during the first reception of radio signals across the Atlantic Ocean

he could transmit and receive signals at distances of about 1.2 mi (2 km). On Dec. 12, 1901, in St. John's, Newfoundland, he successfully received the first transatlantic radio communication.
See also: Telegraph.

Marco Polo *see:* Polo, Marco.

Ferdinand Marcos

Marcos, Ferdinand Edralin (1917-89), president of the Philippines (1965-86). In 1972 Marcos declared martial law in the country and in 1973, under a new constitution, he assumed near-dictatorial authority. Although he lifted martial law in 1981, he retained certain broad martial-law powers. Anti-Marcos forces attracted worldwide attention in Aug. 1983 when returning opposition leader Benigno Aquino was murdered at the Manila airport while in government custody. In Feb. 1986 Marcos was reelected president in an election marked by demonstrations and charges of fraud. His main opponent, Corazon Aquino, the widow of Benigno, refused to recognize the results of the election. After continued popular demonstrations against the government, Marcos and his wife, Imelda, left the country on Feb. 25th to settle in Hawaii. Corazon Aquino replaced him as president. Both Marcos and his wife were indicted by the U.S. government on charges that they embezzled from the Philippine treasury to purchase assets for themselves in the United States. Marcos proved too ill to stand trial and charges against him were dropped; he died in Hawaii. Court actions against Imelda continued into 1991 and ultimately resulted in her acquittal.
See also: Philippines.

Marcus Aurelius (Marcus Aelius Aurelius Antoninus; 121-180), Roman emperor and philosopher. Adopted at 17 by his uncle Antoninus Pius, he succeeded him as emperor in 161, after a distinguished career in public service. During this time he wrote *Meditations*, his spiritual philosophy and a classic work of stoicism. His reign was marred by plague, rebellion, barbarian attacks along the Rhine and Danube, and his own persecution of Christians, considered at that time to be the chief enemies of the empire. His government was otherwise noted for social reform, justice, and generosity.
See also: Rome, Ancient.

Marcuse, Herbert (1898-1979), German-born U.S. political philosopher who combined Freudianism and Marxism in his social criticism. According to Marcuse, modern society is automatically repressive and requires violent revolution as the first step toward a Utopian society. He became a cult figure of the New Left in the United States in the 1960s. His works include *Eros and Civilization* (1954) and *One Dimensional Man* (1964).
See also: Philosophy; Utopia.

Mardi Gras (French, "fat Tuesday"), festivities prior to and on Shrove Tuesday, the last day of carnival before the start of Lent. Celebrated as a holiday in various Catholic countries, it was introduced into the United States by French settlers and is most notably observed in New Orleans.
See also: Shrove Tuesday.

Marduk, highest god of ancient Babylon. Called "lord of the gods of heaven and earth," Marduk rose to power by conquering Tiamat, the monster of chaos. Some of Babylon's most elaborate temples were built to worship Marduk, and, as the conquering armies of the empire overran most of the Middle East, worship of Marduk spread to those lands.
See also: Babylon.

Mariana Islands, group of islands (184 sq mi/476.6 sq km) in the West Pacific, east of the Philippines. Discovered by Magellan in 1521 and owned by Spain until surrendered to the United States, in 1898, they were named the Ladrones (Thieves) Islands until renamed in 1668 by Jesuit missionaries. They were briefly under Japanese occupation (1941-44) and became part of the United Nations Trust Territory of the Pacific Islands in 1947. In 1978 the northern islands became the Northern Mariana Islands and a commonwealth of the United States. The majority of the population lives on the largest and southernmost island, Guam, an outlying U.S. territory. The group's economy rests on subsistence agriculture, copra export, and government and military installations.

Mariana Trench, world's deepest discovered submarine trench 210 mi (338 km) southwest of Guam. More than 1,500 mi (2,414 km) long, it averages over 40 mi (64 km) in width and has a maximum known depth of 36,201 ft (1,034 m).

Maria Theresa (1717-80), archduchess of Austria, queen of Hungary and Bohemia (1740-80), and wife of Holy Roman Emperor Francis I. As a result of the Pragmatic Sanction of 1713, she acquired the Habsburg lands upon the death of her father, Emperor Charles VI (1740); the War of the Austrian Succession, in which she lost Silesia to Prussia but gained the election of her husband, Francis of Lorraine, as emperor, was immediately launched against her. She later allied with France in the Seven Years War against Prussia but was defeated. A capable ruler, she introduced administrative, agrarian, and fiscal reforms and maintained a strong army. After 1765 she shared her powers with son Joseph II, one of 16 children, including Marie Antoinette of France and Emperor Leopold II.

Marie Antoinette (1755-93), queen of France from 1774. Daughter of Maria Theresa and the Emperor Francis I, she married the Dauphin in 1770 to strengthen ties between Austria and France and became queen on his accession as Louis XVI. The unpopular, unconsummated (for 7 yrs) marriage and youthful extravagances made her many enemies, as did her involvement in several scandals. When the French Revolution broke out she advised the attempted escape of the royal family, which ended with its capture at Varennes. She began her own negotiations, independent of her husband, first with comte de Mirabeau, later with Antoine Barnave, and even asked for Austrian intervention in France, to no avail. Imprisoned with Louis, her son, Louis XVIII, taken from her, she was guillotined 9 months after the king, in Oct. 1793.
See also: French Revolution; Louis XVI.

Marie Louise (1791-1847), empress of France (1810-15). Eldest daughter of Francis II of Austria, she married Napoleon after he divorced Josephine (1810) and was the mother of Napoleon II. After Napoleon's exile she became duchess of Parma.

Marigold, annual plant (genus *Tagetes*) with fragrant orange or yellow flowers, native to Central and South America. Two common species, native to Guatemala and Mexico, are the African marigold (*T. erecta*) and the French marigold (*T. patula*).

Marihuana *see:* Marijuana.

Marijuana, or marihuana, nonaddictive drug derived from the hemp plant (*Cannabis sativa*). It is usually smoked, but can also be sniffed or taken as food. It is mainly used for the mild euphoria it produces; other symptoms include loss of muscular coordination, increased heart beat, drowsiness, and hallucination. The most potent form of the drug is hashish. Marijuana's use, the subject of much medical and social debate, is widespread throughout the world. In the United States, use of the drug has been prohibited by federal law since 1937.

Marin, John (1870-1953), U.S. painter and print maker best known for his expressionistic watercolors of Manhattan and the Maine coast. Among his works are *Singer Building* (1921) and *Maine Islands* (1922).

Marine biology, study of the flora and fauna of the sea, from the smallest plankton to massive whales. It includes the study of the complex interrelationship between different marine organisms and between the organisms and their environment. Through experiments with marine organisms, marine biologists can increase our knowledge of human reproduction and development and the nervous system. Scientists have also discovered substances in certain marine animals, such as sponges and seaweeds, that may be used in treating cancer, infections, and pneumonia. These substances might possibly be used as commercial drugs in the future.

Marine Corps, U.S., armed service within the Department of the Navy providing troops trained for land, sea, and air operations. The Corps was founded by the Continental Congress in 1775 and established by act of Congress on July 11, 1798. It served in the Revolutionary War, the naval war with France (1798-1801), and the war with Tripoli (1801-05). Nearly 79,000 Marines served in World War I, and over 475,000 fought in World War II. They played a major role in the Pacific theater in World War II, first with their heroic stands at Wake Island, Guam, Bataan, Corregidor, and Midway and later with the assault at Guadalcanal and the Pacific campaign. Subsequently the Corps fought in Korea (1950-53), preserved order in Lebanon in 1958 and the 1980s, ended fighting in the Dominican Republic in 1965, and served in the Vietnam War (1965-73) and the Persian Gulf War (1991). Between 1943 and 1945, the Marine Corps Women's Reserve numbered over 23,000. With the passing of the Women's Armed Services Integration Act in 1948, the women reservists became full-fledged members of the regular Marine Corps.

Marion, Francis (c.1732-95), guerilla leader in the American Revolutionary War. Commander of the South Carolina troops, he fought at Charleston in 1776. In 1780 he and his men were forced to take refuge in the swamps, from which they waged ceaseless guerilla warfare on Loyalist farms and on British troops, who nicknamed Marion "the Swamp Fox." He served in the state senate (1782-90).
See also: Revolutionary War in America.

Marionette *see:* Puppet.

Mariposa lily, or sego lily (genus *Calochortus*), tuliplike member of the lily family. Taking its name from the Spanish word for butterfly, mariposa lilies bloom in spring in the sandy soil of Western United States. They are perennials, growing from bulbs, and range in color from white or purple to yellow or orange. There are about 60 species, 40 of which are native to the U.S.

Maris, Roger (1934-85), U.S. baseball player. In 1961, Maris made sports history by hitting 61 home runs, breaking Babe Ruth's single season home run mark of 60 set in 1927. Because Maris hit his home runs during a 162-game schedule and Ruth his during a 154-game schedule, both totals are considered records. Maris was also named the American league's most valuable player twice (1960, 61). He played outfield for the Cleveland Indians (1957-58), Kansas City Athletics (1958-59), New York Yankees (1960-66), and St. Louis Cardinals (1967-68).

Marisol (Marisol Escobar; 1930-), Venezuelan-born U.S. sculptor who satirizes and caricatures human society by creating Pop Art-type figures, usually from wood and clay. Reminiscent of South American folk art, her sculptures are stark representations, with many of the details drawn on them.

Maritain, Jacques (1882-1973), leading French neo-Thomist philosopher. He turned to the study of Thomism, the system of philosophy developed by St. Thomas, after his conversion to Catholicism in 1906. He was professor of modern philosophy at the Catholic Institute, Paris (1914-39) and French ambassador to the Vatican (1945-48).
See also: Philosophy.

Maritime law, body of law, based on custom, court decisions, and statutes, seeking to regulate all aspects of shipping and ocean commerce, such as insurance, salvage, and contracts for carriage of goods by sea. It is international to the extent that firm general principles exist, but these have no legal force except as they are incorporated by individual countries into their own legal systems; they are often modified in the process. Many derive from decisions of medieval maritime courts. In the United States, maritime law is administered by the federal district courts.

Maritime Provinces *see:* Atlantic Provinces.

Marius, Gaius (157-86 B.C.), Roman general and politician. After successes on the battlefield, he was elected consul 7 times between 107 and 86 B.C.
See also: Rome, Ancient.

Marivaux, Pierre (1688-1763), French playwright and novelist, best known for his witty comedies. Sparkling dialogue is still termed *marivaudage*. Among his works are the comedy *The Game of Love and Chance* (1730) and the novel *The Successful Peasant* (1735-36).

Marjoram, perennial herb of the mint family, native to the Mediterranean region and Asia. It is cultivated in the United States for flavoring foods and for use in toilet soaps. Sweet marjoram is *Marjorana hortensis*. Common marjoram (*Origanum vulgare*) is also called oregano.

Mark, Saint, or John Mark (fl. 1st century A.D.), Christian evangelist and traditional author of the second Gospel, which derived information from St.Peter in Rome. Mark accompanied Barnabas (his cousin) and Paul on their missionary journeys. His feast day is Apr. 25.
See also: Christianity.

Mark Antony *see:* Antony, Mark.

Marketing, refers to all activities concerned with the flow of goods and services from the producer to the consumer. It includes the various physical movements of the product including the pricing, wholesaling, transporting, and retailing of the product. It also involves packaging, design, and advertising. Marketing may be said to include everything that has to do with *how* a product is sold. In earlier times, when economic activities were simpler, people concentrated on the actual manufacture of the product. The business of taking it to a market and selling it was relatively simple. Today, with a huge range of products to choose from (often almost indistinguishable from each other) marketing is an important operation. Most companies employ a team of people, working under a marketing director, to plan the marketing of a product. They have to decide, on the basis of market surveys, just what the consumer wants. Then they design and package the product to match the requirements of the consumer. Marketing decisions involve a whole complex of considerations: what country and climate, for example, the product will be sold in; which social groupings among the population will buy it; how it will be distributed—through supermarkets, department stores, or mail order; and whether, and how, it should be advertised. Marketing plays a vital role in ensuring prosperity since, it is argued, consumers are given what they want at a convenient location and packaged in the most efficient way possible. On the other hand,however, there is the objection that too much money is spent on marketing and that it is sometimes more concerned with persuading people that they need a certain product, rather than finding out what they want.

Market research, process of gathering and analyzing information for marketing decision making. It dates back to the early 20th century in the United States before spreading to Europe and Japan. Business employs market research to identify customers (markets) for its products, to analyze their needs (through such techniques as polls and surveys), and to suggest strategies to develop interest among those customers for their products.

Markham, Edwin (1852-1940), U.S. poet and lecturer whose poem of social protest, "The Man with the Hoe" (1899), based on a painting by Millet, brought him a fortune and worldwide acclaim.

Markova, Dame Alicia (1910-), leading English ballerina. She was a member of Sergei Diaghilev's Ballets Russes (1925-29) and became a prima ballerina with London's Vic-Wells Ballet in 1932. She founded her own company with Anton Dolin in 1935. This grew into the London Festival Ballet, which they headed from l944-52. She also directed the Metropolitan Opera Ballet (1963-69) and taught at the University of Cincinnati (1969-74).

Marlborough, Duke of (John Churchill;1650-1722), English soldier and politician, one of the country's greatest generals. He helped suppress the Duke of Monmouth's rebellion (1685) for James II, but in 1688 transferred his allegiance to

William of Orange, who made him an earl and a member of the Privy Council. His wife, Sarah Churchill, was the closest friend and attendant of Princess (later Queen) Anne; together they had great influence with the queen. After Anne's accession in 1702 Marlborough commanded English, Dutch, and German forces in the war of the Spanish Succession. In 1704 he won a great victory over the French at Blenheim. Further victories followed at Ramillies (1706), Oudenarde (1708), and Malplaquet (1709). His wife fell from favor with the queen in 1711, and Marlborough was dismissed; in 1714, however, he was restored to favor by George I.
See also: United Kingdom.

Marlin, gamefish related to the sailfish and the swordfish, found in warm oceans. The marlin is armed with a long spike extending from its upper jaw. Most marlins weigh 50-400 lb (23-180 kg), although the blue marlin (genus *Makira*) can reach 1,000 lb (454 kg).

Marlowe, Christopher (1564-93), English poet and dramatist, a major influence on William Shakespeare. He developed the use of dramatic blank verse. His best-known plays are *Tamburlaine the Great* (c. 1587); *Dr. Faustus* (c. 1588), in which he developed a new concept of tragedy, that of a heroic character doomed to failure because of his ambition and power; and *Edward II* (c.1593). He also wrote the unfinished long poem *Hero and Leander* (1598) and the lyric "The Pastoral Sheperd to His Love."

Marmara, Sea of, large body of water lying between the Asian and European sections of Turkey. It is connected to the Black Sea on the northeast by the Bosporus and to the Aegean Sea on the southwest by the Dardanelles. The sea covers 4,300 sq mi (11,100 sq km) and is a key waterway for the passage of ships between the Mediterranean and the southern ports of the USSR.

Marmoset, the world's smallest monkey, usually growing to less than 1 ft (30 cm) long. It is a member of the family Callitrichidae. Some marmosets have striking ear tufts. The pygmy marmoset (*Cebuella pygmaea*) is 5.5 to 6.25 in (14-16 cm). Marmosets live in the forests of South America, feeding on insects, leaves, and fruit.

Marmoset

A market in Marrakech

Marmot, large round squirrel (genus *Marmota*) found in much of the Northern Hemisphere. Marmots dig burrows, where they hibernate in winter, and live in colonies. Most live in hill country, although the woodchuck, or groundhog (*M. monox*), prefers open areas. Marmots grow from 1-2 ft (30-61 cm) long.

Marne, Battles of the, two World War I battles fought in the Marne River area of France. In the first (Sept. 1914), the German advance on Paris was halted by an Allied offensive. The second (July 1918) countered the last German offensive.
See also: World War I.

Marne River, chief tributary of the Seine River, France, rising on the Langres Plateau of eastern France and flowing through 310 mi (500 km) of rich farmland before joining the Seine southeast of Paris. Several key battles fought there during World War I saved Paris from being overrun by the German army.

Marquand, J(ohn) P(hillips) (1893-1960), U.S. novelist best known for his detective stories centered on the Japanese agent Mr. Moto and for his gentle satires of New England society, such as *The Late George Apley* (1937), for which he won a Pulitzer Prize, and *Point of No Return* (1949).

Marquesas Islands, 2 clusters of mountainous and volcanic islands in the South Pacific, about 900 mi (1,400 km) northeast of Tahiti. The islands are governed by France. Their total area is about 492 sq mi (1,274 sq km). The largest islands are Hiva Oa and Nuku Hiva. The population is made up mainly of Polynesians. The islands are fertile, producing breadfruit, coffee, vanilla, and copra (dried coconut meat) for export.

Marquette, Jacques (1637-75), French Jesuit missionary and explorer. With Louis Joliet he traced the course of the Mississippi River, discovering that it flowed into the Gulf of Mexico (1673).
See also: Jesuits.

Marrakech, or Marrakesh (pop. 332,700), city of southwestern Morocco, near the Atlas Mtns. Founded in 1062, Marrakech was the capital of the Berber Empire and a center of commerce and culture in the 15th century. It was captured by the French in 1912. Marrakech is a popular tourist attraction for its fine examples of Islamic architecture and its outdoor markets (*souks*). It is also a food-processing and leather manufacturing center.
See also: Morocco.

Marriage, union between man and woman for the purpose of cohabitation and usually also for raising children. The modern trend is towards monogamy, union between one man and one woman only. Many societies still permit polygamy, but it is increasingly rare. Forms of group and communal marriage have been tried from time to time, though with little success or social acceptance.
Marriage is in some senses a contract, often involving property and in some societies a dowry. In U.S. law marriage creates special ownership rights in marital property. It is still also a religious matter in many countries; marriage is a minor sacrament of the Roman Catholic Church.
Most societies limit marriage in certain ways. It is forbidden in most countries between partners who have too close a blood relationship, although the degree permissible varies widely among countries, religions, and U.S. states. In U.S. common law a purported marriage involving bigamy is void; other conditions, such as non-consummation, render marriage void or voidable, generally through the courts. A marriage is also void if not carried out in the prescribed legal form, although in some states common law marriage may arise after long cohabitation without any formality. Most societies have some provision for divorce. Marriages in the U.S. are performed either by a civil authority or by a religious ceremony with civil authorization; the ceremonies of most denominations are so authorized in most states. In general, a marriage valid in one state is recognized in the others. Some states require banns to be posted.

Marryat, Frederick (1792-1848), English author. An officer in the British Navy who spent 24 years at sea, Marryat's books all had maritime adventure themes. His best-known works are *Frank Mildmay* (1829), *The King's Own* (1830), and *Mr. Midshipman Easy* (1836).

Composite photograph of Mars taken by Viking 2 (1976)

Mars, the fourth planet from the Sun, with a mean solar distance of 141.6 million mi (227.9 million km) and a mean diameter of 4,223 mi (6,796 km). Mars takes about 687 earth-days to orbit the Sun. The planet's temperature ranges from –191° to 81°F (–124° to 27°C), and its tenuous atmosphere consists mainly of carbon dioxide. The distinctive Martian polar caps are composed of frozen carbon dioxide and water ice.

Telescopically, Mars appears as an ocher-red disk marked by extensive dark areas; these latter have in the past been erroneously termed *maria* (seas). Several observers in the past reported sighting networks of straight lines on the Martian surface—the famous canals—but observations with large telescopes and the photographs sent back by the United States' Mariner (1965, 1969, 1971) and Viking (1976) space probes showed these to be an optical illusion. Mars actually has a cratered surface marked with canyons, ancient volcanoes, and jumbled terrains. No probe has yet found evidence that life ever existed on the planet. Mars has 2 satellites (moons), Phobos and Deimos.

See also: Planet; Solar system

Mars, in Roman mythology, the god of war. He was originally the god of agriculture, but later was identified with Ares, the Greek god of war. Second in importance only to his father, Jupiter, Mars had several children by Venus and was also regarded as the father of Romulus, legendary founder of Rome. His altar on the Campus Martius was the scene of festivals in Mar. (his month) and Oct.

See also: Mythology.

Marseille (pop. 874,400), second largest city in France, located in the southeastern part of the country. It serves as France's chief seaport and is a major industrial center. The oldest city in France, was settled by the Greeks c.600 B.C. and annexed by Rome in 49 B.C. The city's expansion began with the conquest of Algeria and the opening of the Suez Canal in the 19th century. Marseille's port handles about one third of French maritime trade.

Marsh, flat wetland area characterized by grassy plant growth. Distinguished from swamps where trees grow, marshes often occur in coastal regions where tidal flows add salt water to fresh water, usually at the mouths of rivers (estuarine marshes). Freshwater marshes occur in low-lying inland areas and both types of marshes are home to a wide variety of fish and wildlife.

Marsh, Reginald (1898-1954), U.S. painter. He began as a newspaper illustrator and later turned to the realistic depiction of New York life in paintings such as *"Why Not Use the 'L' ?"* (1930).

Marshall, Alfred (1842-1924), English economist, professor of political economy at Cambridge (1885-1908). His *Principles of Economics* (1890) systematized economic thought up to that time and was the standard text for many years. Through his work on cost, and value, and distribution Marshall developed a concept of marginal utility.

Marshall, George Catlett (1880-1959), U.S. general and politician. As chief of staff (1939-45) he influenced Allied strategy in World War II. As secretary of state (1947-49) under President Harry S. Truman, he introduced the European Recovery Program, or Marshall Plan, for which he was awarded the 1953 Nobel Peace Prize. As U.S. secretary of defense (1950-51), he was active in the creation of the North Atlantic Treaty Organization (NATO).

See also: Marshall Plan; North Atlantic Treaty Organization.

Marshall, James Wilson (1810-85), discoverer of gold in California. On Jan. 24, 1848, while building a sawmill for John Sutter on the American River, Marshall

Small fishing port at the entrance of the Old Harbor in Marseille

found several gold nuggets in the water. Word of the discovery spread quickly and triggered the California Gold Rush of 1849. *See also:* Gold rush.

Marshall, John (1755-1835), fourth chief justice of the United States, known as the "Great Chief Justice." He established the modern status of the Supreme Court. He served in the Revolutionary War, studied law, and was elected to the Virginia legislature in 1782. A staunch Federalist, he supported acceptance of the Constitution. He declined ministerial posts but became one of the U.S. negotiators who resolved the XYZ Affair (1797-98). Elected to Congress in 1799, he was made secretary of state by President John Adams (1800-01). In 1801 he became chief justice. He labored to increase the then-scant power and prestige of the Supreme Court. In *Marbury* v. *Madison* he established the Court's power to review a law and, if necessary, declare it unconstitutional. An opponent of states' rights, he established in *McCulloch* v. *Maryland* and *Gibbons* v. *Ogden* the superiority of federal authority under the Constitution.
See also: Supreme Court of the United States.

Marshall, Thurgood (1908-93), U.S. judge, first black member of the United States' Supreme Court. He served as chief counsel for the National Association for the Advancement of Colored People (1938-61) and U.S. solicitor general (1965-67), before being nominated to the Supreme Court by President Lyndon B. Johnson in 1967. As associate justice, Marshall was known for his liberal positions on issues as capital punishment and free speech.
See also: Supreme Court of the United States.

Marshall Islands

Capital:	Dalap Uliga Darrit
Area:	70 sq mi (180 sq km)
Population:	50,000
Government:	republic
Independent:	1990
GNP per capita:	U.S. $7,560

Marshall Islands, 2 curving chains, each about 650 mi (1,050 km) in length, of altogether 34 coral atolls and islands in the west central Pacific: the eastern *Radak* (Sunrise) chain and the western *Ralik* (Sunset) chain. Formerly Japanese, the islands were self-governing in free association with the United States from 1986-90, when the islands became independent. Their total land area is 70 sq mi (180 sq km). The main atolls are Majuro, Amo, Ailinglaplap, Jaluit, and Kwajalein, which the United States uses as a missile range. After World War II the United States used the Eniwetok and Bikini atolls as atomic testing grounds. The island's population is predominantly Micronesian. Breadfruit is the main crop, and copra (dried coconut meat) is the chief export. The islands are named for a British sea captain, John Marshall, who discovered them in 1788.

Marshall Plan, or European Recovery Program, program designed to help Europe's economic recovery after World War II, named for its originator, U.S. Secretary of State George C. Marshall. From 1948 to 1948 to 1952, material and financial aid amounting to almost $13 billion dollars was sent by the United States to the 17 European countries who formed the Organization for European Economic Cooperation (OEEC). The plan was administered by the Economic Cooperation Administration (ECA).
See also: World War II.

Marsh gas *see:* Methane.

Marsh hawk *see:* Northern harrier.

Marsh mallow (*Althaea officinalis*), herb found mainly in Europe, although it is now grown in the United States. The marsh mallow grows from 2 to 4 ft (61 to 120 cm) and has large leaves covered by soft hair.

Marsh marigold *see:* Cowslip.

Marston, John (1576-1634), English playwright best known for his comedy *The Malcontents* (1604). His *Antonio's Revenge* (1600) is one of the first examples of English tragedy.

Marsupial, any of an order (Marsupialia) of pouched mammals found mainly in Australia, Tasmania, and New Guinea. With few exceptions, marsupials do not develop placenta. They give birth to undeveloped young that attach themselves to the mother's teats inside a pouch on her abdomen, where they continue their development. Members of the order include the kangaroo, koala, and wombat.

Martel, Charles *see:* Charles Martel

Marten, any of several large mammals (genus *Martes*) of the weasel family with valuable fur. The home of the marten is the pine forests of North America, Europe, and Asia. In Europe martens are also called sables. Their prey is mainly squirrels. American species include the American marten and the larger fisher or pekan.

Martha's Vineyard, island off the coast of southeast Massachusetts. About 100 sq mi (260 sq km) in area, it is separated from Cape Cod by Vineyard Sound. Named by Barthelomew Gosnold (1602), it was settled in 1632. A major whaling center in the 18th and 19th centuries, it is now a popular summer resort.

Martí, José Julian (1853-1895), Cuban poet and hero of the independence movement. While in exile in the United States (1881-95) he founded the Cuban Revolutionary Party. His best known poems appear in *Ismaelillo* (1882), *Versos sencilles* (1891), and *Versos libres* (1913). A leader of the 1895 Cuban rebellion against Spanish rule, Martí was killed at the battle of Dos Rios.

Martial (Marcus Valerius Martialis; C.A.D. 40-104), Spanish-born Latin poet. He lived in Rome 64-98 and was favored by emperors Titus and Domitian. Martial wrote 15 books of epigrams famous for their wit and their unusual poetic meter.
See also: Epigram.

Martial law, temporary superimposition of military on domestic civil government, usually in wartime or other national emergency. The army takes over executive and judicial functions, and civil rights such as habeas corpus may be suspended. When an invading army assumes control of a country, it is said to act not under martial law but as a military government.

Martin, any of several birds of the swallow family. The best-known member of the species is the purple martin (*Progne subis*), valued throughout the Southern United States for its consumption of large quantities of mosquitoes and other insect pests. They are native to most of the United States and the lower portions of Canada and often flock together in large numbers, consuming swarms of winged insects in flight.

Martin du Gard, Roger (1881-1958), French novelist known for his objective but somber exploration of human relationships and the large backgrounds in which he sets them. In *Jean Barois* (1913) it is the Dreyfus Affair; in *The Thibaults* (1922-40), an 8-part novel cycle, it is World War I. In 1937 he won the Nobel Prize for literature.

Martineau, Harriet (1802-76), British writer and social reformer. A writer of fiction as well as nonfiction on many topics, she is best known for her works on economics and social reform, particularly her *Illustrations of Political Economy* (1832-34) and *Illustrations of Taxation* (1834), written for the layperson, and *Society in America* (1837), presenting her antislavery views.

Martinique, island in the Windward group in the east Caribbean, an overseas department of France since 1946. A volcanic island discovered by Columbus c.1502,

Martinique was colonized by France as a sugar-growing center after 1635. Slave labor was used until 1848, and much of the present population is of African descent. The economy still rests on sugar, as well as rum, fruit, and tourism. The island is rugged and mountainous but very fertile. Its main town is Fort-de-France.

Martin of Tours, Saint (c.316-397), bishop of Tours. Son of a pagan, he served in the Roman army but after a vision of Christ sought a religious life. Bishop of Tours from c.371, he encouraged monasticism and opposed execution of heretics.
See also: Tours.

Martins, Peter (1946-), Danish dancer. He danced with the Royal Danish Ballet 1964-67, then joined the New York City Ballet, where he became a leading male dancer in such works by George Balanchine as *Violin Concerto* and *Duo Concertant* (both 1972). In 1983, following Balanchine's death, he became ballet master-in-chief (with Jerome Robbins).
See also: Ballet.

Martin V (Oddone Colonna; 1368-1431), 15th-century Roman Catholic pope. Elected to the papacy in 1417 at the Council of Constance, his accession ended the Great Schism in the church. Martin worked for reforms within the church structure and hierarchy and arranged agreements (concordats) with the most powerful nations of Europe. He also called several councils aimed at receiving input for the continued unity and betterment of the church.

Marvell, Andrew (1621-1678), English metaphysical poet. Assistant to John Milton from 1657, Marvell was also a member of Parliament from 1659. A Puritan, he was known as a wit and satirist, but is best remembered today for his lyric poetry, including such works as "To His Coy Mistress" and "The Garden."

Marx, Karl (1818-83), German philosopher and social and economic theorist, founder of modern socialism. Born in Prussia of Jewish parents, Marx studied philosophy in Bonn and Berlin. When the Cologne newspaper he edited the *Rheinische Zeitung,* was suppressed (1843), he moved with his wife Jenny von Westphalen to Paris, where he met Friedrich Engels in 1844, and later to London, where he spent most of his life in great poverty.
In 1848 Marx and Engels published the *Communist Manifesto,* which established the theoretical basis for a socialist movement based on class struggle and sociological analysis rather than moral appeals to natural rights. Marx and Engels later cofounded (1864) International Workingmen's Association, the first international revolutionary organization. Marx wrote prolifically on questions of philosophy, history, and politics, but his greatest work was *Capital,* his analysis of the system of capitalism. Only the first volume was published in his lifetime (1867). After his death, Engels completed the second (1885) and third (1894) volumes. Building on his criticism of the theories of Adam Smith and David Ricardo, Marx developed the theory of surplus-value to explain the exploitation of workers under capitalism. He predicted that the working class, or proletariat, would grow in numbers and power and would eventually overthrow capitalism, and establish socialism. The economic and political analysis of capitalism was integrated into a broader theory called historical materialism, which analyzed human history in terms of a sequence of kinds of society based on different forms of ownership of the means of production. Marx's influence has been widespread, and he is universally regarded as one of the major thinkers of the 19th century.
See also: Communism; Marxism.

Marx brothers, U.S. comedy team whose main members were Groucho (Julius; 1895-1977), Harpo (Arthur; 1893-1964), and Chico (Leonard; 1891-1961). Gummo (Milton; 1892-1961) left the team after their vaudeville days, and Zeppo (Herbert; 1901-79) left in 1934. The Marx brothers made about a dozen movies (1933-46). Their anarchic humor made hits of such memorable movies as *Duck Soup* (1933) and *A Night at the Opera* (1935).

A Marx brothers movie poster

Marxism, foundation philosophy of modern communism, originating in the work of Karl Marx and Friedrich Engels. Three of its basic concepts are that productive labor is the fundamental attribute of human nature; that the structure of any society is determined by its economic means of production; and that societies evolve by a series of crises caused by internal contradictions, analyzable by dialectical materialism.
Marx held that 19th-century industrial capitalism, the latest stage of the historical process, had arisen from feudalism by class struggle between the aristocracy and the rising bourgeois capitalist class. Dialectical materialism predicted conflict between these capitalists and the working class, or proletariat, on which the new industrialism depended. The triumphant dictatorship of the proletariat, an idea further developed by Lenin, would give way to a classless, stateless communist society where all would be equal, contributing according to their abilities and receiving according to their needs.
A key concept of Marxist economics is the labor theory of value, that value is created by labor and profit is surplus value creamed off by the capitalist. The fact that the capitalist owns the means of production makes this exploitation possible. It also means that the worker cannot own the product of his labor and thus suffers alienation from part of his own humanity and the social system. Marx believed capitalism would be swept away by the last of a catastrophic series of crises.
Among numerous later Marxist theorists are Karl Kautsky and Rosa Luxemburg. In *The Accumulation of Capital* (1913), Luxemburg argued that capitalism was able to adapt and survive by exploitation of its colonial empires. In the USSR Stalin proclaimed Marxist-Leninism an active philosophy of society in forced evolutionary conflict. In China Mao Zedong adapted Marxism to an agricultural peasant situation. Yugoslavia's Tito gave Marxism a nationalist bias, still more marked in the thinking of Fidel Castro of Cuba. Some western economists, sociologists, and historians have been widely influenced by Marxism.
See also: Marx, Karl.

Karl Marx

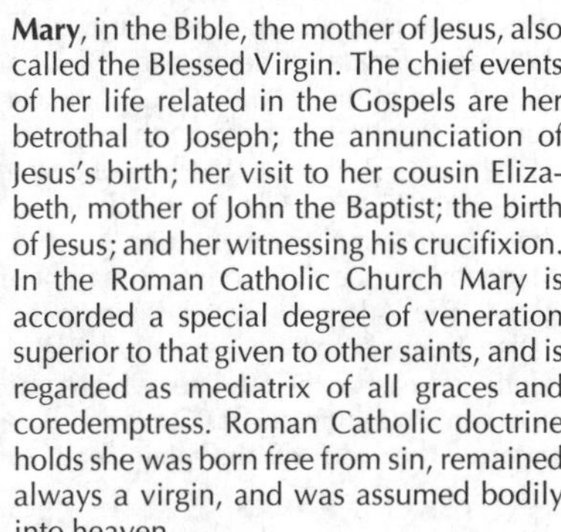

Mary, in the Bible, the mother of Jesus, also called the Blessed Virgin. The chief events of her life related in the Gospels are her betrothal to Joseph; the annunciation of Jesus's birth; her visit to her cousin Elizabeth, mother of John the Baptist; the birth of Jesus; and her witnessing his crucifixion. In the Roman Catholic Church Mary is accorded a special degree of veneration superior to that given to other saints, and is regarded as mediatrix of all graces and coredemptress. Roman Catholic doctrine holds she was born free from sin, remained always a virgin, and was assumed bodily into heaven.
See also: Bible; Jesus Christ.

Mary, name of 2 English queens. **Mary I** (1516-58), daughter of Henry VIII and Catherine of Aragon, succeeded Edward VI in 1553. She strove to restore Roman Catholicism in England. Some 300 Protestants were burnt as heretics—a persecution unparalleled in England, which earned her the name "Bloody Mary." Her unpopular alliance with and marriage to Philip II of Spain (1554) led to war with France and the loss of Calais (1558). **Mary II** (1662-94) was the Protestant daughter of James II and the wife (1677) of her cousin William of Orange, the Protestant ruler of the Netherlands. She helped found the College of William and Mary in Virginia in 1693. In the Glorious Revolution of 1688, William's forces attacked England, causing James to

flee. Mary II was proclaimed joint sovereign with William in 1689.
See also: United Kingdom.

Mary, Queen of Scots, (1542-87), queen of Scotland (1542-67), daughter of James V and Mary of Guise. Brought up in France, she married (1558) the Dauphin, King Francis II (died 1560). Returning to Scotland (1561), she married (1565) Lord Darnley. In 1566 he murdered her counselor, David Rizzio; later Darnley himself was murdered, supposedly by the Earl of Bothwell, whom Mary married. Public outrage and Presbyterian opposition forced her abdication, and in 1568 she fled to England. Mary, heir presumptive of Elizabeth I and a Roman Catholic, soon became the natural focus of plots against the English throne. Parliament demanded her death; only in 1587, after Anthony Babington's plot, did Elizabeth reluctantly agree. Mary's trial and execution at Fotheringay castle inspired Schiller's tragedy *Maria Stuart*.
See also: Scotland; United Kingdom.

Mary, Virgin *see:* Mary.

Maryknoll Fathers, popular name for the Catholic Foreign Mission Society of America. It was founded in 1911 with headquarters at Maryknoll, N.Y. It has sent missions to Asia, Latin America, and the Pacific islands.

Maryland, state in the mid-Atlantic region of the eastern United States; bordered by Pennsylvania to the north, Delaware and the Atlantic Ocean to the east, Virginia and the District of Columbia to the south, and West Virginia to the south and west.
Land and climate. Chesapeake Bay, a jagged arm of the Atlantic Ocean, almost cuts the state in two from north to south. Maryland's 3,190 mi (5,134 km) of coastline—only 31 mi (49 km) of which are on the Atlantic—include many fine harbors. Maryland can be divided into 3 major regions. The Atlantic Coastal Plain (often called Tidewater Maryland) includes land south and east of the fall line, which runs between Washington, D.C., and Baltimore. The part of the plain east of Chesapeake Bay (called the Eastern Shore) is very flat. The part west of the bay (the Western Shore) is fairly flat, but includes some hills. The central Piedmont-Blue Ridge region is an area of foothills and plateaus. The Appalachian-Allegheny area, which stretches from Hagerstown to the western border, is the state's highest region. Maryland's major rivers all flow into Chesapeake Bay. They include the Potomac, Patapsco, and Susquehanna. All Maryland's lakes are artificial. Forest covers approximately 40% of the state. Maryland has hot summers and mild winters. Principal cities are Baltimore, Silver Spring, and Dundalk.
Economy. Maryland's economy is based on service industries. Many federal office buildings and support services are here, due to Maryland's proximity to the U.S. capital. Manufacturing and tourism are the principal industries. Manufactured products include electrical equipment, processed foods, chemicals, printed materials, and transportation equipment. Tourist attractions include horse- and yacht-racing events, shore resorts, and historic Fort McHenry. Maryland's fishing industry is another major source of income. Its production of clams and oysters is one of the nation's highest, and it is known for its crabs and other seafood. About 35% of the state's area is farmland. Broilers (chickens), beef cattle, and milk are the leading livestock products; greenhouse and nursery plants, cotton, soybeans, and rice are the major crops. Mineral products include construction sand and gravel, crushed stone, and coal.
Government. Maryland's present constitution was adopted in 1867. The governor serves a 4-year term. The state legislature, called the General Assembly, consists of 47 senators and 141 delegates; all serve 4-year terms. In the U.S. Congress, Maryland is represented by 2 senators and 8 representatives.
History. Maryland was home to several Native American tribes before Spanish explorers, the first Europeans, arrived in the 1500s. One of the original 13 colonies, Maryland played an active part in the American Revolution. During the War of 1812, a battle at Baltimore's Fort McHenry inspired Francis Scott Key to write "The Star-Spangled Banner," which later became the U.S. national anthem. Maryland officially supported the Union in the Civil War, but its people were sharply divided. Afterward, its economy grew and became more diverse, booming after World War I, crashing in the Great Depression, and rising again after World War II. Today, Maryland is a center of research and development for the U.S. space program.

Maryland

Maryland

Capital:	Annapolis
Statehood:	Apr. 28, 1788 (7th state)
Familiar names:	Old Line State, Free State
Area:	10,577 sq mi (27,394 km); ranks 42nd
Population:	4,798,622 (1990); ranks 19th
Elevation:	Highest—3,360 (1,024 m), Backbone Mountain Lowest—sea level
Motto:	*Fatti Maschii, Parole Femine* (Manly Deeds, Womanly Words)
Flower:	Black-eyed Susan
Bird:	Baltimore oriole
Tree:	White oak
State song:	"Maryland, My Maryland"

Mary Magdalene, in the New Testament, the woman of Magdala from whom Jesus cast out 7 demons (Luke 8:2). She became his devoted follower and may have been present at his death and burial. Mary was the first person to see the risen Jesus.
See also: New Testament.

Masaccio (Tommaso Guidi; 1401-28), Florentine painter of the Renaissance, one of the great innovators of Western art. Possibly a pupil of Masolino, Masaccio produced paintings that inspired such painters as Michelangelo and Raphael. Through austere composition and inspired use of light Masaccio created expressive monumental paintings and frescoes, notably in the Brancacci Chapel of Santa Maria del Carmine in Florence. Other works include the *Trinity* fresco in Santa Maria Novella and the *Virgin with St. Anne* in the Uffizi Palace, both in Florence.
See also: Renaissance.

Masada, mountaintop rock fortress near the southeastern coast of the Dead Sea, Israel. The castle-palace complex, built (37-31 B.C.) largely by Herod the Great, was seized from Roman occupation by Jewish Zealots in A.D. 66. A 2-year seige, 72-73, was needed to recover it, but the Zealots committed suicide rather than surrender. The site has been excavated (1963-65) and restored.

Masai, people of eastern Africa who speak the Masai language of the Sudanic group. The nomadic pastoral Masai of Kenya, the largest Masai tribe, practice polygamy and organize their society on a system of male age sets, graded from junior warrior up to tribal elder. They subsist almost entirely by herding.

Masaryk, name of 2 Czechoslovakian politicians. **Thomas Garrigue Masaryk** (1850-1937), was chief founder and first president of Czechoslovakia (1918-35). Professor of philosophy at the Univ. of Prague from 1882, he was a fervent nationalist. During World War I he lobbied Western statesmen for Czech independence. His son **Jan Garrigue Masaryk** (1886-1948) was foreign minister of the Czech government-in-exile in London in World War II, broadcasting to his German-occupied country. He continued as foreign minister in the restored government (1945). Soon after the Communist coup (1948) he was said to have committed suicide.

Mascagni, Pietro (1863-1945), Italian opera composer of the *verismo* (realist) school, known for the one-act *Cavalleria Rusticana* (Rustic Chivalry, 1890). In 1929 he became musical director of La Scala, Milan. Although he composed 15 operas, among them *L'Amico Fritz* (1891), Mascagni did not repeat his initial success.
See also: Opera.

Masefield, John (1878-1967), English poet, novelist, and playwright. As a youth he served on a windjammer ship, and love of the sea pervades his poems. He won fame with such long narrative poems as *The Everlasting Mercy* (1911), *Dauber* (1913), and *Raynard the Fox* (1919). In 1930 he became poet laureate.

Maser, in technology, acronym for Microwave Amplification by Stimulated Emission of Radiation, a device capable of amplifying or generating radio frequency radiation. Maser amplifiers are used in satellite communication ground stations to amplify the extremely weak signals received from communication satellites.
See also: Laser.

Maseru (pop. 109,400), capital of Lesotho, a landlocked independent state in southern Africa. Standing near Lesotho's northwestern border with the Orange Free State (South Africa), the town is linked by a short railroad with the Bioemfontein-Natal line in South Africa. Maseru has a public library, hospital, and technical training school.
See also: Lesotho.

Maslow, Abraham Harold (1908-70), U.S. psychologist, the major figure in the humanistic school of psychology. Rejecting behaviorism and psychoanalysis, he saw human beings as creative entities striving for self-actualization. His books include *Motivation and Personality* (1954), *Toward a Psychology of Being* (1962), and *The Psychology of Science* (1966).
See also: Psychology.

Mason, Charles *see:* Mason and Dixon's Line.

Mason, George (1725-92), U.S. politician who helped draft the U.S. Constitution, but refused to sign it because of its compromise on slavery and other issues. His Virginia declaration of rights (1776) became the basis for the Bill of Rights. Much of the Virginia Constitution was also his work.

Mason and Dixon's Line, Mason-Dixon Line, traditional dividing line between the northern and southern states of the United States. Surveyed by Charles Mason and Jeremiah Dixon in 1767, the line formed the east-west boundary between Pennsylvania and Maryland and the north-south boundary between Maryland and Delaware. In 1779 the east-west line was extended to form the boundary between Virginia and Pennsylvania.

Mason and Slidell, Confederate diplomats; their seizure while aboard a British vessel nearly touched off a war between the United States and Great Britain during the Civil War. James Murray Mason (1798-1871) served in the U.S. Senate and House of Representatives from Virginia. John Slidell (1793-1871) served in both houses of Congress from Louisiana. On Nov. 8, 1861, they were captured along with the British ship *Trent*, as they sailed toward Europe to seek diplomatic recognition for the confederacy. They were released on Jan. 2, 1862.
See also: Civil War, U.S.

Masonry, or freemasonry, common name for the practices of the order of Free and Accepted Masons, one of the world's largest and oldest fraternal organizations. Members participate in elaborate, secret rituals and are dedicated to the promotion of brotherhood and morality. Membership, of which there are several grades, is restricted to men; allegiance to some form of religious belief is required. Modern Masonry emerged with the Grand Lodge of England, founded in 1717, although masons trace their ancestry to the craft associations or "lodges" of medieval stone masons. The first U.S. lodge was founded in Philadelphia, Pa. in 1730. There are associated organizations for women, boys, and girls. The worldwide membership is more than 6 million.

Masqat *see:* Muscat.

Masque, or mask, dramatic entertainment popular in the early-17th-century English court. It concentrated on spectacle rather than plot. Members of the aristocracy often took part with the actors, and masks were generally worn (hence the name). Ben Jonson was the most famous masque writer, and Inigo Jones designed many of the lavish sets.

Mass, term for the celebration of Holy Communion in the Roman Catholic Church and in Anglo-Catholic churches. Roman Catholics believe that the bread (host) and the wine become Christ's body and blood, which are offered as a sacrifice to God. The text consists of the "ordinary," spoken or sung at every celebration, and the "proper," sections which change according to the day or occasion—for example, the requiem mass has its own proper. In High Mass, celebrated with priest, deacon, and choir, the text is sung to plainsong with choral responses. Medieval choral settings of the mass were the first great masterpieces of Western music, remaining a major musical form into the 20th century. Low Mass, said by a single priest, is the basic Roman Catholic service. In 1965 the Vatican sanctioned the use of vernacular languages in place of Latin.

Mass, in physics, measure of the linear inertia of a body, i.e., of the extent to which it resists acceleration when a force is applied to it. Alternatively, mass can be thought of as a measure of the amount of matter in a body. This view seems validated when one remembers that bodies of equal inertial mass have identical weights in a given gravitational field. The exact equivalence of inertial mass and gravitational mass is only a theoretical assumption, albeit one strongly supported by experimental evidence. According to Einstein's theory of relativity, the mass of a body is increased if it gains energy, according to the equation $E=mc^2$, where m is the change in mass due to the energy change E, and c is the electromagnetic constant. It is an important property of nature that in an isolated system mass-energy is conserved. The international standard of mass is the international prototype kilogram.
See also: Inertia.

Massachusetts

Capital:	Boston
Statehood:	Feb. 6, 1788 (6th state)
Familiar name:	Bay State
Area:	8,284 sq mi (21,456 km); ranks 45th
Population:	6,029,051 (1990); ranks 13th
Elevation:	Highest—3,491 ft (1,064 m), Mt. Greylock; Lowest—sea level, along the Atlantic coast
Motto:	Ense Petit Placidam Sub Libertate Quietem (By the Sword We Seek Peace, But Peace Only Under Liberty)
Flower:	Mayflower
Bird:	Chickadee
Tree:	American elm
Song:	"All Hail to Massachusetts"

Massachusetts, state in New England, the northeastern region of the United States; bordered by Vermont and New Hampshire to the north, the Atlantic Ocean to the east

Massachusetts

and south, Rhode Island and Connecticut to the south, and New York to the west.

Land and climate. Massachusetts can be divided into six land regions. The Coastal Lowlands is a flat or gently sloping plain in the eastern third of the state. Most of the state's people and principal manufacturing centers are here. The hilly Eastern New England Upland extends west of the Lowlands for 40-60 mi (64-97 km). The land then dips into the broad, fertile Connecticut Valley, which is about 20 mi (32 km) wide. West of there, the land rises into the most rugged regions of the state—the Western New England Upland (including Mt. Greylock, the state's highest point), the Berkshire Valley, and the Taconic Mountains.

Although there are more than 4,200 mi of rivers in Massachusetts, the Connecticut River is the state's only major navigable waterway. The Merrimack River furnished the water power for Massachusetts's early industries. The state has more than 1,000 lakes and ponds. The climate is humid, with sharply defined seasons. Western Massachusetts is colder and snowier than the east. Principal cities are Boston, Worcester, and Springfield.

Economy. The state's economy is based on such service industries as banking, health care, real estate, and retail trade. Principal manufactured goods are machinery (particularly computers), electrical equipment, scientific instruments, printed materials, transportation equipment, chemicals, and food, plastic, and paper products. Tourism, an important part of the economy, thrives in Boston, Cape Cod, and the Berkshires. Agriculture, fishing, and mining, once of prime importance, are now minor branches of the economy.

Government. The Massachusetts constitution, the oldest state constitution still in use, was adopted in 1780. The governor serves a four-year term. The state legislature, called the General Court, consists of 40 senators and 160 representatives; all serve 2-year terms. In the U.S. Congress, Massachusetts is represented by two senators and 10 representatives.

History. Native American peoples were the area's first known settlers, more than 3,000 years ago. The first European explorers may have been Vikings, about A.D. 1000. The Pilgrims, who came from England in 1620, built the first European settlement. English Puritans settled at and around Boston. The Massachusetts Bay Colony was one of the original 13 British colonies. Indian opposition culminated in King Philip's War (1675-76). The Boston Massacre (1770) and the Boston Tea Party (1773) helped spark the American Revolution, whose first battles were at Lexington and Concord (1775). The new state's commerce flourished, especially in the major seaport of Boston. In 1814, one of the first U.S. factories was built at Waltham; Massachusetts soon became the most industrialized state in the nation. Massachusetts supported the Union during the Civil War. Between that war and World War I, an immigration boom swelled the state's population and helped power its industrial rise. The state economy suffered during the 1920s and 1930s, but World War II brought recovery. Massachusetts, known for its historic universities and colleges (including Harvard and MIT), attracts research and development industries that supported it during the economic slump of the late 1980s.

Massachusetts Bay Company, English joint stock company set up by royal charter in 1629 and styled the "Governor and Company of the Massachusetts Bay in New England." The charter gave the company self-government, subject only to the king; it effectively became the constitution of the colony. In 1630 almost 1,000 immigrants landed in Massachusetts, led by John Winthrop, who became the first governor. The franchise was then restricted to Puritan "freemen," and the colony became an independent Calvinistic theocracy; it coined its own money and restricted freedom of worship. As a result, the charter was revoked in 1684 and Massachusetts became a royal colony

Massasoit (1580?-1661), powerful Wampanoag chief who signed a treaty with the Pilgrims under Governor John Carver of Plymouth Colony in 1621. He befriended the Plymouth colony, teaching the settlers how to survive, and kept up friendly relations until his death.
See also: Plymouth Colony.

Massenet, Jules (1842-1912), French composer. Best known for his operas *Manon* (1884), *Werther* (1892), and *Thaïs* (1894), he frequently used spoken (accompanied) dialogue in the place of recitative.

Massey, Vincent (1887-1967), Canadian diplomat. The first Canadian-born governor-general of Canada (1952-59), he became Canada's first minister in Washington (1926). From 1935-46 he was high commissioner in London. Massey also became chairperson of the Royal Commission on National Development in the Arts, Letters and Sciences (1949) and chancellor of the Univ. of Toronto (1947-53). In 1961 he founded Massey College. He also published several books of his speeches, and his autobiography, *What's Past Is Prologue* (1963).

Massine, Léonide (1896-1979), Russian-born U.S. ballet dancer and choreographer. He worked with Diaghilev as principal dancer and choreographer (1914-21, 1925-28), and directed the Ballet Russe de Monte Carlo 1932-42. His works include *Parade* (1917) and *Jeux d' Enfants* (1943).

Massinger, Philip (1583-1640), English dramatist known for satirical comedies. Among his works are *A New Way to Pay Old Debts* (1621), *The City Madam* (1632), and the romantic tragedy *The Duke of Milan* (1621). He often collaborated with others, such as John Fletcher. A moralist, he criticized the frivolity in society.

Mass media *see:* Advertising.

Mass number *see:* Atom.

Masson, André (1896-1987), French painter and graphic artist. Influenced by surrealism, he developed a style of drawing ("automatic drawing") intended to be spontaneous and without a specific subject.

Mass production, production of large numbers of identical objects, usually by use of mechanization. The root of mass production is the assembly line, essentially a conveyer belt that transports the product so that each worker may perform a single function on it (e.g., add a component). The advantages of mass production are cheapness and speed; the disadvantages are lack of job satisfaction for the workers and resultant sociological problems.
See also: Assembly line; Machine tool.

Mass spectroscopy, spectroscopic technique in which electric and magnetic fields are used to deflect moving charged particles according to their mass; employed for chemical analysis, separation, isotope determination, or finding impurities. The apparatus for obtaining a mass spectrum (i.e., a number of "lines" of distinct charge-to-mass ratio obtained from the beam of charged particles) is known as a mass spectrometer or mass spectrograph, depending on whether the lines are detected electrically or on a photographic plate. In

essence, it consists of an ion source, a vacuum chamber, a deflecting field, and a collector. By altering the accelerating voltage and deflecting field, particles of a given mass can be focused to pass together through the collecting slit.
See also: Spectrometer.

Masters, Edgar Lee (1869-1950), U.S. poet, novelist, biographer, and playwright whose best-known work is *Spoon River Anthology* (1915), which reveals the life of a small town as seen through the epitaphs of its inhabitants. He also wrote critical biographies of Abraham Lincoln and Mark Twain.

Masters, William H. (1915-), and Virginia E. Johnson (1925-), U.S. sex researchers whose book *Human Sexual Response* (1966) was the first complete study of the physiology and anatomy of sexual activity.

Masterson, Bat (1853-1921), U.S. pioneer and peace officer. He is best known as assistant to Wyatt Earp, a deputy U.S. marshall in Tombstone, Ariz., 1881. Masterson was a deputy marshall in Dodge City, Kans. (1876), sheriff of Ford county (1878-80), and city marshall of Trinidad, Colo. (1882).

Mastodon, any of a genus (*Mammut*) of the extinct mammals resembling elephants. Different from mammoths and elephants because of their molar teeth, they sometimes had 4 tusks (2 on the lower jaw, 2 on the upper jaw). Forest dwellers, mastodons lived in Africa during the Oligocene epoch.
See also: Mammoth.

Mata Hari (Margaretha Geertruida Zelle; 1866-1917), Dutch-born dancer and spy for Germany in World War I. She belonged to the German secret service in Paris. The mistress of many French officials, she passed on military secrets to the Germans, for which she was tried and executed.
See also: World War I.

Maté, also known as yerba maté or Paraguay tea, evergreen tree of the holly family. Its leaves are dried to make a tea containing caffeine that is widely drunk in South America.

Materialism, in philosophy, any view asserting the primacy of physical matter in explaining the nature of the world. The earliest materialists were the classical atomists, e.g., Democritus and Leucippus. Modern science has revived materialism, argued as a prerequisite for scientific thought, particularly in psychology.
See also: Democritus; Leucippus; Marx, Karl.

Mathematics, field of thought concerned with relationships involving concepts of quantity, space, and symbolism. Over the past several centuries mathematics developed to include *axiomatic-deductive reasoning*. This aspect of mathematics is credited to the classical Greeks and is traced back to Euclid, who formalized it in 300 B.C. with his work *Elements*. Axiomatic-deductive systems are based on elementary ideas assumed self-evident (*axioms*) and formal rules governing the mathematical system. Consequences (*theorems*) can then be deduced systematically and logically from axioms. All mathematical systems have this quality. Familiar examples include algebra, where relationships between known and unknown quantities are represented symbolically; arithmetic, the science of quantity and space concerned with numbers and rules for manipulating them such as addition or multiplication; calculus, dealing with relationships involving rates of change; and geometry, concerned with spatial relationships. Mathematics is pursued to solve practical problems as well as to enhance its logical and often abstract nature. Consequently it is often categorized as *applied* and *pure*. The applied mathematician uses or develops mathematics as a tool, solving problems or relationships in other fields. Physicists and engineers often apply calculus to questions of motion, economists apply concepts of linear algebra to determine cost effective solutions, and statistics and probability are frequently used by psychologists. The scholar of pure mathematics investigates logical relationships of abstract quantities or objects. Questions of the completeness and consistency within given mathematical constructs are addressed in pure mathematics.
Major contributions in the development of western mathematics came from Egypt (3000-1600 B.C.), Babylonia (1700-300 B.C.), Greece (600-200 B.C.), and the Hindu and Arab world (600 B.C.-A.D. 1450). Major achievements before modern times have also occurred in China, Japan, and Incan and Aztec empires.

Mather, family of American colonial ministers. **Richard Mather** (1596-1669) fled England (1635) for Massachusetts seeking religious freedom. A Puritan and pastor of Dorchester, he wrote the *Platform of Church Discipline* (1649), the basic creed of Massachusetts Congregationalism. **Increase Mather** (1639-1723), son of Richard, was president of Harvard College (1685-1701). A renowned Puritan pastor and scholar, he helped negotiate the colony's new charter and intervened against witchcraft persecution. **Cotton Mather** (1663-1728), son of Increase, was a famous preacher and scholar who contributed to the witchcraft hysteria. He helped found Yale Univ.; because of his broad scientific interests he was the first American colonist elected to the Royal Society of London.

Mathewson, Christy (Christopher Mathewson; 1880-1925), U.S. baseball player. Mathewson, a right-handed pitcher for the New York Giants (1900-16) and Cincinnati Reds (1916) is considered one of the best pitchers of all time and is credited with developing the screwball. His achievements include being the first pitcher of the 1900's to win 30 games or more for 3 consecutive seasons (1903-05), 373 career wins, and winning 20 games or more for 12 consecutive seasons (1901-14). Mathewson was among the first group of players inducted into the National Baseball Hall of Fame (1936). A victim of poison gas in World War I, he died of tuberculosis.

Matisse, Henri (1869-1954), French painter, sculptor, and lithographer. He is regarded, with Picasso, as one of the 2 most important artists of the 20th century. He was a leader of the fauves and was noted for his brilliant, expressive use of color in such paintings as *The Green Line* (1905) and *Landscape at Callioure* (1905). Earlier he had explored impressionism, as in his painting *The Dinner Table* (1897). In his last years he created abstract compositions out of handpainted cut paper, a technique he called "drawing with scissors." From 1948 to 1951 he designed and decorated the Dominican chapel at Vence, France.

Henri Matisse's Flowering Ivy *(1941)*

Matter, material substance existing in space and time. All matter has inertia, measured quantitatively by its mass and weight, exerting its gravitational pull on other such bodies. There are 3 common states of matter: solid, liquid and gas; scientists consider plasma a fourth. Atoms and molecules make up ordinary matter.

Matterhorn, 14,691-ft (4,478-m) high mountain in the Alps on the Swiss-Italian frontier. It was first climbed by Edward Whymper in 1865.

Matthew, Saint, one of the twelve apostles, traditionally the author of the first gospel. His gospel, the fullest of the 4 gospels, was probably written for Jewish Christians. By its many Old Testament quotes it shows Jesus as the promised Messiah. His feast day is Sept. 12.
See also: Apostles.

Mattingly, Don (Donald Arthur Mattingly; 1961-), U.S. baseball player. As first baseman for the New York Yankees, American League (AL), he distinguished himself as a batter and fielder. He was named AL Most Valuable Player in 1985, and batted over .300 for 6 consecutive seasons (1984-89). In 1991 Mattingly became the tenth captain in New York Yankees history.

Somerset Maugham

Maugham, W(illiam) Somerset (1874-1965), British author. A playwright, short story writer, and novelist, his writing frequently was characterized by irony and cynicism. Maugham's novels include the autobiographical *Of Human Bondage* (1915), *The Moon and Sixpence* (1919), and the satirical *Cakes and Ale* (1930).

Maui *see:* Hawaii.

Mauldin, Bill (1921-), U.S. cartoonist. His cartoons of World War II GIs, Willie and Joe, published in the armed forces newspaper *Stars and Stripes,* became the national embodiment of the American infantrymen. He won the Pulitzer Prize for cartooning in 1945 and 1959. *Up Front* (1945) and *Brass Ring* (1971) are 2 of his books of cartoons.
See also: Cartoon.

Mau Mau, terrorist organization in Kenya (chiefly the Kikuyu tribe) whose main aim was to expel the British. Organized as a secret society, the Mau Mau ran a campaign of murder and sabotage (1952-60); after 1956 the British put an end to most of the bloodshed.

Mauna Kea, dormant volcano in Hawaii. At 13,796 ft (4,205 m) high, Mauna Kea ("white mountain") is the world's highest island mountain. At the top of its snow-covered summit are several astronomical observatories and large telescopes.

Mauna Loa, active volcano in the Hawaii Volcanoes National Park. The world's largest volcano, it erupts every 3.5 years. It is 13,680 ft (4,170 m) high. Kilauea volcano is on its southeastern side.

Maundy Thursday, the Thursday before Easter, commemorating Jesus's washing of his disciples' feet and institution of Holy Communion at the Last Supper.
See also: Holy Week.

Maupassant, Guy de *see:* De Maupassant, Guy.

Mauriac, François (1885-1970), French author. A nonconformist Catholic, his novels concern man's vulnerability to sin and evil. Winner of the 1952 Nobel Prize for literature, his works include *The Desert of Love* (1925), *Thérèse Desqueyroux* (1927), and *The Knot of Vipers* (1932).

Maurice of Nassau (1567-1625), Prince of Orange from 1618, Dutch statesman, and military leader. A son of William the Silent, he conducted a successful war against Spanish rule and was an architect of the emerging Dutch republic. He was virtual ruler of the Netherlands, executing his former ally Johan van Oldenbarneveldt in 1619 and establishing the supremacy of the house of Orange.
See also: Netherlands.

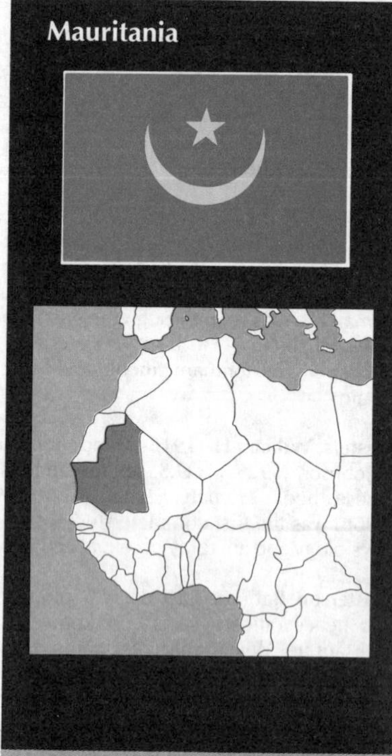

Capital:	Nouakchott
Area:	398,000 sq mi (1,030,700 sq km)
Population:	1,946,000
Form:	republic
Independent:	1960
GNP:	U.S. $8430,000,000
Per capita:	U.S. $450

Mauritania, Islamic Republic of, former French colony in western Africa. Mauritania is some 419,231 sq mi (1,085,808 sq km) in area and is bordered by Morocco and Algeria to the north, Mali and Senegal to the south, Mali to the east, and the Atlantic Ocean to the west.

Land and climate. Mauritania is principally a dry, rocky plateau averaging 500 ft (152 m) above sea level, a southern extension of the Sahara. There is a fertile grain growing district along the Senegal River in the south and cattle raising grasslands in the southeast. The climate is hot throughout the country, but rainfall varies considerably from less than 4 in (10 cm) annually in the north to about 24 in (61 cm) annually toward the south.

People. Some 80% of the population are Berbers or Moors and the remaining 20% are black Africans. Only about 25% of the people live in towns. The Berbers and Moors live a nomadic life principally in the north and the black Africans live in rural villages in the south. The capital is Nouakchott. The official languages are French and Arabic. Islam is the official religion.

Economy. There are large deposits of iron ore, gypsum, and copper, and iron ore accounts for about 80% of all exports. Farmers in the south raise millet, sorghum, rice, and other cereals and vegetables while nomads raise sheep, goats, cattle, and camels. Recent droughts have dealt a serious blow to livestock.

History. In the 11th century, the Ghanaian Empire, to which most of Mauritania then belonged, was invaded by nomadic Berbers of the Almoravid group. In the 13th century South Mauritania fell to the Mali Empire and Islam was firmly established. The Portuguese probed the coast in the 15th century; the French penetrated the

Mauritanian landscape

interior in the 19th century. In 1920 Mauritania became the colony of French West Africa. In 1960 it gained full independence and became a Muslim state under President Mokhtar Ould Daddah. The military seized power in 1968. During the 1970s a war against the Polisario Front guerrillas over claims to the Western Sahara brought political and economic instability. Mauritania relinquished its claim to the territory in 1979. In 1984, Lt. Col. Maaouga Ould Sidi Ahmed Taya replaced Lt. Col. Mohamed Khouma Ould Haidalla as head of state.

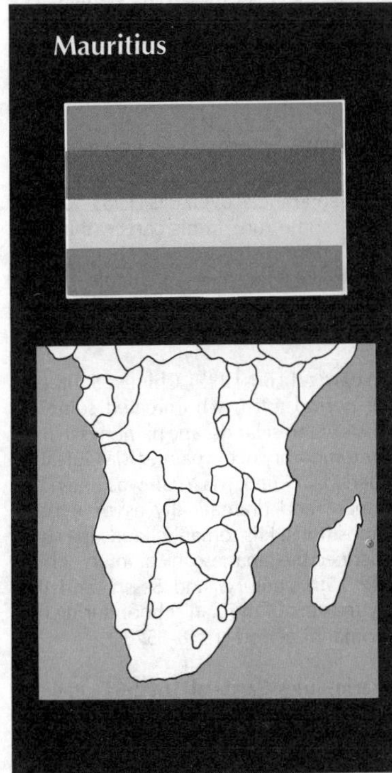

Capital:	Port Louis
Area:	788 sq mi (2,040 sq km)
Population:	1,099,000
Form:	republic
Independent:	1968
GNP:	U.S.$2,965,000,000
Per capita:	U.S.$2,700

Mauritius, island republic 500 mi (805 km) east of Madagascar in the Indian Ocean, comprising the islands of Mauritius, Rodrigues, and associated archipelagos.
Land and climate. The main island, Mauritius, is surrounded by coral reefs. The island is principally a plateau and approximately 788 sq mi (2,040 sq km) in area. The climate is warm and humid with a cyclone season from Dec. to Mar.
People. More than 60% of the population consists of Indians, about 30% are Creole, a mixture of French and black African, and the remainder are principally Europeans, African, and Chinese. Religions reflect the diversity of the people and include the Hindu religion, Christianity, and Islam. The official language is English and the capital is Port Louis.
Economy. Sugar was the single most important export until the 1980s when it was surpassed by textile products. Tea and tobacco are also cash crops and tourism contributes to the economy as well. But with more than 1,000,000 inhabitants, overpopulation and unemployment are persistent problems for Mauritius.
History. Formerly uninhabited, Mauritius was settled by the Portuguese in the early 1500s but soon abandoned. After a period of Dutch occupation in the 17th century, the French settled the island in 1715, founded the sugar industry, and imported slaves from Africa to work the plantations. The British took Mauritius in 1810, during the Napoleonic Wars and when they abolished slavery in the colonies in 1831, the planters resorted to indentured laborers from India. The British first initiated moves toward representative government for the colony in the late 19th century. Mauritius was granted full independence in 1968. Until 1992 Mauritius was a constitutional monarchy in the British Commonwealth, with the British Queen as the head of state. In 1992 the country became a republic with Cassan Uteem as the first elected president.

Maurois, André (Émile Herzog; 1885-1967), 20th-century French author. A soldier in World War I, his earliest works were novels about his war experiences, including *The Silence of Colonel Bramble* (1918) and *Les Discours du Docteur O'Grady* (1921). Maurois is known for his biographies of authors Percy Bysshe Shelley, Lord Byron, George Sand, Victor Hugo, and Alexandre Dumas and politicians George Washington, Benjamin Disraeli, and Chateaubriand. His *Memoirs: 1885-1967* was published posthumously in 1970.

Maury, Matthew Fontaine (1806-73), U.S. naval officer, head of the Depot of Charts and Instruments (1844-61). His study of the bed of the Atlantic Ocean and his *Physical Geography of the Sea* (1855) helped pioneer the science of oceanography.

Maurya Empire, Indian imperial dynasty, 325-183 B.C., founded by Chandragupta Maurya. Its capital was near modern Patna. Chandragupta Maurya's grandson Asoka (d. 232) brought almost the whole subcontinent under one rule and made Buddhism the state religion. Under Mauryan art, there was a flowering of the Indian Buddhist culture.
See also: Asoka; Chandragupta, Maurya.

Maverick, Samuel Augustus (1803-70), Texas politician and cattle rancher. He was a member of the convention that founded the Republic of Texas (1836) and served as a member of the Texas Congress and its first state legislature. Owner of a large cattle ranch, Maverick did not brand his herd, and neighbors called his strays, "mavericks." The word came to mean all unmarked cattle. Today the term applies largely to politicians who have no distinct affiliations or party loyalties.

Maxim, U.S. family of inventors. **Sir Hiram Stevens Maxim** (1840-1916) invented (1854) the automatic, rapid-firing gun (Maxim machine gun) and tested a steam-powered aircraft (it successfully lifted off the ground). **Hudson Maxim** (1853-1927), Sir Hiram's brother, invented an explosive more powerful than dynamite, a smokeless powder, and a torpedo propellant. **Hiram Percy Maxim** (1869-1936), Sir Hiram's son, invented the gun silencer, designed an electric automobile, and helped develop mufflers for automobiles and jet engines.
See also: Explosive; Machine gun.

Maximilian, name of 2 Habsburg Holy Roman emperors. **Maximilian I** (1459-1519) reigned from 1493. He married, first, Mary of Burgundy (1477) and then Bianca, daughter of the Duke of Milan (1494). He arranged other family marriages that brought the Habsburgs much of Burgundy, the Netherlands, Hungary, Bohemia, and Spain. Maximilian I reorganized imperial administration and set up a supreme court of justice. However, he had to recognize Switzerland's independence (1499), and failed to hold Milan. His finances were severely strained by continual warfare in support of his ambitions. **Maximilian II** (1527-76), emperor from 1564, was also king of Bohemia from 1549 and of Hungary from 1563. He was the son and successor of Ferdinand I. A humanist, he adopted a policy of religious toleration. Maximilian II arranged a truce with Turkey, according to which he would pay tribute to the sultan for his part of Hungary.
See also: Holy Roman Empire.

Maximilian I

Maximilian (1832-1867), emperor of Mexico from 1864 until his death. An Austrian archduke, he was given the throne by the French emperor Napoleon III, who hoped to extend his empire. Maximilian believed that the Mexicans would welcome him and attempted to rule liberally and benevolently, but found French troops essential against popular support for President Benito Juárez. After the troops withdrew (1866-67), Maximilian was defeated by Juárez's forces and executed.

Maxwell, James Clerk (1831-79), Scottish theoretical physicist. His most important work was in electricity, magnetism, and his kinetic theory of gases. He also studied color vision, elasticity, optics, Saturn's rings, and thermodynamics. *Maxwell's equations*, 4 linked differential equations, extend the work of Michael Faraday and others and completely define the classical theory of the electromagnetic field. Maxwell's most famous work was *Treatise on Electricity and Magnetism* (1873). Its main concepts are considered to be thebasis for Albert Einstein's theory of relativity and the quantum theory.
See also: Electromagnetic waves.

Maxwell's rule, law stating that every part of an electric circuit is acted upon by a force tending to move it in such a direction as to enclose the maximum amount of magnetic flux.

May apple, or mayapple (*Podophyllum peltatum*), woodland plant native to eastern North America. Also known as mandrake, it produces white flowers between Apr. and June and edible yellow berries often used in jellies. A member of the barberry family, may apple roots are used to manufacture types of herbal medicines.

Mayas, Middle American Indian confederation of Central America, covering the Yucatán peninsula, East Chiapas state in modern Mexico, most of Guatemala, and the western parts of El Salvador and Honduras. Its civilization was at its height A.D. 300-900. A farming people of the rain forests, the Mayas grew corn, cassava, cotton, beans, and sweet potatoes and kept bees for wax and honey. They had a hierarchy of priest-nobles under a hereditary chief. The Mayans developed an involved hieroglyphic form of writing, still undeciphered, and a knowledge of mathematics, astronomy, and chronology superior to that in contemporaneous Europe. The priests devised 2 calendars: a 365-day civil year and a sacred year of 260 days. Mayan art comprises fine sculpture, both in the round and in relief; painted frescoes and manuscripts; ceramics, and magnificent architecture, including the lofty stone pyramid topped by a temple. By 900 their main centers, such as Palenque, Peidras, and Copán, had been abandoned to the jungle for reasons unknown. A "post-classical" tradition, under Toltec influence, sprang up in new centers, notably Chichén Itzá, but in the early 1500s the entire region came under Spanish rule.

Descendants of the Mayas in a shop in Todos Santos, Cuchamatan, Guatemala

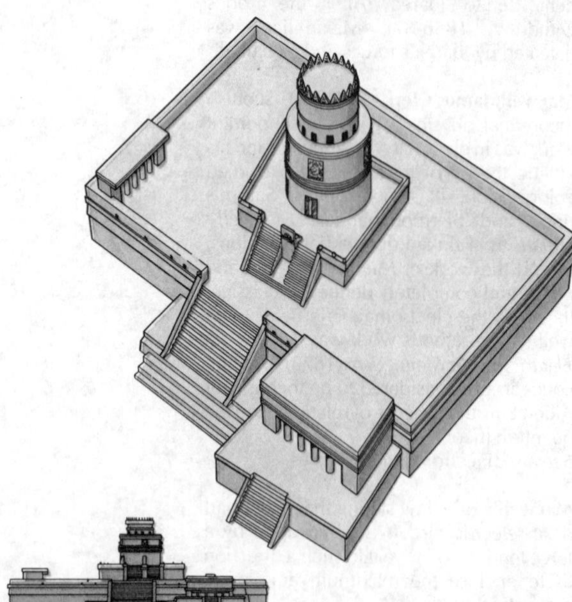

Mayan astronomical observatory at Chichen Itza

May beetle *see:* June bug.

May Day, spring festival on May 1. Traces of its pagan origins survive in the decorated maypoles and May queens of England. Declared a socialist labor festival by the Second International in 1889, it is celebrated, particularly in communist countries, by parades and demonstrations.

Mayer, Julius Robert von (1814-78), German physician and physicist who contributed (1842) to the formulation of the law of conservation of energy.
See also: Heat; Joule, James Prescott.

Mayflower, ship that carried the Pilgrims to America in 1620. It left Plymouth, England, on Sept. 21 and reached Provincetown, Mass., on Nov. 21. The Pilgrims settled what is now Plymouth, Mass., after signing the Mayflower Compact. The *Mayflower* a 2-decker ship, probably 90 ft (27 m) long and about 180 tons (163 metric tons), has not survived, but an English-built replica, *Mayflower II*, sailed the Atlantic in 1957. It is now at Plymouth, Mass.

Mayflower *see:* Arbutus.

Mayflower Compact, agreement signed by 41 of the Pilgrims on Nov. 21, 1620. Having landed outside any civil jurisdiction and fearing that their group might split up, they undertook to form a "civil body politic," governed by majority rule, and to "frame just and equal laws." The compact became the basis of the government of the colony of Plymouth.
See also: Plymouth Colony.

Mayfly, common insect (order Ephemeroptera) of ponds and rivers. The larvae live in the water and emerge to molt as subadults. The subadults immediately molt again into full adults. The adults have 3 fine "tails" (as have the larvae), large transparent forewings, small or no hindwings, and weak legs. The mouthparts are also weak; adult mayflies do not feed during their short life, which may last no longer than an afternoon.

Mayo, U.S. family of surgeons. **William Worrall Mayo** (1819-1911) founded St. Mary's Hospital, Rochester, Minn. (1889), which was to become the famous Mayo Clinic. His sons, **William James Mayo** (1861-1939), and **Charles Horace Mayo** (1865-1939), traveled to many countries to discover new surgical techniques and to attract foreign surgeons to the clinic; in 1915 they set up the Mayo Foundation for Medical Education and Research. Charles's son, **Charles William Mayo** (1898-1968), was also a distinguished surgeon.

Mayo Clinic, one of the world's largest medical centers. It was founded in 1889 at Rochester, Minn., as a voluntary association of physicians. It grew from an emergency hospital set up by Dr. William W. Mayo (1861-1939) to help cyclone victims. The Clinic treats about 175,000 patients a year and is financed by the Mayo Foundation.

Mays, Willie (1931-), U.S. baseball player. An outfielder for the New York (later, San Francisco) Giants (1951-72), he hit 660 home runs in his career (third on the all time list) and was named the National League's most valuable player twice (1954, 65). He was inducted into the National Baseball Hall of Fame in 1979.

Ma Yuan (c.1160-1225), Chinese Southern Sung period artist, who created some of China's greatest landscape paintings in ink. A contemporary of the painter Xia Gui (also spelled Hsia Kuei), Ma Yuan was noted for his spare and dramatically asymmetrical compositions. His romantic landsape style influenced the Japanese ink painters Shbun (early 15th century) and Sessh, and the early masters of the Kan school during the Muromachi period (1338-1573).

Mazarin, Jules Cardinal (1602-61), Italian-born French politician and cardinal. Born Giulio Mazarini, he strengthened the French monarchy and by successful di-

Mayfly

plomacy increased France's influence abroad. After the deaths of Cardinal Richelieu (1642) and Louis XIII (1643), he became the trusted chief minister of the regent, Anne of Austria, and educator of her son, the future Louis XIV. His policy of centralized power and his imposition of taxes provoked the revolts known as the Fronde of the Parlement (1648-53), which he eventually crushed decisively. In foreign policy he gained favorable terms in the treaties that ended the Thirty Years War (1648) and the war with Spain (1659). He was patron of the arts.

Maze *see:* Labyrinth.

Mazepa, Ivan (1640?-1709), Cossack chief who vainly aided Charles XII of Sweden against Peter the Great, hoping to win independence for his native Ukraine. Byron's *Mazeppa* immortalizes a youthful incident in which he is said to have been tied to a wild horse by a jealous Polish nobleman.

Mazzei, Philip (1730-1816), Italian-born U.S. patriot. A physician and wine merchant, Mazzei came to the United States in 1773 and was befriended by Thomas Jefferson. In the years before the American Revolution, he wrote articles calling for independence that Jefferson translated into English. During the war he was sent on an intelligence-gathering mission to Italy. In 1796, while living in France, Mazzei received a letter from Jefferson that was critical of the Federalist government; it caused a political uproar on publication.

Mazzini, Giuseppe (1805-72), Italian patriot and a leading propagandist of the secret society, the Risorgimento, the nationalist involvement that achieved Italian unification. Exiled in 1831, he formed the Young Italy societies, and from France, Switzerland, and England promoted his ideal of a united, democratic Italy. In 1849 he became a leader of the short-lived republic of Rome, but was soon in exile again, continuing his revolutionary propaganda and organizing abortive uprisings. The actual unification of Italy, in which he took little part, fell short of his popular republican ideals.

Mbabane (pop. 38,600), town, administrative capital of Swaziland. Founded as a mining camp in a mountainous region of the former British colony, Mbabane is the center of a prosperous tin mining and agricultural region. Most of the city's residents are Swazi, a Bantu-speaking people of southern Africa, but English is also widely spoken there.

Mboya, Tom (1930-1969), Kenyan political leader. General secretary of the Kenya Federation of Labor (1953-63) and a member of the colonial legislative assembly (1957), he played a key role in securing Kenya's independence. Economics minister from 1964, he was established as a likely successor to Jomo Kenyatta. His assassination (1969) led to rioting and political tension.

McAdam, John Loudon (1756-1836), British engineer and surveyor. He developed a method of paving roads using layers of crushed stone, that revolutionized road building throughout the world. Macadamized roads built in the early 1800s lasted until the 20th century and were the forerunners of many highways still in use today.

McCarran, Patrick Anthony (1876-1954), U.S. Democratic senator from Nevada (1933-54). He sponsored 2 controversial measures, the McCarran-Wood Act (1950), which required the registration of communists, and the McCarran-Walter Act (1952), which tightened controls over aliens and immigrants.

McCarthy, Eugene Joseph (1916-), U.S. Democratic senator from Minnesota (1959-71). A consistent opponent of the Vietnam War, he campaigned for the presidential nomination in 1968 and attracted considerable support. Although he lost the nomination to Hubert Humphrey, his campaign helped to consolidate public opposition to the war.

McCarthy, Joseph Raymond (1908-57), U.S. Republican senator from Wisconsin (1947-57). The "McCarthy era" was born in the early 1950s as a result of his sensational investigations into alleged communist subversion of U.S. life. These investigations were first made (1950) in federal departments, then in the army and among prominent civilians. *McCarthyism* became a word for charges made without proof and accompanied by publicity. After the Army focused national publicity on his activities during the McCarthy hearings (1954), McCarthy was formally censured by fellow senators, and his influence steadily diminished.

McCarthy, Mary (1912-89), U.S. writer, best known for her satirical novel *The Group* (1963), about the lives of a generation of Vassar graduates. Her nonfiction works include *Memories of a Catholic Girlhood* (1957), *Vietnam* (1967), and a body of outstanding literary criticism.

McCarthyism, political movement named after Republican Senator Joseph R. McCarthy of Wisconsin that investigated suspected Communist activities in the United States in the early 1950s. Fearing a Communist takeover of the U.S. government, McCarthy conducted public investigations of suspected officials (and civilians). None of his suspicions were substantiated. He was "condemned" by the Senate in 1954, after having ruined many lives and careers. In contemporary terminology, McCarthyism denotes accusations of disloyalty to the United States or subversive activities based on insufficient evidence.

McCartney, (James) Paul (1942-), English singer, guitarist, and songwriter, member of the Beatles (1959-70). Most of the Beatles' songs were sung and written by McCartney and John Lennon. McCartney's contributions were predominantly ballads, including "Yesterday" (1965), "Hey Jude" (1969), and "Let It Be" (1970). McCartney and his wife, Linda Eastman McCartney, subsequently formed and performed with the rock band Wings (1971-81), recording such albums as *Band on the Run* (1973). His more recent solo albums include *Tug of War* (1982).
See also: Beatles, The.

McClellan, George Brinton (1826-85), controversial Union general in the U.S. Civil War. In July 1861 he was given command of the Army of the Potomac, and later that year the supreme command. His hesitation in taking the offensive and his failure to take Richmond led to his dismissal. After being reinstated, McClellan failed to follow up his success at the Battle of Antietam and was again dismissed in 1862. In 1864 he ran unsuccessfully for the presidency against Abraham Lincoln.
See also: Civil War, U.S.

McClintock, Barbara (1902-), U.S. geneticist. She won the 1983 Nobel Prize in physiology or medicine for her discovery in the 1940s of the mobility within the chromosome of genetic elements that had been believed to be stationary. McClintock found that certain genetic material is transferred unpredictably from generation to generation, and offered a means of understanding cell differentiation. Her work, considered a great contribution to DNA research, led to greater understanding of some human and animal diseases.
See also: Genetics.

Joseph R. McCarthy

McCloskey, John Cardinal (1810-85), U.S. Roman Catholic prelate. He became archbishop of New York (1864) and was created the first U.S. cardinal (1875). He was responsible for the completion of St. Patrick's Cathedral in New York City.

McClure, Samuel Sidney (1857-1949), editor and publisher who founded (1884) the first U.S. newspaper syndicate. *McClure's Magazine*, of which he was founder (1893) and editor, presented many famous writers to the U.S. public.

McClure, Sir Robert John Le Mesurier (1807-73), English arctic explorer and naval officer. On a search (1850-53) in the Arctic Archipelago for Sir John Franklin, he discovered McClure Strait and became the first to prove the existence of the Northwest Passage.
See also: Northwest Passage.

McCollum, Elmer Verner (1879-1967), U.S. biochemist and professor. While teaching at the Univ. of Wisconsin, he pioneered the study of nutrition and was responsible for assigning letters of the alphabet to the individual vitamins (1915). He also studied the role of other minerals in the diet and the effects of Vitamin D. His published works include *The Newer Knowledge of Nutrition* (1918) and *Foods, Nutrition and Health* (1933).
See also: Biochemistry; Vitamin.

John McEnroe

McCormack, John (1884-1945), Irish-American tenor. He began his operatic career in London, first appearing in the U.S. in 1909. He gained his greatest popularity as a concert singer.
See also: Opera.

McCormick, Cyrus Hall (1809-84), U.S. inventor and industrialist. He invented (1831) an early mechanical reaper (patented 1934) that contained innovations used commonly in harvesting machines. The first models appeared under license from 1841 onward.
See also: Reaper.

McCormick, Robert Rutherford (1880-1955), U.S. newspaper editor and publisher who became sole owner of the *Chicago Tribune* after World War I. Pursuing an extreme right-wing policy, it won the largest circulation of any paper in the Midwest.

McCoy, Elijah (1844?-1929), U.S. engineer and inventor. He developed an efficient system of reducing friction on industrial machinery through the invention of the lubricator cup, which fed a continuous supply of lubricants to the moving parts of machinery, thereby enabling factories to increase their productivity. The popular expression, "the real McCoy" originated when buyers of new machinery insisted that they contain real McCoy lubricators.

William McKinley

25th U.S. President	
Born:	Niles, Ohio; Jan. 29, 1843
Term:	Mar. 1897-Sept. 1901
Vice presidents:	Garret A. Hobart; Theodore Roosevelt
Political party:	Republican
Spouse:	Ida Saxton McKinley
Children:	2
Died:	Buffalo, N.Y.; Sept. 14, 1901

McCrae, John (1872-1918), Canadian physician and poet of World War I, famous for his poem "In Flanders Fields," which was written under fire. It was first published in the magazine *Punch* in Dec. 1915.

McCullers, Carson (1917-67), U.S. writer. She is best known for her novels portraying small-town life in the South, and particularly for her lonely, isolated characters, as in *The Heart Is a Lonely Hunter* (1940) and *Member of the Wedding* (1946; adapted by McCullers as a play, 1950). Her *Collected Stories* were published posthumously (1987).

McCulloch v. Maryland, case before the U.S. Supreme Court in 1819, in which Congress was ruled to have implied powers other than those specifically granted by the Constitution. The case involved the Baltimore branch of the Bank of the United States, which refused to pay a tax imposed by Maryland. The court ruled that the tax was unconstitutional because it interfered with Congress, which had the implied power to charter a bank, being responsible for the fiscal operations of the national government.

McEnroe, John (1959-), U.S. tennis player. Known for his powerful serve and speed, he won 4 U.S. Open singles titles (1979-81, 1984) and 3 Wimbledon singles titles (1981, 1983-84).

McGillivray, Alexander (1759?-93), Native American leader of the Creek tribe. During the American Revolution he sided with the British and helped protect Creek tribal lands from encroachment by colonial settlers. Between 1785 and 1787 he led the Creeks (backed by the Spanish) in wars against Georgia and Tennessee, and in 1790 he signed a treaty with the United States guaranteeing the Creeks sovereignty over certain lands they held.

McGovern, George Stanley (1922-), U.S. senator from South Dakota and the 1972 Democratic presidential candidate. A leading advocate of an end to the Vietnam War, he campaigned for a broad program of social and political reforms. He initially attracted substantial support from liberals, but encountered serious party divisions that hurt his campaign. Richard Nixon won with a record 61% of the popular vote. McGovern unsuccessfully sought his party's nomination again in 1984.

McGraw, John Joseph (1873-1934), U.S. professional baseball player and manager. A star third baseman for the American League's Baltimore Orioles, he became manager of the team in 1901. He then managed the New York Giants (1902-32), who won 10 league championships and 3 World Series.

McGuffey, William Holmes (1800-73), U.S. educator and clergyman. His series of 6 *Eclectic Readers* (1836-57) sold an estimated 122 million copies. Almost universally used in elementary schools in the Midwest and South, they had an immense influence on public education. McGuffey was also president of Ohio Univ. (1839-45).

McKay, Alexander (?-1811), early Canadian explorer and fur trader. He was a member of Alexander Mackenzie's first trans-Canadian expedition that reached the Pacific Coast in 1793. As a member of the North West Company (later Hudson's Bay Company), McKay agreed to help John Jacob Astor build Astoria, Ore. in 1810. A year later he brought his ship into the columbia River to begin work on the settlement but hostile Native Americans boarded it, killing everyone on board.

McKay, Claude (1890-1948), U.S. poet and novelist born in Jamaica. His was the first and most militant voice of the New York Negro movement in the 1920s. His works include poetry, *Harlem Shadows* (1922), and the novel *Home to Harlem* (1927).

McKay, Donald (1810-80), Canadian-born U.S. naval architect, master builder of clipper ships. His *Great Republic* (1853) at 4,555 tons (5,020 metric tons) was the biggest clipper ever built. The use of steam brought a decline in business that forced him to close his Boston shipyards in 1855.

McKean, Thomas (1734-1817), U.S. patriot. He as a signer of the Declaration of Independence and Delaware representative to the Continental Congress (1774-1783). He served as president of the Congress (1781), chief justice of Pennsylvania (1777-99), and governor of Pennsylvania (1799-1808). He also wrote most of the Delaware state constitution.

McKim, Charles Follen (1847-1909), U.S. architect, founder of the firm McKim, Mead, and White (1878) and of the American Academy in Rome. His best-known projects, such as the University Club in New York City (1900), are in a neoclassical style.

McKinley, William (1843-1901), 25th president of the United States. McKinley—last in a long line of presidents who had fought in the Civil War—led the U.S. during its war with Spain, and presided over a nation emerging from a period of isolation to become a world power.
Early life. McKinley attended Allegheny College at Meadville, Pa., but illness forced him to return home after a few months. He taught school until the Civil War broke out. McKinley, then 18, enlisted in the 23rd Ohio Volunteers. His bravery in the Battle of Antietam earned him a higher commission; by the war's end, he had reached the rank of brevet major. After studying law in Albany, N.Y., he was admitted to the bar in 1867 and set up a practice in Canton,

Ohio. In 1871, he married Ida Saxton; they had two children.
Political career. McKinley entered Republican party politics soon after moving to Canton. In 1876, he was elected to the U.S. House of Representatives, where he served, except for one term, until 1891. He sponsored the McKinley Tariff Act of 1890, which set record-high protective duties. The tariff's unpopularity contributed to his reelection defeat in 1890, but he was elected governor of Ohio in 1891 and 1893. In 1896, the Republicans nominated him for the presidency. McKinley was elected after a bitter campaign in which opponent William Jennings Bryan, the famous orator, portrayed McKinley and his running mate, Garret A. Hobart, as supporters of "rule of the rich."
President. In his administration's early years, McKinley had to cope with the nation's economic problems. By 1898, however, the depression that had lasted for five years was ending. As the severe economic and social problems of the 1880s and 1890s subsided, U.S. attention turned outward and foreign-affairs problems took center stage. Spanish outrages during a Cuban insurrection that had begun in 1895 aroused indignation in the U.S. war hysteria grew after the battleship U.S.S. *Maine* was blown up in Havana's harbor on Feb. 15, 1898. McKinley hoped to avoid war, but eventually yielded to public opinion and that of many Congress members and other high officials by asking Congress to authorize U.S. intervention in Cuba. On Apr. 24, two days after Congress authorized a U.S. blockade of Spanish ports, Spain declared war on the U.S.
The Spanish-American War, which lasted only 113 days, brought the U.S. into the arena of international politics and made it an imperial power. During the war, the U.S. annexed Hawaii; the following year, the U.S. demanded equal trade opportunities with China.
The war had brought on a period of booming prosperity, helping McKinley and running mate Theodore Roosevelt, who promised "a full dinner bucket" for four more years, to win the 1900 election.
Assassination. In 1901, McKinley took a national speaking tour to call for freer trade and an end to U.S. isolation. As he greeted a crowd in Buffalo, N.Y., he was shot by anarchist Leon Czolgosz. McKinley died eight days later.

McKissick, Floyd Bixler (1922-), African-American political leader. In the 1960s he was the national chairperson and director of the Congress of Racial Equality (CORE) and one of the leading advocates of Black Power. McKissick and other Black Power proponents urged African-Americans to take control over the destinies of their own communities and to foster a greater sense of pride in their social and cultural heritage.

McKuen, Rod (1933-), U.S. poet and songwriter. His poetry collections include *Lonesome Cities* (1968) and *In Someone's Shadow* (1969). He has performed and recorded many of his own songs, and has also written film scores.

McLoughlin, John (1784-1857), Canadian pioneer of the Oregon Territory. Directing (1824-46) the operations of the Hudson's Bay Company in the region of the Columbia River, McLoughlin was credited with achieving peace between Native American tribes and European-American settlers of the Columbia and Willamette river valleys. Often called the "father of Oregon," McLoughlin's efforts contributed to the formation of the Oregon Territory (1848) and the achievement of statehood (1859).
See also: Oregon.

McLuhan, Marshall (1911-80), Canadian professor of humanities and mass communications specialist. He is best known for his influential *Understanding Media* (1964). It contains the famous phrase, "the medium is the message"—that is, the content of communication is determined by its means, with the implication that modern mass communications technology is creating a "global village" and transforming our way of thinking and perceiving.
See also: Communication.

McNamara, Robert Strange (1916-), secretary of defense under presidents Kennedy and Johnson (1961-68), who played an important part in the shaping of U.S. defense policy, including Vietnam War policy. Before this he had been president of the Ford Motor Company, and in 1968 he became president of the World Bank, serving until 1981.

McPherson, Aimee Semple (1890-1944), U.S. evangelist, famed for her flamboyant preaching. She worked as a missionary in China, then returned to the United States to become an itinerant preacher and faith-healer. She opened the Angelus Temple (1923) and founded the International Church of Foursquare Gospel (1927), both in Los Angeles. She was involved in numerous legal actions, including a sensational one for fraud, of which she was acquitted.

McVeigh, Timoty James (1968-), the alledged bomber of the federal office building in Oklahoma City (April 19, 1995). Sentenced to death in 1997.

Mead, Margaret (1901-78), U.S. cultural anthropologist known for *Coming of Age in Samoa* (1928), *Growing Up in New Guinea* (1930), *the Mountain Arapesh* (3 vols., 1938-49), and *Male and Female* (1949), among other works. Her autobiography, *Blackberry Winter*, appeared in 1972. She was adjunct professor of anthropology at Columbia Univ. after 1954, and was associated with New York's American Museum of Natural History from 1926 until her death.
See also: Anthropology

Meade, George Gordon (1815-72), Union general of the U.S. Civil War. He performed with distinction in 1862 at the Seven Days Battles, Bull Run, and Antietam, and afterwards at Fredericksburg and Chancellorville. As commander of the Army of the Potomac, he won the Battle of Gettysburg. Criticized for not following up his victory, he kept his command under Ulysses S. Grant's direction.
See also: Civil War, U.S.

Meadowlark, common North American field bird of the family Icteridae, with a distinctive black V on its yellow underside. It is a relative of the blackbird and oriole. Also called a meadow starling, the meadowlark eats insects rather than grain and builds its nest on the ground. The eastern meadowlark, known for its whistling song, lives in moister areas than the western meadowlark.

Meany, George (1894-1980), U.S. labor leader, president (1955-79) of the American Federation of Labor and Congress of Industrial Organizations (AFL-CIO). He was president of the New York State Federation of Labor (1934) and secretary-treasurer (1939) and president (1952) of the AFL.

Meadowlark

Measles, common infectious disease usually seen in children and caused by a virus. It involves a characteristic sequence of fever, headache, and malaise, followed by conjunctivitis and rhinitis, and the development of a typical rash, with blotchy erythema (redness) affecting the skin of the face, trunk, and limbs. Complications can include pneumonia and encephalitis. Vaccination confers temporary immunity; one attack confers lifelong immunity.

Measuring worm, also known as inchworm or looper, hairless caterpillar, moth larvae found on every continent. Measuring worms move by extending their front end and holding on with their legs, then bringing up the rest of the body in a loop so that the rear end practically meets the front end. They move in this way because they have only 2 or 3 (rather than the usual 5) pairs of leglike structures on the back part of their bodies. Many measuring worms are difficult to detect when not moving, as they often resemble twigs and rest in twiglike positions.

Margaret Mead

The regal pomp of Lorenzo de Medici

Meat packing, industry that involves the butchering and processing of meat-producing animals for human consumption. Meat packing companies purchase large herds of cattle, sheep, and hogs from ranchers and farmers or from terminal markets. In the packing plants, the animals are slaughtered and cut up into their edible sections (dressed). The meat is treated to preserve freshness, frozen to keep it from being spoiled by bacteria, and shipped to consumer markets.

Mecca (Arabic: *Makka*; pop. 463,000), is the chief city of the Hejaz region of Saudi Arabia. It is the birthplace of the prophet Muhammad, the founder of Islam, and the most holy city of Islam. Only Muslims may enter the city. The courtyard of the great Haram mosque encloses the sacred shrine, the Kaaba, which Muslims face when they pray; nearby is the holy Zem-Zem well. Pilgrimage to Mecca, "haji," is a duty of all Muslims able to perform it; each year over a million pilgrims arrive. The economy of Mecca depends on the pilgrims.
See also: Islam; Saudi Arabia.

Mechanical engineering *see:* Engineering.

Mechanics, branch of applied mathematics that deals with the effects of forces on solids, liquids, and gases at rest or in motion. Dynamics studies the way in which forces produce motion; statics addresses the forces acting on a motionless body; kinematics deals with relationships among distance, time, velocity, and acceleration. Solid mechanics examines the motions of rigid bodies and deformable solid bodies and the causative forces. Continuum mechanics addresses deformable bodies, such as gases, liquids, and deformable solids.
See also: Aerodynamics; Hydraulics.

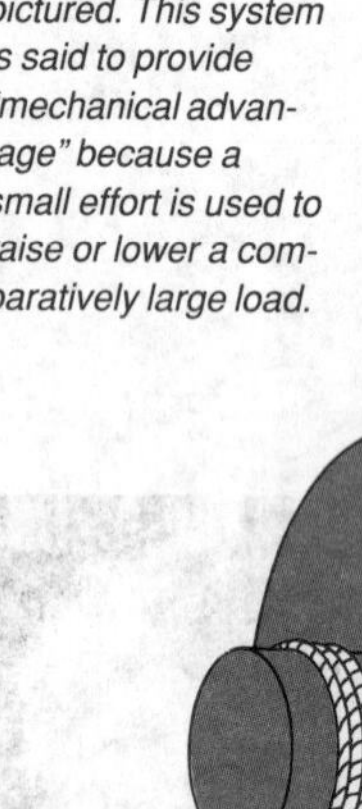

The principles of mechanics were used to design the system pictured. This system is said to provide "mechanical advantage" because a small effort is used to raise or lower a comparatively large load.

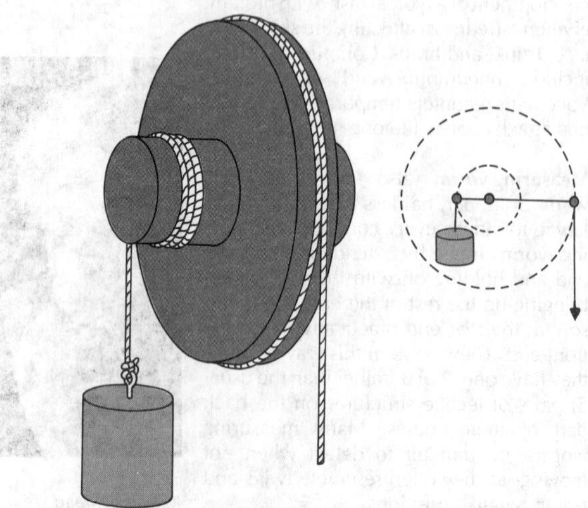

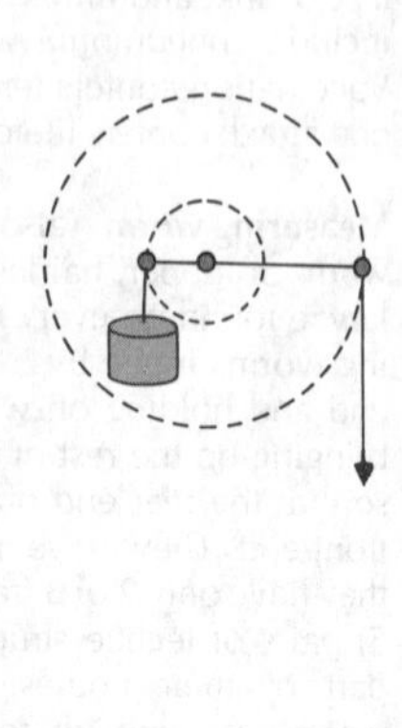

Mecklenburg, German state, renamed Mecklenburg-Western Pomerania upon Germany's reunification (1990). Primarily a farming region along Germany's Baltic coastal plain, Mecklenburg was ruled by powerful German princes and kings throughout the Middle Ages. It was divided many times into separate states, following wars during the 17th through the 19th centuries, and powerful landowners (Junkers) controlled vast estates from the mid-18th century through the end of World War II. Captured by the Communist army in 1945, Mecklenburg was an East German state until 1952, when it was divided into 3 districts.
See also: Germany.

Medal *see:* Decorations, medals and orders.

Medawar, Sir Peter Brian (1915-), Brazilian-born British zoologist who shared with Sir Macfarlane Burnet the 1960 Nobel Prize for physiology or medicine for their work on immunological tolerance. Inspired by Burnet's ideas, Medawar showed that if fetal mice were injected with cells from eventual donors, skin grafts made onto them later from those donors would "take," thus showing the possibility of acquired tolerance and hence, ultimately, organ transplants.
See also: Zoology.

Medea, in Greek mythology, sorceress and princess of Colchis. Through her magical powers she helped Jason obtain the Golden Fleece in Colchis where she was the daughter of King Aites. Returning with Jason to the Greek city of Iolkos where he claimed the throne, Medea conspired to kill King Pelias who had seized the throne from Jason's father. When Jason tried to divorce her, Medea had his bride-to-be killed and after plotting to kill the oldest son of the king of Athens, she was banished.
See also: Mythology.

Medellín (pop. 1,468,000), city in west-central Colombia. Medellín is the capital of Antioquia department and the hub of a rich mining and agricultural region. It was founded in 1675 near several gold mines and later became a textile, manufacturing, and coffee-processing center. Medellín also houses 3 universities and is a major educational center.

Medfly *see:* Mediterranean fruit fly.

Media, homeland of a nomadic people, the Medes, it was located in what is now northern Iran. Its history has been traced back to 836 B.C., when the Assyrians, under King Shalmaneser III, invaded Media in the first of many invasions. The Medes reached their peak under Cyaxares, who reigned from 625 to 585 B.C. His son, Astyages, the last Median king, was defeated by Cyrus the Great of Persia about 550 B.C. Media became a part of the Persian Empire.

Media, the plural form of "medium." The term is used to apply to communication systems, such as books, newspapers, radio, and television.
See also: Newspaper; Radio; Television.

Medicaid, U.S. government-financed system of medical aid to low-income people under 65. It was introduced in 1965 along with the Medicare legislation. The federal government pays from 50% to about 80% of the costs for anyone eligible, as determined by each state separately. To participate, a state must meet the standards of the federal government.

Medical Association, American *see:* American Medical Association.

Medicare, U.S. government-financed system of medical and hospital insurance for people aged 65 and over. It was set up in 1965 by legislation supported by President Lyndon B. Johnson. It was opposed by the American Medical Association, which objected on principle to possible government intervention, although the cost of private treatment had risen beyond the means of most older people. In 1972 Medicare was extended to cover disabled Social Security beneficiaries and persons of any age suffering from chronic kidney disease.

Medici, Italian family of bankers, princes, and patrons of the arts who controlled Florence almost continually from the 1420s to 1737 and provided cardinals, popes (Leo X, Clement VII, and Leo XI), and 2 queens of France. The foundations of the family's power were laid by **Giovanni di Bicci de'Medici** (1360-1429), who achieved wealth through banking and commerce. His elder son, **Cosimo de'Medici** (1389-1464), was effectively ruler of Florence from 1434 and was voted "Father of the Country" after his death. He founded the great Laurentian Library and patronized artists including Donatello and Lorenzo Ghiberti. His grandson **Lorenzo** (1449-92), called "the Magnificent," was Italy's most brilliant Renaissance prince. Himself a fine poet, he patronized Sandro Botticelli, Domenico Ghirlandaio, the young Michelangelo, and many other artists. Lorenzo helped make Florence a powerful and beautiful Italian state, and took over the state government. His son **Pietro** (1471-1503) was expelled from Florence (1494) by a popular rising led by Girolamo Savonarola. The family was restored in 1512; Pietro's son **Lorenzo** (1492-1519) ruled from 1513 under the guidance of his uncle **Giovanni** (1475-1521), who was Pope Leo X and a bountiful patron of the arts in Rome. The ruthless **Cosimo I** (1519-74) doubled Florentine territory and power and was made grand duke of Tuscany in 1569. **Catherine de Médicis** (1519-89) was the wife of Henry II and mother of 3 French kings. She virtually ruled France from 1559. **Marie de Médicis** (1573-1642), the wife of Henry IV, reigned after his death (1610) until her son, Louis XIII, became king. The later Medicis were less distinguished; the line died out with Gian Gastone (1671-1737).
See also: Catherine de' Medici; Clement VII; Leo X.

Medicine, the art and science of treating disease. Within the last 150 years medicine has become dominated by scientific principles. Prior to this, healing was mainly a matter of tradition and magic. The Greeks introduced anatomy and physiology and provided the Hippocratic oath, in use today. In the 17th century, William Harvey researched blood circulation and the heart; in the 18th century, Edward Jenner introduced vaccination; in the 19th century, Louis Pasteur proposed the germ theory and anesthesia made advances in surgery possible. Medicine in the 20th century uses new diagnostic techniques (x-rays, CAT scans, MRIs), organ transplants, a better understanding of nutrition and immunity, and new drugs, especially antibiotics.

Medicine, patent *see:* Patent medicine.

Medieval period *see:* Middle Ages.

Medill, Joseph (1823-99), Canadian-born U.S. editor and publisher of the *Chicago Tribune*, and a builder of the Republican Party. A strong emancipationist and supporter of Abraham Lincoln, he served at the Illinois Constitutional Convention of 1869 and as mayor of Chicago (1872-74).

Medina (pop. 198,200), holy Muslim city and place of pilgrimage in Hejaz, Saudi Arabia, 210 mi (338 km) north of Mecca. The prophet Muhammad came to Medina after his *hegira* (flight) from Mecca (A.D. 622), and the chief mosque contains his tomb. A walled city, Medina stands in a fertile oasis noted for its dates, grains, and vegetables.
See also: Muslims; Saudi Arabia.

Medina, Harold Raymond (1888-1990), U.S. jurist. A Columbia University law professor from 1915 to 1947. Medina was appointed a federal judge in 1947. Two years later he presided over the trial of 11 American Communist party leaders convicted of advocating the overthrow of the U.S. government by force. He stepped down from the bench in 1958.

Mediterranean fruit fly, or Medfly (*Ceratitis capitata*), pest of fruit in Africa, Australia, and the United States, attacking, in particular, peaches, apricots, and citrus fruits. The larvae destroy the fruits, and whole harvests may be lost. The maggots are capable of prodigious leaps of about 4 in (10 cm) high and over distances of 8 in (20 cm).

Mediterranean Sea, intercontinental sea between Europe, Asia, and Africa (over 965,000 sq mi—2,500,000 sq km). It opens into the Atlantic Ocean in the west through the Strait of Gibraltar, and into the Black Sea through the Dardanelles and Bosporus. The Suez Canal provides the Mediterranean Sea's link with the Red Sea and on to the Indian Ocean. Peninsular Italy, Sicily, Malta, and Pantelleria and Tunisia's Cape Bon mark the dividing narrows between the eastern and western basins. The many islands of the western basin include Sicily, Sardinia, Elba, Corsica and the Balearics. Crete, Cyprus, Rhodes, and the numerous Aegean islands are included in the eastern basin. Geologically the Mediterranean Sea is a relic of a sea that separated Eurasia from Africa about 200 million years ago, and was partially uplifted to form the Alps, South Europe, and the Atlas Mountains. The name (Latin, "middle [of the] land"), reflects the sea's central position and importance in the ancient world. Limited access from the Atlantic Ocean and confined entries to both the Black and Red seas have given the Mediterranean Sea great strategic importance throughout history.

Medusa, in Greek mythology one of three equally hideous-looking sisters (Gorgons). She and her sisters, Stheno and Euryale, had snakes growing from their heads in place of hair and fangs for teeth. Anyone looking directly at them turned to stone but Perseus slew Medusa by looking at a reflection of her as he cut off her head. Later he gave the head to Athena.
See also: Mythology.

Medusa *see:* Jellyfish.

Meeker, Ezra (1830-1928), U.S. author and explorer of the Oregon Trail. In 1852, Meeker and his family made an ox-cart journey on the Oregon Trail from Iowa to Portland, Ore. He made the return trip some years later in 1906 and once again by automobile in 1915. His books are *Ox-Team Days on the Oregon Trail* (1922) and *Kate Mulhal* (1926). Meeker was the founder of the Oregon Trail Association.
See also: Oregon Trail.

Meerkat, or suricate (*Suricata suricatta*), small, insect-eating mammal of the family Herpestidae, native to dry regions of southern Africa. The meerkat's slim body and long tail measure about 20 in (51 cm) long, and it weighs about 2 lb (900 gm). It has silvery brown fur with dark markings. Its sturdy hind legs allow it to stand upright to search for predatory birds. Meerkats live in burrows in colonies of up to 30 animals. The name "meerkat" is also sometimes applied to various mongooses.

Mehta, Zubin (1936-), Indian-born U.S. conductor who studied at the Vienna Academy of Music and later became musical director of the Montreal Symphony (1961-67), Los Angeles Philharmonic (1962-78), and New York Philharmonic (1978-91).

Meighen, Arthur (1874-1960), 2-term Canadian prime minister. Elected to the Canadian House of Commons in 1908, Meighen, a Conservative, held 3 Cabinet posts under Prime Minister Sir Robert Borden. Following Borden's retirement in 1920, Meighen took office on July 10. On Dec. 29, 1921, he was replaced by William Lyon Mackenzie King. He won a second term as prime minister in 1926, serving from June 29 to Sept. 25 and was replaced by King again.

Meiji (1852-1912), emperor of Japan (1867-1912); his given name was Mutsuhito. The long isolation of Japan under the shoguns ended in 1868 with the restoration of imperial power. Meiji guided the transformation of Japan from a feudal empire into a modern industrial nation with a central administration. The court was moved from Kyoto to Tokyo.

Mein Kampf (German, "My Struggle"), Adolf Hitler's book detailing his life and beliefs, published in 2 volumes (1925, 1927; English trans., 1933, 1939). The book, which advocates Germany's conquest of the world and expresses Hitler's views on the superiority of the German "master race" and the inferiority and evil of Jews, became the Nazi manifesto.
See also: Hitler, Adolf; Nazism.

Golda Meir

Meir, Golda (1898-1978), Israeli leader, prime minister of Israel (1969-74). Born Golda Mabovitch in Kiev, USSR, she was raised in the United States and emigrated to Palestine in 1921. She was a prominent figure in the establishment of the State of Israel (1948). Elected to the Knesset (parliament) in 1949, Meir became foreign min-

ister in 1956; in 1966 she was elected general secretary of the dominant Mapai party, later the Israel Labor Party (1968). In 1969 she succeeded Levi Eshkol as premier and formed a broad coalition government. During her time in office the Israelis fought off a 1973 Syrian-Egyptian surprise attack (the Yom Kippur War). In 1974 she resigned because of criticism of her lack of preparedness for that war.
See also: Israel.

Meitner, Lise (1878-1968), Austrian physicist who worked with Otto Hahn to discover protactinium (1917). Following the experiments of German physical chemists Hahn and Fritz Strassmann in bombarding uranium with neutrons, Meitner and her nephew, Otto Robert Frish (1904-), correctly interpreted the results as showing nuclear fission and predicted the chain reaction. This work contributed to the development of the atomic bomb and other uses of nuclear energy.
See also: Nuclear energy; Physics.

Mekong River, one of the chief rivers of the southeastern region of Asia, rising in the Tibetan highlands. It flows 2,600 mi (4,180 km) southward through the Yunnan province of China and Laos, along the Thailand border, and through Cambodia to its wide fertile delta in southern Vietnam, on the South China Sea. The lower 340 mi (547 km) can accommodate medium-sized vessels. Phnom-Penh is an important port. The Mekong River's lower valley produces much of the world's rice.

The Mekong River

Melaka (pop. 88,100), Malaysian port city. Located on the strategic Strait of Malacca, Melaka (formerly Malacca) is the capital of the state of the same name. In the 15th century, it was one of the most important ports in Southeast Asia and was captured by Portugal (1511), the Netherlands (1641), and Great Britain (1795). Melaka remained in British hands until Malaysia was granted independence (1957) as the Federation of Malaya.
See also: Malaysia.

Melanchthon, Philipp (1497-1560), German scholar and humanist, second to Luther in initiating and leading the Protestant Reformation in Germany. His *Loci communes rerum theologicarum* (1521), a systematic statement of Lutheran beliefs, was the first great Protestant work on religious doctrine; and his *Augsburg Confession* (1530) was one of the principal statements of faith in the Lutheran Church.
See also: Reformation.

Melanesia *see:* Pacific Islands.

Melanin *see:* Skin.

Melbourne (pop. 2,645,000), second-largest city in Australia and capital of Victoria, on the Yarra River. Founded by settlers in 1835 and named (1837) in honor of the British prime minister Lord Melbourne, the city is now one of the nation's chief ports; it ranks with Sydney as a major industrial center. Manufactures include textiles, leather goods, ships, automobiles, and aircraft; oil refineries also have been built. Melbourne was the seat of the Australian federal government (1901-27).
See also: Australia.

Mellon, Andrew William (1855-1937), U.S. financier, industrialist, U.S. treasury secretary (1921-31), and U.S. ambassador to Britain (1931-32). After taking control of his father's banking firm and founding other banks, he increased his holdings in such companies as oil, coal, locomotives, hydroelectricity, bridge construction, insurance, and steel. He served under 3 presidents, and reduced the national debt by some $9 billion. A multimillionaire himself, he founded the Mellon Institute of Industrial Research. His vast art collection formed the basis (1937) of the National Gallery of Art in Washington, D.C.

Mellon Foundation, Andrew W., philanthropic organization that grants funds to educational, scientific, public affairs and cultural institutions. Named after Andrew W. Mellon, former secretary of the treasury (1921-32), the foundation was started by Mellon's daughter and son in 1969. It is one of the 10 wealthiest foundations in the United States.
See also: Mellon, Andrew William.

Melodrama, originally a term used to refer to a passage in opera spoken over an orchestral accompaniment but more usually used to describe the sentimental drama of the 19th century in which characters were either good or bad. Melodramas were often based on romantic novels or bloodthirsty crimes. Thrills and narrow escapes played an important part in the plot.

Melon, fruit of *Cucumis melo*, a plant of the gourd family that grows wild in Africa and Asia. It is now widely cultivated in the United States, where the climate is hot and dry. The 2 main kinds of melon are the *watermelon* and the *muskmelon*, which includes *honeydews, casabas,* and *Persian melons.* The *cantaloupe* spoils rapidly, whereas the others will last for months, becoming softer as they ripen. The *tsamma melon,* a watermelon, supplies vital water to the Bush people of the Kalahari Desert. The round melons can grow to 1 ft (30 cm) across and vary in color.

Melos *see:* Milos.

Meltdown *see:* Nuclear reactor.

Melville, Herman (1819-91), U.S. writer. His reputation rests mainly on the masterpiece *Moby-Dick* (1851), and the short novel *Billy Budd, Foretopman,* published posthumously (1924). Melville's whaling and other voyages provided material for several of his earlier, popular books. *Typee* (1846), his first, was based on his adventures and capture by cannibals after jumping ship in the Marquesas islands. *Moby-Dick,* a deeply symbolic work, combines allegory with adventure. Too profound and complex for its audience, this great novel was not successful; subsequent books did not recapture Melville's former popularity. Only in the 1930s did his talent receive full recognition.

Melville Island, Canadian island in the Arctic Ocean. Covering an area of 16,369 sq mi (42,396 sq km), Melville Island is one of the Parry Islands, discovered in 1819 by the British explorer Sir William Parry. The straits and seas surrounding the island are frozen most of the year; herds of musk-oxen inhabit the island, which is without human habitation. Melville Island is administered by the District of Franklin, Northwest Territories.

Memel *see:* Klaipeda.

Memling, Hans (1430-94), Flemish painter famous for his portraits and religious works, including the paneled *Shrine of St. Ursula* (1489). The German-born Memling (or Memlinc) worked in Bruges, Belgium, and was probably a pupil of Rogier van der Weyden.

Memorial Day, or Decoration Day, U.S. holiday honoring the dead of all wars, observed on the last Mon. in May. Memorial Day originated in the South after the Civil War when the graves of both Confederate and Union soldiers were decorated.

Memphis, capital of the Old Kingdom of ancient Egypt until c.2200 B.C. Probably founded (c.3100 B.C.) by Menes, the first king of a united Upper and Lower Egypt, the city stood on the West bank of the Nile, about 15 mi (24 km) south of modern Cairo. Excavations have revealed the temple of Ptah, god of the city, and the 2 massive statues of Ramses II; cemeteries and pyramids also remain.

Memphis (pop. 981,747), largest city and chief river port of Tennessee, seat of Shelby County, on the high east banks bluffs of the Mississippi River below the mouth of the Wolf River. It was founded in 1819 and

incorporated in 1826. Memphis is a leading market for cotton, hardwood lumber and livestock, as well as meat packing center and a transportation hub. Its manufactures include cottonseed products, textiles, farm machinery, paper, and drugs. It has foundries and rice mills. The city, noted for its fine churches, also has many educational institutions, including the medical divisions of the University of Tennessee. Memphis is the site of Beale Street, made famous by the composer W.C. Handy, and of Elvis Presley's estate, Graceland, a popular tourist attraction.
See also: Tennessee.

Menander (342-c.291 B.C.), leading Greek writer of New comedy. Of over 100 plays, only *Dyscolos* (The Grouch) survives complete; adaptations of his other plays, by the Roman playwrights Plautus and Terence, influenced 17th-century comedy. His plots are based on love affairs, and he is noted for his elegant style and debt characterization.

Mencius (Mengke; 370-290 B.C.), Chinese philosopher. A follower of Confucius, he was influential in the development of Confucianism. He held that humanity is naturally good and that the principles of true moral conduct are inborn. He was a champion of the ordinary people and exhorted rulers to treat their subjects well.
See also: Confucianism.

Mencken, H(enry) L(ouis) (1880-1956), U.S. journalist and author, caustic critic of U.S. society and literature. He wrote for the *Baltimore Sun* and founded and edited the *American Mercury* (1924). His collected essays appeared in *Prejudices* (6 vols., 1919-27). Among other works, he also wrote an authoritative study, *The American Language* (1919).

Mendel, Gregor Johann (1822-84), Austrian botanist and Augustinian monk who laid the foundations of the science of genetics. His results with experiments on dwarf pea plants provided a mechanism justifying Charles Darwin's theory of evolution by natural selection; however, contemporary lack of interest and his unsuccessful experiments with the hawkweeds discouraged him from carrying this work further. Only in 1900, when scientists found his published results, was the importance of his work realized.
See also: Genetics; Heredity.

Mendeleev, Dmitri Ivanovich (1834-1907), Russian chemist who formulated (1869) the Periodic Law, stating that the properties of elements vary periodically with increasing atomic weight. This work enabled him to draw up the Periodic Table.
See also: Chemistry; Periodic table.

Mendelevium, chemical element, symbol Md; for physical constants see Periodic Table. An artificial radioactive element, mendelevium was discovered by Albert Ghiorso and his co-workers in 1955. Einsteinium-253 was bombarded with helium ions in the 60-inch cyclotron in Berkeley. Mendelevium-256, having a half-life of 76 minutes, was produced. That is the longest-lived isotope of the element known. It is a metallic element and a member of the actinide series. Fourteen radioactive isotopes of mendelevium have been produced.

Mendel's laws *see:* Genetics; Mendel, Gregor Johann.

Mendelssohn, Felix (1809-47), German Romantic composer. He wrote his concert overture to *A Midsummer Night's Dream* at age 17. Other works include his *Hebrides Overture* (also known as "Fingal's Cave," 1830-32), *Scotch* (1842) and *Italian* (1833) symphonies, a violin concerto, chamber music, and the oratorio *Elijah.* He was also a celebrated conductor, notably of the Leipzig Gewandhaus orchestra, and he revived interest in the music of Johann Sebastian Bach.

Felix Mendelssohn at age 12

Mendelssohn, Moses (1729-1786), German-Jewish philosopher and scholar, a leading figure of the Enlightenment in Prussia, and a promoter of Jewish assimilation into German culture. He wrote *Phädon* (1767) and *Jerusalem* (1783).
See also: Age of Reason; Philosophy.

Mengele, Josef (1911-79?), Nazi war criminal. A doctor who conducted often inhuman medical experiments on inmates of Auschwitz, a Nazi concentration camp. Mengele is believed responsible for 400,000 deaths there. Captured by the Allies at the end of World War II, he was inadvertently released and fled to South America. Charged with war crimes by West Germany (1959), Mengele eluded capture for 20 years before dying in Brazil. Remains believed to be his were unearthed in a Brazilian cemetery in 1985.
See also: Auschwitz; Nazism.

Menhaden, marine fish (*Brevoortia tyrannus*) of the herring family. Inhabiting the Atlantic coastal waters from Nova Scotia to Brazil, menhaden measure 12-18 in (30-46 cm) and weigh up to 1 lb (0.5 kg). They are edible but are most often processed for their oil or as livestock feed and fertilizer.

Meningitis (cerebrospinal meningitis), inflammation of the menninges caused by bacteria or viruses. Bacterial meningitis is of abrupt onset, with headache, vomiting, fever, neck stiffness, and sensitivity to light. Early and appropriate antibiotic treatment is essential as permanent damage may occur, especially in children. Viral meningitis is a milder illness with similar signs; only symptomatic measures are required. Tuberculous meningitis is an insidious chronic type that responds slowly to antituberculous drugs. Some fungi, unusual bacteria and syphilis may also cause varieties of meningitis. Diagnosis is made through an examination of the cerebrospinal fluid via a spinal tap.

Menninger, U.S. family of psychiatrists. **Charles Frederick Menninger** (1862-1955), along with his sons **Karl Augustus** (1893-1990) and **William Claire** (1899-1966) established the clinic (1920) and foundation (1941) that bears their name in Topeka, Kans. Karl and William served as officials for the Menninger Foundation which specializes in research, treatment of mentally ill patients, and the training of psychiatric professionals. Published works include Karl's *The Human Mind* (1930), *Man Against Himself* (1938), and *The Crime of Punishment* (1968) and Williams's *Psychiatry in a Troubled World* (1948).
See also: Psychiatry.

Mennonites, Protestant sect originating among the Anabaptists of Zurich, Switzerland. They became particularly influential in the Netherlands, and are named for the Dutch reformer Menno Simons. They base their faith solely on the Bible, believe in separation of Church and State, pacifism, and baptism only for adults who renounce sin. They are known for the strict simplicity of their life and worship. The Amish Church is a well-known, conservative division of the Mennonites in the United States.
See also: Anabaptism.

The Dutch reformer Menno Simons, for whom the Mennonites are named

Menominee, Native American tribe of the Algonquian linguistic group. For more than 5,000 years they lived in upper Michigan and Wisconsin, along the western shore of Green Bay, gathering wild rice (*Menominee* means *wild rice people*). In 1854 they were settled on a reservation on the Wolf and Oconto rivers in Wisconsin, now a county, where their descendants still live and work in the lumber business. In 1953, through the policy of termination, the U.S. government abolished the Menominee reservation, but reestablished it in 1975.

Menotti, Gian Carlo (1911-), Italian-born U.S. composer of operas and founder (1958) of the Festival of Two Worlds at

Spoleto, Italy. His works include *The Medium* (1946) and the television opera *Amahl and the Night Visitors* (1951). *The Consul* (1950) and *The Saint of Bleecker Street* (1954) won Pulitzer prizes for music.

Mensheviks, name for the position of the minority group in the Russian Social Democratic Workers' Party-opposition to the Bolsheviks, the majority group led by Vladimir Ilyich Lenin. Unlike Lenin, the Menshevik theoretician Georgi Plekhanov favored mass membership and believed a spell of bourgeois rule must precede communism. Led by L. Martov (Yuly Osiporich Tsederbaum), the Mensheviks emerged in 1903, backed Aleksandr Feodorovich Kerensky's short-lived government (1917), and opposed the Bolshevik seizure of power. By 1921 they had been eliminated.
See also: Bolsheviks; Russian Revolution.

Menstruation, in women of reproductive age, specifically the monthly loss of blood (period), representing shedding of womb endometrium; in general, the whole monthly cycle of hormonal, structural, and functional changes, punctuated by menstrual blood loss. After each period, the endometrium (womb-lining) starts to proliferate and thicken under the influence of gonadotrophins (follicle-stimulating hormone) and estrogens. In midcycle an egg is released from an ovarian follicle (ovulation). The endometrium is prepared for implantation of a fertilized egg. If the egg is not fertilized, pregnancy does not ensue; then blood-vessel changes that occur lead to the shedding of the endometrium and some blood, sometimes with pain or colic. The cycle then restarts. Cyclic patterns are established at puberty (menarche) and end in middle life (age 45-60) at the menopause, the "change of life." Disorders of menstruation include heavy, irregular, or missed periods; bleeding between periods or after the menopause; and excessively painful periods. These disorders are studied in gynecology.
See also: Reproduction.

Yehudi Menuhin

Mental age *see:* Intelligence quotient.

Mental illness, any of several diseases of the mind manifesting itself as disordered thoughts or feelings, or behavior which is apparently irrational or which deviates from socially and culturally accepted norms. The modern concept of mental illness rests on 3 foundations. The oldest of these consists of norms of feeling, development, and behavior defined by society and prevailing in a culture at a particular time. One example of an important area bearing on an individual's mental health that is strongly defined by custom and belief is sexuality. Our definition of mental illness also proceeds from rationalism, the idea that a healthy mind is predominantly a logical mind. And we rely upon science, particularly neurophysiology and neurochemistry, for research into the organic causes of mental illness. Though it is widely accepted that many, if not most, mental illnesses are caused or can be treated organically, there are many mental disorders that have no known organic cause but whose symptoms may be masked or alleviated by drugs. Organic disorders include delirium, which may be accompanied by illusions or hallucinations, and dementia, characterized by lapses of one or more of the mental faculties. Delirium can be caused by alcoholism or certain illnesses; dementia often accompanies aging. Schizophrenia, a severe form of psychosis, has recently been associated with chemical imbalances in the brain and there are indications it may be hereditary. Affective disorders, including mania, depression, and manic-depression, are profound disturbances of mood which can be managed to some degree with antidepressants or tranquilizers.
Other forms of mental illness include a variety of anxieties such as obsessive-compulsive behavior or phobias (agoraphobia, or fear of public places, and claustrophobia, or fear of closed places, are examples). There are also dissociative disorders in which a person may suffer a change or loss of identity. These can manifest as one of several kinds of amnesia or as multiple personality disorder, in which a person has more than 1 personality with now one, then the other, being dominant. The underlying causes of these conditions are as yet unknown.
There are also certain kinds of mental illness unique to a particular age group. Children, for example, may be hyperactive or they may be afflicted with autism, a disorder in which the child appears remote, expressionless, and unresponsive. Alzheimer's, a disease of the brain cells that leads to impairment of the mental faculties, attacks people in their 40s and older.
The principal health professionals concerned with diagnosing and treating the mentally ill are psychiatrists and psychologists. Psychiatrists are medical doctors; psychologists are usually Ph.D.s in psychology. Treatment for the mentally ill may include drug therapy, various forms of psychotherapy, or periods of institutionalization. In many cases, a combination of therapies is used. For some patients, psychoanalysis is found useful, while others respond best to behavior modification. In extreme cases, electroshock treatments and even psychosurgery may be necessary, though both are highly controversial forms of treatment which now raise fundamental moral, ethical, and legal questions.
For the most part, society's treatment of the mentally ill has not been a bright page in human history. Mental disorders have been seen as curses and the work of malevolent spirits and the mentally ill, as often as not, were shunned, tormented, or persecuted. Among the Greeks, Hippocrates made a major advance in the 5th century B.C. by offering a rational explanation for mental illness as being due to imbalances in certain bodily fluids. But it would be another 2,000 years before humane and rational treatment of the mentally ill became the accepted standard. It was in the 1700s that Philippe Pinel, a French doctor, and the British merchant William Tuke, introduced modern reforms into mental institutions. Their innovations were taken up by Benjamin Rush in America, and reform of the country's mental institutions was hastened by the writings of Dorothea Dix. Reform was also advanced by the work of Clifford W. Beers, a former mental patient, whose book, *A Mind That Found Itself*, helped improve public understanding of the problems of the mentally ill. In 1909, he founded the National Committee for Mental Hygiene, which later became the National Association for Mental Health.
Simultaneously with institutional reform came medical advances and new forms of treatment and therapy. Toward the end of the 19th century, Emil Kraepelin and Eugen Bleuler classified most mental disorders. Early in the 20th century, Sigmund Freud introduced his psychoanalytic method and his ideas on the structure and development of the mind. Research into various forms of psychotherapy, the development of behaviorist theories, research into the physiology and chemistry of the brain and the nervous system, and the development of psychotropic drugs, have all had a significant effect upon the care and treatment of the mentally ill. But they are still, in many ways, feared, ignored, or discriminated against, and problems of care, treatment, and integration of the mentally ill into society are as urgent as the need for continued medical research.

Mental retardation, low intellectual capacity, arising not from mental illness but from impairment of the normal development of the brain and nervous system. Causes include genetic defect (as in Down's syndrome); infection of the embryo or fetus (hydrocephalus or inherited metabolic defects), injury at birth, including cerebral hemorrhage and fetal anoxia (lack of oxygen), and disease in infancy (for example, encephalitis). Retardation is initially recognized by slowness to develop normal patterns of social and learning behavior; it is confirmed through intelligence measurements. Although mental retardation cannot be cured, it is most important that affected children receive adequate social contact and education, for their development is generally retarded, not arrested. Special schooling may help them achieve a degree of learning and social competence. Proper prenatal, perinatal, and postnatal care may help prevent some cases of mental retardation.

Menuhin, Yehudi (1916-), U.S. violinist and conductor. He made his concert debut in San Francisco at age 7, played for Allied forces in World War II, and later performed to raise cash for war victims. He has revived forgotten masterpieces, promoted interest in Eastern music, and toured internationally with the Menuhin Festival Orchestra. In 1963 he opened the Yehudi Menuhin School of Music for musically gifted children in Suffolk, England.

Mephistopheles, in medieval legend, the devil to whom Faust sold his soul. He is primarily a literary creation and appears in

the famous plays by Christopher Marlowe and Johann Goethe.
See also: Devil.

Mercantilism, economic system prevailing in 16th- to 18th-century western Europe that reflected the increased importance of the merchant. Mercantilism was based on the concepts that a country's wealth was founded on its supply of gold and silver, and that in a world of limited resources one nation could prosper only at the expense of another. Mercantilists favored tariffs in order to secure a favorable international trade balance and thereby maintain reserves of previous metals. Their protectionism was succeeded by the free trade arguments of the French physiocrats and later the policy of laissez faire. Today, mercantilism sometimes refers to policies that protect domestic businesses from foreign competition.
See also: Colonialism.

Mercator, Gerardus (Gerhard Kremer; 1512-94), geographer and cartographer best known for his world map. With this map Mercator introduced a new map projection, or method of transferring features of the earth's surface onto a flat sheet of paper. On a map using the so-called Mercator projection, the lines of latitude, which are equidistant on a globe, are drawn with increasing separation as their distance from the equator increases. While this exaggerates the sizes of areas as they move away from the equator, it preserves their shapes. Mercator's method is still in use today by navigators.
See also: Geography.

Merchandising *see:* Marketing.

Merchant marine, commercial shipping operations of a maritime nation and the personnel who operate the ships. Privately-owned cargo ships make up the largest percentage of most nations' fleets, but state-owned vessels are operated in some countries, particularly those of the Communist bloc. Gross tonnage, the total cargo capacity of all ships of a nation's registry, is the figure used to measure a merchant marine's size.

Merchant Marine Academy *see:* United States Merchant Marine Academy.

Mercury, chemical element, symbol Hg; for physical constants see Periodic Table. Mercury was known to the ancient Chinese and Hindus. It is a silvery-white, heavy, liquid metal. Compared with other metals, it is a poor conductor of heat and a fair conductor of electricity. Mercury is the only common metal that is liquid at ordinary temperatures. It easily forms alloys with many other metals. Both the element and most of its compounds are poisonous. Mercury and its compounds are used in electrolytic cells, dentistry, thermometers, barometers, diffusion pumps, electrical switches, mercury-vapor lamps, paint, batteries, explosive detonators, and in medicine.

A map of Flanders (1540) by Gerardus Mercator

Mercury, in Roman mythology, god of commerce and wealth; associated with Hermes in Greek mythology. Known as the messenger of the gods, he delivered his messages with great speed because he wore winged sandals. Mercury was the son of Jupiter, and Maia, a goddess. He was depicted as both crafty and deceptive.

Mercury, in astronomy, planet closest to the sun, with a mean solar distance of 36 million mi (57.9 million km). Its eccentric elliptical orbit brings it within 28.5 million mi (46 million km) of the sun at perihelion (point nearest to the sun) and takes it 43.5 million mi (70 million km) from the sun at aphelion (point farthest from the sun). Its diameter is 3,031 mi (4,878 km), and its mass about 0.054 that of the earth. Mercury revolves around the sun in just under 88 days—faster than any other planet—and rotates on its axis in about 59 days. Albert Einstein's successful prediction that Mercury's orbit would advance by 43 in (109 cm) per century is usually regarded as a confirmation of the general theory of relativity. Night surface temperature on this dry and airless planet is believed to be about –315°F (–°193C), midday equatorial temperature over 648°F (342°C). No plant life is believed to exist. Mercury also has no known satellites. The U.S. *Mariner* space probe revealed (1974-75) that Mercury has a moonlike, heavily cratered surface and a slight magnetic field.
See also: Planet; Solar system.

Mercury program *see:* Space exploration.

Meredith, George (1828-1909), English novelist and poet. His novels include the tragicomic *The Ordeal of Richard Feverel* (1859), *The Egoist* (1879), and *Diana of the Crossways* (1885). The sonnet sequence *Modern Love* (1862) grew out of the breakdown of his marriage. His writing offers piercing character and social analyses.

Merganser, fish-eating duck of the family Anatidae, found in many parts of the world. It is also called the sawbill because of its long serrated bill. Both sexes have a large head crest—the male dark, and the female brown. Mergansers nest in tree holes. They include the American, red-breasted, and hooded mergansers, all of which can be found in North America.

On this ancient vase, Mercury holds an oil lamp, giving light to Jupiter, who is about to climb a ladder to his beloved. In his left hand, Mercury holds his traditional serpent's rod.

Mergenthaler, Ottmar (1854-99), German-American inventor of the Linotype machine, an automatic typesetting device. Patented in 1884 and produced in 1886, the Linotype made the printing process more efficient and cost-effective, thus producing widespread changes in publishing.
See also: Linotype.

Mérida (pop. 250,000), founded in 1542, now the largest city on the Yucatan Peninsula in Mexico. Mérida is surrounded by farmland and is located near the the ancient Mayan sites of Chichén Itzá and Uxmal. The city contains a magnificent cathedral and examples of early Spanish architecture.

Mérimée, Prosper (1803-70), French author, historian, archeologist, and linguist. He is best known for his novelettes (long short stories such as "Mateo Falcone" (1829), "Colomba" (1840), and the romance "Carmen" (1845), which was the source of Georges Bizet's opera. Mérimée also wrote essays and translations in the 1850s intended to interest the French in Russia and its literature.

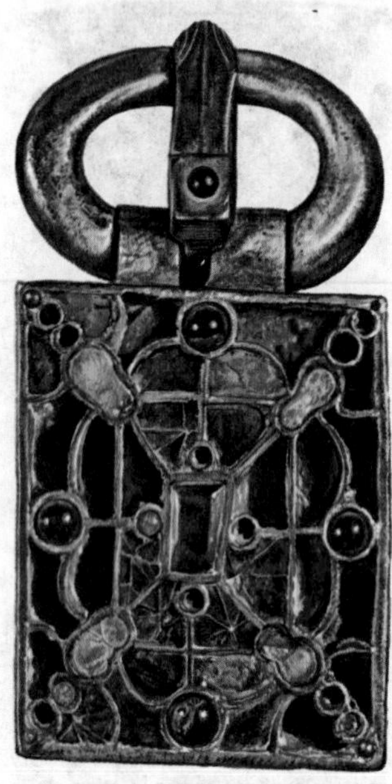

Top: Merovingian bronze ornament (6th century A.D.).
Left: Merovingian arms and armor (helmet, sword, axe, javelin)(6th century A.D.)
Right: Merovingian buckle (6th century A.D.)

Merit badge *see:* Boy Scouts.

Merlin *see:* Round Table.

Merovingian, dynasty of Frankish kings (A.D. 428-751) who governed Gaul. They were named for the 5th-century king Merovech; his grandson Clovis I first united much of France. The kingdom was later partitioned, but enlarged and reunited (A.D. 613) under Clotaire II. The Merovingians governed through the remnants of the old Roman administration and established Catholic Christianity. After Dagobert I in the 7th century, the kings became known as *rois-fainéants* (do-nothings), and power passed to the mayors of the palace, nominally high officials. The last of these, Pepin the Short, deposed the last Merovingian, Childeric III, and founded the Carolingian dynasty.
See also: Carolingian; Gaul.

Merrill, Robert (1919-), internationally acclaimed New York-born baritone opera singer. Known for his powerful voice and technical proficiency, he has performed extensively worldwide, notably with the Metropolitan Opera and on Broadway. Among his famous roles are Renato in Verdi's *Un Ballo in Maschera,* Amonasro in *Aïda,* and Escomillo in Bizet's *Carmen.* He wrote an autobiograhy, *Once More from the Beginning* (1965), and a novel, *The Divas* (1978).

Merrimack *see:* Monitor and Merrimack.

Merrimack River, stream of New England, flows 110 mi (177 km) from the White Mountains of New Hampshire through northeastern Massachusetts to the Atlantic Ocean. The river and its 6 waterfalls provided water power for the first U.S. textile factories; it now is harnessed to produce hydroelectricity. *Merrimack* means "swift water."

Mersey, River, major trade waterway rising in the Pennine Hills of northwest England and entering the Irish Sea. About 70 mi (110 km) long, the river has underwater tunnels for railroads and automotive traffic. Its many docks and basins, serving the cities of Liverpool and Birkenhead, have contributed to the development of Birkenhead as an important market for cattle. A canal connects the river to the city of Manchester.

Merton, Robert King (1910-), U.S. sociologist. His seminal work on the sociology of science produced *Science, Technology and Society in Seventeenth Century England* (1938), expressing the view that English Puritanism helped lead to the modern scientific age. He wrote an analysis of the function of deviant behavior in society (*Social Theory and Social Structure,* 1949), and was instrumental in developing quantitative (statistical) research methods in sociology.
See also: Sociology.

Merton, Thomas (1915-68), U.S. religious writer of poetry, meditative works and an autobiography, *The Seven Storey Mountain* (1948). A convert to Roman Catholicism, he became a Trappist monk (1941) and was later ordained a priest. The French-born Merton also wrote *The Waters of Siloe* (1949) and *The Sign of Jonas* (1953) about the Trappist life.

Merv, ruined city in the Turkmen Soviet Socialist Republic, situated near the modern city of Mary. Since ancient times an oasis in the desert, Merv was once a prosperous city and center of Islamic learning. Destroyed by the Mongols in 1221, it was rebuilt in the 15th century and occupied by the Russians in 1884. Farming is its main occupation.
See also: Turkmenistan.

Mesa (Spanish, "table"), used in the western and southwestern United States for a steep-sided, flat-topped hill or isolated tableland, such as Mesa Encantada (Enchanted Mesa) in New Mexico and Mesa Verde (Green Mesa) in Colorado. Often red or yellow, mesas were long ago part of much larger plateaus of softer rock that were gradually worn down. The mesas escaped erosion because they were capped by hard rock layers protecting the softer strata below.

Mesabi Range, hills in northeastern Minnesota, northwest of Lake Superior from Babbitt to Grand Rapids; highest point is 2,000 ft (610 m). The range is famous for its iron ore deposits, which lie near the surface and have been mined since the 1890s. *Mesabi* means "hidden giant."

Mescaline, nonaddictive hallucinogen derived from the Mexican peyote cactus (*Lophophora williamsii*). Because peyote is bitter-tasting and causes a burning sensation and itching of mucous membranes, the "buttons" are brewed with tea or chewed while drinking beverages. Pure mescaline is more potent than peyote powder, which may be mixed with gelatine or injected intravenously in decoctions. About 10 minutes to 3 hours after taking mescaline, and lasting about 12 hours, one experiences nausea, dizziness, sweating, headache, palpitations, heat or chilliness, and cramps in chest, neck, or abdomen. Effects include multicolored visions; hypersensitivity to sound; disturbed senses of touch, taste, smell, space, and time; and a distorted concept of one's own body. Euphoria and glee are followed by anxiety (sometimes depression and hostility), loss of concentration and control over speech and action, and possibly general but temporary schizophrenic psychosis. U.S. law prohibits the use of mescaline except by members of the Native American Church.
See also: Drug; Drug abuse.

Meshed (pop. 1,120,000), capital city of Khorsn province, northeastern Iran. Meshed, center of the northern wool trade, is also a religious center, visited by over 100,000 pilgrims annually. It contains the tombs of the caliph Hrn ar-Rashd (A.D. 809) and his son-in-law, religious leader Alar-Rid.
See also: Iran.

Mesmer, Franz, or **Friedrich Anton** (1734-1815), Austrian physician who theorized (1775) that a person may transmit universal forces to others through "animal magnetism." Controversy over his unusual techniques and theories, involving the beneficial effects of a magnet upon an occult force within the subject, forced Mesmer to flee Austria (1778) for Paris. Interest in mesmerism led the British surgeon James Braid, the French neurologist Jean Charcot, and the Viennese psychologist Sigmund Freud to develop the ancient practice of hypnotism for the study of psychology.
See also: Hypnosis.

Mesolithic Period *see:* Stone Age.

Meson, subatomic particle of a family called hadrons, which act via a strong nuclear force that holds together an atomic nucleus. Mesons are unstable particles that decay; they carry a positive, negative, or neutral electric charge. They consist of a quark and an antiquark. Mesons include pions (or pi-mesons), upsilon particles, k-mesons (or kaons), and psi particles (or J particles). British physicist Cecil Powell discovered the meson (1947) in cosmic radiation.
See also: Hadron; Quark.

Mesopotamia (Greek, "between the rivers"), ancient region between the Tigris and Euphrates rivers in southwestern Asia. Called "the cradle of civilizations" Mesopotamia mainly lies in Iraq, between the Armenian and Kurdish Mountains in the north and the Persian Gulf in the south. The north is mainly grassy, rolling plateau; the south is a sandy plain leading to marshes. Since ancient times the rivers have been used to irrigate the area; however, the ancient systems degenerated under Mongol invasion and Ottoman rule and were not replaced until the 20th century. Neolithic farming peoples settled Mesopotamia by 6000 B.C. By 3000 B.C. the Sumerians, who created the first system of writing (cuneiform), had developed a civilization of independent city-states in the south. From c.3000-625 B.C. Mesopotamia was dominated successively by Sumer, Akkad, the Sumerian dynasty of Ur, the empires of Babylonia and Assyria, and Chaldea. In 539 B.C. the Persian Empire absorbed Mesopotamia; in 331 B.C. it was conquered by Alexander the Great. It subsequently came under Roman, Byzantine, and Arab rule. The Abbasid caliphs made Baghdad their capital in 762, but prosperity collapsed with the Mongol invasion of 1289. After Ottoman rule (1638-1918), Mesopotamia was largely incorporated into Iraq. Today it is generally barren, but contains rich oil fields.

Mesosphere, layer of the atmosphere immediately above the stratosphere, marked by a temperature maximum (about 10°X/50°Φ) βετωεεν αλτιτυδεσ οφ αβουτ 30 μι–50 μι (58–80 κμ).
See also: Atmosphere.

Mesozoic Era *see:* Dinosaur; Reptile.

Mesquite, or screw bean, tough shrub or tree (genus *Prosopis*) that grows in the stony deserts of the southwestern United States and similar regions. The roots may penetrate as much as 70 ft (21 m) into the ground. It bears spines and small olive-colored leaflets. A member of the pea family, mesquite has seeds that develop into edible pods that can be used to make bread and a fermented beverage. The pods, wood, and gum from the stem have commercial value as food, fuel, and lumber.

Messenia, region in the southern peninsula of Greece and seat of the ancient Mycenaean civilization. Under Spartan domination for hundreds of years, the Messenians were finally freed in the 4th century B.C. by Theben leader Epaminondas. Messenia is noted for its Frankish and Turkish castles, and for its rich farmland.
See also: Mycenae.

Messiaen, Olivier (1908-), French composer, organist, teacher, and theorist. Much of his music, such as *The Ascension* (1935), was influenced by Roman Catholic mysticism. Others are based on Oriental music, such as the *Turangalila* symphony (1949), or on birdsong, such as the *Catalog of Birds* (1959). He influenced many modern composers, among them Pierre Boulez of France and Karlheinz Stockhausen of Germany.

Messiah (Hebrew, "anointed one"), according to Israelite prophets, especially Isaiah, the ruler whom God would send to restore Israel and begin a glorious age of peace and righteousness. He would be a descendant of King David. Christians recognize Jesus of Nazareth as the Messiah (or Christ); his role as "suffering servant" was alien to Jewish hopes of a political deliverer. The concept of a forthcoming divine redeemer is common to many religions.
See also: Religion.

Messier, Charles (1730-1817), French astronomer and compiler of an extensive catalog of celestial sources of light that are not stars. Among these are galaxies, nebulae, and star clusters. In attempting to distinguish between nebulae and comets, he discovered 21 comets and predicted the return of Halley's Comet in 1758-59.
See also: Astronomy.

Messina (pop. 255,900), city on Sicily's northeast coast, on the Strait of Messina. First mentioned in history as an ancient Sicilian colony (c.730 B.C.) it was occupied by the Greeks in the 700s B.C. and became a flourishing Greek colony. Throughout history it has been fought over and survived many rulers. Earthquakes in 1783 and 1908 almost destroyed Messina, which also sustained great damage during World War II. A gateway to Sicily, its principal exports are fruits, wine, olive oil, chemicals, pharmaceuticals, and medicinal products.
See also: Sicily.

Metabolism, sum total of all chemical reactions that occur in a living organism. It can be subdivided into *anabolism*, which describes reactions that build up more complex substances from smaller ones, and *catabolism*, which describes reactions that break down complex substances into simpler ones. Anabolic reactions require energy, while catabolic reactions liberate energy.
Metabolic reactions are set off by enzymes in a highly integrated and finely controlled manner so that there is no overproduction or underutilization of the energy required to maintain life. All this energy is ultimately derived from sunlight by the photosynthesis in plants, and most organisms use the products of photosynthesis either directly or indirectly.

Metal, element that has high specific gravity; high opacity and reflectivity to light (giving a characteristic luster when polished); ability to be hammered into thin sheets and drawn into wires (i.e., is malleable and ductile); and is a good conductor of heat and electricity, its electrical conductivity decreasing with temperature. Roughly 75% of the chemical elements are metals, but not all of them possess all the typical metallic properties. Most are found as ores and in the pure state are crystalline solids (mercury, liquid at room temperature, being a notable exception), their atoms readily losing electrons to become positive ions. Alloys are easily formed because of the nonspecific nondirectional nature of the metallic bond.

Metallurgy, the science and technology of extracting metals from ores, the methods of refining, purifying, and preparing them for use, and the study of the structure and physical properties of metals and alloys. A few unreactive metals such as silver and gold are found native (uncombined), but most metals occur naturally as minerals (i.e., in chemical combination with nonmetallic elements). *Hydrometallurgy* uses chemical reactions in aqueous solutions to extract metal from ore. *Electrometallurgy* uses electricity for firing a furnace or electrolytically reducing a metallic compound to a metal. *Pyrometallurgy* covers roasting, smelting, and other high temperature chemical reactions.

Detail of a Mesopotamian stele (2250 B.C.) depicting the King Naram-Sin

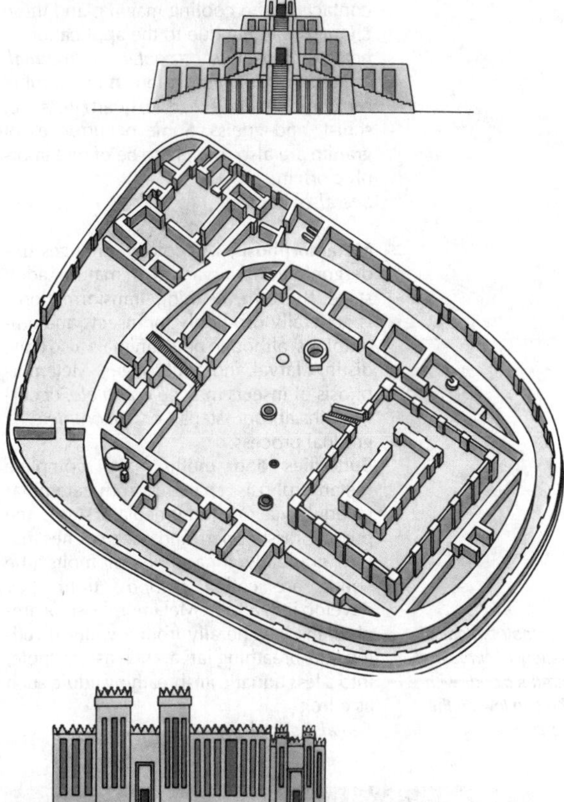

Three examples of Mesopotamian temples: The Ziggurat at Ur-Nammu (top) is characterized by its square shape and ramps, The Temple Oval at Khafaje (middle) by its interior walls, and the Ishtar Temple of Tukulti-Ninurta at Ashur (bottom) its small size.

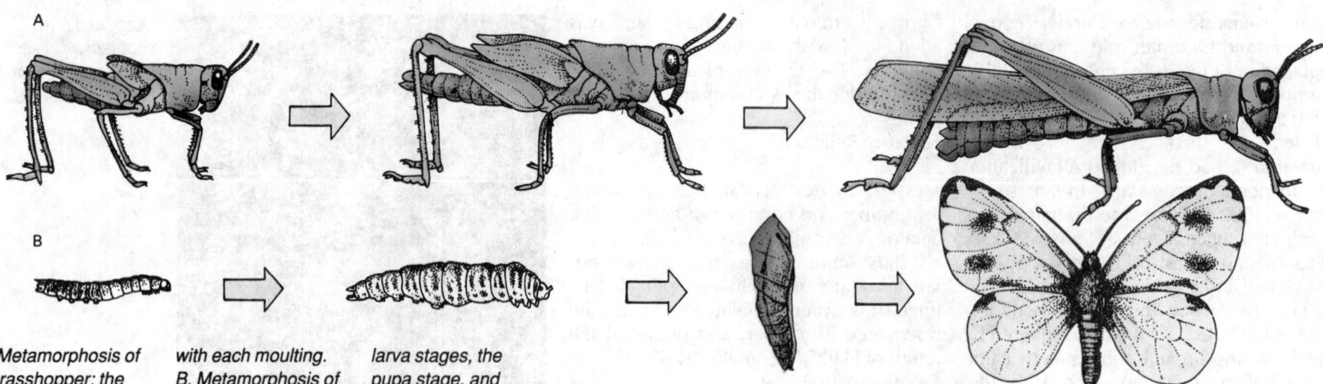

A. Metamorphosis of a grasshopper: the wing pad elongates with each moulting. B. Metamorphosis of a butterfly: the two larva stages, the pupa stage, and adult stage.

Metamorphic rock, one of the 3 main classes of rocks of the earth's crust—the class that has undergone change owing to heat, pressure, or chemical action. In plate tectonic theory the collision of lithospheric plates leads to widespread *regional metamorphism.* Igneous intrusion leads to changes in the rocks close to the borders or contacts of the cooling magma, and these changes, largely due to the application of heat, constitute *contact (thermal) metamorphism.* Common metamorphic rock types include marble, quartzite, slate, schist, and gneiss. Some occurrences of granite are also thought to be of metamorphic origin.
See also: Rock.

Metamorphosis, in zoology, changes undergone from larvae to a mature adult stage. The term, meaning "transformation," is generally used only for insects and amphibians, although other animals also have distinct larval and adult stages. Metamorphosis of insects may be *complete*, occurring in abrupt steps, or *incomplete*, a gradual process.
Butterflies and moths have complete metamorphosis, changing from caterpillar to adult via one intermediate stage, the pupa. Grasshoppers and cockroaches mature gradually in a series of molts (the young are called *nymphs*) until they develop into adults. Metamorphosis of amphibians is generally from a water-dwelling, gill-breathing larva, such as a tadpole, into a less aquatic air-breathing adult, such as a frog.
See also: Zoology.

The meteorological beauty of cirrus and stratus clouds with the sun low on the horizon

Metaphysical poets, early 17th-century English lyric poets whose style relied on the metaphysical conceit, an elaborate metaphorical image. Most famous among them is John Donne; others include Andrew Marvell, George Herbert, Richard Crashaw, Henry Vaughan, and Thomas Carew. The Metaphysical poets (a term first used by Samuel Johnson in 1744) extended the range of lyric poetry by writing about death, decay, immortality, and faith. They declined in popularity after about 1660, but their complex intellectual content and rich exploration of feeling was a major influence on 20th-century poetry.

Metaphysics, branch of philosophy that addresses the fundamentals of existence or reality, such as the existence and nature of God, immortality of the soul, meaning of evil, the problem of freedom and determinism, and relationship of mind and body. Metaphysical systems have included Aristotelian scholasticism and the 17th-century rationalistic systems of Descartes, Spinoza, and Leibniz. Metaphysical thinking was criticized in the 18th century by Immanuel Kant, who claimed that traditional metaphysics, while raising morally necessary questions, sought to go beyond the limits of human knowledge. In the 20th century, the concerns of metaphysics were rejected as being meaningless by the logical positivists.
See also: Philosophy.

Metaxas, Ionannis (1871-1941), Greek general and from 1936 ultraroyalist premier and dictator of Greece. He made important social and economic reforms. He tried to maintain Greek neutrality in World War II, but after successfully resisting the Italian invasion in 1940 joined the Allied powers.
See also: Greece.

Metazoan, in zoology, multicellular animal, member of the group Metazoa, distinguished from single-celled protozoans. With increase in the number of cells comes differentiation of function of cells, tissues, and organs. Many zoologists divide the Metazoa group into sponges (Parazoa) and all other multicelled animals (Eumetazoa).

Metchnikoff, Élie (1845-1916), Russian biologist who shared with Paul Ehrlich the 1908 Nobel Prize for physiology or medicine for his discovery of phagocytes (in humans, called leukocytes) and their role in defending the body from, for example, bacteria.
See also: Biology.

Meteor, small speck of material from space, about the size of a grain of sand. Meteors become visible as they burn up in the earth's atmosphere. Friction with the air causes them to glow and vaporize, resembling a swift streak of light (*shooting star* or *falling star*). When the earth crosses the orbit of a comet, whole swarms of meteors, called *meteor showers*, can be seen burning up in the atmosphere. A *meteorite* is a meteor that reaches the earth's surface before completely burning up in the atmosphere. An estimated 1,000 tons of meteoric material lands on the earth each day

Meteorology, study of the atmosphere and its phenomena, weather, and climate. Based on atmospheric physics, meteorology is mainly applied in weather forecasting and control. The rain gauge and wind vane were known in ancient times. The other basic instruments—anemometer, barometer, hygrometer, and thermometer—were invented by 1790; however, simultaneous observations over a wide area were impracticable until the development of the telegraph. Since World War I, observations of the upper atmosphere have been made using airplanes, balloons, and radiosonde, and since World War II, using radar, rockets, and artificial satellites. Observed phenomena include clouds, precipitation and humidity, wind and air pressure, air temperature, storms, cyclones, air masses, and fronts.
See also: Atmosphere.

Meter, basic unit of length in the metric system. One meter is equal to 39.37 in. and to 1.1 yd.
See also: Metric system.

Methadone, synthetic narcotic used extensively to treat heroin addicts. Methadone causes less severe and dangerous withdrawal symptoms than other narcotic drugs, although it is also addictive. It is also used as an analgesic, particularly in terminally ill patients, and sometimes in very small doses as a cough suppressant.

Methamphetamine, generic name of a powerful drug that is a derivate of and similar to amphetamine. Also known as "speed," methamphetamine enables a user to work and talk for long periods. Legally obtainable only with a doctor's prescription, methamphetamine can be hazardous if misused. Withdrawal symptoms may occur when use is stopped.
See also: Amphetamine.

Methane (CH_4), colorless, odorless gas; the simplest alkane. It is produced by decomposing organic matter in sewage and in marshes (hence the name *marsh gas*), and is the "firedamp" of coal mines. Nontoxic but highly flammable, methane when mixed with air, oxygen, or chlorine is explosive. It is the chief constituent of natural gas, occurs in coal gas and water gas, and is produced in petroleum refining. Methane is used as a fuel, for making carbon-black, and for chemical synthesis.

Methanol (CH_3OH), also called methyl alcohol or wood alcohol, type of alcohol with many industrial uses. Methanol is clear, colorless, flammable, and poisonous. Ways of lowering its manufacturing costs and enlarging its use as an alternate fuel are being sought.

Methodists, doctrine and polity of Protestant churches that originated in the 18th-century evangelical revival led by John and Charles Wesley. The name Methodist was first used in 1729 for members of the "Holy Club" of Oxford University, led by the Wesleys, who lived "by rule and method." Influenced by the Moravian Church, Methodism began as an evangelical movement in 1738 when the Wesleys and George Whitefield began preaching. Banned from most Anglican pulpits, they preached in the open air and drew vast crowds. After Wesley's death in 1791, Methodist societies formally separated from the Church of England and became the Wesleyan Methodist Church. The American Methodist movement was established after 1771 by Francis Asbury and Thomas Coke. Methodist polity in Britain is in effect Presbyterian; in the United States it is Episcopal. Methodism traditionally stresses conversion, holiness, and social welfare.
See also: Protestantism; Wesley, John.

Methuselah, oldest person in the Bible. According to the Bible (Gen. 5.25-27) he lived to the age of 969. He was the grandfather of Noah. The term "old as Methuselah" is a popular expression denoting an old person.
See also: Bible.

Methyl alcohol *see:* Methanol.

Methylbenzene *see:* Toluene.

Metre *see:* Meter; Metric system.

Metric system, decimal system of measurement, first adopted in France during the Revolution (1790s), called the Système International d'Unités, or SI. This simple system is used to measure length and distance, surface, volume and capacity, weight and mass, time, and temperature. The modern version of the metric system currently in use worldwide includes 7 base units: meter (length or distance), kilogram (mass), second (time), ampère (electricity),degrees (temperature, Celsius or Kelvin), candela (light), and mole (chemical substance).

Metropolitan Museum of Art, largest and most comprehensive art museum in the United States, founded in 1870 in New York City. Its collections include art, pottery, jewelry, and sculpture from ancient Egypt, Greece, Rome, Babylonia, and Assyria; Eastern paintings, sculptures, and artifacts; American art, sculpture, and period rooms; African art; and modern art, photography, and industrial design. The Uris Center hosts educational activities. Medieval art is housed in the Cloisters, located in Fort Tryon Park. It features parts of European medieval buildings, outdoor gardens, and medieval art, such as tapestries, ivories, and stained glass.

Metternich (Clemens Wenzel Nepomuk Lothar von Metternich; 1773-1859), Austrian diplomat. After a diplomatic career in Saxony, Prussia, and France he became Austrian foreign minister (1809-48). He gradually dissociated Austria from France and organized an alliance of Austria, Russia, and Prussia against Napoleon. However, at the Congress of Vienna (1814-15) he reestablished a system of power whereby Russia and Prussia were balanced by the combined power of Austria, France, and England. Appointed state chancellor in 1821, his authority declined after 1826, and he was overthrown in 1848. The period 1815-48 is often called the Age of Metternich.
See also: Austria; Vienna, Congress of.

Metz (pop. 118,500), city in northeastern France on the Moselle River, a center for iron and coal mining. Of pre-Roman origin, it became a bishopric and capital of the Frankish kingdom of Austrasia. France annexed it in 1552, and Germany held it from 1871 to 1918.
See also: France.

Meuse River, rises in the Langres Plateau, France, and flows north for about 580 mi (933 km) across Belgium and the Netherlands, where it is named *Maas,* into the North Sea. It is an important thoroughfare and line of defense for France and Belgium.

Mexicali (pop. 361,000), city in Mexico founded in 1903. Mexicali is the capital and second largest city of the Mexican state of Baja California Norte. The name is a combination of the words "Mexico" and "California." Mexicali is a popular tourist attraction that offers beautiful architecture, handicrafts, and exciting sporting events like rodeos and bullfights.
See also: Mexico.

The city of Dinant on the Meuse River

Mexican Americans *see:* Hispanic Americans

Mexican hairless, dog that derives its name because it has no coat of hair. It typically weighs about 12 lb (5 kg) and is pinkish in color. The dog was brought to the New World from China.

Mexican turnip *see:* Jicama.

Mexican War (1846-48), conflict between Mexico and the United States that resulted in the defeat of Mexico and America's acquisition of territory that became California, Nevada, Utah, most of New Mexico and Arizona, and parts of Colorado and Wyoming. The war took place against a background of expansionist sentiment (Manifest Destiny) in the United States, which held that it was destined to become a continental power and the dominant nation of the Western Hemisphere.
Causes of the war. In 1835, when the region comprising Texas, then under control of Mexico, revolted and declared its independence, Mexico warned the United States that it would break off diplomatic relations if Texas were admitted to the union. President James K. Polk, elected in 1844, favored expansionism and backed the annexation of Texas. When Texas was accepted into the union in 1845, Mexico broke relations. The matter could have been negotiated peacefully except that other issues, notably the boundary dispute between Texas and Mexico, stymied agreement. Mexico put the boundary at the Nueces River while Texas claimed it was the Rio Grande farther to the south. In addition, American citizens claimed damages from the Mexican government for losses sustained in Mexico's war of independence from Spain, which ended in 1821. Also, U.S. expansionists had designs on the vast California territory, then under Mexican rule but which had experienced an influx of English-speaking people. Polk sent John Slidell to offer Mexico a solution whereby the United States would pay Mexico $25 million and assume all American claims against it if Mexico, in turn, would

accept the Rio Grande boundary and agree to sell the New Mexico and California regions to the United States. When Mexico declined to deal on these terms, Polk resorted to force.

Outbreak of the war. In April 1846, General Zachary Taylor was ordered to advance his 3,000 troops from the Neuces to the Rio Grande. Mexico saw this as an invasion, and a slight engagement of forces occurred—excuse enough for Polk, on May 13th, to get a declaration of war on Mexico. Even before that reached Taylor, he had won the battles of Palo Alto and Resaca de la Palma, forcing the Mexicans across the Rio Grande.

Course of the war. U.S. strategy involved a 3-pronged attack on Mexico: an invasion of New Mexico and California, a naval blockade of both the Gulf of Mexico and California, and a major thrust from the north. The first 2 objectives were quickly attained. General Stephen W. Kearny, with about 1,700 troops, took New Mexico in August 1846, then moved on to California where, in January 1847, forces under Kearny and Commodore Robert F. Stockton won the Battle of San Gabriel, completing the conquest of California. Taylor took Monterrey in September 1846, but Mexico still refused to negotiate. Polk sent General Winfield Scott to land an army at Veracruz on Mexico's east coast, and to menace Mexico City. Many of Taylor's best troops were transferred to the Veracruz campaign, leaving him vulnerable when challenged by a large Mexican force led by General Antonio López de Santa Ana. In February 1847, Taylor only narrowly won the hard-fought battle of Buena Vista. Scott took Veracruz in March and drove toward Mexico City. In April, his troops defeated Santa Ana at the mountain stronghold of Cerro Gordo; and in August, near Mexico City, after hard fighting they defeated Mexican forces at the battles of Contereras and Churubusco. A 2-week armistice ensued, but when negotiations broke down, fighting resumed. Moving on Mexico City, Scott took the strong points of Casa Mata and Molino del Rey and stormed the fortress of Chapultepec. On September 14, 1847, U.S. troops entered Mexico City, ending the war.

Outcome of the war. By the Treaty of Guadalupe Hidalgo (February 1848), Mexico ceded to the United States two-fifths of Mexican territory (nearly all of present-day Arizona, California, Colorado, Nevada, New Mexico, and Utah)—more than 500,000 sq mi. The United States agreed to pay Mexico $15 million and to assume all outstanding claims of American citizens against Mexico. The war deeply divided the American people, not least because some feared an extension of slavery into the new territories. The Compromise of 1850 made California a free state but allowed the people of the other territories to decide whether they should be slave or free states. Bitter disputes followed, 12 years later contributing to the chain of events that led to the American Civil War.

Mexico, the United Mexican States, a federal republic occupying the southernmost portion of the North American continent. Mexico is bounded by the United States to the north, Guatemala and Belize to the south, the Caribbean Sea and the Gulf of Mexico on the east, and the Pacific Ocean on the west.

Land and climate. Mexico is nearly 1,200 mi/1,930 km long with an area of 761,530 sq mi/1,972,544 sq km. Two mountain ranges run most of the length of the country from northwest to southeast, the Sierra Madre Occidental along the Pacific coast and the Sierra Madre Oriental along the Atlantic coast. Between the two ranges lies

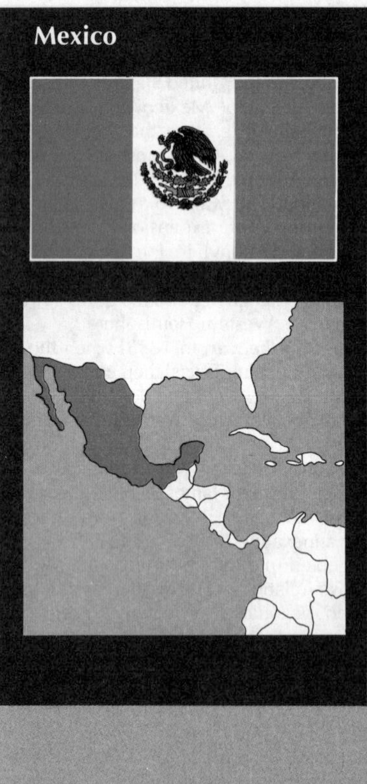

General information	
Capital:	Mexico City
Area:	756,066 sq mi (1,958,201 sq km)
Population:	88,335,000
Official language:	Spanish
Monetary unit:	1 peso = 100 centavos
Main cities:	Mexico City, Guadalajara, Monterrey
Government	
Form:	federal republic
Independent:	1821
Head of state:	President (elected every 6 years)
Head of government:	President
Legislature:	two legislative houses (Senate and Chamber of Deputies)
Executive:	President and Cabinet
Judiciary:	highest court is the Supreme Court of Justice
Political division:	31 states, 1 federal district
National economy	
Gross national product:	U.S. $151,870,000,000
Per capita income:	U.S. $1,820
Agriculture:	cotton, rice, corn, sugar cane, sorghum, wheat, oranges, tomatoes, coffee
Livestock:	cattle, pigs, goats
Fisheries:	1,419,000 metric tons
Mining:	silver, lead, zinc, iron, crude petroleum, gold
Industries:	petroleum products, machinery and transport equipment, food and beverages, chemical products, printed and published materials, textiles, tourism
Main exports:	crude petroleum, metallic products, machinery, and equipment, chemical products
Transportation:	16,341 mi (26,299 km) of railroads, 146,290 mi (235,431 km) of roads, 32 international airports
Trading partners:	U.S., Japan, Germany, France, Canada
People	
Urban:	69%
Ethnic composition:	mestizo 60%, Native American 29%, European 9%
Birth rate:	30 per 1,000 population
Death rate:	6 per 1,000 population
Infant mortality:	42 per 1,000 live births
Life expectancy:	male 68 years, female 74 years

Tzotzil of Chamula, in the Mexican state Chiapas.

The mountain city of Guanajuato, Mexico, is noted for its architecture.

the great central plateau rising 3,000 to 4,000 ft/914 to 1219 m in the north to 8,000 ft/2,438 m in the south. Mexico City, the capital, is situated near the southern end of the plateau at an elevation of about 7,400 ft/2,256 m.

Mexico is a land of dramatic contrasts. Its mountain ranges include the extinct volcanoes Popocatépetl (17,888 ft/5,452 m), Ixtacihuatl (17,343 ft/5,286 m), and Orizaba (18,406 ft/5,610 m). Its high plateau gives way to semi-tropical coastal regions. To the northwest lies Baja California, mountainous desert, and to the southeast the low limestone plateau of the Yucatan which includes tropical forests in the south. As a result, Mexico's climate varies considerably from the mountains to the desert, from the temperate plateau to the tropical lowlands. In all, less than 15% of the land surface is cultivable and most of it is on the central plateau.

People. The majority of Mexicans are mestizos, a mixture of native Americans and Spanish, but nearly one-tenth of the population remains pure native American and many of Mexico's native Americans speak only their native languages. About 10% of the population is of pure Spanish descent. Spanish is the official language and the people are overwhelmingly Roman Catholic.

Economy. Despite considerable industrialization since World War II, agriculture remains the major employer in the Mexican economy with more than 25% of the work force. The chief subsistence crops are corn and beans. The main commercial crops are wheat, corn, beans, cotton, coffee, sugarcane, sisal, and citrus fruits. The country also has valuable forests and fisheries which contribute to its economy. Mexico is rich in minerals and exports silver, zinc, lead, manganese, and sulfur. Abundant reserves of iron ore and uranium await development. Huge petroleum reserves, perhaps the second largest in the world, were discovered in the mid 1970s. Major industries include iron and steel, textiles, chemicals, electric goods, ceramics, paper, footwear, and processed foods. Mexico is plagued by inflation, government debt, and, more recently, a severe drop in world oil prices. Its economic problems are compounded by unemployment and illiteracy.

History. Prehistoric remains indicate that Mexico was inhabited as early as 10,000 B.C. Between A.D. 300 and 800, four classical native American civilizations developed in Mexico including the Maya of the Yucatán Peninsula. By the 15th century the Aztecs established the last Indian civilization in Mexico with its capital at Tenochtitlán, the site of present day Mexico City. It was this empire, under Montezuma, which was conquered by the Spanish under Hernán Cortés in 1521 thereby ushering the Spanish dominion. The Spanish consolidated their rule, exploiting the labor and mineral wealth of the colony they named New Spain. The colony was governed by a line of 62 viceroys appointed by the Spanish throne until independence in 1821. At the same time, the Roman Catholic church pursued a thorough policy of converting the Indians to Christianity and acquired considerable power. In September 1810, Father Miguel Hidalgo raised a rebellion against Spain which was subsequently crushed. another priest, José María Morelos, took up the struggle in 1813, but he too was defeated. Finally, backed by conservative elements seeking independence from a more liberal Spain, the country achieved independence in 1821 under Augustín de Iturbide. Emperor Augustín I was deposed in 1823 by Antonio Lopes de Santa Anna who dominated the turbulent politics of the new federal republic until 1855. During that period, Mexico waged a costly war with the U.S., the Mexican-American War (1846-48), which led to the loss of Texas and Mexico's considerable northwest territories in the U.S.

In 1855 Benito Pablo Juarez overthrew Santa Anna and introduced a more liberal constitution. Civil war between liberals and conservatives followed. In the ensuing turmoil, the French invaded and Napoleon III installed Maximilian of Austria as emperor in 1864. He was overthrown and executed in 1867. From 1876 to 1911 Mexico was governed by Gen. Porfirio Díaz, who brought a measure of stability and economic growth to the country. But his oligarchic regime generated deep and widespread resentment. Pancho Villa, Emiliano Zapata, and Francisco Madero raised rebellions which led to the downfall of Díaz in 1911. In 1917 Venustiano Carranza established control and promulgated a new liberal constitution. President Alvaro Obregon (1920-24) began a program of land redistribution and education and carried on a struggle with the Roman Catholic church which was not settled until 1929 when the church was granted autonomy in religious matters only. In 1929 Plutarco Elías Calles established the Institutional Revolutionary Party (PRI) which has effectively governed Mexico ever since. President Lázaro Cárdenas continued educational reform and nationalized some industries.

Since World War II, Mexico has been politically relatively moderate and stable, concentrating primarily on economic development. Despite progress, significant signs of strain and resistance were apparent under the presidencies of Luis Echeverria and his successor José Lopez Portillo. Mexico's economy suffered in the 1970s, due in part to the worldwide oil glut. Miguel de la Madrid Hurtado was elected president in 1982, promising new programs to deal with Mexico's grave economic problems, such as the crushing foreign debt and high unemployment. De la Madrid's programs failed, and Carlos Salinas de Gortari succeeded him in 1988. Although the rule

The city of Miami is connected to Miami Beach by a series of highways.

of the PRI is challenged since the 1980s, PRI candidate Ernesto Zedillo Ponce de Leon was elected president in 1994. At the end of 1994 Mexico suffered from a severe financial crisis. It took large scale help by the U.S. and international financial institutions to support the peso and the Mexican economy.

Mexico City (pop. 12,061,000), capital and largest city of Mexico. Located at an altitude of about 7,500 ft (2,300 m) and at the southern end of Mexico's central plateau, it is surrounded by the mountain ranges of Ixtacihuatl and Popocatepétl. The climate is cool and dry, but the city has often been damaged by local floods. Mexico City is on the site of the old Aztec capital of Tenochtitlán, founded in 1325. Cortés captured the city in 1521, and for the next 300 years it was the seat of the viceroyalty of New Spain; consequently it possesses some of the finest Spanish colonial architecture. Mexico's leading industrial center, Mexico City, was hit by a severe earthquake in 1985.
See also: Mexico.

Meyer, Julius Lothar (1830-1895), German scientist who developed the periodic chart of the elements which organizes the elements according to atomic weight and property. He also demonstrated the relationship between atomic weights and the properties of elements.
See also: Chemistry; Periodic table.

Meyerbeer, Giacomo (1791-1864), German composer. His romantic and spectacular operas, with librettos by A.E. Scribe, set the vogue for French opera. Most famous are his *Robert le Diable* (1831), *Les Huguenots* (1836), and *L'Africaine* (1865). Meyerbeer's music influenced that of Richard Wagner.

Miami, member of Algonquian-speaking Native American group, of the Great Lakes region. The Miami tribe hunted buffalo and grew crops. In the 18th century enemies drove them to northwest Ohio, where they numbered not more than 1,750. The Miamis were allies of the French during the French and Indian Wars and aided the British during the American Revolution. In 1867 most of the Miami tribe was moved to an Oklahoma reservation.

Miami (pop. 367,000), city in southeast Florida, at the mouth of the Miami River on Biscayne Bay. Its near-tropical climate, fine hotels, beaches, and recreational facilities make it a world-famous resort center. Miami was chartered in 1896, when Henry Flagler brought the railroad to Biscayne Bay. Now an agricultural processing and shipping center, Miami is also a center for aircraft and ship rebuilding and textiles.

Mica, group of minerals that split into thin, flat sheets of aluminum, silicon, and oxygen. Varieties of mica include muscovite, biotite, phlogopite, and lepidolite. Mica can be found in glistening rocks such as igneous and metamorphic. In its sheet, scrap, or ground form, it has a wide variety of industrial uses. Most scrap mica is produced in the United States.

Micah, Book of, sixth of the Old Testament Minor Prophets. These prophets were oracles of the Judean prophet Micah, who flourished in the late 8th century B.C. (Chapters 4 through 7 are believed to have been written later.) Ethical in tenor, the book prophesies judgment for sin and redemption by the Messiah.
See also: Old Testament.

Michaelmas daisy *see:* Aster.

Michel, Hartmut (1948-), German biochemist, head of biophysics division (Frankfurt am Main) of the Max Planck Institute for Biochemistry (1987-). Michel, Johann Deisenhofer, and Robert Huber shared the 1988 Nobel Prize for chemistry for their study of the structure of protein molecules involved in photosynthesis. Michel crystallized the proteins in 1982, enabling Deisenhofer and Huber to analyze them.
See also: Biochemistry; Photosynthesis.

Michelangelo (Michelangelo Buonarroti; 1475-1564), Italian sculptor, painter, architect, and poet. As a child he was apprenticed to the Florentine painter Ghirlandaio; in adolescence he was a protégé of Lorenzo de Medici. He went to Rome in 1496, where his marble *Pietà* in Saint Peter's (1498-99) established him as the foremost living sculptor. In Florence Michelangelo sculpted the magnificent *David* (1501-04). In 1505 he returned to Rome to work on a sepulchral monument tomb for Pope Julius II. There he painted the ceiling of the Sistine Chapel (1508-12), one of the most influential works in the history of art. After living in Florence (1515-34) and building the Medici Chapel and Laurentian Library for the Medici family and assisting as engineer in the defense of Florence, Michelangelo moved permanently to Rome. He painted the *Last Judgment* in the Sistine Chapel (1536-41) and was chief architect of Saint Peter's Basilica (1546-64). His architectural designs were influential throughout Italy and in France and England.
See also: Renaissance.

Michener, James Albert (1907-), U.S. author. His Pulitzer Prize-winning *Tales of the South Pacific* (1947), based on his U.S. Navy experiences in World War II, inspired the famous musical *South Pacific* (1949) by Rodgers and Hammerstein. He also wrote such ambitious, historically based novels as *Hawaii* (1959), *The Source* (1965), *Centennial* (1974), *Chesapeake* (1978), *Poland* (1983), *Texas* (1985), and *Caribbean* (1989).

Michigan, state in the Great Lakes region of midwestern United States; it consists of two separate land masses, the Upper Peninsula and the Lower Peninsula. The Upper Peninsula is bordered by Lake Superior to the north, St. Marys River (dividing it from Canada) to the east, the Straits of Mackinac and Lake Michigan to the south, and Wisconsin to the south and west. The Lower Peninsula is bordered by the Straits of Mackinac to the north; Lake Huron, Canada, and Lake Erie to the east; Ohio and Indiana to the south; and Lake Michigan to the west.

Land and climate. Michigan's two main land regions are the Superior Upland and the Great Lakes Plains. The Superior Upland region, in the Upper Peninsula's western half, is a rugged, forested area possessing some of the nation's richest iron and copper deposits. The Upper

Detail from Michelangelo's Last Judgement *depicting the resurrection of the dead*

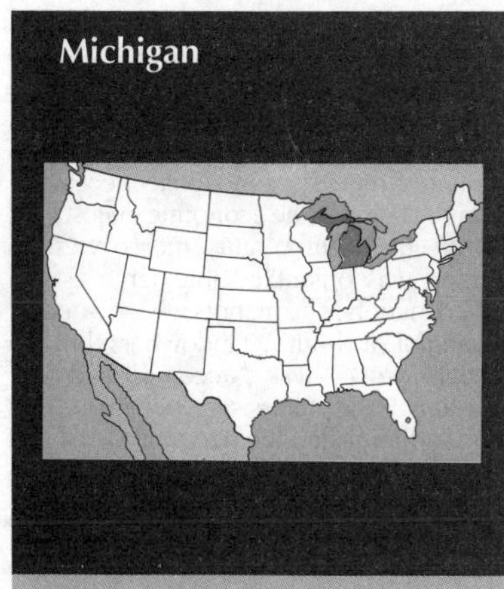

Capital:	Lansing
Statehood:	Jan. 26, 1837 (26th state)
Familiar name:	Wolverine State
Area:	58,527 sq mi (151,586 sq km); ranks 23rd
Population:	9,328,784 (1990); ranks 8th
Elevation:	Highest—1,980 ft (604 m), Mt. Curwood; Lowest—572 ft (174 m) at Lake Erie
Motto:	*Si Quaeris Peninsulam Amoenam, Circumspice* (If You Seek a Pleasant Peninsula, Look Around You)
Flower:	Apple blossom
Bird:	Robin
Tree:	White pine
Song:	"Michigan, My Michigan" (unofficial)

Peninsula's eastern half and the entire Lower Peninsula has thin soil; the northern Lower Peninsula is a rolling and hilly plateau; the southern Lower Peninsula has the best farmland. High bluffs and sand dunes border parts of Lake Michigan. Bordered by four of the five Great Lakes, Michigan has the longest coastline of any inland state: 3,288 mi (5,292 km). It has thousands of lakes and ponds. Most of Michigan's rivers and streams flow into the Great Lakes. Some 500 islands lie off Michigan's shores. Michigan's climate is moist, with cold winters and summers that are cool in the north, warm in the south. Principal cities are Detroit, Grand Rapids, Warren, and Flint.

Economy. Michigan's economy is based on service industries, the most important being wholesale and retail trade. Michigan is one of the foremost manufacturing states, producing transportation equipment, machinery, food products, chemicals, and metal, rubber, and plastic goods. It leads the nation in the manufacture of automobiles; Detroit is called the "Automobile Capital of the World" and "Motor City." The most valuable mineral is petroleum, followed by iron ore, natural gas, salt, limestone, and copper. Michigan is a leading producer of iodine, gypsum, peat, and sand and gravel. The chief livestock product is milk, followed by cattle, hogs, and eggs. The chief crops are corn, wheat, soybeans, dry beans, oats, hay, sugar beets, and fruits. Tourism is a major contributor to the economy.

Government. Michigan's present constitution was adopted in 1964. The governor serves a 4-year term. The state's legislature consists of 38 senators serving 4-year terms and 110 representatives serving 2-year terms. In the U.S. Congress, Michigan is represented by 2 senators and 18 representatives.

History. Native Americans, including the Chippewa, Menominee, and Miami, were Michigan's first settlers. French explorers—the first Europeans—arrived about 1620. France ceded the area to Britain in 1763, after the French and Indian Wars. After the American Revolution, it became part of the United States' Northwest Territory; it became a state in 1837. The Civil War (in which Michigan supported the Union), was followed by rapid expansion. Lumber production was the main industry until the early 1900s, when the automobile industry was established in Detroit. Michigan's economy boomed through World War I, slumped during the Depression of the 1930s, then recovered with World War II. It suffered again during the nationwide recessions of the 1970s and 1980s, when Michigan's unemployment rate led the nation.

Michigan, Lake, third largest of the Great Lakes, in North America. It is the largest freshwater lake wholly within the United States, with an area of 22,178 sq mi (57,441 sq km). Important ports on the lake include Milwaukee, Wis., Chicago, Ill., and Gary, Ind. In the north, Lake Michigan empties into Lake Huron by the Straits of Mackinac. It is part of the navigable Great Lakes-Saint Lawrence Seaway; a series of connections link it to the Mississippi River and the Gulf of Mexico.
See also: Great Lakes.

Micmac, Canadian Native Americans of New France (Nova Scotia, New Brunswick, Prince Edward Island, and coastal Quebec), of the Algonquian language group. They lived by hunting and fishing, using canoes for transportation. They traded with the French explorer Jacques Cartier, who arrived in 1534, and strove unsuccessfully with the French to ward away the British. They numbered about 3,000 in the 17th and 18th centuries. They came under Canadian government in 1867. The Micmacs survive today as a tribal group engaged in guiding and farming.

Microbe see: Microbiology.

Microbiology (formerly called bacteriology), study of microorganisms, including bacteria, viruses, fungi, protozoans, yeasts, and algae. Microbiology includes anatomy, physiology, genetics, taxonomy, and ecology, along with branches of medicine, veterinary sciences, and plant pathology, since many microorganisms are disease causing by nature.
Microbiologists also play an important role in the food industry, particularly in baking and brewing. In the pharmaceutical industry, they supervise the production of antibiotics.
See also: Bacteriology.

Microcomputer, complete small computer system, consisting of hardware and software, whose main processing parts are made of semiconductor integrated circuits. The various applications include video games, traffic control systems, scientific instruments, credit card verification and cash machines, blood analyzers, pinball machines, microwave ovens, flow meters, sewing machines, pollution monitors, and control units for hundreds of other devices.
See also: Computer.

Microelectronics, branch of technology and electronics that deals with the production of miniature electronic devices that use minimal electric power. Approaches include forming integrated circuits, thin-film techniques, and solid logic modules.

Microfiche *see:* Microfilm.

Microfilm, photographic film used for recording and storing graphic information in a reduced size. Microfilm comes in rolls, often called microform, and rectangular sheets called microfiche. It is used extensively in government offices, libraries, banks, and businesses.

While the size of microcomputers gets smaller and smaller, their capacity for data storage gets bigger and bigger. Depicted is the first portable computer equipped with CD-ROM capabilities.

Micronesia

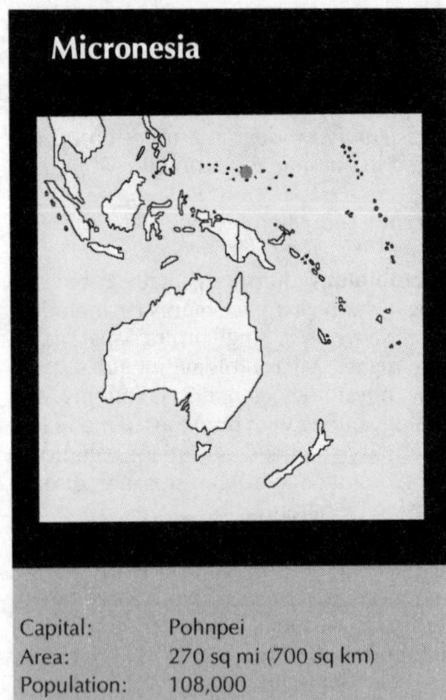

Capital: Pohnpei
Area: 270 sq mi (700 sq km)
Population: 108,000
Government: republic
Independent: 1990
GNP per capita:U.S. $980

Micronesia, Federated States of. Island state of 670 islands and atols in the western Pacific Ocean. Formerly part of the UN Trust Territory of the Pacific Islands, Micronesia became independent in 1990. Despite its independence foreign policy and defense are administered by the US government.

Microorganism *see:* Microbiology.

Microphone, instrument (invented c.1880) for transmitting or intensifying sounds, by means of electricity that converts sound waves into electrical waves. It is used in radio and television broadcasting and the film and recording industries. Types of microphones include carbon, crystal and ceramic, moving coil, ribbon, and capacitor.

Microprocessor, integrated circuit that performs the functions of a large computer on a tiny "chip" of silicon. Unlike a computer, which can be programmed to solve many different problems, a microprocessor is designed for a specific task. Microprocessors are called very large-scale integrated circuits because they may contain more than 100,000 transistors. First produced in 1971, microprocessors today can perform about 66 million functions per second. Microprocessors are used in a variety of "smart" devices, including appliances used at home, businesses, and industrial plants.
See also: Computer; Integrated circuit.

Microscope, instrument for producing enlarged images of small objects. In the compound microscope a magnified, inverted image of an object resting on the "stage" (a platform) is produced by the objective lens, or lens system. This image is viewed through the eyepiece (or ocular) lens, which acts as a simple microscope, giving a greatly magnified image. Generally the object is viewed by transmitted light, illumination being controlled by mirror, diaphragm, and "substage condenser" lenses. Near-transparent objects are often stained to make them visible; phase-contrast microscopy, in which a "phase plate" produces a diffraction effect, is an alternative to staining. Objects too small to be seen directly can be made visible in dark-field illumination, in which an opaque disk prevents direct illumination; the object is viewed in the light diffracted from the remaining oblique illumination. Although theoretically the magnifying power of the optical microscope is unlimited, magnifications greater than about 2,000 offer no improvement in resolving power for light of visible wavelengths. The shorter wavelength of ultraviolet light allows better resolution and hence higher useful magnification. For yet finer resolution, physicists use electron beams and electromagnetic focusing. The field-ion microscope, which offers the greatest magnifications is quite dissimilar from the optical microscope. The compound microscope was invented in the early 17th century.
See also: Leeuwenhoek, Anton van.

Microwave, electromagnetic wave in the superhigh frequency radio spectrum (890 to 300,000 megacycles per sec). Microwaves are electromagnetic radiations of wavelength between .03937 in (1 mm) and 1 ft (30 cm). Microwaves first received attention through the use of radar in World War II (1939-45); today they are used in radar, telecommunications, and spectroscopy and for cooking (microwave ovens).
See also: Radio; Television; Ultrahigh frequency waves.

Midas, in Greek mythology, king of Phrygia who was given the power by the god Dionysus to turn whatever he touched into gold. At first a cause for celebration, this power soon became a curse when even Midas' food turned to gold. With the aid of Dionysus, Midas was able to reverse his powers by bathing himself in the Pactolus River.
See also: Mythology.

Middle Ages (A.D. 400-1500), also known as the medieval period, era in western European history between the fall of the Roman Empire and the beginnings of modern European civilization. By the year 400 A.D., Germanic tribes, called barbarians by the Romans, began to invade the territories of Rome. By this time, the Roman Empire had lost much of its power and could not prevent the invasions. Tribes such as the Visigoths, Angles, Jutes, Saxons, Franks, and Ostrogoths divided the huge Roman Empire into different kingdoms. Because of the primitive legal and economic structures of these tribes, much of the Roman legacy in law, trade, and education was destroyed or lost for centuries. It is for this reason that the term "Dark Ages" is sometimes incorrectly applied to this era. The laws that once provided safety and security to Roman citizens gave way to tribal allegiances and superstitions. The great network of roads built by Rome to maintain trade and communication were destroyed by the barbarians. In the absence of a trade economy, money was no longer necessary. Farming became the economic mainstay of Europe. By the 9th century, most of western Europe was organized into large estates called manors. The manors were owned by a handful of wealthy landowners, but the actual work was accomplished by peasants. The increased power of the manor diminished the need for towns and the need for a merchant class. Consequently, the Middle Ages is characterized by a diminishment in urban life and the loss of culture. Education and cultural institutions were almost totally destroyed during this period. Knowledge of Greece and Rome was lost, the Latin language was unknown to most, and the disciplines of literature, painting, and architecture were forgotten. The sole civilizing force during the Middle Ages was the Christian Church, which saved western Europe from intellectual and cultural oblivion. By the 11th and 12th centuries some powerful lords had succeeded in establishing stable governments that provided peace and security. This, in turn, stimulated thought and economic activities—merchants and towns reappeared, trade routes were established, technological advances occurred, and people ventured far beyond the borders of the manor. This era also experienced remarkable artistic and intellectual achievements such as the cathedral of Notre Dame, the writings of St. Thomas Aquinas, the introduction of the works of Aristotle, and the establishment of universities. Between the 14th and 16th centuries, the Middle Ages slowly yielded to a more modern Europe characterized by the advances of the Renaissance.

Middle East, region, mostly in southwestern Asia but extending into southeastern Europe and northeastern Africa. Today the term usually includes Bahrain, Cyprus, Egypt, Iran, Iraq, Israel, Jordan, Kuwait, Lebanon, Libya, Saudi Arabia and the other countries of the Arabian peninsula, and Sudan. Politically, other countries of predominantly Islamic culture, such as Algeria, Morocco, and Tunisia, are sometimes included. The site of early civilization (including that of Sumer and Egypt, 3500-3100 B.C.), the Middle East was also the birthplace of Judaism, Christianity, and Islam. It has been the seat of many great empires, including the Ottoman Empire, which began in the 14th century and survived until 1923. The Tigris-Euphrates and the Nile are the Middle East's 2 major river systems; agriculture has been its most important economic activity. Today, the Middle East has assumed geopolitical importance as the world's primary oil-producing region; it is also the focus of international tensions and strife.

Middleton, Arthur (1742-87), South Carolina planter and one of the signers of the Declaration of Independence. At the

Above: The art of the Middle Ages is sometimes characterized by representations of death because of the gigantic death toll caused by the Black Death (bubonic plague), which killed one-third of the population of Europe in the 14th century.
Left: The economy of the Middle Ages was primarily agricultural employing over 80% of the population.
Right: Painting depicting a jousting tournament between knights.

center of the struggle for American independence, he served as a delegate to the Continental Congress (1776, 1777) and to the Congress of the Confederation (1781). In 1780, he was captured by the British at the siege of Charleston but was released as a result of a prisoner exchange.

Middleton, Thomas (1580-1627), English dramatist. He wrote lively, naturalistic comedies, the Lord Mayor of London's pageants and various masques, and 2 tragedies concerning human corruption: *The Changeling* (1621) and *Women Beware Women* (1657). *A Game at Chesse* (1624) was his satire on political marriages with Spain, suppressed under James I.

Middle West *see:* United States of America (regions).

Midge, large group (about 2,000 species) of tiny flies belonging to the Chironomidae family. Although related to biting midges and resembling mosquitos, midges do not bite. They often appear in swarms around streams and ponds. Their larvae, found in water, mud, tree bark, or manure, provide food for certain varieties of insects and fish.

Midget, human dwarf having normal body proportions, mental capacity, and sexual development. This type of dwarfism is caused by a deficiency of pituitary growth hormone.
See also: Dwarf.

Midway Island, group of islands (2 sq mi/5.2 sq km) northwest of Honolulu. Annexed by the United States in 1867 and used as a naval base, the island was the site of the Battle of Midway, the first important U.S. naval victory of World War II.
See also: World War II.

Mies van der Rohe, Ludwig (1886-1969), German-born U.S. architect, famous for functional but elegant buildings in the International Style, constructed of brick, steel, and glass. His work includes the Illinois Institute of Technology campus (1939) in Chicago, and the Seagram Building (1958, with Philip Johnson) in New York. Although he had no formal training, he was a director of the Bauhaus school and one of the leading architects.
See also: Architecture; Bauhaus.

Mifflin, Thomas (1744-1800), American soldier and political leader. A member of the First Continental Congress (1774-76, 1782-84) during the Revolutionary War he rose to the rank of quartermaster general (1775-77). He was later a delegate to the Constitutional Convention (1787) and the first governor of Pennsylvania (1790-99).

Mignonette, decorative garden plant belonging to the Resedaceae family. Found in North America and Europe, it has bushy leaves and tall spikes on which appear small, fragrant, yellowish-white or flowers with reddish pollen sacs.

Mikan, George (1924-), U.S. basketball player. Known for his strength and accurate hook shot, he was named the Associated Press' Player of the Half Century. Standing at 6-ft 10-in (208-cm), Mikan became the first center known for scoring (11,764 career points). He played in the National Basketball Association (NBA) for the Minneapolis Lakers (1946-55), and led them to 5 championships (1949, 50, 52-54). In 1967, he was named commissioner of the newly founded American Basketball Association. Mikan was inducted into the Basketball Hall of Fame in 1960.

Mikulic, Branko (1928-), premier of Yugoslavia (1986-88). He joined the League of Communists in 1943 and was a member of the Central Committee Presidium (1984-86). Mikulic was appointed as premier, but he and his entire cabinet resigned Dec. 30, 1988 over disputes with the Yugoslav parliament regarding economic planning.

Milan (pop. 1,635,000), city in northern Italy, capital of Lombardy. An important European trade and transportation hub, it is Italy's major industrial and commercial center, producing automobiles, airplanes, textiles, chemicals, electrical equipment, machinery, and books. Founded by the Celts c.400 B.C., Milan was a major late Roman city; it was the principal city state of Lombardy under the Visconti (1277-1447) and Sforza families. Spanish from 1535, Milan fell to Austria in 1714 and became a center of the 19th-century Risorgimento. Artistic treasures include the Milan Cathedral, Leonardo da Vinci's *Last Supper*, the Brera palace and art gallery, and La Scala opera house.

Milan Decree, order issued by Napoleon I of France in December, 1807. Hoping to bring about a complete economic blockade of Britain, the decree stated that even neutral ships were subject to capture. Although its effect was felt by the neutral nations—including the United States—the decree could not be enforced due to the superior naval strength of the British.
See also: Continental System; Napoleon I.

Mildew, general name for superficial growth of many types of fungi often found on plants and material derived from plants. Powdery mildews, numbering about 50, are caused by fungi belonging to the Asco-

Arthur Miller

mycetes order Erysiphales; the powdery effect is due to the masses of spores. Downy mildews are caused by Phycomycetes. Both types of disease can be controlled by the use of fungicides.

Miles, Nelson Appleton (1839-1925), U.S. soldier, army commander in chief (1895-1903). A Union general in the Civil War, in the Indian Wars he campaigned against the Sioux and also accepted the surrenders of Chiefs Joseph (1877) and Geronimo (1886). He also commanded in Cuba and Puerto Rico (1898).

Milhaud, Darius (1892-1974), French composer, one of the Parisian group called Les Six, noted for his polytonality (the simultaneous use of different keys). His vast output includes the jazz-influenced ballet *Creation of the World* (1923), *Saudades do Brasil* (1921), and various operas, among them *Christophe Colombe* (1930).

Military Academy, U.S *see:* United States Military Academy.

Military service, compulsory *see:* Draft, military.

Milk, liquid secreted by the mammary glands of female mammals. It contains water, protein, fat, sugar, vitamins A, C, and D, and some B vitamins, as well as inorganic salts and minerals (calcium and phosphorus). In any species, milk serves as a complete food for the young of that species until weaning. Milk for human use is commercially produced by cows and water buffalo (especially in India); goat's milk is also commonly used in some areas, particularly the Middle East. An extremely perishable liquid, milk must be cooled to a temperature of not more than 10°C (50°F) within two hours of milking and maintained at that temperature until delivery.

Lateral view (A) and axial view (B) of the Milky Way. The majority of all stellar systems in the universe posses such a structure. The spiral arms consist of young, hot stars and clouds of luminous gas, alternating with dark lanes of light-absorbing dust clouds. The sun (2) is located at a distance of about 30,000 light years from the galactic centre (1), while the outmost spiral arm (3) lies at a distance of about 55,000 light years from it.

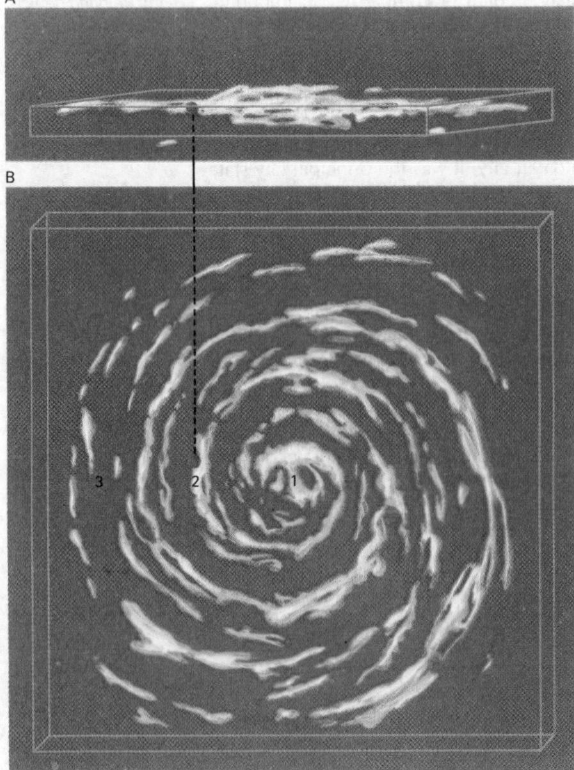

Milk snake, small kingsnake (*Lampropeltis triangulum*), found in North America, from the northeastern United States to Mexico. About 4 ft (1.2 m) long, milk snakes are bright red, black, and yellow when young and gray and brown when adult.

Milkweed, any of various perennial plants (genus *Asclepias*) that secrete latex. They are common in fields and waste areas of North America. Milkweed is poisonous in large quantities especially for children.

Milky Way, spiral galaxy with a radius of about 50,000 light-years, containing some 100 billion stars. The Milky Way is shaped like a flat disk about 10,000 light-years thick in most places, about 30,000 light-years at the center. It is a modest-sized galaxy. Our solar system is in one of its spiral arms, just over 30,000 light-years from the galactic center. The galaxy rotates about a roughly spherical nucleus, the sun circling the galactic center once every 230 million years or so. The Milky Way is surrounded by a spheroidal halo some 165,000 light-years in diameter composed of gas, dust, occasional stars, and globular clusters. The name of the galaxy is derived from its appearance as a hazy, milklike band of stars in the night sky. Irregular dark patches are caused by intervening clouds of gas dust.
See also: Galaxy; Solar system.

Mill, name of British literary family famed for their work in history, philosophy, economics, and psychology. **James Mill** (1773-1836) gained recognition with his book *A History of British India* but whose great contribution came through his work as the disciple of Jeremy Bentham, the father of utilitarianism. Mill was instrumental in explaining the fundamental tenets of the utilitarian doctrine. He also wrote a work on psychology, *Analysis of the Phenomena of the Human Mind* (1829); the first textbook of English economics, *Elements of Political Economy* (1821); and a work on moral philosophy, *Fragment on Mackintosh* (1835). His other accomplishments include being a Presbyterian minister, journalist, and head of the East India Company (1830-36). **John Stuart Mill** (1806-73), son of James Mill, is considered one of the most important thinkers of the 19th century. Mill was the head of the utilitarian movement and worked actively to promote the rights of workers and women. His most important work, *System of Logic* (1834), is a seminal work. Other works include *Principles of Political Economy* (1848), the famous *On Liberty* (1859), *The Subjection of Women* (1869), and *Autobiography* (1873). Mill was a brilliant child, who by the age of 14, mastered Latin, classical literature, history, mathematics, economics, and philosophy. He followed in his father's footsteps and became head of the East India Company but then went on to become a member of Parliament in 1865. **Harriet Taylor Mill** (1807-58), wife of John Stuart Mill, was instrumental in the thinking and writing of her husband's works. Her only work of actual authorship is her essay "Enfranchisement of Women" which appeared in one of her husband's works.
See also: Economics; Philosophy; Psychology.

Millais, Sir John Everett (1829-96), English painter, a founder of the Pre-Raphaelite "brotherhood" (1848). The realism of his *Christ in the Carpenter's Shop* (1850) caused a scandal. Later works such as *The Blind Girl* (1856) and *Bubbles* (1886) were more sentimental.

Millay, Edna St. Vincent (1892-1950), U.S. poet. Her reputation was established with *A Few Figs from Thistles* (1920). *The Harp Weaver* (1922) won a Pulitzer Prize. Other works include *Wine from These Grapes* (1934) and the verse drama *Aria da Capo* (1920).

Miller, Arthur (1915-), U.S. playwright. He has explored individual and social morality in plays like *Death of a Salesman* (1949; Pulitzer Prize); *The Crucible* (1953), about the witch trials in Salem, Mass.; *A View from the Bridge* (1955; Pulitzer Prize); the partly autobiographical *After the Fall* (1964); and the screenplay *The Misfits* (1961), written for his second wife, Marilyn Monroe. His autobiography, *Time Bends,* was published in 1987.

Miller, Glenn (1904-44), U.S. trombonist and bandleader of the big band "swing" era of the late 1930s and early 1940s. His blend of instrumental colors, the "Glenn Miller sound," had great success. Among his most popular recordings were *In the Mood, Moonlight Serenade,* and *Chattanooga Choo-Choo.* He died in a plane crash in Europe during World War II.

Miller, Henry (1891-1980), U.S. writer, noted for his candid treatment of sex and his espousal of the "natural man." *Tropic of Cancer* (1934) and *Tropic of Capricorn* (1939) were banned as obscene in the United States until 1961. Other books include the trilogy *The Rosy Crucifixion* (1949-60). He was a major influence on the Beat Generation of writers.

Miller, Lewis *see:* Chautauqua Movement.

Millerites *see:* Adventists.

Millet, common name for several varieties of cereal that grow on poor soil and ripen rapidly in hot sun. These characteristics have made it a popular crop in hot, dry countries, particularly in Africa and Asia. The grains can be stored for a long time and are richer in protein than rice, though the yield is small. Fermented millet grain is used to make beer in some countries, e.g. South Africa. In western countries millet is generally grown as cattle feed and for cage-birds. The tall elephant grass of Africa is a millet.

Millet, Jean François (1814-75), French painter. His peasant subjects, for example *The Gleaners* (1857) and *The Angelus* (1859), are naturalistic, though romanticized in style.
See also: Barbizon School.

Milligan, ex parte *see:* Ex parte Milligan.

Millikan, Robert Andrews (1868-1953), U.S. physicist. He was awarded the 1923 Nobel Prize for physics for determining the electron's charge and for his work on the photoelectric effect. He also studied and named cosmic rays.
See also: Photoelectric effect.

Milliliter, in the metric system, unit of capacity equal to one-thousandth (.001) of a liter.
See also: Metric system.

Millimeter *see:* Metric system.

Millimicrosecond *see:* Metric system.

Millipede, segmented arthropod having two pairs of legs on each body segment (unlike centipedes, which have only one pair of legs per segment). Millipedes live in damp soil, rotting vegetation, or under stones. They eat mainly decaying vegetation. Some roll into a ball when molested, while others squirt a spray of poison that can burn the skin. Some tropical millipedes grow to several inches in length, and a few are brightly colored. One species, living among the sequoias of California, is luminous.

Mills, C(harles) Wright (1916-62), U.S. sociologist and critic of U.S. capitalism and militarism whose work was influential with radical social scientists of the 1970s. His books include *White Collar* (1951), *The Power Elite* (1956), and *The Sociological Imagination* (1959), which argues that sociologists should not be passive observers but agents of social change.
See also: Sociology.

Mills, Robert (1781-1855), U.S. architect and engineer. Official architect of public buildings in Washington, D.C. (1836-51), he aimed at an American neoclassical style. He designed the Washington Monument, the Treasury, and the Old Post Office building.
See also: Washington Monument.

Milne, A(lan) A(lexander) (1882-1956), English writer and dramatist. His fame rests on stories and poems he wrote for his son Christopher Robin: *Winnie-the-Pooh* (1926), *The House at Pooh Corner* (1928), *When We Were Very Young* (1924), and *Now We Are Six* (1927).

Milo *see:* Sorghum.

Mílos, or Milo, one of the Greek Cyclades islands in the Aegean Sea. The seat of ancient Athenian civilization, it is known as the place where the celebrated statue of Venus de Milo was discovered in 1820. Tourism is important to the economy of the island. Other industries include olive and tobacco production.
See also: Greece.

Miltiades (c.540?-488? B.C.), Athenian general who defeated the invading Persians at the battle of Marathon (490 B.C.). Earlier, he had served the Persian king Darius I against the Scythians.
See also: Greece, Ancient; Marathon.

Milton, John (1608-74), English poet. His blank-verse epic *Paradise Lost* (1667), detailing Lucifer's revolt against God and the fall of Adam and Eve in the Garden of Eden, is one of the masterpieces of English literature. His major early works are the ode "On the Morning of Christ's Nativity" (1629), "L'Allegro" (1630), "Il Penseroso" (c. 1631), *Comus* (c. 1632), and "Lycidas" (1638). A supporter of the anti-monarchists during the English Civil War, he wrote many political pamphlets and a defense of freedom of the press, *Areopagitica* (1644). He retired after the Restoration (1660), and though totally blind, dictated his final great works: *Paradise Lost*, *Paradise Regained* (1671), and *Samson Agonistes* (1671).

Milwaukee (pop. 1,432,149), largest city in Wisconsin, seat of Milwaukee County, in the southeast region of the state. An industrial center and leading Great Lakes port (on Lake Michigan), Milwaukee was incorporated in 1848. Notable landmarks include the Greek Orthodox Annunciation Church, designed by Frank Lloyd Wright; the War Memorial Center, housing the Milwaukee Art Center, designed by Eero Saarinen; the Performing Arts Center (1969); and the Civic Center downtown. The city has many spacious parks. Its educational institutions include the University of Wisconsin at Milwaukee, Marquette University, and 16 other universities and colleges.
See also: Wisconsin.

Mimosa, any of several tropical American plants (genus *Mimosa*) of the pulse family, with pink flowers and small leaves. One variety is called the sensitive plant (*M. pudica*), because its leaves fold together when touched, though after a few minutes they return to the normal position.

Mindszenty, József (1892-1975), Hungarian Roman Catholic cardinal who was sentenced (1949) to life imprisonment for his opposition to communism. Released in the uprising of 1956, he took refuge in the U.S. legation in Budapest. He refused to leave until the charges against him were rescinded. In 1971, after an agreement between the Vatican and the Hungarian government, Mindszenty left for Rome.

A scene from A.A. Milne's Winnie the Pooh *(1926), illustrated by E.H. Shepard*

Mineral, in biology, inorganic element vital to human health. Minerals are usually obtained from food. The essential ones are calcium, chlorine, cobalt, copper fluorine, iodine, iron, magnesium, manganese, phosphorus, potassium, sodium, sulphur, and zinc. Other minerals, known as trace elements, are present in the body in minute quantities and are presumed to be necessary for health: aluminum, boron, bromine, chromium, molybdenum nickel, silicon, and silver.

Mineral, in geology, naturally occurring inorganic substance with a particular chemical composition and definite physical properties. The rocks of the earth's crust are composed of minerals, which are generally classified in order of increasing complexity: elements, sulfides, oxides, halides, carbonates, nitrates, sulfates, phosphates, and silicates

Minerva, in Roman mythology, daughter of Jupiter. She was modeled on the Greek goddess Athena. Worshiped for her skill in handicrafts as well as for her artistic and intellectual gifts, Minerva came to symbolize military prowess and was often depicted wearing a helmet and suit of armor.
See also: Mythology.

Mineworkers of America, United (UMW), U.S. labor union for workers in coal mines and coal industries. The UMW is an industrial union, with membership based on an industry rather than on job skills. Founded in 1890, it was a member of the American Federation of Labor (AFL) until 1936 (rejoining briefly 1946-47). Under the leadership of John L. Lewis, union president 1919-60, it then became a moving force in the formation of the Congress of Industrial Organizations (CIO; 1935). It resigned from the CIO in 1942 and is an unaffiliated union.
See also: Unions, Labor.

Ming dynasty, imperial family that ruled China from 1368-1644. Following years of Mongolian rule, this period was characterized by a return to civil service and an emphasis on scholarship, the arts, and ar-

chitecture. Achievements included the building of the imperial palace in Beijing's Forbidden City and the creation of exquisite porcelain vases.
See also: China.

Miniature schnauzer, dog breed developed in Germany in the 19th century. Standing at 12 to 14 inches (30 to 36 centimeters) and possessing a variety of colorations, it is characterized by wiry hair that bristles out in its spiky eyebrows and beard. It is considered to be intelligent, energetic, affectionate, and a good watchdog and mouser.

Minimalism, art movement initiated in the 1960s that stressed pure color and geometry. In both painting and sculpture—generally executed with great precision—it rejected emotionalism, striving for an "exclusive, negative, absolute, and timeless" quality. Minimalism comprises, among styles and techniques, color-field painting, hard-edge painting, pop art, the shaped canvas, serial imagery, and primary structures.

Mining, extraction of minerals and ores from the earth. There are various types of mines. The open pit mine is used when the desired minerals lie near the surface. It usually consists of a series of terraces that are worked back in parallel so that the mineral is always within reach of the excavating machines. In strip mining a surface layer is peeled off to reach a usually thin mineral seam (often coal). When minerals lie far below the surface, various deep mining techniques must be used. Access to the mineral-bearing strata is obtained through a vertical shaft or sloping incline dug from the surface or through a horizontal adit driven into the side of a mountain. Underground mines require ventilation and lighting, facilities for pumping out any groundwater or toxic gases, and some means (railroad or conveyor) for carrying the ore and waste to the surface. Several serious occupational diseases (e.g., pneumoconiosis, or "black lung") are associated with mining and extractive metallurgy, particularly where high dust levels and toxic substances are involved.

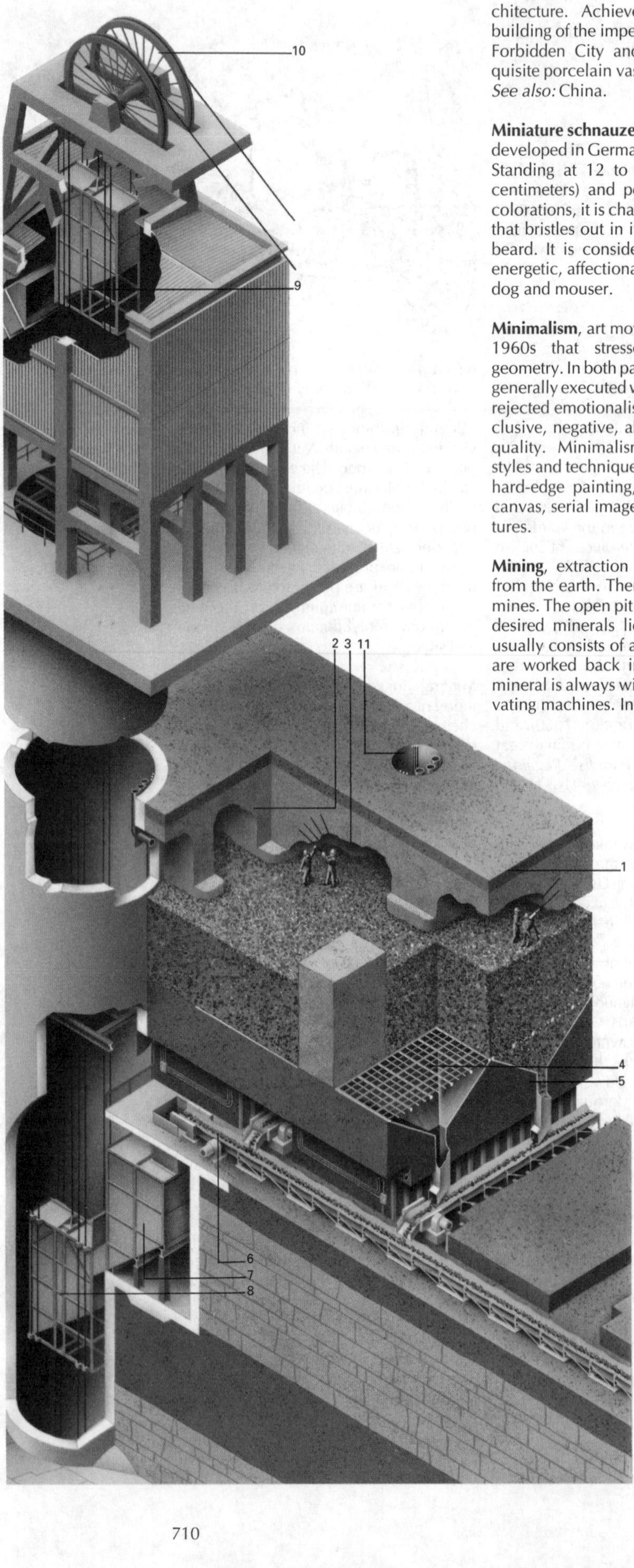

Highly schematic block diagram of an ore mine. The "roof" of the chamber (1), where the ore is extracted, has here been supported by pillars of unremoved ore (2). The ore is removed from the roof and the wall (3); passing along a system of large screens (4) and funnels (5), it reaches a story located below the body of ore (6). Here the ore is carried on conveyor belts (7) along horizontal galleries and tipped down a chute (8) into an elevator (9), which moves up a vertical shaft (10) to the surface. Electricity cables, pipes for the supply and extraction of air, telephone lines etc. are passed through "service holes" (11).

Mink, semiaquatic carnivore (genus *Mustela*) of the weasel family, extensively farmed for its fur. There are two species: *M. lutreola*, of European distribution, and *M. vision*, originating in North America but now widely distributed throughout Europe. Feeding on small fish, eggs, young birds, and small mammals, minks are avid hunters, often killing more than they can eat.

Silver mink

Minneapolis (pop. 2,464,124), largest city of Minnesota and seat of Hennepin County, on the upper Mississippi River, contiguous to its twin city, St. Paul. Minneapolis is a manufacturing, trading, and financial center noted for its many large flour mills and grain elevators. Its products include farm machinery, electronic equipment, linseed oil, paint, precision instruments, and furniture. Site of the University of Minnesota, the city also has an institute of art, a symphony orchestra, and a repertory theater.
See also: Minnesota.

Minnehaha, in Henry Wadsworth Longfellow's poem *The Song of Hiawatha* (1855), a young Native American woman. She became the wife of Hiawatha.

Minnesinger, minstrel-poet of medieval Germany. Minnesingers composed and sang songs of courtly love (*minne*). Heirs to the Provençal troubadours, they flourished from c.1150 to c.1350.

Minnesota

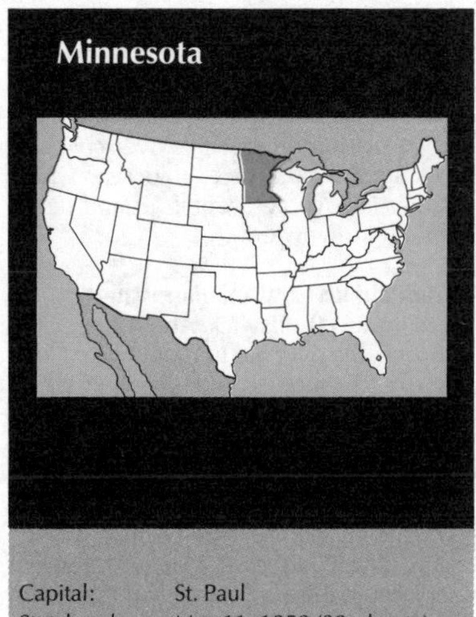

Capital:	St. Paul
Statehood:	May 11, 1858 (32nd state)
Familiar name:	Gopher State
Area:	84,402 sq mi (218,601 sq km);
Population:	4,387,029 (1990); ranks 12th
Elevation:	Highest—2,301 ft (701 m), Eagle Mountain; Lowest—602 ft (83 m), along Lake Superior
Motto:	L'Etoile du Nord (The Star of the North)
Flower:	Pink and white lady's-slipper
Bird:	Common loon
Tree:	Norway pine
Song:	"Hail! Minnesota"

Minnesota, state in the Great Lakes region of the midwestern United States; bordered by Canada to the north, Lake Superior and Wisconsin to the east, Iowa to the south, and South Dakota and North Dakota to the west.

Land and climate. Minnesota's 4 main land regions are the Superior Upland, the Young Drift Plains, the Dissected Till Plains, and the Driftless Area. The Superior Upland, in northeastern Minnesota, includes some of the most rugged and isolated parts of the state. The gently rolling Young Drift Plains cover most of the rest of the state. This region has the state's most important farmlands. In the Dissected Till Plains, at the state's southwestern corner, the soil is a thick mixture of sand, gravel, and clay. Parts of this region are good farmland. The Driftless Area in the southeastern corner is nearly flat in the east, but with deep valleys cut by swift streams in the west. Minnesota has as many as 22,000 lakes; more than 15,000 of them are 10 acres or larger. The nation's greatest river, the Mississippi, has its source in Minnesota. Other major rivers include the Red River of the North, the Rainy River, and the St. Louis River. Minnesota has long, cold winters and warm-to-very-hot summers. Principal cities are Minneapolis, St. Paul, and Duluth.

Economy. Minnesota's principal industries are agri-business, forest products, mining, manufacturing, and tourism. The chief manufactured products are nonelectrical machinery, food products, fabricated metal products, chemicals, paper and paper goods, and adhesive tapes and industrial adhesives. Livestock and dairy products account for about more than half of the state's farm income; chief crops are corn, soybeans, hay, and wheat. Chief mineral products are iron ore, taconite, granite, limestone, and clay.

Government. Minnesota's constitution was adopted in 1858. The governor serves a 4-year term. The state's Legislature consists of 67 senators serving 4-year terms and 134 representatives serving 2-year terms. In the U.S. Congress, Minnesota is represented by 2 senators and 8 representatives.

History. Sioux were living in the region when the first whites arrived in the late 1600s; Chippewa came soon after. French fur traders and missionaries settled the area. At various times, parts of Minnesota were held by France, Spain, and Britain. Some of Minnesota became part of the U.S. after the American Revolution, the rest with the Louisiana Purchase. In 1851, the Sioux were forced to sign treaties that opened most of Minnesota to white settlement, which boomed. Minnesota, which became a state in 1858, supported the Union during the Civil War. In 1862, the Sioux rose in a bloody uprising that the U.S. Army and state militia eventually quashed. After the Civil and Indian Wars, industries developed rapidly and immigration increased. World War I raised demand for Minnesota's iron and steel, but the Depression of the 1930s devastated the state's economy. World War II brought recovery. Since then, industry's importance has grown, while farming's has declined. During the 1970s and 1980s, a major concern was finding ways to develop Minnesota's rich resources without damaging its environment, especially the lakes and rivers, wooded parks, and ski areas that draw millions of vacationers a year.

Minnow, common name for many small freshwater fishes found throughout the world except for South America and Australia. The original minnow is a 3-in (7.6-cm) European fish, but the name has also been extended to its relatives, which include carp, cutlips, shiners, roach, and tench. Minnows feed on insects and crustaceans and are important in the food chain, since larger fish feed on them. The largest American minnow is the squawfish, or Pacific pike, which may grow to several feet. Minnows have long pharyngeal teeth around their gills. They lay their eggs in gravel or in special nests.

Minoan civilization, Bronze Age culture that flourished on the island of Crete during the 3rd and 2nd millenniums B.C. The first great Aegean civilization—with cities, palaces, a highly developed art and architecture, writing, extensive trade, and complex religious beliefs—Minoan culture reached its high point c.2200-1500 B.C. The city of Cnossus on the north coast of Crete was its center, from which the Minoan fleet carried goods to Egypt, Syria, Phoenicia, Asia Minor, Sicily, and Greece. By c.1000 B.C. Minoan civilization had declined, and its remains were incorporated by Greece. The word "Minoan" comes from the legendary King Minos, who was said to have ruled in Cnossus.
See also: Crete; Greece, Ancient.

Minorca, or Menorca, one of the Balearic Islands off the eastern coast of Spain. The second largest of the islands, it was seized several times by France and by England, who eventually ceded it to Spain in 1802. Minorca is known for its farm crops, light manufacturing, lobster fishing, and beaches. Tourism is also important.

Minor leagues *see:* Baseball.

Minos, in Greek mythology, wealthy king of Crete who commanded the artisan Daedalus to construct a labyrinthine prison for a beast called the Minotaur, to whom the young people of Athens were regularly sacrificed. One of these, Theseus, succeeded in killing the Minotaur and running away with Minos' daughter Ariadne. Minos was married to Pasiphaë; his other children included Androgeous, Glaucus, and Phaedra.
See also: Mythology.

Minot, George (1885-1950), U.S. physician who developed a cure for the once-fatal blood disease called pernicious anemia. He found that feeding patients a diet consisting largely of raw liver normalized their red blood count. He was awarded the Nobel Prize for medicine (1934, with G.H. Whipple and W.P. Murphy). Minot wrote numerous articles on blood disorders and dietary deficiency.
See also: Anemia.

Minnesota farmland

Minsk (pop. 1,442,000), capital city of the Byelorussian Soviet Socialist Republic, located on the Svisloch River. After suffering extensive damage during World War II, the city was revitalized by the creation of factories and new housing. Among the goods produced in Minsk are trucks, machine parts, tools, and radios. The city is also noted for its academic and cultural institutions.
See also: Union of Soviet Socialist Republics.

Minstrel, wandering professional entertainers who flourished in medieval Europe. Known variously as *troubadours* or *jongleurs* in France, *bards* in Ireland, *skalds* in Scandinavia, and *minnesingers* in Germany, they were generally singers but also used storytelling and mime. Because they wandered from town to town, they spread local news and helped to preserve oral traditions. They began to die out in the 15th century, largely due to the appearance of the printing press.

These minstrels with flutes are shown in the Tropaire-prosier, an 11th century from around Albi.

Minstrel show, form of entertainment popular in the United States from about 1840 to 1900. White performers blackened their faces in imitation of African Americans and alternated jokes with African American songs, many of which thus became well-known American folk songs. Minstrel shows reinforced negative stereotypes of blacks that lasted for decades after the shows had ceased to exist.

Mint, in botany, family of square-stemmed plants with white, blue, purple, or red flowers in the form of a lipped tube. Many are aromatic. Familiar examples are lavender, sage, oswego tea, marjoram, and thyme. The true mints (genus *Mentha*) include spearmint (*M. spicata*) and peppermint (*M. piperita*).

Minto, Earl of (1845-1914), British governor general of Canada (1898-1904) and viceroy of India (1905-10). As governor general, he was criticized by French-speaking Canadians for sending Canadian troops to South Africa during the Boer War. As viceroy, he angered Indian nationalists by instituting reforms that resulted in the intensification of divisions between Hindus and Muslims.

Minuit, Peter (c.1580-1638), Dutch colonial administrator in North America. He was the first director-general of New Netherland for the Dutch West India Company and is remembered for buying Manhattan island from the Native Americans (1626) for about $24 worth of trinkets. He founded New Amsterdam (now New York City) and later (1638) established New Sweden on the Delaware River.

Minuteman, member of a volunteer militia during the American Revolutionary War, ready to take up arms "at a minute's notice." Massachusetts minutemen fought at the battles of Lexington and Concord (1775). Maryland, New Hampshire, and Connecticut also had such militias.
See also: Revolutionary War in America.

Miocene, last epoch but one of the Tertiary period, which lasted from 25 to 10 million years ago.

Mira, variable star about 270 light-years away from the earth. The German astronomer Fabricius first observed the brightening and dimming of the star in 1596; later, variations in diameter and temperature were also noted. The diameter of Mira can be imagined as equal to that of the sun and all nearby planets, extending to a point somewhere beyond Mars. It is visible to the naked eye for about half the year; otherwise it can be seen through a telescope.
See also: Star.

Mirabeau, Comte de (1749-91), French revolutionary leader. A powerful orator, he became an early leader of the moderate wing of revolutionary forces, representing the third estate (the commoners) in the States-General (the French parliament). He worked secretly to establish a constitutional monarchy but was mistrusted by both revolutionaries and royalists. He was elected president of the National Assembly in 1791 but died a few months later.
See also: French Revolution; Jacobins.

Miracle play *see:* Mystery play.

Mirage, optical illusion in the atmosphere in which the refraction of light passing through air layers of different densities causes non-existent images to be seen. Distant objects may appear to be reflected in water, as light rays traveling initially toward the ground have been bent upward by layers of hot air close to the surface. In some mirages objects seem to float in the air. This commonly occurs over cold surfaces such as ice or a cold sea, where warmer air overlies cooler air and bends light rays downward.

Miramichi River, Canadian waterway located in New Brunswick. About 135 mi (48 km) long, the river has its mouth near Newcastle and empties into the Gulf of St. Lawrence. It is an important source of salmon and provides passage for large ships.

Miranda, Francisco de (1750-1816), Venezuelan patriot who fought for the forces of freedom on 3 continents. While an officer in the army of Spain he served in the American Revolution, receiving the British surrender at Pensacola, Fla. He later joined the French revolutionary forces, fighting in several major battles. When in 1810 patriots in Venezuela formed a provisional government, he returned home, where he and Simón Bolivar proclaimed the first South American republic, in Caracas on July 5, 1811. Captured by royalists, he died in prison in Spain.
See also: Venezuela.

Miranda v. Arizona, U.S. Supreme Court case (1966) establishing the rights of criminal suspects in police custody. In its 5-4 ruling the Court specified that prior to any sort of questioning suspects must be informed of their rights to remain silent and to have a lawyer present. Miranda had been questioned by police in Arizona and had confessed to a crime without having been told of these rights. The Court ruled that the confession was therefore inadmissible evidence.

Miró, Joan (1893-1983), Spanish painter. A pioneer of surrealism, Miró produced freely drawn works characterized by bright colors and clusters of abstract symbolic forms. His work includes murals and large ceramic decorations for UNESCO in Paris.

Joan Miró's Stormy People *(1949)*

Misdemeanor, crime that is not as serious as a felony. In general, offenses punishable only by a fine or short imprisonment in

county jails are misdemeanors. These may include traffic violations, assault and battery, and theft of small amounts of money. Convictions that carry punishment by imprisonment in state penitentiaries are felonies.
See also: Crime.

Mishima, Yukio (Kimitake Hiraoka; 1925-70), Japanese author. His writing is obsessed with the conflict between traditional and post-World War II Japan. He formed a private army devoted to ancient martial arts and committed hara-kiri. His work includes the novels *The Temple of the Golden Pavilion* (1956), *Sun and Steel* (1970), *Sea of Fertility* (4 vols., 1970), and *Patriotism* (1966), on ritual suicide, and modern Kabuki and Noh plays.

Missile, guided *see:* Guided missile.

Missionary, individual sent to a foreign territory or country to educate others in particular religious tradition. While their goal is religious conversion, missionaries also work to provide agricultural information, social services, and literacy skills. The Christian church, with the greatest number of missionaries, sponsors activities in Asia, Latin America, Africa, and the Pacific islands.

Mississippi

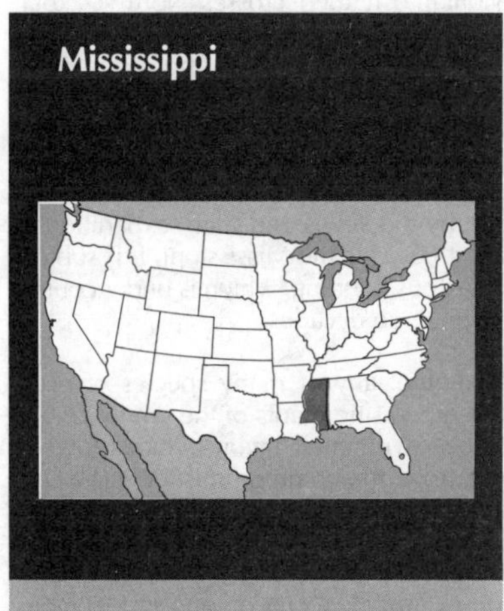

Capital:	Jackson
Statehood:	Dec. 10, 1817 (20th state)
Familiar name:	Magnolia State
Area:	47,689 sq mi (123,515 sq km);
Population:	2,586,443 (1990); ranks 31st
Elevation:	Highest—806 ft (246 m), Woodall Mountain; Lowest—sea level, along the Gulf of Mexico coast
Motto:	Virtute et Armis (By Valor and Arms)
Flower:	Magnolia.
Bird:	Mockingbird
Tree:	Magnolia
Song:	"Go Missisipi"

Mississippi, state in the Deep South region of the United States; bordered by Tennessee to the north, Alabama to the east, the Gulf of Mexico to the south, Louisiana to the south and west, and Arkansas to the west.

Land and climate. Mississippi has 2 main land regions. The Mississippi Alluvial Plain, often called "the Delta," lies on the state's western edge along the Mississippi River. Its rich lowlands, built up by river deposits, support good cotton and soybean crops. Small, slow-moving streams called bayous connect this region's lakes and rivers. The rest of the state lies in the East Gulf Coastal Plain, which consists of low, rolling hills with some prairie and lowland. Pine forests cover much of this region's southern portion; the northeast is a fertile agricultural area. Forests, which originally covered nearly the entire state, now cover more than half of it. Mississippi's complex river system drains into the Gulf of Mexico—directly, or via the Mississippi River. Other large rivers include the Yazoo, Tallahatchie, Tombigbee, Pearl, and Pascagula. A system of *levees* (dikes) helps to control the lower Mississippi River during flood season. All of the state's larger lakes are man-made reservoirs. Mississippi has a warm, humid climate, with long, hot summers and short, mild winters. Principal cities are Jackson, Biloxi, and Meridian.

Economy. Mississippi's principal industries are manufacturing, food processing, seafood, government, and wholesale and retail trade. Cotton, though no longer "king," remains the most important crop. Other important agricultural products include soybeans, catfish, and rice. Timber, petroleum, and natural gas are the main natural resources.

Government. Mississippi's present constitution was adopted in 1980. The governor serves a 4-year term. The state's legislature consists of 52 senators and 122 representatives; all serve 4-year terms. In the U.S. Congress, Mississippi is represented by 2 senators and 5 representatives.

History. Chickasaw, Natchez, and Choctaw were living in Mississippi when the first white settlers arrived. The first European to visit the area was de Soto, a Spanish explorer, in 1540. In 1683, the French explorer La Salle claimed the entire Mississippi Valley for France. In 1763, after the French and Indian Wars, France ceded the region to Britain. After a series of border changes and land conflicts, Mississippi became the Union's 20th state in 1817. Indians had controlled most of the area throughout its territorial days, but whites had full control by 1840. By 1860, black slaves outnumbered the white population and Mississippi had become the Union's top cotton-producing state. The second state to secede from the Union, Mississippi was a leading member of the Confederacy during the Civil War. The state's economy was ruined by the war; Reconstruction and the postwar military government did nothing to restore it. Depression-era programs helped improve Mississippi's agriculture and industry somewhat; modest industrial growth continued during the 1940s and 1950s. During the 1960s, Mississippi was the scene of some of the worst violence in the civil-rights movement. Race relations improved during the 1970s and 1980s—as did the state's economy. But many farm workers are jobless, and many educated young people leave the state to seek employment elsewhere.

Paddle steamer on the Mississippi River

Mississippian *see:* Mound Builders.

Mississippi River, chief river of the North American continent and the longest river in the United States, flowing about 2,350 mi (3,780 km) south from Lake Itasca in northwestern Minnesota to its enormous delta at the Gulf of Mexico, below New Orleans. Called the "father of waters" by Native Americans, the Mississippi drains an area of about 1.25 million sq mi (3,237,500 sq km). With the Missouri and Ohio rivers (its chief tributaries), it forms the world's third longest river system, after the Nile and the Amazon. It receives more than 250 tributaries in all. The Mississippi is noted for sudden changes of course, its length varying by 40-50 mi (64-80 km) per year. The river's average discharge is 1.64 million cu ft (46,412 cu m) per sec, but in high water season this soars to some 2.3 million cu ft (65,090 cu m) per sec. Flooding is a serious problem, but dikes and levees contain its periodic massive overflows. The river is a major transportation artery of the United States and was of fundamental importance in the development of the North American continent.

Missoula (pop. 33,388), large city in western Montana known for its wood products. A regional headquarters for the U.S. Forest Service, it has a training center for *smoke jumpers*—firefighters who descend into remote forest areas by parachute. Founded in the 1860s as a trading post, its growth was triggered by the creation of the Northern Pacific Railway.

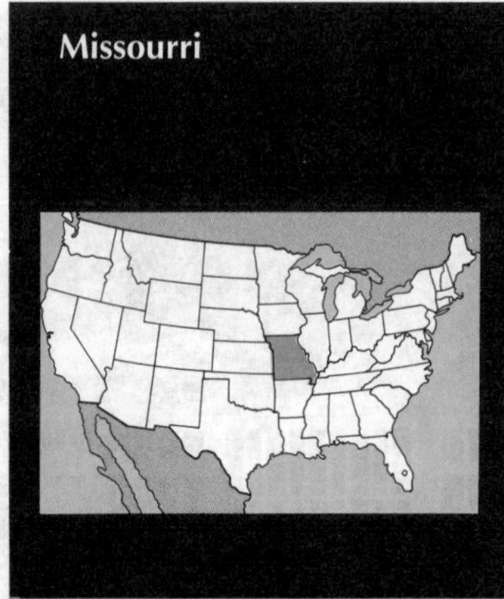

Capital:	Jefferson City
Statehood:	Aug. 10, 1821 (24th state)
Familiar name:	Show Me State
Area:	69,697 sq mi (180,516 sq km); ranks 19th
Population:	5,137,804 (1990); ranks 15th
Elevation:	Highest—1,772 ft (540 m), Taum Sauk Mountain; Lowest—230 ft (70 m) along the St. Francis River near Cardwell
Motto:	Salus Populi Suprema Lex Esto (The Welfare of the People Shall be the Supreme Law)
Flower:	Hawthorne
Bird:	Bluebird
Tree:	Flowering dogwood
Song:	"Missouri Waltz"

Gateway Arch in St. Louis, Missouri

Missouri, state in central United States, considered part of the Midwest; bordered by Iowa to the north; the Mississippi River and Illinois, Kentucky, and Tennessee to the east; Arkansas to the south, and Oklahoma, Kansas, and Nebraska to the west.

Land and climate. Missouri's 4 land regions reflect a unique blending of North, South, East, and West. The state's southeastern corner is part of the rich Mississippi Alluvial Plain. The flattest, lowest, and most fertile part of the state, it recalls the Deep South. The forested Ozark Plateau, in central and southern Missouri, is the state's largest land region. This area of poor, stony soil but great scenic beauty resembles the hill country of eastern Tennessee and Kentucky. The Osage Plains region in western Missouri is a relatively flat prairie area much like the Great Plains. The upper third of the state is part of the fertile Dissected Till Plains region, which is part of the Midwest's Corn Belt. The nation's 2 largest rivers, the Mississippi and the Missouri, enrich the state's soil and make it an important waterway, railroad, and highway hub. Missouri's climate is humid, and the weather is extremely changeable. Summers are long and winters are brisk. Principal cities are St. Louis, Kansas City, and Springfield.
Economy. Missouri's main industries are agriculture, manufacturing, aerospace, and tourism. Soybeans, corn, wheat, and cotton are the main crops. Missouri is a leading beef-cattle state; other important livestock products are dairy cattle, hogs and pigs, sheep, eggs, turkeys, and chickens. Chief manufactured products are transportation equipment, food products, chemicals and related products, and electrical machinery and equipment. The most important mineral resources are lead, crushed stone, limestone, sand and gravel, coal, zinc, and silver.
Government. Missouri's present constitution was adopted in 1945. The governor serves a 4-year term. The state legislature, called the General Assembly, consists of 34 senators serving four-year terms and 163 representatives serving two-year terms. In the U.S. Congress, Missouri is represented by two senators and nine representatives.
History. Native Americans known as Mound Builders lived in Missouri long before the first whites, French explorers Marquette and Joliet, arrived in 1673. France claimed the entire Mississippi Valley after La Salle's voyage down the river in 1682. The U.S. acquired the area in the 1803 Louisiana Purchase. In 1812, Congress created the Missouri Territory. By 1815, fighting between Indians and settlers ended in treaties that followed further white settlement. Most new settlers were slave owners from the South, which caused problems when Missouri requested statehood. After three years of controversy, the Missouri Compromise of 1820 allowed Missouri to enter the Union as a slave state in 1821. Missouri became known as the "Gateway to the West" as thousands of settlers left from Independence to travel west on the Santa Fe and Oregon Trails and St. Joseph became the starting point of the Pony Express. During the Civil War, Missouri was bitterly divided; heavy fighting took place there. Postwar recovery was slow. Since about 1830, manufacturing, rather than agriculture, has been the state's chief source of income. World War II brought new industries. Missouri battled urban problems during the 1970s and a farm crisis and financial problems in the 1980s.

Missouri Compromise, package of measures adopted by the U.S. Congress in 1820-21, to resolve issues relating to the extension of slavery. At the time of Missouri's first petition to become a state (1819), there were 11 free and 11 slave states in the Union. Missouri's addition would have changed the balance of power in the U.S. Senate and reopened the bitterly contested issue of whether slavery should be permitted to spread in the United States. Action on Missouri's petition was delayed until Maine requested admission as a free state, and both were admitted. The compromise also barred slavery from being extended to the rest of the territory of the Louisiana Purchase north of 36°30′ latitude. The compromise was repealed in 1854 by the Kansas-Nebraska Act.
See also: Kansas-Nebraska Act; Slavery.

Missouri River, second-longest river in the United States (about 2,500 mi/4,023 km) and chief tributary of the Mississippi, with which it forms the world's third-largest river system. Rising in southeastern Montana in the Rocky Mountains, the Missouri river flows north and then east through Montana; it then crosses North Dakota, and continues generally southeast until emptying into the Mississippi north of St. Louis. Its main tributaries include the Cheyenne, Kansas, Osage, Platte, Yellowstone, James, and Milk rivers. The Missouri was explored by Joliet and Marquette in 1673 and by the Lewis and Clark expedition in 1804-05. Like the Mississippi, it is subject to serious flooding, which is under control since three decades.

Mistletoe, any of many species of evergreen parasitic plants of the family Loranthaceae with small, inconspicuous flowers. In Europe the common mistletoe (*Viscum album*) grows on apples, poplar, willow, linden, and hawthorns, while common U.S. mistletoes (*Phoradendron flavescens*, for example) occur on most deciduous trees and some conifers. Mistletoes derive some of their nutrients from the host plants, but they also produce some by photosynthesis. Their seeds are spread by fruit-eating birds.

Mistral, Frédéric (1830-1914), French poet. He won the 1904 Nobel Prize for literature and for his work as leader of a movement to restore the former glories of the Provençal language and culture. Among his works are the epic poems *Mirèio* (1859), *Calendau* (1867), *Nerto* (1884), and *Lou Pouémo dúo Rose* (1897).

Mistral, Gabriela (Lucila Godoy Alcayaga; 1889-1957), Chilean poet, educator, and diplomat awarded the Nobel Prize for literature in 1945. Her simple, lyrical poems express sympathy with nature and mankind. Her works include *Desolation* (1922) and *Tenderness* (1924).

Mitanni, kingdom that flourished in northern Mesopotamia (now southeastern Turkey) from about 1500 B.C. A warfaring people renowned for their skills with horses and chariots, the early Mitannians fought the Egyptians for control of Syria, but the threat of a common enemy—the Hittites—caused these empires to form an alliance. Ultimately, the kingdom of Mitanni was captured in 1350 B.C. and became part of the Assyrian Empire.

Mitchell, Billy (1879-1936), U.S. army officer and aviator. After leading U.S. air services in World War I, he became an outspoken champion of a strong air force independent of army or naval control. Court-martialed for insubordination (1925) and suspended from duty for five years, he resigned from the army in 1926.

Mitchell, John Newton (1913-88), U.S. attorney general (1969-72) and convicted Watergate felon. A former law partner of Richard M. Nixon, he served as Nixon's campaign manager in 1968. In 1972, as director of the Committee to Reelect the President, he was involved in the burglary of the Democratic Party headquarters, resulting in his 1977 conviction and prison sentence. He was paroled in 1979 after serving 19 months.
See also: Watergate.

Mitchell, Margaret (1900-49), U.S. writer. Her best-selling and only novel *Gone With the Wind* (1936) won the 1937 Pulitzer Prize and was made into a successful film (1939).

Mitchell, Maria (1818-89), U.S. astronomer who discovered a comet in 1847. She was the first woman to be elected to the American Academy of Arts and Sciences (1848) and was professor of astronomy at Vassar College (1865-88).
See also: Astronomy.

Mitchell, Wesley Clair (1874-1948), U.S. economist and educator. He helped organize the National Bureau of Economic Research (1920), and was its research director (1920-45). He served on many government boards and was a leading authority on business cycles.
See also: Economics.

Mite, tiny arachnid, a relative of the spider, rounded body, four pairs of legs. Mites feed by sucking the juices of plants and animals. Some are pests and may carry diseases, e.g. scrub typhus. Others cause itching and scabs when they get under the skin. Chiggers are the larvae of one form of mite.

Mithra, ancient Indo-Iranian sun-god, one of the ethical lords, or gods, of Zoroastrianism. He was the chief Persian deity during the 5th century B.C., and his cult spread over most of Asia Minor reaching Rome, according to Plutarch, in 68 B.C.. Mithraism was especially popular among the Roman legions. Roman Mithraism, which competed with early Christianity for converts, thought that the forces of good and evil waged a struggle in the world. It made ethical demands on its followers and offered them the hope of immortality. It declined after A.D. 200 and was officially suppressed in the 4th century.
See also: Zoroastrianism.

Mithridates VI (132 B.C.-63 B.C.), king of ancient Pontus, on the Black Sea, who fought three wars against the Roman state. In the first (88-84 B.C.), he overran Asia Minor but was subsequently forced to make peace. He won the second war (83-81 B.C.) but lost the third (74-63 B.C.). Pompey drove him into exile in the Crimea, where he had himself killed by a mercenary.
See also: Pontus.

Mitterrand, François Maurice (1916-96), French politician, president of the republic from 1981-95. A cabinet minister in 11 governments during the Fourth Republic (1946-58), he opposed De Gaulle's establishment of the Fifth Republic in 1958. A socialist and candidate of the non-Communist left, he first ran for the presidency in 1965, but was defeated by De Gaulle. He became head of the Socialist Party in 1971 and ran unsuccessfully for the presidency a second time in 1974, losing to Valéry Giscard d'Estaing. He finally won in 1981. His party also won a majority in the National Assembly and initiated a program of mild nationalization and social reform. In the late 1980s his government became increasingly moderate.
See also: France.

Mix, Tom (1880-1940), U.S. film actor and director whose popular westerns featured spectacular photography and daring horseriding. He starred in the silent films *Desert Love* (1920) and *Riders of the Purple Sage* (1925) and in numerous films of the 1930s.

Moabite stone, ancient, black-basalt stone containing writing in Hebrew-Phoenician characters. Probably inscribed about 865 B.C., the stone stands 3 ft, 8 in (112 cm) high and 2 ft, 3 in (68 cm) wide. Its inscription narrates the deeds of Mesha, king of the Moabites, in his wars against Israel and against the Edomites.

Bronze cast of the Möbius band, (Max Bill, 1953-56, Antwerp)

Mobile (pop. 476,923), city in southwestern Alabama, on Mobile Bay, and connected by a deepwater channel to the Gulf of Mexico. Alabama's only seaport, Mobile exports cotton, iron, steel products, and lumber. The city was settled by the French in 1702, and from 1711 to 1720 was the capital of French Louisiana. It was taken successively by the English and the Spanish and became part of the U.S. in 1813.

Möbius, August Ferdinand (1790-1868), German mathematician and astronomer who developed the field of topology, which derived from his work in geometry. Topology studies the qualities of a geometric form that do not change when subject to twisting, bending, and stretching.
See also: Topology.

François Mitterrand

Mobutu Sese Seko, (1930-), president of the Republic of Zaïre (formerly the Belgian Congo) from 1966-97. He took power in a coup and in 1967 established a dictatorial regime with himself as president. In 1997 he was ousted by Laurent Kabila and went into exile.

Mobutu Sese Seko

Moccasin flower *see:* Lady's-slipper.

Moccasin snake *see:* Water moccasin.

Mockingbird, any of several species of birds of the family Mimidae native to the Americas, with long tails, short rounded wings and well-developed legs. They feed on insects and fruit. The name is derived from their ability to mimic the calls of other birds.

Mock orange, or syringa, small garden bush belonging to the saxifrage family and known for its clusters of tiny, light-colored, often-fragrant flowers. Various hybrids are grown in the United States and Mexico.

Model Parliament, English parliament set up in 1295 by King Edward I. The Model Parliament's wide representation (clergy, earls, barons, two knights from each county, and two burgesses from each borough) was symbolic of Parliament's developing representational role, although the principles of membership were by no means strictly observed through much of the 14th century.

Modigliani, Amedeo (1884-1920), Italian painter and sculptor best known for his nudes and portraits, works characterized by elegant elongated forms. He was influenced by African sculpture and by Constantin Brancusi.

Modoc, Native Americans who occupied parts of what is now California and Oregon. They are closely related to the Klamath, with whom they agreed in 1864 to move to an Ore. reservation. In 1870 a Modoc group, led by Chief Kintpuash (Captain Jack), fled back to northern California. The group was attacked by a U.S. army unit, bringing about the Modoc War (1872-73). Some of the Modoc sub-

The emperor Akbar of the Mogul Empire taming a wild elephant (illustration from the Akbar-name). The emperor sits on a horse, an example of quietness among his frightened subjects.

sequently returned to Oregon; others were sent to Oklahoma.

Moffat Tunnel, U.S. railroad tunnel, one of the longest, running for over 6 mi (9.7 km) through James Peak, Colo. The tunnel shortens the rail distance from Denver to Salt Lake City by 176 mi (283 km).

Mohammad Reza Pahlavi

Mogadishu, or Mogadiscio (pop. 1,000,000), capital and major port city of the Somali Democratic Republic, located on the Indian Ocean. Long under Arab rule, it was made the colonial capital of Italian Somaliland in 1905. When Somalia gained its independence in 1960, Mogadishu remained as its capital. Both Arabic and Italian influences are evident in the city, which was heavily damaged during the civil war in the early 1990s.

Mogul Empire, Muslim empire in northern India (1526-1857), founded by Babur, who invaded India from Afghanistan. His son Humayun was defeated by the Afghan Sher Shah Sur, but Mogul power was restored by Akbar (1556-1605), who established centralized government throughout Afghanistan and northern and central India. The Mogul "golden age" was in the reign of Shah Jehan (1628-58). During this time, the Taj Mahal, the Pearl Mosque of Agra, and many of Delhi's finest buildings were erected. In the 1700s, the rising power of the Hindu Mahratetas weakened the empire. In 1857 the British deposed the last Mogul emperor, Bahadur Shah II.
See also: Akbar; Babur.

Mohammad *see:* Muhammad.

Mohammad Reza Pahlavi (1919-80), shah of Iran (1941-79). The British forced his pro-German father, Reza Pahlavi, to abdicate in 1941. Mohammad Reza Pahlavi left the country briefly during the rule of the left-wing Nationalist Muhammad Mossadegh (1953), but returned with CIA-backing to consolidate his power. He instituted certain western social reforms, but exercised a dictatorship bolstered by a pervasive secret police, the Savak. An Islamic revolution forced him into exile in 1979. He died in exile in Egypt.

Mohawk River, chief tributary of the Hudson River. Formed in Oneida county, central New York State, the Mohawk flows south and east for about 145 mi (233 km) joining the Hudson at Cohoes. The Mohawk Valley, a historic route from the Hudson to the Great Lakes, saw fierce fighting during the French and Indian Wars and the Revolutionary War.

Mohawks, Native American tribe, of what is now New York State, one of the five tribes of the Iroquois League, which had a highly developed culture that flourished through the 17th and 18th century.

Mohegan, North American Indian tribe of the Eastern Woodlands. Mohegans formed a branch of the Mahican group, which occupied southwestern Connecticut in the 17th and 18th centuries. In the 1600s, the Mohegan chief, Uncas, and the settlers formed an alliance against hostile native groups. In the 1700s, however, many Mohegans were driven from the land, had died of disease, or were converted to Christianity. A few remaining descendants still live on a Connecticut reservation. Both Mohegans and Mahicans are sometimes called Mohicans, after the fictional tribe in James Fenimore Cooper's *The Last of the Mohicans*.
See also: Mahican.

Mohican *see:* Mahican; Mohegan.

Moholy-Nagy, László (1895-1946), Hungarian painter, designer, and member of the German Constructivist school. He was professor at the Bauhaus, 1923-28. He founded the Institute of Design at the Illinois Institute of Technology in Chicago in 1939 and was an important influence on U.S. industrial design.

Mohorovicic discontinuity, or Moho, seismic boundary of the earth originally regarded as separating the crust and mantle, evidenced by rapid increase in the velocity of seismic waves.

Moisture *see:* Humidity; Weather.

Mojave Desert, barren area of mountains and desert valley in southeastern California. It includes Death Valley in the north and the Joshua Tree National Monument in the south.

Molar *see:* Teeth.

Mold, general name for a number of filamentous fungi that produce powdery or fluffy growths on fabrics, foods, and decaying plant or animal remains. Best known is the blue bread mold caused by penicillium, from which the antibiotic penicillin was first discovered.
See also: Fungi.

Moldavia, historic region in eastern Romania, divided by the Prut River from the Moldavian Soviet Socialist Republic (MSSR). Moldavia belonged to Romania from 1918 to 1940, when a portion of it was annexed by the Soviets as the MSSR, with Kishinev as its capital. After the collapse of communism in the USSR in 1991 the MSSR became an independent country, named Moldova. Moldavians constitute 65% of the population; Ukrainians and Russians are important minorities. Agriculture and mining are important to the country's economy.
See also: Union of Soviet Socialist Republics; Romania.

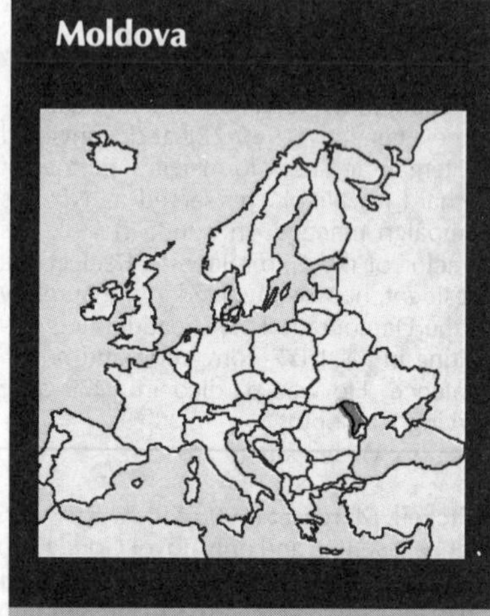

Capital:	Kishinev
Area:	13,010 sq mi (33,700 sq km)
Population:	4,359,000
Government:	republic
Independent:	1991
GNP:	U.S.$5,485,000,000
Per capita:	U.S.$1,260

Mole, any of various small burrowing insect-eating mammals of the family Talpidae native to the Northern Hemisphere. Moles have spade-shaped front feet and long, mobile muzzles. Their eyes are small and often covered with fur, and they have no external ears, though their sense of hearing is acute.

Mole, in chemistry, a quantity of particles equal to Avogadro's number, or 6.02252×10^{23}. One mole of a given compound is that number of molecules of the compound. The gram-atomic weight of an element is the weight, in grams, of a mole of that element. The gram-molecular weight of a compound is the weight in grams of a mole of molecules of that compound.
See also: Chemistry.

Mole, in dermatology, pigmented spot or nevus in the skin, consisting of a localized group of special cells containing melanin. Dramatic change in a mole, such as an increase in size, change of color, or bleeding, may indicate that the mole has developed in to a cancerous tumor called a melanoma, which can spread to other parts of the body.

Molecular biology, study of the structure and function of the molecules that make up living organisms. This includes the study of proteins, enzymes, carbohydrates, fats, and nucleic acids, and their interactions in the life processes.
See also: Biology.

Molecular weight, sum of the atomic weights of all the atoms in a molecule, expressed in atomic mass units.

Molecule, smallest particle of a chemical compound that retains all the chemical properties of that compound. Molecules are made up of atoms joined to one another by chemical bonds. The composition of a molecule is represented by its molecular formula. Molecules range in size from two atoms to macromolecules (chiefly proteins and polymers), which may be composed of 10,000 or more atoms.

Molière (1622-73), French playwright of high comedy and farce, also known for his skills as an actor and director. He was born Jean Baptiste Poquelin. Granted patronage by Louis XIV and given his own theater, Molière wrote satiric plays with controversial themes that often offended religious groups. Among these were *The School for Wives* (1662), *The Imposter* (1664), and *The Misanthrope* (1666).

Mollusk, any of many soft-bodied invertebrate animals (phyllum Mollusca), typically having a shell into which the body can withdraw. Mollusks constitute the second largest phylum of invertebrates. They include slugs and snails, limpets, winkles, clams, mussels, and oysters, as well as octopuses and squids. Mollusks have adapted to niches in the sea, in fresh water, and on land. Major groups of mollusks include bivalves, cephalopods, chitons, and gastropods.

Molly Maguires, secret society of Irish-Americans in the Pennsylvania coal-mining area, 1862-75. The name was borrowed from an Irish anti-landlord organization. Their purpose was to help miners in resisting oppressive conditions and intimidation by mine owners, but they frequently resorted to violence against private police hired by owners. In 1875 the organization was broken by Pinkerton agents who infiltrated the group. Twenty members were executed by hanging.

Molnár, Ferenc (1878-1952), Hungarian author and playwright. His play *Liliom* (1909) was adapted as the musical *Carousel* (1945). He also wrote novels and short stories. He lived in the United States from 1940.

Moloch, or Molech, Canaanite god of fire, to whom children were sacrificed, identified in the Old Testament as a god of the Ammonites. His worship, introduced by King Ahaz, was condemned by the prophets, and his sanctuary at Tophet near Jerusalem later became known as Gehenna.

Molokai *see:* Hawaii.

Molotov, Vyacheslav Mikhailovich (1890-1986), Soviet diplomat and politician. Born Vyacheslav Mikhailovich Skriabin he became a Bolshevik in 1906. After the Russian Revolution of 1917 he quickly rose to power in the ruling Communist Party. He was Soviet Premier (1930-41) under Joseph Stalin. As foreign minister (1939-49 and 1953-56) he negotiated the 1939 nonaggression pact with Germany and played an important role in the USSR's wartime and postwar relations with the West. Expelled from the party central committee in 1957 for opposing Nikita Khrushchev, he held only minor posts. In 1964 he was expelled from the party itself, but he was reinstated in 1984.
See also: Union of Soviet Socialist Republics.

Molting, shedding of the skin, fur, or feathers by an animal. It may be a seasonal occurrence, as a periodic renewal of fur or plumage in mammals and birds, or it may be associated with growth, as in insects or crustaceans. In birds and mammals the molt is primarily to renew worn fur or feathers so that pelage or plumage is kept in good condition for waterproofing, insulation, or flight. It also may serve to shed breeding plumage or to change between summer and winter coats. In invertebrates the rigid external skeleton must be shed and replaced to allow growth within. In larval insects the final molts are involved in the metamorphosis to adult form.

Moltke, Helmuth Karl Bernhard (1801-91), Prussian and, later, German chief of staff (1858-88). A strategist of genius, he won victories against Denmark (1864), Austria (1866), and France (1870), greatly furthering German unification.

Molybdenum, chemical element, symbol Mo; for physical constants see Periodic Table. Molybdenum was discovered by Karl Scheele in 1778. It occurs in nature in the minerals wulfenite and powellite and is obtained principally from molybdenite, a sulfide. Molybdenum is a silvery-white, hard, ductile, unreactive, metal. It is a valuable alloying agent for steels and for nickel-based, heat-resistant, and corrosion-resistant alloys. Molybdenum and its compounds are used in nuclear energy applications, missile and aircraft parts, ultra-high-strength steels, high-temperature lubricants, and as catalysts.

Mombasa (pop. 341,100), large port city in Kenya, on the Indian Ocean, an international center of shipping and industry. It contains an airport, state buildings, an oil refinery, and tourist facilities. Its major industries include cement, food processing, and glass. First settled by the Persians and Arabs in the 8th century, Kenya was later ruled variously by Portugal, Oman, and Great Britain until it was declared independent in 1963.

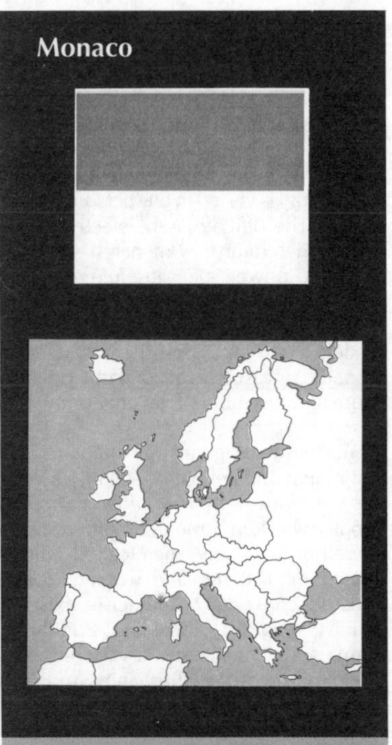

Capital:	Monaco
Area:	0.7 sq mi (1.9 sq km)
Population:	29,100
Form:	constitutional monarchy
Independent:	1489

Monaco

Monaco, independent principality on the Mediterranean near the French-Italian border, about 370 acres (150 hectares) in area. It is a tourist center, with a yachting harbor and a world-famous casino. The reigning constitutional monarch, Prince Rainier III, succeeded to the throne in 1949 and married the U.S. film actress Grace Kelly in 1956. In 1962, after a crisis with France over Monaco's tax-free status, Rainier proclaimed a new constitution, guaranteeing fundamental rights, giving the vote to women, and abolishing the death penalty. The government consists of three councilors, headed by a minister of state who must be French. There is an

18-member National Council, elected for five-year terms by universal suffrage, which shares legislative powers with the Prince.

Mona Lisa *see:* Da Vinci, Leonardo.

Monarchy, form of government in which sovereignty is vested in one person, usually for life. The office may be elective but is usually hereditary. A monarch who has unlimited power is an *absolute monarch*; one whose power is limited by custom or constitution is a *constitutional monarch.* In modern parliamentary democracies a monarch is usually a nonparty political figure and a symbol of national unity

Monasticism, religious way of life, usually communal and celibate, generally involving withdrawal from worldly concerns. People who join a monastic order are secluded from society; men (called monks) live in *monasteries* and women (called nuns) in *convents.* Monasticism exists in various religions, including Buddhism, Islam, and Christianity (also Greek Orthodox church). In Christianity, monasticism is mostly a phenomenon of Catholicism. Monastic orders include Franciscans, Carmelites, and Dominicans.

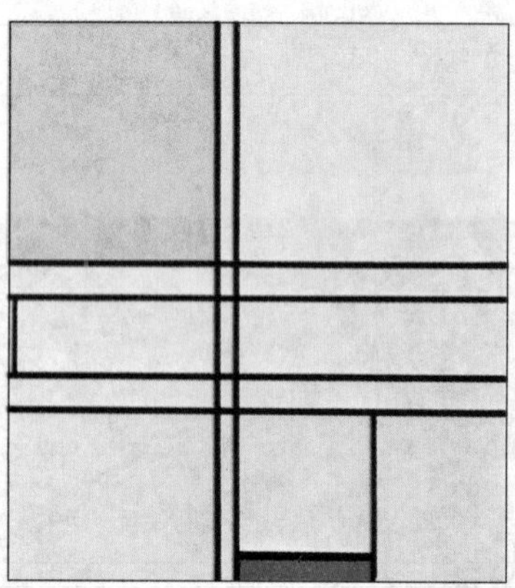

Piet Mondrian's Composition in blue and yellow *(1939)*

Claude Monet's The Saint-Lazare Railway Station *(1876-78)*

Monazite, yellow to brown mineral containing phosphates of the rare earth elements cerium, lanthanum, and neodymium. It also contains yttrium and thorium. Found mainly in India, Brazil, and Australia, monazite is the prime source of thorium, a nuclear fuel. The rare earths, important for the manufacture of glass are also extracted from monazite

Monck, Viscount (1819-94), Irish-born governor general of British North America (1861-67) and first governor general of the Dominion of Canada (1867-68). Monck's support of confederation helped to bring about the establishment of the dominion.

Moncton (pop. 55,500), city in New Brunswick and the center of distribution and transportation for the Maritime Provinces of Canada. It provides railway, ferry, and highway access to Prince Edward Island and Nova Scotia, as well as regular air flights to the Canada mainland and the U.S. Industries include metal products, wood, and textiles.
See also: New Brunswick.

Mondale, Walter (1928-), 41st U.S. vice president (1977-81), under Jimmy Carter. His early career was furthered by Hubert Humphrey. As a Democratic senator from Minnesota (1964-77) he was known as a liberal and populist reformer. Carter and Mondale ran again in 1980 but lost to Ronald Reagan and George Bush. Mondale was the Democratic nominee for president in 1984. His running mate, Geraldine Ferraro, was the first woman to be chosen for the vice presidency by a major U.S. party. Mondale and Ferraro lost to Reagan and Bush.

Mondrian, Piet (1872-1944), Dutch painter and theorist, a founder of the Stijl movement. At first a symbolist, he was later influenced by cubism and evolved a distinctive abstract style relating primary colors, black, white, and gray in gridlike arrangements.

Monera, group of primitive one-celled organisms that have no nucleus. Scientists place monera in the Monera kingdom or in the plant or protist kingdom. Bacteria and blue-green algae comprise the group's single division. Monera, found throughout the world, live in soil (parasitic species live in organisms) and are able to survive the extreme temperatures of hot springs and frozen tundra.

Monet, Claude (1840-1926), French painter, leading exponent of impressionism, a term coined after his picture *Impression, Sunrise* (1872). He painted his landscapes outside, in natural light, applying paint in a multitude of variously colored strokes and swatches, thus conveying the appearance of a subject in a particular light, in a particular season, and at a particular time of day. His last pictures of water lilies are virtually abstract patterns of color.

Monetarism, theoretical position in economics, chiefly associated with the work of Milton Friedman of the University of Chicago. This contemporary theory is based on the 19th-century "quantity-of-money" theory, which directly related changes in price levels to changes in the amount of money in circulation. Monetarism, which stands generally in opposition to Keynesianism, advocates curing inflation and depression not by fiscal measures but rather by control of the nation's money supply—for instance, by varying the interest rate charged by the Federal Reserve System and expanding or limiting the sale of treasury bills.
See also: Economics.

Money, in an economic system, anything accepted as a medium of exchange, measure of value, or means of payment. In primitive societies, barter, or direct physical exchange, was commonly used. The precise origin of money is unknown. It evolved gradually out of the needs of commerce and trade. Many objects have at one time or another been used as money: shells, nuts, wampum, beads, and stones. Gradually, metal was adopted because of its easy handling, durability, divisibility, and—especially with gold or silver—for its own value. The oldest coinage dates back to 700 B.C., when coins of gold and silver alloys were made in Lydia (Asia Minor). Paper money was known in China as early as the 7th century A.D., but it did not develop in Europe until the 17th century. The stability and value of paper currency is usually guaranteed by governments or banks (those invested with legal authority to issue currency) with some bullion holdings.
The monetary system of the United States during most of the 19th century was based on bimetallism, which meant that both gold and silver were legal money. With the passing of the Gold Standard Act of 1900, the dollar was defined only in terms of gold. The Gold Reserve Act of 1934 reduced this dependence on gold, and in 1971 the nation went off the gold standard

altogether. The nation's money supply is controlled by the Federal Reserve System, a central banking system created in 1913. Most currency in circulation today consists of Federal Reserve notes.

Mongol Empire, empire founded in the early 13th century by Genghis Khan (1167?-1227). Superb horseriders and archers, the Mongols of Central Asia were united into a well-disciplined, highly mobile army that conquered northern China by 1215 and then swept west through the Middle East and southern Russia, establishing a vast empire with its capital at Karakorum, in Mongolia. After Genghis Khan's death, the Mongol invasions were continued under his son Ogotai. During 1237-40 the Mongol general Batu Khan, a grandson of Genghis Khan, crossed the Volga, crushed the Bulgars and Kumans, and invaded Poland and Hungary. Baghdad, seat of the Abbasid caliphate, was sacked in 1258. The Mongol troops had a reputation for great ferocity, in particular when attacking and destroying cities.
By about 1260 the Empire was organized into four Khanates, centered in Persia, southern Russia, Turkestan, and China. Kublai Khan's rule in China (1260-94) saw the foundation of the Yüan Dynasty. The Mongol tradition of conquest was revived by Tamerlane in the 14th century and by Babur (founder of the Mogul Empire) in the 16th century.
See also: Genghis Khan; Kublai Khan.

Mongolia

Capital:	Ulaanbaatar (Ulan Bator)
Area:	604,800 sq mi (1,566,500 sq km)
Population:	2,096,000
Form:	people's republic
Independent:	1921
GNP:	U.S. $3,620,000,000

Mongolia, area in east central Asia divided into Outer Mongolia, or the Mongolian People's Republic, and Inner Mongolia, or the Inner Mongolia Autonomous Region of China. Mongolia as a whole is bordered by the Soviet Union to the north and by China to the south, east, and west.
Land and climate. The land is largely a steppe plateau with an average elevation of 3,000 ft/914 m. The Hentiyn, Sayan, and other mountain ranges hem the area to the north and northeast and the Altai Mountains mark the end of the plateau to the southwest. Much of the southeast is part of the Gobi Desert which straddles a large part of Outer and Inner Mongolia. The climate is harsh with great extremes of heat and cold. The capital of the Mongolian People's Republic is Ulan Bator.
People. Although both Inner and Outer Mongolia are communist, many Mongolians continue to practice Tibetan Buddhism (Lamaism). Mongolian is the official language.
Economy. The economy is based upon livestock farming, the principal livelihood of a traditionally nomadic people. There is also some agriculture. Coal, iron ore, gold, and other minerals are mined. Industry is limited to felts, furniture, and other consumer goods. The chief exports are livestock, wool, hides, meat, and ores.
History. Formerly the heartland of the Mongol Empire founded by Genghis Khan in the 13th century, Mongolia became a province of China in 1691. Mongolia declared its independence in 1911, but was reoccupied by China in 1919. With support from the Soviet Union, Outer Mongolia declared its independence again in 1921. In 1924 it became the Mongolian People's Republic, the world's second communist state although China did not recognize Mongolia's independence until 1946. In 1990 the country became a multiparty democracy, and Punsalmaagiyn Ochirbat was elected president.

Mongolism *see:* Down's syndrome.

Mongoose, small carnivorous mammal with a reputation for killing snakes and stealing eggs. There are about 48 species occupying a variety of habitats around the Mediterranean, in Africa, and in southern Asia. Most are diurnal, feeding on lizards, snakes, eggs, and other small mammals. Mongooses generally resemble weasels.

Monitor, any of a family of mostly tropical lizards of the Eastern Hemisphere that includes the world's largest, the 10-ft (3-m) Komodo dragon, of Indonesia.

Monitor and Merrimack, pioneer ironclad warships that fought the world's first battle between iron-armored vessels, at Hampton Roads, Va., on Mar. 9, 1862, during the U.S. Civil War. The *Merrimack* was a scuttled Union steam frigate, salvaged by the Confederates and renamed the *Virginia*. The Union's *Monitor* was equipped with a revolving gun turret. Neither vessel was victorious in the engagement.

Traditional nomadic huts of Mongolia

Monk, Thelonious (1917-82), U.S. composer, pianist, bandleader, and one of the innovators of modern jazz in the 1940s. His compositions "Round Midnight," "52nd Street Theme," "Epistrophy," and "Straight No Chaser" are jazz standards.

Monkey, any of several primates, suborder Anthropoidea. There are two superfamilies of monkeys, New World and Old World. Though there is little uniformity in the group, monkeys have flattened faces, the Old and New World families being distinguished by nose shape. Monkeys are normally restricted to tropical or subtropical areas of the world. Old World forms include langurs, colubuses, macaques, guenons, mangabeys, and baboons. Monkeys of the New World include sakis, uakaris, howlers, douroucoulis, squirrel monkeys, and capuchins.

Monkey bread *see:* Baobab.

Monkey flower, name of large group of herbs and shrubs (genus *Mimulus*) in the figwort family. Found mostly on the western coast of North America in wet areas, these plants grow to a height of 6 to 36 in (15 to 91 cm). The spots on their petals give the impression of a monkey.

Monmouth, Duke of (1649-85), illegitimate son of King Charles II of England. When he did not inherit his father's throne, he invaded England (1685) with his own army and demanded that his father's successor, James II, relinquish the crown to him. Monmouth's army lost the battle that ensued. He was captured and executed.

Monnet, Jean (1888-1979), French economist and politician, known as the architect of a united Western Europe. His Monnet Plan (1947) helped France's economic recovery after World War II. He served as first president of the European Coal and Steel Community (ECSC), and helped organize the Common Market (European Community).
See also: European Community.

Thelonious Monk

Monongahela River, river formed in West Virginia by the junction of the West Fork and Tygart rivers in Marion County. It flows 128 mi (206 km) northeast into Pennsylvania, joining the Allegheny at Pittsburgh to form the Ohio River.

Marilyn Monroe in a scene from Bus Stop *(1956)*

Mononucleosis, also called infectious mononucleosis or glandular fever, infectious disease commonly affecting adolescents and young adults. Symptoms include severe sore throat, headache, fever, and enlargement of the lymph nodes and spleen. It is believed to be caused by a herpes virus. Severe cases may require steroids, and convalescence may be lengthy.
See also: Herpes; Epstein-Barr virus.

Monopoly, economic term describing significant control or ownership of a product or service (and thereby its price) because of command of the product's supply, legal privilege, or concerted action. There are different kinds of monopoly. Patents and copyrights are legal monopolies granted by a government to individuals or companies. A nationalized industry or service, such as the U.S. Postal Service, has a monopoly. A franchise granted by government to a public company to run a public utility (such as an electrical company) creates a monopoly.
Trading and industrial monopolies have the power to decide upon supply and price of goods. Sometimes labor unions act as monopolies in the supply of workers' services. In the case of national monopolies it is considered that they can provide mass-produced goods or services at a lower price, or more efficiently, than could be provided in a competitive situation; in practice this is not always true. Business or manufacturing monopolies may often discourage competitors from entering the field of competition. There is legislation designed to control monopolies that conspire to restrain price or trade.

Monotheism, belief in one God, contrasted with polytheism, pantheism, or atheism. Classical monotheism is held by Judaism, Christianity, and Islam; some other religions, such as early Zoroastrianism and later Greek religion, are monotheistic to a lesser degree. In the theories of Sir Edward B. Tylor, religions have evolved from animism through polytheism and henotheism (the worship of one god, ignoring others in practice) to monotheism. There is, however, evidence for residual monotheism (the "High God") in primitive religions.
See also: Religion.

Monroe, James (1758-1831), fifth president of the United States. Monroe held office during the "Era of Good Feeling," a period marked by the absence of party conflict and by exceptional national growth.
Early years. Monroe entered the College of William and Mary at age 16, but left after 2 years to fight in the American Revolution. In 1780 he began to study law under the direction of Thomas Jefferson, then governor of Virginia.
Public service. Monroe was elected to the Virginia Assembly in 1782, and he later served in the Congress of the Confederation and attended the Annapolis Convention. In 1790 the Virginia legislature chose him to fill a vacancy in the U.S. Senate.
Monroe was U.S. minister to France from 1794 to 1796, under President George Washington. He served as governor of Virginia from 1799 to 1802. In 1803, as President Jefferson's special envoy to France, he helped negotiate the Louisiana Purchase, which doubled the size of the United States.
Monroe's diplomatic service continued with a stint as U.S. minister to Great Britain (1804-7). In 1811, he was once again elected governor of Virginia. Later that year, however, President James Madison appointed Monroe secretary of state, a position he held until 1817.
In 1816 Monroe, a Democratic-Republican, ran for president and defeated his Federalist opponent easily. Four years later, with the Federalist party virtually dead, Monroe was reelected with only a single electoral vote cast against him.
President. Monroe believed that Congress rather than the president should have a leading role in legislative issues. But he did take a strong stand on certain matters, such as the debate over whether Missouri should be admitted to the Union as a slave or a free state. Monroe left Congress to try to resolve the issue, but he made it clear that he would veto any bill that admitted Missouri but prohibited slavery in the state.
It was in foreign affairs that Monroe's administration had the greatest impact. With the help of Secretary of State John Quincy Adams, Monroe reached an agreement with Spain that acquired Florida for the United States and recognized a U.S. border with Mexico all the way to the Pacific Ocean. Monroe also reached agreements with Great Britain banning military installations on the Great Lakes and establishing the border between the United States and Canada as far west as the Rocky Mountains. Monroe was sympathetic to the newly independent states of Latin America and urged that they be recognized. Again with Adams's help, he formulated the famous Monroe Doctrine, which stated U.S. opposition to further interference by European countries in the affairs of the Americas. The Monroe Doctrine became an important foundation for later U.S. foreign policy decisions.
Retirement. Monroe left office at the height of his prestige. He retired to his Virginia estate, but in his last years financial difficulties caused him to move to New York City, where he lived with one of his daughters. He died there on July 4, 1831.

James Monroe

5th U.S. president

Born:	Westmoreland, County, Va.; Apr. 28, 1758.
Term of office:	March 1817-March 1825.
Vice president:	Daniel D. Tompkins.
Party:	Democratic-Republican.
Children:	3.
Died:	New York, N.Y.; July 4, 1831

Monroe, Marilyn (Norma Jean Baker; 1926-62), U.S. movie star who became world famous as a sex symbol. A comic actress of considerable talent, she acted in such films as *Gentlemen Prefer Blondes* (1953), *The Seven-Year Itch* (1955), *Bus Stop* (1956), and *Some Like It Hot* (1959).

Monroe Doctrine, declaration of U.S. policy toward the newly independent states of Latin America, issued by President James Monroe on Dec. 2, 1823. It stated that the United States would not tolerate any European interference with the former colonies of the Americas, which were "henceforth not to be considered as subjects for further colonization by any European powers." President Theodore Roosevelt's corollary to the doctrine (1904) asserted that the United States had the right to intervene to prevent any interference in the affairs of the hemisphere by outside governments and to ensure that acceptable governments were maintained there. This became known as the "big stick" policy and was invoked often by Presidents Taft and Wilson to justify armed U.S. intervention in the Caribbean.

Monrovia (pop. 465,000), capital city of Liberia, in West Africa, on Bushrod Island. Situated on the Atlantic coast at the mouth of the Saint Paul River, it is the administrative, commercial, cultural, and educational center of Liberia. Monrovia's modern harbor is the main source of its revenue. Monrovia, named for the U.S. president James Monroe, was founded in 1822 by the American Colonization Society as a place where freed U.S. slaves could live.
See also: Liberia.

Monsoon, wind system in which the prevailing wind direction reverses in the course of the seasons, occurring where large temperature (hence pressure) differences arise between oceans and large land masses. Best known is that of Southeast Asia. In summer, moist winds, with associated hurricanes, blow from the Indian Ocean into the low-pressure region of northwestern India caused by intense heating of the land. In winter, cold, dry winds sweep south from the high-pressure region of southern Siberia.

Montagnais, tribe of people that dwelled in Canada's Labrador Peninsula. Because the climate was too cold to grow adequate crops, the Montagnais ("Mountaineers") traveled the land in bands of 50-100 people to hunt and fish for their food. Their diet included moose, seals, fish, and small game. In the 1600s, the Montagnais became active in fur trading with the French. By the 1700s, the population of large animals had declined severely, leading to starvation among the Montagnais. Today, approximately 7,000 Montagnais remain, living in Quebec and Labrador.

Montaigne, Michel Eyquem de (1533-92), French writer, generally regarded as the originator of the personal essay. The first two books of his *Essays* (1580), written in an informal style, display insatiable intellectual curiosity tempered by skepticism. A third book of essays, which appeared in 1588, includes his last reflections. The essays deal with a range of subjects, most revolving around the nature of human life and the requirements of knowledge and happiness.

Montale, Eugenio (1896-1981), Italian poet and literary critic. Recipient of the 1975 Nobel Prize for literature, his books of poetry include *Cuttlefish Bones* (1925), *The Occasions* (1939), *Satura* (1971), and *Notebook of Four Years* (1977). In his writings, Montale expressed the complexity of modern life and the difficulty of achieving happiness. Montale also wrote short stories and essays, and translated English writings by Emily Dickinson, T.S. Eliot, and William Shakespeare into Italian.

Montana, state in the northwestern United States in the Rocky Mountain region; bordered by Canada to the north, North Dakota and South Dakota to the east, Wyoming to the south, and Idaho to the south and west.

Land and climate. Montana's two main land regions are separated by the Continental Divide, which marks the division between streams flowing west toward the Pacific and those flowing east toward the Atlantic. The Great Plains, in the eastern three-fifths of the state, are part of the huge Interior Plain of North America. They consist of high flat or gently rolling land: the northern section has numerous lakes. The Rocky Mountains, in the state's western two-fifths, is very high, rugged land with many snow-capped or heavily forested peaks. Montana has many rivers, the two principal ones being the Missouri and the Yellowstone. Grassland covers about half of Montana's area; forests cover another fourth. Many wild animals—including deer, pronghorn antelope, bear, moose, mountain goats and sheep, wolves, coyotes, and elk—live in the state. Montana's varied elevations make for great differences in climate. West of the Continental Divide, summers are cooler and winter's warmer than east of the divide. Principal cities are Billings, Great Falls, and Butte.

Montana

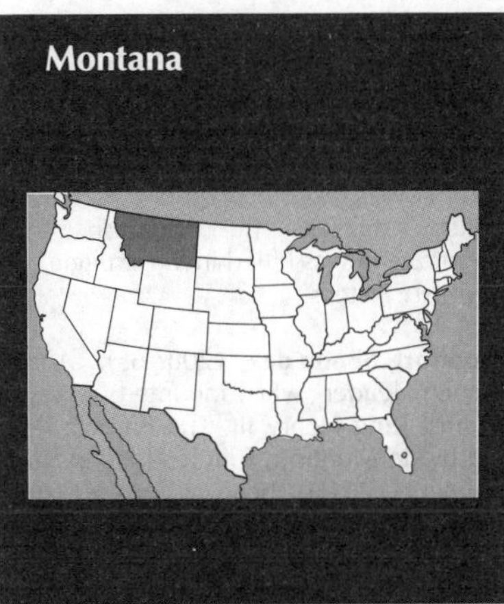

Capital:	Helena
Statehood:	Nov. 8, 1889 (41st state)
Familiar name:	Treasure State
Area:	147,046 sq mi (380,848 sq km); ranks 4th
Population:	803,655 (1990); ranks 44th
Elevation:	Highest—12,799 ft (3,901 m), Granite Peak; Lowest—1,800 ft (549 m) along the Kootenai River in Lincoln County
Motto:	Oro y Plata (Gold and silver)
Flower:	Bitterroot
Bird:	western meadowlark
Tree:	Ponderosa pine
Song:	"Montana"

Economy. Montana's main industries are manufacturing, agriculture, mining, and tourism. Chief manufactured goods are lumber and wood products, petroleum products, primary metals and minerals, farm machinery and processed foods. Chief crops are wheat, barley, sugar beets, hay, and oats; chief livestock products are cattle, hogs, sheep, and wool. Petroleum and coal are the top mineral products, followed by gold, silver, copper, and lead. The manufacture of lumber and wood products is Montana's leading industry, even though trees in the national parks cannot be logged. (The U.S. government owns about 30% of Montana's land.) National parks and forests, fishing, hiking, skiing, and dude ranches are popular with tourists.

Government. Montana's present constitution was adopted in 1973. The governor serves a four-year term. The state's legislature consists of 50 senators serving four-year terms and 100 representatives serving two-year terms. In the U.S. Congress, Montana is represented by two senators and one representative.

History. The area was home to many Native American tribes before the arrival of whites. French trappers probably entered the area in the 1700s, but the Lewis and Clark expedition of 1803-06 was the first recorded visit by whites. For decades after, fur trappers and traders were the only whites in the region. The discovery of gold at Gold Creek in 1852 swelled the white population—as well as lawlessness. To better control the area, Congress created the Montana Territory in 1864. Conflicts between whites and Indians peaked in the 1870s; "Custer's Last Stand" was fought at Montana's Little Bighorn River in 1876. Montana became a state in 1889. During the early 1900s, Montana developed its natural resources. Its economy suffered during the Great Depression of the 1930s, then boomed after World War II. The petroleum industry and tourism expanded in the mid-1900s. During the 1980s, thousands of jobs were lost in Montana's farming, mining, and lumber industries. Today, Montana is working to develop its natural resources, new businesses, and tourism.

State Capitol in Helena, Montana

Montcalm, Marquis de (1712-59), French general, military commander in Canada from 1756 during the French and Indian Wars. He captured Fort Ontario (1756) and Fort William Henry (1757) and repulsed the British at Ticonderoga (1758). He was defeated and killed on the Plains of Abraham (Sept. 13, 1759), while unsuccessfully defending Quebec against the British General James Wolfe, who was also killed.
See also: Quebec, Battle of.

Monte Carlo (pop. 11,600), town in Monaco, on the Mediterranean coast. An international resort with a gambling casino, a yacht harbor, and an annual automobile rally, it is the home (and tax haven) of many international firms.
See also: Monaco.

Monte Cristo, small Italian island. Located in the Tyrrhenian Sea between Italy and Corsica, this mountainous island has an area of 6 sq mi (16 sq km) and rises to 2,116 ft (645 m) above sea level. Ruins of a 13th-century Benedictine monastery abandoned in 1553 after pirates destroyed it still stand there. Alexandre Dumas made the island famous in his novel *The Count of Monte Cristo* (1844).
See also: Italy.

Montenegro, smallest of Yugoslavia's six constituent republics, in the southwestern part of the country. Its capital is Titograd. Its former capital, Cetinje, was absorbed into Serbia after World War I. The area is mountainous with heavy forests. Mining and the raising of livestock are its chief occupations.

Monterey (pop. 27,558), city in northern California on the Pacific coast, situated about 120 mi (193 km) south of San Francisco. Until 1850, Monterey was the capital of California, under Spanish, Mexican, and U.S. rule. The 18th-century Spanish Presidio, formerly the capitol, is now the home of the U.S. Army Language School. The city, with its surrounding area, including Carmel, is a popular tourist resort and artists' colony.

Montesquieu (Charles de Secondat; 1689-1755), French political philosopher. He inherited the title Baron de la Brède et de Montesquieu. His theory that governmental powers should be separated into legislative, executive, and judicial bodies to safeguard personal liberty was developed in his most important work, *The Spirit of Laws* (1748). His ideas influenced the framers of the U.S. Constitution. Montesquieu's *Persian Letters* (1721), which satirized contemporary French sociopolitical institutions, won him early fame.

Montesquieu

Montessori, Maria (1870-1952), Italian psychiatrist and educator. The first woman to gain a medical degree in Italy (1894), she developed a system of preschool teaching, the Montessori Method, which is designed to encourage individual initiative. Children of three to six are given a wide range of materials and equipment that enables them to learn by themselves or with minimal adult intervention. There are about 600 schools in the United States using this method.
See also: Psychiatry.

Monteverdi, Claudio (1567-1643), Italian composer. His innovative operas were the predecessors of modern opera, in which aria, recitative, and orchestral accompaniment enhances dramatic characterization. *Orfeo* (1607) is considered the first modern opera. His other compositions include many madrigals, *Vespers* (1610), much other sacred music, and the operas *The Return of Ulysses to His Country* (1641) and *The Coronation of Poppaea* (1642).
See also: Opera.

Bernard Montgomery

Montevideo (pop. 1,247,900), capital and largest city of Uruguay, located in the south on the Rio de la Plata. It is the country's industrial, cultural, and transportation center, as well as a seaport and popular resort. Founded in 1724, it became the capital in 1828.

Montezuma, or Moctezuma. name of two Aztec rulers of Mexico before the Spanish conquest. Montezuma I (1390-1469) was a successful military leader who ruled from 1440. His descendant, Montezuma II (1466?-1520), was the last Aztec emperor (c.1502-20). When the Spanish conquistadors arrived, Montezuma failed to resist them because he believed Cortés to be the god Quetzalcoatl. When Montezuma was taken hostage, the Aztecs rebelled against the Spanish, and Montezuma was killed in the struggle.
See also: Aztecs.

Montfort, Simon de (1208?-65), Anglo-French leader who mounted a revolt against King Henry III. The Baron's War, led by de Montfort, followed Henry's annulment (1261) of the Provisions of Oxford which he had been forced to sign in 1258. The war was ended with the capture of the king (1264). The parliament of 1265, summoned by Montfort and including representatives from every shire, town, and borough, was a landmark in English history. In subsequent fighting Montfort was killed at the Battle of Evesham.

Montgolfier, Joseph Michel (1740-1810) and **Jacques Étienne** (1745-99), French brothers noted for their invention of the first manned aircraft, the first practical hot-air balloon, which they flew in 1783. Later that same year Jacques Montgolfier assisted Jacques Charles in the launching of the first gas (hydrogen) balloon.
See also: Balloon.

Montgomery (pop. 292,517), capital of Alabama. Lying in the cotton-belt, it is a major Southern agricultural market center. Its other industries include manufacturing of furniture, glass, machinery, paper, and textiles. Named after Brigadier General Richard Montgomery, a Revolutionary War hero, Montgomery played a key role in the Civil War, and is often referred to as the "Cradle of the Confederacy." In 1861, the Confederate States of America were established there, Montgomery was made the first Confederate capital, and Jefferson Davis was inaugurated as president of the Confederacy in its capital. More recently, Montgomery was a focus in the Civil Rights Movement. Dr. Martin Luther King, Jr. led demonstrations there to promote equal treatment for all people. In 1956, Montgomery was one of the first Southern cities to ban racial segregation on buses.

Montgomery, Bernard Law (1887-1976), British field marshal who defeated the Germans by Gen. Rommel at El Alamein (1942), thus driving the Germans out of northern Africa. Montgomery later commanded the British forces in the invasion of Normandy (1944). After the war he served as supreme commander of NATO (1951-58).
See also: North Atlantic Treaty Organization.

Monticello, 640-acre (260-hectare) estate planned by Thomas Jefferson in Virginia, just outside Charlottesville. Construction of the neoclassical mansion atop a small mountain began in 1770; Jefferson moved in before it was completed and lived there for 56 years. His tomb is nearby. The house was declared a national shrine in 1926 and is open to the public.

Montpelier (pop. 8,241), capital of Vermont. Located on the Winooski and North Branch rivers in central Vermont, many of its citizens are employed by the state government and insurance offices in the area. Products manufactured in Montpelier include lumber, granite, plastics, and stone-finishing and sawmill equipment. It is a tourist center.

Montreal (officially Montréal; pop. 1,015,000), city in southern Quebec, Canada, located on the island of Montréal at the confluence of the St. Lawrence and Ottawa rivers. A major inland port on the St. Lawrence Seaway, Montreal is Canada's largest city. It is named for 764-ft (233-m) Mount Royal, which rises in the city's center. A French mission was built on the site in 1642, which soon become an important fur-trading center. Ceded to Britain in 1763, the city has retained much of its French character. In the 19th century Montreal grew into an important transportation and industrial center, aided by its many natural resources and an abundance of hydroelectric power. It is the site of McGill University and the University of Montréal.

Mont Saint Michel, rocky isle off the northwestern French coast. A tourist attraction, it contains a small town and a Benedictine abbey founded in 708. The abbey's church is renowned for its Gothic architecture.

Montserrat, Leeward Island in the West Indies, situated southeast of Puerto Rico. It was discovered and named in 1493 by Christopher Columbus, and colonized by the British in 1632; they took possession of it in 1783. Montserrat contains 3 mountain groups within an area of 38 sq mi (98 sq km). A British dependency, Montserrat has been self-governing since 1960. Plymouth is its capital. Its chief crops include cotton, limes, and vegetables.

Moody, Helen Wills *see:* Wills, Helen Newington.

Moon, natural satellite of the earth. The moon is 2,160 mi (3,476 km) in diameter, or about one-fourth the size of the earth, and has a smaller mass than the earth. It would take 82 moons to tip the scales against the earth. The moon is about 239,000 mi (384,623 km) from earth.
The moon takes just under a calendar month, or 27.322 days, to orbit the earth. In fact, the word "month" is derived from the word "moon." As it orbits the earth, it also rotates on its axis. The result is that the moon always presents the same side toward the earth.
In the course of its orbit, the moon is seen to go through phases. It reflects sunlight and its phases are the result of the progressive increase and decrease of the portions of its surface reflecting sunlight as it orbits the earth. The new moon occurs when the moon's reflecting surface is turned away from the sun and is completely in shadow.

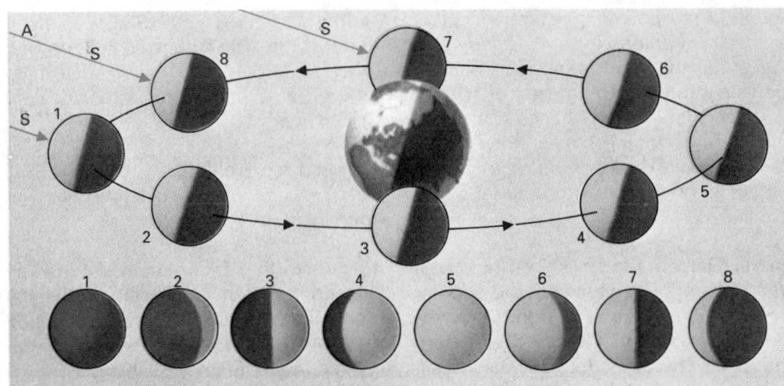

A. As the moon rotates around the earth, it goes through phases. At each phase, the amount of sunlight reflected by the moon towards the earth changes. In position 1, when the moon is between the sun and earth, it is called a new moon, in position 5, it is a full moon, in positions 3 and 7 it is a half moon, and in positions 4 and 6 it is a gibbous moon.
B. The moon rotates on its axis once every 27 1/3 days. Since it rotates around the earth at the same rate, the same moon face always faces towards earth.
C. From point 1 to point 2, the moon makes one complete revolution. To an observer on earth, however, the moon has not made a complete revolution until it reaches point 3, since the earth is itself orbiting around the sun.

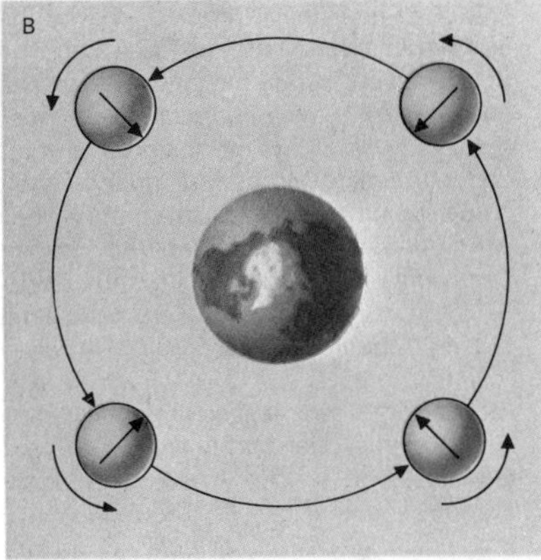

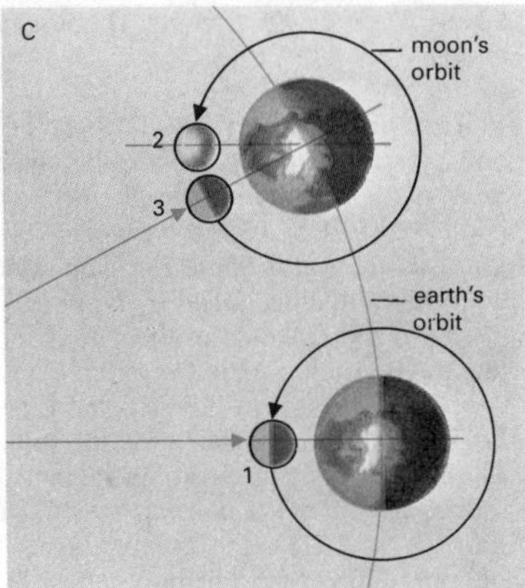

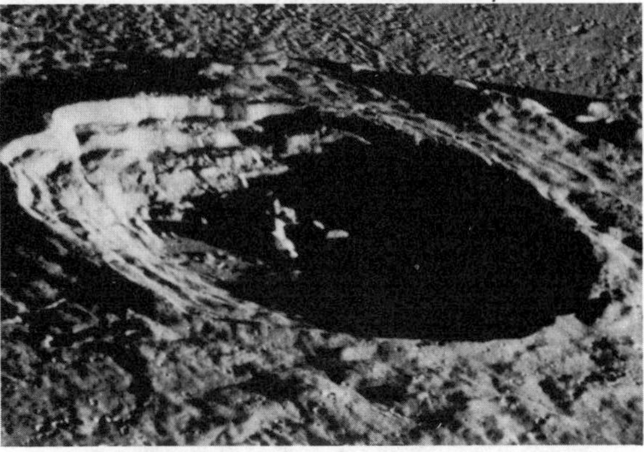

The crater Erastosthenes on the moon, photographed by Apollo 12

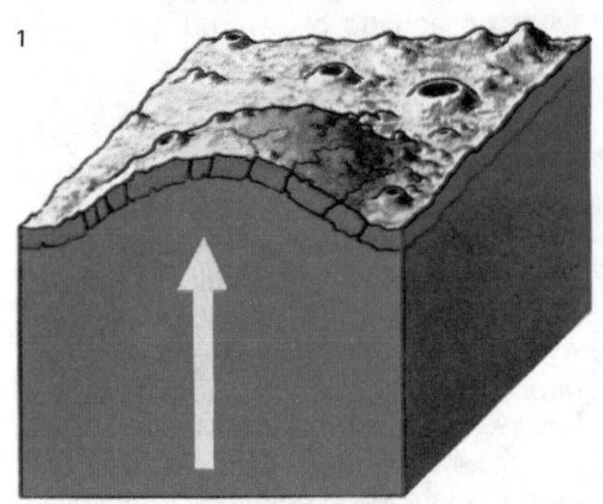

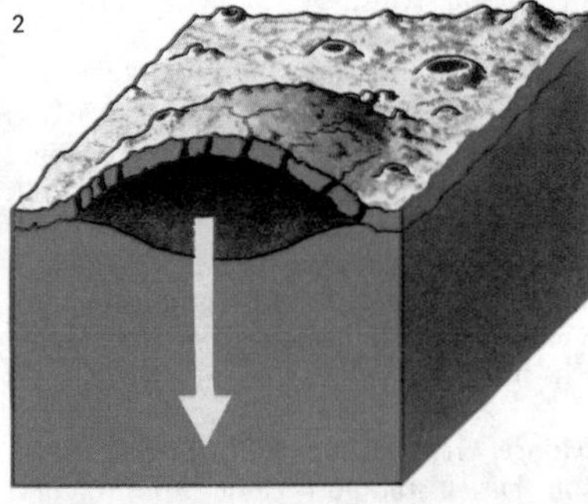

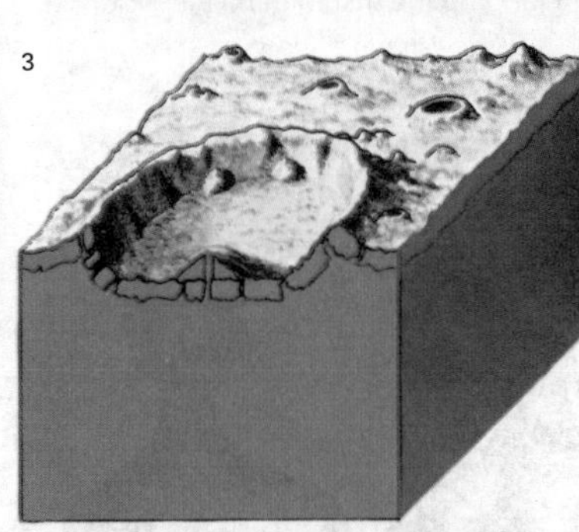

The volcanic theory states the following: Domes formed on the hot lunar crust by such processes as magmatic convection (1). On cooling, the material under these domes descended, leaving a void (2). The surface layer then collapsed, forming a walled plain or crater (3). Central volcanic peaks can also form, as magma penetrates through fissures in the collapsed dome.

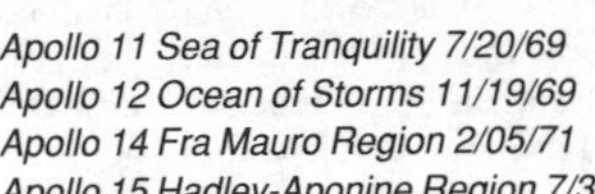

Apollo 11 Sea of Tranquility 7/20/69
Apollo 12 Ocean of Storms 11/19/69
Apollo 14 Fra Mauro Region 2/05/71
Apollo 15 Hadley-Aponine Region 7/30/71
Apollo 16 Descartes 4/16/72
Apollo 17 Taurus-Lithrow 12/72

The lunar rover of the Apollo 15 mission, used to carry the astronauts over 17 mi (27 km) of lunar terrain

The full moon occurs when the whole of the moon's reflecting surface is illuminated by the sun.
With the naked eye, the moon appears to be divided unevenly into bright and dark areas. Through a telescope astronomers are able to identify the bright regions as upland areas and the dark regions as lowlands, plains, or depressions. The plains are called "maria," from the Latin for "seas," because they were once thought to be expanses of water. There are no bodies of water on the moon, although in 1972 Apollo 17 did discover possible traces of water. Neither is there a lunar atmosphere. Without an insulating atmosphere the daytime temperature of the lunar surface reaches 200°F (93°C), and at night it falls to –250°F (–157°C).
The "seas" of the moon are lowland areas that appear to have been flooded with volcanic lava. Scientists reason that the lava has obliterated many craters. But for more than a century, scientists argued about the origin of the moon's many craters. One theory was that the moon's features were the result of explosive impacts by giant meteors. Opponents of that view argued that some form of volcanic action had built up the craters. Closeup photographs by orbiting space probes have provided evidence of both processes. On July 20, 1969, the United States succeeded in landing the first man on the moon.
See also: Solar system.

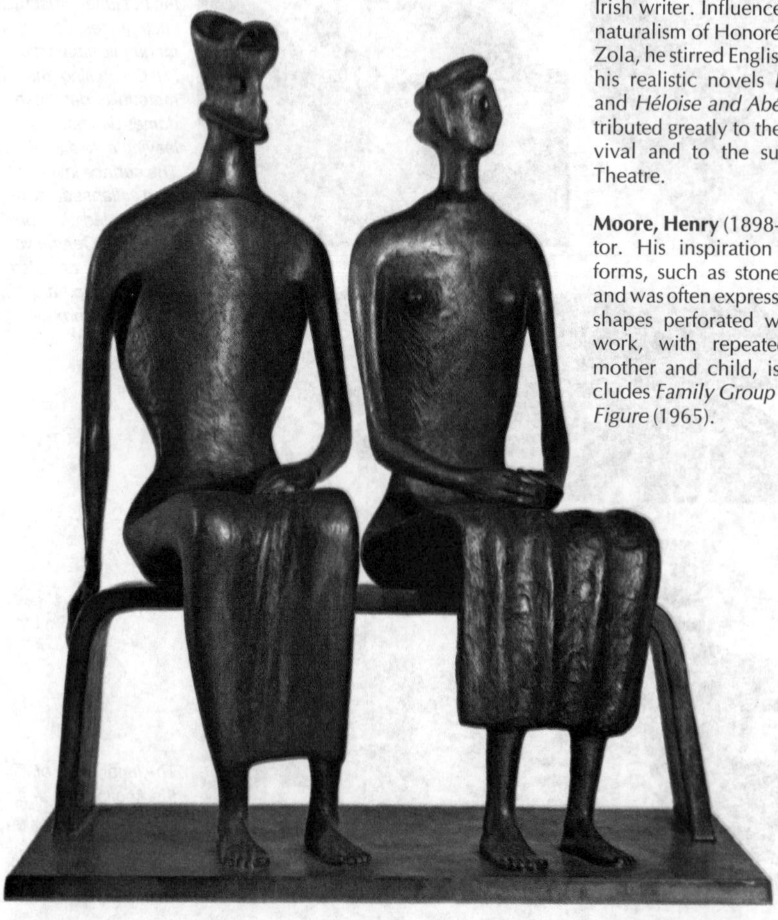

Moonflower, flowering climbing plant (*Ipomaea bona-nox* or *Calonyction aculeatum*) in the morning glory family. The vine can grow to a height of 10 ft (3 m). It bears large, heart-shaped leaves and large, white, funnel-shaped flowers that bloom at night. The flowers have a delicate fragrance and can grow to be from 3 to 6 in (8 to 15 cm) across.

Moore, Clement Clarke (1779-1863), U.S. educator and poet. He wrote the popular Christmas poem "A Visit from St. Nicholas," which begins "'Twas the night before Christmas" (1823), and for 29 years was a professor of Oriental and Greek literature at New York City's General Theological Seminary.

Moore, Douglas Stuart (1893-1969), U.S. composer and teacher. Most of his major works deal with American themes and people. In 1951 he won the Pulitzer Prize for music for *Giants in the Earth*, an opera about the difficulties faced by Norwegian farmers in the Dakotas in the 1800s. His other operas include *The Devil and Daniel Webster* (1939), set in New England, and *The Ballad of Baby Doe* (1956), set in Colorado. He also wrote orchestral pieces, such as *Pageant of P.T. Barnum* (1924) and *Moby Dick* (1928). He taught music at Columbia University. His book *From Madrigal to Modern Music* (1942), is a study of musical styles.

Moore, George Augustus (1852-1933), Irish writer. Influenced by the realism and naturalism of Honoré de Balzac and Émile Zola, he stirred English literary society with his realistic novels *Esther Waters* (1894) and *Héloise and Abélard* (1921). He contributed greatly to the Irish renaissance revival and to the success of the Abbey Theatre.

Moore, Henry (1898-1986), English sculptor. His inspiration came from natural forms, such as stones, roots, and bones, and was often expressed in curving abstract shapes perforated with large holes. His work, with repeated themes, such as mother and child, is monumental. It includes *Family Group* (1949) and *Reclining Figure* (1965).

Henry Moore's King and Queen (1952-53)

Moore, Marianne (1887-1972), U.S. poet, winner of the 1952 Pulitzer Prize for her *Collected Poems*. She edited *Dial* magazine (1925-29) and translated La Fontaine's *Fables* (1954).

Moor hen *see:* Gallinule.

Moorish art *see:* Islamic art.

Moors, North African nomadic people who adopted Islam and became ethnically fused with the Arabs during the expansion of Islam in the 7th century. The Moors went on to conquer much of Spain and Portugal in the early 8th century, crossing into France, where they were stopped by the army of Charles Martel in 732. Their rule in Spain, centered in the cities of Córdoba and Granada, saw an unparalled development of philosophy, the sciences, and architecture. The Moors lost much of their land in Spain by the late 13th century. They were finally driven from the Iberian peninsula (along with the Jews) by Christian forces under King Ferdinand and Queen Isabella in 1492.

Moose, large, long-legged mammal (genus *Alces*) of the deer family, native to cold climates. The species *A. alces*, found in Europe, is called an elk. The males have large, palmate antlers, as wide as 7 ft (2 m) across. Often living near water, the moose feeds on aquatic plants and bushes and mature trees.

Moose Jaw (pop. 35,100), city in Canada, located in southern Saskatchewan, at the point where Thunder Creek and Moose Jaw River meet. Situated on a major railway line, Moose Jaw is an agricultural and livestock processing and distribution center. Available facilities include grain storage, flour milling, stockyards, dairies, slaughterhouses, and meatpacking. Moose Jaw also has several oil refineries. Manufactured products include chemicals, clothing, and lumber.
See also: Saskatchewan.

Moose River, in northeastern Ontario, Canada. The Moose River begins at the confluence of the Mattagami and Missinaibi rivers and flows 75 mi (121 km) into Hudson Bay. Moose River and the streams and rivers that empty into it drain almost the entire northeastern Ontario area.

Mora, Juan Rafael (1814-1860), president of Costa Rica (1849-59). His accomplishments included creating a public school system, building public buildings, establishing the first Costa Rican national bank, and promoting the coffee industry. Considered a hero for his defense of Central America in 1956 and 1957 against William Walker of the United States, he was nevertheless ousted by rebels in 1859 and executed during a revolution in 1860.
See also: Costa Rica.

Morality play, form of drama popular at the end of the Middle Ages, from about the 14th to the 16th century. It was intended to instruct its audience on the eternal struggle between good and evil for human souls. The characters were personifications of virtues and vices. The most noted English example is *Everyman* (from the late 15th century), which is still sometimes performed. Morality plays grew out of earlier religious pageants and were an important step in the secularization of drama.

Moral Majority, strictly, the U.S. religious-political organization headed by the Rev. Jerry Falwell; loosely, the entire religious constituency of the New Right. In this second sense the Moral Majority is the same as the New Christian (or Religious) Right. Led chiefly by TV evangelists, it represents fundamentalist Christian beliefs and proved a potent force in the 1980 presidential and congressional campaigns, especially in the Sun Belt and West.

Moravia, central region of Czechoslovakia, bounded on the west by the Bohemian highlands and on the east by the Carpathian Mountains. Historically the homeland of the Moravian Empire, from 1029 Moravia was a province of Bohemia. In 1526 it passed under Hapsburg rule, and was part of Austria-Hungary until 1918. Moravia is a fertile and now highly industrialized region. Brno, the largest city, is noted for textile manufacturing.
See also: Czechoslovakia.

Moravian Church, Protestant church, also known as the *Unitas Fratrum* (Unity of Brethren), formed in 1457 by Bohemian followers of Jan Hus. They believed in simple worship and strict Christian living, with the Bible as their rule of faith. They broke with Rome in 1467. During the Thirty Years' War (1618-48), they were persecuted almost to extinction, but they revived in Silesia and in 1732 began the missionary work for which they are still known. The first American settlements were in Pennsylvania (1740) and North Carolina (1753). The Moravian church has about 50,000 members in the United States and has been very influential in shaping modern Protestantism.
See also: Hus, Jan; Protestantism.

Moray *see:* Eel.

More, Saint Thomas (1478-1535), English statesman, writer, and saint who was executed for his refusal to take the oath of supremacy recognizing Henry VIII as head of the English church. A man of brilliance, subtlety, and wit, he was much favored by the king. When Cardinal Wolsey fell in 1529, More was made lord chancellor. Probably because of Henry's determination to divorce Catherine of Aragon in defiance of the pope, More resigned only 3 years later. Considered dangerously influential even in silence and retirement, More was condemned for high treason. His best-known work is *Utopia*, a description of an ideal society based on reason. Long recognized as a martyr by the Catholic church, More was canonized in 1935.
See also: Utopia.

Morgagni, Giovanni Battista (1682-1771), anatomist, the first person to make the study of diseases a science. An anatomy professor at the University of Padua, Morgagni believed that the key to diagnosing and treating diseases lay in knowledge of the body and how it functions. He studied hundreds of corpses to find the causes of their deaths. His findings are recorded in *On the Seats and Causes of Diseases* (1761).
See also: Anatomy; Pathology.

Morgan, U.S. banking family famous for its immense financial power and its philanthropic activities. The banking house of J.S. Morgan & Co. was founded by **Junius Spencer Morgan** (1813-90) and developed into a vast financial and industrial empire (J.P. Morgan & Co.) under his son, **John Pierpont Morgan** (1837-1913). Many of J. P. Morgan's commercial activities aroused controversy, and in 1904 his Northern Securities Company was dissolved as a violation of the Sherman Antitrust Act. Notable philanthropic legacies include part of his art collection to the Metropolitan Museum of Art, as well as the Pierpont Morgan Library, which was endowed by his son. **John Pierpont Morgan, Jr.** (1867-1943) was U.S. agent for the Allies during World War I, when he raised huge funds and organized contracts for military supplies. Most of the large postwar international loans were floated by the house of Morgan.

Morgan, John Hunt (1825-64), Confederate general in the U.S. Civil War, famous for his skilled and daring raids behind Union lines. His great raid (1863) through Kentucky, Indiana, and Ohio ended in his capture, but he escaped to resume fighting until killed at Greenville, Tenn.
See also: Civil War, U.S.

Morgan, Sir Henry (1635-88), English adventurer and leader of the West Indies buccaneers. The destruction of Panama City (1671), his most daring exploit, took place after the signing of a treaty between England and Spain. Recalled under arrest, he was subsequently pardoned, knighted (1673), and made lieutenant governor of Jamaica (1680-82).

Morgan, Thomas Hunt (1866-1945), U.S. biologist who, through his experiments with the fruit fly *Drosophila*, established the relation between genes and chromosomes and thus the mechanism of heredity. For his work he received the 1933 Nobel Prize for physiology or medicine. His books include *The Physical Basis of Heredity* (1919), *Evolution and Genetics* (1925), and *Embryology and Genetics* (1934).
See also: Genetics; Heredity.

Morgan's Raiders *see:* Morgan, John Hunt.

Morgenthau, Henry, Jr. (1891-1967), U.S. secretary of the treasury (1934-45). During World War II he raised billions of dollars through the sale of government bonds. In 1945 he helped establish the World Bank and the International Monetary Fund, organizations to help countries develop self-sufficiency and economic prosperity.

Mörike, Eduard (1804-75), German lyric poet. His poetry, first collected in the volume *Gedichte* (1838), is small in quantity but varied in theme and technique. He also wrote a novel *Maler Nolten* (1832) and some short stories.

Morison, Samuel Eliot (1887-1976), U.S. historian and Harvard professor who wrote the official 15-volume history of the U.S. Navy during World War II. He won Pulitzer Prizes for his *Admiral of the Ocean Sea* (1942), a life of Christopher Columbus, and *John Paul Jones* (1959).

Morisot, Berthe (1841-95), French impressionist painter. Her paintings, which often included family members, were noted for the originality of their design and their exquisite color. Morisot was a prominent figure in the Parisian art world, and was good friends with Degas, Renoir, and Eduard Manet, whose brother she married.

Morley, Thomas (1557?-1603?), English composer noted for his madrigals. A pupil of William Byrd and organist of St. Paul's Cathedral, he also wrote *A Plaine and Easie Introduction to Practicall Musicke* (1597), an invaluable source of information on Elizabethan musical practice.

Mormon cricket, insect (*Anabrus simplex*) belonging to the family of grasshoppers and katydids. Found in the Great Plains and Western United States, Mormon crickets grow to a length of approximately 2 in (5 cm) and can be black, green, or brown. Although they have small wings, they cannot fly. In 1848 Mormons in Utah almost lost all their crops to a swarm of these insects. Miraculously, a flock of seagulls appeared in time and ate the crickets. Farmers today use poisons and baits to destroy them.

Mormon monument "This Is the Place", commemorating the selection of the Great Salt Lake region as a place of settlement.

Mormons, members of The Church of Jesus Christ of Latter-Day Saints, founded in 1830 by Joseph Smith. Mormons accept Smith as having miraculously found and translated a divinely inspired record of the early history and religion of America, the *Book of Mormon*. With Smith's own writings and the Bible, this forms the Mormon scriptures. The Mormons' attempts to settle in Ohio and Missouri met with recurrent persecution, culminating in the murder of Smith in 1844. In 1847 Brigham Young led the Mormons west to Salt Lake City (still the location of their chief temple). In 1850 Congress granted them the Territory of Utah, with Young as governor. Hostility to the flourishing agricultural community that developed focused on the Mormon sanction of polygamy and came to a climax with the "Utah War" (1857-58). In 1890 the Mormons abolished polygamy, and Utah was admitted to the Union in 1896. The Mormons have a president and counselors; their membership is about 3 million.
See also: Utah; Young, Brigham.

Morning-glory, common name for herbs, shrubs, and small trees of the family *Convolvulaceae.* Predominantly climbing plants, morning-glories are found in warm climates. Their fast-growing vines bear colorful, funnel-shaped flowers (some of which only open in the morning) and can grow to heights of 10-20 ft (3-6 m). The sweet potato, bindweed, moonflower, and garden morning glory are some plants belonging to this family.

Morning star *see:* Evening star.

The Roman ruins of Morocco are testimony to the Roman province that flourished here in the 2nd century A.D.

Morocco, kingdom in northwest Africa bordered by the Mediterranean Sea on the north, the Atlantic Ocean to the west, Algeria to the east, and Mauritania and the western Sahara to the south.

Land and climate. Morocco occupies an area of c.172,000 sq mi (445,480 sq km). In the north and east of the coastal plain, the ridges of the Rif Mountains form an arc from Ceuta to Melilla, 2 ports under Spanish suzerainty. South of the Rif, the Atlas Mountains extend southwestward across central Morocco. And southeast of the Atlas Mountains is the Sahara Desert and the as yet undefined section of the border with Algeria. The climate of the fertile coastal plain is Mediterranean, with hot dry summers and mild winters. The climate of the interior plains and mountainous regions is harsh. Morocco's capital is Rabat, and its cities include Casablanca, Marrakesh, and Fez.

People. Moroccans are mostly of Arab descent, but about one-third of the people are Berbers, and there are Jewish, French, and Spanish communities. Less than one-third of the people live in the cities and towns. The official language is Arabic.

Economy. Morocco's economy rests primarily on mining and agriculture. Farming accounts for about 30% of the gross national product and wheat, barley, corn, beans, dates, citrus, and other fruits are grown. Coal, manganese, iron ore, lead, cobalt, zinc, silver, and some are produced, but the principal source of export revenue is phosphate. Morocco leads the world in production of this important mineral. Tourism and handicrafts also contribute to the economy.

History. Once ruled by Carthage and then Rome, Morocco was later invaded by the Vandals (429 A.D.). The Arabs conquered in 683 A.D. and Moroccan Berbers helped them in their subsequent conquest of Spain. In the 11th century, Morocco was part of the great Almoravid empire. A haven for pirates in the 18th century, Morocco was coveted by France, Spain, and Germany, and they struggled for dominance throughout the 19th century. In the Algeciras Conference of 1906, the great powers pledged Moroccan independence but ceded special rights to France, enabling that country to establish a protectorate in 1912, part of which was ceded to Spain. The Moroccans resisted and effective French and Spanish control was not complete until 1930. Resistance continued after World War II and Morocco was granted its independence in 1956, though Ceuta, Melilla, and a few small islands remain under Spanish control.

King Muhammed V governed from 1957 to 1961 and was succeeded by his son Hassan II. He reigned as absolute monarch, but his rule was constantly threatened by attempted coups and assassinations. In 1970, a new constitution was adopted and, in 1972, amended to further limit Hassan's powers. Morocco, though not one of the hard-line Arab states, supported Syria in

Morocco

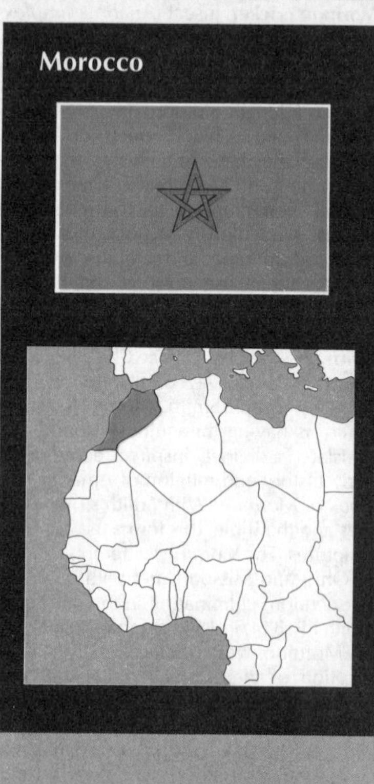

General information	
Capital:	Rabat
Area:	177,117 sq mi (458,730 sq km)
Population:	24,530,000
Official language:	Arabic
Monetary unit:	1 Moroccan dirham = 100 Mor. francs
Main cities:	Casablanca, Rabat, Fes
Government	
Form:	constitutional monarchy
Independent:	1956
Head of state:	King
Head of government:	Prime minister
Legislature:	one legislative house (Chamber of Representatives)
Executive:	King and President with Ministers
Judiciary:	highest court is the Supreme Court
Political division:	35 provinces, 8 prefectures
National economy	
Gross national product:	U.S. $17,830,000,000
Per capita income:	U.S. $750
Agriculture:	wheat, barley, corn, sugar beets, citrus fruits potatoes, tomatoes
Livestock:	sheep, cattle
Fisheries:	591,000 metric tons
Mining:	phosphate rock, coal, iron ore, lead, zinc, copper
Industries:	carpets, minig, tourism
Main exports:	phosphates, phosphoric acid, clothing, citrus fruits, fish
Transportation:	1,176 mi (1,893 km) of railroads,
Trading partners:	France, Spain, Germany, Italy
People	
Urban:	45%
Ethnic composition:	Arab-Berber 99.5%, other 0.5%
Birth rate:	35.3 per 1,000 population
Death rate:	9.7 per 1,000 population
Infant mortality:	79 per 1,000 live births
Life expectancy:	male 62 years, female 65 years

the 1973 Arab-Israeli War. Since the discovery of oil in the Middle Atlas Mountains, Hassan has pressed Morocco's claims to the western Sahara. The Polisario Front has resisted those claims, and with Algerian aid and backing has waged a guerrilla war against the king's forces. Attempts to find a political solution to the dispute have failed so far.

Morpheus, in Greek mythology, one of the many offspring of Hypnos (Somnus), god of sleep. Morpheus and 2 brothers are gods of dreams; while he is responsible for the appearance of humans in dreams, his brothers Phobetor (Ikelos) and Phantasus produce forms of animals and inanimate objects.
See also: Mythology.

Morphine, addictive opium derivative used as a narcotic painkiller. It suppresses anxiety and produces euphoria. Morphine also weakens mental and physical powers and reduces sex and hunger urges. It depresses respiration and the cough reflex, induces sleep, and may cause vomiting and constipation. Medically it is valuable in the treatment of heart failure and as a premedication for anesthetics.
See also: Drug; Drug abuse.

Morris, Gouverneur (1752-1816), U.S. politician responsible for planning the U.S. decimal coinage system. He was a member of the New York provincial congress (1775-77). At the Constitutional Convention of 1787 he argued for a strong, property-based federal government and was responsible for much of the wording of the U.S. Constitution. He was minister to France (1792-94) and later played a leading part in promoting the Erie Canal.

Morris, Lewis (1726-98), U.S. patriot and signer of the Declaration of Independence. A member of the Continental Congress, he helped supervise the storing and distribution of military supplies during the Revolutionary War and also served as a major general of New York State's militia. From 1777 to 1790 he was a member of the New York state legislature.

Morris, Robert (1734-1806), U.S. financier who funded the American Revolution and signed the Declaration of Independence. As superintendent of finance (1781-84) he saved the nation from bankruptcy by raising money (chiefly from the French) to establish the Bank of North America.

Morris, William (1834-96), English artist, poet, and designer. One of the Pre-Raphaelites, he sought to counteract the effects of industrialization by a return to the aesthetic standards and craftsmanship of the Middle Ages. In 1861 he set up Morris and Co. to design and make wallpaper, furniture, carpets, and stained glass. Influenced by John Ruskin, he formed the Socialist League (1884). His founding of the Kelmscott Press (1890) had a primary impact on typographical and book design.

Morrison, Toni (Chloe Anthony Wofford; 1931-), U.S. novelist. She is known for imaginative, poetic, emotional portrayals of individuals in relation to society and the African American experience in such novels as *Song of Solomon* (1977), *Tar Baby* (1981), and the best-seller *Beloved* (1987, Pulitzer Prize).

Morse, Samuel Finley Breese (1791-1872), U.S. inventor of an electric telegraph and portrait painter. Morse spent 12 years developing the range and capabilities of his system; he was granted a U.S. patent for his telegraph in 1840. His famous message—"What hath God wrought!"—was the first sent on his Washington-Baltimore line on May 24, 1844. For this he used Morse code, which he devised in 1838.
See also: Telegraph.

Morse code, telegraphic signal system devised (1838) by Samuel Morse for use in transmitting messages. Letters, numbers, and punctuation are represented by combinations of dots (brief taps of the transmitting key) and dashes (3 times the length of dots).

Morton, John (1724-77), U.S. patriot and signer of the Declaration of Independence. In 1765 he was a Pennsylvania delegate to the Stamp Act Congress, representatives from 9 colonies who protested British taxation of American colonists. From 1774 to 1777 he served in the Continental Congress, representatives from the 13 colonies who founded the U.S.

Morton, William Thomas Green (1819-68), U.S. dentist who pioneered the use of diethyl ether as an anesthetic (1844-46). In later years he engaged in bitter litigation over his refusal to recognize Crawford W. Long's prior use of ether as an anesthetic.
See also: Anesthesia; Ether.

Mosby, John Singleton (1833-1916), Confederate U.S. Civil War hero who led Mosby's Partisan Rangers, a cavalry troop known for its daring raids behind enemy lines in Maryland and Union-occupied Virginia. After the war he became a Republican and entered government service.

Moscow (Russian: *Moskva;* pop. 8,275,000), city, capital of the Union of Soviet Socialist Republics (USSR) and of the Russian Soviet Federated Socialist Republic, on both banks of the Moskva River. It is the USSR's largest city, and its political, cultural, commercial, industrial, and communications center. Some leading industries are chemicals, textiles, wood products, and a wide range of heavy machinery, including aircraft and automobiles. Moscow became the capital of all Russia under Ivan IV in the 16th century. Superseded by St. Petersburg (now Leningrad) in 1713, it regained its former status in 1918, following the Russian Revolution. At the city's heart is the Kremlin, location of government headquarters and a palace housing architectural relics of tsarist Russia. Red Square, the site of parades and celebrations, along with the Lenin Mausoleum and St. Basil's Cathedral, is nearby. Among outstanding cultural and educational institutions are the Bolshoi Theater, the Moscow Art Theater, the Maly Theater, Moscow University, the Academy of Sciences, the Tchaikovsky Conservatory, and the Lenin State Library.

St. Basil's Cathedral in Red Square, Moscow

Moscow Art Theater, influential Russian repertory theater famed for its ensemble acting and its introduction of new techniques in stage realism. Founded in 1897 by Konstantin Stanislavski and Vladimir Nemirovich-Danchenko, it introduced plays by Chekhov, Dostoyevsky, Gorky, and Tolstoy.
See also: Stanislavski, Konstantin.

Moselle, or **Mosel River**, tributary of the Rhine River, about 339 mi (545 km) long, arising in northeastern France; it flows into Germany, where it empties into the Rhine at Koblenz. Along its French banks lie power stations and iron and steel plants. In the German Moseltal, the renowned Moselle wines are produced.

Moses (c.13th century B.C.), Hebrew lawgiver and prophet who led the Israelites out of Egypt. According to the Bible, the infant Moses was found and raised by the pharaoh's daughter. After killing an Egyptian, he fled to the desert. Speaking from a burning bush, God ordered Moses to return and demand the Israelites' freedom under threat of ten plagues. At last, Moses led them out of Egypt (the "exodus"); the Red Sea miraculously parted to let them cross to safety. On Mt. Sinai Moses received the Ten Commandments. After years of ruling

the wandering Israelites in the wilderness, Moses died within sight of the promised land. Traditionally he was the author of the first five books of the Bible, the Torah.
See also: Bible.

Moses, Edwin Corley (1955-), U.S. track and field athlete in hurdling events. He won the 1976 and 1984 Olympic gold medals for the 400-m (438-yd) hurdle, and held the world record in that event from 1983. In 1990 he became eligible to represent the United States in international bobsled competitions.

A painting by Grandma Moses

Moses, Grandma (Anna Mary Robertson Moses; 1860-1961), U.S. artist of the primitive style. Self-taught, she began painting at age 76 and won wide popularity with her lively, unpretentious pictures of rural life in upstate New York.

Moses, Phoebe Ann *see:* Oakley, Annie.

Mosque, Muslim place of worship. The name derives from the Arabic *masjid,* meaning "a place for prostration" (in prayer). Mosques are typically built with one or more *minarets* (towers); a courtyard with fountains or wells for ceremonial washing; an area where the faithful assemble for prayers led by the *imam* (priest); a *mihrab* (niche) indicating the *qiblah* (direction) of Mecca; a *mimbar* (pulpit) and sometimes, facing it, a *maqsurah* (enclosed area for important persons). Some mosques include a *madrasah* (religious school).
See also: Islam.

Mosquitia *see:* Mosquito Coast.

Mosquito, any of 35 genera of small insects belonging to the fly order Diptera of the family *Culicidae.* Mosquitoes have long legs and 2 wings capable of beating about 1,000 times a second. Males survive on plant juices; females feed on the blood of mammals. They are able to pierce skin with needlelike parts in their proboscises. Certain species transmit diseases such as malaria, yellow fever, and encephalitis.

Mosquito Coast, coastal landstrip in Nicaragua and Honduras, along the Caribbean Sea. It begins at the San Juan River on the eastern coast of Nicaragua and continues to the Aguan River on the northeastern coast of Honduras, it is about 40 mi (65 km) wide and 200 mi (320 km) long and is named after the indigenous Mosquito tribe.

Mosquito hawk *see:* Nighthawk.

Moss, primitive plants related to the liverworts. The mosses and liverworts together make up the phylum bryophyta. Of the 2 groups, the mosses are the more advanced because they have a vertical stem with simple leaves and roots. From the tip of the leafcovered stem springs a tall stalk bearing a capsule containing the spores. Mosses display alternation of generations, with both sexual and asexual stages in their life cycles. Mosses are dependent on water for their life and reproduction. They are found in damp woods, crevices, bogs, and a few live underwater in ponds. They play an important part in preventing erosion and in the formation of soil. The peat mosses, are of considerable economic importance. They are extremely absorbent, taking up over 100 times their weight of water, and have been used in surgical dressings. Their rotted remains collect in bogs to form peat, which is used in many parts of the world as fuel and in garden cultivation.

Mössbauer, Rudolf Ludwig (1929-), German physicist. In 1961 he shared the Nobel Prize for physics for his discovery (1957) of the Mössbauer effect, a method of producing gamma rays. Among other applications, Mössbauer's work led to the verification of Albert Einstein's theory of relativity. Mössbauer taught physics briefly at the California Institute of Technology (1961) before returning to Munich to teach at its Technical University.
See also: Gamma rays.

Mossbunker *see:* Menhaden.

Moth, insect that, together with the butterfly, makes up the order *Lepidoptera.* Most moths have intricately patterned, dull-colored wings to camouflage them. When a moth larva, or caterpillar, hatches out from its egg, it eats the leaf, plant, or fabric on which it was laid. Caterpillars cause extensive damage to trees, crops, and clothes. As caterpillars grow, they shed their skin. In the final stage of growth, when it is known as a pupa, the caterpillar changes into an adult moth. Most moths sleep during the day and come out at night. They are drawn by the radiation around bright lights. There are about 120,000 known species of moths, ranging from minute wingless forms to giants several inches across.

Mother Carey's chicken *see:* Petrel.

Mother Goose, fictitious character who wrote many collections of fairy tales and nursery rhymes. The name seems to have been first associated with Charles Perrault's French *Tales of Mother Goose* (1697). Others say the American *Mother Goose Melodies* (1719) was the origin.

Mother Jones *see:* Jones, Mary Harris.

Mother of Canada *see:* Saint Lawrence River.

Mother Teresa *see:* Teresa, Mother.

Motherwell, Robert (1915-), U.S. painter and theoretician, a leading exponent of abstract expressionism. His work is characterized by restrained colors and large, indefinite shapes. His best-known series is *Elegies to the Spanish Republic* (1975).

Motion, perpetual *see:* Perpetual motion machine.

Motion pictures, the art of interpreting reality and presenting entertainment or information by projecting a series of connected photographs in rapid succession onto a screen. The illusion of motion pictures rests upon the eye's tendency to retain an image for a fraction of a second after that image has been withdrawn. If a series of pictures is prepared showing, in gradual progression, the different phases of an action and the pictures are then viewed in rapid succession, the eye tends to connect the pictures, resulting in the illusion of a moving image. In fact, a movie is a series of still photographs printed on a long strip of celluloid. The strip is run through a projector which, by means of a shutter, shows each picture, or frame, for a split second. Modern movies run at a speed of 24 frames per second; silent films ran at 16 frames a second.

Thomas A. Edison and his assistant, W.K.L. Dickson, made the first significant step toward the development of a motion picture camera by exploiting this principle. Dickson, using the new celluloid film developed by another American inventor, George Eastman, contrived a method of moving the film through the camera using sprocket wheels. By 1894, Edison had perfected the Kinetoscope, in which a viewer could see minute-long scenes from vaudeville acts and boxing matches. European inventors, adapting the Kinetoscope, devised a means of projecting pictures onto a screen for public showings, and projectors were developed almost simultaneously by Robert Paul in London and the Lumière brothers in Paris. Nickelodeons were replaced by movie theaters, and soon moving pictures were shown in many of the world's major cities.

Following the work of early pioneers, like the French magician Georges Méliès and the U.S. director Edwin S. Porter, D. W. Griffith brought the art of movie-making to its first maturity. In films such *The Birth of a Nation* (1915) and *Intolerance* (1916), he refined the elements of film language to create a highly effective narrative technique and style. He made conscious use of selective editing, closeups, and carefully considered camera positioning and movement. At about the same time, Mack Sennett produced superb silent comedies starring comedians like Charlie Chaplin, Buster Keaton, and Harold Lloyd. The studio star system developed.

Relying upon an ever more sophisticated technology and the cooperation of large

groups of skilled and semiskilled professionals, the new art form also became a new industry. Until 1912, the U.S. movie industry was dominated by the Motion Picture Patents Company. But as movies attracted rapidly growing audiences, production companies learned they could ensure profits through distributing movies to chains of theaters they had bought or built. Theater owners, for their part, banded together and formed their own studios. Until World War I, the movies were international, but after the war the United States dominated the industry. By 1920, the combination of the star system, distribution monopolies at home, and large markets abroad made Hollywood the world's film capital and the center of a multimillion-dollar industry. Its great stars included Clara Bow, Lon Chaney, Charlie Chaplin, Greta Garbo, Lillian Gish, Tom Mix, Gloria Swanson, and Rudolph Valentino. Westerns and slapstick comedies were the most popular movies.

Europe did less movie-making in this era, but its work was influential. German directors like F. W. Murnau and G. W. Pabst introduced original and highly expressive techniques into film-making, which were studied and adapted by Hollywood. And in Russia, after the revolution, Sergei M. Eisenstein perfected his montage technique in *Battleship Potemkin* (1925).

In the meantime, technicians were advancing the new art form. An American, Lee De Forest, devised a method for recording sound onto the margin of the film alongside the frames. The innovation was demonstrated in 1923, but it was not until 1927, with the release of *The Jazz Singer* featuring two songs sung by Al Jolson, that "talkies" revolutionized the movies. Overnight, silent films were abandoned. Studios embraced talking pictures and, a few years later, the technological breakthrough of color films. Joining the ever-popular dramas, costume epics, and screwball or romantic comedies, the new genres of musical and gangster films dominated the movies in the 1930s and 1940s. Joining Garbo and a few other silent stars who made the transition, a new generation arose, among them Fred Astaire, Humphrey Bogart, James Cagney, Claudette Colbert, Bette Davis, Marlene Dietrich, Judy Garland, Cary Grant, Katharine Hepburn, Edward G. Robinson, and Spencer Tracy; the innovative new directors included George Cukor, Howard Hawks,

Alfred Hitchcock, Preston Sturges, William Wyler, and actor Orson Welles.

The end of World War II and the advent of television brought a period of ferment to the movie industry. Hollywood studios turned to making TV films and shooting their movies throughout the United States and abroad. The studio system's virtual monopoly on the international film scene gave way to foreign influences. The Italians and French broke new ground under directors like Michelangelo Antonioni, Federico Fellini, Roberto Rossellini, Luchino Visconti, Jean-Luc Godard, and François Truffaut, as did the Japanese with Akira Kurosawa and Yasujiro Ozu. Meanwhile, technology continued to redefine the industry and its markets, most recently with the production of videocassettes for home viewing and the construction of multi-theater complexes. The result is an industry and art form that continue to be as dynamic as they were in their formative years.

Motmot indigenous forest-bird family of South America. Motmots are beautiful birds with feathers of blue, black, green, and orange. Motmots possess an unusual tail configuration caused by the loss of feathers which creates paddlelike shapes at the end of the tail.

Motor *see:* Electric motor; Engine; Rocket.

Motor car *see:* Automobile.

Motorcycle, motorized bicycle developed in 1885 by Gottlieb Daimler. The engine of a motorcycle may be either 2-stroke or 4-stroke and is usually air cooled. Chain drive is almost universal. In lightweight machines ignition is often achieved by means of a magneto inside the flywheel. Motorcycles were first widely used by dispatch riders in World War I. Between the wars the motorcycle industry was dominated by simple, heavy British designs. After World War II Italy developed the motor scooter, designed for convenience and economy, with 150cc 2-stroke engines. In the 1960s the Japanese introduced a series of highly sophisticated, lightweight machines that are now used all over the world.

Left: Movie greats D.W. Griffith (left), Mary Pickford, Charlie Chaplin (seated), and Douglas Fairbanks Sr. (right) at the founding of the United Artists Corporation, in 1919. Below: A scene from Orson Welles's Citizen Kane *(1941) Middle: Rudolph Valentino in* The Sheik *(1921) Right: A scene from* Dances with Wolves, *winner of the 1990 Academy Award for best picture*

Mott, Lucretia Coffin (1793-1880), U.S. reformer, pioneer of women's rights. She founded the Philadelphia Female Anti-Slavery Society (1833) and with Elizabeth Cady Stanton organized the first women's rights convention at Seneca Falls, N.Y., in 1848.
See also: Stanton, Elizabeth Cady.

Moultrie, William (1730-1805), patriot general during the Revolutionary War. In 1776 he defeated the British fleet at Charleston harbor in South Carolina, defending a fort that was later named in his honor. In 1779 he drove British troops from Beaufort. He was captured in 1780 when Charleston surrendered to the British, and was freed 2 years later in a prisoner exchange. After the end of the war he served 2 terms as governor of South Carolina (1785-87, 1792-94).
See also: Revolutionary War in America.

Mound bird, any of 12 species of birds in the megapode family. Found from Australia westward to the Nicobar Islands, this bird is also known as mound builder or incubator bird because of the mound in which it incubates its eggs. The male uses his large feet to heap plant matter into a mound, which may take up to 11 months

Louis Mountbatten

to build; the female lays her eggs in it, and then covers them with more matter. As the materials in the mound decay, they release heat. That and the heat of the sun keep the mound warm, and the eggs hatch in 6-7 weeks. Mound birds use the same mound year after year, adding to it each time. A mound can become as large as 14 ft (4 m) high and 70 ft (21 m) across.

Mound Builders, in archeology, early native North Americans who built large mounds, primarily in valleys of the Mississippi and Ohio rivers and the Great Lakes region. The chief mound building peoples were the Adena, the Hopewell and the Mississippian. Mound Builders were active from approximately 5000 B.C. to 600 B.C. Their mounds served as burial places, fortresses, or as platforms for temples or official residences. The pottery, jewelry, weavings, and stone carvings found buried in the mounds show that their builders were skilled craftspeople, and confirm that they were ancestors of Native Americans. Built entirely by human labor, thousands of mounds remain, ranging in size from 1 to 100 acres (0.4 to 40 hectares). Their shapes vary from geometric patterns to those resembling animals.

Mount Aetna *see:* Mount Etna.

Mountain, land mass elevated substantially above its surroundings. Most mountains occur in ranges, chains, or zones. The earth's crust is made up of various moving fragments; hence, land masses are in constant motion. Thus the Andes have formed where the Nazca oceanic plate is being forced under the South American continental plate, and the Himalayas have arisen at the meeting of 2 continental plates.
Mountains are classified as volcanic, block, or folded. Volcanic mountains occur when lava and other debris build up a dome around the vent of a volcano. Block mountains occur where land has been uplifted between earthquake faults. Folded mountains occur through deformations of the earth's crust; when vast quantities of sediments accumulate, their weight causes deformation. Erosion eventually reduces all mountains to plains.

Mountain ash, name for various trees and shrubs of genus *Sorbus*, rose family, native particularly to high elevations in the Northern Hemisphere. The leaves are compound, with leaflets opposite each other on the leaf stem. The white clustered flowers develop into clusters of orange or red berrylike fruit. The mountain ash provides food for wildlife, shade, and wood for implements. The American mountain ash (*S. americana*) grows in eastern Canada and the United States.

Mountain beaver, or sewellel (*Aplodontia rufa*), nocturnal, burrowing rodent of western North America. Perhaps the oldest rodent species on earth still in existence, the mountain beaver has lived in North America at least 60 million years. Unrelated to the beaver, it looks like a vole, with a stout body about 1 ft (30 cm) long, short legs, and very short tail. Colonies of mountain beavers live in burrow systems dug in stream banks.

Mountaineering, climbing of hills, cliffs, or mountains for exploration or sport. There are two types of climbing: *free climbing*, in which the climber ascends by using protrusions and cracks in the rocks as holds; and *artificial climbing*, where ladders and slings are used as aids in climbing difficult places having no natural holds. Mountaineers usually climb in a team, roped together for safety. Depending on circumstances, they will use climbing boots, ropes, pitons (steel pegs), small hammers, carabiners (rings to hold rope), and insulating clothing; in addition, for snow climbing, sunglasses, crampons (spikes attached to boots), and ice axes; and on large mountains, concentrated food, signaling devices, medical supplies, camping and cooking equipment, and oxygen masks. Two of the most famous and challenging objectives for mountaineers have been Mount Blanc in the Alps, first scaled in 1786, and Mount Everest in the Himalayas, first conquered in 1953 by Sir Edmund Hillary and his Sherpa guide Tenzing Norkay.

Mountain goat *see:* Chamois; Ibex; Rocky Mountain goat.

Mountain laurel (*Kalmia latifolia*), evergreen shrub or tree in the heath family. Native to eastern North America, it grows on mountains. A shrub can reach a height of 5 to 10 ft (1.5 to 3 m); a tree can grow to be 33 ft (10 m) tall. Mountain laurels have pink or white clustered flowers and dark, long, oval leaves with pointed ends.

Mountain lion, also known as catamount, cougar, panther, or puma, member of the cat family that inhabited the United States and Canada prior to settlement. The mountain lion can be found in Mexico, Central America, and South America. It has a tawny-colored coat and stands about 5 ft (1.5 m) long. The mountain lion is a hunter that feeds on elk and deer.

Mountain men, pioneer fur trappers and traders in the Rocky Mountains in the 1820s and 1830s. Early mountain men included John Colter, who stayed in the area after the Lewis and Clark expedition of 1804-6, Thomas Fitzpatrick, Jedediah Smith, and W.S. Williams. Many mountain men, including James Bridger, took part in William Ashley's expedition up the Missouri River in 1822. The mountain men were the first to begin opening up the Rockies and make the area's potential known. They were quickly followed by the big fur companies, such as the Rocky Mountain Fur Company and the American Fur Company.

Mountain nestor *see:* Kea.

Mountain sheep *see:* Bighorn.

Mountbatten, Louis (Francis Albert Victor Nicholas, 1st Earl Mountbatten of Burma; 1900-79), English admiral and politician. In World War II he was supreme allied commander in Southeast Asia and liberated Burma from the Japanese. After the war he was the last British viceroy of India (1947), and led the negotiations for India's and Pakistan's independence. He later served as first sea lord, admiral of the fleet, and chief of the defense staff (1959-65). He was killed by Irish Republican Army terrorists.

Mounted Police *see:* Royal Canadian Mounted Police.

Mount Elbrus, highest mountain peak in Europe. Located in the Caucasus Mountains in southwestern USSR, it is 18,481 ft (5,633 m) high and covers an area of 55 sq mi (140 sq km). Covered by approximately 22 glaciers, it is a major tourist and mountain climbing center.

Mount Etna, active volcano on the eastern coast of Sicily. Its height is about 11,000 ft (3,352 m) and its base is approximately 100 mi (160 km) in circumference. It has erupted over 250 times since its first recorded eruption in 700 B.C., some of which have been extremely destructive to nearby inhabitants.

Mount Everest, highest mountain on earth. Located in the Himalayas, in Tibet and Nepal, it rises to a height of about 29,000 ft (8,839 m). Reaching its top has been the goal of many climbing expeditions. The first to succeed were Sir Edmund Hillary and Tenzing Norkay in 1953. Several other expeditions have since been successful. According to the Sherpa tribes of the area, Mt. Everest is the abode of the Abominable Snowman, or Yeti.
See also: Hillary, Sir Edmund Percival.

Mount Fuji, highest mountain in Japan. Situated on Honshu, an island west of Tokyo, it is 12,388 (3,776 m) high. Its slopes create almost a perfect cone. The Japanese revere Mount Fuji as a sacred place; thousands climb to its top yearly. Fuji contains an inactive volcano.

Mount Kilimanjaro *see:* Kilimanjaro.

Mount Fuji in Japan

Mount McKinley, highest mountain in North America, part of Denali National Park. Located in south-central Alaska near the center of the Alaska Range, it has 2 peaks: South Peak, rising 20,320 ft (6,194 m), and North Peak, 19,470 ft (5,934 m). *Denali*, meaning "High One," is the Native American name for the mountain; McKinley was the name given in honor of William McKinley, U.S. president (1897-1901). In the early 1900s, several attempts were made to reach the mountain's summit. The first successful ascent was made in 1913, by Hudson Stuck, Harry P. Karstens, and 2 companions.

Mount Olympus, highest mountain in Greece. It rises 9,570 ft (2,917 m) at the east end of a 25-mi (50-km) range along the Thessaly-Macedonia border. The summit is snowcapped most of the year. The ancient Greeks believed Olympus to be the home of Zeus and most other gods.

Mount Palomar Observatory *see:* Palomar Observatory.

Mount Parnassus *see:* Parnassus.

Mount Rainier, highest mountain in Washington State; also known as Tacoma, its Native American name. Located in Mt. Rainier National Park, it is part of the Cascade Range. The mountain, a dormant volcano, is 14,410 ft (4,392 m) high.

Mount Royal *see:* Montreal.

Mount Rushmore National Memorial, memorial, carved into the northeast side of Mt. Rushmore, of the heads of U.S. Presidents George Washington, Thomas Jefferson, Theodore Roosevelt, and Abraham Lincoln. Located in the Black Hills of South Dakota, it was designed by the sculptor Gutzon Borglum. He and his son supervised execution of the project, which took 6.5 years of actual work to complete, and used dynamite and drills to sculpt the granite. The heads, each about 60 ft (18 m) high, are the largest sculptures in the world and can be easily seen from many miles away.

Mount Saint Helens, active volcano in the Cascade Range of the southwest region of Washington. Long considered dormant, the volcano became seismically active in Mar. 1980 and erupted for the first time in 120 years on May 18, 1980. Preceded by two magnitude-5 earthquakes, the eruption was the first in the 48 coterminous states since Mt. Lassen erupted in 1915. More than 60 people were killed; there were widespread floods and mudslides. Surrounding forests were scorched or devastated, and much of Washington, Oregon, Idaho, and Montana was blanketed with volcanic ash.

Mount Shasta, inactive volcano in northern California. Located in the southern part of the Cascade Range, it is 14,162 ft (4,317 m) high. The sides of its peak are covered with glaciers.

Mount Sinai *see:* Sinai.

Mount Vernon, restored Georgian home of George Washington (1747-99) on the Potomac River in Virginia, south of Washington, D.C. The tomb of Washington and his wife, Martha, is nearby.
See also: Washington, George.

Mount Vesuvius, only active volcano on mainland Europe, in southern Italy near Naples. Its height (about 4,000 ft/6,440 km) varies with each eruption. Capped by a plume of smoke, it is a famous landmark. Its lower slopes are extremely fertile. In A.D. 79 it destroyed the cities of Pompeii and Herculaneum. Recent eruptions occurred in 1906, 1929, and 1944.
See also: Pompeii.

Mount Washington, mountain with the highest peak in northeastern United States. Part of the Presidential Range of the White Mountains, it has two peaks. The higher peak is 6,288 ft (1,917 m) above sea level and is located in northern New Hampshire. The other peak 2,624 ft (799 m) high, is in southwestern Massachusetts.

Mount Whitney, highest mountain in the United States excluding Alaska. Its peak is 14,495 ft (4,418 m) high. Located in Sequoia National Park in central California, it is part of the Sierra Nevada Range.

Mount Wilson Observatory, astronomical observatory located on Mount Wilson 5,710 ft (1,740 m) above sea level, near Los Angeles, California. The observatory's many powerful telescopes, including both solar and reflecting telescopes, have facilitated the work of such astronomers as Edwin P. Hubble, who discovered the expansion of the universe. Founded in 1904 by the astronomer George Hale to study the solar surface, it was operated by the Carnegie Institute and the California Institute of Technology until 1989, when administrative control was assumed by the Mount Wilson Institute.
See also: Astronomy.

Mourning dove (*Zenaida macroura*), bird belonging to the pigeon and dove family. Native to North America, it measures about 12 in (30 cm) long and has a long, tapered tail. It is predominantly grayish brown, with pink and violet marks on its neck and a white border on its tail. Its name is derived from the seemingly mournful calling sound it makes. In the winter, mourning doves migrate south to warmer climates.

Mouse, term applied loosely to many small rodents. The house mouse (*Mus musculus*), found worldwide, is gray-brown with large ears, a pointed nose, and a naked tail. It is about 6 in (15 cm) long and weighs under 1 oz (28 grams). The house mouse eats almost everything, nesting in paper. The field mouse is an important herbivore, and in turn important as prey for many birds and mammals.

Mousorgski, Modest *see:* Mussorgsky, Modest.

Mouth, opening through which humans and animals take food. This cavity contains the jawbone, the teeth and gums, the palate, and the tongue. Food passes through the mouth into the digestive tract. The mouth's tongue is also essential for speaking.

Movie *see:* Motion Pictures.

Moynihan, Daniel Patrick (1927-), U.S. senator from New York since 1977. A politician with roots in academia, Moynihan distinguished himself as an authority on urban problems, serving as head of Harvard University's and Massachusetts Institute of Technology's Joint Center of Urban Studies (1966-69) and as professor at Harvard (1971-76). He was also a consultant to President Richard Nixon (1969-70), U.S. ambassador to India (1973-75), and ambassador to the United Nations (1975-76).

The Cabora Bassa Dam, on the Zambesi River, in Mozambique

Mozambique, country in southeast Africa, bordered on the north by Tanzania, on the northwest by Malawi and Zambia, on the west by Zimbabwe and South Africa, on the southwest by South Africa and Swaziland, and on the east by the Indian Ocean. The capital is Maputo.

Land and climate. Mozambique has an area of 303,075 sq mi (784,964 sq km), mostly fertile low-lying plateau and coastal plain. Of the country's many rivers emptying into the Indian Ocean, the most important, and a source of hydroelectric power, is the Zambezi, some 820 mi (1,320 km) of which flows in Mozambique. The highest peak is Monte Binga (7,992 ft/2,436 m). The climate is predominantly humid; the interior uplands are cooler.

People. The Mozambique people are overwhelmingly Bantu-speaking black Africans. Most practice native religions but there are sizable numbers of Muslims and Christians as well. Portuguese is the official language.

Mozambique

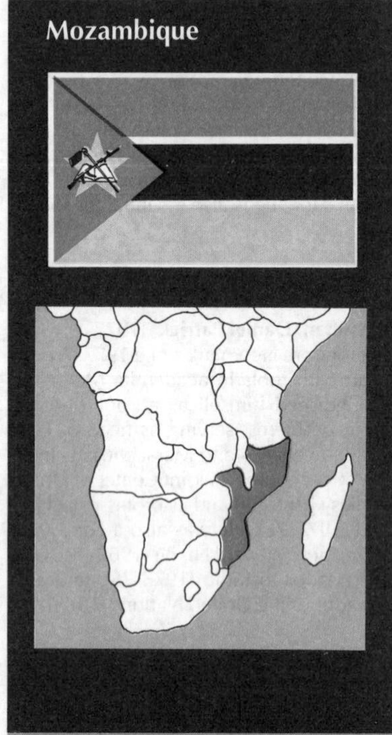

Capital:	Maputo
Area:	308,642 sq mi (799,380 sq km)
Population:	15,293,000
Government:	socialist (one party)
Independent:	1975
GNP:	U.S.$1,550,000,000
Per capita:	U.S.$100

Economy. Mozambique's economy depends principally on agriculture, forestry, and fishing. Principal exports are cashews, seafood, and cotton. Mineral wealth remains underdeveloped and a limited industry engages in food processing and cement and fertilizer manufacturing.

History. The Portuguese explorer Vasco da Gama visited the Mozambique coast in 1498, and the first Portuguese settlement was established in 1505. During the next 2 centuries, colonists exploited the native populace for cheap plantation labor and carried on a lucrative slave trade. From the mid- to late-19th century, Portugal expanded its control and private businesses, like the Mozambique Company, were allowed to rule and exploit large areas. After World War II, Mozambique's territory was increased by the addition of land formerly part of German East Africa. Confronted, as in Angola, with active guerrilla movements for independence, dominated by the Mozambique Liberation Front (FRELIMO), the Portuguese maintained strict control over the native population. After a military coup in Portugal, a decade of warfare in Mozambique ended in 1974 with an agreement for joint Portuguese-Frelimo rule. On June 25, 1975, Mozambique became the 45th African state to achieve full independence. The establishment of a black African, Marxist regime was followed by nationalization and the flight of most Europeans from the country. Mozambique's fledgling government supported Zimbabwe nationalists during the war in Rhodesia, and, despite ideological differences, maintains strong economic ties with South Africa. In 1990 Mozambique adopted a new constitution, and the Front for the Liberation of Mozambique (Frelimo) and the Mozambique National Resistance (Renamo) agreed to a limited ceasefire after 15 years of fighting.

Mozart, Wolfgang Amadeus (1756-91), Austrian composer whose brief career produced some of the world's greatest music. A child prodigy of the harpsichord, violin, and organ at the age of 4, he was concertmaster to the archbishop of Salzburg (1771-81). In 1781 he moved to Vienna, where he became Court Composer to Joseph II in 1787. He became a close friend of Haydn and set Lorenzo Da Ponte's opera librettos *The Marriage of Figaro* (1786) and *Don Giovanni* (1787) to music. In 1788 he wrote 3 of his greatest symphonies (numbers 39 to 41). Mozart composed over 600 works, including 50 symphonies, over 20 operas, nearly 30 piano concertos, 27 string quartets, and about 40 violin sonatas. In all these genres his work shows great expressive beauty and technical mastery.

MS *see:* Multiple sclerosis.

Mswati III (Prince Makhosetive; 1968-), king of Swaziland since 1986, son of King Sobhuza II, whom he succeeded to become the world's youngest head of state. He named himself for 19th-century king Mswati (Mswazi), who unified the nation of the Ngwane (who subsequently became known as the Swazi). Mswati III reconstituted the government, dissolving the 12-member supreme council, appointing a new prime minister, and placing his brothers in key cabinet positions.
See also: Swaziland.

Mubarak, Hosni (1928-), president of Egypt since 1981. A graduate of Egypt's military academy, he was trained as a bomber pilot and rose in rank to air force chief of staff (1969) and air force commander (1972). He launched the surprise air attack in the 1973 war with Israel. Chosen by President Anwar Sadat to be Egypt's vice president in 1975, Mubarak became president, by public referendum, after Sadat was assassinated.

Muckraker, term coined in 1906 by President Theodore Roosevelt to journalists specializing in sensational exposés of corrupt businesses and political procedures. The muckrakers included Lincoln Steffens, who wrote about political corruption, Ida Tarbell, who exposed the exploitative practices of an enormous oil company, and Upton Sinclair, who uncovered deplorable conditions in the Chicago meat-packing industry.
See also: Sinclair, Upton; Steffens, Lincoln.

Mucoviscidosis *see:* Cystic fibrosis.

Mud hen *see:* Coot.

Wolfgang Amadeus Mozart

Hosni Mubarak

Mudpuppy, or water dog (*Necturus maculosus*), salamander growing up to 2 ft (0.6 m) that lives in many North American rivers and streams. It retains its gills even when adult. Mud puppies get their name because they are reputed to emit barking sounds; however, they possess no voice organs of any kind

Mugabe, Robert Gabriel (1924-), prime minister of Zimbabwe since 1980. A Marxist, he and Joshua Nkomo shared leadership of a guerrilla movement against the white leaders of Rhodesia. When Rhodesia achieved legal independence (as Zimbabwe) and black majority rule in 1980, Mugabe became prime minister in a government of national unity. In 1982, however, he expelled Nkomo from his cabinet.
See also: Zimbabwe.

Mughal Empire *see:* Mogul Empire.

Mugwump, term for independent voter or political fence straddler. It was particularly used to describe Republicans who voted for Democrat Grover Cleveland for U.S. president in 1884.

Muhammad (570?-632), prophet founder of Islam. Born in Mecca into the ruling Qureish tribe, Muhammad spent his early years as a merchant. At the age of 40 he had a vision of the archangel Gabriel bidding him go forth and preach. His teachings are recorded in the Koran, which Muslims believe is the word of God. Muhammad proclaimed himself the messenger of the one true god, Allah. At first he made few converts, among them his wife (Khadija), his daughter (Fatima), and her husband (Ali). The Meccan rulers persecuted Muhammad's followers. In 622, he escaped to Yathrib, a nearby city, thereafter called Medinat al-Rasul (City of the Prophet), or Medina, for short. The Muslim calendar dates years from this event, known as the *Hegira* (departure). In Medina, Muhammad formed an Islamic community based on religious faith rather than tribal or family loyalties. He rapidly won converts and his influence grew. In 630, after several years of warfare with Mecca and his victories in the battles of Badr (624) and Uhud (625), he captured Mecca with little bloodshed, making it both the political and religious capital of Islam. By the time of his death, Muhammad had unified the entire Arabian peninsula and the worldwide expansion of Islam had begun. Within a century, the Islamic empire extended from the Iberian peninsula in the west to the borders of India in the east.
See also: Islam.

Muhammad II (1430?-81), sultan and ruler of the Ottoman Empire (Turkey). He founded the Ottoman Empire when he captured Constantinople (1453), which he made his capital. He also conquered other territories in southeast Europe and around the Black Sea. As a ruler, he restructured his government and had government officials trained. He also founded colleges and set up charities, in the interest of his people's welfare.
See also: Ottoman Empire.

Muhammad, Elijah (Elijah Poole; 1897-1975), U.S. Black Muslim leader. In 1931 he met Wali "Prophet" Farad, founder of the first Temple of Islam in Detroit, Mich. Elijah became a prominent disciple, and on Farad's disappearance (1934) he became leader of the movement.
See also: Black Muslims.

Muhammad Ali *see:* Ali, Muhammad.

Muhammadan art *see:* Islamic art.

Muhammad Reza Pahlavi *see:* Mohammad Reza Pahlavi.

Muir, John (1838-1914), Scottish-born U.S. naturalist and writer, an advocate of forest conservation. He described his walking journeys in the northwestern part of the United States and Alaska in many influential articles and books. Yosemite and Sequoia national parks and Muir Woods National Monument in California were established as a result of his efforts.
See also: Sierra Club.

Mukden *see:* Shenyang.

Mulberry, medium-sized deciduous or evergreen tree (family Moraceae) that carries edible fruits, such as berries, figs, and breadfruit. The red mulberry grows in the eastern states and the Mexican mulberry in the southwest. The black mulberry is grown in Asia for its fruit. The leaves of the white mulberry of the Far East form the food of the silkworm.

Mule, infertile offspring of a male donkey and a mare (female horse). Mules have the shape and size of a horse and the long ears and small hooves of a donkey. They are favored for their endurance and surefootedness as draft or pack animals.

Mule deer, medium-sized deer (*Odocoileus hemionus*), of the western United States, closely related to the Virginia, or white-tailed, deer. The two are distinguished by the shape of the antlers and by the Virginia deer's habit of carrying its white tail up when running. Both live in open country and have increased as forests have been cut down. They are the main prey of deer hunters, and in many places their numbers have to be regulated to prevent crop damage.

Mullein, large herbal plants (genus *Verbascum*) of the figwort family. Found in northern regions with mild climates, there are 300 species. The common mullein, which grows to a height of 2 to 7 ft (0.6 to 2 m), has a single stem with large, thick, velvety leaves on the bottom and yellow flowers that grow in clusters, in the form of a spike at the top of the plant. When touched, the mullein's leaves and stem inflame the skin. Its leaves were once used to create a medicinal tea.

Muller, Hermann Joseph (1890-1967), U.S. geneticist awarded the 1946 Nobel Prize for physiology or medicine for his work showing that X-rays greatly accelerate mutation processes.
See also: Genetics.

Müller, Karl Alexander (1797-1840), German philologist and archeologist. He wrote extensively on the ancient Macedonians, Etruscans, and Greeks. His books include *Handbuch der Archaeologie der Kunst* (Handbook on the Archaeology of Art, 1830) and *A History of the Literature of Ancient Greece* (1840).
See also: Archaeology.

Robert Mugabe

Müller, Paul Hermann (1899-1965), Swiss chemist. His discovery of DDT (dichlorodiphenyltrichloroethane) as an insecticide won him the 1948 Nobel Prize for medicine or physiology. The subsequent use of DDT led to increased food production in the world and to a decrease in diseases spread by insects. However, its widespread, long-term use eventually led to a buildup of DDT in the environment that threatened animal life and disrupted ecological food chains. As a result, several countries, including the United States, have banned its use.
See also: DDT.

Mullet, any of several species of fish of either the mullet or goatfish families. Fish in the mullet family (also known as gray mullets) have large scales and silvery, stocky bodies that can reach a length of 1 to 3 ft (30 to 90 cm). Their mouths are small and their teeth weak. Living on a mainly vegetarian diet, they inhabit shallow coastal waters in tropical and temperate regions throughout the world. They are fished commercially for their tasty flavor. The common or striped mullet (*Mugil cephalus*) is the best-known species of this family. Mullets in the goatfish family also live in warm waters.

Mulliken, Robert Sanderson (1896-1986), U.S. chemist and physicist awarded the 1966 Nobel Prize for chemistry for his work on the nature of chemical bonding and hence on the electronic structure of molecules.
See also: Chemistry; Molecule.

Mulroney, Brian (1939-), prime minister of Canada since 1984. He was elected leader of the Progressive Conservative Party in 1983. The Conservatives won a parliamentary majority in the 1984 elections by a landslide victory. Mulroney's reelection (1988) assured passage of the U.S.-Canada Free Trade Agreement.

Multiple sclerosis, degenerative disease of the brain and spinal cord in which myelin sheath around nerve fibers is destroyed. Its cause is unknown, although slow viruses, abnormal allergy to viruses, and abnormalities of fats are suspected. It particularly affects young adults. Episodic symptoms are blurring of vision, double vision, vertigo, paralysis, muscular weakness, and bladder disturbance. Symptoms can disappear and recur over a remission of many years. Steroids, certain dietary foods, and drugs acting on muscles and bladder spasticity can help. The course of the disease is extremely variable, some subjects having only a few mild attacks, others progressing rapidly to permanent disability and dependency.

Mumford, Lewis (1895-1990), U.S. social critic and historian concerned with the relationship between people and environment, especially in urban planning. His books include *The Culture of Cities* (1938), *The Condition of Man* (1944), and *The City in History* (1961).

Mummy, corpse preserved, particularly by embalming. The earliest known Egyptian attempts to preserve bodies were c.2600 B.C., It is believed that the body was being prepared for a reunion with the soul. Natural mummification was seen in bodies buried in Danish peat bogs from 300 B.C. to A.D.300.

Mumps, common viral infection causing swelling of the parotid salivary gland. It can also cause problems in swallowing and fever. Usually occurs in children ages 5 through 15 but can occur in adults. For adults, the condition is more severe and can cause swelling of the testes and sterility. It is highly contagious.

Munch, Edvard (1863-1944), Norwegian painter and printmaker. His work foreshadowed expressionism and was influential in the development of modern art. His powerful, often anguished pictures, for example, *The Shriek* (1893), *The Kiss* (1895), and *Anxiety* (1896) show his obsession with the themes of love, death, and loneliness.

A self-portrait by Edvard Munch

Munich, or München (pop. 1,267,000), capital of Bavaria, southwestern Germany, on the Isar River about 30 mi (48 km) north of the Alps. A cultural center with a cathedral and palace, it is also heavily industrialized (beer, textiles, publishing), and is Germany's third-largest city. Founded in 1158 by Duke Henry the Lion, it was ruled (1255-1918) by the Wittelsbach family (dukes and kings of Bavaria). Munich was the birthplace and headquarters of Nazism and the site of the Munich Agreement in 1938.
See also: Germany.

Munich Agreement, pact signed Sept. 30, 1938, prior to World War II, forcing Czechoslovakia to surrender its Sudetenland to Nazi Germany. The Sudetenland in western Czechoslovakia contained much of the nation's industry and about 700,000 Czechs. The agreement, which allowed an immediate German takeover, was signed by Hitler, Neville Chamberlain (Britain), Edouard Daladier (France), and Benito Mussolini (Italy). Neither the Czechs nor their Soviet allies were consulted. In Mar. 1939 Hitler occupied the rest of Czechoslovakia.
See also: World War II.

Municipal government *see:* City government.

Munro, Hector Hugh (1870-1916), British writer who wrote under the pen name Saki, known for his inventive, satirical, and often fantastic short stories. Among his published works are stories collected in *Reginald* (1904) and *Beasts and Super-Beasts* (1914) and a novel, *The Unbearable Bassington* (1912).

Munsee, Native American group consisting of the Wolf clan of the Delaware tribe. They originally lived around the northern Delaware River and the Hudson River (now southwestern New York State), but were driven to other areas by European settlers in the 18th century, notably to the Susquehanna River (Pennsylvania), the midwestern and southwestern United States, and Ontario, Canada.

Muppets, puppet family created by the master puppeteer Jim Henson in 1955. Henson was strongly influenced by the diversity of the European puppet theater. The first network television appearance of the Muppets occurred on "The Steve Allen Show" in 1956. The Muppets continued to grow in popularity through the early 1960s but it was their appearance on the Children's Television Workshop production of "Sesame Street" that brought them global recognition. The likes of Kermit the Frog, Big Bird, Bert and Ernie, Oscar the Grouch, and Cookie Monster, among many others, provided entertainment and education. In 1976, a new group of Muppets characters that included Kermit began starring in "The Muppet Show," which received a total of 3 Emmy awards during its 5-year run and became the most popular TV show in the world. Another Henson creation, "Fraggle Rock," recently became the first U.S. television series to be broadcast in the USSR. Other Henson creations are the "Muppet Babies" cartoon show, winner of 7 Emmy awards, *The Great Muppet Caper, The Dark Crystal, The Muppets Take Manhattan,* and "The Storyteller." Henson's philanthropic work included the creation of the Henson Foundation and a close affiliation with the United Nations which issued a Kermit the Frog stamp in 1991. He also supported environmental causes. On May 16, 1990, Jim Henson died of a sudden illness.

Murasaki, Shikibu, or Lady Murasaki (978-1026?), pseudonym of Japanese court figure and author of *The Tale of Genji*, one of the first great works of fiction written in Japanese.

Murat, Joachim (1767-1815), French marshal under Napoleon Bonaparte and king of Naples (1808-15). Murat gained his reputation as a brilliant cavalry leader in the Italian and Egyptian campaigns (1796-99), and contributed to French successes in the Napoleonic Wars. He married Napoleon's sister, Caroline. As king of Naples he fostered the beginnings of Italian nationalism. Although he joined the Allies in 1814, he supported Napoleon during the Hundred Days and was executed after an attempt to recapture Naples.
See also: Napoleon I.

Murdoch, Iris (1919-), Irish-born British novelist. Her novels, such as *A Fairly Honourable Defeat* (1970) , *The Sea, the Sea* (1978), *Nuns and Soldiers* (1980), *The Good Apprentice* (1986), and *The Book and the Brotherhood* (1988), display wit and a gift for analyzing human relations.

Muriatic acid *see:* Hydrochloric acid.

Murillo, Bartolomé Estéban (1617-82), baroque painter, Spain's most famous in his time, known as the Raphael of Seville. He produced religious narrative scenes expressing deep piety and gentleness, works of realism, and fine portraits. Among his many paintings are the *Vision of St. Anthony* (1656), *The Ragged Boy* (c.1670), and the *Two Trinities* (known as the *Holy Family*) (1678).
See also: Baroque.

Murmansk (pop. 412,000), city in the northwestern USSR, lying on the Kola Gulf of the Barents Sea, within the Arctic Circle. An important ice-free port since 1916, it served as an Allied supply base during World War II. It is a shipping and fishing center, with lumber and shipbuilding industries, and is connected by rail with Leningrad.
See also: Union of Soviet Socialist Republics.

Murphy, Audie (1924-71), U.S. soldier and actor. The many medals he received for his gallantry in action during World War II (1939-45) made him the most highly decorated hero of the war. Born in rural Texas, he joined the army in 1942 and served in combat for the war's duration, rising from private to lieutenant. He was decorated

several times for his bravery and received the highest military award, the Medal of Honor, for single-handedly holding off 6 German tanks and about 250 German soldiers. His popularity as a war hero led him to embark upon an acting career. *The Red Badge of Courage* (1951) and *To Hell and Back* (1955) were two of his most successful films. He died in a plane crash.
See also: World War II.

Murray, Philip (1886-1952), Scottish-born U.S. labor leader. He was president of the Congress of Industrial Organizations (CIO) from 1940; prominent leader of the United Mine Workers, 1912-42, and organizer and head of the United Steelworkers from 1942. In 1949-50 he helped rid the CIO of communist unions.
See also: Labor movement.

Murray River, Australia's chief river, an important source of irrigation and hydroelectricity. Rising in the mountains of New South Wales, it flows for 1,609 mi (2,589 km), passing through Hume reservoir and Lake Victoria and on to Encounter Bay and the Indian Ocean.

Murre, seabirds (genus *Uria*) in the auk family. They inhabit cliffs on the coasts of the North Atlantic and North Pacific oceans. Murres, approximately 16 in (41 cm) long, are brownish black, with white breasts. In their breeding season, they nest in large numbers, the female in each pair laying one egg on the bare rock.

Murrow, Edward R(oscoe) (1908-65), U.S. newscaster. He was head of Columbia Broadcasting System's European bureau during World War II; from 1947 to 1960 he produced many acclaimed radio and TV programs, including an exposé of Senator Joseph McCarthy (1954). He also directed the U.S. Information Agency (1961-63).

Muscat, or Maskat (pop. 30,000), capital of Oman. A major port and commercial center, it lies on the Gulf of Oman in southeast Arabia. The city has existed since ancient times. Two Portuguese forts testify to Portugal's occupation of Muscat (1508-1648). In 1741 it became Oman's capital. Muscat and its modern suburbs are known as the Capital Area.
See also: Oman.

Muscle, contractile tissue that produces movement in the body. We consciously control striated muscle at will through the central nervous system, such as when we walk or run. We cannot, however, control the smooth muscle lining most organs, such as organs in the digestive system.

Muscular dystrophy, group of inherited diseases in which muscle fibers are abnormal and become wasted. Duchenne dystrophy occurs only in boys, beginning with swelling of calf muscles before age 3. Death often occurs by age 30. A similar disease, Becker dystrophy, can affect females. There are many variants, largely due to structural or biochemical abnormalities in muscle fibers. A waddling gait and exaggerated curvature of the lower spine are typical. If pneumonia and respiratory failure or heart muscle are affected, early death may result.

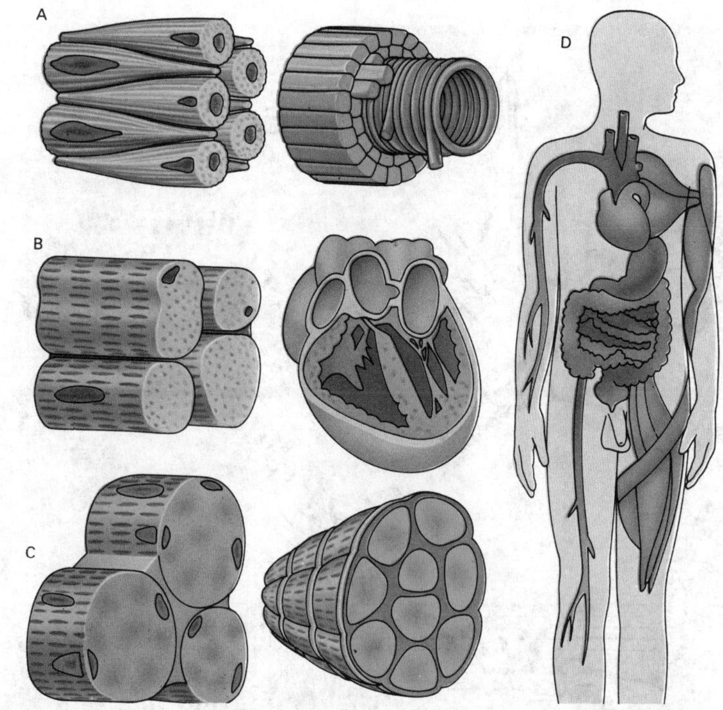

The human body has three types of muscle:
A. Smooth muscles (indicated by the color blue in D) are found in various organs. The muscles consist of fibers, each with one nucleus, which contains growth-producing substances. The fibers are arranged around a tube.
B. Cardiac muscles (green), which make up the walls of the heart, also consist of fibers, each with one nucleus. The fibers have alternating light and dark bands called striations.
C. The fibers of the skeletal muscles (brown), which are also striated, have many nuclei. The fibers are bundled in big bundles.

Muses, in Greek mythology, 9 patron goddesses of the arts, worshiped especially near Mt. Helicon. Daughters of Zeus and the titan Mnemosyne (Memory), they were attendants to Apollo, god of poetry. The chief muse was Calliope (epic poetry); the others were Clio (history), Euterpe (lyric poetry), Thalia (comedy, pastoral poetry), Melpomene (tragedy), Terpsichore (choral dancing), Erato (love poetry), Polyhymnia (sacred song), and Urania (astronomy).
See also: Mythology.

Museum of Modern Art, one of the world's pre-eminent museums of modern art, New York City. Founded in 1929, it is privately supported and has a collection of more than 100,000 objects, including paintings, sculptures, drawings, architecture and design, decorative arts, crafts, industrial design, prints, and illustrated books. Its holdings of film and photography are especially notable. The museum also has programs of loan exhibitions and publications.

Museveni, Yoweri Kaguta (1944-), president of Uganda since 1986. His Front for National Salvation helped overthrow dictator Idi Amin (1979). After a prolonged struggle he overthrew President Milton Obote by force (1985); when his National Resistance Army seized the capital of Kampala, ousting the ruling military council, Museveni was installed as president. Museveni maintains good relations with Europe and the West and has helped stabilize the country, but has been accused of human rights violations.

Mushroom, popular name given to an umbrella-shaped gill fungi. Edible mushrooms have 5% protein and are mostly water. Poisonous, or inedible, mushrooms are called toadstools. The common field mushroom (*Agaricus campestris*) is the wild species most frequently eaten; *bisporus* is the cultivated mushroom. Some mushrooms are parasites of wood, plantation trees, and garden plants.

Mushroom

Musial, Stan(ley) (1920-), U.S. baseball player. An outfielder and first baseman for the St. Louis Cardinals (1941-63), he is acclaimed as one of baseball's great hitters. "Stan the Man" was named the National League's most valuable player 3 times (1943, 46, 48), had a lifetime batting average of .331, hit 475 career home runs, and held the National League record for career hits (3,630) until 1981, when it was topped by Pete Rose. He was inducted into the National Baseball Hall of Fame in 1969.

Music, sound organized and arranged as a means of expression and for sensual and intellectual pleasure. Of the major arts, music may be the most ancient, because the urge to sing and dance in response to feelings of anger, joy, or sorrow springs

Musical notations for a song called "The Heart" *(1400s)*

The "waltz king," Johann Strauss (the Younger), composed over 400 waltzes.

Medieval mural depicting the benificial effect of music

from the body itself. Music may also be described as sound shaped by time. Its 2 most important elements are rhythm and melody, rhythm being organized in terms of intervals of time and beats to the bar, and melody in terms of notes whose pitch is determined by frequency, or the number of sound vibrations per second. These basic characteristics of music can be considered universal, but musical expressions and traditions are quite distinct and diverse. Oriental music, for instance, does not rely upon harmony, a late but significant development in Western music. And although any music can be arranged according to scale and notated, the development of musical notation was gradual and is a relatively recent phenomenon.

Western music evidently originated in the Middle East, was developed by the Greeks, and, in the form of Byzantine ecclesiastical music, was embraced by the early church. Such music was originally limited to plainsong, a form of chant unadorned by any kind of harmony or accompaniment sung by church or monastery choirs. During the 9th and 10th centuries, choirs began to be divided into sections, each with a different melody line. This gave rise to polyphonic music, the so-called *ars antiqua,* which reached its height in the motet in the 13th century. Following this was the *ars nova,* the new art, a style of musical composition that departed from the excessive formalism and complexity of the *ars antiqua* and achieved its finest expression in the madrigal of the 14th and 15th centuries. This period also saw the rise and spread of the first comprehensive system of musical notation.

Though the church dominated ancient and medieval music, alongside the ecclesiastical was a lively secular tradition closely related to sung poetry and represented in the works of minstrels, troubadours, and minnesingers. As in the other arts, the secular would become independent and eventually supplant the ecclesiastical, beginning with the Renaissance.

From c.1400 to 1600, great changes in music occurred. It turned to nonecclesiastical themes. New instruments were developed, played by groups of musicians—the nuclei for the modern orchestra. In the work of Claudio Monteverdi, early opera developed. Other composers of the period were Josquin Desprez and Orlando di Lasso in Flanders, Andrea and Giovanni Gabrieli in Venice, and Thomas Morley and John Dowland in England.

The Baroque period was born with Pierluigida Palestrina (c.1526) and culminated in the works of Johann Sebastian Bach (d.1750). The era saw major improvements in instruments, particularly the violin and cello, inspiring composers like Antonio Vivaldi and Arcangelo Corelli. François Couperin and Domenico Scarlatti exploited the newer keyboard instruments. A new harmonic structure of scales and keys familiar today was finally established, and the music of the period achieved a formal complexity, balance, and richness, above all in the work of Bach, which to many remains the highest achievement of Western music.

The late 18th century saw a new age in music, the classical period, pioneered and perfected in the work of Franz Josef Haydn and Wolfgang Amadeus Mozart. The period was marked by the growth and completion of several musical forms—the sonata, symphony, concerto, *opera buffa*—and by works that, as the result of greater mastery and skill with instruments, were musically richer and contained, particularly in Mozart's, an expressiveness that opened new possibilities for music.

Ludwig van Beethoven seized that opportunity and, in the spirit of the times, revolutionized the concept and the practice of the art of music. In his work and influence, Beethoven, in effect, gave a charter of liberties to individual expression that inspired the Romantic movement and, by extension, modern music as well. Franz Schubert, Robert Schumann, Frédéric Chopin, Franz Liszt, Felix Mendelssohn, and Hector Berlioz, Anton Bruckner, Gustav Mahler, and Jan Sibelius completed the Romantic period in music, each with a signal style and distinct sensibility, and each the heir of Beethoven.

As *ars antiqua* gave rise to the rebellion and innovations of *ars nova,* so the classical and Romantic traditions, particularly in the wake of World War I, gave rise to 20th-century modernism in music. It is heard in the neoclassicism of Paul Hindemith and Igor Stravinsky and the more radical atonalism of Arnold Schönberg, which offered an entirely new set of rules for music and gave rise, in turn, to serial and 12-tone music. Influenced by music of non-Western cultures as well as the innovations of jazz and modern technology, often disturbing and unsettling in the way it deliberately explores the untried and the unconventional, serious modern music defies the kind of clear-cut and comfortable categories that make traditional music seem more comprehensible and familiar.

Musil, Robert (1880-1942), Austrian writer. He is known for *The Man Without Qualities* (3 vols., 1930-42), an encyclopedic novel about the ills of prewar Austria. Posthumous collections include *Tonka and Other Stories* (1965) and *Three Short Stories* (1970).

Musk deer (*Moschus moshiferus*), a deer of the family Cervidae. The musk deer stands about 20-24 in (50.8-60.9 cm) at the shoulder, slightly higher at the rump. It has a coarse, gray-brown coat. The male has long upper canine teeth resembling tusks, no antlers, and a musk gland on its abdomen. The deer marks its territory with the musk; people use musk to scent perfumes and soaps. Unlike most deer, musk deer are solitary. They live in the mountains of Asia.

Muskellunge (*Esox masquinongy*), the largest fish of the pike family. Most muskellunges are 2 1/2-4 ft (6.4-10.2 cm) in length and 5-36 lb (2.3-16 kg) in weight. Its slender body may be brown, gray, green, or silver with dark bars or spots on the side. A distinctive feature of the muskellunge is the absence of scales on its lower head. The muskellunge is solitary and carnivorous. It is found in southern Canada and northern United States. A strong fighter, the muskellunge is sought for sport and food.

Musket, shoulder firearm developed in Spain in the 16th century and used into the 19th century. A musket could be 5.5-7 ft (1.7-2.1 m) long and weigh 20-40 lb (9-18.1 kg). It was loaded from the muzzle with a single ball, or a ball plus small lead shot, and fired by igniting a powder charge. Unlike the rifle, the musket had a smooth bore; this made it an inaccurate weapon against targets beyond 100 yd (91 m). The matchlock, the earliest musket, was succeeded by the flintlock, caplock, and wheel lock.

Musk hog *see:* Peccary

Muskmelon, edible fruit of certain plants (*Cucumis melo*) belonging to the gourd family. Cantaloupes, Persian melons, casabas, and honeydew melons are subspecies of muskmelon. The plants are annual, grow along the ground, and produce hairy, heart-shaped leaves and 5-lobed yellow flowers. The fruit varies: the skin may be smooth, ridged, or latticed, and the flesh white, pale green, or orange. Muskmelons grow best in a hot, dry climate. They are believed to have originated in western Asia.

Musk ox (*Ovibos moschatus*, shaggy-furred, hoofed animal of Arctic America, related to sheep and goats. With a pronounced hump over the shoulders and a musky odor, these highly aggressive animals live in herds of up to 100. When threatened, adults circle the calves, with horns facing outward.

Muskrat, or musquash, aquatic rodent of North America, *Ondrata ziethica*, up to 2 ft (6 m) long. It lives in fresh water or salt marshes, feeding mainly on water plants. The feet are broad; the hindfeet webbed; and the fur is thick and waterproof.

Muslims, practitioners of the religion of Islam as preached by the prophet Muhammad in the 600s. Muslim is an Arabic word meaning one who submits to God. Muslims form the majority of the population of the Middle East, North Africa, Bangladesh, Indonesia, Malaysia, and Pakistan. The Koran, believed to be the revelations of God (Allah) to Muhammad, is the book to which Muslims are devoted. A dispute, dating back to the first centuries of the Muslim era, caused a fundamental division of Muslims into the Sunni and Shi'te sects.
See also: Islam.

Mussel, two-shelled mollusk that lives in masses on most rocky shores and is exposed at low tide. It feeds on minute particles sifted from the sea and is anchored to the rock by the byssus, a series of strong, silky threads.

Musset, (Louis-Charles) Alfred de (1810-57), French romantic poet and playwright. After an affair with George Sand, he wrote *Les Nuits* (1835-37), some of the finest love poetry in French, and the autobiographical novel *Confession of a Child of the Century* (1836). His witty plays, including *Lorenzaccio* (1834), are often produced today.

Mussolini, Benito (1883-1945), founder of Fascism, dictator of Italy (1924-43). Editor of the Socialist party paper (1912-14), Mussolini split with the Socialists when he advocated Italy's entry in World War I. In 1919 he formed a Fascist group in Milan; in 1921 he was elected to parliament and founded the National Fascist party. In 1922 he led the Fascist march on Rome and was made premier. His dictatorship ended parliamentry government in 1928. As *Duce* leader he signed the Lateran Treaty, creating Vatican City, in 1929. He conquered Ethiopia (1935-36) and annexed Albania in 1939. Joining Hitler in 1940, he declared war on the Allies but suffered great military failures in North Africa and Greece. Mussolini was imprisoned by the king (1943), only to be made a puppet ruler in northern Italy by the Germans. He was shot by partisans after the German defeat.
See also: Fascism; World War II; Italy.

Mussorgsky, Modest (1839-81), Russian composer, one of the first to develop a style around characteristically Russian idioms. His *Boris Gudonov* (1874) is one of the finest Russian operas. Other major works include *Night on Bald Mountain* (1860-66), the piano suite *Pictures at an Exhibition* (1874), later orchestrated by Maurice Ravel; and the song cycle *Songs and Dances of Death* (1875-77).

Mustafa Kemal Pasha *see:* Atatürk, Kemal.

Mustard, any of several herbs (genus *Brassica*) of the Cruciferae family. The Cruciferae include food plants (e.g., many cabbage varieties, watercress, turnip, radish, and horseradish) and such condiment plants as the white mustard (*B. alba*) and black mustard (*B. nigra*), native to the Mediterranean region. They are cultivated for their seeds, which are ground and used as a condiment, or used as medicine.

Mustard gas *see:* Chemical and biological warfare.

Mutsuhito (1852-1912), emperor of Japan (1867-1912); his regal title was *Meiji* ("enlightened rule"). The long isolation of Japan under the shoguns ended in 1867 with the restoration of imperial power. Mutsuhito guided the transformation of Japan from a feudal empire into a modern nation. He established industries, promoted education, gave farmers titles to their land, and modernized the armed forces. Japan's defeat of China (1895) and Russia (1905) and its alliance with England (1902) helped to establish the nation as a great power.

Mutual fund, investment company that pools its shareholders' funds and invests them in a broad range of stocks and shares.

Benito Mussolini surrounded by supporters after his march on Rome in 1922

Musk oxen in a protective phalanx formation, which thwarts wolf attacks.

A shareholder receives dividends for his or her shares in the fund, rather than for individual company shares. Mutual funds are popular amongsmall investors because of the low risk involved (due to the variety of stocks invested in by the mutual fund) and the expert management provided.

Myanmar, country in Southeast Asia, formerly called Burma, bordered by India, Bangladesh, and the Bay of Bengal on the west, by China on the north and northeast, by Laos and Thailand on the east, and by the Andaman Sea on the south. The capital is Yangon, formerly called Rangoon.

Climate. Myanmar's climate is typical of the tropical monsoon regions of southeast Asia and India. The rainy season lasts from June to October, and rainfall averages 200 in (508 cm) annually.

The Burmese city of Yangon (Rangoon) has many ancient temples

People. The people are predominantly (about 70%) Burmans, but there are minorities of Karens, Shans, Chins, Kachins, Indians, Chinese, and Bangladeshis. More than 85% are adherents of Theravada Buddhism. Although more than 100 different languages are spoken, the official language is Burmese.

Economy. The majority of Myanmar's work force is engaged in agriculture and forestry. The forests are sources of teak and rubber. There are also rich mineral deposits of oil, silver, tungsten, tin, zinc, and lead. Myanmar is famous for its rubies, sapphires, and rich deposits of jade, but agriculture remains the mainstay of the country's economy.

History. Myanmar was settled in the 9th century by peoples who established a kingdom that reached its height under the Buddhist King Anawrahta in the 11th century. The kingdom and its capital fell to Kublai Khan in 1287, and the area was not reunited until the 16th century. After a series of wars (1826-85), Britain annexed Burma to its Indian empire. It was granted separate dominion status in 1937. The Japanese occupied the country during World War II, and it was not until after the war, with the foundation of the Union of Burma in 1948, that the country became independent. The first prime minister, U Nu, was overthrown by Gen. Ne Win in 1958. In 1960 U Nu returned to power but was again overthrown by Ne Win in 1962. In 1973 a new constitution made Burma a one-party socialist republic. In 1981 Ne Win resigned the presidency but retained control of the Burma Socialist Program Party. Pro-democracy demonstrations were crushed by the military late in 1988. In elections for a National Assembly in May 1990 the National League for Democracy won 80% of the vote, but the military arrested the League's leaders and the country remains under military rule.

Myasthenia gravis, disease of the junctions between the peripheral nerves and the muscles, probably due to abnormal immunity and characterized by muscle fatigue. It commonly affects eye muscles, leading to drooping lids and double vision, but it may involve limb muscles. Weakness of the muscles of respiration, swallowing, and coughing may lead to respiratory failure and aspiration or bacterial pneumonia. Speech is nasal, regurgitation into the nose may occur, and the face is weak, lending a characteristic snarl to the mouth. It is associated with disorders of thymus and thyroid glands. Treatment is with cholinesterase inhibitors; steroids and thymus removal may control the causative immune mechanism.

Myanmar (formerly Burma)

General information	
Capital:	Yangon (Rangoon)
Area:	261,228 sq mi (676,577 sq km)
Population:	40,810,000
Official language:	Burmese
Monetary unit:	1 Myanmar kyat = 100 pyas
Main cities:	Yangon (Rangoon), Mandalay,Moulmein
Government	
Form:	republic
Independent:	1948
Head of state:	Chairman of the State Law and Order Restoration Council
Head of government:	Chairman of the State Law and Order Restoration Council
Legislature:	People's Assembly dissolved in 1990
Executive:	Chairman of the State Law and Order Restoration Council and the Council
Judiciary:	highest court is the Council of People's Justices
Political division:	7 divisions, 7 states
National economy	
Gross national product:	U.S. $7,450,000,000
Per capita income:	U.S. $200
Agriculture:	rice, sugar cane, vegetables, pulses, peanuts, maize, rubber
Livestock:	cattle, pigs, buffaloes
Fisheries:	686,000 metric tons
Mining:	copper, zinc, lead, tin, tungsten, silver, jade, precious stones
Industries:	petroleum products, cigarettes, soap, cement
Main exports:	rice and rice products, teak, base metals and ores, machinery
Transportation:	1,949 mi (3,137 km) of railroads, 14,416 mi (23,200 km) of roads, 1 international airport
Trading partners:	Southeast Asian countries, Japan, EEC
People	
Urban:	24%
Ethnic composition:	Burman 69%, Shan 8.5%, Karen 6%, Rakhine 4.5%, Mon 2.5%
Birth rate:	33 per 1,000 population
Death rate:	13 per 1,000 population
Infant mortality:	99 per 1,000 live births
Life expectancy:	male 53 years, female 56 years

Mycenae, city of Bronze Age Greece. It was founded c. 2000 B.C. by an Indo-European Greek-speaking people on the southern peninsula. Mycenaean culture benefitted from contact with the Minoans on Crete. By 1600 B.C. Mycenae had risen to cultural, political, and commercial prominence in the Mediterranean world. Between 1400 and 1200 B.C. it was at its height. In 1100 B.C. Mycenae was invaded by the Dorians. Mycenae remained unknown to the modern world until Heinrich Schliemann began excavations at the site and discovered 5 royal tombs (1876).
See also: Greece, Ancient.

My Lai, hamlet in South Vietnam where nearly 350 Vietnamese civilians were massacred by U.S. soldiers in 1968. Subsequent revelations led to army and congressional investigations. Lt. William Calley, in immediate command during the incident, was convicted of killing 22 persons and imprisoned for 3 years. Two generals were censured for failing to conduct an adequate investigation.
See also: Vietnam War.

Myna, several birds of the starling family, native to Indian and Asian forests but dispersed to the Pacific tropics. These noisy birds adapt well to living near people and livestock. The hill or talking myna (*Gracula religiosa*) is kept as a pet and can be trained to mimic the human voice. About 12-15 in (30-38 cm), this glossy black bird has yellow feet, wattles, and beak.

Myocarditis, inflammation of the heart muscle (myocardium). It may be due to a variety of diseases, certain chemicals or drugs, or injury—for instance, electric shock or excessive X-ray treatment.

Myoelectricity *see:* Artificial limb.

Myopia, commonly called nearsightedness, inability to clearly see objects at a distance. The image is focused in front of the retina rather than on it, due to an overly strong refractive power of the eye or an eyeball that is too long. Eyeglasses with concave lenses compensate for myopia.

Myrdal, Gunnar (1898-1987), Swedish economist who wrote a classic work on race relations, *An American Dilemma* (1944), an influential study of Third World economic development, *Asian Drama* (1968), and *Challenge of World Poverty* (1970). He won the 1974 Nobel Prize for economics.

Myrtle, common name for the Myrtaceae family of trees and shrubs. Myrtles are native to temperate Asia and tropical America and Australia. They include the clove, eucalyptus, guava, and pimento. Myrtles are valued for their aromatic oils, timber, spices, and fruit. The common or classical myrtle (*Myrtus communis*) grows in the Mediterranean region. The ancient Greeks associated the glossy evergreen with Aphrodite and awarded Olympic athletes wreaths of myrtle.

Mysteries, secret religious cults of ancient Greece and Rome; their rites were revealed only to initiated persons. The mysteries involved purification rites, dance, drama, and the display of sacred objects such as an ear of corn. The Orphic mysteries were also important.

Mystery play, medieval religious drama based on biblical themes, chiefly those concerning the Nativity, the Passion, and the Resurrection. The form is closely related to that of the miracle play, which is generally based on nonbiblical material, for example, the saints' lives. The distinction between the 2 forms is not clear-cut, and some authorities refer to both as miracle plays. Mystery plays, which are liturgical in origin, can be ambitious in scale, treating the whole of spiritual history from the Creation to Judgment Day in vast cycles. Examples are the English York and Wakefield cycles, the French cycle *Miracle of Notre Dame*, and the Oberammergau Passion of Bavaria.

Mysticism, experience of a transcendental union in this life with God, the divine, through meditation and other disciplines. Cleansing away of physical desires, purification of will, and enlightenment of mind are the stages along the path to unification. Mystics suggest either that God is indwelling and can be reached by delving within, or dwells outside the soul and is reached by the soul's rise in successive stages. Mysticism, which has broad association in English to include the occult and magic, is found in Greek Neoplatonism, Christianity, Judaism, Hinduism, Buddhism, Islam, and Taoism.

Mythology, stories or explanations of the origin and meaning of the world and the universe and their relation to a particular culture or civilization. Mythological stories differ from folk tales and legends in that they tend to be integrated in the religious doctrine of a particular culture and are considered sacred and factual. Mythological stories also contain supernatural and divine elements. Folk tales and legends, on the other hand, are more lighthearted, entertaining, and fictive. Though mythological stories are characteristic of the pre-scientific world many aspects and beliefs of the modern world perpetuate the mythic tradition. The most well-known myths in western civilization are those of ancient Greece. The historic sources for our knowledge of this mythology are the *Theogeny* by Hesiod and the *Illiad* and the *Odyssey* by Homer. All three works date from the 8th century B.C. Other significant mythologic systems are Teutonic, or Norse, mythology of Scandinavia and Germany. The sources for this mythology are the *Eddas* (1200s B.C.).The source for the Hindu mythology of Asia and India are the *Vedas* (1200 to 600 B.C.) The basis of Irish Celtic mythology are three cycles of stories—the mythological cycle, the Ulster cycle, and the Fenian cycle. Other significant mythological systems are those of Africa, Native America, and the Pacific Islands.

Many theories have been developed by scholars about how and why myths began. Some of the more significant theories are those of Euhemerus, the Greek scholar (3rd century B.C.) who believed that myths are based on historical fact; Friedrich Max Muller, a German scholar (late 1800s) who held that mythic heroes were representations of nature; Sir Edward Burnett Tylor, an English anthropologist (1800s) who stated that myths were an attempt to explain the unexplainable events in dreams; Bronislaw Malinowski, a British anthropologist (early 1900s), who held a more psychologic perspective; and Sir James George Frazer, a Scottish anthropologist (early 1900s), who concluded that myths reflect the cyclical nature of life—birth, growth, decay, and rebirth. Frazer is the author of *The Golden Bough*, one of the most famous works in the study of mythology. Among modern psychologists, the work of Sigmund Freud and Carl Jung are significant in their interpretation of myths. In more recent times, the work of Joseph Campbell in the area of comparative mythology has also made a contribution to human knowledge.

Zeus, a figure in Greek mythology, depicted on an ancient coin

N

N, 14th letter of the English alphabet, corresponds with the 14th Semitic letter *nun*, denoting a fish. After it was adopted by the Greeks from the Phoenicians, *nun* became *nu*. Its present form is that used by the Romans. When written with a tilde (common in Spanish words), *n* is pronounced as if it were followed by a *y* (*cañon* = canyon). As an abbreviation, *n* represents noun, neuter, name, and north. In mathematics it may stand for any number. It is the chemical symbol of nitrogen.

NAACP *see:* National Association for the Advancement of Colored People.

Nabokov, Vladimir (1899-1977), Russian-born U.S. novelist and critic. Born in St. Petersburg, he came to the United States in 1940 and taught at Cornell (1948-59). Noted for his originality and satiric wit, he published poetry, essays, short stories, and novels in Russian and in English. His first novel in English was *The Real Life of Sebastian Knight* (1938); he became famous

Vladimir Nabokov

after the U.S. publication of *Lolita* (1958), the story of a middle-aged man's passion for a young girl. Other works include *Pnin* (1957), *Pale Fire* (1962), *Ada* (1969), and an English translation of *Eugene Onegin* (1964).

Nadelman, Elie (1882-1946), Polish-born U.S. sculptor. He interpreted the human form through the eyes of 18th-century folk artists and doll makers, but was also influenced by "classic" sculptors such as Auguste Rodin. Among his more amusing sculptures is *Man in the Open Air* (c.1915).

Nader, Ralph (1934-), U.S. consumer crusader and lawyer. The controversy over his book *Unsafe at Any Speed* (1965), a criticism of safety standards in the auto industry, gained him support to investigate other areas of public interest, including chemical food additives, X-ray leakage, and government agencies. His work has resulted in Congressional hearings and remedial legislation. In 1996 Nader ran for the U.S. presidency, with no success.

Nadir, in astronomy, point on the celestial sphere directly opposite the zenith, that is, directly below an observer.
See also: Zenith.

Nadir Shah (1688-1747), shah of Iran (1736-47), often called the Napoleon of Iran. He created an Iranian empire reaching from the Indus River to the Caucasus Mountains by ruthless military conquest, including the capture of the Delhi (and its famous Koh-i-noor diamond and peacock throne).

Nagana *see:* Tsetse fly.

Nagasaki (pop. 439,100), city on western Kyushu Island, Japan, capital of Nagasaki prefecture. A major port on the China Sea, it has been a foreign trading center since 1571. In World War II about 75,000 residents were killed or wounded and much of the city was destroyed when the United States dropped the second atomic bomb (Aug. 9, 1945). Today shipbuilding is the city's major industry.

Nagoya (pop. 2,095,400), capital of Aichi prefecture, Japan, on the island of Honshu. It is a major port and a manufacturing center for textiles, steel, and ceramics. In 1610, the feudal lord Ieyasu Tokugawa built a magnificent castle at Nagoya.

Nagy, Imre (1895?-1958), Hungarian communist leader and premier (1953-55). His criticism of Soviet influence led to his removal from office, but during the Oct. 1956 revolution he became premier again briefly. After Soviet troops crushed the uprising, Nagy was tried and executed in secret.

Nahum, Book of, seventh of the Old Testament Minor Prophets, the oracles of the prophet Nahum. It foretells the fall of Nineveh (612 B.C.).
See also: Bible.

Naiad *see:* Nymph.

Nail, metal shaft, pointed at one end and usually with a head at the other, that can be hammered into pieces of material, usually wood, to fasten them together.

Nail, thin, horny plate growing on the ends of the fingers and toes of humans and other primates. Dead nail cells are pushed outward by dividing cells in the root. Nails are made of a sulfur-containing protein material called keratin.

Naipaul, V(idiadhar) S(urajprasad) (1932-), Indian writer, born in Trinidad, who has lived in England since 1950. A critic and essayist, Naipaul has been especially praised for his novels of life in the Third World, including *A House for Mr. Biswas* (1961), *Guerrilas* (1975), and *A Bend in the River* (1979).

Nairobi (pop. 1,162,200), capital of Kenya. A modern city on the east African plateau, it is Kenya's administrative, commercial, manufacturing, and transportation center. The city encompasses Nairobi National Park, a wildlife reserve. The city was founded in 1899, became a British colonial capital (1905) and railroad center, and then the capital of independent Kenya (1963).

Naismith, James (1861-1939), inventor of basketball. He developed the game (1891) while a physical education teacher at the YMCA in Springfield, Mass. The first game was played indoors with a soccer ball and 2 peach baskets.
See also: Basketball.

Najibullah, Mohammad (1948-96), political leader of Afghanistan (1986-93). He was the leader of the People's Democratic Party. With his election to the presidency of the legislative Revolutionary Council (1987) he officially assumed presidency of the nation. His government was consistently opposed by Muslim factions; he was hung by Taliban rebels in 1996.

Namaliu, Rabbie (1947-), prime minister of the south Pacific nation of Papua New Guinea (1988-92). He became head of the Pangu Pati Party shortly before the party was voted into power.

Namibia, Republic of, in southern Africa, an area covering about 318,261 sq mi (824,292 sq km), bordered by Angola, Zambia, Botswana, South Africa, and the Atlantic Ocean. The capital is Windhoek.
Land and climate. From the Namib Desert, which stretches north-south on the Atlantic coast, the land rises to a plateau averaging 3,500 ft (1,067 m) above sea level covered by rough grass and scrub. The Kalahari, a desert region, lies to the east. The climate is hot and dry. In the north are the Kunene and Okavango rivers, and in the south, the Kwando and Zambezi rivers. The Orange River runs along the southern border. The Etosha Game Park protects elephants, cheetahs, antelope, giraffes, zebras, lions, and rhinoceros.

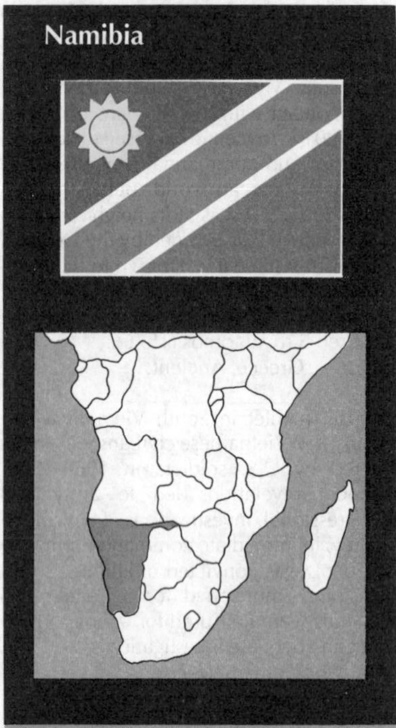

Capital:	Windhoek
Area:	318,261 sq mi (824,292 sq km)
Population:	1,529,000
Form:	republic
Independent:	1990
GNP:	U.S. $2,502,000,000
Per capita:	U.S. $1,610

Mining is the most important industry in Namibia. The major minerals mined are diamond, uranium, copper, lead, zinc, and tin.

People. The population of 1,529,000 (1996 est.) is 86% black, overwhelmingly Bantu, and 7% white. Ovambos (the largest ethnic group), Bushmen, and Kavango live to the north in Ovamboland. The Hereros, Nama, and Damara live in the south plateau, chiefly around Windhoek, home to most of the country's Europeans. About 60% of the population live in urban areas.

The Tswana people live in the east. The Rehoboths, or coloreds, of African and European ancestry, are another important group. Except for the Bushman, these groups mostly farm, raise cattle, or work in mines. In addition to native African languages, Afrikaans, English, and German are spoken. The few black Namibians who go beyond high school may attend the University of Namibia; literacy among nonwhites is 16% (1989).

Economy. Minerals account for most exports, led by diamonds and uranium. Livestock has dominated agriculture, which has been weakened by numerous droughts since the 1970s. Fishing remains important. Railroads connect cities in Namibia and South Africa, and Windhoek has an international airport.

History. The original peoples of Namibia were the Damara and the San; other Africans moved there over the centuries. The territory was annexed as a protectorate in 1884 by Germany, who named it South-West Africa. In 1920 the League of Nations mandated it to South Africa, which refused to place it under UN trusteeship after World War II. An independence move was launched in 1966 by the South-West Africa People's Organization (SWAPO), a Marxist guerilla group. Renaming the country Namibia in 1968, the UN declared (1970) South Africa's occupation of it was illegal, a move backed by the International Court of Justice (1971), pointing to South Africa's practice of apartheid. Through referendums and mediation from 1977, the UN continued to seek the country's freedom in spite of opposition from South Africa and factions of Namibian white voters and black opposition parties. Since Mar. 21, 1990, Namibia has been an independent nation with black majority rule.

Namphy, Henri (1933-), military ruler of Haiti 1986-88. After Jean Claude Duvalier stepped down as ruler of Haiti, a military-civilian council took power, with Lt. Gen. Namphy, then armed forces chief of staff, as its head. Namphy repeatedly promised free elections and the protection of civil rights. Amidst widespread violence and general strikes, repressive measures continued and the elections did not take place until Jan. 1988. The newly elected president, Leslie Mandigat, was ousted by Namphy in June, but Namphy was arrested and exiled in Sept. 1988.

Nan-ching *see:* Nanjing.

Nancy (pop. 96,300), capital of Meurthe-et-Moselle *département* in the Lorraine region of northeastern France, on the Meurthe River. Once an industrial center, Nancy now serves as a financial and administrative center. The city's central plan and civic buildings exemplify 18th-century French architecture.

Nanjing, or Nanking (pop. 2,210,000), industrial and manufacturing city on the Yangtze River in east-central China. Originally the only capital of China, it is now the southern capital, Beijing being its northern counterpart. Oceangoing ships dock at the city's wharves and facilitate transportation of products which include steel, coal, petroleum, tea, grain, and vegetables. The Chinese Communists, the nation's ruling force since 1949, are responsible for greater industrial development. A 3-mi (5-km) bridge crosses the Yangtze at Nanjing.

Nanking *see:* Nanjing.

Nansen, Fridtjof (1861-1930), Norwegian explorer, scientist, and humanitarian. He is best known for his explorations of the Arctic. His attempts at reaching the North Pole by drifting on ice across the polar basin in a crush-resistant ship yielded information on oceanography and meteorology. He was awarded the 1922 Nobel Peace Prize for his work as the League of Nations' high commissioner for refugees.

Nantes (pop. 240,500), port city in western France near the Loire River, capital of the Loire-Atlantique department. It is linked to the Atlantic Ocean through the port of St.-Nazaire and a ship canal. Shipbuilding and transporting food products and farm equipment provide revenue. King Henry IV signed the Edict of Nantes (1598) in the city's 10th-century castle, providing restricted religious freedom for Protestants.

Nantes, Edict of, proclamation of religious toleration for French Protestants (Huguenots) issued in the city of Nantes by Henry IV in 1598. Protestants were granted civil rights and freedom of worship. In 1685 Catholic pressure led Louis XIV to revoke the edict.
See also: Huguenots.

Nantucket Island, island 25 mi (40 km) south of Cape Cod, Mass., across Nantucket Sound. The island, which is 14 mi (23 km) long, has a mild climate and popular beaches. It was a world-famous 18th-century whaling center.

Napalm, mixture of gasoline and thickeners, used in flame throwers and incendiary bombs. It burns relatively slowly, and sticks to its target. Developed in World War II, it was used extensively in the Vietnam War.

Naphtha, volatile inflammable hydrocarbon liquid (distilled from substances that yield carbon). It is used as a solvent, cleaning fluid, or fuel.

Napier, John (1550-1617), Scottish mathematician, the inventor of logarithms. He also developed the decimal point in writing numbers. His *Rabdologiae* (1617) deals with abbreviating mathematical calculations.
See also: Logarithms.

Naples (pop. 1,210,503), third-largest city in Italy, capital of the region of Campania, on the Bay of Naples, 120 mi (193 km) southeast of Rome. Founded by the Greeks (600 B.C.), it was part of the kingdom of Sicily and later capital of the Kingdom of Naples. The historic city has a 13th-century cathedral and university and medieval castles and palaces. Nearby are the ruins of the Roman city of Pompeii. Naples is the financial and intellectual center of southern Italy.

The North Pole expedition of explorer Fridtjof Nansen was made possible by his specially constructed ship, Fram, *which had reinforced sides to resist the pressure of the ice.*

Naples, Bay of, bay of the Tyrrhenian Sea (arm of the Mediterranean west of Italy), southwest of Naples. It is 20 mi (32 km) wide from Cape Miseno to Point Campanella and penetrates the land 10 mi (16 km). Along its shoreline are the ancient Roman ruins of Pompeii and Herculaneum.

Many tourists visit the ancient ruins of Pompeii, along the shoreline of the Bay of Naples. Pictured is a fresco in a villa in Pompeii.

Naples, Kingdom of, region once comprised of all Italy south of the Papal States, including Sicily. It emerged after the conquests by the Norman Robert Guiscard in the 11th century; his nephew, Roger II, took the title King of Sicily and Apulia (1130). Naples was ruled in turn by the Hohenstaufens, the Angevins, the Aragonese, and the Spanish. The Austrians conquered the kingdom in 1707, but it was taken by the Spanish Bourbon kings in 1738. Napoleon I annexed the kingdom to his empire and made his brother, Joseph, king (1806), followed by his brother-in-law, Joachim Murat. In 1815, after Napoleon's defeat, the Bourbon Ferdinand IV was restored; he reunited Naples and Sicily as the Kingdom of the Two Sicilies. Bourbon rule collapsed before the advance of the revolutionary forces of Garibaldi (1860). When Victor Emmanuel was confirmed by the Italian parliament as king of all Italy (1861), Naples became a part of the new Italian state, ending 700 years as an independent kingdom.

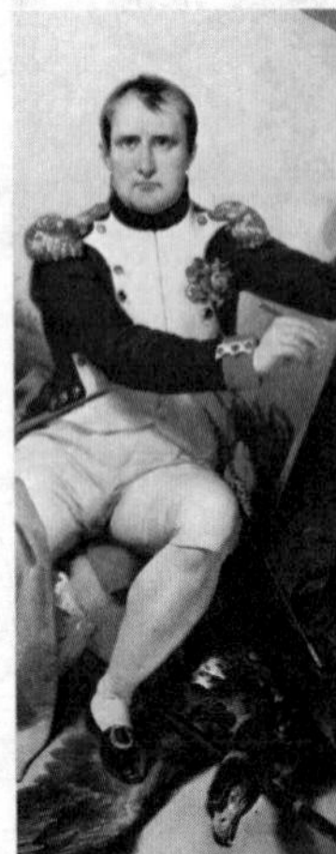

Napoleon I

Napoleon I (1769-1821), general and emperor of France (1804-14). Napoleon Bonaparte was born in Corsica, went to military schools in France, and became a lieutenant in the artillery (1785). He associated with Jacobins on the outbreak of the French Revolution, drove the British from Toulon (1793), and dispersed a royalist rebellion in Paris (Oct. 1795). He defeated the Austro-Sardinian armies in Italy (1796-97) and signed the treaty of Campo Formio, extending French territory. He then campaigned in Egypt and the Middle East, threatening Great Britain's position in India. Although he won land battles, the French fleet was destroyed in the Battle of the Nile in 1798. Returning to Paris Napoleon engineered the coup d'état of Nov. 9, 1799, establishing a Consulate with himself as first consul and dictator. He reorganized the government and established the Bank of France and the Code Napoléon, still the basis of French law.
The Treaty of Lunéville (1801) made peace with Austria; the Treaty of Amiens (1802) made peace with Britain. Napoleon became first consul for life (1802) and crowned himself emperor (1804). In the Napoleonic Wars he won victories over the European alliance at Austerlitz (1805), Jena (1806) and Friedland (1807), dissolving the Holy Roman Empire (1806), and becoming ruler of almost the whole continent. After Jena he inaugurated the Continental System whereby he hoped to keep European ports closed to British trade, but the battle of Trafalger (1805) established the dominance of Britain at sea.
In 1809 Napoleon divorced Joséphine de Beauharnais and married Marie Louise, who bore him an heir, Napoleon II. The Peninsular War revealed growing French weakness, and in 1812 Napoleon began his disastrous campaign against Russia. A new alliance of European nations defeated the French at Leipzig (1813); in 1814, after France was invaded, Napoleon abdicated and was exiled to the island of Elba. In March 1815 he escaped, returned to France, and ruled for the Hundred Days, which ended in French defeat at Waterloo (1815). Napoleon was then exiled to Saint Helena, where he died in 1821.
See also: Napoleonic Wars.

Narcissus depicted in a 17th-century painting by Jan Cossiers

Napoleon II (1811-32), son of Napoleon I and Marie Louise, proclaimed king of Rome at birth. After his father's abdication (1814), he lived in Austria as Duke of Reichstadt. He died of tuberculosis.

Napoleon III (Louis Napoleon Bonaparte; 1808-73), emperor of the French (1852-70); son of Louis Bonaparte (king of Holland), nephew of Napoleon I. He attempted several coups against King Louis Philippe, was jailed, but escaped to England (1846). After the 1848 revolution, he was elected president of France. He then dissolved the legislature and made himself emperor (1852). His regime promoted domestic prosperity, but by the 1860s opposition had grown. Among his military efforts were the Crimean War (1854-56), in which France was a victor, and an intervention in Mexico (1861-67), in which he failed to maintain Maximilian as emperor of Mexico. In 1870 his ill-judged war with Prussia ended in defeat, capture, and the collapse of his empire; he died in exile in England.

Napoleonic Code *see:* Code Napoléon.

Napoleonic Wars (1803-15), fought by France after Napoleon I became emperor. After the Treaty of Amiens (1802), which had ended the French Revolutionary Wars (1792-1802), Britain declared war on France (1803), maintaining that Napoleon was not keeping the treaty. Napoleon planned to invade Britain, but the British fleet proved too strong for him, especially after the Battle of Trafalgar (1805). The British, Swedes, Austrians, and Russians formed an alliance (July 1805); Napoleon defeated the Austrians and Russians at Austerlitz (Dec. 1805), the Prussians at Jena (1806), and the Russians at Friedland (1807); the Peace of Tilsit (1807) left him nearly master of Europe. Meanwhile, Britain had secured supremacy of the seas at Trafalgar. The Continental System begun after Jena was Napoleon's attempt to blockade British trade; on the pretext of enforcing it he invaded Portugal (1807) and Spain (1808). During the defeat of his armies by the British in the Peninsular War (1808-14), he signed the Peace of Schönbrunn (1809) with the defeated Austrians. In 1812 Napoleon invaded Russia with an army of some 500,000. He barely won the Battle of Borodino (1812) and marched unchallenged to Moscow, but his troops suffered from lack of supplies and the cold weather. Their retreat from Moscow and Russia was horrifying; only about 30,000 of Napoleon's soldiers returned. The French, by now drained of manpower and supplies, were decisively beaten at Leipzig (1813). Paris fell, and on April 11, 1814, Napoleon abdicated. The victorious allies signed the Treaty of Paris with the Bourbons. After Napoleon's escape from Elba and return (the Hundred Days) and his defeat at Waterloo (1815), the second Treaty of Paris was signed (1815).

Narayan, R(asipuram) K(rishnaswamy) (1906-), Indian novelist writing in English who created the fictitious town of Malgudi in a series of novels that dealt with the ironies of daily life in contemporary India. These include *The Bachelor of Arts* (1937), *The Financial Expert* (1952), and *The Vendor of Sweets* (1967).

Narcissus, fragrant yellow, white, or pink perennial flower (genus *Narcissus*) of the amaryllis family, named after the youth Narcissus of Greek mythology. Its large, brown, poisonous bulbs are planted in the fall and bloom each spring. The yellow daffodil and jonquil are varieties of narcissus.

Narcissus, in Greek mythology, name of a self-centered, handsome youth loved by many, including the nymph Echo. Having rejected all, he was denounced by the gods and sentenced to reflect upon his own image near a small pool. He gradually deteriorated until just a flower, the narcissus, remained. Echo, too, wasted away, leaving only her voice in the forest.

Narcolepsy, chronic disease marked by uncontrollable attacks of deep sleep of brief duration. The cause of the disease is unknown, although it may be hereditary. There is no cure.
See also: Cataplexy.

Narcotic, drug that induces sleep; specifically, the analgesics (painkilling drugs) opium, codeine, morphine, and heroin. These affect the higher brain centers, numbing the senses, lessening pain, causing mild euphoria and sleep (narcosis). They may act as hallucinogenic drugs and are addictive.
See also: Drug abuse.

Nard *see:* Spikenard.

Narraganset, Native American tribe of the Algonquian linguistic family who inhabited most of Rhode Island. They were friendly to the colonists until King Philip's War (1675-76) resulted in their virtual annihilation.

Narváez, Pánfilo de (c.1470-1528), Spanish conquistador. Under Diego de Velázquez, he played a major role in subjecting Cuba to Spain. In 1520 Velázquez sent him on a punitive expedition against Hernán Cortés in Mexico that failed. To subjugate and exploit Florida, he also led an unsuccessful expedition on which he died.

Narwhal (*Monodon monoceros*), tusked whale native to the Arctic. The body of the narwhal is about 18 ft (2.5 m) long. It is a toothless whale except for the single spiral tusk, present only in males, on the left-hand side of the jaw, up to 8 ft (2.5 cm) long. The function of the tusk is unknown. The narwhal is hunted for the ivory of its tusk and for oil.

NASA *see:* National Aeronautics and Space Administration.

Nash, Charles William (1864-1948), U.S. automobile manufacturer. He influenced the industry as head of Buick Motors (1910-12) and General Motors (1912-16), and as founder and head of Nash Motors, from which he retired in 1932. In 1954 Nash Motors and Hudson Motors became American Motors.

Nash, Ogden (1902-71), U.S. humorous poet. His witty, sometimes satirical style was punctuated by puns, asides, and unconventional rhymes. He published 20 volumes of verse, including *Hard Lines* (1931), *The Private Dining Room* (1953), and *Bed Riddance* (1970).

Nashua (pop. 180,557), city in southern New Hampshire, seat of Hillsborough County, situated on the Merrimack and Nashua rivers. It was settled c.1655 and incorporated in 1853. Originally, river power was used for its textile mills, but its industries now are printing, publishing, paper, leather products, and machinery. Educational institutions include New England Aeronautical Institute, Rivier College, and Daniel Webster College.

Nashville (pop. 985,026), capital city of Tennessee, on the Cumberland River. The last major battle of the Civil War was fought nearby (Dec. 1864). Nashville is a commercial, industrial, and agricultural city, and a religious, educational, and publishing center. It is the center of the country music recording industry, and its "Opryland" is a major entertainment complex.

Naskapi, Native American tribe living in Quebec and Labrador, Canada. Accustomed to fishing and hunting caribou and seals for food, clothing, and other survival needs, most members of the tribe have been forced to seek work in nearby villages because of the decline of the animal population.

Nassau (pop. 132,000), capital city of the Bahama Islands, a port on the northeastern New Providence Island. Long a pirate haunt, it is now a world-famous tourist resort.

Nasser, Gamal Abdel (1918-70), Egyptian president (1956-70) and Arab leader. He led the military coup d'état overthrowing King Farouk (1952), and named himself prime minister (1954). He ended British military presence in Egypt (1954) and nationalized the Suez Canal (1956), precipitating a brief war with Britain, France, and Israel. Elected president of Egypt unopposed (1956), he was also president of the short-lived United Arab Republic (1958-61). His "Arab socialism" policy brought new land ownership laws and agricultural policies, more schools, and the building of the Aswan Dam. He resigned after the disastrous 1967 Arab-Israeli War but resumed office by popular demand.

Nast, Thomas (1840-1902), German-born U.S. cartoonist, creator of the symbols for the Democratic Party (donkey) and the Republican Party (elephant). His attacks on the Tammany Hall politicial machine of New York City, symbolized as a tiger, contributed to its disintegration.

Nasturtium, annual plant (*Tropaeolum majus* and *T. minus*) native to mountainous areas of the American tropics and cultivated in gardens for its red, orange, and yellow flowers. Nasturtiums may be used medicinally for respiratory congestion. Their leaves and flowers are used in salad.

Natal, province of eastern Republic of South Africa, on the Indian Ocean. It is 33,578 sq mi (86,967 sq km) in area, with its capital at Pietermaritzburg. It produces sugar, fruit, cereals, and coal and manufactures fertilizers and textiles, mainly near Durban, the chief city. Natal was a British colony (1856-1910).

Natchez, Muskogean-speaking Native American tribe of southwestern Mississippi. Primarily an agricultural people, they worshipped the sun and maintained a rigid social caste system. Driven from their villages near today's Natchez, Miss., after 3 wars with French settlers (1716, 1723, 1729), they were assimilated by other tribes.

Natchez (pop. 22,209), city of southwestern Mississippi, seat of Adams County, on the bluffs overlooking the Mississippi River. A traditional center of the cotton industry, Natchez is the oldest city along the Mississippi, dating from its beginning as Fort Rosalie, built (1716) by the French.

Nation, Carry Amelia Moore (1846-1911), U.S. temperance agitator. Her campaign against liquor bars began in the "dry" state of Kansas. She became well known by smashing several saloons with a hatchet. Arrested on 30 occasions, she paid fines by selling souvenir hatchets and lecturing. She helped advance the national Prohibition movement that led to the passage of the 18th amendment.
See also: Prohibition.

National Academy of Sciences, private U.S. organization of scientists and engineers, founded 1863 by an act of Congress. It officially advises the government on scientific questions and coordinates major programs. Members are selected for distinguished research achievements.

Nashville. This replica of the Athenian Parthenon (1897), commemorates Tennessee's statehood

National Aeronautics and Space Administration (NASA), U.S. government agency responsible for nonmilitary space exploration and related research. Founded by President Eisenhower (1958), it has numerous research stations, laboratories, and space flight launching centers, including the Kennedy Space center at Cape Canaveral, Fla., the Johnson Space Center at Houston, Tex., and the Jet Propulsion Laboratory in Pasadena, Calif.
See also: Space exploration.

Gamal Abdel Nasser

National Air and Space Museum, part of the Smithsonian Institution, Washington, D.C., devoted to displays and exhibits about the history of air and space travel. The museum, originated by the U.S. Congress in 1946 and housed in its permanent building 30 years later, has 20 galleries, a theater, and a planetarium.

National Alliance of Business, organization whose major goal is to reduce unemployment among the disadvantaged population. Founded in 1968, it has 54,000 involved companies and operates in 11 U.S. cities. Administrators representing industry, government, and organized labor seek job opportunities and then locate unemployed persons for job training and placement.

NASA's Mission Control Center at the Johnson Space Center in Houston during the voyage of the Gemini VIII capsule (1966)

National anthem, official song of a nation, played on state or ceremonial occasions, intended as an expression of unity and loyalty to the country's ideals. One of the best-known national anthems is France's *La Marseillaise*, composed during the French Revolution of 1792. The text of the American anthem, *The Star-Spangled Banner*, was written in 1814 by Francis Scott Key, set to a popular English tune.

National Archives, U.S. governmental organization devoted to preserving archival material (documents, records, the presidential libraries, films, and maps) dating back to 1774 for public viewing and reference at the National Archives Building in Washington, D.C. The Declaration of Independence and the U.S. Constitution are sealed in protective display cases that can be lowered into an underground safe.
See also: Presidential libraries.

National Association for the Advancement of Colored People (NAACP), U.S. interracial organization, founded in New York City (1909) to oppose racism, segregation, and discrimination. It works for the enactment and enforcement of civil rights laws, supports education programs, and engages in direct action. An early success was the ending of lynching, and it was instrumental in desegregating public schools. It was directly responsible for the historic Supreme Court decision in *Brown* v. *Board of Education of Topeka* (1954).

National Gallery of Art, Washington D.C.

National League *see:* Baseball.

National Basketball Association (NBA) *see:* Basketball.

National budget, financial procedure recommended by the U.S. Office of Management and Budget (OMB) for the handling of income and expenditures during a fiscal year. A balanced budget is no longer an annual goal, but, rather, a deficit is desired when the economy lags and a surplus is planned during inflationary years.
See also: Budget; Congressional Budget Office.

National Bureau of Economic Research, organization that studies economic growth, taxation, investments, international trade, employment, and money. Unaffiliated and nonprofit, it provides its research data to the U.S. government, universities, and corporations so that they can better evaluate the economy and plan appropriately for the future.

National Bureau of Standards (NBS), of the U.S. Department of Commerce, established 1901. It determines national weights and measures, tests products and materials, and carries on research in science and technology. It also advises government agencies and U.S. industries on safety codes and technical specifications.

National cemetery, any of a system of burial places operated by U.S. government agencies for the deceased of the U.S. armed forces. Of the 127 national cemeteries, 50 are filled, and spouses or dependent children who wish to be buried there are often placed directly above or below the deceased veteran. Best known are Arlington National Cemetery in Arlington, Va., where John F. Kennedy is entombed, and the Gettysburg National Cemetery in Gettysburg, Pa., part of the Civil War battlefield.
See also: Arlington National Cemetery.

National Collegiate Athletic Association (NCAA), U.S. advisory body founded in 1906 to establish eligibility and competition rules for intercollegiate athletics. The NCAA compiles statistics on college sports and publishes rule books and guides. It has over 980 member institutions.

National Congress of American Indians, U.S. agency devoted to the welfare, benefits, and work opportunities for Native Americans. Property and voting rights are protected, and fair health services, equality in education, and legal aid are sought for the 600,000 Native Americans represented.

National Congress of Parents and Teachers (National PTA), U.S. organization whose major objective is to provide the best possible education for children from elementary grades through high school. Members also work for laws to protect children in the community, for parent education, and for drug and alcohol prevention. PTA groups are in 50 states, Washington, D.C., and in Europe for U.S. military personnel.

National debt, amount of money owed by a government, borrowed to pay expenses not covered by taxes. The U.S. national debt totaled approximately $3 trillion by 1991. National debts are incurred to pay for wars, public construction programs, recessions, etc. To obtain money, governments sell bonds or short-term certificates to banks, other organizations, and individuals. Some governments in crisis have defaulted on their debt or devalued the currency.

National Defense Education Act (NDEA), educational bill passed by the U.S. Congress in 1958 to provide matching funds to states for educational programs, classroom equipment to enrich academic subjects, teacher training, research in communications, counseling and testing, and financial loans to students.

National Educational Association of the United States (NEA), largest U.S. professional organization of educators. Goals are focused on classroom conditions, public school improvements, and increased employee benefits. NEA groups are in 50 states, Puerto Rico, and Washington, D.C., and have U.S. teacher representation overseas. Established in 1857, the NEA was directed mostly by administrators until the mid-1960s, when teachers took the leadership.

National Farmers Organization (NFO), group representing U.S. farmers in seeking the best prices and contracts for farm products and livestock. Negotiations with buyers are based on farm costs and a profit. Remaining NFO funds are used to confirm buyers' credit and protect farmers from invalid contracts.

National Football League (NFL) *see:* Football.

National forest, 186 million acres (75 million hectares) preserved and protected by the U.S. government for controlled use and enjoyment by the public, by ranchers for livestock grazing, and by businesses who harvest wood to make products and perform limiting mining operations. The forests also provide a wildlife sanctuary and safeguard water sources. They are administered by the Forest Service in the Department of Agriculture, an arrangement begun in 1905 under President Theodore Roosevelt.
See also: Forest Service, U.S.

National Gallery of Art, U.S. museum of nationally owned works of art, opened 1941 in Washington, D.C. as a branch of the Smithsonian Institution. The initial col-

lection was donated by Andrew Mellon (1937). The gallery possesses Jan van Eyck's *The Annunciation* and Raphael's *The Alba Madonna*; it includes many works by Italian, French, and American artists.
See also: Smithsonian Institution.

National Geographic Society, nonprofit scientific and educational organization, established in Washington, D.C. (1888) "for the increase and diffusion of geographic knowledge." It publishes *National Geographic* magazine, books, maps, and school bulletins, and sponsors expedition and research projects.

National Guard, volunteer reserve groups of the U.S. Army and Air Force, authorized by the Constitution and organized in 1792. The National Defense Acts of 1920 and 1933 empower the president to call up units in time of national crisis (e.g., the Korean War, 1950-53). Governors may call up state units during strikes and riots (e.g., Detroit and Newark, 1957). In peacetime a guard attends 48 drill sessions initially and a 2-week training camp annually.

National Hockey League (NHL) *see:* Hockey.

National income, total of labor and property earnings from the current production of goods and services by the nation's economy. It is the sum of employee compensation, proprietor's income, rental income, corporate profits, and net interests. The gross national product is the total national output of goods and services valued at market prices.

National Industrial Recovery Act *see:* National Recovery Administration.

National Institute for Occupational Safety and Health (NIOSH), U.S. organization responsible for evaluating all facets of work conditions for employees' benefits. It is a subsidiary of the U.S. Department of Health and Human Services. Safety codes, health hazards, and accident causes are examined, and recommendations for improvements are made. Investigators include all work sites in their research, and report data to the Occupational Safety and Health Administration (OSHA), which enforces judgments made.
See also: Occupational Safety and Health Administration.

National Institute of Standards and Technology, U.S. organization that seeks to preserve a basic system of measurement for the physical sciences, manufacturing enterprises, and general business. It evaluates international means of measurement to align with U.S. industry and publishes research data, which is available to the public.

National Institutes of Health (NIH), research agency of the U.S. Public Health Service. It supports over one-third of the nation's medical research through special-

Nationalism on parade

interest institutes (cancer; heart, lung, and blood disease; dental research; child health; allergy and infectious diseases; aging; and mental health), a clinical center, and fellowships and grants to universities and other private facilities.

Nationalism, political and social attitude of people who share a common culture, language, and territory as well as common aims, and thus feel a deep-seated loyalty to their group. Nationalism had its roots in the rise of strong centralized monarchies, in the economic doctrine of mercantilism, and the growth of a substantial middle class.

Nationalist China *see:* Taiwan.

Nationality, in law, recognized citizenship of a particular country. Two basic principles for deciding nationality are acknowledged by most countries: the right of blood, based on the nationality of a parent, and the right of place of birth.
See also: Citizenship.

Nationalization, governmental control and ownership of an industry. It is often practiced by socialist or communist governments, which believe that a nationalized industry can provide goods and services to the citizenry more efficiently and equitably than private businesses can. Underdeveloped countries have also nationalized industries to remove them from foreign control. Industries commonly nationalized include transportation, electric and gas utilities, and telephone services.
See also: Socialism.

National laboratory, any of 9 U.S. government laboratories devoted to studying a scientific problem such as conservation, energy, nuclear medicine and power, and radiation. During World War II, Los Alamos National Laboratory was responsible for developing the first atomic bomb.

National Labor Relations Act, or Wagner Act, law enacted in 1935 permitting the establishment of unions to protect employees' rights, and requiring employers to participate in collective bargaining with elected union representatives. The act created the National Labor Relations Board (NLRB) to monitor both the union and the employer to counteract unfair practices by either side. In 1947 the Taft-Hartley Act amended the Wagner Act by limiting union strength.
See also: Taft-Hartley Act.

National Labor Relations Board (NLRB), independent U.S. government agency designed to prevent or correct unfair labor practices. Set up to administer the National Labor Relations Act of 1935 and protect fledgling unions from illegal interference, the board has since been granted power to police illegal union and management practices. Its actions are subject to approval by the federal courts.

National League *see:* Baseball.

National League of Cities, agency representing about 15,000 U.S. cities and responsible for improving city life, solidifying power in city government, and occasionally representing cities in federal courts.

City officials attend an annual convention to interact with other city representatives and update municipal policy.

National Library of Medicine, located in Bethesda, Md., the central source of medical data in the U.S. Founded in 1836, the library houses an enormous collection of information in medicine, health sciences, dentistry, public health, nursing, and biomedical research. It maintains subscriptions to 25,000 journals and serials. In l956 the library became a part of the National Institute of Health of the Department of Health, Education, and Welfare (now Health and Human Services).

National Mediation Board, independent U.S. federal agency that mediates and arbitrates in labor disputes threatening to disrupt interstate airline and railroad commerce. Its arbitration decisions are legally binding.

National Motto, United States, "In God We Trust." This phrase, printed on coins since 1864, probably came from the fourth stanza of "The Star-Spangled Banner": "And this be our motto: 'In God is our trust.'" Congress made it the official U.S. motto in 1956.
See also: E Pluribus Unum.

National Museum of African Art, museum of the Smithsonian Institution in Washington, D.C., and the only U.S. museum devoted exclusively to African art. The collection includes more than 6,000 pieces, mainly sculpture, textiles, musical instruments, and everyday items like tools and baskets, coming largely from central and west Africa. The museum also contains a library and photographic archives.
See also: Smithsonian Institution.

National Museum of American Art, collection of more than 32,000 art works by U.S. artists from the mid-18th century to the present, part of the Smithsonian Institution in Washington, D.C. Edward Hopper, Mary Cassatt, and Man Ray are among the numerous artists represented by paintings, drawings, photographs, sculptures, and crafts.
See also: Smithsonian Institution.

Big Bend National Park, Texas

National Museum of American History, bureau of the Smithsonian Institution in Washington, D.C., that houses more than 17 million artifacts relating to the social, cultural, political, and technological development of the United States. Alexander Graham Bell's first telephone and George Washington's Revolutionary War field headquarters are among many displays.
See also: Smithsonian Institution.

National Museum of Natural History, collection relating to the earth, its inhabitants, and outer space, part of the Smithsonian Institution in Washington, D.C. Exhibits ranging from the evolution of humans to moon rocks to a living coral reef are drawn from more than 80 million artifacts housed here.
See also: Smithsonian Institution.

National Naval Medical Center, largest U.S. Navy medical facility for treatment, training, and research, located in Bethesda, Md. It includes a hospital, other medical, dental, and administrative facilities, and a medical research institute.
See also: Navy, United States.

National Oceanic and Atmospheric Administration (NOAA), U.S. government agency set up in 1970 to coordinate scientific research into atmosphere and oceans, focusing on pollution, resources, and weather control. The NOAA now includes the Coast and Geodetic Survey (founded in 1807) and the Weather Bureau (founded in 1870).

National Optical Astronomy Observatories (NOAO), group of 3 U.S. research centers for optical astronomy, established in 1984 and operating under the National Science Foundation, a federal agency. The sun, planets, and other objects in outer space are studied through telescopes. The centers are Kitt Peak National Observatory and the National Solar Observatory, at Tucson, Ariz., and Cerro Tololo Inter-American Observatory, near La Serena, Chile.
See also: Observatory; Telescope.

National Organization for Women (NOW), organization founded by Betty Friedan (author of *The Feminine Mystique*, 1963) in 1966 to promote full equality between men and women in all walks of life. With some 150,000 members, NOW has focused its efforts since 1978 on passage of the Equal Rights Amendment to end sexual discrimination in employment and on the abortion issue in support of the "Pro-Choice" advocates favoring abortion.
See also: Women's movements; Friedan, Betty.

National Park Service, bureau of the U.S. Department of the Interior established in 1916 to manage over 330 national parks and recreation areas, historic sites, and national monuments, which together comprise over 79 million acres (32 million hectares).

National Park System, system instituted by President Woodrow Wilson in 1916, whereby land of outstanding scenic or historical interest is protected "for the benefit and enjoyment of the people." An Act of Congress in 1872 had already created Yellowstone National Park. Today the system administers more than 46,000 sq mi (119,000 sq km) of parkland, comprising about 300 protected areas.

National Primitive Baptist Convention in the U.S.A., organization comprising more than 2,000 black Baptist churches. It was established in 1907 to join black Baptist congregations formed after the Civil War by former slaves. These Baptists follow 3 religious rites: baptism, Holy Communion, and feet-washing. The convention operates a publishing house, women's auxiliaries, training unions, and church schools.
See also: Baptists.

National Radio Astronomy Observatory (NRAO), U.S. observatory for radio astronomy that operates radio telescopes at Kitt Peak National Observatory, near Tucson, Ariz.; in Green Bank, W. Va.; and in Socorro, N.M., which has the Very Large Array, the world's most powerful radio telescope. Radio astronomy uses reflective dishes to collect radio waves that emanate from objects in outer space. The NRAO was founded in 1956 by the National Science Foundation, a federal agency.
See also: Radio telescope.

National Railroad Passenger Corporation *see:* Amtrak.

National Recovery Administration (NRA), government agency (1933-36) set up by the National Industrial Recovery Act to administer codes of fair practice for businesses and industries. By early 1934 the laboriously negotiated codes had become intolerably cumbersome, and in May 1935 the Supreme Court ruled the agency unconstitutional, although many of its codes became part of later legislation.

National recreation area *see:* National Park System.

National Republican Party, 19th-century U.S. political party formed when the Democratic-Republican Party split up in the 1828 presidential election. The party's presidential candidate in 1832, Henry Clay, was defeated by Andrew Jackson. In 1836 the party merged with other political groups to form the Whig Party.
See also: Whig Party.

National Rifle Association of America (NRA), U.S. organization promoting civilian use of firearms, founded 1871. The legally approved, private use of pistols and rifles for hunting, self-defense, safety, and wildlife conservation is the aim of the NRA,

which also maintains all national records of shooting competitions. It is a major lobbying group opposed to gun-control legislation and has 1 1/2 million members.
See also: Gun control.

National Road, U.S. paved road used by settlers emigrating to the West, begun in 1815 and completed in 1833. It ran from Cumberland, Md. to St. Louis, Mo. Today's U.S. Highway 40 closely follows the original route.
See also: Westward movement.

National Science Foundation (NSF), U.S. federal agency, established 1950. It promotes research, education, and international exchange in the sciences, and it funds fellowships, projects such as the International Decade of Ocean Exploration, and several permanent observatories.

National Security Agency/Central Security Agency (NSA/CSA), unit of the U.S. Department of Defense that protects U.S. codes and communications, breaks codes of other countries, and gathers foreign intelligence. The NSA was created in 1952, the CSA in 1972.

National Security Council (NSC), U.S. defense council created by Congress in 1947 as part of the executive office of the president, to advise on matters relating to national security and defense policies. Members include the vice-president and the secretaries of state and defense. Special advisers are the chair of the Joint Chiefs of Staff and the director of the Central Intelligence Agency.
See also: Central Intelligence Agency.

National Wildlife Refuge System, areas designated by the U.S. government to conserve wildlife and its habitat. The system, established in 1966, covers 89 million acres (36 million hectares). In the 410 refuges, most of them open to the public, the dwindling populations of such species as the bison and the trumpeter swan have been rebuilt.
See also: Fish and Wildlife Service; Wildlife conservation.

National Zoological Park, zoo maintained by the Smithsonian Institution in Washington, D.C. The 3 million annual visitors to the 176-acre (71-hectare) zoo can see some 5,000 animals representing 500 species, among them the renowned pandas Ling-Ling and Hsing-Hsing, given to the United States by China in 1972.

Nation of Islam *see:* Black Muslims.

Native Americans, preferred term to designate aboriginal peoples who inhabited the Americas before the arrival of the Europeans. It is generally believed that the ancestors of these first Americans migrated from Asia 26,000 years ago across a land bridge (now the Bering Strait) between Siberia and Alaska. A less popular theory suggests that the Native Americans evolved on the American continent. It is certain that by 6000 B.C. they were distributed widely throughout North and South America.
Central and South American tribes. The major Native American groups in Central and northern South America at the beginning of the European conquest (16th century) included the Caribs, Arawaks, Aztecs, Mayas, and Incas. The Maya civilization had reached its zenith some 700 years before, but the Inca and Aztec were at their peak. The cultures were overthrown and millions were killed by warfare and disease during the 16th-century Spanish conquest. The Spanish government proclaimed the Native Americans to be subjects and not slaves, but the settler community treated them as chattels and subjected them to forced labor. The situation was little better in Portuguese Brazil, though Jesuit-run plantations treated the indigenous population humanely. Where they were able to, Native Americans withdrew physically and psychologically from European culture. South American independence in the 19th century did little to improve their status. Atrocities committed against them by robber barons in the early 20th century brought a degree of government protection. In Mexico Native American influence in the 1910-17 revolution, the restitution of certain Native American property rights, and some integration between Native Americans and European cultures greatly improved the status of Native Americans. In South America progress continues to be fitful, however, for cultural more than racial reasons.
There is still a good deal of exploitation and maltreatment of remote tribes, often by government officials; they are still sometimes brutally driven off their lands or simply massacred.
North American tribes. By the time of the European incursion, there appeared to have been about 900,000 Native Americans north of the Rio Grande. European weapons, diseases, and destruction of natural resources took their toll, however, and the Native American population declined rapidly. Comprising hundreds of peoples and nations, with as many languages, Native Americans can be divided into 6 broad culture areas (the Eskimos are treated separately). (1) Early inhabitants of the Eastern Woodlands region in the eastern part of the United States were the mound builders of the Mississippi Valley. Later tribes in the area belonged to the great Algonquian and Iroquoian linguistic families, which included Cherokee, Chickasaw, Choctaw, and Creek. In the southeast the Seminole were the dominant tribe, living largely by farming. (2) The vast Plains area lay between the Mississippi River and the Rocky Mountains. It was uninhabited until the 1600s, when the introduction of horses and guns by settlers made it possible for tribes to live as nomadic buffalo hunters. These included the Apache, Cheyenne, Sioux, Comanche, Blackfoot, and Arapaho. The Plains tribes maintained a long resistance to white encroachment with skill and courage. (3) The original inhabitants of the Southwest included a group called the basketmakers (A.D. 100-700), who may have been the ancestors of the Pueblos. The peace-loving Pueblo peoples depended on agriculture for food, while their neighbors, tribes of the Apache and Navaho, relied on hunting and marauding. (4) The Plateau region included most of what is now California and the Great Basin between the Rocky Mountains and the Sierra Nevada Rangers. Most tribes lived simply by gathering. Their culture was not sophisticated, and there was little warfare. (5) The tribes of the Northwest Coast, notably the Haida, Kwakiutl, and Nootka, lived along the Pacific coast from southern Alaska to northern California. The area was rich in food, principally fish, freeing the tribes to develop an elaborate and sophisticated culture. Art, particularly carving, was complex and developed; it still flourishes today. The northern tribes retain much of their culture. (6) The peoples of the sparse North, or Subarctic, region from Newfoundland to Alaska belonged to the Athabascan language group in the west and the Algonquian group around Hudson Bay. Warfare played a small part in their seminomadic life styles; too much energy was required in the search for food.
Religion. Most Native American religion reveals a deeply felt communion with nature and a belief in a divine power. Individuals and kin groups of many tribes had spiritual ties with particular totems and animals. Shamans performed sacred rituals and treated the sick. The 1800s saw the tragic rise and fall of another Native American religion, the millenarian Ghost Dance.
North American Native Americans and European Americans. The paternalistic attitudes of the first English colonists did not stop their encroachment on Native American lands, leading to the Indian Wars. Native Americans were caught up in British and French rivalry in the French and Indian Wars. With the Northwest Ordinance (1787), the newly independent United States, in need of Native American support, proclaimed a policy of peaceful coexistence, yet with new expansion hostilities increased. The Indian Removal Act of 1830 was followed from 1850 by campaigns against Plains tribes, which ended in the massacre of Native Americans at Wounded Knee, S. Dak., in 1890. In 1871 Congress ceased to recognize the tribal nations' independent rights; the Dawes Act (1887), by breaking up tribal land into individual grants, deprived the Native Americans of around 86 million acres (35 million hectares), more than half their territory. Reform began with the Indian Reorganization Act of 1934, aimed at increasing Native American autonomy and improving their economic position; it restored some lands. Other reforms followed, but poverty, poor education, and unemployment are still problems on the reservations, where the majority of U.S. Native Americans still live.

Native bear *see:* Koala.

NATO *see:* North Atlantic Treaty Organization.

The ancient Incan city of Machu Picchu was discovered in 1911 by Hiram Bingham.

Toltec statue of the rain god chac-mool, located near the Warrior Temple in Chichen Itza.

Aztec drawing of an encounter between a Spanish man (left) and a messenger of Montezuma II, leader of the Aztecs

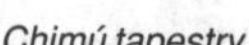

Chimú tapestry

Pre-Columbian gold earring

European painting depicting a battle between two groups of Native Americans. The group on the right is supported by the Europeans (note the gun).

A village of Kitwancool (British Columbia) with totem poles

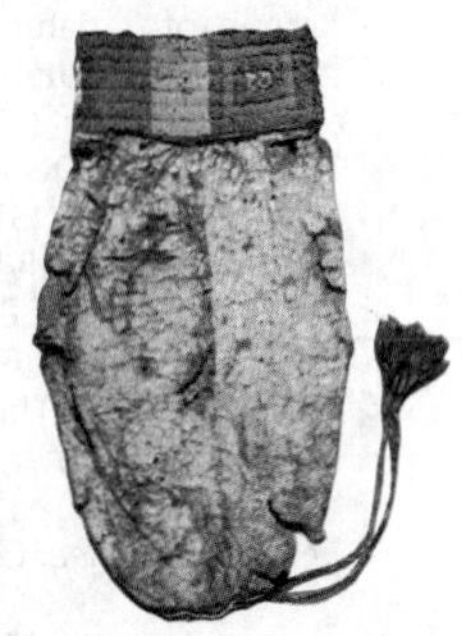

Typical utensils of the Sioux: On the left is a parfleche, a rawhide bag used to carry food; on the right is a water pouch.

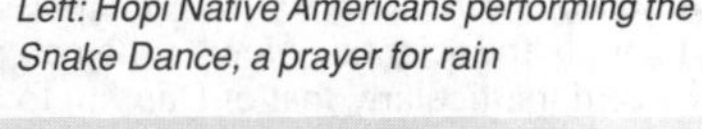

Left: Hopi Native Americans performing the Snake Dance, a prayer for rain

Left: Arapaho women perform the Ghost Dance (1893).

George Catlin's Buffalo Chase

Natural Bridges National Monument, group of 3 natural sandstone bridges in southeastern Utah. The Sipapu, the largest bridge, is 220 ft (67 m) high and spans 268 ft (82 m). The Owachomo, the smallest and oldest, is 106 ft (32 m) high and 180 ft (55 m) long but only 10 ft (3 m) thick. The Kachina, 93 ft (28 m) thick at its smallest point, is 205 ft (62.5 m) high and 204 ft (62.2 m) high. The monument was established in 1908.

Natural gas *see:* Gas.

Natural gas liquids (NGL), chemical compounds in liquid form obtained from natural gas. The main NGL compounds are ethane, butane, pentane, hexane, and heptane. Natural gas liquids (NGL) are light hydrocarbons. The 2 methods of producing NGL are condensation and absorption.
See also: Butane and propane; Gas.

Naturalism, aesthetic movement attempting to apply the scientific view of the natural world (particularly that of Darwin) to the arts. According to naturalism, there is nothing real beyond nature; humans are thus prisoners of their environment and heredity. This movement, inspired by Émile Zola's argument for a scientific approach to literature in *The Experimental Novel* (1880), influenced such writers Guy de Maupassant (France), Stephen Crane and Theodore Dreiser (U.S.), Henrik Ibsen (Norway), August Strindberg (Sweden), and Maxim Gorki (Russia). The naturalist influence is also evident in the work of French painter Gustave Courbet. More recent naturalists are U.S. playwrights Arthur Miller and Tennessee Williams.

Naturalization, process whereby a resident alien obtains citizenship of a country. In the United States, under the Immigration and Nationality Act of 1952, a candidate must be over 18, have entered the country legally and have resided there for at least 5 years, be of "good moral character," be able to read and write English, and take an oath of loyalty and service to the United States.
See also: Citizenship; Immigration.

Natural law, body of law supposed to be innate, discoverable by natural human reason, and common to all people. Under this philosophy, human or positive law, though changeable and culturally dependent, must—if truly just—be derived from the principles of natural law. The concept was rooted in Greek philosophy and Roman law. Particularly in the Christian philosophy of Thomas Aquinas, natural law—the sense of right and wrong implanted in humans by God—is contrasted with revealed law. It lay behind Hugo Grotius's ideas on international law (17th century). It was used as a basis for ethics, morality, and even for protests against tyranny by Spinoza, Leibniz, Locke, Rousseau, and many others, but with the development of scientific philosophies in the 19th century, natural law largely lost its influence.
See also: Aquinas, Saint Thomas.

Natural resources, earth's products or features that support life or are used to make food, fuel, and raw materials. Natural resources include air, water, and sunshine; biological resources like plants and animals; and mineral resources like oil and coal.

Natural selection, mechanism central to Charles Darwin's theory of evolution (1830s). According to Darwin, evolution occurs when an organism is confronted by a changing environment. Organisms able to adapt to this change survive and are thus "naturally selected," passing their useful traits on to offspring. Darwin saw this process as analogous to the artificial selection practiced by animal breeders.
See also: Darwin, Charles Robert; Wallace, Alfred Russel.

Nauru, officially the Republic of Nauru, independent island republic in the western Pacific Ocean. The island is 40 mi (64 km) south of the equator and about 8 sq mi (20 sq km) in area. Revenues come primarily from the export of phosphate rock. Discovered in 1789 and annexed by Germany in 1888, it was captured by Australia in World War I and administered as a trust territory until independence was granted in 1968.

Nausea, feeling of discomfort in the stomach, with a distaste for food and a tendency to vomit. Nausea is a typical symptom of seasickness, the original meaning of the word.
See also: Vomiting.

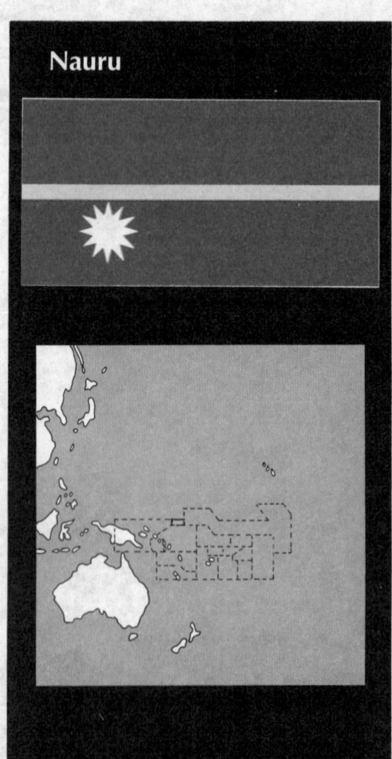

Capital:	Yaren
Area:	8.2 sq mi (21.2 sq km)
Population:	9,100
Form:	republic
Independent:	1968
GNP:	U.S.$160,000,000
Per capita:	U.S.$21,400

Nautilus, or chambered nautilus, genus of shellfish native to the South Pacific and Indian oceans, having a spiral shell divided into chambers. As the nautilus grows it adds on new and larger chambers, sealing off the old ones and living in the new ones. The nautilus breathes by means of gills and uses tentacles to catch the animals on which it feeds. It is a member of the class of cephalopods (which includes squid and octopi), mollusks with a tubular siphon and a circle of tentacles around the head.

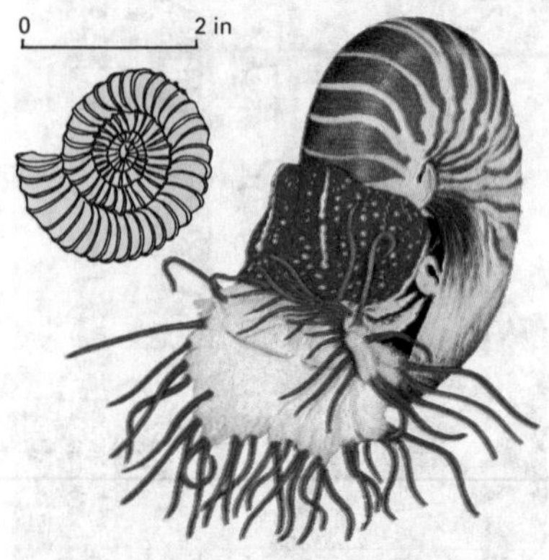

Nautilus

Nautilus, U.S.S., first nuclear-powered submarine, launched Jan. 1955. It was named for one of the first successful submarines (1800-01), invented by Robert Fulton. Capable of submerged speed of over 20 knots, the *Nautilus* made the first transpolar voyage beneath the North Pole on Aug. 3, 1958. It measured 323 ft (98 m) in length and had a crew of over 100.
See also: Submarine.

Navajo, Native American tribe, thought to have migrated from the north to settle in Arizona and New Mexico C.A.D. 1000. They learned agriculture, weaving, and sand painting from the Pueblo. After the Spanish introduced sheep in the 1600s, they became shepherds. Raiders of Spanish settlements in the southwest, they were subdued (1864) by Kit Carson and held at Fort Sumner, N.M., until their resettlement on a reservation (1868), now over 16 million acres in Arizona, New Mexico, and Utah.

Naval Academy, United States *see:* United States Naval Academy.

Naval Observatory, United States, astronomical observatory and source of official standard time in the United States. Founded in Washington, D.C., in 1833, the observatory has moved several times to obtain better observing conditions. Since 1955 its main station has been in Flagstaff, Ariz.
See also: Astronomy.

Navarre, Basque province in northern Spain. Formerly an independent Basque kingdom, it was strategic in international politics as a buffer state between Spain and France because it controlled a principal Pyrenees mountain pass, Roncesvalles, on the border. Most of Navarre was conquered in 1515 by Ferdinand V; it sank to provincial status in 1841. Bordering the province, in France, is Lower Navarre. It remained independent until 1589, when Navarre's ruler became Henry IV of France as well. Today that district is part of the French department of Pyrénées-Atlantiques.
See also: Spain.

Navel *see:* Umbilical cord.

Navigation, science of finding the position and directing a marine, air, or space vessel from one place to another. Ocean navigators were dependent on landmarks and observations of the heavenly bodies until the invention of the compass around the 12th century gave them an independent means of determining direction. Latitude has been found using the astrolabe, cross-staff, and quadrant since the Middle Ages, and longitude has been determined with the chronometer and the sextant since the 18th century. Radio signals and satellites are now used.

Navigation acts, laws regulating navigation at sea or in port or restricting commercial shipping in the national interest—more specifically, regulations promulgated (from 1650) by the British during the American colonial period to try to ensure that benefits of commerce would accrue to England (and to a lesser extent, the colonies) rather than to England's enemies. After 1763 strict enforcement of the acts caused friction between England and the American colonies and was a major factor leading to the outbreak of the Revolutionary War.
See also: Revolutionary War in America.

Navratilova, Martina (1956-), Czechoslovakian-born U.S. tennis player. Known for her aggressive and powerful play, in singles competition she won a record 9 Wimbledons (1978, 79, 82-87, 90), 4 U.S. Opens (1983, 84, 86, 87), 3 Australian Opens (1981, 83, 85) and 2 French Opens (1982, 84). Navratilova defected in 1975 and became a U.S. citizen in 1981.

Navy, seaborne armed force maintained for national defense or attack. In ancient times, Greek and Roman ships ruled the Mediterranean. In Scandinavia the Vikings ravaged the coasts of Europe from C.A.D. 800 for over 200 years. By the later 16th century most western European nations had acquired naval forces. Spain emerged as the leading naval power, but after its Armada was defeated by the English in 1588, England had mastery of the seas. England's naval supremacy was challenged by Holland and France, but the Battle of Trafalgar in 1805 restored it for another 100 years. The submarine and the aircraft carrier have replaced armored battleships. In the post-World War II period, Britain was overshadowed as a leading naval power by the United States and the USSR.

Navy, Department of the, division comprising the U.S. Navy, the U.S. Marine Corps, and during wartime, the U.S. Coast Guard. Established by Congress in 1798, the Department of the Navy became part of the U.S. Department of Defense in 1949.
See also: Defense, Department of.

Navy, United States, branch of the U.S. armed forces designed to maintain command of the sea. The Continental Congress voted (1775) the first naval budget to outfit ships in the American Revolution against the British. By 1798 the Navy Department was established. The Spanish-American War in 1898 brought the United States to the forefront of the world's seapowers, second only to Great Britain. Leading developments after the 2 world wars were the navy's nuclear-powered submarines and guided missiles.

Nazareth (pop. 45,600), historic town in northern Israel, lower Galilee, where Jesus lived as a youth. A place of Christian pilgrimage, the town has many shrines and churches. It also has some light industry and is an agricultural market center.
See also: Israel.

Nazism, or National Socialism, the creed of the National Socialist German Workers' Party (Nazi Party) led by Adolf Hitler from 1921 to 1945. The Nazi movement began (1918-19) when Germany was humiliated and impoverished by defeat in World War I and by the severe terms of the Treaty of Versailles. From a membership of around 100,000 in 1928, the party increased in strength to 920,000 in 1932. The ideas behind the program were rooted in nationalism, racism (especially anti-Semitism), authoritarianism, and militarism, expressed by Hitler in *Mein Kampf* (My Struggle, 1923). Recovery of the German nation was to be accomplished by rearmament, territorial expansion to acquire *lebensraum* ("living space") for the Teutonic master race, and the restoration of self-respect under a unified military regime. With the aid of the secret police (Gestapo), Hitler's Nazi dictatorship exterminated

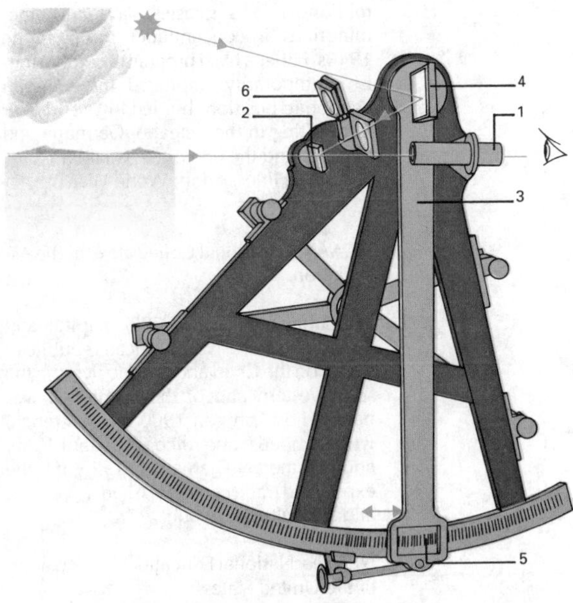

The sextant is a navigation instrument that determines the latitude. It is held so that the horizon is visible through the telescope (1). The moveable arm (2) carries a mirror (3), and the arm is moved so that an image of the sun, reflected from (3) and the half-silvered mirror (5), is aligned with the horizon. The angular distance between the sun and the horizon can be read on the vernier scale (6). There is a piece of dark glass (4) to reduce the intensity of the sun's image.

Naval strategy has been greatly enhanced by the role of the aircraft carrier.

millions of Jews, gypsies, slavs, and other minorities, in concentration camps in the 1940s. Hitler's Nazi program of expansionism temporarily improved the German economic position, but led to World War II, resulting in the defeat of Germany and its allies and the end of the Nazi Party.
See also: Hitler, Adolf; World War II.

NCAA *see:* National Collegiate Athletic Association.

N'Djamena (pop. 511,700), capital and largest city of the North African republic of Chad, on the Chari and Logone rivers in the southwestern part of the country. It was named Fort-Lamy in 1900 by the French, who founded it and ruled Chad until 1960, and renamed N'Djamena in 1973. It is the export and trade center for Chad's livestock and agricultural products.

NEA *see:* National Educational Association of the United States.

Nearsightedness *see:* Myopia.

Nebraska, state in central United States in the Great Plains region; bordered by South Dakota to the north, the Missouri River and Iowa and Missouri to the east, Kansas to the south, Colorado to the south and west, and Wyoming to the west.
Land and climate. Nebraska, which slopes gradually from northwest to southeast, has 2 main land regions. The eastern fifth of the state lies in the Dissected Till Plains. Once covered by glaciers, this region has a fertile, yellowish soil called loess that was built up by winds. The Great Plains region covers the rest of the state. It includes the Sand Hills section, the largest area of sand dunes in North America, whose streams and grasses make it good for cattle grazing; the Loess Plain section, a farming area; and the High Plains and Badlands sections, used mainly for cattle grazing. The state's rivers, which drain into the Missouri, include the Platte (the state's major river), Loup, Elkhorn, Niobrara, Republican, Big and Little Blue, and Big and Little Nemaha. Nebraska's unpredictable climate is marked by extremes of heat and cold. Principal cities are Omaha and Lincoln.

The selling of Texan Longhorns in Nebraska

Nebraska

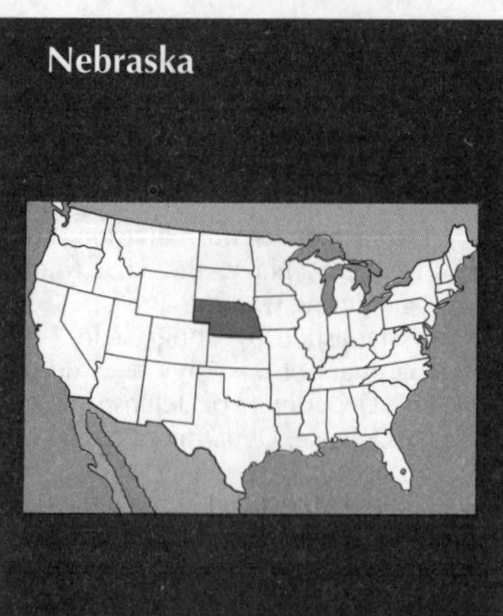

Capital:	Lincoln
Statehood:	Mar. 1, 1857 (37th state)
Familiar name:	Cornhusker State
Area:	77,355 sq mi (200,350 sq km); ranks 15th
Population:	1,584,617 (1990); ranks 36th
Elevation:	Highest—5,424 ft (1,654 m) in Kimball County; Lowest—840 ft (255 m) along the Missouri River in Richardson County
Motto:	Equality Before the Law
Flower:	Goldenrod
Bird:	Western meadowlark
Tree:	Cottonwood
Song:	"Beautiful Nebraska"

Economy. Service industries—wholesale trade, finance, and insurance—are important to Nebraska's economy, as is agriculture. Beef cattle are the chief livestock product; others are hogs and milk. Chief crops are corn, hay, soybeans, wheat, beans, sorghum, sugar beets, and oats. Manufactured goods include processed foods, machinery, chemicals, primary and fabricated metals, and transportation equipment. Nebraska has few minerals.
Government. Nebraska's present constitution was adopted in 1875. The governor serves a 4-year term. Nebraska is the only state with a unicameral (one-house) legislature; it consists of 49 senators serving 4-year terms. In the U.S. Congress, Nebraska is represented by 2 senators and 3 representatives.
History. Prehistoric people probably lived in the area 10,000 to 25,000 years ago. When European explorers arrived in the 1500s, several Indian tribes lived in the area. In 1682, the French explorer La Salle claimed all lands in the Mississippi Valley—including Nebraska—for France. France ceded the area to Spain for a time, then sold it to the U.S. in the 1803 Louisiana Purchase. Soon after, traders established posts there. Until 1854, the U.S. government classified Nebraska as Indian territory, forbidding further white settlement there. However, thousands of white settlers traveled through on the Oregon Trail during the 1830s and 1840s. The slavery debate led to the Kansas-Nebraska Act of 1854, which established the territories of Kansas and Nebraska. (The Nebraska Territory included present-day Nebraska and parts of Montana, North Dakota, South Dakota, Wyoming, and Colorado.)
Railroads and the Homestead Act of 1862 opened Nebraska to expanding white settlement; clashes erupted between ranchers and farmers. The territory supported the Union during the Civil War. Nebraska became a state in 1867. The farm-based economy suffered during the Great Depression of the 1930s but improved during World War II, when the state's food output increased and new industries were developed. The farm crisis of the 1970s and 1980s hit Nebraska hard. Today, it is working to preserve family farms and attract new industries.

Nebuchadnezzar, name of three kings of Babylonia. **Nebuchadnezzar I** (ruled 1124-1103 B.C.) conquered Elam and extended Babylonian rule over most of ancient Mesopotamia. **Nebuchadnezzar II** (605-562 B.C.) waged military campaigns to consolidate the Neo-Babylonian or Chaldean Empire, crushing the kingdom of Judah, destroying Jerusalem (586 B.C.), and taking captive Jews to Babylon. His conquest of the Jews is described in the Old Testament book of Daniel. **Nebuchadnezzar III** (6th century B.C.) usurped the throne from Darius I for 10 weeks before he was killed.
See also: Babylon.

Nebula, enormous interstellar cloud of gas and dust, often luminous. *Diffuse nebulae* can measure 100 light-years in diameter. *Bright nebulae,* such as the Orion Nebula, appear to shine due to nearby bright stars, whose light they either reflect (reflection nebula) or absorb and re-emit (emission nebula). *Dark nebulae,* such as the Horsehead Nebula, are distant from stars, and hence appear as dark patches in the sky obscuring the light from stars beyond them. *Planetary nebulae* are cast off by stars that have exploded. They are usually symmetrical, forming an expanding shell around the central star, often still visible within. The Ring Nebula is an outstanding example.
See also: Solar system.

Nebular hypothesis, theory accounting for the origin of the solar system, developed by Immanuel Kant and given scientific form by P.S. Laplace in the late 1700s. It suggested that a rotating nebula had formed gaseous rings that condensed into the planets and moons, the nebula's nucleus forming the sun.
See also: Solar system.

Necker, Jacques (1732-1804), Swiss-born French banker; finance minister under Louis XVI. In 1777 he tried to raise money to support French involvement in the American Revolution. Later, before the States-General, he proposed sweeping public reforms. His dismissal (1789) led to the storming of the Bastille. Once more he was recalled to office, but he resigned in 1790.
See also: France.

Necrosis, death of a diseased cell, tissue, or organ while still in contact with living cells.

Nectar, in Greek mythology, the drink of the gods, which, along with ambrosia—food of the gods—gave them youth and immortality.
See also: Mythology.

Nectar, sweet substance secreted from the nectaries, or glands, in plant blossoms, stems, and leaves, and from which honeybees make honey. In Greek mythology, the drink of the gods was nectar, which, along with ambrosia—food of the gods—gave them youth and immortality.

Nectarine *(Prunus persica)*, tree in the rose family whose fruit is a smooth-skinned peach. The nectarine and peach trees are very closely related, and both peach and nectarine fruit may grow on either variety of tree.

Needle, long, slender tool used to sew, embroider, crochet, and knit. Needles are generally pointed at one end to allow them to pass easily through material. Most varieties have "eyes," holes near one end through which the thread is passed so as to be pulled through the material, but crocheting and knitting needles are eyeless. Different sizes and shapes of needles are designed for various uses—upholstery, garment creation or repair, decoration, and surgery. A complex manufacturing process produces the steel needle. Predating the modern steel needle were prehistoric bone or horn needles and medieval iron needles.

Needlepoint, canvas work, or tapestry, form of embroidery. Designs for needlepoint are outlined on a box grid of the work surface or *canvas*. A blunt needle and soft yarn are used to create decorative patterns using such stitches as the cross stitch, tent stitch, knotted stitch, and bargello or Florentine stitch. Used to create pictures or patterns for upholstery or clothing garments, needlepoint is classified as *petit point, gros point*, and *quick point*, according to the size of the boxes (and thus the stitches) on the canvas.

Nefertiti, or Nefretete (fl. c.1372-1350 B.C.), queen of ancient Egypt, wife of Ikhnaton (reigned c.1370-50 B.C.), and aunt of Tutankhamen. Nefertiti and Ikhnaton promoted monotheism, and their rule was a time of great social and cultural change.

Negev, or Negeb, triangular region of hills, plateaus, and desert in southern Israel, extending south from Beersheba to Elath on the Gulf of Aqaba. It covers around 5,000 sq mi (13,000 sq km), or more than half of Israel. Irrigation has made many areas fertile. It is rich in mineral and natural gas resources.

Negligence, in law, inadvertent failure to act with the degree of care a situation demands. The degree may be determined by a contractual obligation or what the law defines as the standard of conduct of a "reasonable" person. Conduct of an accident victim that contributed to an accident is contributory negligence and may prevent or reduce compensation. Negligence is usually a civil offense but may lead to a criminal charge, such as manslaughter.

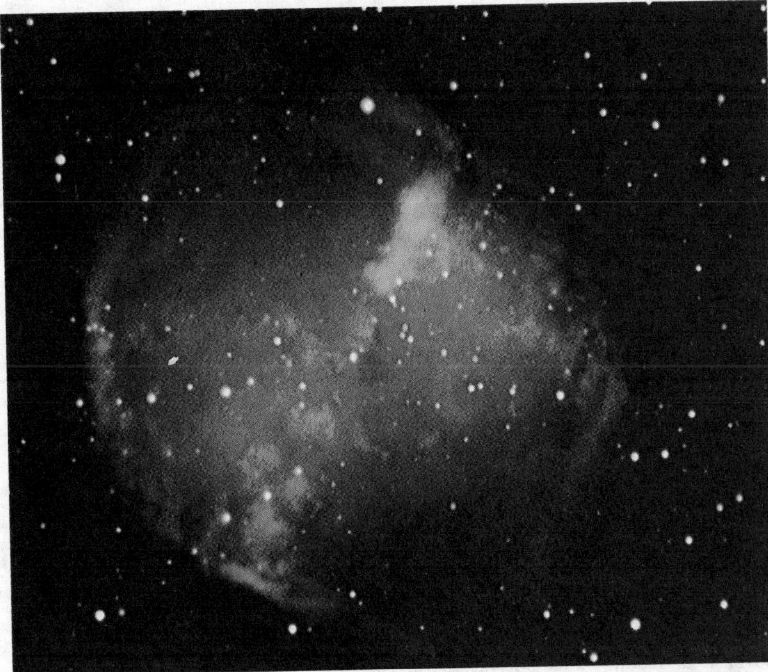

Nebula are made of gas and dust particles. Shown is the Dumbbell nebula (M27) in the constellation Vulpecula.

Negotiable instrument, paper document that represents money. Money orders, checks, and traveler's checks as well as promissory notes, certificates of deposit, and bills of exchange are kinds of negotiable instruments. These documents are endorsed, or signed to indicate to whom or what the money value of the document is to be credited. Negotiable instruments, which must fulfil certain requirements for legal transfer, are regulated by the Uniform Commercial Code in all but one state in the United States—Louisiana.

Negroes *see:* African Americans.

Nehemiah (fl. 5th century B.C.), Jewish leader of the return from the Babylonian Captivity. In the Old Testament book of Nehemiah (written with the Book of Ezra by the author of Chronicles), he rebuilt Jerusalem's walls and enforced moral and religious reforms.
See also: Bible.

Nehru, Jawaharlal (1889-1964), first prime minister of independent India (1947-64). An English-educated lawyer, he embraced the cause of India's freedom after the British massacre of Indian nationalists at Amritsar (1919), becoming president of the Indian National Congress (1929). He spent most of 1930-36 in prison for his part in civil disobedience campaigns. During World War II he and Gandhi united in their opposition to aiding Britain unless India was freed. Released in 1945 after 3 year's imprisonment, Nehru began negotiations with Britain that culminated, in 1947, in the establishment of independent India. Nehru's daughter Indira Gandhi was prime minister of India (1966-77 and 1980-84); his grandson became prime minister in 1984.
See also: India.

Jawaharlal Nehru

Nelson, Horatio (1758-1805), British naval hero who defeated the French and Spanish fleets at the Battle of Trafalgar (1805). His destruction of the French fleet off Aboukir (1798) brought him fame. The scandal of his liaison with Emma, Lady Hamilton, was dispelled by his defeat of the Danes at Copenhagen (1801). The victory at Trafalgar cost Nelson his life, but ensured British naval supremacy for 100 years.
See also: Trafalgar, Battle of.

Nelson, Thomas, Jr. (1738-89), colonial and early U.S. politician. He was a signer of the Declaration of Independence and a representative to the Continental Congress (1775-77), and served as governor of Virginia after the revolution (1781).

Nelson River, longest river (400 mi/640 km) in Manitoba, Canada. Flowing northeast from Lake Winnipeg to Hudson Bay at Port Nelson, it is the outlet for the Winnipeg, Red, and Saskatchewan river systems, and for lakes Winnipeg, Manitoba, and Winnipegosis. Once the transportation route of fur traders, it now provides hydroelectric power at Kelsey Rapids and other points.

Neman River (Lithuanian: *Nemunas;* Polish: *Niemen*), river in the Soviet Union. Approximately 582 mi (937 km) long, the Neman River flows westward from the republic of Byelorussia, then northward through the republic of Lithuania, to empty into Kurland Gulf of the Baltic Sea. Although the river freezes for up to 5 months each year, it is used as a transportation route for timber. The river also supports a dam for a hydroelectric plant.

Nematoda, class of worms known as roundworms. Separate entities within this class are referred to as *nematodes.* Ranging from microscopic size to over 3 ft (1 m) long, these worms live in soil, water, or in plants or animals as parasites. Hookworms, pinworms, and trichinae are all parasitic nematodes that may live in humans or animals.

Nematomorpha *see:* Horsehair worm.

Nemean Games, athletic and musical competition of ancient Greece held every other year at the shrine of Zeus in Nemea, on the Peloponnisos. These games, recorded as early as 597 B.C., along with the Olympic, Isthmian, and Pythian games, made up the national festivals of the ancient Greeks.

Nemerov, Howard (1920-), U.S. poet, novelist, and critic noted for his satiric power. His *Collected Poems* (1977) won a National Book Award and a Pulitzer Prize in 1978. Among his novels are *The Melodramatists* (1949) and *The Homecoming Game* (1957).

Nemertinea *see:* Ribbon worm.

Nemesis, in Greek mythology, goddess of just retribution, avenger of evil. She was the agent of punishment for violations of sacred law. More generally, the word "nemesis" now means any formidable opponent.

Religion in Nepal is intimately entwined with daily life. Although the majority of the people are Hindus, the dominant faith is suffused with Buddhism and animism. In the hills, especially, Buddhist prayer walls are common. Travelers still recite the sacred words as they pass.

Nene, or Hawaiian goose (*Nesochen sandvicensis*), bird that lives among the lava in the hills of Hawaii. Through hunting and the ravages of pigs and dogs, it nearly became extinct. By 1950 only 34 survived, 17 in captivity. These were sent to England, where a small population was built up; some were taken back to Hawaii in 1962.

Neodymium, chemical element, symbol Nd; for physical constants see Periodic Table. Neodymium was discovered by C.F. Auer von Welsbach in 1885 after he separated didymia into earths (oxides) called praseodymia and neodymia. Neodymium is a silvery, soft, reactive metal, belonging to the series of elements known as the rare-earth metals. It occurs in the minerals monazite and bastnasite, the 2 principal sources of the rare-earth elements, and is prepared by reducing the anhydrous chloride with calcium. Neodymium is present to the extent of 18% in misch metal. Ion-exchange and solvent extraction techniques have led to much easier isolation of the rare-earth elements. Neodymium and its compounds are used in laser materials, carbon lighting applications, special glasses and enamels, and refractory materials.

Neolithic Period *see:* Stone Age.

Neo-Malthusianism *see:* Malthus, Thomas Robert.

Neon, chemical element, symbol Ne; for physical constants see Periodic Table. Discovered by William Ramsay and Morris W. Travers in 1898, it occurs in the atmosphere to the extent of 1 part in 65,000. It is obtained by liquefaction of liquid air and separated from other gases by fractional distillation. Neon is an inert gas, but is said to form a compound with fluorine. It belongs to the so-called noble gas group of elements. In a vacuum discharge tube, neon glows reddish-orange and is the most intense of all the rare gases at ordinary voltages and currents. The largest use of neon is in neon advertising signs. It is also used in gas lasers, voltage indicators, lightning arrestors, wave meter tubes, and TV tubes. Liquid neon is an economical cryogenic refrigerant.

Neoplatonism, school of philosophical thought, founded by the Greek philosopher Plotinus, influenced by the late writings of Plato. This mystical belief, popular from the 3rd through the 6th centuries, was based on the concept of *emanation*—a process by which an essential sense of things permeates different levels of existence. A diagram of these levels would show the *One*, that incomprehensible thing beyond being, as uppermost, emanating through to the *Logos* or intellect, where ideas reign, then to the *World Soul*, where the intellect and the material world are linked, and finally to the lowest level, the *Material*, the level from which humanity begins. Philosophers ranging from St. Augustine (3rd-4th century) to St. Thomas Aquinas before his conversion to Christianity (13th century) to G.W.F. Hegel (19th century) were influenced by neoplatonism. *See also:* Plato; Plotinus.

Nepal, kingdom of southern Asia, bordered by India, Sikkim, and China (Tibet). Katmandu is the capital.

Land and climate. Nepal has an area of 56,136 sq mi (145,392 sq km). It is an elongated country on the southern flanks of the towering Himalayas, extending some 500 mi (805 km) westward from its borders with Sikkim to the Sarda River, a tributary of the Ganges.

Along its borders with Sikkim and Tibet are some of the world's loftiest peaks, including Mt. Everest (29,028 ft/8,848 m), the world's highest. The Bheri, Sun Kosi, and other rivers flow through wild gorges between the mountain spurs, forming a series of fertile, longitudinal valleys called *duns.* South of the Dundwa, Sumesar, and Churia Ghati hills (2,000-3,500 ft/610-912 m), are the swampy jungle-plains, called Terai, and the border with India.

Icy-cold temperatures in the high Himalayas sometimes fall to –40°F (1°C). The peaks are always snow-capped. In central Nepal, temperatures average 50°F (10°C) in January and 78°F (25°C) in July. The main rainy season is June through October, the yearly average being about 60 in (152 cm).

People. The population is of mixed Mongolian and Indo-Aryan origin. Its main ethnic groups are the Newars, the Bhotias (who include the Sherpas, well-known mountain guides), and the Gurkhas (noted soldiers). Hinduism, the dominant religion, has long coexisted with Buddhism. About 90% of the people are farmers who live in villages. Although educational programs were begun in the 1950s, only 29% are literate (1989). The official language is Nepali.

Economy. In this predominantly agricultural country, crops include rice, wheat, corn, oilseeds, potatoes, jute, tobacco, opium, and cotton. Livestock is important. The Terai forests provide wood, and medicinal herbs are exported from the Himalayan slopes. Nepal has little industry and only a few paved roads. There are several airports, including an international facility at Katmandu. Tourism is important to the economy.

History. Nepal, the world's only Hindu kingdom, lay isolated from the world until recently. In 1768 Ghurkhas took command of the Nepal Valley, still the home of most Nepalese, but expansion into Tibet was checked by the Chinese. In the south the Nepalese fought the British (1814-16) and were defeated only after a hard struggle, but remained independent. From 1846 the Rana family reigned as a military oligarchy until 1951, when the present Shah family took control, establishing a constitutional monarchy. Polygamy, child marriage, and the caste system were abolished. In 1962 the *panchayat* system of government was established, in which various political leaders, including the king, serve as prime minister. In response to pro-democracy protests, political parties were legalized in

Nepal

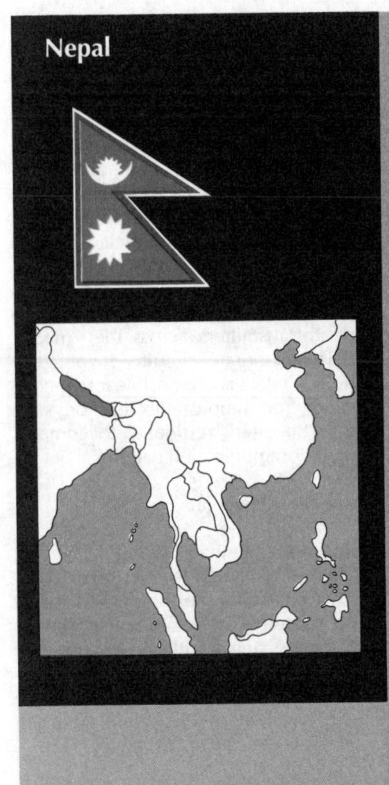

General information	
Capital:	Kathmandu
Area:	56,827 sq mi (147,181 sq km)
Population:	18,452,000
Official language:	Nepali
Monetary unit:	1 Nepalese rupee = 100 paisa
Main cities:	Kathmandu, Biratnagar, Lalitpur
Government	
Form:	constitutional monarchy
Independent:	1769
Head of state:	King
Head of government:	Prime minister
Legislature:	one legislative house (National Panchayat)
Executive:	King and Council of Ministers
Judiciary:	highest court is the Supreme Court
Political division:	14 zones, 5 development regions
National economy	
Gross national product:	U.S. $3,150,000,000
Per capita income:	U.S. $170
Agriculture:	jute, rice, corn, wheat, sugar cane
Livestock:	cattle, goats, buffalo
Fisheries:	11,000 metric tons
Mining:	quartz
Industries:	sugar, jute goods, tourism
Main exports:	food and live animals, basic manufactures, crude materials, animal and vegetable oils and fats
Transportation:	3,918 mi (6,306 km) of roads, 1 international airport
Trading partners:	India, Japan
People	
Urban:	8%
Ethnic composition:	Nepalese 58.5%, Bihari (including Maithili and Bhojpuri) 18.5%, T haru 3.5%, Tamang 3.5%
Birth rate:	39.3 per 1,000 population
Death rate:	14.6 per 1,000 population
Infant mortality:	101 per 1,000 live births
Life expectancy:	male 50 years, female 49 years

1990, and multiparty elections were scheduled for 1991.

Nephrite *see:* Jade.

Nephritis, general term for several diseases, especially glomerulonephritis, involving inflammation of the kidneys caused by infection or degenerative changes in the renal vessels. Acute or chronic renal failure or nephrotic syndrome may result. The treatment is chemicals, drugs, or steroids.

Neptune, in Roman mythology, god of the sea, son of Saturn and Ops. Seafaring Romans prayed to Neptune for safe voyages and returns. He came to be identified with the Greek god Poseidon.
See also: Mythology.

Neptune, fourth-largest planet in the solar system and the eighth from the sun, with a mean distance of 2.7941 billion mi (4.4966 billion km). Its diameter is about 30,760 mi (49,500 km), and it has 2 known moons. Its atmosphere contains hydrogen, helium, methane, and ammonia. Neptune was first discovered in 1846 by Johann Galle using computations by Urbain Leverrier based on the irregularities of Uranus's orbit. Neptune circles the sun once for every 164.8 earth years, and its day (one rotation on its axis) is 15.8 hours.
See also: Planet; Solar system.

Neptunium, chemical element, symbol Np; for physical constants see Periodic Table. Discovered by Edwin M. McMillan and P.H. Abelson in 1940, it was produced by bombarding uranium with neutrons in a cyclotron. Neptunium was the first synthetically produced transuranium element of the actinide series to be discovered. It is produced in nuclear reactors as a by-product of plutonium production. Neptunium is a silvery, radioactive metal. Neptunium-237 has a long half-life (2.14 million years) and is used in neutron detection instruments.

Nereus, in Greek mythology, sea god and father of the sea nymphs known as nereids. He was Homer's "Old Man of the Sea," who had the ability to foretell the future and change his shape. Heracles, a Greek hero, obtained directions to the Hesperides as he successfully held Nereus, who changed into numerous shapes during the struggle. Nereus is also known for his prophecy about the Trojan War.
See also: Mythology.

Neri, Saint Phillip (1515-95), mystical leader and founder of the Congregation of the Oratorians during the Counter-Reformation in Italy. He was ordained in 1551. A room above his church, called an *oratory*, held large audiences for religious conferences and recreation. His congregation is named after this room, as is the musical genre known as oratorio. A spiritual rather than political leader of the church, he claimed to have experienced unusual religious moments, including miracles that are ascribed to him.
See also: Counter-Reformation.

Nernst, Walther Hermann (1864-1941), German physical chemist awarded the 1920 Nobel Prize in chemistry for his discovery of the third law of thermodynamics, dealing with matter at temperatures approaching absolute zero.
See also: Thermodynamics.

Nero (Nero Claudius Caesar, originally Lucius Domitius Ahenobarbus; A.D. 37-68), Roman emperor. He was the adoptive son of the emperor Claudius, whom he succeeded in A.D. 54. Nero had Claudius's son Britannicus murdered in A.D. 55. In A.D. 59 he killed his mother Agrippina, and in A.D. 62 his wife Octavia, Claudius's daughter. Nero rebuilt Rome after the fire in A.D. 64. He accused the Christians of starting it, and the first Roman persecution followed. His cruelty, instability, and imposition of heavy taxes led to a revolt. Deserted by the Praetorian Guard, Nero committed suicide.
See also: Rome, Ancient.

Neptune, god of the sea

Neruda, Pablo (Neftalí Ricardo Reyes Basualto; 1904-73), Chilean poet, diplomat, and communist leader. He won the 1971 Nobel Prize for literature. His verse collections, written in the surrealist vein, include *Twenty Love Poems and One Song of Despair* (1924), the highly regarded *Canto General* (1950), and *A New Decade: 1958-1967* (tr. 1969).

Nerval, Gérard de (Gérard Labrunie; 1808-55), French romantic writer who anticipated the symbolist and surrealist movements in French literature. His works include a collection of sonnets, *Les Chimères* (1854); some short stories, *Les Filles de Feu* (1854); and his autobiography, *Aurélia* (1854-55).

Nerve *see:* Nervous system.

Nerve gas *see:* Chemical and biological warfare.

Nervi, Pier Luigi (1891-1979), Italian civil engineer and architect. In the 1940s he invented *ferrocemento*, a form of reinforced concrete. Notable among his bold and imaginative designs are the Turin exposition hall, the railway station in Naples, and the Olympic buildings in Rome. He also collaborated on the UNESCO headquarters in Paris.
See also: Architecture.

Nervous system, network of specialized tissue that coordinates and controls the various activites of the body, both voluntary and involuntary. The nervous system can be divided into 2 main parts. The central nervous system consists of the brain and spinal cord. It stores and processes information and sends messages to muscles and glands. The peripheral nervous system consists of 12 pairs of cranial nerves located in and near the medulla oblongata at the rear of the brain and 31 pairs of spinal nerves originating in the spinal cord. It carries messages to and from the central nervous system. A third system, the autonomic nervous system, normally considered part of the peripheral nervous system, controls involuntary actions such as heartbeat and digestion. It can be divided into 2 parts: the sympathetic system, which speeds up the heartbeat and prepares the body for "fight-or-flight," and the parasympathetic system, which slows down the heartbeat and controls the body's vegetative functions. The balance between the 2 systems is regulated by the central nervous system. The nervous system transmits messages by means of highly specialized nerve cells, called neurons. Tubelike extensions called axons and dendrites branch out from the neuron cell body. Axons, which vary greatly in length and speed of conduction, carry messages. An axon from one neuron may transmit impulses to as many as 1,000 other neurons. Dendrites receive impulses from axons. Adjacent neurons communicate through specialized contact points, called synapses. Messages are also carried from axon to dendrite by chemical messengers known as neurotransmitters across the synaptic gap. The elaborate circuitry involved in synaptic contact is responsible for much of behavior, from simple reflex reactions such as the "knee-jerk response" to complex thought-communication patterns.

Nestor *see:* Messenia.

Nestorians, members of the heretical Christian sect named for Nestorius (patriarch of Constantinople, 428-431). The sect was condemned by the Council of Ephesus (431) for rejecting the title "Mother of God" for the Virgin Mary, and teaching the existence of 2 persons—divine and human—in Jesus. The modern Nestorian (Assyrian) Church has about 100,000 members.

Netherlands

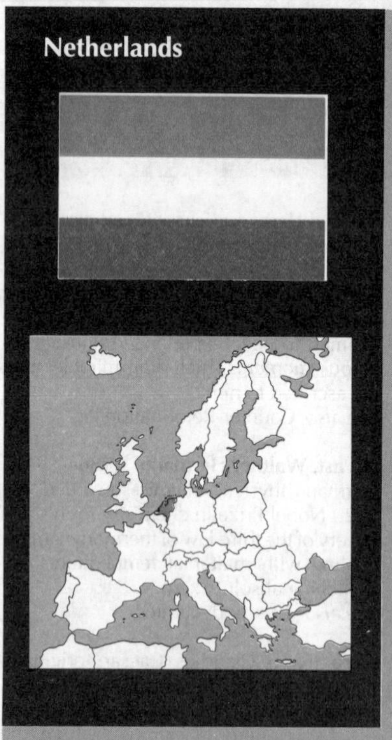

General information	
Capital:	Amsterdam
Area:	16,013 sq mi (41,473 sq km)
Population:	14,846,000
Official language:	Dutch
Monetary unit:	1 Netherlands guilder = 100 cents
Main cities:	Amsterdam, Rotterdam, The Hague
Government	
Form:	constitutional monarchy
Independent:	1814 (constitutional monarchy)
Head of state:	Dutch monarch
Head of government:	Prime minister
Legislature:	two legislative houses (First Chamber and Second Chamber of the States-General)
Executive:	Dutch monarch and Council of Ministers
Judiciary:	highest court is the High Court of the Netherlands
Political division:	12 provinces
National economy	
Gross national product:	U.S.$214,458,000,000
Per capita income:	U.S. $14,530
Agriculture:	sugar beet, potatoes, wheat, barley, flowers, vegetables and fruit
Livestock:	chickens, pigs, cattle
Fisheries:	435,000 metric tons
Mining:	natural gas, crude petroleum
Industries:	foodstuffs, synthetic fibres, electrical machinery, petroleum products, transport equipment
Main exports:	machinery and transport equipment, mineral fuels (natural gas), chemicals, food and live animals, basic manufactures, flowers
Transportation:	1,746 mi (2,809 km) of railroads, 71,718 mi (115,413 km) of roads, 4 international airports
Trading partners:	Germany, Belgium-Luxembourg, France, United Kingdom, U.S.
People	
Urban:	88.5%
Ethnic composition:	Dutch 96%, Turkish 1%, Moroccan 1%
Birth rate:	12.6 per 1,000 population
Death rate:	8.4 per 1,000 population
Infant mortality:	7 per 1,000 live births
Life expectancy:	male 73.5 years, female 80 years

The windmills of the Netherlands have been used for sawing wood, grinding paper, pressing oil, and pounding tobacco.

Netherlands, constitutional monarchy of western Europe bordering the North Sea, Germany, and Belgium. It is popularly but inaccurately called Holland. Amsterdam is the capital; The Hague is the seat of government.

Land and climate. The country is a flat, low-lying area of 15,785 sq mi (40,883 sq km). Most (13,042 sq mi/33,779 sq km) is land: dunes along the sea coast; polders, drained areas below sea level that cover 40% of the country; the sand plains where the Maas (Meuse) and Rhine rivers flow; and the southern plains, a small fertile region. The Dutch reclaim land from the sea by building a dike to seal off an area and pumping out the water. The drained land is then transformed into fertile farmland. Electric pumps keep the polders drained, but some windmills are still used. The climate is damp and mild, averaging 60°-65°F (16°-18°C) in summer and near freezing in winter.

People. The Netherlands is the world's most densely populated country. Nearly half the population lives close to the three largest cities—Amsterdam, The Hague, and Rotterdam, the chief port. There are 11 universities, including the famous public ones at Leiden, Utrecht, Groningen, and Amsterdam. Dutch is the official language. Roman Catholicism and Dutch Reformed are the major religions.

Economy. There are reserves of oil, natural gas, and coal, but most raw materials must be imported for industries; major ones include oil-refining, iron and steel, textiles, machinery, electrical equipment, and plastics. Dairy produce, the basis of The Netherlands' intensive agriculture, sustains a large food-processing industry. International financial services and petroleum interests, the diamond industry, and tourism contribute significantly, as does fishing and the advanced transportation system, which includes the natural waterways and canals that crisscross the country. Rotterdam, at the Rhine's mouth, handles more cargo than any other ocean port in the world. The Netherlands is a member of the European Common Market.

History. After the Romans left the Low Countries in the 5th century, Frankish tribes dominated. Dukes of Burgundy in the later Middle Ages began unifying the regions small principalities, which included Holland, Brabant, and Flanders. Through intermarriage, the Spanish King Phillip II was sovereign until the growing popularity of Calvinism in the late 16th century caused the Dutch to expel the Catholic Spanish, except in the south. Naval and economic eminence made the 17th century a golden age for the independent Dutch republic, then Europe's leading commercial nation. Philosopher Baruch Spinoza and the natural scientist Anton van Leeuwenhoek flourished, as did painters Rembrandt van Rijn and Jan Vermeer (the late-19th-century Dutch painter Vincent van Gogh would equal their fame eventually). Wars and treaties with other European nations brought political confusion and economic decline after 1715. Napoleonic control (1795-1813) and revolutionary ferment ended with the issuance of a constitution (1814) providing a monarchy to rule the United Kingdom of The Netherlands, formed by the Congress of Vienna (1815). The kingdom ended (1830) when the Catholic people of the south seceded, founding modern-day Belgium. But The Netherlands remained a constitutional monarchy and is today a parliamentary democracy. Neutral in World War I but occupied by the Nazis in World War II, The Netherlands afterward became one of NATO's original members. In 1949 the Dutch recognized the independence of Indonesia, their colony since the 17th century, and in 1963 transferred to it another colony, West New Guinea. The Netherlands Antilles—2 groups of Caribbean islands—are still under Dutch control.

Netherlands Antilles

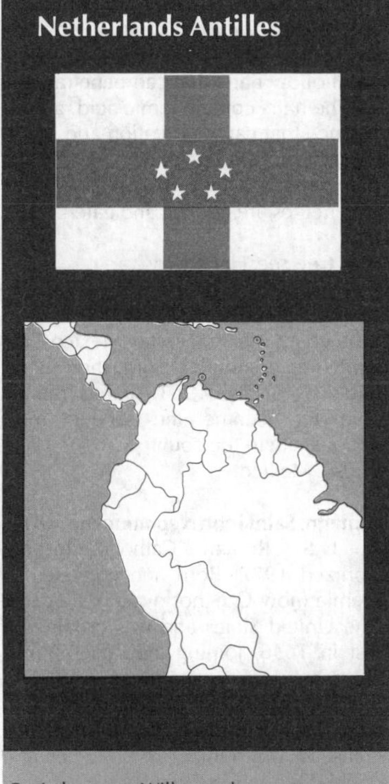

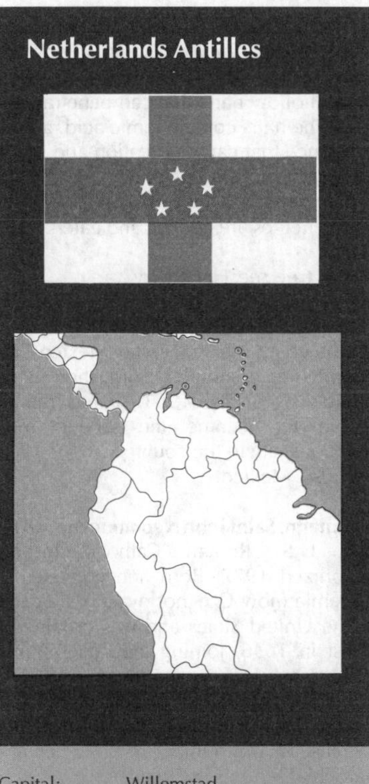

Capital:	Willemstad
Area:	308 sq mi (798 sq km)
Population:	183,000
Form:	nonmetropolitan territory of the Netherlands
Independent:	1954
GNP:	U.S. $1,610,000,000
Per capita:	U.S. $6,810

Netherlands Antilles, St. Anna Bay, Willemstad, Curaçao. In the background is the Queen Juliana Bridge.

Netherlands Antilles, also called the Dutch Antilles or Dutch West Indies, 2 groups of islands in the Caribbean Sea, collectively an autonomous part of the Netherlands since 1954. The southern group—the Leewards—includes Curaçao (location of the capital, Willemstad), Aruba, and Bonaire. They lie off the coast of Venezuela. The northern group—the Windwards—includes Saba, St. Eustacius, and St. Martin, which are east of Puerto Rico. The processing of Venezuelan oil accounts for 98% of export earnings. There is also some tourism. Aruba was constitutionally separated from the other islands in 1986.

See also: Netherlands.

Nettle, common name for a family of plants (Urticaceae) including shrubs and trees, many species of whose leaves bear brittle hollow hairs that can penetrate the skin. The hairs contain fomic acid, a toxic substance that causes irritation and sometimes blistering. Nevertheless, cattle eat stinging nettles, and in parts of Europe young nettles are cooked and eaten.

Nettle tree *see:* Hackberry.

Netzahualcóyotl (pop. 2,068,000), city in south-central Mexico, east of Mexico City. Founded as a suburb (1900), then incorporated as a city (1963), it has rapidly grown to become the second most populous city in the country.
See also: Mexico.

Neumann, Saint John Nepomucene (1811-60), U.S. Roman Catholic bishop, canonized 1977. Born and educated in Bohemia (now Czechoslovakia), he came to the United States and was ordained a priest in 1836, joining the Redemptorist Fathers missionary society in 1840 and appointed bishop of Philadelphia in 1852. Under Neumann there was a substantial increase in the number of churches and parochial schools in Philadelphia.

Neuralgia, severe pain along the course of a nerve, often coming in sharp bursts and normally lasting for a short time. Nerves commonly affected include the digital nerves of toes and facial nerves. Neuralgia may be caused by inflammation or trauma.
See also: Nervous system.

Neuritis, inflammation of a peripheral nerve. More generally, any disorder of the peripheral nervous system that interferes with sensation, muscle control, or both may be considered neuritis. Symptoms include numbness, tingling, weakness, and in extreme cases, paralysis. Neuritis often occurs in patients with rheumatoid arthritis, and various genetic disorders.
See also: Nervous system.

Neurofibromatosis, hereditary disorder that produces pigmented spots and tumors of the skin, tumors of peripheral, optic, and acoustic nerves, and subcutaneous bony deformities. Deep tumors are treated by surgical removal or radiation. The underlying cellular disorder is unknown, and no general treatment is available.

Neurology, branch of medicine concerned with diseases of the brain, spinal cord, and peripheral nervous system, including multiple sclerosis, epilepsy, migraine (headache), stroke, Parkinson's disease, neuritis, encephalitis, meningitis, brain tumors, muscular dystrophy, and myasthenia gravis.
See also: Nervous system.

Neuron *see:* Nervous system.

Neuropathology, study of the intrinsic causes of disorders of the nervous system.
See also: Nervous system.

Neurosis, mild mental disorder involving any of a number of varied symptoms, including phobias, anxiety, psychosomatic illnesses, and compulsive behavior. Neurosis is commonly distinguished from psychosis in that psychosis entails a loss of touch with reality, whereas neurosis does not.
See also: Mental illness.

Neurotransmitters *see:* Nervous system.

Neutra, Richard Joseph (1892-1970), Austrian-born U.S. architect who brought the International style of architecture to the United States. The Tremaine House (1947) in Santa Barbara, Calif., demonstrates his skill in relating a building to its setting.

Neutrality, status of a country that elects not to participate in a war between other countries. Under international law the boundaries and territorial waters of a neutral state must be respected.

Neutrality Acts (1935, 1936, 1937), U.S. legislation banning arms sales and loans to belligerent states. The acts were aimed at keeping the United States out of war. Modified in 1939, they were effectively replaced by the Lend Lease Act of 1941, the purpose of which was to assist the Allies without direct participation in the war.

Neutralization, in chemistry, reaction in which the hydrogen ion of an acid and the hydroxyl ion of a base unite to form water and a salt.
See also: Acid; Base.

Neutrino, elementary particle with no electrical charge emitted during the decay of other particles. The existence of the neutrino was first postulated by Wolfgang Pauli in 1930 to account for the conservation of energy in the beta decay process, but the particle was not actually detected until 1956. There are distinct types of neutrinos associated with the electron and the muon. All 3 are part of the class of elementary particles known as leptons. Each type of neutrino has a corresponding particle, called an antineutrino, which differs from its neutrino only in a quality known as spin. Neutrinos are stable particles, being created or destroyed only in interactions involving the weak nuclear force, one of the 4 fundamental forces of nature. It is not known whether neutrinos have any mass at all.
See also: Lepton.

Neutron, electrically uncharged elementary particle with a mass slightly greater than that of the proton. All elements except hydrogen contain neutrons in their nuclei, along with protons. Free neutrons (those not bound within a nucleus) or excess neutrons in the nucleus of heavy elements are subject to a process called beta decay. In this process the neutron decays in a proton, an electron, and an antineutrino. The neutron is a member of the baryon class of elementary particles. It was discovered by James Chadwick in 1932. Its antiparticle, the antineutron, was discovered in 1956.
See also: Chadwick, Sir James; Quark.

Neutron bomb, variant form of the hydrogen bomb in which an atomic-bomb trigger is surrounded by non-fissionable material, the result being a much smaller blast than in a hydrogen bomb, along with a rain of neutrons that would leave nonliving structures relatively intact while killing living things. Although theoretically feasible, no neutron bomb has ever been tested.
See also: Nuclear weapon.

Neutron star, hypothetical extremely small star, of large mass but very great density. It is believed that when certain stars explode as supernovas their cores collapse and form either a neutron star or a *collapsar* (black hole). Neutron stars are thought to be made up of elementary particles and neutrons created from the compressed protons and electrons of the original supernova core, emitting powerful X-rays and reaching extremely high temperatures in the first few months of their existence. They may be more than 72,000 times smaller in diameter than the sun but with the same mass. In 1938 scientists predicted the existence of neutron stars, and in 1967 astronomers in Great Britain located *pulsars*—objects in space that emit radio waves, believed to be rotating neutron stars.
See also: Pulsar.

Nevada

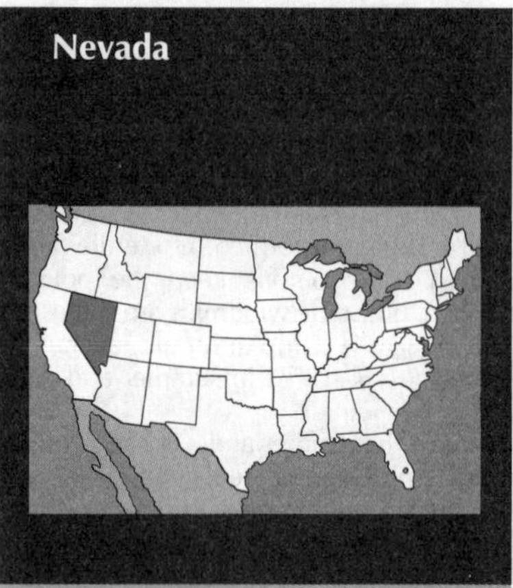

Capital:	Carson City
Statehood:	Oct. 31, 1864 (36th state)
Familiar names:	Silver State, Sagebrush State, Battle Born State
Area:	110,561 sq mi (286,352 sq km); ranks 7th
Population:	1,206,152 (1990); ranks 39th
Elevation:	Highest—13,143 ft (4,006 m), Boundary Peak; Lowest—470 ft (143 m) along the Colorado River in Clark County
Motto:	All for Our Country
Flower:	Sagebrush
Bird:	Mountain bluebird
Tree:	Single-leaf piñon
Song:	"Home Means Nevada"

Nevada, state in western United States in the Rocky Mountain region; bordered by Oregon and Idaho to the north, Utah to the east, Arizona to the southeast, and California to the south and west.
Land and climate. Most of Nevada lies in the Great Basin, a vast desert area. Nevada has 3 main land regions. The Basin and Range region—most of the state—is high, arid plateau broken by many mountain ranges. This region's southeastern corner is a small part of the Mojave Desert. The Columbia Plateau region, in the state's northeastern corner, is an area of deep canyons that flattens into prairie to the north. The Sierra Nevada region, in the state's southwest corner, is rugged, mountainous land. The Humboldt is the state's longest river. Most of Nevada's rivers are small and seasonal. Major lakes are Lakes Mead (created by the construction of Hoover Dam), Tahoe, Pyramid, and Walker. Nevada, which has an arid climate, receives less precipitation than any other state. Average temperatures and rainfall vary, depending on the terrain. Principal cities are Las Vegas and Reno.
Economy. Tourism—to the states's canyons, lakes, ski resorts as well as to its casinos and nightclubs—is Nevada's main source of income. Mining and manufacturing are also important. The most valuable mineral products are gold, diatomite, petroleum, and silver. Chief manufactured products are gaming devices, electronics, chemicals, machinery, processed foods, and stone-clay-glass products. Agriculture accounts for only a small part of the economy. Livestock ranching is the main source of agricultural income. Chief crops are hay, alfalfa, barley, potatoes, and wheat.
Government. Nevada's constitution was adopted in 1864. The governor serves a 4-year term. The state's legislature consists of 21 senators serving 4-year terms and 42 Assembly members serving 2-year terms. In the U.S. Congress, Nevada is represented by 2 senators and 2 representatives.
History. Native Americans were the first inhabitants of what today is Nevada; they lived there more than 20,000 years ago. In 1776, the first Europeans—Spanish explorers—came to the area. In 1848, after the Mexican War, the U.S. acquired the area from Mexico. The first permanent white settlement was established at Mormon Station (now Genoa) by Mormons in 1851. In 1859, the Comstock Lode—one of the world's richest veins of silver ore—was discovered at what today is Virginia City; hundreds of boom towns sprang up. In 1861, the U.S. Congress gave Nevada separate territorial status. During the Civil War, most Nevadans supported the Union. Nevada became the 36th state in 1864. Its economy suffered during the 1870s, when the mines began to give out and the U.S. government adopted the gold standard, limiting the use of silver in its monetary system. During the 1930s, the economy shifted from mining and agriculture to manufacturing and tourism. World War II brought new uses for Nevada's mineral resources. In the 1950s and 1960s, Nevada became a center for testing and research in atomic and nuclear energy. Today, tourism is the mainstay of the economy. The urban centers are struggling with problems caused by increasing populations; air and water pollution are other major concerns.

Nevada Falls, waterfall in Yosemite National Park, east-central California. It is part of a series of drops in the Merced River, which covers 1 mi (2 km) between the Little Yosemite Valley to the floor of Yosemite Valley. Nevada Falls, first named *twisted falls* by Native Americans, drops 594 ft (181 m).

Nevelson, Louise (1900-88), Russian-born U.S. sculptor famous for her intricate wood constructions, both freestanding and wall-hung, that suggest vast ranges of boxlike shelves with found objects placed on them.

Nevins, Allan (1890-1971), U.S. historian whose best-known work is *The Ordeal of the Union* (1947-60) a series of books on the Civil War. Nevins received Pulitzer Prizes for his biographies *Grover Cleveland* (1932) and *Hamilton Fish* (1936). His many other works include the biography *John D. Rockefeller* (1953).

Nevis *see:* Saint Christopher and Nevis.

Nevsky, Alexander (1220-63), Russian national hero. His military victories over the Swedes at the Neva River (1240) and over the Teutonic Livonian knights on the ice of Lake Peipus (1242) made him preeminent among Russian princes. He later became grand duke of Kiev and Novgorod (1252).

Newark (pop. 1,824,321), largest city of New Jersey and the seat of Essex County. Eight miles (13 km) west of Manhattan, Newark is a major transportation, commercial, and industrial center. The port was opened during World War I and became one of the nation's major shipbuilding centers. Industries now include chemicals, alcoholic beverages, automobile parts, electrical equipment, foodstuffs, and paints. Newark also ranks as the third-largest insurance center in the nation, with some 19 companies. Since the 1930s, however, Newark's economic and population growth rates have declined because of urban poverty and decay. Newark is the site of several universities, including Newark Campus of Rutgers University. The huge waterfront development of Port Newark is run by the Port Authority of New York and New Jersey, as is Newark Airport, one of New York City's three major air terminals.
See also: New Jersey.

New Bedford (pop. 175,641), city in southeastern Massachusetts, at the mouth of the Acushnet River on Buzzard's Bay. Once a famous whaling port, it is now a leading textile center. Settled in 1652, it was a privateer port during the Revolutionary War, and was burned by the British (1778). Since World War II, new pulp and paper industries, the discovery of rich mineral deposits, and the completion of several hydroelectric projects, promise brighter economic prospects.
See also: Massachusetts.

Cathedral Gorge, Nevada

New Bern (pop. 14,557), city in eastern North Carolina on the Trent and Neuse rivers; capital of colonial North Carolina. This city was founded by Swiss and German immigrants in 1710 and named after the Swiss city of Bern. Its location on the Neuse River, which empties into Pamlico Sound, inlet of the Atlantic, made it a major port. The need for harbors with deeper waters, coupled with the introduction of the railroad, diminished the commercial importance of this city.
See also: North Carolina.

Newbery, John (1713-67), English publisher and bookseller in the field of children's literature. Known for tiny, colorful books referred to as penny books, such as *A Little Pretty Pocket-Book* (1744) and *Goody-Two-Shoes* (1765), he essentially created the first market for the publication of books for children in English. The Newbery Medal, a yearly prize awarded in the field of children's literature since 1922, is named after him.

Newbery Medal, award presented annually in the field of children's literature. Established in 1921, this award is named after John Newbery (1713-67), first publisher of children's books. It honors the author of the most distinguished children's book published in the preceding year. The Newbery Medal and the Caldecott Medal (for best children's book illustrator) are presented at the yearly American Library Association conference.

New Britain, island in the Bismarck Archipelago east of the island of New Guinea, and part of the nation of Papua New Guinea since 1975. It is approximately 300 mi (480 km) long and 50 mi (80 km) wide, with a center portion containing active volcanic mountains. Previously it was controlled by Germany (1884-1914), Australia (1914-42), and Japan (1942-45). William Dampier, an English navigator, was the first European to reach the island (1700). The people of New Britain, mostly Melanesians, farm and fish.

New Britain (pop. 148,188), city in central Connecticut. Settled in 1686 and named New Britain in 1754, this city was an 18th-century center for metalworking, where small arms parts as well as the first tinware made in North America were produced. Popularly referred to as the *Hardware City*, it is still the leader in the manufacture of hardware, tools for carpenters, and other metal items.
See also: Connecticut.

New Brunswick (pop. 41,442), city in north-central New Jersey on the Raritan River. Named after an English duke of the 18th century, it became an important outpost for colonists setting out to fight British ships docked in New York City as well as the location where Washington's troops retreated from New York (1776). Today it is a manufacturing center, especially for medical supplies and pharmaceuticals. It is the home of Rutgers University, including Douglass College, and the New Brunswick Theological Seminary, the oldest seminary in the United States.
See also: New Jersey.

New Brunswick, second-largest of Canada's 4 Maritime Provinces. The capital is Fredericton; St. John and Moncton are ports.
Land and climate. New Brunswick covers 28,354 sq mi (73,436 sq km) and is bounded by Maine to the west; Quebec and the St. Lawrence River and Gulf to the north and east; the Northumberland Strait, which separates it from Prince Edward Island in the east; and the Bay of Fundy to the south. There, only the Chignecto Isthmus connects the province to Nova Scotia. Of the 10 Canadian provinces, only Nova Scotia and Prince Edward Island are smaller (originally, these 3 provinces formed the French region known as Acadia). Forested land covers much of New Brunswick, and it is well-drained by many swift-flowing rivers and streams. Coastal lowlands slope gently toward the St. Lawrence's waters but become rugged on the coast of the Bay of Fundy, an arm of the Atlantic. By confining the Atlantic's tides, the bay creates the highest tides in the world, often over 50 ft (15 m). The weather ranges from 14°F (—10°C) in winter to 64°F (18°C) in summer. Average precipitation is 44 in (113 cm).
People. About half the total population lives in the cities. Over half the people are of British origin, one-third of French. In public schools, French is the language of instruction.
Economy. Lumber, fisheries (cod, herring, salmon, sardines), dairy, food processing, pulp, paper, and wood-product manufacturing, along with copper, lead, silver, and particularly zinc mining in the northeast, as well as tourism, support the economy. Hydroelectric power is increasingly exploited. Roads, railways, ocean ports, and airports create a good transportation network.
History. Jacques Cartier explored the coastal area in 1534, and settlement began when the sieur de Monts and Champlain established a trading post at Port Royal in 1604. Both France and England disputed this Acadian region, which the British included with present-day Nova Scotia. In 1714 England gained control. In 1755 it expelled the French Acadian people, but some returned to live with the British settlers, and during the American Revolution they were joined by thousands of British Loyalists who fled from New England. As a result, New Brunswick is sometimes called the "Loyalist Province." It became a separate British colony in 1784. Boundary conflicts with Maine provoked the bloodless Aroostook War (settled 1842). Discontentment with the colonial governor's rule resulted in the establishment of a government more responsible to the people in 1849. In 1867 New Brunswick joined with Nova Scotia, Quebec, and Ontario to form the Dominion of Canada.
See also: Canada.

New Caledonia, French island with dependencies, forming a French overseas island territory in the southwest Pacific about 1,115 mi (1,794 km) east of Australia. New Caledonia island is the largest; its dependencies are the Loyalty Islands, the Isle of Pines, Walpole Island, and Huon, Chesterfield, and Belep islands. The territory is administered from New Caldeonia island by a governor with a 5-person council and popularly elected Territorial Assembly. A deputy and senator are elected to the French Parliament.
Land and climate. Altogether, the New Caledonia territory covers 8,548 sq mi (22,139 sq km). New Caledonia island covers 6,530 sq mi (16,913 sq km). It is volcanic, long, narrow, and mountainous. Trade winds moderate the climate. The annual rainfall at Nouméa is 42 in (106 cm).
People. The population includes a majority of Melanesians, with Europeans (mainly French), Polynesians, Vietnamese, and Indonesians. About half the population lives in Nouméa, on New Caldeonia, the territorial capital and chief harbor.
Economy. Resources of nickel, chromium, iron ore, cobalt, manganese, silver, gold, lead, and copper make mining the chief industry. Nickel-smelting plants are at Nouméa, Yaté, and Doniambo. Coffee, copra, bananas, and pineapples are grown for export. Food crops include corn, sweet potatoes, taro, and manoic (cassava). A cattle industry and meat-packing plant thrive.
History. Melanesians (Kanaks) may have inhabited New Caledonia island for over 4,000 years. It was discovered by the English navigator Captain James Cook in 1774. Along with the other islands, it was annexed by France in 1853 and used as a penal colony (1864-94). In World War II, it was a strategic Allied base. Conflicts between France and native groups resulted in a treaty (1988) promising a referendum on independence in 1998.

Newcastle (pop. 255,800), city in New South Wales, southeastern Australia, on the Pacific Ocean, at the mouth of Hunter River. Coal, steel, and other industrial products are produced and transported through this port city. Newcastle was founded as a European convict settlement in 1804 and recognized as a city in 1885.
See also: Australia.

Newcastle upon Tyne (pop. 282,200), city in northern England, on the North Sea and the river Tyne. It is a center for industry, known mainly because of its coal mines, which have been active since the 18th century. It is also a center for education. An ancient Roman community, the city received its current name from the "new castle" built there by William the Conqueror (1080).
See also: England.

Newcomb, Simon (1835-1909), U.S. astronomer. He computed new planetary tables whose data were so accurate that they were used for more than 50 years. He was director of the *American Nautical Almanac* (1877-97) and taught at Johns Hopkins University (1884-94).
See also: Astronomy.

Newcomen, Thomas (1663-1729), British inventor of the first practical steam engine, c.1711. His device, employed mainly to pump water from mines, used steam pressure to raise the piston and, after condensation of the steam, atmospheric pressure to force it down again: it was thus called an atmospheric steam engine.
See also: Steam engine.

New Deal, program adopted by President Franklin D. Roosevelt to alleviate the effects of the Great Depression. During its initial phase, the New Deal was centered on programs designed to stimulate economic activity, reduce unemployment, and introduce regulations to control business practices that threatened to deepen the depression. Measures were also taken to control the Stock Exchange. The National Recovery Administration (NRA) and the Civilian Conservation Corps (CCC) were set up to boost business and provide jobs. The second phase of the New Deal began with the Labor Relations Act (1935) which protected the right of workers to organize unions. This was followed by other steps to aid working people. The Fair Labor Standards Act (1938) set a national minimum wage. The Social Security system was established in 1935, and jobs were created by the Work Projects Administration (WPA), including the massive Tennessee Valley Authority (TVA) project. The Home Loan Corporation and the Federal Housing Administration (FHA) helped homeowners and aided recovery in the construction industry. After its initial popularity, especially among liberal and labor groups, the New Deal met increasing opposition in Congress and the Supreme Court. These controversies were largely superseded when World War II broke out, effectively ending the Great Depression. Though the term "New Deal" fell out of use, much of its legislation has remained, and it altered the direction of social legislation, increasing government intervention into the economy and changing the U.S. public's attitude to the role of the federal government.

New Delhi (pop. 6,200,000), capital of India, on the Jumna River, in the north-central part of the country. It was built by the British in 1912-29 to the south of Delhi, replacing Calcutta as the capital. Designed as a spacious city by the architect Sir Edwin Lutyens, New Delhi is noted for its official buildings, large shops, and industrial quarters.
See also: India.

New Economic Policy (NEP), plan adopted (1921-28) by the USSR to deal with the effects of the previous civil war years. The NEP made concessions to private enterprise in industry, trade, and agriculture and allowed peasants to sell produce profitably. By 1927 the NEP had successfully restored the prewar national income level.

New England, Dominion of, separate colonial government within the colonies established in 1686 by King James II, controlling Connecticut, Massachusetts, New Hampshire, New Jersey, New York, Plymouth, and Rhode Island. Used to further English control of the American colonies, this government was resented by colonists and abolished with the overthrow of King James II (1688).

New England Confederation, alliance organized in 1643 by representatives of the Massachusetts Bay, Plymouth, Connecticut, and New Haven colonies. They formed "the United Colonies of New England" to settle boundary disputes and arrange "mutual safety and welfare." Intercolonial rivalry undermined the confederation, and it was dissolved in 1684.

Newfoundland, province of Canada, far larger than the other Atlantic Provinces. St. John's is the capital and largest city.
Land and climate. The province comprises the island of Newfoundland (43,539 sq mi/112,299 sq km) and the long arm of Labrador (112,825 sq mi/292,218 sq km), which borders eastern Quebec. The island's western shore, in the mouth of the Gulf of St. Lawrence, has a long, indented coastline dotted with small islands. Newfoundland's north, south, and east coast, along the Atlantic Ocean, is rugged, with the land rising to rocky heights and a plateau with lakes and bogs. The longest river is the Exploits (153 mi/246 km). Flanking the western and northern coasts is the forested Great Northern Peninsula, dominated by the Long Range Mountains. In the south is the Burin Peninsula. In the southeast, across a narrow isthmus, is the densely populated Avalon Peninsula and St. John's.
Labrador, across the Strait of Belle Isle to the north of the island, comes within the Canadian Shield, the great plateau of forest-covered ancient rocks that covers about half of Canada. The high, rocky coast on

Newfoundland landscape

the Labrador Sea portion of the Atlantic has many fjords. The largest lake is Lake Melville (1,113 sq mi/2,883 sq km). Emptying into it is the Churchill (formerly Hamilton) River, the longest (600 mi/965 km) in the province. The province's highest mountains are in Labrador; the tallest is Cirque Mountain (5,160 ft/1,573 m).
The northern coasts of both Labrador and Newfoundland island have a harsh climate; it is less severe on the southern coasts. Precipitation averages from 20 in (51 cm) in northern Labrador to 60 in (150 cm) in the southern part of the island.
People. The province is sparsely inhabited, with most people, mainly of Irish, English, or French descent, living on the coasts. Only 3% live in Labrador, and 10% of these are of Native American or Eskimo descent.
Economy. Some of the world's most lucrative fisheries have been operating off Newfoundland in the Grand Banks since the early 18th century, although the island's local economy remained precarious until the 1930s. Its strategic position as the closest North American point (along with Greenland) to Europe makes it a center of transatlantic air service. In Labrador huge iron-ore deposits are mined, and also copper, gold, lead, silver, and zinc. Powered by its hydroelectric plants, service industries, mining, lumbering, food processing, and the manufacture of pulp, paper, steel, textiles, and clothing also support a firmer provincial economy.
History. Remains of 10th-century Viking settlements have been found on the island. John and Sebastian Cabot rediscovered it in 1497, and Sir Humphrey Gilbert claimed it for England in 1583, establishing a settlement at St. John's. England ruled it, though in conflict with the French, who maintained fishing rights until 1904. In 1927, England gave Labrador to Newfoundland as a dependency. They chose to join the Dominion of Canada in 1949, becoming its 10th province.
See also: Canada.

Newfoundland dog, breed of large, heavy dog known for its strength, patience, and intelligence. It weighs up to 150 lb (68 kg) and stands as high as 28 in (71 cm) at the shoulder. Its webbed feet and thick oily black or black-and-white coat aids it in performing water rescues. The breed is most likely a cross between the Great Pyrenees dog of the Basque region of Europe and dogs native to Newfoundland.

New France, North American territories held by France from the 16th century to 1763. These included what is now Quebec. France lost these territories to Britain in a series of colonial wars.

New Frontier, collective name for the policies of the administration of President John F. Kennedy, derived from his acceptance speech after winning the Democratic nomination in 1960, when he said that the nation stood on "the edge of a new frontier." Characteristic New Frontier programs aimed at space exploration, improved science education, extension of civil-rights protections, and better medical care for the elderly.

Newgate Prison, prison in London, England. Begun as a jail above the West Gate to London in the early 15th century, it continued to house hardened criminals along with debtors and minor offenders until its demolition (1902). The public often complained of the unsanitary and unfair conditions of this jail. Early in the 19th century, prison reform allowed debtors to await trial in separate facilities.

New Granada, 16th-century Spanish colony in northwestern South America that included present-day Colombia, Panama, Ecuador, and Venezuela. Named by Gonzalo Jiménez de Quesada in 1537, it was attached to the viceroyalty of Peru until 1717, when it became a viceroyalty itself until independence in 1819.

New Guinea, world's second largest island, in the southwestern Pacific, just south of the equator and separated from northern Australia by the Torres Strait and the Arafura and Coral Seas. The island has an area of 319,713 sq mi (828,057 sq km), being about 1,500 mi (2,410 km) long and 400 mi (640 km) wide. The interior is mountainous, the coastal lowlands densely forested. Djaja Peak is the highest mountain, at 16,503 ft (5,030 m). The western part of

Old religions are still followed in the highland of New Guinea

New Guinea is a province of Indonesia, Irian Jaya. Papua New Guinea, the eastern part, is self-governing since 1973. Melanesians and Papuans are the two largest population groups. In remote mountain areas there are tribes that still practice headhunting. New Guinea was explored by Portuguese in the 16th century and named for Guinea, then a Portuguese colony in West Africa. It was later colonized by the Dutch, Germans, and British. The German sector was taken over by Australia after World War I. The island was bitterly contested by the Japanese and the Allies during World War II.

New Hampshire, state in New England, the northeastern region of the United States; bordered by Canada to the northwest, Maine and the Atlantic Ocean to the east, Massachusetts to the south, and Vermont to the west.

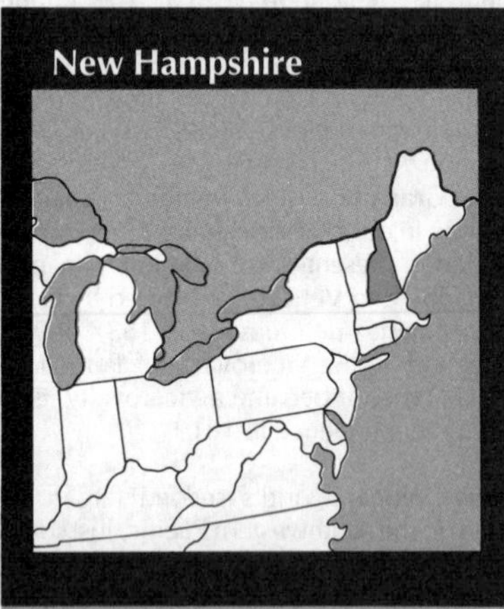

Capital:	Concord
Statehood:	June 21, 1788 (9th state)
Familiar name:	Granite State
Area:	9,297 sq mi (24,032 sq km); ranks 44th
Population:	1,113,915 (1990); ranks 41st
Elevation:	Highest—6,288 ft (1,917 m), Mt. Washington; Lowest—sea level, along the Atlantic coast
Motto:	Live Free or Die
Flower:	Purple lilac
Bird:	Purple finch
Tree:	White birch
Song:	"Old New Hampshire"

New Hampshire

Land and climate. New Hampshire has 3 main land regions: the rugged and wooded White Mountains region in the northern third of the state; the Eastern New England Upland, a rolling plateau that covers the western, central, and southern portions of the state; and the Coastal Lowlands, which occupy the state's extreme southeastern corner. The Connecticut River Valley, a rich farming area, stretches along New Hampshire's western border. Hydroelectric plants along the river power the area's public utilities. The state's major cities line the Merrimack River, the power source for New Hampshire's early factories and cotton mills. Lake Winnipesaukee, in east-central New Hampshire, is the state's largest body of water. New Hampshire has cool summers and long, snowy winters. Principal cities are Manchester, Nashua, and Concord.

Economy. Wholesale and retail trade and other service industries have supplanted manufacturing as New Hampshire's major source of income; however, manufacturing remains important to the state's economy. Major manufactured goods are machinery, electrical and electronic equipment, wood and paper products, fabricated metal products, plastics, and leather products. Mining and agriculture account for only a small part of New Hampshire's economy. Chief mining products are sand and gravel, and stone, particularly granite. Chief livestock products are milk, beef cattle, eggs, and hogs; chief crops are hay, apples, potatoes, sweet corn, greenhouse and nursery products, and maple syrup.

Government. New Hampshire's constitution was adopted in 1784. The governor serves a 2-year term. The state's legislature, called the General Court, consists of 24 senators and 400 representatives. In the U.S. Congress, New Hampshire is represented by 2 senators and 2 representatives.

History. Many Native American tribes lived in the area before the first Europeans arrived. French and English explorers visited in the early 1600s. The first white settlement was established by England in 1623. In 1641, New Hampshire was made part of Massachusetts, but again became a separate colony—one of the original 13—in 1680. From 1689 to 1763, the French and Indian wars were fought in New Hampshire and other parts of New England. New Hampshire residents were among the Minutemen who fought the British at Lexington and Concord, and throughout the American Revolution. Yet New Hampshire was the only colony in which no fighting occurred. New Hampshire became the 9th state in 1788. During the Civil War, in which New Hampshire supported the Union, industry boomed in the state. The plentiful waterpower led to the development of textile and paper mills, Portsmouth became a major shipping port, and shoemaking became an important industry. The nationwide economic hardship of the Great Depression of the 1930s was intensified in New Hampshire by the move of many textile firms to the South. World War II revived New Hampshire's mills and turned Portsmouth's workers to submarine building and warship repair. In the 1950s and 1960s, New Hampshire's urban areas grew. Today, it is attracting new businesses, particularly in the electronics and computer industries.

New Harmony (pop. 945), town in southwestern Indiana, the site of 2 cooperative communities of the early 1800s. Harmonie was founded in 1814 by George Rapp, leader of the Harmony Society. In 1824 the colony was sold to Robert Owen and renamed New Harmony. The new community, based on socialism and Owen's theories of human freedom, became a noted scientific and cultural center, establishing the first U.S. free library, the first kindergarten, and the first public school. The experiment broke down, however, in 1828.
See also: Indiana.

New Haven (pop. 530,180), third largest city in Connecticut, a river port leading to Long Island Sound, and the seat of Yale University. New Haven is noted as a cultural center and is important for its varied industrial products. It was founded in 1638 by Puritans from Boston led by John Davenport and Theophilus Eaton.
See also: Connecticut.

New Hebrides Islands, *see:* Vanuatu.

Ne Win, U (Shu Maung; 1911-), Burmese general, political leader, and president (1974-81). After serving as prime minister, he assumed power in 1962 in an army coup and attempted to establish a form of socialist republic in Burma. After resigning the presidency, he remained head of the ruling party.

New Ireland, island in the Bismarck Archipelago north of New Britain, part of the nation of Papua New Guinea since 1975. It is a narrow and rugged volcanic island, approximately 230 mi (370 km) long. The first European to reach and name the island was Philip Carteret. Germany claimed the island (1884) until, at the end of World War I, Australia took over its control. Except for the Japanese occupation (1942-5), Australia administered the island until the independence of Papua New Guinea (1975).

New Jersey, state in the Middle Atlantic region of eastern United States; bordered by New York to the north; the Hudson River, New York Bay, and the Atlantic Ocean to the east; and Delaware Bay and the Delaware River (which separates New Jersey from Delaware and Pennsylvania) to the south and west.

Land and climate. New Jersey has 4 main land regions. The mountainous Appalachian Ridge and Valley region, in New Jersey's extreme northwest, is the state's most rugged section. Just south of there is the New England Upland, also called the Highlands, which is a rocky, narrow plateau. The Piedmont, only a fifth of New Jersey's land area, is where most of the

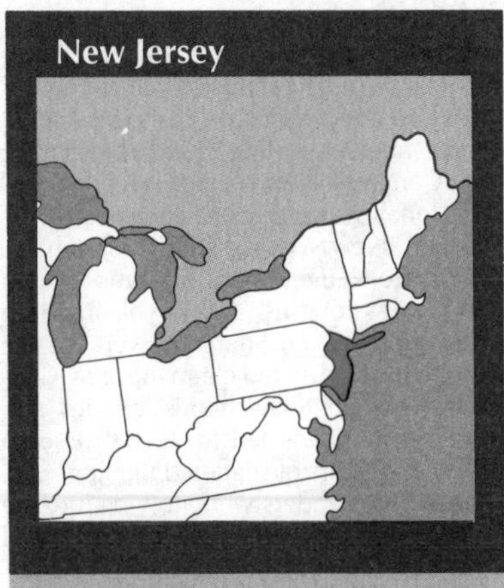

Capital:	Trenton
Statehood:	Dec. 18, 1787 (3rd state)
Familiar name:	Garden State
Area:	7,787 sq mi (20,169 sq km); ranks 46th
Population:	7,748,634 (1990); ranks 9th
Elevation:	Highest—1,803 ft (550 m), High Point; Lowest—sea level, along the Atlantic coast
Motto:	Liberty and Prosperity
Flower:	Purple violet
Bird:	Eastern goldfinch
Tree:	Red oak
Song:	None

state's people and industries are located; this region has many large rivers. Atlantic Coastal Plain, which occupies the southern three-fifths of the state, is a flat or gently rolling lowland. Its eastern half is covered by forests and salt marshes called the Pine Barrens; its western half is a fertile truck-farming area. Two great rivers, the Delaware and the Hudson, flow along New Jersey's borders. The Delaware Water Gap, formed by the Delaware River as it cuts through the Kittatinny Mountains, is one of the most scenic areas in the East. Many beaches and seaside resorts, including Atlantic City and Asbury Park, line the Atlantic coast. New Jersey has warm to hot summers and cold winters. Principal cities are Newark, Jersey City, and Paterson.

Economy. New Jersey is a leading industrial state. Its chief industrial products are chemicals, processed foods, electronic and electrical equipment, nonelectrical machinery, printed materials, and fabricated metal products. Service industries, including tourism, account for a large share of the state's income, agriculture and mining for a small share. Chief crops are greenhouse and nursery products, milk, tomatoes and other vegetables, peaches, blueberries, cranberries, corn, and hay; chief livestock products are eggs, beef cattle, and hogs.

Government. New Jersey's present constitution was adopted in 1947. The governor serves a 4-year term. The state's legislature consists of 40 senators serving 2- or 4-year terms and 80 General Assembly members serving 2-year terms. In the U.S. Congress, New Jersey is represented by 2 senators and 13 representatives.

History. The Lenni-Lenape lived in the area when the first European explorers arrived in the 1500s. Dutch and Swedish traders who arrived in the 1630s were the first European settlers. England won control of the area in 1664. New Jersey, one of the original 13 colonies, became a prosperous farming area. The site of some of the American Revolution's major battles, New Jersey became the nation's third state in 1787. During the Civil War, New Jersey contributed thousands of soldiers to the Union cause, but many of its residents sympathized with the South. Through the 1800s, New Jersey's importance as an industrial and transportation center grew. Widespread unemployment during the Depression was relieved by industrial resurgence during World War II. In the 1970s, 1980s, and early 1990s, New Jersey struggled with the problems of aging and overcrowded urban centers, toxic wastes and other pollution, and heavy taxes.

New Left, loose coalition of political and social groups from the 1960s and 1970s in the United States. Philosophies of the New Left ranged from beliefs in peaceful change to violent overthrow of the government. The coalition fought to end racial discrimination, poverty, and imperialism. Factions of the New Left, many of which were student-based, clashed with police and U.S. law enforcement in demonstrations at the 1968 Democratic convention in Chicago and other demonstrations focused against the war in Vietnam. The New Left is cited as one reason for President Lyndon Johnson's decision not to seek a second term in the 1968 election. Although the New Left coalition dissolved, it influenced later groups that focused on issues of the environment, women's rights, and civil rights.
See also: Students for a Democratic Society.

New London (pop. 266,819), seaport city of southeastern Connecticut, at the mouth of the Thames River, near Long Island Sound. A commercial and distribution center, it is the seat of the United States Coast Guard Academy and also has a U.S. Navy submarine base and the home of the U.S. Underwater Sound Laboratory. Its manufactures include clothing, paper boxes, antibiotics, toothpaste, and food products. It is the home of Connecticut College (1911). Founded by John Winthrop (1646), New London was a whaling port and has whaling and art museums.
See also: Connecticut.

Atlantic City, New Jersey

New London Naval Submarine Base, submarine school and headquarters for Submarine Group Two, in Groton, Ct. The U.S. Navy has used this property since 1872—in particular for submarines since 1900. The U.S.S. *Nautilus,* the world's first nuclear-powered submarine (1954), was built and launched here. Today this base is home to the *Nautilus* as well as the Submarine Force Library and Museum.

Newman, Barnett (1905-70), U.S. painter. He was a member of the abstract expressionist school of painting based in New York City after World War II. Newman's

Barnett Newman's Blue Midnight *(1970)*

large canvases often consisted of a simple, stark vertical image presented on a large field of color. His work influenced the color field movement of the 1960s as well as the minimalist artists.
See also: Abstract expressionism.

Newman, John Henry Cardinal (1801-90), English religious thinker, writer, and founder of the Oxford Movement. Ordained by the Church of England (1824), he became an Oxford Movement leader, calling for an emphasis on traditional belief that was akin to Catholicism. He converted to Catholicism (1845) and later became a cardinal (1879). Outspoken and often controversial both as an Anglican and as a Catholic, his beliefs were expressed in influential writings—his Oxford Movement tracts (*Tracts for the Times,* begun in 1833) and his Catholic autobiography *Apologia pro vita sua* (1864).
See also: Oxford movement.

Newman, Paul (1925-), U.S. film and stage actor, director. Newman first appeared on Broadway in *Picnic* (1953), and on film in *The Silver Chalice* (1955). He appeared in Tennessee Williams's *Sweet Bird of Youth* both on the Broadway stage (1959) and in the film version (1962). He has starred in many films, including *The Hustler* (1961), *Cool Hand Luke* (1967), *The Sting* (1973), and *The Color of Money* (1986; Academy Award). He also directed *Rachel, Rachel* (1968), a film starring his wife, Joanne Woodward.

Paul Newman

New mathematics, educational curricula developed in the 1950s and 1960s, emphasizing knowledge of mathematical concepts and principles over the mastery of mathematical computation. This educational movement, inspired by technological leaps, left many educators and parents confused. While some have acclaimed new math curricula, others have doubted its merits.

New Mexico, state in the southwest region of the United States; bordered by Colorado, Oklahoma, Texas, Arizona, and Mexico. Northwestern New Mexico is one of the "Four Corners": the only place in the United States where 4 states—Utah, Colorado, New Mexico, and Arizona—meet at right angles.

Taos Pueblo in New Mexico

New mexico

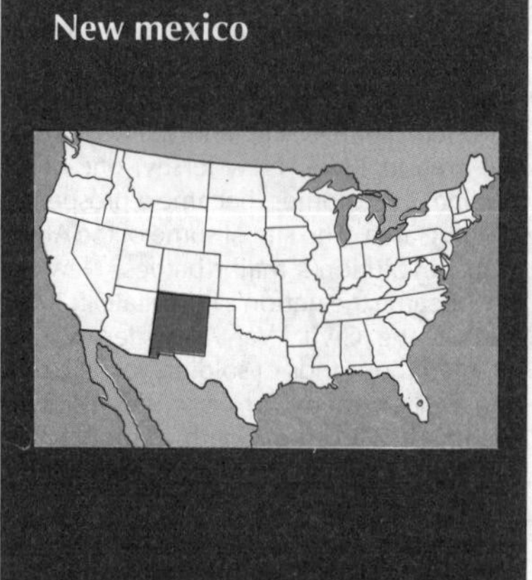

Capital:	Santa Fe
Statehood:	Jan. 6, 1912 (47th state)
Familiar name:	Land of Enchantment
Area:	121,593 sq mi (314,295 sq km; ranks 5th)
Population:	1,521,779 (1990; ranks 37th)
Elevation:	Highest—13,161 ft (4,011 m), Wheeler Peak; Lowest—2,817 ft (859 m), Red Bluff Reservoir
Motto:	*Crescit Eundo* (It Grows As It Goes)
State flower:	Yucca
State bird:	Roadrunner
State tree:	Piñon, or pine nut
State song:	"O, Fair New Mexico."

Land and climate. New Mexico has 4 main land regions. The Colorado Plateau, in the northeast, is an area of deep canyons, wide plains and valleys, and flat-topped hills called mesas. The Rocky Mountains, which extend from Colorado into north-central New Mexico, constitute the highest and most rugged part of the state. The Great Plains, covering the eastern third of the state, are part of the great Interior Plain that extends from Canada to the Gulf of Mexico. The Basin and Range Region, in central and southwestern New Mexico, consists of scattered mountain ranges separated by low-lying desert basins. The state has no natural lakes of consequence, but a number of rivers, the main ones being the Rio Grande and the Pecos. Dams and reservoirs provide irrigation water. Forests cover about one-fourth of the state. Its climate is warm and dry. Principal cities are Albuquerque, Santa Fe, and Las Cruces.
Economy. Service industries employ the greatest percentage of New Mexico's workers. The federal government funds major nuclear and engineering research centers in the state. Mining is a leading economic activity; minerals include natural gas, petroleum, coal, copper, uranium, and potash. Chief manufactured products are refined petroleum, electrical machinery, processed foods, apparel, lumber, printed materials, and transportation equipment. Ranching is the most important agricultural activity; chief agricultural products are beef cattle, hay, milk, wheat, sorghum grain, and corn. Tourism is a major contributor to the economy.
Government. New Mexico's constitution was adopted in 1911. The governor serves a 4-year term. The state legislature consists of 42 senators serving 4-year terms and 70 representatives serving 2-year terms. In the U.S. Congress, New Mexico is represented by 2 senators and 3 representatives.
History. New Mexico's original inhabitants were Native Americans, who lived in the area as long as 20,000 years ago. In 1528, gold-seeking Spaniards were the first Europeans to visit and claim the area. Conflicts between Spanish missionaries and Native Americans led to a 1680 Pueblo revolt and years of scattered fighting. U.S. trappers and traders were flowing into the area by 1821, when Mexico took control of the area.
The United States annexed New Mexico in 1848, after the Mexican War; in 1850, New Mexico became an official U.S. territory that was expanded by the 1853 Gadsden Purchase. Settlers poured in along the Santa Fe Trail. During the 1860s, fierce conflicts between Native Americans and settlers erupted, and New Mexico was briefly occupied by Confederate forces. After the Civil War, expansion of railroads helped development of the mining industry. New Mexico was the scene of a 1916 border conflict with Mexico. During World War II, the first atomic bomb was developed at Los Alamos; after the war, the U.S. government continued nuclear research and development in the state. Today, New Mexico remains a leading area for research and tourism. It reflects a rich mixture of Anglo-American, Spanish, and Native American cultures.

New Netherland, Dutch colonial territory extending roughly from what is now Albany, N.Y., to Manhattan Island, and including parts of New Jersey, Connecticut, and Delaware. It was granted in 1621 by the government of Holland to the Dutch West India Company. In 1626 the company purchased Manhattan Island from Native Americans and named it New Amsterdam. In 1664 the British seized New Amsterdam, changing its name to New York.

New Orleans (pop. 1,238,816), city in Louisiana, between the Mississippi River and Lake Pontchartrain, 107 mi (172 km) from the river's mouth. Called the Crescent City because of its placement on a bend in the river, New Orleans is one of the world's great ports and the business and financial capital of the South. Excellent transport facilities serve the port, and the city is surrounded by oil and natural gas deposits. It is also a center of the aerospace, shipbuilding, oil and chemical industries, and has many manufacturing and processing plants. The city is famed for its French Quarter (Vieux Carré) and the Mardi Gras Carnival. It is also known as the birthplace of jazz. Its varied population includes French-speaking Creoles, who are descended from early French and Spanish settlers. The Creole cookery of New Orleans is world famous.
See also: Louisiana.

New Orleans, Battle of *see:* Jackson, Andrew; War of 1812.

Newport, historic resort city in southeastern Rhode Island, seat of Newport County and an important naval base.
See also: Rhode Island.

Newport News (pop. 144,903), city in southeastern Virginia, on the north shore of the James River estuary. It is one of the ports of the natural harbor called Hampton Roads. A noted shipbuilding center since the 1880s, it also produces electrical machinery, automotive parts, paints, and other products. The city is renowned for its seafood. Landmarks include the Mariners Museum and the War Memorial Museum of Virginia. Settled in 1621, the city was named for Capt. Christopher Newport, who brought supplies and colonists for the Jamestown colony. The Civil War battle between the *Monitor* and the *Merrimack* (1862) was fought off the coast of Newport News.
See also: Virginia.

New South Wales, oldest state of Australia, lying in southeastern Australia between the Great Dividing Range and the Pacific Ocean. Because of its mild climate, good harbors, sandy beaches, and fertile land, it is the most populous state in Australia. Agriculture, mining (coal, silver, zinc), and manufacturing are the major components of the economy. Sydney, its capital and coastal city, contains the majority of the population, made up of people of British and other European descent, native Aborigines, and Asian immigrants. James Cook, an English navigator, was the first European to reach New South Wales (1770). With a group of English convicts, Captain Arthur Phillip established the first English settlement (1788).
See also: Australia.

Newspaper, daily or weekly publication of current domestic and foreign news. In 59 B.C., Julius Caesar ordered the daily publication of a newsheet, the *Acta diurna*. Johann Guttenberg's invention of movable type in the mid-15th century was an important step in the development of newspapers. *The London Gazette* (1665) was the first paper issued regularly in newspaper format. The first American paper was the *Boston Newsletter* (1704). James Gordon Bennett, Horace Greeley, and Adolph Ochs publishing daily penny papers, such as the *New York Sun* (1833), the *New York Herald* (1835), and the *New York Times* (1851). With the end of the Civil War, newspapers became increasingly sensational. In the late 19th and early 20th centuries Joseph Pulitzer and William Randolph Hearst were czars of vast newspaper empires and important forces in international politics. Technological advances in the 1970s, such as photocomposition and satellites, have changed the industry.

Newspaper Guild, labor union that represents workers in journalism enterprises in the United States, Puerto Rico, and Canada—previously called the American Newspaper Guild (1933-71). The union is affiliated with the AFL-CIO and the Canadian Labor Congress. It negotiates for employees in commercial and news departments of journalism ventures such as newspapers, magazines, and news services.

New Sweden, Swedish colony on the Delaware River extending from the present site of Trenton, N.J., to the mouth of the river. Founded by the New Sweden Company in 1638 under the leadership of Peter Minuit, it was taken over by the Dutch, led by Peter Stuyvesant, in 1655.

Newt, any of various small salamanders found in many areas of the Northern Hemisphere. The adults feed on small animals and spend much of their time on land, but they return to water to breed. The male deposits a bag containing the sperm cells that is picked up by the female. She lays her eggs one at a time, wrapping each in the leaf of a water plant. The eggs hatch into larvae that have external gills. By the fall, they emerge onto land as efts, with lungs and rough skins.

New Testament, part of the Bible that is distinctively Christian. It consists of 27 books recording the life and teachings of Jesus Christ and the beginnings of Christianity. The books were written in the popular form of Greek spoken in Palestine since the time of Alexander the Great. They include the 4 Gospels (Matthew, Mark, Luke, and John), the Acts of the Apostles, the Epistles (early evangelical letters), the Book of Revelation, and various others. The earliest fragments of the New Testament date from the early 2nd century. The present canon, used by all major Christian churches, was not decided on until 367, when other early Christian writings were excluded from the compilation.

New Thought, school of religious and philosophical thought originated in the mid-19th century United States and emphasizing the power of the mind to solve problems and heal the body. New Thought was developed mainly by Phineas Quimby (1802-66), who was influenced by New England transcendentalists such as Ralph Waldo Emerson. It influenced the later Christian Science movement, begun by Mary Baker Eddy.
See also: Bible.

Newton, Sir Isaac (1642-1727), English natural philosopher and mathematician, the discoverer of the calculus and author of the theory of universal gravitation. Professor of mathematics at Cambridge University (1669-1701), he wrote *Mathematical Principles of Natural Philosophy* (*Principia*; 1687), covering dynamics, fluid mechanics, and tides. His theory of light was developed in *Optics* (1704). He built the first reflecting telescope (1668). He is best known for his work in gravitation.
See also: Calculus; Gravitation.

New Orleans

Newton's rings, optical phenomenon of *interference* created when light waves travel through a convex piece of glass placed on top of a flat piece of glass. The light reflected from each piece interferes with that reflected from the other, creating patterns of rings. Strong sunlight produces rings in every color of the spectrum. Light of a single color produces rings of that same color. The phenomenon was studied by 17th-century English scientist Sir Isaac Newton.
See also: Newton, Sir Isaac.

New Westminster (pop. 39,972), city in the western Canadian province of British Columbia, southeast of Vancouver on the Fraser River. It serves as an important port and center for marketing and industry (especially the manufacture of timber products). A large hospital and the nearby city of Vancouver are the major sources of employment for the population. Named Queensborough until the current name was established a year later (1859), New Westminster was the first incorporated city in British Columbia.
See also: British Columbia.

New Year's Day, first day of the new calendar year, celebrated since ancient times by many peoples, including Babylonians, Assyrians, Persians, Egyptians, Jews, Greeks, Romans, and Chinese. Rites were usually held on the days of the vernal or autumnal equinox or the winter or summer solstice, when there was feasting and an exchange of gifts. The Julian calendar decreed Jan. 14 as New Year's Day, but when the Gregorian calendar was ordained in the 16th century, the date was changed to Jan. 1. The Jewish New Year (Rosh Hashanah) is in late Sept. or early Oct., at the time of the autumnal equinox. The Chinese base their New Year date on the waning and waxing of the moon, usu-

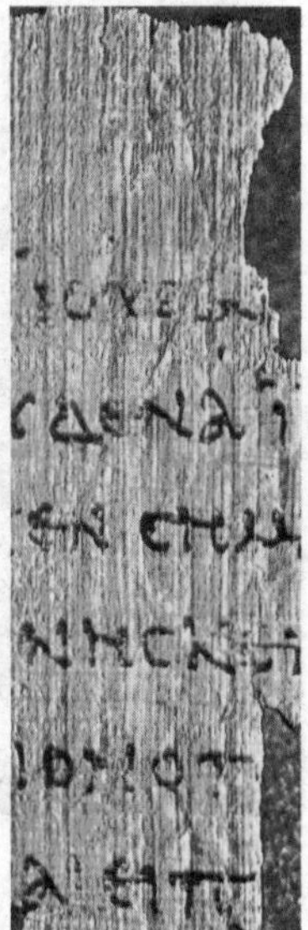
The oldest known fragment of the New Testament (John 18:31-33) was discovered in Egypt in 1920.

ally between the middle of Jan. and the middle of Feb. Christmas Day is now more observed as a festive holiday in many countries, but New Year's Day remains the major occasion in France, Scotland, and Italy.

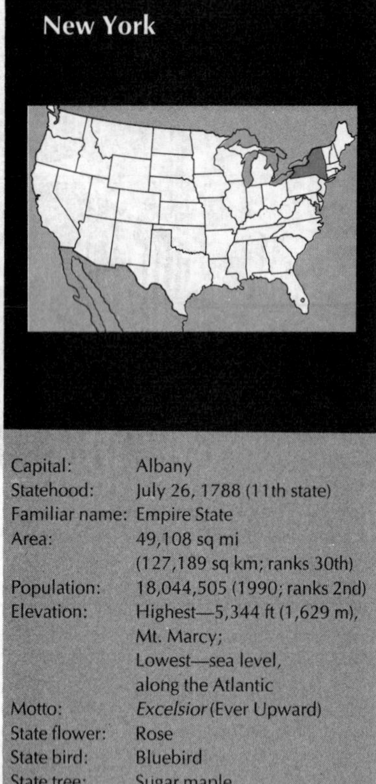

Capital:	Albany
Statehood:	July 26, 1788 (11th state)
Familiar name:	Empire State
Area:	49,108 sq mi (127,189 sq km; ranks 30th)
Population:	18,044,505 (1990; ranks 2nd)
Elevation:	Highest—5,344 ft (1,629 m), Mt. Marcy; Lowest—sea level, along the Atlantic
Motto:	*Excelsior* (Ever Upward)
State flower:	Rose
State bird:	Bluebird
State tree:	Sugar maple
State song:	"I Love New York"

New York, the Brooklyn Bridge (foreground) and the Manhattan Bridge connect Brooklyn and Manhattan

New York, state in the Middle Atlantic region of the United States; bordered by Lake Ontario, the St. Lawrence River, and Canada to the north; Vermont, Massachusetts, and Connecticut to the east; the Atlantic Ocean, New Jersey, and Pennsylvania to the south; and Pennsylvania, Lake Erie, and Canada to the west.

Land and climate. New York has 7 main land regions. The St. Lawrence Upland, in northernmost New York, has level to rolling land. The Adirondack Upland, a region of hills and mountains, includes the state's highest and most rugged land. The Appalachian Plateau, New York's largest land region, consists of broad uplands and deep valleys. To the south and east of Lakes Erie and Ontario is the Erie-Ontario Lowland, a low, swampy plain. Along the southern half of New York's eastern border lies the Hudson-Mohawk Lowland, including the valleys of the Hudson and Mohawk rivers; the hills and low mountains of the New England Upland; and the Atlantic Coastal Plain. New York is the only state to border both the Atlantic Ocean and the Great Lakes. That fact, plus its great rivers—including the Hudson, Mohawk, Genesee, and Susquehanna—and many lakes, make it a major shipping area. The world's most famous waterfall, Niagara Falls, is shared by New York and Canada. New York's climate varies widely. Generally, the north has long, cold winters and short summers, while the south has relatively milder winters and hot, humid summers. Principal cities are New York City, Buffalo, and Rochester.

Economy. New York's broad-based economy is led by service industries, followed by manufacturing, construction, agriculture, and mining. Chief service industries are finance (including the world's largest stock exchange and international banks), insurance, and real estate. Chief manufacturing products are printed materials, scientific instruments, machinery, chemicals, apparel, food products, transportation equipment, fabricated metal products, and lumber and paper products. Chief livestock products are milk and dairy goods, beef cattle, eggs and poultry, hogs, and sheep. Chief crops are hay, corn, fruits and vegetables, greenhouse and nursery products, sorghum, oats, and wheat. Chief mineral products are stone, salt, natural gas, and sand and gravel.

Government. New York's present constitution was adopted in 1894. The governor serves a 4-year term. The state legislature consists of 61 senators and 150 assembly members; all serve 2-year terms. In the U.S. Congress, New York is represented by 2 senators and 31 representatives.

History. Many Native American tribes, including the great Iroquois Nations, lived in the New York area before the first Europeans—with Italian navigator Giovanni da Verrazano—arrived in 1524. In 1609, Samuel de Champlain of France explored northern New York, while Henry Hudson, an Englishman working for a Dutch company, explored southern New York and the river that now bears his name. Dutch and English settlers shared southern New York until the English took it over—as one of the original 13 colonies—in 1664. France claimed the northern area, which England won in 1763 after the French and Indian Wars. During the American Revolution, New York was a major battle site. New York City was the nation's first capital (1785-90). During the Civil War, New York supported the Union. After the war, industry boomed until the crash and hardships of the Great Depression (1930s), but World War II brought recovery. Today, New York is working to provide jobs and social services for its huge population, overcome problems of crime and drug abuse, improve its environment, and repair its aging cities and highway systems.

New York City (pop. 8,546,846), city in the southeastern region of New York state. It is divided into 5 boroughs: Manhattan, the Bronx, Brooklyn, Queens, and Richmond (on Staten Island). The long, narrow island of Manhattan, upon which New York's complex network of bridges and tunnels converges, is the city's economic and cultural heart. New York is the nation's largest port and a world leader in trade and finance. It is also a manufacturing (notably garments), communications (broadcasting, advertising, and publishing), and performing arts center. In 1626, Dutch settlers of New Netherland purchased Manhattan from the resident Native Americans (reputedly for $24 worth of goods), and it became New Amsterdam. The city was surrendered to the British in 1664 and renamed New York. After the defeat (1776) of George Washington at the Battle of Long Island, the city remained in the hands of British troops until the end of the Revolutionary War, after which it served briefly (1789-90) as the nation's capital. As early as the first census of 1790, New York was the largest city in the United States. Population doubled in the wave of immigration between 1880 and 1900. Construction of the first elevated railway (1867), the Brooklyn Bridge (1883), and the first subway system (1904) helped housing and transport. New York's political leadership, at times notoriously corrupt, has included such notable reformers as Theodore Roosevelt and Fiorello La Guardia. Among the points of interest in New York are the Empire State Building, the World Trade Center, the Statue of Liberty, Greenwich Village, and Central Park. The city also houses the Lincoln Center for the Performing Arts, the Metropolitan Museum of Art, and the Museum of Modern Art.

New York State Barge Canal, inland waterway system that connects the Hudson river with the Great Lakes. It was completed in 1918. Its 524-mi (843-km) length includes the Erie Canal.
See also: Erie Canal.

New York World's Fair, 2 fairs in New York City that presented art, culture, science, and technology exhibits. The first fair (1939 and 1940), based on the theme "Building the World of Tomorrow," introduced the public to such new products as television. The second fair (1964-65), based on the theme "Peace Through Understanding," introduced computers and communications satellites. Each fair developed symbolic monuments: An obelisk called the Tryon and a sphere called the Perisphere were erected in 1939 and a steel globe called the Unisphere was erected in 1964.

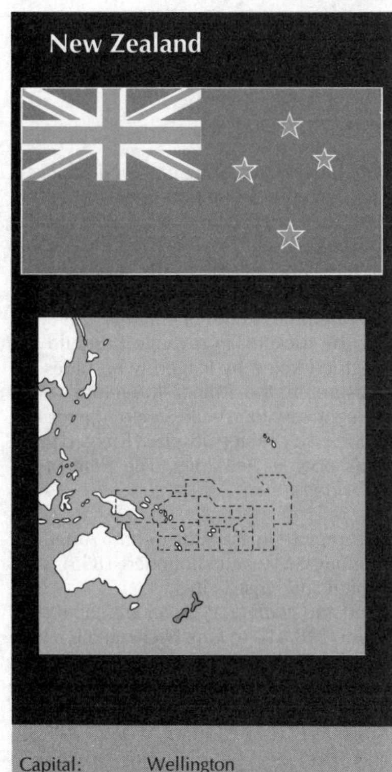

Capital:	Wellington
Area:	103,883 sq mi (269,057 sq km)
Population:	3,371,000
Form:	constitutional monarchy
Independent:	1947
GNP:	U.S. $32,109,000,000
Per capita:	U.S. $9,620

New Zealand, sovereign state within the British Commonwealth situated in the southwest Pacific Ocean. It is administered by a governor general (representing the British sovereign), a prime minister, and a House of Representatives. The capital is Wellington, on North Island.

Land and climate. Lying some 1,200 mi (1,931 km) east of Australia across the Tasman Sea, New Zealand comprises 2 main islands (North, South); Stewart Island; the Chatham Islands, about 400 mi (644 km) east of the South Island; and various minor islands. The total area is 103,736 sq mi (268,676 sq km). The main islands stretch about 1,000 mi (1,609 km) from north to south. They exhibit scenic contrasts ranging from sandy subtropical beaches and smoking volcanoes to lush pastures, majestic forests, placid lakes, glaciers, and snow-capped Alpine peaks.

The North Island (44,281 sq mi/114,688 sq km) is mostly hilly or mountainous. Remarkable thermal springs have been tapped for geothermal power; most of the native Maoris (Polynesians) live in this region. Active volcanoes, such as Mt. Egmont (8,260 ft/2,518 m), are found in Tongariro National Park. The island also has New Zealand's largest lake, Taupo (234 sq mi/629 sq km), and longest, most important river, the Waikato (220 mi/354 km).

The South Island (58,093 sq mi/150,460 sq km), separated from the North Island by Cook Strait, is long and narrow. New Zealand's highest peak, Mt. Cook (12,349 ft/3,764 m) lies in its massive mountain backbone, the Southern Alps. The southwest coast is famed for its fjords. Near Milford Sound are the Sutherland Falls (1,904 ft/580 m), one of the world's highest waterfalls.

Stewart Island (670 sq mi/1,735 sq km) is separated from the South Island by Foveaux Strait. The island is rugged and hilly. The minor islands, except Raoul in the Kermadec group, are uninhabited.

Overall, the climate is pleasant and moderate, without extremes of heat or cold in the lowlands, and rainfall is sufficient.

People. In New Zealand's population, 9% are Maoris and 87% are descended from British settlers. They live and work together as a peaceful, integrated people. Over 80% of the population reside in urban areas, notably Auckland (the leading port, on North Island), Christchurch, and Wellington. The major cities have state university branches; the literacy rate is 99%.

Economy. With only 2% of the land arable, sheep- and cattle-raising are the main sources of income. Principal exports are frozen meat (mainly lamb), wool, and dairy products. Tourism provides income, and privately run industry includes fishing, food processing, textiles, and machinery; mining and forestry are state-owned.

History. The chief Maori migrations were from 1200 to 1400. Abel Janszoon Tasman, a Dutch navigator, was the first European to sight the islands (1642). Although the Maoris would not let him ashore, the islands were named after the province of Zeeland in The Netherlands. The English navigator Captain James Cook claimed the country in 1770, and the first missionaries arrived in 1814. Systematic colonization was begun by the New Zealand Company in 1840, when the Treaty of Waitangi acknowledged British sovereignty. Despite harsh land disputes with the Maoris (1845-70), the country was given a constitution providing for self-government in 1853. Social welfare programs began in the 1890s, and in 1907 Britain made New Zealand a dominion. New Zealanders fought with the Allies in both World Wars and in Vietnam; the country joined the South East Asia Treaty Organization (SEATO) in 1954. Nuclear weapons and nuclear-powered ships have been banned from its ports since 1985.

Ney, Michel (1769-1815), French Napoleonic marshal and military hero. His rear-guard defense during Napoleon's retreat from Moscow (1812) was the most notable achievement of a brilliant career. After helping persuade Napoleon to abdicate in 1814, Ney was made a noble by the Bourbon Louis XVIII. When Napoleon returned from exile, however, Ney supported him, fighting at the battle of Waterloo. When Napoleon was defeated, Ney was condemned for treason by the house of peers and was executed.
See also: Napoleon I.

Fjordland National Park in South Island, New Zealand

Nez Percé, Native American tribe of what is now western Idaho, northeastern Oregon, and southeastern Washington. Noted horse breeders, they ceded (1855) much of their territory to the United States. The fraudulent cession of a further 75% of their land (1863) led to the Nez Percé War of 1877, in which 300 Indians held out for 5 months against 5,000 U.S. troops.

NF *see:* Neurofibromatosis.

Ngo Dinh Diem (1901-63), Vietnamese politician and first president of the Republic of Vietnam (South Vietnam). Born of a royal Roman Catholic Vietnamese family, he fled into exile after arrest by Ho Chi Minh and the Communist forces (1945). With the division of Vietnam into north and south (1954) he returned and was appointed prime minister and later elected to the presidency (1955). Known for his dictatorial rule and cruelty—especially toward Buddhist monks accused of communist Viet Cong sympathy—his popularity waned. He and his brother and sister-in-law (Ngo Dinh Nhu and Madame Nhu) were assassinated when his regime fell in a coup d'état.
See also: Vietnam.

Nguyen Van Linh (1913-), secretary-general of the Vietnamese Communist Party, 1986-90. Nguyen had been active in government 1975-82, but for several years was in political disgrace, and did not reappear in the party organization until 1985.
See also: Vietnam.

Nguyen Van Thieu (1923-), Vietnamese politician and president (1967-75) of the Republic of Vietnam (South Vietnam). Originally a supporter of Ngo Dinh Diem, first president of the Republic of Vietnam, he took part in the 1963 coup d'état that deposed Diem. Elected to the presidency, he ruled with U.S. support. Two years after the withdrawal of U.S. troops from Vietnam (1973), he resigned his office to pro-

mote peace talks between the South and North. Shortly thereafter, in April 1975, Saigon and the rest of South Vietnam fell to the North Vietnamese, and Thieu went into exile in Taiwan and Great Britain.
See also: Vietnam.

Niacin *see:* Vitamin.

Niagara Falls, large waterfall in the Niagara River along the border between western New York state and Ontario, Canada. A world-famous spectacle and an important source of hydroelectric power, the falls are divided by Goat Island into the American Falls (1,060 ft/323 m wide and 167 ft/51 m high) and the Canadian, or Horseshoe Falls (2,600 ft/792 m wide and 158 ft/48 m high). The Niagara Gorge, below the falls, is about 7 mi (11 km) long and is noted for its Whirlpool Rapids and Whirlpool. Some 2,200 cu ft (6,005 cu m) of water pass over the falls every second.

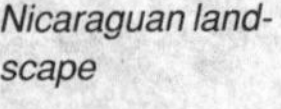

Nicaraguan landscape

Niagara Movement, U.S. civil rights organization led by W.E.B. Du Bois and other African American leaders, precursor to the National Association for the Advancement of Colored People (NAACP). The organization, operational for 5 years (1905-10), blamed European Americans for problems of racism, and fought for school integration, voting rights, and the election of black political candidates. Although the group was short-lived and not strongly supported, its principles influenced later civil rights groups.
See also: Du Bois, W(illiam) E(dward) B(urghardt).

Niagara River, river about 34 mi (55 km) long, flowing north from Lake Erie to Lake Ontario (over Niagara Falls), forming part of the border between the United States and Canada. Water from the river is diverted above Niagara Falls for hydroelectricity.

Niamey (pop. 400,000), capital and largest city of Niger, located on the Niger River in the southwestern part of the country. It serves as Niger's center for the export of peanuts and other agricultural products. Colonized by the French in the late 1800s, it became the capital in 1926.
See also: Niger.

Nibelungenlied ("Song of the Nibelungs"), German epic dating from the early 1200s, partly based on Scandinavian myths. It tells the story of Siegfried, who wins the treasure of the Nibelungen dwarfs and is given Kriemhild in marriage as a reward for helping Kriemhild's brother Gunther win Brunhild by trickery. In revenge Brunhild has Siegfried killed by Hagen, who hides the treasure in the Rhine. Kriemhild's subsequent vow to avenge Siegfried ends in a holocaust. The story inspired Richard Wagner's operatic tetralogy, *The Ring of the Nibelungs.*

Nicaragua, largest of the Central American republics. Managua (founded 1855) is the capital and largest city.
Land and climate. With an area of 49,579 sq mi (128,410 sq km), Nicaragua is a little larger than Illinois. The country is bounded on the north by Honduras, on the south by Costa Rica, has a Caribbean coastline (the Mosquito Coast) of about 300 mi (483 km) and a 200-mi (322-km) Pacific coastline. A narrow volcanic belt runs southwest across the country from Honduras to Costa Rica, between the Pacific and two lakes: Lake

Nicaragua

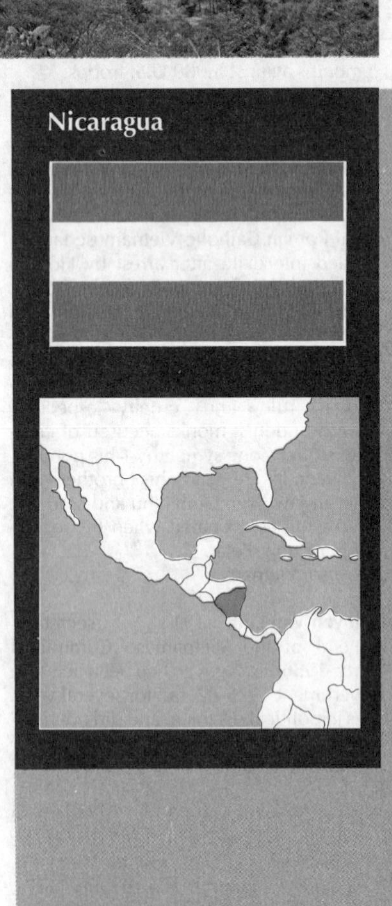

General information	
Capital:	Managua
Area:	50,200 sq mi (130,000 sq km)
Population:	3,745,000
Official language:	Spanish
Monetary unit:	1 Nicaraguan new córdoba = 100 centavos
Main cities:	Managua, León, Granada
Government	
Form:	republic
Independent:	1838
Head of state:	President (elected every 6 years)
Head of government:	President
Legislature:	one legislative house (National Assembly)
Executive:	President and Cabinet
Judiciary:	highest court is the Supreme Court
Political division:	16 departments
National economy	
Gross national product:	U.S. $2,911,000,000
Per capita income:	U.S. $830
Agriculture:	coffee, seed cotton, sugar cane, bananas, rice, cottonseed
Livestock:	cattle, pigs, horses
Fisheries:	5,000 metric tons
Mining:	gold, silver, copper, tungsten
Industries:	processed foods, beverages, metal products, textiles, petroleum products
Main exports:	coffee, cotton, sugar, bananas, seafood
Transportation:	214 mi (344 km) of railroads, 9,319 mi (14,997 km) of roads, 1 international airport
Trading partners:	EEC, Socialist countries, Japan
People	
Urban:	59%
Ethnic composition:	mestizo 67%, European 17%, African 10%, Native American 6%
Birth rate:	39 per 1,000 population
Death rate:	8 per 1,000 population
Infant mortality:	62 per 1,000 live births
Life expectancy:	male 60 years, female 62 years

Nicaragua, Central America's largest at 3,089 sq mi (8,006 sq km), and its connecting Lake Managua (386 sq mi/1,000 sq km), both containing small active volcanos. The country's population and productive wealth are concentrated in this region. Earthquakes, like the one that devastated Managua in 1972, are not uncommon.

North of the region are wedge-shaped, forested highlands. Eastward, these fall away to broad lowlands extending to the coast, where Nicaragua's chief rivers—the Coco, Rio Grande, Escondido, and San Juan—empty into the Caribbean.

The climate of the coastal lowlands is mainly hot and humid, with temperatures averaging 80°F (25°C). The rainy season, May through December, brings plentiful rainfall, especially in the eastern lowlands and slopes of the central highlands.

People. The population is predominantly mestizo (mixed Spanish-Indian descent). Minorities include those of Spanish or African descent, and native Indians. About 80% of the people, poor farmers mostly, live in the Pacific region. Spanish is the official language. Most Nicaraguans are Roman Catholics. Before 1980 the literacy rate was less than 50%, but government-built schools and literacy programs raised it to 66% by 1986. The National University is centered in León and Managua, which also has the Jesuit Central University.

Economy. Only 10% of the land is cultivated, but agriculture is the mainstay of the economy, along with forestry, fisheries, and mining (gold, silver, copper, tungsten). Main exports are coffee, cotton, and sugar.

History. The Nicarao Indians, who probably gave the country its name, were conquered by Spanish conquistador Gil González de vila in 1522; various other Indians had inhabited it previously. Francisco Fernández de Córdoba, after whom Nicaragua's currency is named, founded Léon and Granada (1524). From 1570, the country was ruled as part of Guatemala. Nicaragua won independence from Spain in 1821, but was annexed by Mexico, then became part of the Central American Federation (1825-38). Independent thereafter, the country experienced internal power struggles and conflicts with British and U.S. military and commercial interests. After asking the United States for aid in 1912, it was occupied by U.S. Marines almost continuously until 1933. From 1936, it was ruled dictatorially by the Somoza family until 1979, when Marxist Sandinista guerrillas forced President Anastasio Somoza-Debayle into exile. A socialist Government of National Reconstruction, led by Daniel Ortega, was installed. Domestic reforms helped the Nicaraguan people, but military actions caused turmoil internally (against opposing contra forces), with its neighbors, and in the U.S. government (the Iran-Contra arms scandal). In 1990, elections replaced the Sandinistas with a new, pro-U.S. government led by Violetta Chamorro.

Nice (pop. 337,100), city in southeastern France, on the Mediterranean Sea, capital of the Alpes-Maritimes department. Originally a Greek settlement (from the 5th century B.C.), it is now a favorite vacation spot for tourists visiting the French Riviera. In addition to tourism, the city is known for the manufacture of olive oil and electronic products.

Nicene Councils, first and 17th Ecumenical Councils, held in Nice (modern Iznik, Turkey). The first Nicene Council, called in 325 by the Byzantine Emperor Constantine, condemned Arianism and drew up the Nicene Creed. The second Nicene Council (787) ruled in favor of the restoration of images in churches.

Nicholas, name of 5 popes, especially Nicholas I, Nicholas II, and Nicholas V. **Saint Nicholas I**, or Nicholas the Great (c.825-867), a Roman, was pope from 858 to 867. A strong pontiff, he supported St. Ignatius, Patriarch of Constantinople, after the Byzantine emperor Michael III deposed Ignatius in favor of Photius, and he excommunicated Photius (863). After Nicholas's death Photius counterdeposed the pope (867), an act that culminated in the Photian Schism, a split between the Eastern and Western churches. **Nicholas II** (Gerhard; 1010?-1061), who was French-born, was pope from 1059 to 1061. His papacy is famous for the Lateran synod of 1059, which eliminated the Roman nobility's influence on papal elections. The 7 cardinal bishops were given the power to choose a candidate that the rest of the cardinals would have to approve. The other clergy and the people would be presented with their new pope, and the emperor would be sent notice. This edict was rejected by the German bishops in 1061, ending their alliance with Rome. The council also passed church laws enforcing celibacy, prohibiting the selling of clerical offices, and preventing secular persons from investing members of the clergy with the symbols of their office. **Nicholas V** (Tommaso Parentucelli; 1397-1455), an Italian, was pope from 1447 to 1455; he was the first Renaissance pope. He sought to reestablish Rome's importance in the Christian world. Toward that end, he patronized famous humanists and literary scholars and founded what would became the Vatican Library, an important collection of ancient Greek, Roman, and early Christian manuscripts. He also initiated the restoration of many famous buildings in Rome, including St. Peter's Church.

Nicholas, tsars of Russia. **Nicholas I** (1796-1855), tsar of the Russian empire (1825-55), notorious for his despotic rule. His first action as ruler was to crush the Decembrist Revolt. A determined absolutist, he opposed all liberal political reforms, while expanding Russian territory at the expense of Turkey. He also suppressed an uprising in Poland (1830-31) and aided the Austrian state in crushing the 1849 revolution in Hungary. He died during the Crimean War. **Nicholas II** (1868-1918), who ruled 1894-1917, helped bring about the Russian Revolution through his inflexibility and misgovernment. His wife, the empress Alexandra, filled the court with irresponsible favorites, of whom the monk Rasputin was the most influential. The repression of political oppositionists and of non-Russian nationalists was intensified. Russian defeats in the Russo-Japanese War (1904-05) led to a popular uprising, and Nicholas granted limited civil rights and called the first representative parliament, or Duma (1905). The military defeats of World War I led to the Feb. 1917 revolution and his abdication, in March. He was executed by the Bolsheviks during the civil war that followed the Oct. 1917 revolution.

Nicholas II, depicted on a Fabergé egg

Nicholas, Saint, 4th-century patron saint of children, scholars, merchants, and sailors, traditionally identified with a bishop of Myra in Asia Minor. In many European countries he is said to visit children and give them gifts on his feast day (Dec. 6). The custom was brought to America by the Dutch, whose Sinter Klaas became the Santa Claus of Christmas.

Nicholas of Cusa (1401-64), German theologian and philosopher. He became a cardinal in 1440. Nicholas is better known for his interest in astronomy—he held that the earth rotates on its axis, that space is infinite, and that the sun is a star—and for his neo-Platonist writings on the limits of reason.

Nicholson, Ben (1894-1982), British abstract sculptor and painter of landscapes and still lifes. His reliefs, like *White Relief* (1939), are composed in an elegant, pure, linear style.

Nickel, chemical element, symbol Ni; for physical constants see Periodic Table. Nickel was discovered by Alex Cronstedt in 1751. It is found in most meteorites and occurs in the minerals niccolite, garnierite, millerite, pyrrhotite, and pentlandite, from which it is extracted commercially. Nickel is prepared by concentrating its ores by flotation and roasting to the oxide, which is then reduced with carbon. Nickel is a steel-white, hard, ferromagnetic, corrosion-resistant metal. It strongly resembles iron and cobalt. Most nickel is used to prepare alloys, among them German silver, Monel metal, nichrome, and nickel bronze. Nickel and its compounds are sus-

The U.S. nickel contains only 25% nickel.

Jack Nicklaus

pected carcinogens. Nickel and its compounds are used in stainless steels, coinage metal, batteries, magnets, and catalysts.

Nickel silver, or German silver, silver-colored alloy of copper, nickel, and zinc, first produced in Germany. It is harder than silver, and although it tarnishes easily and has a duller appearance, it can easily be polished. Nickel silver dinnerware is silver-plated, although the silver plating wears off.

Nicklaus, Jack (1940-), U.S. golfer. Before turning professional (1962) he won the United States Amateur tournament 2 times (1959, 61). His professional victories include the British Open (1966, 70, 78), U.S. Open (1962, 67, 72, 80), Masters tournament (1963, 65, 66, 72, 75, 86), and the Professional Golfers' Association (PGA) tournament (1963, 71, 73, 75, 80). Nicklaus became the first golfer to be a repeat winner of all 4 of these major professional tournaments.

Nicolet, Jean (1598-1642), French explorer who was probably the first European to visit the Lake Michigan area. In 1634 he set out by canoe through Lake Huron, entered Lake Michigan and explored Green Bay and the Fox River, making friendly contact with the Winnebago tribe.

Joseph Niépce

Nicolson, Sir Harold (1886-1968), British writer and diplomat, born in Iran. After diplomatic service (1909-29), he was a member of Parliament (1935-45). He published many reviews and biographies of Verlaine, Byron, Tennyson, Swinburne, and King George V.

Nicosia (pop. 163,700), city in north-central Cyprus, capital of the island nation. An ancient agricultural trade center, it is now a center for the manufacture of textiles and other goods and for governmental and commercial business. Ancient artifacts from previous colonists are housed in its museums.
See also: Cyprus, Republic of.

Nicotine, poisonous alkaloid ($C_{10}H_{14}N_2$) found in all parts of the tobacco plant, but especially in the leaves. When pure, it is a colorless oily fluid with little odor, but a sharp, burning taste. On exposure to air it becomes deep brown, with the characteristic tobacco-like smell.
See also: Smoking; Tobacco.

Nictitating membrane, mucous membrane that acts like a third eyelid in many vertebrates. This thin transparent or semi-transparent membrane, located under the outer eyelid of birds and reptiles, pulls down over the animal's eyeball.

Niebuhr, name of 2 U.S. brothers, leading Protestant theologians. **Reinhold Niebuhr** (1892-1971) was an active socialist in the early 1930s. After World War II he turned back to traditional Protestant values, relating them to modern society in his "conservative realism." His *Nature and Destiny of Man* (2 vols., 1941-43) greatly influenced American theology. **Helmut Richard Niebuhr** (1894-1962) Niebuhr taught at Yale Divinity School (1931-62) and wrote on ethics and the history of Christian thought in such books as *The Kingdom of God in America* (1937) and *Radical Monotheism and Western Culture* (1960).
See also: Theology.

Nielsen, Carl August (1865-1931), Danish composer. His 6 symphonies are notable for their original harmonic structure. He also wrote chamber music, operas, and concertos for flute, clarinet, and violin.

Niemeyer, Oscar (Oscar Niemeyer Soares Filho; 1907-), Brazilian architect whose outstanding work in Brazil culminated in that country's capital city, Brasilia (1956-60). His most characteristic style uses curved, sculptural, reinforced concrete.
See also: Brasilia.

Niemöller, Martin (1892-1984), German Lutheran pastor who opposed the Nazis and Adolf Hitler. He was confined in concentration camps (1938-45). He organized the "Declaration of Guilt" (1945), in which German churches admitted their failure to resist the Nazis. He was president (1961-68) of the World Council of Churches.

Niépce, Joseph Nicéphore (1765-1833), French physicist and inventor who produced the first successful permanent photograph (1826). The image, recorded in asphalt on a pewter plate, required an 8-hr exposure in a camera obscura. In 1829 Niepce went into partnership with Louis Daguerre, who later perfected his process, which became widely known as daguerrotype.

Nietzsche, Friedrich (1844-1900), German philosopher. In *Thus Spoke Zarathustra* (1833-92) he introduced the concept of the "superman," who would transcend what he considered the slavish morality of Christianity and whose motivating force would be a "will to power," directed toward creativity, that would set him off from lesser human beings. Nietzsche's ideas, further elaborated in *Beyond Good and Evil* (1886), have been much misrepresented, particularly by the Nazis, who misappropriated the concept of the superman to justify their own concepts of Aryan racial superiority.
See also: Philosophy.

Niger, largest republic (in area) in the interior of northern Africa. The capital is Niamey.

Land and climate. Niger is bordered on the north by Algeria and Libya, on the east by Chad, on the south and southwest by Nigeria, Dahomey, and Burkina Faso, and on the west by Mali. A landlocked desert country, with an area of 489,189 sq mi (1,267,000 sq km). The north is typically Saharan, the northeast virtually uninhabitable. Agadez, in central Niger south of the Aïr Massif (5,905 ft/1,800 m), has an annual rainfall of only 7 in (18 cm), all of it coming in an 8-week period. Temperatures there in May exceed 100°F (37°C). Conditions are better in the south, where rainfall averages 22 in (55.88 cm), and in the southwest, which profits from the seasonal flooding of the Niger River. Most Nigerians live in this region, between Lake Chad and Niamey.

People. Half the population are Hausa peoples; the rest are the Djerma-Songhai and Beriberi-Manga, mainly farmers in the south, and the nomadic Fulani, Tuareg, and others in the north. French is the official language; Hausa and Djerma are also spoken. The literacy rate is 13% (1989). Animism is practiced but Sunni Moslem is the predominant religion.

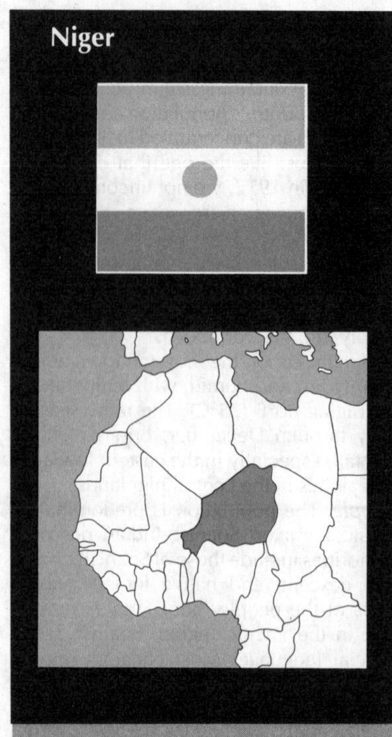

Capital:	Niamey
Area:	489,191 sq mi (1,267,000 sq km)
Population:	7,523,000
Form:	republic
Independent:	1960
GNP:	U.S. $2,190,000,000
Per capita:	U.S. $310

Peanuts are a major crop of Niger. Shown are peanuts ready for transport.

Economy. Though one of the world's poorest countries, Niger is rich in mineral potential. Principal exports are uranium, livestock, and vegetables. Only 3% of the land is arable; chief food crops are peanuts, cotton, millet, cassava, sorghum, vegetables, and rice.

History. Niger was once part of ancient and medieval African empires, such as Mali and Songhai. In the 9th century, a Bornu kingdom was founded near Lake Chad by Berbers from North Africa, who were converted to Islam in the 11th century. In the late 18th century, Europeans explored the region. The French, after defeating Tuareg fighters who had invaded the area from the north a century before, incorporated the territory into French West Africa in 1896, establishing a military rule. It became the colony of Niger in 1921. Electing its first territorial assembly in 1946, Niger acquired self-government in 1956 and became an independent republic in 1960 but maintained close economic and military ties with France. Its first president, Diori Hamani, ruled until 1974, when he was ousted by a military coup. Drought and famine wreaked disaster 1973-5, with half the population reportedly starving, but this eased. In 1989, the drafting of a new constitution provided for a new National Assembly.

Nigeria, federal republic in West Africa. Lagos is the capital.

Land and climate. Nigeria has an area of 356,667 sq mi (923,768 sq km). It is bordered on the north by Niger, on the east by Chad and Cameroon, on the west by Benin, and on the south by the Gulf of Guinea. Its 500-mi (800-km) coastline has sandbars, swamps, mangrove forests, lagoons, and the mouths of several navigable rivers, predominantly the delta of the country's most important river, the Niger. Beyond the coast and rain forests are savannas.

North of the Niger River and its tributary, the Benue, the grass-covered Jos plateau falls away to the sandy high plains of Hausaland. Another watershed lies to the southwest, where the Yoruba highlands, covered with tall grass and hardwood forests, form the divide between northward-flowing rivers and those draining south to the gulf. Other highlands run along Nigeria's border with Cameroon, where Vogel Peak (6,700 ft/2,040 m) is the highest. In the far north, central highlands merge with the Sahara along the Niger border. Annual rainfall in this entirely tropical country, hot the year round, ranges from more than 150 in (381 cm) on the central coast to only 25 in (64 cm) in the northeast.

People. Nigeria is the most populous country on the African continent. Of the 250 ethnic groups that comprise two-thirds of the population, there are 3 major peoples: some 35.7 million Hausa-Fulani live in the Muslim north, and about 44 million Ibo and Yoruba live in the Christian south and east. With 31% of the land arable, more than half the Nigerians are farmers and herders. The country is one of Africa's most urbanized, with Lagos and Ibadan having more than 1 million inhabitants. English is the official language; Hausa, Yoruba, and Ibo are also spoken.

Lagos, Nigeria

Nigeria

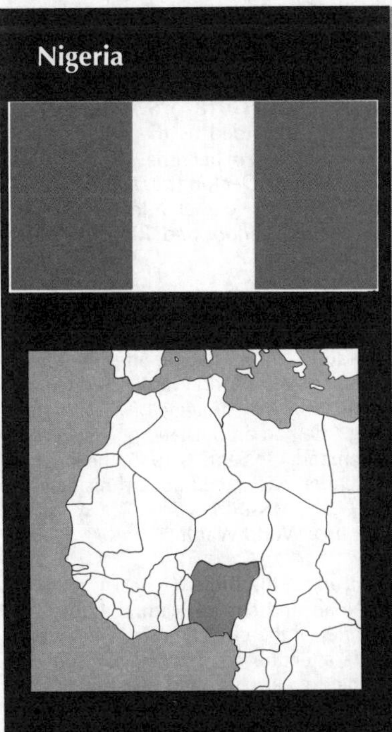

General information	
Capital:	Lagos
Area:	356,669 sq mi (923,768 sq km)
Population:	115,973,000
Official language:	English
Monetary unit:	1 Nigerian naira = 100 kobo
Main cities:	Lagos, Ibadan, Ogbomosho
Government	
Form:	Military
Independent:	1960
Head of state:	President
Head of government:	Chairman of Armed Forces Ruling Council (AFRC)
Legislature:	National Assembly dissolved in 1983
Executive:	President and Commander-in-Chief of the Armed Forces, AFRC and National Council of Ministers
Judiciary:	highest court is the Federal Supreme Court
Political division:	21 states, 1 federal capital territory
National economy	
Gross national product:	U.S. $77,770,000,000
Per capita income:	U.S. $790
Agriculture:	cocoa beans, rubber, palm kernels, cassava, yams, tobacco
Livestock:	goats, sheep, cattle
Fisheries:	268,000 metric tons
Mining:	crude petroleum, tin concentrates, hard coal, natural gas
Industries:	petroleum products, motor vehicles, food products, textiles, chemical products, lumber
Main exports:	mineral fuels, lubricants, food and live animals
Transportation:	2,178 mi (3,505 km) of railroads, 77,067 mi (124,000 km) of roads, 2 international airports
Trading partners:	U.S., EEC
People	
Urban:	29%
Ethnic composition:	Hausa 21.5%, Yoruba 21.5%, Ibo 18%, Fulani 11%, Ibibio 5.5%, Kanuri 4%
Birth rate:	46 per 1,000 population
Death rate:	17 per 1,000 population
Infant mortality:	121 per 1,000 live births
Life expectancy:	male 47 years, female 49 years

Florence Nightingale during the Crimean War

Economy. Oil is the leading export. Its revenues have fueled massive, mostly private development. Other leading exports are cocoa, palm kernels and palm oil, peanuts, soybeans, rubber, cotton, and bananas. Manufacturing includes oil refining, vehicle assembly, food processing, textiles, building materials, and furniture. In the south there are extensive fisheries. A network of railways, roads, and 14 airports serves travelers.

History. The Nok, an advanced Iron Age culture (800 B.C.-A.D. 200), is the earliest known in Nigeria. From about A.D. 1000, small city-states arose. The sacred Yoruba city of Ife in the southwest developed its great culture during the 12th century, and during the 14th century Islam become predominant in the north, where several cities were trans-Saharan trade centers. In the south, the ancient city-state of Benin was a flourishing center when the Portuguese (1483) and the British (1553) arrived and began the trade in Nigerian slaves for Europe and the Americas. By the mid-19th century, palm products replaced slaves as the leading export, and Lagos, the chief port, was ceded to Britain (1861), which made it an outpost to fight the slave trade, and then a colony (1886). Soon the entire country was under control of the British, who made it a protectorate (1914). After World War II, responding to militant nationalists, the British increased self-government, and Nigerians from the 3 major ethnic groups took over by democratic means when the country became a federation of regions (1954), then an independent republic (1963). However, rival ethnic military factions battling for control tore Nigeria apart. Thousands of Ibos were massacred or fled their homeland, Biafra. When the military government reorganized Nigeria into ethnic states (1967), Biafra seceded. The ensuing civil war ended (1970) with Nigeria's unity preserved, but at the cost of perhaps 1 million Ibo dead from starvation. With a new constitution (1976), Nigeria returned to a democratically elected civilian government (1979), but it was ousted in a military coup (1983). A return to civilian rule is promised by 1992.

Poster depicting Vaslav Nijinsky in the ballet Prélude à L'après midi d'un faune *(1912)*

Niger River, third-longest river of Africa. Along with its eastern branch, the Benue, it drains an area of more than 1 million sq mi (2.59 million sq km) in west Africa. Rising in southwestern Guinea, it flows 2,600 mi (4,180 km), curving northeast, east, and then southeast into Nigeria, eventually running south to the Gulf of Guinea, where it forms a delta.

Nighthawk, bullbat, or mosquito hawk (*Chordeiles minor*), nocturnal, insect-eating bird in the goatsucker family (Caprimulgidae), not a true hawk. It measures approximately 10 in (25 cm) long, with white wing bars and a white throat patch on a mottled brown, black, and white body. Nighthawks reside in South America during the winter and the United States and Canada for the rest of the year.

Nightingale, bird (*Luscinia megarhynchos*) of the thrush family, renowned for the male's beautiful song. A small brown bird feeding on insects and other invertebrates, it lives in deciduous woodlands throughout most of Europe.

Nightingale, Florence (1820-1910), English founder of modern nursing, known as the "Lady with the Lamp" because she worked night and day during the Crimean War (1954), establishing sanitary methods and discipline in 2 huge army hospitals. In 1860 she set up a nurses' training school in London. She was the first woman to be awarded the British Order of Merit (1907).
See also: Crimean War; Nursing.

Nightshade, common name for a number of plants (family Solanaceae) with small but distinctive tubular or flared flowers. Some nightshades (e.g., deadly nightshade and Jimson weed) produce rounded fruits that may contain poisons, but many are edible crops, e.g., tomato, potato, red pepper, and eggplant.

Nihilism, doctrine that denies all values, questions all authority, and advocates the destruction of all social and economic institutions. The movement, romantic in origin and anarchist in outlook, arose in 19th-century Russia. Its most noted exponent was Prince Piotr Kropotkin.

Nijinsky, Vaslav (1890-1950), Russian ballet dancer. His career began in St. Petersburg in 1907. His outstanding technique and magnetic stage presence contributed greatly to the impact of Russian ballet in the West when Sergei Diaghilev brought a company to Paris in 1909. With Diaghilev's encouragement, Nijinsky devised original choreography, based on Greek vase paintings, for Claude Debussy's *Afternoon of a Faun.* Mental illness ended his career in 1919.
See also: Ballet.

Nikolais, Alwin (1912-), U.S. dancer and choreographer. He formed his own dance company, now known as the Alwin Nikolais Dance Theatre, in 1949. Nikolais not only choreographs his works, but designs the pieces' other elements, such as the costumes and scenery, and composes the music. Among his works are *Kaleidoscope* (1956), *Imago* (1963), and *Cent Dom* (1980).
See also: Ballet.

Nile River, longest river in the world, flowing generally north about 4,145 mi (6,671 km) from east-central Africa through the Sudan and Egypt to the Mediterranean. Its remote headstream is the Luvironza River in Burundi above Victoria Nyanza (Lake Victoria), where the White Nile originates. The Blue Nile rises above Lake Tana in northwestern Ethiopia and joins the White Nile at Khartoum, Sudan, to form the Nile proper. North of Cairo, Egypt, the Nile fans out into a delta 115 mi (185 km) wide, with principal outlets at Rosetta near Alexandria and Damietta near Port Said. Silt deposited by the Nile's annual overflow brought agricultural prosperity throughout Egypt's history. The river has been harnessed, notably at the Aswan High Dam in Upper Egypt, to supply hydroelectricity as well as constant irrigation. The Nile is navigable the year round from its mouth to Aswan, and in full spate it is generally navigable as far south as Uganda.

Nilsson, Birgit (1918-), Swedish soprano, widely regarded as the greatest Wagnerian soprano of her time. She is famed as Brünnhilde in *Der Ring des Nibelungen* but is also known for her roles in Giacomo Puccini's *Turandot* and Richard Strauss' *Elektra.*

Nimitz, Chester William (1885-1966), U.S. admiral who commanded naval operations in the Pacific after the United States entered World War II. Credited with originating the strategy of "island hopping," he had an outstandingly successful command. On Sept. 2, 1945, the Japanese surrender was signed aboard his flagship, the U.S.S. *Missouri.*
See also: World War II.

Nimrod, in the Bible (Genesis), grandson of Noah and son of Ham, a hunter and founder of the city Nineveh. Living many years after the great flood, Nimrod constructed great cities and became a legendary hunter. Nineveh was located in present-day Iraq.
See also: Bible.

Nin, Anaïs (1903-77), French-born U.S. author whose novels and stories depict the inner worlds of women in surrealistic and psychoanalytic fashion. Her novels include *The House of Incest* (1936) and *Collages* (1964). She is best known for *The Diaries of Anaïs Nin* (7 vols., 1966-80), which span the years 1931-74 and include portraits of such contemporaries as Lawrence Durrell, Henry Miller, William Carlos Williams, and Marguerite Young.

Nineveh, ancient capital of Assyria, on the Tigris River, opposite modern Mosul, Iraq. Invaluable remains survive from its period of greatness under Sennacherib and Assurbanipal, in the 7th century B.C. Its destruction by Babylonian, Medean, and Scythian invaders in 612 B.C. ended the Assyrian Empire.
See also: Assyria.

Ningbo, or Ning-po (pop. 468,200), formerly Ninghsien, port city on the Yung River in northern Zhejiang province, eastern China. In 1843 Ningbo became one of 5 Chinese ports open to foreign trade. Although nearby Shanghai is now the more prominent center of international trade, Ningbo remains a major commercial and manufacturing center for the region. Textiles, food processing, shipbuilding, and machine production are among its chief industries.
See also: China.

Ning-po *see:* Ningbo.

Niobe, in Greek mythology, daughter of Tantalus and wife of Amphion, and a figure of eternal sorrow. Queen Niobe, who had 12 children, claimed that her child-bearing powers were greater than those of the goddess Leto, who had only 2 children. Leto punished Niobe for this boast by having all of her children slain. The gods, pitying the grieving queen, turned her into a weeping rock, which, according to tradition, is on Mt. Sipylon in Turkey.

Niobium, chemical element, symbol Nb; for physical constants see Periodic Table. Niobium was discovered by Charles Hatchett in 1801. It occurs associated with tantalum in the minerals pyrochlore, and euxenite. It is obtained commercially from columbite-tantalite, a mixed oxide with tantalum and iron and manganese. The element is prepared by the high-temperature reaction of niobium oxide with niobium carbide in a vacuum. Niobium is a shiny, soft, white, ductile metal. Ferroniobium is used in arc-welding rods and stainless steels. Niobium is used in high temperature alloys and nuclear applications. Niobium is also known as columbium.

Nippon *see:* Japan.

Nirvana, Sanskrit term used in Buddhism, Jainism, and Hinduism to denote the highest state of existence, reached when all bodily desires have been quelled and the self is free to dissolve into the ocean of peace, or God. It means literally *extinguished*, denoting freedom from ego. Nirvana is the final escape from the cycle of rebirth.
See also: Buddhism.

Nisei (Japanese, "second generation"), those born of immigrant Japanese parents in the United States. After the Japanese attack on Pearl Harbor (1941), some 110,000 Americans of Japanese ancestry were forcibly evacuated from their homes on the West Coast and placed in detention centers, in most cases until World War II had ended.

Nitrate, chemical compound, generally sodium ($NaNO_3$) or potassium nitrate (KNO_3), formed in the soil by bacteria. Plants use nitrates to make protein. Nitrates are used in making explosives, fireworks, heart medicine, and photographic film, and are added to the soil as fertilizers to replace depleted nitrogen.

Nitrate of silver *see:* Silver nitrate.

Nitre *see:* Saltpeter.

Nitric acid, corrosive, colorless liquid (HNO_3) with powerful oxidizing properties, used in the manufacture of medicine, dyes, explosives, and metal products.

Nitrite, salt or esther of nitrous acid. Certain nitrites cause dilation of small blood vessels and thus help to lower blood pressure. Examples are amyl nitrite, sodium nitrite, nitroprusside, and nitroglycerin.

Nitrocellulose *see:* Guncotton.

Nitrogen, chemical element, symbol N; for physical constants see Periodic Table. Nitrogen was discovered by Daniel Rutherford in 1772. It is present in air to the extent of 78% and is commercially obtained by the liquefaction and fractional distillation of air. Nitrogen is a colorless, odorless, and chemically inert gas. When heated, however, it combines directly with magnesium, lithium, or calcium. The largest use of elemental nitrogen is in the Haber process, where nitrogen is heated under pressure to form ammonia. In the Ostwald process it is oxidized to nitric acid. Millions of tons of elemental nitrogen are produced in the United States each year. Nitrogen is used as an inert atmosphere for the production of electronic components and in the annealing of steel. In liquid form it is used as a refrigerant. Nitrogen compounds are used in the manufacture of fertilizers, explosives, and pharmaceuticals.

Nitrogen cycle, cycle of chemical changes that keep nitrogen flowing through the biosphere, in air and soil. Nitrogen is a fundamental part of living protoplasm. In order to be absorbed by living things, however, it has to be combined into hydrogen and oxygen compounds that plants can use. This process, called nitrogen fixation, is carried on by bacteria in the soil that produce ammonia and nitrates. Plants then absorb these from the soil and use them to make protein. When animals eat plants, they convert the plant protein into animal protein. Meanwhile, some of the nitrates present in soils seeps into groundwater and rivers, and the remainder undergoes denitrification, a process that breaks nitrates down into nitrogen and nitrous oxide, which is then released into the atmosphere, soil, and water. When remains of dead animals and wastes decay, nitrogen is put back into the soil in the form of ammonia, which bacteria oxidize to nitrites and then to nitrates, thus beginning the cycle again.

Nitroglycerin, unstable, oily compound ($C_3H_5N_3O_9$) that explodes when exposed to heat or shock. It is used to make dy-

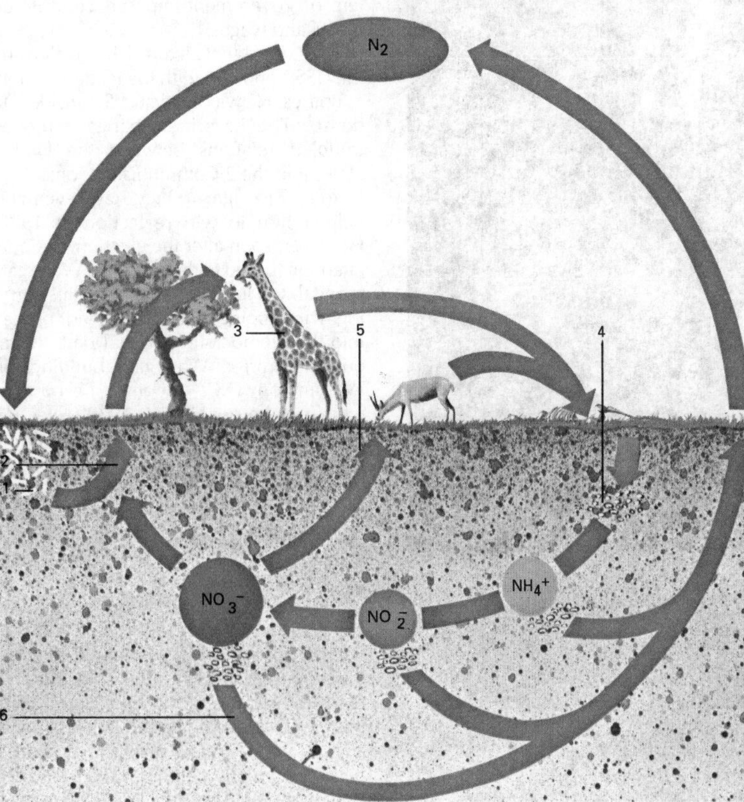

The nitrogen cycle involves the conversion of nitrogen gas in the air (N_2) into nitrates in the soil by nitrogen - fixing bacteria (1). Plants take up the nitrates (2) and use the nitrogen to produce tissues. Herbivorous animals feed on the plants (3). When animals and plants die, their bodies are decayed by bacteria and fungi (4) and ammonium compounds (NH_4^+) are released into the soil. These are converted into nitrites (NO_2^-) and then nitrates (NO_3^-) by nitrifying bacteria, thus making nitrogen available to the plants once more (5). Ammonium compounds, nitrates and nitrites are also converted back to nitrogen by denitrifying bacteria (6) thus completing the cycle.

namite, which is basically nitroglycerin mixed with an absorbing material to make it less easily exploded. Nitroglycerin also causes the dilation of blood vessels and is therefore used in the treatment of angina pectoris.
See also: Dynamite; Glycerol.

Alfred Nobel

Nitrous oxide, colorless, odorless gas (N_2O) first prepared by British chemist Joseph Priestley in 1772. Used by dentists as an anesthetic, it is also called laughing gas because it produces a euphoric effect when inhaled.

Nixon, Richard Milhous (1913-94), 37th president of the United States, who became the only president to resign from office. On Aug. 9, 1974, facing impeachment in the wake of the Watergate scandal, Nixon surrendered the presidency. Although Nixon's presidency ended in disgrace, he effected important breakthroughs in U.S.-Soviet and U.S.-Chinese relations. In addition, in 1973, Nixon signed the ceasefire agreement that ended U.S. participation in the Vietnam War.
Early life. Nixon was graduated from Whittier College in 1934, went to Duke University Law School, and then returned to Whittier to practice law. During World War II he served in the navy.
Politics. Nixon entered the U.S. House of Representatives in 1947. Reelected in 1948, he became well known nationally as a member of the House Committee on Un-American Activities. In 1950, Nixon won election to the U.S. Senate. From 1953 to 1961, he served as vice president under President Dwight D. Eisenhower.
In 1960, Nixon won the Republican nomination for president, but lost the election to Democrat John F. Kennedy. He suffered another defeat in 1962, when he lost a bid for the governorship of California. In 1968, Nixon ran for president a second time. This time, he was successful; in an extremely close race, Nixon defeated the Democratic candidate, Vice President Hubert H. Humphrey.
President. Nixon inherited a nation troubled by serious social and economic problems. The Vietnam War was a source of turmoil and anguish throughout Nixon's first term. The war had been going on for years, with mounting casualties and no end in sight. Many Americans were opposed to the war and held protests and rallies demanding an end to the U.S. role in the fighting. In 1969, Nixon, who had pledged to seek an end to the war, began a program of gradually withdrawing U.S. troops from Vietnam. U.S. military action in Vietnam did not end until 1973, however, when the United States and the other parties in conflict agreed to a ceasefire plan.
In addition to the social upheaval caused by the war, Nixon had to deal with economic worries: rising unemployment, rampant inflation, and sluggish growth. To address these problems, he instituted a system of government-imposed controls on prices and wages.
In 1972, President Nixon visited China and the USSR and met with the leaders of both countries. He was the first U.S. president to do so. The historic meetings improved troubled relations between the United States and the 2 Communist nations.
Nixon's foreign policy achievements helped him to win reelection in 1972. However, soon after the election, national attention turned to the so-called Watergate scandal. On June 17, 1972, burglars carrying wiretapping equipment had broken into the Democratic national party headquarters in the Watergate buildings in Washington, D.C. Although the burglars were members of Nixon's 1972 reelection committee, Nixon denied any White House involvement in the crime. Later investigations revealed, however, that top White House aides had been involved both in planning the break-in and trying to hide evidence concerning it. Ultimately, tapes of White House conversations would prove that Nixon himself had authorized the cover-up. Nixon tried repeatedly to withhold these tapes. He finally released them on Aug. 5, 1974, after being ordered to do so by the U.S. Supreme Court. With this new evidence, Nixon's impeachment, already under consideration in Congress, became virtually certain. Nixon resigned from office on Aug. 9th, 1974. Since leaving office he has spent most of his time golfing, writing, and making some public appearances. In 1978 he published hi memoirs, *RN: The Memoirs of Richard Nixon.*

Richard Milhous Nixon

37th U.S. President

Born:	Yorba Linda, Cal.; Jan. 9, 1913
Term of office:	Jan. 1969-Aug. 1974
Vice presidents:	Spiro T. Agnew, Jan. 1969-Oct. 1973 (resigned); Gerald R. Ford, Oct. 1973-Aug. 1974
Party:	Republican
Spouse:	Thelma (Pat) Ryan Nixon
Children:	Two
Died:	New York City; Apr. 22, 1994

Nkrumah, Kwame (1901-72), African political leader who led his country, Ghana, to independence. A champion of pan-Africanism, he became the first prime minister of independent Ghana (formerly a British colony called the Gold Coast) in 1957. In 1960 he assumed dictatorial powers as president and in 1966 his government was overthrown by a military coup.
See also: Ghana.

NLRB *see:* National Labor Relations Board.

Noah, in the Bible (Genesis 6-10), man who built the ark, at God's direction, that saved human and animal life from the great flood. His sons were Shem, Ham, and Japheth. Shem became the father of the Semitic people, including Jews and Arabs. Ham was the father of the Hamitic people. Japheth was the father of the people of Asia Minor and Europe.
See also: Bible.

Nobel, Alfred Bernhard (1833-96), Swedish chemist and inventor of dynamite and other explosives. About 1863 he set up a factory to manufacture liquid nitroglycerin, but the factory exploded in an accident killing his younger brother. Nobel then set out to find safe handling methods for the substance. In 1867 he developed dynamite, a combination of nitroglycerin and inert, stabilizing filler. Later he invented gelignite (1876) and ballistite (1888). A lifelong pacifist, Nobel wished his explosives to be used solely for peaceful purposes and was embittered by their military use. He left most of his fortune to the Nobel Foundation, which has used the money to reward Nobel Prize winners since 1901.
See also: Dynamite.

Nobelium, chemical element, symbol No; for physical constants see Periodic Table. Nobelium was discovered by Albert Ghiorso and his coworkers at the Lawrence Radiation Laboratory in Berkeley, Calif., in 1958. A target of curium isotopes was bombarded with carbon-12 ions in a heavy-ion linear accelerator (HILAC) to produce nobelium-254. It is a metallic element and a member of the actinide series. Eleven radioactive isotopes of nobelium are now known. Nobelium-259, an alpha-emitter with a half-life of 58 minutes, is the most stable.

Nobel Prizes, annual awards given to individuals or institutions judged to confer "the greatest benefit on mankind" in each of 6 fields: physics, chemistry, physiology or medicine, literature, peace, and economics. Prizes for the first 5 categories have been given since 1901; the economics prize was first awarded in 1969. The winner of the peace prize is decided by a

committee of the Norwegian parliament; the other winners are determined by the corresponding bodies in Sweden: the Royal Academy of Sciences, the Caroline Medico-Chirurigal Institute, and the Academy of Literature. Winners receive a gold medal and a cash payment, now consisting of several hundred thousand dollars. The prize money comes from the foundation set up by Alfred Nobel.
See also: Nobel, Alfred Bernhard.

Nobility, class of people considered to have social prominence. The titles that often accompany high social position, such as *duke*, *count*, or *baron*, may be inherited or granted by monarchs. Great Britain's noble class is called the *peerage*. The U.S. Constitution prohibits government-awarded titles. France, Russia, and Germany no longer recognize titles of nobility.

Noble gas, or inert gas, any of the elements in Group 0 of the Periodic Table, comprising helium, neon, argon, krypton, xenon, and radon. These are colorless, odorless gases whose outermost electrons are complete, making them chemically unreactive. Helium has 2 electrons in its outer shell; all the others have 8.
See also: Periodic table.

Noguchi, Isamu (1904-88), U.S. abstract sculptor whose works, especially those created for specific architectural settings (such as the UNESCO building in Paris), won him international recognition. He was a student of Constantin Brancusi.

Noh, or No, classical drama of Japan, developed under court patronage in the 14th century. Typically, a Noh play dramatizes the spiritual life of its central character, employing speech, singing, instrumental music, dancing, and mime. The play is short but moves slowly in a highly ritualized style. The performers are all male and use traditional wooden masks. Noh gave rise to the more popular Kabuki theater.

Nok, civilization that existed in West Africa from c.500 B.C. to A.D. 200. Its artifacts were found in the village of Nok, Nigeria, in the valley between the Niger and Benue rivers. This farming and hunting society produced stone and iron tools, as well as highly civilized human and animal clay statues.

Noland, Kenneth (1924-), U.S. painter whose work features bands of color. With Morris Louis he developed a technique of employing thinned paints for staining and became one of the best-known color field painters. Typical of his work is *Par Transit* (1966).

Nolde, Emil (Emil Hansen; 1867-1956), German expressionist engraver and painter, notably of landscapes and figures, whose bold, visionary, and highly emotional style is typified in *The Prophet* (1912), *Life of Maria Aegyptiaca* (1912), and *Marsh Landscape* (1916).

Nomad, member of a population group that moves from place to place for subsistence. The nomadic way of life, though fast declining, is still found among some herders, such as the Arab Bedouins, and hunters, such as some groups of Australian aborigines. Some peoples, like the Lapps of northern Scandinavia, are semi-nomadic, residing in one place during the warmer months and moving to another during the winter.

Nome, city and port in western Alaska, on the south coast of the Seward Peninsula overlooking Norton Sound, an arm of the Bering Sea. The city is a commercial and distribution center. Its artificial harbor is open June through Oct. Nome became a boom town after the discovery of gold in 1898. It was incorporated as a city in 1901.
See also: Alaska.

Nonaggression pact, agreement between nations to reconcile differences without the use of force. After World War I, many nations signed nonaggression pacts, most of which were violated during World War II. The pacts became obsolete in 1945, when the United Nations became the forum for peaceful solutions to international conflicts. However, the UN has not resolved whether only military attacks are acts of aggression or if such acts include hostile economic policies and seditious propaganda as well.

Nonaligned nation *see:* Third World.

Nonconformists, in religion, those who will not conform to the doctrine or practice of an established church. Notable were Protestant dissenters from the Church of England, mainly Puritans, who were expelled by the Act of Uniformity (1662). They now include Baptists, Congregationalists, Methodists, Presbyterians, and Quakers.

Nonpartisan League, political association of U.S. farmers and farmworkers founded (1915) to respond to the power of banking, grain, and railroad bosses. The league campaigned for state-run elevators, mills, banks, and insurance. Strongest in the Dakotas and in Minnesota, the league dominated North Dakota's government from 1916 to 1921.
See also: Farmer-Labor Party.

Nonviolent resistance *see:* Gandhi, Mohandas; King, Martin Luther, Jr.

Nootka, Native Americans of Wakashan linguistic stock who lived on the west coast of Vancouver Island and in the northwestern part of Washington. Several families lived together in long wooden houses. The Nootka hunted whales in 60-ft (18-m) seagoing, cedar canoes, used dentalia (tooth) shells for money, and carved puppets and masks with moving parts.

Nopal *see:* Prickly pear.

NORAD, acronym for the North American Aerospace Defense Command, a large defense system set up in 1957 to protect the United States and Canada against air raids. Headquartered at Peterson Air Force Base, Colorado, NORAD is designed to track an air attack and counter with antiaircraft missiles and fighter planes. U.S. and Canadian generals are, traditionally, the first and second in command.

Nordenskjöld, Nils Adolf Erik (1832-1901), Finnish-born Swedish geologist, cartographer, and explorer of Spitsbergen and of Greenland, where he studied inland ice. He was the first to navigate the Northeast Passage (1878-79).
See also: Northeast Passage.

Nordhoff and Hall, U.S. writing team. **Charles Bernard Nordhoff** (1887-1947) and **James Norman Hall** (1887-1951) are best known for a trilogy of novels (*Mutiny on the Bounty*, 1932; *Men Against the Sea*, 1934; *Pitcairn's Island*, 1934) based on the 1789 mutiny against British naval officer William Bligh, who was infamous for his cruelty.

Norfolk (pop. 266,979), city-port of southeast Virginia, on the Elizabeth River and the southern side of Hampton Roads. An industrial and shipping center, Norfolk is the largest city in Virginia. Its port ships coal, chemicals, textiles, food products, and lumber. Norfolk Naval Base (commissioned 1817) is the largest in the United States. Norfolk is also a resort center, with many parks, gardens, and recreational facilities in or near the city. Cultural institutions include Norfolk State College, Old Dominion University, the Museum of Arts and Sciences, and Scope, a new $30 million cultural and convention center.
See also: Virginia.

Norfolk Island, Australian territory in the South Pacific, between New Caledonia and New Zealand. Tourism is the small island's chief industry. The first European on the island was James Cook (1774). It was used as a penal colony, 1788-1814 and 1825-1856. Descendants of the HMS *Bounty* mutineers relocated there from Pitcairn Island in 1856.

Norfolk Naval Base, Virginia, home to the Atlantic Fleet, the Fifth Naval District, NATO (North American Treaty Organization) Allied Command Atlantic, and the Armed Forces Staff College. Among the largest U.S. naval bases, within its 5,000 acres (2,000 hectares) more personnel are employed and more ships are stationed than in any other such base.
See also: Navy, United States.

Norfolk terrier, breed of hunting dog developed in Great Britain. One of the smallest terriers, it is distinguishable from the Norwich terrier only by its forward-bending ears. These affectionate, hardy, and active dogs usually weigh 10-12 lbs (4.5-5.4 kg), stand 10 in (25 cm) tall, and have short legs and a wiry coat.

Isamu Noguchi's The cry *(1959)*

Manuel Noriega

Noriega, Manuel (1938-), Panamanian general, leader of Panama 1985-88. He commanded the National Defense Forces to unseat civilian president Nicolas Ardito Barletta (1985). His 1987 indictment in the United States for violations of racketeering and drug laws was controversial; he had been operating with close ties with the U.S. Central Intelligence Agency (CIA) under William Casey since the 1970s, supplying them with information on the drug trade and other intelligence. The United States offered to drop charges if Noriega stepped down, but he refused (1988). He eluded capture during the 1989 invasion of Panama, but finally surrendered to the United States and was arraigned on charges of cocaine trafficking. Noriega asked for special protection as a prisoner of war, claiming his arrest was a result of the invasion of Panama.
See also: Panama.

Norman architecture, medieval style characterized by massive scale, 6-part vaulted ceilings, and rounded arches. Structures in this style were built in Norman-conquered lands (northern France, England, southern Italy, Sicily), 1066-1154. La Trinité church in France and Ely Cathedral in England are examples.

Norman Conquest, era of English history following the Battle of Hastings (1066), when William, Duke of Normandy, defeated and killed England's Saxon king, Harold. William claimed the English throne and quickly crushed resistance. By 1070 most Anglo-Saxon nobles had been either killed or subjugated, their land distributed to Normans in return for their agreement to supply the king with mounted soldiers. One of the results of the conquest was that French became the language of the royal court and had major and lasting influence on English.
See also: Hastings, Battle of; William I.

Normandy, region of northwestern France facing the English Channel, noted for dairy products, fruit, brandy, wheat, and flax. Le Havre, Dieppe, and Cherbourg are the main ports; Rouen and Caen are historic cathedral and university cities. Shipbuilding, steel, iron, and textiles are the main industries. Home of the Normans, Normandy definitively became part of France in 1450. In World War II it was the site of the D-Day landing on June 6, 1944.
See also: France.

Les Andelys in Normandy

Normandy, Duke of *see:* William I.

Normandy invasion *see:* World War II.

Normans, inhabitants of Normandy, a region and former province of northwestern France, along the English Channel. In 911 Rollo, leader of Viking raider-settlers, was recognized as duke of the area by King Charles III of France. The Normans (the name is derived from "Norsemen") adopted Christianity in the 10th century. In the 11th their duke, William, initiated the Norman Conquest of England. Normans were also active in the Crusades, in the reconquest of Spain, and in southern Italy and Sicily.

Norns, in Scandinavian mythology, 3 sisters who represent past (Urd or Wyrd), present (Verdandi), and future (Skuld). Like the Greek Fates, they spin and cut the thread of life. According to earlier beliefs, there was a lesser Norn that controlled the fate of each individual.

Norodom Sihanouk (1922-), leader of Cambodia (1941-70, 1975-76). Originally installed as king, he abdicated and became premier (1955) while his father ruled. On his father's death he again became head of state (1960). During the French war in Indochina and the Vietnam War he tried to keep Cambodia neutral. He was forcibly overthrown by right-wing military leader Lon Nol (1970). Fleeing to China, he formed a government in exile, and was returned to power when Lon Nol was deposed by the left-wing guerrilla forces known as the Khmer Rouge (1975). He resigned from power April 1976. During the 1980s he remained involved in resistance to the Vietnam-backed government, leading the rebel coalition.
See also: Kampuchea.

Norris, Frank (Benjamin Franklin Norris; 1870-1902), U.S. novelist and newspaper columnist. His best-known novels are *McTeague* (1899), a naturalist account of life in San Francisco slums, and his 2 exposés of the railroad and wheat industries, *The Octopus* (1901) and *The Pit* (1903). These were part of an uncompleted trilogy entitled *The Epic of Wheat.*

Norris, George William (1861-1944), U.S. legislator and reformer. As a liberal Republican U.S. Representative from Nebraska (1903-13), he led the fight to reform House rules and oust Speaker Joseph Cannon. As a U.S. Senator (1914-43), he opposed U.S. entry into World War I, wrote the 20th amendment to the Constitution (1932), helped set up the Tennessee Valley Authority (1933), and cosponsored (1932) the Norris-LaGuardia Act regulating labor disputes. He also supported farm relief and abolition of the poll tax.

Norris-LaGuardia Act, U.S. law (1932) that outlawed "yellow-dog" contracts in which workers promised not to join or encourage others to join labor unions. The act made such contracts unenforceable in federal court. One of the first U.S. laws protecting the right to join and organize unions, it was sponsored by Republicans Sen. George W. Norris (Nebr.) and Rep. Fiorello H. LaGuardia (N.Y.).

Norsemen *see:* Vikings.

Norse mythology *see:* Mythology.

North, Lord (1732-92), Frederick, 2nd Earl of Guilford, British prime minister (1770-82) under King George III. Lord North's colonial policies, such as the tea tax that inspired the Boston Tea Party, were contributing causes of the American Revolution.
See also: United Kingdom.

North, Oliver Laurence (1943-), U.S. Marine lieutenant colonel, involved in the Iran-contra affair of the 1980s. A National Security Council aide under President Ronald Reagan, he was involved in illegal clandestine operations to divert funds raised by arms sales to Iran to aid the right-wing contra rebels seeking to oust the left-wing government of Nicaragua. His activities were investigated by congressional committees, and he was finally convicted of criminal charges (1989), although he retained some support from those who believed him a hero. In 1990 he succeeded in having one of his 3 convictions overturned, and requested appeal of the remaining charges.
See also: Iran-Contra affair.

North America, third-largest continent, situated in the Western Hemisphere and bounded on the north by the Arctic Ocean, on the south by South America, on the west by the Pacific Ocean and Bering Sea, and on the east by the Atlantic Ocean. Besides the area covered by Canada and the United States, it includes Mexico and Central America, the islands of the Caribbean Sea, and Greenland.
Land and climate. North America, roughly triangular in shape, covers about 9,400,000 sq mi (24,346,000 sq km) with a coastline of about 190,000 mi (300,000 km). Hudson Bay in the north and the Gulf of Mexico in the south break into the triangle. The continent contains several regions of coastal and mountain ranges, and interior plains. The Great Divide formed by the crest of the Rocky Mountains creates 2 great groups of rivers. One group, including the Colorado, Columbia, Fraser, and Yukon rivers, flows west into the Pacific; the other, which includes the Mackenzie, St. Lawrence, Rio Grande, Missouri, and Mississippi rivers, drains into the Atlantic Ocean or the Gulf of Mexico.
North America's climate ranges from polar in the north to tropical in the south. Climatic differences account for a wide variety of vegetation on the continent, ranging from arctic tundra in Greenland,

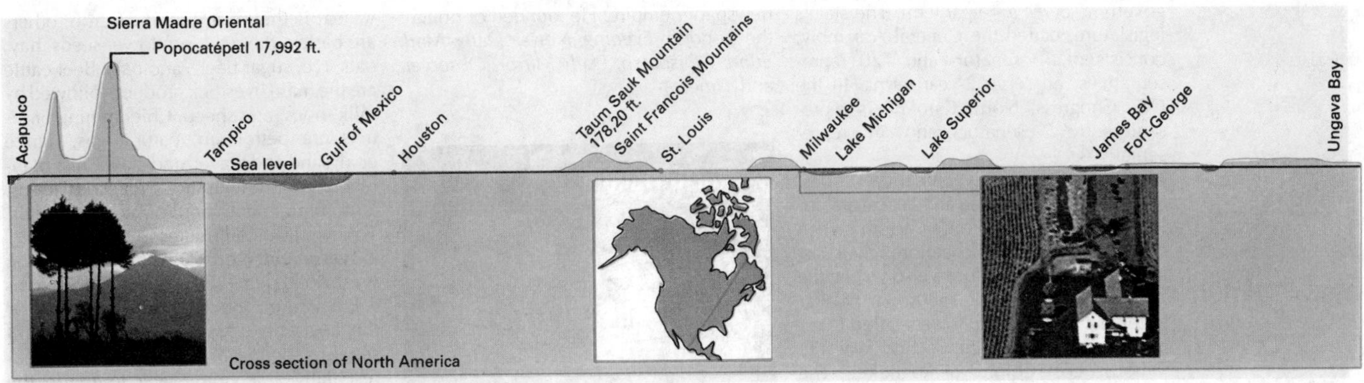

Cross section of North America

northern Canada, and much of Alaska, to desert scrub in the Mojave, Sonora, and other deserts of the southwestern United States and Mexico, to tropical rain forests in the lowlands of Central America. Coniferous forests cover much of Canada, the northern Pacific ranges, and the southeastern United States. In the Appalachians, mixed forests predominate, while deciduous forests are characteristic of the coastal plain and the eastern part of the Interior Plain. Grassland covers vast areas of the rest of it, including the Great Plains.

People. With a total population of about 427,000,000, North America ranks third among all the continents. The most heavily populated regions lie in the eastern United States, southeastern Canada, along the Pacific coasts of both these countries, and in Central America. Indians were North America's first inhabitants; today the largest concentration of Native Americans and mestizos (mixed Indian and Spanish ancestry) is found in mainland Central America. Africans and mulattos (mixed black and white descent), whose ancestors were brought from Africa as slaves, constitute a large proportion of the population of the Caribbean islands. In the United States, about 10% of the population are of African-American descent. Caucasians of European descent form the great majority of North Americans.

Early history. It is thought that about 25,000 years ago peoples from Mongolia moved out of Asia across a natural land bridge that then linked the Asian and North American continents, where the Bering Strait is today. These people are believed to be the ancestors of all Native North American groups. It is known that Eric the Red, a Norseman, reached Greenland from Iceland in about A.D. 980, and Leif Ericsson reputedly landed in Nova Scotia about 1000. The first permanent contacts made by Europeans came in the 15th century, when Christopher Columbus landed on Hispaniola (1492) in the Bahamas, and John and Sebastian Cabot explored the coast of Newfoundland (1497).

North American Aerospace Defense Command *see:* NORAD.

North Atlantic Treaty Organization (NATO), military defense organization of nations established in 1949 by Belgium, Canada, Denmark, France, Great Britain, Iceland, Italy, Luxembourg, the Netherlands, Norway, Portugal, and the United States. Greece and Turkey joined in 1951, West Germany in 1955 and Spain in 1982. Its purpose originally was to protect Western Europe against attack particularly by the Soviet Union and its East European satellites. The falling of the totalitarian regimes in many Eastern European countries and the Soviet policy of glasnost has greatly reduced the military threat to NATO.

North Carolina

Capital:	Raleigh
Statehood:	Nov. 21, 1789 (12th state)
Familiar names:	Tar Heel State, Old North State
Area:	52,669 sq mi (136,413 sq km); ranks 28th)
Population:	6,657,630 (1990; ranks 10th)
Elevation:	Highest—6,684 (2,037 m), Mt. Mitchell; Lowest—sea level, along the Atlantic coast
Motto:	*Esse Quam Videri* (To Be, Rather Than to Seem)
State flower:	Flowering dogwood
State bird:	Cardinal
State tree:	Pine
State song:	"The Old North State"

North Carolina, state in the southeastern United States; bordered by Virginia to the north, the Atlantic Ocean to the east, South Carolina and Georgia to the south; and Tennessee to the west.

Land and climate. North Carolina has 3 main land regions. The eastern Atlantic coastal plain consists of low-lying, swampy marshland covered with trees and shallow lakes and rivers that extends into broad, grassy plains called savannas. The central Piedmont plateau is an area of rolling hills and numerous rivers. The western mountain region includes the Blue Ridge mountain range, as well as other ranges in the Appalachian system. Most of North Carolina's rivers rise in the Piedmont or mountain regions and flow southeast. Above the fall line are many waterfalls and rapids. The Roanoke, Neuse, and Tar are the major rivers. The only natural lakes lie on the coastal plain; the others are formed by dammed rivers. Forests cover about two-thirds of the state. North Carolina's climate is mild, ranging from the cool mountain regions to the subtropical temperatures of the southeast. Principal cities are Charlotte, Greensboro, and Raleigh.

Economy. North Carolina's leading industries are manufacturing, agriculture, and tourism. Chief manufactured goods are textiles, tobacco products, chemicals, electrical and electronic equipment, machinery, food products, and furniture. Tobacco is the most important agricultural product; others are corn, soybeans, peanuts, sweet potatoes, feed grains, vegetables, and fruits. Chief livestock products are broilers (chickens), hogs, and turkeys. The chief mineral products are crushed stone (particularly limestone), clay, sand and gravel, and lithium compounds.

Government. North Carolina's present constitution was adopted in 1971. The

The NATO emblem

governor serves a 4-year term. The state's legislature, called the General Assembly, consists of 50 senators and 120 representatives; all serve 2-year terms. In the U.S. Congress, North Carolina is represented by 2 senators and 11 representatives.
History. Several Native American tribes, including the Cherokee and Tuscarora, inhabited what is now North Carolina when Giovanni da Verrazano explored the coast in 1524. Spanish explorers also visited the region. Twice in the 1580s, Sir Walter Raleigh and English followers failed to establish settlements; the second was the famous "Lost Colony of Roanoke." The next white settlers came in the mid-1600s, from Virginia. In 1712, North Carolina became a separate British colony, one of the original 13. White settlers and Tuscarora Native Americans clashed in the Tuscarora War (1711-13), while settlers on the coast faced raids by pirates. North Carolina supported the colonists cause during the American Revolution. During the mid-1800s national debate over slavery, North Carolina tried to preserve the Union, but seceded when the Civil War broke out in 1861 and was the scene of several battles. After the war, federal troops oversaw the state's government until 1868, when it rejoined the Union. By World War II, North Carolina had become a leading industrial state. In 1960, a lunch counter sit-in staged by black college students in Greensboro sparked a new phase in the U.S. civil-rights movement. Today, the state's tobacco industry has been threatened by evidence of the dangers of smoking. North Carolina is working to improve its public schools, health-care and other social services, highways, and urban areas.

North Cascades National Park, park located in the Cascade Range of northwestern Washington, covering 504,781 acres (370,250 hectares). The alpine scenery includes glaciers, icefalls, jagged mountain ridges, and cedar and fir forests. The park was established in 1968.
See also: National Parks table.

Northcliffe, Viscount (1865-1922), publisher who created modern British journalism. On a base of popular journals, starting with the weekly *Answers to Correspondents* (1888), he built the world's biggest newspaper empire. He founded or bought the London *Evening News, Daily Mail, Sunday Dispatch, Daily Mirror, Observer,* and *Times.*

The plains of North Dakota

North Dakota

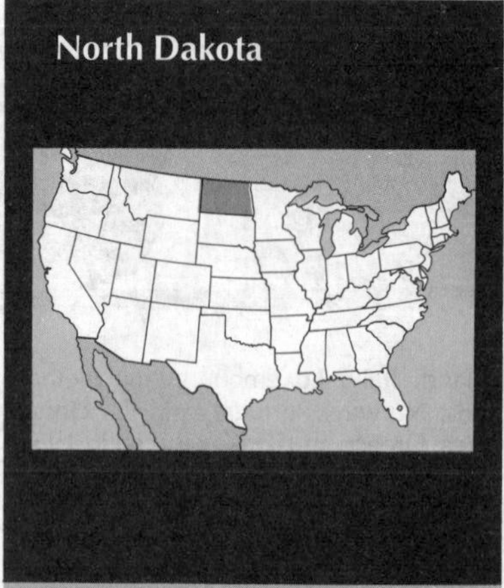

Capital:	Bismarck
Statehood:	Nov. 2, 1889 (39th state)
Familiar names:	Flickertail State, Peace Garden State, Sioux State
Area:	70,702 sq mi (183,119 sq km); ranks 17th
Population:	641,364 (1990); ranks 47th
Elevation:	Highest—3,506 ft (1,069 m), White Butte; Lowest—750 ft (229 m), along the Red River in Pembina County
Motto:	Liberty and Union, Now and Forever, One and Inseperable
Flower:	Wild prairie rose
Bird:	Western meadowlark
Tree:	American elm
Song:	"North Dakota Hymn"

North Dakota, midwestern state in north-central United States; bordered by Canada to the north, the Red River (with Minnesota on the other side) to the east, South Dakota to the south, and Montana to the west.
Land and climate. North America's geographic center is in North Dakota, near Rugby. North Dakota has three main land regions. The fertile Red River Valley, along the eastern border, has the state's lowest, flattest terrain. The land rises into the Drift Prairie (or Drift Plain), a rolling, fertile plateau. The Great Plains (also called the Missouri Plateau) in western and south-central North Dakota, has the state's highest land. This region includes the Missouri Breaks, an area of rugged valleys and steep hills along the Missouri River, and the Badlands, an area of buttes and mesas with exposed layers of vividly colored clays. North Dakota's major rivers are the Missouri River and the Red River, and their tributaries. Devils Lake is the largest natural lake; there are many small lakes. Forests cover about one percent of the state. North Dakota has moderate summers and severe winters. Principal cities are Fargo, Bismarck, and Grand Forks.
Economy. Agriculture and mining are the mainstays of North Dakota's economy. Wheat is the most important crop; others are barley, flaxseed, sunflower seeds, hay, oats, rye, sugar beets, and oats. Beef cattle are the main livestock product, followed by milk, hogs, and sheep. Chief mining products are petroleum, natural gas, lignite coal, sand and gravel, and clay. Chief manufactured products are processed foods, farm equipment, and printed materials. Tourism also contributes to the economy.
Government. North Dakota's constitution was adopted in 1889. The governor serves a 4-year term. The state's legislature, called the Legislative Assembly, consists of 53 senators serving 4-year terms and 106 representatives serving 2-year terms. In the U.S. Congress, North Dakota is represented by 2 senators and 1 representative.
History. Until they gained statehood in 1889, North Dakota shared much of its history with South Dakota. A number of Indian tribes—including the Lakota (or Dakota) Sioux, Mandan, Assiniboine, and Cheyenne—lived in the area before the first Europeans, French explorers, arrived about 1738. The area had already been claimed for France by explorer La Salle in 1682. France ceded it to Spain, 1762-1800, then sold it to the United States under the 1803 Louisiana Purchase. The Lewis and Clark expedition explored North Dakota in 1804-6; the first white settlers arrived in 1812.
The United States gained northeastern North Dakota from Britain in 1818; the Dakota Territory was formed in 1861. The land was opened to homesteaders in 1863, but attacks by the Sioux, who were being displaced, slowed white settlement until the U.S. Army forced Sitting Bull to surrender in 1881. That, plus the spread of railroads, brought rapid settlement—mostly by farmers—and economic growth. North Dakota became the 39th state in 1889. The Depression of the 1930s hit farmers hard, but World War II and the 1951 discovery of oil brought recovery. In 1957, the Economic Development Commission was established to attract new industries. In recent years, North Dakota's industrial growth has been slowed by decreases in oil prices as well as environmental concerns.

Northeast Passage, sea route linking the Atlantic and Pacific oceans. It passes north of the Eurasian mainland along the Arctic coast of Norway and the USSR. Adolf Nordenskjöld, the Swedish explorer, was the first to sail its length (1878-79), although its exploration dates from the 16th century. Area explorers included William Barents, Henry Hudson, James Cook, and Vitus Bering.
See also: Nordenskjöld, Nils Adolf Erik.

Northern harrier, or marsh hawk (*Circus cyaneus*), North American bird of prey. It belongs to the Old World vulture family, Accipitridae. Males are pale gray with a wingspan up to 45 in (114 cm) and a body 19 in (48 cm) long. Females are streaked brown; their bodies are slightly longer than the males'. Both have a white patch above the tail. They feed on snakes and fowl.

Northern Ireland, one of the four countries that make up the United Kingdom of Great Britain, the others being England, Wales, and Scotland. It was established by the Government of Ireland Act of 1920, which separated Northern Ireland from the independent Republic of Ireland. It comprises six of the nine counties that made up the ancient province of Ulster on the northeastern corner of the island of Ireland, with the Republic occupying the rest. Its capital is Belfast.
Land and people. Northern Ireland occupies about a sixth of the entire island. It is bordered by the Republic on the south and west, and it is separated from Scotland to the northeast by the North Channel and from England to the southeast by the Irish Sea. The land itself is made up of low mountains and rolling plains, with few natural resources. About two-thirds of the people of Northern Ireland are descended from English and Scottish Protestants, with the remaining third of Irish Catholic descent. The official language is English, and all the people speak it although Gaelic (the native Irish language) is still taught in Catholic schools.
Economy. About three-fourths of the people in Northern Ireland are employed in service industries. The two other most important industries are farming and manufacturing, with most of the heavy industry situated around Belfast, one of the chief ports of the British Isles. The major manufactured product is Irish linen, which is known throughout the world for its fine quality. Other industries include shipbuilding, and aircraft manufacturing. Agricultural products include: dairy products, cattle, hogs, eggs, and chickens. Coal for industry is imported, but large peat deposits provide fuel for cooking and heating.
History. English rule of parts of Ireland goes back to the 12th century, but it was only in 1541 that King Henry VIII of England declared himself king of Ireland. The Reformation turned England from a Catholic country to a Protestant one, but the change had little effect on the Irish people, who remained Catholic. During the 1600s, the Irish staged a number of rebellions against English rule, but they were suppressed. In 1603, a major rebellion in Ulster was put down, and the defeated Irish chieftains fled. The British Crown confiscated much of the land of the beaten rebels and gave it to English and Scottish settlers. This gave Ulster a distinctly Protestant character as compared with the rest of the country, which remained steadfastly Catholic. When an attempt to restore Catholic power in Ulster in 1690 was defeated by William of Orange in the Battle of the Boyne, Protestants were assured of their domination of Irish government throughout the island. In 1801, the Act of Union abolished the Irish parliament and made Ireland part of Great Britain. In the late 19th century, the British Liberal Party, led by William Gladstone, presented a plan for *home rule* for Ireland, which would have kept Ireland as part of Great Britain but would have allowed it to have its own national parliament for domestic affairs. The Ulster Protestants feared that an all-Ireland parliament would be dominated by the more numerous Catholics of the south, and they formed the Unionist Party to oppose home rule. The plan was defeated, and succeeding schemes to effect some sort of home rule only widened the rift between Ulster and the rest of the country. In 1919, after World War I, Irish members of the British Parliament met in Dublin and declared Irish independence from England. Civil war broke out. In 1920 the British Parliament passed the Government of Ireland Act, which set up separate parliaments for the two parts of Ireland. The northern Ulster Protestants accepted the division, and formed the separate state of Northern Ireland, made up of its present six counties. The southern Catholics refused to recognize the act and pressed for independence. In 1921, leaders of the south concluded a treaty with Britain that created the Irish Free State (made up of 23 southern counties and 3 counties of Ulster). In 1949, this became the Republic of Ireland. Agitation by Irish nationalists in the south, and especially by the Catholics living in Protestant-dominated Northern Ireland, for an end to the separation continues to this day. The Irish Republican Army (IRA), a militant nationalist group, still continues to carry out terrorist bombings and assaults on British troops both in Northern Ireland and in England. Britain took over direct rule of Northern Ireland in 1972 because of continuing violence there. Despite numerous attempts to arrive at a settlement agreeable to both Catholics and Protestants, the problem of separation remains, and sporadic violence on the part of militant nationalists against an English-affiliated Northern Ireland continues.
See also: United Kingdom.

Northern lights *see:* Aurora.

Northern Mariana Islands, commonwealth of the United States, comprising 16 islands in the western Pacific Ocean. Saipan is the capital.
Land and climate. Of these volcanic and coral islands, only 6 are inhabited, with more than 88% of the population living on Saipan, the largest island, which is followed in size by Rota and Tinian. The total area is 183 sq mi (475 sq km). The tropical climate has temperatures 70°-90°F (20°-30°C) and an average rainfall of about 70 in (178 cm). Although Guam is geographically part of the Marianas, it has long been administered separately and is not considered part of the group.
People. About 75% of the people are descended from the Chamorro, the indigenous Micronesian group of the Marianas; most of the others are Caroline Islanders (est. pop. 21,800). Roman Catholicism predominates.
Economy. The U.S. government is the largest employer, as Saipan continues to serve as the administrative center of the Trust Territory of the Pacific Islands, despite the Northern Marianas' separate status. The leading crops include coconuts, sugar, coffee, taro, breadfruit, and yams; cattle raising is increasingly important. Tourism is also a leading source of income.
History. After Spain assumed control of the Marianas in 1565, all the Chamorros were moved to Guam; the other islands remained uninhabited until some resettlement began during the late 17th century. In 1898 control of Guam passed to the United States. The other Marianas were sold to Germany (1899), then occupied in 1914 by Japan, which developed commercial sugar plantations. U.S. forces captured the islands in 1944 after heavy fighting, and they subsequently became part of the U.S. Trust Territory of the Pacific Islands. Northern Mariana voters approved separate status as a commonwealth in 1975, which became effective in 1978.

Northern pike *see:* Pike.

Northern Rhodesia *see:* Zambia.

Northern Territory, north-central region of Australia. Controlled first by New South Wales and then South Australia, it was granted self-government in 1978. Nearly a quarter of the territory is reservation land, home of the Aborigines, Australia's native people. Darwin, on the coast, is the capital and largest city. Numerous cattle and sheep ranches are in the dry interior. Mining, tourism, and pearling are important industries.
See also: Australia.

Northfield (pop. 12,562), city in southeastern Minnesota, on the Cannon River, 40 mi (64 km) south of St. Paul. It was founded by John W. North in 1855. The city annually celebrates the heroism of citizens who thwarted a Jesse James bank robbery. Carleton and St. Olaf colleges were established here in the 19th century. Local industries produce cereal and machinery.
See also: Minnesota.

North Island *see:* New Zealand.

North Korea *see:* Korea.

North magnetic pole *see:* North Pole.

Northmen *see:* Vikings.

North Pacific Current, ocean current fed by the Japan Current, heading east from the region of Japan to the U.S. West Coast, where it becomes the Alaska Current and California Current.

North Platte (pop. 24,509), city in west-central Nebraska, where the North and South Platte rivers join. Founded in 1866, it became the division headquarters of the Union Pacific Railroad and is a major economic center for the region's chief industries, farming and cattle raising. Home to the University of Nebraska's agricultural experiment station, as well as to Buffalo Bill Ranch State Historical Park, the city hosts an annual June rodeo.
See also: Nebraska.

Illustration from a pack of cigarettes depicting Robert Peary's ship *Diana*, in 1909

North Pole, northernmost point of the earth's axis, located at lat. 90°N, long. 0°, some 466 mi (750 km) north of Greenland. The North Pole is a geographical designation that does not coincide with the North Magnetic Pole. The Pole lies roughly in the center of the Arctic Ocean, which is permanently covered with ice. The pole was first reached by Robert E. Peary in 1909.
See also: Peary, Robert Edwin.

Northrop, John Howard (1891-1987), U.S. biochemist who received the 1946 Nobel Prize for chemistry, with James B. Somner and Wendell M. Stanley, for the crystallization of several pure enzymes (proteins that assist the body's chemical reactions). Professor of bacteriology at the University of California at Berkeley during the 1950s, he was a member of the Rockefeller Institute for Medical Research (now Rockefeller University), 1925-87. *Crystalline Enzymes* (1939), written with M. Kunitz and R. M. Herriot, is his most important book.
See also: Enzyme.

North Sea oil platform preparing for installation

North Sea, arm of the Atlantic Ocean lying between Great Britain, Scandinavia, and northwest Europe. Rich in fish, gas, and oil, the sea covers 222,125 sq mi (575,304 sq km), and has an average depth of 300 ft (91 m), falling to 2,400 ft (732 m) off Norway. Major gas and oil deposits have been found off the Dutch, Norwegian, and Scottish coasts.

North Star, also called Polaris, Cepheid variable star (Alpha Ursae Minoris) nearest the north celestial pole. Also known as the Polestar, it has been used in navigation for centuries.
See also: Star.

Northumbria, Anglo-Saxon kingdom of the 7th-10th centuries, extending from the Mersey and Humber rivers in the south to the Firth of Forth in the north. It became the cultural center of England due to the civilizing work of monks. After Danes overran the kingdom, the north remnant became subject to Wessex.

North Vietnam *see:* Vietnam.

North West Company, fur-trading company in Canada, 1783-1821. Nor'Westers (as members were called) such as Alexander Mackenzie and David Thompson were important in the exploration of Canada as far north and west as the Arctic and Pacific oceans. The company was in competition with the Pacific Fur Company and particularly (and sometimes violently) with the Hudson's Bay Company, with which it was forced to merge in 1821.

Northwest Ordinance, measure adopted by the Congress of Confederation in 1787 that established the government of the Northwest Territory and provided a form through which territories could become states. Congress appointed a territorial governor, a secretary, and 3 judges, and the ordinance said that once the territory had a voting population of 5,000, it could elect a legislature and send a nonvoting representative to Congress. When the population reached 60,000, the territory could seek full admission to the Union.

Northwest Passage, inland water routes along the north coast of North America linking the Atlantic and Pacific Oceans. John Cabot explored the coast around Newfoundland in 1497, thinking it was China; Henry Hudson sailed to Hudson Bay and beyond (1609-11); William Baffin and Robert Bylot sailed up Davis Strait an found a passage between Baffin Island and Greenland (1616). Explorations opened up important new lands, but not until Robert McClure's expedition of 1850-54 was the existence of a passage weaving among the Arctic islands proved. The first complete journey was made when Roald Amundsen sailed west from Baffin Bay through Lancaster Sound (1903-06). The first west-to-east journey was accoplished by a ship of the Royal Canadian Mounted Police, *St. Roch*, in 1942.

Northwest Territories, federally administered region of Canada comprising that part of the mainland north of latitude 60°N lying between the Yukon Territory on the west and Hudson Bay on the east. The islands in Hudson Bay, James Bay, and Hudson Strait are included, as are all islands north of the mainland. The territories are divided into 3 districts: Keewatin on the mainland in the east, Mackenzie on the mainland to the west, and Franklin in the north, including all the Arctic islands. About half the region lies north of the Arctic Circle. Two-thirds of the mainland is covered by the Mackenzie River and its tributaries and by lakes like the Great Bear and Great Slave. The Mackenzie Mountains to the west rise to 9,000 ft (2,743 m). More than 60% of the population is composed of Inuit (Eskimo) and Native Americans. The Mackenzie District is the most developed area and has the largest towns: Yellowknife (the capital), Fort Smith, and Inuvik. The principal industries are mining, fishing, and trapping. The territory produce all of Canada's tungsten, 44% of its lead, 26% of its zinc, 20% of its silver, and 13% of its gold. Uranium exploration is continuing. There has also been oil and gas exploration. The region was part of a larger area sold to Canada in 1870 by the Hudson's Bay Company. The Territories' boundaries were established in 1912.
See also: Canada.

Northwest Territory, region between the Ohio and Mississippi rivers, extending north around the Great Lakes. It was the first national territory of the United States, eventually forming Ohio, Indiana, Illinois, Michigan, Wisconsin, and part of Minnesota. Won by Britain (1763) from the French, who had explored it in the 1600s, it was ceded to the United States by the Treaty of Paris (1783). The Ordinance of 1787, or the Northwest Ordinance, provided the region with a governmental system that would eventually allow the different territories to become states.

North Yemen *see:* Yemen.

Norwalk (pop. 77,767), city in southwestern Connecticut, at the mouth of the Norwalk River, on Long Island Sound. On land purchased from the Norwalk tribe, the town was settled by colonists in 1649. An industrial city, it produces textiles, electronic equipment, and hardware. Norwalk Community and Norwalk State Technical colleges were established here in 1961.

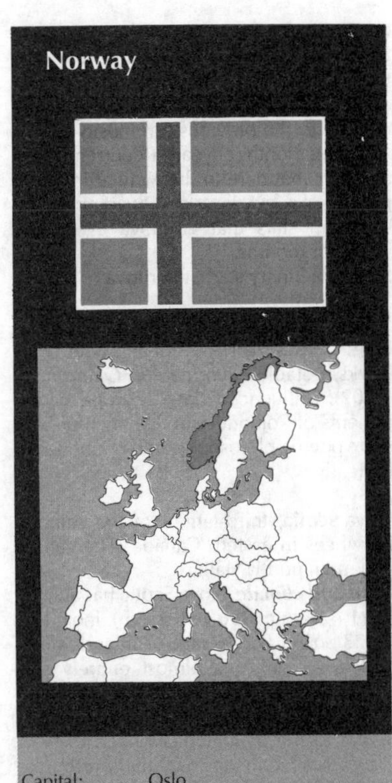

Capital:	Oslo
Area:	125,050 sq mi (323,878 sq km)
Population:	4,228,000
Form:	constitutional monarchy
Independent:	1905
GNP:	U.S. $84,165,000,000
Per capita:	U.S. $20,020

Norway, kingdom of northern Europe, occupying the smaller western portion of the Scandinavian peninsula. It is sometimes called the "Land of the Midnight Sun" since about one-third of it lies north of the Arctic Circle, where from mid-May into July there is continuous daylight; conversely, for part of the winter only twilight occurs at midday. The capital is Oslo.

Land and climate. Covering 125,181 sq mi (326,219 sq km), Norway is slightly larger than New Mexico. It is bordered by the USSR, Finland, and the Barents Sea in the north, Sweden in the east, the Skagerrak arm of the North Sea in the south, and the Atlantic Ocean in the west. Thousands of islands dot the coast, and the Norwegian territory also includes the Svalbard island group 300 mi (483 km) north of the mainland in the Arctic Ocean; also Jan Mayen, 500 mi (805 km) northeast, and Bouvet Island, Queen Maud Land, and Peter I Island in Antarctica.

The extremely fragmented and indented coastline is perhaps Norway's most spectacular feature. Glaciers of the past dug deep valleys as they moved down mountains to the sea. When it flooded these depressions, it created the long indentions called fjords or fiords, which are usually ice-free in winter. Mountains cover almost the entire length of Norway, over half the country. The highest peak (and of Scandinavia) is Galdhpiggen (8,097 ft/2,468 km); west of it lies the largest icecap in mainland Europe, the Jostedalsbreen. Most of Norway's rivers are short and swift, used for logging and dams but with rapids preventing navigation. The longest is the Glomma, flowing 400 mi (644 km) into the Skagerrak. Of the many glacier-formed lakes, the largest is Mjösa (140 sq mi/363 sq km), north of Oslo.

Despite its Arctic proximity, Norway has a relatively mild climate because of its maritime situation and the prevailing on-shore winds, which bring heavy rainfalls. Summers are cool, winters usually below freezing, although temperatures inland and in the mountains are much colder.

People. Scandinavians comprise most of the population, although there are some Lapps and Finns in the north. Most Norwegians live in urban areas. The largest cities are Oslo and Bergen, in the heavily populated south, and Trondheim in the north. There are 2 official Norwegian languages, Nynorsk and Bokmål, although Lapps speak Ugro-Finnic. Oslo and Bergen have universities. The state religion is Evangelical Lutheran.

Economy. Abundant hydroelectric power supports industrialization, giving the Norwegians one of the world's highest living standards. Petroleum output from oil and mineral deposits under the continental shelf provides revenue. Rich coal deposits are mined in Spitsbergen, largest of the Svalbard islands. Although less than 3% of Norway's land is arable, grains, potatoes, fruits, sheep, and livestock are grown. Whaling and fishing, particularly of cod, mackerel, and herring, is a leading industry, as is lumbering, although only 25% of the land is forested. Since World War II, the thriving economy has been developed through restricting imports and promoting industrialization. The chief industries are pulp and paper manufactures, fish canning, electrochemicals, electrometellurgicals, oil and gas refining, and shipbuilding; Norway has one of the world's largest merchant fleets. Thousands of miles of roads and railways plus some 50 airports provide transportation.

History. For 2 centuries after A.D. 800, Vikings from Norway, the Norsemen, raided and occupied European coastal towns, notably Normandy, as well as islands off Scotland and Canada, and parts of England, Iceland, and Ireland. Later, civil wars preoccupied the country, though it enjoyed prosperity too, before it was united with Denmark (1397-1814), then Sweden. In 1905 Norway became a constitutional monarchy under Haakon VII, a Danish prince. Mass emigrations to the United States, arctic explorations, and the socialized government's social welfare legislation have predominated since. Germany occupied Norway throughout World War II. It is a member of NATO and the European Free Trade Association but, in a 1972 referendum, rejected membership in the Common Market. The country has continued to debate since then whether to join the Common Market, and the debate took a sharp turn in 1990 when the Progress Party came out in favor of membership.

Town hall (1950) of Oslo

Norwegian, language of Norway, developed from the Norse and influenced by union with Denmark (1397-1814). There are 2 official versions: *Nynorsk* or *Landsmäl*, based on native dialects, and *Bokmäl* or *Riksmäl*, a Dano-Norwegian used by city dwellers, writers, and the press. Differences between them are diminishing.

Norwegian elkhound, breed of dog originally used by Norwegian hunters and shepherds in the 4000s B.C. At about 50 lb (23 kg) with a thick gray coat, it is a high-spirited dog known for its ability to smell prey from as far away as 3 mi (5 km). It was used to hunt elk, mountain lion, lynx, and game birds.

Norwegian elkhound

Norwich terrier, hunting dog first bred in England around 1880. Characterized as rugged, alert, energetic, and affectionate, it has a stocky build, a thick wiry coat, and stands about 10 in (25 cm) high at the shoulder. It is often used in England in fox hunting and in the United States to hunt rabbits and other small animals.

Nose, organ of breathing and smell, located in the middle of the face. The nose consists of bone and cartilage extension with 2 external openings, or nostrils. These pass into the nasal cavities, which are separated from each other by a septum and contain turbinates that increase the mucous membrane surface and direct the air flow. The chemoreceptors for smell lie mainly in the roof of the nasal cavities, but fine nerve fibers throughout the nose contribute both to tactile sensation and smell.

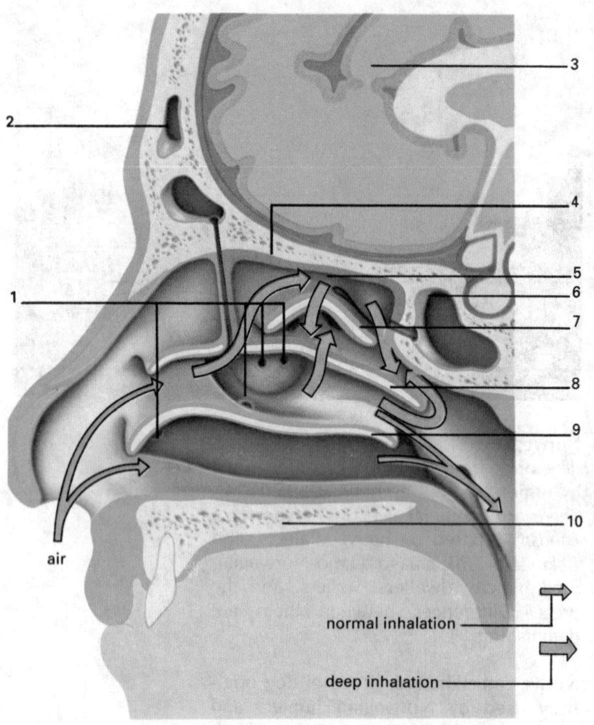

Profile of the human nose. On the side wall of the nasal cavity are three bony protrusions, the nasal conchae. Above the superior nasal concha is situated the nasal mucous membrane, with the sense organ cells of smell. The air reaches this area especially during deep inhalation. The bones of the skull around the nose hold several sinus paranasales.

1. nasal cavity
2. frontal sinus
3. brain
4. ethmoid bone
5. nasal mucous membrane
6. sphenoidal sinus
7. superior nasal concha
8. middle nasal concha
9. inferior nasal concha
10. palate

Nostradamus (Michel de Nostredame; 1503-66), French astrologer, famed for his prophecies published in verse, *Centuries* (1555). He was court physician to Charles IX, and his prediction of Henry II's death 4 years ahead made his name, though his prophecies were generally vague.
See also: Astrology.

Notary public, state-appointed official who certifies the authenticity of documents and takes oaths. Birth certificates, marriage licenses, and property deeds require notarizing, to avoid the possibility of forging. A notary affixes a seal to a document when he or she is certain that the person who signed it is known to him or her and that the signature is genuine. In most states anyone can become a notary with proof of good character, legal age, and residence in the area in which he or she wishes to be appointed.

Notation, in music, method of writing down notes to be read for study or performance. The method was formalized between the 10th and 18th centuries into a system, now in general use, of stave notation. This consists of five horizontal lines, or staves, as the framework on which any of 8 notes can be written: A, B, C, D, E, F, G (in ascending or descending order of pitch), then to A again an octave higher or lower, and so forth. Each note's placement on or between the lines depends on its pitch: if low, in the bass clef of staves; if higher, in the treble clef. A middle, or alto, clef is sometimes used.
The key in which the music is to be performed is indicated by symbols for sharps and flats on the staves next to the clef sign at the beginning of the score. Sometimes such a symbol is placed against a single note on a line to indicate that its pitch is to be momentarily sharped or flatted. The length the notes are to be held, relative to each other, is shown by the form they are notated in. Commonly, there are 7 ways the notes can be formed, from the longest held to the shortest. The beat of the music is shown by dividing the staves with vertical lines into bars and marking at the outset how many beats there are to each bar. This establishes rhythm. Other notations are the *tonic sol-fa*, in which notes are related to each other, not to the established pitch of the written stave; and *tablature*, in which a diagram indicates where to place the fingers on various instruments to obtain notes. For electronic music, new signs are being devised.

Note, or promissary note, written record in which an individual agrees to pay a designated sum of money to a specified individual. Like bank checks, notes are negotiable and can be transferred from one holder to another.

Notre Dame, Cathedral of cathedral church of Paris, on the Île de la Cité in the Seine River. Begun in 1163, it was consecrated in 1183. The nave was completed in 1196. In 1230 flying buttresses were added and the nave was rebuilt. Chapels were later added, and the cathedral was not complete until 1313. It is one of the finest examples of early Gothic architecture, especially for the rose window of the west facade and the sculptured portals. Some restoration was necessary after the French Revolution.

Nottingham (pop. 279,400), city in England, administrative seat of Nottinghamshire. Located on the River Trent, Nottingham is a transportation center and industrial city known for its manufacture of tobacco, pharmaceuticals, hose, lace, and bicycles. The city is noted for its medieval architecture and for its proximity to Sherwood Forest, the legendary home of Robin Hood.

Nouakchott (pop. 450,000), the capital of Mauritania and an important port city on the Altantic coast of West Africa. Once a small fishing village, it became the capital when Mauritania won independence from France in 1957. Severe droughts in rural areas have driven large numbers of people into the city, contributing to serious problems of overcrowding. Its industries include handicrafts, chemical products, and soft drinks.
See also: Mauritania.

Nova, relatively small, very hot variable star that suddenly (usually within a few days) increases up to thousands of times in brightness. It is thought that the increase in brightness is caused by violent explosions that eject some of the star's mass, which escapes the star's gravitational field. The decline to the previous luminosity generally takes months or years. Recurrent novas are stars that flare in this way at irregular periods of a few decades. Dwarf novas are subdwarf stars that go nova every few weeks or months.
See also: Binary star; Supernova.

Novalis (Friedrich Leopold von Hardenberg; 1772-1801), German poet. His works, notably *Heinrich von Offerdingen* (1802), influenced later European exponents of Romanticism. He attempted to unite poetry, philosophy, and science allegorically.

Nova Scotia, third-largest of the Atlantic Provinces in eastern Canada. The capital and main port is Halifax.
Land and climate. Nova Scotia has an area of 21,425 sq mi (56,491 sq km), including 1,023 sq mi (1,646 km) of inland water, and is a peninsula almost entirely surrounded by the sea. Only the narrow land link of the Chignecto Isthmus joins Nova Scotia to the mainland province of New Brunswick, Canada. On the north, the Northumberland Strait divides Nova Scotia from Prince Edward Island in the Gulf of St. Lawrence. Also in the north, the narrow Strait of Canso, crossed by a road and railway causeway, separates Cape Breton Island from Nova Scotia. The Atlantic Ocean bounds Nova Scotia's coasts east and south, the location of Sable Island, called "the graveyard of the Atlantic" owing to numerous ship disasters. On the west coast is the Bay of Fundy, with its great range of tides; on the bay's opposite shore are Maine and New Brunswick. No part of Nova Scotia is more than 50 mi (80.4 km) from the sea, with its rich cod, lobster, and haddock fisheries on the continental shelf or in the Atlantic's Grand Banks.
A distinctive feature of Nova Scotia's landscape is the Atlantic Upland, 5 detached hilly areas of woodlands. More than three-fourths of the province is covered by forests of white pine, spruce, balsam, birch, and maple. The Annapolis Valley and the Cornwallis region support abundant apple orchards. Hay, oats, barley, wheat, and vegetables are grown in fertile meadowlands, site also of dairy farms. Lowlands reclaimed from the bay contain mineral resources. Of Nova Scotia's many rivers, the longest are the Mersey and St. Mary's, both 72 mi (116 km). The province's largest lake is the salt-water Bras d'Or (230 sq mi/370 sq km) on Cape Breton Island.
The cold Labrador Current particularly affects the Atlantic coast. At Halifax, temperatures average 24°F (–1°C) in January and 65°F (20°C) in July. Average precipitation ranges from about 55 in (127 cm) on the ocean coast to about 40 in (102 cm) on the bay coast.
People. Of the total population, most Nova Scotians are of British or French ancestry; some 3,000 are Micmac Native Americans.

Economy. About one-third of Canada's coal supply is mined underwater in northern Nova Scotia. Other mineral resources include gypsum, zinc, barite, salt, and natural gas. Petroleum refining, food and beverage processing, transportation-equipment manufacturing, and pulp and paper production are leading industries. Food, fish, and wood products are leading exports. About half the province's electric power is provided by hydroelectric plants on the Mersey and other rivers. Much tourism takes advantage of the good transportation system.
History. The region that is now New Brunswick and Nova Scotia was the home of the Micmac Native Americans before European exploration. The Nova Scotia peninsula is probably Lief Ericsson's Vinland (c. 1000). In 1497 John Cabot landed on Cape Breton Island, and soon Basque fishermen as well. The entire region became the New France province of Acadia after sieur de Monts's Port Royal (now Annapolis Royal) trading settlement was moved from the mainland to the peninsula's bay shore in 1605. England colonized the peninsula in 1621 and renamed it Nova Scotia (Latin, "New Scotland") after early Scots settlers. Thereafter, territorial warfare ensued between France and England. The Treaty of Utrecht (1713) confirmed British possession, giving Cape Breton and Prince Edward islands to the French. Britain acquired the rest of Acadia in 1717. Tragically, in 1755, it deported Nova Scotia's French settlers, the Acadians. During the Seven Years' War, in 1758, Nova Scotia took Cape Breton Island. That year also the British colonists were granted an elected representative assembly. Nova Scotia annexed (1763) Prince Edward Island, which became a separate colony in 1769. After the American Revolution, thousands of New Englanders who were British Loyalists moved into the region, where they were joined later, in Nova Scotia, by Irish, Germans, and more Scots. In 1784, the region's mainland part separated to become the New Brunswick colony. Under John Howe's leadership, Nova Scotia became the first Canadian colony to achieve government highly responsible to the people (1848). In 1867, it confederated with Quebec, Ontario, and New Brunswick to form the Dominion of Canada. Thereafter, Nova Scotia had Canada's first newspaper, first printing press, and first university.

Novaya Zemlya, group of 2 large islands and several smaller ones in the USSR, in the Arctic Ocean between the Barents Sea on the west and the Kara Sea on the east. Total area is 36,000 sq mi (93,600 sq km). The 2 large islands are separated by a narrow strait, the Matochkin Shar. Used as a Soviet nuclear testing site, the islands have a small native population that fishes and hunts in the southern tundra areas.

Novel, work of prose fiction longer than the short story and novella. Although there were precursors in ancient Greece and Rome and in medieval Japan, the novel arose primarily in late medieval and early Renaissance Europe. The term come from the Italian *novella*, a literary form typified by Giovanni Boccaccio's *Decameron.* François Rabelais' *Gargantua* and *Pantagruel* (1532-52) and Miguel Cervantes' *Don Quixote* (1605-15) are prototypes of the European novel. In English literature the form was established in the 18th century by authors such as Daniel Defoe, Samuel Richardson, and Henry Fielding. In the 19th century the novel became the dominant form of literature in Europe and the Americas. Major authors included Jane Austen and Charles Dickens (England), Victor Hugo, Gustave Flaubert, Emile Zola, and Honoré de Balzac (France), Leo Tolstoy, Fyodor Dostoevski, and Ivan Turgenev (Russia), and Nathaniel Hawthorne, Herman Melville, and Mark Twain (United States). All these novelists told stories of individual characters faced with social and psychological problems that had a universality that went beyond the particular setting. In the 20th century, novelists began experimenting with more varied forms of language, dialogue, and structure. Another development that has enriched the novel in the 20th century was the spread of the form to non-European cultures, such as China, Africa, and the Arab world. Since 1980, the Nobel Prize for literature has been won by novelists from Colombia (Gabriel García Márquez), Nigeria (Wole Soyinka), and Egypt (Naguib Mahfouz).

Novgorod (pop. 215,000), historic city in the northwestern USSR, capital of Novgorod Oblast. Located on the Volkhov River, it long formed a trade link between the Baltic and the Orient and was the capital of the Russian state in 862. Although later superseded as the capital by Kiev, in 1136 it again became the capital of a north Russian state. During the Middle Ages Novgorod was a cultural and a commercial center carrying on trade with the Hanseatic League. Its importance declined after 1703, when the city of St. Petersburg (now Leningrad) was founded. Many of Novgorod's medieval buildings were damaged during the German occupation (1941-44) in World War II, but some remain.
See also: Union of Soviet Socialist Republics.

Novi Sad (pop. 213,900), city in Yugoslavia, transportation center and capital of the autonomous region of Vojvodina, in the Serbian republic. Located on the Danube River and the Belgrade-Budapest railway line, Novi Sad has many cultural institutions serving an ethnically diverse population including Hungarians, Serbs, Croats, and Romanians. Its industries include food processing, textiles, milling, and electrical equipment.
See also: Yugoslavia.

Novocaine *see:* Procaine.

Novosibirsk (pop. 1,384,000), city in southern Siberia, USSR, on the Ob River and the Trans-Siberian railway line. Founded in the late 19th century as a camp for railway workers, Novosibirsk developed into a river, rail, and air transport center during World War II. Its industries include textiles, heavy machinery, metals, and chemicals. Novosibirsk is the also the site of an important Soviet scientific research center.
See also: Union of Soviet Socialist Republics.

Novotny, Antonín (1904-75), president of Czechoslovakia (1957-68) and communist leader. As a Stalinist and supporter of Moscow, Novotny fell from power after years of economic stagnation and political unrest. He was succeeded by a liberal regime led by Alexander Dubek and others.
See also: Czechoslovakia.

NOW *see:* National Organization for Women.

Noyes, Alfred (1880-1958), English poet, a traditionalist known for his popular, vigorous, rhythmic ballads, such as "The Highwayman," and patriotic, blank-verse epics, such as *Drake* (1908), about the Elizabethans, and *The Torch Bearers* (1922-30), a trilogy praising scientific progress. His *Collected Poems* were published in 1950.

Noyes, John Humphrey (1811-86), U.S. religious reformer. He preached a Christian doctrine called perfectionism, which taught that people could regain their innate sinlessness and become perfect. Noyes, believing that the way to achieve perfection was through communal living, founded the Oneida Community (1848) in New York. When this attempt at creating a utopia failed (1879), mainly because of outside opposition to the practice of polygamy within the community, Noyes fled to Canada.

NSC *see:* National Security Council.

Nu, U (1907-), Burmese political leader, prime minister (1948-56, 1957-58, and 1960-62). A founder of the Anti-Fascist People's League after World War II, he was the first prime minister of independent Burma. Twice ousted by army coups, he left Burma in 1969 but continued to support minority rebel groups against the government until 1973. He returned from exile in 1980.
See also: Burma.

Nubia, ancient region of northeastern Africa, now mostly in the Sudan, along both banks of the Nile River from Khartoum in the south to Aswan (Egypt) in the north. In the 8th and 7th centuries B.C. Egypt was ruled by a Nubian dynasty that was ousted when the Assyrians took over c.667 B.C. In the 3rd century A.D. the Nobatae, a black tribe, settled in Nubia and founded a kingdom that lasted for centuries. It was Christianized in the 6th century and disintegrated under Muslim pressure in the late 14th century.

Nuclear bomb *see:* Nuclear weapon.

Nuclear energy, energy released through the fission or fusion of atomic nuclei. In fission, the nucleus of a heavy atom absorbs an extra neutron, which causes it to become unstable and split apart into 2 lighter nuclei plus other subatomic particles, including other neutrons. Fission can occur only in a few of the heaviest, least stable nuclei. The energy released by a fission reaction consists mainly of the transformation of nuclear forces (the forces holding the nucleus together) into heat. Fusion is the opposite process: here the lightest nuclei (usually isotopes of hydrogen) are squeezed together under conditions of extreme heat and pressure until they merge, forming a new nucleus whose mass is very slightly smaller than the total masses of the nuclei that were fused. The extra mass is converted into energy (mostly heat) according to Einstein's formula $E=mc^2$, where E is energy, m is mass, and c is the speed of light. Since c^2 is a very large number, the energy yielded by this reaction is large even when the mass, m, is very small. Fission reactions were first observed in 1938. When the nucleus of Uranium-235 is bombarded with neutrons, it splits apart, releasing an average of 2.5 free neutrons. If these released neutrons collide with other nuclei of U-235, a chain reaction ensues. If this reaction is uncontrolled, the result is an atomic explosion like the one caused by the atomic bombs dropped on the Japanese cities of Hiroshima and Nagasaki in 1945. This is what happens in a nuclear reactor. Fusion, unlike fission, requires very high temperatures. In a hydrogen bomb, these temperature are brought about by a fission explosion, which triggers uncontrolled fusion reactions in the hydrogen that is packed around the fission bomb. So far, attempts to create controlled fusion reactions are only at the research stage. One line of experimentation has been to use magnetic fields to contain hydrogen fuel in the form of a plasma, a fully ionized gas containing equal numbers of positive and negative ions. Another has been to bombard pellets of frozen deuterium (a hydrogen isotope) with high-powered laser beams. The successful control of fusion would be an epoch-making achievement in providing energy. Unlike fissionable fuel and fossil fuels like oil, hydrogen is virtually limitless, and fusion produces far fewer radioactive by-products than fission. This means that fusion reactors, if they are possible, would produce much less radioactive waste than today's fission reactors do.

Nuclear fission *see:* Fission; Nuclear energy.

Nuclear force *see:* Grand unified theories.

Nuclear magnetic resonance (NMR) *see:* Magnetic resonance imaging.

Nuclear medicine, branch of medicine that uses radioisotopes in diagnostic and treatment procedures.

Nuclear physics, study of the physical properties, structure, and laws of the atomic nucleus and subatomic particles. Its primary area of concern is the nature of matter and the behavior of elementary particles. The subject has grown rapidly with the technical exploitation of nuclear energy.
See also: Atom; Particle physics; Radioactivity.

Nuclear power *see:* Nuclear energy.

Nuclear reactor, device containing sufficient fissionable material to produce a controlled chain reaction of neutrons able to split other nuclei. Many types of reactors exist; all produce neutrons, gamma rays, radioactive fission products, and heat. A

Liquid-metal-cooled, fast breeder reactor, a type of nuclear reactor. Fast neutrons are used to produce more fissionable material than is consumed. The reactor is fueled by Uranium-238, which absorbs a neutron to become Neptunium. This decays to Plutonium-239, which in turn absorbs a neutron, giving off fission products and more neutrons. The diagram shows a cutaway of a fast reactor.

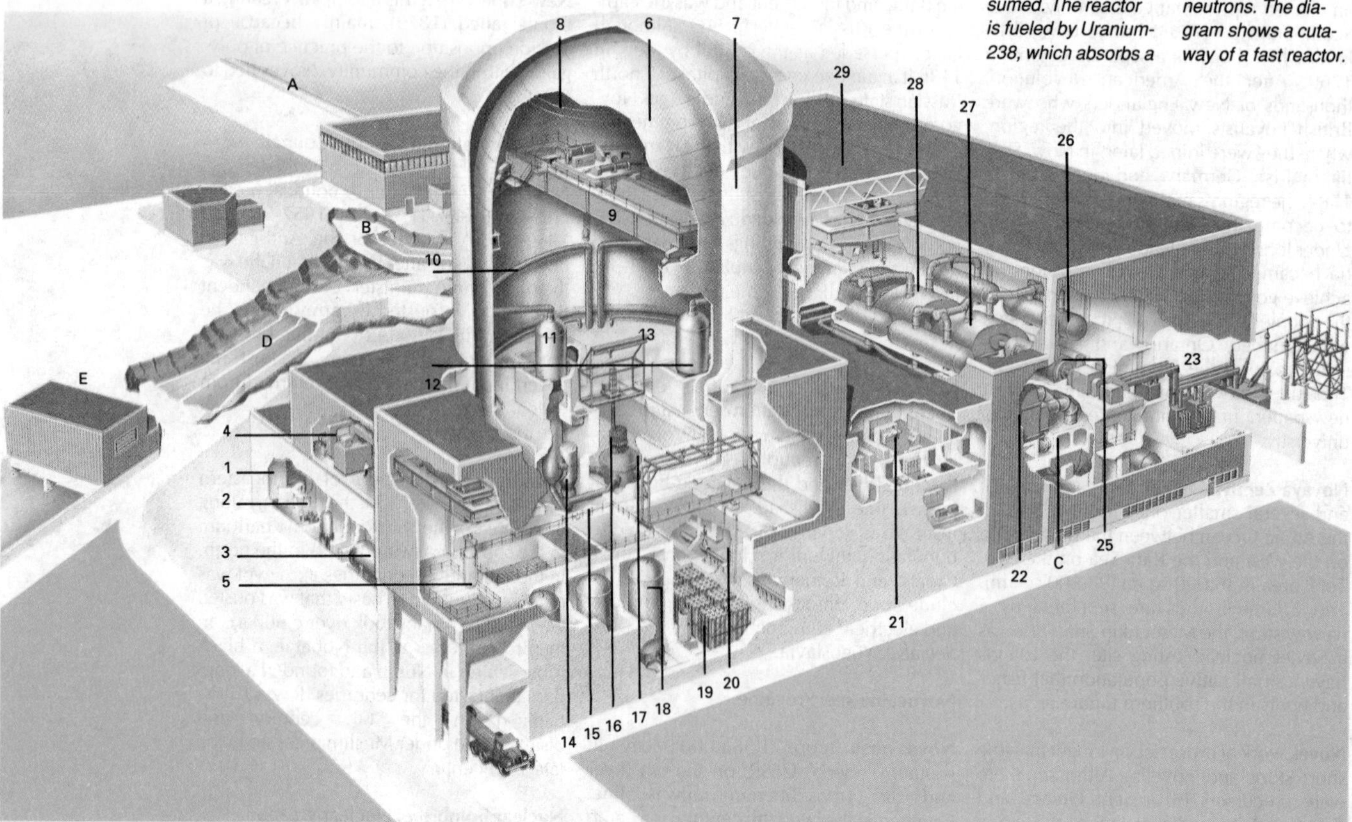

Nuclear power plant with the characteristic dome-shaped reactor building.
Key:
1. *Waste drum loading area*
2. *Drum storage*
3. *Drums for liquid waste*
4. *Auxiliary building ventilation*
5. *Spent fuel cask*
6. *Containment vessel*
7. *Reactor building*
8. *Containment spray system*
9. *Reactor crane*
10. *Steam generator*
11. *Steam generator*
12. *Steam generator*
13. *Fuel handling crane*
14. *Expansion trunk*
15. *Reactor coolant pump*
16. *Operating mechanism for control rods*
17. *Reactor vessel*
18. *Spent fuel cask*
19. *Spent fuel storage rack*
20. *Transfer tube*
21. *Main control room*
22. *Condenser*
23. *Transformer*
24. *Electricity distribution station*
25. *Generator*
26. *Moisture separators*
27. *Low pressure turbine*
28. *High pressure turbine*
29. *Turbine building*

A. Circulating water pump house
B. Circulating water to turbine house
C. Circulating water in
D. Circulating water from turbine house
E. Circulating water discharge house

fission reactor consists of a fuel, a moderator, and a cooling system. The fragments produced by fission of a heavy nucleus have a large amount of energy, and the heat they produce may be used for carrying out a variety of high-temperature processes or for heating a working fluid (such as steam) to operate a turbine and produce electricity. Nuclear reactors are also used to power ships and submarines. The 1979 accident at Pennsylvania's Three Mile Island reactor—involving a partial fuelcore meltdown and the release of radioactive gases into the atmosphere—brought the issue of nuclear safety to the public. Concern for safety increased with the 1986 explosion and fire at a nuclear power plant at Chernobyl in the USSR.

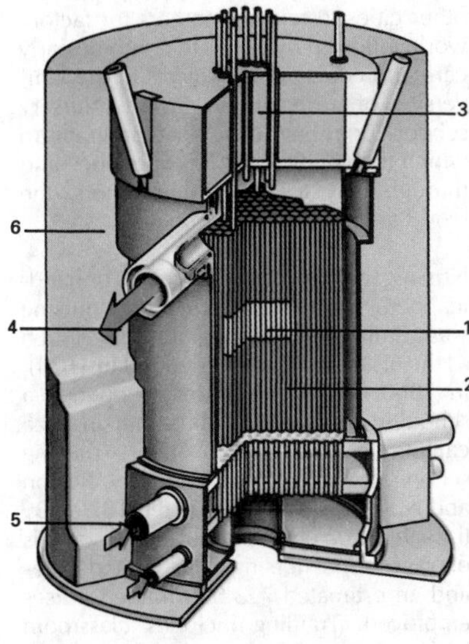

Liquid-metal-cooled, fast breeder reactor, a type of nuclear reactor. Fast neutrons are used to produce more fissionable material than is consumed. The reactor is fueled by Uranium-238, which absorbs a neutron to become Neptunium. This decays to Plutonium-239, which in turn absorbs a neutron, giving off fission products and more neutrons. The diagram shows a cutaway of a fast reactor. Fission reactions take place in the U-235 core (1) and the U-238 blanket (2). Cadmium control rods (3) are interspersed through the core. The fission heat is carried from the reactor by liquid sodium coolant (4, 5). The whole core tank is contained within a thick concrete radiation screen (6).

Nuclear Regulatory Commission (NRC), independent U.S. government agency set up in 1975 to license and regulate the civilian use of nuclear energy. The NRC, successor to the Atomic Energy Commission (founded 1946), sets safety standards for nuclear reactors.
See also: Nuclear energy.

Nuclear submarine *see:* Submarine.

Nuclear weapon, powerful explosive weapon whose power derives from nuclear energy. There are 2 main types of such weapons: fission bombs and fusion, or thermonuclear, bombs. The bombs dropped by the United States on the Japanese cities Hiroshima and Nagasaki in 1945, during World War II, were fission bombs. Fusion bombs (also called hydrogen bombs, or H-bombs) were developed in the early 1950s and have never been used in warfare. Various countries today have fission bombs, but only 5 countries—the United States, the Soviet Union, Britain, France, and China—have produced and tested fusion bombs.
See also: Nuclear energy.

Nuclear winter, term referring to the global environmental catastrophe that might occur as a result of dramatic changes in the earth's atmosphere caused by nuclear war. The theory holds that the dust and debris hurled into the sky by nuclear bombs would remain in the air for years, blocking a large percentage of the sun's light and resulting in freezing temperatures throughout the world. Nearly all crops would die, food chains would be interrupted, and many species of plant and animal life would become extinct. Agriculture as we know it would no longer be possible.
See also: Nuclear weapon.

Nucleic acid, the vital chemical constituents of living things; a ciass of complex threadlike molecules comprising 2 main types: DNA (deoxyribonucleic acid) and RNA (ribonucleic acid). DNA is found almost exclusively in the nucleus of the living cell, where it forms the chief material of the chromosomes. The DNA molecule's ability to duplicate itself (replicate) makes cell reproduction possible; by directing protein synthesis, DNA controls heredity. RNA performs several important tasks connected with protein synthesis, and is found throughout the cell.

Nucleus, in biology, the central part of a cell, containing the genetic material; also, a group of nerve cells or mass of gray matter in the central nervous system. In physics, the central core of an atom, positively charged, containing the vast majority of the atom's mass.
See also: Biology; Cell.

Nuer, people living in southern Sudan on both banks of the Nile River. The raising of cattle for sacrifice is central to their way of life. Because of seasonal flooding, the Nuer spend part of each year on higher ground, where they grow crops such as millet and peanuts.

Nuevo Laredo (pop. 214,200), city in northeastern Mexico, on the U.S.-Mexican border, opposite to Laredo, Tex., to which it is joined by a bridge spanning the Rio Grande. Nuevo Laredo is a main entry point into Mexico for U.S tourists and is a center of tourism, trade, and transportation.
See also: Mexico.

Nullification, in U.S. history, an act by which a state suspends a federal law within its borders. An extreme outgrowth of the doctrine of states' rights, the tactic of nullification was particularly used by southern states before the Civil War. First used in the Kentucky and Virginia Resolutions of 1798-99, the doctrine was invoked in 1832 by John C. Calhoun, who argued that the state of South Carolina could nullify the so-called "Tariff of Abominations." When South Carolina declared the tariff null and void, some opponents of the action urged President Andrew Jackson to enforce the law by military action. Instead a compromise tariff was arranged before the state's nullification order came into effect. The doctrine of nullification died when the South lost the Civil War.

Numbers, Book of, book of the Old Testament, fourth of the 5 books of the Pentateuch (or Torah), describing the 40-year wanderings of the Israelites through the desert after their exodus from Egypt and before their arrival in Palestine.
See also: Bible; Old Testament.

Number theory, branch of mathematics that deals with the integers (or whole numbers), which include zero and the negative whole numbers. One of the important concepts of number theory is that of the prime numbers, those numbers greater than 1 divisible only by 1 and themselves. For instance, 2, 3, 5, and 7 are prime numbers, whereas 9 is not, since it is divisible by 3. One of the best-known theorems of number theory, called *the fundamental theory of arithmetic,* states that every positive integer can be expressed as the product of prime numbers that are unique. For example, the number 15 can be expressed as 3 x 5 and by no other product of primes (except for 5 x 3, which is regarded as the same thing). This theorem is attributed to the ancient Greek mathematician Euclid, who may be considered the founder of number theory.

Numeration systems, or number systems, method of arranging and representing numbers. The most familiar and widely used system today is the decimal system. Based on innovations of Hindu mathematicians of the 4th and 3rd centuries B.C., and introduced to Europe by the Arabs, it uses 10 numerals or digits, 0 through 9, which stand for different values according to whether they represent 1s, 10s, 100s, or other powers of 10. For this reason the decimal system is also called "numbers to the base 10." Originally, numerals 1-9 were combined with words to accomplish this. The number 263 might be read as "2 hundreds, 6 tens, and 3 ones." With the Hindu invention of the zero C.A.D. 600, a more efficient method became possible. Here the position of the digit determines its value. In the number 200, 2 zeros are needed to hold the positions of the tens and ones, so that the digit 2 can be correctly interpreted as 2 hundreds. This system, disseminated by Arab mathematicians, reached Europe in the 12th century. The decimal system was later extended to include a representation of fractions. Positions of digits representing fractions are separated by those representing integers (whole numbers) by a decimal point. Thus, while values to the left of the decimal point represent 10^0 (ones), 10^1 (tens), 10^2 (hundreds), and so on, values to the right of the decimal point represent 10^{-1} (1/10 or tenths), 10^{-2} (1/100 or hundredths), 10^{-3} (1/1,000 or thousandths), and so on. Numeration systems can be based on numbers other than 10 while applying the same principle of positional value. The binary system or base 2, for example, uses only 2 digits, 0 and 1; positional values are based on powers of 2. For instance: in the binary system 1011 means $(1 \times 2^0) + (1 \times 2^1) + (0 \times 2^2) + (1 \times 2^3) = 1 + 2 + 0 + 8 = 11$. Invented by the German mathematician Gottfried

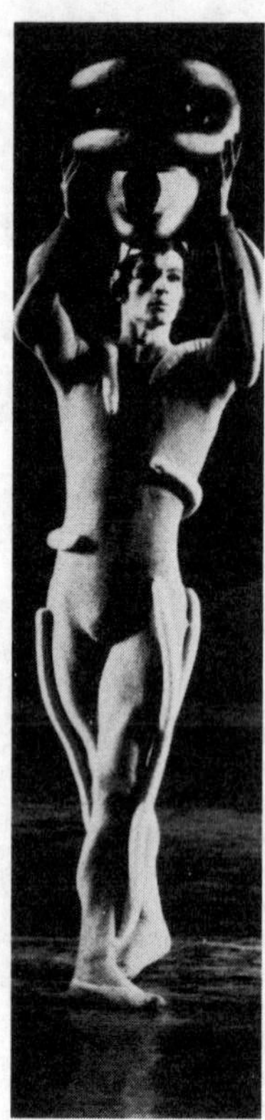

Rudolf Nureyev

Wilhelm Leibniz (1646-1716), the binary system became important in the development of computers, because "on" and "off" switches or electrical circuits could be used to represent 0 and 1. The hexadecimal system, base 16, uses 16 digits (commonly, 0-9 and A-F), with place values equal to powers of 16. It is also of importance in computers. The number system of the ancient Babylonians, which had a base 60, survives in the division of the hour into 60 minutes, each divided into 60 seconds. It is also reflected in the degrees, minutes, and seconds in which angles may be measured.

Numerology, use of numbers to predict future events or provide insight into personality. Numerology translates the letters in particular names and dates into numbers, each of which is claimed to have certain unique properties. There is no evidence whatever that numerology has the slightest validity.

Numidia, ancient region of northern Africa, generally corresponding to present-day Algeria. The Numidian chieftain Massinisa helped the Romans defeat the Carthaginians in the Second and Third Punic wars in the 3rd and 2nd centuries B.C. Julius Ceasar later turned Numidia into a Roman province.

Numismatics *see:* Coin collecting.

Nummulite, single-celled sea organism from the Eocene and Oligocene periods. Nummulite fossils are abundant in rocks from this period, such as the limestone that was used to build the pyramids of Egypt. Nummulites belong to the camarind family.

Nun, woman member of a religious order, who devotes her life to religious service. In Roman Catholic canon law, a nun takes solemn vows of poverty, chastity, and obedience; some orders are devoted to prayer and contemplation.

Nuremberg (pop. 465,300), historic city of Bavaria, southwestern Germany, on the Pegnitz River. Founded in the 11th century, it became a cultural and trading center in the Middle Ages and was the first city to accept the Reformation. Hitler staged annual rallies here in the 1930s and proclaimed anti-Jewish laws in 1934. Now a major manufacturing city, it was the scene of war crimes trials following World War II.
See also: Germany.

Nuremberg Trials, series of war crimes trials held in Nuremberg, Germany (1945-49) by the victors of World War II: the United States, USSR, Great Britain, and France. The accused, including Joachim von Ribbentrop, Hermann Goering, and Rudolf Hess, were tried for crimes against peace, war crimes, and crimes against humanity. In total more than 200 Germans were tried in 13 separate trials from October 1945 until 1949.
See also: International law; War crime; World War II.

Nureyev, Rudolf (1938-), Russian ballet dancer who sought asylum in the West when touring with the Kirov Ballet in 1961. As a guest artist of the Royal Ballet, London, Nureyev was famous as a leading classical and modern dancer and for his partnership with Margot Fonteyn. He also staged several ballets. He has been director of the Paris Opéra since 1983.
See also: Ballet.

Nursery rhyme, short, rhymed poem or tale intended to amuse children. The term nursery rhyme was first used in *Blackwood's Edinburgh Magazine* in 1824. There are 8 types of popular nursery rhymes: lullabies, singing game rhymes, nonsense rhymes, rhyming riddles, counting-out rhymes, tongue twisters, verse stories, and cumulative rhymes. The majority of nursery rhymes were created after 1600 and for many years, nursery rhymes were passed from generation to generation orally. *Mother Goose's Melody* (1781) was one of the first published compilations of nursery rhymes. Other collections include *The Nursery Rhymes of England* (1842) and *The Oxford Dictionary of Nursery Rhymes* (1951).

The Nuremberg Trials

Nursery school, preschool care and early education for children from about 3 to 5 years old. Nursery schools developed from 19th-century infant care programs for factory women's children, launched by Robert Owen (1771-1858) in Great Britain and copied in Europe as the Industrial Revolution spread. Johann Pestalozzi (1746-1827), Friedrich Froebel (1782-1852), and Maria Montessori (1870-1952) pioneered preschool methods of nursery education. The first U.S. nursery schools opened in the 1850s in New York, Philadelphia, and other cities to release mothers for factory work, followed by efforts to combine early care and educational projects at the University of Chicago in 1915. Nursery schools today have developed programs in which the young learn by experience and through play to understand others, the world around them, and themselves.

Nursing, care of the sick, injured, or handicapped. Until the 19th century nursing was administered by religious bodies such as the Sisters of Charity (founded in 1634). In 1860 Florence Nightingale opened a school in London to establish nursing as a career. In the United States, nursing schools opened in New York City, Boston and New Haven, Conn., in the 1870s. By the 1980s there were about 1,350 schools of professional nursing in the United States and an estimated 723,000 trained nurses employed. Training includes classroom and hospital experience.

Nursing home, residential facility for individuals, especially old people, needing medical or other daily assistance. Although some institutions in the United States are publicly funded or sponsored by religious organizations, most are operated on a profit basis by private owners. Laws regulating licensing and inspection are designed to protect residents from fraud and abuse.

Nut, the edible kernel of a dry fruit, such as the walnut or chestnut, enclosed in a hard shell. Nuts are rich in minerals and some vitamins, abundant in carbohydrates and fats. Peanuts, in spite of their name, are legumes.

Nutcracker, any of several birds of the crow family. Found in the mountainous pine regions of North America and Eurasia, nutcrackers feed mainly on nuts, seeds, and pine cones.

Nuthatch, any of various small birds of the family Sittidae, found in temperate climates worldwide. The name derives from the birds' ability to open nuts by wedging them into the bark of trees. Known to be tame and sociable, they will look for food in places inhabited by humans.

O

Nutmeg, evergreen tree (*Myristica fragrans*) grown in the tropics for the sweet, tangy spices it produces. The spice called nutmeg comes from the tree's seed kernels; another spice, mace, comes from the fiber that covers each kernel.

Nutmeg State *see:* Connecticut.

Nutria, large South American water rodent (*Myocastor coypus*), also found in the Mississippi Delta, raised commercially in Europe and North America for its reddish-brown fur, which resembles that of the beaver or muskrat. Because it feeds on water plants, it is considered a threat to the ecology. It is also known to destroy certain crops.

Nutrition, process by which living organisms take in and utilize nutrients, the substances required for growth and for the maintenance of life. Essential nutrients are those that cannot be produced within living cells and must be derived from food. Unlike plants, which can synthesize their nutritional requirements from exposure to sunlight, soil, and air, animals depend largely on the eating of plants or other animals. A broad array of essential nutrients are required by the human body. These include protein, carbohydrates, fats, vitamins, and minerals. Deficiencies in any of these can result in stunted growth or in a variety of illnesses involving malfunctions of organs or systems.

Nutting, Mary Adelaide (1858-1948), Canadian-born U.S. pioneer in the field of professional nursing. The world's first professor of nursing, she worked to improve educational standards for nurses in the United States.
See also: Nursing.

Nyasaland *see:* Malawi.

Nyerere, Julius Kambarage (1921-), founder and first president (1964-85) of the East African state of Tanzania. He led Tanganyika to independence (1961) and united it with Zanzibar. He believed in a one-party socialist democracy and helped overthrow Ugandan dictator Idi Amin. He was succeeded in 1985 by Hassan Mwinyi, former President of Zanzibar, a semiautonomus island off the Tanzanian coast.
See also: Tanzania.

Nylon, heat-resistant, strong, elastic, synthetic material introduced in 1938. Nylon is made into fibers or cast and molded into bearing, gears, zippers, etc.

Nymph, in Greek mythology, female divinity normally considered the guardian of an object or place occurring in nature. Nymphs were depicted as beautiful young women and were named according to the geographic features with which they were associated. Naiads, for example, watched over brooks, rivers, and other bodies of fresh water; nereids were identified with the sea, dryads with trees, and oreads with mountains.

Nystagmus, rhythmic rolling of the eyes that occurs normally when the head rotates. The eyes attempt to focus on a fixed spot, then rapidly move back. Abnormal nystagmus may be caused by nervous system disorders.

Nzinga a Nkuwa (d. 1506), ruler of the Congolese people of west-central Africa. Following the arrival of the Portuguese in 1482, he promoted trade with Europe. Although considered by his people to be divine, he converted to Christianity and was baptized in 1491.

O, 15th letter and 4th vowel of the English alphabet. It was the only Semitic letter (*ayin*) adopted by the Greeks, who called it *omicron*. It passed into the Roman alphabet as the 14th letter and was also used in medieval roman numbering to indicate 11. In chemistry, O is the symbol of the element oxygen.

O. Henry *see:* Henry, O.

Oahe Dam, in South Dakota, one of the world's largest embankment dams. Completed in 1960 by the U.S. Army, it has a volume of 92 million cu yd (70 million cu m). Facilities include seven 150-ft (46-m) high generators that together can produce 595,000 kw of electricity.

Oahu *see:* Hawaii.

Oak, tree that grows in moderate climates and subtropics. There are more than 600 species of oak found in the Northern Hemisphere. Seeds of the oak are called acorns. Oak wood is used in construction and for flooring and furniture. The bark is used for medicinal purposes.

Oakland (pop. 2,082,914), city on the east side of San Francisco Bay in northern California. The port handles over 5 million tons of cargo a year. Much of the farm produce of California's Central Valley passes through Oakland; it is also a major industrial city for shipbuilding, food processing, and oil refining.
See also: California.

Oakley, Annie (Phoebe Anne Oakley Mozee; 1860-1926), U.S. entertainer. Known as "Little Sure Shot," she was a sharpshooter star of Buffalo Bill's Wild West Show.

Oak Ridge National Laboratory, in Tennessee, one of the largest energy research centers in the United States. Founded (1942) by the U.S. government during World War II to develop the atomic bomb, the laboratory is still an important center for nuclear as well as nonnuclear research. Although under contract with the U.S. Department of Energy, the center is now privately operated and connected to a large network of Southern universities.

Oakum, loose fibers of hemp or flax, used to make the seams of wooden ships watertight—a process called caulking. Oakum may be made from tow, a byproduct in the manufacture of linen. The best oakum is made from ships' ropes, picked apart and tarred.

Oarfish, or ribbonfish (*Regalecus glesne*), eellike fish with a flattened body 20 ft (6 m) or more long, 1 ft (1/3 m) deep and only 2 in (5 cm) across. Oarfish are found in all warm and temperate seas.

OAS *see:* Organization of American States.

Julius Nyerere

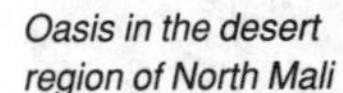

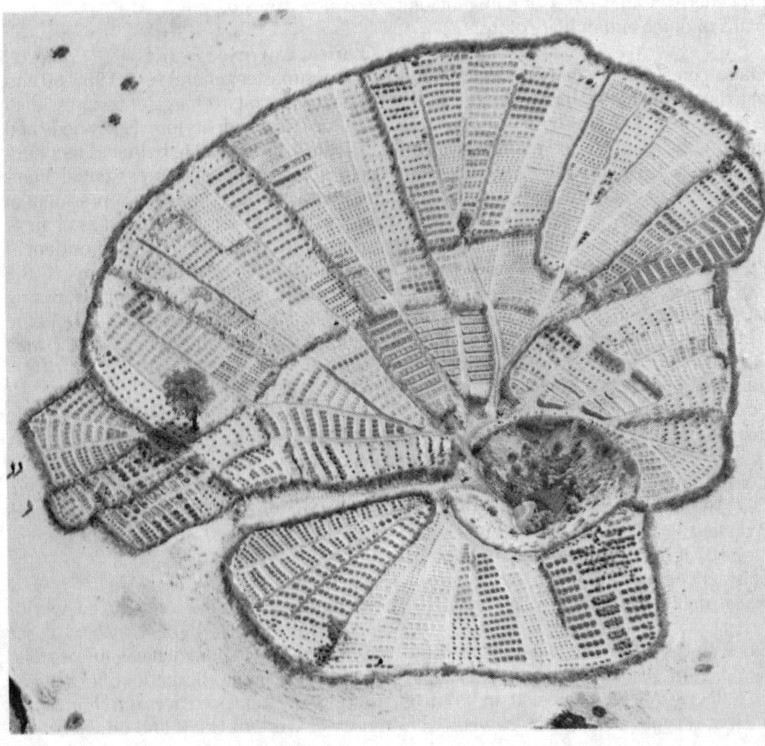

Oasis in the desert region of North Mali

This obelisk was brought to Paris from Luxor, Egypt, in 1836.

Oasis, area in a desert where there is sufficient water for plants to grow. Oases vary in size, from small ponds to vast regions covering thousands of square miles. The Nile Valley, the home of most of Egypt's people, is a large oasis flanked by barren desert. Many oases occur in areas bordering mountain ranges because the rain that falls on the mountains often seeps through porous rock layers under the desert. Oases may also occur around springs where the porous rock comes to the surface, or the water may be tapped through wells. Artificial oases are found in many deserts.

Oates, Joyce Carol (1938-), prolific U.S. novelist, short-story writer, poet, playwright, and critic whose work often deals with insanity, violence, and other nightmarish aspects of society. Among her many books are the novels *A Garden of Earthly Delights* (1967), *Them* (1969; National Book Award, 1970), *Bellefleur* (1980), *Solstice* (1985), and *Because It Is Bitter, and Because It Is My Heart* (1990).

Oates, Titus (1649-1705), English conspirator who in 1678 claimed to have discovered a Roman Catholic plot (called the Popish Plot) against Charles II. No such plot existed, but his story set off a wave of persecution in which some 35 innocent persons were executed. Exposed and imprisoned in 1695, he was freed and pensioned (1689) after the Glorious Revolution.

Oath, pledge used to guarantee the honesty of an individual's statements. In legal situations, a witness can commit the crime of perjury for giving false testimony under oath. Although the oath originally had religious significance, it is used today primarily, but not exclusively, for judicial procedures. Other types of oaths include oaths of office and military oaths.

Oats, cereal plants (genus *Avena*) cultivated in cool, damp climates in the Northern Hemisphere. Rich in starch and protein, the grain is used mainly as a livestock feed; less than 5% is processed for human consumption.

Oaxaca, southern Mexican state bordering the Gulf of Tehuantepec, founded by Aztecs c.1500. Oaxaca de Juárez is the capital. Covering 36,821 sq mi (95,366 sq km), it is mountainous with deep, fertile valleys; farming is the most important activity. Mineral resources include gold and silver. The population is predominantly Indian.
See also: Mexico.

Obadiah, Book of, shortest book of the Old Testament, 4th book of the Minor Prophets. Probably written in the 6th century B.C., its 21 verses foretell the triumph of Israel over its rival Edom.
See also: Bible; Old Testament.

Obelisk, 4-sided pillar tapering to a pyramidal top. Pairs of these, often as tall as 105 ft (32 m), were erected in front of ancient Egyptian temples, carved with hieroglyphs for decorative, religious, and commemorative purposes. Cleopatra's Needles in London and New York City, dating from c.1500 B.C. in Egypt, are notable examples.
See also: Cleopatra's Needles.

Oberammergau (pop. 4,700), village in Germany's Bavarian Alps, famous for its Passion Play. Every 10 years inhabitants of the village reenact the suffering, death, and resurrection of Christ, in fulfillment of a vow made by the villagers during a plague in 1633.
See also: Germany.

Oboe, soprano wind instrument consisting of a double-reed mouthpiece at the end of a conically bored tube. It is controlled by keys and finger holes. Developed in 17th-century France, the oboe is essentially an orchestral instrument.
See also: English horn.

Obote, Apollo Milton (1924-), president of Uganda (1966-71, 1980-5). The first prime minister of independent Uganda (1962), Obote made himself president under a new, centralizing constitution (1966). In 1971 he was overthrown by Idi Amin. After Amin's overthrow in 1979, Obote was reelected president.
See also: Uganda.

Obregón, Alvaro (1880-1928), president of Mexico (1920-4). He joined Carranza in overthrowing President Huberta in 1914, served in Carranza's government, but led the revolt against him in 1920. As president, Obregón promoted economic and educational reforms. Four years after leaving office he was elected again, but was assassinated by a religious fanatic before taking office.
See also: Mexico.

O'Brien, Lawrence Francis (1917-90), U.S. postmaster general from 1965-68 and special assistant in charge of congressional relations to presidents John F. Kennedy and Lyndon B. Johnson. He helped direct Kennedy's senatorial and presidential campaigns, as well as Johnson's presidential campaign. O'Brien also served as chair of George McGovern's 1972 presidential campaign. He was chairperson of the Democratic National Committee during 1968-72. He was also commissioner of the National Basketball Association (NBA) from 1975-84.

O'Brien, Robert C. (Robert Leslie Conly; 1918-73), popular U.S. author of children's fiction. He was the winner of the Newbery Medal in 1972 for his book *Mrs. Frisby and the Rats of NIMH*. His other books include *The Silver Crown* (1968) and *Z for Zachariah* (1974).

Ob River, fourth longest river in the world, located in Siberia, USSR. With about 19,000 m (30,600 km) of navigable waters, the Ob river and its tributaries offer a major route for the transportation and shipping of goods to western USSR and other parts of the world. Major ports are found at Novosibirsk and Barnaul.

Obscenity and pornography, terms referring to material believed to be publicly offensive. Although the terms are used interchangeably, obscenity refers to morally indecent language or behavior, while pornography refers to sexually explicit printed or pictorial material. U.S. antiobscenity laws attempt to inhibit the sale, presentation, or expression of obscenity and pornography, but heated controversy over the legal definitions of these terms makes it difficult to enforce the laws. Many nations have antiobscenity laws while others, such as Denmark in the late 1960s, dropped legal barriers against adult pornography.

Observatory, in astronomy, a scientific site at which systematic observations of the sky are made. The first observatories were set up by ancient civilizations to regulate the calendar and predict eclipses and the rising of the sun and the moon. The sextant, quadrant, and astrolabe were devices for sighting positions of stars and planets. The invention of the telescope in the early 17th century revolutionized observational astronomy. Contemporary observatories contain optical or radio telescopes housed in rotating domes. Satellite telescopes allow X-ray observation.
See also: Telescope.

The ESO-observatory complex on Cerro La Silla, Chile

Obsidian, igneous rock, also called volcanic glass. It is formed from molten lava. Obsidian is composed of the same chemicals as granite, but it solidifies so quickly that there is no time for crystals to form, so it becomes smooth and glasslike. Obsidian is generally black in color, but it can be brown or red. It can be shattered into sharp-edged pieces. The Native Americans of the western United States used such fragments for arrowheads and spear points.

Obstetrics, the care of women during pregnancy and childbirth, a branch of medicine and surgery linked with gynecology. Control of risk factors for both mother and

baby—anemia, toxemia, high blood pressure, diabetes, venereal disease, frequent miscarriage—have greatly contributed to the reduction of maternal and fetal deaths.
See also: Birth; Pregnancy.

O Canada, Canadian national anthem. Composed in 1880 and given French lyrics, the song was given English words in 1908. It was adopted as the national anthem of Canada by the Canadian Parliament in 1908.

O'Casey, Sean (1880-1964), Irish playwright whose sardonic dramas depict the effects of poverty and war. His early plays, such as *Juno and the Paycock* (1924) and *The Plough and the Stars* (1926), are the most highly regarded. His later works, such as *The Silver Tassie* (1929), were written in self-imposed exile due to hostility from Irish nationalists who objected to his unglamorous portrayal of the independence movement.

Occam, William of *see:* William of Ockham.

Occultism, wide range of practices and theories based on belief in the supernatural; among them witchcraft, mind reading, astrology, divination, and telepathy. Definitions of occultism have changed over the years; certain occult practices are now considered to have a scientific base. Although occultism is generally repudiated by the scientific community, there has been much renewed popular interest in occult beliefs and practices.
See also: Parapsychology; Spiritualism.

Occupational Safety and Health Administration (OSHA), U.S. agency of the Department of Labor established in 1970 to regulate health and safety standards in industry. OSHA conducts on-site inspections and promotes public awareness of on-the-job hazards, such as exposure to asbestos and other toxic substances.

Occupational therapy, rehabilitative medicine concerned with practical measures to overcome disability due to disease. It includes work and/or play activities under a therapist's guidance.

Ocean, combined area of interconnected water that covers about 71% of the earth's surface. The salt waters of the earth are divided into 4 main oceans: the Pacific, Atlantic, Indian, and Arctic. Scientists are interested in the food and mineral resources of the oceans. Marine biologists concentrate on the study of the food chain, the distribution of plankton, fish, and aquatic mammals, and the effects of pollution on marine life.

Ocean Drilling Program, geological research program established (1984) by the United States and other nations to determine the composition of the earth beneath the ocean floor. Drilling expeditions provide information on the evolution of life forms, the creation of the earth's land masses, shifts in the earth's climate, and the location of fossil fuels. Cylindrical cores of sediment and hard rock beneath the ocean floor are removed through a drill pipe and studied. The Ocean Drilling Program is operated by Texas A & M Univ. in College Station, Tex.

Oceania, vast section of the Pacific Ocean, stretching roughly from Hawaii to New Zealand and from New Guinea to Easter Island, divided into 3 broad cultural areas: Melanesia, Micronesia, and Polynesia. The area has about 25,000 small islands ranging from large masses of ancient rock to minute coral atolls—many of volcanic origin—and the vegetation varies from lush jungles to scanty palm trees. The native islanders live mainly by fishing and farming.

Ocelot, medium-sized wildcat marked with black spots, rings, and stripes, of forests from the southwestern United States to Paraguay. Although their fur is valuable, the ocelot is abundant. They feed on small animals.

Ochoa, Severo (1905-), Spanish-born U.S. biochemist who shared with Arthur K. Kornberg the 1959 Nobel Prize for physiology or medicine for first synthesizing a nucleic acid (RNA).
See also: Biochemistry; Nucleic acid.

Ochs, Adolph Simon (1858-1935), U.S. newspaper publisher responsible for creating the prestige of the *New York Times.* He became the paper's manager in 1896, adopting the slogan "All the news that's fit to print."

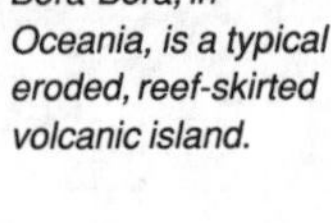

Bora-Bora, in Oceania, is a typical eroded, reef-skirted volcanic island.

Ockham, William of *see:* William of Ockham.

Ockham's Razor *see:* William of Ockham.

Ocmulgee National Monument, in central Georgia, site of prehistoric Native American ruins. Mounds date from 8,000 B.C. and include a council chamber, now reconstructed. The monument, established in 1934, occupies 683 acres (273.2 hectares).

O'Connell, Daniel (1775-1847), Irish statesman, called the Liberator, who led the fight for Catholic emancipation. He founded the Catholic Association (1823) and after his election to Parliament (1828) refused to take his seat until public opinion precipitated the Catholic Emancipation Act (passed in 1829). He contested the 1801 act uniting Ireland with Britain.
See also: Ireland.

Occultism has been practiced since ancient times. Pictured on this 15th century manuscript is a witches' sabbath.

O'Connor, Flannery (1925-64), U.S. fiction writer noted for her brilliant style and grotesque, tragicomic vision of life in the South. Her work includes the novel *Wise Blood* (1952) and the short-story collections *A Good Man Is Hard to Find* (1955) and *Everything That Rises Must Converge* (1965).

O'Connor, Frank (1903-66), Irish short-story writer whose works are admired for their oral quality and portrayals of Irish life. His collections include *Guests of the Nation* (1931), *Bones of Contention and Other Stories* (1936), and *A Set of Variations* (1969). O'Connor also published poetry, criticism, and translations of old Irish literature from the Gaelic.

O'Connor, John Joseph Cardinal (1920-), cardinal of the Roman Catholic Church. The former archbishop of New York City, he was named cardinal (1985) by Pope John Paul II. In 1983, he worked with other bishops to draft a letter, approved by the National Conference of Catholic Bishops, denouncing the nuclear arms buildup. He was an auxiliary bishop (1979) of the Military Ordinariate, serving members of the U.S. armed forces.

O'Connor, Sandra Day (1930-), U.S. Supreme Court Justice (1981-), the first woman appointed to the court. A lawyer, she was assistant attorney general of Arizona and a state senator. She then served as a trial judge on the state court of appeals.
See also: Supreme Court of the United States.

Ocotillo, or coach whip, tall, slender plant of U.S. southwestern deserts that grows new leaves after each rain. When dry, the stems are burnt as candlewood.

Octane, colorless, liquid, highly flammable hydrocarbon, commonly used in gasoline. Since the 18 octane compounds vary in their molecular structure, they have different physical properties.
Octane number is the designation given to gasoline based on the amount of isooctane present. Fuels with a lower octane number have a larger amount of normal heptane and are prone to engine "knock," which decreases the power of the engine.
See also: Hydrocarbon.

Octane number, measure of a liquid fuel's ability to resist premature ignition (knocking) and to burn evenly in an internal combustion engine. Gasolines with higher octane numbers produce less knocking than those with lower octane numbers. Desirable octane numbers range from 90-100.
See also: Gasoline.

Octave, in music, the interval between two pitches, one of which having twice the frequency of the other. In the diatonic scale these are the first and the eighth tones. Because of its unique consonance, the octave gives an aural impression of a single tone duplicated.

Octavia (65?-9 B.C.), wife of Marc Antony and sister of Emperor Augustus of Rome. Her marriage ended hostilities between her husband and brother, but war recommenced when Antony left her for the Egyptian queen Cleopatra in 37 B.C.
See also: Rome, Ancient.

Octavian *see:* Augustus.

Octopus, marine mollusk (genus *Octopus*) with 8 tentaclelike arms that surround the mouth; a cephalopod. Behind the beaked head is a saclike body containing the internal organs. Octopods can change color for camouflage and eject a black pigment which forms a smokescreen to foil predators.

Octopus

Odd Fellows, Independent Order of, secret organization promoting good will and brotherhood and committed to helping its members in time of need, hardship, or sorrow. Created in England in the early 1700s, in 1819 it spread to the United States, where it now claims more than 1 million members. Its logo of 3 links, skull and crossbones, and a single eye represents friendship, love, and truth, our limited state of being, and an omnipotent God. Rebekah lodges of Odd Fellows are mostly women.

Ode, stately lyric poem usually expressing praise. It is often addressed to the person, object, or concept (such as Joy or Autumn) being celebrated. It originated in the ancient Greek choral songs. Pindar used a three-part structure in his odes; strophe, antistrophe (both in the same meter), and epode (in a different meter). Horace's odes were in stanzaic form. English poets of the 19th century, such as John Keats and Percy Shelley, wrote odes with irregular structures.

O'Dell, Scott (1898-), U.S. author of children's historical novels, born in Los Angeles, Calif. Many of his books use California and Mexico as backgrounds for his characters and include the Newbery Medal-winning *Island of the Blue Dolphins* (1961), *The Black Pearl* (1969), and *Sing Down the Moon* (1970).

Oder River, European water route forming a large part of the border between Poland and eastern Germany, economically essential and mostly navigable on its 551-mi (886-km) length. Originating in the Oder Mountains of Czechoslovakia, it joins the Neisse River near western Poland and drains into the Baltic Sea through the Stettin Lagoon. Along the river are major cities in Poland, Germany, and Czechoslovakia.

Odessa (pop. 1,113,000), city and port in the Ukraine, USSR, on the Black Sea. It is a major transportation, industrial, commercial, and cultural center. During World War II about 280,00 residents of Odessa, mostly Jews, were massacred.
See also: Ukraine.

Odets, Clifford (1906-63), U.S. playwright and screenwriter noted for social-protest dramas about ordinary people in the Depression. A leading figure in the Group Theatre in New York City, his works include *Waiting for Lefty* (1935), *Awake and Sing!* (1935), and *Golden Boy* (1937).

Odin, in Germanic mythology, the chief god, also known as Woden (whose name gave us Wednesday). God of war, poetry, wisdom, learning, and magic, he had a single all-seeing eye. He made the world from the body of the giant Ymir, man from an ash tree, and woman from an elm.
See also: Mythology.

Odoacer (435-493), German chief who overthrew the last of the West Roman emperors in 476 and was proclaimed king of Italy. The East Roman Emperor Zeno sent Theodoric the Great to depose him. After a long war, Theodoric killed Odoacer.

Odometer *see:* Speedometer.

Odysseus *see:* Homer; Odyssey; Ulysses.

Odyssey, ancient Greek epic poem ascribed to Homer, one of the masterpieces of world literature. Its 24 books relate the adventures of Odysseus and his companions following the Trojan War. Eventually, Odysseus reaches his home in Ithaca and is reunited with his wife, Penelope.
See also: Homer.

Oedipus, in Greek legend, king of Thebes who was fated to kill his father, King Laius, and marry his mother, Jocasta. When he discovered what he had done, he blinded himself. His story and that of his daughter, Antigone, inspired tragedies by Sophocles: *Oedipus Rex* and *Oedipus at Colonus*.
See also: Mythology.

Oedipus complex, sexual obsession by a son for his mother accompanied by resentment and aggression toward his father. It is named after the mythological Greek hero Oedipus who killed his father and married his mother.

Oersted, Hans Christian (1777-1851), Danish physicist. His discovery (1820) that a magnetized needle can be deflected by

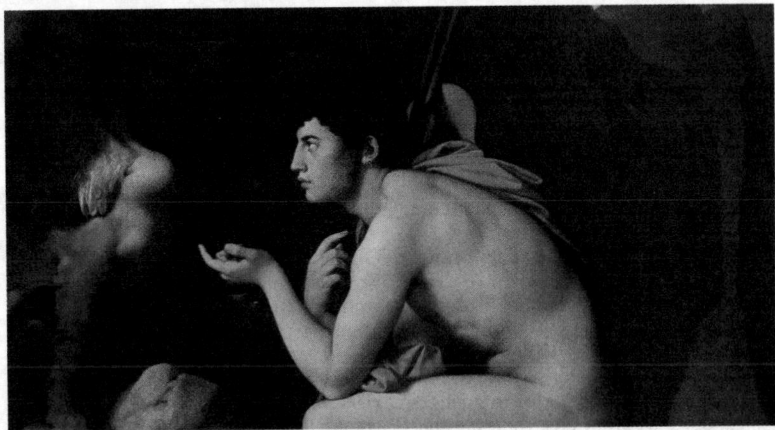

Oedipus and the Sphinx *by Jean Auguste Dominique Ingres (1808)*

an electric current passing through a wire gave birth to the science of electromagnetism. The unit of magnetic field strength, the oersted, is named after him.
See also: Electromagnetism.

O'Faolain, Sean (1900-), Irish short-story writer, novelist, and biographer. Among his works, which often give an unflattering yet sympathetic view of everyday Irish life, are *Midsummer Night Madness and Other Stories* (1932), the novel *A Nest of Simple Folk* (1933), *The Great O'Neill: A Biography of Hugh O'Neill* (1942), and his autobiography, *Vive Moi!* (1964).

Offenbach, Jacques (1819-80), French composer. He wrote over 100 operettas including *Orpheus in the Underworld* (1858), containing some famous can-can music, and *La Belle Hélène* (1864). His masterpiece is considered to be the opera *Tales of Hoffmann* (1881).

Offset, printing process whereby ink is transferred from a chemically treated printing plate, used so that only the printing or design will receive the ink, onto a rubber-covered cylinder, to paper. Offsetting is an improvement over other printing methods in its ability to print on numerous uneven surfaces and textures, such as rough paper, tin, or celluloid. Offset has been used successfully with color printing and rare book reproductions.
See also: Printing.

O'Flaherty, Liam (1897-1984), Irish novelist known for his realistic stories of ordinary people in trouble, such as *The Black Soul* (1924), *The Informer* (1925), and *The Assassin* (1928).

Ogaden *see:* Ethiopia.

Ogden (pop. 64,407), city in Utah, 35 mi (56 km) north of Salt Lake City, established by the Mormons in 1848 and incorporated in 1851. Industries include agricultural products, mineral processing from the Great Salt Lake, and aerospace and defense production.
See also: Utah.

Oglala *see:* Red Cloud; Sioux.

Oglethorpe, James Edward (1696-1785), English philanthropist, general, and member of parliament. He obtained a charter (1732) to found the colony of Georgia as a refuge for jailed debtors from England, and governed it until he returned to England in 1743.

O'Hara, John (1905-70), U.S. journalist and fiction writer known principally for his vigorous accounts of urban and suburban life in the United States. His novels include *Appointment in Samarra* (1934), *Butterfield 8* (1935), and *A Rage to Live* (1949).

O'Hara, John Francis Cardinal (1888-1960), Roman Catholic Church archbishop appointed a cardinal by Pope John XXIII in 1958. Ordained a priest in 1916, he began teaching religion in 1917 at Notre Dame University. He became its religious administrator and founded the College of Commerce. Chosen to be the university's president in 1934, he served for 5 years. He was ordained a bishop in 1940 and an archbishop in 1951.

Ohia, mountain apple tree with evergreen leaves found in many tropical climates, of the family Myrtaceae. Its hard wood is used to produce furniture and railroad ties.

O'Higgins, political family in South America. **Ambrosio O'Higgins** (1720-1801), born in Ireland and educated in Spain, was governor of Chile (1789-96) and viceroy of Peru (1796). **Bernardo O'Higgins** (1778-1842), his son, liberated Chile from Spanish rule and became its dictator (1817). His reforms aroused such opposition that he was exiled to Peru in 1823.

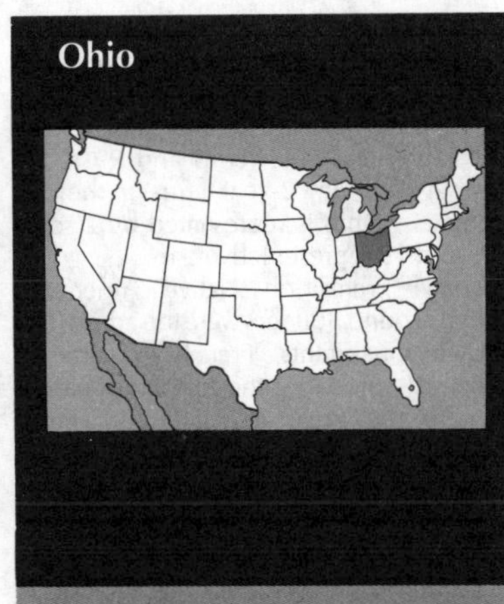

Capital:	Columbus
Statehood:	Mar. 1, 1803 (17th state)
Familiar name:	Buckeye State
Area:	41,330 sq mi (107,044 sq km); ranks 35th
Population:	10,887,325 (1990); ranks 7th
Elevation:	Highest—1,550 ft (472 m), Campbell Hill; Lowest—433 ft (132 m), along the Ohio River in Hamilton County
Motto:	With God, All Things Are Possible
Flower:	Scarlet carnation
Bird:	Cardinal
Tree:	Buckeye
Song:	"Beautiful Ohio"

Ohio, midwestern state in the northern United States; bordered by Michigan and Lake Erie to the north, Pennsylvania to the east, the Ohio River (with West Virginia and Kentucky on the other side) to the southeast and south, and Indiana to the west.
Land and climate. Ohio has four main land regions. The Great Lakes Plains, a narrow, fertile strip of land bordering Lake Erie, is one of the nation's busiest shipping and manufacturing areas. The Appalachian Plateau in the east is a high, rugged area of relatively poor soil but it has the state's largest forests, richest mineral deposits, and most impressive scenery. The Till Plains in the west, an area of gently rolling plains, is the easternmost part of the great, fertile Corn Belt of the Midwest. The Bluegrass Region, a small wedge-shaped area in southern Ohio, has both hilly and flat areas, with relatively thin, poor soil. Ohio's rivers—including the Maumee, Miami, Scioto, and Muskingum—drain into Lake Erie or the Ohio River. Excellent ports on Lake Erie, together with the Ohio River and two major canals, have made Ohio a major transportation hub of the Midwest. Forests cover about one-fourth of the state. Ohio has warm, humid summers and cold, dry winters. Principal cities are Cleveland, Columbus, and Cincinnati.
Economy. Manufacturing is by far the most important economic activity in Ohio, which is one of the nation's leading industrial states. Chief manufactured products are transportation equipment, machinery, primary and fabricated metal products, household appliances, chemicals, processed foods, and rubber products. Wholesale and retail trade is the chief service industry. Mining and agriculture are less important to the economy. Chief mineral products are coal, natural gas, petroleum, sandstone, limestone, and salt. Chief crops are corn, soybeans, hay, wheat, oats, and popcorn. Chief livestock products are beef cattle, hogs, sheep, and eggs and poultry.

Government. Ohio's present constitution was adopted in 1851. The governor serves a 4-year term. The state's legislature, called the General Assembly, consists of 33 senators serving 4-year terms and 99 representatives serving 2-year terms. In the U.S. Congress, Ohio is represented by 2 senators and 19 representatives.

History. Prehistoric Native Americans called Mound Builders were the area's first-known inhabitants. French explorer La Salle was probably the first European to explore the area, about 1670. France claimed the entire Ohio Valley, as did England. The conflicting claims led to the French and Indian wars (1754-63), after which France ceded the area to England. In 1763, Pontiac, an Ottawa chief, launched an Indian rebellion that the British eventually suppressed. Ohio, the scene of some battles during the American Revolution, became part of the U.S.'s Northwest Territory in 1787. In the late 1700s and early 1800s, white settlement increased rapidly, disrupted by a series of Indian uprisings. Ohio became the 17th state in 1803. During the Civil War, Ohio—a key Underground Railroad station—sided with the Union. After the war, Ohio's industries developed rapidly. The state's economy suffered in the Great Depression of the 1930s, but revived during World War II. Urban centers were hard-hit by Ohio's fiscal problems in the 1960s and 1970s. In the 1980s, Ohio sought improvements for its troubled farmers and industries.

Ohio Company, organizations formed to settle the Ohio River Valley. For the Ohio Company formed by Virginians in 1747, King George II deeded 200,000 acres (80,000 hectares) around the forks of the Ohio River (now Pittsburgh) to colonists. They built roads, supply houses, a fort, and a settlement, but the French objected to the British development and destroyed it. After the last French and Indian war (1763), the company closed. The Ohio Company of Associates, formed by New Englanders in 1787, acquired title to 750,000 acres (300,000 hectares) elsewhere on the river. New settlements were established, beginning in 1788 with Marietta. This Ohio Company profited, remaining in business until 1796.
See also: Northwest Ordinance; Putnam, Rufus.

Ohio river

Ohio River, main eastern tributary of the Mississippi River. The Ohio is formed at Pittsburgh, Pa., by the junction of the Allegheny and Monongahela rivers. It flows generally southwest for c.980 mi (1,557 km) and is navigable throughout.

Ohio University, first school of higher education in the Northwest Territory, established in 1804 in Athens, Ohio. The school offers associate, bachelor's, master's, and doctorate degrees, and studies in sciences, education, and the fine arts. There are challenge programs for the gifted and outreach campuses to serve students' needs.

Ohira, Masayoshi (1910-80), Japanese prime minister (1978-80). First elected to parliament as a member of the Liberal Democratic Party (1952), he held numerous ministerial posts before becoming party leader and prime minister. He was unable to hold together antagonistic factions of his party and died ten days before new parliamentary elections.

Ohm, Georg Simon (1787-1854), Bavarian-born German physicist who formulated Ohm's Law, from his studies of electric current. He also contributed to acoustics, recognizing the ability of the human ear to resolve mixed sound into its component pure tones.

Ohm's law, law stating that the electric potential difference across a conductor is proportional to the current flowing through it, the constant of proportionality being known as the resistance of the conductor. It holds well for most materials and objects, including solutions.
See also: Electric current.

Oil, any substance that is insoluble in water, soluble in ether, and greasy to the touch. Mineral oils include gasoline and other fuel oils, heating oils, and lubricants. Fixed vegetable oils change when they absorb oxygen (linseed, tung, and olive oil). Volatile vegetable oils usually have a distinct odor and flavor (peppermint, turpentine).

Oilbird, or guacharo (*Steatornis caripensis*), night-flying bird that lives in caves in northern South America and on Trinidad. It finds its way by echo-location, a batlike sonar device in its ears that emits audible, echoing clicks. It is called the oilbird because Native Americans used the fat of its chicks as cooking oil.

Oilcloth, fabric treated with oil or thick paint to become waterproof. Designs printed on it produce attractive tablecloths and shelf lining. It originated in China c.7th century, was made in England in the 1500s, and in the United States after 1809.

Oil refinery *see:* Petroleum.

Oil shale, fine-grained, dark-colored sedimentary rock from which oil suitable for refining can be extracted. The rock contains an organic substance called kerogen, which may be distilled to yield oil. Significant deposits occur in Wyoming, Colorado, and adjacent states.

Oil well *see:* Petroleum.

Oistrakh, David (1906-74), Russian violinist. His brilliant technique and strong emotional interpretation (especially of the romantic composers) brought him worldwide acclaim. Sergey Prokofiev and Dmitry Shostakovich wrote works for him. His son, **Igor** (1931-), is also a violinist and conductor of world renown.

Ojibwa, or Chippewa, large Algonquian-speaking tribes of Native Americans. Small bands of hunter-gatherers lived in woodland areas around Lakes Superior and Huron, and to the west. They fought with the Sioux, but had little contact with white settlers. Longfellow's *The Song of Hiawatha* was based on Ojibwa mythology. Today some 60,000 Ojibwas live on U.S. and Canadian reservations.

Ojos del Salado ("Salty Eyes"), mountain in the Andes range in northwest Argentina, 22,572 ft (6,880 m) high. The year-round snow on its 4 well-defined peaks gives it its name.

Georgia O'Keeffe's Black Iris *(1926)*

O'Keeffe, Georgia, (1887-1986), U.S. painter noted for her delicate, abstract designs incorporating symbolic motifs drawn from nature such as *Cow's Skull, Red, White, and Blue* (1931). She is also known for sexually symbolic flower paintings such as *Black Iris* (1926). Her paintings were first exhibited in 1916 by photographer Alfred Stieglitz. She was greatly influenced by the geography of the American southwest and was an early settler of the artistic community in Taos, New Mexico.

Okefenokee Swamp, warm, boggy, unsettled region in southeastern Georgia and somewhat into northeastern Florida, covering 700 sq mi (1,800 sq km). A recreation wetland for people, 460 sq mi (1,200 sq

Okefenokee Swamp

km) are designated a wildlife area. Protected are alligators, 50 kinds of fish, countless variations of birds and animals, and lush vegetation on many small islands.

Okhotsk, Sea of, branch of the northern Pacific Ocean, 1,000 mi (1,600 km) long and 600 mi (970 km) wide, along Russia's eastern border and used as a travel and trade route to Soviet ports. It joins the Sea of Japan by way of the Tatar and La Pérouse Straits. Travel is inhibited when severe storms occur between November and April, and ice and fog cover the sea.
See also: Pacific Ocean.

Okinawa, largest (454 sq mi/1,176 sq km) of the Ryukyu Islands in the West Pacific, part of Okinawa prefecture, Japan. Naha is the capital. Mountainous and jungle-covered in the south, hilly in the north, it is fertile—sugarcane, sweet potatoes, and rice are grown, and there are good fisheries. Captured by the United States during World War II, Okinawa was formally returned to Japan in 1972.

Oklahoma, state in the southwestern United States; bordered by Colorado and Kansas to the north, Missouri and Arkansas to the east, the Red River to the south, Texas to the south and west, and New Mexico to the west.

Land and climate. Oklahoma's topography varies immensely. There are broad, flat plains in the west, rolling hills in the center, and mountain ranges in the east. In some areas, the soil is fertile; in others, it is only loose sand. The western panhandle, including the state's highest point, lies in the Great Plains region. From there, the land slopes eastward into a central lowland. In the northeast lies the hilly Ozark Plateau; the Ouachita Mountains lie in the southeast. All of Oklahoma's large rivers—the 2 greatest being the Red and the Arkansas—are part of the Mississippi River system. There are about 300 small lakes, 100 natural and 200 artificial. Forests cover about one-fifth of the state. Oklahoma's climate varies considerably but, in general, it is mild and dry. Principal cities are Oklahoma City and Tulsa.

Economy. Wholesale and retail trade, mining, and manufacturing lead Oklahoma's economy. Chief mining products are natural gas, petroleum, coal, crushed stone, gypsum, iodine, and sand and gravel. Chief manufactured goods are nonelectrical machinery, fabricated metal products, and rubber and plastic products. Agriculture is less important to Oklahoma's economy. Beef cattle are the most important agricultural product; wheat and hay are the chief crops.

Government. Oklahoma's constitution was adopted in 1907. The governor serves a 4-year term. The state's legislature consists of 48 senators serving 4-year terms and 101 representatives serving 2-year terms. In the U.S. Congress, Oklahoma is represented by 2 senators and 6 representatives.

History. Several Indian tribes lived in the area when the first Europeans, led by Spanish explorer Coronado, came through in 1541. Oklahoma was among the lands that La Salle claimed for France in 1682. France ceded it to Spain, 1762-1800, then sold it to the U.S. under the 1803 Louisiana Purchase. In 1819, most of Oklahoma became part of the Arkansas Territory. In 1834, the land was designated as Indian Territory, and several tribes from the East were forced from their homelands to settle there. The arduous 1838 journey of the Cherokee from Georgia to Oklahoma is known as "the Trail of Tears." The immigrant Five Civilized Tribes set up a representative government, schools and churches, and farms. During the Civil War, the Five Civilized Tribes' loyalties were split between the Union and the Confederacy. After the war, railroads and cattle drives brought a boom of white settlers sooner than the law allowed (giving Oklahoma its nickname). Over time, the government opened more Oklahoma land to homesteading whites in great "land rushes." Oklahoma became the 46th state in 1907. During the 1920s, Oklahoma was torn by border disputes and Ku Klux Klan terrorism. During the Great Depression of the 1930s, severe drought forced thousands of farmers—called "Okies"—from the "Dust Bowl." Recovery came with World War II. The 1960s brought new industries and construction projects. The oil boom of the 1970s collapsed during the 1980s, forcing Oklahoma to seek new ways to combat its unemployment problems.

Oklahoma

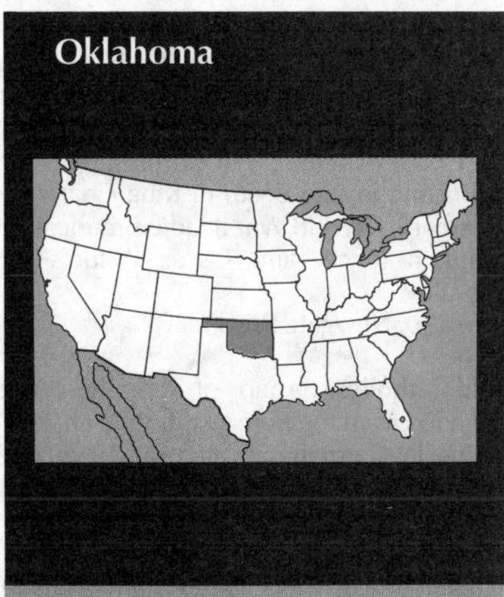

Capital:	Oklahoma City
Statehood:	Nov. 16, 1907 (46th state)
Familiar name:	Sooner State
Area:	69,956 sq mi (181,186 km); ranks 18th
Population:	3,231,000 (1993); ranks 28th
Elevation:	Highest—4,973 ft (1,516 m), Black Mesa; Lowest—287 ft (87 m), along the Little River in McCurtain County
Motto:	Labor Omnia Vincit (Labor Conquers All Things)
Flower:	Mistletoe
Bird:	Scissor-tailed flycatcher
Tree:	Redbud
Song:	"Oklahoma!"

Oklahoma City (pop. 454,000), capital of Oklahoma, on the North Canadian River. It was founded on April 22, 1889, when that portion of Indian territory was first opened for white settlement. For the land-rush some 10,000 people set up tents in the region that day. Incorporated in 1890, it became the state capital in 1910. Oil was discovered in 1928, and the city's large reserves of crude oil and natural gas have made it a major petroleum production area. Industries include farming, ranching, building materials, aircraft production, and electronic and communications equipment. In 1995 a bomb destroyed a federal office building, killing 168.
See also: Oklahoma.

Quachita Mountains, Oklahoma

Okra, or Gumbo, hibiscus plant cultivated in West Africa, India, and the southeastern United States for its fruits, which are pickled or cooked. They contain watery solutions of vegetable gum used to thicken and flavor broths. The seeds yield an oil and are used as a coffee substitute.

Olav V (1903-91), king of Norway (1957-91). After Germany took Norway (1940) in World War II, he was active in the resistance and in 1944 took command of the Norwegian forces.

Old Bailey, main criminal court in London, England, on Old Bailey Street (a bailey was an area between the inner and outer city walls in medieval times). Trials heard in Old Bailey include that of the judges responsible for the death of King Charles I, Germany's World War II radio broadcaster William Joyce, and Oscar Wilde's on morality.
See also: Newgate Prison.

Old Catholics, group of churches that seceded from the Roman Catholic church. Some in Germany, Austria, and Switzerland would not accept the dogmas of papal infallibility and jurisdiction defined by the First Vatican Council (1870). Later, several smaller Slavic churches separated. Virtually high Anglican in doctrine and practice, Old Catholics have been in fellowship with the Church of England since 1932.

Claes Oldenburg's Trowel *(1971)*

Oldenbarneveldt, Johan van (1547-1619), Dutch statesman. As advocate of Holland (from 1586), he supported self-government for the burgher towns of the United Provinces, recently liberated from Spain, and encouraged commerce during the early years of the Dutch East India Company. He came into conflict with Maurice of Nassau and the nobles over the role of the States-General and in the Calvinist-Remonstrants controversy. Oldenbarneveldt was arrested on unfounded treason charges and executed.

Oldenburg, Claes (1929-), Swedish-born U.S. pop artist best known for his soft constructions (sculptures) that satirize America. His hamburgers, ice cream cones, telephones, and bathroom fixtures are usually larger than normal size. His works include *Giant Saw, Hard Version* and *Lipstick.*

Old English *see:* English language; English literature.

Old English sheepdog, working dog that resembles an unshorn sheep. The breed, developed in 19th-century England, has long, abundant, coarse hair and is used to herd sheep and cattle and as a family guard dog. Its colors are gray or blue, with or without white, and as a full adult it weighs 55-65 lbs (24.9-29.5 kg).

Old Faithful *see:* Yellowstone National Park.

Oldfield, Barney (1878-1946), U.S. race car driver. Hired by Henry Ford in 1902 to drive Ford's racing car, the "999", Oldfield became the first person to break the 60 mph (96.56 kmph) barrier (1903). In 1910 he set another speed record of 131.724 mph (211.983 kmph). After retiring from racing in 1918, he worked toward improved auto safety engineering.

Old Ironsides (ship) *see:* Constitution, USS.

Old North Church, name given to the old Christ Church in Boston, Mass., immortalized in Henry Wadsworth Longfellow's poem "Paul Revere's Ride": "Hang a lantern in the belfry arch of the North Church tower as a signal light...," a warning to the town of the British coming. Today the tower has the first church bells cast in the Colonies, in 1744.

Olds, Ransom Eli (1864-1950), pioneer U.S. automobile engineer and manufacturer. His first powered vehicle was a steam-driven 3-wheeler (1886). He established the Olds Motor Vehicle Company in 1889, marketed the first commercially successful American car, an Oldsmobile, in 1901; and established the Reo Motor Car Company in 1904.

Old Spanish Trail *see:* Santa Fe Trail.

Old Testament, or the Hebrew Bible, the first part of the Christian Bible, describing God's covenant with Israel. The Old Testament is traditionally divided into 3 parts: the Law, the Prophets, and the Writings. Christianity regards the Old Testament as an inspired record of God's dealings with his people in preparation for the coming of Christ.
See also: Bible.

Olduvai Gorge *see:* Leakey.

Old World, refers to the Eastern Hemisphere, which includes Europe, Asia, Africa, and Australia. Botanists and zoologists often categorize plants and animals into Old World and New World (Western Hemisphere) terminology.
See also: Hemisphere.

Oleander (*Nerium oleander*), poisonous, evergreen ornamental shrub with roselike flowers. It grows as tall as 30 ft (9 m) high.

Oligocene, third epoch of the Tertiary, c.40-25 million years ago.

Oliphant, Patrick Bruce (1935-), editorial cartoonist whose work is seen in about 500 U.S. newspapers and won a Pulitzer Prize in 1967. Born in Australia, he worked for *The Advertiser* there, and in the United States for the *Denver Post* and the *Washington Star.* His character Punk the Penguin usually delivers Oliphant's mocking comments about the cartoon.

Olive, evergreen tree (*Olea europaea*) growing in Mediterranean climates and one of the world's oldest cultivated crops. Its unripe fruits are pickled, treated with lye solution to remove the bitter taste, and stored in brine. When left to ripen they turn black and are pressed for their oil.

Olive oil, clear edible substance obtained from the fruit of the olive tree. The fruit is pulped, then the pulp is pressed and the oil is expressed. The best quality, virgin olive oil, comes from the first pressing of fruits picked just after ripening.

Olivier, Laurence (1907-89), English actor, producer, and director. Immensely versatile and brilliant in classical as well as modern stage roles, such as John Osborne's *The Entertainer* (1957), he also acted in such films as *Wuthering Heights* (1939) and *Hamlet* (1948; Academy Award). He was director of Britain's National Theatre (1962-72).

Olivine, group of minerals or chemical compounds made from silicon, oxygen, magnesium, and iron, found in igneous rocks (those formed from a molten state), schists, and gray, pink, or white marble. A hard substance, olivine can withstand temperatures of more than 2,700°F (1,500°C) before igniting. It is used in making bricks and glass. Colors vary from clear green to brown; the gemstone peridot is deep, yellowish-green olivine.
See also: Peridot.

Olmec, people of the southeastern coastal lowlands of ancient Mexico (c.500 B.C.-A.D. 1150). Skilled in artistic stone work, they produced huge sculptured basalt heads, beautiful jewelry, fine jade, white ware, and mosaics. They knew how to record time and write in hieroglyphics. Their culture influenced that of the Zapotec and Toltec.

Olmsted, Frederick Law (1822-1903), U.S. landscape architect and writer. With Calvert Vaux he planned Central Park in New York City. He himself designed parks in Philadelphia, Brooklyn, Montreal, and Chicago. In the 1850s he was well known for his perceptive books on the South.

Olson, Charles (1910-70), U.S. critic and poet whose persuasive ideas challenged writers to reexamine their poetic style, structure, and phrasing, to intensify and further project its meaning. His essay *Projective Verse* (1950) describes his complex and distinctive mode of writing. *The Maximus Poems* (1960, 1968), a series of 38 poems, was his major work. He also wrote about the Mayan Indians, U.S. history, and Herman Melville.

Olympia, ancient sanctuary near the confluence of the Alpheus and Cladeus rivers in southwest Greece. The great temple of Zeus, one of the 7 wonders of the world, contained his gold and ivory statue by Phidias. To the north was the temple of Hera (600 B.C.). In the excavation of Olympia in the late 19th century, archeologists found the important statues of the *Nike* (Victory) of Paeonius and the *Hermes* of Praxiteles.
See also: Greece, Ancient; Olympic Games.

Olympia (pop. 161,238), capital of Washington state since 1853, on the southern side of Puget Sound, within sight of Mt. Rainier. The western terminus of the Old Oregon cattle trail, Olympia was founded in 1848, incorporated in 1859. Shipbuilding, food processing, lumber milling, and refining are major industries in Olympia.
See also: Washington.

Museum at Olympia, Greece

Olympiad, ancient Greek method of figuring a 4-year calendar time period. The Olympiad was set in conjunction with the first full moon after the longest day of the year and fell between consecutive Olympic Games. After 304 Olympiads, this way of telling time ceased (C.A.D. 440).
See also: Greece, Ancient.

Olympians *see:* Hera; Zeus.

Olympias (375?-316 B.C.), powerful, influential wife of Philip II of Macedonia, whom she had killed to secure the throne for her son, Alexander the Great. Upon his death in 323 B.C., she tried to ensure the dominion for her grandson, Alexander IV, but failed and was executed when Cassander came to power.
See also: Alexander the Great; Philip II.

Olympic Games, oldest and most famous international sporting contest. Traditionally for amateurs, it is held once every 4 years. The Olympics probably developed from the ancient Greek custom of holding athletic contests in honor of a god or a dead hero. A list of male champions exists from 776 B.C. The Olympics continued through the Roman period in Greece. Gradually, however, they lost their popular esteem, largely through the growth of cheating. In A.D. 394 they were abolished by decree of the Emperor Theodosius.
In 1894 a French nobleman, Pierre de Coubertin, called a meeting in Paris that led to the first modern Olympic Games, held in Athens in 1896. Thirteen nations sent a total of 285 men, and the Games were effectively revived. Since then the Olympics have been held in different cities once every 4 years, with the exception of the war years 1916, 1940, and 1944. Women first competed in 1912. In 1924 the Winter Olympics were instituted at Chamonix, France.
There are more than 20 Summer Olympics sports, including swimming, basketball, soccer, gymnastics, boxing, weightlifting, yachting, cycling, and equestrian events. Skiing, ice-skating, and ice hockey are among the 7 Winter Game sports. A competitor must be a citizen of the country he or she represents. No more than 3 entries from any country are permitted in each event (4 in the winter games). Only 1 team per country is allowed in team sports.

Olympic Mountains, part of the Pacific Coast Range in northwest Washington. The highest point is Mt. Olympus (7,965 ft/2,428 m). More than 100 small glaciers are scattered among the peaks, and at the foot of the southwestern slopes are luxuriant northern rain forests. The mountains' natural beauty and abundance of wildlife caused Theodore Roosevelt to declare the area a national monument in 1909. It is now part of Olympic National Park.

Olympic National Park, scenic region established in Washington State in 1938. The park includes the Olympic Mountains, glaciers, lakes, temperate rain forests, and wildlife sanctuaries.
See also: National Parks.

Omaha, Siouan-speaking Native American tribe of North America. They originally lived in the Ohio valley area, but moved with the Poncas to the Missouri River region and then to what is now the northeastern region of Nebraska. They were an agricultural and hunting tribe and lived mainly in earth lodges. Today 1,000-1,500 live on the Nebraska reservation.

Omaha (pop. 618,262), largest city in Nebraska, on the west bank of the Missouri River, established in 1854 after the Omaha Indians and U.S. government signed a peace treaty (1852). Covering 96 sq mi (249 sq km) surrounded by fertile farmland, it is a natural cattle industry site and expedites meat products via the Union Pacific Railroad. Home offices of the giant Mutual of Omaha insurance company plus 34 other insurance groups are here. Among its schools are the medical college of the University of Nebraska and, just outside the city, Boys Town, for disadvantaged youths.
See also: Nebraska.

Oman (formerly Muscat and Oman), independent sultanate on the southeast coast of the Arabian peninsula. One area of the country, a peninsula separated from the rest of Oman by the United Arab Emirates, juts into the strategic Straits of Hormuz. Oman's area is 82,030 sq mi (212,458 sq km). Its population is 1,389,000. Much of Oman is barren, with little rainfall and temperatures reaching 130°F (54°C). Dates are grown on the Batinah coastal plain, northwest of Muscat (the capital), and Dho-

In the Olympic Games of 1988, Ben Johnson (right), winner of the 100-m sprint, was disqualified after it was discovered that he had taken a banned drug.

Oman

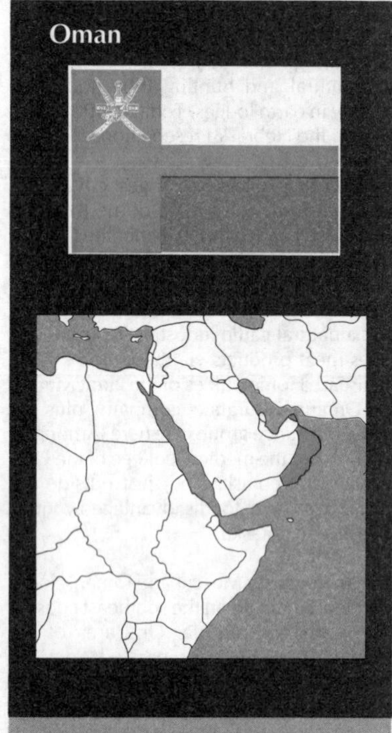

Capital:	Muscat
Area:	82,030 sq mi (212,457 sq km)
Population:	1,647,000
Form:	absolute monarchy
Independent:	1951
GNP:	U.S.$10,683,000,000
Per capita:	U.S.$6,490

New housing in Oman

far province is noted for sugarcane and cattle. Grains and fruits are grown around Jebel Akhdar. Oil was discovered in 1964, and over 100 million barrels are produced yearly. Closely associated with Britain since 1798, Oman has a population that is mostly Arab but includes blacks, Indians, and Pakistanis. In 1970 the reformist Sultan Qabus bin Said ousted his father and has become a prominent moderate in Middle Eastern affairs.

Omar Khayyam (1048-1131), Persian poet, astronomer, and mathematician. His epic poem *Rubaiyat,* dealing with nature and love, is known in the West through its translation (1859) by Edward FitzGerald.
See also: Rubaiyat.

Ombudsman, official appointed to investigate complaints by citizens against government officials or agencies. The office originated in Sweden in 1809 and since 1955 has been adopted by Denmark, New Zealand, and Britain. In the United States ombudsmen operate in some states and localities as well as within businesses and other organizations.

Omdurman (pop. 526,800), largest city in Sudan, on the White Nile, established in 1885 by Muhammad Ahmed, who is entombed here. It is a religious site for Sudan's Muslims and the region's commercial market. Many business people live here and work across the river in Khartoum, Sudan's capital.
See also: Sudan.

Ommatidium *see:* Compound eye.

Omnibus bill, legislation that includes many nonrelated bills lumped into 1 cumbersome package. Inadequate bills, those in dispute, and those of lesser importance are grouped together in hopes of being passed under the guise of propriety.
See also: Compromise of 1850.

Omsk (pop. 1,159,000), industrial city in Siberia, Russian Federation, about 1,360 m (2,190 km) east of Moscow. Commercial development began when the Trans-Siberian Railroad reached Omsk in 1894. Industrial growth spurted during World War II when factories were moved out of war zones to the comparative safety of Siberia. Today Omsk has oil refineries and grain mills and manufactures railroad equipment and farm machinery used nearby.
See also: Russian Federation.

Onager (*Equus hemionus*), wild relative to the donkey found in Asia. It was domesticated long ago and is possibly an endangered species. Colored different shades of brown with a white stomach and a black stripe down its back, it has a short mane and reaches 4 ft (1.2 m) at the shoulder.

Onassis, Aristotle Socrates (1906-75), Greek shipping magnate since the early 1930s. With relatives Stavros Livanos and Stavros Niarchos he developed the world's most powerful shipping partnership. He held citizenships in Greece and Argentina. In 1968 he married Jacqueline Bouvier Kennedy, widow of President John F. Kennedy.

Oñate, Juan de (c.1549-1628), Spanish explorer of the American southwest. He colonized what is now New Mexico from 1598. He led expeditions to the Wichita area of present-day Kansas (1601) and to the Colorado River and Gulf of California (1605).

Oncology, branch of medicine concerned with the diagnosis and treatment of cancer, and research into its causes.
See also: Cancer.

Oneida, smallest of the original 5 nations of the Iroquois Confederacy. They lived in present-day central New York. In the American Revolution they sided with the colonists. About 3,000 remain.

Oneida Community, religious commune founded by J. H. Noyes in 1848 near Oneida, N.Y. The group shared possessions and partners and thought of themselves as a "family" of God. They set up successful businesses in silver and steel products. The flourishing community was made a joint stock company in 1881, and social experiments were ended.

O'Neill, Eugene Gladstone (1888-1952), U.S. playwright, winner of the 1936 Nobel Prize for literature and several Pulitzer Prizes. He started to write plays during a convalescence from tuberculosis and was initially involved in off-Broadway efforts to introduce seriousness into American theater. Whether expressionistic (*The Emperor Jones,* 1920), naturalistic (*Anna Christie,* 1921), symbolist (*The Hairy Ape,* 1922), or updated Greek tragedy (*Mourning Becomes Electra,* 1931), his plays were ambitious in scope and relentlessly tragic (except for the comedy *Ah, Wilderness!,* 1933). His work included the masterpieces *The Iceman Cometh* (1946) and *Long Day's Journey into Night* (1956).

O'Neill, Thomas Philip ("Tip"), Jr. (1912-94), U.S. legislator. Elected to the House of Representatives (1952) as a Democrat from Massachusetts, he became majority whip (1972) and Speaker of the House (1976-86). Liberal, he was an early opponent of the Vietnam War and a critic of budget cuts for domestic programs by Presidents Carter and Reagan.

Onion (*Allium cepa*), biennial or perennial plant of either the amaryllis or the lily family. Onions have a bulb that is edible, as are the leaves. There are many varieties: the red onion, the yellow onion, the white onion, and the larger Bermuda and Spanish onions. Other onions include the garlic, the shallot, the leek, and the chive.

Onondaga, name of one of the original five nations of the Iroquois Confederacy, living in what is now New York. Because of their location, they played an important role in the confederacy and provided the leaders. In the 1700s their loyalties were divided between the French and British.

Ontario, most populous and wealthiest province in Canada. It is the nation's leader in manufacturing, mining, and agriculture. Ottawa, the nation's capital, and Toronto, the province's capital and the nation's second-largest city, are located in Ontario. The economic heart of Canada, Ontario accounts for 40% of the nation's productive capacity. Its industrial output is equal to that of the rest of the country combined.
Land. Ontario can be divided into 4 physical regions. In the north lies the sparsely populated Hudson Bay Lowland, a flat, wet, rocky plain covered with forests, tun-

dra, and swamps. To the south is the Canadian Shield, extending from the Manitoba border to the Ottawa River and covering over half of Ontario's surface with hard rock. Although it supports little agriculture, the Canadian Shield region is one of the greatest sources of mineral wealth in the world. The Great Lakes Lowland lies along Lakes Huron, Erie, and Ontario. Most of Ontario's population, cities, and industries are located on this peninsula, which is also the site of the region's richest farmland. The fourth and smallest land region is the St. Lawrence Lowland, a triangular area of low hills and fertile valleys between the Ottawa and St. Lawrence rivers, in the extreme eastern corner of the province.
Water covers one-sixth of Ontario's surface. On the Ontario-United States border lie 4 of the 5 Great Lakes, the largest group of freshwater lakes in the world. In the interior of the province are some 250,000 lakes, most in the Canadian Shield. The St. Lawrence, the chief river in Ontario, has become a great international seaway since the construction of the St. Lawrence Seaway. The Detroit, St. Clair, and St. Marys rivers, which connect the upper Great Lakes, are important shipping routes. Ontario's rivers supply 90% of the province's electricity.
Economy. Ontario is responsible for about half of Canada's manufactured goods, a third of its agricultural wealth, and a fourth of its mineral production. Highly industrialized cities such as Toronto manufacture cars, iron and steel products, and petrochemicals. In the Great Lakes Lowlands, specialized and highly productive farms grow crops such as hay, tobacco, soybeans, oats, tomatoes, and corn. Rich orchards and vineyards lie in the Niagara fruit belt. In the northeastern part of the Great Lakes Lowlands, beef and dairy cattle are reared. Ontario also provides about 20% of Canada's commercial lumber.
History. Ontario's first significant settlement was in the 1780s, when thousands of American Loyalists made their homes along the Niagara, Detroit, and St. Lawrence rivers. The Constitutional Act of 1791 gave the settlement a British form of government. Struggles for political reform culminated in the Rebellion of 1837-38 and resulted in Britain's decision to reunite the regions of Ontario and Quebec. With the historic British North America Act of 1867, the Dominion of Canada was formed; its 4 original members included Ontario, Quebec, New Brunswick, and Nova Scotia. Ottawa became the first federal capital, and Sir John A. Macdonald of Ontario the first prime minister. During World War II Ontario experienced a great burst of industrial growth, and the pace of development accelerated as huge deposits of uranium, copper, zinc, and silver were found. The province's prosperity has attracted more than half of the 3 million European immigrants that have come to Canada since World War II.

Onyx, hard form of quartz made up of extremely small crystals. Onyx can be recognized by its regular and straight parallel bands of white, black, or brown. The regular banding of onyx distinguishes it from agate, a virtually identical mineral. Black-and-white onyx is a popular material for cameos. Sardonyx, which is commonly used as a gemstone, is a red-brown variety of onyx with white or black bands.

Oostende *see:* Ostend.

Ooze, any mud deposit, but especially that found on the ocean floor, often made up primarily of the remains of plankton (microscopic sea plants and animals that float on the surface of the water).

Opal, cryptocrystalline variety of porous hydrated silica, deposited from aqueous solution in all kinds of rocks, and also formed by replacement of other minerals. Opals are variously colored; the best gem varieties are translucent, with milky or pearly opalescence and iridescence.

Oparin, Alexander Ivanovich (1894-), Soviet biochemist whose hypothesis on the origin of life became rationale for others' research. Presuming that earth's original atmosphere contained no nitrogen or oxygen but instead consisted of ammonia, hydrogen, methane, and water in a gaseous state, he theorized that life formed spontaneously in this type of atmosphere and developed as we know it today. He wrote about his theory in *Origin of Life* (1936). *See also:* Biochemistry.

OPEC *see:* Organization of Petroleum Exporting Countries.

Open-Door Policy, policy of equal commercial rights for all nations involved in an area. The term emerged in the late 19th century when the United States sought trade with China on a basis of equality with other nations, which had divided China into spheres of influence. The Open-Door Policy ended with World War II.

Open housing, enforcement of equal rights provided by fair-housing laws. These prohibit discrimination, in selling homes or renting property, against minorities, the handicapped, or for reasons of religious preferences or national origins.

Open shop, business that does not restrict its employees to labor union members. It is the opposite of a closed shop, where only union members may be employed.

Opera, staged dramatic form in which the text is wholly or partly sung to an instrumental or orchestral accompaniment. It originated in 17th-century Italy, in an attempt to recreate Greek drama. Much early opera was a mere excuse for spectacle, but works by Claudio Monteverdi, Jean Baptiste Lully, and Henry Purcell advanced the art. Dramatic standards declined in the 18th century, despite fine works by George Frederic Handel. Christoph Willibald von Gluck sought to unify plot, music, and staging into a dramatic whole, while Wolfgang Amadeus Mozart introduced greater depth of feeling into the music and realism of character on stage. The form was further enriched by the Romantics: Ludwig van Beethoven and Karl Maria von Weber in Germany and Hector Berlioz and Georges Bizet in France. The great Italians Vincenzo Bellini, Gaetano Donizetti, and Gioacchino Rossini developed the stylized bel canto form to which Giuseppe Verdi, in his later operas, gave depth and naturalism, a trend carried further in the works and theories of Richard Wagner, who sought to add a philosophical basis to Gluck's synthesis by creating *Gesamtkunstwerk,* the total work of art. Wagner influenced such later composers as Richard Strauss and Claude Debussy. The Italian verismo (naturalistic) school produced smaller-scale, often sensational works: Giacomo Puccini mastered both this and a more epic, fantastic style. Among eminent 20th-century opera composers are Leos Janácek, Alban Berg, and Benjamin Britten.

The changing of the guard in front of the parliament building in Ontario

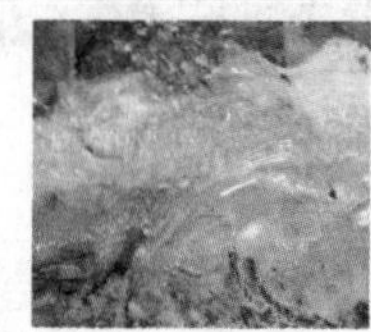

Opal

Operetta, light, amusing, semi-operatic form using spoken conversation and tuneful songs. Most plots deal with human folly, foolishness or romance, remind the listeners of conscience and good behavior, and have happy endings. Some familiar operettas are *Die Fledermaus,* by Johann Strauss, Jr., *The Merry Widow,* by Franz Lehár, *H.M.S. Pinafore,* by Gilbert and Sullivan, and *Naughty Marietta,* by Victor Herbert.

Ophthalmia, disease of the eye tissue, extremely serious and usually occurring from a wound, poison, or contamination, although it can also be acquired through birth. Sympathetic ophthalmia results when the unaffected eye responds to the affected one, causing disease in both eyes. *See also:* Blindness.

Ophthalmology, branch of medicine and surgery concerned with diagnosing and treating diseases of the eye.
See also: Eye.

Ophthalmoscope, instrument for examining the retina and structures of the inner eye. A powerful light and lens system allows the retina and eye blood vessels to be seen at high magnification.

Opiate, potent drug mixed with opium, used to relieve extreme pain, induce sleep, or control coughing. Because they are potentially addictive, opiates are available only through a physician's prescription, except for heroin, the sale of which is forbidden in the United States.
See also: Drug.

Opinion poll *see:* Public opinion.

An opium poppyfield

Opium, narcotic extract derived from the immature fruits of the opium poppy, native to Greece and Asia Minor. The milky juice is refined to a powder that has a sharp, bitter taste. Drugs derived from opium include heroin, morphine, laudanum, and codeine. Because these drugs can cause severe physical and psychologic dependencies, their use outside the pharmaceutical industry is strictly controlled in the West. The period necessary for physical dependency to occur varies with the type of drug and the amount and frequency of dose. With drugs of the morphine type, harm is often experienced indirectly, through preoccupation with drug-taking, personal neglect, malnutrition, and infection. These effects may lead to disruption of personal and family relationships, economic loss, and crime. When opiates use is stopped, withdrawal symptoms may occur, often within a few hours after the last dose and reaching a peak within the next 24-48 hours. The most severe symptoms generally disappear within 10 days. The time of onset, peak intensity, and duration of the withdrawal symptoms vary with the type of drug and degree of dependence. Withdrawal symptoms include alterations in behavior, excitation of the nervous system, and feelings of depression and anxiety. Physical disturbances, such as weight loss, abdominal cramps, nausea, and body aches, are also common.
See also: Drug; Narcotic.

Opium War (1839-42), fought in China by the British, the first in a series aimed at opening ports and gaining tariff concessions. The pretext was the burying of 20,000 chests of opium by the Chinese. China had banned the opium trade in 1799, but with the aid of corrupt Chinese officials British merchants still made enormous profits from it. British troops occupied Hong Kong in 1841, and the fall of Chinkiang (Zhen-jiang) in 1842 threatened Peking (Beijing) itself. The Treaty of Nanking (Nanjing) ceded Hong Kong to Britain and granted British merchants full rights of residence in the ports of Amoy (Xiamen), Canton (Guangzhou), Foochow (Fuzhou), Ningpo, and Shanghai; Britain was also to receive over $50 million war indemnity. The United States gained trade facilities by the 1844 Treaty of Wanghai. Further hostilities, in which French joined British troops (1856), led to more concessions, notably in the Treaties of Tientsin (1858) to which Britain, France, Russia, and the United States were parties, which legalized the opium trade, and when Kowloon was ceded to Britain and part of Manchuria to Russia (1860).

Opossum, primitive arboreal marsupial of the Americas. Opossums are carnivorous and usually have a prehensile tail, which coils around to grasp. The pouch is developed only in some species, but all have an uneven number of teats, as many as 17 in the Virginian opossum. In size, opossums vary from mouselike to the size of a domestic cat.

J.Robert Oppenheimer

Oppenheimer, J(ulius) Robert (1904-67), U.S. physicist who headed the Manhattan Project (1942-45) which developed the atomic bomb. He fought against the construction of the hydrogen bomb but was overruled by President Harry S. Truman in 1949. His main aim was the peaceful use of nuclear power, but because of his leftwing friendships, he was unable to pursue his researches in this direction after being labeled a security risk in 1954. He also worked out much of the theory of black holes in the universe.
See also: Manhattan Project.

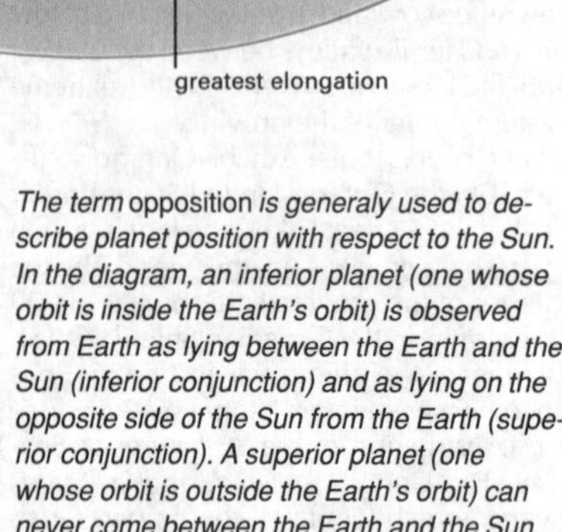

The term opposition *is generally used to describe planet position with respect to the Sun. In the diagram, an inferior planet (one whose orbit is inside the Earth's orbit) is observed from Earth as lying between the Earth and the Sun (inferior conjunction) and as lying on the opposite side of the Sun from the Earth (superior conjunction). A superior planet (one whose orbit is outside the Earth's orbit) can never come between the Earth and the Sun, but it can occupy a position directly opposite the Sun (opposition), when the elongation is 180°.*

Opposition, in astronomy, placement whereby 2 heavenly bodies are aligned with a third in a somewhat straight line. The planet Venus is in opposition when Earth lines up between Venus and the Sun.

Optical disc, thin, flat, circular plastic plate covered with a reflective substance that receives coded information from a laser beam to record sound, data, or pictures. The beam marks the disc, which can be stored or decoded by a weaker laser upon playback. Some optical discs have only prerecorded material, which cannot be erased. Optical discs have a greater storage capacity and wear longer than magnetic discs.
See also: Compact disc; Videodisc.

Optical fiber *see:* Fiber optics.

Optical illusion, visual distortion of reality. To an observer standing at the corner of a street and looking down the row of houses on the street, the closest house will appear to be the biggest, while the house at the end will seem the smallest. Since the houses are all roughly the same size, the perception that the closer ones are large and the further ones are small is an optical illusion. This differs from an illusion, where a person sees an object but it isn't really there.

Optic nerve *see:* Eye.

Optics, branch of physical science that deals with vision and light: its properties and phenomena, its origin and effects, and its role as a medium of sight.

Optometry, measurement and examination of the visual powers; the art and practice of testing the eyes by means of instruments or appliances for defects of vision in order to correct them with eyeglasses.

Oracle, in ancient times, the answer by a god or goddess to a human questioner, or the shrine at which the answer was given, usually through a priest or priestess (also called oracles). There were oracles in Egypt and Rome, but the greatest were in Greece: at Dodona, with Zeus's oracle, and at Delphi, where Apollo spoke through a priestess, the Pythia. Answers, often to important political questions, were obtained directly or derived from dreams, from signs (such as the rustling of leaves in a sacred tree), and from divination by lot.
See also: Mythology.

Oraibi *see:* Hopi.

Oral contraceptive *see:* Birth control.

Oral surgery *see:* Periodontitis.

Oran (pop. 663,500), Algerian port city about 225 mi (362 km) west of Algiers on the Mediterranean Sea. Settled by the Moors in the 10th century, it fell successively to the Spanish (1509 and 1732) and the Turks (1708 and 1791). In the aftermath of an earthquake, it became French (1831), who controlled it during World War II, when it was a U.S. base of operations.
See also: Algeria.

Orange, tree (genus *Citrus*) of the rue family; also, the fruit of the tree. Oranges, which have been cultivated since ancient times, probably originated in tropical regions of Asia. The sweet, or China, orange (*C. sinensis*) and the mandarin orange (*C. reticulata*), the main species in cultivation, are used as dessert fruit and for making orange drinks. The Seville, or sour, orange (*C. aurantium*) is mainly used to make marmalades. The chief orange-growing states are Florida, California, Arizona, and Texas.

Orange Free State, province in the Republic of South Africa, 49,866 sq mi (129,152 sq km), with Bloemfontein as its capital. The region was settled c.1836 by the Boers, South Africans of Dutch descent, who named it in 1854 and remained there, despite strife with native Africans, until defeated in war by the British (1899-1902). Under British rule, the state became part of the Union of South Africa. The majority of the state's people are black Africans, yet the majority of farms, land, and mines are owned by whites.
See also: South Africa.

Orange hawkweed *see:* Devil's paintbrush.

Orangemen, or Loyal Orange Institution, Protestant (chiefly Ulster) society that since the first (1795) lodge has identified with the Protestant ascendancy in Ireland and, more recently, union with Britain. The name is from William of Orange (William III of England, who succeeded the Catholic king James II in 1690).
See also: Protestantism.

Orange River, South African river with dams along its course (1,300 mi/2,090 km) to generate hydroelectric power, plus canals and tunnels that control flooding and bring irrigation water to 750,000 acres (300,000 hectares). It originates in Lesotho's mountains and flows into the Atlantic Ocean but is not navigable because of shallow water and numerous sandbars.

Orange root *see:* Goldenseal.

Orangutan, large, red, anthropoid ape (*Pongo pygmaeus*), native to the rain forests of Sumatra and Borneo. They are truly arboreal apes—walking quadrupedally along branches, or bipedally, with the arms holding on above. Occasionally the orangutans progress by swinging by their arms for short distances. They can move along the ground but rarely descend from the trees. They are vegetarians, feeding mainly on leaves, buds, and fruit.

Oratorio, musical composition for vocal soloists, chorus, and orchestra, usually with a religious subject. The form evolved from medieval sacred drama. Early oratorio composers include Alessandro Scarlatti, Johann Sebastian Bach, and George Frideric Handel, whose *Messiah* is probably the most famous oratorio. Among later oratorio composers are Ludwig von Beethoven, Felix Mendelssohn, and Edward Elgar.

Oratory, also called rhetoric, skill in persuasive speaking, originating in Greece c.460 B.C. Demosthenes, who charged Philip II of Macedonia with menacing Greek independence, was the most famous Greek orator. Aristotle contributed written style to organize a speaker's approach, incorporating ethical, pathetic, and logical means to persuade successfully. Martin Luther and John Calvin were powerful orators on behalf of Protestantism. Daniel Webster and Abraham Lincoln in the 19th century, and Winston Churchill, Franklin D. Roosevelt, and Martin Luther King in the 20th were most effective U.S. orators.
See also: Public speaking.

Orbit, path followed by 1 celestial body revolving under the influence of gravity about another. In the solar system, the planets mainly orbit the sun, and the moons the planets, in elliptical paths. The point in the planetary, asteroidal, or cometary orbit closest to the sun is called its perihelion; the farthest point is termed the aphelion. In the case of a moon or artificial satellite orbiting a planet or other moon, the corresponding terms are perigee and apogee. Celestial objects of similar masses, particularly double stars, may orbit each other.

Orcagna (1308-68), painter, sculptor, and architect of Florence, Italy, leading artist in the Byzantine Gothic style. His work includes the Strozzi Chapel altarpiece in Santa Maria Novella and the Or San Michele tabernacle, and the facade of Orvieto Cathedral.

Orangutan

Orchestra, instrumental group of more than a few players. The modern orchestra dates from the birth of opera, c.1600. The first great operatic composer, Claudio Monteverdi, wrote for orchestra, and for some time opera and orchestra music were closely linked. As the violin family replaced viols, composers like Antonio Vivaldi, Johann Sebastian Bach, and George Frideric Handel began to write purely orchestral music. The symphony was developed around the same time (1700) from the operatic overture. In the 18th century Franz Josef Haydn organized the orchestra into 4 groups: string, woodwind, brass, and percussion—a basic pattern that has not altered. With the great 18th- and 19th-century composers, the orchestra came to dominate the musical scene. New and more numerous instruments were introduced, permanent orchestras were established, and the art of conducting developed. The 20th century has seen a move to return to smaller ensembles.

Orchid, plant of the large family Orchidaceae (15,000-30,000 species) that produces colorful and elaborate flowers.

Orchid

Some species are native to cold and temperate regions, but most occur in tropical, damp climates. Orchid flowers are specially adapted to insect pollination, some requiring a particular species of insect. Orchids are of little economic importance except as curious ornamental plants; cultivation has developed into an extensive hobby throughout the world.

Orczy, Baroness Emmuska (1865-47), Hungarian author best known for the French Revolution adventure novel *The Scarlet Pimpernel* (1905). Her 2 sequels to it did not achieve the acclaim of the original. She also wrote numerous short detective stories.

Order in Council, statement or instruction from the British crown rule usually set forth in times of emergency or great national threat and without initial Parliamentary consent. Orders in Council were issued during World Wars I and II, and when immediate, prudent economic regulations have been needed.
See also: Continental System; Privy Council.

Ordinance, rule, decree, or command usually prepared locally to maintain order and control in cities, towns, or settlements where constitutions or laws of command have not yet been prepared.

Ordovician, second period of the Paleozoic Era, c.500-440 million years ago, immediately following the Cambrian.

Ore, aggregate of minerals and rocks from which minerals (usually metals) can be extracted. An ore has 3 parts: the country rock in which the deposit is found; the gangue, the unwanted rocks and minerals of the deposit; and the desired mineral itself. Mining techniques depend greatly on the form and position of the deposit.

Oregano *see:* Marjoram.

Oregon, Pacific Coast state in the northwestern United States; bordered by Washington to the north, Idaho to the east, Nevada and California to the south, and the Pacific Ocean to the west.

O'Bryant Square in Portland, Oregon

Oregon

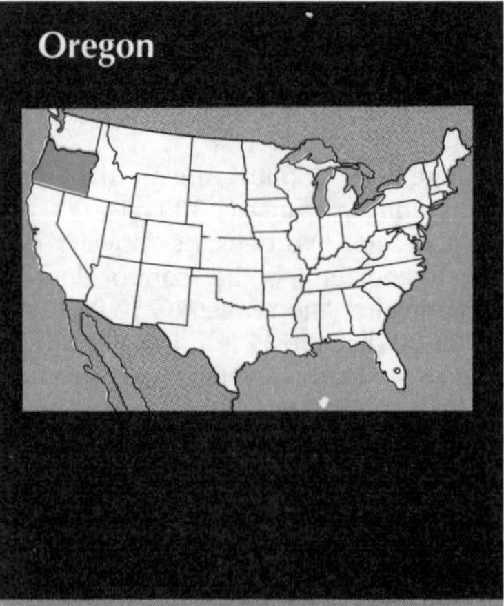

Capital:	Salem
Statehood:	Feb. 14, 1859 (33rd state)
Familiar name:	Beaver State
Area:	97,073 sq mi (251,419 sq km); ranks 10th
Population:	2,853,733 (1990); ranks 29th
Elevation:	Highest—11,239 ft (3,426 m), Mt. Hood; Lowest—sea level, along the Pacific coast
Motto:	The Union
Flower:	Oregon grape
Bird:	Western meadowlark
Tree:	Douglas fir
Song:	"Oregon, My Oregon"

Land and climate. Oregon has 6 main land regions. In the west, along the coast, the Cascade Mountains in the north merge into the Klamath Mountains in the south. Just east of the Coast Range lies the narrow Willamette Lowland, the valley of the Willamette River. East of there, the Cascade Mountains run from north to south, dividing western Oregon from the east. This region's snowcapped volcanic peaks are among the highest in North America. The high Columbia Plateau, which occupies most of Oregon east of the Cascades, is the state's chief wheat-growing area. In southeastern Oregon lies the Basin and Range Region, an area of semiarid land. The Columbia River and its tributary, the Willamette, are Oregon's major rivers. There are many waterfalls along the Columbia River Gorge. In the east, the Snake River cuts Hells Canyon, the deepest chasm in North America. Other rivers include the John Day, in the east, and the Deschutes, in central Oregon. Oregon's volcano-formed Crater Lake is the deepest body of water in the U.S. Forests cover nearly half of the state. Western Oregon has a mild, moist climate; eastern Oregon is drier, with cold winters and hot summers. Principal cities are Portland and Eugene.
Economy. Manufacturing is Oregon's leading economic activity. Chief manufactured goods are lumber and wood products, processed foods, scientific instruments, machinery, paper products, printed materials, primary metals, and fabricated metal products. Wholesale and retail trade is also important. Agriculture and mining are less important to the economy. Agriculture is led by timber. Chief crops are wheat, greenhouse and nursery products, and vegetables; chief livestock products are beef cattle and milk. Sand and gravel are the chief mining products.
Government. Oregon's constitution was adopted in 1857. The governor serves a 4-year term. The state's legislature, called the Legislative Assembly, consists of 30 senators serving 4-year terms and 60 representatives serving 2-year terms. In the U.S. Congress, Oregon is represented by 2 senators and 5 representatives.
History. Many Native American peoples were living in the area when Spanish sailors first sighted Oregon's coast in the 1500s. American Captain Robert Gray sailed into the Columbia River (named for his ship) in 1792. The Lewis and Clark expedition explored Oregon in 1805-6. In the early 1800s, U.S. and British fur traders competed in the region; in 1843, thousands of American settlers began arriving via the Oregon Trail. In 1846, the United States and Britain agreed on a boundary dividing "the Oregon Country" that stretched from Russian Alaska to Spanish California. (The U.S. portion was present-day Washington and Oregon.) Oregon became the 33rd state in 1859. In 1880-90, after a series of Indian rebellions was quelled, white settlement boomed. During the Great Depression of the 1930s, the U.S. government built Bonneville Dam, which provided hydroelectric power for new industries developed during World War II. New uses for wood and paper products, plus new methods of planting and timber conservation, improved lumber-related industries in the 1960s. In the 1980s, nationwide economic problems strained those industries, but growth of the computer and other industries helped to stabilize Oregon's economy.

Oregon Caves National Monument, wildlife preserves and limestone caves located on 480 acres (192 hectares) in the Siskiyou Mountains of Oregon. Vast stalagmites and stalactites fill the limestone caves, which are surrounded by forests with trees as old as 400 years and up to 180 ft (55 m) tall.

Oregon grape, wild, flowering, low-growing evergreen plant producing small blue edible berries in the fall, of the family Berberidaceae (genus *Mahonia*). Also known as the Oregon hollygrape, it is neither a holly nor a grape. Found also in Washington and British Columbia, it is Oregon's state flower.

Oregon Territory, in North American northwest, area south of the 49th parallel, excluding Vancouver Island. It was territorialized in 1848 after the resolution (1846) of a boundary disagreement between the United States and Great Britain, both of whom dominated the region. Oregon joined the Union February 14, 1859.

Oregon Trail, pioneer wagon route between Independence, Mo., on the Missouri River, and the Columbia River region of the

Pacific Northwest. The 2,000-mi (3,200-km) trail was most popular in the 1840s, before the beginning of the California gold rush. In that decade at least 10,000 pioneers made the arduous trek from northeast Kansas along the Platte River in Nebraska, to Fort Laramie, Wyo. From there they crossed the Rocky Mountains at South Pass and proceeded through Snake River country to Fort Vancouver. The journey was recounted in Francis Parkman's classic, *The Oregon Trail* (1849).
See also: Westward movement.

O'Reilly, Leonora (1870-1927), U.S. women's rights activist, instrumental in developing the National Women's Trade Union League for protection of women workers' rights (1903) and in establishing the National Association for the Advancement of Colored People (NAACP). She promoted women's vocational training, fought for increased wages for garment workers, and was active in the Woman Suffrage Party.
See also: Women's movements.

Orellana, Francisco de (c.1511-46), Spanish soldier and explorer of the Amazon River. On an expedition with Pizarro east of Quito, Ecuador, Orellana and a group of soldiers left to search for provisions but never returned. Instead, they continued to the Atlantic Ocean, floating down the river later named the Amazon, after his comparison of tribal women he had seen there to those in Greek myths. On a subsequent expedition to the Amazon, his boat capsized and he drowned.

Orestes, in Greek mythology, son of Agamemnon and Clytemnestra. Orestes killed his mother and her lover, Aegisthus, after they murdered Agamemnon. Thereafter, the Furies, goddesses of vengeance, harassed Orestes. Fleeing to Athens, he was purified and found innocent of the killings by a jury.
See also: Mythology.

Orff, Carl (1895-1982), German composer and music teacher. His works are marked by short melodic motifs and strong rhythms from a large and varied percussion section. His best-known work is the oratorio *Carmina Burana.*

Organ, musical instrument in which air is blown into pipes of different shape and size to produce a range of notes. Organ pipes are of 2 kinds: flue pipes that work like a flute or recorder, and reed pipes that operate on the same principle as a clarinet or oboe. Although organs existed in ancient times, the major developments in organ building took place between the 14th and the 18th centuries. Composers like Jan Pieter Sweelinck and Dietrich Buxtehude paved the way for Johann Sebastian Bach, the greatest of all composers for the organ. Bach and George Frideric Handel wrote for the baroque organ, a relatively small instrument. In the 19th century many great organs were built, precursors of the huge electric-powered instruments built in the 1920s and 1930s in cinemas and theaters. The modern Hammond organ produces its sound electronically. Small electronic organs are now frequently used by popular musical groups.

Settlers on the Oregon Trail, which crossed 2,000 miles of prairie, desert, and mountains

Organic chemistry, branch of chemistry comprising the study of hydrocarbons, or carbon compounds containing hydrogen. (Simple carbon compounds such as carbon dioxide are usually considered inorganic.) Because of carbon's ability to form linked chains of atoms of any length and complexity, there are far more organic compounds than inorganic. Organic compounds form the basic stuff of living tissue. Organic chemistry is also of fundamental importance in the textile, petrochemical, and pharmaceutical industries.
See also: Chemistry.

Organization for Economic Cooperation and Development (OECD), international governmental body representing 24 countries, created in 1961 to develop trade and support and assist in each other's growth and economic welfare. An administrative body, the Council, having representatives from each country, governs OECD. Its headquarters are in Paris, France.

Organization of African Unity (OAU), association of independent African states (excluding South Africa) that aims to promote unity among its members and improve economic and cultural relations in Africa. It has been opposed to the government of South Africa and endorses majority rule for the country. Founded in 1963, the OAU has a permanent secretariat in Addis Ababa, Ethiopia, and has had great influence at the United Nations.

Organization of American States (OAS), association of republics of the Americas that aims to settle disputes peacefully, to create a collective security system, and to coordinate the work of other intra-American bodies. The OAS was founded in Bogotá, Colombia, in 1948 and has a permanent secretariat, the Pan American Union. Its activities have included support for the U.S. blockade of Cuba in 1962 and mediation between Britain and Guatemala in 1972.

Organization of Petroleum Exporting Countries (OPEC), group of 13 oil-producing countries that attempts to control oil prices in world sales. Organized in 1960, its members are Algeria, Ecuador, Gabon, Indonesia, Iran, Iraq, Kuwait, Libya, Nigeria, Qatar, Saudi Arabia, United Arab Emirates, and Venezuela. OPEC's 4 administrative sections, each with its own responsibilities, work toward the common goals of oil pricing and supplying world demands.

Organ Pipe Cactus National Monument, desert region in southwest Arizona named for that cactus which, with additional uncommon plants, is found only in this 517 sq mi (1,339 sq km) U.S. location. Crossing it is part of El Camino del Diablo, a trail where many prospectors and early settlers died.

Organ transplant *see:* Tissue transplant.

Oriental exclusion acts, edicts either limiting or halting immigration of Asians into the United States. Initially, Chinese laborers were welcomed and protected by the Burlingame Treaty (1868), but when the U.S. economy slipped the Chinese were blamed, and the Chinese Exclusion Act of 1882 was passed. Japanese immigration met the same fate when the Immigration Act of 1924 prohibited all Asian immigration. The Immigration and Nationality Act of 1952 gave Asians the same rights as other immigrants, but the U.S. quota system did not end until 1965.

Origami, Japanese form of art made by folding various-sized squares of paper into birds, flowers, fish, and abstract shapes. Pleated ceremonial decorations attached to presents are a form of origami called *noshi.* The decorative folding of paper is not exclusively Japanese; it has thrived in Spain and South America, and in Germany as a teaching tool for commercial design.

Origen (Origines Adamantius; A.D. 185?-A.D. 254?), one of the foremost radical theologians of the early Christian Church. Born in Alexandria, Egypt, Origen tried to reconcile Greek philosophy with Christian theology in works like *De Principalis* (On First Principles) and *Contra Celsum* (Against Celsus), a defense of Christianity.Charles R.; Evolution.

Walt Disney World in Orlando, Florida

Orinoco River, tributary of Venezuela, about 1,700 mi (2,736 km) long. Mostly navigable, it rises in the Parima highlands of southeastern Venezuela and eventually flows into the Atlantic Ocean through a 7,000-sq-mi (18,130-sq-km) delta.
See also: Venezuela.

Oriole, name of several members of the blackbird family. Most species live in tropical America, where both sexes are brightly colored; in temperate regions the females are olive drab or brown. The Baltimore oriole, now called the Northern Oriole, is black and brilliant orange. Orioles build their nests of woven grass, and some build hanging nests or large communal nests occupied by several families.

Northern Oriole

Orion (the hunter), star constellation resembling the shape of a man, named from Greek mythology. Three bright aligned stars make up Orion's belt and a group of fainter stars depict his sword. The yellow-red star Betelgeuse identifies the left shoulder, and the star Rigel his right foot. Innumerable faint stars and luminous masses of gas and dust complete Orion's figure.
See also: Constellation.

Orion, in Greek mythology, giant hunter killed by the goddess Artemis, who then turned him into a constellation.
See also: Mythology.

Orizaba, or Citlaltépetl, Mexico's highest mountain and North America's third tallest, elevation 18,701 ft (5,700 m). The snow-covered extinct volcano is about 30 mi (48 km) west of Orizaba city.
See also: Mexico.

Orizaba (pop. 118,400), Mexican resort city located in a scenic valley between Veracruz and Mexico City. Settled by the Spanish in the 1500s to protect essential travel routes between the 2 cities, it was incorporated in 1774 and developed into an agricultural and industrial site. In 1973, an earthquake devastated the area.

Orkney Islands, group of about 70 islands north of Scotland, of which they are part. Their total area is 376 sq mi (974 sq km) but fewer than half are inhabited. The climate is mild and the soil fertile. Farming is the chief activity (grains, sheep, cattle, poultry), and there is some fishing.

Orlando (pop. 1,072,748), resort city and retirement center in central Florida, with a year-round temperate climate for its fast-growing population. Nearby Walt Disney World, Epcot Center, Disney-MGM Studios, aerospace industries, and a large citrus crop provide employment.
See also: Florida.

Orlando, Vittorio Emanuele (1860-1952), Italian statesman and prime minister (1917-19). He led the Italian delegation at the Paris Peace Conference of 1919-20, but left the conference because of opposition from U.S. President Wilson regarding territorial compensation for Italy. Orlando retired from politics with the advent of Fascism but returned after the fall of Mussolini.
See also: Italy.

Orléans, family name of 2 branches of the French royal line. The house of Valois-Orléans was founded by **Louis, duke of Orléans** (1372-1407), whose grandson ascended the throne (1498) as **Louis XII**. The house of Bourbon-Orléans was founded by **Philippe, duke of Orléans** (1640-1701), brother of King Louis XIV. His son, **Philippe** (1674-1723), was regent of France (1715-23). **Louis Philippe** (1773-1850) was the sole member of the house to become king (1830-48).
See also: France.

Orléans (pop. 102,700), city in the Loire Valley, northwest France. Among the ancient buildings still standing are remnants from the time of Julius Caesar's occupation. When the English attacked it in 1429 during the Hundred Years War, Joan of Arc led French soldiers to victory. Industries include flower production, candies, liqueurs, automobiles, and farm machinery.
See also: France.

Ormandy, Eugene (Eugene Ormandy Blau; 1899-1985), Hungarian-born U.S. symphony conductor, music director of the Philadelphia Orchestra 1938-80. Ormandy originally came to the United States (1921) as a violinist, but began to conduct, becoming conductor of the Minneapolis Symphony Orchestra in 1931. During his tenure with the Philadelphia Orchestra he established its lush sound, particularly that of its string sections, and became a leading interpreter of Romantic music.

Ornithischian *see:* Dinosaur.

Ornithosis *see:* Psittacosis.

Oroville Dam, transversing California's Feather River, providing flood control, irrigation, and hydroelectric power. About 80 million cubic yds (61 million cubic m) of sludge and useless material accumulated from gold mining were used to build the strucure (height, 754 ft/230 m; length, 6,920 ft/2,109 m) from 1957-68.

Orozco, José Clemente (1883-1949), Mexican painter. He exploited the fresco technique in his large-scale murals, which express strong social convictions. His most famous works include the fresco *Prometheus* (1930), *Mankind's Struggle* (1930), and the mural *Epic Culture in the New World* (1932-34).

Orpheus, in Greek mythology, renowned musician of Thrace. Son of the muse Calliope, he could tame wild beasts with his lyre playing. After the death of his wife, Eurydice, Orpheus sought her in Hades. He was allowed to lead her back to earth providing he did not look at her, but he could not resist the temptation, and Eurydice vanished forever. He was regarded as the founder of the Orphic mystery cult, which saw both good and evil in human nature, and followed a strict ethical and moral code.
See also: Mythology.

Orr, Bobby (1948-), Canadian-born, U.S. hockey player. Known for his leadership and scoring, he played in the National Hockey League (NHL) for the Boston Bruins (1967-76), where he was chosen the NHL's most valuable player 3 times (1970, 71, 72) and was named the most outstanding defensemen 8 consecutive times (1968-75). He finished his career with the Chicago Black Hawks (1976-79) after suffering serious knee injuries. Orr was inducted into the Hockey Hall of Fame in 1979.

Bobby Orr

Orrisroot, root body of 3 species of irises, which produce an oil with the fragrance of violets. In powdered form, the substance was once used extensively in perfumes but high costs now limit it to expensive brands. It is also an ingredient in medicine.

Ortega, Daniel (1945-), revolutionary leader of the Sandinista National Liberation Front in Nicaragua (1984-1990). In 1979 Ortega removed Anastasio Somoza-Debayle from power and took control of the government. He improved health, education, and welfare services but controlled the press, several private businesses, and limited civil rights. The contras opposed Ortega's government and engaged in guerrilla warfare until a 1988 cease-fire. The United States cut back trade with Ortega, claiming he formed a Communist government. Lack of U.S. trade, the contra war, and ongoing welfare services presented overwhelming adverse conditions for Ortega, who was defeated by Violeta Chamorro in a general election in 1990.
See also: Nicaragua.

Ortega y Gasset, José (1883-1955), Spanish philosopher whose best-known work, *The Revolt of the Masses* (1929), attributes Western decadence to the revolt of "mass man" against an intellectual elite. His philosophy attempts to reconcile reason with individual lives and needs.
See also: Existentialism.

Orthodontics, in dentistry, correction or prevention of the arrangement or number of teeth in people and animals. Procedures include tooth extractions and using metal or plastic braces and wires to adjust unaligned teeth, a problem which usually occurs during childhood as the teeth develop. These abnormalities in teeth position are called maloclusions.
See also: Dentistry.

Orthopedics, specialty within surgery dealing with bone and soft-tissue disease, damage, and deformity. Its name derives from 17th-century treatments designed to produce "straight children." Treatment of congenital deformity, fractures and tumors of bone, osteomyelitis, arthritis, and joint dislocation are commonly treated by orthopedic professionals. Methods range from the use of splints, physiotherapy, and manipulation, to surgical correction of deformity, the fixing of fractures, and the refashioning or replacement of joints. Suture and transposition of tendons, muscles, and nerves are also performed.

Orwell, George (Eric Arthur Blair; 1903-50), English writer, famous principally for *Animal Farm* (1945), a satire on communist revolution, and *Nineteen Eighty-Four* (1949), which depicts a dehumanizing totalitarian society. Orwell was also a critic and essayist. Other works include the semiautobiographical *Road to Wigan Pier* (1937) and *Homage to Catalonia* (1938), an account of his experiences in the Spanish Civil War.

Oryx, genus of African antelopes with a white or fawn coat and long curving horns. All 5 species have been reduced by hunting.

Osage, Native American tribe of the Siouan language group who lived in what is now western Missouri and Arkansas in the late 17th century. In 1872 they were moved to a reservation in Oklahoma. They became one of the richest communities in the world when oil was discovered on their reservation two decades later.

Osage orange (*Maclura pomifera*), tree originally found only in Texas, Oklahoma, and Arkansas. Its large green fruit is known as a hedge apple, and its elastic timber is used for making archery bows.

Osaka (pop. 2,636,000), Japan's third-largest city, an industrial and commercial center, on Honshu Island at the mouth of the Yodo River on Osaka Bay. Lack of land (it covers only 80 sq mi/206 sq km) has forced a rapidly increasing population into apartments or to the suburbs, and shopping centers underground. It has centuries-old cultural and religious monuments and several universities and museums. Steel, chemicals, and textiles are leading products. A great port, it is connected by the world's fastest railway system to Tokyo and Asia's busiest airport.
See also: Japan.

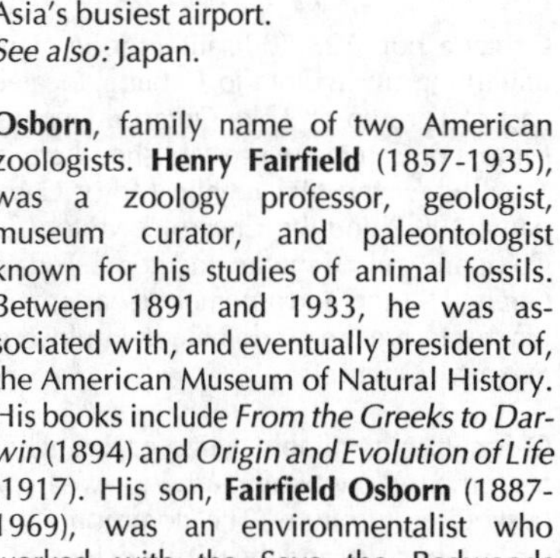

George Orwell

Osborn, family name of two American zoologists. **Henry Fairfield** (1857-1935), was a zoology professor, geologist, museum curator, and paleontologist known for his studies of animal fossils. Between 1891 and 1933, he was associated with, and eventually president of, the American Museum of Natural History. His books include *From the Greeks to Darwin* (1894) and *Origin and Evolution of Life* (1917). His son, **Fairfield Osborn** (1887-1969), was an environmentalist who worked with the Save the Redwoods League, the National Audubon Society, the International Commission for Bird Protection, and was president of the New York Zoological Society.
See also: Zoology.

Daniel Ortega

Osborne, John (1929-), English dramatist whose *Look Back in Anger* (1956) made him the first Angry Young Man of the 1950s and established a new and vigorous realism in the British theater. His later plays include *The Entertainer* (1957), *Luther* (1961), and *Inadmissible Evidence* (1964).

Oscar *see:* Academy Awards.

Osceola (1804?-38), Native American leader in the Second Seminole War against the United States (1835-42). He used guerrilla tactics to resist a U.S. plan to transport the Seminoles from Florida to Oklahoma. Osceola was taken prisoner in 1837 and died in prison.

Osaka Castle (1584), Japan

Oscilloscope, device using a cathode ray tube to produce line graphs of rapidly varying electrical signals. Since nearly every physical effect can be converted into an electrical signal, the oscilloscope is widely used. Typically, the signal controls the vertical deflection of the beam while the horizontal deflection increases steadily, producing a graph of the signal as a function of time.
See also: Cathode ray.

Oshawa (pop. 123,700), automobile-manufacturing city in Ontario, Canada, located east of Toronto on Lake Ontario. General Motors of Canada was established here in 1918 when the McLaughlin Motor Company (1907) and the Chevrolet Motor Car Company of Canada merged. Today, General Motors and automobile parts manufacturers are the predominant employers.
See also: Ontario.

Osier, tough, pliable twigs or branches from the willow family, used for weaving baskets or furniture. The common osier (*Salix viminalis*) and the purple osier (*Salix purpurea*), which originated in Europe and Asia, thrive in the United States beside streams and ponds.

Osiris, ancient Egyptian god, brother and husband of Isis, and father of Horus. He was killed by his evil brother Set but restored to life by Isis. His cult was important in dynastic Egypt and later became popular in the Roman Empire. A benefactor of mankind, Osiris was a ruler of the underworld and also a life-giving power, symbolizing the creative forces of nature.
See also: Mythology.

Osler, Sir William (1849-1919), Canadian-born U.S. physician and educator who taught medical students the value of patient involvement. He was the first to detect platelets in blood, wrote many research papers on diseases and health problems, and helped establish the Association of American Physicians and the American Lung Association.

Lee Harvey Oswald

Oslo (pop. 454,000), capital, largest city and chief seaport of Norway. Founded c.1050, it was rebuilt after the great fire of 1624. Known as Christiania or Kristiania from 1625 to 1925, today Oslo is Norway's chief commercial and industrial center, producing chemicals, paper, textiles, and wood products. The hub of Norways's railroad system, Oslo is also serviced by an international airport located just outside the city. Home to Norway's oldest university, the city also features many fine museums, including the Norwegian Folk Museum and the Viking Ships Museum (which displays Viking ships that date back to the 10th century).
See also: Norway.

Osmium, chemical element, symbol Os; for physical constants see Periodic Table. Osmium was discovered by Smithson Tennant in 1804. It occurs native associated with platinum and in the mineral iridosmine. The element is obtained commercially as a byproduct of nickel-bearing ores. Osmium, a bluish-white, lustrous, dense, hard and brittle metal, is a member of the platinum group of metals, and has the highest melting point of the group. Osmium forms a volatile oxide that is highly toxic. Powdered osmium metal, like palladium, adsorbs large amounts of hydrogen. The primary use of osmium is to harden other platinum metals. It is used in machine bearings, pen points, and as catalyst. Osmium tetroxide is used as an organic reagent to convert olefins to glycols.

Osmosis, diffusion of a solvent through a semipermeable membrane that separates 2 solutions of different concentration. The movement is from the more dilute to the more concentrated solution, because of the thermodynamic tendency to equalize the concentrations. The liquid flow may be opposed by applying pressure to the more concentrated solution; the pressure required to reduce the flow to zero from a pure solvent to a given solution is known as the osmotic pressure of the solution.

Osprey, large fish-eating bird of prey (*Pandion haliaetus*), found worldwide, except in South America. Also known as the fish hawk, the osprey occupies marine and freshwater areas, cruising above the water and plunging to take the fish in its talons.

Ostend (pop. 69,100), port city in northwest Belgium on the North Sea. Its worth as a port has caused it to be attacked by the Dutch, French, Spanish, Germans, British, and Allied Forces over the centuries. Since Belgium's independence in 1803, the city has developed into a significant import-export link with a Channel link to England. Products include tobacco, soap, fish, and oyster cultivation.

Ostend Manifesto, document created in Ostend, Belgium, in 1854 by 3 proslavery U.S. diplomats, James Buchanan, John Y. Mason, and Pierre Soulé. The manifesto implied that if Spain refused to sell Cuba, the United States would forcibly seize the island. The diplomats, who probably hoped to make Cuba a Union slave state, were denounced by the press and most politicians, and the manifesto was repudiated by the U.S. government.

Osteomyelitis, bacterial infection of bone, usually caused by staphylococcus, streptococcus, or salmonella carried to the bone by the blood or through open fractures. It commonly affects children, causing fever and local pain. If untreated or partially treated, it may become chronic.

Osteopathic medicine, method of therapy that concentrates on manipulation of bones and muscles, developed in 1874 by Andrew Taylor Still. The musculoskeletal system is focused upon to treat the whole person rather than an isolated region. Osteopathic physicians are fully qualified to use surgery and all medications as part of their medical care. In the United States, there are 15 osteopathic colleges, 180 osteopathic hospitals, and over 28,000 osteopathic-practicing physicians.

Osteoporosis, loss of bone mass and density. It occurs mainly among older people, especially postmenopausal women. Osteoporosis increases the risk of bone fractures in all parts of the body, can cause a weakening of the jaw and loss of teeth, and contributes to collapse of the spine. Preventive measures include exercise, calcium supplements, and, for older women, estrogen treatments.

Osteosclerosis, abnormal hardening or thickening of the bone, causing brittleness and an inclination to fracture. Called osteopetrosis in children, the disease becomes increasingly serious as growing bone density crowds the bone marrow and limits space for red blood cell production, resulting in extreme anemia.

Ostrava (pop. 325,400), industrial city in northeastern Moravia, Czechoslovakia, about 170 mi (274 km) east of Prague. Industries include coal mining, oil refineries, and chemical factories. Manufactured goods include clothing, building supplies, and food products.
See also: Moravia.

Ostrich (*Struthio camelus*), the largest living bird, at one time found throughout Africa and southwest Asia but now common only in east Africa. Flightless birds, well adapted to a terrestrial life, they have long powerful legs, with two toes on each foot, an adaptation for running over dry grassland.

Ostrogoths (East Goths), branch of the Goths, a Germanic people who originally occupied the lands to the north of the Black Sea. The accession of their king Theodoric the Great (A.D. 471) heralded an alliance with Zeno, emperor of the East Roman Empire. On Zeno's orders, Theodoric invaded Italy in 488, overthrew Odoacer (493), and ruled from Ravenna. The Byzantine generals, Belisarius and Narses destroyed Ostrogothic rule in the 530s; the final Ostrogothic revolt under Totila was swiftly crushed by Narses in 552.

Ostrovsky, Aleksander (1823-86), Russian dramatist whose plays, usually about merchants and minor officials, are marked by powerful characterization and strong drama. His masterpiece is *The Storm* (1860), a domestic tragedy.

Ostwald, Wilhelm (1853-1932), German physical chemist regarded as a father of physical chemistry, awarded the 1909 Nobel Prize for chemistry for his work on catalysis. He also developed the Ostwald process for manufacturing nitric acid.
See also: Chemistry; Catalysis.

Oswald, Lee Harvey (1939-1963), the alleged assassin of President John F. Kennedy in Dallas, Tex., on Nov. 22, 1963. A former marine, he had lived in the USSR (1959-

62). He was shot dead by Jack Ruby while under arrest. The Warren Report (1964) on the investigation of Kennedy's assassination declared Oswald the sole assassin.

Oswego, Great Lakes port city, on Lake Ontario and the Oswego River in New York, originally commanded by the British (1722-96) and incorporated in 1848. Usage of railways and the Erie Canal diminished the city's port value, but the opening of the Oswego Canal made it the northern terminus of the New York State Barge Canal, completed in 1918, and brought industrial development. Products include cement, wood pulp, coal, textiles, and sheet metals. The Nine Mile Point Nuclear Station here provides a major power source for central New York.
See also: New York.

Otis, Elisha Graves (1811-61), U.S. inventor of the safety elevator (1852), first installed for passenger use in 1857.

Otis, James (1725-83), American Revolutionary politician in the colonial conflict for independence from Great Britain. He was instrumental in establishing the Stamp Act Congress of 1765, assisted Samuel Adams in protesting several revenue acts, and published *The Rights of the British Colonies Asserted and Proved* (1764).

Otoscope, instrument for examining the internal parts of the ear.

Ottawa (pop. 300,800), capital city of Canada, located at the junction of the Ottawa and Rideau rivers, near the southeastern tip of the province of Ontario. Across the Ottawa River is the twin city of Hull, Quebec. In 1968 the city of Ottawa was combined with a number of communities to form a regional government area called Ottawa-Carleton. Ottawa is principally concerned with the business of government. Its most striking feature is the group of Parliament buildings in Victorian Gothic style on a bluff (Parliament Hill) overlooking the Ottawa River. The city has numerous educational and cultural institutions. The National Arts Center (1969) contains a theater and an opera house-concert hall. Over a third of the metropolitan area's residents are French Canadians. Ottawa developed in the early 19th century when the Rideau Canal was built by Colonel John By, and was known as Bytown until it was incorporated (1854) as the city of Ottawa. In 1858 Queen Victoria selected the city as the capital of the United Provinces of Canada, and on confederation (1867) it became the national capital.
See also: Canada.

Ottawa

Ottawa, name of large North American Native American tribe of the Algonquian family originally inhabiting, with the Ojibwa and Potawatomi tribes, the region north of the Great Lakes. The Ottawa later moved to Manitoulin Island. They were active traders and negotiated with the French.

Ottawa River, principal tributary of the St. Lawrence River, rising in western Quebec province north of the city of Ottawa. The river flows west 696 mi (1,120 km) through a series of lakes as far as the Quebec-Ontario border, then generally southeast past Ottawa and Hull to empty into the St. Lawrence. Extensive hydroelectric power is developed in its lower reaches. The river is linked with Lake Ontario by the Rideau Canal.

Otter, aquatic or semiaquatic carnivore of the weasel family. The body is lithe and muscular, built for vigorous swimming and covered with thick fur. The paws are generally webbed. The nostrils and eyes may be shut when swimming underwater. Unlike most other wild animals, otters remain playful as adults.

Otter hound, working dog, dating to 14th-century England, used for hunting otters. Its webbed paws and coarse oily skin enable it to swim in chilly waters. It is 24-27 in (61-69 cm) high and weighs 65-100 lbs (29-45 kg). Colors range from dappled blue to light brown to black and tan.

Otto, name of 4 Holy Roman Emperors. **Otto I the Great** (912-73) was founder and first emperor of the Holy Roman Empire from 962. King of Saxony from 936, he invaded Italy and declared himself king of the Lombards (951). He subdued the Poles and Bohemians and routed the Magyars of Hungary (955). Otto was crowned emperor in Rome for helping Pope John XII against an Italian king, Berengar II. **Otto II** (955-83) succeeded his father as emperor (973-83). He crushed the rebellion of Henry, duke of Bavaria, defeated the Danes (974), but failed to extend his empire in Italy and was badly defeated by the Saracens in southern Italy (982). **Otto III** (980-1002) succeeded his father as emperor (996-1002), after a regency. He planned to make Rome the capital of a vast theocratic empire. **Otto IV** (c.1174?-1218), emperor (1209-15), was excommunicated by Pope Innocent II for attempting to master parts of Italy (1210) and later deposed.
See also: Holy Roman Empire.

The coronation of Sultan Selim II, during the flourishing of the Ottoman Empire (16th century)

Otto I (1815-67), Austrian-born king of Greece (1833-62). He was unpopular for many reasons, among them his attempts to discard the constitution, his use of German advisers, the loss of the chief port of Piraeus to France and Britain during the Crimean War, and failure to free Greek prisoners in Turkish-held Crete, Thessaly, and Macedonia. He was deposed by a military revolt.
See also: Greece.

Ottoman Empire, vast empire of the Ottoman Turks that at its height, during the reign of Sultan Suleyman I, stretched from the far shore of the Black Sea and the Persian Gulf in the east to Budapest in the north and Algiers in the west. The Ottoman Turks, led by Osman I, entered Asia Minor in the late 1200s and, expanding rapidly, made Bursa their capital in 1326. They crossed to the Balkan Peninsula (1345), and in 1453 Constantinople fell to Muhammad II. The empire continued to expand in the 16th century under Selim I, the Terrible (1512-20), and reached its zenith under Suleyman I. However, Suleyman failed to capture Vienna (1529) and was driven back to Malta (1565). Directly after his death, the Ottoman fleet was annihilated at the naval battle of Lepanto (1571). During the 1700s and 1800s the decaying empire fought against Russia, and Greece won its independence. The reformist Young Turk movement led the empire into World War I on the German side, with disastrous results. The nationalists, led by Kemal Atatürk, deposed and exiled the last sultan, Muhammad, and proclaimed the Turkish republic in 1922.

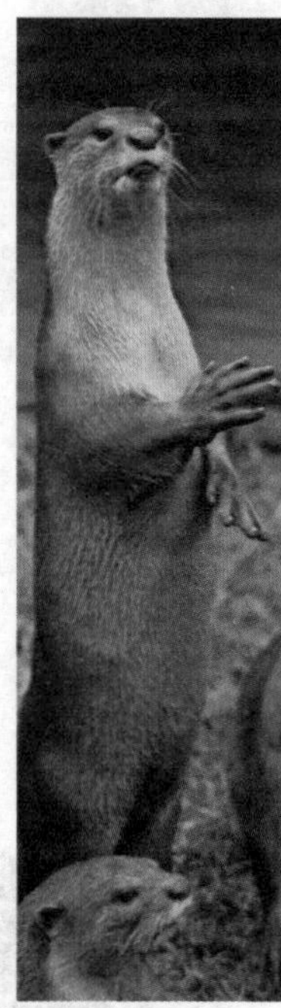
Small-clawed otter

Ouachita River, in western Arkansas and eastern Louisiana, 605 mi (974 km) long, about 350 mi (563 km) of which is navigable. Rising in the Ouachita Mountains, it joins the Tensas River to form the Black River.

Ouagadougou (pop. 442,200), capital of Burkina Faso, land of the Mossi people in western Africa. The city has many mosques, a museum, and a university. An airport and a railroad provide transporta-

tion to the Ivory Coast. Manufactured goods include textiles, building materials, and food processing.
See also: Burkina Faso.

Oubangui River *see:* Ubangi River.

Ouida (Maria Louise de la Ramée; 1839-1908), English novelist. Among her works are *Under Two Flags* (1867), *A Dog of Flanders* (1872), and *Moths* (1880).

Jesse Owens

Outboard motor, high-speed boat motor having 1 to 8 cylinders. Attached outside the stern, it operates an underwater propeller that drives the boat forward. Usually gasoline-powered, it can also use electric power operating off of rechargeable storage batteries.

Outcault, Richard Felton (1863-1928), U.S. cartoonist, originator of the Yellow Kid and Buster Brown comic strips. Joseph Pulitzer's New York *Evening World* published them on yellow newsprint. The strips were so successful that William Randolph Hearst of the New York *Journal* lured Outcault away to draw the Yellow Kid for him. Pulitzer then hired another cartoonist to compete with Outcault. From such unprincipled competitive practices arose the term "yellow journalism."

Ouzel *see:* Dipper.

Ovary, female reproductive organ. In humans it contains the follicles in which the eggs (*ova*) develop.
See also: Reproduction.

Ovenbird (*Seiurus aurocapillus*), member of the wood warbler family, a 6-in (15-cm) long bird whose grassy rounded nest, with a side opening built on the ground, resembles an adobe oven. Sometimes referred to as the teacher bird because its repeated call sounds like the word "teacher," it is dull green with a white flecked breast and a rust crown.

Owl

Overture, independent instrumental musical work, often serving as a prelude to a major musical presentation and including portions of that production's music. In developing the form for French opera, Jean Baptiste Lully wrote the first standardized overture c.1660, and Wolfgang Amadeus Mozart used it as a single movement in the 1700s. Familiar concert overtures, not part of another work, are Tchaikovsky's *1812* and Johannes Brahms's *Academic Festival.*

Ovid (Publius Ovidius Naso; 43 B.C.-A.D. 18), Latin poet. Popular in his time, he was exiled by the Emperor Augustus to the Black Sea in A.D. 8 and died there; his *Sorrows* and *Letters from Pontus* are pleas for his return. He was a master of erotic poetry, as in his *Amores* and *The Art of Love,* but his *Metamorphoses,* a collection of myths linked by the common theme of change, is considered to be his finest work.

Oviparous animal, one hatched from a fertilized egg that matured after being expelled from its parent's body. Most birds, fish, reptiles, and some mammals are oviparous.

Ovulation *see:* Reproduction.

Owen, 2 industrialists and social reformers. **Robert Owen** (1771-1858) was a socialist and pioneer of the cooperative movement. He introduced better conditions in his cotton mills in Scotland and was active in the trade union movement in Britain. In the United States Owen set up short-lived "villages of cooperation," such as that at New Harmony, Ind. **Robert Dale Owen** (1801-77), his son, campaigned in the U.S. for birth control, women's property rights, state public schools, and slave emancipation. He was a member of Congress from Indiana (1843-47).

Owen, Ruth Bryan (1885-1954), first U.S. woman diplomat, as minister to Denmark (1933-36). The daughter of politician William Jennings Bryan, she served in the U.S. House of Representatives (1929-33) and as an alternate at the UN General Assembly (1949).

Owen, Wilfred (1893-1918), English poet, deeply influenced by Siegfried Sassoon, who wrote movingly of the savagery and human sacrifice in World War I. Owen was killed in action a week before the end of World War I. Nine of his poems form the text of Benjamin Britten's *War Requiem* (1962).

Owens, Jesse (1913-80), U.S. African-American athlete. He once broke 3 world records at a single college meet (1935). At the 1936 Berlin Olympics Owens won 4 gold medals (100-meter, 200-meter, 4 x 400 relay, and long jump) breaking olympic records in both the 200-meter and long jump competitions. Owens' record-setting achievements proved to be an embarrassment to German dictator Adolf Hitler, who had hoped to use the Games to prove his theory of Aryan German supremacy.

Owensboro (pop. 87,189), city in Kentucky, originally called Yellow Banks after the color of its site on the Ohio River. Settled in the late 1790s and named after Colonel Abraham Owens, today it is an oil and gas, coal, and agricultural center. Manufactured goods include bourbon whisky, cigars, and food products.
See also: Kentucky.

Owl, nocturnal bird of prey of the family Tytonidae or the family Strigidae. Owls have large eyes, directed forward, and all have pronounced facial disks of feathers. Some species develop ear tufts, and most have extremely sensitive hearing. Many species hunt primarily on auditory cues. Their eyes are also extremely powerful: some 35-100 times more sensitive than our own. All owls are soft-feathered, and their flight is almost silent.

Owyhee Dam, concrete arch gravity dam on Oregon's Owyhee River near the Idaho border, completed by the U.S. Bureau of Reclamation in 1932. The dam, 417 ft (127 m) high and 830 ft (253 m) across, creates a reservoir 52 m (84 km) long and has the capacity to irrigate 16,000 acres (6,400 hectares) of farm land.

Ox, term zoologically applied to many members of the family Bovidae; also, in common usage, a castrated bull used for draft purposes or for its meat.

Oxalic acid, $(COOH)_2 \cdot 2H_2O$, colorless, poisonous, organic acid. Found in many vegetables and in the rumex and oxalis plants, it is also produced by the body. The synthetic type is used to process textiles, as a paint-stripper, and in laundries to remove stains.

Oxalis, group of about 850 kinds of plants of the wood-sorrel family, occurring mostly in South Africa and South America. Most grow from bulbs producing thick tubers bearing both white and pastel-colored flowers and clover-shaped leaves.

Oxbow lake, shallow U-shaped or serpentine lake, formed from a riverbed when the river has changed to a straighter course. The deposits of earth left by the new course help separate the lake from the river. Oxbow lakes are common along the lower Mississippi River.

Oxenstierna, Axel Gustaffson (1583-1654), Swedish politician. As chancellor (1612-54) he served under King Gustavus Adolphus (Gustavus II, r. 1611-32), Queen Christina (1632-54), and Charles X (1654), also acting as head of the regency (1632-44) until Queen Christina came of age. A close friend and adviser of Gustavus II, he was chief administrator during the military conflicts with Denmark and Russia and the Thirty Years War (1618-48). He also wrote the 1634 constitution, which strengthened Sweden's central government.
See also: Sweden.

Oxford (pop. 115,000), city of south-central England, the seat of Oxford University. The city existed in the early 900s. The university began to form in the early 1100s. Standing on the Thames River (known locally as the Isis) where it is joined by the Cherwell, Oxford is rich in historic buildings, including the many colleges, the Ashmolean Museum, the Bodleian Library, the cathedral, and the Norman castle. The city is the county seat of Oxfordshire.
See also: England.

Oxford Movement, religious movement begun in 1833 in Oxford that aimed to revitalize the Church of England by reintroducing traditional Catholic practices and doctrines. Its leaders, John Keble, J. H. Newman, and, later, Edward Pusey, wrote a series of *Tracts for the Times* (1833-41) and became known as the Tractarians. Despite violent controversy, the movement has had great influence in the Anglican Church.
See also: Church of England.

Oxford University, English university in Oxford comprising nearly 50 affiliated but autonomous colleges and halls, a great center of learning since its foundation in the 12th century. The oldest men's college is University (1249), and the oldest women's is Lady Margaret Hall (1879). The major university library is the Bodleian.

Oxidation, any process that increases the proportion of oxygen or acid-forming element or radical in a compound.
See also: Reduction; Rust.

Oxide, chemical compound of oxygen and another element or, in the case of organic oxides, an organic compound. The formation of an oxide, called oxidation, occurs rapidly, in burning, or slowly, as in rusting. Metallic oxides such as quicklime or calcium oxide (CaO) react with water to form alkalis and with acids to form salts. Nonmetallic oxides such as sodium trioxide (SO_3) react with water to form acids and with bases to form salts. Sulfur dioxide and nitrogen oxides are common air pollutants that combine with water to form acid rain. Industrial uses of oxides include the production of acids and the manufacture of glass.

Oxnam, G(arfield) Bromley (1891-1963), U.S. Methodist bishop, teacher, and author. Ordained in 1916, he served as bishop of Omaha (1936-40), Boston (1940-44), New York (1944-52), and Washington, D.C. (1952-60). He voiced his liberal views on social issues in such books as *The Mexican in Los Angeles* (1920), *Russian Impressions* (1927, written following a visit to the Soviet Union), and *Labor in Tomorrow's World* (1945). He was an outspoken opponent of totalitarianism, and defended religious freedom in front of the U.S. House of Representatives' Un-American Activities Committee (1953).

Oxyacetylene *see:* Acetylene.

Oxygen, chemical element, symbol O; for physical constants see Periodic Table. Oxygen was discovered by Joseph Priestley in 1772. It is present in air to the extent of 21% and is commercially obtained from the air by liquefaction and fractional distillation. The element makes up 49.2%, by weight, of the earth's crust and is the most abundant element. Oxygen is a colorless, odorless, reactive gas, capable of combining with most other elements. Ozone, a poisonous allotrope of oxygen, is formed by the action of ultraviolet light, or an electrical discharge on oxygen. The greatest use of the gas is in the oxygen enrichment of steel blast furnaces. Large quantities of oxygen are used in the synthesis of ammonia, methanol, and ethylene oxide, as well as for oxy-acetylene welding, and as rocket propellent. Oxygen consumption in the United States is 20 million short tons per year.

Oxygen tent, enclosed space, often made of plastic, in which a patient is nursed in an atmosphere enriched with oxygen. It is mainly used for small children with acute respiratory diseases and for adults when the use of a face mask is impractical.
See also: Anoxia.

Oyster, bivalve mollusk of shallow coastal waters. While other bivalves are able to move by means of a muscular "foot," oysters have lost this foot, and the animal lives cemented to a hard substrate of rocks or shells. Like all bivalves, oysters feed by removing suspended organic particles from a current of water drawn into the shell. Edible oysters are extensively fished and cultivated worldwide. The pearl oyster is a tropical species.

Oystercatcher, any of a family (Haematopodidae) of shorebirds found in most parts of the world. The oystercatcher is distinguished by a flat, long, sharp orange-red bill, used to open the shells of the mollusks on which it feeds. It measures 16-20 in (40-50 cm) long and is black or white and black.

Oyster plant *see:* Salsify.

Ozalid process, trademarked photocopying process using Ozalid paper, which is chemically treated to receive an impression made by ultraviolet rays, and then developed by the Ozalid machine.

Ozark Mountains, plateau of rugged beauty in southern Missouri, northern Arkansas, and northeastern Oklahoma. The highest peaks in the region, the Boston Mountains in the south, do not reach over 2,350 ft (716 m) above sea level, and the St. François Mountains in the east are less than 1,800 ft (550 m). Taum Sauk in the St. François range is the highest point in Missouri at 1,772 ft (540 m). The heavily forested hills and mountains of the Ozark region are thinly populated. Farming and mining (lead, limestone) are the region's major economic activities. Tourists are attracted by the scenery and clear air.

Ozawa, Seiji (1935-), Japanese conductor, best known for his fiery interpretations of Romantic and modern French composers. He served as director of the San Francisco Symphony Orchestra (1970-6) and of the Boston Symphony Orchestra and the Berkshire Music Festival from 1973.

Ozone, O_3, triatomic oxygen; a blue gas with a pungent odor. It is a very powerful oxidizing agent and decomposes rapidly above 212°F (100°C). The upper atmosphere contains a layer of ozone, formed when ultraviolet radiation acts on oxygen, that protects the earth from the sun's ultraviolet rays. Ozone, made by subjecting oxygen to a high-voltage electric discharge, is used for killing germs, bleaching, removing unpleasant odors from food, and sterilizing water.

P

P, 16th letter of the English alphabet, corresponding with the letter *pe* of the Semitic alphabet, which was represented by a diamond-shaped symbol based on the Egyptian hieroglyph for "mouth." The Greeks adopted the letter as *pi*, and it took its modern form in Latin. As an abbreviation it represents phosphorus in chemistry, pence and peso in currency, and piano (Italian for "softly") in music.

Paca, any of a genus (*Cuniculus*) of large, nocturnal, plant-eating rodents of the tropical forests of North and South America. Pacas measure up to 30 in (75 cm) in length and weigh as much as 22 lb (10 kg). They are hunted as food by humans, and their hides are used for leather.

Paca, William (1740-99), U.S. political leader, signer of the Declaration of Independence. Paca was a member of the Continental Congress (1774-79), a governor of Maryland (1782-85), and a judge of the Court of Maryland (1789-99).

Oyster

Pacemaker, small mass of cells in the right atrium of the heart that gives rise to the electrical impulses that initiate contractions of the heart; also called sinoatrial (S-A) nodes. Under abnormal circumstances, other cardiac tissues may assume the pacemaker role. The artificial pacemaker is a battery-powered device that controls the beating of the heart by a series of rhythmic electrical discharges. If the electrodes that deliver the discharges to the heart are placed on the outside of the chest, it is called an external pacemaker. If they are placed within the chest wall, it is called an internal pacemaker.
See also: Heart.

Pacific Islands, also Oceania, consisting of the 20,000 to 30,000 islands scattered over thousands of square miles of the Pacific Ocean. The outer limits of Oceania, known as the Pacific Rim, are defined by the archipelagos of Indonesia, the Philippines, and Japan on the Asian side, and by the Aleutians, Galapagos, and other island groups close to the northern and southern continents on the American side. The southern limit is Australia. Within the Rim is a vast area of ocean with numerous islands, but divided into three distinct regions: Melanesia, Micronesia, and Polynesia.
Land and climate. Melanesia consists of New Guinea, the Solomon Islands, New Caledonia, Vanuata, and Fiji. Micronesia, consisting of some 2,000 islands, is situated north of Melanesia. Its principal islands include Guam, the Caroline Islands, the Mariana Islands, the Marshall Islands, the Gilbert Islands, and Nauru. Polynesia is the largest division of Oceania. It extends some 5,000 mi (8,047 km) north to south from midway to New Zealand and some 4,000 mi (6,437 km) east to west from Easter Island to New Zealand and includes the Hawaiian Islands, Samoa, the Marquesas, and the Society Islands.
The Pacific islands are of two types, high islands or low islands. High islands are distinguished by hills and mountains, some of them snow covered. New Britain, New Caledonia, New Guinea, and New Zealand are all high islands. Low islands, the type most frequent in Polynesia, are coral islands. Many are atolls, coral reef surrounding a lagoon. They are low-lying islands and some of the lesser ones are only a few feet above sea level. Typical low islands are the Gilbert Islands, the Marshall Islands, Phoenix, Tuamotu, and the Tuvalu groups.
The prevailing climate throughout the Pacific Islands is tropical and it is warm the year round. On high islands, it is cool in the mountains, and the lowlands are often dense with tropical rain forest. Throughout the region, rainfall varies. Most islands have a wet and dry season, and typhoons are frequent.
People. The three divisions of Oceania are ethnically as well as geographically distinct. It is believed that the peoples who originally settled the islands were from southeast Asia. Over the long period of dispersion throughout the islands, different cultures developed, but all of them centered on village life. Kinship bonds have been and remain important and the community was traditionally led by a chief. People's diets were principally fish and native plants. There are some 12,000,000 people living in the islands, many of them still in traditional villages. Throughout the islands some 1,200 native languages are spoken. Of non-native languages, English is the most common in the region, but Japanese, French, and Pidgin English are also used. Christianity is the dominant religion, but in many areas the system of native beliefs remains quite strong, particularly in New Guinea, the Solomon Islands, and Vanuatu. Cannibalism is still practiced among certain of the natives in New Guinea.
Economy. Hawaii, New Zealand, and Nauru have modern economies and most of their people are wage earners. But on the other islands, most people live in traditional and self-sufficient economies and earn little or no money, though recently, more and more islanders have begun moving to towns to join the money economy. Beyond those of Hawaii and New Zealand, there are few towns or cities, principally Port Moresby in Papua New Guinea, Apia in Western Samoa, Nouméa in New Caledonia, Papeete in French Polynesia, and Sura in Fiji.
The islands are, in general, not suitable for farming and have few minerals for export. Among the exceptions are New Caledonia, whose nickel, chromium, and iron ore are mined, Nauru which exports phosphates, and New Guinea. Bougainville, New Guinea, is the site of one of the world's largest copper mines. Otherwise, agriculture is the main industry and copra, dried coconut meat, the main export. Some coffee, sugar, cocoa, and bananas are grown, too.
Tourism is also a source of income, but has met with resistance from people concerned about its adverse effects upon native cultures and the environment.
History. The first European to visit the islands was Ferdinand Magellan in 1521. The Dutchman, Abel Janszoon Tasman, discovered New Zealand in 1642 and the Englishman, James Cook, explored the region in the 18th century. The missionaries followed the explorers and the islands were opened for exploitation which, at the time, included the slave trade. In the 19th century the United States competed with France, Germany, and Spain for dominance in the region. Australia and New Zealand became independent in the early 20th century, and, following World War I and Germany's defeat, Japan took control of its Pacific possessions and became a presence in the region. In World War II Japan made a bid for dominion in the region; its defeat led to major changes. In the decades since the 1960s a number of individual islands and island groups have become independent. Others have joined in what is called free association, an arrangement in which an island is internally self-governing but leaves external affairs to a larger stronger partner such as New Zealand or the United States. After World War II, islands taken from Japan were placed by the United Nations under U.S. administration as the Trust Territory of the Pacific Islands. Since the war, islands within the Trust Territory have become independent within a free-association arrangement wherein the United States retains control over foreign affairs and guarantees the islands' security.

The Pacific Island of Moorea, part of French Polynesia

Pacific Islands, Trust Territory of the, trust territory of the UN administered by the United States (1946-81). There are about 2,180 islands in all (only 96 inhabited) scattered over about 3 million sq mi (7.77 million sq km) of the Pacific Ocean within the area known as Micronesia. The formerly German islands were mandated to Japan in 1922 and, after U.S. occupation in World War II, to the United States. Among constituent territories, the Marianas gained separate status as the Northern Marianas and became a U.S. commonwealth (1978); the Marshall Islands became self-governing (1979); the islands of Truk, Yap, Ponape, and Kosrae became the Federated States of Micronesia (1978); and Palau became self-governing as the Republic of Belau (1981).

Pacific Ocean, world's largest and deepest ocean, extending from the Arctic to the Antarctic oceans and from the Americas to Asia, covering an area of about 70 million sq mi (181.3 million sq km), or one-third of the earth's total surface. The average depth of the Pacific is 14,000 ft (4,267 m); the deepest point is 36,198 ft (11,033 m) in the Challenger Deep, in the Marianas Trench, southwest of Guam. Plateaus, ridges, trenches, and sea mountains make for many variations in depth. Japan, the Philippines, New Zealand, and thousands of islands lie on the connected series of ridges running from the Bering Straits southwest to the South China Sea. Despite its name, the ocean is not generally calm. In the tropical and subtropical zones an average of more than 130 cyclones occur per year.

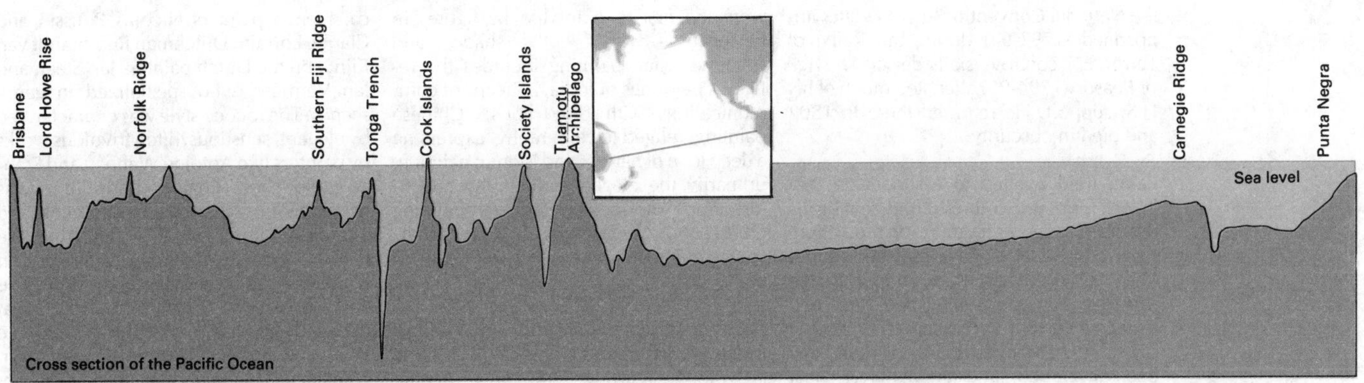

Cross-section of the Pacific Ocean

Pacific scandal (1873), corruption charges against Canadian prime minister John Macdonald. In 1872 he awarded a contract to build the Canadian Pacific Railway to Sir Hugh Allan, who had financed his 1872 election campaign. Denying the charges, Macdonald resigned, and the contract was cancelled.
See also: Macdonald, Sir John Alexander.

Pacifism, belief that violence is never justified and hence that peaceful means should always be employed to settle disputes. A pacifist may refuse not only to use force but also to abet its use, as by refusing to help produce weapons of war. Pacifists who refuse to serve in the armed forces are called conscientious objectors. Supporters of nuclear disarmament or opponents of specific wars are not necessarily pacifists.
See also: Gandhi, Mohandas Karamchand; King, Martin Luther, Jr.

Pack rat *see:* Woodrat.

Paddlefish, any of various freshwater relatives of the sturgeon, resembling a shark with a long, paddlelike snout. A Mississippi River paddlefish, also known as the spoonbill sturgeon, grows to 6 ft (1.8 m) in length, and another, the swordbill sturgeon of the Yangtze River in China, may grow to twice that size. Paddlefish are sometimes eaten, and their large black eggs make caviar.

Paderewski, Ignace Jan (1860-1941), Polish concert pianist, composer, and politician. An internationally acclaimed interpreter of Frédéric Chopin, Franz Liszt, Anton Rubinstein, and Robert Schumann, he frequently toured the United States, where he sometimes gave concerts to raise funds for Polish causes. He was the first prime minister of the Polish republic (1919) and led the Polish government in exile (1940-41). He died in the United States.
See also: Poland.

Padua (pop. 231,300), oldest city in northern Italy, on the Bacchiglione River, 22 mi (35 km) southwest of Venice. Padua is a renowned renaissance center noted for its architecture and art treasures, including works by Giotto, Donatello, and Fra Filippo Lippi.
See also: Italy.

Paducah (pop. 29,315), river port city in southwestern Kentucky, on the Tennessee and Ohio rivers, at the head of the Tennessee-Tombigbee Waterway, which extends to the Gulf of Mexico. Paducah was founded by the explorer William Clark in 1827. It is a market center for the area's coal and agricultural products and a diversified industrial center.
See also: Kentucky.

Paestum, ancient city (fl. 6th century B.C.) situated south of Salerno, southern Italy. Founded by Greek colonists as Posidonia (c.600 B.C.), it became a Roman colony and was renamed in 273 B.C. Over a period of several centuries the silting up of the surrounding River Sele made the vicinity unhealthy, and it was abandoned after being sacked by Saracens in 871. Two 6th-century B.C. Doric temples and one from the 5th century survive; excavations have also revealed a Temple and an amphitheater.

Paéz, José Antonio (1790-1873), Venezuelan soldier and president. He assisted Bolívar in the Spanish defeats at Carabobo (1821) and Puerto Cabello (1823). He led the successful Venezuelan independence movement (1829) and ruled Venezuela (as president or the power behind other presidents) from 1831 to 1846, and, after a period of exile, from 1861 to 1863, before being exiled again.

Pagan, volcanic island in the western Pacific Ocean, one of the Mariana islands. Pagan is only 19 sq mi (49 sq km) in area. Its small population was evacuated when Mount Pagan last erupted (1981). In 1986 it became part of a U.S. commonwealth that includes the Northern Marianas and Guam.

Paganini, Niccolò (1782-1840), Italian virtuoso violinist. By his use of adventurous techniques, such as diverse tuning of strings and the exploitation of harmonics, he extended the range of the instrument. His best-known compositions are his 24 *Caprices.*

Page *see:* Knights and knighthood.

Page, Geraldine (1924-87), U.S. stage, film, and television actress. She made her New York City stage debut in *Seven Mirrors* (1945). Page starred opposite Paul Newman in Tennessee Williams's *Sweet Bird of Youth* both on stage (1959) and on film (1962). Nominated for an Academy Award many times, she won for her role in *The Trip to Bountiful* (1986).

Pagnol, Marcel (1895-1974), French playwright, screenwriter, director, producer, and critic. He wrote the screenplays *Marius* (1930) and *Topaze* (1932), both adapted from his own plays. *Marius* was the first in his Provençal trilogy, which also included *Fanny* and *César.*

Pago Pago *see:* American Samoa.

Pahlavi, Mohammad Reza *see:* Mohammad Reza Pahlavi.

Pahlavi, Reza Shah *see:* Reza Shah Pahlavi.

Paige, Satchel (Leroy Robert Paige; 1906-1982), U.S. baseball pitcher. Barred as an African-American from the major leagues for most of his career, Paige played with the Negro Leagues. He pitched dozens of no-hitters and was considered one of the greatest pitchers in the game by major league players who faced him in exhibition games. Paige was the first African-American pitcher in the American League, playing with the Cleveland Indians (1948-51) and the St. Louis Browns (1951-53). He was inducted into the National Baseball Hall of Fame in 1971.

Paine, Robert Treat (1731-1814), American lawyer, signer of the Declaration of Independence. He was a delegate to the Continental Congress (1774-8), first Massachusetts attorney general (1777-90), and Massachusetts state supreme court judge (1790-1804).

Niccolò Paganini

Paine, Thomas (1737-1809), English-born writer and radical, a leading figure of the American Revolution. His highly influential pamphlet *Common Sense* (1776) urged the American colonies to declare independence. His pamphlet series *The Crisis* (1776-83) inspired the Continental Army. After returning to England, he wrote *The Rights of Man* (1791-92), a defense of the French Revolution and of republicanism. Forced to flee to France, he was elected to the National Convention and was later imprisoned (1793-94) during the Reign of Terror. His controversially deistic *The Age of Reason* (1794-95) alienated much of his U.S. support. He returned there in 1802 and died in obscurity.

Paint, fluid applied to a surface in thin layers, forming a colored, solid coating for decoration, representation, or protection. Paint consists of a pigment dispersed in a "vehicle" or binder that adheres to the substrate and forms the solid film, and usually a solvent or thinner to control the consistency. Many specialized paints have been developed, for example to resist heat or corrosion. After applying a primer, the paint is brushed, rolled, or sprayed on; dip coating and electrostatic attraction are recently developed methods of application.

Painted Desert, brightly colored barren region about 150 mi (241 km) long of mesas and plateaus in north central Arizona, east of the Little Colorado River. Centuries of erosion have exposed red, brown, and purple rock surfaces.

Painted-tongue, or salpiglossis, flowering garden annual (*Salpiglossis sinuata*) of the nightshade family. Its flowers, similar to those of the related petunia, are trumpet-shaped and range from white to yellow, orange, pink, red, or purple.

Painter's colic, or lead colic, symptom of lead poisoning characterized by severe abdominal pain. It is so called because lead may be absorbed into the body by skin contact with paints or by the breathing of vapors from paints.
See also: Lead poisoning.

Painting, depiction by means of line and color of a subject, rendered representationally or abstractly, on a 2-dimensional surface. The art of painting dates from more than 20,000 years ago, with cave paintings of animals and hunters, to ancient Egyptian tomb paintings, Cretan celebratory paintings on buildings, and the painted pottery of the Greeks. The Romans were the first to paint lifelike figures in perspective with depth, shade, and shadow. Asian painting includes the religious paintings of India, a means of communicating with the gods; Chinese painting, related to calligraphy, expressing a deep love of nature; and Islamic painting, primarily the elegant calligraphy and illustrations of books. Medieval painting (300s-1300s) centered on Christianity as its source of inspiration and was expressed in paintings lacking perspective and using symbols to tell stories.
Italian painting, 1300-1600. Giotto's fresco works broke away from Byzantine art with his realistic depiction of people and their emotions. His monumental, sculptural style was generally followed in 14th-century Florence. In Siena, the decorative linear style of Duccio and Simone Martini prevailed. The Florentine discovery of linear perspective was first employed by Masaccio, and the tradition was continued by Fra Angelico, Piero Della Francesca, and Botticelli. Western painting reached an apogee in the High Renaissance works of Leonardo da Vinci, Raphael, and Michelangelo. Mannerism, developed by Giulio Romano and Andrea del Sarto, influenced the arresting style of El Greco. From the mid-15th century a distinct Venetian school emerged, notable for its use of color. The most influential Venetian artists were Titian, Tintoretto, and Veronese.
Painting outside Italy, 1400-1600. Flemish art was finely detailed, as in the work of Jan Van Eyck who, with his brother Hubert, created innovative oil paintings. A more emotional style was developed by Rogier Van der Weyden, while Hieronymus Bosch and Pieter Bruegel developed grotesque fantasy pictures. In the late 15th century, German art became influential with Albrecht Dürer's woodcuts and engravings, Mathias Grünewald's Isenheim Altar piece, and Hans Holbein's portraits.
Painting, 1600-1850. The prominent artists of the baroque period were the Italian painter Caravaggio; the brilliant and imaginative Flemish painter Peter Paul Rubens; the Spaniard Diego Velázquez; the classical French painters Nicolas Poussin and Claude Lorrain; Dutchman Rembrandt van Rijn; and the Dutch painters Jan Steen and Jan Vermeer, who specialized in genre scenes. The rococo style was characterized by elegant, sensuous, often frivolous works by painters like Antoine Watteau and François Boucher. English portraiture was developed by Sir Joshua Reynolds and Thomas Gainsborough, influencing the first important American artists, John Singleton Copley and Benjamin West. The Spanish rococo painter, Francisco Goya, depicted the savagery of the Napoleonic Wars. The first half of the 19th century in France was dominated by the classicism of Jean Auguste Dominique Ingres and the romanticism of Eugène Delacroix.
Painting since 1850. Gustave Courbet rendered large-scale pictures of ordinary life and Édouard Manet influenced impressionism. Claude Monet and Pierre Auguste Renoir pioneered painting outdoors and experimented with the effects of light. The postimpressionists Paul Gauguin and Vincent Van Gogh, through their novel use of paint and simplified forms, greatly influenced expressionism and fauvism. Paul Cézanne's work was crucial to the development of cubism, largely invented by Pablo Picasso and Georges Braque. Wassily Kandinsky and Casimir Malevich developed forms of abstract art. Surrealism used imagery taken from dreams, such as in the works of Salvador Dali and Max Ernst. In the 1960s pop art was developed by Jasper Johns, Robert Rauschenberg, and Andy Warhol. A resurgence of interest in various aspects of realism occurred in the 1970s and 1980s.

Paisley (pop. 203,400), industrial city in western Scotland near Glasgow, on the White Cart River. A medieval village that grew up around an abbey, Paisley became a center for linen weaving in the 18th century. In the 19th-century it was known for its manufacture of paisley shawls. Its industries now include engineering, shipbuilding, and food processing.

Paiute, several Native American tribes of the Shoshone group. They can be divided into the North Paiute, of northern California and Nevada, and the South Paiute, of Arizona and southern Nevada. The Paiute ghost dance religion, which began c.1870, led by the prophet Wovoka, led to violent uprisings against white encroachment. Today about 4,000 Paiute live on reservations.

Pakistan, Islamic Republic of Pakistan, nation state on the Indian subcontinent. Pakistan covers about 310,403 sq mi (803,944 sq km) and is bordered on the west by Iran, on the northwest by Afghanistan, on the southeast by India, and on the south by the Arabian Sea.
Land and climate. Pakistan is dominated by the mountains of the Hindu Kush in the north, but there are fertile valleys in the northwest. The west is arid, but there is arable land in the east, drained by the Indus River.

A village near Rawalpindi, Pakistan

Pakistan

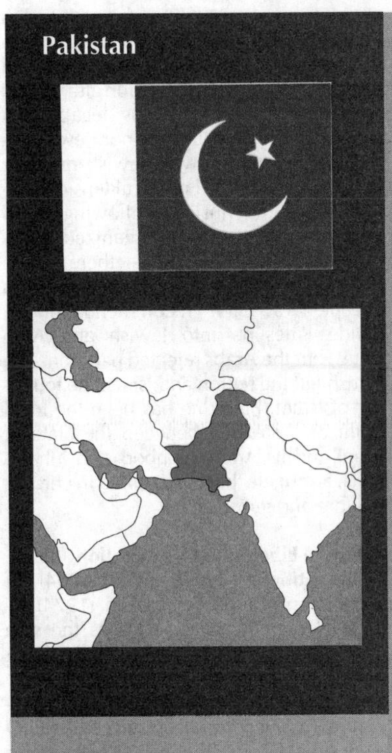

General information	
Capital:	Islamabad
Area:	307,374 sq mi (796,095 sq km)
Population:	119,347,000
Official language:	Urdu
Monetary unit:	1 Pakistani rupee = 100 paisas
Main cities:	Karachi, Lahore, Islamabad
Government	
Form:	federal republic
Independent:	1947 (federal republic)
Head of state:	President (elected every 5 years)
Head of government:	Prime minister
Legislature:	two legislative houses (Senate and National Assembly)
Executive:	President and Cabinet
Judiciary:	highest court is the Supreme Court
Political division:	4 provinces, 1 federal capital area, tribal territories
National economy	
Gross national product:	U.S. $49,477,000,000
Per capita income:	U.S. $410
Agriculture:	wheat, sugar cane, rice, cotton, chickpeas
Livestock:	goats, sheep, cattle, water buffalo
Fisheries:	428,000 metric tons
Mining:	limestone, gypsum, rock salt, silica sand, fireclay, crude petroleum
Industries:	cotton textiles and clothing, cement, chemical fertilizers, refined sugar, chemicals, paper and paperboard
Main exports:	raw cotton, cotton yarn and thread, cotton fabrics, clothing, rice, carpets
Transportation:	7,842 mi (12,620 km) of railroads, 68,430 mi (110,128 km) of roads, 5 international airports
Trading partners:	Japan, U.S. Germany, United Kingdom, Saudi Arabia
People	
Urban:	32%
Ethnic composition:	Punjabi 65%, Sindhi 13%, Pushtun 8%, Urdu 7%, Baluchi 2.5%
Birth rate:	43 per 1,000 population
Death rate:	14 per 1,000 population
Infant mortality:	120 per 1,000 live births
Life expectancy:	male 54 years, female 55 years

People. Most of the people of Pakistan are Punjabis, but other groups include the Pathans and the Baluchi. The people are overwhelmingly Muslim and the official language is Urdu. The capital is Islamabad. Most Pakistanis live in small villages.

Economy. Pakistan's is primarily an agricultural economy. Wheat is the main subsistence crop, and fruit and livestock are important in the north. Pakistan is not yet self-sufficient in food production. Its diverse mineral resources have yet to be fully developed, but low-grade coal and iron ore, chromite, gypsum, and limestone are being mined. Deposits of natural gas and oil are potentially large. Pakistan exports wool and cotton textiles and leather goods and has a growing industrial base.

History. Presentday Pakistan was once at the center of the ancient Indus Valley civilization. It was subsequently invaded by Aryans, Persians, Greeks, and Arabs and became part of the Mughal Empire in the eighteenth century. Dominated for a time by the Sikhs, the area came under British control as part of its Indian empire. The modern state was formed with the partition of India in 1947 into India and Muslim East and West Pakistan under Muhammad Ali Jinnah and his Muslim League. The partition was accompanied by terrific bloodshed and, almost immediately, the new states of Pakistan and India fought bitterly over Kashmir. Separated by 1,000 miles of Indian territory, tensions grew between Bengali East and Punjabi West Pakistan. in 1958 Gen. Muhammad Ayub Khan seized power and instituted a reform program. He was replaced in 1969 by Gen. Agha Muhammad Yahya Khan. In 1969, East Pakistan took its first formal steps toward self government and in 1971 declared its independence. In the ensuing civil war, Indian troops took the side of East Pakistan, now Bangladesh, and West Pakistan was defeated in the fighting. Pakistan formally recognized Bangladesh in 1974, but the loss was a considerable blow to Pakistan's economy and prestige. After the war, separatist violence broke out in the western province. Zulfigar Ali Bhutto succeeded Yahya Khan, and was reelected in 1977. But opposition to his government was intense, the vote was declared fraudulent, and in the ensuing disorder Bhutto was overthrown and Gen. Muhammad Zia al-Haq took control of the government. Bhutto was subsequently tried for treason and other charges and executed in 1979. After postponing elections and constitutional reform, Gen. Zia formally ended military rule in January 1986, but no formal elections were held. Following his death in a plane crash, Gen. Zia was succeeded by Benazir Bhutto, Ali Bhutto's daughter, who was elected prime minister in 1988. In August 1990, Bhutto's government was dismissed by President Ghulam Ishaq Khan, amidst charges of corruption and abuse of power. Following elections that November, Nawaz Sharif took office. However, Bhutto returned to her position as prime minister in 1993.

Palate, bodily structure dividing the mouth from the nose and bounded by the upper gums and teeth; it is made of bone and covered by mucous membrane. At the back of the palate is a soft mobile connective-tissue that can close off the nasopharynx during swallowing and speech. *See also:* Mouth.

Palatinate, 2 regions of Germany: the Lower, or Rhine, Palatinate is on the Rhine River bordering France and the Saar; the Upper Palatinate is in northeastern Bavaria.

Palau Islands (Belau), independent group of coral and volcanic islands in the western Pacific Ocean. Of the nearly 200 islands totaling 196 sq mi (508 sq km) in area, only 8 are inhabited. Babelthaup is the largest; Koror is the capital. The small population lives on subsistence farming and fishing. The islands were under Spanish control for several hundred years before being sold to Germany (1899). Japan seized them during World War I, and the United States took them over during World War II. A UN trust territory 1947-87, they became self-governing in 1981 and remained under

Palau Islands

Capital:	Koror
Area:	196 sq mi (508 sq km)
Population:	15,800
Government:	republic
Independent:	1994
GNP per capita:	U.S. $2.260

U.S. administration until 1994 when they became independent.

Paleocene, first epoch of the Tertiary period, c.65-55 million years ago.

Paleogeography, science of the construction from geologic, paleontologic, and other evidence of maps of the earth's surface at specific times in the past. Paleogeography has been of considerable importance in studies of continental drift.

Paleography, the study of handwritten material from the ancient and medieval times. It deals with writing on papyrus, parchment, paper, and other perishable materials, as opposed to epigraphy, which deals with writing on metal or stone. Paleographers study handwriting to interpret and date events and to trace the evolution of the written alphabet.

The amphitheater of Caesarea, an ancient ruin in Palestine

Paleolithic Period *see:* Stone Age.

Paleontology, study of fossils. The principal branches of study are paleobotany and paleozoology, dealing with plants and animals respectively. These studies are essential in charting the history of the evolution of life and in tracking continental drift.
See also: Fossil.

Paleozoic, earliest era of the Phanerozoic Eon, comprising the Lower Paleozoic (570-400 million years ago), containing the Cambrian, Ordovician, and Silurian periods; and the Upper Paleozoic (400-225 million years ago), containing the Devonian, Carboniferous (Mississippian and Pennsylvanian), and Permian periods.

Palermo (pop. 696,700), capital, largest city, and major port of Sicily, Italy, on the northwestern coast. Shipbuilding, textiles, and chemicals are leading industries. Palermo was founded by Phoenicians between the 8th and 6th centuries B.C. The city was ruled by Byzantines (535-831), Arabs (831-1072), and Normans (1072-1194), and its notable medieval architecture exhibits features of all these cultures.
See also: Sicily.

Palestine, the biblical Holy Land, named for the Philistines and also called Canaan. Its boundaries, often imprecise, have varied widely. Palestine now usually refers to the region bounded by the Mediterranean on the west, the Jordan River and the Dead Sea on the east, Mt. Hermon on the Syria-Lebanon border to the north, and the Sinai Peninsula in the south. It includes almost all of modern Israel and extends, as well, into present-day Jordan and Egypt. There were Paleolithic and Mesolithic cultures in Palestine, and Neolithic Jericho emerged by about 7000 B.C. Semitic peoples arrived about 3000 B.C. and founded a Bronze Age civilization. About 1000 B.C., after warring against Canaanites and Philistines, the Jews succeeded in establishing a kingdom that later split into Israel to the north and Judah to the south. In the eighth century B.C. the Assyrians overran Israel and in the sixth century B.C., Judah was conquered by the Babylonians. Palestine later fell to Alexander the Great, the Ptolemies of Egypt, and the Seleucids of Syria. An independent Jewish state arose again briefly in the second century B.C., but the region was then incorporated into the Roman empire. In the fourth century A.D., control passed to the Byzantines and the conquest of Palestine by the Arabs, beginning in A.D. 630, marked the beginning of 1300 years of Muslim rule, which ended with the collapse of the Ottoman empire in 1918.
In response to Zionism, Jews had been emigrating to Palestine since the 1850s. Seeking to establish a Jewish homeland, the immigrants met with increasing resistance and hostility from Muslim Palestinians. With its Balfour Declaration in 1917, the British government, which had become dominant in the region after World War I, left an ambiguous legacy that satisfied neither Muslims nor Jews. Between the two world wars, Jewish immigration increased as did political tensions between Jews and Muslims. Following World War II and the Nazi-organized mass murders of European Jews, there was a mass exodus to Palestine. In 1948, the Jews accepted a U.N. recommendation to divide Palestine into Jewish and Arab states, but the Arabs rejected partition. The British left the region and, since the founding of Israel, Palestine has been the focal point of a struggle between the State of Israel and its Arab neighbors and inhabitants, a struggle that has resulted in chronic warfare and terrorism.

Palestine Liberation Organization (PLO), coordinating body (founded 1964) of Palestinian groups recognized (1974) by the UN and the Arab states as the sole official representative of the Palestinian people. Of the many groups that make up the PLO, Fatah, led by Yasir Arafat, is predominant. The guerrilla groups of the PLO were driven out of Jordan in 1970, after a bloody civil war. They were next based in Lebanon, until the Israeli invasion (1982) dispersed them to several Arab countries, notably Tunisia and Syria. In 1988 the PLO proclaimed an independent Palestinian state in the West Bank and Gaza Strip, territories occupied by Israel since the June 1967 war. That proclamation was rejected by Israel and the United States, and the occupation continues. The goals of the PLO and its tactics have shifted over the years and are still subject to dispute within the organization. Some factions favor the destruction of the Israeli state, while others have conditionally recognized Israel, demanding a Palestinian state in return. Despite opposition of some Palestinian factions, political negotiations between the PLO and the Israelian government resulted in reproachement in the 1990s and limited Palestinian autonomy in some territories.
See also: Arafat, Yasir.

Palestrina, Giovanni Pierluigi da (c.1525-94), Italian Renaissance composer of unaccompanied choral church music. He wrote over 100 masses and is perhaps best known for his *Missa Papae Marcelli.* He was organist and choirmaster in several Roman churches.
See also: Renaissance.

Palladio, Andrea (Andrea di Pietro; 1508-80), Italian architect, creator of the immensely influential Paladian style. His designs for villas, palaces, and churches stressed harmonic proportions and classical symmetry. Palladio's *The Four Books of Architecture* (1570) helped to spread his style throughout Europe.

Palladium, chemical element, symbol Pd; for physical constants see Periodic Table. Palladium was discovered by William H.

Wollaston in 1803. It occurs native associated with platinum, gold, and silver and also as a selenide. Commercially, it is obtained as a byproduct in the production of platinum, nickel, and copper. It is prepared in sponge form by the thermal decomposition of palladium dichlorodiamine. Palladium is a steel-white, malleable, soft, ductile metal. It is a member of the platinum group of metals and is the least dense, lowest melting, and most readily fused. Palladium metal resists oxidation. It absorbs up to 900 times its volume of hydrogen at ordinary temperatures. Hydrogen gas is purified by diffusing it through heated palladium. Palladium is used in the finely divided state as a catalyst for hydrogenation and dehydrogention reactions. Palladium is used in jewelry, dentistry, surgical instruments, electrical contacts, and high temperature solders. It is the least expensive of the platinum metals.

Pallas *see:* Athena.

Palm, any of over 3,000 species of trees, shrubs, and vines of the family Palmae, native mainly to tropical and subtropical regions. Palms are characterized by an unbranched stem bearing a cluster of featherlike (pinnate) or fanlike (palmate) leaves at its crown. Flowers are greenish, borne in spikes, and the fruits are covered with a leathery, fibrous, outer layer. Palm products are of great economic importance: the coconut and date palms produce staple crops; wax is obtained from the carnauba palm; the African oil palm and the coconut palm yield oil used in food, soap, toiletries, and industrial processes. Fibers yielded include rattan and raffia.

Palmer, A(lexander) Mitchell (1872-1936), U.S. attorney general (1919-21) notorious for the Palmer Raids—mass arrests of supposed subversives, many of whom were deported as aliens. A Democratic U.S. representative (1909-15), Palmer was U.S. alien property custodian in World War I.

Palmer, Arnold (1929-), U.S. golfer. Palmer's playing style and charismatic personality helped make golf a popular spectator sport. Palmer won the U.S. Open (1960), the British Open (1961, 62), and was the first to win the Masters tournament 4 times (1958, 60, 62, 64).

Palmer, Nathaniel Brown (1799-1877), U.S. mariner and explorer, the reputed discoverer of the Antarctic continent. In 1820-21 he sighted Palmer Peninsula (now the Antarctic Peninsula) and discovered the South Orkney Islands.

Palmerston, Viscount (1784-1865), British politician remembered for his successful and often aggressive foreign policy. As foreign secretary (1830-34, 1835-41, 1846-51), he was instrumental in securing Belgian independence and maintaining peace in Europe during the revolutions of 1848. As prime minister (1855-58, 1859-65), he led Britain to victory in the Crimean War, maintained neutrality in the American Civil War, and aided the unification of Italy.
See also: United Kingdom.

Palmetto, any of a genus (*Sabal*) of fan-leaved, usually small, palm trees, common to the southeastern United States and the West Indies. The name refers especially to the cabbage palm (*S. palmetto*).

Palmistry, practice (over 4,000 years old) of reading the markings on a person's palm for the purpose of predicting the future. The various lines on the palm are held to indicate the individual's character and destiny.

Palm oil, substance obtained from the fruit and seed kernel of the African oil palm (genus *Elaeis*). It is used in candles, cosmetics, margarine, lubricants, and soaps.

Palm Springs (pop. 32,359), city in southern California where natural hot springs (for which the Spanish named it Agua Caliente) make it a resort and tourist center. The area was populated by Native Americans before the arrival of the Spanish, and part of it remains reservation land for the Cahuilla tribe.
See also: California.

Palm Sunday, Sunday before Easter and the first day of Holy Week, commemorating Jesus's triumphal entry into Jerusalem, when palm leaves were spread in his path. Palm leaves are blessed and carried in procession.
See also: Holy Week.

Palmyra, ancient city in central Syria. Prominent as a trading center, Palmyra prospered under Roman rule and reached its height (A.D. 30) as an independent state under Queen Zenobia. In 273 it was largely destroyed by the Romans under Aurelian; more than a century later it was sacked by Tamerlane. Imposing ruins remain.

Palmyra palm, tall, fan-leaved tree (*Borassus flabellifer*) of tropical Asia. Its trunk, which may grow to 70 ft (21 m), supplies lumber. The large leaves, which ancient Hindus used as paper, provide thatching. The fiber of the palmyra is used to make rope, and the fruit, seeds, and shoots are edible.

Palo Alto (pop. 55,225), California city about 25 mi (40 km) south of San Francisco, near the southern tip of San Francisco Bay. Stanford University is situated nearby, Palo Alto is one of the leading educational, electronics, medical, and research centers in the U.S.
See also: California.

Palomar Observatory, astronomical observatory on Palomar Mt. 5,660 ft (1,725 m) above sea level, northeast of San Diego, in southern California. Its Hale telescope, with its 200-in (500-cm) reflector, is capable of photographing objects several billion light years away. At the time of its construction (1948), the telescope was the world's largest. The observatory's Schmidt telescopes have photographed all of the northern and half of the southern sky. The Palomar Observatory, the Mount Wilson Observatory, and the Las Campanas Observatory were jointly administered and known collectively as the Hale Observatories until 1980, when the California Institute of Technology assumed separate control of the Palomar Observatory.
See also: Astronomy.

Paloverde, any of a genus (*Cercidium*) of small trees of the pea family native to the southwestern United States and other hot, dry regions of the Americas. A yellow-flowering tree that loses its small leaves in the spring, it gets its name (Spanish, "green tree") from its smooth green bark. The beanlike seeds were an important food for Native Americans.

Palpitation *see:* Tachycardia.

Palsson, Thorsteinn (1947-), Icelandic politician, prime minister since 1987. He was director of the Employer's Federation (1979-83), head of the Independence Party (1983-87), and minister of finance (1985-87).
See also: Iceland.

Palsy, paralysis, especially a progressive form culminating late in life, characterized by tremors of the limbs and muscular weakness and rigidity.
See also: Paralysis.

Pamirs, mountainous region of central Asia, predominantly in Tajikistan, but extending into Afghanistan, China, and Kashmir. The mountains form a hub from which radiate the Hindu Kush, Karakorum, Kunlun, and Tien Shan ranges. Communism Peak (24,590 ft/7,495 m) and Lenin Peak (23,508 ft/7,165 m) are the highest.
See also: Hindu Kush.

Pampa, term for several plains of South America, specifically for the great grass plain of central and northern Argentina. The Pampa covers some 250,000 sq mi (647,500 sq km) and is the economic heart of Argentina, where its livestock and much of its crops are raised. Pampas grass, with its mass of plumed flowers, is often grown as an ornamental.

Pan, in Greek mythology, god of fertility, usually portrayed as a man with the legs, ears, and horns of a goat. All of his myths deal with his many love affairs. Worship of Pan began in Arcadia in southern Greece.
See also: Mythology.

Panama, small Central American republic situated on the Isthmus of Panama, which is a narrow strip of land forming the connecting link between Central and South America that also separates the Atlantic and Pacific Oceans. Panama City is the capital. Panama is bisected by the Panama

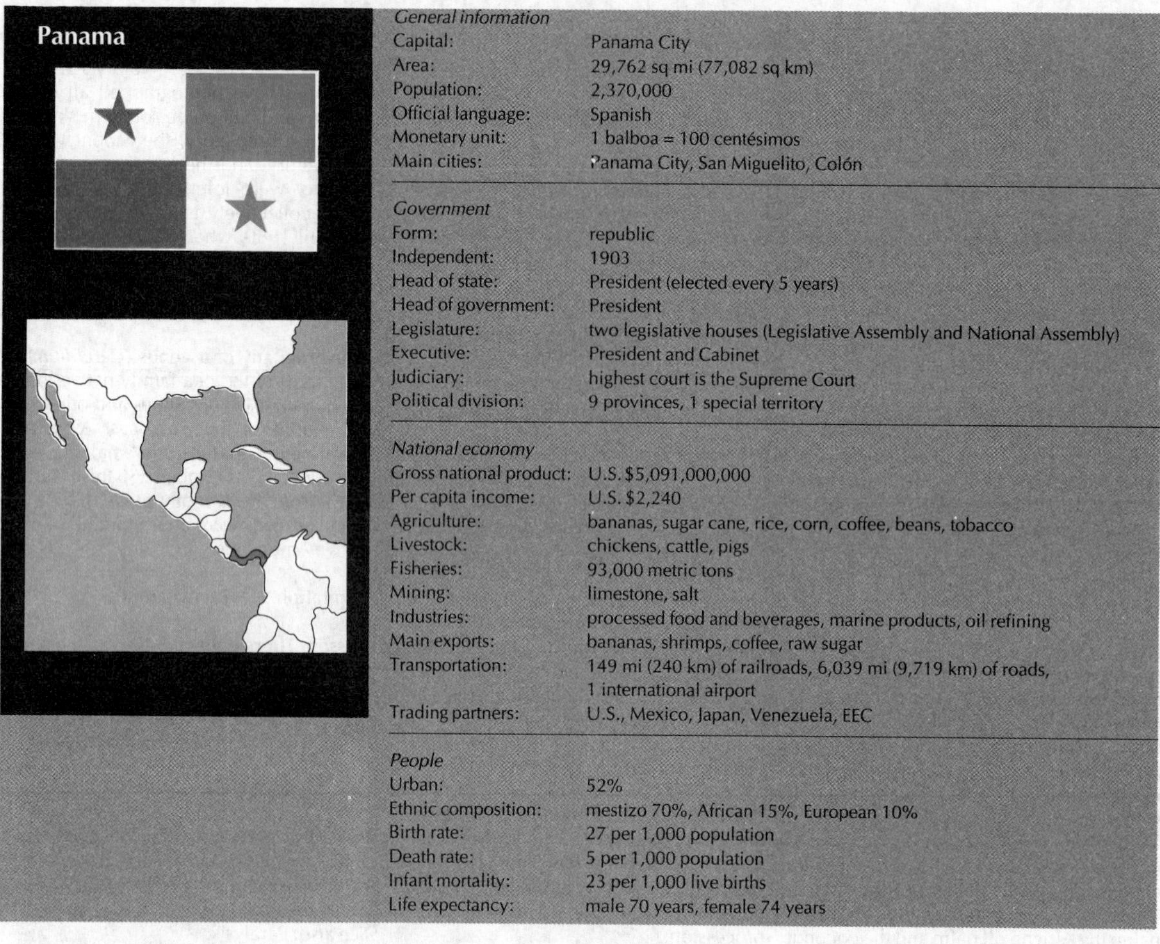

Panama

General information	
Capital:	Panama City
Area:	29,762 sq mi (77,082 sq km)
Population:	2,370,000
Official language:	Spanish
Monetary unit:	1 balboa = 100 centésimos
Main cities:	Panama City, San Miguelito, Colón
Government	
Form:	republic
Independent:	1903
Head of state:	President (elected every 5 years)
Head of government:	President
Legislature:	two legislative houses (Legislative Assembly and National Assembly)
Executive:	President and Cabinet
Judiciary:	highest court is the Supreme Court
Political division:	9 provinces, 1 special territory
National economy	
Gross national product:	U.S. $5,091,000,000
Per capita income:	U.S. $2,240
Agriculture:	bananas, sugar cane, rice, corn, coffee, beans, tobacco
Livestock:	chickens, cattle, pigs
Fisheries:	93,000 metric tons
Mining:	limestone, salt
Industries:	processed food and beverages, marine products, oil refining
Main exports:	bananas, shrimps, coffee, raw sugar
Transportation:	149 mi (240 km) of railroads, 6,039 mi (9,719 km) of roads, 1 international airport
Trading partners:	U.S., Mexico, Japan, Venezuela, EEC
People	
Urban:	52%
Ethnic composition:	mestizo 70%, African 15%, European 10%
Birth rate:	27 per 1,000 population
Death rate:	5 per 1,000 population
Infant mortality:	23 per 1,000 live births
Life expectancy:	male 70 years, female 74 years

Canal, which cuts through the low hills of the country's central area. The canal is the most important feature of Panama, and it has played a major role in the creation of the country and in its subsequent development.

Land and climate. There are highlands in the west and east, wooded hills in the center, and lowland shelves along the Atlantic and Pacific coasts. The climate is tropical, with little variation from season to season. Rainfall is very heavy on the Atlantic side, less so on the Pacific coast.

People. Mestizos and mulattos (people of mixed racial ancestry) make up about 70 percent of the population; the rest is mostly composed of unmixed Indian, white, or black ancestry. Panama is a Spanish-speaking, predominantly Roman Catholic country. Nearly one-third of the population lives in Panama City and Colón.

Economy. Agriculture employs more people than any other economic activity, but the Panama Canal is the major single factor in the country's economy, providing about 25 percent of national income. It also provides many jobs. Exports—bananas, shrimp, sugar, and petroleum products—lag far behind imports, and Panama suffers from a huge trade deficit. Until its recent domestic turmoil, Panama was a center of international banking.

History. Indians were the first inhabitants of what is now Panama, but little is known about them. Spain took control of the region during the early 1500s and established settlements there. In 1513 Vasco Núñez de Balboa crossed the isthmus and became the first European to see the eastern shore of the Pacific. Panama became a springboard for Spanish conquests in the Americas and a route for transshipping Peruvian gold to Spain, but it lost importance in the 18th century after buccaneer attacks forced treasure ships from Peru to sail around South America. In 1819, Colombia broke away from Spanish rule, and in 1821 Panama freed itself from Spain and became part of Colombia. Relations between the two nations, however, were always strained. The California gold rush of 1848 caused many people from the eastern part of the United States to travel to Panama, cross the isthmus, and continue their sea journey on to California, and the idea of a canal across the isthmus took on new significance. In 1903, the United States tried to negotiate a deal with Colombia whereby it would build the canal, but Colombia refused. Panama, with encouragement from the United States, revolted from Colombia, became an independent nation, and agreed to the United States' plan. The completion of the canal in 1914 brought some prosperity to Panama, but also led to discontent with the United States' control of the canal and of the Panama Canal Zone. Those in favor of Panamanian control of the canal rioted in 1959, 1962, and 1964. General Omar Torrijos Herrera seized control of Panama in 1968 and backed the movement to return the canal to Panama. In 1977, Panama and the United States signed a treaty that transferred control of the Canal Zone to Panama in 1979 and provided for full transfer of the canal to Panama in 1999. In 1983, General Manuel Antonio Noriega became head of the army and Panama's most powerful figure. In 1988, grand juries in the United States indicted him for narcotics smuggling and racketeering. The Panamanian president dismissed him, but the military forced the president from office. In 1989, Panama held an election in which Noriega was apparently defeated. The government, under Noriega, declared the election invalid and refused to let the winning candidate, Guillermo Endara, take office. The United States intervened by imposing economic sanctions on Panama. When these failed to change the government, President Bush in 1989 ordered a United States expeditionary force to Panama to oust Noriega and restore the duly elected president. Noriega was captured and brought to the United States to stand trial. Panama's economy, however, remains in a weakened condition, and the political situation continues to be unstable.

Panama Canal, artificial waterway crossing the Isthmus of Panama, linking the Atlantic and Pacific oceans. The canal is 51 mi (82 km) long; traverses 2 natural lakes,

one of which is 85 ft (26 m) above sea level; and has 6 locks. It was built by U.S. military engineers in 1904-14, after U.S. troops helped Panama secede from Colombia. The United States was granted rights in perpetuity to a zone 10 mi (16 km) wide across the isthmus. After World War II there was U.S.-Panamanian friction over canal sovereignty, and in 1977 U.S. and Panamanian representatives signed a new treaty ceding administration of the canal to Panama in 1979 and full control in 2000, with guarantees of its neutral operation.
See also: Clayton-Bulwer Treaty; Hay-Pauncefote Treaties.

The Panama Canal: the Miraflores Lock

Panama Canal Zone, strip of land (553 sq mi/1,432 sq km) extending 5 mi (8 km) on either side of the Panama Canal. The Canal zone was controlled by the United States until Oct. 1979, when Panama took control after U.S.-Panamanian treaties were ratified by the U.S. Senate (1978).

Panama City (pop. 390,000), capital of Panama, on the Gulf of Panama, at the Pacific entrance to the canal. Mainly a modern industrial city, it owes its growth to the building of the canal. The city was founded in 1672, after the original Panama, founded by Pedrarias the Cruel (1519) 4 mi (6.4 km) distant, had been sacked by Sir Henry Morgan (1671). The city also served as port for the shipment of Andean gold during Spanish colonial days.
See also: Panama.

Pan-American conferences, or Inter-American conferences, meetings of representatives of independent nations of the Western Hemisphere to discuss political, legal, military, economic, and social issues. The first such conference, organized largely through the efforts of Simón Bolívar, was held in Panama City in 1826. Further meetings were held throughout the 19th century. A conference in 1889 established the International Union of American Republics, later called the Pan American Union. Conferences organized by F.D. Roosevelt (1938-47) dealt with economic and defense issues. The Organization of American States (OAS), formed in 1948, added anticommunism to the agenda.
See also: Bolívar, Simón; Organization of American States.

Pan American Games, quadrennial amateur sports contest between nations of the Americas. The event is based on the Olympic Games and includes many of the same events. Proposed at the 1940 Pan-American Congress, the games were postponed due to World War II and were first held in 1951.

Pan American Highway, road system linking Latin American countries with each other and with the U.S. interstate highway system. The Pan-American link was conceived at the Fifth International Conference of American States (1923).

Pan American Union, organization of independent states of North and South America founded in 1910. Its stated purpose was to foster economic, political, and social cooperation among member nations. When the Organization of American States (OAS) was founded in 1948, the Pan American Union became its central office. In 1970 the Union was renamed the General Secretariat of the OAS.
See also: Organization of American States.

Pancreas, glandular organ that secretes enzymes and hormones essential to the digestive process. Located beneath the stomach, the pancreas is connected to the small intestine at the duodenum. Powerful digestive-system enzymes (trypsin, lipase, amylase) are produced and secreted to aid in the digestion of proteins, fats, and carbohydrates, respectively. Insulin and glucagon, hormones secreted by the islets of Langerhans, small cell groups in the pancreas, have important roles in glucose and fat metabolism and regulate blood-sugar levels.
See also: Diabetes; Insulin.

Pancreatin, mixture of enzymes from the pancreatic juice, a secretion of the pancreas that helps the body to digest starch, fats, and proteins.
See also: Pancreas.

Panda, either of 2 Asian mammals anatomically similar to raccoons and each having an unusual sixth digit on each hand. This digit has evolved to thumblike size and flexibility in the giant panda of central China (*Ailuropoda melanoleuca*), remaining vestigial in the red, or lesser, panda (*Ailurus fulgens*), found in the Himalayas and the mountains of western China and northern Burma. Though they have evolved from carnivores, both pandas are vegetarians. The giant panda, resembling a bear, with its predominantly white body, black ears, limbs, and eye patches, weighs from 200-300 lb (90-140 kg).

Pandit, Vijaya Lakshmi (1900-), Indian diplomat and political leader. The sister of Jawaharlal Nehru, Pandit was active in the struggle for India's independence and helped implement a postwar policy of nonalignment. She was ambassador to the United States (1949-51) and was the first woman to serve as president of the UN General Assembly (1953-54).
See also: India.

Pandora, in Greek mythology, first woman on earth. Created by Hephaestus on the orders of Zeus, she was given a box that she was ordered never to open. Unable to contain her curiosity, she disobeyed, thus releasing all the evils that plague humanity. The only thing that had not escaped when she closed the lid was hope.
See also: Mythology.

Pangolin, any of a group of mammals found in Asia and Africa whose bodies are covered by hard, overlapping scales. Only their undersides are soft and hairy. Many pangolins (genus *Manis* or related genera of the order Pholidota) climb trees, and some can hang by their tails. They have strong claws for tearing open the nests of termites and ants, and long tongues for drawing them into their mouths.
See also: Anteater.

Pankhurst, English family of women's rights activists. In 1903, **Emmeline Goulden Pankhurst** (1858-1928), a suffragist, and her daughters, **Christabel Pankhurst** (1880-1958) and **Sylvia Pankhurst** (1882-1960), founded the Woman's Social and Political Union, a base for their increasingly militant actions to further women's rights. Emmeline was repeatedly impris-

Panda

oned (1912-13) and conducted several hunger strikes (1908-14). She died a month before British women gained full voting equality with men and was revered nationally for her work during the war and to extend suffrage.
See also: Women's movements.

Panmunjom, village in the demilitarized zone between North and South Korea, where the truce to end the Korean War was negotiated (1951-53) and signed (July 27, 1953). The joint security area was partitioned in 1976 by North Korea and the UN command after the killing of 2 U.S. soldiers by the North Koreans.
See also: Korean War.

Pansy, cultivated plant (*Viola tricolor hortensis*) bred from the European violet. It has variously colored flowers with 5 broad, velvety petals and is a popular garden plant.

Pantheon, historically, temple dedicated to the worship of all the gods. In modern times it refers to a structure in which a nation's heroes are buried or honored. The Pantheon of Rome, a domed, circular temple, was built in 27 B.C. Later destroyed, it was rebuilt C.A.D. 120 by Hadrian. It became a Christian church in 609.

Panther, common name for the black leopard, found in Asia and Africa. The North American puma, also known as the cougar or mountain lion, is sometimes referred to as a panther.
See also: Leopard.

Marcel Marceau, a master of pantomime

Pantomime, drama performed entirely through facial expression, movement, and gesture, without speech. Popular in Roman times, it was developed in Italy by the commedia dell'arte in the 16th century, which created the popular Harlequin and Columbine characters. Popular 20th-century pantomimists include Marcel Marceau and Charlie Chaplin.

Pantothenic acid *see:* Vitamin

Papadopoulos, George (1919-), Greek army officer, prime minister (1967-73) and president (June-Nov. 1973) of Greece under a military junta. Overthrown by a military coup in 1974, he and others were tried and found guilty of crimes against the state. His death sentence was commuted to life imprisonment.
See also: Greece.

Papago, name for North American Native American tribe of southern Arizona and northwestern Sonora, Mexico, related to the Pimas. They rebelled unsuccessfully against the Spanish (1695 and 1751) and in the 1860s joined the U.S. government against the Apaches. Crops and cattle raising remain their primary economic activities, along with income from leases to their mineral-bearing lands.

Papal States, lands in Italy under the rule of the popes from 754 to 1870. The states date from the donation of conquered Lombard lands to the papacy by the Frankish King Pepin the Short. Augmented by later gifts and conquests, the states stretched from coast to coast across central Italy by the early 13th century. Napoleon I conquered the Papal States in 1796, but they were restored to the pope in 1815. King Victor Emmanuel II annexed the Papal States during the Risorgimento, Rome itself coming under Italian rule in 1870. The papacy did not officially accept the loss of its lands until the Lateran Treaty (1929) created an independent Vatican City.

Papandreou, 2 premiers of Greece. **George Papandreou** (1888-1968) was premier from 1964-65. His removal by King Constantine II led to the military coup of 1967 and to the abolition of the monarchy in 1973. His son, **Andreas Papandreou** (1919-96) was premier of Greece from 1981-89 and 1993-96. Imprisoned and then exiled under the military dictatorship (1967-74), he founded in exile the socialist party known as Pasok (for Panhellenic Socialist Movement). As premier, he instituted numerous reforms.
See also: Greece.

Papaw *see:* Papaya; Pawpaw.

Papaya, small, tropical, American fruit tree (*Carica papaya*), widely cultivated for its yellow, oblong, edible fruit of the same name. The juice of the stem, leaves, and unripe fruit contains the protein-digesting enzyme papain. The papaya is sometimes called a papaw.

Papeete *see:* Tahiti.

Papen, Franz von (1879-1969), German diplomat and politician. Lacking support as chancellor (1932), he resigned and helped engineer the appointment of Hitler. He was Hitler's vice-chancellor (1933-34) and as German minister to Austria (1934-38) paved the way for German annexation of Austria. Acquitted of war crimes by the Nuremberg tribunal (1946), he was convicted by a German "denazification court" (1947), but its sentence was rescinded.

Paper, flat sheet, usually made of plant fibers, used for writing and printing, probably invented in China C.A.D. 105, using bark and hemp. Cotton rags and cloth—still used for special high-grade papers—were the raw materials most often used until generally replaced by wood-pulp processes developed in the mid-19th century. In chemical pulping, wood chips are cooked under pressure in a solution (soda, sulfate, or sulfite) that dissolves all but the cellulose. The pulp is then bleached, washed, and refined, the fibers being crushed, frayed, and cut by mechanical beaters. This increases their surface area and bonding power. At this stage various substances are added: fillers (mainly clay and chalk) to make the paper opaque, sizes (rosin and alum) for resistance to water, and dyes and pigments as necessary. The pulp is fed to the paper machine, where it flows onto a moving belt or cylindrical drum of fine wire mesh, and most of the water is drained off by gravity and suction. The newly formed continuous sheet is pressed between rollers, dried by evaporation, and subjected to calendaring. Some paper is coated to give a special surface.

Paper nautilus *see:* Argonaut.

Paperwork, paper designed and used for decorative purposes, including wallpaper and gift wrapping. Although now mostly machine-made, such paper has often been made and decorated by hand. Decorative book endpapers were traditionally used to line the insides of book covers. Origami is the Japanese art of folding paper to represent objects.

Papier-mâché, molding material made of pulped paper mixed with flour paste, glue, or resin. It is usually molded while wet, but in some industrial processes is pressure-molded. The technique of making papier-mâché decorative objects began in the Orient and reached Europe in the 18th century.

Papillon, originally, dwarf spaniel, breed of small dog with a long, silky coat and butterfly-shaped ears. Papillons stand up to 11 in (28 cm) tall and weigh up to 11 lb (5 kg). The breed was developed in 16th-century Spain and later became popular among the French nobility.

Papineau, Louis Joseph (1786-1871), Canadian politician, champion of French-Canadian rights in the English-dominated executive and legislature of Lower Canada (Quebec). While serving in the assembly of Lower Canada (1815-37), he framed the 92 Resolutions, a statement of French-Canadian grievances, passed by the assembly in 1834. In 1837 a revolt broke out, and Papineau, although not an active revolutionist, fled to the United States to avoid arrest. He resettled in Canada in 1845 and served in the assembly from 1848 to 1854.

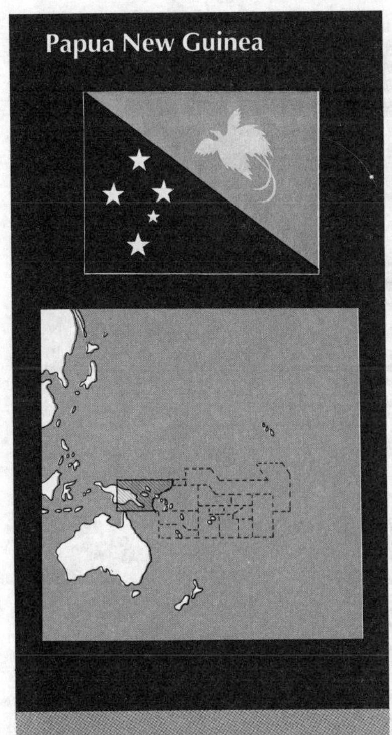

Capital:	Port Moresby
Area:	178,704 sq mi (462,840 sq km)
Population:	3,593,000
Form:	constitutional monarchy
Independent:	1975
GNP:	U.S. $2,920,000,000
Per capita:	U.S. $770

Papua New Guinea, since 1975, independent nation in the Pacific located just north of Australia.
Land and climate. The eastern half of New Guinea Island comprises five-sixths of the nation's territory, which also includes the islands of Bougainville, Buka, and the Bismarck archipelago to the northeast and smaller islands to the southeast. Papua New Guinea is a mountainous, densely forested region with a monsoon climate and a rich variety of plant and animal life. The capital is Port Moresby.
People. The population consists of several distinct ethnic and cultural groups, including Stone Age peoples who inhabit the remote interior. A wide variety of native languages are spoken and Pidgin English is used as a common tongue. Most of the people adhere to traditional animistic beliefs and practices and cannibalism persists among certain groups.
Economy. Plantation farming has replaced traditional subsistence agriculture in some areas. Exports include timber and coconut products, rubber, cocoa, tea, and coffee. Copper and gold are mined.
History. The northern region of present day Papua New Guinea was part of German New Guinea from 1884 to 1914, when it was seized by Australia and became the Trust Territory of New Guinea. The southern region was British New Guinea from 1884 to 1905, then, as the Territory of Papua, it was under Australian rule. The two regions were merged administratively in 1949 as the Territory of Papua and New Guinea and administered by Australia. It was renamed Papua New Guinea in 1971, became self governing in 1973, and independent in 1975. A treaty with Indonesia in 1979 ended efforts by Papuan nationalists in neighboring Irian Jaya to unite with Papua New Guinea. In 1988, an independence movement on the island of Bougainville led to an open rebellion. Despite several cease-fires and rounds of negotiations, fighting has continued throughout 1990.

Papyrus, stout, reedlike plant (*Cyperus papyrus*) of the sedge family widely used in ancient Egypt. Sails, baskets, sandals, and clothing were made from the stem, as was a material for writing on (a predecessor of paper). The pith was eaten, and the roots were used as fuel.
See also: Paper.

Parable, short tale or anecdote designed to make a moral point or to present a spiritual truth, using everyday language and homely imagery. The literature of the ancient Greeks and the Old Testament abound in parables. In the New Testament Jesus conveys much of his most profound teaching in the form of parables. Some of these are the stories of the house built on rock and sand (Matthew 7.24-27), the pearl of great price (Matthew 13.45-46), the talents (Matthew 25.14-29), the sower and the seed (Mark 4.3-8; 14-20), the mote and the beam (Luke 6.41-42), the Good Samaritan (Luke 10.29-37), and the prodigal son (Luke 15.11-32).

Parabola, geometrical curve, similar in shape to the path followed by a projectile when it is fired into the air. A parabola is a conic section, obtained by the intersection of a right circular cone and a plane. If a parabola is rotated about its axis, it traces out a three-dimensional parabolic surface. When a light source is placed at the focus of a mirror with this shape, all the light rays are reflected parallel to the axis. A reflecting telescope uses the principle in reverse, collecting parallel rays of light from space and concentrating them at the focus.

Paracelsus, Philippus Aureolus (1493?-1541), Swiss alchemist and physician who channeled the arts of alchemy into the preparation of medical remedies. Born Theophrastus Bombastus von Hohenheim, he adopted the name Paracelsus, boasting that he was superior to the renowned first-century Roman medical writer Celsus.
See also: Alchemy.

Parachute, collapsible, umbrellalike device used to retard movement through the air. It was invented in the late 18th century by French aeronaut Jacques Garnerin for descent from a balloon. When opened—either manually, by pulling a ripcord, or automatically, by a line attached to the aircraft—the canopy traps a large air mass, which produces the desired drag force. The canopy consists of numerous strong panels of canvas, silk, and nylon and has a series of cords connecting to a harness worn by the user. Parachutes are used for safe descent from airplanes, for dropping cargo from airplanes, and as braking devices for returning space vehicles, rockets, and airplanes. Sport parachuting, or skydiving, is a popular sport.

Melpas live in small family settlements in the central highlands of Papua New Guinea, near Mount Hagan.

Paraguay, landlocked country in South America. Paraguay has an area of 157,047 sq mi (406,752 sq km) and is bordered by Bolivia on the northwest, Brazil on the northeast, and Argentina to the south and southeast.
Land and climate. The Paraguay River, flowing north-south, divides the country into two sharply contrasting regions: the eastern region, sometimes called Paraguay Proper, and the western Chaco region. The Chaco is largely flat, scrub country and is thinly populated. Though some of it is suitable for raising cattle, much of it is arid. The far richer eastern region is divided into two contrasting areas by a clifflike ridge running northward from the Paranà River near Encarnación. West of the ridge, where most of the people live, is rolling hill country that falls away to low-lying areas along the Paraguay River. East of the ridge is the Paraná Plateau, about 2,000 ft (610 m) above sea level and covered by dense tropical forest. The country has a subtropical climate, very like that of Florida, with hot wet summers and warm and drier winters. Thunderstorms are frequent in summer. The capital of the country is Asunción.
People. The majority of the people are mestizo, a mixture of the Spanish and the native Guaraní people. Many people speak Guaraní, but Spanish is the official language and Roman Catholicism the official religion.
Economy. More than 50% of the work force is employed on the land, and over one-third of the gross national product comes from agriculture. Cotton, tobacco,

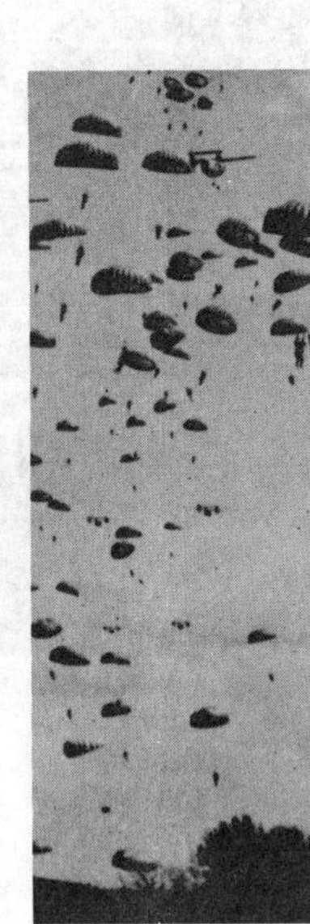

Parachutes are used by paratroopers to drop into battle areas or behind enemy lines.

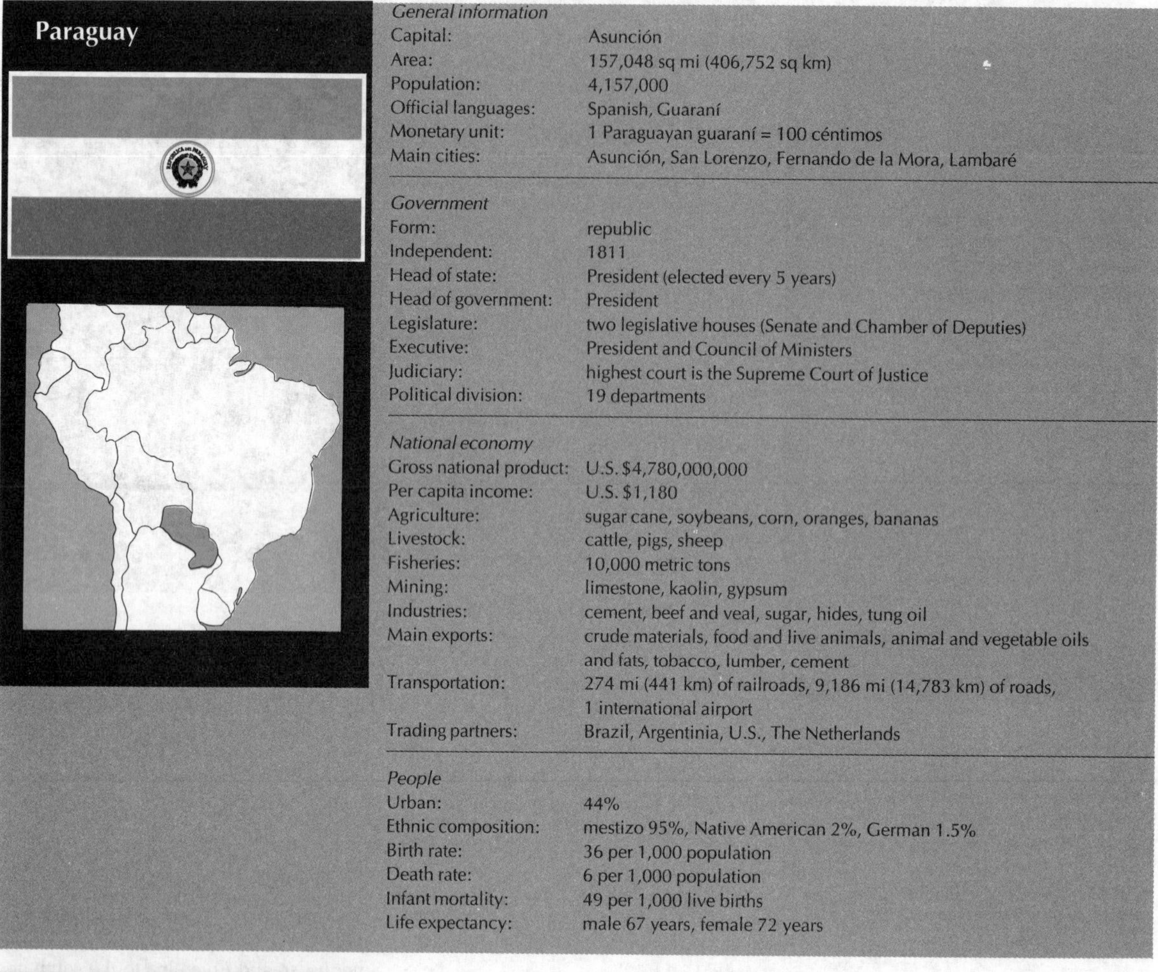

Paraguay

General information	
Capital:	Asunción
Area:	157,048 sq mi (406,752 sq km)
Population:	4,157,000
Official languages:	Spanish, Guaraní
Monetary unit:	1 Paraguayan guaraní = 100 céntimos
Main cities:	Asunción, San Lorenzo, Fernando de la Mora, Lambaré
Government	
Form:	republic
Independent:	1811
Head of state:	President (elected every 5 years)
Head of government:	President
Legislature:	two legislative houses (Senate and Chamber of Deputies)
Executive:	President and Council of Ministers
Judiciary:	highest court is the Supreme Court of Justice
Political division:	19 departments
National economy	
Gross national product:	U.S. $4,780,000,000
Per capita income:	U.S. $1,180
Agriculture:	sugar cane, soybeans, corn, oranges, bananas
Livestock:	cattle, pigs, sheep
Fisheries:	10,000 metric tons
Mining:	limestone, kaolin, gypsum
Industries:	cement, beef and veal, sugar, hides, tung oil
Main exports:	crude materials, food and live animals, animal and vegetable oils and fats, tobacco, lumber, cement
Transportation:	274 mi (441 km) of railroads, 9,186 mi (14,783 km) of roads, 1 international airport
Trading partners:	Brazil, Argentinia, U.S., The Netherlands
People	
Urban:	44%
Ethnic composition:	mestizo 95%, Native American 2%, German 1.5%
Birth rate:	36 per 1,000 population
Death rate:	6 per 1,000 population
Infant mortality:	49 per 1,000 live births
Life expectancy:	male 67 years, female 72 years

Dwellings on the banks of the Paraguay River outside Asunción

coffee, timber, tannin, and oils are the chief exports. Some processing of agricultural products constitutes the country's main industry.

History. Originally inhabited by the Guaranís, by the 1550s the region had become Spain's power base in southeastern South America. Jesuit influence in the 17th century contributed significantly to the merging of Guaraní and Spanish cultures. From 1776 to 1811 Paraguay was part of the Spanish vice-royalty of La Plata. It became independent in 1811 after a relatively peaceful revolt. Following José Gaspar Rodriguez Francia, and Carlos Antonio López, the dictator Francisco Solano López led the country in the disastrous War of the Triple Alliance against Brazil, Uruguay, and Argentina from 1865 to 1870. Paraguay was laid waste and more than half the population died. Clashes with Bolivia over a border dispute led to the Chaco War (1932-35). Political turmoil was followed by the relatively stable regime of Pres. Higinio Morinigó from 1940 to 1948. Civil War followed the overthrow of Morinigo and in 1954 Gen. Alfredo Stroessner seized power and governed ruthlessly until he too was overthrown in 1989. The current government is headed by President Andrés Rodríguez Pedotti.

Paraguay River, chief tributary of the Paraná River, in South America. It rises in the Mato Grosso region of western Brazil and flows about 1,300 mi (2,090 km) southward to join the Paraná near Corrientes. Part of the Río de la Plata system, its chief branches, the Pilcomayo and the Bermejo, enter from the west. It is mostly navigable; Asunción, Paraguay, is its chief port.

Parakeet, popular name for any of various small parrots, usually with green plumage and a long tail, popular as a cage bird and native to the Indo-Malayan region. The best known of the true parakeets is the budgerigar (*Melopsittacus undulatus*), also called the zebra, shell, or grass parakeet.

Parallax, change in the apparent position of an object due to a change in the position of the observer. Parallax in nearby objects may be observed by closing each eye in turn so that a more distant object appears to move relative to a closer one. The brain normally assembles the 2 images to produce a stereoscopic effect. If the length and direction of the line between the 2 points of apparent observation is known, parallax may be used to calculate the distance of an object. In astronomy, the parallax of a star is defined as half the greatest parallactic displacement when the star is viewed from earth at intervals of 6 months.

Paralysis, temporary or permanent loss of muscle power or control. It may consist of the inability to move a limb or part of a limb or individual muscles. Paralysis may be due to brain damage (e.g., from strokes or tumors), diseases of or damage to the spinal cord (poliomyelitis), nerve roots (slipped disk), peripheral nervous system (neuritis), or muscles (muscular dystrophy).
See also: Palsy.

Paramaribo (pop. 150,000), capital and chief port of Suriname, on the Suriname River, 17 mi (27 km) inland from the Carib-

bean Sea. Settled by British from Barbados in the 1630s, Paramaribo was taken over by the Dutch in 1815. Canals from that time give today's city a Dutch character. Paramaribo is an export center for bauxite, sugar, shrimp, rice, rum, molasses, and coffee.
See also: Suriname.

Paramaribo, Suriname

Paramecium, single-cell, microscopic animal (genus *Paramecium*) in the phylum Protozoa. The most complex of one-celled organisms, paramecium live in fresh water and propel themselves by the coordinated beating of minute, hairlike projections called cilia. Paramecium feed on bacteria and algae and reproduce by splitting in 2.
See also: Protozoan.

Paramedic, person who assists medical personnel. Paramedics perform routine medical procedures (X-rays, injections, blood pressure) that allow physicians to treat more critically ill patients. Emergency Medical Technician-Paramedics perform emergency procedures for car crash and heart attack victims and for illnesses of sudden occurrence. They usually travel in ambulances equipped with the appropriate medical equipment for such events and communicate with police and hospital by radio. Paramedic services were introduced by the 1960s.

Paraná (pop. 159,600), river port in northeastern Argentina, capital of Entre Ríos province, on the Paraná River. The city is primarily a shipping center for agricultural products, but also manufactures cement and glass. Founded in 1730, it was capital of Argentina, 1853-62.
See also: Argentina.

Paraná River, southeastern South American river, formed by the confluence of the Rio Grande and the Paranaíba rivers in southeastern Brazil. A commercial artery, it flows some 2,000 mi (3,200 km) south-southwest to meet the Uruguay River in Argentina (at the head of the Río de la Plata estuary). The Paraguay River is its major tributary.

Pará nut *see:* Brazil nut.

Parapsychology, scientific evaluation of ESP (extrasensory perception) and phenomena concerned with life after death, reincarnation, etc., particularly claims to communication with souls of the dead (spiritism, or, incorrectly, spiritualism). Tests of the former have generally been inconclusive; of the latter, almost exclusively negative. But in both cases many believers hold that such phenomena cannot be subjected to laboratory evaluation. Because of the disparity among various accounts of the spirit world, parapsychology is generally treated with skepticism.
See also: Extrasensory perception; Psychical research.

Parasite, organism that is physiologically dependent on another organism, the host, from which it obtains nutrition and to which it gives nothing in return. Most parasites cannot survive if separated from their host, whom they may or may not harm. Besides the viruses (a wholly parasitic group), parasites include bacteria, flatworms, and various invertebrates.

Parathyroid gland, any of 4 small endocrine bodies behind the thyroid that regulate calcium and phosphorus metabolism. Parathyroid hormone, produced when the concentration of calcium ions in the blood is low, takes calcium from the bone and increases absorption of calcium in the intestines and kidneys. The hormone also decreases the phosphate ion concentration. An imbalance in parathormone levels leads to calcium deficiency (low levels) or bone degeneration (high levels).
See also: Gland.

Parchment, skin of sheep, goats, or calves, which is cleaned, stretched, and rubbed with pumice or chalk to make a material that can be written on, used to make drumheads, or bookbinding. Invented in the 2nd century B.C. as a substitute for papyrus, parchment was widely used until superseded by paper in the 15th century. Vellum is fine-quality parchment.
See also: Paper.

Pardon, official act of forgiveness extended to a convicted person, generally by a country's chief executive, and in the United States also by a state's governor. A pardon is usually given because innocence is discovered after a conviction, but it may be used because the law was too harsh. A famous example of a pardon was Governor John P. Altgeld's freeing of the Haymarket Affair participants in 1893.

Paré, Ambroise (1517?-90), French surgeon whose many achievements (e.g., using ligatures of arteries in place of cauterization, introducing the use of artificial limbs) earned him regard as a pioneer of modern surgery.

Parent, biological or social father or mother. Biological parents are those from whose egg and sperm cells the individual was produced. The genetic make-up of the parents is passed on to the offspring, resulting in various combinations of inherited physical and mental traits. Social parents, who may or may not be biological parents, are those who care for the child.

Parent education, instruction in childrearing. Informal instruction from relatives and friends has always been available, but formal parent education began in the United States in the late 1800s. Such formal education has been important in helping people deal with nontraditional family structure, divorce, and child abuse. Federal government programs involving parent education have included the Children's Bureau (est. 1912) and Head Start, a project established in 1964 to help low-income preschoolers.

Pareto, Vilfredo (1848-1923), Italian economist and sociologist. He followed Léon Walras in applying mathematics to economic theory. His theories on governing elites, developed in *Mind and Society* (1916), influenced Benito Mussolini's fascists.
See also: Economics.

Paricutín, volcano in southwestern Mexico. Between Feb. 20, 1943 (its first appearance) and 1952 (when its activity ceased), it rose over 1,700 ft (525 m) and spread lava and ash over 19 sq mi (50 sq km), burying the villages of Paricutin and San Juan Parangaricútiru and destroying farmlands and forests. It is part of Mexico's Volcanic Axis, an east-west line of volcanoes.

Paris, in Greek mythology, son of Priam (king of Troy) and Hecuba. Left alone to die on Mt. Ida because his mother dreamed that she had given birth to the destroyer of Troy, the infant Paris was rescued and raised by shepherds. Years later the gods ordered Paris to judge a beauty contest between Hera, Athena, and Aphrodite. Hera promised him greatness and Athena victory in war, but he awarded the prize, the golden apple of discord, to Aphrodite, who promised to give him the most beautiful of women—Helen, wife of the Spartan king, Menelaus. Paris's abduction of Helen led to the Trojan War, in which Paris was killed.
See also: Mythology.

Paris (pop. 10,000,000), capital and largest city of France, in the north-central part of the country. World-famous for its beauty, historic importance, and social, intellectual, and cultural life, Paris is a major transportation center and France's chief industrial hub. In the city itself, tourism, fashion, and service industries predominate. Heavier industry (chiefly automobile manufacturing) is based farther out in the metropolitan area. The city, made up of 20 *arrondissements* (boroughs), is divided by the Seine River, which flows 110 mi (177 km) northwest to the English Channel; 30 city bridges span the river. Its left (southern) bank is home to government offices and much of the intellectual community. Landmarks here include the Sorbonne, the Pan-

Procession on the Champs Elysées in Paris, on the 200th anniversary of the French Revolution

théon, the Luxembourg Palace, and the well-known Latin Quarter. The right bank, with its fashionable streets and shops, is the site of the Louvre, the Arc de Triomphe, Sacré Coeur, and Place de la Concorde. In the middle of the Seine, on the Île de la Cité, is the Cathedral of Notre Dame de Paris and the Palais de Justice. The island was inhabited by Gauls when Caesar set up a colony at this important crossroads in 52 B.C. In the early 6th century, the Frankish King Clovis I made Paris his capital. It became a national capital in 987 when Huge Capet, count of Paris, became king of France. The city flourished during medieval times as a center of commerce and scholasticism, but suffered greatly during the Hundred Years War. Following the French Revolution (1789) much of Paris was rebuilt, most characteristically during Napoleon III's reign (1852-70), when Georges Haussmann constructed the parks, wide avenues, and tree-lined boulevards. Growth was interrupted (1870-1) by the Franco-Prussian War and the conflict over the Paris Commune. German occupation during World War II (1940-44) inflicted little damage.
See also: France.

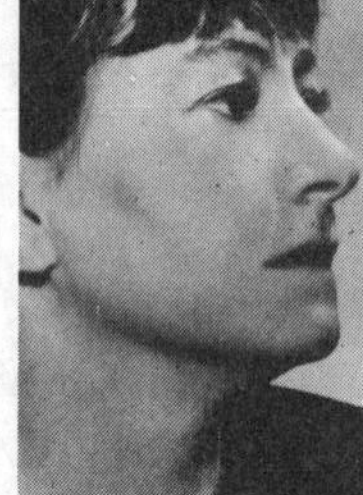

Dorothy Parker

Paris, Pact of *see:* Kellogg-Briand Peace Pact.

Paris, Treaty of, name given to several treaties concluded at or near Paris, France. The **Treaty of Paris, 1763**, along with the Treaty of Hubertusburg, ended the Seven Years War, including the French and Indian Wars in America. France lost its military rights in India (and thus any chance of ousting the British) and its American possessions. Britain gained Canada, Florida, and parts of Louisiana, and Spain regained Cuba and the Philippines. Freed from the French threat, American colonists stepped up the struggle for independence, which was finally confirmed by the **Treaty of Paris, 1783**, ending the Revolutionary War. U.S. boundaries were agreed upon as Canada in the north, the Mississippi in the west, and Florida (regained by Spain) in the south, and the United States won fishing rights off Newfoundland. The **Treaty of Paris, 1814**, attempted to end the Napoleonic Wars after Napoleon Bonaparte's first abdication. France under the restored Bourbon monarchy was allowed to retain its 1782 boundaries and most of its colonies. The **Treaty of Paris, 1815**, signed after Napoleon's final defeat at Waterloo, dealt with France more harshly. French boundaries were reduced to those of 1790, and France had to pay reparations and support an army of occupation for up to 5 years. The **Treaty of Paris, 1856**, ending the Crimean War, was signed by Russia, Britain, France, Turkey, and Sardinia. Designed largely to protect Turkey from Russia, it guaranteed Turkish independence, declared the Black Sea neutral, opened Danube navigation to all nations, and established Moldavia and Walachia (later Romania) as independent states under Turkish suzerainty. The **Treaty of Paris, 1898**, ended the Spanish-American War and effectively ended the Spanish empire. Cuba became independent, and the United States gained Puerto Rico, Guam, and the Philippines. After World War I the treaties of Neuilly, Saint-Germain, Sèvres, Trianon, and Versailles were concluded at the Paris Peace Conference. Treaties were also signed in Paris after World War II.

Paris, University of, France's renowned institution of higher learning. Growing out of the medieval cathedral schools of Notre Dame, it has granted master's degrees since 1170. The Sorbonne (founded 1253) became its single most famous college. Reconstituted during the Napoleonic era as a modern university, it was reorganized again in 1970 into 13 autonomous units.

Parity, in economics, equivalence in the values of currencies or the price of goods over a period of time. If the exchange rate between the currencies of 2 countries is such that the purchasing power of the 2 currencies is equivalent, then they are said to be in parity.
See also: Economics.

Parity, in physics, symmetry between an event and its reflection in a mirror. Physicists say that parity is conserved when an event and its mirror image both satisfy identical laws of nature. In 1956, 2 Chinese physicists, Tsung Dao Lee and Chen Ning Yang conducted experiments which showed that parity is not conserved in a type of nuclear event called a weak interaction. Their work and other experiments demonstrated that conservation of parity is not a universal law of nature.
See also: Physics.

Park, David (1911-60), U.S. painter and art teacher. Park painted human figures in a representational style. He was head of the art department at Windsor School, Boston (1936-41) and later taught at the California School of Fine Arts, San Francisco, and the University of California.

Park, Mungo (1771-1806), Scottish explorer of West Africa. He made 2 exploratory journeys along the Gambia, upper Senegal, and Niger rivers (1795-97 and 1805-06), the former described in *Travels in the Interior of Africa* (1799). He drowned at Bussa during an attack by hostile Africans.

Park, National *see:* National Park System.

Park Chung Hee (1917-79), president of South Korea (1963-79). Leader of the 1961 military coup, he was later elected president 3 times. Increasingly more dictatorial, in 1972 he assumed almost unlimited power, and was a strong ally of the United States. He was assassinated by Kim Jae Kyn, director of the Korean C.I.A.
See also: Korea.

Parker, Alton Brooks (1852-1926), U.S. jurist and Democratic presidential candidate. He was chief justice of the New York court of appeals (1898-1904), and, after losing the presidential election to Theodore Roosevelt in 1904, returned to private practice.

Parker, Charlie (Charles Christopher Parker, Jr.; 1920-55), U.S. jazz musician and composer, known as Bird or Yardbird. An alto saxophonist, he and Dizzy Gillespie were the originators and leaders of the bop movement, an innovative and influential revolution in jazz.
See also: Jazz.

Parker, Dorothy (1893-1967), U.S. writer and critic. She wrote short stories, satirical verse, and newspaper columns, and was a celebrated conversationalist. Her tone is poignant, ironic, and sometimes cruelly witty and cynical. Her story collections include *Laments for the Living* (1930), *After Such Pleasures* (1933), and *Here Lies* (1939); her verse collections include *Enough Rope* (1926) and *Sunset Guns* (1939).

Parker, Ely Samuel (Do-ne-ho-ga-wa; 1828-95), first Native American U.S. Commissioner of Indian Affairs (1869-71). Parker, a Seneca Iroquois, studied law but was not permitted to practice and instead became a civil engineer. He served as Ulysses S. Grant's military secretary during the Civil War and drafted the terms for the Confederate surrender. He became a brigadier general (1867), but resigned his commission when President Grant appointed him Commissioner of Indian Affairs.

Parker, Theodore (1810-60), U.S. liberal preacher and social reformer. A Unitarian pastor in West Roxbury, Mass. (1837-46) and Boston (1846-59), he championed the abolition of slavery, prison reform, temperance, and education for women.

Parkinson's disease, or Parkinsonism, degenerative brain disorder, usually appearing after age 40, characterized by trembling lips and hands, shuffling gait, and muscular rigidity. Causes are often unknown, although in some cases the disorder is a result of carbon monoxide poisoning, influenza, encephalitis, or drugs. Because the disorder is often accompanied by depression, it is hard to measure its effects on mental capacity, which may often be impaired. Named after the English surgeon James Parkinson, who first described it in 1817, the disease is treated with the drugs L-Dopa (and carbidopa for side effects) and amantadine.

Parkinson's law, principle that in any bureaucracy "work expands so as to fill the time available for its completion." This humorous formulation of bureaucratic practices first appeared in C. Northcote Parkinson's *Parkinson's Law and Other Studies in Administration* (1957).

Parkman, Francis (1823-93), U.S. historian of the frontier and of the Anglo-French struggle for North America. Despite a severe nervous affliction, his commitment to his research and writing made him a leading historian. Among his works are *The Oregon Trail* (1849), an enormously popular account of a journey made in 1846; *History of the Conspiracy of Pontiac* (2 vols.; 1851); and his chief work, *France and England in North America* (7 vols.; 1865-92). He was also an expert horticulturalist.

Parks, Rosa Lee (1913-), African American civil rights activist. In 1955, in Montgomery, Ala., she refused to give up her bus seat to a white man, as required by segregation law. Her arrest led to an antisegregation boycott of Montgomery's buses that lasted more than a year and finally succeeded in desegregating the buses. Martin Luther King, Jr. first rose to national prominence for his leadership of the boycott, which inspired the civil rights movement throughout the country. Parks, who lost her job as seamstress as a result of her actions, eventually joined the staff of Detroit congressman John Conyers, Jr. (1967). She won the Spingarn Medal for her contribution to the civil rights movement (1979).
See also: Civil rights.

Parlement, French high court of justice in Paris that operated from the Middle Ages until 1789. It had some political influence through its power of questioning the king's edicts. Membership became a hereditary privilege. There were also 12 provincial parlements. Deemed reactionary and exclusive, they were swept away in the French Revolution.

Parliament, legislative body of Great Britain, technically comprising of the monarch (sovereign in name only), the House of Lords (a relatively powerless body composed of nobles and Anglican prelates), and the 635-member House of Commons, chosen by elections. The term Parliament usually refers to the Commons, the sovereign power of the nation. They elect the prime minister and the nonpartisan speaker who presides over them. The executive head of government also comes from the Commons, and government ministers are selected from either house. The major parties of Parliament today are Labour, Conservative, Liberal Democratic, and Social Democratic. Elections must be held every 5 years, although they may be called more frequently by the prime minister. If the party in power loses its parliamentary majority on a major issue, Parliament is dissolved and new elections held. The beginnings of Parliament go back to medieval times. The Curia Regis (great council), an executive and judicial body gathered from the nobility and the church to aid the monarch, evolved into the House of Lords. Knights and burgesses were summoned to give their approval to royal acts in the 13th century. In the 17th century Parliament won legislative power over taxation and expenditures and then ultimate sovereignty as a result of the Glorious Revolution (1688). The Industrial Revolution brought demands for suffrage from the new classes it created; universal suffrage for men and women was won in the 20th century.

Parliamentary procedure, (parliamentary law, parliamentary practice, rules of order), rules that govern the functioning of legislative bodies and other institutions—such as clubs, political parties, or corporations—that hold meetings that resemble those of legislatures. The most popular book on parliamentary procedure is Robert's Rules of Order, originally compiled in 1876 and frequently revised since then. In the English-speaking world, parliamentary procedure is ultimately derived from the traditions of the British Parliament.

Parma (pop. 176,800), city in the Emilia-Romagna region of northern Italy, capital of Parma province, on the Parma River. The city is an important junction on the Milan-Bologna rail and road route. The surrounding area is primarily agricultural and is known for the production of Parmesan cheese. Other local products include machinery and pharmaceuticals. Parma was founded by the Romans in 183 B.C.
See also: Italy.

Parma (pop. 92.548), city in northeastern Ohio, a southern suburb of Cleveland. Local industries include the manufacture of automobile parts, tools and dies, and metal stamping.
See also: Ohio.

Parmenides (b. c.515 B.C.), Greek pre-Socratic philosopher, founder of the Eleatic school. His philosophy, anchored on the proposition "What is *is*," denied the reality of multiplicity and change, claiming that they were illusions of the senses.
See also: Pre-Socratic philosophy.

Parnassus, or Parnassós, mountain 8,060 ft (2,430 m) high, in central Greece, north of Delphi and the Gulf of Corinth. In ancient times Parnassas was considered sacred to Dionysus and Apollo and celebrated as the home of the Muses.

Parnell, Charles Stewart (1846-91), Irish nationalist, leader of the Irish Home Rule movement. A member of the British Parliament from 1875, he obstructed parliamentary business, demanding attention to Irish land reform, and his supporters' agitation persuaded William Gladstone to adopt a home rule policy. His political career was ruined in 1889 when he was named correspondent in a divorce case.
See also: Ireland.

Parole, system of releasing a convict from prison before the end of a sentence. Generally, parole is granted for good behavior in prison, if the parole board considers a prisoner psychologically and socially ready to readjust to the outside world. A parolee usually must observe certain standards of conduct, stay within certain areas, and report regularly to a parole officer.

Parotid gland *see:* Saliva.

Parotitis *see:* Mumps.

Parrington, Vernon Louis (1871-1929), U.S. educator and literary historian. He stressed the influence of social and economic affairs on American writers and was awarded the Pulitzer Prize for his *Main Currents in American Thought* (3 vols.; 1927-30).

Parrish, Maxfield (1870-1966), U.S. artist, with an elegant, richly decorative style. He is noted for murals, posters, and magazine and book illustrations, e.g., *Arabian Nights.*

Parrot, popular name for about 320 species (family Psittacidae) of brightly colored birds distributed throughout the tropics. Parrots have large heads, short necks, heavy, hooked bills, and strong feet for climbing and grasping. Popular as cage birds (especially those that learn to mimic speech), some species are parakeets, cockatoos, and macaws. Parrots range in size from the pygmy (3.5 in/8.7 cm) of the South Pacific to the Amazon parrot (40 in/100 cm) of South America.

Parrot fever *see:* Psittacosis.

Parry, Sir William Edward (1790-1855), British Arctic explorer. Parry led British naval expeditions in search of the Northwest Passage (1819, 1821, 1824); his *Voyage for the Discovery of a Northwest Passage* (1821) describes these experiences. In *Narrative of an Attempt to Reach the North Pole in Boats* (1828) he recounted his 1827 journey by ship and then by boats equipped with steel runners (to permit travel on ice), finally coming to within 500 mi (800 km) of the pole, 82°45′ north latitude, a record not broken until 1876.
See also: Melville Island.

Parsec, unit of distance in astronomy, equivalent to 3.26 light-years. Nearby stars show a slight shift in position (a parallax) when observed from opposite sides of the earth's orbit. A star with a parallax of one second or arc (1/3,600 of a degree) is said to be one parsec away. Proxima Centauri, the nearest star, is somewhat less than 1 1/3 parsecs away.
See also: Astronomy.

Parsis, or Parsees, religious group centered in Bombay and northwest India, followers of Zoroastrianism. Numbering about 120,000 today, their ancestors came from Persia in the 8th century to escape Muslim persecution. The Parsis, many of whom are traders, are among the wealthiest and best educated groups in India. They revere aspects of nature, especially fire, as manifestations of Ahura Mazdah (the divinity).
See also: Zoroastrianism.

Parsley, biennial or perennial herb (*Petroselinum crispum*) of the carrot family, native to southern Europe. Its leaves are used as seasoning and garnish, the plants and seeds for medicinal purposes.

Parsnip, carrotlike plant (*Pastinaca sativa*) native to Europe, grown for its edible, sweet-flavored, yellowish-white root.

Parsons, Talcott (1902-79), U.S. sociologist. A professor at Harvard University (1927-74), he advocated a structural-functional theory, a framework for classifying the characteristics of a stable social system. Works include *The Structure of Social Action* (1937), *The Social System* (1951), and *Politics and Social Structure* (1969).
See also: Sociology.

Blaise Pascal

Partch, Harry (1901-74), U.S. composer who devised a special notation for his microtonal music, based on an octave divided into 43 intervals instead of the traditional 12. His works received slight public attention as they could only be performed on instruments of his own devising.

Parthenon (Greek, "the virgin's place"), temple to Athena, on the Acropolis. It was built of marble (447-432 B.C.) by the architects Ictinus and Callicrates; Phidias supervised the sculptures. The temple featured 46 Doric columns surrounding a main hall, behind which rested an inner chamber (the Parthenon proper). The main hall was divided by a Doric colonnade into a broad nave and side aisles. Sculptures of Athena's birth and her contest with Poseidon were depicted on the east and west pediments. Of the sculptures on the interior frieze, most of the originals still exist, though some (the Elgin Marbles) are in the British Museum in London. The temple became a Christian church (6th century) and later a mosque (with added minaret). It was well preserved until 1687, when a Venetian bombardment caused the explosion of gunpowder stored within it. Today the temple ruins are threatened by industrial pollution.
See also: Acropolis.

A fragment of a long cavalcade depicted on a frieze in the Parthenon

Parthia, ancient country of Asia, southeast of the Caspian Sea. The Parthian empire was established in 250 B.C., following a revolt, led by Arsace, against the Syrian empire. The Parthian empire reached its zenith under Mithradates I (171-138 B.C.) and II (123-88 B.C.). The Parthians conquered Persia and nearby lands, and their mounted archers successfully withstood Roman attacks until 38 B.C. In A.D. 226 the territory that had been under Parthian rule was taken over by Ardashir I, the founder of the Sassanid dynasty of Persia.

Particle accelerator, research tools used to accelerate electrically charged subatomic particles to high velocities. Physicists can focus the resulting particle beams to interact with othr particles or to break up atomic nuclei, in order to learn more about the fundamental nature of matter. Accelerators use electromagnetic fields to accelerate the particles in a straight line or in a circular or spiral path. The devices are rated according to the kinetic energy they impart, which is measured in electron volts (eV).
The first accelerator, designed by John Douglas Cockcroft and Ernest Thomas Walton in l932, accelerated protons to energies of 700 keV.
The first *linear accelerator*, or *linac*, was built in l928 by R. Wideröe. The largest linear accelerator still in operation, 2 mi long (3.2-km), at Stanford University, can accelerate electrons to energies of 20 GeV. The first *circular accelerator, the cyclotron*, was built by E.O. Lawrence in l931. The particles were accelerated twice in each revolution, spiraling outward and eventually shot out toward a target; however the relativistic gain in mass tended to throw them out of phase with the acceleration pulses. The solution was the *synchrocyclotron*, or *frequency modulated cyclotron*, which varies the acceleration frequencies to keep them in phase with the particles. The largest synchrocyclotron today achieves energies of more than 700 MeV.
As still higher energies continued to be sought, the *synchrotron* was developed, guiding the particles around a ring of magnets through a thin evacuated tube. The largest now operating, at the Fermi National Accelerator Laboratory in Batavia, Ill., achieves energies in excess of 500 GeV.
The latest accelerators are *colliding-beam machines*, in which positive and negative particles circle in opposite directions. The resulting head-on collisions yield much higher effective energies than collisions with stationary targets.

Particle physics, study of subatomic particles (those particles that are smaller than atoms), including protons, neutrons, electrons, and a wide variety of much more unstable particles. Physicists now classify subatomic particles into 4 general classes. The smallest of these are the bosons, which have no mass. They include the photon, which is a packet of energy, and 8 types of gluons. The next class, the leptons, has 12 particles: the electron, which carries a negative electromagnetic charge, the positron, which is identical but carries a positive charge, 2 muons (of opposite charge), and a neutrino associated with each of these 3 pairs. The third class of particles is the mesons, which are larger in mass than the leptons. They are nuclear particles that serve to hold the nuclei of atoms together. The most massive of the 4 classes is the baryons, which include the proton, the neutron, and heavier particles called hyperons. Mesons and baryons, unlike the other 2 classes, are governed by the strong nuclear force, which is one of the 4 fundamental forces of nature (the others being gravity, electromagnetism, and the weak nuclear force). For this reason, these 2 classes of particles are sometimes grouped together under the term hadrons. Many particle physicists today subscribe to a theory first put forward in 1964 by Murray Gell-Mann and George Zweig stating that all the hedrons are ultimately composed of still more elementary particles called quarks. Particle physics studies all these various particles and the relationships and interactions among them.
See also: Atom; Boson; Lepton; Quark.

Partridge, any of several game birds distributed through Europe, Asia, and Africa. Best known is the gray, or common, partridge (*Perdix perdix*) of Europe, with a chestnut horseshoe on its breast. The true partridge belongs to the pheasant family; the name is also applied to the bobwhite, or quail, in the northern and western parts of the United States.

Pasadena (pop. 118,072), city in the foothills of the Sierra Madre Mountains in southern California. Located just above the state's fertile San Gabriel Valley, it was given a Chippewa name meaning "crown of the valley." A marketing center for the valley's abundant agricultural output, it is also a center of electronic and aerospace components. The California Institute of Technology (with its NASA Jet Propulsion Lab.) is in the city, which is also host to college football's postseason Rose Bowl game.
See also: California.

Pascal, Blaise (1623-62), French scientist and religious philosopher. A mathematical prodigy, discoverer of the properties of the cycloid, and founder of the modern theory of probability, his work also contributed to the formulation of differential calculus. In physics he pioneered hydrodynamics and fluid mechanics, discovering Pascal's Law, the basis of hydraulics. His religious thought, influenced by Jansenism and by a religious experience (1654) that led him to enter the convent of Port-Royal, emphasizes "the reasons of the heart" over those of logic and intellect. It is expressed in his *Provincial Letters* (1656) and his posthumously published *Pensées* (1670).

Pascal's law, in fluid mechanics, states that the pressure applied to an enclosed body of fluid is transmitted equally in all directions with unchanged intensity. The application of Pascal's law may be seen in hydraulic presses, jacks, and elevators.
See also: Pascal, Blaise; Pressure.

Paschal II, or Pascal II (d.1118), pope, 1099-1118. During his reign he was involved in the investiture controversy, a power struggle to determine whether kings or popes had the right to appoint ecclesiastical authorities. The Holy Roman Emperor Henry V invaded Italy and kidnapped Paschal to force him to renounce the papal right of investiture. Paschal later repudiated the renunciation.

Pasqueflower, common name for spring-flowering anemones of the buttercup family. The North American pasqueflower (*Anemone patens*) is abundant in the prairies, and the European pasqueflower (*A. pulsatilla*) grows in chalky pastures.

Passamaquoddy Bay, inlet of the Bay of Fundy between Maine and New Brunswick, Canada, at the mouth of St. Croix River. The bay, which extends inland about 15 mi (24 km) and is about 10 mi (16 km) wide, is characterized by a powerful tidal flow.

Passenger pigeon, extinct bird (*Ectopistes migratorius)* of the pigeon family, extremely common until the 19th century throughout most of North America. Highly gregarious and social birds that migrated in huge flocks, passenger pigeons fed on invertebrates, fruits, and grain, often doing extensive damage to crops. Hunted both as pests and for food, they became extinct.

Passionflower, any of a group of tropical climbing plants (genus *Passiflora*) grown for the juice of their berries and for their ornate flowers. The name is derived from the religious symbolism attributed to the flowers: the 3 stigmatas are considered to represent the Holy Trinity, while the hairy corona recalls the crown of thorns. The 5 petals and sepals represent the 10 Apostles present at the Crucifixion.

Passion play, dramatic presentation of Jesus's suffering, death, and resurrection. It was one of the popular medieval mystery plays that were performed by amateurs at religious festivals. The most famous passion play still performed is that at Oberammergau, Germany, staged every ten years since 1633.

Passover, or Pesach, major Jewish festival held for 8 days from the 14th to the 22nd of the month of Nisan (March/April). It celebrates the Israelite's escape (led by Moses) from Egypt. At the *seder* feasts on the evenings of the first 2 days, special dishes symbolize the hardships of the escape, and the story of the exodus is read from the Haggadah.
See also: Judaism.

Pasternak, Boris (1890-1960), Russian novelist, poet, and translator. His poetry *Over the Barriers* (1916) and *My Sister, Life* (1922) brought him his first successes. During the Stalinist repression of the 1930s, he stopped publishing his own work and turned to translating the works of Shakespeare and Goethe. *Doctor Zhivago,* his epic novel of 20th-century Russian history, was denied publication in the USSR but was published in Italy (1957) to worldwide acclaim. Awarded the Nobel Prize in literature (1958), Pasternak was forced to decline it as a result of Soviet pressure. *Doctor Zhivago* was finally published in the USSR in the late 1980s, under Mikhail Gorbachev's policy of glasnost.

Pasteur, Louis (1822-95), French microbiologist and chemist. He conducted important studies on fermentation and bacteria (which resulted in his theory that living germs spread disease). He disproved the theory of spontaneous generation and popularized the sterilization of medical equipment, which saved many lives. He discovered anthrax and rabies vaccines and developed pasteurization (the use of heat to kill germs), a process of great economic import. The Pasteur Institute (Paris) was founded in 1888 as a teaching and research center on contagious and virulent diseases.
See also: Bacteria; Fermentation.

Pasteurization, process for partially sterilizing milk, originally developed by Louis Pasteur for improving the storage qualities of wine and beer. The milk was held at 145°F (63°C) for 30 min in a vat, but today is usually held at 162°-185°F (72°-85°C) for 16 sec. Disease-producing bacteria, particularly those causing tuberculosis, are thus destroyed with a minimum effect on the flavor of the product. Since the process destroys a majority of the harmless bacteria that sour milk, the milk's keeping properties are also improved.
See also: Pasteur, Louis.

Pastoral, literature idealizing simple shepherd life, free of the corruption of the city. Typical forms are the verse elegy, prose romance, and drama. Originating with Theocritus in the 3rd century B.C., the form was used by many ancient authors, including Vergil in his *Bucolics* (eclogues). In England, after a Renaissance revival, it was used by William Shakespeare (in *As You Like It*), Sir Philip Sidney (in *Arcadia*), and John Milton (in *Comus*).

Patagonia, dry plateau of about 300,000 sq mi (777,000 sq km) in southern Argentina, between the Andes Mountains and the Atlantic Ocean. Sheep-raising is the main activity of the few inhabitants. There are oil, iron ore, and coal deposits, as well as other untapped mineral resources.

Patagonia

Patchen, Kenneth (1911-72), U.S. poet, novelist, and painter who often illustrated his own work. *The Collected Poems of Kenneth Patchen* appeared in 1969. His novels include *The Memoirs of a Shy Pornographer* (1945).

Patent, in law, governmental grant of the exclusive right to make, use, or sell an invention or grant others that right. In the United States a patent is valid for 17 years and may be requested to cover any useful and original device or process. The term derives from the medieval "letters patent"—public letters by which a sovereign conferred monopolistic control of certain goods on a subject. The first patent legislation in the United States was passed in 1790; the U. S. Patent Office was established in 1836.

Boris Pasternak

Patent medicine, or proprietary medicine, over-the-counter drugs that can be sold without prescription. Patent medicines include aspirin, acetaminophen, ibuprofen, mouthwash, antiseptics, and laxatives. The term "patent" is outdated, referring to a time when the formulas for such products were kept secret. "Proprietary" trade names of many preparations are registered, but some (like Aspirin) pass into common usage. Both patent and prescription medicine in the United States are regulated by the Food and Drug Administration.
See also: Pure food and drug laws.

Louis Pasteur

Paterson (pop. 137,970), city in northeastern New Jersey, seat of Passaic County. Founded in 1791 at the falls of the Passaic River, Paterson was the site of the Society for Establishing Useful Manufactures, an

industrialization program initiated by Alexander Hamilton to build an independent American manufacturing industry. The small settlement soon became an industrial city, specializing in silk manufacture during the 19th century. Locomotives and Colt revolvers were also made there. Today the city is a major producer of textiles, machinery, and plastics.
See also: New Jersey.

Paterson, William (1745-1806), U.S. jurist and politician. A delegate from New Jersey, he was author of the New Jersey plan at the Constitutional Convention (1787), a U.S. senator (1789-90), governor of New Jersey (1790-93), and from 1793 associate justice of the U.S. Supreme Court. Paterson, N.J. is named for him.
See also: Supreme Court of the United States.

Pathans *see:* Pushtuns.

Saint Paul

Pathology, study of the causes of diseases and of the changes they produce in the body. Techniques include X-rays and biopsies (removal and microscopic examination of tissue, fluid, or cells).
See also: Disease.

Patmos, northernmost of the Dodecanese Islands of Greece, in the southeast Aegean Sea, near Turkey. Patmos is a barren volcanic island 13 sq mi (34 sq km) in area. Grapes, citrus fruits, olives, and cereals are grown, but the economy is dependent mainly on tourism and sponge fishing. Its 11th-century monastery contains an important library.
The island was settled in ancient times by the Dorians and Ionians, and was used as a place of exile by the Romans. It was while in exile on Patmos that the apostle John is said to have written the Fourth Gospel and the Book of Revelation of the New Testament. Patmos was controlled by Turkey (1537-1912) and Italy (1912-47) before it returned to Greek rule.

Paton, Alan Stewart (1903-88), South African writer. His novel *Cry, the Beloved Country* (1948), drawing on his experience as principal of a reform school for Africans, describes apartheid. In 1953 he became president of the Liberal Party, which was banned in 1968.

Patriarch, Old Testament title for the head of a family or tribe, especially the Israelite fathers, Abraham, Isaac, Jacob, and Jacob's sons. The title was adopted by the early Christian bishops of Constantinople, Rome, Alexandria, Jerusalem, and Antioch, and now extends to certain other sees, especially of the Eastern Orthodox churches. It implies jurisdiction over other bishops.
See also: Eastern Orthodox Church.

Patricians (Latin, "of the fathers"), in ancient Rome, members of the aristocratic class. In the early Republic the heads of the chief families dominated political power in the Senate. The plebeians fought for equality (500-300 B.C.), until the term "patrician" eventually became an honorary title.
See also: Rome, Ancient.

Patrick, Saint (c.385-461), Christian missionary, patron saint of Ireland. Controversy surrounds his identity, dates, and works. In the popular version he was born in Roman Britain, was captured by pagan Irish, and was enslaved for 6 years. After escaping to Gaul and studying there, he returned (432) to convert Ireland, winning spectacular success in Ulster. He founded an archiepiscopal see in Armagh (444 or 445). Author of the autobiographical *Confessions,* he died in a Christianized Ireland. His feast day is March 17.

Patterson, family of U.S. newspaper publishers and editors. **Joseph Medill Patterson** (1879-1946) was coeditor (from 1910) and copublisher (1914-25) of the *Chicago Tribune* (with Robert McCormick). He was cofounder (1919), coeditor, and publisher of the *New York Daily News*, the largest-circulation tabloid in the United States. His sister, **Eleanor Medill Patterson** (1884-1948), edited the *Washington Herald* (from 1930), leased it and the *Times* (1937-39), and published the merged *Washington Times-Herald* (1939-48). His daughter, **Alicia Patterson** (1906-63), founded (with her husband, Harry F. Guggenheim), published, and edited, from 1940, the Long Island, N.Y., newspaper *Newsday,* which she developed into one of the largest suburban dailies in the United States.

Patton, George Smith, Jr., (1885-1945), U.S. general whose ruthlessness and tactical brilliance as a tank commander in World War II won him the nickname Old Blood and Guts. He was highly successful in North Africa and led the Third Army's liberation of France (1944) and thrust into Germany (1945).
See also: World War II.

Paul (1901-64), king of Greece 1947-64, successor to his brother, George II. He was succeeded by his son, Constantine II.
See also: Greece.

Paul, name of 6 Italian popes. **Paul III** (Alessandro Farnese; 1468-1549), pope (1534-49), encouraged the first major reforms of the Catholic Reformation, recognized the Jesuit order, and convened the Council of Trent (1545). **Paul IV** (Giovanni Caraffa; 1476-1559), reigned (1555-59), increased the powers of the Inquisition, enforced segregation of the Jews in Rome, and introduced strict censorship. His fanatical nepotism created widespread hostility. **Paul V** (Camillo Borghese; 1552-1621), pope (1605-21), clashed with the Venetian Republic over papal jurisdiction; a member of the Borghese family, he too was notorious for nepotism. **Paul VI** (Giovanni Montini; 1897-1978), pope (1963-78), continued the modernizing reforms of his predecessor, John XXIII, including vernacularization of the liturgy, relaxing of rules regarding fasting and abstinence, and reversal of some restrictions on intermarriage. He also reaffirmed the church's ban on contraception. The first pope to travel outside Italy in more than 150 years, Paul made a pilgrimage to the Holy Land (1964), followed by trips to India, the United States, Africa, and Southeast Asia. He also helped to forge limited doctrinal agreements with Lutherans and Anglicans. Though criticized by both liberals and traditionalists, Paul was widely respected for his spirituality, intellect, and compassion.

Paul, Alice (1885-1977), U.S. leader of the women's movement for equal rights. A founder of the National Woman's Party (1917) and the World Woman's Party (1938), she was active in the struggle for passage of the 19th Amendment to the U.S. Constitution, giving women the right to vote. After it was ratified (1920), she worked for the Equal Rights Amendment, first submitted to Congress in 1923.
See also: Equal Rights Amendment.

Paul, Saint (d.A.D.64? or 67?), apostle to the Gentiles. The son of a Roman citizen, Paul was a zealous Jew who was active in the persecution of Christians until a vision of Christ seen on the road to Damascus made him a fervent convert to the new faith. After being baptized, Paul began preaching. He went on extensive missionary journeys (A.D.47-59) to Cyprus, Asia Minor, and Greece. Returning to Jerusalem, he was violently attacked by the Jews and imprisoned for 2 years. Claiming his Roman citizen's right, he was transferred (A.D. 60) to Rome, where he was imprisoned again. His final fate is uncertain. His tomb and shrine are in Rome at St. Paul's Without the Walls. His life is recorded in the Acts of the Apostles and the Pauline Epistles. The epistles attributed to Paul are Romans, Corinthians, Galatians, Philippians, Colossians, First Thessalonians, and Philemons; also generally accepted to be his work are Ephesians and Second Thessalonians.
See also: New Testament.

Paulding, James Kirke (1778-1860), U.S. writer and public official. He satirized British colonialism in works like *John Bull in America* (1925) and did much to encourage the development of distinctively American literature. His novels include *Westward Ho!* (1832). He served as secretary of the navy (1838-41).

Pauli, Wolfgang (1900-58), Austrian-born U.S. physicist awarded the 1945 Nobel Prize in physics for his discovery of the exclusion principle, which stated that no 2 electrons in any atom could be in the same quantum state. He also postulated the existence of the neutrino before it was actually observed.
See also: Neutrino.

Pauling, Linus Carl (1901-), U.S. chemist and pacifist, awarded the 1954 Nobel Prize in chemistry for his work on chemical bonding and the 1962 Nobel Peace Prize for his support of the campaign for nuclear disarmament. Other contributions include

his work in molecular biology, his support in advancing the use of chemotherapy for mental diseases, and the use of Vitamin C in the treatment of the common cold.
See also: Quantum mechanics.

Paulist Fathers, officially the Society of Missionary Priests of St. Paul the Apostle, an evangelical order of Roman Catholic priests in the United States founded by Isaac Hecker (1858).

Pavarotti, Luciano (1935-), Italian tenor. A leading singer internationally since his Italian debut (1961) as Rodolfo in *La Bohème*, he has performed regularly at New York City's Metropolitan Opera (N.Y.C.) since his 1968 debut there. He is noted for his interpretations of the works of Puccini, Verdi, Donizetti, and Bellini.

Pavlov, Ivan Petrovich (1849-1936), Russian physiologist and experimental psychologist. For his studies of the physiology of the digestive system of dogs, he received the 1904 Nobel Prize in physiology or medicine. Continued experiments with dogs, this time involving the stimulation of gastric secretions, led to his discovery of the conditioned reflex (physiological reaction to environmental stimuli), which in turn influenced the development of behaviorism. His major work was *Conditioned Reflexes* (1926).
See also: Physiology; Psychology.

Pavlova, Anna (1881-1931), Russian ballerina, considered the greatest of her time. After her debut (1899) in St. Petersburg, she danced with Diaghilev's Ballets Russes before forming her own company. She was famed for her interpretations of *The Dying Swan*, choreographed for her by Michel Fokine, and of the title role in *Giselle*.
See also: Ballet.

Pawnee, Native American tribe of Caddoan linguistic stock who inhabited river valleys of what is now Nebraska and Kansas (16th-19th centuries). They had an elaborate religion, including a supreme being, and for a time performed human sacrifice to their god of vegetation. They lived by farming and buffalo hunting. By 1876 they had ceded all their land to the U.S. government and were settled on a reservation in Oklahoma.

Pawpaw, or papaw, tree (*Asimina triloba*) of the custard-apple family, whose fruits have a creamy edible pulp. Most pawpaws are grown in tropical countries, but the North American pawpaw thrives along streams in many parts of the eastern United States.

Payne, John Howard (1791-1852), U.S. playwright and actor. He wrote his first play, *Julia, or, The Wanderer*, at age 14 and first appeared on stage at age 17. Payne lived in London and Paris 1813-32, during which time he studied and adapted many French plays and met and collaborated with Washington Irving. After his return to the United States (1832), he was an advocate for Native American rights. He also served as U.S. consul in Tunisia (1842-45, 1851-52). Payne's most important works include *Brutus, or, The Fall of Tarquin* (1818) and *Clari, or, The Maid of Milan* (1823), for which he wrote the words to the song "Home, Sweet Home."

Payton, Walter (1954-), U.S. football player. Known for his powerful running and ability to break tackles, he holds the National Football League (NFL) record for yards rushed in a single game with 275 (1977) and career rushing yards (16,726). Payton played for the Chicago Bears (1975-87) of the NFL, and led them to a Super Bowl victory (1985).

Paz, Octavio (1914-), Mexican poet and essayist. His writings are known for their synthesis of many influences, including Aztec and Mexican culture, French surrealism, and Tantric and Buddhist thought. Paz traveled to Spain as a left-wing activist in the Spanish Civil War (1930s) and then to Paris (1940s). He lived in the United States during the 1940s, returning in the 1970s to teach in universities. He also traveled to India and Japan (1952) and became Mexican ambassador to India (1962-68). His writings include the poetry collections *Liberty Under Oath* (1960) and *The Collected Poems of Octavio Paz, 1957-1987* (1987) and the essay collections *The Labyrinth of Solitude* (1950) and *One Earth, Four or Five Worlds* (1985).

PCB *see:* Polychlorinated biphenyl.

Pea, herbaceous annual leguminous plant of the pulse family cultivated mainly for its edible seeds. Peas have white or purple flowers and a many-seeded fruit pod, or legume, which is high in protein. The garden pea (*Pisum sativum*) is native to Middle Asia and is now widely cultivated in North America, Europe, and Asia. The field pea (var. *arvense*) provides split peas. The sweet pea and chick-pea are of different genera.

Peabody, Elizabeth Palmer (1804-94), U.S. educator, author, and publisher. She started one of the first U.S. kindergartens (1861) and introduced Friedrich Froebel's methods of education to the United States. She wrote widely on educational theory, published *Dial* magazine and early works of Nathaniel Hawthorne, and was an exponent of transcendentalism.
See also: Education; Kindergarten.

Peabody, George (1795-1869), U.S. financier and philanthropist. From 1837 he lived in London, where he set up an immensely prosperous investment banking house. His donations made possible such foundations as the Peabody Institute of Baltimore and the George Peabody College in Nashville, Tenn., as well as museums at Harvard and Yale.

Peace, condition that exists when nations or other groups are not fighting; the treaty that ends a war; harmony; tranquility.

Walter Payton

Peace Corps, agency of the U.S. government established to help raise living standards in developing countries and to promote international friendship and understanding. Peace Corps projects, ranging from farm assistance to nursing instruction, are established at the request of the host country. Its volunteers normally serve for 2 years. The program was initiated by President John F. Kennedy in 1961 and transferred to ACTION, the agency coordinating federal volunteer programs in 1971.
See also: Shriver, Sargent.

Peace River, largest branch of the Mackenzie River, in northwestern Alberta and eastern British Columbia, Canada. The river, formed at Williston Lake from the Finlay and Parsnip rivers, crosses the Rocky Mountains north and east and joins the Slave River at Lake Athabasca. It is about 1,000 mi (1,600 km) long. It was explored in 1792-93 by Sir Alexander Mackenzie.

Peach, tree (*Prunus persica*) of the rose family; also, its fuzzy-skinned fruit. Native to China, it is now cultivated in warmer regions throughout the world (notably in California). There are several thousand varieties, divided into freestone or clingstone types according to the ease with which the flesh comes away from the pit. The nectarine is a smooth-skinned variety of peach.

Peach moth (*Grapholitha molesta*), small brown moth whose larvae are major fruit tree pests. Each year the adult deposits eggs on the leaves of peach and other fruit trees. The larvae feed on new twigs and on fruit. Growers attempt to control the peach moth with natural predators (parasitic wasps and flies) and with chemical sprays such as malathion.

Peach State *see:* Georgia.

Peacock, or peafowl, large ground bird of the pheasant family, native to east Asia; there are 2 genera, *Pavo* and *Afropavo*. The common peacock male (*P. cristatus*) has a

White peacock

train of up to 150 colorful tail feathers, which he displays to the peahen during courtship.

Peacock, Thomas Love (1785-1866), English novelist and poet, a satirist of contemporary intellectual trends. He was a close friend of Percy Bysshe Shelley and an able administrator in the East India Company. His best poetry is contained in his novels, which he described as comic romances. They include *Headlong Hall* (1816), *Nightmare Abbey* (1818), and *Crotchet Castle* (1831).

Peale, family of early U.S. painters. The prolific and versatile **Charles Willson Peale** (1741-1827) is best known for his portraits of Washington and other leading figures of the American Revolutionary period. He studied with J.S. Copley and Benjamin West in London and in 1784 founded a museum in Philadelphia. Also a scientist, he invented false teeth, the velocipede (an early bicycle), and (with Thomas Jefferson) the polygraph. Other interests included taxidermy and paleontology. His younger brother, **James Peale** (1749-1831), was known mainly for his portrait miniatures. Charles's many sons included **Raphaelle Peale** (1774-1825), a pioneer of still-life painting; **Titian Peale** (1799-1885), an animal painter; **Rubens Peale** (1784-1865), a still-life painter; and **Rembrandt Peale** (1778-1860), a portraitist and founder of the Peale Museum, Baltimore. His most famous work is a portrait of Thomas Jefferson (1805).

Former U.S. president Jimmy Carter on his Georgia peanut farm.

Peale, Norman Vincent (1898-), U.S. clergyman. He is well known through his popular writings, particularly *The Power of Positive Thinking* (1952), and his radio and television broadcasts. Since 1932 he has been pastor of the Marble Collegiate Reformed Church, New York City.

Peanut, also known as goober or groundnut (*Arachis hypogaea*), low, bushy, leguminous plant cultivated in tropical and subtropical regions. The "nut," the most popular in the United States, is a protein-rich fruit containing 1-3 seeds, and is produced when the yellow flowers grow down into the ground to mature after pollination. Peanuts are eaten fresh or roasted, are ground to make peanut butter, and yield an oil used for cooking oil, margarine, industrial purposes, and soap manufacturing.

Pear, tree (*Pyrus communis*) of the rose family; also, the oval-shaped, soft-fleshed fruit produced by the tree. Bartlett, Bosc, Anjou, and Seckel are among the fruit's hundreds of varieties. Pears are eaten fresh, dried, or canned, and the wood of the tree is used in cabinetmaking. A close relation of the apple, pear trees are occasionally cultivated as ornamentals.

Pearl, hard, rounded gem produced by certain bivalve mollusks, particularly pearl oysters (*Pinctada*) and the freshwater pearl mussel (*Margaritifera margaritifera*). In response to an irritation by foreign matter within the shell, the mantle secretes calcium carbonate in the form of nacre (mother-of-pearl) around the irritant body. Over several years, this encrustation forms the pearl. Cultured pearls may be obtained by "seeding" the oyster with an artificial irritant such as a small bead. Pearls are variable in shape and may be black or pink as well as the usual white.
See also: Oyster.

Pearl Harbor, natural landlocked harbor on Oahu island, Hawaii. Of great strategic importance, it is best known as the target of the Japanese surprise bombing of the U.S. Pacific fleet on Dec. 7, 1941. Damaged or sunk were 19 ships; 188 planes were destroyed on the ground at Wheeler Field. The raid caused more than 2,200 casualties with negligible losses to the Japanese and brought the United States into World War II. Today it is a national historic landmark.
See also: Hawaii; World War II.

Pearson, Karl (1857-1936), English mathematician best known for his pioneering work on statistics (e.g., devising the chi-square test), *The Grammar of Science* (1892), and his contributions to the philosophy of mathematics. He was also an early worker in the field of eugenics.
See also: Statistics.

Pearson, Lester Bowles (1897-1972), Canadian diplomat, prime minister (1963-68), and winner of the 1957 Nobel Peace Prize for his mediation in the Suez crisis (1956). In 1928 he joined the Department of External Affairs, becoming the first secretary, and in 1945 he was appointed ambassador to the United States. As secretary of state (1948-57) he made notable contributions in the creation of the UN and NATO. In 1958 he became the Liberal leader. After resigning as prime minister, he headed the World Bank commission, which produced the Pearson Report on developing countries.
See also: Canada.

Peary, Robert Edwin (1856-1920), U.S. Arctic explorer who discovered the North Pole. He entered the U.S. Navy in 1881 and first journeyed to the interior of Greenland in 1886. On leaves of absence from the Navy he led a series of exploratory expeditions to Greenland that culminated in his reaching the North Pole on Apr. 6, 1909. Peary's books, including *The North Pole* (1910) and *Secrets of Polar Travel* (1917), give an account of his extraordinary stamina and courage. In recent years his claim of reaching the North Pole has been challenged by some scholars.
See also: North Pole.

Peasants' War, popular revolt (1524-26) that began in southwestern Germany and spread to many parts of Germany and Austria. The social turmoil created by the Reformation and the decay of Feudalism seems to have been at the root of the discontent. The movement collapsed when Martin Luther denounced the uprising and supported its ruthless suppression.

Peat, partially decayed plant material found in layers, usually in marshy areas. It is composed mainly of the peat mosses sphagnum and hypnum, but also of sedges, tress, etc. Under the right geological conditions, peat forms coal. It is used as a mulch and burned for domestic heating.

Peat moss, moss (genus *Sphagnum*) that grows and accumulates on the surface of freshwater marshes in Canada, northern Europe, and Siberia. Peat moss grows up to 20 in (50 cm) high, forming a spongy mat without true roots. Its ability to absorb and hold water makes it commercially useful as a mulch (soil covering to prevent drying).

It is also used as a growth medium for mushrooms and orchids and as a packing material.

Pecan, nut-bearing tree (*Carya illinoensis*) of the walnut family native to North America, a member of the genus that also includes the hickory. It has furrowed bark and groups of long, thin leaflets. The tree, which grows up to 180 ft (55 m) high, takes 10 years to become a prolific nut-bearer. Nuts are harvested from both wild and orchard pecan trees. The tree is also valued for its wood, which is used for flooring and furniture.

Peccary, pig-like mammal of the southwestern United States and northern South America, inhabiting bushy thickets or forests. There are two species within the family Tayassuidae, the collared peccary (*Pecari tajacu*) and white-lipped peccary (*Tayassu pecari*). Both are long-legged, with thick bristly hair and an erectile mane along the back.

Peckham, Rufus W. (1838-1909), U.S. jurist and associate justice of the Supreme Court (1896-1909), member of the New York supreme court (1883-86), and state court of appeals (1889-95). Peckham defended property rights and opposed government intervention in business and is known for his opinions in *Allgeyer* v. *Louisiana* (1897) and *Lochner* v. *New York* (1905), in which the legal concept of due process became standard doctrine.
See also: Supreme Court of the United States.

Pecos River, originates in New Mexico's Sangre de Cristo mountains and flows southeast more than 800 mi (1,300 km) through New Mexico and Texas. The longest tributary of the Rio Grande, it is controlled by several dams of the Carlsbad Reclamation Project and drains nearly 35,000 sq mi (91,000 sq km).

Pectin, substance found in many fruits, especially apples. Pectin is available in tablet form as a digestive aid.

Pederson, Charles John (1904-89), U.S. chemist. Pederson, Donald J. Cram, and Jean-Marie Lehn won the 1987 Nobel Prize for chemistry for their discovery of simple molecular structures that mimic the behavior of the complex molecules produced by living cells. Pederson was a researcher in the laboratories of du Pont, 1927-69.
See also: Chemistry.

Pediatrics, branch of medicine concerned with the care of children. This care starts with the newborn, especially with premature, babies for whom intensive care is required. An important aspect is the recognition and treatment of congenital diseases or disease acquired during development of the embryo or fetus. Pediatricians also deal with infectious disease, growth or development disorders, mental retardation, diabetes, asthma, and epilepsy.

Pedro, two emperors of Brazil. **Pedro I** (1798-1834) was the son of John VI of Portugal, who fled with his family to Brazil when Napoleon Bonaparte invaded his homeland in 1807. On his father's return to Portugal in 1821, Pedro remained in Brazil, declared Brazilian independence (1822), and was crowned emperor. His subsequent mismanagement led to his abdication (1831). He was succeeded by his son **Pedro II** (1825-1891), declared of age in 1840, who gave Brazil over half a century of stable government. But his liberal policies, especially his attempt to abolish slavery, alienated the Brazilian landowning classes. They organized a bloodless coup in 1889 and made Brazil a republic.
See also: Brazil.

Peel, Sir Robert (1788-1850), English statesman. As home secretary in the 1820s Peel set up the British police force (thereafter called Bobbies) and sponsored the Catholic Emancipation Act (1829). Though he opposed the Reform Bill (1832), became more progressive, and after a brief term (1834-35) as prime minister, he organized the new Conservative Party out of the old Tory Party, aided by young politicians like Benjamin Disraeli and William Gladstone. His second term in office (1841-46) saw the introduction of an income tax, banking controls, and Irish land reforms, and the further removal of discriminatory laws against Roman Catholics. The repeal of the Corn Laws (1846) led to an era of free trade but caused a party split that led to his resignation.
See also: Conservative Party; United Kingdom.

Peeper *see:* Tree frog.

Peerce, Jan (1904-84), U.S. opera singer and violinist. A tenor, Peerce made his opera debut (1938) in *Rigoletto* and appeared with the Metropolitan Opera in Verdi's *La Traviata* (1941).

Peewit *see:* Lapwing.

Pegasus, in Greek mythology, the winged horse, represented by a large constellation of stars whose most famous feature is the Great Square, picked out by four bright stars, one at each corner, appearing high in the sky during fall in the Northern Hemisphere. Springing from the blood of the beheaded Medusa, Pegasus caused the fountain of Muses to flow and was associated with poetry. The hero Bellerophon rode Pegasus but was thrown to his death when he tried to reach heaven.
See also: Mythology.

Pegmatite *see:* Beryl; Feldspar.

Pei, I.M. (1917-), Chinese-born U.S. architect of public buildings and urban complexes, e.g., the Mile High Center in Denver, Place Ville Marie in Montreal, the John Hancock Tower in Boston, and the National Gallery's East Wing in Washington, D.C. Most are noted for their simplicity and environmental harmony.
See also: Architecture.

Peiping *see:* Beijing.

Peirce, Charles Sanders (1839-1914), U.S. philosopher, a pioneer of pragmatism. He is also known for his work on the logic of relations, theory of signs, and other contributions in logic and the philosophy of science. He wrote no comprehensive work but published numerous articles in philosophical journals, some of which were collected posthumously in *Chance, Love and Logic* (1925).
See also: Pragmatism.

Peking *see:* Beijing.

Pekingese, toy dog of Chinese origin with a flat, wrinkled face, protruding eyes, and bowed legs. The Pekingese has a long, thick coat of any color with longer hair around the neck and on the tail. It is 6-9 in (15-23 cm) at the shoulder and weighs 6-10 lbs (2.7-4.5 kg). Sacred to Chinese nobility from the 8th century, the breed reached Europe in the 1860s.

Peking man (*Sinanthropus pekinensis*), prehistoric upright human of the species *Homo erectus* whose first fossil remains were discovered near Beijing, China (1929). Intermediate between Java man (*Pithecanthropus erectus*) and Neanderthal man, Peking man lived between 500,000 and 250,000 years ago, had less brain development than modern humans, and reached about 5 ft (1.5 m) in height. Peking man used fire and developed stone tools.
See also: Prehistoric people.

Pelé (Edson Arantes do Nascimento; 1940-), Brazilian soccer player. Often rated as the best player of all time, he was known for his precise passing and shooting and led the Brazilian national team to 3 World Cup titles (1958, 62, 70). In 1975 Pelé joined the N.Y. Cosmos of the North American Soccer League (N.A.S.L.) and led them to a championship in 1977, after which he retired. He scored 1,281 goals.

Pelée, active volcano in Martinique, an island in the French West Indies. Rising 4,583 ft (1,397 m) above sea level, it had minor eruptions in 1702 and 1851. In 1902 a major eruption occurred, destroying the port of St. Pierre and killing approximately 38,000 people. Between 1929 and 1932 there were several milder eruptions. A volcano observatory on top of the volcano monitors its activity.

Peleliu, Pacific island of the Palau group, 500 mi (800 km) east of Mindanao, the Philippines. Peleliu is surrounded by coral reefs and covers 5 sq mi (13 sq km). The island exports phosphate, ebony, and pearls. Discovered in 1543, Peleliu was owned by Japan between World War I and World War II and was the site of heavy fighting from Sept.-Nov., 1944. It has been a U.S. protectorate since 1947, as part of the Trust Territory of the Pacific.

Pelican, large aquatic bird (genus *Pelecanus*) found in warm climates. The pelican's long bill is provided with an expansible pouch attached to the lower mandible, used not for storage, but simply as a catching apparatus, a scoop-net. Pelicans are social birds, breeding in large colonies. Most species also fish in groups, swimming together, herding the fish in horseshoe formation. All are fine fliers.

Pelican flower (*Aristolochia grandiflora*), woody flowering vine of the birthwort family Aristolochiaceae. The Pelican flower grows wild, has heart-shaped leaves, and the yellow-green blossoms may grow as wide as 18 in (46 cm) across.

Pellagra, vitamin deficiency disease (due to lack of niacin), often found in maize- or millet-dependent populations. A dermatitis, initially resembling sunburn but followed by thickening, scaling, and pigmentation, is characteristic; internal epithelium is affected (sore tongue, diarrhea). Confusion, delirium, hallucination, and ultimately dementia may ensue.

Pelopidas (410?-364 B.C.), military leader and politician instrumental in establishing Theban authority in mainland Greece. In 379 B.C. he and 6 compatriots assassinated the Spartan dictators and reasserted Theban liberty. Pelopidas was named boeotarch (leader), and, with his friend Epaminondas, developed Theban military supremacy. They defeated Sparta at the decisive battle of Leuctra (371 B.C.). Pelopidas was ambassador to Artaxerxes II of Persia (367 B.C.) and defeated the despot Alexander of Pherae at Cynoscephalae, Thessaly (364 B.C.), but died in the battle.
See also: Greece, Ancient.

Peloponnesian War, (431-404 B.C.) war between the rival Greek city-states, Athens and Sparta, that ended Athenian dominance and marked the beginning of the end of Greek civilization. The first phase (431-421) was inconclusive because Athenian sea power was matched by Spartan land power. A stalemate was acknowledged by the Peace of Nicias, named for the third Athenian leader in the war, following Pericles and Cleon. His leadership was then challenged by Alcibiades, who initiated the second and decisive phase of the conflict (418-404). In an attack on Syracuse in 413, the Athenians suffered a major defeat. The Spartans, with Persian aid, built up a powerful fleet under the leadership of Lysander, who blockaded Athens and forced the final surrender.
See also: Athens; Greece, Ancient; Sparta.

White pelican

Peloponnesus, peninsula forming the southern part of the Greek mainland, linked with the north by the Isthmus of Corinth. It is mostly mountainous, but its fertile lowlands provide wheat, tobacco, and fruit crops. Its largest city and port is Patras. In ancient times it was the center of the Mycenaean civilization and later was dominated by Sparta in the southeast.
See also: Greece.

Pelvis, lowest part of the trunk, bounded by the pelvic bones and in continuity with the abdomen. The principal contents are the bladder and lower gastro-intestinal tract (rectum) and reproductive organs, particularly in females the uterus, ovaries, fallopian tubes, and vagina. The pelvic floor is a powerful muscular layer that supports the pelvic and abdominal contents and is important in urinary and fetal continence. The pelvic bones articulate with the legs at the hip joints.
See also: Human body.

Pemmican, concentrated food, used by Native Americans on journeys, consisting of buffalo meat, venison, or fish, dried and ground to paste, then mixed with fat and dried fruit and packed in hide bags. Hunters and expeditions still use a beef, suet, and raisin version of pemmican.

Penal colony, overseas settlement in which convicts were isolated from society. The forced labor that was part of their punishment was often used for colonial development. All colonial powers had penal colonies, as had Russia in Siberia. Britain transported large numbers of convicts to the American colonies and to Australia.

Penderecki, Krzysztof (1933-), Polish composer. His innovative works used such unorthodox sounds as sawing and typing, scraping instruments, and hissing singers and include *Threnody for the Victims of Hiroshima* (1960) and *St. Luke Passion* (1965).

Pendulum, rigid body mounted on a fixed horizontal axis that is free to rotate under the influence of gravity. Many types of pendulum exist, the most common consisting of a large weight (the bob) supported at the end of a light string or bar. An idealized simple pendulum, with a string of negligible weight and length, l, the weight of its bob concentrated at a point, and a small swing amplitude, executes simple harmonic motion. The time, T, for a complete swing (to and fro) is given by Huygens' formula $T=2\pi\sqrt{l/g}$, depending only on the string length and the local value of the gravitational acceleration, g. Actual physical or compound pendulums approximate this behavior if they have a small angle of swing. They are used for measuring absolute values of g or its variation with geographical position and as control elements in clocks (Huygens, 1673).
See also: Foucault, Jean Bernard Leon; Galileo Galilei.

Penelope, in Greek mythology, wife of Odysseus and symbol of faithfulness and domestic virtue. In Homer's *Odyssey* Penelope is besieged by suitors during her husband's long absence. Wishing to remain faithful to Odysseus, she refuses to remarry until she can weave her father-in-law's shroud, but she unravels her work each night. Eventually Odysseus returns, and they are reunited.
See also: Mythology.

P'eng-hu *see:* Pescadores.

Penguin, the most highly specialized of all aquatic birds, with 17 species in the order Sphenisciformes, restricted to the southern hemisphere. Completely flightless, the wings are reduced to flippers for "flying" through the water. Ungainly on land, penguins only leave the water to breed. The nest is usually a skimpy affair, emperor and king penguins brood their single eggs on their feet, covering them with only a flap of skin. Most species nest in colonies, some with as many as 500,000 members. Penguins are long-lived birds: the yellow-eyed penguin may live for 20 years or more.

Penguins

Penicillin, substance produced by a class of fungi that interferes with cell wall production by bacteria and was one of the first, and remains among the most useful, antibiotics. The property was noted by A. Fleming in 1928, and production of penicillin for medical use was started by E.B. Chain and H.W. Florey in 1940. Staphylococcus, streptococcus, and the bacteria causing the venereal diseases of gonorrhea and syphilis are among the bacteria sensitive to natural penicillin, while bacilli negative to Gram's stain, which cause urinary tract infection, septicemia, etc., are destroyed by semisynthetic penicillins like ampicillin, oxacillin, and methicillin.
See also: Antibiotic; Fleming, Sir Alexander.

Peninsular Campaign, in the U.S. Civil War, unsuccessful Union campaign against the Confederate capital of Richmond, Va., Apr.-July 1862, led by General George B. McClellan across the peninsula between the James and York rivers. Although the Union troops, 100,000 strong, initially inflicted severe losses on the rebels, they were heavily defeated in the Seven Days Battles (June 26-July 2) by Confederate forces under General Robert E. Lee.
See also: Civil War, U.S.

Peninsular War (1808-14), part of the Napoleonic Wars, in which the French, fighting against the British, Portuguese, and Spanish, were driven out of the Iberian Peninsula. To increase his security in Europe, Napoleon sent General Andoche Junot to occupy Portugal (1807), and in 1808 dispatched Joachim Murat to occupy his ally, Spain. The Spanish and the Portuguese soon rebelled, and, with the aid of the British under Arthur Wellesley (later duke of Wellington), the French were driven out of Portugal (1809). In the long struggle that followed, the British, aided by Portuguese and Spanish guerrillas, gradually gained the upper hand, despite many reverses. By 1813 the French forces in Spain had been defeated, and Wellesley invaded southern France. The war ended on Napoleon's abdication.
See also: Napoleonic Wars.

Peninsula State *see:* Florida.

Penis, male reproductive organ for introducing sperm and semen into the female vagina and uterus; its urethra also carries urine from the bladder. The penis is made of connective tissues and specialized blood vessels which become engorged with blood in sexual arousal and which cause the penis to become stiff and erect; this facilitates the intromission of semen in sexual intercourse. A protective fold, the foreskin, covers the top and is often removed for religious or medical reasons in circumcision.
The penis has a fixed root situated in the urogenital triangle of the perineum and a free shaft. At the root of the corpora cavernosa diverge to be attached to the boney structure of the pelvis. The corpus spongiosum expands to form the bulb of the penis. The skin of the shaft of the penis forms a fold, the prepuce, which projects from a sulcus to cover the glans. The skin of the penis is thin, distensible, devoid of fat, and closely attached to the underlying fascia. On one end it is continuous with the skin of the abdominal wall, and the scrotum and peritoneum.
See also: Reproduction.

Penn, John (1740-88), U.S. Revolutionary leader, delegate from North Carolina to the Continental Congress, signer of the Declaration of Independence. Penn was admitted to the Virginia bar (1762) and practiced law there until he settled in North Carolina (1774).

Penn, William (1644-1718), English Quaker, advocate of religious tolerance, and founder of Pennsylvania. He wrote numerous tracts on Quaker beliefs and was several times imprisoned for his nonconformity. In 1681, he and 11 others bought the rights to eastern New Jersey, and he received a vast province on the west bank of Delaware River in settlement of a debt owed by Charles II to Penn's father. Thousands of European Quakers emigrated there in search of religious and political freedom. In 1682 Penn visited the colony and witnessed the fulfillment of his plans for the city of Philadelphia. He returned in 1699 to revise the constitution.
See also: Quakers.

William Penn making a treaty with the Native Americans of Pennsylvania

Pennsylvania

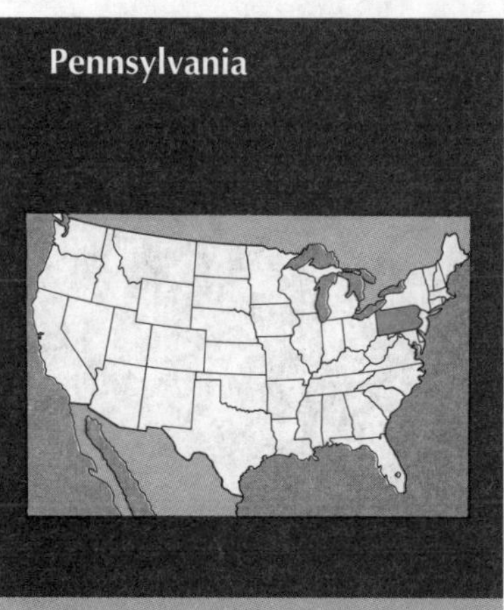

Capital:	Harrisburg
Statehood:	Dec. 12, 1787 (2nd state)
Familiar name:	Keystone State
Area:	45,308 sq mi (117,348 sq km); ranks 33rd
Population:	11,924,710 (1990); ranks 5th
Elevation:	Highest—3,213 ft (979 m), Mt. Davis; Lowest—sea level, along the Delaware River
Motto:	Virtue, Liberty and Independence
Flower:	Mountain laurel
Bird:	Ruffed grouse
Tree:	Hemlock
Song:	None

Pennsylvania, state in the Middle Atlantic region of eastern United States; bordered by Lake Erie and New York to the north; the Delaware River (with New York and New Jersey on the other side) to the east; Delaware, Maryland, and West Virginia to the south; and West Virginia and Ohio to the west.
Land and climate. Pennsylvania has seven main land regions. The Erie Lowland, in the northwest corner, is a strip of flat land along Lake Erie's coast. It abuts the Appalachian (or Allegheny) Plateau, which covers most of northern and all of western Pennsylvania, stretching south and east as well. This region is generally hilly and marked by deep, narrow valleys. The Appalachian Ridge and Valley Region has long, parallel ridges separated by narrow valleys. To its southeast lies a small extension of the New England Upland; to its southwest is a small extension of the Blue Ridge, part of the Blue Ridge Mountains. The Piedmont is a region of rolling plains and rich farmland. The Atlantic Coastal Plain, a narrow strip in the state's southeastern corner, has low-lying, fertile land. Pennsylvania's major rivers are the Allegheny, Ohio, Monongahela, Susquehanna, Schuylkill, and Delaware. Forests cover about three-fifths of the state. Pennsylvania's climate is humid, with warm summers and cold winters. Principal cities are Philadelphia, Pittsburgh, and Erie.
Economy. Manufacturing is the mainstay of Pennsylvania's economy. Chief manufactured products are processed foods, chemicals, machinery, electrical equipment, fabricated metal products, and primary metals (mainly steel). Tourism and other service industries also are important. Less important are agriculture and mining. Chief livestock produce are milk and beef cattle; chief crops are corn and hay. Chief mining products are coal, natural gas, and limestone.
Government. Pennsylvania's present constitution was adopted in 1968. The governor serves a 4-year term. The state's legislature, called the General Assembly, consists of 50 senators serving 4-year terms and 203 representatives serving 2-year terms. In the U.S. Congress, Pennsylvania is represented by 2 senators and 21 representatives.
History. Algonquin and Iroquois Indians were living in the area when English explorer Henry Hudson arrived in 1609.

Amish Fields near Lancaster, Pennsylvania

Swedes built the first permanent European settlement in 1643, near present-day Philadelphia. The Dutch took control of the area in 1655, but lost it to the British in 1664. In 1681, it was granted to William Penn, an English Quaker. Pennsylvania became one of Britain's 13 American colonies. The French and Indian wars disrupted the peace forged between Penn's followers and the Native Americans. Pennsylvania played a vital role during the American Revolution and the founding of the nation. The Declaration of Independence and the Constitution were signed in Philadelphia, which was the nation's capital from 1790 to 1800. During the Civil War, Pennsylvania, whose many Quakers opposed slavery, supported the Union. From the Civil War's end until that of World War II, the state's prosperity grew, broken only by severe floods (1889) and the Great Depression (1930s). But during the 1950s, the economy went into a decline, and the state's aging urban areas suffered from unemployment and overpopulation. In recent years, Pennsylvania has moved toward newer technologies and service industries.

Pennsylvania Dutch (from German *Deutsch*, "German"), descendants of German-speaking immigrants who came to Pennsylvania during the 17th and 18th centuries in search of religious freedom. They were mainly Lutheran and Reformed Protestant but included such Pietist sects as the Amish, Dunkers, Mennonites, and Moravians, who still retain their original culture.
See also: Amish; Mennonites.

Pennyroyal (*Mentha pulegium*), any of 4 species of low-growing herb of the mint family Labiatae native to Europe, Asia, and North America. Pennyroyal has purple flowers on prostrate stems. The oval leaves are cultivated for their oil, used in medicine, perfume, and insect repellents.

Penobscot River, longest river in Maine. From the head of its longest branch it runs 350 mi (563 km) to its mouth at Penobscot Bay on the Atlantic Ocean. The Penobscot rises near the Canadian border and flows east and then south past Bangor. During the 19th century it was used for transporting timber to the coast for shipment to eastern cities.

Penology *see:* Criminology.

Pensacola (pop. 344,406), city, northwest Florida, seat of Escambia County, seaport on Pensacola Bay of the Gulf of Mexico. Pensacola was settled by Spain (1559), though not continuously inhabited, and belonged at various times to Spain or England before being purchased by the United States (1821). It is the site of the U.S. Naval Air Training Station and the University of West Florida. Pensacola manufactures wood and paper products and chemicals.
See also: Florida.

Pension, regular payment received after retirement from employment because of age or disability, from the government under Social Security programs, or from private employers, or both. In the U.S. almost all large corporations provide pension plans for their employees, based on salary and length of service and financed either by the company alone or jointly by company and employee (contributory plans). There are individual pensions as well. Individual retirement accounts (IRA), offered by banks and other financial institutions, are accounts which are specially structured to help working individuals save money over a long period of time, with different types of tax shelters and special interest rates. Another type is the Keogh plan, which is similar to an IRA, but is used by self-employed people or business owners.
See also: Social security.

Penstemon *see:* Beardtongue.

Pentagon, The, five-sided building in Arlington, Va., that houses the U.S. Department of Defense, built in 1941-43. The largest office building in the world, it consists of five concentric pentagons covering a total area of 34 acres.
See also: Defense, U.S. Department of.

Pentagon Papers, 2.5-million-word, top-secret history of U.S. involvement in Indochina from 1945 to 1968, compiled by order of Secretary of Defense Robert S. McNamara, and leaked by Daniel Ellsberg, a former government researcher, to the *New York Times*. A court order secured by the Justice Department barring publication was overturned by the U.S. Supreme Court in June 1971. Later attempts to prosecute Ellsberg were thrown out of court because evidence against him was obtained by wiretaps and other illegal means (May 1973).

Pentateuch (Greek, "five books"), the first five books of the Old Testament: Genesis, Exodus, Leviticus, Numbers, and Deuteronomy. They were traditionally assigned to Moses, but are now regarded as a compilation of four or more documents dating from the 9th to the 5th centuries B.C. and distinguished by style and theological bias.
See also: Old Testament.

Pentathlon, track and field competition that consists of 5 events. The ancient Greek contest included jumping, racing, wrestling, discus, and javelin. The modern pentathlon, part of the Summer Olympic Games since 1924, consists of horseback riding, shooting, fencing, swimming, and cross-country running.

Pentecost (Greek, "50th"), Jewish and Christian festivals. The Jewish Pentecost, called Shavuot, celebrated on the 50th day after Passover, is a harvest feast. The Christian Pentecost (Whitsunday in England), the 50th day inclusively after Easter, commemorates the descent of the Holy Spirit upon the Apostles, marking the birth of the Christian Church.

Pentecostalism, Protestant fundamentalist and revivalist movement that emphasizes holiness and spiritual power as initiated by an experience ("baptism in the Spirit") in which the recipient "speaks in tongues." The Pentecostal churches base their distinctive doctrines and practice of charismata on New Testament teachings and accounts of the bestowal of the Holy Spirit. Pentecostalism began c.1906 and spread rapidly; it is now influential in many major denominations. The largest Pentecostal churches in the United States are the Assemblies of God and the United Pentecostal Church.
See also: Protestantism.

Pentothal *see:* Thiopental.

Penzias, Arno Allan (1933-), German-born U.S. physicist who shared (with Robert Wilson) the 1978 Nobel Prize in physics for discovering cosmic microwave radiation emanating from outside of the galaxy, providing evidence for the big bang theory of the origins of the universe.

The Pentagon

Peonage, form of coercive servitude by which a laborer (*peon*) works off debts—often inescapable and life-long—to a creditor-master. In Spanish America, where it was most prevalent, and in the southern states of the United States (in a modified form as sharecropping), peonage did not end until the 20th century.

Peony, cultivated member of the buttercup family (genus *Paeonia*) with large showy blossoms. Most peonies are herbaceous plants that sprout new stems each year, but the tree peony (*P. suffricosa*) has a woody trunk that grows to 5 ft (1.5 m).

Peoria (pop. 339,172, industrial city in north-central Illinois, the third largest city in the state and the seat of Peoria County. Peoria is a transportation and distribution center for a large surrounding area. Among its products are tractors and other farm machinery, earth-moving equipment, fencing, masonry, alcoholic beverages, foodstuffs, radio equipment, and power. A government agricultural research laboratory and Bradley University also have their homes here. The town developed in the early 19th century on the site of an old French and Indian settlement. It became a city in 1845.

Pepin the Short (c.714-768), first Carolingian king of the Franks, who succeeded on the deposition (751) of Childeric, the last of the Merovingian kings. He was the younger son of Charles Martel and father of Charlemagne. In return for papal recognition he helped to establish the temporal power of the papacy.
See also: Carolingian; Charlemagne.

Pepper (*Capsicum frutescens*), woody plant of the family Solanaceae; also, its edible fruit. Commercial garden, or bell, peppers are grown in warm regions of the United States. Red peppers are widely distributed and have been cultivated since pre-Incan times. They include the mild peppers grown and dried for paprika and pungent Chili peppers. Garden peppers are also marketed as unripe green peppers.

Pepper, pungent spice obtained from the black pepper (*Piper nigrum*) plant, a woody climbing vine of the family Piperaceae native to Java. The unripened berries of the plant are dried and ground to make the black pepper common in every household; white pepper is made from the ripened berries of the same plant.

Pepperell, Sir William (1696-1759), American colonial leader and soldier who, backed by a British fleet, conquered (1745) the reputedly impregnable French fortress of Louisburg in Cape Breton, Canada, during the French and Indian Wars. He was the first American to be created baronet.
See also: French and Indian Wars.

Peppermint (*Mentha piperita*), wild herb of the family Labiatae whose leaves contain an oil widely used for flavoring. Menthol, derivative, is used in medicines.

Peppertree (*Schinus molle* and *S. terebinthifolius*), tropical ornamental tree of the cashew family Anacardiaceae. It bears yellow-white flowers in clusters and red berries that are used medicinally. The long thin leaves store a volatile oil. The peppertree grows to about 50 ft (15 m).

Pepsin, enzyme secreted by glands in the walls of the stomach to break down and digest protein.
See also: Enzyme.

Peptide, compound containing from 2 to as many as 50 amino acids linked through the amino group of one acid and the carboxyl group of the other. The linkage is termed a peptide bond. Peptides containing 2 amino acids are called dipeptides; with 3, tripeptides, and so on; those with many acids are polypeptides.

Pepys, Samuel (1633-1703), English diarist. Although he was a successful reforming naval administrator and president of the Royal Society (1684-85), it is his talent in recording contemporary affairs and the events in his own private life for which he is famed today. His diary, written in cipher (1660-69) was not decoded and published until 1825.

Pequot, Native Americans of the Algonquian language group who lived in southern New England. Their murder of a colonial trader by whom they had been mistreated led to the Pequot War (1637), the first major European massacre of Native Americans in North America, in which almost the entire tribe was slaughtered or enslaved. The Pequot were resettled (1655) on a Connecticut reservation.

Percentage, literally by the hundred, numerical computation indicating the ratio of a given number to a total number when the total number is compared to 100, shown by the symbol %. One hundred percent of something is all of it; 1 percent of something is one hundredth part of it. To find what percentage a number is of another, divide the number being compared by the number it is compared to, and multiply the quotient by 100. For instance, in a class of 80 students, 20 are men. To determine the percentage of men in the class, divide the number of men by the number of students and multiply by 100:

$20/80 \times 100 = 25\%$.

Percentages are commonly used to express interest rates, scientific data, statistics, market and production figures, and taxes.
See also: Fraction.

Perception, recognition or identification of something. External perception relies on the senses, internal perception, on the consciousness. Some psychologists hold that perception need not be conscious; in particular, subliminal perception involves reaction of the unconscious to external stimuli and its subsequent influencing of the conscious.
See also: Senses.

Perch, freshwater fish of the family Percidae, often having colorful striped bodies. They live in slow-flowing rivers and lakes and feed on other fish. The smallest perch is little more than 1 in (2.5 cm) long. The largest are the walleyes or pike perch which are fished commercially on the Great Lakes. Many perches are also caught by sport fishers. Yellow perch is particularly tasty. It breeds so prolifically that it may sometimes crowd out other fish and even outrun the supply of food.

Percussion instrument, musical instrument from which sound is produced by striking. These are divided into 2 main classes: idiophones, (e.g., bells, castanets, cymbals) and gongs, whose wood or metal substance vibrates to produce sound, and membranophones, chiefly drums and tambourines, in which sound is produced by vibrating a stretched skin. Although the celesta, triangle, xylophone, and glockenspiel can be classed as percussion instruments, the term commonly denotes those instruments used for rhythmic effect.

Peregrine falcon *see:* Falcon.

Perelman, S.J. (1904-79), U.S. humorous writer noted for his collaboration as screenwriter on several Marx Brothers' films, humorous books like *The Rising Gorge* (1961), and many articles that appeared in *The New Yorker.*

Samuel Pepys, painted by John Hayls (1666)

Perennial, any plant that continues to grow for more than two years. Trees and shrubs are perennials whose woody stems thicken with age. The herbaceous perennials, such as the peony and daffodil, have stems that die down each winter and regrow in the spring from underground perennating organs, such as tubers and bulbs.

Peres, Shimon (1923-), prime minister (1985-86) of the National Unity government of Israel. He was instrumental in the withdrawal of the Israeli troops from Lebanon in 1985.
See also: Israel.

Pérez de Cuéllar, Javier (1920-), secretary general of the United Nations since 1982, successor to Kurt Waldheim. As a Peruvian diplomat, he had represented Peru as ambassador to the USSR (1969-71) and to the United Nations (1971-75).
See also: United Nations.

Perfume, blend of substances made from plant oils and synthetic materials that produce a pleasant odor. Perfumes were used in ancient times as incense in religious rites, in medicines, and later for adornment. Today they are utilized in cosmetics, toilet waters, detergents, soaps, and polishes. A main source of perfumes is the essential oils extracted from parts of plants, e.g., the flowers of the rose, the leaves of lavender, cinnamon from bark, and pine from wood. The development of synthetic perfumes began in the 19th century. There are now a number of synthetic chemicals with flowerlike fragrances.

Pergamum, ancient capital of Mysia in Asia Minor, now western Turkey. An independent kingdom from 282 B.C. and a sovereign monarchy from 262 B.C., Pergamum was Hellenistic in culture and orientation. It sided with Rome under the Attalid kings (263-133 B.C.) and received large holdings in Asia Minor as a reward. Pergamum achieved its peak as a center of art and learning during the rule of Eumenes II (197-159 B.C.). Its public buildings, particularly its library, were among the greatest in the Greek world. Eumenes's successor, Attalus II, doubted his heirs' ability to maintain Pergaman liberty and at his death (133 B.C.), he willed the kingdom to Rome. Pergamum was famed for the manufacture of textiles, parchment, perfumes, tiles, and bricks. It was a seat of early Christianity.

Pergolesi, Giovanni Battista (1710-36), Italian opera composer famed for his comic intermezzo *The Maid as Mistress* (1733). He also composed serious opera and religious music, such as the *Mass in F* (1734) and *Stabat Mater* (1736).
See also: Opera.

Pericles (c.495-429 B.C.), Athenian general and statesman. A strong critic of the conservative and aristocratic council, he obtained (461) the ostracism of Cimon and became supreme leader of the Athenian democracy. The years 462-454 saw the furthering of that democracy, with salaried state offices and supremacy of the assembly. Pericles's expansionist foreign policy led to a defeat of Persia (449), truce with Sparta (445), and the transformation of the Delian League into an Athenian empire. The peace of 445-431 was the height of Athenian culture under his rule. The Parthenon and Propylaea were both built at Pericles's request. One of the instigators of the Peloponnesian War, he was deposed but re-elected in 429; his death in a plague soon after may have lost Athens the war.
See also: Athens; Peloponnesian War.

Peridot, transparent green olivine of gemstone quality. Deposits of the mineral occur on Saint John's Island in the Red Sea, Burma, and the southwest United States. Most peridots used in jewelry are faceted.

Perigee *see:* Orbit.

Periodic table, table of the elements listed in order of increasing atomic number, arranged in rows and columns to illustrate periodic similarities and trends in physical and chemical properties. In 1869 Dmitri Mendeleev published the first fairly complete periodic table, which was later revised by Henry Moseley. The numbers and arrangement of the electrons in the atom are responsible for the periodicity of properties; hence the atomic number is the basis of ordering. Each row, or period, of the table contains elements that have the same number of electron shells. The number of electrons in these shells equals the element's atomic number; these numbers increase from left to right within each period. The elements are arranged in vertical columns, or groups, containing elements of similar atomic structure and properties, with regular gradation of properties down each group. The longer groups, with members in the first three (short) periods, are known as the main group; they are usually numbered IA to VIIA, and 0 for the noble or inert gases. The remaining groups, the transition elements, are numbered IIIB to VIII, IB, and IIb. The elements in group IA are called The alkali metals; in group IIA, the alkaline-earth metals; and in group VIIA, the halogens.
See also: Mendeleev, Dmitri Ivanovich.

Periodontitis, or *pyorrhea alveolaris*, disease of the gums and bones surrounding the teeth. Caused by inadequate hygiene or nutrition, periodontitis is symptomized by inflamed, bleeding, or receding gums and loose teeth. It may be treated by plaque removal or oral surgery.
See also: Dentistry.

Peripatetic philosophy, method of teaching philosophy attributed to the ancient Greek philosopher Aristotle. The word *peripatetic* is derived from the Greek term for walking. This refers to Aristotle's practice of strolling with his students under the portico of his school in Athens, the Lyceum, as he gave his lectures.
See also: Aristotle.

Peritonitis, inflammation of the peritoneum (abdominal lining), usually caused by bacterial infection or chemical irritation of peritoneum when internal organs become diseased (as with appendicitis) or when gastrointestinal tract contents escape (as with a perforated peptic ulcer). Characteristic pain, sometimes with shock, fever, and temporary cessation of bowel activity, is common. Urgent treatment of the cause is required, often with surgery; antibiotics may also be needed.

Periwinkle, any of a genus (*Littorina*) of edible snails found in northern Europe and on the Atlantic coast of the United States. The periwinkle has a thick, spiral shell that ranges in color from grayish-brown to black. It feeds on algae and seaweed.

Perjury, willful false statement made under oath during judicial or administrative proceedings. In a U.S. federal court a false statement must be relevant to the object of the enquiry in order to constitute perjury. As a criminal offense perjury is usually a felony punishable by imprisonment or a substantial fine. Subornation to perjury, the act of getting someone else to lie under oath, is also punishable as a crime.
See also: Felony.

Perkins, Frances (1882-1965), U.S. Secretary of Labor (1933-45), first U.S. woman cabinet member. From 1910 she was active in New York State factory and labor affairs. Appointed labor secretary by President F.D. Roosevelt, she administered New Deal programs.

Perlman, Itzhak (1945-), U.S.-Israeli violinist. Although partly crippled by polio in childhood, he quickly became an accomplished musician, performing publicly from the age of 10. He made his professional New York debut in 1963 and won the Leventritt Competition in 1964. Known for his tone and technical excellence, and supported professionally by violinist Isaac Stern, he has become one of the world's leading violin soloists. His many recordings include works of the standard repertoire as well as Scott Joplin rags. He has also premiered many new works, including concertos by Earl Kim and Robert Starer.

Permafrost, permanently frozen ground, typical of the treeless plains of Siberia, though common throughout polar regions.

Permalloy, alloy that may be temporarily magnetized by electric current. Developed by G.W. Elmen, an engineer for Western Electric Company (1916), permalloy is an important component in transformers. It is made of nickel and iron.

Permian, last period of the Paleozoic era, stretching between c.280 and 230 million years ago.

Permutations and combinations, mathematical term for ways of counting out, arranging, and choosing objects in a group. A permutation is simply a way in which the elements of a set can be ordered. For instance, a set of 3 objects—say the numbers 1, 2, and 3—can be arranged in 6 different ways: 123, 132, 231, 213, 312, and 321. Each of these is a permutation. A combination is a choice of a certain number of elements from a larger set, without regard to the order of the elements. For instance, given the same set—1, 2, and 3—we may be asked to pick 2 out of the 3 numbers. Here there are 3 possibilities: 1 and 2, 1 and 3, 2 and 3. In other words, there are 3 different ways of picking 2 elements out of a set of 3 elements. Each different way is a combination. The techniques of permutations and combinations are of central importance in problems of probability and statistics.

Perón, Eva Duarte de (1919-52), popularly known as Evita, second wife of Argentina's President Juan Perón. A powerful presence in the politics of Argentina, she ran the ministry of labor in her husband's first government (beginning in 1946). She attempted to run for the vice presidency (1951), but leading Argentine military officers blocked her bid for that position. Her background was humble—she was an actress from a poor family. She died of cancer in 1952.
See also: Argentina.

Perón, Juan Domingo (1895-1974), president of Argentina (1946-55, 1973-74) as head of an army clique, he helped overthrow Ramón Castillo in 1943. He won union loyalty as secretary of labor. Elected president (after police intervention), he began with his second wife Eva (1919-52)

a program of industrialization and social reforms. Church and army opposition to corruption and repression forced him into exile. Peronist influence survived, however; he returned in 1973 and was reelected president. He served until his death and was succeeded by his third wife, Isabel.
See also: Argentina.

Perpetual motion machine, concept of a machine that would work continuously without external interference, or at least with 100% efficiency. Perpetual motion machines of the first kind do work without energy being supplied, they are disallowed by the first law of thermodynamics. Those of the second kind take heat from a reservoir (such as the ocean) and convert it wholly into work, although energy is conserved, they are disallowed by the second law of thermodynamics. Those of the third kind do no work merely continuing in motion forever; they are not achievable, because some energy is always dissipated—as heat by friction, for example. However, electric current flowing in a superconducting ring continues undiminished indefinitely and is in a sense a perpetual motion machine of the third kind.
See also: Thermodynamics.

Perrault, name of two French brothers. **Claude Perrault** (1613-88), architect, scientist, and physician, is remembered for his buildings, notably the colonnade of the Louvre (1667-70), and the Paris Observatory (1667-72), and for his translation of the works of Vitruvius (1673). **Charles Perrault** (1628-1703), poet, fairy-tale writer, and belle lettrist, is best known for his *Comtes de ma mére l'Oye* (Tales of Mother Goose; 1697), which includes "Little Red Riding Hood," "Cinderella," "Puss in Boots."
See also: Mother Goose.

Perret, Auguste (1874-1954), French architect known for his use of reinforced concrete in housing projects (Paris, 1903), in the Théâtre des Champs Élysées (1913), and in the church of Notre-Dame, Le Raincy (1922-23).
See also: Architecture.

Perry, name of two U.S. brothers who became distinguished naval officers. Oliver Hazard Perry (1785-1819), became a hero of the War of 1812. After assembling a fleet of nine ships at Erie, Pa., he defeated six British warships on Sep. 10, 1813, off Put-in-Bay, Ohio, the Battle of Lake Erie. He announced his victory in the famous message, "We have met the enemy and they are ours." **Matthew Calbraith Perry** (1794-1858) was instrumental in opening Japan to the U.S. and world trade. He commanded the first U.S. steam warship, the *Fulton II* (1838) and led U.S. naval forces suppressing the slave trade; he also fought in the Mexican War. In 1853 Commodore Perry took four vessels into Tokyo Bay and remained there until a Japanese envoy agreed to receive President Millard Fillmore's request for a diplomatic and trade treaty. He returned in Feb. 1854 to conclude the treaty, which was a turning point in U.S.-Japanese relations.
See also: Navy, U.S.

Perse, Saint-John (1887-1975), French poet and diplomat whose real name was Alexis Saint-Léger. Under his real name, he was the secretary-general of the ministry of foreign affairs (1933-40). When the Nazis occupied France, he went into exile in the United States. Under his pseudonym he authored many books of lyrical poetry, including the long poem *Anabasis* (1924). Other works written in his exile include *Exile* (1942) and *Seamarks* (1957). He returned to France in 1959 and won the Nobel Prize in literature for 1960.

Persephone, in Greek and Roman mythology, goddess of the underworld; the Romans called her Proserpina. The daughter of Demeter (Ceres in Roman mythology) and Zeus (Jupiter), Persephone was kidnapped by Hades (Pluto) and taken to the underworld. Demeter refused to allow anything on earth to grow until Persephone was returned; Zeus then worked out a compromise where Persephone would stay with Hades for half the year and with Demeter the other half. The Greeks and Romans used this myth to explain the seasons: when Persephone was with Hades, nothing grows (autumn and winter), and when she was with Demeter, crops flourish (spring and summer).
See also: Mythology.

Persepolis, ancient ceremonial capital of the Achaemenian kings of Persia, lying 30 mi (48 km) northeast of Shiraz, southwestern Iran. It flourished under Darius I (d. 486 B.C.) and his successors but was later destroyed by Alexander the Great in 330. In 1971 the 2,500th anniversary of the Iranian monarchy was celebrated among the ruins of the city.
See also: Persia, Ancient.

Perseus, in Greek mythology, son of Zeus and Danaë, a mortal. His grandfather, King Acrisius, set him adrift at sea with his mother after learning from an oracle that his grandson would one day kill him; King Polydectus rescued them. Perseus beheaded Medusa, the Gorgon, and saved Andromeda from being sacrificed to a sea monster. Perseus later accidentally killed his grandfather, realizing the oracle's prediction.

Perseus, in astronomy, constellation containing the variable star Algol. The Perseid meteors appear to radiate from the constellation during the first two weeks of Aug. Perseus is high in the sky during the Northern Hemisphere fall and winter.
See also: Constellation.

Pershing, John Joseph (1860-1948), U.S. general. After distinguished service in the Indian Wars (1886, 1890-91), the Spanish-American War (1898), and the Philippines (1899-1903), he was promoted to brigadier general (1906). He led a punitive expedition to Mexico against U.S. Villa (1916) and a year later became commander of the World War I Expeditionary Force in Europe. In 1919 he became general of the armies, and he was chief of staff from 1921 until his 1924 retirement.
See also: Army, U.S.

Persia *see:* Iran; Persia, Ancient.

Persia, Ancient, ancient high plateau of Iran, home of several great civilizations. In 2nd millennium B.C. the literate civilization of Elam developed in the southwest of the plateau, with its capital at Susa. It was ended in 639 B.C. by the invasion of Ashurbanipal of Assyria. Assyrian downfall followed in 612 after the sacking of Nineveh by the Babylonians and the Medes. The area of Parsumash to the south of the Medes was ruled by the Achaemenians. Cyrus the Great expanded the Achaemenid empire, and at his death (529) he c
led the Middle East from the Medite
to the Indus River. Under Darius
486) a road system linked the great empire and a canal linked the Nile and Red Sea. Flourishing trade, commerce, and public works continued under Xerxes I (586-465). Xerxes' murder by his son was followed by intrigues and rebellions that weakened the Achaemenians. In 330 the empire was conquered by the Parthians. The empire of Parthia (3rd century B.C. to 3rd century A.D.) halted the nomads in the northeast and the Romans in the west, defeating Crassus in 53 B.C. and later Mark Antony. In c.A.D. 224, a successful revolt by Ardashir, ruler of the Fars (the southern Persian homeland), established the vigorous Sassanian empire. Arts, architecture, and religion (Zoroastrianism) revived, the wars with Rome continued, and in 260, Shapur, the son of Ardashir, captured the Emperor Valerian. After constant struggles with the Byzantines, the Sassanian empire was overwhelmed by the Arabs and converted to Islam in 651.

Juan Domingo Perón

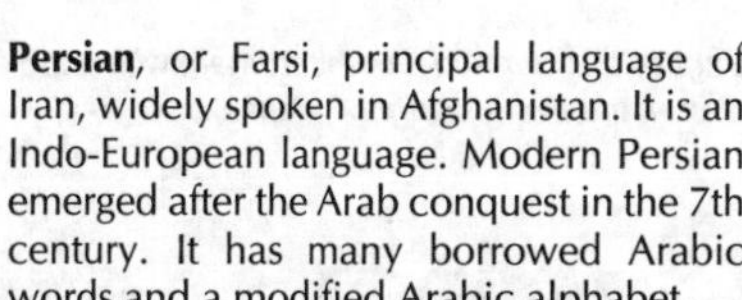

Persian, or Farsi, principal language of Iran, widely spoken in Afghanistan. It is an Indo-European language. Modern Persian emerged after the Arab conquest in the 7th century. It has many borrowed Arabic words and a modified Arabic alphabet.

Persian Gulf, or Arabian Gulf, arm of the Arabian Sea between Iran and Arabia. About 550 mi (855 km) long and 120 mi (193 km) wide, the gulf is entered from the Gulf of Oman by the Straits of Hormuz. The bordering regions of Iran, Kuwait, Saudi Arabia, Bahrain, Qatar, and the United Arab Emirates contain more than half the world's oil and natural gas resources. The effects of the Persian Gulf War (1991) caused serious environmental damage to gulf waters because of enormous oil spills.

Persian Gulf War, conflict (January-February 1991) initiated by Iraq's invasion of Kuwait and its announced annexation of that country. A coalition of forces led by the United States was assembled, first to

(Left) Generals Colin Powell and Norman Schwarzkopf
(Right) Saddam Hussein

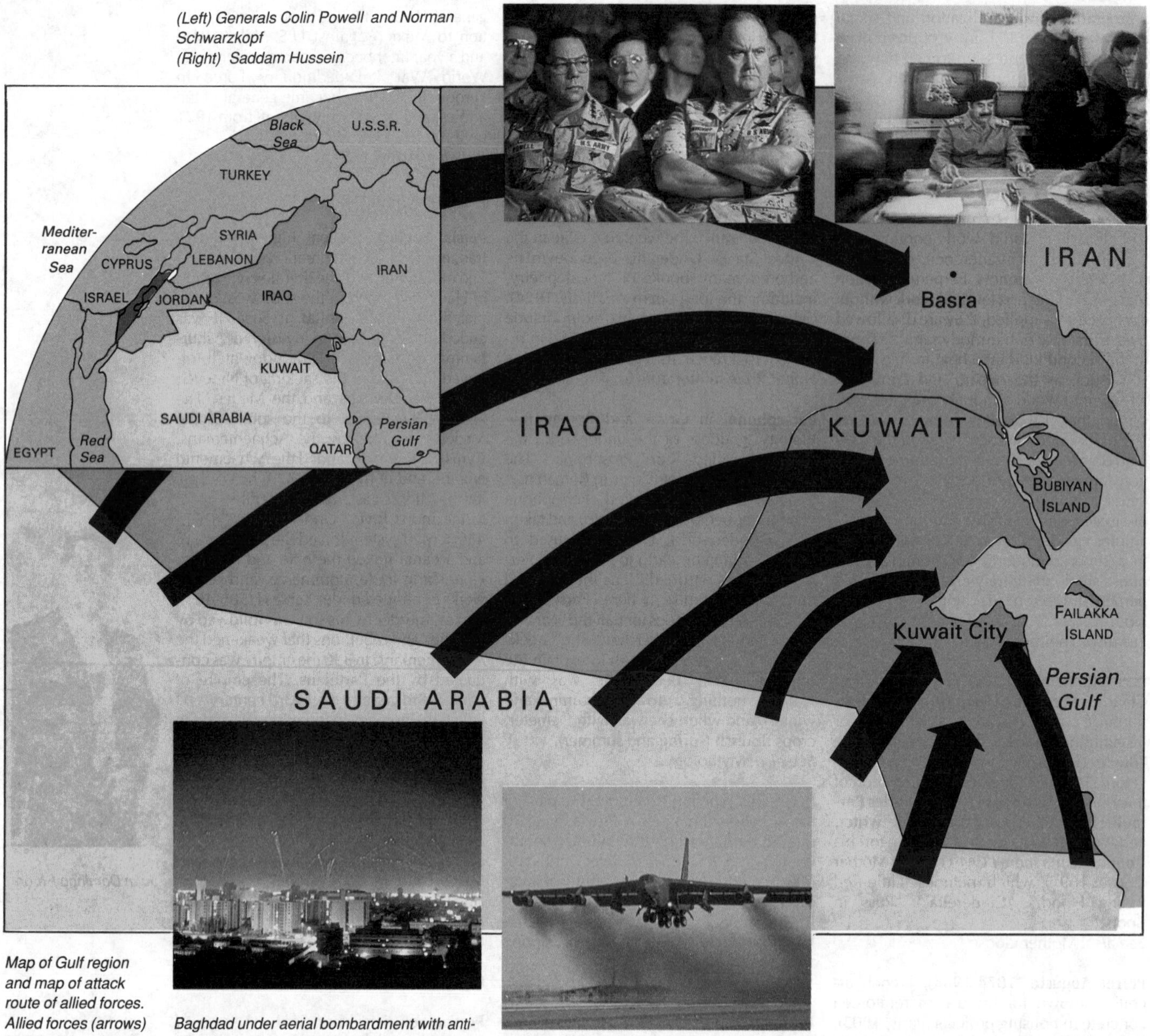

Black Sea
U.S.S.R.
TURKEY
Mediter-ranean Sea
CYPRUS
SYRIA
LEBANON
ISRAEL
JORDAN
IRAQ
IRAN
KUWAIT
SAUDI ARABIA
Persian Gulf
EGYPT
Red Sea
QATAR

IRAN
Basra
IRAQ
KUWAIT
BUBIYAN ISLAND
FAILAKKA ISLAND
Kuwait City
Persian Gulf
SAUDI ARABIA

Map of Gulf region and map of attack route of allied forces. Allied forces (arrows) invaded Kuwait and Iraq and encircled the Iraqi forces. The entire war took 43 days.

Baghdad under aerial bombardment with anti-aircraft fire illuminating the night sky

A B-52 takes off on a bombing mission.

Allied tanks roll into Kuwait. Oil well fires are seen on the horizon.

forestall further incursions of Iraq into Saudi Arabia or other Gulf states and second to reverse Iraq's takeover of Kuwait, as called for in a series of 12 UN resolutions.
Beginning of the war. After his fruitless but costly war with Iran, Iraqi leader Saddam Hussein turned to oil-rich Kuwait as a way of replenishing his spent treasury. Using earlier disputes with Kuwait as pretexts, Saddam ordered his troops into the country on August 2, 1990, and soon overran it. Saudi Arabia and other Gulf states, alarmed that Iraq might go on to move against them, called on the UN and the United States for help. President George Bush dispatched a U.S. force, code-named Desert Shield, to Saudi Arabia to block further Iraqi military thrusts. At the same time, he persuaded the UN to condemn the Iraqi action and to vote for a total embargo of all goods to or from Iraq. He also forged a coalition of some 30 nations, including Arab states like Saudi Arabia, Egypt, and Syria, to send forces and other kinds of aid to help the United States meet the military threat.
Freeing Kuwait. The UN voted a deadline of January 15, 1991, for total Iraqi pullout from Kuwait. Despite a last-minute flurry of diplomatic activity, Saddam stood firm, and on January 16 (early January 17th in Iraq) the coalition changed from the defensive posture of Desert Shield to the aggressive stance of Desert Storm by launching a massive air war against Iraq and its forces in Kuwait. The air war involved the newest and most sophisticated high-tech weapons in today's arsenal. The first "shot" in the war was a laser-guided "smart" bomb dropped from a U.S. F-117A Stealth fighter-bomber. The Tomahawk cruise missile, launched from warships in the Gulf, was another precision-guided weapon that proved its value in the war. Iraqi forces in Kuwait dug in behind tank barriers, called *berms*, and extensive mine fields. Many tanks and heavy artillery pieces were buried in sand bunkers to ward off frontal attacks. More mobile units, including the elite Republican Guards, were held in reserve to counterattack in case the allied forces breached the frontline fortifications. The coalition, using its complete air superiority, maintained an unprecedented bombardment of military targets in Iraq and Kuwait, and pummeled the dug-in defenses. Iraq's only answer to the air war was sporadic attacks by its Scud ground-to-ground missile. These were largely neutralized by the American-made Patriot missile, which destroyed most of the Scuds in the air. Iraq's attempt to draw Israel into the war by random strikes with Scuds failed.
The end of the war. After 40 days of air bombardment, coalition forces began the ground war on February 25th. Allied forces punched through defensive barriers along the Kuwaiti front in several places and moved on Kuwait City. An enveloping movement involving massive armored columns struck Iraq itself far to the west in a successful attempt to encircle the Iraqi forces in Kuwait and along the Iraqi/Kuwait border and to cut off their supply lines and escape routes. The destruction of the entire Iraqi forces in the south was accomplished in a matter of days. The problems of making peace in the area, however, and providing for future stability remain.

Persian lamb *see:* Karakul.

Persian wars (500-449 B.C.), wars between Greek states and the Persian Empire. Athenian support of the revolt of Greek states within the empire precipitated three Persian offensives in Greece. The 2nd Persian expeditionary force was forced back by the Athenians at the Battle of Marathon (490). The 3rd expedition is famous for the resistance at Thermopylae, at which 300 Spartans fought to the death, holding off the overwhelming Persian force. By 449 B.C. Greek strength had secured Europe from further Persian invasions.

Persimmon, any of several trees (genus *Diospyros*) of the ebony family. These trees are grown especially for their fruit of the same name. The kaki persimmon *(D. kaki)*, produced for commercial purposes, is native to Asia, while the common persimmon *(D. virginiana)* is native to the United States. When ripe, persimmon fruit is sweet, with a wrinkled or brown-streaked reddish-orange skin.

Personality, in psychology, characteristics and ways of behavior that define the uniqueness of an individual. Most studies conclude that the formation of personality is a complex process, influenced by a variety of factors both inherent and learned.

Perspective, method of producing the appearance of three dimensions on a flat surface. Linear perspective, developed during the Renaissance, exploits the fact that the size of an object seems to shrink to a point as its distance increases. Lines in a picture would, if extended, meet a vanishing point which is always on the horizon line, one the level of the observer's eye. Depending on the view, there may be more than one vanishing point in a picture. Aerial perspective, depends on the fact that the atmosphere disperses the light from distant objects. An artist paints features fainter and bluer to convey the impression of distance.

Perspiration, watery fluid secreted by the skin as a means of reducing body temperature. Sweating is common in hot climates, after exercise, and in the resolution of fever; the evaporation of sweat allows the skin and thus the body to be cooled. Humid atmosphere and high secretion rates delay evaporation, leaving perspiration on the surface. Excessive fluid loss, and of salt in cystic fibrosis, may lead to sunstroke. Most sweating is regulated by the hypothalamus and autonomic nervous system, but there is also a system of sweat glands, especially on the palms, that secretes at times of stress. Hyperhidrosis is a condition of abnormally profuse sweating.
See also: Skin; Temperature, Body.

Perth (pop. 895,700), capital of Western Australia, a western state with a coast on the Indian Ocean. Located on the Swan River, Perth is a port that supports industry (especially mining) as well as business, education, and recreation. A goldrush in the 1890s encouraged its development and growth. It was founded by James Sterling, an officer in the British Navy (1829).
See also: Australia.

Pertussis *see:* Whooping cough.

Peru, third largest country in South America. With an area of 496,225 sq mi (1,285,210 sq km), Peru is bordered on the north by Ecuador and Colombia; on the east by Brazil and Bolivia; on the south by Chile; and on the west by the Pacific Ocean.
Land and climate. The 1,400 mi (2,253 km) long coastal strip, a central mountain region, and the eastern Amazonian plains are the country's main regions. The coastal zone is mainly desert, but the sands are very fertile when irrigated and the region supports agriculture and contains about 35% of the population. Most of Peru's important cities are also located on the coast. The mountainous region consists of parallel ranges of the Andes with intervening deep valleys and mountain bases. Among the lofty peaks in this part of Peru is Huascarán (22,205 ft/6,768 m). Straddling the border with Bolivia is also Lake Titicaca at 12,500 ft (3,810 m) above sea level, the highest navigable body of water in the world. Although conditions are harsh and the soil mostly poor, more than half of Peru's people live in the region. It is also susceptible to earthquakes and on May 31, 1970, a devastating quake took the lives of some 50,000 Peruvians and left some 800,000 homeless. The lush eastern slopes of the Andes with their heavy rainfall give way to the dense tropical forests of the eastern plains draining into the Amazon River. The climate of the coastal area is dominated by the Humboldt Current that comes northward from the Antarctic Ocean. In the mountains, the western slopes are generally dry while the northern and eastern areas have heavy rainfall from October to April. The climate of the eastern plains is tropical. The capital of Peru is Lima.

The Central Railway of Peru climbs higher than any other railroad in the world.

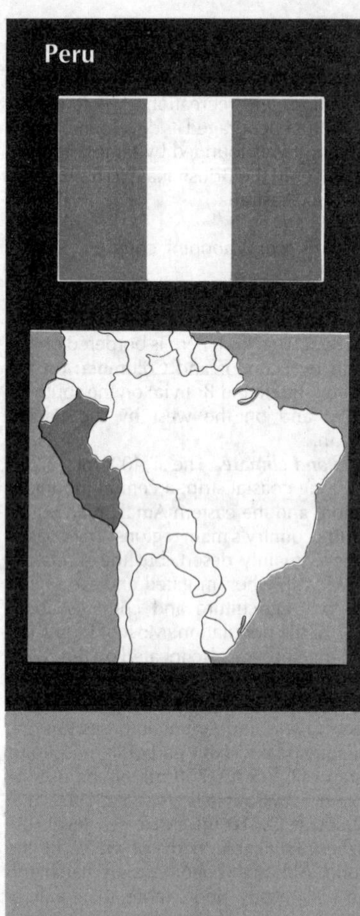

General information	
Capital:	Lima
Area:	496,225 sq mi (1,285,216 sq km)
Population:	21,792,000
Official languages:	Spanish, Quechua
Monetary unit:	1 Inti = 100 céntimos
Main cities:	Lima, Arequipa, Callao
Government	
Form:	republic
Independent:	1827
Head of state:	President (elected every 5 years)
Head of government:	President
Legislature:	two legislative houses (Senate and Chamber of Deputies)
Executive:	President and Council of Ministers
Judiciary:	highest court is the Supreme Court
Political division:	24 departments, 1 constitutional province
National economy	
Gross national product:	U.S. $20,185,000,000
Per capita income:	U.S. $1,440
Agriculture:	cotton, sugar cane, corn, coffee, plantains, potatoes, rice
Livestock:	cattle, sheep, pigs
Fisheries:	4,584,000 metric tons
Mining:	crude petroleum, gold, tin, copper, lead, silver, zinc, iron
Industries:	fishmeal, cement, wheat flour, refined sugar, iron and steel
Main exports:	fishmeal, copper, silver, petroleum and derivatives, lead, zinc
Transportation:	2,144 mi (3,451 km) of railroads, 43,460 mi (69,942 km) of roads, 4 international airports
Trading partners:	U.S., Japan, EEC
People	
Urban:	69%
Ethnic composition:	Quechua 47%, mestizo 32%, European 12%, Aymara 5.5%
Birth rate:	29 per 1,000 population
Death rate:	8.7 per 1,000 population
Infant mortality:	69 per 1,000 live births
Life expectancy:	male 61 years, female 66 years

People. The people are about 50% Native American, 40% mestizo (a mixture of Spanish and Native American), and 10% Spanish. The majority of the mestizos and Spanish are Roman Catholic. The official languages are Spanish and Quechua.

Economy. Cotton, sugarcane, and coffee are grown for export. Fishing is a major industry and processed fish meal is the country's chief export. Copper, iron, silver, phosphates, and other minerals are mined and exported; some are also processed and refined in Peru.

History. The Inca empire, the last of several great indigenous cultures, was conquered by the Spanish conquistador Francisco Pizarro beginning in 1532. Spanish rule, based in Lima, continued until the revolution led by Simon Bolívar and José de San Martín from 1820 to 1824. After independence, power continued to be concentrated in the hands of a small number of wealthy landowners. Attempts to redress inequalities or retrench privilege have dominated Peru's politics since its independence and throughout the twentieth century, leading to unstable regimes and military coups. In 1968 Gen. Juan Velasco Alvarado instituted a program of social reform, suspended the constitution, and seized U.S. owned companies. Gen. Alvarado was overthrown by military coup in 1975 under the leadership of Francisco Morales Bermudez. The country returned to constitutional rule in 1980 and on July 28, 1985, Alan Garcia Peres was elected president in a democratic election. He was succeeded by Alberto Fujimori in 1990.

Peru Current, or Humboldt Current, cold ocean current originating in the South Pacific and flowing north along the coasts of north Chile and Peru, whose climates it moderates, before turning west to join the South Equatorial Current.
See also: Humboldt, Friedrich Heinrich Alexander, Baron von.

Perugino (Pietro Vannucci; 1446-1523), Italian Renaissance painter, teacher of Raphael. His frescoes in the Vatican's Sistine Chapel, including *Christ Giving the Keys to St. Peter* (1481), established his fame. He worked much in Florence and later in his native Umbria.
See also: Renaissance.

Perutz, Max Ferdinand (1914-), Austrian-born English biochemist who shared with J.C. Kendrew the 1962 Nobel Prize for chemistry for their research into the structure of hemoglobin and other globular proteins.
See also: Biochemistry; Hemoglobin.

Pescadores, group of about 64 small islands c. 50 sq mi (130 sq km) of land area belonging to Taiwan, in the Formosa strait. The chief occupations are fishing and farming.

Pestalozzi, Johann Heinrich (1746-1827), Swiss educator. At his school at Yverdon he stressed the importance of the individual and based his methods on the child's direct experience, rather than on mechanical learning. *How Gertrude Teaches Her Children* (1801) was his most influential work.
See also: Education.

Pesticide, substance used to kill plants or animals responsible for economic damage to crops or ornamental plants or that prejudice the well-being of humans and domestic or conserved wild animals. Pesticides are subdivided into insecticides (which kill insects), miticides (which kill mites), herbicides (which kill plants), fungicides (which kill fungi), and rondeticides (which kill rats and mice). A major question with all pesticides is the possibility of unfortunate environmental side effects.

Pétain, Henri Phillippe (1856-1951), French World War I hero who became chief of state in the collaborationist Vichy regime (1940). Famous for his defense of Verdun (1916), he was made chief-of-staff (1917), and subsequently held important military offices. In 1934 he served briefly as war minister. Recalled from his post as ambassador to Spain in June 1940, he became premier and negotiated an armistice with the Nazis. As head of the Vichy government, he aided the Nazis, and in

1945 was convicted of treason and sentenced to life imprisonment.
See also: Vichy; World War II.

Peter I (1844-1921), king of Serbia. A Serbian prince, he spent years in exile, and joined the anti-Turkish Herzegovinian revolt in 1875. He became an honorary senator of Montenegro in 1883 and was elected king of Serbia in 1903.
See also: Serbia.

Peter I, the Great (1672-1725), became joint tsar in 1682 and sole tsar in 1696. He traveled in western Europe (1697-98), learning techniques of war and industry and recruiting experts to bring back to Russia. He warred against Turkey to gain access to the Mediterranean, and his Northern War with Sweden (1700-21) led to Russian domination of the Baltic Sea. He established his new capital of St. Petersburg on the Baltic as a symbol of his policy of westernization. Domestically he introduced sweeping military, administrative, and other reforms. A man of enormous size, strength, and energy, Peter was also savage in the exercise of power, and although he modernized, reformed, and strengthened Russia, it was at great human cost.

Peter II (1923-70), king of Yugoslavia. On the death of his father Alexander I, his cousin governed as regent (1934-41). Peter fled to London after the Nazi invasion (1941) and set up an exile government. In 1945 Yugoslavia became a republic, and Peter a pretender.
See also: Yugoslavia.

Peter, Epistles of, 2 New Testament letters, traditionally attributed to St. Peter. The first is written to encourage persecuted Christians in Asia Minor; the second closely parallels the Epistle of Jude and refers to the Second Coming. Authorship is doubtful, particularly of the second, which some scholars date C.A.D. 150 and which was admitted late to the canon.
See also: New Testament.

Peter, Saint (Simon Peter; d. C.A.D. 64), leader of the 12 Apostles, regarded by Roman Catholics as the first pope. A Galilean fisherman when Jesus called him to be a disciple, he was a dominating but impulsive figure, and he denied Jesus after his arrest. He played a leading role in the early Church, especially in Jerusalem, as related in the Acts of the Apostles. By tradition, he died a martyr at Rome and is buried beneath St. Peter's church in Rome.
See also: Apostles.

Peterborough (pop. 61,000), city in southern Ontario, Canada, on the Otonabee River. Known for the Trent Canal—the tallest hydraulic lift lock in the world, 65 ft (20 m)—Peterborough is also a center for manufacturing and farming. Located 70 miles northeast of Toronto, the provincial capital, it was settled in the 1820s, mostly by Irish immigrants.
See also: Ontario.

Petersburg (pop. 41,055), city in southeastern Virginia, on the Appomattox River. The city was burned by British troops (1781) under Benedict Arnold during the American Revolution. During the Civil War it was the scene of major battles (1864-65) between the armies of Robert E. Lee and Ulysses S. Grant. Lee surrendered at the Appomattox courthouse. Today the city is noted for tobacco manufacturing as well as the often-visited National Battlefield (established 1926).
See also: Virginia.

Petersburg, Siege of *see:* Civil War, U.S.

Petipa, Marius (1819-1910), French dancer and choreographer who created the modern classical ballet. An outstanding dancer and mime, he joined the Russian ballet at St. Petersburg in 1847, becoming chief choreographer in 1869. There, he created over 60 full-length ballets, including *The Nutcracker*, *Swan Lake*, and *The Sleeping Beauty*.
See also: Ballet.

Petit, Roland (1924-), French dancer and choreographer. A founder (1945) and premier danseur of Les Ballets des Champs-Elysées, in 1948 he formed Les Ballets de Paris. He choreographed *Carmen* (1949), *La Croqueuse de diamants* (1950), and many other ballets for stage and film. Since 1972 he has directed Ballets de Marseilles.
See also: Ballet.

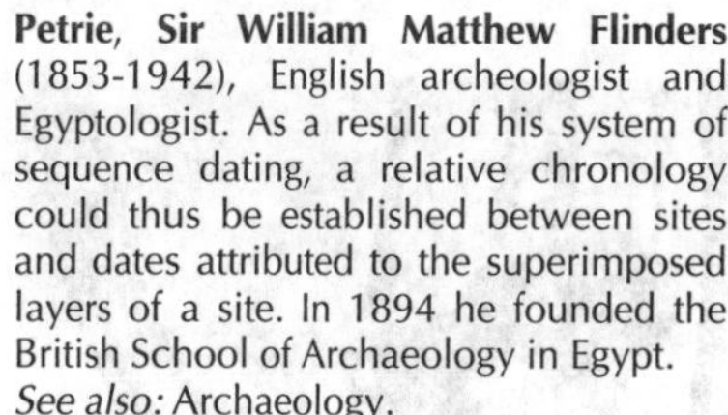

Petitgrain oil, oil manufactured from parts of the bitter orange tree, produced abundantly in Paraguay, South America. It is used in the making of perfume. The highly-valued petitgrain bigrade is produced from another variety of bitter orange tree in the Mediterranean countries of Europe.

Petition of Right, document presented to Charles I of England by Parliament (1628) in protest against his arbitrary fiscal methods. It asserted four principles: no taxation without parliamentary consent, no imprisonment of subjects without due legal cause, no billeting of soldiers in private houses without payment, and no declaring of martial law in peacetime. Accepted (although later disregarded) by the king, it represents a landmark in English constitutional history.
See also: United Kingdom.

PETN, common designation for the explosive pentaerythritol tetranitrate, an organic compound essential to the detonation system of certain explosive devices. Introduced after World War I, it is more powerful than TNT. It also serves as a medication for certain heart disorders.
See also: Explosive.

Petoskey stone, fossilized coral and state stone of Michigan, found outside the town of Petoskey. Valued by mineral collectors, Petoskey stones reveal a 6-sided shape with a pattern of lines radiating from the center. The column-shaped formation of this coral is the result of the actions of natural forces on deposited limestone over 350 million years.

Petra, ancient city in south-western Jordan. Famous for its tombs and temples cut into sandstone cliffs, it was the capital of the Nabataeans, prospered under the Romans, but lost its trade to Palmyra. Its decline continued under Muslim rule. Its ruins were discovered by Burckhardt in 1812.

Petrarch (Francesco Petracco; 1304-74), Italian poet and early humanist. Supported by influential patrons, he spent his life in study, travel, and writing. He wrote poetry, epistles, and other prose works in Latin, but also much in the vernacular Italian, of which he is one of the earliest masters. He himself rated his Latin works highest, but his fame now rests on the Italian *Canzoniere*, mostly sonnets inspired by his love for the enigmatic Laura, who died of plague in 1348.

Peter the Great

Petrel, name for seabirds of the tubenosed-bird order Procellariformes, particularly the typical petrels and shearwaters of the families Procellariidae and Hydrobatidae. All have webbed feet and hooked bills, with nostrils opening through horny tubes on the upper mandible. They swim and fly expertly, feeding far from the shore on fish, squid, and offal. Normally they go ashore only to breed.

Petrie, Sir William Matthew Flinders (1853-1942), English archeologist and Egyptologist. As a result of his system of sequence dating, a relative chronology could thus be established between sites and dates attributed to the superimposed layers of a site. In 1894 he founded the British School of Archaeology in Egypt.
See also: Archaeology.

Petrified forest, stone-covered trunks of coniferous trees. The trunks were buried in mud, sand, or volcanic ash and mixed with running water, which carried dissolved minerals. The result is stone that shows the detail of the original wood. Many logs are rainbow colored as a result of oxidation. The most famous such forest is in Petrified Forest National Park in eastern Arizona.
See also: Fossil.

Petrified Forest National Park, park of 147 sq mi (381 sq km) in eastern Arizona. The fossil remains of a Triassic forest are exposed on the surface, creating the largest display of petrified wood in the world.
See also: National Parks.

Petrochemical, any chemical made from petroleum or natural gas; includes organic chemicals, plus the inorganic substances carbon black, sulfur, ammonia, and hydrogen peroxide. Polymers, detergents, solvents, and nitrogen fertilizers are major products.

Petrograd *see:* Leningrad.

Petrol *see:* Gasoline.

Saint Peter was crucified upside down C. A.D. 64.

When petroleum is formed it migrates until it accumulates in "traps", wich may be either structural, reflecting the geological structure of the locality, or stratigraphic, reflecting the nature of the beds.

A. Structural traps.
1. Anticline or dome. The oil migrates upward under the influence of hydrostatic forces until it reaches an impermeable layer like anhydrite or shale and it can rise no further. It then accumulates at the highest part of the bed beneath - called the reservoir rock - and fills the spore-spaces of the rock above a water-saturated region (blue). Natural gas (violet) accumulates above this.
2. Occasionally the upward migration of oil and gas is halted when the reservoir bed is truncated at a fault. Such a trap may be indicated by an oil seep forming a pool on the surface.
3. When a layer of salt is found at depth it may become plastic due to hydrostatic pressure. When it does it rises in a salt dome, twisting the surrounding beds upward to form high points in reservoir rocks which may act as traps.
4. Tilted beds may give rise to traps.

B. Stratigraphic tramps.
5. Reservoir rocks may pinch out at their highest points and form traps here.
6. When no water is present the oil may migrate downward to collect in hollows in a basement rock.
7. Limestone may act as a reservoir in, for example, a reef structure.
8. A shoestring oil trap is formed from a fossil river channel of coarse material.

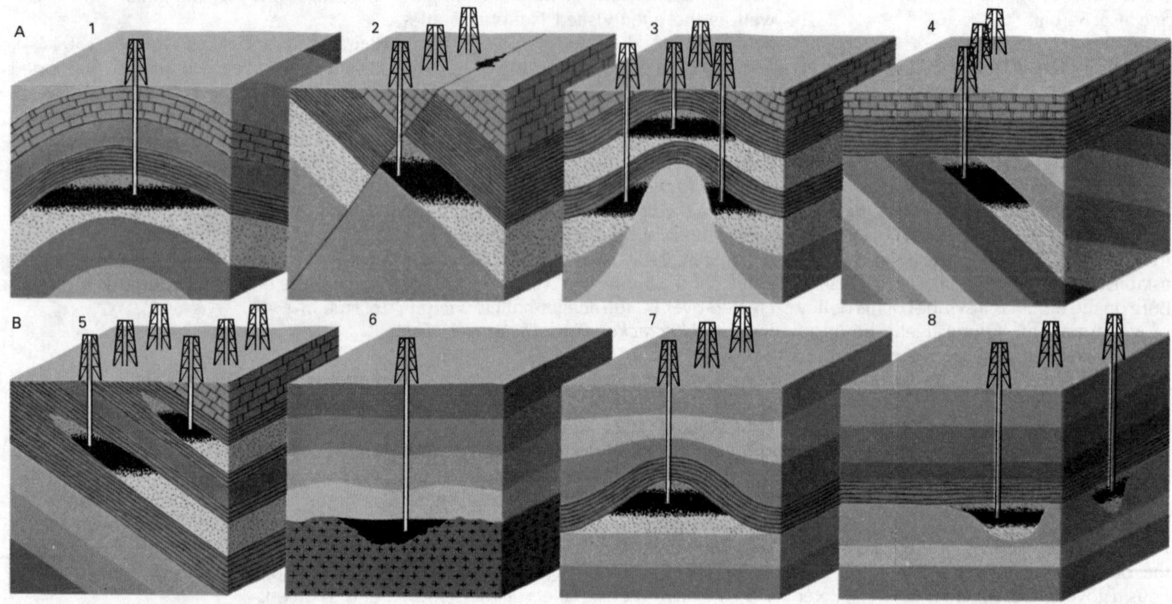

The drilling platform of a petroleum drilling tower

Petroleum, naturally occurring mixture of hydrocarbons, usually liquid "crude oil," but sometimes taken to include natural gas. Petroleum is believed to be formed from organic debris, chiefly of plankton and simple plants, which was rapidly buried in fine-grained sediment under marine conditions unfavorable to oxidation. After some biodegradation, increasing temperature and pressure caused cracking, and oil was produced. As the source rock was compacted, oil and water were forced out and slowly migrated to porous reservoir rocks, chiefly sandstone or limestone. Finally, secondary migration occurred within the reservoir as the oil coagulated to form a pool, generally capped by impervious strata and often associated with natural gas. Some oil seeped to the earth's surface; this was used by the early Mesopotamian civilizations. The first oil well was drilled in western Pennsylvania in 1859. The industry now supplies about half the world's energy, as well as the raw materials for petrochemicals. The chief world oil-producing regions are the Persian Gulf, the U.S., the USSR, northern and western Africa, and Venezuela. After the removal of salt and water, the petroleum is refined by fractional distillation, producing the fractions natural gas, gasoline, naphtha, kerosene, diesel oil, fuel oil, lubricating oil, and asphalt. Undesirable compounds may be removed by solvent extraction, treatment with sulfuric acid, etc., and less valuable components converted into more valuable ones by cracking, reforming, alkylation, and polymerization.

Petroleum coke, byproduct of the process of refining crude oil. Petroleum coke is used in the production of flashlight batteries, drycells, and the synthetic graphite required for nuclear reactors. It is also used in the manufacture of certain abrasives, heat resistant materials, and chemicals.

Petronius Arbiter, Gaius (d.A.D. 66), Roman satirist. He became Nero's "arbiter of taste," but fell from favor and committed suicide. "Trimalchio's Dinner" is the best known fragment of his *Satyricon*, a sensual, amoral, often obscene, and satirical romance, considered the first Roman novel.

Petunia, group of popular herbs (genus *Petunia*) from South America. They belong to the nightshade family, but the flowers differ from the basic pattern of the family. Each plant bears a succession of white to red or blue funnel-shaped blooms; these are pollinated by hawkmoths and hummingbirds. In the U.S. it is grown for its beautiful flower.

Pevsner, Antoine (1886-1962), Russian-born sculptor who studied in Paris (1911-13) and settled there from 1922. In 1920 he launched constructivism with his brother Naum Gabo in Moscow. Light and space play important roles in his sculptures.

Pewter, class of alloys consisting chiefly of tin, now hardened with copper and antimony, and usually containing lead, which increases malleability. Today lead is now omitted because it can be toxic. Pewter has been used in the west since Roman times for bowls, drinking vessels, and candlesticks.

Peyote *see:* Mescaline.

pH, measure of hydrogen gas in a solution. a pH of 7, which is neutral (neither acid nor alkaline), means there are 100 nanoequivalents of hydrogen ions per liter of blood. The human body functions best when the blood pH is 7.40, that is, when it contains about 40 nanoequivalents of hydrogen ions per liter. Therefore, the blood is normally very slightly alkaline. When the pH goes below 7.38, normal body functions are disrupted and the pathological, possibly fatal conditions of acidemia (acidosis) exists. Should hydrogen ions be lost from the body (or neutralized) and the blood pH rise above 7.44, alkalemia (alkalosis) occurs. Either condition reflects an acid-base balance disturbance. Breathing out carbon dioxide (which is acid) helps keep the pH properly balanced. The pH is measured in blood, urine, spinal fluid, lung fluid, semen, and many other body secretions.

Phaëton, or Phaëthon, in Greek mythology, mortal son of the sun god Helios and the sea goddess Clymene. Helios granted him his wish to drive the chariot of the sun, but he was unable to control it. He first flew it too high, freezing the earth and creating the scar in the sky known as the Milky Way, and then too low, burning and nearly destroying the earth. Zeus was forced to kill him with a thunderbolt to protect the earth.
See also: Mythology.

Phalanx, ancient Greek infantry formation, consisting of rows of eight men, each heavily armed with an overlapping shield and long pike. Philip II of Macedon developed a phalanx of 16 men, which his son Alexander the Great used in defeating the Persians. After defeat by Rome in 168 B.C. the phalanx became outmoded.
See also: Greece, Ancient; Infantry.

Phalarope, any of various small seabirds of the family Phalaropodidae. They fly to the Southern Hemisphere in winter but breed in Arctic regions during the summer. The females court and establish territory. Their eggs are incubated by the smaller, less colorful males, who are also the nest builders. The birds resemble sandpipers and are up to 10 in (25 cm) long.

Pharaoh, Hebrew form of the title of the kings of ancient Egypt. The term (actually *per'O*: great house) described his palace and, by association, the king. The Egyptians believed the pharaoh to be the personification of the gods Horus and, later, Amon.
See also: Egypt, Ancient.

Pharaoh hound, breed of hunting dog originating in ancient Egypt. It is built for speed, standing 21-25 in (53-64 cm) at the shoulder and weighing 35-50 lb (16-23 kg). It has a short, tan, glossy coat, with white markings on the toes, chest, tail, and face, and distinctive amber eyes. It is pictured in Egyptian paintings dating to 2300 B.C.

Pharisees, member of an ancient Jewish sect devoted to strict observance of the holy law and strongly opposed to pagan practices absorbed by Judaism and to the Sadducees. Their moral fervor and initially progressive nature made them an important political force. Tradition has made them synonymous with hypocrisy and self-righteousness, but Jesus only attacked the debasement of their ideals.

Pharmacology, study of drugs, their chemistry, mode of action, routes of absorption, excretion, metabolism, drug interactions, toxicity and side effects. The dispensing of drugs is called pharmacy.
See also: Drug.

Pharmacopoeia, text describing all available drugs and pharmacological preparations. It includes the properties and formulation, routes and doses of administration, mode of action, metabolism, and excretion, known interactions, contraindications and precautions, and toxicity and side effects of drugs. The first pharmacopoeia appeared in the 16th centruy in Germany (The Nuremberg pharmacopoeia). In the United States the first *United States Pharmacopoeia* (USP) was published in 1820. In 1888 the *National Formulary* was created. The two publications merged in 1980 and continue to be published.
See also: Drug.

Pharmacy, preparation or dispensing of drugs and pharmacological substances used in medicine; also, the place where this is practiced. Most drugs are now formulated by drug companies, and the pharmacist only measures them out and instructs the patient in their use. The first U.S. pharmacy school was established in Philadelphia, Pa., in 1821.

Pharos of Alexandria *see:* Seven Wonders of the Ancient World.

Pharyngeal tonsils *see:* Adenoids.

Pharynx, part of the digestive system, back of the throat where the mouth (oropharynx) and nose (nasopharynx) pass back into the esophagus. It contains specialized muscle for swallowing. The food and air channels are kept functionally separate so that swallowing does not interfere with breathing and speech.
See also: Digestive system.

Pheasant, game bird of the 16 genera of subfamily Phasianidae, including partridges and the peacock. They originated in Asia, but are now found all over the world. Pheasants are ground birds that scratch the earth for seeds and insects. When they fly, they rise almost vertically on short, broad wings. Males are usually brightly colored, and many species are kept as ornaments.

Phenology, science studying the effects of climate on biological phenomenon. Cycles of animal migration or hibernation and of plant flowering are dependent on climate and are therefore studied by phenologists. Among other results, phenology helps farmers correctly time procedures such as planting and harvesting. Phenologists also develop phenological maps that chart global phenological events.
See also: Biology; Climate.

Phenolphthalein, white or yellowish white chemical compound ($C_{20}H_{14}O_4$) used medicinally as a laxative and as an indicator of alkalies and acids. (Its solution is bright red in alkalies and colorless in acid.) The German chemist Adolf von Baeyer discovered the compound (1871).

Phenomenology, modern school of philosophy based largely on a method developed by Edmund Husserl. Unlike the naturalist, who describes objects without subjectivity, the phenomenologist attempts to describe the "invariant essences" of objects as objects "intended" by consciousness. The first step is "phenomenological reduction," a suspension of all preconceptions about experience.
See also: Husserl, Edmund.

Phenylketonuria (PKU), inborn error of metabolism, characterized by a virtual absence of phenylalanine hydroxylase activity and an elevation of plasma phenylalanine, that frequently results in mental retardation. Early and well-maintained treatment, which consists in limiting the phenylalanine intake of the child so that the essential amino acid requirement is met but not exceeded, makes normal development possible and prevents involvement of the central nervous system. Treatment must be intiated during the first days of life to prevent mental retardation. Some clinicians believe that treatment must be continued for life; others think that it can be terminated when myelinization of the brain is virtually complete, at about five years of age.

Pheromone, chemical substance secreted by animals and serving to stimulate behavioral responses by other individuals of the same species. Some pheromones are alarm siganls or mark territory, but many are sex attractants, especially among insects.

Phi Beta Kappa, most prestigious U.S. honor society for college and university students in the liberal arts and sciences. Members are generally elected in their third or fourth year on the basis of academic achievements. The fraternity was founded at William and Mary College, Va., in 1776.

Phidias, or Pheidias (500-432 B.C.), perhaps the greatest Greek sculptor, whose work showed the human form idealized and with great nobility. None of his work survives; his reputation rests on contemporary accounts, Roman copies, and on the Parthenon statues made under his direction. Under Pericles he had artistic control over the Acropolis.
See also: Parthenon.

Philadelphia, name of several ancient Greek cities. One, founded in the 2nd century B.C., was in Amman, now the capital

A relief of a pharaoh standing in traditional pose

of Jordan. It was renamed Philadelphia in the 3rd century B.C. by Ptolemy II, one of the successors of Alexander the Great. The name is Greek for "brotherly love."

Philadelphia (pop. 4,856,881), historic city in the southeastern region of Pennsylvania, the fourth largest in the United States. It is a key shipping port, with important metal, machinery, clothing, petroleum, chemical, and food industries and has long been a center for publishing, education, and the arts. It was one of the first planned cities. Its founder, William Penn, created his colony in 1682 as a "holy experiment" in which all sects could find freedom. Philadelphia (Greek, "brotherly love") attracted immigrants and brought commerce that made it the largest and wealthiest of New World cities. In the Old City, near Delaware River, is the Independence National Historic Park, whose buildings include Independence Hall, where both the Declaration of Independence and the Constitution were adopted. The city was U.S. capital, 1790-1800; corruption in government and growth of slums accompanied a decline. In the 1950s massive urban renewal projects were initiated. Today the city has the world's largest freshwater port, linked with the Atlantic by the Delaware River.
See also: Pennsylvania.

Philip II of Spain

The port of Philadelphia

Philanthropy, acts of charity meant to improve the welfare of people. Philanthropy has been a part of many cultures, from the ancient Hebrews (who introduced a tax to help the poor) to the Greeks, Egyptians, Muslims, and Europeans of the Middle Ages. In the United State, philanthropy is often carried out through charitable foundations established by wealthy families.

Philemon, Epistle to, New Testament letter written c.A.D. 61 by St. Paul to Philemon, a Colossian Christian, asking him to forgive his runaway slave Onesimus, who had become a Christian and who carried the letter.
See also: New Testament.

Philip, name of six kings of France. **Philip I** (1052-1108) reigned from 1060. He enlarged his small territories and prevented the union of England and Normandy. His practice of simony and his disputed second marriage led him into conflict with the papacy. **Philip II**, or Philip Augustus (1165-1223), reigned from 1180 and established France as a European power. He joined the Crusades, only to quarrel with Richard the Lion Heart and seize his French territories. By 1204 he had added Normandy, Maine, Anjou, Touraine, and Brittany to his domain, in which he set up new towns and a system of royal bailiffs. **Philip III**, or Philip the Bold (1245-85), reigned from 1270 and secured Auvergne, Poitou and Toulouse for France. **Philip IV**, or Philip the Fair (1268-1314), reigned from 1285 and added Navarre and Champagne to the kingdom, but his attempts to overrun Flanders led to his defeat at Courtrai in 1302. He seized Pope Boniface VIII in a quarrel about taxation of clergy, obtained the election of Clement V, a puppet pope residing at Avignon, and seized the land of the crusading order of the Knights Templar. **Philip V**, or Philip the Tall (1294-1322), reigned from 1317, having invoked the Salic Law of male succession, and carried out reforms to strengthen royal power. The succession in 1328 of **Philip VI** (1293-1350) through the Salic Law was disputed and led to the Hundred Years War against England.

Philip, name of five kings of Spain. **Philip I**, or Philip the Handsome (1478-1506), was archduke of Austria, duke of Burgundy, and inheritor of the Netherlands. He became first Habsburg king of Castile in 1506, ruling jointly with his wife Joanna. **Philip II** (1527-98), crowned in 1556, united the Iberian peninsula and ruled an empire that included Milan, Naples, Sicily, the Netherlands, and vast tracts of the New World. Though son of the Holy Roman Emperor Charles V, he never became emperor. A fanatical Catholic, he married Mary I of England, supported the Inquisition, and tried in vain to crush the Protestant Netherlands. He was recognized king (Philip I) of Portugal in 1580 but lost naval supremacy to England after the defeat of the Armada (1588). His son **Philip III** (1578-1621), crowned in 1598, made peace with England and the Netherlands but was frustrated in Italy by the Thirty Years' War. **Philip IV** (1605-55), crowned in 1621, son of Philip III and the last Habsburg king of Spain, was the patron of Diego de Velázquez. He attempted unsuccessfully to dominate Europe by fighting France, Germany, and Holland in the Thirty Years' War, and lost Portugal in the process (1640). **Philip V** (1683-1746), crowned in 1700, founder of the Bourbon line, restored influence, but his accession led to the war of the Spanish Succession. By the Treaty of Utrecht (1713) his title was recognized, though he ceded possessions in Italy and the Netherlands to Austria.

Philip II (382-386 B.C.), king of Macedonia from 359 and father of Alexander the Great. His powerfully reorganized army conquered northern Greece, acquiring the gold mines of Thrace and advancing south as far as Thermopylae, the key to central Greece. He defeated Athens and Thebes at Chaeronea (338) and became ruler of all Greece. His reign marked the end of the independent, warring city-states.
See also: Greece, Ancient.

Philip, Prince (1921-), consort of Queen Elizabeth II of England. The son of Prince Andrew of Greece and Princess Alice of Battenberg, he renounced his Greek title, became a British subject, and married Elizabeth in 1947. He was created duke of Edinburgh in 1947 and prince in 1957.
See also: United Kingdom.

Philip, Saint, one of the Twelve Apostles. Born in Bethsaida, he was martyred at Hierapolis in Phrygia, according to legend.
See also: Apostles.

Philippi, ancient city of Macedonia, in present-day Greece, named for Philip II of Macedon. It was there Brutus and Cassius were defeated (42 B.C.) by Mark Antony and Octavian, and where St. Paul first preached the gospel in Europe.

Philippians, Epistle to the, New Testament letter written by St. Paul from prison in Rome (A.D. 62) to the Christians at Philippi, whom he himself had converted. He encourages them affectionately and quotes an early hymn on Christ's humility.
See also: New Testament.

Philippines, archipelago and republic in the southwest Pacific Ocean.
Land and climate. The Philippines consists of more than 7,000 islands with a total area of 115,830 sq mi (299,999 sq km). A far-flung archipelago, the Philippines is bounded by the China Sea to the west, the Celebes Sea to the south, the Philippine Sea

Rice terraces in the mountains of Luzon, Philippines

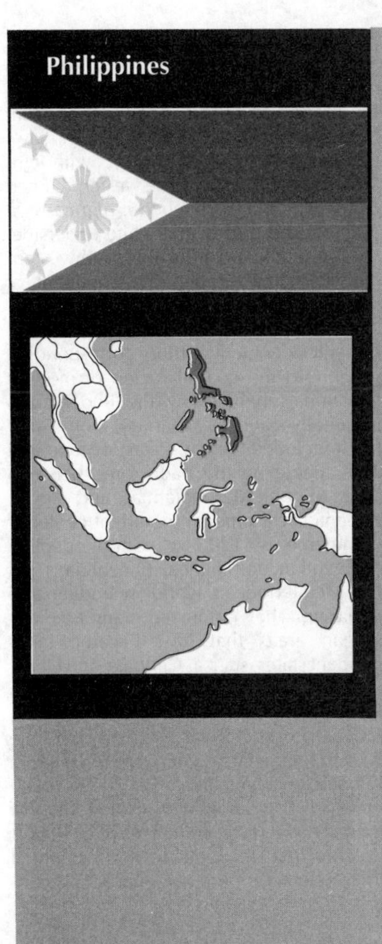

General information	
Capital:	Manila
Area:	115,830 sq mi (300,000 sq km)
Population:	64,187,000
Official languages:	Pilipino, English, Spanish
Monetary unit:	1 Philippine peso = 100 centavos
Main cities:	Manila, Quezon City, Cebu
Government	
Form:	republic
Independent:	1946
Head of state:	President (elected every 6 years)
Head of government:	President
Legislature:	two legislative houses (Senate and House of Representatives)
Executive:	President and Cabinet
Judiciary:	highest court is the Supreme Court
Political division:	73 provinces
National economy	
Gross national product:	U.S. $49,462,000,000
Per capita income:	U.S. $770
Agriculture:	sugar cane, coconuts, rice, corn, pineapples, bananas
Livestock:	pigs, buffalo, goats, poultry
Fisheries:	1,989,000 metric tons
Mining:	copper, nickel ore, silver, coal, gold, cobalt, manganese
Industries:	food and beverages, petroleum products, tobacco, industrial chemicals
Main exports:	food and live animals, miscellaneous manufactured articles (clothing), machinery and transport equipment, crude materials, basic manufactures
Transportation:	658 mi (1,059 km) of railroads, 98,058 mi (157,810 km) of roads, 2 international airports
Trading partners:	U.S., Japan, Germany, Hong Kong, Taiwan
People	
Urban:	41%
Ethnic composition:	Tagalog 25%, Cebuano 24%, Ilocano 10.5%, Hiligaynon Ilongo 9%, Bicol 5.5%
Birth rate:	35.9 per 1,000 population
Death rate:	7.8 per 1,000 population
Infant mortality:	53 per 1,000 live births
Life expectancy:	male 63 years, female 69 years

to the east and, in the north, the Bashi Channel separates the Philippines from Taiwan. The islands range in size from tiny rocks and islets to Luzon, the largest of them, with an area of 41,845 sq mi (108,378 sq km). Only 2,870 of the islands are named, about 730 are inhabited, and 11 account for most of the total land area and most of the population.

The landscape of the Philippines is characterized by coastal mangroves, fertile plains, luxuriant tropical jungles, rugged mountains, and active volcanoes and hot springs. The area is prone to earthquakes. Each island has its own distinct features. Luzon is mountainous, but has fertile plains and rolling hills. Among its many fine harbors is Manila Bay, site of the nation's capital, Manila. Mindanao, the archipelago's second largest island with an area of 36,381 sq mi (94,227 sq km) is even more mountainous, but also has the Cotabato Valley, an important agricultural area. The Philippines has a consistently hot and humid monsoon climate and is exposed to destructive Pacific typhoons.

People. The Philippine people are predominantly of Malay origin, but also include Chinese, Indonesians, Moros, and Negritos, pygmies who are descendants of the island's original inhabitants. Pilipino was adopted as the national language in 1946, and many other native languages are also spoken. The majority of the people are Roman Catholic, but there is also a sizeable Muslim minority.

Economy. About 45% of Philipinos work on the land. The leading crops are rice, coconut, corn, and sugar. Abaca (Manila hemp) and lumber are important exports. The islands are rich in mineral resources, in particular lead, nickel, zinc, copper, and cobalt. Manila is the main industrial center and manufacturing includes wood products, textiles, aluminum, and tobacco.

History. The islands were first visited by Europeans on Magellan's expedition of 1521, and were later named in honor of the future Philip II of Spain. By the 1570s Spanish rule was secure and lasted until the end of the Spanish-American War in 1898, after which the Philippines were ceded to the United States. A revolutionary nationalist movement under the leadership of Emilio Aquinaldo helped the United States defeat Spain. The issue of independence loomed large in U.S. relations with the Philippines until the establishment, in 1935, of the internally self-governing Commonwealth of the Philippines, with Manuel Quezon as president. Occupied by the Japanese during World War II, the country was made an independent republic in 1946, with Manuel Roxas and later Ramon Magsaysay as presidents. Communist revolutionary movements have been active since 1949. The powers of the presidency were greatly increased in 1972 with the imposition of martial law under President Ferdinand Marcos. Martial law was nominally ended in 1981.

The murder of Benigno Aquino and charges of fraud in the presidential elections of February 7, 1986, led to the ouster of Ferdinand Marcos. Corazon Aquino, wife of Benigno Aquino, claimed victory in the elections and accused Marcos forces of manipulating election returns. After weeks of political turmoil the army took the side of Mrs. Aquino, and Marcos and his wife Imelda fled the country. Under Aquino, a new constitution was ratified in 1987. Based on a three year phased-out withdrawal agreement, the U.S. navy closed it Subic Bay base on September 30, 1992.

Under Fidel Ramos, who was elected president in May 1992, political stability led to economic growth. Liberalized economic policies, deregulation, and privatization produced consumer confidence and attracted substantial foreign investment. In 1995, Ramos signed a peace agreement with military rebels, and another peace agreement was signed in 1996 with the Moro National Liberation Front.

Philip the Evangelist, also called Philip the Deacon, early Christian preacher chosen by the apostles to work in the church of

Jerusalem. He is said to have preached in Judea and Samaria and later became bishop of Tralles, in Asia Minor.

Philistines, non-Semitic people who lived in Palestine from the 12th century B.C. They were hostile to the Israelites and for a time held considerable power. The term *philistine* may nowadays denote an uncultured person.

Phillips, Wendell (1811-84), U.S. orator and social reformer. He gave up law in 1835 to campaign with W.L. Garrison for the abolition of slavery. He attended as a delegate the World Anti-Slavery Convention in England (1840). After the Civil War he worked for blacks' civil rights, women's suffrage, and other reforms.

Philodendron, genus of South American evergreen plants frequently grown as greenhouse and house plants. Many are vigorous climbers and produce attractive foliage, but they rarely flower in cultivation. The most popular climbing species are *Philodendron oxycardium* (heart-leaf philodendron), *P. sodiroi* (silver-leafed), and *P. panduraeforme* (fiddle leaf, or horsehead), while *P. bipinnatifidum* and *P. selloum* are self-heading cut-leaved types, closely resembling monstera except for their nonclimbing habit. Propagation is by shoot cuttings or air layering.

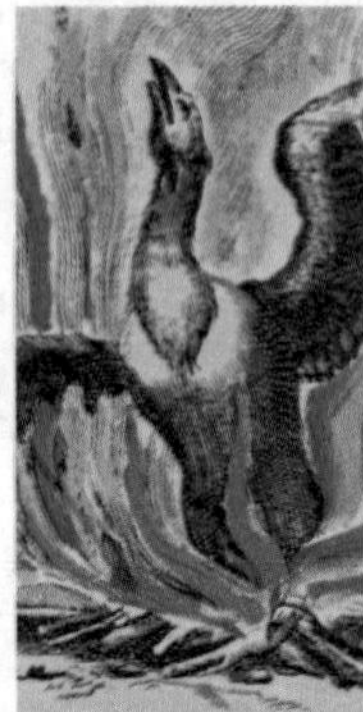

Phoenix

Philo Judaeus (c.20 B.C.-C.A.D. 50), Egyptian-born Jewish philosopher, "the Jewish Plato." His attempt to fuse Greek philosophical thought with Jewish biblical religion had a profound influence on both Christian and Jewish theology.
See also: Philosophy; Theology.

Philosophe, member of the 18th-century French school of thinkers, scientists, and belles lettrists who believed that the methodology of science should be applied to contemporary social, economic, and political problems. Inspired by René Descartes and the school of Skepticism, they included Montesquieu, Voltaire, Denis Diderot, and Jean-Jacques Rousseau.

Philosophy, study of the nature of being and thinking, and more specifically of the human experience. Traditionally, philosophers have focused on four main areas: (1) logic, or the study of the formal structure of truthful arguments; (2) metaphysics, or the study of the nature of "being" or ultimate reality; (3) epistimology, or the theory of knowledge; (4) ethics, or moral and political philosophy. The earliest known attempts to raise distinctively philosophical questions go back to the 7th century B.C., when the pre-Socratic Greek philosophers were active. Their intellectual heirs were Socrates, Plato, and Aristotole. Later ancient philosophies included epicureanism, stoicism, and neo-Platonism. Foremost among medieval philosphers in the West were St. Augustine and St. Thomas Aquinas. Modern philosophy, identified by the parallel development of rationalism and empiricism, began with René Descartes and culminated in the philosophy of Immanuel Kant. The idealism of G.F.W. Hegel and the positivism of August Compte were major forces in 19th-century philosophy, forming a basis for the philosophy of dialectical materialism espoused by Karl Marx. The philosophical orientations of most 20th-century philosophers have their roots in Marxism, Kantianism, logical positivism, pragmatism, phenomenology, or existentialism. Although at one time areas such as the natural sciences, psychology, sociology, logic, and mathematics were all considered to be within the domain of the philosophers, today's philosophers tend to concentrate on more specialized areas of inquiry, such as the philosophy of logic, the philosophy of science, and the philosophy of religion.

Phlebitis, inflammation of the veins, usually causing a blood clot, or thrombosis (thrombophlebitis), and obstruction to blood flow. Pain, swelling, and redness over the vein are typical, with the vein's becoming a thick, tender cord. Occasionally, phlebitis indicates systemic disease (for instance, cancer). Treatment includes anticoagulant medication.
See also: Embolism.

Phlogiston, elementary substance (without color, weight, taste, or odor) postulated by G.E. Stahl and Johann Becher to be lost from matter when it is burned. The phlogiston concept provided 18th-century chemistry with its unifying principle. The phlogiston theory of combustion found general acceptance until displaced by its inverse, Antoine Lavoisier's oxygen theory.

Phlox, genus of plants of North America and eastern Siberia that are grown in gardens around the world. The plants are either low-growing or upright and bear masses of tubular flowers that open to a flat whorl of petals.

Phnom Penh (pop. 700,000), capital and river port of Cambodia, on the Tônlé Sap River, where it joins the Mekong. It is the country's administrative, commercial, communications and cultural center. Founded in the 14th century, it was first made Khmer capital in the 1430s. Phnom Penh was the focus of a massive civil war campaign in 1970-75 in which almost the entire population was evacuated and put to forced labor. In 1979 the city was conquered by a Vietnamese invasion.
See also: Kampuchea.

Phobia, inordinate and overwhelming fear of certain events, situations, and objects. Some common fears include fear of heights (acrophobia), small spaces (claustrophobia), water (hydrophobia), foreigners (xenophobia), spiders (arachnophobia), and open spaces (agoraphobia). Phobias can severely restrict an individual's daily life and prevent the execution of daily routines. Phobias are considered a psychological disorder and treatment usually requires psychoanalysis or behavior therapy.
See also: Neurosis.

Phoebe, any of several small birds (genus *Sayornis*) in the flycatcher family. The eastern phoebe *(S. phoebe)*, with its pale yellow breast and dull green back, is prevalent in the northeastern United States. The say's phoebe (*S. saya*), slightly larger with light tan undersides, lives in the western United States. The black phoebe (*S. nigricans*), a dark-backed bird with a white underside, ranges southward from the southwestern United States through the continent of South America.

Phoenicia, ancient territory corresponding roughly to the coastal region of modern Lebanon, inhabited by the Phoenicians (originally called Canaanites) from 3000 B.C. It included the city-states of Sidon and Tyre. Being on the trade route between Asia Minor, Mesopotamia, and Egypt, Phoenicia became an important center of commerce. By 1200 B.C. with the decline of Egyptian dominance, Phoenicians led the Mediterranean world in trading and seafaring. They colonized many Mediterranean areas that later became independent states, such as Carthage and Utica. From the 9th century B.C. Phoenicia was intermittently dominated by Assyria, and in 538 came under Persian rule. By the time Alexander the Great conquered Tyre (332) Phoenician civilization had largely been eclipsed. The Greeks were the inheritors of their outstanding cultural legacy—most notably their alphabetic script, from which the modern Western alphabet is descended.

Phoenix (pop. 2,122,101), largest city in and capital of Arizona and the seat of Maricopa County. Phoenix lies in the Salt River Valley in south-central Arizona, in the heart of an irrigated area that contains the state's most productive cropland. Industries include the processing and shipping of the cotton, vegetables, fruit, hides, and other products of the nearby farms, metal processing, and the manufacture of electronic equipment, aircraft parts, and air conditioners. Tourism is also important.
See also: Arizona.

Phoenix, symbol of rebirth. Originally a mythical bird of ancient Egypt, it was sacred to the sun god Ra and worshipped at Helipolis. There was said to be only one phoenix in the universe at any one time; large as an eagle, brilliantly plumed, it lived 500 or more years, then made a pyre of aromatic boughs, consumed itself in the fire and rose reborn from its own ashes.
See also: Mythology.

Phonetics, systematic examination of the sounds made in speech, concerned with the classification of these sounds, the physical and physiological aspects of their production and transmission, and their reception and interpretation by the listener. Phonology, the study of phonetic patterns in languages, is of importance in comparative linguistics.

Phonograph, or record player, instrument for reproducing sound recorded mechani-

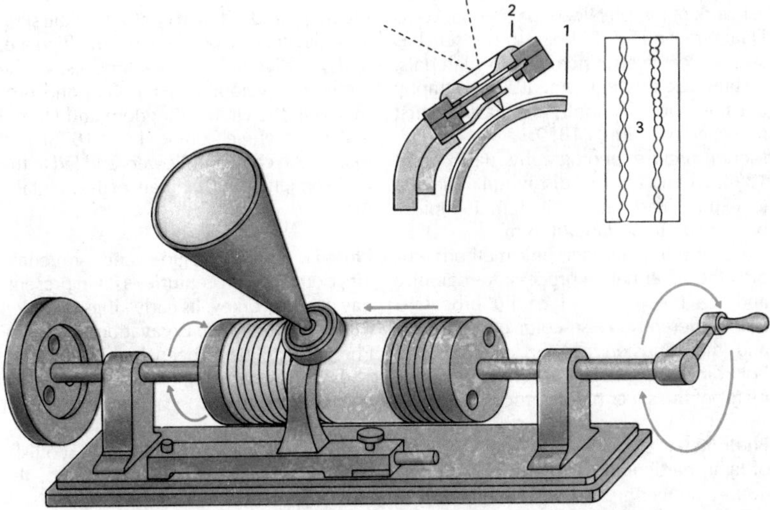

An early phonograph. It consists of a brass cylinder (1) cut on its surface with spiral grooves. Over this is wrapped a sheet of thin foil. The conical mouthpiece focuses the sound onto a metal diaphragm (2), behind which the steel stylus is mounted on a flat spring and connected to the center of the diaphragm by a wire. The cylinder keeps the needle engaged as it is turned by the handle, keeping a steady speed by virtue of the flywheel. When the sound causes the diaphragm to vibrate, the needle traces the vibrations onto the metal film (3), leaving permanent indentations. After the cylinder is returned to its original position, the sounds are reproduced when the handle is cranked.

cally as modulations in a spiral groove. It was invented by Thomas Edison (1877), whose first machine had a revolving grooved cylinder covered with tinfoil. Sound waves caused a diaphragm to vibrate, and a stylus on the diaphragm made indentations in the foil. These could then be made to vibrate another stylus attached to a reproducing diaphragm. Wax disks and cyclinders soon replaced tinfoil, then when metal master disks could be made by etching or electroplating, copies were mass-produced in rubber, wax, or plastic. The main parts of a phonograph are the turntable, to rotate the disk at constant angular velocity; the stylus, which tracks the groove and vibrates with its modulations; the pickup, or transducer, which converts these movements piezoelectrically or electromagnetically into electrical signals; the amplifier; and the loudspeaker.
See also: Edison, Thomas Alva

Phosphate, derivative of phosphoric acid, either a phosphate ester or a salt containing phosphate ions. Of many phosphate minerals, the most important is apatite, which is treated with sulfuric acid or phosphoric acid to get superphosphate, the major phosphate fertilizer. Phosphates are used in making glass, soaps, and detergents.

Phosphor, substance emitting light (or other electromagnetic radiation) on nonthermal stimulation. Important phosphors include those used in television picture tubes (where stimulation is by electrons) and those coated on the inside wall of fluorescent lamp tubes to convert ultraviolet radiation into visible light.

Phosphorescence, light produced by certain substances after the absorption of certain forms of energy, especially radiant energy. The light is produced when the electrons of the substance, excited by the radiation, drop back to lower energy levels. Phosphorescence is similar to fluorescence except that fluorescence occurs *while* the substance is subject to radiation, whereas phosphorescence continues even after the radiation has stopped. Natural forms of phosphorescence occur in gems and minerals. Some insects, such as fireflies, exhibit it too. Scientists use phosphorescent substances to track and examine body systems with X-rays. Manufacturers use phosphorescence in clock faces, computer monitors, and other products.
See also: Fluorescence; Luminescence.

Phosphoric acid, also called orthophosphoric acid, syrupy acid (H_3PO_4) produced from phosphate rock or, in purer form, from white phosphorus. This acid has various applications in the manufacture of fertilizers, flavored syrups, dental adhesives, detergents, water softeners, and anti-corrosive coatings for metals.

Phosphorus, chemical element, symbol P; for physical constants see Periodic Table. Phosphorus was discovered by Hennig Brand in 1669. The element is found in nature as phosphate rock containing *apatite*, an impure tri-calcium phosphate. It is prepared by heating tri-calcium phosphate with carbon in an electric furnace, with the vapor being collected under water. Phosphorus, a nonmetallic element, exists in three or more allotropic forms, white, red, and black. It catches fire spontaneously in air and must be kept under water. It may cause severe burns to the flesh and must be handled with forceps. It is an essential component of animal tissue and bone. Phosphorus and its compounds are used in fertilizers, fine china, safety matches, pesticides, incendiary weapons, cleaning agents, and water softeners.

Phosphorus cycle, the cycling and recycling of phosphorus in the living world, or biosphere. Phosphates (the natural occurring salt-form of phosphorus) are absorbed by plant life and later released into the atmosphere and the sea. In time, decayed matter containing phosphates returns to the soil. In this way phosphorus, a substance necessary for life, works its way through the living matter of the earth.
See also: Phosphorus.

Photochemistry, branch of physical chemistry dealing with chemical reactions that produce light or are initiated by (visible or ultraviolet) light. Important examples include photosynthesis, photography, and bleaching by sunlight.

Photocomposition, also called phototypesetting, system by which words are arranged for printing on photographic film or paper. In the past typesetters hand placed and arranged metal dies with letters on them for the printing of newspapers, magazines, and books. Today this job is done quickly and efficiently through a keyboard connected to a photographic device, both of which are controlled by a computer. Computers allow instantaneous changes of typeface, or font. The computer can also automatically reposition an entire body of type whenever a change is made.
See also: Printing; Type.

Photoconductive cell *see:* Electric eye.

Photocopying, duplication of printed images or words through a process involving photographic techniques. The most popular of these techniques, *Xerography* (1938), is a dry process in which light-sensitive material is charged with static electricity to produce an image when a toner (powdered ink) adheres to heated paper and recreates the original image. Older processes depended on liquid developers, such as photostats and blueprints. Libraries and other document storage facilities use microfilming to make miniature copies, up to 1/100th the original size.

Photoelectric cell *see:* Electric eye.

Photoelectric effect (properly photoemissive effect), the emission of electrons from a surface when struck by electromagnetic radiation, such as light. In 1905 Albert Einstein laid one of the twin foundations of quantum theory by explaining photoemission in terms of the action of individual photons, which are quanta of light. The effect is used in phototubes (electron tubes having a photoemissive cathode), often employed as "electric eye" switches.

Photoengraving and photolithography, processes by which plates or cylinders containing matter for printing are created. Techniques of photographing and etching (acid engraving) replicate illustrations and drawings to be printed in the photoengraving process. In this method line engravings reproduce lines and halftone engravings reproduce continuous ranges of tone. Photography is used to transfer printed matter to the printing plate. The body of text to be printed is then treated with water that will accept the oily ink from the rollers, while the unprinted portions of the plate are treated with an oil that accepts only water from the rollers.
See also: Engraving; Lithography; Printing.

Photogrammetry, method for making measurements for maps or surveys through photographs. Cameras—often mounted on aircraft or space vehicles—take 2 or more shots of the same area from different angles. Land masses as well as the moon are

subjects for photogrammetry. A stereoplotter corrects errors in measurements due to photographic distortions. Photogrammetry was developed by a French colonel, Amie Laussedat (1859).
See also: Map; Surveying.

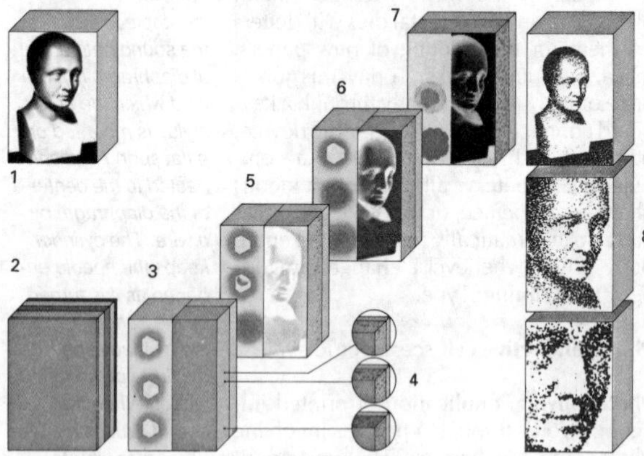

When exposed to light, silver bromide crystals (contained in the emulsion of the film) undergo a partial chemical change and are ready to be acted on by the developer. The developer separates the crystals, which form the dark parts of the image, and bromine, which combines with the developer.
1. subject to be photographed
2. film consisting of a protective layer and emulsion on the base
3. exposed film consisting of sensitized silver bromide crystals
4. the longer the exposure, the longer the number of sensitized grains
5. film developed for short time
6. longer development gives denser negative
7. very long period of development
8. the final image, magnified in three stages

Photography, use of light sensitive material to produce permanent visible images (photographs). In the most familiar processes a photographic emulsion is a preparation of tiny silver halide crystals suspended in a thin layer of gelatin coated on a glass, film, or paper support. On brief exposure to light in a camera or other apparatus, a latent image in activated silver salt is formed wherever light has fallen on the emulsion. This image is made visible in development when the activated silver halide crystals (but not the unexposed ones) are reduced to metallic silver (black) using a weak organic reducing agent (the developer). The silver image is then made permanent by fixing with agents that dissolve out the silver halide crystals that were not activated on exposure. The image is a "negative" one. To produce a positive image, the negative is itself made the original in the above process, the result being a positive "print," usually on a paper carrier. An alternative method of producing a positive image is to bleach away the developed image on the original film or plate before fixing, and reexpose the unactivated halide in diffuse light. This forms a second latent image that on development produces a positive image of the original subject (reversal processing).
The history of photography from the earliest work of Joseph Nicéphore Niepc, Louis Daguerre, and Fox Talbot to the present has seen successive refinements in materials, techniques, and equipment. Photography became a popular hobby after Eastman first marketed roll film in 1889.
Motion-picture photography dates from 1890, when Thomas Edison built a device to expose Eastman's roll film. It rapidly became an important art form.
Not all modern photographic methods employ the silver halide process; Xerography and the blueprint and ozalid processes work differently. False-color photography and the diffusion process used in the Polaroid Land camera are both developments of the silver halide process.

One of the founders of photography, Fox Talbot

Photometry, science of the measurement of light, particularly as it affects illumination engineering. The brightness experienced when light strikes the human eye depends not only on the power but also on the wave-length of the light. In SI (international system) units, the photometric base quantity is luminous intensity, which measures the intensity of light radiated from a small source. The base unit of luminous intensity is the candela (cd). The illuminance falling on a surface (formerly known as its illumination) is measured in luxes (lx). Up to the 1970s scientists were not in agreement about the concepts and terminology to be used in photometry, so many alternative units—apostilbs, blondels, foot-candles, and lamberts—are still encountered.

Photon, quantum of electromagnetic energy, often thought of as the particle associated with light or other electromagnetic radiation. Its energy is given by hv, where h is the Planck constant and v the frequency of the radiation.
See also: Light; Quantum mechanics; Radiation.

Photosynthesis, process by which green plants convert the energy of sunlight into chemical energy that is stored as carbohydrate. The process can be written as: $6CO_2+6H_2O \rightarrow C_6H_{12}O_6+6O_2$ ($\rightarrow$ = *light*)
In the "light reaction," chlorophyll (the key chemical in the whole process) is activated by absorbing a quantum of light, initiating a sequence of reactions in which the energy-rich compounds (ATP) adenosine triphosphate and the reduced form of triphosphopyriden nucleotide (TPNH) are made, water being decomposed to give free oxygen in the process. In the second stage, the "dark reaction," the ATP and TPNH provide the energy for the assimilation of carbon dioxide gas, yielding a variety of sugars from which other sugars and carbohydrates, including starch, can be built up.

Phrenology, theory that the various faculties of the mind occupy distinct and separate areas in the brain cortex and that the predominance of certain faculties can be predicted from modifications of the parts of the skull overlying the areas where these faculties are located. Phrenologists studied the shape and detailed contours of the skull as indicators of personality, intelligence, and individual characteristics. The method, developed by F.J. Gall and promoted in the United Kingdom and United States by George Combe (1788-1858), had many 19th century followers and led to the more enlightened treatment of the mentally ill.

Phrygia, ancient region and sometime kingdom (8th-6th centuries B.C.) in present-day central Turkey. Its early kings included Midas and Gordius. Excavation shows the Phrygians to have been highly cultured. The Phrygian worship of Cybele was taken over by the Greeks.

Phyfe, Duncan (c.1768-1854), Scottish-born U.S. cabinetmaker, designer of the most distinctive U.S. neoclassical furniture. He based his work on European styles such as the Sheraton and the Empire style.

Phylloxera, louse resembling an aphid that is a serious pest in vineyards. In North America, where phylloxera originated, the native grapes are resistant to it, but when it was imported into Europe in the middle of the 19th century this insect nearly caused disaster in some of the most famous wine-making regions. The problem was solved by grafting plants onto American grape rootstocks.

Phylum *see:* Classification.

Physical chemistry, branch of chemistry in which the theories and methods of physics are applied to chemical systems. Its main divisions are the study of molecular structure, colloids, crystals, electrochemistry, chemical equilibrium, gas laws, chemical kinetics, molecular weight determination, photochemistry, solution, spectroscopy, and chemical thermodynamics.

Physical education, instruction designed to further the health, growth, and athletic capacity of the body. It may include gymnastics, sports, and Asian techniques like yoga. Culturally important in ancient China and ancient Greece, physical education later had a primarily military application until the 19th century, when it began to be incorporated into school programs in Europe and the United States.

Physical therapy, or physiotherapy, system of physical treatment for disease or disability. Techniques include active and passive muscle movement, electrical stimulation, balancing exercises, heat, ultraviolet, or shortwave radiation; and manual vibration of the chest wall with postural drainage. Rehabilitation after fracture, surgery, or stroke or other neurological disease, training unimpaired muscles to compensate for those whose function has been lost, and the treating of lung infections such as pneumonia and bronchitis are among the aims.

Physics, science that deals with the interaction of matter and energy. Physics attempts to explain the nature of the physical world from the movements of planets to the smallest sub-atomic particles. Physics is important because many of the conclusions drawn from scientific study are applied to medicine and technology. Physics is usually divided into 2 large categories-classic physics and modern physics. Classic physics is primarily concerned with matter, motion, and energy. It can be subdivided into other areas of investigation which include mechanics, thermodynamics, acoustics, optics, and electromagnetism. The outstanding contributions to classical physics are found in the works of Archimedes, Copernicus, Galileo, Kepler, Descartes, Huygens, and Newton. Modern physics is primarily concerned with the structure of the physical world and contains a number of different disciplines including, atomic, nuclear, particle, solid state, and fluid physics. The major contributions to modern physics can be found in the works of Max Planck, Niels Bohr, and Albert Einstein, Enrico Ferni, Theodore H. Maiman, Murray Gell-Mann, George Zweig, Burton Richter, Samuel C.C. Ting, and Carl Rubbia.

Physiocrat, member of 18th century French school of economists founded by François Quesnay, who held that agriculture, rather than industry or commerce, was the basis of a nation's prosperity, and that land alone should be subject to tax. The physiocrats' belief in a natural economic law, which merely required non-interference to be successful, is reflected in their famous formula *laissez faire* (let it be). The physiocrats influenced Adam Smith.
See also: Economics.

Physiology, study of function in living organisms. Based on knowledge of anatomy, physiology seeks to demonstrate the manner in which organs perform their tasks and in which the body is organized and maintained in a state of homeostasis. Normal responses to stress are studied. Branches deal with respiration, blood circulation, the nervous system, the digestive system, the kidneys, the fluid and electrolyte balance, the endocrine glands, and metabolism.

Three types of piano:
1. Italian Cristofori piano (1720)
2. modern grand piano
3. giraffe piano (1800s)

Physiotherapy *see:* Physical therapy.

Pi, in mathematics, name of the symbol π, which denotes the ratio of the circumference of a circle to its diameter (3.1416).

Piaf, Edith (Edith Giovanna Gassion; 1915-63), French cabaret and music-hall singer. She began singing for a living at 15 and won international fame with stirringly interpreted songs like *Milord* and *Je ne regrette rien.*

Piaget, Jean (1896-1980), Swiss psychologist whose theories of the mental development of children, though now often criticized, have been of paramount importance. He held that children develop intellectually in clear stages and that the ability to reason logically is absent from the early stages. His many books include *The Psychology of the Child* (1969), and *Biology and Knowledge* (1971).
See also: Psychology.

Piankashaw *see:* Miami (Native American tribe).

Piano, or pianoforte, musical stringed keyboard instrument. Depression of the keys causes the strings to be struck with felt-tipped hammers; these hammers rebound immediately after striking, so the strings go on sounding their notes until the keys are released, at which point the strings' vibrations are stopped with dampers. Bartolomeo Cristofori made the first piano in 1709, and by 1800 it had overtaken the harpsichord and the clavichord, whose plucked strings offered less volume and expressiveness, in popularity. Today the two basic types of piano are the upright piano, with vertical strings, and the grand piano, with horizontal strings, which has a range of seven octaves. Composers noted for their writing for the piano include Bach, Mozart, Beethoven, Chopin, Liszt, and Rachmaninov.

Piatigorsky, Gregor (1903-76), Russian-born U.S. cellist. He made his debut as a concert cellist in the United States in 1929 and became a U.S. citizen in 1942. Together with the violinist Jascha Heifetz and violist William Primrose, he was esteemed for his performance of chamber music.

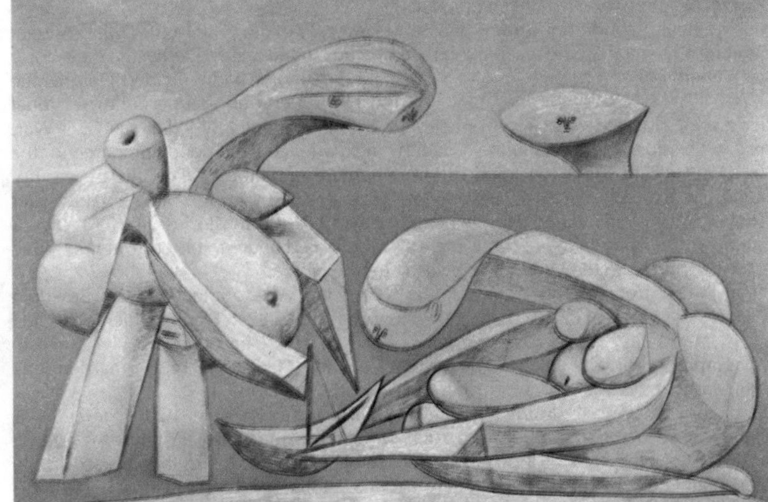
Pablo Picasso's La Baignade *(1937)*

Picasso, Pablo (Pablo Ruiz y Picasso; 1881-1973), Spanish-born French painter, sculptor, graphic artist, and ceramist, considered by many the greatest artist of the 20th century. A precocious painter, after his melancholy "blue period" and his lyrical "rose period" (1901-6), he was influenced by African and primitive art, as shown in *Les Demoiselles d'Avignon* (1907). Together, he and Georges Braque created cubism (1907-14), its principles seen already in *Demoiselles.* His friends at this time included the poet and critic Apollinaire, the ballet impresario Serge Diaghilev (for whom he made stage designs), and the expatriate author Gertrude Stein, who acted as a patron for modernist artists. In 1921 he painted both the cubist *Three Musicians* and the classical *Three Women at the Fountain.* In the 1930s he

Mary Pickford

adopted the style of surrealism, using it to horrify in the large antiwar canvas *Guernica* (1937). His later work employed both cubist and surrealist forms and could be beautiful, tender, or grotesque. His output was enormous, and near the end of his life he produced a brilliant series of etchings.

Piccalilli, relish made from chopped and pickled vegetables (green pepper, onion, cucumber, among others) and spices (mustard seed, celery seed, etc.).

Piccard, name of Swiss scientists who were twin brothers. **Auguste** (1884-1962), a physicist, set a world ballooning altitude record (1931), and an ocean-depth record (1953) in the bathyscaphe, which he designed. **Jean Felix** (1884-1963), a chemist, measured cosmic radiation during a 57,000-ft (17,374-m) balloon ascent (1934).
See also: Bathyscaphe.

Piccolo, small woodwind instrument resembling a flute. Measuring 12 in (30 cm), the piccolo plays an octave higher than the concert flute. Developed in the late 1700s in Europe, it is used in concert bands, military bands, and orchestras.

Franklin Pierce

14th U.S. President	
Born:	Hillsboro, N.H.; Nov. 23, 1804
Term:	Mar. 1853-Mar. 1857
Vice president:	William R.D. King
Political party:	Democratic
Spouse:	Jane Means Appleton Pierce
Children:	3
Died:	Concord, N.H.; Oct. 8, 1869

Pickerel, carnivorous freshwater fish, smaller relative of the pike (family Esocidae), also with a snout like duck's bill. The grass's, or redfin, pickerel, found from Nova Scotia to Texas, grows up to 2 ft (0.6 m), and the chain pickerel, of the eastern United States grows to 14 in (36 cm).

Pickering, Timothy (1745-1829), U.S. politician. After a distinguished military career in the Revolutionary War, he served as postmaster general (1791-95), secretary of war (1795), secretary of state (1795-1800), senator (1803-11), and representative (1813-17).

Pickett, George Edward (1825-75), Confederate general in the U.S. Civil War who led the disastrous assault (July 3, 1863) on Cemetery Ridge in the Battle of Gettysburg. Of the 15,000 Confederate troops who charged the Union line, some 6,000 were killed. Pickett later suffered a second major defeat at the Battle of Five Forks (Apr. 1, 1865).
See also: Civil War, U.S.; Gettysburg, Battle of.

Pickford, Mary (Gladys Smith; 1893-1979), Canadian-born U.S. movie actress. Her roles in films like *Daddy Long Legs*, under D. W. Griffith, won her the title "America's Sweetheart." In 1919 she and her husband, Douglas Fairbanks, helped found United Artists.
See also: Fairbanks, Douglas, Sr.

Pickle, food preserved in vinegar or brine to prevent the development of putrefying bacteria. Spices are usually added for flavor. Cucumbers, onions, beets, tomatoes, and cauliflowers make popular pickles. Pigs' feet and corned beef are also sometimes pickled.

Picotte, Susan La Flesche (1865-1915), first Native American woman to become a physician. A member of the Omaha tribe and daughter of the chief, she became the leading physician on the tribe's Nebraska reservation (1891-94) after earning her M.D. (1889) from the Women's Medical College of Pennsylvania. She worked to improve health conditions for her people, founding a hospital on the reservation that was named for her (1913).

Picric acid, also known as trinitrophenol, toxic, explosive, crystalline acid ($C_6H_3N_3O_7$) with industrial applications. Originally an explosive, it is now more commonly used in textile dyes, electric batteries, burn ointments, and the manufacture of glass. Peter Woulfe, a British chemist, first isolated this acid solid in 1771.

Pictography, writing by means of pictures, particularly ancient methods of using actual pictures as symbols. Many alphabetic symbols have been simplified from such pictures. over the course of time. For instance, our letter *A*, which developed from the Greek *alpha* and the Hebrew *aleph*, was adapted from a pictograph showing the horns of an ox.

Pictou (pop. 4,400), town and port in northern Novia Scotia, Canada, on Northumberland Strait. First settled in 1767, it is now known mainly for its abundant lobster harvest and lobster carnival, which takes place each summer.
See also: Nova Scotia.

Picts, ancient inhabitants of Scotland whose forebears probably came from the European continent c.1000 B.C. By the 8th century A.D. their kingdom extended from Fife to Caithness. In 843 they united with the kingdom of the Scots (Dalriada) and were assimilated into the Scottish nation.
See also: Scotland.

Pidgin, language of simplified grammar and vocabulary, most often based on a western European language, with some vocabulary from or based on another or several other languages. Pidgins originate as a means of communication (e.g., for trading purposes) between peoples with different mother tongues.

Piedmont, region in northwestern Italy, including both mountainous terrain—the Alps and the Appenines—and the upper Po River valley, a rich farm area. Turin, the capital city, is a leading industrial center, the home of Fiat. The Savoy family was powerful in the region beginning in the 11th century. France ruled the region from 1798 to 1814 and had a lasting influence on local cultures. Piedmont was a center of Italian nationalism during the 19th century and played a leading role in the Risorgimento, the movement for Italian unification. Turin became the first capital of the united kingdom of Italy in 1861.
See also: Italy.

Piedmont Region, region of the United States from New Jersey in the north to Alabama in the south, from the Appalachian Mountains in the west to the Atlantic coastal plains in the east.

Pieplant *see:* Rhubarb.

Pierce, Franklin (1804-69), 14th president of the United States. Pierce, the dark-horse candidate of a badly divided Democratic Party, served during a period of sectional strife that eventually led to the Civil War. Inexperienced and poorly prepared for the burdens of national office, Pierce was unable to cope with the bitter conflict over slavery in the territories. He left office a discredited figure in his party and in much of the nation.
Early life. After graduating from Bowdoin College in 1824, Franklin Pierce studied law; in 1827, he opened a law office in Concord, N.H. In 1834, he married Jane Means Appleton.
Political career. In 1829, Pierce was elected to the state legislature, where he served until 1833. He then served in the U.S. House of Representatives (1833-37) and the U.S. Senate (1837-42). In 1842, he

resigned and resumed his law practice. When the Mexican War broke out in 1846, Pierce saw active duty as a commissioned officer. After it ended, he returned to his law practice.
At its 1852 national convention, the Democratic Party, deeply divided over slavery, could not nominate one of three favored candidates. Pierce was nominated on the 49th ballot. Fellow Northerners accepted him, and Southerners accepted him for his support of the Compromise of 1850. He and running mate William R.D. King defeated the Whig candidates, Winfield Scott and William A. Graham.
President. Pierce was a pliable and vacillating chief executive. He formed a Cabinet of inharmonious sectional spokesmen rather than a politically coherent team. Subservient to warring party managers, Pierce was conciliatory, bland, and yielding to all sides.
Pierce pledged loyalty to the Compromise of 1850 and expressed hope that the slavery issue could be removed from national politics. Partly to divert attention from domestic problems, he also promised an expansionist foreign policy. However, under Pierce, U.S. plans to annex Hawaii and to acquire Cuba from Spain failed.
On the domestic scene, Pierce encouraged development of the West. In 1853, his administration acquired the Gadsden Purchase—with its right-of-way for a southern route to the Pacific—from Mexico. Pierce was pressured into supporting the Kansas-Nebraska Act of 1854. It repealed the Missouri Compromise (which had prohibited slavery in the region), leaving the question of allowing slavery in the territories to be decided by the settlers. The Kansas-Nebraska Act upset the careful balance between North and South, reopened the bitter slavery controversy, and wrecked Pierce's administration. The bitter divisions would deepen until they erupted into the Civil War in 1861.
Pierce's handling of the slavery issue made him unacceptable for renomination at the 1856 Democratic convention; it nominated James Buchanan instead.
Retirement. After leaving office, Pierce traveled abroad for several years. An outspoken critic of President Lincoln's conduct in the Civil War, he became more disliked than ever in the North. He gradually withdrew from public life and died in virtual obscurity.

Piero della Francesca (c.1420-92), Italian painter, one of the greatest Renaissance artists. His concern for the harmonious relationship of figures to their setting was expressed through simple, elegant forms, clear colors and tones, atmospheric light, and perspective, as seen in his fresco *Legend of the True Cross* (1452-59) in Arezzo.
See also: Renaissance.

Pierre (pop. 11,973), capital city of South Dakota, in the central part of the state. A Native American settlement in the 1820s, it became a European fur trading post named after one of the traders, Pierre Chouteau. In the late 19th century, it became known as the terminus of the Chicago and North Western railroads. Today it houses the state government and supports a prosperous livestock industry.
See also: South Dakota.

Pietermaritzburg, also called Maritzburg (pop. 126,300), capital of Natal Province in northeastern South Africa. The city was founded by Boers (Dutch settlers in South Africa) after a Zulu defeat (1839). It is known for manufacturing, higher education, and its parks and gardens.
See also: South Africa.

Piezoelectricity, reversible relationship between mechanical stress and electrostatic potential exhibited by certain crystals with no center of symmetry, discovered in 1880. When pressure is applied to a piezoelectric crystal, such as quartz, positive and negative electric charges appear on opposite crystal faces. Replacing the pressure by tension changes the sign of the charges.
If an electric potential is applied across the crystal, its length changes. A piezoelectric crystal placed in an alternating electric circuit will alternately expand and contract. Resonance occurs in the circuit when its frequency matches the natural vibration frequency of the crystal. This way of coupling electrical and mechanical effects is used in microphones, phonograph pickups, and ultrasonic generators.
See also: Quartz.

Pigeon, name for family (Columbidae) of some 255 species of birds, with worldwide distribution. The typical pigeon is pastel gray, pink, or brown with contrasting patches of brighter colors. The body is compact, the neck short, and the head and bill fairly small. Most species are gregarious, and many are seen in very large flocks. The food may be stored in a distensible crop. The name *dove* is synonymous with *pigeon*.

Pigeon guillemot *see:* Guillemot.

Pigfish *see:* Grunt.

Pig iron *see:* Iron and steel.

Pigment, coloring substance. Pigments differ from dyes, which dissolve in a medium and stain the upper layers of a surface. Pigments are finely ground insoluble substances that are suspended in a medium and form a colored layer on top of the surface to which they are applied. Paints consist of pigments suspended in liquids, such as resins. Many of the pigments used in paints consist of oxides of various metals. The colors of animals and plants are caused by pigments in their skins or outer tissues. Human skin and hair contains malanin, and plants contain the green pigment chlorophyll.
See also: Color.

Pigmy *see:* Pygmy.

Pigweed, any of several weeds of the Amaranth family. This weed is easy to grow because of its strong roots. It rises to 3 ft (91 cm) in height and displays large coarse leaves and heads of small green hair-covered flowers.

Pika, group of small mammals (family Ochstonidae) related to the hares and rabbits, also known as mousehares, whistling hares, and rock conies. They look like rabbits but have short ears and lack tails. Two species live in the Rocky Mountain regions, and the rest live in mountainous parts of Asia. Pikas are known for their piping calls and for "making hay": rather than hibernate, they survive the winter by feeding on grass and herbs that they cut, dry in the sun, and store under a rock or log.

Pike, carnivorous freshwater fish (family Esocidae) with ducklike snout and sharp teeth. The northern pike, or jackfish (*Esox lucius*), lies in the rivers and lakes of the Northern Hemisphere. It grows up to 4.5 ft (1.4 m) long and a weight of 53 lb (24 kg). Northern pike are green with yellow spots, a color scheme that harmonizes with the weeds in which they lurk, ready to shoot out and snap up another fish, a duck, or even a muskrat. Other pikes are the muskellunge and pickerel.

Pike, Zebulon Montgomery (1779-1813), U.S. general and explorer, best known as the discoverer (1806) of the Colorado mountain thereafter called Pikes Peak.

Pikes Peak, mountain, 14,110 ft (4,301 m) high, in east-central Colorado, part of the Rocky Mountains, near Colorado Springs. It was first explored by Zebulon Pike in 1806. Its solitary position and commanding vistas make it a popular tourist attraction.
See also: Pike, Zebulon Montgomery.

Pilate, Pontius, Roman procurator of Judea (A.D. 26-36) who ordered the crucifixion of Christ, afterward washing his hands to declaim responsibility. Hated by the Jews, he was recalled to Rome after his behavior provoked a riot that had to be put down by troops.
See also: Jesus Christ; Rome, Ancient.

Piles *see:* Hemorrhoid.

Pilgrimage *see:* Hajj; Lourdes.

Pilgrims, English settlers who first landed in New England in 1620 in the location now known as Plymouth, Mass. Fearing religious persecution in England, these Pilgrims first fled to Holland but could not tolerate the cultural differences. With the support of English merchants, they set sail in the *Mayflower* on September 1620. Upon their arrival they established the Plymouth colony. The origin of the word "Pilgrim" to designate these settlers is not certain, but it is often attributed to William Bradford, a governor of Plymouth Colony, who referred to the settlers as "Pilgrims."
See also: Brewster, William; Colonial life

in America; Massachusetts Bay Colony; Plymouth Colony.

Pilotfish (*Naucrates ductor*), fish (family Carangidae) once believed to guide sharks and even ships. Pilot fish grow to 2 ft (0.6 m) and are patterned with conspicuous bands. When young, they shelter under jellyfish or pieces of floating seaweed and driftwood. As adults, they swim very close to sharks, whales, sailing ships, or manta rays. It is thought that they feed on scraps from the shark's meals, but this does not explain why they follow ships or whales.

Pilotweed *see:* Compass plant.

Pilot whale, also called blackfish, any of several species of smalltoothed whales (genus *Globicephala*) of the dolphin family. Pilot whales are named after those members that lead the large schools—sometimes in the hundreds or thousands—in which they travel. They can detect obstacles in the water through a fatty organ called the melon. Black with white on the underside, pilot whales can weigh up to 2.5 tons (2.3 m tons) and are about 20 ft (6 m) in length. They live mainly in warmer oceans.

Pilsen *see:* Plzen.

Pilsudski, Józef (1867-1935), Polish general and politician. Imprisoned several times for his nationalism, he led a private army against Russia in World War I and directed the Russo-Polish War. He was president of the new Polish republic (1918-22). After a coup d'état in 1926 he became virtual dictator.
See also: Poland.

Piltdown man (*Eoanthropus dawsoni*), fraudulent human ancestor whose "remains" were found (1908-15) under Piltdown Common, Sussex, United Kingdom. These consisted of a skull with an apelike jaw but a large, human cranium and teeth worn down unlike those of any extant ape, surrounded by fossil animals that indicated an early Pleistocene date. In 1953 the fraud was exposed: The skull was human but relatively recent; the even more recent jaw was that of an orangutan; the teeth had been filed down by hand; and the fossil animals were not of British origin. The remains had been artificially stained to increase confusion. The hoax has been attributed to Sir Arthur Conan Doyle, among others.

Pima, Native American peoples living with the Maricopas on the Gila River and Salt River reservations in southern Arizona. A sedentary agricultural group, they are related to the Papagos and descended from the Hohokam peoples. The Pimas were noted for their dome-shaped houses and basketry.

Pimento, tree (*Pimenta officinalis*) of the myrtle family whose small berry-like fruit is used to make the spice allspice. The pimento is native to the Caribbean island of Jamaica. It grows 20-40 ft (6-12 m) tall; the small black fruits appear on the slender top branches. When dried, these fruit become allspice. This tree should not be confused with the red pepper commonly called pimento or pimiento.

Pimpernel (*Pimpinella magna*), perennial plant that grows along the edges of woods and in many meadows; the rootstock is used for medicinal purposes, in treating sore throats, colds, bronchitis, and inflammation of the larynx.

Pinching bug *see:* Stag beetle.

Pinchot, Gifford (1865-1946), U.S. politician and conservationist who was largely responsible for making conservation a public issue. He headed the Division of Forestry, U.S. Department of Agriculture (1898-1910), and influenced President Theodore Roosevelt to transfer millions of acres of forest land to public reserves. He was a founder of the Progressive Party (1912) and twice governor of Pennsylvania (1923-29, 1931-35).
See also: Conservation.

Pinckney, South Carolina family whose members were notable in the founding period of the republic. **Elizabeth Lucas** (1722-93), a rich planter, was a patriot and champion of independence. Her son **Charles Cotesworth** (1746-1825) was a soldier in the Revolutionary War and a member of the Constitutional Convention. He is best known for his part in the XYZ Affair. His brother **Thomas** (1750-1828), soldier and statesman, arranged Pinckney's Treaty with Spain (1795). He was governor of South Carolina and was, like his brother, an unsuccessful Federalist Party candidate for the vice-presidency. Their cousin **Charles** (1757-1824) brought the "Pinckney Draft" to the Constitutional Convention of 1787. Most of its clauses were adopted. He was 3 times governor of South Carolina, U.S. minister to Spain (1801-5), and a member of Congress (1819-21).
See also: XYZ Affair.

Pinckney Treaty (1795), negotiated with Spain by Thomas Pinckney, establishing commercial relations with Spain, opening the entire Mississippi River to U.S. navigation, granting Americans the right of deposit at New Orleans, and fixing the boundaries of Louisiana and east and west Florida.

Pindar (518-438 B.C.), ancient Greek lyric poet, inventor of the Pindaric ode, a poetic form in which complex rhythms in a series of stanzas hailed the victors in national athletic contests such as the Olympics. His odes were actually sung by a choir. The Pindaric ode influenced later English poetic forms developed by poets such as John Dryden and Thomas Gray.

Pine, common name for the evergreen conifer trees of the family Pinaceae. Pines have needlelike leaves and reproduce through wind-dispersed seeds contained in pine cones. These trees are found in many places in the Northern Hemisphere. They are commercially valuable for their timber (used in the making of furniture, cabinetry, and paper pulp) and their resin (used in the making of paint, soap, and turpentine). Some western pines, such as the *Pinus Ponderosa,* grow as tall as 130 ft (40 m). Some pine cones, such as those of the Sugar pine, can be as long as 30 in (76 cm). One species, the Bristlecone pine, live over 4,000 years. Existing bristlecones are some of the oldest living things on earth.

Pineal gland, pea-sized glandlike structure situated over the brain stem that appears to be a vestigial remnant of a functioning endocrine gland in other animals. It has no known function in humans, although Réné Descartes thought it to be the seat of the soul. It has a role in pigmentation in some species; calcium deposition in the pineal makes it a useful marker of midline in skull X-rays.

Pineapple, short-stemmed plant (*Ananas comosus*) with pointed, spiny leaves. At the tip there is a dense head of flowers that form a single compound fruit, the sweet, juicy pineapple Columbus found in the West Indies. Pineapples were transported from mainland South America to European colonies in Africa and Asia. The British developed new varieties in greenhouses. Hawaii's pineapples, now 75% of the world's crop, came from England via Australia.

Pinero, Sir Arthur Wing (1855-1934), British playwright known both for his farces and for his plays based on social realism. *Dandy Dick* (1887) is an example of the former, while *The Second Mrs. Tanqueray* is an instance of the latter.

Pine siskin, North American bird (*Spinus pinus*) of the finch family, measuring about 5 in (13 cm) in length. It summers in northern regions and winters as far south as Mexico. Yellow wing and tail markings stand out from the gray to brown colored bird when it is in flight.

Pink, common name for various flowering plants in the family Caryophyllaceae. These flowers bloom from white to pink to purple. They are appreciated for their scent. Among them are the carnation *(Dianthus caryophyllus),* the common pink *(D. plumarius),* and sweet William *(D. barbatus).*

Pink bollworm, small, dark-brown moth *(Pectinophora gossypiella)* of the gelechiid moth family. The larvae dig into cotton plants, on which they feed, destroying the plants. The adult develops within a cocoon inside or near the cotton plant. Introduced into the Americas at the beginning of the 20th century, the pink bollworm has caused serious problems for farmers.

Pinkerton, Allan (1819-84), Scottish-born U.S. founder of a pioneer detective agency.

He organized a Civil War espionage network that became the Federal Secret Service. "Pinkerton Men" broke up the Molly Maguires, and they were used to break the Homestead Strike in 1890.

Pink-eye *see:* Conjunctivitis.

Pinochet Ugarte, Augusto (1915-), president of Chile (1973-88). A right-wing general, he led a bloody coup overthrowing Marxist president Salvador Allende (1973). His authoritarian regime was affirmed by a plebiscite in 1980, but he was ousted (1988) because of his government's economic incompetence despite increasingly repressive measures.
See also: Chile.

Pinochle, card game played with a 48-card deck containing 2 each of the cards 9, 10, jack, queen, king, and ace in each of the 4 suits. In the most popular version of the game, 3 players engage in a series of bids before playing the hand. Other versions of the game—developed in the United States in the 19th century—depend upon different methods of gaining points.

Piñon, small, low-growing nut pines (genus *Pinus*) of the southwestern United States and northern Mexico. The 4 main species are noted for the edible seeds—called pine nuts—found in their cones.

Pinta *see:* Columbus, Christopher.

Pintail, duck (*Anas acuta*) of the family Anatidae. Living in fresh waters throughout the Northern Hemisphere, it is so named because of its long, pointed tail. It has a brown head and neck, and a white breast that continues into a white line on each side of the neck. The rest of the plumage on the male is predominantly gray, whereas that of the female is brown.

Pinter, Harold (1930-), English dramatist and stage director. His "comedies of menace" have intricate and oblique human relationships, ambiguous and deceptively casual dialogue, and a fine balance of humor and tension. Notable are *The Caretaker* (1960), *The Homecoming* (1965), and *No Man's Land* (1974). His successful screenplays include *The Servant* (1963) and *The French Lieutenant's Woman* (1981).

Pinworm, parasitic nematode worm (family Oxyuridae) that infests the intestines of vertebrates. An infestation by *Enterobius vermicularis* in humans is characterized by perianal itching. The pinworm is the most common parasite infecting children in temperate climates. The parasitic relationship is seldom harmful, and treatment is usually not indicated. However, pyrantel pamoate will eradicate pinworms in about 90% of cases.

Pinzón, family of 3 Spanish brothers, navigators who took part with Columbus in discovering America. **Martín Alonso** (1440?-93) commanded the *Pinta*; he left Columbus after reaching Cuba and unsuccessfully tried to reach Spain first. **Francisco Martín** (c.1441-93?) served under his brother on the Pinta. **Vicente Yáñez** (c.1460-1524?) commanded the *Niña* and stayed with Columbus; he went on to discover Brazil (1500) and to explore the coasts of Central and northern South America.
See also: Columbus.

Pion *see:* Meson.

Pioneer life in America, way of life characteristic of the people who first settled the western reaches of the continental United States. Pioneer life in America has two aspects. It is the story of migration and settlement. It is also an important part of American identity, one of the fundamental images Americans have of themselves, and an important part of the development of the country's values and customs.

In one sense, the pioneering life was characteristic of America from the beginning. The country's original settlers faced the same challenges, risks, and opportunities the pioneers later faced. But there are at least two important differences. America's original settlers were colonists and, to one degree or another, most came to America seeking refuge from Europe. By contrast, the pioneers were Americans or inspired by the optimism of a new nation. They were taking possession of a continent driven by the desire to own their own land, to make real the American promises of individual liberty and unlimited opportunity.

Pioneer life developed in two great migrations between 1760 and 1850. The first extended American settlement to the Mississippi Valley. It lasted from the late 1700s to the early 1800s and took in areas of what are now the states of Kentucky, Tennessee, Ohio, and Illinois. The second migration, which continued into the 1850s, settled California, the Northwest, the Southwest and, eventually, the Great Plains. These migrations coincided with and were often triggered by political events, among them, the Louisiana Purchase, the Mexican-American War, and the acquisition of Oregon. The Gold Rush of 1848 was a powerful motivating force in the settlement of California. Settlement was also encouraged by generous federal land grant programs.

The focus of the first migration was the land beyond the Appalachian Mountains. The Appalachian barrier was breached by settlers using the Cumberland Gap and by trappers and frontiersmen who opened the Wilderness Road. In New York State, settlers followed the Mohawk Trail west and, as settlement progressed, steamboats carried settlers on the Ohio and Mississippi rivers beginning in 1811. The Erie Canal, opened in 1825, also made it easier for settlers to get to new lands.

The usual patterns of these migrations began with the trailblazing of frontiersmen, fur trappers, or explorers, men like Daniel Boone or Lewis and Clark. They were followed by the first wave of settlers, principally small farmers, who cleared the land.

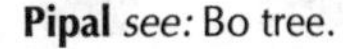

These settlers would often move on to virgin land and their places were taken by a second wave of settlers who established more permanent communities and, eventually, towns. The process was completed when towns were connected by roads, the post, and, above all, by the railroads. Upon arrival in a particular area, settlers might take possession of the land by purchase from a private company or from a federal land agent, or else by squatting.

The second great migration was undertaken by wagon trains called prairie schooners, larger versions of the older Conestoga wagons. A wagon train heading west would start in the spring in time to pass the Rocky Mountains before winter set in. Several known trails were followed, among them the Oregon Trail across the Great Plains, the South Pass across the Rockies to California, the Santa Fe Trail to the Southwest, and the Old Spanish Trail to Los Angeles. It was a difficult and dangerous journey, hard on animals and people alike. Indians were a constant threat, especially as settlers began to clear and farm the Great Plains.

Both migrations were marked by frequent bloody episodes between settlers and Native Americans and by warfare that eventually decimated the latter. Blacks also participated in the settlement of the west. Freed or escaped slaves helped settle the Northwest Territories comprising the states of Ohio, Illinois, Michigan, Wisconsin, parts of Minnesota, and later Oregon. Slavery was forbidden in the Northwest Territory and black pioneers had an opportunity to begin new lives in those frontier regions.

The pioneers lived a rough, dangerous, and demanding life. The men had to be farmers, hunters, trappers, skilled carpenters, and skillful with weapons, especially the rifle. The women did much heavy farm work, raised and cared for the children, cooked, spun yarn, and wove cloth. There were no doctors and medical care had to be improvised. A serious illness or injury often meant death and epidemics were devastating. The pioneer diet was simple, consisting primarily of corn and game. Corn was preferred because it could be easily preserved and salt was used to preserve meat. Eventually, as conditions improved, so did diet, clothing, and the availability of other essentials. Pioneers built their own homes (often helping one another in the hard work), grew and hunted their own food, made their own yarn and cloth, bullets, candles, medicines, shoes, and other necessities. Their way of life fostered values of independence and self-reliance that were reinforced by religion and a strong sense of community.

The struggles, hardships, and experiences of the first settlers continued to influence the later community. Values and attitudes were transmitted through stories that have become an essential part of American self awareness from the Leatherstocking novels of James Fennimore Cooper to the movies of John Ford.

Pipal *see:* Bo tree.

Harold Pinter

Pipe, musical instrument consisting of a tube of wood or metal, that produces sounds when air is blown through it. Holes along the pipe's length are covered and uncovered by fingers to produce a variety of notes. The length of the pipe, as well as whether it is stopped or open at one end, also affects the sounds it creates. The pipe was one of the first musical instruments. Other wind instruments—such as the flute, oboe, clarinet, trumpet, and pipe organ—developed from it.

Pipe, long hollow tube that transports gas, steam, or liquids. Networks of pipes distribute materials such as water and natural gas in residential communities. They also take away waste, such as sewage. Pipes also have many industrial functions. They carry oil from wells to and through refineries, and in factories they move materials through the manufacturing process. Pipes may be made of metal, wood, concrete, or plastic. The diameter and the material varies according to the purpose.

Pipe, hollow stem connected to a small bowl used for smoking tobacco. Tobacco is placed in the bowl and ignited, and its smoke is drawn into the mouth through the stem. Pipes have been used in many cultures for thousands of years. They are often named for the material used to create the bowl; a corncob pipe, for instance, has a bowl made of a corncob. Other kinds of pipes include meerschaum (a clay-like material), briarwood, and porcelain.

Pipefish, eellike fish with tubular mouth of the family Syngnathidae. They live in tropical seas and estuaries, feeding on minute plankton. The U.S. species can change color to match their backgrounds and swim vertically so that they look like waving weeds. Like the related sea horses, the male carries the eggs and babies.

Pipeline, tube for conveying fluids—liquids, gases, or slurries. Pipes vary in diameter considerably, according to the flow rate required and the pressure gradient. Materials used include steel, cast iron, other metals, reinforced concrete, fired clay, plastic, bitumenized-fiber cylinders, and wood. They are often coated inside and out with bitumen or concrete to prevent corrosion. Concrete, plastic, and steel pipes can now be made and laid in 1 continuous process, but most pipes still need to be joined by means of welding, screw joints, clamped flange joints, couplings, or bell-and-spigot joints caulked with lead or cement. Pipelines, consisting of long lengths of pipe with valves and pumps at regular intervals (about 60 mi/98 km for oil pipelines), are used chiefly for transporting water, sewage, chemicals, foodstuffs, crude oils, and natural gas.

Piranhas

Pipit, small songbird (family Motacillidae) of open country that looks and sings rather like a lark. Pipits nest under clumps of vegetation. They are found all over the world, including the subantarctic island of South Georgia. The water pipet and Sprague's pipit are the only North American species.

Piraeus (pop. 196,400), city in Greece. It is the port for Athens and the largest Greek port, handling most of Greece's importing and exporting. The port is very modern, and is linked by railway and highway to Athens. Piraeus is also a manufacturing center, producing cloth, leather-goods, soaps, metals, and alcohol. Athenians created a port in Piræus in the 5th century B.C. The arrangement of streets in modern Piræus is based on a city plan developed in 460 B.C. Romans destroyed Piræus in 86 B.C. Piræus' harbors remained unused until A.D. 1834, when the Greeks rebuilt it. It has been an important port ever since. Artifacts from early Greek and Roman times are on display in the Archeological Museum in Piræus.
See also: Greece.

Pirandello, Luigi (1867-1936), Italian dramatist and author, winner of the 1934 Nobel Prize for literature. He is noted for his grimly humorous treatment of psychological themes and of the reality of art compared with "real" life, as in his best-known play, *Six Characters in Search of an Author* (1921).

Piranesi, Giovanni Battista (1720-78), Italian etcher, draftsperson, and architect, known for his prints of old and contemporary Roman buildings, *Views of Rome* (begun 1748), and for a series of fantastic *Imaginary Prisons* (c.1745). They are notable for their grandeur and lighting contrasts.

Piranha, or caribe, small, extremely ferocious, shoaling freshwater fish (family Characidae) of South America. The jaws are short but powerful, armed with sharp cutting teeth. They quickly strip the flesh from other fish and mammals and have been known to attack humans.

Pirate, person who robs ships at sea. Pirates were active in the sea routes of trading ships. They also attacked and plundered coastal villages. Although piracy still occurs in such waters as the South China Sea and the Gulf of Thailand, it no longer occurs on the scale it once did. In Roman times, pirates along the Eastern Mediterranean Sea robbed ships from importing goods into Rome. From the 1500s through the 1700s, pirates from the Barbary Coast of northern Africa roamed the Mediterranean to plunder European ships. During that same period, English, Dutch, and French pirates sailed the Caribbean to rob Spanish ships carrying goods from the Spanish-controlled West Indies islands and South America. During the 1700 and 1800s pirates attacked ships carrying cargo between North America and Europe. By the mid-1800s, the navies of various countries successfully rid the sea of pirate ships.

Pirates from the Barbary Coast of Northern Africa

Pisa (pop. 104,300), historic city in the northwestern region of central Italy, on the Arno River in Tuscany. Galilei Galileo was born at Pisa. The city is famous for its marble campanile (the Leaning Tower) and rich in architecture and art.
See also: Leaning Tower of Pisa.

Pisa, Council of (1409), uncanonical Roman Catholic Ecumenical Council of 500 prelates and delegates from throughout Europe that met to try to heal the Great Schism. It deposed the rival popes of Rome and Avignon and elected a 3rd pope, Alexander V. This, however, merely created 3 separate parties.

Pisa, Leaning Tower of *see:* Leaning Tower of Pisa.

Pisano, Nicola (1210?-1278), Italian sculptor. Inspired by ancient Roman sculpture, he worked in a classical style that anticipates the Renaissance movement. The reliefs he created for the six-sided baptistry in Pisa showing events in Christ's life was his first masterpiece. Other important works include the eight-sided pulpit for the Cathedral of Siena and the fountain at Perugia. His son, Giovanni, helped him de-

sign and execute some of his works. Pisano lived in Pisa.
See also: Relief.

Pisistratus, or Peisistratus (600-527 B.C.), tyrant of Athens, whose benign rule and fostering of commerce and the arts made Athens the foremost city in Greece. In 560 B.C. he seized power in a popular coup d'état. Aristocrats, having returned from exile, ousted him in 552, but in 541 he established himself firmly. He enforced Solon's laws, promoted public works, and was succeeded by his sons.

Pissarro, Camille (1830-1903), French impressionist painter. Influenced by the Barbizon School at first, he was, with Cézanne, Monet, and Renoir, a founder of impressionism. His works, especially landscapes and street scenes, are noted for their freshness, vividness, and luminous color.

Pistachio nut (*Pistacia vera*), seed of the pistachio tree in the cashew family. Pistachio trees grow in western Asia, the Mediterranean, and southwestern U.S. The nut, which is about 1 in (2.5 cm) long, consists of a hard shell, smooth husk, and an edible green kernel. The kernel, which has a mild flavor, can be eaten whole. When ground, kernels are used to flavor foods; when pressed, they produce a cooking oil.

Piston, Walter (1894-1976), U.S. neoclassical composer, professor of music at Harvard (1926-60). His austere but dynamic music incorporates complex rhythms and harmonics in traditional forms. His *Symphony No. 7* (1961) won a Pulitzer Prize.
See also: Counterpoint.

Pit bull, any of several breeds or crossbreeds of dogs having a mixture of bulldog and terrier. The American pit bull terrier, bull terrier, bulldog, and Staffordshire bull terrier are breeds of pit bulls. They have strong muscular bodies, and are very courageous fighters. When trained properly, they are excellent guard dogs as well as obedient, affectionate companion dogs. However, pit bulls can become dangerous when their owners abuse them or train them to be aggressive. Then they become capable of attacking and even killing other dogs, as well as people. This has led some communities to enact laws regulating pit bulls to ensure that the dogs will not threaten public safety.

Pitcairn Island, British colony (2 sq mi/4 sq km) in the Pacific Ocean midway between New Zealand and Panama, famous as the uninhabited island settled by *Bounty* mutineers and Tahitian women (1790). Its present English-speaking islanders are descended from them.

Pitch, frequency of the vibrations constituting a sound. The frequency associated with tones of the musical scale has varied over the years. The present international standard sets Concert A (A above middle C) at 440 cycles per sec.
See also: Music; Vibration.

Pitchblende, or uraninite, brown, black, or greenish radioactive mineral, the most important source of uranium, radium, and polonium. The composition varies between UO_2 and $UO_{2.6}$; thorium, radium, polonium, lead, and helium are also present. Principal deposits are in Zaire and Czechoslovakia, at Great Bear Lake in Canada, and in the U.S. Mountain States.

Pitcher, Molly (Mary Ludwig McCauley; 1754-1832), heroine of the American Revolution. She carried water for the Continental soldiers during the battle of Monmouth, hence her nickname. According to legend, she also took over her husband's rifle when he collapsed.
See also: Revolutionary War in America.

Pitcher plant, name given to several insect-eating plants of 3 different families (North American, Old World, and Australian) in which the leaves form a pot-shaped trap for insects. Unwary insects make their way into the pitcher and are drowned in the water that collects there. Among the pitcher plant's many local names are huntsman's-cup and sidesaddle flower.

Pitt, name of 2 English statesmen. **William, 1st Earl of Chatham** (1708-78), known as Pitt the Elder and a noted orator, was war minister during the Seven Years' War (1756-63). Through defeating the French, by 1761 he had gained imperial supremacy for Britain in Europe, Canada, and India, and made the British navy a formidable force. Out of office after 1768, he opposed taxing American colonists and defended their rights, but was against granting them independence. His second son, **William** (1759-1806), known as **Pitt the Younger**, at 24 became Britain's youngest prime minister. He dominated British politics until his death. From 1784, supported by a weakened George III, Pitt's ministry strengthened national finances and the government's power in India, but agitation by radicals at home forced him to suppress some civil rights (1794) and shelve parliamentary reforms. Continental wars waged, and lost (1793-1805), by coalitions of Britain's allies against Napoleon I required Pitt's financial support, which he raised through higher taxes. To quell continuing Irish rebellions, Pitt proposed a parliamentary union with England and Catholic Emancipation (1798), but King George refused it. Pitt resigned in 1801, then returned to office in 1804 when Napoleon threatened to invade England—prevented, evidently, by Britain's sea victory at Trafalgar in 1805. But Napoleon's defeat of Britain's allies at Austerlitz later that year proved a death blow to Pitt politically.
See also: United Kingdom.

Pitti Palace, palace in Florence, Italy. Currently, it is an art museum housing an extensive collection of Renaissance art. It was originally built for the wealthy merchant Luca Pitti and later became the home of several Italian kings. The structure was begun in 1458, and major expansions were added subsequently. As the largest palace in Florence, it is impressive for its size and for the beautiful gardens (Boboli Gardens) located behind it.

Pittsburgh (pop. 2,056,705), steel-producing city in southwestern Pennsylvania, seat of Allegheny County, and the state's 2nd-largest city. Settled in 1758 as Fort Pitt and incorporated as a city in 1816, it now occupies over 55 sq mi (142 sq km) around its business center, the Golden Triangle, where the Allegheny and Monongahela rivers meet to form the Ohio. The city's economic wealth is based on steel mills, coke from Allegheny coal, pig iron, glass, and various manufactured products. The University of Pittsburgh and the Carnegie Institute are among its educational institutions.
See also: Pennsylvania.

Pituitary gland, major endocrine gland, situated just below the brain, under the control of the adjacent hypothalamus and in its turn controlling other endocrine glands. The posterior pituitary is a direct extension of certain cells in the hypothalamus and secretes vasopressin and oxytocin into the bloodstream. The anterior pituitary develops separately and consists of several cell types that secrete different hormones, including growth hormone, follicle-stimulating hormone, luteinizing hormone, prolactin, thyrotrophic hormone (which stimulates thyroid gland), and adrenocorticotrophic hormone (ACTH). Feedback from organs occurs at both the hypothalamic and pituitary levels. Pituitary tumors or loss of blood supply may cause loss of function; however, some tumors may be functional and produce syndromes like gigantism or acromegaly (due to growth hormone imbalance).
See also: Human body; Hypothalamus.

Pit viper, predominantly New World venomous snake (family Crotalidae). Pit vipers have a pit on each side of the head, each containing a temperature-sensitive organ that can detect the minute changes in temperature caused by the presence of other animals, enabling the snake to detect and strike at its prey. Pit vipers have fangs that fold back when not in use. Most species give birth to live young. Pit vipers include the copperhead, water moccasin, fer-de-lance, and rattlesnake.

Pius, name of 12 popes. Saint **Pius V** (Michele Ghislieri; 1504-72), an Italian, was elected in 1566. With some severity he restored a degree of discipline and morality to the papacy in the face of the Protestant challenge and organized the Spanish-Venetian expedition that defeated the Turks at Lepanto in 1571. **Pius VII** (Gregorio Luigi Barnaba Chiaramonti; 1740-1823), an Italian, was elected in 1800. Under an 1801 concordat French troops were withdrawn, but the Papal States were later annexed by Napoleon I, whom Pius had consecrated emperor in 1804. **Pius IX** (Giovanni Maria Mastai-Ferretti; 1792-1878), an Italian, began the longest papal

Pius IX

reign, in 1846, with liberal reforms but became an extreme reactionary in both politics and dogma after the revolution of 1848. The Immaculate Conception became an article of dogma (1854), and papal infallibility was proclaimed in 1870 by the 1st Vatican Council. In 1871 the new kingdom of Italy passed the Law of Guaranties, defining relations between the state and the papacy, but Pius refused to accept the position. **Saint Pius X** (Giuseppe Melchiorre Sarto; 1835-1914), an Italian, was elected in 1903. He condemned modernism in the church. **Pius XI** (Ambrogio Damiano Achille Ratti; 1857-1939), an Italian, was elected in 1922. He concluded the Lateran Treaty (1929) with the Italian state and issued encyclicals condemning communism, fascism, and racism. **Pius XII** (Eugenio Pacelli; 1876-1958), a Roman, was elected in 1939. He was an active diplomat in a difficult period and undertook a considerable amount of humanitarian work during World War II, although he was criticized for refusing to condemn Nazi policy toward the Jews. His encyclical *Mediator Dei* led to changes in the Masses.

Pizarro, Francisco (c.1474-1541), Spanish conquistador who destroyed the Inca empire in the course of his conquest of Peru. He was with Vasco de Balboa when he discovered the Pacific Ocean (1513). In 1524 and 1526-7, Pizarro attempted, with Diego de Almagro and Fernando de Luque, to conquer Peru. In 1531, with royal assent, he began a new campaign and found Peru in an unsettled state under the Inca emperor Atahualpa. At Cajamarca in the Andes, Pizarro's small band, at first pretending friendship, kidnapped Atahualpa and massacred his unarmed followers. Pizarro, a vicious and greedy man, forced the emperor to pay a massive ransom, then executed him. Turning on Almagro, Pizarro cheated him and eventually had him killed; Almagro's followers assassinated Pizarro.
See also: Conquistadors.

PKU *see:* Phenylketonuria.

Placebo, tablet, syrup, or other form of seeming medication that is inactive, prescribed in lieu of active preparations. Placebos are prescribed for psychological purposes and are used as controls in experimental studies of drug effectiveness.

Placenta, specialized structure derived from the uterus lining and part of the embryo after implantation. It separates and yet ensures a close and extensive contact between the maternal (uterine) and fetal (umbilical) blood circulations. This allows nutrients and oxygen to pass from the mother to the fetus, and waste products to pass in the reverse direction. Gonadotropins produced by the placenta prepare the maternal body for delivery and the breasts for lactation. The placenta is delivered after the child at birth (the afterbirth) by separation of the blood-vessel layers.
See also: Reproduction.

Max Planck

Placentia (pop. 2,000), town in southeastern Newfoundland, Canada. Founded in 1662 by the French who used it as headquarters for their troops fighting against the British, it became a British possession in 1713. Its old ruins and proximity to salmon fishing waters make it a popular tourist area.
See also: Newfoundland.

Plagiarism, the act of copying another's work (ideas, writings, or other creative work) and presenting it as one's own. As it is in essence stealing, plagiarism is unethical. Copyright laws make plagiarism a punishable crime in many countries. However, the borrowing of ideas or thoughts and expressing them in one's own words is not considered plagiarism.
See also: Copyright.

Plain, expanse of nearly level land, usually surrounded by higher land forms. About half of the world's land area is made up of plains, and they are found on ocean and sea floors as well. On land, there are three major kinds of plains: coastal, inland, and flood. Coastal plains stretch along seacoasts and often slope from sealevel to higher land. Inland plains are found in the interior of continents. Flood plains occur along rivers and are formed by materials (silt, sand, mud) deposited when the rivers overflow during floods. Depending on the climate, plains can be very fertile areas conducive to farming. A large percentage of the world's population lives on plains because they are food-producing, easy to build on, and to travel across.

Planarian, type of flatworm (turbellarian) having a flat, long body and broad head. Planarians are found in fresh or salt water, as well as in moist earth. Depending on the species, they are white, gray, brown, or black, and range in size from $^1/_4$ in to $1^1/_2$ in (7 mm to 35 mm) long. Some planarians living in tropical soil may grow as long as 2 ft (60 cm). Planarians are meat eating, and feed on small animals and dead bodies of larger animals. They can reproduce by laying eggs or by dividing their bodies into parts, each part then becoming a complete body.

Planck, Max Karl Ernst Ludwig (1858-1947), German physicist whose quantum theory, with Albert Einstein's theory of relativity, ushered physics into the modern era. Initially influenced by Rudolf Clausius, he made fundamental researches in thermodynamics before turning to investigate blackbody radiation. To describe the electromagnetic radiation emitted from a blackbody, he evolved the Planck radiation formula, which implied that energy, like matter, can exist only as quanta (discrete amounts).
Planck himself was unconvinced of this, even after Einstein had applied the theory to the photoelectric effect and Bohr in his model of the atom, but Planck received the 1918 Nobel Prize for physics for his achievement.
See also: Quantum mechanics; Radiation.

Plane, in mathematics, surface having only length and breadth, any 2 points of which can be joined by a straight line composed entirely of points also in the plane. A plane may be determined by 2 intersecting or parallel lines, by a line and a point that does not lie on the line, or by 3 points that do not lie in a straight line. The intersection of 2 planes is a straight line; the intersection of a plane and a line in a different plane is a point. An infinite number of planes may pass through a single point or line. A plane is parallel to another plane if all perpendiculars drawn between them are of equal length.

Planet, in the solar system, 1 of the 9 major celestial bodies (Mercury, Venus, Earth, Mars, Jupiter, Saturn, Uranus, Neptune, and Pluto) orbiting the sun; by extension, a similar body circling any other star. In 1963 it was discovered that Barnard's Star has at least 1 companion about 1.5 times the size of Jupiter, and in 1983 scientists detected possible evidence of an evolving planetary system around the star Vega.
See also: Solar system.

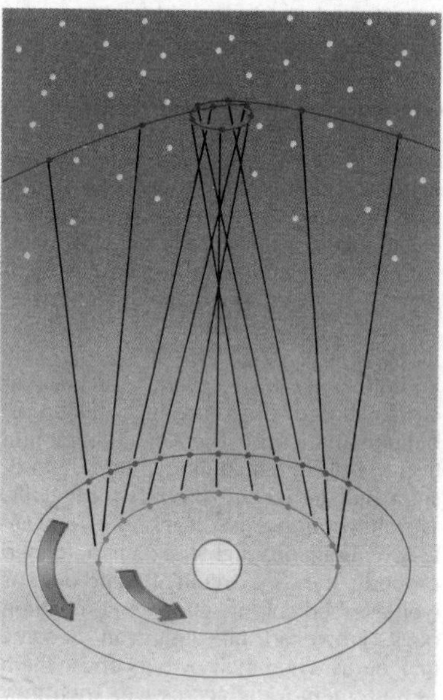

The celestial motion of a planet is seen from earth as an apparent movement, depending on the direction in which the planet moves in relation to the movement and position of the earth. Thus the planet may at times appear to stand still, or to move "backward".

Planetarium, optical device representing the relative positions and motions of celestial objects on the interior of a hemispherical dome. Of great assistance to students of astronomy and celestial navigation, planetariums also attract large public audiences. The 1st modern planetarium, built in 1923 by the firm of Carl Zeiss, is still in use at the Deutsches Museum, Munich, Germany.

Planetoid *see:* Asteroid.

Plane tree *see:* Sycamore.

Plankton, microscopic marine animals and plants. They drift under the influence of ocean currents and are vitally important links in the marine food chain. A major part of plankton comprises minute plants (phytoplankton), mainly algae but including dinoflagellates and diatoms. Phytoplankton may be so numerous as to color the water and cause it to have a "bloom." They are eaten by various animals (called zooplankton) that are in turn an important food for large animals, such as whales, and countless fishes. Phytoplankton is confined to the upper layers of the sea, where light can reach, but zooplankton has been found at great depths.

Planned Parenthood Federation of America, organization that promotes voluntary family planning in the United States and developing countries. Through a network of clinics staffed by some 27,000 volunteers, it provides counseling and distributes information on birth control and other health issues. Abortions are performed at some clinics. Founded in 1916 by Margaret Sanger, a U.S. nurse, Planned Parenthood promotes government legislation supporting family planning and reproductive rights for women. It is a member organization of the International Planned Parenthood Federation, headquartered in London.

Plant, living organism belonging to the plant kingdom (Planta). Green plants are unique in being able to synthesize their own organic molecules from carbon dioxide and water, using light-energy, by the process known as photosynthesis. Mineral nutrients are absorbed from the environment. Plants are the primary source of food for all other living organisms.

The possession of chlorophyll, the green photosynthetic pigment, is probably the most important distinction between plants and animals. Plants are generally stationary and have no nervous system, and the cell wall generally contains large amounts of cellulose. Some insectivorous plants obtain their food by trapping insects.

The higher plants (gymnosperms and angiosperms) are much the same in their basic anatomy and morphology. In a typical angiosperm, 4 main regions can be recognized: root, stem, leaf, and flower. Each region has one or more basic functions.

Plants cells are not all alike, and each one is adapted to do a certain job, but all are derived from a basic pattern. This basic plant cell tends to be rectangular and has a tough wall of cellulose, which gives it its shape. The cell membrane is inside the wall. Inside the membrane is the protoplasm, which contains the nucleus and chloroplasts and many other microscopic structures. In the center of the protoplasm there is a large sap-filled vacuole that maintains the cell's shape and plays an important part in the working of the whole plant. Both sexual and asexual reproduction are widespread throughout the plant kingdom. Many plants are capable of both forms, and in some cases the life cycle of the plant may involve the two different forms.

Plantagenet, name given to the branch of the Angevin dynasty descended from Geoffrey Plantagenet that ruled England from 1154 to 1485. From Henry II until the deposition of Richard II in 1399 the succession was direct. Thereafter, the crown passed to other branches of the family until the defeat of the Yorkist Plantagenet, Richard III, at the hands of Henry Tudor (Henry VII), who had remote Plantagenet connections.
See also: United Kingdom.

Plantain, group of herbs in the family *Plantaginaceae*. Growing close to the ground, they have spikes growing out of a circular cluster of leaves. Many plantains are weeds and are undesired by gardeners. Some plantain plants, however, are grown for their medicinal value. Plantain is also the name of a tropical plant related to the banana. Hard and full of starch, this plantain is eaten cooked and is a major food in some tropical regions.

Plantain lily *see:* Day lily.

Plantation, large farm on which a crop is planted, tended, and harvested by workers who live there. Plantations are most often in tropical or semitropical regions. Crops raised on plantations include cotton, tobacco, coffee, cocoa, tea, rubber, sugarcane and tropical fruits. Most plantations specialize in one product. Many plantations developed by Europeans who colonized regions throughout the world, including America, were once worked by slaves and by servants who were indebted to the plantation owner.

After slavery was abolished, plantations hired laborers who were paid very little or else received a share of the crop for their work. In modern times, the development of agricultural techniques has led many plantations to use more farm machinery and fewer workers.

Planting *see:* Agriculture.

Plant louse *see:* Aphid.

Plasma, in physics, almost completely ionized gas containing equal numbers of free electrons and positive ions. Stars and interstellar gas consist of plasma. Unlike un-ionized gas, plasma conducts electricity and is affected magnetically. Plasma may be a 4th state of matter (besides gases, liquids, and solids). Because the temperature of a plasma is theoretically high enough to support a controlled nuclear fusion reaction, plasmas are being widely studied as a means to contain such a reaction to create energy. Plasmas are formed by heating low-pressure gases until the atoms have sufficient energy to ionize each other. Unless the plasma can be successfully contained by electric or magnetic fields, rapid cooling and recombination occur.
See also: Physics.

Plasma, in biology, fluid portion of the blood, including fibrinogen; distinguished from serum, from which fibrinogen has been separated.
See also: Blood.

A flowering plant such as the wallflower is divided into a root (1) and stem (2). The root grows from its apex (11), which is protected by a root cap (10). Both main (9) and branch (8) roots are covered in root hairs (7) and are supplied with water-conducting xylem (13) and food-conducting phloem (12). These conducting tissues form a ring of bundles just below ground level. This ring divides the stem into cortex (14) and pith (15). Leaves and axillary buds (5) are found at nodes (6). Axillary buds produce branch stems (16) if the terminal bud (18) is damaged. The flower (17) is the reproductive structure, which, when fertilized, produces a fruit (3) containing seeds (4).

Plaster, mixture of water, sand, and lime used to coat walls and ceilings. Applied as a wet paste, it hardens as it dries. Plaster can be applied to various bases, such as brick, stone, or thin strips of wood or metal that are laid out parallel. It creates an airtight and durable finished surface. Several coats of plaster are usually necessary to build up the surface to the desired thickness. Materials such as hair or fiber can be added to plaster to make it stronger. Other kinds of materials can be added to make it fire resistant or sound absorbing.

Plastic, material that can be molded (at least in production) into desired shapes. A few natural plastics are known, e.g., bitumen, resins, and rubber, but almost all are synthetic, made mainly from petrochemicals. They have a vast range of useful properties, including hardness, elasticity, transparency, toughness, low density, insulating ability, inertness, and corrosion resistance. Plastics are high polymers with carbon skeletons, each molecule being made up of thousands or even millions of atoms. Thermoplastics soften or melt reversibly on heating; they include celluloid or other cellulose plastics, Lucite, nylon, polyethylene, styrene polymers, vinyl polymers, polyformaldehyde, and polycarbonates. Thermosetting plastics, although moldable when produced as simple polymers, are converted by heat and pressure, and sometimes by an admixed hardener, to a cross-linked, infusible form. These include Bakelite and other phenol resins, epoxy resins, polyesters, silicones, urea-formaldehyde and melamineformaldehyde resins, and some polyurethanes.

Centrifuges are widely used in obtaining plasma.

Plastic explosive, puttylike, flexible explosive. Because it can be molded into any shape and is weather resistant, it can be placed and hidden easily and is difficult to detect. Developed by the U.S. Army during World War II, it has since become a powerful weapon often used by political terrorists.
See also: Explosive.

Plastic surgery, branch of surgery devoted to reconstruction or repair of deformity, surgical defect, or the results of injury. Using bone, cartilage, tendon, and skin from other parts of the body, or artificial substitutes, the surgeon can restore function and appearance in many cases. In skin grafting, the most common procedure, a piece of skin is cut, usually from the thigh, and stitched to the damaged area. Bone and cartilage (usually from the ribs or hips), or sometimes plastic, are used in cosmetic remodeling and facial reconstruction after injury. Congenital defects such as harelip and cleft palate can be treated in infancy. "Face lifting," the cosmetic removal of excess fat and tightening of the skin, is a delicate and often unsuccessful operation, carrying the added risk of infection.
See also: Skin grafting.

Plateau, high plain. A plateau is formed by the erosion of lands bordering it, a build-up of recurrent lava flows, or the earth's upward movements. Heights of plateaus vary. Lower altitude plateaus, such as some in Australia and the U.S., can be valuable to people because they are often excellent grazing lands for livestock. High altitude plateaus, such as those in the Himalayas, have climates not suitable for human habitation.
See also: Plain.

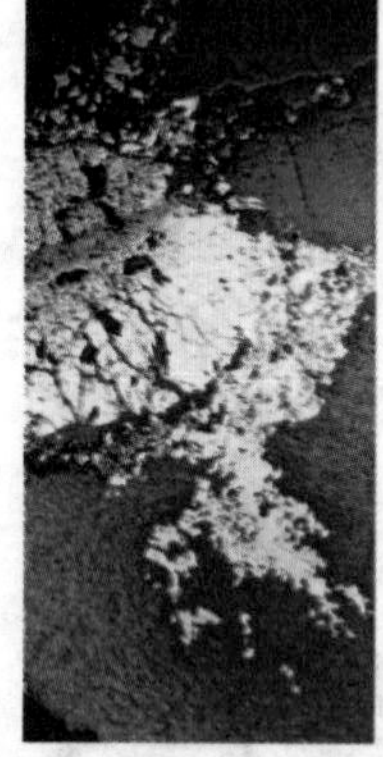
Platinum ore

Plate tectonics *see:* Tectonics; Volcano.

Platform tennis, game resembling tennis in which players use paddles to hit a sponge rubber ball back and forth over a net. It is played on an outdoor elevated court 44 ft (13 m) long and 20 ft (6 m) wide surrounded by a wire fence 12 ft (3.7 m) high. Usually two pairs of players play against each other. In platform tennis, a player has one serve per point, and may return balls that have bounced off the fence. Created in 1928, platform tennis was devised so that it could be played in the winter. The court allows for the easy removal of snow.

Plath, Sylvia (1932-63), U.S. poet whose taut, melodic, highly imagistic works explore the nature of womanhood and her fixation with death. *Ariel* (1965), published after Plath's suicide, won her international acclaim as a major U.S. "confessional" poet. Her other works include *The Bell Jar* (1963), a semiautobiographical novel about a young woman's emotional breakdown, and *Complete Poems* (1981), edited by her husband, Ted Hughes.

Platinum, chemical element, symbol Pt; for physical constants see Periodic Table. Platinum was discovered by Julius Scaliger in 1557. It is a metallic element occurring native, and as the mineral sperrylite, an important source of the element. Platinum is a silver-white, malleable, ductile metal. The element does not oxidize in air at any temperature, but reacts with halogens, cyanides, sulfur, and caustic alkalis. The metal absorbs large volumes of hydrogen at ordinary temperatures. It is used in resistance wires for constructing high-temperature electric furnaces. In the finely divided state the metal is used as a catalyst. Platinum and its compounds are used in plating, jewelry, wire, corrosion-resistant apparatus, magnetic alloys, electrical contacts, and dentistry.

Bust of Plato

Plato, Greek philosopher (c.427-347 B.C.). A pupil of Socrates, he founded (c.385 B.C.) the Academy, where Aristotle studied. His early dialogues present a portrait of Socrates as critical arguer, but in the great middle dialogues he develops his own doctrines—such as the theory of Forms (*Republic*), the immortality of the soul (*Phaedo*), knowledge as recollection of the Forms by the soul (*Meno*), virtue as knowledge (*Protagoras*)—and attacks hedonism and the idea that "might is right" (*Gorgias*). The *Symposium* and *Phaedrus* sublimate love into a beatific vision of the Forms of the Good and the Beautiful. The late dialogues (*Sophist, Theaetetus, Politicus, Philebus, Parmenides*) deal with problems of epistemology, ontology, and logic; the *Timaeus* contains cosmological speculation. In the *Republic* Plato posits abstract Forms as the supreme reality. The highest function of the human soul is to achieve the vision of the Form of the Good. Drawing an analogy between the soul and the state, he presents his ideal state ruled by philosophers, who correspond to the rational part of the soul. In the late *Laws* Plato develops in detail his ideas of the state. His idealist philosophy, his insistence on order and harmony, his moral fervor and asceticism, and his literary genius have made Plato a dominant figure in Western thought.
See also: Philosophy.

Platt Amendment, provision forced through Congress and into the Cuban constitution by Senator Orville Platt in 1901. Setting out conditions for U.S. intervention, it made Cuba virtually a U.S. protectorate. It was abrogated in 1934.
See also: Cuba, Republic of.

Platte River, river in Nebraska, U.S. It begins at North Platte, Nebraska, at the joining of the North Platte and South Platte rivers, flows 310 mi (500 km) east, and empties into the Missouri River at Plattsmouth. The Platte and its tributaries drain approximately 90,000 sq mi (233,000 sq km) of land. The river's abundant waters are used to irrigate farms, as well as to provide water for communities. It is too shallow to navigate, but the river's valley has been used as a transportation route for land travel since pioneer days.

Plattsburgh (pop. 21,057), largest city in northeastern N.Y. Located on Lake Champlain 22 mi (35 km) south of the Canadian border, it is named after Zephaniah Platt who founded it in 1784. During the War of 1812 it was the scene of a decisive battle between the British and Americans which resulted in U.S. victory. Plattsburgh's economy relies on its many industries, which include the manufacturing of wood and paper products, dairy products, and plastics. Plattsburgh was a village from 1785 to 1902, when it became a city.
See also: New York.

Platyhelminth *see:* Flatworm.

Platypus, or duck-billed platypus (*Ornithorhynchus anatinus*), amphibious monotreme (egg-laying mammal) found in Australia and Tasmania. The platypus has webbed feet and thick fur (equipping it for an aquatic life); a short, thick tail, and a flat, toothless, bill-like mouth used for taking insects and crustaceans off the surface of the water. Like echidnas, the other monotreme group, they retain many reptilian characteristics.

Platypus

Plautus (c.254-184 B.C.), Roman writer of comedies, 21 of which have survived. He based them on Greek New Comedy, especially Menander, but adapted them to Roman tastes and situations, and added his own brand of lively, bawdy humor. Popular in his time, he influenced William Shakespeare, Ben Jonson, and Molière, among others.

Play, in animals, a distinctive type of behavior of both adults and juveniles, of unknown function and involving the incomplete, ritualized expression of normal adult behavior patterns. Play occurs particularly in carnivores, primates, and certain birds.

Plea bargaining, agreement between the accused and the prosecutor under which the accused agrees to plead guilty to a lesser offense in order to receive a lighter sentence from the judge. Plea bargaining has been accepted by judges, prosecutors, and lawyers as necessary though undesirable, saving time and speeding up the work of overcrowded courts, but denying the accused a fair trial and not requiring the prosecutor to prove the accused's guilt beyond a reasonable doubt.

Plebeians, nonaristocratic classes in ancient Rome. In their continual rivalries with the ruling patrician aristocracy, they created their own assemblies and officers, and gained full political and civil rights by c.300 B.C.
See also: Rome, Ancient.

Plebiscite, in Roman history, law enacted by the plebeian *comitia*, or assembly of tribes. In modern times a plebiscite is a direct vote of a whole body of citizens on a specific issue.

Plecoptera, or stonefly, order of insects that lays eggs in water. When the young hatch, they live along the rocky edges of ponds, lakes, and streams. Although adults have wings, they are poor fliers and so tend to live on rocks near the water. Larvae and adults constitute a large percentage of the diet of freshwater fish.

Pledge of Allegiance, promise of loyalty to the United States. It is recited as follows: *I pledge allegiance to the flag of the United States of America and to the Republic for which it stands, one Nation under God, indivisible, with liberty and justice for all.* The pledge was originally written in 1892 by Francis Bellamy (1855-1931) for the National Public School Celebration of the 400th anniversary of Christopher Columbus's discovery of America. The pledge underwent several slight revisions in 1923, 1924, and 1954. In 1942, Congress officially sanctioned the recitation of the pledge to be a customary part of flag use.

Pleistocene Epoch, also known as the Great Ice Age, an earlier epoch of the Quaternary Period, stretching from between c.2 million and 3 million through 10,000 years ago.
See also: Ice Age.

Plekhanov, Georgi Valentinovich (1857-1918), Russian Marxist thinker. Always opposed to political terror, he at first supported V. I. Lenin, but after 1903 he espoused Menshevik views and, during World War I, supported military defense of Russia. After the successful Bolshevik-led revolution, he retired from public life.
See also: Marxism; Russian

Plesiosaur, huge, prehistoric marine reptile now extinct. It lived approximately 200 million years ago in what is currently Europe and North America. It resembled a large whale with paddlelike limbs.

Plessy v. Ferguson, U.S. Supreme Court ruling on segregation (1896) which held that the provision of "separate but equal" accommodations for blacks on railroad trains did not violate the "equal protection of the laws" clause of the 14th Amendment. This decision was reversed in 1954 when the Supreme Court unanimously ruled against segregation in the case of *Brown* v. *Board of Education.*
See also: Segregation.

Pleura, thin connective membrane that covers the inside of the thorax (chest cavity) and the lungs in mammals.

Pleurisy, inflammation of the pleura, the thin membrane covering the outer lung surface and the inner chest wall. It causes a characteristic chest pain, which is often worsened by deep breathing and coughing. It may be caused by infection (e.g., pneumonia, tuberculosis) or by tumors and inflammatory diseases.

Plexiglas, trademarked name of a type of plastic. Made from acrylic it is very clear and does not break easily. Because of its transparency and durability, Plexiglas is widely used instead of glass in such things as aircraft windows, picture frames, eyeglasses, appliances, and light fixtures.
See also: Plastic.

Plexus, network of stringlike structures, such as of nerves or blood vessels. A plexus can consist of interweaving fibers, such as the nerve fibers in a nerve plexus. In a blood carrying plexus, veins or arteries intertwine, opening into each other in many different places.
See also: Solar plexus.

Plimsoll mark, line or series of lines on the side of a seagoing ship indicating the safe loading limit. Samuel Plimsoll (1824-98) first secured the compulsory marking of British ships in 1876.

Pliny, name of 2 Roman authors. **Gaius Plinius Secundus**, or **Pliny the Elder** (C.A.D. 23-A.D. 79), is known for his *Natural History,* a vast compendium of ancient sciences, which though of little scientific merit was popular throughout antiquity and the Middle Ages. He died attempting to help the citizens of Pompeii in the eruption of Vesuvius. **Gaius Plinius Caecilius Secundus**, or **Pliny the Younger** (A.D. 61?-c.113), a nephew of Pliny the Elder, was a lawyer, politician, and administrator, primarily known for his elegant *Letters.*
See also: Rome, Ancient.

Pliocene, final period of the Tertiary, immediately preceding the Quaternary, c. 5-1.8 million years ago.

PLO *see:* Palestine Liberation Organization.

The asphalt deposits of La Brea Tar Pit, in southern California, have yielded fossils of numerous animals of the Pleistocene epoch, including the giant ground sloth, (3); a cottontail rabbit, (1); a weasel, (2); a lionlike cat, (4); the emperor mammoth, (5); the American mastodon, (6); a stork, (7); a condor-like vulture, (13), with a 12-ft (3.6-m) wingspan; a camel, (8); the dire wolf (9); the western horse (10); a saber-toothed cat, (12); and the ancient bison (11).

Ploiesti (pop. 232,500), large city in southeastern Romania, center of the Romanian oil industry. One of the world's first oil refineries started operations there in 1856. Besides refining and storing oil, Ploiesti produces oil-mining equipment as well as chemicals derived from petroleum. Other industries include textile manufacturing and food processing.

Plotinus (205?-270?), Greek philosopher, founder of Neoplatonism. Born in Egypt, he moved to Greece to study philosophy. His learning led him to develop Neoplatonism and to found a school where he taught that philosophy. Based on the philosophy of Plato and other Greek philosophers, as well as on Indian philosophy, Neoplatonism is the belief that the material world is an unimportant illusion, and that reality is spiritual and can only be experienced by those whose souls are pure. After 244, Plotinus moved to Rome to continue his teachings there. His beliefs were popular with many Romans, and he inspired early Christians, particularly St. Augustine. *The Enneads* is a collection of some of his lectures.
See also: Neoplatonism.

Plovdiv (pop. 350,400), second-largest city in Bulgaria, situated on the Maritsa River. Plovdiv is a major industrial, agricultural, and marketing center and is the site of a biannual international trade exhibition. Its products include textiles, metals, leather, and dairy products. Founded by the Thracians before the 4th century B.C., it was held successively from the 4th century B.C. to the 8th century A.D. by Macedonia and by the Roman Empire. Around 1360 it was captured by the Turks; in 1877 it became part of the Russian empire. It became annexed to Bulgaria in 1885.
See also: Bulgaria.

Plover, common name for various small or medium-sized wading birds of the family Charadriidae, which includes the lapwings and the true plovers. Most plovers have an olive or brown back, with lighter underparts. Typically they have a dark band across the belly and a white band on a black head. Plovers feed on insects or crustacea in mud and sand.

Plow, implement for tilling the soil: breaking up the surface crust for sowing and turning under stubble and manure. Essentially it is a horizontal blade (the share) that cuts the furrow and a projecting moldboard to turn the soil over. Plows have been used since the Bronze Age. Roman plows had an iron-shod share with a beam to draw it. Wheels were used in Saxon plows, and developments after 1600 led eventually to the steel plow of the U.S. engineer John Deere (1837), disk plows with revolving concave disks instead of shares and moldboards, and tractor-drawn plows that make multiple furrows.
See also: Deere, John.

Plum, common name for many species of trees (genus *Prunus*) of the rose family that produce soft-fleshed fruits enclosing a single pit. The European plum (*P. domestica*) has been cultivated for 2,000 years. Wild species of North American plum include the American plum and the Canada plum. Wild species have been crossed with the European plum to make hardy varieties. Prunes are plums that have been preserved by drying.

Plumbago, any of several plants and shrubs belonging to the leadwort family, grown mostly in warm climates. The plumbago's clusters of white, blue, or purple flowers make it an attractive garden plant. It has shiny, dark-green, oval leaves.

Plumbing, system of pipes and fixtures through which water and drainage flow into and out of a building. Water travels through large underground pipes called *mains.* These connect with smaller pipes called service lines which bring the water into buildings. A network of pipes distributes the water to fixtures and appliances, providing cold water. One pipe carries water to a hot-water heater, which is connected to pipes that distribute the heated water to fixtures and appliances. The water in pipes is constantly kept under pressure, so that when the faucets or valves are opened, the water will flow out. Drainage pipes carry used water and wastes from sinks, toilets, and appliances, such as washing machines, from a building to a sewer or septic tank. Because they may carry solid materials, drainage pipes are larger than water pipes.

Plutarch (C.A.D. 46-C.A.D. 120), Greek philosopher and biographer. His *Parallel Lives* of famous Greeks and Romans, paired for comparison, exemplifies the private virtues or vices of great men; it has had great influence on European literature, notably on William Shakespeare (in *Julius Caesar, Antony and Cleopatra,* and *Timon of Athens*).
See also: Greece, Ancient; Philosophy.

Pluto, in astronomy, ninth planet of the solar system, orbiting the sun at a mean distance of 3.67 billion mi (5.9 billion km) once every 248.4 years. Pluto was discovered in 1930 following observations of perturbations in Neptune's orbit. Little is known of Pluto's composition, atmosphere, or mass. Its diameter is estimated to be between 1,500 mi (2,400 km) and 2,400 mi (3,800 km). Its orbit is very eccentric, occasionally bringing it closer to the sun than Neptune. It may have originated as a satellite of Neptune. In 1978 the U.S. astronomer James Christy discovered that Pluto had a satellite, named Charon, with a diameter perhaps as large as a third of Pluto's itself.
See also: Planet; Solar system.

Pluto, in Greek and Roman mythology, ruler of the underworld and god of the dead. The Greeks also called him *Hades;* the Romans also called him *Dis Pater* and *Orcus.* He was originally a Greek god. The Romans incorporated him and the myths about him into their religion during the 7th century B.C.
See also: Mythology.

Plutonium, chemical element, symbol Pu; for physical constants see Periodic Table. Discovered by Glenn Seaborg and coworkers in 1940. It was produced by bombarding uranium with deuterons in a cyclotron. It exists in trace quantities in nature in uranium ores. It is produced in large quantities in nuclear reactors from uranium-238. Plutonium is prepared by the reduction of its trifluoride with alkaline-earth metals. It is a silvery, radioactive, toxic metal, a member of the actinide series. Plutonium is used as an explosive in nuclear weapons and as nuclear reactor fuel. Plutonium-238 is used as a thermoelectric generator and heat source. In handling plutonium and its compounds, care must be taken to ensure that a critical mass is not formed, especially in liquid solution. Plutonium is the most important of the transuranium elements.

Plymouth (pop. 35,913), town in southeastern Massachusetts, the site where the Pilgrims came ashore from the *Mayflower* on Dec. 21, 1620, and where they established the second permanent English settlement in America. Among the town's historic sites are Plymouth Rock, the *Mayflower II* (a replica of the colonists' ship), and Plimouth Plantation, a reconstruction of the original settlement.
See also: Massachusetts.

Plymouth (pop. 253,400), city in Devon county, southwest England, on Plymouth sound, from which the *Mayflower* sailed in 1620. It was also the home port of Sir Walter Raleigh's and Sir Francis Drake's expeditions to the Americas and was the launching point of the British fleet in its attack on the Spanish Armada in 1588. It is now an important maritime center and naval base.
See also: England.

Plymouth Colony, first English settlement in what is now New England, second permanent English settlement in America, founded by the Pilgrims in 1620. In 1691 it was merged with Massachusetts Bay Colony to form Massachusetts. The Pilgrims were Puritan Separatists from the Church of England who were bound for Virginia when their ships were blown off course. Under the Mayflower Compact they agreed to form a "civil body politic" that became a virtual theocracy. The original settlers included John Carver and William Bradford, the first 2 governors. Half the colony died during a bitter first winter, but the survivors were helped by the friendly chief Massasoit. By 1624 Plymouth was thriving.

Plymouth Company, speculative joint-stock company founded in 1606 by a group of English "merchant adventurers." Its purpose was to colonize the coast of North America and thus increase English wealth and trade. It had exclusive rights to the region between Latitude 45° and 41°N. After the failure of its first and only colony on the Kennebec River in Maine (1607-08), the company was reorganized in 1620 as the Council for New England.

Plymouth Rock, granite boulder off the shore at Plymouth, Mass., on which, according to tradition, the Pilgrims first set foot in America in 1620. There is no documentary evidence confirming the legend.

Plywood, strong, light wood composite made of alternate layers of veneer glued together with their grain at right angles. Thick plywood may have a central core of sawn lumber. It is made of an odd number of layers and is termed 3-ply, 5-ply, etc., depending on the number of layers. Strong and almost free of warping and splitting, plywood is used for construction of all kinds.

Plzen (pop. 174,600), city in Bohemia, a western region of Czechoslovakia. Situated at the junction of the Radbuzza and Me rivers. Plzen is a leading industrial, economic, and cultural center. Skoda Works, a factory noted for its production of military aircraft, automobiles, machinery, and locomotives, operates there. Its other products include paper products, chemicals, and metal hardwares. Pilsner, a world-renowned beer, has been brewed there since the Middle Ages. Founded before the 10th century, Plzen was a Roman Catholic stronghold during the religious wars of the 15th century. Its town square dates back to medieval times.
See also: Bohemia.

Pneumoconiosis *see:* Black lung.

Pneumonia, inflammation and consolidation of lung tissue (giving it a solid consistency). It is usually caused by bacteria (pneumococcus, staphylococcus, Gram's stain negative bacilli); it results rarely from pure virus infection (influenza, measles); other varieties occur if food, secretions, or chemicals are aspirated or inhaled. In response to inflammation, lung tissue fills with exudate and pus, which may center on the bronchi (bronchopneumonia) or be restricted to a single lobe (lobar pneumonia).
Cough, with yellow or green sputum (sometimes containing blood), fever, malaise, and breathlessness are common. The involvement of the pleural surfaces causes pleurisy. Antibiotics and physiotherapy are essential in treatment for the bacterial forms, which are generally the more severe.

Pneumothorax, condition in which air is present in the pleural space between the lungs and the chest wall. This may result from trauma, rupture of lung bullae in emphysema or in asthma, tuberculosis, pneumoconiosis, cancer, etc. Drainage of the air through a tube inserted in the chest wall allows reexpansion of the lungs.

Pnom Penh *see:* Phnom Penh.

Pocahontas (1595-1617), Native American who strove to improve relations between Native Americans and English settlers in Jamestown, Va. The daughter of chief Powhatan, she is credited with saving the colonist John Smith's life just as her father was about to execute him. When fighting broke out between Native Americans and colonists, she was captured by the English. During her captivity, she fell in love with John Rolfe. She became a Christian and married him in 1614. In 1616, she accompanied Rolfe to England, where she was favorably received. She died of smallpox the following year and was buried in England.

Pocatello (pop. 46,340), city in southeast Idaho. Located in a rich agricultural area, it is the market center and shipping point for livestock and farm products. Its industries include phosphate mining, cement, steel, dairy products, and animal feed. Pocatello was founded in 1882 when it became a railroad center. Its proximity to attractions such as Caribou National Forest, Yellowstone National Park, and Harriman State Park, to name a few, makes it a much-visited tourist site. Idaho State University is situated there.
See also: Idaho.

Podgorny, Nikolai Viktorovich (1903-83), Soviet political leader. After rising through the Communist Party ranks in the Ukraine, he was named to the party secretariat of the Soviet Union (1963). After Nikita Khrushchev's fall, he became (1965) chairman of the Presidium of the Supreme Soviet, or head of state, holding that post until his demotion to deputy of the Supreme Soviet (1977).
See also: Union of Soviet Socialist Republics.

Podiatry, science of disorders and diseases of the feet. Podiatrists, who are licensed practitioners in the United States, treat nails, corns, calluses, bunions, and toe deformities and may prescribe orthopedics and perform minor surgery.

Poe, Edgar Allan (1809-49), U.S. short-story writer, poet, and critic, famous for his tales of mystery and the macabre, such as "The Murders in the Rue Morgue" (1841) and "The Purloined Letter" (1844), prototypes of the detective story, and "The Fall of the House of Usher" (1839). His poems, including "The Raven" (1845) and "Annabel Lee" (1849), are musical and striking in imagery. Poe discussed beauty and form in art in "The Philosophy of Composition" (1846), which influenced Charles Baudelaire and the French Symbolists.

Poet laureate, royal appointment held by a British poet who writes poems for state occasions. The title is now largely honorific. John Dryden first had the title in 1668, but the custom started when Ben Jonson received a royal pension in 1616. In the U.S., the poet laureates have been appointed by the Library of Congress. Robert Penn Warren was the first (1986), Richard Wilbur (1987), Howard Nemerov (1988), Mark Strand (1990), and Joseph Brodsky (1991), who is the first foreign-born poet to be named laureate.

Edgar Allan Poe

Poetry, meaningful arrangement of words into an imaginative or emotional discourse, with a strong rhythmic pattern. The language, seeking to evoke image and idea, uses imagery and metaphor. Rhyme or alliteration may also be important elements. The length of poems varies from brief lyric poems to long narrative poems or epic poems, with the length and scope of the novel. The kind of forms and devices used (for example, alliteration, assonance, onomatopoeia) depends on the tone and intentions of the poet. Since the sense of poetry is intimately tied to its sound, it is extremely difficult to translate. In most cultures poetry, linked by its rhythmic elements to music and dance, develops before prose literature; the poetic form aids memory in oral transmission. Eventually poetry is written down; a "higher" form then develops—poetry carefully crafted for the printed page and intensely involved reader. Even such written poetry, however, must remain to some extent "musical."

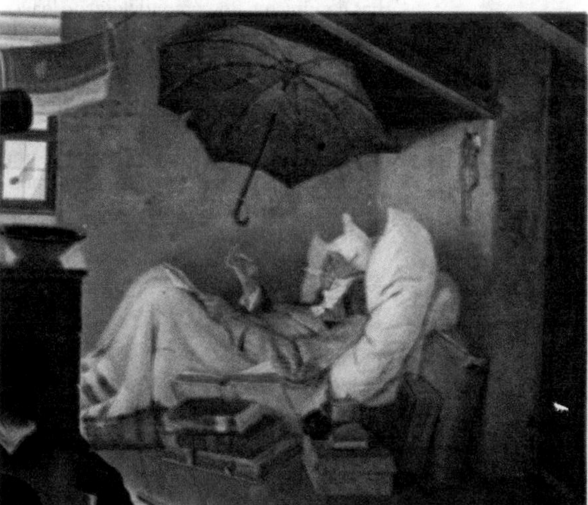
Nineteenth century Romantic picture of an impoverished poet

Pogrom (from Russian for "devastation" or "riot"), term for the officially condoned mob attacks on Jewish communities in Russia between 1881 and 1921. More generally, it is used to describe any massacre of a defenseless minority, particularly Jews, such as those organized by the Nazis. The pogroms were a major factor in the large-scale emigration of European Jews to the United States.
See also: Jews.

Pohnpei, island in the western Pacific Ocean. The largest of the eastern Caroline Islands, Pohnpei has an area of approximately 129 sq mi (334 sq km). Many tropical crops are raised there, including yams, bananas, taros, and breadfruit. It has been controlled successively by Spain, Germany, Japan, and the United States. Pohnpei and the other Caroline Islands currently make up the self-governing Federated States of Micronesia.

Poincaré, Jules Henri (1854-1912), French mathematician, cosmologist, and scientific philosopher, best known for his many contributions to pure and applied mathematics and celestial mechanics.
See also: Cosmology; Mathematics.

Poincaré, Raymond (1860-1934), French politician, three times premier (1912-13, 1922-24, 1926-29) and president (1913-20). A strongly nationalist conservative, he ordered the French occupation of the Ruhr (1923). His financial policies succeeded in stabilizing the currency (1928).
See also: France.

Poinciana, any of various tropical flowering trees in the pea family. The poinciana has large red or orange flowers that grow in clusters. Each flower has 5 petals and ranges in size from 3 to 4 in (8 to 10 cm) across. The royal poinciana (*Delonix regia*), which grows in southern Florida, has flaming red flowers and delicate leaves made up of small leaflets. Royal poinciana trees can grow to a height of 40 ft (12 m).

Poinsettia, name for a variety of spurges (genus *Euphorbia*) with colorful, attractive bracts (whorled leaves that enclose the small flower). A popular indoor ornamental plant with red, yellow, or white bracts, *E. pulcherrima,* native to Mexico and Central America, grows up to 10 ft (3 m) high in the wild. Propagation is by shoot tip cuttings taken in the spring.

Pointer, large hunting dog. It uses its keen sense of smell to hunt game birds. When the pointer detects a bird, it stands absolutely still and points its nose towards the bird to show the hunter where it is. A pointer has a short white coat with black, yellow, orange, or reddish-brown marks. Its shoulder height ranges from 23 to 28 in (58 to 71 cm), and it weighs from 45 to 75 lb (20 to 34 kg).

Pointillism was developed by the impressionist Georges Seurat

Point Four Program, technical assistance plan for less developed nations proposed by President Harry Truman in his inaugural address, Jan. 1949, so named because it was the fourth point in the speech. Launched in 1950 and later merged with other aid programs, it provided technical, educational, and health assistance and aimed to encourage private investment and increase U.S. influence during the cold war.

Pointillism, painting technique in which tiny paint dots of color are juxtaposed on a canvas to build up the form. This method was developed by the post-impressionist painters Georges Seurat and Paul Signac to achieve more luminosity and greater control of tone.

Poison, substance that causes illness or death when it is eaten or absorbed into the body. There are many different kinds of poisons. Some are found in nature. For example, some plants contain poison. Caution should always be taken before eating wild foods, such as mushrooms or berries. Some animals eject poison when they bite, such as rattlesnakes, wasps, and scorpions. In the home, various products contain poisonous chemicals, such as cleaning fluids and insect sprays. Such products should always be used according to instruction and should be kept away from children. Medicines taken in large doses can become poisonous. Gases such as carbon monoxide are deadly when inhaled in large amounts. Drugs called *antidotes* can be taken to reverse the harmful effects of some poisons.
See also: Toxin.

Poison gas *see:* Chemical and biological warfare.

Poison ivy, vine that grows plentifully in the United States and southern Canada. Its leaves appear red in early spring, turn shiny green later in spring, and red or orange in autumn. It contains a poisonous oil that is extremely irritating to the skin, causing blisters and red, itching spots.

Poison oak, vine similar to poison ivy and poison sumac. It contains an irritant, urushiol, which causes skin eruptions and watery blisters.

Poisonous plant, any plant that produces harmful effects to people or animals. The harmful effects of a poisonous plant range from minor irritation to death, depending on the plant. Some plants are poisonous when eaten, such as poisonous mushrooms, and others when merely touched, such as poison ivy. Some plants have parts that are safe to eat and other parts that are poisonous. Potatoes, for example, have poisonous leaves. It is not possible to make general statements about the appearance, taste, and smell of poisonous plants. The poison from some plants is used to create medicines, which are prescribed in controlled doses. For example, the leaves of the foxglove, a tall plant with bell-shaped flowers, is used to create digitalis, a medicine used to stimulate the heart.

Poison sumac *see:* Sumac.

Poitier, Sidney (1927-), U.S. film and stage actor. He was the first African American actor to become accepted as a star in films made for largely white audiences. Many of these films (e.g., *The Blackboard Jungle*, 1955; *In the Heat of the Night*, 1967) deal specifically with racial issues. Poitier directed and starred in *A Patch of Blue* (1965), played Porgy in *Porgy and Bess* (1959), and won an Academy Award for his role in *Lilies of the Field* (1963).

Poitiers, Battle of, English victory in the Hundred Years' War, fought in 1356, near Poitiers in west-central France. The English, led by Edward the Black Prince, were outnumbered four to one by their French opponents but won a brilliant victory over John II and Philip the Bold.
See also: Edward, the Black Prince; Hundred Years' War.

Poker, card game whose earliest forms date back to 520 in Europe, developing into bet-and-bluff games like **brag** in England, **pochen** ("bluff") in Germany, and **poque** in France. The French brought **poque** to America (1800), where it was developed and reexported to Europe as poker (1870). It is now one of the world's top 3 card games. There are many variations, but basically 5 or 7 cards are dealt, and each player tries to make up a winning combination, on which he or she bets and bluffs in a contest of skill and nerves against the unknown combinations ("hands") of his opponents. The winner either has the best hand or has bluffed all opponents into "folding" (dropping out of the game).

Pokeweed (*Phytolacca americana*), tall, herbal plant belonging to the pokeweed family. Native to North America, it is also known as *poke, pigeonberry, pokeberry, pokeroot,* and *inkberry.* Pokeweed has small white flowers and berries that ripen to a deep red-black color. Its stem is red and grows to a height of 4 to 10 ft (1.2 to 3 m). The root, stem, leaves, and seeds of the pokeweed are poisonous, but its young shoots can be eaten if properly prepared.

Poland, former communist state in central Europe.
Land and climate. Poland is bordered by the Baltic Sea on the north, the Soviet Union on the east and northeast, Czechoslovakia on the south, and Germany on the west. The land is generally low, with about 90% of it less than 1,000 ft/305 m above sea level, but in the south are the peaks of the Sudeten and Carpathian

Poland

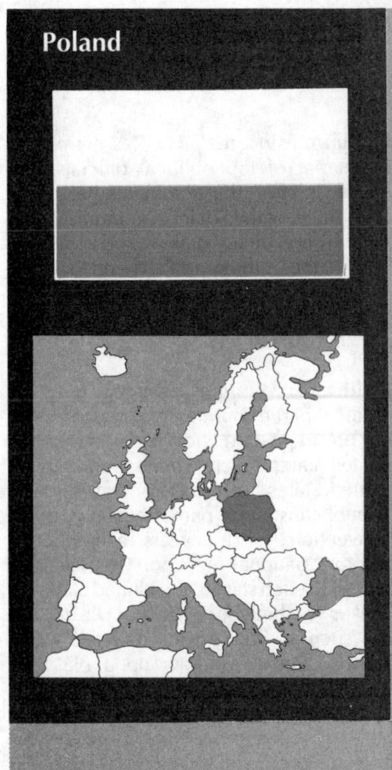

General information	
Capital:	Warsaw
Area:	120,727 sq mi (312,683 sq km)
Population:	37,875,000
Official language:	Polish
Monetary unit:	1 zloty = 100 groszy
Main cities:	Warsaw, Lódz, Kraków
Government	
Form:	socialist republic
Independent:	1918
Head of state:	President
Head of government:	Prime minister
Legislature:	two legislative houses (Sejm and Senate)
Executive:	President and Council of Ministers
Judiciary:	highest court is the Supreme Court
Political division:	49 provinces
National economy	
Gross national product:	U.S.$258,970,000,000
Per capita income:	U.S.$1,850
Agriculture:	potatoes, sugar beets, wheat, rye, barley
Livestock:	chickens, cattle, sheep
Fisheries:	671,000 metric tons
Mining:	hard coal, salt, natural gas, sulfur, copper, zinc
Industries:	shipbuilding, machinery and transport equipment, food, textiles, chemicals
Main exports:	machinery and transport equipment, chemicals, fuel and power (hard coal), metals, textiles and clothing
Transportation:	16,552 (26,637 km) of railroads, 211,395 (340,191 km) of roads, 1 international airport
Trading partners:	USSR, Germany, Czechoslovakia, United Kingdom, Yugoslavia
People	
Urban:	61%
Ethnic composition:	Polish 98.5%, Ukrainian 0.5%, other 0.5%
Birth rate:	16.1 per 1,000 population
Death rate:	10.1 per 1,000 population
Infant mortality:	21 per 1,000 live births
Life expectancy:	male 67 years, female 75 years

Poland is a Roman Catholic country, more than 90% of the people follow the faith.

mountains, forming a natural border with Czechoslovakia. Poland's climate is moderate, with cool summers and cold winters.

People. World War II saw the destruction of Poland's ethnic minorities; the country is now almost entirely Polish. The official language is Polish and the people are overwhelmingly Roman Catholic.

Economy. Until World War II, Poland was an agricultural country; since then it has been rapidly industrialized. The former communist regime attempted to impose collectivized farms, but was effectively resisted by the peasantry. The chief agricultural products are wheat, rye, barley, oats, potatoes, and sugar beets. Poland's industries produce coal, zinc, steel, petroleum, and sulfur. Its manufactures include machinery, textiles, cement, and chemicals with a sizeable shipbuilding industry at Gdansk. The country's principal exports have been coal, textiles, metal products, and processed meat. With the end of communist control of the economy, Poland faces the massive task of shifting to privately owned enterprises and must simultaneously cope with sudden and acute shortages of essential goods, a weak currency, and a critical need for investment capital.

History. Poland's recorded history dates back to the 10th century when local Slavic tribes first united. Later, Germans settled in Poland, particularly on the Baltic coast. From the 14th through the 16th centuries Poland was governed by the Jagiello dynasty and flourished in its most sustained period of freedom and independence. But the country was invaded by both Swedes and Russians in the 17th century, and then divided among Austria, Prussia, and Russia in 1772, 1793, and again in 1795. In 1919 the Treaty of Versailles established a new Poland that survived barely twenty years before it was invaded by Nazi Germany in 1939. The USSR occupied the eastern part of the country until 1941 when Germany invaded the USSR and took control of all of Poland. As a result of the German invasions and occupation, the population was decimated by massacres, starvation, and imprisonment in death camps like Auschwitz. After the last Germans were expelled early in 1945, a provisional government was set up under Soviet auspices. The communists dominated the 1947 elections, gained control of the government and, in 1952, declared the country a people's republic modeled on Soviet lines. With the death of Stalin, opposition to Soviet control led to widespread rioting in 1956, and Wxadys-Xaw Gomutka became leader of the anti-Soviet revolt. But by the early 1960s, Gomutka was following Russian policies. In 1970 Edward Gierek replaced Gomutka, instituted many reforms, and sought to control inflation. In the late 1970s, a new wave of unrest swept the country, stimulated primarily by the higher food prices. Polish workers formed the independent trade union Solidarnosé (Solidarity) in 1980, headed by Lech Walesa, and sought a greater measure of worker control in industry. Gierek fell from power that same year and Gen. Wojciech Jaruzelski took the

The lakes of the Tatra Mountains in Poland

reins of government. In 1981 Gen. Jaruzelski imposed martial law, arrested Solidarity's leaders, and banned the trade union in 1982. Within a year of the ban, martial law gradually came to an end. By 1984, martial law had ended and by 1986 the imprisoned members of Solidarity had been released. As a result of the liberalization of domestic politics within the Soviet Union and its decision to relinquish much of its former empire, Poland found itself free to chart its own course. In 1989, the ban on Solidarity was lifted and free elections were held. Lech Walesa, the Solidarity leader, was elected president in 1990.

Polanyi, John Charles (1929-), Canadian chemist. He shared the 1986 Nobel Prize for chemistry with U.S. collaborators Yuan T. Lee and Dudley Herschbach for his work in chemiluminescence, the faint infrared light emitted by molecules as they recombine. He is the son of noted chemist Michael Polanyi.
See also: Chemistry.

Polar bear, large (up to 1,650 lb/750 kg), white-furred, arctic bear (*Thalarctos maritimus*). It can swim strongly and is also agile on land. It hunts seals, whale calves, fish, and, on land, arctic foxes and even lemmings.

Polar bears

Polaris *see:* North Star.

Polarized light, light that exhibits unmixed properties (a particular vibration) in a given direction at a right angle to the line of propagation.
See also: Land, Edwin Herbert.

Polecat, small carnivore of the weasel family (*Mustela putorius*), found throughout northern and central Europe. It feeds at night on birds, small mammals, frogs, other animals, and eggs. In the United States the name is sometimes given to the skunk, a close relative.

Polestar *see:* North Star.

Pole vault, sporting event in which an athlete jumps over a crossbar using a pole to push him- or herself off the ground. The crossbar is supported by 2 uprights and is set at a specified height. The pole is usually made of fiberglass and is from 12 to 16 1/2 ft (3.7 to 5 m) long. The vaulter grips one end of the pole, runs at top speed, and plants the other end of the pole into the take-off box. The pole bends and catapults the vaulter upwards towards the crossbar as it straightens again. The vaulter pulls his or her body up into a handstand position at the top of the pole, swings his or her feet over the crossbar, pushes the pole away, travels across the bar, and drops down. The vaulter lands onto a soft area called a pit. The vaulter has been successful when he or she has cleared the crossbar without dislodging it.

Police, civil body charged with maintaining public order and protecting persons and property from unlawful acts. Most modern forces are descended from the Metropolitan Police established in London by Sir Robert Peel in 1829. In the United States, Boston introduced a similar force in 1836, and New York City soon afterward. Today in the United States the police are organized into around 40,000 separate forces, consisting of local, district, county, and state police and the sheriffs and deputies of around 35,000 towns and villages. There are also federal police agencies, such as the FBI, the Bureau of Narcotics and Dangerous Drugs, the Border Patrol, and the Internal Revenue Service, each responsible to its own civil governing authority. Police powers are in most countries strictly circumscribed by law and constitution. In the United States and Great Britain police are obliged to inform an arrested person of his or her rights.
See also: Peel, Sir Robert.

Polio *see:* Poliomyelitis.

Poliomyelitis, or infantile paralysis, viral disease causing muscle paralysis as a result of direct damage to motor nerve cells in the spinal cord. Current polio vaccine (Sabin vaccine) is a live strain taken by mouth that induces immunity. Poliomyelitis vaccination, originally developed by Jonas Salk (using a killed-virus vaccine), has been one of the 20th century's chief successes in preventive medicine.
See also: Sabin, Albert Bruce; Salk, Jonas Edward.

Polish, West Slavic language, the official and literary language of Poland. Modern literary Polish, dating from the 16th century, was originally based on dialects in the vicinity of Porzna.

Polish Corridor, strip of Polish land about 25-65 mi (40-105 km) wide and 90 mi (145 km) long. Formerly German, it was granted to Poland in 1919 to give it access to the Baltic Sea. The predominantly German port of Danzig (now Gdansk) adjoining the corridor was declared a free city. The separation of East Prussia from the rest of Germany by the corridor precipitated the German invasion of Poland (1939).
See also: World War II.

Polishing *see:* Grinding and polishing.

Polish Succession War *see:* Succession wars.

Politburo, in the USSR, permanent secretariat of top political officials, first formed in 1917, that dominates the Central Committee of the Soviet Communist Party. It is the chief policy-making and governing body of the Communist Party and to a large extent of the USSR. Its size varies; usually it has about 11 voting members and 9 nonvoting members.

Political convention, gathering at which political parties nominate their candidates for president and vice president of the United States. The two major parties in the United States are the Democrats and the Republicans. Each party holds a political convention every four years, in the summer before a national election. The delegates represent each state in the United States, as well as Washington, D.C., and U.S. territories such as Puerto Rico and the Virgin Islands. Delegates draw up a platform, which is a description of the party's goals and positions on current issues of importance. They then nominate presidential and vice presidential candidates who will run in the national election using that platform.

Political party, body or organization that puts forward candidates for public office and contends for power in elections. Parties pose alternative programs and candidates and provide a means by which voters can make their desires and opinions felt.
The U.S. has a two-party system. In European legislatures, representatives are generally chosen under the system of proportional representation, which allows the election of candidates from a number of parties in exact proportion to their popular strength. If no party has a simple majority, a coalition is necessary. Communist states and many newly independent states have a single-party system in which the political party is in effect part of the state apparatus.

Political science, study of government and political institutions and processes. It was initiated by Plato's *Republic* and Aristotle's *Politics*, and well-known political theories have included those of Niccolò Machiavelli, Jean Bodin, Thomas Hobbes, John Locke, Montesquieu, Jeremy Bentham, Jean-Jacques Rousseau, and Karl Marx. Traditionally, the study was primarily concerned with the nature of the state, sovereignty, and government. Today greater emphasis is placed on the human associations, the behavior of interest groups, and the decision-making processes. Past theories cannot provide for the complexity of modern society; a standard view today regards society as a set of interacting interdependent systems.

Polk, James Knox (1795-1849), 11th president of the U.S. Polk was elected on a pledge to extend the nation's existing territory. During his presidency, the United

States—in accordance with the doctrine of "manifest destiny"—expanded across the entire continent and, as part of that expansion, fought the Mexican War.

Early life. Polk graduated from the University of North Carolina in 1818, then studied law. Admitted to the bar in 1820, he set up a practice in Columbia, Tenn. In 1824, Polk married Sarah Childress.

Political career. Polk became active in the Democratic party. He served in the Tennessee House of Representatives (1823-25), then in the U.S. House of Representatives (1825-39). In 1839, he was elected governor of Tennessee on a slavery-and-states'-rights platform, but lost reelection bids in 1841 and 1843. At the 1844 Democratic national convention, the most pressing political issue was the annexation of Texas. The country as a whole—particularly the South and West, on whose votes the Democrats relied—wanted territorial expansion. The leading Democratic candidate, Martin Van Buren, opposed the annexation of Texas. Polk, proposed as a compromise candidate, became the first "dark horse" (or little-known) presidential candidate in U.S. politics. Besides favoring annexing Texas, Polk pledged to extend the Oregon Territory's boundary to a latitude of 54°40'; his campaign slogan was "54-40 or Fight!" He soundly defeated Henry Clay, the Whig candidate, who had vacillated on the annexation issue.

President. By the time Polk took office, the annexation issue had been settled. (Texas had been admitted to the Union as a slave state under John Tyler, the outgoing Whig president.) As for the "54-40 or Fight!" pledge, Polk had to compromise. In June 1846, the Oregon Treaty established the boundary between the U.S. and British America (now Canada) at the 49th parallel. Polk offered to buy from Mexico the territory of California and New Mexico (present-day Arizona, California, Utah, and New Mexico) and to settle Texas's boundary at the Rio Grande. Mexico refused. Polk sent troops to the Mexican border, then, when a small Mexican force attacked, told Congress that the U.S. had been "invaded." On May 13, 1846, Congress declared war. The Mexican War (1846-48) ended with Mexico recognizing the Rio Grande border and with the U.S. annexing California and much of the Southwest.

Keeping a campaign pledge to the South, Polk pushed for a lower tariff; it was not raised again till after the Civil War. Other voters fared less well during his administration. Westerners accused Polk of favoring the South, arguing that his major achievement had been to acquire territory that benefited slave owners.

Retirement. Polk chose not to run for reelection, and retired in 1849. He lived for only a few months after his term ended. Polk died at his home in Nashville, Tenn., on June 15, 1849.

Polk, Leonidas (1806-64), first bishop of Louisiana (1841-61). He abandoned the ministry to fight in the Confederate Army in the Civil War. He served as a major general in the Army of Tennessee and fought at Shiloh, Murfreesboro, and Chickamauga before being killed in action at Pine Mountain, Ga.

Poll *see:* Public opinion.

Pollack *see:* Pollock.

Pollaiuolo, Antonio Del (1429?-98), Italian painter, sculptor, and goldsmith. His knowledge of the human anatomy and his mastery in portraying figures in action inspired Renaissance artists such as Michelangelo and Leonardo da Vinci. He used Hercules as the subject of some of his most famous works; including several paintings and a bronze piece. He created the bronze tombs of Popes Sixtus IV and Innocent VIII in Rome.

Pollen, fine yellow powder produced in the male part of flowers and in the male cone of conifers (cone-bearing plants). The male organs of flowers are called *stamens*; the female parts are called *pistils*. Pollination is the transference of pollen from the plant's stamen to its pistil. In conifers, pollination occurs when pollen is transferred from the male pollen cone to the female seed cone. Pollen can be transferred by the wind or by birds or insects who come into contact with the flowers. The pollen clings to them and is transferred as they move from flower to flower. After a plant is pollinated, it becomes fertile and begins seed production.

Pollination, in plants, the transfer of pollen from the male stamen of a flower to the female pistil of the same or another flower for fertilization. Wind-pollinated plants, such as grasses, produce inconspicuous flowers with large, feathery stamens and stigmas and usually large quantities of pollen. Insect- or bird-pollinated flowers have large, conspicuous, and colorful flowers, produce nectar, and have small stigmas.

Pollinosis *see:* Hay fever.

Polliwog *see:* Tadpole.

Pollock (*Pollachius virens*), fish belonging to the codfish family. A valuable food fish, it is found in the northern Atlantic Ocean. It grows to a length of 2 to 3 1/2 ft (61 to 107 cm) and has a protruding lower jaw. Pollocks move in schools and feed on smaller fish.

Pollock, Jackson (1912-56), U.S. painter, leader of abstract expressionism. Influenced by surrealism, he developed "action painting": dripping paint on canvas placed flat on the floor, and forming marks in it with sticks, trowels, and knives. His work, such as *Number 32* (1950) and *Blue Poles* (1953), comprises intricate networks of lines.

See also: Abstract art.

Poll tax, tax collected from every adult in a community. All people pay the same amount, no matter what their incomes or what properties they own. This kind of taxation is controversial because many feel that it places an unfair burden on the poor and that a fairer way would be to tax according to how much a person owns. There is no national poll tax in the United States. Several U.S. states in the South enacted poll taxes. Those who could not pay them were not allowed to vote. The 24th Amendment (1964) to the U.S. Constitution and action taken by the Supreme Court in 1966 declared that states could not require the payment of poll taxes as a prerequisite for voting in any election.

See also: Taxation.

James Knox Polk

11th U.S. president	
Born:	near Pineville, N.C.; Nov. 2, 1795
Term:	Mar. 1845-Mar. 1849
Vice president:	George M. Dallas
Political party:	Democratic
Spouse:	Sarah Childress Polk
Children:	None
Died:	Nashville, Tenn.; June 15, 1849

Pollution *see:* Environmental pollution.

Pollux *see:* Castor and Pollux.

Polo, game played on horseback (polo ponies), with a ball and mallets. It is played between two teams of four on a field 300 yd (271 m) long and 200 yd (183 m) wide, with a goal at each end. The object is to score points by striking the 3-3.5 in (7.6-8.9 cm) diameter ball into the goal with the mallet, which is 48-54 in (122-137 cm) long. The game originated in Persia and spread through Turkey, Tibet, India, China, and Japan. It was revived in 19th-century

India and learned by British army officers, who introduced it into England in 1869 and into the United States in 1876.

Polo, Marco (1254?-1324?), Venetian explorer famous for his overland journey to China (1271-95). Reaching China in 1275, he served as an envoy of the ruler, Kublai Khan. He was appointed governor of Yangchow for 3 years and assisted in the capture of the city of Sainfu. He returned home to Venice (1295) laden with a treasure in precious stones. Commanding a galley against the Genoese at the battle of Curzola (1298), he was captured. In prison he wrote an account of his travels that later inspired explorers like Christopher Columbus to search for a sea passage to the East.

Polonium, chemical element, symbol Po; for physical constants see Periodic Table. Discovered by Marie Curie in 1898. Polonium was the first element to be discovered by virtue of its radioactivity. It occurs in pitchblende and other uranium minerals in minute amounts. The element is a decay product of radium and is also called Radium F. It is produced artificially by irradiating bismuth-210 with neutrons in a high-flux nuclear reactor. Polonium is a low-melting metalloid. It resembles tellurium and bismuth. Several compounds have been synthesized, including a polonide. Polonium-210 is a powerful α-emitter and is dangerous to handle even in small amounts. It is alloyed with beryllium as a neutron source. Polonium is used in devices for removing dust particles and static electricity. It is one of the most toxic substances known.

Polyandry *see:* Polygamy.

Polychlorinated biphenyl (PCB), any of several compounds formed by substituting hydrogen (H) atoms in biphenyl ($C_6H_5C_6H_5$) with chlorine (C1) atoms. PCBs were once widely used in the manufacture of many products, including lubricants, paints, and adhesives. However, scientific studies have concluded that PCBs are a poisonous threat to the environment, killing wildlife and creating health problems for people. Their use has been banned in the United States.

Polyester comes in three basic varieties—fiber, film, and plastic. Shown is a boat made of polyester plastic.

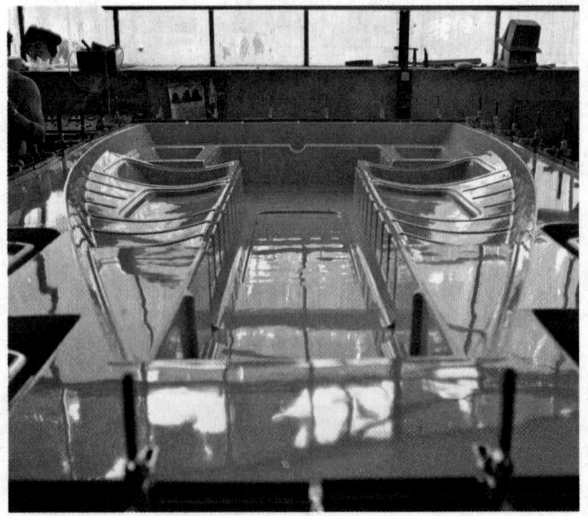

Polyclitus, name of 2 Greek sculptors. **Polyclitus the Elder** (5th century B.C.) was renowned for bronze statues of athletes, of which numerous marble copies survive. His most famous works, a colossal statue of Hera, now lost, and the *Doryphorus* (Spear Bearer), became the models for ideal proportion. **Polyclitus the Younger** (4th century B.C.) was known primarily as an architect but also produced figures of athletes.

Polyester, any of several strong, light synthetic products made from chemical substances derived from petroleum. Polyesters are manufactured in 3 forms: textiles, plastics, and films. Products made from polyester have great strength and durability. Polyester textiles are colorfast and wrinkle-resistant and are widely used in the creation of clothing and home furnishings. Polyester plastics are used to manufacture such products as bottles, household fixtures and appliances, boats, and automobile parts. Polyester films are used to create Mylar, insulation wires, sealing tapes, computer tapes, and other items.

Polyethylene *see:* Plastic.

Polygamy, marriage in which a man has more than one wife at one time (polygyny), or a woman has more than one husband (polyandry). It is still practiced in parts of Asia and Africa; both the Muslim and Hindu religions permit polygyny. It was once also a custom of U.S. Mormons but is now forbidden by them.

Polygon, closed plane figure bounded by three or more straight lines, such as triangles (3 sides), pentagons (5 sides), and dodecagons (12 sides). Convex polygons have interior angles that are all either acute or obtuse; in concave polygons one or more of these angles is reflex. A polygon with equal angles and sides equal in length is called a regular polygon. A *spherical polygon* is a closed figure on the surface of a sphere bounded by arcs of great circles.

Polyhedron, three-dimensional figure bounded by 4 or more polygon sides. There are only 5 types of convex polyhedron that can be regular (i.e., have faces that are equal regular polygons, each face being at equal angles to those adjacent to it); the tetrahedron, the octahedron, and the isocahedron, with 4, 8, and 20 faces, respectively, each face being an equilateral triangle; the hexahedron, with 6 square faces; and the dodecahedron, with 12 pentagonal faces. Regular polyhedrons may be circumscribed about or inscribed in a sphere.

Polymer, substance composed of very large molecules (macromolecules) built up by repeated linking of small molecules (monomers). Natural polymers include proteins, nucleic acids, polysaccharides, resins, rubber, and many minerals. The ability to make synthetic polymers (e.g., plastics and synthetic fibers) lies at the heart of modern technology. Polymerization, which requires that each monomer have two or more functional groups capable of linkage, takes place by condensation, with elimination of small molecules, or by simple addition. Catalysis is usually required, or the use of an initiator to start a chain reaction of free radicals. If more than one kind of monomer is used, the result is a copolymer with the units arranged at random in the chain.

Polymerization, chemical process in which many small molecules, called monomers, are joined together to produce a large molecule, called a polymer. The monomers combined can be all of one kind or of many different kinds. The characteristic of the polymer is determined by what monomers are combined. Some polymers, such as starch and rubber, are found in nature; others, like plastic and paint, are synthetically produced.

Polymorphism, in zoology, the existence of more than two forms or types of individual within the same species of animal. An example is seen in some social insects, such as ants and bees, in which many different types of worker are structurally adapted for different tasks within the colony.
See also: Zoology.

Polynesia *see:* Pacific Islands.

Polyphony (Greek, "many sounds"), music made up of several independent melodic lines linked harmonically through counterpoint.

Polytheism, belief in many gods, as opposed to monotheism or dualism; characteristic of most religions, notably Hinduism and Greek and Roman religion. It may arise from the personification of forces worshiped at a more primitive level in animism. One god may dominate the others (e.g., Zeus); sometimes a supreme being is recognized, transcending the gods.
See also: Gods; Religion.

Pomegranate, family of tropical shrubs and small trees native to Asia and India and cultivated in the United States. Pomegranates in the wild are shrublike; when cultivated, they grow as trees and can reach a height of 15 to 20 ft (4.6 to 6 m). A pomegranate is valued for its golden red fruit. The fruit is the size of a large apple and has a tough rind. Inside are many small seeds, each of which is enclosed by fleshy pulp. The pulp has a pleasant flavor and is eaten fresh or used to create syrup for drinks.

Pomerania, region in north-central Europe, south of the Baltic Sea. The greater part of Pomerania lies in Poland; the rest lies in Germany. Pomerania is mostly made up of fertile lowlands. Agriculture is the main occupation. Industries in the area include the manufacture of metals, ships, and paper. Pomerania was first settled as early as A.D. 100 by Germanic tribes. It has been occupied and governed by Slavs, Germans, Prussians, and Swedes. After World War II, it was divided between Germany and Poland.

Pomeranian, small dog, weighing from 3 to 7 lbs (1.4 to 3.2 kg) and standing approximately 6 in (15.3 cm) tall at the shoulder. The Pomeranian has long, fluffy hair on its body and a furry collar around its neck. Its face has sharp, foxlike features. Related to large dogs of the Arctic, the pomeranian became a popular "toy dog" pet in the late 1800s.

Pomo, Hozan-speaking tribe living in North California, noted for their intricate basket making. A wealthy tribe with many natural resources, they used shells as currency.

Pompadour, Marquise de (1721-64), mistress of King Louis XV of France from 1745. She was a patroness of the arts and had much influence on the political and artistic life of France.

Pompano, any of several saltwater fishes belonging to the jack family. Found in warm waters throughout the world, the pompano is valuable as a delicious food fish. Pompanos vary in size, shape, and color, depending on the species. The size range is 1 ft to 3 ft (46 cm to 114 cm); the weight range is from 3 lbs to 50 lbs (1.4 kg to 23 kg). Some of the species found along the Atlantic coast include the common pompano, the great pompano, and the palometa.

Pompeii, ancient Roman city in southern Italy, buried by an eruption of Mt. Vesuvius (A.D. 79). It was rediscovered in 1748. Excavations have revealed a town preserved much as it was on the day of its destruction, even to several bodies. The site has yielded invaluable information on Roman urban life and beautiful examples of Roman art.
See also: Rome, Ancient.

Pompey the Great, (106-48 B.C.), Roman general and political leader. He started his career in 83 B.C. when he helped Lucius Sulla win a war against Gaius Marius. A few years later, he was sent to Spain to end a rebellion by Marius' supporters. In 72 B.C. he suppressed the slave revolt led by Spartacus. He was elected a Roman consul in 70 B.C. In 67 B.C. he was given the task of ridding the Mediterranean Sea of pirates. The next year he fought and defeated Mithridates VI of Pontus, conquering Palestine, Syria, and parts of Asia Minor. When the senate disapproved of some of his actions, Pompey united with Julius Caesar, a senate opponent. In 60 B.C., Pompey, Caesar, and Marcus Crassus formed the First Triumvirate (a triumvirate is a trio who head a government together), which ruled for several years. However, Pompey became competitive for Caesar's power and consequently broke with him. Pompey went over to senate's side and became a consul again in 52 B.C. In 49 B.C., Caesar defied the senate and initiated military action that resulted in civil war. Pompey was defeated at Pharsala. He fled to Egypt and was captured and executed there by the Roman-controlled Egyptian government.
See also: Caesar, (Gaius) Julius.

Pompidou, Georges Jean Raymond (1911-74), president of France from 1969 to 1974. He was a literature professor before he began his political career in 1944 as an aide to Charles De Gaulle. De Gaulle was at that time a general and head of a temporary government. Pompidou's subsequent political career consisted of various posts in connection with De Gaulle. De Gaulle was elected president in 1958. When he resigned his presidency, Pompidou was elected to take his place. As president, Pompidou strove to better France's economy.
See also: France.

Ponape *see:* Pohnpei.

Ponce (pop. 161,700), city in Puerto Rico. Located in the south, near the coast, it is an important port through which a major portion of the island's imports and exports pass. Its other industries include liquor distilling, sugar refining, and tourism.
See also: Puerto Rico.

Ponce de León, Juan (c.1460-1521), Spanish discoverer of Florida. He sailed with Christopher Columbus in 1493, and in 1508 he conquered Puerto Rico and became its governor. Leading an expedition, possibly to find the mythical Fountain of Youth, he discovered and named Florida in 1513, but when he attempted to colonize it in 1521, he was driven off and mortally wounded by Indians.
See also: Florida.

Ponchielli, Amilcare (1834-86), Italian opera composer. His best-known works are *I Promessi Sposi* (1856) and *La Gioconda* (1876), with its famous ballet, *Dance of the Hours.*
See also: Opera.

Pond, still body of water smaller than a lake. Ponds can be natural or artificial. Ponds are located in many different kinds of terrain, form arctic to tropical regions. Their location, depth, soil, and water level and quality determine the kind of plant and animal life found in them.
See also: Marsh; Swamp.

Pond lily *see:* Water lily.

Georges Pompidou

Pondweed, name for freshwater plants (genus *Potamogeton*) that sometimes clog streams and ponds. Their leaves may lie flat on the surface of the water or be completely submerged. The sago pondweed has branching stems and hairlike leaves. Like all pondweeds, its flowers open above the water. Its fruits are an important food for migrating ducks.

Ponomarev, Boris Nikolaevich (1905-), prominent official in Soviet Communist Party. He first became prominent in 1956 when he was voted into the party's Central Committee. In 1961, he became a secretary of the Central Committee. Ponomarev has also been a member of the Soviet Union's parliament since 1958.
See also: Union of Soviet Socialist Republics.

Ponselle, Rosa Melba (1897-1981), U.S. soprano, born Rosa Ponzillo. She sang in vaudeville before her sensational Metropolitan Opera debut in 1918 opposite Enrico Caruso in Verdi's *La Forza del Destino.* Until retiring in 1936, she was one of the company's leading dramatic sopranos.

Ponta Delgada (pop. 21,800), city on Saö Miguel Island, the largest of the Portuguese Azores islands. Its harbor is the main port of the Azores, exporting tropical fruits, vegetables, tea, and other products from

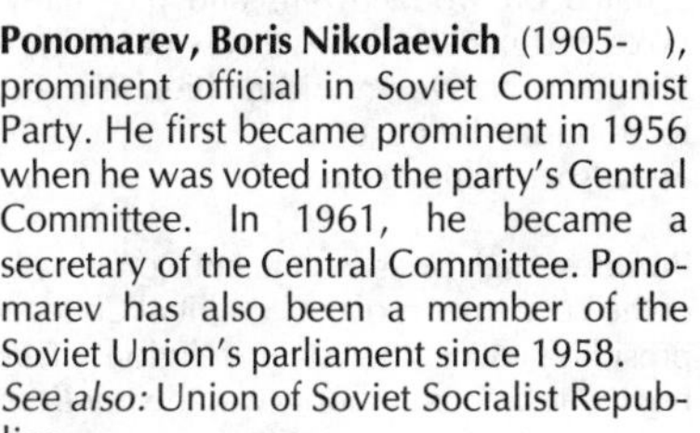

Still life from a wall in Pompeii (50 B.C.)

the area. Other important industries in Ponta Delgada include sugar refining and liquor distilling. Its beautiful setting and favorable climate also makes it an active tourist resort.

Pontiac (1720-69), chief of the Ottawa Indians. He opposed the English during the French and Indian Wars, and was one of the leaders of an unsuccessful war against them, called Pontiac's Rebellion (1763-65), in which Pennsylvania, Virginia, and Maryland were seriously threatened. He signed a peace treaty in 1766.

Pontiac (pop. 76,715), city in southeastern Michigan. It lies on the Clinton River. Pontiac was founded in 1818 and became a city in 1861. In its early days, Pontiac was a leading manufacturing center of wagons and carriages. That developed into automobile manufacturing, which is still its major industry. Its plants produce many cars, trucks, and buses annually. Pontiac is situated on wooded hills and has many lakes and parks nearby. It was named for Pontiac, a Native American chief believed to be buried in the area.
See also: Michigan.

Pontifex, high priest of ancient Rome, one of the 16 members of the Pontifical College presiding over the state religion. The highest religious authority was the *pontifex maximus* (supreme pontiff); this title was adopted by the emperors and later by the popes.
See also: Rome, Ancient.

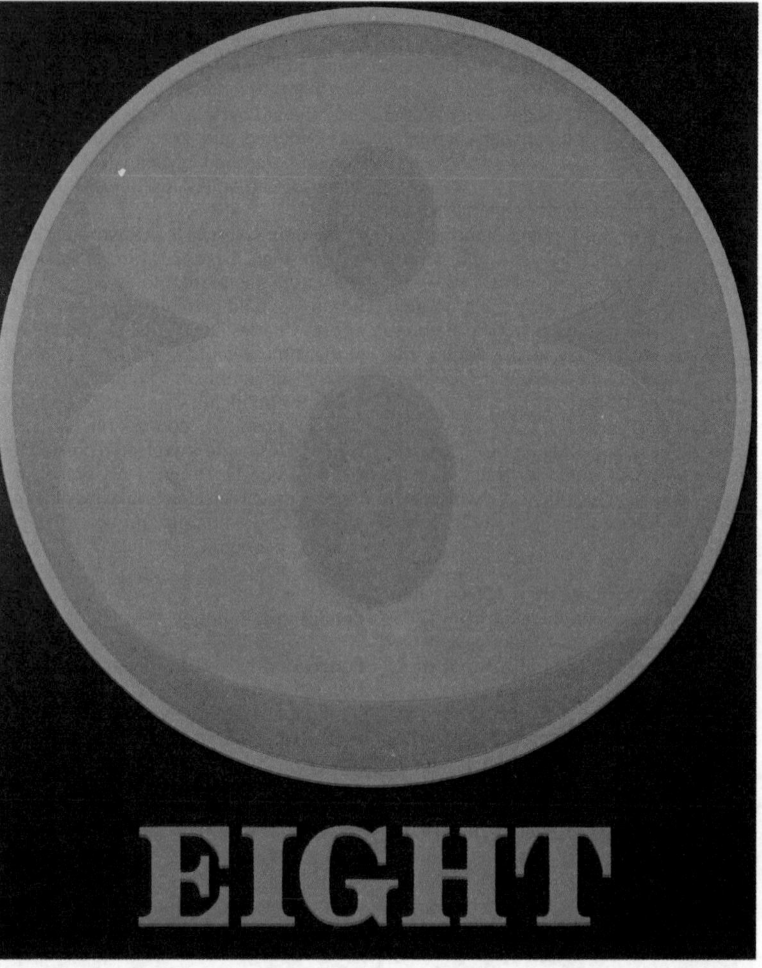

Pop artist Robert Indiana's Eight *(1965)*

Pontiff *see:* Pope.

Pontine Marshes, swamp region in Italy. Located in central Italy, it covers an area of about 175,000 acres (70,820 hectares). The hills and mountains around this area prevent its water from being drained into the sea, creating an unhealthy environment. For centuries, it was the cause of malaria epidemics. Attempts to drain the area by digging waterways date back to as early as 312 B.C. In 1926, Benito Mussolini initiated a project that successfully drained the marshes. The reclaimed land has become a fertile agricultural area with several cities.

Pontoon bridge, bridge held up by pontoons (flat-bottomed boats), sealed metal tubes, or other floating objects. Because it can be built relatively quickly and is made up of materials that are transportable, it is especially convenient for military purposes. An army can set it up when invading or defending a territory to transport troops and equipment across a river when no bridge exists, or when the enemy has destroyed a once-existing bridge. A pontoon bridge was used as early as 480 B.C. by the Persian army. More recently, pontoon bridges were important to U.S. troops in Europe during World War II, where many bridges had been annihilated. Because a pontoon bridge blocks navigation, it is not a viable permanent structure. However, several long-span permanent concrete pontoon bridges exist. Washington has three, and Tasmania and Istanbul have one each.

Pontus, ancient kingdom in northeastern Asia Minor by the Black Sea. Dating from the 4th century B.C., it reached its height under Mithridates VI, who was, however, defeated by the Roman general Pompey in 65 B.C. Pontus was annexed by the Roman Empire in 9 B.C. after it had challenged Roman power.
See also: Mithridates VI.

Pony *see:* Horse.

Pony express, famous relay mail service between St. Joseph, Mo., and Sacramento, Calif. (Apr. 1860 to Oct. 1861). It used horses, not ponies, with riders chosen for their small size. The route covered 1,966 mi (3,164 km), with stations at 10-15 mi- (16-24 km-) intervals. The goal of 10-day delivery was often met. The pony express was superseded by the transcontinental telegraph.

Poodle, breed of intelligent dogs. Poodles have curly hair that can be trimmed in various styles. Their coats are of one solid color, and can be white, black, gray, brown, orange, or blue. There are three varieties of poodles. The *toy poodle* has a shoulder height of up to 10 in (25.4 cm) and weighs up to 6 lbs (2.7 kg). The *miniature poodle* has a shoulder height of 10 to 15 in (25 to 38.1 cm) and weighs 14 to 16 lbs (6.4 to 7.3 kg). The *standard poodle* has a shoulder height of over 15 in (38.1 cm) and weighs 40 to 60 lbs (18.1 to 27 kg). Poodles originated in Germany and were once used to retrieve game. However, they are no longer hunting dogs.

Pool *see:* Billiards.

Poor Richard's Almanac, almanac, written and published by Benjamin Franklin. The almanac was published annually from 1732 to 1757. It included weather predictions, poetry, astrological signs, as well as proverbs and advice. Franklin wrote the almanac under the pen name Richard Saunders. In the early almanacs, Richard had a foolish, dull personality, but in subsequent almanacs he developed into a witty, clever character who promoted thrift, simplicity, and hard work as the keys to success.
Some of his now famous proverbs were: "God helps those who help themselves" and "a penny saved is a penny earned." The almanac was popular in its time, and the philosophies it expressed continue to be relevant.
See also: Franklin, Benjamin.

Poorwill *see:* Whippoorwill.

Pop art, modern art movement dating from the mid-1950s, based on images of advertising, commercial illustration, and mass-produced objects. Developed in England and the United States, it included the artists Richard Hamilton, David Hockney, Andy Warhol, and Robert Rauschenberg, among others.

Popcorn (*Zea mays everta*), type of corn that opens and puffs open when it is heated. It belongs to the family Gramineae. A popular snack, it is a good source of fiber and does not contain many calories. A popcorn kernel contains moist starch. When the kernel is heated, the moisture turns into steam that creates pressure and causes the kernel to burst and the starch to puff out. Native to America, popcorn was cultivated by Native Americans for thousands of years before they introduced it to settlers.

Pope, head of the Roman Catholic church and head of state of Vatican City. The pope is the bishop of Rome, successor in a long line that Roman Catholics believe began with St. Peter, the first bishop of Rome. Basing their authority upon Peter and, ultimately, upon the words of Jesus of Nazareth, the popes, as early as Clement I (c. 92-101), claimed paramount authority over all Christians and primacy over all other bishops. In succeeding centuries, the popes would maintain and extend their claim to absolute spiritual authority and eventually, to political authority as well. But over the centuries, the content and extent of papal authority, power, and prestige, spiritual and political, has varied considerably and was contested almost from the outset. The early church had been governed loosely and informally as a community of believers and bishops who were the equals of each other. The memory of that tradition persisted in Eastern Orthodoxy and when the capital of the Roman empire was moved east to Constantinople in the fourth century, the ground was laid for a contest between east and west for supreme authority over Christendom. That contest, begun in the fourth century, culminated in 1054 during the papacy of Leo IX in a complete schism, or break, between the Roman Catholic and Eastern Orthodox churches. The pope eventually faced two greater challenges to his claims in the Protestant Reformation of the 16th century and the rise of nationalism beginning in the Renaissance. The one effectively put an end to the pope's hitherto unchallenged spiritual authority among Western Christians and the other put an end to his once considerable political power. At the height of political power under Pope Innocent III (1198-1216) the popes claimed to have the power to elevate and depose monarchs as well as bishops and cardinals and the Holy See included considerable territories and drew upon revenues from throughout Europe. The rise of nationalism and the loss of church property and income eventually reduced the pope's domain. The Papal States, founded in 756 and at one time quite extensive, were all part of Italy by 1870, and what was left to the pope, Vatican City, was eventually created an independent state by the Lateran Treaty of 1929. While the modern papacy is vastly reduced politically, the popes continue to enjoy and exercise considerable political influence and prestige. As a head of state, the pope sends ambassadors, or *nuncios*, throughout the world to represent the position and policies of the papacy on a wide range of issues affecting Roman Catholics.

The history of the papacy is a story of popes who were great administrators, visionaries, saints, jurists, and politicians. Among them, too, were diplomats and scholars, discerning patrons of arts and letters, sensualists, weaklings, and scoundrels. The fall of Rome and the subsequent power vacuum ushered in a centuries' long period of lawlessness in the West known as the Dark Ages. For most of that period, the popes took a leading role in the struggle to restore order and civilized life to the West. Pope Gregory I, the Great (590-604) defended Italy from barbarian attack and imposed a measure of enduring order upon the chaos. In the 9th and 10th centuries, the pope's influence declined but was restored by a powerful reform movement. Pope Gregory VII (1073-85) established the pope's authority over clerics and kings and ushered in the greatest years of papal power and prestige. Decline set in with the capture of Pope Boniface VIII by troops of the French King Philip IV in 1303. The pope had become just one more of the many players in the ruthless game of politics. From 1309 to 1377 the popes resided in Avignon, France, and the result was the Great Schism in the western church that lasted from 1378 to 1417, a period in which rival popes claimed to be Peter's true heir and successor. The period raised fundamental questions about the papacy and church governance. In the centuries that followed the popes rapidly lost ground to the Reformation and nationalism.

Wealth and power had corrupted the ecclesiastical bureaucracy and hierarchy and many popes, among them Borgias and Medicis, led lives that scandalized pious Christians, particularly those who lived outside of Italy. But among these Renaissance popes were outstanding men, like Pope Sixtus IV (1471-84), a patron of arts and letters, and Pope Julius II (1503-13), patron of Raphael and Michelangelo. But the popes were not to recover lost ground. Despite the internal reforms and the work of the Counter-Reformation, through the 1700s and 1800s the popes were clearly taking a rear guard action, supporting politically conservative forces, and widely perceived as reactionary. Ideologically, the popes retrenched. They claimed infallibility in matters of faith and morals and there have since, for the most part, appeared departures from orthodoxy and the influences of modern thought.

The pope is elected for life. Upon his death, a conclave, or gathering, of cardinals is called to convene within 20 days. Voting is usually by ballot and for a man to be declared pope he must win a 2/3 majority plus one vote. A woman may not be pope. After a man is elected and accepts, a coronation ceremony is held. The current pope, John Paul II, was elected in 1978. He is the first non-Italian pope since Adrian VI (1522-23). John Paul II is Polish; Pope Adrian II was Dutch. The pope receives an annual salary and, in the course of discharging his many duties and responsibilities, leads a busy, demanding, and relatively spartan life absorbed in administrative, theological, ceremonial, and political matters bearing on the lives of Roman Catholics throughout the world.

See also: Roman Catholic Church.

Popé (d. c.1692), medicine man of the Pueblo Indians who organized the so-called Pueblo Revolt in 1680 against the Spanish in New Mexico. He succeeded in driving them out of Santa Fe and temporarily destroyed Spanish practices, restoring the Pueblos' ancient traditions.

Pope, Alexander (1688-1744), the greatest English poet and satirist of the Augustan Age. He was 4 ft 6 in (1.4 m) tall and partly crippled by tuberculosis. He first set out his literary ideals in his *Essay on Criticism* (1711), written in rhymed (heroic) couplets. His best-known works are the mock epic *The Rape of the Lock* (1712), his translations of the *Iliad* (1720) and the *Odyssey* (1726), *The Dunciad* (1728, 1743), a satirical attack on literary critics, and his essays on moral philosophy, *An Essay on Man* (1733-34) and *Moral Essays* (1731-35).

Poplar, name of group of trees belonging to the willow family. Poplars are found in Europe, Asia, and North America. They grow quickly and produce a soft, light wood used in the manufacture of crates and boxes. Depending on the species, they may be heart-shaped, triangular, or diamond-shaped. The name of some poplars are: balsam poplar, white poplar, white or silver poplar, and Carolina poplar.

Popocatépetl, volcanic mountain in Mexico. Its name is the Aztec word for "smoking mountain." With an altitude of 17,887 ft (5,452 m), it is one of the highest mountains in North America, and the second-highest mountain in Mexico. Its peak is always snow-covered. "Popo," as it is sometimes called, has not had a major eruption since 1702. It does occasionally emit smoke clouds and sulfur gas, and, less frequently, ashes and stones.

Popper, Sir Karl Raimund (1902-), Austrian-born English philosopher, best known for his theory of falsification in the philosophy of science. Popper contends that scientific theories are never more than provisionally adopted and remain acceptable only as long as scientists are devising new experiments to test (falsify) them. He attacks the doctrine of historicism (presuming to understand phenomena entirely through their development) in *The Open Society and Its Enemies* (1945) and *The Poverty of Historicism* (1957).

See also: Philosophy.

Pope John Paul II

Poppy, name for annual or herbaceous perennial plants of the genus *Papaver* and related genera. There are about 100 species, which are mostly native to temperate and subtropical areas in Eurasia and northern Africa. The flower bud is enclosed by two thick, green sepals that drop off to allow the thin petals to unfold. The seeds are enclosed in a capsule. The sap of the unripe capsules of the opium poppy (*P. somniferum*) yield opium; its seeds (poppyseed) are not narcotic.

Popular music, term used to describe several kinds of music that are not classical. Classical music includes symphonies, operas, and ballet works performed by an orchestra. Popular music includes rock and roll, country and folk music, jazz, and other styles and blendings of styles. It is called "popular" because it is usually appreciated by a large number of the general public.

Prince, popular performer/writer/producer

Population, number of or term for all the inhabitants of a designated territory. For the world as a whole, population doubled between 1930 and 1975, from 2 to 4 billion, and increased to 4.7 billion by mid-1983, with a possible 6 billion forecast for the year 2000. The sharpest increases have been in developing nations, which are least able to provide food, education, and jobs for all. Averting world famine depends on the few countries able to export food. Many nations now have population-control programs, but the control of infectious diseases and increases in the food supply because of modern growing techniques have combined to encourage population growth. In some societies, however, fertility rates have declined somewhat, and an increase in abortions, approaching the number of live births in a few countries, has helped defuse the population bomb, though not without great controversy. In the United States, a "baby boom" occurred after World War II, but after 1957 the birth rate declined and by the 1980s gave indications of approaching zero population growth.

Populism, "grass roots" agrarian political movement incorporating a farmer-labor coalition. Specifically, it refers to the doctrines of the U.S. People's Party. The post-Civil War farm depression had created agrarian reform movements like the Grange and the Farmers' Alliance. In 1891-92 delegates from the Farmers' Alliance and labor organization set up the People's Party, which espoused an eight-hour day, government ownership of railroads, graduated income tax, government postal savings banks, direct election of senators, increase of the money supply, and free silver. At first the party gained support rapidly. However, the People's Party declined following the 1896 presidential election, when the Democratic candidate, W.J. Bryan, captured most of the populist vote. The term *populism* is also applied to any policies appealing to the common citizen, such as those advocated by Huey Long and George Wallace.

Poquelin, Jean Baptiste *see:* Molière.

Porcelain, a kind of white earthenware. It is hard, fine, and translucent. Porcelain is made from a mixture of kaolin (a pure white clay) and petuntse (a hard mineral). After the mixture is shaped, it is fired at an extremely high temperature that causes the petuntse to melt into glass that is fused to the kaolin which retains the shape. Porcelain is used to create such items as tableware, vases, and figurines. It is most often decorated with painted designs. Because it was first developed by the Chinese (7th century), it is sometimes referred to as china. Europe, Japan, and the United States produce most of the world's porcelain.

Porcupine, name for large, spiny vegetarian rodents of two distinct families: Erithizontidae, confined to the Americas, and Hystricidae, to the tropics of the Old World. Old World forms, including about a dozen species in Africa and South Asia, are among the largest rodents, and the entire body is covered with spines. The American porcupines have an equal armory of spines, but when relaxed, these are concealed in a thick underfur.

Porcupinefish, slow-moving tropical fish that can blow up its body when alarmed. It takes in water through the mouth to swell

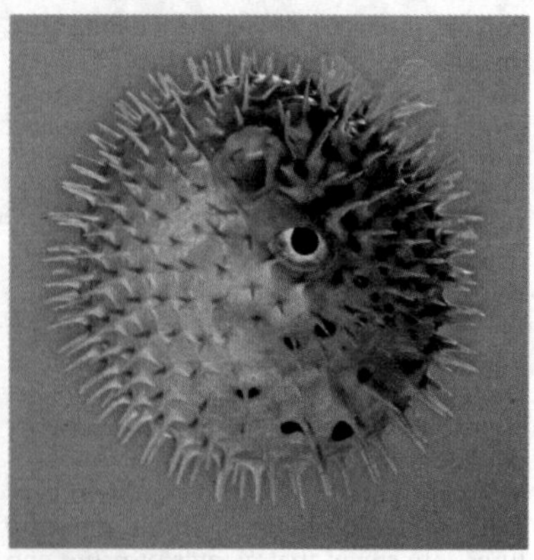

Porcupinefish

its body into a sphere; at the same time, sharp spines are raised, making it very difficult to handle. Porcupinefish feed on shellfish and coral. Pacific Islanders used to make the skins into helmets.

Pore, minute opening of a gland in skin. Skin has many small glands that produce perspiration and oil. Pores serve as an outlet for the perspiration and oil. When pores are blocked up, skin becomes inflamed, resulting in a skin rash or acne.

Porgy, deep-bodied fish (family Sparidae) with powerful teeth. Porgies are found in shallow tropical and temperate seas. The largest is the 100-lb (45-kg) South African mussel-cracker. On the Atlantic coast of America there are the northern porgy, the sheepshead, and the pinfish.

Porifera *see:* Sponge.

Po River, longest river in Italy. Beginning in the Cottian Alps, it flows east for 405 mi (652 km) and drains into a huge delta in the Adriatic Sea. Most rivers in northern Italy empty into it, as do the Garda, Como, Maggiore, Lecco, and Iseo lakes. The Po carries a tremendous amount of water and has created many devastating floods. Efforts were made as early as 300 B.C. to control the river by building embankments. Several large Italian cities are situated on the Po, such as Cremona and Turin. From the mouth of the Po to Turin, the river is deep and wide enough for the navigation of freight ships transporting cargo. On the upper section of the river are several electric power plants.

Pork, pig flesh used for food. Pork may be eaten cooked. It may also be cured with salt and then smoked or dried. Smoking and drying cured pork prevents the meat from spoiling, and gives it an added flavor. Ham and bacon are cured pork. Pork may contain small worms that, when consumed, create a disease called trichinosis. Fresh pork should always be thoroughly cooked until the meat becomes gray—this kills any worms that may be in it.

Pork barrel, pejorative U.S. term for government spending on local, presumably unnecessary, projects. The term, which originated in the 19th century and derives from the practice of salting pork to store in barrels, is used to indicate the wastefulness and selfishness of legislators who vote on such expenditures to reward political allies and direct funds into their districts.

Pornography, term applied to materials, including books, pictures, magazines, and films, with obscene or offensive content designed to cause sexual excitement. The term is derived from the Greek *pornographos* ("writing of harlots") and most often refers to sexual material, though it is now sometimes applied to other forms of offensive material, such as that which portrays gratuitous violence. In the United States each state has laws concerning the publication and distribution of obscene material; these are backed up by extensive international agreements designed to inhibit the import and export of pornography.

Porphyry (A.D. 233-304), ancient Greek philosopher, author of *Introduction to the Categories*, a book which discussed how the qualities of things could be put into categories and groups. He studied in Athens before moving to Rome, where he became a member of the Neoplatonic group led by Plotinus.
See also: Neoplatonism.

Porpoise, small toothed whale (family Phocaenidae), distinguished from dolphins in being smaller and having a rounded head with no projecting beaklike mouth. They feed mainly on shoaling fishes. The name is sometimes loosely applied in the United States to the various species of dolphin.

Porsche, Ferdinand *see:* Volkswagen.

Port, sweet wine, usually red, fortified with brandy. It comes from grapes grown in the Douro Valley, Portugal, and is shipped from Oporto, whence its name.

Portage la Prairie (pop. 13,198), city of southern Manitoba. Situated between the Assiniboine River and Lake Manitoba, it was founded in 1738 by the French who built Fort LaReine there. French fur traders carried their canoes across the prairie between the river and the lake, thus giving the city its name. Today it is a key agricultural market city and food processing center for the Portage Plains region.

Port-au-Prince (pop. 738,000), capital, largest city, and leading port of Haiti. It stands on a sheltered bay facing the Caribbean Sea. In spite of local industries, including textile, flour, and sugar milling, some imposing buildings, and a modern airport, the city is one of the Western Hemisphere's poorest capitals. French colonists founded Port-au-Prince in 1749.

Port Authority of New York and New Jersey, governing agency for port-owned facilities in New York City and adjacent New Jersey. Incorporated in 1921 to develop and improve commerce in and around New York Harbor, the Port Authority operates bridges, tunnels, marine terminals, airports, and buildings such as the "twin towers" of the 1,350 ft (411 m) World Trade Center. It is governed by 12 commissioners, 6 from each of the 2 states, and maintains trade development offices in major United States and foreign cities.

Portcullis *see:* Castle.

Port Elizabeth (pop. 281,600), city in South Africa. Situated on a bay of the Indian Ocean, it was founded in 1799. The modern city was laid out in 1820 by Sir Rufane Donkin, who named it for his wife, Lady Elizabeth. Port Elizabeth is a major seaport and manufacturing center with important rubber and automobile industries.

Porter, U.S. naval officers, father and son. **David Porter** (1780-1843) took part in the war against Tripoli (1801-5) and during the War of 1812 he became the first United States naval officer to operate a warship in the Pacific Ocean. He was also the foster father of David G. Farragut, one of the greatest Union naval commanders of the Civil War. **David Dixon Porter** (1813-91) served under Farragut in the Civil War and played key roles in the captures of New Orleans, Vicksburg, and other major Southern ports.

Porter, Cole (1893-1964), U.S. popular song composer. After World War I he achieved great success as a writer of sophisticated songs and musical comedies, providing both the words and music. His prolific output includes *Anything Goes* (1934), *Kiss Me Kate* (1948), *Can-Can* (1953), the film score for *High Society* (1956), and many classic songs.

Porter, Fitz-John (1822-1901), U.S. Army officer. During the Civil War, he served as a corps commander in the Army of the Potomac and fought in the Shenandoah Valley and Peninsular campaigns. During the second Battle of Manassas (Bull Run) in 1862, the Union commander, Gen. John Pope, accused him of failing to carry out orders. Porter was court-martialed, found guilty, and discharged from the army in 1863. In 1879 his case was reviewed and he was exonerated. He was restored to his rank 7 years later.

Porter, Katherine Anne (1890-1980), U.S. short-story writer and novelist who won the 1966 Pulitzer Prize for her *Collected Short Stories* (1965). Her collections of short stories include *Flowering Judas* (1930) and *Pale Horse, Pale Rider* (1939). *Ship of Fools* (1962) is her only novel.

Porter, William Sydney *see:* Henry, O.

Portland (pop. 215,281), largest city in Maine. Located on Casco Bay, Portland was founded in 1632 and has one of the finest harbors along the Atlantic Coast. It is a major shipping center for pulpwood and other agricultural products and oil bound for the Portland-Montreal pipeline is unloaded there. Portland is also an important seafood processing hub and its downtown business district features many good examples of Victorian architecture.
See also: Maine.

Portland (pop. 1,239,842), largest city in Oregon, a leading West Coast port. It stands in northwestern Oregon on the Willamette River near its junction with the Columbia River, c.60 mi (97 km) due east of the Pacific Ocean. Ocean-going ships reach Portland by river, enabling it to handle more dry cargo than any other Pacific port. Lumber, fruit, and wheat are the main exports. Important educational institutions include the University of Oregon's schools of medicine and dentistry, Portland State College, and the Roman Catholic University of Portland. The city's rose gardens are nationally famous.
See also: Oregon.

Portland, Oregon, with Mount Hood in the background

Portland cement *see:* Cement.

Port Louis (pop. 138,000), capital and largest city of the island nation of Mauritius. Located on a sheltered harbor of the Indian Ocean on the northwestern shore of the country's main island, Port Louis is a key agricultural and industrial export center. It was founded by the French in 1735 and named for King Louis XV.

Port Moresby (pop. 122,800), capital and largest city of Papua New Guinea. It lies on a harbor of the Coral Sea in the southeastern part of the country and was founded in 1873 by the British explorer Capt. John Moresby. During World War II (1939-45) Port Moresby served as an Allied military operations center for the South Pacific.

Porto, or Oporto (pop. 330,200), second largest city in Portugal. Situated on the Douro River near its mouth at the Atlantic Ocean, Porto was founded during the Roman Empire and several of its medieval landmarks, including a cathedral, survive today. Porto is the major commercial and industrial hub of northern Portugal and is famous for its port wines. Fishing and food processing also contribute greatly to the city's economic base.

Pôrto Alegre (pop. 1,109,000), city in southeastern Brazil. It is located on the Guaíba River near the Atlantic Ocean and is the capital of the state of Rio Grande do Sul. Pôrto Alegre is a key shipping and commercial port, as well as an important cultural and educational center.

Portobelo (pop. 550), village in Panama. Named by Columbus in 1502 and founded as a Caribbean shipping port, Portobelo was often the starting point for Spanish treasure ships bound for Spain from its New World colonies. Repeated attacks by English pirates in the 17th and 18th centuries destroyed much of the town and its importance declined after the opening of the Panama Railroad in the 1850s.

Port-of-Spain (pop. 150,000), capital and largest city of Trinidad and Tobago. Situated on the northwest coast of the island of Trinidad, Port-of-Spain was founded by the Spanish around 1560 and was briefly the capital of the Federation of the West Indies (1958-62), a group of British-owned Caribbean islands. It is a major agricultural export center for the nation and the southern Caribbean region.

Portolá, Gaspar de (1723?-?84), Spanish colonizer of California. In 1769, as governor of the Californias, he mounted an expedition from Mexico that founded San Diego and Monterey. He was governor of Puebla, Mexico, from 1776.
See also: California.

Porto-Novo (pop. 144,000), capital and second largest city of Benin. Lying on the Gulf of Guinea, it was founded and named by the Portuguese in the 17th century and became a hub for the West African slave trade. Captured by the French in 1883, Porto-Novo was made the capital of the colony of Dahomey and remained the capital when independence was granted in 1960. It is a major port and rail terminal for the rest of the nation.

Port Said (pop. 399,800), port city in Egypt. Located on the Mediterranean Sea at the northern terminus of the Suez Canal, Port Said was founded in 1859 as a camp for workers building the canal. Because of its key location, it is a major commercial center for ships using the canal and the site of a free trade zone established by the Egyptian government to encourage commerce.
See also: Egypt.

Portsmouth (pop. 187,900), major port and naval center in southern England. Situated on the English Channel, Portsmouth was founded in the 1100s and became a key shipbuilding city in the 16th century. Shipbuilding and naval activity provide the city with much of its economic base and its busy harbor handles much of the country's import and export trade. Historic sites there include the 12th century cathedral, the birthplace of Charles Dickens, and Lord Nelson's flagship, *Victory.*
See also: England.

Portsmouth (pop. 26,254), New Hampshire, major seaport on the state's Atlantic coast. Founded in the early 1600s at the mouth of the Piscataqua River, Portsmouth is the site of an important naval shipyard and Air Force base. It is the oldest settlement in New Hampshire and the site of its first capital. The Treaty of Portsmouth, ending the Russo-Japanese War, was signed at the naval base in 1905.
See also: New Hampshire.

Port Sudan (pop. 206,700), chief port city of Sudan. It is on the Red Sea and was built between 1905 and 1909 to replace an earlier Arab port that became choked off by coral reefs. With modern harbor facilities, Port Sudan handles most of the nation's overseas trade and is the fourth largest city in Sudan.
See also: Sudan.

Portugal

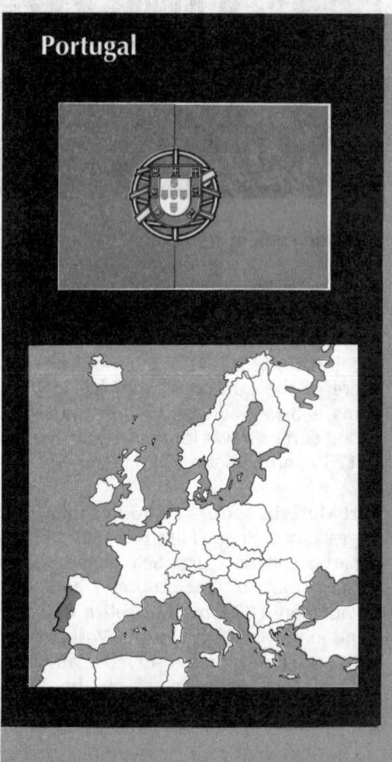

General information	
Capital:	Lisbon
Area:	35,672 sq mi (92,389 sq km)
Population:	10,372,000
Official language:	Portuguese
Monetary unit:	1 escudo = 100 centavos
Main cities:	Lisbon, Porto, Amadora
Government	
Form:	republic
Independent:	1910 (republic)
Head of state:	President (elected every 5 years)
Head of government:	Prime minister
Legislature:	one legislative house (Assembly of the Republic)
Executive:	Prime minister and Council of Ministers
Judiciary:	highest court is the Supreme Court
Political division:	18 districts, 2 autonomous regions
National economy	
Gross national product:	U.S. $37,260,000,000
Per capita income:	U.S. $3,670
Agriculture:	grapes, potatoes, corn, tomatoes, wheat, olives
Livestock:	sheep, pigs, cattle, poultry
Fisheries:	395,000 metric tons
Mining:	iron, anthracite, tungsten, copper, gold and silver sulfides
Industries:	cotton and synthetic fibers, cork products, refined petroleum, clothing, knitted fabrics, motor vehicles, tires, wine
Main exports:	miscellaneous manufactured articles (clothing), machinery and transport equipment, crude materials, food and live animals
Transportation:	2,241 mi (3,607 km) of railroads, 32,282 mi (51,953 km) of roads, 5 international airports
Trading partners:	Germany, France, Spain, United Kingdom, Italy, U.S.
People	
Urban:	30%
Ethnic composition:	Portuguese 99%, Cape Verdean 0.5%, Brazilian 0.5%
Birth rate:	15 per 1,000 population
Death rate:	8.4 per 1,000 population
Infant mortality:	15 per 1,000 live births
Life expectancy:	male 70 years, female 77 years

Portugal, republic on the Iberian peninsula in the extreme southwest of continental Europe.

Land and climate. Excluding the Azores and Madeira, Portugal covers an area of 34,340 sq mi/88,941 sq km and is bordered by Spain to the east and north and by the Atlantic Ocean to the west and south. Portugal lies at the point where the western ridge of the high Spanish plateau slopes downward towards the Atlantic Ocean. Most of the highest land lies in the northeast gradually giving way to undulating hills and low fertile plains. Three large rivers, all rising in Spain, cross the country: the Douro, the Tagus, and the Guadiana. Coastal Portugal has a mild climate; the interior has colder winters and is often subject to drought. The capital is Lisbon.

People. The Portuguese people are a mixture of the original inhabitants of the land and successive waves of invaders. The Portuguese language is closely related to Spanish and almost everyone in Portugal is Roman Catholic.

Economy. Portugal is one of Europe's poorer countries. Most of the people live in villages and small towns and agriculture is the principal occupation. Most farms are small and poor. Portuguese raise livestock, olives, grapes, citrus fruits, and almonds and produce wine and olive oil. Portugal is the world's major producer of cork. Fishing is important, the chief catches being sardines and tuna. Industries include food processing, textiles, metals, mining, and hydroelectricity.

History. Over the centuries, the area that is now Portugal was invaded by Celts, Greeks, and Romans and later by Visigoths, Berbers, and Moors. The Moors arrived in 711 and remained until 1249. Their influence upon Portuguese culture has been deep. Portugal became an independent Christian kingdom in 1143 under Alfonso I and over the next century the country was completely reconquered from the Moors. In 1385, John I founded the Aviz dynasty and by the second half of the 16th century, Portugal was at the pinnacle of its power with an empire that included much of South America, Africa, and South and Southeast Asia. Philip II of Spain seized Portugal in 1580 and the Spanish ruled until a successful revolt established the ruling house of Braganza in 1640. By then, Portugal had lost most of her former power and influence. During the Napoleonic Wars, Portugal was invaded by both the French and the Spanish. By 1825 Brazil had become an independent empire. A Portuguese republic was declared in 1910 and after a military coup in 1926 Antonio de Oliveira Salazar rose to power and became virtual dictator until he was succeeded by Marcello Caetano in 1968. A coup in 1974 ushered in a government that brought democratic reforms. Subsequently, Portugal shed virtually all of its overseas territories. Guinea-Bissau became independent in 1974, followed by Angola, the Cape Verde Islands, Mozambique, and São Tomé and Príncipe in 1975. In 1976 Portuguese Timor became part of Indonesia and Macao will revert to China in 1999. In the process, Portugal has also recovered a measure of political stability. The current government, headed by Premier Anibal Cavaco Silvas, was democratically elected in 1987.

Portuguese, official language of Portugal and Brazil. It is one of the Romance languages and developed from the Latin spoken in Roman Iberia. Brazilian Portuguese has absorbed words and phrases from the languages of the Native American and African slave populations.

Portuguese Guinea *see:* Guinea-Bissau.

Portuguese man-of-war (*Physalia physalis*), colorful jellyfish of the order Siphonophora. It consists of an assemblage of four kinds of polyps, the most obvious of which is a gas-filled bladder about 1 ft (30.5 cm) long, which carries a high crest and is colored blue or purple. Below this float are supported other polyps, including the long, stinging tentacles used for catching prey. The sting can be painful to humans.

Portuguese water dog, web-footed dog capable of swimming great distances. Portuguese fishermen trained and used the dogs to retrieve fish and nets from the water and they have also been used to carry messages between ships. Males range from 20 to 23 in (51 to 59 cm) tall and weigh between 42 and 60 lb (19-27 kg), while females are smaller.

Portulaca, flower of the purslane family. Producing colorful blossoms that open only in full sunlight, portulacas are cultivated in gardens and several species are used as potted plants. The petals are most commonly red, yellow, pink, white, or purple and the plant may grow from 1 to 1.5 ft (30-46 cm) tall.

Poseidon, in Greek mythology, god of the sea. The son of Cronus and Rhea and brother of Zeus, Poseidon was also the god of horses, earthquakes, and sea storms. He was often pictured with a long white beard driving a chariot and wielding a trident with which he stirred up the earth or sea when venting his wrath. His Roman counterpart was Neptune.

Positivism, philosophical theory of knowledge associated with the 19th-century French philosopher Auguste Comte. It holds that the observable, or "positive," data of sense experience constitute the sole basis for assertions about matters of fact; only the truths of logic and mathematics are additionally admitted. The speculative claims of theology and metaphysics, regarded as the primitive antecedents of "positive" thought, are discounted.
See also: Comte, Auguste.

Positron emission tomography (PET), technique used to study brain activity. A person undergoing a PET scan is injected with a glucose solution containing low-level radioactive particles that produce positrons, electrically charged particles that help produce gamma rays. The person places his or her head inside a ring containing sensors that measure gamma ray signals from the brain, and these signals are translated by colors onto a screen. Scientists reading the screen can interpret the colors in a way that measures brain activity.
See also: Brain.

Wine kegs being transported on sailing ship in Porto, Portugal

Possum, tree-dwelling mammal of the family Phalangeridae, native to Australia and New Guinea. There are about 40 species of possums, ranging in weight from 1/2 oz (14 grams) to 11 lb (5 kg). They are nocturnal animals, foraging through forests and garbage cans for their food. As with other marsupials, the babies are born prematurely and are nurtured in the mothers' pouches. Their practice of lying absolutely still when frightened gives rise to the term "playing possum."

Post, Emily Price (1872-1960), U.S. writer, accepted authority on correct social behavior because of her book *Etiquette* (1922).

Post, Wiley (1899-1935), U.S. aviator. In 1933 he was the first person to fly solo around the world, a feat he accomplished in a little over a week (July 15-22). During this flight, which covered 15,596 mi (25,099 km), Post proved the effectiveness of an automatic pilot system that enabled the plane to stay aloft while he rested. On Aug. 15, 1935 he was killed in a plane crash near Point Barrow, Alaska.

Postal Service, U.S., independent federal agency that provides mail service nationwide. The Postal Service began operation on July 1, 1971, replacing the United States Post Office Department founded in 1775. The current arrangement calls for an 11-member independent board of governors, headed by the Postmaster General, to oversee all facets of the postal system's operations. They set postage rates, appoint postmasters, and set salaries for employees. There are about 30,000 post offices in the United States and the USPS employs about 730,000 people.

Postal Union, Universal (UPU), United Nations agency governing the international flow of mail. Begun in 1874 with 22 nations attending the first International Postal Congress in Berne, Switzerland, the UPU became a UN agency in 1947. Today it includes all 170 member nations. The UPU sets policies and uniform procedures for the exchange of mail and parcels between countries and establishes reasonable postal rates. It also provides technical assistance and advice to its members and strives toward the improvement of all services under its supervision.

Postimpressionism, term coined by critic Roger Fry to describe the work of certain painters (1880-90) whose styles, though dissimilar, flowed from, and were a reaction to, impressionism. Paul Cézanne, Paul Gauguin, Georges Seurat, and Vincent Van Gogh are considered the principal postimpressionists.

Post mortem *see:* Autopsy.

Pot *see:* Marijuana.

Potash, potassium-based salts used in fertilizers. Most potash comes from the mineral sylvite and is often found in underground salt beds or in salt lakes. Potassium chloride (KCl) is the most important type of potash but another type, potassium carbonate (K_2CO_3), can be manufactured by running water through wood ashes and boiling the solution in large iron pots.

Potato beetle

Potassium, chemical element, symbol K; for physical constants see Periodic Table. Potassium was discovered by Sir Humphrey Davy in 1807. It was the first metal isolated by electrolysis. It is found mainly as *sylvite* (potassium chloride) but occurs in many other minerals. It is obtained commercially by electrolysis of the hydroxide. Potassium is a silvery-white, soft, reactive metal of the alkali metal group. It catches fire spontaneously in water and oxidizes rapidly in air and must be stored in a dry oxygen-free liquid such as mineral oil. It is essential to plant growth and is found in most soils. Potassium and its compounds are used in fertilizers, photography, organic synthesis, and heat transfer media.

Potassium nitrate *see:* Saltpeter.

Potato (*Solanum tuberosum*), herbaceous plant of the nightshade family, with an edible, fleshy, tuberous, underground stem. It originated in the South American Andes. The tubers became a popular European foodstuff in the 18th century, the Irish in particular becoming dependent on the high-carbohydrate crop.

Potato beetle (*Lema trilineata*), destructive insect of the leaf beetle family. The larvae feed on the leaves and stems of potato plants, causing extensive damage and diseases that harm proper potato tuber growth. The most common type is the Colorado potato beetle (*Leptinotarsa decemlineata*), which measures 1/2 in (13 mm) long and is yellow with black stripes on its wing covers.

Potato famine, in 19th-century Ireland, famine caused by potato blight. In 1845 and 1846 potato crops failed; in the subsequent famine nearly a million people died, and over a million emigrated, particularly to the United States. Ireland's population fell from about 8.5 million in 1845 to 6.55 million in 1851.
See also: Ireland.

Potawatomi, North American tribe of the Algonquian language family. In the 18th century they lived around the south shore of Lake Michigan. They allied with the French colonists and joined Pontiac in his rebellion (1763). They later supported the British in the Revolutionary War and in the War of 1812. Coming under pressure from settlers, they moved west, and in 1846 most of them were forced into a reservation in Kansas. The Potawatomi in Kansas have preserved much of the aboriginal culture.

Potemkin, Grigori Aleksandrovich (1729-91), Russian soldier and favorite of Catherine the Great. For the last 20 years of his life, he was the most powerful man in Russia. He enlarged the Russian army and navy, and annexed (1783) and administered the Crimea.

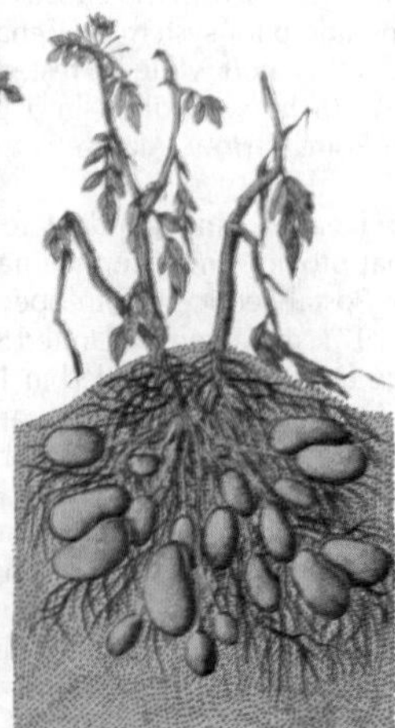

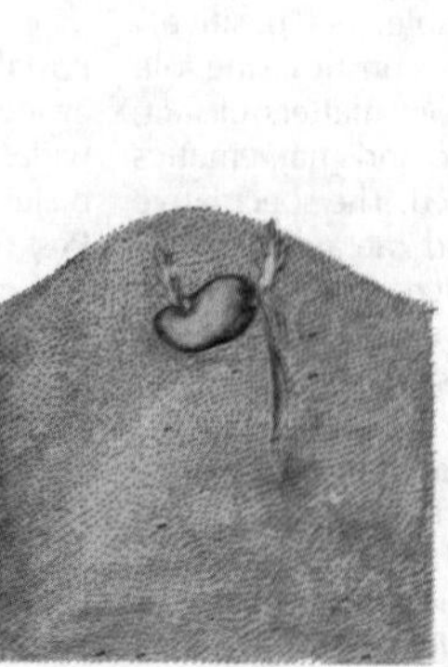

The potato plant develops from the seed potato, reaching full leaf during the summer. When the stem and leaves wither, the tubers, which are thickenings of underground stems, are ready for harvest.

Potential, electric, work done against electric fields in bringing a unit charge to a given point from some arbitrary reference point (usually earthed), measured in volts (i.e., joules per coulomb). Charges tend to flow from points at one potential to those at a lower potential; potential difference, or voltage, thus plays the role of a driving force for electric current. In inductive circuits, the work done in bringing up the charge depends on the route taken, and potential ceases to be a useful concept.

Potentiometer, device used to obtain a precise measure of the electromotive force (emf), or voltage, of an electrical cell. It employs a special circuit incorporating a variable resistor (rheostat) and a galvanometer. Using a standard cell of known emf, the rheostat is adjusted until no current flows in the circuit, as indicated by the galvanometer. The cell of unknown emf is then placed in the circuit instead of the standard cell, and the rheostat is adjusted again so that no current flows. The difference in the 2 settings of the rheostat indicates the emf of the unknown cell. The potentiometer can be used to calibrate electrical instruments and as a variable resistor. The volume control in a radio is a type of potentiometer.

Potlatch, in many tribal cultures, especially among the Native Americans of the Northwest Coast, an elaborate ceremonial feast at which the host distributes or destroys his own wealth to gain status or office in his tribe. Wealthier guests are expected in turn to match or exceed this in future potlatches. Although banned for a while in Canada, the potlatch is still an important tribal institution.

Potomac River, U.S. river flowing through Washington, D.C. Formed by the confluence of the 110-mi (177-km) long northern branch and the 140-mi (125-km) long southern branch, it flows 287 mi (462 km) into Chesapeake Bay. Navigation for large ships is prevented above Washington, D.C., by the Great Falls. The river is noted for its scenic attraction.

Potsdam (pop. 138,700), city in eastern Germany, near Berlin. In the 18th century it was chosen by Frederick II as his principal residence and became a center and symbol of Prussian militarism. Noted for its royal palaces, it is now also an industrial city. It was the site of the 1945 Potsdam Conference.

Potsdam Conference, (July 17 to Aug. 2, 1945), a summit meeting at Potsdam, Germany, between Premier Joseph Stalin, President Harry S. Truman, and in succession, Prime Ministers Winston Churchill and Winston Attlee. They agreed that a four-power Allied Control Council would rule defeated Germany, disarming it and fostering democratic government; Poland would gain part of East Germany; the Ger-

man economy would be decentralized; Germans in Hungary, Poland, and Czechoslovakia would be repatriated. The conference also discussed reparations payments and issued an ultimatum to Japan. Almost all the agreements were breached as the Cold War hardened.
See also: World War II.

Potter, Beatrix (1866-1943), English author and illustrator of children's books. Her works, illustrated by herself, have become classics, including *The Tale of Peter Rabbit* (1902), *The Tailor of Gloucester* (1903), *Benjamin Bunny* (1904), *Mrs. Tiggy-Winkle* (1905), *Jemima Puddle-Duck* (1908), and *Pigling Bland* (1913).

Pottery and porcelain, ceramic articles, especially vessels, made of clay (generally kaolin) and hardened by firing. In the manufacture of pottery the clay is made plastic by blending with water. The article is then shaped—traditionally by hand, by building up layers of strips (coiled pottery), by "throwing" on the potter's wheel, or by molding, industrially by high-pressure molding or by a rotating template. The clay is fired in a kiln, slowly at first, then at higher temperatures to oxidize and consolidate it. The glaze (if desired) is then applied by spraying or dipping and the article is refired.

Potto (genus *Perodicticus*), various slow-moving African primates related to the lorises. The potto has large, staring eyes, thick, woolly fur, and a short tail; spines from the neck bones protrude through the skin. It leads a solitary life, emerging at dusk to search for fruit, insects, lizards, or birds' nests.

Poulenc, Francis (1899-1963), French composer, member of the post-World War II group of composers called *Les Six*. His music is light in texture, although serious. His best-known works include *Mouvements perpetuels* for piano (1918), the ballet *Les Biches* (1924), and the opera *Dialogue des Carmélites* (1957). He was also a notable songwriter.

Potto

Poultry farming, rearing of all types of domesticated farm fowls for eggs and flesh. Chickens are the most popular bird, followed by turkeys, ducks, geese, and other types. Important chicken breeds are the leghorn and Rhode Island Red for eggs and the Plymouth Rock and Cornish for meat. Nearly all economically valuable fowls live in controlled environments, with artificial lighting and heating and small pens for individuals or groups. Chickens are hatched in incubators, reared in brooders and transferred to laying or fattening quarters. An annual output of 200-250 eggs per bird is essential for good profits. Marketing is organized through farmers' cooperatives and marketing boards.

Pound, Ezra Loomis (1885-1972), U.S. poet, critic, and translator. A gifted linguist, he went to Europe in 1908 and soon won recognition. His most important works are *Homage to Sextus Propertius* (1918), *Hugh Selwyn Mauberley* (1920), and the epic *Cantos* (1925-60). He championed the imagist and vorticist movements, and influenced T.S. Eliot, Robert Frost, and W.B. Yeats, among others. He supported Benito Mussolini, and after broadcasting pro-Fascist propaganda during World War II, he was indicted for treason by the United States; he was found unfit to plead and confined to a mental institution until 1958.

Pound, Roscoe (1870-1964), U.S. jurist and educator who championed flexibility in the law and efficiency in court administration. Professor of law at Harvard (1910-37), he advocated a "sociological jurisprudence" that would adapt the law to changing social and economic conditions.

Poussin, Nicolas (1594-1665), greatest 17th-century French Baroque painter. He worked mostly in Rome and based his style on Raphael and antiquities. He was first painter to Louis XII. His classical and religious subjects, such as *Shepherds of Arcadia* (1629), *The Rape of the Sabine Women* (1635), and *The Seven Sacraments* (1644-48) are rich in color, austere in handling, dramatic, and evocative in mood. He influenced Jacques-Louis David, Paul Cézanne, and Pablo Picasso.

Poverty, shortage of come or resources necessary for a minimum standard of living in a particular society. In the United States, where a poor minority exists in the midst of an affluent society, a major element in poverty is the feeling of psychological deprivation. In the poor countries of Asia, Africa, and Latin America, where the poor constitute a majority of the people, poverty consists more of physical deprivation, but even in the third world the economic expectations of the poor have been substantially raised by exposure to the mass media.

Powder metallurgy, process of reducing metals into powder. The process is used to make metal alloys by mixing them as powder and heating them to bind the powders together. They are then pressed into the desired shape or form. Metals can be broken down into powders by crushing them or by submittting them to intense heat. They can also be reduced through electrolysis or by atomization of the metal in molten form.

Powder River, river of western United States. From its source in the foothills of Wyoming's Bighorn Mountains, the Powder River flows northward into Montana and joins the Yellowstone River near Terry, Mont. It is 486 mi (782 km) long.

Ezra Pound

Powell, Adam Clayton, Jr. (1908-72), U.S. politician. Minister of the Abyssinian Baptist Church, he was New York's first black city council member (1941). He founded *The People's Voice* (1942) and, as the flamboyant "Voice of Harlem," was a Democratic representative (1945-70). Excluded from Congress for alleged misuse of public funds (1967), the expulsion was overturned by the U.S. Supreme Court and he was reelected twice until he was defeated in 1970.

Powell, Anthony Dymoke (1905-), English novelist, best known for his contemporary comedy of manners *A Dance to the Music of Time*, a 12-volume series of novels starting with *A Question of Upbringing* (1951) and ending with *Hearing Secret Harmonies* (1976).

Colin Powell

Powell, Colin (1938-), youngest person and first black officer ever to become Chair of the Joint Chiefs of Staff (appointed 1989), the highest-ranking military post in the United States. Powell, a 4-star general, co-directed (with Secretary of Defense Dick Cheney) the allied effort during the Persian Gulf War (1991).
See also: Persian Gulf War.

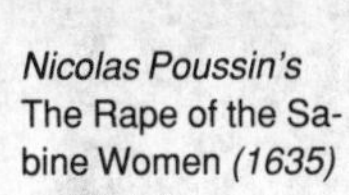

Nicolas Poussin's The Rape of the Sabine Women *(1635)*

Powell, John Wesley (1834-1902), U.S. geologist and ethnologist best known for his geological and topographical surveys and for his anthropological studies of Native Americans. He helped establish and headed the U.S. Geological Survey (1881-94).
See also: Geology.

Powell, Lewis Franklin, Jr. (1907-), associate justice of the U.S. Supreme Court (1971-87). A lawyer and former president of the American Bar Association, he was appointed to the court by President Richard M. Nixon.
See also: Supreme Court of the United States

Power, in physics, the time rate at which work is done. The amount of power that is put forth determines the amount of work that can be done per unit time. Power can be calculated with the following formula:

$$P=\frac{W}{t}$$

In this formula, P stands for power, W for work, and t for time. Work is measured by multiplying the force times the distance. The formula for power is then written:

$$P=\frac{Fd}{t}$$

In this formula, F stands for force and d stands for distance.
The basic unit of power in the English system of measurement is *foot-pounds per second*. When a force of 1 pound moves an object 1 foot, 1 foot-pound of work is done. In the metric system, the customary unit of power is the watt. A watt is the power needed to do 1 joule of work per second.
See also: Mathematics.

Power, in the social sciences, the ability to exercise control over others. Power is most often exerted by individuals, groups, or nations through superior physical strength, social position, or intellect. Greater resources or attributes usually give a person or entity power to impose penalties on those who fail to yield to their demands. Fear of the imposition of those penalties is what most often keeps weaker individuals or nations from rebelling against those holding power over them.

Alchemist Street in Prague: the home of Franz Kafka is in the foreground.

Power, in mathematics, the total of a number multiplied by itself a given number of times. It was developed as a shortcut to having to write the same number multiplied by itself many times, for example, 5 to the fourth power means that the number 5 is multiplied by 5 four times. It is written as a cardinal number with a superior number to the upper right of it (5^4=625). In the example, 5 is called the base and 4 is the exponent.

Power of attorney, in U.S. law, legal document authorizing a person to act on behalf of the signatory, usually in business and financial matters. To be officially recorded, it usually must be certified by a notary public. A general power allows the agent to act for the signatory in all circumstances, while a special power covers only specified items.

Powers, Hiram (1805-73), U.S. sculptor. He worked in Florence, Italy, from 1837. His work includes the neoclassical *Greek Slave* (1843) and busts of eminent Americans, including Andrew Jackson, Thomas Jefferson, and Benjamin Franklin.

Powhatan (c.1550-1618), personal name Wahunsonacock, chief of the Powhatans and head of the Powhatan Confederacy of tribes, which he enlarged until it covered most of the Virginia tidewater region and part of Maryland. He befriended the Jamestown settlers under their leader John Smith (1608). Later hostilities were settled when his daughter Pocahontas married John Rolfe (1614).

Powhatan, North American tribe in eastern Virginia, of Algonquian linguistic stock. They grew corn, hunted, fished, and lived in villages with palisades. Under Powhatan their confederacy dominated some 30 tribes. After his death (1618) violent clashes with encroaching settlers led to their defeat. Some 3,000 Powhatan live in Virginia today.

Poznan (pop. 575,100), city in Poland. Located on the Warta River in the west-central part of the country, it was founded in the 9th century A.D. It became part of Poland in 1919 when the national boundaries were realigned following World War I. In 1956 labor riots against communist government policies there led to major reforms for the Polish people. Today, Poznan is an important industrial and educational center.

PR *see:* Public relations.

Prado *see:* Madrid.

Praetor, in ancient Rome (from 366 B.C.), a magistrate elected annually to administer justice, 2nd in rank to the consul. By 197 B.C. there were six praetors; four were responsible for provincial administration.

Praetorian Guard, elite household troops of the Roman emperors, consisting of 9 (later 10) cohorts of 1,000 foot soldiers with higher rank and pay than ordinary troops. Instituted by Augustus in 2 B.C., they assumed enough power to overthrow emperors. Constantine disbanded them in 312.

Pragmatic sanction, edict by a ruler pronouncing on an important matter of state, such as the succession. The most famous was issued by the Holy Roman Emperor Charles VI in 1713 (published 1718), declaring that his eldest daughter, Maria Theresa, would inherit the Austrian throne in the absence of a male heir. This resulted in the War of the Austrian Succession (1740-48).

Pragmatism, philosophical method whose criterion of truth is relative to events and not, as in traditional philosophy, absolute and independent of human experience. A theory is pragmatically true if it "works"—if it has an intended or predicted effect. All human undertakings are viewed as attempts to solve problems in the world of action; if theories are not trial solutions capable of being tested, they are pointless. The philosophy of pragmatism was developed in reaction to late 19th-century idealism, mainly by the U.S. philosophers C.S. Peirce, W. James, and John Dewey.
See also: Dewey, John; James, William; Peirce, Charles Sanders.

Prague, or Praha (pop. 1,190,000), capital and largest city of Czechoslovakia, on the Vlatava River. One of Europe's great historic cities, it became prominent under Emperor Charles IV, who founded the university in central Europe (1348). The Hapsburgs ruled Prague for nearly 300 years, beginning in 1526, until Czechoslovakia's independence after World War I. Prague was invaded by the Nazis in 1939 and by Warsaw Pact countries in 1968. The city has great cultural, commercial, and industrial importance and is the center of the country's manufacturing industries.
See also: Czechoslovakia.

Prairie, rolling grassland that once covered much of interior North America. There are three types of prairie: tall-grass, midgrass (or mixed-grass), and shortgrass, which is found in the driest areas. Typical prairie animals are the coyotes, badgers, prairie dogs, and jackrabbits and the now largely vanished bison and wolf.

Prairie chicken, name for two species of grouse (genus *Tympanuchus*) that were once common in the eastern half of North America. Plowing of the prairies and cutting down of the woodlands have destroyed their homes. The males have airsacs on their throats for making booming calls. The airsacs are orange in the greater prairie chicken and violet in the lesser prairie chicken. The heath hen, which was a race of the greater prairie chicken, has been extinct since 1932.

Prairie dog, ground squirrel of the genus *Cynomys*. Social animals of the open plains of North America, they live in large colonies in connected burrows. They are short-tailed, marmot-like creatures, active by day, feeding, grooming, or sunbathing near their burrows. They frequently raise themselves on their hindlegs to watch for danger. A sharp whistle, given as warning, sends the colony dashing into the burrows.

Prairie Provinces, popular name for the Canadian provinces of Manitoba, Saskatchewan, and Alberta.

Prairie wolf *see:* Coyote.

Praseodymium, chemical element, symbol Pr; for physical constants see Periodic Table. Praseodymium was discovered by C.A. von Welsbach in 1885 after he separated didymia into earths (oxides) called praseodymia and neodymia. The element occurs in the minerals monazite and bastnasite, the two principal sources of the rare-earth elements. It is prepared by reducing the anhydrous chloride with calcium. Praseodymium is a silvery, soft, reactive metal, belonging to the series of elements known as the rare-earth metals. Ion-exchange and solvent extraction techniques have led to much easier isolation of the so-called rare-earth elements. Praseodymium and its compounds are used in carbon lighting applications, special glasses and enamels, and refractory materials.

Prawn *see:* Shrimp.

Praxiteles (active c.370-330 B.C.), greatest Greek sculptor of his time. Of his major works, which introduced a new delicacy, grace, and sinuosity of line, only the marble statue *Hermes with the Infant Dionysus* survives. There are Roman copies of his *Aphrodite of Cnidus* and *Apollo Sauroctonus.*

Prayer book, collection of commonly used prayers in Judeo-Christian religious services. They contain statements of doctrine, ordinances, and explanations of the sacraments, in addition to prayers. The Church of England developed its *Book of Common Prayer* in 1549 and other Christian faiths have devised similar concepts. Prayer books are also widely used in Jewish temple (synagogue) services and ceremonies.

Preble, Edward (1761-1807), U.S. naval officer. He commanded the first U.S. warship to go beyond the Cape of Good Hope (1799) and in 1804 led the unsuccessful assault on Tripoli.

Precambrian, whole of geological time from the formation of the planet Earth to the start of the Phanerozoic (the eon characterized by the appearance of abundant fossils in rock strata), thus lasting from about 4.55 billion to 570 million years ago. It is essentially equivalent to the Cryptozoic eon.

Precipitation, in meteorology, all water particles that fall from clouds to the ground, including rain and drizzle, snow, sleet, and hail. Precipitation is important in the hydrologic cycle (the circulation of water between the surface of the earth and the atmosphere).

Pre-Columbian art, art of what is now Latin America prior to Columbus' discovery of the Americas (1492). The two main cultural areas were the central Andes (southern Colombia, Ecuador, Peru, Bolivia, northwestern Argentina and northern Chile) and Meso-America (Mexico and Central America). In both areas artistic development took place after 3000 B.C. Monochrome-decorated pottery, female figurines, and elaborately designed textiles have been discovered in Ecuador and Peru dating from 3000-2500 B.C. The great Andean classical period noted for textiles, ceramics, gold and silver work, jewelry, and stone masonry took place in 1000 B.C.-A.D. 800, prior to the Inca kingdom. The great city buildings at Cuzco, Machu Picchu, and Tiahuanaco are striking achievements. The Meso-Americans excelled in the graphic and plastic arts. From about A.D. 1000 the illuminated codex writings of the Mayas, Mixtecs, and Aztecs recorded mythological stories. Their temples, as at Chichén Itzá, are decorated with elaborately carved stone sculptures and reliefs, with wall frescoes inside. The Olmecs made small jade carvings and colossal stone heads. In Colombia the Chibcha Indians were skilled in ceramics, textiles, and jewelry.

Predestination, in theology, doctrine that through God's decree the souls of certain persons (the elect) are destined to be saved. Premised on God's omniscience and omnipotence and buttressed by the doctrines of God's providence and grace, predestination was taught especially by St. Paul and was elaborated by St. Augustine in opposition to Pelagianism (which denied Original Sin and asserted that people are free to do good or evil). Calvinism taught additionally the predestination of the nonelect to damnation, denying individual free will and regarding saving grace as irresistible and wholly gratuitous. Jansenism was a similar Roman Catholic movement. Islam likewise teaches absolute predestination.
See also: Religion; Theology.

Pre-emption, right of individuals to purchase land or goods before others and the act of such purchases. During the 1800s more than 200 million acres (81 million hectares) of government-owned land in the United States passed into private hands through pre-emption. Squatters settled lands they didn't own and usually built homes there. The federal government passed laws allowing them to purchase the land cheaply before it was offered for sale to anyone else. The practice was abolished in 1891.

Pregnancy, time between conception and birth. In the human female this takes about 39 weeks, or 9 months. The first symptom of pregnancy is usually a missed menstrual period (though this in itself is not proof) followed perhaps by "morning sickness," which can continue for some weeks. Tenderness of the breasts and darkening of the nipples usually occur, and frequent urination is common.
As the fetus develops, swelling of the abdomen can first of all be felt and then seen. Inside the womb the fetus develops rapidly, and is well formed by 3 1/2 months. After the 28th week, the child is capable of surviving outside the womb, but infant mortality is higher in premature babies than in those carried to full term.
See also: Reproduction.

One of the great monuments of pre-Columbian art: an Olmec colossal head

Prehistoric animal, animal that became extinct before human beings began to produce written records. Our knowledge of these animals is therefore derived almost completely from fossils. Although scientists believe life on earth began over 3 billion years ago, few fossils have been found that are more than 600 million years old. The earliest are all invertebrates, or animals without skeletal backbones. These include ammonites, snails, clams, worms, and animals resembling jellyfish. The most common prehistoric invertebrate seems to have been the trilobite—a kind of flat shellfish with jointed legs. The first fishes appeared about 480 million years ago. They had no jaws and were covered with heavy, bony armor. Fishes as we know them did not appear until about 130 million years later. Some of these had fleshy fins that probably evolved into legs. The first amphibians appeared about 400 million years ago.

An extensive fossil record indicates that the first land vertebrates—the reptiles—evolved about 290 million years ago. They were bigger and more powerful than the amphibians, and were able to hatch their eggs on land. Reptiles dominated the earth for about 100 million years. Dinosaurs are perhaps the best known of the prehistoric animals. Although some grew to enormous size and were very powerful, they all became extinct, although the reason why remains a subject of controversy. Among the dinosaurs was the carnivorous Tyrannosaurus rex, the 85-ton Brachiosaurus, the 87-foot-long Diplodocus, the horned Triceratops, and the armored vegetarian Stegosaurus.

Flying reptiles began to appear during the Jurassic period. One of these—the Archaeopteryx—is believed to be the earliest ancestor of modern birds.

Placental mammals, or animals who carry their young within their bodies, have been on earth for about 65 million years. Later, when mammals came to dominate the land, larger variants of modern-day mammals existed. Megatherium was a 20-foot-long mammoth that resembled a large, hairy elephant. Some of these prehistoric mammoths have been found deep-frozen in the icy soil of Siberia.

The Hortus Cave, near Montpellier in southern France, was used as a summer shelter about 40,000 years ago by the prehistoric human population known as the Neanderthalers. The reconstruction shows a hunter sharpening a wood spear. Behind him a young man is making fire with the help of an elder, and a woman is scraping hides.

Prehistoric people, general term for a variety of species of human ancestors. Humans and apes, who share common ancestors, began to diverge in their evolutionary development about 14 million years ago. The first certain ancestor of modern humans is *Australopithecus afarensis,* discovered in 1978, a species that flourished in Ethiopia and Tanzania 3.8-2.5 million years ago. Adult individuals walked upright and had a brain size of about 400 cc. They inhabited grasslands and ate a wide variety of food, including some meat. There were other species within the genus *Australopithecus,* but they are believed to have left no descendants. *Homo habilus,* the earliest true human being, dates back about 2 million years. They used primitive tools, hunted in groups, and had a brain capacity of 500 to 750 cc. *Homo erectus,* whose earliest remains date back about 1.5 million years, had a brain size of 800 cc, which increased to 1,300 cc over the next million years. *Homo erectus* lived originally in Africa and used fire and the ax. This species evolved into an early form of *Homo sapiens* some 400,000 years ago. These ancestors of ours cooked meat, wore clothes, made wooden tools, and built huts. It is unknown whether the Neanderthal, who flourished about 75,000 to 35,000 years ago, was within the human line of descent or represented a competitor exterminated by the expansion of modern humans. There is much evidence that *Homo sapiens sapiens,*modern humans, first appeared about 40,000 years ago. Cro-Magnon, an example of this modern species, used a variety of tools, domesticated animals and plants, and created cave paintings.

Prejudice, opinions and attitudes formed by individuals or groups about other individuals or groups, usually without ample sustaining evidence. Most forms of prejudice are unfavorable or even hostile, based on fears or preconceived notions against a religious, ethnic, or national group. Extreme forms have resulted in persecution or acts of violence by one group of people against another. Prejudice can be overcome or eliminated through openmindedness, understanding, education, and interaction with groups or individuals targeted for discrimination.

Premature birth, birth of a baby before the 40th week of pregnancy. A birth before the 28th week of pregnancy, when the fetus is not viable, is a miscarriage.
See also: Birth.

Prendergast, Maurice Brazil (1859-1924), U.S. painter influenced by postimpressionism, a member of the ashcan school founded by 8 U.S. painters in 1908. His works include *Umbrellas in the Rain* (1899) and *Central Park* (1901).
See also: Ashcan School.

Presbyterian Church (U.S.A.), largest Presbyterian denomination in the United States, formed in 1983 when the Presbyterian Church in the United States and the United Presbyterian Church in the U.S.A. were united. Local congregations are organized into regional groups called presbyteries, which, in turn, are organized into larger synods.

Presbyterianism, form of Christian church government based on bodies of clergy and lay presbyters. Midway between episcopacy and congregationalism, it was espoused at the time of the Reformation by the reformed churches, which viewed it as a rediscovery of the apostolic practice of church government. There is a hierarchy of church courts. The lowest is the kirk-session, composed of the minister and elders elected by the local congregation. This is followed by the presbytery, including representative ministers and elders from a given area, the synod, composed of members chosen from several presbyteries, and the general assembly, the supreme body, consisting of ministers and elders from all the presbyteries. (Various names are used for these courts.) Presbyterian doctrine is biblical Calvinism.

Prescott, William (1726-95), American Revolutionary colonel. He commanded the militia in the Battle of Bunker Hill (1775) and took part in the battles of Long Island (1776) and Saratoga (1777).
See also: Bunker Hill, Battle of.

Prescott, William Hickling (1796-1859), U.S. historian. Despite the handicap of near blindness, he became an authority on Spain and the Spanish conquest of America. His *History of the Reign of Ferdinand and Isabella the Catholic* (1837), *History of the Conquest of Mexico* (1843), and *His-*

tory of the Conquest of Peru (1847) became classics, admired for their narrative skill as well as their historical rigor.

Presidential libraries, collections of documents, personal papers, and other memorabilia of former U.S. presidents. There are nine such libraries in the United States preserving the historical records of former presidents Rutherford B. Hayes, Herbert Hoover, Franklin D. Roosevelt, Harry Truman, Dwight Eisenhower, John F. Kennedy, Lyndon B. Johnson, Gerald Ford, and Jimmy Carter. Scholars and historians use these libraries and their adjoining museums to do research; audio-visual aids and newspaper articles are also on file.

Presidential Medal of Freedom *see:* Decorations, medals, and orders.

Presidential succession, system of selecting a new U.S. president when the incumbent dies in office, resigns, is removed from office, or is unable to discharge his duties. Under Article II of the Constitution, the vice president is next in line for the presidency and the 20th and 25th Amendments further ensure that the succession will continue through a vice president or vice president-elect. The Presidential Succession Act of 1886, amended in 1947, specifies that the Speaker of the House, the president pro tempore of the Senate, and the 14 members of the president's Cabinet follow the vice president in line to succeed the president.

President of the United States, elected official, head of the executive branch of the U.S. government. The office of president derives its authority from the U.S. Constitution. In order to avoid concentration and abuse of political power, the Constitution established a system of checks and balances whereby power in the U.S. government is divided among the Congress, an independent judiciary, and the president. Defined by the Constitution in less detail than the other two branches, the presidency was given its fundamental form and character by George Washington, but its role and the range of its powers have changed with the nation and with the men who have held the office. To date, no woman has yet been elected to the presidency.

The president's basic roles and duties include being the country's chief executive in charge of enforcing federal law, commander in chief of the armed forces responsible for the country's defense, the formulator of foreign policy, lawmaker, head of a political party, a popularly elected leader, and head of state.

In most cases, presidents have been nominated by one of the major political parties and have won the presidency in contested elections. A majority of popular votes generally translates into a majority of votes in the electoral college. The electoral college consists of 538 delegates, selected by state and according to the number of representatives and senators in that state. To win the presidency, the successful candidate must have 270 electoral votes. The electoral vote is the last formal step in the process of a president's election and can almost always be determined by the outcome of the popular vote. A person can also become president by succeeding to the presidency from the vice presidency. And, in the event no candidate in an election receives a majority of electoral votes, the president is elected by a vote of the House of Representatives. To be eligible for president, one must be a natural-born citizen, at least 35 years of age, and living in the United States 14 years. In the event the office is vacant between elections, succession to the presidency is to the vice president, followed by the Speaker of the House, the president *pro tempore* of the Senate, then to the various secretaries of the president's cabinet beginning with the secretary of state. Presidents serve for a term of 4 years and, since the 22nd Amendment in 1961, no one can serve more than two terms. Presidents may also be removed from office. The process requires first that a president be impeached, that is, charged with some offense or offenses. The president is then tried by the Senate, the chief justice of the Supreme Court presides, and the outcome is determined by vote. A two-thirds majority is required for conviction.

The office of the presidency is supported by a vast bureaucracy consisting of 14 departments, more than 100 separate agencies, and more than 5 million civilian and military employees. The executive departments are headed by secretaries, who are members of the president's cabinet. They include the Secretaries of State, the Treasury and Defense, Justice (headed by the Attorney General), the Interior, Agriculture, Commerce, Labor, Health and Human Services, Housing and Urban Development, Transportation, Energy, Education, and Veterans' Affairs. Among the more important agencies in the executive branch are the Council of Economic Advisers, the National Security Council, the Office of Management and the Budget, the Federal Reserve System, and the Federal Communications Commission. The president also has the power to appoint judges to the federal bench, including the Supreme Court, though these appointments must be approved by the Senate.

Up to the Civil War, strong personalities defined and strengthened the office of president. Thomas Jefferson, Andrew Jackson, and Abraham Lincoln greatly enhanced the power of the office. In the decades between the end of the Civil War (1865) and the Spanish American War (1898), Congress became the dominant branch of government. But the presidency of Theodore Roosevelt (1901-9) marked the beginning of the rise of America as a major military power and player on the international political scene. With this change, a greater measure of power and prestige returned to the presidency. The trend increased under Woodrow Wilson (1914-18), who led the country through its involvement in World War I and culminated in the presidency of Franklin D. Roosevelt (1933-45), the most powerful president of modern times. The end of World War II found the United States at the pinnacle of international power and prestige and the presidency, though a troubled office, has retained its place as the focus of power and decision making within the government. But there have been setbacks and there continues to be debate over the limits of presidential power. At the heart of the debates have been the legacies of Roosevelt's presidency, Truman's decision to use the atomic bomb, the debacle of the Korean War and defeat in the Vietnam War, the Watergate scandal, and the Iran-contra scandal.

Presley, Elvis (1935-77), U.S. singer, first major rock star, and present-day cult hero. From 1956 to the mid-1960s, Presley's versions of rhythm-and-blues songs ("Hound Dog") and ballads ("Love Me Tender") were instant hits, as were his 33 films. His Memphis, Tenn., home, Graceland, became a shrine for his many fans.

Elvis Presley

Pre-Socratic philosophy, general term applied to the thought of the early Greek philosophers (c.600-400 B.C.) who lived before Socrates. Their writings survive mostly in obscure fragments, but their fame and importance lie in their being the first to attempt rational explanations of the universe. Some of the major pre-Socratics were Anaximander, Anaxagoras, Heraclitus, Parmenides, and Pythagoras.
See also: Philosophy.

Press *see:* Journalism; Newspaper; Printing.

Pressburg *see:* Bratislava.

Pressure, force acting on a surface per unit of area. All liquids and gasses exert pressure on any body immersed in them and on the walls of their containers, if any. According to the kinetic theory of matter, the pressure in a closed container of gas arises from the bombardment of the container walls by gas molecules: it is proportional to the temperature and inversely proportional to the volume of the gas.
See also: Physics.

Prester John, legendary Christian priest-king. A purported letter from "Presbyter John," probably of Western authorship, reached the papal court in 1165. It described a great Christian utopia in the "three Indies," identified in later legend as Ethiopia.

Pretoria (pop. 435,100), administrative capital of South Africa. It is also the capital of the province of Transvaal. Founded by the Boers in 1855, the city was named for Andries Pretorius, who defeated the Zulus in 1838. It became the administrative capital of the Union of South Africa when it was formed in 1910 and is a major manufacturing and cultural center.
See also: South Africa.

Pretorius, Andries Wilhelmus Jacobus (1799-1853), commandant of the Boers and Great Trek leader. His defeat of the

Zulus at Blood River (1838) led to the founding of the Republic of Natal. He led the 1848 trek into the Transvaal.

Pretzel, popular snack biscuit. Pretzels are made from twisted dough that is usually glazed, salted, and baked until hardened, but some varieties are large and soft. They are believed to have originated in southern Europe where monks gave them to children as a reward for learning their prayers, and the name comes from a Latin word meaning "small reward." Its popularity spread to the United States in the 1860s and is a favorite snack food today.

Prévert, Jacques (1900-77), French writer. His popular poems, sometimes satirical, sometimes melancholy, include *Paroles* (1946). Among his screenplays is that for Marcel Carné's *Les Enfants du Paradis* (1944).

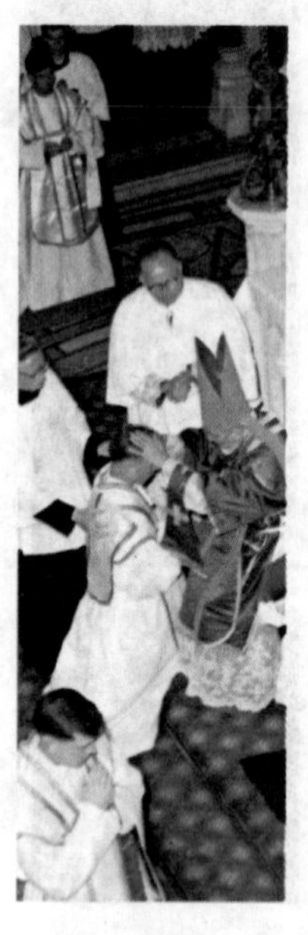

A priest's ordination

Previn, André (1929-), German-born U.S. musician. Originally an adapter of stage musicals for the screen, he won Academy Awards for his arrangements in the films *Kiss Me Kate* (1953) and *Gigi* (1958). As a jazz pianist he made several successful recordings and is also a classical composer and pianist. Principally a symphony conductor since 1960, he has led seasons of the Houston Symphony, the London Symphony, and the Pittsburgh Symphony, recording widely as well.

Prévost d'Exiles, Antoine François, or Abbé Prévost (1697-1763), French writer, priest, and adventurer. *Manon Lescaut* (1731), a love story, is the masterpiece among his novels. It is the basis of operas by Jules Massenet and Giacomo Puccini.

Pribilof Islands, group of 4 small islands of volcanic origin in the Bering Sea, about 300 mi (483 km) southwest of Alaska. St. Paul and St. George are the largest. Every spring some 80% of the world's fur seals visit the islands to breed. Since 1911 the seal herds have been protected, and the United States, which acquired the islands in 1867, regulates the harvesting of seals.

Price, Leontyne (1927-), U.S. soprano. Her first success was as Bess in Gershwin's *Porgy and Bess* (1952-54). She made debuts in televised operas (1955), at the San Francisco Opera (1957), and at the New York Metropolitan Opera (1961), winning international fame for her performances in works by Verdi and Puccini. She retired from opera in 1985 but continues as a recitalist.
See also: Opera.

Prickly ash, shrub or tree (*Zanthoxylum americanum*) growing in damp soils. The bark and fruit are used for medicinal purposes in the treatment of rheumatism and such stomach problems as flatulence and poor digestion.

Prickly heat, or heat rash, uncomfortable itching sensation caused by excessive sweating in hot weather.

Prickly pear, any of a genus (*Opuntia*) of branching cactus with flat stems and yellow flowers. It is found in most of the southern United States and grows farther north (into New England) than other cacti. Prickly pears are grown in many places as hedges. Introduced to Australia, they spread so rapidly as to become a pest, but were brought under control by introducing a moth whose caterpillars burrowed into the stems.

Priest, in most religions, a cultic officer who communicates the sacred to the followers; a spiritual leader expert in ritual and generally the offerer of sacraments.

Priestley, J(ohn) B(oynton) (1894-1984), English writer and critic. Besides many plays, he wrote popular novels such as *The Good Companions* (1929) and *Angel Pavement* (1930), and criticism, of which his major work is *Literature and Western Man* (1960).

Priestley, Joseph (1733-1804), British theologian and chemist. Encouraged and supported by Benjamin Franklin, he wrote *The History and Present State of Electricity* (1767). His most important discovery was oxygen (1774; named later by Lavoisier), whose properties he investigated. He later discovered many other gases—ammonia, carbon monoxide, hydrogen sulfide—and found that green plants require sunlight and give off oxygen. His association in the 1780s with the Lunar Society brought him into contact with scientists such as James Watt and Erasmus Darwin. Priestley's theological writings and activity led some English Presbyterians into Unitarianism, and he is regarded as a principal architect of the Unitarian church. He was also an opponent of the slave trade and a supporter of the French Revolution. When his house and laboratory were destroyed by people enraged by these ideas, he emigrated to the United States (1794).
See also: Oxygen; Unitarianism.

Primary color *see:* Color.

Primary election, in the United States, an election in which supporters of a political party elect candidates to run in a subsequent general election. Primary elections are used throughout the United States to select candidates for Congress, state offices, and local government posts. In some states the candidates are proposed by petition; in others they simply file for the office. Most states operate "closed" primaries in which only registered party members may vote. Presidential primaries are a prelude to a party's national convention. Although some states choose delegates to the national convention by the caucus system, most have adopted the primary in one form or another. Voters indicate their preference either directly or by voting for delegates who are pledged to support a particular presidential candidate.

Primate, member of an order of mammals including humans, anthropoid apes, monkeys, tarsiers, pottos, galagos, and lemurs. Compared with most mammal groups, primates are anatomically less specialized; the brain, however, is larger and more developed.

Prime meridian, meridian that indicates zero degree longitude. Meridians are imaginary lines drawn on the earth's surface from the North to the South Pole. The prime meridian passes through Greenwich, England. All other longitudes are identified in degrees by their distance from the prime meridian.
See also: Longitude.

Prime minister, or premier, head of the government in a parliamentary system. The prime minister appoints and directs his or her own cabinet, which is the source of all major legislation, and also has the power to make and dismiss ministers and to call an election before the full term of a government. The office developed in 18th-century England under Robert Walpole. Most parliamentary democracies distinguish between the head of state (a monarch or president) and the prime minister, who is head of the government.

Prime minister of Canada, highest-ranking elected official of Canada and leader of the government. The prime minister is traditionally the leader of the majority party in the Canadian House of Commons and is responsible for directing the affairs of the government and the nation's foreign and domestic policies. A prime minister must have the support of a majority of the House to remain in office and if the House passes a vote of no confidence, he or she must resign or call a new election. Since independence in 1867, 18 men have held the office.

Primo de Rivera, Miguel (1870-1930), Spanish general and politician. Supported by King Alfonso XIII, he overthrew the government in 1923 and became dictator. Popular discontent, economic failure, and loss of army support forced him to resign in 1930. His son, **José Antonio Primo de Rivera**, founded the Falanga (a Fascist political party) and was executed by Loyalists (republicans) in 1936.

Primogeniture, law by which the eldest son inherits all the lands of a family. It originated in medieval Europe as a reward for the son who gave military service to his king. Never widely established in the United States, primogeniture is still customary in England.

Primrose, perennial plant (*Primula officinalis*) growing in dry meadows, lightly wooded areas, and along forest edges; the flowers, herb, and rootstock are used for medicinal purposes.

Primrose, William (1904-82), Scottish violist, U.S. resident from 1937. He cofounded the Festival Quartet in 1956. Several composers, including Béla Bartók, wrote works especially for him.

Prince Albert (pop. 33,700), city in central Saskatchewan. Situated on the North Saskatchewan River, it was founded in 1866 and named for Queen Victoria's prince consort. It is an important lumbering and manufacturing center and due to its location near the entrance to Prince Albert National Park, it is a major tourist center as well.
See also: Saskatchewan.

Prince consort, husband of a reigning queen. A prince consort is not given the title of king in European countries where the sovereign's daughter may inherit the throne and he has no place in the royal succession under ordinary circumstance. These rules apply in the monarchies of Denmark, the Netherlands, and the United Kingdom.

Prince Edward Island, one of Canada's maritime provinces, and the smallest of all Canada's provinces both in area and population.
Land and climate. Prince Edward Island is about 10 mi/16 km from the mainland, separated from it by the Northumberland Strait. The maximum length is about 145 mi/233 km and its greatest width about 55 mi/89 km. The shoreline is deeply serrated with tidal inlets. The surface of the island is gently rolling, with some small hills in the center and southeast. Because of its agricultural resources, it is sometimes called the "Garden of the Gulf" and "The Million Acre Farm."
The island's climate is variable but generally milder than that of the mainland. The capital is Charlottetown.
People. Some 80% of the population are descendants of British and Scots settlers, about 15% are descendants of Acadian French settlers, and the balance are Micmac Indians living on reservations.
Economy. Prince Edward Island's economy is based upon farming, fishing, tourism, and light industry. Tobacco, strawberry, and blueberry crops are exported. Potatoes are an important crop and about half of the crop is processed, mainly into frozen French fries. Processing of lumber is important to the island as is lobster fishing. There is also manufacturing of fisheries' products.
History. Prince Edward Island was originally inhabited by nomadic Micmacs, Native Americans of the Algonquian tribe. Jacques Cartier landed in 1534, becoming the first European to explore the island for France, and named it Île Saint-Jean. Some 2,000 Acadians, French settlers expelled from Nova Scotia by the British, settled on the island between 1749 and 1755. With the Treaty of Paris in 1763, the island became British, most of the French settlers were expelled, and its name was changed to St. John's Island. Originally annexed by the British to Nova Scotia, St. John's Island became a separate colony in 1709. In 1799, the British changed the name of the island to Prince Edward Island in honor of the Duke of Kent. In 1851, the island won control of its local affairs. After some hesitation, Prince Edward Island decided to join the Dominion of Canada and on July 1, 1873, became the seventh province.
See also: Canada.

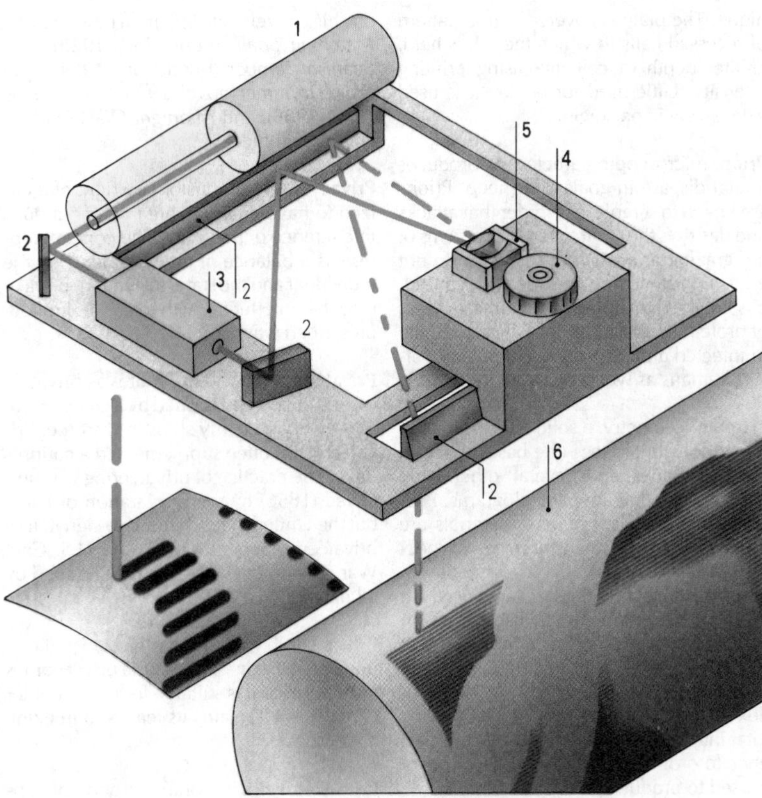

The working of a printer directed by laser:
A beam of light from a laser (1) is mirrored (2) through a modulator (3), in which the strength of the beam is regulated. By way of a series of mirrors the beam comes through a system of lenses (4) to a scan prism (5), after which it is sent back through the system of lenses to an opposite mirror, to be reflected to the photosensitive cylinder (6).

Prince George (pop. 67,600), city of central British Columbia. Located at the junction of the Fraser and Nechako rivers, the city was founded in 1807 by Simon Fraser as a fur-trading post named Fort George. It is the site of several major pulp mills and is a major manufacturing and energy center for the province.
See also: British Columbia.

Prince Rupert (pop. 15,800), port on the west coast of British Columbia. Lying on an island at the mouth of the Skeena River, Prince Rupert developed in the early 1900s as a western rail terminus for the Grand Trunk Railway. It is a major fishing, lumbering, and pulp processing center, and its ice-free harbor makes it a key Canadian west coast port.
See also: British Columbia.

Princeton (pop. 25,718), borough and township in central New Jersey, site of Princeton University, Princeton Theological Seminary, and the Institute for Advanced Study. The region was settled by Quakers in 1696. In 1777 it was the scene of a Revolutionary War battle in which George Washington defeated British forces. The Continental Congress met in Princeton for 5 months in 1783.
See also: New Jersey.

Princeton University, private university in Princeton, N.J. Chartered as the College of New Jersey in 1746, it was renamed in 1896, when it became a university. A leading U.S. educational institution, it includes world-famous graduate schools of public and international affairs, architecture, and scientific research. It has admitted women since 1969.

Príncipe Island *see:* São Tomé and Príncipe.

Printing, reproduction of words and pictures in ink on paper or other suitable media. Despite the advent of information retrieval systems, the storage and dissemination of knowledge are still based primarily on the printed word. Modern printing began with the work of Johann Gutenberg, who invented movable type and type metal in the 15th century. Individual characters could be used several times. The process was little changed for 400 years, until the invention of machines that could cast type as it was required.
Letterpress and lithography are today the two most used printing techniques. Letterpress uses raised type that is a mirror image of the printed impression. The type is inked and the paper pressed to it. Lithography depends on the mutual repulsion of water and oil or grease. In fine art a design is drawn with a grease crayon on the surface of a flat, porous stone, which is then wetted. Water is repelled by the greasy areas; but ink is repelled by the damp and adheres to the greasy areas. Modern mechanized processes use the same principle. Commonest is photo-offset, where the copy to be printed is photographed and the image transferred to a plate such that the part to be printed is oleophilic (oil-loving), the rest hydrophilic (water-loving). Gravure is another major printing tech-

nique. The plate is covered with a pattern of recessed cells in which the ink is held, greater depth of cell increasing printing intensity. Little-used for books, it is used extensively in packaging.

Prion, microscopic particle that produces a fatal disease in goats and sheep. Prions are linked to scrapie, a disorder that attacks and destroys the central nervous systems of the grazing animals, but scientists do not fully understand how the disease is caused. It is believed that prions contain an excess of protein that disrupts normal cell activity in infected animals and might possibly affect humans as well.

Prism, in geometry, a solid figure having 2 equal polygonal faces (the bases) lying in parallel planes and several others (the lateral faces) that are parallelograms. Prismatic pieces of transparent materials are much used in optical instruments. In spectroscopes and devices for producing monochromatic lights, prisms are used to produce dispersion effects, just as Newton first used a triangular prism to reveal that sunlight could be split up into a spectrum of colors. In binoculars and single-lens reflex cameras, inflecting prisms (employing total internal reflection) are used in preference to ordinary mirrors. The Nicol prism is used to produce polarized light.

Prison, institution for confining people convicted of breaking a law. There are three types of prisons in the United States: jails and lockups, run by city and county governments mainly for those awaiting trial; state prisons, operated by the individual states containing the majority of convicted criminals, and federal prisons, which house society's most violent offenders and those who break federal laws. By the early 20th century imprisonment had replaced corporal punishment, capital punishment, and exile as the chief method of dealing with criminals. The purpose of prisons is threefold: to punish the wrongdoer; to protect society; and to act as a deterrent. Overpopulation is a serious problem in modern prisons, leading to the 1981 Supreme Court ruling that two prisoners may be kept in a cell built for one if prison conditions on the whole are humane. At the end of 1989 U.S. federal and state prisons held about 710,000 inmates; nearly 0.3% of the U.S. population.

Prisoners of war, combatant who has been captured by or has surrendered to an enemy state. The Hague Convention of 1907 and the Geneva Conventions of 1919 and 1949 established rules in international law for the protection of such prisoners, notably that they should not be maltreated nor required to give any information other than their name, rank, and serial number, and that they should be repatriated upon the cessation of hostilities.
See also: Geneva conventions.

Pritchett, V(ictor) S(awdon) (1900-86), English novelist, short-story writer, and literary critic. Many of his works are based on his travels in Spain. They include *Marching Spain* (nonfiction, 1928), *The Spanish Temper* (nonfiction, 1954), and *Clare Drummer* (novel, 1929). *A Cab at the Door* (1968), and *Midnight Oil* (1971) are autobiographical.

Privacy, Right of, customary right of a citizen to have a private life free of "undue" interference or publicity. The concept represents a balance of interests between the individual and the state. In general, privacy may be interfered with only in limited, prescribed ways.

Privateer, armed vessel that was privately owned but commissioned by a government to prey upon enemy ships in wartime. Privateers thus often supplemented a nation's navy. The practice of privateering was outlawed (1856) by the Declaration of Paris, but the United States refused to sign it, and privateers operated during the U.S. Civil War. The practice has been abandoned by all nations.

Privet, shrub whose dense growth makes it popular for hedges. California privet comes from Japan and is suitable for use in colder climates, as it retains its leaves in freezing conditions.

Privy Council, honorary group of appointed advisers to the reigning sovereign of Great Britain. Instituted by William the Conqueror (William I) in the late 11th century, the privy council once had the important function of advising the king on matters of national importance. As parliament and the prime minister replaced the monarchy in the nation's governing structure, the privy council declined in importance. Today it serves a largely ceremonial function, overseeing matters of commerce, scientific research, and the arts.

Probability, branch of mathematics that deals with the likelihood that an event will occur. Most commonly, the number of possible outcomes is counted, and the probability of any particular outcome is expressed as a fraction between 0 and 1. For instance, in rolling 2 dice there are 36 possible outcomes. Only one of these is that a 12 will turn up (a 6 on each die). The chance of rolling a 12 is therefore 1/36. On the other hand, there are 6 possible ways of rolling a 7: 1-6, 6-1, 5-2, 2-5, 3-4, 4-3. The chance of rolling a 7 is therefore 1/6. As more complicated theories and problems arise, more sophisticated techniques arise, such as permutations and combinations. Probability theory has contributed vital understanding in many fields of physics, including statistical mechanics. Its importance in science has risen dramatically in recent decades. Statistics, a related field, is the application of probability theory to data collected from research samples.
See also: Mathematics.

Probate, legal process of proving that a will is valid. Before a will can take effect, it must be shown that it is genuine, that it was the deceased's last will, that he or she signed it voluntarily and was of sound mind. Probate requires all possible heirs of the testator's property to be notified before a special hearing is held in a probate court, where objections can be lodged.
See also: Will.

Probation, alternative to prison, whereby convicted offenders are placed under the supervision of a probation officer, on condition that they maintain good behavior. The aim is to encourage reform, particularly for the young, when a spell in prison might simply reinforce criminal tendencies.

Proboscis monkey, large monkey (*Nasalis larvatus*) native to Borneo. They are herbivores (plant eaters), feeding on leaves that they shred easily with well-developed back teeth. Males may weigh up to 52 lb (24 kg) and females about half that. They stand about 21-30 in (53-76 cm) tall and live in trees near rivers, which they swim easily.

Procaine, or novocaine, pain-killing drug used as an anesthetic. Developed by German chemist Alfred Einhorn in 1905, procaine is injected into a designated area of the body to deaden nerve sensitivity prior to a surgical procedure being performed. It has been largely replaced by more effective nerve blocks in recent years but it remains popular with dentists, who inject it into the gums of patients whose teeth they are preparing to work on.
See also: Anesthesia.

Proclamation of 1763, statement issued by the British government at the end of the French and Indian Wars, establishing territorial rights for North American Native Americans. It aimed both to appease the Native Americans and to prevent land disputes, but it angered (and was in many respects disregarded by) the colonists.
See also: French and Indian Wars.

Profit, amount of money a company or individual engaged in business makes after all costs have been subtracted. Profit is the chief motivation for the establishment of all businesses in a free enterprise economic system and the goal of all employers and individuals seeking monetary gain. Profits can be increased by keeping production costs, including labor, as low as possible and employers are constantly seeking means of generating greater profits than others engaged in competing businesses and industries.

Profit sharing, incentive developed by businesses and employers to give workers a share of the extra money a company makes. It was devised to instill workers with greater company loyalty and motivate them toward higher productivity. Profit sharing provides workers with a source of income above their regular wages and may be disbursed in the form of direct cash payments, shares of company stock, or deferred payments made in lieu of pension plans.

Progeria, or Hutchinson-Gilford syndrome, rare disease that causes premature aging in children and early death. Sir Jonathan Hutchinson researched the disease in 1886 and there is no cure or treatment for it. Symptoms begin appearing by the second year of life; they include hair loss, wrinkled skin, stunted growth, and other signs of aging normally associated with older persons. Half of all progeria deaths occur by age 13 and the oldest known victim lived only to 27.

Progesterone, female sex hormone that causes changes in the womb lining necessary for the implantation of a fertilized egg. *See also:* Hormone; Reproduction.

Programmed learning, teaching method whereby matter to be learned is arranged in a coherent sequence of small, clear steps (programmed), enabling the student to instruct, test, and, if necessary, correct him or herself at each step. The learning program is usually embodied in a book or booklet or adapted for use in conjunction with a teaching machine. The linear program, based on the work of psychologist B.F. Skinner, obliges the student to compare his or her own response at each step with the correct response. The intrinsic (or branching) program offers a limited choice of responses at each step. The correct response is immediately reinforced; an incorrect response obliges the student to follow a corrective subprogram leading back to the point at which the error occurred.

Progression, in mathematics, a sequence of numbers (terms) that have a direct relationship to one another. The most common types are arithmetic, which involves addition; geometic, which involves multiplication; and harmonic, which involves fractions. Each successive term in a progression is added by or multiplied by the same number all the way through the sequence. An arithmetic progression that begins with 2, 4, and 6 will continue with 8, 10, and all successive numbers that are 2 larger than the preceding number. The same principle applies to all other types of progressions.
See also: Mathematics.

Progressive Conservative Party, one of Canada's two major political parties. It is generally more conservative on most issues than Canada's Liberal party. Called the Conservative Party from its formation in 1854, it was the nation's dominant political party for nearly a century. After changing its name in 1942, the party has won only two national elections and has governed Canada only twice, in 1957-63 under John G. Diefenbaker and for six months in 1979 under Joe Clark. His Progressive Conservative-Social Credit coalition was forced to resign after losing a vote of confidence in the House of Commons on Clark's austerity budget.

Progressive education, reform movement that grew from the idea that schooling should cater to the emotional as well as the intellectual development of the child and that the basis of learning should be the child's natural and individual curiosity, rather than an enforced discipline. In the United States the movement, led by John Dewey, was most active from 1890-1950. *See also:* Education.

Progressive movement, campaign for political, economic, and social reform in the United States, which began in the depression of the 1890s and ended in 1917 with U.S. involvement in World War I. *See also:* Addams, Jane; Roosevelt, Theodore.

Progressive Party, name of three 20th century U.S. political organizations. Each was largely characterized by programs of social and economic reform. The Progressive Party of 1912 (better known as the Bull Moose Party) chose ex-President Theodore Roosevelt as its nominee. It left the Republican Party after the nomination of William Taft, but they were reunited during the campaign of 1916.
The Progressive Party of 1924 was formed by farm and labor leaders dissatisfied with the conservatism of the Republican administration. Its position, like that of the Bull Moose Party, was that there should be governmental control of trusts, and it upheld the right of government intervention in private wealth. Its presidential nominee was Robert La Follette, who received almost five million votes. The Progressive Party of 1948 nominated former Democratic vice president Henry A. Wallace for the presidency. The party sought better relations with the USSR and an end to the Cold War. It had support from many left-wing groups and was labeled by some a Communist-front organization. It polled little more than one million votes out of 48 million.

Prohibition, restriction or prevention of the manufacture and sale of alcoholic drinks. It refers in particular to the period from 1919 to 1933, when (by means of the 18th Amendment to the Constitution) there was a federal prohibition law in the United States. In spite of the intensive economic and group pressures that had brought it about, it soon became apparent that the law was too unpopular and too expensive to enforce. A notorious era of gangsterism followed, with a vast illegal liquor business (the activities involved were known as bootlegging) under the control of men such as Al Capone. Prohibition was repealed (1933) by the 21st Amendment. A few U.S. states maintained local prohibition laws as late as 1966.
See also: Capone, Al; Volstead Act.

Prohibition Party, minor U.S. political party. It was founded in 1869 to prohibit the manufacture and consumption of alcohol and has fielded candidates for president and vice president in every national election since 1872. Its greatest showing was in 1892 when Gen. John Bidwell received 271,000 votes. Pressure from the party and other anti-alcohol crusaders led to the imposition of nationwide prohibition (1919-33) through passage of the 18th Amendment.

A Prohibition-era speakeasy

Projector, machine that passes light through film to show pictures on a screen. Lenses magnify the images on the film, showing them larger than they appear on the film itself. Projectors consist of several types—slide projectors that show still photos, movie projectors that show continuously moving film, and overhead projectors such as those used in planetariums that show images in all directions above the viewers.

Prokhorov, Aleksandr Mikhailovich (1916-), Soviet physicist awarded, with N.G. Basov and C.H. Townes, the 1964 Nobel Prize for physics for work with Basov leading to development of the maser.
See also: Maser.

Prokofiev, Sergei Sergeyevich (1891-1953), Russian composer who created a fierce, dynamic, unemotive style that later became somewhat softer and more eclectic. His works include seven symphonies, the operas *The Love for Three Oranges* (1921) and *War and Peace* (1943); *Peter and the Wolf* (1936), for narrator and orchestra; *Romeo and Juliet* (1936), a ballet; concertos for piano, violin, and cello; film scores; and chamber music.

Proletariat, name given to industrial employees as a social and economic class. In Marxist theory, the proletariat is exploited by and must inevitably overthrow the bourgeois class, made up of employers and property owners.
See also: Marxism.

Prometheus, in Greek mythology, one of the Titans and a brother of Atlas. He was sometimes said to have created humankind out of earth and water and to have stolen fire from the gods for the benefit of mankind. Zeus punished Prometheus by having him bound to a rock, whereupon his liver was devoured by an eagle.
See also: Mythology.

Promethium, chemical element, symbol Pm; for physical constants see Periodic Table. Branner, in 1902, predicted the existence of an element between neodymium and samarium. This element, promethium, was discovered by J.A. Marinsky, Lawrence E. Glendenin, and Charles D. Coryell in 1945 by fission of uranium and neutron bombardment of neodymium with neutrons. This was the first chemical identification by use of ion-exchange chromatography. Promethium is not found in the earth's crust but is obtained from nuclear reactors as a fission byproduct. Promethium-145, the most stable isotope, has a half-life longer than 17.7 years. Promethium, a metallic element, has been prepared by the reduction of the fluoride with lithium metal. It is a member of the rare-earth series of metals. Promethium isotopes are used in thickness gauges, self-luminous compounds, nuclear-powered batteries, portable X-ray sources, and auxiliary power sources.

Pronghorn, resembling an antelope (*Antilocapra americana*) the only horned animal that sheds its horn sheath and the only one with branched horns as distinct from antlers. They live in groups in arid grasslands and semi-desert of western North America, feeding on weeds and browse plants. Conservation efforts have restored numbers from an estimated 30,000 in 1924 to a present 400,000.

Pronghorn

Proofreading, reading and correcting of printed matter prior to publication. It is done by skilled proofreaders using universally understood marks and symbols on the copy itself to indicate what corrections need to be made on the final draft. Newspapers, magazines, and printing shops employ proofreaders to check over all copy before it is published, in an effort to eliminate or minimize errors that might appear in print. Book publishing companies also use proofreaders, who mark up authors' original manuscripts as well as typeset copy (galley proofs) before they appear in book form.

Propaganda, selected information, whether true or false, designed to persuade people to adopt a particular belief, attitude, or course of action. During the 20th century all the major political ideologies have employed propaganda and made use of

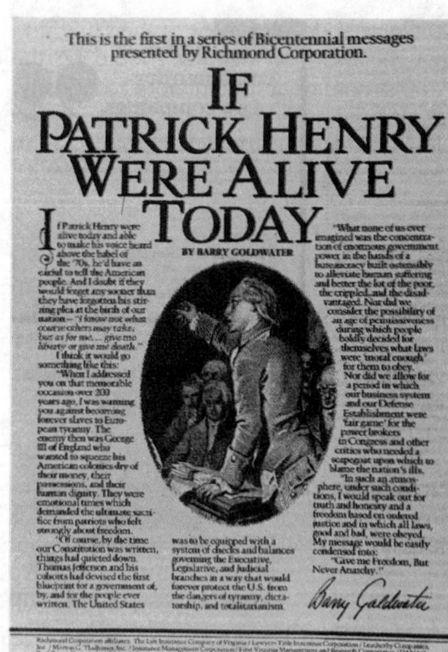

U.S political propaganda of the 1970's

modern media to reach a mass audience. It plays an important role in modern warfare, and during World War II separate offices and ministries were established to promote morale and subvert the enemy. The Nazi Ministry of Propaganda, headed by Joseph Goebbels, was one of the most active. In the business world, professional propagandists—communicators in public relations and advertising—are increasingly in demand.

Propane *see:* Butane and propane.

Propeller, mechanical device designed to impart forward motion, usually to a ship or airplane, operating on the screw principle. It generally consists of two or more inclined blades radiating from a hub, and the amount of thrust it produces is proportional to the product of the mass and the fluid it acts on and the rate at which it accelerates the fluid. The inclination, or pitch, of the propeller blades determines the theoretical distance moved forward with each revolution. A variable-pitch propeller can be adjusted while in motion, to maximize its efficiency under different operating conditions; it may also be possible to reverse the propeller's pitch, or to feather it—i.e., minimize its resistance when not rotating. John Fitch developed the first marine screw propeller in 1796; John Ericsson perfected the first bladed propeller in 1837.

Propertius, Sextus (50?-16 B.C.), Roman elegiac poet, whose poems center on his love affair with his mistress Cynthia. Though often obscure, he is vivid and imaginative.

Property, social concept and legal term indicating the ownership of, or the right to enjoy, something of value; it may also be an interest in something owned by another. Under some systems such as feudalism or communism, ownership of some or all kinds of property is vested not in the individual, but in the state or its head. The U.S. Constitution establishes the individual's right to property. Common law distinguishes between real property (land and generally nontransportable goods, such as houses and trees) and personal property) (all other kinds). Financial rights, such as copyrights or patent holdings, are personal.

Property tax, money collected by state and local governments from owners of property. It is levied upon land, homes, buildings, and in some cases on farm equipment, based on a fixed percentage of the property's estimated (assessed) valuation. Monies collected from property taxes are usually used to pay for government services such as road repair, schools, and police and fire protection.
See also: Taxation.

Prophet, in the Old Testament of the Bible, a man who by special revelation proclaimed the word of God by oracles and symbolic actions; originally a seer or ecstatic. Often a scourge of the establishment, prophets were religious and social reformers who called for righteousness and faithfulness to God and pronounced judgment on the ungodly. In the early Christian Church prophecy was a recognized charisma, but soon died out except in Montanism, a heretical sect. It was revived among Anabaptists, Quakers, Mormons, and Pentecostals. In Islam Muhammad is the last and greatest prophet. Oracular prophets are found in many religions.
See also: Old Testament.

Prophylaxis, general term for the prevention of diseases. This is most often done through preventative treatments given prior to a person's contracting a disease. Vaccinations are a form of prophylaxis that build up immunities within the human body against certain types of disorders. Pasteurization of milk and milk products is another form of prophylaxis, as is proper sanitation on a community-wide scale.

Proportion, in mathematics, equality of two ratios. The numbers a, b, c, and d are said to be in proportion if $a/b = c/d$. The expression may also be written as $a{:}b{::}c{:}d$. The term *proportion* is useful in describing the relationship between quantities whose ratio is constant—for example, the ratio between the radius and circumference of a circle. If there are two circles with circumferences c_1, c_2 and radii r_1 and r_2 then $c_1 = 2\pi r$, and $c_2 = 2\pi r_2$. This can be written $c_1/r_1 = 2\pi = c_2/r_2$. The figures c_1, r_1, c_2 and r_2 are in proportion, and we say that the circumference of a circle is proportional to its radius.
See also: Mathematics.

Proportional representation, system of electing members to a legislature in which political parties or groups contesting the election are awarded a number of seats in the legislature more or less proportional to the number of votes they get. For instance, if 3 parties are running for seats in a 300-member legislature, and one party gets half the vote while the others roughly split the remaining half equally, the largest party would be allotted about 150 seats, the 2 others about 75 each. There are various ways of organizing such elections and of calculating the results. The system is generally used in places where there are more than 2 significant-sized parties. Supporters of proportional representation argue that it is the most democratic system, since it most accurately reflects the political desires of the population. Opponents argue that it can give unreasonable power to small groups, which can sometimes gain decisive leverage in a divided multiparty assembly.

Proslavery movement, U.S. movement to justify and expand the practice of slavery prior to the Civil War. It gained strength and prominence in the American South in direct response to the abolitionist movement that began to take hold in the northern states in the 1830s. Proslavery advocates used biblical and economic justifications for the ownership of slaves and they constituted a large and influential voting bloc in the United States Congress. The Civil War ended slavery and the proslavery movement.
See also: Abolitionism; Slavery.

Prospecting, process of searching for minerals worth exploiting economically. The simplest technique is direct observation of the local surface features characteristically associated with specific mineral deposits. This is often done by prospectors on the ground, but aerial photography is increasingly employed. Other techniques include examining the seismic waves caused by explosions (which supply information about the structures through which they have passed); testing local magnetic fields to detect magnetic metals or the metallic gangues associated with nonmagnetic minerals; and, especially for metallic sulfides, testing electrical conductivity.

Prosser, Gabriel (c.1775-1800), black American slave who planned a slave revolt in Virginia, intending to create an independent black state and to become its king. Prosser was born in Henrico County, Va., to an African woman. He was owned by Thomas H. Prosser. In the attack planned for Richmond, Virginia's capital, Prosser and his followers were to seize the arsenal and kill all whites except Frenchmen, Methodists, and Quakers. Then the rebels would proceed to take over the state. On Aug. 30, 1800, an army numbering 1,000-50,000 gathered outside Richmond. But heavy rain had washed out the bridges to the city, thwarting the army's approach. The revolt was doomed when two slaves betrayed the plot to their owner, who then informed Gov. James Monroe. Prosser and about 34 supporters were captured, tried, and hanged.
See also: Slavery.

Prostaglandin, variety of naturally occurring aliphatic acids with various biological activities including increased vascular permeability, smooth muscle contraction, bronchial constriction, and alteration in the pain threshold. Seminal fluid contains lipid-soluble substances that stimulate smooth muscle, and it has been suggested that the active principle should be called prostaglandin. Although prostaglandins are present in highest concentration in seminal fluid, they have been found in numerous other tissues, such as the kidney, iris, pancreas, lung, and brain.

Prostate gland, male reproductive gland that surrounds the urethra at the base of the urinary bladder and that secretes prostatic fluid. This organ is formed of fibrous muscular and glandular tissue. It is described as having the shape of a chestnut and as being an inverted pyramid whose base is applied to the neck of the bladder. The normal gland usually measures about 1 in (2.54 cm) from front to back, 1 1/4 in (3.18 cm) from above downward and nearly 2 in (5 cm) from side to side. The connective tissue around the gland is condensed to form a fibrous capsule. There is a groove between the neck of the bladder and the base of the prostate that contains a venous plexus.
The prostate is traversed from top to bottom by the urethra. The glandulary tissue consists of secretory acini. After middle age, acini may contain concretions of secretion and desquamated cells.
The glands of the median lobe and mucosal glands constitute the glands of the inner zone, in which penile enlargement usually starts. Cancer of the prostate usually starts in the outer zone which consists of the main prostatic gland.
See also: Reproduction.

Prosthetic, mechanical or electrical device inserted into or onto the body to replace or supplement the function of a missing, defective, or diseased organ. Artificial limbs were among the first prosthetics, but metal or plastic joint replacements and bone fixations are now also available. Replacement teeth are also prosthetics. The valves of the heart may be replaced with mechanical devices, and electrical pacemakers can be implanted to stimulate the heart muscle at a set rate.

Prostitution, practice of exchanging sexual favors for material profit, usually money. Prostitution is as old as civilization and has flourished throughout history, especially in urban centers, which generate demand and provide conditions of relative anonymity. Although there is some male prostitution, the term usually refers to the practice as performed by women.

Protactinium, chemical element, symbol Pa; for physical constants see Periodic Table. Discovered in 1917 by 2 teams of scientists working independently; Otto Hahn and Lise Meitner of Germany and Frederick Soddy and John Cranston of Great Britain. It is found in the mineral *pitchblende* in minute quantities. Protactinium is a lustrous, radioactive metal, and a member of the actinide series. The element was initially prepared by decomposing its iodide in a vacuum with an electrically heated filament. The longest lived is an alpha emitter with a half-life of 32,500 years. It is a dangerous and toxic material.

Protagoras (c.490-421 B.C.), Greek Sophist, remembered for the maxim "Man is the measure of all things." A respected figure in Athens, where he spent most of life, he taught rhetoric and the proper conduct of life ("virtue"), and was appointed lawmaker to the Athenian colony of Thurii in 444 B.C. Little is known of his teaching, but he is thought to have been a relativist concerning knowledge and a skeptic about the gods, although he upheld conventional morality.
See also: Sophist.

Protective coloration, adaptation of coloration by animals, often providing a means of defense against predators. Except where selection favors bright coloration for breeding or territorial display, most higher animals are colored in such a way that they blend in with their background: by pure coloration, by disruption of outline with bold lines or patches, or by a combination of the two. The most highly developed camouflage is found in ground-nesting birds, or insects. Associated with this coloration must be special behavior patterns enabling the animal to seek out the correct background for its camouflage and to "freeze" against it. Certain animals can change their body texture and coloration to match different backgrounds: octopuses, chameleons, and some flatfishes. An alternative strategy adopted by some animals, particularly insects, is the use of shock-coloration: when approached by a predator, these insects flick open plain wings to expose bright colors, often in the form of staring "eyes," to scare the predator.

Protective coloring exhibited by the pine weevil

Protectorate, country that is nominally independent but surrenders part of its sovereignty, such as control over foreign policy, in return for protection by a stronger state. The degree of control and dependency varies.

Protein, high-molecular-weight compound that yields amino acid through hydrolysis. Although hundreds of different amino acids are possible, only 20 are found

Marcel Proust

in appreciable quantities in proteins, and these are all alpha-amino acids. Proteins are found throughout all living organisms. Muscle, the major structural material in animals, is mainly protein; the 20% of blood that is not water is mainly protein. Enzymes may contain other components, but basically they, too, are protein. Approximately 700 proteins are known; of these, 200-300 have been studied and over 150 obtained in crystalline form. Some are very stable, while others are so delicate that even exposure to air will destroy their capability as enzymes. The best food sources for proteins are meat, fish, eggs, milk, and cheese. These foods provide all the essential aminoacids and are known as complete proteins. Vegetables and nuts do provide proteins but are not complete proteins. The absence of protein in the diet can diminish growth and reduce energy levels.

Protestant ethic, set of values that esteems hard work, thrift, duty, efficiency, and self-discipline. The Protestant ethic follows from the beliefs, identified with Calvinism, that a person's time and talents are gifts from God and that prosperity is a sign of piety and salvation. The concept of a protestant ethic was formalized by the German sociologist Max Weber in his essay, "The Protestant Ethic and the Spirit of Capitalism" (1904-5). He attributed the economic success of Protestant groups to Protestant values.
See also: Weber, Max.

One of the leaders of the Protestant Reformation: John Calvin

Protestantism, principles of the Reformation. The name derives from the *Protestatio* of the minority reforming delegates at the Diet of Speyer (1529). Protestantism is characterized by subordinating tradition to the Bible as the basis for doctrine and practice, and stresses justification by faith, biblical preaching, and a high personal morality. In reaction to Roman Catholicism it rejects papal claims, the mass, and the worship of saints. The main original branches were Lutheranism, Calvinism, Anglicanism, and Zwinglianism, with small Anabaptist sects. Exercise of the right of privacy judgment in interpreting Scripture led to fragmentation, a trend reversed in recent decades by the Ecumenical Movement. Later Protestant churches include the Congregational churches, Baptists, Quakers, Methodists, the Moravian Church, and the Pentecostal churches.
See also: Reformation.

Protista, members of a proposed group of organisms having characteristics of both the plant and the animal kingdoms. The classification usually includes single-celled organisms that have a distinct nucleus and organelles (structures that perform specific functions): protozoans, diatoms, bacteria, and some algae. Some scientists consider multicelled fungi and seaweeds as protista. The classification was proposed by the German zoologist Ernst H. Haeckel (1866).

Proton, elementary particle having a positive charge equivalent to the negative charge of the electron but possessing a mass approximately 1,837 times as great. A member of the baryon class of elementary particles, the proton was discovered in 1919 by Ernest Rutherford. The proton is, in effect, the nucleus of the hydrogen atom. Every atomic nucleus contains at least one proton.
See also: Atom.

Protoplasm, basic substance of which all living things are made up. Mostly water, protoplasm also contains proteins, fats, and inorganic salts. It is present in all cells, usually differentiated into the nucleus and the cytoplasm. The latter is generally a transparent viscous fluid containing a number of specialized structures; it is the medium in which the main chemical reactions of the cell take place. The nucleus contains the cell's genetic material.

Protozoan, single-celled organism belonging to the phylum Protozoa. Protozoans fall into 4 classes: flagellates, sarcodines, sporozoans, and ciliates. Most are aquatic, living in fresh or salt water. Some live in plants or animals and cause serious diseases. A few protozoans contain chlorophyll and make their own food, but the majority must ingest their food. They reproduce in many ways, including undergoing fission (cell division) or budding. Protozoans tend to be solitary; a few cluster in colonies.

Protractor, semicircular device used to measure or to construct angles. The curve is usually marked in degrees, (0-180), or sometimes in mils (0-3,200). A plane protractor is used to measure angles within a plane. A spherical protractor is used in navigation and astronomy to measure spherical angles.
See also: Angle.

Proudhon, Pierre Joseph (1809-65), French social thinker. He first gained notoriety with his book *What is Property?* (1840). He advocated a society in which property would be distributed among free individuals who cooperated spontaneously outside a framework of state authority—a philosophy he called *mutualism*. In 1847 he clashed with Karl Marx, thus starting a struggle between libertarian and authoritarian views on socialism which continued long after his death.

Proust, Joseph Louis (1754-1826), French chemist who established the law of definite proportions, or Proust's law.
See also: Chemistry.

Proust, Marcel (1871-1922), French novelist whose seven-part work *Remembrance of Things Past* is one of the greatest novels of the 20th century. It was written during the period 1907-19, after Proust, who suffered continually from asthma, had retired from Parisian high society and become virtually a recluse. A semiautobiographical exploration of time, memory, and consciousness, with an underlying theme of the transcendency of art over the futility of one's best efforts, it broke new ground in the art of the novel and was enormously influential.

Provençal, or langue d'oc, Romance language developed from the Latin spoken in southern France, principally Provence. During the Middle Ages, Provençal produced a notable literature that reached its highest point with the courtly love poetry of the troubadours.

Provence, region and former province of France, embracing the lower Rhone River (including the Camargue) and the French Riviera. The chief cities are Nice, Marseilles, Toulon, Avignon, Arles, and Aix-en-Provence (the historic capital). It is a sunny and picturesque region, famous for historical associations and its fruit, vineyards, and olives. It was the first transalpine Roman province (hence the name), and later it became an independent kingdom (879-933), finally passing to the French kings in 1486.
See also: France.

Lavender fields in Provence

Proverbs, Book of, book of the Bible's Old Testament; an example of the "wisdom literature" popular in post-exilic Judaism. Its eight sections, attributed in their headings to various authors, including Solomon, consist of numerous pithy proverbs and mostly unconnected moral maxims, probably dating between the 9th and 2nd centuries B.C.
See also: Old Testament.

Providence (pop. 654,854), capital of Rhode Island, on the Providence River at the head of Narragansett Bay. The second-largest city in New England (after Boston), Providence is an important industrial, commercial, and education center. Its port is among the busiest in New England. Its major industries include jewelry, silverware, textiles, machinery, and metal products. Brown University is located here, as are the famous Rhode Island School of Design, Bryant College, Catholic Teacher's College, Providence College, Providence-Barrington Bible College, and Rhode Island College.
Providence is among the oldest cities in the

United States, founded by Roger Williams in 1636 after his expulsion from the Plymouth Colony. Williams and his followers named it for "God's merciful providence" and made it a haven for religious dissenters. Toward the end of the century, Providence became a major port and commercial center. In the 18th and 19th centuries manufacturing (especially textiles) developed strongly. The city maintains a number of historic old homes and public buildings, many of which date from colonial times.
See also: Rhode Island.

Province, region governed or administered by a country, empire, or diocese. Some nations are formed by a union of provinces, while others are divided into provinces, e.g., Canada. To the Romans, a province was a conquered land ruled from Rome as a self-contained unit.

Provincetown *see:* Cape Cod; Mayflower.

Provo (pop. 263,590), a city in Utah and the seat of Utah County. Named for Étienne Provost, a fur trapper, it was founded by Mormons (1849) and incorporated in 1851. Its products include fruit, steel, and iron. Brigham Young University is in Provo.
See also: Utah.

Prud'hon, Pierre Paul (1758-1823), French painter. His best-known works are the portrait of the Empress Josephine (1805) and *Crime Pursued by Vengeance and Justice* (1808). His painting, influenced by Correggio, is soft and sensual in character.

Prune, dried plum. Certain plum varieties, especially French prune plums, are suited for prune production. The ripe fruit is dried in a dehydrator for 14-24 hours, dipped in a lye solution, and allowed to cure for at least 2 weeks.

Pruning, the cutting away of a plant's branches, shoots, buds, or roots. Pruning is done to shape a plant, increase air and light circulation among the branches, increase fruit and flower quality, remove dead, diseased, injured, or hazardous parts, retard water loss after transplanting, or renew growth. A gardener prunes certain plants according to the season and makes the cut at a prescribed place and angle.

Prussia, state in north central Europe that became the foundation of the modern state of Germany. At the height of its strength it stretched from west of the Rhine to Poland and Russia. The Baltic territory later known as East Prussia was Germanized by the Teutonic Knights in the 1200s and later became the duchy of Prussia. In 1618 it came under the rule of the Electors of nearby Brandenburg, the Hohenzollerns; and Frederick I declared himself king of Prussia in 1701. Under his successors, particularly Frederick the Great, the Prussian state expanded to become the strongest military power in northern Europe. In 1862 Bismarck became premier, and as a result of a planned series of wars and skillful diplomacy conducted under his direction, King William I of Prussia was declared Emperor of Germany in 1871. Prussia was the largest and most powerful of the states of the united Germany until 1934, when by a decree of Hitler the separate German states ceased to exist as political entities. After World War II former Prussian territory was divided among East Germany, Poland, and the USSR.
See also: Germany.

Prussian blue, category of deep-blue pigments containing ferrocyanide. It is used to color paint, enamel, lacquer, printing ink, and carbon paper. Some Prussian blue is prepared from sodium ferrocyanide that has been oxidized in the presence of sodium chlorate, sodium chromate, or other reagent. Others are made by oxidizing a mixture of ferrous sulfate and potassium ferrocyanide. Prussian blue was first made in 1704.

Prussic acid (HCN), also called hydrocyanic acid, a colorless, highly toxic, aqueous solution of hydrogen cyanide. The acid is flammable and evaporates readily. It is used in the manufacture of plastics, fumigants, and dyes. Prussic acid was first derived from the pigment Prussian blue.

Przewalski's horse, or Eastern wild horse, last remaining race of true wild horses. Of the three subspecies of *Equus przewalskii*, two—the steppe tarpan and forest tarpan—were exterminated by the middle of the 19th century. Only Przewalski's horse remained, undiscovered until 1881. Ancestors of domestic horses, they are about the size of a pony, yellow or red-brown, and with an erect mane. It is probable that they, too, are now extinct in the wild. Today it is an endangered species with less than 200 animals living in zoos and fewer than 50 living in the wild.

Psalms, Book of, collection of 150 songs in the Old Testament, used as the hymn book of Judaism since the return from exile and prominent in Christian liturgy. Metrical psalms are sung in the Reformed churches. Many psalms are traditionally ascribed to David; modern scholars date them between the 10th and 2nd centuries B.C. Their fine poetry embodies a rich variety of religious experience, both national and individual.
See also: Old Testament.

Psi particle, subatomic particle consisting of a charmed quark and an anticharmed quark bonded by their opposite electric charges and a strong nuclear force, or strong interaction. The psi particle itself has no electric charge. The psi particle, also called a J particle, was discovered in 1974 by two separate teams of U.S. physicists.
See also: Quark.

Psittacosis, infectious atypical form of pneumonia caused by *Chlamydia psittaci* and transmitted by certain birds. Human infection usually occurs by inhaling dust from feathers or excreta of infected birds; it may also be transmitted to humans by a bite from an infected bird or, rarely, by cough droplets of infected bird or, rarely, by cough droplets of infected persons. The onset may be insidious or abrupt, with fever, chills, general malaise, and anorexia. The temperature gradually rises and a cough develops, initially dry but at times becoming mucopurulent. During the second week pneumonia and frank consolidation may occur with secondary purulent lung infection. Convalescence is gradual and may be prolonged, especially in severe cases. Tetracycline is an effective treatment.
See also: Pneumonia.

Psoriasis, skin condition characterized by patches of red, thickened, and scaling skin. It often affects the elbows, knees, and scalp but may be found anywhere. Several forms are recognized, and the manifestations may vary over time in each individual. Coal tar preparations are valuable in treatment, but steroid creams and cytotoxic chemotherapy may be needed. There is also an associated arthritis.

Psychedelics *see:* Hallucinogenic drug.

Psychiatry, field of medicine concerned with the study and treatment of mental disorders, including neurosis and psychosis. Its major branches are psychotherapy, the application of psychological techniques to the treatment of mental illness where a physiological origin is either unknown or does not exist; and medical therapy, where attack is made either on the organic source of the disease or on its physical or behavioral symptoms.
See also: Mentall illness.

Psychical research, field of study concerned with the evaluation of phenomena having to do with so-called extrasensory perception. So far, no scientific evidence for such phenomena has been found.
See also: Extrasensory perception; Parapsychology.

Psychoanalysis, system of psychology having as its base the theories of Sigmund Freud; also the psychotherapeutic technique based on that system. The distinct forms of psychoanalysis developed by Carl Jung and Alfred Adler are more correctly termed *analytical psychology* and *individual psychology*, respectively. Freud's initial interest was in the origins of neuroses. On developing the technique of free association to replace that of hypnosis in this therapy, he observed that certain patients could in some cases associate freely only with difficulty. He decided that this was due to repression, where memories of certain experiences being held back from the conscious mind, and noted that the most sensitive areas were in connection with sexual experiences. He thus developed the concept of the unconscious (later to be called the *id*) and suggested (for a while) that anxiety was the result of repression of the libido. He also defined *resistance* by the conscious mind to accep-

tance of ideas and impulses from the unconscious, and *transference*, the idea that relationships with other people or objects in the past affect the individual's relationships with other people or objects in the present.
See also: Freud, Sigmund; Psychology.

Psychological warfare, various propaganda methods directed at a nation's enemy. The objective is to demoralize the enemy's people, break their will, and discredit their leaders. Civilians, soldiers, and prisoners of war may be subjected to psychological warfare.
See also: Propaganda.

Psychology, originally the branch of philosophy dealing with the mind, then the science of mind, and now, considered in its more general context, the science of behavior, whether human or animal, and of human thought processes. Psychology is closely connected with medicine, psychiatry, and sociology. There are a number of closely interrelated branches of human psychology. *Experimental psychology* embraces all psychological investigations undertaken by the psychologist. The experiments may center on the individual or on a group, in which latter case statistics will play a large part in the research. *Social psychologists* use statistical and other methods to investigate the effect of the group on the behavior of the individual. In *applied psychology*, the discoveries and theories of psychology are put to practical use, as in industrial psychology. *Comparative psychology* deals with the different behavioral organizations of animals, including humans. *Physiological psychology* attempts to understand the neurology and physiology of behavior. *Clinical psychologists* diagnose and treat mental disorders, principally using psychological tests, psychotherapy, and behavior therapy. They also do research on psychological factors affecting mental illness.

Ptarmigan

Psychosis, any mental disorder that, whether neurological or purely psychological in origin, renders an individual incapable of distinguishing reality from fantasy. Symptoms may include delusions and hallucinations, severe mood swings, dissociation, etc. If the loss of mental capacity is progressive, the illness is termed a deteriorative psychosis. Today, the term is less often used in psychiatric diagnosis.
See also: Mental illness; Schizophrenia.

Psychosomatic medicine, that aspect of medical treatment that considers the emotional and mental component of physical illness. Emotional and mental disturbances undermine a person's physical health. They can also make a person feel sick when there is no physical cause. Disorders linked with emotional disturbances include asthma, headache, ulcers, hypertension, neurodermatoses (chronic skin disorders), sexual dysfunction, gastrointestinal upsets, and rheumatoid arthritis, among others. A patient whose complaint is determined to be psychosomatic may be treated by a physician, psychiatrist (or other therapist), or both.

Psychotherapy, application of the theories and discoveries of psychology to the treatment of mental illness, particularly in the form of some sort of relationship between the therapist and the patient. Psychoanalysis, the technique pioneered by Sigmund Freud, was the first form of psychotherapy. Since then many others have been developed, including behavior therapy and Gestalt therapy. Most approaches to psychotherapy involve some type of support, confrontation, or interpretation. Any approach may be applied in a group setting of 5 to 12 people. Group therapy enables a therapist to serve more people, and members of a group can learn from and provide support for one another.
See also: Behavior therapy; Gestalt psychology; Psychology.

Psyllium, herb belonging to the plantain family, Plantagnaceae. *Plantango psyllium* and *P. ovata* are common species. An annual, the plant may grow 20 in (51 cm) high. It has narrow leaves, 1-2$^{1}/_{2}$ in (2.5-6.4 cm) long, and tiny flowers along spikes. Psyllium is cultivated in southern Europe and India for the medicinal, especially laxative, properties of its seeds.

Ptarmigan, any of several birds of the grouse family that can be identified by their white wings and underparts. The willow ptarmigan and rock ptarmigan live in Arctic regions, while the white-tailed ptarmigan is found above the treeline of the Rocky Mountains. Ptarmigans turn white in winter. They have feathered toes that act as snowshoes, and they can burrow under snow for food.

PT boat, small, manueverable boat used by the U.S. Navy to torpedo enemy ships. Its full name is *patrol torpedo boat.* The PT boat was used to advantage during World War II but taken from the active list in 1959. PT boats were 77-80 ft (23-24 m) long. Powered by 3 supercharged gasoline engines, a PT boat could travel at 43 knots, or 49 mi (79 km) per hr. The near-flat hull, which allowed the PT boat to skim over smooth water, handicapped the boat in rough waves.
See also: Navy, U.S.

Pteranodon *see:* Pterosaur.

Pteridophyte, class of plants that produce spores and have roots, stems, and leaves. Having vascular tissue places pteridophytes in the division, or phylum, Tracheophyta. Among other plants, the class includes ferns, horsetails, club mosses, and numerous species known from fossils. The pteridophyte's life cycle is one of alternating generations and asexual (with spores) and sexual (with egg and sperm) reproduction. Spores released from spore cases develop into a plant unlike the parent. This second form develops male and female reproductive organs. These produce eggs and sperm that unite to begin the first form of the plant. Pteridophytes that lived millions of years ago are the source of today's coal.

Pterosaur, member of a group of flying reptiles that lived 195-65 million years ago, during the Mesozoic era. The compact body had a pointed head with powerful, toothed jaws. Skin between the hindlimb and the forelimb's 4th finger served as a wing. The other 3 fingers were clawed and free for clutching. The slender hindlimbs seem to have been adapted for suspending the animal. Scientists believe that the pterosaur, besides gliding and soaring, flapped its wings. There are 2 known groups of pterosaurs: the earlier rhamphourhynchoids, the size of a sparrow; and the various sized pterodactyls. The *Pteranodon*, a pterodactyl descendant, had a wingspan estimated at up to 51 ft (15.5 m), making it the largest flying reptile.

Ptolemy, or Claudius Ptolemaeus (2nd century A.D.), Alexandrian astronomer, mathematician, and geographer. Most important is his book on astronomy, now called *Almagest* ("the greatest"), a synthesis of Greek astronomical knowledge, especially that of Hipparchus. His geocentric cosmology dominated Western scientific thought until the Copernican Revolution of the 16th century. His *Geography* gave rise to Columbus' belief in the westward route to Asia. In his *Optics* he attempted to solve the astronomical problem of atmospheric refraction.
See also: Astronomy.

Ptolemy, name used by all 15 Egyptian kings of the Macedonian dynasty (323 B.C.-30 B.C.). **Ptolemy I Soter** (367 B.C.-283 B.C.) was one of Alexander the Great's generals. He secured Egypt for himself after Alexander's death and defended it in a series of wars against Alexander's other generals. He founded the library of Alexandria, which became a center of Hellenistic culture. **Ptolemy II Philadelphus** (308 B.C.-246 B.C.) succeeded in 285. Under him Alexandria reached its height; he completed the Pharos lighthouse and appointed Callimachus librarian. **Ptolemy III Euergetes** (c.280-221 B.C.) Succeeded in 246. He extended the empire to include most of Asia Minor, the eastern Mediterranean, and the Aegean islands. After 221 the Ptolemaic empire entered a long period of decline, gradually losing its overseas possessions. **Ptolemy XV Cesarion** ("son of Caesar"; 47-30 B.C.) ruled from 44 B.C. jointly with his mother, Cleopatra VII. On their defeat at the battle of Actium (31 B.C.), Egypt became a Roman province.
See also: Egypt, Ancient.

Ptomaine poisoning, type of food poisoning caused by spoiled foods.

Puberty *see:* Adolescence.

Public domain, in U.S. law, ownership of a property or resource by the people. In 1980 public domain or public land made up 34% of U.S. land. Processes, plans, and creative works not protected by patent or copyright are said to be in the public domain.

Public health, organization and practice of preventative medicine within a community. Many threats to health are beyond individual control: Disease, epidemics, pollution of the air, and purity of water can only be effectively regulated by laws and health authorities. Among the strictest controls are those on sewage and waste disposal. Most advanced countries have pure-food laws controlling food purity, freshness, and additives. In the United States, these controls are the responsibility of the Food and Drug Administration. The work of individual countries in the public-health field is coordinated by the World Health Organization. Some countries have complete public-health services that provide free or low-cost medical treatment of all kinds.

Public lands, land areas owned by the U.S. government, especially those it sells or leases to individuals. The government uses public lands for parks, forests, cemeteries, wildlife refuges, federal buildings, and defense installations. Congress determines how to use or dispose of public lands; the Bureau of Land Management in the Department of the Interior administers public lands. About 762 million acres (308 million hectares) are public lands.

Public opinion, opinions held by many people on issues of local, national, or worldwide importance. Public opinion is shaped by factual information and individuals' values and emotions. It is circulated and further influenced by conversation, fora, the media, schools, public figures, and special interest groups, such as political parties, labor unions, religious organizations, and businesses. Public opinion polls survey the range of public opinion within a group. In a democratic society, government and private institutions are responsive to public opinion and divergent public opinion is permitted.

Public opinion poll, technique for measuring the range of opinions held by the general public or by specifically limited groups of people. It developed during the 1920s. Opinion polls rely on certain statistical laws that show that small, carefully chosen samples of any group can accurately represent the range of opinions of the whole group, or population. The population in question, known as the "universe," may be a general one (all voters in the United States) or a limited one (all car workers in Detroit). Accuracy depends on the care with which the sample is constructed and on the size of the sample. Since 1944 all polls have adopted the method of random selection pioneered by the U.S. Census Bureau in which each member of the "universe" has an equal chance of being questioned. Pioneers in U.S. public-opinion polling include George Gallup, Louis Harris, and Elmo Roper.

Public relations (PR), general term for fostering goodwill for a person, corporation, institution, or product without actually paying for advertisements. Practitioners of PR supply information to the media in the hope that the media will not bother to make any changes in what they want to have said. PR people suggest improvements in behavior, grooming, packaging, etc., to a client or employer. The term *public relations* is thought to have been used first by Ivy L. Lee, who styled himself an "adviser" on "public relations" as early as 1919.

Public utility, business that performs a service for the public and is subject to government regulation. Companies that supply electricity, water, and natural gas and provide sewage treatment, waste disposal, telephone service, and transportation are examples of public utilities. In Canada and Europe, the state owns the public utilities. In the United States, most public utilities are privately owned; some are owned by municipalities and counties. Government regulation assures that the public utility, a monopoly, charges a reasonable fee and supplies adequate and safe service to all who apply for it.

Public Works Administration (PWA), or Federal Emergency Administration of Public Works, a New Deal agency set up in 1933 to stimulate employment and purchasing power. Under H.L. Ickes it made loans and grants, mainly to governmental bodies, for projects which included the Grand Coulee and Bonneville dams. The PWA was phased out from 1939.

Publishing, preparation, manufacture, and distribution of printed materials. In Europe, publishing became distinct from printing and bookselling soon after the introduction of printing (15th century). By the 1800s, book publishing was an important industry. Today, large publishers are often owned by conglomerates. Many publishers specialize as to subject matter; type of book: trade, text, or reference; and means of distribution. Trade books (fiction and nonfiction) are sold to readers through stores; textbooks reach students through school purchases; reference books are sold to libraries and individuals. Some books are sold by subscription or through book clubs. In a publishing house, the steps needed to bring a manuscript to book form are carried out by separate departments: editorial, production, promotion, and distribution.
See also: Printing.

Puccini, Giacomo (1858-1924), Italian opera composer. His first international success, *Manon Lescaut* (1893), was followed by *La Bohème* (1896), *Tosca* (1900), *Madama Butterfly* (1904), and *Turandot* (uncompleted at Puccini's death, produced 1926). A lyric style and strong orchestration are characteristic of his operas, which have great dramatic and emotional power. Puccini's works are among the most popular in the operatic repertoire.
See also: Opera.

Pudding stone, kind of conglomerate rock. It consists of pebbles and gravel embedded in a fine-grained, loosely cementing matrix. The term is chiefly British.

Puebla (pop. 646,600), capital of Puebla, Mexico. The city, one of Mexico's largest, was founded in 1531. It is known for its architecture, much of which is decorated with colored tiles. Puebla's products include pottery, glass, tiles, cotton textiles, fruits, and vegetables.
See also: Mexico.

Puebla, state of Mexico, in central Mexico, near Mexico City. It produces agricultural products and textiles. Three of Mexico's highest mountains, Orizaba (Citlatltépetl), Popocatépetl, and Ixtacihuatl, are within Puebla. Its capital is the city of Puebla.
See also: Mexico.

Pueblo (pop. 123,051), city in southeastern Colorado and the seat of Pueblo County. It lies on the Arkansas River in the foothills of the Rocky Mountains. Among its products are steel, timber, and coal. It was built on the site of a frontier trading post and fort (1842).
See also: Colorado.

Pueblo, several Native American tribes living in southwestern United States (Arizona and New Mexico) in permanent villages (*pueblos*). They have the oldest and most developed pre-Columbian civilization north of Mexico. The various tribes, which include the Hopi and Zuñi, are de-

Pueblo people of Taos, New Mexico

scended from the basket makers and cliff dwellers. Pueblo Indians are noted for their handiworks; their social system and religious practices remain largely intact today.

Puerto Rico, officially the Commonwealth of Puerto Rico, island in the Caribbean Sea.

Land and climate. Puerto Rico is the smallest and easternmost island of the Greater Antilles, the other members of which are Cuba, Jamaica, and Hispaniola. It is about 950 mi (1,529 km) southeast of Miami, Florida and 550 mi (885 km) north of Caracas, Venezuela. A number of offshore islands, including Vieques, Culebra, and Mona, also belong to Puerto Rico, bringing the commonwealth's total area to about 3,435 sq mi (8,897 sq km). Along the coast is a narrow fertile plain from 1 to 12 mi (19 km) wide. In the center of the island is a chain of mountains that roughly divides it into two distinct northern and southern regions. Puerto Rico has a tropical climate, but the effects of high temperature are moderated by the trade winds. Tropical hurricanes frequently bear down on the island, especially between August and October. The capital city is San Juan. The official language is Spanish, but English is also spoken.

San Juan, Puerto Rico

People. The people of Puerto Rico are a mixture of Spanish and African. Some two-thirds of the population lives in the cities of San Juan, Ponce, and Mayagüez. Most Puerto Ricans are Roman Catholic.

Economy. Puerto Rico's was formerly a single-crop economy based upon sugar, but it now depends largely upon manufacturing. Metals, chemicals, oil refining, textiles, and sugar products account for most manufacturing and provide the principal exports. Coffee, tobacco, and tourism are also important. The United States is Puerto Rico's main trading partner.

History. Puerto Rico was discovered in 1493 by Christopher Columbus. In 1508, Juan Ponce de Leòn founded a colony. The native Arawak people perished under Spanish rule and, from 1510, black African slaves were imported to work on sugar plantations. The island was ceded to the United States in 1898 following the Spanish American War. In 1917, the Puerto Ricans received U.S. citizenship. U.S. economic dominance resulted in economic dislocation and political tension. In 1952, Puerto Rico became a commonwealth in free association with the United States. Under the arrangement, Puerto Ricans remain U.S. citizens, though they cannot vote in U.S. elections and are not obligated to pay U.S. taxes. Following World War II and Operation Bootstrap, a program for strengthening the island's economy, Puerto Rico experienced increased investment that spurred economic growth and diversification. However, high unemployment coupled with a high birth rate have led large numbers of Puerto Ricans to emigrate to the United States. The island's relationship to the United States remains a political issue. Mainstream political parties are divided between those favoring statehood and those favoring the commonwealth arrangement. A nationalist minority outside the mainstream seeks in-

Puerto Rico

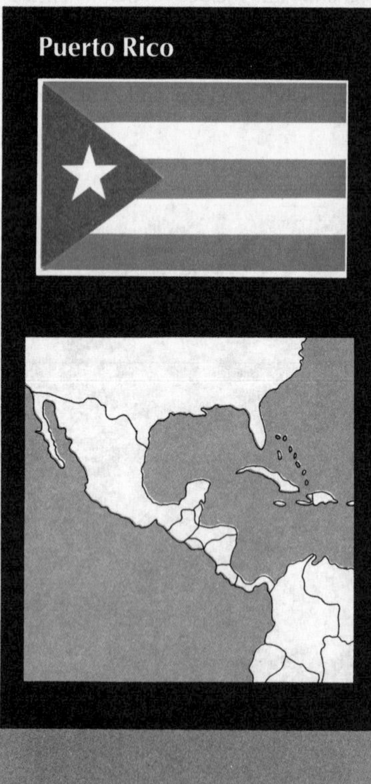

General information	
Capital:	San Juan
Area:	3,515 sq mi (9,104 sq km)
Population:	3,308,000
Official languages:	English, Spanish
Monetary unit:	1 U.S. dollar = 100 cents
Main cities:	San Juan, Bayamón, Ponce
Government	
Form:	self-governing commonwealth associated with the United States
Independent:	dependent
Head of state:	Governor (elected every 4 years)
Head of government:	Governor
Legislature:	two legislative houses (Senate and House of Representatives)
Executive:	Governor and Executive Officials
Judiciary:	highest court is the Supreme Court
Political division:	78 municipio
National economy	
Gross national product:	U.S. $18,520,000,000
Per capita income:	U.S. $5,540
Agriculture:	coffee, sugar cane, bananas, plantains, pineapples, tobacco
Livestock:	cattle, pigs, poultry
Fisheries:	1,000 metric tons
Mining:	stone
Industries:	chemicals, pharmaceuticals, electrical and nonelectrical machinery and equipment, food products, tourism
Main exports:	chemical and related products, metals and metal products, animal and vegetable products
Transportation:	59 mi (96 km) of railroads, 5,810 mi (9,351 km) of roads, 2 international airports
Trading partners:	U.S., Japan, Venezuela, Dominican Republic, Brazil
People	
Urban:	70%
Ethnic composition:	European 80.0%, African 20.0%
Birth rate:	19.4 per 1,000 population
Death rate:	7.1 per 1,000 population
Infant mortality:	15 per 1,000 live births
Life expectancy:	male 71 years, female 79 years

dependence. The issue dominates Puerto Rico's political life.

Puff adder *see:* Adder.

Puffball, fungus of the family Lycoperdaceae. Puffballs produce a roundish fruiting body (basidiocarp) that contains spores. Before maturity, the basidiocarp is firm and edible. The dry, mature puffball often has cracks from which the powdery spores issue.

Puffer, or globe fish, fish that blows up its body like a balloon. It is found in warm and temperate seas, and some grow to 3 ft (0.91 m) long. The bodies of some puffers contain a deadly poison, tetradontoxin. In Japan they are a delicacy, but a cook has to have a license to prepare puffers, for it is necessary to remove the poison parts.

Puffin, any of several stubby seabirds of the auk family. Black or black-and-white, they are characterized by their large, laterally compressed bills, which become further enlarged and brightly patterned at the beginning of the breeding season. Puffins live in colonies on sea cliffs, nesting in burrows.

Pug, breed of toy dog. It has a squarish build, wrinkled face, short muzzle, and curled tail. Adults stand 10-11 in (2.5-2.8 cm) and weigh 13-18 lb (6-8 kg). The pug probably originated in China.

Pugachev, Emelian Ivanovich (1742-75), Cossack leader of the great Urals peasant revolt (1773-74). Claiming to be Peter III, murdered husband of Catherine II of Russia, he declared serfdom abolished and led an army of serfs and Cossacks that seized several cities and killed thousands before he was captured, sent to Moscow in an iron cage, and executed.
See also: Cossacks.

Puget, Peter (1762?-1822), British naval officer and explorer. As a lieutenant with Captain George Vancouver, he explored Puget Sound (1792) and other coastal areas of northwest North America.

Puget Sound, irregular inlet of the Pacific Ocean in northwestern Washington. It extends south about 100 mi (161 km) to Olympia and is navigable by large ships (U.S. navy yard at Bremerton). Seattle and Tacoma lie on its shores, and the state's fish and lumber industries are centered in the area. It was explored by George Vancouver in 1792 and named by him.
See also: Pacific Ocean; Puget, Peter.

Pulaski, Casimir (c.1748-79), Polish soldier, hero of the anti-Russian revolt of 1768 who, exiled from Poland, fought in the American Revolutionary War. He fought at the battles of Brandywine and Germantown. In 1778 he formed his own cavalry unit, the Pulaski Legion. He was mortally wounded at the siege of Savannah.
See also: Poland; Revolutionary War, American.

Pulitzer, Joseph (1847-1911), Hungarian-born U.S. publisher who created the Pulitzer Prizes. In 1883 he bought the New York *World* and raised the circulation tenfold in seven years by aggressive reporting (the term *yellow journalism* was coined to describe its style). In the 1890s Pulitzer was involved in a circulation war with William Randolph Hearst's New York *Journal*. He regularly ran liberal crusades. He also endowed the school of journalism at Columbia University.

Pulitzer Prizes, awards for achievement in U.S. journalism and letters, given every May since 1917 through a foundation created by the estate of Joseph Pulitzer and administered by Columbia University. There are eight cash awards for journalism ($1,000 each), five for literature ($500 each), and four traveling scholarships. An award for music was added in 1943.
See also: Pulitzer, Joseph.

Pulley, grooved wheel mounted on a block with a cord or belt passing over it. A pulley is a simple machine applying the equilibrium of torque to obtain a mechanical advantage. Thus the block and tackle is a combination of ropes and pulleys used for hoisting heavy weights. A belt and pulley combination can transmit motion from one part of a machine to another. Variable speed can be obtained from a single-speed driving shaft by the use of stepped or cone-shaped pulleys with diameters that give the correct speed ratios and belt tensions. To help prevent excessive belt wear and slipping, the rim surface of a pulley is adapted to the material of the belt used.

Pullman, George Mortimer (1831-97), U.S. industrialist and inventor of the first modern railroad sleeping car, the Pullman (patented 1864). In 1880 he built a model company town, Pullman, Ill. (now part of Chicago), later site of the Pullman Strike.
See also: Railroad.

Pullman Strike (May-July 1894), famous boycott of rolling stock of the Pullman Palace Car Co., Pullman, Ill., by E.V. Dees's American Railway Union to protest the company's wage cuts and victimization of union representatives. After the owners obtained a federal injunction the strike was broken by federal troops and the U.S. labor movement suffered a major setback.

Pulsar, short for *pulsating radio star*, a celestial radio source emitting brief, extremely regular pulses of electromagnetic radiation. Each pulse lasts a few hundredths of a second, and the period between pulses is of the order of one second or less. The pulse frequency varies from pulsar to pulsar. The first pulsar was discovered in 1967 by Anthony Hewish and S.J. Bell. The fastest pulsar yet observed has a period of 0.033 sec, emitting pulses of the same frequency in the X-ray and visible regions of the spectrum. It is likely that there are some 10,000 pulsars in the Milky

Pulses of radio and light emissions from pulsars. It seems almost certain that they must be generated by continuously emitting, fast-spinning, compact bodies called neutron stars.

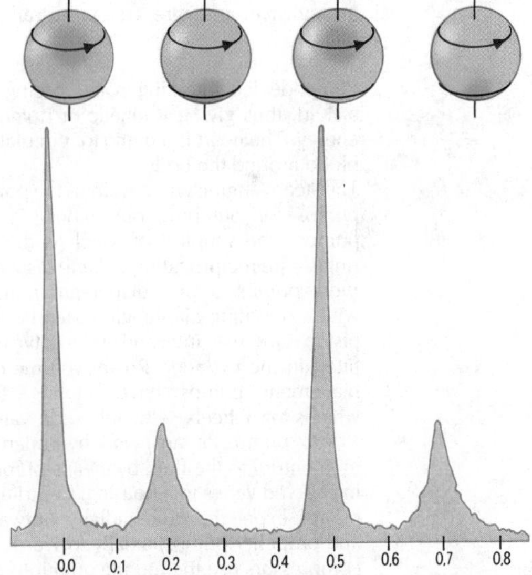

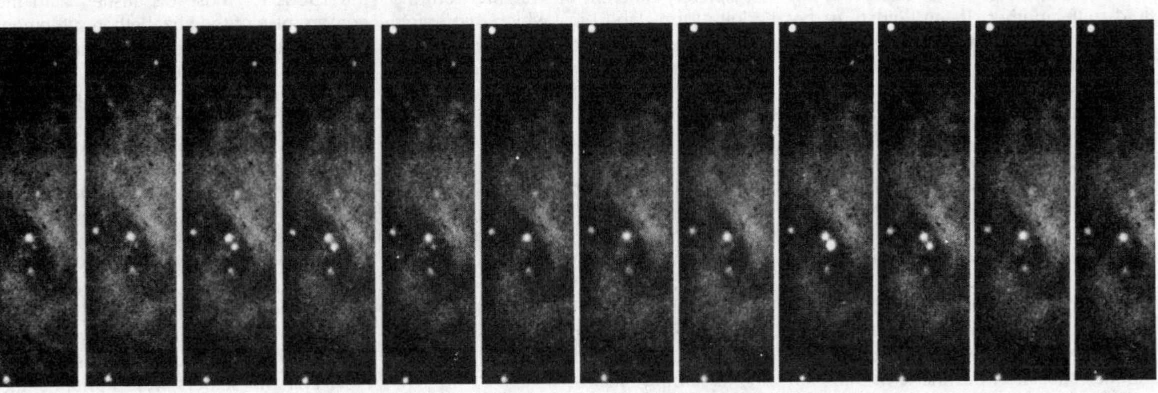

A radio pulsar in the Crab nebula: In order to make the pulse visible a type of stroboscopic effect is applied with the pulsar being photographed during many short intervals.

Henry Purcell

Way, though fewer than 100 have as yet been discovered. It is believed that pulsars are the neutron star remnants of supernovas, rapidly spinning and radiating through loss of rotational energy.
See also: Astronomy.

Pulse, throb in the artery walls due to the beating of the heart. The walls expand when the heart contracts and contract when the heart relaxes. This creates a wave of pressure that can be felt externally. The pulse is usually counted on the thumb side of the wrist, but it may be taken over any artery that can be felt. A doctor takes the pulse to determine if the heart is beating normally.
See also: Artery; Heart.

Puma, cougar, panther, or mountain lion (*Felis concolor*), the most widespread of the big cats of the Americas, occupying an amazing variety of habitats. Powerful cats, resembling a slender and sinuous lioness with a small head, they lead solitary lives, preying on various species of deer. The lifespan of a puma in the wild is about 18 years. A puma can cover up to 20 ft (6.1 m) in a bound and will regularly travel up to 50 mi (80.5 km) when hunting.

Pumice, porous, frothy, volcanic glass formed by the sudden release of vapors as lava cools under low pressure. It is used as an abrasive, an aggregate, and a railroad ballast.

Pump, device for taking in and forcing out a fluid, thus giving it kinetic or potential energy. The heart is a pump for circulating blood around the body.
The steam engine was developed to power pumps for pumping out mines. Piston pumps—the simplest of which is the syringe—are reciprocating *volume displacement pumps*, as are diaphragm pumps, with a pulsating diaphragm instead of the piston. One-way inlet and outlet valves are fitted in the cylinder. Rotary volume displacement pumps have rotating gear wheels or wheels with lobes or vanes. *Kinetic pumps*, or fans, work by imparting momentum to the fluid by means of rotating curved vanes in a housing: Centrifugal pumps expel the fluid radially outward; and propeller pumps, axially forward. Air compressors use the turbine principle. *Air pumps* use compressed air to raise liquids from the bottom of wells, displacing one fluid with another. If the fluid must not come into direct contact with the pump, as in a nuclear reactor, *electromagnetic pumps* are used. An electric current and a magnetic field at right angles induce the conducting fluid to flow at right angles to both; or the principle of the linear induction motor may be used. To achieve a very high vacuum, the *diffusion pump* is used, in which atoms of condensing mercury vapor entrain the remaining gas molecules.

Pumpkin, plant (genus *Cucurbita*) of the gourd family. The genus includes winter squashes (*C. maxima* or *C. moschata*) and summer squashes, but the term *pumpkin* usually refers to the round, orange-skinned fruit of the vine *C. pepo*. The pumpkin's stringy pulp is used as food and pie filling. The seeds, which fill the pumpkin's cavity, are also eaten. At Halloween, pumpkins are carved into jack-o'-lanterns. The pumpkin probably originated in North America.

Punch and Judy, leading characters in a children's handpuppet show of the same name. Punch, descended from Pulcinella (Punchinello) of the Commedia Dell'Arte, is a hooknosed, hunchbacked, wife-beating rogue who usually ends on the gallows or in a crocodile's mouth. He is accompanied by his shrewish wife, Judy (originally called Joan), and their dog, Toby. The Devil, Baby, Hangman, Policeman, and Doctor may also appear.

Punic Wars, 3 conflicts between Carthage and Rome. Rome emerged from the Punic Wars as the dominant Mediterranean power. The **First Punic War** (264-241 B.C.) involved a local dispute over the control of the Strait of Messina, between Sicily and Italy. Carthage, led by Hamilcar Barca, and the Sicilian town Syracuse fought well on land but yielded to Rome's greater sea power. During the **Second Punic War** (218-201 B.C.), Hannibal, the Carthagenian general, crossed the Alps into Italy. The Romans struggled to contain him and finally defeated him (202 B.C.) in Africa. Rome gained Carthage's Spanish provinces. The **Third Punic War** (149-146 B.C.) resulted from Carthage's alleged violation of the 201 B.C. treaty. Rome blockaded Carthage and sacked the city.
See also: Carthage; Hannibal; Rome, Ancient.

Punishment *see:* Capital punishment.

Punjab (Sanskrit, "five rivers"), large wheat-growing region in the northwest of the Indian subcontinent, on the upper Indus River plain. Formerly the British Indian province of Punjab, it was divided in 1947 into what became known as Punjab (Pakistan) and Punjab (India). In 1966 Punjab (India) was divided into two further provinces, Punjab and Haryana.
See also: India.

Pupa, immature stage in the development of those insects whose larval form is completely different in structure from the adult form and in which complete metamorphosis occurs. The pupa normally is a resting place in which the larval structure is reorganized to form the adult. Everything but the nervous system changes, and feeding and locomotion are suspended.

Pupfish, about 30 species of fish (genus *Cyprinodon*) belonging to the killifish family. Pupfish live in the southwestern United States and Mexico, in springs and streams. A few species can tolerate water temperatures of 108°F. (42°C) and thrive in hot springs. Some pupfish are endangered or extinct. Efforts are being made to protect the remaining species.

Pupil *see:* Eye.

Puppet, figure of a person or animal manipulated in dramatic presentations. There are hand (or glove) and finger puppets; jointed marionettes string-controlled from above; and rod puppets, often used in shadow plays. Puppetry, with which ventriloquism is associated, is an ancient entertainment, popular in many countries.

Purcell, Edward Mills (1912-), U.S. physicist who shared the 1952 Nobel Prize for physics for his discovery of nuclear magnetic resonance (NMR) in solids.

Purcell, Henry (c.1659-95), English composer, the foremost of his time. A master of melody and counterpoint, he wrote in every form and style of the period: odes and anthems for royal occasions, many choral and instrumental works, and music for plays and masques, including his opera *Dido and Aeneas* (1689).

Pure food and drug laws, in the United States, general term for laws such as the Federal Food, Drug and Cosmetic Act (1938) prohibiting the distribution of impure foods and drugs and the false or misleading labeling of such products. The Food and Drug Administration (FDA) enforces these laws and publishes explanatory regulations.

Purgatory, in Roman Catholicism, the place where Christians after death undergo purifying punishment and expiate unforgiven venial sins before admission to heaven. Indulgences, masses, and prayers for the dead are held to lighten their suffering.

Purim (Feast of Lots), Jewish festival of the 14th day of Adar (Feb.-Mar.), a celebration of the deliverance from massacre of Persian Jews through intervention by Esther and Mordecai. The story is told in the Book of Esther.

Puritans, English reforming Protestants who aimed for a simpler form of worship expressly warranted by Scripture, devout personal and family life, and the abolition of clerical hierarchy. They stressed self-discipline, work as a vocation, and the Christianizing of all spheres of life. Most were strict Calvinists. The term was first used in the 1560s for those dissatisfied with the compromise of the Elizabethan settlement of the Church of England; under James I, after their unsuccessful pleas for reform at the Hampton Court Conference (1604), some separated from the Church of England. Archbishop Laud set about systematic repression of Puritanism, causing some to emigrate to the colonies. The English Civil War—known also as the Puritan Revolution—led to the establishment of Presbyterianism, but under Oliver Cromwell Puritan dominance was weakened by internal strife. Most Puritans were forced to leave the Church after the Restoration (1660), becoming Nonconformists. Many New England settlers were Puritans, and

their influence on the colonies was profound, especially their concern for education and church democracy.
See also: Protestantism.

Purple Heart *see:* Decorations, Medals and orders.

Purus River, third-longest river in South America and a major tributary of the Amazon River. It rises in the Andes in Peru and meanders 1,956 mi (3,148 km) in a northeasterly direction into Brazil.

Pusan (pop. 3,517,000), second-largest city in South Korea, in the southeast. Having an excellent natural harbor, it is a major port and a center for commerce, shipbuilding, and the fishing industry. It is also a manufacturing and transportation center. Visitors come to its religious and historic landmarks, beaches, and hot springs. During the Korean War, it was South Korea's capital and a landing site for men and arms.
See also: Korea.

Pushkin, Alexander (1799-1837), poet, widely recognized as the founder of modern Russian literature. A sympathizer of the Decembrist Revolt, he spent his adult life in exile or under police surveillance. His poetic range included the political, humorous, erotic, lyrical, epic, and verse tales or novels like *Russlan and Ludmilla* (1820), *The Prisoner of the Caucasus* (1822), and his masterpiece *Eugene Onegin* (1833). Other works are the great drama *Boris Godunov* (1831) and such prose works as "The Queen of Spades" (1834) and *The Captain's Daughter* (1836).

Pushtuns, ethnic group comprising about one half the population of Afghanistan and one fifth the population of Pakistan. They are also called Pathans, Pashtuns, Pakhtuns, and Pukhtuns. Their language, called Pashto, Pushtu, or Pukhtu, is related to Persian. Most Pushtuns live as farmers or nomadic herders and follow Islam. The group is divided into about 40 tribes. Each consists of groups of extended families and is governed by a democratic council. Ancestors of the Pushtuns can be traced to 4000 B.C. During the Soviet invasion of Afghanistan (1979-89), guerrilla bands of Pushtuns resisted the Soviets.

Pussy willow, small tree (*Salix discolor*) particular to North America and characterized by a silky, often drooping flower cluster called a catkin, produced in the early spring.

Putnam, Israel (1718-90), U.S. patriot and general in the Revolutionary War. A veteran of the French and Indian Wars, he was prominent in the Battle of Bunker Hill, but had less success as commander of Continental forces at the Battle of Long Island.
See also: French and Indian Wars; Revolutionary War in America

Putnam, Rufus (1738-1824), U.S. pioneer who served in the French and Indian Wars and in many of the engagements of the Revolutionary War. He emerged a brigadier general and chief engineer of the army and in 1786 helped organize the Ohio Company of Associates.
See also: French and Indian Wars; Revolutionary War in America

Pu Yi (1906-67), as Hsuan T'ung, the last emperor (1908-12) of China. The Japanese installed him as Emperor K'ang Te of the puppet state Manchukuo (1934-45). He was captured by the Soviets and returned to China (1950), where he was imprisoned until 1959.

PVC *see:* Vinyl.

Pygmalion, in Greek mythology, king of Cyprus who carved a statue of a beautiful woman and then fell in love with it. The goddess Aphrodite brought the statue (named Galatea) to life as an answer to Pygmalion's prayer for a wife just like her, and they were married. The Pygmalion theme has been used by many authors, particularly George Bernard Shaw in his play *Pygmalion* (1913).

Pygmy, term used to denote those people whose adult males are on average less than 5 ft (1.52 m) tall. Some Kalahari desert Bushmen are of pygmy size, but the most notable pygmies are the Mbuti, or Bambuti, of the Ituri Forest, Zaïre, who, through their different blood type, skin color, thick lips, and scant body hair but thick head hair, are regarded as distinct from the surrounding peoples and were probably the original inhabitants of the region. A Stone Age people, they are nomadic hunters, living in groups of 50 to 100. Asian pygmies are generally termed *Negritos*. Peoples rather larger than pygmies are described as pygmoid.

Pyle, Ernie (Ernest Taylor Pyle; 1900-45), U.S. journalist and war correspondent. He accompanied U.S. troops to all the major fronts in North Africa and Europe during World War II, and his popular news column won a Pulitzer Prize in 1944. He was killed by Japanese machine-gun fire during the Okinawa campaign.
See also: World War II.

Pyle, Howard (1853-1911), U.S. writer and illustrator of children's books, such as *The Merry Adventures of Robin Hood* (1883) and *The Story of King Arthur and His Knights* (1903).

Pylos (modern Greek Pilos, formerly Navarino), ancient port in the southwestern Peloponnese, Greece, site of a Mycenaean palace of the 13th century B.C., associated with king Nestor. In the modern Greek War of Independence, it was the site of the Battle of Navarino (1827).
See also: Greece.

Pym, John (1584-1643), English statesman. A Puritan, he led parliamentary opposition to Charles I and organized the impeachment of the Duke of Buckingham (1626). Dominating the Short and Long Parliaments, he narrowly escaped arrest by the king in 1642 and then arranged an alliance with the Covenanters in 1643.

Pynchon, Thomas (1937-), U.S. novelist whose works, influenced by James Joyce and Vladimir Nabokov, are noted for their ingenious wordplay and complexity. His novels include *V* (1963), *The Crying of Lot 49* (1966), *Gravity's Rainbow* (1973), a National Book Award winner, and *Vineland* (1990).

Pyongyang (pop. 1,283,000), capital and largest city of North Korea. It lies on the Taedong River in an important coal-mining area and is a major industrial center producing iron, steel, machinery, and textiles. An ancient settlement, it was the capital of the Choson kingdom in the 3rd century B.C. The city was severely damaged during the Korean War.
See also: Korea.

Pyorrhea *see:* Periodontitis.

Pyramid, polyhedron whose base is a polygon and whose sides are triangles having a common vertex. A pyramid whose base is triangular is termed a tetrahedron (or triangular pyramid); one whose base is a regular polygon is termed regular; one with a square base, square; one with a rectangular base, rectangular.

Alexander Pushkin

Pyramids, structures built by the Egyptians and other ancient peoples as royal tombs or temples; they are composed of square bases and 4 triangular faces that meet at a common point, the apex. The Egyptian pyramids, erected around 4,500 years ago, are the largest and most notable. The first pyramid dates back to the Old Kingdom and was built by the architect Imhotep for King Zoser c.2650 B.C. The largest pyramid was constructed for King Khufu (reigned c.2589-c.2566 B.C.), also known as Cheops. It is 13 acres (5.3 hectares) in area and 482 ft (147 m) high. It is considered one of the Seven Wonders of the Ancient World. Pyramidal structures were also constructed by the native peoples of Central and South America. The Mayan pyramids were characterized by level tops that were probably used as pulpits.
See also: Egypt, Ancient.

Pyrenees, mountain range between France and Spain, stretching 270 mi (435 km) from the Bay of Biscay to the Mediterranean and rising to Pico de Aneto (11,168 ft/3,404 m) in the central section. The average height is about 3,500 ft (1,067 m) and the maximum width about 50 mi (81 km). The range includes extensive forests and pasture land. Its mineral deposits include iron, zinc, bauxite, and talc, and there are sports and health resorts and a growing tourist industry.

Pyrethrum, any of a group of flowers (genus *Chrysanthemum*) that produce insect powder. Similar in appearance to the daisy, pyrethrums have stems measuring

Q

up to 1 ft (30 cm). The insecticide is developed from the powdered or dried flowers and is considered one of the least harmful to humans and animals. Kenya is the world's chief exporter of pyrethrum.

Pyridoxine *see:* Vitamin (B complex).

Pyrite, or iron pyrites (FeS_2, iron (II) disulfide), hard, yellow, common sulfide known as fool's gold for its resemblance to gold. Of worldwide occurrence, it is an ore of sulfur that crystallizes in the isometric system, usually as cubes. It alters to goethite and limonite.

Pyromania, recurring impulse to set fire to objects or buildings.

Pyrometry, process of measuring exceedingly high temperatures through the use of a pyrometer, an instrument that can function in heat far hotter than that tolerated by ordinary thermometers. Most pyrometers measure temperature by detecting the rise in electrical resistance in a metal, by the increase in the intensity of light, or by similar electrical or radiation techniques.

Muammar Muhammad al-Qadhafi

Pyroxene, general term for a group of crystalline silicate minerals containing iron, calcium, and magnesium, prevalent in igneous, metamorphic, and lunar rocks. The color of pyroxenes ranges from black and brown to colorless.

Pyrrho of Elis (360-270 B.C.), Greek philosopher, the founder of skepticism. He taught that because nothing can be known with certainty, suspension of judgment and imperturbability of mind are the true wisdom and source of happiness.
See also: Skepticism.

Pyrrhus (c.318-272 B.C.), king at the age of 12 of Epirus, northwestern Greece, he served with Demetrius I of Macedonia in Asia Minor, was helped by Ptolemy I of Egypt to regain his throne, and later won and lost Macedonia. His costly victory over the Romans at Asculum (279), gave rise to the term *Pyrrhic victory.* Further campaigns in Macedonia and Sparta failed. He was killed in Argos.
See also: Greece, Ancient.

Pythagoras (c.582-507 B.C.), Greek philosopher who founded the Pythagorean school. Attributed to the school are: the proof of the Pythagorean theorem (the suggestion that the earth travels around the sun, the sun in turn around a central fire); observation of the ratios between the lengths of vibrating strings that sound in mutual harmony, and ascription of such ratios to the distances of the planets, which sounded the "harmony of the spheres"; and the proposition that all phenomena can be reduced to numerical relations. The Pythagoreans were also noted for their concept of the soul, the life of moderation, and their interest in medicine. They exerted great influence on Plato and ancient philosophy generally.
See also: Philosophy.

Pythagorean theorem, statement that, for any right-angled triangle, the square of the hypotenuse is equal to the sum of the squares of the other two sides. The earliest known formal statement of the theorem is in the *Elements* of Euclid, but the basis of it was known long before this time.
See also: Geometry.

Pythias *see:* Damon and Pythias.

Python, Old World equivalent of the New World boa, a snake bearing small spurs as the vestiges of hindlimbs. These two groups are clearly the closest relatives of the ancestral snake type. Like boas, pythons are nonvenomous constrictors. They are found from Africa to Australia in a wide variety of habitats. All have bold color patterns in browns and yellows. The largest species, the reticulate python of Asia, reaches 33 ft (10.1 m). Pythons feed on small mammals, birds, reptiles, and frogs; the larger African species also feed on small antelopes.

Q, 17th letter of the alphabet, can be traced back to the letter *koph* in the Semitic alphabet and *koppa* in ancient Greek, on through the Etruscan alphabet, taking its modern form in Latin, usually followed by *u.* As an abbreviation, a capital *Q* is used for "Quebec" and for "queen" in titles such as Q.C. (Queen's Counsel). A lower-case *q* may stand for "quart," "question," and is part of *q.v.* for the Latin phrase *quod vide* (which see), meaning "refer to."

Qadhafi, Muammar Muhammad al- (1942-), Libyan leader. One of a group of army officers who deposed King Idris I in 1969, he became chairman of the ruling Revolutionary Command Council and commander-in-chief of the armed forces. One of the world's most controversial heads of state, he has been vehemently anti-Israel and supported several insurgent and terrorist groups around the world. In response to his support of terrorists, in 1986 U.S. planes attacked Tripoli, destroying a military camp.
See also: Libya.

Qandahar, or Kandahar (pop. 191,300), city in southern Afghanistan, second largest Afghan city, and major international trade center. Industries include farming and fruit processing and exportation.
See also: Afghanistan.

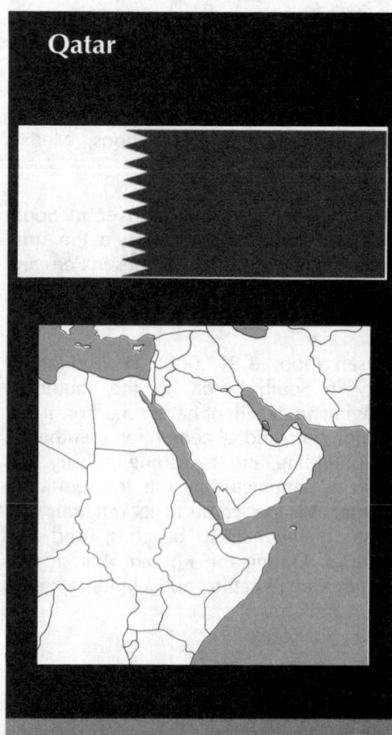

Capital:	Doha
Area:	4,377 sq mi (11,337 sq km)
Population:	427,000
Government:	emirate (monarchy)
Independent:	1971
GNP:	U.S. $4,060,000,000
Per capita:	U.S. $17,610

Qatar, the State of, oil-rich emirate in Arabia. It comprises a low limestone peninsula, about 120 mi (193 km) long, that juts north into the Persian Gulf from eastern Saudi Arabia. Its 4,416 sq mi (11,437 sq km) consist of barren desert that receives under 4 in (10 cm) of rainfall a year. The only natural vegetation is scrub. Oil accounts for more than 90% of exports and government income. Most of Qatar's workers are employed in the oil fields; others are goat and camel herders, fishers, or pearl divers. The merchants and industrial workers live in Doha, the capital, in eastern Qatar. Industry has expanded since 1939, when an oil strike led to the growth of the Dukhan oil field in western Qatar, one of the richest in the Middle East. In 1971 Qatar ceased to be a British protectorate and became a fully independent member of the UN.

Qin dynasty, also Ch'in dynasty, era of totalitarian Chinese rule dating from 221 B.C.-206 B.C. Under the rule of Shi Huangdi, the Chinese regions and regional chiefs were unified into one central empire. The dynasty is noted for advancing national unity and for the building of China's Great Wall.
See also: Great Wall of China; Shi Huangdi.

Quadhafi, Muammar Muhammad al- *see:* Qadhafi, Muammar Muhammad al-.

Quadrilateral, in geometry, plane 4-sided polygon. Quadrilaterals with 2 pairs of sides parallel are called parallelograms; with one pair of sides parallel, trapezoids; with no 2 sides parallel, trapeziums (the word *trapezium* is often used as a synonym of *trapezoid*). Parallelograms whose sides are all of equal length are termed rhombuses. Each side of a parallelogram is equal in length to the side parallel to it, and each interior angle is equal to the interior angle diametrically opposite it. A parallelogram whose interior angles are each 90° is a rectangle; a special case of this is the square, all of whose sides are equal. The sum of the interior angles of a quadrilateral is always 360°.

Quadruple Alliance, alliance of 4 countries. Historically, the most famous are (1) alliance among Britain, France, Austria, and the Netherlands (1718) to prevent Spain from changing the terms of the Peace of Utrecht (Spain later joined the alliance), (2) alliance among Britain, Austria, Russia, and Prussia (signed 1814, renewed 1815) to defeat Napoleon and, after his defeat and first abdication, to ensure that France abided by the terms of the 1815 Treaty of Paris, and (3) alliance among Britain, France, Portugal, and Spain (1834), supporting Queen Isabella II of Spain.

Quail, name for 2 distinct groups of game birds of the pheasant family. About 45 species of quail exist. Small ground birds of open country, quail are found on every continent except Antarctica. They feed on insects, grain, and shoots and rarely fly, even when disturbed. Quail live in groups called coveys in the fall and winter. The tiny painted quail was carried by Chinese mandarins to warm the hands.

Quaker-ladies *see:* Bluet.

Quaker meeting in London, 1737

Quakers, or Society of Friends, church known for its pacifism, humanitarianism, and emphasis on inner quiet. Founded in 17th-century England by George Fox, it was persecuted for its rejection of organized churches and any dogmatic creed. Many Quakers emigrated to America, where in spite of early persecution they were prominent among the colonizers. In 1681 William Penn established his "Holy Experiment" in Pennsylvania; from that point the church's main growth took place in America. The early Quakers adopted a distinctive, simple style of dress and speech; simplicity of manner is still a characteristic Quaker Trait. They have no formal creed and no clergy, putting their trust in the "inner light" of God's guidance. Their meetings for worship, held in "meeting houses," follow a traditional pattern of beginning in silence, with no set service and no single speaker. The Quakers have exercised a moral influence disproportionate to their numbers through practicing what they believe, particularly pacifism. In the United States they were prominent abolitionists and have been among the pioneers of social reform.
See also: Fox, George; Penn, William.

Quanah, or Quanah Parker (1845-1911), North American Comanche chief and leader of a brief uprising against settlers in an effort to end their slaughter of the buffalo in Texas. Quanah was the son of Chief Peta Nokoni and Cynthia Ann Parker, who was captured as a child by the Comanches. Quanah became an advocate of education and agricultural training for members of his tribe, who moved to a reservation (1875) near Fort Sill, Oklahoma.

Quantico Marine Corps Development and Education Command, training center for U.S. Marine Corps officers at Quantico, Va. The Quantico facility houses various schools including the Basic School for Commissioned Officers, The Woman Officer School, the Command and Staff College, and training schools for communications, ordnance, and computer sciences. Quantico also has a U.S. Navy hospital and a Marine air installation.
See also: Marine Corps, U.S.

Quantrill, William Clarke (1837-65), Confederate guerrilla leader in the U.S. Civil War. A criminal before the war, Quantrill was made a Confederate captain in 1862. In 1863, with a force of 450 men he attacked the town of Lawrence, Kans., and slaughtered 150 civilians. He was killed by Union troops while on a raid in Kentucky.
See also: Civil War, U.S.

Quantum electrodynamics, or QED, concept in theoretical physics. It concerns the motions and relationships between charged electrical particles including electrons, positrons, and photons and their interaction with electrical and magnetic fields. QED allows highly accurate predictions of changes in the properties of these particles. Physicists Richard P. Faynman and Julian S. Schwinger of the United States and Sin-itiro Tomonaga of Japan contributed in the 1940s to the development of QED.
See also: Feynman, Richard Phillips.

Quantum mechanics, fundamental theory of small-scale physical phenomena (such as the motions of electrons within atoms). This theory was developed during the 1920s, when it became clear that the existing laws of classical mechanics and electromagnetic theory were not successfully applicable to such systems. French physicist Louis De Broglie suggested (1924) that particles have a wavelike nature, with a wavelength h/p (h being the Planck constant, and p the particle momentum). This wavelike nature is significant only for particles on the molecular scale or smaller. These ideas were developed by Erwin Schrödinger and others into the branch of quantum mechanics known as wave mechanics. Werner Heisenberg of Germany worked along parallel lines with a theory incorporating only observable quantities, such as energy, using matrix algebra techniques. His uncertainty principle (that a subatomic particle's momentum and position cannot both be accurately known) is fundamental to quantum mechanics, as is Wolfgang Pauli's exclusion principle (that each electron in an atom is in a quantum state shared by no other electron in that atom). Paul Dirac incorporated relativistic ideas into quantum mechanics.
See also: Atom; Physics.

Quantum theory *see:* Quantum mechanics.

Quapaw, North American Plains Indians of the Siouan language group. By the 17th century they had migrated from the Ohio valley to near the mouth of the Arkansas River. They relinquished most of their lands to the United States in 1818.

Quarantine, period during which a person or animal must be kept under observation in isolation from the community after having been in contact with an infectious disease. The duration of quarantine depends on the disease(s) concerned and their maximum length of incubation. The term derives from the period of 40 days that ships had to wait before their crews could disembark at medieval European ports, due to fear of their carrying plague.
See also: Epidemic.

Quark, particle believed by physicists to be the basic subunit of neutrons and protons. The quark theory was first proposed by 2 American physicists, Murray Gell-Mann and George Zweig in 1964. The theory holds that neutrons and protons consist of even simpler particles called quarks. Scientific studies have indicated evidence of quarks since 1971.
See also: Gluon; Hadron.

Quarles, Benjamin Arthur (1904-), U.S. historian, teacher and writer of the impact of African-American culture on U.S. history. Quarles was professor (1939) and dean (1945-53) at Dillard Univ., and headed the department of history at Morgan State College (1953-74). His writings include *Frederick Douglass* (1948), *The Negro in the Civil War* (1953), *The Negro in the American Revolution* (1961), and *The Negro in the Making of America* (1964).

Quarrying, excavation, from open-pit mines, of dimension stone (cut stone) or crushed stone to be used for building projects or ornamentation. The 3 major methods of quarrying are the plug and feather method, by which rock is loosened by applied pressure; the use of explosives; and channeling with special machinery.

Quartering Act *see:* Revolutionary War in America.

Dan Quayle

Quartz, rhombohedral form of silica, usually forming hexagonal prisms, colorless when pure. A common mineral (SiO_2), it is the chief constituent of sand, sandstone, quartzite, and flint and an essential constituent of high-silica igneous rocks, such as granite, rhyolite, and pegmatite. It also occurs as the gems chalcedony, agate, jasper, and onyx. Quartz is piezoelectric and is used to make oscillators for clocks, radio, and radar and to make windows for optical instruments. Crude quartz is used to make glass, glazes, and abrasives, and as a flux.

Quartzite, hard metamorphic rock composed of and cemented by recrystallized quartz grains. The fracturing of quartzite takes place through the grains, rather than between them, due to the extreme strength of the bonding.

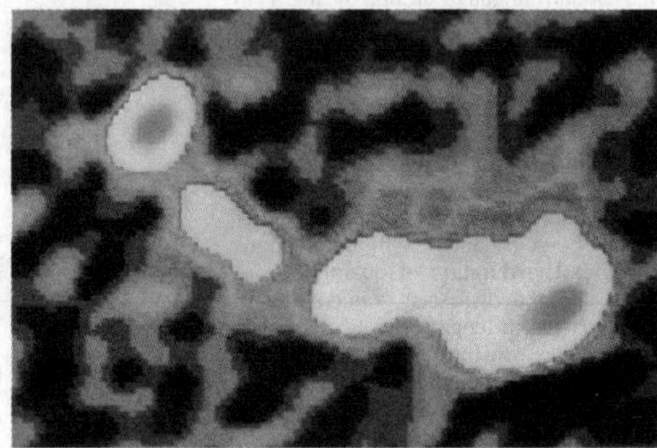

Quasar

Quasar, or quasi-stellar object, a starlike celestial object whose spectrum seen telescopically shows an abnormally large red shift. Quasars may be extremely distant objects—perhaps the inexplicably bright cores of galaxies near the limits of the known universe—receding from Earth at high velocities (which would account for the red shift). Quasars also show variability in light and radio emission. (Although the first quasars were discovered by radio astronomy, not all are radio sources. These phenomena might indicate that quasars are comparatively small objects comparatively close to us (large and more distant objects being unlikely to vary in this way). There are about 200 quasars in each square degree of the sky.
See also: Astronomy; Red shift.

Quasimodo, Salvatore (1901-68), Italian poet and translator of poetry awarded the 1959 Nobel Prize for literature. During and after World War II he turned (originally because of his opposition to fascism) from a complex, introverted, "hermetic" style to social protest and examination of the plight of the individual, as in *Day after Day* (1947). His first poems were collected in *Waters and Lands* (1930).

Quaternary Period, period in geologic time, of the Cenozoic era whose beginning is marked by the advent of humans. It has lasted about 4 million years, up to and including the present.

Quayle, Dan (James Danforth Quayle; 1947-), U.S. vice president, elected 1988 with George Bush. Quayle served as U.S. senator from Indiana (1981-89), following two terms in the House of Representatives (1976, 1978). Quayle and Senator Edward M. Kennedy of Massachusetts developed (1982) the Job Training Partnership Act .

Quebec, largest province in Canada, second-largest in terms of population. Its capital is Quebec City, one of the oldest cities in North America. About 80% of the people of Quebec are of French descent and speak French. Montreal, on the St. Lawrence River, is the second-largest French-speaking city in the world.
Land and climate. The enormous land area of Quebec can be divided into 3 well-defined regions: the Canadian Shield, the St. Lawrence Lowlands, and the Appalachian Uplands. Over 90% of the area of Quebec lies within the Canadian Shield, a rocky plateau filled with uninhabited forests, lakes, and streams. The St. Lawrence Lowlands, including the St. Lawrence River Valley, has been smoothed out by glacial action and erosion. The Appalachian Uplands, which lie partly along the New Brunswick border and partly along the U.S. border, is part of the Appalachian Chain, which runs from the Gaspe Peninsula in Quebec as far south as Alabama in the United States. Much of this region has been smoothed out by erosion to form a rolling plateau. The St. Lawrence River, which links the Great Lakes and the Atlantic Ocean, is Quebec's most important river. Numerous rivers in northern Quebec flow west into the Hudson Bay or north into the Ungava Bay. The largest lake in the province is Lake Mistassini in south-central Quebec. More than half the total area of Quebec is forested. Above the 52nd parallel, west of the Ungava Peninsula, is a tundra region. In general, the climate of Quebec is continental, with severe winters and cool to hot, humid summers. In southern Quebec, precipitation averages 35 to 45 in (889 to 1,143 mm) a year, while the Laurentian Mountains receive well over 100 in (2,540 mm) of snow per year, making skiing a popular sport.
People. Most of the population of Quebec is concentrated in a relatively narrow strip of land along the St. Lawrence River and close to the U.S. border. About 85% are urban dwellers. French Canadians, mostly descended from 17th- or 18-century settlers, constitute 80% of the population. Separate radio and television stations and newspapers exists for the French- and English-speaking communities. French was made the official language of education, business, and government by the French Language Charter of 1977. Roman Catholicism dominates the religious life of the province.
Economy. Quebec has vast supplies of raw materials and almost limitless hydroelectric power. Industries include aluminum processing, foodstuffs, textiles, chemicals, and metal products. Montreal and Quebec City are the leading manufacturing centers; ships, aircraft, and railway rolling stock are the chief products. The principal mineral products are iron ore, asbestos, and copper. Dairying is the most important branch of agriculture, and Quebec's forestry industry accounts for nearly half of Canada's wood and paper products. The development of iron ore mines in the northeast has encouraged development of a steel industry. Construction began in 1979 on La Grande Complex, on La Grande River, scheduled to be the world's second-largest hydroelectric plant.
History. The first permanent settlement in Quebec dates from 1608, when the French explorer Samuel de Champlain built a trading post at the site of Quebec City. From then until defeat by the British in the French and Indian War (1754-63), the region was controlled by the French. Since the beginning of British rule in 1763, Quebec's history has been dominated by its effort to preserve its French identity. Its attempts to maintain its cultural identity led to prolonged conflict with "English" Canada. In 1867 Quebec became a founding province of the Dominion of Canada, and as such was given considerable autonomy. In the 1960s a French separatist movement emerged, and the Canadian government has since made several concessions to French Canadians in the field of education.

Quebec

When the issue of constitutional reform was raised in the early 1980s, Quebec was the focus of the debate on national unity. In 1990, an attempt was made to amend the Canadian constitution in the Meech Lake Accord, which, if approved, would yield greater autonomy and additional rights to Quebec. While the initial discussions for the amendments indicated possible ratification, the Meech Lake Accord eventually failed because a political consesus could not be reached. The failure to reach an accord has further complicated an already complex issue between English-speaking Canadians and Quebec.
See also: Canada.

Quebec (pop. 645,500), capital of Quebec province, situated on the St. Lawrence River. Founded in 1608 by Samuel de Champlain, it is Canada's oldest city. Despite British dominance since 1759, Quebec has remained essentially French, and more than 90% of its citizens claim French ancestry. Today it is a leading manufacturing center and transatlantic port. Industries include shipbuilding, paper milling, food processing, machinery, and textiles.
See also: Quebec.

Quebec, Battle of, most important battle of the French and Indian War, whose outcome transferred control of Canada from France to Britain. French troops under General Louis Joseph de Montcalm were defending Quebec City. On the night of Sept. 12, 1759, British troops under General James Wolfe silently scaled the cliffs west of the city to the Plains of Abraham. After a short, bloody battle the French fled. Both Wolfe and Montcalm were mortally wounded.
See also: French and Indian Wars.

Quebec, University of, also Université du Québec, largest Canadian university, founded 1969. The university has 6 campuses, in Chicoutimi, Hull, Montreal, Rimouski, Rouyn, and Trois-Riviéres. All instruction is in French.

Quebec Act, passed by the British Parliament in 1774, one of the Intolerable Acts that led to the American Revolution. It guaranteed the use of the French civil code and established religious freedom for the Roman Catholic Church in Quebec. It also extended Quebec's boundary to the Ohio and Mississippi rivers.
See also: Intolerable Acts.

Quebec Conference (1864), conference in the city of Quebec that laid the foundations of the Canadian Confederation. Representatives from the British provinces in North America produced a series of 72 resolutions outlining a centralized federal union. This union was desirable in that it promoted better defense and economic growth, and eased friction between French- and English-speaking groups. The Quebec Conference became the basis of the British North America Act (1867), which created the Dominion of Canada.
See also: Confederation of Canada.

Quebec separatist movement, various French-Canadian political factions in Quebec, Canada, which demand that French be the sole language of Quebec and that Quebec separate from Canadian rule and become an independent nation. The movement, begun in the early 1960s as the Quiet Revolution, and furthered by legislator René Lévesque and his Parti Québécois, stemmed from anger with British-centered policies, and governmental discrimination against French-speaking peoples. Despite the terrorist tactics of some groups, the separatist movement is growing in popularity. Nevertheless a popular referendum held in 1995 indicated that a majority of the electorate was against separation from Canada.

Quebracho, South American hardwood tree (genus *Schinopsis*) of the cashew family, with a high content of tannin, an extract used to tan leather. The quebracho grows mainly in Paraguay and Argentina. *Quebracho* means *ox-breaker* in Spanish.

Quechua, also Kechua or Quichua, linguistic family belonging to natives of South America. They were once part of the Inca Empire and now live mostly as peasants in the Andean highlands from Colombia to North Chile. Quechua is also the name of the family to which the official language of the Incas belonged; some 28 languages of the family are still spoken.

Queen, female monarch or the wife of a king, with all the powers allowed by the country that she rules. A queen regnant rules in her own right, by virtue of her birth; a consort is the wife of a king; and a dowager queen is the widow of a king.
See also: Monarchy.

Queen, Ellery, pen-name and fictional hero of American detective writers Frederic Dannay (1905-82) and Manfred B. Lee (1905-72). Their successful *The Roman Hat Mystery* (1929) was followed by over 100 other novels characterized by complexity of plot. *Ellery Queen's Mystery Magazine* was founded in 1941.

Queen Anne's lace *see:* Wild carrot.

Queen Anne's War *see:* French and Indian Wars.

Queens, largest and second most populous of the 5 boroughs that make up the city of New York. Queens is located at the western end of Long Island and is linked to Manhattan by an intricate network of tunnels and bridges crossing the East River. A largely middle-class area of small homes, Queens includes such residential neighborhoods as Forest Hills, Flushing, and Kew Gardens, as well as the industrial and commercial centers of Long Island City and Astoria, directly opposite Manhattan. In the southern part of the borough are a racecourse (Aqueduct), several beaches, and the John F. Kennedy International Airport. Flushing Meadow was the site of the 1939-40 and 1964-65 World's Fairs. Queens was founded by the Dutch in 1635, became part of the British province of New York in 1683, and became part of New York City in 1898.
See also: New York City.

Queensberry rules, basic rules of modern boxing, drawn up in 1865 under the auspices of John Sholto Douglas, 8th Marquess of Queensberry, supplanting London prize-ring rules. Innovations included the use of padded gloves instead of bare fists, a 10-sec count to determine a knockout, and the division of the bout into rounds with intermissions.
See also: Boxing.

Queensland, second largest Australian state, in the northeastern region of Australia, covering 667,000 sq mi (1,727,530 sq km). Tropical and eucalyptus forests in the rugged east contrast with pasture and desert on the vast western plain. It produces sheep, nearly half of Australia's cattle, and such crops as sugarcane, wheat, cotton, and fruit. It has valuable oil and mineral deposits. Founded as a penal colony (1824-43), Queensland became a state of the Commonwealth in 1901.
See also: Australia.

Quemoy, or Chin-men, island group on the Formosa Strait off southeastern China. The islands have a combined area of about 58 sq mi (150 sq km), with 2 large islands and 12 islets. The Quemoy Islands remained a Chinese Nationalist garrison after the communist takeover in 1949.

Querétaro, state in central Mexico, on the Mexican Plateau, 6,119 ft (1,865 m) above sea level. Querétaro covers about 4,420 sq mi (11,450 sq km) of land, which includes mountainous areas, plains, and fertile valleys. Industries include farming and the mining of opals, silver, iron and copper. The Mexican constitution was drafted there (1916-17).
See also: Mexico.

Quesnay, François (1694-1774), French economist and a leader of the physiocrats. Although trained in medicine (he was physician to Louis XV), his fame rests on his essays in political economy, which first began to appear in 1756 in Denis Diderot's *Encyclopédie*, and on his *Economic Table* (1758), which influenced Adam Smith.
See also: Physiocrat.

Quetzal (*Pharomacrus mocinno*), bird in the trogon family. Compared to the cream-colored females, the resplendent quetzal males display long tails—up to 3 ft (91 cm)—and brilliant feathers colored green on their backs, gold on their heads, with deep red on their undersides. The national bird of Guatemala, the quetzal lives in countries of Central and South America as well as in Mexico.

Quetzalcóatl (Nahuatl, "plumed serpent"), ancient Mexican god identified with the

Quetzalcóatl

morning and evening star. He is said to have ruled the pre-Aztec Toltec empire and to have invented books and the calendar. He represented the forces of good and light; whether he was an historical leader or merely mythological is not certain. The Aztec leader Montezuma II welcomed Hernándo Cortés, believing him to be descended from the god.
See also: Mythology.

Francisco de Quevedo Villega

Quevedo Villega, Francisco de (1580-1645), Spanish satirist, poet, and prose writer. Master of the *conseptismo* style of terse and arresting intellectual conceits, he is best known for *the Life of a Swindler* (1626), a parody of the picaresque novel, and *Visions* (1627), a bitter, fantastic view of Spanish society.

Quezon City (pop. 1,166,000), Philippine city on Luzon Island, near Manila. Once the capital of the Philippine Islands (1948-76), Quezon City is primarily a residential area. It is the seat of Ateneo de Manila University and the University of the Philippines.
See also: Philippines.

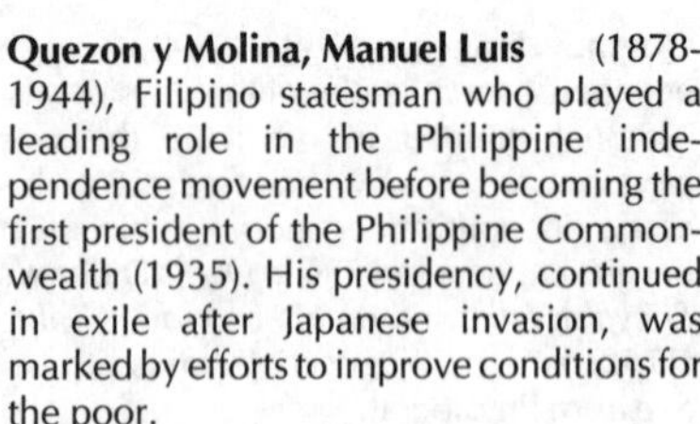

Quezon y Molina, Manuel Luis (1878-1944), Filipino statesman who played a leading role in the Philippine independence movement before becoming the first president of the Philippine Commonwealth (1935). His presidency, continued in exile after Japanese invasion, was marked by efforts to improve conditions for the poor.
See also: Philippines

Quicksand, sand saturated with water to form a sand-water suspension possessing the characteristics of a liquid. Quicksands may form at rivermouths or on sandflats; they are dangerous because they appear identical to adjacent sand. In fact, the density of the suspension is less than that of the human body, so a person who does not struggle may escape being engulfed.

Quicksilver *see:* Mercury (chemical element).

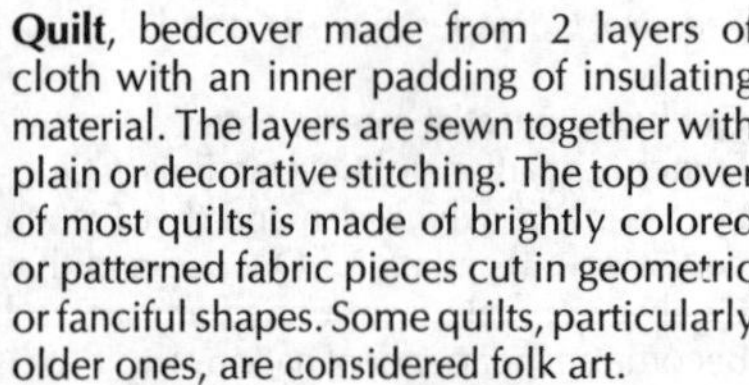

Quilt, bedcover made from 2 layers of cloth with an inner padding of insulating material. The layers are sewn together with plain or decorative stitching. The top cover of most quilts is made of brightly colored or patterned fabric pieces cut in geometric or fanciful shapes. Some quilts, particularly older ones, are considered folk art.

Quincy (pop. 42,554), westernmost city in Illinois, located on the Mississippi River. The development of meat packing, brewing, grain milling, and manufacturing industries and easy access to river transportation made Quincy a commercial center beginning in the 1850s. The city was the site of the sixth Lincoln-Douglas debate (1858), and is the home of Quincy College.
See also: Illinois.

Quincy (pop. 84,743), city in eastern Massachusetts, the birthplace of Presidents John Adams and John Quincy Adams and an important industrial and shipbuilding center. Situated in Boston Harbor about 8 mi (13 km) south of Boston, Quincy was incorporated in 1888. The Fore River shipyards at Quincy are among the most important in the United States. Other industries include dairy products, gears, riveting machinery, detergents, and television tubes.
See also: Massachusetts.

Quine, Willard Van Orman (1908-), U.S. philosopher and logician. He rejected the long-standing philosophical claims that analytic ("self-evident") statements are fundamentally distinguishable from synthetic (observational) statements and that the concept of synonymy (sameness of meaning) can be exemplified.
See also: Philiosophy.

Quinine, alkaloid derived from cinchona bark from South America, long used in treating a variety of ailments (now rarely used). It was preeminent in early treatment of malaria until the 1930s, when atabrine was introduced. Quinine is also a mild analgesic and may prevent cramps and suppress heart rhythm disorders. Its side-effects include vomiting, deafness, vertigo, and vision disturbance.
See also: Cinchona; Malaria.

Quinsy, acute complication of tonsillitis in which abscess formation causes spasm of the adjacent jaw muscles, fever, and severe pain. Incision and drainage of the pus produce rapid relief; antibiotics are helpful; and the tonsils may be removed when the infection diminishes.
See also: Tonsillitis.

Quintana Roo, state in southeastern Mexico on the Yucatán Peninsula, whose capital is Chetumal. The state, covering an area of about 19,387 sq mi (50,212 sq km), is a flat plain covered by dense jungle, with a hot and humid climate. Population is sparse. Quintana Roo became a Mexican territory in 1902 and a state in 1974.
See also: Mexico.

Quintilian (Marcus Fabius Quintilianus; A.D. 35?-95?), Roman rhetoric teacher, whose famous 12-volume *Institutio Oratoria,* covering rhetorical techniques, educational theory, literary criticism, and morality, deeply influenced Renaissance culture.

Quirinal Hill, one of the famous 7 hills of Rome. The hill was named for Quirinus, a mythological deity, and was the habitation of the Sabines. Many temples, gardens, and a public bath were built there.
See also: Sabines.

Quirinus, in Roman mythology, god responsible for the well-being and prosperity of the community. Believed by some to be either Mars in a different bodily form, or the divine incarnation of Romulus, Quirinus lost importance after about 200 B.C.
See also: Mythology.

Quisling, Vidkun Abraham Lauritz (1887-1945), Norwegian fascist leader who assisted the German invasion of Norway (1940) during World War II and was afterward appointed premier of Norway's puppet government (1942-45) by Adolf Hitler. He was executed for treason. His name has come to mean "traitor." He had formed his own political party, the National Union, in 1936, and contacted German Nazi leaders.
See also: World War II.

Quito (pop. 866,500), capital and second largest city of Ecuador and oldest capital in South America. It is located just south of the equator at the foot of the Pichincha volcano, at an altitude of 9,350 ft (2,850 m). Seized from the Incas by a Spanish conquistador in 1534, it is famous for its Spanish colonial architecture.
See also: Ecuador.

Quixote, Don *see:* Don Quixote.

Qumran, village on the northwestern shore of the Dead Sea, on the West Bank of Jordan, near the caves where the Dead Sea Scrolls were found (1947). Built by Essenes (130-110 B.C.), it was destroyed by an earthquake (31 B.C.), rebuilt, and destroyed again by the Romans (A.D. 68).

Quoits, game similar to horseshoes in which 2 players alternately attempt to toss a ring (quoit) around a stake (hob or mott). The quoit is metal and has 1 rounded and 1 flat surface and weighs at least 3 lb (1.5kg). The distance between the hobs is 54 ft (16 m). Points are scored by circling or touching the hob. A game is 21 points.

Quorum, minimum number of members who must be present before an organization can legally transact business. This number, or proportion, varies with the constitution or by-laws of the organization concerned; legislative bodies usually cannot pass laws unless a majority of their members is present (but all are not necessarily voting).

Qur'an *see:* Koran.

R

R, 18th letter of the English alphabet, corresponding to the Semitic letter *resh*, meaning "head," and represented by a sign based on an ancient Egyptian picture symbol for a human head. R is *rho* in the Greek alphabet and the 17th letter of the Roman alphabet. The present form of the capital R comes from classical Latin, the small r from Carolingian script.

Ra *see:* Re.

Rabat (pop. 1,472,000), capital city of Morocco, in the north, on the Atlantic Ocean. Dating from the Phoenician civilization, the city was founded in the 12th century and presently is a governmental center. Industries include textile, brick, and cement production.
See also: Morocco.

Rabbi (Hebrew, "my master" or "my teacher"), leader of a Jewish religious congregation with the role of spiritual leader, scholar, teacher, and interpreter of Jewish law. The term originated in Palestine, meaning merely religious teacher, after the return from exile and destruction of the hereditary priesthood (1st century A.D.).
See also: Judaism.

Rabbit, herbivorous lagomorph (gnawing) mammal (family Leporidae), usually with long ears and a white scut for a tail. Best known is the European rabbit (*Oryctolagus cuniculus*), which lives in discrete social groups in colonial burrows. Territory is defended by all members of the group, and within the group there is distinct dominance ranking. It attains maturity at three months and can breed every month thereafter.

Rabbit fever *see:* Tularemia.

Rabelais, François (1492?-1553), French monk, doctor, and humanist author. With his *Gargantua and Pantagruel* (five books, 1532-62), an exuberant mixture of popular anecdote, bawdiness, • and erudition, Rabelais created a comic masterpiece that is also an important social vehicle for exploring the important issues of society: education, law, philosophy, and religion. It is considered one of the great masterpieces of world literature.
See also: Humanism.

Rabi, Isidor Isaac (1898-1988), U.S. physicist whose discovery of new ways of measuring the magnetic properties of atoms and molecules paved the way for the development of the maser and the atomic clock. His work earned him the 1944 Nobel Prize in physics.
See also: Maser; Physics.

Rabies, or hydrophobia, acute infectious disease of mammals, characterized by irritation of the central nervous system, followed by paralysis and death. The cause is a virus often present in the saliva of rabid animals. These animals transmit the infection by biting animals or humans. In humans, the incubation period varies from

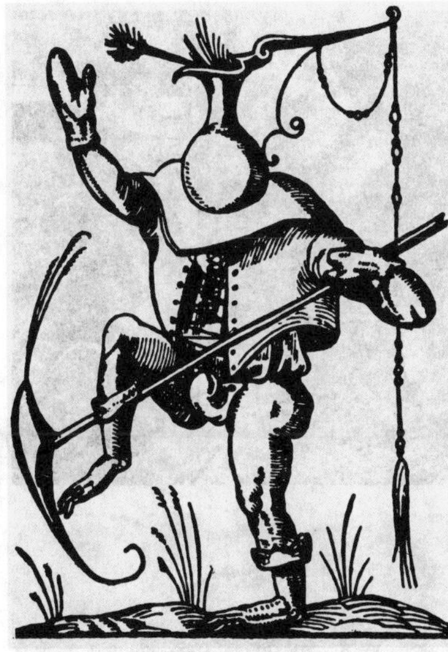

An illustration of Rabelais's character Gargantua

10 days to over a year. The disease commonly begins with a short period of mental depression, restlessness, malaise, and fever. Restlessness increases to uncontrollable excitement, with excessive salivation and painful spasms of the laryngeal and pharyngeal muscles. As a result, the person cannot drink (hence hydrophobia: fear of water). Rabies rarely occurs in humans if proper treatment (vaccination) is carried out immediately after exposure.
See also: Pasteur, Louis.

Rabin, Yitzhak (1922-95), late prime minister of Israel (1974-77, 1992-95) and Israeli military leader. Rabin, after distinguished service in and after World War II, commanded Israel's defense forces from 1964-67, including the Six-Day War. He served as ambassador to the United States (1968-73), as minister of labor (1974), and as minister of defense (1984-90). During his second office as premier he successfully

Rabies can be spread by the fox.

negotiated with the PLO on peace measures in the occupied territories. For their efforts Arafat, Peres, and Rabin won the Nobel Peace Prize in 1994. Rabin was killed in 1995 by a right extremist Israeli.
See also: Israel.

Rabinowitz, Soloman *see:* Sholem Aleichem.

Raccoon, stout, bearlike, nocturnal mammal (genus *Procyon*), with a distinctive black mask and five to eight black bands on the bushy tail. Raccoons are found in North and South America. They live in trees, alone or in small family groups, descending at night to forage for crayfish, frogs, and fish in shallow pools.

Raceme, type of flower cluster characterized by multiple flowers with separate short stems ranging along a common stalk (or peduncle). Racemous flowers multiply along the main stalk as it grows.

Racer, any of several species (family Colubridae) of swift North American snakes. Racers are broad-headed, varied in color, and measure from 3 1/2 ft (107 cm) to 6 ft (1.8 m) in length.

Races, human, subdivisions of the species *homo sapiens.* The concept of race provides distinctions that are useful in the scientific study of the human species, its dissemination and adaptation to various environments and conditions throughout the world. It can also provide useful clues and insights for historians and cultural anthropologists into a people's development. Like Darwin's theory of evolution, the concept of race has a history outside of science, in social and political thought and mass psychology. Racism is any ideology which assigns superiority to one group of people and inherent inferiority to others on the basis of certain physical characteristics. Both the scientific concept of race and the ideology of racism have histories.
In the West, by late medieval and modern times, all human beings were considered divisible into people of white, black, or yellow skin. A fundamental distinction was observed among humans based upon a leading physical characteristic. By the 19th century, this elementary classification was filled in with more study and research and the three basic races were held to be Caucasoid, Negroid, and Mongoloid. These distinctions were based upon observed physical differences characteristic of each group or race, including skin color, hair, stature, body proportions, skull shape, and facial features. Advances in science have significantly changed the content of the term *race.* It was discovered that the groupings are more than three and the traits that distinguish peoples are more mutable, or changeable, and more subtle than was formerly known. For example, the study of blood types has revealed not only significant differences among Europeans, Asians, and Africans, but within the group that was classified Negroid, there are significant differences among Australian Aborigines,

Far left: Native American of Mexico
Left: Asians of North Laos
Below, center: Indian of Kashmir
Below: Africans of Nigeria

Above: African of Sudan
Above, center: Australian Aborigine
Right: Asians of Mongolia
Far right: Europeans of The Netherlands

Micronesians, and Negritos of the Philippines.
Most anthropologists now understand races as geographical and local groups and identify nine instead of three. The nine in the current classification are African, American Indian, Asian, Australian, European, Indian, Melanesian, Micronesian, and Polynesian. The geographical groups are defined by major blood types and genetic groups whereas local races are defined by more restricted gene pools. Examples of local races in Europe are the Basques and Lapps.
Human races develop as a result of evolution and in response to the environment. In addition to the obvious inherited differences, such as melanin or inner eyefolds, modern science has discovered the importance of blood types. In some races, certain blood types are dominant, and certain races are susceptible to particular blood disorders. Africans, for instance, may succumb to sickle cell anemia. But scientists have determined that the same trait in the blood responsible for the anemia also makes Africans relatively immune to malaria, suggesting an inherited trait formed by natural selection and conditioned by a specific environment. Human races are understood as less static and more in flux not only as the result of natural selection, gene mutation, and changes in which genes dominate in a group's gene pool, but also as the result of war, migrations, and intermarriage. Rather than providing any evidence for the notion of superior and inferior groups, scientific study indicates the basis for physical differences among humans and studies the remarkably wide and varied adaptations of a single highly successful species.
Ideologies of race, though they claim to be scientific, are not, but they remain potent. Though not unique to the West, ideologies of race have claimed scientific authority in the West beginning with the theories of Joseph Arthur Gobineau in the 19th century and later with Huston Stewart Chamberlain, the anti-Semitism of Nazis, and theories of the inherent racial inferiority of blacks. At bottom, all these theories of race advance the same propositions: that certain peoples are inherently superior and certain others inherently inferior, and that these qualities of superiority or inferiority are inherited, characteristic of an entire group and each of its individual members, and readily identifiable by certain physical traits. Growing and flourishing side by side with advances in modern science and claiming to be grounded in science, theories of race persist in spite of the fact that there is no scientific basis for their claims.
See also: Racism.

Rachel, in the Old Testament, daughter of Laban, wife of Jacob, and mother of Joseph and Benjamin. Rachel was one of the four Jewish matriarchs.
See also: Bible; Old Testament.

Rachmaninoff, Sergei Vassilievich (1873-1943), Russian composer and virtuoso pianist. After a successful career in Russia he left in 1917, settling in Switzerland (until 1935) and then the United States. His extensive output of piano music, symphonies, songs, and choral music incudes such popular works as *Prelude in C Sharp Minor* (1892) and *Second Piano Concerto* (1901).

Racial segregation *see:* Segregation.

Racine (pop. 84,298), industrial city of southeastern Wisconsin, situated on Lake Michigan at the mouth of the Root River. Founded in 1834, it was a major grainshipping area before the railroads were built, and it is still a depot for the dairy and agricultural products of the outlying farm areas. Racine is one of the leading manufacturing cities in Wisconsin.
See also: Wisconsin.

Racine, Jean (1639-99), French tragic dramatist. After a Jansenist education at Port Royal schools, he surpassed his rival Pierre Corneille with seven tragedies, from *Andromaque* (1667) and *Britannicus* (1669) to *Phèdre* (1677), possibly his masterpiece. His greatness lies in the beauty of his verse, expressing both powerful and subtle emotions, and the creation of tragic suspense in a classically restrained form. Racine's work are the epitome of French classical theater.

Racing, contest of speed in both individual and team competition, popular throughout history. The ancient Greek Olympics (700s B.C.) featured only a foot race. The marathon, a race of 26 mi 385 yds (42.2 km), is a test of both speed and endurance. Among the many types of races, which can involve machine operation or animals, are swimming, skiing, walking, roller skating, motorboat racing, and dog racing.
See also: Automobile racing; Horse racing; Track and field.

Racism, belief that some races are inherently superior to others. Racism in the early 19th century was an offshoot of nationalism, placing emphasis on the differences among cultures. Also, the study of human types revealed some physical differences among the races. Despite the theories of Carolus Linnaeus and J.F. Blumenbach, that environment rather than heredity molded intellectual development, many associated culture with race, assuming white superiority. Guided by thinkers like Joseph Arthur Gobineau (1816-82), the concept of "tribal nationalism" began to appear. It was used to justify imperialism, the imposition of colonial status on less technologically accomplished peoples, and finally the concept of the "master race" fostered by the Nazis. Horror at the mass exterminations before and during World War II, together with greater understanding through the social sciences, such as anthropology, discredited racism.
See also: Prejudice; Races, human; Segregation.

Rack, implement of torture made of a wooden structure with rollers at two ends. The rollers were wound, pulling the attached legs and arms of a victim from their joint sockets.

Rackham, Arthur (1867-1939), English artist best known for his fanciful, delicately colored illustrations for children's books, such as *Grimm's Fairy Tales* (1900), *Peter Pan* (1906), and *A Wonder Book* (1922).

Racquetball, fast-paced indoor court game played by 1-4 players with 18-in (45.7-cm) racquets and a hollow rubber ball. Played on a 4-sided handball court, racquetball basically follows the same rules as 4-wall handball.
See also: Handball.

Radar (*r*adio *d*etection *a*nd *r*anging), system that detects long-range objects and determines their positions by measuring the time taken for radio waves to travel to the objects, be reflected, and return. Radar is used for navigation, air control, fire control, storm detection, in radar astronomy, and for catching speeding drivers. It developed out of experiments in the 1920s that were measuring the distance to the ionosphere by radio pulses. R.A. Watson-Watt showed that the technique could be applied to detecting aircraft, and from 1935 Britain installed a series of radar stations that were a major factor in winning the Battle of Britain in World War II. From 1940 the United Kingdom and the United States collaborated to develop radar. *Continuous-wave radar* transmits continuously and detects the signals received by their instantaneously different frequency.

A game of racquetball in progress

A radar installation at an airport is monitored by an air traffic controller.

Pulsed radar has a highly directional antenna, alternately a transmitter or a receiver. As a transmitter, it scans the area systematically or tracks an object, emitting pulses, typically 400 per second. As a receiver, the antenna amplifies and converts echo pulses to a video signal that is displayed on a cathode-ray tube. The time-lag between transmission and reception is represented by the position of the pulse on the screen. Various display modes are used: commonest is the plan-position indicator (PPI), showing horizontal position in polar coordinates.

Radcliffe, Ann (1764-1823), English novelist remembered for her Gothic novels, notably *The Mysteries of Udolpho* (1794) and *The Italian* (1797).

Radcliffe-Brown, A(lfred) R(eginald) (1881-1955), British anthropologist and author of studies of kinship and social organization. His *Andaman Islanders* (1922; rev. 1948) was a pioneering work.
See also: Anthropology.

High levels of radioactive particles were detected in the atmosphere of Western Europe after the Chernobyl disaster. This led to the temporary prohibition of vegetable consumption.

Radcliffe College, private liberal arts college affiliated with Harvard University, in Cambridge, Mass. Established in 1879 for women undergraduate students, Radcliffe maintains its own board of trustees while sharing faculty and facilities with Harvard.

Radian, in geometry, metric unit for measuring angles, used to simplify calculations. The radian measure of an angle is the ratio a/r; a being the length of the arc intercepted by the given angle; and r being the radius of the circle. An angle of approx. 57.3 (or 360° divided by 2 pi) = 1 radian.
See also: Angles.

Radiant energy *see:* Star; Sun.

Radiation, emission and propagation of energy through space or through a material medium in the form of waves. The term may be extended to include streams of subatomic particles—alpha-rays or beta-rays—and cosmic rays. In the case of electromagnetic radiation (light), energy is transmitted in bundles (photons). Acoustic radiation is made up of sound waves.
See also: Radioactivity.

Radiation belt *see:* Van Allen belts.

Radiation detector *see:* Geiger counter.

Radiation sickness, malaise, nausea, loss of appetite, and vomiting occurring several hours after exposure to ionizing radiation in large doses. This occurs as an industrial or a war hazard or more commonly following radiation therapy for cancer, lymphoma, or leukemia. Large doses of radiation may cause bone marrow depression, or gastrointestinal disturbance. Skin erythema and ulceration, lung fibrosis, nephritis, and premature arteriosclerosis may follow radiation, and there is a risk of malignancy.
See also: Fallout.

Radiator, device in which steam or hot water circulates and gives off heat. Through a process called convection, hot air expands and rises as surrounding cooler air is drawn in. This constant circulation of air can take place within the radiator tubing in convector radiators; radiators also heat air via direct radiation. Radiators are found in homes, offices and stores, as well as in automobiles and other engine-powered vehicles.

Radical, atom or group of atoms having an unpaired electron. Most radicals combine with other atoms to form compounds or ions, although free radicals, those remaining unbound to others, may exist briefly.
See also: Atom.

Radicalism, political philosophy whose purpose is to root out economic, political, and social injustices. Radicals may support different causes in different societies at different times. An English radical reform movement in the 18th to 19th centuries called Radicalism or Utilitarianism supported suffrage and greater democracy. In the 20th century, prodemocracy movements in Communist countries and procommunist movements under noncommunist governments are referred to as groups based on radicalism. Official radical political parties exist in some countries, but not the United States.

Radical Republican *see:* Reconstruction.

Radio, communication of information between distant points using electromagnetic radiation (radio waves). Radio waves are often described in terms of their frequency, which is measured in hertz (Hz) and found by dividing the velocity of the waves by their wavelength. Radio communications systems link transmitting stations with receiving stations. In a transmitting station a piezoelectric oscillator generates a steady radio-frequency (RF) "carrier" wave, which is amplified and "modulated" with a signal carrying the information to be communicated. The simplest method of modulation is to pulse (switch on and off) the carrier with a signal in, for example, Morse code. Speech and music enter the modulator as an audiofrequency (AF) signal from tape or a microphone, and can also interact with the carrier. The modulated RF signal is then amplified to a high power and radiated from an antenna. At the receiving station, another antenna picks up a minute fraction of the energy radiated from the transmitter, together with some background noise. This RF signal is amplified, and the original audio signal is recovered (demodulation, or detection). In point-to-point radio communications most stations can both transmit and receive messages, but in radio broadcasting a central transmitter broadcasts program sequences to a multitude of individual receivers. Because there are potentially so many users of radio communications, use of the RF portion of the electromagnetic spectrum is strictly controlled to prevent unwanted interference between signals having adjacent carrier frequencies. The International Telecommunication Union (ITU) and national agencies like the U.S. Federal Communications Commission (FCC) divide the RF spectrum into banks that they allocate to the various users.

Radio, amateur, hobby practiced throughout the world by enthusiasts ("hams") who communicate with one another on short-wave radio, by voice "phone," or by using international Morse code. In the United States, the various grades of license may be obtained by passing tests of progressively greater difficulty. Citizens' Band (CB) radio, a more informal kind of "ham" radio, became popular in the United States in the late 1970s, with a vast network of amateur radio operators.

Radioactive fallout *see:* Fallout.

Radioactivity, spontaneous disintegration of unstable atomic nuclei, accompanied by the emission of alpha particles (weakly penetrating helium nuclei), beta rays (more penetrating streams of electrons), or

gamma rays (electromagnetic radiation capable of penetrating up to 4 in/100 mm of lead). In 1896, Antoine Becquerel noticed the spontaneous emission of energy from uranium compounds (particularly pitchblende). The intensity of the effect depended on the amount of uranium present, suggesting that it involved individual atoms. The Curies discovered further radioactive substances such as thorium and radium; about 40 natural radioactive substances are now known. Their rates of decay are unaffected by chemical changes, pressure, temperature, or electromagnetic fields, and each nuclide (nucleus of a particular isotope) has a characteristic decay constant, or half-life (amount of time for half of a substance to decay). Rutherford and F. Soddy suggested in 1902 that a radioactive nuclide decays to a further radioactive nuclide, a series of transformations that ends with the formation of a stable "daughter" nucleus. A large number of induced radioactive nuclides have been formed by nuclear reactions taking place in accelerators or nuclear reactors.
See also: Radiation.

Radiocarbon, or Carbon 14, naturally occurring radioactive isotope of carbon. With an atomic weight of 14, it is heavier than ordinary carbon, which has an atomic weight of 12. Radiocarbon is produced when cosmic rays disturb nitrogen atoms in the upper atmosphere, causing them to gain a neutron and lose a proton. Radiocarbon, found in 1.1% of CO_2 (carbon dioxide) molecules, is absorbed by plants in CO_2 gas and passed on to animals and humans. Radiocarbon dating, developed in the 1940s by U.S. chemist Willard F. Libby, can calculate the age of organic matter to about 50,000 years, by comparing its remaining amount of radiocarbon to that in a contemporary radiocarbon sample. Radiocarbon breaks down by releasing particles over a period measured by the half-life (the time it takes half the isotope to decay)—5,700 years. Counting radiocarbon involves burning a portion of it to release the CO_2 gas; today a particle accelerator and a magnetic field are used to separate out the carbon 14 atoms. Artificially produced radiocarbon is used medically as a "tracer" to study biological functions. The artificial isotope was first produced (1939) in the United States by chemists Martin D. Kamen and S. Ruben.

Radiochemistry, use of radioisotopes in chemistry, especially in studies involving chemical analysis. Tracer techniques, in which a particular atom in a molecule is "labeled" by replacement with a radioisotope, are used to study reaction rates and mechanisms.

Radio Free Europe/Radio Liberty (RFE/RL), radio broadcasting networks based in Munich, Germany. It was originated in 1950 to broadcast political, social, and cultural information to people in Communist nations of Central Europe. Privately owned and run, it is supported by the U.S. government.

Radiogeology, branch of geology in which scientists measure radioactive elements in rocks, fossils, and other geological specimens to determine their age. The measurement that enables this determination is called half-life—the time it takes one-half of the atoms of a radioactive isotope to decompose and form a different isotope. Radioactivity, found in all living things, is caused by uranium and thorium and their decay products: radioactive potassium, samarium and rubidium, and raciocarbon.

Radioisotope *see:* Isotope; Radioactivity; Radiochemistry.

Radiology, in medicine, diagnosis and treatment through the use of radioactivity, gamma rays, and X-rays.

Radiosonde, meteorological instrument package attached to a small balloon capable of reaching the earth's upper atmosphere. The instruments measure the temperature, pressure, and humidity of the atmosphere at various altitudes, the data being relayed back to earth via a radio transmitter.

Radio telescope, basic instrument of radio astronomy. The receiving part of the equipment consists of a large dish that operates on the same principle as the parabolic mirror of a reflecting telescope. The signals that it receives are amplified and examined. It is possible to build radio telescopes far larger than any possible dish by using several connected dishes; this is known as an array.
See also: Jansky, Karl Guthe; Lovell, Sir Bernard.

Radio waves *see:* Electromagnetic waves; Radio.

Radish, herb (*Raphanus sativus*), relative of mustard whose edible root looks like a small white to red turnip and has a burning flavor. A native of Europe, it was introduced as a garden plant but has become a weed. Radishes are eaten raw but the related *horseradish*, not a true radish, is ground up and served as a condiment.

Radisson, Pierre Esprit (1636?-1710), French fur trader who worked for both French and British in the exploration of parts of present-day Minnesota and Wisconsin. His reports of the wealth of furs obtainable prompted the creation of the Hudson's Bay Company.
See also: Hudson's Bay Company.

Radium, chemical element, symbol Ra; for physical constants see Periodic Table. Radium was discovered by Pierre and Marie Curie in 1898. It occurs in the minerals carnotite, uraninite, and pitchblende. Radium is produced by electrolysis of its chloride. Radium is a brilliant, white, radioactive, reactive metal. It is decomposed by water and turns black in air. It is a member of the alkaline-earth metals. Its salts color a flame carmine red. Radium is radioactive and emits alpha, beta, and

Radish

gamma rays. The curie (Ci), a unit of radioactivity, is defined as the amount of radioactivity that has the same disintegration rate as 1 g of radium-226 (3.7×10^{10} disintegrations/second). Radium and its compounds are used in medicine, neutron sources, and self-luminous paints. Radium is a source of the element radon.

Radon, chemical element, symbol Rn; for physical constants see Periodic Table. Radon was discovered by Friedrich E. Dorn in 1900. Radon is present in the air to the extent of one part in 10^{21} and occurs in some spring waters, such as those at Hot Springs, Ark. Radon is a colorless, odorless, and chemically inert gas. It is a radioactive byproduct of the alpha-decay of radium, thorium, and actinium and is a member of the noble, or inert gases. It is the heaviest known gas. It has been reported that fluorine reacts with radon to form radon fluoride. Radon is a radiation hazard, and remedial action is recommended for homes where the activity is greater than 4 picocuries/liter.

Raeburn, Sir Henry (1756-1823), Scottish painter. He was a lesser known portraitist than his famous English contemporary, Sir Joshua Reynolds. He painted directly on canvas with strong brush strokes and without the assistance of preliminary sketch marks. These portraits, mostly of well-to-do Scots, also were painted so that light and color produced dramatic effects.

Raffia, Asian palm (*Raphia ruffia*) whose long, tough leaf fibers are used for making baskets and tying up plants.

Raffles, Sir Stamford (1781-1826), British colonial administrator who refounded the ruined city of Singapore (1819). He persuaded the British government to seize Java, which he governed from 1811 to 1815. His career was marked by his liberalism, especially in his opposition to slavery.
See also: Singapore.

Rafflesia, genus of parasitic Indonesian plants with the largest flower in the world, up to 1 yd (0.9 m) across. The flower lacks petals but bears broad fleshy sepals. It smells of decaying meat, which attracts flies to pollinate it. It is named for Sir Thomas Raffles, the founder of Singapore.

Raft, simple platform, usually square or rectangular, that floats on water. One of the earliest forms of water travel, rafts originally were made from logs, reeds, or animals skins tied with vines. Today they are often constructed from synthetic materials that are inflated for buoyancy. Rafts travel on water currents, often aided by the use of poles, paddles or sails; they have been used as a means to cross wide rivers, such as the Mississippi. Adventurers, including Thor Heyerdahl of Norway (1947) and William Willis of the United States (1963-64) have successfully crossed oceans on simple rafts.

Rafting, water recreation that gained popularity in the 1960s. On inflatable rafts, usually 12-16 ft (3.7-5 m) long, people travel the rapid currents, or white water, of rivers. A 6-person crew guides the raft with paddles as the passengers enjoy the ride and scenery. The Colorado River, where it cuts through the Grand Canyon, is among the most popular rafting sites in the United States.

Ragtime, style of piano playing in which the left hand provides harmony and a firm beat, while the right hand plays the melody, usually syncopated. Famous exponents of the style, which was the immediate predecessor of jazz, are Scott Joplin and Jelly-Roll Morton.
See also: Jazz.

Ragweed, or hogweed, composite weedy herb (genus *Ambrosia*) with inconspicuous flower heads. The giant ragweed, or bufaloweed, grows up to 18 ft (5.5 m) high. Ragweed pollen is an important cause of hay fever. Some ragweeds have tiny seeds, others have spiny burs that catch in hair and clothing.

Rail, family of marsh birds, including gallinules, coots or mud hens, and rails proper. Protected by their camouflage coloring, rails eat seeds, grasses, worms, and insects. These extremely slender birds are often classified by their long or cone-shaped short bills. They lay their eggs in nests built on the ground or among grass in or near a marsh. Types of rails, found throughout the world, include the water rail, land rail (corncrake), king rail, black rail, yellow rail, VIrginia rail, sora rail, and clapper rail.

Rail

Railroad, land transportation system in which cars with flanged steel wheels run on tracks of two parallel steel rails. Railroads are economical in their use of energy because the rolling friction of wheel on rail is very low; however, costs of maintenance are high, so high traffic volume is needed. Costs, rising competition and overmanning led to the closure of many minor lines in the United States and Europe. Maintenance, signaling, and many other functions are now highly automated.
Railroads developed out of the small mining tracks or tramways built in the United Kingdom and Europe from the mid-16th century. They used gravity or horse power, and the cars generally ran on flanged rails or plateways. The first public freight railroad was the Surrey Iron Railway (1801). The modern era of mechanized traction began with Richard Trevithick's steam locomotive *New Castle* (1804). The first public railroad to use locomotives and to carry passengers was the English Stockton and Darlington Railway (1825). The boom began when the Liverpool and Manchester Railway opened in 1830 using George Stephenson's *Rocket*, a much superior and more reliable locomotive. In the 1880s track gauges were standardized at 4 ft 8 1/2 in (1.435 m), allowing various lines to use one another's rails. After ever-increasing development in the 2nd half of the 19th century, railroads began to decline in the 1920s because of competition from other forms of transportation, such as air travel, trucking, and passenger cars. The sharp increases in oil prices in the early 1970s appeared to give railroads a new lease on life; however, railroads were limited mostly to commuter lines, rather than to hauling freight. In the United States the national Amtrak system survived with the aid of federal subsidies.

Railroad, electric *see:* Electric railroad.

Railroad, model, hobby in which a miniature railroad system is developed. The model railroader, who often uses kits with to-scale (size proportionate to the original) parts, assembles and then operates the cars, tracks, signals, bridges, and other railroad equipment. Miniature towns accompanied by scenery are also developed. Carpentry, electrical skills, and imagination are involved in building and operating a model railroad. Demand for manufactured model railroad products in the United States arose after model railroads were exhibited at the Century of Progress Exposition in Chicago (1933-34). The National Model Railroad Association was formed (1935) to create standards for model railroad materials.

Railway brotherhoods, unions for railroad workers in the United States and Canada. Because railway work—originally viewed as dangerous— was uninsured, these unions formed (1863) to insure workers. The unions generally operated through collective bargaining rather than strikes, since the railroads were strictly controlled by the government. By the 1950s the unions in this brotherhood joined the American Federation of Labor and Congress of Industrial Oranizations. By 1969 the four unions of the Railway brotherhoods merged to form the United Transportation Union.

Railway Labor Act, legislation passed by the U.S. Congress (1926) to settle labor disputes in the railway and later the airline industries. This act was created to avoid strikes by the well-organized railroad unions that might jeopardize the national economy. A 60-day period after a fact-finding board is appointed is required before a strike may commence; employees may reject the board's recommendations and strike after 60 days. The federal National Mediation Board and the National Railroad Adjustment Board administer the Railway Labor Act.
See also: National Mediation Board.

Rain, water drops falling through the atmosphere, the liquid form of precipitation. Raindrops range in size up to 0.16 in (4 mm) in diameter; if they are smaller than 0.02 in (0.5 mm), the rain is called *drizzle.* The quantity of rainfall is measured by a *rain gauge*, an open-top vessel that collects the rain, calibrated in inches or millimeters and so giving a reading independent of the area on which the rain falls. Light rain is less than 0.1 in (2.5 mm) hr, moderate rain up to 0.3 in (7.6 mm) hr, and heavy rain more than 0.3 in/hr. Rain may result from the melting of falling snow or hail, but it is commonly formed by direct condensation. When a parcel of warm air rises, it expands, almost without loss of heat; thus its relative humidity rises until reaching saturation, water vapor begins to condense as droplets, forming clouds. These droplets coalesce into raindrops chiefly through turbulence and nucleation by ice particles (and also cloud seeding). Moist air may be lifted by convection, producing *convective rainfall*; by forced ascent of air as it crosses a mountain range, producing *orographic rainfall*; and by the force within cyclones, producing *cyclonic rainfall.*

Rainbow, arch of concentric spectrally-colored rings seen in the sky by an observer looking at rain, mist, or spray with his or her back to the sun. The colors are produced by sunlight's being refracted and internally reflected by spherical droplets of water. The primary rainbow, with red on the outside and violet inside, results from one total internal reflection. Sometimes a dimmer secondary rainbow with reversed colors is seen, arising from a second total internal reflection.

Rainbow Bridge National Monument, largest and one of the most perfectly arched natural bridges in the world, situated slightly north of the Arizona-Utah border in Utah's Escalante Desert. Its 278-ft (85-m) span arches 309 ft (94 m) above a deep gorge. It was made a national monument in 1916.

Rain dance, ritual Native American dance ceremony performed to induce rain. These various ceremonial dances are performed by different tribes (mainly the Pueblos) during the planting and growing seasons, to help provide rainfall necessary for good harvests. The dances are directed at spirits that control natural phenomenon.

Rain forest *see:* Tropical rain forest.

Rain gauge, instrument that measures accumulated rainfall in a specific location during a particular period. The open vessel is calibrated to measure linear units. These devices vary in type: some collect the water in an inner tube marked with measurements, some empty and simultaneously record the amount of collected rainwater, some collect and weigh falling rain. Computer analysis is used to calculate the amount of rainfall.

Rainier III (Rainier Louis Henri Maxence Bertrand de Grimaldi; 1923-), prince of Monaco since 1949. He married the U.S. actress Grace Kelly (1929-82) in 1956.
See also: Monaco.

Rainmaking, method by which cloud precipitation is increased. Modern techniques of cloud seeding create conditions within clouds in which crystals, or water drops, become heavy and large enough to fall to earth as rain. Generators or airplanes inject the bottoms of clouds with substances called seeding agents—such as ammonium nitrate and urea, silver iodide crystals, or dry ice—to begin this crystal-making process. Rainmaking can increase an area's water supply or reduce the intensity of an approach storm.

Rain tree, or monkeypod tree (*Pithecellobium saman*), shade tree found in tropical climates of the Americas. This short tree has branches that may span 100 ft (30 m) or more. Monkeys often eat its black seed pods. The rain tree has pink to white flowers, as well as a transparent fluid—rainlike in appearance—that drips from its branches.

Rainy Lake, island-studded lake on the U.S.-Canadian border, between Minnesota and Ontario, located 125 mi (201 km) north of Duluth. It covers 350 sq mi (906.5 sq km) and forms a 56 mi (90 km) long and 5 mi(8 km) wide area flanked by rocky, pine-covered, and deeply serrated shores. It drains into the Lake of the Woods by way of the Rainy River.

Raisin, dried grape. Ripe grapes that are 20% sugar by weight are picked and then laid out in the sun to dry for 10-14 days on brown paper. Machines help stem, grade, rinse, and package the raisins. Raisins are mainly produced in California, Australia, Greece, Iran, and Turkey. A delicacy since ancient times, raisins are noted for their natural sugar content and various vitamins and minerals. Requiring no preservatives, they are eaten as is or used in cooking or baking. Thompson Seedless grapes are most commonly used; other types are Muscat of Alexandria, Black Corinth, and Sultana.

Raja, or Rajah (from Sanskrit *rjan*, "king"), Indian or Malay prince (extended to other men of rank during British rule). Higher-ranking princes were called *maharajas* (or *maharajahs*). A *raja's* wife is a *rani*.

Rajputs (Sanskrit, "kings' sons"), military and landowning caste mostly of the Rajasthan (now Rajputana) region, India. Their origins date back nearly 1,500 years. Although their influence in northern and central India has waxed and waned and at times has been considerable, since India's independence (1947) it has steadily declined.

Rake, tool with large teeth that gathers hay or leaves. As part of a tractor system, modern rakes gather large amounts of cut hay and place them in piles called windrows. Hand rakes with long handles are used to collect smaller amounts of material, usually lawn leaves. Rakes may also be used to break up top soil.

Rákóczy, Francis II (1676-1735), prince of Transylvania who led a Hungarian rising against the Habsburg Empire. Initially successful, he was elected prince (1704), but after several crushing defeats he left the country (1711) and died in exile in Turkey.
See also: Transylvania.

Raleigh (pop. 150,255), capital of North Carolina and seat of Wake County. Named for the English colonizer, Sir Walter Raleigh, it was incorporated as the state capital in 1792. The city supports a variety of light industry, including the manufacture of chemicals, electronics, textiles, processed foods, and building products. It also serves as the marketing and distribution center for the surrounding agricultural region. Raleigh is the home of North Carolina State University, St. Augustine's College, Meredith College, and Shaw University. North Carolina Museum of Art was opened at Raleigh in 1955.
See also: North Carolina.

Raleigh or **Ralegh, Sir Walter** (1554?-1618), English adventurer and poet, a favorite of Queen Elizabeth I. His efforts to organize colonization of the New World resulted in the tragedy of the Lost Colony of Roanoke Island, Va. In 1589 he left court and consolidated his friendship with Sir Edmund Spenser, whose *Faerie Queene* was written partly under Raleigh's patronage. Returning, he distinguished himself in raids at Cadiz (1596) and the Azores (1597). James I imprisoned him for treason in the Tower of London (1603-16), where he wrote poetry and his uncompleted *History of the World*. After two years' freedom, during which he made an unsuccessful expedition to the Orinoco River, he was executed in England under the original treason charge.

Ram *see:* Battering ram; Sheep.

Ramakrishna Paramahansa (1836-86), Indian saint whose teachings, now carried all over the world by the Ramakrishna Mission (founded in Calcutta in 1897), emphasize the unity of all religions and place equal value on social service, worship, and meditation.

Raman, Sir Chandrasekhara Venkata (1888-1970), Indian physicist awarded the 1930 Nobel Prize in physics for his discovery of the *Raman effect*: When molecules are exposed to a beam of infrared radiation, light scattered by the molecules contains frequencies that differ from that of the beam by amounts characteristic of the molecules. This is the basis for Raman spectroscopy.
See also: Physics.

Ramapithecus, prehistoric ape. Its remains were discovered in Pakistan (1932) by the U.S. anthropologist George E. Lewis. Named after a mythological Indian prince, Ramapithecus lived approximately 8 to 14 million years ago. Its remains have also been found in China, Kenya, Greece, and Hungary. In the late 1970s, scientists came to believe that Ramapithecus is most likely related to the orangutan rather than being a hominid, of the human family.
See also: Prehistoric people.

Ramayana, major Hindu epic poem, composed in Sanskrit in about the 3rd century B.C., concerning the war waged by the legendary hero Rama against Ravana, the demon-king of Lanka. Helped by Hanuman, king of the monkeys, Rama eventually rescues his wife, Sita, abducted by Ravana, and slays the demon, enabling the righteous once more to live in peace.

A dramatization of Ramayana performed on the island of Bali

Rameau, Jean Philippe (1683-1764), French composer and one of the founders of modern harmonic theory. He achieved recognition with his *Treatise on Harmony* (1722) and composed some 30 operas, among them *Hippolyte et Aricie* (1733) and *Castor et Pollux* (1737).

Rameses II *see:* Ramses II.

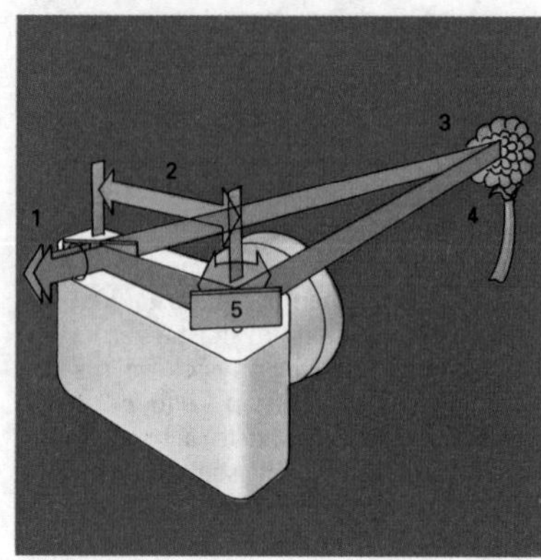

The range finder of many cameras is of the "split image" type. Light from the object on which the camera is focused enters the finder through two windows (1). The direct ray (3) travels straight to the eye. The indirect ray (4) is reflected in a pivoting mirror (5), travels a distance across the camera (2), and is reflected in the same path as the direct ray. In general, a double or split image will be seen in the range finder.

Ramie (*Boehmeria nivea*), perennial plant of the nettle family, grown for its fiber. Native to Asia, it is now also grown in Florida. Stalks grow from 3-7 ft (1-2 m) high and produce large leaves. When the plants are mature, the fiber is stripped from the stalks, washed to remove impurities, and dried. Ramie is one of the oldest sources of fiber and is ideal for the manufacture of canvas, ropes, and nets because its strength increases when it is wet.

Ramp, or wild leek (*Allium tricoccum*), wild plant considered a member of either the amaryllis or lily family. The ramp, which smells and tastes like onion, grows in great abundance in the Midwest United States. The leaves appear in early spring, after which green-to-white tiny flowers appear.

Rampal, Jean-Pierre (1922-), French flutist. A virtuoso known for his pure luxuriant tone, he revived interest in the flute as a solo instrument.

Ramsay, Sir William (1852-1916), British chemist awarded the 1904 Nobel Prize in chemistry for his discovery of helium, codiscovery (with Lord Rayleigh) of argon, and codiscovery (with Morris Travers) of krypton, neon, and xenon.
See also: Chemistry; Helium.

Ramses II (c.1304-1237 B.C.), called "the Great," Egyptian pharaoh, 4th king of the 19th dynasty, who built hundreds of temples and monuments, probably including Abu Simbel and the columned hall at Karnak. He campaigned against the Hittites, and celebrated a battle at Kadesh (1300 B.C.) on many of his monuments, but was eventually obliged to make peace (c.1283). His long reign marked a high point in Egyptian prosperity. He may have been the Pharaoh who allowed the Hebrews to leave Egypt, as told in Exodus in the Bible.
See also: Egypt, Ancient.

Ranching, breeding and raising usually of cattle or sheep on large tracts of land; in California also the name for farms smaller than 10 acres. Ranches, called stations in Australia, exist throughout the world. Land boundaries for U.S. ranches in the West were established in the mid 1800s. Cowboys (sometimes cowhands or cowpunchers), brand young animals with the farm insignia, oversee grazing cattle, and round up and lead animals in a cattle drive to market. Sheep ranchers harvest sheered wool from sheep as well as manage the herds. Today, in addition to horses, ranchers use trucks, jeeps, and sometimes helicopters to increase production.

Rand, Ayn (1905-82), U.S. writer. Her "objectivist" philosophy—individualistic, egoistic, and capitalist in inspiration—is at the core of such novels as *The Fountainhead* (1943) and *Atlas Shrugged* (1957). She also wrote nonfiction, including *For the New Intellectual* (1961) and *Capitalism, the Unknown Ideal* (1966).

Randolph, name of a prominent Virginia family. **William Randolph** (1651?-1711) was attorney general for Virginia (1694-98). The post was also held by his son **Sir John Randolph** (1693?-1737) and his grandson **Peyton Randolph** (1721?-75), who was also president of the 1st Continental Congress. **Edmund Jennings Randolph** (1753-1813), a nephew of Peyton, became attorney general (1776-86) and then governor (1786-88) of Virginia. At the Constitutional Convention (1787) he drafted the Virginia Plan, calling for representation in Congress to be related to state population. He did not sign the Constitution but later urged its ratification. He became the first U.S. attorney general (1789-94) and secretary of state (1794-95). **John Randolph of Roanoke** (1773-1833), great-grandson of William Randolph, entered the U.S. House of Representatives in 1799. A much-feared orator and champion of States' Rights, he led Southern opposition to the Missouri Compromise in 1820. **George Wythe Randolph** (1818-67), great-great-great grandson of William Randolph and grandson of Thomas Jefferson, became Confederate secretary of war in 1862.

Randolph, A(sa) Philip (1889-1979), U.S. African-American labor and civil rights leader. He organized the Brotherhood of Sleeping Car Porters (1925), then an all-black union, and served as its president until 1968. His influence was instrumental in the setting up of the Fair Employment Practices Committee in 1941. He became a vice president of the American Federation of Labor and Congress of Industrial Organizations (AFL-CIO) in 1955. In 1963 he directed the March on Washington for Jobs and Freedom.
See also: Labor movement; Civil rights.

Randolph, Edward (1632?-1703), British colonial agent whose reports led to the Massachusetts charter being revoked in 1684. He was secretary and registrar of the Dominion of New England (1685-9) and in 1691 became surveyor general of customs for North America.

Randolph Air Force Base, center for recruiting, assigning, and training of personnel for the United States Air Force; Air Training Command headquarters. Founded in 1930, this base is located in south central Texas, near the city of San Antonio. It occupies about 3,000 acres (1,200 hectares).
See also: Air Force, U.S.

Range, or stove, appliance that creates heat for cooking and area warming. U.S. cast iron ranges were first produced in the mid-1600s; Europeans developed ranges in the 15th century, while the Chinese invented them in the 8th century. Modern ranges provide individual cooking units on top, and one or more ovens within. They are fueled by gas or electricity; some ovens use microwaves.

Range finder, instrument used to ascertain the distance of an object from the observer. In *coincidence* range finders, used in many cameras, light from a distant object passes through two separate apertures, forming a double image that can be viewed through the eyepiece; a mirror in one aperture can be rotated by a knob until both images coincide exactly, and a calibrated scale on the knob indicates the distance of the object. In the *stereoscopic* range finder, which has mainly military uses, adjustment is made until a stereoscopic image produced by a special optical system coincides with the image of a reference mark; the range may then be read from a calibrated scale.
See also: Radar.

Rangoon *see:* Yangon.

Ranjit Singh (1780-1839), ruler of India who united many Sikhs in a great kingdom. As head of the Sikhs, a religious group of India that lives mainly in the northwest state of Punjab, he began his rule upon his father's death (1792). He conquered neighboring Indian states and overthrew Afghan control, gaining the title "Lion of the Punjab." Through treaties signed with British colonists, Ranjit kept the peace in India, although his efforts to unite all Sikhs were curtailed.
See also: India; Sikhism.

Rank, military, designation of position in the military service. Often called grade when associated with salary level and lower-level personnel, rank also refers to an officer's authority. In the U.S. titles for rank include the President as commander in chief, commissioned officers, and noncommissioned officers, which include warrent officers and enlisted personnel.

Rank, Otto (1884-1939), Austrian psychoanalyst and pupil of Sigmund Freud, best known for his suggestion that the trauma of birth is the basis of later anxiety neurosis and for applying psychoanalysis to artistic creativity.
See also: Psychoanalysis.

Ranke, Leopold von (1795-1886), German historian, one of the founders of modern historical research methodology. Professor of history at Berlin (1834-71), Ranke insisted on objectivity and the importance of original documents.

Rankin, Jeannette (1880-1973), pacifist, feminist, social reformer, and first woman elected to the U.S. Congress. She became Republican Congresswoman at large for Montana in 1917-19 and returned to the House in 1941, when she cast the only vote against entering World War II. In the 1960s she reemerged as a leader of the campaign against the war in Vietnam.

Ransom, John Crowe (1888-1974), U.S. poet and proponent of the New Criticism, which emphasized textual, rather than social or moral, analysis. Professor of poetry at Kenyon College, Ohio (1937-58), he founded and edited the *Kenyon Review* (1939-59). His poetry includes *Chills and Fever* (1924).

Rape, crime of forced sexual intercourse without the consent of the subject, who may be male or female. Statutory rape refers to sexual intercourse with someone who is under the legal age of consent (age 12-16 in the United States), is mentally defective, or does not comprehend the physical or other consequences of the act. In most societies of the world, rape is considered a serious crime. Rape crisis centers offer counseling for rape victims and encourage them to report the crime to the police. Some psychologists hold that rape is an antisocial act that is only peripherally sexual.
See also: Crime.

Rape, flowering plant in the mustard family. Rape is used for animal feed; its seed is used in the production of a cooking oil. This deep green plant, originally from Europe, has jagged leaves and clusters of tiny yellow flowers. The plant may grow up to 3 ft (91 cm) tall and may be an annual or biennial.

Raphael (Raffaello Santi or Sanzio; 1483-1520), Italian High Renaissance painter and architect. He was early influenced by Perugino, as in *Marriage of the Virgin* (1504). In Florence (1504-8) he studied the work of Michelangelo and Leonardo da Vinci, being influenced especially by the latter, and painted his famous Madonnas. From 1508 he decorated the Vatican rooms for Julius II; the library frescoes, masterly portrayals of symbolic themes, use Raphael's new knowledge of classical art. His Sistine Chapel tapestries (1515-16) and his sympathetic portraits were much imitated. Chief architect of the Vatican (from 1514), he worked at rebuilding Saint Peter's Basilica.
See also: Renaissance.

Rapid City (pop. 81,343), second-largest city in South Dakota, situated on Rapid Creek near the Black Hills. It was established when gold was found in the area in the 1870s and grew with later discoveries of uranium and other minerals. Its economy has since diversified to include marketing and processing for local agricultural and lumbering industries and the production of cement. It is the home of the South Dakota School of Mines and Technology, which has a well-known Museum of Geology.
See also: South Dakota.

Rapid Deployment Force, special U.S. military unit trained to act quickly upon command. Called the RDF, the force was founded in 1980 particularly to protect U.S. interests in oil-rich regions of the Middle East. Headquartered in Tampa, Fla., the RDF has ships and personnel stationed on the Diego Garcia Island in the Indian Ocean. The island location helps this force move swiftly when necessary to areas around the globe.

Rappahannock River, river flowing 212 mi (341 km) southeast from the Blue Ridge Mountains of Virginia to Chesapeake Bay. It is joined by its main tributary, the Rapidan, above Fredericksburg near the Salem Church Dam.

Rare earth, name for the elements scandium and yttrium and the lanthanide series, Group IIIB of the Periodic Table, occurring throughout nature as monazite and other ores. They are separated by chromatography and ion-exchange resins. Rare earths are used in alloys, including misch metal, and their compounds (mixed or separately) are used as abrasives, for making glasses and ceramics, as "getters," as catalysts in the petroleum industry, and to make phosphors, lasers, and microwave devices.
See also: Berzelius, Jöns Jakob, Baron.

Rasmussen, Knud Johan Victor (1879-1933), Danish explorer and ethnologist. From Thule, Greenland, he undertook many expeditions to study Eskimo culture, including the longest dog-sled journey known, from Greenland to Alaska (1923-24), described in his *Across Arctic America* (1927).
See also: Eskimo; Ethnography.

Raspberry, fruit-bearing bushes (genus *Rubus*), including some 200 species. European cultivated red-fruited varieties are derived from *B. idaeus*, while North American varieties, including a number that are black-fruited, are derived from three species.

Rasputin, Grigori Yefimovich (1872-1916), Russian mystic (the "mad monk") who gained influence over the Tsarina Alexandra Fyodorovna after supposedly curing her son's hemophilia in 1905. The scandal of his debaucheries, as well as his interference in political affairs, contributed to the undermining of the imperial government in World War I. He was assassinated by a group of ultraconservatives.

Ras Tafari *see:* Rastafarians; Haile Selassie.

Rastafarians, world-wide religious group founded in Jamaica in the 1920s. Its original members, of African descent, believed that Haile Selassie (Ras Tafari)—who ruled Ethiopia 1916-74—was a messiah who would return all African descendants to the continent of Africa. Reggae music and hair worn in dreadlocks (long ropes of curls) are part of Rastafarian culture.
See also: Haile Selassie.

Raphael's The School of Athens, *depicting the Greek philosopher Plato and his disciple Aristotle*

Rasputin (left)

Rat, name for numerous species of rodents belonging to many different families, largely Muridae and Cricetidae. The brown (*Rattus norvegicus*) and black (*R. rattus*) rats are familiar farmyard and warehouse pests. A strong exploratory urge and an ability to feed on almost anything make them persistent pests; in addition, they transmit a number of serious diseases, such as typhus and plague. Rats native to the New World include wood rats or pack rats, cotton rats, and the rice rats.

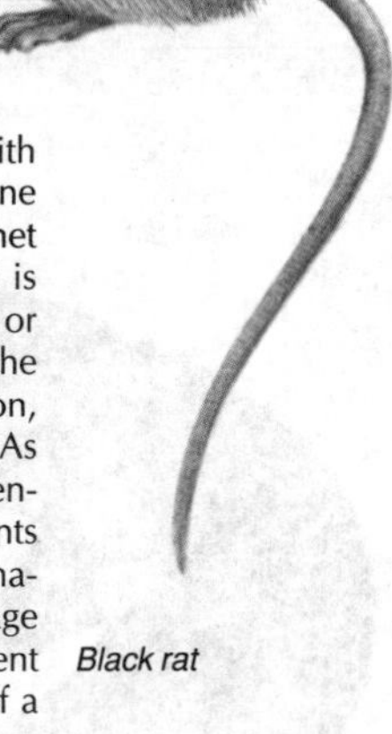
Black rat

Ratchet, toothed wheel that operates with a catch, or *pawl*, so as to rotate in only one direction. Typically, the toothed ratchet wheel is rotated by a handle. The pawl is curved and pivoted so that it rests on or presses against the wheel teeth. When the wheel rotates in the permitted direction, the teeth can move beneath the pawl. As soon as the rotation ceases, the pawl engages one of the wheel teeth and prevents any motion backward. A release mechanism is usually incorporated to disengage the pawl when required. The escapement in clocks and watches is an example of a ratchet.

Ratel, or honey badger, carnivorous nocturnal African mammal (genus *Mellivora*) with distinctive grayish back and black

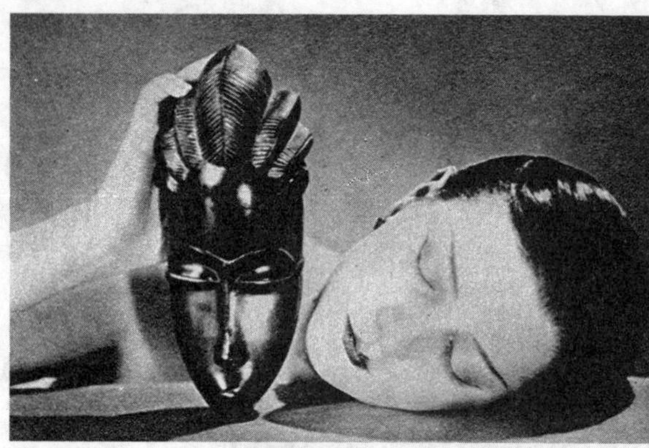
Man Ray's portrait of Kiki de Montparnasse holding a mask (1926)

underparts. It has powerful legs and strong claws and eats almost anything, even pythons. Its fondness for honey has led to a close association with the honeyguide, a bird that directs it to bees' nests.

Rate of exchange *see:* Exchange rate.

Rationalism, philosophical doctrine that reality has a logical structure accessible to deductive reasoning and proof. Against empiricism, it holds that reason unsupported by sense experience is a source of knowledge not merely of concepts (as in mathematics and logic) but of the real world. Major rationalists in modern philosophy include Descartes, Spinoza, Leibniz, and Hegel.
See also: Age of Reason.

Rationing, method by which distribution of food and other important products are controlled. Governments usually impose rationing policies in times of large demand and short supply, such as war or severe inflation. Rationing was used in the United States, among other countries, during World War II. Coupons or a point system are allocated to families to obtain rationed products. Rationed products bought outside of the rationing system are considered black market products.

Rattan, stems from any of 200 species of climbing palm of the genus *Calamus*, family Palmaceae. The stems are strong and pliant and are used to make furniture, baskets, canes, rope, and umbrellas. Rattan palms are native to the East Indies and Africa, and some are edible or have medicinal or veterinary uses. The stems may grow to 500 ft (150 m).

Timber rattlesnake

Rattlesnake, any of two genera (*Crotalus* and *Sistrurus*) of pit vipers of the Americas, referring to a rattle, composed of successive pieces of sloughed-off dead skin, at the end of the tail. Rattlers have moveable fangs that fold up into the roof of the mouth when not in use and are shed and replaced every three weeks. They are extremely venomous snakes, with the diamondback rattler being the largest and most dangerous.

Ratzel, Friedrich (1844-1904), German geographer. With works such as *Anthropogeography* (1882-91), *Political Geography* (1897), *The History of Mankind* (1896-98), and *Lebensraum* (1901), he strongly influenced later German geopolitics.
See also: Geopolitics.

Rauschenberg, Robert (1925-), U.S. artist, an initiator of the Pop Art of the 1960s. His "combines" (collages) use brushwork along with objects from everyday life, such as pop bottles and news photos.

Rauschenbusch, Walter (1861-1918), U.S. Baptist minister, reformer, and theologian. A leader of the Social Gospel movement, he became a national spokesman for social evangelism with his *Christianity and the Social Crisis* (1907).
See also: Baptists.

Rauwolfia serpentina *see:* Reserpine.

Ravel, Maurice (1875-1937), French composer, known for his adventurous harmonic style and the combination of delicacy and power in such orchestral works as *Rhapsodie Espagnole* (1908) and *Bolero* (1928), and the ballets *Daphnis and Chloé* (1912) and *La Valse* (1920). *Gaspard de la Nuit* (1908) is among his many masterpieces for the piano, his favorite instrument.

Raven, largest member of the crow family, with a wedge-shaped tail. The common raven (*Corvus corax*) is found in the United States and in the Old World, where it appears in many European legends as a prophet of doom. Ravens eat many things but are particularly fond of carrion.

Ravenna (pop. 101,000), city in northeastern region of Italy, famous for its superb mosaics, notably in the 5th-century mausoleum of Galla Placidia and 6th-century churches (notably San Vitale and Sant'Apollinare Nuovo). Emperor Honorius made Ravenna his capital; it was seized by Odoacer in 476 and was later seat of the Byzantine exarch. It was given to the Pope in the 8th century by the Carolingean King Pepin the Short. Papal control was lost and not regained until the 16th century. Modern Ravenna, an agricultural and manufacturing center, has a port and petrochemical plants.
See also: Italy.

Rawlings, Marjorie Kinnan (1896-1953), U.S. novelist. With a dramatic change in lifestyle from urban journalist to Florida back-country resident, she began to write fiction about life in her new home of Cross Creek. Her novel *The Yearling* (1939) won the Pulitzer Prize for fiction. Her stories were collected in *When the Whippoorwill* (1940). *Cross Creek* (1942), a nonfiction book of essays, humorously describes her life on her Florida farm.

Rawlinson, Sir Henry Creswicke (1810-95), British soldier and archeologist who deciphered the cuneiform inscriptions of King Darius I of Persia.
See also: Archaeology.

Ray, any of a group of more than 400 species of flat-bodied marine fish (order Rajiformes) with a boneless skeleton made from a tough, elastic substance called cartilage. Rays resemble sharks in having gill slits, but under the pectoral fins. Most rays live on the sea floor and feed on smaller species. Rays eggs are fertilized and hatched inside the female. The largest rays are the mantas, which may grow to 22 ft (7 m) wide and weigh up to 3,000 lbs (1,360 kg).

Ray, John (1627-1705), English naturalist, who, with Francis Willughby (1635-72), made important contributions to taxonomy, especially in *A General History of Plants* (1686-1704).

Ray, Man (1890-1976), U.S. abstract artist and photographer, a founder of the Dada movement. He recreated several "lost" photographic techniques and produced surrealist films.
See also: Dada

Ray, Satyajit (1921-), Indian film director. *Pather Panchali* (1954) was his acclaimed debut. His many other films include *Aparajito* (1956), *The Music Room* (1958), and *The World of Apu* (1959).

Rayburn, Sam (1882-1961), longest-serving U.S. House of Representatives speaker (17 years from 1940) and congressman from 1913. A dedicated Democrat, he helped build New Deal policy.

Rayleigh, John William Strutt, 3rd Baron (1842-1919), English physicist awarded the 1904 Nobel Prize in physics for his measurements of the density of the atmosphere and its component gases, work that led to his isolation (with William Ramsay) of argon.
See also: Atmosphere; Physics.

Raymond, Henry Jarvis (1820-69), cofounder and editor of the *New York Times* from 1851 who took an active part in forming the Republican Party. He was in the House of Representatives for one term (1865-67), losing renomination because of his moderate stand on Reconstruction.

Rayon, synthetic cottonlike fiber with a sheen. Patented in 1884 by the French inventor, Hilaire Chardonnet, it was named rayon in 1924. Rayon is produced from cellulose fiber of wood pulp or cotton.

Chemicals reduce the cellulose to a thick liquid, which is forced under pressure into a metal spinneret and emerges as filaments. The filaments are twisted into silky yarn or cut and spun. Spun rayon can be treated to simulate wool, linen, or cotton. The 3 main processes for making rayon are viscose, cuprammonium, and acetate.

Razor, sharp-edged instrument used to shave hair from the skin. Razors in crude forms, such as clam shells and flints, have been used since prehistoric times. They evolved into the 3 basic types in use today. Straight-edged razors (blades 3-4 in (8-10 cm) long encased in a safety handle) and safety razors (hoe-shaped with shorter blades and protected cutting surface) manually remove hair from a lathered surface. Electric razors, powered by motors, move a series of small, sharp blades over unlathered skin. Many electric razors are "cordless," able to operate on batteries.

RCMP *see:* Royal Canadian Mounted Police.

RDX, or Research Department Explosive ($C_3H_6O_6N_6$), powerful explosive used in bombs. Discovered by Hans Henning in Germany (1899), RDX was used extensively by the air forces of both sides in World War II. Known also as hexogen and cyclonite, it is a white, insoluble, crystalline solid. RDX is produced by the action of nitric acid on a product of formaldehyde and ammonia. Its chief nonmilitary use is in blasting caps, detonators, and fuses. RDX can also be mixed with trinitrotoluene (TNT) to form a more powerful explosive known as Composition B.
See also: Explosive.

Re, or Ra, in Egyptian mythology, the sun god. Worshipped as the creator of the entire earth, Re evolved into the chief deity of ancient Egypt. Many myths and legends came to be associated with Re; early pharaohs claimed to be descended from him. Re has appeared in Egyptian hieroglyphics as the sun, lion, cat, or bird, and is symbolized by a pyramid.
See also: Mythology.

Reaction, chemical *see:* Chemical reaction.

Reactor, nuclear *see:* Nuclear reactor.

Read, George (1733-98), American Revolutionary leader. As a representative of Delaware, he signed both the Declaration of Independence and the Constitution, one of only 6 people to do so. After serving as Delaware's attorney general (1763-74) and legislator (1765-77), Read represented the state in the first 2 Continental Congresses (1774-77). At the Constitutional Convention of 1787, he was an outspoken proponent of the rights of smaller states; his efforts helped Delaware become the first state to ratify the Constitution and enter the Union. He served as one of Delaware's first 2 U.S. senators and served (1789-93) until he was named chief justice of the Delaware Supreme Court, a position he held until his death.

Reading, process of assimilating language in the written form. Initial language development in children is largely as speech and has a primarily auditory or phonetic component; the recognition of written letters, words, and sentences represents a transition from the auditory to the visual mode. In reading, vision is linked with the system controlling eye movement, so that the page is scanned in an orderly fashion. Reading is represented in essentially the same areas of the brain as are concerned with speech, and disorders of the two often occur together. In dyslexia, pattern recognition is impaired, and a defect of reading and language development results.

Reading (pop. 336,523), city on the Schuylkill River in southeast Pennsylvania. It is surrounded by rich farmland and the state's famous "Pennsylvania Dutch" colony, but it is best known as a major manufacturing center. The town was laid out in 1748 and named after the Penn family's home city in England. Reading was one of the first places in the United States to manufacture iron products and supplied cannon for the Revolution.
See also: Pennsylvania.

Reagan, Ronald Wilson (1911-), 40th president of the United States. Reagan's administration strengthened the U.S. military presence in Europe, increased support for anti-Communist forces in Central America, and signed a nuclear-arms-reduction treaty with the Soviet Union. It also made large cuts in federal income taxes while sharply reducing spending on domestic programs. Although Reagan's two terms brought lower unemployment and a temporarily stronger economy, social programs suffered and the federal budget deficit grew larger than ever in U.S. history.
Early life. Reagan attended Eureka (Ill.) College. After graduating in 1932, he worked as a radio sports announcer in Iowa. In 1937, he began a successful new career as a film actor. In 1940, he married actress Jane Wyman. They had one child and adopted another, but divorced in 1948. During World War II, Reagan served in the Army Air Forces (1942-45), making training films. He then returned to acting and served as president of the Screen Actors Guild (1947-52; 1959). In 1952, he married actress Nancy Davis; they had two children.
Political career. Once a liberal Democrat, Reagan became a conservative Republican. He was elected governor of California in 1966 and reelected in 1970. In 1976, he ran for the Republican presidential nomination, but lost.
In 1980, Reagan did get the nomination. He and running mate George H.W. Bush won a landslide victory over the Democratic incumbents, President Jimmy Carter and Vice President Walter Mondale.
President. Reagan immediately called for tax cuts combined with reductions in social and other domestic programs. Congress passed most of the proposed cuts. The business failures and higher unemployment of a recession, coupled with increased military spending, made the federal budget deficit soar and the economy weaken. Reagan's administration met with rising public criticism, particularly from blacks, women, and environmental groups. By 1984, however, the economy seemed to recover and Reagan and Bush were reelected in another landslide, defeating Democratic candidates Walter Mondale and Geraldine Ferraro. In Reagan's second term, the economy took another beating: a stock-market crash in October 1987.
Reagan faced a number of foreign-relations crises. In 1983, he sent U.S. troops to invade Grenada and to join a multinational peacekeeping force in Lebanon. In Central America, Reagan's administration supported anti-Communist forces in El Salvador and the "contras" opposing Nicaragua's government. Over the course of Reagan's two terms, U.S.-Soviet relations worsened, then slowly improved. Reagan met several times with Mikhail Gorbachev, the Soviet leader, and they signed a nuclear-arms-reduction treaty in 1987.

Ronald Wilson Reagan

40th U.S. president

Born:	Tampico, Ill.; Feb. 6, 1911
Term:	Jan. 1981-Jan. 1989
Vice president:	George H.W. Bush
Political party:	Republican
Spouses:	Jane Wyman; Anne Frances (Nancy) Robbins Davis Reagan
Children:	4

Dubbed "the Teflon president" for his ability to withstand criticism and scandal, Reagan's popularity remained high throughout his presidency. He survived a 1981 assassination attempt, as well as the Iran-contra affair, a major domestic crisis (1986-87). It was revealed that Reagan's administration had sold weapons to Iran in exchange for the release of hostages held in Lebanon (contradicting Reagan's public statements against dealing with terrorists), then used the money to illegally fund the Nicaraguan contras.
Retirement. When his second term ended in 1989, Reagan retired to California.

Real estate, term used to describe land and that which is attached to it, including buildings, trees, and underground resources, such as minerals or water. Real estate is generally sold by plots of ground (parcels), which are surveyed, sized, and registered with the particular governing agency for that area. Real estate properties for sale can be listed with agencies and sold by brokers or realtors, but often the owners of the property sell it themselves. The U.S. real estate industry employs about 1.8 million brokers; many more are involved in subsidiary businesses such as construction, financing (mortgage lending), appraising, and property management. In all 50 states, real estate agents must pass tests and be licensed before they can legally sell properties.
See also: Property.

Realism, in art and literature, the faithful imitation of real life; more specifically, the artistic movement which started in France c.1850 in reaction to the idealized representations of romanticism and neoclassicism, with a social dimension derived from scientific progress and the revolutions of 1848. In France the leading painters were Jean-Baptiste Corot, Gustave Courbet, Honoré Daumier, Jean François Millet, and its main literary expression was in the novels of Honoré de Balzac, Gustave Flaubert, and Emile Zola. In the United States, Thomas Eakins, Winslow Homer, and members of the Ashcan School were realistic painters, and Stephen Crane, Theodore Dreiser, William Dean Howells, Henry James, and Frank Norris led the literary movement.

Recife

Reaper, machine for harvesting grain. The U.S. inventor Cyrus Hall McCormick's horse-drawn reaping machine (1831) consisted simply of a long knife, or cutter bar, a platform, and a rotating reel to bend the grain back against the knife and knock it onto the platform. The modern reaper, or self-binder, cuts the standing grain, binds it into sheaves with twine, and then ejects the sheaves onto the ground. Reapers are seldom used today for cutting grain, however; the harvesting of grain is done mostly with combine harvesters, machines that combine reaping and threshing.
See also: McCormick, Cyrus Hall.

Reapportionment *see:* Apportionment, legislative.

Reasoning *see:* Logic.

Rebecca *see:* Isaac.

Rebellion of 1837-1838, 2 unsuccessful and parallel uprisings against British colonial rule in Canada, prompted by an economic depression and desire for local self-government. A subsequent report by Lord Durham, English governor general in Canada, urged the union of Upper and Lower Canada, which became law with the 1840 Act of Union.
See also: Canada.

Recall *see:* Initiative, referendum, and recall.

Receiver, in law, person, bank, or trust company appointed by a court and paid a fee to take charge of a company or a person's assets, most frequently in cases of bankruptcy. The receiver maintains existing assets in good order, since creditors will ultimately have a claim on them and may also carry on the business, collecting money that is due, paying out salaries, and dealing with suppliers.
See also: Bankruptcy.

Recession, extended period of economic decline. In the United States, a recession is defined as a drop in the gross national product (GNP) over 2 consecutive quarterly periods. During recessions, business activities such as buying, selling, and overall productivity decline, causing increases in unemployment and unpredictable fluctuations in stock markets. Until the 1970s, recessions caused prices to fall, but since then they have continued to increase despite several recessions. A sudden shortage of vital goods, such as oil and petroleum-based products, often triggers recessions and accompanying rising prices, which result in decreased consumer spending. A pattern is formed in which manufacturers decrease production to keep pace with reduced demands for their goods, and fewer workers are needed to produce those goods. Recessions are often worldwide; an extended period of recession could develop into a depression. Short-term recessions are called economic slumps.
See also: Business cycle; Depression.

Recife (pop. 1,184,000), capital of Pernambuco, state in northeastern Brazil. Located at the mouths of the Capibaribe and Berberibe rivers on the Atlantic Ocean, the city was settled by the Portuguese in 1535. The British held it briefly (1595), as did the Dutch (1630-54). In 1710 Recife became a Brazilian town, and in 1823 a city. Part of Recife is on an island; because of many intersecting waterways, is often called the Brazilian Venice. Manufactured goods include textiles, ceramics, synthetic rubber, paper and leather products, and agricultural goods. Its port exports large quantities of bananas, sugar, coffee, and cotton. Recife is an educational center with 4 universities.
See also: Brazil.

Reciprocal trade agreement, mutual tariff reduction pact enacted between 2 or more nations. Such agreements began in response to the trend toward protectionism that prevailed throughout most of the 19th century, in which steadily increasing tariffs on imported goods hampered international trade. Bilateral trade agreements were worked out in the early 20th century, when 2 nations consented to lower import duties on certain goods they exchanged. Such pacts were later expanded to include other nations. The United States passed the first Reciprocal Trade Agreements Act in 1934; in 1947, 23 countries ratified the General Agreement on Tariffs and Trade (GATT), which reduced tariffs on specified goods by rates believed to be beneficial to all the signatory nations. Today, reciprocal trade agreements are universal, although worldwide economic conditions are continually requiring changes in the nature of these agreements. Industrially developed nations have been encouraging developing countries through modified trade agreements.
See also: Tariff.

Reclamation, Bureau of, agency of the Department of the Interior created to administer the Reclamation Act of 1902 for reclaiming arid land by irrigation in the 16 western states. Its responsibilities were later progressively expanded.

Reconstruction, period (1865-77) when Americans tried to rebuild a stable Union after the Civil War. The deadlock inherited by President Andrew Johnson on Abraham Lincoln's death, over who should control Reconstruction, hardened with increasing congressional hostility toward restoring the South to its old position. Republicans wanted to press home the Union victory by following the 13th Amendment abolishing slavery (1865) with full civil rights for blacks, including the vote. While Congress was not in session, Johnson implemented Lincoln's policy of lenience by giving amnesty to former Confederates in return for a loyalty oath. He also condoned the Black Codes, which practically reintroduced slavery in another guise. Reconvening (1866) with a landslide victory, however, the Radical Republicans took control. Their first Reconstruction Act of 1867 divided ten southern states into five mili-

tary areas, with a major general for each. Under army scrutiny, black and white voters were registered, and constitutions and governments were instituted. In 1868 six southern states were readmitted to the Union, followed in 1870 by the other four. By ratifying the 14th Amendment (1868) on black civil rights, Tennessee escaped the military phase. There were no mass arrests, no indictments for treason, and the few Confederate officials jailed were (except for Jefferson Davis) soon released. Apart from slaves, the property of the confederate leaders was untouched, although no help was given to rescue the ruined economy. On readmission, the southern governments were Republican, supported by enfranchised blacks, Scalawags (white Republicans), and Carpetbaggers (Northern profiteers). Constructive legislation was passed in every state for public schools, welfare taxation, and government reform, although the governments were accused of corruption and incompetence. The Freedmen's Bureau lasted only four years, but it did help to found Atlanta, Howard, and Fish universities for blacks. Southern conservatives, hostile to Radical Republican policies, turned to the Democratic Party; terrorist societies like the Ku Klux Klan crusaded against blacks and radicals. Full citizenship for blacks, though legally assured by the 14th and 15th (1870) amendments, was denied by intimidation, unfair literacy tests, and the Poll Tax. The Republican Party, secure in the North, abandoned the black cause. In 1877 when federal troops withdrew from the South, the last Republican governments collapsed, and Reconstruction was over.
See also: Civil War, U.S.

Recorder, wind instrument related to the flute but held vertically, with a mouthpiece that channels the airstream and without keys. Relatively easy to play, soft and sweet in tone, it was most popular about 1600-1700 and is again popular today. There are soprano, alto, and (with some keys) tenor and bass recorders.

Recording industry, group of businesses that produce and sell sound recordings. The industry records primarily popular forms of music, as well as verbal communication such as speeches and seminars. The industry began with Thomas Edison's invention of the phonograph (1877), which pushed a sound-sensitive needle along the grooves of a cylinder to reproduce sound. The cylinder was replaced by flat disc—the phonograph record—in the early 1900s; this evolved into today's compact disc, which plays recorded sounds by means of a laser beam. Invention of magnetic recording tape in the 1940s enabled the development of cassette tapes. In the United States, the industry employs more than 30,000 people, among them musicians, composers, arrangers, and engineers. Most recordings today are done in studios.

Record player *see:* Phonograph.

Recreation, leisure activities that people enjoy. Recreation has become an important aspect of modern life that often relieves stress; many businesses and hospitals provide various forms of recreation for their workers and patients. These activities can be passive ones, such as reading or watching television or movies, or participatory forms ranging from hobbies and games to strenuous amateur sports. Donation of time by volunteers to help others is another form of recreation. Commercial recreation includes watching sporting, cultural, and other entertainment events, or active forms, such as tourism or visiting theme parks. State, national, and local agencies set aside scenic or historic lands for public recreational use, usually financed through taxes and user fees. In the United States, recreation is a multibillion-dollar business.

Recreational vehicle (RV), temporary living quarters on wheels, used for traveling or camping. Five basic types of RVs are in use today. Motor homes contain an engine and living quarters, which have conveniences such as running water and facilities for cooking, heating, and food-storage. This type includes vans adapted for overnight use. Travel trailers are not motorized and must be pulled by another vehicle, as must campers (camping trailers), which are smaller than these trailers. They have collapsible sides that can fold out to provide extra sleeping or storage space. Truck campers are adapted to fit over the bed and cab of a pickup truck. Pickup covers enclose only the bed of a pickup truck.

Rectangle, 4-sided plane figure with sides that meet at 4 right-angles. Rectangles are classified as special cases of parallelograms, in that the opposite sides are parallel and of equal length, but all 4 sides are not necessarily equal. When they are equal, rectangles are called squares. The word is derived from the Latin *rectus angulus*, meaning *straight angles*.

Rectum *see:* Colon; Intestine.

Recycling, recovery and use of waste material. Paper, aluminum cans, and glass are the most commonly recycled materials and can be used to make insulation, new cans and glass containers, and material for road construction. As concern over the earth's environment increases, recycling has emerged as an effective method for cutting down on pollution and conserving important natural resources. It has also become an increasingly vital source of material for modern industry.

Red Baron *see:* War aces.

Redbreast *see:* Robin.

Redbud, flowering tree (genus *Cercis*) of the pea family, native to North America, southern Europe, and Asia. Redbuds display their pink blossoms in early spring before their heart-shaped leaves unfold. The flowers ripen into seed pods that wild game feed on. The reddish-brown trees grow as high as 40 feet (12 m) and thrive on fertile, sandy soil. Redbuds are sometimes called Judas trees because, according to legend, Judas Iscariot hanged himself from a redbud tree after betraying Jesus.

With the increased cooperation of government and industry, spurred on by environmental activists, the U.S public is becoming more aware of the benefits of recycling. Pictured is a road sign urging people to cash in their metal cans rather than throw them away.

Red cedar *see:* Juniper.

Red Cloud (1822-1909), chief of the Oglala Sioux and leader of the Native American struggle against the opening of the Bozeman Trail. The trail was closed in 1868 following the Fetterman Massacre (1866).

Red Cross, international agency for the relief of victims of war or disaster. Its two aims are to alleviate suffering and to maintain a rigid neutrality so that it may cross national borders to reach those otherwise unaidable. An international committee founded by J.H. Dunant and four others from Geneva secured 12 nations' signatures to the first of the Geneva Conventions (1864) for the care of the wounded. Aid was given to both sides in the Danish-Prussian War the same year. During World Wars I and II the Red Cross helped prisoners of war, inspecting camps and sending food and clothing parcels; it investigated about 5 million missing persons and distributed $200 million in relief supplies to civilians. The International Red Cross won the Nobel Prize in 1917 and 1944. It works through the International Committee (1880), made up of 25 Swiss citizens. Over 100 national Red Cross societies (Red Crescent in Muslim countries) carry out peacetime relief and public health work.

Red deer (*Cervus elaphus*), member of the deer family, native to Europe, Asia, and North Africa. They are named for the color of their coat, which is reddish-brown in summer, fading to grayish-brown in winter. The American elk is classified as a subspecies of red deer. Male red deer are called harts, standing 3.5-4.5 ft (1.-1.4 m) tall, weighing 250-350 lb (113-159 kg), and sporting multibranched antlers, which are shed each year. Female red deer, called hinds, are smaller than harts and do not have antlers.

Red drum *see:* Redfish.

Redfield, Robert (1897-1958), U.S. cultural anthropologist best known for his comparative studies of cultures, and for his active support of racial integration.
See also: Anthropology.

Redfish, name for several types of popular gamefish found off the Atlantic coasts of North America. Known as red drum, channel bass, California sheepshead, red (sockeye) salmon, or by other names, the most popular types of redfish are found in the Gulf of Mexico and adjoining waterways. The gulf species are marked by a distinctive red spot near the base of the tail; they grow to 5 ft (1.5 m) long and usually weigh up to 40 lb (18 kg). Widespread restaurant demand for redfish in the late 1980s resulted in such large commercial catches that federal restrictions were imposed to protect the species.

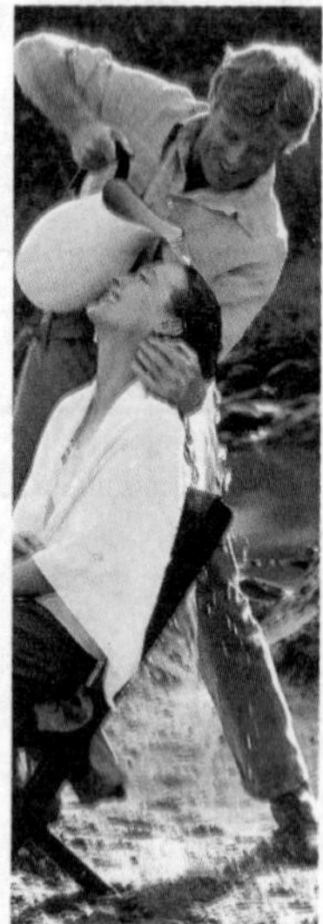
Robert Redford with Meryl Streep in a scene from Out of Africa *(1985)*

Redford, Robert (1937-), U.S. actor and director, winner of the Academy Award for best director (1980) for *Ordinary People.* He made his film debut in *War Hunt* (1962), and his best-known roles include *Butch Cassidy and the Sundance Kid* (1969), *The Sting* (1973), *All the President's Men* (1976), *The Electric Horseman* (1979), *The Natural* (1984), *Out of Africa* (1985), and *Havana* (1990). His Utah ranch, Sundance, is a ski resort and school for film arts.

Red fox *see:* Fox.

Redgrave, Sir Michael (1908-85), English actor. An accomplished Shakespearean performer, Redgrave was a noted stage director and appeared in many contemporary plays and more than 50 movies, including *The Lady Vanishes* (1938), *Dead of Night* (1946), *The Importance of Being Earnest* (1952), and *The Loneliness of the Long Distance Runner* (1962). Redgrave was knighted by Queen Elizabeth II in 1959. He was married to Rachel Kempson, a popular stage actress; their daughters, Vanessa and Lynn, became famous actresses in their own right.

Red gum *see:* Sweet gum.

Red Jacket (Sagoyewatha; 1758?-1830), Seneca chief named for the red coat he wore when an English ally in the Revolution. Later an ally of the United States in the War of 1812, he strongly opposed European customs and Christianity for his people in New York.

Redmond, John Edward (1856-1918), Irish politician. He succeeded Charles Stewart Parnell as Irish nationalist leader in the British parliament and secured the passage of the 1914 Home Rule bill. After the repression of the 1916 Easter Rising, he lost power to the revolutionary Sinn Fein movement.
See also: Ireland; United Kingdom.

Redon, Odilon (1840-1916), French painter and engraver associated with the Symbolists. His oil paintings, usually of flowers and full of color and light, contrasted with bizarre lithographs such as *The Cyclops* (1898).

Red pepper *see:* Capsicum.

Redpoll, small bird (*Acanthis flammea*) of the finch family. Redpolls are commonly found in northern North America and migrate as far south as California and the Carolinas. Both males and females have reddish crowns; the male also has a rosy-pink breast. Adult redpolls feed on plant buds and insects. They build their nests in bushes and small trees and line them with feathers. Usually 5-7 blue speckled eggs are laid at a time.

Red River, river that rises in northern Texas and flows southeast to join the Mississippi River between Natchez and Baton Rouge, forming most of the Oklahoma-Texas boundary. Named for its red sediment, it drains about 90,000 sq mi (233,100 sq km) and is 1,222 mi (1,967 km) long.

Red River of the North, river formed at Wahpeton, N. Dak., by the junction of the Bois de Sioux and Otter Trail rivers. About 540 mi (866 km) long, it flows north as the North Dakota-Minnesota boundary and enters Manitoba, Canada, emptying into Lake Winnipeg. It drains some 43,500 sq mi (112,665 sq km) of rich wheatlands.

Red Sea, sea separating the Arabian Peninsula from the northeastern region of Africa. It extends some 1,300 mi (2,090 km) from the Bab al-Mandab strait by the Gulf of Aden in the south to the gulfs of Suez (with the Suez Canal) and Aqaba in the North. It is up to 250 mi (402 km) wide and up to 7,800 ft (2,377 m) deep.

Red shift, increase in wavelength of the light from an object (toward the red end of the visible spectrum), usually caused by its rapid recession. The spectra of distant galaxies show marked red shifts; this is usually, though far from always, interpreted as implying that they are rapidly receding from us.
See also: Quasar.

Red snapper *see:* Snapper.

Red Square *see:* Moscow.

Redstart, bird (*Setophaga ruticilla*) of the wood warbler family. Adult males have black plumage with brilliant orange-red or salmon-red streaks; females and young birds are brown and dull yellow. They are found throughout most of North America and in winter migrate to the Caribbean region and northern South America. Eggs, usually laid in groups of 4 or 5, are creamy white with reddish-brown markings. Redstarts' diets consist mostly of insects.

Red tape, expression used to describe inaction or delay caused by official or bureaucratic inefficiency, inflexibility, or complexity, so called for the red string once used by lawyers to bind legal documents. Scottish author Thomas Carlyle (1795-1881) made the term popular.

Red tide, natural phenomenon caused by a sudden increase of microscopic reddish organisms on the surface of a body of water. Under optimum conditions, one celled organisms called dinoflagellates multiply by the millions and float on rivers, lakes, oceans, and arms of the oceans. Most red tides are harmless, but some types kill large fish and marine life by poisoning the water or using up the available oxygen supply. Why the dinoflagellate population suddenly proliferates is not completely understood, but scientists theorize that a combination of factors such as temperature, amount of sunlight, water currents, and availability of nutrients create ideal conditions for spawning. Some sea creatures feed off large numbers of the dinoflagellate colonies or eat the food the colonies thrive on, thus decreasing or ending the red tide.

Reduction, in chemistry, any process that increases the proportion of hydrogen or base-forming elements or radicals in a compound. Reduction is also the gaining of electrons by an atom, an ion, or an element, thereby reducing the positive valence of that which gained the electron.
See also: Oxidation.

Red-winged blackbird *see:* Blackbird.

Redwood (*Sequoia sempervirens*), world's tallest living tree. Growing primarily in a narrow, mountainous strip along the Pacific Ocean from northern California into southern Oregon, redwoods thrive in the region's cool, foggy climate. They are closely related to the giant sequoias that grow further inland along the western slopes of the Sierra Nevadas. Coast redwoods average 200-275 ft (61-84 m) high; the tallest measured tree in the world is a redwood standing 368 ft (112 m) along Redwood Creek in Humboldt County, Calif. Redwood trunks average 8-12 ft (2.4-3.7 m) in diameter, and the wood, resistant to decay and insects, is valued by the lumbering industry for its durability. Redwoods are also among the world's oldest living things, some trees being an estimated 3,500 years old.

Redwood National Park, area in northern California of 109,207 acres (44,196 hectares), including 40 mi (64 km) of Pacific Ocean coastline, established in 1968 to preserve groves of ancient redwood trees.
See also: National Parks.

Reed, name for cosmopolitan grasses of wet ground and shallow water. They have feathery flowers, give shelter to many birds, and are used in thatching. They grow from a tangled mass of rhizomes that are hard to uproot.

Reed, John (1887-1920), U.S. journalist and radical, author of the eyewitness *Ten Days That Shook the World* (1919), which recounts the Russian October Revolution. Reed was instrumental in the creation of

the Communist Labor Party in the United States. Reed is buried in front of the Kremlin in Moscow.
See also: Russian Revolution.

Reed, Thomas Brackett (1839-1902), U.S. Republican speaker of the House of Representatives (1889-91, 1895-9) called Tsar Reed for his strong control. His "Reed Rules" (1890) are still the basis for procedure in Congress. He supported high tariffs and opposed the Spanish-American War and the annexation of Hawaii.

Reed, Walter (1851-1902), U.S. Army pathologist and bacteriologist who demonstrated (1900) the role of the mosquito *Aëdes aegypti* as a carrier of yellow fever, so enabling the disease to be controlled.
See also: Pathology; Yellow fever.

Reef *see:* Atoll; Coral.

Reference book *see:* Almanac; Dictionary; Encyclopedia.

Referendum *see:* Initiative, referendum, and recall.

Refining *see:* Metallurgy; Petroleum; Sugar cane.

Reflection, bouncing back of energy waves (e.g., light radiation, sound or water waves) from a surface. If the surface is smooth, "regular" reflection takes place, the incident and reflected wave paths lying in the same plane as, and at opposed equal angles to, the normal (a line perpendicular to the surface) at the point of reflection. Rough surfaces reflect waves irregularly, so an optically rough surface appears matt or dull, whereas an optically smooth surface looks shiny. Reflected sound waves are known as echoes.

Reflex action, automatic response of the human body to stimuli. If a part of the body such as the hand touches a hot object, it pulls away involuntarily, without conscious decision. Reflex action is caused by sensitive nerve endings transmitting messages to the brain which, in turn, sends a message about corrective action to the body part receiving the stimuli. Reflex action involves 4 stages—reception, conduction, transmission, and response—all occurring in a fraction of a second. Often the action is taken before pain is felt. Some types of reflex action can become "conditioned reflexes," in which association or anticipation, rather than actual stimulus, causes a certain reaction in the body.
See also: Nervous system.

Reformation, religious and political upheaval in western Europe in the 16th century. Primarily an attempt to reform the doctrines of the Roman Catholic church, it led to the establishment of Protestantism. Anticlericalism spread after the movements led by John Wycliffe and the Lollards in 14th-century England and by John Hus in Bohemia in the 15th century. At the same time the papacy had lost prestige due to its 70-year exile, the Babylonian Captivity at Avignon, and the 50-year Great Schism. Renaissance thought, particularly humanism, stimulated liberal views, spread by the invention of printing. Many, like Martin Luther, criticized the low moral standards of Rome and the sale of indulgences. Luther also challenged papal authority and the accepted Roman Catholic doctrines, such as transubstantiation and celibacy, and argued strongly for justification by faith. Luther's ideas spread in Germany after the Diet of Worms (1521) and after the Peasants' War, when Luther won the support of many German princes and of Denmark and Sweden. The protest made by the Lutheran princes at the Diet of Speyer (1529) provided the term *Protestant.*
The Swiss divine Huldreich Zwingli won a large following in Switzerland and southwestern Germany. He carried out radical religious reforms in Zürich, abolishing the mass. After his death (1531), John Calvin led the Swiss reform movement and set up a reformed church in Geneva. Calvin's *Institutes of the Christian Religion* (1536) had great influence, notably in Scotland, where Calvinism was led by John Knox. In France Calvin's religious followers, the Huguenots, were involved in the complex political struggles leading to the Wars of Religion (1562-98).
The Protestant movement in the Low Countries was linked with the national revolt that freed the Dutch from Roman Catholic Spain. The English Reformation was initiated by Henry VIII, who denied papal authority, dissolved and seized the wealth of the monasteries, and made the Church of England autonomous. Henry remained in doctrine a Catholic, but the influence of reformers such as Nicholas Ridley and Hugh Latimer established Protestantism under Edward VI, when Thomas Cranmer issued a new prayer book (1549). There was a Roman Catholic reaction under Mary I, but in 1558 Elizabeth I established moderate Protestantism as the basis of the English Church. The religious position of Europe as a whole, however, was not settled for another century.
See also: Luther, Martin; Protestantism.

Reform bills, 3 acts of Parliament passed in Britain during the 19th century to extend the right to vote. The first (1832) abolished rotten boroughs (localities that sent members to Parliament long after their populations had disappeared) and enfranchised industrial cities, such as Birmingham and Manchester, and the propertied middle class. The second bill (1867) gave the vote to urban dwellers, and the third (1884) extended it to agricultural workers.

Reformed churches, Protestant churches arising from the Reformation that adhere to Calvinism doctrinally and to Presbyterianism in church polity and are thus distinct from the Lutheran churches and the Church of England. They grew up especially in Switzerland, Germany, France, Holland, Scotland, Hungary, and what is now Czechoslovakia. Each had its own simple formal liturgy, and all acknowledged the Reformed Confessions. There are several Reformed Churches in the United States, the largest being the Christian Reformed Church.
See also: Calvinism; Presbyterianism; Reformation.

Reformed Church in America, offshoot of the Dutch Reformed Church of the Netherlands, based on the doctrines of John Calvin. It was formed on Manhattan Island (1628) by Dutch and Walloon settlers, and received a charter from King William III of England (1696). The Reformed Church founded Hope College in Holland, Mich.; Central College, in Pella, Ia.; and Northwestern College in Orange City, Ia. It maintains seminaries in New Brunswick, N.J. and Holland, Mich.
See also: Calvin, John.

Refraction, deviation of a ray of light passing through one transparent medium to another of different density, as for instance an object that is half in and half out of water.
See also: Light.

Refractory, nonmetallic materials that can withstand high temperatures without losing their hardness. Refractory substances include magnesite, dolomite, silica, alumina, chromite, and zirconia. Firebrick or fire clay is a common refractory, using aluminum silicates and other substances to retain their original properties. Refractories are used industrially in kilns, furnaces, and crucibles, where they line or insulate the walls of these high-heat chambers or containers. Refractories are also required in nuclear power plants, where high levels of radioactivity are capable of generating intense heat.

The appearance of reflected light depends on the surface reflecting the light. A mirror of polished metal or silvered glass reflects light in a regular manner called specular reflection (A). If the mirror has a rough or irregular surface, the reflected light wille be scattered and blurred (B).

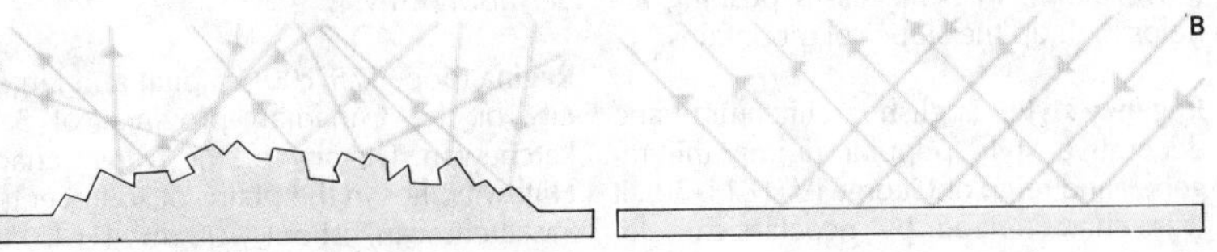

Refrigeration, removal of heat from an enclosure in order to lower its temperature. It is used for freezing water or food, for food preservation, for air conditioning, and for low-temperature chemical processes and cryogenics studies and applications. Modern refrigerators are insulated cabinets containing a compressor, which forces a refrigerant gas, such as ammonia or freon, to pass through a condenser; losing heat through condensation, the refrigerant gas goes through refrigeration coils, where it vaporizes, removing heat from the coils, and returns as a gas to the compressor for another cycle. In another system compression is accomplished by absorbing the refrigerant in a secondary fluid, such as salt water, and pumping the solution through a heat exchanger to a generator, where it is heated to drive off the refrigerant at high pressure. Other cycles, similar in principle, using steam or air, are also used.

Refugee, or displaced person, person fleeing a native country to avoid a threat or restriction. In the 20th century refugees have created a world problem. Pogroms forced Jews to leave Russia (1881-1917). In World War I Greeks and Armenians fled Turkey. About 1.5 million Russians settled in Europe after the Russian Revolution. In the 1930s Spaniards and Chinese left their respective homelands. The World War II legacy of about 8 million refugees led to the United Nations Relief and Rehabilitation Administration, replaced in 1946 by the International Refugee Organization, which in turn was succeeded by the Office of the United Nations High Commissioner for Refugees. They resettled millions of homeless from, for example, the Korean war. Many thousand Arabs who were displaced when Israel was created in 1948 still live in Middle Eastern refugee camps and are a serious political problem. The 1971 war between India and Pakistan over Bangladesh produced 9 million refugees, most of whom subsequently settled in Bangladesh. During the 1970s thousands of refugees from Southeast Asia—the "boat people"—fled to neighboring countries, many later emigrating to the United States. The refugee population of the United States was further increased in the 1980s by boatloads of Cubans and Haitians seeking asylum or economic opportunity.

Regelation, melting of ice under pressure and refreezing when the pressure is removed. When compressed, ice changes into water; when temperature conditions are at or below 32°F (O°C), it freezes again when the pressure is taken off. A large rock on frozen water gradually sinks as the pressure melts the ice directly below it, but as the rock sinks the water refreezes around it. Glaciers undergo a slow process of regelation, melting and refreezing as they move along, in some cases pushing ice fields high up the slopes of mountains.

Regency style, English architectural and decorative style popular during the regency and reign of George IV (1811-30). It was characterized by neoclassical elegance, refinement, and the use of Egyptian and Oriental forms. John Nash was the foremost architect of the period. The term also refers to the elaborate decorative style of the French Régence (1715-23).

Regeneration, in biology, regrowing of a lost or damaged part of an organism. In plants this includes the production, for instance of dormant buds and adventitious organs. All animals possess some power to regenerate, but its extent varies from that in sponges, in which all the cells in a piece of the body, almost completely separated, will come together to build up new but smaller sponges, to that in the higher animals, in which regeneration is limited to the healing of wounds.
See also: Biology.

Regent, in monarchies, person designated to rule when the rightful ruler is absent, ill, mentally incapable of ruling, or a minor. A regent may be a single member of the nation's royal family or a council of several persons in line for the succession to the crown. Throughout the history of England and other European monarchies, regents often directed the affairs of state when a child of a deposed or deceased king succeeded to the throne; other regents ruled when the rightful monarch was in exile or judged to be mentally unstable. Prior to passage of the Regency Act in England (1937), no specific guidelines existed governing the selection of a regent, and past regents were acknowledged by common consensus. In the United States, members of governing bodies of schools, higher learning facilities, and other institutions are often called regents.
See also: Monarchy.

Reggae, popular Jamaican musical style that combines U.S. rock and soul music with calypso and other Latin American rhythms. The 1973 film *The Harder They Come* introduced reggae to the United States, where performers such as Bob Marley (1945-81) won huge audiences.

Regiment, military term for what was once the largest infantry and armored division unit in an army. Regiments today, largely administrative units not assigned to combat duty, have been replaced by more mobile units called brigades. A regiment generally has groups of battalions and squadrons under its aegis, assigned to other units called divisions. The earliest units to be called regiments were French cavalry soldiers in 1558; regiments initially recruited, equipped, and trained troops for combat. In the early United States and 19th-century Europe, each regiment usually contained 10 smaller units or companies; in the 20th century companies were phased out as war became more mechanized.
See also: Army.

Regina (pop. 175,100), capital and largest city of the Canadian province of Saskatchewan. The city, on the Trans-Canada Highway, lies in the plains of southcentral Saskatchewan, about 100 mi (161 km) from the U.S. border. Founded in 1883 as the new capital of the Northwest Territories, it became the capital of the new province of Saskatchewan in 1905. The community originally bore the picturesque name Pile O'Bones, but was renamed Regina in honor of Queen Victoria. Major industries include steel and steel products, agricultural machinery, meat packing, and oil refining. The city is also the headquarters of the Saskatchewan Wheat Pool.
See also: Saskatchewan.

Regina Medal, children's literature award. Presented annually by the Catholic Library Association, the Regina Medal is awarded to an individual for a lifetime contribution to children's literature. Award winners do not have to be Catholic or American to receive the honor. The first winner was Eleanor Farjeon (1959). Other distinguished recipients have been Frederic Melcher (1962), Lois Lenski (1969), Beverly Cleary (1980), Dr. Seuss (1982), and Tomie DePaola (1983).

Regulators, movement in the western part of North Carolina (1764-71) that resisted extortion and oppression by colonial officials. After failing to effect reforms, they rose in revolt but were defeated at Allemance Creek (1771), and 6 leaders were hanged for treason.

Regulus, Marcus Atilius (d. c.249 B.C.), roman general captured in the first Punic War (255 B.C.). He was sent to Rome to deliver Carthage's peace terms, under parole to return if they were rejected. He nevertheless urged their rejection, returned, and was apparently tortured to death.
See also: Punic Wars.

Rehnquist, William Hubbs (1924-), U.S. jurist. After serving as assistant attorney general, he was appointed (1971) by President Richard M. Nixon to the U.S. Supreme Court as an associate justice, where he became a voice of conservatism. He was made chief justice in 1986.
See also: Supreme Court of the United States

Reich, German term used to designate an empire. Derived from the Old High German word *rihhi*, meaning realm, the term came into widespread use during Adolf Hitler's proclamation of a Third Reich (1933-45). The First Reich was considered to be the Holy Roman Empire (9th century-1806). The Second Reich was the German empire built by Chancellor Otto von Bismarck and Kaisers Wilhelm I and Wilhelm II (1871-1919).
See also: Germany.

Reich, Wilhelm (1897-1957), Austrian psychoanalyst who broke with Sigmund Freud over the function of sexual repression, which Reich saw as the root of neurosis. He held the controversial theory that there exists a primal life-giving force called orgone energy. His design and sale of "orgone boxes" for personal therapeutic use

led to his imprisonment for violating the Food and Drug Act.
See also: Psychoanalysis.

Reichstag, imperial parliament of the Holy Roman Empire and, from 1871 to 1945, Germany's lower legislative house (the upper house was called the Reichsrat). The ruling body of the Weimar Republic, the Reichstag lacked real power under the Nazi regime.
See also: Holy Roman Empire; Weimar Republic.

Reichswehr, German term meaning "army of the state." Set up by the German republic after World War I, it had 300,000 troops until the Treaty of Versailles reduced it to 100,000. During the Wiemar Republic (1919-33), the Reichswehr developed into a training program that enabled its ranks to swell and its combat efficiency to increase after Adolf Hitler came to power. In World War II, the Reichswehr made up the core of Hitler's army, which overran most of Europe.

Reid, Whitelaw (1837-1912), U.S. journalist, ambassador to Britain (1905-12). Editor of the *New York Tribune*, (1872-1912) he was the Republican vice-presidential candidate in 1892.

Reign of Terror, period (1793-94) during the French Revolution when fanatical Jacobin reformers, including Maximilien Robespierre, Georges Jacques Danton, and Jacques René Hébert, seized control from the Girondists. They guillotined over 2,600 "counterrevolutionaries" (including Danton and Hebert, eventually) in Paris and sanctioned "Terrors" elsewhere, notably in Nantes. The Terror ended with the guillotining of Robespierre himself in 1794.
See also: French Revolution.

Reims, or Rheims (pop. 177,200), city in northern France, about 100 mi (161 km) east of Paris on the Besle River. Dating from Roman times, it is famed for its Gothic cathedral (built 1211-1430). All but two French kings were crowned in Reims (1179-1825). Center of champagne and woolen production, it also produces chemicals, machinery, and paper.

Reincarnation, or transmigration of the soul, belief that the soul survives death and is reborn in the body of another person or living thing. It is an important concept in Buddhism, Hinduism, Jainism, Sibhism. In India, reincarnation is related to the law of karma, which dictates that a person's actions in life determine the type of body the soul will enter during reincarnation.
See also: Karma.

Reindeer, deer (genus *Rangifer*) widely distributed in arctic and subarctic regions of Europe, Asia, and North America, closely related to the caribou. Reindeer stand about 3-4 ft (90-120 cm) tall and can weigh up to 400 lb (180 kg). The Lapps of northern Scandinavia have used reindeer for food, clothing, and transportation for centuries.

Reindeer Lake, natural body of water on the Manitoba-Saskatchewan border in Canada. It is a major commercial and recreational fishing site covering 2,444 sq mi (6,330 sq km). Reindeer Lake lies 1,150 ft (350 m) above sea level in a sparsely settled region near the furthest northern reaches of the coniferous forests. Once a major link in the waterborne transit route of fur trappers and traders, the lake feeds into the Reindeer River, a tributary of the Churchill River, which flows into Hudson Bay. Important lakeshore towns are Brochet, Manitoba, and Southend and Kinoosao, Sask.

Reindeer moss (*Cladonia rangiferina*), type of lichen commonly found in the Arctic. It is a principal food source for reindeer, moose, caribou, and musk oxen; in northern Scandinavia people have used it to make bread and alcohol. A short, multi-branched plant that covers vast areas sufficient to feed large herds of grazing mammals, it grows more rapidly during the spring and fall months, aided by cool temperatures and high levels of humidity.

Reiner, Fritz (1888-1963), U.S. conductor, director of the Cincinnati Symphony (1922-31), Pittsburgh Symphony (1938-48), Metropolitan Opera (1948-53), and Chicago Symphony (1953-62).

Reinforcement *see:* Learning.

Reinhardt, Max (Max Goldmann; 1873-1943), Austrian theatrical director famous for his vast and spectacular productions—especially of *Oedipus Rex* and *Faust*—and for his elaborate and atmospheric use of stage machinery and management of crowds.

Relapsing fever, bacteria-transmitted ailment that may recur several times in the same person. Usually occurring in the tropics, relapsing fever is caused by spirochetes carried by lice and ticks, which thrive on unsanitary living conditions. Symptoms of the disease include fever, chills, headaches, muscular pain, and sometimes vomiting. An infected person may be violently ill for several days or a week, return to good health, but if not treated properly have a relapse—as many as 10-12 times. The body's natural defenses may successfully combat the disease for a time, but infected spirochetes still in the body may reinvade the bloodstream, causing relapses when the body's defenses weaken. Penicillin and other antibiotics combined with extensive bed rest is effective treatment.

Relativity, theory of the nature of space, time, and matter. Albert Einstein's special theory of relativity (1905) is based on the premise that different observers moving at a constant speed with respect to each other find the laws of physics to be identical, and,

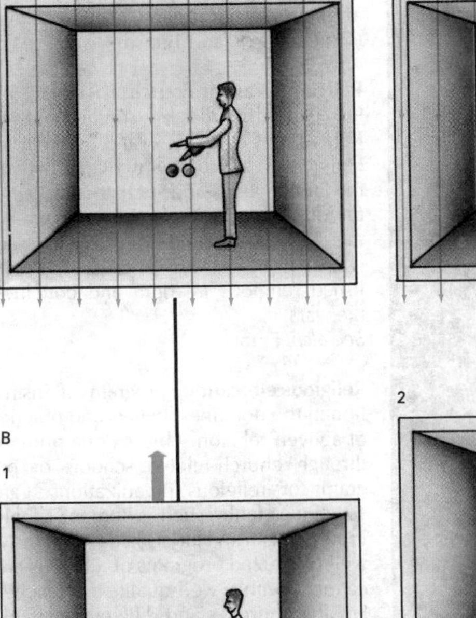

Albert Einstein's general relativity theory is a highly complex mathematical creation of the human intellect. It attempts to explain the perceptual phenomena of space, time, gravity, mass, and motion in a 4-dimensional world. It is a new way of looking at the world and has opposed some of Isaac Newton's gravitational theories. Depicted is an elementary example of how relativity works and how it differs from Newton's theories.
A1 and 2. An observer is assumed to be inside a closed, empty compartment suspended on a rope. In order to test gravity, he releases two objects and concludes that the force of gravity made both objects fall to the floor at the same speed.
B1 and 2. With relativity, one can state that if this same compartment were to rise at a constant speed, and gravity was not present at all, the observer inside would still see the objects fall to the floor. However, to an observer outside the compartment (not shown) it would appear that the rising compartment was responsible for the objects hitting the floor—not gravity. Both explanations are plausible. Einstein called this phenomena the Principle of Equivalence.

in particular, find the speed of light waves to be the same (the principle of relativity). Among its consequences are (1) that events occurring simultaneously according to one observer may happen at different times according to an observer moving relative to the first (although the order of two causally related events is never reversed), (2) that a moving object is shortened in the direction of its motion, (3) that time runs more slowly for a moving object, (4) that the velocity of a projectile emitted from a moving body is less than the sum of the relative ejection velocity and the velocity of the body, (5) that a body has a greater mass when moving than when at rest, and (6) that no massive body can travel as fast as, or faster than, the speed of light. These effects are too small to be noticed at normal velocities; they have nevertheless found ample experimental verification and are common considerations in many physical calculations.

The relationship between the position and time of a given event according to different observers is known (for H.A. Lorentz) as the Lorentz transformation. In this, time mixes on a similar footing with the three spatial dimensions, and it is in this sense that time has been called the fourth dimension. The greater mass of a moving body implies a relationship between kinetic energy and mass; Einstein made the bold additional hypothesis that *all* energy is equivalent to mass, according to the famous equation $E = mc^2$. The conversion of mass to energy is now the basis of nuclear reactors and is indeed the source of the energy of the sun itself.

Einstein's general theory (1916) is of importance chiefly to cosmologists. It asserts the equivalence of the effects of acceleration and gravitational fields and that gravitational fields cause space to become "curved," so that light no longer travels in straight lines, while the wavelength of light falls as the light falls through a gravitational field. The direct verification of these last two predictions, among others, has helped deeply to entrench the theory of relativity in the language of physics.

See also: Einstein, Albert.

Rembrandt's Saskia as Flora *(1634)*

Relief, form of sculpture in which the elements of the design, whether figures or ornament, project from their background. In *high relief* the elements stand out prominently and may even be undercut; in *low*, or *bas, relief* they hardly emerge from the plane of the background.

Relief *see:* Welfare.

Religion, system of belief to which a social group is committed, in which there is a supernatural object of awe, worship, and service. It generally provides a system of ethics and a worldview that supply a stable context within which each person can relate to others and to the world and can understand his or her own significance. Religions are found in all societies and are generally dominant (modern secularism being an exception).

Some form of religion seems to fulfill a basic human need. Some features are common to most religions: the recognition of a sacred realm from which supernatural forces operate, a mediating priesthood, the use of ritual to establish a right relationship with the holy (though ritual used to manipulate the supernatural becomes magic), and a sense of group community. Some religions have no deity as such, but are natural philosophies (e.g., Buddhism, Confucianism, and Taoism.)

Religion, Wars of, French civil wars (1562-98) caused partly by conflict between Roman Catholics and Protestant Huguenots, and partly by rivalry between the French kings and such great nobles as the dukes of Guise. The worst event was the St. Bartholomew's Day Massacre (1572). The Edict of Nantes (1598) established religious freedom and concluded the wars.

See also: France.

Religious education, program of instruction in the doctrines, beliefs and practices of a given religion. This is done primarily through church-related schools or programs or religious organizations. Large sanctioned faiths, such as Roman Catholic, Protestantism and Judaism, have extensive, well-organized programs of religious education with well-qualified teachers. Smaller churches and religious sects may offer informal systems of teaching their beliefs, often in members' homes. Religious education usually uses books (primarily the Bible), visuals, and oral transmissions of doctrine. Persons planning to teach religious education must often undergo a formal program of study.

Religious festivals *see:* Holiday.

Religious life, lifestyle voluntarily chosen by persons to enhance their own spirituality. People who adopt this way of life for becoming holy and for being of the greatest service to others include monks, nuns, brothers, sisters, priests, and ministers. A religious life may be followed and practiced by individuals on their own, or within the organized framework of an established practice or religious order. Roman Catholic religious followers take vows of poverty and chastity and may belong to a religious order to practice their beliefs in a public place, such as a church. Other religions, such as Hinduism and Buddhism, sponsor monastic orders, although many Hindu and Buddhist holy men and women practice a religious life as individuals. Some Protestant faiths have established orders, but most Protestant ministers, as do Islamic and Jewish religious leaders, impart the knowledge acquired during their religious lives to their congregations.

Religious Society of Friends *see:* Quakers.

Remarque, Erich Maria (1898-1970), German-born novelist famous for his powerful antiwar novel *All Quiet on the Western Front* (1929), describing the horror of the trenches in World War I. In 1932 Remarque emigrated to Switzerland, later becoming a U.S. citizen. Other works include *Arch of Triumph* (1946).

Rembrandt (Rembrandt Harmenszoon van Rijn; 1606-69), Dutch painter and etcher. Born and trained in Leiden, he moved to Amsterdam in 1631 and achieved recognition with a group portrait, *The Anatomy Lesson* (1632). Adapting the styles of Caravaggio, Hals, and Rubens, his painting became, during 1632-42, Baroque in style, as in *Saskia as Flora* (1634), *Blinding of Samson* (1636), and *The Night Watch* (1642). The years 1643-56 were notable for his magnificent drawings and etchings, predominantly of New Testament themes, such as *The Three Crosses* (1653-61). From the mid-1650s his painting was more solemn and spiritual in mood and richer in color, as shown in portraits (*Jan Six*, 1654, *The Syndics of the Amsterdam Cloth Hall*, 1662), a series of moving self-portraits, and religious paintings like *David and Saul* (c.1658).

Remington, Frederic (1861-1909), U.S. painter, sculptor and writer chiefly known for his portrayals of the Old West, where he traveled extensively. His paintings, usually of Native Americans, cowboys, and horses, skillfully convey violent action and are notable for authenticity of detail.

Remora, warmwater fish (family Echeneidae) that feeds off other marine animals. A remora uses an oval disc at the top of its head as a suction cup to attach itself to a host animal—usually a shark, whale, sea turtle, or other large marine animal—and is carried along with them as they swim. Ranging 7 in (17 cm) to 3.5 ft

(110 cm) in length, remoras enjoy a symbiotic relationship with the animals they attach themselves to, eating leftover scraps of food not eaten by the hosts while removing parasites from the hosts. Some remoras cling to the hulls of ships and boats.

Remote control, control of a system from a distance. It can range from a television set to a guided missile or satellite, over a few feet or thousands of miles. Types of remote control include radio, infrared, ultrasonic, laser, electrical, human voice, and mechanical. Radio-controlled motorboats used by the German Navy in World War I (1914-18) were the first machines operated by remote control. Today some robots are run by remote control.

Remote sensing, information-gathering process that operates independently of physical contact with the object being studied. Modern technology has developed complex forms of remote sensing through the use of electronic sensors that pick up and transmit visual images. Television is a form of remote sensing, and TV cameras are used in spacecraft to receive and translate visual data about Earth or the celestial body being studied. Satellites convey meteorologic conditions of the atmosphere or geologic conditions of the earth's surface or underground resources. Radar and sonar use sound to detect physical objects. Some sensors detect infrared (heat) rays sent out by the earth; the information is translated by computer into color images that scientists can interpret.

REM sleep *see:* Sleep.

Remus *see:* Romulus and Remus.

Renaissance (French, "rebirth" or "revival"), transitional period between the Middle Ages and modern times (1350-1650). The term was first applied by the Swiss historian Jakob Burckhardt in 1860. The Renaissance saw the Reformation challenge the unity and supremacy of the Roman Catholic Church, along with the rise of humanism, the growth of large nation-states with powerful kings, far-ranging voyages of exploration, and a new emphasis on the importance of the individual.
The origins of the Renaissance are disputed, but its first flowering occurred in Italy. In the world of learning a new interest in secular Latin literature can be detected in early 14th century, and by the middle of the century Petrarch and Giovanni Boccaccio were searching for old texts and self-consciously cultivating a prose style modeled on Cicero. They inaugurated an age of research and discovery in which the humanists ransacked the monastic libraries of Europe for old manuscripts, and scholars like Desiderius Erasmus set new standards in learning and critical scholarship. Greek was also studied, particularly after the fall of Constantinople (1453) drove many Greek scholars to the West. The invention of printing (1440) and the discovery of the New World (1492) by Columbus gave further impetus to the search for knowledge.
The Renaissance marked the end of feudalism and the rise of national governments, for example, in Spain under Ferdinand II of Aragon, in France under Francis I, in England under Henry VIII and Elizabeth. In Italy, however, independent city states engaged in fierce rivalry, providing Niccolò Machiavelli with his notorious "ideal" of a Renaissance prince. Prosperous trading provided money for the arts, and princes like Cosimo de'Medici eagerly patronized artists, musicians, and scholars. Renaissance painting and sculpture flourished in Florence and Rome with the works of Sandro Botticelli, Leonardo da Vinci, Michelangelo, and Raphael. Literary revivals occurred in England, France, and Spain; William Shakespeare and Edmund Spenser were prominent in Renaissance English literature, and some of the finest French writing came from François Rabelais and Pierre de Ronsard. In science the findings of the astronomers Nicolaus Copernicus and Galileo Galilei were the basis of modern astronomy and marked a turning point in scientific and philosophical thought.

René of Anjou (1409-80), duke of Anjou and Provence. He inherited a claim to the kingdom of Naples (1435) but was defeated by Alfonso V of Aragon in 1442. His daughter, Margaret of Anjou, married Henry VI of England. René's court at Angers in France was a brilliant cultural center.

Reni, Guido (1575-1642), Italian baroque painter. He developed an elegant classical style, using light tones, for religious and mythological themes, such as *Aurora* (1613) and *Baptism of Christ* (1623).
See also: Baroque.

Reno (pop. 254,667), second-largest city in Nevada and a major resort and gambling center. Situated on the Truckee River, 14 mi (22.5 km) from the California state line, the city was founded in 1868 and incorporated in 1879. Legalized gambling in Nevada brings thousands of tourists to Reno every year, and liberal Nevada laws on divorce have also made Reno a well-known divorce center. The main campus of the University of Nevada is located on hills overlooking the city. Not far from Reno are Lake Tahoe and a number of other noted recreation areas.
See also: Nevada.

Reno, Marcus Albert (1834-89), U.S. Army officer during and after the Civil War. Reno was supposed to go to the aid of Colonel George A. Custer in the Battle of the Little Bighorn (1876). After Custer's defeat Reno was accused of cowardice. Reno claimed that he had been forced to retreat and was thus unable to help Custer. A military court exonerated him (1879), but one year later Reno received a dishonorable discharge for conduct unbecoming of an officer. In 1967 the Army reversed the decision and changed the record to reflect an honorable discharge.

Renoir, Jean (1894-1979), French film director, son of Pierre Auguste Renoir. His motion pictures are characterized by a sensitive feeling for atmosphere and a strong pictorial sense. *La Grande Illusion* (1937) and *The Rules of the Game* (1939) are two of his most important works.

Renoir, Pierre Auguste (1841-1919), French Impressionist painter. He started painting—with Claude Monet, Camille Pissarro, and Alfred Sisley—scenes of Parisian life, such as *La Grenouillère* (1869) and *The Swing* (1876), using vibrant luminous colors. Later he became mostly interested in figure painting, usually large female nudes set in rich landscapes. One of his best-known works is *Luncheon of the Boating Party* (1881).

Pierre Auguste Renoir

Rent, in law, the price a tenant pays for the use of another's property. In economics, rent means any income or yield from something capable of producing wealth. In general usage, the term covers the monetary return from anything from real estate to cars and computers.

Reparations, term applied since World War I to monetary compensation demanded by victorious nations for material losses suffered in war. In 1919 Germany was required to pay enormous reparations to the Allies (although the United States subsequently waived all claim). After World War II, reparations were exacted from Germany and Japan.

Repeal, act of nullifying or removing a law or constitutional amendment from the books. This can be done by legislative action in several ways—either by directly stating that a certain law is repealed (express repeal) or by passing a new law that makes clear it supercedes the previous one (repeal by implication). Sometimes legislative bodies employ both types of repeal to avoid confusion. In U.S. history, the 18th Amendment (1919) that prohibited the sale and manufacture of alcoholic beverages was repealed through the enactment of the 21st Amendment (1933).

Repin, Ilya Yefimovich (1844-1930), Russian painter. His realistic paintings often expressed criticism of the Russian social order during the late 19th century.

Representative government *see:* Democracy; Republic.

Representatives, House of *see:* House of Representatives.

Repression *see:* Psychoanalysis.

Reprieve, in criminal law, the postponement of a sentence that has been imposed by the courts. The term is usually used to refer to a stay of execution when the death sentence is involved and is often granted to allow the investigation of new evidence in a case.

Renaissance religious reform without the approval of the pope was a dangerous activity. A painting depicting the burning of the Dominican monk Girolamo Savonarola and two of his followers in the Piazza della Signoria in Florence on May 23, 1498.

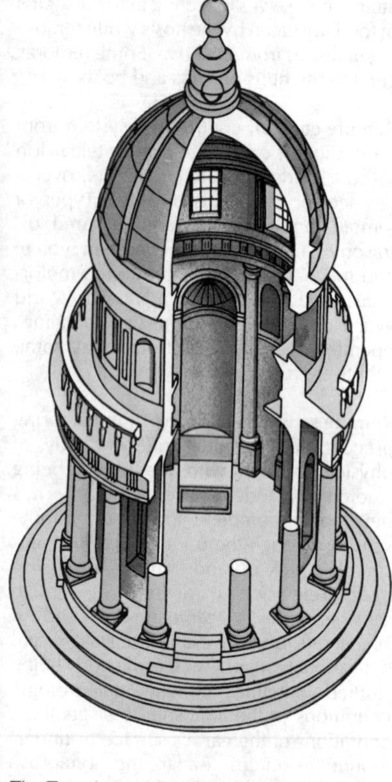

The Tempietto of San Pietro in Montorio, Rome, designed by Donato Bramante. This chapel was built to commemorate the site of St. Peter's crucifixion. With its emphasis on architectural volume, not space, it marks the beginnings of High Renaissance in Rome.

A perspective study by the greatest intellect of the Renaissance Leonardo Da Vinci

One of the most important thinkers of the Renaissance, the Christian humanist Desiderius Erasmus. Portrait of Erasmus painted by his friend Hans Holbein the Younger

Great patron of Renaissance scholars, the Florentine grand duke Cosimo de' Medici, depicted in a bronze bust by Benvenuto Cellini (1450)

The Villa Rotunda (16th century) in Vicenza, Italy, designed by Andrea Palladio (1508-80). The columns and triangular keystones of this building were influenced by the architecture of the ancient Greeks, a major inspiration for Renaissance architects.

Reproduction, process by which an organism produces offspring. In asexual reproduction parts of an organism split off to form new individuals; the process is found in some animals but is more common in plants: e.g., the fission of single-celled plants; the budding of yeasts; the fragmentation of filamentous algae; spore production in bacteria, algae, and fungi; and the production of vegetative organs in flowering plants (bulbs, rhizomes, and tubers). In sexual reproduction, special (haploid) cells containing half the normal number of chromosomes, called gametes, are produced: in animals, sperm by males in the testes and ova by females in the ovary; in plants, pollen by males in the stamens and ovules by females in the ovary. The joining of gametes (fertilization, or conception) produces a (diploid) cell with the normal number of chromosomes, the zygote, which grows to produce an individual with genes inherited from both parents. Fertilization may take place inside the female (internal fertilization) or outside (external fertilization). Internal fertilization demands that sperm be introduced into the female —insemination by copulation— and is advantageous because the young spend the most vulnerable early stages of their life histories protected inside the mother.

Reptile, cold blooded vertebrate with dry, scaly skin. Reptiles can be found in a wide variety of habitats, including the sea and points north of the Arctic Circle, but most live in the tropics. There are no reptiles in Antarctica. There are about 6,000 species of reptiles. They range in size from 2 in (5 cm) to 30 ft (9 m). They breathe through lungs and are cold blooded, meaning that their body temperatures vary with external conditions making it necessary for reptiles to seek conditions favorable to their metabolisms. Most reptiles lay eggs. Certain snakes and lizards retain the eggs in their bodies until the young hatch, and they are born live. The major species of reptiles are lizards and snakes, turtles, crocodilians, and tuatoras. The last are related to the now-extinct dinosaurs and live on islands off the coast of New Zealand. Lizards and snakes account for some 3,000 species, among them certain venomous types. The turtles comprise some 250 species and some are among the longest lived of all animals. Crocodilians include alligators, caymans, crocodiles, and gavials, about 20 species altogether. Most reptiles live by eating other animals and are descendants of the dinosaurs, or giant reptiles.

Reptiles, Age of *see:* Dinosaur; Prehistoric animal.

Republic (from Latin *res publica*, "thing of the people"), form of government in which the head of state is not a monarch (and today is usually a president). Popularly, the idea of a republic includes the notion of elected representation and democratic control by the people, although many present-day governments that do not meet this requirement call themselves republics.
See also: Democracy.

Republican Party, one of the two major political parties of the United States. It is sometimes called the G.O.P., which stands for Grand Old Party, a nickname dating from the 19th century. It was founded in 1854 by dissidents of the Whig, Democratic, and Free Soil parties to unify the growing antislavery forces. Its first national nominating convention was held in 1856; J.C. Frémont was adopted as presidential candidate. Campaigning for the abolition of slavery and of polygamy in the territories, he captured 11 states. Abraham Lincoln became the first Republican president, and in spite of the unpopularity of the post-Civil War Reconstruction policies and the secession of the Liberal Republican Party in 1872, the Republicans remained dominant in U.S. politics, winning 14 out of 18 presidential elections between 1860 and 1932. In an era of scandal, the Republicans consolidated a "probusiness" and "conservative" reputation with the nomination and election of William McKinley in 1896. His successor, Theodore Roosevelt, adopted a progressive stance; he defected to the Bull Moose Party in 1912. In 1932 the Democrats swept to power, not to be dislodged until the election of the Republican Dwight D. Eisenhower in 1952. His successors, John F. Kennedy and Lyndon Johnson, were Democrats, but Richard Nixon's landslide victory in 1972 marked a zenith of party strength. The Watergate scandal shattered this, contributing to the defeat of Gerald Ford in the 1976 elections. The Republicans rallied again in 1980 to elect Ronald Reagan president and to capture control of the Senate. In 1988 the Republican George Bush was elected president. Bush was succeeded by the Democrat Bill Clinton in 1993, who had to face a Republican majority in Congress from 1994. In 1996 the Republican candidate Bob Dole lost the presidential elections against Clinton.

Research, use of appropriate methods to discover new knowledge, develop new applications of existing knowledge, or explore relationships between ideas or events. Scientific discoveries, technological achievements, and scholarly publications are the fruits of research. Research always involves three basic steps; the formulation of a problem, the collection and analysis of relevant information, and an attempt to discover a solution or otherwise resolve the problem based on evidence.

Reserpine ($C_{33}H_{40}N_2O_9$), tranquilizing drug used to treat mild forms of hypertension (high blood pressure). Extracted from the roots of the Rauwolfia serpentina plant of India and Southeast Asia, reserpine was isolated in 1952. It came into Western medical usage to calm mental patients in 1953. For centuries, the powdered whole root had been used in India to treat the mentally ill. Since the 1960s, more effective drugs have superseded it, but low doses of reserpine are still used to relieve minor cases of hypertension.

Reservation *see:* Indian reservation; Native Americans.

Reserve Officers Training Corps (ROTC), U.S. Army recruiting project that holds courses in military leadership in schools and colleges. It grew out of the Land Grant Act of 1862 and began operating full scale under the National Defense Act of 1916. It comprises two to four years of course work and drill plus several weeks of field training. The U.S. Navy and Air Force have similar programs.
See also: Army, U.S.

Reservoir, body of water or receptacle used for storing large supplies of water. Reservoirs are most often manmade lakes, caused by damming up rivers and streams or dredging a basin into a flat stretch of land; water towers and holding tanks atop buildings are also reservoirs. Whether manmade or natural lakes, reservoirs usually supply drinking water to cities and towns, and are used to irrigate, supply power, or control flooding. Water is drawn from reservoirs through pipes (aqueducts) and in some cases is pumped hundreds of miles away.

Resin, high-molecular-weight substance characterized by its gummy or tacky consistency at certain temperatures. Naturally occurring resins include congo copal and bitumen (found as fossils), shellac (from insects), and rosin (from pine trees). Natural Resins have for the most part been replaced by synthetic resins.
See also: Resin, synthetic.

Resin, synthetic, industrial chemical compound made up of many simple molecules linked together to form large, complex molecules. Most plastics and polymers are a form of synthetic resin. Complicated chemical processes are used to convert petroleum, coal, water, air, and wood into more complex chemicals, such as alcohol, phenol, ammonia, and formaldehyde; these, in turn, are combined to form synthetic resins. The first totally synthetic resin was Bakelite, which was produced by L.H. Baekeland in 1910 from phenol and formaldehyde. The work in the 1920s of H. Staudinger on the polymeric nature of natural rubber and styrene resin, which laid the theoretical basis for polymer science, was a major factor in stimulating the extremely rapid development of a wide range of synthetic plastics and resins. Resins have a wide variety of uses in manufactured goods for which durability and flexibility are required, and are also used in paints, adhesives and coatings for cloth, metal, and paper.
See also: Plastic.

Resorcinol ($C_6H_4[OH]_2$), compound used to manufacture resins, dyes, medical products, and other chemical compounds. A phenol, it is produced by fusing benzenedisulfonic acid with sodium hydroxide (caustic soda). A key agent in commercial skin-treatment products, resorcinol is often added to external skin-treatment lotions and ointments and is an effective antibacterial, antifungal treatment. Dermatologists use it to treat acne and eczema. Resorcinol is also used to make eosin, a dye used in red ink, and is useful in photographic developers.

Resources, natural *see:* Natural resources.

Respighi, Ottorino (1879-1936), Italian composer, director (1924-26) of the Accademia di Santa Cecilia in Rome. He is best-known for tone poems, such as *The Fountains of Rome* (1917) and *The Pines of Rome* (1924).

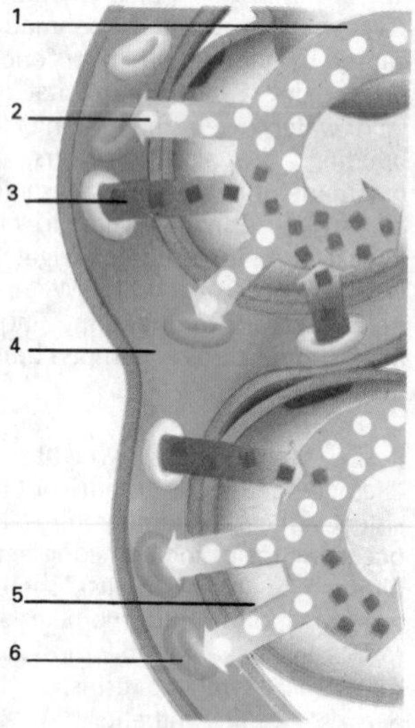

Human external respiration (the exchange of oxygen and carbon dioxide between the lungs and the blood) takes place in tiny air sacs called alveoli (5), which are found in the lungs. Within the walls of each alveolus are tiny blood vessels called capillaries (4). The alveoli's air stream (1) contains much oxygen (2) and little carbon dioxide (3), while the blood entering the capillaries is low in oxygen and high in carbon dioxide. The carbon dioxide is exhaled with the air, and the inhaled oxygen passes into the blood (6). The arrows indicate this exchange through the walls of the capillaries.

Respiration, term applied to several activities and processes involving the exchange of gases with the environment, occurring in all animals and plants. Breathing movements, if any, and the exchange of oxygen and carbon dioxide, may be called external respiration, while energy-releasing processes at the cellular level are termed "internal respiration," or tissue respiration. Air, which contains about 20% oxygen, is drawn into the lungs (inspiration) via the nose or mouth, the pharynx, trachea, and bronchi. Expiration is usually a passive process of relaxation of the chest wall and diaphragms allowing the release of the air, which is depleted of oxygen and enriched with carbon dioxide. Exchange of gases with the blood circulating in the pulmonary capillaries occurs by diffusion across the lung alveoli. Disorders of respiration include lung disease (e.g., emphysema, pneumonia and pneumoconiosis), muscle and nerve disease (e.g., brain-stem stroke, poliomyelitis, myasthenia gravis, and muscular dystrophy, skeletal deformity, asphyxias, and disorders secondary to metabolic and heart disease. Tissue respiration involves the combination of oxygen with glucose or other nutrients to form high-energy compounds. This reaction also produces carbon dioxide and water.

Respirator, machine that aids the respiratory process in human beings, especially in extreme circumstances when a patient has difficulty breathing normally or if breathing stops altogether. Some respirators administer oxygen directly to the patient. Hospitals, mobile medical units, and other treatment facilities constantly monitor respirators to ensure proper breathing in patients hooked up to them. Portable respirators, attended by qualified personnel, may be used in a patient's home or room in an extended-care facility (nursing home). Positive-pressure respirators force or assist the flow of air into the lungs. Negative-pressure types, such as the "iron lung," create a vacuum that causes the chest to expand, thus inhaling air.

Respiratory distress syndrome *see:* Hyaline membrane disease.

Respiratory system *see:* Respiration.

Restaurant, food-and-drink facility that serves the public. Some 130 million meals are served daily in the United States 300,000 restaurants. Table-service restaurants seat patrons; they have a meal brought to them or can serve themselves at a buffet (cafeteria). Ethnic restaurants are table-service facilities that specialize in the food of a particular country or ethnic group. Other unusual (gourmet) food is sold in more highly specialized restaurants. Fast-service restaurants are characterized by large-scale production of food items, inexpensive prices, and quick service. Some provide tables but no table service for their customers. Food is ordered and paid for at a counter.

Restigouche River, river in northeastern Canada, more than 100 mi (160 km) long, forming part of the boundary between Quebec and New Brunswick. Abundant trout and salmon attract many commercial and sports fishermen to the Restigouche. The name is derived from a Native American term, translated as "the river that divides like a hand," referring to the five main branches of the river. Much of it flows swiftly through dense, sparsely inhabited wilderness before widening into a broad estuary at its mouth in Chaleur Bay, an arm of the Gulf of St. Lawrence.

Restoration, name given to the return of Charles II as king of England in 1660, after the fall of the protectorate. Coinciding with a national mood of reaction against the Puritans, the Restoration was widely popular. The Restoration period (1660 to the fall of James II, in 1688) was one of irreverent wit, licentiousness, and scientific and literary achievement. Politically, it was a period of uneasy relations between king and parliament, culminating in the Glorious Revolution (1688-89).
See also: Glorious Revolution.

Resurrection, act of God believed to restore life in perfected form to the dead. Many faiths believe resurrection—in physical or spiritual form—will come in the final days of the earth's existence when all people will stand as equals before God and be judged for their deeds in life. In Christianity, the Resurrection refers specifically to the return of Jesus after his crucifixion and the belief that his triumph over death was a spiritual redemption for all humanity. Those who follow his beliefs and practices in their own lives expect to be similarly resurrected and redeemed after their deaths. Easter is a Christian celebration of Jesus's resurrection, said to have occurred 2 days after his death on Good Friday.
See also: Religion.

Resurrection plant, one of several species of plants that curl up when dry but turn green when exposed to water. The rose of Jericho (*Anastatica hierochuntica*), a member of the mustard family, grows from seeds and, when dry, loses its leaves and curls up into a ball. The wind carries the balls, thus scattering the seeds. Another plant, also called the rose of Jericho (*Selaginella lepidophylla*), a member of the selaginella family, is most commonly found in the arid regions of the Middle East and North Africa. It reproduces by microscopic spores.

Resuscitator *see:* Respirator.

Retailing, selling of merchandise or services to the public. When a business sells at retail prices, that means it buys its goods or services from a supplier, usually a wholesaler, or directly from the factory. The business then sells the goods to consumers at a higher price designed to make a profit for the business. Specialty stores sell particular types of product and accessories, such as shoes, clothes, jewelry, or books. Department stores offer a wide variety of items in separate areas (departments) of the store. Discount stores sell their inventory at prices below normal retail prices. Supermarkets sell food and other household products. Chain stores are those under the same name or ownership in 2 or more locations. Nonstore retailing involves selling goods by mail order, telephone, vending machines, and door-to-door methods.

Retainer, in law, agreement between an attorney and client for legal representation. A retainer can be a formal or special type, in which the lawyer agrees to represent a client on a particular case, or it can be a special retainer, in which the lawyer agrees to act on behalf of the client when necessary. A retaining fee paid by a client to an attorney is also called a retainer. Once a retainer, either general or special, is agreed to, the attorney has a legal obligation to represent the client to the best of his or her abilities. The attorney cannot act on behalf of the opposing party or parties in a legal action.

Retardation *see:* Mental retardation.

Retina *see:* Eye.

Retriever, breed of sporting dog trained to search out and bring back small game shot by hunters. Easily trainable, retrievers are excellent swimmers with water-resistant coats and a highly developed sense of smell. The popular golden retriever and the Labrador retriever can also be trained as guide dogs for blind persons and the hearing-impaired. Other recognized breeds are the Chesapeake Bay, curly-coated, and flat-coated retrievers.

Reunion, volcanic island covering 970 sq mi (2,512 sq km) in the West Indian Ocean. Discovered in the early 1500s by the Portuguese, Reunion has been a French possession since 1642 and an overseas department of France since 1946. The islanders, mostly of mixed descent, are nearly all Roman Catholic and speak a Creole patois. Its products include sugar, rum, corn, and vanilla. The capital is Saint-Denis. A 36-member elected council governs the city.

Reuter, Baron de (Paul Julius von Reuter; 1816-99), German-born founder of Reuters, the worldwide news agency. He pioneered the use of the newly invented telegraph to transmit news between major European cities and, later, to other continents via underseas cables. In 1849 he set up a carrier pigeon service between Aachen, Germany, and Brussels, Belgium. In 1851 he moved to London, where he opened a telegraph office near the Stock Exchange and reported on European financial news, expanding to other types of news events. Several major daily newspapers subscribed to his supplying service, and over the years he expanded it throughout Europe and the world.

Reuters, one of the largest international news agencies, based in Britain, that distributes information to local agencies, newspapers, television, and radio to more than 150 countries. Founded by Baron de Reuter in Germany in 1849, it moved to London in 1851. Reuters expanded its coverage from financial to general news in 1858. Today it is a trust owned mainly by the British press.
See also: Reuter, Baron de.

Reuther, Walter Philip (1907-70), U.S. labor leader, president of the United Automobile Workers from 1946 until his death, and important labor spokesperson. Reuther was president of the Congress of Industrial Organizations (CIO, 1952-56) and one of the architects of its merger with the American Federation of Labor (AFL), becoming vice president of the combined organization.

Revelation, Book of, or Apocalypse, the last book of the New Testament. Traditionally ascribed to St. John the Apostle, it was probably written by another John, and dated c.96. It is addressed to people being persecuted. After 7 letters to the Asia Minor churches, it contains a series of apocalyptic visions in Old Testament imagery, giving a Christian philosophy of world history.
See also: New Testament.

Revels, Hiram Rhodes (1827-1901), pastor, educator, and first black U.S. senator. Elected by the Republicans in Mississippi for 1870-71, he was subsequently involved in state politics and became president of Alcorn College, Lorman, Miss. As a minister (1845) of the African Methodist Episcopal Church, Revels helped establish black churches and schools in the Midwest and South.

Revenue, internal *see:* Internal revenue.

Revenue sharing, return of U.S. tax revenues to the state and local governments. The State and Local Fiscal Assistance Act of 1972, supported by President Richard M. Nixon, appropriated $30.1 billion for this financial aid. No conditions were attached to state uses; local governments chose from 7 broad categories. The program, representing a political revolution in the relationship between the federal and state governments, was renewed in 1976 and 1980.

Revere (pop. 42,423), resort suburb on Massachusetts Bay, north of Boston. Primarily a residential city, Revere has popular beach attractions, including a dog-racing track, but little industry. Founded in the late 1620s as Rumney Marsh, it was part of Boston (1632-1739), then Chelsea, until it became the incorporated city of North Chelsea (1846). To honor the celebrated Boston patriot Paul Revere, it was renamed in 1871.
See also: Massachusetts.

Revere, Paul (1735-1818), American Revolutionary hero, immortalized by the poet Henry Wadsword Longfellow for "Paul Revere's Ride" from Boston to Lexington (April 18, 1775) to warn the Massachusetts minutemen that the British were coming. A silversmith and engraver, he joined in the Boston Tea Party in 1773. During the Revolutionary War he served the new government, designing and producing the first Continental money, casting official seals, and supervising gunpowder and cannon manufacture. After the War he became a prosperous merchant known for his copper and silver work, much of which is still copied today, and his bronze bells. Revere also was the first American to discover the method of rolling sheet copper, and constructed the first U.S. copper-rolling mill.
See also: Revolutionary War in America.

Reversing Falls of Saint John, natural wonder at the mouth of the St. John River in Saint John, New Brunswick, Canada. High tide in the Bay of Fundy at the river's mouth forces the water's current to flow backward over the falls, a 14-ft (3.7-m) drop in the river's elevation. During low tide, the river flows over the falls through a narrow gorge into the bay. But at high tide, when the water in the bay reaches its maximum level, a rushing tide (bore) sweeps in and raises the level of the river to the exact height of the drop. The rush of water backward over the falls gives the site its name.

Revivalism, in religion, emphasis on personal experience and salvation of the soul. This form of worship is often characterized by emotionally charged gospel preaching that is extemporaneous and requires audience participation. Revivalism began in Europe in the 1700s and spread quickly to North America in a series of "Great Awakenings." Prayer meetings, outdoor services, often called camp meetings, and tent meetings, or chautauquas, were practiced widely in the 1800s and early 1900s, much less so today. Itinerant preachers would travel from town to town with their entourages, set up tents, and exhort congregations to receive eternal salvation for their souls. Today, revivalism is practiced primarily by organized, denominational churches, principally Baptist and Methodist, many of whom broadcast their congregations' services to at-home audiences as well.
See also: Great Awakening.

Revolution, fundamental change in the form or nature of a government or societal way of life. A revolution can be a violent one that completely changes a form of government, such as the Russian Revolution (1917). It can also be nonviolent yet have a profound effect on the lives of people, such as the Industrial Revolution or other great changes brought on by technological innovations. Political revolutions usually occur when an outspoken leader or faction is able to capitalize on widespread dissatisfaction with an existing ruler or governing system. Some political revolutions have been nonviolent, with popular opposition forcing a decisive change, while other revolutions have resulted in large numbers of casualties and extensive property damage.

Revolutionary War in America (1775-1783), also known as the American Revolution, in which Britain's 13 North American colonies lying along the Atlantic seaboard won their independence. It was a minor war at the time that had immense consequences later—the founding of a new nation, the United States of America.
The background. Differences in life, thought, and interests had developed between England and its small colonies in America throughout the 18th century. Beginning in 1763, after the French had been defeated in the New World, Britain took steps to increase its control over the colonies and to enforce more strictly the Navigation Acts, which had been designed to regulate colonial commerce in Britain's favor. England did this in conformity with the prevailing theory of the time that colonies existed solely for the benefit of the mother country (*mercantilism*). In addition, the Proclamation of 1763, issued by King George III, limited the expansion of the American colonies to the Appalachian Mountains. In 1764, the British Parliament, led by the king's chief minister George Grenville passed the Sugar Act, which put levies on all molasses and sugar coming into the colonies from Britain. Even more unpopular were the Stamp Act (1765) and the Quartering Act (1765), which sought to raise revenue from the colonies and force the colonists to supply living quarters for

The Boston Tea Party

British soldiers. Outraged colonists, near rebellion, drew upon liberal ideas from England and the continent to assert the principle of no taxation without representation in the English Parliament. The meeting in 1765 in New York City of delegates from the nine colonies to protest the act (the Stamp Act Congress) was the first united action of the colonies to protest their treatment by Britain. The Stamp Act was indeed repealed, but the Declaratory Act (1766), which gave the king and Parliament full legislative authority over the colonies, and the Townshend Acts (1767), which taxed tea and other imports into the colonies, further inflamed colonials, leading to a protest in Boston, Ma. On March 5, 1770, British troops fired on the demonstrators killing five, including the black patriot Crispus Attucks (the Boston Massacre). Duties were dropped, except for tea, but the colonists still fumed. The Tea Act of 1773, designed to help the East India Company financially, aroused patriots like Samuel Adams of Boston. Colonists, disguised as Indians, raided English ships in Boston Harbor and dumped their tea overboard (the Boston Tea Party, 1773). Britain's response to the raid was a series of punitive laws called the Intolerable Acts (1774), which closed Boston Harbor until the colonists reimbursed England for the lost tea. It also restricted the Massachusetts legislature. Colonial resistance was prompt. *Committees of correspondence* were formed by patriots to exchange information, and these led to the First Continental Congress (September to October 1774) to protest the Intolerable Acts. Another congress was planned for May 1775, but by then war had begun.

Outbreak of the War. In April 1775, colonial volunteer soldiers known as *minutemen* engaged British troops at Lexington, Ma. The troops were on their way to destroy colonial arms stores at Concord, and the minutemen had been alerted to the the British action by Paul Revere and William Dawes.

The Battles of Lexington and Concord were the opening shots in the war. Boston was under siege by the British, and the colonials flocking to its defense formed the Continental Army. The Second Continental Congress, meeting in Philadelphia, named George Washington as commander-in-chief of the continental forces (June 15, 1775). Two days later the British won a costly victory in Boston (the Battle of Bunker Hill) and took over the city. Washington arrived outside Boston on July 3, 1775 and began plans to retake the city. Earlier (May 1775) Benedict Arnold and Ethan Allen had captured British posts at Fort Ticonderoga and nearby Crown Point in New York. These victories secured much-needed heavy artillery for the continental forces. The guns were moved by sled to the Boston area, and by Mar. 1776, General William Howe, commander of the British army, realized he could not hold the city. He evacuated Boston on March 17 and sailed for Canada. Washington went to New York.

Declaration of Independence. Prior to open hostilities, colonists had been most concerned that their rights as English citizens were being trampled, but by 1776, the idea of complete independence from Britain was gaining support. Thomas Paine's immensely popular pamphlet *Common Sense* (published January 1776), urging the patriot cause, was a major contributing factor to the change. In June, Richard Henry Lee introduced a resolution to the Congress calling for independence; on July 2, Congress approved; and on July 4 it adopted the *Declaration of Independence*, almost exactly as drafted by Thomas Jefferson.

The War of Independence. Much hard fighting remained to make the independence real. Britain committed more troops and a large fleet to the war.

By late 1776, Howe had taken New York City and driven Washington and his small, discouraged forces into winter quarters at Valley Forge, Pa. At year's end, Washington, in a stunning Christmas night (Dec. 25, 1776) surprise attack at Trenton and Princeton N.J., achieved two of the most important victories of the war. A down-and-out colonial army turned its fortunes around by dealing the best army in the world two crushing defeats. The tide also turned in the north with Arnold's major victory at Saratoga, N.Y. (Sept. 1777) over British forces under General John Burgoyne, who had advanced down New York State from Canada.

The Saratoga victory helped persuade France that it could now openly commit forces to aid the embattled Americans. In 1778, it commenced operations in the West Indies, forcing Britain to spread its forces thin. With stalemate in the north, British forces concentrated on the southern states, winning victories at Savannah (1778) and Charleston (1780).

The colonial cause was further damaged in 1780 by the treason of the disaffected Arnold, who had attempted to turn over a military post he commanded at West Point to the British. In 1781, General Charles Cornwallis headed an unsuccessful British campaign to take the Carolinas. He was thwarted by colonials under Nathaniel Greene and Daniel Morgan. Cornwallis turned to Virginia, where in the Spring of 1781 he was preparing to launch a campaign to conquer the south. He was ordered, however, to take up defensive positions along the Virginia coast, and prepare to return north where General Clinton feared a colonial attack on New York City. Cornwallis moved his troops to Yorktown on Chesapeake Bay. In July, Washington learned that a large French fleet, under Admiral François de Grasse, was planning to block Chesapeake Bay and trap Cornwallis's forces at Yorktown. Washington rushed his forces from New York to Yorktown to seal off Cornwallis by land. Cornwallis, besieged by colonials on land and blocked by the French from an escape by sea, surrendered to Washington on October 19, 1781. The war was essentially over.

Treaty of Paris (1782). Britain opened peace negotiations with the Americans in Paris in April 1782. An agreement was struck in November, and Congress approved it in April 1783.

The treaty, which recognized the independence of the United States and established the new nation's borders, was signed on September 3, 1783.

Revolution of 1848, series of unsuccessful revolutionary uprisings in France, Italy, the Austrian Empire, and Germany in 1848. Each was relatively spontaneous and self-contained, but all had a number of common causes: the successful example of the French Revolution of 1789, economic unrest due to bad harvests and unemployment, and a growing frustration, fired by nationalist fervor, about the repressive policies of conservative politicians like Prince von Metternich and François Guizot. In 1848, a major uprising in Paris overthrew King Louis Philippe and Guizot, but it was suppressed and the Third Republic proclaimed. In Italy, during the Risorgimento, short-lived republics were proclaimed, and there was agitation to secure independence from Austria, which was itself shaken by revolutions in Vienna, Prague, and Hungary. The demand for a representative government led to an all-German Diet in Frankfurt that failed in its efforts to unite Germany. In England there was working-class agitation (Chartism), and other European countries were also affected.

Revolver, pistol with semiautomatic action made possible by the incorporation of a revolving cylinder carrying several bullets. In 1835 Samuel Colt patented the first practical revolver. The modern revolver is based on the Colt design and is used by police and other armed forces throughout the world.
See also: Colt, Samuel.

Rexroth, Kenneth (1905-82), U.S. poet. In the 1940s and 1950s he developed a style that broke with traditional forms of poetry and became the forerunner of what is now considered the "Beat generation" of San Francisco poets and writers. His best-known works are *In What Hour* (1940), *The Dragon and the Unicorn* (1952), and *In Defense of the Earth* (1956). *The Collected Shorter Poems* (1967) and *The Collected Longer Poems* (1968) further enhanced Rexroth's literary reputation, as did a collection of his essays, *The World Outside the Window* (1987). He was also a gifted painter and translator of Chinese, Latin, and Greek poetry.

Reye's syndrome, rare disease that attacks the liver and central nervous system of children age 4-15. Of unknown cause, it is contracted by most victims following a viral illness, such as chicken pox or the flu. Aspirin use may be associated with the syndrome. Symptoms include vomiting and may progress into convulsions, disorientation, and possible brain damage and comas. Treatment is with glucose and other nutrients or with drugs and surgery when pressure within the skull reaches dangerous levels. About 3-5% of victims die. It was named (1963) after Australian pathologist R.D.K. Reye, who researched it.

Reykjavik (pop. 91,400), capital of Iceland and its chief port, commercial and industrial center, and home of its cod-fishing fleet. Settled in A.D. 877, Reykjavik means "smoking bay," from the nearby hot springs that provide the city with central heating.
See also: Iceland.

Reynard the Fox, leading character in a popular medieval series of fables. Appearing first in the area between the Flanders and Germany in the 10th century, the tales, with their cunning but sympathetic hero and biting satire, became popular in France, Germany, and the Low Countries.

Reynaud, Paul (1878-1966), French statesman. After holding a number of cabinet posts (from 1930), he became premier (1940). An opponent of the Nazis, he spent World War II in prison. Afterward he held several posts and helped draft the constitution of the Fifth Republic (1958).
See also: France.

Reynolds, Sir Joshua (1723-92), perhaps the most famous English portrait painter. Ambitious and popular, he became first president of the Royal Academy of Arts (1768). He held that great art is based on the styles of earlier masters and espoused the "Grand Style." He painted nearly all his notable contemporaries, including his friend Samuel Johnson (1772). His works also include William Robertsen (1772) and Sarah Siddons as the Tragic Muse (1784). He also published influential essays on art education called *Discourses* (1769-90). Reynolds was influenced by the paintings of Anton Van Dyck, Tintoretto, Titian, Paolo Veronese, and Peter Paul Rubens.

Reza Shah Pahlavi (1877-1944), shah of Iran (1925-41). An army officer, he led a coup in 1921, becoming prime minister and later (1925) founder of the Pahlavi dynasty. He made important military, administrative, and economic reforms, but the Allies forced him to resign in World War II for refusing to allow them to use Iran as a supply route.
See also: Iran.

Rhea, large flightless South American bird of the order Rheaformes. Closely resembling the ostrich, the rhea is smaller, with larger wings, more head and neck feathers, and 3 rather than 2 toes on each foot. Rheas generally stand 5 ft (1.5 m) tall and weigh up to 55 lb (25 kg). They are plains-dwellers in the temperate region south of the equator, usually flocking together in groups of 5-30. Often found grazing with cattle, they feed on leaves, roots, and insects. The male rhea digs a hole in the ground for a nest, where several females may lay as many as 30 eggs; the male sits on the eggs until they hatch.

Rhea, in Greek mythology, wife and sister of Cronus (ruler of the Titans), daughter of Gaea (the earth) and Uranus (the sky). She became queen of the gods after Cronus defeated Uranus. She had 6 children: Zeus, Poseidon, Pluto, Hestia, Hera, and Demeter. She later helped Zeus overthrow Cronus.
See also: Mythology.

Rhee, Syngman (1875-1965), president of South Korea. A leader in the movement to win Korean independence from Japan, he was in exile in Honolulu from 1910 to 1945, serving as president of the Korean Provisional Government for 20 years. Returning to Korea after World War II, he became the first president of the Republic of Korea (South Korea) in 1948. He resigned from office in 1960 because of corruption and mismanagement by some of his appointees. He wrote *Spirit of Independence* (1904) during his imprisonment (1897-1904) for heading demonstrations for independence.

Rhenium, chemical element, symbol Re; for physical constants see Periodic Table. Rhenium was discovered by Walter Noddack, Ida Tacke, and Otto Berg in 1925. It occurs in the minerals columbite, wolframite, gadolinite, and molybdenite. It is prepared by the high-temperature reduction of ammonium with hydrogen. Rhenium is a silver-white, ductile, high-melting, dense metal. It is resistant to wear and electrical corrosion. Rhenium and its compounds are used in alloys for electrical contacts and filaments, electron tube and semiconductor applications, high-temperature thermocouples, and poison-resistant catalysts. Dmitri Mendeleev predicted this element, which he called *dwi-manganese*.

Joshua Reynolds's Portrait of Augustus Keppel *(1753-54)*

Rheostat, variable resistor used to control the current drawn by an electric motor to dim lighting. It may consist of resistive wire wound in a helix, with a sliding contact varying the effective length, or of a series of fixed resistors connected between a row of button contacts. For heavy loads, electrodes dipped in solutions can be used, the resistance being controlled by the immersion depth and separation of the electrodes.

Rhesus monkey (*Maccaca mulatta*), monkey found in southern and southeastern Asia. Its use in medical and behavioral research led to the discovery of the Rh factor, a substance found in human red blood cells. Rhesus monkeys measure 18-25 in (48-64 cm) and weigh from 9-22 lb (4-10 kg) with a tail of 7-12 in (18-30 cm). They live in deserts, farm areas, forests, mountains and swamps. They eat birds, fruit, insects, leaves, roots, and farm crops.

Rhetoric *see:* Oratory.

Rheumatic fever, feverish illness, following infection with *streptococcus* and leading to systemic disease. It occurs mainly in children age 5-15. Symptoms include skin rash, subcutaneous nodules, and a migrating arthritis. Involvement of the heart (rheumatic heart disease) may lead to palpitations, chest pain, cardiac failure, myocarditis, inflammation of the pericardium, and permanent heart damage. Treatment includes bed rest, aspirin, and steroids. Penicillin treatment of this noncontagious disease may prevent recurrence.

Rheumatism, term popularly applied to pain affecting muscles, tendons, joints, bones, or nerves, in such widely varied disorders as rheumatoid arthritis, degenerative joint disease, spondylitis, bursitis, fibrositis, myositis, neuritis, lumbago, sciatica, and gout.

Rh factor, protein substance appearing on the surface of red blood cells of most people (85% or more), capable of inducing an immune response. It was first detected in a rhesus monkey in 1940 by Karl Landsteiner and Alexander Weiner.
See also: Landsteiner, Karl.

Rhineland, region of Germany along the Rhine River and its tributaries. From the Roman Empire through World War II, the Rhineland was strategically important; whoever controlled the river often exercised power over Western Europe. During the Middle Ages, Rhineland cities were political and religious centers of the Holy Roman Empire and, later, for the breakaway Protestant churches. For protection against raiding armies, heavily fortified castles—now tourist attractions—were built on hills overlooking the Rhine. In the Napoleonic Wars, the Franco-Prussian War, and both world wars, the Rhineland was a key battleground. Rich mineral deposits there, especially iron and coal, led to Germany's development as a world power in the late 19th and early 20th centuries. The Rhineland is still a key industrial region, and has some the world's most productive vineyards.
See also: Germany.

Rhine River, longest river in western Europe, rising in Switzerland and flowing 820 mi (1,320 km) through Germany and the Netherlands into the North Sea near Rotterdam. It is of great historical and commercial significance, being navigable by seagoing ships up to Cologne and by large barges as far as Basel. Canals link it to the Rhône, Marne, Ems, Weser, Elbe, Oder, and Danube rivers. Some of its finest scenery is along the gorge between Bingen and Bonn, with terraced vineyards, ruined castles, and famous landmarks like the Lorelei rock.

Rhode Island

Rhinitis, most frequent of the acute upper respiratory infections, characterized by edema, swelling and widening of the blood vessels of the mucous membrane of the nose, nasal discharge, and obstruction. It can result from infections, allergic reactions, hay fever, and unknown stimuli.
See also: Cold, Common.

Rhinoceros, any of 5 species of heavy land mammals (family Rhinocerotidae) characterized by one or two nasal "horn" or "horns," formed of a mass of compacted hairs. They are bulky animals with poor vision and thick, hairless skin, often falling in heavy, loose folds. They live in transitional habitats between open grassland and high forest, grazing or browsing at night on bushes or shrubs. All 5 species— the white rhinoceros (*Ceratotherium simum*), the black (*Diceros bicornus*), the Indian (*Rhinoceros unicornis*), the Sumatran (*Dicerorhinus sumatrensis*), and the Javan (*R. sondaicus*)—have been hunted for their horns to the verge of extinction.

Rhizoid *see:* Moss.

Rhizome, or rootstock, swollen horizontal underground stem of certain plants, such as ginger. The rhizome acts as an organ of perennation (ability to live over from season to season), and vegetative propagation lasts for several years. New shoots appear each spring near the scale leaves. If split, the rhizome lives on as numerous individuals.

Rhode Island

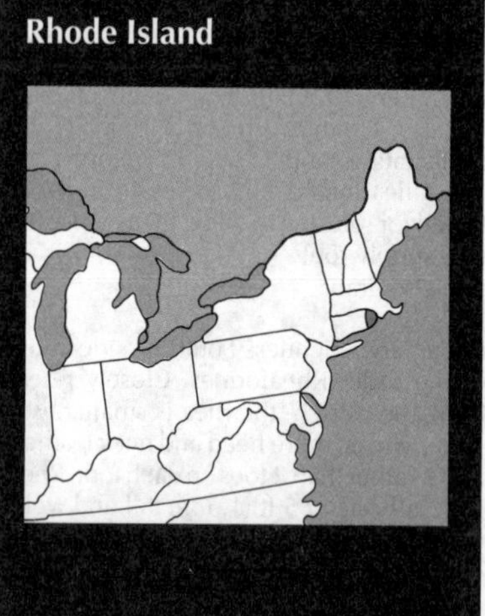

Capital:	Providence
Statehood:	May 29, 1790 (13th state)
Familiar names:	Ocean State, Little Rhody
Area:	1,212 sq mi (3,140 sq km); ranks 50th
Population:	1,005,984 (1990); ranks 43rd
Elevation:	Highest—812 ft (247 m), Jerimoth Hill; Lowest—sea level, along the Atlantic coast
Motto:	Hope
Flower:	Violet
Bird:	Rhode Island Red
Tree:	Red maple
Song:	"Rhode Island"

Rhode Island, state in New England, the northeastern region of the United States; bordered by Massachusetts to the north and east, the Atlantic Ocean to the south, and Connecticut to the west.

Land and climate. Rhode Island has two main land regions. The Coastal Lowlands cover roughly half of the state's mainland, plus the islands in Narragansett Bay and all the land to the east of the bay. Low inland hills slope downward toward the coast, which is lined by sandy beaches and salt ponds. The New England Upland, covering the northwestern third of the state, is a hilly area with higher elevations than along the coast. The Providence, Seekonk, and Sakonnet rivers are saltwater arms of Narragansett Bay. Major freshwater rivers are the Pawtuxet, Pettaquamscutt, Woonasquatucket, and Potowomut. Rhode Island has many lakes, ponds, and reservoirs. Forests cover about three-fifths of the state. Rhode Island's climate is kept mild by the ocean and the waters of Narragansett Bay. Principal cities are Providence and Warwick.

Economy. Rhode Island's most important economic activity is manufacturing, followed by tourism and service industries. Chief manufactured goods are jewelry, silverware, fabricated metal products, electrical equipment, machinery, and textiles. Agriculture, of minor importance to the state's economy, is led by greenhouse and nursery products and milk. Chief crops are potatoes, hay, and apples. Mining, also of little importance, is led by construction sand and gravel.

Government. Rhode Island's present constitution was adopted in 1843. The governor serves a 2-year term. The state's legislature, called the General Assembly, consists of 50 senators and 100 representatives; all serve 2-year terms. In the U.S. Congress, Rhode Island is represented by 2 senators and 2 representatives.

History. Algonquian peoples lived in the area before the first European explorers arrived in the early 1500s. In 1636, the first permanent white settlement was established at Providence by Roger Williams, a religious exile from the Massachusetts Bay Colony. In following years, other seekers of religious or political freedom established settlements in the area. Relations between Indians and settlers were peaceful until the spread of settlements began forcing Indians from their lands, sparking an Indian uprising known as King Philip's War (1675-6). Rhode Island prospered in the early 1700s. Large plantations run by slave labor lined the fertile coastal plain, and trade with other colonies and nations was brisk. (Slave trade was abolished in Rhode Island in 1774.) On May 4, 1776, Rhode Island became the first of the 13 colonies to declare independence from Britain; Rhode Islanders supported the American side during the American Revolution. Rhode Island became the 13th state in 1790. From 1790, when the first water-powered spinning machines were built at Pawtucket, textile and other industries grew rapidly; urbanization also increased. During the Civil War, Rhode Island supported the

Union. Industry continued to grow in Rhode Island; the state's shipyards and factories were of great importance during World Wars I and II. During the 1950s and 1960s, Rhode Island's textile industry suffered a decline as more textile manufacturers moved to the South. Rhode Island recovered somewhat in the 1980s with growth in tourism and U.S. government contracts for developing submarines.

Rhodes, or Ródhos, Greek island covering 540 sq mi (1,399 sq km), off the southwest coast of Turkey. The capital city is also called Rhodes. The island's exports include wine, fruit, and olive oil; tourism is its main industry. Rhodes was a prosperous city-state in the 3rd century B.C. At the harbor stood the Colossus of Rhodes, a statue that was one of the Seven Wonders of the ancient world.

Rhodes, Cecil John (1853-1902), English politician and business magnate who first opened up Rhodesia to European settlement. Having made a fortune in diamond mining, he founded the De Beers Mining Company in 1888 at Kimberly in South Africa. After helping bring about the British annexation of Bechuanaland (1884), he also obtained the territory to the north, later called Rhodesia (now Zimbabwe) in his honor, which he managed until 1890. Prime minister of the Cape Colony from 1890, he was forced to resign because of complicity in the Jameson raid (1896) into the Transvaal. Much of his £6 million fortune went to found the Rhodes scholarships.
See also: Rhodes Scholarship.

Rhodes, John Jacob (1916-), U.S. political leader. A lawyer in Mesa, Ariz., he was the first Republican ever elected by Arizona to the U.S. House of Representatives. He chaired the Republican House Policy Committee (1965-73) and served as House Minority Leader (1973-81), replacing Gerald R. Ford, who was chosen vice president by President Richard Nixon. Rhodes was a fiscal conservative who supported federal projects aimed at increasing Arizona's water supply.

Rhodesia *see:* Zimbabwe.

Rhodesia and Nyasaland, Federation of, British federation in central Africa created in 1953 that included Southern Rhodesia, Northern Rhodesia, and Nyasaland. In 1963 Great Britain agreed to break up the federation and give the colonies their independence, largely as a result of widespread opposition by the black majority to the white-dominated government. The new nations of Malawi, Zambia, and Zimbabwe were later formed.
See also: Malawi; Zambia.

Rhodesian ridgeback, also called African lion hound, hunting dog that originated in southern Africa. Hunters value its ability to find and hold off lions; it is also known as a good watchdog and companion. Ridgebacks are named for the ridge of hair that grows on their backs in the opposite direction from the rest of the coat, which is yellowish to reddishbrown. They have the drooping ears typical of most hounds, stand 24-27 in (61-69 cm) high, and weigh 65-75 lb (30-34 kg).

Rhodes Scholarship, award instituted (1902) at Oxford University by the bequest of Cecil John Rhodes, English politician and business magnate, for students from the Commonwealth, the United States, and Germany. The scholarship, awarded for 2 and sometimes 3 years, provides the student's university tuition and fees as well as living allowance. Elections are based on general grounds as well as on academic ability.

Rhodium, chemical element, symbol Rh; for physical constants see Periodic Table. Rhodium was discovered by William H. Wollaston in 1803. It occurs in the minerals sperrylite, iridosmine, and in some copper-nickel sulfide ores. Rhodium is a silver-white, high-melting, unreactive metal, a member of the platinum family of elements. It is one of the few substances that is not attacked by fluorine. The metal is used to harden platinum and palladium. Plated or evaporated coatings of the element have high reflectance and are used in optical instruments. Rhodium and its compounds are used in thermocouples, crucibles, electrodes, and electrical contacts and as catalysts.

Rhododendron, genus of mostly evergreen shrubs (family Ericaceae) found mainly in forests of the arctic and north temperate zones. They bear leathery dark-green leaves and, in late spring, masses of fragrant blossom. North American species include the great rhododendron, also known as great laurel or rosebay (*R. maximum*), and the mountain rosebay (*R. catawbiense*).

Rhombus, parallelogram in which the sides are of equal length but usually not at right angles to each other. Its area can be computed by using the formula $A = bh$, where b is the base and h is the height.

Rhône River, important European river, 507 mi (816 km) long, rising in Switzerland and flowing through Lake Geneva and then southwest and south through France into the Mediterranean Sea. With its tributaries, particularly the Isère and the Saône, it has a large flow of water, which has been harnessed in major hydroelectric schemes. Navigable in part, it is linked by canal to the Camargue region.

Rhubarb, name for plants (genus *Rheum*) of the buckwheat family. First cultivated in China for its purgative medicinal rootstock, it is also used for food. The pink, fleshy leaf-stalks, or petioles, sprout from underground rhizomes and bear large green leaves that can be poisonous.

Rib, in humans, one of the 24 long, flat, curved bones forming the wall of the chest.
See also: Human body.

Rhodes

Ribaut or **Ribault, Jean** (1520?-65), French mariner who helped colonize Florida. On present-day Parris Island, S.C., he set up a colony in 1562. He fled to England to escape persecution as a Huguenot. In 1565 he was shipwrecked off Florida and killed by Spanish forces.

Ribbentrop, Joachim von (1893-1946), German Nazi leader, ambassador to the United Kingdom (1936-38) and foreign minister (1938-45). He helped to negotiate the Rome-Berlin Axis (1936) and the Russo-German nonaggression pact (1939) and to plan the invasion of Poland, but he wielded little influence in World War II. He was hanged for war crimes.
See also: Nazism; World War II.

Ribbon Falls, in the Yosemite Valley, one of the highest waterfalls in the world. Fed by the melting snows of the Sierra Nevadas, it drops 1,612 ft (491 m) and empties into the Merced River. In early August, the snow dries up and the falls cease. Its name derives from its ribbonlike appearance.

Ribbon worm, any of a group of elongated marine worms (phylum Nemertina), ranging in size from less than 1 in (2.5 cm) to 90 ft (27 m) long. Most live in the open sea, but some live in fresh water or on land. They all have a long proboscis, sometimes spiked and poisonous, that can be thrown out with great accuracy to capture worms and other small animals.

Rhododendron

Ribera, Jusepe de (c.1590-1652), Spanish painter who lived after 1618 in Naples. His work, influenced by Caravaggio, combines naturalism and mysticism, as in the *Martyrdom of St. Sebastian* (1630) and *The Penitent Magdalen* (c.1640).

Ribicoff, Abraham A. (1910-), U.S. public official, widely known as a champion of consumer protection. A Democrat, he was a Connecticut representative (1949-53), governor (1955-61), and senator (1963-81). Under President Kennedy he was secretary of health, education, and welfare (1961-62).

Riboflavin *see:* Vitamin.

Ricardo, David (1772-1823), English economist, founder, with Adam Smith, of the classical school. He made a fortune as a stockbroker and then devoted his time to economics and politics, becoming a member of Parliament (1819-23). His main work, *Principles of Political Economy and Taxation* (1817), pioneered the use of theoretical models in analyzing the distribution of wealth.
See also: Economics.

Ricci, Matteo (1552-1610), Italian Jesuit missionary. He entered China in 1583, learned Chinese, and eventually won acceptance. He introduced Western mathematics, astronomy, and geography to the Chinese, and sent the first detailed reports of China to the West.
See also: Jesuits.

Rice (*Oryza sativa*), grain-yielding annual plant of the grass family (Graminae). It is grown chiefly in southern and eastern Asia, where it is the staple food of hundreds of millions of people. Rice needs hot, moist conditions to grow, which historically made it highly dependent on monsoon rainfall. Improved irrigation, fertilizers, pesticides, and the development of improved varieties have enormously increased the yield. Machinery for planting and harvesting rice is used in the United States and parts of South America, but in Asia rice farming uses hand labor. Rice has a reasonable nutrient value, but when brown rice is "polished" (to make white rice), much of its vitamin B_1 content is lost.

Rice farmers transplanting germinated rice plants into flooded patties.

Rice, Elmer (1892-1967), U.S. dramatist. His plays on social themes include *The Adding Machine* (1923), an expressionist fantasy; *Street Scene* (1929), a Pulitzer Prize-winning portrait of life in a tenement; and the romantic comedy *Dream Girl* (1945).

Rice, Grantland (1880-1954), U.S. journalist known as the first famous sportswriter. Rice covered sporting events in the 1920s and 1930s and also produced poetry and his autobiography, *The Tumult and the Shouting* (1954).

Ricebird *see:* Bobolink.

Rice weevil *see:* Grain weevil.

Rich, Adrienne (1929-), U.S. feminist poet whose primary themes are women's issues and sexuality and the problem of human communication. Her works include *Diving into the Wreck* (1973), *Of Woman Born* (1976), *The Dream of a Common Language* (1978), *Time's Power: Poems 1985-1988*, and several volumes of selected prose.

Richard, name of three kings of England. **Richard I** (1157-99), called Coeur de Lion (the Lion Heart), was the third son of Henry II, whom he succeeded in 1189. He spent all but six months of his reign out of England, mainly on the Third Crusade. After taking Cyprus and Acre in 1191 and recapturing Jaffa in 1192, he was captured while returning to England and handed over to Holy Roman Emperor Henry VI, who held him for ransom until 1194. After a brief spell in England, he spent the rest of his life fighting against Philip II in France. **Richard II** (1367-1400), son of Edward the Black Prince, succeeded his grandfather Edward III in 1377. In his minority the country was governed by a group of nobles dominated by his uncle John of Gaunt. Richard quarreled with them but only began to assert himself after 1397; he executed his uncle the Duke of Gloucester and banished Henry Bolingbroke, Gaunt's son, and confiscated his estates. Bolingbroke returned in 1399 to depose Richard and imprison him in Pontefract castle, where he died. Bolingbroke succeeded as Henry IV. **Richard III** (1452-85), third son of Richard Plantagenet, Duke of York, and the younger brother of Edward IV, usurped the throne in 1483. The traditional picture of him as a hunchbacked and cruel ruler who murdered his nephews in the Tower has little historical backing. He instituted many reforms and encouraged trade but had little hope of defeating his many enemies gathering in France under Henry Tudor (later Henry VII). They defeated and killed Richard at Bosworth Field, ending the War of the Roses.
See also: England; United Kingdom.

Richard, Maurice (1921-), Canadian-born hockey player. Known for his fast skating and blistering shots, "The Rocket" was the first National Hockey League (NHL) player to score 50 goals in a 50-game season. Richard, named the NHL's most value player in 1947, played right wing for the Montreal Canadiens (1942-1960) and led them to 8 Stanley Cup championships (1944, 46, 53, 56-60). He was inducted into the Hockey Hall of Fame in 1961.

Richards, Dickinson Woodruff (1895-1973), U.S. physiologist awarded, with A.F. Cournand and Werner Forssmann, the 1956 Nobel Prize in physiology or medicine for his work with Cournand using Forssmann's catheter technique to probe the heart, pulmonary artery, and lungs.
See also: Physiology.

Richards, Ivor Armstrong (1893-1979), English literary critic. He developed with C. K. Ogden the concept of Basic English, a primary vocabulary of 850 words. His books include *The Meaning of Meaning* (with Ogden, 1923) and *Principles of Literary Criticism* (1924).

Richardson, Elliot Lee (1920-), U.S. lawyer and government official. After serving as assistant secretary of health, education and welfare (1957-67), Massachusetts lieutenant governor (1965-67), attorney general (1967-69), and secretary of health, education, and welfare (1970-73), he was appointed secretary of defense and then attorney general (1973) but resigned over the Watergate Scandal. He was also ambassador to the United Kingdom (1975-76) and U.S. secretary of commerce (1976-77).

Richardson, Henry Hobson (1838-86), U.S. architect who pioneered an American Romanesque style. Among his important buildings are the Trinity Church in Boston and the Marshall Field Wholesale Store in Chicago.
See also: Architecture.

Richardson, Samuel (1689-1761), English novelist, best known for his novels in epistolary form, especially *Pamela; or, Virtue Rewarded* (1740-41), the story of a servant girl's moral triumph over her lecherous master, and *Clarissa Harlowe* (1747-48), his tragic masterpiece, also on the theme of seduction. *The History of Sir Charles Grandison* (1753-54) portrays a virtuous hero, in contrast to the amoral hero of Henry Fielding's *Tom Jones*.

Richard the Lion-Hearted *see:* Richard (I).

Richelieu, Cardinal (Armand Jean du Plessis, Duc de Richelieu; 1585-1642), French cardinal, statesman, and chief minister to Louis XIII for 18 years. By a mixture of diplomacy and ruthlessness he helped make France the leading power in Europe, with a monarchy secure against internal revolt. He destroyed Huguenot power by 1628, foiled an attempt by the king's mother, Marie de Médicis, to oust him in 1630, and suppressed the plots of the Duc de Montmorency in 1632 and of Cinq-Mars in 1642, at the same time reducing the power of the nobles. In foreign policy he opposed the Habsburgs, intervening against them in the Thirty Years' War. Richelieu strengthened the navy, encouraged colonial development, and patronized the arts (founding the Académie Française).
See also: France.

Richelieu River, river in Quebec known for its scenic beauty. It was named after Cardinal de Richelieu, prime minister of France under Louis XIII. It rises from Lake Champlain near the Vermont border and it flows about 80 mi (130 km) northward to meet the St. Lawrence River. It is used for boating and as a transportation link between New York City and Montreal.

Richfield (pop. 5,482), in central Utah, seat of Sevier County and site of various federal and state governmental agencies. Agriculture, livestock, and dairy products are its major economic activities. Located in Richfield are the offices of the Forest Service and the Bureau of Land Management.
See also: Utah.

Richland (pop. 33,578), city in Washington and site of the U.S. Department of Energy's Hanford Atomic Energy Plant. The city's population increased dramatically as a result of The Hanford Project, created during World War II to develop nuclear weapons. In addition to the plant, economic activity also includes farming and ranching.
See also: Washington.

Richler, Mordecai (1931-), Canadian writer. His novels, especially *The Apprenticeship of Duddy Kravitz* (1959) and *Cocksure* (1968), are noted for their wry wit and biting satire.

Richmond (pop. 219,214), state capital of Virginia; capital of the Confederacy (1861-65). Located at the navigation head of the James River, it is a port and a financial and distribution center, as well as being an important industrial city, with tobacco and food processing, chemicals, metals, and wood products. It has many historic buildings and sites, including the Capitol (1785), designed by Thomas Jefferson, and Hollywood Cemetery, where some 18,000 Confederate soldiers are buried. Richmond National Battlefied Park contains several Civil War battle sites.
See also: Virginia.

Richmond (pop. 74,676), Calif., major West Coast port on the northeast shore of San Francisco Bay. Richmond has more than 120 industries, including oil refining, steel fabrication, chemicals, and food processing. Settled in 1899, it has a council-manager government. Among the world's largest high-level bridges is the San Rafael-Richmond Bridge, spanning 5.5 mi (8.9 km).
See also: California.

Richmond (pop. 41,349), city in Indiana and the seat of Wayne County, located on the Whitewater River. Founded by Quakers who traveled from North Carolina in 1806, it remains a center of Quaker activity. Economic activities include metalwork and the manufacture of machine parts.
See also: Indiana.

Richmondtown, area in Staten Island, New York City, and county seat of Richmond County. Developed in 1939 as a historic site, the area includes many restored buildings dating back to the 17th century. The restoration, which is financed by the City of New York and independent sponsors, is expected to be completed in the late 1990s.

Richter, Conrad (1890-1968), U.S. writer of fiction and nonfiction known for his novels about life on the American frontier. In 1961 he won the National Book Award for his novel *The Waters of Kronos.* He is best known for his trilogy, *The Awakening Land (1940-50),* the story of a pioneer family living in Ohio; the third novel, *The Town*, won the 1950 Pulitzer Prize for literature.

Richter, Hans (1843-1916), German conductor who presented the first performance of Wagner's *Ring* cycle at Bayreuth in 1876. A Brahms specialist also, he conducted in England for many years.

Richter, Johann Paul Friedrich (1763-1825), German humorous and sentimental novelist, who wrote as Jean Paul. He achieved popularity with such works as *The Invisible Lodge* (1793), *The Life of Quintus Fixlein* (1796), and *Titan* (1800-3).

Richter scale, scale devised by C.F. Richter (1900-85), used to measure the magnitudes of earthquakes in terms of the amplitude and frequency of the surface waves. The largest recorded earthquakes are about 8.5. A great earthquake of magnitude 8 occurs only once every 5-10 years. An increase of one unit corresponds to a tenfold increase in the size of an earthquake.
See also: Earthquake; Seismograph.

Richthofen, Manfred von (1892-1918), German aviator, nicknamed the Red Baron. Known for the daring and chivalry with which he led his squadron in World War I, he shot down about 80 opponents before being killed in action.
See also: World War I.

Rickenbacker, Eddie (Edward Vernon Rickenbacker; 1890-1973), U.S. air ace of World War I. He shot down 26 aircraft. He served as president of Eastern Airlines from 1938 to 1953.
See also: World War I.

Rickets, deficiency disease of infancy due to lack of vitamin D, characterized by poor nutrition and changes in the bones (bowleggedness, knock-knees, etc.). There is slight fever and sweating along with general symptoms.

Rickettsia, name for organisms partway between bacteria and viruses. Often borne by ticks or lice, they are responsible for a number of diseases, including typhus, scrub typhus, and Rocky Mountain spotted fever.

Rickover, Hyman George (1900-86), Russian-born U.S. admiral who brought nuclear power to the U.S. Navy. Head of the navy's electrical division in World War II, he moved to the Atomic Energy Commission (AEC) in 1947 and developed the first nuclear-powered submarine, the *Nautilus* (1954). He attained the rank of full admiral at the age of 73 and retired in 1982.

Ricksha *see:* Jinrikisha.

Ride, Sally Kristen (1951-), U.S. astronaut and astrophysicist. In 1983, she became the first American woman in space when she made a 6-day shuttle flight on the *Challenger.* On this and a second shuttle flight, she used the spacecraft's remote manipulator arm, a device she helped design. After the *Challenger* explosion in 1986, she was appointed to the presidential commission created to conduct an investigation.

Rideau Canal, waterway in Ontario and Canadian historic site. It serves as a link between Ottawa on the Ottawa River and Kingston on Lake Ontario. It is nearly 125 mi (200 km) long and consists of 47 locks. Completed in 1832, it was originally intended to carry military supplies from the Great Lakes region to Montreal. Instead, it was used to transport settlers.

Cardinal Richelieu

Ridgway, Matthew Bunker (1895-1985), U.S. military leader. During World War II he led the first full-scale U.S. airborne attack in the invasion of Sicily (1943) and took part in the invasion of France (1944). He became commander of the United Nations forces in Korea (1951), supreme commander of NATO Allied Forces in Europe (1952-53), and U.S. army chief of staff (1953-55).
See also: Korean War; World War II.

Ridley, Nicholas (c.1500-55), English Protestant martyr. Under Thomas Cranmer's patronage he became a chaplain to Henry VIII and bishop of Rochester (1547) and London (1550). He helped compile the Book of Common Prayer. On the accession of the Roman Catholic Mary I (1553) he was imprisoned and burned at Oxford, with Hugh Latimer, for heresy.
See also: Book of Common Prayer; Protestantism.

Riel, Louis (1844-85), Canadian rebel leader. In 1869 he organized the *métis* (people of mixed native Canadian and French descent) of Red River, now in Manitoba, to oppose Canada's annexation of the Northwest Territories. He fled to the United States after government troops moved in (1870). In 1884 he led another Indian uprising in Saskatchewan but was captured. His execution for treason was a cause of friction between English and French Canadians.
See also: Canada.

Riemann, Georg Friedrich Bernhard (1826-66), German mathematician, whose best-known contribution is the initiation of studies of non-Euclidean geometry. Elliptic geometry is often referred to as Riemannian geometry.
See also: Geometry.

Riemenschneider, Tilman (c.1460-1531), German Gothic sculptor in wood and stone. He worked in Würzburg, where many of his works survive, and carved the marble tomb of Emperor Henry II and his wife in Bamberg Cathedral (1499-1513).

Rienzi, Cola di (1313-54), Italian popular leader. With papal support, he became "Tribune" of a popular republic in Rome (1347), but his plans for restoring the Roman Empire led to his overthrow and exile.

Rifle, strictly, any firearm with a "rifled" bore—i.e., with shallow helical grooves cut inside the barrel. These grooves, by causing the bullet to spin, steady it and increase its accuracy, velocity, and range. The term "rifle" is more narrowly applied to the long-barreled hand weapon fired from the shoulder. Rifles are generally classified by caliber or decimal fractions or by mode of action.

Rift Valley *see:* Great Rift Valley.

Riga (pop. 875,000), capital of the Latvian Soviet Socialist Republic. Located near the Gulf of Riga at the mouth of the Daugava River, it is an important center of shipping and industry as well as the hub of Latvian cultural and political activity. The city, founded in 1201 and variously under the control of Poland, Sweden, and Russia, was incorporated into the USSR in 1940.
See also: Latvia.

Rigel, one of the brightest stars in the galaxy. Located in the constellation Orion, it is about 50 times as large as the sun, with a diameter of about 40 million mi (64 million km). Its distance from the earth is about 900 light-years.
See also: Orion; Star.

Rigging *see:* Sailing.

Right of privacy *see:* Privacy, Right of.

Right of search, international law under which nations at war are allowed to search the vessels of neutral nations for contraband. Ships may also be searched during times of peace. Regulations regarding a ship's distance from the coast depend on the nature of the particular search. During Prohibition, some nations consented to extend the number of miles. This practice is still in effect.
See also: Contraband.

Right of way *see:* Easement.

Rights, Bill of *see:* Bill of rights.

Rights of Man, Declaration of the *see:* Declaration of the Rights of Man and the Citizen.

Right-to-work laws, laws enforced in 19 U.S. states requiring companies to maintain an "open shop" in which a person may not be prevented from working because he does not belong to a union.

Right whale *see:* Whale.

Right wing, conservative faction within a political group or party. The term derives from the custom—first used in revolutionary France—of seating nobility on the right side of the king. This convention is still used by some organizations.
See also: Conservatism.

Riis, Jacob August (1849-1914), U.S. journalist and social reformer whose book *How the Other Half Lives* (1890) drew attention to slum conditions in New York City. He worked as a police reporter on the *New York Tribune* (1877-88) and the *New York Evening Sun* (1888-99).

Riley, James Whitcomb (1849-1916), U.S. poet, known as the "Hoosier Poet." *The Old Swimmin' Hole and 'Leven More Poems* (1883) was the first of his many popular collections of humorous and sentimental dialect poems.

Rilke, Rainer Maria (1875-1926), German lyric poet. His complex, symbolic poetry is preoccupied with spiritual questioning about God and death, as in the *Book of Hours* (1905) and *New Poems* (1907-8). The poems in his later *Duino Elegies* (1923) and the *Sonnets to Orpheus* (1923) are considered his finest work.

Rillieux, Norbert (1806-94), U.S. engineer who developed an improved method of manufacturing sugar (1846). His vacuum evaporator made it possible to cheaply and effectively dehydrate sugar cane and turn it into granules.

Rimbaud, Arthur (1854-91), French poet. His vivid imagery and his "disordering of consciousness," reflected in such poems as "The Drunken Boat" (1871), have had an enormous influence on modern poetry. He published *A Season in Hell* in 1873, after which he denounced his poetry and became an adventurer. His major collection, *Les Illuminations*, was published in 1886. Rimbaud was closely associated with the poet Paul Verlaine.

Rimsky-Korsakov, Nikolai (1844-1908), Russian composer. While still a naval officer he started teaching composition at the St. Petersburg Conservatory (1871). He wrote scores for the operas *The Snow Maiden* (1882) and *The Golden Cockerel* (1909) and a colorful symphonic suite, *Scheherezade* (1888).

Rinderpest, acute virus disease of cattle, common in North Africa and South Asia.

Rinehart, Mary Roberts (1876-1958), U.S. writer of popular detective stories, including *The Circular Staircase* (1908). She also wrote an autobiography, *My Story* (1931).

Ring, small circular band worn on the body as decoration. It is often made of metal and sometimes engraved or set with gems. Rings are most common on the fingers and ears, but are also worn on the nose or toes. Its symbolic value has been recognized throughout the ages. Rings have been used to show position or social status, designate membership in an organization, and denote friendship.
See also: Jewelry.

Ringette, sport similar to ice hockey created for women. Invented in Canada in 1963, its popularity has spread to the northern United States and some parts of Europe. Although many of its rules are similar to those of hockey, ringette does not allow body contact. Players use a bladeless stick and a hollow circular puck made of rubber.
See also: Hockey.

Ringling brothers, five U.S. brothers who created the world's largest circus. Led by John Ringling (1866-1936), they started with a one-wagon show and became Barnum & Bailey's chief rival, buying them out in 1907. The combined Ringling Bros. and Barnum & Bailey Circus was the world's largest by 1930. It remained in the family's hands until 1967.
See also: Barnum, P(hineas) T(aylor); Circus.

Ringtail, or cacomistle, member of the raccoon family found in North and Central America. About 12-15 in (30-38 cm) long, ringtails generally have grayish brown fur and long, black-and-white striped tails. They are nocturnal and subsist mainly on rodents. North American ringtails live in the deserts and forests of the West and Southwest.

Ringworm, common fungus disease of the skin of humans and animals; it may also affect the hair and nails. Ringshaped raised lesions occur; temporary baldness is seen on hairy skin, and the nails may disintegrate. Athlete's foot is ringworm of the toes, while tinea cruris is a variety that affects the groin. Treatments include topical ointments and systemic antifungal antibiotics.

Rio de Janeiro (pop. 5,093,000), second largest city of Brazil, on the Atlantic coast about 200 mi (322 km) east of São Paulo. Located in a picturesque setting, the city is

a leading resort, as well as a center for the manufacture of clothing, furniture, glassware, and foodstuffs. The area was settled by the French (1555-67) and then by the Portuguese. It was the Brazilian capital from 1763 to 1960, when it was supplanted by Brasília.
See also: Brazil.

Río de la Plata, estuary formed by the Paraná and Uruguay rivers, separating Argentina and Uruguay. It flows 171 miles (275 km) southeast into the Atlantic.

Rio Grande, one of the longest rivers in North America, known in Mexico as the Rio Bravo del Norte. It rises in the San Juan Mountains in southwestern Colorado and flows 1,885 (3,034 km) southeast and south to the Gulf of Mexico at Brownsville, Tex., and Matamoros, Mexico. From El Paso, Tex., to its mouth, it forms the U.S.-Mexico border.

Rio Madeira *see:* Madeira River.

Riot, unlawful rebellion against a public authority by a group of people, involving breach of the peace, destruction of property, and/or violence. Riots are defined variously around the world, and punishment differs accordingly. Riots can be spontaneous or planned. They often break out during a protest, due to the heightened emotions of demonstrators and authorities. Although the U.S. Constitution protects the right of its citizens to group together for the purposes of peaceful dissent, such gatherings are considered riots when they involve breach of peace, destruction of property, or violence.

Riparian rights, privileges accruing to owners of land on the edges of streams, rivers, and lakes. These "water rights" allow a landowner to use the water for domestic, agricultural, or commercial purposes, usually with the provision that such use should not infringe on the rights of other riparian owners.

The Rio Grande

Ripley, George (1802-80), U.S. social reformer and critic. A transcendentalist, he founded and ran the Brook Farm community (1841-47). Later (1849-80) he became an influential literary critic with the *New York Tribune*.

Rip Van Winkle, folk tale by U.S. author Washington Irving from his collection, *The Sketch Book of Geoffrey Crayon, Gent.* (1819-20). The story concerns a cheerful but unsuccessful farmer who, while hunting in the Catskill Mountains, meets some quaintly dressed men playing ninepins. After he drinks from their keg of liquor he falls asleep and wakes to find his dog gone and his gun rusted. He makes his way home and discovers that he has slept for 20 years, his children have grown, and he has become a citizen of the United States instead of a subject of King George III. He later finds that the men he encountered were the ghosts of Henry Hudson and his crew.

Rite of passage, ceremony within a community to mark an individual's achievement of a new stage in life (e.g., birth, puberty, marriage) and consequent change of role in the community.

Rittenhouse, David (1732-96), U.S. astronomer and mathematician who invented the diffraction grating, built two orreries, discovered the atmosphere of Venus (1768) independently of Lomonosov (1761), and built what was probably the first U.S. telescope.
See also: Astronomy; Telescope.

Ritual *see:* Religion.

River, long channel of water. The ground beneath is called the bed; to either side are its banks. Rivers begin as headwaters overflowing from lakes or running down mountains as the snow melts, forming rills, brooks, and streams. The amount of river water depends on rainfall, since the river system provides the drainage for the surrounding land. The water runs downward to sea level, taking the shortest, steepest route; the river's upper course has the swiftest currents, as well as any waterfalls or rapids. The force of the current may erode the valleys or cut into rock, forming canyons. The river's lower course usually flows through a flat area called the flood plain until it reaches the mouth, the point where the river reaches the coast. The mouth may form a delta (a triangular deposit of sediment), or an estuary (a deep, wide mouth filled with fresh and salt waters). Rivers, important routes of transportation, can provide power for industry and help irrigate crops. At 4,145 mi (6,671 km), the Nile River in Africa is the longest in the world.

Rivera, Diego (1886-1957), Mexican mural painter. He painted large murals of social life and political themes throughout Mexico and in the United States, where his Marxist views aroused controversy.

Rio de Janeiro

River dolphin, any of four species of freshwater whales found in the waters of South America and Asia, belonging to the family Platanistidae. River dolphins differ from marine dolphins in that they have longer snouts, more teeth, poorer vision, and a lower level of activity. They measure up to 9 ft (2.7 m) long, and can be black, white, yellow, pink, gray, or brown in color.

River horse *see:* Hippopotamus.

Rivers, Larry (1923-), U.S. painter. He adapted the style of abstract expressionism to the popular imagery of well-known pictures and commercial advertisements, as in *Dutch Masters Series* (1963).

Riveting, joining of machine or structural parts, usually plates, by rivets. Rivets are headed bolts, usually made of steel, that are passed through the plates, a second head then being formed on the plain end by pressure, hammering, or an explosive charge. Large rivets are heated for satisfactory closing. Although riveting can be automated, it is slowly being displaced by arc welding.

Riviera, coastal region of the Mediterranean Sea in southeastern France and northwestern Italy. It is a major tourist center, noted for its scenery and pleasant climate. The Riviera's fashionable resorts include Cannes, Nice, and St. Tropez in France; Monte Carlo in Monaco; and Bordighera, Portofino, Rapallo, and San Remo in Italy.

Roadrunner

Riyadh (pop. 1,380,000), Saudi Arabian city and seat of the Saudi royal family, about 240 mi (386 km) west of the Persian Gulf. It is an important commercial center and has rapidly expanded because of the oil trade.
See also: Saudi Arabia.

Rizal, José (1861-96), Philippine writer and patriot. His novels *The Lost Eden* (1886) and *The Subversive* (1891) denounced Spanish rule in the Philippines. His execution by the Spanish on charges of instigating insurrection led to a full-scale rebellion.

Rizzio, David (c.1533-66), Italian musician, favorite of Mary, Queen of Scots. He became Mary's secretary in 1564. Scottish nobles, including Lord Darnley, Mary's husband, assassinated him.

RNA *see:* Nucleic acid.

Roach, fish belonging to the carp and minnow family, commonly found in the lakes and rivers of Europe. Measuring from 6 to 16 in (15 to 40 cm) in length, it is yellow-green in color, with red eyes. It is often used as bait or caught for food. The name also refers to certain varieties of North American fish, notably the golden shiner.

Roach *see:* Cockroach.

Road, surfaced or unsurfaced path over which vehicles travel. Roads include streets; local and secondary thoroughfares linking rural areas and communities; primary highways, including freeways and expressways, connecting larger communities; and in the United States the Federal Interstate Highway System, a system of freeways connecting most cities larger than 50,000. The first roads appeared around 3000 B.C., soon after the invention of the wheel. Later the Chinese and Egyptians built roads, but the Romans are generally considered the first really knowledgeable road builders. In the United States, roads remained crude, unsurfaced or covered with gravel or wood planks, until the beginning of the 20th century; the invention and growing popularity of the automobile aided road development around this time. Today, the United States has almost 4 million mi (6.5 million km) of roads.

Roadrunner (*Geococcyx californianus*), large, slenderly built bird of the cuckoo family, found in arid regions in the southwestern United States and Mexico. Roadrunners fly weakly but have strong legs and run very rapidly, up to 15 mph, catching lizards and small rodents.

Roanoke (pop. 224,477), industrial, trade, transportation, and medical center, and one of the largest cities in Virginia. Roanoke comes from the Indian word *Rawenoke*, meaning *shell money*. Schools in Roanoke include Hollins College, Roanoke College, and Virginia Polytechnic Institute. The Norfolk and Western Railroad and the Appalachian Power Co. have headquarters there. Roanoke was also the childhood home of black educator Booker T. Washington. Settled in 1881 as Big Lick and renamed Roanoke in 1882, it has a council-manager form of government.
See also: Virginia.

Roanoke Island, island off the northeastern coast of North Carolina, 12 mi by 3 mi (19.3 km by 4.8 km) site of the first English settlement in North America (1585). Its economy depends on fishing and tourism.

Roaring Twenties, period of the 1920s in the United States identified with restlessness and social reform. After years of involvement with the war in Europe, the nation experienced a surge of economic prosperity that resulted in dramatic shifts in American attitudes and culture. This period, also called the Dollar Decade and the Jazz Age, inspired many in the arts to rebel against narrow-mindedness and traditional values. The period is often associated with bootleg liquor, short skirts, women smoking cigarettes, and sexual permissiveness.

The Charleston, regarded as indecent by most parents, was a popular dance during the Roaring Twenties.

Robbe-Grillet, Alain (1922-), French novelist, originator of the French "new novel." In works such as *The Voyeur* (1955), *Jealousy* (1957), and the screenplay for *Last Year at Marienbad* (1960), structure, objects, and events displace character and story.

Robber crab *see:* Hermit crab.

Robbins, Frederick Chapman (1916-), U.S. virologist who shared the 1954 Nobel Prize in physiology or medicine with J. F. Enders and T. H. Weller for their cultivation of the poliomyelitis virus in non-nerve tissues.
See also: Physiology; Poliomyeletis.

Robbins, Jerome (1918-), U.S. choreographer and director. He danced major roles with the American Ballet Theatre (1940-44), where he created his first ballet, *Fancy Free* (1944). With the New York City Ballet he was associate artistic director (1950-59), a ballet master after 1968, and from 1983 ballet master-in-chief (with Peter Martins). For motion pictures, television, and Broadway he choreographed and directed such productions as *West Side Story* (1957) and *Fiddler on the Roof* (1964).

Roberts, Kenneth Lewis (1885-1957), U.S. writer and *Saturday Evening Post* correspondent. His series of popular historical novels, including *Arundel* (1930), *Rabble in Arms* (1933), and *Northwest Passage* (1937), received a special Pulitzer Prize citation (1957). He also wrote travel books.

Roberts, Owen Josephus (1875-1955), associate justice of the U.S. Supreme Court (1930-45). He was a prosecuting attorney in the Teapot Dome scandal (1924) and was involved in economic legislation in the Depression. He led the inquiry into the Pearl Harbor disaster (1941).
See also: Supreme Court of the United States.

Roberts, Sir Charles George Douglas (1860-1943), Canadian writer. His simple, descriptive poems of the Maritime provinces contributed to an emerging Canadian consciousness. Among his works are animal stories, such as *Red Fox* (1905).

Robertson, Oscar (1938-), U.S. basketball player. Nicknamed the "Big O" and renowned for his passing and scoring ability, Robertson played for the National Basketball Association (NBA) Cincinnati Royals (1960-70) and Milwaukee Bucks (1971-74). His achievements include NBA Rookie of the Year (1961), 4 Most Valuable Player awards—1 regular season (1964) and 3 All-Star (1961, 64, 69), and ranking fourth on the all time regular season scoring list (26,710 career points). Robertson is the only player to average a triple-double (10 or more assists, points, and rebounds per game) for an entire season (1961-62). In 1979 he was inducted into the Basketball Hall of Fame.

Robertson, Rev. Pat (1930-), U.S. evangelist and politician who established the first television station for Christian broadcasting (the Christian Broadcasting Network, 1960) at Portsmouth, Va. Robertson was an unsuccessful presidential candidate in the 1988 election.

Robert's Rules of Order *see:* Parliamentary Procedure.

Roberval, Sieur de (Jean François de la Rocque; 1500?-60?), French explorer who led one of the first expeditions to colonize Canada. He was named lieutenant general and viceroy of Canada by Francis I. In 1542 he and a group of 200 settlers landed in the supposedly mineral-rich territory of Newfoundland previously explored by Jacques Cartier. Many of the colonists did not survive the year, and no mineral riches were found. A later expedition also proved unsuccessful. His death was the result of murder.
See also: Canada.

Robeson, Paul (1898-1976), U.S. singer and stage and film actor. A basso, he made his concert debut in 1925 and became known for his renditions of spirituals. Son of a former slave, his most famous song was "Ol' Man River" from the musical *Show Boat* (1928). Robeson starred in the play and film of *Emperor Jones* (1925; 1933) and in Shakespeare's *Othello.* As a collegiate athlete Robeson was twice named an All-American end in football. He also starred in 3 other sports. He was also valedictorian of his class. Ostracized in the United States for his communist beliefs, he lived and sang in Europe between 1958 and 1963.

Robespierre, Maximilien Marie Isidore (1758-94), fanatical idealist leader of the French Revolution. A lawyer, he was elected as a representative of the third estate to the States-General (1789) and rose to become leader of the radical Jacobins in the National Convention (1793). He liquidated the rival moderate Girondists and as leader of the Committee of Public Safety initiated the Reign of Terror. The National Convention rose against him, alienated by his increasing power. He was arrested, summarily tried, and executed.
See also: French Revolution.

Robin, vernacular name for various unrelated species of small birds with red breasts. They include the European robin (*Erithacus rubecula*), American robin (*Turdus migratorius*), Pekin robin (*Leiothrix lutea*), and Indian robin (*Saxicoloides fulicata*). Most familiar are the European robin (robin redbreast), an insectivorous thrush noted for its beautiful song, and the American robin, a common garden and woodland bird of the United States.

Robin Hood, legendary medieval English hero. He is usually depicted as an outlaw, living with his band of followers, including Little John and Friar Tuck, in Sherwood Forest in Nottinghamshire. He robbed the Norman overlords to give to the poor.

Robinson, Bill (1878-1949), popular U.S. dancer and entertainer, nicknamed "Bojangles." He won national and international acclaim as a musical comedy performer and was featured in numerous Broadway shows and Hollywood films, including those in which he starred with Shirley Temple. He was especially known for his "stair tap" dance, which he claimed to have invented when he danced up a staircase to receive an award from the king of England.

Robinson, Eddie (Edward Gay Robinson; 1919-), the most victorious coach in college football history. In 1985, Robinson guided Grambling State University to its 324th win, surpassing the record of 323 wins held by Paul (Bear) Bryant. Grambling State has captured 14 Southwestern Athletic Conference championships under Robinson and more than 200 of his players have gone on to professional football teams.

Robinson, Edwin Arlington (1869-1935), U.S. poet, known for his series of terse, sometimes bitter, verse characterizations of the inhabitants of the fictitious Tilbury Town. His *Collected Poems* (1921), *The Man Who Died Twice* (1924), and *Tristam* (1927) won Pulitzer Prizes.

Robinson, Frank (1935-), U.S. baseball player and manager. Known as an excellent outfielder, Robinson won the Rookie of the Year award (1956) and was the first player to be named Most Valuable Player in both the National and American Leagues (1961 and 66, respectively). He played for the Cincinnati Reds (1956-65), Baltimore Orioles (1966-71), Los Angeles Dodgers (1972), California Angels (1973-74), and Cleveland Indians (1974-76). Robinson became the first African-American manager of a major league baseball team, as player-manager of the Cleveland Indians (1975-77). He also managed the San Francisco Giants (1981-84) and Baltimore Orioles (1988). Robinson was inducted to the National Baseball Hall of Fame in 1982.

Robinson, Jackie (Jack Roosevelt Robinson; 1919-72), U.S. baseball player. A lettermen in 4 sports at UCLA, Robinson became the first African-American to be admitted into baseball's major leagues (1947). Known for his exceptional hitting and base-stealing ability, he was named Rookie of the Year and won the National League's Most Valuable Player award once (1949). Robinson played for the Brooklyn Dodgers (1947-56) and led them to a championship in 1955. He was inducted into the National Baseball Hall of Fame in 1962.

Robinson, James Harvey (1863-1936), U.S. historian. He was one of the founders of the "new history," studying the intellectual, social, and scientific development of humankind rather than only the narrow range of political events.

Robinson, Joan Violet (1903-83), British economist, writer, and advocate of Keynesian economics. A colleague of John Maynard Keynes, she worked with him to provide a new economic model based on increased government spending as a solution to depression and unemployment. Her work helped to shape the economic policies of the 1930s and has been an important influence on economic thought.

Robinson, Sir Robert (1886-1975), English organic chemist awarded the 1947 Nobel Prize in chemistry for his pioneering studies of the molecular structures of alkaloids and other vegetable-derived substances.
See also: Chemistry.

Robinson, Sugar Ray (Walter Smith; 1921-89), U.S. boxer. Considered one of the greatest fighters of all time, Robinson won the world welterweight title (1946) and the middleweight title (1951). He retired in 1952, but returned in 1955 to regain the middleweight title. In 1958 Robinson won his fifth middleweight title, becoming the first boxer to win a divisional world championship 5 times. He retired in 1965.

Robot, mechanical device equipped with sensing instruments for detecting input signals or environmental conditions, with a calculating mechanism for making decisions, and with a guidance mechanism for providing control.
See also: Automation.

Rob Roy (Robert MacGregor; 1671-1734), Scottish outlaw, romanticized in Sir Walter Scott's *Rob Roy* (1818). He was outlawed for cattle theft in 1712 by the duke of Montrose, whose tenants he then plundered. Hunted for many years, he surrendered in 1722 but was pardoned in 1727.

Robusti, Jacopo *see:* Tintoretto.

Rocard, Michel Louis Leon (1930-), French prime minister (1988-91). Rocard is a socialist who served as secretary to the Unified Socialist Party (1967-73). He was elected to 2 terms in the National Assembly (1969-73 and 1978-81) and held several government positions.

Rochambeau, Comte de (Jean Baptiste Donatien de Vimeur; 1725-1807), French general who commanded French troops sent to help General George Washington in the American revolution. Involved in the French Revolution, he narrowly escaped execution in the Reign of Terror.
See also: France.

Roche, Mazo De la *see:* De la Roche, Mazo.

Rochester (pop. 1,002,410), large industrial city in upstate New York, on the banks of the Genesee River, near its confluence with Lake Ontario. The community was laid out by Col. Nathaniel Rochester in 1811, and it became a commercial and industrial center within 20 years. Modern Rochester is known for the manufacture of cameras and film equipment, a variety of consumer goods, and machinery and precision instruments. The city is the home of the University of Rochester and the Eastman School of Music.
See also: New York.

Rock, hard, solid matter of the earth's crust, sometimes a combination of one or more minerals. Rock may occur close to the

Paul Robeson

Jackie Robinson

earth's surface or deep underground. Rocks are classified according to their origin. Igneous rock forms when magma (molten material deep within the earth) rises toward the surface and cools. Intrusive igneous rock, such as granite, results if the magma solidifies before it reaches the earth's surface. Extrusive igneous rock, such as obsidian, occurs when magma reaches the surface, as it does in a volcano eruption. Sedimentary rock, such as sandstone, gypsum, and chalky limestone, forms when sediments, or parts of other rocks, mix together and harden. These sediments can be formed by erosion, chemical action, or an accumulation of plant and animal parts. Metamorphic rock, such as marble and slate, occurs when igneous or sedimentary rocks are exposed to intensive pressure or heat and subsequently change their form. Rock is used primarily as a building material and is an important component of concrete.

Rockefeller, family of U.S. financiers and politicians. **John Davison Rockefeller** (1839-1937) entered the infant oil industry in Cleveland, Ohio, at the age of 24 and ruthlessly unified the oil industry into the Standard Oil Trust. He devoted a large part of his later life to philanthropy, creating the Rockefeller Foundation. **John Davison Rockefeller, Jr.** (1874-1960), only son of John D. Rockefeller, followed his father's business and charitable interests. He donated the land for the UN headquarters and helped found the Rockefeller Center in New York City. **John Davison Rockefeller, 3rd** (1906-78) first son of John, Jr., helped establish New York City's Lincoln Center for the Performing Arts and the United Negro College Fund. **Nelson Aldrich Rockefeller** (1908-79), second son of John, Jr., governor of N.Y. 1959-73, was appointed U.S. vice president in 1974. He sought presidential nomination in 1960, 1964, and 1968. He expanded transportation, welfare, housing, and other social services in N.Y. **Winthrop Rockefeller** (1912-73), fourth son of John, Jr., was Republican governor of Arkansas (1967-71). **David Rockefeller** (1915-), youngest son of John, Jr., was president of the Chase Manhattan Bank and chairman of Rockefeller University. **John Davison "Jay" Rockefeller, 4th** (1937-), grandson of John D. Rockefeller, Jr., became Democratic governor of West Virginia in 1977 and 1980 and was elected to the U.S. Senate in 1985.

Nelson Rockefeller

Knute Rockne

Rockefeller Foundation, U.S. philanthropic foundation. Founded in 1913 by John D. Rockefeller, it supports research in three main areas: medical and natural sciences, agricultural sciences, and the humanities and social sciences.

Rocket, form of jet-propulsion engine in which the substances (fuel and oxidizer) needed to produce the propellant gas jet are carried internally. Working by reaction, and being independent of atmospheric oxygen, rockets are used to power interplanetary space vehicles. In addition to their chief use to power missiles, rockets are also used for supersonic and assisted-takeoff airplane propulsion, and sounding rockets are used for scientific investigation of the upper atmosphere. The first rockets—of the firework type, cardboard tubes containing gunpowder—were made in 13th-century China, and the idea quickly spread to the West. Their military use was limited, guns being superior, until military rockets were developed by Sir William Congreve (1772-1828). The 20th century saw the introduction of new fuels and oxidants, e.g., a mixture of nitrocellulose and nitroglycerin for solid-fuel rockets, or ethanol and liquid oxygen for the more efficient liquid-fuel rockets. The first liquid-fuel rocket was made by R.H. Goddard, who also invented the multistage rocket. In World War II Germany, and afterward in the U.S., Wernher von Braun made vast improvements in rocket design. Other propulsion methods, including the use of nuclear furnaces, electrically accelerated plasmas and ion propulsion, are being developed.

Rocket launching

Rocket, model, or space model, small-scale working replica of the kind of rocket used in military and space programs. Weighing under 1 lb (0.45 km) and measuring 8-24 in (20-61 cm), these models have fuel-burning engines that allow them to travel distances of up to 2,000 ft (610 m) at a speed of 300 mph (480 kmph). Model rocketry kits are commercially available to hobbyists. Associations, clubs, and competitions exist throughout the world.

Rocket, The, first locomotive powered by steam. It was invented by George and Robert Stephenson of Britain in 1829 to provide a railway link between the cities of Liverpool and Manchester. The name derives from a response by the Stephensons to a public jibe that the locomotive was as hazardous to ride as a space rocket. The speed of *The Rocket* reached as high as 36 mph (57.9 kmph).
See also: Locomotive.

Rock festival *see:* Rock music.

Rockford (pop. 283,719), second-largest city in Illinois. It lies on the Rock River in the north-central area, about 17 mi (27 km) south of the Wisconsin state line and less than 100 mi (161 km) northwest of Chicago. Rockford is one of Illinois' major industrial centers and is known for the manufacture of machine tools, hardware, heavy earth-moving equipment, automobile parts, paint, and farm and household goods. The city is the seat of Winnebago County and the home of Rockford College (founded in 1847). Rockford was founded in 1834 at the site of a stagecoach ford and became a city in 1852.
See also: Illinois.

Rock music, the dominant popular music since the late 1950s. Rock music first emerged in the mid-1950s as rock 'n' roll, a hybrid evolving from a sophisticated blues style called rhythm and blues, which often used amplified instruments to produce a heavy beat. The first national rock 'n' roll hit—and the one that probably gave the genre its name—was "Rock Around the Clock," by Bill Haley and His Comets (1955). Rock 'n' roll's first superstar, Elvis Presley, hit on a riveting combination of harddriving rhythm and blues with country and western music. Other important performers includeed Chuck Berry and Buddy Holly. Rock 'n' roll, with its exciting beat and lyrics about school, cars, and love, was especially popular with adolescents. The impetus for the transformation of rock 'n' roll into rock music came from England, where, in the early 1960s, bands like the Beatles and the Rolling Stones remixed the original ingredients, adding new musical textures, forms, and rhythms and more sophisticated lyrics. The 1960s also saw the emergence of soul music, a product of rhythm and blues and gospel styles, which would add its sound to rock; folk rock, as in the later work of Bob Dylan; and acid rock, an attempt to reproduce musically the hallucinogenic drug experience. In the 1970s acid rock was followed by hard rock or heavy metal, which was louder and more repetitive and by eclectic mixtures of the rock sound with country, jazz, calypso, and other styles. Another 1970s innovation was disco, repetitive dance music with a rock beat. In the mid-1970s punk rock, an angry, harsh, sometimes violent style, emerged out of the postindustrial despair of working-class youth in England. Punk rock, also reflected young people's disillusionment with the so-called rock establishment and the overcommercialization of what had been a rebellious art form. The 1980s were dominated by rock videos, short films that feature acting, dancing, and effects as well as music.

Rockne, Knute Kenneth (1888-1931), U.S. football coach. Known for his inspirational talks, and use of great speed and variety on the field, Rockne helped make football a more entertaining sport. While coaching for Notre Dame (1918-30) he achieved a record of 105 wins, 12 losses, and 5 ties, giving him a winning percentage (.881) that is the best in college football history.

Rock oil *see:* Petroleum.

Some of rock music's great superstars: Bill Haley (above), Tina Turner (upper right), Buddy Holly (below right), and the Rolling Stones.

Rockwell, Norman (1894-1978), U.S. illustrator, known for his realistic and humorous scenes of U.S. small town life. His work includes magazine covers for *The Saturday Evening Post* and a series of paintings of the Four Freedoms.

Rocky Mountain goat (*Oreamnos americanus*), goatlike herbivorous mammal closely related to the antelope. It is found in the coastal mountain ranges of North America. An excellent climber, it is considered to be fairly unintelligent. It has curved horns, dense whitish fur, black hoofs, and a long beard in the male of the species.

Rocky Mountain National Park, natural wild area in north central Colorado, in the heart of the Rocky Mountains. Founded in 1915, the park is dominated by Longs Peak (14,225 ft/4,345 m) and has many glaciers.
See also: National Parks.

Rocky Mountains, principal range of the western region of North America. Extending from north Alaska for more than 3,000 mi (4,800 km) to New Mexico, they form the Continental Divide; rivers rising on the eastern slopes flow to the Arctic or Atlantic Ocean, and those rising on the western slopes flow toward the Pacific. Rivers originating in the Rockies include the Missouri, Rio Grande, Colorado, Columbia, and Arkansas. A relatively new system, the Rockies were formed by massive uplifting forces that began about 70 million years ago.

Rocky Mountain spotted fever, acute febrile disease caused by *Rickettsia rickettsii* and transmitted by ixodid ticks. The onset is abrupt, with severe headache, chills, and muscular pains. Fever reaches 40°C (104°F) within several days and remains high for 10 to 15 days. Untreated patients may develop pneumonia, tissue necrosis, and circulatory failure, with resulting brain and heart damage. Starting antibiotic therapy early has significantly reduced mortality, formerly about 20 percent.
See also: Rickettsia.

Rococo, 18th-century European artistic and architectural style. The term derives from *rocaille* (French, "rock work"), whose arabesque and ingenious forms are found in many rococo works. The style, characterized by lightness and delicacy, emerged c.1700 in France, finding expression in the works of François Boucher, Jean-Honoré Fragonard, and others. Some of the greatest achievements of rococo sculpture and decoration are found in the palaces and pilgrimage churches of Austria and southern Germany.

Rodent, largest order of mammals, including some 1,500 species of mice, rats, porcupines, and squirrels. Rodents have a single pair of incisors in the upper and lower jaws that continue to grow throughout life. Behind the incisors is a gap to allow recirculation of food in chewing. The cheek skin can be drawn across the gap, in front of the molars and premolars, leaving the incisors free for gnawing. Rodents are predominantly eaters of seeds, grain, and other vegetation.

A U.S. rodeo

Rodeo, in the United States and Canada, contest and entertainment based on ranching techniques; it derives from late-19th-century cowboy meets held to celebrate the end of a cattle drive. It usually comprises 5 main events: calf-roping, in which a mounted cowboy must rope a calf, dismount, throw the calf, and tie 3 of its legs together; steer-wrestling, in which the cowboy jumps from a galloping horse and wrestles a steer to the ground by its horns; bareback riding on an unbroken horse for 8 to 10 secs; saddle-bronc riding; and bull-riding.

Auguste Rodin's The Age of Bronze *(1876)*

Rodgers, Richard (1902-79), U.S. songwriter and composer. He collaborated with librettist Lorenz Hart on *A Connecticut Yankee* (1927), *Pal Joey* (1940), and many other Broadway musicals containing dozens of enormously popular songs. Later he teamed up with Oscar Hammerstein II on the Pulitzer Prize-winning *Oklahoma!* (1943), *South Pacific* (1949), *The King and I* (1951), and *The Sound of Music* (1959), among other shows.

Rodin, Auguste (1840-1917), French sculptor. He rose to fame in the late 1870s and in 1880 began the never-completed *Gate of Hell,* the source of such well-known pieces as *The Thinker* (1880) and *The Kiss* (1886). His works, in stone or bronze, were characterized by energy and emotional intensity, as in *The Burghers of Calais* (1884-94).

Rodney, Caesar (1728-84), American statesman. He was Delaware's delegate to the Continental Congress, signed the Declaration of Independence, and was president of Delaware (1778-82).

Rodrigo Díaz *see:* Cid, El.

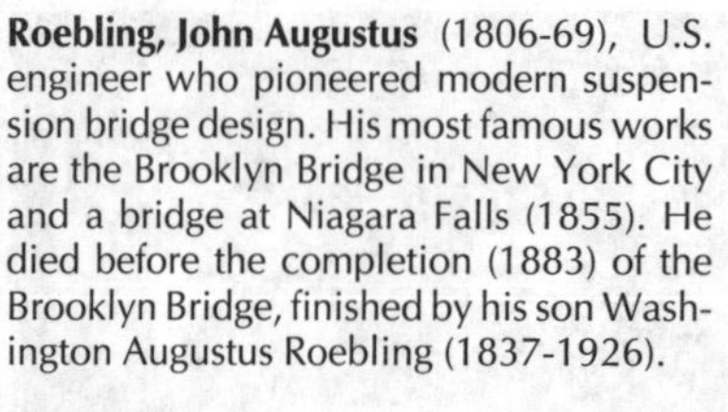

Roebling, John Augustus (1806-69), U.S. engineer who pioneered modern suspension bridge design. His most famous works are the Brooklyn Bridge in New York City and a bridge at Niagara Falls (1855). He died before the completion (1883) of the Brooklyn Bridge, finished by his son Washington Augustus Roebling (1837-1926).

Roemer, Olaus (1644-1710), Danish astronomer, the first to show that light has a finite velocity. He noticed that Jupiter eclipsed its moons at times differing from those predicted and correctly concluded that the discrepancy resulted from the finite nature of light's velocity, which he calculated as 141 mi per sec (now calculated as about 186,282 mi per sec/299,792.458 km per sec).
See also: Astronomy.

Roentgen, Wilhelm Conrad (1845-1923), German physicist, recipient (1901) of the first Nobel Prize in physics for his discovery of X rays.
See also: X rays.

Roethke, Theodore (1908-63), U.S. poet who won a Pulitzer Prize for *The Waking* (1953) and a National Book Award for *Words for the Wind* (1958). Much of his imagery is drawn from nature.

Roe v. Wade, landmark decision (1973) by the U.S. Supreme Court ruling that a state may not prohibit a woman's right to have a medically initiated abortion during the first 6 months of pregnancy. A Texas waitress ("Jane Roe") began the case in 1970, when she challenged a state law that denied her a lawful abortion. The court came to this decision by determining that a fetus was not a living person and was therefore not entitled to constitutional protection.
See also: Abortion.

Rogers, Carl Ransom (1902-87), U.S. psychotherapist, who instituted the idea of the patient determining the extent and nature of his course of therapy, the therapist following the patient's lead.
See also: Psychotherapy.

Rogers, John (1829-1904), U.S. sculptor known for realistic figural groups, such as *The Slave Auction.* His extremely popular works were often mass-produced.

Rogers, Will (William Penn Adair; 1879-1935), U.S. humorist known for his homespun philosophy and mockery of politics and other subjects previously considered "untouchable." Part Irish and part Cherokee, he became famous in the Ziegfeld Follies of 1916. He wrote a syndicated column that appeared in 350 newspapers.

Rogers' Rangers, U.S. commando unit that fought on the side of the British during the French and Indian War. Led by the Loyalist Robert Rogers (1731-95), the rangers were responsible for daring raids on French settlements during the years 1758-63.
See also: French and Indian Wars.

Roget, Peter Mark (1779-1869), English scholar and physician, author of the definitive *Thesaurus of English Words and Phrases* (1852).

Rohrer, Heinrich (1933-), Swiss physicist, winner with Gerd Binnig and Ernst Ruska of West Germany of the Nobel Prize for physics (1986) for his contribution to the development of the scanning tunneling microscope (STM) that allows scientists to view individual atoms.
See also: Physics.

Roh Tae Woo (1932-), South Korean president (1988-) and general. Roh Tae Woo led the Defense Security Council (1979-81) under President Chun Doo Hwan. He retired from the military (1981) and organized the Summer Olympic Games held at Seoul (1988). He was active in the Democratic Justice Party before his election.

Roland, one of Charlemagne's commanders, hero of the *Song of Roland.* Ambushed by Basques at Roncesvalles in A.D. 778, he and his men were massacred because he was too proud to summon help.
See also: Charlemagne.

Roland de la Platière, husband and wife French revolutionaries. **Marie Jeanne Roland de la Platière** (1754-93) was hostess and adviser to the Girondists. Madame Roland, as she was known, became involved in a power struggle between the Girondists and the Jacobins, for which she and other leaders of the Girondists were arrested and sent to the guillotine. **Jean Marie Roland de la Platière** (1734-93) was leader of the Girondists (1791) and minister of the interior (1792-93). He committed suicide on hearing of the execution of his wife.
See also: French Revolution.

Rolfe, John (1585-1622), early English settler in Virginia who married the Indian princess Pocahontas (1614). His methods of curing tobacco made it the basis of the colony's later prosperity.
See also: Pocahontas.

Rolland, Romain (1866-1944), French writer, who won the 1915 Nobel Prize for literature. He is best known for his biographies, including *Beethoven* (1903), his pacifist articles *Above the Battle* (1915), and the novel-cycle *Jean Christophe* (1904-12).

Roller, species of bird belonging to the roller family. Flocks of rollers can be found in southern Europe during the warm season and northern Africa during the cold season. Standing at 10-16 in (25-40 cm), the roller resembles—but is not closely related to—the jay. Its name derives from the mating dance of the male, which consists of a series of airborne dives and tumbles.

Roller skating, popular source of sport and recreation. Traditional skates consist of four wheels fitted with ball bearings attached, 2 in front and 2 in back, to a shoe or to a steel platform that can be attached to a shoe. Clamp-on skates with metal wheels are generally worn out-of-doors while bootskates are most often used on rinks. For racing, wooden wheels are favored; for figure skating and roller hockey, wheels are usually made of plastic. In the late 1980s, a new type of skate, the roller blade, was introduced, with four wheels placed front to back to form a single line, or blade, of wheels.

Rolling Stones, influential rock band from Britain. Renowned for their hard-driving, blues-inspired, often sexually explicit songs, the band has influenced the course of popular music since the mid-1960s. Original band members include Mick Jagger (1943-), Keith Richard (1943-), Bill Wyman (1936-) and Charlie Watts (1941-). Guitarist Brian Jones left the band shortly before his death and was replaced by Mick Taylor in 1969 and then by Ron Wood in 1974. In addition to their many recordings,the Stones are known as one of the world's most exciting performance bands.

Rölvaag, Ole Edvart (1876-1931), Norwegian-born novelist, who came to the United States in 1896 and wrote in Norwegian. His trilogy *Giants in the Earth* (1927-31) is the story of Norwegian settlers in the United States.

Romains, Jules (Louis Farigoule; 1885-1972), French author and exponent of unanimism, or the collective personality. He is known for his plays and his 27-volume cycle *Men of Good Will* (1932-46).

Roman Catholic Church, major branch of the Christian church consisting of Christians in communion with the pope. It comprises the ecclesiastical organization that remained under papal obedience at the Reformation, consisting of a hierarchy of bishops and priests, with other officers such as cardinals. Roman Catholicism stresses the authority of tradition and the church (through ecumenical councils and the papacy) to formulate doctrine and regulate moral and spiritual life. Members participate in grace, mediated through the priesthood, by means of the seven sacraments. The mass is central to Roman Catholic life and worship. Doctrinally, Roman Catholic theologians emphasize the role of the Virgin Mary and the authority and infallibility of the pope. Other distinctive doctrines include clerical celibacy, limbo, and purgatory. Those held in common with the orthodox churches (but rejected by Protestants) include the invocation of saints, veneration of images, acceptance of the Apocrypha, the sacramental system, and monasticism. Since the Second Vatican Council, there has been a movement toward accommodation with the modern world, cautious dealings with the ecumenical movement, and encouragement of lay participation and vernacular liturgy. There are about 600 million Roman Catholics worldwide.
See also: Christianity.

Romance, literary term identified with fiction usually depicting idealized love. Romances typically contain nonrealistic characters and plots and use elements of fantasy or adventure. The ancient Greek romance, *Daphnis and Chloë,* written c.A.D. 200, is considered to be the first great romance. The genre reached its height in the Middle Ages with the tales of King Arthur. In the 19th century, romances contained a strong element of mystery and the supernatural.

Romance languages, one of the main groups of the Indo-European languages. It comprises those languages derived from the vernacular Latin that was spread by Roman soldiers and colonists, and that superseded local tongues. The languages include Italian, the Rhaeto-Romanic, Provençal, French, Walloon, Spanish, Catalan, Portuguese, and Romanian. The languages share a similar vocabulary and grammatical development.

Roman Circus *see:* Rome, Ancient.

Roman Empire *see:* Rome, Ancient.

Romanesque art and architecture, artistic style prevalent in Christian western Europe from c.A.D. 950 to 1200. Romanesque preceded Gothic art and architecture and is so called because its forms are derived from Roman art and architecture. The architecture, based on the round Roman arch and improvised systems of vaulting, was characterized by a massive, simple, and robust style with great vitality, particularly in the case of Norman architecture. Churches had immense towers; interiors were decorated with frescoes depicting biblical scenes. The sculptural style was varied, vigorous, and expressive, with carved, sculptured scenes on column capitals, and larger reliefs and figures on exterior portals and tympanums.

Roman Forum *see:* Forum.

Roman gods *see:* Mythology.

Romania, or Rumania, republic in southeastern Europe occupying the northeastern part of the Balkan Peninsula and bordering the Black Sea. Once part of the Roman Empire, its language is directly descended from Latin and closely resembles modern Italian. Although Romania is a communist country and a member of the Warsaw Pact, its foreign and economic policies have been independent of those of the Soviet Union. Romania has worked to advance its own agriculture and industry, seeking relations with nations of the West as well as the East. However, the Communist Party is still all-powerful, and pressure to conform to the official party line remains considerable.
Land and climate. The Carpathian Mountains are Romania's dominant geographical feature. They cross the forested southern Bukovina region and divide Moldavia in the east from Transylvania in the west. Moldavia extends east from the mountain highlands and sheltered valleys

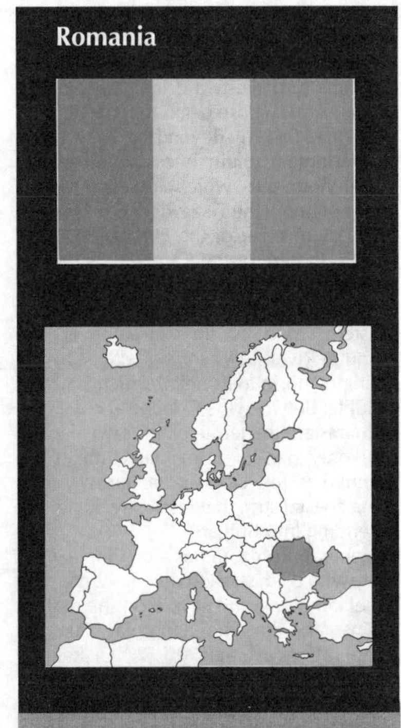

Capital:	Bucharest
Area:	91,699 sq mi (237,500 sq km)
Population:	23,168,000
Government:	republic
Independent:	1878
GNP:	U.S.$148,048,000,000
Per capita:	U.S. $6,400

Most of Romania's main oil wells are found in the lower Carpathians around the industrial city of Ploiesti.

to the Prut River, forming the Moldavian "platform"—an unrelievedly flat plain covered by loess. Around Brasov, the Carpathians turn westward into the Transylvanian Alps, whose peaks reach heights of 8,347 ft (2,541 m). Beyond the Timis River, the mountain chain is continued by the Banat Mountains, which slope down to the fertile plains of the Tisza River Lowlands on the eastern edge of the Hungarian Plain. Within the arc of the Carpathians lies the Transylvania Plateau, a region of low hills, fertile valleys, and alluvial plains. At the western edge of the Carpathians, the Danube River flows south and east before swinging north to its delta, which is rich in wildlife. Between the Danube and the Carpathians are the fertile plains of Walachia. The only part of Romania south of the Danube is the Dobruja, a narrow, low-lying coastal strip that is marshy but fertile, extending into Bulgaria.

In general, Romania has a continental climate with cold, snowy winters. Winters are especially long and severe on the eastern plains and in the Dobruja. Summer temperatures average 70°F (20°C). Rainfall averages 25 in on the plains and 10 in in parts of the Dobruja. The high west-facing mountain slopes receive more than 60 in of rain and snow annually.

People. Over 60% of the population of Romania live in rural areas. About 85% are Romanians, with Hungarian and German minorities. The largest cities are Bucharest, Brasov, Iasi, Timisoara, Constantsa, Cluj-Napoca, and Galati. Bucharest is the capital city.

Economy. Over 60% of the land area of Romania is agricultural, but industry provides two thirds of the national income. More than 90% of the farmland is collectivized. About 25% of the land is covered by forests. With large oil fields in the Prahova Valley, Romania is the second-largest producer of petroleum and natural gas in Europe. Copper, lead, coal, iron ore, and lead are mined. Principal industries are iron and steel, machinery, textiles, and chemicals. The main exports are oil-field equipment, furniture, agricultural machinery, and textiles.

History. Most of modern Romania was once part of ancient Dacia, thoroughly imbued with the language and culture of Rome. After the 13th century the two principalities of Moldavia and Walachia emerged, existing as dependencies of Turkey until 1829, then as Russian protectorates. United in 1861, Romania gained its independence in 1878. After World War I the Romanian-speaking province of Transylvania was acquired from Austria-Hungary. In the 1930s the country was dominated by Fascist rule; in 1941 dictator Ion Antonescu sided with the Axis powers. Overrun by the USSR in 1944, Romania became a satellite state. After King Michael's abdication in 1947 it became a republic. In the 1960s and 1970s Romania worked to establish diplomatic and economic relations with the West. In the 1980s, Nicolae Ceausescu, Romania's ruler since 1965, began a "modernization" program to industrialize urban communities. Romania's subsequent debt to Western European banks has slowed its economic growth. In December 1989, an anti-communist revolution resulted in Ceausescu's ouster and subsequent execution. On May 20, 1990 Ion Iliescu was elected president and Petre Roman became prime minister. While trying to modernize its economy, Romania has adopted harsh economic measures, which have led to continued political and social unrest.

Roman numerals, system of numerical representation based on symbols invented by the ancient Romans c.500 B.C. The early Roman system—with some modification—was commonly used for simple calculations as late as the 16th century, when it was eclipsed by the Arabic system. It is used today primarily for notational and decorative purposes, and to record dates. In the Roman system, the symbols I, V, X, L, C, D, and M stand for the numbers 1, 5, 10, 50, 100, 500, and 1,000, respectively.
See also: Numeration systems.

Romanov, ruling dynasty of Russia (1613-1917). The first Romanov tsar was Michael. The last of the direct Romanov line was Peter, but succeeding tsars retained the name of Romanov, down to Nicholas II (r. 1894-1917).

Romanov, Grigoriy Vasilyevich (1923-), USSR Communist Party official and member of the Politburo (1976-1985). He was previously a member of the Secretariat and the Presidium. Although he ostensibly quit his post for medical reasons, it is believed his removal was political.
See also: Union of Soviet Socialist Republics.

Roman Republic *see:* Rome, Ancient.

Romans, Epistle to the, New Testament book written by Saint Paul to the Christians of Rome (A.D. 58). It presents his major statement of justification by faith, and the Christian's consequent freedom from condemnation, sin, and the law. It stresses God's sovereignty and grace.
See also: New Testament.

Romanticism, 19th-century European artistic movement. Its values of emotion, intuition, imagination, and individualism were in opposition to the ideals of restraint, reason, and harmony promoted by classicism. The word "romantic" was first applied to art by Friedrich von Schlegel in 1798. It was later used as a label for works emphasizing the subjective, spiritual, or fantastic; those concerned with wild, uncultivated nature; and those that seemed fundamentally modern rather than classical. The evocative qualities of nature inspired poets such as William Wordsworth, Samuel Taylor Coleridge, and Alphonse Lamartine, and painters such as Joseph Turner and Caspar Friedrich. William Blake and J.W. von Goethe sought to develop new spiritual values; individualism concerned artists as disparate as Walt Whitman and Francisco Goya. The lives of Lord Byron and Frédéric Chopin seemed to exemplify the romantic myth. Among the greatest romantic composers were C.M. von Weber, Hector Berlioz, Felix Mendelssohn, Franz Liszt, and Richard Wagner.

Roman walls, walls constructed by the ancient Romans in what is now Germany, Romania, and northern England. They served to protect the Romans against invasion as well as to facilitate trade and the collection of taxes. The ruins of Hadrian's Wall, built c.A.D. 120, still exist today. It was built primarily of stone and had ditches both in front of the wall and behind. Forts and watchtowers were placed along the wall at regular intervals.
See also: Rome, Ancient.

Romberg, Sigmund (1887-1951), Hungarian-born U.S. composer. He wrote over 70 operettas and musicals, including *The Student Prince* (1924) and *The Desert Song* (1926). He went on to write many film scores.

Rome (Italian: *Roma*; pop. 2,820,000), capital and largest city of Italy, located on the rolling plain of the Roman Campagna, 15 mi (24 km) from the Thyrrenian Sea. Rome has been a center of Western civilization for over 2,000 years. "The Eternal City" was capital of the Roman Empire and is of unique religious significance as the site of the headquarters of the Roman Catholic Church in Vatican City. Administration (of the Italian government as well as of Roma province and the region of Latium), religion, and tourism are the most important activities of modern Rome, which is also a center for commerce, pub-

The "Spanish Steps," on Rome's Piazza di Spagna, lead to the Trinita dei Monti Church.

lishing, movies, and fashion. A great transportation hub, the city has relatively little industry. The site of ancient Rome is the Seven Hills. The Tiber River flows through the city, which contains many important relics of classical Rome, such as the Forum, the Colosseum, the *Domus Aurea* (Golden House), the baths of Caracalla, and the Pantheon. Rome is famous for its squares, Renaissance palaces, churches, basilicas, catacombs, and fountains. There are also many fine museums, art collections, and libraries; the Rome opera house; and the Santa Cecilia music academy, the world's oldest (1584). The University of Rome was founded in 1303.
See also: Italy.

Rome (pop. 43,826), city in Oneida County in central New York State. The location of important battles fought during the American Revolution, it is known as the site of the first raising of the American flag. The building of the Erie Canal began in Rome in 1817. Major industries are copper production and machinery. It is the home of the Griffiss Air Force base.
See also: New York.

Rome, Ancient, city-state in central Italy that grew into a vast empire. At its height, in A.D. 117, it comprised most of the known Western world. The ancient Romans made great advances in the fields of law, civil engineering, standardization in coinage and measurement, philosophy, architecture, and literature. The region was controlled by the Etruscans until Romans established an independent republic in 500 B.C. Throughout the period of the republic (500-31 B.C.), warfare was almost continuous. Under a government controlled by consuls and the senate, Rome overran central and southern Italy and defeated Carthage. Expansion continued to Greece, Asia Minor, Syria, Palestine, and Egypt, Gaul, and England. From about 100 B.C., Rome began to move steadily toward disaster. Civil wars arose from conflicts between senatorial factions, and between rich and poor. The army leaders Pompey and Julius Caesar arose to form the first Triumverate with Crassus. After the assassination of Caesar, Caesar's nephew Octavian defeated Antony and became the first emperor of Rome, renaming himself Augustus. For more than 200 years (27 B.C.-A.D. 180) the empire flourished. The establishment of trade routes throughout the empire lead to the spread of new ideas, particularly Christianity. From about A.D. 200 the period was characterized by internal strife and barbarian raids. Under Constantine I (emperor 306-337) the capital was moved to Byzantium (renamed Constantinople), and Christianity was officially recognized. At the beginning of the fifth century, the empire was divided into East and West, and a period of barbarian invasion and vandalism followed.

Rommel, Erwin (1891-1944), German field marshal, named the "Desert Fox" for his tactical genius as commander of the Afrika Korps (1941-43). His advance ended with the battle of El Alamein (1942). He commanded Army Group B in northern France when the Allies landed in Normandy (1944). He was implicated in the July 1944 plot to assassinate Hitler. Given the choice of suicide or trial, he took poison.
See also: World War II.

Romney, George (1734-1802), English portrait painter, rival of Sir Joshua Reynolds in late-18th-century London. Influenced by classical sculpture, he tended to flatter his subjects, among whom was Lady Emma Hamilton.

Romulo, Carlos Pena (1901-85), Filipino journalist and statesman. His World War II broadcasts during the Japanese occupation of the Philippines were known as "The Voice of Freedom." He won a Pulitzer Prize (1941) and was ambassador to the United States and president of the UN general assembly (1949-50).
See also: Philippines.

Romulus and Remus, mythical founders of Rome (by tradition in 753 B.C.), twin sons of Rhea Silvia, descendant of Aeneas, by the god Mars. Abandoned as infants, they were suckled by a she-wolf until adopted by a herdsman. After a long rivalry, Remus was killed by Romulus, who became the first king of Rome and was later worshiped as the god Quirinus.
See also: Mythology; Rome.

Romulus Augustulus (b. c.A.D. 461), last Western Roman emperor (475-6), puppet of his father Orestes. The end of the Western Roman Empire dates from his overthrow by Odoacer.
See also: Rome, Ancient.

Rondo, musical form in which a main theme is repeatedly stated between two contrasting sections. The rondo generally consists of five or seven parts and has a fixed pattern (ABACA or ABACABA). It was frequently used by composers of the late 18th and early 19th centuries as the last movement of a larger work. Wolfgang Amadeus Mozart and Franz Josef Haydn often concluded their symphonies with a rondo section.

Ronsard, Pierre de (1524-85), French "Prince of Poets," leader of the influential group of poets called Pléiade. Best known as a lyric poet, as in *Sonnets for Hélène* (1578), he also wrote lofty *Hymnes* (1556) on more public subjects and an epic, *La Franciade* (1572).

Ronstadt, Linda (1946-), U.S. singer. Ronstadt began her musical career with the rock group Stone Poneys (1967). She achieved solo success and starred as Mabel in the Broadway production and film of *The Pirates of Penzance* and sang the lead in Puccini's *La Bohème* in New York (1983).

Roof, cover for the top of a building. A roof encloses and protects a building from the

The Via Appia Antica, in the southern part of Rome

elements, and helps drain water from rainfall. Large beams (often called joists), timbers, and rafters support a roof. Metal, concrete, or composite materials are used to build a roof or smaller roofing units called shingles. Flat and lean-to roofs consist of designs of one flat plane. Roofs in which the design consists of two joined flat planes are the gable roof and its inverted design, the butterfly roof. The hip, gambrel, and mansard roofs are more sophisticated designs, in which more than two flat planes are joined at various angles. The design of the roof and the choice of roofing materials are based on the function of the building as well as the climate.

Erwin Rommel

Rook (*Corvus frugilegus*), European bird in the crow family. The rook is about 18 in (45 cm) long. A purple gloss on the black back, white skin next to the bill, and gray to white feathers on the face of an adult are its distinguishing features. It eats insects, worms, and grain. Some rooks native to Europe do not migrate while others in more northern locations migrate south in winter. Rookeries are enormous groupings of rooks—often in the hundreds—that gather during the mating season.

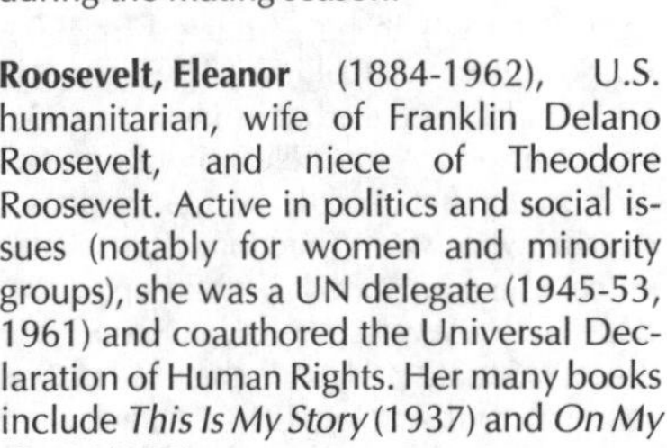

Roosevelt, Eleanor (1884-1962), U.S. humanitarian, wife of Franklin Delano Roosevelt, and niece of Theodore Roosevelt. Active in politics and social issues (notably for women and minority groups), she was a UN delegate (1945-53, 1961) and coauthored the Universal Declaration of Human Rights. Her many books include *This Is My Story* (1937) and *On My Own* (1958).
See also: Human Rights, Declaration of.

Roosevelt, Franklin Delano (1882-1945), 32nd president of the United States. Roosevelt was elected to four terms, more than any other U.S. president, and led the nation through two major crises: a severe depression and a global war. His flexible, experimental approach to politics enabled him to lead the U.S., with widespread support of the people, through one of the most formative periods in U.S. history.

Franklin Delano Roosevelt

32nd president of the United States

Born:	Hyde Park, N.Y.; Jan. 30, 1882
Term:	Mar. 1933-Apr. 1945
Vice presidents:	John N. Garner; Henry A. Wallace; Harry S. Truman
Political party:	Democratic
Spouse:	Anna Eleanor Roosevelt Roosevelt
Children:	6
Died:	Warm Springs, Ga.; Apr. 12, 1945

Early life. Roosevelt was born into a wealthy New York family and brought up—as was his fifth cousin, Theodore Roosevelt—in a restricted social circle that was the closest to an aristocracy the United States ever had. Educated at home until age 14, he attended private school and Harvard, from which he graduated in 1903. Roosevelt entered Columbia Law School in 1904 and passed the bar in 1907. In 1905, he married Anna Eleanor Roosevelt (known by her middle name), a distant cousin who was Theodore Roosevelt's niece. The couple had six children.

Politics. Roosevelt served as a Democrat in the N.Y. Senate (1910-13), then as assistant secretary of the Navy (1913-21), gaining a national reputation as a capable administrator. In 1920, he ran for vice president with presidential candidate James M. Cox. They lost to the Republican ticket of Warren G. Harding and Calvin Coolidge.

While on vacation in Aug. 1921, Roosevelt suffered a severe attack of polio, which partially paralyzed his arms and legs. His mother urged him to retire, but his wife and his secretary, Louis Howe, encouraged him to work to regain some use of his limbs—and reenter politics. He did both. Roosevelt was elected governor of New York in 1928 and 1930. In 1932, he ran for president against incumbent Herbert Hoover. Roosevelt promised a "New Deal" to bring the nation out of its worsening depression, but it was Hoover's unpopularity that most helped Roosevelt win the election.

President. By the time Roosevelt took office in 1933, the U.S. economy was near collapse. More than 13 million people were unemployed, many farmers and city workers were homeless, and thousands of banks were closing daily. Two days after his Mar. 4 inaguration, Roosevelt ended a run on the banks by declaring a "bank holiday." He closed all banks, then had the Treasury Dept. examine their books and resupply funds where possible. Public confidence was restored by the time the banks reopened. On Mar. 9, Congress met in a special session to pass Roosevelt's call for emergency legislation. On Mar. 12, he gave the first of his many "fireside chats"—radio addresses to the nation, explaining his policies. Four days later, he began sending his New Deal proposals to Congress, beginning the "Hundred Days" in which many new programs were established to rebuild the economy and put people back to work. Among Roosevelt's ground-breaking New Deal programs were the Agricultural Adjustment Administration (AAA), which paid farmers to voluntarily reduce production in order to raise prices; the National Recovery Administration (NRA), which included minimum wages and maximum hours for workers; the Civilian Conservation Corps (CCC), which put young men to work in reforestation and other public works; and the Tennessee Valley Authority (TVA), a model for interstate conservation projects of the future. The New Deal also brought in the Wagner Act of 1935, which aided labor; the Work Projects Administration (WPA), a massive new relief program; and a tax-reform bill, social-security act, and youth administration act. In 1936, Roosevelt won reelection in a landslide. However, the economy was not yet under control. When the Supreme Court nullified some New Deal acts, Roosevelt attempted to "pack" the court with additional justices who would support him, but Congress denied him that power. Full economic recovery came only with the war. Until 1937, Roosevelt had paid relatively little attention to foreign affairs. Then World War II broke out in Europe in 1939. In 1940, Roosevelt was reelected to a third term, promising to keep the nation out of war. But on Dec. 7, 1941, Japan struck the U.S. fleet at Pearl Harbor, Hawaii, in a surprise attack. Four days later, the U.S. was at war with Japan, Germany, and Italy. Roosevelt, who directed the immense U.S. war effort and conferred with Allied leaders, was elected to an unprecendented fourth term in 1944. But he did not live to see the war's end. He died suddenly on Apr. 12, 1945, of a cerebral hemorrhage.

Roosevelt, Nicholas J. (1767-1854), U.S. engineer who, at the request of Robert Fulton and Robert Livingston, built and operated the *New Orleans*, the first Mississippi paddle-wheel steamer (1811).

Roosevelt, Theodore (1858-1919), 26th president of the United States. Widely known as "Teddy" or "T.R.," he was one of the most popular, colorful, and controversial presidents, and the youngest (at 42) ever inaugurated. He also was a prolific writer.

Early life. Roosevelt was born into a well-to-do family. A sickly child, he built up his strength through strenuous exercise. In 1880, he graduated from Harvard University and married Alice Hathaway Lee. Roosevelt became involved in Republican politics and served in the N.Y. State Assembly (1882-84). In 1884, his wife died soon after the birth of their child; his mother died the same day. Roosevelt gave up his political career and moved to Dakota Territory to become a rancher and to write.

In 1886, Roosevelt returned to New York, married Edith Kermit Carow (the couple had five children), and built his famous home at Sagamore Hill.

Politics. Roosevelt reentered politics, losing a race for mayor of New York City (1886), and serving on the U.S. Civil Service Commission (1895-97), as president of the Board of Police Commissioners (1897-98), and as assistant secretary of the Navy (1897-98).

During the Spanish-American War, Roosevelt led the 1st Volunteer Cavalry Regiment, known as the Rough Riders. In Cuba in 1898, he led a victorious U.S. attack up Kettle Hill in the battle of San Juan Hill. Returning home a national hero, he was elected governor of New York (1898-1900), then was persuaded to run as vice president in President William McKinley's 1900 reelection campaign. The McKinley-Roosevelt ticket won. On Sept. 6, 1901, McKinley was shot by an assassin; eight days later he died, and Roosevelt became president.

President. Roosevelt, long known as a reformer, used his executive power to control the growing industrial and financial monopolies and regulate the railroads. His "trust buster" administration broke up the powerful Northern Securities Co. and other big-business trusts (monopolies). Roosevelt also intervened in a dangerously stalemated coal strike. Returned to the presidency by a wide margin in the 1904 election, he won passage of the 1906 Hepburn Act to prevent abuses in railroad-shipping rates, and of the 1906 Pure Food and Drug Act, which began U.S. regulation and inspection of foods, drugs, and medicines. He also added about 150 million acres to the national forests, established the U.S. Forest Service (1905), and created other conservation programs.

Roosevelt pursued an aggressive foreign policy. He issued the "Roosevelt Corollary" (1904) to the Monroe Doctrine, warning European nations against intervening in Latin American affairs while reserving that right for the U.S. He pushed the U.S. to build the Panama Canal and sent the U.S. fleet around the world (1907-1909) to show off its strength. In 1905, he helped mediate peace between Russia and Japan, which won him the Nobel Peace Prize.

Retirement. Roosevelt chose not to run for reelection. After his handpicked successor, William Howard Taft, took office in 1909, Roosevelt went big-game hunting in Africa. In 1912, he returned to politics, forming the "Bull Moose" (Progressive) party and losing a bid for the presidency. Retiring to private life, he remained interested in world affairs, opposing U.S. isolationism in World War I.

Roosevelt, Theodore, Jr. (1887-1944), U.S. politician, explorer, soldier, and author; son of President Theodore Roosevelt. He participated in the founding of the American Legion (1919). As a politician, he was a representative in the New York Assembly, assistant secretary of the Navy in the 1920s, and governor of Puerto Rico (1929-32). As an explorer he traveled through Asia for the Field Museum and subsequently wrote about his experiences. He wrote other books, including *Colonial Policies of the United States* (1937). As a soldier he served as a commander in both world wars; he died in France during World War II.

Roosevelt Campobello International Park, jointly administered by the United States and Canada, covers about 2,700 acres (1,090 hectares) on Campobello Island, southwest New Brunswick, Canada.

Root, quantities that when taken a designated number of times will result in a specific quantity. Some roots are the second (square) or third (cube) time a number is designated; for example, the square of 25 is 5, because the root 5 is designated twice: 5 x 5 = 25. Similarly the cube of 27 is 3, because the root 3 is designated three times: 3 x 3 x 3 = 27. The number of times a root is designated is called its index. In algebra, the number that may stand for *x* and satisfy the equation is also called a root.
See also: Algebra; Factor.

Root, part of a plant that absorbs water and nutrients and anchors the plant. Water and nutrients enter a root through minute root hairs sited at the tip of each root. There are two main types of root systems; the taproot system, in which smaller secondary and tertiary roots branch out from a strong main root; and the fibrous root system, in which a mass of equal-sized roots are produced. In plants such as the sugar beet, the taproot may become swollen with stored food material. Adventitious roots anchor the stems of climbing plants, such as ivy. Epiphytic plants such as orchids have roots that absorb moisture from the air. The roots of parasitic plants such as mistletoe and dodder absorb food from other plants.

Root, Elihu (1845-1937), U.S. statesman. He reorganized the command structure of the army as war secretary (1899-1904) under President William McKinley, and as Theodore Roosevelt's secretary of state (1905-9) he oversaw administration of the new possessions won from Spain. A champion of the League of Nations and the World Court, he won the 1912 Nobel Peace Prize. He was a New York Republican senator (1909-15).

Root, John Wellborn (1850-91), U.S. architect, member of the Chicago School. Along with the architect Daniel Hudson Burnham, he was a leader in technical innovations and design of early skyscrapers. The use of heavy, load-bearing mason walls and iron frame interior supports were used to construct the Montauk Block office building (1881-82) and the Rookery (1885-88). The Monadnock Building (1889-91) is still the highest building with load-bearing walls and a steel interior frame. The Rand McNally Building (1889-90) used a steel-frame construction, still important in modern architecture. Root also designed the tallest building in the world for its time, the 22-story Masonic Temple (1890-92).
See also: Architecture; Burnham, Daniel Hudson.

Rope, thick, strong cord made from twisted lengths of fiber. It can be made from manila hemp, henequen, sisal, true hemp, coir (coconut palm fiber), flax, jute, and cotton. Synthetic fibers, particularly nylon and polyesters, are used for lighter and more durable rope. Other ropes, such as for suspension cables in bridge building, are made from wire.

Rorem, Ned (1923-), U.S. composer of melodic art-songs whose texts are drawn from the works of 20th-century U.S. poets. His *Air Music* won the 1976 Pulitzer Prize. He has published 5 volumes of diaries (1966-78).

Rosario (pop. 875,600), city in east-central Argentina on the Paraná River. The third largest city in the country, it developed as a shipping and processing center for the many food products from the Pampa, the fertile plains of Argentina, which Rosario borders to the east. Water and railway transportation make Rosario an important inland port city. Chemical, textile, and metal manufacturers as well as petroleum refiners are also located here. Founded in 1730, it became an important city in the 1800s when the Pampas began developing agricultural products.
See also: Argentina.

Rosas, Juan Manuel de (1793-1877), Argentine dictator, governor of Buenos Aires province (1835-52), who built up a private army of *gauchos* (cowboys). Bribery, force, expansionism, and continuous revolt marked his rule, which nevertheless contributed to Argentine unification.
See also: Argentina.

Roscius, Quintus (Quintus Roscius Gallus; d. 62 B.C.), Roman actor of such renown that "Roscius" was long a compliment for actors.

Rose, popular name for various woody shrubs and vines of the genus *Rosa*, with tough thorns and colorful flowers. There are some 100 wild rose species native to the Northern Hemisphere, but only 9 have been involved in the breeding of the hundreds of varieties now available. In many cultivated varieties the stamens become petaloid, producing double flowers. The rose family contains many important cultivated plants, including the apple, cherry, plum, and strawberry.

Theodore Roosevelt

26th president of the United States	
Born:	New York City, N.Y.; Oct. 27, 1858
Term:	Sept. 1901-Mar. 1909
Vice president:	Charles W. Fairbanks (Mar. 1905-Mar. 1909)
Political party:	Republican
Spouses:	Alice Hathaway Lee Roosevelt; Edith Kermit Carow Roosevelt
Children:	6
Died:	Oyster Bay, N.Y.; Jan. 6, 1919

Rose, Ernestine Potowski (1810-92), advocate for women's rights. Born in Poland, she lived in the United States for more than 30 years before retiring to England. In New York State, she fought for and won legislation that allowed women the control of properties they had obtained before marriage (1848). Along with Elizabeth Cady Stanton and Susan B. Anthony, she founded the National Suffrage Association (1869), a group that fought for women's rights—including the right to vote. She was also an active abolitionist and prohibitionist.
See also: Women's movements.

Rose, Pete (1941-), U.S. baseball player. Known for his aggressiveness, he earned the nickname "Charlie Hustle." He holds the all time major league record for hits (4,256) and was named the National

League's Most Valuable Player in 1973. He played several positions while a member of the Cincinnati Reds (1963-78), the Philadelphia Phillies (1979-83) and the Montreal Expos (1984). In 1984, Rose returned to the Reds as a player-manager for 3 years, after which he continued to serve as manager until 1989, when he was suspended (later banned for life) from baseball for alleged gambling on baseball games.

Roseau (pop. 11,000), capital city of Dominica, one of the Windward Islands in the Caribbean Sea. It is a port city, located on a river by the same name. Its exports include spices and lime products. Before its independence (1978), Dominica was ruled by the British (1759-1978) after the original European colonization by the French (mid-17th century).
See also: Dominica.

Rose chafer, or rose bug (*Macrodactylus subspinosus*), beetle found in the eastern and central regions of the United States. The rose chafer feeds on and destroys rose, grape, and apple blossoms. It measures about 1/3 in (8 mm) long, is light brown to gray, and has long legs with tiny spines. Special cultivating techniques used by commercial growers, cloth coverings used by home gardeners, and insecticides used by both help rid plants of these beetles.

Rosecrans, William Starke (1819-98), Union general in the U.S. Civil War. After early successes in West Virginia and Mississippi, he was given command of the Army of the Cumberland (1862) but was heavily defeated at the Battle of Chickamauga (1863) and relieved of command.
See also: Civil War, U.S.

Rosefish, or Norway Haddock, important food fish of the family Scorpaenidae. The orange-to-red colored rosefish is abundant in the North Atlantic, especially between the New England coast and Greenland. It is also plentiful off the North Atlantic coast of Europe. It may grow up to 2 ft (61 cm) in length.

Rosemary (*Rosmarinus officinalis*), evergreen shrub of the mint family, found in southern Europe and western Asia. It has blue flowers and grayish leaves and produces a pungent, refreshing perfume.

Rosenberg, Alfred (1893-1946), Nazi propagandist and newspaper editor, early associate of Adolf Hitler. In his *Myth of the 20th Century* (1930) he outlined a theory of Nordic racial superiority that was used to justify Nazi anti-Semitism and German world conquest. After the Nuremberg Trials, he was executed for war crimes.
See also: Nazism; Propaganda.

Rosenberg, husband and wife, the only U.S. citizens put to death in peacetime for espionage. **Julius** (1918-53) and **Ethel** (1915-53) were convicted in 1951 for passing atomic secrets in World War II to the USSR, then a U.S. ally. They were electrocuted on June 19, 1953.

Rosenquist, James Albert (1933-), U.S. painter who turned his early billboard-painting career into a style of art. His gigantic images of movie stars, such as Kirk Douglas, and objects of cultural impact, such as *F-111*, put him in the vanguard of pop art.
See also: Pop art.

Rose of Jericho *see:* Resurrection plant.

Rose of Lima, Saint (1586-1617), born in Lima, Peru, first canonized saint in the New World (1671) and patron saint of South America.

Rose of Sharon, or Althaea (*Hibiscus syriacus*), shrub in the mallow family. The rose of Sharon, a native of Asia, is abundant in North American gardens. It is grown indoors in pots and often transplanted to the outdoors. The late purple through white and blue blooms of September are about 3 in (8 cm) wide. This shrub often reaches a height of 12 ft (3.7 m).

Rosetta Stone, inscribed basalt slab, discovered in 1799, that provided the key to Egyptian hieroglyphics. About 4 ft (1.2 m) long and 2.5 ft (0.75 m) wide, it is inscribed with identical texts in Greek, Egyptian demotic, and Egyptian hieroglyphs. Found near Rosetta, Egypt, the stone is now in the British Museum.
See also: Egypt, Ancient; Hieroglyphics.

Rose window *see:* Stained glass.

Rosewood, any of a genus (*Dalbergia*) of trees in the pea family. All species are located in tropical climates. Rosewood from Honduras and Brazil, in particular, is valuable in the commercial manufacture of fine furniture and musical instruments. The color ranges from a deep brown to purple, with attractive blackish streaks and grain markings. When cut, rosewood has a scent similar to that of garden roses.

Rosh Ha-Shanah (Hebrew, "head of the year"), Jewish New Year, observed on the 1st and 2nd days of the 7th Jewish month, Tishri (Sept.-Oct.). It is considered the Day of Judgment, when each person's fate is inscribed in the Book of Life. On Rosh Hashanah the *shofar* (ram's horn) calls Jews to 10 days of penitence ending with Yom Kippur.
See also: Yom Kippur.

Rosin, resin derived from certain pine trees from North America and Europe. A distilling process makes the resin collected from live trees usable in the manufacture of various products, from paints and paper sizing to adhesives and inks. String bows and dance shoes are treated with dried rosin to prevent slipping. Rosins range in color from black to deep red amber, and yellow. The cluster and scotch pines of Europe and the longleaf and loblolly pines of the United States produce most resins for rosin. Three main types of rosin include gum, wood, and sulfa.
See also: Resin.

Ross, Betsy (1753-1836), U.S. seamstress who is said to have made, to George Washington's design, the first U.S. flag (1776).

Ross, George (1730-79), colonial politician and lawyer from Pennsylvania. He was a signer of the Declaration of Independence (1776) while a member of the Continental Congress (1774-77). He helped write the Constitution for Pennsylvania (1776) and also served as a member of the Pennsylvania assembly (1768-76). His last political post was as one of Pennsylvania's admiralty judges (1779).

Ross, Harold Wallace (1892-1951), founder (1925) and lifetime editor of the *New Yorker* magazine. Originally conceived as basically by and for New Yorkers, the magazine won national prestige and has had an enduring effect on American journalism and literature.

Ross, John (1790-1866), Cherokee chief and, from 1839, chief of the united Cherokee nation. He opposed the U.S. government's attempt to move his people west of the Mississippi River, but in 1838 he was forced to lead them to Oklahoma on a difficult journey known as the "trail of tears."

Ross, Nellie Tayloe (1876-1977), U.S. public official. Elected to succeed her husband, who had died, she was the first woman governor (Wyoming, 1925-27). She was director of the U.S. Mint (1933-53).

Ross, Sir James Clark (1800-62), British polar explorer who reached a point farther south (78°10'S) than any explorer until 1900. He made a number of Arctic expeditions, some with his uncle, Sir John Ross, and with William Parry. He located the north magnetic pole in 1831. In the historic 1839-43 Antarctic expedition, he discovered the Ross Sea and Victoria Land.
See also: Antarctica.

Ross, Sir John (1777-1856), British explorer whose first, unsuccessful expedition in search of the Northwest Passage was made in 1818 with James Ross and William Parry. In a return voyage (1829-33), he discovered and surveyed Boothia Peninsula, the Gulf of Boothia, and King William Island.
See also: Northwest Passage.

Ross, Sir Ronald (1857-1932), British physician awarded the 1902 Nobel Prize in physiology or medicine for his investigations of the *Anopheles* mosquito in relation to the transmission of malaria.

Ross Dependency, section of Antarctica on the Ross Sea. Science personnel are located on bases here. The base established by the U.S. explorer Richard E. Byrd in 1928 is also here. This New Zealand-administered dependency covers about 160,000 sq mi (414,000 sq km) of land uninhabited except for the bases. An ice shelf takes up approximately 130,000 sq mi (337,000 sq

km). McMurdo Sound is also found within its borders.
See also: Antarctica.

Rossellini, Roberto (1906-77), Italian film director. His *Open City* (1945), partly made up of footage of the Italian resistance during World War II, established him as a leader of the neorealist movement. Among his other films are *General della Rovere* (1959), *The Rise of Louis XIV* (1966), and *Socrates* (1970).

Rossetti, two leading English artists, brother and sister. The poems of **Christina Georgina Rossetti** (1830-94) range from fantasy (*Goblin Market*, 1862) to religious poetry. Her brother, **Dante Gabriel Rossetti** (1828-82), was a founder of the Pre-Raphaelites. His paintings, of languid, mystical beauty, depict subjects from Dante and medieval romance. He excelled as a poet, notably in his love sonnets.

Rossini, Gioacchino Antonio (1792-1868), Italian composer best known for his comic operas, especially *The Barber of Seville* (1816). The dramatic grand opera *William Tell* (1829), with its famous overture, was his last opera.

Rosso, Il (Giovanni Battista di Iacopo di Gasparre; c.1495-1540), Italian painter, one of the founders of mannerism. *The Deposition* (1521) exemplifies the elongated figures, hectic color, and emotionalism of his paintings.

Rostand, Edmond (1868-1918), French dramatist, best known for his play *Cyrano de Bergerac* (1897), which led a romantic revival.

Rostock (pop. 242,700), city in eastern Germany, located on the Baltic Sea and the Warnow River. It is an important port city through which ships, machinery, and supplies for the petroleum industry are transported. Founded in 1218, it became an important member of the medieval Hanseatic League. The University of Rostock (1419) is also located here.
See also: Germany.

Rostov-on-Don, or Rostov (pop. 983,000), important city in the USSR, near the Sea of Azov on the Don River. Rostov-on-Don is known mainly for farm products, coal, and farm machinery. Founded in 1780, it is an active port and railway center, as well as an industrial city at the foot of the Caucasus Mountains. It is also the site of a World War II battle (1942) in which German forces defeated the Soviet army, until the city was retaken by the Soviets a year later.
See also: Union of Soviet Socialist Republics.

Rostropovich, Mstislav Leopoldovich (1927-), Soviet cellist, who has had works created for him by many composers. Since the mid-1970s he and his wife, the soprano Galina Vishnevskaya, have lived outside the USSR. He became conductor of the National Symphony Orchestra, Washington, D.C., in 1977.

Roszak, Theodore (1907-81), U.S. sculptor. Best known for his sinister, birdlike figures in steel and bronze, he also designed the 45-ft (14 m) spire of the Massachusetts Institute of Technology chapel.

Rot, the name given to several fungi and bacteria that destroy plants. Root rot attacks various root crops, sugarcane, and peas. Brown rot is either a cup fungus or a bacterial attack on tobacco, peas, and beans. Black rot attacks cabbages and cauliflower heads.

Rotary engine, internal-combustion engine that uses rotors instead of pistons. The most important parts of this type of engine are the triangle-shaped rotor and the chamber. The movement of the rotor keeps the chamber divided into three sections in which different stages of the combustion process occur. Depending on the engine, there may be several rotors, each containing its own chambers. The rotary engine works on a four-stroke cycle of induction, compression, combustion, and exhaust. In the induction stage a mixture of air and gas enters the chamber. The mixture is then compressed in the second stroke of the cycle. The mixture is then ignited by spark plugs in the combustion stroke. This creates gases which cause the rotor to move. The exhaust stroke forces the burnt gases to leave the engine. Although it consists of fewer parts than equally-powered piston engines, it emits more pollution and burns more fuel. At low speeds, but not high speeds, it emits a loud noise. Felix Wankel of Germany created the most popular rotary engine design in the 1950s.
See also: Internal combustion engine.

Rotary International, worldwide service organization, consisting of members from various professions and businesses. The organization originally met in a rotating basis at the homes of its members in Chicago, where it was founded (1905) by Paul P. Harris. The club provides scholarships and business exchanges as well as health programs in communities around the world. It has member clubs in over 150 countries.

Rotary wing aircraft *see:* Autogiro; Helicopter; V/STOL.

ROTC *see:* Reserve Officers Training Corps.

Rotenone, naturally occurring insecticide. This substance is extracted from the root of the tropical derris and cube plants. Harmless to humans and other warm-blooded animals, it poisons cold-blooded animals, especially insects. Rotenone protects garden plants and vegetable crops from insect destruction and protects farm animals from certain parasites, such as fleas.
See also: Insecticide.

Roth, Mark (1951-), U.S. professional bowler. He set the record for the highest average, 221.662, in 1979. Roth's achievements include winning a record 8 Professional Bowlers Association (PBA) titles (1978), and the U.S. Open and Touring Players Championship (1984). A member of the PBA since 1970, Roth was selected as Player of the Year 4 times (1977-79, 84).

Roth, Philip (1933-), U.S. writer. His protagonists agonize between a traditional Jewish upbringing and modern urban society. He became recognized with the novella and stories in *Goodbye Columbus* (1959). His best-known novel is *Portnoy's Complaint* (1969), a hilarious, bitter account of sexual frustration. Among his other works are the novels *The Ghost Writer* (1979), *Zuckerman Unbound* (1981), and *The Anatomy Lesson* (1983), later reissued in a single volume as *Zuckerman Bound* (1985), and an autobiography, *The Facts* (1988).

Gioacchino Rossini

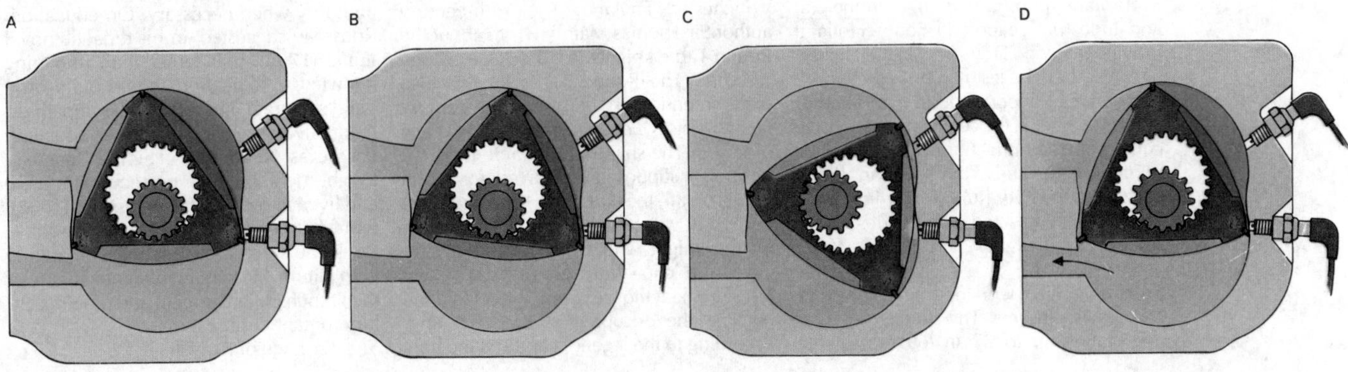

The rotary engine works in a four-stroke cycle: (A) induction, (B) compression, (C) combustion, and (D) exhaust.

Mark Rothko's Blue, Orange, Red *(1961)*

Rothko, Mark (1903-70), U.S. painter, a leading abstract expressionist. On large canvases he used rich and somber colors to create designs of simple, lightly painted rectangular shapes.

Rothschild, family of European Jewish bankers who wielded considerable political influence for nearly two centuries. The founder of the house was **Mayer Amschel Rothschild** (1743-1812), who established banks at Frankfurt, Vienna, London, Naples, and Paris, with his sons as managers. The financial genius who raised the business to dominance in Europe was his son **Nathan Mayer Rothschild** (1777-1836), who handled Allied loans for the campaign against Napoleon. His son, **Baron Lionel Nathan de Rothschild** (1808-79), was the first Jewish member of the British Parliament.

Henri Rousseau's Self-Portrait in Landscape *(1890)*

Rotifer, or wheel animal, microscopic roundworm only a fraction of an inch long. Rotifers are plentiful in fresh water, a few live in the sea, and others live in damp moss. They may be fixed in one place or able to swim. At the head end is the "wheel organ," a delicate ring of rapidly beating hairs that is used for movement or feeding.

Rotterdam (pop. 558,800), commercial and industrial seaport in South Holland province, second largest city in the Netherlands, and the largest harbor in the world. Site of the Europoort industrial and harbor complex, it lies at the center of an extensive canal system connecting with other parts of the Netherlands, the German Rhine ports, and the river Ruhr. Major industries include shipyards and oil refineries.
See also: Netherlands.

Rottweiler, large work dog, ancestor to the Doberman pinscher. This strong, muscular dog stands up to 27 in (69 cm) at the shoulder and weighs up to 90 lb (41 k). It is a short-haired black dog with brown markings at the legs, chest, neck, and face. In Roman times, these dogs guarded herds for the army; in medieval times, they served as guard dogs. They are named for the German town, Rottweil, in which they were developed as a breed.

Rouault, Georges (1871-1958), French artist known especially for his intense religious paintings such as *The Three Judges* (1913). Influenced by medieval stained glass work, he developed a distinctive style with the use of thick black outlines around primary colors.

Rouen (pop. 102,000), city and major port on the Seine River, industrial and commercial center, capital of historic Normandy and of today's Seine-Maritime department, northwestern France. Joan of Arc was burned at the stake here, and Champlain and La Salle sailed from Rouen to explore the New World.
See also: France.

Rough Riders (1st Regiment of U.S. Cavalry Volunteers), unit comprising cowboys, miners, and college athletes among others, organized by Theodore Roosevelt and Leonard Wood (commander of the unit) at the outbreak of the Spanish-American War (1898). They fought mainly in Cuba and are renowned for their success at San Juan Hill.
See also: Spanish-American War.

Roulette, game of chance. The roulette wheel is divided into a series of small compartments, alternatively black and red, numbered 1 to 36 with an additional zero (the U.S. game sometimes has two zeros). A croupier spins the wheel and releases into it a small ivory ball. Players bet on where the ball will settle.

Roumania *see:* Romania.

Roundheads, derogatory name for Puritans in the Parliamentary forces in the English Civil War (1642-8). Many wore their hair closely cropped, in sharp contrast to their royalist opponents, called Cavaliers.
See also: Puritans.

Round Table, table at which the medieval King Arthur and his knights sat. The actual table is claimed as an artifact that can be seen in the remains of a castle in Winchester, England. The 15th-century author Sir Thomas Malory wrote about the Round Table knights in his book *Le Morte d'Arthur.* The Round Table knights also were mentioned in the 12th-century French history *Le Roman de Brut* by Wace of Jersey. The shape of the table (with 12 positions) supposedly allowed for equal status of all the knights. A position left purposely vacant (*Siege Perilous*) was left for the knight who would eventually recover the cup—holy grail—from which Jesus drank at the Last Supper. Sir Galahad became the occupant of that seat and, according to the legend, captured the holy grail along with Sir Bors and Sir Perceval. The knights of the Round Table included, among others, Sir Gawain, Lancelot, Ban, Gareth, Bedevere, Ector, Launfal, Palomides, and Sagramore. One of the major figures in the legends of the knights of the Round Table was the sorcerer Merlin who, according to one legend, had the table constructed for Uther, King Arthur's father.
See also: Arthur, King.

Roundworm, or nematode, any of more than 10,000 species of worms making up the phylum Nematoda, found in terrestrial, freshwater, and marine forms. All roundworms are long and thin, tapering at each end, and are covered with a complex cuticle. The internal organs are suspended within a fluid-filled cavity pseudocoeom. The free-living and plant-parasitic forms are usually microscopic, but animal-parasitic species may reach up to 3.5 ft (1.07 m). Rotifers, and horsehair worms are in the same phylum.

Rous, Francis Peyton (1879-1970), U.S. physician. He shared (with C.B. Huggins) the 1966 Nobel Prize in physiology or medicine for his discovery (1910) of a tumor-causing virus in chickens.

Rousseau, Henri (1844-1910), self-taught French primitive painter much admired by Gauguin, Picasso, and others. Rousseau is known mainly for his portraits, landscapes, and jungle paintings, such as *The Sleeping Gypsy* (1897) and *The Hungry Lion* (1905).

Rousseau, Jean-Jacques (1712-78), Swiss-born French writer, philosopher, and political theorist. Greatly influenced by Denis Diderot, Rousseau first gained fame from his essay *Discourse on the Sciences and the Arts* (1750), an attack on the arts as a source for the increased wealth of the rich and an instrument of propaganda. In his *Discourse on Inequality* (1755), he professed the equality and goodness of "natural man" and asserted that the golden age of humanity occurred before the formation of society, which bred competition and the corrupting influences of property, commerce, science, and agriculture. *The Social Contract* (1762), influential during the French Revolution, claimed that when human beings formed a social contract to live in society, they delegated authority to a government; however, they retained sovereignty and the power to withdraw that authority when necessary. On education, Rousseau suggested, in his didactic novel *Emile* (1762), that rather than imparting knowledge, education should build on a child's natural interests and sympathies, gradually developing his or her potential. For the last 10-15 years of his life, Rousseau fought mental illness (persecution mania) and lived in seclusion. *Confessions* (1782), written shortly before his death, describes Rousseau's romantic feelings of affinity with nature. He was an influential figure of the French Enlightenment and of 19th century romanticism.
See also: Age of Reason.

Rousseau, Théodore (1812-67), French landscape painter, a leader of the Barbizon school. His scenes of wooded landscapes at sunset include *Coming out of the Fontainebleau Woods* (c.1850).
See also: Barbizon school.

Roussel, Albert Charles Paul Marie (1869-1937), French composer. His music was based on contrapuntal rather than tonal construction, varying in style from *The Feast of the Spider* (1912) to *Padmavati* (1918).

Rowan, Carl Thomas (1925-), U.S. journalist and statesman. He was the first member of the National Security Council who was of African American descent. He headed the U.S. Information Agency (1964-65). Rowan has also served as ambassador to Finland (1963-64) and deputy assistant secretary of state for public affairs (1961-63). As a journalist he worked for the *Minneapolis Tribune* (1948-61) and the *Chicago Daily News* (1965-78); he has been a columnist at the *Chicago Sun-Times* since 1978. Rowan received Sigma Delta Chi national journalism awards in 1954, 1955, and 1966.

Rowing, propelling a boat by means of oars operated by hand. In sport there are 2 types: sculling, in which each member of the team (2, 4, or 8 people) uses 2 oars, and sweep rowing, in which each has 1. In the United States competitive team rowing is known as crew. For speed, the craft (shells) are long, narrow, and light. The team may be steered by a coxswain, who also sets the rhythm and speed for the crew's strokes. The first recorded race was held on the Thames River, London (1716). The annual Oxford-Cambridge race (England) began in 1829, and the Yale-Harvard race in 1852.

Rowland, Henry Augustus (1848-1901), U.S. physicist and engineer. He developed the concave diffraction grating in which lines are ruled directly onto a concave spherical surface, thus eliminating the need for additional mirrors and lenses. He also determined the mechanical equivalent of heat and of the ohm.

Rowlandson, Thomas (1756-1827), English caricaturist. His satirical work is a valuable record of contemporary English life. It includes *The English Dance of Death* (1815-16) and illustrations for *The Tour of Dr. Syntax in Search of the Picturesque* (text by William Combe, 1812-21).

Roxas y Acuña, Manuel (1894-1948), Philippine politician. He was a member of the Japanese-sponsored Philippine puppet government in World War II while aiding the Philippine underground. He became the 1st president (1946-48) of the Republic of the Philippines, leader of an administration marked by corruption.
See also: Philippines.

Roy, Gabrielle (1909-), French-Canadian novelist noted for her portrayals of poor urban workers in *The Tin Flute* (1947) and *The Cashier* (1955). Some of her novels, such as *Street of Riches* (1957), are set in the isolated rural landscape of her native Manitoba.

Royal Canadian Mounted Police (RCMP), Canadian federal police force. It was formed in 1873 as the Northwest Mounted Police to bring law and order to the new Canadian territories. In 1874, the persistence and determination of the 300 men on the force became legendary: "The Mounties always get their man." In 1920 it absorbed the Dominion Police and received its present name and duties. The Royal Canadian Mounted Police serves as a provincial police force in the nation's provinces (excluding Ontario and Quebec).
See also: Canada.

Royal Gorge, canyon created by the Arkansas River in south-central Colorado, also known as the Grand Canyon of the Arkansas. It is about 10 mi (16 km) long, with steep granite walls rising more than 1,000 ft (305 m) above the river. The highway bridge over the gorge, with a main span of 880 ft (268 m), is the highest suspension bridge in the United States.

Royal Household of Great Britain, those who administer the private business and court life of the monarchy of Great Britain. Many of these positions, established in the Middle Ages, are hereditary. Today these offices are ceremonial. Over the centuries British monarchs have adjusted the roster of royal attendants. Among the many positions, the lord chamberlain administers ceremonial affairs and is head of the Royal Household; the lord steward governs financial matters of the Royal Household; and ladies of the bedchamber, ladies in waiting, and the mistress of the robes are the Queen's attendants.

Royal palm, tree (genus *Roystonea*) in the palm family, found in the southeastern United States, the West Indies, and Central America. Royal palms have column-shaped trunks with feathery palm fronds gathered at their tops.

Royce, Josiah (1855-1916), U.S. philosopher, a major proponent of idealism. Influenced by Hegel and Schopenhauer, his philosophy emphasized will and purpose rather than intellect, as expressed in *The World and the Individual* (2 vols., 1901-02). Among his other major works was *The Problem of Christianity* (2 vols., 1913), in which he developed his metaphysic of interpretation and community.
See also: Idealism.

Ruanda-Urundi, Belgium-supervised United Nations territory (1946), which later became the independent nations of Rwanda and Burundi (1962). Pygmies called Twa, a Bantu people called Hutu (or Buhutu), and Watusi are the native inhabitants of this area. The Germans laid claim to Ruanda-Urundi in the late-19th century. The Belgic gained a mandate here through the League of Nations (1923). This area is bordered by Zaïre to the west, Uganda to the north, and Tanzania to the east. Lake Tanganyika borders Burundi to the south.

Rubaiyat, collection of quatrains written by Omar Khayyám, an 11th century Persian poet, and translated to English by Edward Fitzgerald (1859). The oldest known manuscript of the original is housed at the Bodleian Library, Oxford and is dated 1460. *The Rubaiyat* views sensual pleasure as the purpose of life, and it heavily influenced post-Victorian English poetry.

Rubber, elastic substance; that is, one which quickly restores itself to its original size after it has been stretched or compressed. Natural rubber is obtained from many plants, and commercially from *Hevea brasiliensis*, a tree native to South America and cultivated also in southeast Asia and West Africa. A slanting cut is made in the bark, and the milky fluid latex, occurring in the inner bark, is tapped off. The latex—an aqueous colloid of rubber and other particles—is coagulated with dilute acid, and the rubber creped or sheeted and smoked. Natural rubber is a chain polymer of isoprene, known as caoutchouc when pure; its elasticity is due to the chains being randomly coiled but tending to straighten when the rubber is stretched. Known to have been used by the Aztecs since the 6th century A.D., and first known in Europe in the 16th century, it was a mere curiosity until Goodyear invented the process of vulcanization. Synthetic rubbers have been produced since World War II. Some latex (natural or synthetic) is used as an adhesive and for making rubber coatings, rubber thread, and foam rubber. Most, however, is coagulated, and the rubber is treated by vulcanization and the addition of reinforcing and inert fillers and antioxidants, before being used in tires, shoes, rainwear, belts, hoses, insulation, and many other applications.

A rubber tree on a plantation in Sumatra, Indonesia

Rubber plant, any of several plants, including the Ceará tree, Pará rubber tree, and guayule, that are sources of latex, a milky fluid used to make rubber. The India rubber fig (*Ficus elastica*), a popular house plant native to India and the East Indies, was once grown for its gum, which was made into erasers.

Rubella, or German measles, contagious viral disease that presents little danger unless contracted in the first trimester of pregnancy, when it may cause serious damage to a fetus. The disease, whose symptoms include rash and fever, usually affects children and young adults. Vaccination against rubella has proven effective.

Rubens, Peter Paul (1577-1640), Flemish artist, one of the greatest baroque painters. Influenced by Tintoretto, Titian, and Veronese, he developed an exuberant style depending on a rich handling of color and sensuous effects. His workshop, an organization of skilled apprentices and talented associates, completed an impressive body

Peter Paul Rubens's Self-Portrait with Isabella Brant *(1609)*

of work, designed by Rubens (who also added the final touches) but largely developed by others. These works include portraits and mythological, allegorical, and religious subjects such as *Raising of the Cross (1610), Descent from the Cross* (1611), *History of Marie de Médicis* (1622-25), *Judgment of Paris (c.1638),* and portraits of his wife. His works influenced many artists.
See also: Baroque.

Rubicon, Italian stream, famous for the crossing made by Julius Caesar in 49 B.C. As commander of Roman troops in Gaul, Caesar crossed this stream—once the border between Rome and Gaul—in reaction to the order for him to give up his power. Today the saying "to cross the Rubicon" indicates that something irreversible has occurred. In 49 B.C. this crossing eventually led to the rule of Rome by Julius Caesar.
See also: Caesar, (Gaius) Julius.

Rubidium, chemical element, symbol Rb; for physical constants see Periodic Table. Rubidium was discovered spectroscopically by Robert Bunsen and Gustav Kirchhoff in 1861. It occurs in lepidolite and several other minerals. The element is prepared by reducing the chloride with calcium. Rubidium is a silver-white, soft, low-melting, reactive metal of the alkali metal group. It can be liquid at room temperature and ignites spontaneously in air. Rubidium and its compounds are used in ion propulsion systems, vapor turbines, thermoelectric generators, batteries, photo cells, and special glasses.

Rubinstein, Anton Gregor (1829-94), Russian piano virtuoso and composer. In 1862 he founded the St. Petersburg Conservatory, where he was director 1862-67 and 1887-91. His brother, Nicholas Grigoryevich Rubinstein (1835-81), also a pianist, founded (1864) and served as director of the Moscow Conservatory.

Rubinstein, Arthur (1889-1982), Polish-born U.S. pianist who remained at the top of his profession for over 70 years. He was well known for his interpretations of Chopin.

Ruby, deep-red gemstone, a variety of corundum colored by a minute proportion of chromium ions, found in Upper Burma, Thailand, and Sri Lanka. Synthetic rubies, used to make ruby lasers, have been produced by the Verneuil flame-fusion process (1902).

Rudolf I (1218-91), German king, elected in 1273, who established the Habsburg dynasty by gaining control of Austria and Styria. The Diet of Augsburg (1282) invested his two sons with these duchies.

Rudolf II (1552-1612), king of Bohemia and Hungary. He succeeded his father Maximilian II as Holy Roman Emperor (1576-1612). His religious persecutions and a Hungarian rebellion led to his replacement by his brother Matthias.
See also: Holy Roman Empire.

Rudolph, Paul (1918-), U.S. architect, connected with Yale University (1958-65). He rejected the international style to experiment with externally visible ducts, a futuristic parking facility, and stacking mobile-home frames. His campus buildings include a controversial art-and-architecture building.
See also: Architecture.

Ruff (*Philomachus pugnax*), bird in the sandpiper family. The term *ruff* refers to the male, while the term *reeve* refers to the female. The male measures about 12 in (30 cm) long and the female measures 10 in (25 cm) long. Both ruff and reeve are gray in appearance during the winter months. In spring, when courtship begins, the male displays a cluster of feathers on his head and neck of red, brown, black, and white feathers. The male uses these feathers in an elaborate courtship performance. Mostly an inhabitant of Europe and Asia, the ruff has been spotted in North America.

Ruffed grouse (*Bonasa umbellus*), bird in the grouse subfamily, Tetraoninae, in the family Phasianidae. When the grouse beats it wings in the air, a loud drumming sound is created that can be heard far away. These birds, which measure up to 17 in (43 cm) long, display a white neck collar of thick feathers on an otherwise brownish body. In winter their legs grow thick feathers for warmth, and their feet develop webs for walking on top of the snow. They reside in the forests of North America. The ruffed grouse is the state bird of Pennsylvania.

Ruffin, Edmund (1794-1865), U.S. planter, father of soil chemistry in the United States. A strong supporter of slavery and secession, Ruffin is said to have fired the first shot on Fort Sumter, S.C., at the outbreak of the Civil War. He committed suicide rather than submit to the U.S. government. A noted agriculturalist, he pioneered crop rotation and founded the *Farmer's Register* (1833).

Rugby, ball game that originated (1823) at Rugby School in England during a soccer match. Somewhat similar to soccer and American football, rugby is played in two 40-minute halves on a field 75 yd (69m) wide by 160 yd (146 m) long. Goal lines are 100 yd (101 m) apart and there are 2 in-goals (equivalent to end zones in football). Each side, comprised of 15 in amateur play and 13 in Rugby league, attempts to move the oval, leather-covered ball beyond the opponents' goal; kicking, carrying, and passing the ball (to the side or rear) is permitted, as is tackling. Blocking, however, is not. Little protective equipment is worn and play is almost continuous.

Rugs and carpets, thick, heavy fabric, most often used as a floor covering. Carpet weaving with sheep's wool was first highly developed in the Near East. By A.D. 600 Persian carpets were internationally famous. Their vivid, long-lasting dyes came from natural materials, e.g., bark and roots. Persian designs influenced the 16th- and 17th-century carpets of India's Mogul courts and the beautiful Chinese carpets produced from the 14th to 17th centuries. Carpet weaving spread in the West, particularly in the 17th century, via France, Belgium, and England. Oriental carpets were woven on looms, still the basic technique of carpet making. But as of 1841, power-driven looms began to mechanize the industry. Classifications of carpets include Oriental, chenille, velvet, hooked, European handwoven, straw, and rag.

Ruhr, important coal-mining and industrial region in Germany, east of the Rhine River, between the valleys of the Ruhr and Lippe rivers. It has more than 30 large cities and towns including Düsseldorf, Essen, Gelsenkirchen, and Dortmund.
See also: Germany.

Ruhr River, river and tributary of the Rhine River in Germany. Through reservoirs and lakes created by dams, this river furnishes water for a densely populated industrial area of Westphalia. The river flows through the industrial Ruhr Valley for over 140 miles before it joins the lower Rhine.

Ruisdael or **Ruysdael, Jacob van** (1629-82), celebrated Dutch landscape painter and etcher. A great influence on English and French landscapists for 2 centuries, he favored a new heroic-romantic style in which small human beings were dwarfed by forests, stormy seas, and magnificent cloudscapes. His works include *Wheatfields* and *Jewish Cemetery.*

Ruiz Cortines, Adolfo (1891-1973), Mexican president (1952-58). During his presidency, corruption was curbed and the March to the Sea to aid the maritime industry was initiated; in addition, the implementation of widespread irrigation boosted agricultural productivity and women were given the vote.

Rules of order *see:* Parliamentary procedure.

Rumania *see:* Romania.

Rumba, or rhumba, ballroom dance of Afro-Cuban origin popular in the 1930s and 1940s. The dancers take 3 steps to each bar, 2 fast side steps and 1 slow forward step in 4/4 time. The rumba is noted for the dancers' side-to-side hip motions with the torso erect and the knees relaxed. Rumba music is performed chiefly with percussion instruments.

Rumford, Benjamin Thompson, Count (1753-1814), U.S.-British scientist best known for his recognition of the relation between work and heat (inspired by observation of heat generated by friction during the boring of a cannon). He played a primary role in the founding of the Royal Institution (1799).

Rumi, Jalal-ed-Din or **Jalal-ud-Din** (1207-73), Sufi poet and mystic of Persia. His major work was the *Mathnawi*, a poetic exposition of Sufi wisdom in some 27,000 couplets.

Ruminant, any of a group of even-toed, hoofed mammals (e.g., giraffes, camels, goats, cows) that regurgitate and rechew their food after swallowing it. They feed by filling one compartment (the rumen) of a 3- or 4-chambered stomach with unmasticated food; the food is mixed with fluid which creates a soft pulp (cud or bolus), and then is regurgitated, rechewed, and sent to the other stomach chambers for digestion.

Rummy, group of card games, all of which, including gin rummy and canasta, are variants on a set of fundamental rules. Rummy is derived from the Spanish game of *conquian* and was called "rum" (queer) poker by the English. Basic rummy was devised about 1895. The object of the game is to lay down as many sets, or melds, of cards as possible; the first player to get rid of all the cards in his hand is the winner. Melds may consist of 3 or 4 cards of the same value in different suits, or sequences of 3 or 4 cards in the same suit.

Rump Parliament, in English civil war, remaining members of Parliament after "Pride's Purge" (led by Col. Thomas Pride) ejected all opposition to Oliver Cromwell's army (1648). These 60 members created a high court that tried King Charles I and had him executed (1649), abolished the House of Lords and monarchy, and established a ruling Council of State. The Rump Parliament itself was dissolved (1653) by Cromwell in his consolidation of power.
See also: Cromwell, Oliver.

Rumsfeld, Donald Henry (1932-), powerful U.S. politician and businessman. He served in the House of Representatives (1963-69). He worked for the Nixon administration, including an appointment as ambassador from the United States in Brussels, Belgium, for the North Atlantic Treaty Organization (NATO). During the administration of President Gerald Ford, he served as chief of staff (1974) and secretary of defense (1975-77). He was involved in Middle Eastern negotiations through appointment by President Ronald Reagan (1983-84). In business, he has headed G.D. Searle & Company (1977) and has been a member of the William Blair & Company investment bank (1985-).

Rundstedt, Karl Rudolf Gerd von (1875-1953), German field marshal. In World War II he was the leader of army groups in Poland, France, and Russia; military ruler of France and commander on D-Day (June 6, 1944) on the western front and during the Battle of the Bulge.
See also: World War II.

Runes, characters of a pre-Christian writing system used by the Teutonic tribes of northern Europe from as early as the 3rd century B.C. to as late as the 10th century A.D. and sometimes after. The three distinct types are Early, Anglo-Saxon, and Scandinavian. The Runic alphabet is sometimes known as Futhork for its first six characters.

Running, pastime and popular sport since ancient times. Running can be divided into 3 basic classes: sprinting, middle-distance running, and long-distance running. Subclasses include relay racing, steeple-chasing, and cross-country running. Sprints, fueled by continuous bursts of speed, generally cover distances of 100, 220, and 440 yds (91, 201, and 402 m). At peak speed a champion sprinter may reach 26 mph (42 kmph). The mile (1.6093 km) is the traditional middle-distance race for British and U.S. runners. In long-distance running, defined as 2 miles (3.2 km) and farther, the emphasis is on endurance and pace. The marathon (26 mi, 385 yd/42.2 km) is a popular long-distance race run annually in many cities worldwide.

Runnymede, or Runnimede, meadow in Surrey, South England, on the southern bank of the Thames River. Here (or at nearby Magna Carta Island), King John conceded the barons' demands embodied in the Magna Carta (1215).
See also: Magna Carta.

Runyon, Damon (1884-1946), U.S. journalist and writer. His entertaining stories of tough-talking gangsters, Broadway actors, and the sporting underworld are written in the colorful vernacular of New York City. *Guys and Dolls* (1931), the first of several collections, became the basis for the successful musical (1950).

Rupert's Land, vast, mineral-rich region of northwest Canada granted to the Hudson's Bay Company in 1670 by Charles II. Named for Prince Rupert (first governor of the company), it comprised the basin of Hudson Bay. In 1818, the United States acquired the portion south of the 49th parallel. In 1869-70, the remainder of the land was sold back to Canada.
See also: Hudson's Bay Company.

Rupture *see:* Hernia.

Rural Electrification Administration (REA), U.S. Department of Agriculture agency that helps provide loans and expertise for electric and telephone development in rural communities. Established by President Franklin Delano Roosevelt (1935), this agency loans money mainly to organized state cooperatives. Both state and federal regulations determine the stipulations of the individual loans. The Congress yearly determines the monies available and interest rates for the REA. In the beginning, about 10% of rural farms had electricity and about 30% had modern telephone service. REA loans have helped increase those percentages to almost 100%.

Rush, tall, grasslike plant (of various genera) in the family Juncaceae, found in marshes, on lake edges, and in paths and ditches. The green stem of the rush bears small scales, which are the leaves, and near the tip is a tuft of brownish or greenish flowers. Rushes are used for floor mats, chair seats, and baskets. The stems, when peeled of their outer covering, are used as wicks.

Rush, Benjamin (1745-1813), U.S. physician and political leader. Signer of the Declaration of Independence and member (1776-77) of the Continental Congress, he established the first American antislavery society and was treasurer (1797-1813) of the U.S. mint (Philadelphia). Among his scientific accomplishments, he was the first professor of chemistry in the colonies (College of Philadelphia), established (1786) the first free dispensary in the United States, and was a pioneer in psychiatry. He held the conviction that insanity is a disease. His *Medical Inquiries and Observations upon the Diseases of the Mind* (1812) was the first U.S. book on psychiatry.
See also: Psychiatry.

Rush-Bagot Convention (1817), negotiations, after the War of 1812, between U.S. diplomat Richard Rush and the British minister to Washington, Sir Charles Bagot, which agreed to mutual U.S.-British disarmament on the Great Lakes.
See also: War of 1812.

Rushdie, Salman (1947-), British writer and critic born in India. Rushdie has written both non-fiction and novels. His fiction often combines fantasy and folklore with realism. His works include *Grimus* (1975), *Midnight's Children* (1981), *Shame* (1983), *Jaguar Smile: A Nicaraguan Journey* (1987), and *The Satanic Verses* (1988), an allegorical novel that so offended Muslims that he was condemned to death by the Ayatollah Khomeini and forced into hiding. Rushdie has since published *Haroun and the Sea of Stories* (1990).

Rushmore, Mount *see:* Mount Rushmore National Memorial.

Dean Rusk

Rusk, Dean (1909-94), U.S. politician and educator. He was secretary of state (1961-69) in both the Kennedy and Johnson administrations, and he was outspoken against the Vietnam War. Serving the state department, he worked for the United Nations and the implementation of both the Marshall Plan and North Atlantic Treaty Organization after World War II. As an educator he has served as president of the Rockefeller Foundation (1952), a "distinguished fellow" at that same institution, and as professor of law at the University of Georgia since 1970.

Ruska, Ernst August Friedrich (1906-88), German physicist and teacher, winner, with Gerd Binnig of Germany and Heinrich Rohrer of Switzerland, of the Nobel Prize (1986) for inventing the electron microscope, allowing scientists to study single atoms. He was named director of the Institute of Electron Microscopy at the Fritz Haber Institute of the Max Planck Society (1955).
See also: Microscope; Physics.

Ruskin, John (1819-1900). English art critic, writer, and social reformer. The first volume of his *Modern Painters* (1843) championed J.M.W. Turner over the old masters; the subsequent 4 volumes (1846-60) expanded his views of the principles of true art, based on integrity and morality. He went on to apply these ideas to architecture in *The Seven Lamps of Architecture* (1849), which stimulated a Gothic revival, and *The Stones of Venice* (1851-53). *Unto This Last* (1860), first of his "letters" to workmen, began his attacks on laissez-faire philosophy. *Sesame and Lilies* (1865) continued to address social and political issues, offering such social reforms as nationalization of education and organization of labor that came to be widely accepted.

Bertrand Russell

Russell, prominent family in British politics. The first member to gain national fame was **John Russell** (c.1486-1555), created first earl of Bedford for helping Edward VI to quell a 1549 rebellion. The family fortune, including Woburn Abbey, Bedfordshire, was acquired during this period. **Francis Russell** (1593-1641), fourth earl, built the square of Covent Garden (c.1631) and was active in Parliament's effort to contain the power held by Charles I. **William Russell** (1613-1700), fifth earl, was a parliamentary general in the Civil War. He was created first duke of Bedford in 1694, partly because of the fame, as a patriotic martyr, of his son **Lord William Russell** (1639-83), first notable Whig in the family. The title of Lord John Russell, first earl Russell, was inherited by his grandson **Bertrand Russell**. **Hastings William Sackville Russell** (1883-1953), a pacifist, defended some of Adolf Hitler's policies in World War II. **John Robert Russell** (1917-) is journalist and farmer in South Africa. In 1955 he turned his land at Woburn into a public park.

Russell, Bertrand (1872-1970), British philosopher, mathematician, and man of letters. Initially a subscriber of idealism he broke away in 1898 and eventually became an empiricist. His most important work was relating logic and mathematics. Russell endeavored to reduce all mathematics to logical principles. His results appeared in *The Principles of Mathematics* (1903) and, in collaboration with A.N. Whitehead, *Principia Mathematica* (3 vols., 1910-13). This work particularly influenced mathematics' set theory, logical positivism, and 20th-century, symbolic logic. Russell was a vehement pacifist for much of his life, especially during World War I and after, in the "ban the bomb" movement, and in his active opposition in Europe to U.S. involvement in Vietnam in the 1960s. His views twice earned him prison sentences (1918, 1961): during the former he wrote his *Introduction to Mathematical Philosophy* (1919). His other works include *Marriage and Morals* (1929), *Education and the Social Order* (1932), *An Inquiry into Meaning and Truth* (1940), *History of Western Philosophy (1945), and popularizations such as The ABC of Relativity* (1925), as well as his *Autobiography* (3 vols., 1967-69). He received the 1950 Nobel Prize for literature and founded the Bertrand Russell Peace Foundation.

Russell, Bill (1934-), U.S. basketball player and coach. Known for strong rebounding and shot blocking, the 6-ft 10-in (208-cm) center is considered one of the best players of all time. Russell's achievements include winning 6 Most Valuable Player awards—5 regular season (1958, 61-63, 65) and 1 All-Star (1963), and being named an All-Star 11 times. He played in the National Basketball Association (NBA) for the Boston Celtics (1956-68) and led them to 11 NBA championships (1957, 59-66, 68, 69). Russell became the first major-league head coach of African American descent in U.S. professional sports (1966) as player-coach of the Boston Celtics. He was inducted into the Basketball Hall of Fame in 1974.

Russell, Charles Marion (1864-1926), U.S. cowboy painter, sculptor, and author. He translated his great love for the West into his many canvases of frontier life, horses, Native Americans, and cattle camps, usually set in Montana.

Russell, George William (1867-1935), Irish poet, nationalist, mystic, and painter, known by the pseudonym A.E. A theosophist, he was, with W.B. Yeats, a leader of the Celtic Renaissance and a cofounder of Dublin's Abbey Theatre.

Russell, Henry Norris (1877-1957), U.S. astronomer. His theory of stellar evolution led to the construction of the Hertzsprung-Russell diagram, work done independently of Ejnar Hertzsprung, showing the relation between a star's brightness and color. He also determined the chemical-element content of the solar atmosphere and analyzed the spectra of various chemical elements.
See also: Astronomy.

Russell, Lord John (1792-1878), British political figure, leader of the British reform movement. As a member of the House of Commons, he helped bring about the repeal of the Test and Corporation acts, which enabled Protestants who did not belong to the Church of England to participate in politics for the first time. He also helped extend the right to vote to more middle-class men through the Reform Bill of 1832. Russell later served as prime minister (1846-52, 1865, 1866).
See also: United Kingdom.

Russell, Lillian (Helen Louise Leonard; 1861-1922), U.S. singer, actress, and flamboyant beauty of the "Gay Nineties." She became a star in the show *The Great Mogul* (1881). She married 4 times, but her affair with "Diamond Jim" Brady spanned 40 years.

Russell, Richard Brevard (1897-1971), influential U.S. Democratic senator (1933-71) from Georgia. Governor of Georgia (1931-33), he was twice candidate for the presidential nomination. As a senator he served as chairman of the Armed Services Committee, the Appropriations Committee, and as president *pro tempore*.

Russell Cave National Monument, location of artifacts related to pre-Columbian man in northeastern Alabama. This cave offers information about ancient peoples, from a fire built about 9,000 years ago to evidence of human habitation from 3 to 4 centuries ago. As part of the National Parks System, it was made a national monument in 1961.

Russia *see:* Union of Soviet Socialist Republics; Russian Federation.

Russian, chief official language of Russia, member of the East Slavic Indo-European languages (Byelorussian and Ukrainian diverged c.1300). Russian is written in the 33-character Cyrillic alphabet introduced in the 800s by Christian missionaries. By combining colloquialism with the formal Church Slavonic, the poet Pushkin did much to shape modern literary Russian, which is based on the Moscow dialect.

Russian Federation, or Russia, largest country in the world. Its 6,592,850 sq mi (17,075,400 sq km) cover Asia's north and a major part of eastern Europe. The capital is Moscow. The federation consists of 21 republics, one autonomous province, 10 autonomous regions, and 55 dependent provinces. After the disintegration of the USSR in 1991 the federation replaced the Russian Federal Soviet Republic (RSFSR) and is considered to be successor to the USSR. (For history before 1991, see Union of Soviet Socialist Republics). Boris Yeltsin, who was president of the RSFSR since 1990, kept his position and replaced Gorbachev. Yeltsin faced severe economic crises and political division with respect to the future development of the country. The political division culminated in the temporary occupation of the Russian White House in 1993. The economic and political liberalization progressed slowly, and by the mid-1990s communism regained popularity.

See also: Union of Soviet Socialist Republics.

Russian Federation

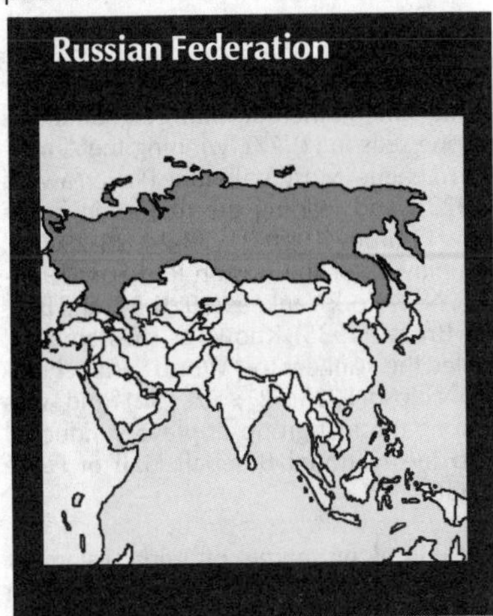

Capital:	Moscow
Area:	6,592,850 sq mi (17,075,400 sq km)
Population:	148,920,000
Government:	republic
Independent:	1991
GNP:	U.S.$397,786,000,000
Per capita:	U.S.$2,680

Russian literature, fiction, poetry, prose, and religious writings written in the Russian language. Throughout its history, Russian literature has been characterized by a deep concern for moral, religious, and philosophical problems.

Early literature. The Byzantine influence that accompanied Russia's conversion to Christianity in the late 900s A.D. also caused Church Slavonic to be adopted as the language of religion and literature. Church Slavonic was used in the Balkans and Russia as the language of secular and religious writings and served in much the same way as Latin did in the West. The earliest writings were primarily the works of clergymen and were religious in content and didactic in purpose although the *chronicles*, records of historic events attributed to the friar Nestor, were nonreligious and had some literary quality. More important than these were the *blyiny*, oral folk lays with a mixture of pagan and Christian themes, that sometimes attained the level of epic poetry. The finest piece of early Russian literature was *The Song of Igor's Campaign* (c. 1187, author unknown), describing an unsuccessful campaign by a Russian prince against an Asian tribe, the Polovtsians.

Beginning of modern Russian literature. Western influence became important in the 17th century when numerous translations appeared and the first theater in Russia was established (1662). The most notable writer of the period was the conservative priest Avvakum (martyred 1682), who opposed the changes in the ritual of the Russian Orthodox Church in the 1650s that led to the great schism. Under Tsar Peter I (the Great), European influence increased, the Russian alphabet was revised, and Russian works were printed in the vernacular. A monk, Simeon Polotsky, introduced a rigid syllabic system of verse, whereby each line of poetry contained a fixed number of syllables with regularly placed pauses. Prince Antioch Kantemir (1703-44) wrote verse satires supporting Peter the Great's reforms, using the syllabic system. Mikhail Lomonosov, a trained scientist, was a noted writer and poet. He was most noted as the founder of modern Russian literature and a precursor of classicism. In his odes, he used the new tonic form of versification (regular patterns of stressed and unstressed syllables) which was more suitable to Russian than the strict syllabic system, and he thereby changed the nature of Russian prosody.

Classicism in Russian literature. Inspired by Lomonosov and influenced by Western models, Russian writers such as Alexander Sumarokov mixed European style with Russian themes. This is especially true of his fables and his plays, which helped begin Russian drama. His *Khorev* (1747) was the first classical tragedy in Russian. The plays of Denis I. Fonzivin (1745-92) mixed satire with more realistic concerns while the outstanding poet of the period, Gavril R. Derzhavin, wrote odes praising Catherine and ridiculing the vices of the court around her, as in his "Ode to Felitsa" (1783). Toward the end of the 18th century, Ivan A. Krylov (1768-1844) wrote many fables, some of them adapted from Aesop and La Fontaine, but most were original.

Romanticism in Russian literature. Vasili Zhukovsky and Konstantin Batyushkov were the leading poets of the preromantic period. In the 1820s, a new group of poets introduced the Golden Age of Russian poetry. The greatest of these was Alexander Sergeyevich Pushkin (1799-1837), who wrote the remarkable historical play *Boris Godunov* in 1825. Other poets of the age included Yevgeny Baratynsky, Baron Anton Delvig, and Wilhelm Kuchelbecker. By the end of the romantic period, Russian writers turned more to social criticism, even under the strict censorship of Tsar Nicholas I. Among these were Mikhail Lermontov, whose *A Hero of Our Times* (1840) was the first psychological novel in Russian literature. The poet Fyodor Tyutchev wrote pessimistic verse, as exemplified in his "A Vision" (1829) and "Holy Night" (1849). The most important writer of this time was Nikolai Vasilyevich Gogol (1809-52). He is best known for his socio-political satires, such as his famous play *The Inspector General* (1836), still performed in many countries today.

Realism in Russian literature. Around mid-19th century began the period of great Russian novels, which attempted to depict Russian life, customs, and politics in a realistic manner. Ivan Turgenev's *A Sportsman's Sketches* (1852) and *Fathers and Sons* (1862) showed his interest in social themes and particularly in character analysis, as did his gentle comedy *A Month in the Country* (completed 1850). Count Leo Tolstoy (1828-1910), one of the greatest of Russian novelists, expanded the form to include deep philosophical probing as well as realistic depictions of Russian life and people, as exemplified in his two great works *War and Peace* (1869) and *Anna Karenina* (1875-77). The other great Russian novelist of the period, Fyodor Dostoevsky (1821-81), wrote novels of extraordinary psychological penetration. Among his most famous works are *Crime and Punishment* (1866), *The Possessed* (1871-72), and *The Brothers Karamazov* (1879-80). Toward the end of the century, the playwright and short story writer Anton P. Chekhov (1860-1904) portrayed Russian life with a kind of lyric realism in such plays as *Uncle Vanya* (1899), *The Three Sisters* (1901), and *The Cherry Orchard* (1904). Prefiguring the Russian Revolution was the playwright and novelist Maxim Gorki (1868-1936) whose works depicted the terrible plight of the Russian poor and downtrodden. His most famous play is *The Lower Depths* (1902).

Russian literature in the 20th Century. The unsettled times before and during the revolution in 1917 spawned new literary trends like symbolism, as exemplified in the poets Alexander Blok and Andrey Bely. Post-symbolist poets included Anna Akmatova and Osip Mendelstam, and futurists found a strong voice in the remarkable poet Vladimir Mayakovsky. Boris L. Pasternak was also associated with the futurists, but is most known for his lyric poetry and his later novel *Doctor Zhivago* (begun 1948, published 1957) for which he won the Nobel Prize. The terrible years of Stalin's repressive rule took a toll on Russian literature, but in the 1960s a new generation of writers moved to reassert liberal ideas. Among them are Yevgeny Yevtushenko and Andre Voznesensky (poets) and prose writers Vasily Aksyonov and Vasily Shukshin. Alexander Solzhenitsyn, an outspoken critic of communism, wrote about the Stalin repression (*The Gulag Archipelago, 1918 to 1956*, published in the West from 1973 to 1976). He was exiled, but with the changes in Russia in the late 1980s, the banishment was revoked. It is hoped that a more liberal Russia will encourage a free and creative literature.

Russian Orthodox Church *see:* Union of Soviet Socialist Republics; Eastern Orthodox Church.

Russian Revolution, momentous political upheaval that changed the course of world history. It destroyed the autocratic tsarist regime and culminated in the establishment of the world's first Communist state, the Soviet Union (1922). Its roots lay in the political and economic backwardness of Russia, the chronic poverty of most of the people, and rising discontent in the middle and lower classes.

The Revolution of 1905. On "Bloody Sunday," Jan. 22, troops fired on a workers' demonstration in St. Petersburg. Wide-

Babe Ruth

spread disorders followed, including mutiny on the battleship *Potemkin* and a national general strike organized by the St. Petersburg *soviet* (workers' council). These events, coupled with the disastrous Russo-Japanese War, forced Nicholas II to grant civil rights and set up an elected duma (parliament) in his October Manifesto. Repression continued until late in World War I, during which Russia suffered severe reverses.

***The* February Revolution (1917).** Food shortages and strikes provoked riots and mutiny. A provisional government under the progressive Prince Georgi Lvov was set up, and Nicholas II abdicated.

***The* October Revolution (1917).** The Bolsheviks, led by V.I. Lenin, staged an armed coup. Moscow was seized, and the remnants of the provisional government were arrested. The constitutional assembly was dispersed by Bolshevik ("Red") troops, and the Cheka (political police) was set up. A Council of People's Commissars was established, headed by Lenin and including Leon Trotsky and Joseph Stalin. In the civil war (1918-20), the anticommunist "Whites," commanded by A.I. Denikin, A.V. Kolchak, and P.N. Wrangel were defeated. Russian involvement in World War I ended with the Treaty of Brest-Litovsk. The tsar and his family were murdered at Ekaterinburg (July 1918), and the new Soviet constitution made Lenin and the Communist (formerly Bolshevik) Party all-powerful.

See also: Communism; Lenin, V.I.; Marxism.

Russian wolfhound *see:* Wolfhound.

Russo-Finnish wars, conflicts during World War II. The first, the Winter War (1939-40), arose from rejection of Russian demands for military bases in Finland, territorial concessions, and the dismantling of the Mannerheim line, Finland's defense system across the Karelian Isthmus. When the Russians attacked (Nov. 30), the Finns unexpectedly threw them back. But in Feb. 1940 the Mannerheim line was broken and Finland signed the Peace of Moscow (March 12), surrendering about 10% of its territory. In the Continuation War (1941-44), Finland fought alongside Nazi Germany, and was forced to pay reparations to the USSR and to lease it the Porkkala Peninsula (returned in 1956).

See also: World War II.

Russo-Japanese War (1904-05), culmination of rivalry in the Far East between powers who sought expansion at the expense of the decaying Chinese empire. Russia occupied Manchuria during the Boxer Rebellion and coveted Korea, dominated the region and refused to share with Japan its position of influence. As a result, the Japanese attacked the Russian naval base of Port Arthur (now Lüshun, China), defeated the Russians at Mukden (now Shenyang) in Manchuria, and destroyed the Russian Baltic fleet in the Battle of Tsushima. Mediation by U.S. president Theodore Roosevelt ended the war in the Treaty of Portsmouth (1905). Russia ceded territory to Japan, recognized Japan's dominance in Korea, and returned Manchuria to China. Russia's disastrous defeat was one immediate cause of the 1905 Russian Revolution.

Russo-Turkish wars (1697-1878), conflicts resulting in Russian expansion into Ottoman territory. The first Russian success was the capture of Azov by Peter I (the Great) in 1696; it was subsequently recaptured (1711) by the Turks and lost again (1739). The 2 earliest major wars (1768-74, 1787-92), the first was declared by Sultan Mustafa III with France's encouragement, were against Catherine the Great. Allied with Austria, Russia gained the rest of the Ukraine, the Crimea, an outlet to the Black Sea, and the straits, and adopted the role of protector of Christians in the declining Ottoman Empire. Western concern over this major gain came to be known as the Western Question. Russia won Bessarabia in the war of 1806-12 and rose to the height of its power in the war of 1828-29. When Russia next pressured the Turks, France and Britain intervened, defeating Russia in the Crimean War (1853-56). The Congress of Paris, which ended that war, marked a major setback for Russia in the Middle East. The last war (1877-78), which began with an anti-Turkish uprising (1875), brought more territory to Russia in the Treaty of San Stefano. Alarmed Western powers revised the treaty in the Congress of Berlin (1878). Russia and Turkey were opponents again in World War I.

See also: Ottoman Empire.

Russwurm, John Brown (1799-1851), Jamaican-born U.S. abolitionist who led a "back to Africa" movement in the 1820s and eventually settled in Liberia (1829). He founded (1827) and edited *Freedom's Journal*, the first black-owned U.S. newspaper.

See also: Abolitionism.

Rust, brownish-red substance that forms on the surface of iron or steel when exposed to oxygen in the air. Rust both corrodes and weakens metal. It is brittle and easily flakes off the metal. Rust can be prevented by coating metal objects with heavy greases or spray-on plastics.

See also: Oxidation.

Rust, in botany, fungi of the order Uredinales and the plant diseases they cause. Rusts infect their hosts by forming orange or red spots, their spore-bearing organs, on their host's leaves. Some rusts are heteroecious: they alternate between host plants of 2 different species (e.g., the cedar rust, which infects apple and cedar trees). One crucial rust fungus (*Puccinia graminis*) attacks grain crops, causing black-stem rust of wheat. Rusts also attack ornamentals, fruits, and vegetables.

Rustin, Bayard (1910-87), U.S. civil rights activist and pacifist. He helped found the Southern Christian Leadership Conference and was chief organizer of the 1963 civil rights march on Washington.

See also: Civil rights.

Ruth, Babe (George Herman Ruth; 1895-1948), U.S. baseball player. Known as the first great power hitter in the major leagues, he is second on the all time home run list (714). Originally an outstanding pitcher (won 94 games, lost 46 for his career), Ruth was switched to the outfield and became a prolific hitter (.342 career average). Ruth's achievements include hitting 60 home runs in one season (1927), winning the American League Most Valuable Player award (1923), and leading the majors in home runs 11 times (1918-21, 23-24, 26-29, 31). He played for the Boston Red Sox (1914-20), New York Yankees (1920-34) and Boston Braves (1935). Known as The Bambino, he led the Yankees to 4 World Series championships (1923, 27, 28, 32) and was among the first group of players inducted into the National Baseball Hall of Fame (1936).

Ruth, Book of, name of Old Testament book in the Bible. It focuses on the love and loyalty of Ruth, described as a descendant of King David and the royal family of Israel. As a widowed non-Israelite, she gave up her home in Moab to follow Naomi, her mother-in-law, to Bethlehem. There, after working to secure a life for both herself and Naomi, she married Boaz, a kinsman to Naomi. Through the sacrifice and effort of Ruth, an Israelite family line continued. This Old Testament book, completed c. 2,500 years ago, is appreciated for its vivid characterization of Ruth and for its literary qualities.

See also: Bible; Old Testament.

Ruthenia, region in western Ukraine, southwest of the Carpathian Mountains, covering 4,940 sq mi (12,800 sq km). Formerly part of Hungary, then of Czechoslovakia (from 1919), it was ceded to the USSR (1945). The region came under independent Ukrainian rule in 1991. Uzhgorod is capital of this mountainous and densely forested region.

See also: Ukraine.

Ruthenium, chemical element, symbol Ru; for physical constants see Periodic Table. Ruthenium was discovered by Karl Klaus in 1844. It occurs in nature associated with native platinum and also with copper-nickel ores. It is obtained in commercial quantities from the mineral pentlandite. The element is prepared by the reduction with hydrogen of the oxychloride. Ruthenium is a hard, lustrous, white metal and is a member of the platinum group of elements. It is used to harden other metals and improve their wear-resistance and resistance to corrosion. It is also a versatile catalyst.

Rutherford, Ernest (1871-1937), New Zealand-born English physicist. He taught at McGill University (Montreal, 1898-1907) and the University of Manchester (1907-19); in 1919 he became director of the Cavendish Laboratory, Cambridge. In studying uranium he discovered and

named alpha and beta radiation. For his theory concerning the radioactive transformation of atoms he was awarded the 1908 Nobel prize in chemistry. In 1911 he proposed his nuclear theory of the atom, on which Bohr based his celebrated theory years later. In 1919 Rutherford announced the first artificial disintegration of an atom. His work was commemorated (1969) by the naming of rutherfordium, a chemical element.
See also: Atom; Physics.

Rutherfordium *see:* Element 104.

Rutile, mineral (TiO_2) found in the United States, Brazil, Europe, Australia, and India. It is a red to brown or black crystal. The titanium of this titanium-oxide mineral is refined for use as pigment in white paint. Porcelain as well as coating for welding rods are also colored with rutile.

Rutin, yellow pigment used as a medicine to treat problems in the circulatory system. Found in such plants as tobacco, rue, and buckwheat, among others, rutin helps make weak capillaries strong.

Rutland (pop. 18,436), second largest city in southwestern Vermont. The area of Vermont surrounding Rutland has an economic base in tourism, especially through the ski industry and other recreation derived from the region's forests, water resources, and mountains. The region contains some industry and marble quarries.
See also: Vermont.

Rutledge, family of U.S. politicians. **John Rutledge** (1739-1800) was a U.S. politician and jurist. Active in South Carolina politics, he was twice delegate to the Continental Congress (1774-76, 1782-83) and a delegate to the 1787 Federal Constitutional Convention. He helped frame South Carolina's constitution (1776) and was governor from 1779 to 1782. Rutledge served as associate justice of the U.S. Supreme Court (1789-91), but George Washington's nomination of him for chief justice (1795) was not confirmed by the Senate. His brother **Edward Rutledge** (1749-1800) was delegate to the Continental Congress (1774-76), a signer of the Declaration of Independence, and South Carolina governor (1798-1800).

Rutledge, Ann (c.1813-35), daughter of an innkeeper at New Salem, Ill., where Abraham Lincoln lived 1831-37. Her early death deeply grieved Lincoln, but stories of a romance or even engagement are probably incorrect.

Ruwenzori Range, east-central African mountain range between Uganda and Zaïre. These mountains, slightly north of the equator, rise to a snowy height of 16,763 ft (5,109 m) at Margherita Peak on Mount Stanley. The range was given its present name by the European explorer Henry Stanley (1889). In ancient times it was named Mountains of the Moon by the geographer Ptolemy. These non-volcanic mountains consist of glaciated masses of crystalline rock. The range has deep chasms and deeply carved river valleys. The rainfall and snow melt from these mountains are considered a source of the Nile River.

Ruysdael, Jacob van *see:* Ruisdael, Jacob van.

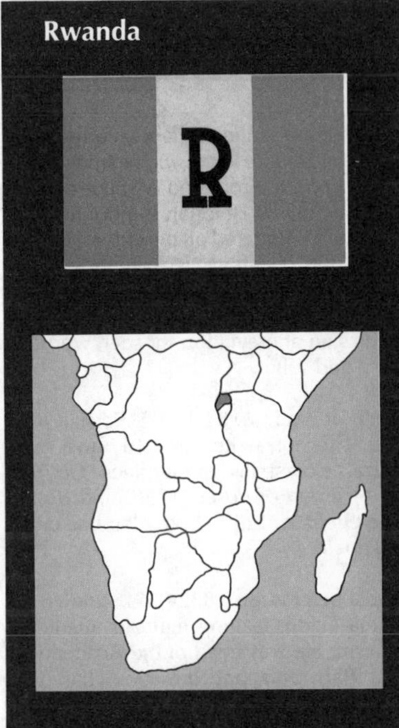

Capital:	Kigali
Area:	10,169 sq mi (26,338 sq km)
Population:	7,310,000
Government:	republic
Independent:	1962
GNP:	U.S.$1,813,000,000
Per capita:	U.S. $250

Rwanda, small independent republic in east-central Africa. It is one of the most densely populated counties in Africa.
Land and climate. The land of Rwanda is dominated by the Rift Valley Highlands. From the high volcanic Virunga Mountains in the northwest, the land falls away southeastward in a series of steeply sloping flat-ridged hills. The forests that once covered these hills have been largely cleared for farming. Marshy plains form the bottoms of the deep, intersecting valleys. In the west, the land rises sharply from Lake Kivu. Chief rivers include the Nyabarongo, the Kagera, the Akanyaru, and the Ruzizi. Because it lies on high plateaus, Rwanda has a cool climate.
People. The population is comprised of three main ethnic groups: 85% are Bantu farming people known as the Hutu, 14% are a pastoral people known as the Tutsi, and a small percentage are the Twa, a pygmy people who live by hunting. The people live mostly in small villages. Kigali is the capital and largest center.
Economy. Agriculture and mining provide nearly 80% of the gross national product. The chief crops are coffee, pyrethrum, and tea. Efforts are being made to expand production. Agricultural output is insufficient to provide enough food for the people.
History. The earliest inhabitants of Rwanda, the Twa pygmies, were long ago driven into the forests by the Hutu, who came from the Congo. In the 16th century

Rwanda farmers

the Hutu were conquered by the tall, cattle-rearing Tutsi. The Tutsi established a feudal state and remained in control until 1959, when the Hutu liberation party known as Parmehutu set up a republican regime that was later recognized by the United Nations. The country was granted full independence in 1962. An attempted invasion of Rwanda from Burundi was bloodily repulsed in 1963. Military leaders took control of the government in 1973, and Major General Juvenal Habyarimana declared himself president. While he at first filled cabinet posts with military leaders, he gradually replaced them with civilians during the 1970s. With civilian rule restored under the new constitution of 1978, Habyarimana was elected president. His death in 1994, resulting from an aircrash, led to a violent and bloody strife between the two main ethnic groups, leading to the murder of over 500,000 people, mainly Tutsi citizens. Coming from Uganda, Tutsi forces took control.

R/x, symbol used on medical prescriptions. It is believed to have evolved from the Latin word recipe (meaning take), or from the ancient symbol for Jupiter that when placed on a prescription became a plea for hasty remedy.

Ryan, Nolan (1946-), U.S. baseball player. Known for his blazing fastball (clocked at a record 100.8 mph/161.3 kmph), he is considered one of the greatest pitchers of all time. At the end of the 1990 season, Ryan had 302 career wins and held the records for career strikeouts (5,308), strikeouts in a single season (383 in 1973), and career no-hitters (6). He pitched his seventh no-hitter early in the 1991 season. Ryan played in the major leagues for the New York Mets (1966-71), California Angels (1972-79), Houston Astros (1980-88), and Texas Rangers (1989-).

Nolan Ryan

S

Ryan, Thomas Fortune (1851-1928), U.S. financier and businessman. With an initial fortune made as a stockbroker, he went on to buy and sell businesses mostly involved in transportation, insurance, and banking. He amassed one of the greatest fortunes in U.S. history, valued at more than $200 million. His prosperous company, Metropolitan Traction Company, was established after he acquired the newly built New York City subway lines (1886). A later company, Consolidated Tobacco Company, was dissolved by order of the government (1911) when it was judged to be a monopoly.

Ryder, Albert Pinkham (1847-1917), U.S. painter, noted for his darkly poetic landscapes, seascapes, and allegorical scenes such as *Toilers of the Sea* (1884), *The Flying Dutchman* (1890), and *The Race Track* (1895). Ryder's body of work (only about 160 canvases) is considered among the finest of American art.

Rye, (*Secale cereale*), grain of the grass family, hardiest of all cereal crops. It can grow in poor, sandy soils in cool and temperate climates. Most rye is used for human consumption, e.g. pumpernickel and light-colored rye bread or to make gin and whiskey, but rye grain and middlings (a by-product of milling) are also fed to livestock and used for cattle pasturage. The leading producer of rye is the USSR. If rye is infected with ergot, a poisonous fungus, it becomes unsafe for use.

Rykov, Aleksei Ivanovich (1881-1938), Russian communist leader. Active in the October Revolution (1917), he was Soviet Premier (1924-30) after Lenin's death. Opposed to Stalin's policies, he was dismissed from office until he recanted (reinstated 1931-36). Due to involvement in an assassination plot against Stalin, he was executed after a show trial.
See also: Russian Revolution; Union of Soviet Socialist Republics.

Ryukyu Islands, archipelago, of approximately 1,850 sq mi (4,790 sq km), forming a 650-mi (1,050-km) arc between Japan and Taiwan. Dividing the East China and Philippine seas, the 100-plus islands comprise 3 groups: the Amami Islands in the north; the central Okinawa Islands, including Okinawa; and the Sakishima Islands in the south. Many have coral reefs and some have active volcanoes. Climate is subtropical; the economy is supported by agriculture and fishing. The Ryukyus became part of Japan in 1879; they passed to the United States after World War II. The northern islands were returned in 1953, and the remainder in 1972.

Ryun, Jim (1947-), U.S. athlete who set world records for middle-distance running. In 1966 he ran the mile in 3 minutes 51.3 seconds and 880 yards in 1 minute 44.9 seconds; in 1967 he ran 1,500 meters in 3 minutes 33.1 seconds. He also broke his own mile-run record by 0.2 seconds.

Ryzhkov, Nikolai Ivanovich (1929-), former prime minister of the USSR (1985-91). He left office when the restructuring of the Soviet government reduced the scope of the position. After his admittance into the Communist Party (1956), he rose through the ranks of the government, becoming deputy minister of heavy machinery (1975), chairman of the Soviet economic planning commission, called Gosplan (1979), Secretariat of the Central Committee involving economic concerns (1982), then full member of the Communist Party Politburo (1985).
See also: Union of Soviet Socialist Republics.

S, 19th letter in the alphabet, corresponding to the Semitic letter *sin*, meaning *tooth*, represented by a rounded W shape derived from an ancient Egyptian symbol for *tusk*. Phoenicians squared off the curves; Greeks turned the resulting sign on its side (as *sigma*); and, as the 18th letter of the Roman alphabet, S assumed its present form. S is used as an abbreviation for such words as south and sulfur.

Saadi, or **Sadi**, (1184-1292), Persian lyric poet. This Sufi writer is best known for 2 ethical works: his masterpiece *Gulistan* (*The Garden of Roses*, 1258) and *Bustan* (*The Orchard*, 1257), both blending prose and poetry.

Saadia ben Joseph (882-952), known as Saadia Gaon, leading figure in medieval Judaism. He was head of the Academy at Sura, Babylonia, and orthodox champion against the ascetic Karaites. He wrote a Hebrew grammar and lexicon, an Arabic translation of the Bible, created the *siddur*, or prayer book, and the *Book of Beliefs and Opinions* (933).
See also: Judaism.

Saar, or Saarland, state in southwest Germany, 991 sq mi (2,567 sq km), bordering France. Its capital is Saarbrücken. It is a major coal-mining, iron, and steel region whose control has historically alternated between France and Germany. After World War I, it was administered by France under the League of Nations. It was reunited with Germany after a plebiscite (1935), occupied by France after World War II, and instated as a German state in 1957.
See also: Germany.

Saarinen, 2 modern architects, father and son. **Eliel Saarinen** (1873-1950), the leading Finnish architect of his day, designed the influential Helsinki railroad station (1905-14). In 1923 he emigrated to the United States, where he designed numerous structures in the Midwest, including the Gateway Arch in St. Louis, Mo. **Eero Saarinen** (1910-61) collaborated with his father (1938-50). His outstanding works include the General Motors Technical Center in Warren, Mich. (1951-5); Massachusetts Institute of Technology's circular chapel and concrete-dome auditorium (1955); and the Trans World Airline Terminal in New York City. He also designed Dulles International Airport in Chantilly, Va., which was completed posthumously.
See also: Architecture.

Saavedra Lamas, Carlos (1880-1959), Argentinian lawyer and statesman. As Argentina's foreign minister (1932-8), he presided over the conference that ended the Chaco War (1935). He won the 1936 Nobel Peace Prize.
See also: Argentina.

Sabah, formerly North Borneo, state in the Federation of Malaysia, on the northern tip of the island of Borneo, Malay archipelago. It lies on the South China and Sulu seas, with Kalimantan (Indonesian Borneo) to the southwest and Brunei to the west. Sabah and Sarawak (also on the island of Borneo) became British protectorates in 1882 and then crown colonies in 1946. In 1963 they joined the newly formed Federation of Malaysia. Sabah's capital is Kota Kinabalu. It has a tropical climate and is largely mountainous (highest peak, Mt. Kinabalu, 13,432 ft/4,094 m). Main exports are timber, rubber, and copra (dried coconut).
See also: Malaysia.

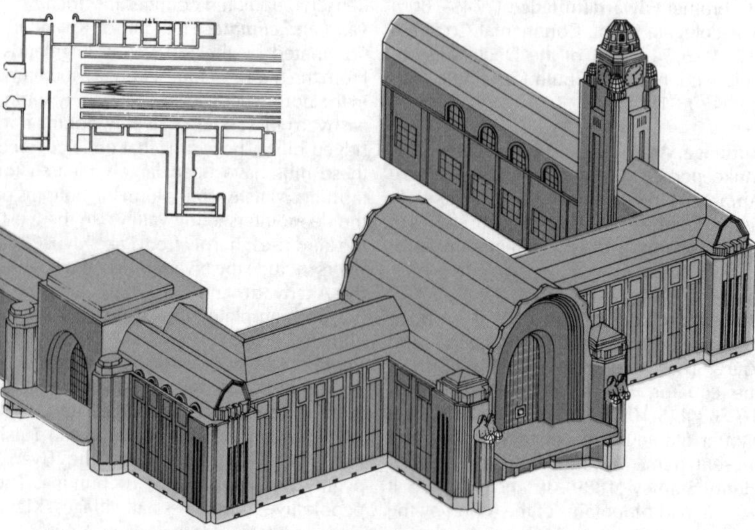

Station at Helsinki, built to a revised design by Eliel Saarinen (1906-14)

Sabatier, Paul (1854-1941), French chemist who shared with Victor Grignard the 1912 Nobel Prize in chemistry for his work on catalyst action in organic syntheses; especially his discovery that finely divided nickel accelerates hydrogenation.
See also: Chemistry.

Sabbath, seventh day of the Hebrew week. The Jews observe it as the day of rest laid down in the Fourth Commandment to commemorate the Creation. It starts at sunset on Friday and ends at sunset on Saturday. Christians adopted Sunday as the Sabbath to commemorate the Resurrection.
See also: Judaism.

Sabbatical year, among ancient Jews every seventh year was a year of rest for the land, ordered by the law of Moses. Crops were to be unsown and unreaped, and debtors were to be released. Today a professor's sabbatical is for rest or research.

Saber-toothed cat, either of 2 genera of extinct cats of the Cenozoic: *Smilodon* of North America and *Machairodus* of Europe and Asia. Slightly smaller than lions but similar in build, saber-toothed tigers had enormous upper canines, up to 10 in (254 mm) long, which they probably used as daggers to pierce the skin of their prey.

Sabin, Albert Bruce (1906-), U.S. virologist best known for developing an oral poliomyelitis vaccine, made from live viruses (1959).
See also: Poliomyelitis.

Sabine River, in northeast Texas, rises in Hunt County and flows about 360 mi (580 km) east and southeast to form the southern part of the Texas-Louisiana boundary. Near its mouth on the Gulf of Mexico it widens into Sabine Lake.

Sabines, ancient people of the Sabine Hills (Apennines) in central Italy, northeast of Rome. The legend of the abduction of the Sabine women by the Romans is fictitious, but there were numerous Roman-Sabine wars. Though there were Sabines in Rome from the earliest times, they became Roman citizens c.268 B.C. and disappeared as a separate people.

Sable (*Martes zibellina*), carnivorous furbearing mammal related to the martens. Sable live on the ground of coniferous forests, now restricted to parts of North Asia. About 20 in (508 mm) long, they prey on small rodents.

Sable Island, small north Atlantic island about 95 mi (150 km) southeast of Nova Scotia, Canada. The island, about 24 mi (38 km) long and 1 mi (1.6 km) wide, consists of sand dunes and is surrounded by *shoals* (sand bars). Before modern radar-aided navigation it was a serious navigational hazard and was known as the "graveyard of the Atlantic." Lighthouses were established in 1873, and it is now the site of a Canadian weather station. The island is partly covered by grasses and shrubs and inhabited by birds and, since the 18th century, wild horses.

Sac *see:* Sauk.

Sacagawea, or **Sacajawea** (1787?-1812?), guide and interpreter (1804-5) for the Lewis and Clark expedition. Sacagawea means "Bird Woman." A member of the Shoshone tribe, she was captured by a hostile tribe and sold to Toussaint Charbonneau, who became interpreter for the expedition. Her help was invaluable in obtaining supplies from the Shoshone.
See also: Lewis and Clark expedition.

Saccharides, or carbohydrates, chemical compounds composed of simple sugar or sugars in combination, including table sugar, starch, and cellulose. Saccharides, fats, and proteins are the 3 main classes of food. *Monosaccharides*, including glucose ($C_6H_{12}O_6$), are sugars that cannot be further digested to yield simpler sugar molecules. *Disaccharides*, including sucrose or table sugar ($C_{12}H_{22}O_{11}$), are composed of 2 linked monosaccharide molecules. *Polysaccharides*, including starch and cellulose, are complex molecules consisting of many linked monosaccharides.

Saccharin, calorie-free sweetening agent, much sweeter than sucrose, normally used in its soluble sodium salt form. Not absorbed by the body, it is used by diabetics and in low-calorie dietetic foods.
See also: Artificial sweetener.

Sacco-Vanzetti case, famous legal battle (1920-21) that polarized opinion between U.S. liberal-radicals and conservatives. In 1921, Nicola Sacco and Bartolomeo Vanzetti were found guilty of murdering a paymaster and his guard in South Braintree, Mass. When arrested, they were armed and gave false statements, many say out of fear of deportation due to their alien status. By 1927, opponents of the verdict claimed that there had been insufficient evidence, and that the trial had been unduly influenced by the fact that Sacco and Vanzetti were aliens, anarchists, and draft evaders. The supreme court of Massachusetts and the governor ruled that the trial was fair. The 2 were executed on Aug. 22, 1927, preceded by demonstrations around the world. Public debate continued for years.
See also: Anarchism.

Sachs, Hans (1494-1576), most popular German poet and dramatist of his time, one of the Meistersingers, and by trade a shoemaker. His prolific output included "The Nightingale of Wittenberg" (1523), which honors Martin Luther. Sachs was the model for a leading character by the same name in Richard Wagner's *Die Meistersinger (1868).*

Sachs, Julius von (1832-97), German botanist. Sachs studied plant metabolism and respiration, the role of minerals in plant nutrition, and the location of chlorophyll within plant cells. His *The Textbook of Botany* (1868) and *History of Botany* (1875) are among the most comprehensive and influential books in the field of botany.
See also: Botany.

Sachs, Nelly (1891-1970), German-born Swedish poet who fled Nazi Germany in 1940. Her poems deal with the sufferings and destiny of her Jewish people (*O the Chimneys*, 1967). She shared the 1966 Nobel Prize for literature with S. Y. Agnon of Israel.

Sackville, Thomas, 1st Earl of Dorset (1536-1608), English statesman and poet. He was coauthor (with Thomas Norton) of the first English blank-verse tragedy, *Gorboduc* (1561). He is also noted for his poems "Induction" and "Complaint of Buckingham" in the collection *A Myrrovre for Magistrates* (1559-63). Sackville was raised to peerage status in 1567 and also had the dubious distinction of announcing the death sentence to Mary, Queen of Scots (1586).

Sackville-West, Victoria Mary (1892-1962), English poet, novelist, and biographer, associated (like her husband, Sir Harold Nicolson) with the Bloomsbury Group. Her works include the poem *The Land* (1926) and the novels *The Edwardians* (1930) and *All Passion Spent* (1931).

Sacrament, in Christian theology, visible sign and pledge of invisible grace, ordained by Jesus Christ. The traditional 7 sacraments (first listed by Peter Lombard) are baptism, Holy Communion, confirmation, penance, ordination, marriage, and extreme unction, of which only the first two are accepted as sacraments by many Protestants. In Roman Catholic theology the

The Passion of Sacco and Vanzetti *(1931-32), by Ben Shahn*

Anwar el-Sadat

sacraments, if validly administered, convey grace objectively to the believing recipients; Protestants stress the joining of Word and sacrament and the necessity of faith.
See also: Christianity.

Sacramento (pop. 382,800), capital city of California since 1854, and seat of Sacramento County, at the confluence of the Sacramento and American rivers in central California. Its economy is based primarily upon the business of government, military manufactures, and agriculture, for which it is a shipping, marketing, and processing center. Its history dates back to 1839, when John Sutter established a colony there on a land grant from Mexico. After the discovery of gold at nearby Sutter's Mill, Sacramento became a boom town.
See also: California.

Sacramento River, longest tributary in California, rising in the Klamath Mountains in the north, flowing southwest for about 380 mi (610 km) to join the San Joaquin River in the Central Valley, before exiting at San Francisco Bay. It is navigable for large vessels as far as Sacramento, 67 mi (108 km) upstream, the major port and largest city on the river. Shasta and Keswick are the chief dams of the Sacramento, which contributes its water to the Central Valley Project (irrigation for the southern part of the state).

Sacrifice, cultic act found in almost all religions, in which an object is consecrated and offered by a priest in worship to a deity. It often involves the killing of an animal or human being and thus the offering up of its life; sometimes a communion meal follows. Sacrifice may also be seen as the expiation of sin, the sealing of a covenant, or a gift to the god that invites blessing in return. Ancient Israel had an elaborate system of sacrifices (chief being that of Passover) that ceased when the Temple was destroyed (A.D. 70). In Christianity, Jesus' death is viewed as the one perfect and eternal sacrifice for sin.
See also: Religion.

Habitat, the experimental cluster of apartments, designed by Moshe Safdie for Expo 67 in Montreal

Sadat, Anwar el- (1918-81), president of Egypt (1970-81). An army officer, he was active in the coup that overthrew King Farouk in 1952. As vice president, he became president on Nasser's death, expelling Soviet military advisers. His war with Israel and support of an Arab oil boycott against the West (both 1973) were followed by a policy reversal. Establishing close ties with the United States, he took initiatives leading to an Egyptian-Israeli peace treaty (1979). He shared the Nobel Peace Prize with Menachem Begin in 1978. Sadat was assassinated by a group of Muslim army officers.
See also: Egypt.

Saddle, seat to support a rider on the back of an animal. Most horse saddles are leather and are held in place by a girth (strap) passing underneath the horse. Two stirrup-leathers (straps) support the stirrups in which the rider places his or her feet. The English saddle is light, almost flat, and often used by jockeys and horse-show riders. The Western saddle is heavier, has a raised frontal horn to which a lariat may be attached, and is most often used by cowhands and rodeo riders.

Sadducees, Jewish sect active in Judea, Palestine, during the 1st century B.C. and active until the destruction of the Second Temple in Jerusalem, A.D. 70. The sect, associated with priests and the upper class, claimed the Old Testament alone as the source of Jewish law. With their dismissal of Jewish Oral Law they dismissed the beliefs in immortality, resurrection, and angelic beings, beliefs all held by the opposing Pharisee sect.
See also: Sanhedrin.

Sade, Marquis de (Comte Donatien Alphonse François de Sade; 1740-1814), French soldier and writer. He proposed that the existence of sexual deviation and criminal acts prove they are natural. He was charged with many sexual offenses and spent much of his life in prisons, writing sexually explicit romances, e.g., *Justine* (1791). He lived his last 11 years in Charenton lunatic asylum. The word *sadism* (infliction of pain to attain sexual pleasure) was named for him.

Sadi *see:* Saadi.

Safdie, Moshe (1938-), Israeli architect. His best known project is Habitat, a modular housing project designed for Expo '67, the 1967 Montreal exposition, and later reproduced in Israel, New York City, Puerto Rico, and the Virgin Islands. Other designs by Safdie include the Yeshivat Porat Joseph Rabbinical College in Jerusalem (1971-79) and the National Gallery of Canada in Ottawa (1988). Safdie became a Canadian citizen in 1959.
See also: Architecture.

Safety, protection from harm, injury, or loss. In a modern, technological society the risks of injury or accidental death caused by machines are very high. Every year in the United States there are over 100,000 deaths from accidents and around 50 million people are injured severely enough to require medical attention. This works out to 1 accidental death every 5 minutes and an injury every 3 seconds. Apart from the immense personal suffering these figures represent, the cost to the economy is enormous. The prevention of accidents is a major concern of all governments.

Safety lamp, oil-burning lamp used in coal mines that indicates the presence of explosive methane gas without igniting it. Designed in 1815 by English chemist Sir Humphry Davy, it uses a double wire gauze cylinder to enclose the flame, preventing heat from escaping and causing an explosion. In the presence of *firedamp*, the methane-air mixture commonly released in coal mining operations, the flame burns with a blue center, warning miners to leave the mine immediately. The safety electric lamps now used to light mines are designed so that if the bulb is broken the current shuts off, thus preventing ignition of firedamp. But although electric lamps are safe, they do not indicate the presence of the gas, and Davy lamps are still used to warn miners of the danger.
See also: Mining.

Safety valve, relief device that automatically opens to allow excess pressure to escape. Sealed by a compressed spring or a weight, it is held open until the pressure has fallen by a predetermined amount. Safety valves are used on all pressurized vessels (e.g., steam boilers) to prevent explosion.

Safflower, thistlelike herb (*Carthamus tinctorius*) that grows in most warm regions. Safflowers are grown by farmers for the oil and meal that can be made from the seeds. Safflower oil has uses in medicine and is used to make varnishes. The safflower's bright red flowers are used as a substitute for true saffron dye.

Saffron, purple-flowered Asian crocus (*Crocus sativus*) of the iris family; also, the yellow dye extracted from it. The orange-yellow stigmas of its pistils yield saffron powder, which is used for flavoring food and in medicine and perfume.

Saga, epic narrative, in prose or verse, of Old Norse literature (11th to mid-14th century). Subjects of sagas range from history (*Sturlungasaga*) to histories of mythical heroes (*Volsungasaga*) or families (*Njala*). One of the greatest saga authors was Snorri Sturluson, whose *Heimskringla* (1230) traced the history of the kings of Norway.

Sagan, Carl Edward (1934-96), U.S. astronomer, educator, and popular science writer. Since 1968 a professor at Cornell University, he has worked on NASA space probe projects and conducted research into the possibility of extraterrestrial life. He helped popularize science through his public television series *Cosmos* (1980). Sagan's books include the Pulitzer Prize-

winning *The Dragons of Eden* (1977) and the novel *Contact* (1985).
See also: Astronomy.

Sagan, Françoise (Françoise Quoirez; 1935-), French novelist best known for the precocious and highly successful *Bonjour Tristesse* (1954), written when she was 18, and *A Certain Smile* (1956), both of which deal with the disillusion of gilded youth.

Sage, aromatic herb or shrub of the mint family. There are several North American species, including the crimson and purple sages of California and the lyre-leaved sage of New England. Cultivated sages include bright-flowered ornamentals known by their scientific name, *salvia*. The common garden sage (*Salvia officinalis*), native to Southern Europe and Asia Minor, has grayish leaves that are used to make tea and as a seasoning.

Sage, Russell (1816-1906), U.S. financier who amassed a fortune from the wholesale grocery, railroad, and other businesses. From his $70-million estate, his widow used $10 million to establish the Russell Sage Foundation (1907) to better U.S. social conditions.

Sagebrush, small aromatic shrub (genus *Artemisia*) of the composite family, native to the plains and mountains of western North America. These deciduous shrubs grow anywhere from 2 to 12 ft (0.6 to 3.7 m) high and have white or yellow flowers. Sagebrush is unrelated to true sage. It is the state flower of Nevada.

Sagebrush State *see:* Nevada.

Saginaw (pop. 77,508), city in southern Michigan, seat of Saginaw County, located on the Saginaw River about 85 mi (137 km) northwest of Detroit. The original settlements of Saginaw (1820) and East Saginaw (1849) were expanded to form the city (1889). A fur trade center from the early 19th century, it was also a lumber center until the lumber supply was exhausted in the late 19th century. The city now manufactures automobiles and machinery and processes sugar beets and other agricultural products. The Saginaw River connects the city with Saginaw Bay, part of Lake Huron.
See also: Michigan.

Sago, starch derived from the coontie or sago palm. The starch is found in the fibrous tissue at the base of the tree's stem. Sago is used to make sago flour, one of the principal foods of East Indian people.

Saguaro, or giant cactus (*Cereus giganteus* or *Carnegiea gigantea*), large member of the cactus family native to the deserts of the U.S. Southwest and Mexico. The plant uses a shallow, wide network of roots to collect moisture, which it then stores in the ribbed, spiny trunk, 1-2.5 ft (30-76 cm) in diameter. The plant may reach the age of 150-200 years, growing to a height of nearly 40 ft (12 m) and occasionally up to 60 ft (18 m). The white night-blooming flowers form at the ends of the trunk and the large branches in late spring, attracting bats, birds, and insects. The red, egg-shaped fruit is eaten by humans and desert animals.

Sahara Desert, largest desert in the world, covering about 3,500,000 sq mi (9,065,000 sq km) of North Africa from the Atlantic Ocean to the Red Sea, about 3,000 mi (4,830 km) by 1,200 mi (1,930) north to south. The terrain includes sand hills, rocky wastes, tracts of gravel, and fertile oasis. The central plateau, about 1,000 ft (305 m) above sea level, has mountain groups (Ahagger, Aïr, and Tibesti), some of which rise well over 6,000 ft (1,829 m). Rainfall averages from less than 5 in (12.7 cm) to 10 in (25 cm) annually (dry periods may last for several years), and temperatures may soar higher than 135°F (57°C) and plunge below freezing at night. Natural resources include oil, iron ore, natural gas, and phosphates. Also underground are vast aquifers holding water thought to date from the Pleistocene epoch.

Sahel, semiarid region south of the Sahara Desert, extending across north-central Africa from Senegal in the west to Ethiopia in the east. The land supports a grazing and agricultural economy with savanna-type grassland and scrub. Rainfall is 8-16 in (20-40 cm) annually, from June to August. A severe drought (1967-74) caused mass migration and the starvation of hundreds of thousands of people.

Saigon *see:* Ho Chi Minh City.

Sailfish, food and game fish of the family Istiophoridae, related to the marlin and swordfish. The sailfish has a pointed beak on the snout and a high, wide dorsal fin sail. Averaging 6 ft (180 cm) in length and 60 to 100 lb (27 to 45 kg), they feed on fish and squid and are highly prized by anglers for their fighting qualities.

Sailing, popular pastime or sport involving the navigation of a boat powered primarily by wind. The earliest known sailing vessels evolved in the Mediterranean region, particularly among the Upper Nile dwellers of ancient Egypt. These sailboats had a mast with 1 sail hung from a fixed yardarm. The Chinese developed the movable yardarm, which allowed vessels to sail with the wind across their bows as well as before the wind. In recent history, boats of varying lengths, with multiple sales and masts, gather to compete with other like vessels. The most prestigious of these races is the *America's Cup*, an international series of races begun in 1851 and dominated by the United States until 1983. Major competitors include the USSR, Australia (winner of the Cup in 1983), and Great Britain. Boats often used for racing include schooners and ketches (2 masts/5 sails) and yawls (2 masts/4 sails). Recreational cruises are often one-design boats, 16-23 ft (4.88-7.01 m) long, such as the Star, Mercury, Comet, Lightning, and Snipe.
See also: America's Cup.

Date palms in the Sahara

Saint, in Christian theology, person pre-eminent for holiness. The term was used in the New Testament to refer to all the faithful. It is now used to designate those recognized by a church as occupying an exalted position in heaven and being worthy of veneration due to martyrdom, holiness of life, miracles during life or after death, or a popular cult. All angels are saints, and the Virgin Mary is chief among them. Feast days in the Anglican, Orthodox, and Roman Catholic liturgies commemorate those canonized with sainthood.
See also: Christianity.

Saint Andrews (pop. 16,000), town in eastern Scotland on the North Sea, in the district of Fife, between the firths of Forth and Tay. The University of St. Andrews is Scotland's oldest (founded 1411). The town, known as the birthplace of golf, is home to the Royal and Ancient Golf Club (founded 1754).
See also: Scotland.

Saint Augustine (pop. 11,985), city, seat of St. John's County, on the Atlantic coast of northeast Florida. The oldest city in the United States (founded 1565), its strategic location was coveted and often fought over (Sir Francis Drake attacked it first in 1586). It did not become part of the union until 1821 (inc. 1824). Today it is a tourist center with light industry and 2 national monuments: the Castillo de San Marcos (1672-96) and Fort Matanzas (1742).
See also: Florida.

Saint Bartholomew's Day, Massacre of, the killing of French Huguenots (Protestants) by Roman Catholics, beginning in

Paris on Aug. 24, 1572. Jealous of the influence of the Huguenot admiral Coligny on her son King Charles IX, Catherine de Médicis plotted to assassinate him. When this failed, Catherine, fearing Huguenot reaction, persuaded Charles to order the deaths of all leading Huguenots. On the morning of St. Bartholomew's Day thousands were slaughtered. Despite government orders to stop, the murders continued in the provinces until October. The Wars of Religion (1562-98) resumed as a result.
See also: Huguenots.

Saint Bernard, breed of large, stout dog developed as a rescue dog at the Alpine monastery of St. Bernard, Switzerland, in the 17th century. It measures up to 30 in (76 cm) at the shoulder and 180 lb (82 kg), and has a white and red or white and brown coat. Its acute sense of smell has helped it locate people buried in snow and makes it a valued guide dog.

Saint Bernard Passes, routes through the Alps. The Great St. Bernard (8,100 ft/2,469 m) links Martigny, Switzerland, with Aosta, Italy. The Little St. Bernard (7,177 ft/2,188 m) connects France's Isère Valley with Aosta.
See also: Alps.

Saint Christopher and Nevis, officially St. Christopher-Nevis, Caribbean island state of the British West Indies, in the Leeward Islands. The area is 101 sq mi (262 sq km); the capital is Basseterre, on Saint Christopher (commonly known as Saint Kitts). Discovered (1493) by Columbus, the islands were awarded to Britain (1783) after struggles with France. Autonomy in internal affairs was granted in 1967, followed by full independence in 1983.

Saint Christopher and Nevis

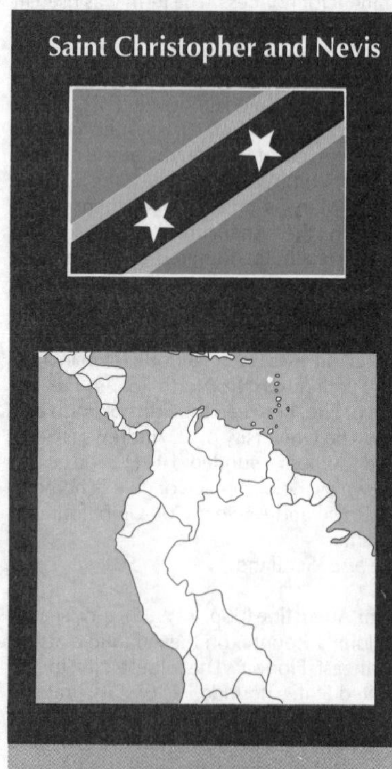

Capital:	Basseterre
Area:	101 sq mi (262 sq km)
Population:	46,000
Government:	constitutional monarchy
Independent:	1983
GNP:	U.S.$120,000,000
Per capita:	U.S.$2,770

Fishermen on Saint Christopher

Saint Clair, Arthur (1743-1818), U. S. soldier and politician. He served in the Revolutionary War and in 1787 became president of the Continental Congress, then first governor of the Northwest Territory (1787-1802). His military career ended with defeat by Native American tribes in 1792. Unpopular as governor, he was removed from office in 1802.

Saint Cloud (pop. 190,921), city in central Minnesota, seat of Stearns County, located on the Mississippi River about 70 mi (110 km) northwest of Minneapolis. Named for a French city, it was a fur-trading center and a stage coach terminus from the mid-1850s. Its granite quarries were opened in 1870, and the city is still a center for the granite industry. Other industry includes the manufacture of optical lenses, railroad cars, and refrigeration equipment. It is the home of St. Cloud State University.
See also: Minnesota.

Saint Croix, largest island of the U.S. Virgin Islands. It is a tourist center and markets sugarcane and rum.
See also: Virgin Islands.

Saint Denis, Ruth (Ruth Dennis; 1878?-1968), U.S. dancer, choreographer, and teacher, whose work strongly influenced modern dance. Deeply interested in ethnic and U.S. dances, music visualizations, and Hindu and other Eastern philosophies, she staged her first major success, the solo *Radha*, in 1906. She and her husband, Ted Shawn, ran the influential Denishawn School and widely touring Denishawn Company (both, 1915-32).
See also: Shawn, Ted.

Sainte-Anne-de-Beaupré, village and Roman Catholic shrine in Montmorency County, southern Quebec, Canada, on the St. Lawrence River near the mouth of the Ste.-Anne River. The village was first settled in 1650. A chapel was built there in 1658 by shipwrecked French sailors who believed they were saved from death by their prayers to Saint Anne, patron saint of sailors. There were subsequent reports of miracle cures in the area, and the village became a pilgrimage center. A basilica was built as a shrine in 1876 and rebuilt after a fire destroyed it in 1922.
See also: Quebec.

Saint Elias Mountains, part of the Pacific Coast Ranges, in eastern Alaska and the southwestern Yukon Territory, Canada. The range is extremely rugged, with many high peaks; Canada's Mount Logan (19,524 ft/5,951 m) and Alaska's Mount St. Elias (18,008 ft/5,489 m) are the second and fourth highest peaks in North America. Its ice fields are the most extensive outside of the polar ice caps.

Saint Elmo's fire, glowing electrical discharge seen at the tips of tall, pointed objects—e.g., church spires, ship masts, and airplane wings—in stormy weather. The negative electrical charge of the storm clouds induces a positive charge on the prominent structures. The impressive display is named (corruptly) for St. Erasmus, patron of sailors.

Saint-Exupéry, Antoine de (1900-44), French aviator and author. After serving in the French Army Air Force (1921-23), he flew commercial routes between France, West Africa, and South America. Most of his writing gives accounts of his flying experiences (*Southern Mail*, 1928) and the philosophical and spiritual meaning he found in its challenges (*Wind, Sand and Stars*, 1939). His most famous work, however, is the fantasy *The Little Prince* (1943). Saint-Exupéry flew reconnaissance missions during World War II, disappearing over Europe on one such mission in 1944.

Saint-Gaudens, Augustus (1848-1907), U.S. sculptor famed for his heroic public monuments, including Abraham Lincoln (Lincoln Park, Chicago), the Robert G. Shaw monument on the Boston Common, and the equestrian statue of General William Sherman (Central Park, N.Y.C.).

Saint George Island *see:* Pribilof Islands.

Saint George's (pop. 7,500), capital, chief port, and industrial center of Grenada, in the West Indies. Originally settled by the French in 1650 at a location near present-day St. George's, the current site was established in 1705. In 1783 control of the town, on the southwestern coast, passed to the British, who soon made it the government headquarters for all of the Windward Islands. A center of tourism, St. George's gained its independence in 1974.

Saint-Germain, Treaty of, treaty signed by the United States and other World War I Allies and the Republic of Austria in France (1919-20), limiting Austrian powers and redistributing some of the lands of the Austro-Hungarian Empire. The treaty resulted in the complete independence of Poland, Czechoslovakia, and Hungary, and the creation of the independent state of Yugoslavia. Austria's army and war industry were restricted, and the country was required to pay reparations to the Allies. The treaty's provision prohibiting the unification of Austria and Germany was violated by Adolf Hitler in 1938.
See also: World War I.

Saint Helena, British island (47 sq mi/122 sq km) in the South Atlantic Ocean, 1,200 mi (1,931 km) west of Africa. Discovered by the Portuguese in 1502, its capital is Jamestown, where Napoleon I died in exile in 1821. With Tristan da Cunha and Ascension, it comprises the British dependency of St. Helena.

Saint Helens, Mount *see:* Mount Saint Helens.

Saint James's Palace, former royal residence (1698-1837), London, England, situated in Pall Mall. Royal gatherings are still held here and foreign ambassadors to Britain are received at its court.

Saint John (pop. 76,381), city in eastern Canada, located in southern New Brunswick on the Bay of Fundy, at the mouth of the St. John River. It is one of the only 2 ice-free ports of Canada's Atlantic coast and is New Brunswick's center of transportation, commerce, and industry, including large shipyards, oil and sugar refineries, and pulp and paper mills. Originally a French trading post (1631-35), it passed between French and English control until 1758, when the English became the permanent rulers. The growth of the city escalated rapidly when the United Empire Loyalists arrived from the United States in 1783. Known as Paar Town, the city was incorporated as St. John 2 years later.
See also: New Brunswick.

Saint John River, tributary (418 mi/673 km long) that rises in northwestern Maine and flows northeast to New Brunswick, where it makes up about 80 mi (129 km) of the U.S.-Canadian border. The river then turns south and east, flowing through New Brunswick to empty into the Bay of Fundy at St. John. It is famous for its "reversing falls," made possible by exceptionally high Fundy tides.

Saint John's (pop. 96,216), largest city and capital of Newfoundland, Canada, situated on a well-protected harbor near the Grand Banks. The site was discovered by John Cabot in 1497 and is believed to have been settled shortly after. The city's key location has made it into an important docking port for fishing boats from around the world. St. John's stands as Newfoundland's chief cultural, educational, and commercial center.

Saint-John's-wort, name generally given to over 400 species of low shrubs of the family Hypericaceae, native to temperate and tropical regions. The flowers, which include both wild and cultivated varieties, are generally yellow, with 5 petals.

Saint Joseph (pop. 83,083), city in northwest Missouri, located on the east bank of the Missouri River about 55 mi (88.5 km) northwest of Kansas City. Saint Joseph was a frontier town, established in 1826 by a French-Canadian trapper, Joseph Robidoux. It became famous as the starting station for the pony express in 1860. The modern city is a distribution center for the meat-packing industry and other regional farm products and manufactures drugs and chemicals, paper products, and other goods.
See also: Missouri.

Saint Kitts *see:* Saint Christopher and Nevis.

Saint Laurent, Louis Stephen (1882-1973), prime minister of Canada (1948-57). Internationally, St. Laurent played an important role in the founding of the United Nations (1945). As prime minister he strengthened Canada's position in the Commonwealth of Nations and was instrumental in founding the North Atlantic Treaty Organization (NATO). Domestically, he achieved the incorporation of Newfoundland as a Canadian province in 1949.
See also: Canada.

Saint Lawrence River, largest tributary in Canada, flowing 744 mi (1,197 km) northeast from Lake Ontario to the Gulf of St. Lawrence. It forms 120 mi (193 km) of the U.S./Canadian border. Canalized as part of the Saint Lawrence Seaway, it serves as the chief outlet for Great Lakes shipping (although it is closed from mid-December to mid-April due to ice).

Saint Lawrence Seaway and Great Lakes Waterway, U.S./Canadian inland waterway for oceangoing vessels connecting the Great Lakes with the Atlantic Ocean, and comprising a system of natural waterways, canals, locks, dams, and dredged channels (including the Welland Ship Canal) 2,342 mi (3,769 km) long. A joint venture between the United States and Canada, it was completed in 1959.

Saint Louis (pop. 2,444,099), city in eastern Missouri, on the Mississippi River. Founded as a fur-trading post by the French in 1764, it was ceded to Spain in 1770, reverting briefly to the French before passing to the United States as part of the Louisiana Purchase in 1803. The city expanded rapidly after the War of 1812 and became a major inland port, transportation center, and market. Products include beer, machinery, chemicals, and basic metals. St. Louis' Gateway Arch (630 ft/192 m high), designed by Eero Saarinen, is the city's most famous landmark. It is also known for its symphony orchestra and Washington University.
See also: Missouri.

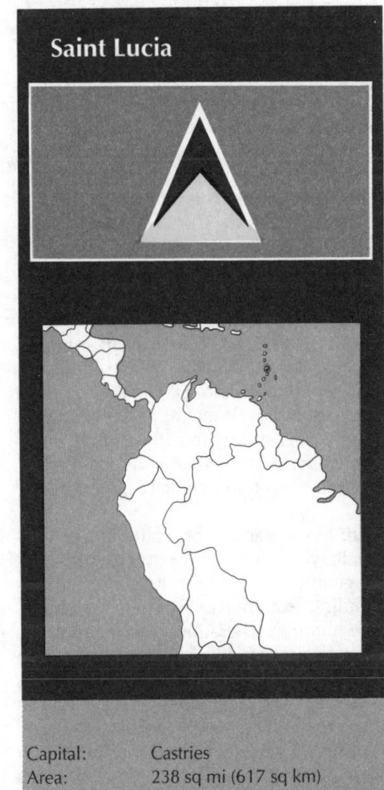

Capital:	Castries
Area:	238 sq mi (617 sq km)
Population:	150,000
Government:	constitutional monarchy
Independent:	1979
GNP:	U.S. $167,000,000
Per capita:	U.S. $1,370

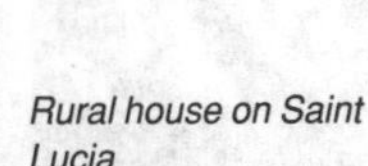
Rural house on Saint Lucia

Saint Lucia, independent West Indies island nation (238 sq mi/616 sq km) in the Windward Islands in the Caribbean Sea.
Land and Climate. St. Lucia, 27 mi (43 km) long and 14 mi (23 km) wide, is of volcanic origin with 1 active volcano. The terrain is

hilly, with Morne Gimie reaching 3,145 ft (959 m), and the interior is covered with tropical rain forests. The average annual temperature is 79°F (26°C).

People. Most of the inhabitants are of black African heritage. Roman Catholicism is the religion of nearly 90% of the population, and English is the official language. However, a French patois is widely spoken.

Economy. Small-scale agriculture is the principal economic activity, with bananas, coconuts, cocoa beans, oil, and citrus fruits grown for export. Industry, including food processing, electrical components, and garments, is being diversified to include an ambitious oil complex and free-trade zone. Although tourism is growing, imports exceed exports by 300%, and the country is heavily dependent upon foreign aid.

History. Though the island was probably sited by Columbus in 1502, the Carib were able to prevent several settlement attempts by the British and French from the early 17th century until 1803, when the island was ceded to Britain. St. Lucia was part of the West Indies Federation from 1958 until it was dissolved in 1962. Full independence from Britain was granted in 1979. It has a parliamentary government.

Saint Mark, Basilica of, cathedral in Venice, Italy, named for the city's patron saint. Originally Romanesque, it became an outstanding example of Byzantine architecture through alterations made from the 12th century on. It is built in the form of a Greek cross surmounted by 5 large domes (1 in the center, the others on the 4 arms of the cross). The richly constructed and sculptured west façade, facing the Piazza San Marco, has Gothic additions. Its famous 4 bronze horses were taken from Constantinople in 1204.

A caricature of Camille Saint-Saëns by the French cartoonist Bils

Saint Marys River, river on the border between Ontario and Michigan that drains Lake Superior, then flows less than 70 mi (110 km) to empty into Lake Huron. The river is part of the St. Lawrence and Great Lakes Waterway, which links the Great Lakes with the Atlantic Ocean. The St. Marys Rapids near Lake Huron make the river impassable for large boats; these are diverted to the Sault Ste. Marie (or Soo) Canals. Saint Marys River is a source of hydroelectric power.

Saint Moritz (pop. 5,263), alpine resort town in southeastern Switzerland, Graubünden (Grisons) canton. The original Roman settlement dates from 50 B.C. The town became a resort in the 19th century, and was home to the 1928 and 1948 Winter Olympics. Saint Moritz is located in the region where Romansh, an Italic language (of Latin derivation) and one of Switzerland's official languages, is spoken.

Saint Nicholas, Feast of, festival on Dec. 6 in honor of a 4th-century bishop of Asia Minor. Saint Nicholas, later known also as Santa Claus, is patron saint of children, and the festival is celebrated as a children's holiday, with rewards and punishment according to the children's behavior. Although Santa Claus became identified with Christmas, the Feast of Saint Nicholas continues to be celebrated by some on Dec. 6.

Saint Patrick's Cathedral, largest U.S. Roman Catholic cathedral, seat of the New York Archdiocese. The Gothic Revival structure was designed by James Renwick and built between 1858 and 1879. It is located on 5th Avenue and 50th Street, New York City.

Saint Patrick's Day, March 17, celebrated as the anniversary of the death (C.A.D. 461) of Patrick, Ireland's patron saint. The Irish celebrate the day by wearing leaves of shamrock (Ireland's national flower) or green-colored items of clothing and by staging colorful parades.

Saint Paul (pop. 270,230), capital of Minnesota and seat of Ramsay County, located in the eastern part of the state on the Mississippi River. St. Paul and neighboring Minneapolis together form the Twin Cities. The site was occupied by U.S. Army Fort St. Anthony from 1819; the settlement of St. Paul was established in 1840 and became an important commercial port and fur-trading center. Railroad lines reached the city by the 1860s, extending to Puget Sound, on the west coast, by the 1890s. While the more industrial Minneapolis flourished, St. Paul suffered an economic decline starting in the 1920s, but it has undergone extensive redevelopment since the mid-1960s. Cultural assets now include 2 major performance centers (Landmark Center, 1978; Ordway Music Theatre, 1984) and the St. Paul Chamber Orchestra.
See also: Minnesota.

Saintpaulia *see:* African violet.

Saint Petersburg (pop. 238,647), city on the central west coast of Florida, situated on the Pinellas peninsula opposite Tampa, on Tampa Bay of the Gulf of Mexico. Native Americans lived in the area since 5000 B.C. It was explored by the Spanish in the 1500s, but was first settled by European Americans in the 1840s. Russian-born Peter A. Demens, who built the railroad that connected the settlement to central Florida (1888), named the city for his birthplace. The location and unusually sunny climate have made the city a major resort and retirement community since the early 1900s. Major attractions include yacht races and spring training camps for professional baseball teams. Eckerd College and St. Petersburg Junior College are located in the city.
See also: Florida.

Saint Petersburg *see:* Leningrad.

Saint Peter's Church, or Saint Peter's Basilica, church in Vatican City, Rome. The world's largest Christian church, it is built over the tomb thought to hold the remains of St. Peter, the first pope. The original church was built by the emperor Constantine the Great in the 4th century A.D. but demolished by Pope Julius II in the 16th century to make way for the new building. Among the successive architects to be involved in the creation of the current church were Donato Bramante, who developed the original design on the shape of a Greek cross (from 1506); Michelangelo Buonarroti, who created the great dome (from 1547); and Carlo Maderno, who added the façade and altered the overall proportions to arrive at the shape of a Latin cross (1607-14). The church was dedicated in 1626, but further work continued, most notably by Gian Lorenzo Bernini, who created the great elliptical piazza in front of the church (completed 1667) as well as much of the interior detail. The church measures nearly 700 ft (210 m) long and is 450 ft (137 m) at its widest. The nave (main aisle) is 150 ft (46 m) high, while the dome is over 400 ft (120 m) high.

Saint Pierre and Miquelon, groups of French islands in the Atlantic Ocean, south of Newfoundland. The capital is Saint Pierre. First visited in the 17th century by Breton and Basque fishermen, the islands' ownership was long disputed between France and England. They became France's in 1814 and are now an overseas department, electing a deputy and senator to parliament. Fisheries (for cod and others), fox- and mink-farming, and tourism are important industries.

Saint-Saëns, Camille (1835-1921), French composer. He wrote many large-scale symphonies, piano concertos, symphonic poems, operas, including *Samson et Dalila* (1877), and such short works as *La Danse Macabre* (1874), and *Carnival of the Animals* (1886).

Saint-Simon, Comte de (Claude Henri de Rouvroy; 1760-1825), French philosopher and early socialist. According to his theories, voiced in *The New Christianity* (1825) and other influential writings, all people would be treated as economic equals—no wealth would be inherited, everyone would work, and compensation would be commensurate with labor. He believed that science could be used to create a fair and harmonious society. Saint-Simon fought on the side of the colonies in the American Revolution.
See also: Socialism.

Saint Sophia *see:* Hagia Sophia.

Saint Thomas, mountainous, heavily cultivated, tropical island (32 sq mi/83 sq km) of the U.S. Virgin Islands, West Indies, in the westernmost part of the Lesser Antilles in the Caribbean Sea. The economy rests on tourism but includes cattle-raising and meat-packaging. St. Thomas was settled by the Danish in 1672. The islanders have been U.S. citizens since 1927 and are administered by the U.S. Department of Interior. They are governed by a locally elected governor and senate.

Saint Vincent and the Grenadines, island nation in the West Indies, part of the Windward Islands in the Caribbean Sea.

St. Vincent and the Grenadines

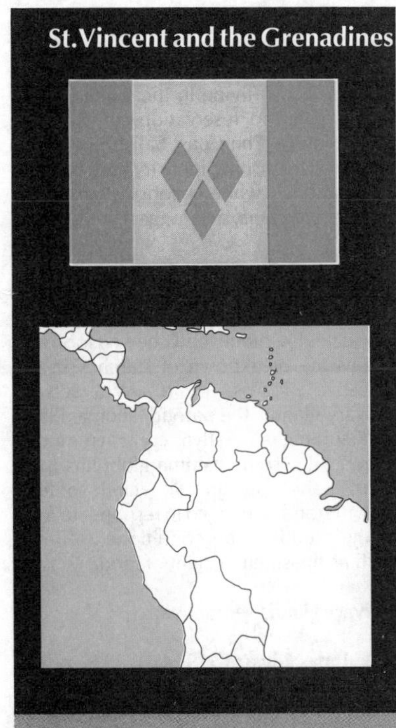

Capital:	Kingstown
Area:	150 sq mi (389 sq km)
Population:	114,000
Government:	constitutional monarchy
Independent:	1979
GNP:	U.S.$130,000,000
Per capita:	U.S.$1,100

St. Vincent's cocoa plantations thrive on the upland slopes.

Land and climate. The principal island, St. Vincent (133 sq mi/344 sq km), is of volcanic origin, with a forested, mountainous spine running down the center of the island. It reaches 4,000 ft (1,219 m) at Soufrière, an active volcano peak that erupted in 1979, causing extensive crop damage and the evacuation of 20,000 people. The 5 small, main islands of the Grenadines extend to the southwest. The climate is tropical.

People. The majority of the inhabitants are descendants of slaves brought from Africa. Most of the population belongs to the Anglican church; English is spoken.

Economy. Agriculture provides all exports, principally arrowroot and bananas, followed by spices and cacao. The small industrial sector mostly processes food crops. Tourism is also important.

History. St. Vincent was discovered by Christopher Columbus in 1498. Although both Britain and France subsequently contested control of the island, it was left largely to the Carib Indians until 1797 when, following a war with both the French and Caribs, the British deported most of the Indians. Full independence was achieved in 1979.

Saint Vitus's dance *see:* Chorea.

Saipan, island, capital of the Northern Mariana Islands and headquarters of the U.S. Trust territory of the Pacific Islands. It is mountainous and fertile. Copra, bananas, and breadfruit are important crops.
See also: Northern Mariana Islands.

Sake, or saki, alcoholic drink made from fermented rice. It is Japan's national beverage and contains 12-16% by volume of ethanol.

Sakhalin (formerly Saghalien), USSR island off the coast of eastern Siberia, in the Sea of Okhotsk, north of the Japanese island of Hokkaido. It measures about 600 mi (970 km) long and 16-100 mi (26-160 km) wide, and contains coal and iron deposits and lumber. Fishing and fur trading are also important economic activities. Ownership of the island, which was originally discovered by the Dutch, was disputed by Japan and Russia—from 1905 it was divided between the 2 countries. The Ainu people were the original inhabitants; Soviet colonization dates from the discovery of oil in 1931. By 1951 Japan had given up all claims to the island.

Sakharov, Andrei Dmitriyevich (1921-90), Soviet physicist and human-rights proponent. He played a prominent part in the development of the first Soviet hydrogen bomb (1948-56). He subsequently advocated worldwide nuclear disarmament (for which he was awarded the 1975 Nobel Peace Prize) and became a leading Soviet dissident. His subsequent banishment (1980) to the city of Gorki provoked international protest. He was pardoned in 1986.
See also: Nuclear weapon.

Saki *see:* Munro, Hector Hugh.

Saladin (1138-93), Muslim ruler and warrior who fought against the Crusaders. He united the Shiite and Sunnite Muslims in 1171 and thus became sultan of Egypt and Syria. In 1187 he led the capture of Jerusalem from the Christians. The Third Crusade that followed resulted in a lengthy siege of the city (1189-91). Saladin finally surrendered to England's King Richard I and entered into a truce ceding coastal lands to the Christians and giving pilgrims access to Jerusalem. Saladin was a noted patron of learning and the arts.
See also: Crusades.

Salamander, tailed amphibian (order Vrodela) related to frogs and toads. Salamanders' weak limbs, which are not used for locomotion to any great extent, are small and can regenerate. These mostly nocturnal creatures range in size from under 6 in (15 cm) to 5 ft (1.5 m) and are abundant in damp areas of the northern temperate zone. Some species are aquatic, most are terrestrial, and a few are arboreal. Salamanders feed on insects and other invertebrates.

Salamis, or Koulouri (Greek, "baker's crescent"), Greek island in the Saronic Gulf (arm of the Aegean Sea between Attica and the Peloponnisos), about 10 mi (16 km) west of Athens. The rocky, crescent-shaped island, 37 sq mi (95 sq km) in area, supports little agriculture, and most residents now work in the shipping industry or in businesses in Athens. In the Battle of Salamis (480 B.C.), fought at sea by the Persians and the Athenians, Themistocles led the Greeks to a decisive victory.

Andrei Sakharov

Salazar, António de Oliveira (1889-1970), dictator of Portugal (1932-68). He reorganized public finances as finance minister (1926, 1928), and achieved certain modernizations as premier. Education and living standards, however, remained almost static, and political freedom was restricted, both at home and in Portugal's African colonies, where he actively suppressed revolts. A stroke in 1968 led to his replacement as premier.
See also: Portugal.

Salem (pop. 278,024), capital and third-largest city of Oregon, in the fertile Willamette Valley about 50 mi (80.5 km) south of Portland. Founded in 1840 by Methodist missionaries, it was the territorial capital in the 1850s and became the state capital when Oregon was admitted to the Union in 1859. Salem is a food-processing and distribution center. Willamette University, founded as Oregon Institute in 1842, is the oldest university in the Pacific Northwest.
See also: Oregon.

Salem (pop. 38,264), manufacturing city in northeast Massachusetts, seat of Essex County, on an inlet of Massachusetts Bay. Founded in 1626, it soon became a major port, crucial for trade with China. Today tourists appreciate it as the site of witchcraft trials (1692), and as the birthplace of Nathaniel Hawthorne, whose home has

been preserved. Other sights include Pioneer Village, a reproduction of a 1630 settlement, and the House of the Seven Gables (1668), about which Hawthorne wrote his novel of the same name.
See also: Massachusetts.

Salem, Peter (1750?-1816), former black slave, American Revolutionary soldier. Salem obtained his freedom by enlisting in the colonial army. He distinguished himself at the Battle of Bunker Hill, near Boston, June 17, 1775, saving the colonial troops from surrender by shooting British Major John Pitcairn, thus giving the troops time to retreat.
See also: Bunker Hill, Battle of.

Salem witchcraft trials, trials held in Salem, Massachusetts Bay Colony, in 1692, as a result of hysteria. The accusations of innocent townspeople began when 3 young girls claimed possession by the devil. The special court sentenced 19 men and women to death by hanging and imprisoned about 150 more. The witch hunt was brought to a halt and those imprisoned were freed in 1693. Samuel Sewall, one of the 3 judges, apologized publicly, and the colony's legislature made payments to families of those who were executed. In Arthur Miller's play *The Crucible* (1953) the events in Salem were used to symbolize the persecution of individuals as alleged communists by Senator Joseph McCarthy's House Un-American Activities Committee.
See also: Sewall, Samuel.

Salerno (pop. 154,900), city and tourist center in Campania, on the Gulf of Salerno in southern Italy. Founded by Romans in 197 B.C., it was occupied by the Norman conqueror Robert Guiscard in 1076 and was the site of a fierce beach battle between the Allies and Germans in World War II. Salerno's medical school, founded in the 9th century and at its peak in the 12th, was the first of its kind, with teachings influenced by the leading Mediterranean cultures.
See also: Italy.

Sales, Saint Francis de *see:* Francis de Sales, Saint.

Salic law, from the 14th century, law to prevent women and those descended from female lines from inheriting the throne and other titles and offices. It was not part of the Germanic *Lex Salica* (laws regarding the penal code and succession to property), as it is sometimes mistaken to be. Salic law was used into the 19th century in France and Spain, where it was rescinded for Queen Isabella II.

Salicylic acid ($C_7H_6O_3$), white crystalline solid made from phenol and carbon dioxide. It is used in medicine against calluses and warts and to make aspirin and dyes. Its sodium salt is an analgesic and is used for rheumatism.
See also: Aspirin.

Salinas de Gortari, Carlos (1948-), president of Mexico from 1988. As secretary of planning and the budget in the cabinet of President Miguel de la Madrid Hurtado, Salinas managed Mexico's economy from 1982 to 1987. He was elected on the ticket of the ruling party, the Institutional Revolutionary Party (PRI), to succeed Madrid.
See also: Mexico.

Salinger, J(erome) D(avid) (1919-), U.S. author. His only novel, *The Catcher in the Rye* (1951), became one of the most popular postwar books, and its adolescent hero, Holden Caulfield, was accepted as a spokesperson of his generation. Salinger's short stories include *Nine Stories* (1953) and *Franny and Zooey* (1961).

Salisbury, or New Sarum (pop. 102,500), town in Wiltshire, southern England, 80 mi (130 km) southwest of London. The original town of Old Sarum was rebuilt as New Sarum when it became a bishopric in the 13th century; Salisbury's main tourist attraction, its cathedral, dates from this time. The famous prehistoric stone circle known as Stonehenge lies 7 mi (11 km) north.
See also: England.

Salish, group of Native American tribes of the U.S. Northwest and British Columbia, Canada. Two groups are distinguished. The Coast Salish, including the Quinault and Tillamook, traditionally lived by salmon fishing and hunting and gathering. The Interior Salish, including the Flathead, Spokan, and Wenatchee, lived east of the Cascade and Coast Range mountains. Those living nearest the Pacific were culturally much like the Coast Salish, while those living farther east lived much like the Plains tribes, hunting on horseback. At the time of the arrival of European settlers, many were fur trappers and traders. Most of those Salish living in the United States were moved to reservations in the mid-19th century. The Coast Salish now work largely in the fishing industry and in urban occupations, while Interior Salish are farmers, ranchers, and loggers.

Saliva, watery secretion of the salivary glands, partly controlled by the parasympathetic autonomic nervous system, that lubricates the mouth and chewed food and begins the breakdown of starches in the digestive process. There are 3 sets of salivary glands: the parotid, submaxillary, and sublingual. Saliva contains mucin, water, salts, some gamma globulins (proteins), and ptyalin (a starch-splitting enzyme) and is secreted in response to food in the mouth or by conditioned reflexes such as the smell or sight of food.

Salivary glands *see:* Saliva.

Salk, Jonas Edward (1914-), U.S. physician and microbiologist. He is best known for developing the first poliomyelitis vaccine, made from killed viruses (1952-54). He served as director of the Salk Institute for Biological Studies at the University of California, San Diego (1963-75).
See also: Poliomyelitis.

Salmon, large, silver, soft-finned game and food fish of the family Salmonidae. Salmon are born in fresh water, spend most of their lives in the ocean, and return to fresh water to breed. The most commercially important salmon is the Pacific salmon (genus *Oncorhynchus*), of which there are 5 species. The largest is the chinook, which reaches up to 100 lb (45 kg); the blueback is the source of most canned salmon. The Atlantic salmon (*Salmo salar*), endangered due to overfishing and pollution, lives in the North Atlantic and reaches only 15 lb (6.8 kg), feeding on crustaceans and small fish. All salmon return to their natal streams to breed, spawning in the sand or gravel of the stream bed.

Salmonellosis, common type of food poisoning caused by the *Salmonella* bacteria. Poultry, milk, eggs, and egg products often carry the bacteria. Salmonellosis is usually confined to the intestines, where it causes

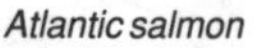
Atlantic salmon

nausea, abdominal pain, diarrhea, and fever. Treatment includes rest, replacement of body fluids and, in severe cases, the use of antibiotics.
See also: Food poisoning.

Salome (fl. 1st century A.D.), daughter of Herodias and stepdaughter of Herod Antipas (governor of Galilee), described in the New Testament (Matthew 14:6-12, Mark 6:22-28). She is said to have danced for Herod, for which she was granted a wish. At the urging of her mother, Herodias, she requested the head of the imprisoned John the Baptist. Oscar Wilde's play *Salome* (1893), which gives an erotic interpretation of these events, formed the basis for Richard Strauss's opera (1905). Another biblical Salome, possibly mother of the apostles James and John, appears in Mark 15:41 and 16:1.
See also: Bible; New Testament.

Salomon, Haym (1740-85), Polish-born U.S. financier, patriot, founder of the first Philadelphia synagogue. Salomon was active in the Polish independence movement before emigrating to New York in 1772. He was a major financial supporter of the American Revolution, lending large sums of money to the colonial government, giving money outright to equip troops, and making interest-free loans to Thomas Jefferson and other prominent statesmen. He was twice arrested and imprisoned for treason by the British (1776, 1778). Salomon challenged the Pennsylvania rule that civil servants swear belief in the New Testament, a rule that was later changed.

Salon, reception hall or drawing room often used for gatherings of society figures, intellectuals, politicians, or artists and their work. Salons can also be fashion establishments offering products or services to customers.

Salonika (pop. 406,400), port city in northern Greece, on the Salonika Gulf, established c.316 B.C., by the Macedonian king Cassander. Known as Thessaloniki in Greek, the city is now an industrial center producing textiles, soap, tobacco, minerals and leather products. It is also the second most important home of modern Greek culture, after Athens.
See also: Greece.

Salpiglossis *see:* Painted-tongue.

Salsify, or oyster plant (*Tragopogon porrifolius*), purple flowering plant of the composite family whose edible root has a flavor similar to oysters.

SALT *see:* Strategic Arms Limitation Talks.

Salt, common name for sodium chloride (NaCl), a chemical compound with an equal number of sodium ions (+) and chlorine ions (–). It is found in seawater and in solid deposits (rock salt, or halite). Pure salt forms colorless-to-white odorless cubic crystals. An essential in the diet of humans and animals, salt is most familiarly used to flavor food. It is also used in much larger quantities to preserve hides in leathermaking, to manufacture soap, as a food curative and preservative, to keep highways ice-free in winter, and in the manufacture of sodium, chlorine, and sodium hydroxide.

Salt, chemical, compound that is formed by a chemical reaction between an acid and a base. When a base totally neutralizes the acid with which it combines, a normal salt results. If neutralization is less than total, an acid salt or basic salt is produced. Table salt (sodium chloride) is a simple salt, a compound of a metal and a non-metal. When simple salts combine with other simple salts, double salts result.

Salter, Susanna Madora (1860-1961), first woman to be elected mayor of a U.S. town (Argonia, Kans.; 1887). Opponents of Prohibition had nominated Salter, a Woman's Christian Temperance Union officer, as a joke.

Salt Lake *see:* Great Salt Lake.

Salt Lake City (pop. 1,072,227), capital of Utah, seat of Salt Lake County, on the Jordan River in north-central Utah, near the Great Salt Lake. Founded in 1847 by Brigham Young, who led a band of Mormons from persecution, it is the world center of the Church of Jesus Christ of Latter-Day Saints. The city surrounds the Temple (1853-93) at its center. It is a commercial and industrial center for minerals, electronics, oil refining, and chemicals. Other sights include the State Capitol (1914) and the Brigham Young Memorial (1897).
See also: Utah.

Salton Sea, large saline lake in southeastern California. Until flooded by the Colorado River in 1905, it was a depression, known as the Salton Sink, 280 ft (85 m) below sea level. It now covers 370 sq mi (958 sq km) and is 232 ft (71 m) below sea level.

Saltpeter, or potassium nitrate (KNO_3), chemical compound occurring as a colorless crystal or white powder. It is found in limestone caves or can be produced by combining potassium chloride with sodium nitrate. It is used for explosives, matches, fertilizer, and to preserve food.
See also: Explosive.

Salts, any of various chemical salts used as agents for cleansing the intestines or as laxatives. Epsom salt, Glauber's salt, and Rochelle salt are examples.

Saluda Dam, large, earth-filled dam on the Saluda River, near Columbia, S.C. The dam, completed in 1930, is 211 ft (64 m) high and 8,650 ft (2,637 m) long.

Saluki, lean, fast-running working hound first bred c.5000 B.C. in Arabia and Egypt to hunt gazelle. The dog has long, silky ears and weighs about 60 lb (27 kg); it stands

The Mormon Temple, Salt Lake City, Utah

23 to 28 in (58 to 71 cm) high at the shoulders. Its colors are light tan, white, brown, or black and tan.

Salute, formal greeting to honor another person, flag or nation, done by raising the hand to the head, by firing guns or presenting arms. Salutes can include dipping of flags, tilting of airplane wings or raising a clenched fist or outstretched palm. Salutes are used mostly in the military or to show respect to a visiting dignitary.

Salvador, or Bahia (pop. 1,496,276), third largest city in Brazil, after São Paulo and Rio de Janeiro. An Atlantic port, Salvador's main industries include food and tobacco processing, textile manufacturing, petrochemical production, and oil exploration equipment. Its exports include cacao, fruit and fruit juices, petroleum, sugar, tobacco and vegetable oils. Founded in 1549, Salvador is the home of the University of Bahia, the Catholic University, and the city's 16th-century cathedral.
See also: Brazil.

Salvage, in maritime law, either the rescue of life and property (a ship and its cargo) from danger on water or the reward given by a court to those who effect a rescue (called *salvors*). Under the law of the sea, it is the duty of a ship's master to go to the aid of an imperiled vessel. If life or property are saved, the owner of the rescue ship, the master, and the crew share in the salvage award. These awards are generous in order to encourage sailors and shipowners to risk their lives and property in rescue operations.
See also: Flotsam, jetsam, and lagan.

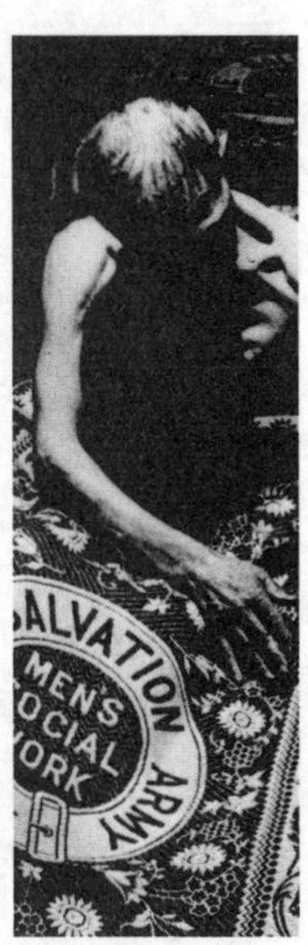

The Salvation Army provides beds and shelter for the homeless.

Salvation Army, nonsectarian, Christian organization founded in London as the Revival Society by William Booth (1865). In 1878 the mission became the army, with Booth as general. Under strict, quasimilitary discipline, the members seek to strengthen Christianity and help the poor and destitute. The army now operates 8,000 centers in the United States alone. Its official journal is *War Cry*.

Salvia

Salvia, any of various plants (genus *Salvia*) of the mint family, that thrive in tropical climates. Some are used as food seasonings, others for ornamental purposes. The 700 species of woody plants vary in size and height and produce flowers of many colors, including brilliant reds, blues, whites, yellows, and violets. Salvia originates in Brazil but grows throughout the world.

Salween River, or Salwin River, river in eastern Burma, originating in eastern Tibet and flowing south 1,500 mi (2,400 km) to empty into the Bay of Bengal. A gorge makes the river largely unnavigable, but the Salween is important agriculturally, providing irrigation and flowing through a fertile delta.

Salzburg (pop. 138,200), historic city in central Austria, on the Salzbach River. The birthplace of Wolfgang Amadeus Mozart, it is world famous for its annual music festival (begun 1917).
See also: Austria.

Samaria, city in ancient central Palestine built by King Omri c.800 B.C. as the capital of northern Israel; also, the region surrounding the city. It fell to Assyria c.722 B.C. and to Alexander the Great in 331 B.C.. John Hyrcanus destroyed Samaria in 120 B.C., but it was rebuilt by Herod the Great. Samaria is the traditional burial site of St. John the Baptist.

Samaritans, members of a religious sect residing in the ancient district of Samaria, central Palestine. Originally non-Jewish colonists from Assyria, the Samaritans intermarried with the Israelites and accepted the Jewish Torah. However, they were not socially accepted—hence the significance of the Good Samaritan in Luke's Gospel.

Samarium, chemical element, symbol Sm; for physical constants see Periodic Table. Samarium was discovered spectroscopically in 1879 by Paul Émile Lecoq de Boisbaudran in the mineral samarskite. It is found in the minerals monazite and bastnasite, which are commercial sources. It is present to the extent of 1% in misch metal. The metal is prepared by reducing the oxide with barium. Samarium is a silvery, reactive metal. Ion-exchange and solvent extraction techniques have led to much easier isolation of the so-called rare-earth elements. An alloy of samarium with cobalt is used to make a permanent magnet with the highest resistance to demagnetization of any known material. Samarium and its compounds are used in carbon-arc lighting applications, permanent magnets, special glasses, and organic catalysts and as a neutron absorber in nuclear reactors.

Samarkand (pop. 515,000), city in the central Asian part of the USSR, formerly the capital of Uzbekistan, one of the 15 Soviet republics. One of the world's oldest cities, Samarkand was a stopover on the ancient trade route between China and the Middle East. In 329 B.C. it was conquered by Alexander the Great. In the 8th century it was taken by the expanding Arab empire, and by the 9th century it had become a center of Asian Islamic culture. It was destroyed by Genghis Khan in 1220. Rebuilt, it became the capital of Tamerlane's empire in the 14th and 15th centuries. The Uzbeks conquered it in the 1500s, and Russia took it over in 1868. Today its industries include cotton and silk goods, wine, tea, and radio and automotive parts.

Samnites, ancient tribe of the mountains of southern Italy who fought 3 wars with the Romans (343-341 B.C., 316-304 B.C., 298-290 B.C.) before being conquered and almost totally destroyed. In 80 B.C. the Romans completely suppressed the remaining Samnites in the Social War, and the few survivors blended into Roman culture.

Samoa, chain of 10 islands and several islets in the South Pacific, midway between Honolulu and Sydney. Volcanic and mountainous, their total area is about 1,200 sq mi (3,108 sq km.). The people are mostly Polynesians. The soil is fertile, producing cacao, coconuts, and bananas. The climate is tropical. Savai'i (the largest), Upolu, and the other Western islands constitute independent Western Samoa. The capital is Apia, on Upolu. American Samoa consists of the eastern islands: Tutuila, the Manua group, and the Rose and Swains islands. The capital is Pago Pago, on Tutila. Discovered by the Dutch in 1722, Samoa was claimed by Germany, Great Britain, and the United States in the mid-19th century, but in 1899 the United States acquired sole rights to what is now American Samoa.
See also: American Samoa; Western Samoa.

Sámos, one of the Sporades islands, southeastern Greece, in the Aegean Sea, separated from Turkey by the Sámos Strait. The island, 184 sq mi (476 sq km), yields crops of olives and grapes. For a time under Turkish control, it became part of Greece in 1913. It was the birthplace of the mathematician and philosopher Pythagoras and is known as the home of Aesop, the semi-legendary creator of fables.

Samoset (1590?-1655), Pemaquid chief who welcomed, assisted, and became a staunch friend of the Plymouth Pilgrims. In 1625 Samoset presented John Brown with 12,000 acres of Pemaquid land for the colonists' use and settlement.
See also: Massasoit.

Samothrace, mountainous Greek island in the northeastern Aegean Sea. About 70 sq mi (180 sq km) in area, Samothrace has hot springs, clay deposits, and one high mountain, the Fengári, near its center. Its many Hellenistic artifacts and ruins date back to the 4th century B.C. Industries today include sponge fishing and sulfur production.

Samoyed, strong working dog of northern Siberia used to pull sleds and oversee reindeer herds. Its heavy white or cream colored coat protects it from severe weather and moisture. It weighs 35-65 lb (15.9-29.5 kg) and stands 19-23.5 in (48.3-59.7 cm) high at the shoulder. The Samoyed people of Siberia developed the breed thousands of years ago.

Sampras, Pete (1971-), U.S. tennis player, youngest ever to win the men's singles title in the United States Open tennis tournament (1990). He is known for his powerful serve, one-handed backhand, and serve-and-volley style of playing.

Sampson, Deborah (1760-1827), schoolteacher from Plympton, Mass., who disguised herself as a man to fight in the Revolutionary War. Wounded twice before her identity was discovered, she was given an honorable discharge by Gen. George Washington. The U.S. Congress granted her a military pension in 1805.
See also: Revolutionary War in America.

Sampson, William Thomas (1840-1902), U.S. admiral, commander of the North Atlantic Squadron in the Spanish-American War.

Samson, in the Bible, hero in ancient Israel known for his extraordinary strength, which came from his long hair. During Israel's war with the Philistines, Samson killed a thousand Philistines with the jawbone of an ass. His love for a Philistine woman, Delilah, became his downfall when she learned the secret of his strength and cut his hair as he slept. Samson was captured and imprisoned. When his hair grew back, he tore down the pillars of the temple, killing both himself and the Philistines inside.
See also: Bible.

Samuel, Books of, Old Testament books (known to Catholics as 1 and 2 Kings) that tell of the statesman, general, and prophet Samuel (11th century B.C.). He united the tribes under Saul and chose David as Saul's successor.
See also: Bible; Old Testament.

Samuelson, Paul Anthony (1915-), U.S. economist, adviser to Presidents John F. Kennedy and Lyndon B. Johnson, and winner of the 1970 Nobel Prize in economics. His widely used college textbook, *Economics* (1948), has been translated into 21 languages.
See also: Economics.

Samurai, hereditary military class of Japan. From A.D. 1000 the samurai dominated Japan, though after 1600 their activities were less military than cultural. They exerted influence through bushido, a code that demanded feudal loyalty and placed honor above life. The class lost its power in the reforms of 1868.
See also: Shogun.

Sana (pop. 427,185), capital and largest city of the Yemen Arabic Republic, in southern Arabia on a high inland plain. The city, a trade center for grapes and other

crops as well as the economic, political, religious, and educational center of Yemen, is linked to the Red Sea port of Hodeida by road. Sana, which is shaped like a figure eight and surrounded by a wall 20-30 ft (6-9 m) high, is noted for the architectural splendor of the Bab al-Yaman (Yemen Gate) and the 7-story Republican Palace, as well as some 50 mosques. Originally a pre-Islamic settlement, it was subsequently ruled by the Ethiopians (6th century) and the Ottoman Turks (17th century and 1872-1918) before Yemen's independence (1918).
See also: Yemen.

San Andreas Fault, break in the earth's crust running 600 mi (965 km) from Cape Mendocino, northwestern Calif., to the Colorado desert. It was the sudden movement of land along this fault that caused the San Francisco Earthquake of 1906. The fracture, and the motion responsibile for this and other quakes, is a result of the abutment of the eastern Pacific and North American plates.
See also: Earthquake.

San Antonio (pop. 1,302,099), city in south-central Texas, seat of Bexar County, on the San Antonio River 150 mi (241 km) north of the Gulf of Mexico. Founded in 1718 by the Spanish, who built a series of missions in the area over the next 13 years, it was an important settlement in early Texan history. Captured (1835) by the Texans during the Texas Revolution, its Alamo was attacked by Mexicans in 1836. It is one of the largest military centers in the United States and the site of a major medical complex. Its manufactures include clothing, chemicals, and processed food; San Antonio is well known for its artists' colonies, museums, and historical sites.
See also: Texas.

San Blas, 4 tribes of about 20,000 Native Americans living on the San Blas Islands off the eastern coast of Panama. The most heavily populated of the tribes is the Cuna. San Blas still practice traditional customs. About 7 out of 1,000 San Blas are albinos.

Sánchez, George Isidore (1906-72), U.S. educator and spokesman for educational reform in the Spanish community. He advocated that schools in Spanish-speaking communities offer bilingual classes, using Spanish-speaking teachers and teaching subjects in Spanish. His book *Forgotten People: A Study of New Mexicans* (1940) is a classic sociological study. Sanchez received a doctorate in education from the University of California at Berkeley in 1934. He was a professor of Latin-American education at Texas University.
See also: Education.

Sand, in geology, collection of rock particles with diameters in the range 0.125-2.0 mm. It can be graded according to particle size: fine, medium, coarse, and very coarse. Sands result from erosion by glaciers, winds, or ocean or other moving water. Their chief constituents are usually quartz and feldspar. Sand's uses include making bricks, cement, glass, and concrete.

Sand, George (Amandine Aurore Lucie Dupin; 1804-76), French novelist. Her novels, at first romantic, later socially oriented, include *Indiana* (1832) and *The Haunted Pool* (1846). Her life-style—coupled with her ardent feminism—caused much controvery. Her lovers included Frédéric Chopin and Alfred de Musset. Her memoirs, *The Story of My Life* (1854-55), provide a graceful justification of her views.

Sandalwood, any of several parasitic trees of the family Santalaceae (especially *Santalum album*), native to India, whose timber exudes a fragrant odor; also, the wood obtained from the trees. Sandalwood oil is used in perfumes and medicines.

Sandbur, or bur grass, any of several species of prickly weed (genus *Cenchrus*) that grow in wasteland. Sandbur is native to the western United States. The prickly fruits cause painful wounds when they catch onto flesh.

Sandburg, Carl (1878-1967), U.S. poet and biographer who won Pulitzer prizes for *Abraham Lincoln: The War Years* (1940) and *Complete Poems* (1951). He left school at 13 and at 20 fought in the Spanish-American war. While a journalist in Chicago, he wrote vigorous earthy free verse, as in *Chicago Poems* (1916) and *Smoke and Steel* (1920). He was also a notable folk-song anthologist.

Sand dollar (*Echinarachnius pama*), marine invertebrate animal that lives in the sand in shallow coastal waters. It has a thin circular body about 2-4 in (5-10 cm) wide. The sand dollar has tiny, movable spines that it uses to dig and crawl. It feeds on aquatic organisms that it finds in the sand.

Sanderling, shorebird (*Calidris alba*) belonging to the snipe and sandpiper family. It stands about 8 in (20 cm) high. Sanderlings breed on Arctic beaches and migrate south in winter to sandy beaches everywhere. They feed on small shellfish and insects that wash up on the shore. Their feathers are rust or gray on the upper parts and pure white underneath.

Sand fly, any of various minute, biting, 2-winged flies (families Psychodidae, Simuliidae, and Ceratopogonidae) found in the southern United States and the tropics. Sand flies are a major health hazard. They carry several diseases, including kalazar.

Sandhill crane *see:* Crane.

Sandia National Laboratories, nuclear weapon research laboratory located in Albuquerque, N. Mex. Sandia researches, engineers, and produces all components of nuclear weapons systems, except explosives. Its technicians design and produce arming and firing systems and safety systems that prevent weapon use by unauthorized persons. Founded in 1945, Sandia employs 8,400 people. It is operated by American Telephone & Telegraph (AT&T) for the U.S. Department of Energy.
See also: Nuclear weapon.

Sana, Yemen

San Diego (pop. 2,498,016), city in southern California; seat of San Diego County, located on the Pacific Coast close to the Mexican border. A center for oceanography, culture, medicine, and research, its natural harbor houses a great navy base, a large fishing fleet, and lumber and shipbuilding yards. Its heavy industries include aircraft, missiles, and electronics; its economy is also supported by tourism and convention business. San Diego was explored and claimed in 1542 by Spain, who later built (1769) the Presidio (historic fort) and the first of Father Junípero Serra's missions. It is also the site of the Cabrillo National Monument, an enormous zoo, and a well-known aquatic park.
See also: California.

The Interstate 880 in San Francisco after the 1989 earthquake

San Diego Naval Base, center of operations for many Pacific-based fleet commands. Established in 1917, the base is a training and supply center and has an antisubmarine-warfare school, a hospital, and a recruiting station. The 11th Naval District Headquarters is located there.
See also: Navy, U.S.

Sandiford, Lloyd Erskine (1937-), prime minister of Barbados since 1987. Deputy prime minister, minister of education, and leader of the House of Assembly, he assumed the post of prime minister on the death of predecessor Errol W. Barrow. Previously he served as minister of education and community development (1967-75) and minister of health and welfare (1975-86).
See also: Barbados.

Sandinistas, leftist Nicaraguan revolutionary movement that overthrew the Somoza family dictatorship in 1979. Named after César Sandino, a Nicaraguan patriot and guerrilla leader of the 1920s, it assembled a broad coalition in the country to defeat Anastasio Somoza and his hated Civil Guard. After the revolution the Sandinista National Liberation Front (FSLN) ruled through a 5-man junta.
See also: Nicaragua.

San Domingo *see:* Santo Domingo.

Sand painting, highly developed art form among the Navajo and Pueblo peoples of the southwestern United States, used in connection with rites of healing. Painting designs are made from crushed, colored sandstone. When the painting is completed, the person needing healing sits on it and has sand from it applied to his or her body. When the ritual is completed, the painting is destroyed.

Sandpiper, any of several small to medium-sized wading birds forming part of the family Scolopacidae and found in all parts of the world. Most are slim birds with long straight bills and dull brown, gray, or white plumage. Among the species found in North America are the spotted sandpiper (*Actitus macularia*) and the upland sandpiper (*Bartramia longicauda*).

San Francisco as seen from Alcatraz

Sandstone, sedimentary rock consisting of consolidated sand, cemented after deposition by such minerals like quartz, calcite, or hematite or set in a matrix of clay minerals. The sand grains are chiefly quartz. Sandstone beds may bear natural gas or petroleum, and they are commonly aquifers (water-bearing). Sandstone is quarried for building and crushed for use as an agglomerate.

Sandstorm, storm in which wind drives masses of coarse sand through the air a few feet above the ground. Sandstorms are powerful agents of erosion and can damage crops.

Sand verbena, low-growing summer annual plant (genus *Abronia*) native to western North America. The plants have fragrant pink, white, or yellow flowers and grow best in open, sunny places and light soils. There are about 25 species of sand verbena.

Sanford, Maria L. (1836-1920), one of the first female professors in the United States. A leading educator of African Americans, Native Americans, and exceptional students, she taught at the University of Minnesota for 30 years.

San Francisco (pop. 1,603,678), western California city and seaport on the Pacific coast, on a peninsula between the Pacific and San Francisco Bay. Its economy is based on shipping and shipbuilding, with exports of cotton, grain, lumber, and petroleum products. It is also the financial, cultural, and communications center for the Northwest Coast. The city, noted for its cosmopolitan charm, has many tourist attractions including cable cars, Chinatown, Fisherman's Wharf, the Nob Hill mansions, and Golden Gate Park. There are several museums, art galleries, and a famous opera house. Founded by the Spanish (as Yerba Buena) in 1776, the city passed into U.S. hands in 1846 and was named San Francisco (1847). The gold rush (1848) soon attracted thousands of settlers to the area, which grew even more during World War II when the city served as an embarkation and supply point for the Pacific theater. Parts of the city were rebuilt after the earthquake of Apr. 18-20, 1906, and more recently, the earthquake of 1989, which occurred on the 84th anniversary of the 1906 quake and measured from 3.3-5.4 on the Richter scale.

San Francisco Conference, conference (April-June 1945) to set up the UN. The conference was sponsored by the United States, Great Britain, the USSR, and China and attended by 50 nations.
See also: United Nations.

San Francisco-Oakland Bay Bridge, series of connected suspension bridges that join Oakland, California to Buena Yerba Island and Buena Yerba Island to San Francisco. Over 8 mi (13 km) long, it is one of the longest constructed spans over water in the world. Each part of the full span consists of a 2-tiered suspension bridge. In addition, a tunnel and a viaduct lead to Oakland. The earthquake of 1989 collapsed part of the bridge, built in the 1930s.

Sanger, Frederick (1918-), British biochemist awarded the 1958 Nobel Prize in chemistry for his work on proteins, particularly for first determining the complete structure of bovine insulin (1955). He shared the 1980 Nobel Prize in chemistry with Paul Berg and Walter Gilbert of the United States for research on nucleic acids (DNA), the carriers of genetic traits. His work helped develop a process for analyzing the structure of DNA. Sanger is one of a handful of people to receive 2 Nobel prizes.
See also: Biochemistry; Deoxyribonucleic acid.

Sanger, Margaret (1883-1966), U.S. pioneer of birth control and feminism who set up the first birth-control clinic in the United States (1916), founded the National Birth Control League (1917), and helped organize the first international birth-control conference (1927).
See also: Planned Parenthood Federation of America.

Sanhedrin, supreme Jewish legislative and judicial court in Roman times. Some scholars hold that there were two Sanhedrin, one religious and one political. Jesus was tried by the religious Sanhedrin while Saints Peter, John, Stephen, and Paul appeared before it on charges of religious error. It ceased to exist in Jerusalem after the Romans put down a rebellion by the Jews in A.D. 66-70.

Sanitation, field of public health dealing with environmental control and the prevention and control of disease. In the United States, government agencies establish and enforce laws that promote a healthful environment. Sanitation activities include food processing and distribution, to prevent contamination of food products through various stages of handling; water and sewage treatment, to treat bacteria, viruses, etc. in water and to remove solid wastes and harmful chemicals from sewage that would contaminate the lakes, rivers, and other bodies of water (and their inhabitants) that receive it; solid waste disposal, also known as refuse disposal, to prevent environmental damage and the fostering of disease; and measures to control air pollution, rodents, and noise.

San Jacinto, Battle of, decisive engagement (Apr. 21, 1836) in the war for Texan independence. It was won by General Sam Houston, whose troops, though outnumbered, surprised and defeated the Mexicans under General Antonio López de Santa Anna, thereby establishing Texas as an independent republic.
See also: Texas.

San Joaquin River, river in central California rising from the junction of 2 forks in the Sierra Nevada, south of Yosemite

National Park. It flows 350 mi (563 km) southwest,then northwest across the San Joaquin Valley to reach the Pacific at Suisun Bay (eastern arm of San Francisco Bay). The very fertile San Joaquin Valley and the Sacramento River Valley to the north together constitute the Central Valley, a rich agricultural region. The 2 rivers have a joint delta east of Suisun Bay.

San José (pop. 241,500), capital and largest city of the Central American nation of Costa Rica. It is a center for government, industry, and finance, and is the location of the nation's largest agricultural market. San José is situated at the center of the country in a valley. It was founded by Spanish settlers in the mid-18th century.
See also: Costa Rica.

San José (pop. 1,497,577), western Californian city (incorporated 1850) about 50 mi (80 km) southeast of San Francisco in the Santa Clara Valley, the seat of Santa Clara County. The economy has long been centered around fruit processing; since World War II heavy industry has also been developed, including aerospace, chemical and electronics firms. San Jose State College (founded 1857) is the oldest state-run college of California. Founded in 1777, San Jose was the first state capital of California (1849-52).
See also: California.

San Jose scale (*Aspidiotus perniciosus*), insect in the armored scale family. Although small as a pinhead, this insect causes mass destruction to a wide variety of trees and their fruit. The wind blows the scales from tree to tree, and upon arrival, they begin to eat a tree's sap. Native to China, they have been found throughout the United States and Canada since their discovery in the San Jose area of California around 1880. Oil spray and natural enemies such as the Chinese ladybird beetle help protect trees from this insect.
See also: Scale insect.

San Juan (pop. 434,800), capital and chief port of Puerto Rico on the northeastern coast of the island. Ponce de León named its bay (Puerto Rico) in the early 1500s, prior to the founding of the city in 1521. The city, which has retained its colonial atmosphere, is known for its fine beaches and exceptional harbor. It is now a trade center producing sugar, rum, metal products, textiles, and furniture, and has a strong tourist industry. Among its landmarks is El Morro castle (begun 1539).
See also: Puerto Rico.

San Juan Hill, Battle of *see:* Spanish-American War.

San Marino, world's smallest republic and possibly the oldest state in Europe, southwest of Rimini, Italy. Built on 3 peaks of Mount Titano, its townships include San Marino (the capital) and Serravalle. Tradition reports that San Marino was founded as a refuge for persecuted Christians in the 4th century. A.D. The area is 24 sq mi (62 sq km). San Marino's chief sources of income are tourism and the sale of postage stamps. The republic is governed by 2 captains-regent assisted by a 60-member council of state. Since 1978 power has been held by a Communist-led coalition.

San Marino

Capital:	San Marino
Area:	24 sq mi (61 sq km)
GNP:	U.S. $188,000,000
Per capita:	U.S. $8,590

San Martín, José de (1778-1850), Argentine patriot and hero of South American struggles for independence. Under his military leadership, Argentina fought successfully for its independence from Spain (1812). San Martín also, with the aid of Bernard O'Higgins, freed Chile (1817-18) and helped Simón Bolívar gain independence for Peru (1821-22). San Martín was born in Argentina but raised mainly in Spain, where he was educated as a professional soldier. After the struggles for South American independence were fought and won, he went to Europe (1824).
See also: Argentina; Chile; Peru.

San Quentin, California's oldest prison, opened in 1852. Its normal capacity is 2,700 inmates, but it has held as many as 3,900 prisoners. Located about 10 mi (16 km) from San Francisco, San Quentin is a maximum security prison for prisoners convicted of violent crimes. The prison administration provides counseling, education, and work-release programs.

San Salvador (pop. 452,600), capital and largest city of El Salvador, about 25 mi (40 km) from the Pacific Ocean. Because it is situated in a volcanic region, it has suffered many earthquakes. The city was founded in 1525 by Spanish explorer, Pedro de Alvarado. It is now a trade center, producing textiles, tobacco and soap.
See also: El Salvador.

Sanskrit, classical language of the Hindu peoples of India and the oldest literary language of the Indo-European family of languages. Some early texts date from 1500 B.C., including the Vedic texts. Vedic Sanskrit was prevalent roughly 1500-150 B.C., classical Sanskrit roughly 500 B.C.-A.D. 900. Sanskrit gave rise to such modern Indian languages as Hindi and Urdu and is distantly related to the Celtic, Romance, and Slavonic languages.

Santa Ana (pop. 135,186), second-largest city in El Salvador. It is a major coffee processing center with one of the world's largest coffee mills. Its other industrial activities include sugar milling, brewing, and the manufacture of cotton textiles, footwear, and furniture.

Santa Anna, Antonio López de (1794-1876), Mexican general and dictator who tried to suppress the Texan revolution and fought U.S. troops in the Mexican War. He helped establish Mexican independence (1821-29) and became president (1833). When the Texan settlers revolted against his tyranny (1836), he defeated them at the Alamo but lost the battle of San Jacinto (1836), was captured, and had to resign. He gained and lost the presidency 3 further times (1841-44, 1846-47, 1853-55). He spent most of his final years in exile.
See also: Mexico.

Santa Claus, Christmastide bearer of gifts to children. The jolly fat man who is transported by flying reindeer and drops presents down chimneys is a comparatively recent (19th-century) legend derived from St. Nicholas (introduced as *Sinter Klaas* to the New World by Dutch settlers), whose feast day (Dec. 6) is a children's holiday. A drawing by cartoonist Thomas Nast is believed to have helped fix the image of a rotund, white-bearded Santa Claus in the popular imagination after such a figure was described in Clement Moore's 1822 poem, "An Account of a Visit from St. Nicholas."
See also: Christmas.

San Marino

Santa Fe (pop. 117,043), capital of New Mexico and seat of Santa Fe County, in the north-central part of the state on the Santa Fe River. The elevation of about 7,000 ft (11,265 km) above sea level provides a bracing climate. Tourism is the major source of income, with the Spanish colonial architecture and numerous cultural attractions drawing many visitors. Santa Fe was founded in 1609-10 as capital of the large but unsettled Spanish territory known as New Mexico. It was under Spanish and Mexican authority until the Mexican War, after which it was ceded to the United States (1846). In the 19th century it was the western terminus of the important wagon route known as the Santa Fe Trail.
See also: New Mexico.

Santa Fe Trail, overland trade route between the western part of Missouri and Santa Fe, N.M., in use from its opening (1821) until the coming of the Santa Fe Railroad (1880). Manufactured goods passed west, furs and bullion, east.

Santa María *see:* Columbus, Christopher.

Santayana, George (1863-1952), Spanish-born U.S. philosopher, writer, and critic. He was an influential writer on aesthetics in books like *The Sense of Beauty* (1896). In *The Life of Reason* (1905-06) he emphasized the importance of reason in understanding the world, but was skeptical of what one can really know. *Skepticism and Animal Faith* (1923) suggests a relationship between faith and knowledge.

Santiago (pop. 4,225,000), capital and principal industrial, commercial, and cultural city of Chile, on the Mapocho River. Industries include textiles, foodstuffs, and iron and steel foundries. It was founded in 1541 by Pedro de Valdivia. Numerous earthquakes destroyed most of the colonial buildings, and Santiago is now a modern city with parks and wide avenues.
See also: Chile.

Santiago (pop. 278,600), second-largest city in the Dominican Republic, lying on the Yanque del Norte River. Santiago is a distribution center for cacao, coffee, fruits, sugar cane, and tobacco, and manufactures cigars, cigarettes, dolls, and clothing. It was founded c. 1500 by Bartholomew Columbus, a brother of Christopher Columbus.
See also: Dominican Republic.

Santiago de Cuba (pop. 345,800), second-largest city in Cuba, founded in 1514 by Diego de Velazquez de Cuellar, and capital of Oriente province. The center of Cuba's mining industry, Santiago is also a shipping center for iron, manganese, sugar, coffee, and tobacco. The Morro Castle is one of its landmarks.
See also: Cuba.

Santo Domingo (pop. 1,313,000), capital and chief port of the Dominican Republic, at the mouth of the Ozama River. Its official name was Ciudad Trujillo (1930-61). Founded by Columbus's brother Bartholomew (1496), it is the oldest continuously inhabited European settlement in the Western Hemisphere, with a university dating from 1538. It was the site of the first Church in the New World.
See also: Dominican Republic.

Santo Domingo, University of, oldest university in the Western Hemisphere, located in the Dominican Republic. It was established by Pope Paul III in 1538 as the Univ. of St. Thomas Aquinas. A lay institution since 1815, the university offers courses in agronomy, architecture, business, engineering, law, medicine, philosophy, and veterinary medicine. It has an enrollment of about 50,000 students.

Santos (pop. 411,000), one of Brazil's major port cities, and the world's leading coffee port. Cotton, sugar, bananas, castor oil, beef, oranges, hides, and manufactured goods are also exported. Its industries include sawmills, canneries, and the manufacture of candy, soap, soft drinks, and canvas. Santos has two airports and a railroad link to São Paulo.
See also: Brazil.

Santos-Dumont, Alberto (1873-1932), aviation pioneer in both lighter-than-air and heavier-than-air machines. Born in Brazil of wealthy parents, he was educated in France, where he spent most of his life. His "Demoiselle" (Grasshopper) monoplane was the forerunner of the modern light plane. He was awarded the Deutsch-Archdeacon Prize (1906) for the first observed power flight in Europe. Depressed over the use of aircraft in war, Santos-Dumont took his own life.
See also: Aviation.

Sanzio, Raffaello *see:* Raphael.

Saône River, waterway of eastern France. The Saône flows some 268 mi (431 km) and connects with the Rhône River at Lyon. The industrial city, Chalon-sur-Saône, lies on its banks. It is navigable for 233 mi (375 km) and has 30 locks. Barge traffic is heavy along its lower course.

São Paulo (pop. 7,034,000), largest city and industrial center of Brazil; capital of São Paulo state, it lies 225 mi (362 km) southwest of Rio de Janeiro. Founded in 1554, it grew rapidly with the development of the coffee industry in the 1880s (it still sends coffee to the port of Santos), and its other industries are diverse. It is the site of 4 universities and numerous cultural institutions.
See also: Brazil.

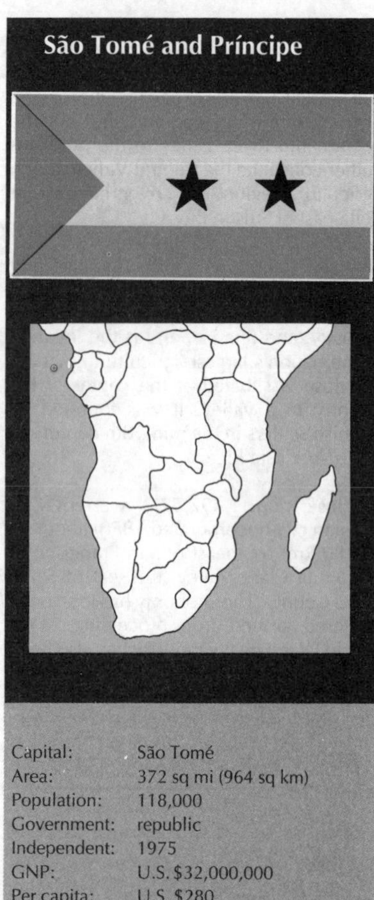

Capital:	São Tomé
Area:	372 sq mi (964 sq km)
Population:	118,000
Government:	republic
Independent:	1975
GNP:	U.S. $32,000,000
Per capita:	U.S. $280

The jagged peaks of Príncipe, one of the islands of São Tomé and Príncipe

São Tomé and Príncipe, republic in the Gulf of Guinea, off the west coast of Africa, comprising 2 main islands and several islets; total area is 370 sq mi (958 sq km). The capital, São Tomé, lies 190 mi (306 km) west of Libreville, Gabon.
Land and climate. São Tomé Island accounts for almost 90% of the country's area and holds about 90% of its population. The land (volcanic rock) slopes downward to fertile volcanic soil on the east coast. Forests grow near the west shore. Príncipe is similar in land pattern. The islands have a tropical climate.
People and economy. The country depends heavily on cocoa for its income.

Copra, coconuts, palm kernels, bananas, and coffee are also important exports. Most of the inhabitants are of mixed African and Portuguese ancestry.
History. Discovered in the 1400s by the Portuguese, the islands achieved independence in 1975. The withdrawal of skilled Europeans after independence seriously disrupted the former plantation economy.

Sap, in botany, the watery fluid in the stems and roots of plants. There are two kinds of sap. One consists of water and dissolved minerals and travels from the roots of the tree to the leaves, moving through a layer in the stem and trunk called the xylem. The other consists of water carrying dissolved plant foods, moving from the leaves to other parts of the plant for storage. It passes through a layer called the phloem.

Sapir, Edward (1884-1939), U.S. anthropologist, poet, and linguist, whose most important work was on the relation between language and the culture of which it is a product. He suggested that one's perception of the world is dominated by the language with which one articulates it.
See also: Anthropology.

Sapodilla, evergreen tree (*Achras zapota*) found in tropical America; also, the fruit of the tree. The bark and fruits contain a milky latex (chicle) that is collected in Central America to provide the raw material for chewing gum. When ripe, the flesh of the fruit is brown and has the consistency of a pear.

Saponin *see:* Soapberry.

Sapphire, any gem variety of the mineral corundum (except those that are red, which are called ruby); blue sapphires are best known, but most other colors of the spectrum are included. The highest-quality sapphires come from Kashmir, Burma, Thailand, Sri Lanka, and Australia. Synthetic stones made by flame-fusion are used for jewel bearings, phonograph styluses, etc.

Sappho (6th century B.C.), Greek poet born in Lesbos. Surviving fragments of her work, mainly addressed to young girls, are among the finest classical love lyrics. The terms *sapphism* and *lesbianism*, meaning female homosexuality, derive from Sappho and Lesbos.

Sapporo (pop. 1,543,000), capital of Hokkaido, the northernmost island of Japan. Laid out in 1871 with wide, tree-lined boulevards intersecting each other at right angles, Sapporo serves as the island's manufacturing and cultural center, and its products include hemp cloth and rubber goods. Sapporo was the site of the Winter Olympics of 1972.
See also: Japan.

Saprophyte, plant that gets its food from dead and decaying material. Saprophytes do not carry out photosynthesis. Most fungi, including molds, mildews, and rusts, are saprophytes. Their fine threads creep over the food, secreting digestive juices and absorbing the resulting solution. Some flowering plants, such as the pinesap, are known as saprophytes, but in fact they rely on a fungus in their roots to absorb food from dead leaves.
See also: Fungi.

Sapsucker, bird of the woodpecker family. Sapsuckers drill neat rows of holes in the bark of trees and lick up the sap that oozes out, but their main food is insects, which they catch in the air or on trees. The 3 North American sapsuckers are the widely distributed yellow-bellied sapsucker (*Sphyrapicus varius*), and the red-breasted (*S. ruber*) and Williamson's sapsucker (*S. thyroideus*) of the Western and Pacific states.

Saracens, Muslims who invaded parts of the Christian world in Asia, Africa, and Europe from the 600s to the 1000s. They consisted of people of Palestine and Syria, the Arab Moors, and the Seljuks. The term *Saracen* was first used by Greek and Roman writers to describe wandering Arab tribes.
See also: Muslims.

Saragossa (pop. 596,100), industrial and trading center located in northeast Spain. The city has metalworks, sugar refineries, chemical plants, and factories that manufacture electrical equipment, farm machinery, and furniture. The city's name comes from Caesarea Augusta, the name that Roman Emperor Augustus gave it in 25 B.C.
See also: Spain.

Sarah *see:* Ishmael; Isaac.

Sarajevo (pop. 447,700), capital and cultural center of Bosnia and Hercegovina, Yugoslavia. It retains a strong Muslim character and is famous for its many Muslim mosques. Sarajevo's industry includes a sugar beet refinery, brewery, furniture factory, tobacco factory, hosiery works, communication plants, and an agribusiness combine. Austrian Archduke Francis Ferdinand was assassinated at Sarajevo in 1914, precipitating World War I.
See also: Yugoslavia.

Saranac Lakes, group of lakes in the Adirondack Mountains of northeastern New York. The region of these glacial lakes is a popular recreation area. The 3 lakes are Upper Saranac (8 mi/13 km long, 2 mi/3.2 km wide), Middle Saranac or Lake Saranac (3 mi/4.8 km long, 1 mi/1.6 km wide), and Lower Saranac (5 mi/8 km long, 1 mi/1.6 km wide).

Sarasota (pop. 277,776), city in southwestern Florida, on the Sarasota Bay of the Gulf of Mexico. Founded in the 1880s, it has become a popular tourist spot. It is home to New College of the Univ. of Southern Florida and to the Mote Marine Laboratory. From 1927 to 1960 it was also the winter home of the Ringling Brothers and Barnum & Bailey Circus.
See also: Florida.

Saratoga Springs (pop. 23,906), city in eastern New York, in the southeastern foothills of the Adirondack Mountains. A flourishing resort since the 19th century, its tourist attractions include mineral springs, thoroughbred racing, and the Saratoga Performing Arts Center, summer home of the New York City Opera, New York City Ballet, and Philadelphia Orchestra. It is also home to Skidmore College.
See also: New York.

Saratov (pop. 893,000), one of the chief ports on the Volga River. Petroleum, natural gas, and power from the Balakovo hydroelectric station form the basis of oil-refining and chemical industries. Manufactures of this industrial complex include machinery, machine tools, ball bearings, flour milling, and consumer products.
See also: Union of Soviet Socialist Republics.

Sarawak, state of Malaysia on the northwestern coast of Borneo. It has a tropical climate, and much of its area, 48,050 sq mi (131,582 sq km), is covered by a primary rain forest. Sarawak became self-governing and joined Malaysia in 1963 after having been occupied by the Japanese during World War II. For 100 years prior to this, Sarawak was governed by an Englishman, James Brooke, and his heirs. The people of Sarawak are Dyaks, Malays, Melanaus, and Murits. Its products include sago palm, timber, rubber, pepper, coconuts, and camphor.
See also: Malaysia.

Sapphire

Sarazen, Gene (Eugene Saraceni; 1902-), U.S. golfer. He won the Professional Golfers Association (PGA) tournament in 1922, 1923, and 1933; the U.S. Open in 1922 and 1932; and the British Open in 1932. He also played 6 times in the Ryder Cup competition between U.S. and British players. Sarazen's outstanding 235-yd (215-m) shot helped win him the 1935 Masters tournament.

Sarcoidosis, chronic disease characterized by fibrous and inflammatory nodules principally affecting lymph glands, skin, lungs, and bones, but arising in any tissue of the body. The cause of the disease is uncertain.
See also: Lymphatic system.

Sarajevo, Yugoslavia

Jean-Paul Sartre

Sarcoma, form of tumor derived from connective tissue, usually of mesodermal origin in embryology. It is often distinguished from cancer because its behavior and natural history may differ, although it is still a malignant tumor. It commonly arises from bone (*osteosarcoma*), fibrous tissue (*fibrosarcoma*), or cartilage (*chondrosarcoma*). Excision is required, though radiation therapy may be helpful.

Sarcophagus, stone coffin. The ancient Egyptians were probably the first to use sarcophagi for the burial of kings and important persons. Some were shaped like small houses, others like human forms with facial features. The best-known modern examples of sarcophagi include those built for George Washington in Mt. Vernon, Napoleon Bonaparte in Paris, the duke of Wellington in London, and V.I. Lenin in Moscow.

The marble sarcophagus of Junius Bassus (c.360, Vatican Museum, Rome), designed in the Roman tradition. Each panel describes a story from the Bible.

Sardine, name for the young of members of the herring family, particularly the European sardine, or pitchard (*Sardina pilchardus*). Sardines get their name from the fact that they were originally caught near Sardinia. They are usually preserved in oil and canned as food.

Sardinia, Italian island in the Mediterranean, 120 mi (193 km) to the west of mainland Italy and just south of Corsica. It is a mountainous area of 9,301 sq mi (24,090 sq km), with some agriculture on the coastal plains and upland valleys. Wheat, olives, and vines are grown, and sheep and goats raised; fish and cork are also exported. Zinc, antimony, and lead are extracted from the ancient mines, and tourism is growing in importance. The island is an autonomous region of Italy, with its capital at Cagliari.

Sardinia, Kingdom of, kingdom founded in 1720 when the Treaty of London awarded the island of Sardinia to Savoy. The kingdom included Sardinia, Savoy, Piedmont, and Nice. Napoleon annexed Sardinia to France in 1802, but it was restored after his defeat in 1815, and Genoa and Liguria were added to it. In 1861 Victor Emanuel II was proclaimed king of a united Italy that included Sardinia.

Sardis, capital of the ancient kingdom of Lydia. Its remains go back to at least 1300 B.C., but it may be even older. It was the first city to mint gold and silver coins. Destroyed by an earthquake in A.D. 17, Sardis was later rebuilt. It was destroyed and rebuilt several times until its final destruction by the Sassanian Persians c. A.D. 615.

Sardonyx, form of the mineral quartz. It is one of the less expensive gemstones. Found in Brazil, Uruguay, and India, sardonyx has bands of reddish-brown and white. It is used in rings and cameos.

Sargasso Sea, oval area in the North Atlantic, of special interest as the spawning ground of American eels, many of whose offspring drift across the Atlantic to form the European eel population. Bounded on the east by the Canaries Current, on the south by the North Equatorial Current, and on the west and north by the Gulf Stream, it contains large masses of seaweed.

Sargent, John Singer (1856-1935), U.S. painter famous for his many flattering portraits of high-society figures in the United States and United Kingdom. A master of the brushstroke, he is distinctive for his treatment of texture. One of his most notable works, *Madame X* (1884), showing the alluring Parisian Madame Gautreau, created a furor that obscured the painting's brilliance.

Sargon of Akkad, king who founded the first great empire in history c. 2300 B.C. An outstanding military leader and administrator, he was the first king to maintain a permanent army. Sargon built a magnificent capital city called Akkad in central Mesopotamia. He reigned for 56 years.
See also: Mesopotamia.

Sark, one of the Channel Islands and the smallest self-governing unit in the United Kingdom. Located in the English Channel, 22 miles (35 km) off the coast of France, it has an area of 2 sq mi (5 sq km).

Sarney, José (1930-), Brazilian politician, president (1985-90). He served as governor of the state of Maranhao, 1965-70, was elected vice president in 1985, and assumed the presidency in Apr. 1985 upon the death of President Tancredo Neves. His Cruzado Plan was an effort to control Brazil's severe inflation and foreign debt.
See also: Brazil.

Sarnoff, David (1891-1971), Russian-born U.S. radio and television pioneer. Starting his career as a telegraph messenger boy, he became president of RCA and later founded NBC, the first commercial radio network (1926).

Saroyan, William (1908-81), U.S. author known for combining patriotism with emotional idealism. Among his many works are *The Daring Young Man on the Flying Trapeze* (1934), a collection of short stories; the novel *The Human Comedy* (1943); and the play *The Time of Your Life* (1939). He won the Pulitzer Prize for the latter but turned it down because he disapproved of literary awards.

Sarton, May (1912-), U.S. writer. Her books include the poetry collections *Inner Landscape* (1939) and *Halfway to Silence* (1980), the novels *The Bridge of Years* (1946) and *The Magnificent Spinster* (1985), and the journals *Recovering* (1980) and *May Sarton: A Self Portrait* (1986). Sarton has taught at Harvard University and Wellesley College.

Sartre, Jean-Paul (1905-80), French philosopher, novelist, and playwright, exponent of existentialism. His writings reflect his vision of the human being as master of his or her own fate, with each life defined by a person's actions: "Existence precedes essence." His works include *Being and Nothingness* (1943); the novels *Nausea* (1938) and *The Roads to Freedom*, a trilogy (1945-49); and the plays *The Flies* (1943) and *No Exit* (1944). Sartre founded the review *Les Temps Modernes* in 1945. A close associate of Simone de Beauvoir and a Communist who spoke eloquently for the left, his influence was international. In 1964 he refused the Nobel Prize for literature.
See also: Existentialism.

Saskatchewan, 1 of the 3 prairie provinces of Canada. The principal wheat-growing province, it produces about one-third of the nation's wheat. It is also a rich source of minerals such as potash and petroleum. Most of Saskatchewan's resources are processed within the province.
Land and climate. Saskatchewan can be divided into 2 major portions: the Canadian Shield, which covers the northern third of the province; and the plains and lowlands, which make up the southern two-thirds. The Canadian Shield is a rough, rocky, mineral-rich terrain that contains many lakes, swamps, and small streams. The plains and lowlands are mostly flat or gently rolling, with black, fertile soil. Most of the province's 20,000 lakes are found north of Prince Albert. The largest is Lake Athabasca, about two-thirds of which lie in the northwest corner of Saskatchewan, the rest in the province of Alberta. The principal river is the Saskatchewan. Divided into the South Saskatchewan and the North Saskachewan, the 2 branches join just east of Prince Albert and flow eastward into the province of Manitoba. Much of the province, especially the northern half, is covered by forests. Numerous commercial forests include valuable supplies of spruce, poplar, and pine. Saskatchewan's inland location gives it a continental climate. Winters are cold, with average January readings of 10°F (–12°C) in the southwest and –23°F (–31°C) in the northeast. Average July temperatures range from 57°-67°F (14°-19°C). Precipitation is light; most of it falls during the growing season, which in the south lasts about 100 days.
People. The population of Saskatchewan is concentrated in the southern half of the province, which has become markedly

urban. Today over 75% of the people live in communities of more than 1,000 inhabitants. Over 25% live in the 2 largest cities, Saskatoon and Regina, the capital. Saskatchewan is the only province in which the people have a variety of ethnic inheritances, rather than a majority of French or British.
Economy. The economy of the province is heavily dependent on farming. Wheat is the main crop; barley, rye, and flax also are grown. Since the discovery of oil and the development of service-supply industries, agriculture has declined in relative importance. Service industries now account for 50% of the total gross domestic product. Food processing and distribution as well as the manufacture of farm machinery are increasing in importance. The province also produces a significant proportion of Canada's crude oil. Oil refining and steel manufacturing can be found in Regina and other northern cities. Lignite coal, mined since the 1880s, has been strip-mined since 1956.
History. It is believed that the first people to inhabit the land of Saskatchewan were the Paleo-Indians, who came from Asia 20,000-30,000 years ago. European-American traders from the Hudson's Bay Company first arrived in 1690. The region was explored some 40 years later by Sieur de la Verendrye. After the purchase of the Northwest Territories by the new Dominion of Canada in 1870, farming settlements spread; they grew rapidly after Saskatchewan joined the Confederation and became a province in 1905. The Great Depression and World War II brought hardship and discontent that led to the formation of the Cooperative Commonwealth Federation (1944-64). In the 1970s and 1980s, petroleum and petroleum-based industries brought new wealth and prosperity to the province.
See also: Canada.

Saskatchewan River, river system in the provinces of Alberta and Saskatchewan, Canada. The North Saskatchewan flows east 760 mi (1,223 km) from the glaciers of the Rocky Mountains. The South Saskatchewan flows east 550 mi (885 km) from the combined waters of the Bow and Oldman rivers. The rivers then join and flow 340 mi (547 km) to empty in Lake Winnipeg, Manitoba. The river system, first explored by Henry Kelsey (1690), became an important fur trade route. It is now important in the irrigation of southern Alberta and as a source of hydroelectric power. Among the cities lying on the Saskatchewan River and its tributaries are Edmonton, Calgary, Saskatoon, and Prince Albert.

Saskatoon (pop. 177,600), largest city of the province of Saskatchewan, on the South Saskatchewan River, western Canada. Founded by John Lake and members of the Temperance Colonization Company in 1883, it was joined to the Canadian Pacific Railway in 1890. It is now a major trading center, and has stockyards and other agriculture-related industry. The economy is also supported by oil refineries and, since the 1950s, potash mining.
See also: Saskatchewan.

Sassafras, tree (*Sassafras albidum*) of the laurel family, found in the eastern half of North America. In the northern states it is usually little more than a shrub, but it grows to 100 ft (30.5 m) in the south. Oil of sassafras, used to flavor foods and perfume soap, is extracted from its bark and roots. Sassafras tea is also made from the roots.

Sassoon, Siegfried (1886-1967), English poet and novelist. Decorated for bravery in World War I, he wrote bitterly satirical poetry such as *The Old Huntsman* (1917) and *Counter Attack* (1918), which shocked the public with their graphic portrayal of trench warfare, their attacks on hypocritical patriotism, and their pacifist conclusions. His novels include *Memoirs of a Fox-Hunting Man* (1928).

Satellite, in astronomy, celestial object that revolves with or around a large celestial object. In our Solar System this includes planets, comets, asteroids, and meteoroids, as well as the moons of the planets, although the term is usually restricted to this last sense. Of the dozens of known moons, the largest is Callisto (Jupiter IV); the smallest, Phobos (the inner moon of Mars). The earth's moon is the largest known satellite relative to its parent planets; indeed, the earth-moon system is often considered a double planet.
See also: Astronomy.

Satellite, artificial, object placed in orbit as a satellite. First seriously proposed in the 1920s, they were impracticable until large enough rockets were developed. The first artificial satellite, Sputnik 1, was launched by the USSR on Oct. 8, 1957, and was soon followed by a host of others, mainly from the USSR and the United States, but also from the United Kingdom, France, Canada, West Germany, Italy, Japan, and China. These satellites have many scientific, technological, and military uses. Astronomical observations (notably X-ray astronomy) can be made unobscured by the atmosphere. Studies can be made of the radiation and electromagnetic and gravitational fields in which the earth is bathed and of the upper atmosphere. Experiments have been made on the functioning of animals and plants in space (with zero gravity and increased radiation). Artificial satellites are also used for reconnaissance, surveying, and meteorological observation, as navigational aids (position references and signal relays), and in communications for relaying television and radio signals. Manned satellites, especially the historic Soyuz and Mercury series, have paved the way for space stations, which have provided opportunities for diverse research and for developing docking techniques; the USSR Salyut and U.S. Skylab projects are notable. The basic requirements for satellite launching are determined by celestial mechanics. Launching at various velocities between that required for zero altitude and the escape velocity produces an elliptical orbit lying on a conic surface determined by the latitude and time of launch. To reach any other orbit requires considerable extra energy expenditure. Artificial satellites require a power supply—solar cells, batteries, fuel cells, or nuclear devices; scientific instruments; a communications system to return encoded data to earth; and instruments and auxiliary rockets to monitor and correct the satellite's position. Most have computers for control and data processing, thus reducing remote control to the minimum.
See also: Satellite.

Satie, Erik (Eric Alfred Leslie Satie; 1866-1925), French composer and pianist. Satie was the philosophical leader of "Les Six," a group of French composers including Darius Milhaud, Arthur Honneger, and Francis Poulenc who rejected the impressionist style of Claude Debussy and Maurice Ravel. He was deliberately eccentric, rejecting convention and popular acceptance. He best-known works include the ballet *Parade* (1917) and pieces for solo piano. His *Gymnopédies* (1888) for solo piano were made famous in their orchestrated version by Debussy.

Self-portrait by Erik Satie

Satinwood, East Indian tree (*Chloroxylon swietenia*) or shrub of the citrus family. Their wood is very hard and is used for inlays on furniture. West Indian satinwood, or yellow wood, so-called for its color, is found in Florida, as is wild lime, a close relative.

Satire, in literature or cartoons, on stage or screen, use of broad humor, parody, and irony to ridicule a subject. More serious than burlesque, it often contains moral or political criticism. In literature, classical satirists Aristophanes, Horace, and Juvenal were followed by such writers as Rabelais, Daniel Defoe, Jonathan Swift, Voltaire, Oscar Wilde, and Mark Twain.

Sato, Eisaku (1901-75), prime minister of Japan (1964-72). A Liberal-Democrat, he presided over the reemergence of Japan as a major economic power and was active in foreign affairs. He won the 1974 Nobel Peace Prize for work on deterring the proliferation of nuclear weapons.

Saturation, in chemistry and physics, term applied to a state in which further increase in a variable above a critical value produces no increase in a resultant effect. A saturated solution will dissolve no more solute, an equilibrium having been reached. Raising the temperature usually allows more to dissolve; cooling may produce supersaturation, in which sudden crystallization depositing the excess solute occurs if a seed crystal is added. In organic chemistry a saturated molecule has no double or triple bonds and so does not undergo additional reactions.

Saturn, in early Roman mythology, god of fertility and planting, eventually identified with the Greek god Cronus as father of

Saturn

Jupiter, Juno, Ceres, Pluto, and Neptune. In ancient Rome he was honored in the Saturnalia festival, a period of revelry and gift-giving starting Dec. 17, during which business, school, and war were suspended.
See also: Mythology.

Saturn, second-largest planet in the Solar System, the sixth from the sun. Until the discovery of Uranus (1781), Saturn was the outermost planet known. It orbits the sun in 29.46 years at a mean distance of 886.7 million mi (1.427 billion km). Saturn has the lowest density of any planet in the Solar System, less than that of water, and may contain over 60% hydrogen by mass. Its total mass is about 95 times that of the Earth. Saturn has 17 known satellites; the largest, Titan, about the same size as Mercury, has a cold nitrogen atmosphere with traces of methane and other gases. Other major satellites include the Mimas, Enceladus, Tethys, Dione, Rhea, Iapetus, Phoebe, and Hyperion. The most striking feature of Saturn is its ring system, composed of countless tiny particles of ice and rock. Three or four major ring divisions are visible from Earth; space probes (1980, 1981) revealed the rings to consist of hundreds of narrow ringlets. The rings are about 10 mi (16 km) thick.
See also: Planet; Solar system.

Saturnalia, in ancient Rome, festival honoring Saturn, god of fertility and planting. The annual festival, which started Dec. 17, originated as a 2-day celebration of the winter planting, but became a week-long period of feasting and gift-giving, the cessation of business and a brief time of freedom for slaves. Its observances are thought to have eventually been absorbed into the celebration of Christmas. "Saturnalia" has become a generic term for any period of wild revelry.
See also: Saturn.

Satyr, in Greek mythology, male spirit of the forests and mountains, often shown as part man and part goat, with hooves, tail, and pointed ears. Companions of Dionysus, satyrs played an important part in his festivals.
See also: Mythology.

Saucer, flying *see:* Unidentified flying object.

Saudi Arabia, desert kingdom occupying most of the Arabian Peninsula of southwestern Asia.

Land and climate. Parts of the frontiers of Saudi Arabia have yet to be accurately determined. Estimates of the country's area vary from about 830,000 sq mi (2,149,700 sq km) to 927,000 sq mi (2,400,930 sq km). It is bordered on the north by Jordan, Iraq, and Kuwait; on the east by the United Arab Emirates, the Persian Gulf, and Qatar; on the south by Oman, Yemen, and Southern Yemen; and on the west by the Red Sea and the Gulf of Aqaba. Most of the country is desert. Rising steeply from the narrow, barren Red Sea coastal plain are the western highlands of the Hejaz in the north and the Asir Highlands bordering Yemen in the south. Eastward sloping desert plateaus of sand and rock cover the interior of the country. The Rub al Khali (Empty Quarter) is a great, southern sand desert of some 250,000 sq mi (647,500 sq km). The An

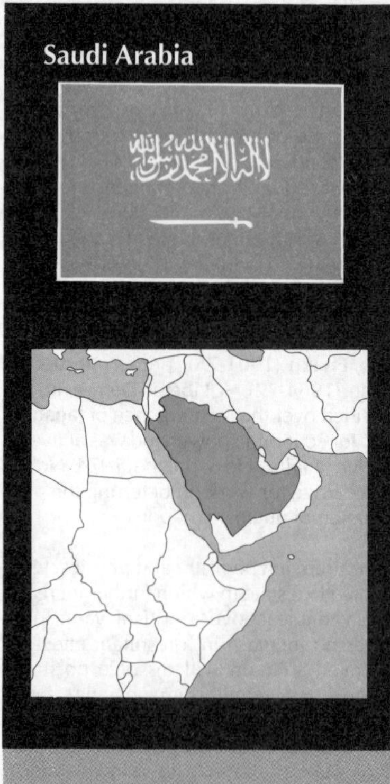

General information	
Capital:	Riyadh
Area:	865,000 sq mi (2,240,000 sq km)
Population:	13,612,000
Official language:	Arabic
Monetary unit:	1 Saudi riyal = 100 halalah
Main cities:	Riyadh, Jidda, Mecca
Government	
Form:	monarchy
Independent:	1932
Head of state:	King
Head of government:	King
Legislature:	no legislative body
Executive:	King and Council of Ministers
Judiciary:	highest court is the Supreme Council of Justice
Political division:	14 administrative districts, 5 regions
National economy	
Gross national product:	U.S. $86,527,000,000
Per capita income:	U.S. $6,170
Agriculture:	wheat, dates, tomatoes, barley, grapes, citrus fruit
Livestock:	sheep, goats, cattle
Fisheries:	46,000 metric tons
Mining:	natural gas, crude petroleum, gypsum, lime
Industries:	petroleum products, cement, steel rods and bars, gypsum
Main exports:	crude petroleum, refined petroleum
Transportation:	544 mi (875 km) of railroads, 57,664 mi (92,802 km) of roads, 2 international airports
Trading partners:	Japan, U.S., Germany
People	
Urban:	73%
Ethnic composition:	Saudi 82%, Yemeni 9.5%, other Arab 3.5%
Birth rate:	37.3 per 1,000 population
Death rate:	7 per 1,000 population
Infant mortality:	74 per 1,000 live births
Life expectancy:	male 64 years, female 67 years

Nafud, the northern sand desert, covers almost 25,000 sq mi (64,750 sq km). In the east, the Hasa Lowlands, mostly sand or gravel, fall away gradually to the sands, lagoons, and occasional coral reefs along the Persian Gulf. There are oases where date palms, tamarisks, and acacias grow, but there are neither lakes nor rivers. The coastal regions have an oppressively humid climate. The interior deserts are hot and dry, and summer temperatures in some areas exceed 120°F (49°C). In winter, however, frosts are common on the plateaus and in the mountains. Some desert areas go without rain for several years in succession.

People. The people of Saudi Arabia are almost entirely Arab. Riyadh, the capital, the Red Sea port of Jiddah, and the Muslim holy cities of Mecca and Medina are the main centers. Islam is the state religion: 90% of the people belong to the Sunni branch of Islam.

Economy. Saudi Arabia's rich oil fields, discovered in 1936, represent nearly one-fifth of the world's known reserves, and the oil and natural gas industry dominates the economy. The Arabian American Oil Company (Aramco) is chiefly responsible for oil operations in Saudi Arabia, although other U.S. and some Japanese concerns also have concessions. Since 1974, Saudi Arabia has held 60% of the ownership of these foreign concessions. Petro dollars are used for industrial development, especially oil refining, ambitious irrigation projects, and foreign investments. Saudi Arabia also produces limestone, gypsum, and salt. Its chief crops are sorghum, dates, wheat, barley, coffee, citrus fruits, and millet.

History. In the 7th century, the formerly disparate Semitic nomadic tribes of the Arabian Peninsula were united for the first time under Islam. In succeeding centuries rival sheikdoms rose and fell. In the 1500s Arabia came under the Ottoman Turks as part of the Ottoman empire. Between 1750 and 1800 the fundamentalist Wahabi sect led by the Saudi rulers of Dariya reconquered most of the Arabian Peninsula. Modern Saudi Arabia was founded by Ibn Saud, who, between 1902 and 1932, conquered Hijd and the Hejaz, joining them with Hasa and Asir and establishing a hereditary monarchy. Ibn Saud died in 1953 and was succeeded by Saud IV, who was deposed in 1964. King Faisal succeeded to the throne and reigned until his assassination in 1975. He was succeeded by King Khalid, who began programs of industrialization and social welfare before he died in 1982; he was followed by the current monarch, King Fahd. Saudi Arabia, through its oil wealth, has considerable political influence in the Middle East and has supported Arab countries and the Palestinians in their conflict with Israel. At the same time, as an ally of the United States, Saudi Arabia also has been something of a moderate voice in the region. Saudi Arabia asked for U.S. military assistance and joined forces with the U.S. and other allies in the Persian Gulf War against Iraq (1990-91). Saudi Arabia plays a major role in the Organization of Petroleum Exporting Countries (OPEC).

Saudi Arabia grows a small portion of its food supply in oases or on irrigated land. Because of the dry terrain, it is less expensive to import food than to produce it.

Sauk, or Sac, Native American tribe of the Algonquian language group. Encountered by the French near Green Bay, Wis. (1667), they later lived along the Mississippi River, hunting and farming. Many took part in the Black Hawk War (1832) rather than move west, but they were eventually resettled in Oklahoma and Iowa.

Saul, first king of Israel (1000 B.C.). The son of Kish of the tribe of Benjamin, he was annointed by Samuel after the tribes decided to unite under a king. His reign was generally successful, but he killed himself after a defeat by the Philistines. His rival, David, succeeded him. (1 Sam,10-31.)

Sault Sainte Marie (pop. 80,900), French settlement founded (1668) on the north bank of the St. Mary's River, which connects Lakes Superior and Huron. Sault is French for "rapids", which provide hydroelectric power for the city and the iron and steel, pulp, paper, and lumber industries. An international railway bridge linking the cities of Sault Ste. Marie in Michigan and Ontario was built in 1887. A U.S. canal and a Canadian canal were constructed in 1895 to link the St. Lawrence and Great Lakes Waterway.

Saurischian *see:* Dinosaur.

Sauvé, Jeanne Mathilde (1922-), first woman to serve as Speaker of the House of Commons (1980-84) and governor general (representative of the British monarch; 1984-89) of Canada. Sauvé worked for UNESCO (from 1950) and as a journalist and broadcaster (1952-72) before being elected to the House of Commons (1972). She served under Prime Minister Pierre Trudeau as minister of state for science and technology (1972), of the environment (1974), and of communications (1975).

Savanna, tropical grassland of South America and particularly Africa, lying between equatorial forests and dry deserts.

Savannah, name of 2 historic U.S. steamships. The first *Savannah* was the first steamship to cross the Atlantic (1819), sailing from Savannah, Ga. to Liverpool, England in 24 days, powered by sails as well as steam. The second, built by the U.S. government and launched in 1959, was the first nuclear-powered cargo ship. This 595.5-ft (195-m)-long ship, which can carry 60 passengers and 9,400 tons of cargo, proved commercially impractical.

Savannah (pop. 242,622), port city in southeastern Georgia near the mouth of the Savannah River, seat of Chatham County. The town was established by James Oglethorpe when he founded Georgia colony in 1733. Its capture (1864) ended General William T. Sherman's march to the sea during the Civil War. In addition to being a major Southern port, Savannah has become a center for agricultural trade and for the production of wood pulp and paper. The city is home to several colleges, and a U.S. Army training center for helicopter pilots is located nearby. Since 1955 it has attracted tourists with its restored historic buildings.
See also: Georgia.

Savannah River, river forming the Georgia-South Carolina border, arising from the confluence of the Tugaloo and Seneca rivers and flowing southeast into the Atlantic Ocean. The 314-mi (505-km) river is used for flood control and hydroelectric power. It is navigable by oceangoing vessels for about 23 mi (37 km) and by smaller vessels for about 230 mi (370 km), as far as Augusta, Ga.

Savings and loan association (S&L), or thrift institution (formerly, building and loan association), U.S. financial institution that accepts private savings of depositors, investing them primarily in home mortgages. Such institutions, the first of which was founded in Pennsylvania in 1831, originally were *mutual*, that is, owned and operated by the depositors. They are now predominantly *capital-stock* institutions, owned and operated by stockholders. They operate under federal and state charters, with deposits insured by the Savings Association Insurance Fund (SAIF). Many S&L's failed during the Great Depression of the

1930s. In the 1980s a combination of deregulation, mismanagement, criminal conduct, competition for depositors' funds from commercial banks and other financial institutions, and loan defaults due to recession resulted in a major crisis in the industry. It is estimated that the costs to taxpayers to "bail out" the S&L's will total $500 billion.
See also: Federal Home Loan Bank Board.

Savings bank, financial institution that encourages saving by individual depositors, paying them interest or dividends, while providing funds to borrowers, who pay interest. In the United States savings banks originated in the early 19th century as charitable nonprofit institutions. Such institutions, which are concentrated in the northeast, are now mostly nonprofit *mutual saving banks*, run by a board of directors. They now provide the additional service of *negotiable order of withdrawal* (NOW) accounts, which function like checking accounts.

Savings bond, interest-bearing bond issued to an individual by the government in specific denominations, functioning as a loan to the government for a fixed term. U.S. savings bonds were first issued to raise money during World War I. Series E, issued from 1941 to 1979, helped finance World War II. The current Series EE is issued in denominations from $50 to $10,000, sold for 50% of face value. Bonds reach maturity (come due) in 12 years. While earlier bonds had fixed interest rates, government savings bonds since Nov. 1982 have market-based rates. U.S. savings bonds are issued by the Department of the Treasury.

Savonarola, Girolamo (1452-98), Italian religious reformer. A friar of the Dominican order living in Florence, he was a powerful and outspoken critic of the Church, preaching against the corruption of the court of Pope Alexander VI and predicting that the Church would be punished. When he refused the pope's order to present himself in Rome, he was forbidden to preach (1495), the violation of which order led to his excommunication (1496). Savonarola remained unrepentant, and he was tried by an ecclesiastical court and executed by civil authorities.

Savoy, powerful dynasty of northwestern Italy that at times ruled portions of Italy, France, and Switzerland. It was founded in the 11th century by Humbert, whose holdings were in the regions of Savoy and Piedmont. Savoy holdings extended into France and Switzerland by the 15th century. Its control in Italy expanded in the 18th and 19th centuries, helping to consolidate rule of the peninsula, and a member of the family, Victor Emmanuel II, became king of Italy in 1861. Victor Emmanuel II was succeeded by his son Humbert I, who was assassinated (1900), Victor Emmanuel III, who abdicated after World War II, and Humbert II, whose brief reign ended (1946) when Italy became a republic.
See also: Italy.

Saw, cutting tool consisting of a flat blade or circular disk, having on its edge a row of sharp teeth of various designs, usually set alternately. The first true saws (copper and bronze) were used in Egypt c.4000 B.C., but only with the use of steel did they become efficient. Hand saws include the crosscut saw for cutting wood to length, the backsaw for joints, the coping saw for shaping, and the hacksaw for cutting metal. Power saws include circular saws, band saws (with a flexible endless steel band running over pulleys), and chain saws.

Sawfish, any of a family (Pristidae) of shark-like fish having "saws" of cartilage set with 2 rows of teeth on their snouts. Sawfish are found in all warm seas and may swim up rivers. The common sawfish of the Gulf of Mexico swims up the Mississippi. Sawfish can grow up to 30 ft (9 m) in length. They use the saw to dig up shellfish or to kill small fish. Although they are reported to be docile, fishers treat them with considerable respect.

Sawfly, insect related to the wasps. Sawflies often have striped bodies. They are harmless to humans, although they do serious damage to plants. They have a long, tubular egg-laying organ with which they drill holes in the leaves of plants or in wood to lay their eggs. The larvae, which look like caterpillars, eat the plants' tissues.

Saw Maung (1928-), president of the Union of Myanmar (Burma) since 1988. Armed forces chief of staff and a close associate of former ruler Ne Win, he led the coup that placed him in office, ousting President Maung Maung. He then abolished parliament and formed the National Unity Party.
See also: Burma; Myanmar.

Saxifrage, any of a genus (*Saxifraga*) of small rock plants whose leaves grow in a rosette at the base of the stem and whose flowers grow in clusters at the tip of the stem. Many of them produce a small bulb at the base of each leaf. The usual place to find saxifrages is in crevices and ledges of rocky cliffs in cold and temperate regions of the Northern Hemisphere. Several species are native to the United States, including the early saxifrage (*S. virginiensis*) and the umbrella plant (*S. peltata*).

Saxons, Germanic people who, with the Angles and the Jutes, founded settlements in Britain from A.D. 450 supplanting the Celts. The 3 peoples eventually formed the Anglo-Saxon kingdom. From modern Schleswig (northern Germany) the Saxons also spread along the coast to northern France before being conquered by Charlemagne (804).

Saxony, state in eastern Germany. Saxony was established as a duchy in the late 9th century. Its size and boundaries shifted as it was broken up and then reestablished as Electoral Saxony (1356). From 1697 to 1763 the elector of Saxony was also king of Poland; during this time the state and its capital city of Dresden were an important center of culture. Saxony was made a kingdom by Napoleon I (1816), but upon his defeat half of its lands became part of Prussia. After World War II Saxony became part of East Germany but was abolished as a political unit by the Communists. In 1990, with the reunification of Germany, Saxony was reestablished as a state.

Saxophone, brass musical instrument, classified as a woodwind since its sound is produced by blowing through a reed. Patented by the Belgian Adolphe Sax in 1846, the saxophone exists in soprano, alto, tenor, and baritone forms; the bass is rare. Sometimes used in the symphony orchestra, the saxophone is better known for its important role in jazz, where it is a leading solo and ensemble instrument.

Sayers, Dorothy (1893-1957), English writer of detective stories and creator of the popular, impeccably aristocratic and erudite Lord Peter Whimsey. He is the hero of some 16 books, beginning with *Whose Body?* (1923). Sayers also wrote religious essays and dramas.

Scabies, infectious skin disease caused by a mite (*Sarcoptes scabiei*) that burrows under the skin, often of the hands or feet; it causes an intensely itchy skin condition that is partly due to allergy to the mite. The disease is spread through contact. Treatment is with ointments.

Scalawag, in U.S. history, derisive term employed by Southern Democrats for Southern whites who cooperated with Republican Reconstruction governments after the Civil War. Although some scalawags sought personal gain, many sought to bring about educational and social reforms, including laws beneficial to blacks. The Southern Democrats gradually regained control in the 1870s.
See also: Reconstruction.

Scale, weighing, instrument for measuring weight. *Balance scales,* which date to about 2500 B.C. and are still in use, measure an unknown quantity by balancing it against established weights. *Mechanical scales,* which date from the 18th century, use beams, springs, or pendulums to convert the measurement of weight into a precise reading on a graduated scale. For example, *spring scales,* including the ordinary bathroom scale, measure weight according to the tension created when the weight stretches or compresses a spring. *Electronic scales,* which have been in commercial use since the 1950s, convert the force exerted by the weight into an electronic signal.

Scale insect, any of various small insects of the order Homoptera (especially family Coccidae) with a flattened body covered by a layer, or "scale," of waxy secretion. There are more than 2,000 species. They live on plants, and many are serious pests. The *cottony cushion scale* did immense damage to the Californian orange plantations after its introduction from Australasia. The *elm scale* kills trees. Other scale insects are collected for their secretions. The dye cochineal is obtained from a scale insect, and the lac insect used to be collected by the millions—its "scale" turned into shellac.

Scalia, Antonin (1936-), U.S. Supreme Court justice, appointed 1986 by President Ronald Reagan. Scalia practiced law in Cleveland and taught at the Univ. of Virginia and Chicago law schools. He then served as U.S. assistant attorney general in the 1970s, and as judge of the U.S. Court of Appeals for the District of Columbia 1982-86. Scalia, who is known for his politically and socially conservative views, his advocacy of judicial restraint, and a narrow interpretation of the Constitution, is the first associate justice of the Supreme Court of Italian descent.
See also: Supreme Court of the United States.

Scallop, bivalve mollusk (family Pectinidae) distinguished by a shell whose valves are rounded, with a series of ribs radiating across the surface in relief. Scallops are used for food. Unique among bivalves, scallops swim extremely well, propelled by jets of water expelled in snapping the shell shut. There are about 300 species. Chief among the commercial species is the common bay scallop (*Argopecten irradians*), found in North America.

Scandinavia, region of northwestern Europe. Geographically it consists of the Scandinavian peninsula (about 300,000 sq mi/777,000 sq km), occupied by Norway, Sweden, and Denmark. Because of close historical development, Finland, Iceland, and the Faeroe Islands are also covered by the term in matters of language, culture, peoples, and politics.

Scandinavian literature, literature of Scandinavia (Denmark, Norway, and Sweden) and usually including Finland and Iceland, from the end of the Viking Age (c.1100) to the present. The peoples of Scandinavia speak closely related North Germanic languages, except those of Finland, whose language is related to Hungarian. Early literature of the 12th and 13th centuries captured works of the oral tradition in writing. These included heroic ballads of Denmark and Sweden, Icelandic poetry collected in the *Poetic Edda*, and heroic *sagas* of Iceland and Norway. There followed a period during which most writing was in Latin and was technical or religious. Literature in the vernacular and about everyday life reemerged in the 18th century, including writings of Swedish poet Carl Michael Bellman and Danish playwright Johannes Ewald. The interest in folk tales shown by the romantic movement of the early 19th century is evident in the epic poem *Kalevala* (1835; derived from Finnish legend), collections of tales in Norway, and the original tales of Hans Christian Andersen in Denmark. Other writers of the romantic movement were Norway's Bjørnstjerne Bjørnson (*A Happy Boy*, 1860) and Finland's Aleksis Kivi (*Seven Brothers*, 1870). Henrik Ibsen of Norway and August Strindberg of Sweden were playwrights of the realist movement of the late 19th century who had international influence. The modern period includes writings of Knut Hamsun of Norway (*Hunger*, 1890) and Selma Lagerlöf of Sweden (*Gösta Berling's Saga*, 1891), and more recently, Isak Dinesen of Denmark (*Winter's Tales*, 1942) and Nobel Prize winners Sigrid Undset of Norway (*Kristin Lavransdatter* trilogy, 1920-22) and Pär Fabian Lagerkvist of Sweden (*Barabbas*, 1950).

Parts of a saxophone:
1. mouthpiece
2. reed
3. crook
4. bell

Scandium, chemical element, symbol Sc; for physical constants see Periodic Table. Scandium was discovered in 1876 by Lars Nilson in the minerals euxenite and gadolinite. It occurs in nature in over 800 mineral species in minute amounts. Scandium is obtained from thortveitite or uranium mill tailings. It is prepared by reducing the fluoride with calcium metal. Although not a member of the rare earth series of metals, it is chemically similar and often considered with them. It is a soft, silvery, reactive metal resembling yttrium and the rare-earth metals (more than aluminum or titanium), and is often associated with tin and zirconium. It is used to produce high-intensity lights. Scandium-46 is used as a radioactive tracing agent. Scandium is the ekaboron predicted by Dmitri Mendeleev (1869).

Scapegoat, in the Old Testament (Leviticus 16:8), goat designated by the Jewish high priest on Yom Kippur (Day of Atonement) to bear the sins of the people and to be sent out into the wilderness. Similar practices existed in ancient Greece and Rome. By extension, the term also refers to a person or group unfairly blamed for the ills of others.
See also: Old Testament.

Scar, mark resulting from the healing of a wound or disease process in a tissue, especially the skin. Also called a cicatrix. The presence of excessive scar tissue is called a keloid.

Scarab, family (*Scarabaeidae*) of beetles that includes the dung beetles, chafers, and dor beetles. Most of the 20,000 species are scavengers of decaying organic matter, especially dung, or they feed on the foliage and roots of growing plants, as do the chafers, many of which may become agricultural pests.

Scarlatti, name of 2 Italian composers of the baroque period. **Alessandro Scarlatti** (1660-1725) was a leading musical scholar, teacher, and composer of hundreds of church masses, cantatas, and oratorios, as well as more than 100 operas. Although few of his works are now performed, he is important for innovations in harmony, thematic development, and the use of instruments. His son **Domenico Scarlatti** (1685-1757) also composed operas and church music but is known for his many brilliant sonatas for harpsichord. An influence upon Franz Joseph Haydn and W.A. Mozart, he is still widely played.
See also: Baroque.

Scarlet fever, infectious disease caused by certain strains of streptococcus. It is common in children and causes sore throat with tonsillitis, a characteristic skin rash, and mild systemic symptoms. Penicillin and symptomatic treatment are required. Scarlet fever occurs in epidemics; some infections are followed by rheumatic fever or nephritis.
See also: Impetigo.

Schacht, Hjalmar Horace Greeley (1877-1970), German financier and banker. He helped halt post-World War I inflation in Germany and was finance minister (1934-37) and Reichsbank president (1923-30; 1933-39). Conflict with Goering and Hitler led to imprisonment in a concentration camp. He was acquitted at the Nuremberg Trials (1946).
See also: Germany.

Schaller, George Beals (1933-), U.S. zoologist and advocate for the protection of endangered species. Schaller's field research includes studies of the daily life and environment of lions and mountain gorillas of East Africa and giant pandas of China. He is author of *The Year of the Gorilla* (1964), *The Deer and the Tiger* (1967), and *The Serengeti Lion: A Study of Predator-Prey Relations* (1972), for which he won the 1973 National Book Award for the sciences. In 1972 he became research associate and coordinator at the Center for Biology and Conservation, New York Zoological Society. In 1980 Schaller, another U.S. conservationist, and a group of Chinese scientists went on a World Wildlife Fund mission in China to locate and rescue pandas.
See also: Zoology.

Schally, Andrew Victor (1926-), Polish-born U.S. medical researcher who shared the 1977 Nobel Prize in physiology or medicine with Rosalyn S. Yalow and Roger C. L. Guillemin for the discovery and synthesis of hormones produced by the hypothalamus. The analysis of these hormones, which control body chemistry, had a revolutionary effect on the study of brain functioning.
See also: Hypothalamus.

Schapiro, Meyer (1904-), Lithuanian-born U.S. art historian and critic. One of the most highly regarded and influential art scholars in the United States, he taught for many years at Columbia Univ. Among his books are *Romanesque Art* (1977) and *Modern Art: 19th and 20th Centuries* (2 vols., 1978-9). He also wrote important essays, e.g., "The Nature of Abstract" (1937) and "Leonardo and Freud" (1956).

Schawlow, Arthur (1921-), U.S. physicist who did pioneering work in the 1950s that led to the construction of the first laser. He shared the 1981 Nobel Prize in physics with Nicolass Bloembergen (of the United States) and Kai M. Siegbahn (of Sweden) for contributions to the development of laser spectroscopy.
See also: Laser.

Schechter v. United States, Supreme Court decision (1935) that ruled unconstitutional the 1933 National Industrial Recovery Act (NIRA), an important part of President Franklin D. Roosevelt's New Deal program. The Schechter Poultry Co. had been convicted of violating an NIRA code regulating interstate commerce. The Court ruled that the NIRA delegated too much legislative power to the U.S. president.
See also: National Recovery Administration.

Scheele, Carl Wilhelm (1742-86), Swedish pharmacist and chemist. He was the discoverer of chlorine and isolated oxygen, although credit went to English scientist Joseph Priestley, who published findings before Scheele. He also isolated many acids, and made significant discoveries regarding nitrogen and manganese, conducting his experiments in the restricted environment of the apothecaries where he was employed.
See also: Chemistry; Chlorine.

Schelde River, important navigable waterway of northwestern Europe. Rising in northwestern France, it flows 270 mi (434.5 km) north and northeast to Antwerp, Belgium, then northwest, as the East Schelde and West Schelde rivers, through the Netherlands to the North Sea. There are canal links to the Rhine and Meuse rivers.

Schelling, Friedrich Wilhelm Joseph von (1775-1854), German philosopher. Influenced by Baruch Spinoza, J.G. Fichte, and others, he developed a concept of an absolute unity of mind and matter toward which all history and nature progressed. Although once a close friend of G.W.F. Hegel, he became an opponent and rival. His view of art as the union of the natural and the spiritual influenced Samuel Taylor Coleridge, Schelling's contemporary and an English poet and philosopher.
See also: Philosophy.

Scherzo (Italian, "joke"), light, lively musical composition. The term most often refers to a movement in 3/4 meter (usually the third) of a sonata, symphony, or similar composition of the late 18th or 19th century; it developed from the minuet but was characterized by a much faster tempo and, frequently, a display of rhythmical humor and surprise (especially in the works of Ludwig van Beethoven). Some light vocal and instrumental compositions of the Baroque period, as well as some dramatic piano pieces by Frederick Chopin and Johannes Brahms, were also named scherzo.

Schiele, Egon (1890-1918), Austrian artist. A leader of the Austrian expressionists, he was influenced by the French impressionists and by Austrian artist Gustav Klimt. His paintings exhibit decorative qualities and a strong sense of line, but also an eroticism and emotional intensity that the public sometimes found disturbing. He is best known for self-portraits and paintings of nude or partly clothed women.

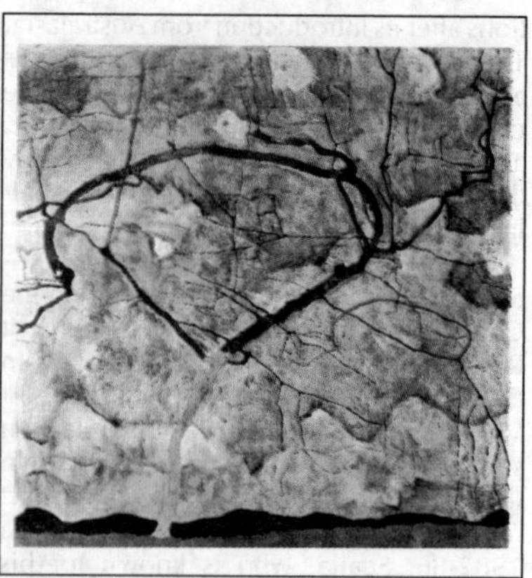

Egon Schiele's Autumn Tree *(1912)*

Schiller, Johann Christoph Friedrich von (1759-1805), German playwright, poet, writer on philosophy, history, and aesthetics. Schiller's highly successful early plays, including *The Robbers* (1781) and *Don Carlos* (1787), articulated his violent opposition to tyranny. In Weimar he became professor at the Univ. of Jena (1789) and married writer Charlotte von Lengefeld. At this time he also began his important friendship with Johann Wolfgang von Goethe, with whom he shared many values and ideas. In 1787 Schiller began writing historical works, as well as works on philosophy and aesthetics, heavily influenced by Emmanuel Kant. He and Goethe also edited the literary magazines *Horen* and *Musenalmanach.* Some of his most important works were historical dramas, including *Wallenstein* (1798-99), *Mary Stuart* (1800), and *William Tell* (1804). He also translated works of Shakespeare and Racine. Schiller is acknowledged to be a leading figure of German literature, second only to Goethe. Beethoven used Schiller's poem "Ode to Joy" (1785) as the text for the final movement of his Ninth Symphony.

Schipperke (Flemish; "little skipper"), Belgian breed of dog once used to guard canal barges. Descended from the Leauvenaar, a black sheep dog, it is a short, stout dog, often tailless, with a foxlike head and a thick black coat, standing 12-13 in (30.5-33 cm) and weighing about 15 lb (7 kg).

Schirra, Walter Marty, Jr. (1923-), U.S. astronaut, 1959-69. Schirra, whose parents were both stunt fliers, attended the U.S. Navel Academy and flew combat missions in the Korean War. In 1959 he became one of the 7 original U.S. astronauts. In his first mission in the Mercury space program, Oct. 3, 1962, he circled the earth 6 times in *Sigma 7.* He and Thomas P. Stafford piloted Gemini 6 in the first space rendezvous (with Gemini 7, Dec. 15, 1965) and was command pilot for Apollo 7 (Oct. 11-22, 1968). Schirra retired from the Navy and the space program and entered private business in 1969.
See also: Astronaut.

Schism, Great *see:* Pope.

Schist, common group of metamorphic rocks that have acquired a high degree of schistosity, i.e., the parallel arrangement of sheety, or prismatic, minerals resulting from regional metamorphism. Schistosity is similar in nature and origin to cleavage in slate but is coarser. The major constituents of most schists are either mica, talc, amphibole, or chlorite.

Schistosomiasis, or bilharziasis, parasitic disease caused by the schistosome, a type of flatworm. The disease is usually acquired by bathing in infected water. The schistosome larvae enter the body through the skin and live in the blood as parasites. As adults they lay eggs that cause infection and destroy the kidneys, liver, and other organs. The disease can ultimately cause death. It afflicts more than 200 million people in Africa, Asia, and Latin America.

Schizophrenia (formerly called dementia praecox), type of psychosis characterized by confusion of identity, hallucinations, delusion, and illogical thought. The 3 main types of schizophrenia are catatonia, in which the individual oscillates between excitement and stupor; paranoid schizophrenia, which is similar to paranoia except that the intellect deteriorates; and hebephrenia, which is characterized by withdrawal from reality, bizarre behavior, delusions, hallucinations, and self-neglect.
See also: Psychosis.

Schlesinger, name of 2 famous 20th-century U.S. historians. **Arthur Meier Schlesinger** (1888-1965) is best known for his U.S. history *The Rise of the City, 1878-1898* (1933) from the series he edited, *A History of American Life.* He stressed the cultural, social, and economic context of history. **Arthur Meier Schlesinger, Jr.** (1917-), his son, won Pulitzer prizes for both *The Age of Jackson* (1945) and *A Thousand Days* (1966), the latter written after a period as special assistant to President John F. Kennedy.

Schleswig-Holstein, state in northern Germany, 6,046 sq mi (15,660 sq km) bordering Denmark. The capital, Kiel, lies at the eastern end of the Kiel Canal, which links the North and Baltic seas. The main economic activities are dairy farming, fishing, shipbuilding, and engineering. Schleswig was a Danish fiefdom from the 12th century. Holstein came under Danish control in the 15th century. Disputes with the German states led to the Austro-Prussian War in 1864. Prussia annexed these 2 Danish duchies in 1866. North Schleswig was reunited with Denmark in 1920.

Schliemann, Heinrich (1822-90), German archeologist, best known for his discoveries of Troy (1871-90) and Mycenae (1876-78).
See also: Archeology.

Schmalkaldic League, alliance of German Protestant states during the Reformation, formed in 1531 for defense against the Catholic Holy Roman emperor Charles V. Member states included Hesse, Saxony, Brunswick, Anhalt, Mansfeld, Magdeburg, Bremen, Strassburg, and Ulm. The Protestants were defeated in 1547 in the War of the Schmalkaldic League, but the subsequent Peace of Augsburg (1555) gave Lutheran churches the right to exist.
See also: Reformation.

Schmidt, Helmut (1918-), chancellor of West Germany (1974-82). A Social Democrat, he was party floor leader in the Bundestag (1962-69), defense minister (1969-72), and finance minister (1972-74). He succeeded Willy Brandt as chancellor when the latter resigned amid a spy scandal. In a continent plagued with economic difficulties, Germany under Schmidt remained stable and prosperous. However, violent radical groups asserted themselves in the early 1980s, and he stepped down after losing a confidence vote in 1982.

Schmitt, Harrison Hagan (1935-), geologist, astronaut, politician. Schmitt joined the National Aeronautics Space Administration (NASA) as an astronaut in 1964. In Dec. 1972 he flew on the Apollo 17 lunar-landing mission, becoming the first U.S. scientist to fly in space and, with Eugene A. Cernan, spent 3 days on the surface of the moon. He was elected to the U.S. Senate in 1976 as a Republican from New Mexico, and became a staunch backer of President Ronald Reagan; however, he lost the 1982 election. In 1989 President George Bush named him to serve on an 8-member commission on government ethics.
See also: Astronaut.

Schnauzer *see:* Giant schnauzer; Miniature schnauzer; Standard schnauzer.

Schnitzler, Arthur (1862-1931), Austrian playwright. He wrote about love and the personality basis of racism, particularly anti-Semitism, in the Vienna of Sigmund Freud. His work included *Anatol* (1893), *Playing with Love* (1896), and *Merry-Go-Round* (1897).

Schoenberg, Arnold (1874-1951), German composer, theorist, and teacher who revolutionized music by introducing serial, or 12-tone, music. His string sextet *Transfigured Night* (1899), with harmonic clashes, was followed by the declaimed songs of *Pierrot Lunaire* (1912) and experiments in whole-tone and finally 12-tone music, culminating in his unfinished opera *Moses and Aaron* (1930-51). Schoenberg emigrated to the United States in 1933.

Schofield, John McAllister (1831-1906), U.S. Union general in the Civil War, from 1864 commander of its Army of the Ohio in the Atlanta Campaign. He was secretary of war (1868-69) and commander of the U.S. Army (1888-95).
See also: Civil War, U.S.

Scholarship, grant-in-aid awarded to a student. In the United States scholarships are awarded by schools, states, the federal government, and private organizations on the basis of financial need, for scholastic excellence or ability or athletic prowess, to aid special groups such as those with particular disabilities, or to encourage students to enter particular fields of study. Under the Servicemen's Readjustment Act (GI Bill of Rights), World War II veterans were given federal tuition grants and stipends to attend college or vocational school; similar acts were passed for veterans of the Korean and Vietnam wars. Rhodes and Fulbright scholarships are among the important awards for U.S. students to study abroad.

Scholasticism, philosophical system of medieval Church teachers, or scholastics, who applied philosophic (primarily Aristotelian) ideas to Christian doctrine. They held that although reason was always subordinate to faith, it served to increase the believer's understanding of what was believed. Typical scholastic works are the commentary on an authoritative text and the *quaestio,* in which the writer sets out opposing authorities and then reconciles them in answering a question. St. Thomas Aquinas's *Summa Theologica* consists of a systematically constructed series of *quaestiones.* The influence of Aristotle on medieval thought was enormous but was not available in the West until a Latin translation appeared in the 13th century.

Schongauer, Martin (1450?-91), German painter and engraver. He was one of the first engravers to use copper plates, and his delicate, skillful work influenced Albrecht Dürer and other German artists. His works include the engravings *The Death of the Virgin Mary* and *Christ Bearing the Cross,* the painting *The Virgin in the Rose Arbor* (1473), and the mural in Breisach, *Last Judgment* (c.1491).

School, institution whose primary purpose is to impart knowledge. The most numerous and the most important kinds of

Arnold Schoenberg, painted by Oskar Kokoschka

schools are those used to educate the young, from early childhood to early adulthood, preparing them for the roles they will play in society, the economy, and in political life. Schools provide students with knowledge, from the basics of reading, writing, and reasoning, to the most sophisticated branches of the arts and sciences. Schools also reflect society and transmit its values and norms.

Before the 1800s in the West, education was reserved for a relatively privileged few. Among the Assyrians, Babylonians, and Egyptians, organized knowledge was largely dominated by priests. Much of what was known was deliberately kept secret and obscure to enhance the power and prestige of a privileged few. Masters of arts and crafts passed on their techniques directly from one generation to the next; the process of teaching and learning was more restricted, personal, and direct. The ancient Greeks marked a significant departure from this approach. Politically independent, socially mobile, free of the dominance of a priesthood, they used their own senses and reason to question what they saw and heard. The spirit of free, rational inquiry among the Greeks led to a free exchange of ideas, the growth of rival world views, the gathering of organized bodies of knowledge, the appearance of the Western world's first teachers for hire, and the first schools open to free inquiry. Education was still a privilege, but the Greeks made learning a goal in its own right and the mark of a truly free individual. The Romans were deeply influenced by Greek practice and ideals.

After the fall of the Roman Empire, education at first declined and then was revived and transformed by the Christian church. It was no longer necessary to educate citizens but to preserve and spread the faith. What little education there was took place in monasteries and was almost wholly religious. Over the centuries, bodies of knowledge accumulated and new needs had to be met. Busy with war and politics, the aristocracy could not read or write, but they needed clerks; in the early days they used men trained by the church. In time, education moved from the monastery schools to schools in the great cathedrals that developed into universities. The upper classes began to cultivate and patronize learning and schools.

In the Renaissance, from the 14th to the 16th centuries, scholars recovered and began to read the works of Greeks and Romans and aspired to their learning and level of culture. Education and the schools began to break away from the church and its priesthood. The Renaissance was followed by the Protestant Reformation and the invention of the printing press. The former challenged the authority of the Roman church, the latter made books available to all who could read, leading to profound changes in education and in schools. The modern state, modern commerce and finance, the rise of a more complex urban society dominated by the middle class and the advent of modern science and technology revolutionized education and schools. Learning was no longer a luxury, privilege, or virtue; it had become a necessity. School systems were established, theories of education were developed, and the modern profession of teaching had its beginnings.

In the United States today, in addition to pre-schools and kindergartens, there are elementary schools, many of them public; middle schools; junior public high schools; and public high schools. Education generally proceeds on a two-track system—vocational or academic. For higher education, students may go on to community college, three-quarters of which are public, or to one of the nation's colleges and universities. There are also many schools for advanced training and retraining of highly skilled professionals, as well as correspondence schools, night schools, and special and vocational education schools.

In the United States, schools are run by elected school boards of education or by local boards composed of parents and teachers. Schools deal with questions of curricula, libraries and censorship, and teachers and their qualifications, as well as questions of the separation of church and state that arise over school prayer and religious instruction. Fundamental issues of conflicting moral values and public health must be addressed in dealing with drugs in the schools. In the universities, corporate and government grants providing badly needed funds for scientific research often generate controversy. In the United States, Japan, Africa, and Europe, schools and particularly colleges and universities not only are places for study and research, but also play vital roles in their relation to the leading issues in their societies.

Franz Schubert and his circle of friends, the Schubertians, as depicted by Leopold Kupelwiesser

Schopenhauer, Arthur (1788-1860), German philosopher, noted for his doctrine of the will. In *The World as Will and Idea* (1819), his main work, he argued that will is the ultimate reality, but advocated the negation of will to avoid suffering. He encouraged the contemplation of philosophy and the arts as a haven of relief from the insatiable strivings of will. Schopenhauer's ideas influenced Friedrich Nietzsche and modern existentialism.
See also: Philosophy.

Schrieffer, John Robert (1931-), U.S. physicist who shared with Leon Cooper and John Bardeen the 1972 Nobel Prize in physics for their work on superconductivity.
See also: Superconductivity.

Schrödinger, Erwin (1887-1961), Austrian-born Irish physicist and philosopher of science who shared with Paul Dirac the 1933 Nobel Prize in physics for his discovery of the Schrödinger wave equation, describing the wavelike behavior of electrons, which is of fundamental importance in studies of quantum mechanics. It was later shown that his theories of wave mechanics were equivalent to the matrix mechanics theories of Werner Heisenberg.
See also: Quantum mechanics.

Schubert, Franz Peter (1797-1828), Viennese composer. He wrote nine symphonies, of which the Fifth (1816), Eighth (1822), and Ninth (1828) are among the world's greatest. He is also famous for his piano pieces and chamber music (especially his string quartets), but above all for his over 600 *lieder* (songs). In addition to individual lieder such as "The Erl King" and "The Trout," he wrote song cycles, among them *The Maid of the Mill* and *Winter's Journey*.

Schulz, Charles Monroe (1922-), U.S. cartoonist, creator of "Peanuts." The "Peanuts" series, which Schulz began in 1950, is about young children but appeals to adults as well in its benign humor and insight into human foibles. The characters of the comic strip, including the insecure Charlie Brown, the bossy Lucy, and the beagle Snoopy, have become the subjects of television programs, an Off-Broadway play, and many books and greeting cards. The comic strip appears in thousands of newspapers throughout the world.
See also: Cartoon.

Schuman, Robert (1886-1963), French politician. Prime minister (1947-48) and foreign minister (1948-52), he launched the Schuman Plan, which resulted in the European Coal and Steel Community, precursor of the European Economic Community.
See also: France.

Schuman, William (1910-), U.S. composer. His symphonies, chamber music, ballets, and operas are known for their rhythmic vivacity and their debt to jazz. His cantata *A Free Song* won the first Pulitzer Prize in music (1943). He was president of the Juilliard School of Music (1945-62) and of Lincoln Center for the Performing Arts (1962-69).

Schumann, Clara (1819-96), German pianist and composer. The daughter of the important piano teacher Friedrich Wieck, she became a well-known soloist and the first to perform entirely from memory. She married pianist and composer Robert Schumann over strenuous objections of her father, and became one of the chief exponents of his piano compositions. After her husband's death in 1856 she continued performing widely, touring frequently to England. A close friend of Johannes Brahms, she also was one of the main interpreters of his compositions. In her later years she was active as a piano teacher, heading the piano department of the Frankfurt Conservatory (1878-92). Her compositions include a piano concerto, smaller piano compositions, songs, and cadenzas for Beethoven's 3rd and 4th piano concertos.

Schumann, Robert (Alexander) (1810-56), German composer and critic, a leader of the romantic movement. His early work, until 1840, comprises inspired piano pieces (e.g., *Symphonic Études, Papillons*). He then turned his attention to music for orchestras (e.g., *Piano Concerto in A Minor*, 1841-45), achieving great heights of emotional intensity, and to songs, uniting voice and piano in beautiful classical compositions. He was an ardent advocate for and influence on new composers, such as Brahms and Chopin. In the 1840s he began to show signs of mental illness and, after a suicide attempt in 1854, was placed in an asylum, where he remained until he died.

Robert and Clara Schumann, by Erald Kaiser

Schumpeter, Joseph Alois (1883-1950), Moravian-born U.S. economist. Schumpeter emigrated to the United States in 1932, when he joined the faculty of Harvard University. His major works were on the importance of entrepreneurs (*The Theory of Economic Development*, 1911) and the inevitability of business cycles and the unequal distribution of wealth (*Capitalism, Socialism, and Democracy*, 1942) in the healthy capitalist economy.
See also: Economics.

Schurz, name of German-born U.S. couple prominent in public life. **Carl Schurz** (1829-1906) came to the United States after fighting in the 1848-49 revolution in Germany. An antislavery activist, he was a supporter of Abraham Lincoln and later a brigadier general in the Civil War. He served in the U.S. Senate as a Missouri Republican (1869-75), helped found the Liberal Republican Party, and was secretary of the interior (1877-81). Schurz wrote biographies of Henry Clay (1887) and Abraham Lincoln (1889). He was editor of the *New York Evening Post* and *The Nation* in the early 1880s, and chief editorial writer for *Harper's Weekly* from 1892 to 1898. **Margaretha Meyer Schurz** (1833-76), a student of the German educator Friedrich Fröbel, was influential in the establishment of kindergartens in the United States, and worked with her husband, assisting him in his social reform and political activities.

Schuyler, Philip John (1733-1804), American soldier and politician who served as major-general in the Continental Army during the Revolutionary War. He served three terms in the New York senate between 1780 and 1797, and was one of the first two U.S. senators from New York (1789-91 and 1797-98).
See also: Revolutionary War in America.

Schuylkill River, river rising in east-central Pennsylvania and flowing southeast 130 mi (210 km) into the Delaware River near Philadelphia. The river is used for hydroelectric power, for Philadelphia's water supply, and as a route for coal barges.

Schwartz, Delmore (1913-66), U.S. poet admired for his rhapsodic yet philosophic style. His works include *In Dreams Begin Responsibilities* (1938), *Summer Knowledge* (1959), and *Last and Lost Poems of Delmore Schwartz* (1979). He also wrote short stories, a play, and a children's book.

Schwartz, Melvin (1932-), U.S. physicist. Schwartz, Leon Lederman, and Jack Steinberger won the 1988 Nobel Prize in physics for their work in using streams of subatomic neutrinos and their discovery of the muon neutrino. The work was conceived at Columbia Univ. in 1960 and executed at Brookhaven National Laboratory in 1962.
See also: Neutrino.

Schwarzkopf, Elisabeth (1915-), German soprano noted for performances in Mozart and Strauss operas in Europe, and later for her expressive *Lieder* recitals there and in the United States.
See also: Opera.

Schwarzkopf, H. Norman (1935-), commander in chief, U.S. Central Command (CENTCOM), responsible for the planning and direction of all U.S. and coalition armed forces in the Persian Gulf War (1991). He was Deputy Chief of Staff for Operation and Plans (1986-87) and Deputy Commander, Joint Task Force, in Grenada (Oct. 1983). He served two consecutive tours in Vietnam. Schwarzkopf graduated from the U.S. Military Academy at West Point (1956). He has received numerous awards and decorations, including 2 Distinguished Service Medals, 3 Silver Stars, and 3 Bronze Stars with a "V" for valor.
See also: Persian Gulf War.

Schweitzer, Albert (1875-1965), German physician, theologian, missionary, musician, and philosopher. He was an authority on Bach and a noted performer of Bach's organ music. He abandoned an academic career in theology to study medicine and became (1913) a missionary doctor in French Equatorial Africa (now Gabon). He devoted his life to the hospital he founded there. His many writings include *The Quest of the Historical Jesus* (1906), and *The Decay and Restoration of Civilization* and *Civilization and Ethics* (1923), the first two volumes of his *Philosophy of Civilization*. Schweitzer won the 1952 Nobel Peace Prize for his inspiring humanitarian work.

Schwinger, Julian Seymour (1918-), U.S. physicist who shared with Richard P. Feynman and Japan's Shinichiro Tomonaga the 1965 Nobel Prize in physics for independent work in formulating the theory of quantum electrodynamics.
See also: Quantum electrodynamics.

Sciatica, pain in the distribution of the sciatic nerve in the leg caused by compression or irritation of the nerve. The pain may resemble an electric shock and be associated with numbness and tingling in the skin area served by the nerve. One of the most common causes is a slipped disk in the lower lumbar spine.
See also: Nervous system.

Science, systematic study of nature and of individual and social human behavior. Science is distinguished from other intellectual disciplines, like the arts and humanities, by several key characteristics. It is based upon observation, either by the unaided senses or with the help of instruments that increase the power of the senses, like microscopes or telescopes. Science requires the careful collection and organization of data. Above all, science employs a rigorous method of reasoning about what it observes. The scientific method relies upon logic to draw conclusions from evidence and tests its reasoning with experiments. As study progresses, a larger pattern or underlying law begins to emerge that helps explain phenomena like the formation of gases, the motion of planets, or the division of cells. Scientists attempt to state those laws or patterns in the form of theories or hypotheses, and those statements are also subjected to experiments. Some hypotheses prove useful and enduring, others are refuted or superseded by new experiments or new findings. Finally, science expresses itself mathematically, in formulas that state numerically the dynamics or relations underlying what we see. Neither the arts nor the humanities are rigorous in the way that science is; the questions they ask, the methods they use, and their findings and results are different. The scope of science is vast. It is broken up into a great many fields and specialties. But a few major divisions are still useful for an overview. The physical sciences are, historically, probably the oldest and include astronomy, meteorology, chemistry, physics, and geology. These fields cover inanimate nature. Life and living beings are studied by the life sciences, including biology, zoology, botany, physiology, and paleontology. The social sciences study human beings as they reveal themselves in individual behavior and in society and its institutions. Such studies include political science, economics, psychology, anthropology, and sociology. To the extent that these disciplines are less successful than the natural sciences in expressing their findings mathematically, they have been criticized for lacking the rigor of pure science. Finally, although they are not themselves sciences in the strict sense, mathematics and logic are essential to science. Though in many ways the two overlap, mathematics provides science with symbols and procedures for measuring and for calculating relations. Logic discovers the ratio and procedures of accurate reasoning.

A scene from the 1966 science fiction film Fahrenheit 451 *based on Ray Bradbury's 1951 novel*

The development of science has led to an explosion of knowledge unprecedented in human history. Allied with mechanical ingenuity, it led to technology, the application of scientific knowledge to practical problems. The results have completely transformed the world. In partnership with modern industry, finance, and the state, science has produced a mixed legacy, creating tools that heal and destroy, that enhance life and threaten it with annihilation.

History. Science's earliest manifestation was among the Greeks who were the first people to reason logically about the natural world. Instead of accepting occult explanations for what they observed, the Greeks tried to discover intelligible laws underlying things. They developed logic and mathematics and made impressive contributions to human knowledge. In the 4th century B.C., Hippocrates laid down elementary principles for the practice of medicine. One hundred years later, Aristotle attempted an exhaustive classification of phenomena based upon logical categories and direct observation. Euclid and Archimedes were great mathematicians and Ptolemy's description of the motion of the planets would not be improved upon for nearly 1,500 years.

With the fall of the Roman Empire and the onset of the Middle Ages in the West, it was left to Islam to pursue some of the promise of the Greeks. To mention only a few great Muslim thinkers, Alhazan in optics, Aricanna in medicine, and Al-Khwarizmi in algebra made important contributions that had their greatest impact on Christian Europe in the late Middle Ages. Schooled in logical rigor by the Scholastics and with access to Islamic work and the Hindu-Arabic numerical notation, Europe was ripe for intellectual change. It came first in Italy between the 14th and 16th centuries in the Renaissance. The use of perspective in painting and architecture that explored principles laid down by the Greeks and Romans fostered a spirit of inquiry that led to detailed studies of human anatomy and innovations in mechanics and virtually every branch of human knowledge. Men like Galileo and da Vinci pointed the way for the rest of Europe. Nicolaus Copernicus, the Polish astronomer, put an end to the medieval view of the world with his theory, based upon careful telescopic observation, that the earth was not the center of the universe but only one of several planets that revolves around the sun. The Copernican revolution sent profound shock waves throughout Europe, and combined with the impact of the discovery of the Americas, inspired the best minds of Europe to turn to science.

In the 17th century, Descartes in France laid the philosophical foundations of the scientific method. In the same century, the Englishman Newton and the German Leibniz simultaneously discovered calculus, and Newton wrote the *Principia Mathematica* in which he proposed his law of universal gravitation. His countryman, William Harvey, described the circulation of blood and Robert Boyle advanced the science of chemistry.

Building upon the work of the previous century, the 18th century saw rapid advances. In chemistry came the discoveries of gases, among them chlorine, hydrogen, and carbon dioxide. Carolus Linnaeus developed a system for the classification of animals and Luigi Galvani, Alessandro Volta, and Benjamin Franklin made advances in the study of electricity. In addition, the sciences had an impact outside of the laboratory in the rationalisms and skepticism of Voltaire, Hume, Diderot, and the work of Adam Smith, whose *Wealth of Nations* marked the advent of the modern study of economics. In the 19th century, Darwin did his pioneering work on natural selection and evolution, presenting theories that would have almost as profound an effect upon social and political thought as they did in science. Michael Faraday and Joseph Henry pioneered work in electromagnetism. James Clark Maxwell studied the laws of electricity and magnetism, and great advances were made in modern medicine, typified by the work and career of Louis Pasteur. Progress in medicine and in the care and treatment of the sick led to a dramatic increase in life expectancy.

Much of the early optimism felt about science began to be lost in the era of World War I, a grim demonstration of what the new knowledge and technology could do when applied to war. But the decades between World War I and World War II saw perhaps the most fertile and creative years of 20th-century science with the work of Einstein, who proposed his theory of relativity, as well as Max Planck and Nils Bohr, who deepened our understanding of the structure and mechanics of the atom. It was their work that made possible the creation of the atomic bomb, a weapon which revolutionized both war and peace.

In the latter half of the 20th century, science has become a highly complex and competitive intellectual pursuit, engaging the talents of many of the best minds throughout the world and tackling problems as diverse as the origin's of the universe to the perfecting of high-definition TV or the next generation of high-speed computers. Modern science is pursued almost entirely in the laboratories of universities, governments, or private industries, and research and development commands billions of dollars every year. But no matter how large or complex the facilities and supporting institutions, the basic work of science requires a combination of intellectual rigor, intuitive power, ambition, and a desire to know that are the characteristics of the individuals who pursue science.

Science fiction, literary genre based on speculation about scientific or social development. With the works of Jules Verne and H.G. Wells, science fiction broke from supernatural fantasy. In the United States in the 1920s "pulp" magazines popularized but all too often debased the form. John W. Campbell's magazine *Astounding* (founded 1937, now called *Analog*) revitalized the genre through its consistently high literary standards; it nurtured writers who today lead the field, among them Isaac Asimov, Robert Heinlein, Poul Anderson, Hal Clement, and Eric Frank Russell. Many science fiction writers, such as Asimov, Arthur C. Clarke, Ray Bradbury, Kurt Vonnegut, and John Wyndham, are well known outside the field. The critical acclaim they and writers no less accomplished but less well known receive indicates that the best science fiction may be considered to rank with the best contemporary general fiction.

Science project, independent project in which the student studies, explores, and demonstrates principles of science. Such projects include building models of anatomical structures or machines, collecting plant or animal specimens, demonstrating chemical reactions, or conducting controlled experiments on heredity in insects. The subject of these studies is not only the area of science involved but also the scientific method itself.

Scientific creationism, belief that current forms of life did not evolve from simpler forms over millions of years but were created more or less as they exist now. According to scientific creationists, neither logic nor physical evidence (fossils) supports the ideas of differentiation and transitions between life forms that are central to the theory of evolution. The scientific creationist movement developed in the mid-20th century, particularly with the activities of Henry M. Morris, cofounder of the Creation Research Society (1963) and founder of the Institute for Creation Research (1970s).

Scientology, religio-scientific movement stressing self-redemption, which originated in the United States in the 1950s and was incorporated as a church in 1965. It was founded by L. Ron Hubbard. Based on Hubbard's theory of dianetics, a "modern science of mental health," scientology holds that all aspects of individual human behavior are linked and must be harmonized; it also posits a life energy in the universe at large that affects human behavior.

Scipio, Publius Cornelius (Scipio Africanus Major, Scipio the Elder; 234?-183? B.C.), Roman general. Scipio defeated the Carthaginian forces under Hannibal in the Second Punic War (218-201 B.C.), fighting in Spain and winning decisively at Zama, in North Africa (202 B.C.). In 199 B.C. he was elected to public office, serving until 184 B.C.
See also: Punic Wars.

Scissors, cutting tool made of 2 metal blades joined at a pivot point. Cutting occurs between the blades as they are brought together when the handles at one end are squeezed together. Scissors may have been invented as early as the Bronze Age. They were in use in ancient Rome, China, Japan, and Korea, and came into regular domestic use in Europe in the 16th century. Among specialized scissors are *shears* (large scissors) and *pinking shears* (sawtooth scissors that cut fabric leaving zigzag edges).

Scoliosis, curvature of the spine to one side, with twisting. It occurs as a congenital defect or may be secondary to spinal diseases. Severe scoliosis causes hunchback deformity and loss of height, and may restrict cardiac or lung function. Scoliosis becomes apparent in adolescence or earlier, and it occurs more often in girls than in boys. Severe cases may require surgery, after which a body cast is worn for several months.
See also: Spine.

Scone, Stone of, ceremonial stone in Westminster Abbey, London, on which British monarchs are crowned. The stone originated in the village of Scone, Scotland, where it was used to crown Scottish kings. It was brought to London by Edward I of England in 1296.
See also: Westminster Abbey.

Scopes trial, 1925 prosecution of a biology teacher, John T. Scopes, for breaking a Tennessee law forbidding the teaching of evolution in state-supported schools. For the defense Clarence Darrow unsuccessfully pitted himself against the orthodoxy of William Jennings Bryan; the Tennessee supreme court reversed the conviction on a technicality, but the law was not repealed until 1967.
See also: Evolution.

Scopolamine, or hyoscine, alkaloid drug derived from plants of the Solenaceae (nightshade) family (especially genus *Scopolia*) and used as a depressant. Toxic unless given in very small quantities, it is administered to control tremors of Parkinson's disease and other disorders, to combat motion sickness, and in combination with morphine, as an analgesic and amnesic drug (reducing pain and inducing forgetfulness) before childbirth or surgery.

Scorpion, any of an order (Scorpionida) of terrestrial arachnids having two claws held in front of the head and a stinging tail curled forward over the back. All scorpions have a poisonous sting but few are dangerous to humans. The sting is usually used in defense or, with the palps, in catching prey. Scorpions are restricted to dry, warm regions of the world and feed on grasshoppers, crickets, spiders, and other arthropods.

Scorpionfly, harmless insect (family Panorpidae) with transparent or colored wings and long, dangling legs. Some species are wingless. The long legs are used to trap smaller insects, which are then bitten and eaten. The caterpillar-like larvae are also flesh eaters.

Scorsese, Martin (1942-), U.S. film director. His first and somewhat experimental feature-length film, *Who's That Knocking at My Door?* (1968), was followed by the semi-autobiographical *Mean Streets* (1973), which he co-wrote. Other films include *Taxi Driver* (1976), *Raging Bull* (1980), the controversial *The Last Temptation of Christ* (1988), based on a novel by Nikos Kazantzakis, and *GoodFellas* (1990).

Scotland, former kingdom now part of the United Kingdom. It is bounded by England in the south, the Atlantic Ocean in the north and west, and the North Sea in the east.
Land. Covering northern Britain and the Hebrides, Orkney, and Shetland islands, Scotland is 30,414 sq mi (78,772 sq km) in area. It is divided into 3 main land regions: the Highlands, the Central Lowlands, and the Southern Uplands. Great Britain's highest peak, Ben Nevis (4,406 ft/1,343 m) is located in the Highlands. Scotland's most important river is the River Clyde.
People. Over 50% of the population is urban; major cities include Edinburgh, the capital and cultural center; Glasgow, the industrial center; Aberdeen; and Dundee. English is spoken everywhere, but some 77,000 Scots in the northwest also speak Gaelic.
Economy. Scotland was one of the first industrialized countries; its economy rests on iron and steel, aluminum, shipbuilding, chemicals, North Sea oil, and the whiskey industry. Agriculture, mainly grain, sheep and cattle, and fishing are also important.
History. Scotland's original inhabitants were the Picts, displaced by the Scots, Britons, and Angles. United under Kenneth I MacAlpin (9th century A.D.) the country maintained an embattled independence from England, ensured by Robert the Bruce (Robert I; r. 1306-29). A brief Renaissance under James IV (r. 1488-1513) ended in disaster at Flodden Field. In the turmoil of the Reformation, James VI (James I of England) united the crowns of Scotland and England, but union of government came only in 1707. It was widely resented, and England fueled this by attacking Scottish autonomy and prosperity; this helped incite the two Jacobite rebellions (1715 and 1745). A great cultural rebirth followed, but also the hardships of the Industrial Revolution and Highland depopulation for sheep farming. Devolution (i.e., greater autonomy) was defeated by referendum vote in 1979, although there continues to be a movement for greater autonomy.
See also: United Kingdom.

The Scottish Highlands

Scotland Yard, headquarters of the Criminal Investigation Department (CID) of the London Metropolitan Police since 1829. Its jurisdiction covers 786 sq mi (2,036 sq km) containing more than 8 million people. It also coordinates police work throughout Britain and provides national and international criminal records.

Scott, Barbara Ann (1928-), Canadian figure skater. In 1947 she became the first non-European to win a world title in figure skating, and in 1948 she won the Olympic gold medal. She then became a professional skater, featured in *Hollywood Ice Revues,* and subsequently, a competitor in equestrian events.

Scott, Robert Falcon (1868-1912), English explorer remembered for his fatal attempt, on his second antarctic expedition, to be the first to reach the South Pole. In 1911 he led 4 men with sleds 950 mi (1,529 km) from the Ross Ice Shelf to the South Pole. They arrived on Jan. 18, 1912, only to discover that Roald Amundsen had reached the Pole a month before. Scurvy, frostbite, starvation, and bitter weather hampered the grueling 2-month return journey, and the last 3 survivors died in a blizzard, only 11 mi (18 km) from the next supply point.
See also: South Pole.

Scott, Sir Walter (1771-1832), Scottish poet and the foremost romantic novelist in the English language. Scott was the inventor of the historical novel, and his vivid recreations of Scotland's past were widely read throughout Europe. He started by writing popular narrative poems, including *The Lay of the Last Minstrel* (1805). After these successes he turned to fiction and completed 28 novels and many nonfiction works. His novels included *Waverly* (1814), *The Heart of Midlothian* (1818), and *Ivanhoe* (1819).

Scott, Winfield (1786-1866), U.S. political and military leader, known as "Old Fuss and Feathers" for his obsession with procedure and detail and for his elaborate uniforms. Scott became a hero in the War of 1812. He was active in the Indian wars and

in 1846 was appointed a commander in the Mexican War. He captured Mexico City. In 1852 he was the unsuccessful Whig presidential candidate. He commanded the Union Army until 1861.
See also: Mexican War; War of 1812.

Scottish deerhound, dog bred by the Scottish nobility since the 16th century to hunt deer. It stands 30 in (76 cm) or more and weighs 76-110 lb (34-50 kg), with a frame much like the greyhound but more heavily built. Its wiry coat is light gray to yellow brown. In the United States the breed is used to hunt wolves.

Scottish terrier, or Scottie, breed of dog with short legs, stocky body, large head, and a gray, tan, or black wiry coat. Scotties originated in the Scottish highlands in the 19th century, where they were used to hunt small game. They average 10 in (25 cm) at the shoulder and 18-22 lb (8-10 kg).

Scottsboro Cases, U.S. legal cases involving nine black youths accused in 1931 of raping two white women on a freight train in Alabama. Indicted and tried in Scottsboro, all the youths were found guilty, and eight were sentenced to death. They had no defense counsel until two lawyers volunteered to aid them on the day of the trial. The first Scottsboro case, *Powell* v. *Alabama*, reached the U.S. Supreme Court in 1932. The court reversed the convictions on the ground that failure to provide adequate counsel for the boys violated the due process clause of the 14th Amendment. Three years later the second case, *Norris* v. *Alabama*, reached the U.S. Supreme Court; it reversed the convictions because blacks had been excluded from the grand jury that indicted the youths. By 1976 all of the youths but one (who had escaped in 1948) were released from prison.

Scottsdale (pop. 88,622), city in south-central Arizona and now a suburb of Phoenix. First settled in 1888 by Major Winfield Scott, a Union chaplain during the Civil War, it became a stagecoach stop and agricultural community. It grew rapidly after World War II with the local development of the electronics industry. Scottsdale is a center for artists and craftspeople, and Frank Lloyd Wright's architecture school, Taliesin West, is located nearby. In the winter its desert climate attracts many tourists.

Scotus *see:* Duns Scotus, John.

Scouring rush *see:* Horsetail.

Scout *see:* Boy Scouts; Girl Scouts and Girl Guides.

Scranton (pop. 88,117), city in northeastern Pennsylvania, situated on the Lackawanna River near the Pocono Mountains. Permanent settlements date to the 1780s. It is located near large coal deposits, which helped make it a center for the iron industry; George W. Scranton, for whom it was named, established an iron works there in 1840. As coal mining declined in the 1950s, the city went into an economic decline, and has worked to attract textile and other industries. Scranton's educational institutions include Marywood College and the Univ. of Scranton, and it shares with the neighboring city of Wilkes-Barre the Northeastern Pennsylvania Philharmonic orchestra.
See also: Pennsylvania.

Scranton, William Warren (1917-), entrepreneur and politician, governor of Pennsylvania, 1963-67. He studied law before serving as a pilot in World War II. A member of the family for which the city of Scranton was named, Scranton became a businessman in that city. Before his governorship he served in the U.S. House of Representatives (1961-63). He lost a bid for the Republican presidential nomination in 1964. He was named by Richard Nixon as head of the Presidential Commission on Campus Unrest in 1970, and served as ambassador to the UN (1976-77).

Screw, simple machine consisting of a cylindrical or conical body around which is wrapped a spiral plane or thread, and used as a fastener, propeller, and part of many more complex machines. Screws were developed by the ancient Greeks and used in presses (to extract oil or juice) and weight-lifting devices. They came into wide use as fasteners in the 1500s, with major refinements in the 1800s including the development of the sharp-tipped wood screw. Screws that modify force and motion, such as are used in vises and drilling tools, are called power screws.

Scriabin, Alexander (1872-1915), Russian composer and pianist. He wanted performances of his tone poem *Prometheus* (1911) to be accompanied by a play of colored lights corresponding to the musical tones.

Scribe (Latin *scrivere*, "to write"), person hired to write out letters, books, and documents by hand. Scribes were particularly important in ancient times, as most people were illiterate. They were involved in legal, political, and business transactions as well as personal communication. In Europe, before the widespread use of the movable-type printing press, many books were copied out by monks, one of the most literate segments of the population. Highly trained scribes are still used to copy out Jewish sacred texts according to precise ritual standards.

Scribe, Augustin Eugène (1791-1861), French playwright and opera librettist. His "well-made plays," realistic dramas constructed according to a formula including a climactic revelation that dictates consequences of the characters' actions, influenced such modern playwrights as George Bernard Shaw and Arthur Miller. Among his works are the plays *Adrienne Lecouvreur* (1849) and *The Ladies' Battle* (1851) and the opera librettos for Auber's *Fra Diavolo* and Meyerbeer's *The Huguenots.*

Scribner, family name of U.S. book publishers. **Charles Scribner** (1821-71) co-founded the publishing company in New York City in 1846. His 3 sons served in turn as president of Charles Scribner's Sons, as the firm became known, but **Charles** (1854-1930) held the position the longest, from 1879 to 1928, during which time it published such major U.S. and British authors as Henry James, Ernest Hemingway, Ring Lardner, and Rudyard Kipling. The founder's grandson **Charles** (1890-1952) and great-grandson **Charles** (1921-) also served as company presidents.

Scripps, Edward Wyllis (1854-1926), U.S. newspaper publisher, founder of the first newspaper chain and of the wire service that eventually became United Press International (UPI). Beginning in the Midwest and West, his chain spread into 15 states by 1922, when Roy Howard, manager of UPI, became a partner. The Scripps-Howard organization subsequently acquired newspapers in nearly every state in the Union.

Scripps Institution of Oceanography, center for advanced study and research in oceanography, in La Jolla, Calif. Founded in 1903, it became part of the Univ. of California in 1912.
See also: Ocean.

Scrofula, tuberculosis of the lymph nodes of the neck, usually acquired by drinking infected milk. The eradication of tuberculosis in cattle and the pasteurization of milk have substantially reduced the incidence of scrofula. Treatment includes antituberculous chemotherapy.
See also: Lymphatic system; Tuberculosis.

Scruple, in the system of apothecaries' weights, unit equal to 20 grains (1.296 g). Three scruples equal 1 dram. These measures are used by pharmacists to measure drugs.

Scuba diving *see:* Diving, deep-sea; Skin diving.

Sculpin, bullhead, or sea scorpion, family of bottom-dwelling fishes (Cottidae) distinguished by a long body, large, wide head, and spiny gills and dorsal fin. Sculpins are found most often in the shallows of seas in northern regions. Bony and sometimes covered with spines, they have little food value, and sometimes steal bait and eat shrimp and young food fish. They are sometimes used as bait. The miller's thumb (*Cottus goblo*) is a common freshwater sculpin of Europe that grows to about 4 in (10 cm). The bullrout (*Myoxocephalus scorpius*) is a larger marine sculpin of Europe, North America, and the Arctic. The largest species grow to a length of 2 ft (60 cm).

Sculpture, artistic creation of three-dimensional forms in materials such as stone, metal, wood, or even foam rubber.
High cost and durability tended to make ancient sculpture an official and conserva-

tive art form. This is evident in the monumental sculpture of Egypt, which changed little in 2,000 years. Greek sculptors aimed to portray beauty of soul as well as body, and idealized the human form. In the archaic period (about 630-480 B.C.) Egyptian influence is evident in the frontal, stylized figures, showing little movement or emotion. Greater realism led to the classical perfection of Phidias, and in the 4th century to Praxiteles, with his more sensuous forms and wider range of expression. The Hellenistic Age favored an exaggerated style, of which the *Laocoön* sculpture and the *Winged Victory of Samothrace* are fine examples. Roman sculpture was deeply indebted to Greek art but was also under Etruscan influence and excelled at realistic portraiture.
The Western tradition revived about A.D. 1000 with the elongated, stylized figures of Romanesque art leading to the more graceful and expressive sculptures of Gothic art. Renaissance sculpture, starting about 1350, was dominated by the Italians. Lorenzo Ghiberti and Donatello treated classical models in a new spirit, and Michelangelo gave to works, such as his *David*, an inner tension quite foreign to classicism. The elegant mannerism of Benvenuto Cellini and the elaborate baroque style of Gian Bernini gave way about 1800 to the neoclassical reaction of Jean-Antoine Houdon, Antonio Canova, and Bertel Thorvaldsen. The great 19th-century sculptor Auguste Rodin created a style of partially unworked figures, such as his *Balzac*, influencing Jacob Epstein. This century has seen the abstract art of Constantin Brancusi and Jean Arp, while Henry Moore and Alberto Giacometti showed interest in the human form. Outstanding U.S. sculptors are David Smith and Alexander Calder, who utilized mobiles to create movable sculpture.

Scurvy, disease caused by the gross deficiency of vitamin C. It is characterized by extreme weakness, spongy gums, and a tendency for hemorrhages to occur under the skin, membranes, and periosteum (the membrane covering the bones).

Scylla and Charybdis, in Greek mythology, perils faced by Odysseus in the Straits of Messina. Scylla was a six-headed monster who ate all within reach and Charybdis was a whirlpool. The phrase "between Scylla and Charybdis" means a straight, narrow course between two dangers.
See also: Mythology.

Sea anemone, cylindrical marine polyp with a ring of tentacles, belonging to the division of the animal kingdom known as Cnideria, or Coelenterata. Anemones are related to the jellyfish. The body of the anemone consists of a hollow sac with a mouth at one end. The base of the sac is fastened to a rock and the mouth is surrounded by a ring of tentacles armed with stinging cells, or *nematocysts*. Sea anemones feed on fish and other small animals, which they catch with their tentacles and force into their mouths. While most anemones are fixed to rocks, some burrow in the sand, some can float free, and many can creep over the rocks. Certain sea anemones live on the shells of hermit crabs. Sea anemones reproduce by laying eggs that develop into minute, floating larvae. They can also split in two.

Seabees (from CB, Construction Battalion), members of the U.S. Navy battalions that build, maintain, and defend overseas bases for the Navy and Marines. The Seabee battalions first came into existence in 1942, and were particularly active in the Pacific theater during World War II.
See also: Navy, U.S.

Seaborg, Glenn Theodore (1912-), U.S. physicist who shared the 1951 Nobel Prize for physics with E.M. McMillan for his work in discovering several actinides: americum and curium (1944), berkelium and californium (1949). Later discoveries were einsteinium (1952), fermium (1953), mendelevium (1955), and nobelium (1957).
See also: Element; Physics.

Sea cow, any of an order (Sirenia) of tropical, herbivorous, aquatic mammals. Probably evolved from a marsh-dwelling ancestor related to the elephant, all sereniáns are completely seal-like with forelimbs modified into flippers and hindlimbs fused into the horizontal flukes of a whalelike tail. Genera include *Trichechus* (the manatee) and *Dugong* (the dugong).

Sea cucumber, any of a class (Holothuroidea) of sea animal of the echinoderm group, which also contains sea urchins and starfish. The leathery, flexible, cucumber-shaped animals grow up to 3 ft (1 m) in the tropics but are smaller in cooler waters. Tentacles around the mouth of the sea cucumber are used to catch food, and suction disks on the tube feet along the body provide locomotion. The animal can eject internal organs to distract attackers, regenerating these organs later.

Sea elephant *see:* Seal.

Sea fan, colony of coral animals called polyps (genus *Gorgonia*) common to shallow, warm waters of the Atlantic and Pacific oceans. The tiny, cylindrical polyps grow together in a flat, treelike form 2-24 in (5-60 cm) across. Coloration commonly ranges from yellows to reds to purples.

Sea gull *see:* Gull.

Seahorse, small marine fish of the Syngnathidae family (genus *Hippocampus*) found mostly in tropical waters, the head and forepart of which strongly resemble the head and neck of a horse. The seahorse is generally under 6 in (15 cm) long, with a body covered with bony plates and a long prehensile tail used to anchor the fish to plants. The female lays eggs in a pouch on the underside of the male, where they are fertilized and mature until they are released as live young.

Sea anemone

Sea Islands, chain of more than 100 islands off the coasts of South Carolina, Georgia, and Florida. Settled by the Spanish in the 16th century, the islands were the first important North American cotton-growing region in the early 19th century. Many are now resorts or wildlife sanctuaries.

Seal, stamping device with an inscription or emblem in relief or cut into its surface, used to make impressions in wax, paper, or other materials, for certification or authentication of documents. "Seal" also refers to the impression made, as well as to the proprietary design itself.

Seal, fin-footed mammal of the order Pinnipedia, which includes both the sea lions (family Otariidae) and the true seals (Phocidae). True seals have no external ears and have a thick coat of strong guard hairs. Seals are animals of the colder seas of both hemispheres. Northern species (subfamily Phocidae) include the bearded seal, the gray seal, and the common, or

Seals

harbor, seal. Southern species (subfamily Monachinae) include the monk seals, elephant seals, crabeater, and Weddell seals. Most seals are gregarious; all live on the open seas and many go ashore only to breed. A single, light-colored pup is born, and further mating takes place immediately afterward. Males form harems of females on the breeding grounds. Many species are now endangered, having been extensively hunted for their skins and meat.

Sea lily, delicate, deep-sea echinoderm (class Crinoidea) shaped like a plant. It is related to the starfishes. Its body has a skeleton of chalk and consists of a stalk with five arms at one end. The arms branch repeatedly so that the animal has a feathery appearance and is often called the feather star. The largest star lily is 2 ft (61 cm) long, but 70-ft (21-m) fossils have been found. They used to be thought rare, but now they are sometimes dredged up by the ton.

Sealing wax, wax once used for sealing letters and still used for taking impressions from seals and for sealing bottles. Sticks of sealing wax, originally made of beeswax, turpentine, and coloring, are held over the material to be sealed and heated by a flame. The wax drips onto the paper or other surface; an impression can be made in the drops before they cool and harden. *See also:* Wax.

Sea lion, fin-footed seal (family Otariidae) differing from the true seals in having external ears and an almost hairless body. Sea lions are found in the northern Pacific Ocean and oceans of the Southern Hemisphere. Males may measure between 6 and 10 ft (1.8 and 3.0 m). They are active marine carnivores, feeding on fishes, squids, and other mollusks.

Sealyham terrier, short-legged dog originally bred in 19th-century Wales for hunting small burrowing animals. The terrier is of sturdy build, about 11 in (28 cm) tall and 23-25 lb (10-11 kg), with a large head and strong jaws. Its wiry coat is white, sometimes with darker markings around its head.

Seaman, Elizabeth Cochrane *see:* Bly, Nellie.

Sea onion *see:* Squill.

Sea otter (*Enhydra lutris*), marine mammal of the weasel family that lives near shores in the North Pacific Ocean. The animal averages 4-5 ft (1.2-1.5 m) and 60-85 lb (27-39 kg), and is covered with a thick, soft brown fur that insulates it against cold. It swims on its back, paddling with its hind feet, the pup carried on the chest of the female, sleeping in masses of kelp. Sea otters dive to a depth of 180 ft (55 m) for food, consisting of shellfish and other sea animals. They eat on their backs, breaking open shells by pounding them together. Sea otters have been hunted for their fur since the 1700s; a 1911 treaty saved them from extinction.

Search warrant, in law, court order issued to give law officers the authority to enter and search private premises for evidence, persons, contraband goods, or illegal equipment, such as counterfeiting machinery. "Unreasonable searches and seizures" are forbidden in the Fourth Amendment to the U.S. Constitution, and the scope of such a warrant is severely limited.

Sears, Roebuck and Company, large U.S. retail firm. Originally a mail-order company, it was founded in Chicago in 1893 by Richard W. Sears and Alvah C. Roebuck. Its mail-order business flourishing, the company began opening retail stores in 1925. It now also includes the Sears Financial Network, comprising the Allstate Insurance Company, the Coldwell, Banker & Company real estate brokerage, and the Dean Witter Reynolds stock brokerage firm, all operating out of Sears retail stores.

Sears Tower, in Chicago, Ill., tallest building (1,454 ft/443 m) in the world. It is over 100 ft (30 m) taller than the World Trade Center in New York City. Designed by Skidmore, Owings and Merrill, the office building was erected in the mid-1970s as the headquarters of Sears, Roebuck and Company. Prefabricated welded steel frames form a vertical core for the 110 stories.
See also: Skyscraper.

Sea serpent, in myths and legends from many parts of the world, large, snakelike sea animal. Sea monsters of various description appear in ancient myths of the Middle East. Sightings of sea serpents, especially in the North Atlantic, have been common but have never been confirmed by material evidence. It is thought that what have appeared to be sea serpents have actually been giant squid, masses of seaweed, schools of porpoises, and other natural phenomena. The Loch Ness Monster is a similar freshwater creature thought to inhabit a lake in northern Scotland.

Seashore, land at the edge of a sea, alternately submerged and exposed by the tides. This land-water environment produces a rich variety of life forms. Tiny plankton (animals and plants floating in the tides) are the basis of shore life, both as larvae for shore animals and as food near the bottom of the food chain. The mollusks, sponges, and other animals that feed on plankton serve as food for shorebirds and other larger animals. Rocky seashores provide surface for seaweeds, mussels, sea urchins, and other organisms to attach themselves. Tide pools left by retreating tides shelter fish and other aquatic animals. Sandy shores are less hospitable, but some clams and crabs can make their home in the loose sand. Where protected bays create muddy shores and sea water mixes with fresh river water, plants thrive and crabs and turtles are common.

Season, one of several divisions of the year, characterized by cyclical changes in the predominant weather pattern. In the temperate zones there are four seasons; spring, summer, autumn (fall), and winter. These result from the constant inclination of the earth's polar axis as the earth orbits the sun: during summer in the Northern Hemisphere the North Pole is tilted toward the sun; in winter, when the solar radiation strikes the hemisphere more obliquely, it is tilted away from the sun. The summer and winter solstices (about June 21 and Dec. 22), popularly known as midsummer and midwinter, mark the beginnings of summer and winter, respectively. Spring begins on the day of the vernal equinox (about Mar. 21) and autumn at the autumnal equinox (about Sept. 23).

Sea squirt, any of a group of marine animals (class Ascidiacea), also known as ascidians, that squirt water when squeezed. The sea squirt's body is enclosed in a jellylike coat; there are two openings, at the top and side, from which the water squirts. When the sea covers it, the sea squirt takes water in through one opening sieving off minute food particles. The waste water is passed out of the other opening. Sea squirts are found alone or in clusters, sometimes with individual animals joined together. Each sea squirt is both male and female; in the larval stage it looks like a tadpole.

SEATO *see:* Southeast Asia Treaty Organization.

Seattle (pop. 1,972,961), largest city in Washington, situated on hills between Elliott Bay (Puget Sound) and Lake Washington; seat of King County. Seattle is the financial, cultural, commercial, industrial, and transportation center of the Pacific Northwest. Its chief industries are aerospace production, steel, shipbuilding, food processing, and chemicals. Settled in 1852, Seattle rapidly expanded with the coming of the railroad, the 1897 Alaska gold rush, and following the boom created by World War II. Its port is important in trade with Asia and serves as the main connection with Alaskan oil. This scenic city has a thriving recreational industry and is a cultural hub for theater, music and art. Seattle, host of the 1962 World's Fair, still boasts the landmark Space Needle, a 600-ft (183-m) structure built for the fair.

Sea urchin, any of a class (Echinoidea) of spiny marine animals related to the starfish and the sand dollar, occurring worldwide. The basic structure of the sea urchin is a sphere of 20 columns of calcareous plates, the "test," within which the gut, gonads, and water-vascular system are looped around the inside wall. The center of the sphere is empty. The test bears tubercles and short spines, and pedicellaria—pincer-like organs that clear the surface of detritus. Tube feet protrude through pores in the test, arranged in double rows down the sides.

Seaweed, algae found around coasts from the shore to fairly deep water. Most common are the brown algae, or wracks. Some, such as bladderwrack, clothe the rocks between tides; others live up to 40 ft (12m) deep. The large brown algae (kelps) sometimes form thick beds of long, tangled fronds, with tough, well-anchored stems. Gulfweed is another widespread species. Delicate green and red seaweeds live mainly in rock pools. Seaweeds provide oxygen through photosynthesis. Some seaweeds also provide food and shelter for sea animals, and many are used for food, fertilizer, iodine, and gelatin.

Sebastian, Saint (d. A.D. 288), early Christian martyr. Stories about him are mostly legends. According to these legends, Sebastian joined the Roman army with the intention of helping Christians. He became popular with Emperor Diocletian, who made him a military commander. When his religious faith was discovered, Sebastian was tied to a tree and shot with arrows. Left for dead, he recovered only to be captured later and put to death in the Roman amphitheater. Scenes of his martyrdom were popular subjects of early Italian painters. His feast day is January 20.

Sebastopol *see:* Sevastopol.

Secession, in U.S. history, withdrawal of the Southern states from the Federal Union, 1860-1. A right of secession, arising from a states' rights interpretation of the Constitution, was claimed in the early 19th century by the defeated Federalist Party in New England. The concept died in the United States when the Civil War ended in the Southern states' defeat.
See also: Civil War, U.S.

Second, measurement of time and angles in the metric system. In time, 60 seconds make up 1 minute; 60 minutes make up 1 hour. In measuring angles, 60 seconds make up 1 minute and 60 minutes make 1 degree. According to the standard established by use of an atomic clock, a second is defined as 9,192,631,770 times the vibration of radiation from a cesium atom.
See also: Metric system.

Secretariat, U.S. thoroughbred racehorse. Born in 1970, he raced only in 1972 and in 1973, when he became the first horse since Citation (1948) to win the racing Triple Crown (Kentucky Derby, Preakness, and Belmont Stakes; Affirmed became the next Triple Crown winner, in 1978). Secretariat retired from racing with lifetime winnings of $1,316,808.

Secretary bird (*Sagittarius serpentarius*), tall bird of prey of the dry African plains. It nests in trees but is the only predatory bird to hunt on the ground, using its long legs to stalk and stamp on snakes and other prey. Standing over 40 in (1 m) tall, it is mostly gray above and black below, with a red or orange face. The black feathers that stand out from the back of its head resemble quill pens, thus its name.

Secretion, complex substance produced in certain cells or glands in the body and discharged into or expelled from the body; also, the process of forming and discharging the substance. External secretions, those released through ducts from the exocrine glands onto an internal or external surface of the body, include tears, mucous, sweat, bile, saliva, and pancreatic juice. Internal secretions, or hormones, are released from the endocrine glands directly into the blood or lymph and effect processes distant from the point of origin. These include thyroxine, insulin, epinephrine, androgens, and estrogens.

Secret Service, United States, branch of the U.S. Treasury Department. Established 1865 to suppress the counterfeiting of currency, it became responsible for protecting the president after the assassination of President William McKinley (1901). It now also guards the vice president, the president-elect, presidential candidates, and former presidents.

Securities and Exchange Commission (SEC), independent agency of the U.S. government set up in 1934 to protect investors in securities (stocks and bonds). It requires disclosures of the structure of all public companies and registration of all securities exchanged. Its 5-member panel, appointed by the U.S. president, hears complaints, initiates investigations, issues brokerage licenses, and has broad powers to penalize fraud.
See also: Stock exchange.

Securities Exchange Act, U.S. law passed in 1934. The Securities Exchange Act established the Securities Exchange Commission, a federal agency charged with regulating the issuance and trade of corporate stocks and bonds. The Securities Exchange Act also allows the Federal Reserve to set margin requirements, the amount a buyer of securities must pay before receiving credit. The Securities Exchange Act replaced the Securities Act of 1933. Its purpose is to prevent the fraud and other financial practices that led to the Great Depression.
See also: Securities and Exchange Commission.

Security Council *see:* United Nations.

Sedative, any of several drugs that reduce anxiety and induce relaxation without causing sleep. Many are also hypnotics, drugs that in adequate doses may induce sleep. Barbiturates, among the earlier drugs used in sedation, have fallen into disfavor because of addiction, side-effects, dangers of over-dosage, and the availability of safer alternatives. Benzodiapezines (e.g., Valium, Librium), classified as minor tranquilizers, are now used more often.
See also: Barbiturate.

Seddon, James Alexander (1815-80), U.S. politician, Confederate secretary of war (1862-65). He was a close friend of Jefferson Davis, the Confederate president, but unpopular with the Confederate Congress. He supported an offensive military effort in the West and the conscription act. Seddon was born in Fredericksburg, Va., studied law at the Univ. of Virginia, and served in the U.S. House of Representatives before the Civil War.
See also: Civil War, U.S.

Sea urchin

Sedge, any of a family (Cyperaceae) of grasslike plants found in damp places worldwide in temperate regions. They have triangular, flattened or cylindrical stems, and the leaves arise from sheaths that enclose the stem. The flowers are in clusters grouped in a spikelet. True sedges have triangular stems. Some are used for making matting. Other sedges include the bulrushes (genus *Scirpus*), cotton grass (genus *Eriophorum*), and papyrus (*Cyperus papyrus*).

Sedimentary rock, one of three main rock classes of the earth's crust; the others are igneous rock and metamorphic rock. Sedimentary rocks consist of weathered fragments of rock transported usually by water and deposited in distinct strata. They may also be of organic origin, as in coal and some organic limestone, or they may be formed by chemical processes, as in the evaporites. About three-quarters of the earth's land area and most of the ocean floor are covered by sedimentary rock. Most common are shale, sandstone, and limestone. Sedimentary rocks frequently contain fossils as well as most of the earth's mineral resources.

Sedition, incitement of the violent overthrow of the government. During World War I Congress passed sedition and espionage acts that banned communications attacking the U.S. government. In appealing convictions under these acts to the U.S. Supreme Court, defendants claimed a violation of their freedom of speech and press. The Court paid some attention to Justice Oliver Wendell Holmes's "clear and present danger" test but gave more weight to the "evil intent" of the defendants and, without exception, upheld their convictions.

George Segal's Restaurant Window *(1967)*

Sedum, genus of succulent plants of the Crassulaceae family. Sedums are native to the temperate zone and tropical mountains of the Northern Hemisphere. Low-grading sedums are planted as ground and rock cover. Sedums are also called stonecrops and live-forevers.

See, Holy *see:* Pope.

Seed, mature reproductive body of angiosperms and gymnosperms (seed-bearing plants). It also represents a resting stage that enables plants to survive through unfavorable conditions. Seeds develop from the fertilized ovule. Each seed is covered with a tough coat called a testa, and contains a young plant or embryo. In most seeds three main regions of embryo can be recognized: a radicle, which gives rise to the root; a plumule, which forms the shoot; and one or two seed leaves, or cotyledons, which may or may not be taken above ground during germination. Plants that produce one seed leaf are called monocotyledons and those that produce two, dicotyledons. The seed also contains enough stored food to support embryo growth during and after germination. It is this stored food that is of value to animals. Flowering plants produce their seeds inside a fruit, but the seeds of conifers lie naked on the scales of the cone. Distribution of seeds is usually by wind, animals, or water, and the form of seeds is often adapted to a specific means of dispersal.
See also: Reproduction.

Seeger, Alan (1888-1916), U.S. poet. He joined the French Foreign Legion at the outbreak of World War I and was killed in France. Among his *Collected Poems* (1916) is the well-known "I Have a Rendezvous with Death."

Seeger, Pete (1919-), U.S. folksinger and conservation activist. A master of the 5-string banjo and 12-string guitar, he led the 1950s revival of interest in folk music with his group the Weavers. Many of his own songs, including "Where Have all the Flowers Gone?" (1961), have become classics of folk music.

Seeing Eye dog, animal trained to guide the blind. Most U.S. guide dogs are German shepherds and are schooled by The Seeing Eye Inc., founded (1929) by Dorothy Harrison Eustis.

Segal, George (1924-), U.S. sculptor. He is best known for his life-size white figures, resembling plaster casts of his subjects, placed in natural settings, such as a doorway or behind a steering wheel.

Sego lily, one of the mariposa lilies (*Calochortus nuttallii*) native to the dry areas of western North America. Its long stems (18 in/46 cm) grow from corms and bear narrow leaves and large 3-petaled flowers. The white petals are marked with yellow-green, purple, or lilac, with a purple spot at the center. The Mormon settlers in Utah used the edible corms as food. The sego lily is Utah's state flower.

Segovia, Andrés (1893-1987), Spanish classical guitarist, most celebrated of modern players. He did much to revive serious interest in the guitar, transcribing many pieces for it. Manuel de Falla, Heitor de Villa-Lobos, and others have composed works for him.

Segregation, separation of people according to race, religion, or ethnic origin. Custom or law may restrict the group's place of residence, use of public facilities and institutions, employment, movement, ownership of property, marriage, and the exercise of citizenship. Segregation has occurred throughout history and in most multiracial societies, especially those in which one group has seized or attained social, economic, and political dominance. In the United States from the early 1800s to the mid-1900s, laws required blacks and whites to use separate public facilities. This is known as *de jure* (by law) segregation. From the mid-1950s on, several Supreme Court decisions were made and federal laws passed that forbade segregation in voting, education, and the use of public facilities, and prohibited job discrimination in federally funded programs. While legal reforms and social patterns have made racial segregation less common in the world, it has not been eradicated. *De facto* segregation—segregation passed along through customs, not laws—actually increased in the mid-1900s and was one of the main causes of the race riots of the 1960s and early 1980s.

Seiche, standing wave that occurs in a lake, bay, or similar basin. A seiche is most often started by wind or a change in air pressure, and sometimes by an earthquake or ocean swell, that suddenly alters the basin's surface. While the surface regains stability, a simple harmonic wave is set in motion along the length of the basin. This wave is reflected by the basin's walls, creating interference. The repeated reflections produce a standing wave, a wave having fixed points with no vertical motion, with a wavelength equal to twice the length of the basin. Lasting a few minutes to an hour, seiches can interfere with shipping, damage property, and imperil lives.

Seifert, Jaroslav (1901-85), Czechoslovakian poet who was awarded the 1984 Nobel Prize in literature. His early work concentrated on revolutionary themes. *City in Tears*, his first book of poems, was published when he was 20.

Seigneurial system, feudal system of landholding practiced in France and in the French colonies in eastern Canada. Beginning in the early 1600s, the French king granted land in Canada to nobles, religious groups, merchants, and military officers. The *seigneury*, often narrow strips of land touching the St. Lawrence River, generally covered 12-100 sq mi (31-259 sq km). The owners, or *seigneurs*, rented the land to farmers in return for an annual payment, a share of the harvest, and several days' free labor. The seigneurs and tenants provided the king with military service and contributed material and labor to such works as the building and maintenance of public roads. The seigneurial system at first spurred French settlement of Canada, but it later proved an impediment to industrialization and urban expansion. The system was abolished by the Canadian government in 1854.
See also: Feudalism.

Seine River, France's principal waterway. Rising on the Langres Plateau 18 mi (29 km) northwest of Dijon, it winds 475 mi (764 km) northwest to Paris, where over 30 bridges span it, through Rouen and Normandy, to the English Channel. It is the main artery of a far-reaching river system converging on Paris. Canals link it to the Loire, Rhône, Rhine, and Schelde rivers.

Seismograph, instrument used to detect and record seismic waves caused by earthquakes, nuclear explosions, etc.; the record it produces is a seismogram. The simplest seismograph has a horizontal bar, pivoted at one end with a recording pen at the other. The bar, supported by a spring, bears a heavy weight. As the ground moves, the bar remains roughly stationary owing to the inertia of the weight, while the rest of the equipment moves. The pen traces the vibrations on a moving belt of paper. Seismographs are used in seismic prospecting.
See also: Richter scale.

Seismology, branch of geophysics concerned with the study of earthquakes, seismic waves and their propagation through the earth's interior. Seismologists use seismographs to detect the location and severity of earthquakes and to locate oil and minerals.
See also: Geophysics.

Selassie, Haile *see:* Haile Selassie.

Selective Service System *see:* Draft, military.

Selene, in Greek mythology, goddess of the moon, called Luna in Roman mythology. At night, her crescent-shaped crown shining gold, she drove a 2-horse chariot across

the sky. She figures in magic rituals held at the full and new moons. There are few myths about her and her relationship to the other Greek gods and goddesses is unclear. Helios, the sun god, was her brother, or possibly her father. She was the daughter of Hyperion and Theia or Zeus and Leto. Some Greek writers added to the confusion by identifying Selene with Artemis, a goddess also associated with the moon.
See also: Mythology.

Selenium, chemical element, symbol Se; for physical constants see Periodic Table. Selenium was discovered by Jöns J. Berzelius in 1817. It occurs in nature in the minerals crooksite and clausthalite. It is obtained commercially from the anode muds left from electrolytic copper refining, from which selenium is prepared by roasting with soda or sulfuric acid. Selenium is a lustrous gray metalloid which exists in several allotropic forms. It can be amorphous or crystalline. The most stable form is the crystalline hexagonal form. Selenium is an essential trace element for humans, however selenides resemble arsenic in their extreme toxicity. Selenium and its compounds are used in photocells, light meters, solar cells, rectifiers, special glasses, and xerography.

Seleucid dynasty (312-64 B.C.), dynasty in southwestern Asia, founded by Seleucus I (c.358-354 B.C.-218 B.C.). A general under Alexander the Great, Seleucus gained control of the eastern part of the Macedonian empire following Alexander's death (323 B.C.). The Seleucids came to rule the area between what is now Turkey and India. In the 200s B.C., the Parthians overran their eastern lands. In the 100s B.C., the Romans began to take over their western regions and brought the dynasty to a close with the occupation of Syria (64 B.C.). The Seleucids helped to spread Greek culture to western Asia.

Seljuks, members of the ruling family of Ouz Turkmen tribes. The warlike and nomadic Seljuks originated in Turkestan, in central Asia, and were named for Seljuk, their first leader. The Seljuks invaded western Asia in the mid-11th century. By 1092 they controlled most of Iran and all of Mesopotamia, Syria, and Palestine. But the Seljuks' territory soon was splintered into small states, one of which, in Anatolia, gave rise to the Ottoman Turks and the modern Turkish state. During the Crusades of the 11th, 12th, and 13th centuries, the Islamic Seljuks defended the Holy Land against the European Christians.

Selkirk Mountains, subdivision of the Columbia Mountains and considered part of the Rocky Mountain system. Mostly in British Columbia, Canada, and touching Idaho and Montana in the United States, the Selkirk Mountains extend for 200 mi (322 km) between the Columbia River, on the west and north, and the Purcell Mountains, on the east. The Selkirk's higher northern peaks include Mt. Sir Sanford (11,590 ft/3,533 m), the range's highest. Glacier and Mt. Revelstoke national parks are also in the northern end. Illecillewaet is the Selkirk's largest glacier.

Selye, Hans (1907-82), Austrian-born Canadian physician best known for his work on the physiological effects of environmental stress, which he suggested might cause certain diseases.
See also: Physiology.

Semantics, study of meaning, concerned both with understanding the relationship of words and symbols to the ideas or objects that they represent and with tracing the histories of meanings and changes that have taken place in them. Semantics is thus a branch both of logic and linguistics. General semantics, propounded primarily by Alfred Korzybski, holds that habits of thought have lagged behind the language and logic of science.
See also: Linguistics.

Semaphore, system of visual signaling using flags or lights to represent letters and numbers. The first such system was introduced by Claude Chappe (1763-1805) used 5-10 mi (8-16 km) apart. Semaphore is still used for signaling between ships and on some railroads.

Semiconductor, solid with an electrical conductivity that lies between the high conductivity of metals and the low conductivity of insulators. A semiconductor device is an electronic element fabricated from crystalline materials, such as silicon or germanium, that in the pure state, are neither good conductors nor good insulators and are unusable for electronic purposes. When certain impurity atoms, such as phosphorus or arsenic, are diffused into the crystal structure of the pure metal, the electrical neutrality is upset, introducing positive or negative charge carriers.

Seminole, last Native American tribe to make peace with the U.S. government. Seminole formed in Florida out of an alliance including refugee Creek from Georgia, native Apalachee and runaway slaves. They fought Andrew Jackson's troops in 1817-18 while Florida was still a Spanish territory. The major Seminole War began in 1835 when the U.S. government ordered their removal to west of the Mississippi. A fierce guerrilla war against overwhelming odds ended in 1842, after which most Seminoles were moved to Oklahoma. However, a small band held out in the Everglades until 1934, when they agreed to a settlement.

Semiramis, mythical Assyrian queen who supposedly founded the city of Babylon. Born of the union of a Syrian youth and a fish goddess, she was raised by doves. She married King Ninus of Assyria, and became queen when he died. During her long reign, she conquered Persia and Egypt. She was overthrown by her son and became a dove. Her story may be based on the life of Sammuramat, regent of Assyria (810-805 B.C.).
See also: Babylon.

Semites, in the Old Testament, the "sons of Shem" (who was the son of Noah). The term now generally applies to speakers of

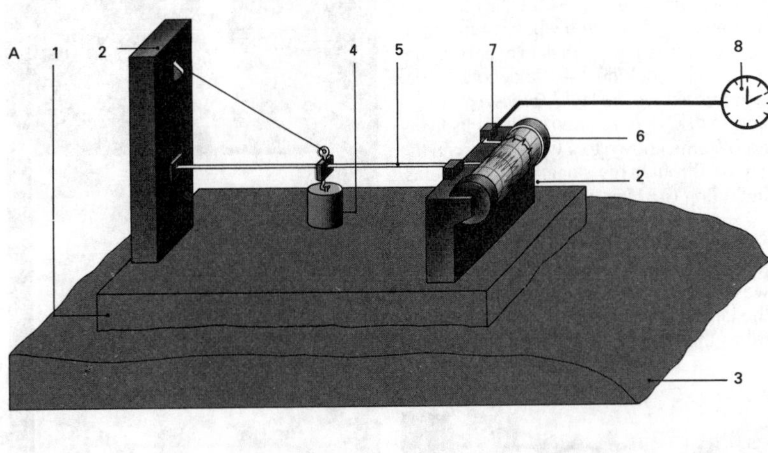

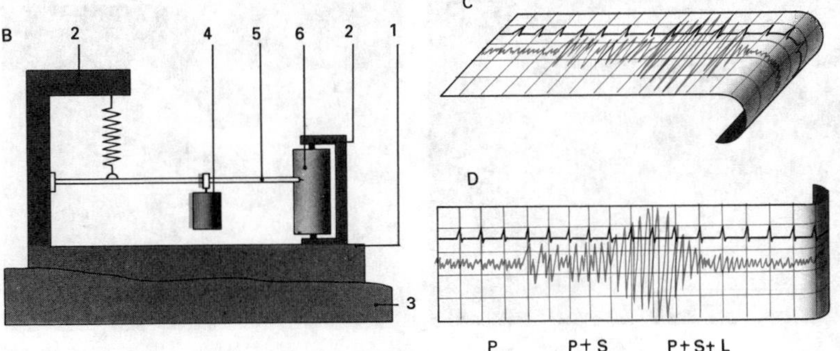

Seismographs locate and record the severity of earthquakes by detecting horizontal (A) or vertical (B) movements of the earth's crust. Both types are attached to concrete bases (1) and pillars (2) that are anchored to bedrock (3). A heavy weight (4) is suspended on a pivoted bar (5) that moves only horizontally (A) or vertically (B). During an earthquake the weight stays still and the rest of the seismograph, including a rotating drum and chart (6), moves with the bedrock. A pen on the suspension bar records the earthquake's primary (P), secondary (S), and long(L) waves on the chart (C, D). A second pen (7) records the time (8).

Semitic languages, including ancient Akkadians, Babylonians, Assyrians, and Phoenicians and modern Arabs and Israelis.
See also: Old Testament.

Semitic languages, group of the Hamito-Semitic language family found in the Near East and North Africa. Most of the group is now extinct; extant members include Hebrew, Arabic and Maltese. A few were written in cuneiform, but most used alphabets. Most of the letters of the Latin alphabet have descended from the North Semitic alphabet, the first fully formed alphabetical writing system.

Semmelweis, Ignaz Philipp (1818-65), Hungarian obstetrician. He was the first doctor to use antiseptic methods in childbirth, after his discovery that puerperal fever was transmitted by obstetricians who had failed to thoroughly clean their hands after performing autopsies on mothers who had died of the disease and then had made examinations of living mothers.
See also: Obstetrics.

Senate, one of the two lawmaking bodies in the United States. It consists of two senators from each state who serve six-year terms. Every two years, one-third of the Senate is elected. The presiding officer of the Senate is the vice president. Both the House of Representatives and the Senate have an equal voice in legislation. The Constitution requires that a U.S. senator be at least 30 years old, be a citizen for at least nine years, and maintain legal residence in the state represented.
See also: Congress of the United States.

Sendak, Maurice (1928-), U.S. illustrator and author of children's books whose inventive renderings both delight and startle. His works include the Caldecott Medal winners *Where the Wild Things Are* (1963) and *In the Night Kitchen* (1970). His lively art became known to a wider public in the 1980s through his stage sets for operas, including *Così fan tutte*.

Seneca, Native American tribe (*O-non-dowanagh*, "people of the great hill") of western New York and eastern Ohio, once the largest nation of the Iroquois League (5 tribes that banded together in the 1400s). The Seneca built their villages on hills above a river and surrounded them with tall wooden stake fences for protection. They lived in large rectangular dwellings (longhouses), 30-50 per village, which gave shelter to several related families. Today most Seneca live on 3 reservations in western New York; they make up the Seneca Nation (a republic) and the Tonawanda Band of Seneca (ruled traditionally by chiefs).

Dakar, Senegal

Seneca, Lucius Annaeus (4 B.C.?-A.D.65), Roman statesman, philosopher, and writer. As Nero's tutor, he restrained the worst excesses of the young emperor. Writing in highly rhetorical, epigrammatic style, Seneca advocated stoicism in his *Moral Letters*, essays, one masterly satire, and nine bloody, intense tragedies. After implication in a conspiracy, he was commanded to commit suicide.
See also: Nero; Rome, Ancient.

Senefelder, Alois (1771-1834), German lithographer. He invented the process of lithography in Munich when he inked and printed some wax crayon marks he had made on a stone slab (c.1796). He published a history of the method in 1818. Senefelder was also a playwright.
See also: Lithography.

Senegal, westernmost country in Africa, formerly part of French West Africa.

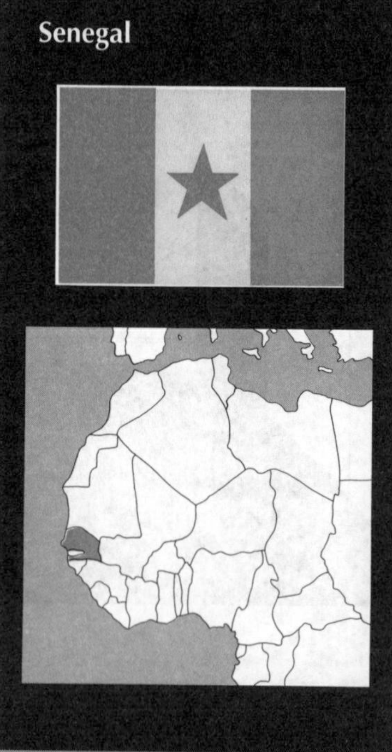

Capital:	Dakar
Area:	75,955 sq mi (196,722 sq km)
Population:	7,400,000
Government:	republic
Independent:	1960
GNP:	U.S.$4,520,000,000
Per capita:	U.S. $630

Land and climate. Bordering on the Atlantic Ocean, Senegal is flanked on the north by Mauritania, on the east by Mali, and on the south by Guinea. The small independent country of Gambia cuts deeply into southern Senegal from the Atlantic coast, forming a long, narrow enclave along the Gambia River. Senegal has an area of 75,750 sq mi (196,192 sq km). The country is mostly plain, with the semidesert Ferlo area in the northeast and savanna grassland elsewhere. In the north, the Senegal River has a broad flood plain which is cultivated. The south is drained by the Gambia, Casamance, Sine, and Saloum rivers. The coastline is sandy in the north and muddy in the south. Climate varies, but is relatively cool along the coast most of the year. Inland temperatures are much higher, especially in the northeast.
People. The people are black African, the most numerous ethnic groups being the Wolof, Fulani, Serer, Toucouleur, and Diola peoples. More than 80% of the people are Muslim. Dakar, the capital, is a modern port city. The official language is French.
Economy. The majority of the people are employed in agriculture, the mainstay of Senegal's economy. Peanuts are the major crop, and peanut processing is the leading industry. Senegal's industrial sector is growing. Limestone and phosphates are important mineral exports, and oil and natural gas deposits have yet to be exploited.
History. Parts of Senegal were within the medieval empires of Ghana, Mali, and Songhai. Under French control and part of French West Africa from 1895, Senegal became part of the Federation of Mali from 1959 to 1960, but declared independence in 1960. Under the presidency of Leopold-Sédar Senghor for two decades following independence, Senegal elected Abdou Diouf to succeed Senghor in 1981. Diouf was reelected in 1988.

Senghor, Léopold Sédar (1906-), Senegalese statesman and poet, Senegal's first president (1960-80), and first black member of the French academy (1984). He became known for his philosophy of *négritude*, a concept of socialism incorporating black African values and rejected the French policy of assimilation.
See also: Senegal.

Senility, general mental and physical deterioration often (but not always) seen in the elderly. Because the term refers to several conditions and causes, experts on the elderly avoid using it. Failure of recent memory, dwelling on the past, episodic confusion, and difficulty in absorbing new information are common conditions associated with so-called senility. Permanent damage can be caused by the brain diseases multi-infarct dementia and Alzheimer's disease.
See also: Alzheimer's disease; Geriatrics.

Senna (*Cassia marilandica*), perennial plant of which the leaves are used for medicinal purposes. Senna is an effective laxative when combined with other herbs.

Sennacherib (d.681 B.C.; r.704-681 B.C.), Assyrian king who succeeded his father, Sargon II. Sennacherib's reign was characterized by war. He put down a revolt by the Elams and the Babylonians led by Merodach-Baladan, the former Babylonian king (703 B.C.). He defeated Egypt and, except for Jerusalem, crushed revolts in Syria and Palestine (701 B.C.). He again fought Babylon and razed the city in 689 B.C. He made Nineveh the Assyrian capital and a magnificent city. Sennacherib was murdered by his sons.
See also: Assyria.

Sennett, Mack (1884-1960), Canadian-born U.S. silent movie director-producer, a pioneer of slapstick humor on the screen. After working with D.W. Griffith, he formed his own Keystone Co. and made over 1,000 short subjects ("shorts") with his Keystone Kops, Bathing Beauties, and stars like Charlie Chaplin, W. C. Fields, and Gloria Swanson.

Senses, media through which stimuli in the environment of an organism act on the organism (external senses); also, the internal senses, which report on the the internal state of the organism (through thirst, hunger, pain, etc.). The organs of sense—the eye ear, skin, etc.—contain specialized cells and nerve endings that communicate with centers in the nervous system. Sense organs may be stimulated by pressure (in touch, hearing, and balance), chemical stimulation (smell, taste), or electromagnetic radiation (vision, heat sensors).

Sensitive plant, small shrub (*Mimosa pudica*) of the pea family. Its leaves and stems curl toward the main stem when touched or exposed to fumes. The plant is native to the tropics of the Western Hemisphere and is grown in greenhouses.

Sensitivity training, technique using group discussion and interaction intended to increase one's awareness of self and others and how one behaves with others. Sensitivity training takes many forms and goes by many names: encounter group, T-group, human relations, and group dynamics training. The group has 8-20 participants. The leader, who is trained in psychotherapy, establishes a psychologically safe environment and encourages participants to speak frankly about their feelings and each other, but remains neutral and outside the discussion. The participants choose the topics and direct the discussion. They examine their reactions to each other and test new ways to communicate. The goal of sensitivity training is to develop trust and improve communication and intrapersonal behavior. The techniques of sensitivity training have been applied to education and to training businesspeople. Sensitivity training was developed at the Esalen Institute, Big Sur, Calif., and was popular in the 1960s.

Seoul (pop. 9,646,000), or Kyongsong, capital, largest city, and industrial and cultural center of South Korea, on the Han River, 25 mi (40 km) east of Inchon, its seaport. It was founded in 1392 as capital of the Yi dynasty, and remained so until 1910. Seoul changed hands several times in the Korean War and suffered great damage. Largely built, it has grown rapidly. The 1988 Summer Olympic Games were held in Seoul.
See also: Korea.

Separation of powers, political theory developed by Montesquieu from his studies of the British constitution, arguing that the arbitrary exercise of government power should be avoided by dividing it between distinct departments: the executive, legislature, and judiciary. This was a basic principle of the Founding Fathers in producing the U.S. Constitution; legislative powers were vested in Congress, judicial powers in the Supreme Court and subsidiary courts, and executive powers in the president and his governmental machinery. Each branch was to have its functions, duties, and authority, and in theory no branch could encroach upon another. In practice there has always been a degree of necessary overlap. The legislature can oppose and impeach members of the executive, the president can veto legislation, and the Supreme Court can adjudicate the actions of the other branches; its members, in turn, are presidential appointees subject to congressional approval. In U.S. history one branch has always tended to dominate others for long periods, but this "checks and balances" ensures that power can and does shift between them.
See also: Montesquieu.

Separatists, in religion, English Christian congregations that sought independence from the state and Established Church, beginning in 1580 with the Norwich Brownists. John Robinson led refugee Separatists in Leyden, the Netherlands, who were later prominent among the Pilgrims.

Sepoy Rebellion, or Indian Mutiny, mutiny of Sepoys (Hindi, "troops") in the Bengal Army of the East India Company. It began at Meerut, near Delhi, in May 1857 and spread over northern India. The immediate cause was the issuing of cartridges greased with the fat of cows (sacred to Hindus) and pigs (unclean to Muslims), but the underlying cause, years of increasing British domination, led to a general revolt that was not suppressed until Mar. 1858. As a result, the British government took over the rule of India.
See also: India.

Septicemia *see:* Blood poisoning.

Septuagint, oldest Greek translation of the Hebrew Old Testament, probably from an older source than any now extant. The Pentateuch was translated in Alexandria at the behest of Ptolemy II (250 B.C.), according to legend by 70 scholars (hence the name *septuagiht*, Latin for "seventy"). It was completed, including the Apocrypha in 130 B.C.
See also: Old Testament.

Sequoia, genus including the two largest trees, the redwood (*Sequoia sempervirens*) and the giant sequoia (*Sequoiadendron giganteum*), both found only in the Pacific Northwest of the United States. Only the bristlecone pine lives longer. The largest living organism in the world is the General Sherman giant sequoia in Sequoia National Park, which is over 270 ft (82 m) high with a circumference at the base of over 100 ft (30.5 m).

Sequoia National Park, park in south-central California (administered with the adjacent Kings Canyon National Park), established in 1890 to preserve the groves of giant sequoia. It covers 402,482 acres (162,879 hectares). Lying in the southern Sierra Nevada, it includes Mount Whitney, the highest U.S. peak outside Alaska.
See also: National Parks.

Sequoyah (c.1770-1843), Cherokee silversmith who devised an alphabet whose 85 characters represented every sound in the Cherokee language, enabling thousands of Cherokee to read and write. The sequoia tree is named for him.

Serapis, Egyptian god, worshipped also in Greece and Rome. He ruled the underworld and the universe and was lord of the Nile. He was a source of fertility and healing and gave the oracles speech. The god may have derived his traits and name from the more ancient gods Osiris and Apis. Osiris was also a fertility god, ruled the underworld, and associated with Isis. Apis was the earthly form of Osiris. The Ptolmaic rulers of Egypt (323-330 B.C.) built temples to Serapis and encouraged his worship.
See also: Mythology.

Serbia, Balkan state, since World War II the easternmost of the six constituent republics of Yugoslavia. The Serbs were Slavs who settled the Balkans from the 600s onward. Stephen Nemanja (r.1168- 96) created the first united kingdom, which became a great empire under Stephen Dushan (r.1331-55), but after the battle of Kosovo (1389) Serbia remained under Turkish rule until independence was restored in 1878. After World War I occupation by Austria, it became the core of the kingdom of Yugoslavia. Serbia (34,00 sq mi/88,060 sq km) is mountainous and mainly agricultural. Its capital is Belgrade.
See also: Yugoslavia.

Serf, medieval peasant generally bound to the land. A serf held the lowest status in the feudal hierarchy and owed allegiance, service, and often certain payments to the lord. The serf retained a number of hereditary rights that were usually determined by local custom. With the development of a money economy and the growth of towns, many serfs escaped or purchased their freedom, and by the 18th century serfdom had largely died out. In Russia and parts of eastern Europe, however, forms of serfdom survived into the 19th century.
See also: Manorialism.

Serval

Sergeant at arms, officer who preserves order in a legislative, judicial, or social organization. The sergeant at arms has the power to execute commands, such as serving legal papers, and to require the body's members to attend meetings. Anyone who disregards the sergeant at arms is guilty of contempt. Each house of the U.S. Congress has a sergeant at arms. The office of sergeant at arms is believed to have been instituted by Richard I of England.

Series, in mathematics, sum of a sequence of terms (numbers or algebraic expressions). The terms in a sequence have a specific relationship and order based on how the terms are formed. The series may be finite (with a definite sum), or infinite. As more terms from an infinite series are added, the sum may approach a value called the limit. Series with a limit are said to converge; those without a limit diverge. Mathematicians have devised formulas and notations to express the values of a series and individual terms in a series.
See also: Mathematics.

Serkin, Rudolf (1903-91), Bohemian-born U.S. pianist. He studied with Arnold Schoenberg in Vienna, made his U.S. debut in 1933, and joined the Curtis Institute of Music, Philadelphia, in 1939. A noted Beethoven interpreter, he played in concerts all over the world. His son Peter (1947-) is also a prominent pianist.

Sermon on the Mount *see:* Beatitudes; Golden Rule.

Serpentine, hydrous magnesium silicate mineral, $Mg_3(Si_2O_5)(OH)_4$, that occurs in 2 forms: chrisotile, the fibrous variety which is the primary source of asbestos, and antigorite, the flaky variety. Serpentine, usually green, may also be black, red, yellow, gray, or white. It is used as an indoor building or decorative stone or as a gemstone. Serpentine is widely distributed and is quarried in Quebec, the USSR, South Africa, and the United States.

Serra, Junípero (1713-84), Spanish Franciscan missionary who founded 9 of California's 21 missions. Serra was ordained (1738) and taught philosophy on the island of Majorca, Spain. He traveled to Mexico City (1749) and then to Sierra Gorda, Mexico to help staff the mission there (1750-59). He joined Gaspar de Portolá's expedition to upper California (1769) and established the mission of San Diego de Alcalá, now the city of San Diego. Between 1770 and 1782 Serra ordered the founding of 8 more missions, including San Luis Obispo and San Juan Capistrano.
See also: Franciscans.

Serum, clear yellowish fluid that separates from blood, lymph, and other body fluids when they clot. It contains water, proteins, fat, minerals, hormones, and urea. Serum therapy involves injecting serum (obtained from humans or horses) containing antibodies (globulins) that can destroy particular pathogens. Occasionally injected serum gives rise to an allergic reaction known as serum sickness; a second injection of the same serum may induce anaphylaxis (hypersensitivity).
See also: Gamma globulin; Plasma.

Serval (*Felis capensis*), large, black spotted, nocturnal wildcat of Africa. It has long legs, a small head, and pointed ears. Its prey is mainly rodents and sometimes birds, reptiles, or insects.

Servetus, Michael (Miguel Serveto; 1511-53), Spanish theologian and physician whose religious work *Christianismi restitutio* (1553) contains the earliest known description of the pulmonary circulation of blood. As a theologian, Servetus antagonized Roman Catholics and Protestants alike by denying the doctrines of the trinity (*De trinitatus erroribus*, 1531), transubstantiation, and original sin. He eventually embraced pantheism, believing that a supreme intelligence orders the universe. He was tried for heresy by the Inquisition (1553) and condemned to death, but escaped from prison. Passing through Geneva, Switzerland several months later, Servetus was arrested on the orders of John Calvin, retried, and burned at the stake.
See also: Inquisition.

Serviceberry, also called shadbush, shadblow, or Juneberry, wild rose tree or shrub found in many parts of North America and in the Mediterranean region and eastern Asia. It bears clusters of small white flowers and blue fruits.

Service industries, commercial, government, or nonprofit occupations performed without involving the sale of commodities. Service industries may be classified as several types: business services, including advertising, bookkeeping, or banking; personal services which might include recreation, travel, housekeeping, and beauty or barbershops; art, including theaters and museums; the professions, including legal, medical, or educational services; and government.
Economists consider service occupations an indicator of a country's economic development: the greater the growth, the more advanced the nation. In the late 1950s services accounted for 25% of the U.S. gross national product, and in the 1980s for 66%.

Servomechanism, or feedback control system, automatic device that detects and corrects errors and maintains constant performance of a mechanism, for example an automatic pilot.
See also: Automation.

Sesame (*Sesamum indicum*), tropical plant cultivated mainly in China and India for its flat seeds; also, the seeds themselves. Sesame seeds yield an oil used as a salad or cooking oil and in margarine, cosmetics, and ointments. The residue left after oil extraction is used as a cattle feed and fertilizer.

Sesshu (1419-1506), Japanese Buddhist monk and landscape artist. Combining Chinese ink-painting technique with Japanese aesthetics, Sesshu's style is characterized by strong composition, straightforward forms, and vigorous brushstrokes. He produced his greatest works, including screens, scrolls, and religious paintings, after 1469, following a period of study in China.

Sessions, Roger (1896-1985), U.S. composer, winner of the Pulitzer Prize for music (1982). He was professor of music at the University of California, Berkeley (1945) and Princeton University (1935-45, 1953-65). Sessions's compositions include operas, symphonies, piano sonatas, and chorus music. He is best known for *The Black Maskers* (1923) and *Concerto for Orchestra* (1981). His written works include *The Musical Experience of Composer, Performer and Listener* (1950) and his collected essays, *Roger Sessions on Music* (1979).

Sessions, William Steele (1930-), U.S. Federal Bureau of Investigation (FBI) director since 1987. After practicing law, he worked as a criminal prosecutor for the U.S. Justice Department (1969-71), actively prosecuting Vietnam draft evaders. He was named by President Richard Nixon as a district attorney for western Texas

(1971-74) and by President Gerald Ford as a U.S. district judge (1974-87).
See also: Federal Bureau of Investigations.

Seth, or **Set**, in Egyptian mythology, god of evil, represented with an ass's head and a pig's snout. Originally a royal deity, he came to personify evil as killer of Osiris, god of goodness. Osiris's son Horus fought and killed Seth.
See also: Mythology.

Seti I, Egyptian ruler of the 19th dynasty who reigned about 1303-1290 B.C. Seti I established his seat of government at Memphis and directed several military campaigns into Syria against the Hittites. He built his mortuary temple at Abydos in the Valley of the Kings and continued work on the temple of Amon at Karnak. Seti I was the father of Ramses II.
See also: Egypt, Ancient.

Seton, Saint Elizabeth Ann, or Mother Seton (1774-1821), first native-born U.S. saint. A devout Episcopalian, she was widowed at 28 with five children. In 1805, she converted to Catholicism. She opened an elementary school (1808), regarded as the basis of the U.S. parochial school system, and in 1813 founded the first U.S. religious society, the Sisters of Charity. She was canonized in 1975. Her feast day is Jan. 4.

Setter, 3 breeds of long-haired dog used in bird hunting: the English, the Gordon, and the Irish setter. Classified in the United States as sporting dogs, setters are derived from the medieval setting spaniel. They have long heads and tails, silky coats, and hanging ears. A setter is trained to locate game by smell, come to a point with its nose directed toward the bird, and retrieve the game after the shot.

Set theory, branch of mathematics or symbolic (mathematical) logic in which systems are analyzed by membership in and exclusion from *sets.* A set is any specified collection of *elements* or *members.* In the notation of set theory, members of a set are enclosed in braces as, {a,b,d,x}. Alternatively, a rule defining inclusion in the set may appear in braces. The expression {xx is a U.S. state bordered by 3 or more other states} defines the set of all U.S. states bordered by 3 or more other states; this is a *finite set,* having a definite number of members. The set of all positive even numbers is an example of an *infinite set,* one with an infinite number of members. It might be represented as {2,4,6,8,...} or as {xx/2 is an integer greater than 0}. *Null sets,* those with no members (e.g., all U.S. presidents who are female, nonwhite, or non-Christian) are represented as { }. Sets that have exactly the same members (the set of all U.S. presidents who have served more than 2 terms, the set of all presidents crippled by polio) are said to be *equal sets,* while those with the same number of members but not necessarily the identical membership are *equivalent.* Set A is a *subset* of set B if all of the members of set A are contained in set B. (The set of all equal sets is thus a subset of the set of all equivalent sets, but not vice versa). The *union* of 2 sets A and B (A B) is the combined membership of those 2 sets. The *intersection* of sets A and B ($A \cap B$) is the set of those elements belonging to both set A and set B. *Disjoint* sets have no common members and thus their intersection is a null or empty set (the set of all women, the set of all U.S. presidents). If A is a subset of B, the *complement* of A consists of all members of B not in A. Set theory, which owes much to the techniques of symbolic logic established by 19th-century English mathematician George Boole, was developed by 19th-century German mathematician Georg Cantor. It is of particular importance in representing logical relationships and approaches to algebraic solutions.
See also: Mathematics.

Settlement house, neighborhood center established to provide social services to inner-city communities and usually staffed by social workers. Samuel A. Barnett, an English clergyman, founded the first settlement house, Toynbee Hall (1884) in London, to restore the neighborhood order disrupted by the Industrial Revolution. The original U.S. settlement house was University Settlement, founded (1886) by Stanton Coit, in New York City. Jane Addams's Hull House in Chicago began (1889) as a settlement. Settlement house programs include counseling, rehabilitation for the disabled, child welfare, athletics and recreation, hobby and interest groups, classes in citizenship and English, and manual training. Originally privately funded, settlement house services were forerunners of tax-supported public welfare programs. There are now some 300 settlement houses in the United States overseen by the United Neighborhood Centers of America.
See also: Hull House.

Seurat, Georges (1859-91), French painter, one of a small group representing neoimpressionism or postimpressionism. Interested in color both scientifically and artistically, he invented pointillism, in which discrete points of color are placed to create patterns that are perceived at a distance as complex tones. His works include *A Sunday Afternoon on the Island of La Grande Jatte* (1884-46)
See also: Impressionism.

Seuss, Dr. (Theodor Seuss Geisel; 1904-), U.S. author-illustrator of children's books. His many imaginative verse tales—*Horton Hears a Who* (1954), *How the Grinch Stole Christmas* (1957)—and humorous pictorial fantasies are tremendously popular. In 1984 he was acknowledged by the Pulitzer committee for having contributed for nearly half a century to the education and reading enjoyment of U.S. children.

Sevastopol (pop. 335,000), Black Sea port of the Crimea peninsula in the Ukraine, southeast European USSR. Now a major Soviet naval base, industrial city, and railroad terminal with lumber milling and shipbuilding industries, the city suffered long sieges in the Crimean War (349 days; 1854-55) and World War II (8 months; 1941-42). Sevastopol is situated near the site of the ancient Greek colony Chersonesus, founded in 421 B.C. It eventually became part of the Roman Empire (first century B.C.) and Byzantine Empire (4th century A.D.).

Seven Cities of Cibola *see:* Cibola, Seven Cities of.

Seven seas, archaic collective term for the world's large bodies of water. The term is usually thought to refer to the Arctic, Antarctic, North and South Atlantic, Indian, and North and South Pacific oceans.

Seventh-day Adventists, Christian religious group, organized in 1863 in both Europe and the United States, who believe that Christ will return in person. They observe the Sabbath on Saturday, the seventh day of the week. There are about 4 million members throughout the world.
See also: Christianity.

Seven Weeks' War (Austro-Prussian War, June 16-August 23, 1866), conflict between Austria (and its German allies), led by Field Marshal Lieutenant von Benedek, and Prussia (and its Italian ally) under Helmuth Karl von Moltke, over control of the Danish duchies of Schleswig and Holstein. Austria declared war on Prussia on June 14, 1866, and the decisive battle was fought July 3 at Königgrätz in Bohemia, resulting in a Prussian victory. The war ended formally on Aug. 23 with the Treaty of Prague. It gave Prussia undisputed leadership of the new North German Confederacy, effectively ending Austrian influence in German affairs.

Detail from A Sunday Afternoon on the Island of La Grande Jatte *by George Seurat*

Seven Wonders of the Ancient World, seven magnificent structures of the ancient world, as listed by Greek scholars. The oldest and only to survive are the pyramids of Egypt. The others were the Hanging Gardens of Babylon, the 30-ft (9-m) statue of Zeus at Olympia, the great temple of Artemis at Ephesus, the mausoleum at Halicarnassus, the Colossus of Rhodes, and the Pharos lighthouse of Alexandria.

Seven Years' War (1756-63), war between Austria, France, Russia, Saxony, Sweden (from 1757), and Spain (after 1762) on the one side and Britain, Prussia, and Hanover on the other. In the United States the struggle centered on colonial rivalry between Britain and France, and formed part of the French and Indian Wars. In Europe the main dispute was between Austria and Prussia for supremacy in Germany. Austria's Maria Theresa aimed to recover Silesia (lost in the War of the Austrian Succession). This provoked Prussia to attack Saxony and Bohemia. Although severely pressed, the Prussians avoided complete defeat. By the treaties of Hubertusberg and Paris (1763), Britain emerged as the leading colonial power and Prussia as a major European force.

Severn, River, Britain's longest river, 220 mi (354 km) long. It rises in eastern Wales and flows east and south into the Bristol Channel. The Severn Bridge is one of the world's longest suspension bridges.

Sevier, John (1745-1815), U.S. pioneer and first governor of Tennessee (1796-80, 1803-09).He was prominent in the Carolina Campaign of the Revolutionary War and became head of the temporary state of Franklin (1785-88). He represented Tennessee in the U.S. Congress (1789-91, 1811-15).
See also: Franklin, State of.

Seville (pop. 668,400), city of southwest Spain, capital of Seville province, and an important industrial center and port on the Guadalquivir River. Seville produces tobacco, machinery, and perfume, among other products, and exports wine and olives. The city is famous for its historic buildings, including the Gothic cathedral (1401-1519), and Holy Week processions. It was the birthplace of the painters Diego Velázquez and Bartolomé Murillo.
See also: Spain.

Sèvres, Treaty of (1920), peace pact between the Allies and Turkey after World War I, signed at Sèvres, France. It redistributed almost all of the Turkish Ottoman Empire, leaving only Istanbul and Anatolia under Turkish control. Though signed by the representatives of Sultan Mohammed VI, the treaty was never ratified by the Turkish National Assembly. After the overthrow of the government by Kemal Atatürk and the nationalists (1922), the Treaty of Sèvres was superseded by the Treaty of Lausanne (1923), which offered Turkey more acceptable terms.
See also: World War I.

Sewage, liquid and semisolid wastes from dwellings and offices, industrial wastes, and surface and storm waters. Sewage systems collect the sewage, transport and treat it, then discharge it into rivers, lakes, or the sea. Vaulted sewers had been developed by the Romans, but from the Middle Ages until the mid-19th century sewage flowed through the open gutters of cities, constituting a major health hazard. Later sewage was discharged into storm-water drains that were developed into sewers. Because the dumping of large amounts of untreated sewage into rivers led to a serious water pollution, modern treatment methods arose, at least for major cities. An early solution (still sometimes practiced) was sewage farming, in which raw sewage was used as fertilizer. Noting that natural watercourses can purify a moderate amount of sewage, sanitary engineers imitated natural conditions by allowing atmospheric oxidation of the organic matter by the activated-sludge process, in which compressed air is passed through a sewage tank, where the sludge is decomposed by the many microorganisms that it contains. A by-product is sludge gas, chiefly methane, burned as fuel to help power the treatment plant. Sedimentation is carried out before and after decomposition; the filtered solids are buried, incinerated, or dried for fertilizer. Dwellings not connected to the sewers have their own septic tanks.

Sewall, Samuel (1652-1730), colonial American politician and jurist best known as one of the judges in the Salem, Mass., witchcraft trials (1692). He was also justice of the colony superior court (1692-1718) and chief justice of the province (1718-25). A liberal, Sewall later publicly repented his part in the witchcraft trials, in which 19 people were condemned to death. His writings include an early antislavery tract *The Selling of Joseph* (1700), *A Memorial Relating to the Kennebeck Indians* (1721), and his 3-volume *Diary* (1878-82).
See also: Salem witchcraft trials.

Seward, William Henry (1801-72), U.S. politician famous for his purchase of Alaska from Russia in 1867. A prominent antislavery senator, he was appointed secretary of state by President Abraham Lincoln in 1861. He did much to keep Britain out of the Civil War. Seward survived an assassination attempt by an accomplice of John Wilkes Booth, and served as President Andrew Johnson's secretary of state.

Sewing, use of a needle and thread to attach, repair, fasten, or decorate fabric or other materials. Sewing dates from the second Stone Age period, when stone or bone needles and hair or animal ligament thread were used to stitch pieces of skin together. Sewing now may be accomplished by hand or machine. The most basic hand-sewing stitches are basting, running, slipstitch, blindstitch, overcast, and catch stitch. Isaac Merritt Singer, improving on earlier inventions, produced the first sewing machine practical for home use (1851). Singer's machine used a top thread with a bobbin thread, allowing continuous stitching. Modern machines commonly provide 3 types of stitches: straight, zigzag, and embroidery. Mechanical sergers can sew, trim, and finish straight seams in a single operation.

Sewing machine, machine for sewing cloth, leather, or books. There are two main types: chainstitch machines, using a needle and only one thread, with a hook that pulls each looped stitch through the next, and lockstitch machines, using two threads, one through the needle eye and the other interlocking with the first in the material, from a bobbin/shuttle system. Chain-stitch machines—the first to be invented, by Barthélemy Thimmonier (1793-1859)—are now used chiefly to make sacks or bags. The lockstitch machines now in general use are based on the one invented by Elias Howe (1846). Isaac M. Singer invented the foot treadle and the presser foot (1850), which holds the fabric down. Zigzag machines differ from ordinary straight-stitch machines in having variously shaped cams that move the needle from side to side. Almost all U.S. machines are electrically powered, but foot-treadle machines are common elsewhere.

Sex (sexual behavior), term covering a wide range of behavior derived from or analogous to sexuality and sexual drive. To the psychologist "sex" and "sexual behavior" are used in connection with human drives linked to reproduction, including fantasies, sensations, etc. To the psychoanalyst, sexual behavior has its roots in infantile sexuality as well as instinct.

Sex education, study of human sexuality and how it is acquired and expressed. Sex education begins in early childhood when children first show curiosity about their sexuality and body processes. Until the mid-20th century, satisfaction of that curiosity was solely a function of a child's parents, and information from outside the family was discouraged. Today children may receive sexual information from their peers, the media, churches, or schools and rely less on traditional sources. Sex education has generated controversy between those who believe that home sex education may be inadequate and those who believe it may encourage premarital sex or fail to teach moral responsibility. Many sex education curricula are available to schools and other agencies, beginning with programs for kindergarten and continuing through high school. They cover aspects of human sexuality including social, physical, and psychological aspects, rudimentary anatomy, marriage, and parenthood.
See also: Calderone, Mary Streichen.

Sextant, instrument for navigation, invented in 1730, superseding the astrolabe. The sextant is named for its shape ($^1/_6$ of a circle). A fixed telescope is pointed at the horizon, and a radial arm bearing a mirror is moved against an arc graduated in

degrees. The mirror reflects an image of a known star or the sun down the telescope to coincide with the image of the horizon. The angular elevation of the star, with the exact time, gives the latitude. The air sextant is a similar instrument, usually periscopic, designed for use in aircraft; it has an artificial horizon, generally a bubble level.
See also: Navigation.

Sexton, Anne (1928-74), U.S. poet. Her work was largely confessional and explicitly personal (*To Bedlam and Part Way Back*, 1960; *Live or Die*, 1966, Pulitzer Prize). *Transformations* (1971) is her ironic retelling of Grimms' fairytales. Sexton struggled with mental illness, ultimately committing suicide.

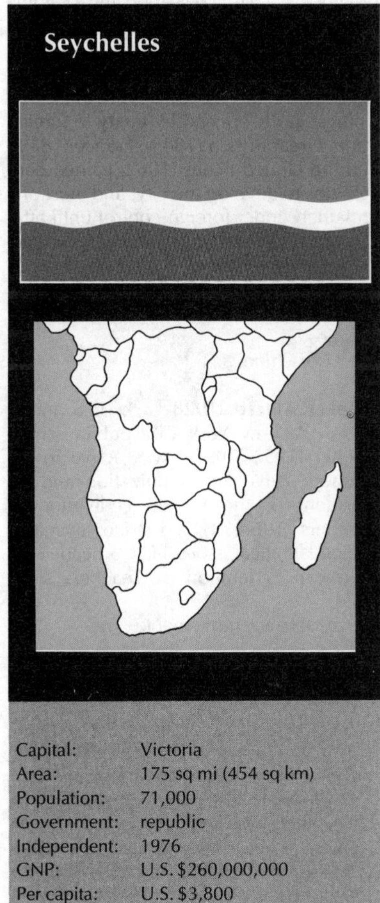

Seychelles, African republic consisting of about 85 islands in the Indian Ocean 1000 mi (1600 km) east of Kenya. Seychelles's total area is 175 sq mi (453 sq km) scattered over 400,000 sq mi (1 million sq km) of ocean. The climate is tropical. Victoria, on Mahé Island, is the capital and only city. Most of the population is Roman Catholic, of African and French descent, and speaks Creole, a French patois. Tourism, construction, agriculture, and fishing are the primary occupations. Cinnamon, coconuts and copra, vanilla, livestock, and poultry are the chief products. Portuguese explorer Vasco da Gama discovered Seychelles (1502), and French planters began colonizing the area in 1768. Britain controlled the islands from 1794 to 1976, when they achieved independence. A one-party government was established in 1979.

Seymour, Horatio (1810-86), U.S. politician. As Democratic governor of New York (1862-64), he declared the Emancipation Proclamation unconstitutional and opposed national conscription, although he encouraged voluntary enlistment. He was defeated by Ulysses S. Grant in the 1868 presidential election.
See also: Copperheads.

Seymour, Jane (1509?-37), third wife of England's Henry VIII (from 1536). She died soon after the birth of her son, Edward VI.

Seyss-Inquart, Arthur von (1892-1946), Austrian Nazi leader, governor of Austria (1938-39), and deputy governor of Poland (1939-40). As a high commissioner for the Netherlands (1940-45), his cruelty was notorious. He was executed for war crimes.
See also: Nazism.

Shabuot *see:* Shavuot.

Shackleton, Sir Ernest Henry (1874-1922), Irish explorer who commanded 3 Antarctic expeditions (1907, 1914, 1921), the first of which came within 97 mi (156 km) of the South Pole and located the south magnetic pole. His 1914 expedition was marked by an open-boat crossing from Elephant Island to South Georgia Island and a winter traverse of that island's crest after his ship was crushed by ice. Written works include *Heart of the Antarctic* (1909), *South: The Story of Shackleton's 1914-1917 Expedition* (1919), and *Adventure* (1928).
See also: Antarctica.

Shad, deep-bodied food fish of the herring family (genus *Alosa*), which grows to about 3 lb (1.4 kg) and 2 ft (61 cm). Native to Atlantic waters from Newfoundland to Florida, the shad was successfully introduced to Pacific waters (c.1871). Characterized by bluish coloring with silver sides and a spineless upper fin, it swims up freshwater rivers to spawn. Some shad is smoked and sold as kippers. The roe is valued as a substitute for caviar.

Shadow, reduction of light on an area caused when an opaque object interrupts the light source. The shadow appears on the side of the body away from the source; the brighter the light, the darker and crisper the shadow seems. A very dark shadow, called an umbra, occurs when the light is completely obstructed. A lighter area surrounding the umbra, called the penumbra, occurs when the light source is larger than the interrupting object, allowing some light to shine beyond it. A solar eclipse is an example of this effect.

Shadow matter, in science, term to describe a theoretical form of matter that neither reflects nor absorbs light and interacts with ordinary matter only through the force of gravity. The existence of shadow matter (a type of dark matter) has not been proved, but physicists theorize that as much as 90% of the mass of the universe may be comprised of this kind of invisible particle.
See also: Dark matter.

Shafter, William Rufus (1835-1906), U.S. soldier. In the Spanish-American War, he led the U.S. expeditionary force that eventually gained the surrender of Santiago, Cuba (1898).
See also: Spanish-American War.

Shaftesbury, 3 important English earls, each bearing the name **Anthony Ashley Cooper**. The **1st earl** (1621-83) was a founder of the Whig Party and a staunch Protestant. After supporting both Cromwell and the Restoration, he became Lord Chancellor (1672) but was dismissed (1673) for supporting the Test Act. He then built up the Whig opposition to Charles II, supporting the duke of Monmouth, the pretender, and opposing James II's successor. He was acquitted of treason (1681) but fled to the Netherlands (1682). The **3rd earl** (1671-1713), grandson of the 1st, was a moral philosopher and pupil of John Locke. He aimed to found an ethical system based on an innate moral sense. The **7th earl** (1801-85) was a politician and leading evangelical Christian who promoted legislation to improve conditions in mines and factories and supported movements for better housing and schools.

Shah (Persian, "king"), title borne by the rulers of Middle Eastern and some Asian countries. It is used especially to refer to rulers of Iran (Persia) until 1979.

Shah Jahan (1592-1666), fifth mogul emperor of India (1628-58), under whose rule the Moguls achieved their cultural peak. He built New Delhi and is best known for construction of lavish buildings, particularly the Taj Mahal (1632-45) at Agra, a tomb for his wife, Mumtaz Mahall. He was deposed (1658) by his son Aurangzeb and imprisoned at Agra until his death.
See also: India.

Shahn, Ben (1898-1969), Lithuanian-born U.S. artist whose realistic works treated social and political themes. Influenced by Diego Rivera and painters of the Parisian school, Shahn's style is characterized by harsh colors and simplified linear forms. Shahn created his own murals, posters, advertising art, and photography. He is particularly known for his series of political paintings on the Dreyfuss Affair, the Sacco-Vanzetti trial, and the Tom Mooney labor disputes. His lectures on art were published in *The Shape of Content* (1957).

Shah Namah *see:* Firdausi.

Shakers, originally an abusive term for the United Society of Believers in Christ's Second Appearing, a religious sect whose members shook with ecstatic emotion in their worship. Originating among the

Quakers of England, they were brought by "Mother" Ann Lee to the United States in 1774, where they formed celibate communes that flourished until the mid-19th century. There are still a few remaining Shakers living in Maine and New Hampshire.

William Shakespeare by Martin Droeshout

Shakespeare, William (1564-1616), English playwright and poet, considered the greatest dramatist ever as well as the finest English language poet.
Shakespeare was born of middle class parents in Stratford-upon-Avon where he spent his school years. At 18 years of age he married Anne Hathaway, with whom he had 3 children. In the years 1594 to 1608, Shakespeare was heavily involved in the world of London theater as a stockholder and an actor in the Lord Chamberlain's Company—renamed the King's Men in 1603—which performed at the Globe Theater. He also wrote an average of 2 plays a year in this period, including several comedies and virtually all of his famous tragedies.
All of Shakespeare's plays have been grouped into 4 periods reflecting general phases of his artistic development. In the first period (1590-94) he wrote comedies, histories, and tragedies. *The Comedy of Errors, Henry VI* (parts I, II, and III) *Richard III, The Taming of the Shrew, Titus Andronicus, The Two Gentlemen of Verona,* and *King John* were all written in the first period.
The second period (1595-1600) consists primarily of historical drama and romantic comedies. Included in this period are *A Midsummer Night's Dream, Richard II, Love's Labour's Lost, Romeo and Juliet, The Merchant of Venice, Henry IV* (parts I and II), *As You Like It, Julius Caesar, Much Ado About Nothing, Twelfth Night,* and *The Merry Wives of Windsor.*
Shakespeare's great tragedies were written in the third period (1601-08). At the height of his artistry his writing now moved back and forth easily between verse and prose in portraying his characters. *Hamlet, All's Well That End's Well, Measure for Measure, Othello, King Lear, Troilus and Cressida, Macbeth, Timon of Athens, Pericles, Antony and Cleopatra,* and *Coriolanus* all were written in this period.
In the fourth and final period (1609-13) Shakespeare wrote 3 comedies and a history. They are *Cymbeline, The Winter's Tale, The Tempest,* and *Henry VIII.*
Shakespeare began to write poems between 1592 and 1594 partly because poetry was considered to be of greater importance than drama by the Elizabethans. His 2 long narrative poems were *Venus and Adonis* (1593) and *The Rape of Lucrece* (1594).
The sonnets were probably written over a period of several years. The first 126 are addressed to a young nobleman and the next 26 to a young woman with whom Shakespeare may have been having a love affair. The common theme of the sonnets concerns the destructive effects of time, the quickness of physical decay, and the loss of beauty, vigor, and love. Although the poems celebrate life, they do so with a keen sense of death.
Shakespeare shaped and used language with great power. He invented, changed, and borrowed words from other languages and employed rhetorical devices such as alliteration and repetition to produce dramatic effect.
Shakespeare's plays and poems have been the subject of critics and scholars who have examined every aspect of the man himself, his works, and his influence. His works have long been a required component of liberal education. His brilliant portrayal of historical figures and events has caused many people to visualize the likes of Julius Caesar, Mark Antony, and Cleopatra not as they have been described in history books but as Shakespeare envisioned them.
Shakespeare was knowledgeable in a wide variety of subjects, including music, the law, the Bible, military science, the stage, art, politics, history, hunting, woodcraft, and sports. He displayed a keen sense of human nature with vivid characters, including kings, pickpockets, drunkards, generals, hired killers, and philosophers. His genius seems all the more amazing considering that as far as scholars have been able to determine, Shakespeare had no experience in any field other than theater.

Shale, fine-grained sedimentary rock formed by compaction and drying-out of mud (clay and silt). Shales are sometimes rich in fossils and are laminated (they split readily into layers, or laminae). Their metamorphism produces slate.

Shallot, edible hardy perennial (*Allium ascalonicum*) of the Liliaceae family, used in cooking. The plant has edible stems, bulbs, and leaves, and grows like garlic or onions. The bulb, composed of cloves attached to a common disk, is green, shading to lavender with a thick grayish skin. Shallots probably developed by cultivation as early as the 9th century.

Shamanism, primitive religious system centered around a shaman, or medicine man. (The word *shaman* is from the language of the Tungus of Siberia). In a trance state, he is believed to be possessed by spirits who speak and act through him; he is expected to cure the sick, protect the tribe, and foretell the future, among other mystical activities.
See also: Religion.

Shamir, Yitzhak (1915-), prime minister of Israel (since 1983), successor to Menachem Begin. Born in Poland, he went to Palestine in 1935, where he joined the underground military organization Irgun Zvai Leumi and later the more radical Stern Gang in combating British rule. From 1955 to 1965 he worked for the Israel intelligence agency. As foreign minister (1980-83), he was identified as a strong supporter of Begin's policies. In 1984 and 1988 his Likud Party formed coalition governments with the Labour Party.
See also: Israel.

Shamrock, popular name in Ireland for several leguminous plants, the trifoliate leaves of which were cited by St. Patrick as a symbol of the Christian Trinity. Among the plants called shamrock are the wood sorrel (*Oxalis acetosella*), white clover (*Trifolium repens*), and black medic (*Medicago lupulina*).

Shang dynasty, first historic Chinese dynasty, traditionally said to have lasted from 1766 to 1122 B.C. The legendary founder was T'ang. The Shang civilization was agriculturally and technically advanced and is famed for the artistic quality of its bronzes.
See also: China.

Shanghai (pop. 6,880,000), China's largest city, in the southeastern region of Jiangsu province. It is a major seaport and a leading commercial and industrial center, producing textiles, iron and steel, ships, petroleum products, and a wide range of manufactured goods. In 1842 it was one of the first Chinese ports opened by treaty to foreign trade. Great Britain (1843), France (1849), and the United States (1862) gained concessions to develop the city, and most of it remained under foreign control until after World War II. The British and U.S. concessions were renounced in 1945. Shanghai is now China's film capital and the home of 190 research institutes, colleges, and universities.
See also: China.

Shanker, Albert (1928-), U.S. labor leader. A New York City public school teacher (1952-59), he was active in the teachers' drive for unionization and, as president of the United Federation of Teachers (1964-74), led strikes over pay and pedagogical issues. He has headed the American Federation of Teachers since 1974.
See also: Labor movement.

Shannon River, chief river in Ireland and longest (240 mi/386 km) in the British Isles. It rises in northern Cavan county, Ulster, and flows south and west through several loughs (lakes) into the Atlantic Ocean. From Limerick westward, it is navigable by all but the largest vessels.

Shapiro, Karl Jay (1913-), U.S. poet and literary critic. His early poetry, such as *V-Letter and Other Poems* (1944; Pulitzer Prize), shows the influence of W. H. Auden and was admired for its verbal conceits. Later work, such as *The Bourgeois Poet* (1964), became more Whitmanesque. His *Collected Poems: 1948-1978* appeared in 1978.

Shapley, Harlow (1885-1972), U.S. astronomer whose work on pulsating stars (Cepheid variables) and globular clusters established the position of the sun in the galaxy and the size of the Milky Way. Shapley discovered 2 star systems in distant galaxies and was director of the Harvard Observatory (1921-52). Shapley's written works include *Star Clusters* (1930), *Gala-*

xies (1943), and *Cosmic Facts and the Human Response* (1957).
See also: Astronomy.

Sharaku (fl. late 1700s), professional name of a Japanese woodcut artist known for color portraits of Kabuki actors, produced in 1794 and 1795. The actors, shown dressed for their roles, have enlarged heads and exaggerated expressions. The backgrounds are plain. Little is known about the artist.

Sharecropping, arrangement whereby a share of a tenant farmer's yearly land yield (usually 50%) went to the landowner in lieu of rent. The tenant provided the labor, while the landowner provided land, equipment, and often loans to buy seed. The system was notorious for its abuses.

Sharif, Nawaz (1949-), prime minister of Pakistan (1990-), president of the Islamic Democratic Alliance (IDA), a right-wing Pakistani coalition. He has shown special interest in accelerating Pakistan's economy while at the same time reducing the country's dependence on foreign aid. He served as Punjab's finance minister under former President Zia ul-Haq (1981).

Shark, any of about 250 species of cartilaginous fishes of marine and fresh waters, order Selachii. Sharks, with the related rays and chimeras, have a skeleton formed entirely of cartilage rather than bone. Other distinguishing features are that the gills open externally through a series of gill slits, rather than through a single operculum, and reproduction is by internal fertilization, unlike that of bony fishes. The body is fusiform, and the upper lobe of the tail is usually better developed than the lower lobe. Sharks swim by sinuous movements of the whole body; there is no swim bladder, so they must swim constantly to avoid sinking. All are extremely fast swimmers and active predators. Despite a universal reputation for unprovoked attack, only 27 out of the 250 known species have been definitely implicated in attacks on humans.

Kinds of sharks:
1. porbeagle shark
2. mako shark
3 .thresher shark
4. blue shark

Shar-pei, dog of Chinese origin first bred from c.200 B.C. as a guard or fighting dog. The Shar-pei is characterized by a compact body, small flat ears, and a loose, wrinkled skin. It grows 16-20 in (41-51 cm) high and weighs 35-55 lb (16-25 kg). The coat is short, of a solid color, and may be tan, black, cream, or red.

Shavuot, Jewish holiday known as the Festival of Weeks, held on the sixth and seventh days of the month of Sivan (May-June). Originally an agricultural celebration of the harvest, it was observed by presenting the season's first fruits and bread baked from the first wheat at the Temple in Jerusalem. Later it came to commemorate the receipt of the Ten Commandments.
See also: Passover.

Shaw, Anna Howard (1847-1919), English-born U.S. leader of women's suffrage and temperance movements. Shaw became a Methodist minister (1880) and a medical doctor (1886). An associate of Susan B. Anthony, she worked for the passage of an amendment to the United States Constitution that would secure voting rights for women. Shaw served as president of the National American Woman Suffrage Association (1904-15).
See also: Woman suffrage.

Shaw, George Bernard (1856-1950), Irish dramatist, critic, and political propagandist whose witty plays contained serious philosophical and social ideas. Born in Dublin, he moved to London (after 1876), where he became a music and theater critic and a leader of the Fabian Society. He began writing his brilliantly witty, ironical, and polemical comedies in the 1890s. Success came with such plays as *Major Barbara* (1905), *Caesar and Cleopatra* (1906; written 1899), *Androcles and the Lion* (1912), and *Pygmalion* (1913; adapted as the musical *My Fair Lady*, 1956). He lost popularity for his opposition to World War I, but regained it with *Back to Methuselah* (1921). *Saint Joan* (1921), his greatest success, was followed by the 1925 Nobel Prize in literature.

Shaw, Robert Gould (1837-63), Union hero of the U.S. Civil War. Colonel Shaw led the first regiment of black troops (54th Massachusetts volunteers) to be mustered in a free state. He was killed attacking Fort Wagner, S.C. (July 18, 1863). The heroic deeds of Shaw and his men were retold in the motion picture *Glory* (1990). A statue of Shaw by Augustus Saint-Gaudens stands in his honor in the Boston Commons.
See also: Civil War, U.S.

Shawn, Ted (Edwin Meyers Shawn; 1891-1972), U.S. dancer, choreographer, and teacher. With his wife, Ruth St. Denis (1877-1968), he founded the Denishawn school and company. He led an all-male company of dancers (1933-40), and in 1941 established an international dance center at Jacob's Pillow, in Massachusetts.

George Bernard Shaw

Shawnee, Native North Americans of the Algonquian language group. They settled in the Ohio Valley during the 18th century, hunting and cultivating maize. In 1811 the Shawnee chief Tecumseh attempted to unite the Native Americans of the region, but his plan failed when the Shawnee were defeated at Tippecanoe by Gen. William

Henry Harrison's army. The Shawnee were eventually resettled in Oklahoma, where about 2,250 still live.

Shawnee Prophet (1775?-1837), Shawnee religious leader who (c.1805) had visions that led him to take the name Tenskwatawa, meaning "the open door." He began to preach to Native Americans, urging them to quit alcohol and to rededicate themselves to their own traditions. Members of many tribes rallied behind him and his brother, the chief Tecumseh. Tenskwatawa and his followers were defeated in the Battle of Tippecanoe (1811).
See also: Indian wars.

Shays, Daniel *see:* Shays' Rebellion.

Shays' Rebellion, uprising in Massachusetts that lasted intermittently from Aug. 1786 to Feb. 1787. At that time the country was suffering a postwar depression, and taxes in Massachusetts were very high and unequally levied. After the legislature ignored local petitions for tax reductions, an easing of legal action against debtors, a halt to mortgage foreclosures, and a proposal to inflate currency by printing paper money, many rebelled. Led by Daniel Shays, they threatened several local courthouses and forced them to close, attempted to capture a state armory, and resisted the state militia until a final defeat by Maj. Gen. Benjamin Lincoln on Feb. 2. Shays escaped and was later pardoned. The uprising led to some of the reforms that farmers had demanded. It also helped bring about the Constitutional Convention of 1787 by pointing up the need for a strong national government and army, because many of the local militia had either deserted to the rebels or refused to fight them.
See also: Annapolis Convention.

Shcharansky, Anatoly Borisovich (1948-), Soviet mathematician and political dissident. Jailed in 1974, he was sentenced in 1978 in Moscow to 13 years in a labor camp for anti-Soviet agitation, espionage, and treason. In 1986 he was released as part of a "spy trade" and was welcomed in Israel as a hero.

This shell from the family Tridactinae is found in the Indian Ocean.

Shearwater, any of about 12 species of oceanic birds related to the petrel and the albatross. They are brown or dark gray, sometimes with a white belly, 10-26 in (25-66 cm) in length with long, slender wings. Shearwaters land only to reproduce, congregating in huge colonies on offshore islands and the rugged coasts of the Atlantic and Pacific oceans and the Mediterranean. They nest in burrows. The female lays one egg, and the chick is tended by both parents.

Sheeler, Charles (1883-1965), U.S. painter and photographer whose linear treatment of architectural forms, interiors, and industrial settings shows the influence of cubism. In 1913, six of Sheeler's paintings were shown at the New York Armory Show, the exhibition that first introduced European modernism to Americans. Among his paintings are *Upper Deck* (1929) and *American Interior* (1934).

Sheen, Fulton John (1895-1979), U.S. Roman Catholic archbishop widely known for his popular inspirational radio and TV talks and for his conservative stances on many issues.

Sheep, diverse genus of mammals best known in the various races of domestic sheep (*Ovis aries*), bred for both meat and wool. Wild sheep are a diverse group of mountain-dwelling forms with about 37 races alive today, divided into 2 large groups: the Asiatic sheep, which include the mouflons, urials, and argalis; and the American sheep, the thinhorns and bighorns. Asiatic sheep are long-legged, lightly built animals that prefer a gently rolling terrain. American-type sheep by comparison are heavyset and barrel-chested and characteristic of steep slopes and rocky areas, in part filling the role played in Europe and Asia by the ibex. Sheep are social animals; males usually form bands following a dominant ram, and females form separate parties following a mature ewe. The rams use their horns and the specially thickened bone of their foreheads for combat, not only when sexually excited but also in dominance struggles.

Sheepdog, type of dog bred to herd and protect sheep. The American Kennel Club lists these 9 breeds of sheepdogs: Belgian sheepdog, Briard, collie, German shepherd, Great Pyrenees, Komondor, old English sheepdog, puli, and Shetland sheepdog.

Sheffield (pop. 538,700), city in South Yorkshire, northern England. Known worldwide for its high-grade steel, metal products, cutting tools, cutlery, and silverware, Sheffield probably began as an Anglo-Saxon farming settlement in the 1000s. It grew into a center of steel production during the Industrial Revolution.
See also: England.

Sheik (more properly spelled "sheikh"), Arabic term for the leader or elder of a family, tribe, or village, also applied to some Muslim religious leaders.

Shell, any hard external covering secreted by an invertebrate, enclosing and protecting the body. The term is used particularly for the coverings of mollusks, but it also refers to those of foraminifers and may be used loosely to describe the exoskeleton of crustaceans and insects.

Shellac, resin produced by the lac insect (*Laccifer lacca*). It softens when it is heated to about 158° F (70° C), a property that makes it useful for making sealing wax. Shellac is also used as a binder in the manufacture of mica board and stiffening materials, and to make polishes, varnishes, and insulating materials. Shellac once had many uses, including the manufacture of phonograph records, but it has mostly been superseded by plastics.

Shelley, Mary Wollstonecraft (1797-1851), English writer, daughter of philosophical radical William Godwin and Mary Wollstonecraft and wife of poet Percy Bysshe Shelley. Her best-known work is the Gothic horror story *Frankenstein* (1818). She wrote several other novels and edited her husband's works (1839-40).

Shelley, Percy Bysshe (1792-1822), English romantic poet whose work reflects his revolutionary political idealism and his strong faith in the spiritual power of the imagination. It includes long narrative poems, such as *Queen Mab* (1813), *The Revolt of Islam* (1818), and *Epipsychidion* (1821); the verse drama *Prometheus Unbound* (1820); and such famous lyrics as "Ode to the West Wind" (1819) and "To a Skylark" (1820). He was drowned in a boating accident in Italy, were he had settled with his second wife, Mary Wollstonecraft.

Shelter, structure to protect people from the weather, animals, insects, and other threats. A shelter can be a house, tent, cave, houseboat, or a lean-to. Shelters have been made from animal skins, cloth, grass, vines, timber, stones, mud, clay, brick, glass, steel, concrete, and plastic. The materials, forms, and method of construction vary worldwide.

Shelter belt, planted or natural line of trees that protects soil and crops from wind erosion. In 1934 the U.S. government started a program under the Forest Service called the Shelter Belt Project and later the Prairie States Forestry Project. Under this program, trees were planted as wind barriers in the farmlands of the Dakotas, Nebraska, Kansas, Oklahoma, and Texas, areas that had been badly damaged by erosion and dust storms. In 1942 the program was transferred to the Soil Conservation Service.

Shenandoah National Park, area in the Appalachian Mountains, northern Virginia. Covering approximately 300 sq

mi (777 sq km) along the crest of the Blue Ridge Mountains, it is heavily crested and affords magnificent views along the Skyline Drive, which runs its whole length.
See also: National Parks.

Shenandoah River, river in Virginia and West Virginia, a major tributary of the Potomac. Its North Fork, 117 mi (188 km) long, and South Fork, 155 mi (249 km) long, meet at Riverton, Va., to form the Shenandoah proper, which flows 55 mi (88 km) to the Potomac at Harper's Ferry, W. Va.

Shenandoah Valley, area between the Allegheny and Blue Ridge mountains in northeastern Virginia. About 150 mi (241 km) long and up to 25 mi (40 km) wide, it is a rich farming area famed for its natural beauty. During the Civil War it was the site of the Shenandoah Valley campaign (1862-64).

Shenyang (pop. 4,130,000), formerly Mukden, capital of Liaoning province in northeastern China, on the Hun River. A major industrial city, its products include steel and steel products, tools, chemicals, and processed food. It is also a transportation hub. The city dates from the Middle Ages. It was the capital of Manchu China and the site of the Japanese invasion of Manchuria (1931).
See also: China.

Shepard, Alan Bartlett, Jr. (1923-) first U.S. astronaut in space (May 5, 1961). He was later grounded for medical reasons but overcame them to command the *Apollo 14* moon landing (1971).
See also: Astronomy.

Shepard, Sam (1943-), U.S. actor and playwright noted for almost cinematic inventiveness in such plays as *Buried Child* (1978; Pulitzer Prize), *True West* (1980), and *Lie of the Mind* (1987). Other works are collected in *Mad Dog Blues and Other Plays* (1972). Shepard appeared in the films *Frances* (1982), *The Right Stuff* (1983), and *Country* (1984).

Sheraton, Thomas (1751-1806), English furniture designer. Sheraton's furniture is noted for its delicacy and simplicity of shape. It may be decorated with inlays, oval or diamond shapes, or classical motifs such as lyres and urns. Sheraton published his designs in *The Cabinet-Maker and Upholsterer's Drawing Book* (1791-94). His style of furniture was popular in England (1790-1805) and in the United States (1795-1810).

Sheridan, Philip Henry (1831-88), U.S. general and Union Civil War hero. After successes in the Chattanooga and Wilderness campaigns, he commanded the army that defeated Gen. Jubal Early and devastated the Shenandoah Valley (1864). In 1865 he won the Battle of Five Forks in Virginia and helped end the war by cutting off Robert E. Lee's line of retreat from Appomattox. He became commander of the U.S. Army in 1884.
See also: Civil War, U.S.

Sheridan, Richard Brinsley (1751-1816), Irish-born English dramatist and politician famous for his witty comedies of manners, including *The Rivals* (1775), *School for Scandal* (1777), and *The Critic* (1779). A Whig member of Parliament (1780-1812), he played a leading part in the impeachment trial (1787) of Warren Hastings.

Sheriff, executive officer of a county, a post that has existed in England since before 1066. Today the duties of a sheriff entail the execution of writs, the preparation of jurors, and the custody of prisoners. In the United States a sheriff functions as a peace officer in areas of a county not protected by city police. The office of sheriff is also found in Canada, Scotland, and Northern Ireland.

Sherman, brothers important in the U.S. Civil War era. **William Tecumseh Sherman** (1820-91) was a Union commander, second in importance only to Gen. Ulysses S. Grant. He fought in the battles of Bull Run (1861) and Shiloh (1862) and in the Vicksburg campaign (1862-63). He was given command of the Army of Tennessee and, with Grant, took part in the Chattanooga campaign (1863). As supreme commander in the West (1864) he invaded Georgia, capturing Atlanta and marching on to Savannah. Turning north, he pushed Gen. Joseph Johnston's army before him and accepted its surrender at Durham, N.C. (1865). The destruction Sherman wrought in obliterating Confederate supplies and communications and breaking civilian morale made him a hero in the North and a villain in the South. He was U.S. Army commander 1869-84. **John Sherman** (1823-1900) was a founding member of the Republican Party. A senator (1861-77, 1881-97) and secretary of the treasury (1877-81), he introduced the Sherman Antitrust Act and the Sherman Silver Purchase Act.
See also: Civil War, U.S.

Sherman, James Schoolcraft (1855-1912), U.S. Republican politician, member of the House of Representatives (1887-91, 1893-1909) and vice president under William H. Taft (1909-12).
See also: Antitrust laws.

Sherman, Roger (1721-93), American patriot who helped draft and signed the Declaration of Independence. He was a member of the 1787 Constitutional Convention and, with Oliver Ellsworth, introduced the Connecticut Compromise. He was a member of the House of Representatives (1789-91) and Senate (1791-93) from Connecticut.

Sherman Silver Purchase Act (1890), compromise measure aiming to placate mine-owners and the advocates of free silver, which required the U.S. government to double its monthly silver purchases. It threatened to undermine gold reserves and was repealed when the panic of 1893 began.

Percy Bysshe Shelley, by Joseph Severn

Sherpas, Buddhist people of northeast Nepal, famous as Himalayan guides. Of Tibetan origin and speaking a Tibetan language, they number some 85,000 and raise cattle, grow crops, and spin wool in the high valleys of the Himalayas.

Sherrington, Sir Charles Scott (1857-1952), British neurophysiologist who shared with Edgar D. Adrian the 1932 Nobel Prize in physiology or medicine for studies of the nervous system that form the basis of our modern understanding of its action. He established the use of the word "synapse," explained the functions of the spinal cord, and made vital contributions to the understanding of muscles. He is the author of *The Integrative Action of the Nervous System* (1906).
See also: Nervous system.

General William Sherman

Sherry, alcoholic beverage named for Jérez de la Frontera, Spain, where it originated. It is an aperitif wine, matured in wooden casks and fortified with brandy to bring the alcohol level to 15%-23% by volume.

Sherwood, Robert Emmet (1896-1955), U.S. playwright. His plays *Idiot's Delight* (1936), *Abe Lincoln in Illinois* (1938), and *There Shall Be No Night* (1940), and his biography *Roosevelt and Hopkins: An Intimate History* (1948) won Pulitzer Prizes for drama or biography.

Shetland Islands, archipelago of about 200 islands, covering 550 sq mi (1,425 sq km) northeast of Scotland's mainland, constituting its northernmost county. Lerwick, on Mainland Island, is the chief port and administrative center. Along with the Orkneys, the Shetlands are the center of the North Sea oil industry. Fishing and cattle and sheep raising are the main occupations of the some 18,500 Scots on the 24 inhabited islands. The Shetlands are noted for their knitted woolen goods and the Shetland pony.

Shetland pony, smallest of the ponies, probably a relic of prehistoric British and Scandinavian horses. Tiny, shaggy, and once restricted to the Shetland Islands, it has now been widely bred as a riding pony for children.

Shetland sheepdog, small dog, developed (19th century) in the Shetland Islands to herd sheep. Measuring 13-16 in (33-41.6 cm) at the shoulder and weighing about 15 lb (7 kg), the Shetland sheepdog resembles a miniature collie. Agile and hardworking, it can cover great distances without tiring and is also kept as a pet or watchdog.

Eduard Shevardnadze

Shevardnadze, Eduard Amvroslyevich (1928-), Soviet politician and diplomat, USSR foreign minister 1985-90. He was head of the ministry of internal affairs of the Republic of Georgia, 1965-72. He became foreign minister after being promoted to a full voting member of the Politburo in 1985. Shevardnadze was known as a liberal on friendly terms with the West. He resigned Dec. 20, 1990 over disagreements with other members of the Soviet government.
See also: Union of Soviet Socialist Republics.

Shevchenko, Taras (1814-61), Ukrainian patriot and poet. He was also a realist painter and a publisher of Ukrainian ballads in Russian. He opposed serfdom and was active in the Ukrainian independence movement. As punishment, the Russian government sentenced him to military service in the Ural Mountains (1847-57). His nationalistic poems include *Katerina* (1840), *Haydamaki* (1841), and *The Dream* (1844). He was born in Kiev.

Shield, defensive armor, usually carried on the left arm to leave the right arm free for fighting. The ancient Greeks and early Romans used large, circular wooden shields covered with bronze. The later Romans, for the sake of greater mobility, switched to smaller, rectangular shields that were curved to half encircle and thus protect the body more effectively. Kite-shaped shields were employed during the Middle Ages. The introduction of body armor and then firearms (requiring the use of both hands) gradually made the shield obsolete. In modern times shields have been reintroduced by riot police as protection against urban rioters.

Shih Huang-ti *see:* Shi Huangdi.

Shih Tzu

Shih Tzu, breed of toy dog. It stands 8-11 in (20-28 cm) at the shoulder and weighs 9-18 lb (4-8 kg). The dog has a broad head, a short, square muzzle, and drooping ears. The thick coat varies in color. The breed originated in Tibet and is related to the Pekingese and Lhasa apso.

Shi Huangdi (259?-210 B.C.), emperor of the first Chinese empire and founder of the Qin dynasty. He became ruler of the kingdom of Qin (246 B.C.), conquered Qin's rival states, and declared himself emperor of China (221 B.C.). He established a strong central government. He had his opponents executed and potentially inciteful books burned. He ordered the construction of roads and canals and the completion of the Great Wall of China, a defense along China's northern frontier.
See also: Qin dynasty.

Shiloh, Battle of, major conflict of the U.S. Civil War, fought at Pittsburgh Landing, Tenn. (Apr. 6-7, 1862). The Union army under Gen. Ulysses S. Grant was forced back by a surprise onslaught of the 40,000-strong Confederate army under Gen. Albert S. Johnston. The reinforced Union army routed the Confederates in a counterattack the next day. On each side casualties were over 10,000.
See also: Civil War, U.S.

Shingles, or herpes zoster, viral disorder of a nerve center, characterized by pain, a vesicular rash, and later scarring of the skin of the abdomen or trunk. The disorder is caused by the same virus that causes chickenpox. Predominantly striking people past age 50, it leads to an acute skin eruption that follows the path of the nerve involved.
See also: Herpes.

Shinn, Everett (1876-1953), U.S. painter, member of the Ashcan School. He is best known for his pictures of the theater and music hall world, such as *Revue* (1908).
See also: Ashcan School.

Shinto (Japanese, "way of the gods"), indigenous religion of Japan originally based on worship of nature's forms and forces. As this worship evolved, entering a stage of polytheism, its most revered deity became the sun goddess, Ama terasu-o-mi-kami, from whom it was believed the emperors descended. They were regarded as chief priests by divine right, until the disavowal of divinity by Emperor Hirohito in 1946. The blending of church and state occurred in 1882, when the religion was organized into state shrines (supervised by the government) and sectarian shrines. (The imperial shrine is at Ise.) State Shinto was used by the militarists of Japan until its dismantling after World War II. Shinto beliefs, rituals, and prayers, transmitted orally before the introduction of writing by the Chinese in the 5th century, are recorded in 3 texts: the *Kojiki*, the *Nihongi*, and the *Yengishiki*. Today Shinto, influenced by Buddhism and Confucianism, is practiced through rituals and customs involving celebration of festivals, pilgrimages to shrines, and the honoring of ancestors. The practice of pure Shinto involves prayer, food offerings, and dances.
See also: Religion.

Ship, large seagoing vessel for transport of people and goods. The wooden ships of ancient times were propelled by oars, sails, or a combination of the two. In the history of ships, highlights include the triremes (warships) of the Greeks and Romans, the Viking ships of the Middle Ages, and the ships of such powers as Spain, Portugal, and England during the 1400s and 1500s. Transoceanic voyages (of Columbus and others), made possible by improved navigational instruments, and the continued use of the seas to conquer new lands and expand empires prompted a booming shipbuilding industry of a wide variety of ships. With the introduction of steel, as well as the steam engine, the steam turbine, and then the diesel engine of the 20th century, the endurance and speed of ocean craft improved markedly. Nuclear engines for ships came into use in the 1950s. Despite competition from the airplane, railroad, and truck, ships still transport the bulk of the world's freight. Half the cargo at sea is oil, carried by supertankers that can hold millions of gallons of crude oil. Luxury cruise ships continue to hold their own in the travel/vacation industry. Ships, including destroyers, cruisers, and frigates, have also maintained an important position in the defense forces of many nations.

Ship, model, small copy of a ship. Some models are built and sailed by hobbyists for pleasure. Historically, shipbuilders have made models as plans for a larger ship's construction. Ship models also are made so the hull's design can be tested in different wave conditions.

Shipworm, bivalve mollusk (*Teredo navalis*) notorious for burrowing into the timbers of piers and wooden ships. The body is long and wormlike, with the shell reduced to a tiny pair of abrasive plates at the head end. These are used for rasping into wood—at a rate sometimes exceeding 1 ft (30.5 cm) per month.

Shire, administrative division in Great Britain. The Anglo-Saxon shires, first organized in the A.D. 800s, were made up of smaller divisions called *hundreds*. A shire was headed by an ealdorman and a sheriff. The term *shire* was eclipsed in the 1400s by the word *county*.

Shi'te (Arabic, "sectarian"), member of one of Islam's two great sects, the other being the orthodox Sunni. The schism arose over disagreement about Muhammad's successor. The Shi'te reject the first 3 caliphs and recognize Ali (Muhammad's son-in-law) and his descendants as rightful successors. They are concentrated principally in Iran, but also with communities in Iraq, Yemen, Pakistan, Oman, and Lebanon.
See also: Islam; Sunni.

Ancient Egyptian ships were characterized by square sails, oars, and a curved hull similar to that of a reed boat.

Unlike earlier galleys, Venetian galleys of the 16th century had fewer oars and more men working each oar.

The cog, a broadly built ship with bluff prow and stern, was used primarily for commercial transport from the 13th to the late 14th century.

The Sea Witch*, built in New York in 1846 for the China trade, was one of the earliest clippers: sleek, light ships built for speed.*

Steam-operated paddleboats, such as John Fitch's 1786 model, were superseded by rudderboats.

The Queen Elizabeth II*, built in 1967, operates as a transatlantic liner and a cruise liner.*

Sculpture of Shiva

Shiva, Hindu deity representing that aspect of the Godhead connected with the destruction necessary for renewal of life. He is sometimes depicted as an ascetic youth. In the role of re-creator he is called "the happy one." His phallic emblem is worshipped.
See also: Brahmanism; Hinduism.

Shock, specifically refers to the development of low blood pressure, inadequate to sustain blood circulation, usually causing cold, clammy, gray skin and extremities, faintness, mental confusion, and decreased urine production. It is caused by acute blood loss, burns with plasma loss, acute heart failure, massive pulmonary embolism, and septicemia. If untreated, death ensues. Early replacement of plasma or blood and administration of drugs to improve blood circulation are necessary to prevent permanent brain damage and acute kidney failure.

Shock absorber, any mechanism used to lessen impact in vehicles, aircraft, or stable structures. Most shock absorbers are hydraulic: They operate by forcing liquid through a small opening, an action that sets up resistance to both contraction and expansion of the spring mountings. In automobiles, shock absorbers control up-and-down vibrations and absorb impact on the car body. They are made of a piston inside an oil-filled cylinder. When the piston slides, it allows the fluid to flow through a spring-loaded valve.

Shockley, William (1910-), U.S. physicist who shared with John Bardeen and Walter H. Brattain the 1956 Nobel Prize in physics for their joint development of the transistor. He is also known for promoting the erroneous belief that black people are intellectually inferior to Caucasians.
See also: Transistor.

Shock treatment, any of several types of therapy for mental illness that involve subjecting the patient to convulsions or seizures produced by electricity. It is now generally used only for hospitalized patients who are suicidal or severely depressed. Controversial because of its negative side effects, particularly amnesia and cardiac damage, shock therapy has been widely replaced by the use of tranquilizers.

Shoe, protective covering for the foot. The various types include the boot, whose upper extends above the ankle; the clog, a simple wooden-soled shoe; the moccasin, a hunting shoe whose sole extends around and over the foot; the sandal, an open shoe whose sole is secured to the foot by straps; and the slipper, a soft indoor shoe. Shoes have been made from earliest times, the type depending mainly on the climate; clogs, sandals, and moccasins predominated until the early Middle Ages. Since then boots and typical shoes in widely varying styles have been most popular. Leather has always been the main material used, shaped on a wood or metal form (*last*) and hand sewn, the sole being nailed to the upper. In the mid-19th century the sewing machine was adapted for sewing shoes, and nailing and gluing were also mechanized, allowing mass production. Other materials have to some extent displaced leather: natural and synthetic rubber for the sole and heel and various plastics and synthetic fibers for the upper.

Shoebill, African wading bird (*Balaenicips rex*), native to the White Nile area of the Sudan. The shoebill is gray, long legged, and has a large, wide bill ending in a hook. It stands 3-4 ft (90-120 cm) high and eats small frogs and shallow-water fish. Shoebills live in pairs and nest on the ground in grass-lined reed platforms.

Shoemaker, Willie (William Lee Shoemaker, 1931-), U.S. jockey. The most successful jockey in U.S. history, he rode 4 Kentucky Derby winners (1955, 59, 65, 86) and was the first jockey to win more than $2 million in a single year (1956). Shoemaker began his career at age 18 and had ridden nearly 9,000 winning mounts when he retired in 1990. He was elected to the National Racing Hall of Fame in 1958.

Shogun, title of the hereditary military commanders of Japan who usurped the power of the emperor in the 12th century and ruled the country for about 700 years. In 1867 the last Tokugawa family shogun was forced to resign and restore sovereignty to the emperor.
See also: Japan.

Sholem Aleichem (Solomon Rabinovitz; 1859-1916), Russian-born Yiddish humorous writer. His pseudonymous first name is Hebrew for "Peace be unto you." He was an immensely prolific and popular author, and his novels, short stories, and plays tell of the serious and absurd aspects of Jewish life in Eastern Europe. His works include *The Old Country* and *Tevye's Daughters* (1894; the basis for the musical *Fiddler on the Roof*, 1964).

Sholes, Christopher Latham (1819-90), U.S. inventor (with Carlos Glidden and Samuel Soulé) of the typewriter (patented 1868). He sold his patent rights to the Remington Arms Co. in 1873.
See also: Typewriter.

Sholokhov, Mikhail (1905-84), Russian novelist awarded the 1965 Nobel Prize in literature. He is best known for his stories about the Don Cossacks of southern Russia. His greatest work is *And Quiet Flows the Don* (1928-40).

Shooting star *see:* Meteor.

Shoplifting, crime of stealing displayed items from a store. It is estimated that $8 billion worth of merchandise is shoplifted in the United States annually, and that fewer than one shoplifter in 1,000 receives a jail sentence. The merchandise most frequently stolen is beauty and health aids, cigarettes, and fresh meat.
See also: Crime.

Shoran, acronym for short-range navigation, an electronic system for establishing the position of a ship or aircraft. The craft being monitored sends a radio signal to 2 separate land stations, and the stations return the signals. Shoran calculates the distance to the craft by the time between transmission and reception of the signal. It can pinpoint the craft's position to within 1 part in 10,000. Its range is limited to 500 mi (800 km). First used during World War II, shoran has largely been replaced by more accurate systems.
See also: Navigation.

Shore Patrol, military police of the U.S. Navy, Marines, and Coast Guard. The Shore Patrol enforces laws involving military personnel while they are ashore. It is made up of trained officers and enlisted personnel empowered to arrest suspected offenders, who are then placed in the custody of their commanding officers. The Shore Patrol has no authority to try or punish those it arrests.

Shorthand, or stenography, any writing system permitting the rapid transcription of speech. Most used today are Speedwriting, which uses abbreviations; (Isaac) Pitman shorthand, the first to be commercially developed (1837); and Gregg shorthand, by John Robert Gregg (published 1888). Pitman and Gregg shorthands are both phonetic, using symbols to represent recurring sounds. Shorthand is much used by secretaries, journalists, and court reporters.
See also: Speedwriting.

Shorthand machine, any of several mechanical devices that use keyboards to record dictation. Invented (1912) by a court stenographer, Ward Stone Ireland, the shorthand machine is used chiefly to record court testimony, legislation, and speeches. The operator works by touch, typing words phonetically while watching the speaker. The keyboard is arranged to allow any number of the 21 lettered keys

to be struck simultaneously, so that an entire word or phrase can be typed with 1 stroke. The shorthand machine is portable and operates silently.
See also: Court reporter.

Short story, form of prose fiction, usually limited in character and situation and between 500 and 20,000 words long. Chaucer's *Canterbury Tales* and Boccaccio's *Decameron* of the 14th century are prototypes of short stories. The art form was revived in the 19th century, and prominent short-story writers include Anton Chekhov, O. Henry, Ernest Hemingway, Henry James, Katherine Mansfield, Guy de Maupassant, John O'Hara, Edgar Allen Poe, Jean Stafford, and Eudora Welty.

Short waves, electromagnetic (radio) waves having a wavelength from about 32 to 328 ft (10 to 100 m) and a frequency between about 3,000 and 30,000 kilohertz—shorter and of higher frequency than the wavelengths of amplitude modulation (AM) transmissions. Short waves are used to carry international broadcasting, FM (frequency modulation) radio stations, and transoceanic telephone calls. Shortwave radios that can receive and transmit signals are used by pilots, the police, and amateur and citizens band operators.
See also: Radio, Amateur.

Shoshone, group of Native North Americans originally inhabiting the territory between southeastern California and Wyoming. The Shoshone of eastern Utah and Wyoming were typical buffalo hunters of the plains. In the 18th century the Comanche split off and moved south to Texas. There are about 8,000 Shoshone on reservations.

Shostakovich, Dmitri (1906-75), Soviet composer. His works include the opera *Lady Macbeth of Mtsensk* (1930-32) and 15 symphonies, the most famous of which are the Fifth (1937), the Seventh—"Leningrad," written during the siege of the city (1941)—and the Tenth (1953). Some of his music is notably patriotic. The Piano Quintet (1940) is one of his leading chamber music pieces.

Shotgun, smoothbore shoulder firearm that discharges pellets (shot) designed to disperse as they leave the gun muzzle. Used primarily in hunting small game and birds and in skeet, or trapshooting, the shotgun evolved from the early fowling guns of 16th century Europe, becoming lighter and shorter and benefitting from the addition of a choke to control the spread of the shot and from the patent of the shotgun cartridge (1831). The repeating shotgun appeared c.1880. A shotgun's caliber is measured by its gauge, the most popular U.S. gauges being 12, 16, 20, and the 410 bore. Models may be single or double barreled.

Shot-put, track-and-field competition in which a weight, generally a solid metal ball, is thrown one-handed from the shoulder, using the whole weight of the body in the heave. Dating from ancient times, when stones were used as shots, the shot-put was made an official event of the first modern Olympic Games (1896). The shot is tossed (or put) from a 7-ft (2.1-m)-diameter circle and weighs 16 lb (7.3 kg) in men's competitions and 8 lb 13 oz (4 kg) in women's. The distance of the put is measured from the inside edge of the throwing circle to the nearest edge of the shot's first ground contact. The put is disqualified if the athlete steps on or outside the circle or allows the shot to fall below shoulder level.

Shoulder, term for the area of the body between the trunk and the arm, including bones, joints, and the adjacent tissue. There are 2 bones in the shoulder: the clavicle (collarbone), which is the horizontal bone that connects to the breastbone, and the scapula (shoulderblade), the flat triangular bone of the back. The upper arm bone (humerus) fits into the socket formed by the scapula. There are several muscles in the shoulder, primarily the trapezius, which helps turn the scapula, and the deltoid, which moves the upper arm. In primates the shoulder protrudes; in other mammals, it slopes.

Shoveler (*Anas clypeata*), common duck of the family Anatidae native to marshes and lakes of North America, particularly west of the Mississippi River. The shoveler also lives in Asia and Europe and migrates to the Southern Hemisphere. The shoveler has a broad bill longer than its head. The drake has a green head and neck, a white breast, and a black tail. The female is mottled brown. The shoveler feeds in shallow water and nests on the ground. It migrates in small flocks of 5 to 10 birds.

Shrapnel, type of antipersonnel artillery shell made of a hollow metal sphere filled with musket balls or other large shot and an explosive charge detonated by an adjustable fuse. Shrapnel was invented by Lt. Henry Shrapnel (1761-1842) and first used (1804) by British forces in the Napoleonic Wars. Since World War II, the term *shrapnel* has usually been understood to mean exploded fragments of the shell casing.
See also: Artillery.

Shreveport (pop. 334,341), city in northwest Louisiana on the Red River, seat of Caddo Parish. A major industrial and agricultural center with more than 250 factories, Shreveport produces primary and fabricated metals, telephones, glassware, timber and wood products, cotton, beef, petroleum products, and natural gas. It is the site of Centenary College (1825), Saint Vincent's Academy, and a branch of Louisiana State University.
See also: Louisiana.

Shrew, small, mouselike, insect-eating mammal with short legs, and long, pointed nose. Shrews have narrow skulls and sharp, rather unspecialized teeth for feeding on insects, earthworms, and small-mammal carrion. They are highly active creatures. The somewhat indigestible nature of their food combined with the high energy consumption of their constant activity means that they may eat 2-3 times their own weight of food in a day. Having a pulse rate that sometimes approaches 1,000 beats a minute, few shrews live longer than a year.

Shrike, aggressive and predatory passerine bird of the family Laniidae that kills insects, birds, or small mammals with its hooked bill. Because shrikes store their victims impaled on thorns like the carcasses hung in a butcher's shop, they are often called butcherbirds. They live on the edges of woods and forests worldwide.

Shrimp, decapod crustacean (suborder Natantia) that uses its abdominal limbs to swim instead of crawling like a lobster or crab. The body, more or less cylindrical and translucent, bears 5 pairs of walking legs and 2 pairs of very long antennae. The eyes are stalked. Shrimp are mostly scavengers or predators and may be found in the open ocean, near shore, in estuaries, and even in fresh water. They are fished for food worldwide.

Shrimp

Shrine, The, fraternal order and service branch of the Masons (officially called the Ancient Arabic Order of Nobles of the Mystic Shrine for North America) open to men who have achieved the rank of Knights Templar or the 32nd Masonic degree. Founded in 1872, the Shrine supports a number of philanthropies, including 22 hospitals offering free services to burned and crippled children. There are over 800,000 North American Shriners.
See also: Masonry.

Shriver, Sargent (1915-), U.S. politician, first Peace Corps director (1961-66), head of the Office of Economic Opportunity (1964), ambassador to France (1968-70), and unsuccessful Democratic candidate for vice president (1972).
See also: Peace Corps.

Shroud of Turin, linen cloth bearing the image of a crucified man, believed to be Jesus' burial cloth. Stored at the Cathedral of Turin since 1578, the shroud measures 14 ft 3 in by 3 ft 7 in (434 cm by 109 cm). It received publicity in the 1970s and 1980s when it became available for scientific research. Tests proved that the negative image was not painted but did not determine how it was produced. They also showed, from pollen and dust samples, that the linen could have been in the Palestine area where Jesus died and that bloodstains on the fabric were genuine. However, radiocarbon dating (1988) seemed to prove that the cloth is no older than about 500 years. Theologians, historians, and scientists have sustained the controversy surrounding the shroud, particularly since no early accounts of an imaged burial cloth exist. Historians usually agree that the shroud's whereabouts can be traced from the 500s with a gap from 1204 to 1355.

Shrove Tuesday, last day before Lent begins. It is a traditional day for Mardi Gras (Fat Tuesday) carnivals, such as those in New Orleans, Rio de Janeiro, and Nice.
See also: Lent.

Shrub, term for a woody plant that is shorter than a tree and usually has branching stems that give it a bushy appearance.

Shuffleboard, game played by 2 or 4 persons who use cues (long sticks) to slide disks down a long, narrow court, 52 x 6 ft (15.8 x 1.8 m), that has a triangular scoring area at either end. The game is generally played outdoors on pavement, a ship deck, or other smooth surface. Players try to knock their opponents' disks into the penalty section, while leaving their own disks in one of the scoring positions on the triangle.

Shultz, George Pratt (1920-), U.S. secretary of state (1982-89). A former dean of the Graduate School of Business at the University of Chicago, in Pres. Richard Nixon's administration he was secretary of labor (1969-70), director of the Office of Management and Budget (1970-72), and secretary of the treasury (1972-74). He was president of the Bechtel Corp. when Pres. Ronald Reagan appointed him to succeed Alexander Haig as secretary of state.

George Shultz

Shumway, Norman Edward (1923-), U.S. surgeon who performed the first adult cardiac transplant in the United States, Jan. 6, 1968, at Stanford Medical Center. Shumway is also known for pioneering research in measuring and combating rejection of transplanted hearts and in other open-heart surgery, such as valve transplantation.

Shush *see:* Susa.

Siam *see:* Thailand.

Siamese fighting fish *see:* Fighting fish.

Siamese twins, identical twins joined most commonly at the hip, chest, abdomen, buttocks, or head. Some share one internal organ, such as the heart or the liver. Originating from a single fertilized egg that has developed imperfectly, Siamese twins occur about once in every 50,000 births. Surgery in some cases can successfully separate these twins.

Sibelius, Jean (Julius Christian Sibelius, sometimes Jan; 1865-1957), Finnish composer. His best-known work is *Finlandia* (1900), which expressed his country's growing nationalist feeling. He composed several tone poems, such as *En Sagà* (1892), that evoke the physical beauty and ancient legends of Finland. He wrote 7 symphonies and many violin and piano pieces.

Siberia, vast, indefinite area of land (about 2.9 million sq km/7.5 million sq km) in northern USSR between the Ural Mountains in the west and the Pacific Ocean in the east, forming most of the Russian Republic. The landscape varies from the Arctic tundra to the great forest zone in the south and the steppes in the west. Summers are mild in most parts, winters extremely severe (as low as –90° F/–67.8° C in some parts). Most of the people are Russian or Ukrainians; Yakuts, Buryats, and Tuvans form autonomous republics. The largest cities are Novosibirsk, Omsk, Krasnoyarsk, and Novokuznetsk. Siberia has rich natural resources—farmland, forests, fisheries, natural gas, and such minerals as coal, iron ore, tungsten, and gold. Industrial centers have developed in the regions of Krasnoyarsk and Lake Baikal (the world's deepest lake), and one of the world's largest hydroelectric plants is near Bratsk. Siberia was inhabited in prehistoric times. Russians conquered much of Siberia by 1598. Political prisoners were first sent to Siberia in 1710 and forced-labor camps still exist. The Trans-Siberian Railroad (completed 1905) led to large-scale colonization and economic development.
See also: Union of Soviet Socialist Republics.

Siberian husky, arctic working dog bred to pull sleds. The husky stands 20-23 in (51-58 cm) high at the shoulder and weighs 35-60 lb (16-27 kg). It has a dense undercoat and a smooth outercoat, of colors ranging from white through tan and gray to black. Originally raised by the Chukchi tribe of northeastern Siberia, the husky was introduced to Alaska (1909) as a sled-racing dog. It is related to the Samoyed and the malamute.

Siberian husky

Sibyl, in Greek and Roman mythology, female prophet, usually divinely inspired and associated with a shrine or temple. There were sibyls throughout the ancient world, the most famous being the Cumaean sibyl, who accompanied Aeneas to Hades and sold the books of the Sibylline Prophecies to King Tarquin of Rome. Her caverns still exist in Mount Cuma in southern Italy. Medieval monks adapted the sibyls to Christianity, making them 12 in number and giving each a separate prophecy regarding Jesus.
See also: Mythology.

Sicilies, Kingdom of the Two, name taken by the kingdoms of Sicily and Naples when they merged in 1816 under Ferdinand I. The Two Sicilies were conquered by the Italian revolutionary leader Guiseppe Garibaldi in 1860, and subsequently absorbed, by popular vote, into the kingdom of Italy.
See also: Italy.

Sicily, largest Mediterranean island (9,925 sq mi/25,706 sq km), part of Italy, but with its own parliament at the capital, Palermo. Its most notable feature is the active volcano, Mt. Etna (height varies around 10,750 ft/3,277 m). Much of the island is mountainous, but there are lowlands along the coasts. About half the population live in the coastal towns Palermo, Catania, Messina, and Siracusa. Agriculture is the mainstay of the economy, though hampered by the low rainfall and feudal land tenure system. Wheat is the staple crop; grapes, citrus fruits, and olives are also grown. Main exports, from Ragusa, are petroleum products. Sicily was the site of Greek, Phoenician, and Roman colonies before conquests by the Arabs, who in turn were ousted by Robert Guiscard, the Norman conqueror. The Sicilian Vespers rebellion (1282) led to Spanish rule, ended by Garibaldi (1860), when Sicily became part of the kingdom of Sardinia, then of unified Italy. In World War II, Sicily was conquered by the Allies (1943) and used as a base for attack on Italy.

Sickle-cell anemia, one of many hereditary blood diseases caused by chemically abnormal hemoglobin in the red blood cells, occurring almost exclusively among blacks. Rather than the normal disk shape, the red cells have distorted (crescent) shapes when their oxygen supply is low. It is from this unusual appearance of the red blood corpuscles that the disease and its abnormal hemoglobin derive their names, the hemoglobin being known as the sickle hemoglobin, or hemoglobin S. The disease was first described by J. B. Herrick in 1910, but it was not until 1949 that Linus Pauling and his associates demonstrated the basic defect to be in the hemoglobin molecule of the red blood cells. Since the discovery of the sickle hemoglobin, more than 100 other abnormal hemoglobins have been described. Characteristics of the disease, for which there is no cure, include fever, anemia, and pain in the joints and abdomen.

Siddhartha Gautama *see:* Buddha, Gautama.

Sidereal time, time as measured by the rotation of the earth relative to the fixed stars rather than relative to the sun. The sidereal day is the time it takes the earth to complete one rotation on its axis, such that a given star reappears on the observer's celestial meridian. The sidereal day (23 hr, 56 min, 4 sec) is slightly shorter than the solar day. The difference is caused by the earth's movement around the sun.

Sidewinder, any of several species of snake, especially rattlesnakes, that exhibit a peculiar sideways looping motion when moving rapidly. The name is particularly applied to the horned rattlesnake (*Crotalus cerastes*) of the southwestern United States.

Sidney, Sir Philip (1554-86), Elizabethan poet and courtier, a favorite with Queen Elizabeth I and a classic example of Renaissance chivalry. He had great influence on English poetry, both through his poems, of which the best known are *Arcadia* (1590) and the love sonnets *Astrophel and Stella* (1591), and through his critical work *The Defence of Poesie* (1595), all published posthumously.

Sidon, or Saida (pop. 80,000), city in southern Lebanon, on the Mediterranean Sea. Founded by the ancient Phoenicians, Sidon was prominent in shipbuilding and trade, and was famous for its bronzeware and purple dyes. The art of glassblowing probably originated in the city. Today, as a result of conflict within Israel, it has a large population of Palestinian refugees.

SIDS *see:* Sudden infant death syndrome.

Siegbahn, Karl Manne Georg (1886-1978), Swedish physicist who was awarded the 1924 Nobel Prize in physics for his pioneer work in X-ray spectroscopy. He devised a way of measuring X-ray wavelengths with great accuracy and developed an account of X-rays consistent with the Bohr theory of the atom. His son, **Kai M. Siegbahn** (1918-), also a Swedish physicist, and a professor at Uppsala University (from 1954), shared the 1981 Nobel Prize in physics with U.S. physicists Nicolass Bloembergen and Arthur Schaalow for work in developing high-resolution electron spectroscopy.

Siegfried, or Sigurd, legendary figure of Germanic mythology possessing outstanding strength and courage. He appears in both the Icelandic *Edda* and the 13th-century German *Nibelungenlied*, and is the hero of Richard Wagner's "Ring" operas *Siegfried* and *Die Götterdämerung*.
See also: Nibelungenlied.

Siegfried Line, defensive line of fortifications built on Germany's western frontier. The first Siegfried Line was constructed in the winter of 1916-17 and ran through northern France and Belgium. The Allies called it the Hindenburg Line and finally breached it at the end of World War I. The second line, built in the 1930s along the German-French border, was smashed by the Allies in World War II.
See also: World War II.

Siemens, German family of technologists and industrialists. **Ernst Werner von Siemens** (1816-92) invented, among other things, an electroplating process (patented 1842), a differential governor (c.1844), and a regenerative steam engine. The principle for it was developed by his brothers **Friedrich** (1826-1904) and then **Karl Wilhelm** (1823-83) to form the basis of the open-hearth process. Karl later became Sir Charles William Siemens after obtaining British citizenship (1859). He and Ernst both made many innovative contributions to telegraph science, culminating in the laying of the Atlantic Cable (1874) by the company Sir William owned—done from the *Faraday*, a ship he designed.

Siena's Gothic cathedral

Siena (pop. 61,900), city in Tuscany, central Italy. Siena is an agricultural and tourist center and produces wine, cotton goods, marble, and chemicals. An ancient Etruscan settlement, Siena was occupied by the Gauls (c.400 B.C.) and became a free commune in the 12th century. It was attached to Tuscany after 1555. Home to the medieval Sienese school of painting (13th-14th centuries), its attractions include the public square (Piazza del Campo), the 14th-century cathedral, and the Piccolomini Library. It is the scene of 2 medieval, pageant-like horseraces, known as the Palio, held every summer.

Sienkiewicz, Henryk (1846-1916), Polish novelist awarded the 1905 Nobel Prize in literature. His greatest works are a trilogy about 17th-century Poland—*With Fire and Sword* (1883), *The Deluge* (1886), and *Pan Michael* (1887-88)—and the internationally famous *Quo Vadis?* (1896).

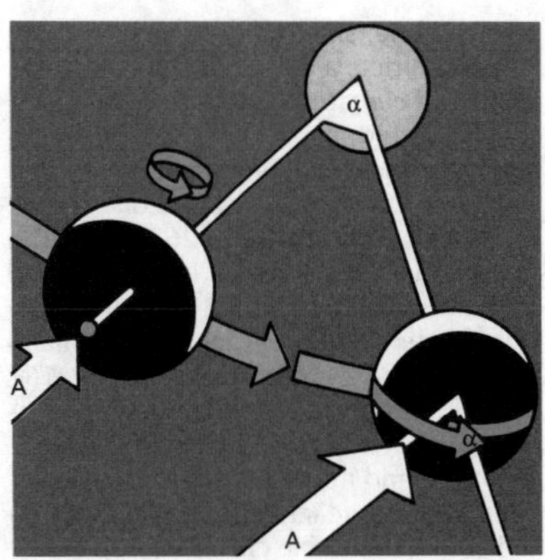

A sidereal day is slightly shorter than a solar day. The difference is caused by the earth's movement around the sun. A = the light from a star.

Sierra Club, environmental organization of North America. Various committees and publications of the Sierra Club work to educate the public and protect the environment. Its founder, the naturalist John Muir, held that its purpose was to protect the Sierra Nevada mountain range of California, but today the club, with a main office in San Francisco, has branches across the United States and Canada. Total membership is about 350,000. The Sierra Club organizes outdoor recreational activities such as mountain climbing and wilderness trips. The club also sponsors lectures, films, and special exhibits and publishes beautifully illustrated books and calendars to promote an appreciation of wildlife and conservation.

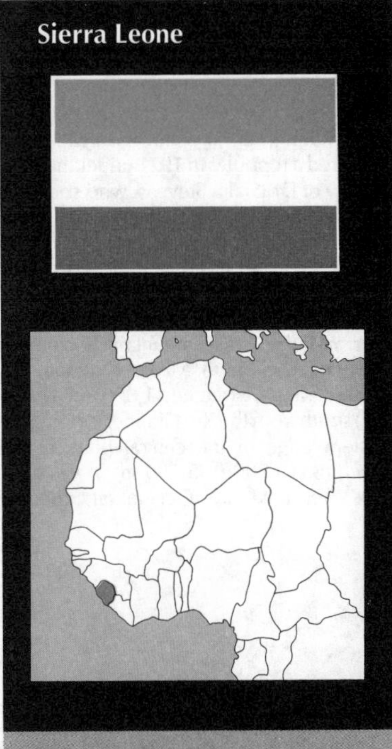

Capital:	Freetown
Area:	27,699 sq mi (71,740 sq km)
Population:	3,957,000
Government:	republic
Independent:	1961
GNP:	U.S. $930,000,000
Per capita:	U.S. $240

Sierra Leone, small, independent country in West Africa; a former British colony.
Land and climate. Bordering on the Atlantic Ocean and situated between the republics of Guinea, to the north and east, and Liberia, to the south, Sierra Leone has an area of 27,925 sq mi (72,326 sq km). The coastal area consists of mangrove and freshwater swamps that are gradually being transformed into rice fields. The inland plains, in places as much as 100 mi (161 km) wide, are crossed by many rivers draining westward to the Atlantic. The land to the north and northeast rises in a series of irregular steps reaching 6,390 ft (1,948 m) in Loma Mansa. The climate is tropical.
People. The population is mostly black African with the Mende people of the south and the Temne people of the north predominating. Creoles, descendants of freed slaves, mainly from the Americas, live around Freetown, the country's capital and chief port. Most of the people adhere to traditional beliefs, but there are also sizable minorities of Christians and Muslims. The official language is English.
Economy. Sierra Leone's economy is heavily dependent for export revenue upon diamond mining and the production of cocoa and coffee. Rice is the chief food crop. Cattle are raised in the north, pigs and poultry in the west. Fishing and tourism also contribute to the economy.
History. Named by the Portuguese who first arrived in 1460, the coastal area of present-day Sierra Leone was long the haunt of slavers. In 1787 the English abolitionist Granville Stamp settled freed slaves there. In 1808 Sierra Leone became a British colony, and in the years following thousands more freed slaves settled there. Independent since 1961, Sierra Leone has seen much internal political unrest. It was declared a republic in 1971 under the presidency of Dr. Siaka Stevens, who sought to establish a one-party regime in the face of more than a decade of protest and resistance. In 1985 Maj. Gen. Joseph Saidu Momoh was elected president.

Sierra Madre, vast mountain system of Mexico. The Sierra Madre Oriental, the eastern range, stretches 1,000 mi (1,609 km) south from the Rio Grande, forming the eastern edge of the central plateau and reaching 18,700 ft (5,700 m) in Orizaba. The Sierra Madre Occidental, running southward from Arizona and New Mexico, borders the plateau on the west, rising to over 10,000 ft (3,048 m). The Sierra Madre de Sur parallels the southwest coast.
See also: Mexico.

The Sierra Madre

Sierra Nevada, mountain range, 420 mi (676 km) long, in eastern California, including Mt. Whitney (14,494 ft/4,418 m), the highest mountain in the United States outside Alaska.

Sieve of Eratosthenes, mathematical process for discovering prime numbers. The ancient Greek mathematician Eratosthenes worked out this method by which whole numbers are eliminated—as if filtered through a sieve—until only prime numbers (those that can be divided evenly by themselves and 1) remain. The sieve starts as a string of consecutive whole numbers, beginning with 2. Every even number (except 2 itself) is eliminated, since each of them can be divided by 2. Next, beginning after the first untouched number after 2 (namely 3), every third number is eliminated, because they can all be divided evenly by 3. The next prime is the next untouched number. Since there is no largest prime number, the process can go on indefinitely.
See also: Eratosthenes.

Sieyès, Emmanuel Joseph (1748-1836), French revolutionary, legislator, and author. He participated in drafting such basic documents of the French revolution as the Declaration of the Rights of Man and Citizen and the Constitution (1791). His pamphlet *What is the Third Estate?* (1789) helped inspire the revolution. He served in various legislative bodies throughout the changing post-revolutionary governments, and he ended his life as an exile in Brussels, Belgium, following the Bourbon restoration in France.
See also: French Revolution.

Sight *see:* Eye.

Sigismund (1368-1437), Holy Roman emperor (1433-37), king of Germany (1410-37), Hungary (1387-1437), and Bohemia (1419-37). His coronation as German king was challenged by his half-brother, the former King Wenceslaus of Germany. Sigismund was an important organizer of the Council of Constance (1417), which ended the Great Schism in the Catholic church over papal elections. His coronation as king of Bohemia was contested by the Czech religious reformer John Hus. When Sigismund offered Hus safe-conduct and then went back on the pledge and had Hus executed, the Hussite Wars broke out.
See also: Holy Roman Empire; Hus, Jan.

Sigma Xi, honorary scientific society founded at Cornell University in 1886. It encourages the study of both pure and applied science.

Signac, Paul (1863-1935), French painter, leading theorist of neoimpressionism. A friend of Georges Seurat, he developed pointillism and painted many views of ports, like *Port of St. Tropez* (1916).

Signaling, any of various methods of nonverbal communication. Early visual and sound signals included smoke signals, drum calls, whistles, torch fires, and buoys. Sailors position flags in specific arrangements to communicate through the international flag code. Electrical signals are transmitted through various electronic devices, including radios, radar, computers, and telephone-operated facsimile (FAX) machines.

Sign language, any system of communication using gesture (usually of the hand and arm) rather than speech. The most comprehensive sign language in modern use is that employed by the hearing- or sight-impaired, but sophisticated sign languages are also used by many primitive peoples to communicate with one another.

Sihanouk, Norodom (1922-), political leader of Cambodia. King from 1941, he abdicated in 1955, became premier, then chief of state (1960-70). Deposed by a Lon Nol coup, he returned from exile in 1975 as figurehead of the Communist victors, but resigned 6 months later.
See also: Kampuchea.

Sikhism, religion combining elements of Hindu and Muslim beliefs. Founded by the guru Nanak at the turn of the 16th century, Sikhism is a monotheism whose teachings are embodied in its holy book, *The Adi Granth*. The word *sikh* means "disciple." Among the beliefs of the Sikhs is the Hindu concept of reincarnation. Their tenth and final guru, Gobind Singh (1666-1708), led

Sikh leader Harchant Singh Longowal makes a speech prior to his assassination.

a fight against Muslim persecution, creating the warrior image with which Sikhs are still identified today. Additional characteristics are their turbans and their uncut hair. After the partition of India (1947), a war between Sikhs and Muslims resulted in the transfer of several million Sikhs from the western Punjab, which became part of Pakistan, to the eastern Punjab, in India. There the Sikhs, numbering some 14 million, have played a major role in the economy and in politics, often clashing with the central government in New Delhi. The Indian government's 1984 military occupation of the Golden Temple, the major shrine of Sikhism, has led to continuing conflict.
See also: Punjab; Ranjit Singh.

Sikkim, state in northeast India, located in the Himalaya Mountains, bordered by Tibet on the north, Nepal on the west, and Bhutan on the east. The altitude of the state ranges from sea level rain forests to Mount Kanchenjunga, at over 28,000 ft (8,530 m), the world's third tallest mountain. The capital city, Gangtok, is also the only significant town. The official religion is Buddhism, although many practice Hinduism. Major products of the country are agricultural, although there is some mining of copper, lead, and zinc. A Sikkim monarchy was established by neighboring Tibet in 1642 and lasted until Indian statehood (1975), functioning under British rule from 1861 to 1947.
See also: India.

Sikorsky, Igor Ivanovich (1889-1972), Russian-born U.S. aircraft designer best known for his invention of the first successful helicopter, flown in 1939. He also designed several airplanes, including the first to have more than one engine (1913).
See also: Helicopter.

Silanpää, Frans Eemil (1888-1964), Finnish novelist awarded the 1939 Nobel Prize in literature. His best-known works are *Meek Heritage* (1919) and *The Maid Silja* (1931).

Silesia, region of central Europe, mostly in Poland but extending to Czechoslovakia and eastern Germany. Known for the mineral and coal deposits of heavily industrialized Upper Silesia, the region is heavily forested and traversed by the Oder River. The Sudetes Mountains rise in the south. The largest cities are Polish: Wroclaw and Katowice. Silesia became part of Poland in the 10th century. It was later conquered by Austria (1526) and Prussia (1742). The present borders were redrawn at the end of World Wars I and II.

Silica, chemical compound (SiO_2), properly called silicon dioxide. Sand, clay, granite, and sandstone contain forms of silica, which is also the major ingredient in glass. Quartz is an important crystalline form of silica used in optical tools and communications instruments. Opals are forms of amorphous silica polished and used in jewelry.

Silica gel, chemical substance (SiO_2) forming a noncrystalline form of silica. Silica gel absorbs moisture and this is its prime use. It was used in World War I in gas masks and now serves to dehumidify foods.

Silicate, any of various metallic compounds containing silicon and oxygen, generally with tetrahedral structures. This material makes up 95% of the earth's crust, including soil and rocks. Its basic structure consists of 4 oxygen atoms forming a pyramid-type shape with a silicon atom at the center. This structure may adhere to metals with positively charged ions.

Silicon, chemical element, symbol Si; for physical constants see Periodic Table. Silicon was isolated by Jöns J. Berzelius in 1823. It occurs in nature as sand, quartz, granite, feldspar, asbestos, and many other minerals. It is the second most abundant element and makes up 25.7% of the earth's crust by weight. Silicon is prepared by heating silicon dioxide in an electric furnace, using carbon electrodes. Silicon is a gray, lustrous, unreactive metalloid. It can be amorphous or crystalline. Silicon transmits more than 95% of all wavelengths of infrared radiation. Single crystals of silicon are used for solid-state or semiconductor devices. Silicones, a class of compounds prepared by hydrolyzing organic chlorides, are numerous with hundreds of useful properties, especially in the form of pottery, glass, and building materials. Silicon and its compounds are used in steel, as abrasives, and in lasers.

Silicone, polymer with alternate atoms of silicon and oxygen and organic groups attached to the silicon. Silicones are resistant to water and oxidation and are stable to heat. Liquid silicones are used for waterproofing, as polishes and antifoam agents. Silicone greases are high- and low-temperature lubricants, and resins are used as electrical insulators. Silicone rubbers remain flexible at low temperatures.

Silicon Valley, area around Sunnyvale, in the Santa Clara Valley, Calif., where many semiconductor manufacturers are located. More generally, it contains the greatest concentration of electronics industries in the United States. The region acquired the name because silicon is a material used in the fabrication of electronic equipment.
See also: Semiconductor.

Silicosis, form of pneumoconiosis, or fibrotic lung disease, in which long-standing inhalation of fine silica dusts in mining causes a progressive reduction in the functional capacity of the lungs. The normally thin-walled alveoli and small bronchioles become thickened with fibrous tissue, and the lungs lose their elasticity. Characteristic X-ray appearances and changes in lung function occur.
See also: Pneumoconiosis.

Silk, natural fiber produced by certain insects and spiders to make cocoons and webs, a glandular secretion extruded from the spinneret and hardened into a filament on exposure to air. Commercial textile silk comes from various silkworms. The cocooned pupae are killed by steam or hot air, and the cocoons are placed in hot water to soften the gum (sericin) that binds the silk. The filaments from several cocoons are then unwound together to form a single strand of "raw silk," which is reeled. Several strands are twisted together (thrown) to form yarn. At this stage, or after weaving, the sericin is washed away. The thickness of the yarn is measured in denier. About 70% of all raw silk is produced in Japan.

Silk-screen printing, method of printing derived from the stencil process. A stencil is attached to a silk screen, or fine wire mesh, or formed on it by a photographic process or by drawing the design in tusche (a greasy ink). The screen is sealed with glue and then the tusche and its covering glue are washed out with an organic solvent. The framed screen is placed on the surface to be printed, and viscous ink is pressed through by a rubber squeegee. Each color requires a different screen. The process, which may be mechanized, is used for printing labels, posters, and fabrics, and on bottles and other curved surfaces. Since 1938 it has been used by painters, who call it *serigraphy.*

Silkworm, caterpillar of a moth (*Bombyx mori*) that, like many other caterpillars, spins itself a cocoon of silk in which it pupates. The cocoon is, however, especially thick and may be composed of a single thread commonly 3,000 ft (915 m) long. This is unraveled to provide commercial silk. Originally a native of China, *B. mori* has been introduced to many countries. The caterpillar, which takes about a month to develop, feeds on the leaves of the mulberry tree.

Silky terrier (formerly called Sydney Silky), breed of toy dog from Australia. Weighing up to 10 lb (4.5 kg), the silky terrier has long dark hair with tan markings. The tail is normally cut, or "docked," and the ears are erect and pointed. It was bred in the early 20th century from the Yorkshire and Australian terriers. Like most terriers, it is attentive and friendly.

Silliman, Benjamin (1779-1864), U.S. chemist and geologist who founded *The American Journal of Science and Arts* (1818). The mineral sillimanite is named for him.
See also: Geology.

Sillimanite, relatively rare silicate mineral (Al_2SiO_5) found in France, Madagascar, Brazil, and the eastern United States. It is glassy in appearance, white, green, or brown in color, and often located in areas where metamorphic rock has formed under thermal pressure.

Sills, Beverly (Belle Silverman; 1929-), U.S. coloratura soprano. She made her debut at the New York City Opera in 1955, and ultimately became internationally acclaimed both as a singer and an actress in a broad variety of roles, ranging from bel canto to modern works. After retiring she was general director of the City Opera (1979-89).

Silo, structure used on farms to preserve grasses, or silage, for livestock feed. Most silos are cylindrical and up to 50 ft (15 m) high. They are made of an air-tight material, such as glass or porcelain on the inside, and a sturdy material such as metal, brick, tile, concrete, or wood on the outside. The sweetness of certain grasses or the addition of a solution (such as sulfur dioxide) promotes fermentation, a natural process that prevents spoilage. Steady deposit and removal of silage keeps the grasses in the silo fresh for year-round feeding of livestock.

O.J. Simpson

Silone, Ignazio (Secondo Tranquilli; 1900-78), Italian writer and social reformer. Opposed to fascism, he spent 1931-44 in exile in Switzerland. His novels include *Fontamara* (1933), *Bread and Wine* (1937), and *A Handful of Blackberries* (1952).

Silt, fine deposit, or sediment, found on river or lake bottoms. Over long periods of time, natural forces break down rock into silt, which generally has a diameter of 0.00008 to 0.002 in (0.002-0.05 mm), approximately half that of a grain of sand. During floods, silt is deposited on land, helping to make it fertile.

Silurian, third period of the Paleozoic era, which lasted between c.435 and 395 million years ago.

Silver, chemical element, symbol Ag; for physical constants see Periodic Table. Silver has been known and used since ancient times. It occurs in nature as argentite and horn silver, and is sometimes found uncombined. The element is produced as a byproduct from ores. It has the highest electrical and thermal conductivity of all metals. In the past silver was used as a coinage metal, but its value as bullion has driven silver coins from circulation. Silver is the best reflector of visible light known and a poor reflector of ultraviolet. Silver and its compounds are used in photography, jewelry, for mirrors and in dentistry.

Silverfish

Silverfish, any of various wingless insects of the order Thysanura. One common variety, *Lepisma saccharina,* has 2 long antennae, 3 barbed tail parts, and silver-to-gray scales. It is a pest that lives in damp areas of houses, feeding on wallpaper, books, clothes, or food.

Silver nitrate, chemical compound ($AgNO_3$) made from silver and nitric acid, used medically and industrially. As a medicine it helps prevent blindness in newborn babies and works as an antiseptic. In the form of lunar caustic, a crystalline mass, it helps cauterize wounds and ulcerations. The material called emulsion that coats photographic film is made from silver nitrate, which is also used in the manufacture of silver-plated mirrors and indelible ink.

Simenon, Georges (Georges Joseph Christian Sim; 1903-89), Belgian-born French author of over 200 novels and thousands of short stories. He is best known for his detective novels about Inspector Maigret, works of tightly plotted suspense and psychological insight.

Simhat Torah, Jewish holiday celebrated on either the 22nd or 23rd day of the Hebrew month of Tishri. It marks the end of the annual cycle of Sabbath readings from the Torah in the Jewish house of worship, the synagogue. The festival falls in September or October of the Roman calendar. The Saturday morning Torah readings recommence the Saturday after Simhat Torah.
See also: Bible; Sukkot.

Simms, William Gilmore (1806-70), U.S. author whose writings on the South include historical novels, short stories, biographies, and poetry. His most important work was *The Yemassee* (1835).

Simon, Claude (Eugene-Henri) (1913-), French writer. Author of *Le tricheur* (1945), *L'herb* (1958), and *Tryptyque* (1973), he won the 1985 Nobel Prize for literature as a major figure in France's *nouvelle roman* ("new novel") movement of the 1950s and 1960s.

Simon, Neil (1927-), U.S. playwright whose career began with successful comedies such as *Come Blow Your Horn* (1961), *Barefoot in the Park* (1963), and *The Odd Couple* (1965). Many of his plays are autobiographical—including the trilogy made up of *Brighton Beach Memoirs* (1983), *Biloxi Blues* (1985), and *Broadway Bound* (1986)—and several have been made into movies. Simon has also written lyrics for Broadway musicals, such as *Sweet Charity* (1966) and *They're Playing Our Song* (1979). He received the Pulitzer Prize for *Lost in Yonkers* (1991).

Simon, Saint, one of the twelve disciples (apostles) of Jesus. Called Zelotes, he may have been associated with the fanatical Zealots. His feast day is Oct. 28.
See also: Apostles.

Simplon Pass and Tunnel, Alpine route, 6,590 ft (2,009 m) high and 29 mi (46.7 km) long, between Brig, Switzerland, and Isella, Italy. Napoleon I built a road across it (1800-06).

Simpson, O.J. (Orenthal James Simpson; 1947-), U.S. football player. Known for his speed and elusive running style, he won the Heisman Trophy as top national college player (1968). Simpson led the National Football League (NFL) in rushing 4 times (1972, '73, '75, '76), and is 6th on the alltime rushing list (11,236 career yards). He played in the NFL for the Buffalo Bills (1969-77) and San Francisco 49ers (1978-79) and was inducted into the Pro Football Hall of Fame (1985). In 1994 he was charged with the brutal slaying of his ex-wife, Nicole Brown Simpson, and Ronald L. Goldman. After an extensive 9-month-long trial and accompanying media frenzy, he was declared not guilty in October of 1995. However, in 1997 a civil trial jury declared Simpson liable and awarded large compensatory damages against him.

Simpson, Wallis Warfield *see:* Edward (VIII).

Sin, or transgression, in Judeo-Christian tradition, unethical act considered as disobedience to the revealed will of God. Sin may be viewed legally as crime—breaking God's commandments—and so deserving punishment, or as an offense that grieves God the loving Father. According to the Bible, sin entered the world in Adam's fall and all humankind became innately sinful. Both for this and for actual sins committed, people become guilty and in need of salvation. Since sin is rooted in character and will, each sinner bears personal responsibility; hence the need for repentance, confession, and absolution. Views as to what constitutes sin vary, being partly determined by church authority, social standards, and one's own conscience. The traditional "7 deadly sins" are pride, covetousness, lust, envy, gluttony, anger, and sloth. The Roman Catholic church defines a mortal sin as a serious sin committed willingly and with clear knowledge of its wrongness; a venial sin is less grave, does not wholly deprive the perpetrator of grace, and need not be individually confessed.

Sinai, in the Bible, mountain on the Sinai Peninsula where Moses received the Ten Commandments.

Sinai Peninsula, triangular desert-mountain area, nearly 150 mi (241 km) at its widest and about 230 mi (370 km) north to south, bounded by the northern arms of the Red Sea, i.e., the Gulf of Suez on the west and the Gulf of Aqaba on the east. It is believed that the Bible's Mt. Horeb, where Moses is said to have received the Ten Commandments, is one of the granitic southern peaks, either Jebel Serbal or Jebel Musa (Arabic, "mount of Moses"; also named Mt. Sinai).

Sinatra, Frank (Francis Albert Sinatra; 1915-), U.S. singer and film star. A master of timing and communication, he achieved fame as a crooner with Tommy Dorsey's band, and then as a solo performer was a teen-age idol during World War II. He starred in several movie musicals, then became a dramatic actor of note in *From Here to Eternity* (1953), for which he received the Academy Award for best supporting actor, as well as other films. He has remained one of the world's most popular vocalist-entertainers.

Sinclair, Upton (1878-1968), novelist and social reformer. He is best known for *The Jungle* (1906), a muckraking expose of the horrors of the Chicago meat-packing industry, and for an 11-novel cycle, beginning with *World's End* (1940), about world events and centered on the fictional Lanny Budd. *Dragon's Teeth* (1942), the cycle's third novel, won a Pulitzer Prize.

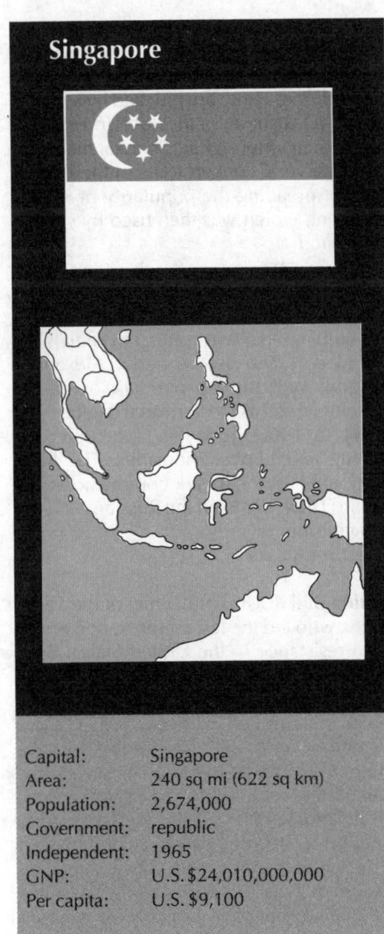

Singapore, small island republic in southeast Asia lying at the southern end of the Malay Peninsula.

Land and climate. Consisting of Singapore Island and several adjacent islets, Singapore has a total area of about 238 sq mi (616 sq km). Singapore Island is separated from the Malay Peninsula by the narrow Johore Strait crossed by a road and a railroad causeway that also has a pipeline bringing fresh water to the island. South of the island is the Singapore Strait. Mostly fringed by mangrove swamps, Singapore Island is largely low-lying, but has a central plateau bounded on the west by low hills. The climate is hot and humid and has no distinctive seasons.

People. The people of Singapore are predominantly Chinese with large Malay and Indian minorities. Principal religions are Buddhism, Islam, Hinduism, and Christianity. Malay, Tamil, Chinese, and English are spoken.

Economy. The capital of the republic, Singapore city, has a fine natural harbor and is southeast Asia's foremost commercial and shipping center, conducting a flourishing international trade as a free port. It trades in textiles, rubber, petroleum, timber, and tin and produces electrical goods, petroleum products, and textiles. Shipbuilding and repair are also important industries.

History. Singapore was founded as a trading port by Sir Thomas Raffles in 1819 and became part of the Straits Settlements in 1826. Occupied by the Japanese during World War II and self-governing since 1959, Singapore joined the Federation of Malaysia in 1963 but withdrew and has been independent since 1965, under the leadership of its controversial prime minister, Lee Kuan Yew.

Singer, Isaac Bashevis (1904-86), Polish-born U.S. Yiddish novelist and short-story writer, known for his portrayal of European Jewish life. His work includes *The Family Moskat* (1950), *The Magician of Lublin* (1960), *The Estate* (1969), and *The Collected Short Stories of Issac Bashevis Singer* (1981). He was awarded the 1978 Nobel Prize in literature.

Singer, Isaac Merrit (1811-75), U.S. inventor of the first viable domestic sewing machine (patented 1851). Although he lost a legal battle with the earlier inventor, Elias Howe, the Singer sewing machine soon became the most popular in the world.
See also: Sewing machine.

Singer, Israel Joshua (1893-1944), Polish-born U.S. Yiddish novelist, playwright, and journalist, best known for his epic novel *The Brothers Ashkenazi* (1936). He was the brother of novelist Isaac Bashevis Singer.

Singing, music created with the voice. In humans, vibrations of the vocal cords in the throat result in sounds whose mechanics are similar to those of wind instruments. The length and thickness of vocal cords as well as their tension in the throat affect the kind of sound that is made. Classifications of women's voices—from highest to lowest in pitch—are soprano, mezzo-soprano, and contralto. For men the classifications are tenor, baritone, and bass.

Singing Tower, tower in central Florida with the biggest bell chimes in the world. Located in Mountain Lake park, which also serves as a bird sanctuary, the tower, designed by Milton B. Medary with doors and railings by Samuel Yellin, stands 205 ft (62 m) high. Marble bridges cross a surrounding moat to allow access to it.

Singapore

Single tax, proposed reform that tax on land value should be a government's sole revenue, stated by Henry George in *Progress and Poverty* (1879). He argued that economic rent of land results from the growth of an economy, not from an individual's effort; therefore, governments are justified in approaching all economic rents, thus eliminating the need for other taxes. The proposal was never enacted in the United States.

Sing Sing, state prison in the city of Ossining, N.Y. Built in 1925 under a program that employed inmates as laborers, the prison has been expanded with the addition of later buildings.
See also: Prison.

Sinhalese, also Singhalese or Sinhala, Indo-Aryan language derived from Sanskrit, spoken by the majority of the people of Sri Lanka. Most other Sri Lankans (or Sinhalese) speak Tamil.

Sinn Féin (Irish, "we, ourselves"), Irish nationalist movement formed by Arthur Griffith in 1905. It secured wide support in 1916, when most of the leaders of the Easter Rebellion against English suppression were martyred. Led by Eamon De Valera, the Sinn Féin set up a separate Irish Parliament, the Dáil Éireann, which declared Irish independence (1918). Sinn Féin guerrilla activity was countered by British Black and Tans military terrorists (1920), but Irish resolve strengthened to the point of war. Britain negotiated a peace treaty with De Valera, and the result was the establishment of the Irish Free State in 1922. The treaty split the Sinn Féin into factions; civil war ensued. Eventually the majority of the Irish backed De Valera's party, the Fainna Fáil, and he became president of the Irish Free State in 1932. With independence, the Sinn Féin movement ended—except for that faction called the Irish Republican Army, which was outlawed.
See also: De Valera, Eamon.

Sintering, process by which powdered metal is used to form solid objects. The particles of the powdered metal are heated until they adhere one to the other to form solid objects.

Sinus, body cavity, usually containing air or blood. Generally, this term refers to the large air space connected with the nose that may become infected and obstructed after upper respiratory infection and cause facial pain and fever (sinusitis). The major nasal sinuses are maxillary, frontal, ethmoid, and sphenoid.

Sioux, or Dakota, confederation of Native American peoples in the North American plains. There were 7 main Sioux tribes, including the Santee, or Dakota, of what is now Minnesota, and the Lakota, or Teton, of the western Dakotas and Nebraska. There were about 30,000 Sioux; 15,000 of these were Lakota, of whom 3,000 were Oglala. The Sioux lived in tepees, and their principal activities were buffalo hunting and raiding. Their most famous ceremony was the sun dance. First noted in the Great Lakes region, the Sioux slowly moved westward after the introduction of the horse in the 17th century, and by the 18th century they roamed the plains of the upper Midwest. They fought on the side of the British in both the American Revolution and the War of 1812. In 1862 a serious revolt of the Sioux led by Little Crow occurred in Minnesota, and 800 European-Americans were massacred, but by 1867 the Sioux had given up their lands and moved to reservations in the Black Hills. The discovery of gold there brought an influx of prospectors and further trouble erupted, resulting in the Sioux's famous defeat of Gen. George Custer and his troops in the Battle of Little Bighorn (1876). After repeated revolts against European-American misrule and treachery, the Sioux were finally defeated at Wounded Knee, S.D. (1890). About 40,000 Sioux now live on reservations in Minnesota, Nebraska, the Dakotas, and Montana.

Sioux City (pop. 115,018), city in western Iowa, on the Missouri River near where the borders of Iowa, Nebraska, and South Dakota meet. Settled in 1854 by John K. Cook, Sioux City was incorporated in 1857. It is the market, meat-packing, and major distribution center for the surrounding agricultural area, which includes parts of the 3 states. The city's industries also produce automobile parts, farm machinery, and clothing.
See also: Iowa.

Sioux Falls (pop. 123,809), largest city in South Dakota, on the Big Sioux River in the southeastern corner of the state. Incorporated as a city in 1883 it is the seat of Minnehaha County. Sioux Falls is the livestock and poultry center for the surrounding area. Its chief industries are meat packing, food processing, and the manufacture of metal and wood products.
See also: South Dakota.

Siphon, device, usually consisting of a bent tube with 2 legs of unequal length, that utilizes atmospheric pressure to transfer liquid over the edge of one container into another at a lower level. The flowing action depends on the difference in the pressures acting on the 2 liquid surfaces and stops when these coincide.

Siple, Paul Allman (1908-68), U.S. geographer and explorer of Antarctica. He was a member of 2 expeditions led by Richard E. Byrd (1928, 1933-35), heading the biology department for the later one. He also served as geographer for the 1939-41 U.S. expedition. He continued his exploration of Antarctica from 1946 to 1957, serving as scientific leader of the South Polar Station 1956-67.
See also: Antarctica.

Siren, device used to create loud, shrill warning signals. Foghorns are sirens that warn of low visibility due to foggy weather conditions. Electronic devices are now often used as sirens. Older ones worked mechanically, one cylinder or disk rotating within another punctured with air holes. The motion created the sound waves.
See also: Civil defense.

Sirenian, or sea cow, any of an order (Sirenia) of aquatic mammals. These large, shy animals feed on plant life in shallow tropical seas. The manatee of Florida, a sirenian, is an endangered species. The name comes from the sirens, sea creatures of Greek mythology.

Sirens, in Greek mythology, sea nymphs whose irresistible singing lured sailors to their deaths on rocky coasts. Sirens appear in ancient stories, including Homer's *Odyssey*, whose hero, Odysseus, had himself tied to a mast and his men's ears plugged as they sailed past the sirens' coast in order to resist.
See also: Mythology.

Sirius, Alpha Canis Majoris (Dog Star), brightest star in the night sky. About 8.8 light years distant from the earth, it is 20 times more luminous than the sun and has an absolute magnitude of +1.4. A double star, its major component is twice the size of the sun; its major component (the Pup), the first white-dwarf star to be discovered, has a diameter only 50% greater than that of the earth but is extremely dense, its mass being just less than that of the sun.
See also: Binary star.

Sirocco, in southern Europe, warm, humid wind from the south or southeast, originating as a dry wind over the Sahara and gaining humidity from passage over the Mediterranean.

Sisal, any of various plants of the agave family, genus *Agave*. Two types of sisal, *A. sisalana*, found in eastern Africa and Brazil, and *A. fourcroydes*, found in Mexico, El Salvador, and Cuba, contain long fibers used to manufacture twine and hemp.

Sisley, Alfred (1839-99), Anglo-French painter, a founder of impressionism. His fine landscapes and snow scenes, painted in the 1870s, often show London and Paris neighborhoods; for example, *Effet de neige* (1874). His work achieved wide recognition only after his death.
See also: Impressionism.

Sistine Chapel, papal chapel in the Vatican Palace, Rome, renowned for its magnificent frescoes by Michelangelo and other Renaissance artists like Perugino, Botticelli, and Ghirlandaio. It is named for Pope Sixtus IV, who began its construction in 1473, and is used by the College of Cardinals when it meets to elect a new pope.

Sisyphus, in Greek mythology, founder and king of the ancient city-state of Corinth. Zeus, the head of the gods, was angered at Sisyphus and condemned him to push a heavy rock to the top of a hill. When it reached the top, it rolled back down, and Sisyphus was compelled to repeat the task for all eternity.
See also: Mythology.

Sitar, Indian stringed instrument with a long neck and smallish, rounded soundbox. There are usually 7 strings—5 melody and 2 drone. These are plucked by a player seated on cushions or the floor. In 1957 the Indian sitar virtuoso Ravi Shankar made the first of several concert tours of the United States, spreading the popularity of the instrument, which was then used by several rock bands.

Sitka (pop. 7,803), city in southeastern Alaska, on Baranof Island, west of British Columbia. Sitka was a Russian settlement founded (1799) by the trader Alexander Baranof. With the U.S. purchase of Alaska, the city served as the territorial capital from 1884 to 1900. Today it is a center for fishing and lumber industries. The Sitka National Historical Park commemorates a battle (1804) between the Russians and the Tlingit tribe.
See also: Alaska.

Sitting Bull (c.1831-90), chief of the Teton Sioux who led the last major Native American resistance in the United States. Born in South Dakota, he became head of the Sioux nation and inspired the 1876 campaign that resulted in the massacre of Gen. George Custer and his troops at Little Bighorn. Escaping to Canada, he was pardoned and returned to the Standing Rock reservation, N.D. (1881). He continued to support his people's causes, including their practice of the messianic Ghost Dance religion. At a performance of it he was killed by Native American police who were attempting to arrest him.

Sitwell, Dame Edith, (1887-1964), British poet and critic. A master technician of sound, rhythm, and symbol, she helped launch *Wheels* (1916), a magazine of experimental poetry, and wrote the satirical *Façade* (1922; music by William Walton).

Six, les, term coined in 1920 for a group of French composers: Georges Auric, Louis Durey, Arthur Honegger, Darius Milhaud,

Francis Poulenc, and Germaine Tailleferre, inspired by the anti-impressionist work of Erik Satie. They also worked with the writer Jean Cocteau.

Sixtus, name of 5 popes. **Sixtus IV** (1414-84) succeeded in 1471 and built the Sistine Chapel. His reign was characterized by nepotism and simony. **Sixtus V** (1521-90) succeeded in 1585 and brought the Papal States to order and made the pope one of Europe's richest princes. His reforms of church administration were part of the Counter-Reformation.

Skagerrak, also spelled Skager-Rak and Skagerrack, arm of the North Sea that separates Denmark from Norway and Sweden. About 130 mi (209 km) long, the Skagerrak joins the North Sea and the Kattegat.
See also: North Sea.

Skate, any of various fish (genus *Raja*) similar to rays. A popular skate used for food is the little skate (*R. erinacea*), which measures up to 2 ft (61 cm) long and is caught along the U.S. and Canadian Atlantic coast. Along the Pacific coast, the big skate (*R. binoculata*), which can measure up to 8 ft (2.5 m) long, are found. The pectoral fins of skate look and act like underwater wings, spanning the length of the fish from head nearly to its rudderlike tail. The wings move up and down to move the fish along. Skates generally feed on smaller animals, such as snails.

Skateboard, small board with plastic wheels, forming a kind of surfboard to be used on land. Professional and experienced skateboard riders can turn in circles on one wheel (endovers), travel on just 2 of the 4 wheels (wheelies), and jump over a multitude of objects during a ride.

Skeena River, river in British Columbia, Canada, rising in the Stikine mountains and flowing about 360 mi (580 k) to the Pacific Ocean. The river is known for the numerous salmon that are caught in its waters. Canneries are located near the mouth of this river, at Hecate Strait.

Skeet, sport in which the competitor shoots at clay disks mechanically thrown into the air. The disks are tossed to imitate the flight of certain birds. Shooters, using modified shotguns, stand at specific stations from which they shoot at the disks, which may be tossed individually or in pairs.

Skeleton, in vertebrates, framework of bones that supports and protects the soft tissues and organs of the body. It acts as an attachment for the muscles, especially those producing movement, and protects vital organs such as the brain, heart, and lungs. It is also a store of calcium, magnesium, sodium, phosphorous, and proteins, while its bone marrow is the site of red blood corpuscle formation. In the adult human body there are about 206 bones, to which more than 600 muscles are attached.
The skeleton consists of the axial skeleton (the skull, backbone, and ribcage) and the appendicular skeleton (limbs). The function of the *axial skeleton* is mainly protective. The skull consists of 29 bones, 8 being fused to form the cranium, protecting the brain. The *vertebral column*, or backbone, consists of 33 small bones (or vertebrae). The upper 25 are joined by ligaments and thick cartilaginous disks, and the lower 9 are fused. It supports the upper body and protects the spinal cord, which runs through it. The *ribcage* consists of 12 pairs of ribs forming a protective cage around the heart and lungs, and assists in breathing. The *appendicular skeleton* is primarily concerned with locomotion and consists of the arms and pectoral girdle and the legs and pelvic girdle. The limbs articulate with their girdles in ball-and-socket joints that permit the shoulder and hip great freedom of movement but that are prone to dislocation. In contrast, the elbows and knees are hinge joints that permit movement in one plane only but that are very strong.

Skepticism, philosophical attitude of doubting all claims to knowledge, chiefly on the ground that the adequacy of any proposed criterion is itself questionable. Examples of thoroughgoing skeptics, wary of dogmatism in whatever guise, were Pyrrho of Elis (*Pyrrhonism* and *skepticism* are virtual synonyms) and David Hume. Other thinkers—among them St. Augustine, Desiderius Erasmus, Michel de Montaigne, Blaise Pascal, Pierre Bayle, and Sören Kierkegaard—sought to defend faith and religion by directing skeptical arguments against the epistemological claims of rationalism and empiricism. Pragmatism and Immanuel Kant's critical philosophy represent two influential attempts to resolve skeptical dilemmas.
See also: Carneades; Pyrrho of Elis.

Skew line, in geometry, line that neither intersects nor runs parallel to another line in the same plane; in statistics, a line, as on a graph, indicating that the measured quantity departs from a normal distribution to the right or left of the curve.
See also: Geometry.

Skidmore, Louis (1897-1962), U.S. architect and cofounder of the firm of Skidmore, Owings and Merrill (1936), which designed such government and corporate projects as Oak Ridge, Tenn. (1943-45), the U.S. Air Force Academy in Colorado Springs (1954-62), and the Sears Tower in Chicago (1971-73).
See also: Architecture.

Skiing, sport of gliding over snow on long, thin runners called skis. It began some 5,000 years ago in northern Europe as a form of transport and became a sport in the 19th century. In 1924 the Fédération Internationale de Ski was formed and the first Winter Olympics held. It has increased enormously in popularity, either for pleasure or through participation in such Olympic-style activities as Alpine downhill slaloms, giant slalom obstacle races, Nordic cross-country skiing, or ski-jumping.

The human skeleton
1. parietal bone
2. frontal bone
3. temporal bone
4. cheek bone
5. nasal bone
6. upper jaw
7. lower jaw
8. spinal column
9. first thoracic vertebra
10. collar bone
11. rib
12. shoulder blade
13. breast bone
14. costal arch
15. humeral bone
16. radial bone
17. ulnar bone
18. carpal bones
19. meacarpal bones
20 . phalangeal bones of the hand
21. lilac bone
22. sacral bone
23. pubic bone
24. pubic symphysis
25. ischium
26. thigh bone
27. knee cap
28. shin bone
29. leg bone
30. outer ankle
31. inner ankle
32. tarsal bones
33. metatarsal bones
34. phalangeal bones of the foot

Skis are generally made of laminated wood, fiberglass, plastic, metal, or a combination of these. They have safety bindings attaching the specially made boot firmly to the ski; ski poles are used for balance.

Skimmer, seabird whose lower half of its bill is longer than the upper half. It flies low over the water with its bill cutting through the water to catch fish. Skimmers are found mainly along tropical coasts, but the black

Skimmer

skimmer comes up the western Atlantic as far as Massachusetts. They live in flocks, and their calls sound like a pack of hounds.

B.F. Skinner

Skin, tissue that forms a sensitive, elastic, protective, and waterproof covering of the body, together with its specializations (e.g., nails, hair). In the adult human it weighs 6.1 lb (2.75 kg), covers 18.3 sq ft (1.7 sq m), and varies in thickness from .04 in (1mm) in the eyelids to .12 in (3 mm) in the palms and soles. It consists of 2 layers: the outer, epidermis, and the inner, dermis, or true skin. The outermost part of the epidermis, the stratum corneum, contains a tough protein called keratin. Consequently, it provides protection against mechanical trauma, a barrier against microorganisms, and waterproofing. The epidermis also contains cells that produce the melanin responsible for skin pigmentation and that provide protection against the sun's ultraviolet rays. The unique pattern of skin folding on the soles and palms provides a gripping surface and is the basis of identification by fingerprints. The dermis is usually thicker than the epidermis and contains blood vessels, nerves, and sensory receptors, sweat glands, sebaceous glands, hair follicles, fat cells, and fibers. Temperature regulation of the body is aided by the evaporative cooling of sweat, regulation of the skin blood flow, and the erection of hairs that trap an insulating layer of air next to the skin. The rich nerve supply of the dermis is responsible for the reception of touch, pressure, pain, and temperature stimuli. Leading into the hair follicles are sebaceous glands that produce the antibacterial sebum, a fluid that keeps the hairs oiled and the skin moist. The action of sunlight on the skin initiates the formation of vitamin D, which helps prevent rickets.

Skin diving, underwater swimming and diving with or without selfcontained underwater breathing apparatus (SCUBA). The simplest apparatus is the snorkel, generally used with goggles, or mask, and flippers. An aqualung consists of compressed-air cylinders with an automatic demand regulator that supplies air at the correct pressure according to the diver's depth. "Closed-circuit" SCUBA contains a chemical that absorbs carbon dioxide from exhaled air.

Skin grafting, application of portions of skin, either the outer layers or the full thickness, to a raw surface to promote healing or to replace a defect.
See also: Plastic surgery.

Skink, slender lizard found in many of the warmer parts of the world. Skinks are abundant in Africa and 50 species live in the Americas. Some have rough scales, but the rest have very flat scales, sometimes so small that they are hard to see. Skinks may be aquatic or tree dwellers, and many have taken up burrowing, like the Florida sand skink. The largest skink is the 2-ft (0.61-m) giant zebra skink of the Solomon Islands, which has a prehensile tail. Skinks eat plants or small animals. Most lay eggs that are guarded by the mother; others bear live young. Young skinks often have blue tails that break off when they are attacked.

Skinner, B. F. (1904-90), U.S. psychologist and author whose advocacy of behaviorism helped it gain acceptance in 20th-century psychology. His best-known books are *Science and Human Behavior* (1953); *Walden Two* (1961), a Utopian novel based on behaviorism; and *Beyond Freedom and Dignity* (1971).
See also: Developmental psychology.

The human skull
A. side view
B. front view
C. back view
D. upper view
E. bottom view
1. frontal bone
2. parietal bone
3. occipital bone
4. temporal bone
5. sphenoid bone
6. maxilla
7. palate bone
8. mandible
9. zygomatic bone
10. ethmoid bone
11. nasal bone
12. occipital hole

Sklodowska, Marie *see:* Curie, Marie Sklodowska.

Skryabin, Alexander *see:* Scriabin, Alexander.

Skua, any of various sea birds (genus *Stercorarius*) known for stealing food from other sea birds, such as gulls, terns, petrels, and penguins. The skua lives in arctic and antarctic regions. Similar in looks to a sea gull, it is normally reddish to brown, with white patches on the wings. Skuas are strong fliers who harass weaker birds, causing them to drop their prey.

Skull, bony structure of the head and face situated at the top of the vertebral column. It forms a thick, bony protection of the brain, with small apertures for blood vessels, nerves, the spinal cord, and the thinner framework of facial structure.

Skunk, carnivorous mammal of the weasel family renowned for the foul stink it produces when threatened. There are 10 species distributed throughout the Americas. All are boldly patterned in black and white. Most are nocturnal and feed on insects, mice, and eggs. For defense, a skunk can expel fine jets of foul-smelling liquid from scent glands under the tail to a distance of 10 ft (3 m) with a remarkably accurate aim.

Skunk cabbage, either of two plant species (*Symplocarpus foetidus* or *Lysichitum americanum*), of temperate regions named for the foul smell that comes from the plant when the tissues are squeezed. Apart from the smell, the skunk cabbage is a welcome addition to the damp woods and fields of the eastern United States for its purple and green arum-type flower, which appears in late winter. The leaves appear after the flowers have died. A third species, *Veratrum californicum*, also called false hellebore or corn lily, grows in western North and Central America and is poisonous.

Sky *see:* Atmosphere.

Skydiving, popular name for sport parachuting. Skydivers reach speeds of up to 100 mph (160 kmph) after jumping out of planes at altitudes of up to 15,000 ft (4,600 m). The last 3,000 ft (920 m) or so of the fall is slowed by a parachute. Skydivers who aim for a ground target are called accuracy skydivers. Those that fall in formation with other divers are called relative work skydivers.

Skye terrier, breed of dog named after the Isle of Skye, Scotland, where it was first bred, in the 17th century. A work dog, good rat hunter, and pleasant companion, this terrier stands up to 10 in (25 cm) high at the shoulder and has a long body. Ears may be floppy or erect.

Skylab *see:* Space exploration.

Skyscraper, extremely tall building. In the mid-19th century the rising cost of land in big cities made building upward rather than outward worthwhile, and this became practicable with the development of safe electric elevators. The first skyscraper was the 130-ft (39.6 m) Equitable Life Assurance Society Building in New York (1870). A major design breakthrough was the use of a load-bearing skeletal iron frame, first used in the 10-story Home Insurance Building in Chicago (1883). The tallest skyscrapers are the Sears Tower in Chicago and the World Trade Center in New York City, with more than 110 stories.

Slag, residual material produced during the manufacture of pig iron and the smelting of metals, such as copper or lead. Slag is used in the making of concrete, road-building materials, and fertilizer. Its composition depends on the metallurgical process that produced it, though all slag contains silicates.

Slander, false statements intended to damage a person's reputation. A slanderous statement that is written or printed is called libel. The civil laws of the United States allow people to sue for libel.
See also: Libel.

Slang, informal and innovative use of language. Slang generally expresses new ideas or variations of old ones, most often in spoken speech. The particular words and expressions used tend not to remain popular for long, and slang often changes from region to region or from one ethnic or class group to the next.

Slate, fine-grained, low-grade metamorphic rock formed by the regional metamorphism of shale. The parallel orientation of platy minerals in the rock causes it to split evenly (slaty cleavage) in a plane that is perpendicular to the direction of the compressive metamorphic stress.

Slater, Samuel (1768-1835), British-born originator of the U.S. textile industry. As an employee of a company using the Richard Arkwright spinning machine, Slater learned about this revolutionary textile manufacturing process. Once in the United States, Slater reconstructed the Arkwright spinning machine from memory for Almy & Brown, a Rhode Island firm. Eventually he opened his own companies throughout New England, beginning with one in Rehoboth, Mass. (1798).
See also: Textile.

Slavery, practice found at different times in most parts of the world, now condemned in the UN's Universal Declaration of Human Rights. Slavery generally means enforced servitude, along with society's recognition that the master has ownership rights over the slave and his or her labor. Some elements of slavery can be found in serfdom, as practiced during the Middle Ages and in Russia up to 1861; in debt bondage and peonage, both forms of enforced labor for the payment of debts; and in forced labor itself, exacted for punishment or for political or military reasons (examples being the "slave" labor used by the Nazis in World War II and the Soviet labor camps). In some places a form of slavery, or bondage, is still practiced today, under the guise of exacting a bride price, or the "adoption" of poor children by wealthier families for labor purposes. While peonage is still rampant in South America, actual slavery is reputed to exist in Africa, the Arabian Peninsula, Tibet, and elsewhere. Slavery in Saudi Arabia was officially abolished only in 1962.
Warfare was the main source of slaves in ancient times, along with enslavement for debt or as punishment and the selling of children. But there was not necessarily a distinction in race or color between master and slave. Manumission (the granting of freedom) was commonplace, and in Greece and Rome many slaves or freedmen rose to influential posts. A slave dynasty, the Mamelukes, ruled Egypt (1250-1517). Germans enslaved many Slavic people (hence *slave*) in the Dark Ages. By the 13th century feudal serfdom was widespread in Europe. Slavery increased when the Portuguese, exploring the coast of Africa, began to import slaves in 1433. With the European discovery of the Americas and the development of plantations, the need for cheap, abundant labor encouraged slave trade. The British abolished its own slave trade in 1807 and slavery in 1833. By constitutional provision, the U.S. slave trade ended in 1808, but not the practice. The abolition issue ignited the U.S. Civil War in 1861. President Lincoln's Emancipation Proclamation (1863) took full effect with the end of the war in 1865.

Slavonic, 3 groups of Indo-European languages spoken by about 440 million people in central and eastern Europe and Siberia. The groups are West Slavonic (Polish, Czech, Slovak), South Slavonic (Slovene, Serbo-Croatian, Macedonian, Bulgarian), and East Slavonic (Russian, Ukrainian, Byelorussian). Byzantine missionaries in the 9th century first developed written Slavic, using a modified Greek alphabet known as Cyrillic. Today Slavs converted by the Orthodox church use Cyrillic characters, and Slavs converted by the Roman church use the Latin alphabet.

Slavs, largest European ethnic group, living today in central and eastern Europe and Siberia, all speaking Slavic languages.
About 4,000 years ago they migrated to land north of the Black Sea and later split into 3 groups: the East Slavs (Byelorussians, Russians, and Ukrainians), the West Slavs (Czechs, Poles, Slovaks, and Sorbs (Wends), and the South Slavs (Bulgarians, Macedonians, Serbs, Croats, and Slovens). By the 9th century Slavic nations were formed, but almost all were overwhelmed by Turkish or Mongol invaders. In the 15th century Russia gained national independence, but other Slavic nations did not regain their national identities until World War I.

Slayton, Donald Kent (1924-), U.S. astronaut. In a cooperative venture between the United States and the USSR (Apollo-Soyuz Test Project, 1975), Slayton and his Apollo crew (Thomas P. Stafford and Vance D. Brand) orbited the earth while docked with a Soviet spacecraft and its crew. Slayton was later director of flight crew operations for the NASA.
See also: Astronaut.

A 19th-century colored print of the cramped slave quarters below a ship's deck during the long journey from Africa to the Caribbean

Sled, transportation vehicle that moves over ice and snow on runners. Early sleds were made from joined logs. Some Native American tribes developed toboggans—sleds shaped like canoes. Today in Alaska and other ice-covered regions, sleds with thin, parallel runners pulled by dogs help to transport people and goods. Bobsleds are fiberglass-and-steel sleds ridden on special courses for speed.

Sleep, state of relative unconsciousness and inactivity. The need for sleep recurs periodically in all animals. If deprived of sleep, humans initially experience hallucinations and acute anxiety and become highly suggestible. Eventually coma and sometimes death result. During sleep, the body is relaxed and most bodily activity is reduced. Cortical, or higher, brain activity, is measured by the electroencephalograph; blood pressure, body temperature, and rate of heartbeat and breathing are decreased. However, certain activities, such as gastric and alimentary activity, are increased. Sleep tends to occur in daily cycles that exhibit up to 5 or 6 periods of deepness—alternating with periods of paradoxical, or rapid-eye-movement (REM), sleep, characterized by restlessness and jerky movements of the eyes. Paradoxical sleep occurs only when we are dreaming and occupies about 20% of total sleeping time. Sleepwalking (somnambulism) occurs only during orthodox sleep, when we are not dreaming. Sleeptalking occurs mostly in orthodox sleep. Many theories have been proposed to explain sleep. Separate sleeping and waking centers in the hypothalamus cooperate with other parts of the brain in controlling sleep. Sleep as a whole—and particularly paradoxical sleep, when dreaming occurs—is essential to health and life. Consequently, the key to why animals sleep may reside in a need to dream.

Sleeping sickness, serious disease caused by protozoan parasites and transmitted by the bite of the tsetse fly. Sleeping sickness is common in many areas of Africa. Symptoms include fever, headache, skin rash, swollen lymph nodes, and lethargy. The disease is named after the comalike state that may eventually result. Early diagnosis and drug treatment can lessen the sometimes fatal effects.

Sleepwalking (somnambulism), condition in which a partly awakened sleeper performs physical activities during a period of tension or worry. It occurs during deep sleep, early in the night. Most sleepwalkers do not remember their activities upon awakening. Sleepwalking is generally harmless, although injury can occur.

Sleet, partially frozen, transparent bits of ice, falling initially as rain or melted snowflakes and freezing as they travel through parts of the atmosphere below 32°F (0°C).

Slime mold, organism classified as a fungus but that resembles an animal in its ability to move. A slime mold is a yellowish mass, like the raw white of an egg, that is found in damp, dark woods, where it oozes over rotten logs and decayed leaves. It moves like an amoeba, sweeping up particles of dead leaves and bacteria as it goes.

Sling, device used to hurl stones or other objects. In ancient slings, a stone was placed on a strap and spun quickly above the head before being let loose to fly through the air with great force. The biblical hero David killed Goliath with a stone from a sling. Soldiers from the armies of ancient Egypt through those of medieval Europe used slings in combat. Another form of sling, the bola, is tossed along with the stone. Thrown at an animal, it will entangle its legs as well as forcefully hit it.

Slipperwort, or slipper flower, any of a group of 300-400 evergreen plants belonging to the figwort family found in Mexico and South America. Its name derives from the slipperlike shape of its flowers, which are variously colored.

Sloan, Alfred P. (1875-1966), U.S. industrialist, president (1923-37) and chairman of the board (1937-56) of General Motors. His Sloan Foundation (1934) finances social and medical research, particularly through the Sloan-Kettering Institute for Cancer Research in New York City.

Sloan, John (1871-1951), U.S. painter, member of the Ashcan School and influential in the development of modern art. He is noted for his paintings of nudes and of urban scenes, such as *McSorley's Bar* (1912) and *Wake of the Ferry* (1907).
See also: Ashcan School.

Sloe, or blackthorn, spiny shrub (*Prunus spinosa*) of the rose family found in some parts of North America, Asia, and Europe. Its plumlike fruits are used to make a variety of products, such as dyes, jellies, and wine.

Sloth, slow, tree-dwelling, toothless mammal. There are 2 genera of modern tree sloths; 2-toed sloths (*Choloepus*) and 3-toed sloths, or ai (*Bradypus*), descending from the giant ground sloths (*Megatherium*) of the Pleistocene epoch. The arms and legs are long and the digits are bound together by tissue and terminate in long, strong claws. With these the sloth can suspend its body from branches. All sloths are South American in origin and vegetarian, feeding on fruits, shoots, and leaves.

Sloth bear, or honey bear, slow-moving mammal of the bear family found in the warm forest regions of India and Sri Lanka. Although its sense of smell is highly developed, the sloth bear has poor vision and hearing. A staple of its diet is insects, which it ferrets out with its long claws and snout, then sucks in through spaces between the teeth. It is also known to like honey. A sloth bear stands about 5 ft (1.5 m) tall and can weigh up to 250 lb (113 kg). Unlike some other bears, it does not hibernate during the winter months.

Slot machine, mechanized gambling device first developed in 1899. Coins are inserted through a slot, a handle is pulled, and a series of reels, visible through a window, spin for a while before coming to a halt. The player wins if the reels show a certain number of identical symbols.

Slovakia, or Slovak Republic, independent country in central Europe. It is mostly mountainous, but the heights slope down to plains and the Danube River in the south and southwest. Slovakia has rich farmlands and mineral deposits; shipbuilding and metal processing are leading industries. The capital, Bratislava, is a prominent Danube port. Slovakia was principally under Hungarian rule from the early 10th century to 1918. Slovakia then became part of Czechoslovakia until it became a German protectorate in 1939. After World War II Slovakia was reincorporated into Czechoslovakia until its independence in 1993.
See also: Czechoslovakia.

Slovakia

Capital:	Bratislava
Area:	18,933 sq mi (49,036 sq km)
Population:	5,346,000
Government:	republic
Independent:	1993
GNP:	U.S. $10,249,000,000
Per capita:	U.S. $1,920

Slovaks, Slavic people who settled in central Europe during the 5th and 6th centuries. Slovakia was dominated by Hungary from about 900 until the 1800s, when the Slovaks began a struggle for autonomy. Together with the more numerous Czechs, they formed the independent nation of Czechoslavakia in 1918.
See also: Slavs.

Slovenia

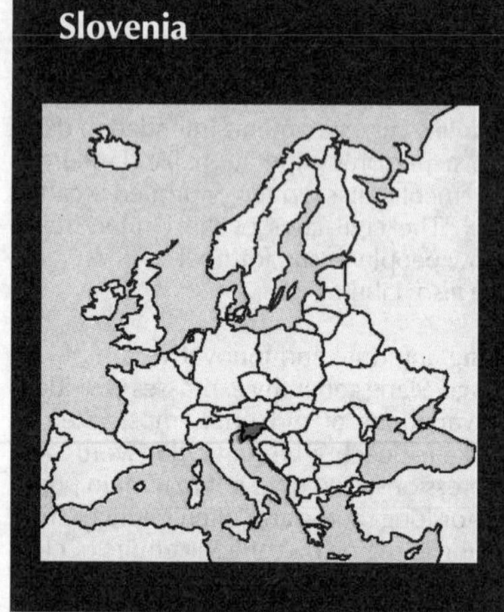

Capital:	Ljubljana
Area:	7,820 sq mi (20,253 sq km)
Population:	2,071,000
Government:	republic
Independent:	1991
GNP:	U.S. $12,744,000,000
Per capita:	U.S. $6,330

Slovenia, independent country in central eastern Europe, bounded by the Adriatic Sea, Italy, Austria, Hungary, and Croatia. Its capital is Ljubljana. From the 13th century until the end of World War I Slovenia was ruled by Austria. In 1918, it became part of Yugoslavia. Slovenia was the most industrialized of the former 6 Yugoslavian republics and had the highest standard of living. Industries currently include chemicals, textiles, iron, and steel. Ski resorts, beaches, and caverns contribute to an active tourist trade. In recent years Slovenia sought increasing independence from Yugoslavia and finally declared its own sovereignty in 1991.
See also: Yugoslavia.

Slug, mollusk best described as a snail without a shell or with a tiny shell inside the body. An exception is the roundback slug, which has an outside shell. Behind the head, with its 4 tentacles, is an oval shield containing a pore that leads to the lungs. Slugs creep over the ground like snails and leave a trail of slime. As they have no shell to retire into, they have to live in moist places to escape drying up. Some slugs eat fungi, others eat green plants and are garden pests.

Small Business Administration, independent agency of the U.S. government that furnishes small businesses with practical advice and low-cost loans. The agency also helps small businesses obtain government contracts and aids minority-owned firms.

Small-claims court, U.S. court set up to resolve lawsuits involving claims of less than $ 5000. First begun in 1913 in Cleveland, Ohio, small-claims courts now exist in every state. Cases frequently pertain to unpaid bills or debts, inferior product performance, or poorly provided services.

Smallpox, acute, highly contagious viral disease, initiated by sudden severe constitutional symptoms and characterized by a progressive skin eruption that often results in permanent pits and scars. The disease is of historical interest only, for the World Health Organization declared the world free of smallpox in 1980.
See also: Jenner, Edward.

Smartweed, weed belonging to the buckwheat family and found in the lowlands and marshes of North America. It can grow up to 5 ft (1.5 m) tall. It is recognized by its small white, pink, or green flowers. The name derives from its sharp, bitter taste.

Smell, sense that enables humans and animals to perceive and identify odors. The organ of smell is the nose. Respiratory air is drawn into the nostrils and passes across a specialized receptor surface—the olfactory epithelium. Receptor cells detect the tiny concentrations of odors in the airstream and stimulate nerve impulses that pass to olfactory centers in the brain for coding and perception. It is not possible to classify odors in the same way as the primary colors in vision, and it is probable that pattern recognition is more important. Certain animals depend mainly on the sense of smell, while humans are predominantly visual animals. But with training, humans can achieve sensitive detection and discrimination of odors.

Smelling salts, chemical stimulant used to alleviate faintness. It consists of a mixture of ammonium carbonate, alcohol, and fragrance. When fumes are inhaled, nasal membranes are irritated and breathing becomes more rapid, resulting in a feeling of clear-headedness.
See also: Ammonia.

Smelt, small, silvery fish that lives in large shoals in the colder waters of the Northern Hemisphere. Smelts range from 3 to 12 in (7.6 to 30.5 cm) and are an important food for other fishes. Like the related salmon and trout, they have a fleshy fin on the back. The American smelt is caught in large numbers as it ascends Atlantic Coast rivers to spawn. Pacific smelt are not often eaten because of their oily flesh.

Smelting, in metallurgy, process of extracting a metal from its ore by heating the ore in a blast furnace or reverberatory furnace (one in which a shallow hearth is heated by radiation from a low roof heated by flames from the burning fuel). A reducing agent, usually a coke, is used, and a flux is added to remove impurities.
See also: Metallurgy.

Smetana, Bedrich (1824-84), Czech composer. Many of Smetana's compositions reflect his ardent Bohemian nationalism; best known are the comic opera *The Bartered Bride* (1866) and the symphonic poem *Má Vlast* (*My Fatherland*; 1874-79), which contains *Vltava* (*The Moldau*).

Smilax, any of many species of woody vines (genus *Smilax*) found in temperate or tropical areas. There are about 300 different species, including the common greenbrier. Smilax typically have prickly stems, veined leaves, white or yellow-green flowers, and bluish-black or red berries.

Smith, Adam (1723-90), Scottish economist and philosopher. The free-market system he advocated in *Inquiry into the Nature and Causes of the Wealth of Nations* (1776) came to be regarded as the classic system of economics. Smith drew on the ideas of his friends D. Hume, A. R. Turgot, F. Quesnay, and C. Montesquieu, and argued that if market forces were allowed to operate without state intervention "an invisible hand" would guide self-interest for the well-being of all. His concept of the division of labor and the belief that value derives from productive labor were major insights. An earlier work, *Theory of Moral Sentiments* (1759), contrasts with *The Wealth of Nations* in its emphasis upon sympathy rather than self-interest as a basic force in human nature.
See also: Economics.

Smith, Alfred Emanuel (1873-1944), U.S. politician elected governor of New York 4 times (1918, 1922-26). He was a Tammany Hall politician and a leading Democrat. Although supported by Franklin D. Roosevelt, Smith, the first Roman Catholic to run for the presidency, failed to be nominated in 1924 and was beaten by Herbert Hoover in 1928. When Roosevelt became president, Smith opposed the New Deal.

Smith, Bessie (1894-1937), U.S. jazz singer. "The Empress of the Blues" came from a poor Tennessee home and first recorded in 1923; later she performed with many leading musicians, including Louis Armstrong and Benny Goodman.

Smith, David (1906-65), influential U.S. sculptor, famous for his constructions of wrought iron and cut steel. His late works, like *Cubi XVIII* (1964), comprised burnished or painted cubic forms dramatically welded together.

Smith, Edmund Kirby (1824-93), U.S. general who served in the Confederate army during the Civil War, having previously fought in the Mexican War. He is known as the last Southern general to surrender to the North at the end of the war.
See also: Civil War, U.S.

Smith, Ian Douglas (1919-), Rhodesian prime minister (1964-79). As leader of a white minority government, he declared unilateral independence from Great Britain and made Rhodesia a republic in 1970. Civil strife ensued. In 1978 Smith and 3 black leaders agreed to share control until power was transferred to the black majority, but guerrilla nationalists rejected the plan. A British cease-fire was accepted in 1979, and complete independence came in 1980 with the formation of a black regime in Rhodesia, renamed Zimbabwe. Under the black majority rule Smith remained active in politics.

Smith, James (1719?-1806), Irish-born U.S. lawyer and legislator and one of the signers of the Declaration of Independence. He was a member of the Continental Congress from 1776 to 1778.

Smith, Jedediah Strong (1799-1831), U.S. pioneer who led fur-trapping expeditions to the Missouri and Wind rivers and in 1824 discovered the South Pass route across the Rocky Mountains to the far West. Smith was the first white man to cross the Sierra Nevada and the Great Salt Desert and to explore the California-Oregon coast by land. He was killed by Comanches.
See also: Pioneer life in America.

Smith, John (1580?-1631), English soldier who helped found the first successful English colony in America, in 1607. As president of the colony—Jamestown, Va.—Smith enforced organization and discipline among the settlers. His harsh treatment of Native Americans, however, contributed to hostilities between the groups. Late in life, he wrote several books about his experiences, one of which was the source of the story of his capture by Powhatan and last-minute rescue by Pocahontas.

Smith, Joseph (1805-44), founder of the Church of Jesus Christ of Latter-Day Saints in Fayette, N.Y., in 1830. Its doctrine and organization are derived from several texts, principally the *Book of Mormon* (1830), which is based on golden tablets inscribed with sacred writings that Smith claimed to have found and translated with miraculous help. Community opposition caused him to move his colony to the Midwest, where it flourished despite schisms. But when Smith announced his candidacy for the US presidency in 1844, non-Mormons arrested both him and his brother, Hyrum, for conspiracy and treason. Taken from jail at Carthage, Ill., by a mob, they were shot.
See also: Mormons.

Smith, Kate (Kathryn Elizabeth Smith; 1909-86), singer and radio and television personality. Although she appeared on the New York stage, she made her reputation on radio in the 1930s. She is associated with Irving Berlin's song "God Bless America," to which she had exclusive radio rights. Smith entertained during World War II, selling war bonds and appearing for the troops. She appeared regularly on television from 1950 to 1956.

Smith, Margaret Chase (1897-), U.S. legislator, first woman to serve in both the House of Representatives and the Senate. She was named to replace her husband (a representative from Maine) when he died in office in 1940, and was later elected for 4 full terms. As a senator, she was one of the first opponents of Senator Joseph McCarthy. In 1964 she became the first woman from a major party to campaign for the presidency.

Smith, Walter Bedell (1895-1961), U.S. Army chief of staff in Europe in World War II. He negotiated the surrenders of Italy (1943) and Germany (1945), was ambassador to the USSR (1946-49), CIA director (1950-53), and undersecretary of state (1953-54).
See also: World War II.

Smith Act (1940), federal U.S. law making it a criminal offense to advocate the violent overthrow of the government or to belong to any group advocating this. Used to convict Communist Party leaders, the act also required registration and fingerprinting of aliens.

Smith-Hughes Act, congressional act adopted in 1917 providing eligible states with funds for job-training programs. State proposals must be submitted and approved prior to the allocation of funds.

A smog-cloaked city

Smithson, James (1765-1829), British chemist and mineralogist. Though he never visited the United States, he bequeathed to it his entire fortune of over £100,000 (then about $500,000) to found the Smithsonian Institution in Washington, D.C.

Smithsonian Institution, world's largest museum complex, known as the "nation's attic," comprising 14 U.S. government-sponsored museums and the National Zoo. All of these are in Washington, D.C., except for the Cooper-Hewitt Museum in New York City, and hold perhaps 100 million artifacts illustrating both scientific and artistic culture. Founded with a bequest from James Smithson, the institution was established by Congress in 1846. The Smithsonian undertakes considerable scientific research, but is popularly known for its National Air and Space Museum, National Museum of Natural History, National Gallery of Art, National Portrait Gallery, and National Museum of American Art. The institution is governed by a board of regents comprising the U.S. vice president and chief justice, 3 senators, 3 representatives, and 9 private citizens appointed by Congress.
See also: Smithson, James.

Smog, term first used in 1905 to describe the combination of smoke and thick fog that hung over London and other cities in Great Britain. London-type fog occurs when moisture in the air condenses on smoke particles produced by burning coal. Sulfur dioxide, the dangerous part of London-type smog, attacks the lungs. Petrochemical smog results from the action of sunlight on hydrocarbons and nitrogen oxides in the air that are formed by burning gasoline and petroleum products. It can irritate the eyes, nose, throat, and lungs. Smog is poisonous in heavy concentrations and can be fatal. It also destroys plant life and deteriorates building materials.
See also: Air pollution.

Smoke, vapor consisting of fine carbonaceous particles suspended in a gas, produced by the burning of fuel. Smoke can harm the lungs as well as cause damage to property and vegetation. It is used commercially in agriculture and in the preservation of meats.
See also: Air pollution.

Smoke detector, or smoke alarm, device placed in a room or floor of a building to signal the presence of smoke or fire. When smoke passes through the device, a loud, high-pitched sound is triggered. The 2 basic types are photoelectric detectors and ionization detectors.

Smoking, habit of inhaling the smoke of dried tobacco or other leaves from a pipe or a cigarette. Smoking has been practiced for centuries in various communities, often using plants with hallucinogenic or other mood-altering properties. The modern habit of smoking began in America and spread to Europe in the 16th century. Mass production of cigarettes began in the 19th century.
Researchers have noted an uneqivocal association between smoking and such life-threatening diseases as lung cancer, chronic arthritis, emphysema, and diseases of the arteries and heart. Smoking appears to play a part in other forms of cancer and peptic ulcers, and is responsible for 2-2.5 million deaths each year. It is not yet clear what part of the smoke is responsible for promoting disease. Nonsmokers may be affected by environmental smoke; passive smokers are perhaps 3 times more likely to die of lung cancer than they would be otherwise. Smoking causes both physical and psychological addiction.
The health hazards resulting from the practice of smoking have generally been recognized by the public. Filter cigarettes and then low-tar and low-nicotine cigarettes have gained popular acceptance. Behavioral scientists have devoted much attention to helping people stop smoking. Although many people have successfully quit, many others have had great difficulty ending the habit. Efforts to educate the public have concentrated on presenting negative images of smoking, regulating the advertising of cigarettes, limiting the public spaces in which smoking is permitted, and increasing the cost of cigarettes by taxation. Some controversy exists between those who believe smoking is an individual choice and those who believe society has the right to act on its own behalf.

Smuggling, unlawful conveyance of goods or individuals across a border. Legitimate goods are often smuggled to avoid payment of a duty; illegal goods—such as drugs—are smuggled. Nations have varying laws regulating the importation of goods, and penalties vary as well. In the United States, proof of intent is a necessary precondition for conviction.

Smut, fungi named for the masses of sooty spores formed on the surface of the host plant. Within the plant the smut develops a network of threads that take nutrients from it and cause stunting. Smuts attack wheat, corn, and other cereals, onions, sunflowers, and a few other plants. Smuts are hard to control because their spores can survive in the ground over the winter.

Smuts, Jan Christiaan (1870-1950), Afrikaaner soldier and politician, prime minister of South Africa (1919-24 and 1939-48). A general in the South African War against the British, Smuts later cooperated with them to found the Union of South Africa (1910). He was made a field marshal during World War II and participated in the British military leadership.
See also: South Africa.

Snail, herbivorous gastropod mollusk with, typically, a spirally coiled shell, found on land, in fresh water, or in the sea. The shell is secreted by the underlying mantle and houses the internal organs. The internal structure is similar in all groups, though land snails (pulmonates) have air-breathing lungs instead of gills. Nonpulmonate snails are mostly unisexual, while pulmonates are typically hermaphrodite.

Snake, legless reptile related to the lizards. There are about 2,700 species, most of which live in tropical countries, though a few survive in nearly arctic conditions. Snakes do not have legs, although the boas and pythons have the remains of a hind pair of legs. It is thought that they evolved from burrowing, legless lizards. Snakes, unlike lizards, do not have eardrums and are deaf to airborne sounds (they cannot hear the snake charmer's flute), but they can sense sounds coming through the ground by their vibrations. Locomotion is achieved by several methods. In the common serpentine movement, the body is pushed forward in S-shaped waves. In concertina movement the body is thrown forward in loops. Large snakes can push themselves along by movements of the belly scales. The sidewinder and the horned viper move over loose sand by throwing the body into S-shaped waves in side-winding locomotion. Snakes feed on live animals or eggs. They kill their prey by constriction—preventing it from breathing but not crushing it—or by biting. Poisonous snakes inject venom through grooved or hollow fangs from modified saliva glands. Hematoxic venoms attack the blood and nervous system; and neurotoxic venoms attack the nerves. The young hatch from eggs or are born alive. The mother may look after the eggs; otherwise they are left in a nest in soil or under a log. Snakes grow throughout their lives and shed their skins every year or so.

Snakebird *see:* Anhinga; Wryneck.

Snakebite, bite of a snake that, when poisonous, can be fatal. Sometimes it may be necessary to cut and suction the wound, and many first-aid kits contain a syringe for this purpose.

Snake charming, folk art originating in northern Africa and southern Asia in which a charmer uses rhythmic body movements to encourage similar swaying movements by a snake, usually a cobra. Although snakes cannot hear, the charmer typically plays a flute while swaying.

Snake dance, religious ceremony of the Hopi tribe of Native Americans in the Southwest. It is part of a larger ceremony held every year to ensure peace, health, and good crops. At the climax of the snake dance, which lasts 9 days, the men hold live rattlesnakes in their mouths as they dance.

Snake killer *see:* Roadrunner.

Snake River, large branch of the Columbia River in the Pacific Northwest, made up of the Upper, Middle, and Lower Snake rivers. Each one has many tributaries. The river has great importance as a generator of hydroelectric power, and its tributaries are used for irrigation. Streams of the Upper Snake River sink beneath the ground to form a huge subterranean reservoir. The river is navigable and is used as a trade link between the Pacific Ocean and inland areas.

Snakeroot, any of a group of unrelated plants found in the prairies and wooded areas of North America and believed to be useful in curing snakebite. Black snakeroot, Virginia snakeroot, and button snakeroot were used to treat a variety of ailments. Texas snakeroot was used as an anesthetic and stimulant.

Snapdragon, plant (genus *Antirrhinum*) of the figwort family whose flowers have the upper and lower petals pressed together like an animal's jaws. Only strong insects, such as bumblebees, can force their way inside the petals to pollinate the flower, but butterflies can insert their tubular tongues between the "lips" to suck nectar. Snapdragons came from the Mediterranean and are a favorite garden flower.

Snapper, large-headed fish with a long dorsal fin and a deep body. There are over 250 warm water species. They live in shoals and feed on almost anything edible. Many have red bodies, and several kinds are marketed as red snapper. The fish is good to eat, and some of the inshore species are caught by anglers. Snappers get their name from a habit of suddenly shutting their mouths when dying—which can be painful for someone who has a finger in the way, for they have sharp teeth.

SNCC *see:* Student Nonviolent Coordinating Committee.

Snead, Sam (1912-), U.S. golfer. Known for his strong drives and fluent swing, "Slamming Sammy" won a record 84 Professional Golfers' Association (PGA) tournaments between 1936 and 1965. His achievements include winning the PGA championship (1942, 1949, 1951), the Masters Tournament (1949, 1952, 1954) and the British Open (1946).

Sneeze, explosive expiration through the nose and mouth stimulated by irritation or inflammation in the nasal epithelium. It is a reflex attempt to remove the source of irritation.

Sneezewort (*Achillea ptarmica*), perennial plant of Europe and Asia, a species of yarrow, whose leaves are used to make sneezing powder.

Snipe, long-billed bird of the family Scolopacidae with flexible bill tips that can be opened below ground to grasp food items. Active mainly at dawn and dusk, snipes are birds of marshy areas or open moorland with large eyes set far back on the head. Extraordinarily well camouflaged, they rise sharply if disturbed at close quarters and escape with an erratic zigzag flight. In courtship many species produce loud whistling or drumming noises by vibration of the primaries or tail coverts in rapid dives.

Sniperscope, device developed during World War II to enable soldiers to aim rifles accurately at night. The scope emits invisible infrared rays whose reflection off objects the shooter can see by looking through the scope. It had limited effectiveness and has since been replaced by the starlight scope.

Snooker *see:* Billiards.

Snoring, rough, hoarse respiration of certain persons during sleep; the noise is caused by vibration of the soft palate. It is predisposed to by the shape of the pharynx and by the sleeping position.

Snow, precipitation consisting of flakes or clumps of ice crystals. The crystals are plane hexagonal, showing an infinite variety of beautiful, branched forms; needles, columns, and irregular forms are also found. Snow forms by direct vapor-to-ice condensation from humid air below 32°F (0°C). On reaching the ground, snow crystals lose their structure and become granular. Fresh snow is very light (specific gravity about 0.1) and is a good insulator, protecting underlying plants from severe cold. In time, pressure, sublimation, melting, and refreezing lead to compaction into névé.

Snow, C(harles) P(ercy) (1905-80), English physicist, government official, and author, many of whose works deal with the widening gap between art and technology. He is best known for his *Strangers and Brothers* series: 11 novels (1940-70) about the English professional classes.

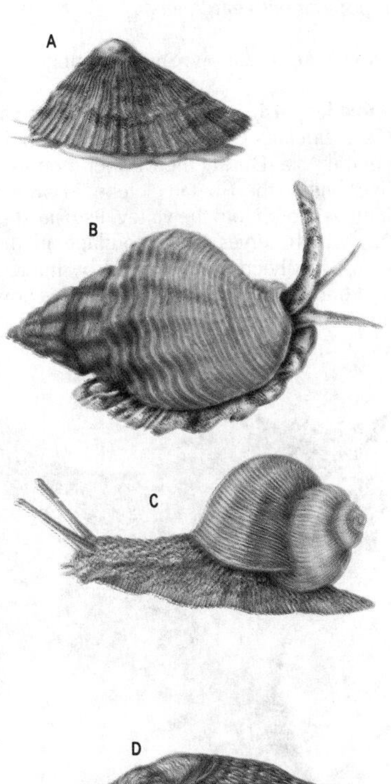

Kinds of snails:
A. limpets
B. whelks
C. land snails
D. slugs

Snow, Edgar (1905-72), U.S. journalist and author. The first Westerner to visit the Chinese Communists in their remote headquarters in Yanan (1936), he wrote a sympathetic account of their programs and idealism in *Red Star over China* (1937). A personal friend of Mao Zedong and Zhou Enlai, he was one of the few U.S. citizens to visit China regularly after the 1949 revolution, about which he wrote *The Other Side of the River* (1962) and *The Long Revolution* (1972).

Snowball, or European cranberry bush, any of various berry-producing shrubs (genus *Viburnum*) of the honeysuckle family native to Gelderland province, the Netherlands. They have clusters of large white flowers. When cultivated, they do not bear fruit and can grow as high as 12 ft (3.7 m).

Snow blindness, temporary loss of vision with severe pain, tears, and swelling due to excessive ultraviolet light reflected from snow. Permanent damage is rare; protective polarized glasses helps prevent snow blindness.

Snow bunting, or snowflake, bird of the finch family found in Arctic regions. It resembles a sparrow except that it has a white head and breast in winter. During the coldest months, it migrates south into Canada and occasionally the United States.

Snowdrop, flowering herb (*Galanthus nivalis*) of the amaryllis family found predominantly in Eurasia. Each plant consists of a leaved stalk topped by a drooping, fragile-looking white flower resembling a snowdrop. A hardy and attractive plant, it is popular with gardeners.

Snowflake *see:* Snow; Snow bunting.

Snow leopard, or ounce, large mammal (*Felis uncia*) of the cat family found in central Asia. During the warmer months it lives high in the Tibetan plateau; in winter, it moves south into the valley. Its pale gray fur, which serves as camouflage in the snow, has been much valued by hunters and traders, and the snow leopard is now an endangered species.

Snow leopard

Snow line, uneven line along mountain slopes marking areas of permanent snow. Since its position depends on many factors, it varies greatly from place to place. Snow lines can be used to evaluate global climatic shifts.

Snowmobile, engine-driven sled used for transport over large areas of ice and snow. An early, more cumbersome form of the vehicle was used in the 1920s. Today snowmobiling is a popular sport in many parts of North America and northern Europe. The snowmobile is also used by hunters, fishers, rescue workers, forest rangers, and power companies. In some areas its use has been restricted because of criticisms from environmentalists.

Snow-on-the-mountain, annual plant (*Euphorbia marginata*) of the spurge family found predominantly in the central plains of the United States. Popular with gardeners and florists, it grows to about 2 ft (61 cm) in height and has small, white flowers.

Snowshoe, oval-shaped wooden frame with crosspieces strung with thongs, attached to the foot to distribute body weight so as to make it easier to walk on snow without sinking. Snowshoes were invented by Native Americans. Today they are used by loggers, hunters, and farmers. They are made of light wood and leather, and are at least 3 ft (91 cm) long and 1-1.5 ft (30-46 cm) wide.

Snowshoe hare, or varying hare, North American mammal of the rabbit family. A hare of medium size, it is recognized by its large, thickly furred hind feet, which allow it to hop effortlessly over snow. It sheds its brown coat in winter and grows a white one. It is prey for the lynx, snowy owls, and hunters.

Snowy egret *see:* Egret.

Snuff, pulverized, fermented tobacco leaves ground into a powder and inhaled, chewed, or placed in the mouth. The taking of snuff was popular in the 18th century, and decorated snuffboxes were commonly worn as jewelry. Today the practice is believed to pose substantial health risks.

Soapberry, species of trees and shrubs belonging to the soapberry family, grown in tropical and subtropical areas of the Americas and Asia, as well as on Pacific islands. When rubbed in water, the leaves and leathery fruits, which contain saponin, produce a soapy lather.

Soap Box Derby, downhill coasting race for small racing cars without motors or pedals, open to young people from 9 to 16 years. Using homebuilt cars that must comply to rules for size, weight, and cost, contestants first race in local competitions. Winners are eligible to compete in the All-American Soap Box Derby held annually in August in Akron, Ohio.

Soap plant, herb (*Chlorogalum pomeridianum*) of the lily family, native to California. It can grow to a height of 8 ft (2.4 m). The soap plant's small, white flowers open in late afternoon or evening and close in the morning. It grows from a large bulb, which was once used by Native Americans as soap and roasted for food.

Soap sculpture, raised design or figure sculpted from a bar of soap. The design, traced in carbon on the soap, may be cut with a sharp knife and smoothed with a nail file. It may be lacquered or painted with acrylic or poster paints.

Soapstone, or steatite, metamorphic rock consisting largely of compacted talc with some serpentine and carbonates, formed by alteration of peridotite. Soft and soapy to the touch, soapstone has been used from prehistoric times for carvings and vessels. When fired it becomes hard and is used for insulators. The chief deposits are in the United States, Canada, and Norway.
See also: Talc.

Soares, Mário Alberto Nobre Lopes (1924-), Portuguese politician, premier (1976-78 and 1983-85) and president since 1986. An opponent of dictator António Salazar, he was repeatedly imprisoned and exiled. Under Soares, Portugal entered the European Community (EC) in 1986.

Sobieski, John *see:* John III Sobieski.

Soccer, national sport of most European and Latin American countries, and rapidly increasing in popularity in the United States. It is played with an inflated leather ball 27-28 in (68.6-71.1 m in circumference) on a field measuring 115 yd by 75 yd (105.2 m by 68.6 m); the goal is 8 yd (7.3 m) wide and 8 ft (2.4 m) high. Two 45-min halves make a game, supervised by 1 referee and 2 lines officials. The aim of each 11-player team is to score by kicking or heading the ball into the opponent's goal. To advance the ball, a player may dribble it (repeatedly kick it while running with it) or kick it to a teammate. The ball may not be touched with the hand or arm, except by the goalkeeper in the penalty area in front of the goal. Modern professional soccer began in the United Kingdom in 1885, in the United States in 1967. The major international competition is the World Cup, held every 4 years.

Social class, group of people with a similar social standing based on factors such as wealth, ancestry, or occupation. The different social classes recognized by members of a society form a hierarchy. This hierarchy may be an informal one, such as exists in democracies like the United States, or it may be rigidly delineated, as is the case of the caste system in India. In the United States, social class is popularly determined by income; people are grouped into upper, middle, and lower classes, with subdivisions of each main category.

Social contract, in political philosophy, concept of the formation of society in which people agree to surrender part of their "natural" freedom to enjoy the security of the organized state. The idea, though of ancient origin, was first fully formulated in the 17th and 18th centuries by Thomas Hobbes (in *Leviathan*, 1651), John Locke, and Jean Jacques Rousseau, and was then controversial because it suggested that heads of state ruled only by their subjects' consent.

Social Credit Party, Canadian party formed (1935) by William Aberhart. It aimed to implement Clifford Douglas's policy of avoiding economic depression by distributing surplus money as a "social dividend" to increase purchasing power. It failed in this but governed Alberta (1935-71) and British Columbia (1952-72). The party failed to win seats in the 1980 federal parliamentary elections.

Social Darwinism, late-19th-century school of thought that held that society evolved on Darwin's biological model. Social inequalities were explained (and made to seem natural and inevitable) by the principle of "survival of the fittest." Its chief theorist was Herbert Spencer.
See also: Darwin, Charles Robert; Spencer, Herbert.

Socialism, economic philosophy and political movement that aims to achieve a just, classless society through the collective or governmental ownership of all property and means of manufacture and distribution of goods. Socialism was born out of the hardships of capitalism and the Industrial Revolution (late 18th-early 19th centuries). The ideas of class war, first put forth by F.N. Babeuf (and rejected by Utopian socialists such as Robert Owen and Charles Fourier), were later elaborated upon by Karl Marx and Friedrich Engels in their *Communist Manifesto* (1848). They suggested that revolution, led by the workers of the world, was inevitable. The first workers' party had already been founded by this time—in Germany in 1863 by Ferdinand Lasalle. This example was soon followed throughout Europe (1870s). Disagreement between gradualists and revolutionists soon emerged and was highlighted in 20th-century Russian socialism, eventually resulting in a split from which Bolshevism and Menshevism emerged. This was the forerunner to the worldwide break that occurred between socialism and communism after the Russian Revolution (1917). Socialism today, as well as its established place in the electoral politics of Europe, is especially active in the Third World, where its focus is on land reform and centralized economic planning.

Brazilian soccer star Pelé

Socialist realism, compulsory artistic doctrine since the early 1930s and until recently the dominant philosophy and style in most Communist countries. The doctrine holds that, in order to serve the people and the revolution, artistic and literary works should be realistic (representational), yet portray, with "positive" heros, the workers' progress toward socialism.
See also: Communism.

A social realist sculpture, The Worker and the Woman of the Collective Farm *by Vera I. Moechina (1937)*

Dutch soccer star Marco van Basten during the European championship of 1988

Socialization, in psychology and sociology, process by which individuals are indoctrinated by parents, teachers, and peers into accepting and following the written and unwritten rules of conduct of a particular society.

Socialized medicine *see:* Health insurance, National.

Social psychology, branch of psychology concerned with group processes and interactions among individuals. Subjects studied by social psychologists include conformity, altruism, interpersonal attraction, and the development of values.
See also: Psychology.

Social sciences, group of studies concerned with humanity in relation to its cultural, social, and physical environment; 1 of the 3 main divisions of human knowledge, the others being the natural sciences and the humanities. The social sciences usually include anthropology, archeology, demography, economics, political science, psychology, and sociology. Social scientists model their disciplines on the natural sciences in order to achieve a similar level of consensus, but can be frustrated by conceptual tools that are limited in relation to the complexity of their subject matter and by controlled experiments of limited scope.

Social security, government programs for protecting people from hardship due to loss of income through old age, disability, unemployment, injury, sickness, etc. State social security systems developed in Europe after 1883, when Germany started a compulsory health insurance scheme. In 1911 Great Britain adopted an unemployment insurance program. In the United States in the Depression, the Social Security Act (1935) established a federal program of old-age insurance and a federal-state program of unemployment insurance. It also provided federal grants for public assistance, public health, and child welfare services. The federal plan has become compulsory, except for railway and government workers, who have their own schemes, and special types of workers who are not regularly employed.

The plan is financed by equal employer and employee contributions. Old-age and survivor benefits are paid to retired workers and their dependents or to survivors of workers who have died. The amount people receive is related to their average monthly earnings over a number of years. The aging of the U.S. population has recently threatened the solvency of this system. The social security tax has become a heavy burden for workers as the ratio of retirees to taxpayers has increased in favor of the former.

In the early 1980s the Reagan administration considered alternatives for reforming the system: reducing benefits, raising the retirement age, or funding the social security program from general revenues.

Disability benefits are paid to workers and dependents in the event of disability lasting over a year. Health insurance for the aged was added in 1965. Those over 65 are automatically helped with payment for hospital and post-hospital care; a supplementary medical insurance scheme, at an extra voluntary premium, covers 80% of doctors' and some other bills.

A claimant of unemployment insurance is usually eligible for about half his earnings. Public assistance, which in some states predates 1935, differs in being financed through federal grants (largely) and state revenues, rather than individual contributions. It goes to the care of the elderly, disabled, the blind, and their dependents. Workmen's compensation, dating from the early 1990s and varying widely between states, aids those employees injured at work or with industrial disease.

A few states administer sickness insurance plans. Government social insurance schemes are more comprehensive in most western European and Communist countries. In the United States private insurance companies play a more prominent role.

Social studies, elementary and secondary educational course designed to give students a knowledge of how people and institutions function in different societies and to promote understanding of both Western and non-Western cultures. The course typically is a combination of several disciplines, including history, economics, and geography.

Social work, activity of trained social workers that has as its aim the alleviation of social problems. Casework, group work, and community organization are employed. Casework involves close cooperation with individuals or families who are under mental, physical, or social handicaps. Group work developed from that in early social settlements and involves group education and recreational activities. Community organization involves the identification of community problems and the coordination of local welfare services, both public and private, in solving them. A social worker's training may include psychology, sociology, law, medicine, and criminology. The person might specialize in family service, child welfare, or medical, psychiatric, or correctional social work.

Society for the Prevention of Cruelty to Animals (SPCA), organizations promoting humane treatment of animals. These various societies aim to educate the public, introduce legislation, and assure the enforcement of laws that protect animals. Many societies maintain animal shelters and provide adoption and neutering services. There are about 1,000 local anti-cruelty societies in the United States today.

Society Islands, southern Pacific islands covering about 650 sq mi (1,684 sq km) in western French Polynesia, comprising the Windward and Leeward archipelagoes. Discovered in 1607 by the Portuguese but named for Britain's Royal Society, which explored the mountainous, volcanic, and coral islands in 1768, the 450-mi (724-km)-long chain has been France's since 1843. Most of the Polynesian population (about 100,000) live on the largest island, Tahiti, in the Windwards. Copra, sugar, and tourism are important industries.

Society of Friends *see:* Quakers.

Society of Jesus *see:* Jesuits.

Sociobiology, controversial theory that attempts to prove the influence of natural selection on human and animal behavior. The theory postulates that genes can influence behavior as well as physiology and that behavior may therefore be as subject to the laws of evolution as is the physical development of the species.

Sociology, systematic study that seeks to describe and explain collective human behavior—as manifested in cultures, societies, communities, and subgroups—by exploring the institutional relationships that hold between individuals and so sustain this behavior. Sociology shares its subject matter with anthropology, which traditionally focuses on small, relatively isolated societies, and social psychology, where the emphasis is on the study of subgroup behavior. The main emphasis in contemporary sociology is on the study of social structures and institutions and on the causes and effects of social change. Some current areas of inquiry are the family, religion, work, politics, urban life, and science.

Sociologists attempt to model their investigations on those of the physical sciences. Mainly because of the complexity of its subject matter and the political implications of social change, questions as to its proper aims and methods remain far from settled. There is little doubt, however, that sociological concepts such as internalization—the processes by which the values and norms of a particular society are learned by its members—and institutionalization—the processes by which norms are incorporated in a culture as binding rules of behavior—do often illuminate important social problems. The 2 great pioneers of modern sociology were Émile Durkheim and Max Weber. Leading U.S. sociologists include the pioneers William Sumner and George Mead, and Talcott Parsons and Daniel Bell.

Socrates (469-399 B.C.), Greek philosopher and mentor of Plato. Born in Athens and the son of a sculptor, Sophroniscus, Socrates became a self-appointed guide to the improvement of the intellectual and moral lives of the Athenians. His search for wisdom about right conduct used the method of discussing virtue, justice, and piety with his many listeners. He wrote nothing, but much of his life and thought is vividly recorded in the dialogues of Plato. The exact extent of Plato's indebtedness to Socrates is uncertain—e.g., it is still disputed whether the doctrine of the forms is Socratic or Platonic; but Socrates made at least 2 fundamental contributions to Western philosophy: by shifting the focus of Greek philosophy from cosmology to ethics, and by developing the "Socratic method" of inquiry. He argued that the good life is the life illuminated by reason and strove to clarify the ideas of his interlocutors by leading them to detect the inconsistencies in their beliefs. His doctrines are the basis of idealistic philosophy. Socrates' passion for self-consistency was evident even in his death. Ultimately condemned for "impiety," he decided to accept the lawful sentence—and so remain true to his principles—rather than make good an easy escape. In prison, surrounded by disciples, he drank hemlock.

See also: Philosophy.

Soda, any of a group of sodium compounds derived from common salt (NaCl). This group contains sodium carbonate (Na_2CO_3), or sal soda, a crystalline or powdered product with strong, acid-neutralizing, alkaline properties used in the production of paper and glass; sodium bicarbonate ($NaHCO_3$), or baking soda, which is used in cooking and for the relief of stomach distress; and sodium hydroxide (NaOH), or caustic soda, which is used in the manufacture of chemicals, soap, aluminum, and paper.

Soddy, Frederick (1877-1956), British chemist awarded the 1921 Nobel Prize in chemistry for his research in radioactive decay and particularly for his formulation (1913) of the theory of isotopes. His many scientific books range from *The Interpretation of Radium* (1922) to *Atomic Transmutation* (1953), and his views on technocracy and the social credit movement are found in *Money versus Man* (1933), among others.
See also: Chemistry; Isotope.

Sod house, ancient northern European type of house made from strips of turf that were used like bricks, the roof being reinforced with wood. Sod houses were also built by early settlers on the Great Plains of the United States and in western Canada.

Sodium, chemical element, symbol Na; for physical constants see Periodic Table. Sodium is the sixth most abundant element on earth. The free element was obtained by Sir Humphry Davy in 1807 by electrolysis of caustic soda (sodium hydroxide). It is found most commonly as common salt, but it occurs in many other minerals. It is obtained commercially by the electrolysis of dry fused sodium chloride. Sodium is a silvery-white, reactive metal, the most abundant of the alkali metal group. It is essential in human and animal nutrition. Sodium and its compounds are used in the paper, glass, soap, textile, petroleum, chemical, and metal industries. It is the cheapest of all metals.

Sodium chloride *see:* Salt.

Sodium hydroxide *see:* Lye; Soda.

Sodium nitrate *see:* Saltpeter.

Sodium nitrite *see:* Nitrite.

Sodium pentothal *see:* Thiopental.

Sodom and Gomorrah, in Old Testament history, cities probably in the southern region of the Dead Sea. According to Genesis, these 2 of the 5 cities on the Jordan plain were destroyed by God for their carnal wickedness. Only Lot and his family were spared, although Lot's wife turned into a pillar of salt.
See also: Old Testament.

Soeharto *see:* Suharto.

Soekarno *see:* Sukarno.

Sofia (pop. 1,057,000), capital, largest city, and commercial and cultural center of Bulgaria, in west-central Bulgaria between the Balkan Mountains in the north and the Vitosa Mountains in the south. Its industry includes machinery, textiles, and electrical equipment. Landmarks include the former royal palace, the parliament building, old mosques, churches, and synagogues. Sofia was settled by the Thracians; between the 1st and 4th centuries, Rome, Byzantium, and the first and second Bulgarian kingdoms were the ruling powers. In 1832 Turkish rule took hold until Russian's ascendance in 1878. Bulgaria achieved independence in 1879, with Sofia as its capital. Occupied by the Germans in World War II, it was taken by Soviet troops in 1944, and a Communist government was established.

The Death of Socrates, *by Jacques-Louis David*

Softball, type of baseball played with a softer, larger ball (12 in/30.5 cm in circumference) and a modified bat. The bases are 60 ft (18.3 m) apart and the pitcher stands 46 ft (14 m) from the home plate (40 ft/12 m in women's games). The ball is pitched underhand, and a game lasts 7 innings. Softball was developed in Chicago in 1888 by G. W. Hancock as an indoor form of baseball. Many countries, particularly in the Americas, now compete in the annual amateur world championships.
See also: Baseball.

Soft-coated wheaten terrier, sporting dog of Irish origin, used for hunting, herding, and as a guard dog. This terrier has a strong, compact body about 19 in (48 cm) high, weighs about 40 lb (30 kg), and has a shaggy coat of soft, wavy hair.

Soft drink, nonalcoholic beverage generally containing fruit acids, sweetening agents, and natural or artificial flavorings and colorings. In the early 19th century carbonated water (soda water) was developed in imitation of effervescent spa, or mineral, water; this was the antecedent of carbonated soft drinks, made by absorption of carbon dioxide under pressure. The dissolved gas gives a pleasant, slightly acid taste and acts as a preservative. Soft drinks without carbon dioxide are frozen or subjected to pasteurization.

Softwood *see:* Wood.

Soil, uppermost surface layer of the earth, in which plants grow and on which, directly or indirectly, all life on earth depends. Soil consists, in the uppermost layers, of organic material mixed with inorganic matter resultant from weathering. Soil depth (where soil exists) may reach to many meters. Between the soil and the bedrock is a layer called the subsoil. Mature (or zonal) soil may be described in terms of 4 soil horizons. The uppermost layer, containing organic components, is a continuous stream to which is added an "active" component produced by bursts of activity on the sun's surface.

Solanum, group of herbs, shrubs, and trees belonging to the nightshade family. Solanum grows worldwide, particularly in the temperate regions of South and North America. Many of the members of this family are important for food and medicinal purposes, although all contain some amounts of poisonous alkaloids such as atropine, nicotine, and solanin. Included in this group are the potato, tomato, eggplant, tobacco, bittersweet, common nightshade, and horse nettle. The fruit may be either capsulated (tobacco) or in berry form (potato and eggplant).

Solar eclipse *see:* Eclipse.

Solar energy, power derived from the sun. Because the earth's supplies of coal, petroleum, and other fossil fuels will eventually be exhausted, while the sun's energy will not, several methods of using solar energy have been developed. One is the solar furnace, basically a huge parabolic mirror that focuses the sun's heat onto a small area. Temperatures of more than 7,232°F (4,000°C) may be produced by this method. The heat can be used to raise steam and generate electricity, or for scientific research. In the Soviet Union a solar power station has been built with a system of 1,300 moving mirrors covering an area of 5 acres (about 2 hectares). It produces 2

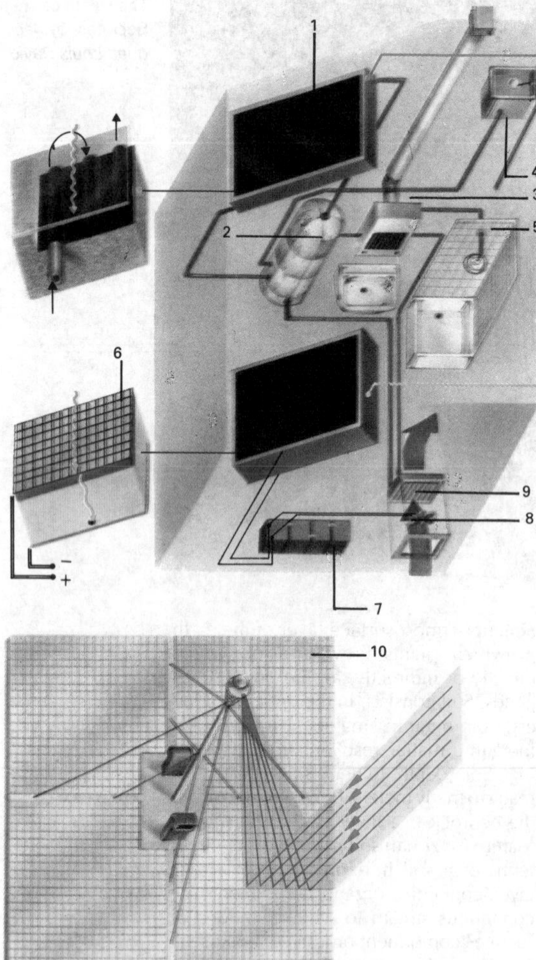

Examples of solar energy: Through a collector (1), water in a boiler (2) is heated for use in a bathroom (5) or radiator (9). For sunless periods there is a supplementary installation (3) with expansion tank (4). Solar cells (6) produce electricity directly for the battery (7), which, for example, powers a ventilator (8). Solar mirrors can convert water into steam (10) for the generation of electricity.

1/2 million kilowatt-hours of electricity annually.

Solar energy is used increasingly for domestic heating. Heat is collected by exposing a large, darkened metal plate, covered with 1 or more layers of glass, to the sun. Water or air is passed through tubes attached to the plate and either circulated through the building or stored. Hot water is stored in insulated tanks. Hot air is passed through a tank full of rocks, which hold the heat until it is required to warm up air for circulation around the house.

Sunlight can also be converted directly into electricity in a solar cell, and there is research into the possibility of using sunlight to produce chemical energy by the same sort of reaction as photosynthesis in plants.

See also: Radiation.

Solar plexus, ganglion of nerve cells and fibers situated at the back of the abdomen that subserve the autonomic nervous system function for much of the gastrointestinal tract. A sharp blow on the abdomen over the plexus causes visceral pain and the sensation that all the "wind" has been knocked out of the lungs.

See also: Nervous system.

Solar System, the sun and all the objects orbiting it, including the planets, asteroids, comets, and meteors. There are 9 known planets in the Solar System. Mercury, Venus, Earth, Mars, and Pluto make up the terrestrial (Earthlike) planets. Jupiter, Saturn, Uranus, and Neptune are giants largely made of gas. All but 3 planets have their own moons orbiting them. There are at least 66 known moons in the Solar System. Astronomers estimate that the Solar System contains at least 100,000 asteroids and about 100 billion comets. But the combined mass of all these bodies is little more than 1/1000th the mass of the Sun.

The Solar System is vast. Pluto, usually the outermost planet (sometimes Neptune is), moves as far as 4 1/2 billion mi (7.2 billion km) from the Sun, while comets move even farther than this.

Origin of the Solar System. From the dating of meteorites (pieces of rock from the Solar System that have hit the earth), scientists believe that the Solar System formed about 4 1/2 billion years ago. No one knows exactly how the planets originated. The first scientific theories were developed in the 18th century by the philosopher Immanuel Kant and the mathematician Pierre Simon Laplace. They believed that the Sun and planets formed together from a cloud of gas or dust. Early in the 20th century a rival theory gained favor. This suggested that a star passed close to the Sun and pulled out some of its material. Part of this material fell into orbit around the Sun, forming planets. Modern theories have returned to Laplace's idea. Astronomers now believe that stars form when giant, diffuse clouds of gas condense. As the cloud contracts, a star forms at its center. Around the rapidly spinning star is a disk of material that slowly spirals away. Most of the disk is lost into space, but at certain points the material of the disk starts to collide and build into lumps. These lumps sweep up more of the surrounding material, eventually forming planets.

Other Solar Systems. The above theory suggests that Solar Systems form naturally around most stars. Although planets are far too faint to be seen going around other stars, they will exert a slight gravitational tug on those stars. By looking at the slight movements of nearby stars, observers have found that some stars have dark companions revolving around them. Astronomers now think that Solar Systems are common in the universe and that perhaps half the stars in the sky have planets orbiting them.

Solar wind, gases in the Sun's corona that escape from its gravitational field. Made of electrically charged particles, particularly ions, and expanding under the high temperatures of the corona, about 4,000,000°F (2,200,000°C), the solar wind accelerates to a velocity of about 310 m/s (500 km/s), a speed that allows escape from the solar gravitational field. The solar wind causes deflection of the tail of Earth's magnetosphere and comet's tails away from the sun. A shock wave results when the solar wind encounters the Earth's magnetic field. The portions of the solar wind that do not encounter either the Earth or other obstacles continue to travel at supersonic velocities until they eventually lose their supersonic characteristics and pour out into galactic space.

Soldering, joining metal objects using a low-melting-point alloy, solder, as the adhesive. Soft solder, commonly used in electronics to join wires and other components, is an alloy of mainly lead and tin. The parts to be joined are cleaned and then heated by applying a hot soldering iron (usually having a copper bit). A flux is used to dissolve oxides, protect the surfaces, and enable the solder to flow freely. The solder melts when applied, solidifying again to form a strong joint when the iron is withdrawn. Solder is often applied as wire with a core of noncorrosive rosin flux. Soldering at higher temperatures is termed *brazing*.

Sole, any of several species (family Soleidae) of flatfishes found in temperate seas and fresh water. Soles are commonly brown with dark patches, have flattened bodies about 10-25 in (25-66 cm) long, weigh about 1 lb (0.5 kg), and have both eyes on the right side of the head. Sole is a valued food fish, particularly the European or Dover sole and the American hogchoker.

Solenodon (genus *Solenodon*), rare, nocturnal, insect-eating mammal of Cuba and Haiti. It looks like a long-nosed rat, measuring about 2 ft (61 cm) long and 2 lb (1 kg), with long claws, a stiff tail, and short, coarse hair. Its saliva is poisonous.

Soleri, Paolo (1919-), Italian-born U.S. architect. A visionary planner and once an apprentice of Frank Lloyd Wright, Soleri published in *Sketchbooks* (1971) his designs for Mesa City, a solar-powered desert metropolis. He began work on Arcosanti, a scaled-down version of it near Scottsdale, Ariz., in 1970. His buildings include Domed Desert House (1951) near Cave Creek, Ariz., and the Solimene Ceramics factory in Vietri sul Mare, Italy, near Salerno.

See also: Architecture.

Solid, one of 3 states of matter possessing the property of excluding all other bodies from the space occupied by itself; it has a definite volume and definite shape. As a result of heating, the molecules of a solid begin to vibrate more rapidly, eventually breaking out of their fixed positions (at the melting point) and becoming a liquid.

Solidarity *see:* Walesa, Lech.

Solid-state physics, branch of physics concerned with the nature and properties of solid materials, many of which arise from the association and regular arrangements of atoms or molecules in crystalline solids. The term is applied particularly to studies of semiconductors and solid-state electronic devices.

See also: Quantum mechanics.

Solitaire, or Patience, any of several card games played by 1 person. Solitaire has countless varieties, but all are played with

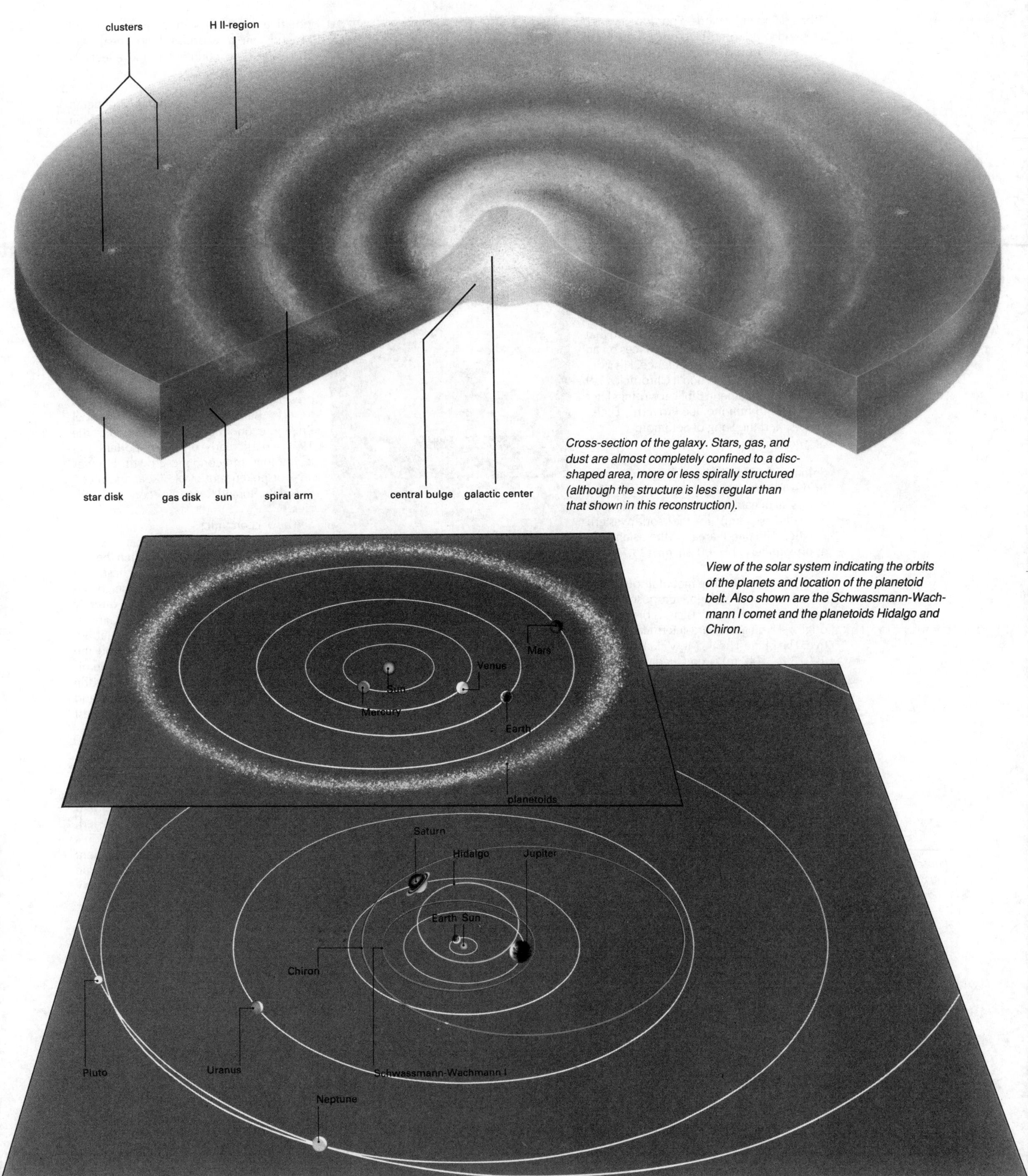

Cross-section of the galaxy. Stars, gas, and dust are almost completely confined to a disc-shaped area, more or less spirally structured (although the structure is less regular than that shown in this reconstruction).

View of the solar system indicating the orbits of the planets and location of the planetoid belt. Also shown are the Schwassmann-Wachmann I comet and the planetoids Hidalgo and Chiron.

1 or 2 decks of 52 cards, a portion of which are laid out, some face-up, others face-down, to form a foundation (tableau) of cards, upon which the game is played. Play resumes when one card is played out onto another in a prescribed manner. The purpose of the game is to play each card out, thus successfully completing the foundations.
Canfield, Klondike, Accordion, Napoleon at St. Helena, Spider, and Pyramid are a few of the games of solitaire.

Solomon (d.922 B.C.), second son of David and Bathsheba. He ruled ancient Israel c.970-933 B.C. at the height of its prosperity, and gained a reputation for great wisdom. His success in establishing lucrative foreign trade and his introduction at home of taxation and forced labor enabled him to finance a massive building program that included a temple and royal palaces on an unprecedented scale of opulence. His story is told in I Kings 1-11 and II Chronicles 1-9 of the Old Testament. Biblical writings later attributed to him include Proverbs, Ecclesiastes, and the Song of Solomon.
See also: Old Testament.

Solomon Islands, independent democracy in the British Commonwealth, extending across an ocean area of over 232,000 sq mi (600,880 sq km) in the southwestern Pacific. The land area of the islands is approximately 11,500 sq mi (29,785 sq km).
Land and climate. The mountainous Solomon Island archipelago, composed of 21 large islands and many islets, is of volcanic origin; 4 volcanoes are intermittently active. The highest peak, Mt. Makarakombou (8,028 ft/2,447 m) is on Guadalcanal, the largest island, where Honiara, the capital, is located. The Solomons are well watered and covered with dense tropical rain forests, with grasslands on the northern plains of Guadalcanal. The climate is equatorial, and temperatures vary little during the year; rainfall, averaging 120 in (305 cm) annually, is concentrated from Nov. to Apr.
People and economy. The population is 95% Melanesian, with Polynesian, Micronesian, European, and Chinese minorities. Most follow tradition, living in small villages, fishing, and growing coconuts, taro, yams, and cassava. Exports, formerly exclusively copra, now also include fish and timber. Tourism is increasingly important.
History. In 1568 a Peruvian expedition sighted the Solomons but they were ignored by Europeans until the 19th century, when islanders were forcibly recruited to labor overseas. By 1900 Great Britain had established a protectorate over the islands. Invaded by the Japanese in 1942, the Solomons were recaptured by U.S. forces only after heavy fighting in 1943. Since independence in 1978, the Solomons have been plagued by regional disputes.

A house built on stilts in the Solomon Islands

Solomon Islands

Capital:	Honiara
Area:	10,639 sq mi (27,556 sq km)
Population:	308,000
Government:	constitutional monarchy
Independent:	1978
GNP:	U.S. $130,000,000
Per capita:	U.S. $430

Solomon Islands, island chain in the South Pacific Ocean. The islands are divided into 2 countries, one at the southern end and one at the northern end of the group. The southern portion, including Choiseul, Guadalcanal, Malaita, New Georgia, San Cristobal, Santa Isabel, and numerous smaller islands, is part of the nation of the Solomon Islands. The northern portion, including Bougainville, Buka, and various smaller islands, is part of Papua New Guinea. Together they cover a land area of about 15,700 sq mi (40,663 sq km). The Solomon Islands were the scene, during World War II (1942-44), of numerous battles between the Japanese and the Allied forces.
See also: Papua New Guinea.

Solomon's seal, perennial plant that grows in woods and thickets. The rootstock, used for medicinal purposes, makes a good poultice for bruises, inflammations, and wounds; in a wash, it helps heal skin blemishes and counteracts the effects of poison ivy.

Solon (c.640-559 B.C.), Athenian politician and poet, and one of the Seven Wise Men of Greece (Seven Sages). Solon gained fame in 612 B.C. with his poems, which compelled the Athenians to recover the Island of Salamis. He was elected leader (archon) of the government in 594 B.C. During his leadership many political and economic reforms were initiated. They included the abolition of unfair debt laws, the institution of habeas corpus, emancipation of slaves, and reforms in the representation of the common citizens in the assembly and in courts of law.
See also: Athens; Greece, Ancient.

Solow, Robert Merton (1924-), U.S. economist. Senior economist (1961-68) on the Council of Economic Advisors and president (1975-80) of the Boston Federal Reserve Bank, he won the 1987 Nobel Prize in economics for work he did in the 1950s, particularly on the importance of technology in economic growth. He was an outspoken critic of "Reagonomics," President Ronald Reagan's economic policies.
See also: Economics.

Solstice, two times each year when the sun is on the points of the ecliptic farthest from the equator. At the summer solstice, in late June (about June 22), the sun is directly overhead at noon on the Tropic of Cancer; at winter solstice, in late December (about Dec. 22), it is overhead at noon on the Tropic of Capricorn. In the Northern Hemisphere these celestial events are used as the traditional commencement of summer and winter. They are also the days of the longest and shortest daylight hours.
See also: Equinox.

Solti, Sir Georg (1912-), Hungarian-born British conductor. He is noted for his recordings of works by Richard Wagner and Richard Strauss, and performances he led, usually as musical director, at London's Covent Garden (1961-71), the Paris Opera (from 1973), the London Philharmonic (1979-83), and the Chicago Symphony (1969-91).

Solution, in chemistry, homogeneous molecular mixtures of 2 or more substances (solid, liquid, gas), commonly of a solid and a liquid, though solid/solid solutions also exist. The liquid component is usually termed the *solvent*; the other component (solid, liquid, or gas), which is dissolved in it, the *solute*. The solubility of a solute in a given solvent at a particular temperature is usually stated as the mass that will dissolve in 3.53 oz (100 g) of the solvent to give a saturated solution. Solubility generally increases with temperature. Two common examples of solutions include vinegar (a solution of a liquid, acetic acid, in water) and syrup (a solution of a solid, sugar, dissolved in water).

Solvent, liquid capable of dissolving a substance to form a solution. Generally "like dissolves like"; thus a nonpolar covalent solid such as naphthalene dissolves well in a hydrocarbon solvent. Overall, the best solvents are those with polar molecules and high dielectric constant; water is the most effective known.

Solzhenitsyn, Alexander Isayevich (1918-), Russian writer. His own experience of Stalin's labor camps was described in *One Day in the Life of Ivan Denisovich* (1962), acclaimed in the USSR and abroad. But *First Circle* and *Cancer Ward* (both 1968) were officially condemned. He accepted the 1970 Nobel Prize in literature by letter. His expulsion from the USSR to West Germany in 1974 and his warnings on the moral and political fate of the West drew worldwide publicity. He has resided in the United States since 1976. Solzhenitsyn's work includes *August 1914* (1971), *The Gulag Archipelago* (1973-75), and *October 1916* (1985).

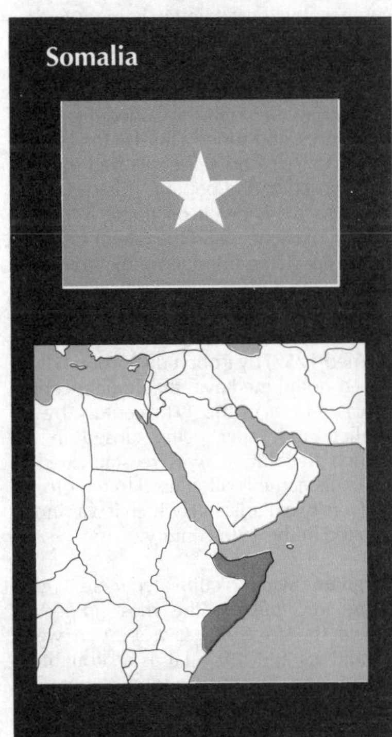

Capital:	Mogadishu
Area:	246,091 sq mi (637,541 sq km)
Population:	8,302,000
Government:	republic
Independent:	1960
GNP:	U.S. $946,000,000
Per capita:	U.S. $150

Somalia, or Somali Democratic Republic, republic occupying the horn, or northeastern tip, of Africa. The capital is Mogadishu.

Land and climate. Covering 246,091 sq mi (637,541 sq km), Somalia is bounded on the north by the Gulf of Aden, on the west and southwest by Ethiopia and Kenya, on the east by the Indian Ocean, and on the northwest by Djibouti. In the north, a narrow, barren coastal plain is hemmed in by mountains rising to more than 8,000 ft (2,438 m) with high plateaus and dry savannas extending inland. Plateaus, plains, and valleys extend westward from a wider coastal plain bordering the Indian Ocean. Flowing southeastward from the Ethiopian highlands are Somalia's only two permanent rivers, the Wabe Shebele and the Juba. The prevailing climate is hot.

People. The population consists mainly of Somalis belonging to northern nomadic or southern farming clans. Somali, the national language, lacks a written form; Arabic, Italian, and English are the chief written languages. Sunni Islam is the country's official religion.

Economy. Most Somalis are nomadic pastoralists moving from place to place with their herds and portable wood-frame huts. Agriculture accounts for the economy's major revenues, with bananas and sugarcane the cash crops. There is a small mining and oil-producing sector of the economy.

History. The British, French, and Italians colonized Somalia in the late 1800s, with the British establishing a protectorate in the region in 1887 and the Italians in 1889. Independent since 1960, Somalia was heavily dependent upon foreign aid. In 1969 Pres. Shermarke was assassinated, and a revolutionary council headed by Maj. Gen. Muhammad Siyad Barre took control, declaring the Somali Democratic Republic a Socialist state. Armed conflict erupted with Ethiopia in 1963-64 and again in 1977-78 over the disputed territory of the Ogaden. As a result, hundreds of thousands of refugees streamed into Somalia, straining the country's meager resources. After Siyad Barre was disposed in 1991 a power struggle between rivaling factions developed. In 1992 US troops launched a military operation, which was set up to improve the food situation, but proved to be inadequate.

Somaliland, *de facto* independent northwestern part of Somalia.

Somerset, Edward Seymour, 1st duke of (1500-52), protector of England (1547-49) on the death of Henry VIII and accession of Edward VI. He used his great power to repeal heresy and treason laws and with Thomas Cranmer introduced the first *Book of Common Prayer* for the Church of England. Falsely accused of treason by his rivals, he was executed.

Alexander Isayevich Solzhenitsyn

Somme River, river rising in northern France near Saint-Quentin, flowing west about 152 mi (245 km) to the English Channel. The Somme was the scene of major fighting with heavy casualties in World War I (1914-17). The Somme's upper valley has canals to the Oise and Escaut rivers.

Somnambulism *see:* Sleepwalking.

Somoza, Nicaraguan political family, 3 members of which controlled Nicaragua from 1936 to 1979. In 1936 **Anastasio Somoza Garcia** (1896-1956) deposed his uncle, President Juan Sacasa, and became president in a nepotistic dictatorship (1937-47; 1950-56) ending in assassination. He was succeeded by his son **Luis Somoza Debayle** (1922-67), who held formal office until 1963. In 1967 Anastasio's second son, **Anastasio Somoza Debayle** (1925-80), was elected president. Replaced by a puppet triumvirate in 1972, he retained control of the army and was reelected president in 1974. His corrupt rule led to a revolt in 1977 by leftist Sandinista guerrillas, who gradually gained broad support and forced him to flee into exile in Paraguay in 1979. A year later he was assassinated in Asunción.
See also: Nicaragua.

Sonar, acronym for Sound Navigation and Ranging, technique used at sea for detecting and determining the position of underwater objects (e.g., submarines, shoals of fish) and for finding the depth of water under a ship's keel. Sonar works on the principle of echolocation. High-frequency sound pulses are beamed from the ship, and the direction of and time taken for any returning echoes are measured to give the direction and range of the reflecting objects.

Sonata, in music, term used in the 17th and early 18th centuries to describe works for various small groups of instruments, as opposed to the cantata, originally for voices only. Since the late 18th century the term

Somalian coastal towns originally settled by Arab merchants have been integrated with the culture and population of nomadic Somali society.

has been restricted to works for piano or other solo instruments (the latter usually with keyboard accompaniment), generally in 3 movements.

Sondheim, Stephen (1930-), U.S. composer and lyricist, whose work is characterized by sophisticated lyrics and intricate music that enriches a storyline. Sondheim began his career as the lyricist for *West Side Story* (1959). He was awarded the Pulitzer Prize in drama in 1985 for *Sunday in the Park with George.* Other works include *Gypsy* (1959), *A Funny Thing Happened on the Way to the Forum* (1962), *Do I Hear a Waltz?* (1965), and *A Little Night Music* (1973).

Song, musical setting of words, usually a short poem, often with instrumental accompaniment. There are 2 basic kinds: songs in which each verse repeats the same tune, and songs with a continuous thematic development. The origins of the song are lost in the history of folk music and poetry (poetry was originally sung); it became a mature art in Western cultures in opera arias, German *Lieder*—those of Schubert are supreme examples—and the French *chanson.* The song forms that have most influenced 20th-century popular music are probably the ballad and the blues.

Sorghum

Song dynasty (960-1279), period of Chinese rule and cultural advancement, founded by Zhao Kuangyin, who became the first emperor. The dynasty encompassed most of China. During this era of enlightenment trade, education, sculpture, painting, and literature flourished; a humane welfare system was instituted; and Confucian philosophy was organized into a cohesive doctrine. The Song dynasty was ended when it was conquered by the Mongols in 1279.
See also: China.

Songhai Empire, West African trading state created by the Songhai people of the Middle Niger. Founded in the 700s and flourishing in the 1400s, Songhai was a powerful and wealthy empire in control of trans-Saharan trade. At the height of power, during the reign of Sunni Ali (1464-92) and that of Askia Muhammad (1493-1528), the Songhai Empire extended west to the Atlantic Ocean and encompassed roughly what is now Mali, Nigeria, and portions of Senegal. Gao, on the Niger River, was the capital. Most of the Songhai people farmed, fished, or were traders. Askia Muhammad was deposed by his 3 sons and by 1591 the empire was defeated by Moroccans at the Battle of Tondibi.

Song of Roland *see:* Roland.

Song of Solomon, or Song of Songs, book of love poems in the Old Testament of the Bible. Although spoken between a man and a woman and sensual in content, the poems are usually interpreted as allegorical and dramatic descriptions of God's love for the Hebrew people.
See also: Old Testament.

Sonic boom, loud noise generated in the form of a shock-wave cone when an airplane traveling faster than the speed of sound overtakes the pressure waves it produces. Because of sonic-boom damage, supersonic planes are confined to closely defined flight paths.

Sonnet, lyric poem of 14 lines with traditional rules of structure and rhyme scheme. There are two traditional types of sonnets: The Petrarchan is comprised of an octave and sestet (rhyming scheme *abbaabba cdecde*) and the Shakespearean comprising three quatrains and a couplet (rhyming scheme *abab cdcd efef gg*). Devised in 13th-century Italy and perfected by Petrarch, it entered English literature in the 16th century and was adopted by such poets as William Shakespeare, John Milton, John Keats, and William Wordsworth as a vehicle for concentrated thought and feeling, very often of love.

Sons of the American Revolution, patriotic organization for male descendants of Revolutionary War veterans or of those who furthered independence in other ways. This group, founded in 1889, seeks to preserve patriotic ideals and American traditions, and to protect the U.S. Constitution. Members also encourage historical research and the conservation of documents and artifacts of the Revolutionary period. The organization is headquartered in Washington, D.C.
See also: Revolutionary Warin America.

Sontag, Susan (1933-), U.S. novelist, short-story writer, filmmaker, and essayist. Her best-known books include *Against Interpretation* (1966), *On Photography* (1977), *Illness as Metaphor* (1978) coupled with *AIDS and Its Metaphors* (1989), and *Under the Sign of Saturn* (1980).

Soo Canals, or Sault Sainte Marie Canals, waterways on the U.S.-Canada border linking Lake Superior and Lake Huron. The U.S. canal has 2 channels and 4 locks, the Canadian canal has 1 lock. About 85 million short tons (77 million metric tons) of cargo are shipped through the canals annually. Cargo is comprised mainly of iron ore, coal, oil, stone, and grain. By using these canals, which are icebound during the winter months, ships may bypass the dangerous rapids on St. Mary's River.

Sooners, Oklahoma homesteaders who entered the Indian Territory in advance of the date of the first official "run" for property: Apr. 22, 1889. Oklahoma is still familiarly known as the Sooner State.
See also: Oklahoma.

Soong Ching-ling (1892-1981), deputy head of state of the Chinese Communist government (1949-75). She also headed the Sino-Soviet Friendship Association, and was awarded the Stalin Peace Prize in 1951. Soong Ching-ling was the wife of the left-wing revolutionary leader Sun Yat-sen. When he died in 1925, she continued his work in the Kuomintang (Nationalist Party). In 1927 when Chiang Kai-Shek, then president of the Chinese Nationalist government, broke with the Chinese Communists, she went into self-exile, living in Moscow until 1937. During the Sino-Japanese War, having returned to China, Soong was the organizer of the China Defense League.

Sophist (Greek, "wise men"), name given to certain teachers in Greece in the 5th and 4th centuries B.C., the most famous of whom were Gorgias and Protagoras. They taught rhetoric and the qualities needed for success in political life. Plato attacked them for taking fees; for teaching skepticism about law, morality, and knowledge; and for concentrating on how to win arguments regardless of truth—attacks still reflected in the modern word *sophistry.*
See also: Greece, Ancient.

Sophocles (c.496-406 B.C.), great Athenian dramatist (also, priest and general), who, together with contemporaries Aeschylus and Euripides, was one of the founders of Greek tragedy. Only 7 of about 123 plays survive, the best known being *Oedipus Rex, Oedipus at Colonus, Antigone,* and *Electra.* Sophocles, who won many dramatic competitions, introduced scene painting to the stage, expanded the size of the chorus, and added a third actor. He also chose to focus on self-contained tragedy, as opposed to the popular trilogies of his day. His plays dwell on tragic ironies of human existence, and the fate of his characters are determined more by their faults than by the gods.

Sorbonne, college founded in Paris in 1253 (named 1257) by Robert de Sorbon (1201-74). A noted medieval theological center, it was rebuilt in the 17th century by Richelieu and, after being closed in the French Revolution, was reestablished in 1808. Its name is often used to refer to the University of Paris, into which it was incorporated in the 19th century.

Sorghum, widely cultivated cereal crop (*Sorghum vulgare*), the most important grown in Africa. It grows best in warm conditions and it is vital as a drought-resistant crop. For human food, the grain is first ground into a meal and then made into porridge, bread, or cakes. Some varieties yield molasses from the cane's juice. The grain is also used as a cattle feed and the whole plants as forage. Many types are in cultivation, including durra and kaffir.

Sorokin, Pitirim Alexandrovich (1889-1968), Russian-U.S. sociologist. He distinguished between sensate (empirical, scientific) and ideational (mystical, authoritarian) societies and wrote *Social and Cultural Dynamics* (1937-41).
See also: Sociology.

Sorrel, plant (genus *Rumex*) of the buckwheat family. This herbaceous perennial has sour, succulent, arrow-shaped leaves and stems that are used in soups and salads. The common American sorrel (sheep sorrel or red sorrel) grows in acid soil.

Sound, sensation produced by stimulation of the organ of hearing; instrument for insertion into a cavity to detect a foreign body or stricture; or noise, normal or abnormal, heard within the body.

Sound, in geography, any of several types of waterways, most commonly a long arm of ocean, larger than a strait or channel, that runs parallel to a mainland coast. A sound may rest between the mainland and an island or peninsula, connect an ocean and a sea, or be a fjord or lagoon.

Sour gum *see:* Tupelo.

Sourwood, or sorrel tree, ornamental deciduous tree (*Oxydendrum arboreum*) of the heath family. The sourwood is native to the United States and grows in the woods of the southern states and in Pennsylvania, Indiana, and Ohio. The trees grow to about 75 ft (23 m) in height, have small, fragrant, white flowers, and oval, sour-tasting leaves that turn bright red in the autumn.

Sousa, John Philip (1854-1932), U.S. bandmaster and composer. He wrote many light operas but is best remembered for his military marches, including "The Stars and Stripes Forever" and "The Washington Post." Sousa was leader of the U.S. Marine Band (1880-92) before forming a world-tour band of his own.

Souter, David Hackett (1939-), associate justice of the Supreme Court of the United States (1990-). He was appointed by President George Bush as a replacement for Justice William J. Brennan, Jr., who retired. His judicial approach is considered conservative.
See also: Supreme Court of the United States.

South Africa, independent republic occupying most of the southern tip of the African continent.

The Cape of Good Hope in South Africa

South Africa

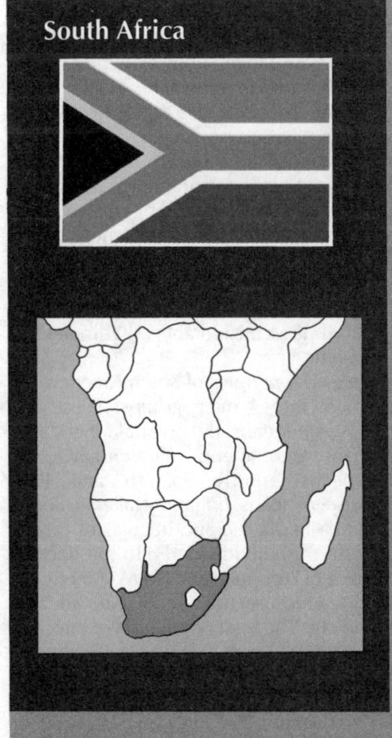

General information	
Capitals:	Bloemfontein, Pretoria, Cape Town
Area:	471,320 sq mi (1,221,037 sq km)
Population:	39,763,000
Official languages:	Afrikaans, English, 9 African languages
Monetary unit:	1 rand = 100 cents
Main cities:	Cape Town, Johannesburg, Pretoria
Government	
Form:	republic
Independent:	1931
Head of state:	State president
Head of government:	State president
Legislature:	three legislative houses (House of Assembly, House of Representatives, and House of Delegates)
Executive:	State president and Cabinet
Judiciary:	highest court is the Appelate Division of the Supreme Court
Political division:	9 provinces
National economy	
Gross national product:	U.S.$106,019,000,000
Per capita income:	U.S.$2,670
Agriculture:	apples, grapes, sugar cane, corn, wheat, potatoes, tobacco, tomatoes
Livestock:	sheep, cattle, goats
Fisheries:	902,000 metric tons
Mining:	gold, diamonds, hard coal, uranium, tin, chromium, asbestos, platinum, silver, iron ore, manganese
Industries:	metal products, chemicals, food and beverages, machinery and transport equipment, textiles
Main exports:	mineral products, metal and metal products, precious stones, food and tobacco
Transportation:	14,669 mi (23,607 km) of railroads, 113,691 mi (182,968 km) of roads, 1 international airport
Trading partners:	U.S., Japan, Germany, United Kingdom
People	
Urban:	56%
Ethnic composition:	African 73% (of which Zulu 29%, Sotho 24%, Xhosa 25%, Tswana 10%) European 14%, coloreds 9%, Asian 3%
Birth rate:	35 per 1,000 population
Death rate:	9.8 per 1,000 population
Infant mortality:	72 per 1,000 live births
Life expectancy:	male 57.5 years, female 63.5 years

Land and climate. South Africa covers 471,320 sq mi (1,221,037 sq km). It is bordered by the Atlantic Ocean on the west, the Indian Ocean on the east and south, Namibia to the northwest, Botswana and Zimbabwe to the north, and Mozambique and Swaziland to the northeast. Geographically, South Africa is a vast system of plateaus separated from narrow coastal plains by the ranges of the Great Escarpment. The plateaus are mostly flat and undulating, their monotony occasionally varied by kopjes (low, flat-topped hills) and low ridges. From the southwestern coastal plain in Cape Province the land rises in a series of steps to the dry valleys of the Little Karroo and the plateau of the Great Karroo, bounded by the ranges of the Great Escarpment. Among these ranges are the lofty Drakensberg Mountains. Beyond the Great Escarpment is the Northern Karroo, or High Veld, the highest and most fertile of the plateaus. The westward flowing Orange River rises in the Drakensberg Mountains and drains most of the interior plateau. The South African climate is mainly subtropical with dry, sunny winters and hot summers. The country is divided into nine provinces: Eastern Cape, Western Cape, Northern Cape, Northwest, Pretoria-Witwatersrand-Vereeniging, Northern Transvaal, Eastern Transvaal, Kwazulu Natal and Orange Free State. Its principal cities are Pretoria, the administrative capital; Cape Town, the legislative capital; Bloemfontein, the judicial capital; and Johannesburg and Durban.

People. The population of South Africa is about 70% black African, principally Zulu and Xhosa peoples, about 14% white, 9% of mixed white and African descent, and 3% Asiatics. Some two-thirds of whites are Afrikaners, descendants of Dutch settlers. Until 1993 South Africa's government and economy were dominated by whites. Blacks were excluded from the franchise, and the government ruthlessly and efficiently pursued a rigorous policy of racial segregation and systematic subjugation of black Africans known officially as apartheid. Christianity is the dominant religion, with the majority of whites adhering to the Dutch Reformed Church. There are also Hindus and Jews. The official languages are Afrikaans, English and nine African languages. The most important African languages are Xhosa, Zulu and Sesotho. Literacy among whites is 95% and among blacks 30%.

Economy. South Africa produces most of the world's gem diamonds and gold, has large coal reserves, and is also rich in uranium, iron ore, asbestos, copper, manganese, nickel, chrome, titanium, and phosphates. Mining contributes the major share of export earnings, but accounts for only 10% of the gross domestic product. The largest contribution is from manufacturing, which includes food processing, iron, steel, and oil from coal production, engineering, and textiles. South Africa is self-sufficient in food production and is a major exporter of food to neighboring countries. Nonwhites comprise more than 75% of South Africa's work force.

History. South Africa was already inhabited by San (Bushmen), Khoikhoi, and Bantu peoples from the north when white settlement began in 1652 with the establishment of a Dutch colony at Cape Town. The British came to the area in 1795, and from 1835 to 1843 the Boers, descendants of Dutch settlers, moved inland on the Great Trek to escape British dominance. They founded the Boer republics and eventually fought the British in the Boer War (1899-1902). The bitter contest was eventually won by the British, and in 1910 the Union of South Africa was formed. During World War I, South West Africa (Namibia) was wrested from the Germans and placed under a mandate. In 1931 South Africa became independent. Since 1948 it has been ruled by the Afrikaner-led National Party and committed to the policy of apartheid. In 1961 under H.F. Verwoerd, South Africa became a republic and left the Commonwealth largely because of differences over apartheid. Succeeding governments under B.J. Vorster (1966-78) and P.W. Botha (1978-89) continued to enforce apartheid, and in the 1980s, met with increasingly determined and often violent resistance internally, engaged in armed conflicts in Namibia and Angola, and were subject to greater and greater international pressure and censure. As a result, the government, headed by Willem de Klerk, gradually took steps toward ending apartheid, a change of policy signalled by the release from prison of Nelson Mandela in 1990. Mandela's release triggered the democratization proces and in 1994 the white minority government was replaced by a democratically chosen black government headed by president Mandela.

South America, southern of the 2 continents comprising the Western Hemisphere. South America is separated from North America at the Isthmus of Panama. Covering an area of 6,880,000 sq mi (17,819,000 sq km), South America contains the 12 independent republics of Argentina, Bolivia, Brazil, Chile, Colombia, Ecuador, Guyana, Paraguay, Peru, Suriname, Uruguay, and Venezuela. There also remains one European possession on the continent, French Guiana.

Land and climate. Roughly triangular in shape, South America extends some 4,750 mi (7,640 km) north to south and, at its widest, is 3,300 mi (5,300 km) east to west. It is surrounded by the Caribbean Sea on the north, the Atlantic Ocean on the east, Drake Passage on the south, and the Pacific Ocean on the west. The continent contains 3 main river basins, the Amazon, Paraná, and Orinoco. The Amazon, the world's most voluminous river, forms a basin containing the world's largest tropical rain forest. The Andes Mountains run in a nearly continuous chain from north to south. Other major topographical features include the grasslands of the pampas, the Gran Chaco, and the Patagonian plateau. The climate ranges from extreme cold in the high Andes to tropical heat and humidity in the lowlands and rain forests at the equator.

Economy. South America is rich in unique varieties of plant and animal life as well as mineral resources, including oil, iron ore, copper, tin, lead, zinc, manganese, gold, nitrate, and bauxite. Much of South America's natural wealth remains to be fully developed. The continent has very little coal, but considerable hydroelectric potential.

People. The peoples of South America are divisible into 4 main groups. These are Native Americans, the original inhabitants of the continent; descendants of Europeans, mostly Spanish and Portuguese; Africans, originally taken to South America as slaves; and peoples of mixed ancestry, usually divided into mestizos, a mixture of European and Native American, or mulattoes, a mixture of African and European. The total population of the con-

Cross section of South America

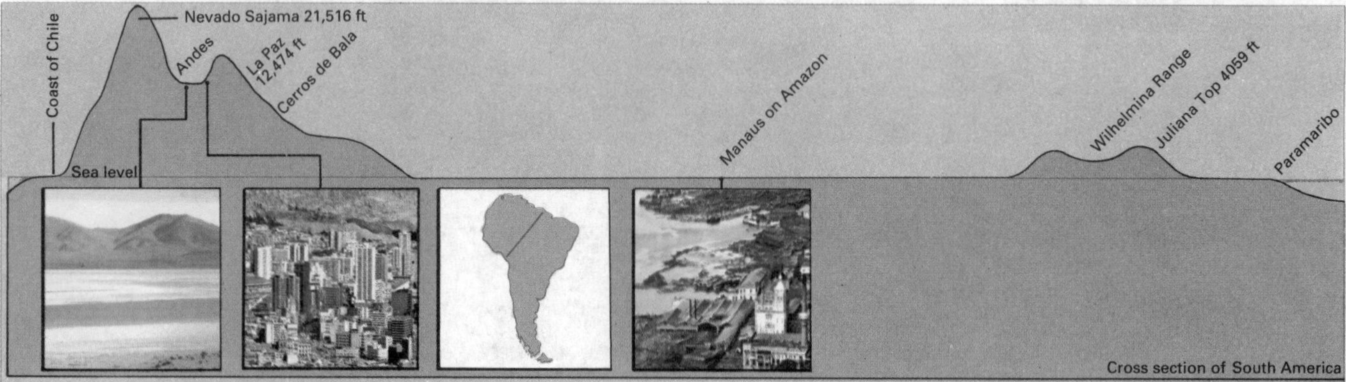

tinent is about 250 million with about one-half that number in Brazil. The chief official languages are Spanish and Portuguese, the latter spoken in Brazil. In Guyana, Suriname, and French Guiana, the official languages are, respectively, English, Dutch, and French. The most widely spoken of the Native American languages are Guaraní in Paraguay; Quechua in Peru, Bolivia, and Ecuador; and Aymará in Bolivia. About 90% of South Americans are at least nominally Roman Catholic.

Complex of falls and rapids in the River Iguaçú on the border of Argentina and Brazil in South America

Southampton (pop. 203,300), English seaport city, on the River Test, near the English Channel. The city is England's chief passenger port. Founded as a Roman settlement by A.D. 43, Southampton's modern industries include ship building and repair, construction, harbor services, and tobacco processing. Of interest to visitors are various medieval structures, including Bar Gate, a portion of wall from the Middle Ages, and the priory of St. Denys (1124).
See also: England.

South Arabia, Federation of, previously an English protectorate of the crown colony of Aden and several Arab states including Alawi, Aqrabi, Audhali, Upper and Lower Aulaqi, Fadhli, Haushabi, Lahej, Mufhahi, Shaibi, Wahidi, and Lower Yafa. At the southern point of the Arabian peninsula, the federation covered about 60,000 sq mi (160,000 sq km) and was controlled economically and politically by England. On Nov. 30, 1967, the alliance gained independence and with the islands of Kamaran, Perim, and Socotra, became the Republic of South Yemen.

South Australia, state in south-central Australia, with an area of 380,070 sq mi (984,381 sq km). Wheat, barley, wool, and wine are produced in the fertile southeast. Minerals include iron ore, opals, salt, gypsum, and coal. Major industries, centered in Adelaide, the capital and chief port, include smelting, chemicals, fertilizers, engineering, and automobiles.
See also: Australia.

South Bend (pop. 247,052), city in northern Indiana, seat of St. Joseph County. Founded as a fur trading post on the St. Joseph River at the site of a Miami Native American village in the early 1820s, South Bend is now a center for commerce and education. It is the seat of the University of Notre Dame, Indiana University-South Bend Campus, and St. Mary's College. Industries include the production of automotive parts, plastics, and machinery.
See also: Indiana.

South Carolina, state in the southeastern United States; bordered by North Carolina to the north, the Atlantic Ocean to the southeast, and Georgia to the southwest.
Land and climate. South Carolina has 3 main land regions. The Blue Ridge, a narrow region in the state's northwestern corner, is part of the Blue Ridge Mountains, which extend into the state. The Piedmont covers most of northwestern South Carolina. This region's rolling land slopes from high in the northwest to low in the southeast, making for swift-flowing rivers and streams. The Atlantic Coastal Plain, in the southeastern two-thirds of the state, has long, sandy beaches in the north; southward, it becomes increasingly swampy, with salt marshes, pine barrens, bays, and tidal rivers.
South Carolina has many large rivers, the main ones being the Santee, Pee Dee, and Savannah. There are many rapids and waterfalls, but no large natural lakes. Forests cover nearly two-thirds of the state. South Carolina has a warm climate, with hot summers and mild winters. Principal cities are Columbia, Charleston, and North Charleston.

South Carolina

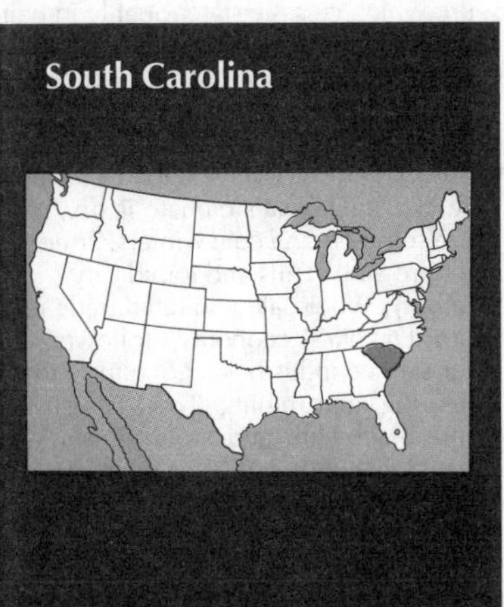

Capital:	Columbia
Statehood:	May 23, 1788 (8th state)
Familiar name:	Palmetto State
Area:	31,113 sq mi (80,582 sq km); ranks 40th
Population:	3,505,707 (1990); ranks 25th
Elevation:	Highest—3,560 ft (1,085 m), Sassaras Mountain; Lowest—sea level, along the Atlantic coast
Mottoes:	Animis Opibusque Parati (Prepared in Mind and Resources); Dum Spiro Spero (While I Breathe, I Hope)
Flower:	Carolina jessamine
Bird:	Carolina wren
Tree:	Palmetto
Song:	"Carolina"

Economy. South Carolina's economy is led by manufacturing, followed by various service industries, including tourism. Chief manufactured goods are textiles, chemicals, machinery, and apparel. Agriculture and mining account for minor shares of the economy. Chief farm products are tobacco, soybeans, corn, cotton, and peaches; chief livestock products are eggs, milk, and beef cattle. Chief mining products are granite, limestone, crushed stone, and cement.
Government. South Carolina's present constitution was adopted in 1895. The governor serves a 4-year term. The state's legislature, called the General Assembly, consists of 46 senators serving 4-year terms and 124 representatives serving 2-year terms. In the U.S. Congress, South Carolina is represented by 2 senators and 6 representatives.
History. Many Native American tribes were living in the area when the first Europeans—Spanish explorers—arrived in 1521. In 1670 the first permanent non-native settlement was established near pre-

Simón Bolívar played an important role in the history of South America.

South Carolina

sent-day Charleston by English colonists. In 1719 the settlers revolted against the colony's proprietors; the province became a royal colony in 1729. South Carolina was one of the 13 British colonies that broke from Britain and fought the American Revolution; in 1788 it became the eighth state. In 1861 South Carolina—a strong proponent of states' rights, free trade, and slavery—became the first state to secede from the Union; the war's first shots were fired at Fort Sumter. Much of the state was damaged during the Civil War. During Reconstruction, federal troops occupied the state, which suffered agricultural depression and political corruption. South Carolina was readmitted to the Union in 1868.

In the late 1800s and early 1900s, industrial growth aided recovery. The widespread unemployment of the Great Depression (1930s) was alleviated by World War II, and industry expanded in the 1950s and 1960s. In the 1960s and 1970s, the state's black majority, disenfranchised during Reconstruction, began voting in larger numbers, and integration, which met strong resistance at first, began taking hold. Today South Carolina seeks new industries as its key tobacco industry faces growing opposition to smoking.

South Dakota, midwestern state in north-central United States; bordered by North Dakota to the north, Minnesota and the Big Sioux River (with Iowa on the other side) to the east, the Missouri River and Nebraska to the south, and Wyoming and Montana to the west.

Land and climate. The geographic center of the United States is in South Dakota, near Castle Rock. South Dakota has 4 main land regions. The Black Hills, a small region on the state's west-central border, is mountainous, with deep canyons and huge rock formations. The Great Plains, covering most of the state's western two-thirds, has rolling, grassy plains and rugged canyons and buttes. The Drift Prairie, in eastern South Dakota, is a low-lying region of rolling hills. The Dissected Till Plains, in the state's southeastern corner, is rolling land cut by glacial streams.

South Dakota's main rivers are the Missouri, which cuts the state roughly in half, and its branches—the Grand, Moreau, Cheyenne, White, James, and Big Sioux. There are no large natural lakes, but artificial ones were created by damming the Missouri. Forests cover less than 4% of the state. South Dakota's climate is dry, with warm summers and cold winters. Principal cities are Sioux Falls and Rapid City.

Mt. Rushmore, in South Dakota

South Dakota

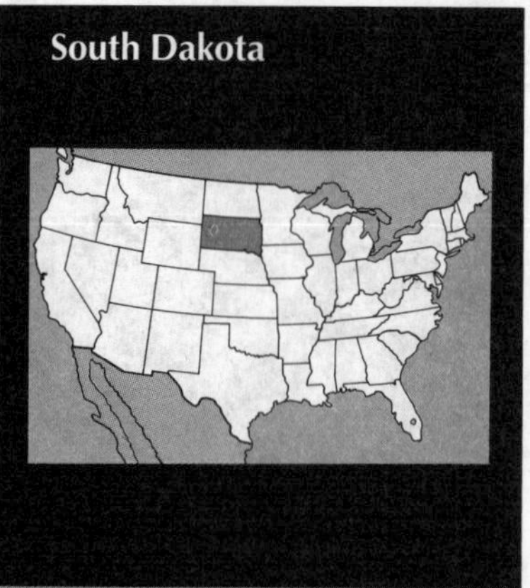

Capital:	Pierre
Statehood:	Nov. 2, 1889 (40th state)
Familiar names:	Sunshine State, Coyote State
Area:	77,116 sq mi (119,730 sq km); ranks 16th
Population:	699,999 (1990); ranks 45th
Elevation:	Highest—7,242 ft (2,207 m), Harney Peak; Lowest—962 ft (293 m), Big Stone Lake
Motto:	Under God the People Rule
Flower:	American pasqueflower
Bird:	Ring-necked pheasant
Tree:	Black Hills spruce
Song:	"Hail, South Dakota"

Economy. Wholesale and retail trade lead South Dakota's economy, followed by other service industries, agriculture, manufacturing, and mining. Tourists visit the scenic Black Hills and Mount Rushmore, into which huge heads of Presidents Washington, Jefferson, Lincoln, and Theodore Roosevelt were carved. Beef cattle, hogs, sheep, and wool lead the agricultural share of the economy. Chief crops are corn, wheat, sunflower seeds, rye, flaxseed, and soybeans. Chief manufactured goods are processed foods, machinery, surgical instruments, and electrical equipment. Chief mining products are gold, petroleum, and crushed stone.

Government. South Dakota's constitution was adopted in 1889. The governor serves a 4-year term. The state legislature consists of 35 senators and 70 representatives; all serve 2-year terms. In the U.S. Congress, South Dakota is represented by 2 senators and 1 representative.

History. Until both gained statehood in 1889, South Dakota shared much of its history with North Dakota. Cheyenne and Arikara peoples lived in the area before the first Europeans, French explorers, arrived about 1743. The area had been claimed for France by explorer Robert La Salle in 1682. France ceded it to Spain in 1762, regained it in 1800, then sold it to the United States under the Louisiana Purchase (1803). The Lewis and Clark expedition explored the area from 1804 to 1806. European-American settlement, at first by fur traders, was dominated by farmers by the 1850s. In 1861 Congress created the Dakota Territory. During the 1860s wars with Native Americans led to the Laramie Treaty (1868), which created the Great Sioux Reservation. In the 1870s a gold rush to the Black Hills violated the treaty, sparking new Native American resistance that ended only with the 1890 massacre of the Sioux at Wounded Knee Creek. Railroads brought rapid settlement to South Dakota, which became the 40th state in 1889. During the Great Depression (1930s), farmers suffered; World War II brought higher farm prices, but mechanized farming put many farmers out of work. Although South Dakota has since broadened its economic base, it was hard hit by the farm crisis of the 1980s.

Southeast Asia, region of Asia south of the southernmost boundaries of China and India, including Brunei, Burma, Cambodia, Indonesia, Laos, Malaysia, the Philippines, Singapore, Thailand, and Vietnam. The area covers about 1,740,000 sq mi (4,506,600 sq km) and is comprised mostly of areas of rich agricultural lands that produce rubber, rice, tea, coffee, tobacco, pepper, and coconut oil. There are also abundant teak forests, petroleum deposits, tin and gem mines, and fish. Southeast Asia is a land of diverse cultural backgrounds influenced in part by Europeans, who as early as the 16th century were drawn by the area's resources. Cities include Bangkok, Thailand; Ho Chi Minh City, Vietnam; Jakarta, Indonesia; Manila, the Philippines; and Singapore.
See also: Asia.

Southeast Asia Treaty Organization (SEATO), defense treaty signed by Australia, France, Great Britain, New Zealand, Pakistan, the Philippines, Thailand, and United States after France withdrew from Indochina in 1954. Headquarters were at Bangkok, Thailand. Although there were no standing forces, its aim was to prevent Communist expansion. The treaty was invoked by the United States in the Vietnam War (1964-73). Pakistan withdrew in 1972. SEATO dissolved in 1977.

Southern Baptist Convention, largest Baptist association. The organization was established in Georgia (1845) by Baptists in the southern states who differed in opinion with northern Baptists on the question of slavery. Theologically more conservative than other Baptist conventions, and more centralized, the Southern Baptist Convention, in part to maintain that conservatism, developed extensive missions, schools, colleges, seminaries, hospitals, and specialized homes of its own. The convention now has over 37,000 churches, and is headquartered in Nashville, Tenn.
See also: Baptists.

Southern Christian Leadership Conference (SCLC), U.S. civil rights organization. The group was established (1957) by the Rev. Martin Luther King, Jr., and his coworkers to coordinate localized groups working for equal rights for African Americans and other minorities. Adhering to King's doctrine of nonviolent civil protest, the SCLC organized numerous marches and voter-registration drives that, in the early 1960s, led to passage of the Civil Rights Act of 1964 and the Voting Rights Act of 1965. Rev. King led the group until his assassination in 1968. Headquarters are in Atlanta, Ga.
See also: King, Martin Luther, Jr.

Southern Cross, or Crux, constellation visible in the Southern Hemisphere, defined by 4 stars in the shape of a cross. In ancient Babylonia and Greece it was part of the constellation Centaurus.
See also: Constellation.

South Island *see:* New Zealand.

South Korea *see:* Korea.

South Pole, point in Antarctica through which passes the earth's axis of rotation. It does not coincide with the earth's south magnetic pole. It was first reached by Roald Amundsen in 1911.
See also: Antarctica.

South Vietnam *see:* Vietnam.

South West Africa *see:* Namibia.

South Yemen *see:* Yemen.

Sovereignty, ultimate political power in a state. In political theory, debates on sovereignty center on the role of the sovereign and on the nature of supreme power—by what rights, and by whom, it should be wielded. A sovereign state is one that is independent of control by other states. The modern theory of sovereignty was developed by Jean Bodin and Thomas Hobbes (1756), who studied the sovereignty of monarchs. The extension of their thought has been applied to the modern state.

Soviet (from Russian *sovet,* "council"), the fundamental political unit of the USSR. The soviets, ranging in importance from rural councils to the Supreme Soviet, the major legislative body of the Soviet Union, are elected policy-making and administrative units. The first soviets were the strike committees set up during the 1905 revolution and others developed during the 1917 revolution. Lenin institutionalized the soviet with the Bolshevik victory.

Soviet Union *see:* Union of Soviet Socialist Republics.

Sow bug *see:* Wood louse.

Soybean (*Glycine soja* or *Glycine max*), annual legume that is one of the best sources of complete protein, as well as being a good source of calcium, phosphorus, magnesium, and virtually all other minerals, plus vitamins A, B, and C and lecithin. Most of the world's soybeans are grown in China and the United States. In Asia, the soybean seed is sometimes ground into a meal, fermented, or dried, and used as a substitute for meat. In the United States, soybeans are generally made into oil or ground for animal feed; soybeans are also used in adhesives and for waterproofing and in many industrial products.

Soyer brothers, family name of 2 U.S. artists. Twins **Raphael** (1899-1987) and **Moses** (1899-1974) emigrated from Russia in 1912. They were impressed by U.S. realist artists and began to paint scenes of everyday life and of common people. Raphael, whose works include *Mission* (1935), *Office Workers* (1936), and *Avenue of the Americas* (1970), was called the "dean of American realism." Moses painted with a more vigorous style, using sharp contrasts and vibrant colors. His works include *Out of Work* (1937) and *Ballet Studio* (1955).

Soyinka, Wole (1934-), Nigerian writer, first African to win a Nobel Prize in literature (1986). His works include the novel *The Interpreters* (1965) and the memoir *Ake: The Years of Childhood* (1981). He has been president of the International Theater Institute since 1985. Soyinka has been jailed for his activities on behalf of black political freedom.

Spaak, Paul Henri (1899-1972), Belgium's first Socialist premier (1938-39, 1946, 1947-50), and deputy premier (1961-65). He was the first president of the UN General Assembly (1946). He was influential in setting up the European Economic Community and was secretary-general of the North Atlantic Treaty Organization (NATO; 1957-61).

Spaatz, Carl (1891-1974), U.S. Army commander, first chief of staff of the United States Air Force. He led the U.S. Strategic Air Forces in Europe for the final attack on Germany (1944-45) during World War II.
See also: World War II.

Space *see:* Space exploration.

Spacecraft *see:* Space exploration.

Space exploration, investigation of planets, stars, and space through the use of satellites, spacecraft, and probes built by human beings. At 10:56 P.M. (E.D.T.) on July 20, 1969, Neil Armstrong stepped off Apollo 11 and became the first human to set foot on the moon. This was the climax of an intensive U.S. space program sparked by the successful launch of the Soviet artificial satellite Sputnik 1 in 1957 and accelerated by Yuri Gagarin's flight in Vostok 1, the first spacecraft flown by a human, in 1961. Later that year Alan Shepard piloted the first U.S. spacecraft, and President John F. Kennedy set the goal, to be realized within the decade, of landing astronauts on the moon and returning them safely to earth.
On Feb. 20, 1962, John Glenn orbited the earth 3 times in the first Mercury craft to be boosted by an Atlas rocket. The next Soviet mission, in June 1963, involved 2 craft. Piloting Vostok 5, Valery Bykovsky set the 1-person endurance record with a 5-day mission; and piloting Vostok 6, Valentina Tereshkova became the first woman cosmonaut. Aleksei Leonov completed the first space walk in Mar. 1965. But then it was the turn of the Gemini missions to break all records. Both countries lost men, on the ground and in space: among them Virgil Grissom, Edward White, and Roger Chaffee (in a fire on board Apollo during ground tests in 1967) and the crew of Soyuz 11, killed during reentry in 1971. Earlier Soyuz missions had docked successfully with the first space station and set new records.
Meanwhile unpiloted probes—such as Orbiter, Ranger, and Surveyor—were search-

Space exploration (from left to right): Russian Sputnik (first artificial satellite), U.S. Apollo (moon landing), U.S. Mariner (first planet exploration), and U.S. Voyager (planet exploration)

ing out Apollo moon-landing sites; teams preparing the Soviet Luna and Lunokhod craft were also studying the moon. In 1968 Apollo 7 carried out an 11-day earth-orbit flight, and at Christmas Apollo 8 made 10 lunar orbits. The lunar landing craft was tested on the Apollo 9 and Apollo 10 missions, opening the way for the triumphant success of Apollo 11.

Apollo 12 was equally victorious, landing only 600 yards from the lunar probe Surveyor 3, but Apollo 13's aborted mission in 1970 was a near disaster. An explosion damaged the craft on its way to the moon, and reentry was achieved only with great difficulty. Apollo 14 had no such problems in 1971, visiting the moon's Fra Mauro area and collecting a wide range of lunar samples. Apollo 16 brought back 213 lb (96.6 kg) of moon rock, and in Dec. 1972 Apollo 17 made the last lunar landing, remaining on the moon for a record 75 hours.

In 1973 the United States launched the Skylab space station, a kind of satellite designed so that astronauts can live and work in orbit for several weeks. The station serves as a laboratory and as a base for other spacecraft.

Exploration of the planets has been carried out by unmanned probes: the Mariner series to Mars, Venus, and Mercury, and the Pioneer missions to the outer planets. There have been a number of Soviet contributions, such as the Venera soft-landing missions to Venus, the Zond bypass probe, and the Mars soft-landing craft. Results from the 2 U.S. Viking probes that soft-landed in Mars in 1976 did not show conclusively existence of life there. Voyagers 1 and 2 (1977) revealed a wealth of new information about Jupiter and Saturn.

The United States launched the first reusable manned space vehicle, the space shuttle Columbia, in 1981. In 1983 Sally K. Ride, one of five crew members aboard the space shuttle Challenger, became the first U.S. woman in space. In the 25th space shuttle mission (1986), the shuttle Challenger exploded immediately after its launch, killing all seven crew members. A commission appointed by President Ronald Reagan to investigate the accident criticized NASA's decision to launch the shuttle and made several recommendations regarding safety measures to be used in future missions.

The United States' Magellan space probe (launched 1989) reached Venus in 1990 and relayed to the earth clear images of Venus's surface. The Ulysses probe, launched by the United States in 1990, is due to reach the sun's south pole in 1994.

Space shuttle *see:* Space exploration.

Space station *see:* Space exploration.

Space telescope *see:* Hubble Space Telescope.

Space-time, concept of the physical universe arising from Einstein's special theory of relativity. Space and time are considered as a single 4-dimensional continuum rather than as a 3-dimensional space with a separate, infinite, 1-dimensional time. Time thus becomes the 4th dimension. Events in space-time are analogous to points in space and invariant space-time intervals to distances in space.
See also: Relativity.

Spahn, Warren (1921-), U.S. baseball player. Considered one of the greatest pitchers of all time, Spahn's achievements include winning the Cy Young award (1957) and setting a record for left-handed pitching in victories (363) and shutouts (63). He played in the major leagues for the Boston (Milwaukee) Braves (1942-64), New York Mets (1965), and San Francisco Giants (1965). Spahn was inducted to the National Baseball Hall of Fame in 1973.

Spaight, Richard Dobbs (1758-1802), North Carolina legislator and a signer of the U.S. Constitution. After the ratification of the Constitution he was governor of North Carolina (1792-95) and served in the U.S. House of Representatives (1798-1801).

Narrow street in the Spanish town of Jimena de la Frontera

Spain, country occupying about four-fifths of the Iberian Peninsula south of the Pyrenees in southwestern Europe.

Land and climate. Including the Balearic and Canary islands, Spain covers 194,884 sq mi (504,750 sq km). Peninsular Spain is bounded on the north by the Bay of Biscay. On the northeast, the Pyrenees mark the borders with France and Andorra. On the west, Spain is bounded by Portugal and the Atlantic Ocean, and to the east and south, by the Mediterranean Sea and the Strait of Gibraltar.

About three-quarters of Spain is the great interior plateau called the Meseta, extending from the Cantabrian Mountains and the Ebro River in the north to the Sierra Morena and the Guadalquivir River in the south. In the west the plateau continues into Portugal; in the east low ranges separate it from the coastal plain. The Meseta is higher in the north than in the south, the dividing line being the central cordillera. It is traversed by the Douro, Tagus, and Guadiana rivers, which flow into the Atlantic. Except for irrigated areas and fertile valleys, the Meseta is mostly arid and large areas are barren. In the southeast, beyond the Guadalquivir River, are the Andalusian Mountains, which contain Spain's highest mountain range, the Sierra Nevada. Spain's coastal plains are mostly narrow, becoming broadest along the Gulf of Cádiz in the south. The north and northwest coasts, hemmed in by mountains, have rocky cliffs and long inlets providing good harbors and some fine beaches. The Mediterranean coast is also rocky but there are fine sand beaches north of Barcelona along the famed Costa Brava. Spain is mainly a dry country with hot summers and cool winters. But great extremes occur on the Meseta. The climate of northern Spain is more equable. Along the south and east coasts, winters are mild and summers hot.

People. The Spanish people are in many ways homogeneous, but certain traditional and ethnic differences distinguish several groups. The Basques are an ethnically distinct people and, together with the Catalonians and Galicians, have preserved their own languages. The official language is Castilian Spanish. The capital of the country is Madrid and Roman Catholicism is the established religion.

Economy. Tourism makes the most important contribution to Spain's income, followed by industry and agriculture. Mineral wealth includes mercury, iron ore, coal, pyrites, potash, and salt. Oil was found near Borgos in 1964. Manufacturing includes textiles, chemicals, iron and steel, paper, explosives, and armaments. Agriculture is about equally divided between crops and livestock. Oranges, olive oil, wine, and cork are exported. Fishing is also important.

History. Present-day Spain was settled successively from prehistoric times to the 3rd century B.C. by Celts, Phoenicians, Greeks, and Carthaginians. A more enduring influence was that of the Romans, who conquered Spain in the Second Punic War in the 2nd century B.C. and remained dominant until the Vandals and Visigoths in-

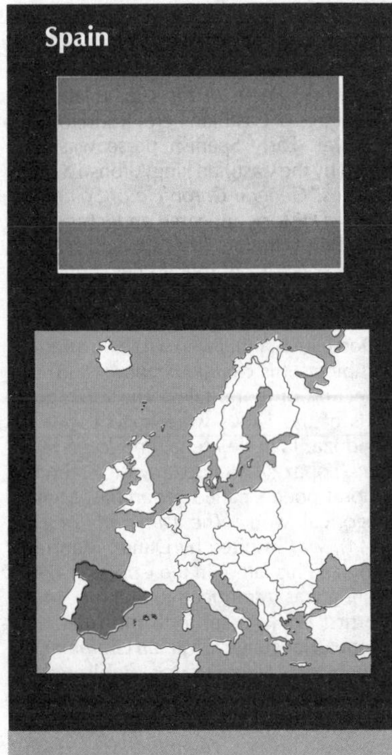

Spain

General information	
Capital:	Madrid
Area:	194,898 sq mi (504,783 sq km)
Population:	39,159,000
Official language:	Castilian Spanish
Monetary unit:	1 peseta = 100 céntimos
Main cities:	Madrid, Barcelona, Valencia
Government	
Form:	constitutional monarchy
Independent:	1492
Head of state:	King
Head of government:	Prime minister
Legislature:	two legislative houses (Senate and Chamber of Deputies)
Executive:	Prime minister and Cabinet
Judiciary:	highest court is the Supreme Court
Political division:	50 provinces, 2 territories, 3 islands
National economy	
Gross national product:	U.S.$301,829,000,000
Per capita income:	U.S.$7,740
Agriculture:	barley, olives, sugar beets, grapes, wheat, corn, oranges
Livestock:	sheep, pigs, cattle, poultry
Fisheries:	1,393,000 metric tons
Mining:	lignite, hard coal, anthracite, gypsum, salt
Industries:	electrical equipment, transport equipment, food and beverage products, chemicals and chemical products, iron and steel, tourism
Main exports:	transport equipment, machines and apparatus, electrical equipment, base metals and their manufactures, vegetable products
Transportation:	7,898 mi (12,710 km) of railroads, 197,609 mi (318,022 km) of roads, 32 international airports
Trading partners:	France, Germany, United Kingdom, Italy, U.S, Mexico, The Netherlands, Saudi Arabia
People	
Urban:	76%
Ethnic composition:	Spanish 73%, Catalan 16.5%, Galician 8%, Basque 2.5%
Birth rate:	11.2 per 1,000 population
Death rate:	7.9 per 1,000 population
Infant mortality:	9 per 1,000 live births
Life expectancy:	male 73.5 years, female 79.5 years

vaded in the 5th century A.D. The last invaders were the Moors, who advanced in A.D. 711. The Christian kingdoms that remained, all in the north, undertook the gradual reconquest of the peninsula, which was not completed until 1492 with the fall of Granada in the reign of Ferdinand V (Ferdinand II of Aragon) and Isabella of Castile (1474-1504). The same monarchs financed the voyages of Columbus, expelled the Jews from Spain, and sponsored the Inquisition. Within a brief period, Spain acquired a vast empire in the New World and North Africa and became rich, particularly in gold and silver from the Americas. Spain's new holdings were augmented by Habsburg lands when Charles I (1516-56) was elected Holy Roman Emperor as Charles V. Under his son and successor, Philip II (1556-98), Spain was at the height of its political and cultural power, as evidenced in the works of Cervantes, Lope da Vega, Velásquez, and El Greco. But Philip's reign also saw the onset of Spain's decline. The Netherlands revolted in 1568, and the Armada was defeated by the English in 1588. The War of the Spanish Succession at the beginning of the 18th century resulted in huge losses for Spain. The French, under Napoleon, invaded in 1808 and were driven out in the Peninsular War, but with revolutions in the Latin American colonies and defeat in the Spanish-American War (1898), the empire was finished. Political division in the early 20th century culminated in the Spanish Civil War (1936-39) between leftists and Fascists, which was won by the right wing under General Francisco Franco, who subsequently became dictator. After Franco's death in 1975, Juan Carlos de Bourbon restored the Spanish monarchy and also encouraged parliamentary democracy. In 1982 Socialists won the elections to lead the first leftist government in Spain since the Civil War.

Spaniel, one of a large family of sporting dogs, probably descended from a Spanish dog, hence the name. Spaniels make good pets and companions as well as good hunters. Most spaniels have silky coats, long ears, and sturdy bodies and legs. The American Kennel Club recognizes these 10 breeds of spaniels: American water, clumber, cocker, English cocker, English springer, field, Irish water, Sussex, Welsh springer, and Brittany.

Spanish, Romance language spoken by about 341 million people, primarily in Spain and Latin America. Modern Spanish arose from the Castilian dialect centered in the town of Burgos, in north-central Spain.

Old Castile, a barren region on the dry, central northern Spanish plateau

Spanish-American War (1898), fought between the United States and Spain, initially over the conduct of Spanish colonial authorities in Cuba. Strong anti-Spanish feeling was fomented in the United States by stories of the cruel treatment meted out to Cuban rebels and the hardships suffered by U.S. business interests. Though President Grover Cleveland took no action, his successor, President William McKinley, had promised to recognize Cuban independence. He succeeded in obtaining limited self-government for the Cubans, but an explosion aboard the U.S. battleship *Maine* (1898), from which 260 died, was blamed on the Spanish. McKinley sent an ultimatum, some of whose terms were actually being implemented when Congress declared war on Apr. 25 (Spain had declared war the previous day). On May 1 Admiral George Dewey destroyed the Spanish fleet in Manila harbor. What remained was trapped in the harbor at Santiago, Cuba, and destroyed on July 3 by U.S. forces that had already shattered Spanish land forces in several battles, including the Battle of San Juan Hill (July 1), famed for the charge of the Rough Riders, led by Theodore Roosevelt, up Kettle Hill. Santiago surrendered on July 17. General Nelson A. Miles occupied Puerto Rico, and on Aug. 13 troops occupied Manila. The Treaty of Paris (Dec. 10, 1898) ended Spanish rule in Cuba. The United States gained the islands of Guam, Puerto Rico, and the Philippines, thus acquiring an overseas empire with accompanying world military power and responsibilities.

Spanish Armada, naval fleet from Spain that attacked England in 1588. At that time the Catholic monarchy of Spain, under King Philip II, wielded great power through its wealthy colonies in the Americas and its control over Portugal and the Netherlands in Europe. Philip wanted to invade and control England, a Protestant country under the rule of Queen Elizabeth I. Sir Francis Drake, encouraged by the Queen, successfully raided Spain and Spanish holdings, which provoked Philip II to attack England from the English Channel. The smaller, swifter ships of the English navy drove the larger Spanish boats away from the coast, sunk 2 Spanish vessels, and damaged many others. Bad weather conditions also wrecked many ships of the Armada as they fled the English coast. Only about half the ships of the Spanish Armada returned to Spain.

Spanish bayonet, plant in the agave family, of the genus *Yucca*. The Spanish bayonet *(Y. aloifolia)* is about 25 ft (8 m) in height. Its name refers to the shape of its leaves, which are like slender, pointed bayonets. This plant can be found in the United States, the West Indies in the Caribbean, and Mexico.

Spanish Civil War (1936-39), one of the most violent and bloody conflicts in Spanish history, between the liberal second republic and conservative forces in Spain. After the bloodless overthrow of the monarchy in 1931, the democratic republican government proposed far-reaching reforms that alienated conservatives. On the election (1936) of the Popular Front, a left-wing coalition, the rightists under Gen. Francisco Franco resorted to force. Supported by Hitler and Mussolini, Franco was on the verge of shattering the republicans when the Soviet Union began to send them aid. Madrid and Barcelona fell to Franco in 1939. Over 600,000 died in the war, many of them foreign volunteers, and the country suffered massive damage. Franco's dictatorship remained in power until his death in 1975. The Luftwaffe's systematic destruction of the Basque town of Guernica, a preview of Hitler's blitzkrieg, shocked the world.

Spanish fly, beetle found mainly in southern Europe. It is the source of cantharidin, which causes blistering and bleeding of the skin and was a fashionable remedy for many diseases in the 19th century. It was also alleged to be an aphrodisiac. When taken by mouth, it is poisonous.

Spanish Inquisition *see:* Inquisition; Torquemada, Tomás de.

Spanish literature, European literature containing elements of the Western traditions of Europe and the Eastern traditions of North Africa. The heritage left behind when the Romans occupied the Spanish peninsula was the vernacular Latin, the foundation for the Romance languages, three of which became the most common Spanish dialects—Castilian, Galician-Portuguese, and Catalan. The long struggle from the A.D. 700s to 1400s between the Christians and the Muslim Moors created a religious patriotism that inspired some of the finest poetry and prose.

The battle of English and Dutch ships against the Spanish Armada off the shore of Dover on August 22, 1588

The Middle Ages. The first lyric poems, called *jarchas*, appeared in the A.D. 900s, expressing themes of longing for love. The epic work, *Poem of the Cid*, relates the adventures of Castilian hero, Rodrigo Díaz de Vivar. Early Spanish prose was promoted by the Castilian king Alfonso X. Two histories, *General Chronicle of Spain* and *General History*, appeared under his direction. Prose fiction first appeared about 1100 in a series of moral tales written by Pedro Alfonso entitled *Scholar's Guide*. The first distinctive prose writing was that of Don Juan Manuel who wrote on a variety of subjects; his *Count Lucanor* (1335) is a collection of moral tales. The three great poets of the 1400s were Iñigo López de Mendoza, Juan de Mena, and Jorge Manrique. López de Mendoza wrote elaborate pastoral poems called *serranillas*. Mena's allegorical work, *The Labyrinth of Fate* (1444), was inspired by Dante. Manrique eulogized his father in the *Coplas* (1476). Printing was introduced to Spain c. 1473. The first book to set forth the rules of a European language, *Castilian Grammar*, by Antonio de Nebrija, was published in 1492. Other prose works such as Diego de San Pedro's *The Prison of Love* (1492) and a book of chivalry, *Tirant lo Blanch* (1490) appeared at this time. A novel about chivalry, *Amadís of Gaul*, was the masterpiece of the period. *La Celestina*, appeared as an anonymous novel in the late 1400s; it combines medieval theology with Renaissance concern for life and love. The story, probably written by Fernando de Rojas, features a witch, Celestina, who unites two lovers, Calisto and Melibea.

The Golden Age. The two main schools of poetry were the Castilian school of Salamanca and the Andalusian school of Seville, both of which followed the style of the Italian poet Petrarch. Writers of the Salamanca school adopted a cautious use of metaphor, while the poets of the Seville school developed a formal use of language that led to the Baroque style of the 1600s. The mystic poets wrote lyrically of a union with God, while the epic poets glorified people and events in long works. The pastoral novel, glorifying the simple life, became popular during the Renaissance. The picaresque novel presented life in satiric fashion through the eyes of a rogue.

Playwriting developed more slowly during the 1500s. The actor-playwright Lope de Rueda created short, farce works called *pasos* that ridiculed the everyday life of his time.

In the 1600s the picaresque novel quickly became a tradition. Mateo Aleman's *Guzmán de Alfarache* presents a bitter, pessimistic view of life in which neither human nature nor the conditions of life can be changed. Francisco López de Beda created a female rogue in *La pícara Justina* (1605). In contrast to the picaresque novel, Cervantes's masterpiece novel, *Don Quixote*, contrasts the ideal and the practical. His characters present universal themes and qualities that extend to all humanity.

Lope de Vega was the leading dramatist of the Golden Age, presenting love and honor as sources of conflict, especially in his two

greatest dramas, *Fuenteovejuna* (1619) and *Justice Without Revenge* (1634).
Two literary examples of the Baroque (ornamental) style of writing of the 1600s were *conceptismo* and *culteranismo.* Conceptismo writers used metaphors to create complicated, original views of life. Culteranismos such as Pedro Soto de Rojas created lyric poetry in full color and imagery.
In drama, Pedro Calderon de la Barca's brilliant work *Life Is a Dream* (1635) was written in the Baroque style. He used symbolism to express in verse philosophical explorations of life and death, original sin, and free will.
Neoclassicism, romanticism, and realism. Neoclassicism, stressing the ideas of reason, proper behavior, and moral sense, became the important literary trend of the 1700s. A Benedictine monk, Benito Jerónimo Feijoo, covered almost every branch of learning in the 9-volume *Universal Theatre of Criticism* (1726-40) and the 5-volume *Erudite and Interesting Letters* (1742-60). In the 1800s the most accomplished writer of neoclassical comedy was Leandro Fernández de Moratín, whose most famous play was *The Maiden's Consent* (1806).
Romantic literary forms intensified after the death of King Ferdinand VII in 1833. Ángel de Saavedra's drama *Don Ivaro or The Force of Destiny* (1835) was a successful romantic tragedy. Antonio García Gutiérrez's historical tragedy *The Troubadour* (1836) was a triumph. Francisco Martínez de la Rosa and Juan Eugenio Hartzenbusch wrote plays reflecting rebellion, melancholy, and the passion of Spanish romanticism. José de Espronseda's poems *The Student from Salamanca* (1836-39) and *Devil World,* unfinished, are rich expressions of Spanish romantic anguish and social protest. Gustavo Adolfo Bécquer's light, airy poetry contains elements of romanticism, and he is often considered the most sensitive poet of the 1800s.
Short prose sketches, called *costumbrismo,* led to the development of the realistic Spanish novel in the mid-1800s. José María de Pereda's *The Upper Cliffs* (1895) was a costumbrista novel describing life on Spain's northern coast. Emilia Pardo Bazán's *The Ulloa Estate* (1886) narrated local traditions and politics in the interior of Galicia. Vicente Blasco Ibáñez's novel *The Cabin* (1898) described life in Valencia. Ibáñez gained international popularity for his novel about the terror of World War I, *The Four Horsemen of the Apocalypse* (1916).
The 1900s. The loss of the last remnants of Spain's empire during the Spanish-American War (1898) led to a resurgence of creative genius that dominated Spanish letters in the early 1900s. Miguel de Unamuno's essay *The Tragic Sense of Life* (1913) was an expression of romantic and philosophical grief. He is often considered the forerunner of the existential movement. Antonio Machado's poetry expresses the severe spirit and landscape of Castile. Ramón María del Valle-Inclán's *Bohemian Lights* (1924) was a picture of Spain as a grotesque distortion of normalcy. Scholars also rediscovered Spain's literary past, and interpreted, edited, and published works at the Center of Historical Studies in Madrid.
The short-lived age of modernism was represented by Manuel Machado and Gregorio Martínez Sierra. It inspired poetry of unequaled quality and intensity in Spanish literature. In Spanish drama, the best-known works are the comedy *The Bonds of Interest* (1907) and the domestic tragedy *The Passion Flower* (1913), by Jacinto Benavente.
The poets of the Generation of 1927 turned to the traditional ballad for inspiration. Their members included Pedro Salinas, Jorge Guillén, León Felipe, Gerardo Diego, Federico García Lorca, and others.
The Spanish Civil War (1936-39) caused a disruption in Spanish literature. Some writers were killed, and others continued to work in exile. The dark novel *The Family of Pascual Duarte* (1942) by Camilo José Cela was followed by Carmen Laforet's existential novel *Nothing* (1944).
Major novels since the mid-1950s have included *The Jarama River* (1956) by Rafael Sanchez Ferlioso, *Time of Silence* (1962) by Luis Martín Santos, and *Soldiers Cry at Night* by Ana María Matute.
Playwrights wrote in a variety of styles. Miguel Mihura wrote farces about everyday life. Antonio Bueno Vallejo promoted interest in serious drama with *History of a Staircase* (1949). The poets who wrote after 1939 used simpler forms of expression than the Generation of 1927. Some, including Claudio Rodríguez and Carlos Bousoño, were less interested in social realism. The newest generation of poets, called *novisimos,* reject social concerns and show interest in more personal, intimate, and intellectual concerns.

Spanish Main, former name of the north Caribbean coast of South America, from Panama to the Orinoco River in Venezuela. It was the hunting ground of the English pirates and buccaneers who attacked the Spanish treasure fleets.

Spanish moss, or Florida moss, epiphyte (*Tillandsia usneoides*) that can be found festooning trees, such as oaks and cypresses, and even telephone poles and wires in the southeastern United States. It is not a true moss. It absorbs water through scaly hairs on the leaves and stem, and is used as a substitute for horsehair stuffing and for insulation.

Spanish Succession, War of the (1701-14), conflict between France and the Grand Alliance of England, the Netherlands, Austria, and the smaller states of the Holy Roman Empire over control of the Spanish Empire. The childless Charles II of Spain willed his kingdom and its empire to France on his deathbed. The alliance sought to prevent France from becoming the dominant European power. Though the decisive battles were fought in Europe, there were also engagements overseas, including North America. The duke of Marlborough and Prince Eugene of Savoy won remarkable victories at Blenheim (1704), Ramillies (1706), and Malplaquet (1709), but Louis XIV fought on. The accession of Charles VI as the new Holy Roman emperor removed obstacles to the recognition of Philip of Anjou as Philip V of Spain. England made a separate peace in 1712, and a general settlement of differences in the Peace of Utrecht followed in 1713.

Spark, Muriel (1918-), Scottish writer best known for her witty, often satirical novels, including *Memento Mori* (1959), *The Prime of Miss Jean Brodie* (1961; later a play and film), *The Mandelbaum Gate* (1965), and *Loitering with Intent* (1981).

Sparks, Jared (1789-1866), U.S. historian best known for *Writings of George Washington* (12 vols., 1834-37). He edited the *North American Review* (1824-30) and was president of Harvard University (1849-53).

Sparrow, gregarious, seed-eating bird of the subfamily Passerinae of the weaverbird family. There are 8 genera: 5 confined to Africa, the other 3—the true sparrows, rock sparrows, and snow finches—are also found in the Palearctic. Of the true sparrows, one species, the house sparrow (*Passer domesticus*), has been successfully introduced to the Americas. Closely associated with human habitation, it is the only bird not known to occur in a "natural" habitat but always with human beings. In the United states some small finches are called sparrows (song sparrow, tree sparrow, field sparrow, etc.).

Sparrowhawk, name for small birds of prey (genus *Accipiter*). They eat insects and small birds and mammals and often hunt by hovering. Upper feathers range from gray to rusty brown. In the United States the kestrel, a small falcon, is called the sparrow hawk.

Sparta, or Lacedaemon, city of ancient Greece, capital of Laconia in the Peloponnesus, on the Eurotas River. A center for culture and wealth, its society was divided into 3 classes: the helots (serfs bound to the land); the free perioeci (freemen allowed to take part in commerce and crafts); and the Spartiates, citizens with legal and civil rights, whose rigorous military training led to the word *Spartan.* There were 2 hereditary kings, though real power resided with the 5 annually elected ephors (magistrates). Founded in the 13th century B.C., Sparta dominated the Peloponnesus by 550 B.C. Despite alliance with Athens in the Persian Wars, Sparta fought and won the Peloponnesian War against Athens (431-404 B.C.), but a series of revolts and defeats destroyed Spartan power, and in 146 B.C. the city became subject to Roman rule. It prospered under the Romans but was destroyed by the Goths in A.D. 395.
See also: Greece, Ancient.

Spartacus (d.71 B.C.), leader of the Gladiators' War, a slave revolt against ancient Rome (73-71 B.C.). With an army of run-

away slaves, Spartacus heavily defeated forces sent against him and gained control of southern Italy, but after his death in battle the revolt was quickly crushed and 6,000 slaves were crucified along the Appian Way.
See also: Rome, Ancient.

Spastic paralysis, form of paralysis due to disease of the brain (e.g., stroke) or spinal cord (e.g., multiple sclerosis), in which the affected muscles are in a state of constantly increased tone (or resting contraction). Spasticity is a segmental motor phenomenon where muscle contractions occur without voluntary control.
See also: Cerebral palsy.

Speaker, in U.S. government, officer presiding in the U.S. House of Representatives. Formally elected by the whole House, the speaker is in fact selected from the majority party by its members and holds powers of recognition, referral of bills to committee, and control of debates. Other, wider powers were stripped from the speaker after the term of Joseph G. Cannon (Rep., Illinois; 1903-11). During the long service of Sam Rayburn (Dem., Texas) as speaker (1940-47, 1949-53, 1955-61), he effectively advanced party programs by maintaining firm discipline. Thomas S. Foley (Dem., Washington) became speaker in 1989.
See also: House of Representatives.

Speaker, Tristram E. (1888-1958), U.S. baseball player. Known for his outstanding defense and speed, Speaker holds the American League record for putouts by an outfielder (6,794 career). He compiled a lifetime batting average of .344 and set a major league record for doubles (793). Speaker played for the Boston Red Sox (1907-15) and Cleveland Indians (1916-26), managing the Indians as well (1919-26). He was inducted into the National Baseball Hall of Fame in 1937.

Spear, weapon on which a point tops a long shank. Spears have been constructed and used by humans since primitive times. The points of spears have evolved from the earliest ones made of wood to those crafted from bones, stones, bronze, and iron. Whether used in hunting or warfare, spears may be thrown toward their targets or used by their owners to stab the intended targets. In the 17th century, the bayonet took over the popular role of the spear in combat.
See also: Javelin.

Spearfishing, sport in which fish are caught underwater with the use of spears. An underwater slingshot device called a Hawaiian sling, a simple spear with a metal tip called a pole spear, and various kinds of spearguns are used to catch the fish. People spear fish from the surface or dive underwater, using breathing equipment, such as snorkels or scuba gear. In official meets, divers must breathe on their own underwater. After a fish is caught, the diver must gain control of it, with the help of a line that connects the spear to the spearing apparatus.

Spearmint, herb in the mint family. Spearmint (*Mentha spicata*), originally from Europe and Asia, is plentiful in North America. It grows to about 2 ft (61 cm) high and displays white to light purple flowers. The leaves, when dried, are used for cooking, baking, and flavoring beverages. Oil extracted from the leaves is used in perfume.

Special education, instruction designed for the special needs of certain students, both gifted and handicapped. Mainstreaming refers to the time spent by these exceptional students in a regular classroom; special instruction takes place in "resource rooms." Over 10% of U.S. schoolchildren need special education programs (approximately 8% are handicapped, including physical and mental impairments; 3-5% are considered gifted). Students of both average and above-average intelligence may need special education, due to learning disabilities from minor disorders. Hyperactive children also participate in special education programs. The Education for All Handicapped Children Act (1975) provides for their education.

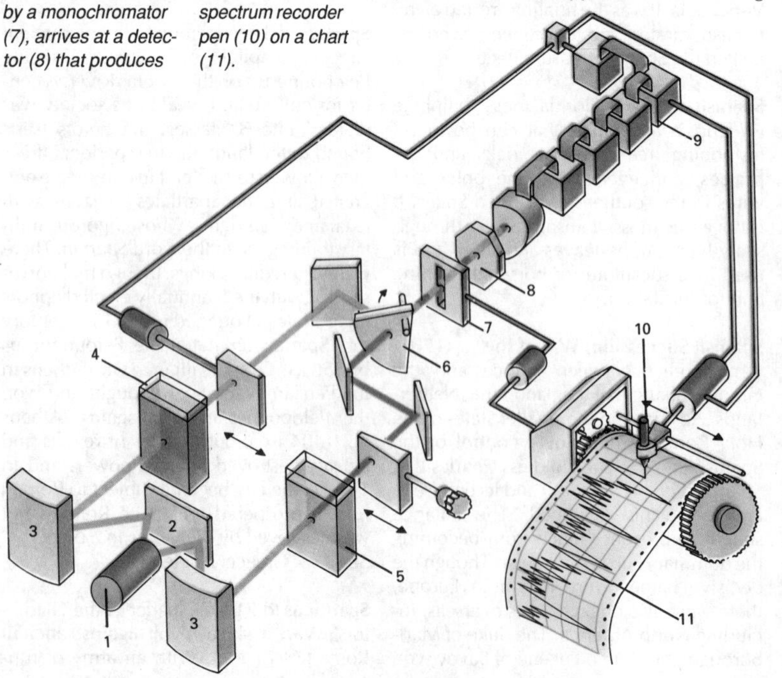

Special effects, in cinema, technique developed to enhance visual illusion, especially important in "disaster movies" and ambitious science fiction films, such as *Star Wars.* Most effects are produced in special studios and are added to the film after it is shot. A great many techniques are employed, including animation, the use of miniature models, and slow-speed or fast-speed photography. An important and increasingly sophisticated technique is the creation of a composite picture—using several different images superimposed within a single frame—often with the aid of electronic memories and timers to match perspectives, light, and camera angles.

Special Olympics, international sporting program designed for participation by mentally retarded people. This program is active in summer and winter sports year round through communities and schools. Like the Olympics, an international winter and summer Special Olympic event takes place every 4 years. The program develops events according to the age and ability of its participants. Headquartered in Washington, D.C., the Special Olympics were founded (1968) and are sponsored by the Joseph P. Kennedy, Jr., Foundation.

Species *see:* Classification.

Specific heat, warmth required to raise the temperature of 1 kg (2.2 lb) of a substance through 1 kelvin; measured by calorimetry. The concept was introduced in 1760 by Joseph Black (1728-99). Subsequently, P. L. Dulong and A. T. Petit evolved a law in 1819 showing that the specific heat of elements is inversely proportional to their atomic weights, which could thus be roughly determined, and the product of the atomic weight and the specific heat is a constant for all solid elements.
See also: Black, Joseph.

Spectrometer, tool that analyzes an object through a spectrum of light. This device can be used to examine evidence at crime scenes, to determine the composition of celestial bodies, and to detect pollution in the sky or water. Spectroscopes allow a scientist to view the light spectrum of an object, which for every object is different. Sometimes photographs of the light spectrum are taken by a spectrograph. The brightness of light in an object may be determined through a spectrophotometer.

Spectrophotometers are used to determine the nature and amounts of a substance in a sample by measuring its absorption of electromagnetic radiation of a specific wavelength. Light from a source (1) is split in half by a plane mirror (2) and two concave mirrors (3). One beam is led through the test sample (4), and the other through a known reference sample (5). A rotating sector mirror (6) switches the light paths from one sample to the other. Light of one wavelength, selected by a monochromator (7), arrives at a detector (8) that produces a electrical signal. The amplified signal (9) is used to drive a spectrum recorder pen (10) on a chart (11).

Spectrum, array of light in the form of different colors produced when a ray of plain white light passes through a prism by a process known as dispersion. The different colors of light are created by different wavelengths, which are forms of electromagnetic radiation. The short-wave lengths (low frequency) create indigo and violet on one end of the spectrum; the long-wave lengths (high frequency) produce red, orange, and yellow on the other end of the spectrum.

Speculation, practice of entering into business transactions in order to make a quick profit from an anticipated substantial price fluctuation. Speculation is also applied to investment in any undertaking when the risks and the potential profit are both high. Most speculation, however, involves the buying of commodities or stocks and bonds.
See also: Stock exchange.

Speech and speech disorders, communication through spoken words and the impairments of this ability. Speech can be subdivided into conception, or formulation, and production, or phonation and articulation. Speech development in children starts with associating sounds with persons and objects, comprehension usually predating vocalization by some months. Nouns are developed first, often with 1 or 2 syllables only; later acquisition of verbs, adjectives, etc., allows the construction of phrases and sentences. A phase of babbling speech, where the child toys with sounds resembling speech, is probably essential for development.
Reading is closely related to speech development and involves the association of auditory and visual symbols. Speech involves coordination of many aspects of brain function (hearing, vision, etc.), but 3 areas particularly concerned with aspects of speech are located in the dominant hemisphere of right-handed persons and in either hemisphere of left-handed people.
Disease of these parts of the brain leads to characteristic forms of dysphasia or aphasia alexia, etc. Development dyslexia is a childhood defect of visual pattern recognition. Stammering or stuttering, with repetition and hesitation over certain syllables, is a common disorder, in some cases representing frustrated left-handedness. Dysarthria is disordered voice production and is due to disease of the neuromuscular control of voice. In speech therapy, attempts are made to overcome or circumvent speech difficulties, which is particularly important to address in children.

Speech therapy, detection and correction of speech problems. Speech-language pathologists work with people who, for various reasons, cannot speak at all (asphasiacs), cannot speak clearly or easily, stutter or have a problem with voice pitch or volume. The most common problem dealt with in speech therapy is that of articulation, the way in which sounds are produced. Speech problems may be physical, environmental, or emotional in origin. Many speech-language professionals belong to The American Speech and Hearing Association (founded 1925).

Speed *see:* Methamphetamine.

Speedometer, instrument for indicating the speed of a motor vehicle. The common type works by magnetic induction. A circular, permanent magnet is rotated by a flexible cable geared to the transmission. The rotating magnetic field induces a magnetic field in an aluminum cup, thus tending to turn it in the same direction as the magnet. This torque, proportional to the speed of rotation, is opposed by a spiral spring. The angle through which the cup turns against the spring measures the speed. The speedometer is usually coupled with an odometer, a counting device geared to the magnet, that registers the distance traveled.

Speed reading, mastery of reading material in terms of both speed and comprehension. Mental training helps quicken the reading pace more than do exercises that improve visual focus, according to experts in this field. A combination of complete concentration, attention to a specific reading purpose (pleasure, fact-finding), and continual reading without pause (regardless of multisyllabic vocabulary or total speed comfort) often yield increased comprehension simultaneously with increased speed.

Speedwriting, writing method that uses the letters of the alphabet in a shortened form. Each letter corresponds with a sound, which in longhand often is made up of a cluster of letters. For example, the letter *a* is pronounced like the word *ate*; therefore, *fa* would stand for *fate*, *stra* would stand for *straight*, etc. Because of fewer (though familiar) letter and sound relationships employed, a person may write what is dictated quickly. Emma B. Dearborn invented this trademarked method of shorthand writing in 1923.
See also: Shorthand.

Speer, Albert (1905-81), German architect and Nazi leader. For his organization of slave labor for Germany during World War II, the international tribunal at Nuremberg sentenced him to 20 years' imprisonment in Spandau. After his release he wrote revealingly of the inner workings of the Nazi regime in *Inside the Third Reich* (1972).
See also: Nazism; World War II.

Speleology, scientific study of caves. The world's first speleological society was founded in France in 1895, and interest soon became worldwide. The U.S. National Speleological Society was founded in 1939. Nonacademic cave exploration is called *spelunking*.
See also: Cave.

Spelling, often referred to as orthography, manner in which letters represent words in writing. Orthographers study sound and letter relationships, base words and affixes (which include prefixes and suffixes), preferred spellings of words, spelling rules and exceptions, homophones, and word pronunciation. Individuals devise their own methods for correct spelling, which may include word visualization, spoken pronunciation, syllabic division of words, repeat writing of the word, and using the word in context.

Spencer, Anna Garlin (1851-1931), U.S. religious and political leader, educator, and author, especially in the field of women's rights. She was the first woman in Rhode Island to become a minister (1891), at the Bell Street Chapel in Providence. She taught sociology in universities and was a leader in the New York School of Philanthropy. She supported woman suffrage, prohibition, world peace, and family unity. Her vision of equal rights for women was expressed in her book *Woman's Share in Social Culture* (1913).
See also: Woman suffrage.

Spencer, Herbert (1820-1903), English philosopher, social theorist, and early evolutionist. In his multivolume *System of Synthetic Philosophy* (1855-93) he expounded a world view based on a close study of physical, biological, and social phenomena, arguing that species evolve by a process of differentiation from the simple to the complex. Spencer coined the phrase "survival of the fittest." His political individualism deeply influenced the growth of Social Darwinism, and, in general, U.S. social thinking.
See also: Social Darwinism.

Spender, Sir Stephen Harold (1909-), English poet and critic, coeditor of the literary magazine *Encounter* (1953-65). His poetry collections include *Poems* (1933), *Ruins and Visions* (1941), and *Generous Days* (1971).

Spenser, Edmund (1552?-99), English poet. His most famous poem, *The Faerie Queene* (1590, 1596), considered a classic in English literature, is an allegory—a story in which people or personified things represent qualities and virtues in addition to their human character. Spenser projected that his masterpiece would contain 12 sections, or books, but at the time of his death only 6 of those books were completed. He lived in the Elizabethan age, under the reign of Queen Elizabeth I. Through her, monies and political position (sheriff of Cork, in Ireland, 1598) were granted to Spenser. Some of his other poems include *The Shepheardes Calendar* (1579), *Colin Clouts Come Home Againe* (1595), and *Amoretti* (1595)—a collection of sonnets that includes a famous poem about marriage, "Epithalamion." Although born and educated in England, Spenser lived his adult life in Ireland.

Sperm *see:* Reproduction.

Sperm whale, family of toothed whales, with 2 species: the cachalot (*Physeter catodon*) and pigmy sperm whale (*Kogia breviceps*). They are among the best known of all whales because of their enormous, squared heads. The front of the head contains a huge reservoir of spermaceti oil, perhaps used as a lens to focus the sounds produced by the whales in echolocation. Spermaceti solidifies in cool air to form a wax once used for candles and cosmetics. Sperm whales are also the source of ambergris, a secretion in the gut produced in response to irritation by the beaks of squids, an important prey. Ambergris is used as a fixative in perfumes. Sperm whales are found in all oceans, migrating from the poles into warmer waters during the breeding season. They are deep-water whales, capable of diving to 1,650 ft (503 m) or more. Female and young form large schools of up to several hundred animals. Males tend to travel alone or in small groups.

Sperry, Elmer Ambrose (1860-1930), U.S. inventor and manufacturer. Although he began his career with inventions in the field of lighting (in particular, arc lamps and searchlights), he is known mainly for his invention of and work with the gyroscope (1911)—a device that always points to the true north. His gyrocompass enabled steel ships to navigate without interference from magnetic fields. He further developed devices based on the gyroscope that stabilized ships and allowed planes to fly on automatic pilot. The gyroscope also made possible advanced weaponry used in World War II, such as naval gunsights and the aerial torpedo. The Sperry Gyroscope Company (1910) was founded and is still located outside New York City.
See also: Gyroscope.

Sphagnum moss *see:* Peat moss.

Sphalerite, also called zinc blende, zinc ore and sulfur ore. It is the major mineral ore of zinc. Sphalerite appears in a variety of colors—brown, red, black, yellow—but is always opaque and dark. When it is abraded by a sharp metal object, an orange flash appears in this ore. The sulfur content may release the scent of rotten eggs. Sphalerite is found in the United States, Mexico, northern Europe, and northern Africa.
See also: Zinc.

The Great Sphinx, near Giza, Egypt, was built c.4500 years ago. It is believed to have the face of King Khafre, who probably commissioned the statue's construction

Sphere, surface produced by the rotation of a circle through 180° about one of its diameters. The intersection of a sphere and any plane is circular; should the plane pass through the center, the intersection is a great circle. The surface area of a sphere is $4\pi r^2$, where *r* is the radius; its volume $4/3\pi r^3$. If mutually perpendicular *x*-, *y*-, and *z*- axes are constructed such that they intersect at the center, the sphere's equation is $x^2 + y^2 + z^2 = r^2$.

Sphinx, mythical monster of the ancient Middle East, in Egypt portrayed as a lion with a human head and used as a symbol of the pharaoh. In Greek mythology the sphinx propounded a riddle to travelers on the road to Thebes: When Oedipus answered correctly the sphinx threw herself from her rocky perch.
See also: Mythology.

Sphinx moth *see:* Hawk moth.

Spice, one of a large number of aromatic plant products that have a distinctive flavor or aroma and are used to season food. Most spices are obtained from tropical plants and were once highly valued as a means of making poor-quality food more palatable.

Spider, any of an order (*Araneida*) of arachnids, with a body of 2 main parts, 4 pairs of legs, and 4 pairs of eyes. Unlike insects, spiders have no antennae and no larval or pupal stages. Their abdominal spinnerets produce silk thread that is used to make cocoons for their eggs and nests, to capture their prey, and as a means of travel. They are a diverse group of some 26,000 species, including jumping spiders, wolf spiders, and trapdoor spiders. They paralyze their prey with poison, which in several species (e.g., black widows) is dangerous to humans.

Spider monkey, slender, pot-bellied monkey found in the forests of central and northern South America. It has a prehensile tail with a naked patch at the end that is ridged like a fingerprint. Spider monkeys swing through the trees by their long forearms and tails. The 2 species, the common and the woolly spider monkeys, live in small groups and feed solely on fruit.

Spiderwort, or Job's tears, family of plants found in the tropical and temperate Americas and cultivated as house plants. Spiderworts have hairy stems that exude a sticky substance that can be drawn into a thread as fine as a spider's web. The leaves are grasslike, and the clusters of 3-petaled flowers open in the morning and die in the afternoon. Spiderwort can be found wild in woods across the country. As house plants they are usually known by their scientific name of *Tradescantia*. Wandering Jew, a house plant from Mexico, belongs to the same family.

Spielberg, Steven (1947-), U.S. film director, writer, and producer. Many of his films have been box office hits, such as *Jaws* (1975), *Close Encounters of the Third Kind* (1977), *Raiders of the Lost Ark* (1981), *E.T.: The Extra-Terrestrial* (1982), and *The Color Purple* (1985). Brilliant technical special effects plus a romantic and heroic quality are signature characteristics of his films.

A scene from Steven Spielberg's E.T. The Extra Terrestrial *(1982)*

Spikenard, flowering plant in the Valerianaeceae family (*Nardostachys jatamansi*) or in the ginseng family (*Aralia racemosa*). The oriental, or "true" spikenard, from India, has a thick stem and a root shaped like an ear of corn; it is valued for its perfume. The American spikenard, or Indian root, is an herb often used in place of sarsaparilla for flavor.

Spina bifida, congenital deformity in which a fissure in the lower part of the spine allows the spinal membranes to protrude. The condition leads to a variable degree of leg paralysis and loss of urine and feces sphincter control; it may be associated with other malformation, particularly hydrocephalus. Mild cases can be treated by surgical closure of the defect, and orthopedic procedures can be applied to balance muscle power.

Spinach (*Spinacia oleracea*), leafy annual plant widely cultivated as an edible vegetable. Spinach leaves have a relatively high content of iron and vitamins A and C.

Spinal cord and spinal nerves, that part of the central nervous system contained within the spinal column and extending from the skull to the level of the first or second lumbar vertebra; the nerve structures and nerve pathways within the vertebral canal, extending from the skull opening to the second lumbar vertebra. These nerves carry sensory information from the body to the brain, and then return

with commands from the brain to the rest of the body.
See also: Nervous system; Spine.

Spinal tap, or lumbar puncture, procedure to remove cerebrospinal fluid (CSF) from the lumbar spinal canal using a fine needle. It is used in diagnosis of meningitis, encephalitis, multiple sclerosis, and tumors. In neurology it may be used in treatment, by reducing CSF pressure or allowing insertion of drugs.

Spine, spinal column or vertebral cord, vertical structure of bone, nerves and nerve fibers, ligaments, and cartilage that act as a skeletal support and transmission center for the nervous system in vertebrate animals. Vertebrae are the flexible, bony joints that make up the spinal column; they number 33 in humans. The spinal cord, where bundles of nerve fibers are found, is encased in the spinal column. The human spine extends from the brainstem to the tailbone region, or coccyx. Sensory impulses travel up the spinal column to the brain; in turn, the brain sends its commands down the spinal column to voluntary muscles used for motion and balance. Paralysis occurs when an injury to the spine interrupts the transmission of these messages between the brain and limbs.
See also: Skelton

Spinning, craft of twisting together fibers from a mass to form strong, continuous thread suitable for weaving. The earliest method was merely to roll the fibers between hand and thigh. Later 2 sticks were used: the distaff to hold the bundle of fibers, and a spindle to twist and wind the yarn. Mechanization began with the spinning wheel, which was invented in India and spread to Europe by the 14th century. Improved weaving methods in the Industrial Revolution caused increased demand, which in turn provoked several inventions. The spinning jenny, invented by James Hargreaves (1767), spun as many as 16 threads at once. Richard Arkwright's "water frame" (1769), so-called from being water-powered, produced strong thread. Then Samuel Crompton produced (1779) a hybrid of the two—his "mule," which had a movable carriage. One modern spinning machine is the ring-spinning frame (1828) in which the strands, drawn out by rollers, are twisted by a "traveler" that revolves on a ring around the bobbin on which they are wound.

Spinoza, Baruch or **Benedict de** (1632-77), Dutch philosopher who held that God is nature or all that is, an interpretation that brought him expulsion from the Amsterdam Jewish community. He claimed that matter and mind are attributes of the one substance: God. His most famous work, *Ethics* (1677), contains the development of his pantheism, which is both rationalist and mystical.
See also: Philosophy.

Spiny anteater *see:* Echidna.

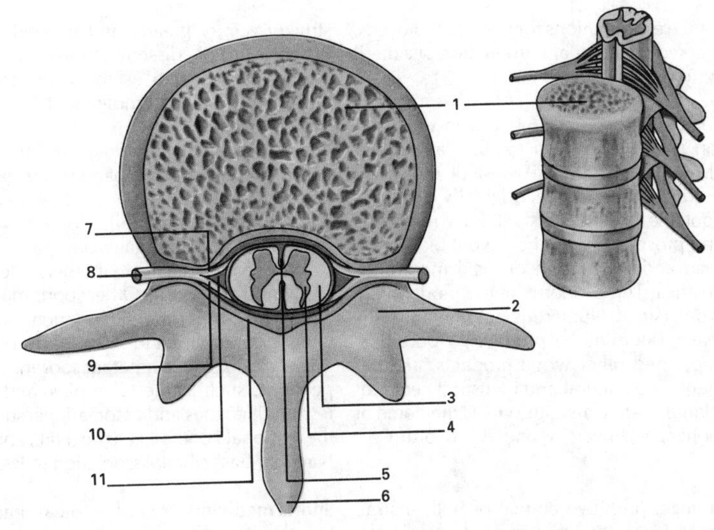

The spinal cord is found in the vertebral canal formed by the openings in the column vertebrae. Between the main vertebra body is the foramen (1) and the neural arch (2); the neural arch has several projections, which include the spinous process (6). The three membranes which cover the spinal cord (5, 10 and 11) consist of white matter (3) and gray matter (4). The spinal nerves (8) leave the vertebral canal through an opening between two neural arches. Near the spinal cord the emerging nerve consists of ventral root (7) and a dorsal root (9).

Spiraea, any of several shrubs with tall clusters of pink or white flowers. They grow wild in the Northern Hemisphere, and several are grown in gardens. Meadowsweet, staplebush, and queen-of-the-meadow are wild American species. The cultivated forms, of which bridal wreath is the most popular, come mainly from the Far East.

Spirit of '76, popular image of the American Revolution, depicted in a painting by Archibald M. Willard. Willard, a U.S. artist, created this image originally as a cartoon (c.1875). Later it was painted and displayed in the Philadelphia Centennial Exhibition (1876). The image of a fife player and 2 drummers leading troops of the American army was modeled by acquaintances and relatives of the artist.
See also: Revolutionary War in America.

Spiritual, form of emotional, often sorrowful, religious folk song using syncopation, a variety of rhythms, and the pentatonic scale (5 whole tones). It usually consists of a number of verses for solo voice, often with biblical text, and a rhythmic choral refrain. Originally though to have been developed solely by African-American slaves and their descendants in the southern United States, it is now believed to be a form that combined African musical systems with those of 19th-century white Southerners (i.e., revival meeting songs).

Spiritualism, belief in the survival of the human personality after death and its ability to communicate with those left behind, usually through a medium.

Spitz, family of dogs, distinguished by their thick, long coats, curly tails, and pointed ears. Breeds in the spitz family include small dogs, such as the Pomeranian; medium-size dogs, such as the Samoyed and chow chow; and large dogs, such as the Alaskan malamute and Akita. Spitz dogs are native to northern climates in the Americas, Europe, and Asia.

Spleen, spongy vascular organ between the stomach and diaphragm on the left side of the abdomen. It eliminates foreign organisms and worn-out red blood cells, recycling their iron. Most of its functions are duplicated by other organs.

Split (pop. 235,400), city in the Croatian republic of Yugoslavia, in the southwestern region of Dalmatia on the Adriatic Sea; known as Spalato in Italian. The remains of the palace of the Roman emperor Diocletian (A.D. 245-313) are central to this modern port city. The tomb of the emperor, within the palace walls, became the Cathedral of Split (A.D. 653). Many have ruled this city, including the Byzantine Empire (mid-4th century to early 12th century), Venice (1420-1797), and Austria (1797-1918). It became part of Yugoslavia after World War I. Today it supports many industries, including chemicals, plastics, aluminum, and shipbuilding.

Spock, Benjamin McLane (1903-), known as "Dr. Spock," U.S. pediatrician and pacifist noted for his best-selling *Common Sense Book of Baby and Child Care* (1946) and *Bringing Up Children in a Difficult Time* (1974). He ran for president in 1972 as candidate of the People's Party.
See also: Pediatrics.

Spode, British family of potters. **Josiah Spode I** (1733-97) founded the Spode works at Stoke-on-Trent and introduced transfer decoration and oriental motifs. His son, **Josiah Spode II** (1754-1827), developed stone china, porcelain, and bone china. He popularized the willow pattern and gained royal patronage.
See also: Pottery and porcelain.

Spoils system, use of appointments to public offices to reward supporters of a victorious political party. With the growth of a 2-party system in the United States, political patronage increased. It was Pres. Andrew Jackson's friend, Sen. William L. Marcy, who said in 1832 that "to the victor belong the spoils," and the system soon operated on every political level. Reforms began with the creation of the Civil Service Commission in 1871, and the Pendleton Act of 1883, introducing competitive entrance examinations for public employees, marked the gradual introduction of a merit system.

Spokane (pop. 361,364), city in Washington state, located on the Spokane River, about 15 mi (24 km) west of the Idaho border. The town site, originally known as Spokane Falls, was first settled in the 1870s and prospered with the advent of the railroad and the growth of local mining industries. The economy of the modern city is diversified. Numerous factories and mills make aluminum products, foodstuffs, paper and other wood products, and cement. The cultural and industrial center of a large, 2-state area, the city is the home of Gonzaga University and Whitworth College.

Sponge, primitive animal of both marine and fresh water. Sponges are true animals, although they have only a simple body wall and no specialized organ or tissue system. They may be solitary or live in colonies. They are filter-feeders, straining tiny food particles out of water drawn in through pores all over the body surface and expelled through one or more vents. The body wall is strengthened by spicules of calcite or silica, or by a meshwork of protein fibers called spongin. Sponges with spongin skeletons are fished for use as bath sponges.

Spontaneous combustion, or spontaneous ignition, phenomenon in which material suddenly bursts into flame without apparent cause but resulting from a slow build-up of heat. The chemical process of oxidation naturally produces heat. If that heat is trapped, oxidation becomes more rapid, and heat builds up quickly. A critical temperature may be reached, causing ignition.

Spontaneous generation, or abiogenesis, theory that living creatures can arise from nonliving matter. Dating from the writings of Aristotle, the idea remained current even after it had become clear that higher orders of life could not be created in this way. It was only with the work of Francesco Redi (1626-97), showing that maggots did not appear in decaying meat protected from flies, and Louis Pasteur (1822-95), who proved that the equivalent was true of microorganisms (i.e., bacteria), that the theory was finally discarded.

Spoonbill

Spoonbill, bird in the ibis family. The Roseate spoonbill *(Ajaia ajaja)* lives in warm locations in the Americas. The spoonbill can grow to 32 in (80 cm) long, with rose to red coloring on its body and white on and around its head. The bill is dipped and then moved through water in search for water insects, crabs, and fish. Other kinds of spoonbills are found in southern regions on all continents.

Spore, minute single- or multicelled body produced during the process of reproduction of many plants, particularly bacteria, algae and fungi, and some protozoa. Their structures vary greatly and depend upon the means of dissemination from the parent. Some, such as the zoospores of algae, are capable of movement.

Sports, organized athletic events in which people are either participants or spectators. Some sporting activities include team playing, such as baseball, football, and basketball; others engage one participant in competition against another, such as tennis and ping-pong. Other sports may not necessarily be competitive, such as jogging, swimming, and horseback riding. There are organized amateur sporting competitions, such as the Olympics, and professional leagues and associations, such as the National Football League (NFL) and the National Basketball Association (NBA).

Sports medicine, area of medical practice based on the effects of sports on the human body. Physicians who practice sports medicine develop preventive treatments, exercises, and mechanical devices for individual athletes and specific activities, as well as treatment for specific injuries. Coaches work with sports medicine professionals to maximize the output of athletes, while minimizing the physical stress experienced by those participating in sports. Sports medicine grew as a separate branch of medicine beginning in the 1970s, through the work of doctors attached to professional teams.

Spot, fish in the croaker family. The spot *(Leiostomus xanthurus)* inhabits the coastal waters of the Atlantic Ocean and the Gulf of Mexico. It is caught for sport and has a commercial value because it is edible. A dark spot at the pectoral fin, or shoulder, of this fish is its most prominent characteristic. It is 6-10 in (15-25 cm) long and weighs about 0.5 lb (0.2 kg).

Spotted fever, Rocky Mountain
see: Rocky Mountain spotted fever.

Spotted Tail (Sioux: *Sinte-galeshka*; 1823?-81), Brulé Sioux leader. Unlike his nephew Crazy Horse or such contemporaries as Red Cloud and Sitting Bull, Spotted Tail worked hard for peaceful solutions to Sioux conflicts with the settlers and the U.S. government. He had a reputation when a young man as a warrior, but he believed compromise would best serve his people, who he knew could not win against the U.S. government. Spotted Tail kept his people out of the war with the U.S. Army resulting from the 1874 gold rush in the Black Hills, where the Sioux lived. This war included the famous battle of the Little Big Horn. In order to keep peace, Spotted Tail signed treaties with the U.S. government that forced the Sioux onto the Rosebud reservation in South Dakota. Spotted Tail was killed by a Sioux assassin, possibly in an effort to further weaken branches of the Sioux nation.
See also: Sioux

Sprague, Frank Julian (1857-1934), U.S. inventor and engineer of the high-speed electric elevator and the electric railroad system, including that now used in the New York City subway.
See also: Elevator; Railroad.

Sprain, injury to a ligament (which connects bone to bone in a joint). The symptoms are rapid swelling and inflammation and some initial pain and stiffness around a joint. Swelling and pain seem worse 24 to 48 hours after injury occurs. Discoloration and limitation in motion and function may also take place.
A ligament is like a rope that, when stretched beyond resting length, is susceptible to injury, and with a severe enough force it may be torn apart. This usually occurs when turning and twisting are involved, especially very quick, sudden motions that twist the joint. The disability depends on the degree of damage. It can be as minor as swelling and inflammation only, causing minimal discomfort, or as severe as a rupture of the ligament(s).
Treatment is with cold compresses (not heat) after the injury occurs and elevation of the injured joint, if possible. The joint should be immobilized and a compression wrap used. If quite painful, inflamed, or swollen, a doctor should be consulted. Some sprains resolve themselves with rest and immobility, while others require splinting, casting, or bracing. With very serious sprains, surgical repair may be required.
See also: Ligament.

Sprat (*Clupea sprattus*), small marine food fish of the herring family native to coastal waters of Europe. Sprats have a flat body and grow to 8 in (20 cm). Canned sprats are sometimes known as brisling sardines.

Spring, mechanical device that exhibits elasticity according to Hooke's Law. Most springs are made of steel, brass, or bronze. The most common type is the *helical spring*, a coil of stiff wire, loose wound if to be compressed, tight wound if to be extended under tension. Helical springs have many uses, including closing valves, spring balances, and accelerometers. The *spiral spring* is a wire or strip coiled in one plane, responding to torque applied to its inner end, and used to store energy, notably in clocks and watches. The *leaf spring*, used in vehicle suspension systems, consists of several steel strips of different lengths clamped on top of each other at one end. When deformed, springs store potential energy, and exert a restoring force. Hydraulic and air springs work by compression of a fluid in a cylinder.
See also: Hooke, Robert.

Spring, in geology, naturally occurring flow of water from the ground. Some are outflows from underground streams, but most often a spring occurs when an aquifer (a layer of water-bearing porous rock or sediment) intersects with the earth's surface. Such an aquifer may travel for hundreds of kilometers underground before emerging to the surface. Spring water is generally fairly clean, since it has been filtered through permeable rocks, but all spring water contains some dissolved minerals.

Spring beauty, wild flowers in the purslane family. This North American wild flower grows in forests. It has white to pink blooms and slender, lengthy leaves on stems up to 12 in (30 cm) high. The Virginia spring beauty (*Claytonia virginica*)—sometimes called the Mayflower—and the Carolina (*C. caroliniana*) are found from Canada through Georgia in the east and Texas in the west.

Springbok, animal in the cattle family, also called springbuck. The springbok *(Antidorcas marsupialis)* inhabit the plains of South Africa, for which area they are considered an emblem. They are a kind of antelope, unusual because of their ability to spring into the air 6.5-11.5 ft (2-3.5 m) as a defensive action to detract predators, such as cheetahs. These red to brown slim-legged animals stand about 32 in (80 cm) at the shoulder and weigh 73-95 lb (33-43 k). Males and females have curved horns. Their once-enormous herds were greatly reduced by hunters.

Springbok

Springer spaniel *see:* Spaniel.

Springfield (pop. 189,550), capital of Illinois. It lies near the Sangamon River in the central part of the state, c.100 mi (160 km) northeast of St. Louis, Mo. The economy of the city is based upon government, a variety of manufactures, and the marketing and processing of regional agricultural products. Springfield was founded in 1818, and in 1837 it became the capital of Illinois. Abraham Lincoln had come to Springfield that year, and he made the city his home until he became president in 1861. Lincoln, his wife, and 3 of their children are buried in the Lincoln Tomb State Memorial in Springfield, and the only house Lincoln ever owned is also preserved there as a memorial. Other Springfield landmarks include the old state capitol (1837-53), the new statehouse (1868-88), and the Centennial Building (1918-23) with its collection of Lincoln artifacts.
See also: Illinois.

Springfield (pop. 529,519), city in Massachusetts. Located on the east bank of the Connecticut River, near the Connecticut state line, it is a commercial and industrial center. Springfield is basically a manufacturing city; its factories turn out machinery, chemicals, electrical equipment, and a wide variety of other goods. It has long been a center of firearms manufacture. Springfield was first settled in the 1630s. It is the home of the Basketball Hall of Fame and of Springfield College, American International College, and Western New England College.
See also: Massachusetts.

Springfield (pop. 240,593), city in southwestern Missouri, the seat of Greene County. Located at the edge of the Ozark Mountains, the city is the principal distribution and processing center for the Ozark region's mines, orchards, farmland, and timber resources, and produces a variety of related manufactures. The town was first settled in 1829.
See also: Missouri.

Springfield (pop. 70,487), city in west-central Ohio, on the Mad River about 45 mi (72.5 km) west of Columbus. The city serves as a marketing and processing center for the surrounding agricultural region and also produces a wide variety of machinery and other manufactured products. First settled in 1799, Springfield is the home of Wittenberg University (chartered 1845) and the seat of Clark County.
See also: Ohio.

Springhare, or springhaas (*Pedetes capensis*), small, nocturnal, herbivorous rodent of eastern and southern Africa, resembling a rabbit with a long tail but belonging to the family Pedetidae. Springhares grow to a body length of 17 in (43 cm) and a weight of 9 lb (4 kg). Their large hind legs enable them to jump up to 10 ft (3 m). They live singly or in small families in burrows and feed on roots and bulbs.

Springsteen, Bruce (1949-), U.S. rock singer, songwriter, and guitarist, known as "The Boss." He has performed with his E Street Band since the early 1970s, recording such albums as *Born to Run* (1975) and *Born in the U.S.A.* (1984), which sold 15 million copies. His lyrics are often topical and idealistic.

Spruance, Raymond Ames (1886-1969), U.S. naval officer known for victories in the Pacific theater during World War II under the command of Admiral Chester W. Nimitz. His first notable victory took place at Midway Island (1942), after which he became Nimitz's chief of staff. From 1943-44 he won victories in islands throughout the central Pacific, including the Gilbert Islands, the Marshall Islands, the island of Truk in Micronesia, Guam, Saipan, and the battle of the Philippines. Spruance also led the victory at Okinawa (1945). He was promoted to commander in chief of the U.S. Pacific Fleet (1945). He took over the presidency of the Naval War College (1946) and served as the U.S. ambassador to the Philippines (1952-55).
See also: World War II.

Spruce, evergreen coniferous tree of the genus *Picea*, with a conical form. There are some 40 species, all of which grow in the cooler regions of the Northern Hemisphere. Among the species found in the United States are the black (*P. mariana*), blue (*P. pungens*), and white (*P. glauca*) spruces.

Spruce budworm, destructive insect in the Tortricidae family. This insect *(Choristoneura fumiferana)* lives in the northern United States and Canada. It destroys evergreen trees—particularly the spruce—by feeding on the needles and pollen each spring for 3-6 years while in the caterpillar stage. Each summer the small moths that display dark markings lay their eggs in the trees, which in turn spin cocoons. Methods of forest management and other biological controls check the spread of these insects more effectively than do pesticides. In the past devastating outbreaks of these pests have occurred approximately once every half century.

Spurge family, group of plants that include herbs, shrubs, and trees that grow mainly in tropical climates throughout the world. These plants provide castor oil, cassava, and rubber; some are poinsettias. Commercial applications for waterproofing, polishes, candle waxes, and other products are derived from a species of the spurge family (*Euphorbia antisyphilitica*) native to Mexico.

Sputnik, series of unmanned satellites launched by the Soviet Union. The first was launched on Oct. 4, 1957. It circled the earth once about every 95 minutes at a speed of 18,000 mph (29,000 kmph) until it fell to earth on Jan. 4, 1958. Nine more Sputnik missions were carried out from 1957 to 1961.
See also: Space exploration.

Bruce Springsteen

Squanto (d.1622), Native American of the Pawtuxet tribe, who befriended the newly arrived settlers of the Plymouth colony, acting as their interpreter in dealing with the powerful chief Massasoit and teaching them how to grown corn.

Square dancing, popular, lively U.S. folk dance in which 4 couples formed in a square carry out steps and formations under the direction of a caller. It dates back to the quadrille dances of 15th-century Europe.

Square Deal, policy of Theodore Roosevelt when, as presidential candidate (1912), he sought to reconcile the demands of both workers and industrialists.
See also: Roosevelt, Theodore.

Squash, any of several edible plants in the Cucurbitaceae family. These vegetables, related to the pumpkin, are eaten cooked or raw. Different species both look and taste different from one another; they have in common a 5-pointed leaf that grows from either a bush or vine. Summer squash (zucchini, crookneck, pattypan) are harvested when immature, about 2 months after planting. Winter squash (Hubbard, acorn, butternut) are harvested when mature, up to 4 months after planting, and can be stored. Squash, popular with home gardeners and truck farmers, were introduced to settlers by Native Americans.

Squash, game played on a 4-walled court with a small, hard-rubber ball and 27-in (68-cm) rackets. Singles squash is played on an indoor court that measures 18.5 ft x 32 ft (5.6 m x 9.75 m); doubles squash requires a larger court. The ball may be hit against any of the 4 walls as long as it bounces on the front wall before striking the floor. The opponent must then hit the ball before it touches the floor twice.

Squeteague *see:* Weakfish.

Squid, shell-less cephalopod mollusk, order Teuthoidea. Although a few species live in coastal waters, the majority inhabit the open ocean. The squid is a streamlined animal with 10 arms around the head, facing forward. The mantle at the rear of the body houses the gills and the openings of the excretory, sex, and digestive organs. Sudden contraction of the mantle cavity produces a blast of water that can be directed forward or backward, providing the main means of propulsion. All squid can swim very rapidly and are active predators of fish, shooting out their long arms, provided with suckers and hooks, to grab their prey.

Squill, plant in the lily family. The sea onion *(Urginea maritima)*, like other squill, is a plant with a bulb root; it is used as medicine. Other species of squill ornament gardens with their clusters of tiny white to blue leafless flowers *(Scilla peruviana)*.

Squire *see:* Knights and knighthood.

Flying squirrel

Squirrel, member of one of the largest families, Sciuridae, of rodents. The name commonly refers only to tree squirrels, found in most forested parts of the world. Typically they have long, bushy tails and short muzzles. They are diurnal and feed on seeds, nuts, and leaf buds, with some insect and other animal food. A number of temperate species, while not true hibernators, store food for the winter and enter deep torpor. The family includes the chipmunk, woodchuck, and prairie dog.

Squirrel monkey, primate of the New World monkey family, Cebidae. They live in the rain forests in Central and South America. Small in size, no longer than 1 ft (30 cm), they weigh no more than 2 lb (0.9 kg). They use their dark-tipped tail for balance as they travel in large groups, single file behind a leader, on paths through the forest trees. Squirrel monkeys have white fur on their undersides and faces, dark facial features, and large eyes. Their fur color ranges from black to gray or reddish brown and olive green to yellow. They are used as laboratory animals and make good pets when kept with other squirrel monkeys.

Sri Lanka, formerly Ceylon, officially the Democratic Socialist Republic of Sri Lanka, independent island republic in the Indian Ocean.

Land and climate. Sri Lanka is separated from southeastern India by the Gulf of Mannar, Palk Strait, and Adam's Bridge, a 30-mi (48-km)-chain of shoals. With an area of 25,332 sq mi (65,610 sq km), Sri Lanka extends 270 mi (435 km) north to south and 140 mi (225 km) east to west. The south-central area of the island is mountainous and its major rivers, including the Mahaweli Ganga, rise in this region, which is dominated by Mt. Pidurutalagala (8,281 ft/2,524 m) and Adam's Peak (7,360 ft/2,243 m). Around the mountains extends a coastal plain up to 100 mi (161 km) wide in the north. Originally dense with tropical forest, much of the plain has been cleared for agriculture. The climate is tropical, but due to its situation the island enjoys more equable temperatures than those prevailing in southernmost India.

People. Buddhist Sinhalese make up 75% of the population. The Hindu Tamils, people of South Indian origin living mainly in the north and east, are the principal minority, but there are also Veddas, probably the island's original inhabitants, and Burghero, Christian descendants of Dutch-Sinhalese forebears. The capital of Sri Lanka is Colombo and Sinhalese is the official language, though English and Tamil are also widely spoken.

Economy. Sri Lanka produces about one-third of the world's tea and over 150,000 tons of rubber a year. Coconuts are commercially grown for their oil, but rice, the main food crop, often has to be supplemented by imports. The country is the world's chief producer of high-grade graphite.

History. The island was settled around 550 B.C. by the Sinhalese, a people from the

Sri Lanka

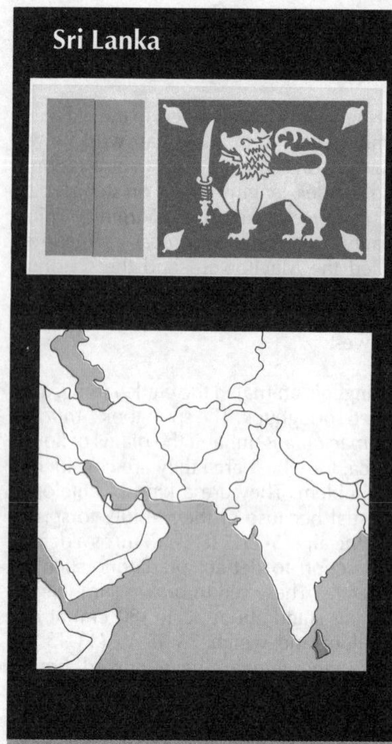

Capital:	Sri Jayawardenepura Kotte (Colombo)
Area:	25,332 sq mi (65,610 sq km)
Population:	16,842,000
Government:	republic
Independent:	1948
GNP:	U.S. $7,020,000,000
Per capita:	U.S. $420

Adam's Peak in Sri Lanka

Indian subcontinent, who built Anuradhapura and made the island a center of Buddhist thought after the religion was introduced there in the 3rd century B.C. The Tamil people held the northern part of the island from the 12th to the 16th centuries. Lured by the spice trade, Europeans began arriving in the 16th century. They called the island Ceylon, and it was held successively by the Portuguese, who landed in 1505, the Dutch, who came after 1658, and finally the British, who came in 1796. Ceylon gained its independence in 1948, and it became a republic in 1956. In 1972 a new constitution was adopted and Ceylon was given the Sinhalese name Sri Lanka. In the late 1970s and early 1980s violence flared up between the Sinhalese and Tamil separatists. The conflict remains unresolved and has been accompanied by charges that India has secretly financed and armed separatist forces.

Staël, Madame de (Anne Louise Germaine Necker; 1766-1817), French-Swiss novelist and critic, celebrated personality, and liberal opponent of Napoleon I's regime. A noted interpreter of German Romanticism, she maintained brilliant salons in Paris until her exile to Geneva. Her major work, *On Germany* (1810), influenced European culture. She also wrote the novels *Delphine* (1802) and *Corinne* (1807). Her memoirs, *Ten Years of Exile* (1818), is a fascinating account of her times. She had liaisons with Talleyrand and the writer Benjamin Constant.

Stafford, Jean (1915-79), U.S. author noted for her sensitive, well-crafted novels and short stories. Her *Collected Stories* (1969) won a Pulitzer Prize. Her novels include *Boston Adventure* (1944) and *The Catherine Wheel* (1952).

Staffordshire bull terrier, also known as pit bull terrier, breed of dog. These muscular dogs stand up to 19 in (48 cm) and weigh up to 50 lb (23 k). They may be any color, solid in patches, or brindled. They are named after the town in which they were bred in early 19th-century England. Their original purpose was to fight other dogs—usually in pits—or bears.

Stag beetle, also called pinching bug, beetle in the Lucanidae family. These beetles are named for the jaws, or mandibles, of the males, which greatly resemble the horns of the male deer, or stag. These mandibles may be from half to the entire length of the body, which ranges from 1.5-2 in (3.8-5 cm). A bite by a toothed mandible can cause bleeding. Stag beetles feed on tree sap, and live and breed among decomposing trees.

Stained glass, pieces of colored glass held in place by a framework usually of lead strips, to form patterns or pictures in a window. The earliest Western windows date from the 5th century, but the art reached its highest development in the period of Gothic architecture (1150-1500): The series of windows made (1200-40) for the cathedral at Chartres is a well-known example. Huge circular windows became common during this period. These windows, because of their flowerlike shape, were known as rose windows. Interest revived in the 19th and 20th centuries with the work of Edward Burne-Jones, Louis Comfort Tiffany, and John La Farge. Later masters of stained glass were the painters Henri Matisse, Fernand Léger, Georges Rouault, and Marc Chagall. The glass is colored during manufacture by mixing it with metallic oxides, then cut according to full-scale cartoons. Details may be painted onto the glass with colored enamels, which fuse to the surface when it is heated.

Stainless steel, corrosion-resistant steel containing more than 10% chromium, little carbon, and often nickel and other metals. There are 4 main types: ferritic, martensitic, austenitic, and precipitation-hardening. Stainless steel is used for cutlery and many industrial components.

Stalactite and **stalagmite**, rocky structures found in limestone caves. Rainwater (containing atmospheric carbon dioxide) percolates through the rocks above limestone caves, dissolving some calcium carbonate, a major component of limestone. Upon reaching the cave, some of the water that drips from the roof evaporates, leaving a little of the calcium carbonate as calcite on the roof; repetition of this process forms a stalactite. The water that continues to drip to the floor leaves a small amount of calcium carbonate (as calcite) on the floor; repetition of this process forms a stalagmite. The two structures often meet to form pillars.

Stalin, Joseph (Josif Vissarionovich Dzhugashvili; 1879-1953), ruler of the Soviet Union from 1924 until his death. A Georgian village shoemaker's son intended for the priesthood, he joined the Georgian Social Democratic Party in 1901. In 1912 V. I. Lenin placed him on the Bolshevik central committee. (Around this time he took the name Stalin, "man of steel.") After the Russian Revolution (1917) he advanced rapidly. In 1922 he was elected general secretary of the Russian Communist Party. In the struggle for the leadership after Lenin's death (1924), he eliminated all opposition and established himself as virtual dictator. In 1928 he launched a vast development and industrialization program that involved the forced collectivization of agriculture and intensive industrialization.
Stalin sought to "Russianize" the Soviet Union, attempting to eradicate by force the separate identities of minorities. Dissent was met with a powerful secret police, informers, mass deportations, executions, and show trials. In 1935 he initiated the first of the great "purges," which spared neither his family nor former political associates. Equally ruthless in foreign affairs, he partitioned Poland with Germany (1939) and imposed Communist rule on the Baltic states (1940). The reversal of German fortunes on the eastern front during World War II strengthened his hand. In 1945 at Yalta he sealed the postwar fate of Eastern Europe to his satisfaction. Thereafter, he pursued Cold War policies abroad and supported rapid industrial recovery at home until his death from a brain hemorrhage. Almost immediately a process of "destalinization" began, culminating in Nikita Khrushchev's 1956 attack on the Stalinist terror and personality cult.
See also: Union of Soviet Socialist Republics.

Joseph Stalin

Stalingrad *see:* Volgograd.

Stalingrad, Battle of, decisive engagement in World War II, fought in the vicinity of Stalingrad (since 1961, Volgograd) from Aug. 1942 to Feb. 1943. The 500,000-man German 6th army surrounded the city on Sept. 14, 1942, but was itself encircled early in 1943 by a Russian army, and forced to surrender. The battle wrested the psychological initiative from the Nazis for the remainder of the war.
See also: World War II.

Stalino *see:* Donetsk.

Stamford (pop. 102,466), U.S. city in Connecticut. Located on the Long Island Sound, Stamford is considered a suburb of New York City, a short distance away. It also is an active city in its own right, with many corporate headquarters located in the new buildings that were constructed as part of an urban renewal project begun in the 1960s. Settlers founded the city in 1641 and named it after an English counterpart. It was incorporated in 1893.
See also: Connecticut.

Stained-glass windows designed by Marc Chagall for the synagogue at the Hadassah-Hebrew University Medical Center in Jerusalem

Stamp Act (1765), first direct tax imposed by the English Parliament on the 13 North American colonies. All legal and commercial documents, pamphlets, playing cards, and newspapers were to carry revenue stamps, which would help finance the British army quartered in America. The colonists balked at the idea of "taxation without representation," and delegates from 9 colonies met in the Stamp Act Congress held in New York to protest the law. A boycott of British goods finally led Parliament to repeal the act in Mar. 1766.
See also: Taxation.

Stamp collecting, or philately, popular worldwide hobby. The first postage stamps were issued in England on May 1, 1840. The first in the United States appeared in 1847, and by 1860 most countries had adopted the prepaid postage stamp system. Today stamp catalogs list more than 200,000 items. Serious collectors, who generally specialize in particular countries, periods, or themes, make a close study of each stamp's paper, ink, printing method, perforations, cancellation, design, information content, and historical occasion. Stamps can also be a good investment; large sums of money have been paid for rare specimens.

Stamp weed *see:* Indian mallow.

Standard of living, statistical measure that attempts to rate the quality of life in a nation or a group in terms of its level of consumption of food, clothing, and other basic goods and services, including transportation, education, and medical care.

Standard & Poor's indexes, U.S. stock market statistics prepared by the Standard & Poor's Corporation. These averages are calculated each business day at 5-min. intervals. They are based on the price-per-share of 500 companies (industrial firms, public utilities, financial institutions, and transportation companies) in comparison to price per share information from the years 1941-43, considered the base period for the U.S. stock market. This information helps investors make decisions in both the buying and selling of stocks. In addition, *The Outlook,* a weekly publication, presents statistics on 100 companies and is used as an overview for the stock market.
See also: Dow Jones Industrial Average.

Standard schnauzer, breed of dog originally from Bavaria, Germany, in the 15th century. These dogs stand up to 19.5 in (50 cm) at the shoulder and weigh up to 40 lb (18 kg). They have short, gray to black, wiry coats, short docked ears and tail, shaggy whiskers, and bushy eyebrows. They were originally used as herders and rodent killers. Later, in the 18th century they were used as carriage and guard dogs for stables. Today they are kept as pets.

Standard time, time kept in the time zones of the world. In the United States the zones are called Eastern, Central, Mountain, and Pacific. The standard time in each zone lags Greenwich mean time (GMT) by 5, 6, 7, and 8 hours respectively. Standard time in Hawaii and Alaska is 10 hours behind GMT. The zones depend on the fact that the earth takes an hour to rotate 15°. Therefore the sun rises an hour later for every 15° west. Each time zone is roughly centered on a meridian (line of longitude) 15° farther west than its predecessor.
See also: Fleming, Sir Sandford.

Standish, Miles (1584?-1656), English passenger on the *Mayflower* and colonist. Unlike most of his fellow travelers from England in 1620, Standish was not a Puritan and did not come to the New World as a religious exile. He led successful military operations for the Plymouth Colony against hostile Native American tribes. He took over ownership of stock from a London-based investment group that financed the Plymouth Colony (1627). Standish participated in the colonial government as assistant governor (beginning in either 1624 or 1633) and treasurer (1652-55). He helped found Auxbury, Mass., where he went to live (c.1632). Although his courtship is the subject of a famous poem by Henry Wadsworth Longfellow, the details are not based in fact.

Stanford-Binet test, adaptation of the Stanford Revision of the Binet-Simon Intelligence Tests introduced by Lewis Madison Terman (1916; 2d revision, 1937), and used primarily to determine the Intelligence Quotient (IQ) of children.
See also: Intelligence quotient.

Stanford University, leading U.S. educational and research center. Stanford was founded by Leland and Jane Lathrop Stanford in 1885 as a memorial to their son who died of typhoid fever. Located in Stanford, Calif., Stanford is a private, coeducational university that offers both undergraduate and graduate courses of study.

Stanislavski, Konstantin (Konstantin Sergeyevich Alekseyev; 1863-1938), Russian-born stage director, teacher, and author. Stanislavski and Vladmir Nemirovich-Danchencko founded the Moscow Art Theater (1898); they used a new acting technique called the *method,* in which actors drew upon personal experiences to bring out the emotions of the characters they portrayed. This technique, outlined in Stanislavski's book *An Actor Prepares* (1926), is often used by actors today.

Stanley and Livingstone, British explorers in Afica. David Livingstone (1813-73) traveled to southern Africa as a missionary and remained on the continent for the rest of his life. His interest in geography ignited a coast-to-coast journey in which he followed the Zambezi River (1853-56). Victoria Falls was named by him, the first European to see it (1855). He met Henry Morton Stanley (1841-1904) while on Lake Tanganyika (1871). Stanley was a reporter employed by the *New York Herald* (1869) to find Livingstone, believed lost in the interior of Africa. Upon discovering Livingstone, Stanley, instead of returning with him to New York, joined Livingstone in a search for the source of the Nile River. After Livingstone's death, Stanley explored the Congo River (1874-77) in a grueling journey that ended up on the Atlantic coast. He helped found the Free Congo State for the king of Belgium, recognized in 1885. He described his African experience in 2 books, *In Darkest Africa* (1890) and *Through South Africa* (1898). He served in the British Parliament (1895-1900) and was knighted (1899).

Stanley brothers, U.S. inventors and twins; **Francis Edgar Stanley** (1849-1918) and **Freeland Oscar Stanley** (1849-1940). Their first company manufactured their inventions related to the field of photography and was eventually sold to Eastman Kodak Company (1904). Their experimentation with steam engines led to building the Stanley Steamer (1897). Their Stanley Motor Carriage Company (1901) produced a steam engine that traveled 128 mph (206 km), breaking the existing speed record (1906). With the manufacture of gasoline-engine automobiles, Stanley Steamers became far less popular; they were discontinued in 1924.

Stanley Cup, trophy presented annually to the winner of the National Hockey League (NHL) postseason playoffs. Lord Stanley, governor general of Canada (1888-1893), first presented the award to the Canadian amateur hockey champion in 1893. From 1918-26, the NHL competed with the Pacific Coast Hockey Association (PCHA) for the Stanley Cup. Since 1926, when the PCHA disbanded, the trophy has been identified solely with the NHL.

Stanton, Edwin McMasters (1814-69), U.S. politician, secretary of war during the Civil War (1862-68), and important ally of the Radical Republicans during Reconstruction. As U.S. attorney general in the last months of President James Buchanan's cabinet, he stood against Southern secession. He resigned following President Andrew Johnson's narrow escape from impeachment (1868). Stanton was appointed to the Supreme Court but died prior to assuming the post.

Stanton, Elizabeth Cady (1815-1902), U.S. abolitionist and feminist. With Lucretia Mott, she organized the first women's rights convention in the United States (1848). She founded the National Woman Suffrage Association with Susan B. Anthony (1869).
See also: Mott, Lucretia Coffin; Woman suffrage.

Staphylococcus, bacterium responsible for numerous skin, soft tissue, and bone infections, less often causing septicemia, pneumonia, bacterial endocarditis, and enterocolitis. Boils, carbuncles, impetigo, and osteomyelitis are commonly caused by staphylococci. Treatment usually requires antibiotics and drainage of pus from abscesses.

Star, large incandescent ball of gases held together by its own gravity. The sun is a fairly normal star in its composition, parameters, and color. It is believed that stars originate as condensations out of interstellar matter. In certain circumstances a protostar will form, slowly contracting under its own gravity, part of the energy from this contraction being radiated, the remainder heating up the core; this stage may last several million years. At last the core becomes hot enough for thermonuclear reactions to be sustained and stops contracting. Eventually the star as a whole ceases contracting and radiates entirely by the thermonuclear conversion of hydrogen into helium; it is then said to be on the main sequence. When all the hydrogen in the core has been converted into helium, the now purely helium core begins to contract while the outer layers continue to "burn" hydrogen; this contraction heats up the core and forces the outer layers outward, so that the star as a whole expands for some 100-200 million years until it becomes a red giant star. Although the outer layers are comparatively cool, the core has become far hotter than before, and thermonuclear conversions of helium into carbon begin. The star contracts once more (though some expand still further to become supergiants) and ends its life as a white dwarf star. It is thought that more massive stars become neutron stars, whose matter is so dense that its protons and electrons are packed together to form neutrons; were the sun to become a neutron star, it would have a radius of less than 12.5 mi (20 km). Finally, when the star can no longer radiate through thermonuclear or gravitational means, it ceases to shine. At this stage some stars may undergo ultimate gravitational collapse to form black holes.

The animals in this 18th-century map represent constellations, which are made up of stars.

Starbuck Island, South Pacific island. This coral island, covering about 1 sq mi (2.6 sq km), claims no human population. Guano, a natural material used in fertilizer, was mined off this island until the resource was depleted (1870-1920). Starbuck Island is located 2,000 mi (3,000 km) south of Hawaii. Now part of the country of Kiribati (1979), it was formally discovered (1823) and appropriated (1866) by Britain.
See also: Kiribati.

Starch, white, odorless carbohydrate powder, essential to both plants and animals as a source of energy (it is converted to glucose when needed). It is made naturally in green plants during photosynthesis; commercially, it is made chiefly from potatoes and corn. Cornstarch is used to make corn syrup and corn sugar, both of which are used to sweeten food products. Starch is also used to size paper and textiles and to stiffen shirts and other laundered items.

Star Chamber, in early English history, meeting room for the King's advisors. The room was located in Westminster Palace, London, and derives its name from the stars which decorated the ceiling of the chamber. During the 1400s these advisors evolved into a powerful council that assumed courtlike powers. It was officially set up in 1487. Operating outside common law, with no jury, it was speedy and efficient but also arbitrary and cruel, particularly under James I and Charles I. It was abolished by the Long Parliament (1641) for its abuses.
See also: United Kingdom.

Starfish, member of a class, Asteroidea, of star-shaped marine echinoderms, with 5-fold symmetry. A starfish consists of a central disk surrounded by 5 or more radiating arms. There is a dermal skeleton of calcite plates, and a water-vascular system gives rise to rows of tube feet on the lower surface by which the animal moves about. The mouth is on the lower surface. Most species are carnivorous or omnivorous scavengers. Starfishes can regenerate lost or damaged parts.

Stark, Johannes (1874-1957), German physicist who received the Nobel Prize (1919) for his discovery that light was uniquely affected by an electrical field, in that the field would cause spectral lines to split. Stark also discovered the laboratory basis (as opposed to celestial observation) of the Doppler effect in optics, in which the light frequencies of moving atoms dispensed in a gas-charged tube changed. Stark was a professor of physics at the Universities of Greifswald (1917-20) and Wurzburg (1920-22). He served as president of Reich Physical-Technical Institute (1933-39). He served 4 years in a labor camp, beginning in 1947, for his Nazi participation.
See also: Relativity.

Stark, John (1728-1822), American Revolutionary soldier. After distinguishing himself at the battles of Bunker Hill and Trenton, he was made a brigadier general of the New Hampshire militia. Stark won a crucial battle at Bennington, Vt., and was instrumental in forcing the surrender at Saratoga. He was made a major general in 1783.
See also: Revolutionary War in America.

Starling, member of a family, Sturnidae, of more than 100 species of songbirds. They have slender bills, an upright stance, and smooth, glossy plumage. Found worldwide, they feed on insects, invertebrates, and seeds. They flock for feeding and roosting, with communal roosts of up to 500,000 birds.

Star-of-Bethlehem, flower in the lily family. This flower (*Ornithogalum umbellatum*) assumes a star shape with 6 white petals. It grows from a bulb, which is poisonous. Star-of-Bethlehem flowers have green stripes on their undersides, while the green leaves have white stripes. They bloom in May and June, often in home gardens or window boxes.

Star of David, known also as Shield of David, symbol of Judaism and the state of Israel. This star is comprised of 2 triangles, one inverted and superimposed over the

Starfish

other. The Hebrew title *Magen David* originates from the late A.D. 200s. Its first recorded appearance is from as long ago as 960 B.C.
See also: Judaism.

Starr, Belle (1848-89), U.S. outlaw. Legend has it that Starr started her career as a horse and cattle thief called Bandit Queen. She served 9 months in prison (1883) for stealing horses. She was killed by a gunman while her companion, Bill July, was being tried in court.

Starr, Ringo *see:* Beatles, The.

Star-spangled Banner, U.S. national anthem, officially adopted by an act of Congress in 1931. Francis Scott Key wrote the words in 1814, near the end of the so-called War of 1812, and they were later set to the tune of an old English drinking song.
See also: Key, Francis Scott.

Starter, device that causes the crankshaft in an engine to turn and operate. Different kinds of engines require different kinds of starters. For example, the starter in an automobile receives electric current from the battery, which, in turn, starts the starter motor: This rotates the crankshaft and ignites the spark plugs in the engine. Diesel-powered engines, including those found on many railroad cars, sometimes inject compressed air into cylinders that start the engine. The air turbine starters or jet turbine starters on airplanes use high-pressure air to start the engine; a separate device on the aircraft or ground—the auxiliary power unit (APU)—ignites the starter.
See also: Kettering, Charles Franklin.

Star Wars *see:* Strategic Defense Initiative.

State, U.S. Department of, oldest executive department of the U.S. government. Originally in charge of domestic as well as foreign affairs, it now conducts U.S. foreign policy. It collects and analyzes information from abroad, gives policy advice to the president, and negotiates treaties and agreements. The Department of State is in charge of the U.S. Foreign Service, which maintains some 280 diplomatic and consular offices. The secretary of state is a senior member of the president's cabinet.

State government, body that administers laws and regulations within a state. Under the U.S. federal system, each state government has its own constitution and consists of an executive branch headed by a governor, a legislative branch, and a judicial branch. State governments have powers that are independent from those of the federal government and can set policy as long as there is no breach of constitutional law. Powers overlap in some areas, however, and it becomes necessary for the state and federal governments to work closely together.

Staten Island, in New York Harbor, 5 mi (8 km) southwest of the Battery tip of Manhattan Island. Staten Island, with an area of more than 60 sq mi (155 sq km), comprises the whole borough and county of Richmond, one of the 5 boroughs of New York City. The island is connected with Manhattan by ferry, with Brooklyn by the Verrazano-Narrows Bridge, and with New Jersey by several bridges. The first permanent settlements on Staten Island were established in the 1660s. It is now a residential suburb and industrial area.

State press, system of publishing owned and controlled by a government or dominant political party. The opposite of a free press, a state press is common in dictatorships, and is used by the state to shape popular opinion and to conceal or manipulate the flow of information to the public.

States' rights, power allowed by the U.S. Constitution to individual states, other than those rights vested in the federal government.

Static, interference in a radio or television signal caused by disturbance in the electrical charge of the receiver. The motion of charged dust particles or drops of water can result in static. More serious static may occur in the event of such natural disasters as earthquakes, volcanoes, and tornadoes.
See also: Frequency modulation.

Statics, branch of mechanics dealing with systems in equilibrium, i.e., those in which all forces are balanced and there is no motion.

Statistics, branch of mathematics that collects, tabulates, and analyzes data by a numerical system which, in turn, is used to make predictions and projections about situations that are uncertain. The process usually involves the acquisition of data from a small group that is used to make predictions about the behavior of a larger group. For example, in a presidential campaign most candidates take polls indicating their level of popularity. These polls do not survey every person in the country, but are based on a sample from a much smaller number of people. Essential to such calculations is the theory of probability, which is utilized to judge the soundness of the numerical assumptions. Statistics plays a significant role in many areas, including scientific research, business (insurance), and politics.

Statuary Hall, domed chamber in the U.S. Capitol building in Washington, D.C., in which statues of important Americans are displayed. Created in 1870, the hall contains at least 1 statue from each of the 50 states. Because of space, some of the statues have been placed in other areas of the Capitol. Statuary Hall is the former site of the House of Representatives.

Statue of Liberty, colossal bronze female figure rising more than 300 ft (91 m) above the sea, on Liberty Island in New York Harbor. She bears in one hand a tablet marked "July 4, 1776" and in the other a torch. Designed by the sculptor Frédéric Bartholdi, the statue was given to the United States by France on the 100th anniversary of U.S. independence. The U.S poet Emma Lazarus epitomized the statue's meaning in an inscription on its base, which reads in part:
"Give me your tired, your poor,
Your huddled masses yearning to breathe free,
The wretched refuse of your teeming shore.
Send these, the homeless, tempest-tost to me,
I lift my lamp beside the golden door!"

Statue of Liberty National Monument, on New York City's Ellis and Liberty islands, 58-acre (23 ha) monument. It includes the Statue of Liberty on Liberty Island, a massive copper work given to the United States by the people of France on July 4, 1884. It was created by the sculptor Frédéric-Auguste Bartholdi to commemorate the friendship between the 2 nations. Ellis Island, an immigration station until 1954, was made part of the national monument in 1965; from 1892 to 1943 it was the chief entry station for thousands of immigrants seeking a new life in the United States.
See also: Ellis Island.

Statute of limitations, law that prevents suits from being filed after a certain period has elapsed. Time limits differ according to the type of claim. Statutes of limitations vary from state to state. The U.S. federal government has its own set of statutes. Crimes such as murder are not affected by these laws.

STD *see:* Venereal disease.

Steamboat, any steam-powered sailing vessel. The term is commonly used to identify the kind of riverboat used in the United States in the 1800s, particularly along the Mississippi. The steamboat was a primary means of transportation before the advent of the railroad. The most famous of the U.S. steamboats was the *Clermont,* which sailed along the Hudson River from New York to Albany in about 30 hours in 1807.
See also: Fulton, Robert.

Steam engine, first important heat engine, supplying the power that made the Industrial Revolution possible. It was the principal power source for industry and transport (notably railroad locomotives and steamships) until the 20th-century advent of steam turbines and internal-combustion engines. The steam engine is an external-combustion engine, the steam being raised in a boiler heated by a furnace. The first working example was that of Thomas Newcomen (1712). Steam was admitted to a cylinder as a piston moved up and was condensed by a water spray inside the cylinder, whereupon the air pressure outside forced the piston down again. James Watt radically improved Newcomen's engine (1769) by condensing the steam outside the cylinder (thus no longer having to reheat the cylinder at each stroke) and by using the steam pressure to force the piston up. Watt also invented the double-

action principle—both strokes being powered by applying the steam alternately to each end of the piston—and devices for converting the piston's linear motion to rotary motion. The compound engine (1781) made more efficient use of the steam by using the exhaust steam from one cylinder to drive the piston of a second cylinder. Later developments included the use of high-pressure steam.
See also: Newcomen, Thomas; Watt, James.

Stearic acid, or octadecanoic acid, common fatty acid derived from animal or vegetable fats. A waxy, colorless solid, it has a wide variety of industrial uses, including the manufacture of soap, cosmetics, and pharmaceuticals.

Steatite *see:* Soapstone.

Steel, alloy of iron and up to 1.7% carbon, with small amounts of manganese, phosphorous, sulfur, and silicon. These are termed carbon steels; those with other metals are termed alloy steels—low-alloy steels if they have less than 5% of the alloying metal, high-alloy steels if more than 5%. Carbon steels are far stronger than iron, and their properties can be tailored to their uses by adjusting composition and treatment. Alloy steels—including stainless steels—are used for their special properties. Steel was first mass-produced in the mid-19th century and is now basic to all industrial economies. The United States, the USSR, and Japan are the major producers. All steelmaking processes remove the impurities in the raw materials—pig iron, scrap steel, and reduced iron ore—by oxidizing them with an air or oxygen blast. Thus most of the carbon, silicon, manganese, phosphorus, and sulfur are converted to their oxides and, together with added flux and other waste matter present, form slag. The main processes are the Bessemer process; the Linz-Donawitz, or basic oxygen, process, and the similar electric-arc process, used for highest-quality steel; and the open-hearth process. When the impurities have been removed, desired elements are added in calculated proportions. The molten steel is cast as ingots that are shaped while still red-hot in rolling mills, or it may be cast as a continuous bar (strand casting). The properties of carbon steels may be greatly improved by heat treatment: annealing, casehardening, and tempering.

Steele, Sir Richard (1672-1729), Irish-born English essayist, playwright, and poet. His first play was *The Funeral* (1701) and his last, *The Conscious Lovers* (1722). He founded a periodical *The Tatler* (1709-11) and soon began collaborating with Joseph Addison. Together they founded the *Spectator* (1711-12). *The Tatler* and the *Spectator* contained their essays on theater, literature, and family life.

Steelworkers of America, United (USWA), large U.S. labor union affiliated with the American Federation of Labor and Congress of Industrial Organizations (AFL-CIO) and consisting mainly of workers in the steel, iron, metal, aluminum, and chemical industries. Founded in 1936, the USWA has since merged with 4 other unions. It has its headquarters in Pittsburgh, Pa., with local chapters throughout the United States and Canada.
See also: Labor movement.

A steam locomotive is powered by a reciprocating double-acting engine. (A) Steam entering the cylinder drives the piston and simultaneously exhausts steam from the other side of the piston. (B) shows the mid-position, with both inlet valves closed. In (C), steam is admitted to the other side of the piston and the cycle is repeated. The exhaust steam is then discharged directly to the atmosphere.

Steen, Jan (c.1626-79), Dutch painter, a master of color and facial expressions. His almost 900 surviving works include jovial scenes of eating, drinking, and revelry, such as *St. Nicholas' Feast* and *As the Old Sing, the Young Pipe*; portraits; landscapes, such as *The Game of Skittles*; and classical and biblical scenes.

Steenbok, or steinbok, small African antelope belonging to the family Bovidae. It lives alone in wooded areas. A distinctive feature is its ability to obtain all the water it needs from the plants it eats. It stands about 21 in (53 cm) high and is reddish in color; the male has small, pointed horns.

Steeplechasing, horse-racing over a course with such obstacles as fences, hedges, and water. It originated in England as a race from one church steeple to another. The world's most famous steeplechase is the Grand National, first run in 1839 and held annually near Liverpool, England. U.S. steeplechases are normally held at racing tracks or hunts.

Steffens, Lincoln (1866-1936), U.S. writer, lecturer, and political critic. Identified with a group of journalists called muckrakers, he worked to expose the corrupt connection between government and private self-interest. He later developed an interest in revolutionary politics. He wrote numerous magazine articles for *McClure's Magazine, American Magazine,* and *Everybody's Magazine,* as well as his *Autobiography* (1931).
See also: Muckraker.

Stegosaurus *see:* Dinosaur.

Steichen, Edward (1879-1973), U.S. photographer known for his sharp, realistic portraits. He was a member of the Photo-Secession Group, founded (1902) by Alfred Steiglitz to advance the cause of photography as a fine art. An air force photographer during World War I (1914-18), he later became known for his fashion work and celebrity portraits. He directed the photography department of the Museum of Modern Art (1947-62) in New York City. For its popular 1955 exhibit "The Family of Man," he selected and assembled photographs of people from around the world.

Stein, Gertrude (1874-1946), U.S. writer who lived in Paris from 1903. Author of short stories, long narratives, critical essays, "cubist" poetry, and operas, her first important work was *Three Lives* (1909). Stein is best known for her experimental syntax and her influence on such figures as Pablo Picasso, Ernest Hemingway, Henri Matisse, and André Gide. These friendships are described in Stein's *The Autobiography of Alice B. Toklas* (1933).

Gertrude Stein

John Steinbeck

Steinbeck, John (1902-68), U.S. author who came to the fore in the 1930s with his novels about poverty and social injustice. *The Grapes of Wrath* (1939), about Depression-era farm workers migrating from the Midwest's Dust Bowl to California, won a Pulitzer Prize. Other works include *Tortilla Flat* (1935), *Of Mice and Men* (1937), *Cannery Row* (1945), *East of Eden* (1952), and *The Winter of Our Discontent* (1961). He was awarded the 1962 Nobel Prize in literature.

Steinberger, Jack (1921-), U.S. physicist. Steinberger, Leon Lederman, and Melvin Schwartz won the 1988 Nobel Prize in physics for their work on the use of the subatomic particles known as neutrinos to study other subatomic particles, and their discovery of the muon neutrino. He worked at the University of California, Berkeley (1948-50), Columbia University (1950-71), and the European Laboratory for Particle Physics (1968-).
See also: Neutrino.

Steinbok *see:* Steenbok.

Steinem, Gloria (1934-), U.S feminist and writer. A founding editor of *New York* magazine and cofounder (1971) of the National Women's Political Caucus, she also founded (1972) and edited *Ms.* magazine. *Outrageous Acts and Everyday Rebellions* is a collection of her writings.

Steiner, Rudolf (1861-1925), Austrian founder of anthroposophy, an attempt to recapture spiritual realities ignored by modern man. He founded the Waldorf School movement and stressed music and drama as aids to self-discovery. Works include *The Philosophy of Spiritual Activity* (1922).

Frank Stella's The Lamp *(1987)*

Steinmetz, Charles Proteus (1865-1923), German-born U.S. mathematician, electrical engineer, and politician. He is best known for his calculation of hysteresis loss (loss of efficiency from certain magnetic effects in alternating current). A Socialist, Steinmetz was forced to emigrate to the United States in 1889. He began his career as a researcher for General Electric Company in 1892. He also held U.S. political office as a Socialist.

Steinway, U.S. family of piano manufacturers. **Henry Engelhard Steinweg** (1797-1871), who changed his name to Steinway after emigrating from Germany to the United States in 1851, founded Steinway & Sons in 1853 in New York City. It was carried on by his sons, notably **Christian Friedrich Theodore** (1825-89) and **William** (1835-96).

Stella, Frank (1936-), U.S. painter. Stella developed the abstract style called minimalism in the 1960s, and he began using 3-dimensional canvases in the 1980s. His paintings are usually large with angular or curved shapes. Often the canvases themselves are irregularly shaped to conform to the shape of the image in the painting.

Stem, part of a plant from which the leaves and flowers sprout. Formed by the growing tip as it emerges from the seed after germination, it may divide repeatedly to produce branches and twigs. A stem may be very short, as in low-growing plants in which the leaves appear to sprout directly from the roots. In trees the stem is represented by the trunk, which may be over 100 ft (30 m) high. Stems are responsible for support and contain strengthening tissues, such as wood. They also carry food and water between the leaves and roots. Green stems carry out photosynthesis; modified stems, such as the tuber, act as food stores.

Stendhal (Marie Henri Beyle; 1783-1842), French pioneer of the psychological novel. *The Red and the Black* (1831) and *The Charterhouse of Parma* (1839) explore the search for happiness through love and political power, with minute analysis of the heroes' feelings. His treatment of the figure of the "outsider," his social criticism, and brilliant ironic prose style make him one of the greatest and most "modern" of French novelists.

Stengel, Casey (c.1890-1975), U.S. baseball manager. A popular and garrulous figure, he managed the Brooklyn Dodgers (1934-36), Boston Braves (1938-43), New York Yankees (1949-60), and New York Mets (1962-65). Stengel led the Yankees to 7 World Series championships (1949-53, 56, 58) and was inducted to the National Baseball Hall of Fame in 1966.

Stephen, name of 9 popes. **Stephen I** (reigned 254-57), who died during Emperor Valerian's persecutions, defended the validity of the baptism of heretics, a stance St. Cyprian of Carthage denounced. **Stephen II** (reigned 752-57) was supported by Pepin the Short in his defeat of the Lombards. The Papal States were founded with land gifts from Pepin. Controversy over papal elections dominated the reign (768-72) of **Stephen III**. **Stephen IV** (reigned 816-17) crowned Louis I emperor (establishing a prerogative of the papacy) and strengthened links with the Franks. **Stephen VI** (reigned 896-97) declared void the reign of his predecessor, Formosus, but was himself imprisoned and strangled. His rule marked the papacy's lowest point. **Stephen IX** (b.1000; reigned 1057-58) continued the reforms of Leo IX, enforcing priestly celibacy and attacking simony. But he failed to stop the rift between the Eastern and Western churches.

Stephen (c.1097-1154), king of England (1135-54). A nephew of Henry I, he was briefly supplanted (1141) by Matilda, Henry's daughter. Though a just and generous ruler, he was not strong enough to govern the warring factions of his realm.

Stephens, Alexander Hamilton (1812-83), vice president of the Confederate States of America (1861-65). A representative from Georgia (1843-59), he opposed secession but stayed loyal to his state in the Civil War. He served in Congress (1873-82) and as governor of Georgia (1882-83).
See also: United Kingdom.

Stephenson, British family of inventors and railroad engineers. **George** (1781-1848) first worked on stationary steam engines. His first locomotive, the Blucher, took to the rails in 1814; it traveled at 4 mph (6.5 kmph). In 1825 his Locomotion carried 450 people at a rate of 15 mph (25 kmph), and the modern railroad was born. In 1829 the Rocket ran the 40 mi (65 km) of his new Manchester-Liverpool line at speeds up to 30 mph (48 kmph). His only son, **Robert** (1803-59), is best known as a bridge builder, notably for the tubular bridges over the Menai Straits, North Wales (1850), and the St. Lawrence River at Montreal, Canada (1859).

Steppe, extensive temperate grasslands of Europe and Asia (equivalent to the North American prairies and South American pampas). They extend from southwest Siberia to the lower reaches of the Danube River.

Stereoscope, optical instrument that stimulates binocular vision by presenting slightly different pictures to the 2 eyes so that an apparently 3-dimensional image is produced.

Stereotyping, in printing, process in which a metal plate is made from a mold of typeface or art. The same plate is then used to print many pages. Use of this method speeds up the printing process and lowers

its cost. Although largely replaced in the United States by offset lithography, stereotyping is still used in other parts of the world.
See also: Printing.

Sterility, condition of being incapable of producing offspring; freedom from germs. In human beings, the inability to reproduce can have several causes, including defects in the reproductive organs, hormonal imbalance, and surgical sterilization.

Sterilization, surgical procedure designed to prevent conception. In females, the fallopian tubes are cut and tied to prevent eggs reaching the womb, thus providing permanent contraception. The procedure is essentially irreversible. In males, sterilization may be achieved by vasectomy, an operation in which the vas deferens on each side is tied off and cut to prevent sperm from reaching the seminal vesicles. Sterilization is also the name of the process of treating medical equipment to ensure that it is not contaminated by bacteria and other microorganisms. Metal and linen objects are often sterilized by heat. Chemical disinfection is also used, and plastic equipment is exposed to gamma rays.

Stern, Isaac (1920-), U.S. violinist. A child prodigy born in the USSR, he came to the United States as a baby, where he studied and made his debut in 1931 in San Francisco. A noted virtuoso, he has recorded extensively and concertized worldwide.

Sternberg, Joseph von (1891-1969), Austrian-born German-U.S. film director. He is most famous for the films he made with Marlene Dietrich, notably *The Blue Angel* (1930), *Morocco* (1930), and *Shanghai Express* (1932).

Sterne, Laurence (1713-68), British clergyman who became known as a novelist, largely because of the popularity of his book *The Life and Opinions of Tristram Shandy, Gentleman* (1760-67). In it, Sterne was thought to anticipate the work of post-Freudian stream-of-consciousness writers. Sterne drew on the ideas of philosopher John Locke to give form to this impressionistic, unconventionally structured novel about life as seen through the eyes of a young boy. Sterne also wrote a work of satire and a book about his experiences and reflections while traveling.

Steroid, hormone produced in the body from cholesterol, mainly by the adrenal glands. Cortisol is the main glucocorticoid (steroids that regulate glucose metabolism) and aldosterone, the main mineralocorticoid (regulating salt, potassium, and water balance). Increased amounts of cortisol are secreted during times of stress, such as shock, surgery, and severe infection. Sterols, mainly of the glucocorticoid type, are also given in doses above normal hormone levels to obtain other effects, e.g., the suppression of inflammation, allergy, and immunity. High-dose systemic steroids may have adverse effects if used for long periods; they may cause acne, osteoporosis, hypertension, fluid retention, altered facial appearance, and growth retardation in children.
See also: Hormone.

Stethoscope, instrument devised (1819) by René T. H. Laënnec (1781-1826) for listening to sounds within the body, especially those from the heart, lungs, abdomen, and blood vessels.

Stettin *see:* Szczecin.

Stettinius, Edward Riley, Jr. (1900-49), U.S. businessperson and politician. By age 35, he was chairman (1935-39) of the finance committee of the U.S. Steel Corp. and president at 39 (1939). In government he was lend-lease administrator (1941-43), undersecretary and then secretary of state (1943-45), and a founder-delegate and U.S. representative to the UN (1945-46).
See also: Lend-Lease.

Steuben, Friedrich Wilhelm Augustin, Baron von (1730-94), Prussian soldier who helped train the Continental army. Arriving in America in 1777 with an introduction from Benjamin Franklin, he was appointed inspector general of the army by Congress in 1778. He organized Washington's troops at Valley Forge into an effective fighting force, which was apparent at the Battle of Monmouth (1778) and siege of Yorktown (1780).
See also: Revolutionary War in America.

Stevens, U.S. family of inventors and engineers. **John** (1749-1838) built the first steamboat with a screw propeller (1802) and the first seagoing steamboat (1809). He also built the first U.S. steam locomotive (1825). His son **Robert Livingston** (1787-1856) invented the inverted T-rail still used in modern railroads (1830). Another son, **Edwin Augustus** (1795-1868), also made contributions to railroad technology.
See also: Railroad.

Stevens, John Paul (1920-), U.S. jurist. He served on the U.S. Court of Appeals and then, by appointment of President Gerald Ford, on the U.S. Supreme Court as an associate justice (1975-).
See also: Supreme Court of the United States.

Stevens, Thaddeus (1792-1868), militant member of the U.S. House of Representatives (1849-53, 1859-68) from Pennsylvania, and an aggressive opponent of slavery. After the Civil War he supported radical measures, such as the confiscation and redistribution of Southern planters' lands, and proposed the Fourteenth Amendment, guaranteeing civil rights. In 1867 he headed the committee to impeach President Andrew Johnson.

Stevens, Wallace (1879-1955), U.S. poet. Working for a Connecticut insurance company, he achieved wide literary recognition with the 1955 Pulitzer Prize for his *Collected Poems*. Rich in imagery and vocabulary, his verse explores the use of imagination to give meaning to life.

Stevenson, family of U.S. Democratic politicians. **Adlai Ewing** (1835-1914) was elected U.S. vice president (1893-97). His grandson **Adlai Ewing** (1900-65) was elected governor of Illinois (1949-53). He was chosen as his party's presidential candidate in 1952 and 1956 but lost to Dwight D. Eisenhower. His positions on halting the arms race and promoting the economies of Africa and Asia were unpopular. He lost the 1960 nomination to John F. Kennedy. From 1961 until his death he was U.S. ambassador to the UN. His son **Adlai Ewing III** (1930-) was elected from Illinois to the U.S. Senate (1970-81) and ran unsuccessfully for governor in 1982 and 1986.

Stevenson, Robert Louis (1850-94), Scottish author, essayist, and poet who was one of the most successful writers of his day. Critically acclaimed for his exceptional ability as a prose stylist, his novels of adventure and romance—among them *Treasure Island* (1883) and *The Strange Case of Dr. Jekyll and Mr. Hyde* (1886)—are known worldwide. He also wrote a popular book of children's poems, *A Child's Garden of Verses* (1885).

Steward, Julian Haynes (1902-72), U.S. anthropologist. A major exponent of cultural evolution, he was among the first anthropologists to emphasize ecology as a determinant of culture. He edited the *Handbook of South American Indians* (7 vol., 1946-59) and wrote *The Theory of Culture Change* (1955).
See also: Anthropology.

Stewart, James (1908-), U.S. popular screen actor acclaimed for his sympathetic portrayals of the American common man. He is known for his lanky build, midwestern drawl, and folksy charm. Stewart starred in several films directed by such cinematic pioneers as Frank Capra and Alfred Hitchcock. Among his most well-known films are *It's a Wonderful Life* (1946) and *Rear Window* (1954).

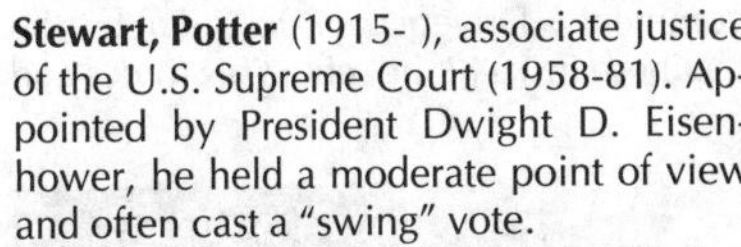

Stewart, Potter (1915-), associate justice of the U.S. Supreme Court (1958-81). Appointed by President Dwight D. Eisenhower, he held a moderate point of view and often cast a "swing" vote.
See also: Supreme Court of the United States.

Stibnite *see:* Antimony.

Stickleback, small fish with spines on its back that lives in fresh and salt waters of the Northern Hemisphere. There are sticklebacks with 3, 4, and 10 spines and the marine stickleback has 15. Sticklebacks are very abundant. They feed on small animals. The male builds a nest of waterweed and entices several females to lay their eggs in it. He stays with the young and drives away enemies.

Isaac Stern

Robert Louis Stevenson

Wallace Stevens

Stickseed, North American wild plant belonging to the borage family. Its name derives from the stickiness of its fruit, which adheres to clothing and animal fur. It has small white, lavender, or blue flowers.

Stieglitz, Alfred (1864-1946), U.S. photographer and founder of Photo-Secession (1902), an organization dedicated to the promotion of photography as a fine art. His magazine *Camera Work* (first published in 1903) as well as his gallery "291" helped introduce the work of many avante-garde artists, critics, and photographers. His wife was the painter Georgia O'Keeffe, a frequent subject of his photographic compositions.
See also: Photography.

Still, Clyfford (1904-80), one of the first abstract expressionist painters in the United States, known for his dramatic use of color. He abandoned his landscape paintings in the late 1940s and began experimenting with large jagged shapes and abstract themes. Still significantly influenced the work of younger abstract painters.
See also: Abstract expressionism.

Stillwater (pop. 12,290), historic city in Minnesota, located on the boundary between Minnesota and Wisconsin and known as the "birthplace of Minnesota." Founded in 1839, it was one of the earliest settlements in the state and the site of a convention that led to the formation of Minnesota territory. Once a major lumbering center, its chief industries are dairy processing and manufacturing.
See also: Minnesota.

Stilt, bird belonging to the stilt and avocet family, commonly found in warm pond areas throughout the world. It is known for its long, thin legs and bill. It measures from 14-18 in (35-45 cm) and usually has black and white feathers and pink legs. It wades in the water and feeds on the small creatures it finds there.

Stilwell, Joseph Warren (1883-1946), U.S. commander of the Allied forces in the Far East in World War II, sometimes referred to as "Vinegar Joe" because of his acerbic comments. Driven back to India by the Japanese in 1942, he rebuilt his forces and counterattacked through Burma to China (1943-4). He was recalled in 1944 after disagreeing with Chiang Kai-shek, under whom he was serving. An excellent history of his era is recounted in *Stilwell and the American Experience in China* (1971) by the historian Barbara Tuchman.
See also: World War II.

Stockholm, Sweden

Stimson, Henry Lewis (1867-1950), U.S. politician, author of the Stimson Doctrine. As secretary of state (1929-33), he declared at the time of Japan's invasion of Manchuria that the United States would not recognize any territorial changes that impaired U.S. treaty rights or were brought about by force. As secretary of war (1940-45), he advocated development and use of the atomic bomb.

Stimulant, drug that stimulates an organ. Nervous system stimulants range from amphetamines and hallucinogenic drugs to drugs liable to induce convulsions. Cardiac stimulants such as digitalis and adrenaline are used in cardiac failure and resuscitation, respectively. Bowel stimulants have a laxative effect. Womb stimulants (oxytocin and ergometrine) are used in obstetrics to induce labor and prevent postpartum hemorrhage.
See also: Drug.

Stingray, one of 100 species of flat, disk-shaped fish belonging to the family Dasyatidae. On its tail are poisonous spines that can cause serious injury to swimmers. Although some varieties can be found in rivers, most live in saltwater. Stingrays vary in size; the largest can measure up to 14 ft (4 m).

Stink bug, shield-shaped insect belonging to the stink bug family, known for the unpleasant odor it emits when disturbed. It feeds on plants and insects. Some varieties are pests that destroy cabbage and rice crops and cause damage to certain kinds of garden plants.

Stirling engine, type of external-combustion engine invented in Scotland by the Rev. Robert Stirling in 1816. Long in disuse, the Stirling engine has recently been reinvestigated as a possible substitute for the gasoline engine, but so far has not proved practical. Different versions of the Stirling engine exist, but all involve a gas (usually air) circulating in a closed system of cylinders and pistons and deriving energy from an external source of heat.

Stoat *see:* Ermine.

Stock, group of about 50 varieties of fragrant garden flowers belonging to the family Cruciferae. Common types are the Virginia stock, the Grecian stock, and the Brampton, or common, stock. They are variously red, white, lilac, or yellow in color.

Stock, capital, ownership in a corporation. A corporation allows stockholders to purchase stock certificates to represent shares of the corporation they own. Stocks can be sold by the stockholders, often for a profit. The value of the stock fluctuates according to such factors as the success of the corporation or the general state of the economy. There are various kinds of stock; a newly formed corporation decides which kinds of stock will be issued.

Stock exchange, auction for the sale and exchange of stock, which is a certificate of ownership in a corporation. Stock markets exist in all major industrial states; stock market proceedings are published in most large daily newspapers. The price of each stock is determined each hour of the trading day, according to the laws of supply and demand. Factors that influence stock prices include the state of the economy, the public confidence in the economy, the amount of profit a company has made or is predicted to make, the rate of a company's growth or decline, and the market for a particular product.
Stocks bought and sold most actively are usually listed on the New York Stock Exchange (NYSE) in New York City. This market, established in 1792, is the leading exchange in the United States. Housed in a large building on Wall Street, the NYSE trades more than 22,000 common and preferred stocks and has a membership of 1,567, most of whom represent brokerage houses. The exchange serves as a place where such brokers can buy and sell stock for their clients, who pay them a commission. Information on stock market transactions and prices are transmitted by computer to every brokerage office in the nation.
In addition to the NYSE there are 12 other exchanges in the United States. The second largest is the American Stock Exchange (AMEX), also in New York City. Other important exchanges include the Midwest Stock Exchange in Chicago and the Pacific Exchange in San Francisco and Los Angeles. The largest securities market in the world is the over-the-counter (OTC) market, which exists primarily as a communications network. It is subject to the rules and regulations of the National Association of Security Dealers, Inc., which has the power to expel dishonest companies or dealers, or corporations that are insolvent.

Stockhausen, Karlheinz (1928-), German composer and theorist. An experimenter with a variety of avant-garde musical techniques, including electronic, 12-tone, and aleatory music, he studied with Frank Martin, Olivier Messiaen, and Darius Milhaud, and was much influenced by Anton Webern. He has produced works like *Gruppen* (1959), in which 3 orchestras play "groups" of sounds against each other, and the electronic *Kontakte* (1959-60).

Stockholm (pop. 653,500), capital of Sweden, located on a network of islands on the country's eastern coast. It is Sweden's major commercial, industrial, cultural, and financial center, and an important port. Chief industries are machinery, paper and print, shipbuilding, chemicals, and food-

stuffs. Founded in the 13th century, it was long dominated by the Hanseatic League. It became the capital in 1634.
See also: Sweden.

Stock market crash of 1929 *see:* Great Depression.

Stock ticker, teletype device for recording the buying and selling of stock. The machine prints transactions on a continuous strip of tape, with symbols to refer to the names of the corporations. First used by the New York Stock Exchange in 1867, the stock ticker became widely used during the early 20th century. It is now almost obsolete, having been largely replaced by electronic devices.

Stockton, Richard (1730-81), member of the Continental Congress and one of the signers of the Declaration of Independence. A lawyer from New Jersey, he was appointed chief justice of his state's Supreme Court in 1776. Soon after, he was captured and imprisoned by the British.

Stoicism, ancient Greek school of philosophy founded by Zeno of Citium, who taught in a stoa (portico) in Athens c.300 B.C. The Stoics believed that man should live rationally and in harmony with nature, and that virtue is the only good. In performing his duty the virtuous man should be indifferent to pleasure and misfortune, thus rising above the effects of chance and achieving spiritual freedom and conformity with the divine reason controlling all nature. Famous Stoics include Seneca, Epictetus, and Marcus Aurelius.
See also: Zeno of Citium.

Stoke-on-Trent (pop. 248,700), city in England known for its pottery, located on the River Trent. Created in 1910 by the confederation of 5 ceramic-producing towns called The Potteries, it achieved status as a city in 1925. It still exists as the pottery center of England. Its other industries include coal mining and steel and iron production.

Stoker, Bram (1847-1912), British author who won notoriety for his book *Dracula* (1897), a tale of horror about a Transylvanian vampire with supernatural abilities. He wrote a sequel, *Dracula's Guest* (1927), as well as other novels. Stoker spent many years as the manager and companion of actor Sir Henry Irving.

Stokes, Carl Burton (1927-), mayor of Cleveland (1967-71) and first African-American mayor of a large U.S. city. He became a lawyer in 1957 and served for 3 terms in the Ohio House of Representatives. After running unsuccessfully as an Independent, he won the mayoral election as a Democrat in 1967. Stokes was reelected in 1969.

Stokowski, Leopold (Boleslawowicz Stanislaw Antoni; 1882-1977), U.S. conductor. He gained his early reputation as musical director of the Philadelphia Orchestra (1912-36), which he conducted in recording the soundtrack for Walt Disney's *Fantasia* (1940). He was noted for innovative orchestrations and championing modern music in his repertoire.

Stol *see:* V/STOL.

Stomach, large organ of the digestive system. It receives food from the esophagus and mixes it with hydrochloric acid and the stomach enzymes; fats are partially emulsified. After some time, the pyloric sphincter relaxes and food enters the duodenum and the rest of the gastrointestinal tract.
See also: Digestive system.

Stone, Edward Durell (1902-78), U.S. architect whose works include the U.S. pavilion for the Brussels World's Fair (1958), the U.S. Embassy in Delhi (1958), and the Kennedy Center for the Performing Arts in Washington, D.C. (1971).
See also: Architecture.

Stone, Harlan Fiske (1872-1946), U.S. jurist. Appointed attorney general (1924) to restore confidence in the scandal-ridden Justice Department, he became associate justice (1925-41) and chief justice (1941-46) of the U.S. Supreme Court. He was noted for his dissenting opinions, many supporting New Deal legislation.
See also: Supreme Court of the United States.

Stone, Lucy (1818-93), U.S. reformer and feminist. A fervent abolitionist, she helped to found the American Woman Suffrage Association (1869) and edited its magazine, *Woman's Journal* (1870-93).
See also: Woman suffrage.

Stone, Oliver (1946-), U.S. film director and screenwriter. He won an Academy Award for direction of *Platoon* (1987), for which he also wrote the screenplay, based on his own experiences serving in the Vietnam war. He also directed *Wall Street* (1987) and *Born on the Fourth of July* (1989).

Stone, Thomas (1743-87), Maryland lawyer and one of the signers of the Declaration of Independence. Although an advocate of colonial independence, he favored a peaceful settlement to America's conflicts with Britain. He died during his third term in the Maryland Senate.

Stone Age, stage of earliest human cultural development, preceding the Bronze Age and Iron Age. It is characterized by the nearly exclusive use of stone tools and weapons and is divided into 3 periods. The Paleolithic period, or Old Stone Age, began with the emergence of *Homo sapiens*. These nomadic hunters and gatherers lived in caves, used fire, and made tools of chipped stone (some relics have been dated at 2.5 million years old). By the end of this period, known as the Upper Paleolithic, it is believed hunting was communal, shelter was manmade, and belief in the supernatural, or magic, had been born. The Mesolithic period, or Middle Stone Age, was confined exclusively to northeastern Europe where, between 10,000 B.C. and 3000 B.C., various peoples enjoyed a culture that showed similarities with those of both the Paleolithic and Neolithic periods. There were the beginnings of settled communities and domesticated plants and animals; hunting was expanded to include use of the bow; and the making of pottery was introduced. The Neolithic, or New Stone Age, began in Asia c.8000 B.C. and spread through Europe between 6000 B.C. and 2000 B.C.; it was signaled by the development of agriculture, with a consequent increase in the stability of the population and hence elaboration of the social structure. The tools of this period were of polished stone. In addition to farming, men also worked mines. The Neolithic period merged slowly into the Early Bronze Age.

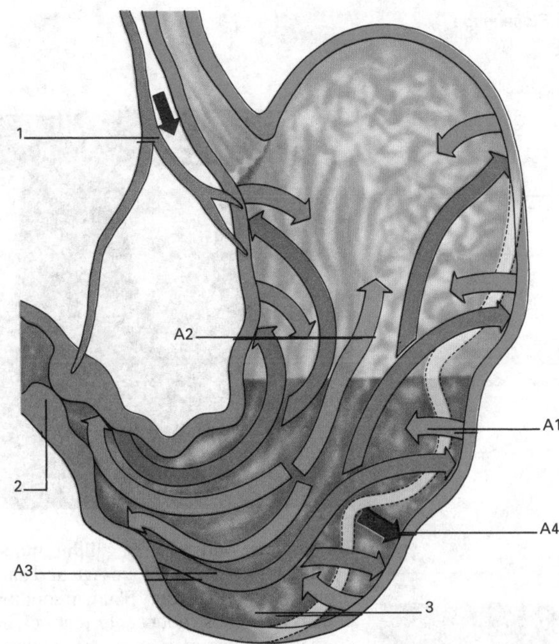

Stomach: Nerve impulses (1) signal the secretion of gastric juices (A1) when a person smells or tastes food. The ingested food (A2) causes the stomach cells in the pylorus (2) to produce gastrin (A3) which then stimulates the stomach wall to secrete gastric acid. The stomach secretes mucus as the stomach enlarges (A4) from the entry of food (3).

Stonechat (*Saxicola torquata*), small bird of the thrush subfamily native to the Eastern Hemisphere, named for the percussive sound of its call. The male is black and chestnut in color, the female somewhat duller. The bird nests on the ground and feeds on insects and seeds.

Stonefly, any of approximately 1,550 species of insects of the order Plecoptera. Stoneflies range in length from 0.25 in (6 mm) to 2.5 in (60 mm). Their gray, black, or brown coloration blends with their environment. Although they have 2 pairs of wings, they do not fly well, and are often found on rocks close to the water. Females drop their eggs—up to 6,000 at a time—into small bodies of water. Fish eat many of them before they have a chance to develop into stonefly nymphs, which have gills and live in the water for 1 to 4 years before becoming adults and developing wings.

Stonehenge

Stonehenge, ruins of a megalithic monument, dating from the Stone Age and early Bronze Age, on Salisbury Plain, in southern England. Its most noticeable features are concentric rings of stones surrounding a horseshoe of upright stones, and a solitary vertical stone, the Heel Stone, to the northeast. Stonehenge was built between 1900 B.C. and 1400 B.C. in 3 distinct phases. It appears to have been both a religious center and an astronomical observatory.

Harriet Beecher Stowe

Stone Mountain, granite dome, 650 ft (198 m), near Atlanta, Ga. A portion of the north face has been sculpted as a memorial to the heroes of the Confederacy. It is part of Stone Mountain Memorial Park.

Stone Mountain Park, Georgia

Stoneware, durable kind of pottery with a variety of industrial and aesthetic applications. Because it is nonporous, it is used to store food and chemicals and to create art objects, such as statues. It is produced by subjecting a mixture of clays to temperatures as high as 2,200°F (1,200°C). The art of making stoneware was developed in China in the 5th century. The technique achieved popularity throughout Europe and was widely used by the early American colonists.
See also: Pottery and porcelain.

Stoppard, Tom (1937-), English playwright best known for *Rosencrantz and Guildenstern Are Dead* (1966), an existentialist drama centering on 2 minor characters from Shakespeare's *Hamlet*. Critics admire his scintillating dialogue in plays such as *Travesties* (1974) and *Hapgood* (1988).

Storey, David (1933-), English playwright and novelist. *This Sporting Life*, his novel (1960) and film (1963), and the play *The Changing Room* (1971), his best-known works, are based on his years as a professional rugby player.

Stork, large, heavily built bird, family Ciconiiodae, with long legs and neck, a long, stout bill, and usually black-and-white plumage. The stork's long legs and slightly webbed feet are adaptations for wading in shallow water, where it feeds on freshwater animals and large insects. Storks tend to be gregarious. They mainly live in the tropics, though some spend part of the year in temperate zones.

Story, Joseph (1779-1845), associate Supreme Court justice (1812-45). He was the author of an extensive series of essays that significantly influenced legal thought in the United States and in other parts of the world. He worked with Chief Justice John Marshall to extend the powers of the federal government under the Constitution.
See also: Marshall, John; Supreme Court of the United States.

Storytelling, folk art practiced throughout the ages whose forms include the reciting of folk tales, myths, legends, epics, and fables. Some stories are handed down through the generations; others are created by an author. Storytelling has been used to transmit information about culture and history, explain the nature of existence, expand the imagination, entertain, and reinforce moral values. The earliest forms of storytelling combined narrative, music, and dance. Since the 1970s there has been a resurgence of interest in the art of storytelling.

Stoss, Veit (1440?-1533), influential German sculptor and wood carver who created dramatic, detailed religious statues in the late Gothic style. His most ambitious work, a carved and painted altar depicting the life of Mary, is located in the Church of St. Mary's in Krakow, Poland; it measures over 42 ft (13 m) high and 36 ft (11 m) wide.

Stowe, Harriet Beecher (1811-96), U.S. writer, author of the antislavery novel *Uncle Tom's Cabin* (1852). From her home in Cincinnati, Ohio, she learned about slavery in nearby Kentucky. Her other books include the documentary *Key to Uncle Tom's Cabin* (1853) and the novels *Dred: A Tale of the Great Dismal Swamp* (1856) and *The Minister's Wooing* (1859). She was also committed to the temperance and woman suffrage movements.
See also: Abolitionism.

Strabismus, condition in which the 2 eyes do not see the identical image simultaneously; usually one eye is directed in a slightly different direction from the other. Most often this condition is the result of an eye muscle weakness (eye movement is controlled by 6 different muscles); it can also come from brain and nerve involvement. Forms of strabismus include heterotropia (squinting); esotropia (cross-eyes), where one or both eyes look inward; exotropia (walleyes), where one eye looks outward; and diplopia (double vision).

Strabo (63 B.C.?-A.D. 24?), ancient Greek geographer and historian known for his massive *Geographical Sketches*, a detailed description of the geography of the known world of his day. His work is a chief source of ancient knowledge on people and places in Europe, Asia, and Africa. He also wrote a 47-volume work, *Historical Sketches*, which has not been recovered.
See also: Geography.

Strachey, Lytton (1880-1932), English critic and biographer who belonged to the famed circle of artists and intellectuals known as the Bloomsbury group in London. He revolutionized biographical writing with his imaginative, irreverent, and psychologically astute sketches of famous Victorian figures. He is best known for his biographies *Eminent Victorians* (1918) and *Queen Victoria* (1921).
See also: Bloomsbury Group.

Stradivari or **Stradivarius, Antonio** (1644-1737), Italian violin maker, most famous of a group of fine craftspeople who worked in Cremona. Stradivarius violins, violas, and cellos are highly prized.

Strait, narrow water channel that joins 2 larger bodies of water, such as an ocean or a sea. Major straits include the Bosporous Strait, the Strait of Magellan, and the Strait of Gibraltar. Considered strategically advantageous, they have been the focus of many of history's great battles.

Strand, Paul (1890-1976), U.S. photographer whose work helped raise photography to an art. He was best known for his photographs of modern machinery and of scenes of life in Manhattan. Later on in his

life, Strand took nature photographs and worked a motion pictures.
See also: Photography.

Strasbourg (pop. 248,700), commercial and industrial city in northeastern France, famed for its Gothic cathedral. A major river port linked with the Rhine and the Rhône, it has metallurgical, petroleum, heavy-machinery, and food-processing industries. Seat of the Council of Europe, it was a free imperial city until the French seized it in 1681. Strasbourg was under German rule from 1871 to 1919.

Strassmann, Fritz, (1902-), German physical chemist who, with Otto Hahn, split the uranium atom (1938). He briefly joined the staff at the Kaiser Wilhelm Institute for Chemistry, taught inorganic and nuclear chemistry at the University of Mainz, and became the head of the Max Planck Institute for Chemistry. In 1966 the U.S. Atomic Energy Commission presented him, Hahn, and Lise Meitner with the Fermi Award.
See also: Chemistry; Uranium.

Strategic Air Command (SAC), main U.S. nuclear striking force, containing U.S. land-based ballistic missiles and long-range bombers. SAC is linked to U.S. warning systems and is a specified command under the Defense Department.
See also: Nuclear weapon.

Strategic Arms Limitation Talks (SALT), negotiations between the United States and the USSR aimed at preventing the expansion of strategic weapons in both countries. Salt I (1969-72) achieved an antiballistic missile treaty and an interim agreement on some offensive nuclear weapons. Salt II was initiated in 1972. A treaty was signed in 1979, but ratification by the U.S. Senate was shelved (1980) after the USSR invaded Afghanistan. In 1982 the United States and USSR initiated a new series of negotiations called the Strategic Arms Reduction Talks (START). A treaty to eliminate intermediate-range nuclear weapons was signed in 1987 by Pres. Ronald Reagan and Soviet Premier Mikhail Gorbachev. The treaty was ratified by the U.S. Senate and the Soviet Presidium in 1988.

Strategic Defense Initiative (SDI), controversial program developed by the U.S. government in 1983 to develop a space-based shield against nuclear missile attack. Commonly called "Star Wars," the program was to rely on satellites and lasers to destroy incoming missiles. Its opponents argued that it was impractical and costly. Funding for research on the project continues, although at a reduced rate.

Strategic Services, Office of (OSS), U.S. government organization founded during World War II (1942) to gather intelligence. It was headed by William J. Donovan, working under the authority of the Joint Chiefs of Staff. With the end of the war the agency was dismantled, its tasks being distributed to the War Department and the Department of State. In 1947 the Central Intelligence Agency (CIA) became the successor to the OSS.
See also: Central Intelligence Agency.

Stratemeyer, Edward (1862-1930), U.S. writer of popular children's literature. His Stratemeyer Syndicate was established in New York City in 1906 with a large staff of writers to develop new productions. The author of more than 160 books (many published under other names), Stratemeyer commonly invented teenage heroes and heroines in adventure-filled tales, including the stories of the Hardy Boys ("Franklin W. Dixon") and the Nancy Drew books ("Carolyn Keene").

Stratford-upon-Avon (pop. 104,600), market town in west-central England, home of William Shakespeare. A tourist mecca, it contains his birthplace (now a museum), his tomb, and the riverside theater where the Royal Shakespeare Company performs.
See also: England.

Stratosphere, layer of the atmosphere that extends upward from the tropopause (upper level of the troposphere) to approximately 18 mi (29 km) above the earth's surface. Its upper level is called the stratopause, which includes the ozone layer.
See also: Atmosphere.

Stratus *see:* Cloud.

Straus, Oscar (1870-1954), Austrian composer of about 50 operettas, notably *A Waltz Dream* (1907; film, 1926) and *The Chocolate Soldier* (1908; film, 1941), performed internationally. In the 1930s he wrote a half-dozen Hollywood film scores.

Strauss, Viennese composers, father and son. **Johann, the Elder** (1804-49), achieved immense popularity and established the distinctive light style of the Viennese waltz. His son, **Johann, the Younger** (1825-99), wrote many favorites, including the waltzes *The Blue Danube* (1866) and *Tales from the Vienna Woods* (1868), and the operetta *Die Fledermaus* (1873).

Strauss, Levi (1829-1902), German-born U.S. clothing manufacturer, founder of Levi Strauss & Co. (1853). The company began making denim work clothes in 1874, and was the world's first manufacturer of denim jeans.

Strauss, Richard (1864-1949), German composer and conductor, the last of the great Romantic composers. He leapt to fame with the tone poem *Don Juan* (1888). Other symphonic poems include *Till Eulenspiegel's Merry Pranks* (1895), *Thus Spake Zarathustra* (1896), *Don Quixote* (1898), and *A Hero's Life* (1898). After 1900 he concentrated on vocal music, and with Hugo von Hofmannsthal as librettist, produced brilliantly scored and popular operas, including *Salome* (1905), *Elektra* (1909), *Der Rosenkavalier* (1911), and *Die Frau ohne Schatten* (1919).

Stravinsky, Igor (1882-1971), Russian-born U.S. composer. He caused a sensation with his scores for the ballets *The Firebird* (1910), *Petrouchka* (1911), and *The Rite of Spring* (1913). Living in France from 1920, he adopted an austere neoclassical style, as in *Symphonies of Wind Instruments* (1920), the opera *Oedipus Rex* (1927), and *Symphony of Psalms* (1930). As a U.S. resident after 1939, he wrote many works, including *Symphony in Three Movements* (1945) and the opera *The Rakes' Progress* (1951). He adopted 12-tone composition for such late pieces as *Agon* (1957) and *Threni* (1958).

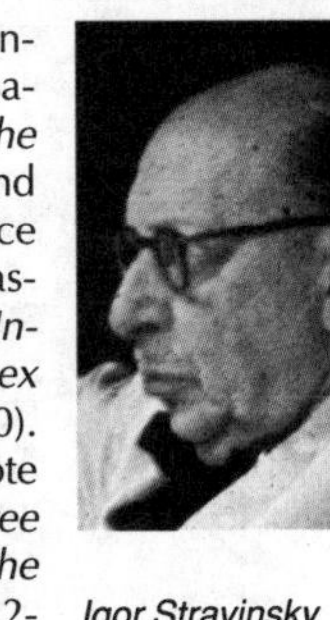

Igor Stravinsky

Straw, dried stalks of several kinds of grain, including wheat, barley, oats, rye, and buckwheat. Straw is employed on farms for litter or bedding. It can also be used as livestock feed although it is inferior to hay in feeding value. Straw forms an important ingredient of farmyard manure and garden composts. In some parts of the world, houses are still thatched with straw.

Strawberry, fruit-bearing plant of the genus *Fragaria*, native to the Americas, Europe, and Asia. Strawberries have been cultivated locally for many centuries; most modern varieties originated in crosses between New World species.

Strawflower, any of various tall annual plants, originally grown in Australia, particularly the *Helichrysum bracteatum*, which measures up to 3 ft (91 cm). This plant produces a variously colored, paper-like flower that is commonly dried and used in winter bouquets.

Streamlining, process of contouring a body to minimize its drag as it travels through a fluid, whether liquid or gas. At subsonic speeds turbulent flow is minimized by using a rounded shape in the front of the body and tapering to a point in the rear. At supersonic speeds a different shape is needed, thin and pointed at both ends.
See also: Aerodynamics.

Richard Strauss

Stream of consciousness, literary technique in which a character's thoughts are presented in the jumbled, nonsequential manner of real life, apparently without the author imposing any order on them. Its best-known exponents are Marcel Proust, James Joyce, and Virginia Woolf.

Streep, Meryl (Mary Louise Streep; 1949-), U.S. actress. Streep made her New York stage debut in 1975. She has appeared in many successful films, including *The Deer Hunter* (1978), *Kramer vs. Kramer* (1979; Academy Award, best supporting actress), *Sophie's Choice* (1982; Academy Award, best actress), *Silkwood* (1983), and *A Cry in the Dark* (1988).

Street, public road in a town or city. A street within an urban area usually has a sidewalk and buildings on one or both sides. Streets are part of a network of thoroughfares that include roads, highways, and expressways connecting communities and cities. Most modern streets are paved with tar or asphalt mixed with sand and crushed stone, although some may be paved with cobblestones, bricks, or concrete.

Streetcar, passenger vehicle that rides on rails laid in the pavements of city streets. Horse-drawn streetcars (horsecars) were first used in New York City in 1852. Electrified streetcars (trolley cars), developed in 1888, drew power from overhead lines by means of a trolley, a device consisting of a pole attached to a wheel that ran along the lines. Although internal combustion buses replaced U.S. streetcars during the mid-1900s, the use of streetcars may be on the increase because they are more energy-efficient and less polluting.

Strep throat, infection affecting the throat and tonsils. Its symptoms include fever and a reddening and swelling of the tonsils. The infection is caused by bacteria called *streptococci*, treatable with penicillin. Left untreated, the bacteria may spread from the throat to other parts of the body, such as the lungs, nose, and ears, causing greater health problems.

Streptococcus, any of a genus of bacteria responsible for many common infections, including sore throat, tonsilitis, scarlet fever, and other ailments. Penicillin is the antibiotic of choice.

Streptomycin, strong antibiotic acquired from a fungus that lives in soil. Streptomycin has the ability to hinder bacteria's protein-creating process. Its discovery in 1943 led to its widespread use to treat infectious diseases, such as tuberculosis, pneumonia, typhoid fever, and spinal meningitis. However, it was found that with continued use, streptomycin loses its effectiveness and some bacteria become resistant to it. Streptomycin today has been replaced by more powerful antibiotics.
See also: Antibiotic; Waksman, Selman Abraham.

19th-century illustration of a violent confrontation during a strike

Stress, in medicine, physical, chemical, or emotional factor that causes tension, whether physical or mental, and may result in disease or malfunction.

Strike, cessation of work by a group of employees to achieve certain goals. Reasons for a strike may include demands for higher wages, better working conditions, shorter work hours, and more benefits. Trade unions may play a role in strikes. Workers may strike to force the employer to recognize a certain union as their bargaining representative. Strikes are intended to create a financial loss for the company in goods produced or services rendered, thus prompting earnest negotiations. The first nationwide strike in the United States occurred in 1877, by railroad workers. As organized labor grew stronger in the late 19th century and strikes occurred more frequently, employers sometimes responded with harassment, engaging police or armed guards to disperse striking workers or to protect strike breakers. In Europe strikes involving all the workers of a nation or region are common.

Strindberg, Johan August (1849-1912), Swedish playwright and novelist, widely considered the leading author in the Swedish language. His biting, pessimistic plays, such as *Master Olof* (1873), *The Father* (1887), and *Miss Julie* (1888), have made a deep mark on modern drama. His novel *The Red Room* (1879), about injustice and hypocrisy, won international acclaim. Later plays, such as *The Ghost Sonata* (1907), combine dream sequences with Swedenborgian religious mysticism.

Stringed instruments, musical instruments whose sound is produced by vibrating strings or wires, the pitch being controlled by their length and tension. In the balalaika, banjo, guitar, harp, lute, mandolin, sitar, ukulele, and zither, the vibration is produced by plucking with the fingers or a plectrum. The strings of the dulcimer are struck with 2 small, light hammers. In the keyboard instruments—clavichord, harpsichord, piano, spinet, virginal—the strings are either plucked or struck by hammers operated by depressing the keys. The violin, viola, cello, and bass are played with a horsehair bow, which is drawn across the strings, or the strings are plucked.

Strip mining, technique used where ore deposits, such as coal, lie close enough to the surface to be uncovered merely by removal of the overlying material.

Stroessner, Alfredo (1912-), president of Paraguay (1954-89). An army commander, he took power in a coup and established a totalitarian dictatorship that proved one of Latin America's most stable. He was ousted in a coup in 1989 during his eighth term as president.

Stroheim, Erich von (1885-1957), German-born U.S. film director. Working under D. W. Griffith, Stroheim became known for his realism, careful construction, and attention to detail, as in *Greed* (1924) and *The Wedding March* (1928), in which he also acted. Other distinguished screen performances were in *Grand Illusion* (1937) and *Sunset Boulevard* (1950).

Stroke, or cerebrovascular accident (CVA), sudden loss of some aspect of brain function due to lack of blood supply to a given area. Stroke may result from embolism, arteriosclerosis and thrombosis, or hemorrhage (in which case it is termed apoplexy). Areas with permanent loss of blood supply do not recover, but other areas may take over their function.

Stromboli, Italian island located in the Tyrrhenian Sea, off northeastern Sicily. It has an area of approximately 5 sq mi (13 sq km) and contains an active volcano, which is 3,031 ft (924 m) high. The volcano produces a continuous flow of lava that pours into the sea. Its volcano, as well as its climate and beaches, make Stromboli a popular tourist attraction.

Strontium, chemical element, symbol Sr; for physical constants see Periodic Table. Strontium was discovered by Adair Crawford in 1790. In nature it is found as celestite and strontianite. Strontium is prepared by electrolysis of its fused chloride mixed with potassium chloride. Strontium is a silvery-white, soft, reactive metal, a member of the alkaline earth metals. It reacts with water more vigorously than calcium, and quickly oxides in air. Strontium-90, present in nuclear fallout, is a strong, long-lived beta emitter and is of potential use in nuclear-electric power devices. Strontium and its compounds are used in fireworks, flares, glass for color television picture tubes, and optical materials.

Struve, Otto (1897-1963), U.S. astronomer. Struve studied the wavelengths of the light emitted from stars to help him draw conclusions about the stars—such as their size, and gases and elements in or surrounding them. Struve was born in the Soviet Union and came to the United States in 1921. He became the director of the Yerkes Observatory in 1932. In 1939 he founded the McDonald Observatory at the University of Texas. Struve subsequently held various important posts at other observatories throughout the United States, and wrote *Stellar Evolution* (1950) and *The Universe* (1962).
See also: Astronomy; Star.

Strychnine, poisonous alkaloid produced from the seeds of the *Strychnos nux vomica* tree, which grows in India, Sri Lanka, and Australia. It can cause violant spinal convulsions and asphyxia, which can be fatal if not treated swiftly with barbiturate sedatives.

Stuart, Charles Edward (1720-88), pretender to the throne of England. The grandson of James II, he was known as the Young Pretender and, in Scotland, as Bonnie

Prince Charlie. After the French refused to support his cause, he rallied the Highland clans to invade England, but was defeated at Culloden Moor in 1746.
See also: United Kingdom.

Stuart, Gilbert Charles (1755-1828), U.S. portrait painter, best known for the portrait of George Washington (1796) reproduced on the one-dollar bill. Praised for his use of color, technique, and psychological insight, he painted nearly 1,000 portraits and created a distinctive U.S. portrait style.

Stuart, House of, royal family of Scotland (1371-1714) and England (1603-1714). The first Stuart king, **Robert II** (r. 1371-90) was a hereditary steward of Scotland whose father had married a daughter of Robert the Bruce. A descendant, **James IV** (r. 1488-1513), married Margaret, daughter of Henry VII of England (r. 1567-1625). Their grandson, **James VI** (r. 1603-25), became James I of England. Between 1603 and 1714, six Stuarts ruled: James I, his son Charles I (r. 1625-49), Charles II (r. 1660-85), James II (deposed 1688), Mary II, wife of William III (r. 1689-94), and Anne (1702-14).
See also: Scotland.

Stuart, James Ewell Brown "Jeb" (1833-64), Confederate cavalry officer. Upon resigning from the U.S. Army, he won command of a Confederate brigade after the first Battle of Bull Run (1861) and began his famous cavalry raids in 1862. Promoted to command all the cavalry in the North Virginia army, he led the cavalry force at Gettysburg (1863). He was killed in the Wilderness campaign.
See also: Civil War, U.S.

Studebaker, family name of 5 brothers (Clement, Harry, John Mohler, Peter Everst, and Jacob Franklin) whose company was the largest producer of horse-drawn wagons in the United States and was also a leading manufacturer of automobiles and trucks. Originally a blacksmith and wagon shop (1852) in South Bend, Ind., the company subsequently expanded (becoming the Studebaker Brothers Manufacturing Co., 1868) as a result of the growing demand for wagons created by the agricultural development of the Midwest. Near the end of the 19th century, the company began developing automobiles, creating an electric vehicle in 1902 and producing gasoline-powered cars in 1904. After chganging its name to the Studebaker Corporation (1911), it eventually produced only cars and trucks and merged with Packard Motors, Inc. in 1954. In 1966 it discontinued production of automobiles, and in 1967 it became part of Studebaker-Worthington, Inc.
See also: Automobile.

Student Nonviolent Coordinating Committee (SNCC), U.S. civil rights organization in the 1960s. It originally consisted of both black and white college students who demonstrated to end segregation in the South. In 1966 Stokely Carmichael became the leader of SNCC. Carmichael, frustrated with the slow progress that SNCC's nonviolent approach was having, began his Black Power campaign and rejected most of SNCC's white support.
See also: Civil rights.

Students for a Democratic Society (SDS), left-wing U.S. student organization founded in 1960 as the youth group of the Social Democratic organization of the League for Industrial Democracy. As SDS became more radical, it broke from its parent organization and began championing the ideas that came to be considered characteristic of the New Left. The influence of SDS spread widely through U.S. universities, and it helped launch the movement against the Vietnam War (1965), as well as providing support for the civil rights movement. In 1969 it split into many competing factions.

Sturgeon, fish of the north temperate zone whose eggs are eaten as caviar. Sturgeon have a row of bony plates down the side of the body and sharklike tailfins; toothless, they suck their food (mostly crayfish) from the water bottom. Most of the 2 dozen or so species are marine but breed in fresh water. The largest is the Russian sturgeon, or belluga (*Acipenser huso*), which grows to 13 ft (4 m) and can weigh 2,000 lb (908 kg). This species, which lives entirely in fresh water, provides half the world's caviar. The white sturgeon of the U.S. Pacific Northwest has been overfished and is now much reduced in number.

Sturges, Preston (1898-1959), U.S. playwright, screenwriter, and film director. His films, many of them witty satires of U.S. life and values, include *The Great McGinty* (1940), *Sullivan's Travels* (1941), and *The Miracle of Morgan's Creek* (1944).

Sturm und Drang (German, "storm and stress"), name given to a period of literary ferment in Germany (1770-84). Influenced by Jean Jacques Rousseau, its leading figures—Johann Gottfried von Herder, Johann Wolfgang von Goethe, and Friedrich von Schiller—espoused an antirationalist and rebellious individualism in opposition to the prevailing classicism.

Stuttering, speech impairment characterized by repeated attempts to pronounce a syllable or word.

Stuttgart (pop. 561,600), capital of Baden-Württemberg, a state in southwest Germany. Stuttgart is a major governing, industrial, and cultural center in West Germany. Once the capital of the Württemberg kingdom, Stuttgart is situated on the Neckar River, in a rich farm and vineyard region. Besides producing wines and fruits, Stuttgart manufactures automobiles, machines, precision instruments, tools, computers, musical instruments, beer, and paper. It has more than 200 publishing houses. A powerful manufacturing center, Stuttgart was severely bombed by the Allies during World War II; it has since been rebuilt. Some of the many historic buildings in Stuttgart are notable for their fine architecture. Two examples are the Old Palace, which was built in the Renaissance style, and the New Palace, which was built in the baroque and rococo styles; both were the homes of rulers of Württemberg. Stuttgart is culturally active with museums and an opera house, as well as schools for art, architecture, and music.
See also: Germany.

Stuyvesant, Peter (c.1610-72), Dutch director-general (1647-64) of New Netherland, Holland's North American colony, which included the city of New Amsterdam, later renamed New York. Autocratic and unpopular, he lost Dutch territory to Connecticut in 1650, conquered and annexed New Sweden in 1655, and finally surrendered New Netherland to England in 1664, after his citizens failed to support him against a surprise English attack. He retired to his farm, "the Bouwerie," now New York's Bowery.

Peter Stuyvesant

Sty, infection in an eyelash follicle or in a gland in the eyelid. A sty is usually caused by staphylococcus bacteria. Sties are treated with antibiotics and, in some cases, with surgery.

Styron, William (1925-), U.S. novelist and winner of the 1968 Pulitzer Prize for *The Confessions of Nat Turner* (1967), a first-person novelization of an 1831 slave rebellion. Other novels include *Lie Down in Darkness* (1951) and *Sophie's Choice* (1979).

Styx, in Greek mythology, river of the underworld. The souls of the dead had to cross the Styx to reach Hades, the underworld. For payment, the boatman Charon would ferry them across. *Styx* in Greek means "hateful." The Greeks abhorred death. According to the Greek poet Homer, the gods made their most important oaths in the name of the Styx. If a god lied, he or she would be punished severely by being banished to a deep pit in the underworld for nine years. The Styx was thought to begin at a waterfall in Arcadia, an ancient Greek region.
See also: Mythology.

Suárez, Francisco (1548-1617), Spanish Jesuit philosopher who represented a late flowering of Scholasticism. He was an influential political and legal theorist, attacking the divine right of kings and arguing that international law was based on custom, not natural law.
See also: Scholasticism.

Sublimation, in chemistry, act of changing a solid into a gas, or a gas into a solid, without going through a liquid stage. Some substances when heated vaporize and become a gas, without melting into a liquid first. When the gas is cooled, the substance returns directly to a solid state. Examples of such substances are dry ice and iodine crystals. Sublimation is used to purify substances: When the solid is heated, only the substance that is pure becomes a gas—the impurities remain solid. When the impurities are removed the substance becomes refined.

Submarine, ship capable of sustained underwater operation. The first working craft, built by the Dutch inventor Cornelis Drebbel (1620), was a wooden rowboat covered with greased leather that could remain submerged for as long as 15 hours. The first submarine used in warfare, designed by David Bushnell of the United States (1776), was a one-man, hand-powered, screw-driven vessel designed to attach mines to enemy ships. In the Civil War the Confederate states produced several submarines. Later (late 1800s and early 1900s) John P. Holland and his rival Simon Lake designed vessels powered by gasoline engines on the surface and by electric motors when submerged. The forerunners of modern submarines, they were armed with torpedoes and guns. Great advances were made during World War I and World War II. German U-boats introduced snorkels to hinder detection while recharging batteries. The first nuclear-powered submarine was the USS *Nautilus* (1955), which made the first voyage under the polar ice-cap (1958). Modern submarines are streamlined vessels, generally with a double hull, the inner one a pressure hull separated from the outer one by fuel and ballast tanks. The submarine submerges by flooding the ballast tanks to displace its own weight of water. It uses hydrofoil diving planes. Besides their military applications, submarines are used for oceanographic research and exploration, salvage, and rescue.

Suburb, community that lies on the outskirts of a city. Suburbs can be residential or industrial, or a combination of both. A city may have any number of suburbs surrounding it. A suburb may be self-governing, or be governed by the city near it, or by the county in which it lies. Suburbs began in the late 19th century when railroad expansion enabled people to work in a city and commute to homes outside of it. Suburbs blossomed further with the development of automobiles and roads. Now, more people live in suburbs than in cities.

Subway, underground railroad system designed for urban and suburban passenger transport. The first subway, known as the Underground, was built in London (1860-63) and used steam trains. From 1886 to 1890 a 3-mile section of the London subway was built using a large, cylindrical steel tube (developed by J.H. Greathead) that was forced forward through the earth by hydraulic jacks; tunnel walls were then built around it. This technique made deep tunnels possible without surface disturbance. The London "tube" thus constructed was the first to use electrically-powered trains, which soon replaced steam trains everywhere. Many cities throughout the world then followed London's lead, notably Paris (begun 1898) and New York (begun 1900). The New York subway, using multiple-unit trains developed by Frank Sprague, is now the largest in the world. The Moscow subway (begun 1931) is noted for its palatial marble stations. Many cities have extended, improved, and automated their subway systems to reduce surface congestion. Some, such as Montreal, have introduced quieter rubber-tired trains that run on concrete guideways.
See also: Railroad.

Succession wars, conflicts that result from disagreements about who should inherit a throne, or who should succeed a monarch. These disputes usually arise when a monarch has no child, or son, to whom to pass the throne. Europe has experienced 4 succession wars, all during the 18th century. They were the War of Spanish Succession (1701-14), the War of Polish Succession (1733-38), the War of Austrian Succession (1740-48), and the War of Bavarian Succession (1778-79).

Succot *see:* Sukkot.

Succulent, category of plants whose leaves or stems are covered with a waxy substance that reduces water loss and enables them to live in arid regions. Cacti are the most familiar, but aloes and yuccas are other examples. Many succulents have attractive foliage and colorful flowers.

Sucker, any of various freshwater fishes (family Catostomidae) related to the minnows. Most suckers live in North America, but there are a few in Asia. They have thick lips and feed by sucking food from the bottoms of lakes and rivers. Some suck up mud and eject inedible matter, while others turn over pebbles and suck the animals attached to the underside. A few have hard lips for scraping rocks.

Suckling, Sir John (1609-42), poet and playwright. Suckling belonged to a troup known as the Cavalier poets, associated with the court of the British king Charles I. Born into a wealthy family in Middlesex, he was knighted at the age of 21 and became a familiar figure at court, where he was a colorful, witty, gallant character. Suckling was a friend of the king, whom he accompanied in the war against the Scots in 1639. In 1641 Suckling fled to Paris when he was suspected of taking part in a scheme to free the earl of Strafford from prison. He died shortly thereafter, perhaps by suicide. Suckling's works include the plays *Aglaura* (1637), a tragedy, and *The Goblins* (1638), a comedy. He also wrote *A Session of Poets* (1637), an entertaining verse about famous poets much admired by his contemporaries.
See also: Navy

Submarines are used in oceanographic exploration. Shown is the yellow research submarine Nautile.

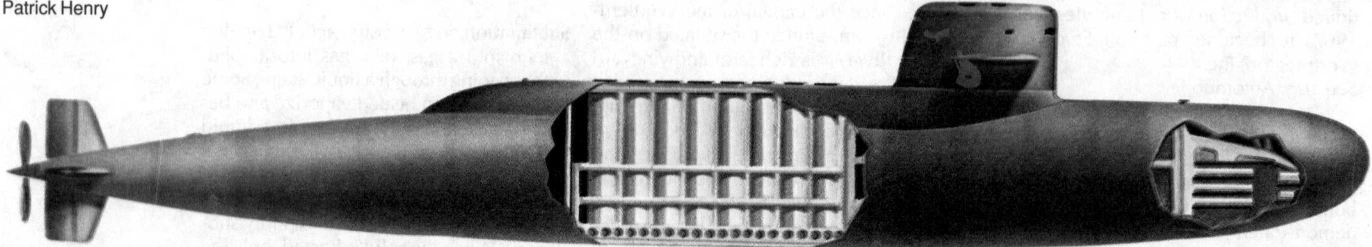

A nuclear-powered submarine, the USS Patrick Henry

Sucre (pop. 88,800), city in central Bolivia, founded as La Plata in 1538 and renamed for Antonio José de Sucre in 1839. A commercial and agricultural center and the seat of the national university and the Supreme Court, Sucre is the judicial capital of Bolivia. It is 250 mi (400 km) southeast of La Paz, which is the administrative capital of the country.
See also: Bolivia.

Sucre, Antonio José de (1795-1830), important leader in Latin American wars against Spanish rule and first president of Bolivia (1826-28). Born in Venezuela, he joined the revolutionary army at age 15 and soon displayed great military skills. He gained the respect of the Venezuelan leader of the Latin American revolution, Simón Bolívar, who made him a general. In the course of several battles, Sucre successfully drove the Spanish from Ecuador and Bolivia. Bolívar appointed Sucre lifetime president of Bolivia (1826). Sucre agreed to serve 2 years, after which time he wanted to retire to Ecuador. Although he was a skillful executive, his attempts to set up a strong Bolivian government were thwarted by other political groups. He resigned his office in 1828 and withdrew to Ecuador when the Peruvian army invaded Bolivia. The next year he returned to drive away the Peruvian invaders. Sucre was assassinated the following year by what were believed to be opponents of Simón Bolívar. He is considered a Latin American hero. The capital of Bolivia is named after him.
See also: Bolivia.

Sucrose, white, crystalline disaccharide carbohydrate ($C_{12}H_{22}O_{11}$) commercially obtained from sugar beet, sugarcane, and sweet sorghum. Common table sugar, sucrose is composed of a glucose unit joined to a fructose unit. Sucrose is produced from juice or sap, which is evaporated to form molasses. Additional evaporation yields brown-colored sugar, which is whitened through further refining.
See also: Sugar.

Sudan, Republic of the Sudan, largest country in Africa, located in the northeast of the continent.
Land and climate. Sudan occupies 967,494 sq mi (2,505,813 sq km) and is bounded on the north by Egypt; on the west by Libya, Chad, the Central African Republic, and Zaire; on the south by Uganda and Kenya; and on the east by Ethiopia and Eritrea. It has a 400-mi (644-km) coastline on the Red Sea. Sudan may be divided into two main regions: the barren desert region north of Khartoum, comprising about one-third of the country, and the well-watered region of the south. The Nile River enters

The Karthoum Mosque in Sudan

Sudan

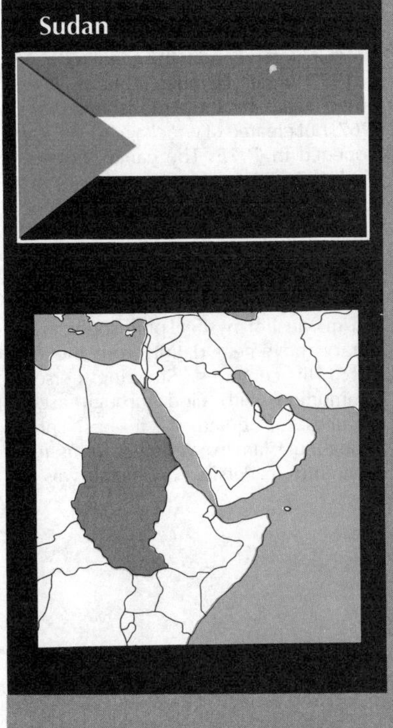

General information	
Capital:	Khartoum
Area:	966,472 sq mi (2,503,813 sq km)
Population:	26,587,000
Official language:	Arabic
Monetary unit:	1 Sudanese pound = 100 piastres
Main cities:	Omdurman, Khartoum, Port Sudan
Government	
Form:	islamic republic
Independent:	1956
Head of state:	President
Head of government:	President
Legislature:	unicameral (National Assembly)
Executive:	President and Council of Ministers
Political division:	26 states
National economy	
Gross national product:	U.S.$10,107,000,000
Per capita income:	U.S. $400
Agriculture:	gum arabis, sugar cane, cotton, peanuts, cottonseed, sesame, coffee, rice
Livestock:	cattle, sheep, goats
Fisheries:	24,000 metric tons
Mining:	chromium ore, copper
Industries:	petroleum products, refined sugar, wheat flour, cement, plastics
Main exports:	cotton, livestock, sesame seed, gum arabic
Transportation:	3,420 mi (5,503 km) of railroads, 4,101 mi (6,599 km) of roads, 3 international airports
Trading partners:	Saudi Arabia, United Kingdom, Germany, PRC
People	
Urban:	29%
Ethnic composition:	Sudanese Arab 40%, Dinka 11.5%, Nuba 8%, Beja 6.5%, Nuer 5%,
Birth rate:	44.6 per 1,000 population
Death rate:	15.8 per 1,000 population
Infant mortality:	98 per 1,000 live births
Life expectancy:	male 51 years, female 55 years

River enters Sudan from Uganda in the south and crosses the entire length of the country on its way to Egypt and the Mediterranean. In the far south is a region of tropical forest and to the southeast wooded grassland. Further north is the Sudd region, a great marshy area where the river is congested with floating vegetation. Between the Sudd and Khartoum, the central area of the Sudan is grasslands. At Khartoum the White Nile is joined by the Blue Nile, both branches of the Nile flowing north to form a triangle of land between them whose apex is at Khartoum, where the rivers meet. The land between them is the Gezira plain, the most fertile part of the Sudan. Beyond Khartoum to the north, the Nile flows through the Libyan and Nubian deserts. In the northeast there are mountain ranges bordering the Red Sea coastal plain. The prevailing climate of the Sudan is hot with rainfall increasing in frequency toward the south. The capital is Khartoum.

People. The people are divided into Arab-speaking Muslims in the north and black African and Nilotic peoples of the south and west. The Muslims are 75% of the population and profess Islam. The black Africans are mainly animists.

Economy. The Sudan is basically agricultural, and most people live by subsistence farming. The chief cash crops are cotton, gum arabic, and peanuts. Domestic crops include millet, sorghum, wheat, and sugar cane. Livestock are raised in large numbers. Manufacturing is limited and there is a small mining industry. The only port is Port Sudan on the Red Sea.

History. Called Nubia in ancient times, North Sudan was colonized by Egypt in 2000 B.C. By 800 B.C. it had come under the Cush kingdom, which by A.D. 600 had given way to independent Coptic Christian states. In the 13th to 15th centuries they collapsed under Muslim expansion, and the Muslim Funj state was established, lasting until Egypt invaded the Sudan in 1821. The nationalist Mahdi led a revolt in 1881, after which a series of campaigns resulted in joint Anglo-Egyptian rule in 1899. Since independence in 1956, the country has been racked by civil war pitting southerners fearful of Muslim dominance against northerners. By 1972 1.5 million southerners had died in the fighting but some autonomy had been achieved for the south. Hostilities have continued and Sudan has been additionally burdened in recent years by an influx of nearly half a million refugees fleeing war and famine in neighboring countries.

Sudan grass (*Sorghum vulgare*, variety *sudanese*), hay plant in the grass family. Native to Sudan, in northeastern Africa, this grass was brought to the United States in 1909 to be planted in dry areas because it needs very little water to grow. Farmers grow it to feed their livestock. Sudan grass, first grown in the South and Southwest, now is found throughout the United States.

Sudbury (pop. 88,700), city in Ontario, Canada. In 1883 rich deposits of copper and nickel were discovered there by workers building the Canadian Pacific Railway. Since the early 1900s, Sudbury has been a major producer of nickel for the world. Sudbury also produces most of the copper used in Ontario. Other metals mined there include gold, silver, platinum, and iron ore. The city suffers from heavy concentration of air pollution created by the metal plants. To help spread the pollution over a greater area, one mining company built a smokestack 1,250 ft (381 m) high—the tallest one in the world.
See also: Ontario.

Sudden infant death syndrome, sudden, unexpected death of an apparently healthy infant, also known as SIDS, crib death, or cot death. It usually occurs while the baby is asleep during the night. Victims' ages range from 2 weeks to 1 year. More crib deaths occur during cold than warm weather. SIDS strikes approximately 1 out of every 350 babies in the United States. It kills more boys than girls, and claims more children born prematurely and those born in poverty. The causes for crib death are difficult and sometimes impossible to determine. A baby dying of SIDS will first turn blue and then stop breathing. Investigation of cases has led to the belief that victims of SIDS may have a slightly defective nervous system that stops their breathing and heart.

Sudetenland, region of northern Czechoslovakia. Originally designated as the area of the Sudetes Mountains on the Bohemia-Silesia border, it came to apply to all the German-speaking Bohemian and Moravian borderlands incorporated into Czechoslovakia in 1919. The Sudetenland was ceded to Nazi Germany by the Munich Pact in 1938 and restored to Czechoslovakia in 1945.
See also: Czechoslovakia.

Suez (pop. 326,800), city in Egypt located at the top of the Gulf of Suez. The southern entranceway into the Suez Canal, it is an important Egyptian port and major industrial center. Railways and roads connect it to Cairo, 80 mi (130 km) west. Its major industries are oil refinement and the manufacture of artificial fertilizer. Suez has been a port since ancient times. Its economy and industries blossomed with the opening of the Suez Canal in 1869. Suez's industries suffered much destruction during the Arab-Israeli War, causing the canal to be closed. Since then, the industries have been rebuilt, and the canal was reopened in 1975.
See also: Egypt.

Suez Canal, canal in Egypt linking the Gulf of Suez (an arm of the Red Sea) to the eastern Mediterranean. About 100 mi (160 km) long, the canal cut over 4,000 mi (6,400 km) from the route from Britain to India and has been a major commercial waterway since its opening in 1869. It has a minimum width of 179 ft (54 m), a dredged depth of almost 40 ft (12 m), and no locks. Work began in 1859 under Ferdinand de Lesseps. In 1875 Britain acquired the canal from the Ottoman ruler of Egypt. In 1956 it was nationalized by President Gamal Abdel Nasser, prompting an invasion by Britain, France, and Israel. After UN intervention, the canal reopened in 1957 under Egyptian control. It was closed again by the Arab-Israeli War of 1967, but cleared of wreckage in 1974 and reopened in 1975. The canal was deepened (1976-80) to permit the passage of oil tankers up to 500,000 tons (453,600 metric tons) and 53 ft (16 m) in draft.

Suffrage *see:* Woman suffrage.

Sufism, Muslim mystical philosophical and literary movement dating from the 10th and 11th centuries. Stressing personal communion with God through ascetic practices or quietism, it has spread throughout Islam in a variety of forms, most apparently in Persia. Al-Ghazali was Su-

Suez Canal

fism's greatest philosophical exponent, and among its great literary exponents are the poets Omar Khayyam and Hafiz.
See also: Omar Khayyam.

Sugar, sweet, soluble compound of carbon, hydrogen, and oxygen. There are 3 groups of sugars. Monosaccharides (such as fructose and glucose) are called simple because they contain a single chain of carbon atoms. Disaccharides (such as lactose and sucrose) contain 2 monosaccharide units joined by an oxygen bridge. Their chemical and physical properties are similar to those of monosaccharides. Trisaccharides (such as raffinose) are composed of 3 monosaccharide units.

Sugar beet, plant (*Beta vulgaris*) whose swollen root provides almost half the world's sugar. It was first extensively grown in Europe to replace cane sugar from the West Indies, supplies of which were cut off during the Napoleonic Wars. Sugar beet is grown in all temperate areas in which cool summers ensure good sugar formation.

Sugar cane (*Saccharum officinarum*), tall plant of the grass family. It grows in tropical and semitropical regions throughout the world. The plant is made up of a solid stalk with joints at regular intervals. Each joint has a single bud. Stalks grow to a height of 7-26 ft (2-8 m), with a diameter of 1.5-2 in (3.5-5 cm). The color of the stalk ranges from yellow to green, violet, or red, depending on the variety. Long, thin leaves grow from the stalk, which contains a juice from which sugar and syrup is made. It was grown as early as 8,000 years ago in the South Pacific. The leading producers of sugar cane are Brazil, India, and Cuba. Sugercane by-products include molasses, rum, alcohol, fuel, and livestock feed.

Sugar maple *see:* Maple.

Suharto (1921-), president of Indonesia since 1968. A general, he defeated an attempted Communist coup in 1965, in the process overthrowing the government of Sukarno and killing as many as 500,000 people. He became acting president in 1967 and president in 1968.
See also: Indonesia.

Suicide, act of voluntarily taking one's own life. In some societies (notably Japan's) suicide is accepted or even expected in the face of disgrace. Judaism, Islam, and Christianity, however, condemn it. Until 1961 the United Kingdom sought to discourage it by making it a crime, and it is still illegal in some U.S. states. Suicide attempts are often considered by psychologists implicit pleas for help and may result from extreme depression.

Sui dynasty, dynasty (ruling family) that governed China from A.D. 581-618. Its first ruler, **Yang Jian**, united North and South China, which had been involved in a lengthy civil war. After his death in 604, his son **Sui Yangdi** worked to strengthen the unified territory's government and economy. One of his most outstanding projects was the building of the Grand Canal, a waterway system over which products could be shipped between northern and southern China. Yangdi suffered military defeats, however, when he tried to overtake Korea and Manchuria, and when he fought Eastern Turks. He was overthrown and assassinated. The Sui dynasty ended with his death in 618. The T'ang dynasty, which began that same year, adopted many of the policies and systems established by the Sui dynasty.
See also: China.

Suite, musical form developed in Germany and France in the 17th and 18th centuries, originally inspired by dance. By the 19th century it had lost its connection to dance. The Baroque suite and its component movements—allemande, courante, sarabande, and gigue—is the more well-known suite form.

Sukarno (1901-70), first president of independent Indonesia (1945-65). A leader of the independence movement from 1927, he was instrumental in creating the republic in 1945. His flamboyant rule turned dictatorial in 1959 and in 1963 he proclaimed himself president for life. In 1965 an attempted coup by the Communist Party, which had been his ally, was crushed by Gen. Suharto who assumed de facto power from Sukarno, formally removing him from the presidency in 1966. Sukarno was placed under house arrest until his death.
See also: Indonesia.

Sukkot, or Feast of Tabernacles, 8-day autumn Jewish festival, during which meals are taken in a hut (sukkah) roofed with branches and fruits to symbolize the shelters used by the ancient Hebrews during their wanderings after the Exodus from Egypt.
See also: Simhat Torah.

Suleiman I, or **Sulayman** (1494-1566), sultan of Ottoman Empire from 1520-1566. He was also known as The Magnificent and The Lawgiver. His reign was marked by his numerous successful military campaigns and the legal, literary, and artistic achievements of his empire. He waged ground and naval wars in parts of Europe, Asia Minor, and Africa, enlarging his territory with each successive victory. During a brief period his navy dominated the Mediterranean Sea, the Red Sea, and the Persian Gulf. He did not succeed, however, in his naval warfare against Holy Roman Emperor Charles V and Venice. His court included lawyers, artists, writers and architects, whom he engaged to help him create his vision of a magnificent and sophisticated empire.
See also: Ottoman Empire.

Sulfa drug, any of various synthetic compounds derived from sulfanilimide that inhibit the multiplication of invading bacteria, thus allowing the body's cellular defense mechanisms to suppress infection. The first sulfa drug was synthesized in 1908 and used widely as a dye before Gerhard Domagk reported its effectiveness against streptococci (1938). In recent years many sulfa drugs have been replaced by antibiotics in the treatment of bacterial infections.

Sulfate, chemical mixture containing sulfur and oxygen. Sulfates are usually formed in crystals. Epsom salt and gypsum are two common sulfates. Most sulfates are water soluble, but some, such as lead sulfates, are not. Industrial uses for sulfates include fabric printing and dying and the manufacture of medicine and varnishes.

Sulfide, compound of sulfur and another element or elements. The element—made up of atoms that are alike and cannot be changed chemically—may be a metal, such as silver or gold, or a gas, such as oxygen or hydrogen. Sulfides have various industrial uses. When sulfur burns, it produces a poisonous gas. A mixture of carbon and sulfur is used as an insecticide. In small doses, it s used as an anesthetic. Some sulfides are used to create color in paints.

Sulfur stored in the open air in Alberta, Canada

Sulfur, chemical element, symbol S; for physical constants see Periodic Table. Sulfur has been known and used for thousands of years. It is referred to in the bible as brimstone. As a mineral, it occurs in iron pyrites, galena, sphalerite, Epsom salts, barite, and many others. It occurs free in nature in the vicinity of volcanoes and hot springs. Sulfur is also found in the atmosphere of Venus and in meteorites and interstellar clouds. It is produced commercially using the Frasch process in which heated water is used to melt underground sulfur that is then brought to the surface. Sulfur is a yellow, brittle, low melting, reactive nonmetal. It readily forms sulfides with many elements. Hydrogen sulfide is poisonous and can cause death by respiratory paralysis. Sulfur forms several allotropes amorphous and crystalline. Sulfur is essential to human and animal life. Sulfur and its compounds are used in gunpowder, in the vulcanization of rubber, as a fungicide, in making sulfite paper, as a fumigant, and in bleaching dried fruits. It is used to produce sulfuric acid, the most important manufactured chemical.

Sulfur dioxide (SO_2), colorless, poisonous gas that has a sharp smell. It is released naturally in gases emitted during volcanic eruptions. Factories or refineries that burn oil or coal also release sulfur dioxide into the atmosphere, creating the potential for human health problems. Sulfur dioxide in the atmosphere may form acid rain when it dissolves in water droplets. Acid rain is damaging to the environment, killing animals and plants. For this reason, many nations are concerned about how much sulfur dioxide their industries should be allowed to release into the air.
See also: Acid rain.

John L. Sullivan

Sulfuric acid, chemical compound (H_2SO_4) that is a colorless, oily liquid that corrodes materials. Exposure to it or its fumes can damage a person's nose, lungs, and skin. Sulfuric acid has been used since the 15th century. In the 19th century it was discovered that adding sulfuric acid to soil made the soil more fertile for plant growth; this discovery led to improved methods of manufacturing sulfuric acid. Besides being used in the manufacture of fertilizer, sulfuric acid is used in steel processing, petroleum refining, and the manufacture of other acids. Because it is so strong and potentially dangerous, great caution must be taken when handling sulfuric acid.

Sulgrave Manor, home of the ancestors of George Washington, first President of the United States. It is located in Sulgrave, a village in Northamptonshire, England. Built by Lawrence Washington, Sulgrave Manor remained in the family from 1539 to 1610. It is now a museum, furnished and restored to reflect the period when the Washingtons lived there.

Sulla, Lucius Cornelius (138-78 B.C.), Roman general and ruler. Sulla was born into the Roman upper class and entered politics as a praetor in 94 B.C. In 88 B.C., after fighting in the Social War, he became one of two consuls ruling Rome. As a military leader, he successfully fought armies of King Mithridates VI of Pontus that were attempting to overtake Roman territories (87-85 B.C.). After Mithridates surrendered, Sulla returned to Rome to confront his opponents, headed by Marius, who accused him of being an enemy of Rome (83 B.C.). He won the civil war against them the following year and became a dictator. Sulla initiated many reforms, such as restoring power to the Senate, but his reign was known for cruelty and illegality. He retired in 79 B.C.
See also: Marius, Gaius; Rome, Ancient.

Sullivan, Anne (1866-1936), U.S. teacher of Helen Keller. Partially blind herself, in 1887 she taught Keller to read and communicate through the touch alphabet and became her life-long companion.
See also: Keller, Helen Adams.

Sullivan, Harry Stack (1892-1949), U.S. psychiatrist and head of William Alanson White Institute and Washington School of Psychiatry, who contributed to the study of schizophrenia and originated the idea that psychiatry depends on study of culture and its influence on behavior.
See also: Psychiatry.

Sullivan, John L., U.S. boxing champion. Sullivan was the last bare-knuckle heavyweight champion, winning the title from Paddy Ryan in 1882 and defending it again in 1888 and 1889. He then boxed with gloves under the Queensbury Rules, losing his title to James J. Corbett in 1892.

Sullivan, Leon Howard (1922-), Baptist minister whose numerous projects have improved economic opportunities for African Americans. Acting on his belief that unemployment was a major reason for crime, he initiated a 1959 boycott of Philadelphia firms that did not hire African Americans. After 3 years, these companies made jobs available to African Americans. In 1964 Sullivan founded a center (Opportunities Industrialization Center) in Philadelphia at which members of minority groups could receive job training. The center was so successful that others were opened throughout the United States as well as in Africa. The following year Sullivan founded a corporation (Zion Investment Associates) that established several diverse African-American businesses. In 1971 Sullivan became a member of the board of directors of General Motors, the first African American ever to do so. In 1977 he initiated a plan for equal treatment of black Africans in South Africa. His Sullivan Principles urged firms there to ban segregation, provide greater opportunities for blacks, and pay blacks and whites equally for equal work. Although many U.S. companies operating in South Africa agreed to the principles, discrimination continued, causing Sullivan to conclude that U.S. firms should not remain in South Africa.

Sullivan, Louis Henri (1856-1924), U.S. architect whose office buildings pioneered modern design. In partnership with Dankmar Adler in Chicago (1881-95), he championed the view that a building's form should express its function. His works include the Auditorium (1889) and the Carson Pirie Scott building (1899-1904) in Chicago, and the Guaranty Building in Buffalo (1894-95). Frank Lloyd Wright was his pupil.
See also: Architecture.

Sullivan, Sir Arthur Seymour (1842-1900), English composer. He was born in London and studied at the Royal Academy of Music. He first met with success for the music he wrote for the Shakespeare play *The Tempest* (1862). Sullivan is perhaps best known for his collaborations with the playwright Sir William Gilbert in which he produced many operettas. Gilbert and Sullivan first became a team with *Thespis* (1871), an operetta that was not very successful. Their next work, *Trial by Jury* (1875), became an instant hit. Other successful collaborations include *The Pirates of Penzance* (1880), *The Mikado* (1885), and *The Gondoliers* (1889). Sullivan also collaborated with other writers and wrote several works alone, including classical music, operas, and hymns. One of his most famous songs is "Onward Christian Soldiers." Sullivan taught at and was later the principal of the Royal Academy of Music. He was also an organist and conductor.

Sully, Thomas (1783-1872), English-born U.S. portrait painter who studied briefly under Gilbert Stuart. Queen Victoria (1839) and several U.S. presidents sat for him, including Jefferson and Monroe. He also painted the well-known picture *Washington's Passage of the Delaware.*

Sully-Prudhomme, René François Armand (1839-1907), French Parnassian poet, winner of the first Nobel Prize in literature, in 1901. His philosophical poems include *Justice* (1878) and *Happiness* (1888).

Sulphur *see:* Sulfur.

Sulu Sea, also known as the Sea of Mindoro, sea located between Borneo and the Philippine Islands. It is bounded by many other islands as well, including the Sulu Islands and the Visaya Islands, and is used for trade among them. The sea has an area of approximately 100,000 sq mi (260,000 sq km). Narrow bodies of water connect the sea to the Pacific Ocean and the South China Sea.

Sulzberger, name of 2 publishers of The *New York Times.* **Arthur Hays Sulzberger** (1891-1968) was the publisher of the *Times* from 1935 to 1961. He printed more editorials than ever before in the paper's history and greatly increased circulation. **Arthur Ochs Sulzberger** (1926-) became publisher of the *Times* in 1963. He expanded coverage of business news and started printing national editions in several cities outside New York.

Sumac, common name for trees, shrubs, and vines (genus *Rhus*) with resinous, sometimes bitter sap. Members of the group include the staghorn sumac, used by Native Americans to make an acidic but pleasant drink, and the Sicilian sumac, whose bark is used for tanning leather. Sumacs, however, are often poisonous: poison oak, poison sumac, and poison ivy. They can be recognized by their white or gray berries.

Sumatra, second-largest island of Indonesia, about 183,000 sq mi (473,970 sq km) in area. Lying on the equator, with a hot, wet climate, Sumatra is heavily forested and rich in oil, bauxite, and coal; it produces 70% of Indonesia's export wealth.

Crops include rubber, coffee, pepper, and tobacco. Medan and Palembang are the chief cities.
See also: Indonesia.

Sumer, southern region of ancient Mesopotamia (presently southern Iraq). From c.3000 B.C.-2400 B.C. it was dominated by several small kingdoms, the first civilizations in the world. The kingdoms had developed from cities founded in the fertile valley between the Tigris and Euphrates rivers, a setting ideal for farming and raising cattle. The Sumerians created an advanced civilization, building palaces and temples and constructing irrigation canals in their fields. Their craftspeople were skilled weavers, potters, jewelers, and stonecarvers. Sumerians traded their goods with regions surrounding the Persian Gulf and promoted the practice and study of medicine, astronomy, mathematics, economy, law, and politics. One of their most noteworthy achievements was the development of the first writing system, known as cuneiform, consisting of wedge-shaped characters pressed into clay tablets. Other civilizations that took control of Sumer absorbed the knowledge and skills developed by them.
See also: Mesopotamia.

Sumner, Charles (1811-74), U.S. political leader and opponent of slavery. He was a senator from Massachusetts from 1851 to 1874. As an active abolitionist, he denounced slavery and the South. In 1856 he made a speech in which he accused Senators Andrew P. Butler and Stephen A. Douglas of suppporting slavery. A few days later, Representative Preston S. Brooks, Butler's nephew, accused Sumner of slander and beat him with a cane, wounding him severely. After the Civil War, Sumner proposed stiff treatment of the South, demanding that Southern states could join the Union only after they allowed freed slaves voting rights. He was active in the impeachment of Andrew Johnson.

Sumter, Thomas (1734-1832), partisan of the American Revolution who formed a guerrilla band and harassed the British in the Carolina campaign (1780-81). He had notable successes at Hanging Rock, Fishdam Ford, and Blackstock. Later he was a South Carolina member of the House of Representatives (1789-93; 1797-1801) and Senate (1801-10). Fort Sumter in Charleston harbor was named for him.
See also: Revolutionary War in America.

Sun, star at the center of our Solar System, a luminous sphere of gas about 865,000 mi (1.4 million km) in diameter and 93 million mi (150 million km) from earth. The sun in 332,000 times as massive as earth, and its volume is 1.3 million times greater. The temperature in its center is about 15,000,000°K. The source of its energy is a series of nuclear fusion reactions in which hydrogen is converted into helium—light, heat, and gamma rays being produced in the process. Light from the sun takes about 8 minutes to reach earth. Although the sun is entirely gaseous, its bright surface looks like a kind of skin. This outer layer is called the photosphere, whose temperature is about 6,000°K. Above the photosphere lies the chromosphere, an irregular layer of gases, sunspots, flares, and prominences visible to the naked eye only during eclipses. The corona is the sparse outer atmosphere.
See also: Solar system.

Sunbelt and Frostbelt, popular terms designating, respectively, the southern tier of states stretching from North Carolina to California and the states of the Northeast and Midwest. The Frostbelt states, besides their more rigorous climate, are characterized by aging industrial plants and urban infrastructures, unionized labor, high rates of unemployment and poverty, static or declining populations, and the severe fiscal problems these conditions impose on state and local governments. By contrast, the Sunbelt states are usually characterized by burgeoning economic development, expanding cities, rising populations (due to migration from the Frostbelt states), and increasing political importance.

Sunbird, any of approximately 115 species of songbirds in the sunbird family. Sunbirds are found in Africa, Southeast Asia, and the Pacific islands. They range in size from 3.5-6 in (9-15 cm). Their plumage may be yellow or gray. Breeding male birds have brilliantly colored feathers of various combinations of red, blue, purple, green, and yellow. Sunbirds resemble hummingbirds, but the two are not related. Like hummingbirds, sunbirds feed on nectar. But whereas a hummingbird hovers in the air as it extracts a flower's nectar, a sunbird perches on a flower or stalk while feeding.

Sunburn, burning effect on the skin caused by exposure to ultraviolet radiation from the sun. First-degree burns may occur, but usually only minor discomfort results, with skin sensitivity. Repeated sunburns may cause skin cancer, including melanoma, the most dangerous variety.

Sun dance, religious ceremony observed by a number of Plains tribes of Native Americans during the summer. It involves eight days of fasting, self-torture (as penance), and the seeking of visions. Common during the 19th century, the ceremonies were discouraged by the U.S. government and have almost died out.

Sunday, Billy (William Ashley Sunday; 1862-1935), U.S. revivalist preacher noted for his flamboyance and his vivid version of fundamentalist theology. He claimed to have saved over a million souls.

Sundew, any plant in the sundew family. Sundews have leaves that produce a sticky fluid enabling them to trap and digest insects. (This same fluid makes the leaves glisten like dew—hence their name.) Sundews are found throughout the world in regions with mild or tropical climates. The round-leaved sundew (genus *Drosera*) is the most common, thriving in wet marshy areas. Its thin, curving stem grows to a height of 4-10 in (10-25 cm) and has small white or pinkish flowers on top. The base of the stem has flat round leaves covered with gland-tipped hairs, which produce the sticky fluid that attracts insects. When an insect lands on the leaf, the tiny hairs curve around it and hold it while the fluid engulfs and suffocates it. Enzymes in the fluid digest the insect, after which the hairs unfold, ready to trap the next victim.

Sundial, ancient type of clock, consisting of a stylus (called a gnomon) parallel to the earth's axis that casts a shadow on a calibrated dial plate, which may be horizontal or vertical. Sundials usually show local time, but they may be calibrated to show standard time.

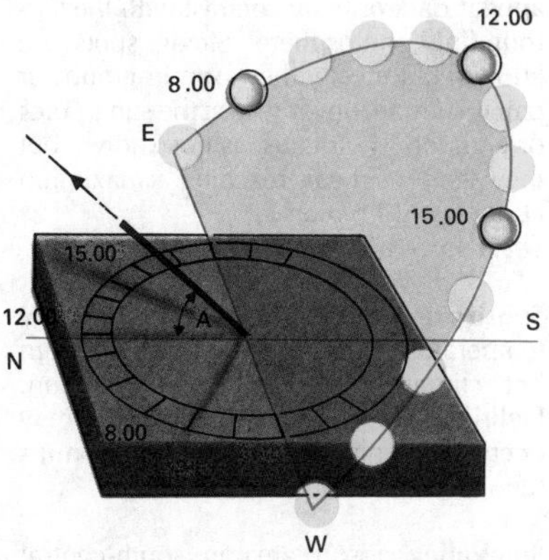

The traditional gnomon, the pointer on a sundial, is set at the latitude of the site (angle A) pointing to the celestial pole. In sunlight its shadow describes a semi-ellipse on the dial graduated in 12 equal parts (hours). At midday the shadow falls due north; before and after midday it falls westward and eastward respectively.

Sunfish, popular fresh water sports fish of the bass family, found in North America. The body is perchlike: deep and flattened, and with a long dorsal fin. Male sunfish dig nests in sand and guard the eggs. They feed on small animals and other fish and are active only during periods of sunshine. Ocean sunfish (*Mola mola*) are unrelated fish that live in the sea.

Sunflower, any of various tall plants (genus *Helianthus*) with large, disk-shaped yellow and brown flowers that twist to face the sun. Most of the 60 species are native to the United States. The common sunflower (*Helianthus annuus*) is cultivated in many parts of the world. The seeds yield an oil and the remainder becomes cattle feed.

Sunflower State *see:* Kansas.

Sung dynasty *see:* Song dynasty.

Sunni, followers of the majority branch of Islam, as distinct from the Shi'te. The term refers to the tradition (Sunna) of the prophet Muhammad. About 85% of the world's Muslims are Sunni, considered the orthodox or traditionalists. Within the Sunni currently, there are four recognized schools of Islamic law and ritual: Hamafi, Maliki, Shafi, and Hambali.
See also: Islam; Shi'te.

Sunset laws, U.S. laws that require regular periodic review of government agencies.

The review determines whether the agency is to be restructured or discontinued. These laws were enacted to attempt to create greater efficiency in government agencies.
See also: Zero-base budgeting.

Sunshine laws, U.S. laws that require government agencies to permit the public to attend their meetings. These laws were enacted to prevent secrecy in government. In those cases where agencies need to discuss matters of security or sensitive issues, the law may permit a closed meeting to be held.
See also: Freedom of Information Act.

Sunshine State *see:* Florida; South Dakota.

Sunspot, apparent dark spot on the surface of the sun. Vortices of gas associated with strong electromagnetic activity, sunspots appear dark only by contrast with the surrounding photosphere. Single spots are known, but mostly they form in groups or pairs. They are never seen at the sun's poles or equator. Their cause is not known, but they seem cyclical, reaching a maximum about every 11 years.
See also: Sun.

Sunstroke, or heatstroke, rise in body temperature and deficiency of sweating in hot climates, often following exertion. Delirium, coma, and convulsions may occur suddenly, and rapid cooling must then be effected.

Sun Valley, resort area in south-central Idaho, in the Sawtooth Mountains on the Big Wood River. The area was developed in 1936 by the Union Pacific Railroad because its climate, snowfall, and terrain were ideal for skiing and winter sports. There are numerous ski slopes and cross-country trails throughout the area. In the summer the recreations it offers are mainly golf and tennis.

Sun worship, reverence for the sun, as for a god or goddess. Sun worship was practiced by peoples throughout the world, especially in agricultural communities in which the sun was necessary for crop growth. Cultures in which sun worship was prevalent include those of ancient Egypt, Persia, India, and Rome. Native Americans and the Aztecs, Incas, and Mayas of Central and South America also considered the sun sacred.

Sun Yat-sen (1866-1925), Chinese political leader, regarded as the "father of modern China." Born in the Guangdong province, he spent most of his youth in Hawaii, where he learned about Western thought and politics. He then studied medicine in Hong Kong, becoming a doctor in 1892. In 1894 Sun founded a political group and attempted his first revolution against the Manchu dynasty. It failed and Sun left China in 1895. He traveled throughout Europe, the United States, and Japan, trying to gain support for his cause. In 1911, the Manchu dynasty was overthrown during a revolt, and Sun returned to China. He was elected temporary president and tried to unite China under a strong government. Some considered his ideas too extreme, however, and after 6 weeks he turned his presidency over to Yüan Shikai. Sun remained committed to his vision of a unified China. In 1923 he and his Kuomintang Party took control of China with assistance from the Soviet Union (Shih-kai had become increasingly dictatorial). He died 2 years later. The Communists and the Kuomintang, who eventually dissolved their partnership, both claimed his legacy to be their inheritance. *Three Principles of the People*, his writings in which he summarized his political doctrines, inspired and guided subsequent developments in China.
See also: China.

Superconductivity, complete disappearance of resistance to electricity in a wire or other electric circuit, which allows a current to continue without any driving voltage. Superconductivity was discovered in 1911 and was long thought to be possible only in certain metals at very low temperatures (close to absolute zero, a total absence of molecular movement). This severely limited the possible applications of superconductivity. In recent years, however, researchers have made considerable progress in inducing superconductivity in some materials at the relatively "high" temperature of about 125°K, or –243°F.
See also: Bardeen, John.

Superego, term coined by Sigmund Freud meaning the mostly subconscious dimension of personality that represents moral and cultural standards established by society. The superego (ego ideal and conscience) develops as a result of the child's identification with parental standards.
See also: Freud, Sigmund.

Superman *see:* Nietzsche, Friedrich.

Supernova, exploding star that may increase in brightness by as much as a billion times its original state in just a few days, after which it gradually fades back to less than its original brightness. It is thought that supernovas are caused by the gravitational collapse of extremely massive stars. Although many presumed remnants of supernovas have been detected, only four of these have been definitely matched to explosions that were seen and recorded in human history. These occurred in 1006, 1054, 1572, and 1604. In more recent times (since the 19th century) many supernovas have been observed by astronomers.
See also: Nova; Star.

Superstition, belief or practice that is not based on reason. Some superstitions involve the belief that an incident will have certain results, or foretell an event—for example, believing that walking under a ladder will bring bad luck. Other superstitions attribute qualities and powers to objects, such as a rabbit foot bringing luck. The origins of superstitions vary, but they have probably existed in every culture since ancient times. They arise out of uncertainty and fear and the desire to empower oneself somehow. Some superstitions are part of a cultural or religious tradition and are believed by a number of people, such as the belief that a groom should not see his bride before the ceremony on their wedding day. Other superstitions may be personal, such as having a lucky number.

Supply and demand, in economics, central concepts that explain changes in prices, production, and consumption of goods and services. Demand refers to the quantity of a product desired by consumers. Supply is the quantity available. Normally, if demand increases relative to supply, the price will rise. If supply rises relative to demand, the price will fall. Competition is the mechanism through which supply and demand tend to reach an equilibrium. In practice, however, such factors as monopolization, state interference, and other variables generally prevent this equilibrium from ever being reached.
See also: Economics.

Supply-side economics, theory of economic management that focuses on stimulating production through tax reduction, which is intended to inspire increased investment in business, leading to higher employment. The theory also calls for a cutback in government spending to achieve a balanced and much smaller budget, thus eliminating deficit spending, which causes inflation and drains funds from the private sector. Inspired by laissez-faire economic thought, the leading theorists of supply-side thinking include Milton Friedman, Arthur B. Lafter, Jack Kemp, and David Stockman. Supply-side economics dominated President Ronald Reagan's economic policies (1981-89).
See also: Economics.

Suprematism, art movement (1913-19) originated by the Russian-Polish painter Kasimir Malevich (1878-1935), establishing a system of nonrepresentational composition in terms of pure geometric shapes and patterns. The movement's influence on graphic design and typography has been significant.

Supreme Court of the United States, highest court of the United States, with the authority to adjudicate all cases arising under U.S. law, including treaties and constitutional matters. The number of justices is set by statute and so has varied; since 1869 the Court has comprised a chief justice and 8 associate justices, appointed for life by the president as vacancies arise. Nominees must be confirmed by majority vote of the Senate. Although theoretically above politics, the Court alone can determine the constitutionality of state and federal laws and interpret acts of Congress. Cases are brought before the Court by appeal (if, after being seen before the highest state court, there are questions concerning the constitutionality of the state's statutes) or by writ of certiorari (granted by discretion of the Court). The power of judicial review is not explicitly stated in the Constitution but is rather an operational precedent established by Chief Justice John Marshall in the case of *Marbury* v. *Madison* (1803). The Court may also overrule its own previous decisions, allowing it to change with the times. An example of this is the decision in *Brown* v. *Board of Education* (1954), which declared racial segregation in education unconstitutional, overturning *Plessy* v. *Ferguson* (1896). The Court of the 1950s and 1960s, under Chief Justice Earl Warren, was generally regarded as judicially liberal; it became more conservative under Chief Justice Warren Burger (1969-86). The first woman was appointed to the Court in 1981 by Pres. Ronald Reagan. Today's Court is headed by William Rehnquist (since 1986).

Surabaya, or Surakaja (pop. 2,028,000), city in Indonesia, located on the northeastern coast of Java at the mouth of the Mas River. Surabaya's port is the second busiest in Indonesia (Jakarta has the busiest). It exports Indonesian products, including sugar, coffee, tobacco, spices, oils,and petroleum. The port is also home to Indonesia's main naval base. Surabaya is a busy industrial center. Its industries include shipbuilding and repair, textiles, chemicals, rubber, and cigarettes. Surabaya's educational facilities include a large university and a naval college.
See also: Indonesia.

Surface tension, property that makes the surface of a liquid act as if it were an elastic film. The molecules in a liquid stay together because they are pulled towards each other equally. This force is called cohesion. The molecules at the surface of a liquid have no molecules above them to attract and pull them; these molecules are pulled only by those beside and below them. This continuous sideward and downward pull creates tension at the surface, making it act as if it were a resilient film. A razor blade placed flatly on the surface of water does not sink because the surface tension supports it. Because of surface tension some birds are able to stand on water.
See also: Capillarity; Cohesion.

Surfer off the coast of Oahu, Hawaii

Surfing, sport of riding a wooden or foam plastic surfboard on the incline of a wave. It requires balance, timing, and coordination. Surfing originated in Hawaii and is the oldest sport in the United States. With worldwide competitions organized by the International Surfing Committee, surfing has gained widespread popularity, particularly in the United States, Australia, Brazil, France, Japan, Mexico, and Peru.

Surgeon general of the United States, chief medical adviser of the United States. The surgeon general commissions studies and research regarding health issues, informs the public about the findings, makes recommendations as to how health problems may be alleviated, and warns the public about health hazards.

Surgery, branch of medicine chiefly concerned with manual operations to remove or repair diseased, damaged, or deformed body tissues. The origins of surgery go back to ancient times, and there is evidence that the Egyptians, Greeks, and Romans achieved some impressive results. Infections and gangrene were major problems resulting from surgery during the Middle Ages in Europe, but this began to change in the 19th century. The development of techniques of sterilization and anesthetics allowed for the expansion of modern surgery under much safer conditions, and the invention of new diagnostic tools, such as X-rays and CAT scans, has made surgery more effective.

Suriname, republic on the northeastern coast of South America, bordered by Guyana on the west, Brazil on the south, and French Guiana on the east. The capital is Paramaribo.
Land and climate. The country consists largely of unexplored forested highlands and the flat Atlantic coast. The climate is tropical, with heavy rains.
People and economy. The population is about 38% East Indian, 31% Creole, and 15% Indonesian. Other groups include Europeans, Chinese, and Native Americans. The official language is Dutch, but most people speak the Creole Sranang Tongo. Hindi, Javanese, Chinese, English, French, and Spanish are also spoken. The most important product of the economy is bauxite. The main crops are rice, sugar, fruits, coffee, and bananas.
History. England ceded Suriname to the Dutch (1667) in exchange for New Amsterdam (now New York City), and the country was subsequently known as Dutch Guiana. It became a self-governing part of the Netherlands in 1954 and gained full independence in 1975. The first years of independence were marked by an exodus of some 40,000 Surinamese to the Netherlands and by border disputes with French Guiana and Guyana. A bloodless military coup took place in 1980, but the country returned to democratic rule in 1988.

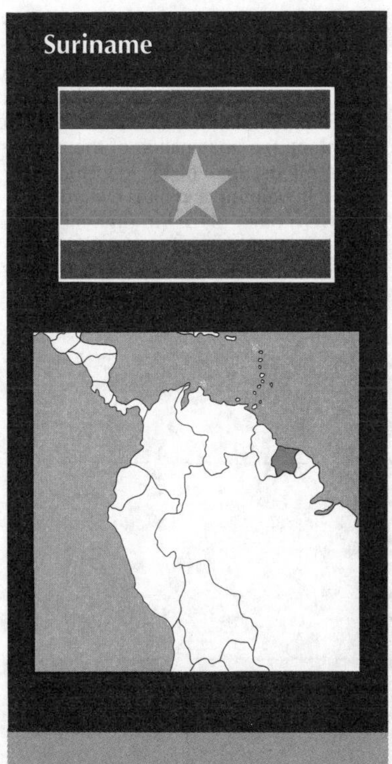

Capital:	Paramaribo
Area:	63,251 sq mi (163,820 sq km)
Population:	395,000
Government:	republic
Independent:	1975
GNP:	U.S.$1,050,000,000
Per capita:	U.S.$2,450

Suriname River

Surratt, Mary Eugenia (1820-65), boardinghouse keeper in Washington, D.C., unjustly hanged for complicity in the assassination of Abraham Lincoln. She was accused because of contact with the assassin John Wilkes Booth, who met in her house with his conspirators, including her son, John H. Subsequent revelations proved that her trial was flagrantly unjust and that she was innocent.

Surrealism, movement in literature and art that flourished between World War I and World War II, especially in Paris; influenced by Freudianism. Writers associated with surrealism include André Breton, Louis Aregon, and Jean Cocteau; surrealist artists include Salvador Dali, Joan Miró, René Magritte, Yves Tanguy, and Max Ernst. The movement was devoted to unleashing the imagination of the unconscious minds, free of the constraints of reason. In painting and films everyday objects were often placed in dreamlike settings; apparently unrelated objects were juxtaposed, and incongruous images were dominant.

René Magritte's surrealist painting, The Red Model *(1937)*

Surrey, Earl of (1517?-47), English poet. Surrey was born into the English nobility and received a classical education in France. He was knighted in 1541 and was a member of the court of King Henry VIII. Surrey's friendship with King Henry's illegitimate son, the duke of Richmond, created speculation that he was part of a treason plot against the king. This led to his arrest and beheading. Surrey's major achievement is his contribution of verse styles to English poetry. His translation of *The Aeneid* was the first English usage of blank verse. Together with Sir Thomas Wyatt (1503-42), Surrey introduced to English poetry the Petrarchan sonnet form used in Italy. Surrey and Wyatt's *The Book of Songs and Sonnets* was published in 1557. Many English poets and writers subsequently wrote in blank verse and the sonnet form, creating an age of high poetic achievement in England.

Surveying, process of measuring distances and features on the earth's surface for map preparation and locating boundary lines. Geodetic surveying, which covers large areas, takes the earth's curvature into account. After a base line of known length is established, the positions of other points are found by triangulation (measuring the angles of the point from each end of the base line) or by trilateration (measuring all the sides of the triangle formed by point and base line). Distances are measured by tape or by electronic means. Instruments for measuring angles are the theodolite and the alidade. Vertical elevations are determined by levels. Much modern surveying is done by photogrammetry, using the stereoscope to determine contours.

Susa (also called Shush), capital of the ancient Middle East country of Elam and later of the Persian Empire. Its ruins are located in southwestern Iran, just north of the Persian Gulf. Susa was an active community as early as biblical times. Archeological digs in the region have unearthed remains of many civilizations. Elam reached the peak of its power after 1300 B.C., after overthrowing Babylonia.
See also: Persia, Ancient.

Suslov, Mikhail Andreyevich (1902-82), Communist Party official in the USSR. An orthodox Stalinist during Stalin's lifetime, Suslov rose steadily through the party ranks, helping to form the Cominform in 1947 and serving as editor of the party newspaper, *Pravda* (1949-50). A member of the ruling Politburo from 1955, he became one of its most rigid ideologues. With an instinct for survival, he at first supported Nikita Khrushchev and then helped overthrow him in 1964. He opposed any suggestion of relaxing party rule in the country.
See also: Union of Soviet Socialist Republics.

Suspension, in chemistry, mixture in which solid particles hang in a liquid or gas. The suspension is maintained by the continued movement of the molecules of the liquid or gas, which bump the molecules of the particles. Two examples of suspensions are dust (solid in a gas) and muddy water (solid in a liquid).
See also: Solution.

Suspension bridge *see:* Bridge.

Susquehanna River, river in the eastern United States, rising in Otsego Lake in central New York state and flowing southward 444 mi (715 km) across Pennsylvania and Maryland, emptying into Chesapeake Bay, Maryland. The Susquehanna's shallow, rapid water flow and many rock obstructions make it unsuitable as a shipping waterway, but it is an important source of waterpower. Several hydroelectric and other energy plants have been built along it.

Sussex spaniel, strong, short, stocky dog originally bred in Sussex, England. It weighs 35-45 lb (16-20 kg) and has a dark gold coat.

Sutherland, Dame Joan (1926-), Australian soprano, one of the foremost exponents of the art of bel canto. She made her debut in Sydney (1950), her U.S. debut in Dallas (1960), and her N.Y. Metropolitan debut (1961) in *Lucia di Lammermoor.*
See also: Opera.

Suva (pop. 64,000), capital of Fiji, a country made up of more than 800 islands in the South Pacific. Suva is located on the southeast coast of Viti Levu, the fifth-largest Fijian island. Its harbor is the country's main port. It is also an educational center, with the University of Fiji and the Fiji School of Medicine located there.
See also: Fiji.

Suwannee River, river rising in the Okefenokee swamp of southeastern Georgia and flowing 250 mi (400 km) generally south through Florida to the Gulf of Mexico. It is the "Swannee River" of Stephen Foster's song, "The Old Folks at Home."

Suzuki method, style of musical instruction begun in the 1940s to teach very young children to play musical instruments. The method was initiated by Shinichi Suzuki, who believed that children could aquire musical skills as they do language, by listening and imitating. Parent involvement is an important component of the method.

Svalbard, or Spitsbergen, island group in the Arctic Ocean 400 mi (640 km) north of Norway and officially belonging to that country since 1920. The 5 main islands are Spitsbergen, North East Land, Edge Island, Barents Island, and Prince Charles Foreland. They were known to the Norwegians by the Middle Ages. Formerly of importance in the whaling and fur trading industries, since the 1890s they have been mined for coal, largely by companies of the Soviet Union.

Svedberg, Theodor (1884-71), Swedish chemist awarded the 1926 Nobel Prize in chemistry for inventing the ultracentrifuge, important in studies of colloids and large molecules.
See also: Chemistry.

Sverdlovsk (pop. 1,286,000), industrial city in the eastern Ural Mountains of the USSR. The western terminus of the Trans-Siberian railroad, Sverdlovsk is a major industrial center, with over 200 factories producing machinery, turbines, diesels, and a variety of engineering products. There are 12 schools of higher education including those for law, medicine, and education. The city was founded in 1721 and called Ekaterinburg, after Tsarina Catherine I. It was renamed in 1924 after Sverdlov, a Bolshevik leader. It was in Sverdlovsk that Tsar Nicholas II and his family were executed in 1918, during the Russian civil war.
See also: Union of Soviet Socialist Republics.

Swahili, Bantu language of East Africa, widely spoken in Kenya, Uganda, Tanzania, and parts of Zaire. Swahili is heavily influenced by Arabic in its vocabulary, the name of the language itself coming from the Arabic word for "coasts."

Swallow, common name for various small birds of the family Hirundinidae. There are at least 78 species; all have long, sickle-shaped wings and long, forked tails. The plumage is generally dark, often with a metallic sheen. Many species have lighter underparts. The legs and feet are small and weak. Swallows can perch on wires or tree branches but are adapted to spend most of their time on the wing, feeding on insects. Many species are migratory.

Swammerdam, Jan (1637-80), Dutch entomologist, zoologist, and anatomist, who made major contributions to research on insect metamorphosis, life cycles, and anatomy. He also studied red blood cells and the working nerves and muscles in animals, showing that muscles change their configuration but not their size when contracting. His written works include *A General History of Insects*, and the *Bible of Nature*.
See also: Entomology; Zoology.

Swamp, area of poorly drained, low-lying land saturated with water. Swamps normally covered by water are called marshes. The obstruction of drainage that causes swamps to form may result from the flatness of the land, the presence of impermeable rock beneath the surface, or the growth of dense vegetation. Lakes that are filled in by sediment may develop into swamps. When drained, swamps usually make fertile farmland. Large swamps in the United States include the Everglades (Florida), the Dismal (North Carolina), and the Okefenokee (Georgia and Florida).

Swan, any of various large, long-necked aquatic birds related to ducks and geese. There are eight species, seven within the genus *Cygnus*. Five of these are found in the Northern Hemisphere; all are white in adult plumage but have different-colored bills. The two remaining species are the black swan of Australia and the black-necked swan of South America. Most feed on vegetation.

Swanscombe man, prehistoric human dating back to the Second Interglacial Period about 350,000 years ago. Three parts of a skull were discovered 3 consecutive years (1935, 1936, 1937) in Swanscombe, England at the River Thames. A better specimen, found in Steinheim, Germany, in 1933, dates back 375,000 years.
See also: Prehistoric people.

Swansea (pop. 183,500), industrial seaport in Wales, originally settled in the 1000s. Its 281 acres of waterfront docks on Swansea Bay export the products of nearby oil refineries, aluminum factories, nickel and zinc refineries, and coal mines. In the 1800s the city was a major copper trading center and produced great amounts of tin plate for cans.
See also: Wales.

Swastika, ancient symbol of well-being and prosperity employed by such diverse peoples as Greeks, Celts, Native Americans, and the Hindus of India, where it apparently arose. The word comes from the Sanskrit for "good fortune." In the 20th century the symbol became infamous as the emblem of Nazism.

Swaziland

Swaziland

Capitals:	Mbabane, Lobamba
Area:	6,704 sq mi (17,364 sq km)
Population:	746,000
Government:	monarchy
Independent:	1968
GNP:	U.S. $580,000,000
Per capita:	U.S. $790

Swaziland, country in southeastern Africa, bordered by Mozambique on the east and the Republic of South Africa on the other three sides. The capital is Mbabane.
Land and climate. There are three main regions: the mountainous High Veld in the west, the lower Middle Veld, and the Low Veld rising in the east to the narrow Lebombo range. The four major rivers, running west to east, are being developed for irrigation and could provide abundant hydroelectricity.
People and economy. Swazis and a smaller number of Zulus constitute 97% of the population. "Coloreds" (of mixed ancestry) and Europeans make up the rest. Agriculture, including forestry, is the largest single sector in the economy. Sugar, wood pulp, asbestos, fruits, iron ore, and canned meats are the main exports. Swaziland has close communication, economic, and trade links with South Africa.
History. Settled by the Swazis, a Bantu people, and unified as a kingdom in the 1800s, Swaziland was taken over by Britain in 1903 and later fell under South African influence. The country became self-governing in 1963 and fully independent in 1968 under King Sobhuza II. Mawati III has ruled since Sobhuza's death in 1982.

Sweat gland *see:* Perspiration.

Sweatshop, place of work with long hours, poor pay, and bad conditions. Such places often exploit those who find difficulty in obtaining employment, such as women, unskilled laborers, newly arrived immigrants, and children. Sweatshops have been curbed by the growth of organized labor.

Sweden, kingdom in northern Europe, occupying most of the eastern and southern portion of the Scandinavian peninsula.
Land and climate. Sweden has an area of 173,648 sq mi (449,750 sq km). It is bounded on the west and north by Norway; on the northeast by Finland; on the east and south by the Baltic Sea; and on the southwest by the Öresund, Kattegat, and Skagerrak, the narrows linking the Baltic with the North Sea. At its northernmost, it lies within the Arctic Circle and includes part of Lapland. Sweden may be divided into four main regions: Norrland, the northern two-thirds of the country; the central lowlands; southern Sweden; and Skåne. Barren heights, high lakes, peat bogs, and great forests of spruce, pine, and larch cover most of the thinly populated Norrland. Sweden's rivers and lakes make up nearly 10% of the country's area and some of the largest of its lakes are in the central low-

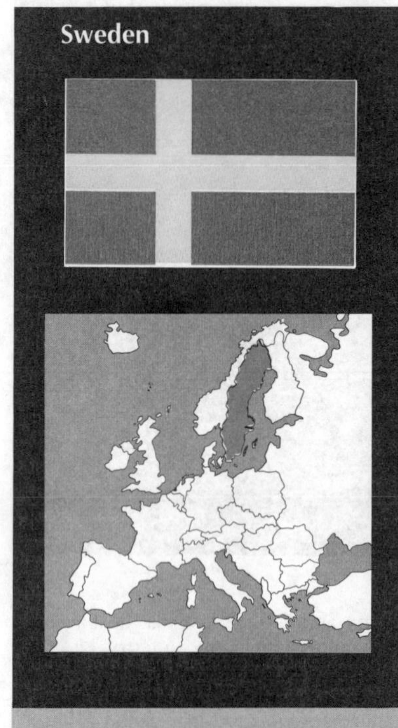

Capital:	Stockholm
Area:	170,250 sq mi (440,945 sq km)
Population:	8,498,000
Government:	constitutional monarchy
Independent:	1917 (constitutional monarchy)
GNP:	U.S.$160,029,000,000

Forest in Darlarna Province, Sweden (left), and village in northern Sweden (right)

lands. Most of the people live in this area and it is also the site of the country's two largest cities, Stockholm and Göteborg. Southern Sweden is a fertile, coastal lowland region, and Skåne is the low-lying agricultural region in the extreme south. Northern Sweden has long, cold winters and brief, cool summers. The south enjoys longer summers and milder winters. The capital of the country is Stockholm.

People. The population is almost entirely Swedish, except for a minority of Lapps in the north. The official language is Swedish, and almost everyone is Lutheran.

Economy. Sweden has extensive forests, rich deposits of iron ore, abundant hydroelectric power, and enough good farmland to be nearly self-sufficient in food production. Metals and metal products dominate industry. Main exports are machinery, iron, steel, paper, wood pulp, timber, and motor vehicles. Sweden enjoys one of the highest living standards in the world with relatively low unemployment and extensive social services, including free education, retirement pensions, and comprehensive medical care. An economic downturn in the 1970s and 1980s partly eroded Swedish prosperity, slowing economic growth and leading to unemployment and inflation.

History. Mention of the Swedes is first recorded by the Roman historian Tacitus in the 1st century A.D. In the 9th and 10th centuries A.D., Vikings from Sweden known as Varangians pioneered trade routes through Russia as far as the Black Sea. Throughout the Middle Ages, the history of the Swedes was tied to that of Norway and Denmark. The Danes, dominant in the Kalmar Union of Denmark, Norway, and Sweden, which was founded in 1397, were driven out of Sweden in 1523. In the 17th century, Gustavus II (Gustavus Adolphus) made Sweden a leading European power, but the rise of Russia in the 18th century checked Swedish ambitions. In 1809 the monarchy became constitutional; a new constitution took effect in 1975. Sweden took no part in World War I or World War II. The Social Democrats have been the predominant political party through much of Sweden's 20th-century history, architects of the country's social welfare system and its policy of neutrality. Sweden opposed the U.S. war in Vietnam and in 1969 recognized North Vietnam, thereby marking the high point of a period of strained relations with the United States. Swedish domestic politics have been free of violence with the sole exception being the assassination of Prime Minister Olof Palme (1986), a murder that remains unsolved.

Swedenborgians, followers of the religious ideas of the Swedish theologian Emanuel Swedenborg (1688-1772). A scientist and engineer, Swedenborg became a Christian mystic in 1747. He believed that the Second Coming of Christ occurred in 1757. After his death, his followers founded the Church of the New Jerusalem, first organized in London in 1787 and introduced in the United States in 1792.

Swedish, one of the North Germanic or Scandinavian languages, spoken by about 9 million people in Sweden, Finland, Estonia, the United States, and Canada. Old Swedish developed from Old Norse and gave place to modern Swedish (1500) with the onset of standardization.

Sweet alyssum, vigorous, low-growing perennial herb (*Lobularia maritima*) of the mustard family, originating in the Mediterranean area. It produces sweet, mostly white but sometimes lavender or pink flowers. Plants can grow to 9 in (23 cm) high.

Sweetbrier *see:* Eglantine.

Sweet flag, tall, straight, perennial marsh herb (*Acorus calamus*) of the arum family, growing in moist areas near streams and ponds. Its fat root is edible and is also used in medicines and perfumes. Flat leaves grow 2-6 ft (61-180 cm) high from the root rather than the stem.

Sweet gum, any of various tall shade trees (genus *Liquidambar*) of the hazel family named for the sweet-smelling gummy substance they produce, called storax. Sweet gums have star-shaped leaves that turn brilliant colors in the fall. Storax is used for perfumes, adhesives, and ointments. Brown, spiny seed balls are produced as fruit and remain on the tree most of the winter.

Sweet pea, fragrant, annual garden plant (*Lathyrus odoratus*) native to Italy and thriving in numerous temperate countries where there is rich soil and abundant sunshine. Flowers grow to 2 in (5 cm) across, either individually or in small clusters.

Sweet potato, trailing creeper plant (*Ipomoea batatas*) of the morning glory family, native to tropical America. It produces a tuberous root that is sweet-tasting when cooked. In the United States an orange variety is grown, with roots rich in carotene.

Sweet William, Eurasian pink biennial (*Dianthus barbatus*), also known as Newport pink. Originating in Europe and Asia, the plant produces thick clusters of white, pink, or purple ringed flowers.

Swift, any of several highly mobile, small, insect-eating lizards (genus *Sceloporus*) found in dry temperate regions of the United States, Mexico, and Central America. Most swifts reproduce by laying eggs, while others give birth to live young.

Swift, small, fast-flying insectivorous bird, similar to a swallow but classed with the hummingbirds in the order Apodiformes. Both swifts and hummingbirds have very small feet and extremely short arm bones, the major flight feathers being attached to the extended hand bones. Entirely aerial, most species feed and even sleep on the wing.

Swift, Gustavus Franklin (1839-1903), U.S. businessperson. The first to slaughter cattle in Chicago for shipment east (1875), he introduced refrigerated railroad cars, founded Swift & Co., and pioneered the manufacture of meat by-products.

Swift, Jonathan (1667-1745), Anglo-Irish writer, journalist, poet, and prose satirist. Two of his satires were published in 1704: *The Battle of the Books* and *The Tale of a Tub*. He became a Tory in 1710, taking over *The Examiner*, the Tory journal. From 1714 he lived in Ireland, as dean of St. Patrick's, Dublin. He deplored the plight of the Irish poor in the *Drapier's Letters* (1724). His masterpiece is *Gulliver's Travels* (1726), a political and social satire that has been adapted as a children's classic.
See also: Gulliver's Travels.

Swigert, John Leonard, Jr. (1931-82), U.S. astronaut who participated in the 1970 Apollo 13 moon mission, which was aborted in space after life-support systems failed. The astronauts returned to earth safely by relying on the lunar module's life systems. Swigert left the space program in 1977 and was elected to the U.S. House of Representatives.
See also: Astronomy.

Swimming and diving, popular water sports. Common swimming styles include the side stroke, a simple sidewise propulsion for distance swimming and lifesaving; the breaststroke, a froglike arm-and-leg thrust; backstroke, either overarm or, for distance endurance, an inverted breaststroke; and the crawl, the most common freestyle form, using an overarm pull and a flutter kick. The butterfly, a modified breaststroke that thrusts the head and arms up from the water and incorporates a dolphin kick, has become a popular competitive style. Distance swimming has produced many well-publicized attempts to cross the English Channel and other large bodies of water. Organized, artistic diving dates back to 17th century Sweden and Germany. Competitions include forward, backward, reverse, inward, twisting, and armstand dives in layout (extended), tuck (rolled in a ball), pike (bent at waist, legs straight), and free positions, from a platform or springboard. Various swimming and diving events are part of the Summer Olympic Games and other competitions.

Swinburne, Algernon Charles (1837-1909), English poet and literary critic. He established his reputation as a writer with the verse play *Atalanta in Calydon* (1865). Other important works were 2 volumes of *Poems and Ballads* (1866, 1878) and the long poem *Tristram of Lyonesse* (1882). His knowledge of literary works of classical Greece and Rome, Shakespeare and other Elizabethans, and French poetry informed his work. His own poetry is known both for its sensuality and its exploration of complex meters and rhyme schemes.

Swing *see:* Jazz.

Swiss chard, green leafy vegetable (*Beta vulgaris cicla*) similar to the beet but with an inedible root. Its large leaves, rich in vitamins A, B complex, and C, grow throughout the summer.

Swiss Family Robinson *see:* Wyss family.

Swiss Guard, member of the Swiss mercenary soldiers who served in various European armies from the 15th to the 19th centuries, most notably as bodyguards to the French monarch (1497-1792 and 1814-30). The colorfully uniformed Papal Swiss Guard at the Vatican Palace in Rome dates back to the late 1400s. It is the only surviving branch of the Guard.

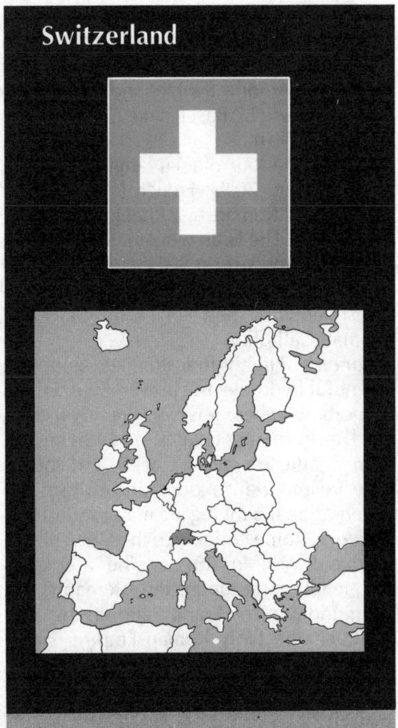

Capital:	Bern
Area:	15,943 sq mi (41,293 sq km)
Population:	6,689,000
Government:	federal republic
Independent:	1499
GNP:	U.S. $178,442,000,000
Per capita:	U.S. $27,260

Bern, Switzerland (left) and the Swiss Alps (below)

Switzerland, officially the Swiss Confederation, federal republic situated in the Alps in central Europe.

Land and climate. Switzerland covers 15,941 sq mi (41,287 sq km). It is bounded by Germany on the north, Austria and Liechtenstein on the east, Italy on the south, and France on the west. Lying almost entirely within the western Alps, Switzerland has three main regions: the Jura Mountains of the western Alps, the Swiss Foreland or Plateau, and the Swiss Alps. The parallel ranges and narrow valleys of the Jura run southwest to northeast along the Swiss-French border from Lake Geneva to the Rhine River at Basel. The long, narrow Swiss Foreland or Plateau, between the Jura Mountains and the Swiss Alps, extends from Lake Geneva to Lake Constance. The plateau is Switzerland's major agricultural area. It contains most of Switzerland's large cities and important manufacturing centers, and is home to about 60% of the population. The outer ranges of the Swiss Alps stretch from Lake Geneva to Lake Thun. They are succeeded by much higher ranges culminating in the Perrine Alps in the south where Monte Rosa soars to 15,203 ft (4,634 m) and the Matterhorn rises to 14,701 ft (4,481 m). Covering more than half of Switzerland, the region contains less than 20% of the population. There are many lakes in the Alps, and both the Rhine and the Rhône have their sources in its mountains. There are great variations of climate in Switzerland, due mainly to differences in altitude. Much of the country has a typically Central

European climate. Sheltered valleys in the south have hot summers and mild winters. Elsewhere winters are cold, with heavy snowfall. Among Switzerland's major cities are Zurich, Basel, and Geneva. The capital is Bern.
People. The four official language groups are German (70%), French (19%), Italian (10%), and Romansh, a Rhaeto-Roman dialect (1%). The Latin word for Switzerland, *Helvetia,* appears on Swiss currencies and postage stamps. The Swiss are divided almost equally between Protestant and Roman Catholic.
Economy. Highly industrialized and with plentiful hydroelectric power, Switzerland exports watches, jewelry, precision tools and instruments, textiles, and chemicals. Dairy cattle are raised. Cheese and chocolate are important exports, and tourism and international banking are major industries.
History. Rome conquered the Helvetii, the native Swiss, in 58 B.C. The area subsequently came under the Alemanni, the Burgundians, the Franks, and, in the 10th century, the Holy Roman Empire. Habsburg oppression led to the Perpetual Covenant among the cantons or states of Uri, Schwyz, and Unterwald in 1291, the traditional beginning of the Swiss Confederation. Wars against Austria resulted in virtual independence in 1499. During the Protestant Reformation, the country was divided by religious civil wars, but it remained neutral throughout the Thirty Years' War and its independence was formally recognized in the Peace of Westphalia of 1648. French revolutionary armies imposed a centralized Helvetic Republic from 1798 to 1803. In 1815 the Congress of Vienna restored the Confederation. After a three-week civil war, a federal democracy was established in 1848. Switzerland remained neutral in both world wars and is not a member of the UN. As presently constituted, the republic is a federation of 22 cantons, or states, with Bern as the federal capital. Women have had the right to vote on federal matters since 1971.

Sydney, Australia

Sword, ancient weapon consisting of a handle and a metal blade with a sharp point and one or two cutting edges. Leaf-shaped Bronze Age swords gave way to short, flat blades in Rome, and these to longer laminated iron (in Damascus) and tempered steel (notably in Toledo). Asian curved cutting blades (the Turkish scimitar) inspired the cavalry saber. The Japanese samurai used a longer, two-handed version. The thrust-and-parry rapier became the weapon of the duel and of fencing.

Swordfish, or broadbill, large, streamlined food and game fish (*Xiphias gladius*) of tropical seas, having a swordlike upper jaw. The maximum length is 16 ft (4.9 m); the maximum weight 1,500 lb (680 kg). Swordfish can swim extremely fast and, when hooked, will leap high out of the water. They eat fish that they kill with strokes of their swordlike jaw.

Sycamore, popular name for a number of deciduous trees. In North America the name is applied to a plane tree (*Platanus occidentalis*), the bark of which flakes off. In Europe the sycamore is a maple (*Acer pseudoplatanus*). The sycamore of ancient times is a fig (*Ficus occidentalis*) that is now seldom cultivated.

Sydenham, Thomas (1624-89), English physician, considered a founder of modern medicine. He pioneered the use of quinine for treating malaria and of laudanum as an anesthetic. He was the author of an important treatise on gout, and first described Sydenham's chorea (St. Vitus's Dance).

Sydney (pop. 2,989,000), oldest and largest city in Australia, capital of New South Wales, in southeastern Australia on the Port Jackson inlet of the Pacific Ocean. Famous for its natural harbor, Harbour Bridge, and opera house, Sydney was founded as a penal colony in 1788, and gold rushes of the 1850 spurred its growth. It is now a major commercial, industrial, shipping, cultural, and recreational center. Manufactures include ships, textiles, chemicals, and refined petroleum.
See also: Australia.

Syllogism, in logic, term for a form of argument consisting of 3 statements: 2 premises and a conclusion. The conclusion of a valid syllogism follows logically from the premises and is true if the premises are true. Aristotle first formulated the concept of syllogistic logic that has served as the basis for logical thought in the West for more than 2,000 years.

Sylvester I, Saint (d.335), pope who reigned from 314 to 335. During his reign the Council of Nicaea declared Arius a heretic for arguing that the Son was unequal to God. Many legends associate Sylvester I with the Donation of Constantine, a document supposedly granting him control of church property. He is thought to be buried in the Cemetery of Saint Priscilla in Rome.
See also: Arianism.

Sylvester II (940-1003), first Frenchman to serve as pope (999-1003), known for his learning, his close links to the Holy Roman emperor Otto III, and his support of the Christianization of Poland and Hungary. Before being elected pope, he was superior at the monastery of Bobbio, Italy, and archbishop of Reims, France.

Symbiosis, also called mutualism, relationship between 2 dependent organisms of different species in which mutual benefit is derived by both participants. Other types of symbiotic relationships are commensalism which denotes independence of the symbiotes; parasitism, which implies potential injury to the host organism, and helotism, which denotes a master-slave relationship.

Symbolism, in literature, movement begun by a group of French poets in the late 19th century in opposition to naturalism. Prominent poets associated with symbolism include Jules Laforgue, Stéphane Mallarmé, Paul Valéry, and Paul Verlaine. Influenced by Charles Baudelaire, the symbolists aimed to create poetic images, or symbols, that would be apprehended by the senses and reach into the preconscious world of the spirit. Though short-lived as a movement, symbolism influenced such major writers as James Joyce, Marcel Proust, R.M. Rilke, and W.B. Yeats.

Symphonic poem, or tone poem, form of orchestral music in one movement that describes a story or scene. Popular with composers c.1850-1900, the form was originated by Franz Liszt and perfected by Richard Strauss.

Symphony, major form of music for orchestra. Developed from the overture, by 1800 it had 4 movements: a fairly quick movement in sonata form; a slow movement; a minuet and trio; and a quick rondo. Haydn and Mozart played a central role in developing the classical symphony. Beethoven introduced the scherzo movement and a new range of emotion. Major symphonic composers include Schubert, Berlioz, Mendelssohn, Brahms, Bruckner, Dvorák, and Mahler in the 19th century, and Stravinsky, Prokofiev, Shostakovich, Vaughan Williams, Elgar, Sibelius, and Nielsen in the 20th century.
See also: Orchestra.

Synagogue (Greek, "house of assembly"), Jewish place of worship. The synagogue became the center of communal and religious life after the destruction of the Temple in Jerusalem (A.D. 70) and dispersal of the Jews. Most synagogues have an ark containing the Torah, an "eternal light," 2 candelabra, pews, and a platform (bimah) for readings and conduct of services. Orthodox synagogues segregate women.
See also: Judaism.

Synchro-cyclotron, cylindrical-shaped particle accelerator designed to accelerate protons. A cylindrical magnet bends the particle beams into a circular path, as in a cyclotron, an electric field being applied to accelerate the protons each time they come around the circle. In the synchro-cyclotron the frequency of the electric field steadily decreases to compensate for the increasing mass acquired by the protons as they approach the speed of light.
See also: Lawrence, Ernest Orlando.
See also: Particle accelerator.

Synchrotron, type of particle accelerator in which a doughnut-shaped ring of magnets around a vacuum produces a magnetic field that rises in intensity as the accelerated protons rise in velocity. This keeps the particles moving in circular orbits whose radii remain constant. The design, which requires no magnet in the center, allows rings to be built of several miles in diameter.
See also: Particle accelerator.

Syndicalism (French: *syndicat,* "labor union"), revolutionary labor movement that aimed at seizing control of industry through strikes, sabotage, even violence, and, as its ultimate weapon, the general strike. It originated in late-19th-century France from the theories of Pierre Joseph Proudhon and Georges Sorel. Syndicalists agreed with Marxist class analysis but like anarchists rejected any state organization. Syndicalism was strong in France and Italy in the early 1900s and found U.S. expression in the industrial unionism of the Industrial Workers of the World. World War I and the advance of communism overtook the syndicalists; their influence lasted longest in Spain, where it was destroyed in the civil war (1936-39).
See also: Labor movement.

Synge, John Millington (1871-1909), Irish poet and playwright. His plays often portray rural Irish life of his times. Among his best-known and most-respected works are the tragedy *Riders to the Sea* (1904) and the comedy *Playboy of the Western World* (1907). Some of his plays were produced in the Abbey Theatre, Dublin, which he and W.B. Yeats helped to found (1904).

Synoptic Gospels, in the New Testament, comprehensive view of the life of Jesus according to Matthew, Mark, and Luke, which contain a high level of agreement on subject matter and phraseology. Modern scholars commonly regard Mark as having written his gospel first and suppose that Matthew and Luke also used *Q*, a now-lost source containing the non-Marcan material common to them.
See also: New Testament.

Synthesizer, electronic musical device able to produce and change the timbre, quality, and frequency of sounds generated. First developed in 1955 and increasingly complex since the advent of microprocessors, the instrument has enabled composers and entertainers to create new works using isolated sounds or various sound combinations.

Synthetic, substance created by chemical processing and used as a substitute for naturally occurring substances. Synthetic fibers such as acrylic and nylon are used as substitutes for silk, cotton, linen, and wool. Plastics, which are all synthetics, replace glass, wood, metal, and other materials. Synthetics are often produced from carbon, hydrogen, oxygen, and other elements by polymerization, which creates extremely large molecules. Rayon, a synthetic fiber, results from dissolving and extruding cellulose, which is one of the main components of wood. Properties of synthesized materials can be controlled to suit their intended form and function.

Synthetic fuels, combustible matter that can replace crude oil and natural gas. Sources for synthetic fuels include plant and animal matter, coal, oil shale, and bituminous sands.

Syphilis, highly contagious venereal disease, caused by a spirochete, *Treponema pallidum*, and characterized by a variety of lesions (chancres, mucous patches, and skin ulcers) at the point of infection. If untreated, syphilis can cause degeneration of the central nervous system resulting in death. It is most often transmitted by sexual contact, but can also be passed on by transfusions of infected blood. Once a widespread cause of death, syphilis is now relatively easily treatable with penicillin, if detected before major damage to the nervous system occurs.
See also: Venereal disease.

Syracuse (pop. 659,864), city in central New York, seat of Onondaga County, situated on Onondaga Lake. The original inhabitants of the area were the Onondaga, an Iroquois tribe. Although French explorers arrived in the 17th century, discovering its economically important salt springs, it was not until 1786 that Ephraim Webster established a permanent settlement. In 1825 the settlement was named for the ancient Greek city of Syracuse, which was also situated on salt springs. In addition to having saltworks, the city was a trade center along the Erie Canal (completed 1825) and a rail center. Manufactures now also include machinery, electronics, and chinaware. Syracuse is home to Syracuse University and the State of New York Upstate Medical Center, and hosts many conventions as well as the annual New York State Fair.

Syracuse, city in southeastern Sicily, on the Ionian Sea. Founded by Corinthians (734 B.C.), it became a brilliant center of Greek culture, notably under Hiero I (r.478-466 B.C.) and Dionysius the Elder (r.405-367 B.C.). Syracuse was defeated by Rome in 212 B.C. Later conquerors included the Arabs (878) and Normans (1085). The modern provincial capital, a port and tourist center, has many ancient monuments.
See also: Sicily.

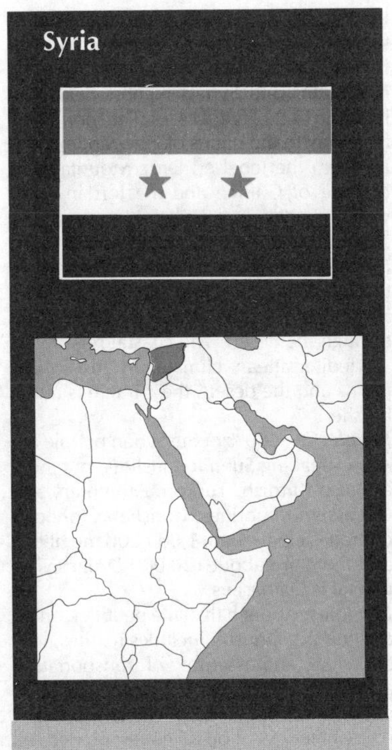

Capital:	Damascus
Area:	71,498 sq mi (185,180 sq km)
Population:	11,719,000
Government:	republic
Independent:	1946
GNP:	U.S.$19,540,000,000

Damascus, Syria

Syria, Arab republic in southwest Asia. ***Land and climate.*** Syria covers about 71,498 sq mi (185,180 sq km) and is bounded by Turkey on the north, Iraq on the east and southeast, Jordan and Israel on the south, and Lebanon and the Mediterranean Sea on the west. Syria has a 100-mi (161-km)-long coastline on the Mediterranean. The coastal plain is separated from the inland reaches by a coast range, the

Jebel Ansariya, part of the Lebanon Mountains. In the southwest, the border with Lebanon is marked by the Anti-Lebanon Mountains and Syria's highest peak, Mt. Hermon (9,232 ft/2,814 m). The mountains fall away to the plains of Hawran, extending from the Jebel ed Druz Mountains to the Sea of Galilee and the Jordan River valley. To the east and southeast are the arid wastes of the Syrian Desert, dominating most of the country and extending through Jordan and Iraq into Saudi Arabia. Syria's largest river, the Euphrates, flows through the desert. The coastal region has a Mediterranean climate. In the inland plains and the desert, the climate is much harsher.

People. Over 80% of the Syrian people are Arab-speaking Sunnite Muslims, but there are also Kurdish, Turkish, Armenian, and Circassian minorities. Christian Orthodox churches claim some 1,000,000 members, and there are about 120,000 Druzes. The capital is Damascus.

Economy. About half of the people work in agriculture. Industry includes textiles, iron and steel, and assembly of transportation and electrical equipment. Exports include cotton, fruits and vegetables, and phosphates. Most oil revenues are derived from pipe lines crossing the country, but income from oil drilled in the northeast is increasing. The large Euphrates Dam power station, completed with aid from the Soviet Union, was opened in 1978.

History. Part of the Hittite Empire in the second millennium B.C., Syria was conquered in succeeding centuries by Assyrians, Babylonians, Persians, and Greeks. Under the Seleucids in the 4th century B.C., it was incorporated into the Roman Empire by Pompey in 63 B.C. Governed by the Byzantines from the 5th to the 7th centuries A.D., Syria was conquered by the Arabs in the 7th century A.D. and, in the centuries that followed, it was governed by the Umayyad caliphs, the Seljuk Turks, the Mongols, and the Mameluks. Part of the Ottoman Empire from 1516, Syria was mandated to the French after World War I and became fully independent in 1946. It joined with Egypt in the United Arab Republic from 1958 to 1961. The ruling Baathist Party, which assumed control of the government in 1963, favors socialism and pan-Arab nationalism. Its foreign policy aligns it with the Soviet Union and against the state of Israel. In the early 1980s, the Baathist regime under Hafez el-Assad faced a period of growing unrest and challenge to its authority from the fundamentalist Muslim Brotherhood. As a result of its participation against Israel in the Six-Day War of 1967, Syria lost control of the Golan Heights to an Israeli occupying force. In 1981 the Israelis annexed the area and tensions between the two countries increased. In 1976 Syrian troops intervened in the Lebanese civil war in support of Palestinians, and since then Syria has retained a force in Lebanon. Syrian forces suffered serious losses when Israel invaded Lebanon in 1982. Syria continues to maintain close ties with the Soviet Union and, although the regime has been linked to international terrorist organizations, its cooperation was sought by the United States in the Persian Gulf War (1990-91). Syrian troops were part of the international force created for the liberation of Kuwait.

Syriac, Aramaic language of the northwestern Semitic group. It was used in early Christian writings but was largely superseded by Arabic after the spread of Islam. Closely related to Hebrew, Syriac is still spoken by a few groups in the Middle East.

Syrian Desert, triangular desert plateau covering much of the Arabian Peninsula, including portions of present-day Saudi Arabia, Jordan, Syria, and Iraq. Al-Hamad, the name of the western part of the desert, is sometimes used as a name for the entire expanse. The northern portion is a flat plain, while the southern portion is rocky, with a mountainous central region. The extreme aridity has made the desert nearly uninhabitable, although there are remains of ancient oasis towns, including the caravan city of Palmyra. The desert is now crossed by 2 highways and by oil pipelines from Iraqi oilfields.
See also: Arabian Peninsula.

Syringa *see:* Mock orange.

Systems analysis, method of studying the interactions of humans, machines, and other elements engaged in activity through the creation of mathematical models. The system is a particular environment of physical and social interaction (e.g., school, factory, economy) viewed as an abstraction so that it can be translated into mathematical statements describing its operation. These are then subject to logical analysis, which can be used to improve the efficient operation of the system. The field, developed in the 1930s, now makes extensive use of computers.

Systolic pressure *see:* Blood pressure.

Szczecin (German: *Stettin*; pop. 392,300), city in northwestern Poland, capital of Szczecin province, on the Baltic Sea at the mouth of the Oder River. It is the main port for Poland, and also an important shipping center for goods in and out of Czechoslovakia, Hungary, and Germany. Szczecin was a fishing settlement by the 8th century. Its status changed a number of times between the 10th century, when it was annexed to Poland, and 1720, when it came under Prussian control. It then remained in German hands until 1945, when it was made part of post-World War II Poland. In addition to shipping, its economy is based on shipbuilding and manufacturing.
See also: Poland.

Szell, George (1897-1970), Hungarian-born U.S. conductor. He established his reputation in Germany but emigrated to the United States when the Nazis rose to power. Szell's performances and recordings with the Cleveland Orchestra (1946-70) gained international acclaim.

Szent-Györgyi, Albert (1893-1966), Hungarian-born U.S. biochemist awarded the 1937 Nobel Prize in physiology or medicine for his work on biological oxidation processes and his discovery of ascorbic acid in the adrenal glands. He was also the first to isolate vitamin C.
See also: Biochemistry.

Szilard, Leo (1898-1964), Hungarian-born U.S. physicist who helped pioneer the U.S. atomic bomb project. Along with Enrico Fermi, he designed the first self-sustaining uranium fission reactor. After 1945 he became a leader of the movement against using the bomb. Later he also made contributions in the field of molecular biology.
See also: Manhattan Project.

Szold, Henrietta (1860-1945), founder (1912) of the Women's Zionist Organization of America (Hadassah). She moved to Palestine in 1920 and directed medical and rehabilitation work, particularly for children.
See also: Hadassah.

T, 20th letter in the English alphabet, corresponding with the Semitic letter *taw*, meaning "mark," it is represented by an upright cross and is probably derived from an ancient Egyptian symbol for a check mark. The Greeks raised the horizontal cross-stroke to produce a capital *T*, which they called *tau*, and which became the 19th letter of the Roman alphabet. The small letter *t* developed from 6th century Roman script. *T* is used as an abbreviation for *testament, tablespoon,* and *township,* and *t* for words including *teaspoon, tempo, tense,* and *ton*.

Tabasco, southwestern state in Mexico on the Bay of Campeche of the Gulf of Mexico. The capital city is Villahermosa. Petroleum is the major resource of this flat, marshy region. Food crops, such as bananas and sugar cane, along with rubber, resins, and hardwoods constitute the important products of this state. Conflicts between native Mexicans (the Olmec) and the Spanish explorer Hernando Cortés took place here in the early 1500s.

Tabernacle, portable temple carried by the Israelis during their nomadic period. According to Exodus its design was given to Moses on Mt. Sinai. The inner chamber contained the Ark of the Covenant, which held the Ten Commandments.

Tabernacles, Feast of *see:* Sukkot.

Table tennis, or ping-pong, indoor game played with a ball, rackets ("paddles"), and a net, a miniature version of tennis. The 9-ft (3-m) table on which it is played is laid out like a tennis court, its 5-ft (150-cm) width spanned by a small net over which the players hit the hollow celluloid ball. The game is played by 2 players, one at either end, or by 4 players, as *doubles.* It originated in England in the late 19th century and is now popular in many countries, particularly in Asia.

Taboo, or **tabu**, prohibition linked to an object, place, or person by law or social custom. The word taboo comes from the Polynesian word *tapu*, meaning something sacred, dangerous, or unclean. In Polynesia, violation of a taboo requires a ritual purification and at times may even warrant the death of the offender (to save the community from suffering ill consequences). In most western societies incest is considered taboo. This taboo was established hundreds of years ago to promote genetic and cultural exchanges between members of clans and tribes by prohibiting the intermarriage of close family relations.

Tabriz (pop. 852,300), city in northwestern Iran, capital of East Azerbaijan province, on the Aji Chai (Talkheh) River. Once called Tauris, it was the capital of Armenia in the 3rd century A.D. It was also briefly the capital of Iran (16th century). Tabriz is surrounded by mountains and has been repeatedly damaged by earthquakes. It produces Persian rugs and other textiles, and is a resort and trade center.
See also: Iran.

Tabularium, library of ancient Rome, used to store records. Erected in 73 B.C, . tt was located on Capitoline Hill, the historic center of ancient Rome.

Taché, Sir Étienne-Paschal (1795-1865), Canadian politician. During Canada's pre-independence years, he served twice as prime minister (1856-57, 1864), an office held jointly with John A. Macdonald. In 1864 Taché presided over the Quebec Conference, which led to Canada's independence 3 years later.
See also: Canada; Macdonald, Sir John Alexander.

Tachometer, instrument that measures the speed at which a wheel or shaft spins. This measurement, usually given in terms of revolutions per minute (rpm), helps gauge the efficiency and power of an engine. Tachometers are used in automobiles, ships, and aircraft.

Tachycardia, abnormally fast heartrate. Generally, anything over 100 beats per minute is considered a tachycardia.
See also: Heart.

Tachyon, subatomic particles that in theory move faster than the speed of light. According to Albert Einstein's theory of relativity (1905), all matter moves slower than the speed of light (186,282 mi per sec/299,792 km per sec). Theoretically, tachyons gain energy as they slow down; it would take massive amounts of energy to slow them down to approximately the speed of light. Physicists today believe that the existence of tachyons fits into Einstein's theory, even though experiments have not as yet proved their existence.

Tacitus, Cornelius (C.A.D.55-120), Roman historian. His most famous works are critical studies of the 1st-century empire, the *Histories* and *Annals*. A son-in-law of Agricola, of whom he wrote a biography, he rose to consul (97) and proconsul (112) of Asia. His *Germania* is the earliest study of the Germanic tribes.

Tacoma (pop. 158,501), port and industrial city of Washington State, on Puget Sound, about 25 mi (40 km) south of Seattle. It is the third-largest city of the state and the seat of Pierce County. The community developed in the 1850s and 1860s and became a terminus of the Northern Pacific Railway (1873). In 1884 two small towns were amalgamated to form Tacoma. Industries in Tacoma include shipbuilding, chemicals, clothing, and metal and wood products. The port can handle oceangoing ships. The University of Puget Sound and the Pacific Lutheran University are in Tacoma. Fort Lewis, an army post, lies 15 mi (24 km) to the south.
See also: Washington.

Taconite, rock containing about 30% iron ore, from which iron is made. The noniron-bearing part of taconite is called chert. Because taconite is very hard, it takes a number of steps to extract the iron ore material, which is speckled throughout the chert. After the rock is initially blasted or cracked, it is broken down further and crushed. Magnets then can attract the iron ore and separate it from the pulverized chert. A large deposit of taconite is found in the Mesabi Range in Minnesota. Taconite is named after the Taconic Mountains of southern New England, where taconite is also found.

Tadpole, or polliwog, larval amphibian hatched from transparent, jellylike eggs laid on the water. Tadpoles have the physical characteristics of fish (tail and gills). Through metamorphosis (a stage that can last from 10 days to 2 years, depending on the species) legs appear, the digestive system develops, the tail begins to shrink, and lungs develop as the gills disappear. In the adult frog or toad, the tail also disappears.

Tadzhikistan *see:* Tajikistan.

Taft, Robert Alphonso (1889-1953), U.S. senator from Ohio (1938-53). Eldest son of President William H. Taft, he studied law, served in the Ohio legislature, and became a leading conservative Republican. Taft was a fiscal conservative, an opponent of the New Deal, and an isolationist. His most famous congressional achievement was the Taft-Hartley Act.

Taft, William Howard (1909-13), 27th president of the United States. Taft was an imposing figure—he stood 6 ft tall and weighed more than 300 lbs. A good-natured, self-effacing man, he had the misfortune to follow the flamboyant Theodore Roosevelt in office—and suffered in the comparison. In his own time, Taft was judged one of the weakest of U.S. presidents, yet the achievements of his administration were substantial.

Early life. Taft's father, Alphonso Taft, was secretary of war and attorney general under President Ulysses S. Grant, then minister to Austria-Hungary and Russia. William graduated from Yale University in 1878 and, in 1880, earned his degree from the Cincinnati Law School and was admitted to the Ohio bar. In 1886, he married Helen (Nellie) Herron. They had three children.

Law and politics. Taft was appointed a state superior court judge (1887), U.S. solicitor general (1890), and a federal circuit judge (1892). He loved the law, but his

Table-tennis match

William Howard Taft

27th president of the United States

Born:	Cincinnati, Ohio; Sept. 15, 1857
Term:	Mar. 1909-Mar. 1913
Vice president:	James S. Sherman (Mar. 1909-Oct. 1912; died in office)
Political party:	Republican
Spouse:	Helen (Nellie) Herron Taft
Children:	3
Died:	Washington, D.C.; Mar. 8, 1930

father's influence in the Republican Party pushed him into politics. Taft served as the first civil governor of the Philippine Islands (1901-04), then as President Theodore Roosevelt's secretary of war. He became a valued troubleshooter, helping to reorganize the building of the Panama Canal, settle the Russo-Japanese War, and avert a revolution in Cuba.

Roosevelt, who chose not to run for reelection in 1908, pushed Taft as his successor—although Taft would have preferred an appointment to the U.S. Supreme Court. Taft easily defeated his opponent, William Jennings Bryan.

President. Taft resolved to carry on "the same old plan" of the Roosevelt administration: domestic reform, the curbing of big business, and conservation of the nation's resources. Taft's administration won twice as many antitrust suits against business monopolies as Roosevelt's. Taft believed that somewhat lower tariffs would help control trusts, but could get only limited tariff reduction passed. He greatly strengthened the powers of the Interstate Commerce Commission (ICC) in regulating transportation rates. He saved the government millions of dollars by instituting strict accounting, and laid the basis for a national budget. He also broadened the Civil Service, instituted the Dept. of Labor, pushed through a bill requiring disclosure of campaign expenses in federal elections, and drafted income-tax amendments. In foreign affairs, Taft was less successful. He and his secretary of state initiated "dollar diplomacy"—a policy of using trade and commerce to enhance the nation's influence abroad. It poisoned foreign relations, particularly with Latin America, for more than a generation. Taft's tariff and conservation policies put him at odds with Republican progressives. Theodore Roosevelt ran against him in 1912, splitting the Republican vote and allowing Democrat Woodrow Wilson to win the presidency.

Later life. Taft became a professor of constitutional law at Yale in 1913 and was co-chair of the National War Labor Board (1914-18). In 1921, President Warren G. Harding appointed him chief justice of the U.S. Supreme Court—the job Taft had always wanted. Taft served in that role until Feb. 1930, when ill health forced him to retire.

Taft-Hartley Act, the Labor-Management Relations Act of 1947, sponsored by Senator Robert A. Taft and Representative Fred Hartley. It was passed over the veto of President Harry S Truman and amended the Wagner Act. The act defined "unfair labor practices" and banned boycotts, sympathy strikes, and strikes in interunion disputes. A federal arbitration service was set up, and states were empowered to prohibit union shop agreements. A further controversial provision was presidential power to seek an 80-day injunction against a strike in cases of "national emergency."

Taglioni, Marie (1804-84), Swedish-born Italian ballerina. Trained from an early age by her father, Filippo Taglioni, she gained worldwide renown for her dancing in *La Sylphide* (1832) at the Paris Opéra. Taglioni was noted for her innovative style and was considered a major figure during ballet's romantic era, which lasted until the mid-1840s.
See also: Ballet.

Tagore, Sir Rabindranath (1861-1941), Bengali Indian writer, painter, musician, and mystic who founded what is now Visva-Bharati University to blend the best in Indian and Western culture. His literary work includes many songs, poems, plays, novels, short stories, and essays. He received the 1913 Nobel Prize for literature.

Tagus River, or Tajo River, river that runs 626 mi (1,007 km) from central eastern Spain west through Portugal to the Atlantic Ocean. The mouth of the river opens into the harbor at Lisbon, Portugal.

Tahiti, largest (400 sq mi/1,036 sq km) of the Society Islands in the South Pacific, the center of French Polynesia. The island is mountainous and rich in tropical vegetation. The people are mostly Polynesians, with some French and Chinese. Papeete is the capital. Tahiti, claimed for France by Bougainville in 1768, was visited by James Cook and William Bligh. Its beauty inspired the painter Paul Gauguin.

Tahiti

Taine, Hippolyte Adolphe (1828-93), French writer and intellectual concerned with aesthetics—the nature of art and artistic judgments. He approached his study of art as a scientist. Taine concluded that the artist's art was determined by influences such as the artist's heredity, environment, and aesthetic training. His belief in determinism supported the French philosophical movement of Positivism—a school of thought developed in 19th and 20th century Europe. It also influenced the artistic movement of naturalism in France, of which the 19th-century novels of Emile Zola are examples. Taine's books include *History of English Literature* (1863), *Philosophy of Art* (1865-69), and *Origins of Contemporary France* (1875-93). He was a professor at the École de Beaux-Arts in Paris (1864-83).
See also: Naturalism; Positivism.

Taipei (pop. 2,696,100), capital and largest city of Taiwan, lying to the north on the Tanshui River. A major industrial city, with steel plants, oil refineries and glass factories, Taipei is also the cultural and educational center of Taiwan. Founded in the early 1700s, it became capital of the Nationalist Chinese government in 1949.

Taiwan, formerly Formosa, island in the western Pacific Ocean, formally Republic of China. Together with the Pescadores, Quemoy, and Matsu groups, it is the official seat of the Republic of China government, which claims to be the legal ruler of all China. Taiwan is separated from mainland China by the Formosa Strait, about 90 mi (145 km) wide. The capital is Taipei.

Land and climate. With an area of 13,900 sq mi (36,000 sq km) the island of Taiwan is forested and mountainous, with extensive plains in the west. Its highest point is Yü Shan (13,113 ft/3,997 m). The monsoonal climate is tropical in the south, subtropical in the north, and makes possible 2 rice harvests a year.

People. Most of the people of Taiwan are Chinese and come largely from the Fukien province on the mainland. The major religions are Buddhism and Taoism. The official language is Chinese.

Economy. Once predominantly agricultural, Taiwan's economy has become heavily industrialized. Major industries include steel, aluminum, textiles, metals, machinery, and chemicals, but the mainstay of its manufacturing and exports is in electronics. Irrigation is vital for growing rice, sweet potatoes, soybeans, sugar, tea, fruits, and cotton; sugar and tea are exported. There are rich fisheries and the island has much timber. Its natural resources include coral, natural gas, some oil, gold, copper, and silver.

History. Named Formosa by the Portuguese, who arrived in 1590, the island came under the control of the Dutch in 1624. It subsequently fell to a Ming general in 1662 and then to the Manchus in 1683. Taiwan was ceded to Japan in 1895 as part of the settlement of the First Sino-Japanese War and remained in Japanese hands until the end of World War II. In 1949, it became a refuge and stronghold for Chiang Kai-shek's Nationalists after they were driven from the mainland by Communist forces under Mao Zedong. The Nationalists turned the island of Formosa into the Republic of China, and declared it the legitimate government of China under the presidency of Chiang Kai-shek. Between 1951 and 1965, Taiwan was supported with the help of substantial subsidies from the U.S. government. But eventually the United States decided to recognize Mao's government, and in 1971 Taiwan was expelled from the UN and its seat given to the government of the People's Republic of China. From 1954 to 1980, Taiwan was protected by the United States under the terms of the Mutual Defense Treaty of 1954, but in the years following U.S. recognition of the mainland government,

Taiwan

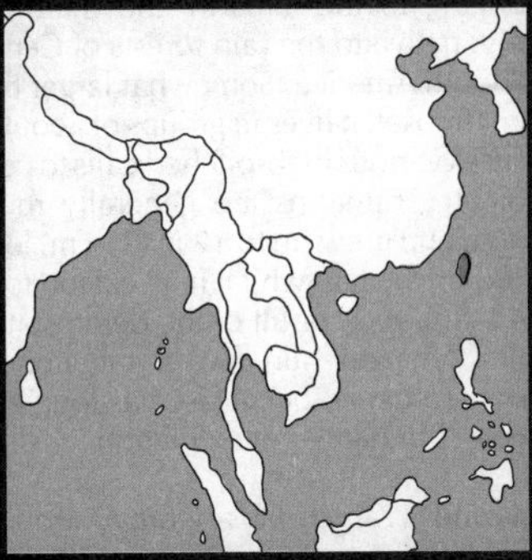

General information

Capital:	Taipei
Area:	13,900 sq mi (36,000 sq km)
Population:	20,800,000
Official language:	Mandarin Chinese
Monetary unit:	1 New Taiwan dollar = 100 cents
Main cities:	Taipei, Kaohsiung, Taichung

Government

Form:	republic
Independent:	1950
Head of state:	President (elected every 6 years)
Head of government:	Prime minister
Legislature:	one legislative house (National Assembly) and Legislative Yuan
Executive:	President and Executive Yuan
Judiciary:	highest court is the Judicial Yuan
Political division:	16 counties, 7 municipalities

National economy

Gross national product:	U.S. $210,722,000,000
Per capita income:	U.S. $10,202
Agriculture:	sugar cane, vegetables, rice, citrus fruit, sweet potatoes, corn, pineapples, bananas
Livestock:	chickens, ducks, pigs
Fisheries:	1,236,000 metric tons
Mining:	coal, marble, limestone
Industries:	cement, steel ingots, paperboard, synthetic fiber, fertilizers, textiles, plastics, electronics
Main exports:	plastic articles, calculating machines, thermionic articles, valves, tubes, photocells, transistors, etc., synthetic fabrics,
Transportation:	2,983 mi (4,800 km) of railroads, 12,394 mi (19,945 km, paved 85%) of roads, 2 international airports
Trading partners:	U.S., Japan, Hong Kong

People

Urban:	75%
Ethnic composition:	Chinese 98%, aborigine 1%
Birth rate:	17 per 1,000 population
Death rate:	5 per 1,000 population
Infant mortality:	5 per 1,000 live births
Life expectancy:	male 71 years, female 76.5 years

Taiwan found itself increasingly isolated. The death of Chiang Kai-shek in 1975 dealt a further blow to Taiwan's political aspirations. Chiang was succeeded by his son, Chiang Ching-kuo, who died in 1988. From 1949 to 1987, Taiwan was under martial law, but with its suspension there arose opposition parties on the island in addition to the dominant Kuomintang of the Nationalists and their supporters. In 1990 Chiang Ching-kuo's successor, Lee Teng-hui, a native Taiwanese, was elected without opposition to a 6-year term.

Tajikistan, also Tadzhikistan, independent country in central Asia, bordering China, Afghanistan, Kirghizstan, and Uzbekistan. Its capital is Dushanbe. Most of its inhabitants are Tajiks, a people related to Sunni Muslim Iranians. Farming and mining are the region's chief industries. Cotton, barley, rice, and wheat are important crops. Major products from mining include fluorite, lead, uranium, zinc, and tungsten. Formerly one of the 15 constituent republics of the USSR, Tajikistan became independent in 1991.
See also: Union of Soviet Socialist Republics.

Taj Mahal, mausoleum built by the Mogul emperor Shah Jahan for his wife Mumtaz-i-Mahal at Agra in North India. Faced in white marble, the central domed tomb stands on a square block with a minaret at each corner, surrounded by water gardens, gateways, and walks. It took some 20,000 workers over 20 years to complete (1630-50).
See also: Shah Jahan.

Takeshita, Noboru (1924-), Japanese politician, prime minister 1987-89. He was elected to parliament in 1858, subsequently serving as chief cabinet secretary (1971-72, 1974), construction minister (1976), and finance minister (1979-80, 1982-86). He became head of the Liberal-Democratic Party in 1987. In a major upheaval, Takeshita and many other high officials of the Japanese government were implicated in a stocktrading scandal, and he resigned as prime minister in 1989.
See also: Japan.

Talbotype, or calotype, early photographic process invented by the English scientist W.H. Fox Talbot in the 1830s. Talbot first made the photographic paper light-sensitive by treating it with sodium chloride and silver nitrate solution. When he then placed the treated paper in a camera and exposed the paper to light, a negative image formed on it, which he then

Tajikistan

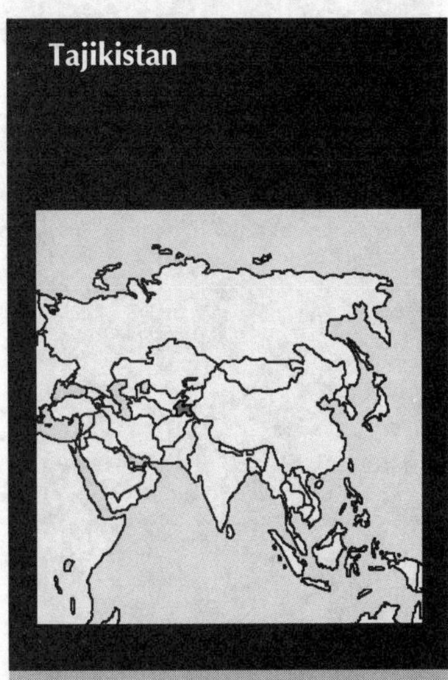

Capital:	Dushanbe
Area:	55,251 sq mi (143,100 sq km)
Population:	5,634,000
Government:	republic
Independent:	1991
GNP:	U.S. $2,723,000,000
Per capita:	U.S. $480

developed in gallo-nitrate of silver to produce the talbotype. Though this method did not produce pictures as clear as the daguerreotype, any number of prints could be made from the talbotype negative.
See also: Photography.

Talc [$Mg_3Si_4O_{10}(OH)_2$], hydrous magnesium silicate mineral occurring in metamorphic rocks, chiefly in the United States, USSR, France, and Japan. It has a layer structure resembling that of mica, and is extremely soft. Talc is translucent but not transparent. It is used in ceramics, roof insulation, cosmetics, as an insecticide carrier, and as a filler in paints, paper, and rubber. Impure, massive talc is called soapstone.

Tallahassee (pop. 233,598), capital of Florida, located in the panhandle just south of the Georgia border. Tallahassee became the territorial capital in 1824 and the state capital when statehood was granted in 1845. The state government and 3 colleges are among the city's largest employers. The area, visited by the Spanish explorer Hernando DeSoto in 1539, was named for the Native American word for "old town." During the Civil War (1861-65) it was the only Confederate capital not to fall into Union hands. Today it is a seafood-processing, printing, and wood-product manufacturing center.
See also: Florida.

Tallchief, Maria (1925-), U.S. ballet dancer, of Native American and European ancestry. With her debut as a dancer for the Ballet Russe de Monte Carlo (1942), she became the first U.S. dancer of prominence in Europe—then the ballet center of the world. As a dancer with the New York City Ballet (1947-65), she performed the female lead in many of the ballets choreographed by George Balanchine. The ballet *Firebird* (1949) became her signature role. The Chicago City Ballet was established by her (1980), and for the first 7 years she was its artistic director.
See also: Ballet.

Tamerlane during a hunting expedition

Talleyrand (Charles Maurice de Talleyrand-Périgord; 1754-1838), French politician. A member of the clergy, he represented them in the French parliament (States-General) in 1789 and became a moderate leader and influential spokesperson for the French Revolution in its early years. A fall from favor with the new leadership in 1792 led to a 4-year exile. Appointed an adviser by Napoleon I, Talleyrand rose to the rank of foreign minister until mutual mistrust between the 2 men led to his resignation in 1807. After Napoleon's first exile (1814), Talleyrand helped restore the Bourbon monarchy and was a key negotiator at the Congress of Vienna (1815). In 1830 he helped lead the overthrow of the last Bourbon king, Charles X, and became the ambassador to England under King Louis Philippe. He helped steer the negotiations that resulted in the independence of Belgium (1830).
See also: France.

Tallinn (pop. 458,000), capital city of Estonia, on the Gulf of Finland, an arm of the Baltic Sea. Tallinn, which dates from the Middle Ages, was a member of the Hanseatic League from the late 1200s to the mid-1300s. Many churches, castles, and buildings survive from that time. From 1346 to 1710, control of Tallinn and the surrounding area passed from the Livonian Knights to Sweden and then Russia. In 1919 it became the capital of an independent Estonian republic, which was overrun in 1940 by the Soviet Union, along with the rest of Estonia and the other 2 Baltic republics, Latvia and Lithuania. Tallinn today is the capital of the Estonian Soviet Socialist Republic and is an important seaport and shipbuilding center.
See also: Estonia.

Tallowtree, any of several trees of the family Euphorbiaceae producing a waxy substance that can be used to produce tallow for candles. The Chinese tallowtree (*Sapium sebiferum*) has also been planted as a shade tree in the southeastern United States.

Talmud (Hebrew, "teaching"), compilation of Jewish oral law and rabbinical teachings begun in the 5th century A.D. It has two parts: the Mishnah (oral law), written between A.D. 70 and 200, and the Gemara (commentary on the Mishnah), written between 200 and 500. In addition to commentary and debates on the details of Jewish law, the Gemara contains many traditional legends and stories. The Talmud consists of 63 sections (*tractates*), which are divided into 6 orders. Each order deals with a different subject, such as civil and criminal law and cleanliness. The study of the Talmud has been the core of Jewish education for over 1,000 years. After the Bible, the Talmud stands as the second most important and influential written work of the Jewish religion.

Tamarack *see:* Larch.

Tamarin, one of 14 monkey species belonging to the tamarin and marmoset family, native to the rain forests of Central and South America. Somewhat larger than the marmoset, it lives in groups of about 40 and uses various high-pitched calls to communicate. Tamarins are generally multicolored and grow up to 12 in (31 cm) long, excluding the tail, which may extend to 17 in (44 cm). As a result of the deforestation of the Amazon rain forest, the lion tamarin—so-called because of its long gold mane—is in danger of extinction.

Tamarind (*Tamarindus indica*), tropical tree belonging to the pea family. The fruits are made into preserves and laxative drinks. The wild tamarind of Florida is the only native representative of related trees from the U.S. tropics.

Tambourine, percussion instrument comprising a skin stretched across a hoop fitted with bells, or "jingles," that rattle as it is tapped or shaken. Originating in the Middle East, it is used in folk and popular music and in some orchestral scores.

Tamerlane, or Timur the Lame (c.1336-1405), Mongol conqueror, descendant of Genghis Khan. Tamerlane succeeded to the throne of Turkestan in 1369 and from his capital at Samarkand set out on a series of conquests, including Afghanistan, Persia, and southern portions of what is now the USSR. In 1398 he invaded India and sacked Delhi, where it is believed he and his troops massacred 80,000 people. Three years later he moved against Syria and captured Baghdad. The following year (1402) his armies defeated the Ottoman Turks and captured their sultan, Beyazid I. After capturing Damascus and defeating the Egyptian army, he plotted to overrun China but died before he could implement his plans. His empire, centered in Turkestan, crumbled after his death.
See also: Mongol Empire.

Tamil, Dravidian language spoken by some 40 million people, principally in southeast India and northeast Sri Lanka. It is the main language of Tamil Nadu (formerly Madras) state. Tamil has its own script and a rich ancient literature.

Tammany, Society of, or the Columbian Order, New York City Democratic political organization. Founded in 1789 as a "fraternity of patriots" dedicated to preserving the nation's independence, it evolved into the most powerful political machine in New York City's Democratic party. Tammany Hall, as it came to be known, drew much

of its strength from newly arrived immigrants willing to pledge their votes for services and political favors. Scandals clouded much of its existence, the most infamous being the corruption of William M. "Boss" Tweed, convicted of defrauding the city of millions of dollars in 1871. Tammany Hall regained much of the power it lost after Tweed's conviction, but in the early 1930s state investigations weakened it, and the organization suffered defeats in the 1932 elections. It had a brief resurgence following World War II but, by the 1970s, ceased to exist as a political force.
See also: Bucktails; Nast, Thomas; Tweed, William Marcy "Boss".

Tampa (pop. 271,523), city in Florida, at the head of Tampa Bay, an arm of the Gulf of Mexico. Inhabited by Native American tribes when Spanish explorer Hernando De Soto landed there in 1539, the area did not see European settlement until 1823. In the late 19th century Tampa grew as a manufacturing center and as home to a prosperous cigar industry; it became a tourist center following the arrival of the railroad. Today Tampa is a major seaport, industrial hub, and retirement center, and houses 2 universities and numerous cultural and tourist attractions, including Busch Gardens and the Florida State Fair.
See also: Florida.

Tanaka, Kakuei (1918-), Japanese prime minister (1972-74). He built up a construction business, headed the Liberal Democratic Party from 1965, and held cabinet posts from 1968. He was forced to resign in 1974 because financial misconduct and was convicted in 1983 of having accepted bribes from Lockheed Corporation.
See also: Japan.

Taney, Roger Brooke (1777-1864), chief justice of the U.S. Supreme Court (1836-64) whose decision in the Dred Scott case (1857) helped bring on the Civil War. As President Andrew Jackson's secretary of the treasury (1833-35), he crushed the Second Bank of the United States. As chief justice, he steered a middle course on States' Rights and continued Chief Justice John Marshall's liberal interpretation of the Constitution.
See also: Dred Scott case; Supreme Court of the United States.

Tang dynasty, rulers of China from A.D. 618 to 907. The Tang period is regarded as the golden age of Chinese civilization by many historians. During this period, Tang rulers centralized the government and unified the country. The capital city, Chang'an (now Xian), served as a worldwide center for scholarship and the arts. During this time, the Chinese invented block printing and produced the first block-printed book (A.D. 868). Emperor Tang Taizong, who ruled for 22 years, led the rise of the Tang dynasty. He conquered foreign lands and opened trade routes that brought the country great wealth and prosperity. Empress Wu followed Emperor Taizong's rule with great skill and came to be known as the second greatest Chinese leader. An 80-year war with the Tibetans in northwestern China, coupled with years of internal fighting, weakened the Tang dynasty, and it came to an end in 907.
See also: China.

Statuette of a polo player on horseback, from the Tang dynasty

Tangelo, citrus fruit produced by crossing a tangerine with a grapefruit. The name *tangelo* is a combination of *tangerine* and *pomelo* (another word for grapefruit). Like the tangerine, the tangelo has a thin peel and sweet pulp. The Minneola and the Orlando are North American varieties, and the Ugli is a Jamaican strain common to the West Indies.

Tangerine, fruit in the rue family, related to the orange. In shape, color, and taste the tangerine resembles the orange, but is smaller and easier to peel. Although originated in Southeast Asia, tangerines are grown in the southeast and western United States and Brazil, Italy and Spain. Clementine and Dancy are two popular varieties of tangerine.

Tangier (pop. 266,300), seaport and residential and commercial city of Morocco, facing the Strait of Gibraltar. Tangier is a major center of tourism and shipping and is considered Morocco's main passenger-vessel port. It is heavily populated by Arabs and Berbers. The city has its origins in the settlements built by the Phoenicians and Romans in ancient times. It was under Arab control in the 700s. From the 1400s to the late 1600s, when the sultan of Morocco acquired the power to guide Tangier, it was held, at different times, by France, Portugal, and England. In 1912 the city again fell under the control of Spain and France, and in 1923 it was put under international control. In 1956 Tangier became fully independent of France and Spain, gave up its international status, and came under the full control of Morocco.
See also: Morocco.

Tank, combat vehicle, armed with guns or missiles, and self-propelled on caterpillar treads; the chief modern conventional ground assault weapon. Tanks were first built in 1915 by Britain and used from 1916 against Germany in World War I. These early tanks were very slow, and development between the wars greatly improved speed and firepower. The Spanish Civil War and World War II showed the effectiveness of concentrated tank attacks. Amphibious and airborne tanks were developed. Heavy tanks proved cumbersome and were generally abandoned in favor of the more maneuverable (though more vulnerable) light and medium tanks. Improved models are now used where heavy guns are needed. Light tanks (less than 25 tons/23 metric tons) are used mainly for infantry support.
See also: Army.

Tanker, ship designed to carry liquid cargo in bulk, notably crude oil, gasoline, or natural gas. The first tanker (1886), a 300-ft (90-m) vessel, carried 3,000 tons (272 metric tons) of oil. Some tankers today hold 100 times as much: a 483,939-ton (439,029-metric ton) vessel (the *Globtik London*, 1975) has been built in Japan. Ships this size greatly reduce per-ton transport costs but cannot enter many ports; some large tankers transfer their cargo to smaller tankers offshore. In gross tonnage tankers account for over a third of all merchant shipping.

Tannhäuser (c.1200-70), German poet and legendary character who wrote poems that were sung. A number of dance songs, love songs, and lyric songs of his still exist. He supposedly participated in the Crusades (1228-29) and traveled widely throughout Europe. The composer Richard Wagner based his opera *Tannhäuser* on the poet's life. As legend has it, Tannhäuser lived in a mountain with the goddess Venus for 7 years. During a visit to Rome, Tannhäuser asked the pope to forgive his sins, but the pope responded that just as his staff could never blossom, never could Tannhäuser's sins be forgiven. Dejected, Tannhäuser returned to Venus. Three days later the pope's staff blossomed into flowers.

Tannic acid, or tannin ($C_{76}H_{52}O_{46}$), organic substance extracted from the bark of certain trees (e.g., oak, hemlock, and chestnut). In a process known as tanning, tannin is added to animal hides to resist decomposition. Tannin is also used to manufacture inks and is used as a fixative (mordant)

U.S. Army combat tank

for dyes. It can also be used as a medicine for treating burns and as an astringent. Most of the tannin used in the United States today is obtained from the quebracho trees of Argentina and Paraguay.

Tantalum, chemical element, symbol Ta; for physical constants see Periodic Table. Tantalum was discovered by A.G. Ekeberg in 1802. It occurs in the mineral microlite. It is obtained commercially from columbite-tantalite, a mixed oxide with niobium and iron and manganese. The element is prepared by the high-temperature reaction of tantalum (V) oxide with tantalum carbide in a vacuum. Tantalum is a gray, hard, malleable, ductile metal. It is high-melting and resistant to chemical attack. A tantalum carbide-graphite composite is one of the hardest materials ever made. Tantalum and its compounds are used in laboratory apparatus, surgical prostheses, special glasses, electrolytic capacitors, nuclear reactors, aircraft, missiles, and catalysts.

Tantalus, in Greek mythology, king of Lydia and son of Zeus and the nymph Pluto. Zeus banished him to Hades because of his cruel sacrifice of his son Pelops. Tantalus was punished by being forced to stand chin-deep in water under hanging fruit, each of which receded just beyond his reach whenever he wanted to eat or drink. The word *tantalize* is derived from his name.
See also: Mythology.

Zanzibar, Tanzania

Tanzania, independent republic in East Africa consisting of the mainland, formerly Tanganyika, and the islands of Zanzibar and Pemba. The mainland of Tanzania has Mozambique, Malawi, and Zambia to its south; Zaïre, Burundi, and Rwanda to the west; Uganda and Kenya on the north; and the Indian Ocean to the east. Zanzibar and Pemba are separated from the mainland by the 22-mi- (35-km)-wide Zanzibar Channel. The capital is Dodoma.
Land and climate. Mainland Tanzania covers an area of 362,821 sq mi (939,706 sq km), including 20,650 sq mi (53,484 sq km) of inland water. The islands cover an area of 1,021 sq mi (2,644 sq km). A coastal belt, fringed by sand beaches, coral reefs, and mangrove swamps, leads inland to plains and plateaus 2,000 to 4,000 ft (1,219 km) above sea level with vast expanses of grasslands and open woodlands, as well as

Tanzania

General information	
Capital:	Dar es Salaam; Dodoma designated
Area:	364,881 sq mi (945,040 sq km)
Population:	23,729,000
Official languages:	English, Swahili
Monetary unit:	1 Tanzanian shilling = 100 cents
Main cities:	Dar es Salaam, Mwanza, Zanzibar, Tanga
Government	
Form:	federal republic
Independent:	1961: Tanganyika; 1963: Zanzibar; 1964: combined as United Republic of Tanzania
Head of state:	President (elected every 5 years)
Head of government:	Prime minister (1 of 2 Vice-Presidents)
Legislature:	one legislative house (National Assembly)
Executive:	President and Cabinet
Judiciary:	highest court is the Court of Appeal
Political division:	25 regions
National economy	
Gross national product:	U.S. $3,780,000,000
Per capita income:	U.S. $160
Agriculture:	coffee, tea, bananas, sugar cane, sisal, cotton, tobacco
Livestock:	cattle, goats, sheep
Fisheries:	314,000 metric tons
Mining:	gold, diamonds, salt
Industries:	fertilizer, food processing, clothing
Main exports:	coffee beans, raw cotton, tobacco, tea, cloves
Transportation:	1,603 mi (2,580 km) of railroads, 51,025 mi (82,114 km) of roads, 3 international airports
Trading partners:	United Kingdom, Germany, Japan
People	
Urban:	18%
Ethnic composition:	Nyamwezi and Sukuma 21%, Swahili 9%, Hehet and Bena 7%, Makonde 6%, Haya 6%
Birth rate:	50.5 per 1,000 population
Death rate:	14 per 1,000 population
Infant mortality:	106 per 1,000 live births
Life expectancy:	male 49 years, female 54.5 years

isolated hills and hill ranges. In this area is the Serengeti Plain, site of one of several national parks. To the north is Lake Victoria, and above the plateaus rise the Usambara, Pare, Kilimanjaro, and Meru mountains. Mt. Kilimanjaro (19,340 ft/5,895 m) is Africa's highest peak. The uplands extend to the south where they meet Lake Nyasa and the Ufipa Highlands. To the west lies Lake Tanganyika. Zanzibar and Pemba are coral islands and fertile. Their climate, like that of the coastal belt, is tropical. The inland climate is hot and dry for most of the year, and most humid in the highlands and along the western shore of Lake Victoria.

People. The vast majority of the people are black Africans, but there are also people of Asian, Arab, and European descent. Christianity and Islam, in roughly equal proportions, account for some three-quarters of the population. The rest of the people adhere to traditional beliefs. The official languages are Swahili and English.

Economy. Tanzania's economy is chiefly agricultural. Coffee and cotton are primary exports, but other important exports include cloves from Zanzibar, pyrethrum, sisal, tobacco, and tea. Manufacturing is limited principally to processing agricultural products and industry is dominated by mining. Tanzania is a leading producer of diamonds.

History. Olduvai Gorge in North Tanzania is the site of the fossil remains of the earliest hominid. The remains have been dated to some 1.7 million years ago. In historical times, the coast and Zanzibar came under Arab control some time in the 8th century A.D. The Portuguese established a presence in the 16th and 17th centuries and introduced the slave trade, but were driven out by natives in 1698. Arabs from Oman established control of Zanzibar and set up on the mainland as well, conducting a flourishing trade in slaves and ivory throughout the 18th and 19th centuries. The Germans established a mainland protectorate in 1891, but, after World War I, the regions passed to Britain through a League of Nations mandate. Tanganyika gained its independence in 1961 and was joined with Zanzibar in 1964. The capital was transferred from Dar-es-Salaam to Dodoma in 1975. Tanzania was directly involved in the overthrow of the regime of Idi Amin Dada in neighboring Uganda in 1978-79. During the 1980s, Tanzania's economic difficulties, brought about by trade deficits and debt, resulted in a decreased emphasis on a government-controlled economy. In 1985 Nyerere left office and was replaced by his recommended successor, Ali Hassan Mwinyi.

Tanzanite, zoisite mineral and semiprecious gem unearthed in Tanzania (1967). This stone is popular for use in jewelry because its polished surfaces, created through a cutting process, reflect beautiful color. When a heat process is applied to tanzanite, it reflects a blue color. Before the heat treatment, tanzanite shines purple, blue, or yellow, depending upon the way light hits it.

Taoism, or Daoism (from Chinese *tao* or *dao*, "the way"), philosophy that originated in China (c.300 B.C.); also, a religion that had its beginnings c.100 B.C. Taoism as a philosophy is chiefly derived from 2 books: the *Lao-tzu* (renamed *Tao Te Ching, The Classic of the Way and the Virtue*), traditionally ascribed to Lao-tzu, and the *Chuang-tzu*. The *Lao-tzu* is a collection of writings by several unknown authors containing ideas that are in direct opposition to the Confucian philosophy. Confucianism stresses a life guided by definite rules of conduct, whereas Taoism emphasizes simplicity and spontaneity. Tao was considered impossible to describe save in cryptic imagery. Chinese literature and art were greatly influenced by Taoism.

Taos (pop. 3,369), historically significant city in New Mexico, located at the base of the southern Rocky Mountains, 75 mi (121 km) north of Santa Fe. It was the site of an ancient Pueblo Indian village as well as a farming center for early Spanish settlers. Taos was also a Spanish and Indian trading post and the center of the Pueblo Revolt of 1680. During the 1900s, the city achieved popularity as an artists' colony. Taos is frequently visited by artists and tourists.
See also: New Mexico.

Tao Te Ching *see:* Taoism.

Tape recorder, instrument for sound recording on magnetic tape and subsequent playback. A microphone changes sound to an electric current, which is in turn changed in the recording head into magnetic flux variations. The tape, consisting of small particles of iron oxides on a thin plastic film base, is wound from the supply reel to the takeup reel by a rotating capstan that controls the speed. The tape passes in turn: the erase head, which by applying an alternating field reduces the overall magnetization to zero; the recording head, which magnetizes the particles; and the playback head. Most recorders use two, four, or even more tracks side by side on the tape. The most common form of audio tape recorder is the cassette recorder, in which the cassette (a small plastic case) is simply snapped into a recorder and is ready to be played.

Tapestry, fabric woven with colored threads to form a design and used to cover walls and furniture. Vertical threads, which make up the warp are stretched on a loom, and horizontal threads, which make up the weft, are woven over and under them and then compacted. Tapestries were known in ancient Egypt, Syria, Persia, and China. North Europe's great era of tapestrymaking began in the 1300s, notably at Arras in Flanders. It reached a peak in the Gobelin tapestries of the 1600s. Great painters who have made tapestry designs include Raphael and Rubens. The Peter Paul Bayeux tapestry is in fact embroidery.

Tapeworm, any of numerous flatworms (class *Cestoda*) that live as parasites in the intestines of humans and other animals. Some tapeworms measure less than 1 in (2.5 cm) long, while others reach 30 ft (9 m) or more. A person can be infected by a tapeworm by eating undercooked meat or fish containing tapeworm larvae. An adult tapeworm can sometimes cause diarrhea, nausea, and other ill effects in a person. Tapeworm larvae pose a more serious threat because they can develop into young worms and spread to other organs of the host body.

Tar, thick, dark, viscous liquid obtained through distillation of organic matter, primarily coal, petroleum products, and wood. Coal tar, obtained at high temperatures and condensed from vapors given off during the manufacture of coke from bituminous (soft) coal, is used for roofing and waterproofing materials, synthetic drugs, disinfectants, dyes, perfumes, and plastics. Coal gassifier tar, a source of organic chemicals, is a byproduct of the process that converts coal into a natural gas substitute. Wood tar is made from the condensed vapors created during the woodburning process; pine tar, the major derivative, is used to manufacture soap, disinfectants, and turpentine. Other types of coal- or petroleum-derived tar are used to seal road surfaces and produce asphalt paving material.
See also: Pitch.

Tarabulus *see:* Tripoli.

Tarantula, popular name, originally of the large wolf spider (*Lycosa tarantula*), but now used for various unrelated giant spiders throughout the world. All are long and hairy and eat large insects or small vertebrates. Their venom seldom has serious effects on humans.
See also: Spider.

Tarascan, Native American tribe of Mexico. The Tarascan controlled a powerful empire from the late 14th to the early 16th century. With early settlements dating to c.500 B.C., their tribal holdings bordered the Aztec Empire at the time of the Spanish arrival in the 1520s. Along with the Aztecs, they were conquered by the Spanish, but only after great resistance. Hunters, farmers, and fishermen, many of the 60,000 Tarascans surviving today, inhabitants of the state of Michoacán, follow traditional ways of life. They are skilled craftspeople, weavers, and woodcarvers. Many still speak the Tarascan language, which bears no relationship to any other known language.

Tarbell, Ida Minerva (1857-1944), U.S. author and reformer. She was one of the leading muckrakers of the late 19th and early 20th centuries, exposing corruption and unsafe or unsanitary working conditions. Her *History of the Standard Oil Company* (1904) blasted monopoly practices in major industries and helped lead to reforms in corporate practices. Other writings include biographies and an autobiography, *All in a Day's Work* (1929).
See also: Muckraker.

Tarragon

Tariff, customs duty on an export or, more commonly, an import. The aim is generally to protect home industries from foreign competition, though it may be merely to provide revenue. During the 17th and 18th centuries the European powers created tariff systems that gave their colonies preferential treatment, but Britain's tariffs, by limiting North America's trade, helped provoke the Revolutionary War. In the early 1800s the free trade movement, bolstered by the economic philosophy of laissez-faire, helped limit the spread of tariffs. However, U.S. federal tariffs imposed to aid Northern industry damaged the South and contributed to the Civil War. U.S. and European tariffs were moderate in the early 1900s but, after the Great Depression, both the United States and the United Kingdom adopted high tariffs, with a consequent decline in international trade. In 1947 the United States and 22 other nations signed the General Agreement on Tariffs and Trade (GATT), aimed at reducing trade discrimination. GATT and the Common Market have been responsible for generally lower tariffs throughout the world.
See also: Taxation.

Tarkenton, Fran (Francis Asbury Tarkenton; 1940-), U.S. football player. A quarterback known for his passing and scrambling ability, Tarkenton holds the career records for pass attempts (6,467), pass completions (3,686), touchdown passes (342), and passing yards (47,003). He played in the National Football League (NFL) for the Minnesota Vikings (1961-66, 1972-79) and New York Giants (1967-71). Tarkenton was inducted into the Pro Football Hall of Fame in 1986.

Tarkington, (Newton) Booth (1869-1946), U.S. writer noted for novels reflecting midwestern life and character, for example, *Penrod* (1914). He won Pulitzer prizes for *The Magnificent Ambersons* (1918) and *Alice Adams* (1921). Tarkington also served as an Indiana state representative (1902-03).

Taro, plant (*Colocasia esculenta*) of the arum family whose rhizomes provide a starch food for millions of people in eastern Asia and the Pacific. Taros have to be peeled to remove a poisonous acid compound, and they do not provide an adequate diet by themselves. In Hawaii taro is fermented to make poi.

Tarot, pack of 78 playing cards used mainly for fortune-telling. There are four suits (cups, pentacles, swords, and wands), each of 14 cards and a major arcana (heavily symbolic "picture cards") of 22 cards. There are various systems of interpretation.

Tarpon (*Tarpon atlanticus*), game fish that can survive in salt or fresh water. Tarpon of over 100 lb (45 kg) are often caught, and they can grow up to 840 lb (381 kg). The body bears large, silvery scales up to 2 in (5 cm) across, and the dorsal fin has a long ray protruding from the rear end. Tarpon live in warm seas from Florida to Brazil and also off West Africa. The eggs are laid in shallow water and the larvae grow up in stagnant lagoons and marshes.

Tarragon (*Artemisia dracunculus*), plant whose aromatic leaves provide a pleasant characteristic flavor to various meats, vegetables, sauces, and stuffings.

Tarsus (pop. 146,500), city in central Turkey on the Mediterranean coast. Archeological studies date the city to Neolithic times. The Assyrians built here in the early 8th century B.C. The Romans once took control of Tarsus (67 B.C.). The city claims to be the place of the first meeting of Antony and Cleopatra (41 B.C.) and the birthplace of St. Paul. Cotton and agriculture are products of the modern city and were the foundation of the ancient economy of Tarsus.

Tartan, checkered fabric of Scotland's native dress. Each clan is ascribed a particular tartan, though often in more than one variety: the hunting tartans are usually somber blues and greens, while reds generally predominate the dress tartans. The authenticity of ascriptions to clans is questioned, and some tartans are of comparatively recent origin.

Tartaric acid ($C_4H_6O_6$), naturally derived plant acid, used extensively for making jellies, jams, and carbonated drinks. There are tartaric salts—cream of tartar, Rochelle salt, and tartar emetic. The first is used in baking powder, hard candies, and for cleaning brass. Rochelle salt is used to silver mirrors and electronically cover metals with gold or silver; tartar emetic (antimony potassium tartrate) is used in medicines. Tartaric acids and their salts are solids, colorless, and water soluble.

Tartars, or **Tatars**, people of Turkish descent who live in the USSR, Bulgaria, Romania, China, and Turkey. Originally a nomadic people, they turned to agriculture in the 16th century and have since figured prominently in the history of the Russian people. Many Tarters now live in the Tatar Autonomous Soviet Socialist Republic; most are Sunni Muslims.

Tartu (German: *Dorpat*), city in eastern Estonia, USSR, lying on the Emajogi River. It was a fortified settlement in the 5th century A.D. From the 11th century it was at different times held by the Russians, Swedes, and Poles; Russian control was established in 1704. Its university, founded 1632, is now an important center for the study of botany and agriculture.
See also: Estonia.

Tashkent (pop. 1,986,000), capital of the Uzbek Republic and fourth-largest city in USSR, located in Chirchik Valley west of the Chatkal Mountains. One of the oldest cities in Asia, it was an important trading center for Arab, Muslim, and Mongol empires. Major products are textiles and agricultural machinery. Rebuilt after a devastating earthquake in 1966, it is an important cultural center.
See also: Union of Soviet Socialist Republics.

Tasmania, smallest Australian state (26,383 sq mi/68,332 sq km). The 150-mi (253.5-km) Bass Strait separates Tasmania from the southeastern mainland. It includes King, Flinders, and Macquarie islands, as well as the main island. Tasmania's forests contain two unique marsupials, the Tasmanian devil and the thylacine. Chief cities are Hobart (the capital), Launceston, Burnie, and Devonport. Important industries are livestock (dairying, wool), horticulture, lumber and newsprint, mining, and mineral processing (zinc, copper, and lead).
See also: Australia.

Former convicts' quarters in Port Arthur, Tasmania

Tasmanian devil (*Sarcophilus harrisi*), mammal of the marsupial family, native to the Australian island of Tasmania. This nocturnal, 4-legged animal measures 3-4 ft (0.9-1.2 m) long. Like other marsupials, the female gives birth to underdeveloped babies who grow to maturity in pouches on the mother's belly. Noted for their fierceness, they have been known to attack livestock and poultry, and have been hunted for that reason.

Tasman Sea, arm of the South Pacific Ocean, between Australia and Tasmania (east) and New Zealand (west). Named for the Dutch explorer Abel Tasman, the Tasman Sea is about 900,000 sq mi (2.3 million sq km). An underwater cable on its floor provides a key communication link between Australia and New Zealand.

TASS (Telegraph Agency of the Soviet Union), state monopoly news agency of the USSR. Founded in 1925, it is managed by the Propaganda Department of the Communist Party's Central Committee.

Taste, special sense concerned with the differentiation of basic modalities of food or other substances in the mouth; receptors are distributed over the surface of the tongue and are able to distinguish sweet (generally at tip), sour, salt (along the sides), bitter (mainly at the back), and possibly water as primary tastes. Much of what is colloquially termed taste is actually smell perception of odors.

Tate, (John Orley) Allen (1899-1979), U.S. writer, critic, and teacher. He edited the literary magazine *Fugitive* (1922-25) and later *Sewanee Review* (1944-46) and advocated the "New Criticism," with its stress on a work's intrinsic qualities. His own work includes several collections of poetry and essays, biographies, and a novel.

Tatum, Art (1910-56), U.S. jazz pianist. With the physical handicap of only slight vision, he became a master of piano technique and various forms of jazz. As an accompanist to jazz singers and as a member of his own jazz trio, he performed mainly in New York City nightclubs, beginning in 1932.
See also: Jazz.

Tatum, Edward Lawrie (1909-75), U.S. biochemist awarded the 1958 Nobel Prize for physiology or medicine, with G.W. Beadle and J. Lederberg, for work with Beadle showing that individual genes control production of particular enzymes (1937-40) and for work with Lederberg showing genetic recombination in the bacterium *Escherichia coli* (1947).
See also: Biochemistry; Genetics.

Taube, Henry (1916-), Canadian-born U.S. chemist who won the 1983 Nobel Prize for chemistry for his work in the mechanisms of electron transfer reactions, especially in metal complexes.
See also: Chemistry.

Taussig, Helen Brooke (1898-1986), U.S. pediatrician and cardiologist. With Alfred Blalock she developed the "blue baby operation" (1945), which increases blood circulation to the lungs and stimulates research on the surgical correction of congenital heart defects.
See also: Blue baby.

Tautog *see:* Blackfish.

Tawney, Richard Henry (1880-1962), English historian and social theorist. His best-known book, *Religion and the Rise of Capitalism* (1926), connects the hard work and individualism of the Protestants of North Europe in the 16th and 17th centuries with the growth of capitalism there.

Taxation, raising of revenue to pay for government expenditure. Broadly speaking, a tax can be described as direct or indirect: income tax is paid directly to the government, but sales taxes are collected indirectly through government charges on goods or services. A tax is progressive or regressive; income tax is usually progressive (its rate rises as the taxable sum increases); sales taxes tend to be regressive (their burden decreases as the taxpayer's income increases).

Taxation without representation *see:* Revolutionary War in America.

Taxco (pop. 27,100), town in Mexico, 70, mi (113 km) southwest of Mexico City. A replica of an early Spanish town, it attracts many tourists and people in the arts. Founded (1529) by Hernando Cortés, it has been an important silvermining town since pre-Columbian times; it is still the center of Mexico's silver industry. Other minerals, such as copper, lead, and zinc are also mined there. Taxco also serves as a commercial center for the region, which is largely agricultural.

Taxidermy, stuffing and mounting animal skins to make lifelike replicas. Taxidermy is now practiced mainly in large museums, though it originated in the production of hunting trophies; in modern taxidermy, rather than stuffing, the animal's skin is streched over an artificial skeleton.

Taxonomy *see:* Classification.

Taylor, Elizabeth (1932-), English-born U.S. film actress. Beginning her career as a child actress (*Lassie Come Home*, 1943; *National Velvet*, 1944), she went on to become a major Hollywood star in such films as *Little Women* (1949) and *A Place in the Sun* (1951). She received Academy Awards for her roles in *Butterfield 8* (1960) and *Who's Afraid of Virginia Woolf?* (1966); in the latter she co-starred with her then-husband, British actor Richard Burton.

Taylor, George (1716-81), Irish-born member of the Continental Congress and signer of the Declaration of Independence. Taylor emigrated to Pennsylvania in 1736, serving there in the provincial assembly (1764-69, 1775) the militia (1775), and the First Supreme Executive Council (1777).

Taylor, John (1753-1824), U.S. political theorist and agricultural reformer, known as John Taylor of Caroline. An early exponent of States Rights, he was elected three times as U.S. senator from Virginia (1792, 1803, 1822).

Taylor, Lawrence (1959-), U.S. football player. A linebacker known for his quickness and powerful hits, he was the National Football League (NFL) Player of the Year (1986) and the National Football Conference (NFC) defensive player of the year 3 times (1981, 82, and 86). Taylor plays for the New York Giants (1981-) and has led the team to 2 Super Bowl victories (1987, 1991).

Taylor, Maxwell Davenport (1901-87), U.S. Army general who largely organized the U.S. Army's first airborne units in World War II. He commanded the 8th Army in Korea (1953-55), headed the U.S. and UN Far East commands (1954-55), was U.S. Army chief of staff (1955-59), and served as ambassador to Vietnam (1964-65).

Taylor, Paul (1930-), U.S. modern dance choreographer. He debuted with Merce Cunningham in 1953 and danced with Martha Graham's company (1955-61) before founding the Paul Taylor Dance Company in the mid-1950s. His work includes *3 Epitaphs* (1956), *Aureole* (1962), *Esplanade* (1975), and *Last Look* (1985).

Elizabeth Taylor

Taylor, Zachary (1784-1850), war hero and 12th president of the United States. Taylor was a bold and resourceful general in the Mexican War and one of the most popular presidents of the period. His brief term in office—he died 16 months into his term—has been all but forgotten. However, he took a bold stand on the extension of slavery, the burning issue of his day, and—had he lived and prevailed—the Civil War might have broken out 11 years earlier than it did.

Early life. Taylor grew up on a wilderness farm. There were no schools, but his parents and tutors gave him some educa-

Zachary Taylor

12th president of the United States

Born:	Orange Co., Va.; Nov. 24, 1784
Term:	Mar. 1849-July 1850
Vice president:	Millard Fillmore
Political party:	Whig
Spouse:	Margaret Mackall Smith Taylor
Children:	6
Died:	Washington, D.C.; July 9, 1850

tion. In 1810, he married Margaret Mackall Smith. They had six children, two of whom died in infancy.

Military career. In 1808, Taylor became a 1st lieutenant in the U.S. Army. During his 40-year army career, he moved from one end of the nation to the other, and did a great deal to open the West to settlement. He fought Native Americans and the British in the Northwest Territory during the War of 1812, served in the Black Hawk Indian War (1832), and spent three years fighting the Seminole in the Florida Everglades. He commanded Army posts, built roads and forts, and—along the way—purchased land and slaves for himself in Mississippi and Louisiana. "Old Rough and Ready," as his troops affectionately called him, won a reputation for skill, daring, and fairness as a commander and fighter.

The Whig Party, which saw the war hero as a sure winner, nominated Taylor as its presidential candidate in 1848. Taylor and the Democratic candidate each took a two-sided stand on slavery; the Free-Soil Party's candidate opposed slavery in new territories. Taylor and his running mate, Millard Fillmore, won the election.

Peter Tchaikovsky

President. In Dec. 1849, Congress was faced with California's request to enter the Union as a free state. Unexpectedly, Taylor urged Congress to accept California and New Mexico as free states. This, coming from a Southerner and slave owner, outraged militant Southerners. There was talk of secession, but Taylor declared that, if there was any rebellion, he would personally lead the army to put it down. Like many older-generation Southerners, Taylor believed that the Union must be preserved, even if it meant slavery would be kept from expanding beyond its existing borders. He probably was also swayed by the anti-slavery attitudes of his Whig advisers.

Senator Henry Clay offered a set of bills—later called the Compromise of 1850—that would admit California as a free state, with no provisions against slavery in Utah and New Mexico, and would prohibit the slave trade in the District of Columbia. To appease the South, they provided a rigorous law for the return of fugitive slaves. There was a great debate in the Senate; Taylor held firm and tensions grew. Then on July 9, 1850, Taylor died suddenly of acute gastroenteritis. Had Taylor lived, his uncompromising stand might have provoked a war by Aug. However, Millard Fillmore, his successor, allowed the compromise bills to go through, postponing the conflict.

Tay-Sachs disease, inherited disorder that occurs primarily in Jewish people from eastern Europe. Children born with the disease have little or no active hexosaminidase enzyme, the lack of which causes fat to accumulate in the brain's ganglions (bundles of nerves). The consequences are mental retardation, paralysis, blindness, and cherry-red spots on the retina of the eye. The disorder is usually fatal before the child reaches the age of four.

TB *see:* Tuberculosis.

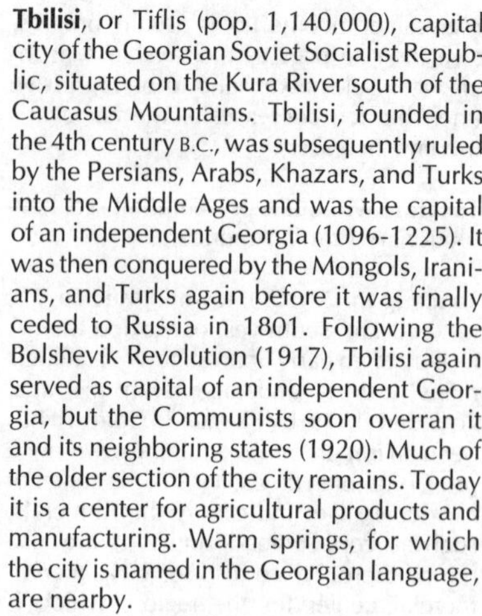

Tbilisi, or Tiflis (pop. 1,140,000), capital city of the Georgian Soviet Socialist Republic, situated on the Kura River south of the Caucasus Mountains. Tbilisi, founded in the 4th century B.C., was subsequently ruled by the Persians, Arabs, Khazars, and Turks into the Middle Ages and was the capital of an independent Georgia (1096-1225). It was then conquered by the Mongols, Iranians, and Turks again before it was finally ceded to Russia in 1801. Following the Bolshevik Revolution (1917), Tbilisi again served as capital of an independent Georgia, but the Communists soon overran it and its neighboring states (1920). Much of the older section of the city remains. Today it is a center for agricultural products and manufacturing. Warm springs, for which the city is named in the Georgian language, are nearby.

See also: Union of Soviet Socialist Republics.

Tchaikovsky, Peter Ilich (1840-93), Russian composer. He studied with Anton Rubinstein, became professor at Moscow Conservatory, and gave concerts of his own music in Europe and the United States. His gift for melody and brilliant orchestration, plus the drama, excitement, and emotional intensity of his music, place him among the most popular composers. Orchestral works include *Violin Concerto in D Major* (1878) and *Symphony No. 6*, or the the "Pathétique" (1893). His ballets, *Swan Lake* (1876), *Sleeping Beauty* (1889), and *The Nutcracker* (1892), have become classics. His operas include *Eugene Onégin* (1879) and *The Queen of Spades* (1890).

Tea (*Camillia sinensis*), evergreen shrub, related to the camellia; also, the leaves of the plant and the beverage made from the leaves. The drink is prepared by pouring boiling water over dry processed tea leaves. Types of tea drunk include green, black (which is fermented), and oolong (which is partly fermented). Tea has been drunk in China since early times, but it was not until the early 1600s that the Dutch introduced it into Europe. Although expensive, it soon became fashionable. In the United Kingdom and the British colonies, the East India Company enjoyed a monopoly of the China tea trade until 1833; it was the attempt of the British government to levy a tax on tea imports into the American colonies that led to the Boston Tea Party of 1773. Today, the chief producers are India and Sri Lanka (Ceylon). Tea contains the stimulant caffeine. The term *tea* is also used to describe many other local drinks produced from the leaves of a vast array of plants.

Teach, Edward *see:* Blackbeard.

Teaching, range of activities used to demonstrate skills, impart information, and guide individuals in learning. Informal teaching, which takes place in any setting and without any requisite structure, may come from parents, employers, colleagues, or other persons. Formal teaching generally occurs in a structured setting and is administered by professional teachers. In the United States since the beginning of the 19th century, teaching procedures for elementary and secondary schools have been increasingly formalized by teacher-training programs and state certification (varying from state to state). Training in education includes general coursework in the subject areas the teacher will specialize in, special courses in educational theory and practice, and practice or student teaching in real classrooms. Both training programs and certification are particular to the grade level and the subject area. Uncertified support personnel are known as teacher aides or paraprofessionals. State certification requirements vary widely, and many states do not accept certificates issued in other states. Many school systems now require evaluations of professional teachers to maintain their level of competence. Teachers are generally hired by the local school board, often under regulation of the master agreement between the board and the teachers' union. In some states teachers are then protected by tenure agreements and cannot easily be fired. The National Education Association (NEA) and the American Federation of Teachers (AFT) are the main professional organizations that deal with working conditions and salaries.

Teak (*Tectona grandis*), deciduous tree whose wood is among the most valuable. Teaks grow in tropical climates from India to Malaysia. The hard, oily (thus water-resistant) wood is used for house construction, furniture, railroad ties, etc. Several other trees produce a similar hardwood also called teak.

Teal, name for various species of river ducks (genus *Anas*) related to the mallard. The blue-winged teal of North America is one of the fastest flying migratory ducks, able to travel over 3,500 mi (5,632 km) in a month. Other teal include the Cape teal of Africa and the Laysan teal, which lives only on the island of Laysan, west of Hawaii.

Teamsters Union (International Brotherhood of Teamsters, Chauffeurs, Warehousemen and Helpers of America), largest U.S. labor union, whose members are largely truckers. Formed by an amalgamation in 1903, the union grew during the presidency of Daniel Tobin (1907-52). Two of his successors, Dave Beck and J.R. Hoffa, were jailed for corruption, and in 1957 the Teamsters were expelled from the AFL-CIO.

See also: Labor movement.

Teapot Dome, scandal over government malpractice under President Warren G. Harding. The naval oil reserve at Teapot Dome, Wyo., was leased in 1922 by agreement of Secretary of the Interior Albert Fall to the Mammoth Oil Co. with no competitive bidding. A Senate investigation followed, and the lease was canceled. Fall was later convicted of receiving another bribe in a similar transaction.

Tears, watery secretions of the lacrimal glands situated over the eyes, which provide continuous lubrication and protection of cornea and sclera. A constant flow runs across the surface of the eye to the nasolacrimal duct at the inner corner, where tears drain into the nose. Excess tears produced in states of high emotion or because of conjunctival or corneal irritation overflow over the lower eyelid.

Teasel, or **teazel** (*Dipsacus fullonum*), European plant found in fields in North America. The small blue flowers grow on a conical head that remains as a prickly head after they have died. It was formerly cultivated, its dead heads used to raise the nap on cloth (fuller's teasel).

Tebaldi, Renata (1922-), Italian operatic soprano. A major rival of Greek-American soprano Maria Callas, she was known for the beauty and purity of her tone. She made her operatic debut in Italy in 1944 and her U.S. debut in 1950. Tebaldi, who performed many roles in the repertoire of Italian opera, sang frequently at the Metropolitan Opera in New York from 1955 to 1973.
See also: Opera.

Technetium, chemical element, symbol Tc; for physical constants see Periodic Table. Technetium was discovered by C. Perrier and E.G. Segrè in 1937. It was the first element to be produced artificially. It was produced in the Berkeley cyclotron by bombarding molybdenum with deuterons. It is present in some stars. It has not been found in any ores on earth. Technetium is prepared by reducing the sulfide with hydrogen at 1,100°C. Technetium is a silvery-gray, reactive metal. Its chemistry is said to be similar to that of rhenium. Potassium pertechnetate is a corrosion inhibitor for steel. Technetium and its compounds have limited commercial use because of its high radioactivity.

Technology, application of science to practical human ends—particularly, to increase productivity and the availability of leisure and to improve the quality of life. Although technology includes developments since ancient times, such as occurred in the metallurgy involved in tool making, the term generally refers to industrial technology of the past 200 years. In agriculture, technology has improved crop yields and reduced the need for labor with the advent of farm machinery. Technology applied to manufacturing has made available goods in large numbers at the same time that industrial labor has become less strenuous and hazardous and work hours have been reduced. Major technological innovations of the past century have included the internal combustion engine used in automobiles and the harnessing of electricity for light, heat, and power. In the 20th century radio communication and powered flight, and more recently, the computer, laser, and atomic fusion and fission have created profound changes in many aspects of life. Technology applied to the field of medicine has greatly increased life expectancy. The extremely rapid changes caused by technology have also created serious problems. Population shifts to cities result in overcrowding. Natural resources have been depleted due to the industrial use of raw materials and the population explosions made possible by technology. Segments of the labor force are suddenly unemployed due to mechanization and automation, in a phenomenon known as technological unemployment. The assembly line that has made possible efficient production has also created boring and repetitive jobs, and the resulting loss of pride in work has created quality problems in U.S. industries. Most seriously, technology has resulted in many forms of environmental pollution, including toxic industrial waste, air pollution from motor vehicles, noise pollution, and the destruction of ecosystems by the use of insecticides.

Tectonics, branch in geology that studies the earth's structural deformations, the forces involved, and the resulting forms. The most popular theory used to explain the origin of tectonic forces is the plate tectonic theory, developed in the 1960s. This theory holds that the movement of the rigid plates that line the surface of the earth's outer shell (either aigainst one other or away from one another) produces the crustal deformations in the earth. A second theory contends thet the earth originated from molten rock, which cooled as it shrunk; this shrinking in turn produced the tectonic forces. A third theory maintains that the earth began as a cold mass, and as it warmed it produced forces that fractured the crust.
See also: Volcano.

Tecumseh (1768?-1813), Shawnee chief. From their home in Ohio, Tecumseh and his brother Tenskwatawa (the Prophet) attempted to unite the Native American tribes of the upper Midwest in a confederacy, calling upon them to maintain their ancient culture and beliefs and to oppose, by force if necessary, all attempts by European-Americans to settle on tribal lands. At the Battle of Tippecanoe (Indiana) in 1811, the Prophet was defeated by a U.S. force led by Gen. William Henry Harrison, a victory that led to Harrison's election as president in 1840. Tecumseh, noted for his military prowess, joined the British army against the United States in the War of 1812 and was made a brigadier general. He was defeated and killed at the battle of the Thames River in Ontario.

Teeth, specialized hard structure used for biting and chewing food. The number of teeth varies from species to species and from age to age, but in most cases an immature set of teeth (milk teeth) is replaced during growth by a permanent set. In humans the latter consists of 32 teeth, comprising 8 incisors, 4 canines, 8 premolars or bicuspids, and 12 molars, of which the rearmost are the late-erupting wisdom teeth. Each tooth consists of a crown (the part above the gum line) and a root (the insertion into the bone of the jaw). The outer surface of the crown is covered by a thin layer of enamel, the hardest animal tissue. This overlies the dentine, a substance similar to bone, and in the center of each tooth is the pulp, which contains blood vessels and nerves. The incisors are developed for biting off food with a scissor action. The canines are for maintaining a hold on an object. The molars and premolars are adapted for chewing and macerating (separating) food. The most common disease of the teeth is dental decay, ot caries, in which acid produced by bacteria dissolves the tooth enamel, causing a cavity.

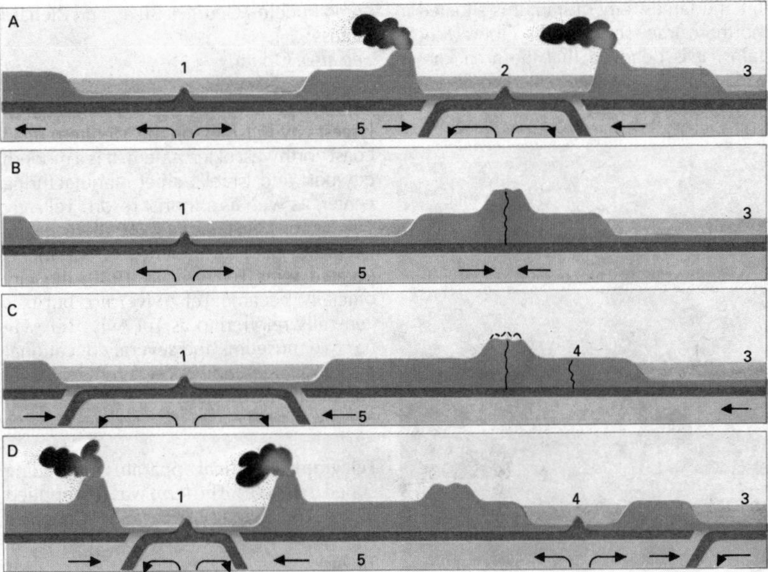

The theory of tectonics and the rise and fall of oceans. A. shows Ocean 1 growing larger as a mid-ocean ridge expands and produces more sea floor. Ocean 2 is disappearing as its sea floor is forced down at the trenches by the continents moving together, while Ocean 3 is beginning its period of expansion. In B, Ocean 1 has reached its peak of development, Ocean 2 has vanished as the continents have come together, and Ocean 3 is still expanding. C shows Oceans 1 and 3 beginning to grow smaller and a crack forming at 4. In D, Oceans 1 and 3 are declining further while the newly formed Ocean 4 begins to expand.

Tegu, or **Teju**, bold, quick and muscular South American lizard (genus *Tupinambis*). They weigh about 5 lb (2.3 kg) and grow up to 4 ft (1.2 m) in length. They have small square scales on their black-colored bodies with yellow horizontal bands over their backs.

Tegucigalpa (pop. 571,400), capital and largest city of Honduras, situated on the Choluteca River and on the slopes of Mt. Picacho in southern-central Honduras. Founded by the Spaniards in the late 1570s as a gold- and silver-mining center, in 1880 Tegucigalpa replaced Comayagua as the national capital. The 2 cities, on opposite banks of the Choluteca, merged in 1938. Today Tegucigalpa is a major manufacturing and agricultural hub, as well as the governmental center. The National University of Honduras is on the outskirts of the city.
See also: Honduras.

Teheran's main highway

Teheran, or **Tehran** (pop. 5,734,000), capital and largest city of Iran. It is situated in northern Iran, south of the Elburz Mountains. It is believed that the area known today as Teheran was settled some 3,000 years ago; it began as a small town, but by the 1200s it had grown significantly. It received prominence after the Mogol destruction of nearby Ragy (1220) and became capital of Iran in 1788. Teheran is Iran's chief center of commerce and industry, employing a majority of the Iranian working population. Under Reza Shah Pahleve the city was modernized and is considered today to be one of the most modern cities in the Middle East. Teheran has two major universities.
See also: Iran.

Tel Aviv

Teheran Conference, inter-Allied conference of World War II, held in Teheran (Nov.-Dec. 1943) and attended by Soviet premier Joseph Stalin, U.S. president Franklin D. Roosevelt, and British prime minister Winston Churchill. Important items were the coordination of landings in France with a Soviet offensive against Germany from the east, future Soviet entry into the war against Japan, agreement on Iran's future independence, and international cooperation after the war.
See also: World War II.

Teilhard de Chardin, Pierre (1881-1955), French Jesuit, philosopher, and paleontologist. In China (1923-46) he studied Peking Man (*Homo erectus*). *The Phenomenon of Man* (1938-40, published 1955) attempted to reconcile Christianity and science with a theory of human evolution toward final spiritual unity. His superiors held his views to be unorthodox and warned against them; fame came to him and his ideas only posthumously.
See also: Paleontology.

Teju *see:* Tegu.

Te Kanawa, Dame Kiri (1944-), New Zealand operatic soprano. Her portrayal of the Countess in Mozart's *The Marriage of Figaro* won her international acclaim in 1971. She made her Metropolitan Opera debut in 1974 as Desdemona in Giuseppe Verdi's *Othello*. Widely recorded, she is known for her roles in works by Wolfgang Amadeus Mozart, Giuseppe Verdi, Giacomo Puccini, Georges Bizet, and Richard Strauss.
See also: Opera.

Tel Aviv-Jaffa (pop. 1,350,000), second-largest city in Israel, on the Mediterranean coast northwest of Jerusalem. It is a modern city-port and Israel's chief manufacturing center, as well as a tourist resort. Tel Aviv was Israel's first capital (1948-49). Jaffa (Hebrew: *Yafo*), an ancient port, was incorporated with Tel Aviv in 1950; the city officially became Tel Aviv-Yafo, but it is generally referred to as Tel Aviv. Tel Aviv has two museums and several educational institutions, including Tel Aviv University and Bar Ilan University.
See also: Israel.

Telegraph, electrical apparatus for sending coded messages. The term was first applied in the 18th century to Claude Chappe's semaphore. Experiments began on electric telegraphs after the discovery (1819) that a magnetic needle was deflected by a current in a nearby wire. In 1837 W.F. Cooke and Charles Wheatstone patented a system using six wires and five pointers that moved in pairs to indicate letters in a diamond-shaped array. It was used on English railroads. In the same year Samuel Morse, in partnership with Alfred Vail and helped by Joseph Henry, patented a telegraph system using Morse code in the United States. The first intercity line was inaugurated in 1884. In 1858 Wheatstone invented a high-speed automatic Morse telegraph, using punched paper tape in transmission; the telex system, using teletypewriters, is now most popular. In 1872 Jean-Maurice-Emil Baudot invented a multiplexing system for sharing the time on each transmission line between several operators. Telegraph signals are now transmitted not only by wires and land lines, but also by submarine cables and radio.
See also: Morse, Samuel Finley Breese; Wheatstone, Sir Charles.

Telegraph plant (*Desmodium motorium*), plant of the pea family, native to tropical Asia. It is sometimes cultivated for its unusual behavior in response to touch—the leaves droop abruptly, like the arms of a railroad semaphore signal (hence its name). The plant grows about 4 ft (1.2 m) high and bears small purple flowers.

Telemann, Georg Philipp (1681-1767), German composer. He was a prolific composer who worked well with musical forms popular in his day. He wrote operas, including *Der geduldige Socrates* (1721) and *Pimpinone* (1725); orchestral music, including *Musique de Table* (1733); concertos; and cantatas. His work was influenced by Italian opera as well as by earlier baroque composers, principally Johann Sebastian Bach. He served as musical director for the 5 churches of Hamburg (1721) and the Hamburg Opera (1722-38).

Teleology (from Greek *telos*, "end"), study of an action, event, or thing with reference to it's purpose or end. Plato and Aristotle argued that the purpose, perfection, and good of a thing, which Aristotle called its "final cause," was the ultimate explanation of the thing. The teleological view of nature has declined since the rise of science. The teleological argument, or argument "from design," argues that the order and perfection of nature requires the existence of a divine Creator who effected that order.

Telephone, apparatus for transmission and reproduction of sound by means of frequency electric waves. The telephone was invented in 1876 by Alexander Graham Bell. Bell's transmitter worked by the voltage induced in a coil by a piece of iron attached to a vibrating diaphragm; the same apparatus, working in reverse, was used as a receiver. The carbon microphone (invented by Thomas Edison, 1878) provided a more sensitive transmitter. In 1878 the first commercial exchange was opened

in New Haven, Conn.; local telephone networks spread rapidly in the United States and elsewhere. Repeaters, or amplifiers, made long-distance telephone calls possible. Today, microwave radio links, communications satellites, and optical fibers are used. Telephone subscribers are connected to a local exchange, these in turn being linked by trunk lines connecting a hierarchy of switching centers so that alternative routes may be used. When a call is dialed, each digit is coded as pulses or pairs of tones that work electromechanical or electronic switches.
See also: Bell, Alexander Graham.

Telescope, instrument used to detect or examine distant objects. It consists of a series of lenses and mirrors capable of producing a magnified image and of collecting more light than the unaided eye.
The refracting telescope (refractor) essentially consists of a tube with a lens system at each end. Light from a distant object first strikes the objective lens, which produces an inverted image at its focal point. In the terrestrial telescope the second lens system, the eyepiece, produces a magnified, erect image of the focal image, but in instruments for astronomical use, where the image is usually recorded photographically, the image is not reinverted, thus reducing light losses.
The reflecting telescope (reflector) uses a concave mirror to gather and focus the incoming light. The various types of instruments use different combinations of mirrors and lenses to view the focal image with fewer optical aberrations.
The size of a telescope is measured in terms of the diameter of its objective. Up to about 12 in (30 cm) diameter, the resolving power (the ability to distinguish finely separated points) increases with size, but for larger objectives the only gain is in light gathering. A 200-in (508-cm) telescope can thus detect much fainter sources but resolve no better than a 12-in (30-cm) instrument. Because mirrors can be supported more easily than large lenses, the largest astronomical telescopes are all reflectors.
See also: Galileo Galilei.

Television, communication of moving pictures between distant points over wire or by means of electromagnetic waves. In television broadcasting, centrally prepared programs are transmitted to millions of individual receivers. Closed-circuit transmissions, which rely upon signals carried over wire rather than electromagnetic waves broadcast at large, are most often used for industrial and educational applications.
The moving picture on a television screen originates with a television camera, which forms an optical image of the scene to be transmitted and then breaks the image down into electrical signals. The signals may be amplified and transmitted directly over a cable, or they can be converted into electromagnetic waves. As electromagnetic waves, they are transmitted by antennas, like radio waves, picked up by receiving antennas, and then conveyed to a television set equipped to reconstitute the electromagnetic waves into an optical image on the screen of a cathode-ray tube.
In the early days of television technology, most cameras used the iconoscope, but the iconoscope technology has since been replaced by orthicon or vidiscope. In order for an image to be transmitted and received electronically, it must be broken down into discrete but organized electrical signals and then reassembled or reconstructed by the receiver.
The image formed by the optical lens system of a television camera is scanned as a sequence of 525 horizonal lines. As an image is scanned, variations in the light intensity along each line are converted into a fluctuating electrical signal, the brightness signal, which gives the image its gradations from light to darkness. Each scan is then repeated 30 times a second to create the illusion that the image is moving and without noticeable flicker. When reassembled on the television screen, the image appears whole and in fluid motion because of the persistence-of-vision effect of the human eye.
In color television, the image is not only resolved into brightness, but into hue and saturation as well. The light entering the camera is analyzed into red, green, and blue components, the 3 primary colors. Both hue and saturation are converted to electronic information, which is added to the brightness signal and transmitted. In the color receiver, this information is recovered and used to control 3 electron beams fired within the television set. The beams are projected through a shadow mask, a screen containing some 200,000 minute, precisely positioned holes, and they excite the mosaic of red, green, and blue phosphor dots, which reproduce the color image on the television screen.
The possibility of television was conceived in the early days of the electric telegraph, but the realization had to await several key developments. First was the discovery of the photoconductive properties of selenium, followed by the development of the cathode-ray tube in 1897 and the electron tube in 1904. Crucial to both systems and at the heart of television technology was scanning. The first practical television system, demonstrated in London in 1926 by J. L. Baird, used a mechanical scanning method devised by Paul Nipkow in 1884. Electronic scanning dates from 1923 when Vladimir Zworykin filed a patent for his iconoscope camera tube. Television broadcasting began in London in 1936 using a 405-line standard. In the United States, public broadcasting began in 1941, and regular color broadcasting in 1954. U.S. television broadcasts are made in the VHF (Channels 2-13) and UHF (Channels 14-83) regions of the RF spectrum.
Recent technology, both in Japan and the United States, has led to the development of High Definition TV with greatly increased scanning capacities making possible images that are much cleaner and much larger.
See also: Sarnoff, David; Videodisc; Videotape recorder

Overhead telephone and electric wires crisscrossing Broadway, New York (1889). The cables were later installed underground.

The original apparatus used by John Logie Baird in 1925 to complete the first television transmission

Tell, William, legendary 14th-century Swiss hero. Ordered by the Austrian bailiff Gessler to bow to a hat on a pole as a symbol of Austrian supremacy, he refused and was forced to shoot an apple from his son's head, using a cross-bow; in this almost impossible task he succeeded. Later he killed Gessler, starting a revolt that overthrew the bailiffs. The story was the basis of a drama by Friedrich von Schiller and an opera by Giacomo Rossini in the early 19th century.

Teller, Edward (1908-), Hungarian-born U.S. nuclear physicist who worked with Enrico Fermi on nuclear fission at the start of the Manhattan Project, but is best known for his fundamental work on, and advocacy of, the hydrogen bomb. He also helped create the Strategic Defense Initiative (SDI) program in the 1980s.
See also: Manhattan Project; Nuclear weapon.

Shirley Temple

Tellurium, chemical element, symbol Te; for physical constants see Periodic Table. Tellurium was discovered by Franz von Reichenstein in 1782. It occurs in nature as metallic tellurides. It is obtained commercially from the anode mud obtained in the electrolytic refining of copper. Tellurium is a silvery-white, brittle, reactive metalloid. It can be amorphous or crystalline and is a *p*-type semiconductor. Tellurium and its compounds are used in alloys with copper, steel, and lead, blasting caps, ceramics, and thermoelectric devices. Tellurium and its compounds are probably toxic.

Telstar, U.S. artificial satellite, launched July 10, 1962. The first to relay television signals across the Atlantic Ocean. Telstar weighed 170 lb (77 kg). Broadcasts ended (Feb. 1963) after Van Allen belt radiation damaged some of the 1,000 transistors.

Temperature, degree of hotness or coldness, as measured quantitatively by thermometers. The various scales used are arbitrary: the Fahrenheit scale was originally based on the values 0°F for an equal ice-salt mixture, 32°F for the freezing point of water, and 96°F for normal human body temperature. There are certain primary calibration points corresponding to the boiling, freezing, or melting points of particular substances, whose values are fixed by convention. The thermodynamic, or absolute, temperature scale, is not arbitrary; starting at absolute zero, at which there is no kinetic energy, and graduated in kelvins, it is defined with respect to an ideal reversible heat engine working on a Carnot cycle between two temperatures, T_1 and T_2. If Q_1 is the heat received at the higher temperature T_1, and Q_2, the heat lost at the lower temperature T_2, then T_1/T_2 is equal to Q_1/Q_2. Absolute temperature is independent of a body's mass or nature; it is thus only indirectly related to the heat content of the body. Heat always flows from a higher temperature to a lower. On the molecular scale, temperature may be defined in terms of the statistical distribution of the kinetic energy of the molecules.

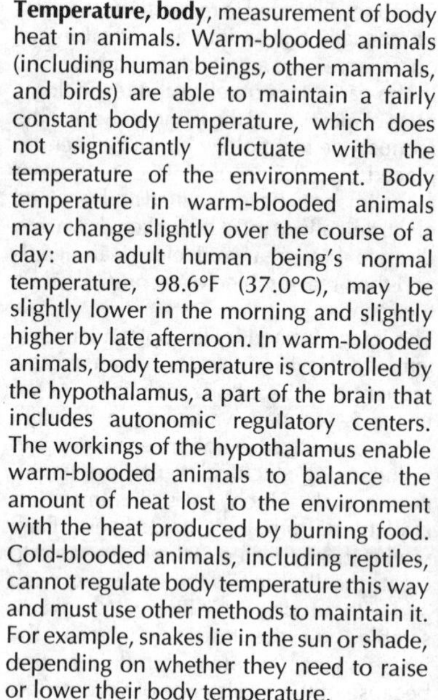

Temperature, body, measurement of body heat in animals. Warm-blooded animals (including human beings, other mammals, and birds) are able to maintain a fairly constant body temperature, which does not significantly fluctuate with the temperature of the environment. Body temperature in warm-blooded animals may change slightly over the course of a day: an adult human being's normal temperature, 98.6°F (37.0°C), may be slightly lower in the morning and slightly higher by late afternoon. In warm-blooded animals, body temperature is controlled by the hypothalamus, a part of the brain that includes autonomic regulatory centers. The workings of the hypothalamus enable warm-blooded animals to balance the amount of heat lost to the environment with the heat produced by burning food. Cold-blooded animals, including reptiles, cannot regulate body temperature this way and must use other methods to maintain it. For example, snakes lie in the sun or shade, depending on whether they need to raise or lower their body temperature.

Templars, Knights *see:* Knights Templars.

Temple, building or place dedicated to the worship of a deity. Temples have been common to most religions; they date back to c.2000 B.C. in Egypt. In Eastern Asia, temples (pagodas) are towerlike structures built with many stories, each story a symbolic representation of a different level in the Buddhist religion. Worship in temples usually involves traditional ceremonies and at times may even contain sacrifices. The first of the three successive temples built by Solomon in ancient Jerusalem became the central shrine where sacrifice could be legally offered. This First Temple, destroyed in the Babylonian invasion 586 B.C., is considered the most important temple in Western history.

Temple, Shirley (1928-), U.S. child film star, later a politician. She made her movie debut at 3 and became phenomenally popular through such films as *Little Miss Marker* (1934) and *The Little Colonel* (1935). She retired from films in 1949. After working on television in the 1950s, Shirley Temple Black (her married name) took up Republican politics. She became a U.S. delegate to the United Nations (1969), ambassador to Ghana (1975), and U.S. chief of protocol (1976).

Tenant farming, system by which agricultural land holders, known as landlords, rent land to farmers, known as tenants, to produce crops. Landlords may either collect an agreed-upon payment for rental of the farm land and buildings or they may share other production costs and investments, as well as the harvested crop, with the farmer. This method of farming has been especially successful in the British Isles and the United States.

Ten Commandments, or the *Decalogue*, moral laws delivered by God to Moses on Mt. Sinai, as recorded in the Bible (Ex. 20:2-17; Deut. 5:6-21). They provide the foundation for Jewish, Christian, and Muslim teaching.
See also: Bible.

Tendon, fibrous structure at the ends of most muscles that transmits the force of contraction to the point of action (usually a bone). Tendons facilitate mechanical advantage and allow bulky power muscles to be situated away from small bones concerned with fine movements, as in forearm muscles acting on the hands.
See also: Muscle.

Teng Hsiao-p'ing *see:* Deng Xiaoping.

Tennessee

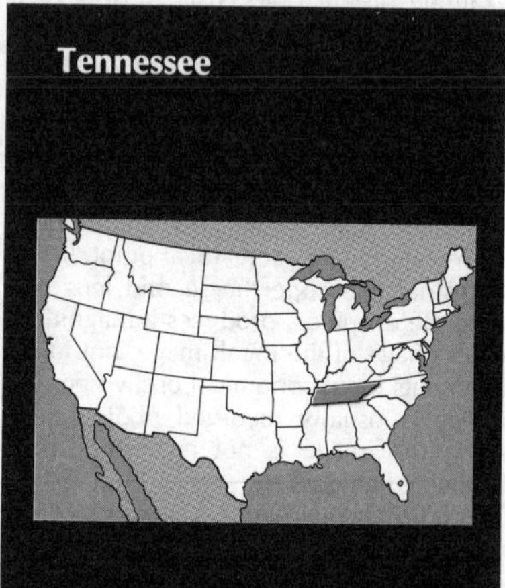

Capital:	Nashville
Statehood:	June 1, 1796 (16th state)
Familiar name:	Volunteer State
Area:	42,114 sq mi (109,152 km); ranks 34th
Population:	4,896,641 (1990); ranks 17th
Elevation:	Highest—6,643 ft (2,025 m), Clingmans Dome; Lowest—182 ft (55 m), along the Mississippi River
Motto:	Agriculture and Commerce
Flower:	Iris
Bird:	Mockingbird
Tree:	Tulip poplar
Songs:	"The Tennessee Waltz" and "Rocky Top"

Tennessee, state in the south-central United States; bordered by Kentucky and Virginia to the north, North Carolina to the east, Georgia, Alabama, and Mississippi to the south, and the Mississippi River (with Arkansas and Missouri on the other side) to the west.

Land and climate. Tennessee has seven main land regions. The Blue Ridge region, a narrow strip along the state's eastern border, is a heavily forested, mountainous area. To its west is the Appalachian Ridge and Valley Region, a fertile farming area of minor ridges and wide valleys. The next westward region, the Appalachian (or Cumberland) Plateau, has flat-topped peaks, rocky cliffs, and narrow valleys. From there, the land drops into a high-plain region called the Highland Rim. In the center of the Highland Rim lies a region of

Memphis, Tennessee

fertile farmland and plain called the Nashville Basin. The westernmost region, the Gulf Coastal Plain, stretches from the Tennessee River to the Mississippi River. Its terrain ranges from rolling hills to a low, flat, narrow area called the Mississippi Alluvial Plain. Tennessee is drained by three major river systems: the Cumberland, Tennessee, and Mississippi. Most of the larger lakes were formed by dams built on the Tennessee and Cumberland rivers. Forests cover about half of the state. Tennessee has a humid, temperate climate. Principal cities are Memphis and Nashville.

Economy. Manufacturing leads Tennesee's economy, followed by wholesale and retail trade and other service industries. Chief manufactured goods are chemicals, processed foods, nonelectrical machinery, electric and electronic equipment, apparel, fabricated metal products, transportation equipment, and rubber and plastic products. Agriculture and mining are less important to Tennessee's economy. Chief crops are soybeans, tobacco, cotton, corn, and wheat. Chief livestock products are beef and dairy cattle and hogs. Chief mining products are coal, marble, limestone, and zinc.

Government. Tennessee's present constitution was adopted in 1870. The governor serves a 4-year term. The state's legislature, called the General Assembly, consists of 33 senators serving 4-year terms and 99 house members serving 2-year terms. In the U.S. Congress, Tennessee is represented by 32 senators and 9 representatives.

History. About 1,000 years ago, an ancient Native American tribe known as the Mound Builders lived in the area. When the first Europeans, Spanish explorers, arrived in 1540, it was populated by the Cherokee, Chickasaw, Shawnee, and other tribes. The area, claimed by France in 1682, was ceded to Britain in 1763. European settlers began building permanent settlements; in 1772 the Watauga Association was established to govern the area. Some of the area, considered part of North Carolina, broke away to form the independent state of Franklin (1784-8). In 1796, Tennessee became the 16th state. Bitterly divided over slavery, Tennessee was the last state to join the Confederacy (June 8, 1861) and the first readmitted to the Union (July 24, 1866). More Civil War battles were fought in Tennessee than in any other state except Virginia. In the first half of the 1900s, industry developed rapidly, aided by the 1933 establishment of the Tennessee Valley Authority (TVA). A plant built in the 1940s at Oak Ridge became an important center for atomic-energy research during World War II. Today, Tennessee seeks new industries to boost its flagging economy.

Tennessee River, principal tributary of the Ohio River. Formed by the junction of Holston and French Broad rivers near Knoxville, Tenn., it flows southwest into Alabama, then northwest and north across Tennessee and into Kentucky. The Tennessee is 652 mi (1,049 km) in length, and it drains some 40,000 sq mi (103,600 sq km). The river's many dams and power facilities are under the control of the Tennessee Valley Authority (TVA).

Tennessee Valley Authority (TVA), U.S. federal agency responsible for developing the water and other resources of the Tennessee River Valley, established (1933) as one of the early measures of President Franklin D. Roosevelt's New Deal. The TVA has 26 major dams on the Tennessee River and its tributaries. The dams and reservoirs have made it possible to eliminate major flooding. Locks make the Tennessee navigable throughout, and TVA hydroelectric and steam plans provide most of the region's electricity. TVA projects have also involved conservation, agriculture, and forestry.
See also: New Deal.

Tennis, racket game played on a rectangular court by two or four players. The court, divided by painted lines into sections (78 ft-23.8 m long and 27-31.5 ft-8.2-9.6 m wide) is bisected by a net 3 1/2 ft (107 cm) high. The object is to hit the hollow ball of cloth-covered rubber, about 2 1/2 in (6.4 cm) in diameter and 2 oz (57 g) in weight, over the net into the opposite court such that the opposing player is unable to return it. The racket has a metal or laminated wood frame, with gut or nylon strings forming an oval "head"; it is about 27 in (69 cm) long and weighs 12 oz (340-454 g). Tennis originated in 15th-century France as indoor court tennis and took its present form, lawn tennis, in 1870. It was first played in the United States in 1874. In 1877 England held the first Wimbledon Championship. Dwight Davis donated the Davis Cup in 1900. The International Lawn Tennis Federation regulates rules and play in over 80 countries.

Tennyson, Alfred, Lord (1809-92), English poet. His *Poems* (1842) established him as a major poet. His philosophic elegy *In Memoriam* (1850) became the favorite of Queen Victoria, who appointed him poet laureate. *Idylls of the King* (1842-85) is an epic based on the legends of King Arthur. Tennyson's mastery of sound and rhythm is perhaps best seen in haunting lyrics like "The Lotus-Eaters" and "The Lady of Shalott," which appear in *Poems* (1832).

Tenochtitlán, capital of the Aztecs, now in Mexico City. Founded c. 1325 on an island in Lake Texcoco, connected to the mainland by causeways, it was a rich city of brick houses, palaces, canals, aqueducts, and a great square of temple-topped pyramids. It was destroyed by Hernán Cortés in 1521.
See also: Aztecs; Cortés, Hernando.

Tenpins *see:* Bowling.

Tenskwatawa *see:* Shawnee Prophet.

Tent caterpillar, larval stage of moths (genus *Malacosoma*) in the Lasiocampidae family. Striped, colorful, and hairy, the tent caterpillar is so-called because most of its species spin communal, tentlike webs in the forks of trees. Notorious for damaging trees in which they live, these caterpillars are capable of killing a small tree by eating all of its leaves. The female moth lays 150-350 eggs during the summer that hatch the following spring. Common to the southeastern and central United States, these caterpillars feed on oaks and other shade trees, as well as on conifers and fruit trees.

Terbium, chemical element, symbol Tb; for physical constants see Periodic Table. Terbium was discovered by C.G. Mosander in 1843. It is found in cerite, and gadolinite and is obtained commercially from monazite. The metal is prepared by reducing the anhydrous fluoride with calcium. Terbium is silvery-white, soft, malleable, ductile metal. Ion-exchange and solvent extraction techniques have led to much easier isolation of the so-called rare-earth elements. Terbium and its compounds are finding use in laser materials, solid-state devices, color TV phosphors, and fuel cells.

Terence (195?-159? B.C.), playwright of Roman comedies, written in Latin. His 6 plays, based on earlier Greek comedies, still exist: *The Woman of Andros, The Self-Tormentor, The Eunuch, Phormio, The Mother-in-Law,* and *The Brothers.* These plays display his wit and his realistic understanding of human nature. He was brought from his native Carthage as a slave to Rome, and a Roman senator secured his education.

Teresa, Mother (1910-), Roman Catholic nun, Albanian parents, who works as a missionary in Calcutta, India. For her work with the poor of India, which began in 1950, she was awarded the Nobel Peace Prize (1979). The religious order she joined (1928) sent her to India, where she at first worked as a teacher. Her convent later permitted her to work among the poor people of Calcutta (1948), and she became an Indian citizen. She has received global recognition for her work, including the Pope John XXII peace prize (1971) and the Jawaharlal Nehru award for international understanding (1972).

Mother Teresa

Teresa, or **Theresa, Saint** (1515-82), also known as Theresa of Ávila, Spanish nun and Doctor of the Church. She worked toward reforming the Carmelite order, which she believed was lacking in self-denial and austerity, and in 1562, with approval from the pope, established her own convent. She was a leading figure in the Catholic Reformation. Her writings rank among the greatest in mystical literature. St. Teresa was considered a miracle worker and was canonized in 1622. Her feast day is Oct. 15.

Tereshkova, Valentina Vladimifouna (1937-), Soviet cosmonaut, the first woman to orbit the earth. Simultaneously with a fellow cosmonaut, Very F. Bykovsky, she circled the earth 45 times in her spacecraft *Vostok VI* (June 16-19, 1963). Her orbits, which she controlled manually, took less than 1 1/2 hours each.

Terman, Lewis Madison (1877-1956), U.S. psychologist. The popular term *IQ* (intelligence quotient) is a result of his development of an English-language version of the French Binet-Simon intelligence tests (1916, revised in 1937 and 1960). Terman's studies concluded that gifted children with high intelligence experienced healthy and stable development from childhood to adulthood. The findings were discussed in his book *Genetic Studies of Genius* (1925-59). He was a professor at Stanford University (1921-42).
See also: Intelligence quotient.

Termite, or white ant, primitive insect (order Isoptera) closely related to the cockroach, found in all warm regions. Termites have a complicated social system and live in well-regulated communities, with different castes taking distinct roles. They build large nests of soil mixed with saliva, in which the colony of king, queen, workers, soldiers, and juveniles live. Soldiers and workers are sterile individuals, their development arrested at an early stage. Termites feed on wood and vegetation, digesting the food with the aid of symbiotic protozoa or bacteria in the gut.

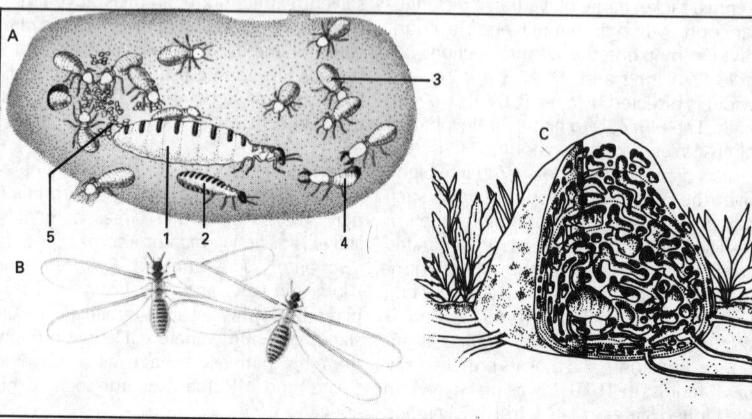

A: Cross-section of a termite colony showing different castes:
1. Queen (reproductive female)
2. King (reproductive male)
3. Worker
4. Soldier with enlarged head and mandibles
5. Eggs
B: Winged reproductive males and females, which are produced and leave the colonies to swarm and mate once a year
C: Termite mound

Tern, or sea swallow, slender, graceful seabird related to, but smaller than, the gull. Terns have a bounding, butterfly-like flight and feed on small fish that they catch by diving from the air. They are found in all seas from the Arctic to the Antarctic and also on some lakes and marshes. They nest on the ground in large, noisy colonies. The Arctic tern migrates from the Arctic to the fringes of the Antarctic.

Terra cotta (Italian, "baked earth"), any fired earthenware product, especially one made from coarse, porous clay, red-brown in color and unglazed. Being cheap, hard, and durable, it has been used from ancient times for building and roofing, and for molded architectural ornament and statuettes. Its use for sculpture and plaques was revived in the Renaissance and in the 18th century.

Terrapin, turtle (family Testudinidae) of fresh or brackish water, with diamond-shaped plates on its shell. It grows to 8 in (20 cm) and is found from Massachusetts to Mexico. At one time a cheap food for slaves, it became a luxury dish as *Terrapin à la Maryland.* The name is sometimes given to all brackish and freshwater turtles.

Terrell, Mary Church (1863-1954), U.S. activist in the movement for equal rights for African Americans. The daughter of a wealthy ex-slave, she graduated from Oberlin College (1884) before settling in Washington, D.C. She became one of the first 2 women and the first African American on the city's school board (1895), and helped found the National Association of Colored Women (1896). Throughout her life she continued to act as an adviser and advocate on racial issues and helped end the city's racial discrimination in public facilities in 1953. Much of her life is detailed in her autobiography, *A Colored Woman in a White World* (1940).

Terrier, class of dogs. Most of the 24 kinds of terrier were originally bred in England. They were developed specifically to hunt or flush out from the ground rats and burrowing animals. Terrier breeds include the fox terrier, the schnauzer, and the Scottish terrier.

Territoriality, behavioral drive causing animals to set up distinct territories defended against other members of the same species (conspecifics) for the purposes of establishing a breeding site, home range, or feeding area. It is an important factor in the spacing out of animal populations. Territoriality is shown by creatures of all kinds: birds, mammals, fish, and insects. A territory may be held by individuals, pairs, or even family groups.

Territorial waters, in international law, the belt of sea adjacent to a country and under its territorial jurisdiction. Important for control of shipping, seabeds, and fisheries, such limits used to extend 3 mi (4.8 km), and more recently 12 mi (19.3 km), from low-water mark. A 200-mi (322-km) limit has been accepted by some countries.
See also: High seas.

Territory, in politics, area under a government's control, but with limited self-government. Territories have lower status than the states of the mother country. All but 19 U.S. states were first territories; Alaska and Hawaii were the last incorporated territories (with full Constitutional rights) to gain statehood. U.S. territories include the Virgin Islands, Guam, and American Samoa. Federated States of Micronesia, formerly a UN Trust Territory administered by the United States, became a self-governing territory in association with the United States in 1981.

Terrorism, actual or threatened violence for political ends. The level of terrorism increased markedly in the 1970s as antigovernment groups throughout the world turned to violent acts such as bombing, hijacking, kidnapping, and murder. Terrorism attracted increased international attention through the stepped up activities of Palestinians and their allies, who gave up hope of defeating Israel by conventional military tactics after the rout of the Arab nations in the 1967 war. The more active terrorist groups of the period included the Provisional wing of the Irish Republican Army, the Japanese Red Army (3 of whose members killed 28 people and wounded 76 at Tel Aviv's Lod airport in 1972), the Palestinian Black September group (responsible for the deaths of 11 Israeli athletes at the 1972 Munich Olympics), the Baader-Meinhof Gang in Germany, the Italian Red Brigades (who kidnapped and killed the former Italian premier, Aldo Moro, in 1978), the Tupamoros in Uruguay, and the Weathermen in the United States. While receiving much publicity—one of their aims—terrorists actually account for relatively few deaths (less than 2,000 in the 1980s) compared with other causes (nearly 10 times as many people are murdered every year by ordinary criminals in the U.S. alone). Terrorists are very hard to catch, however, because their groups are small, tightly organized, and highly mobile. As a major measure to curb the involvement of Libya in terrorism worldwide, President Ronald Reagan on January 8, 1984, issued an executive order severing virtually all U.S. economic ties to Libya.

The aftermath of a terrorist attack by the Irish Republican Army (IRA) on British Prime Minister John Major

Terry, Dame Ellen Alicia (1848-1928), English actress. Throughout more than 50 years on the stage, she performed often as Sir Henry Irving's leading lady, and is remembered for her roles as Beatrice in *Much Ado About Nothing*, Juliet in *Romeo and Juliet*, and Desdemona in *Othello*.

Tertiary Period, the lower division of the Cenozoic era, extending from the end of the Cretaceous to the beginning of the Quaternary, from 70,000,000 to 2,000,000 years ago. It is divided into 5 epochs: Paleocene, Eocene, Oligocene, Miocene, and Pliocene. The early Tertiary period was characterized by a large amount of mountain building (Andes, Alps, Hymalayas). In this period marsupials and placental mammals diversified and began to take a more modern appearance. Also during this time, worldwide climates began to gradually change into today's climatic zones.

Tesla, Nikola (1856-1943), U.S. electrical engineer, inventor of the induction motor. His innovative motor used alternating electric current. This concept, purchased by a George Westinghouse company, was used to develop a successful commercial motor. Tesla worked on other successful inventions, including the Tesla coil, an arc-lighting system, and various generators and transformers. He was a forerunner in the field of communications with his work on wireless radio transmissions. He was born in Croatia, now part of Yugoslavia, and moved to the United States in 1884.
See also: Electric motor.

Testes *see:* Testicle.

Testicle, or testis (plural: testes), one of paired male sex glands. The testes are contained in the scrotal sac just between the legs. They have two functions. As ductless glands, they secrete testosterone, the male sex hormone. This substance is responsible for maintenance of the accessory reproductive organs and also for the secondary sexual characteristics—deep voice, strong muscles, and facial hair. Their other function is to produce the sperm needed to fertilize the female egg. Sperm is produced in a series of long coiled tubes called seminiferous tubules. In higher mammals, this process requires a temperature lower than normal body temperature, a condition provided by having the scrotal sac outside the body cavity. Mature sperm are stored in a coiled tube, the epididymis, up to 20 ft (6 m) long, which leads from the rear of the testis to the ejaculatory duct.

Testing, in education and psychology, procedures to evaluate individuals with respect to intelligence, skills, perceptions, or other parameters. Testing in the classroom is generally nonstandardized, designed by the teacher to measure the achievements of the students in assimilating subject matter. Standardized testing in education is used to compare individuals to group norms, as in Graduate Record Examinations (GREs), or to measure them against predetermined standards, as in tests used to license professionals in law and medicine. Achievement tests measure learning in specific subject areas. Aptitude tests, which include intelligence tests that measure intelligence quotient (IQ), attempt to evaluate potential while eliminating factors of previous experience. Psychologists use a variety of personality tests, including both standardized tests that determine categories of personality profile and projective tests, like the Rorschach inkblot test, which can be evaluated only by a trained professional. Because test results are widely used to determine an individual's future in education and work, the validity of test procedures and contents must be scrutinized. Testing may inadvertently favor those of particular socioeconomic groups or otherwise express cultural biases.

Testosterone, androgen steroid produced by the testes under the control of luteinizing hormone. It is responsible for most male sexual characteristics—voice change, hair distribution, and sex organ development.
See also: Steroid.

Tetanus, or lockjaw, disease of the nervous system caused by toxins produced by the bacterium *Clostridium tetani*. The bacteria enter the body through breaks in the skin. The first symptom is often painful contraction of jaw and neck muscles; trunk muscles, including those of respiration, and muscles close to the site of injury are also frequently involved. Untreated, many cases are fatal, but artificial respiration, antiserum, and penicillin have improved the outlook. Regular vaccination and adequate wound cleansing are important in prevention.

Tet Offensive, in the Vietnam War, a coordinated cluster of attacks against cities and bases in South Vietnam by Vietcong and North Vietnamese forces, beginning on Jan. 30, 1968, the first day of the Tet (New Year) holiday. The offensive, which included a brief occupation of part of the U.S. embassy in Saigon, was costly to the

enemy; nevertheless, it converted many Americans to the view that the war could not be won.
See also: Vietnam War.

Teton, Grand *see:* Grand Teton National Park.

Teton Range, mountain range located in Wyoming and Idaho in Grand Teton National Park. This rugged range, part of the Rocky Mountains, stretches for 40 mi (64 km) in length and up to 15 mi (24 km) in width. Grand Teton (13,770 ft, 4,197 m) is the highest peak. John Colter, part of the Lewis and Clark expedition, discovered (1808) the Teton Range.

Tetracycline, name for broad-spectrum antibiotics that can be given by mouth. They are useful in bronchitis and other minor infections and especially valuable in diseases due to rickettsia and related organisms; they can also be used in acne.
See also: Antibiotic.

Teutonic Knights, group of German crusaders. Founded in the Middle East at the end of the 12th century, this organization of knights worked to conquer and convert areas of central and eastern Europe to Christianity. Prussia was converted in the 1200s as were the neighboring countries of Estonia and Livonia, where the Livonian Knights were founded. Lithuania was eventually converted (1387), but with Poland later defeated the Teutonic Knights (1410). The order continued to weaken and, beginning in Prussia (1525), its various branches were eventually dissolved.
See also: Knighthood, Orders of.

Teutons, Northern European tribes that attacked the Roman empire early in the 1st century B.C. Though the Teutons, with the Cimbri, were badly beaten by the Romans under General Gaius Marius, both Caesar and the historian Tacitus wrote of the Teutons' warlike nature. As the Teutons moved south, southeast, and west, what is known as the Teutonic languages came to encompass the Scandinavian as well as Germanic languages, including Dutch, English, and Flemish.

Big Bend National Park, Texas

Texas

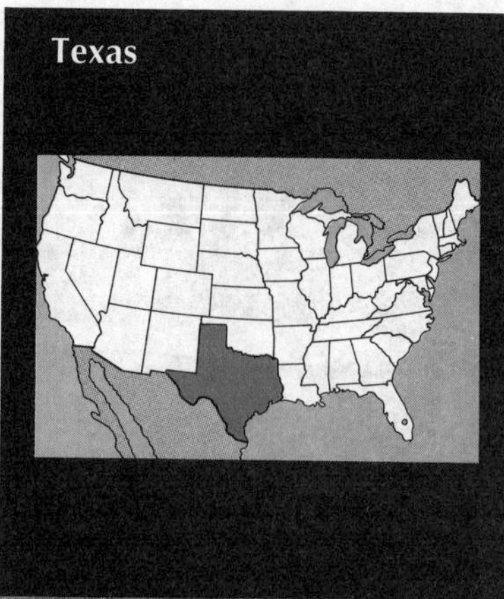

Capital:	Austin
Statehood:	Dec. 29, 1845 (28th state)
Familiar name:	Lone Star State
Area:	266,807 sq mi (691,030 sq km); ranks 2nd
Population:	17,059,805 (1990); ranks 3rd
Elevation:	Highest—8,751 ft (2,667 m), Gaudalupe Peak; Lowest—sea level, along the Gulf of Mexico
Motto:	Friendship
Flower:	Bluebonnet
Bird:	Mockingbird
Tree:	Pecan
Song:	"Texas, Our Texas"

Texas, the largest state in the southwestern region of the United States and the second-largest state in the nation; bordered by Oklahoma and the Red River to the north, Arkansas, Louisiana, and the Sabine River to the east, the Gulf of Mexico to the southeast, the Rio Grande (with Mexico opposite) to the south and southwest, and New Mexico to the west.
Land and climate. Texas has five main land regions. The Gulf Coastal Plains in the east and the southern horn cover a low-lying area with timberland in the northeast and fertile farmland in the south. West of that timberland is the Prairie Plains, a hilly, forested region. In the Rolling Plains region, another hilly area, elevations rise from east to west. The Great Plains, stretching southward from the northern Panhandle, is a high, level, grassland. In Texas's extreme southwest is the Basin and Range Region, a high, dry area that includes high spurs of the Rocky Mountain range. The Rio Grande, which forms the entire border between Texas and Mexico, is one of the largest in the nation. Other major rivers include the Pecos, Brazos, Red, Canadian, Colorado, Nueces, and Trinity. Forests cover about 14% of the state. Texas's climate ranges from temperate in the Panhandle region to subtropical in the Rio Grande delta. Principal cities are Houston, Dallas, and San Antonio.
Economy. Texas's economy depends heavily on its oil and natural gas resources, among the richest in the world. Other mineral resources include sulfur, helium, coal, clay, salt, asphalt, limestone, gypsum, and sand and gravel. Service industries and manufacturing are also important to the economy. Chief manufactured goods are nonelectrical machinery, chemicals, processed foods, oil and coal products, electrical equipment, fabricated metal products, transportation equipment, and apparel. A leading agricultural state, Texas produces beef cattle, cotton, grain sorghum, rice, wheat, vegetables, and citrus and other fruits.
Government. Texas's present constitution was adopted in 1876. The governor serves a 4-year term. The state legislature consists of 31 senators serving 4-year terms and 150 representatives serving 2-year terms. In the U.S. Congress, Texas is represented by 2 senators and 30 representatives.
History. Several Native American peoples were living in Texas when Spanish gold-seekers, the first Europeans in the area, arrived in the early 1500s. In 1685, the French explorer La Salle arrived and claimed the area, which France sold to the United States as part of the 1803 Louisiana Purchase. In 1821, Texas became part of the newly independent Empire of Mexico. But U.S. settlement in the area continued to grow; the Texas Revolution—a rebellion of U.S. settlers against Mexico—began in 1835. In 1836, after the famous battle at the Alamo, the independent Republic of Texas was formed. It became the 28th state in 1845. The Mexican War (1846-48) ended all Mexican claims to Texas. In 1861, Texas seceded from the Union and fought on the Confederate side during the Civil War; it was readmitted to the Union in 1870. Texas played a major role in the expansion of the western frontier during the late 1800s. The 1901 discovery of oil near Beaumont spurred rapid industrial growth, as did World War II. During the 1960s and 1970s, growth was centered in the U.S. space program and the oil and oil-related industries. Falling oil prices during the mid-1980s dealt Texas a heavy blow; it has been working to diversify and attract new industries.

Texas fever *see:* Cattle tick.

Texas Rangers, law enforcement body, part of the Texas department of public safety. The first Rangers were 10 men employed (1823) by S.F. Austin to protect settlers from Native American and Mexican raiders. In 1935 the Rangers were merged with the state highway patrol.

Textile, fabric made from natural or synthetic fibers, whether knitted, woven, bonded, or felted. The fibers (silk, wool, cotton, linen, or synthetics) are prepared and spun into yarn, which is formed into fabric by weaving or other methods. Finished processes include bleaching, calendering, mercerizing, dyeing, brushing, sizing, fulling, and tentering. Chemical processes are used to impart crease-resistance, fireproofing, stain resistance, waterproofing, or non-shrink properties.

Thackeray, William Makepeace (1811-63), English novelist, essayist, and illustrator. He did much to shape *Punch* and was first editor of *the Cornhill Magazine* (1860). His best-known novel is *Vanity Fair* (1848), a gentle satire of the early 19th-century middle classes. His other novels include *Barry Lyndon* (1844), *Pendennis* (1850), and *Henry Esmond* (1852).

Thailand, Kingdom of Thailand, formerly Siam, constitutional monarchy in Southeast Asia. Thailand is bordered by Myanmar (Burma) to the west and northwest, Laos in the north and east, Cambodia to the southeast, and Malaysia and the Gulf of Siam to the south. The capital is Bangkok.
Land and climate. Thailand takes up an area of 198,455 sq mi (514,000 sq km) and is divisible into 3 main areas. The principle region is a fertile plain approximately in the center of the country. It is here that most of the people live. To the north and northeast is a region sometimes called the Khorat Plateau. It is a high red sandstone plateau that drains eastward to the Mekong. It has poor clay, sand soils, and scrub vegetation and is dry and dusty about half of the year. The region is thinly populated. To the south, Thailand extends into the long narrow Malay Peninsula, which it occupies with Myanmar and Malaysia. In places where it borders Myanmar, Thailand's peninsular territory is not more than 10 mi (16 km) wide. The region is mostly mountainous and forested, but has rice-producing plains and mineral deposits. The many islands along its coast include Phuket, important for its tin. The climate of Thailand is monsoonal.
People. The Thai people are of Mongol origin. Ethnic Chinese are an important minority, and there are hill peoples in the north and Malays, most of them Muslim, in the south. Hinayana Buddhism is the official religion and Thai, a Sino-Tibetan language is the official language.
Economy. Rice is the chief crop in Thailand's predominantly agricultural economy, but sugarcane, cotton, corn, coconuts, rubber, and tobacco are also cultivated. Fishing is important and forestry yields teak, oils, resins, and bamboo. Among the few manufactures is quality silk production. Thailand is one of the world's

(Left) The Royal Chapel with the "Emerald Buddha," part of the Royal Palace in Thailand. (Right) In Thailand, trained elephants are used for a variety of tasks. Here they are shown leading an attack.

Thailand

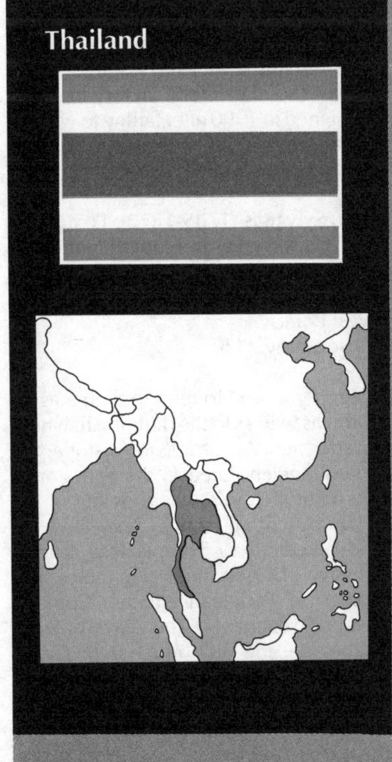

General information	
Capital:	Bangkok
Area:	198,115 sq mi (513,115 sq km)
Population:	55,258,000
Official language:	Thai (Siamese)
Monetary unit:	1 Thai baht = 100 stangs
Main cities:	Bangkok, Chiang Mai, Hat Yai
Government	
Form:	constitutional monarchy
Independent:	1939 (as Thailand)
Head of state:	King
Head of government:	Prime minister
Legislature:	two legislative houses (National Assembly: Senate and House of Representatives)
Executive:	Prime minister and Council of Ministers
Judiciary:	highest court is the Supreme Court
Political division:	72 provinces
National economy	
Gross national product:	U.S. $54,550,000,000
Per capita income:	U.S. $1,000
Agriculture:	rice, cassava, sugar cane, corn, pineapples, bananas
Livestock:	buffalo, cattle, pigs
Fisheries:	2,165,000 metric tons
Mining:	tin, bauxite, iron ore, lead, precious stones, natural gas
Industries:	cement, refined sugar, paper, textiles, automobiles and motorcycles, tourism
Main exports:	food and live animals, basic manufactures, machinery and transport equipment, teak, tin
Transportation:	2,321 mi (3,735 km) of railroads, 52,670 mi (84,764 km) of roads, 4 international airports
Trading partners:	Japan, U.S., Singapore
People	
Urban:	20%
Ethnic composition:	Thai 79.5% (of which Siamese 52.5%, Lao 27%), Chinese 12%, Malay 3.5%, Khmer 2.5%
Birth rate:	22.1 per 1,000 population
Death rate:	7 per 1,000 population
Infant mortality:	50 per 1,000 live births
Life expectancy:	male 63 years, female 67.5 years

largest exporters of rice. Other exports include corn, rubber, and teak. Tourism is also important to the economy.
History. The Thai people migrated from South China c.1000 B.C. The center of their culture and civilization moved south under the successive dynasties of the Sukho Thai (c.1220-1350), Ayuthai (1350-1778), and Chakri (1782-). The coming of the Portuguese in the 16th century eventually led to an enduring association between the kingdom of Siam and the Western powers. The only country of Southeast Asia that has never been a colony of a European power, Siam lost territorial influence in the 1800s to the British in Burma and Malaya and to the French in Laos and Cambodia, but kept its independence. Thailand was invaded and occupied by the Japanese in World War II. In the early 1950s it sent troops to Korea and joined the South East Asia Treaty Organization (SEATO) in 1954, which is headquartered in Bangkok. Thailand supported the United States in Vietnam, providing troops as well as air bases. King Prajadhikop was forced to grant the country a constitution in 1932 and Siam became Thailand in 1939. The post-World War II years saw political instability and military coups. A new constitution was promulgated in 1978 and general elections were held in 1979, but in 1991 the government was again brought down by a military coup.

Thalassemia, inherited blood disorder in which hemoglobin is not adequately produced. Without hemoglobin—the red pigment in blood that carries oxygen through the body—children become sick and, with some varieties of the disease, die. This disorder most often affects people from the Mediterranean, along with Asian and Middle Eastern people as well as Black Americans. A mild form of the disease called thalassemia minor may cause a person to transmit the disorder to the next generation. With thalassemia major, or Cooley's anemia, a child may suffer various symptoms that often become fatal by early adulthood. Thalassemia intermedia is a serious but not always fatal variation of the disorder. Although not a cure, blood transfusions may relieve symptoms if administered on a regular basis.

Thales (625?-546? B.C.), first known Greek philosopher. His ideas are known to us through the writings of others, such as the Greek philosopher Aristotle. Thales approached subjects through what he could scrutinize and logically reason about them—an approach quite different from the Greek tradition of explanations through supernaturally directed myths. Because of this approach, he is considered the first philosopher in the Western tradition. His observations led him to the conclusion that water was the cornerstone of all things on earth. He also introduced geometry to Greece. His school of thought is called either Milesian (based on Miletus, his birth place) or Ionian (based on Ionia, city-state of Greece in which Miletus was located).
See also: Pre-Socratic philosophy.

Thalidomide, mild sedative introduced in the late 1950s and withdrawn a few years later when it was found to be responsible for congenital deformities in children born to mothers who took the drug. This was due to an effect on the embryo in early pregnancy, in particular causing defective limb bud formation. Stricter regulations for testing new drugs in the United States resulted.

Thallium, chemical element, symbol Tl; for physical constants see Periodic Table. Thallium was discovered spectroscopically by William Crookes in 1861. It occurs in crookesite, loandrite, orbaite, and other minerals. It is obtained commercially from flue dusts remaining from pyrite calcination. Thallium is a tin-white, soft, reactive metal. It is soft enough to be scratched with the finger nail. The metal oxidizes in air and should be kept covered by an inert liquid. Thallium is a suspected carcinogen. The element and it compounds are poisonous, and contact with the skin should be avoided. The sulphate has been used as an insecticide and rodenticide, but its use in the United States is now prohibited. Thallium and its compounds are used in photo cells, infrared detectors, low-temperature mercury switches, and special glasses.

Thames River, England's chief waterway, winding east from the Cotswolds to its North Sea estuary. The Thames is 210 mi (338 km) long. On its banks lie Oxford, Reading, Eton, Windsor Castle, Runnymede, Hampton Court Palace, and Greenwich. Canals link it to the West and Midlands. Above London it displays fine, gentle scenery; below London it is of considerable importance for shipping. It is tidal up to Teddington (10 mi/16 km west of London).
See also: England.

Thanksgiving Day, since 1863, an annual U.S. national holiday to give thanks for blessings received during the year. It is celebrated on the fourth Thursday in November with feasting and prayers. The tradition was begun by the colonists of Plymouth, Mass., in 1621, and can be traced back to the English harvest festivals. In Canada, it is celebrated on the second Monday in October.

Thant, U (1909-74), Burmese diplomat, United Nations secretary-general (1961-71). A cautious and unassertive negotiator, he was involved in the Cuban missile crisis (1962), and in peace negotiations in Indonesia (1962), the Congo (now Zaïre; 1963), Cyprus (1964), and the India-Pakistan war (1965).
See also: United Nations.

Thar Desert, also called the Indian Desert, located in northwest India and eastern Pakistan. This desert covers 74,000 sq mi (192,000 sq km). Even though rainfall is scarce (10 in/25 cm per year on average), the Indian government has developed the Indian Gandhi canal for irrigation (completed 1986), so that crops and people may thrive in this arid region. Nuclear power facilities of India are located within the desert in Kota.

Tharp, Twyla (1941-), U.S. choreographer and dancer. After 2 years as a dancer with the Paul Taylor Company (1963-65), she began to create original, expressive dances for her own company (founded 1965) and later the American Ballet Theater (joined in 1988). She uses various aspects of dance genres (ballet, tap-dance, social dance) and genres of music (classical, jazz, rock and roll). Some of her well-known dances are *Re-Moves* (1966), *Deuce Coupe* (1973), *Short Stories* (1980). She has also choreographed movies, such as *Hair* (1979) and *Amadeus* (1984).

Thatcher, Margaret Hilda (1925-), English prime minister (1979-90). She entered Parliament in 1959 and served (1970-74) as secretary of state for education and science. In 1975 she was elected Conservative Party leader, and in 1979, when the Conservatives won a parliamentary majority, Mrs. Thatcher became Britain's first female prime minister. To fight inflation she introduced austerity measures, but this kept unemployment high and contributed to domestic unrest. She took a firm line against the hunger strikes and terrorist tactics of the Irish Republican Army. Her vigorous defense of the Falkland Islands against Argentina in 1982 contributed to her party's solid electoral victory in 1983. She resigned in 1990 after failing to win the Conservative Party's leadership election.
See also: United Kingdom.

Thayer, Sylvanus (1785-1872), U.S. Army officer. He served as the superintendent of the U.S. Military Academy at West Point (1817-33), becoming known as the father of West Point.
See also: Army, U.S.

Theater, term used to refer to drama as an art form, as well as to the building in which it is performed. According to Aristotle, the drama of ancient Greece, the ancestor of modern European drama, grew out of the dithyramb (choral song). The form of tragedy credited to Thespis was refined successively by Aeschylus, Sophocles, and Euripides in Periclean Athens. Comedy developed separately. The plays of Aristophanes are the only remains of Greek Old Comedy (5th century B.C.), a form that was extremely licentious and close to its ritual origins. Middle and New comedy (4th and 3rd centuries B.C., respectively) became increasingly sentimental. Greek drama was performed at religious festivals in amphitheaters built into hillsides; that at Epidaurus is still used each summer.
The Roman plays of Plautus, Terence, and Seneca were influenced by Greek theater. However, mime and pantomime were the popular theatrical forms in the Roman Empire. After the fall of the Empire, theater was banned by the Church until the 9th century. Medieval drama evolved from musical elaborations of the church service. Eventually these developed into mystery

plays and were moved outdoors onto play wagons. Miracle plays, based on the lives of the saints and on scripture, also developed; cycles of plays were performed at religious festivals. Morality plays (such as *Everyman*) and interludes (comic plays) appeared in the 15th century.
During the Renaissance the rediscovery of Greek and Roman dramatic texts led directly to the growth of secular drama. Buildings for the performance of plays were erected in Elizabethan times. One of the most famous was the Globe Theatre (associated with Shakespeare), a multistory roofed building inside which the audience ranged around an open stage.
The modern form of the stage, with painted scenery and a proscenium arch across which a curtain falls between acts, was established by the 17th century. However, in the 20th century attempts have been made to eliminate the distancing of audience from the dramatic action, using such new theatrical designs as theater in the round.

One of the most important theaters in history, the Italian Comedia dell'Arte (16th century)

Theater of the Absurd, term to describe plays in which traditional values are unable to fulfill emotional and spiritual needs. Human experience is seen as chaotic and without purpose, and people are often depicted as victims of technology and bourgeois values. Samuel Beckett, Eugéne Ionesco, Jean Genet, Edward Albee, and Harold Pinter have been identified with this genre.

Thebes, ancient Greek city located on same site as the modern-day Greek city of Thivai. It headed an alliance, or confederacy, of Greek city-states called Boeotia. As a rival of Athens—a southeastern neighbor about 30 miles away—Thebes supported an invasion of Athens by Persia (480 B.C.). Thebes also sided with Sparta against Athens in the Peloponnesian War (431-404 B.C.). After this war Thebes was dominated by Sparta until a Theban victory by Epaminondas (371 B.C.) made Boeotia powerful once again. Thebes was controlled by other city-states after the death of Epaminondas. Alexander the Great sacked Thebes (336 B.C.); the city was rebuilt 20 years later.
See also: Greece, Ancient.

Thebes, southern city in ancient Egypt, located on the Nile River; present-day city of Luxor. Temples to the god Amon-Re as well as elaborate pyramids constructed for the burial of kings from the Eighteenth Dynasty (1554-1304 B.C.) are found here. The temples of Karnak and Luxor still stand. Thebes served as the capital for many of these rulers, including Tutankhamen, whose remains were unearthed in the 20th century (1922). Remnants of tombs are still apparent in the nearby Valley of the Kings. Thebes was destroyed by the Assyrians (661 B.C.) and the Romans (29 B.C.).
See also: Egypt, Ancient.

Theism, philosophical system, as distinguished from deism and pantheism, that professes the existence of a personal, transcendent God who created, preserves, and governs the world. Orthodox Christian philosophy is a developed form of theism.
See also: Religion.

Themistocles (514?-449? B.C.), ancient Greek politician and military strategist of Athens. He endorsed the development of the Athenian navy, which helped bring victory to Athens in their war against Persia. Themistocles is best known for his participation in the Athenian victory against the Persians in the battle at Salamis (480 B.C.). Suspicions due to political intrigues resulted in his exile to Persia, where he died on an estate presented to him by the Persian king.
See also: Salamis.

Theocracy, government in which power and authority are seen as derived directly from God and rulers are considered either incarnations or representative of divine power. In ancient times theocracy was widespread. During the Middle Ages in Europe the pope claimed ultimate authority in governing based on his religious authority, and later kings used the "divine right of kings" to justify their absolutist rule. Early Puritan colonies in New England like Massachusetts Bay and New Haven had leaders who claimed to derive their authority from God. While today secular and religious authority are for the most part separated in the Western democracies, their fusion in such political units as the Iranian Islamic Republic is still strong.

Theocritus (c.3rd century B.C.), poet of ancient Greece. He expressed himself through the idyll—a short, lyrical and emotional poem that describes the virtues and beauty of the countryside. This form of poetry is also called a pastoral. He worked in Alexandria, Egypt, a literary center of his time. Of his life's work, 30 written poems remain. Theocritus was influenced by the Alexandrian librarian and poet Callimachus, and in turn influenced the work of the Roman poet Vergil.

Theodoric (A.D. 455?-526), conqueror of Italy, king of Ostrogoths. He inherited the crown from his father Theodemir (A.D. 471). With the help of the Byzantine emperor, Zeno, Theordoric and his barbarians defeated Odoacer, the ruling barbarian of Italy (A.D. 493). Rather than tyrannize the Italians, Theodoric respected Roman citizens and used their political and legal institutions during his peaceful rule. He allowed Catholics to practice their religion even though his Arian beliefs conflicted with the beliefs and doctrines of the church. His elaborate tomb is located in Ravenna, Italy. Theodoric was known in Germanic legends as Dietrich of Bern.
See also: Ostrogoths.

Theodosius I (A.D. 346-395), emperor of Rome. Theodosius was of Armenian descent, born in Spain. He rose through the ranks of the Roman military. Later with Emperor Gratian he ruled Rome, becoming responsible for provinces in the east (A.D. 379). He would not allow religious practices that were not Christian, but he did allow the formation of an independent nation for the non-Christian Visigoths (A.D. 382) within the eastern provinces. He became emperor of all of Rome when he conquered the non-Christian peoples that populated the west (394 A.D.).
See also: Rome, Ancient.

Theology, science of religious knowledge; the formal analysis of what is believed by adherents of a religion, making its doctrine coherent, elucidating it logically, and relating it to secular disciplines. Most religions have no well-developed theology. The concept arose in Greek, but its elaboration took place only in Christianity. The early Church Fathers and Doctors formulated doctrine in contemporary philosophical terms, and major advances were made by resolving controversies. In the Middle Ages Scholasticism developed, partly in reaction to the influence of Neoplatonism, and divided theology into natural theology and revealed theology. From the Reformation

each branch of Protestantism began to develop its own distinctive theology. From the Enlightenment rationalist theology became dominant, leading to modernism and the modern critical view of the Bible. Partly in reaction, neo-orthodoxy and the existentialist theology of Reinhold Niebuhr and Paul Tillich arose.
See also: God; Religion.

Theorell, Axel Hugo Teodor (1903-82), Swedish biochemist awarded the 1955 Nobel Prize for physiology or medicine for his studies of enzyme action, specifically the roles of enzymes in biological oxidation and reduction processes.
See also: Biochemistry; Enzyme.

Theorem *see:* Geometry; Pythagorean Theorem.

Theosophy (Greek, "divine wisdom"), mystical system of religious philosophy claiming direct insight into the divine nature. The speculations of such philosophers as Plotinus, Jakob Boehme, and Emanuel Swedenborg are often called theosophical, as are many Eastern philosophies. The Theosophical Society was founded in 1875 by Madame Helena Petrovna Blavatsky.
See also: Besant, Annie (Wood).

Theotokopoulos, Domenikos *see:* Greco, El.

Therapy *see:* Occupational therapy; Physical therapy; Psychotherapy.

Theresa, Saint *see:* Teresa, Saint.

Thermal pollution, ecologically harmful warming of rivers, lakes, or oceans. In the past, this pollution was most often caused by heated wastewater discharged from nuclear power plants or factories into streams, rivers, or other bodies of water, resulting in elevated water temperature that endangered both plant and animal life in the water. The Environmental Protection Agency (EPA) established regulations requiring such parties either to cool the heated wastewater before discharging it or to release small amounts of it into many different places. Both precautions are aimed at maintaining normal temperatures in rivers and lakes to protect the life in them.
See also: Pollution.

Thermal springs *see:* Hot springs.

Thermocouple, electric circuit involving two junctions between different metals, or semiconductors. These junctions create a small electromotive force (emf) in the circuit (known as the Seebeck effect). Measurement of this electromotive force provides a sensitive, if approximate, temperature reading ranging from 70°K to 1,000°K. Thermocouples can be run in reverse as small refrigerators. A number of thermocouples connected in series with one set of blackened junctions form a thermopile, which measures radiation. Thermoelectricity embraces the Seebeck and other effects relating heat transfer, thermal gradients, electric fields, and currents.
See also: Electric current.

Thermodynamics, division of physics concerned with the interconversion of heat, work, and other forms of energy, and with the states of physical systems. *Classical thermodynamics* is basic to engineering, parts of geology, metallurgy, and physical chemistry. Building on earlier studies of temperature and heat, Sadi Carnot pioneered the science with his investigations of the cyclic heat engine (1824), and in 1850 Rudolf Clausius stated the first two laws. Thermodynamics was further developed by J.W. Gibbs, H.L.F. von Helmholtz, Lord Kelvin, and J.C. Maxwell. In thermodynamics, a system is any defined collection of matter: a *closed system* is one that cannot exchange matter with its surroundings; an *isolated system* can exchange neither matter nor energy. The *state* of a system is specified by determining all its properties, such as pressure, volume, etc. A *process* is a change from one state to another, the path being specified by all the intermediate states. A *state function* is a property or function of properties that depends only on the state and not on the path by which the state was reached.
See also: Physics.

Thermography, method to measure the slightest variations in temperature of soft tissue in the body using infrared heat sensors. The technique is often used in mammography (breast examination) to detect any growth in the breast (the mass will have a different temperature from other breast tissue). Thermography can also be used on an extremity, particularly the leg, to help diagnose a thrombus (clot) in a vein. The area of the body to be tested is usually placed on a heat-detection device that reacts to specific temperatures, either by color changes or by a direct display of temperatures.

Thermometer, instrument for measuring the temperature of a substance or object. Clinical thermometers are made of a glass tube with a bulb containing liquid (usually mercury) that expands and rises in the tube as the temperature increases. A scale on the tube indicates the object's temperature by measuring how high the liquid rises. The type of thermometer used in a given application depends on the temperature range.

Thermopylae (Greek, "hot gates"), narrow mountain pass that in ancient Greece led from the north to the south. This pass between Mt. Oeta and the Maliac Gulf was the scene of a famous battle from the Persian Wars (480 B.C.) that the Spartans lost against the invading Persian forces. Although this area is a marshy plain rather than a mountain pass, it contains hot springs as it did in ancient times.

Thermosphere, outermost layer of the earth's atmosphere, at altitudes between approximately 53 mi (85 km) and 300 mi (480 km). The heat, caused by radiation of the sun, varies from –135°F (–93°C) at the lowest altitude to 2,700°F (1,500°C) and more at the highest altitude. The thermosphere is different from the layers of the atmosphere closest to earth in that the pressure is much lower (1 million times lower than at sea level) and the chemical makeup includes mostly atoms of helium and hydrogen.
See also: Atmosphere.

Thermostat, device for maintaining a material or enclosure at a constant temperature by automatically regulating its heat supply, which is cut off if the temperature exceeds and reconnected if it falls below that required. A thermostat comprises a sensor whose dimensions or physical properties change with temperature and a relay device that controls a switch or valve accordingly.

Theropod *see:* Dinosaur.

Theseus, in Greek mythology, son of King Aegeus and princess Aethra, renowned for his heroism. As a youth he went to Crete with other youths to be sacrificed to the Minotaur, but instead succeeded in killing the beast. On his voyage back to Athens, he failed to fly his ship's white sails, a symbol of his safe return. Aegeus thought his son was dead and killed himself in his grief. Theseus was then declared king.
See also: Mythology.

Thespis (c. 6th century B.C.), ancient Greek actor. Among his many innovations was that of allowing a character to speak dialogue separately from the words spoken by the chorus. The use of make-up and masks is also attributed to him. Most importantly, through an innovative performance in honor of the Greek god Dionysus at an Athenian festival (c.534 B.C.), Thespis became known as the originator of tragedy. A word for actors, thespians, honors his contributions to drama.

Thessalonians, Epistles to the, books 13 and 14 of the New Testament Bible. After the founding of the church at Thessaloniki in Greece, the apostle Paul wrote a letter (c.A.D. 50) to its members, explaining the purpose of the resurrection of Christ. A second letter, attributed to Paul but more likely written by one of his followers, indicated the lengthy time that would elapse before Christ's second coming. These letters represent the first Christian writings.
See also: Bible; New Testament.

Thessaloniki *see:* Salonika.

Thessaly, northeast region of Greece in which Mount Olympus of ancient Greek legend is located. This region was the home of the legendary Achilles, hero of the Trojan War, and Jason, head of the Argonauts. Lack of cooperation among its own people kept Thessaly weak militarily. It was conquered (344 B.C.) by Philip of Macedon, father of Alexander the Great. Later rulers included the Romans (146 B.C.), the Turks

(1355), and the Greeks (1878). In ancient times, Pherae, Crannon, and Larisa were its major cities. Today, its major cities are Volos and Larisa.
See also: Greece.

Thiamine *see:* Vitamin.

Thibault, Jacques A.F *see:* France, Anatole.

Thiers, Louis Adolphe (1797-1877), French author and diplomat. Among his writings are *History of the French Revolution* (1823-27), a 10-volume study, and *History of the Consulate and the Empire* (1845-62). He helped organize the July Revolution (1830), which opposed the rule of Charles X. He served in the government of Louis Philippe, successor of Charles X. He opposed the rule of Napoleon II in the Second Empire. Later, after the Franco-Prussian War, he served 2 years as the first president of the Third Republic of France (1871-73).
See also: France.

Thieu, Nguyen Van (1923-), president of South Vietnam (1967-75). An army officer, he helped overthrow Ngo Dinh Diem (1963), becoming premier in 1965 and president in 1967. He was re-elected (1971), but after U.S. troops were withdrawn his dictatorial regime gradually collapsed, and he resigned in April 1975. He fled to Taiwan and later to Great Britain, after South Vietnam fell to the North.
See also: Vietnam.

Thiopental, drug used in general anesthesia. It is commonly known by its trade name, Pentothal or Sodium Pentothal. It was first demonstrated in 1934. Because it will not burn or explode, it is preferred over combustible anesthetics, such as ether. It is often used, usually by injection, to begin the anesthesia process. Small doses tend to release emotional inhibitions, and it is sometimes used in the treatment of psychiatric patients.
See also: Anesthesia.

Third International *see:* International, The.

Third Reich *see:* Germany; Reich.

Third World, term often applied to the nonaligned (and mostly developing) nations of Africa, Latin America, and Asia as opposed to Western and Eastern (Communist) countries.

Thirty-Nine Articles, doctrine issued by the Church of England to bridge the gap between Roman Catholic and Protestant Reformation groups in 16th-century England. The Articles, approved by Parliament in 1571, are still accepted today by the Anglican Church. Among the tenets are the condemnation of such Roman Catholic beliefs as purgatory, transubstantiation, and reverence for saints. Because the language of the Articles is intentionally vague, interpretations have been various.
See also: Anglicans.

Thirty Tyrants, or The Thirty, term used to identify the group of Athenians who ruled Athens after it fell to Sparta (404 B.C.). The oligarchy was set up by the Spartan general Lysander. Under the leadership of the Athenian politician Critias, the group terrorized the Athenian citizenry and seized their property. In 403 B.C., Sparta reinstated Athens's democratic form of government.
See also: Athens; Greece, Ancient.

Thirty Years' War, series of European wars (1618-48). Partly a Catholic-Protestant religious conflict, they were also a political and territorial struggle by different European powers, particularly France, against its greatest rivals, the Habsburgs, rulers of the Holy Roman Empire. War began when Bohemian Protestants accused 2 government ministrers of wrongdoing and threw them out a window (a customary Bohemian punishment for offending officials). This event became known as the Defenestration of Prague (from Latin *fenestra*, "window") and triggered a civil war in Bohemia that rapidly spread to all of western Europe. The Bohemians were defeated by General Tilly (1620), who went on to subjugate the Palatinate (1623). In 1625 Denmark, fearing Habsburg power, invaded North Germany but was defeated in 1629. The emperor Ferdinand II issued the Edict of Restitution, restoring lands to the Roman Catholic Church. In 1630 the Swedish king Gustavus Adolphus led the Protestant German princes against Ferdinand. He was killed at Lützen (1632). By 1635 the Swedes had lost support in Germany, and the German states concluded the Peace of Prague. But now France, under Cardinal Richelieu, intervened. Further wars ensued, with France, Sweden, and the German Protestant states fighting in the Low Countries, Scandinavia, France, Germany, Spain, and Italy against the Holy Roman Empire, Spain (another Habsburg power), and Denmark. Peace negotiations, begun in 1640, were completed with the Peace of Westphalia (1648).

Thistle, common name for many prickly, herbaceous plants (family Compositae). They normally have purple or yellow flowers. When the seeds are ripe, they are dispersed as fluffy thistledown. Thistles normally produce a thick taproot that can be eaten or used as a coffee substitute.

Thomas, Dylan (1914-53), Welsh poet who first achieved recognition with *Eighteen Poems* (1934). His prose includes the quasi-autobiographical *Portrait of the Artist as a Young Dog* (1940) and *Adventures in the Skin Trade* (1955); his poetry includes *Deaths and Entrances* (1946) and *Collected Poems* (1952). His drama *Under Milk Wood* (posthumously published, 1954) was originally a radio play.

Thomas, George Henry (1816-70), U.S. Union general victorious at Mill Springs (1862) and dubbed the "Rock of Chickamauga" for his stand at that battle (1863). His Army of the Cumberland destroyed General John Hood's army at Nashville, Tenn. (1864).
See also: Civil War, U.S.

Thomas, Isaiah (1749-1831), U.S. printer and publisher. He printed books and magazines, and published the *Massachusetts Spy* (1770-1802), a colonial newspaper criticizing British policy before and throughout the Revolutionary War. He printed the first Bible and dictionary in the United States. His *The History of Printing in America* (1810) remains an informative work.

Thomas, Martha Carey (1857-1935), U.S. leader in higher education and women's suffrage movement. She served as president of Bryn Mawr College (1894-1922), following 9 years as a dean and professor of English. The rigorous student requirements and course curriculum she endorsed upgraded academic possibilities for women in the United States. She also served as president of the National College Equal Suffrage League (1908-17), working to gain women the right to vote. Thomas earned a PhD at the University of Zurich in Switzerland, because few U.S. graduate schools accepted women at that time.
See also: Woman suffrage.

Thomas, Norman Mattoon (1884-1968), U.S. socialist leader who ran six times (1928, 1932, 1936, 1940, 1944, 1948) for the presidency of the United States as a Socialist Party candidate. He helped found the American Civil Liberties Union (1920) and the League for Industrial Democracy (1922). An ardent pacifist, he tried to keep the United States out of World War II. Many of his then radical proposals eventually became law.
See also: Socialism.

Thomas, Saint, one of the 12 apostles, known as "Doubting Thomas" because he would not believe Jesus' resurrection until he put his fingers in Jesus' wounds. His subsequent career and martyrdom at Madras are recounted in the apocryphal *Acts of Thomas*.
See also: Apostles.

Thomas à Becket *see:* Becket, Saint Thomas à.

Thistle

Thomas à Kempis (Thomas Hermerken von Kempen; 1380-1471), German religious writer and Augustinian friar at Zwolle in the Netherlands. He is the probable author of *The Imitation of Christ* (c.1427), one of the most widely read works of Christian literature.

Thomas à Kempis

Thomas Aquinas, Saint *see:* Aquinas, Saint Thomas.

Thompson, Sir John Sparrow David (1844-94), Canadian diplomat and prime minister (1892-94). He had previously served as justice of the Nova Scotia Supreme Court and minister of justice in the Cabinet of prime minister John MacDonald. He was renowned for his diplomatic skills and his successful negotiation of many treaties and controversies. He was named prime minister following the death of MacDonald and the resignation of MacDonald's successor.
See also: Canada.

Henry David Thoreau

Thomson, Charles (1729-1824), signer of the Declaration of Independence and secretary of the Continental Congress throughout its existence (1774-89).
See also: Declaration of Independence.

Thomson, Sir Joseph John (1856-1940), British physicist. The Nobel Prize in physics (1906) was awarded to him for his discovery of the electron. This discovery was made as he studied rays—known as cathode rays—that occurred in a vacuum in a glass tube when electric current was introduced. Eventually he proved that this phenomenon was due to moving particles rather than light rays; those particles were later named electrons. As professor of physics at Cambridge in England, he helped develop their atomic research facilities. His son, Sir George Paget Thomson, also won the Nobel Prize for physics (1937), along with Clinton Davisson of the United States.
See also: Electron.

Thomson, Virgil (1896-1989), U.S. composer and music critic. Influenced by The Six in Paris, he became a leading "Americanist." His works include the operas *Four Saints in Three Acts* (1928) and *the Mother of Us All* (1947), in collaboration with Gertrude Stein, symphonies, and instrumental, chamber, and film music. He won a 1949 Pulitzer Prize for his *Louisiana Story* score.

Thor, in Norse mythology, god of thunder. Son of Odin, the king of the deities, Thor is depicted as a powerful warrior with a huge appetite. The fiercest adversary of the giants, Thor's strength is symbolized by his weapon, a magical hammer called Mjollnir, which unerringly hits its target and flies back to Thor. According to Norse myth, the world will be destroyed in a great war between the giants and the gods, which will also kill Thor. Thursday is named after Thor (Thor's day).
See also: Mythology.

Thoreau, Henry David (1817-62), U.S. writer, naturalist, and abolitionist. His book *Walden* (1854) was a philosophical essay that recounted Thoreau's experiences living close to nature in a cabin at Walden Pond, near Concord, Mass. His influential essay "Civil Disobedience" promoted the concept of passive resistance that inspired leaders such as Mohandas K. Gandhi and Martin Luther King, Jr. Thoreau's place in literature is as a major voice among the New Transcendentalists, led by his mentor Ralph Waldo Emerson. Self-direction and an intimate understanding of nature, as found within and outside of the individual, were Thoreau's consistent themes.

Thorium, chemical element, symbol Th; for physical constants see Periodic Table. Discovered by Jöns Jakob Berzelius in 1828. The element occurs in the minerals thorite, thorianite, orangite, yttrocrasite, and monazite and is obtained commercially from the latter. Thorium is obtained as a powder by reduction of its oxide with calcium. It is a gray-white, radioactive metal. It is pyrophoric in powder form and burns in air to form the oxide, which has the highest melting point of all oxides. It is a member of the actinide series. Thorium is used as a nuclear fuel source and for incandescent lamp mantles. It is estimated that the energy available from thorium in the earth's crust is probably greater than that from uranium and fossil fuels combined.

Thorn apple *see:* Jimsonweed.

Thorndike, Edward Lee (1874-1949), U.S. psychologist best known for devising tests to measure intelligence, learning, and aptitude. His system of psychology, *connectionism*, had a profound influence on U.S. school education techniques, especially his discovery that the learning of one skill only slightly assists in the learning of another, even if related.
See also: Psychology.

Thornton, Matthew (1714?-1803), signer of the Declaration of Independence. A New Hampshire delegate to the Continental Congress in 1776 and 1778, he previously had been the president of the first New Hampshire Provincial Congress.

Thorpe, Jim (James Francis Thorpe; 1888-1953), U.S. athlete. Known for his all-around athletic ability, he played major league baseball (1913-19), professional football (1915-30), and was the first athlete to win both the decathlon and pentathlon at the Olympic Games (1912). Thorpe was stripped of his gold medals after a controversy arouse involving his amateur status; the International Olympic Committee restored these medals in 1982. Thorpe was inducted into the Pro Football Hall of Fame in 1963.

Thoth, Greek name for Djhowtey, an ancient Egyptian moon god who became associated with civilization, learning, and healing. His sacred animals are the ibis and the baboon, and he is often depicted as a human with the head of an ibis or a baboon with the head of a dog. Said to be the inventor of writing, he was often considered the representative on earth and the scribe of the sun god, Re.
See also: Mythology.

Thothmes III *see:* Thutmose III.

Thousand and One Nights *see:* Arabian Nights.

Thousand Islands, group of over 1,500 islands—some Canadian, some U.S.—in the St. Lawrence River at the outlet of Lake Ontario. St. Lawrence Islands National Park includes 13 of them. Thousand Islands International Bridge (actually five bridges) is 8 1/2 mi (13.7 km) long and carries traffic across the river.

Thrace, ancient region in the eastern part of the Balkan Peninsula, southeastern Europe, bordering the Black and Aegean seas. It includes modern northeastern Greece, southern Bulgaria, and European Turkey.

Thrasher, any of 17 U.S. bird species belonging to the mockingbird family. A brownish, long-tailed bird, it is known for its raucous call. It forages on the ground for insects, worms, seeds, and fruit. The most familiar is the brown thrasher, found east of the Rocky Mountains.

Three Mile Island, site in the Susquehanna River, near Middletown, Penn., of a nuclear reactor that, on March 28, 1979, began to emit "puffs" of radiation as a result of malfunction of the cooling system, aggravated by problems with the computer monitors and some human error. Initial reports downplayed the crisis, but it developed that a core meltdown was a possibility and that a large, potentially explosive hydrogen bubble had formed in the reactor; also, it was learned that no workable plans existed for evacuating the area.

Luckily, catastrophe was averted without fatalities or known injury.
See also: Nuclear reactor.

Three-mile limit *see:* Territorial waters.

Three Wise Men *see:* Magi.

Thrombosis, formation of a clot (thrombus) in the heart or blood vessels. It commonly occurs in the legs and is associated with varicose veins (thrombophelotist), but is more serious if it occurs in the heart or in the brain arteries. Detachments from a thrombus in the legs may be carried to the lungs as an embolus; this may have a fatal outcome if large vessels are occluded. Treatment includes anticoagulants.

Thrush, name for a family (Turdidae) of slender-billed songbirds found in most parts of the world. The plumage is often gray or red-brown, and many species have speckled or striated breasts. The tail is usually rounded or square and is held erect in some species. Birds of worldwide distribution, they feed largely on insects, worms, and snails, but many species also take fruit and berries. Species include the robin, the nightingale, the hermit thrush, and the bluebird.

Thrush, infection due to the fungus *Candida albicans.* It occurs usually in children and is characterized by small whitish spots on the tip and sides of the tongue and the lining membrane of the mouth.

Thucydides (460?-400 B.C.), historian of ancient Greece. His work *History of the Peloponnesian War* (441-404 B.C.) eloquently communicates an unbiased and accurate account of events in the first 30 years of that war. Both sides in the conflict are quoted, analyzed, and described in detail. Thucydides was an Athenian naval general who, upon failure to defeat the Spartan troops at Amphipolis in the Peloponnesian War, was exiled (424-404 B.C.).
See also: Greece, Ancient; Peloponnesian War.

Thugs, members of an Indian religious sect (13th-19th centuries) who murdered and robbed to honor the goddess Kali. All victims, usually wealthy travelers, were systematically strangled because the spilling of blood was forbidden. In 1831, British and Indian regimes collaborated to eliminate thug activities.

Thulium, chemical element, symbol Tm; for physical constants see Periodic Table. Thulium was discovered in 1879 by P.T. Cleve in crude erbium oxide. It occurs in the minerals gadolinite, euxenite, ytterspar, and monazite and is obtained commercially from the latter. It is prepared by reducing the anhydrous chloride with calcium. Thulium is a silvery, soft, reactive metal belonging to the series of elements known as the rare-earth metals. Thulium salts have a characteristic absorption spectrum. Ion-exchange and solvent extraction techniques have led to much easier isolation of the rare-earth elements. Thulium and its compounds are used in carbon-arc lighting, glass, and refractory materials.

Thunder Bay (pop. 112,300), city in Ontario, Canada, on the northwestern shore of Lake Superior. It has an excellent harbor, which makes it a major shipping center for grain and ore from western Canada. It is also the home of Lakehead University and of Confederation College of Applied Arts and Technology.
See also: Ontario.

Thurber, James (1894-1961), U.S. humorist and cartoonist. The sophisticated humor of his writing contrasts with the simplicity of his line drawings. Several stories, such as "The Secret Life of Walter Mitty" (1942), were filmed. He contributed to *The New Yorker* from 1927. His collections include *My Life and Hard Times* (1933) and *The Thurber Carnival* (1945).

Thurmond, (James) Strom (1902-), U.S. political leader, senator from South Carolina since 1954. A hardline supporter of States Rights, he opposed federal civil rights legislation and federal welfare. He served as South Carolina's governor (1947-51) and was the 1948 States' Rights Democratic presidential candidate, carrying four states. During his Senate career he shifted to the Republican party. He served as chairman of the Senate's Judiciary Committee (1981-87).

Thutmose III, or **Thothmes III** (d.1450 B.C.), king (c.1490-36 B.C.) of ancient Egypt. Upon accession to the throne, his half sister and wife, Queen Hatshepsut, acted forcefully as his governing ruler. Upon her death he became sole ruler and a brilliant leader and conqueror, expanding Egypt's boundaries, increasing its wealth, improving its manpower, and building and enlarging numerous temples, including the temple at Karnak.
See also: Egypt, Ancient.

Thyme, pungent, aromatic herb (genus *Thymus*) of the mint family. It has pale purple flowers. *T. vulgaris* is commonly used in seasoning.

Thyme

Thymus, lymphoid organ situated in humans in the chest cavity, behind the breastbone, and extending into the neck. It reaches its maximum weight at about puberty and then undergoes involution (shrinks). It is necessary in early life for the development of immunological functions.

Thyroid gland, ductless two-lobed endocrine gland lying in front of the trachea in the neck. The principal hormones secreted by the thyroid play a crucial role in regulating the rate at which cells oxidize fuels to release energy and thus strongly influence growth. Thyroid stimulating hormones (TSH) are released by the pituitary gland. Undersecretion (hypothyroidism) in adults leads to myxedema, with mental dullness and cool, dry, puffy skin. Oversecretion (thyrotoxicosis) produces nervousness, weight loss, and increased heart rate. Goiter, an enlargement of the gland, may result when the diet is deficient in iodine.
See also: Gland; Hormone.

Tianjin, or Tientsin (pop. 5,300,000), international port city on the Hai River in northeastern China. One of China's largest cities and Beijing's major port, it is a viable industrial center producing machinery, textiles, chemicals, and consumer products, in addition to offshore oil production. Tianjin was occupied by Western powers during the Boxer Uprising (1900) and was controlled by Japan from 1937 until the end of World War II. A major earthquake inflicted serious damage to Tianjin in 1976.
See also: China.

Tian Shan, or Tien Shan, major mountain system of central Asia. It runs some 1,500 mi (2,410 km) through the USSR and China. Its highest peak, the Pobeda Peak, stands 24,406 ft (7,439 m) above sea level.

Tiberias, Lake *see:* Galilee, Sea of.

Tiberius (Tiberius Julius Caesar Augustus; 42 B.C.-A.D. 37), Roman emperor, successor of his stepfather, Augustus, upon his death in A.D. 14. Tiberius oversaw tax collections and selected capable administrators to supervise his provinces. However, due to unpopular financial reforms and his growing tyranny, he retired to the island of Capri, where he ruled until his death.
See also: Rome, Ancient.

Tiber River, river in central Italy, flowing 252 mi (405.5 km) from the Appenines south through Umbria and Latium and southwest through Rome to the Tyrrhenian Sea near Ostia. Ancient Rome was built on its east bank.

Tibet, autonomous region of China in central Asia, bordering Myanmar (Burma), India, Nepal, Bhutan, and Sikkim. The capital is Lhasa.
Land and climate. Tibet's area is 471,662 sq mi (1,221,600 sq km), and the region averages 15,000 ft (4,570 m) in altitude. Tibet is often called the "Roof of the World." The tallest mountain in the world,

Mt. Everest (29,028 ft/8,848 m above sea level), is in the Himalaya, the world's tallest mountain chain. The Himalaya rise along the southern end of the Plateau of Tibet. The Kunlun Mountains in the north are almost as high as the Himalayas. The Brahmaputra, Indus, and Yangtze rivers rise in Tibet. The winters are dry and intensely cold; summers, hot and humid.

People. Tibetans follow Buddhist Lamaism, headed by the Dalai Lama and the Panchen Lama. Until 1965 there were many monasteries, involving 20% of the male population as monks. After 1965, the Chinese Communists decreased emphasis on religion.

Economy. The pastoral, livestock-based economy has been affected by roadbuilding and new cement, chemical, paper, textile, and other industries. Tibet has deposits of coal and iron (exploited in the northeast) and other minerals.

History. Tibet was a powerful kingdom during the A.D. 600s, flourishing until the early eighteenth century, when it fell under Chinese control. In 1911 Tibet expelled the Chinese, but friction remained between the 2 countries until 1950, when China invaded again. An agreement signed in 1951 ended Tibetan sovereignty, but allowed self-government and freedom of religion and speech. However, Chinese rule became steadily more oppressive, and y the mid-1950s Chinese rule in eastern Tibet caused open dissent and a revolt (1959) that was ruthlessly suppressed. The Dalai Lama fled from the capital Lhasa to India, and in 1965 Tibet became an autonomous region. After 20 years of periodic rioting and unrest in Tibet, the Chinese began a policy of liberalization, decentralizing the economy and allowing a degree of freedom of religion. However, massive rioting again erupted during the late 1980s and the Chinese declared a state of matrial law and sent in troups. Unrest continues in Tibet today.

See also: China.

Tick, name for a group of parasitic arthropods (order Acarina). Unlike most other arthropods, ticks have no head, and the thorax and abdomen are fused. All ticks are bloodsucking external parasites of vertebrates. They are divided into two main families: the soft ticks, Argasidae, and hard ticks, Ixodidae. Ticks transmit more diseases to humans and domestic animals than does any other arthropod group except the mosquitoes.

Tickseed *see:* Coreopsis.

Ticonderoga, village in northeast New York, near Lake George, site of Fort Ticonderoga, which commanded the route between Canada and the Hudson River valley. Taken (1759) by the British in the French and Indian Wars, it fell (1775) in the Revolutionary War to the Green Mountain Boys, led by Ethan Allen and Benedict Arnold. It was recaptured (1777) by General Burgoyne. The fort is now a museum.

See also: New York.

Tide, periodic rise and fall of land and water on the earth. Tidal motions are primarily exhibited by water: the motion of the land is barely detectable. As the earth-moon system rotates about its center of gravity, which is within the earth, the earth bulges in the direction of the moon, as well as in exactly the opposite direction owing to the moon's gravitational attraction and the centrifugal forces resulting from the system's revolution. Since the moon orbits the earth in the same direction that the earth rotates, the bulge "travels" round the earth each lunar day (24.83 hr); hence most points on the earth have a high tide every 12.42 hr. The sun produces a similar though smaller tidal effect. Exceptionally high high tides occur at full and new moon (spring tides), particularly if the moon is at perigee; exceptionally low high tides (neap tides), at first and third quarter. The friction of the tides causes the day to lengthen 0.001 sec per century.

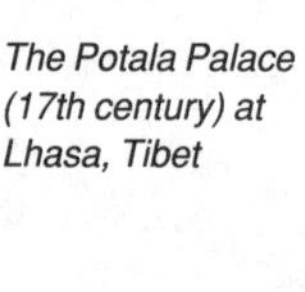

The Potala Palace (17th century) at Lhasa, Tibet

Tien Shan *see:* Tian Shan.

Tientsiu *see:* Tianjin.

Tiepolo, Giovanni Battista (1696-1770), most renowned Venetian painter of his time, a capable craftsman, decorator, and artist of vivid, large murals. His frescoes in Labia Palace brought him widespread recognition. As a result he was commissioned by Emperor Frederick I of Bavaria and by the Spanish royalty of Madrid, where his work included the *Apotheosis of Spain*.

Giovanni Battista Tiepolo's painting of the meeting between Antony and Cleopatra

Tierra del Fuego (Spanish, "Land of Fire"), several small islands (28,476 sq mi/73,753 sq km) separated from the southern coast of South America by the Strait of Magellan. Named by Ferdinand Magellan in 1520, the islands belong to Chili and Argentina. The small population is supported by income from sheep and petroleum.

See also: Cape Horn.

Tiffany, Charles Lewis (1812-1902), U.S. jeweler and retailer. The stock in his first store, opened in 1839, was limited mainly to ordinary glassware and stationery, but it soon included bohemian glass, jewelry, silverware, and rare porcelain. Tiffany began manufacturing his own jewelry in 1848, and by 1870 had extended his operations to Paris and London.

Tiffany, Louis Comfort (1848-1933), U.S. artist and designer, a leader of Art Nouveau; son of jeweler Charles Tiffany. He created decorative objects of iridescent "favrile," or Tiffany glass.

See also: Art nouveau.

Tiflis *see:* Tbilisi.

Tiger (*Panthera tigris*), major cat of Asia with distinct races in different parts of that continent. Closely related to lions, they are the largest of all the cats. A tawny coat broken with dark, vertical stripes provides excellent camouflage against natural patterns of light and shade. Tigers do not chase after food, but prefer to stalk and spring. For the most part they are solitary animals, hunting in the cool of the day and otherwise lying in the shade to rest.

Tiger lily (*Lilium tigrinum*), plant of the lily family originating in eastern Asia and grown widely as a garden flower. The dark stem, 2-6 ft (0.6-1.8 m) tall, supports large red-orange flowers with black markings. The plant propagates by means of small, black, berrylike bulbs that form where the leaves join the stem and fall to the earth to produce new plants.

Tiglath-pileser, rulers of ancient Assyria. **Tiglath-pileser I** ruled from 1115-1077 B.C. A great military leader, he conquered territories from the Mediterranean coast to what are now Turkey and Iran. Historians know little about **Tiglath-pileser II**, who ruled from 967-935 B.C. during a seemingly stable reign. **Tiglath-pileser III**, who ruled from 744-727 B.C., founded the Assyrian Empire. He led a massive military and diplomatic campaign that extended into parts of what are now Iraq, Syria, and Turkey. In 728 B.C., he united the kingdoms of Assyria and Babylonia and declared himself king of Babylonia.
See also: Assyria.

Tigris River, easternmost of the two great rivers of ancient Mesopotamia. The Tigris-Euphrates valley was the cradle of Middle East civilizations. Baghdad, city of the Abbasids, now capital of Iraq, stands on its banks. It rises in the Taurus Mountains in Turkey and flows 1,180 mi (1,900 km) southeast through Iraq to join the Euphrates at Basra.

Tijuana (pop. 535,000), city in Mexico, near the U.S. border. Tijuana, its name derived from the Tia Juana (Spanish, "Aunt Jane") ranch in the area, was settled in the early 1900s. It is a popular tourist town, noted for its bullfights and racetracks.
See also: Mexico.

Tikhonov, Nikolai Aleksandrovich (1905-), soviet premier (1980-85). In 1940 Tikhonov joined the Communist Party. During the 1950s-70s he rose in the Soviet government, becoming a member of the Politburo in 1979. Failing health caused him to resign in 1985.
See also: Union of Soviet Socialist Republics.

Tilden, Bill (William Tatem Tilden, Jr.; 1893-1953), U.S. tennis player. Known for his powerful serve and strong forehand, from 1920 to 1930 he was the top-ranked U.S. player, and led the U.S. team to 7 Davis Cup titles (1920-26). Other victories include 3 Wimbledon titles (1920, 21, 30) and 7 U.S. Open titles (1920-25, 29).

Tilden, Samuel Jones (1814-86), U.S. lawyer and politician. An early leader of the Barnburners faction of the New York Democratic Party and of the Free Soil Party, he proved that there was corruption among New York City politicians led by William ("Boss") Tweed. He was governor of New York (1875-76). Even though he won more popular votes, Tilden lost the hotly contested 1876 presidential election to Republican Rutherford B. Hayes by one electoral vote.

Tilefish, colorful ocean fish belonging to the tilefish family, found along the New England coastline. It is about 3 ft (91 cm) in length and can weigh over 30 lb (14 km). It eats mostly crabs and other fish, and is considered to be a good food fish.

Tillich, Paul Johannes (1886-1965), German-born theologian and teacher. He attempted to synthesize Christianity and classical and modern existentialist philosophy in works like *Systematic Theology* (1951-63), *The Shaking of Foundations* (1948), and *The Courage to Be* (1948). Dismissed from Frankfurt University because of opposition to the Nazis, he taught at the Union Theological Seminary, New York (1933-59) and at Harvard and Chicago universities (1954-62 and 1962-65, respectively).
See also: Theology.

Timbuktu (pop. 20,500), city in central Mali, in the southern Sahara. It was settled in the 1100s by the Tuareg and used by merchants of the 14th century as a major trading center for gold, salt, ivory, and slaves. The 15th and 16th centuries saw the rise of the Songhai Empire and Timbuktu became a center of Muslim learning. It was sacked by the Moroccans (1593), and French rule was established in 1894. Today it continues to be an important marketplace (salt, handicrafts) for the nomads of the Sahara.
See also: Mali.

Time, measure of duration, whether past, present, or future; a particular portion or part of duration; period at which any definite event occurred or person lived; prevailing state or circumstances. Absolute time is time considered without relation to bodies or their motions. Relative time is the sensible measure of any portion of duration. Astronomical time is mean solar time reckoned through the 24-hour cycle. Civil time is mean time adapted to civil uses and distinguished into years, months, days, etc. A timetable is a table or register of times, as of the hours to be observed in a school, of the departure and arrival of railroad trains, buses, etc. Time-sharing is a method of operation in which a computer facility is shared by several users for different purposes at the same time. A time quantum, in a time-sharing system, is a unit of time allotted to each user. Time slicing is the allotment of a portion of processing time to each program in a multiprogramming system to prevent the monopolization of the central processing unit by any one program.

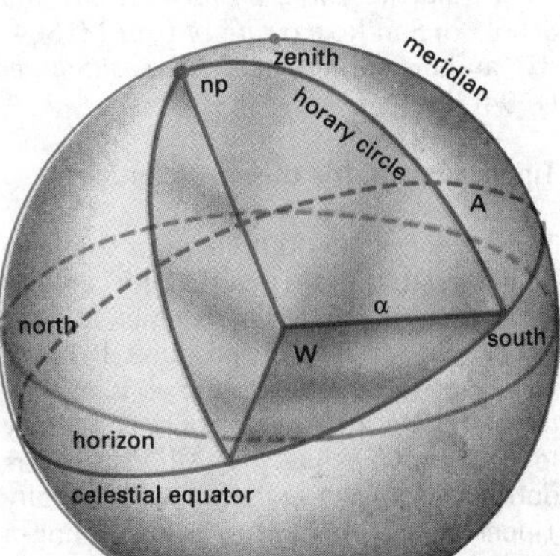

A fixed point (A) in the firmament is taken as a reference point when rotation of the Earth is to be used as the basis for measuring time. This point then determines the horary circle that passes through the point and the northern and southern celestial poles (np and sp, respectively). The horary circle seems to revolve once per day, and thus passes the observer's local meridian (the circle passing through the two celestial poles as well as the zenith and nadir of the observer) at daily intervals.

Tiger

Timor, largest and easternmost of the Lesser Sunda Islands, 400 mi (644 km) northwest of Australia. Since Dec. 1975, when the former Portuguese (eastern) Timor was occupied by Indonesian troops, the whole island has been under Indonesian control. The terrain is largely mountainous. Crops include coffee, coconuts, and rice, and cattle are raised.

Effects of time shown in a piece of tree in a petrified forest

Tintoretto's Saint Mark Rescuing a Slave *(1548)*

Timothy (*Phleum pratense*), perennial coarse grass grown for hay harvesting and animal grazing. Its nutritional value is increased when alfalfa or clover seed is added to its fields. Also known as herd's-grass, it grows 1.5-3.5 ft (46-107 cm) high and thrives in the northern United States (especially New York state) and Canada.

Timothy, disciple of the Apostle Paul; also, 2 epistles of the New Testament addressed to Timothy. They became part of the Pastoral Epistles, providing guidelines and advice on governing a church.
See also: New Testament.

Timpani, or kettledrums, drums having a calfskin head over a hollow brass or copper hemisphere. They were first used in orchestral music in the 1600s. A set of timpani usually consists of three drums. Pitch is governed by the tension of the head, which can be adjusted. Tone may be varied by the type of stick used for play and by the region of the head struck.

Timur the Lame *see:* Tamerlane.

Tin, chemical element, symbol Sn; for physical constants see Periodic Table. Tin was known to the ancients. It occurs in cassiterite, stannite, and tealite. The element is produced by reducing the oxide with coal in a reverberatory furnace. Tin is a silver-white, soft, malleable, ductile metal. It is resistant to corrosion and is used extensively for coating other metals. Tin exists in 2 forms: alpha (gray) and beta (white). Change to the unusable gray form, called tin pest, is prevented by the addition of small amounts of antimony or bismuth. Pewter, bronze, type metal, and soft solder are some important tin alloys. Stannous chloride is an important reducing agent. Tin and its compounds are used in electrically conductive coatings, dyeing, and super-conductive magnets.

Jan Tinbergen

Tinbergen, Jan (1903-), Dutch economist who in 1969 shared the first Nobel Prize for economic science with Ragnar Frisch for work in developing dynamic models (econometrics).
See also: Economics.

Tinbergen, Nikolas (1907-), Dutch ethologist awarded, with Konrad Lorenz and Karl von Frisch, the 1973 Nobel Prize for physiology or medicine for their individual, major contributions to the science of animal behavior.
See also: Ethology.

Tinnitus, sensation of sounds not derived from the outer environment, such as ringing, roars, or banging in the inner ear. It is a common symptom of most ear disorders. Tinnitus is not a severe or disabling problem, but a medical diagnosis is important in determining whether an underlying cause requires treatment.

Tintoretto (Jacopo Robusti; 1518-94), Venetian mannerist painter of the Renaissance. His popular name, Tintoretto ("Little Dyer"), refers to his father's occupation. Influenced by Titian and Michelangelo, Tintoretto's paintings and frescoes are characterized by free brushwork, dramatic viewpoint, movement, monumental figures, and rich colors. He sought to express drama through color and light, as in *Saint Mark Rescuing a Slave* (1548), the Scuola di San Rocco *Life of Christ* (1564-87), and his masterpiece, *The Last Supper* (1594).

Tippecanoe, Battle of *see:* Indian wars.

Tipperary (pop. 5,000), town in southern Ireland established in the late 12th century, located on the Ara River. Its chief industry is the processing of dairy products. Its name was made famous due to the popularity of the marching song "It's a Long, Long Way to Tipperary," sung by Allied soldiers during World War I (1914-18). Originally Tipperary was a small town encircling a castle built by the man who became King John of England.

Tiranë, or **Tirana** (pop. 260,000), capital of Albania, located about 20 mi (32 km) east of the Adriatic Sea. It was founded in the early 17th century and became the capital city in 1920. After the proclamation of Communist rule in 1946, the city grew as an industrial center. It is the home of many of Albania's cultural and educational institutions as well as the center of the country's publishing and broadcast industries. Most residents are Muslim.
See also: Albania.

Tirso de Molina (1584-1648), pen name of Spanish author and playwright, Gabriel Tellez. He is known as one of the greatest playwrights of the Golden Age of Spain. Among the hundreds of plays he wrote, 86 survive, most notably *The Deceiver of Seville* (1630), which introduced the legendary character of Don Juan. A friar and a respected theologian, he wrote plays, stories, and poetry that reflected his knowledge and understanding of history, religion, and human nature. These include *The Gardens of Toledo* (1624) and *Pleasure with Profit* (1635).

Tissue, in biology, similar cells grouped together in multicellular animals and plants. These cells are usually specialized for a single function; thus muscle cells contract but do not secrete, and nerve cells conduct impulses but have little or no powers of contraction. The cells are held together by intercellular material. Having become specialized for a single or at most a very narrow range of functions, they are dependent upon other parts of the organism for necessities like food and oxygen. Groups of tissues, each with its own functions, make up organs. Connective tissue refers to the material in which all the specialized body organs are embedded and supported.

Tissue transplant, permanent transfer of tissue or organs from one part of a body to another. It may involve transplanting tissue, such as skin or bone, within the same body (autografts); or it might involve more than one body, as when one person donates an organ to another person (allografts). Autografts are usually successful because the body normally does not reject its own tissues. Allografts, however, are often unsuccessful because the transplant recipient may reject the donor's tissue or organ. To avoid such rejections, physicians try to match donors and recipients with compatible tissues. People who have a number of similar proteins (HLA antigens) in the cells of the tissues to be exchanged are more likely to achieve a successful tissue transplant. Because HLA antigens are inherited, siblings have a higher rate of tissue transplant success.

Titanic, 46,328-ton British liner that sank in 1912 after hitting an iceberg on its maiden voyage. At least 1,500 of the 2,200 aboard drowned. After the disaster (caused mainly by excessive speed), lifeboat, radio watch, and ice patrol provisions were improved.

Titaniferous ore, blend of minerals rich in the metal titanium. The ore is black and granular and is usually composed of ilmenite and magnetite.

Titanium, chemical element, symbol Ti; for physical constants see Periodic Table. Titanium was discovered by William Gregor in 1791 (named after the Titans). It occurs in the minerals rutile, ilmenite, and sphene. Titanium is the ninth most abundant element in the earth's crust. It is prepared by reducing titanium tetrachloride with magnesium. Titanium is a white, lustrous, strong, corrosion-resistant metal. It is the only element that burns in nitrogen. It is as strong as steel, but 45% lighter. Titanium and its compounds are used in heat-resistant alloys, paint pigments, and chemical smoke screens.

Titans, in Greek mythology, offspring of Uranus and Gaea, including Cronus, Hyperion, Iapetus, Oceanus, Coeus, Creus, Theia, Rhea, Mnemosyne, Phoebe, Tethys, and Themis, as well as their descendants (e.g., Atlas, Prometheus). Cronus and his siblings overthrew Uranus. In turn one of Cronus's offspring, Zeus, led the Olympians to defeat Cronus and become rulers of the universe, banishing the Titans, except for Cronus (who ruled the Isle of the Blessed) and Atlas (who held up the sky), to Tartarus. Prometheus, who aided Zeus, was also allowed to remain.
See also: Mythology.

Titchener, Edward Bradford (1867-1927), English-born U.S. psychologist. A disciple of Wilhelm Wundt, he played a large part in establishing experimental psychology in the United States, especially through his *Experimental Psychology* (2 vol., 1901-05).
See also: Psychology.

Titi, small tree-dwelling monkey belonging to the New World monkey family Cebidae and found in Brazil's Orinoco River Basin. It lives in 2-parent family units and subsists on fruit, leaves, small birds, and insects. A characteristic of the titi is its habit, with others of its kind, of winding its tail around a tree branch when asleep or at rest.

Titian (Tiziano Vecellio; 1487-1576), Venetian painter, leading Renaissance artist. He worked for Giovanni Bellini and Giorgione, who influenced his early work, before becoming Venice's official painter (1516). His perceptive portraits, monumental altarpieces, and historical and mythological scenes are famous for their energetic composition, use of rich color, and original technique. Among his works are *La Gloria* (1554), *Rape of Europe* (1562), and *Adam and Eve* (1570).
See also: Renaissance.

Titmouse, forest bird of the family Pariclae, found mainly in the Northern Hemisphere. Related to the nuthatch and the chickadee, these small, brown-and-gray birds travel with other birds in flocks and are easily trained to do tricks.

THE MAGNIFICENCE OF THE TITANIC: PORTRAITS OF NOTABLE PASSENGERS ON BOARD THE ILL-FATED VESSEL.

A story about the Titanic *was published in the* Daily Mirror *on April 16, 1912, one day after the ship sank.*

Tito, Josip Broz (1892-1980), president of Yugoslavia (1953-80), founder of the post-World War II republic. He became a Communist while a World War I prisoner of war in Russia, and later spent several years in Yugoslav jails. General secretary of the Communist Party from 1937, Tito organized partisan resistance to the Nazis in World War II, eclipsing the Chetniks, and after the war established a Socialist republic. He served as prime minister (1945-53) before becoming president. Tito broke with Joseph Stalin in 1948. He suppressed home opposition but worked for workers' self-management and the reconciliation of national minorities. Later years saw a substantial liberalization of his policies. On the international scene, Tito became an organizer and leading representative for Third World or neutralist countries.
See also: Yugoslavia.

Titus (Titus Flavius Sabinus Vespasianus; A.D.39-81), Roman emperor, successor (79) to his father Vespasian. A successful soldier, he captured (70) Jerusalem in the Jewish revolt (66-70). He was popular for lavish entertaining and for aiding victims of the eruption of the Vesuvius (79) and the fire at Rome (80).
See also: Rome, Ancient.

Titus, early Christian follower of St. Paul. He traveled with Paul to the Council of Jerusalem, and later went with him to Greece. Appointed by Paul as a special representative to the church in Corinth, he was later made the first archbishop of Crete. Paul's epistle to Titus, the 17th book of the New Testament, believed to have been written in A.D. 65 or 66, gave Titus instructions on how to organize the church in Crete.
See also: Paul, Saint.

TNT, or trinitrotoluene, $[CH_3C_6H_2(NO_2)_3]$, pale yellow crystalline solid made by nitration of toluene. It is the most extensively used high explosive, being relatively insensitive to shock, especially when melted by steam heating and cast.
See also: Explosive.

Toad, name strictly referring only to members of the family Bufonidae, but generally distinguishing warty-skinned, tailless amphibians from smoother-skinned types, which are called frogs. Toads range in size from 1 to 7 in (2.5 to 18 cm). They are independent of water except for breeding, the larvae—tadpoles—being purely aquatic. Most toads feed nocturnally on insects.

Toadstool *see:* Mushroom.

Tobacco, plant of the nightshade family (especially genus *Nicotiana*); also, the dried and cured leaves of the plant, used for smoking and chewing and as snuff. Native to America, tobacco was introduced to Europe by the Spanish in the 16th century and from there spread to Asia and Africa. Today the United States remains the world's largest producer, followed by China, India, and the USSR. Consumption is increasing despite the health hazards of smoking. Tobacco is grown in alluvial or

Josip Broz Tito

Titian's Danaë *(1553/4)*

sandy soils and may be harvested after about 4 months. Cultivation is dependent on hand labor.

Tobago *see:* Trinidad and Tobago.

Tobey, Mark (1890-1976), U.S. painter. Strongly influenced by Chinese calligraphy and Zen Buddhism, he developed his "white writing" style in the 1930s in small abstracts representing street scenes. His later, delicately colored abstracts have more intricate linear rhythms.

Tobin, Daniel Joseph (1875-1955), Irish-born U.S. labor leader. As president of the Teamsters Union (1907-52), he built it into one of the most powerful unions in the United States. He was also vice-president of the American Federation of Labor (1933-52).
See also: Labor movement.

Tobin, James (1918-), U.S. economist. He won the 1981 Nobel Memorial Prize in economic science for his research in relating the effects of financial markets to consumption, prices, production, and investment, as well as his studies of government monetary policies and budgets. He had served as one of President John F. Kennedy's economics advisors.
See also: Economics.

Tobit, or **Tobias, Book of**, in the Apocrypha, account of how Tobias, son of the devout but blinded Jew Tobit (or Tobias), successfully undertook a dangerous journey, helped by the angel Raphael, to exorcise a demon from, and marry, Sara. He then helped Tobit regain his sight.
See also: Old Testament.

Tobogganing, sport of riding down snow or ice slopes on a sled or toboggan. Although sleds with runners are sometimes called toboggans, the term usually refers to runnerless sleds such as were originally developed by Native American hunters. The modern toboggan is generally 6-8 ft (1.8-2.4 m) long and 1 ft (46 cm) wide, and carries 4 people, one behind another. Artificial chutes for the initial acceleration have allowed high speeds. Bobsledding, a type of tobogganing, is a sport of the Winter Olympics.

Tocopherol *see:* Vitamin.

Tocqueville, Alexis de (1805-59), French historian and writer best known for the 2-volume *Democracy in America*, written after visiting the United States in the early 1830s. The book made him a leading European advocate of democracy, a system he believed would eventually replace the European monarchies and aristocracies. A philosopher, Tocqueville also saw the pitfalls of democracy, warning against a "tyranny of the majority" in which conformity would discourage individualism. He served in the French legislature (1839-51) and was foreign minister following the Revolution of 1848.
See also: France.

Todd, Mary *see:* Lincoln, Mary Todd.

Tofu, or bean curd, soft, white, cheeselike food made by treating soybean milk with coagulants and pressing the curds into cakes. It originated in China more than 1,000 years ago and is widely used in Asia. Tofu is bland, high in protein, low in salt and calories, and cholesterol-free. It has thus become popular in the West as a substitute for cheese, cream, and other animal fat products.

Toga, robe worn in ancient Rome. Originally worn by both men and women, it gradually fell out of favor with women. Made of soft wool, it was loosely draped in abundant folds over an undergarment called a tunic. Its color delineated the status, rank, or age of the wearer. Because it limited movement, it eventually came to be worn by the upper classes and politicians.

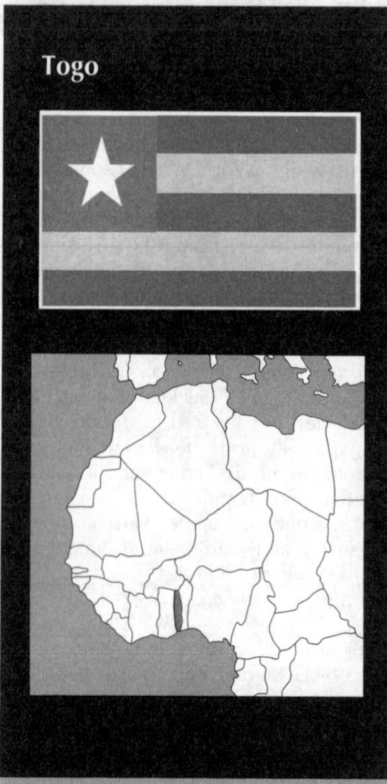

Capital:	Lomé
Area:	21,925 sq mi (56,785 sq km)
Population:	3,622,000
Government:	republic
Independent:	1960
GNP:	U.S.$1,240,000,000
Per capita:	U.S.$370

Togo, republic in West Africa. Bordered by Ghana on the west, Benin on the east, Burkina Faso on the north, and the Gulf of Guinea on the south, Togo has an area of 21,853 sq mi (56,599 sq km) and is 340 mi (547 km) long and 70 mi (113 km) wide. The capital is the seaport of Lomè.
Land and people. From the central Togo Mountains a grassy plateau slopes east to the Mono River and south to the sandy coastal plain. North of the mountains is the savanna of the Oti Plateau. The climate is hot and humid. The people of Togo are almost entirely black Africans of the Ewe, Ouatchi, Mina, and Kabre ethnic groups. There are Christians and Muslims, but most people follow traditional beliefs. French is the official language, but Ewe is the most widely used.
Economy. Over 90% of the people live in rural areas, mostly in the south, and the economy is primarily agricultural. The chief exports are cocoa and coffee, but cassava, corn, and cotton are also important. Large phosphate deposits discovered northeast of Lomè have proven profitable and Togo ranks fourth in world production.
History. Togo was settled in the 1300s by a group of Ewe-speaking people, then further populated by invaders and refugees from various wars north of the area. As the slave trade grew, Togo became an important center for the buying and selling of slaves. Germany set up a protectorate (known as Togoland) in 1884; after World War I, it was administered by the French. Togo became an independent nation in 1960 with Sylvanus Olympio as president. After a long period of political turmoil, a military coup in 1967 installed Lt. Col. Gnassingbe Eyadema as the country's leader. He received popular support in a 1972 presidential vote and was reelected in 1979.

Tojo, Hideki (1884-1948), Japanese military and political leader. He became minister of war in 1940, premier in Oct. 1941, and approved the bombing of Pearl Harbor on Dec. 7, 1941, leading Japan into World War II against the United States. Assuming totalitarian control over Japan during the early years of the war, Tojo was responsible for atrocities and the torture of Allied prisoners of war. He was forced to resign as premier in 1944 but continued to advocate a "no surrender" policy. After the war he was captured, tried as a war criminal, and hanged on Dec. 23, 1948.
See also: World War II.

Tokyo (pop. 8,354,000), capital of Japan. It lies at the head of Tokyo Bay on the southeastern coast of Honshu Island and contains over 10% of Japan's population. Founded in the 12th century as Edo, it became capital of the Tokugawa shoguns in 1603; it was renamed and made imperial capital in 1868. Reconstruction after earthquake and fire (1923) and the air raids of World War II transformed much of Tokyo. It is today a center of government, industry, finance, and education. The National Diet (parliament) meets here; most of Japan's great corporations have their head offices in the Maurunochi district; Tokyo University (founded 1877) is one of hundreds of educational institutions. Tokyo has many parks, museums, and temples, the Imperial Palace, and the Kabukiza theater. Industries (with large complexes to the west) include printing, shipbuilding, metal manufactures, automobile, chemicals, and textiles. The harbor and airport are Japan's busiest.
See also: Japan.

Ginza, the entertainment district of Tokyo

Toledo (pop. 614,128), city in northwestern Ohio, at the mouth of the Maumee River on Lake Erie. It was settled in the early 19th century after Gen. Anthony Wayne's victory over Native American forces at the nearby Battle of Fallen Timbers (1794) and the establishment of Fort Industry (1795). The settlements of Port Lawrence and Vistula, built near the site of Fort Industry, merged in 1833 to form Toledo. Today Toledo is an important Great Lakes port and manufacturing center (e.g., glass, oil products, machines), and a cultural center with 2 universities, a major art museum, symphony, opera, and one of the nation's best zoos.
See also: Ohio.

Toledo (pop. 62,800), city in central Spain 40 mi (64 km) southwest of Madrid, seat of Toledo province, former Roman and Visgoth capital. Possessing minimal industry, Toledo produces textiles, sabers, and firearms. The entire city has been declared a national monument and contains beautiful examples of medieval and Renaissance art and architecture. Toledo's many landmarks include the Alcázar (citadel), Gothic cathedral (the archbishop is Spain's primate), and El Greco's house, which serves as a museum for several of his paintings.
See also: Spain.

Tolkien, J(ohn) R(onald) R(euel) (1892-1973), English author and scholar, celebrated for *The Hobbit* (1937) and the trilogy *The Lord of the Rings* (1954-56), which present a mythical world of elves and dwarfs, partly based on Anglo-Saxon and Norse folklore. Tolkien was professor of Anglo-Saxon, then of English, language and literature at Oxford University.

Tolstoy, Aleksei Nikolaevich (1882-1945), Russian novelist and playwright, best known for his trilogy *The Road to Calvary* (1921-40), the novella *Nikita's Childhood* (1922), and the novel *Peter the First* (1929-45). A nobleman distantly related to Leo Tolstoy, he left Russia in 1917 but returned in 1922 and became a supporter of Joseph Stalin's regime.

Tolstoy, Leo (1828-1910), Russian novelist. Educated at Kazan University, he served in the army, married in 1862, and spent the next 15 years on his estate at Yasnaya Polyana near Moscow. In this period he produced his masterpieces, including *War and Peace* (1865-69), an epic of vast imaginative scope and variety of character, telling the story of five families against the background of the Napoleonic invasion of Russia. *Anna Karenina* (1875-77), the tragic story of an adulterous affair, is remarkable for its psychological portrayal. In later years Tolstoy experienced a spiritual crisis, recounted in his *Confession* (1882), and embraced an ascetic philosophy of Christian anarchism. His other works include *Childhood* (1852), *The Cossacks* (1863), and *Resurrection* (1899).

Toltec, Native American civilization dominant in the central Mexican highlands between the 900s and 1100s. The Toltec god was Quetzalcoatl, for whom they performed human sacrifice. The Toltecs, sophisticated builders and artisans, erected their capital at Tollán (ruins near modern Tula, 60 mi [96.5 km] north of Mexico City). The dominant group were Nahuati speakers. Aztecs and others overran the area and adopted various aspects of Toltec culture.

Toluene ($C_6H_5CH_3$), liquid hydrocarbon related to benzene. Made from treated petroleum or distilled coal tar, it is commonly used in the production of a wide range of industrial chemicals, such as the preservative benzoic acid and the explosive trinitrotoluene (TNT). Because it is toxic, federal guidelines exist to regulate its use in the workplace.
See also: Benzene.

Tomato (*Lycopersicon esculentum*), herbaceous plant of the nightshade family, native to South America but introduced to Europe in the 16th century and now cultivated worldwide; also, the fruit of the plant. Most of the crop is canned or processed to make prepared foods, a relatively small proportion being grown for salad use. In northern latitudes, tomatoes are grown under glass, but the bulk are grown as a field crop. Italy, Spain, Brazil, and Japan are among the leading producers.

Ruins of Tula, the religious center of the Toltecs

Tombstone (pop. 1,632), city in southeastern Arizona, founded in 1879 after the discovery of silver veins in the nearby mountains. Once billed as "the town too tough to die," Tombstone was one of the most notoriously lawless settlements of the American West. In Oct. 1881 Tombstone's O.K. Corral was the site of a famous gunfight pitting Wyatt Earp, 2 of his brothers, and Doc Holliday against a rival faction. Today Tombstone is a major tourist attraction and in 1962 was designated a national historic landmark.
See also: Arizona.

Tom Thumb, General (1838-83), stage name for the U.S. entertainer Charles Sherwood Stratton. Stratton, a midget whose adult height was 40 in (101.5 cm), toured Europe and the U.S. with P.T. Barnum.

Tonegawa, Susumu (1939-), Japanese biologist. An expert in immunology, he won the 1987 Nobel Prize for physiology or medicine for his discovery of techniques to study the response of the body's immune system in order to protect against new disease agents. Formerly at the Basel Institute for Immunology in Switzerland, he has worked at the Massachusetts Institute of Technology since 1981.
See also: Biology; Immunity.

Leo Tolstoy

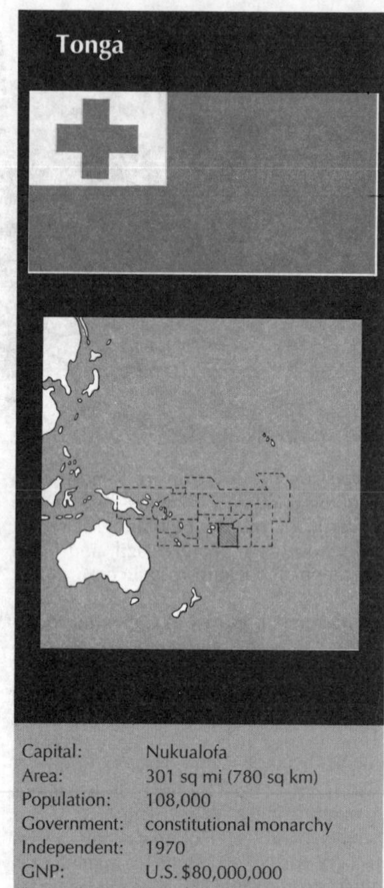

Capital:	Nukualofa
Area:	301 sq mi (780 sq km)
Population:	108,000
Government:	constitutional monarchy
Independent:	1970
GNP:	U.S. $80,000,000
Per capita:	U.S. $800

Tonga, or Friendly Islands, constitutional monarchy in the South Pacific. The kingdom comprises over 150 islands of which the chief groups are Tongatapu, Háapai, and Vaváu. The climate is tropical. The capital is Nukùalofa on Tongatapu. The population is mainly Polynesian, with a small number of Europeans. The economy is agricultural, with copra, banana, and vanilla the chief exports. Promising petroleum deposits were located near Tongatapu in 1977. The islands were discovered in 1616 by the Dutch explorer Jakob Lemaire and later visited by Abel Tasman (1643), and James Cook (1773), who named them the Friendly Islands. The present kingdom was founded in 1845 by George Tupou I and became a British protectorate in 1900. It achieved independence in 1970. The present king (since 1967) is Taufaahau Tupou IV.

Topaz

Tongue, muscular organ in the floor of the mouth, concerned with the formation of food boluses and self-cleansing of the mouth, taste sensation and voice production. In certain animals, the tongue is used to draw food into the mouth from a distance.

Tonkin, historic region of Southeast Asia, now comprising most of northern Vietnam. It was the European name for the region around the Red River delta, which became a French protectorate in 1883, part of French Indochina. Under Japanese occupation during World War II and thereafter a French protectorate again, Tonkin became part of independent North Vietnam with the departure of the French in 1954.

Tonsil, name for either of two small oval-shaped, fleshy bodies, situated on each side of the back of the throat (palatine tonsils). They act as filters of disease organisms. Similar lymphoid masses are the phalangeal tonsils (adenoids) between the back of the nose and throat, and the lingual tonsils, on the back of the tongue.
See also: Adenoids.

Tonsillitis, inflammation of the tonsils due to virus or bacteria infection. It may follow sore throat or other pharyngeal disease, or it may be primary tonsil disease. Sore throat and red swollen tonsils, which may exude pus or cause swallowing difficulty, are common; lymph nodes at the angle of the jaw are usually tender and swollen. Quinsy is a rare complication. Antobiotic treatment for the bacterial cause usually leads to a resolution, but removal of the tonsils is needed in few cases.

Topaz, aluminum silicate mineral of composition $Al_2SiO_4(F,OH)_2$, forming prismatic crystals (orthorhombic) that are variable and unstable in color and valued as gemstones. The best topazes come from Brazil, Siberia, and the United States.

Topeka (pop. 160,976), state capital of Kansas, located on the Kansas River in the northeastern part of the state. Topeka was laid out by Free Staters in 1854, following passage of the Kansas-Nebraska Act that opened the territory to popular sovereignty, and in 1861 was chosen as the state capital. Headquarters of the Atchison, Topeka & Santa Fe Railroad, Topeka is also a major agricultural, livestock, and manufacturing center, and is home to the Menninger Foundation, one of the world's leading psychiatric facilities and research centers.
See also: Kansas.

Topology, branch of mathematics that studies properties of geometrical figures or abstract spaces that are independent of shape or distance. Point-set topology deals with ways of defining "nearness" of elements, or points, of a set without necessarily assigning numerical distances to pairs of points. Such a definition is called "a topology on the set," and the set is called a topological space. The topology makes it possible to define continuous functions on the space. Algebraic topology, or combinatorial topology, uses abstract algebra to treat the ways in which geometrical figures fit together to form figures of higher dimension, disregarding shape. For example a sphere is topologically the same as a cube, but it is distinct from a torus (doughnut) because if the surfaces of the figures are divided into triangles, the algebraic relationships between the triangles will be different in the two cases.

Torah (Hebrew: "law, teaching"), the Pentateuch (first five books of the Bible) kept in the ark of every synagogue. In a wider sense it is the whole body of the oral and written teaching central to Judaism and includes the rest of the Hebrew Bible, rabbinic codes, the Talmud, and the Midrash.
See also: Bible.

Tornado, violent whirlwind cloud of small diameter, extending downward from a convective cloud in a severe thunderstorm, generally funnelshaped. Air rises rapidly in the outer region of the funnel, but descends in its core, which is at very low pressure. The funnel is visible owing to the formation of cloud droplets by expansional cooling in this low-pressure region. Very high winds spiral in toward the core. There is almost total devastation and often loss of life in the path of a tornado, which may move at speeds up to 656 ft (200 m) per sec. Though generally rare, tornadoes occur worldwide, especially in the United States and Australia in spring and early summer.

Toronto (pop. 612,300), capital of Ontario province and York County, second-largest city in Canada (after Montreal), on the northwestern shore of Lake Ontario. It is a major port, as well as a commercial, manufacturing, and educational center. The cultural focus of English-speaking Canada, Toronto is home to the Royal Conservatory of Music, the Canadian Music Center, the Royal Ontario Museum, and a parks system that covers 6,000 acres (2,400 hectares). Its industrial products include chemicals, machinery, electrical goods, and clothing. The French settled the area and built Fort Rouillé (1750), which was replaced by the English city of York (1793). Sacked in the War of 1812, York was renamed Toronto in 1834.
See also: Ontario.

Nathan Phillips Square, Toronto

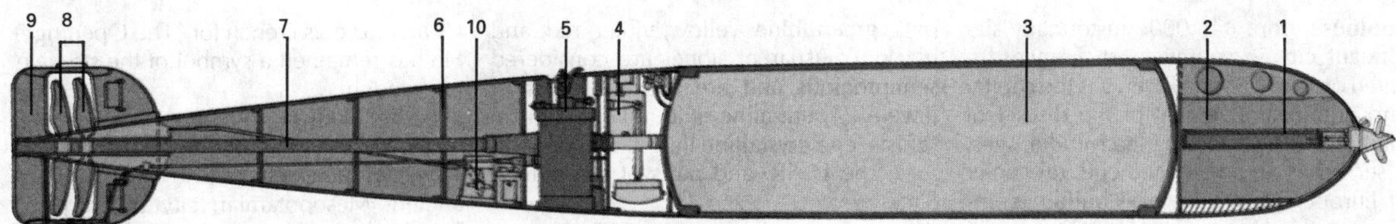

The Mark II 1891 Witehead torpedo.
Key:
1. ignition
2. explosive
3. air chamber
4. balance chamber
5. engine
6. watertight partition
7. propeller shaft
8. propellers
9. rudder
10. gyro mechanism

Torpedo, flat, broad fish of the Torpedinidae family, found in tropical and temperate regions of the Atlantic and Pacific oceans. Also known as the electric ray, it emits electricity to stun fish for food and to protect itself. The shock from the torpedo is not lethal to humans but has been known to stun them.

Torpedo, self-propelled streamlined missile that travels underwater, its explosive warhead detonating when it nears or strikes its target. The torpedo was invented (1866) by Robert Whitehead, a British engineer. Torpedoes are now chiefly antisubmarine weapons.

Torpedo boat *see:* PT boat.

Torquemada, Tomás de (1420-98), Spanish Inquisition leader. A Dominican monk, he became the confessor to Queen Isabella and was named inquisitor general (1483), responsible for the executions of more than 2,000 people considered heretics (primarily Muslims and Jews). He was largely responsible for the expulsion of more than 200,000 Jews from Spain in 1492. Torquemada established rules and procedures for the Inquisition, some of which involved torture and other cruel methods of execution; his name has become synonymous with excessive cruelty.
See also: Inquisition.

Torricelli, Evangelista (1608-47), Italian physicist and mathematician who invented the barometer in 1643. He also improved the effectiveness of the telescope and the microscope. His work in the field of pure mathematics was influential in the development of integral calculus. He was inspired by the work of his friend and mentor, Galileo.
See also: Barometer.

Torsion balance, device for measuring the force of a twisting motion. These measurements are registered on a gauge that is calibrated—readings adjusted for correct measurement. In a torsion bar, stretched fibers (usually gold, quartz, or steel) are attached to heavy noncorrosive balls (usually gold, lead, or stainless steel) that twist and turn to compensate for the introduced push-and-pull actions. A balanced zero reading is the desired result. In automobiles, a torsion bar, through torsion balance, compensates for bumps and holes experienced on the road.

Torsion bar suspension, system designed to absorb front-end shock in automobiles. There is one torsion bar for each of an automobile's 2 front wheels. One end of the torsion bar is attached to the car's frame. The other end is attached to the axle near the wheel. When the car hits a bump, the torsion bar, which somewhat resembles a straightened spring, twists and then untwists. This movement absorbs the shock and makes the ride smoother.
See also: Shock absorber.

Tort (French, "wrong"), in law, a wrongful act against a person or their property for which that person can claim damages as compensation. It is distinguished from a crime, which the state will prosecute; it is up to the injured party to sue for redress of a tort. The same wrongful act, an assault for example, may be both actionable as a tort and prosecuted as a crime. Torts range from personal injury to slander or libel; they include trespass and damage or injury arising through negligence. Wrongful breach of an agreement, however, is covered by the law of contract.

Tortoise, name for slow-moving, herbivorous, heavily armored terrestrial reptiles of the family Testudinidae, found in the tropics, subtropics, and warmer temperate regions. The body is enclosed in a boxlike shell into which the head and limbs can be withdrawn. The shell is covered with horny plates, or scutes. Toothless, the tortoise's jaws are covered to form a sharp, horny beak. There are many species, ranging from the familiar garden tortoises to the 5-ft (1.5-m) giant tortoises of the Galapagos and Seychelles.

Tory Party, popular name of the Conservative and Unionist Party, one of Britain's two chief parties. The term (originally describing Irish highwaymen) was applied in 1679 to supporters of the future James II of England. In the main, Tories became staunch royalists and supporters of the Church of England. "Tory" was applied to Loyalist colonists in the American Revolution. Taking a reactionary stance because of the threat to authority posed by the French Revolution, the party lost its support after the Reform Bill of 1832 and became the Conservative Party.

Toscanini, Arturo (1867-1957), Italian conductor, one of the greatest of his time. He became musical director of La Scala in Milan (1898) and went on to conduct the New York Metropolitan Opera (1908-14) and New York Philharmonic orchestras (1926-36). The NBC Symphony Orchestra was created for him in 1937.

Totalitarianism, system of government in which the state exercises wide-ranging control over individuals within its jurisdiction. Usually, a totalitarian state has only one political party, led by a dictator, and an official ideology; dissent is suppressed. Nazi Germany epitomized the repression of totalitarian states.

Totem, object, animal, or plant toward which a tribe, clan, or other group feels a special affinity, often considering it a mythical ancestor. Killing of the totemic animal or animals by members of the group is taboo, except, with some peoples, ritually during religious ceremonies. Totem poles, on which human and animal shapes representing a particular warrior's heritage, were common among the Native Americans.

Toucan, exotic bird of the family Ramphastidae, native to the tropical regions of Latin America. It is noted for its huge, brightly colored bill. About forty varieties exist, ranging in size from 13-25 in (33-64 cm). It subsists on fruits, often using its saw-edged bill to tear off small pieces. It lives in small flocks and is believed to be highly social.

Touch, sensory system concerned with surface sensation, found in all external body surfaces including the skin and some mucous membranes. Functional categories of touch sensation include light touch (including movement of hairs), heat, cold, pressure, and pain sensation. Receptors for all the senses are particularly concentrated and developed over the face and hands. When the skin receptors are stimulated, they activate nerve impulses in cutaneous nerves; these pass via the spinal cord and brain stem to the brain, where coding and perception occur.
See also: Senses.

Touch-me-not, wild flower of the balsam family, related to the impatiens. Its seed pods pop open when touched, hence its name. It grows in damp, shady regions of the eastern and central United States, reaches 3-5 ft (0.9-1.5m) tall, and bears pale yellow or spotted flowers. The pale yellow variety is thought to prevent poison ivy rashes when the juice from its stems and leaves are rubbed on the skin.

Toulon (pop. 179,400), port city in southeastern France. It is the administrative seat of the district of Var and an important French naval base. Historic landmarks include medieval churches and a 16th-century fish market. Toulon is the site of a Roman colony founded in the 100s B.C. Chief economic activities include shipbuilding, fishing, wine making, and chemical and machine manufacturing.
See also: France.

Tourmaline

Toulouse (pop. 348,000), historically significant city in southwestern France, located on the Garonne River. It is the capital and administrative seat of the district of Haute-Garonne. During the Middle Ages, it served as an artistic and cultural center of Europe. Many medieval buildings, including the University of Toulouse, still stand. The city supports many economic activities, including the manufacture of electronics, aircraft, chemicals, and textiles.

Toulouse-Lautrec, Henri de (1864-1901), French painter and lithographer who portrayed Parisian nightlife. Born into an old aristocratic family, he was crippled at 15, studied art in Paris, and settled in Montmartre to paint the entertainers and circus performers who lived there, such as Jan Avril and Aristide Bruant. Influenced by Edgar Degas and by Japanese prints, his work did much to popularize the lithographic poster.

Touré, Sékou (1922-84), president of the Republic of Guinea (1958-84). A labor leader in French colonial times, a Marxist, and a political writer, Touré was the winner of the 1960 Lenin Peace Prize.
See also: Guinea.

Tourette syndrome, disorder of the central nervous system characterized by muscular tics, or twitches, and uncontrollable vocalizing. Symptoms first appear in childhood between 2 and 15 years and, if not treated, continue throughout the person's life, sometimes becoming more severe and other times less so. People with Tourette syndrome may also suffer from hyperactivity. Though no cure is yet known, symptoms can be alleviated by drug therapy.

Tourmaline, hard, complex silicate mineral containing such elements as boron, aluminum, and silicon. Colors include pink, green, blue, yellow, violet, red, and black. Transparent stones are considered semiprecious and are used as gems in jewelry. Tourmaline is found in granites, schists, and crystalline limestone of Brazil, Asia, the USSR, and parts of the United States.

Tournament, or tourney, series of games; originally a combat between armored knights, usually on horseback. Popular in Europe in the Middle Ages, it provided both entertainment and training for war. In the 13th century the dangerous melée was replaced by the joust contest between only two knights, who tried to unhorse each other with lance, mace, and sword.

Tours (pop. 132,200), city in west-central France along the Loire River. Established by the Romans in 50 B.C., it served in medieval times as a center for Christian learning. The great Battle of Tours was fought nearby in 732 by the Christian Franks and Muslim armies, effectively stopping the Moorish advance in Europe. During World War II the city became the French government's headquarters. Today Tours is an important wine market and tourist and business center, with banking, insurance, medical- and electrical-equipment manufacturing industries.

Toussaint L'Ouverture (Pierre Dominique Toussaint-Bréda; c.1774-1803), emancipated Haitian slave who led the 1791 slave rebellion on the island of Haiti. The slaves won their freedom in 1793, while the French in Haiti were fighting against British and Spanish troops there. Toussaint, who joined forces with the French and forced the British to evacuate, became ruler of the island in 1799. He suppressed a mulatto uprising (1799) and resisted Napoleon's attempt to reimpose slavery on Haiti. Ultimately, Toussaint was captured and imprisoned until his death. His popular name, L'Ouverture, is French for "The Opening." He has remained a symbol of the struggle for freedom.
See also: Haiti.

Tower of Babel, mythical tower built in the ancient Mesopotamian city of Babylon. The myth popularly connected with it is related in the Bible (Genesis 11.1-9). According to this version the tower was built by the descendants of Noah and was intended by these peoples to reach heaven. God, however, disapproved of the tower and, as a consequence, confused the builders by causing them to speak in different languages. As a result of their confusion, the people stopped work on the tower and wandered off to various parts of the world. Many people believe today that the myth was an attempt by ancient peoples to explain the origin of different languages.

Tower of London, ancient fortress on the Thames River in the eastern part of London. Built 1078-1300, mainly by William the Conqueror and Henry III, its massive stone buildings are enclosed by high walls and a moat. It has been palace, prison, arsenal, and mint. Today it houses the crown jewels and an armor museum. Here Thomas More, Anne Boleyn, and Roger Casement were executed. Convicted Nazi war criminal Rudolf Hess was its last prisoner.

Townes, Charles Hard (1915-), U.S. physicist awarded the 1964 Nobel Prize for physics, with Nikolai Basov and Aleksander Prokhorov, for independently working out the theory of the maser and, later, the laser. He built the first maser in 1951.
See also: Laser; Maser.

Town meeting, direct democratic form of local government, mainly in New England (Massachusetts, New Hampshire, and Vermont). In colonial days, all enfranchised citizens met to choose officials, decide taxes, and discuss affairs. In the 1800s meetings became an annual event called by warrant. Today, many town meetings are attended only by officials and elected representatives, but others are fully attended by the public when significant local issues are discussed.

Townsend, Francis Everett (1867-1960), U.S. reformer, author of the Townsend Plan (1933), a share-the-wealth program by which citizens over 60 were to receive $200 a month, the money to be raised by a federal tax. Townsend claimed supporters of the plan numbered 5 million, but Congress rejected it.

Townsend, Willard Saxby (1895-1957), one of the first African-American labor leaders. He served as the first president of the Auxiliary of Redcaps (1936), a union that represented railroad baggage porters. In 1955, when the American Federation of Labor (AFL) merged with the Congress of Industrial Organization (CIO) to form the AFL-CIO, Townsend became the new union organization's first vice president.
See also: Labor movement.

Henri de Toulouse-Lautrec's Au Salon de la Rue des Moulins *(1894)*

Toxemia of pregnancy, or preeclampsia, disease caused by bacterial toxins or other toxic substances in the blood, usually referring to a condition that attacks women in the last stages of pregnancy or just after childbirth. It occurs in about 5% of all pregnancies and, unless treated, may lead to eclampsia (convulsions and coma) and other complications, including death of the mother and fetus. Toxemia is characterized by an increase in blood pressure, excessive protein in the urine, and swelling of the body, and can be treated by drugs if diagnosed in time.

Toxic shock syndrome (TSS), rare and sometimes fatal bacterial disease associated with the use of tampons. TSS is characterized by high fever, vomiting, and diarrhea, followed by a sharp drop in blood pressure that may bring on fatal shock. At greatest risk are women under 30 during their menstrual periods. The incidence is low, with a frequency of about 3 cases per 100,000 women annually in the United States, and the mortality rate is about 10%.

Toxic wastes *see:* Hazardous wastes.

Toxin, poisonous substance produced by a living organism. Examples of toxin-producing organisms include fungi, which secrete substances that destroy bacteria (and provide antibiotics), and poisonous spiders and snakes, which deliver their toxin via fangs. The symptoms of many infectious diseases (e.g., cholera, diphtheria, tetanus) are due to the release of toxins by the bacteria.

Toy dog, any of several small breeds of dogs kept as pets. Toy dogs are either naturally small or selectively bred to keep them small. In most cases they do not constitute a separate genus or species, but are related to larger dogs of various species. Examples include the Maltese, chihuahua, Pekingese, Pomeranian, shih tzu, toy poodle, and Yorkshire terrier.

Toynbee, Arnold Joseph (1889-1975), English historian. His principal work, *A Study of History* (12 vol., 1934-61), divides the history of the world into 26 civilizations and analyzes their rises and falls according to a cycle of "challenge and response."

Trace elements, minerals that make up all human, animal, and plant life. Small quantities of trace elements are needed to ensure the normal action of enzymes and hormones. In humans, lack of essential minerals such as iron may result in conditions such as pernicious anemia and goiter. Necessary minerals can generally be obtained from a healthy diet. Requirements vary among the different human, animal, and plant species.

Trachea, conduit by which air reaches the lungs from the pharynx. Air is drawn in through the mouth or nose and passes via the larynx into the trachea, which then divides into the major bronchi. It may be seen below the Adam's apple. In a tracheostomy, it is incised to bypass any obstruction to respiration.
See also: Respiration.

Trachoma, chronic conjunctivitis caused by *Chlamydia trachomatis*. Tetracycline eye ointments are usually effective.

Track and field, athletic sports including running, walking, hurdling, jumping for distance or height, and throwing various objects. The revival of the Olympic Games in 1896 gave international and national competition an enormous boost, and in 1912 the International Amateur Athletes Federation was set up.
Track events. Distances raced vary from the 50-m sprint to the 5,0000-m run. Hurdlers and steeplechasers have to clear a set number of obstacles. In relay races a baton is passed from one runner to the next.
Field events. In high jump and pole vault the contestant who clears the greatest height with the least number of attempts wins. A long jump running or triple jump (hop, step and jump) competitor is permitted six jumps. Throwing events also permit six throws. The javelin is a spear thrown by running up to a line and releasing. The shot, a solid iron ball, is "put" from the shoulder. The discus is a circular plate released with a sweeping sidearm action. The hammer throw consists of throwing an iron ball attached to a handle by a wire. All-around events include the 10-event decathlon and the 5-event pentathlon.

Tracy, Spencer (1900-67), U.S. film actor. During his career he appeared in more than 70 films over 37 years and won Academy Awards for *Captains Courageous* (1937) and *Boys' Town* (1938). His pairing with Katharine Hepburn in several movies, including *Woman of the Year* (1942) and *Adam's Rib* (1949), made them one of Hollywood's most famous cinematic couples.

Trade, buying and selling of commodities. It can take place within a nation (domestic trade) or between nations (foreign or international trade). Trade occurs because the people of a particular community or country do not produce all the goods they need. As a consequence, they must purchase these goods from another community or country. They may in turn sell their products to other communities or countries that need them. Trade among early peoples and civilizations usually involved an exchange of one product or service for another. For example, one group might have traded wood to another group for grain. As populations grew and their needs became more complicated, money became the medium of exchange and the boundaries of trade expanded. During the 13th, 14th, and 15th centuries, European merchants traveled to the Middle East and China in search of exotic goods. Overseas exploration created important trade between Europe and Africa and India, and between Europe and the colonies in both North and South America. Today in many countries, including the United States, trade occurs on many levels. People exchange money for services (subway or bus rides) and for goods (food, clothes, radios, and so on). Communities and states trade among one another, which explains why people in Ohio can buy California oranges. The United States also maintains a vast and active foreign trade with countries all over the world.

Trademark, name, symbol, or other device that identifies the product of one company. Strong trademarks, such as Tonka, are words with no apparent meaning which lessen the chance of them being used by another company. Weak trademarks, such as Bubbles, are ordinary words that often communicate the main feature of the product. Trademarks do not need to be registered with the U.S. Patent and Trademark Office to protect them from being duplicated, but such registration makes it easier to sue for infringement if the trademark is copied.

Arnold Toynbee

Trade route, land or water route used to transport goods from one area to another. Trade routes have historically led to the development of civilizations, the growth of cities, and the interchange of ideas. They have existed since ancient times and have increased in number and importance as civilizations have grown. The search for trade routes has contributed to the exploration of new territories and the establishment of colonial empires. Today an extensive network of air, land, and water routes covers all parts of the globe.

Trade union *see:* Labor movement.

Trade winds, persistent warm moist winds that blow westward from the high pressure zones at about 30°N and °S latitude toward the doldrums (intertropical convergence zone) at the equator. They are thus northeasterlies in the Northern Hemisphere and southeasterlies in the Southern Hemisphere. They are stronger and displaced toward the equator in winter.
See also: Horse latitudes.

Trafalgar, Battle of, decisive naval engagement of the Napoleonic Wars, fought on Oct. 21, 1805. The British fleet of 27 warships under Admiral Horatio Nelson met a combined French and Spanish fleet of 33 ships off Cape Trafalgar (southwestern Spain). By attacking in an unorthodox formation, Nelson surprised the enemy, sinking or capturing 20 vessels without loss, but was himself killed.
See also: Napoleonic Wars; Nelson, Horatio.

Roman sculpture of an actor in a tragedy (2nd century B.C.)

Tragedy, form of drama originating in ancient Greece, in which exceptional characters are led, by fate and by the very qualities that make them great, to suffer calamity and often death. Aristotle, in his famous definition, spoke of purification (*catharsis*) through the rousing of the emotions of pity and fear. The great classical tragedians were Aeschylus, Sophocles, and Euripides. Supreme in modern times is William Shakespeare. Great tragedians include Félix Lope de Vega, Pedro Calderón de la Barca, Pierre Corneille, Jean Racine, Johann Wolfgang von Goethe, and Friedrich von Schiller. In the 19th and 20th centuries, in which the heroic dimension of tragedy in drama is often shunned, the greatest exponents are probably Henrik Ibsen and Eugene O'Neill.

Tragopan, any of 5 species of birds in the pheasant family. These inhabitants of central and southern Asia mainly live on forested mountains. During courtship the colorful feathered folds of throat skin (the lappet) and blue fleshy horns on the sides of the head of the males enlarge for a brilliant display. Unlike many other kinds of pheasants, tragopans nest in trees rather than on the ground.

Trail of Tears *see:* Oklahoma.

Trajan (A.D. 53-117), Roman emperor responsible for great extensions of the empire and vast building programs. He conquered Dacia (Romania) and much of Parthia and rebuilt the Roman Forum. Adopted heir by Nerva (97), he became emperor in 98. He was known as a capable administrator and a humane and tolerant ruler.
See also: Rome, Ancient.

Tranquilizer, any of the agents that induce a state of quietude in anxious or disturbed patients. Minor tranquilizers are sedatives (e.g., benzodiazepines) valuable in treating anxiety. In psychosis, especially schizophrenia and (hypo) mania, major tranquilizers are required to suppress abnormal mental activity, as well as to sedate; phenothiazines (e.g., chlorpromazine) are often used.
See also: Depressant.

The transcendentalist Ralph Waldo Emerson

Transcendentalism, philosophical and literary movement that flourished in New England c.1835-60. Regarding rationalist Unitarianism and utilitarian philosophy as morally bankrupt and shallow, the transcendentalists took their inspiration from the German idealists, notably Immanuel Kant, from Samuel Coleridge, and from Eastern mystical philosophies. They believed in the divinity and unity of humankind and nature, and in the supremacy of intuition over sense perception as well as reason as a source of knowledge. The major figures were Ralph Waldo Emerson and Margaret Fuller, who edited *The Dial* (1840-44), Henry David Thoreau, and Amos Bronson Alcott. The movement had considerable influence on U.S. literature (Nathaniel Hawthorne, Herman Melville, Walt Whitman) and politics (abolitionism, Brook Farm).

Transcontinental treaty *see:* Adams-Onís Treaty.

Transducer, device for converting an input of energy or information of one form into an output of another. Passive transducers require only the input signal to produce the output signal; active transducers require an additional source of energy. The light bulb and the microphone are examples of transducers.

Transformer, device for moving an alternating current by increasing or decreasing the voltage. This is an easy, inexpensive way for power companies to transport electricity over long distances. Transformers work by electromagnetic induction, where a magnetic field alters the voltage of the electric current. The current goes through a step-up transformer, which increases the voltage. High voltage electricity loses very little power when transported over long distance wires. When the current reaches its destination, step-down transformers are used to decrease the voltage to the level where it can be used to decrease the voltage to the level where it can be used by customers.

Transfusion, blood *see:* Blood transfusion.

Transistor, device in electronic equipment thast regulates the flow of electricity in such equipment. It works by controlling the flow of current between two terminals, the emitter and collector, by means of variations in the current flow between a third terminal, the base, and one of the other two. Transistors lower the voltage of the electricity to be used by a piece of electronic equipment, but keep the current strong. This provides items such as calculators, which require small voltages, with enough power to perform complex calculations. Transistor-transistor logic is a family of integrated circuits characterized by relatively high speed and low power consumption. Transistors are used in radios, television sets, and computers to control the flow of electric current.

Transkei, homeland established by South Africa for the black Xhosa-speaking people. Located between the Indian Ocean and the Republic of Lesotho, it is 15,831 sq mi (41,002 sq km) and its capital is Umtata. Transkei, granted independence in 1976, is not recognized by any nation except South Africa. It is governed by a 150-member National Assembly, half of whom are appointed chiefs. South Africa provides about 75% of the nation's budget and about 70% of its employment. Many of Transkei's people are farmers and herders living in small villages, but the mining of the nation's rich mineral deposits is on the increase.

Transmigration of the soul *see:* Reincarnation.

Transmission, automobile part that transmits the power generated by the engine to a driving axle. The power travels from the transmission to the drive shaft, then to the final drive. These 3 parts make up the drive train of an automobile. The transmission has several gears, which regulate the speed of the automobile by controlling the amount of power delivered to the driving axle. There are 2 types of automobile transmissions: manual, where the driver is responsible for shifting the gears, and automatic, where a device automatically shifts the gears when necessary.

Transmutation of elements, conversion of an atom of one element to an atom of another. Since atoms are identified by their atomic number (number of protons), any change in the number of protons will result in a different element. Atoms may change their number of protons by giving off or taking in atomic particles. Transmutation occurs naturally as a result of radioactive decay. Radioactive atoms are very unstable and give off atomic particles in order to become more stable. With one form of radioactive decay, alpha decay, the atom emits an alpha particle (2 protons and 2 neutrons). With beta decay the atom emits an electron, resulting in the production of a proton and the loss of a neutron. Sometimes, but less often, a positron (a positively charged electron) is emitted, so that a proton is lost and a neutron gained. Artificial transmutation may be accomplished by bombarding atoms with alpha particles so that the atom accepts an extra proton (1 of the 2 is immediately expelled). Transmutation is a by-product of fission (the splitting of nuclei) and fusion (the joining of nuclei).
See also: Radioactivity.

Transpiration, loss of water by evaporation from the aerial parts of plants. Considerable quantities of water are lost in this way, far more than is needed for the upward movement of solutes and for the internal metabolism of the plant alone. Transpiration is necessary for photosynthesis: In order to obtain sufficient carbon dioxide from the air, considerable areas of the plant's wet surface have to be exposed. But as a result, much water is lost through evaporation.

Transplant, organ removed from one person and surgically implanted in another to replace a lost or diseased organ. Autotransplantation is the moving of an organ from one place to another within a person, where the original site has been affected by local disease (e.g., skin grafting). Blood transfusions between those with compatible blood groups was the first practical form of transplant. In organ transplantation, tissue compatibility typing as well as blood grouping are needed to minimize the risk of rejection. Immunosuppressive drugs are also given to block the creation of antibodies that would attack the donor tissue. The most important, and now most successful, of organ transplants is that of the kidney. A single kidney is transplanted from a live donor who is a close relative or from a person who has recently suffered sudden death. Heart transplantation has been much publicized, but is limited to a few centers, and many problems remain. Liver and lung transplants have also been attempted, but there are still numerous difficulties. In corneal grafting the cornea of the eye of a recently dead person replaces that of a person with irreversible corneal damage leading to blindness. The lack of blood vessels in the cornea reduces the problem of rejection. Grafts from nonhuman animals are occasionally used (e.g., pig skin as temporary cover in extensive burns). Both animal and human heart valves are used in cardiac surgery.

Transportation, Department of, executive department of the U.S. government responsible for the development and coordination of national transport policies and agencies. Set up by the Department of Transportation Act (1966), it began operating the following year. It reports to Congress on the optimum use of federal transportation funds. It supervises the federal aviation, highway, railroad, and urban mass transportation administrations, the U.S. Coast Guard, the Saint Lawrence Seaway Development Corporation, and the National Transportation Safety Board.

Transsexualism, condition in which a person has a psychological urge to belong to the opposite sex. People who experience this condition are called transsexuals. In most cases, therapy is not an effective treatment. Surgical techniques in conjunction with certain hormones can be used to make transsexuals physically resemble a member of the opposite sex. Transsexuality is not the same as homosexuality.

Trans-Siberian Railroad, railroad in the USSR, the longest in the world, stretching 5,787 mi (9,313 km) from Moscow to Vladivostock on the Sea of Japan. Its construction (1891-1916) had a dramatic effect on the development of Siberia.

The Trans-Siberian Railroad

Transuranium elements, elements of atomic number above 92. All transuranic elements are radioactive and are products of artificial nuclear changes. All are members of the actinide group.

Transvaal, second-largest province in the Republic of South Africa, between the Vaal and Limpopo rivers in the northeast. It is mainly high veld, 3,000-6,000 ft (914-1,829 m) above sea level. The capital is Pretoria and the largest city is Johannesburg. Mineral wealth includes gold, silver, diamonds, coal, iron ore, platinum, asbestos, and chrome. Its farmlands are noted for their cattle, corn, and tobacco.
See also: South Africa.

Transylvania, province in central Romania near the Hungarian border, situated between the Transylvanian Alps and the Carpathian Mts. Transylvania has been in dispute between Romania and Hungary for several hundred years. Once part of the Roman Empire, Transylvania was conquered and ruled by the Magyars (Hungarians) from the 11th to the 16th centuries. The Ottoman Turks took control in 1526 but vied with Austria for prominence until 1711, when Austria dominated. From 1867 to 1918, it was part of the Austro-Hungarian Empire. Transylvania was absorbed by Romania after World War I and, though a portion of it went to Hungary in 1940, Romania regained control after World War II. The province is rich in iron and other minerals and is a fertile farming, grazing, and wine-making area. It is famous as the setting of the legend of Dracula, written by English author Bram Stoker in 1897.
See also: Romania.

Trappists, members of the clan of the Reformed, or Strict, Observance, a Roman Catholic monastic order founded (1664) by Armand de Rancé, abbot of La Trappe in Normandy, France. He instituted a rigorous discipline of silence, prayer, and work. There are 12 U.S. abbeys. The abbot general lives in Rome.
See also: Cistercians.

Travertine, type of limestone that forms in dense layers. It is easily cut and often used in construction for decorative purposes. It is found in places where limestone is in contact with evaporated water containing calcium carbonate, and around hot springs and streams. Stalactites and stalagmites are chiefly comprised of travertine, which is mostly white or cream colored.

Treason, behavior by a subject or citizen that could harm the sovereign or state. In many countries treason has been loosely defined and used as a political weapon. The U.S. Constitution, however, states that treason consists only in levying war against the United States or in adhering to it enemies, "giving them Aid and Comfort"; evidence of two witnesses or confession in open court is necessary to secure a conviction.

Treasury, Department of the, executive department of the U.S. government, established in 1789, responsible for federal taxes, customs, and expenditure. It also plays a major role in national and international financial and monetary policies. Its head, the secretary of the treasury, the second-ranking member of the president's cabinet, is an *ex officio* governor of the International Monetary Fund. The department's other responsibilities include the U.S. Secret Service and the bureaus of Customs, Mint, Engraving and Printing, Internal Revenue, and Narcotics.

Treaty, agreement between states. Treaties are bilateral (between two states) or multilateral (between several states), and cover matters such as trade, tariffs, taxation, economic and technical cooperation, diplomatic relations, international boundaries, extradition of criminals, defense, and control of arms and aggression. Some treaties, for example the North Atlantic Treaty Organization (NATO), are military; others set up international organizations, which have become an important part of modern international relations.

The Peles Castle in Transylvania

Treaty of 1783 *see:* Revolutionary War in America.

Tree, woody perennial plant with a well-defined main stem, or trunk, that either dominates the form throughout the life cycle (giving a pyramidal shape) or is dominant only in the early stages, later forking to form a number of equally important branches (giving a rounded or flattened form to the tree). The trunk of a tree consists almost wholly of thick-walled water-conducting cells (xylem) that are renewed every year, giving rise to annual rings. The older wood in the center of the tree (the heartwood) is much denser and harder than the younger, outer sapwood. The outer skin, or bark, insulates and protects the trunk and often shows characteristic cracks or falls off, leaving a smooth skin. Trees belong to the two most advanced group of plants. The gymnosperms include the cone-bearing trees such as pine, spruce, and cedar; they are nearly all evergreens and most live in the cooler regions of the world. The angiosperms (flowering plants) have broader leaves and much harder wood; in tropical climates they are mostly evergreen, but in temperate regions they are deciduous.

Tree frog, or tree toad, one of several hundred types of frogs belonging to the family Hylidae, commonly found in North and South America. Many varieties have adhesive pads on their fingers and toes that stick to trees and facilitate climbing and leaping. Males have a characteristic high-pitched call, which they use to attract their mates. Tree frogs are about 1-5 in (2.5-13 cm) long, eat insects, and change color.

Tree frog

Tree shrew, small, squirrel-like arboreal insectivore (family Tupaiidae) with a pointed snout. Tree shrews were once thought to be primates, related to the lemurs, but they are now considered a group of their own. They live in trees and bushes from India and China to the Philippines and Borneo. Except for the pen-tailed tree shrew they come out by day, and most species live in family groups. They feed on leaves, fruit, and small animals. The babies are born in a nest of leaves, and the mother visits them every two days to feed them.

Tree toad *see:* Tree frog.

Trench mouth, or Vincent's infection, disease of the mouth and throat, probably caused by bacteria, poor oral hygiene, and malnutrition. Initial symptoms include pain and bleeding of the gums and bad breath. Chewing and swallowing food is also painful. If not treated, trench mouth can lead to gum destruction and eventual tooth loss.

Trent, Council of, series of 3 conferences held in Trent, Italy, by leaders of the Roman Catholic church in the mid-16th century. Convened by Pope Paul III in 1545 to counteract the Protestant Reformation in Europe, the council did much to define Catholic doctrine and bring about a Counter-Reformation. The first council, which lasted until 1547, established the Catholic church's sole right to interpret the Scriptures and took issue with the Protestant interpretations of sin and salvation. The second council (1551-52) defined the nature of the sacraments and reaffirmed the validity of the rituals practiced in Holy Communion. The third council (1562-63) defended the controversial granting of pardons (indulgences) for the commission of certain sins, approved prayers to the saints, and established seminaries for training the priesthood. The council's actions became part of the Catholic doctrine by papal confirmation in 1564.
See also: Counter-Reformation.

Trent Affair, naval incident in the U.S. Civil War that nearly brought Britain to militarily support the South. In Nov. 1861, Charles Wilkes, commanding the Union ship *San Jacinto* stopped the British ship *Trent* and seized two southern agents, J.M Mason and John Slidell. Britain demanded an apology for this violation of the freedom of the sea and ordered 8,000 troops to Canada. The southerners were freed in December.
See also: Civil War, U.S.

Trenton (pop. 92,124), capital (since 1790) of New Jersey, situated at the head of navigation on the Delaware River, opposite Pennsylvania. The city was settled in 1679 by Quaker farmers under Mahlon Stacy. In 1714 Stacy's son sold part of the property to William Trent, for whom the city was named. During the American Revolution, Trenton was the site of Gen. George Washington's famous crossing of the Delaware at the head of his troops and the site of their victory over the Hessians (Battle of Trenton, 1776). Trenton, which served as the capital of the United States Nov.-Dec. 1784, developed as an industrial, transportation, and trade center in the 20th century.
See also: New Jersey.

Trenton, Battle of, American victory in the Revolutionary War, fought on Dec. 26, 1776. To forestall a British attack on Philadelphia, George Washington crossed the Delaware River at night and surprised a British force of 1,500 Hessians at Trenton, N.J. The battle was won in 45 minutes, rallying Washington's army and the American cause.
See also: Revolutionary War in America.

Trephining, surgical removal of a small, circular piece of skull. An ancient, even prehistoric, practice, it was probably first performed to release evil spirits from a person's head. Today it is used primarily to open the way for certain brain surgeries and to relieve pressure caused by bleeding between the brain and the skull. The operation is performed with a small saw called a trephine.

Trevelyan, George Macauley (1876-1962), English historian who rejected the "scientific" approach to history in favor of a more humanistic and literary approach. He taught at Cambridge (1927-51) and was best known for a colorful study of Garibaldi (3 vols., 1907-11), a one-volume *History of England* (1926), *England Under Queen Anne* (3 vols., 1903-34), and *English Social History* (1942).

Triage (French, "sorting"), allocation of limited medical or food resources by selecting those in need who would most benefit in the long run. During World War I (1914-18) the word was introduced to describe the classification of wounded soldiers. Medical help was first administered to those who would survive only with immediate treatment; help was delayed or, if necessary, withheld from those who were expected to die or to recover with or without treatment. By extension, a triage system is suggested to determine what countries in need of food are to receive supplies. A system of triage also is used in hospital emergency rooms to determine the order in which patients are attended.

Trial, method of settling disagreements of determining criminal guilt. In the United states, this involves a hearing before a judge, with or without a jury. In the United States the right of an accused person to a speedy and public trial by a jury of peers is guaranteed in the Constitution. Trials in common law countries, such as the United Kingdom and United States, are "adversary" proceedings, in which the court impartially decides between the evidence of two parties. Under civil law systems trials tend to be more "inquisitorial," allowing the court itself a greater role in the gathering of evidence. Under both systems the judge ensures that procedure is followed and that the rules of evidence are observed, and determines the guilty offender's sentence. Questions of fact are left to a jury, if there is one; jury trial is more expensive and time-consuming, and so it is reserved for more serious offenses.

Trial by combat, medieval method of settling disagreements. According to its tenets, the two disputing parties fought hand-to-hand combat, the belief being that God would intervene on behalf of the just participant. Nobles, women, and priests were usually represented by substitute fighters. Eventually the method was replaced by trial by jury.
See also: Divination.

Triangle, three-sided polygon. There are three main types of plane triangle: scalene, in which no side is equal in length to another; isosceles, in which two of the sides are equal in length; and equilateral, in which all three sides are equal in length. A right (or right-angled) triangle has one interior angle equal to 90° and may be either scalene or isosceles. The "corners" of a triangle are termed vertices (singular: vertex). The sum of the angles of a plane triangle is 180°. A spherical triangle is an area of the surface of a sphere bounded by arcs of three great circles, each arc being less than 180°, each side and interior angle being termed an element. The sum of the three sides is never greater than 360°; the sum of the three angles is always in the range of 180°-540°.

Trianon, Treaty of, World War I treaty that reduced Hungary's territory by almost two-thirds as punishment for its part in the war. Signed June 4, 1920 by Hungary and the Western Allies, including the United States, the treaty forced Hungary to relinquish almost 90,000 sq mi (233,100 sq km) to Romania, Czechoslovakia, and what is

now Yugoslavia. As a result, the country lost all of its seaports as well as about 12 million inhabitants.
See also: World War I.

Triassic Period, first period of the Mesozoic Era (c.225-190 million years ago).

Tribe, people who live in a community in a particular area, sharing the same language, culture, and often kinship. The tribal system is one the earliest forms of society and still exists in most of Africa, on many Pacific islands, and among Australian aborigines and Native Americans. Tribes may be made up of only 50 to 60 people or, like the Kikuyu of East Africa, have more than a million members. Tribal rule may be by a local chief or, as in some large African tribes, by a king and councillors. Native American Plains tribes, such as the Arapaho and Cheyenne, were ruled by a council of chiefs. In earlier times, the kingdom of Israel united a number of Jewish tribes.
See also: Ethnic group.

Trichina, parasitic roundworm, belonging to the trichina family, that causes an infection known as trichinosis. Larval worms that infect the muscles of animals usually die by themselves; if an infected animal is eaten, however, the larvae can be set free from their cysts (sacs) to invade the intestine of the host and reproduce more larvae. The degree of infection in these cases ranges from mild to fatal. Preventative measures include sufficient cooking and freezing of meat.

Trichinosis *see:* Trichina.

Trier (pop. 93,500), city in southwestern Germany, on the Moselle River. Named for the Treveri, a people of ancient Gaul, the city produces steel, leather goods, and textiles. It is also an important railroad junction and the center of a famous wine district. Trier has been a center of Roman Catholic tradition since the Renaissance.
See also: Germany.

Trieste (pop. 251,380), city-seaport in northeastern Italy at the head of the Adriatic Sea, with steel, oil, and shipbuilding industries. A busy port in Roman times, it was part of Austria (1382-1919) and then of Italy. Claimed by Yugoslavia in 1945, it was made a Free Territory (1947-54), then restored to Italy.
See also: Italy.

Triggerfish, fish belonging to the Balistidae family, found in tropical coastal waters. It measures less than 1.5 ft (46 cm) in length, is colorful, and has a round, flat body. When threatened, it uses one of its spines to "trigger" a spinal enlargement, thus allowing it to lock itself into tight spaces.

Trigonometry, branch of geometry that deals with the ratios of the sides and angles of triangles, particularly of right-angled triangles and the applications of these ratios. Plane trigonometry deals with these relationships mapped on a plane surface. The principle ratios, when considering angle A of right-triangle ABC whose sides opposite the angles A, B, and C respectively are a, b, and c, and where c is the hypotenuse, are:

name	*abbreviation*	*ratio*
tangent	tan A	a/b
sine	sin A	a/c
cosine	cos A	b/c
cotangent	cot A	b/a
cosecant	cosec A	c/a
secant	sec A	c/b

As can be seen, the cotangent is the reciprocal of the tangent, the cosecant that of the sine, and the secant that of the cosine. The basis of trigonometric calculations is Pythagoras's theorem, $a^2 + b^2 = c^2$, which in trigonometric form reads $\sin^2 A + \cos^2 A = 1$; this is true for angle A. From these ratios are derived the trigonometric functions, setting y equal to tan x, sin x, etc. These functions are termed transcendental (nonalgebraic). Of particular importance is the sine wave, in terms of which many naturally occurring wave motions, such as sound and light, are studied. Spherical trigonometry studies triangles lying on a sphere, and thus can be used to calculate distances on a globe.

Trillium, colorful wildflower (genus *Trillium*) of North American woodlands and eastern Asia. A member of the lily family, trilliums have 3 sepals, petals, and leaves on each stem. They bloom in early spring, and are also called wake-robins because their flowers appear at the same time robins return north. Colors of the more than 40 varieties include white, pink, dark red, yellow, green, or a painted variety.

Trilobite, extinct marine animal (phylum Arthropoda) from the Paleozoic Era (570-240 million years ago). Scientists have identified about 10,000 species from the fossilized remains of these small (4 in/10 cm) invertebrates. Their name (Latin, "3 lobes") refers to the 3 sections created by 2 lengthwise grooves across their soft, horny shells. The thorax contained many sections, each bearing legs that had gills, enabling the trilobites to breathe.

Trinidad and Tobago, officially Republic of Trinidad and Tobago, independent republic in the West Indies, consisting of 2 separate islands in the Caribbean Sea north of Venezuela. The island of Trinidad is 1,864 sq mi (4,828 sq km) and Tobago is 116 sq mi (300 sq km). The capital is Port of Spain, on Trinidad.

Land and people. Trinidad is very fertile and mainly flat, rising to c.3,000 ft (914 m) above sea level in the north. Tobago is densely forested and is dominated by a mountain ridge some 1,800 ft (549 m) high. The climate of both islands is tropical. The majority of the people are of black African descent, but more than one-third are East Indian. The principal languages are English and a French patois.

Economy. The country is one of the more prosperous in the Caribbean, producing and exporting sugarcane, cocoa, and bananas, as well as chemicals and petroleum products. Tourism is a growing industry.

History. Trinidad was discovered by Christopher Columbus in 1498 and settled by the Spanish, but British rule was established in 1802. Tobago, once held by the Dutch and French, went to the British in 1803. Combined politically in 1888, Trinidad and Tobago joined the West Indies Federation in 1958 but left in 1962. Eric Williams was premier from independence in 1962 until his death in 1981. During this term, Trinidad and Tobago became a republic (1976). In 1990, a coup attempt against the government of Prime minister Arthur Napoleon Raymond Robinson was diffused when the government

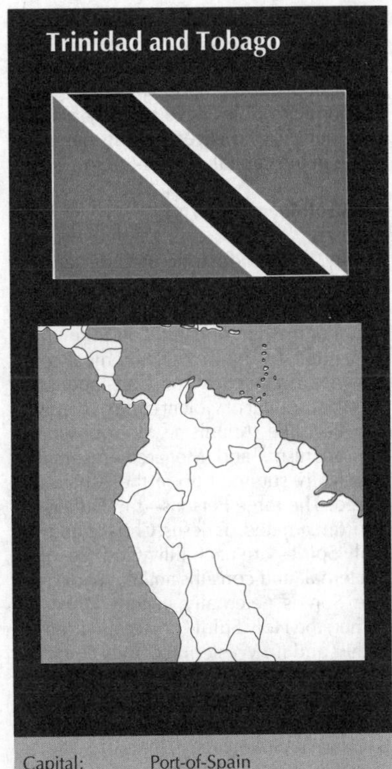

Capital:	Port-of-Spain
Area:	1,980 sq mi (5,128 sq km)
Population:	1,285,000
Government:	republic
Independent:	1962
GNP:	U.S.$4,160,000,000
Per capita:	U.S.$3,350

Oil wells in Trinidad and Tobago

promised new elections and amnesty for the rebels. However, rebel leader Iman Yasin Abu Bakr and many of his followers were imprisoned upon their surrender. Economic troubles have recently plagued the country, and severe rioting has taken place in the capital, Port-of-Spain.

Trinitrotoluene *see:* TNT.

Trinity, central doctrine of Christian theology, that there is one God who exists in three Persons and one Substance. The definition of the doctrine, implicit in the New Testament, by the early ecumenical councils (notably Nicaea and Constantinople) was the product of violent controversy with heresies like Arianism, Monophysitism, Nestorianism, and Monarchianism. It is classically summed up in the Athanasian Creed. The three Persons—the Father, the Son (incarnated as Jesus Christ), and the Holy Spirit—are each fully God: coequal, coeternal, and consubstantial, yet distinct. The Son is "eternally begotten" by the Father; the Holy Spirit "proceeds" from the Father and (in Western theology) from the Son. The doctrine is a mystery, being known by revelation and being above reason (though not unreasonable). Hence it has been challenged by rationalists and by sects like the Jehovah's Witnesses and the Mormons.
See also: Christianity; Religion.

Triple Alliance, defense arrangement between Austria-Hungary, Germany, and Italy in the late 19th and early 20th centuries. In 1882 the 3 nations pledged mutual help if any of them were attacked by 2 or more other nations. Germany and Austria-Hungary signed an agreement in 1879 at the prompting of German chancellor Otto von Bismarck, and Italy joined them 3 years later. Serbia also joined in 1882 and Romania in 1883; the name remained Triple Alliance because the 2 Balkan nations were not considered major powers. The alliance was renewed several times before the outbreak of World War I in 1914, but actually broke up when the war started: Italy and Romania fought on the side of the Allies—France, Great Britain, and Russia (the Triple Entente).
See also: World War I.

Triple Entente, defense pact originally formed between France and Russia in 1890 to counterbalance the threat posed by the Triple Alliance—Germany, Austria-Hungary, and Italy—8 years earlier. In 1907 Great Britain joined. Each nation agreed to help the others if attacked by any or all of the Triple Alliance nations. After World War I broke out in 1914, the Triple Entente nations became known as the Allies; they signed the Declaration of London in which each ally agreed not to make a separate peace with the Central Powers, as the Triple Alliance nations came to be called.
See also: World War I.

Tripoli (pop. 175,000), city located in northwestern Lebanon, second largest in the country. A manufacturing center and seaport, its industries include petroleum refining, sponge fishing, textiles and the growing of citrus fruits. The name Tripoli comes from the Arabic *Tarabulus* ("Three Cities") because the city was founded in the 300s B.C. by explorers from 3 different Phoenician cities.
See also: Lebanon.

Tripoli(pop. 990,700), capital and largest city of Libya, located in northwest Libya on an arm of the Mediterranean Sea. Founded in the 600s B.C. by the Phoenicians, it was captured by the Romans in the 1st century B.C. Control passed to the Vandals in the 4th century A.D., the Arabs in the 7th century, the Spanish in 1510, and the Ottoman Turks in 1551. In the early 1800s, Tripoli was a stronghold for the Barbary Pirates, who attacked ships in the Mediterranean and exacted money from their captains in exchange for their freedom. The United States went to war against Tripoli (1801-05) to end the practice. Tripoli was conquered by Italy in 1911 and remained in Italian hands until freed by the Allies during World War II. Today it is a major manufacturing center, shipping port, and oil-refining center. The city was bombed by the United States in 1986 as a result of Libya's alleged condoning of terrorist activities.
See also: Libya.

Triticale (genus *Triticosecale*), hybrid grain produced by crossbreeding wheat with rye. When developed by botanists in 1876, it could not produce seeds; the development of seed-bearing triticale in the 1930s suggested commercial uses. It has a high yield and is high in protein. It can be bred for special soil and climatic conditions and resistance to disease, and may become an important food for humans and animals.

Tritium, hydrogen isotope that is 3 times heavier than ordinary hydrogen. One of 3 hydrogen isotopes (the others are protium and deuterium), tritium contains 1 proton and 2 neutrons in its nucleus. It is used in the release of nuclear energy through the fusion process. A radioactive gas and a key component of the hydrogen bomb, it is also used in luminous paints and as a tracer. Helium is formed when tritium decays.

Triton, in Greek mythology, sea god with human head and chest and a fishlike tail. Son of the sea god Poseidon and Amphitrite, he lived in a golden palace on the sea floor and stirred or calmed the seas by blowing on a conch shell. He is credited with helping Jason's Argonauts on their journey and with befriending sailors in the seas around ancient Greece. In Virgil's *Aeneid,* Triton is accused of drowning Misenus, a human trumpeter who challenged Triton's skill on the conch shell.
See also: Mythology.

Triumph, Arch of *see:* Arc de Triomphe.

Trogon, bird of the family Trogonidae. Male trogons have dark feathers of green, blue, or violet on their heads and backs and bright feathers of red, orange, or yellow on their undersides. Female trogons are similar but duller in color. Trogons inhabit warm regions in both the Western and Eastern hemispheres.

Trojan horse *see:* Trojan War.

Trojan War, conflict between Greece and Troy, made famous by Homer's *Iliad.* Paris, son of Priam of Troy, carried off Helen, wife of Menelaus of Sparta, and took her to Troy. The Greeks, led by Agamemnon, Menelaus, Odysseus, Achilles, and other heroes, swore to take revenge. They besieged Troy for 10 years; in seeming defeat they pretended to sail away, leaving a huge wooden horse outside the city, with Greek soldiers concealed in its belly. The Trojans took it into the city, and that night the soldiers opened the city gates to the Greek army. Most of the Trojans were killed, the city was burnt, and Helen reclaimed. The legend is thought to have been based on an actual conflict of 1250 B.C.
See also: Greece, Ancient.

Trollope, Anthony (1815-82), English author. His series of 6 books, known as "the Barsetshire novels," (1855-67) are satires that portray the lives of ordinary people in a fictional county (Barsetshire): *The Warden, Barchester Towers, Doctor Thorne, Framley Parsonage, The Small House at Allington,* and *The Last Chronicle of Barset.* In all he wrote more than 50 books, including *The Bertrans* (1859), *The Eustace Diamonds* (1873), *The Way We Live Now* (1875), and *Cousin Henry* (1879).

Trombone, musical instrument, one of the brass wind instruments. It has a slide mechanism to alter the length of the playing tube and increase the note range. Developed from a sackbut, it was first used in a symphony by Ludwig van Beethoven in 1808. There is also a valve trombone, similar to the trumpet.

Trona, carbonate mineral found in dry regions of the world or extracted from evaporated brine. It is light-colored, has crystal formations, and is soluble in water. Trona is a source of soda ash, which is used to manufacture paper, glass, and chemicals.

Tropical fish, any of a variety of marine and freshwater fish native to the tropics, but particularly those valued for use in aquariums because they are ornamental, small, and able to reproduce quickly and easily. The tropical fish most commonly found in home aquariums are guppies and other freshwater fish of the Poeciliidae family, bearing live young (rather than eggs). Some other popular aquarium fish are cichlids, which are egg bearing, and clownfish, a saltwater species. Tropical fish range in size from 1-12 in (2.5-30 cm) and generally eat food made from grains, as well as insects, fish, aquatic plants, and dried fish.

Tropical rain forest, regions of the world near the equator characterized by high levels of rainfall and humidity. Vast numbers of unique animal and bird species

Tropical rain forest
1. *Epiphytic orchid (Oncidium spp.)*
2. *Vochysia tree*
3. *White-headed capuchias*
4. *Scarlet macaw*
5. *Three-toed sloth*
6. *Howler monkeys*
7. *Common opossum*
8. *Epiphytic orchid (Cattleya spp.)*
9. *Bromeliad*
10. *Rare tiger*
11. *Cecropias tree*
12. *Brocket deer*
13. *Tamandua*
14. *Termite nest*
15. *Scarlet ibis*
16. *Brown coati*
17. *Epiphytes*
18. *Great anteater*
19. *Roseate spoonbill*
20. *Keel-billed toucan*
21. *Liara flowers*
22. *Ruby and topaz hummingbird*
23. *Capybara*
24. *South American river turtle*
25. *Arrow-poison frog*
26. *Paca*
27. *Bird-eating spider*
28. *Tapir*
29. *Jaguar*
30. *Giant lily*
31. *Red and blue leafhopper*
32. *Leafcutter ants*

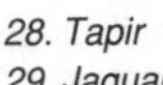

inhabit these regions. Vegetation includes many trees that have significant commercial value. This has resulted in extensive deforestation, especially in the Amazon rain forest region of South America. This practice endangers many plant and animal species and poses a threat to the world's climate system. The temperature in a rain forest ranges from 68°F (20°C) to 93°F (34°C).

Tropic bird, graceful seabird (genus *Phaethon*) with long, trailing tail feathers. Tropic birds are found in all tropical oceans and are often seen far out to sea. Their food is fish and squids, which they catch by diving. They nest under rocks or in crevices on islands. Plumage is generally satiny and white, with some black.

Tropic of Cancer, imaginary line of latitude showing the northernmost point on the earth at which the sun can appear directly overhead. The sun's rays shine straight down on the Tropic of Cancer on June 20 or 21, which is the summer solstice and the first day of summer in the Northern Hemisphere. Lying 23°27′ north of the equator and encircling the earth, the Tropic of Cancer also represents the northern boundary of the Tropical Zone.
See also: Latitude; Tropics.

Tropic of Capricorn, imaginary line of latitude showing the southernmost point on the earth at which the sun can appear directly overhead. The sun's rays shine straight down on the Tropic of Capricorn on December 21 or 22, which is the winter solstice and the first day of winter in the Northern Hemisphere. Lying 23°27′ south of the equator and running completely around the earth, the Tropic of Capricorn also marks the southern boundary of the Tropical Zone.

Tropics, land and water 1,600 mi (2,570 km) north and south of the equator, as defined by the Tropic of Cancer (23°27′ north latitude) and the Tropic of Capricorn (23°27′ south latitude). Because the sun's rays are more direct in these latitudes, the tropics generally have warm to hot climates year round with little variation in temperature, and receive sunshine for longer hours each day. Elevation, wind, and proximity to the ocean are also factors that affect weather conditions in the tropics, creating several climatic types, including tropical rain forests, steppes, deserts, and savannas.

Tropism, movement of a plant in response to external directional stimuli. If a plant is laid on its side, the stem will soon start to bend upward again; this movement (geotropism) is a response to the force of gravity. The stem is said to be negatively geotropic. Roots are generally positive geotropic and grow downward. Phototropisms are bending movements in response to the direction of light. Stems are generally positive phototropic (bend toward the light). Most roots are negatively phototropic. Some roots exhibit positive hydrotropism: They bend toward moisture. This response is more powerful than the response to gravity. Tropisms are controlled by differences in concentration of growth hormones.

Troposphere, lowermost zone of the earth's atmosphere, extending from the earth's surface up to 5-6 mi (8-9 km) over the poles and 8-10 mi (12.8-16 km) over the equator. In this zone normal lapse rates prevail, i.e., temperatures decrease with altitude. The top of the troposphere is called the tropopause.
See also: Atmosphere.

Trotsky, Leon (Lev Davidovic Bronstein; 1879-1940), Russian revolutionary Communist, a founder of the USSR. President of the Petrograd (Leningrad) soviet in the abortive 1905 revolution, he escaped from prison to France, Spain, and New York. In 1917 he returned, went over to Bolshevism, and led the Bolshevik seizure of power in the October Russian Revolution. As commissar of foreign affairs (1917-18) he resigned in protest over the Treaty of Brest-Litovsk and became commissar of

Leon Trotsky

war (1918-25), organizing the Red Army into an effective force. After V.I. Lenin's death (1924), he lost power to Joseph Stalin and was deported (1929). Bitterly opposed to Stalin's "socialism in one country," he continued to advocate international revolution, founded the Fourth International, and attacked Stalinism in *The Revolution Betrayed* (1937). He was murdered in Mexico City by a Stalinist agent.
See also: Russian Revolutionary; Union of Soviet

Pierre Trudeau

Troubadour, name for courtly poet-musicians of Provence, southern France (1100-1300). Their poems, written in Provençal, mostly on the theme of love, were sung. Troubadours developed the conventions of courtly love, and influenced poetry and music in Germany, Italy, Spain, and England. Courtly poets in northern France were called *trouvéres.*

Trout, any of several relatives of the salmon, native to the Northern Hemisphere. Trouts are prized as game and food fishes. Like salmon, trout can be recognized by the fleshy, adipose fin. Some trout spend all their lives in fresh waters, favoring clear, well-aerated streams or lakes, but others live in the sea and return to river beds to breed. Various species include the brown trout, imported from Europe, the rainbow trout of western states, and the red-spotted Dolly Varden. The lake, or mackinaw, trout of deep lakes used to be netted by the ton in the Great Lakes until the arrival of lampreys.

Trout lily *see:* Dogtooth violet.

Troy, city of ancient northwestern Asia Minor, near the Dardanelles, described in Homer's *Iliad* and rediscovered by Heinrich Schliemann in 1870. The earliest site (Troy I) dates from 3000 B.C. Troy II contained an imposing fortress and had wide trade contacts. Its famous treasure of gold, copper, and bronze indicates a wealthy community. Troy VI (2000-1300 B.C.) had a citadel surrounded by huge limestone walls and large houses built on terraces; it was destroyed by earthquake. The rebuilt Troy VIIa was probably Homer's Troy. It was looted and destroyed by fire (c.1250 B.C.). Troy VIII was a small Greek village. Troy IX was the Greek and Roman city of Ilium, or Ilion.
See also: Trojan War.

Trucial states *see:* United Arab Emirates.

Trudeau, Edward Livingston (1848-1915), innovator of tuberculosis treatment in the United States. He founded the Trudeau Sanitarium and in 1894, the Saranac Laboratory, the first U.S. laboratory for tuberculosis research.
See also: Tuberculosis.

Trudeau, Pierre Elliott (1919-), Canadian prime minister (1968-79, 1980-84). A law professor, he entered parliament in 1965, became minister of justice in 1967, and succeeded Lester Pearson as prime minister and Liberal Party leader (1968). He sought to promote a dialogue between the provincial and federal governments and to contain the Quebec separatist movement, giving the French language equal status with English. In 1970 he recognized the People's Republic of China. Briefly out of office (1979-80), he returned to cope anew with the constitutional issue that resulted in the Constitution Act (1982), giving Canada its independence from Great Britain.
See also: Canada.

Truffaut, François (1932-84), French film director and critic. A leading New Wave director, he attracted attention for his series of semi-autobiographical films, including *The 400 Blows* (1959) and *Stolen Kisses* (1968). His other films include *Jules and Jim* (1961), *Day for Night* (1973), and *The Last Métro* (1980).

Truffle, underground fungus (genus *Tuber*) that has long been regarded as a delicacy. Pigs and dogs are trained to find them by scent. Some grow up to 2.2 lb (1 kg) and resemble potatoes; most are much smaller. They have not yet been cultivated on a wide scale, but there are attempts underway.

Trujillo Molina, Rafael Leonidas (1891-1961), Dominican Republic dictator (1930-61) and president (1930-38, 1942-52). He introduced much material progress but savagely suppressed political opposition and feuded with neighboring countries. He was assassinated.
See also: Dominican Republic.

Truk Islands, group of islands in the western Pacific, part of the Caroline Islands. All of the major islands and many smaller ones lie within a lagoon almost 40 mi (64 km) wide surrounded by a coral reef. Nearly 40,000 people live on the islands, which were first explored by Europeans in 1825. Possession of the islands passed from Spain to Germany to Japan. After World War II, they came under U.S. control. Today, along with other Caroline Islands, they make up the Federated States of Micronesia.

Truman, Harry S. (1884-1972), 33rd president of the United States. The challenges of Truman's presidency, which began after the sudden death of Franklin D. Roosevelt, included the end of World War II, use of the first atom bomb, the Cold War, the Marshall Plan and NATO, the controversial McCarthy hearings, and the Korean War.
Early life. Truman's poor eyesight kept him out of West Point, so he worked at odd jobs in Kansas City, then on the family farm. During World War I, he served in France as a member of the Missouri National Guard. In 1919, he married Elizabeth Wallace, known as Bess; they had one child. Truman co-owned a men's clothing store that failed in the 1921 farm depression.
Politics. Truman left business to serve as a Jackson Co. judge (1922-24), attend Kansas City School of Law (1923-25), and serve as a chief judge (1926-34). As a U.S. senator (1934-44), Truman chaired a defense-related Senate committee, gaining influence and respect in Congress. In 1944, when a three-way contest developed, Truman became the compromise Democratic vice-presidential candidate. He was elected with incumbent Franklin D. Roosevelt. Only 83 days into his fourth term, President Roosevelt died and Truman became president.
President. Truman's first task was the resolution of World War II. With Stalin and Churchill, he made postwar arrangements for Europe. To end the war in Asia, he twice used the atom bomb on Japan—the first and only times that devastating weapon has been used in war.
Domestically, Truman's conflict with Congress contributed to rising inflation and a wave of strikes. Congress passed the antilabor Taft-Hartley Act over Truman's veto, and buried his ambitious Fair Deal program, which included civil rights proposals, a medical insurance plan, and federal aid to education. But eventually he won a higher minimum wage, increased social security, and was able to pass aid-for-housing laws.
Overseas, a "cold war" was growing as the Soviet Union expanded its control over Eastern Europe. Truman announced the Truman Doctrine and the Marshall Plan, which pledged aid for nations resisting Communist takeover. He also supported the 1949 creation of the North Atlantic Treaty Organization (NATO), a military alliance that would defend Western Europe from Eastern-bloc attack.
Truman won the 1948 election to remain in office. In 1950 Sen. Joseph McCarthy launched a campaign to drive Communists, real and imagined, out of government. The investigations grew in fervor until it was finally discredited, but for a time it all but overwhelmed Truman's domestic attention. Also in 1950, Communist North Korea invaded South Korea.

Brown trout

Truman immediately sent U.S. troops to Korea, winning UN approval of the "police action." His policy disputes with Gen. Douglas MacArthur, commander of the UN forces (of which 90% were from the United States), led him to dismiss MacArthur in 1951, sparking controversy at home. The Korean War ended by armistice in July 1953; loss of life was heavy on both sides.

Truman survived an assassination attempt in Nov. 1950 and, in 1950-51, congressional exposures of corruption and wrongdoing in some executive agencies. In 1952 he announced that he would not run for reelection.

Retirement. Truman retired to his home in Independence, Mo., to write his memoirs and plan Independence's Harry S. Truman Library and Museum. He died Dec. 26, 1972, in Kansas City, Mo.

Truman Doctrine, U.S. declaration (1947) stating the United States would "support free peoples who are resisting attempted subjugation by armed minorities or by outside pressures." Aimed at halting communist expansion and aggression, the Truman Doctrine provided substantial aid to Greece and Turkey, helping those nations defeat communist guerrillas.

Trumbull, John (1756-1843), U.S. painter. He studied with Benjamin West in London, where he started *The Battle of Bunker's Hill* (1786). He made 36 life-portrait studies for his best known work, *The Signing of the Declaration of Independence* (1786-94), one of his four monumental pictures on Revolutionary themes for the U.S. Capitol rotunda (1817-24). He is also well known for his portraits of George Washington.

Trumbull, Jonathan (1710-85), governor of Connecticut (1769-84). The only governor to support the patriotic cause before the Revolutionary War, he later helped supply colonial troops with ammunition, food, and clothing. A statue of Trumbull was installed at the Capitol Building in Washington, D.C., in 1872.

Trumbull, Lyman (1813-96), U.S. senator from Illinois who supported antislavery legislation. He was one of the originators of the Thirteenth Amendment, which made slavery unconstitutional. He also played an influential role in the passage of the Fourteenth Amendment, which guaranteed the rights of blacks.

Trumpet, musical instrument, one of the brass wind instruments. The modern trumpet comprises a cylindrical tube in a curved, oblong form that flares out into a bell. Three piston valves (first introduced in 1815) regulate pitch. The trumpet is a popular dance and jazz-band instrument, as well as an orchestral instrument.

Trust, in law, legal relationship in which property is administered by a trustee, who has some of the powers of an owner, for the benefit of a beneficiary; the trustee is obliged to act only in the beneficiary's best interest and can derive no advantage except an agreed upon fee. The trustee may be an individual, perhaps looking after the property of a child until it comes of age, or a corporate body; banks and trust corporations often act as trustees of larger properties. Under specialized form, called corporate trust, a group of trustees may hold the stock and thus control the operations of companies that would normally be competitors. The Sherman Antitrust Act (1890) attacked such trust, but enforcement was weakened by U.S. Supreme Court decisions. Enforcement of antitrust legislation has become complicated by the growth of huge conglomerates, which control many companies in different industries.

Trust territory, formerly dependent territory administered under United Nations supervision. A trustee nation was responsible for developing the trust territory and assisting it to independence. The Trusteeship Council helped the General Assembly and Security Council supervise trust territories. Of the 11 trust territories (mostly former mandates of the League of Nations), the U.S.-administered Pacific Islands was the last to be terminated.

Truth, Sojourner (1797?-1883), U.S. abolitionist and feminist. Born into slavery in New York State as Isabella Baumfree, she escaped shortly before slavery was declared unlawful in the state (1828). In 1843, after taking the name Sojourner Truth, she became a traveling preacher. Soon after, she began to speak out against slavery, the first black woman to do so. She was known for her passionate oratorial style, her great energy, and her ready wit. In 1864 she went to Washington, D.C., to work for improved living and working conditions for the black people who settled there after fleeing the South. In the 1870s she tried unsuccessfully to convince the U.S. government to set apart undeveloped land for farms for blacks.
See also: Abolitionism.

Truth table, systematic tabulation of all the possible input/output combinations produced by a binary circuit.

Trypanosome, microscopic unicellular parasite that infests the blood plasma of animals and humans, producing disease; it is transmitted by insects. Trypanosome protozoa are responsible for trypanosomiasis of the African (Changas's disease) varieties, carried by the tsetse fly and certain other bugs. They are relatively insensitive to chemotherapy in established cases; prevention is therefore important.

Tsar, or czar, English spellings of the Russian word for "emperor." The term is used for the rulers of Russia from 1547 to 1917. The last tsar, Nicholas II, was executed in 1918, during the civil war that followed the October 1917 revolution.

Tschaikowsky, Peter Ilich *see:* Tchaikovsky, Peter Ilich.

Harry S. Truman

33rd president of the United States

Born:	Lamar, Mo.; May 8, 1884
Term:	Apr. 1945-Jan. 1953
Vice president:	Alben W. Barkley (Jan. 1949-Jan. 1953)
Political party:	Democratic
Spouse:	Elizabeth (Bess) Virginia Wallace Truman
Children:	1
Died:	Kansas City, Mo.; Dec. 26, 1972

Tsetse fly, name for 20 species of muscoid flies (genus *Glossina*). They are true winged flies very like houseflies, except that the mouthparts are adapted for piercing the skin of mammals and sucking blood. Widespread in tropical Africa, some species act as vectors of the trypanosomes that cause sleeping sickness.

Tshombe, Moise Kapenda (1919-69), president (1960-63) of the Congolese breakaway state of Katanga. Backed by Belgian interests, he unsuccessfully opposed Prime Minister Patrice Lumumba and the UN. He returned from exile to be premier (1964-65) of the Congo (Zaïre). He died in prison in Algeria.

Tsimshian, Native American tribe, residing in British Columbia along the Nass and Skeena rivers. Known for their seaworthy canoes and elaborate totem poles, the tribe became wealthy during the late 18th and early 19th centuries through trade with European sea merchants exploring the west coast of North America. Tsimshian are known for the potlatch, a complex ceremony marking important events, such as marriages or deaths. There are about 12,000 Tsimshian in British Columbia today.

Saint Xavier del Bac in Tucson, Arizona

Tuamotu Islands, group of 75-80 small islands and atolls spanning nearly 1,000 mi (1,609 km) in the South Pacific Ocean. The first European to see the islands (1606) was Pedro Fernandes de Queivós, a Portuguese explorer in the service of Spain. Annexed by France in 1881, the islands now are part of French Polynesia. About 11,000 Polynesians inhabit the Tuamotu Islands, making their living primarily from the sale of pearls and coconut oil.

Tuareg, Berber tribe in the Sahara. Its people are fair skinned and its social system comprises noble families, a large number of vassal tribes, and black slaves. Adult men, but not women, wear a blue veil. Tuareg script is like that of the ancient Libyans.

Tuatara (*Sphenodon punctatus*), reptile resembling the lizard. Inhabitants of a few small islands off the coast of New Zealand, they are the last surviving members of the order Rhynchocephalia, which lived on earth more than 200 million years ago. Green-skinned tuataras have a row of scales down their backs and tails and grow to 2 ft (60 cm) in length. Females carry their eggs for up to a year before depositing them in the ground, where they take another year to hatch. Some tuataras live as long as 77 years.

Tuba, low-pitched brass musical wind instrument with three to five valves. It is held vertically. There are tenor, baritone, euphonium, bass, and contrabass tubas. They are included in symphony orchestras and in marching bands.

Tuatara

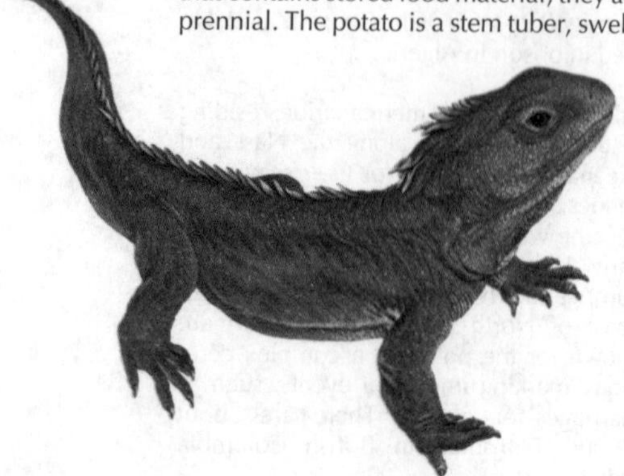

Tuber, swollen, underground stem or root that contains stored food material; they are prennial. The potato is a stem tuber, swells at the tip of a slender underground stem (stolon) and gives rise to a new plant the following year. Dahlia tubers are swollen roots.

Tuberculosis (TB), group of infectious diseases caused by the bacillus *Mycobacterium tuberculosis*, which kills some 3 million people every year throughout the world. TB may invade any organ but most commonly affects the respiratory system, where it has been called consumption or phthisis. In 1906 it killed 1 in every 500 persons in the United States, but today it leads to only 1 in 30,000 deaths because of effective drugs and better living conditions. Symptoms of pulmonary tuberculosis include fatigue, weight loss, persistent cough with green or yellow sputum and possibly with blood. Treatment is mainly by triple drug therapy, with streptomycin, para-aminosalicylic acid (PAS), and isoniazid, together with rest. Recovery takes about 2 years. The tuberculin skin test can show whether a person has some immunity to the disease, though the detection of the disease in its early stages, when it is readily curable, is difficult. Control of the disease is accomplished by preventive measures such as X-ray screening, vaccination, isolation of infectious people, and food sterilization.

Tuberose (*Polianthes tuberosa*), tropical plant of the agave family, native to Asia and America but cultivated elsewhere for its use in perfumes and other products. The tube-shaped root produces a long stem up to 3 ft (91 cm) tall, with sword-shaped leaves and waxy, white, heavily fragrant flowers.

Tubman, Harriet (c.1820-1913), U.S. abolitionist. Born a slave in Maryland, she escaped in 1849. Using her wits, her knowledge of the woods, and her trusted contacts on the Underground Railroad, Tubman conducted 19 rescue missions that freed more than 300 slaves from Maryland. Despite a $40,000 reward for her capture, she was never caught. During the Civil War (1861-65) she served as a nurse and spy for the Union army in South Carolina; after the war, she helped raise money for African-American schools in Auburn, N.Y., and in 1908 she established a home for elderly and needy African Americans.
See also: Abolitionism; Underground railroad.

Tubman, William Vacanarat Shadrach (1895-1971), president of Liberia (1944-71). He made extensive economic, social, and educational reforms and extended the rights of tribespeople and women.
See also: Liberia.

Tucker, Richard (1914-75), U.S. opera singer. In 1945 Tucker, a lyric tenor, made his debut at the New York Metropolitan Opera as the lead in Amilcare Ponchielli's *La Gioconda*, and went on to sing in the leading opera houses of North America and Europe. Equally versatile in French and Italian, he was a star at the Metropolitan until his death.
See also: Opera.

Tucson (pop. 666,880), city in southeast Arizona, inc. 1877. Founded as a Spanish presidio (walled military outpost) in 1776 by Juan Bautista de Anza, Tucson became part of Mexico in 1821, and, in 1853, control passed to the United States as a result of the Gadsden Purchase. A major research and educational center, Tucson is also a popular tourist destination, transportation hub, and home of the University of Arizona, several museums, and the San Xavier del Bac Mission, dating from the earliest days of the town. Situated in a valley with mountains on 3 sides, Tucson enjoys a year-round hot, dry, sunny climate that has made it a popular retirement center.
See also: Arizona.

Tudor, Antony (1909-87), English choreographer who introduced dramatic, emotional themes into U.S. ballet. Founder (1939) of the American Ballet Theatre (ABT), his works for the company include *Dark Elegies* (1937) and *Pillar of Fire* (1942). He was also ballet director of the Metropolitan Opera (1957-63) and associate director of the ABT (1974-80).

Tudor, House of, reigning dynasty of England (1485-1603). Of Welsh descent, Henry Tudor, earl of Richmond and heir to the House of Lancaster, ended the Wars of the Roses by defeating Richard III in 1485; he became Henry VII, first Tudor king. The succession included Henry VIII (r.1509-47), Edward VI (r.1547-53), Mary I (r.1553-58), and Elizabeth I (r.1558-1603). Under the Tudors England became a major power and enjoyed a flowering of the arts.
See also: England; United Kingdom.

Tuileries, former royal palace in Paris. Situated on the right bank of the River Seine, the palace was built by order of Catherine de Medici (1564) and was completed in the 1600s. Forced into use as a residence by King Louis XVI and his queen, Marie Antoinette, during the French Revolution (1789), it was also used during the 1790s by revolutionary leaders to hold session and by Napoleon, who made it his primary residence after taking power. After the Bourbon restoration (1814-15) it once again became a royal residence before being destroyed by fire during the Paris Commune uprisings of 1871. The 75-acre (30-hectare) Tuileries Gardens remain affiliated with the Louvre museum.

Tularemia, or rabbit fever, infectious disease due to bacteria (*Pasteurella tularensis*), causing fever, ulceration, lymph node enlargement, and sometimes pneumonia. It is carried by wild animals, particularly rabbits, and insects. Antibiotics are fully effective in treatment.

Tulip, name for plant (genus *Tulipa*) native to Europe and Asia, grown from bulbs. Cultivated tulips were introduced to

Europe via Holland in the 16th century and have become popular spring-flowering garden and pot plants. They have deep, cup-shaped flowers; new varieties are continually being bred. Tulips come in a variety of colors and in some instances in a combination of colors.

Tuliptree *see:* Yellow poplar.

Tulsa (pop. 708,954), city in northeast Oklahoma, on the Arkansas River. Settled in the 1830s by members of the Creek tribe, Tulsa grew rapidly after the discovery of oil in 1901. Oil is still a major industry, along with airline, aerospace, and construction-material industries. Completion of the McClellan-Kern Arkansas River Navigation System in 1971, connecting Tulsa with the Gulf of Mexico, made Tulsa a major inland port. The city is also a major education and cultural hub, with 4 colleges, 2 prominent museums, a ballet company, opera company, and philharmonic orchestra.
See also: Oklahoma.

Tumbleweed, common name for several plants native to North America that grow in clumps on waste land and dry into loose balls. These break from the soil and are blown by the wind, scattering seeds. Examples are the so-called Russian thistle (*Salsola kali*) and *Amaranthus albus*.

Tumboa *see:* Welwitschia.

Tumor, or neoplasm, abnormal overgrowth of tissue. These may be benign proliferations, such as fibroid of the womb, or they may be forms of cancer (lymphoma or sarcoma), which are generally malignant. The rate of growth, the tendency to metastasize (spread locally and to distant sites via the blood vessels and lymph system), and systemic effects determine the degree of malignancy. Tumors may present as a lump, by local compression effects (especially with brain tumors), or by systemic effects, including anemia, weight loss, false hormone actions, neuritis, etc. Treatments include surgery, radiation therapy, and chemotherapy.
See also: Cancer.

Tuna, high-speed fish with rows of finlets on the tail. Also called tunnies, they live in shoals in the warmer seas of the world. The bluefin tuna (*Thunnus thynnus*) of the North Atlantic and Mediterranean grows to 14 ft (4.3 m) long and weighs up to 1,800 lb (816.5 kg). Others, such as the Pacific albacore and yellow-fin tuna, are smaller, but all are important commercial fish. They are caught by net, hook, and harpoon, and their "white meat" is canned. Tuna feed on small fish, eating considerable amounts during the summer months in the northern parts of their ranges before migrating southwards to spawn.

Tundra, plains of the Arctic Circle. For most of the year the temperature is less than 32°F (0°C), and even during the short summer it never rises above 50°F (10°C). The soil is a thin coating over permafrost. Tundra vegetation includes lichens, mosses, and stunted shrubs. Similar regions on high mountains (but generally without permafrost) are called alpine tundra.
See also: Permafrost.

Tungsten, or wolfram, chemical element, symbol W; for physical constants see Periodic Table. Tungsten was discovered by brothers Fausto and Juan José de Elhuyar in 1783. It occurs in wolframite, scheelite, huebnerite, and ferberite. The element is prepared by reduction of the oxide with hydrogen or carbon. It is a steel-gray, hard, ductile, unreactive metal, and has the highest melting point and lowest vapor pressure of all metals. Alloys of tungsten have many high-temperature applications. Tungsten and its compounds are used in filaments for electric lamps and television tubes, fluorescent lighting, glass-to-metal seals, and high-speed tool steels.

Tunis (pop. 596,700), capital city of Tunisia, on the Lake of Tunis, in northeastern Tunisia. Probably established before Carthaginian times, the city was part of the ancient Carthaginian empire until Carthage was destroyed by the Romans in 146 B.C. Later rebuilt, Tunis became a major trading port that was captured by the Moslems in the 7th century. It was established as the country's capital by the Hafsid dynasty (13th-16th centuries) and was under Turkish rule from 1534 to 1881, when it became a center for piracy as well as trade. The French occupation of Tunisia lasted 1881-1956, after which time the country gained its independence. Today it thrives as a major port and is active in the manufacture of olive oil, textiles, and carpets. Since 1979 it has been the headquarters for the Arab League.
See also: Tunisia.

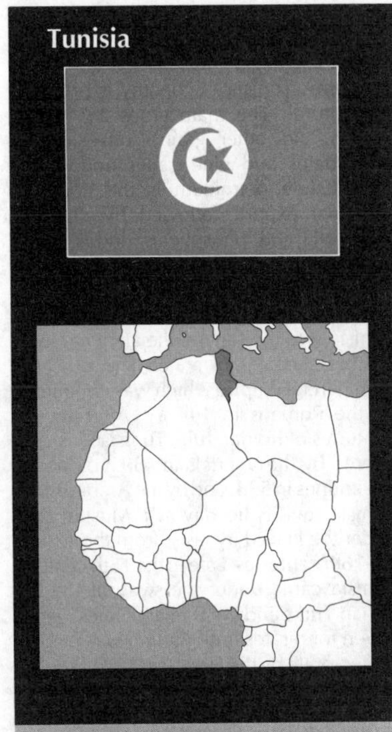

Capital:	Tunis
Area:	63,170 sq mi (163,610 sq km)
Population:	7,973,000
Government:	republic
Independent:	1956
GNP:	U.S. $9,610,000,000
Per capita:	U.S. $1,230

Tunisia, republic in North Africa. With an area of some 63,378 sq mi (164,149 sq km), Tunisia is bounded on the south by Libya, on the west by Algeria, and on the north and east by the Mediterranean Sea. The Cape Bon peninsula, in the extreme northeast, is only 96 mi (153 km) from Sicily. Tunis is the capital and chief port.

Land. Tunisia's irregular coastline has several good harbors, among them Bizerte. In the northwest, spurs of the Atlas Mountains enter the country from Algeria. The Medjerda River, Tunisia's only permanent river, flows through the northern mountains on its way to the Gulf of Tunis. The Medjerda River valley is a major wheat-producing area. The northern highlands also have dense forests of oak and cork oak, pines, and junipers. The Tabassah Mountains rise in west-central Tunisia and include the country's highest peak, Mt. Sha'nab (5,066 ft/1,544 m). In north-central Tunisia, the dry plain of the Sahel lies between the Atlas and Tabassah mountains and gives way to Tunisia's fertile, heavily populated coastal plain. To the south of the Sahel, beyond the Chott Djerid and other salt lakes, are the Saharan sands and date-palm oases of southern Tunisia. In coastal Tunisia, summers are generally hot and dry; winters are warm and wet. The Sahel has less than 10 in (25 cm) of rain yearly. Rainfall can be irregular and there are sometimes droughts.

In Tunisia, a farmer uses his camel to get water from a well.

People. The people of Tunisia, predominantly Berber and Arab, include small French, Italian, and Maltese minorities. Most people live in the fertile north and some 40% of the population live in towns.

The people are overwhelmingly Muslim, and French is spoken, though Arabic is the official language.

Economy. Tunisia's economy is primarily agricultural. The main crops are wheat, barley, and other grains; olives, citrus fruits, dates, and wine grapes; and vegetables. Crude petroleum is the country's principal export, followed by clothing, olive oil, and phosphates. Industry has traditionally centered around food processing, but is expanding.

History. Once a colony of the Phoenicians, Tunisia was the state of the ancient city of Carthage, center of a rich and powerful commercial empire which was conquered by the Romans in 146 B.C. After several centuries of Roman rule, Tunisia was conquered by the Vandals in 439 A.D., by the Byzantines in 533, and by the Arabs in 670. Tunisia saw its heyday as a Muslim state under the Hafsid dynasty, from the 13th to the 16th centuries. Late in the 16th century, Tunisia came under the sway of the Ottoman Turks and the Barbary States were a haven for pirates until Tunisia was made a protectorate by the French in 1881. Tunisia achieved its independence from France in 1957 and became a republic under the presidency and virtual one-man rule of Habib Bourguiba. Bourguiba's dominance was not effectively challenged until 1987, when he was replaced by Gen. Zine al-Abidine Ben Ali.

Ivan Turgenev

Tunnel, underground passageway usually designed to carry a highway or railroad, to serve as a conduit for water or sewage, or to provide access to an underground working face. Although tunnels have been built since prehistoric times, tunneling methods remained primitive and hazardous until the 19th century. Modern softground tunneling was pioneered by Marc Brunel, who invented the "tunneling shield" (1824), a device subsequently improved (1869-86) by James Greathead, whose shield is basically a large steel cylinder with a sharp cutting edge driven forward by hydraulic rams. Tunneling through hard rock is facilitated by an array of pneumatic drills mounted on a "jumbo" carriage running on rails. Explosives are inserted in a pattern of holes drilled in the rock face and then detonated. Increasingly, however, automatic tunneling machines called moles, with cutting heads consisting of a rotating or oscillating wheel that digs, grinds, or chisels away the working face, are employed. Another common tunnel-building method—used in constructing the New York subway—is "cut-and-cover," which involves excavating a trench, building the tunnel lining, and then covering it. The world's longest vehicular or railroad tunnel is the 12.3-mi (19.8-km) Simplon II in the Alps, completed in 1922.

Tunney, Gene (James Joseph Tunney; 1898-1978), U.S. world heavyweight boxing champion (1926-28). In 1926 he beat Jack Dempsey in the controversial fight of the "long count." He retired in 1928, having lost only one of his professional bouts.

Tunny *see:* Tuna.

Tupelo, name of several trees belonging to the Nyssaceae family, found in Southeast Asia and in North America. The trees produce small white flowers and fruits, which provide food for many species of birds. The wood of the tupelo is used for making boxes, baskets, and other wooden products. The black tupelo, or Blackgum (*Nyssa sylvatica*), is found in moist areas of the United States and in parts of Canada and Mexico. It grows from 35-80 ft (11-24 m) tall. The water tupelo, or sourgum (*N. aquatica*), is found in swamps in the southeastern United States. It grows as tall as 115 ft (35 m).

Tupí-Guaraní, group of Native American tribes from central and eastern South America. The tribes inhabiting Paraguay and southern Brazil are called Guaraní; those in the Amazon Basin are of the Tupí, or Tupinabá, stock. Practitioners of ritual cannibalism in ancient times, they developed into farmers, hunters, fishers, and fruit gatherers. Under Spanish and Portuguese rule, which began in the 16th century, Jesuit missionaries organized the Tupí-Guaraní people into agricultural settlements, where many of them were converted to Christianity and assimilated into the Western cultural mainstream. Guaraní is still one of the major languages spoken in Paraguay today.

Tupper, Sir Charles (1821-1915), Canadian politican and one of the founders of the Dominion of Canada. He served temporarily as prime minister in 1896 following the resignation of Mackenzie Bowell; however, he lost the election largely due to his support of the reestablishment of French-language schools in Manitoba. Tupper was known as a skilled speaker and politician.
See also: Canada.

Turbine, machine for directly converting the kinetic and/or thermal energy of a flowing fluid (air, hot gas, steam, or water) into useful rotational energy. The working fluid either pushes against a set of blades mounted on the drive shaft (impulse turbines) or turns the shaft by reaction when the fluid is expelled from nozzles (or nozzle-shaped vanes) around its circumference (reaction turbines). Water turbines include the vast inward-flow reaction turbines used in the generation of hydroelectricity and the smaller-scale tangential-flow "Pelton wheel" impulse types used when exploiting a very great head of water. In the 1800s, Charles Alernon Parsons (1854-1931), a British engineer, designed the first successful steam turbines, having realized that the efficient use of high-pressure steam demanded that its energy be extracted in a multitude of small stages. Steam turbines thus consist of a series of vanes mounted on a rotating drum with sator vanes redirecting the steam in between the moving ones. They are commonly used as marine engines and in thermal and nuclear power plants. Gas turbines are not as yet widely used except in airplanes and for peak-load electricity generation.

Turbojet *see:* Jet propulsion.

Turbot (*Psetta maxima*), large flatfish found in the North Sea and Icelandic waters. It has an almost circular body up to 3 ft (91 cm) long, with a warty upper surface. Its an important food fish in Europe. Two American Pacific flatfish are also known as turbot: the curlfin turbot and the "C-O" sole.

Turgenev, Ivan (1818-83), Russian writer whose realistic portrayals of the peasants and nobility of his country helped bring about social reforms and influenced later Russian writers. *A Sportsman's Sketches* (1852), one of his earliest works, is believed to have led to Czar Alexander II's emancipation of the serfs. Other major works include *Rudin* (1856), *A Nest of Gentlefolk* (1859), *On the Eve* (1860), *Fathers and Sons* (1861), *Smoke* (1867), and *Virgin Soil* (1877). Also a playwright, his best-known drama is *A Month in the Country* (1850), which influenced Anton Chekhov. A member of the landowning class who spent much of his time in Western Europe, Turgenev was one of a group of reformers who believed that Russia should adopt some of the best attributes of Western culture.

Turin (pop. 1,104,000), city in northwestern Italy. It is a major industrial center, with automobile (Fiat, Lancia), machinery, chemical and electrical industries. It was the capital of the kingdom of Sardinia (1720-1861) and the first capital of united Italy (1861-64).
See also: Italy.

Turkestan, or **Turkistan**, large region in Asia covering parts of China, the USSR, and Afghanistan. It is so-called because peoples of Turkic ancestry have inhabited this region since the 6th century A.D. From the time of Marco Polo, the area has served as an important trade link between the Asian and European continents. The region, which has no distinct boundaries, has been officially divided into Chinese, Soviet, and Afghan Turkestan. Many of the region's people are Muslim.

Turkey, republic occupying Asia Minor and a small part of southeastern Europe. Lying between the Black and the Mediterranean seas, the Asian and European parts of Turkey are separated by the Straits, a waterway consisting of the Bosporus, the Sea of Marmara, and the Dardanelles. The Straits strategically link the Black Sea with the Mediterranean Sea. Covering 301,382 sq mi (780,574 sq km), Turkey is bounded by Iraq, Syria, and the Mediterranean Sea on the south; the Aegean Sea on the west; Greece and Bulgaria on the north; and the USSR and Iran in the east. The capital is Ankara.

Land. Asian Turkey is mountainous inland and has an extensive semiarid plateau giving way to narrow coastal lowlands. Mt.

General information

Capital:	Ankara
Area:	300,948 sq mi (779,452 sq km)
Population:	55,541,000
Official language:	Turkish
Monetary unit:	1 Turkish lira = 100 kurus
Main cities:	Istanbul, Ankara, Izmir

Government

Form:	republic
Independent:	1923
Head of state:	President (elected every 7 years)
Head of government:	Prime minister
Legislature:	one legislative house (Grand National Assembly)
Executive:	Prime minister and Cabinet
Judiciary:	highest court is the Court of Cassation
Political division:	67 provinces

National economy

Gross national product:	U.S. $68,600,000,000
Per capita income:	U.S. $1,280
Agriculture:	wheat, sugar beet, barley, corn, melons and watermelons, tomatoes, potatoes, tobacco, cotton
Livestock:	sheep, goats, cattle
Fisheries:	626,000 metric tons
Mining:	lignite, coal, iron ore, crude petroleum, chromium ore
Industries:	petroleum products, cement, commercial fertilizers, iron, steel, machinery
Main exports:	textiles, agricultural products, mining products
Transportation:	5,076 mi (8,169 km) of railroads, 198,293 mi (319,133 km) of roads, 6 international airports
Trading partners:	Germany, Iraq, U.S., Italy, United Kingdom

People

Urban:	46%
Ethnic composition:	Turkish 85.5%, Kurdish 10.5%, Arab 1.5%
Birth rate:	28.4 per 1,000 population
Death rate:	8.4 per 1,000 population
Infant mortality:	84 per 1,000 live births
Life expectancy:	male 62.5 years, female 66 years

Ararat, at 16,945 ft (5,165 m), is Turkey's highest peak, and the Tigris and Euphrates rivers rise in the east. Earthquakes are frequent. European Turkey, which is actually eastern Thrace, is fertile hill country and the site of the city of Istanbul, formerly Constantinople. The climate is Mediterranean around the coastal lowlands and the European section, but drier and subject to greater extremes inland on the Asian side, with harsh winters toward the northeast.

People. The Turks are largely descended from the Tatars, who entered Asia Minor in the 11th century A.D. There are small Kurdish, Arab, and Orthodox Christian minorities. The people are overwhelmingly Muslim. The official language is Turkish.

Economy. Agriculture is the basis of the economy. The chief crops are grains, cotton, fruits, and tobacco. Cattle are raised on the Anatolian plateau, in the western reaches of Asian Turkey. Turkish industry has been developed greatly since World War II and includes steel, iron, and textile manufacturers. There are large deposits of coal, iron, and other metals, and some oil.

History. Anatolia was the cradle of ancient civilizations, dating back to at least 7000 B.C. Its famous sites include Troy, Ephesus, and the Hittite capital of Hattusas. Turkey was, successively, part of the Hittite, Persian, Roman, Seljuk, and Ottoman empires. Its western coast was, for a time, the site of some of the most brilliant city-states of the ancient Greeks, including Halicarnassus and Miletus. The Ottoman Empire, with its center in Turkey, was founded in the 13th century and endured until it was formally dissolved after World War I. Modern Turkey was largely the work of Mustafa Kemal Atatürk, who declared the republic in 1923. Atatürk initiated an ambitious program of reform and modernization aimed at establishing Turkey as a modern nation-state on the European model. His reforms ranged from changing the alphabet to emancipating women. Atatürk died in 1938 and Turkey remained neutral for most of World War II. Afterwards, the country joined NATO and received substantial U.S. aid. Turkey has undergone 2 major military coups since the end of World War II, one in 1960 and another in 1980. Tension with Greece has almost led to war on several occasions. In 1974, Turkey invaded and occupied the northern third of the island of Cyprus. The central government has also fought intermittently with Kurds in Anatolia. Civilian rule returned to Turkey in 1983 with the election of Turgut Ozal to the presidency.

Turkey, name of two species of large New World game birds, family Meleagrididae. The common turkey (*Meleagresi gallopavo*) is found in the open woodland and scrub of North America, and is the ancestor of the domestic turkey. The head and neck of both species are naked and have wattles; a fleshy caruncle overhangs the bill. The naked skin in the common turkey is red; in the ocellated turkey, blue.

Rock houses built amid conical limestone formations in the Turkish region of Cappadocia

Turkish, Turkic language, official language of Turkey, also spoken by minorities in eastern Europe and southwestern Asia.

Evolved during the Ottoman Empire, it was written in Arabic script until Atatürk introduced a modified Latin alphabet in 1928.

Turkmenistan, independent country in central Asia, bordering Kazakhstan and Uzbekistan in the north, Afghanistan in the southeast, Iran in the south, and the Caspian Sea in the west. The Kara Kum desert covers about 90% of the landmass in this region. Most of the population are Muslims, who speak a Turkic language. Russians, Uzbeks, and Kazakhs are important minorities. The majority of the population lives in the southeast, where the capital city of Ashkhabad is located. The major products are related to their herds of Karakul sheep and Turkoman horses. In the late 19th century Turkmenistan came under Russian rule; it became part of the USSR in 1920 and a constituent republic in 1925. Turkmenistan declared its sovereignty in 1990 and became fully independent in 1991.
See also: Union of Soviet Socialist Republics.

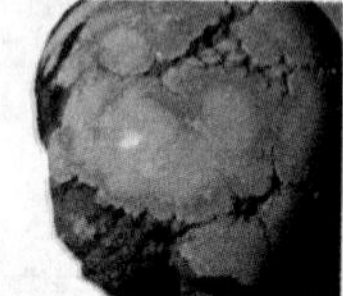

Turquoise

Turks, family to Turkic-speaking, chiefly Muslim people extending from Sinkiang (west China) and Siberia to Turkey, Iran, and former East European USSR. They include the Tatars, Kazakhs, Uzbeks, Kirghiz, Turkmens, Vighurs, Azerbaijanis, and many others. The Turks spread through Asia from the 6th century onward and were converted to Islam in the 10th century. In the west they controlled vast lands under the Seljuks (1000s-1200s) and the Ottoman Empire (1300s-1923).

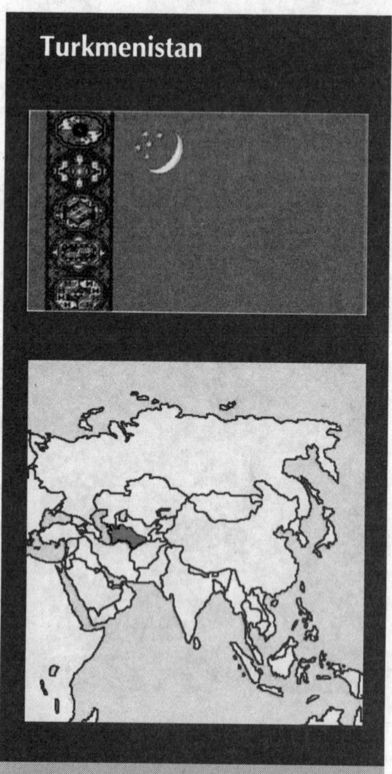

Capital:	Ashkhabad
Area:	188,456 sq mi (488,100 sq km)
Population:	3,852,000
Government:	republic
Independent:	1991
GNP:	U.S. $4,895,000,000
Per capita:	U.S. $1,270

Turks and Caicos Islands, two British colonial island groups in the West Indies. They cover 166 sq mi (430 sq km) of land in the southeastern part of the Bahama Islands group. The chief economic activity is the exportation of lobster, hemp, and sponges. Many of the region's inhabitants fish for a living.

Turner, Frederick Jackson (1861-1932), U.S. historian. His view of the role of the frontier in shaping U.S. individualism and democracy was influential. *The Frontier in American History* (1920) reprinted earlier papers. He won a Pulitzer Prize for his study of sectionalism in the United States (1932).

Turner, John Napier (1929-), prime minister of Canada following the resignation of Prime Minister Pierre Trudeau. In 1984, after having served 2 1/2 months, Turner called a general election and lost to Progressive Conservative candidate Brian Mulroney. Turner had previously held a variety of posts in the cabinets of prime ministers Lester Pearson and Pierre Trudeau. A Liberal Party member, he was interested in developing social programs to help the nation's poor and unemployed.
See also: Canada.

Turner, J(oseph) M(allard) W(illiam) (1775-1851), English Romantic landscape painter. His work is famous for its rich treatment of light and atmosphere, in oil, watercolor, or engraving. His paintings include *The Fighting Téméraire* (1839) and *Rain, Steam and Speed* (1844).

Turner, Nat (1800-31), U.S. slave and revolutionary. Born on a plantation in Southampton County, Va., he believed that God had chosen him to free the slaves. He gathered 60-70 other slaves and led them in what came to be known as the most serious slave rebellion in the nation's history. About 60 whites were killed, including the family of Turner's owner, Joseph Travis, before the Virginia militia suppressed the revolt 6 weeks later, capturing and hanging Turner and about 20 of his followers. Although the rebellion led to reprisals and stricter laws against slaves, Turner became a symbol for the abolitionist movement.

Turnip, plant (genus *Brassica*) native to Europe and Asia. It was developed into a root crop, mainly for cattle feed, in the 19th century. Its swollen, yellowish-white taproot is packed with starch and is fit for human consumption. If left in the ground over the winter, the turnip sends up a flowering stem, using food stored in the root during its first year.
See also: Starch.

Turnstone, one of two types of shore birds belonging to the sandpiper family. It characteristically uses its short bill to turn over stones in search of food. The ruddy turnstone is found in arctic regions of the world. The black turnstone is native to the Bering Sea region and migrates to southern Alaska and California for the winter.

Turquoise, $AL_2(OH)_3PO_4H_2O+Cu$, igneous (volcanic) mineral containing aluminum, copper, and phosphorus, found in arid regions of the earth, especially Iran, the Sinai Peninsula, and the North American Southwest. Varying in color from light blue (gem quality) to greenish-gray, turquoise has been used to make jewelry for thousands of years. Native American tribes of the Southwest, especially the Navajos, became skilled in fashioning turquoise-and-silver jewelry.

Turtle, reptile (order Chelonia) with a shell that almost encloses the body. A land turtle is sometimes called a tortoise, and some freshwater turtles are given the name terrapin. The turtle has existed for more than 175 million years, and there are now about 230 species spread over the warmer parts of the world, 44 of them in the United States. Some species are becoming rare because they are hunted for their flesh or for their shells. The turtle's shell is made of two parts—the upper carapace and the lower plastron. The vertebrae and ribs are fused to the carapace. The shell is covered with horny plates, except in the soft-shell and the leathery turtle, where it has a leathery covering. There are five kinds of marine turtles: the leathery turtle and the green, hawksbill, loggerhead, and ridley turtles. Except for the last, all are found in North American waters. All come ashore to lay their eggs in sandy beaches: Freshly hatched turtles have to rush down to the shore after hatching to avoid predators. The green turtle is the species most used for turtle soup, and the hawksbill provides tortoise shells. The land and freshwater turtles are smaller than the marine turtles. They range from 2-in (5-cm) mud turtles to the 2-ft (61-cm) 100-lb (45-kg) alligator snapping turtle or "stinkpot", the reptilian equivalent of the skunk. The box turtles have a hinged plastron so that they can completely shut themselves in their shells.

Turtledove, woodland bird belonging to the pigeon and dove family. It is native to Europe and parts of Asia and Africa. During the winter, it migrates south to the sub-Saharan continent. A small, shy bird, it is often recognized by its sad, cooing song.

Tuscany, region in west-central Italy, extending from the Apennine Mountains to the west coast. It is mostly mountainous, with fertile river valleys and coastal strip. Agricultural products include cereals, olive oil, and Chianti wine. Iron and other minerals are mined; the chief manufactures are textiles, chemicals, and machinery. Center of the ancient Etruscan civilization, Tuscany has many famous cities, including Florence, Lucca, Pisa, and Siena.

Tuscarora, North American Native American tribe. Driven from their lands in North Carolina by European-American settlers, the Tuscaroras joined the Iroquois League in 1722. Some hundreds now live in New York State and Ontario, Canada.

Tussock moth, type of moth belonging to the Lymantriidae family. Caterpillars of the species have brightly colored hair, but adults are whitish-gray in color. Some varieties, such as the gypsy moth, were brought to the United States from Europe. Tussock moths often cause extensive damage to trees and orchards.

Tutankhamen, (fl.c.1350 B.C.), Egyptian pharaoh. Though he died at 18, he gained modern-day fame when his tomb was discovered in Thebes by Howard Carter and the earl of Carnarvon in 1922 with its treasures intact. His solid gold coffin, gold portrait mask, and other treasures are housed in the Cairo museum.
See also: Egypt, Ancient.

Tutankhamen

Tutu, Desmond (1931-), South African black minister, recipient of the 1984 Nobel Peace Prize. In 1957 Tutu was named the first black Anglican dean of Johannesburg. In 1978 he was appointed general secretary of the South African Council of Churches, elected bishop of Johannesburg in 1984, and archbishop of Cape Town in 1986. He has been a consistent opponent of apartheid.

Archbishop Desmond Tutu

Tutuila *see:* American Samoa.

Tuva, republic of the USSR between Siberia and Mongolia. Formerly a Russian protectorate, the region became the autonomous republic of Tannu Tuva in 1921. In 1944, it was annexed by the USSR and its name changed to Tuva. Most of the region's inhabitants are descended from Turkic-speaking peoples and raise animals for a living. Tuva exports animal hides and wool; its mineral resources include gold, asbestos, and cobalt.
See also: Union of Soviet Socialist Republics.

Tuvalu (formerly Ellice Islands), independent Commonwealth nation composed of nine small atolls spread over more than 500,000 sq mi (1,295,000 sq km) in the West Pacific. The capital is Fongafale on Funafuti.
Land and climate. The largest island, Vaitupu, covers only 2 sq mi (5.2 sq km). No spot on these coral atolls rises more than 16 ft (4.9 m) above sea level. The soil is poor and there are no rivers and little vegetation besides coconut palms. The average annual temperature is 86°F (30°C); most of the rainfall occurs between Nov. and Feb.
People and economy. The inhabitants are Polynesian, with almost 30% living on the island of Funafuti. Copra is the only export, although the sale of postage stamps abroad also produces income.
History. The islands were largely ignored by Europeans until the 19th century, when whaling began in the area. The population was reduced from 22,000 to 3,000 between 1850 and 1875 because of disease and forcible recruitment for labor abroad. A British protectorate over both the Ellice and Gilbert (now Kiribati) islands was established in 1892. In 1974 Ellice Islanders voted for separate status, achieving independence in 1978.

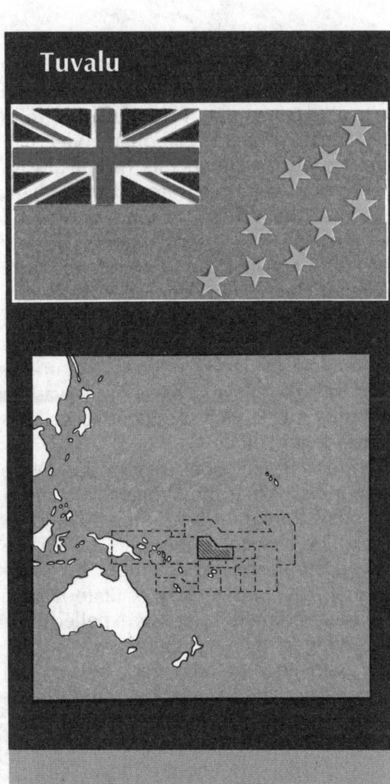

Capital:	Funafuti
Area:	10 sq mi (26 sq km)
Population:	8,900
Government:	constitutional monarchy
Independent:	1978
GNP:	U.S. $3,427,000
Per capita:	U.S. $420

TV *see:* Television.

TVA *see:* Tennessee Valley Authority.

Twain, Mark (Samuel Langhorne Clemens; 1835-1910), U.S. author and popular humorist and lecturer. After being a printer's apprentice (1848-53), he led a wandering life, becoming a Mississippi river pilot (1857-61) and then a journalist, establishing a reputation with his humorous sketches. In 1869 he produced his first best-seller, *The Innocents Abroad,* followed by *The Adventures of Tom Sawyer* (1876), *The Prince and the Pauper* (1882), his masterpiece *Huckleberry Finn* (1884), and the satirical *A Connecticut Yankee in King Arthur's Court* (1889). In later life, Twain lost most of his money through speculation and suffered the loss of his wife and daughters. His works became increasingly pessimistic and bitingly satirical, as in *The Tragedy of Pudd'nhead Wilson* (1894) and *The Man Who Corrupted Hadleyburg* (1899).

Tweed River, waterway forming part of the Scotland-England border. It rises in southeastern Scotland and flows into the North Sea. In the 19th century, mills were built along the river to produce water power for local textile factories. The name of the cloth known as tweed may come from the name of the river.

Tweed, William Marcy "Boss" (1823-78), U.S. politician. Born in New York City, Tweed was a member of the U.S. House of Representatives (1853-55). Afterwards, he held various powerful positions in New York City politics, including New York City school commissioner (1856-57) and commissioner of public works (1870). Through his control of the Tammany organization, he affected nominations and patronage in New York City Democratic politics. From 1867 to 1871, he served as a state senator. He is best known as the leader of the Tweed Ring, a group of New York City politicians infamous for swindling the city treasury out of millions of dollars through contracts for city improvements. Due in large part to the efforts of the magazine *Harper's Weekly* and political cartoonist Thomas Nast, the Tweed Ring was finally exposed, and Tweed himself was convicted and jailed in 1873 on charges of corruption. He died in jail.
See also: Tammany, Society of.

Twelve Tables, Laws of the, earliest Roman code of laws. Created by decemvirs (members of a council of 10 men) who based the laws on earlier Roman customs, the Laws of the Twelve Tables were written on tablets (450 B.C.) and displayed in the forum. They contained civil, criminal, and sacred legal precepts and became revered as a prime source of law. Only fragments survive.
See also: Rome, Ancient.

Twelve-tone music, or serial music, type of music developed in the 1920s that rejects tonality as the basis for composition. Its most famous exponent, Arnold Schoenberg, laid down a method of composition that attempted to free music from the 8-note octave and its associated conventions. Twelve-tone compositions are constructed around a specific series of the twelve notes of the chromatic scale. Later 20th-century composers have used the twelve-tone construction with greater freedom. Composers of twelve-tone music include Igor Stravinsky, Roger Sessions, Walter Piston, Ernst Krenek, Domitry Shostakovich, and Schoenberg's pupils Anton von Webern and Alban Berg.

Twelve Tribes, twelve family groups into which the ancient Hebrews were divided. According to the Bible they were descended from and named for ten sons of Jacob and two sons of Joseph. Those descended from Jacob's sons were Asher, Benjamin, Dan, Gad, Issachar, Judah, Naphtali, Reuben, Simeon, and Zebulun; the two from Joseph's sons were Ephraim and Manasseh. When the Hebrews finally reached the Promised Land, they divided the country

Mark Twain

among these twelve family groups. A thirteenth tribe, Levi, third son of Jacob, had no portion of land set aside for it.

Tyler, John (1790-1862), 10th president of the United States. Tyler, the first United States vice president to step into the presidency on a president's death in office, entered politics as a Democrat but was elected as a Whig. As president, however, he so opposed the Whigs' program that he was expelled from the party, burned in effigy, and threatened with impeachment. Most of his cabinet resigned in anger.

Early life. Tyler graduated from William and Mary College in 1807; studied law under his father, a former Virginia governor; then was admitted to the Virginia bar in 1809. At age 21, he was elected to the Virginia House of Delegates. In 1813, Tyler married Letitia Christian; they had eight children.

Politics. Tyler served in the U.S. House of Representatives (1816-21), in the Virginia legislature (1823-25), as governor of Virginia (1825-1827), and as a U.S. senator (1827-36). A political conservative, Tyler believed in a narrow interpretation of the Constitution, and that the powers of the federal government should be strictly limited. In 1836, when the Virginia legislature instructed him to support President Andrew Jackson, who stood for a powerful federal government, Tyler resigned from the Senate instead. Although Tyler had broken with the Democrats, he had always opposed favorite measures of the Whigs. Even so, the Whigs, seeking to rally all anti-Jackson forces, nominated Tyler for the vice presidency in 1840. He ran with William Henry Harrison under the slogan "Tippecanoe and Tyler too." The Whig ticket won. Within a month after the inauguration in 1841, however, Harrison died and Tyler became president. It was the first time a U.S. vice president succeeded a president in office.

President. Tyler soon angered his Whig supporters. When the Whigs presented a nationalist program, including a National Bank, Tyler vetoed the bill. When he vetoed another bill in September, his entire cabinet, except Secretary of State Daniel Webster, resigned. Tyler was expelled from the Whig party and there was an unsuccessful attempt to impeach him.

Under Tyler, the United States and Britain signed the Webster-Ashburton Treaty defining the Canadian border and committing both nations to police the illegal African slave trade. Tyler ended the Seminole War in Florida, backed Morse's telegraph system, reorganized the Navy, and signed the Preemption Act that helped settle much of the Midwest.

Tyler's determination to bring Texas into the Union reopened the slavery controversy, as the North opposed its entry as a slave state. With no hope of reelection in 1844, Tyler pushed hard to win annexation for Texas. On Mar. 1, 1845, after much debate and political wrangling, he signed the bill admitting Texas to the Union. Two days later, on his last day in office, he signed another bill, admitting Florida.

Retirement. Tyler's wife, Letitia, had died in 1842. In 1844, he had married Julia Gardiner; the couple had seven children. Tyler retired to Virginia, but continued to take part in politics. In 1861, he led a peace conference in Washington, hoping to avert civil war. When the Senate rejected the Southerners' terms, he returned to Virginia and voted for itss secession. He was elected to the Confederate House of Representatives in Nov. 1861, but died on Jan. 18, 1862, before taking his seat.

John Tyler

10th president of the United States

Born:	Charles City Co.; Mar. 29, 1790
Term:	Apr. 1841-Mar. 1845
Vice president:	None
Political party:	Whig
Spouses:	Letitia Christian Tyler; Julia Gardiner Tyler
Children:	15
Died:	Richmond, Va.; Jan. 18, 1862

Tyler, Moses Coit (1835-1900), critic and historian of early U.S. literature. He was appointed professor of American history at Cornell University in 1881, the first such position in the United States. He helped to found the American Historical Association in 1884. His books include the 2-volume *The Literary History of the American Revolution 1763-1783*, published in 1897.

Tyler, Wat (d. 1381), leader of the English Peasant's Revolt (1381), England's first popular rebellion. Protesting high taxation after the Black Death, Tyler and his Kentish followers captured Canterbury, then took the Tower of London. Richard II promised abolition of serfdom and feudal service. At a second meeting with the king, Tyler was stabbed, and the revolt was brutally crushed.

Tylor, Sir Edward Burnett (1832-1917), British anthropologist. A pioneer in the field, he was an authority on animism and primitive mentality. His books *Research into the Early History of Mankind* (1865) and *Primitive Culture* (1871) were among the earliest works on anthropology as a social science. Additional theories were expounded in *Anthropology* (1881).
See also: Anthropology.

Tyndale, William (c.1494-1536), English biblical translator. A Roman Catholic priest, he translated the New Testament from Greek and Hebrew to the English vernacular in his effort to stem church corruption, but he was unable to get his work published in England. He left for Germany in 1524, where he succeeded; he then had copies smuggled into England. While in Germany, he befriended Martin Luther and was strongly influenced by him. Despite the ban on his translated Bibles in England, Tyndale wrote tracts defending the English Reformation. In 1535 he was arrested by Roman Catholic authorities in Antwerp, Belgium, tried and convicted of heresy, and the following year was executed. His translations form the basis of the King James (Authorized) Version of the Bible, which is in common usage today.
See also: Bible

Type, characters, including letters, numbers, and punctuation marks, assembled to form words and sentences in the printing of books, magazines, and newspapers. Type consists of thousands of styles, or type faces (fonts), that fall into 4 categories: Roman type, with small finishing strokes (serifs) that extend outward from the characters; sans-serif type, lacking the serifs; script type, which closely resembles actual handwriting; and italic type, which is slanted to the right. Type size is measured by "points" in North America and England. One point equals 0.012837 in (0.3514598 mm) and most type ranges from 6 to 72 points. Movable type was invented in Asia in the 11th century and was introduced to Europe by Johannes Gutenberg in the 1440s. Type was later cast in lead and set by hand or machine. Today most type is set on computers programmed for correct size, style, and line width.
See also: Printing

Typewriter, writing machine activated manually or electrically by means of a keyboard. In the classic model, when a key is depressed, a pivoted bar bearing a type character strikes an inked ribbon against a sheet of paper carried on a cylindrical rubber "platen." The platen carriage then automatically moves a space to the left. In some electric models all type is carried on a single rotatable sphere that moves from left to right and strikes a fixed platen. The first efficient typewriter was developed in 1868 by C.L. Sholes.
See also: Sholes, Christopher Latham.

Typhoid fever, infectious disease due to *Salmonella typhosa*, causing fever, a characteristic rash, lymph node and spleen enlargement, gastrointestinal tract disturbance with bleeding and ulceration, and usually marked malaise or prostration. It is contracted from other cases or from disease carriers, with contaminated food and water as major vectors. Carriers must be treated with antibiotics (and have their gall bladder removed if this site is the source); they must also stop handling food until they are free of the bacteria. Vaccination may help protect high-risk persons; antibiotics (e.g., chloramphenicol) form the treatment of choice.

Typhus, infectious disease caused by rickettsia and carried by lice, leading to a feverish illness with a rash. Severe headache typically precedes the rash, which may progress to skin hemorrhage; mild respiratory symptoms of cough and breathlessness are common. Death ensues in a high proportion of untreated adults, usually with profound shock and kidney failure. Recurrences may occur in untreated patients who recover from their first attack, often after many years. A similar disease due to a different but related organism is carried by fleas (murine typhus). Chloramphenicol or tetracyclines provide suitable antibiotic therapy.

Tyrannosaurus *see:* Dinosaur; Prehistoric animal.

Tyre, or Sur (pop. 23,000), town in southwest Lebanon, situated on the eastern end of the Mediterranean Sea. A thriving seaport under the Phoenicians, Tyre was ruled by Egypt before 1000 B.C. From 1100 to 573 B.C. it enjoyed its most prosperous period, which included the founding of Carthage (9th century), and was a major cultural, intellectual, and commercial center, famous for its purple dye and high-quality ceramics. In 332 B.C. Alexander the Great conquered Tyre and built a causeway that connected what was then the island of Tyre to the mainland, creating a peninsula, site of the present-day city of Tyre. The city later fell under the control of the Roman and Byzantine empires and was captured by the Crusaders in 1124, before being overrun and destroyed by the Muslims in 1291. Tyre was taken by Israeli forces in 1982 during their invasion of Lebanon.

Tyrol, or Tirol, state in western Austria. Over half its original area was ceded to Italy in 1919. Austria's highest peak, Grossglockner (12,461 ft/3,798 km), is located there. Farming, lumber, and tourism are its main sources of income. The capital is Innsbruck.

Tyron, William (1729-88), English governor of North Carolina (1765-71). In 1771, after harshly crushing the revolt of the Regulators at the Battle of Alamance, he was appointed governor of New York.

Tyrrhenian Sea, part of the Mediterranean Sea bounded by the west coast of Italy and by the islands of Corsica, Sardinia, and Sicily. The Strait of Messina in the south connects it with the Ionian Sea. Its ports include Naples and Palermo.

Tyson, Mike (1966-), U.S. boxer. He won the World Boxing Council heavyweight title in 1986 to become the youngest winner of a boxing championship to date. In 1987 he went on to win the World Boxing Association (WBA) and International Boxing Federation (IBF) titles. He lost his heavyweight titles after being knocked-out by James "Buster" Douglas in 1990.

U, 21st letter of the English alphabet, corresponding to the Semitic letter *waw*, meaning "hook," represented by a tenthook symbol and probably derived from an ancient Egyptian symbol for a pole support. The Greeks altered it to *Y*, and as the 20th letter of the Roman alphabet it became *V*, representing both *U* and *V* sounds. The use of *U* for the *U* sound dates from the Middle Ages. *U* is also the chemical symbol for the element uranium.

U-2, U.S. spy plane used during the 1950s and 1960s. The U-2 was effective because it could fly at extremely high altitudes of 70,000 ft (21,100 m) and photograph military installations on the ground. It became the focus of international attention when a U-2 was shot down while flying over the USSR in 1960, at the height of the Cold War between the United States and the USSR.
See also: Cold War.

U-235, any of the different forms of an isotope of the element uranium with a mass number of 235 (the number of protons and neutrons in the atom's nucleus). When found in minerals, U-235 is always combined with the isotopes U-234 and U-238. Separating the natural U-235 from the other isotopes produces a more potent form of U-235, which is used in atomic bombs and nuclear reactors because it easily undergoes fission. The use of U-235 in nuclear reactors produces extremely toxic isotopes of other elements, such as strontium 90. Disposing of such nuclear waste is an important environmental concern. U-235 was used in the atomic bombs that the United States dropped on Hiroshima and Nagasaki, Japan, in 1945.
See also: Nuclear energy; Radioactivity.

U-238 *see:* Uranium.

U.A.R. *see:* United Arab Republic.

U.S. *see:* United States of America.

U.S.A. *see:* United States of America.

Ubangi River, chief northern tributary of the Zaïre (Congo) River, in central Africa. Formed by the junction of the Mbomu and Uele rivers, it flows 700 mi (1,130 km) west and south, forming part of Zaïre's northwest border with the Central African Republic.

U-boat *see:* Submarine.

U

Ucayali River, chief headstream of the Amazon, in northern Peru. Formed by the junction of the Urubamba and Apurímac rivers in central Peru, it flows 1,000 mi (1,600 km) north to the Marañón River southwest of Iquitos.
See also: Amazon River.

Uccello, Paolo (c.1397-1475), Florentine early Renaissance painter, noted for his use of perspective. His best-known works are the *Creation* and *Noah* scenes (1431-50) in Santa Maria Novella, Florence, and the three richly decorative panels of *The Battle of San Romano* (1455-60).
See also: Renaissance.

Udall, Nicolas (1505-56), English schoolmaster, scholar, and playwright. Headmaster of Eton (1534-41) and of Westminster (1554-56), he wrote the first known English comedy, *Ralph Roister Doister* (c. 1553).

Uffizi Palace, 16th-century palace in Florence, Italy, built by Giorgio Vassari for Cosimo I de' Medici as a public office building. It houses one of the world's finest art collections, rich in classical, Dutch, Flemish, and Italian Renaissance paintings and sculptures.
See also: Florence.

UFO *see:* Unidentified flying object.

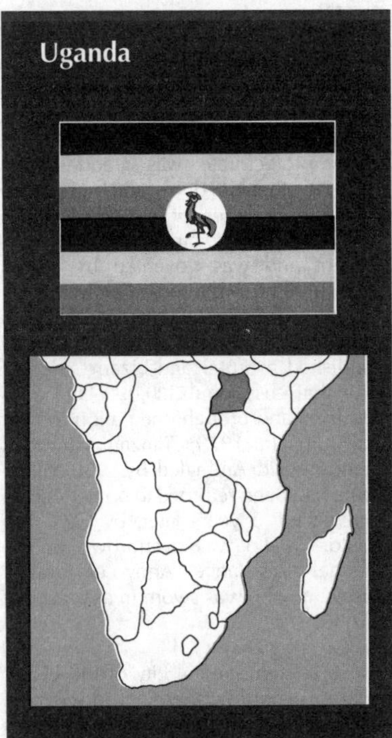

Capital:	Kampala
Area:	93,070 sq mi (241,040 sq km)
Population:	16,452,000
Government:	military
Independent:	1962
GNP:	U.S.$4,480,000,000
Per capita:	U.S. $280

Uganda, landlocked republic in east-central Africa. Covering 93,070 sq mi (241,040 sq km), Uganda is bordered by Tanzania and Rwanda in the south, Sudan in the north, Zaïre in the west, and Kenya in the east. The capital is Kampala.
Land and People. More than 80% of the land area of Uganda consists of a fertile plateau some 3,000 to 5,000 ft (914-1,524 m) above sea level, with highlands to the east and west. About 16,386 sq mi (42,440 sq km) of Uganda consists of freshwater lakes and swamps. At the center of the plateau that dominates the country is Lake Kyoga. Other lakes are lakes Edward, Albert, George, and Victoria. Although Uganda is a tropical country, crossed by the equator, its altitude ensures a comparatively mild climate. Almost all Ugandans are black Africans, the majority belonging to one of several Bantu-speaking groups. The Baganda people of the south are the most numerous of these. More than half of the people are Christians, with a small minority of Muslims; the rest of the people adhere to animist beliefs. The official languages are English and Swahili.
Economy. Uganda's economy is agricultural and most farms are small, growing subsistence crops and raising livestock. Despite severe economic dislocation under Idi Amin Dada, Uganda remained one of the world's major producers of coffee, which accounts for almost all of its export earnings. Copper is the principal mineral.
History. The Bunyoro Kingdom of Bantu-speaking people that flourished in the 16th and 17th centuries and dominated Uganda was succeeded by the Baganda Kingdom, which came under the British in 1894. The British protectorate was gradually extended to other kingdoms, and by 1914 the present boundaries of Uganda became fixed. In 1962, Uganda became independent and was governed by Milton Obote until he was deposed by Maj. Gen. Idi Amin Dada in 1971. In 1972, Amin expelled Uganda's Asian population and established a brutal and bizarre reign of terror that cost some 300,000 Ugandans their lives and brought the nation to near total ruin. In 1979, Tanzania invaded Uganda and Idi Amin fled. By 1980, Milton Obote had been returned to power only to be replaced, 3 years later, by Gen. Tito Okello. Okello was overthrown by the National Resistance Army of Yoweri Museveni, who was sworn in as president in 1986.

Ugarit, ancient capital city of the Ugarit Kingdom of northwestern Syria, discovered in 1929 by French archeologists. Settled in the 5th millennium B.C., it flourished in the 15th and 14th centuries B.C. Numerous cuneiform tablets have revealed much information about the Ugarit language, related to biblical Hebrew.

UHF waves *see:* Ultrahigh frequency waves.

Ukraine, independent country in eastern Europe, bordered by Poland to the northwest; by Slovakia, Hungary, Romania, and Moldavia to the southwest; by the Black Sea and the Sea of Azov to the south; by Russia to the northeast and east; and by Byelorussia to the north. The capital is Kiev. About 75% of the population is Ukrainian, and Russians form the largest minority. The economy is based on heavy industry. Principal crops are sugar beets and potatoes. Important industrial cities include Kharkov, Donetsk, and Dnepropetrovsk. The chief Black Sea port is Odessa. The region was ruled by the Mongols in the 13th century and by Poland and Lithuania from the 14th to the 17th centuries. In the late 18th century it came under Russian rule. After a brief period of independence (1918-22), it became part of the Soviet Union. It was almost completely destroyed by the Nazi occupation during World War II (1941-44), after which it was wholly rebuilt. In the 1980s there was a rise in nationalist sentiment, especially in the western Ukraine. Together with the collapse of communism this resulted in independence in 1991.
See also: Union of Soviet Socialist Republics.

Ukraine

Capital:	Kiev
Area:	233,090 sq mi (603,700 sq km)
Population:	52,118,000
Government:	republic
Independent:	1991
GNP:	U.S.$87,025,000,000
Per capita:	U.S.$1,670

Ukranian, East Slavic language of the Slavonic group, closely related to Russian, from which it diverged c.1200. Written in a modified Cyrillic alphabet, it emerged as a literary language in the 18th century. It is the official language of the Ukraine.

Ukulele, small guitarlike instrument. Modeled after a small guitar of Portuguese origin, the ukulele became popular in Hawaii during the late 19th century. It was widely used throughout the United States and Europe in jazz bands and as accompaniment in folk songs.

Ulan Bator (pop. 619,000), capital and largest city of Mongolia. Located in the northeastern part of Mongolia along the Tuul Gol River, the city developed around a famous Buddhist monastery built in 1639. For years it served as an important trade center along a route between Russia and China. The city was known as Urga and Niislel Khureheh until it was renamed in 1924 in honor of the famous Soviet revolutionary leader Sukhe Bator. Today, Ulan Bator is Mongolia's cultural and industrial center. It is the home of the Mongolian State University and a science academy. Meat packing is an important industry along with the manufacture of furniture, textiles, and pharmaceutical products.
See also: Mongolia.

Ulanova, Galina (1910-), Russian prima ballerina of the Bolshoi Theater, Moscow (1944-62). She excelled as a dramatic and lyric dancer, notably in Tchaikovsky's *Swan Lake* and Prokofiev's *Romeo and Juliet.*

Ulbricht, Walter (1893-1973), leader of post-World War II East Germany. A founding member (1918) of the German Communist Party, he spent 1933-45 in exile in the USSR. He became first deputy premier (1949) and head of state (1960-73) of the German Democratic Republic. An uncompromising Stalinist, he headed the Socialist Unity Party from 1950 until his replacement (1971) by Erich Honecker. He ordered the building of the Berlin Wall (1961) and had Eastern German troops participate in the invasion of Czechoslovakia, in 1968.
See also: Germany.

Ulcer, pathological defect in skin or mucous membrane caused by inflammation due to infection, loss of blood supply, failure of venous circulation, or cancer. Peptic, gastric, and duodenal ulcers may cause pain or acute hemorrhage, and may lead to perforation and peritonitis. Antacids usually provide effective treatment.

Ultima Thule, ancient Greek and Roman name for lands of the far north. Scholars believe that the Greek term referred to Norway, Iceland, and possibly the Shetland Islands. The Greek sailor Pytheas mentions the icy waters and long nights and days of a region he reached sometime during the 4th century B.C., but the location is not specified.

Ultrahigh frequency waves (UHF), radio waves with frequencies from 300 to 3,000 megahertz (1 megahertz equals 1 million cycles per second) and with short ranges, usually less than 50 mi (80 km). They are used primarily for television broadcasting, but are also used for air and naval navigation, for police radios, and for tracking spacecraft.
See also: Short waves.

Ultramicroscope, special microscope used for studying colloidal particles (particles in

solution or suspension) too small to be seen with a regular-light microscope. A high intensity light beam originates not from the bottom of the instrument as with an ordinary microscope, but from the side. As this beam passes through the solution or suspension, the colloidal particles scatter the light, producing tiny dots of light that then can be seen against a dark background. The ultramicroscope, however, cannot provide the viewer with any structural detail of the particles.
See also: Microscope.

Ultrasonics, science of sound waves with frequencies above those that humans can hear (above 20,000 cycles per second). Modern piezoelectric techniques generate ultrasonic waves with frequencies above 24,000 cycles per second. These exhibit the normal wave properties of reflection, refraction, and diffraction, and are used to clean fine machine parts and, in medicine, to examine internal organs non-surgically.

Ultraviolet rays, invisible light lying beyond the violet end of the spectrum. It is produced naturally by the sun and lightning. Prolonged exposure to the sun's ultraviolet rays can result in sunburn and over a period of years, can cause skin cancer. Plants and animals are partially protected from the sun's ultraviolet rays by ozone, a form of oxygen formed in the upper atmosphere. Ultraviolet rays can, however, be beneficial. They are used by physicians to destroy some bacteria and viruses and by food manufacturers to disinfect food containers. Special lamps that produce ultraviolet rays have been successfully used to treat acne and other skin disorders.

Ulysses, or Odysseus, legendary hero of ancient Greece, son and successor of King Laertes of Ithaca, and husband of Penelope. He was the crafty counselor of the Trojan War (described in Homer's *Iliad*) and the subject of Homer's *Odyssey*, a recount of 10 years of adventures and obstacles faced by Ulysses in his effort to return home after the war.

Umbilical cord, in mammals, tubelike structure linking the developing embryo, or fetus, to the placenta through most of pregnancy. It consists of blood vessels that carry blood to and from the placenta, along with a gelatinous matrix. In humans, the cord is clamped at birth to prevent blood loss. It undergoes atrophy and its remains become the navel.

Umbrellabird, any of several crowlike birds (genus *Cephalopterus*) of tropical American forests, especially *C. ornatus*, whose crest can be expanded into an "umbrella." It also has a lappet of feathers hanging from the throat.

UN *see:* United Nations.

Un-American Activities Committee (HUAC), committee of the U.S. House of Representatives formed in 1938 to investigate subversive activities in the United States. The committee (officially designated the House Committee on Un-American Activities) won notoriety after World War II for its witch-hunt investigations of alleged Communist influence in government, unions, education, and the film industry. It was renamed Committee on Internal Security in 1969, but has been largely inactive.

Unamuno, Miguel de (1864-1936), Spanish philosopher and writer, rector of Salamanca University from 1900 to his death. Influenced by Kierkegaard, he explored the faith-reason conflict and the desire for immortality in *The Tragic Sense of Life in Men and Nations* (1913) and in essays and novels, such as *Mist* (1914). "The Christ of Velázquez" (1920) is his best-known poem.
See also: Philosophy.

Uncas (1588?-1683), chief of the Mohegans of Connecticut, celebrated in James Fenimore Cooper's *The Last of the Mohicans* (1826). He supported the British colonists in the 1637 war against the Pequot Native Americans.

Uncle Sam, popular figure developed by 19th-century cartoonists and officially adopted as a U.S. national symbol in 1961. He is portrayed as a white-haired, bearded gentleman dressed in the Stars and Stripes. The name possibly derives from Samuel "Uncle Sam" Wilson, an inspector of Army supplies in Troy, N.Y., during the War of 1812.

Unconscious, in psychology, that part of the mind the individual is unable to recall at will. The concept of the unconscious, or subconscious, was developed and studied by Sigmund Freud, the founder of psychoanalysis. He believed the unconscious included instinctual drives and repressed memory and desires. To this foundation of belief, C.G. Jung added the idea that there is also a collective unconscious, universal or cultural mental patterns and acts.
See also: Freud, Sigmund.

Underground, term generally used for any secret political movement that seeks to overthrow a country's existing government or military authority. Though undergrounds have operated in many nations throughout history, they came to wide public attention during World War II (1939-45). They were especially effective in German-occupied countries such as Yugoslavia, Poland, France, and the Netherlands.
See also: Guerrilla warfare.

Underground Railroad, secret network that helped U.S. slaves to escape from the South to the northern states and to Canada before the Civil War. Neither underground nor railroad, it was named for its necessary secrecy and for the railroad terms used to refer to its operation. Most of the "conductors" were slaves themselves, Harriet Tubman being one of the best known. Abolitionists, notably Quakers such as Levi Coffin, ran "stations" providing food and shelter along the way. Some 40,000-100,000 slaves escaped in this way.
See also: Abolitionism; Slavery.

Undset, Sigrid (1882-1949), Norwegian novelist. Largely known for her epic trilogy set in medieval Norway, *Kristin Lavransdatter* (1920-22), she won the 1928 Nobel Prize in literature. Her contemporary novels dealt with the position of women in society and with Roman Catholicism.

Undulant fever *see:* Brucellosis.

Unemployment, situation in which people who are normally part of the labor force are unable to find jobs. Seasonal layoffs occur because certain jobs are not available year round. Cyclical unemployment occurs during economic depressions or recessions, when production declines. Structural unemployment refers to permanent shifts in a nation's productive system such that certain groups become permanently unemployed.

Unemployment insurance, type of Social Security providing income to people involuntarily unemployed. Most modern industrial nations have programs of this kind, financed by the governmnent, employers, employees, or a combination of these. In the 1800s some labor unions initiated unemployment benefits for out-of-work members. France introduced a voluntary national scheme in 1905, and Britain introduced the first compulsory insurance program in 1911. In the United States the first unemployment insurance law was passed in Wisconsin in 1932; three years later the Social Security Act established a federal-state program, now administered by the Department of Labor.
See also: Welfare.

UNESCO *see:* United Nations Educational, Scientific, and Cultural Organization.

Ungulate, term for any mammal with hoofs. Ungulates evolved to stand on their toes, and the toenails have become solid hoofs. The odd-toed ungulates (order Perissodactyla), with one or three toes per foot, include horses, rhinoceroses, and tapirs; the even-toed ungulates (order Artiodactyla), with two or four toes, include pigs, deer, antelopes, camels, cattle, and hippopotamuses.

UNICEF *see:* United Nations Children's Fund.

Unicorn, mythical creature with the body of a horse and one horn on its forehead. Unicorns have appeared in the art and legends of India, China, the Middle East, and medieval Europe, where they were associated with the Virgin Mary and Christ.
See also: Mythology.

Unicycle, single-wheeled vehicle with pedals, a seat mounted above the wheel, and no handlebars. The rider moves it by pedalling and can change direction by pedalling backward or forward or by shifting his or her weight. Unicycles were first used in the 19th century by circus performers, who often juggled objects as they rode.

Unidentified flying object (UFO), object or light reprotedly seen in the air during day or night that cannot always be explained by conventional phenomena. Though many UFOs are found to be objects, such as weather balloons or satellites, or the result of atmospheric conditions, there are certain sightings that do not fall into any known-phenomena categories. The U.S. government continues to investigate thousands of such reports and to sponsor scientific studies on the subject.

Unification Church, religious organization of Korean origin that became highly visible in the United States in the late 1960s. Based on the ideas of the Reverend Sun Myung Moon, who represents himself as an elect leader and seer, the organization recruits and regiments young people to dedicate their lives to the church in a highly disciplined fashion. Accused of "programming" its adherents ("Moonies") by brainwashing techniques, the Unification Church was investigated by Congress in 1977 and has been attacked by both business competitors and parents of involved youths. In 1982 Moon was convicted of conspiracy to evade taxes.

Uniform Code of Military Justice, body of law governing all members of the U.S. armed forces. It sets out procedures for court-martial and military justice. Enacted in 1950, it unified the codes of the army, navy, air force, and coast guard.

Uniformitarianism, doctrine in geology originally opposed to Catastrophism. Originated (1785) by James Hutton and championed by Charles Lyell in the 19th century, it holds that the same geologic processes are at work today as have always existed thoughout geologic time. Uniformitarianism emphasizes the relative slowness and gradual nature of geological change.
See also: Geology.

Union, Act of, British Parliamentary act of 1840 that officially united Upper Canada and Lower Canada. Two separate Canadas had originally been established to appease the English and French inhabitants. The act not only joined the two Canadas but also stipulated that a government should be formed, consisting of a colonial governor and a legislative assembly composed of members elected by the people. Under the act, English became the official government language.
See also: Canada.

Union of South Africa *see:* South Africa.

Union of Soviet Socialist Republics (USSR), also known as the Soviet Union. Name of a union of 15 Soviet republics that desintegrated in 1991. Now independent countries, the constituent republics were Armenia, Azerbaijan, Byelorussia, Estonia, Georgia, Kazachstan, Kirgizstan, Latvia, Lithuania, Moldova, Russian Federation, Tajikistan, Turkmenistan, Ukraine and Uzbekistan. The union covered more than half of Europe and two-fifths of Asia. The capital was Moscow.

Land and People. The country comprises 15 constituent republics divided into 4 regions—European, Central Asian, Siberian, and Far Eastern. The Ural Mountains separate the European (west) sector from the Asian (east) sector. Most of the European sector is flatland, broken by the Urals, the Caucasus, and other highlands. To the east

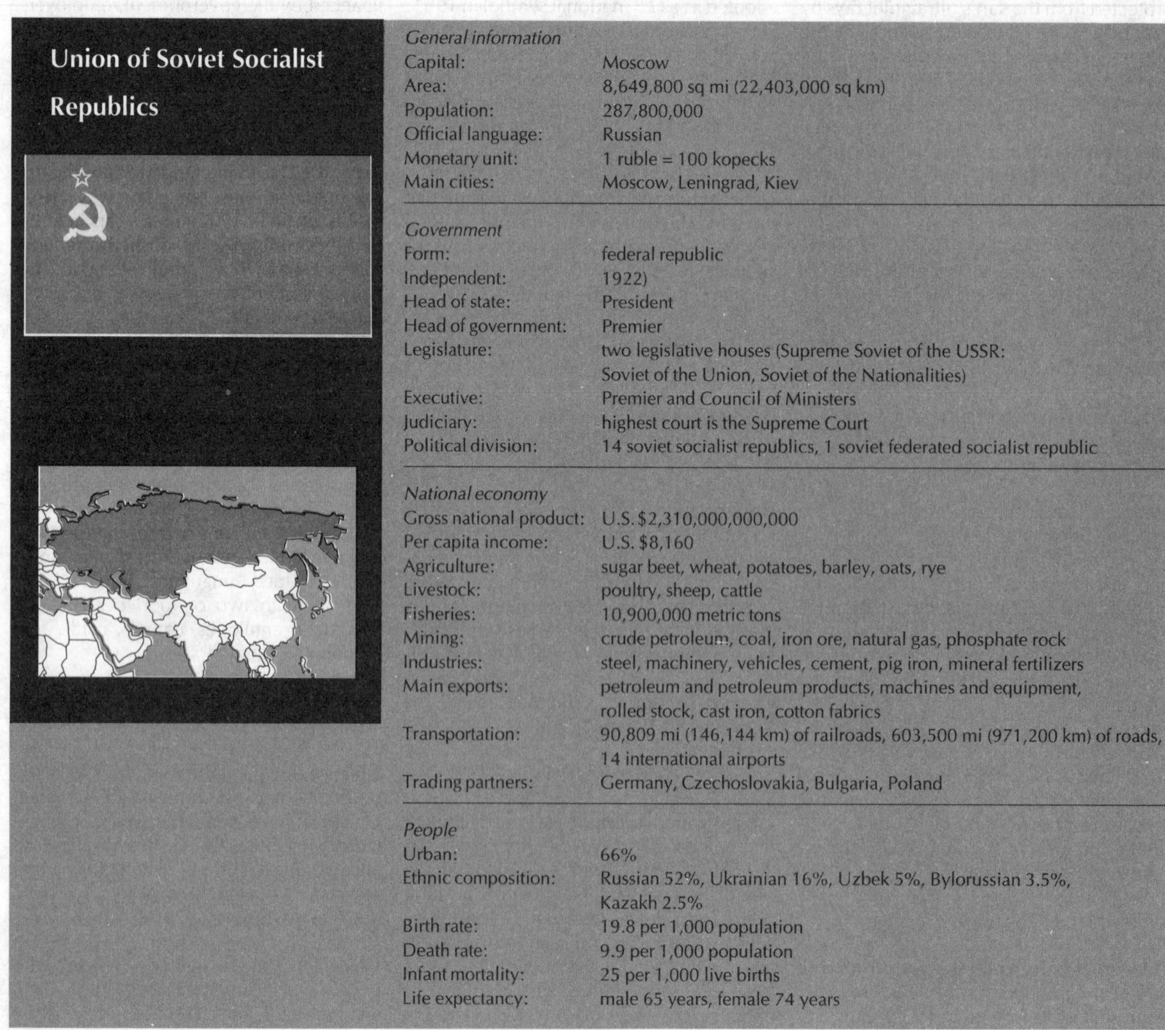

Union of Soviet Socialist Republics

General information	
Capital:	Moscow
Area:	8,649,800 sq mi (22,403,000 sq km)
Population:	287,800,000
Official language:	Russian
Monetary unit:	1 ruble = 100 kopecks
Main cities:	Moscow, Leningrad, Kiev
Government	
Form:	federal republic
Independent:	1922)
Head of state:	President
Head of government:	Premier
Legislature:	two legislative houses (Supreme Soviet of the USSR: Soviet of the Union, Soviet of the Nationalities)
Executive:	Premier and Council of Ministers
Judiciary:	highest court is the Supreme Court
Political division:	14 soviet socialist republics, 1 soviet federated socialist republic
National economy	
Gross national product:	U.S. $2,310,000,000,000
Per capita income:	U.S. $8,160
Agriculture:	sugar beet, wheat, potatoes, barley, oats, rye
Livestock:	poultry, sheep, cattle
Fisheries:	10,900,000 metric tons
Mining:	crude petroleum, coal, iron ore, natural gas, phosphate rock
Industries:	steel, machinery, vehicles, cement, pig iron, mineral fertilizers
Main exports:	petroleum and petroleum products, machines and equipment, rolled stock, cast iron, cotton fabrics
Transportation:	90,809 mi (146,144 km) of railroads, 603,500 mi (971,200 km) of roads, 14 international airports
Trading partners:	Germany, Czechoslovakia, Bulgaria, Poland
People	
Urban:	66%
Ethnic composition:	Russian 52%, Ukrainian 16%, Uzbek 5%, Bylorussian 3.5%, Kazakh 2.5%
Birth rate:	19.8 per 1,000 population
Death rate:	9.9 per 1,000 population
Infant mortality:	25 per 1,000 live births
Life expectancy:	male 65 years, female 74 years

Top left: Volgograd railway station. This city (formerly Stalingrad), which was almost destroyed during World War II, was rebuilt after the war in the style of the late-Stalinist period. Bottom left: Winter landscape in Siberia. Right: Horsemen in a cornfield south of the Caucasus. Mt. Elbrus is in the background.

lie the great Siberian Plain and the deserts of central Asia; beyond them are the Siberian highlands and the Far Eastern mountains. Because it occupies about one-sixth of the land area of the world, the USSR has several different climatic regions, ranging from the polar north to the subtropical south. Long, cold winters and short summers are characteristic of much of the USSR's climate. Over 100 ethnic groups and nationalities make up the people of the country. Chief among them are Slavic-speaking peoples (Russians, Ukrainians, and Byelorussians); Turkic-speaking peoples (Uzbeks, Tatars, Kazakhs, and Azerbaijani); and the Armenians, Georgians, Lithuanians, and Moldavians. The official language is Russian. Approximately 75 percent of the people live in the European sector of the country. Religion is officially discouraged, but many people still follow the Russian Orthodox church. Other religions include Roman Catholicism, Protestantism, Islam, Judaism, and Buddhism. The ban on religion may be relaxed in the 1990s.

Economy. Under Communism, all industry is owned and operated by the government. Agriculture is organized around state farms (*collective farms*), with some small private plots permitted to farmers. A centralized economy has been a feature of the Soviet Union since 1917, but in the latter part of the 1980s, dissatisfaction with the performance of the economy has led to a time of turmoil and change. The USSR is a major producer of oil, coal, iron ore, natural gas, and timber, and it possesses a wealth of other natural resources. It is a major military power in the world, and a leader in space exploration and scientific research. In the 1990s the Soviet Union has begun to move away from top-down, centralized management in an attempt to form a market economy. Widespread strikes and demonstrations have been an early result of this transition.

History. Russia was ruled by tsars (emperors) for hundred of years in an extremely autocratic manner. Under them the country was largely cut off from the industrially developing West. There were sporadic uprisings in the 19th and early 20th centuries against this despotic rule, and finally, due in large measure to the horrendous losses suffered by the Russians in World War I, the Russian Revolution of 1917 forced Tsar Nicolas II to abdicate. He was replaced by a provisional government, led by Alexander F. Karensky, a Socialist. The government proved ineffective and was itself overthrown in November 1917 by the Marxist Bolsheviks led by Vladimir I. Ulyanov, who took the name of Lenin. He was helped by Leon Trotsky in organizing the takeover and in successfully prosecuting the following civil war. Lenin and the Bolsheviks set Russia on the course of state ownership of the means of production (farms, factories, mills, mines, etc.). In 1922, the Communist government established the Union of Soviet Socialist Republics (then 4 union republics) with the Russian Republic the first and the largest, which it remains to this day.

Lenin died in 1924, and, after some jockeying for power among his successors, Joseph Stalin emerged in 1927 as undisputed leader. He embarked on a far-reaching policy of collectivizing the farmland and of securing total government control over all economic planning. The followers of Trotsky and many other opponents of Stalin's rule were purged in the fierce repression of the 1930s. In 1941, Germany invaded the USSR despite having signed a nonaggression pact with it in 1939. The Great Patriotic War, as the Russians call World War II, lasted until the defeat of Germany in 1945, in which the Russian forces played a key role despite having sustained fearful losses. After World War II, the Soviet Union went on to establish Communist governments throughout eastern Europe and in Soviet-held East Germany. Friction between the Soviet Union and the United States and other West European democracies led to the Cold War, which effectively divided the world into competing East and West blocs, led by the Soviet Union and the United States, respectively. Stalin died in 1953 to be replaced by Nikita S. Khrushchev, who denounced the worst excesses of the Stalin era but who also continued the rivalry with the United States.

Partly as a result of the dangerous confrontation with the United States over Soviet missiles in Cuba in 1962, where Russia was forced to turn back, Khrushchev was ousted by the party in 1964, replaced by Leonid I. Brezhnev. Relations with the West improved somewhat under Brezhnev (the period of détente), but the Soviet economy continued to stagnate and even deteriorate. The era of the old Bolsheviks, trained under Stalin, was coming to an end. Brezhnev died in 1982, to be replaced by Yuri V. Andropov. Andropov died in 1984 and was succeeded by Konstantin V. Chernenko, who died in 1985. Mikhail S. Gorbachev, at age 54, became head of the Communist Party, the first of the new generation of Soviet leaders to head the country. Faced with an unpopular war in Afghanistan, begun in the Brezhnev years, and with dire economic problems at home, Gorbachev embarked on a series of reforms he hoped would revitalize the country. He ended the Afghan war, allowed non-Communist governments to take power in Eastern Europe, approved the reunification of Germany by relinquishing control of East Germany, and set in motion new domestic policies such as *glasnost* (openness or freedom of expression for the people) and *perestroika* (reforms designed to transform the command economy of the USSR into one more receptive to free market forces). All these changes led to turmoil, where long-simmering disputes between ethnic groups and rival republics of the union broke into the open. With non-Communist parties allowed to participate in elections, various republics clamoring for independence, ethnic strife, and challenges mounted by powerful political leaders, the future existence of the Union of Soviet Socialist Republics was threatened and the union collapsed in 1991.

John Unitas

Unions, labor, workers' organizations formed to improve pay, working conditions, and benefits through collective power. Modern labor unions arose out of the concentrations of workers created by the Industrial Revolution. A craft (horizontal) union organizes workers by their particular skill; an industrial (vertical) union includes all workers in an industry. Unions negotiate contracts with employers by the process of collective bargaining. A closed (or union) shop increases bargaining strength by requiring that all workers belong to a union. Some states prohibit union shops by law. A dispute with employers may be referred to arbitration, or union members may resort to strikes, slowdowns, boycotts, or, more rarely, sit-downs. In the United States, local craft unions existed from the late 1700s. The influence of the socialistic Knights of Labor (1869-1917) gave way to that of the craft unions of the American Federation of Labor (AFL; founded 1886). In the early 1900s a wave of radicalism resulted in the formation of the Industrial Workers of the World, a revolutionary union across all industries. The industrial union-based Congress of Industrial Organizations (CIO) was formed in the 1930s, during the Depression. The AFL and CIO merged in 1955. The Taft-Hartley Act (1947) placed restrictions on unions, and the Landrum-Griffin Act (1959) curbed union corruption. In recent years, union organizing has lagged as the U.S. economy has become more service-oriented. Britain has a single Trades Union Congress, but many countries have rival unions with differing political outlooks.

Dubai, United Arab Emirates

Unitarianism, unorthodox Protestant faith that rejects the Trinity and the divine nature of Christ, and asserts the unipersonality of God. It developed out of views of such Reformation figures as Faustus Socinus, who influenced many 18th-century English Presbyterians to become Unitarians. Joseph Priestley gave it a great impetus in the United States, where liberal, rationalist Unitarianism, preaching toleration and universal salvation, developed among Congregational churches. The American Unitarian Association, led by William Ellery Channing, was founded in 1825. In 1961 the Unitarian and Universalist churches merged, creating the Unitarian Universalist Association.
See also: Protestantism.

Unitas, John (1933-), U.S. football player. A quarterback known for his accurate passing, he threw at least one touchdown pass in 47 consecutive National Football League (NFL) games. His achievements include 40,239 career passing yards (third on the all time list) and 253 career touchdown passes (second on the all time list). He played for the Baltimore Colts (1956-1973), winning 2 world championships (1958, 59) and 1 Super Bowl (1971). He finished his career with the San Diego Chargers (1974) and was inducted into the Pro Football Hall of Fame in 1979.

United Arab Emirates, federation of emirates in the eastern Arabian Peninsula, bordered in the north by the Persian Gulf, in the east by the Gulf of Oman, in the south by Oman, in the south and west by Saudi Arabia, and in the northwest by Qatar. It comprises Abu Dhabi, Ajman, Dubai, Fujairah, Ras al-Khaimah, Sharjah, and Umm al-Qaiwain. The city of Abu Dhabi is the capital. The indigenous population is Arab, and Arabic is the official language. Islam is the state religion, and most of the people are Sunni. The majority of inhabitants, however, are foreign workers, mostly from Asia. The country has a 400-mi (644-km) coastline and is mostly desert. In the east mountains rise to over 8,000 ft (2,438 m), giving way to a fertile coastal strip where dates, grains, and tobacco are cultivated. Herding, fishing, and pearling were the traditional occupations, but since the 1960s the country and its economy have been dominated by oil. The large oil income and small native population have made the Emirates one of the world's richest countries. Abu Dhabi, the largest emirate, is the site of the bulk of the oil production, but Dubai and Sharjah are significant oil exporters, too. Historically, the Emirates were dominated by Britain, to which they were bound by a formal truce (1820) that gave them the name Trucial States. After World War II, Britain granted the Trucial States autonomy. At that time they included Qatar and Bahrain, which chose separate statehood when the United Arab Emirates was formed as an independent state (1971).

United Arab Emirates

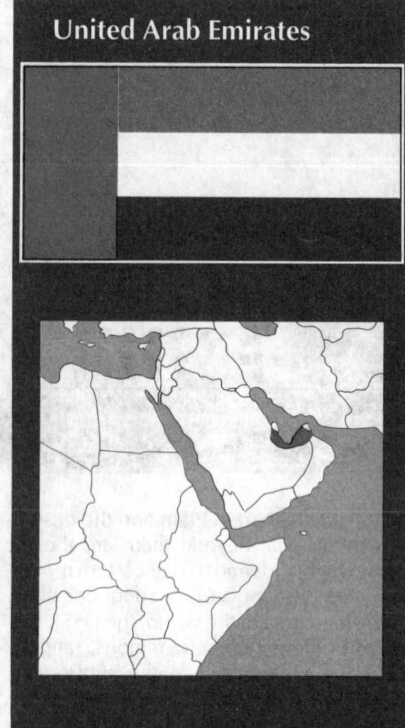

Capital:	Abu Dhabi
Area:	29,992 sq mi (77,700 sq km)
Population:	1,668,000
Government:	federal union of seven states
Independent:	1971
GNP:	U.S. $37,068,000,000
Per capita:	U.S. $22,220

United Arab Republic (UAR), union of Egypt and Syria proclaimed in 1958 as a step toward Arab unity. Cairo was the capital, and Egyptian president Gamal Abdul Nasser was president. The UAR effectively collapsed in 1961, when Syria withdrew. A 1963 attempt to unite Egypt, Syria, and Iraq failed. Egypt was still called the UAR until 1971, when its name was changed to Egyptian Arab Republic.

United Automobile Workers (United Automobile, Aerospace and Agricultural Implement Workers of America), second-

largest U.S. industrial labor union, with local affiliates in Canada. Founded in 1935, it won recognition at General Motors, Chrysler, and Ford after major strikes and struggles (1937-41). Its members work in the automobile, space, aviation, and metal industries. The UAW cofounded the CIO, but left the AfL-CIO in 1968. Presidents have included Walter Reuther (1946-70), Leonard Woodcock (1970-77), and Douglas Fraser (1977-). UAW headquarters are in Detroit.
See also: Unions, labor.

United Church of Canada, Protestant church formed in 1925 by the union of Methodist and most Presbyterian and Congregationalist churches. Ecumenical, national, and missionary, it has a Presbyterian form of organization, stresses the rights of congregations, and has male and female ministers. It was joined in 1966 by Canada's Evangelical United Brethren Church, and has over a million adult members.

United Church of Christ, U.S. Protestant denomination set up by the 1957 union of the Congregational Christian Churches and the Evangelical and Reformed Church. It combines strong local autonomy with national services and organization.
See also: Congregational Church.

United Empire Loyalists, term for people of the original 13 American colonies who remained loyal to Britain during the Revolution and who emigrated to Canada. The largest group, some 50,000, left New York City in 1783 and founded New Brunswick (1784) and Upper Canada (now Ontario, 1791).

United Farm Workers of America (UFW), U.S. farm workers union. Several associations of agricultural workers merged in 1973 to form the UFW, which fights for better living and working conditions for farm workers, especially migrant workers in the southwest, south, and northeast, trying to ensure job security and better wages. The founding president is Cesar Chavez. To bring public attention to the needs of its members, the UFW of America often urges consumer boycotts of non-union products.
See also: Chavez, Cesar Estrada; Unions, labor.

United Food and Commercial Workers International Union (UFCW), large U.S. labor union formed in 1979 by the merger of the Amalgamated Meat Cutters and Butcher Workmen of North America and the Retail Clerks International. UFCW members include butchers, meat packers, canners, supermarket employees, department store clerks, and employees of pharmacies, shoe stores, hospitals, and nursing homes.
See also: Unions, labor.

United Kingdom, officially, United Kingdom of Great Britain and Northern Ireland, commonly known as Great Britain, constitutional monarchy consisting of most of the British Isles located off the northwestern coast of Europe. With a total area of 94,226 sq mi (244,044 sq km), the United Kingdom is entirely surrounded by water, bounded on the east by the North Sea, on the west by the North Atlantic Ocean, and on the south by the English Channel. The island of Great Britain is separated from Northern Ireland, located in the northeast part of the island of Ireland, by the North Channel and the Irish Sea. The Strait of Dover is the narrowest part of the English

United Kingdom

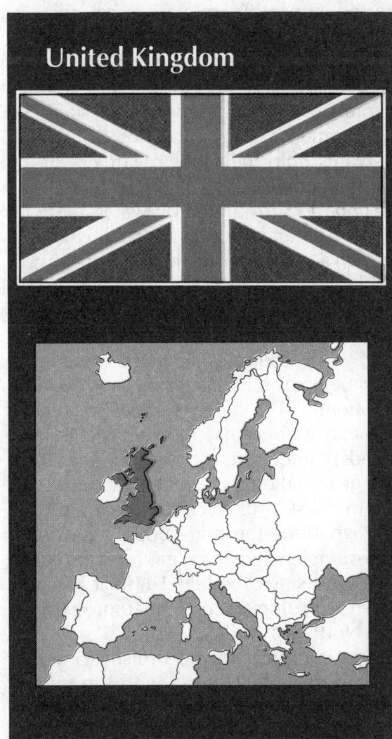

General information	
Capital:	London
Area:	94,251 sq mi (244,110 sq km)
Population:	57,218,000
Official language:	English
Monetary unit:	1 pound sterling = 100 new pence
Main cities:	London, Birmingham, Glasgow
Government	
Form:	constitutional monarchy
Independent:	1801
Head of state:	British monarch
Head of government:	Prime minister
Legislature:	two legislative houses (House of Lords and House of Commons)
Executive:	Monarch and Ministry
Judiciary:	highest court is the House of Lords
Political division:	54 counties, 9 regions, 26 districts
National economy	
Gross national product:	U.S. $730,038,000,000
Per capita income:	U.S. $12,800
Agriculture:	wheat, barley, sugar beet, potatoes, cabbages and savoys, carrots
Livestock:	chickens, sheep, cattle, pigs
Fisheries:	955,000 metric tons
Mining:	crude petroleum, common sand and gravel, limestone, hard coal, natural gas
Industries:	motor vehicles and parts, aerospace equipment, electronic data processing and telecommunications equipment, radios and electronic goods, banking, tourism
Main exports:	machinery and transport equipment, basic manufactures, chemicals and related products, miscellaneous manufactured articles, mineral fuels, lubricants
Transportation:	23,900 mi (38,464 km) of railroads, (352,295 km) of roads 218,906 mi, 28 international airports
Trading partners:	Germany, U.S., France, The Netherlands
People	
Urban:	91%
Ethnic composition:	European 94%, Asian Indian 1.5%, West Indian 1%, Pakistani 1%
Birth rate:	13.8 per 1,000 population
Death rate:	11.1 per 1,000 population
Infant mortality:	9 per 1,000 live births
Life expectancy:	male 71.5 years, female 77.5 years

The house of Mary Arden (the mother of Shakespeare) in Wilmcote, England, United Kingdom

Left: Annual games in Braemar, Scotland, United Kingdom Right: Minster Cathedral in York, England, United Kingdom

Channel and is a passage of 21 mi (34 km) between Great Britain and France. In addition to Great Britain and Northern Ireland, the British Isles consists of thousands of smaller islands, including the Shetland Islands, the Orkneys, the Outer Hebrides, the Isle of Man, and the Scilly Islands. The capital is London.

Land and People. Geographically, the island of Great Britain is divisible into 7 distinct zones. The northernmost section of the island is the Scottish Highlands, a mountainous area and the site of Britain's highest mountain, Ben Nevis, 4,400 ft (1,343 m). Most of Scotland's people and its best farmland are in the Central Lowlands, a fertile plain just south of the Highlands. The Southern Uplands are the southernmost part of Scotland. It is hilly country culminating in Cheviot Hills, which separates England from Scotland.

The hilly country continues south of the Cheviot Hills in the Pennines of England, an area that includes England's famous Lake District. Below the Pennines and extending to the Channel are the English Lowlands. It is on this undulating plain that most of England's farms, villages, mines, industries, and major cities are located. West of the Central Lowlands lies Wales, dominated in the north by the Cambrian Mountains and in the south by fertile river valleys. The Bristol Channel separates Wales from the Southwest Peninsula, an uneven plateau that ends in cliffs facing the open seas. Northern Ireland, situated at the northeast end of the island of Ireland, has fertile land somewhat similar to the Central Lowlands of Scotland. Great Britain contains many bays and inlets, several navigable rivers, and numerous lakes. Though Britain is located in a relatively high northern latitude, its climate is comparatively mild, moderated by the influence of the Gulf Stream. In addition, the island gets regular and adequate rainfall.

The people of Great Britain have a mixed ancestry of Celtic peoples and Romans, as well as Germanic, Scandinavian, and Norman peoples. Over the centuries, the population has tended toward a certain homogeneity, but clear distinctions are still discernible and are reinforced by differences in language, religion, and custom. Welsh remains a distinct Celtic language. The native Scots and Irish speak varieties of Gaelic. And even the dominant English language has strong regional variants, though they began to disappear with the advent of television. Since World War II England has also become a racially varied society, thanks to a large influx of immigrants in the 1950s and 1960s, mostly from Asia, Africa, and the West Indies. The established church in England is the Church of England, headed by Archbishop of Canterbury. In Scotland, the established church is the Church of Scotland. Both churches are Protestant, but there are sizable minorities of Roman Catholics and Jews.

The United Kingdom is governed as a constitutional monarchy. In modern times, England's monarchs have reigned, but they have not governed. The monarch's role, though almost entirely symbolic, is important to England's social and political system and to the maintenance of the traditions that are the sources of authority. Power resides in the Parliament, a representative body divided into an upper and lower house. Members of the upper house, the House of Lords, hold their seats as privileges attached to rank; they are not elected. Members of the House of Commons must be elected. Effective political power is in the House of Commons. Elections must be held at least once every five years, but are usually held more often, and can be called at any time. After an election, the head of the winning party is designated prime minister and forms a government of ministers from among the most important members of the party. These leading ministers make up the cabinet, or inner council. Although Great Britain has a constitution, it is not in the form of a single written document as it is in the United States. It is made up, in part, of certain documents, like the Magna Carta, and, more loosely, of the vast body of Common Law, but it also consists, to a very large degree, of traditions that have continued over many generations. The British people are at liberty to reconstitute their government at any time. In addition to the monarchy and parliament, the system relies upon an independent judiciary with courts of appeal and judges who are appointed for life. It also relies upon a professional civil service to staff the government's many ministries. British civil servants hold their jobs regardless of the party in power.

Economy. Surrounded by water and with limited natural resources, England has long grown accustomed to and made a virtue of looking beyond its own borders for its economic well-being. Though not nearly as rich and powerful as it was in the 18th and 19th centuries, England remains a competitive manufacturing and trading economy. The country does not have enough arable land to meet all its farm needs: Agriculture accounts for just 2% of the gross national product. It has also used up the best of its once-rich coal reserves, though since the mid-1960s it has been self-sufficient in natural gas from the North Sea, and since the late 1970s it has also been self-sufficient in petroleum, also from the North Sea wells.

Trade is critical to the British economy. Britain ranks fifth in the world in foreign trade, after the United States, Germany, Japan, and France, and trades principally in manufactured goods, though one-third of its trade volume is given to food and raw materials. Britain has one of the world's largest merchant marine fleets. The country also continues to be a leading manufacturer, producing steel, automobiles and other vehicles, heavy machinery, appliances, machine tools, products of advanced technology (including jet engines and aircraft for military and civilian use), and electronic equipment. The economy is aided by advanced scientific and technological research at its great universities. Great Britain also supplies markets in the chemical industries, pharmaceuticals, textiles and apparel, and food processing and beverages. Worldwide printing and publishing concerns are headquartered in England.

Government continues to be a strong presence in the British economy, and service industries are the major part of its economy, employing some two-thirds of its work force. The service sector includes education and the health-care system. It also includes wholesale and retail trade and the various institutions that provide financial services, including banks and insurance companies. The financial services industry contributes substantially to Great Britain's economy, and London continues to be one of the world's leading financial centers.

History. Evidence of Bronze Age civilization in England can be seen in the ruins of Stonehenge, but comparatively little is known about England before the arrival of the Romans in the 1st century B.C. The Romans were followed in the 5th century A.D. by Germanic tribes, the Angles, Saxons, and Jutes, who set up petty kingdoms. These in turn were overrun by Vikings, chiefly Danes, in the 9th and 10th centuries. The last successful invasion of England was in 1066, under William the Conqueror, of Normandy. The political and social organization the Normans imposed upon England laid the foundations of customs and traditions that would prove remarkably durable over the centuries and contribute much to the distinctive character of the people. In the 13th century, a group of English barons won concessions from King John set forth in the Magna Carta in 1215, marking an important development in the growth of Britain's unique political institutions. The 14th century was dominated by the Hundred Years War and the final unsuccessful bid by England's monarchs to establish effective control over their French lands and vassals. The 15th century witnessed the turmoil of the Wars of the Roses, dynastic struggles, which led to the rise of the Tudors, Henry VIII and Elizabeth I, whose combined reigns embraced the 16th century. Henry VIII embodied the English Renaissance and established England's independence from the papacy by seizing all church properties and establishing the Church of England. Elizabeth presided over the England of William Shakespeare and Sir Francis Drake. England, after destroying the Spanish Armada in 1588, claimed supremacy at sea and began expanding its overseas colonies and markets, an expansion that was to lead to a great empire. This was after nearly a century of civil and religious warfare centered upon the throne and, in particular, the Stuarts. The issue was finally put to rest with the Glorious Revolution and the accession of William III and Mary II in 1689, but only after bitter fighting and the Protectorate of Oliver Cromwell, leader of the Puritans. It was in the course of the conflicts of the 17th century that Parliament rose to prominence as a governing institution and the groundwork was laid for the governance of England in modern times. Modern Great Britain, with sovereignty residing in Parliament, was born with the Act of Union of 1707, which joined the formerly separate kingdoms of England and Scotland to form the United Kingdom. Through the laws of succession, the heirs to the British throne in the 18th century were German and this, as well as George III's disastrous policy leading to the loss of the American colonies, contributed to the reduction of the monarch to a symbolic head of state. Sovereignty resided in Parliament and the official leader of the government became the prime minister.

In the 18th century, Great Britain increased its power tremendously by using both the raw materials and markets of its growing empire to fuel the Industrial Revolution. Using modern technology, especially the steam engine, to build the first modern industries and turning its populace from agricultural work to industrial labor, Great Britain rapidly increased its wealth and power. At the end of the century, Great Britain faced a determined adversary in Napoleon Bonaparte of France. Defeated first at sea by Admiral Nelson in 1805 and on land by Lord Wellington at Waterloo in 1815, Napoleon, in fact, marked Britain's passage to world dominance. The 19th century also saw England's attempt to resolve the centuries' old hostilities with the Irish with the Act of Union of 1800, which created the United Kingdom of Great Britain and Ireland.

The 19th century was a period of political conflict and reform occasioned by Great Britain's wealth and power. There were bitter debates in Parliament over laws to ameliorate the harsh conditions in factories, and equally bitter disputes over the Corn Laws and the franchise. These debates would lay the foundations for the political parties that would dominate British politics throughout the 20th century, with the Whigs representing Liberal policies and the Tories conservative policies. These differences developed at the height of Britain's empire under Queen Victoria, who reigned from 1837 to 1901 and the rival views of politics were embodied in her two brilliant prime ministers, Benjamin Disraeli, the conservative, and William Gladstone, the liberal. By the time of Queen Victoria's death, the British empire consisted of about one-quarter of the world.

The 20th century proved much harder on England's fortunes. Great Britain entered World War I in 1914 against its economic rival, Germany. Great Britain helped win the war but lost 750,000 men in the fighting and did not adequately recover economically. The Irish problem continued to vex England, and in 1921 the British agreed to the independence of southern Ireland, but retained Northern Ireland. The worldwide depression hit England hard, and the 1930s saw the rise of fascism and the Nazis. Neville Chamberlain's policy of appeasing Hitler proved disastrous, and, led by Winston Churchill, England resisted Nazi ambitions. The English not only defended their own country, but in union with the United States and other allies, they destroyed the Nazis. England lost 360,000 men in World War II and its economy was in decline. In 1945, the Labour Party acceded to power and established England's welfare state with unemployment benefits, a comprehensive program of national health insurance, and the nationalization of key industries. The changes were dramatic, but the economy continued to lag. The same period saw the beginning of the breakup of Britain's empire. In 1947, India and Pakistan became independent, then in succession, one foreign policy and possession after another asserted its independence in Africa, Asia, and the Pacific.

In the 1950s Great Britain decided not to join the European Coal and Steel Community, nor would it join the European Economic Community, the Common Market. These proved costly decisions. The British economy expanded for a time but began to contract in the 1960s, and in 1963 and 1967 bids by Britain to gain admission to the Common Market were rejected, principally by France. Britain finally succeeded in joining the EEC in 1973, in the grip of the deepest economic downturn in the postwar years. In addition, the conflict in Northern Ireland turned violent. In May 1979 the Conservative Party, led by Margaret Thatcher, the first woman prime minister, came to power. The Conservatives drastically reduced government holdings, curbed the power of the unions, and strove to increase investment, all with some positive results. But after 11 years as prime minister, Mrs. Thatcher resigned in Nov. 1990 after losing Conservative Party leadership over her opposition to England's participation in the European Union. Thatcher was succeeded by John Major as Conservative leader and prime minister. In 1997 Major and the Conservatives lost the general election to Labour's Tony Blair.

Snowdon mountain railway in Wales, United Kingdom

United Methodist Church, largest Protestant denomination in the United States. Formed when the Methodist Church joined with the Evangelical United Brethren Church in 1968, it is the latest permutation of Methodism, a religious movement founded in England by John Wesley (1703-91). The church has around 10 million members nationwide and supports seminaries and colleges throughout the United States. It also supports many missionaries

in foreign countries. A governing body made up of members from the laity and clergy meets every four years to elect bishops and determine church policy. The church opposes racism and the consumption of alcoholic beverages and supports the United Nations' peace-keeping efforts around the world.
See also: Methodists.

United Mineworkers of America
see: Mineworkers of America, United.

Emblem of the United Nations

United Nations (UN), international organization of the independent states founded after World War II, with the declared goals of promoting peace and international cooperation. It was launched at the 1945 San Francisco Conference prepared by the "Big Three" Allied Powers of World War II (the United States, Britain, and the USSR), and 51 states signed the charter. Membership had grown to 160 by 1989. The headquarters are in New York City. The UN has six major organs. The General Assembly, composed of delegates from all member states, meets once a year and provides a general forum but has little actual power. The Security Council has five permanent members, (China, France, Great Britain, the United States, and the USSR), each of which has the right to veto any resoltion, and ten rotating members. The Economic and Social Council, with 54 elected members, deals with "nonpolitical" matters, coordinating the work of the specialist agencies and operating commissions, such as those on children, refugees, and human rights. The Trusteeship Council is responsible for UN Trust Territories. The International Court of Justice, in The Hague, Holland, is the UN's principal organ of international law. The Secretariat is the administrative body headed by the Secretary General. Other UN institutions include the United Nations Conference on Trade and Development, the Office of the United Nations High Commissioner for Refugees, and the United Nations Children's Fund.
Major specialized agencies affiliated with the UN include the Food and Agriculture Organization (FAO), General Agreement on Tariffs and Trade (GATT), International Atomic Energy Agency (IAEA), International Civil Aviation Organization (ICAO), International Labor Organization (ILO), International Monetary Fund (IMF), International Telecommunication Union (ITU), United Nations Educational, Scientific, and Cultural Organization (UNESCO), Universal Postal Union (UPU), World Bank (IBRD), World Health Organization (WHO), and World Meteorological Organization (WMO).

United Nations Children's Fund (UNICEF), UN organization formed (1946) as the UN International Children's Emergency Fund to help in countries devastated by World War II. It became a permanent body in 1953, retaining the UNICEF acronym and specializing in child welfare, family planning, and nutrition programs in disaster areas and in many poorer countries. It is financed voluntarily. In 1965 UNICEF was awarded the Nobel Peace Prize.
See also: United Nations.

United Nations Educational, Scientific, and Cultural Organization (UNESCO), UN agency established in 1946 to promote international collaboration through scientific, educational, and cultural activities. Its policy-making general conference meets biennially at its Paris headquarters. UNESCO has helped develop education in poorer countries and arranges scientific and cultural exchanges. Both the United States and Britain withdrew from UNESCO in 1985, charging that the organization was being manipulated for political purposes with an anti-American slant.
See also: United Nations.

United Nations University, research and training institution chartered in 1973 by the United Nations (UN). It is actually an agency through which institutions coordinate educational programs. Its aims are to provide information, research, and training opportunities for scholars and organizations around the world. Projects usually focus on the management of natural resources, hunger, and developing societies. University headquarters are in Tokyo.
See also: United Nations.

United Negro College Fund, nonprofit organization, founded 1944, that raises money to operate private colleges and universities for African Americans. It also provides counseling for students and staff for the member schools. The money comes from corporations, foundations, and individuals.

United Parcel Service (UPS), U.S. package delivery company. UPS delivers packages by truck or plane throughout the United States, Puerto Rico, and parts of Canada. Air service to Europe is also offered. The small delivery company that eventually became UPS was started in 1907 by James Casey and Claude Ryan to serve the Seattle area.

United Press International (UPI), world's largest independent news agency, created by the 1958 merger of United Press (founded 1892 by Edward W. Scripps) and the International News Service (founded by William Randolph Hearst in 1906). At its height in the 1950s, UPI had some 200 bureaus (half in the United States) that sent news and pictures to over 5,000 clients.

United Service Organizations (USO), independent, nonprofit grouping of organizations founded in 1941 to provide recreational, entertainment, religious, and social facilities for members of the U.S. armed forces. It is recognized by the U.S. Department of Defense and supported by contributions and volunteers.

United Society of Believers *see:* Shakers.

United States, government of the, consisting of various democratically elected governmental bodies in a federated union, with a judiciary both elected and appointed. The U.S. government relies for its day-to-day administration upon millions of employees and civil servants in numerous bureaucracies. Civil order is maintained by police forces, and national defense is the responsibility of the military. In the United States, both the police and the military as organs of government are under the ultimate authority and control of civilians holding elective office.
The government of the United States owes its fundamental character to the political practice and experience of the 13 original colonies. The colonists, in turn, were deeply influenced by their European heritage. The 3 major traditions that influenced the colonists in their political thinking were the parliamentary tradition of self-government and the principles of common law they brought with them from England; principles of governance contained in the Protestant, especially the Puritan, tradition of Biblical study; and the history of the ancient Roman republic. Against the background of the Europe they left behind, most of the early settlers were nonconformists. Their relation to the European tradition tended to be radical and unorthodox. Added to this was the experience of the New World. Its very existence was a challenge to assumptions and knowledge that had been taken for granted for centuries. It was separated from Europe by a long and dangerous ocean voyage.
The country was wild. Settling and cultivating the land required hard work and resourcefulness, which eventually developed certain habits of mind, an independence from authority, practicality, and ingenuity, a willingness to experiment, and an openness to novelty. Well before the Revolutionary War, the American colonists had become a people with a separate and distinct character and sensibility, and with considerable experience in governing themselves. Added to that experience was confidence in their judgment, enough to pit themselves against the accumulated authority and force of a major European power. All these elements are the historical foundations of government in the United States.
The Revolution established that, for Americans, power and authority did not proceed from a monarch or a privileged aristocracy.

Rather, government proceeded from the people. After the Revolution, America consisted of 13 independent states loosely united in a confederation. The arrangement did not work. A constitutional convention was called and the U.S. Constitution was drawn up, leaving substantial authority in each state but also establishing a central federal government. The principles of the Constitution are simple to state but were subject to intense debate and different interpretations even as they were being given their definitive written form. Government proceeds from the will of the people. The people have the right to make and unmake their government as they see fit. Power is divided so that it cannot easily be concentrated. The government is divided among a legislature that makes law, an executive that enforces it, and an independent judiciary that interprets the law when its meaning is in dispute. These branches check one another in various ways. Congress passes laws, but a president can veto. The president is commander-in-chief of the armed forces, but only Congress can levy taxes and declare war. No matter how promising the arrangement looked on paper, there were those who remained fundamentally critical and wary of concentrated governmental power. At their insistence, the constitution came to include the Bill of Rights with its list of basic liberties. Also firmly established in the Constitution were the strict separation of church and state and the supremacy of civilian authority over the armed forces. Profoundly influenced by English law and political traditions, the U.S. Constitution was a radical and revolutionary departure from the English model and, for that matter, from all others. It was ratified by two-thirds of the states and George Washington became the nation's first president. In doing so he not only filled a political office, but also fundamentally defined it. The Constitutional Convention was convened in Philadelphia in 1787 and went into effect on June 21, 1788.

Government in the United States is divided among several jurisdictions. There is the federal government, each separate state government, and local governments. The federal government has the power to collect taxes and custom duties, issue currency through the mint, borrow money, and issue bonds. It determines official weights and measures, issues patents and copyrights, controls immigration, and determines and confers citizenship. The federal government alone determines foreign policy, declares war, or negotiates with foreign states. Through its bureaucracies, it performs a wide range of regulatory functions touching on many industries and many aspects of the lives of its citizens. It has authority over interstate commerce, the environment, the national parks, labor-management disputes, and social security. Above all, and in the most basic terms, it is responsible for protecting the lives, property, rights, and liberties of its citizens. These include the right to vote, the right to trial by a jury of one's peers, freedom of speech and association, and freedom from arbitrary arrest or imprisonment.

Despite the considerable power and dominance of the federal government, authority is shared with the states, each of which has its own legislature, executive, and judiciary, each with its own written constitution and body of law.

Government has expanded and changed in the United States as rapidly as the country itself. Westward expansion in the 19th century required greater centralization of authority. The secession of the southern states provoked a constitutional crisis that ended in civil war. The South was defeated and the federal government emerged with more power and authority. Before the Civil War, Thomas Jefferson, Andrew Jackson, and James K. Polk enhanced the power of the presidency. During the Civil War, Abraham Lincoln became the most powerful president the republic had seen. For the balance of the 19th century, power shifted to Congress, but continued to accrue to Washington, D.C. The Spanish-American War in 1898, World War I, and World War II, under the successively more powerful presidencies of Theodore Roosevelt, Woodrow Wilson, and Franklin D. Roosevelt, saw the ascent of the United States as an international power and then a superpower. With the wars came a corresponding expansion in governmental power and responsibility. The U.S. government is now supported by vast bureaucracies, its budgets detail annual expenditures in the billions, it maintains huge standing military forces at home and around the world, but it continues to operate on much the same principles and organizational lines laid down in the Constitution.

The Congress makes laws; the executive branch, under the leadership of the president, enforces the laws and formulates national policies; the judiciary settles disputes at law. The relations within and among the branches of government are complex and change with new administrations and personalities, but the basic mechanics and principles remain much the same. Law is shaped by the needs or demands of organized citizens. Today there are many special interest groups (i.e., major industries, environmental groups), with money to employ lobbyists; these groups are outside of the main political parties and have some special policy goal or agenda. They influence lawmaking through newspapers, books, magazines, and television, demonstrations, and the use of lobbyists—paid professionals who actually seek out individual lawmakers and seek to persuade them to introduce certain legislation or to vote one way or another on pending legislation.

It is the elected congressional representatives and senators who draft bills and submit them to Congress for consideration. Bills are then assigned to various committees for study. Once out of a committee, a bill is returned for consideration and debate in the House or Senate before being voted upon. A simple majority is required to pass it. Then it must be signed by the president, who can veto the bill. The Congress may override the president's veto with a two-thirds majority. The process is lengthy, and from the time it is introduced to the time it becomes law, a bill goes through many changes, or amendments, in response to all of the competing and often conflicting interests that may be affected by the new law. The process has often been described as cumbersome and inefficient, but it was devised to ensure that laws would be made thoughtfully and with maximum input from those most affected. A more telling criticism of the current system is that in a society as large and complex as that of 20th-century United States, the only voices heard are those with the money needed to participate in government. More and more, it requires substantial sums of money to be elected to public office or to influence legislation.

In addition to elected officials, the government consists of vast bureaucracies without which the country could not function and elected officials could not effectively govern. In the executive branch, the major bureaucratic bodies include the departments of State, the Treasury, Defense, Justice, the Interior, Agriculture, Commerce, Labor, Health and Human Services, Housing and Urban Development, Transportation, Energy, Education, and Veterans' Affairs. The heads of these departments constitute what is known as the president's cabinet. In addition, there are a large number of independent agencies with various regulatory responsibilities, such as the Interstate Commerce Commission, the Federal Reserve, the Federal Communications Commission, the Selective Service System, and the National Labor Relations Board. The Congress also has a network of supporting bureaucracies that include 8 major administrative agencies. They are the Congressional Budget Office, the General Accounting Office, the Government Printing Office, the Library of Congress, the Office of Technology Assessment, the Copyright Royalty Tribunal, the Architect of the Capitol, and the U.S. Botanic Garden.

The House of Representatives has 435 members and the U.S. Senate has 100

President George Bush delivering the State of the Union address before the U.S. Congress (January 29, 1991)

members. Representatives sit for 2 years, senators for 6. Presidents are elected for 4 years with a maximum of 2 terms. The number of representatives a state has depends upon its population. Population is determined by a census and reapportionment takes place every 10 years. Tax bills can only be initiated in the House of Representatives. The Senate has the authority to approve treaties and presidential appointments to major federal posts, including the Supreme Court. The federal judicial system is organized into 95 district courts, 13 federal appeals or circuit courts, and the Supreme Court. Federal judges are appointed for life by the president, but must be approved by the Senate. Nine justices sit on the Supreme Court. The United States has been traditionally a 2-party political system. Unlike other representative democracies, the U.S. system confers elective office upon the winner of a majority of the voters in a contested election. In proportional systems of representation, minority parties hold seats based upon the percentage of the electorate that supports them. In the United States the influence of third or minor parties tends to be temporary and usually takes the form of bringing forward to public attention and debate new grievances or political programs that are then taken up by one or another of the major parties.

United States Air Force *see:* Air Force, United States.

United States Air Force Academy, federal institution for educating and training young men and women to be officers in the U.S. Air Force. Located in Colorado Springs, Col., and authorized by Congress in 1954, the academy offers a 4-year program consisting of academic work leading to a Bachelor of Science degree, military training (including flying instruction), physical education, and courses in ethics and honor. Candidates for the academy must be nominated by elected (or some appointed) U.S. officials.
See also: Air Force, U.S.

United States Army *see:* Army, U.S.

United States Border Patrol *see:* Border Patrol, United States.

United States Botanic Garden, national plant collection in Washington, D.C. Begun by a private organization in 1820, it was taken over by the government in 1843. The collection, which is open to the public, consists of over 10,000 plants, from the common to the rare and exotic. Guided tours and education courses are available.

United States capitals, cities that served as seats of the U.S. government until 1800, when Washington, D.C., became the permanent capital. After the Declaration of Independence (1776), the Continental Congress and subsequently the U.S. Congress met in various cities, moving every few years. Among these cities were Baltimore, Philadelphia, and New York City. Eventually, Virginia and Maryland negotiated with Congress to be the site of a permanent capital. In 1791, both states donated land to be set aside for its construction. The new capital was named after the nation's first president and is under direct federal jurisdiction, not being part of any state.

United States Coast Guard *see:* Coast Guard, United States.

United States Coast Guard Academy, federal institution for the education and training of young men and women as commissioned officers in the U.S. Coast Guard. Created in 1876, it now is located in New London, Conn., on the Thames River. Candidates compete nationally on the basis of college entrance exams. The students, or cadets, participate in a 4-year program, during which they receive military training, training at sea, and academic instruction in courses ranging from marine engineering to government.
See also: Coast Guard, U.S.

United States Congress *see:* Congress of the United States.

United States Constitution *see:* Constitution of the United States.

United States Forest Service *see:* Forest service, U.S.

United States literature, literary works in English beginning in the original 13 English colonies and continuing in the present-day United States. Although the United States is a large continental country with varied influences, several strands or themes characterize its literature. The pioneer heritage of the country left its mark on later writers, primarily in their concern with individual values and liberties and a certain pervasive skepticism toward authority. Perhaps aligned with this, U.S. writers have shown a consistent tendency to break with literary traditions and strike out in new directions.

Colonial literature. The first writings in English in North America were by adventurers and colonists for readers back in England. While few of these could be called literature, some journals and accounts did manifest a lasting quality and interest. Capt. John Smith's vigorous *True Relation of Such Occurrences and Accidents...as Hath Happened in Virginia* (published in England in 1608) was the first personal account of life in the colonies. More sober histories of the period included John Winthrop's *Journal,* which described life in the Massachusetts Bay Colony from 1630 to 1649, and William Bradford's *History of Plimoth Plantation.* Religious and instructional works, however, dominated colonial writing, with sermons and religious tracts making up most of the colonists' reading matter. The first book published in the Puritan colonies was the *Bay Psalm Book* (1740). The most important of the early religious writers were Cotton Mather (a 2-volume ecclesiastical history of New England), Jonathan Edwards (sermons and books), and John Woolman (a journal reflecting on his life in the Quaker belief). Poetry in colonial times also largely reflected religious and pious themes. Among the early poets were Mi-

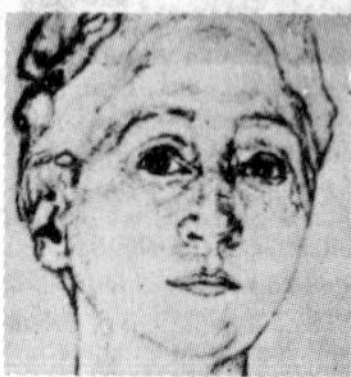

20th-century U.S. writers. Above left: Marianne Moore; above center: Truman Capote; above right: Edmund Wilson; bottom left: Sherwood Anderson; and bottom right: Mary McCarthy

chael Wigglesworth, Anne Bradstreet, and Edward Taylor.

Revolutionary period literature. Not surprisingly, writing during the period of the Revolution concentrated on politics and on political philosophy. Benjamin Franklin encouraged writers by acting as a publisher and founder of newspapers. He also wrote political and satirical works, with his witty *Poor Richard's Almanac* (1733-58), one of the period's most popular publications. Political writing during this time reached new heights as men like Thomas Paine, Thomas Jefferson, Alexander Hamilton, and John Madison examined the nature of society. A formidable female writer of the late 18th century, Mercy Otis Warren, wrote not only plays and poetry but a history of the American Revolution—one of two contemporary histories considered significant. At war's end, as the new nation struggled to discover its identity, Hamilton, Madison, and John Jay wrote a brilliant series of letters called *The Federalist* in support of the new constitution. For style and content they are scarcely rivaled in political discourse.

Literature in the New Nation. The first U.S. novel was William Hill Brown's *The Power of Sympathy* (1789). Charles Brockten Brown, the first professional U.S. novelist, modeled his work after the English gothic romances, as exemplified in *Wieland* (1798) and *Edgar Huntly* (1799). Fame both in the United States and Europe was gained by Washington Irving with his *Sketch-Book* (1819-20) and by James Fenimore Cooper with his *Leatherstocking Tales* (1823-41). The leading poet of this time was William Cullen Bryant, who became known as the American Wordsworth for his deeply felt nature poems. Among his most important lyrics are "Thanatopsis" (1811), "To a Waterfowl" (1818), and "To the Fringed Gentian" (1832). Also notable was Henry Wadsworth Longfellow (*Evangeline*, 1847). The nation's attention turned to the problem of slavery in the 1830s with William Lloyd Garrison and his newspaper, *The Liberator*, leading the antislavery movement. The most influential antislavery work was Harriet Beecher Stowe's novel *Uncle Tom's Cabin* (1851-52), the best-selling book of the time.

Literature at mid-19th century. By the middle of the 19th century, U.S. literature had come of age. The transcendentalists were a group of New England writers who displayed in their works characteristics thought to be specifically American. They espoused a high moral seriousness and a sense that the individual was superior to tradition and social customs. They also called for a distinctly American literature, quite independent of European models. Chief among them was Ralph Waldo Emerson, who presented the group's theories in *Nature* (1836) and in his brilliant essays (e.g., "Self-Reliance," and "The Over-Soul," both 1841). Henry David Thoreau (*Walden*, 1855) was another transcendentalist who wrote observant, thought-provoking, and beautifully styled prose. Utterly American was the poet Walt Whitman (*Leave of Grass*, first edition published 1855), writing a free-form verse that broke with European models and celebrated the new country in the New World. Quite different, but equally untraditional, were the compact, emotionally intense lyrics of Emily Dickinson, almost all of which were published after her death in 1886. A darker strand in U.S. literature was evident in the eerie, haunting poetry and short stories of Edgar Allen Poe, for example, in lyrics such as "The Raven" (1845) and the sinister *Tales* (1840). Nathaniel Hawthorne's masterpiece *The Scarlet Letter* (1850) probed the psychological aspects of sin in the closed society of early New England Puritanism. In *Moby Dick* (1852), Herman Melville created an American epic, at once an adventure tale of the sea and a deep, enigmatic allegory.

Literature in the second half of the 19th century. After the Civil War, literature in the United States took on a national aspect in that writings of distinct regions gained a nationwide audience. The country eagerly read about the California gold rush and life in the West in the short stories of Bret Harte. Joel Chandler Harris retold the old black tales of the South. The greatest of the regionalist writers, however, Mark Twain, surpassed the genre and in *The Adventures of Tom Sawyer* (1876) and *The Adventures of Huckleberry Finn* (1884) wrote two American classics. By century's end, a new realism was taking hold in U.S. literature as was a reaching-out to European models and culture. Stephen Crane's *Red Badge of Courage* (1895), set in the Civil War, won acclaim for its realistic portrayal of warfare. Henry James went to Europe where he wrote novels of rare psychological insight about the clash of U.S. and European cultures (*The Portrait of a Lady*, 1881, and *The Golden Bowl*, 1904). William Dean Howells set out to depict the lives of average Americans (*The Rise of Silas Lapham*, 1885). Other noted realists included Frank Norris, Harold Frederick, Theodore Dreiser, Hamlin Garland, Jack London, and James T. Farrell. A group of journalists and writers known as "muckrakers" employed realism to examine corruption and fraud in U.S. society. Among them were Lincoln Steffins, Ida M. Tarbell, and Upton Sinclair, whose novel *The Jungle* (1906) was instrumental in bringing about food and drug laws.

Literature after World War I. Disillusionment with the war stirred a generation of U.S. writers to become expatriates in Europe, in search of something to believe in. Labeled the "lost generation" by Gertrude Stein (*The Autobiography of Alice B. Toklas*, 1933), the group included Ernest Hemingway (*The Sun Also Rises*, 1925), F. Scott Fitzgerald (*The Great Gatsby*, 1925), and John Dos Passos (*U.S.A.*, 1930-36). One of the most powerful of U.S. novelists was William Faulkner (*The Sound and the Fury*, 1929). Social criticism continued with such writers as critic H. L. Mencken and Edmund Wilson and novelists Sherwood Anderson and Sinclair Lewis. Other novelists of the period include Willa Cather, Thomas Wolfe, and Nathanael West. The Great Depression fostered more socially aware writing, as evidenced in the works of John Steinbeck (*The Grapes of Wrath*, 1939). Notable U.S. poets of the 20th century include Edward Arlington Robinson, Edna St. Vincent Millay, Robert Frost, T.S. Eliot, Carl Sandburg, Hart Crane, Marianne Moore, Wallace Stevens, e.e. cummings, Langston Hughes, and, more recently, Robert Lowell, Elizabeth Bishop, Sylvia Plath, John Berryman, and John Ashberry. Among the most important playwrights of this period were Eugene O'Neill (*Long Day's Journey Into Night*, first produced in 1956), Elmer Rice, Maxwell Anderson, Lillian Hellman, Tennessee Williams, Arthur Miller, William Inge, and, in recent years, Edward Albee, David Rabe, Sam Shepard, and Neil Simon. Major novelists include Flannery O'Connor, Eudora Welty, J.D. Salinger, Norman Mailer, Saul Bellow, Philip Roth, Ralph Ellison, James Baldwin, Truman Capote, Mary McCarthy, Joyce Carol Oates, Thomas Pynchon, John Barth, Toni Morrison, and John Updike.

United States Marine Corps *see:* Marine Corps, U.S.

United States Merchant Marine Academy, government-sponsored educational institution (since 1943), located in Kings Point, N.Y. The academy prepares young men and women to become officers in the U.S. Merchant Marine. To be considered for admission into the school, a candidate must be nominated by a U.S. senator or representative and pass a competitive examination. The school program involves a 4-year undergraduate education, with some technical and naval training, as well as training on board a ship.
See also: Merchant marine.

United States Military Academy, oldest government-sponsored educational facility (founded in 1802), located in West Point, N.Y. The academy trains young men and women to become officers in the U.S. Army. An applicant must be nominated by an elected or appointed U.S. official, and must pass certain academic, medical, and physical requirements. The academy offers a 4-year undergraduate education with strong emphasis on military training.
See also: Army, U.S.

United States Naval Academy, federally funded and operated college for training men and women to be officers in the U.S. Navy and Marine Corps. Founded in 1845, it is located at Annapolis, Md. Candidates must be nominated by elected or appointed officials, such as senators and representatives, and must be between the ages of 17 and 21 years. The four-year program includes academic studies leading to a bachelor of science degree, as well as required participation in varsity or intramural sports and training in professional skills such as navigation and sailing.
See also: Marine Corps, U.S.; Navy, U.S.

United States Navy *see:* Navy, United States.

United States of America, country whose territory is principally on the continent of North America, but which includes islands of the Hawaiian archipelago in the Pacific Ocean. The United States is organized into 50 political subdivisions, or states, and the District of Columbia. In addition, the U.S. government maintains special political associations with various overseas territories including Puerto Rico and the U.S. Virgin Islands in the Caribbean, and Guam, American Samoa and Belau, the Marshall Islands, the Federated States of Micronesia, and Northern Marianas, all formerly parts of the Trust Territory of the Pacific Islands. Johnson, Midway, and Wake islands, also in the Pacific, are also dependent upon the United States. The contiguous states of the United States are bounded by the Atlantic Ocean to the east, the Pacific Ocean to the west, Canada to the north, and Mexico, the Gulf of Mexico, and the Caribbean Sea to the south. Alaska is separated from the 48 contiguous states by Canada and bounded by that country as well as the Pacific and Arctic oceans. The Hawaiian islands are in the central Pacific Ocean c.2,100 mi (3,380 km) from San Francisco, Calif. The nation's capital is Washington, D.C.

Land and People. With an area of 3,618,770 sq mi (9,372,143 sq km), the United States is geographically varied, and can be divided into approximately 6 regions. The Atlantic and Gulf Coastal Lowlands stretch south from Long Island to Florida and then west to Mexico. They extend inland an average of 200 mi (322 km) with many lagoons, sandbars, and good natural harbors. In southern Florida they include the Everglades and, on the Gulf Coast, the Mississippi River delta. The Appalachian mountain chain separates the Atlantic Lowlands from the western interior. The Appalachians run northeast to southwest from Nova Scotia in Canada to the southern United States. A low mountain system, the Appalachians include the White Mountains of New Hampshire, the Great Smoky Mountains, and the Blue Ridge Mountains of North Carolina, and give way to the Allegheny Plateau. The north-central section of the United States has the Great Lakes, among the world's largest freshwater lakes. The Great Lakes region forms a natural boundary between the eastern and western United States, and between the United States and Canada. Beyond the Alleghenies are the Central and Interior Plains, stretching to the Rocky Mountains and drained by the Mississippi-Missouri river system and its branches. Its uplands include the Ozarks in Arkansas and Missouri, and the Black Hills of South Dakota and Wyoming. The Rocky Mountains mark the western barrier of the Great Plains and are part of a mountain system extending from Alaska, through Canada and the United States and continuing down the length of South America. The highest mountain in the United States is Mt. McKinley in Alaska at 20,320 ft (6,194 m). Between the Rocky Mountains and the mountains of the Cascade and Sierra Nevada ranges farther west lies the Western Plateau and Basin, or the Intermontane Region. It contains the Great Salt Lake and Grand Canyon. Finally, beyond the western mountains, are the Pacific Coastlands extending south from Puget Sound in the state of Washington to Central Valley in California. The lowest point in the United States is Death Valley in California, one of several desert regions to be found in the southwestern United States.

Climate in the continental United States is greatly influenced by geographic position. Winter temperatures vary greatly, being relatively high along the sheltered Pacific coast, but often extremely low in the interior and the east. Summer temperatures are mainly high in most areas with the southeast becoming subtropical and humid. Tornadoes can occur in spring, especially in the Mississippi valley, and summer thunderstorms and hurricanes are frequent along the south Gulf and Atlantic coasts.

The original inhabitants of the Unites States were the Native Americans, racially distinct and consisting of various peoples of

United States of America

General information	
Capital:	Washington, D.C.
Area:	3,618,770 sq mi (9,372,614 sq km)
Population:	248,777,000
Official language:	English
Monetary unit:	1 dollar = 100 cents
Main cities:	New York, Los Angeles, Washington D.C.
Government	
Form:	federal republic
Independent:	1776
Head of state:	President (elected every 4 years)
Head of government:	President
Legislature:	two legislative houses (Senate and House of Representatives)
Executive:	President and Cabinet
Judiciary:	highest court is the Supreme Court
Political division:	50 states, 1 district
National economy	
Gross national product:	U.S. $4,863,674,000,000
Per capita income:	U.S. $19,780
Agriculture:	cereals, oranges and tangerines, grapefruit, potatoes, lemons, sugarbeets
Livestock:	cattle, pigs, poultry
Fisheries:	3,235,000 metric tons
Mining:	coal, iron, molybdenum, phosphate rock, silver, crude petroleum
Industries:	crude steel, paper and paper products, cement, wood pulp, pig iron
Main exports:	machinery and transportation equipment, chemicals, crude materials, miscellaneous manufactured articles, food and livestock, coal
Transportation:	184,235 mi (296,497 km) of railroads, 3,879,538 mi (6,243,340 km) of roads, 52 international airports
Trading partners:	Canada, Japan, Mexico, United Kingdom
People	
Urban:	76%
Ethnic composition:	European 84.5%, African 12.5%, other 3%
Birth rate:	16 per 1,000 population
Death rate:	8.7 per 1,000 population
Infant mortality:	10 per 1,000 live births
Life expectancy:	male 71.5 years, female 78.5 years

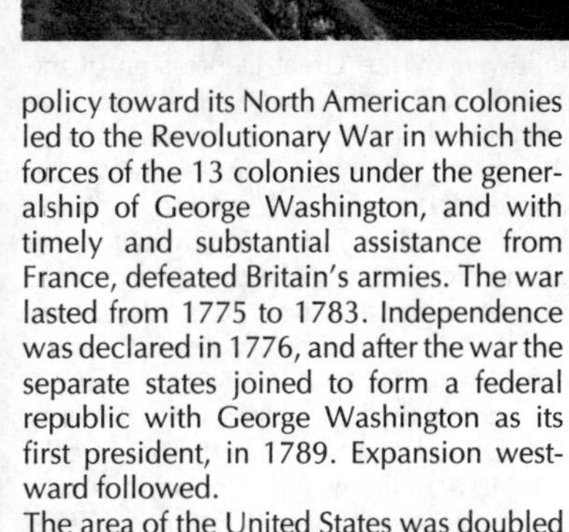

different languages and cultures. Displaced and decimated by successive waves of migration from Europe beginning in the 16th and 17th centuries, remnant populations now live for the most part on reservations, principally in the Great Plains and Western states. The majority of the people of the United States are immigrants or descendants of immigrants who came to the United States in 2 distinct groups. From 1600 to 1820, most settlers were from England and Scotland. From the 1820s to the present, newcomers arrived from Ireland, Germany, and Scandinavia before the U.S. Civil War, then from Eastern Europe, the Mediterranean, and Asia. The U.S. population also includes a significant number of citizens who are descendants of the Mexicans who originally settled what is now the U.S. Southwest. African Americans are the descendants of men and women who were brought to North America as slaves as early as 1619. An exhaustive list of the origins of all U.S. citizens would include peoples from all over the world. Despite their varied origins, they have combined sufficiently to constitute an identifiable people with a common language, culture, and outlook. There is no established religion in the United States, but a majority of the people are Christians, chiefly Protestants but also Roman Catholics. The country's language is English, though many immigrants speak their own native languages.

Economy. In 1989, the gross national product of the United States was in excess of $5.2 trillion dollars, making it by far the world's richest country. The United States can grow nearly all temperate and subtropical crops and is not only self-sufficient in essential foods but regularly produces surpluses. About half the land surface is given to farming, including dairy farming and the raising of livestock. The country contains valuable forests, particularly in the northwest and Alaska, and rich fisheries in the Atlantic, the Pacific, and the Gulf. Its considerable mineral wealth includes coal, iron ore, petroleum, and natural gas, but the needs of its vast economy and the consumption it generates have led to a decline in the reserves of some minerals, and the United States has increasingly become an importer of ores and of oil. Its enormous manufacturing sector produces steel, automobiles, aircraft, and aerospace technology, electronic equipment, textiles, and most kinds of consumer goods. The United States not only manufactures in quantity, but it also has long been a leader in setting standards for quality and efficiency in modern industrial production. In addition, a large sector of the economy is committed to research, development, and production in sophisticated weaponry and aerospace systems. Banking and the interrelated institutions that provide financial services and products worldwide are also major contributors to the economy.

History. The first permanent European settlement in the United States was St. Augustine, Fla., founded by the Spanish in 1565. Early English settlements were in Jamestown, Va., in 1607; Plymouth, Mass., in 1620; Maryland in 1634, Connecticut in 1636, and Pennsylvania in 1681. There were also French, Dutch, and Swedish settlements. By the 18th century, Britain was the paramount power on the new continent with prosperous, flourishing colonies in what was later to become the United States. Opposition to Britain's policy toward its North American colonies led to the Revolutionary War in which the forces of the 13 colonies under the generalship of George Washington, and with timely and substantial assistance from France, defeated Britain's armies. The war lasted from 1775 to 1783. Independence was declared in 1776, and after the war the separate states joined to form a federal republic with George Washington as its first president, in 1789. Expansion westward followed.

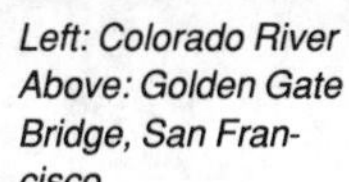

Left: Colorado River
Above: Golden Gate Bridge, San Francisco

The area of the United States was doubled by the Louisiana Purchase, made in 1803. Florida was purchased from Spain in 1819. U.S. ambitions for expansion into Canada ended with the War of 1812 between Britain and the United States. Settlers moved over the Alleghenies and west over the Great Plains. Texas was annexed in 1845 and much of the territory of the U.S. Southwest was acquired through the Treaty of Guadalupe Hidalgo, which ended the Mexican-American War of 1848. Five years later, southern New Mexico and southern Arizona were added to the United States with the Gadsden Purchase in 1853 and, at the other end of the continent, Alaska was purchased from Russia in 1867. As the country expanded, differences deepened between the cultures and economies of the northern and southern states. The southern states eventually elected to secede from the union and the result was the Civil War (1861-65), the bloodiest single conflict in the nation's history. Following the war came a period known as Reconstruction (1865-77). What was Reconstruction for the South was develop-

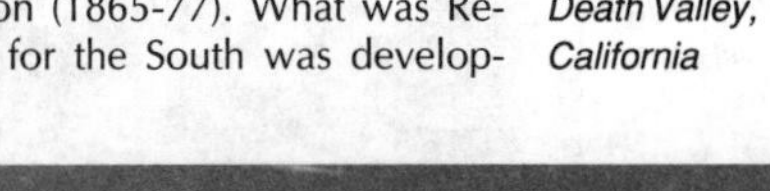

Death Valley, California

ment and expansion for the rest of the country. The North became more and more industrialized and urbanized and the settlement of the West was hastened with the completion of the transcontinental railroad in 1869. As the nation became richer, more powerful, and more self-confident, its presence began to be felt abroad.

In 1898 Hawaii was annexed and other overseas territories came under U.S. control as a result of its victory in the Spanish-American War. The United States completed its entry into international affairs by participating (from 1917) in World War I (1914-18) and tipping the scales in favor of the Allies, the British and the French. Power and prosperity were soon followed by the Great Depression of the 1930s, an economic breakdown so complete that many felt the country was on the brink of revolution. Franklin D. Roosevelt became president and instituted his New Deal reforms, which halted the economic decline. Worldwide economic frustration and ambition led to World War II (1940-45) and the Japanese attack on Pearl Harbor on Dec. 7, 1941, marked the entrance of the United States into the war. The United States emerged from World War II a military and economic superpower, leader of the Western, or free, world, and locked in rivalry with the Communist bloc led by the Soviet Union. With an ideology of anti-communism, which it pursued relentlessly at home and abroad, and a policy of resisting and containing what it saw as the spread of communism, the United States committed itself to the Cold War. It participated in the Korean War (1950-53) and, later, in the Vietnam War (1961-73).

Domestically, the Congressional hearings and investigations of Sen. Joseph McCarthy and his staff into Communist subversion, the unofficial purges of people who had been slandered or blackballed, and the trial and execution of Ethel and Julius Rosenberg for spying for the Soviet Union dominated much of the postwar decade. In the 1960s, at the same time the country was engaged in the Vietnam War, the government pursued its war on poverty, a combination of programs meant to alleviate poverty and equalize access to equal economic opportunity. The country also faced the profound social and legal crisis generated by the civil rights movement led by the Rev. Martin Luther King, Jr. The turmoil and unrest of the period was marked at the very outset by the assassination of President John F. Kennedy and later of Dr. King, and then Robert Kennedy.

Richard Nixon's election to the presidency signalled the end to the Vietnam War, but not before Cambodia had been embroiled in the widening regional disaster. Defeat in Vietnam was followed by economic recession at home. The Nixon presidency saw a major diplomatic breakthrough in its recognition of Communist China, but lost its credibility and authority with the Watergate domestic political scandal. Rather than face impeachment, Nixon resigned the presidency in disgrace. Both Gerald Ford and his Democratic successor, Jimmy Carter, worked to restore the sagging economy. The last year of Carter's presidency witnessed a further blow to the international standing of the United States with the ouster of the Shah of Iran by Iranian Muslim fundamentalists under the leadership of Ayatollah Khomeini, whose followers held the U.S. embassy staff in Teheran hostage for more than a year.

The Republican administration of Ronald Reagan sought to revive the economy by radically reducing governmental regulation. The policy proved stimulating in the short run, but left the nation deep in debt, with a great part of its banking system in disarray, and the gap between rich and poor wider than it was before Reagan's program was initiated. Internationally, the Reagan presidency struck a more militant anti-Communist tone. Defense spending was increased and the administration was determined to regain ground from communism, particularly in Nicaragua. The result was the Iran-contra scandal, in which it was discovered that the executive branch had been selling arms to Iran to finance forces seeking to overthrow the Marxist regime in Nicaragua. The president denied knowledge of the transactions or involvement in any wrongdoing, but the hearings into the matter raised serious questions, among them, whether or not the president was competent to govern.

Ronald Reagan was succeeded by George Bush, whose administration inherited the severe economic consequences of his predecessor's policies, in particular the collapse of the savings and loan institutions and the weakening of the U.S. banking system. In foreign policy, President Bush urged a continuation of normalizing relations with China despite pressure from many quarters to censure China for the Tiananmen Square massacre of dissident students and workers. In 1993 Bush was succeeded by the Democrat Bill Clinton. Clinton stood for a better social policy, but was often frustrated by the Republican majority in the Congres and Senate. Clinton was re-elected in 1996.

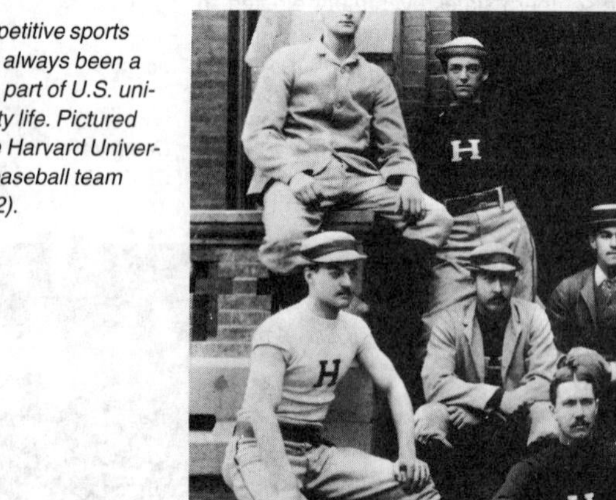

Competitive sports have always been a large part of U.S. university life. Pictured is the Harvard University baseball team (1882).

United States Postal Service *see:* Postal Service, U.S.

United States President *see:* President of the United States.

United States Seal *see:* Great Seal of the United States.

United States Supreme Court *see:* Supreme Court of the United States.

United Steelworkers of America *see:* Steelworkers of America, United.

United Way of America (UWA), U.S. umbrella organization founded in 1918 to raise funds for charitable agencies working on health, recreation, and welfare projects. Over 200 major national organizations have been helped by the United Way's funds. It has 1,200 local chapters.

Unit rule, U.S. voting rule used at many political conventions. Under the rule, all the votes in a state delegation are thought of as a single unit. When a majority of the delegation members vote for a certain candidate during a convention, all the delegation votes go to that candidate. Unit rule was used by the Democratic party until 1968.

Universalism, Christian doctrine that holds that everyone will ultimately be saved by divine grace. The Universalist Church in the United States, initially Calvinistic, was formed (1779) by Hosea Ballou and other New England nonconformists. Liberal and syncretist, in 1961 it joined the Unitarians to form the Unitarian Universalist Association.
See also: Unitarianism.

Universal language, proposed language that people of all nations could speak and understand. Since the 1600s, the idea of a universal language has attracted philosophers, educators, politicians, and businesspersons alike. Its advocates believe that it would aid both cultural and political understanding among the disparate nations of the world. Its detractors claim that the idea of such a language is impractical. Several universal languages, including Volapuk and Esperanto, have been developed and used with some success. During the Middle Ages and Renaissance, Latin almost achieved the status of a universal language as it was used as a common language by diplomats and other educated people throughout Europe. Today, English is fast becoming a universal language.

Universe, general term for all of space and everything in it.

Universities and colleges, schools that are designed for the continuation of education beyond high school and that emphasize the study of liberal arts, arts, and sciences. A university generally offers courses in many subjects, including agriculture, art, history, literature, philosophy, and science. It may be divided into different departments, or colleges. For example, a university may have a College of Education within it. A college may also be a separate school, which usually emphasizes study in one area, such as liberal arts. Most U.S. universities and colleges are sponsored either privately (often by a church) or by local, state, or federal government. Most universities and colleges offer students a course of study leading to an undergraduate degree, a bachelor of arts or science degree. Most also have various graduate programs in which a student may continue to work toward a master of arts or science degree or a doctor's degree. Though the oldest university in the world is probably Al-Azhar University in Egypt (founded in A.D. 970), the prototypes for U.S. universities sprang up in Europe during the 12th century. These universities were usually associated with the Church, though by the 14th century, they were designed to train students in medicine and law as well as theology. The earliest U.S. university is Harvard, which was founded in 1636. Like their European models, the first U.S. universities and colleges were training centers for ministers. They soon, however, expanded their curricula to include engineering, art, medicine, science, and law. Today the population of the student body in these schools can range from several hundred, as might be found in a small liberal college, to many thousands (Ohio State University in Columbus, Ohio, has an enrollment of over 50,000).

Unknown soldier, in the United States and some European countries, an unidentified soldier killed in action in war whose tomb serves as a national shrine honoring all war dead. Unknown soldiers of World War I, World War II, the Korean War, and the Vietnam War are buried in the Tomb of the Unknown Soldier in Arlington National Cemetry, Arlington, Va.

UN Peacekeeping Forces, multinational forces under UN command, deployed around the world since 1948 to settle conflicts between and within countries. Such forces include armed troops as well as unarmed observers monitoring the implementation of political agreements. Peacekeeping forces are put in place when requested by the countries in conflict, with the agreement of the UN Security Council; personnel is then supplied voluntarily by UN member states. Primary areas of activity have been the Congo, Central America, and the Middle East. UN forces have been active in the Israeli-Arab conflict and in conflicts between Iran and Iraq, India and Pakistan, and parties within Cyprus and Angola.
See also: United Nations.

Untermeyer, Louis (1885-1977), U.S. writer and editor. Though he published many volumes of poetry and two novels, he is better recognized today as having been the editor of several poetry anthologies: *Modern American Poetry* (1919 and subsequent revision), *Modern British Poetry* (1920), and *A Treasury of Great Poems, English and American* (1942). From 1961 to 1963, he served as the poetry consultant for the Library of Congress.

Upanishads, group of philosophical treaties that make up the final part of the Veda, a collection of Hindu scriptures. They are thought to have been written from 900 to 600 B.C. Most of the existing 112 Upanishads are in dialogue form, and their speculative nature has inspired the formulation of several concepts central to the Hindu religion. One puts forth that the soul of an individual is one with the soul of the universe, or God.
See also: Hinduism; Vedas.

Upas, forest tree (genus *Antiaris*) of tropical Asia and Indonesia. Ancient tales describe this tree as yielding a juice that was used as arrow poison by ancient peoples; this accounts for a lot of the superstition and mysticism that surrounds this tree.

Updike, John (1932-), U.S. novelist, short-story writer, poet, and critic. He has dealt with the trials of contemporary life in such novels as *Rabbit, Run* (1960), *Couples* (1968), *Bech: A Book* (1970), *The Coup* (1978), *Rabbit is Rich* (1981, Pulitzer), *The Witches of Eastwick* (1984), *S.* (1988), and *Rabbit at Rest* (1990; Pulitzer). He published a book of memoirs, *Self-Consciousness*, in 1989.

Upjohn, Richard (1802-78), English-born U.S. architect, noted for his Gothic Revival churches, such as Trinity Church, New York City (1846). He was one of the founders and the president of the American Institute of Architects (1857-76).
See also: Architecture.

Upland sandpiper (*Bartramia longicauda*), also called upland plover, North American bird of the sandpiper family. For most of the year, it lives on the prairies and meadows of Canada and the northern United States, but it migrates for the winters to the grassy plains of Argentina and Brazil. It is usually about 12 in (30 cm) long, with dark- and light-brown feathers and a white belly. It eats locusts and other insect pests.

Upper Volta *see:* Burkina Faso.

UPS *see:* United Parcel Service.

Upshaw, Eugene, Jr. (1945-), U.S. football player. Upshaw played for the Oakland Raiders (1967-81) and was captain of the team (1970-81). Upon retirement as an active player, he became president of the National Football League Players' Association (1981-83). He was appointed to executive director in 1984 and supported the players in the football strike of 1987. He was inducted into the Pro Football Hall of Fame in 1987.

Upsilon particle, unstable subatomic particle without electrical charge. With a mass almost 10 times that of a proton, it is the heaviest known subatomic particle.
See also: Quark.

Ur, ancient Sumerian city that lay in what is now southern Iraq along the Euphrates River. An important port as well as religious and trade center, Ur thrived from about 3500 B.C. until the 4th century B.C. At that time, the Euphrates River changed its course and the then useless port city was abandoned. According to the Bible, the Hebrew leader Abraham was born in Ur. Some important architectural ruins of Ur have been found in southern Iraq. These ruins include the remains of a ziggurat, an ancient pyramid-like structure.
See also: Sumer.

Votive relief of Ur-Nanshe and his family (c.2500 B.C.), rulers in Ur

Ural Mountains, mountain chain about 1,500 mi (2,400 km) long in the western USSR, running north-south from the Kara Sea toward the Caspian. The Urals are the traditional boundary between Europe and Asia. Mt. Narodnaya (6,214 ft/1,894 m), in the northern section, is the highest peak. The Urals are heavily forested and rich in minerals.

Ural River, USSR river. Originating in the Ural Mountains of the west-central USSR, it flows some 1,570 mi (2,527 km) south to the Caspian Sea. Several important Russian cities lie along it, including Magnitogorsk, a steel-making center. It is a rich source of salmon and sturgeon.

Uranium, chemical element, symbol U; for physical constants see Periodic Table. Discovered by Martin H. Klaproth in 1789, it occurs in the minerals pitchblende, uraninite, carnotite, autunite, and uranophane, among others. It is prepared by reduction of the tetrafluoride in a Thermit type of reaction. Uranium is a silver-white, lustrous, radioactive, reactive metal, a member of the actinide series. It is pyrophoric. Uranium-235 is fissionable and is used as fuel in nuclear reactors, and in atomic and hydrogen bombs. One pound of uranium has the fuel value of 1,500 tons of coal. Uranium-238 is fertile and used to produce plutonium-239, which is fissionable in breeder reactors. Uranium and its salts are highly toxic.

Uranium-235 *see:* U-235.

Uranus, third-largest planet in the Solar System and the seventh from the sun. Physically very similar to Neptune, but rather larger, Uranus orbits the sun every 84.02 years at a mean distance of 1.78 billion mi (2,87 billion km), rotating on its axis once every 10.75 hours. Since the plane of its equator is tilted 98° to the plane of its orbit, the rotation of the planet and the revolution of its five known moons (Titania, Oberon, Ariel, Umbriel, and Mirando), which orbit closely parallel to the equator, are retrograde. In 1977 the planet was found to have five rings, like those of Saturn but much fainter.
See also: Planet; Solar System.

Uranus, god of the sky in Greek mythology. His union with Gaea, the earth, produced a race of giants known as the Titans. Because Uranus hated and feared his offspring, he forced them to live deep within the earth. The Titan Cronus rebelled against his father's decree, attacking and emasculating Uranus, a wound that separated Uranus from Gaea. (The myth may have originated as an explanation for the separation of the sky and earth.) The function of Uranus as god of the sky was eventually taken over in Greek mythology by Zeus, a son of Cronus.
See also: Mythology.

Urban, name of eight popes. **Urban II** (c.1042-99; r. 1088-99) continued the struggle against the emperor Henry IV begun by his predecessor, Gregory VII. At the Council of Clermont (1095) he initiated the Crusades. **Urban III** (r. 1185-87) was absorbed in a struggle with Emperor Frederick Barbarossa and his son Henry IV. **Urban IV** (c.1200-64; r. 1261-64) continued the struggle against the Hohenstaufen emperors and gave the crown of Naples and Sicily to Charles I. **Saint Urban V** (c.1310-70; r. 1362-70) attempted to return the papacy to Rome from Avignon and to effect a reconciliation with the Eastern Church. **Urban VI** (1318?-89; r. 1378-89) was involved in disputes with his cardinals that precipitated the Great Schism. **Urban VIII** (1568-1644; r. 1623-44) played an ambiguous role in the Thirty Years War through political opposition to the Roman Catholic Hapsburgs.

Urban Coalition, National, U.S. organization that works to solve problems of city dwellers. Formed in 1970, members include religious and civic leaders as well as business and labor representatives. Members identify problems related to education, health care, housing, and employment, and try to make local, state, and federal governments, as well as private organizations, aware of them. The coalition has about 40 local chapters operating throughout the United States.

Urban League, or National Urban League, voluntary organization established to end racial discrimination and to help minorities achieve political equality. Founded in 1910, the League works through its more than 100 local groups throughout the United States to provide job training and employment opportunities for minorities. It also implements health care and counselling programs. It funds research aimed at identifying the problems facing minorities and works to ensure that state and national governments are made aware of such problems. Headquarters are in New York City.

Urban renewal, removal of city slums and their replacement with improved residential or commercial facilities. Ideally, the federal government grants a city a certain amount of money to replace a slum neighborhood. The city then uses the funds to buy and demolish derelict property, relocating families and businesses to new areas. Next, the land is sold to private or public developers at a low price. Schools, parks, office centers, and so on are then to be built where the slum once stood. The program as a whole has been only moderately successful. In many cities cleared land has remained unsold and undeveloped for years. Federal funding of urban renewal has also been greatly cut, shifting the financial burden to the state and city governments.

Urea, organic compound, $CO(NH_2)_2$, that is the end product of the metabolism of nitrogen in protein in many animals. It is excreted in the urine. Urea's major uses are as a nitrogenous fertilizer and to make urea-formaldehyde resins.

Uremia, biochemical disorder often seen in cases of kidney failure, consisting of high levels of urea and other nitrogenous waste products entering the blood. Nausea, vomiting, malaise, itching, pigmentation, anemia, and acute disorders of fluid and mineral balance are common.
See also: Kidney.

Urey, Harold Clayton (1893-1981), U.S. chemist awarded the 1934 Nobel Prize in chemistry for his discovery of deuterium, an isotope of hydrogen. He was a leading theorist of the nature and origin of the moon.
See also: Deuterium.

Urine, waste product consisting of a dilute solution of excess salts and nitrogenous material, such as urea and deaminated protein, excreted by many animals. The wastes are filtered from the blood by the kidneys or equivalent structures and stored in the bladder until excreted. The passage of urine not only serves to eliminate wastes, but also provides a mechanism for maintaining the water and salt concentrations and pH of the blood. While all mammals excrete nitrogenous wastes in urine, other animals—birds, insects, and fish—excrete them as ammonia or in solid crystals as uric acid.

Uris, Leon (1924-), U.S. author of modern historical fiction. His most famous novel, *Exodus* (1958), follows the development of the state of Israel. His first novel, *Battle Cry* (1953), is a personalized account of service in the Marine Corps during World War II. Other works include *QB VII* (1970), *Trinity* (1976), and *Mitla Pass* (1988). Uris, in collaboration with his wife, Jill, has also written two photoessays, *Ireland: A Terrible Beauty* (1975) and *Jerusalem: Song of Songs* (1981).

Ursa Major and Ursa Minor *see:* Big and Little Dippers.

Ursulines, Roman Catholic religious order of women, the first devoted exclusively to the education of girls. The order was founded in Brescia, Italy (1535), by St. Angela Merici, with St. Ursula as patron saint.
See also: Roman Catholic Church.

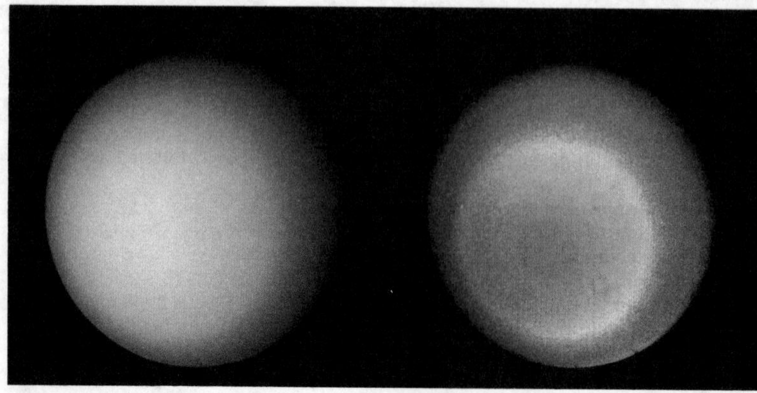

Picture of the planet Uranus made by Voyager 2 (January 17, 1986)

Uruguay

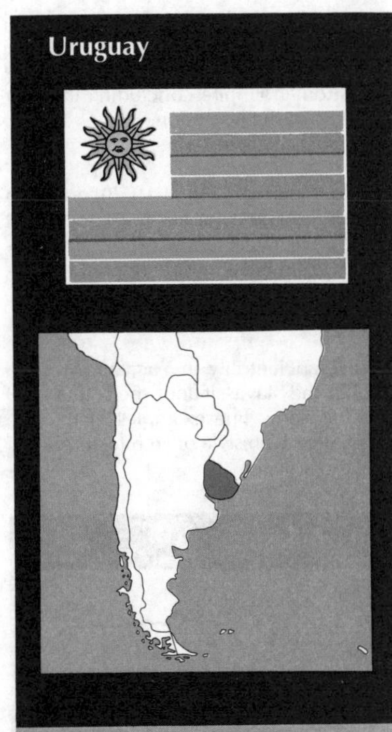

Capital:	Montevideo
Area:	68,037 sq mi (176,215 sq km)
Population:	3,058,000
Government:	republic
Independent:	1828
GNP:	U.S.$7,430,000,000
Per capita:	U.S.$2,470

Uruguay, officially the Oriental Republic of Uruguay. Covering 72,172 sq mi (186,925 sq km), which makes it the smallest republic in South America, Uruguay is bordered by Brazil to the north and northeast, the Atlantic Ocean to the east, Argentina to the west, and the Rio de la Plata to the south. The capital and chief port is Montevideo, where about 40% of the people live.

Land and People. Uruguay is a country of rolling grasslands and low hills, fringed by sands, lagoons, and bays. In the south, the Rio de la Plata estuary forms an alluvial plain called the Banda Oriental. From the narrow coastal plain the land rises gently to the Cuchilla Grande and other highlands, reaching their highest point in the Sierra de las Animas at 1,644 ft (501 m). Uruguay has a pleasantly mild climate. The people are mostly of Spanish and Italian descent with some 300,000 mestizos, persons of mixed European and Native American descent, forming a significant minority. Spanish is widely spoken, and most people are Roman Catholic.

Economy. The economy of Uruguay is based on cattle and sheep raising with meat, wool, and hides providing 80% of the country's exports. Wheat, oats, flax, oilseeds, grapes, fruit, and sugarbeets are grown. Meat packing and tanning are the chief industries. There are important fisheries, but few mineral resources.

History. The region was visited by the Spanish in 1516 and settled by them in 1624. Resisting Portuguese incursions, they founded Montevideo in 1726. José Artigas led the independence movement from 1810 to 1820. Uruguay was then occupied by Brazil for several years, but finally expelled the invaders and became independent in 1828. A period of prolonged political instability was followed, in the early 20th century, by government under José Battle y Ordóñez. His economic and social reforms made Uruguay one of the most developed Latin American countries with a comprehensive social welfare system and advanced labor legislation. Labor unrest and the terrorism of the leftist Tupamaro guerrillas in the late 1960s led to a military takeover in 1973. Repression in the decade following was widespread, but eventually gave way to a return to civilian government in 1985.

Cattle in Uruguay

Uruguay River, southern South American river. Originating in southern Brazil, it flows for 1,000 mi (1,600 km) first west and then south before finally emptying into the Rio de la Plata, a huge estuary on the Atlantic coast. It forms part of the Argentine-Brazil border and all of the Argentine-Uruguay border.

USO *see:* United Service Organizations.

USSR *see:* Union of Soviet Socialist Republics.

Utah

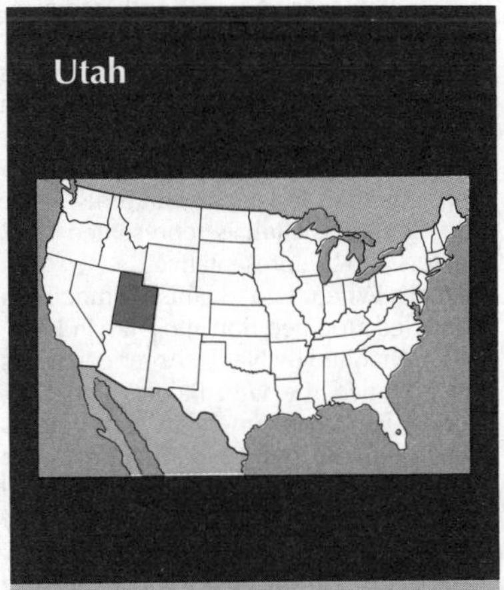

Capital:	Salt Lake City
Statehood:	Jan. 4, 1896 (45th state)
Familiar name:	Beehive State
Area:	84,899 sq mi (219,889 sq km); ranks 11th
Population:	1,727,784 (1990); ranks 35th
Elevation:	Highest—13,528 ft (4,123 m), Kings Peak; Lowest—2,000 ft (610 m), Beaverdam Creek
Motto:	Industry
Flower:	Sego lily
Bird:	Sea gull
Tree:	Blue spruce
Song:	"Utah, We Love Thee"

Utah, state in the Rocky Mountain region of the western United States bordered by Utah to the north, Wyoming to the northeast, Colorado to the east, Arizona to the south, and Nevada to the west.

Land and climate. Utah has three main land regions. The state's northeast corner is part of the Rocky Mountains, primarily the Uinta and Wasatch ranges. Eastern and southern Utah lie in the Colorado Plateau region, where rivers have cut hundreds of deep canyons and erosion has created spectacular land formations.

The Basin and Range Region of western Utah, one of the nation's driest areas, has dry plains and the broad, barren salt flats of the Great Salt Desert. The Colorado and the Green are the state's chief rivers. Great Salt Lake, the largest natural lake west of the Mississippi River, is saltier than the ocean; only the Dead Sea is saltier. Deserts cover about a third of the state and forests another third. Utah has cold winters and warm summers.

Principal cities are Salt Lake City, Provo, and West Valley City.

Economy. Manufacturing and service industries are the economy's mainstays, and Utah is a leading mining state. Chief manufactured goods are machinery, transportation equipment, processed foods, electrical equipment, and fabricated metals. Chief mining products are oil, coal, natural gas, uranium, copper, gold, magnesium, and natural salts. Agriculture is less important than in the past. Chief farm products are beef and dairy cattle, turkeys, hay, wheat, barley, corn, apples and other fruits, potatoes, and greenhouse and nursery products.

Government. Utah's constitution was adopted in 1895. The governor serves a 4-year term. The state legislature consists of 29 senators serving 4-year terms and 75 representatives serving 2-year terms. In the U.S. Congress, Utah is represented by 2 senators and 3 representatives.

History. When two Spanish Franciscan monks led an expedition into Utah in 1776, it was inhabited by Native American tribes that included the Ute, Paiute, and Shoshone. European-American fur traders soon followed, but no permanent white settlement occurred until the Mormons, led by Brigham Young, arrived at present-day Salt Lake City in 1847. The Mormons, members of the Church of Jesus Christ of Latter-Day Saints, sought refuge from religious persecution. In 1848, the United States acquired Utah as part of the settlement of the Mexican War. Utah applied for statehood as the state of Deseret in 1849, but Congress refused, instead creating the Utah Territory (which was larger than present-day Utah). In the 1850s and 1860s, fighting—including the Black Hawk War—erupted between Mormons and the Native Americans they displaced. The first transcontinental railroad, completed at Promontory Point, Utah, in 1869, brought new settlers. Utah won statehood in 1896, after clashes between Mormons and U.S. authorities, especially over the practice of polygamy, which the Mormons discontinued in 1890. Utah was hit hard by the Great Depression, but World War II renewed demands for its mining and manufacturing. Industry's importance grew in the 1950s and 1960s, as did the rise of tourism. In recent years, Utah has sought new businesses to avoid too much dependence on oil and mining. It also has worked to clean up pollution and protect its deserts and other land and water resources.

Ute, Native American tribe speaking a Shoshonean language and having a nomadic culture common in the Western plains, particularly Utah, Colorado, and New Mexico. Originally peaceful hunter-gatherers, they became marauders and buffalo hunters after obtaining Spanish horses in the 1800s. Some 4,000 now live in Colorado and Utah.

Uterus, or womb, female reproductive organ that is specialized for implantation of the fertilized egg and development of the embryo and fetus during pregnancy. The regular turnover of its lining under the influence of estrogen and progesterone is responsible for menstruation.
See also: Reproduction.

U Thant *see:* Thant, U.

Utica (pop. 75,632), industrial city of central New York State and the seat of Oneida County. Lying in the Mohawk River Valley, Utica is an important terminal on the New York State Barge Canal System. Its factories turn out electrical tools and machinery, textiles, metal products, foodstuffs, paper products, and clothing. The city is also an important market for the surrounding farm region.

Utica, ancient Phoenician colony on the coast of North Africa on the Mediterranean Sea. Founded about 1100 B.C., it was an important port and helped give the Phoenicians control over sea trade on the Mediterranean. A rival of its neighbor Carthage, Utica sided with Rome against Carthage in the Third Punic War (149-146 B.C.). With the Roman victory and the destruction of Carthage, Utica became the capital of the province. It fell to the Vandals (A.D.439), was recaptured by the Byzantine Empire (534), and destroyed by the Arabs (c.700).

Utilitarianism, theory of ethics that holds that the rightness or wrongness of an action is determined by the happiness its consequences produce. The theory dates from the 18th-century thinker Jeremy Bentham, who believed that actions are motivated by pleasure and pain and that happiness can be assessed by the quantity of pleasure. His follower John Stuart Mill later argued in *Utilitarianism* (1863) that some pleasures should be sought for their intrinisic quality. He interpreted the principles of utilitarianism as a basis for the struggle for political and social reforms.
See also: Bentham, Jeremy; Mill, John Stuart.

Utopia, term used to denote any imaginary ideal state. Based on the Greek words meaning "no place," it was coined by Sir Thomas More as the title of his *Utopia* (1516), in which he described a just society free of internal strife.

Utrecht (pop. 235,700), city in the central Netherlands. Built on the site of a Roman fort, it was during its early history the residence of several German emperors. Until the 15th century, it was the region's most important cultural and industrial center, a role eventually taken over by Amsterdam. In 1579, representatives from the northern provinces met in Utrecht and signed the Union of Utrecht, uniting them against Spain and setting up the eventual formation of what is now the Netherlands. Today Utrecht is an important cultural center and the site of many historical buildings, medieval churches, museums, and universities. It is also the headquarters of the Netherland's rail network. Chief industries include construction and metalworking.
See also: Netherlands.

Utrecht, Peace of (1713-14), series of treaties among England, France, the Netherlands, Portugal, Prussia, Spain, and the Holy Roman Empire concluding the War of the Spanish Succession.
See also: Succession wars.

Utrillo, Maurice (1883-1955), French painter best known for his Paris street scenes. His finest works capture in modified cubism the atmosphere of old Montmartre, as in *Sacré Coeur de Montmartre* (1937).

Uxmal, ancient city in Yucatán, Mexico. Built by the Mayas, it flourished c.600-900 and has some fine examples of the late classical Mayan style of architecture.
See also: Mexico

Uzbekistan

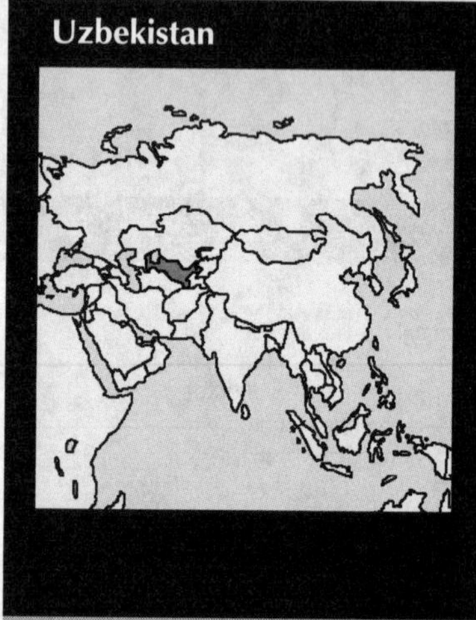

Capital:	Tashkent
Area:	172,740 sq mi (447,400 sq km)
Population:	21,285,000
Government:	republic
Independent:	1991
GNP:	U.S.$18,377,000,000
Per capita:	U.S. $860

Uzbekistan, independent country in central Asia, surrounded by Kazakhstan, Kirghizstan, Tajikistan, Afghanistan, and Turkmenistan. The capital is Tashkent. The inhabitants are mostly Uzbeks, an Islamic people. Russians, Tartars, Kazakhs, and Tajiks are minorities. Before the 4th century, it was a province of the Persian Empire. Control of the region then shifted to the Arabs and to other groups, including the Turks, until it finally fell to the Russians toward the end of the 19th century. In 1991 the country gained independence. Since then the government has pursued a policy to liberalize the economy. Farming (especially cotton, rice, and fruit), horse breeding, and cattle raising are its chief industries. This country also has rich deposits of coal and oil.
See also: Union of Soviet Socialist Republics.

V

V, 22nd letter in the English alphabet, corresponding with the Semitic letter *waw*, meaning "hook," represented by a tent-hook symbol probably derived from an ancient Egyptian symbol for a pole support. The Greeks altered it to *Y*, and as the 20th letter of the Roman alphabet it became a *V*, representing both *V*, and *U* sounds. The use of *V* for the *V* sound dates from the Middle Ages, though the old confusion persisted longer. *V* represents 5 in Roman numerals, and serves as an abbreviation for words including *vanadium, verb, versus,* and *volt.*

Vaccination, method of inducing immunity to infectious disease due to bacteria or virus.Early methods of inducing immunity consisted of the deliberate innoculation of material from a mild case. The vaccinated body forms antibodies and is able to produce large quantities of them rapidly thereafter. This gives protection equivalent to that induced by an attack of the disease. It is occasionally followed by a reaction resembling a mild form of the disease, rarely by the serious manifestations. Persons on steroids, with immunity disorders, or eczema may suffer severe reactions and should generally not receive vaccinations.
See also: Immunity.

Vacuum, region of space devoid of matter. Such a region will neither conduct heat nor transmit sound waves. Because all materials that surround a space have a definite vapor pressure, a perfect vacuum is an impossibility and the term is usually used to denote merely a space containing air or other gas at very low pressure.

Vacuum cleaner, electric appliance that cleans dirt from surfaces such as carpets, rugs, and bare floors by suction. The first vacuum cleaning machines were developed about 1900 by several different inventors.

Vacuum tube, glass or metal envelope that controls electronic currents that are necessary to operate electronic equipment like radios, televisions, and computers. It gets its name from the fact that almost all air is removed from the tube for it to work. Between 1920 and 1950, all electrical equipment used vacuum tubes. They have now been replaced by a newer device, the transistor, which is smaller and more reliable and consumes less power.

Vaduz (pop. 4,900), capital of Liechtenstein, a principality in the Alps between Switzerland and Austria. Many medieval buildings still stand. Within walking distance of the picturesque town is the famous castle of the Liechtenstein princes.

Vagina, female reproductive organ consisting of a tubeshaped canal leading from the external genital orifice to the uterus. It measures 4 in (10 cm). The muscular walls, which are covered with a mucous membrane, fall together to give the vagina a slitlike appearance. During sexual intercourse, the male's penis is inserted into the vagina. During birth the vagina serves as the passage through which the baby leaves the mother's body.
See also: Reproduction.

Vaginitis, inflammation of the vagina, occurring particulary in women of childbearing age. Under normal circumstances, balanced quantities of various bacteria, fungi, and protozoa are present in the vagina. When the balance of these organisms is disrupted and larger amounts of organisms are allowed to reproduce at larger and faster rates, vaginitis occurs. Vaginitis can be triggered by pregnancy, lack of sleep, and poor health and diet. Common symptoms include swelling, itching, and vaginal discharge.

Valence, ability of an atom to form compounds, expressed as the number of electrons an element gives up or accepts from other elements. The meaning of the term has undergone several changes over the past century. One of the first definitions of valence referred to the number of hydrogen atoms with which an atom of a different element could combine. The term then came to encompass the bonding capabilities of ionized (electrically charged) atoms.
See also: Bond, Chemical.

Valencia (pop. 738,600), third-largest Spanish city, in eastern Spain on the Turia River. A Roman settlement (138 B.C.), it came under the rule of the Moors (750-1238). Today it is a commercial and industrial center.

Valens (A.D. 328-378), Roman emperor from 364 to 378. He was actually co-emperor, ruling the eastern part, while his brother Valentinian ruled the western part. During his reign the Visigoths, a tribe living along the empire's northern borders, rebelled against the Romans. The Visigoths met and defeated the Romans in the battle of Adrianople. Valens was killed during the fighting.
See also: Rome, Ancient.

Valentine, Saint (d.A.D. 270), Roman martyred priest. His traditional association with love probably reflects the near-coincidence of his feast day (Feb. 14) with the ancient Roman fertility festival of Lupercalia (held Feb. 15). The practice of sending Valentine cards dates from the 19th century.

Valentinian I (A.D. 321-375), Roman emperor who ruled 364-375 in conjunction with his younger brother Valens. Valentinian succeeded the Emperor Jovian and appointed his brother to rule the eastern part of the empire while he ruled the west. During his reign, he subdued the Germanic tribes threatening the western provinces and built fortifications along the Rhine.
See also: Rome, Ancient.

Valentinian III (A.D. 419-455), Roman emperor 425-455. Though declared emperor at the age of 6; he never ruled the empire in his own right, since political power was wielded in his youth by his mother, Galla Placidia, and later by the patrician Flavius Aëtius. The invasion of the Vandals and Huns occurred during his reign. Hostilities between Valentinian and Aëtius led to the murder of Aëtius by Valentinian (454), who was himself murdered the following year.
See also: Rome, Ancient.

Valentino, Rudolph (Rodolfo d'Antonguolla; 1895-1926), Italian-born U.S. film star, one of the greatest romantic male stars of the silent film era. Valentino's films included *The Four Horsemen of the Apocalypse* (1921), *The Sheik* (1921), and *Blood and Sand* (1922).

Valera, Eamon de *see:* De Valera, Eamon.

Valerian (d.A.D. 269), Roman emperor 253-60. In 257 he campaigned against the Persians, but was defeated and captured (260) by the Persian emperor, Shapur I, and died in captivity.
See also: Rome, Ancient.

Valéry, Paul (1871-1945), French poet, essayist, and critic. His early verse, *Album de Vers Anciens* (1920), was influenced by Stéphane Mallarmé. His best-known works are *La Jeune Parque* (1917) and *Le Cimetière Marin* (1920). He wrote on poetry in *Monsieur Tetse* (1896) and also on philosophical and critical themes.

Valhalla, in Scandinavian mythology, paradise hall of the dead where slain warriors live under the leadership of the god Odin. Valhalla is depicted as a magnificent palace built of battle shields, spears, and gold. The chosen heroes are wounded in battle daily and are restored each evening, until led by Odin to battle the giants at the time of Ragnarok, or Doomsday.
See also: Mythology.

Valkyrie, in Scandinavian mythology, warriorlike maidens sent by Odin to escort dead heroes to Valhalla. The armored

Plaza del Caudillo, the center of Valencia, Spain

Valkyries rode on horseback to the battlefields to choose slain warriors worthy of afterlife. Valkyries were often portents of war in a supernatural or a human form who had the power to cause death.
See also: Mythology.

Valle, José Cecilio Del (1780-1834), Guatemalan political leader and author of the Central American Declaration of Independence (1821). Valle led Guatemala's fight for independence from Spain, and when the country was annexed by Mexico (1822), he was imprisoned. Although elected vice president of the Central American Confederation (1823), Valle declined to serve.
See also: Guatemala.

Valletta (pop. 14,200), seaport capital of Malta, on the northeastern coast of the island. A commercial and cultural center, Valletta is the site of the Royal Malta Library, the Royal University of Malta, and the Manoel Theatre.
See also: Malta.

Valley, long, narrow depression in the earth's surface, usually formed by glacier or river erosion. Young valleys are narrow, steep-sided, and V-shaped; mature valleys are broader, with gentler slopes. Rift valleys are the result of collapse between faults. A hanging valley, of glacial origin, is a side valley whose floor is considerably higher than that of the main valley.

Valley Forge, area in Pennsylvania about 21 mi (34 km) north of Philadelphia where George Washington and his Revolutionary troops camped during the winter of 1777-78, often called "The Winter of Despair." Washington had suffered defeats at Brandywine and Germantown, Pa., and Philadelphia was under British control. The Continental Congress was unable to keep his troops supplied, and about 10,000 men endured cold and near starvation. Although publicly criticized for holding this position, Washington remained steadfast, and with Baron von Steuben, a Prussian military expert, reorganized the Continental Army. The soldiers were taught new drills and troop formations, and by winter's end the army was highly disciplined. Valley Forge National Historic Park now covers the campsite.
See also: Revolutionary War in America.

Valley of the Kings

Valley of the Kings, or Valley of the Tombs of Kings, narrow canyon on the west bank of the Nile near Thebes, Egypt. It is the site of over 60 ancient tombs, including the burial places of most of the Pharaohs of the 18th, 19th, and 20th dynasties (1550-1085 B.C.). Among the tombs are those of Tutankhamen, Set I, Thutmose III, Ramses II, Ramses III, and Queen Hatshepsut.
See also: Egypt, Ancient.

Valois, royal house of France that ruled 1328-1589. The first Valois king was Philip VI; under his rule and that of his descendants, the Valois region of France was a Duchy held by family members. The rule of the Valois Dynasty survived the Hundred Years War (1337-1453), and other conflicts. With the death of Henry III (1589), the crown passed to the house of Bourbon.
See also: France.

Valparaíso (pop. 266,900), seaport city in central Chile, capital of Valparaíso province. The city, founded in 1536, lies on the Pacific Ocean about 70 mi (110 km) northwest of Santiago. It is a major center for manufacture. Chief products include chemicals, textiles, tobacco, sugar and machinery.

Value added by manufacture, statistical measurement of the gain in value of raw materials after being processed into a finished commodity. This is computed by subtracting the overall cost of manufacture—including materials, supplies, storage, fuel, and labor—from the value of the finished product.

Value-added tax (VAT), tax on the value added to goods or services at each stage in their production and distribution. It originated in France in 1954 and was later extended throughout the European Economic Ccommunity; it has been considered at various times in the United States. In effect, VAT is a sales tax computed on the difference between what a producer pays for a raw material or semi-finished product and what he or she sells it for. The cost of the tax is borne ultimately by consumers. It is a regressive tax because it bears most heavily on low-income people, who spend more and save less than those with high incomes. For government, VAT has the advantage of being broader than most sales taxes and thus producing large revenues even at low rates. The tax is virtually self-enforcing; producers who make tax payments submit claims for credit for the taxes included in their suppliers' prices, and this tends to discourage nonpayment along the line.
See also: Taxation.

Valve, mechanical device that, by opening and closing, enables the flow of fluid in a pipe or other vessel to be controlled. Common valve types are generally named after the shape or mode of operation of the movable element—cone, or needle, valve; gate valve; globe valve; poppet valve; and rotary plug cock. In the butterfly valve a disk pivots on one of its diameters. Self-acting valves include safety valves, usually spring-loaded and designed to open at a predetermined pressure; nonreturn valves,

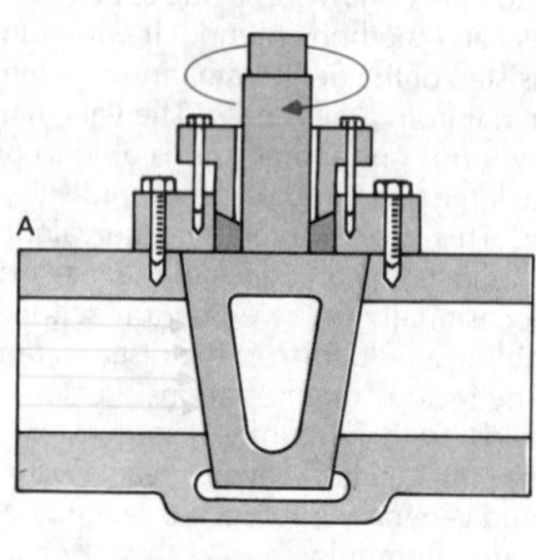

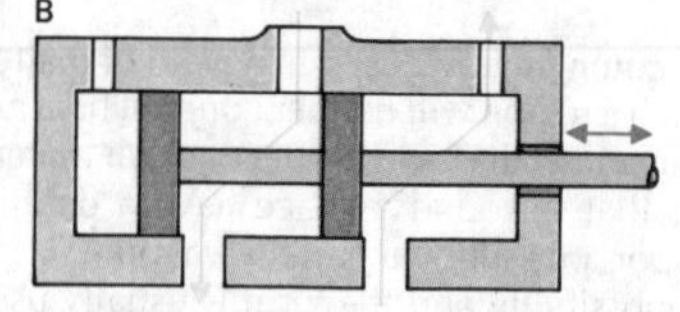

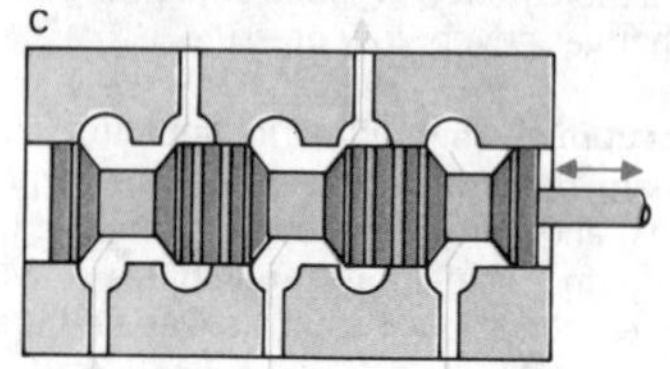

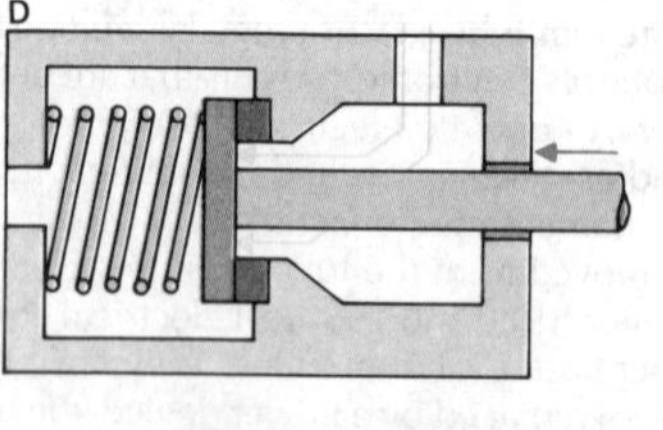

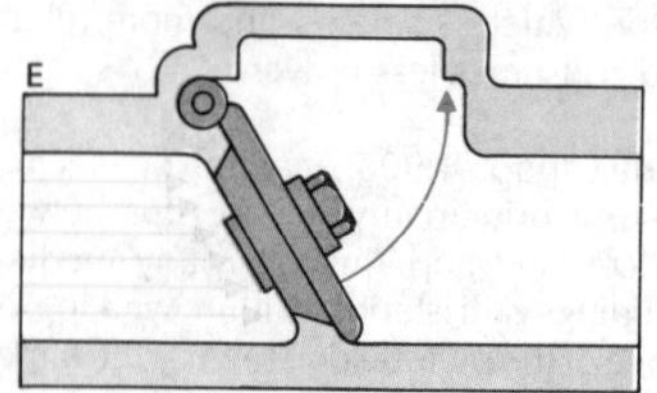

Types of valves :
A. plug valve
B. slide valve
C. spool valve
D. poppet valve
E. check valve

which permit flow in one direction only; and float-operated valves, set to shut off a feeder pipe before a container overflows.

Vampire, in folklore, spirit of the dead that leaves its grave at night to suck the blood of living persons. A victim who dies must be decapitated or buried with a stake through his or her heart, to keep from becoming a vampire.
See also: Dracula.

Vampire bat, South and Central American bat (genera *Desmodus* and *Diphylla*) that feeds on the blood of larger mammals and birds; the only parasitic mammal. The bat cuts a slit with its teeth and laps blood from the wound; anticoagulants in its saliva ensure a constant flow.

Vanadium, chemical element, symbol V; for physical constants see Periodic Table. Vanadium was discovered by A.M. del Rio in 1801. It occurs in the minerals carnotite, roscoelite, vanadinite, and patronite. It is obtained commercially from patronite, a sulfide. The element is prepared by reduction of the trichloride with magnesium. Vanadium is a bright white, soft, ductile metal, resistant to corrosion. It has a low thermal neutron cross section. It is used to bond titanium to steel. Vanadium and its compounds are used in special steels and ceramics and as catalysts and superconductive magnets. Vanadium and its compounds are toxic.

Van Allen, James Alfred (1914-), U.S. physicist and inventor who discovered two zones of radiation surrounding the earth (1958). This led to new knowledge of the effects of cosmic radiation on the earth. Van Allen developed the research rocket Aerobee. He was also instrumental in organizing the International Geophysical Year (1957-58), a program promoting worldwide cooperation in research.

Van Allen belts, 2 belts of high-energy charged particles, mainly protons and electrons, surrounding the earth, named for U.S. physicist James Van Allen, who discovered them in 1958. They extend from a few hundred to about 40,000 mi (65,000 km) above the earth's surface and radiate intensely enough that astronauts must be specially protected from them. The mechanisms for their existence are similar to those involved in the production of the aurora borealis.
See also: Radiation; Van Allen, James Alfred.

Van Buren, Martin (1782-1862), eighth president of the United States. Van Buren was a shrewd judge of people and affairs and a consummate politician who virtually created the Democratic party and made Andrew Jackson president. Van Buren's skill in political maneuvering and in using patronage and the power of the press earned him the nickname "The Little Magician" and "The Fox of Kinderhook." But what he could do for others, he could not do as well for himself. His presidency did not lack achievement, but his do-nothing attitude in the face of the United States' first major depression cost him reelection.

Early life. With a rudimentary education, Van Buren studied law from an early age under a local lawyer. He was admitted to the bar in 1803. He began a successful legal career in Kinderhook, N.Y., entering local politics at about the same time. In 1807, he married Hannah Hoes; the couple had 4 sons. She died in 1819; he never remarried.

Politics. Van Buren served as surrogate of Columbia County, N.Y., then as New York senator and attorney general. His industry and political astuteness soon won him influence within the Republican Party. In 1821, he was elected to the U.S. Senate.

Van Buren, who stood for state's rights and opposed a strong central government, began to bring together other powerful Republicans who shared his sentiments. These "new" Republicans became the Democratic Party.

In 1828, the year Jackson won the presidency, Van Buren was elected governor of New York. But within a few months, he resigned to become Jackson's secretary of state (1829-31). He served Jackson more as a political manager than as a cabinet member and became one of the most powerful men in Washington. He drafted Jackson's speeches, smoothed his relations with Congress, and continued to build up the Democratic Party.

When Jackson won reelection in 1832, Van Buren was his running mate. In 1836, Jackson supported Van Buren for the presidency as his "hand-picked" successor; Van Buren defeated Whig candidate William Henry Harrison.

President. Within days of Van Buren's inauguration, the Panic of 1837 broke. Banks and business failed, specie payments were suspended, and rents and fuel and food prices soared. The Panic had been caused by unchecked speculation in western lands, manufacturing, transportation, and banking. A firm hand was needed to control it, but Van Buren, who believed that "the less government interferes with private pursuits the better for the general prosperity," did almost nothing. Inevitably, he was blamed for the depression, as well as for the costly war against the Seminoles in Florida. He also antagonized the South by opposing the annexation of Texas. Van Buren was nominated for reelection in 1840, but had little chance of winning. The rough campaign tactics used to elect Jackson were used against Van Buren, and he lost to William Henry Harrison.

Retirement. Van Buren retired to his country estate at Kinderhook. He ran for president as a Democrat in 1844 but failed to win nomination; he ran again in 1848 on the Free-Soil ticket and lost. He died on July 24, 1862.

Martin Van Buren

8th president of the United States

Born:	Kinderhook, N.Y.; Dec. 5, 1782.
Term:	Mar. 1837-Mar. 1841.
Vice president:	Richard M. Johnson.
Political party:	Democratic.
Spouse:	Hannah Hoes.
Children:	4.
Died:	Kinderhook, N.Y.; July 24, 1862.

Vance, Cyrus (1917-), U.S. public official. A Wall Street lawyer, he was secretary of the army (1962-63) and deputy secretary of defense (1964-67). An experienced diplomatic troubleshooter, he served as President Jimmy Carter's secretary of state (1977-80), resigning in protest over the abortive attempt to rescue U.S. diplomatic hostages in Iran.

Vancouver (pop. 42,800), city in southwestern Washington, seat of Clark County. Founded by the Hudson's Bay Company as a trading fort (1825), the city is a port on the Columbia River. Industries include lumber, shipping, and paper. Vancouver is the site of Clark College.
See also: Washington.

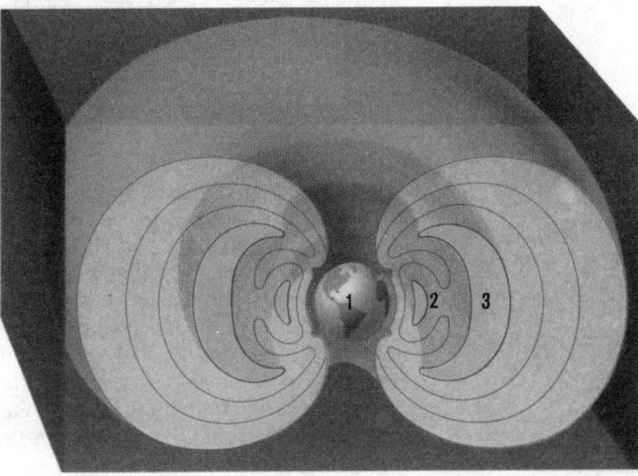

Model of the magnetosphere with the earth (1) and the two Van Allen belts (2, 3)

Vancouver

Vancouver (pop. 431,100), largest city in British Columbia and third-largest in Canada, located on the Burrard Inlet, Strait of Georgia. Originally known as Granville, in 1886 it was renamed for the English explorer George Vancouver. It is an important Pacific port and a major manufacturing center for wood, paper, iron, steel, and chemical products. Other industries are shipbuilding, oil refining, and fish processing. After becoming the terminus of the trans-Canada railroad (1886), it rapidly expanded.
See also: British Columbia.

Vancouver, George (1757-98), English explorer. He took part in Captain Cook's voyages (1772-80) and in 1791-94 led an expedition that explored the Pacific and surveyed the American coast from San Luis Obispo, Calif., to British Columbia. He made surveys of Vancouver Island and the Strait of Georgia, visited Cook's Inlet, Alaska, and failed to find a Northwest Passage. The city of Vancouver, in British Columbia, Canada, was named after him in 1886.

Vancouver Island, largest island on the Pacific North American Coast, off southwestern British Columbia, Canada. Vancouver is separated from mainland Canada by a series of straits. The island is the southernmost end of a partially sunken mountain range called the Vancouver Range. It has a particularly mild climate due to the flow of the Japan Current. The mountain slopes are covered with extensive cedar and fir forests. Major industries include lumber, farming, and tourism. Victoria, Vancouver Island's largest city, is the capital of British Columbia.

Vandals, ancient Germanic people. They gradually migrated from south of the Baltic to Pannonia and Dacia. In the 5th century they invaded the Roman Empire, ravaging Gaul and Spain. Under Genseric they established a strong Vandal kingdom in northern Africa (429) that extended to Sicily, and in 455 they sacked Rome. The Vandals were finally defeated by the Byzantine Belisarius, after which they disappeared as a unified people.

Van de Graaff, Robert Jemison (1901-67), U.S. physicist and inventor of the electrostatic generator, used in nuclear research. While a student at the Sorbonne, Van de Graaff attended lectures given by Marie Curie. He formed the idea for his generator when he realized that the study of atomic behavior requires a source of energetic beams of subatomic particles. In 1946 he became a founder of the High Voltage Engineering Corporation (HVEC).

Van de Graaff generator, or electrostatic generator, device for generating a high voltage charge, important in the study of nuclear power. Invented in the 1930s by Robert Van de Graaff, the machine operates by carrying electrical charges from a collection of high-voltage points on a moving belt into a hollow metal casing. A metallic brush transports the charge to the surface of the casing, and as the charge accumulates, the voltage increases.
See also: Particle accelerator; Van de Graaff, Robert Jemison.

Vanderbilt, Cornelius (1794-1877), U.S. transportation mogul. Known as Commodore, he began with a ferry service that grew into an international steamship business. In the 1860s, he purchased a number of small eastern railroads. His group dominated the Northeast by the 1870s and controlled the New York-Chicago route. He established Vanderbilt University at Nashville, Tenn.

Van der Goes, Hugo (1440?-82), Flemish painter of religious subjects. He was influenced by Jan van Eyck and Rogier van der Weyden. Among his works are the *Portinari Altarpiece* (c.1476) and *Death of the Virgin* (c.1480).

Van der Meer, Simon (1925-), Dutch physicist who shared the 1984 Nobel Prize for physics with Carlo Rubia for their leading roles in planning and executing the experiments, reported in 1983, that demonstrated the existence of the elementary particles called intermediate vector bosons.
See also: Boson; Physics.

Van der Waals, Johannes Diderik (1837-1923), Dutch physicist who investigated the properties of real gases. Noting that the kinetic theory of gases assumed that the molecules had neither size nor interactive forces between them, in 1873 he proposed **Van der Waals' equation**, in which allowance is made for both these factors. The weak attractive forces between molecules are therefore named Van der Waals forces. He received the 1910 Nobel Prize for physics.
See also: Physics.

Van der Weyden, Rogier (1399?-1464), Flemish painter of religious subjects. He was probably influenced by Robert Campin and Jan van Eyck. He masterfully captured intangible emotion, while also distancing the viewer, in such works as *The Descent from the Cross* (c.1435).

Van Devanter, Willis (1859-1941), associate justice of the U.S. Supreme Court (1911-37). His opinions were staunchly conservative, and he was opposed to social welfare legislation and the New Deal.
See also: Supreme Court of the United States.

Van Doren, Carl (1885-1950), U.S. author, educator, and literary critic. Van Doren taught at Columbia University (1911-30) and was an editor of the *Cambridge History of American Literature* (1917-21); *The Nation* (1919-22); and *Century Magazine* (1922-25). He is best known for his biographies, including *Swift* (1930), *Sinclair Lewis* (1933), and *Jane Mecom* (1950). He was awarded the Pulitzer Prize in 1939 for his biography *Benjamin Franklin* (1938).

Van Doren, Mark (1894-1972), U.S. poet and critic. His *Collected Poems* (1939) earned him the Pulitzer Prize in 1940. As a critic, Van Doren began his career with a study of Henry David Thoreau in 1916. His major critical writings appear in *Private Reader* (1942) and *The Happy Critic* (1961). Van Doren was a renowned professor of English at Columbia University (1920-59), where his students included John Berryman and Lionel Trilling. He also wrote plays, novels, and short stories.

Van Dyck, Sir Anthony (1599-1641), Flemish baroque portrait and religious painter. He was a pupil of Peter Paul Rubens, and his portrait style, influenced by Venetian art, was one of elegantly posed figures and rich but refined color and handling, particularly of materials. He painted Italian and English nobility and was court painter from 1632 to Charles I of England.
See also: Baroque.

Van Eyck, Jan (1390-1441), Flemish painter. The first leading artist from the Netherlands, he collaborated with his older brother, Hubert (c.1370-1426), on the Ghent altarpiece. Completed in 1432, it comprises more than 250 figures in 20 panels. Van Eyck's other important works include a number of portraits, such as *Giovanni Arnolfini and His Bride* (1434). All are remarkable for realistic, closely observed details. He was the first painter to develop effects of richness, brilliance, and intensity in oil paint.

Van Gogh, Vincent (1853-90), Dutch postimpressionist painter. His early, dark-toned work, done in the Netherlands, fo-

Portrait of the art dealer Père Tanguy by Vincent van Gogh

cuses on peasant life. Later (1886-88), in Paris, he met Paul Gauguin and Georges Seurat. In 1888 he moved to Arles, in southern France, where—among many other paintings—he produced the brilliantly colored *Sunflowers* in a direct style and the symbolic *The Night Café*, using color suggestively. After a fit of insanity, in which he cut off his left ear (1889), he painted at the asylums of St. Rémy and Auvers. In *Portrait of Dr. Gachet* (1890) he attempted to express ideas and emotion in and through paint. He committed suicide.

Vanilla, any of various tropical vines (genus *Vanilla*) of the orchid family; the term also refers to the extract made from the vine's pods and used for flavoring. The plants grow to about 50 ft (15.2 m) and bear yellow-green flowers that produce the pods, 5-10 in (13-25 cm) in length. Vanilla extract is obtained by a process of pulverization of the cured vanilla pods which are then heated in alcohol and water. Vanilla is widely used to flavor chocolate, candy, ice cream, baked goods, and beverages.

Van Leeuwenhoek, Anton *see:* Leeuwenhoek, Anton van.

Van Leyden, Lucas (1494?-1533), Dutch engraver and painter. Van Leyden's engravings are finely executed compositions without any particular central character. His engraving technique, utilizing precise cutting strokes, created depth and the illusion of light and shadow. His works include *Abraham and Isaac, Ecce Homo,* and *The Milkmaid* (all early 1500s).

Van Rensselaer, Kiliaen (1595-1643), Dutch colonizer and leading *patroon* (landowner). A member of the Dutch West India Company, he established the manor of Rensselaerswyck on the banks of the Hudson River, south of Albany.

Vanuatu, officially the Republic of Vanuatu, formerly the New Hebrides, independent republic consisting of 80 small islands, situated east of Australia and extending over some 500 mi (805 km) of the South Pacific Ocean.

Land. The overall area of the islands of Vanuatu is 5,570 sq mi (14,426 km). Espíritu Santo, the largest island, has an area of 1,542 sq mi (3,994 sq km). The capital, Vila, is on the second-largest island, Efâte. The islands are of volcanic origin and there are 6 active volcanos. The rugged mountainous interiors, densely covered with tropical rain forests, give way to narrow coastal strips where most of the islands' inhabitants live.

People. Almost all the people of Vanuatu are Melanesians. There are also small Chinese, British, and French minorities. The official languages are Bislama, English, and French.

Economy. About 70% of the people live in rural villages and pursue traditional subsistence farming. They grow coconuts and other fruits, yams, and taro; pigs are raised for food and ceremonial purposes. Local industries process copra, fish, and beef for export. Manganese has been mined since 1961, and tourism is increasing. Special tax laws have made Vanuatu a banking center and corporate haven.

History. There is evidence of human settlements on the islands as early as 1300 B.C., but the islands were not discovered by Europeans until the arrival of the Portuguese in 1606. The British and French explored the islands in the 18th century. During the 19th century, strife broke out between native inhabitants and British and French settlers. In 1906 a joint British-French condominium was established to rule the islands. In 1980, on the eve of independence, fighting broke out on Espíritu Santo where guerrillas were mounting an armed struggle for that island's secession. The fighting ended after British peacekeeping forces arrived. A 1987 hurricane caused much death and destruction.

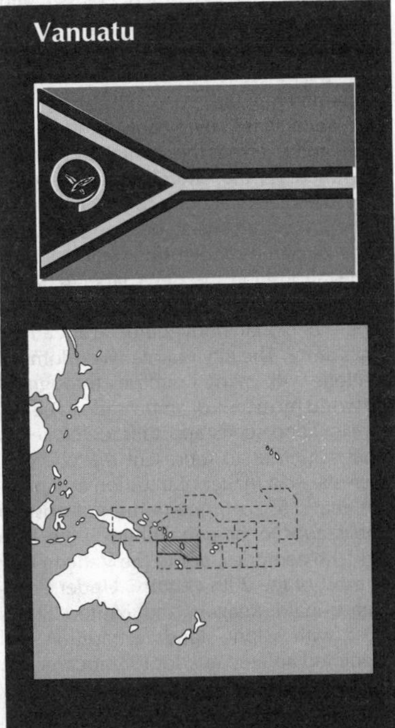

Capital:	Port Vila
Area:	4,707 sq mi (12,190 sq km)
Population:	154,000
Government:	republic
Independent:	1980
GNP:	U.S. $120,000,000
Per capita:	U.S. $820

Vanzetti, Bartolomeo *see:* Sacco-Vanzetti case.

Vapor, substance that, though present in the gaseous phase, generally exists as a liquid or solid at room temperature.
See also: Evaporation.

Varanasi (pop. 708,600), formerly Benaras, ancient city in Uttar Pradesh State, on the Ganges River in northern India. The city is of great religious import as a center for Hindu pilgrimage, with over 1,500 temples and shrines. Varanasi has miles of riverfront ghats, or stairways, from which pilgrims may bathe in the holy Ganges River before praying. Industries include textiles and brassware. Varanasi is the site of Benaras Hindu University (1916) and the Mosque of Aurangzeb.
See also: India.

Varèse, Edgard (1883-1965), French-born U.S. composer of non-traditional music and sound techniques. *Ionisation* (1931), his most famous composition, is written for numerous percussion instruments and two sirens. Other works include *Hyperprism* (1923), and *Density 21.5* (1935). After 1950 Varèse concentrated mainly on electronically produced music.

Vargas, Getúlio Dornelles (1883-1954), president of Brazil (1930-45,1951-54). He set up a "New State" (1937), strongly centralized government-promoted industrial, economic, and social development. Opposition from the army during his second term led him to commit suicide.
See also: Brazil.

Vargas Llosa, Mario (1936-), Peruvian author of novels depicting modern Peruvian social and political life. His novels include *The Time of the Hero* (1962), *The Green House* (1966), *Conversations in the Cathedral* (1969), *The War of the End of the World* (1984), *Who Killed Palomino Molero?* (1987), and *The Storyteller* (1989). Vargas Llosa was an unsuccessful candidate for the presidency of Peru in 1990.

Varicella *see:* Chickenpox.

Varicose vein, enlarged or twisting vein, usually occuring in the legs, resulting from incompetent or damaged valves in the veins. Unpleasant in appearance, they cause venous stagnation, with skin eczema

and ulcers on the inside of the ankle, hemorrhage, and edema (swelling). Treatment includes support stockings and, in more serious cases, removal through surgery.
See also: Vein.

Varnish, solution of resin that dries to form a hard, transparent film. It is widely applied to wood, metal, and masonry to improve surface properties without changing appearance. There are two main types: spirit varnishes, consisting of natural or synthetic resins dissolved in a volatile solvent such as alcohol, and oleoresinous varnishes—more resistant to heat and weather—which are mixtures of resins and drying oils dissolved in turpentine or a petroleum oil. Lacquer, the original wood varnish, is the sap of the varnish tree.
See also: Resin.

Varying hare *see:* Snowshoe hare.

Vasco Da Gama *see:* Da Gama, Vasco.

Vasectomy, sterilization procedure for men. The vas deferens are cut to prevent sperm from reaching the seminal vesicles and hence the urethra of the penis. It does not affect ejaculation.
See also: Sterilization.

Vásquez de Coronado, Francisco *see:* Coronado, Francisco Vásquez de.

Vassal *see:* Feudalism.

Vatican City, independent state, the world's smallest. It occupies 108.7 acres (44 hectares) of territory within the city of Rome, Italy. Vatican City serves as the spiritual, administrative, and political center of Roman Catholicism, and it is ruled by the pope, as head of the Roman Catholic church. It has a population of c.1,000 and its official languages are Italian and Latin. Vatican City is dominated by Saint Peter's basilica and the Vatican Palace, the world's largest residential palace. Among the city's treasures are the frescoes of the Sistine Chapel executed by Michelangelo Buonarroti as well as the paintings, sculpture, and other artifacts in the Vatican Museum collection. The Vatican Archive and Library contain many priceless manuscripts and, reputedly, the world's most extensive holdings of erotic literature, including a collection that once belonged to Benjamin Franklin.

The Vatican has its own bank, mints its own coins, and oversees the administration and investment of the church's assets worldwide. The city has no income tax and no restriction on the import or export of funds. It has its own broadcasting facilities, railroad station, and the newspaper *L'Osservatore Romano.* The Swiss Guard, the pope's personal bodyguard, are Vatican City's army. The city maintains diplomatic relations with many countries throughout the world by means of ambassadors, called nuncios, and sends apostolic delegates to other countries to represent the church's interests. As a matter of tradition and practice, the U.S. government did not post an ambassador to the papal court in the 18th and 19th centuries, nor to the Vatican City for most of the 20th century. Under President Ronald Reagan, the United States broke with a long-standing tradition and appointed an ambassador to Vatican City. The official independence of Vatican City from Italy was established in 1929 following a long period of estrangement between the papacy and Italy over the papacy's loss of its once extensive territorial holdings, known as the Papal States, on the Italian peninsula. The issue was finally resolved in the Lateran Treaty negotiated that year between Cardinal Pietro Gasparri for the papacy and the Fascist dictator Benito Mussolini.
See also: Roman Catholic Church.

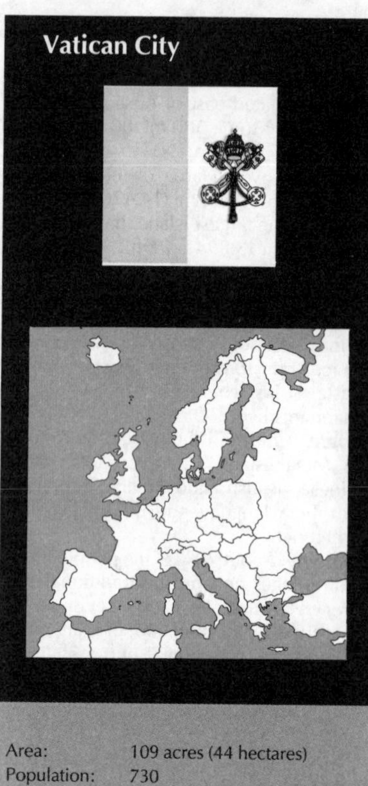

Area: 109 acres (44 hectares)
Population: 730

St. Peter's Square in Vatican City, where tens of thousands of people gather to receive the Pope's Easter blessing

Vatican Councils, the two most recent Roman Catholic ecumenical councils, held at the Vatican. Vatican Council I (1869-70), summoned by Pius IX, restated traditional dogma against materialism, rationalism, and liberalism. It also declared the pope to be infallible when, speaking *ex cathedra*, he defines a doctrine of faith or morals. Some dissenters seceded as Old Catholics. Vatican Council II (1962-65), summoned by John XXIII, aimed at renewal of the church, the updating of its organization and attitude to the modern world, and the ultimate reunion of all Christian churches. Protestant and Orthodox observers attended. Along with calling for a reform of the ministry and liturgy, including increased lay participation and use of vernacular languages, the council decreed that the bishops with the pope form a body ("collegiality") and that the Virgin Mary is "Mother of the Church."

Vatican Library, official library of the Roman Catholic Church in Vatican City. It was founded by Pope Nicholas V (r.1447-55) as a library for handwritten manuscripts. Open to scholars, the library contains about 1 million printed books and more than 70,000 manuscripts.

Vaudeville, term for variety shows deriving from Vau de Vire, a French valley and source of 15th-century songs, or from *voix de ville*, French street songs. It was applied from the 1880s to U.S. shows with musical, comic, dramatic, acrobatic, and juggling acts. Noted artists included Eddie Cantor, Will Rogers, and W. C. Fields. Vaudeville declined in the 1930s.

Vaughan Williams, Ralph (1872-1958), English composer famous for his use of traditional English folk music. The three *Norfolk Rhapsodies* (1906) were the first major works characteristic of his distinctive style. Other works include nine symphonies.

VD *see:* Venereal disease.

Veal, meat of young cattle or calves. The calves are fed on milk and the meat is drained of blood. As a result, veal is light in color and in flavor. Consumption in the United States averages about 4 1/2 lb (2 kg) per person yearly.

Veblen, Thorstein Bunde (1857-1929), U.S. economist and author. A social theorist known for his study of economic evolution and social change, Veblen produced sharp analyses of the wealthy classes. His *Theory of the Leisure Class* (1899), coined such terms as "conspicuous consumption" and "pecuniary emulation." Other works include *The Theory of Business Enterprise* (1904), a criticism of capitalism; and *The Engineers and the Price System* (1921).
See also: Economics.

Vecellio, Tiziano *see:* Titian.

Vector *see:* Force.

Vedanta (Sanskrit, "end of knowledge"), system of Hindu philosophy, based at first on the Upanishads (the final part of the Veda) and later on the Brahma Sutras, commentaries on the Upanishads, that date from the 1st century A.D. The Vedanta concern the relation of the individual (*atman*) to the Absolute (*Brahman*).
See also: Upanishads.

Vedas (Sanskrit, "knowledge"), most ancient of Indian scriptures, believed to have been inspired by God and basic to Hinduism. There are 4 *Samhitas* or collections of mantras (hymns)—the *Rig, Yajur, Sama,* and *Atharva-Veda.* The oldest may date from 1500 B.C. Vedic literature consists of the Veda itself, the *Brahmanas* and *Aranyakas*, and the Upanishads.
See also: Hinduism.

Veery (*Catharus fuscescens*), brownish bird of the thrush family, found in the northeastern United States and Canada. It is about 7 in (18 cm) long and nests in the lower branches of bushes or small trees.

Vega, or Alpha Lyrae, brightest main-sequence star in the constellation Lyra in the northern hemisphere, the fourth-brightest star in the night sky. The star is surrounded by a shell of solid particles indicating that it may be a solar system in a formative state. Vega is 26 light years away and is expected to become earth's polar star C.A.D. 14,000.
See also: Star.

Vega, Lope de (1562-1635), Spanish dramatist and poet credited with founding Spain's national drama. A prolific writer, Lope produced 426 plays of which 42 short ones survive. He also wrote narrative poetry, prose romances, and a poetical essay, *The New Art of Writing Plays* (1609), that expounded his theories of drama. His main themes were the friction between the masses and a corrupt nobility and the conflicts of honor and passion.

Vegetable, general term for the edible part of a plant. Vegetables are excellent sources of vitamins, iron, and calcium. They are sometimes grouped according to the part of the plant they represent: flower clusters (e.g. cauliflower), fruits (tomatoes), leaves (spinach), roots (carrots), seeds (peas), stems (asparagus), tubers (potatoes), and bulbs (onions).

Vegetable oil, substance obtained from the seeds of plants and the fleshy part of fruits. It consists almost entirely of fat, an important part of a healthy diet. It is used in both the production and the cooking of many foods. Soybean oil is the most commonly used vegetable oil in the United States, followed by corn, cottonseed, olive, peanut, safflower, and sunflower oil. Most margarines are made with soybean or sunflower oils as the main ingredient.

Vegetarianism, restriction of one's food to substances of vegetable origin. Vegetarianism is practiced variously for health and fitness and because of ethical or religious beliefs. A vegetarian is a person who abstains from eating meat, either keeping strictly to a diet of vegetables, grains, nuts, and fruit, or including eggs, milk, butter, and cheese. The latter is called an ovo-lacto-vegetarian.

Vein, thin-walled collapsible vessel that returns blood to the heart from the tissue capillaries. Veins contain valves that prevent back-flow, especially in the legs. Blood drains from the major veins into the inferior to superior vena cava.

Velázquez, Diego (1599-1660), Spanish painter. In 1623, he became court painter to King Philip IV of Spain. His style was influenced strongly by his Flemish contemporary, Peter Paul Rubens, and also by Italian artists of the High Renaissance. His masterpieces include *The Drunkards, Christ on the Cross,* and *The Maids of Honor.*
See also: Renaissance.

Velocity, vector quantity expressing the direction and speed of any moving object. Velocity may be uniform, in which case both speed and direction remain constant, or variable, in which case speed and/or direction change.
See also: Falling bodies, Law of.

Velvet leaf *see:* Indian mallow.

Venerable Bede, The *see:* Bede, Saint.

Venereal disease, name for infectious diseases transmitted mainly or exclusively by sexual contact. *Gonorrhea* is an acute bacterial disease that is frequently asymptomatic in females, although they may suffer mild cervicitis or urethritis. In males it may be asymptomatic also, but it usually causes a painful urethritis with urethral discharge of pus. Gonorrhea is best treated with penicillin. *Syphilis*, due to *Treponema pallidum*, a spirochete, is a disease with 2 stages. A painless genital ulcer, or chancre, develops in the weeks after contact. Secondary syphilis, starting weeks or months after infection, involves fever, malaise, and a characteristic rash, as well as organ disease (hepatitis, meningitis). If the disease is treated with a full course of penicillin in the early stages, its progression is prevented. Tertiary syphilis takes several forms. Gummas—chronic rubbery tumors affecting skin, epithelium, bone, or internal organs—may develop. Tertiary syphilis causes heart disease. Syphilis of the nervous system may cause tabes dorsalis, primary eye disease, chronic meningitis, or paralysis, with mental disturbance, personality change, failure of judgment, and muscular weakness. Penicillin may only partially reverse late syphilis. Other venereal diseases include Reiter's disease (in males only), genital trichomoniasis, thrush, *Herpes simplex* virus, and "non-specific urethritis." Tropical venereal diseases include chancroid, lymphogranuloma venereum, and granuloma inguinale.

Diego Velázquez's Portrait of Felipe Prospero *(c.1659)*

Venezuela, republic in northern South America. Covering an area of 352,134 sq mi (912,050 sq km), Venezuela extends along the Caribbean coast from Colombia in the west and southwest to Guyana in the east. It is bordered by Brazil to the south and the Caribbean Sea in the north. The capital is Caracas.

Land. Venezuela may be divided into 4 contrasting geographical regions: the Venezuelan Highlands in the west and north; the coastal lowlands; the great central plain called the Llanos, dominated by the Orinoco River; and the Guiana Highlands. The Venezuelan Highlands are an extension of the Andes. Entering the country in the southwest, they contain Venezuela's highest mountains, including Pico Bolivár rising to 16,411 ft (5,002 m) to dominate the Sierra Nevada de Mérida. The central highlands with their fertile valleys form the most important part of the country and contain several large cities, including the capital, Caracas. The coastal lowlands, almost completely enclosed by mountains and centered on swamp-fringed

Lope de Vega

Caracas, Venezuela

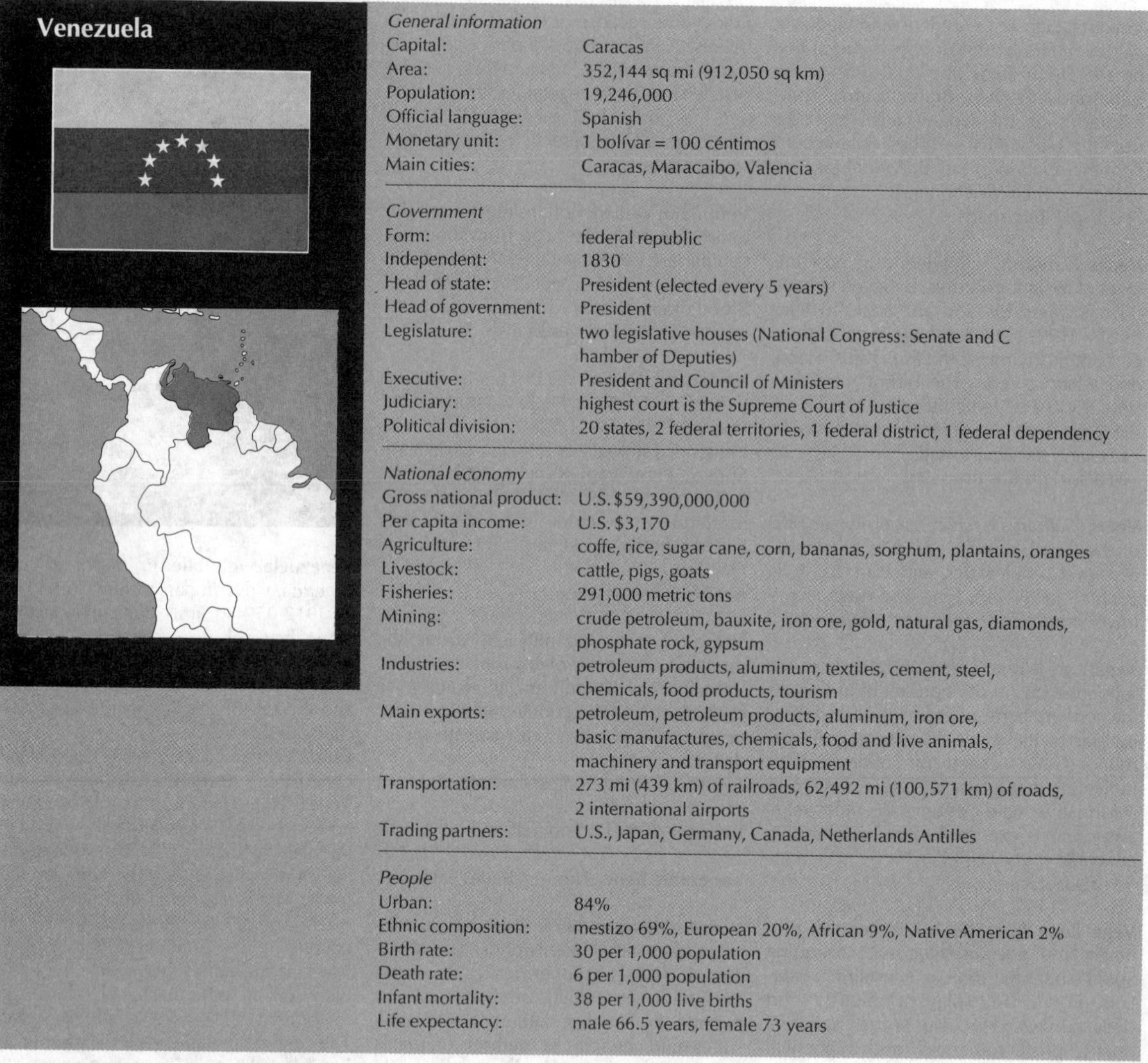

Venezuela

General information

Capital:	Caracas
Area:	352,144 sq mi (912,050 sq km)
Population:	19,246,000
Official language:	Spanish
Monetary unit:	1 bolívar = 100 céntimos
Main cities:	Caracas, Maracaibo, Valencia

Government

Form:	federal republic
Independent:	1830
Head of state:	President (elected every 5 years)
Head of government:	President
Legislature:	two legislative houses (National Congress: Senate and C hamber of Deputies)
Executive:	President and Council of Ministers
Judiciary:	highest court is the Supreme Court of Justice
Political division:	20 states, 2 federal territories, 1 federal district, 1 federal dependency

National economy

Gross national product:	U.S. $59,390,000,000
Per capita income:	U.S. $3,170
Agriculture:	coffe, rice, sugar cane, corn, bananas, sorghum, plantains, oranges
Livestock:	cattle, pigs, goats
Fisheries:	291,000 metric tons
Mining:	crude petroleum, bauxite, iron ore, gold, natural gas, diamonds, phosphate rock, gypsum
Industries:	petroleum products, aluminum, textiles, cement, steel, chemicals, food products, tourism
Main exports:	petroleum, petroleum products, aluminum, iron ore, basic manufactures, chemicals, food and live animals, machinery and transport equipment
Transportation:	273 mi (439 km) of railroads, 62,492 mi (100,571 km) of roads, 2 international airports
Trading partners:	U.S., Japan, Germany, Canada, Netherlands Antilles

People

Urban:	84%
Ethnic composition:	mestizo 69%, European 20%, African 9%, Native American 2%
Birth rate:	30 per 1,000 population
Death rate:	6 per 1,000 population
Infant mortality:	38 per 1,000 live births
Life expectancy:	male 66.5 years, female 73 years

Lake Maracaibo, are known as the Maracaibo Lowlands. They constitute one of the world's great oil-producing regions. The lowlands are known for their hot and humid climate. Inland lies the great central grassland plains called the Llanos. Covering some 120,000 sq mi (310,800 sq km) and drained by many streams descending from the mountains to the Orinoco River, they are the great cattle-grazing region of Venezuela. Finally, the Guiana Highlands, south of the Orinoco River, cover about half of Venezuela and are very thinly populated. Much of the region is covered with tropical forests and parts have yet to be explored. Angel Falls, the highest falls in the world at a height of 3,212 ft (979 m), are located in the Guiana Highlands.

People. Nearly 70% of the people of Venezuela are mestizo, a mixture of whites and Native Americans. About 20% of the population is white, mostly of Spanish descent; another 10% of the people are of black African descent; and 2% are Native Americans. The official language is Spanish and the dominant religion is Roman Catholicism.

Economy. Oil was first discovered in Venezuela in 1918. Since then, the country has been a major oil producer, although its share of the world market declined in the 1970s. Venezuela now accounts for 14% of the world's output. It also produces natural gas and iron ore. The country's chief agricultural products are coffee, rice, and cocoa. Oil revenues have been used to finance irrigation projects, industrial diversification, public works, and social welfare programs.

History. Venezuela was discovered by Columbus in 1498, but may have been named by the Italian navigator Amerigo Vespucci, who sailed the north coast of South America in 1501. When the first Spanish settlement was founded at Cumaná in 1521, the country was inhabited by Arawaks and Caribs. The Spanish had to overcome fierce resistance in establishing dominion. Venezuelan independence, unsuccessfully attempted by Francisco de Miranda in 1806, was proclaimed by a national congress in 1811. Miranda became dictator in 1812, but was imprisoned by the Spanish. Simón Bolívar, who was born in Venezuela, led the independence struggle and triumphed in 1821. He made the country part of Greater Colombia, but it later broke free and became an independent republic in 1830 under José Antonio Páez. Dictatorships followed, the longest and most successful under Juan Vicente Gómez, who ruled the country from 1908 to 1935. It was under Gómez that Venezuela's oil riches were first developed and concessions granted to foreign companies. In 1958, the corrupt dictatorship of Marcos Pérez Jiménez was brought down by a military junta under Rómulo Betancourt and the country was restored to democracy. The petroleum industry was nationalized peacefully in 1976. Venezuela's economy suffered in the early 1980s with the drop in oil prices, but new discoveries of oil fields and higher oil prices brought on by the crisis in the Persian Gulf (1990) have led to a boost in oil production.

Venezuela Boundary Dispute, chiefly from 1841, Anglo-Venezuelan dispute over the location of the British Guiana-Venezuela border. In 1895 U.S. president Grover Cleveland, invoking the Monroe Doctrine, demanded arbitration supervised by the United States. This initially strained Anglo-U.S. relations almost to the point of war, but Britain submitted to arbitration, and a boundary was agreed upon in 1899.
See also: Monroe Doctrine.

Venice (pop. 332,800), city in northeastern Italy, seaport capital of the Veneto region and Venezia province. It comprises 118 islands in the Lagoon of Venice at the head of the Adriatic Sea. Transport is mainly along the famous canals by motorboat and gondola. Venice is built on piles sunk deep into the mud and is linked by a causeway to the mainland. The first *doge* (duke) was elected in 697. Venice rose to control trade between Europe and the East. At its height (15th century), Venice ruled many areas along the coast of the eastern Mediterranean, the Aegean, and parts of the Black Sea. Its power weakened during the long struggle with the Ottoman Empire (1453-1718). It fell to Napoleon Bonaparte in 1797 and became part of Italy in 1866. Venice is now a major tourist resort, boasting unique beauty and a magnificent cultural heritage.
See also: Italy.

Venkataraman, Ramaswamy (1910-), Indian statesman and president of India (1987-). Venkataraman was an attorney and pro-labor advocate and social worker who was elected to parliament (1950). He served as minister of finance (1980-84), and as minister of defense (1982-84). He was active in the United Nations and then served as Indira Gandhi's vice president (1984-87).
See also: India.

Ventricle *see:* Heart.

Ventris, Michael George Francis (1922-56), English architect and cryptographer who deciphered (1953) Linear B, a semipictorial Minoan-Mycenaean script, and showed it to be an ancient form of Greek. Following World War II, during which he was trained as a decoder, Ventris established a Committee of Correspondents, a group of scholars worldwide. With their advice, he set about deciphering the script, discovered on a number of clay tablets at Knossos, Crete (1900-08). Ventris used statistical analysis to plot a tentative syllabary. The results were published as "Evidence for Greek Dialect in Mycenaean Archives" (1953) and are significant for proving the Greek world to be literate some 500 years before Homer.

Venturi, Robert (1925-), U.S. architect. A controversial critic of the purely functional and spare designs of modern orthodox architecture, he set forth his "counterrevolutionary" views in *Complexity and Contradiction in Architecture* (1966) and *Learning from Las Vegas* (1972).
See also: Architecture.

Venus, in Roman mythology, goddess of love and beauty. Originally a minor deity associated with gardens, fruits, and flowers, Venus was adopted by Latin soldiers (c.217 B.C.) who enlarged her image to symbolize the life force. Venus was closely identified with the Greek Aphrodite. The Julii family, ancestors of Julius Caesar, were her priests.
See also: Mythology.

Venus, second planet from the sun in the solar system. Its diameter is 7,700 mi (12,392 km), slightly smaller than that of the earth. Its face is completely obscured by dense clouds containing sulfuric acid, although the USSR's spaceprobes *Venera-9* and *Venera-10* (Oct.1975) landings provided photographs of the planet's rocky surface. Venus revolves about the sun at a mean distance of 67.2 million mi (108.2 million km) in 225 days, rotating on its axis in a retrograde direction in 243 days. Its atmosphere is 97% carbon dioxide, and its surface temperature is c.850°F (455°C). Venus has no known moons and could not support life.
See also: Planet; Solar system.

Venus de Milo, armless statue of the Greek goddess Aphrodite. It was carved in marble c.150 B.C. and was discovered (1820) on the island of Melos. It is now in the Louvre in Paris.

Venus's-flytrap (*Dionaea muscipula*), insect-catching plant that lives in the sandy country of the Carolinas and neighboring states. Its leaves form a rosette against the ground, and the outer part of each forms a pad hinged in the middle. Around the edge of the pad are stiff teeth and 3 spines stick up from the middle of the pad. When an insect brushes the spines, the pad rapidly folds up so that the insect is caught behind the teeth. Secretions digest the soft parts of the insect's body. The Venus-flytrap's speed is remarkable. It has even been recorded catching a small frog.

Veracruz (pop. 295,300), port city in east central Mexico on the Gulf of Mexico. Once the site of a Native American village, Veracruz is now an important shipping center handling much of Mexico's foreign trade. It exports sugar, coffee, vanilla, chicle, and petroleum products. The city manufactures tiles, chocolate, liquor, footwear, and textiles. Gallega Island protects the harbor and is the site of the Spanish fortress of San Juan de Ulua (1565).
See also: Mexico.

Verbena, genus (*Verbena*) of the vervain family of herbaceous plants, especially several cultivated species with blue, white, crimson, purple, or striped flowers.

Verdi, Giuseppe (1813-1901), Italian opera composer. He rose to fame during the struggle for Italian unification and independence; early operas, such as *Nabucco* (1842), express these political ideals. By the time of *Rigoletto* (1851), *Il Trovatore* (1853), and *La Traviata* (1853), he had developed his powerful individual style well beyond the conventions inherited from Gioacchino Rossini, Gaetano Donizetti, and Vincenzo Bellini. *Don Carlos* (1867), *Aïda* (1871), and the *Requiem* (1874) honoring the novelist Alessandro Manzoni are works of his maturity. The 2 great Shakespearian operas of Verdi's old age, *Otello* (1887) and *Falstaff* (1893), were written to libretti by Arrigo Boito.
See also: Opera.

Venice

Verdin (*Auriparus flaviceps*), songbird common in low deserts and brushlands of the U.S. Southwest and northern Mexico. The verdin is gray, with a yellow head, long tail, and sharp, black bill. It makes an oblong, thorny nest with a small side opening and the female lays 3 to 6 blue-green eggs. The verdin feeds on small insects and is usually seen singly but may travel in pairs or small family groups.

Verdun, Battle of (Feb.-Dec. 1916), major World War I engagement. The Germans launched a concentrated offensive against the fortified line of Verdun. The French logistically could not abandon this position, and the Germans hoped to exhaust France's forces during the battle. Total casualties were well over 700,000. No significant advantage was gained by either side.
See also: World War I.

Verdun, Treaty of, pact (A.D. 843) concluding the civil war between the heirs of Louis I, by which Charlemagne's empire was divided between his 3 grandchildren (Louis's sons). Lothair I kept the title emperor and received Italy and a narrow strip of land from Provence to Friesland. Louis the German received the lands between the Rhine and Elbe. Charles the Bald held the area west of the Rhine.
See also: Charlemagne.

Vergil, or **Virgil** (Publius Vergilius Maro; 70-19 B.C.), Roman poet. Maecenas became his patron and Octavian (later the Emperor Augustus) his friend. He won recognition with his *Eclogues* or *Bucolics*, pastoral poems reflecting the events of his own day. The *Georgics*, a didactic poem on farming, uses the world of the farmer as a model for the world at large. His last 10 years were spent on his epic masterpiece, the *Aeneid*, about the wanderings of the Trojan War survivor Aeneas and his struggle to found Rome.

Verlaine, Paul (1844-96), French poet, an early and influential exponent of symbolism. While imprisoned (1873-75) for shooting and wounding his friend and lover, the poet Arthur Rimbaud, he wrote *Romances sans Paroles* (1874), one of his finest volumes. After a period of religious piety, he returned to his life of bohemian dissipation and died in poverty.

Vermeer, Jan (1632-75), Dutch painter who spent his entire life in Delft. His interior scenes are noted for superb control of light, precise tonality, cool harmonious coloring, and classical composition. Of the fewer than 40 works attributed to him, his masterpieces include *The Letter* and *Head of a Girl* (both 1665).

Vermiculite, foliated clay mineral formed as a change in biotite. Vermiculite is soft, yellow or brown in color, with a monoclinic crystal structure. When heated, it can expand to a lightweight, highly absorbent, fireproof material about 16 times its original volume. Deposits occur in the United States, Australia, the USSR, South Africa, and Brazil. Vermiculite is used in construction as a sound and thermal insulator, as a fireproofing element, and as a potting medium for plants.

Vermont, state in New England, the northeastern region of the United States; bordered by Canada to the north, the Connecticut River (with New Hampshire on the other side) to the east, Massachusetts to the south, and New York and Lake Champlain to the west.

Vermont

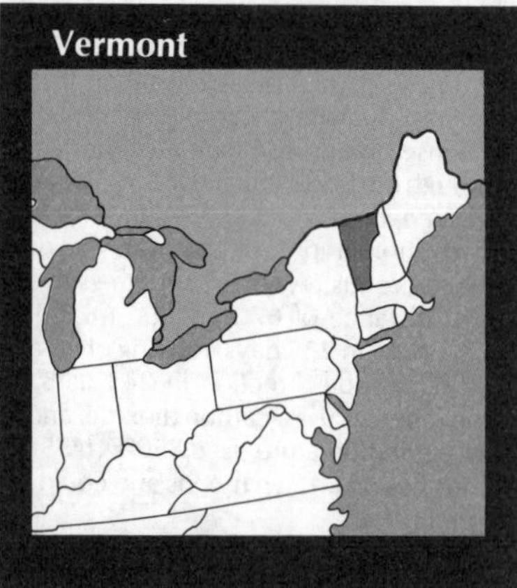

Capital:	Montpelier
Statehood:	Mar. 4, 1791 (14th state)
Familiar name:	Green Mountain State
Area:	9,614 sq mi (24,900 sq km); ranks 43rd
Population:	564,964 (1990); ranks 48th
Elevation:	Highest—4,393 ft (1,339 m), Mt. Mansfield; Lowest—95 ft (29 m), Lake Champlain
Motto:	Freedom and Unity
Flower:	Red clover
Bird:	Hermit thrush
Tree:	Sugar maple
Song:	"Hail, Vermont"

Land and climate. Vermont has 6 main land regions. The Northeast Highlands are part of the White Mountain range of New Hampshire. In the Western New England Upland, which lines most of the state's eastern border, lies the broad, fertile Connecticut River Valley. In the Green Mountains region, rounded peaks run north-south through the center of the state. The Champlain Valley is a fertile lowland area bordering Lake Champlain. In the southwest lie the Taconic Mountains region, part of a mountain range running from Massachusetts into Vermont, and the Vermont Valley, a narrow region of river valleys. The Connecticut is the state's major river; others include Otter Creek and the Winooski, Missisquoi, and Lamoille rivers. Forests cover about four fifths of the state. Vermont has short, cool summers and long, cold winters. Principal cities are Burlington and Rutland.

Vermont

Economy. Vermont's economy is led by service industries and manufacturing. Chief manufactured goods are electrical equipment, fabricated metal products, books and other printed materials, processed foods, transportation equipment, and furniture. Agriculture and mining account for a small share of the state's economy. Chief farm products are milk and dairy products, apples, maple syrup, potatoes, corn, and hay. Granite is the chief mining product.

Government. Vermont's present constitution was adopted in 1793. The governor serves a 2-year term. The state's legislature, called the General Assembly, consists of 30 senators and 150 representatives; all serve 2-year terms. In the U.S. Congress, Vermont is represented by 2 senators and 1 representative.

History. Several Native American tribes lived in the area before the first Europeans—an expedition led by French explorer Samuel de Champlain—arrived in 1609. The first permanent white settlement was established at present-day Brattleboro in 1724. Parts of Vermont were battlegrounds during the French and Indian wars. In 1770, Ethan Allen organized the Green Mountain Boys to resist New York's claims to Vermont lands. When the American Revolution broke out, the Green Mountain Boys joined other patriots to fight the British. In 1777, Vermont's settlers declared it an independent territory; it is one of 3 states (with Texas and Hawaii) that were recognized by the U.S. government as being independent republics before they joined the Union. Vermont's 1777 constitution prohibited slavery and was the first to provide for universal male suffrage (the right to vote). After the War of 1812, which was unpopular in Vermont, hard times drove many Vermonters to the Midwest. During the 1800s, Vermont switched from a sheep-raising to a dairying state. During the Civil War, Vermont supported the Union cause. From the late 1800s until the Great Depression (1930s), the importance of agriculture and the state's textile industries declined while that of tourism and manufacturing grew. World War II revived manufacturing. In the 1960s, 1970s, and 1980s, Vermont sought new industries while trying to preserve the scenic beauty that attracts tourists to the area.

Vernal equinox *see:* Equinox.

Verne, Jules (1828-1905), French novelist, pioneer of the genre of science fiction. He often incorporated genuine scientific principles in his imaginative adventure fantasies and anticipated the airplane, submarine, television, space travel, etc. His most famous novels include *Journey to the Center of the Earth* (1864), *Twenty Thousand Leagues Under the Sea* (1870), and *Around the World in Eighty Days* (1873).

Verrazano, Giovanni da (1485?-1528?), Italian navigator and explorer in the service of France. Verrazano explored the Atlantic coast of North America from Newfoundland to the Carolinas (1524). He is believed to have been the first European to explore the Hudson River and Manhattan Island regions.

Verrazano-Narrows Bridge, world's longest suspension bridge (4,260 ft/1,298 m), spanning the Narrows at the entrance to New York harbor, completed in 1964.

Verrocchio, Andrea del (1435-88), Italian sculptor, painter, and architect. Verrocchio trained as a goldsmith and probably learned painting under Fra Filippo Lippi. Many of Verrocchio's sculptures survive, but only 1 or 2 paintings are positively identified as his. His works are characterized by naturalistic poses, strong forms, and careful craftsmanship. His most famous works include the bronze sculptures *Christ and Saint Thomas* and *David* and an equestrian statue, the Colleoni Monument. Leonardo da Vinci and Il Perugino were among Verrocchio's students.

Versailles (pop. 91,500), French city, residential suburb 12 mi (19 km) southwest of Paris, capital of Yveline department. It is world-famous for its magnificent Palace of Versailles, built for King Louis XIV in the mid-1600s. The seat of the French court for over 100 years, it was made a national museum in 1837, and the palace and its formal gardens are among France's greatest tourist attractions.
See also: France.

Versailles, Treaty of, agreement ending World War I, imposed on Germany by the Allies on June 28, 1919. It set up the League

of Nations. Under the treaty, Germany lost all her colonies and Lorraine was given to France, Eupen-Malmédy to Belgium, and Posen and West Prussia to Poland. Gdansk became a free city, the Saar (with its coalfields) was to be under international administration for 15 years, and the Rhineland was to be demilitarized and occupied by the Allies for 15 years at German cost. Heavy reparations were imposed, and Germany's armed forces were drastically reduced. German resentment of the treaty's harshness was a factor in the rise of Nazism and the eventual outbreak of World War II.
See also: World War I.

The signing of the Treaty of Versailles.

Vertebra *see:* Spine.

Vertebrate, subphylum of the chordates, containing all those classes of animals that possess a backbone—a spinal column made up of bony or cartilaginous vertebrae. The classes of vertebrates are fish, amphibians, reptiles, birds, and mammals.

Vertical take-off aircraft *see:* V/STOL.

Vertigo, disturbance in which the individual has a subjective impression of movement in space or of objects moving around him or her, usually with a loss of equilibrium. As distinguished from faintness, lightheadedness, or other forms of dizziness, vertigo results from a disturbance somewhere in the body's equilibratory apparatus, e.g., the inner ear.

Vervain *see:* Verbena.

Verwoerd, Hendrik Frensch (1901-66), Dutch-born South African politician and premier (1958-66). A professor of psychology from 1927, he became editor of the Afrikaans nationalist newspaper *Die Transvaaler* (1937). A senator from 1948, he was appointed minister of native affairs (1950), and enforced apartheid rigorously, stressing "separate development" and creating the homelands. He was assassinated.

Very high frequency waves (VHF), electromagnetic radio waves falling between high frequency and ultra high frequency. VHF waves are from 30 million to 300 million cycles per second, and the wavelengths range from 1 to 10 meters. They are used for television and FM (frequency modulation) radio broadcasts and by amateur radio operators.
See also: Radio.

Vesalius, Andreas (1514-64), Flemish biologist regarded as a father of modern anatomy. After considerable experience of dissection, he became one of the leading figures in the revolt against Galen. In his most important work, *On the Structure of the Human Body* (1543), he described several organs for the first time.
See also: Anatomy.

Vesey, Denmark (1767?-1822), free African American who planned a slave revolt at Charleston, S.C. (1822). Vesey was a carpenter who had purchased his freedom with money won in a street lottery. Dissatisfied with his inability to achieve full citizenship, with his children's status as slaves, and with the oppressive treatment of slaves in general, he gathered as many as 9,000 slaves and free blacks, who armed themselves with homemade weapons and prepared to attack Charleston. The plot was betrayed, and Vesey and 35 other leaders were hanged; 32 others were exiled.
See also: Slavery.

Vespasian (Titus Flavius Vespasianus; A.D. 9-79), Roman emperor from 69. The son of a tax collector, he rose in the army under Nero and was sent in 66 to suppress a rebellion in Judaea. His reign began an era of order and prosperity. He began the building of the Colosseum.
See also: Rome, Ancient.

Vespucci, Amerigo (1454-1512), Italian navigator for whom America was named. In 2 voyages (1499-1500, 1501-2) he explored the coast of South America and deduced that the New World must be a continent and not part of Asia. The name *America* first appeared on a map published in 1507.
See also: America.

Vessel, Blood *see:* Artery; Blood; Vein.

Vesta, in Roman mythology, goddess of the hearth and home. She was the daughter of Saturn and Ops and the sister of Jupiter and is portrayed as young and virginal. Vesta's symbol, that of fire, evolves from the Roman necessity of maintaining a perpetual fire in the home as a sacred obligation. Vesta's temple, in the Forum in Rome, housed a public flame guarded by the six vestal virgins.
See also: Mythology.

Vestal virgins, in ancient Rome, priestess, chosen very young, who served the shrine of Vesta, goddess of the domestic hearth, for 30 years. Punishment for breaking the vow of chastity was burial alive. The virgins' chief responsibility was to tend to the sacred flame in Vesta's temple.
See also: Vesta.

Vetch, climbing or trailing vine (genus *Vicia*) of the pea family. At the tip of each leaf stem is a pair of slender tendrils that curl around other plants. They have attractive flowers like those of peas, and their seeds are carried in pods. There are several native vetches in North America, but the most common ones are of European origin. In Europe they are grown as crops for hay or pasture or to hold the soil on embankments.

Veterans Administration *see:* Veterans Affairs, Department of.

Veterans Affairs, Department of (VA), formerly the Veterans Administration, U.S. government executive department consolidated (1989) to administer the various health, rehabilitation, education, loan, compensation, and insurance programs provided to veterans of the military services. The VA operates hospitals throughout the country, provides educational assistance and training programs under various GI Bills, lends money for home purchases, and administers 113 national cemeteries.

Amerigo Vespucci

Veterans Day, U.S. holiday, celebrated on Nov. 11, to honor the members of the U.S. military forces, past and present. Originally known as Armistice Day, it was designated by President Woodrow Wilson to commemorate the end of World War I.

Veterans of Foreign Wars of the United States (VFW), one of the largest veterans' organizations in the United States. It assists needy veterans and their families, fosters patriotism, promotes community service, and lobbies for legislation. The VFW was formed in 1913. There are some 2.1 million members in about 9,800 local posts. Officers and enlisted men and women on active duty or honorably discharged, who have fought in any foreign military campaign of the United States, are eligible to join the VFW.

Veterans' organizations, groups formed to foster the spirit of comradeship developed during war and to demonstrate support for the government. The groups are politically influential due to the size of their memberships, and they lobby for legislation beneficial to veterans such as pensions, education, and services for disabled veterans. In the United States, the first veterans' organization was the Society of the Cincinnati. Formed in 1783, with George Washington as its first president, it consisted of veterans who had fought in the Revolutionary War. The Grand Army of the Republic, formed in 1866, was an organization of veterans of the Union Army that wielded great political power for over 40 years. The American Veterans of World War II, Korea and Vietnam (AMVETS) was founded in 1944.

Veterinary medicine, medical care of sick animals, sometimes including the delivery of their young. It is practiced separately from human medicine since animal diseases differ largely from those affecting humans. Veterinarians treat domestic, farm, sport, and zoo animals. General medical advances—e.g., in vaccines and antibiotics—have been aided by veterinary research.

Veto, in politics, the power of the executive to reject legislation. It is a Latin word meaning "I forbid," pronounced by the Roman tribunes when they exercised their right to block laws passed by the Senate. Under the U.S. Constitution (Art. I, Sect. 7), the president can veto any bill passed by Congress, but this can be overridden by a two-thirds majority in both houses. In the Security Council of the United Nations, the 5 permanent members (China, France, Great Britain, the United States, and the USSR) possess a veto over proceedings.

VFW *see:* Veterans of Foreign Wars of the United States.

VHF waves *see:* Very high frequency waves.

Vibraphone, electric percussion instrument resembling a xylophone but having metal rather than wooden bars. The vibraphone has 37 bars (keys), each attached to a frame above a tuned resonator that can be opened or closed to produce a vibrating note. The player uses hard or soft cloth-headed beaters to strike the keys and can control the length and loudness of the notes with a sustaining pedal. The vibraphone was invented (1921) by Hermann Winterhoff and was first used orchestrally in the opera *Lulu* (1937).

Vice president of the United States, second-highest elected official. Constitutionally and politically, this office does not carry great power. The vice president was originally intended as the neutral presiding officer in the Senate and as the constitutional successor on the death or resignation of the president. Eight vice presidents have succeeded to the presidency during their time in office, taking over for presidents who have died or resigned. The increase in presidential duties with World War II has been partly responsible for giving the vice president a greater share in political and legislative matters, in particular as a member of the National Security Council. The 25th Amendment (1967) permits the president to fill a vacancy in the office of vice president, subject to the approval of Congress. The amendment permits the vice president to act as president when the president is disabled. For 8 hours in 1985, while President Reagan was in surgery, Vice President George Bush served as acting president, the first vice president to do so.

Vice-presidential seal

Vichy (pop. 30,500), health resort in south-central France, famous for its mineral springs. Its chief industry is bottling Vichy water. In World War II it was the seat of the Vichy government of Marshal Henri Pétain, which was set up in unoccupied France in 1940. After Germany occupied the whole of France in 1942, the Vichy government under Pierre Laval continued to collaborate with the Nazis, until the Allies liberated France.
See also: France.

Vicksburg (pop. 25,434), city in western Mississippi, seat of Warren County and site of a crucial campaign in the U.S. Civil War. Built in 1791 on the site of a Spanish outpost on the Mississippi River, it had a strategic position that made it a key Confederate bastion, until it was taken by Union forces under Gen. Ulysses S. Grant in 1863 after a 6-week siege. The port produces chemicals, machinery and metal, lumber and food products.

Vicksburg, Battle of *see:* Civil War, U.S.

Victor Emmanuel, name of 3 Italian kings. Victor Emmanuel I (1759-1824) was king of Sardinia (1802-21). He recovered his mainland possessions after Napoleon I's fall (1814), but his harsh rule provoked a revolt in Piedmont led by the Carbonari, and he abdicated. Victor Emmanuel II (1820-78) was king of Sardinia (1849-61) and the first king of united Italy (1861-78). With the Conte di Cavour and Giuseppe Garibaldi he played a major part in Italy's unification. Victor Emmanuel III (1869-1947) was king of Italy (1900-46), emperor of Ethiopia (1936-43), and king of Albania (1939-43). After appointing Benito Mussolini premier in 1922, he became a mere figurehead. His unpopular association with Fascism ultimately obliged him to abdicate.

Victoria (1819-1901), queen of Great Britain and Ireland from 1837 and empress of India from 1876. As a young queen she depended heavily on the counsel of Lord Melbourne. Her life was transformed by marriage in 1840 to Prince Albert, who became the greatest influence of her life. She mourned for the rest of her life after his death in 1861. She had strong opinions and believed in playing an active role in government, and her relations with a succession of ministers colored the political life of her reign. Her dislike of Palmerston and Gladstone and fondness for Disraeli, for example, were notorious. In old age she became immensely popular and a symbol of Britain's imperial greatness.
See also: United Kingdom.

Victoria (pop. 66,300), city in southwestern British Columbia, Canada, on the southeastern tip of Vancouver Island. Victoria is the capital of British Columbia, a tourist and retirement center, and a shipping point for the island's products. It is the site of the University of Victoria and the Royal Roads Military College. The Dominion Astrophysical Observatory and the British Royal Navy base at Esquimalt Harbor are nearby.

Victoria (pop. 1,184,000), capital of the colony of Hong Kong. The city is located on the slopes of Victoria Peak on the island of Hong Kong. It is commonly referred to as the Central District or merely as Hong Kong. Victoria is the government, banking, and commercial center of the island and home to the University of Hong Kong.
See also: Hong Kong.

Victoria, state in southeast Australia, the second-smallest and most densely populated in the country. It is divided east-west by an extension of the Australian Alps, with lowlands, hills, and valleys in the south and low plains north and west. The climate is temperate. Agriculture is important: wheat, oats, barley, and grapes are grown, and cattle and sheep are raised. Automobiles, textiles, and processed foods are produced, and coal and some gold are mined. Melbourne is the capital and largest city.
See also: Australia.

Victoria Falls, waterfall on the Zambesi River in south-central Africa between Zimbabwe and Zambia, where the 1-mi- (1-km-) wide river plunges 400 ft (122 m) into a narrow fissure. The falls were named for Britain's Queen Victoria by the explorer David Livingston in 1855.

Vicuña (*Lama vicugna*), member of the camel family living in the western High Andes at up to 16,400 ft (c.5,000 m). They are believed to be the original of the domesticated alpacas. Vicuñas are graceful animals living in family groups of a stallion and up to 20 mares, occupying a fixed territory.

Video camera, device that converts images into electronic signals for television viewing. The first video cameras, developed in the 1930s, were used for live telecasts. Color video cameras were developed in the 1950s. By the 1970s portable video cameras were being manufactured for use

Victoria Falls on the Zambesi River

in the home. In the mid-1980s the videotape recorder was small enough to be combined with a video camera in a single unit.

Video cassette recorder *see:* Videotape recorder.

Videodisc, flat, round, plastic platter on which both picture and sound are reproduced on a television set. Unlike a video cassette recorder (VCR), a videodisc cannot record television programs off the air. Videodiscs do, however, offer superior picture and sound quality. There are 2 different videodisc systems: one employs a mechanical stylus and the other a laser. Originally developed in the 1970s for use as home entertainment, videodiscs are now used widely in education and industry.

Videotape, magnetic tape used to record television programs. In order to record the vast amounts of information necessary to reconstruct a television picture, 2-in- (5-cm-) wide tape must be run through the tape heads at 15 in (38 cm) per sec. The tape heads rotate to record the track crosswise on the tape.

Videotape recorder (VTR), mechanism that records visual images and sounds on magnetic tape. The recorded picture and sound can be played back and seen on the television screen. Home videotape recorders, also known as video cassette recorders (VCRs), are used largely by a consumer population to record television programs.

Vienna (German: *Wien*; pop. 1,516,000), capital of Austria, on the Danube River, one of the world's great cities. Associated with Josef Haydn, W. A. Mozart, Ludwig von Beethoven, and the various Strausses, it is a celebrated musical, theatrical, and cultural center and has many famous buildings and museums, including the Hofburg, Schönbrunn, and Belvedere palaces, the Cathedral of St. Stephen, the State Opera, the Art History Museum, and the City Hall. A Roman town, it became the residence of the Hapsburgs in 1282. It was besieged by the Turks in 1529 and 1683. A great period of prosperity and building began in the 18th century, and Vienna was capital of the Austro-Hungarian empire until 1918, when the modern republic of Austria was formed. In World War II it was occupied by the Nazis and bombed by the Allies. The modern city, population 1,500,000 (1987 est), is also a commercial and industrial center, producing machinery, metals, textiles, chemicals, furniture, handicrafts, and food products.
See also: Austria.

Vienna, Congress of, assembly held in Vienna (1814-5) to reorganize Europe after the Napoleonic Wars. Effective decision making was carried out by Metternich of Austria, Tsar Alexander I of Russia, Castlereagh and Wellington of Britain, von Humboldt of Prussia, and Talleyrand of France. Among other territorial adjustments, the Congress established the German Confederation and the kingdoms of the Netherlands and Poland (under Russian rule), and restored the Papal States and the kingdoms of Sardinia and Naples. Austria gained parts of Italy, Prussia gained parts of Austria, and Britain gained overseas territories to achieve a new balance of power, ignoring the nationalist aspirations of the peoples concerned.
See also: Napoleonic Wars.

Vientiane (pop. 264,300), capital and largest city of Laos, located on the Mekong River. Vientiane is the commercial center of Laos and produces livestock, rice, cigarettes, silk and other textiles, and plastics. It is the site of the Royal School of Medicine and the Royal School of Public Administration and is noted for its many Buddhist pagodas.
See also: Laos.

Vienna

Vietnam, officially the Socialist Republic of Vietnam, located in southeast Asia. With an area of 128,401 sq mi (332,559 sq km), Vietnam is bordered by Kampuchea (formerly Cambodia), and Laos on the west; China to the north and east; and the Gulf of Tonkin, the South China Sea, and the Gulf of Thailand to the east and south. The capital is Hanoi.

Land and climate. Narrow and S-shaped, Vietnam is a 1,000-mi (1,609 km)-long strip on the Indo-China peninsula. The country's major cities and economic centers are located in the Red River delta in the north and the Mekong River delta in the south. More than 90% of the people live in the delta regions. Between them lies a heavily forested mountainous backbone giving way to a narrow coastal strip along the South China Sea and the Gulf of Tonkin. Vietnam has a tropical monsoon climate with high humidity and rainfall.

People. About 85% of the people are Vietnamese. There are also urban Chinese minorities, though many Chinese fled the country in 1979 when hostilities flared up between Vietnam and China. There are also several distinct peoples in the highlands, such as the Meo, also called the

Typical modes of Vietnamese transportation

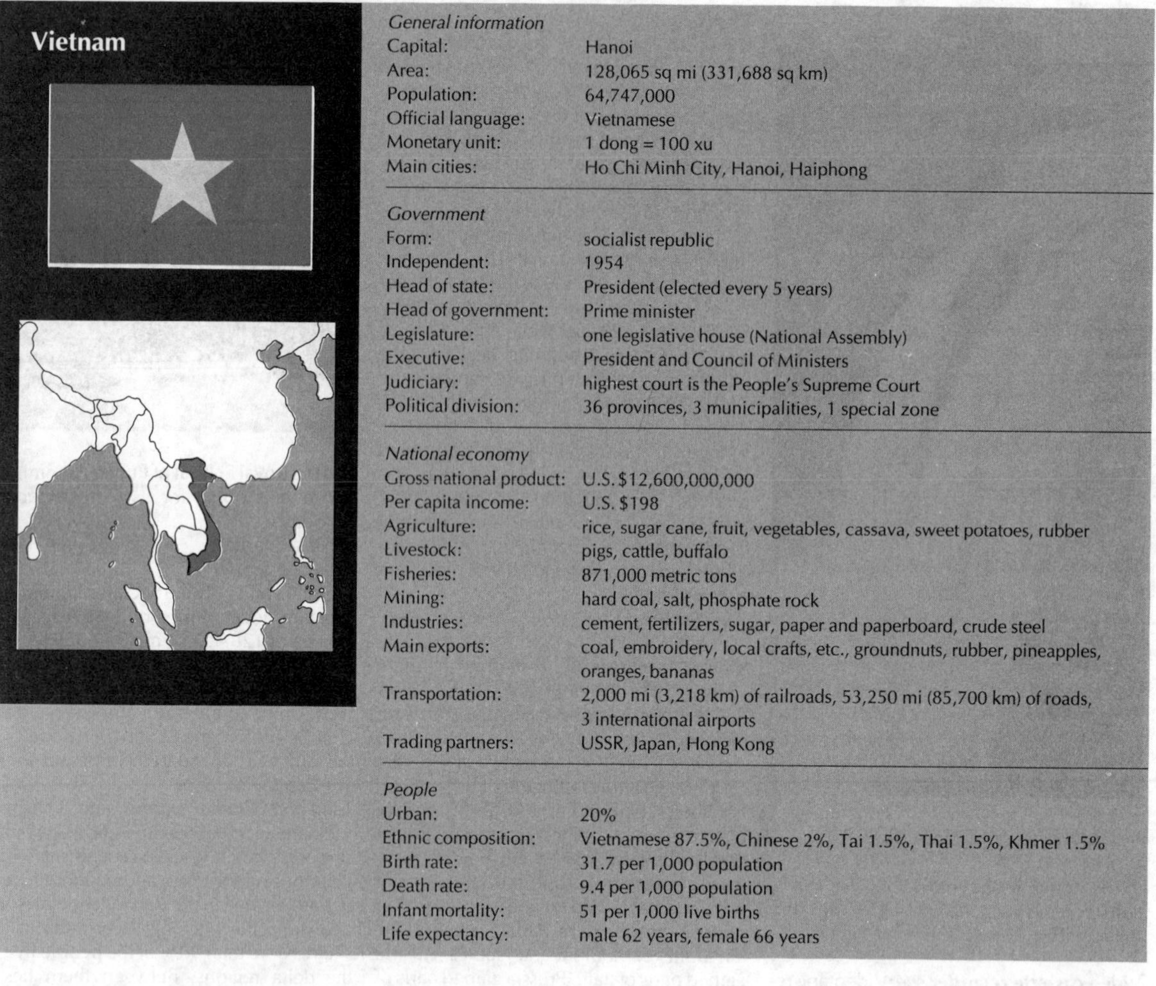

Vietnam

General information	
Capital:	Hanoi
Area:	128,065 sq mi (331,688 sq km)
Population:	64,747,000
Official language:	Vietnamese
Monetary unit:	1 dong = 100 xu
Main cities:	Ho Chi Minh City, Hanoi, Haiphong
Government	
Form:	socialist republic
Independent:	1954
Head of state:	President (elected every 5 years)
Head of government:	Prime minister
Legislature:	one legislative house (National Assembly)
Executive:	President and Council of Ministers
Judiciary:	highest court is the People's Supreme Court
Political division:	36 provinces, 3 municipalities, 1 special zone
National economy	
Gross national product:	U.S. $12,600,000,000
Per capita income:	U.S. $198
Agriculture:	rice, sugar cane, fruit, vegetables, cassava, sweet potatoes, rubber
Livestock:	pigs, cattle, buffalo
Fisheries:	871,000 metric tons
Mining:	hard coal, salt, phosphate rock
Industries:	cement, fertilizers, sugar, paper and paperboard, crude steel
Main exports:	coal, embroidery, local crafts, etc., groundnuts, rubber, pineapples, oranges, bananas
Transportation:	2,000 mi (3,218 km) of railroads, 53,250 mi (85,700 km) of roads, 3 international airports
Trading partners:	USSR, Japan, Hong Kong
People	
Urban:	20%
Ethnic composition:	Vietnamese 87.5%, Chinese 2%, Tai 1.5%, Thai 1.5%, Khmer 1.5%
Birth rate:	31.7 per 1,000 population
Death rate:	9.4 per 1,000 population
Infant mortality:	51 per 1,000 live births
Life expectancy:	male 62 years, female 66 years

Hmong, who preserve their own cultures. The major cities are Hanoi, Ho Chi Minh City (formerly Saigon), Hue, Da Nang, and Haiphong. The official language is Vietnamese and the dominant religions are Buddhism and Roman Catholicism, though the Vietnamese government discourages both.

Economy. Vietnam has an agricultural economy based principally upon rice growing in the Mekong and Red River deltas. Other crops include corn, cotton, hemp, sugarcane, rubber, coffee, and tea. Fishing and forestry are locally important. Minerals, including coal, iron, tin, zinc, lead, and phosphates are found mainly in the north, where most of the country's industry, chiefly the manufacture of iron and steel, chemicals and textiles, is concentrated. There is also some manufacturing around Ho Chi Minh City. Offshore oil deposits have been found.

History. Established as a distinct people by the 2nd century B.C., the Vietnamese now occupy what were formerly the distinct regions of Tonkin in the north, Annam in the center, and Cochin China in the south of their country. Tonkin and Annam were conquered by China in 111 B.C. In the 2nd century A.D., the Champa kingdom emerged in central Vietnam. The Chinese were eventually driven out in 939. The Annam empire then grew, eventually defeating and displacing the Champas in 1471 and expanding south into Cochin China. European traders and missionaries began arriving in the 1500s. French forces captured Saigon in 1859 and in 1862 the French annexed Cochin China and merged it with present-day Kampuchea to form French Indochina. During the Japanese occupation of Indochina (1941-45), the Vietnamese resisted. After the defeat and withdrawal of the Japanese, a republic was proclaimed under Ho Chi Minh in 1945. The French attempted to reassert their authority by establishing Bao Dai as emperor and became embroiled in a war between nationalist and communist guerrillas beginning in 1946. The French were finally defeated in 1954 at Dien Bien Phu. At the Geneva Conference held that same year, the country was divided, pending nationwide free elections, into Communist North Vietnam under Ho Chi Minh, and non-Communist South Vietnam. The French withdrew and, with U.S. backing, the regime of Ngo Dinh Diem declared an independent republic in South Vietnam in 1955 and, in 1956, refused to hold free elections. The Vietnam war ensued with South Vietnam being aided by the United States. At the height of its involvement, the United States had committed some 550,000 ground troops to the war. Despite a major military effort, the United States was unable to contain or defeat the Viet Cong guerrillas consisting of South Vietnamese opposed to the regime and North Vietnamese guerrillas reinforced by regulars of the North Vietnamese army. Successive South Vietnamese regimes proved unable to win popular backing and to provide the necessary political and military leadership. In addition, the United States suffered substantial setbacks to its international standing as the object of widespread criticism and resistance to the war at home and abroad. A cease-fire agreement was finally signed in 1973 and U.S. troops were withdrawn, but only at the end of a prolonged bombing campaign and the invasion of Cambodia. Upon the withdrawal of U.S. troops, Communist forces launched a major offensive and by 1975 had won control of all of South Vietnam, effectively ending 35 years of fighting. The unified Socialist Republic of Vietnam was proclaimed in 1976. Since then, Vietnam has attempted to rebuild its society and economy but was further distracted by war with neighboring Kampuchea in 1979 when its forces overthrew the regime headed by Pol Pot. Years of war and economic dislocation have resulted in living conditions so harsh for so many of its people that large numbers have fled or attempted to flee the country, creating a major refugee problem in the area.

Vietnam Veterans Memorial *see:* Washington, D.C.

Vietnam War, conflict in South Vietnam (1957-75) between South Vietnamese government forces, backed by the United States, and Communist guerrilla insurgents, the Vietcong, backed by North Vietnam. The conflict originated in 1941 when a Viet-minh guerrilla force was formed under Hi Chi Minh to fight the Japanese. After 1946 it fought the French colonial government, defeating them at Dien Bien Phu. The Geneva Conference then temporarily divided Vietnam at the 17th parallel between the Communists (North) and the Nationalists (South). Ngo Dinh Diem, the South Vietnamese premier, canceled national elections and declared the South independent in 1956. The Viet Nam Cong San (Vietnamese Communists), or Vietcong, was then formed to oppose his increasingly corrupt regime. The Vietcong fought a ferocious guerrilla campaign that led Diem to call in U.S. support forces under the U.S.-South Vietnamese military and economic aid treaty of 1961. In 1963 he was overthrown by his officers; after a period of turmoil, Nguyen Van Thieu became president in 1967. In 1965 the United States had begun bombing the North in retaliation for the use of northern troops in the South. Increasing numbers of U.S. combat troops, many of them drafted, began to arrive in 1965 and totaled nearly 550,000 by 1968, when fruitless peace talks began in Paris. The large-scale U.S. campaign proved unable to do more than hold back the highly motivated Vietcong. Vietnamese civilians suffered terribly at the hands of both sides. The American people were sharply divided by severe uncertainties about U.S. goals and participation in the war. In November 1969 President Richard M. Nixon announced the "Vietnamization" of the war by building up South Vietnamese forces and withdrawing U.S. combat troops, but ever mounting, sometimes violent U.S. anti-war demonstrations reached their peak later that month when 250,000 protesters marched on Washington. The war had spread to Cambodia and Laos before a cease-fire was signed in Jan. 1973, followed by the total withdrawal of U.S. troops a few months later. The South was then overrun by Vietcong and North Vietnamese forces; the war effectively ended with the fall of the South Vietnamese capital of Saigon in May 1975. In the late 1980s the government began an economic restructuring plan with the purpose of stimulating private enterprise. In 1990 the Vietnamese Foreign Minister, Nguyen Co Thach, met with U.S. Secretary of State James A. Baker III in the first high-level meeting since the 1970s. They discussed Vietnam's involvement in Cambodia and U.S. MIAs, 2 issues that have kept the countries from establishing diplomatic relations.

Vikings, or Norsemen, Norwegian, Swedish, and Danish seafarers who raided Europe from the 9th to the 11th centuries. Expert shipbuilders and navigators, they were capable of long sea voyages, and their ferocity made them the terror of Europe. The Norwegians raided Scotland, Ireland, and France and colonized the Hebrides, Orkneys, the Faroes, Iceland, and Greenland. They may also have discovered America. The Danes raided England, France, the Netherlands, Spain, and Italy. The Swedes went down the eastern shores of the Baltic, through what is now western Russia, and reached the Bosporus and Byzantium. In addition to being raiders, the Vikings traded and created permanent settlements. They united the Hebrides and the Isle of Man into a kingdom. The Shetlands, the Orkneys, and Caithness became an earldom. Kingdoms were also set up in Ireland and Russia.

Villa, Pancho (Francisco Villa; 1877-1923), Mexican revolutionary leader. Originally a bandit in northern Mexico, Villa joined (1910) the insurgent forces of Francisco Madero fighting against the dictator Porfirio Díaz. After the successful campaign, he remained in the irregular army. When Madero was assassinated (1913), Villa joined forces with another revolutionary, Venustiano Carranza, and together they took Juárez (1914). Villa became governor of the state of Chihuahua and with Carranza continued his rebellion against Madero's successor, Gen. Victoriano Huerta (1914). In 1914-15 Villa and Emiliano Zapata took control of Mexico City but were later defeated by Gen. lvaro Obregón. Competition between Villa and Carranza forced a break in their alliance, and Villa, embittered by U.S. recognition of Carranza's government, attacked and burned the town of Columbus, N.M., killing 16 people. U.S. Gen. John Pershing then led an unsuccessful 11-month expedition into northern Mexico in pursuit of Villa. The invasion strained U.S.-Mexican relations, and Pershing was recalled. When Carranza's government was overthrown (1920), Villa was awarded a grant of land. He was assassinated at his ranch (1923).
See also: Mexico.

Villa-Lobos, Heitor (1887-1959), Brazilian composer, conductor, and teacher, known for his research on and use of folk music. He composed over 2,000 works, many of which combine indigenous melodies with the counterpointing of Johann Sebastian Bach. His compositions include 9 instrumental suites called the *Bachanias Brasileiras* (1930-45), 14 *Serestas* (1925-41) for voice and piano, 12 symphonies, and 16 string quartets. Villa-Lobos founded the Brazilian Academy of Music (1945).

Villard, Henry (1835-1900), German-born U.S. journalist and financier. Correspondent for the *New York Herald* and *New York Tribune* in the Civil War, he later (1881) acquired the New York *Evening Post* and *The Nation*. Entering the railroad business in 1873, he created the Oregon Railway and Navigation Co. (1879), and became president of Northern Pacific (1881-84, 1888-93). In 1890 he formed the Edison General Electric Co.

Villella, Edward Joseph (1936-), U.S. dancer who performed his first solo within a year of joining the New York City Ballet (1957). He is noted for his bravura style, with powerful leaps. Villella's most famous performances include the title role in Balanchine's *The Prodigal Son*, and Oberon in *A Midsummer Night's Dream*.
See also: Ballet.

Vietnam veteran looking for names of killed comrades on the Vietnam Veterans Memorial in Washington, D.C.

Vilnius, or Vilna, capital and largest city of Lithuania. Settled in the 10th century, Vilnius was named the Lithuanian capital in 1323. The city later came under Polish rule (1569) and then was annexed by Russia (1795) which retained power until 1918. Between that year and 1938, control was contested by Poland and Lithuania. In 1939 Lithuania recovered control, but the country (and the city) was occupied by the USSR. The Nazi occupation (1941-45) destroyed the large Jewish population. Today Vilnius is an important trade center for grain, timber, chemicals, machinery, leather goods, paper, and textiles. It is noted for its public buildings and churches reflecting Roman, Byzantine, and Gothic influences.
See also: Lithuania.

Vimy Ridge, Battle of, World War I battle (April 9, 1917) in which the Canadian Corps of the British Army impressively defeated the German forces in northern France. The capture of Vimy Ridge by the Canadian forces helped to symbolically identify Canada as an independent nation.
See also: World War I.

Viña del Mar, leading resort and second largest city in Chile, located on the Pacific coast just northeast of Valparaíso. The city is noted for its pleasant climate, beaches, hotels, and nightclubs.

Vincennes, city on the Wabash River in southwestern Indiana. Founded in 1732 by François-Marie Bissob, sieur de Vincennes, the city was Indiana's first permanent settlement. In 1779 it was taken over by U.S. forces under George Rogers Clark. The Northwest Ordinance (1787) brought settlers from Kentucky, Virginia, and Pennsylvania. Today, Vincennes is the seat of Knox County. It is an agricultural, industrial, and coal-mining center.
See also: Indiana.

Vinci, Leonardo da *see:* Da Vinci, Leonardo.

Pancho Villa

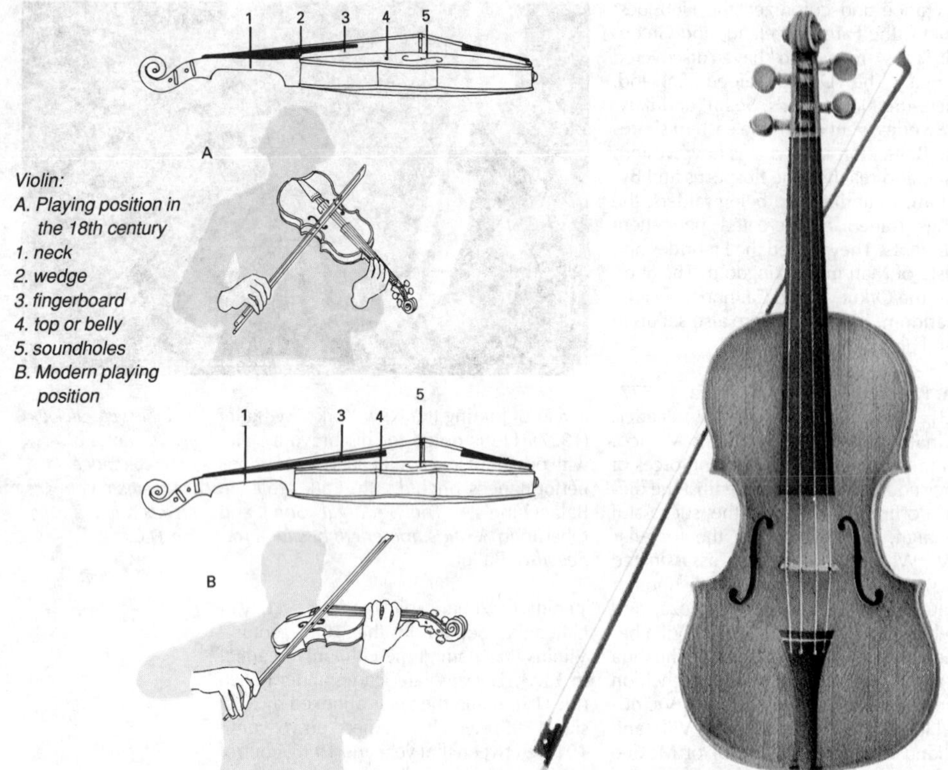

Violin:
A. Playing position in the 18th century
1. neck
2. wedge
3. fingerboard
4. top or belly
5. soundholes
B. Modern playing position

Viola, stringed musical instrument, the tenor voice of the violin family. It is 14.5-17 in (37-43 cm) long, has 4 strings, and is played with a bow. The viola originated in the 1500s. The composers Hector Berlioz, Richard Strauss, and Sir William Walton wrote for the viola as a solo instrument.

Violet, low herbaceous plants (genus *Viola*) that produce characteristically shaped flowers on slender stalks. Most species occur in the Andes, but many are found in North America and Europe. Several species, including the pansy, are cultivated as garden ornamentals. They grow mainly in moist woods.

Violin, smallest, most versatile member of the bowed, 4-stringed violin family (violin, viola, cello, double bass). Violins succeeded the viol in the 17th century, differing in their flexibility, range of tone and pitch, arched bridge, squarer shoulders, narrower body, and lack of frets. The violin proper, derived from the 16th-century arm viol, is tuned in fifths and ranges over 4 1/2 octaves above G below middle C. Perfected by the craftsmen of Cremona, it became a major solo instrument. The principal violinist leads the orchestra. Classical string quartets have 2 violins.

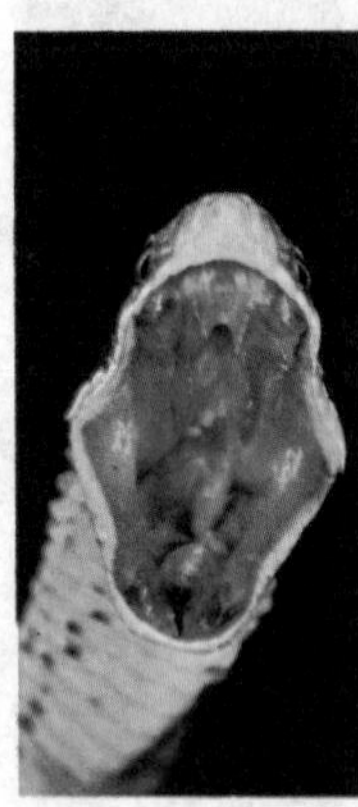
Viper

Vine, general name for plants with climbing or trailing stems that cannot grow upright without support. Vines have either woody or herbaceous (nonwoody) stems. They can be evergreen or deciduous. Some have tendrils (the sweet pea, the grapevine, and the cucumber), and others have adhesive disks (the woodbine or Virginia creeper) or small roots (English ivy) to anchor them to their support. Some twine their stem around the support (the convolvulus and hop), and others simply ramble over the surrounding area, with no means of holding themselves up (the blackberry and the rambler rose). By far the most important vine economically is the grapevine, from which the wine grape is harvested.

Vinegar, sour liquid, consisting mainly of acetic acid and water, used for seasoning and preserving foods. Vinegar is produced by the action of yeast and bacteria on fruits and grains. It is made from alcoholic beverages such as wine and cider.

Vinegar eel (*Turbatrix aceti*), tiny roundworm, about 1/16 in (1.6 mm) in length, found in fermenting cider vinegar. Vinegar eels feed on fruit pulp and the bacteria that produce the vinegar from the cider. They are harmless if swallowed.

Vinland, region of eastern North America discovered A.D. 1000 by Viking explorers, probably led by Leif Ericson, and briefly settled (1004) by Thorfinn Karlsefni. Some scholars believe it was in New England, others favor Newfoundland (where Viking remains have been found). The Norse sagas describe the discovery of a fertile region where grapes grew, hence "Vin(e)land."

Vinson, Frederick Moore (1890-1953), chief justice of the U.S. Supreme Court (1946-53). A Kentucky Democrat, he was a member of the House of Representatives (1923-9, 1931-7) and secretary of the treasury (1945-6). While he was chief justice, the Supreme Court made important civil liberty rulings.
See also: Supreme Court of the United States.

Vinyl, durable and useful plastic material used in making a variety of products. Vinyl plastics were first manufactured commercially in 1927. By 1973 the production of vinyl plastics in the United States totaled 4.6 billion lb (2.1 billion kg). One of the strongest vinyl plastics is polyvinyl chloride (PVC), produced by combining vinyl with chloride to form vinyl chloride gas, and then putting the gas through a process known as polymerization. Research in the 1970s showed that serious illness, including a form of liver cancer, can result from breathing air polluted by vinyl chloride. The Environmental Protection Agency now requires that manufacturers install equipment to eliminate vinyl chloride from the air breathed by workers.

Vinyl chloride *see:* Vinyl.

Viol, forerunner (15th-17th centuries) of the violin. Viols have sloping shoulders, frets, a low bridge, and a soft, mellow tone. The 6 strings are tuned in fourths. The treble, alto, tenor, and bass (*viola da gamba*) viols are all held upright, as was the double-bass *violone*, which became today's double-bass. Interest in the viol has revived in the 20th century.

Violoncello *see:* Cello.

Viper, family of snakes with highly developed venom apparatus, found in Europe, Africa, and Asia. Vipers are short, stoutly built, and typically terrestrial. One of the best-known species is the common European viper, or adder (*Vipera berus*).

Viper's bugloss, or blue thistle (*Echium vulgare*), plant found in dry areas of the eastern United States. It has bright blue flowers and grows to about (90 cm) tall. It was once thought to be a cure for viper bites.

Virchow, Rudolf (1821-1902), Pomeranian-born German pathologist. His most important work was to apply knowledge concerning the cell to pathology. He was the first to document leukemia and embolism. He was also distinguished as an anthropologist and an archeologist.
See also: Leukemia; Pathology.

Vireo, small, greenish, insectivorous bird (family Vireonidae) of tropical and temperate America. Vireos live in thick undergrowth except for the red-eyed vireo. This species is also noted for its rambling song. The white-eyed vireo mimics other birds. The nest is built near the ground and is anchored by cobwebs. Most species are migratory.

Virgil *see:* Vergil.

Virginal, type of small harpsichord, its strings parallel to the single keyboard. There is 1 wire per note. Encased in a small rectangular box, the virginal was popular c.1550-1650.

Virginia

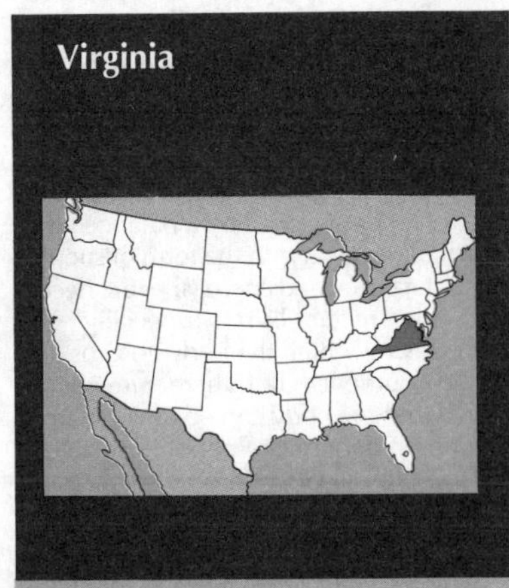

Capital:	Richmond
Statehood:	June 25, 1788 (10th state)
Familiar name:	Old Dominion
Area:	40,767 sq mi (105,586 sq km); ranks 36th
Population:	6,216,568 (1990); ranks 12th
Elevation:	Highest—5,729 ft (1,746 m), Mt. Rogers; Lowest—sea level, along the Atlantic coast
Motto:	Sic Semper Tyrannis (Thus Always to Tyrants)
Flower:	Flowering dogwood
Bird:	Cardinal
Tree:	Flowering dogwood
Song:	"Carry Me Back to Old Virginia"

Virginia, state in the southeastern United States; bordered by Maryland to the northeast, the Atlantic Ocean to the east, North Carolina and Tennessee to the south, Kentucky to the west, and West Virginia to the west and northwest.

Land and climate. Virginia has 5 main land regions. The Atlantic Coastal Plain, also called the Tidewater, is a low-lying area of tidal waterways with some swamps or salt marshes. Covering most of central Virginia is the Piedmont, a low, rolling plateau that rises into the mountain peaks and valleys of the Blue Ridge region. The Appalachian Ridge and Valley region, covering most of western Virginia, consists of a series of parallel ridges separated by river valleys and lowlands. The rugged Appalachian Plateau, in the state's southwestern corner, contains extensive coal deposits. Virginia's major rivers are the James, Rappahannock, and Potomac. The state's largest lake, Kerr Reservoir, is artificial. Forests cover nearly two thirds of the state. Virginia has mild winters and warm summers. Principal cities are Norfolk, Virginia Beach, and Richmond.

Economy. Virginia's economy is based on service industries and manufacturing. Chief manufactured goods are chemicals, tobacco products, processed foods, electrical and transportation equipment, and textiles. Agriculture and mining account for a small share of the state's economy. Chief livestock products are beef and dairy cattle and turkeys; chief crops are tobacco, soybeans, peanuts, corn, and hay. Chief mining products are coal and crushed stone. Virginia is the nation's leading producer of kyanite.

Government. Virginia's present constitution was adopted in 1971. The governor serves a 4-year term. The state's legislature, called the General Assembly, consists of 40 senators serving 4-year terms and 100 delegates serving 2-year terms. In the U.S. Congress, Virginia is represented by 2 senators and 11 representatives.

History. The Virginia area was home to various Native American tribes when the first European settlers—Spanish Jesuits—arrived in 1570. In 1607, the first permanent English settlement in the New World was established at Jamestown. In 1612, John Rolfe, a Jamestown settler, began raising tobacco, which became the basis of Virginia's economy. The first blacks came to Virginia as indentured servants in 1619; by 1715, blacks constituted about 25% of the population. Also in 1619, the House of Burgesses, the country's first representative legislature, was established. Virginia became a royal colony in 1624. It took a leading role in the American Revolution and events leading to it; distinguished Virginia patriots included Patrick Henry, Thomas Jefferson, George Washington, and James Madison. In 1776, Virginia became the first American colony to adopt a constitution and a declaration of rights. During the Civil War, a Virginia convention voted to secede, but western Virginians supported the Union. The split led to the 1863 formation of the state of West Virginia. Virginia was readmitted to the Union in 1870. In the late 1800s and early 1900s, Virginia became industrialized and urbanized. Desegregation and school integration became major issues in the 1950s and 1960s. In the 1970s and 1980s, major issues included antipollution and conservation efforts and problems related to falling demand for coal and tobacco, once key to Virginia's economy.

Virginia Beach (pop. 262,199), resort city on the southeastern edge of Virginia, bordered by the Atlantic Ocean and Chesapeake Bay. Over 2 million tourists visit its warm climate and attractive beaches annually. Many of its residents are employed at 4 nearby military installations. Virginia Beach was incorporated in 1963 and has a council-manager form of government.
See also: Virginia.

Virginia City, "ghost town" in western Nevada, a leading tourist attraction, c.20 mi (32 km) south of Reno. The town was founded in 1859, and the exploitation of the Comstock Lode of gold and silver turned the community into a boom town overnight. A fire destroyed most of it in 1875, and the ore gave out by the 1890s.
See also: Nevada.

Virginia Company, name of 2 companies of merchant-adventurers granted patents by the English crown (1606) for colonizing America. The London Company, authorized to settle anywhere from present-day South Carolina to New York, founded Jamestown (1607). The Plymouth Company, granted rights from present-day Virginia to Maine, fared badly. It was reorganized (1620) into the Council for New England, which made the original grant to the Pilgrim Fathers and the Puritan settlers.

Virginia creeper (*Parthenocissus quinquefolia*), rambling, viny plant that grows in eastern North America. A member of the vine family, it resembles poison ivy. Its leaves turn red and yellow in autumn.

Virginia Resolutions *see:* Kentucky and Virginia Resolutions.

Virgin Islands, westernmost group of the Lesser Antilles in the West Indies, east of Puerto Rico. The western islands belong to

Virginia

the United States and the eastern group to Britain. Discovered and claimed for Spain by Christopher Columbus (1493), the Virgin Islands were settled chiefly by English and Danes in the 1600s. England secured the British Virgin Islands in 1666. The Danish West Indies were acquired by the United States for strategic reasons in 1917 and became the U.S. Virgin Islands. The economy of both groups now depends on tourism, but farming (food crops, livestock) and fishing are also important. The Virgin Islands of the United States, a U.S. territory covering 133 sq mi (344.5 sq km) include St. Thomas, St. John, St. Croix, and some 65 islets. Charlotte Amalie, the capital and only city, stands on St. Thomas. The British Virgin Islands are separated from the American islands by a strait called The Narrows. Covering 59 sq mi (153 sq km), the group consists of about 30 mainly uninhabited islands. The largest island is Tortola, which has the capital and chief port, Road Town.

Virgin Islands National Park, national park, authorized in 1956, located on most of St. John (19 sq mi/49 sq km) Virgin Island of the United States, comprising 15,000 acres (6,070 hectares) with interesting marine flora and fauna and remnants of prehistoric Native American civilization.
See also: National Parks.

Virginius Massacre, seizure of a merchant ship, the *Virginius* (1873), by Spain during its conflict with Cuba. Spanish authorities executed 53 passengers and crew members, including the commander, John Fry, a U.S. citizen. The event almost involved the United States in a war with Spain. It was later discovered that the *Virginius* was a Cuban-owned ship fraudulently flying the U.S. flag and carrying a U.S. registration. Spain returned the ship, paid an indemnity to the families of those executed, and denied any hostile intent.

Virgin Mary *see:* Mary.

Viroid, class of infectious agents, causing several plant diseases. Made up of a complex chain of RNA (ribonucleic acid) molecules, they are replicated by the host cell's enzymes. Viroids affect such plants as potatoes, tomatoes, hops, and avocadoes, among others.

Relief of Vishnu at rest

Virus, submicroscopic parasitic microorganism comprising a protein or protein/lipid sheath containing nucleic acid (DNA or RNA). Viruses are inert outside living cells, but within appropriate cells they can replicate (using raw material from the cell), causing viral diseases in the host organism. Various viruses infect animals, plants, and bacteria (in which case they are bacteriophages). Few drugs act specifically against viruses, although immunity can be induced against particular viruses. Various pathogenic organisms formerly regarded as large viruses are now distinguished as *bedsonia*.

Viscosity, resistance of a fluid to shape change or relative motion within itself. All fluids are viscous, the viscosity arising from internal friction between molecules. The viscosity of liquids decreases as they are heated, but that of gases increases.

Vishinsky, Andrei Yanuarievich (1883-1954), Soviet diplomat and jurist. Chief state prosecutor in the purge trials of 1936-38, he was deputy commissar (1940-9) and commissar (1949-53) for foreign affairs, and USSR's chief UN delegate (1953-54).
See also: Union of Soviet Socialist Republics.

Vishnu, in Hinduism, second deity in the Trimurti (divine trinity, including Brahma, the creator, and Shiva, the destroyer), representing the preserving and protecting aspect of the godhead. The ancient *Vishnu Purana* text describes him as the primal god, as do his followers (Vaishnavas), who also worship his many avatars, such as Rama, Buddha, and Krishna. Vishnu is often represented dark blue in color, holding in his 4 hands a lotus, mace, discus, and conch. His consort is Lakshmi.
See also: Hinduism.

Visigoths (West Goths), Germanic people. In the 3rd century A.D. they invaded Roman Dacia (Romania). Under Fritigern they defeated the Romans at Adrianople (378) and, led by Alaric I, they invaded Thrace and Italy, sacking Rome (410). They founded a kingdom in Gaul and Spain (419), but Alaric II lost the northern lands to Clovis, king of the Franks (507). Roderick, last Gothic king of Spain, lost his throne to the Moors (711).

Vision *see:* Eye.

Vistula River, largest (678 mi/1,091 km long) and most important river in Poland. Through a system of canals, it connects the Oder, Dmepr, and Neman rivers, all of which are navigable. It empties into the Baltic Sea. The Vistula is frozen 2 to 3 months of the year.

Vital statistics, data related to the important events, such as birth, marriage, and death, in a person's life. Registration of many such statistics, including birth dates filed on birth certificates, is required by law. The Vital Statistics Division of the National Center for Health Statistics, a division of the U.S. Dept. of Health and Human Services, analyzes and publishes U.S. data.

Vitamin, specific nutrient compounds essential for body growth or metabolism and which can be supplied by a balanced diet or, when necessary, in the form of supplements. Enzymes and coenzymes are necessary for metabolism, especially the processes by which the body absorbs and utilizes nutrients. But there are certain coenzymes the body can obtain only from vitamins. Vitamins are denoted by letters and are often divided into fat-soluble and water-soluble kinds. Fat-soluble vitamins can be stored in the body's fat; water-soluble vitamins pass out of the body through urine. The A, D, E, and K vitamins are fat soluble; the B and C vitamins are water soluble.
Vitamin A, or retinol, is essential for skeletal growth, healthy epithelial tissue, and eyesight. It is found in milk, butter, and egg yolks. Green leafy or yellow vegetables contain a substance called carotene, which the body converts to Vitamin A. Vitamin A deficiency can cause skin, eye, or mucous membrane lesions. Overdoses can be harmful to the skin. Vitamin D, or calciferol, is a crucial factor in calcium metabolism, especially the growth and maintenance of bone. It is found in human skin and is activated with exposure of the skin to sunlight. Vitamin D deficiency can cause rickets or bow legs. An overdose can cause kidney damage. Vitamin E, or tocopherol, appears to play a role in blood cell and nervous system tissues, but its precise functions and properties have yet to be determined. It is found in peanuts, vegetable oils, wheat germ, and green leafy vegetables. Vitamin K provides essential cofactors for the production of certain clotting factors in the liver. It is used to treat some clotting disorders. Vitamin K is contained in liver and green leafy vegetables. Important members of the B group include B_1 or thiamine; B_2 or riboflavin; niacin; B_6 or pyridoxine; folic acid; and B_{12} or cyanocobalamin. Thiamine acts as a coenzyme in carbohydrate metabolism. It occurs naturally in whole grains, yeast, nuts, and lean pork. Its deficiency, seen in rice-eating populations and alcoholics, causes beriberi. Riboflavin is also a coenzyme active in oxidation reactions. It is found in milk, green leafy vegetables, and liver and organs. A deficiency will cause lesions of the skin, mouth, or eyes. Niacin is a general term for nicotinic acid and nicotinamide, coenzymes in carbohydrate metabolism. Niacin occurs in wheat germ, lean meat, fish, and peanuts. A deficiency causes pellagra and, if the deficiency is extreme, it can cause death. Pyridoxine provides an enzyme important in energy storage and its deficiency can lead to anemia. It occurs naturally in lean meat, whole grains, milk, and egg yolks. Folic acid is an essential cofactor in the metabolism of nucleic acid and a deficiency of the vitamin, which is not uncommon in pregnancy, can cause anemia. Folic acid occurs naturally in yeast and in green leafy vegetables. Cyano-

cobalamin is essential for all the body's cells and a deficiency can lead to pernicious anemia. It occurs naturally in bivalves and fish, eggs and lean meat, and rigorous vegetarians are at particular risk of deficiency. Pantothenic acid, biotin, choline, inositol, and para-aminobenzoic acid are other members of the B-group. Vitamin C, another of the water-soluble vitamins, is also known as ascorbic acid and plays an important role in the healing process, blood cell formation, and bone and tissue growth. It occurs naturally in citrus fruits, cabbage, berries, peppers, and tomatoes. Deficiency leads to scurvy, and extreme and prolonged deficiency causes death. The beneficial effects of Vitamin C in the prevention and treatment of the common cold have yet to be conclusively determined.

Vivaldi, Antonio (c.1680-1741), Venetian baroque composer. He wrote vocal music, sonatas, some 450 concertos for violin and other instruments (helping establish the 3-movement form), and *concerti grossi*, including the famous *Four Seasons*. His work has a sparkling clarity, strong rhythms, and a wealth of melody.
See also: Baroque.

Antonio Vivaldi

Vivisection, dissection of living animals, usually in the course of physiological or pathological research; the use of the term is often extended to cover all animal experimentation. The practice remains the subject of considerable public controversy.

Vizsla, or Hungarian pointer, breed of hunting dog. It was probably first brought to central Europe by the Magyars about 1,000 years ago. The vizsla weighs about 50 lb (23 kg) and has a rusty or sandy yellow coat.

Vladimir I (?-1015), Russian grand duke who established Christianity as the country's official religion. Born a pagan, he converted to Christianity about 988. He built churches, schools, and libraries and promoted trade with European countries. He was declared a saint after his death.

Vladivostok (pop. 590,000), capital of Primorski Kray, East Russian SFSR, USSR, chief Pacific naval port of the USSR, on Peter the Great Bay near North Korea. Founded in 1860, it has shipbuilding, manufacturing, chemical, and fish-canning industries. It is the east terminus of the Trans-Siberian Railway.
See also: Union of Soviet Socialist Republics.

Vlaminck, Maurice de (1876-1958), French artist who, along with André Derain and Henri Matisse, was a leader of the fauvist movement. Vlaminck was strongly influenced by Vincent van Gogh and adopted his slashing brushstrokes and brilliant colors for dramatic effect. He moved gradually to a style close to that of Paul Cézanne. Notable works include *The Storm.*

Vocal cord *see:* Larynx.

Vocational education, courses of study that prepare students for a range of occupations that do not require baccalaureate or higher degrees, in areas such as agriculture, business, trades, industry, health services, home economics, and various technical fields. Instruction takes place in high schools, trade schools, community colleges, and correspondence schools and through formal apprenticeship programs and on-the-job training. Many vocational education programs have been funded by the U.S. government.

Vocational rehabilitation, service designed for persons, usually 16 years of age and older, with mental and/or physical handicaps, to become employable. The three components of vocational rehabilitation are rehabilitation counseling, vocational evaluation, and job placement. Specialists in each of these areas work as a team, matching job skills and performance against standards in a career field. In the United States, vocational rehabilitation first developed in the late 1800s to assist disabled veterans. In Canada, the Vocational Rehabilitation of Disabled Persons Act of 1961 established vocational rehabilitation guidelines. Counselors in vocational rehabilitation are usually required to have a bachelor's degree and preferably a master's degree with a concentration in counseling, human relations, industrial psychology, statistics, and testing.

Vogelweide, Walther von der *see:* Walther von der Vogelweide.

Voice, sound emitted in speech, the method of communication exclusive to *Homo sapiens*. Dependent upon the passage of air from the lungs through the trachea, larynx, pharynx, and mouth, its quality is largely determined by the shape and size of these structures and the resonance of the nose and nasal sinuses. Phonation is the sounding of the elements of speech by the action of several small muscles on the vocal cords of the larynx. Articulation consists in the modulation of sounds by the use of the tongue, teeth, and lips in different combinations. Vowels are produced mainly by phonation, while consonants derive their characteristics principally from articulation.

Voice of America (VOA), radio division of the International Communications Agency (formerly the U.S. Information Agency), established in 1942 to explain the U.S. role in World War II. Its network now broadcasts, in English and other languages, a favorable view of life in the United States to many (chiefly Communist) countries.
See also: Information Agency, U.S.

Voiceprint, or speech spectrogram, visual record of the sound waves of a human voice made by running a tape recording of a voice through an instrument called a sound spectrograph. The sound spectrograph was developed in the 1940s by U.S. scientists at Bell Research Laboratories. Voiceprints are used in the study of speech and hearing disorders. Police use voiceprints for evidence in the prosecution of criminal cases.

Volapük, universal language created in 1879 by Johann Martin Schleyer, a German priest. It combined elements of English, German, Latin, French, and Italian. It proved difficult to learn because of the unfamiliar appearance of the words and its grammatical complexity. Few people speak Volapük today.

Volcano, fissure or vent in a planet's crust through which magma and associated material may be extruded onto the surface. This may occur with explosive force. The extruded magma, or lava, solidifies in various forms soon after exposure to the atmosphere. In particular it does so around the vent, building up the characteristic volcanic cone, at the top of which is a crater containing the main vent. There may be secondary vents forming "parasitic cones" in the slopes of the main cone. If the volcano is dormant or extinct, the vents may be blocked with a plug (or neck) of solidified lava. Classifying volcanoes in order of increasing violence, the main types are Hawaiian, Strombolian, Vulcanian, Vesuvian, and Peléan. Volcanoes are generally restricted to belts of seismic activity, particularly active plate margins, but some intraplate volcanic activity is also known, as in the case of Hawaii. At midocean ridges magma rises from deep in the mantle and is added to the receding edges of the plates. In mountain ranges, where plates are in collision, volatile matter ascends from the subducted edge of a plate, perhaps many kilometers below the surface, bursting through the overlying plate in a series of volcanoes. Around 500 active volcanoes are known of on earth; active volcanoes have also been found on Mars and on Jupiter's satellite Io.

The eruption of lava and hot ash from the ocean floor lead to the formation, in 1963, of Surtsey, a volcanic island to the south of Iceland.

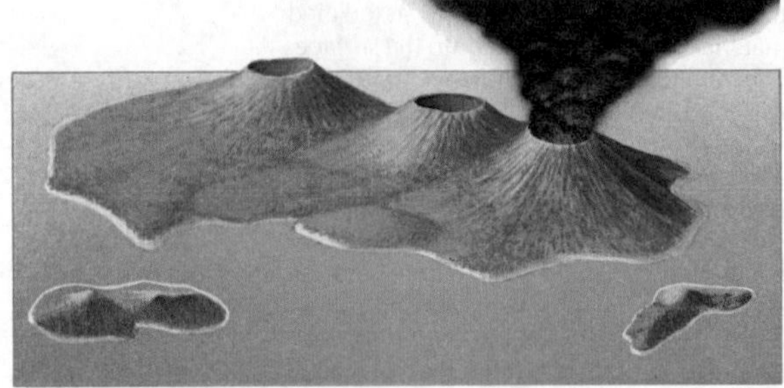

Before the great eruption in 1883, Krakatoa was a small volcanic island in the Sunda Strait of Indonesia consisting of three volcanic cones: Perbuwatan (northwest), Danan (middle), and Rakata (south). At the termination of the 1883 activity, it was discovered that Perbuwatan, Danan, and half of Rakata had been destroyed, leaving only a sterile, ash-covered islet some 59 ft (18 m) higher than its predecessor.

According to the theory of plate tectonics, the earth's outer shell is divided into sections called plates, which move continuously. Most volcanoes occur where two plates collide.

When two plates move away from each other they form an oceanic ridge; when two plates slide past each other, the dipping plane forms the subduction zone.

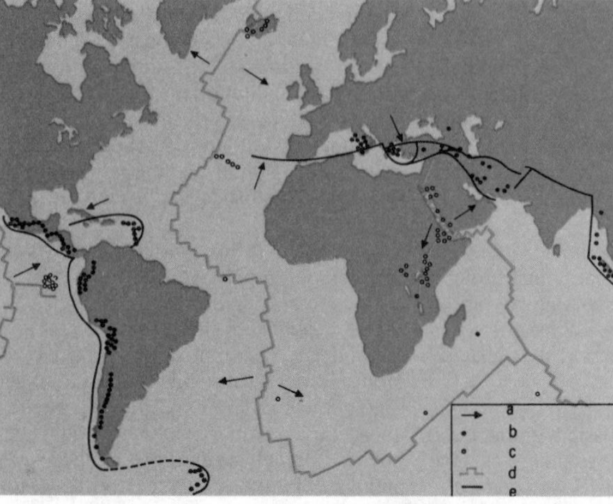

Key:
a. movement of plates
b. volcanoes in subduction zones
c. volcanoes on mid-oceanic ridges
d. mid-oceanic ridge
e. subduction zone

Volcker, Paul Adolph (1927-), U.S. economist and chairman of the Federal Reserve Board (1979-87). He served as undersecretary for monetary affairs in the Treasury Department (1969-74) and president of the New York Reserve Bank (1975-9) before being appointed to head the Federal Reserve by President Jimmy Carter. He was architect of the Board's tight-money policy, which kept interest rates on borrowing high in order to contract the money supply and dampen inflation. In 1983 President Ronald Reagan appointed him to a second term.
See also: Economics.

Vole, mouselike member of the New World rat and mouse family, closely related to the lemming. Voles are about 5 in (13 cm) long with short, shaggy, grayish-brown fur. Most inhabit fields and meadows. There are over 40 species of vole. The most common North American species is the meadow vole (genus *Microtus*).

Volga River, chief tributary of Russia and the longest in Europe. It rises in the Valdai Hills, northwest of Moscow, and flows 2,293 mi (3,690 km) through Gorki, Kazan, Kuibyshev, Saratov, Volgograd, and Astrakhan to its Caspian Sea delta. Draining an area of some 530,000 sq mi (1,372,700 sq km) it is the main artery of the world's greatest network of commercial waterways linking the White, Baltic, Caspian, Azov, and Black seas.

Volgograd (pop. 969,000), important manufacturing city in the Soviet Union, located on the west bank of the Volga River. It was founded in the 1200s as Tsaritsyn and renamed Stalingrad (after Joseph Stalin) in 1925. During World War II the city was devastated by the battle between the advancing German army and the defending forces. It was completely rebuilt after the war and renamed Volgograd in 1961, after Stalin was downgraded.

Volkswagen (German, "the people's car"), one of the world's largest producers of passenger cars. It was established by the German government in 1937 and is now owned privately. The Volkswagen beetle, designed by the Austrian engineer Ferdinand Porsche in the mid-1930s, became the most popular car ever built. Volkswagen builds over 2.5 million cars annually in countries throughout the world.

Volleyball, game for 2 teams of 6, who volley (using any part of the body above the waist) an inflated ball (8.25 in/21 cm in diameter) across an 8-ft (2.4-m) high net, conceding points by failing to return the ball or by hitting it out of bounds. Invented at the Holyoke (Mass.) YMCA in 1895 by W. G. Morgan, it became an Olympic event in Tokyo (1964).

Volstead Act, law passed by the Congress of the United States in 1919 to enforce the 18th Amendment to the Constitution, which prohibited the manufacture, sale, or transportation of alcoholic beverages within the United States. The amendment was introduced by Representative Andrew J. Volstead of Minnesota. The 21st Amendment repealed the Volstead Act (1933).
See also: Prohibition.

Volta, Alessandro (1745-1827), Italian physicist. The volt was named for him. He invented (1800) the voltaic pile (the first battery) and thus provided science with its earliest source of continuous electric current. Volta's invention demonstrated that "animal electricity" could be produced using solely inanimate materials, thus ending a long dispute with the supporters of Luigi Galvani's view that it was a special property of animal matter.
See also: Electric current.

Voltaire (François-Marie Arouet; 1694-1778), French author, philosopher, and major figure of the Enlightenment. An enemy of tyrants, he spent much of his life in exile, including 23 years at his property on the Swiss border. His *Letters Concerning the English Nation* (1733) extolled religious and political toleration and the ideas of Sir Isaac Newton and John Locke. The satire *Candide* (1759), a rational skeptic's attack on the optimism of Gottfried von Leibniz, shows Voltaire's astringent style at its best. A friend of Frederick II of Prussia, Voltaire contributed to Denis Diderot's *Encyclopedia* and wrote his own *Philosophical Dictionary* (1764).
See also: Age of Reason.

Volunteers of America, voluntary philanthropic society founded in New York City (1896) by Ballington and Maud Booth after a split with the Salvation Army. It aims to win converts to Christianity and provides many social services. Though it retains military forms and titles, it is run democratically.

Vomiting, return of food or other substance (e.g., blood) from the stomach. It may be induced by drugs, motion sickness, infection, uremia, or stomach or pyloric disorders. Morning vomiting may be a feature of early pregnancy. Drugs may be needed to control vomiting, along with fluid and nutrient replacement.

Von Braun, Wernher (1912-77), German rocket engineer who designed the first self-contained missile, the V-2, which was used against the United Kingdom in 1944. In 1945 he was brought to the United States, where he led the team that put the first U.S. artificial satellite in orbit (1958). He later developed the Saturn rocket used in the Apollo moon-landing program, and he pioneered the concept of the space shuttle.
See also: Rocket.

Vonnegut, Kurt, Jr. (1922-), U.S. fiction writer. Vonnegut writes dark and humorous science-fictionalized novels of life with little purpose. His works portray societal, religious, political, and scientific systems as unavoidably destructive. His first novel, *Player Piano* (1952), is a study of technology in modern society. *Mother Night* (1961), *Cat's Cradle* (1963), and *God Bless You, Mr. Rosewater* (1965), explore the morals and social conventions in America. *Slaughterhouse Five* (1969), ruminates on the compulsion humans have to impose devastation on themselves, and suggests that this be accepted with resignation and humor. Other works include *Breakfast of Champions* (1973), *Deadeye Dick* (1982), *Galapagos* (1985), *Bluebeard* (1987), and *Hocus Pocus* (1990).

Von Neumann, John (1903-57), Hungarian-born U.S. mathematician who put quantum mechanics on a rigorous mathematical foundation. He created game theory, and made important contributions to the theory of computers, as well as to many branches of abstract mathematics.
See also: Quantum mechanics.

Von Sternberg, Josef (1894-1969), Austrian-born U.S. motion-picture director famous for his films starring Marlene Dietrich. The first film, *The Blue Angel* (1930), was made in Germany. It was followed by *Morocco* (1930), *Dishonored* (1931), *Shanghai Express* (1932), *Blond Venus* (1932), *The Scarlet Empress* (1934), and *The Devil Is a Woman* (1935), all filmed in Hollywood.

Von Willebrand's disease, hereditary disease in which there is prolonged bleeding when the skin is injured. Unlike hemophilia, Von Willebrand's disease causes external bleeding; internal bleeding is rare. It affects both males and females and occurs most commonly in Scandinavian countries. The disease is caused by the absence of one of the clotting factors in the blood. Erik von Willebrand, a German professor of medicine, first identified the disease in 1926.

Voodoo, folk religion, chiefly of Haiti, with West African and added Roman Catholic and native West Indian elements. It involves worship of the spirits of saints and ancestors, who may "possess" participants. Prayers, drumming, dancing, and feasts are part of the ritual. A cult group's priest or priestess is believed to act as a medium, work charms, lay curses, and recall zombies (the "living dead").
See also: Religion.

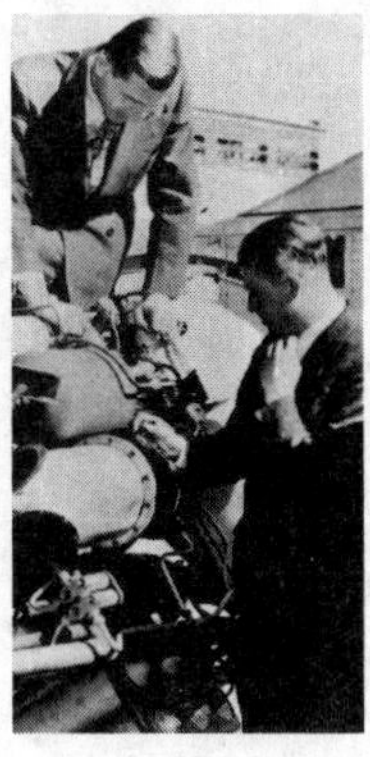
Wernher von Braun

Vorster, Balthazar Johannes (1915-83), South African political leader and prime minister (1966-78). On the right of the Nationalist Party, he was in charge of education (1958-61) and minister of justice (1961-66), responsible for some of the most repressive of the apartheid laws. He sought later to improve relations with black Africa. Elected president in 1978, he resigned in 1979 after being accused of false testimony on expenditure of government funds.
See also: South Africa.

Voting, formal collective expression of approval or rejection of a candidate for office or a course of action. The election of of-

W

ficers is a basic feature of democracy, but universal adult suffrage is recent: U.S. women obtained the vote only in 1920. Sometimes voting is compulsory, as in Australia and in Communist states. In the United States, voting originally followed English parliamentary practice, with the addition of the New England town meeting. Ballot papers first appeared in Massachusetts in 1634. Most U.S. states now use voting machines to ensure secrecy, speed, and accuracy.

Voting Rights Act of 1965, U.S. law aimed at eliminating local laws and practices that served to prevent blacks and other minorities from voting. It was strongly backed by President Lyndon B. Johnson, who signed it into law.

Voyager Program, two unmanned U.S. probes of the outer solar system. *Voyager 1* made close approaches to Jupiter in March 1979 and to Saturn in Nov. 1980. *Voyager 2* bypassed Jupiter in July 1979, swung around Saturn in Aug. 1981, continued to Uranus in 1986 and Neptune in 1989. The probes provided remarkable close-up views of the two giant gas planets and their satellites, revealing, among other things, the existence of a ring around Jupiter, active volcanoes on Jupiter's moon Io and a completely unexpected complexity in Saturn's ring system.
See also: Space exploration.

Voyager

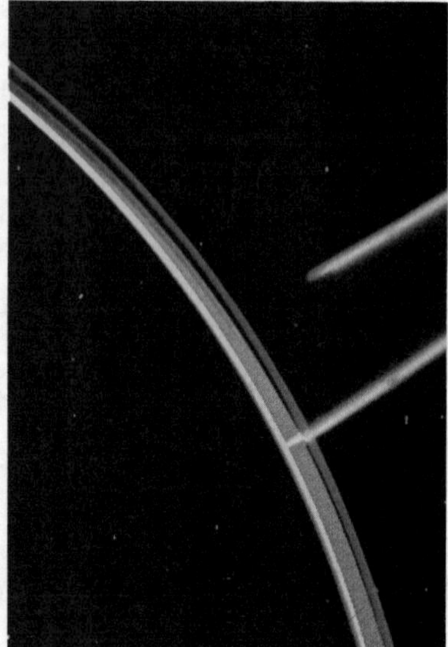

Part of the ring of Jupiter, photographed by Voyager *2 on July 10, 1979*

Voyageurs National Park, scenic 219,431-acre (88,804-hectare) park in northern Minnesota (authorized in 1971), with lakes, forests, and interesting glacial features.
See also: National Parks.

V/STOL (*V*ertical/ *S*hort *T*ake-*O*ff and *L*anding), type of aircraft that can take off and land vertically or on a short runway. While large conventional planes need about 5,000 ft (1,500 m) of runway, a V/STOL plane needs less than 500 ft (150 m). V/STOLs have great military value because they can land on small airfields near the scene of battle as well as on small aircraft carriers and military ships without large flight decks. Both the United States and Great Britain have a combat V/STOL called the Harrier. There are commercial STOLS that can operate from small airports.
See also: Airplane.

Vuillard, Édouard (1868-1940), French painter, printmaker, and decorator who, along with his friend Pierre Bonnard, developed the intimist style of painting. His subjects were scenes from his private world, chiefly domestic scenes from his mother's home. Vuillard received commissions to do decorative works also. He painted the foyer of the Théatre des Champs-Elysées (1913) and the murals in the Palais de Chaillob (1937) and the League of Nations, Geneva (1939).

Vulcan, in Roman mythology, god of fire. He was also the blacksmith of the gods, skilled in metalworking. Vulcan is identified with the Greek god Hephaestus. He was a son of Jupiter and Juno and was married to Venus.
See also: Mythology.

Vulgate, Latin version of the Bible, so called because it became the most widespread (Latin: *vulgata*) in use. Largely the work of St. Jerome, who revised earlier Old Latin translations, it was collected in the 6th century and universally established by 800. In 1546 the Council of Trent confirmed the Vulgate as the sole official version of the Roman Catholic church.
See also: Bible.

Vulture, any of 2 families of large, soaring, diurnal birds of prey. The New World vultures are a primitive family, Cathartidae; the Old World vultures are a branch of the Accipitridae, being most closely related to certain eagles. All vultures are adapted to feed on animal carrion. Their heads and necks are wholly or partially naked; several have specialized tongues to feed rapidly on liquid flesh or bone marrow.

W, 23rd letter of the English alphabet. Its origins have been traced to the Semitic letter *waw* (meaning "hook"), which was a symbol resembling a tent peg or hook, itself perhaps derived from a *y*-shaped Egyptian hieroglyph. This letter reached the Roman alphabet as a *v*, though it was used both for *u* and *v*. Medieval Norman scribes began writing *vv* or *uu* ("double *u*") to represent the Anglo-Saxon *w* sound for which Norman French had no equivalent.

Wabash River, river running through Ohio, Indiana, and Illinois. Rising in Grand Lake, in western Ohio, the Wabash flows west and southwest across Indiana for about 475 mi (764 km) before emptying into the Ohio River in southwestern Indiana. The river forms a major segment of the border between Indiana and Illinois. The Wabash was used as a transportation route by Native Americans as early as the 12th century.

Waco (pop. 189,123), industrial city in central Texas, situated on the Brazos River nearly 100 mi (161 km) south of Dallas. Besides being a major market for cotton and other agricultural products, Waco is home to factories producing clothing, glass products, textiles, and machinery. Waco was the residence of the Branch Davidians, a religious cult that made headlines in 1993, when, after a 6-week standoff with the FBI , its compound was burned and at least 75 cultists died.

Wages and hours, income derived from labor, figured on the basis of the number of hours worked. Wages, the rate of which is determined by supply and demand, are the leading source of income in the United States and may be calculated for work completed by the hour, day, week, month, or by individual job or service performed. In addition to wages, workers may also receive remuneration in the form of overtime payments, bonuses, paid vacations, holidays, sick or maternity leave, and retirement benefits. Wages are categorized as either money wages or real wages. Money wages are the actual amount paid to workers; real wages represent the buying power of the money wages. Economists gauge economic change by investigating the fluctuations in money wages and making real-wage comparisons.

Wagner, Honus (John Peter Wagner; 1874-1955), U.S. baseball player. Wagner, considered to be baseball's greatest shortstop, won 8 National League batting titles (1900, 03, 04, 06-09, 11) and holds the National League record for triples (252 career). Wagner's hit over .300 for 17 consecutive seasons (1897-1913), a major league record. He played for the Louisville Colonels (1897-99) and Pittsburgh Pirates (1900-17) and was among the first group of players inducted into the National Baseball Hall of Fame (1936).

Wagner, Richard (1813-83), German composer. His adventurous and influential music marks the high point of German romanticism. A conductor in provincial opera houses, he achieved his first successes as a composer with the operas *Rienzi* (1838-40), *Der Fliegende Holländer* (1841), *Tannhäuser* (1844), and *Lohengrin* (1846-48), in which he pioneered his new ideas in fusing music and drama. The culmination of his creative principles is found in the myth cycle, *Der Ring des Nibelungen,* comprising *Das Rheingold* (1853-54), *Die Walküre* (1854-56), *Siegfried* (1856-69), and *Götterdämmerung* (1874). Involved in the 1848 Dresden revolution, Wagner fled (with the help of Franz Liszt) to Switzerland, where he wrote *Tristan und Isolde* (1857-59) and the comic opera *Die Meistersinger von Nürnberg* (1862-67), in addition to part of the Ring cycle. He next moved to Bavaria (1872), where Ludwig II helped him found the Bayreuth Festival. *Parsifal* (1877-82) was his last opera. His second wife, **Cosima** (1837-1930), the daughter of Liszt, was largely responsible for the continuing success of the Bayreuth Festival.

Wagner, Robert Ferdinand (1877-1953), German-born U.S. politician. As a Democratic senator (1927-49) from New York, he helped create the New Deal program, particularly influencing programs involving labor, social security, and housing.

Wagner, Robert Ferdinand, Jr. (1910-91), U.S. politician and administrator. Son of senator Robert F. Wagner, he served 3 terms as mayor (1954-66) of New York City, introducing controversial reforms in housing, education, and civil rights. He was U.S. ambassador to Spain (1968-69).

Wagner Act *see:* National Labor Relations Act.

Wagon, wheeled vehicle of primary importance to transportation and commerce. The invention of the wagon coincided with that of the wheel, over 5,000 years ago, when solid wooden wheels were fixed to a simple axle attached to a sledge. Wheeled transport vehicles, hauled by oxen, developed in Mesopotamia. The Greeks and Romans improved vehicle design until after the fall of the Roman Empire, when little was done to advance the design of wheeled conveyance. Farm carts remained the most widely used transport until the development of 4-wheeled coaches in Germany in the Middle Ages. By the 17th century, in western Europe, a period of mechanical and scientific enlightenment had begun. Spring suspension came into use permitting longer-distanced travel at higher speeds. This led to development and improvement of commercial and passenger coaches and carriages, freight-transport vehicles, and ultimately to the invention of the automobile.

Wagtail, any of several small Old World birds (family Motacillidae) related to the pipits. Wagtails have long tails that they wag up and down to keep their balance. The yellow wagtail has spread across the Bering Strait and nests in Alaska.

Wahoo, swift-swimming sport and food fish (*Acanthocybium solandri*), of the mackerel family. The wahoo is found worldwide in warm waters, particularly tropical areas of the Atlantic, Pacific, and Indian oceans. The wahoo has a slender, elongated body with a pointed nose, long backfin, and crescent-shaped tail. Its back is dark gray-blue, with silvery, irregularly striped sides. Wahoos may grow to 8 ft (2.4 m) in length and attain a weight of about 180 lb (82k).

Wailing Wall, part of the western wall of the ancient Temple in Jerusalem, destroyed by the Romans in A.D.70. It is held sacred by the Jews, who gather there to pray and mourn the Temple's destruction.
See also: Jews.

Wainwright, Jonathan Mayhew (1883-1953), U.S. general. A veteran of World War I, he was commander of the defense of the Philippines during World War II. Despite great courage, he had to surrender Bataan and Corregidor to the Japanese in 1942, upon which he was taken as a prisoner of war until 1945. He was awarded the Medal of Honor on his return.
See also: World War II.

Waite, Morrison Remick (1816-88), seventh chief justice of the U.S. Supreme Court (1874-88). Appointed by Pres. Ulysses S. Grant, Waite became the principal interpreter of post-Civil War amendments to the Constitution, including that of the due process clause of the 14th Amendment, limiting state power. In the Granger Cases (1877), which involved state legislation intending to establish maximum rates charged by the operators of grain elevators and railways, he maintained that only businesses that were "affected with a public interest" could be subject to state regulation. In several cases concerning newly freed slaves, Waite held that the privileges and immunities due U.S. citizens under the 14th and 15th amendments had not provided Congress the power to safeguard civil rights, but that suffrage for freed slaves must come from the states. Waite was one of the founders of the Republican Party.
See also: Supreme Court of the United States.

Wake, tradition in which people gather at the home of a dead person before burial. This is a popular custom, especially in Western cultures. Its purpose in part is to console the family and friends of the deceased, but it is also assumed that long ago a consensus of people was needed to confirm the status of the corpse.

Wake Island, atoll in the central Pacific Ocean, an unincorporated territory administered by the U.S. Air Force. An important commercial and military airbase, it consists of 3 islets (Wake, Wilkes, and Peale), totalling 3 sq mi (7.8 sq km) situated around a shallow lagoon. It was occupied by Japan from 1941 to 1945.

Wake-robin *see:* Trillium.

Waksman, Selman Abraham (1888-1973), U.S. microbiologist. Waksman, an authority on soil microbiology, developed a controlled system to discover antibiotics among microbes, particularly actinomycetes. Antibiotic activity was tested on about 10,000 soil microbes, leading to the discovery of the antibiotic streptomycin (1943), the first truly effective agent in the treatment of tuberculosis. Waksman was awarded the Nobel Prize in physiology or medicine in 1952.
See also: Microbiology.

Walata, important trade city of West Africa in the 11th-16th centuries, now the town of Oualata in Mauritania. Settled by the Muslims in the late 11th century, it was successively controlled by the Mali Empire, the Tuareg, and the Songhai Empire. Trade was conducted in copper, gold, swords, and slaves.

Wald, George (1906-), U.S. chemist and prominent pacifist. His work on the chemistry of vision brought him a share, with Haldane K. Hartline and Roger A. Granit, of the 1967 Nobel Prize in physiology or medicine.
See also: Chemistry.

Wald, Lillian D. (1867-1940), U.S. nurse, public health services pioneer, and social worker, founder of the Henry Street Settlement (1893). Wald organized a visiting nurse service that led to the inception of the first public school nursing system. She became an advocate for children and others with special health needs, and was responsible for initiating both an American Red Cross nursing service to rural areas (1912) and The Children's Bureau (1912), a national group. Wald, as a member of the American Union Against Militarism as well as several other national and international commissions of the same nature, promoted world peace, public welfare, and supported worker's unions. Written works include *The House on Henry Street* (1915) and *Windows on Henry Street* (1934).
See also: Nursing.

Waldenses, or Waldensians, reforming Christian sect founded by Peter Waldo in Lyons, France, in the 12th century. They preached poverty, rejected the papacy, and took the Bible as their sole authority, for which they were excommunicated (1184) and persecuted. The survivors united with the Protestants in the Reformation. The Waldensian Church still exists, with several offshoots in the United States.
See also: Protestantism.

Waldheim, Kurt (1918-), Austrian diplomat and minister of foreign affairs (1968-70), and secretary general of the United Nations (1972-81). As secretary general he worked to strengthen the UN's peacekeeping role and to increase aid to poor countries. In 1986 he was elected to the Austrian presidency, in spite of his history as a German intelligence soldier and Nazi officer (World War II).
See also: Austria; United Nations.

Richard Wagner

Wales (Welsh: *Cymru*), historic principality of Great Britain, politically united with England since 1536. It is a large, roughly rectangular peninsula projecting into the Irish Sea west of England. Covering 8,016 sq mi (20,761 sq km), it is dominated by the Cambrian Mountains (Mt. Snowdon, 3,500 ft/1,085 m), and its rivers include the Severn, Wye, Usk, Taff, Dee, and Teifi. The climate is mild and wet. The majority of the population lives in the south, near the rich coalfields. Less than 20% speak both Welsh and English. The largest cities are Cardiff, the capital, and Swansea. Major industries, including coal mining, steel, oil refining, manmade fibers, and electronics, are also concentrated in the south. Agriculture, mostly cattle and sheep raising, predominates elsewhere.
See also: England.

Wales

Walesa, Lech (1943-), president of Poland (1991-). In 1980 he led the Polish labor movement in its struggle to win government recognition of Solidarity (an umbrella labor group composed of about 50 trade unions)—the first time a Communist government had recognized an independent labor organization. In a 1981 military crackdown, the Polish government banned Solidarity and interned Walesa. He was released in 1982 and awarded the Nobel Peace Prize in 1983. In the upheavals of 1989, Solidarity was revived, and Walesa played a key role in establishing the new non-Communist Polish government.
See also: Poland.

Lech Walesa

Walker, Alice (1944-), U.S. author of poetry and novels examining the life experiences of African Americans. Walker was awarded the Pulitzer Prize for *The Color Purple* (1982), the story of Celie, a poor girl growing up in the rural South. Other works include *Once* (1968) and *Revolutionary Petunias and Other Poems* (1973), both volumes of poetry; a biography, *Langston Hughes, American Poet* (1974); and the novel *The Third Life of Grange Copeland* (1970).

George Wallace

Walker, David (1785-1830), radical African-American abolitionist. Walker, a free man, educated himself, became an abolitionist speaker, and contributed to *Freedom's Journal*, a newspaper dedicated to the anti-slavery movement. In 1829 Walker wrote the anti-slavery tract *An Appeal to the Colored Citizens of the World*, which was a strong indictment of all proslavery advocates, and which exhorted slaves to revolt against their bondage. Copies of Walker's treatise were smuggled into Southern states in the pockets of second-hand clothing. Legislation was soon introduced outlawing the circulation of all abolitionist literature and making it illegal for slaves to be educated.
See also: Abolitionism.

Walker, Herschel, Jr. (1962-), U.S. football running back. Walker, a 3-time All-American player from the Univ. of Georgia, won the Heisman Trophy in 1982. He played for the New Jersey Generals (U.S. Football League), the Dallas Cowboys, and the Minnesota Vikings.

Walker, Mary Edwards (1832-1919), U.S. physician, writer, and advocate of women's rights. The Medal of Honor bestowed upon Walker (1865) for her work as a surgeon for the Union forces during the Civil War was revoked (1917) because of her official non-military status. The medal was rightfully reinstated many years later (1977). To protest restrictions placed upon women, she chose to wear clothes unacceptable in her time—trousers. She further discussed women's rights in her books *Hit* (1871) and *Unmasked, or the Science of Immortality* (1878).
See also: Women's movements.

Walkie-talkie, portable 2-way radio frequently used by police, hunters, and others on the move to communicate over short distances (up to a few kilometers). In the United States, walkie-talkies operate on 1 or more of 23 channels lying between 26.960 MHz and 27.255 MHz.

Walking, or race-walking, competitive track-and-field sport. This form of racing utilizes a precise heel-and-toe gait: The leading foot touches the ground heel first advancing the walker quickly forward onto the toe, which provides a pushing momentum to each stride. The leg is locked in a straight position momentarily while the foot is still touching the ground. An expert race-walker can walk 1 mi (1.6 km) in about 6.5 minutes while an ordinary walker would take about 15-20 minutes to cover the same distance. Walking competitions, particularly in the Olympic Games, are held at distances of about 12-31 mi (20-50 km).

Walking stick, or stick insect, insect (*Diapheromera femorata*) that resembles a twig, camouflaging it from its enemies. There are several species of these insects of the family Phasmidae; the common walking stick has long, slender legs and a body of about 2-3 in (5-8 cm). They are usually a green or brownish color, may have sharp spines, and release a noxious scent. Walking sticks harm trees by eating the leaves; however, few survive the larval stage because the female lays her eggs where she stands and most fall to the ground.

Wallaby, rabbit-sized member of the kangaroo family (especially genus *Macropus*), native to Australia, Tasmania, and New Guinea. Like kangaroos, wallabies have large, strong hind feet and limbs and long tails. They are herbivores. All wallabies produce a single offspring, suckling it in the marsupium, or pouch.

Wallace, Alfred Russel (1823-1913), English naturalist and evolutionist. He formulated a theory of natural selection (survival of the fittest) simultaneously with, but independent of, Charles Darwin. Wallace explored at length the Malay Archipelago and the Amazon, where the idea of natural selection occurred to him, and where he formulated a basis for geographically categorizing animals. Wallace published "On the Law Which Has Regulated the Introduction of New Species" (1855), which he shared with Darwin. Together they presented their theory before the Linnaean Society (1858). Other works include *The Malay Archipelago* (1869), *Contributions to the Theory of Natural Selection* (1870), and *The Geographical Distribution of Animals* (2 vols, 1876), a systemization of the science of biogeography.
See also: Darwin, Charles Robert.

Wallace, George Corley (1919-), U.S. political leader, governor of Alabama (1963-67, 1971-79, 1983-86). Wallace, a segregationist, achieved notoriety in 1963 with his unsuccessful attempt to prevent racial integration at the University of Alabama. He ran for president 3 times, and in 1972 was shot and paralyzed in an attempted assassination while campaigning for the Democratic presidential nomination. Unable by Alabama law to succeed himself as governor, he had his wife, Lurleen, run for office to replace him (she won the election). He won the 1982 gubernatorial election with black support, and retired in 1986.

Wallace, Henry Agard (1888-1965), 33rd vice president of the United States (1941-45). A distinguished agricultural economist and plant geneticist, he was secretary of agriculture under President Franklin D. Roosevelt (1933-41). His success with New Deal farm programs led to the vice presidency. He became secretary of commerce (1945) but was dismissed (1946) for criticizing Truman. He ran unsuccessfully in 1948 as presidential candidate of the Progressive Party.

Wallace, Lew (Lewis Wallace; 1827-1905), U.S. military leader, lawyer, and author. Wallace is best known for his novels, particularly *Ben Hur* (1880), about the advent of Christianity in the Roman Empire. Wallace served in the Mexican War, and while a Union Army major general in the Civil War, captured Fort Donelson, Tenn. Wallace had studied law before the wars and became a practicing attorney in Indianapolis after military service. He headed courts of inquiry investigating wartime conduct of some Union and Confederate leaders, and served on the trial of Abraham Lincoln's assassins. He was appointed governor of New Mexico (1878-81) and minister to Turkey (1881-85).

Wallboard, fibrous building material made in rigid sheets and used to cover walls and ceilings for temperature and sound insulation, fire protection, and decoration. Types of wallboard include *fiberboard*, made of compressed cane or wood fibers; *hardboard*, a denser, more compressed board of similar composition; and *plasterboard*, used in building as a substitute for plaster, made of heavy paper, fiberboard, or other material bonded to a gypsum core.

Wallenberg, Raoul (1912-47?), Swedish diplomat. While representing Sweden in Budapest during World War II, he issued Swedish passports to 20,000 Hungarian Jews to prevent their deportation into Nazi hands. Soviet authorities arrested him as a spy in 1945 and reported his death in prison in 1947. In 1981 an international association found evidence indicating he might be alive and urged the Soviet Union to investigate (his death was never verified). In the same year the U.S. Congress declared him an honorary U.S. citizen.
See also: Sweden.

Waller, Fats (Thomas Wright Waller; 1904-43), U.S. jazz and blues pianist, composer, and entertainer. Waller began his career working in cabarets and theaters, where he accompanied various singers. He was one of few jazz musicians to become widely popular, and by the late 1920s his music, which was often witty and animated, was heard in many Broadway revues. From 1929 to 1943 Waller recorded hundreds of songs, including "Ain't Misbehavin'," "Honeysuckle Rose," and "Blue Turning Gray Over You." Waller also appeared in films, including *Stormy Weather* (1943).
See also: Jazz.

Walleye *see:* Perch.

Wallflower, or gillyflower, fragrant flowering plant (*Cheiranthus cheiri*) of the mustard family. Wallflowers, native to southern Europe and now widely cultivated, are so named for their tendency to grow on walls or on the sides of cliffs. The plants are biennial or perennial, grow to about 28 in (70 cm), and have stalks bearing clusters of maroon or purple flowers. The western wallflower (*Erysimum asperum*), a perennial, produces golden, orange, or brown flowers.

Walloons, French-speaking people (chiefly Celtic), inhabitants of southern Belgium and adjacent areas of France. The Walloons, who make up about 44% of Belgium's population, have often been at odds with the Flemish-speaking majority, who have resented French political and cultural domination. Separate regional administrations were set up in 1974.

Wallpaper, printed, painted, or embossed wall covering used to finish interior walls. Wallpaper, which is hung with glue or paste on the undecorated side, is utilized mainly as a decorative feature, and may be from any of 5 categories: ceiling papers, border papers, scenic or panel papers, papers of imitative design, or relief-surfaced papers made of ricepaper, burlap, straw fibers, or thin wood. It is thought that wallpapers originated in Europe in the 1500s to imitate expensive tapestries. Other wallpapers evolved in China (1600s) and in France (1700s). The first U.S. wallpapers were produced in Philadelphia (1739).

Wall Street, financial center of the United States, located in lower Manhattan, New York City. Wall Street is the home of the New York Stock Exchange, many other commodity exchanges, and head offices of many banks and insurance and brokerage firms. The term "Wall Street" also refers to the nation's aggregate financial interests.
See also: Stock exchange.

Walnut, deciduous tree of the genus *Juglans*, prized for its wood and nuts. In the United States the black walnut (*J. nigra*) grows to 150 ft (45.7 m), its wood being used for furniture, musical instruments, and gun stocks. The English walnut (*J. regia*), which provides edible walnuts, is naturalized throughout the world. The walnut tree is a member of the family Juglandaceae and is related to the hickory and pecan.

Walpole, Sir Robert (1676-1745), English politician often described as Great Britain's first prime minister. A Whig, he held ministerial posts from 1708 to 1717. He was rewarded for his role in salvaging the government from the South Sea Bubble (a speculation scandal) with an appointment as first lord of the treasury and chancellor of the exchequer (1721), during which time he dominated Parliament and created political and financial stability. Facing opposition and unpopularity as Britain became involved in European wars from 1739, he resigned in 1742, becoming first earl of Orford.
See also: United Kingdom.

Walrus, either of 2 subspecies of seal-like marine mammals (*Odobenus rosmarus*), distinguished by upper canines that extend into long tusks (up to 3.5 ft/1.1 m) and wrinkled brown hides. Adult males may weigh up to 3,000 lb (1,400 kg). Walruses are found in shallow waters around Arctic coasts, often hauling themselves out onto rocks or ice floes to bask. They feed almost exclusively on mollusks.

Walter, Bruno (Bruno Walter Schlesinger; 1876-1962), German-born U.S. conductor. He was a protégé of Gustav Mahler, but his career in Europe was cut short by the Nazis (they forced him to leave), and he lived in the United States from 1939. He was renowned for his interpretations of Mahler, Wagner, Beethoven, and Brahms with the Metropolitan Opera and the New York Philharmonic.

Walter, Thomas Ustick (1804-87), U.S. architect known for the classical Greek influence in his designs. Walter was professor of architecture at Franklin Institute in Philadelphia; president of the American Institute of Architects (1876-87), and designer of Founder's Hall, Girard College, Philadelphia. Walter is best known for his designs of the additions and new dome for the U.S. Capitol in Washington, D.C. (1851-65). Other examples of his architectural designs are Andalusia, the home of Nicholas Biddle, and Moyamensing, a Philadelphia county prison.
See also: Architecture.

Fats Waller

Walter Reed Army Medical Center, military hospital and care facility in Washington, D.C. The center, named for U.S. Army pathologist Walter Reed, researcher of typhoid and yellow fevers, provides medical care for military personnel and their families; conducts medical and scientific research; and provides advanced education for medical personnel. The center covers a combined area of 253 acres (103 hectares) in Washington, and Forest Glen and Glenhaven, Md. Facilities include the Walter Reed Army Inst. of Research, the Armed Forces Inst. of Pathology, and the Inst. of Dental Research.
See also: Reed, Walter.

Walther Von der Vogelweide (c.1170-c.1230), most renowned medieval German lyric poet, or minnesinger. Walther's

Wall Street around the middle of the 19th century

poetry was more politically oriented than that of other minnesingers, with about one-half of his 200 poems being moral, political, or religious in nature. These didactic poems encouraged such virtues as self-discipline, charity, and fidelity, and extolled the benefits of pilgrimage. The other half were love poems, which were fresh in their appraisal of courtly love and of the society of his time. Walther was a poet in the Viennese court of Leopold V, and later wandered from court to court until German Emperor Frederick II granted him a small fief in Wurzburg, where it is assumed that he lived out the remainder of his life.

Walton, Ernest Thomas Sinton (1903-), Irish nuclear physicist. He shared with John D. Cockcroft the 1951 Nobel Prize in physics for their development of the first particle accelerator, with which they initiated the first nuclear-fission reaction applying non-radioactive substances.
See also: Cockcroft, Sir John Douglas; Particle accelerator.

Walton, George (1741-1804), colonial politician from Georgia. He signed the Declaration of Independence and served on the Continental Congress (1776-81). While defending Savannah against the British, he was taken prisoner (1778). He served his state as a chief justice and governor as well as a senator in the federal government (1795-96).

Izaak Walton

Walton, Izaak (1593-1683), English writer. His famous *The Compleat Angler* (1653), written as a dialogue between a fisherman, Piscator, and a hunter, Venator, combines praise for simple living with sound advice on the sport of fishing. His biographies include *John Donne* (1640), *Sir Henry Wotton* (1651), *George Herbert* (1670), and *Bishop Sanderson* (1678).

Walton, Sir William Turner (1902-83), English composer. He had a brilliant early success with *Façade* (1923), a chamber work set to poems by Edith Sitwell. Other works include the oratorio *Belshazzar's Feast* (1931), film scores (notably for films of Shakespeare plays), and the opera *Troilus and Cressida* (1954).

Waltz, ballroom dance in 3/4 time, probably originating from the *ländler*, a folk dance; also, music in 3/4 time. Its popularity in the 19th century was due largely to the music of the Strauss family.
See also: Strauss.

Walvis Bay, or Walvisbaai, South African exclave district within Namibia's boundaries, on the Atlantic coast. Walvis Bay has an area of about 434 sq mi (1,124 sq km) and is Namibia's only deep-water seaport. The harbor is a major one with links to most leading overseas shipping centers, and has been a point of controversy since the 1970s, with South Africa and Namibia in dispute over the area's jurisdiction. When Namibia became independent of South Africa (March 21, 1990), Walvis Bay was adjudged to remain under the dominion of South Africa. Industries include fishing and fish processing.
See also: Namibia; South Africa.

Wampanoag, Native Americans of the Algonquian language family who lived east of Narragansett Bay, R.I. Their chief, Massasoit (c.1580-1661), made friends with the Pilgrims (1620). His second son, known as King Philip, was the leader during King Philip's War (1675), his attempt to rid his land of foreign settlers. After their defeat the Wampanoag were nearly exterminated. Descendants live in Martha's Vineyard, Mass.

Wampum, strings of shell beads and disks made by Native Americans, used as ornaments and as money in trading. Early European settlers accepted wampum as currency (a purple variety was especially valuable), but the production of counterfeit glass beads undermined their value in the early 18th century.

Wandering Jew, or striped inch plant, any of several trailing plants that are grown indoors for their flowers and foliage. *Tradescantia fluminensis variegata* has green leaves, irregularly striped with white; *Callisia elegans* has green leaves with white pinstripes; and *Zebrina pendula* has purple, green, and silver striped leaves. They grow best in sunny windows and are extremely easy to propagate by taking cuttings and rooting them in water and wet sand.

Wandering Jew, legendary man (identified as a Jew in the 17th century) doomed to wander the earth until the Second Coming of Christ as punishment for taunting Jesus as He struggled to His Crucifixion. This tale has been chronicled several times, in the medieval tale *Flores historiarum*; in "A Brief Description and Narration Regarding a Jew Named Ahasuerus" (1602); and in the play "Le Juif errant" (1844-45).

Wang Wei (699-759), Chinese poet, landscape painter, and calligrapher of the T'ang dynasty (618-907). Wang Wei is credited with the creation of the broken ink (*p'o-mo*) method of wash brushstrokes, and was a master of monochromatic landscape paintings, particularly snowscapes. The lyric poetry of Wang Wei often related nature's attributes. He was revered in later years, probably for uniting poetry, painting, and calligraphy in a single art form.

Wankel engine, internal-combustion engine that produces rotary motion directly. Invented by the German engineer Felix Wankel, who completed his first design in 1954, it is used in automobiles and airplanes. A triangular rotor with spring-loaded sealing plates at its apexes rotates eccentrically inside a cylinder, while the 3 combustion chambers formed between the sides of the rotor and the walls of the cylinder successively draw in, compress, and ignite a fuel-and-air mixture. The Wankel engine is simpler in principle, more efficient, and more powerful weight-for-weight than a conventional reciprocating engine, but it is more difficult to cool.
See also: Internal combustion engine.

Wapiti (*Cervus canadensis*), North American subspecies of the red deer, called elk in the United States. It is larger than the typical European red deer, and, unlike the red deer, the terminal points of its antlers are in the same plane as the beam and do not form a crown. Once the most abundant deer in North America, wapiti are now severely reduced in number and range.

War, organized armed conflict between groups of people or states. War is not found elsewhere in the animal kingdom. Since recorded history began, people have been involved in hostility for different aims: power, territory, wealth, ideological domination, security, or independence. Until modern times most wars were fought with limited means for limited aims, but modern weapons threaten mass destruction with their ability to eliminate whole populations, thus endangering the survival of the human race.

War aces, combat pilots with at least 5 "victories" or "kills," confirmed downings of enemy aircraft. Famous aces of World War I, the first air war, included Baron Manfred von Richthofen of Germany (the "Red Baron") and Captain Eddie Rickenbacker of the United States. The leading ace of World War II was Captain Erich Hartmann of Germany (a record 352 kills); Lieutenant Colonel Heinz Bär of Germany was the first jet ace.

War Between the States *see:* Civil War, U.S.

Warble fly, also cattle warble or heel fly, large, beelike fly of the family Hypodermatidae that deposits its eggs on the legs or feet of cattle. There the larvae (cattle grub) enter the skin and migrate within the body for several months. This produces a characteristic painful lump, or warble. At maturity, the cattle grub emerges and pupates wherever it drops. The warble fly is a pest in Europe and North America, causing economic losses due to damaged hides and meat.

Warbler, small songbird native to the Americas. Warblers (family Parulidae) are seen throughout the United States and Canada during the temperate months, and migrate south to winter in South and Central America. Among the many species of warblers are the American redstart (*Setophaga ruticilla*), the yellow warbler (*Dendroica petechia*), and the hooded warbler (*Wilsonia citrina*). The feathers of warblers vary in color. The birds grow to about 3.5-10 in (9-25 cm), and they are noted for their lively movements and song. Warblers are beneficial to farmers and gardeners as they feed on harmful insects.

Warburg, Otto Heinrich (1883-1970), German biochemist. He was awarded the 1931 Nobel Prize in physiology or medi-

cine for discovering the chemistry of cell respiration. He was director of the Kaiser Wilhelm (now Max Planck) Institute for Cell Physiology, Berlin, from 1931 to 1953.
See also: Biochemistry; Cell.

War correspondent, news reporter who sends information from a war front to print or broadcast media, to provide accurate, up-to-date coverage. The Mexican War (1846-48) was probably the first war to be reported on systematically by getting information immediately from the front. U.S. writers who have been important war correspondents include Walt Whitman (Civil War, 1861-65) and Stephen Crane (Spanish-American War, 1898).

War crime, in international law, violation of the laws and rules of war. The first systematic attempt to frame laws for warfare was by Hugo Grotius (1625). Since 1864 various agreements have laid down principles for the treatment of combatants and civilians and have attempted to outlaw certain weapons. Among the few people convicted of war crimes was Confederate officer Henry Wirz, executed in 1865. An attempt was made to try the German Kaiser after World War I, and some German officers were tried (mostly acquitted) by a German court. One major war crimes trial, conducted by the United States, USSR, France, and Britain, was at Nuremberg, Germany, in which 3 categories of war crimes were defined: crimes against peace (planning and waging aggressive war); "conventional" war crimes (murder of civilians or prisoners of war, plunder, etc.); and crimes against humanity (murder, enslavement, or deportation of whole populations). The principle of individual responsibility was also established. A tribunal of 11 nations in Tokyo, Japan (1946-47), sentenced alleged Japanese war criminals.
See also: Nuremberg Trials.

Ward, Aaron Montgomery (1843-1913), U.S. businessperson. In 1872, with capital of $2,400, he and his partner, George Thorne, started the mail-order house that became the vast firm of Montgomery Ward & Co. Annual sales had risen to $40 million at the time of his death.

Ward, Artemus (1727-1800), leader in the American Revolutionary War. As governor of Massachusetts (1774-75), he besieged Boston until George Washington arrived, and he was second in command of the Continental army (1775-76). He served in Congress (1791-95).
See also: Revolutionary War in America.

Ward, Barbara (1914-81), British writer, economist, and commentator on the relations between the Western powers and developing nations. She was foreign editor of *Economist* magazine (from 1946), governor of British Broadcasting Corp. (1946-50), and a professor at Columbia Univ. (N.Y.C.; 1968-73). In her writings she stressed the importance of economic aid and international cooperation in such books as *The Rich Nations and the Poor Nations* (1962), *Nationalism and Ideology* (1967), and *Progress for a Small Planet* (1979).
See also: Economics.

Ward, Joseph (1838-89), U.S. educator, Congregational minister, and missionary. As a young minister he moved to the Dakota Territory (1869) and worked as a missionary. In conjunction with the Congregational Church, he established Yankton College (1881). For the duration of his life he was president and professor of philosophy of the college. He worked for the statehood of South Dakota and organized a group to pursue that goal (1879).

Ward, Lynd Kendall (1905-85), U.S. artist, writer, wood engraver. His works include *God's Man* (1929) and other novels created in woodcut (the first such text-less novels published in the United States), and watercolors, oil paintings, and lithographs. He illustrated such children's books as *The Little Red Lighthouse and the Great Gray Bridge* (1942) and *The Biggest Bear* (1952), for which he won the 1953 Caldecott Medal.

Ward, Robert (1917-), U.S. composer. He studied at both the Eastman and Juilliard schools of music. The influence of jazz and U.S. folk melodies is heard in his works, which include the Pulitzer Prize-winning opera *The Crucible* (1961).

War debt, financial obligations to the United States incurred by foreign countries during World War I. The United States lent its allies $11.5 billion when the expense of war became unaffordable for many of them. The war debt was paid in part by reparations levied against Germany at the Treaty of Versailles, and in part by the borrower nations. The entire war debt was never paid due to worldwide post-war economic depression.
See also: World War I.

War Department, United States, former executive department (1789-1947) created to govern all phases of the military. The War Department was headed by the secretary of war, an administrator who was under military advisement by the War Council. The principal task of the War Department was to ensure the proper functioning of the Army, including recruitment, transportation, weapon maintenance, and education and welfare of the troops. At times the War Department was involved in nonmilitary functions, such as managing the U.S. Island possessions and supervision of Reconstruction in the post-Civil War South. In 1947 the Natl. Military Establishment came into being (it later became the Dept. of Defense) and the War Department became the Dept. of the Army, within the Dept. of Defense.
See also: Defense, U.S. Department of.

Warhol, Andy (1930?-87), U.S. artist and filmmaker, famous for his pop art silkscreen paintings that incorporated everyday objects (e.g., soup cans). His highly innovative, often erotic, and often lengthy films include *Chelsea Girls* (1966) and *Lonesome Cowboys* (1969).

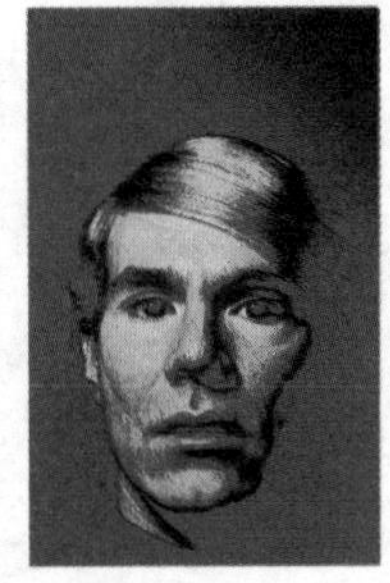
Andy Warhol

Warm-blooded animal, or homoiotherm, animal whose body temperature is not dependent on external temperature but is maintained at a constant level by internally generated metabolic heat. This constant temperature enables the chemical processes of the body, many of them temperature dependent, to be more efficient. Mammals and birds have developed this homoiothermy, and it is now believed that pterodactyls, therapsids, and many other extinct reptiles may also have been warm-blooded.

Warner, Jack L. (1892-1978), U.S. film producer who, with his 3 brothers, founded Warner Brothers, one of the largest and most successful Hollywood film studios. Warner Brothers produced the first sound film, *The Jazz Singer* (1927), and was the first studio to produce for television.

Warner, Pop (Glenn Scobey Warner; 1871-1954), U.S. football coach. He coached at Georgia (1895-96), Cornell (1897-98), Carlisle (1899-1903), Cornell (1904-06), Carlisle (1907-14), Univ. of Pittsburgh (1915-23), Stanford (1924-32), and Temple (1933-38), winning 313 games (third winningest coach in Division I-A). Warner pioneered both the single- and double-wing formation and led Standford to a Rose Bowl victory (1928).

Warner, Seth (1743-84), hero of the American Revolutionary War and a leader of the Green Mountain Boys. He helped capture Fort Ticonderoga, took Crown Point, N.Y. (1775), and was largely responsible for the victory at Bennington (1777).
See also: Green Mountain Boys; Revolutionary War in America.

War of 1812, conflict between the United States and Great Britain (1812-15). Due to the maritime policies of Britain and France

The burning of Washington, D.C., by the British in the War of 1812; the White House is in the background.

during the French Revolutionary Wars and the Napoleonic Wars, U.S. trade slumped. At the same time, the British were confiscating U.S. ships and impressing U.S. crewmen (as in the *Chesapeake* incident, when the British impressed 4 crew members from a U.S. frigate), to which the United States responded with the Embargo Act (1807) and the Noninterference Act (1809), banning trade with the belligerents. Anti-British feeling, fed by war hawks and by the conviction that British support of the Native Americans in the West was hindering U.S. expansion, led to declaration of war on June 18, 1812. However, the United States was unprepared for such a conflict, and its attempted invasion (1812) of Canada (Britain's main North American possession) was a failure. Early U.S. naval successes, which led to a retaliatory British blockade, include Capt. Oliver Perry's victory in 1813 at the battle on Lake Erie. In 1814 U.S. troops held their own at Chippewa and Lundy's Lane, and the victory of the Battle of the Thames at Plattsburgh halted a British advance on the Hudson Valley. In Chesapeake Bay a British force that had captured and sacked Washington, D.C., was repelled in its attempt to take Baltimore. There was a military stalemate, and peace negotiations were begun in June 1814. The Peace of Ghent, signed on Dec. 22, 1814, was essentially a return to the situation before the war. Two weeks later, Andrew Jackson defeated the British at the Battle of New Orleans, which took place before word of the treaty reached the United States. The war had several far-reaching effects on the United States: The military victories promoted national confidence and encouraged expansionism, while the trade embargo encouraged home manufactures.

Earl Warren

War on Poverty *see:* Johnson, Lyndon Baines.

War Powers Resolution, also called War Powers Act, U.S. law that describes the procedure that both the President and the Congress must follow in order to legally declare war. According to this law, the President may send military forces to an area where conflict arises, but the legislative branch must be informed by the executive branch within 48 hours. For the forces to remain in place for more than 90 days, the President must seek approval from the Congress. The law was created in response to the Vietnam War (1957-75), during which time both President Nixon and President Johnson approved military actions without the consent of Congress. This law was employed to initiate military action in the Persian Gulf (1991).

18th-century painting of Krakowski Street in Warsaw

Warrant, judicial order (signed usually by a judge or court clerk) authorizing arrest of a suspect, seizure of goods, or search of premises. Strict procedures govern the issuing of a warrant. There are also tax warrants and warrants of attorney and of attachment.

Warren, Earl (1891-1974), chief justice of the U.S. Supreme Court (1953-69). Attorney general (1939-43) and governor (1943-53) of California, he was Republican vice presidential candidate in 1948. Appointed to the Supreme Court by President Eisenhower, his leadership of the court resulted in a number of landmark liberal judgments concerning individual and civil liberties, notably *Brown* v. *Board of Education of Topeka* (1954), declaring racial segregation in schools unconstitutional. Warren also led the commission assigned to investigate Pres. John F. Kennedy's assassination.
See also: Supreme Court of the United States.

Warren, Joseph (1741-75), U.S. politician and physician. A patriot, he became a leader in the Revolutionary War when his sympathies for the effort were aroused by the passage of the Stamp Act. Warren became a Whig in Massachusetts and spoke and wrote in protest of unfair parliamentary actions. He was selected president of the Provincial Assembly (1775) and was major general of the Massachusetts troops. Warren was killed at the Battle of Bunker Hill.
See also: Revolutionary War in America.

Warren, Mercy Otis (1728-1814), U.S. author of patriotic works. Warren, who knew several Revolutionary War leaders, wrote to express her own political beliefs. She encouraged pro-Revolutionary sympathy with her satirical, anti-Tory plays: *The Adulateur* (1773), *The Defeat*, and *The Group* (1775). Her major work was a history of the American Revolution titled *History of the Rise, Progress, and Termination of the American Revolution* (3 vols., 1805). Warren advocated equal rights for women and the conservation of rights of individuals.

Warren, Robert Penn (1905-89), U.S. novelist, poet, and critic. One of the poets associated with the *Fugitive* magazine (1922-23), Penn's poetry and novels are often set in the South and address political and moral themes. He won Pulitzer prizes for his novel *All the King's Men* (1946), and his poetry collections *Promises* (1957) and *Now and Then* (1979). In 1986 he was appointed the first U.S. poet laureate.

Warren Report, findings of the commission established (Nov. 1963) by President Lyndon Johnson to investigate the assassination of President John F. Kennedy. The commission comprised Supreme Court Chief Justice Earl Warren, U.S. Representatives Hale Boggs and Gerald Ford; U.S. Senators Richard Russell and John S. Cooper; Allen Dulles; and John J. McCloy. The report, released in Sept. 1964, concluded that neither assassin Lee Harvey Oswald nor his killer, Jack Ruby, was part of a conspiracy. It criticized the FBI and Secret Service and recommended reforms in presidential security. The work of the commission has been widely challenged since its findings were published, and in 1979 a congressional committee announced its determinations, based on acoustical evidence, that 2 gunmen had shot at Kennedy.

Warsaw (pop. 1,659,000), largest city and capital of Poland, on the Vistula River. It is a commercial, industrial, cultural, and educational center, and transportation hub. Chief products are machinery, precision instruments, motor vehicles, electrical equipment, textiles, and chemicals. Warsaw has frequently been a focal point in European history. It replaced Kraków as Poland's capital in 1596 and subsequently fell into Swedish, Russian, Prussian, and German hands. Much of the city, which was razed in World War II, has been carefully reconstructed, including Warsaw's medieval old town, Stare Miasto.
See also: Poland.

Warsaw Pact, or Warsaw Treaty Organization, mutual defense pact signed in 1955 in Warsaw by the USSR and its Communist neighbors (Albania, Bulgaria, Czechoslovakia, East Germany, Hungary, Poland, and Romania) after the formation of the North Atlantic Treaty Organization (NATO). Its unified command has headquarters in Moscow. In 1968 (when Albania formally withdrew) pact forces invaded Czechoslovakia to overthrow its independent-minded regime. In 1980-81 the USSR used pact maneuvers and threats of intervention by pact members to discourage labor unrest in Poland. Following the conventional arms treaty signed with NATO (1990), which drastically reduced the number of soldiers and weapons on the European continent, and the breakup of the Soviet-led Communist bloc, the Warsaw Pact was officially dissolved (1991).
See also: North Atlantic Treaty Organization.

Warship, ship armed and employed for combat. Ships have been used in battle since antiquity, when cargo carriers became warships when necessary. The oar- and sail-powered galley ships of the Romans and Greeks, and the Viking long ships attacked enemy vessels by ramming them. By the 1500s ships were larger and heavier, and when armed became floating artillery depots. Spain had such a fleet—galleons built for their explorers' long expeditions; however, when England, with lighter galleons, destroyed the Spanish Armada, heavier-armed but more maneuverable warships (called capital ships) were built and ruled the seas for the next 200 years. In the early 1800s steam-powered warships with rotating gun turrets were invented and outfitted with explosive shells, which replaced cannonballs. But ironclad ships, the precursors of modern warships, proved able to withstand their attack, as was attested in the Civil War battle between the *Monitor* and the *Merrimack* (neither lost in battle). The English ship *Dreadnought* was the first truly modern battleship, and in the early 1900s designers improved battleship capabilities using it as a model. This type of massive battleship, as well as the submarine, were the most effective of the World War I warships. By the end of World War II there were great advances in the design and capabilities of combat ships. Aircraft carriers, destroyers, cruisers, frigates, amphibious ships, and minesweepers led the way into modern warfare. Advances in technology yielded further specialization, and with the advent of the *Nautilus* submarine, warships entered the nuclear age.

Wars of Succession *see:* Succession wars.

Wars of the Roses, fight between the House of Lancaster and the House of York for the English throne (1455-85). A white rose stood for the House of York and a red rose stood for the House of Lancaster. The throne of England changed hands 5 times after the beginning of the war, at which time Henry VI, a Lancaster, ruled. When Henry Tudor, King Henry VII, took the throne (1485), he married Elizabeth, a York. This union dissolved the conflict between both houses and created a new dynasty, the House of Tudor.

Wart, scaly excrescence on the skin caused by a virus. Warts may arise without warning and disappear equally suddenly. Numerous remedies have been suggested, but local freezing or cauterization are often effective. Warts that grow on the soles of the feet, pushed inward by the weight of the body, are called verrucas.

Wart hog, wild hog (genus *Phacochoerus*) distinguished by large, gristly facial warts and 1-ft (30.5-cm) curling tusks. Wart hogs are found in Africa south of the Sahara. They prefer plains and open scrub and live in family groups, feeding on grass, leaves, sometimes fruit, roots, and carrion.

Warwick (pop. 87,123), city in east-central Rhode Island, on Pawtuxet River and Narragansett Bay. The township government of Warwick was organized in 1647, and became an industry-based settlement when mills were built on the Pawtuxet River. The city's major industries include production of textiles, clothing, and metal products.
See also: Rhode Island.

Warwick, Earl of (Richard Neville; 1428-71), British soldier and influential leader. He is known as "the Kingmaker" for having put Edward IV and Henry VI on the throne. In 1453 Warwick aided the duke of York in his attempt to seize the power of the Lancastrian duke of Somerset, chief adviser to Henry VI. In 1455, during the War of the Roses, when the 2 sides fought at the Battle of Saint Albans, Warwick and the Yorkists were victorious over the Lancastrians. In 1460 the 2 sides fought again at the Battle of Northampton. Warwick won again, this time capturing the king, who was allowed to keep his throne because he was deemed such an ineffectual leader. Later that same year, the Lancastrians captured and killed York, and a few months later, regained King Henry. Warwick managed to enter London with York's son, Edward, proclaim him king in March of 1461, and, in effect, rule England for the first 3 years of Edward's reign. That same month Warwick and Edward defeated the Lancastrians at the Battle of Towton. Warwick gradually became disenchanted with the independent-minded Edward, who married against his wishes, and so in 1470, Warwick teamed with Lancastrian Henry VI and his wife, Margaret, in France and brought them back to England, where he deposed Edward and restored the crown to them. In 1471 Warwick was killed at Barnet in a battle against Edward.
See also: United Kingdom.

Wasatch Range, part of the Rocky Mountains that stretches southward from northern Utah into southern Idaho. The range is about 140 mi (225 km) long and its height averages about 10,000 ft (3,000 m). Its highest peak is Mt. Timpanogos, at 11,750 ft (3,581 m). West of the Wasatch Range lies a lake valley in which the Great Salt Lake and Salt Lake City are located. Streams from the Wasatch Range are used to irrigate farmlands in the valley.
See also: Rocky Mountains.

Washakie (1804?-1900), chief of Eastern Shoshone Indians, a tribe from Utah and Wyoming. Because the Sioux, Cheyenne, and Blackfoot, among other tribes, were already the enemies of the Eastern Shoshone, Washakie and his people became allies of the U.S. government during the Indian Wars of the 1870s. He signed a treaty with the United States to allow the railroad through his tribe's territory. Later he voluntarily moved his people to the Wind River Reservation of Wyoming.

Washburn, Sherwood Larned (1911-), U.S. anthropologist. An expert on ape behavior and anatomy, he was one of the first scientists to study apes in their natural environments. Washburn was editor of *American Journal of Physical Anthropology* (1955-57). Previously on the faculties of Columbia University and the University of Chicago, he has been on the faculty of University of California, Berkeley, since 1959.
See also: Anthropology.

Washing machine, machine that washes clothes. Most washing machines work automatically through the power of an electric motor. The temperature and amount of wash and rinse water as well as the strength of agitation used to clean the clothes is controlled through settings selected by the operator. The last cycle of most washing machines removes excess water by spinning the clothes. Although an electric-powered machine was invented in 1910, it took 27 more years to develop the automatic washer. The first patented washing machines (1860s) mechanically pushed clothes through water by use of a paddle.

Washington

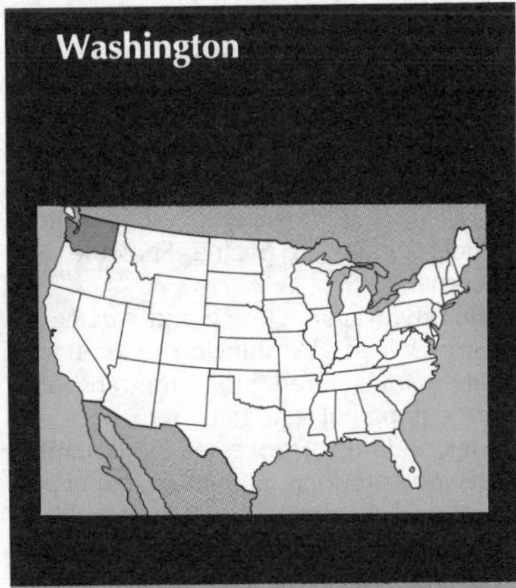

Capital:	Olympia
Statehood:	Nov. 11, 1889 (42nd state)
Familiar name:	Evergreen State
Area:	68,139 sq mi (176,479 sq km); ranks 20th
Population:	4,887,941 (1990); ranks 18th
Elevation:	Highest—14,410 ft (4,392 m), Mt. Rainier; Lowest—sea level, along the Pacific coast
Motto:	Alki (Bye and Bye)
Flower:	Coast rhododendron
Bird:	Willow goldfinch
Tree:	Western hemlock
Song:	"Washington, My Home"

Seattle, Washington

Washington, Pacific Coast state in northwestern United States; bordered by Canada to the north, Idaho to the east, Oregon and the Columbia River to the south, and the Pacific Ocean and Puget Sound to the west.
Land and climate. Washington has six main land regions. The Rocky Mountains, in the northeast, is an area of mineral-rich

ridges and valleys. The Columbia Plateau, in central and eastern Washington, is a semiarid, treeless lava basin with many coulees (steep, dry canyons). The Cascade Mountains, which split the state in two, has high, rugged peaks and volcanoes (most long-extinct) covered by glaciers and snowfields. The Puget Sound Lowland, between the Cascades and the Pacific coast, is a fertile, low-lying plain. The Olympic Mountains region, in the northwestern corner, has high, rugged, snowcapped peaks, many of which are still unexplored. The hilly, heavily forested Coast Range lies in the southwestern corner. The vast Puget Sound, dotted with more than 170 islands, cuts deep into western Washington. The Columbia is the state's major river. Forests cover more than 50% of the state. Western Washington has cool summers and relatively mild winters; eastern Washington has warmer summers and colder winters. Principal cities are Seattle, Spokane, and Tacoma.

Economy. Manufacturing and service industries lead Washington's economy. Chief manufactured goods are transportation equipment (aircraft, aerospace vehicles, and ships), processed foods, lumber and wood products, aluminum, paper products, and chemicals. Agriculture and mining account for a small share of the state's economy. Lumber is the most valuable agricultural product; chief crops are wheat, apples, potatoes, hops, hay, and flower bulbs; chief livestock products are dairy and beef cattle. Chief mining products are sand and gravel and coal.

Government. Washington's constitution was adopted in 1889. The governor serves a 4-year term. The state legislature consists of 49 senators serving 4-year terms and 98 representatives serving 2-year terms. In the U.S. Congress, Washington is represented by 2 senators and 9 representatives.

History. The area was long-populated by various Native American peoples, including Nez Percé, Spokane, and Chinook, before the first Europeans—Spanish and English explorers—sailed along the coast in the 1500s. The first recorded European landing was in 1775, by the Spanish. The Lewis and Clark expedition explored the area in 1805; fur traders gradually moved in. In 1846, the 49th-parallel boundary with Canada was established. The area was included in the Oregon Territory (1848); Washington Territory (larger than present-day Washington) was created in 1853. War raged between European-American settlers and the area's Native Americans (1855-58); the coming of the railroad (1883) brought new white settlement. In 1889 Washington became the 42nd state. The Alaska and Klondike gold rushes (1897-98) brought new prosperity, as did World War I. The Great Depression (1930s) caused economic collapse, but World War II and new hydroelectric plants attracted the airline, aerospace, and other new industries. An economic slump in the 1970s forced state leaders to seek more diverse industries. In 1980 a devastating volcanic eruption at Mt. St. Helens killed 57 people and caused billions of dollars' worth of damage. In recent years, Washington has worked to attract new industries, and to conserve its natural resources without damaging valuable lumber-related industries.

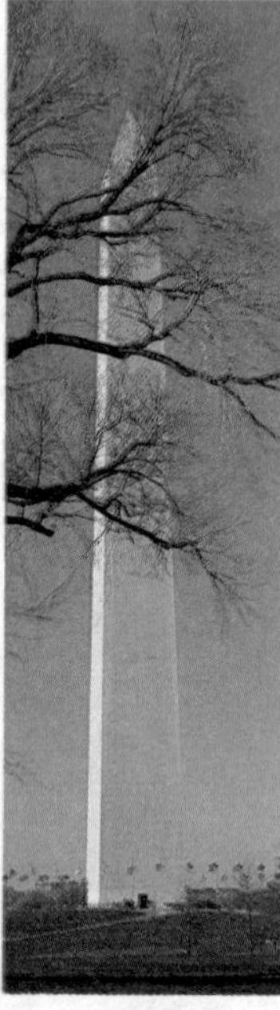

Washington Monument, the tallest building in Washington, D.C.

Washington, Booker T. (1856-1915), U.S. educator. Born into a Virginia slave family, he was educated and chosen in 1881 to head a new school for blacks, the Tuskegee Institute, Ala. Under his guidance the institution expanded from 2 unequipped buildings to a complex with over 100 buildings and 1,500 students. Washington urged industrial education as the way to economic independence, which he believed to be an essential prerequisite to the demand for social equality. His writings included an autobiography, *Up from Slavery* (1901).

Washington, D.C

Area:	69 sq mi (179 sq km)
Population:	638,000 in the city
Motto:	Justitia omnibus (Justice for All)
Flower:	American beauty rose
Bird:	Wood thrush
Tree:	Scarlet oak

Washington, D.C. (pop. 3,923,574), capital of the United States, coextensive with the federal District of Columbia, which is the seat of the U.S. federal government. (The "D.C." in the city's name stand for District of Columbia.) It lies in the eastern United States on the west-central edge of Maryland on the Potomac River, with Virginia on the river's opposite side.

Important sites. The city's focal point is the domed Capitol, home of the Congress of the United States. The Capitol lies on a small rise; for this reason the area is referred to as Capitol Hill. To the northwest lies the White House, official office and residence of the President. Other important buildings are the headquarters of government departments and agencies, the U.S. Supreme Court, the Federal Bureau of Investigation (FBI), and the Library of Congress. Also a cultural and educational center, Washington, D.C., is the site of the Smithsonian Institution, the National Gallery of Art, the John F. Kennedy Center for the Performing Arts, the National Archives, and the Folger Shakespeare Library. Among the city's famous monuments, parks, and memorials are the Lincoln Memorial, the Washington Monument, the Jefferson Memorial, and the Vietnam Veterans Memorial.

Economy. The city's economy is based largely on the federal government and related services; many important organizations also have offices there. There is little industry.

Government. The city's present system of government was established in 1973 by an act of Congress and approved by the people in 1974. Washington, D.C., is run by an elected mayor and city council. However, the federal government has final authority over all the city's government concerns. The mayor serves a 4-year term. The city council consists of 13 members serving 4-year terms. Washington, D.C., is represented in the U.S. Congress by 1 non-voting representative.

History. In 1783 the Continental Congress voted for a federal city. In 1791 President George Washington chose the present site as a compromise between North and South. Washington, D.C., is one of the few cities to be planned before being built. In 1800 Congress moved to Washington, which replaced Philadelphia as the national capital. In 1814, during the War of 1812, the government buildings were burned down by British troops; new and more splendid plans were made and carried out. Since then, the city's population has risen steadily. Washington has long served as a gateway for blacks emigrating north; since the 1950s, blacks have made up a majority of the city's population. Since the 1970s, there has been a growing call among Washingtonians for statehood for the District of Columbia, but the U.S. Congress would have to vote approval of statehood and the proposed state constitution written by a 1982 constitutional convention. As the nation's capital, Washington, D.C., is a focal point for tourism, government, and political demonstrations.

Washington, George (1732-99), first president of the United States. As a soldier, Washington led the Continental Army in the revolution to win American independence from Britain. As one of the founders of the new republic, he headed the Constitutional Convention. He was president during the most crucial years of his country's formation as a new nation. Washington's reputation for honesty, his strength of character, and his qualities as a leader won him the admiration of all Americans and a permanent place in history as "the Father of Our Country."

Early life. Washington spent his first 11 years on the family estate near Fredericksburg, Va. In 1743, after his father's death, George moved to Mount Vernon, home of his half-brother, Lawrence. Educated at home, Washington became interested in land management and surveying. At age 16 he went on an important surveying expedition of the Shenandoah Valley. The next year he was appointed surveyor of Culpeper Co. After Lawrence's death in 1752, Washington managed Mount Vernon, inheriting the estate in 1760.

In 1753 Virginia's Governor Dinwiddie

sent Washington on military missions against the French. When the French and Indian War broke out in 1754, Washington served the British side with distinction. At age 23 he was appointed commander in chief of Virginia's colonial troops.
In 1758 Washington returned home and resigned from the military. In Jan. 1759 he married Martha Dandridge Custis, a widow with two children, and settled down to run Mount Vernon. He served in the Virginia House of Burgesses and as justice of the peace. Although he did not support calls for independence at first, he came to oppose severe measures imposed by Britain and became a representative to the First Continental Congress. On June 15, 1775, he was elected commander in chief of the Continental Army.
The American Revolution. When the war for independence began, the forces under Washington's command were poorly trained and armed. In spite of the odds against him, Washington proved to be an able commander and was a constant source of inspiration to his troops. Alliances with France (1778) and Spain (1779) greatly relieved America's position, and the decisive victory against Britain came in Oct. 1781 when Washington and the French joined to defeat General Cornwallis at Yorktown. In Dec. 1783 Washington bid his troops an emotional farewell and went back to Mount Vernon.
A new nation. In 1787 Washington chaired the Constitutional Convention, at which the nation's leaders sought a way to strengthen the weak confederation of states. Under the new constitution, members of the first Electoral College voted Washington president in Feb. 1789.
President. Washington was determined to establish a strong central government. His first administration established a federal judiciary (1789), a national bank (1791), and far-reaching measures by which the national government assumed responsibility for state debts and imposed wide-ranging taxes. In fact, his government assumed responsibilities far greater than some of the nation's founders had intended; the split that developed led to the formation of the first national political parties. Washington reluctantly accepted a second term in 1792. Determined to keep the United States free of foreign influence, he declared it neutral in France's war with Britain and its allies. In spite of this, Washington's second term was largely devoted to foreign affairs, particularly the strained U.S. relations with Britain, France, and Spain. He also had to prove the federal government's power to enforce its laws by putting down the Whiskey Rebellion (1794) against a federal excise tax.
Retirement. Washington refused to accept a third term. He retired to Mount Vernon in Apr. 1797 and died there on Dec. 14, 1799.
See also: Revolutionary War in America.

Washington, Harold (1922-87), U.S. lawyer, politician, first black mayor of Chicago, elected 1983 and 1987. Washington served in the Illinois House of Representatives (1965-76), the Illinois Senate (1976-80), and the U.S. House of Representatives (1981-83). In the racially charged 1983 Democratic primary for mayor he defeated Mayor Jane M. Byrne and Richard M. Daley (son of former mayor and party boss Richard J. Daley) and went on to defeat Republican Bernard E. Epton.

Washington, Martha Custis (1731-1802), wife of President George Washington and first First Lady of the United States. At 17 she married a wealthy planter, Daniel Parke Custis, who died in 1757. She married George Washington in 1759 and moved with her 2 children to Mt. Vernon, which she supervised during Washington's absences.

Washington, Treaty of (1871), agreement between the United States and Great Britain, signed in Washington, D.C., to arbitrate the Alabama claims of the U.S. Civil War and the U.S.-Canadian boundary and fishing disputes. It was largely brought about by Hamilton Fish, U.S. secretary of state.

Washington Cathedral, or National Cathedral, officially, Cathedral Church of Saint Peter and Saint Paul, Episcopal church in Washington, D.C. Built in the early 20th century (starting 1907), it incorporates stones from historic buildings from around the world. It measures 525 ft (160 m) long and 275 ft (84 m) wide at the widest point of its transept.

Washington Conference, post-World War I disarmament meetings convened by Pres. Warren Harding in Washington, D.C., 1921-22. Agreements between the United States, Great Britain, Japan, France, and Italy included a limit on each navy's capital ships, restrictions on submarine warfare, and a ban on the use of poison gas. France, Japan, Great Britain, and the United States also agreed to respect each other's Pacific territories. A 9-power treaty, with the additional signatures of Belgium, China, the Netherlands, and Portugal, guaranteed China's territorial integrity.

Washington Monument, stone obelisk in Washington, D.C., honoring George Washington. Begun in 1848, it was completed in 1884 and opened to the public in 1888. Faced with white marble, it is 555.5 ft (169.3 m) high. Visitors may go to the top by elevator or by climbing 898 steps.

Washington's Birthday, federal holiday celebrated on the third Monday in February in honor of the first president of the United States, George Washington. He was born Feb. 11, 1732, but the 1752 calendar reform changed the date to Feb. 22. In some states the Monday holiday also honors President Abraham Lincoln, who was born on Feb. 12; it is then called *President's Day.*

Wasp, stinging winged insect, banded black and yellow, related to bees and ants in the order Hymenoptera. There are a number of families; most are solitary, but members of the Vespoidea are social, forming true colonies with workers, drones, and queen(s). Most of the solitary species are hunting wasps. These make nest cells in soil or decaying wood, in which they place one or more paralyzed insects before the egg is laid, to act as a living larder for the larva when it hatches. Social wasps congregate to form a permanent colony with both adults and young. The nest is usually constructed of wasp paper, a thick pulp of wood fibers and saliva. The adults feed the developing larvae on dead insects that have been killed by a bite on the neck; the sting, which in solitary wasps is used to paralyze prey, is reserved for defense. Adult wasps feed on carbohydrates: nectar, aphid honeydew, or jam.

Wasserman, August von (1866-1925), German physician and scientist. In 1906 he developed a process, known as the Wasserman test, which indicated syphilis infection through the testing of blood or spinal fluid. Earlier, Wasserman had developed inoculations against cholera, diphtheria, and tuberculosis.
See also: Venereal disease.

George Washington

1st president of the United States

Born:	Westmoreland Co., Va.; Feb. 22, 1732.
Term:	Apr. 1789-Mar. 1797.
Vice president:	John Adams.
Political party:	None.
Spouse:	Martha Dandridge Custis Washington.
Children:	None (2 stepchildren).
Died:	Mount Vernon, near Alexandria, Va., Dec. 14, 1799.

Water beetle

Waste disposal, disposal of such matter as animal excreta and the waste products of agricultural, industrial, and domestic processes, where an unacceptable level of environmental pollution would otherwise result. Where an ecological balance exists, wastes are recycled naturally or by technological means before accumulations affect the quality of life or disrupt the ecosystem. The most satisfactory waste disposal methods are therefore probably those that involve recycling, as in manuring fields with dung, reclaiming metals from scrap, or pulping waste paper for remanufacture. Recycling, however, may be inconvenient, uneconomic, or not yet technologically feasible. Many popular waste disposal methods consequently represent either an exchange of one form of environmental pollution for another less troublesome one, at least in the short term—e.g., the dumping or burying of nondegradable garbage or toxic wastes—or a reducing of the rate at which pollutants accumulate—e.g., by compacting or incinerating bulk wastes before dumping. Urban wastes are generally disposed of by means of dumping, sanitary landfill, incineration, and sewage processing. Agricultural, mining, and mineral-processing operations generate most solid wastes—and some of the most intractable waste disposal problems: the "factory" farmer's problem of disposing of surplus organic wastes economically without resorting to incineration or dumping in rivers; the problems created by large mine dumps and open-cast excavations; and the culm dumps that result from the processing of anthracite coal. Another increasingly pressing waste disposal problem is presented by radioactive wastes. Those with a "low" level of radioactivity can be safely packaged and buried; but high-level wastes, produced in the course of reprocessing the fuel elements of nuclear reactors, constitute a permanent hazard. Even the practice of encasing these wastes in thick concrete and dumping them on the ocean bottom is considered by many environmentalists to be an inadequate long-term solution.

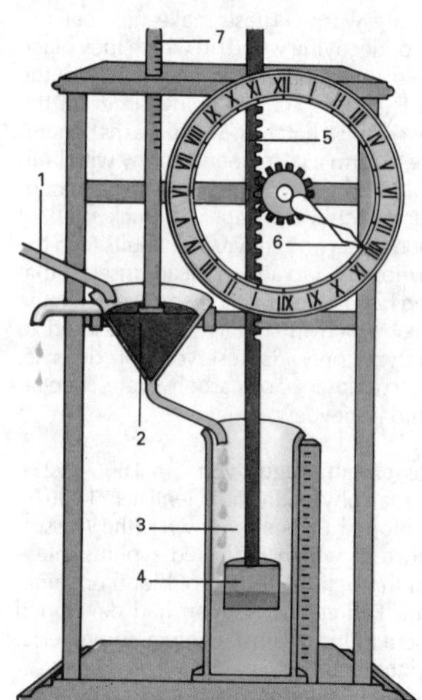

How water clocks worked: Water was supplied to the funnel (1) and passed to the cylinder (3), in which a piston (4) floated. The piston was connected to a rack (5) and pinion, which actuated the hour hand (6). To account for varying day length, according to time of year and latitude, the rate of water flow was varied by means of the stopper (2), which could be raised or lowered by an amount previously determined and marked on the stopper rule (7). The excess water escaped through the waste tube in the funnel.

Watauga Association, government (1772-75) set up on land leased from the Cherokee along the Watauga River in eastern Tennessee. The settlers, from Virginia and (after suppression of the Regulators) North Carolina, joined North Carolina (1775), became part of the State of Franklin (1784-88), and finally part of Tennessee (1796).

Watch, small, portable timepiece. It is usually worn around the wrist, but may also be carried in a pocket or purse, or be worn as part of jewelry, such as a ring, necklace, or pin. Watches have been in use since the early 1500s when a method was discovered whereby a mainspring could be used to power a clock instead of falling weights; this made it possible to create portable clocks. Most modern watches are electronic, powered by small quartz crystals. After running a year, an electronic watch may be off fewer than 60 seconds.

Water (H_2O), transparent, odorless liquid that in liquid form and solid form (ice) covers about 74% of the earth's surface. Water is essential to life, which began in the oceans. Water is also humanity's most precious natural resource. The advent of desalination technology has made sea water, which accounts for 97% of the total water on earth, available for use as fresh water. Chemically, water is a compound of hydrogen and oxygen. It is a good solvent for many substances, especially ionic and polar compounds; it is ionizing and itself ionizes to give a low concentration of hydroxide and hydrogen ions. It is thus also a better conductor of electricity than most pure liquids. Water is a polar molecule and shows anomalies due to hydrogen bonding, including contraction when heated from 0°C to 4°C (32°F to 39.2°F). Formed when hydrogen or volatile hydrides are burned in oxygen, water oxidizes reactive metals to their ions and reduces fluorine and chlorine. It converts basic oxides to hydroxides and acidic oxides to oxyacids.

Water beetle, any of a number of families of oval insects, in the order Coleoptera, that live in or near water and propel themselves by fringed hind legs. Three of the most common water beetles are the giant water scavenger beetle (family Hydrophilidae), predaceous diving beetle (family Dytiscidae), and whirligig (family Gyrinidae). The predaceous diving beetle and water scavenger beetle feed on small fish and insects.

Water boatman *see:* Water bug.

Water buffalo, any of several oxen in the family Bovidae, most common of which is the Indian buffalo (*Bubalus bubalis*), standing 6-6.5 ft (1.5-2 m) at the shoulder. Bulls have curved horns that may measure as wide as 12 ft (3.7 m) along the curve. The fierce-tempered water buffalo feeds on grass and has very little hair on its dull, bluish-black hide. Domesticated, the water buffalo is a strong and helpful farm animal, used throughout China, southeast Asia, Egypt, Europe, and the Philippines.

Water bug, name given to a number of insects that live on or below the surface of fresh water, especially the giant water bug, which may grow up to 4 in (10 cm) long. Water bugs feed on small aquatic animals, including fish. Backswimmers, water boatmen, and water scorpions are also water bugs.

Waterbury (pop. 221,629), city (inc. 1853) in Connecticut, situated on the Naugatuck River. Once a leading manufacturer of brass products (from the 18th century through World War II), items produced in Waterbury today include timepieces and metal products. Banking and insurance are among its other industries.

Water chestnut, name of 2 different plants that grow in subarctic and temperate wetlands. The Oriental water chestnut (*Eleocharis tuberosa*) is in the sedge family and is native to China. Some of its tubelike stems, which may grow to a height of approximately 5 ft (1.5 m), grow upward out of the soil and water. However, some of the stems grow underground and have small, round, edible bulblike swellings at the end called corms. The water caltrop (genus *Trapa*) also belongs to the water-chestnut family. It is native to tropical and subtropical areas of Africa, Europe, and Asia, and bears edible, nutlike fruits.

Water clock, also called clepsydra, ancient instrument that measured time by the amount of water flowing from it. Used as early as the 14th century B.C. by the Egyptians, it consisted of a hollow container, such as a cylinder or a glass jar, with measuring lines. Water was poured into the container and then allowed to flow out. The lines indicated how much water had escaped, and from this it could be determined how much time had passed. Water clocks were used by Greeks and Romans as well. Among its various purposes was the timing of orators' speeches.

Watercolor, painting technique in which the pigment is mixed with water before application, such as fresco and tempera, but more particularly the aquarelle technique of thin washes. Ancient Egyptians produced watercolor paintings, and the medium was used during and after the Renaissance by, among others, Rembrandt and Van Dyck. The aquarelle technique was mastered by such English artists as John Cotman and J.M.W. Turner around 1800. Watercolor permits powerful effects of transparency, brilliance, and delicacy. Important U.S. watercolorists include Winslow Homer and John Marin.

Water dog *see:* Mudpuppy.

Waterfall, vertical fall of water formed where a river flows from hard rock to an area of more easily eroded rock, or where there has been a rise of the land relative to sea level or a blockage of the river by a landslide. The power of waterfalls often provides energy for the many cities that have sprung up around them. The highest waterfall in the world is Angel Falls, Venezuela (3,212 ft/979 m).

Water flea, any of a group of small animals belonging to the class Branchiopoda. Most species live in fresh water and are anywhere from 1/125-3/4 in (0.2-18 mm) long. Their bodies are covered by a transparent shell, exposing their organs for easy viewing. Water fleas move through water by jumping in jerky motions resembling those of fleas—hence their name.

Waterford (pop. 39,500), port city in southeastern Ireland, located on the River Suir near the point where it flows into the Waterford Harbour. Waterford was first settled in the A.D. 800s by Vikings. It was captured by the English in 1170. Waterford became prominent during the latter part of the 18th century because of the well-known Waterford crystal glassware manufactured there. The city remains an important export center of locally produced items, including canned fruits and meats, beer, paper, chemicals, furniture, and electrical products.
See also: Ireland.

Watergate, series of scandals involving Pres. Richard Nixon and his administration. On June 17, 1972, 5 men from Nixon's reelection committee were arrested as they tried to plant electronic eavesdropping equipment in the headquarters of the Democratic Party national committee in the Watergate office building, Washington, D.C. As a result of their convictions and the suspicions of Judge John Sirica, who tried the case, that a conspiracy was being covered up, investigations were opened that led to Nixon's inner councils. Though Nixon easily won reelection in Nov. 1972, his public support eroded as a televised U.S. Senate investigation continued. Newspaper revelations (notably by Carl Bernstein and Bob Woodward in the *Washington Post*) and testimony of Republican Party and former governmental officials clearly implicated him and his senior aides in a massive abuse of power and the obstruction of justice involving campaign contributions, the CIA, the FBI, the Internal Revenue Service, and other government agencies. The House of Representatives Judiciary Committee voted to impeach Nixon in July 1974, and his ouster from office became inevitable; on Aug. 9, 1974 he resigned—the only U.S. president to do so. One month later he was granted a full pardon by Pres. Gerald Ford. Almost 60 individuals, including former U.S. Attorney General John Mitchell and senior White House staff were convicted of Watergate crimes.
See also: Nixon, Richard Milhouse.

Water glass, also known as soluble glass, colorless lump made up of sodium, silicon, and oxygen that resembles glass. Water glass is soluble in water, turning into a thick liquid. It has many industrial uses: as adhesive in fiberboard boxes, glass, and porcelain; to manufacture concrete and cement; and to fireproof and waterproof materials.

Water hyacinth, South American floating plant (*Eichhornia crassipes*). The plants, which have attractive purple or yellow flowers growing on erect stems, float on air-filled bladders, trailing their roots in the water, or in mud where the water is very shallow. Water hyacinths grow wild in South America but have been introduced into other tropical areas. They frequently clog waterways, as in the southern United States.

Water lily, aquatic plant of the genus *Nymphaea* (unrelated to true lilies). They grow in calm, shallow fresh water, with stems rooted in the mud and floating leaves. Many hybrids are used as ornamentals in water gardens. The most well known of the species is the blue or white Egyptian lotus, Egypt's national emblem.

Water lily

Waterloo, Battle of (June 18, 1815), final engagement of the Napoleonic Wars. Having escaped from exile on Elba and having reinstated himself with a new army, Napoleon returned to face a coalition of Austria, Great Britain, Prussia, and Russia. On the offensive, he advanced into Belgium to prevent an Anglo-Dutch army under Wellington from uniting with the Prussians. After separate battles with the British and Prussians on June 16, the French army, led by Marshall Ney, attacked Wellington's strongly defended position at Waterloo, south of Brussels. The intervention of a Prussian force under Blücher allowed Wellington to take the offensive. The French were routed, losing some 25,000 men. Napoleon abdicated on June 22, 1815.
See also: Napoleon I; Napoleonic Wars.

Watermelon, plant (*Citrullus vulgaris*) and its edible fruit, with a thick rind, juicy pulp, and many seeds. A member of the gourd family native to Africa, the watermelon has been cultivated for at least 4,000 years. Watermelons, so named because more than 90% of their substance is water, may weigh from 5-40 lb (2.3-18.1 kg) or more and are rich in vitamins A and C. They grow on vines and their pulp is red to pink, yellow, or white.

Water meter, device to measure the quantity of water flowing through a pipe or other channel. Such meters, connected with registers that display numerical readings indicating gallons, cubic feet, or other quantities, are used to measure home or business use of water from public water systems or other sources, or to monitor flow in rivers and other moving bodies of water. Quantity may be measured by the water's motion or pressure, or by using magnetism, sound waves, or other energy affected by the rate of flow.

Water moccasin, also called cottonmouth or moccasin snake, poisonous snake in the viper family. This species *(Agkistrodon piscivorus)* lives in the southeastern United States in swampy or marshy areas of rivers, streams, and lakes. It may grow between 3 1/2 ft (107 cm) and 5 ft (1.5 m) long. It is considered a pit viper because of a hollow pit located between the eye and nostril on the side of its head. Its often fatal bite may be preceded by a warning, which involves the exposure of the white, cottonlike inside of its mouth.

Water pipit *see:* Pipit.

Water plant, also called aquatic plant or hydrophyte, any of several plants classified as those that live on the surface or below the surface of water. Water lilies, sedges, and cattails are common water plants. Water bladders, or pores that contain air, are found in submerged water plants to support their upright position. Water plants most often grow in lakes and ponds.

Water pollution, contamination to water systems as a direct result of the discharge of harmful products. There are 3 main sources of water pollution: industrial waste, sewage, and chemical and agricultural wastes. Environmental concern has grown through the years, and government agencies worldwide have helped pass laws that limit the amount of wastes that may be dumped into our waters. Billions of dollars a year are spent to clean up the diseased waters, yet specialists doubt that the natural state of the waters will ever be fully restored. Water pollution has become a grave environmental problem that increasingly threatens lakes, rivers, and oceans.

Water polo, game played in a swimming pool in which 2 teams try to pass or throw a ball into the opponent's goal. The game began in England in the 1870s. Each team consists of 7 players—6 in the field and 1 goalkeeper. Fieldplayers may use head, feet, or 1 hand to manage the ball; goalkeepers may use both hands while in the goal area. The team with the ball is allowed 35 seconds to get the ball across the opponent's goal and score. If the team is unsuccessful, the ball goes to the other team. Water polo is played in an area 66-98 ft (20-30 m) long and 26-66 ft (8-20 m) wide. A men's game lasts 28 minutes, and is divided into 7-minute quarters. A women's game lasts 24 minutes and is divided into 6-minute quarters.

Water power, energy obtained from flowing or falling water used to run machinery or create electrical power. Water has been used to drive devices since ancient times, beginning with the invention of the water wheel. Streaming water flowing over the blades of a wheel caused the wheel to rotate, setting in motion other mechanisms—thus creating the energy that drove the mechanisms. Water was first used to power grinding stones that ground grains. Water power was very important during the Industrial Revolution, when it was used to operate factory machines. The most important modern use of water power is the generating of electricity. Hydroelectric power plants producing electrical energy have been built on rivers in many parts of the world. The largest U.S. power plant is the Grand Coulee on the Columbia River in Washington.
See also: Turbine.

Waters, Ethel (1900-77), African-American singer and actress. She started singing the blues and popular music in clubs when she was 17 and went on to star in musicals, including *Africana* (1927), *At Home Abroad* (1935), and *Cabin in the Sky* (1940). She popularized several songs from the musicals, such as "Heat Wave," and "Taking a Chance on Love." Her singing style was greatly acclaimed, and she recorded with jazz musicians such as Benny Goodman and Duke Ellington. Waters had dramatic roles in several films, including *Pinky* (1949), for which she was nominated for an Academy Award as supporting actress, and *The Member of the Wedding* (1950). She recounted her life in her autobiography, *His Eye Is on the Sparrow* (1951).

Water-skiing, sport in which a person wearing a pair of ski-like runners glides over water while being pulled by a motorboat moving at speeds of 15-35 mph (24-56 kmph). Water skiing is done for recreation as well as for competition events, which include jumping, slalom, and trick riding. In the jumping competition, skiers ski jump off a ramp 24 ft (7.3 m) long and 6 ft (1.8 m) high in an attempt to achieve the greatest distance. In the slalom competition, a skier negotiates through a course of buoys as quickly as possible. For trick skiing, skiers perform intricate actions, such as jumps and turns.

Water snake, any of nearly 80 species of nonvenomous snakes of the genus *Natrix*, including the European grass snake. Water snakes live in fresh waters and feed on fish and amphibians.

Water softening, process of removing calcium and magnesium from hard water. These insoluble minerals, when left in water, form scale in pipes and prevent the dissolution of cleansers, such as soap. Hard water may be softened by adding soda ash and lime to it. The soda ash and lime join with the calcium and magnesium, making them settle to the bottom of the water container. Water may also be softened by filtering it through zeolites, minerals that contain sodium ions. The sodium ions change places with the calcium and magnesium ions, thereby softening the water. When the zeolites become depleted of sodium ions, a strong solution of common salt can be placed in the filter to replenish the sodium.

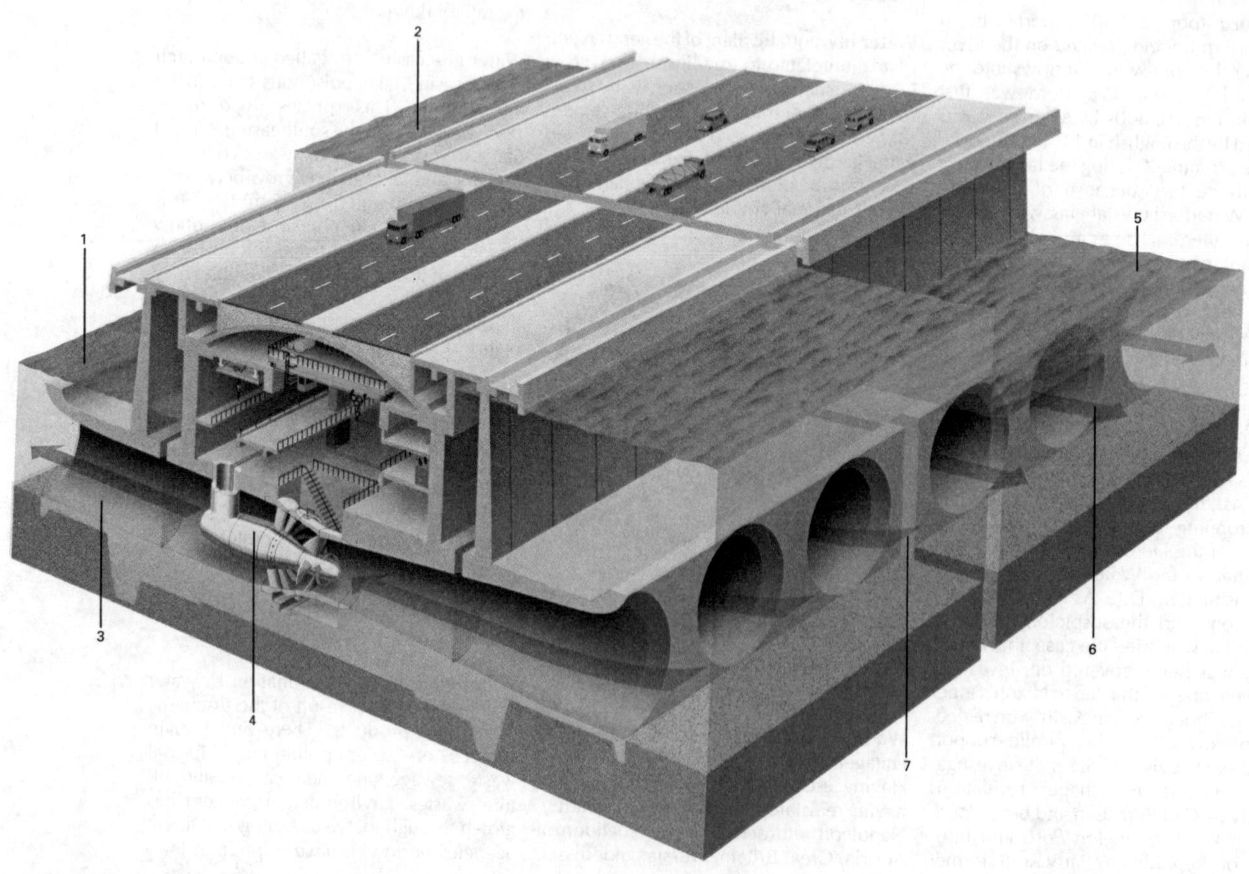

This water-power plant uses the difference in the height of the sea at high tide and low tide to generate electrical power.
Key:
1. low tide
2. high tide
3. tunnel
4. entrance to generator
5. basin
6. At high tide the water flows from the sea into the basin.
7. At low tide the water flows from the basin into the sea.

Waterspout, rotating column of air, or tornado, as it passes over water. A funnel-like cloud of condensed water vapor extends from a parent cumulonimbus cloud to the water surface, where it is surrounded by a sheath of spray.

Water wheel, wheel that is turned by flowing water, providing power to operate a device. The running water may come from rivers or waterfalls. Water wheels were used by ancient Romans to grind grain and in time were developed to run other devices, such as machinery. There are 2 basic types: vertical and horizontal. Vertical water wheels often have containers around the wheel. Water usually flows into a container at the top of the wheel, the weight of the water causes the container to fall, and the water flows into the next container, creating a constant motion. Horizontal water wheels have vertical blades. Water strikes the blade on one side of the wheel, causing the wheel to turn to the next blade, thus creating continual motion. Horizontal water wheels are capable of converting more water power into energy and have greater use in the modern world.
See also: Water power.

Watie, Stand (1806-71), Native American brigadier general in the Confederate Army. This Cherokee leader volunteered for the Confederate Army in 1861 and led a Cherokee regiment known as the Cherokee Mounted Rifles.
See also: Civil War, U.S.

Watson, James Dewey (1928-), U.S. biochemist. He shared with Francis Crick and Maurice H.F. Wilkins the 1962 Nobel Prize in physiology or medicine for his work with Crick establishing the double-helix molecular model of DNA. His personalized account of the research, *The Double Helix* (1968), became a best-seller.
See also: Biochemistry; Deoxyribonucleic acid.

Watson, John Broadus (1878-1958), U.S. psychologist who founded behaviorism, which states that a person's behavior is a result of stimuli in his or her environment. It rejects the idea of inborn emotions, with the exceptions of fear, anger, and love. While Watson's work helped lead to the development of psychology as a science, his views are not widely held today.
See also: Psychology.

Watson, Thomas Edward (1856-1922), U.S. author and political leader from Georgia. He attacked blacks, socialists, Catholics, and Jews. A Farmers' Alliance representative (1891-93) and Democratic U.S. representative (from 1920), he ran as a populist vice presidential and presidential candidate (1896, 1904, respectively). He became a champion of the Ku Klux Klan.

Watson, Thomas John (1874-1956), U.S. business executive and philanthropist. He took over an ailing computing company (1914), changed its name to International Business Machines Corp. (IBM; 1924), and built it into one of the world's largest corporations. Under his presidency (1914-49) and chairmanship (1949-56), IBM became the leader in electronic data-processing equipment, with sales in 82 countries and assets of more than $600 million at the time of his death.

Watson-Watt, Sir Robert Alexander (1892-1973), Scottish scientist and inventor. His research into radio led to his creation (1935) of a radar device capable of detecting and tracing the movements of flying airplanes. He received many honors for his work, including knighthood, medals, and honorary degrees.
See also: Radar.

Watt, James (1736-1819), Scottish engineer and inventor. His first major invention (patented 1769) was an improved steam engine, with a separate condenser air pump, and insulated engine parts. For the manufacture of such engines he entered into partnership with John Roebuck and later (1775), more successfully, with Matthew Boulton. Between 1775 and 1800 he invented the sun-and-planet gear wheel, the double-acting engine, a throttle valve, a pressure gauge, and the centrifugal governor—as well as taking the first steps toward determining the chemical structure of water. He also coined the term *horsepower* and was a founding member of the Lunar Society.
See also: Steam engine.

Watteau, Jean-Antoine (1684-1721), French draftsperson and painter, strongly influenced by Peter Paul Rubens. A masterful colorist, he specialized in small, gay paintings called *fêtes galantes* ("elegant parties") or *fêtes champêtres* ("country parties"). He also painted theater scenes. His works include *The Embarkation for Cythera* (1717), based upon a play of the day, and *Gilles* (c.1718).
See also: Rococo.

Wattmeter, instrument that measures electric power in watts, kilowatts, or megawatts.

Watusi (Swahili: *Watutsi*), Tutsi people of Burundi and Rwanda in central Africa (formerly Ruanda-Urundi). In the 1400s and 1500s the invading Watusi imposed a feudal system on the native Hutu, who revolted in 1959 and drove their cattle-raising rulers to what is now Burundi (the 2 parts became independent nations in 1962). The Tutsi king of Burundi was deposed in 1966. An unsuccessful Hutu rebellion in Burundi in 1972-73 left 10,000 Tutsi and 150,000 Hutu dead. The Watusi, probably originally from Ethiopia, differ ethnically from other African peoples, and many attain a height of over 7 ft (2.13 m).

Waugh, name of 3 English writers, the sons and grandson of journalist and publisher Arthur Waugh (1886-1943). **Alexander Raban (Alec) Waugh** (1898-1981) wrote over 40 novels and travel books, including *Loom of Youth* (1918) and *Island in the Sun* (1956). **Evelyn Arthur St. John Waugh** (1903-66) wrote mainly satire, both elegant and biting. His conversion to Roman Catholicism in 1930 had a deep affect on his work. His novels include *Decline and Fall* (1928), *Vile Bodies* (1930), *Put Out More Flags* (1942), *Brideshead Revisited* (1945), *The Loved One* (1948), and his World War II trilogy, *The Sword of Honour* (1952-61). Evelyn's son **Auberon Alexander Waugh** (1939-) is a novelist whose works include *Bed of Flowers* (1972).

Wave, in physics, energy that travels in rhythmical motions. Waves may travel on a substance (waves on water), through a substance (the waves of an earthquake through the earth), or in a space devoid of matter (radio waves through space). The top of a wave is the crest, the bottom of a wave is the trough. Wavelength refers to the distance between 2 consecutive crests. There are 3 kinds of waves: transverse, standing, and longitudinal. In transverse waves the energy flows in a steady forward direction and causes the medium through which it travels to move up and down, like water waves. Standing waves are created by 2 identical waves moving in opposite directions, creating a series of loops. Longitudinal waves travel in a forward direction in a series of short back-and-forth motions, like the coils of a spring.
See also: Physics.

James Watt

Wavell, Archibald Percival, 1st earl (1883-1950), British field marshal. He was British commander-in-chief in the Middle East during World War II, defeating the Italians in North Africa (1940-41). He served as viceroy and governor general of India from 1943 to 1947.
See also: World War II.

Wax, moldable, water-repellent solid, of which there are several entirely different kinds. *Animal waxes* were the first known: Wool wax when purified yields lanolin; beeswax, from the honeycomb, is used for some candles and as a sculpture medium (by carving or casting); spermaceti wax, from the sperm whale, is used in ointments and cosmetics. *Vegetable waxes*, like animal waxes, are mixtures of esters of long-

Jean-Antoine Watteau's The Embarkation for Cythera *(1717)*

chain alcohols and carboxylic acids. Carnauba wax, from the leaves of a Brazilian palm tree, is hard and lustrous and is used to make polishes; candelilla wax, from a wild Mexican rush, is similar but more resinous; Japan wax, the coating of sumac berries, is fatty and soft but also tough and kneadable. *Mineral waxes* include montan wax, extracted from lignite, which is bituminous and resinous; ozokerite, an absorbent hydrocarbon wax obtained from wax shales; and paraffin wax, or petroleum wax, the most important commercially, obtained from the residues of petroleum refining by solvent extraction. Some of its uses are to make candles, to coat paper products, in the electrical industry, and to waterproof leather and textiles. Various *synthetic waxes* are made for special uses.

Wax myrtle, tree in bayberry or wax myrtle family. The common wax myrtle (*Myrica cerifera*) grows to about 35 ft (11 m) high. It has thick leaves with small brown dots and small green flowers that bloom between April and June. As an ornamental tree wax myrtle are found along the east coast of the United States.

Waxwing, any of 3 species of starling-sized birds (genus *Bombycilla*) named for the red, waxlike marks on their wings. Found in the Northern Hemisphere, they are the Bohemian waxwing, the cedar waxwing, and the Japanese waxwing (of northeastern Asia). Waxwings feed largely on berries but feed their chicks on insects. They move their nesting grounds from place to place, and in some years migrate en masse southward in the fall.

John Wayne

Wayne, Anthony (1745-96), American Revolutionary general whose daring tactics earned him the name "mad Anthony Wayne." In 1779 he executed the brilliant victory of Stony Point over the British, and he was with Lafayette at the siege of Yorktown (1781). During the wars with Native Americans out West, his success at Fallen Timbers in 1794 led to his negotiation of the Treaty of Greenville (1795) in which most of Ohio was ceded to the U.S.
See also: Indian wars; Revolutionary War in America.

Wayne, John (Marion Michael Morrison; 1907-79), U.S. film actor, known mostly for his tough hero roles. He acted in low-budget westerns until his big break in 1939 in *Stagecoach.* Over the course of his career, Wayne appeared in over 175 films, including *Red River* (1948), *She Wore a Yellow Ribbon* (1949), *Sands of Iwo Jima* (1950), and *The Quiet Man* (1952). He received an Academy Award for his acting in *True Grit* (1969).

Carl Maria von Weber

Weakfish, or squeteague, any of a genus (*Cynoscion*) of saltwater fishes used for food, measuring 1-2 ft (30-61 cm) long or more. Its name comes from the fact that it has a weak, fleshy mouth that is easily torn. It is found along the Atlantic and Gulf coasts of the United States.

Weapon, any device used to attack or defend. Throughout human history, weapons have been used to kill animals for food, to protect people in wilderness, and to wage wars. Bows and arrows, slings, swords, blowguns, rifles, guns, bombs, torpedoes, and hand grenades are examples of weapons. As technology has become more sophisticated, destructive power has increased, e.g., nuclear bombs capable of killing millions of people and destroying the planet.

Weasel, small, carnivorous mammal (*Mustela nivalis*) related to the skunk, wolverine, and mink. A slender, lithe, red-brown creature, which often kills prey many times its own size, it measures only up to 10-11 in (25.4-27.9 cm) in the male, 8 in (20.3 cm) in the female. The normal diet is mice, voles, and fledgling birds, though rabbits may be taken. The many races of weasel are distributed throughout Eurasia, Africa, and the Americas.

Weather, variations in atmospheric conditions (temperature, precipitation, wind, humidity, air pressure, and cloudiness) experienced at a given place over a short period of time. Longer periods of data fall under the term *climate.*
See also: Climate.

Weather Service, National, part of the Environmental Science Services Administration (ESSA), in the U.S. Department of Commerce. Its head office in Washington, D.C., near the National Meteorological Center, is where data from 300 weather stations in the United States and from many other sources, including aircraft, satellites, and balloons, are coordinated and incorporated into charts for distribution to the 30 forecast centers across the country. Here long- and short-range forecasts are prepared and warnings of hurricanes, flooding, and other weather hazards given. Research to improve forecasting accuracy is also undertaken.

Weather vane, instrument used to perceive the direction in which the wind is moving. The vane is built in the form of an arrow, so as to pick up even the smallest breeze. Often the vane has electrical connections by which it can communicate the wind movement to areas that might be far from the device itself.

Weaver, Robert Clifton (1907-), U.S. economist, and secretary of housing and urban development (HUD; 1966-68). He was the administrator of the N.Y. Rent Commission (1955-59) and led the federal Housing and Home Finance Agency (1961-66) before his appointment by Pres. Lyndon Johnson as secretary of the newly formed HUD—a job that made him the first black member of a presidential cabinet.

Weaverbird, small, seed-eating bird (family Ploceidae) of Africa and Asia. Weaverbirds are related to the English sparrow and are usually drab, though during the nesting season many males develop bright plumage. They are named for their elaborate flask-shaped nests, woven from strips of palm fronds or grasses. Weavers live in flocks and are often pests when they descend on crops.

Weaving, process of making a fabric by interlacing 2 or more sets of threads. In plain, or tabby, weave, 1 set of threads (the warp) extends along the length of the fabric; the other set (the woof, or weft) is at right angles to the warp and passes alternately over and under it. Other common weaves include twill, satin, and pile. In basic twill, woof threads pass over 2-4 warp threads, producing diagonal ridges, or wales, as in denim, flannel, and gaberdine. In satin weave, a development of twill, long "float" threads passing under 4 warp threads give the fabric its characteristically lustrous and smooth appearance. Pile fabrics, such as corduroy and velvet, have extra warp or weft threads woven into a ground weave in a series of loops that are then cut to produce the pile. Weaving is usually accomplished by means of a hand- or power-operated machine called a loom. Warp threads are stretched on a frame and passed through eyelet in vertical wires (heddles) supported on a frame (the harness). A space (the shed) between sets of warp threads is made by moving the heddles up or down, and a shuttle containing the woof thread is passed through the shed. A special comb (the reed) then pushes home the newly woven line.

Webb, name of 2 English social reformers and economists. **Beatrice Webb** (née Potter, 1858-1943) studied working life for her *Life and Labour of the People in London* (1891-1903). Her husband, **Sidney James Webb** (1859-1947), was a Labour member of Parliament (1922-29) and held several cabinet posts. The couple were leading intellectuals of the Labour movement and wrote together *The History of Trade Unionism* (1894). They were Fabians and helped found the London School of Economics in 1895 and the left-wing journal *The New Statesman* in 1913.

Weber, Carl Maria von (1786-1826), German composer, pianist, and conductor who established the romantic opera and paved the way in Germany for Richard Wagner. His operas include *Der Freischütz* (*The Marksman*; 1821), *Euryanthe* (1823), and *Oberon* (1826). He wrote a number of orchestral and chamber works, notably for the piano, including the well-known *Invitation to the Dance* (1819).

Weber, Max (1881-1961), U.S. painter. He introduced European modern art movements, such as Fauvism and Cubism, to America by incorporating the styles into his own work. His works between 1912 and 1919 were abstract, becoming more representational from 1919 on. Weber was born in Russia and came to the United States when he was 10. He studied art at the Pratt Institute in Brooklyn, N.Y., at the Académie Julian in Paris, and with the renowned

French artist Henri Matisse. Weber was an influential teacher at the Art Students League. Among his students there was Mark Rothko, who later became an important abstract artist.

Weber, Max (1864-1920), German economist and sociologist. His theories contributed to the formation of modern sociological theory. Weber considered bureaucracy the crucial component of society and created an ideal type method for examining different societies. His most influential work, *The Protestant Ethic and the Spirit of Capitalism* (1904-05), deals with Protestantism's economic aspects. Other works include *From Max Weber: Essays in Sociology* and *The Theory of Social and Economic Organization.*

Webern, Anton (1883-1945), Austrian composer. He studied with Arnold Schoenberg and developed 12-tone music. His works include *Five Pieces for Orchestra* (1911-13), 2 symphonies, 3 string quartets, and a number of songs.

Webster, Daniel (1782-1852), U.S. politician, lawyer, and orator whose advocacy of strong central government earned him the name "defender of the Constitution." Early in his career he eloquently defended states' rights and championed New England's interests, first as a New Hampshire member of the House of Representatives (1813-17), and Massachusetts representative (1823-27) and senator (1827-41; 1845-50). As New England's interests changed from shipping to industry, Webster became nationalistic and supported protective tariffs despite his earlier castigation of trade restrictions. His battle against nullification began in 1830 and continued throughout the crisis of 1832-33. In his efforts to preserve the Union, he supported the Compromise of 1850. He was twice secretary of state.

Webster, Noah (1758-1843), U.S. lexicographer whose works—such as *The Elementary Spelling Book*, called the "Blue-Backed Speller" (1829; earlier versions, 1783-87)—helped standardize American spelling. He also compiled a grammar (1784) and a reader (1785). Working on dictionaries from 1803, he published *An American Dictionary of the English Language* (1812), with 70,000 entries and 12,000 new definitions. Today his name is often applied to dictionaries that are in no way based on his work.
See also: Dictionary.

Webster, William Hedgecock (1924-), U.S. jurist and director of the Central Intelligence Agency (CIA). Webster was appointed to the U.S. District Court for the Eastern District of Missouri (1971) by Pres. Richard M. Nixon. In 1973 he began serving in the U.S. Court of Appeals, and in 1978 he was appointed director of the Federal Bureau of Investigation (FBI) by Pres. Jimmy Carter. An expert on terrorist tactics, Webster was made director of the CIA in 1987. He retired in 1991.

Webster-Ashburton Treaty, 1842 agreement between the United States and Great Britain. It settled boundary disputes between Canada and the United States, established a cooperative effort toward ending the slave trade, and provided for the extradition of criminals. The treaty was signed by Secretary of State Daniel Webster and Lord Ashburton.

Weddell Sea, arm of the Atlantic Ocean in Antarctica between Palmer Land and Coats Land. At its southern end are the Ronne and Filchner ice shelves. It was named for James Weddell, who claimed to have discovered it in 1823.
See also: Atlantic Ocean.

Wedding anniversary, celebration that takes place at the yearly return of an original wedding date. In Western society it has become common practice to commemorate this event with a characteristic gift, symbolic of the number of years a couple has been married; e.g., silver represents a 25th wedding anniversary; gold, a 50th anniversary.

Wedekind, Frank (1864-1918), German playwright and actor. His work denounced a corrupt bourgeois society that had no interest in the arts or learning, and that was stifling the freedom of individuals. His plays include *The Awakening of Spring* (1895), *Earth Spirit* (1895), and *Pandora's Box* (printed 1904). Although Wedekind was considered scandalous by many in his time, he had a strong following and inspired modern dramatists, including Bertolt Brecht.

Wedge, device with 2 or more surfaces that slope and taper to a thin edge. A wedge may be made of wood, metal, or other material and is used to split something apart. The wedge's thin edge is forced into a narrow opening of the object. The top of the wedge is hammered, driving the wedge further down, thereby piercing the object. A wedge may also be used to move a heavy object.

Wedgwood, Josiah (1730-95), English potter, inventor of Wedgwood ware. Famous for his cream-colored queen's ware, patented in 1765, he frequently employed artists such as John Flaxman for the designs on his blue-and-white jasper ware. Wedgwood, who introduced new materials and machinery to the craft of pottery-making, was the first to acquire steam engines at his factory in Etruria, Staffordshire, and contributed much to improve the standard of living of his workers.

Wedgwood ware, fine English pottery first created by Josiah Wedgwood (1730-95). Wedgwood comes in various styles, including a cream-colored stoneware called creamware (also called queen's ware because Queen Charlotte was so pleased with her set of creamware), a black stoneware called Egyptian black or black basalt, and colored stoneware that often had white designs or figures in relief called Jasperware. Wedgwood ware's durability and beauty made it very popular. Production of it has continued to present time, and it still has a world market.

Weed, any plant that is useless or destructive, or that grows where it is not desired. A plant that grows abundantly in an area where it is not wanted crowds out and takes nutrition, water, and space away from plants that are being cultivated. Injurious plants may be considered weeds. For example, poison ivy and oak can produce a skin rash; goldenrod and ragweed can cause hay fever; and thistles have prickly leaves that can hurt skin. Herbicides and soil cultivation are among methods developed to control the proliferation of weeds.

Weed, Thurlow (1797-1882), U.S. journalist and Whig political leader. He used his Albany *Evening Journal* to promote the Antimasonic party. He supported the presidential campaigns of William Harrison, Henry Clay, and Zachary Taylor, and the career of his friend, William H. Seward. He joined the Republicans in 1855 and under President Lincoln served as a special agent to England.

Weems, Mason Locke (1759-1825), U.S. Anglican Church minister, writer, and traveling bookseller. He wrote popular biographies of noted Americans that were more entertaining than accurate. His biography of George Washington, *The Life and Memorable Actions of George Washington,* contained the fictitious tale about George Washington chopping down a cherry tree.

Weevil, any of 35,000 species of oval- or pear-shaped beetles (from the largest animal family, Curculionidae), having a greatly drawn-out head that ends in a pronounced snout. They feed on hard vegetable matter, seeds, and wood; the larvae, which develop within seeds, are

Wedgwood vase (c.1785)

legless. Weevils are pests of such important economic crops as cotton and grain and of stored peas, beans, and flour.

Weight, gravitational force experienced by an object in relation to another massive body (planet). The weight of a body (measured in newtons) is equal to the product of its mass and the local acceleration due to gravity. Weight differs from mass in being a vector quantity.
See also: Gravitation.

Weight, Atomic *see:* Atom.

Weight control, method by which a person maintains a healthy weight. The medical as well as social and emotional well-being of a person is based in part on the maintenance of proper weight. A person must take in 3,500 calories of food to gain 1 lb (0.45 kg). In turn the human body burns up calories during exercise. Therefore food intake and physical exercise are important factors in weight control. Not all weight gain is unhealthy, since exercise often encourages a gain in muscle mass and weight. However, too much weight, based on fat, can cause health problems and, in the extreme, *obesity*—a state of being extremely overweight. Some studies indicate that weight may be related to heredity. In general, underweight people are considered healthy as long as they do not have a disease or serious eating disorder and people who are somewhat overweight are also considered healthy if they maintain a balanced diet and exercise.
See also: Diet.

Weightlessness, condition that arises in the apparent absence of gravitational pull. Experienced by astronauts in space, weightlessness occurs when the centrifugal force of the astronauts and spacecraft in forward motion exactly cancels the force of gravity.

Weight lifting, bodybuilding exercise and competitive sport. As a contest, it has long been popular in Turkey, Egypt, Japan, Europe, and the USSR, and has been a regular event in the Olympics since 1920. There are 3 basic lifts: the snatch (from the floor to over the head in a single motion); the clean-and-jerk (2 movements—first to the chest and then over the head); and the military, or 2-hand, press (similar to the clean-and-jerk but performed while maintaining a "military" stance).

Weights and measures, units of weight, length, area, and volume commonly used in the home, in commerce, and in industry. Although, like other early peoples, the Hebrews used measures such as the foot, the cubit (the length of the human forearm), and the span, which could easily be realized in practice by using parts of the body, in commerce they also used standard containers and weights. Later, weights were based on the quantity of precious metal in coins. During and after the Middle Ages each region evolved its own system of weights and measures. In the 19th century these were standardized on a national basis, and then in turn were superseded by standards of the metric system. In the Western world, only the British Empire and the United States retained their own systems (the Imperial System and the U.S. Customary System, respectively) into the mid-20th century. With the United Kingdom's adoption of the International System of Units (SI units), the United States remains one of the few countries that does not use metric units, although, as has been the case since 1959, the U.S. customary units are now defined in terms of their metric counterparts and not on the basis of independent standards. In the United States the administration of weights and measures is coordinated by the National Bureau of Standards.

Weil, Simone (1909-43), French philosopher, religious mystic, and left-wing intellectual. She was active in the Spanish Civil War and the French resistance in World War II. She converted from Judaism to Roman Catholicism in 1938. Among her books to be translated into English are *Waiting for God* (1951) and *The Need for Roots* (1952).

Weill, Kurt (1900-50), German-born U.S. composer. His most well-known music is for the 2 satirical operas on which he collaborated with Bertolt Brecht, *The Threepenny Opera* (1928) and *The Rise and Fall of the City of Mahagonny* (1927, rev. 1930). Unpopular with the Nazis, he came to the United States in 1935 and became a successful Broadway composer, creating the music for such musicals as *Knickerbocker Holiday* (1938, with Maxwell Anderson) and *Street Scene* (1947). He was married to singer Lotte Lenya.

Weimar (pop. 63,400), city in east-central Germany, on the Ilm River. Weimar is a center for manufacturing agricultural machinery, electrical equipment, and chemicals. It was capital of the Saxe-Weimar duchy from 1547, and its court became the German cultural and intellectual center in the 18th and 19th centuries. Weimar was the site of the national assembly that established the so-called Weimar Republic in 1919. Buchenwald concentration camp was located nearby (1937-45).

Weimaraner, hunting dog developed in the early 19th century in Weimar, Germany. First used to hunt large animals such as deer, it was later used to hunt game. The Weimaraner has a smooth, short, gray coat and amber eyes. It weighs 55-85 lb (25-39 kg), and is 23-27 in (58-69 cm) high. Weimaraners are graceful, affectionate, and obedient companions and watchdogs.

Weimar Republic, German government (1919-33) based on the democratic republican constitution adopted at Weimar in 1919. The constitution provided for a parliament of 2 houses and a popularly elected president. President Paul von Hindenburg made Adolf Hitler chancellor in 1933, whereupon Hitler suspended the constitution.

Weinberg, Steven (1933-), U.S. physicist who shared the 1979 Nobel Prize in physics for work demonstrating that 2 of the basic forces of nature, electromagnetism and weak interaction (the cause of radioactive decay in certain atomic nuclei), are aspects of a single interaction.
See also: Physics.

Weinberger, Caspar (1917-), U.S. government official. He served as secretary of health, education, and welfare (1973-75) under Pres. Richard M. Nixon and as secretary of defense (1981-87) under Pres. Ronald Reagan.

Weisgard, Leonard (1916-), U.S. artist and children's book writer and illustrator. He illustrated over 20 books by Margaret Wise Brown (pseud. Golden MacDonald), including *The Little Island*, for which he won the 1946 Caldecott Medal. Among the books he both wrote and illustrated are *My First Picture Book* (1953) and *The Plymouth Thanksgiving* (1967).

Weismann, August (1834-1914), German biologist. He is renowned for his work on and theories about evolution. Weismann was interested in how a species passed to its offspring various traits, which traits could be inherited, and which could not. He wrote several books, the most famous being *The Germ Plasm: A Theory of Heredity* (1893).
See also: Biology; Evolution.

Weiss, Peter (1916-82), German-Swedish playwright, artist, and filmmaker. He fled Nazi Germany in 1934. With his innovative play *The Persecution and Assassination of Jean Paul Marat as Performed by the Inmates of the Asylum of Charenton Under the Direction of the Marquis de Sade*, or *Marat/Sade* (1964), Weiss was acclaimed the successor of Bertolt Brecht. His other dramas include *The Investigation* (1965), and *Trotsky in Exile* (1970).

Weizmann, Chaim (1874-1952), Polish-born scientist and Zionist leader, first president of Israel (1948-52). He emigrated to England in 1904 and became an eminent biochemist and director of the British Admiralty laboratories in 1916. He helped secure the Balfour Declaration (1917), which promised a Jewish state in Palestine. He was head of the World Zionist Organization (1920-29) and of the Jewish Agency (1929-31, 1935-46). He also founded what is known today as the Weizmann Inst. of Science.
See also: Zionism.

Welding, process of bringing pieces of metal together under conditions of heat or pressure, or both, until they coalesce at the joint. The oldest method is forge welding, in which the surfaces to be joined are heated to welding temperature and then hammered together on an anvil. The most widely used method today is metal-arc welding: An electric arc is struck between an electrode and the pieces to be joined, and molten metal from a "filler rod"—usu-

ally the electrode itself—is added. Gas welding, now largely displaced by metal-arc welding, is usually accomplished by means of an oxyacetylene torch, which delivers the necessary heat by burning acetylene in a pure oxygen atmosphere. Sources of heat in other forms of welding include the electrical resistance of the joint (resistance welding), an electric arc at the joint (flash welding), a focused beam of electrons (electron-beam welding), and friction (friction welding). Some more recently applied heat sources include hot plasmas, lasers, ultrasonic vibrations, and explosive impacts.
See also: Soldering.

Welfare, direct government aid to the needy. In the United States various programs, operated by the social security office and by state and local governments, provide aid to the handicapped, aged, poor, and unemployed. Benefits to the aged are more-or-less standardized nationally, but the form of, amount of, and qualifications for other benefits differ from state to state. Benefits fall under many programs, such as veterans' aid and workmen's compensation. All welfare programs are linked to programs that do not give direct financial assistance, such as housing, food stamps, and medical aid. The Reagan administration made significant cuts in federal welfare programs.

Well, manmade hole in the ground used to tap water, gas, or minerals from the earth. Most modern wells are drilled and fitted with a lining, usually of steel, to forestall collapse. Though wells are sunk for natural gas and petroleum oil, the most common type yields water. Such wells may be horizontal or vertical, but all have their innermost end below the water table. If it should be below the permanent water table (the lowest annual level of the water table), the well will yield water throughout the year. Most wells require pumping, but some operate under natural pressure.

Welland Ship Canal, Canadian waterway running 27.6 mi (44.4 km) from Port Colborne on Lake Erie to Port Weller on Lake Ontario to form a major link of the Saint Lawrence Seaway and Great Lakes Waterway. The canal was built 1914-32, modernized in 1972, and has a minimum depth of about 30 ft (9.1 m). It has 8 locks to overcome the 326-ft (99.4-m) difference in height between Lakes Erie and Ontario.
See also: Saint Lawrence Seaway and Great Lakes Waterway.

Weller, Thomas Huckle (1915-), U.S. bacteriologist and virologist who shared with John F. Enders and Frederick C. Robbins the 1954 Nobel Prize in physiology or medicine for their cultivation of poliomyelitis viruses on tissues of human embryos outside the body.
See also: Poliomyelitis.

Welles, Gideon (1802-78), U.S. secretary of the navy in Pres. Abraham Lincoln's cabinet. During the Civil War, he directed the navy to block off the Confederate coast and to patrol the Mississippi River. Originally a newspaper editor, Welles left the Democrats in disagreement over slavery to help found (1856) the Republican Party.

Welles, Orson (1915-85), U.S. actor, director, and producer. In 1938 his realistic radio production of H.G. Well's *War of the Worlds* caused thousands of listeners to panic, fearing the account of the alien attack was a genuine news report. His first motion picture, of which he was director, cowriter, and star, was *Citizen Kane* (1940), loosely modeled on the life of newspaper magnate William R. Hearst. Innovative camera work and film editing continued to characterize his work in such films as *The Magnificent Ambersons* (1942), *The Lady from Shanghai* (1947), *Macbeth* (1948), and *Touch of Evil* (1962).

Wellington (pop. 325,700), capital city of New Zealand since 1865, at the southern end of North Island. Founded in 1840, it is the nation's second-largest city and an important port and transportation center. Manufactures include processed food, transportation equipment, textiles, and clothing.
See also: New Zealand.

Wellington, Arthur Wellesley, 1st duke of (1769-1852), British general and politician, "the Iron Duke," who defeated Napoleon I at the Battle of Waterloo. After distinguished military service in India (1796-1805), he drove the French from Spain and Portugal in the Peninsular War and entered France in 1813. After being created duke, he led the victorious forces at Waterloo (1815). Serving the Tory government (1819-27), he became prime minister (1828-30), and passed the Catholic Emancipation Act; however, he opposed parliamentary reform. In 1842 he became commander-in-chief for life.
See also: Napoleonic Wars.

Wells, Fargo & Company, U.S. banking company. Founded in 1852 by Henry Wells and William G. Fargo as a bank and a delivery company servicing the route from San Francisco to New York, the company expanded with the purchase of the Pony Express (1861) and the Holladay Overland Stage Company (1866), in time servicing the entire West Coast as well as parts of Canada, Mexico, and Central America. Wells Fargo transported passengers, mail, money, and cargo, including gold. In 1905 Wells Fargo gave up its banking operations to the Wells Fargo Nevada National Bank. In 1918 the remainder of the company merged with other companies to form the American Railway Express Company.
See also: Fargo, William George.

Wells, H. G. (1866-1946), British writer and social reformer. A draper's apprentice, he studied science and became a teacher. After such early science fiction as *The Time Machine* (1895) and *The War of the Worlds* (1898), he wrote novels on the lower middle class, including *Kipps* (1905) and *The History of Mr. Polly* (1910). A founder of the Fabian society, he became a social prophet (*A Modern Utopia*; 1905). After World War I he popularized knowledge in *Outline of History* (1920) and *The Science of Life* (1931).

Wells, Henry (1805-78), U.S. pioneer businessperson. With William G. Fargo, he founded Wells, Fargo & Co. (1852), which carried people, freight, and mail from New York City to California. With the acquisition of Benjamin Holladay's mail and stagecoach business (1866), Wells, Fargo & Co. became the most powerful firm in the Far West.
See also: Wells, Fargo & Company.

Wells-Barnett, Ida Bell (1862-1931), African-American reformer and journalist known for her anti-lynching efforts in the late 1800s and early 1900s. In 1909 she helped establish the National Association for the Advancement of Colored People (NAACP). She also participated in the campaign aimed at giving women the right to vote.

Welsbach, Baron von (1858-1929), Viennese chemist and inventor who worked on artificial lighting. He developed the Welsbach mantle (1885), a gas lamp that produced brighter light than previous gas lamps. A few years later, he created the filament for an incandescent lamp that led to the development of the modern light bulb. He also created a metal, called Auer's metal, which, when struck, creates a spark. It is used in modern-day cigarette lighters.
See also: Chemistry.

Welsh *see:* Wales.

Welsh corgi *see:* Cardigan Welsh corgi.

Welsh springer spaniel, breed of dog. This sporting dog can withstand long hours, poor weather, and rough terrain as a re-

REWARD!

WELLS, FARGO & CO'S

Express was Robbed this Morning, between Ione Valley and Galt, by two men, described as follows:

One elderly, heavy set, and sandy complexion. The other tall, slim, and dark complexion.

$200 Each and one-fourth of the Treasure recovered, will be paid for the *arrest* and *conviction* of the robbers.

JNO. J. VALENTINE, Gen. Supt.

San Francisco, May 3d, 1875.

Wells, Fargo & Co. poster

trieving companion to a hunter. Welsh spaniels need careful training, though, because of their tendency to roam. They stand up to 17 in (43 cm) at the shoulder and weigh from 35-45 lb (15.75-20.25 kg). Their fur, including that on their tail, legs, and chest, is white with red patches or spots.

Welsh terrier, small dog native to Wales, used to hunt foxes. The Welsh terrier has a wiry coat with black and reddish-tan markings. It weighs approximately 20 lb (9 kg) and is about 15 in (38 cm) high. The Welsh is a very lively and spirited dog.

Welty, Eudora (1909-), U.S. novelist and short-story writer, known for sensitive tales of Mississippi life. She superbly depicted atmosphere and characters in *The Wide Net* (1943), *The Ponder Heart* (1954), *The Optimist's Daughter* (1972; Pulitzer Prize), and others.

Welwitschia, also known as tumboa, family of desert plants (*Welwitschia mirabilis*) that grow in Africa. The Welwitschia is a large, slow-growing plant that lives 100 or more years, and may reach an age of 1,000-2,000 years. Its long main root extends into a short, cone-shaped trunk that spreads to a width of 5-6 ft (1.5-1.8 m). At the base of the trunk grow a pair of leaves 2-3 ft (61-91 cm) wide and 4-6 ft (1.2-1.8 m) long. These leaves, which grow for the entire life of the plant, are usually shredded into thinner strips by strong desert winds and sand.

Mae West

Wen, or sebaceous cyst, blocked sebaceous gland, often over the scalp or forehead, that forms a cyst containing old sebum under the skin. Should it become infected, its excision is a simple procedure.

Werewolf, in folklore, a man who can supernaturally turn into a wolf and devour humans. The belief dates from Greek legend and was widespread in medieval Europe and in the 19th-century Balkans. The psychiatric condition of lycanthropy involves the belief that one is a werewolf or other beast.

Werfel, Franz (1890-1945), Austrian novelist, poet, and playwright. His early plays and poetry, such as *Der Spiegelmensch* (1920), were important works of German expressionism. He fled Nazi-occupied Austria (1938) and later settled in the United States. His novels include *Embezzled Heaven* (1939), *The Song of Bernadette* (1941), and *Jacobowsky and the Colonel* (1944).

Wergeland, Henrik Arnold (1808-45), Norwegian writer and nationalist. He promoted Norwegian independence from Sweden and inspired Norwegians to feel pride in their own culture. He produced much poetry, drama, and prose, but it is his poetry that received the most acclaim. *Creation, Humanity, and Messiah* (1830), *Jan van Huysum's Flower Piece* (1840), and *The English Pilot* (1844) are some of his best-loved poems. He was dedicated to the causes of liberty, democracy, and international cooperation.

Wertheimer, Max (1880-1943), German psychologist who founded (with Kurt Koffka and Wolfgang Köhler) the school of Gestalt psychology. He taught at Frankfurt and Berlin and emigrated to the United States in 1933.
See also: Gestalt psychology.

Weser River, major German river whose source is the junction of the Fulda and Werra rivers at Munden. The Weser is about 273 mi (440 km) long and flows into the North Sea near Bremerhaven. About 45 mi (72 km) of the river, from its North Sea mouth to Bremen, is navigable by large ships.

Wesker, Arnold (1932-), English playwright, one of the so-called angry young men to emerge in England in 1956. His early plays, such as the trilogy *Chicken Soup with Barley* (1958), *Roots* (1959), and *I'm Talking About Jerusalem* (1960), are committed to the ideals of socialism. The later, more introspective *Chips with Everything* (1962) and *The Friends* (1970) explore themes of private pain.

Wesley, name of 2 English evangelistic preachers who, with George Whitefield, founded Methodism. **John Wesley** (1703-91) and his brother **Charles** (1707-88) formed an Oxford Holy Club of scholarly Christians, known as Methodists for their "rule and methods." In 1738 the brothers were profoundly influenced by the Moravian Church in Georgia and, John in particular, by Luther's *Preface to the Epistle to the Romans.* Aiming to promote "vital, practical religion," the Wesleys took up evangelistic work by field, or open-air, preaching. Rejected by the Church of England, they were enthusiastically received by the people, and they organized conferences of itinerant lay preachers. Charles composed some 6,500 hymns, including "Hark! The Herald Angels Sing."
See also: Methodists.

Wesleyan Church, U.S. Protestant church formed in 1968 by the merger of the Wesleyan Methodist Church of America and the Pilgrim Holiness Church. Members attempt to live a life free of sin or indulgences such as alcohol or tobacco. The church, headquartered in Marion, Indiana, operates several educational facilities and has missionaries working in areas throughout the world.
See also: Protestantism.

West, Benjamin (1738-1820), U.S.-born painter. After studying in Rome he settled in London (1763) and was appointed the official historical painter (1772) to King George III. He was also a founder of the Royal Academy of Arts. His best-known works are *Death of General Wolfe* (1771) and *Penn's Treaty with the Indians* (1776). Gilbert Stuart and J.S. Copley were among his students.

West, Dame Rebecca (Cicily Isabel Fairfield; 1892-1983), British novelist, critic, and journalist. *Black Lamb and Grey Falcon; A Journey through Yugoslavia* (1941) is perhaps her finest work. Her novels include *The Return of the Soldier* (1918) and *Birds Fall Down* (1966).

West, Jerry (1938-), U.S. basketball player and coach. Known for his high scoring as well as ball-handling and defense, he scored 25,192 regular-season points in his National Basketball Association (NBA) career. His achievements include 2 Most Valuable Player awards—1 Playoff (1969) and 1 All-Star (1972)—and appearing in 13 All-Star games. West played for the Los Angeles Lakers (1960-74), leading them to a championship (1972) and, after retiring, became the team's head coach (1976-79) and later, general manager (1982-). He was inducted into the Basketball Hall of Fame in 1979.

West, Jessamyn (1907-84), U.S. author. A Quaker whose writings often reflect the ideals of the Quaker religion, West's most famous book is *Friendly Persuasion* (1945), a view of life in a rural Quaker family in the 1800s (she later adapted this book for the 1956 film of the same name). Other works include *The Witch Diggers* (1951), *Cress Delahanty* (1953), and *Except For Thee and Me* (1969), which chronicles the lives of various characters in *Friendly Persuasion.*

West, Mae (1892-1980), U.S. stage and screen actress. This sultry mistress of provocative innuendo and sex symbol of Hollywood films of the 1930s was frequently at odds with the censors. She immortalized the phrase "come up 'n' see me sometime," and starred in such movies as *She Done Him Wrong* (1933), *I'm No Angel* (1933), and *My Little Chickadee* (1940).

West, Nathanael (Nathan Wallenstein Weinstein; 1903-40), U.S. author. His acerbic novels about the American dream include *The Dream Life of Balso Snell* (1931); *Miss Lonelyhearts* (1933), a gloomy satire about a lovelorn columnist; *A Cool Million* (1934), a lampoon of the rags-to-riches theme; and *The Day of the Locust* (1939), a surrealistic view of life and failure in Hollywood.

West, The, western portion of the United States, formerly the region west of the Appalachian Mountains; presently, the territory west of the Mississippi River, in particular the northern part of this area. In U.S. history, the West was a region that lay at the rim of the settled land. This unsettled area was a place where unlimited land was available at a very cheap price to anyone willing to lead a life on the frontier.

West Bank, land to the west of the Dead Sea and the Jordan River, between Israel and Jordan. A part of Palestine, the area was annexed by Jordan following the partition of Palestine and the formation of the state of Israel (1948). It has been occupied by Israel since 1967, despite a call for withdrawal from the United Nations. Historically known as Judaea and Samaria, the West Bank contains such famous cities as Bethlehem, Jericho, Hebron, and the Old City of Jerusalem. The status of the West Bank, along with that of the Gaza Strip in southwestern Israel, has become an important issue in the Arab-Israeli disputes. The Camp David Agreement of 1978, between Egypt and Israel, specified that the 1.3 million Palestinian Arabs, who are the great majority of inhabitants in the 2 areas, would be given "full autonomy and self-government" for a 5-year period, during which the ultimate sovereignty of the territories would be determined. The parties, however, failed to agree about the details of self-government. At the same time, Israel increased its settlements there. Hostility between Israel and the Palestinians escalated in the late 1980s during the *intifada*, a Palestinian uprising marked by boycotts, demonstrations, and stone-throwing. In 1988 Jordan gave up the West Bank and Jericho attained limited Palestinian self-government in 1994.

The West Bank

West Berlin *see:* Berlin.

Western Australia, largest Australian state (975,290 sq mi/2,527,633 sq km), first settled 1826-29, covering the western third of the country. Beyond the narrow coastal strip and fertile southwest, it is mostly dry plateau with vast desert wastes. Major products are wool, wheat, and lumber, and chief minerals are gold, coal, and iron.

Western European Union (WEU), defensive economic, social, and cultural alliance among Belgium, France, Great Britain, Italy, Luxembourg, the Netherlands, and Germany, formed in 1955. Spain and Portugal joined in 1988 and Greece in 1991. Comprising most of the members of the North Atlantic Treaty Organization (NATO), the organization works to strengthen the European part of NATO.
See also: North Atlantic Treaty Organization.

Western frontier life, folklore and reality of the lives of the men and women who participated in the last phase of the settlement of the U.S. frontier. The western territories of the United States were settled in several stages. After pioneers had settled lands from the Appalachians to the Mississippi and the Old Northwest territory around the Great Lakes, they headed for the Far West, chiefly California and Oregon. The Great Plains, stretching from west of the Mississippi to the Rocky Mountains, were a passage to be crossed, not land to be settled. That changed after the 1850s and, in particular, after the Civil War. The vast expanses of the Great Plains and the intermontane region, between the Rocky Mountains and the Sierra Nevada, were the last frontier, and the area was settled between 1850 and 1890. Within that 40 years, the United States completed its drive to subdue and fill the entire expanse of land between the Atlantic and Pacific oceans. The nation succeeded in fixing and defining its continental boundaries. But the people who did it, the men and women who went out to settle the last frontier, lived lives that would decisively shape the American character. In the process, their lives became the stuff of folklore and the imagination; the land became the setting, the people the characters, and the settlement the taming of the wild west. The 19th century was the age of imperialism. The great European powers, particularly Great Britain, France, and Germany, struggled for markets, territory, and domination in Africa and Asia. The first half of the century had been absorbed with the military ambitions of Napoleon Bonaparte and the political repercussions of the French Revolution. The general failure of the revolutions of 1848 left the industrialized nation states dominated by a socially and politically conservative but ambitious middle class. With Europe temporarily stable, energy was directed outward and fortunes and reputations were sought in the colonies. The United States, was influenced by these developments. Proud of its separation and isolation from Europe, it was not a party to the competition for foreign colonies. The Great Plains remained unsettled and the United States turned to the task with a deliberate sense of itself that took the form of a political purpose and program articulated by the central government and different from the country's previous pioneering efforts. Much more than its earlier pioneering drives, the settlement of the frontier was more frankly driven by the profit motive, more centrally directed by a successful partnership between central government and private enterprise, and inspired by the ideology of Manifest Destiny. While Europeans made their fortunes and reputations in far-off Africa and Asia, U.S. citizens pursued the work and adventure of subduing their country's last frontier.

The people who settled the Great Plains were a varied lot. Most were farmers, skilled and unskilled laborers, miners and prospectors, and, after the Civil War, former soldiers all looking for a better life. Among them were drifters and those with criminal records or a past they wanted to escape. Many were blacks who were attracted to the greater opportunity and freedom from prejudice they hoped to find in the frontier. Among the blacks were men who became well-known cowboys, like the ranchhand Nat Love, famous for his horsemanship, or the former slave, Base Ikard, who rose to become foreman of one of the biggest ranches in Texas. Many European immigrants came to settle the West, too. Some were miners from England or Wales. Many others, especially Germans, came to the United States after the failed revolutions of 1848. Scandinavians also came in large numbers. And in California, the Chinese came to work as laborers on the transcontinental railroad. The major divisions among all these people were the miners and prospectors, the ranchers and cowboys, and the farmers.

The miners and prospectors went west to find gold. The first great gold rush was in the Far West in 1848 triggered by the discovery of gold at Sutter's Mill in California. In succeeding decades, strikes were made farther inland. From 1856 to 1875 silver was found in southern Arizona, then Colorado and Nevada. Eventually, mining prospered in Idaho, Montana, Washington, and the Black Hills of South Dakota. Mining gave rise to boom towns, some of which eventually became stable and prosperous towns and cities, but many of which became ghost towns when the mines gave out. Tucson, Tombstone, Denver, Central City, and Leadville were all, at one time, mining towns.

The ranchers went west to raise cattle. The open plains were ideal for grazing huge herds, and the completion of the transcontinental railroad in 1869 made it possible to ship the cattle to market in large and profitable numbers. Cattle ranching was a tough business that gave the West its cowboys. Cowboys tended the herds while

It took six months to cover the 2,000-mi (3,200-km) Oregon Trail, which was used to reach the Oregon Territory

Above: The pony express lasted only two years (1860-61), ending two days after the first transcontinental telegraph line was completed.

Right: Pony express relay riders could travel the distance between Missouri and California in about nine days.

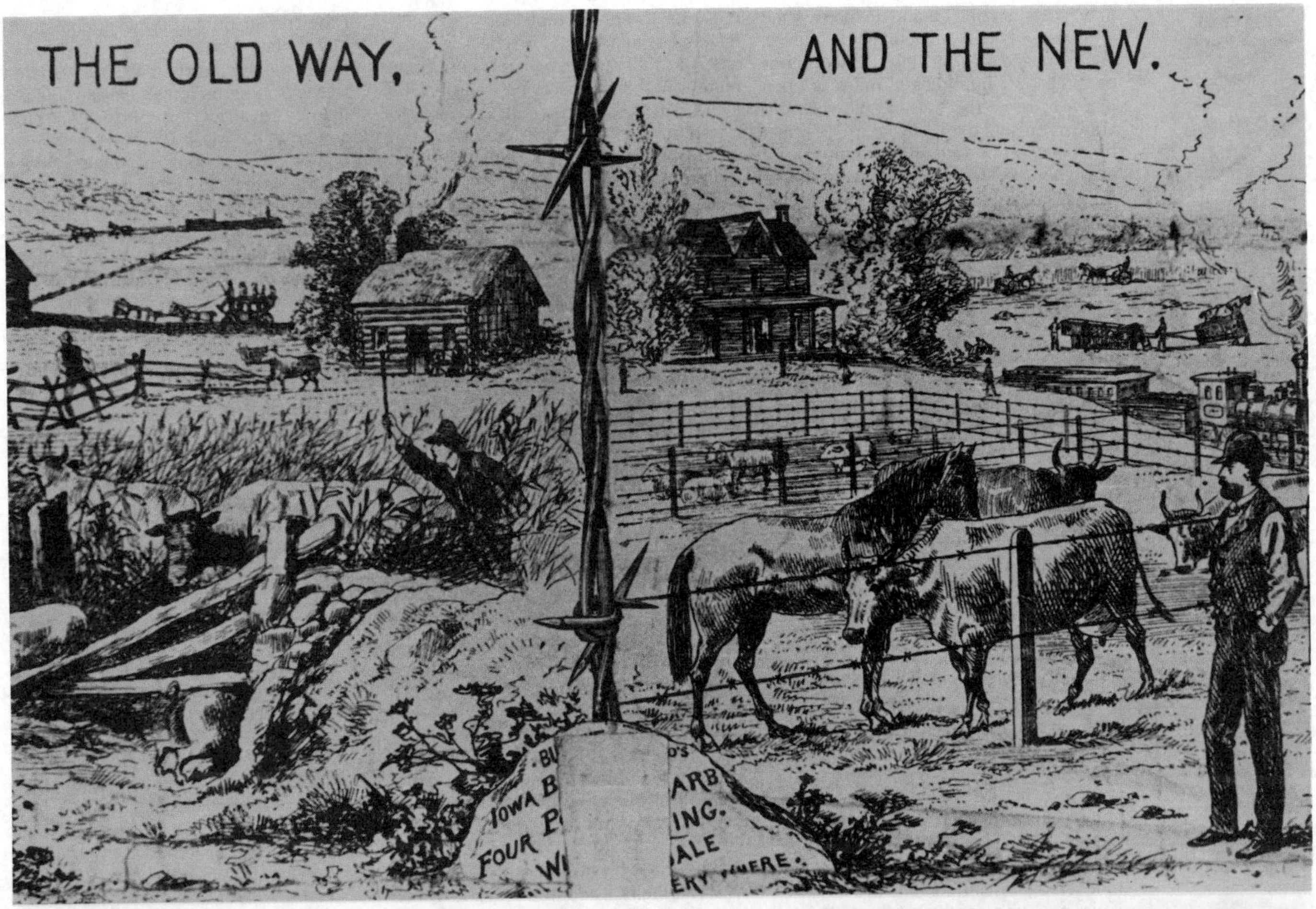

THE OLD WAY, AND THE NEW.

The Dodge City Peace Commission (1882).

The gold rush brought many settlers to the West. Shown is a Klondike prospector panning for gold.

Top. Barbed wire not only replaced the wooden fence, it helped lead to the demise of the U.S. cowboy

they were grazing, branded them when they were of age, fought off cattle thieves, and managed the long drives of thousands of cattle over hundreds of miles of open prairie to the railroads. They followed well-known trails, like the Chisholm Trail, that have become a part of the landscape of U.S. folklore. The cattle business made towns like Abilene, Kans., and Dodge City. But eventually boom went to bust. The cattle market became glutted, the blizzards of 1886 and 1887 wiped out many ranchers, and competition with farmers for the open range also took its toll.

Farmers had been reluctant, at first, to settle the Great Plains, and the homesteaders formed the last wave of settlers. At first the land was considered unsuitable for farming. There was little water and there were no trees. On top of that, the Native Americans were hostile. But several developments in the 1870s changed the prospects for homesteaders. Barbed wire was invented, so wood was no longer necessary for poling and fencing. New methods of dry farming were invented and windmills were developed to draw water from underground. Homesteaders moved west. They faced harsh conditions. Their houses were built of sod, blocks of compacted soil cut out of the prairie. They had to deal with hot summers and ice-cold winters, infestations of grasshoppers, prairie fires, and possible confrontations with Native Americans. They also had to contend with ranchers, whose herds and livelihoods were threatened when barbed wire put an end to the open range. Bloody range wars pitted ranchers against farmers and in some cases it was necessary for the U.S. army to intervene. But in the end, the farmers prevailed.

Settling the frontier brought out the best and the worst in people. For miners and ranchers, farmers and cowboys, and the skilled and semi-skilled professionals who helped build and settle the towns, life could be harsh, there were few comforts, and a rough-and-ready democracy prevailed. Men who were poor prospectors one day became fabulously rich the next. Many drank or gambled their money away. Some built prosperous farms and ranches, while others were wiped out. In the early days, there were few women and little of the social stability that comes with family life. Those who settled the West lived by a rough-hewn code made up in part of values they brought with them and values that arose from the lives they lived. Men were prized for their self-reliance, survival skills, and reliability. A man's word was more binding than any written law. Though not nearly as violent as one would believe by watching movies or reading Zane Grey, the West saw more than its share of violence and bloodshed and tested man's capacity to fight and endure. These values were rooted in the day-to-day living conditions. Transportation was uncomfortable and often dangerous. Stagecoaches ran over uneven ground and passengers sat on rough wooden benches for long, dusty, cold rides during which they had often to stay alert for Native Americans or bandits. People traveled by wagon trains before the railroads were completed, and they traveled regularly by horseback. Eventually, the railroads expanded, connecting more towns and improving transport, but in the early days even camels were used for transport over the dry prairies. Communication was no less difficult, though the problem was met with characteristic ingenuity and energy. For 19 months, between Apr. 1860 and Oct. 1861, the Pony Express, a relay system of horseback riders, covered the distance between St. Joseph and Sacramento in about 10 days. The system was replaced by the telegraph.

The 3 great threats to the lives of the settlers on the frontier were nature and the elements, Native Americans, and lawbreakers. Men like Bat Masterson and Wyatt Earp became famous for enforcing the law, and theirs was a daunting task. Everyone was armed and a single lawman was often the only law for 200 or 300 miles around. Judges, like the famous Roy Bean, dispersed law on a circuit and conducted hearings in local saloons with a law book in one hand and a pistol in the other. Desperadoes were not always the colorful or spectacular kind. Most crime had to do with swindles and thefts, the work of claim jumpers, confidence men, card sharps, and rustlers. If caught, these men often faced rough justice, if not at the hands of an individual, then at the hands of vigilantes or a lynch mob. But the Old West had a deep ambivalence about the law. It admired tough and independent characters, gamblers who took chances and won, people who knew how to fight for and keep what was theirs. It admired a tough lawman but was suspicious of government. That ambivalence is apparent in the reputations enjoyed by men like the Dalton boys, Billy the Kid, Sam Bass, and Frank and Jesse James, notorious outlaws who were feared but, in a sense, also admired.

Finally, there were the Native Americans. The Comstock Lode produced $300 million worth of silver ore (1860-80). Cattle ranching made men fortunes. And eventually, farmers turned the Great Plains into the world's greatest bread basket. In this scheme of things there was finally no room for buffalo or tribes of nomadic hunters. The Native Americans occupied the land of the last frontier, presumably protected by treaties, but the treaties gave way to the overwhelming drive for riches, land, and the territorial ambitions of a growing nation-state. The Native Americans resisted and the settlers and the government fought back. The U.S. Army established forts and outposts to protect settlers and subdue the Native Americans. In the process, both fear and greed combined to weave into the ethos of the West the conviction that the only good Indian was a dead Indian. The result was the systematic reduction, the demoralization and decimation, of the Native American peoples, in open warfare or in massacres, like the one near Sand Creek, Col., in 1864. Nonetheless, the Native Americans left a mixed legacy among the people who settled the frontier. There were many who admired their courage and skills and there were those, among them agents of the Indian Bureau, who attempted to mitigate their destruction.

In 1890 the Bureau of the Census declared that the frontier no longer existed. Buffalo Bill Cody began touring with his Wild West Show in 1883. Mark Twain wrote *Roughing It.* Nearly 450 books have been written about Billy the Kid alone, not to mention the works of Zane Grey, Walter Van Tilburg Clark, and A.B. Guthrie. Western frontier life has inspired works in the opera, ballet, and musical theater, and was long a staple of movies that became popular throughout the world. The actual settlement of the frontier was undertaken by individuals and by the country as a whole, driven by the desire for wealth, a better life, and a belief in the country's political destiny. In the process, it shaped people's lives and gave birth to values and a folklore that continue to influence the nation and the people's sense of itself, even though values are critically examined and re-examined, long after the official declaration that the frontier had disappeared.

Western Isles *see:* Hebrides.

Western Reserve, northeastern region of Ohio on the south shore of Lake Erie. In 1786 Connecticut refused to cede this area, which covered 3,667,000 acres (1,483,982 hectares), to the Northwest Territory. In 1792, 500,000 acres were granted to Connecticut citizens whose land was destroyed during the American Revolution. The region joined the Northwest Territory in 1800.

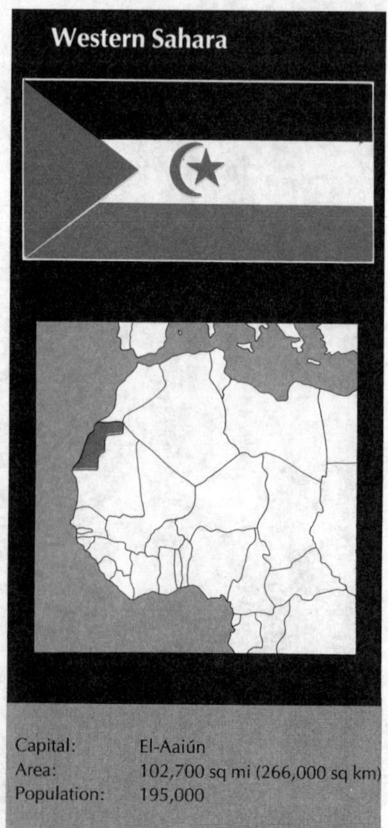

Capital: El-Aaiún
Area: 102,700 sq mi (266,000 sq km)
Population: 195,000

Western Sahara, formerly Spanish Sahara, area in northwest Africa, comprising 102,680 sq mi (265,941 sq km) of mainly desert; bordered by the Atlantic Ocean in the west, Morocco in the north, Algeria in the northeast, and Mauritania in the east and south. Western Sahara is rich in phosphate deposits. The people are Arabs and Berbers. Western Sahara was a Spanish province from 1958 to 1976, when the territory was transferred to Morocco and Mauritania. Mauritania gave up its claim in 1979, following guerrilla action by nationalists seeking self-government of the Saharans, but Morocco continues to occupy the area, with U.S. arms support. The nationalists have renamed the area the Sacharawi Arab Democratic Republic.

Western Samoa

Capital:	Apia
Area:	1,093 sq mi (2,831 sq km)
Population:	164,000
Government:	consitutional monarchy
Independent:	1962
GNP:	U.S. $100,000,000
Per capita:	U.S. $580

Western Samoa, officially the Independent State of Western Samoa, independent state in the southwestern Pacific Ocean, comprising 2 large islands, Savai'i and Upolu, and 7 smaller islands, only 2 of which are inhabited. Its area is 1,133 sq mi (2,934 sq km).

Land and climate. Most of the islands are mountainous, volcanic, forested, and fertile. The climate is rainy and tropical.

People and economy. The people are Polynesian, and the majority live in Upolu, where Apia, the capital and chief port, stands. Samoans speak probably the oldest Polynesian language in use. The economy is agricultural, the main exports being copra, bananas, and cacao. Tourism is important. The current development program, backed by foreign aid, aims to expand agriculture and encourage modest industrialization (e.g., soap, lumber).

History. The islands were probably discovered by the Dutch explorer Jacob Roggeveen (1722). Germany, Great Britain, and the United States jointly administered the islands (1889-99), and agreed in 1899 that Samoa should be divided between the United States and Germany. In 1914 New Zealand seized German Samoa, later administering it by League of Nations mandate and, later, as a UN Trust Territory. It became independent as Western Samoa in 1962. It joined the UN in 1976.

Western Union, shortened name for Western Union Telegraph Company, U.S. communications company. When the company was founded (1851), it telegraphed information from location to location in the eastern half of the United States. By the end of its first decade, a transcontinental telegraph system was in place. At the turn of the century, transatlantic telegraph cables existed. As a means of communication, telegraphs allowed for immediate transmittal of messages. To keep up with technological advances, Western Union has developed transmitting towers that communicate messages through radio beams (beginning in 1945), satellite communications (beginning in 1974), telex services (beginning in 1982), and an electronic mail service called *EasyLink* (beginning in 1982), which allows computers to communicate with each other. Today this company, based in New Jersey, is called Western Union Corporation (1970).
See also: Telegraph.

West Germany *see:* Germany.

West Highland white terrier, small, white Scottish dog. About 11 in (27.9 cm) high and weighing 13-20 lb (5.9-9.1 kg), its coat is thick and wiry. This terrier was once used to hunt small birds and animals.

West Indies, chain of islands extending about 2,500 mi (4,020 km) from Florida to Venezuela, separating the Caribbean Sea and the Gulf of Mexico from the Atlantic Ocean. An alternative name (excluding the Bahamas) is the Antilles. The West Indies comprises 4 main groups: the Bahamas to the northeast of Cuba and Hispaniola; the Greater Antilles (Cuba, the largest island in the West Indies, Hispaniola, Jamaica, and Puerto Rico); the Lesser Antilles (Leeward and Windward islands, Trinidad and Tobago, and Barbados); and the Netherlands Antilles (Aruba, Bonaire, Curaçao) as well as other islands off the Venezuelan coast. Many of the islands are mountainous and volcanic with lagoons and mangrove swamps on their coastlines. The climate is warm, but there are frequent hurricanes. The principal crop is sugarcane and tourism is an important industry. After Columbus reached the West Indies (1492), they were settled by the Spanish, followed by the English, French, and Dutch, who exploited the spices and sugar, using African slaves. The political status of the islands varies widely.

Gatavai, on the Western Samoan island of Savai'i

Westinghouse, George (1846-1914), U.S. engineer, inventor, and manufacturer. In 1869 he founded the Westinghouse Air Brake Company to develop the air brakes he had invented for railroad use. From 1883 he did pioneering work on the safe transmission of natural gas. He also pioneered the use of high-voltage AC electricity and in 1886 founded the Westinghouse Electric Company to develop AC induction motors and transmission equipment. The company was largely responsible for the acceptance of AC in preference to DC for most applications, in spite of opposition from the influential Thomas Edison.
See also: Brake.

Westminster, Statute of (1931), British parliamentary act abolishing Great Britain's power to legislate for its dominions. It gave the dominions complete independence in the commonwealth of nations, although they owed common allegiance to the British crown.

Westminster Abbey, officially the Collegiate Church of Saint Peter, English Gothic church in London, a national shrine. The Abbey has been the traditional scene of English coronations since that of William the Conqueror, and is a burial place for English monarchs and famous subjects, including many of England's

Westminster Abbey

greatest poets, who lie in the Poets' Corner. The present building, begun in 1245 by Henry III, is on the site of a church built (1065) by Edward the Confessor.

Westminster Choir, U.S. chorus founded at Dayton Westminster Church, Ohio, in 1921, and since 1932 a part of Westminster Choir College, Princeton, N.J.

Westminster Hall, building that serves as an entranceway to Britain's House of Parliament (Westminster Palace) in London. Westminster Palace was the royal residence before it became the home of Parliament (16th century), and the rulers of Britain held court in its Great Hall. Westminster Hall is all that remains of the Great Hall, which was built in the late 11th century but mostly destroyed by German fire bombs during World War II. Westminster Hall measures 240 ft (73 m) long, 68 ft (21 m) wide, and 89 ft (27 m) high.
See also: Parliament.

Westmoreland, William Childs (1914-), U.S. general, army chief of staff (1968-72). He was superintendent of West Point (1960-63) and the U.S. commander (1964-68) in Vietnam.
See also: Army, U.S.

Weston, Edward (1886-1958), U.S. photographer, winner of the Guggenheim Fellowship (1937). Originally a producer of hazy, unclear pictures, popular in the late 1800s, Weston switched in the 1920s to crisp, focused photographs of simple subjects, a stlye known as straight photography. His pictures emphasized the form and texture of objects and centered predominantly on nature scenes.
See also: Photography.

Westphalia (German, "western plain"), region in Germany, located just east of the Netherlands. Westphalia was first settled C.A.D. 700 by a group of Saxons. It came under the control of the archbishops of Cologne in 1180. During the 18th century, Prussian rulers steadily acquired the region. Napoleon transferred portions of Westphalia to his brother and to the duchy of Berg. However, the Congress of Vienna (1814-15) reestablished Prussian rule of the region. It came under German control in 1946.

West Point, site of, and common name for, the U.S. Military Academy in southeast New York, an institute of higher education that trains officers for the regular army. Established by an Act of Congress in 1802, its training methods and traditions were set down by Col. Sylvanus Thayer, superintendent of the academy from 1817 to 1833. Candidates for entry (since 1976, of either sex) to the academy must be unmarried U.S. citizens age 17-22 and must meet minimum academic requirements. Cadets are enlisted in the regular army on entrance. Graduates are awarded a B.S. degree and a commission as second lieutenant.
See also: United States Military Academy.

West Virginia

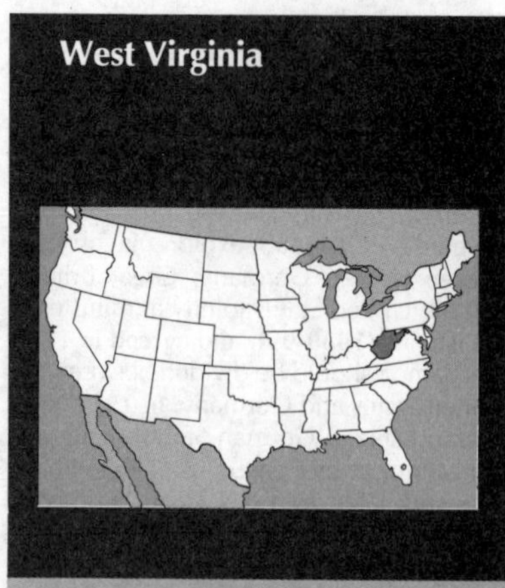

Capital:	Charleston
Statehood:	June 20, 1863 (35th state)
Familiar name:	Mountain State
Area:	24,231 sq mi (62,759 sq km); ranks 41st
Population:	1,801,625 (1990); ranks 34th
Elevation:	Highest—4,863 ft (1,482 m), Spruce Knob; Lowest—240 ft (73 m), along the Potomac River
Motto:	Montani Semper Liberi (Mountaineers Are Always Free)
Flower:	Rhododendron
Bird:	Cardinal
Tree:	Sugar maple
Songs:	"The West Virginia Hills," "This Is My West Virginia," "West Virginia, My Home, Sweet Home"

West Virginia, state in east-central United States; bordered by Pennsylvania and Maryland to the northeast, Virginia to the east and south, Kentucky to the southwest, and the Ohio River (with Ohio on the opposite side) to the west and northwest.
Land and climate. West Virginia has three main land areas. A tiny strip at the state's northeastern corner is part of the Blue Ridge Mountains, a region of fertile slopes and river valleys. In the Appalachian Ridge and Valley Region, which runs in a narrow band along the state's eastern border, high ridges of hard rock are separated by parallel valleys with streams or rivers flowing in them. The Appalachian Plateau, which covers most of the state, is a rugged area of flat highlands, narrow stream valleys, and sloping hills; most of the state's coal deposits are in this region. The Ohio is the state's major river; other important waterways are the Kanawha and the Potomac. There are no large natural lakes; artificial ones have been formed by damming the rivers. Forests covers about four-fifths of the state. West Virginia has warm, humid summers and cold winters.
Principal cities are Charleston, Huntington, and Wheeling.
Economy. West Virginia's economy is led by mining, manufacturing, and wholesale and retail trade. Coal is the chief mining product; others are natural gas, crushed stone, sand and gravel, clays, and salt. Chief manufactured goods are chemicals; primary metals; stone, clay, and glass products; plastic and hardwood products; and fabricated metal products. Agriculture accounts for less than half of 1% of West Virginia's gross state product; beef and dairy cattle and hay are the chief agricultural products.
Government. West Virginia's present constitution was adopted in 1872. The governor serves a 4-year term. The state legislature consists of 34 senators serving 4-year terms and 100 delegates serving 2-year terms. In the U.S. Congress, West Virginia is represented by 2 senators and 3 representatives.
History. West Virginia's history until 1861 is essentially the same as Virginia's, although West Virginia was distinguished by its isolation from the state capital, by the fact that few West Virginians owned slaves, and by its economy (small-scale farming and industries based on mineral resources). In 1861, when a Virginia convention voted to secede from the Union, West Virginians refused to do so. They declared their independence, adopted a constitution (1862), and became the 35th state in 1863. In the early 20th century, West Virginia's rapid expansion in the coal, gas, and steel industries was accompanied by severe labor-management conflicts and by riots. The formation of the National Recovery Administration (1933) improved miners' wages and working conditions. World War II brought industrial growth to the state but, from the 1950s onward, demand for the state's mining products fell. West Virginia remained poor, its land and water resources damaged by strip mining, and many people left the state. The energy shortage of the 1970s temporarily boosted the state's economy, but coal prices dropped in the early 1980s; by the mid-1980s, West Virginia's unemployment rate was the nation's highest. In recent years state leaders have worked to attract tourism and more diverse industries to West Virginia.

Westward movement, in the United States, events and conditions comprising the several major migrations by which the country was settled. The exploration and settlement of the U.S. frontier was an ongoing process that began with the first communities founded on the Atlantic seaboard in the 17th century and ended in the 1890s with the settlement of the Great Plains between the Mississippi River and the Rocky Mountains. Whereas the history of European countries is the story of gradual accretion of territories and extension of authority over centuries, involving many peoples with deep and sharply differing regional loyalties, the establishment and settlement of the territories that now make up the continental United States was swift and dynamic. The previous occupants of the land, the Native Americans, largely nomadic peoples, were unable to mount any long-term effective resistance and, in the end, proved to be more victims than adversaries. The United States was a new land. Its government was revolutionary, its

society democratic, its spirit pragmatic and forward looking. All these factors fed into and were fed by its westward expansion.
The first settlers of what was to become the United States came to the Atlantic coast early in the 17th century. Jamestown, Va., was established in 1607, becoming the country's first English settlement. In Massachusetts, other settlers from England founded Plymouth Colony and Boston, and the Dutch established New Amsterdam, later to become New York City.
Colonial America, beginning as it did, at the very edge of a literally uncharted continent, retained close ties with Europe in certain respects while in other ways it began breaking ties from the outset. Many who came to America were religious dissenters, like the Puritans and Quakers. Others came as indentured servants willing to pay their way for the chance for a new life in exchange for their labor. Still others came with royal charters, while black Africans, beginning in 1619, were imported as slaves. In the end, one of the common elements among all these different people and the waves of immigrants who would follow was the attraction of the nearly limitless opportunity of the new continent's open lands. From the original settled towns and communities, the expanding ranks of the colonists spread out, at first along the valleys of the James, York, Rappahannock, and Potomac rivers. By the end of the 17th century, the colonial Americans had expanded from the Atlantic coast to the low hills of the Appalachians. The following century, the 18th century, would culminate in the Revolutionary War, but throughout the century, before the war and after, the colonists would settle the Old West, consisting of the back country of New England, the Piedmont, and the valleys of the Appalachians. With fresh influxes of Germans, Scots-Irish, and Scandinavians, colonists settled the Shenandoah Valley of Virginia, Pennsylvania, North Carolina, South Carolina, and Georgia.
Colonial expansion was both aided and hindered by the British. While still British colonists, the Americans fought in the French and Indian War (1754-63), and Great Britain won territory from France between the Appalachians and the Mississippi. In 1763 Britain put a temporary halt to westward expansion in order to keep peace between the Native Americans and expansionist colonials. Eventually, treaties had to be renegotiated and in any case they proved ineffective in stopping the settlement of Kentucky and Tennessee under the leadership of adventurers like Daniel Boone, who opened the Cumberland Gap in 1775. During the Revolutionary War, America's military successes led it to claim the Old Northwest territories, between the Ohio River and the Great Lakes. After the war, settlers moved to the area and to the old Southwest, including Kentucky, Tennessee, and lands toward the Gulf of Mexico. The U.S. government took an active part in aiding, organizing, and encouraging the settlements.
The Ordinance of 1785 divided the land of the Old Northwest into salable parcels. Large tracts were bought from the government by speculators who then sold them in lots to settlers. The Northwest Ordinance of 1787 settled the political organization of the territories. A territory's original officials would be appointed by Congress. When the population reached 5,000, the adult males elected an assembly and sent a nonvoting representative to Congress. When the population reached 60,000, a territory could apply for statehood. With these ordinances, the U.S. government laid the groundwork for the organized settlement of its expanding territories. Kentucky joined the Union in 1792 and Tennessee in 1796.
As the Old Northwest and the Old Southwest were being rapidly settled, the United States expanded its territory by 827,987 sq mi (2,144,476 sq km) at a cost of $15 million paid to France. The Louisiana Purchase, completed by Thomas Jefferson, expanded U.S. territory from the Mississippi River to the Rocky Mountains. The area would be explored by Merriwether Lewis and William Clark (1803-05), by Zebulon Pike (1806), and by Major Stephen H. Long (1820), but would not actually be settled until the latter half of the 19th century. In the meantime, America fought the British in the War of 1812, bringing an end to British power in America and an end, as well, to effective resistance from Native Americans in the region who had largely sided with the British. The attempt by Tecumseh and his brother, the Shawnee Prophet, to unify the Native Americans from the Great Lakes to the Gulf of Mexico had already been undone by their defeat at the Battle of Tippecanoe in 1811. After the War of 1812, the defeated Native Americans were consigned to an Indian Territory west of the Mississippi in what is present-day Oklahoma. Thousands died of disease and starvation on their way west.
With the threats of the British and the Native Americans eliminated, the Old Northwest was settled rapidly. By 1820 there were 792,000 settlers in the region, and the completion of the Erie Canal in 1825 hastened the development of towns and cities. In the meantime the Adams-Onís Treaty with Spain (1819) opened up Florida, Alabama, and Mississippi. Aided by the river traffic of the Mississippi, the area became home to huge and successful cotton plantations. In the decades before the Civil War, the westward expansion had taken possession of lands from the Great Lakes to the Gulf of Mexico, from Maine to Florida, and from the Atlantic coast to the Mississippi. The last large area of settlement before the Civil War was the Far West.
Originally attracted by the reports and surveys of John C. Fremont in the early 1840s, settlers began moving to California. The first to come were usually trappers and traders, followed by the wagon trains that crossed the prairies over the Oregon Trail that branched into the Santa Fe or Spanish Trails to California. Settlers had already begun moving into Oregon as early as 1835. At first the British were a residual presence in Oregon and contested U.S. expansion, but the Oregon Treaty of 1846 settled all claims between the United States

Family of settlers headed west in a covered wagon (1886)

Western pioneers on the Santa Fe Trail (1855).

and Britain and established the territory that now comprises the states of Oregon and Washington and the northwestern border with Canada. Two years later, in 1848, gold was discovered at Sutter's Mill in California, and the first gold rush brought California's population from 15,000 in 1848 to 100,000 in 1849. Eventually, gold and silver fever would contribute to the settlement of South Dakota, Montana, Arizona, and Nevada. The decades before the Civil War also saw the settlements of Texas, the Southwest, and Utah.

Originally settled by Stephen F. Austin in the 1820s with the permission of the Mexican government, Texas was Mexican territory. But less than 20 years after Austin's settlement, the settlers were strong enough to contest Mexican authority and, under Samuel Houston, defeat the Mexicans at the Battle of San Jacinto, declaring Texas an independent republic. It joined the union as a state in 1845. Three years later, the United States ended its war with Mexico with the Treaty of Guadalupe Hidalgo and gained California, Nevada, Utah, most of Arizona, and parts of Colorado, New Mexico, and Wyoming. The Gadsden Purchase of 1853 completed the acquisition of the lands that now form the border between Arizona and New Mexico and Mexico.

Sam Houston, first president of the western republic of Texas

Within the same period, Utah was settled by Mormons. They first settled the Great Salt Lake region in 1847. By dint of remarkable industry, the Mormons succeeded in settling arid country. Persecuted for their religious beliefs, the Mormons at first proved hostile to other settlers. In order to discourage outsiders, they even disguised themselves as Native Americans and attacked several wagon trains until they were stopped by the U.S. Army.

An anomaly in some ways, the conduct of the Mormons was not completely without precedent. The original colonists had, with few exceptions, fled governments inimical to them. They became self-reliant and self-governing and defeated a major European power in armed struggle over the issue of governance. The Constitutional Convention was marked from beginning to end with a certain hostility toward and suspicion of centralized governments. The settlers carried these same attitudes to the frontier where experience tended to confirm and deepen them. Backwoods and frontier citizens resented the more settled people of the East and, above all, the constraints of authority. The most common grievance was over taxes to be paid to a government that was remote, did little to better their daily lives, and was dominated by people who seemed alien to the plain-spoken, straightforward westerner. That there was much romanticizing and self-serving talk in all of this should not disguise real differences in outlook that bound in common the men who led the Whiskey Rebellion, Sam Houston's Texas Republic, the Mormons in Utah, and the general suspicion of and contempt for Washington, D.C., its politicians and bureaucrats, that has deep roots among western citizens.

Begun before the Civil War and completed by 1890, the last frontier to be settled was the Great Plains, the land west of the Mississippi and extending to the Rocky Mountains, and the intermontane region between the Rocky Mountains and the Sierra Nevada. Gold and silver were the leading inspiration for the last stage of the U.S. westward movement. Rich strikes were made in Nevada and Arizona and also helped open South Dakota, Montana, and Idaho. In the meantime the railroads crossed the plains completing the transcontinental line in 1869. The railroads provided the transport necessary for commerce and the development of towns and cities. But in the beginning, they brought the cattle boom. Taking advantage of the vast stretches of open prairie ideal for grazing livestock, ranchers hurried west to take part in the boom that would last nearly 20 years, 1867-87. At the same time, the U.S. government encouraged settlement with the Homestead Act of 1862. Anyone who would improve the land over 5 years could have 160 acres of it free. At first the farmers had a hard time of it. The Great Plains were treeless and dry. But in the 1870s several developments brought dramatic changes. Barbed wire made it possible to fence off land without wood. Dry farming techniques made raising crops viable, and wind mills provided a means for drawing underground water. The farmers went west. They fought the elements, the Native Americans, and the ranchers, and turned the Great Plains into the country's bread basket.

According to the U.S. census of 1890, there was no more frontier. But it was the last frontier, the last of the westward movement, that would prove in many ways the strongest and most enduring in the country's imagination, peopled with cowboys and outlaws, vigilantes, Native Americans, lawmen, and the cavalry. But for all its robust energy, vitality, and ruthless optimism, the last of the U.S. westward expansion also marked the end of the Native Americans as independent peoples. In the mid-1860s the Sioux were defeated in order to open the Bozeman Trail through their hunting grounds in Wyoming. They were defeated again when gold was discovered in 1874 in the Black Hills of South Dakota. The Arapaho and Cheyenne, the Kiowa, Comanches, and other Native American peoples were in turn subdued, and when they resisted being moved to reservations, they were defeated again in the Red River War of 1874-75. The Indian Territory, which had been established in present-day Oklahoma, proved no more secure than the open plains. Giving in to land-hungry settlers, the government opened the Indian Territory to settlement in 1898. The last armed encounter between the United States and Native Americans occurred in 1890 at Wounded Knee Creek in S. Dak.

In one sense, the entire history of the United States can be seen as a series of westward movements, beginning with the original colonies and ending with the last frontier in 1890. Fed by successive waves of immigrants seeking new lands and new opportunities, these westward movements not only settled the land but also indelibly stamped the character of the people. Energetic, restless, and impatient with authority, they are distinct from the peoples of Europe and Asia. Less regional, they are defined by the nation more than the place, and by ideals and outlooks more than religions or creeds. In many ways, U.S. citizens continue to see themselves in terms whose origins are in its westward movements.

Wetland, area of land where the earth is continuously saturated with water. Three major types of wetlands are bogs, swamps, and marshes, each supporting a different kind of plant life. Bogs, usually located in cooler climates, have acidic soil that appears dry but is not. Bogs are dominated by mosses, which, when they decay, turn into peat. (Peat is valuable because, when dried, it can be burned as a fuel.) Swamps and marshes have mineral soils and are found mostly in warmer climates. Wetlands support a variety of valuable bird and mammal life.

Weymouth (pop. 55,601), city on Massachusetts Bay, southeast of Boston. Founded in 1622 and incorporated in 1635, it is the second-oldest settlement in Massachusetts, after Plymouth. Primarily a residential community, Weymouth has some industry, including the manufacture of fertilizer, lacquers, and electrical equipment.

See also: Massachusetts.

Whale, one of the order Cetacea of large, wholly aquatic mammals. All are highly adapted for life in water, with a torpedo-shaped body, front limbs reduced and modified as steering paddles, and hind limbs absent. They have a tail of 2 transverse flukes and swim by up-and-down movements of this tail. Most species have a fleshy dorsal fin that acts as a stabilizer. The neck is short, the head flowing directly into the trunk. The body is hairless, and the smooth skin lies over a thick layer of blubber that has an insulating function but also acts to smooth out the passage of water over the body in rapid swimming. The nose, or blowhole, is at the top of the head, allowing the animal to breathe as soon as it breaks the surface of the water.

Modern whales divide into 2 suborders, the whalebone whales and the toothed whales. Whalebone whales feed on plankton, straining the enormous quantities they require from the water with special plates of whalebone, or baleen, developed from the mucus membrane of the upper jaw. Whalebone whales—the right, rorqual, and gray whales—are usually large and slow-moving. The group includes the blue whale (*Balaenoptera musulus*), the largest animal of all time (up to 100 ft/30.5 m long). Toothed whales, equipped with conical teeth, feed on fishes and squids. The group includes the dolphins and porpoises, the sperm whale (*Physeter macrocephalus*), and the narwhal (*Mmonodon monoceros*). Many species of whale are endangered.

See also: Whaling.

Whaling, hunting of whales, originally for oil, meat, and baleen (whalebone), practiced since the 10th century. The Basques and Dutch hunted from land and pioneered methods of flensing (stripping of blubber) and boiling whale meat. U.S. whaling started in the 1600s, and whaling ports such as Nantucket and New Bedford, Mass., grew to great size in the 1700s. Whaling became safer for the hunters after the invention (1856) of harpoons with explosive heads that caused instantaneous death and avoided the dangerous pursuit of a wounded whale. From the 1800s whalers moved south in pursuit of the sperm whale. Development of factory ships that processed the catch on board facilitated longer expeditions. In the 20th century whaling has centered on Antarctic waters. Reconnaissance aircraft and electronic aids are now used. Whale products include oils, ambergris, spermaceti, meat, and bone meal. Despite the voluntary restrictions of the International Whaling Convention, whales are still overfished, and many species face extinction.

Wharton, Edith (1862-1937), U.S. novelist, poet, and short-story writer. She wrote subtle and acerbic accounts of society in New York, New England, and Europe, including *The House of Mirth* (1905), *Ethan Frome* (1911), and *The Age of Innocence* (1920; Pulitzer Prize).

Wheat, cereal plant (genus *Triticum*) of the grass family, the world's main cereal crop; about 300 million tons are produced every year, mostly used to make flour for bread and pasta. Wheat has been in cultivation since at least 5000 B.C. and grows best in temperate regions of Europe, North America, China, and Australia. The USSR is the largest producer, followed by the United States and Canada. There are many varieties of wheat, and different parts of the grain are used to produce the various types of flour. Grains comprise an outer husk called bran and a central starchy germ (which is embedded in a protein known as gluten). Wheat is graded as hard or soft depending on how easily the flour can be separated from the bran. Wheat for bread is hard wheat and contains a lot of gluten. Soft wheat flours containing more starch and less protein are used for pastries. There are 2 main types of wheat; these are sown either in the fall (winter wheat) or in the spring (spring wheat). Harvesting is carried out by combine harvesters that cut and thresh the crop in one operation. Wheat is vulnerable to several diseases, including smut, rust, army worm, and Hessian fly.

Wheatley, Phillis (1753?-84), U.S. poet. Brought to Boston from Africa as a slave, she was educated by her owners, John Wheatley and his wife, and began writing poetry. A collection of her verse *Poems on Various Subjects, Religious and Moral* was published in 1773. Her work deals with her joy about converting to Christianity, as well as her concerns about slavery. She is regarded as the first important black U.S. writer.

Beluga whale

Wheatstone, Sir Charles (1802-75), British physicist and inventor. He popularized the "Wheatstone bridge" for measuring voltages and, with W.F. Cooke, invented the electric telegraph at about the same time as U.S. inventor Samuel F.B. Morse (1837).
See also: Telegraph.

Wheatstone bridge, electric circuit used for comparing or measuring resistance. Four resistors, including the unknown one, are connected in a square, with a battery between one pair of diagonally opposite corners and a sensitive galvanometer between the other. When no current flows through the meter, the products of opposite pairs of resistances are equal. Similar bridge circuits are used for impedance measurement.
See also: Electric circuit; Wheatstone, Sir Charles.

Wheel and axle, disklike mechanical device consisting of a wheel mounted on an axle of smaller diameter; the wheel and axle turn on the same axis. A first-class lever, it is used to facilitate the movement of heavy objects. The wheel and axle is one of the classic simple machines, along with the pulley and the screw.

Wheelbarrow, boxlike device used to move small loads. The load is carried in a box or tub at the front, below which there is a wheel. The box or tub is lifted and pushed by 2 handles at the rear.

Wheeler, Burton Kendall (1882-1975), U.S. senator from Montana (1923-47). A Democrat, he ran in 1924 as vice presidential candidate, with Robert M. LaFollette, for the Progressive Party. He helped uncover the scandals of Pres. Warren G. Harding's administration. In World War II he advocated isolationism.

Wheeler, Earle Gilmore (1908-75), U.S. Army general. He served in Europe in World War II and in 1962 was appointed army chief of staff by Pres. Lyndon B. Johnson. He was chairman of the Joint Chiefs of Staff (1964-70).
See also: Army, U.S.

Wheeler, William Almon (1819-87), vice president of the United States from 1877 to 1881. A Republican, he served under Pres. Rutherford B. Hayes. He began his career as a lawyer, and from 1861 to 1863 and 1869 to 1877 he represented New York in the House of Representatives. In 1875 he was part of a committee formed to settle a dispute over an election in Louisiana. His "Wheeler Adjustment" was a compromise that gave the Democratic and Republican parties control of the Louisiana state government.

Wheeling (pop. 159,301), city in northern West Virginia, located on the Ohio River. Wheeling is a highly industrial city, producing products such as coal and natural gas, metals, glass, plastics, textiles, and tobacco. The city is also a shipping and educational center. Wheeling College, Bethany College, and West Liberty State College are located in and around the area. Wheeling was founded in 1769 by the Zane family. In time, it became a trading center. During the Civil War, it was the headquarters for Virginians who opposed the withdrawal of the South from the Union.

Wheelwright, William (1798-1873), U.S. businessperson and promoter who opened the first steamship line between South America and Europe. He was responsible for building the first railroad and telegraph lines in Argentina, Chile, and Peru. Shipwrecked near Buenos Aires in 1823, he settled in South America, where he recognized the vast commercial possibilities and natural resources. A native of New England, Wheelwright was born in Newburyport, Mass.

Whelk, spiral-shelled sea snail found worldwide. It feeds off other mollusks and fish caught in commercial traps. The northern whelk, found in North Atlantic waters, has a shell about 3 in (8 cm) long. Most are edible.

Whetstone, natural or artificial abrasive stone used for sharpening and grinding tools. Quartz is the abrasive agent that makes whetstones effective.

Whig Party, English and U.S. political party. In England the term was applied in 1679 to Protestant opponents of the English Crown. The Whigs enjoyed a period of dominance c.1714-60, notably under Robert Walpole. Largely out of office when led by Charles James Fox, they were increasingly associated with Nonconformism, mercantile, industrial, and reforming interests. After the Whig ministries of the 2nd earl Grey and Lord Melbourne (1830-41), during which the Reform Bill of 1832 was passed, the Whigs helped form the Liberal Party in the mid-1800s.
The U.S. Whig Party was formed c.1836 from diverse opponents, including the National Republicans, of Andrew Jackson and the Democrats. Its leaders were Henry Clay and Daniel Webster, and a national economic policy was its principal platform. Whig President William Henry Harrison died after one month in office and was succeeded (1841) by John Tyler, who was disowned by the Whigs when he vetoed their tariff and banking bills. Clay, the next Whig candidate, lost the 1844 election. The second Whig president, Zachary Taylor, died in office (1850) after serving 1 year. He was succeeded by a loyal Whig, Millard Fillmore, but the party was by then divided by the issues of slavery and national expansion; the Compromise of 1850 did not last, and Winfield Scott was heavily defeated in the 1852 election. The party never recovered, and many of the Northern Whigs joined the new Republican Party, while the Cotton (Southern) Whigs joined the Democratic Party.

Whip, in U.S. and British politics, party member of a legislative body chosen to enforce party discipline in attendance and voting. The first U.S. whip, Republican congressperson James E. Watson, was appointed in 1899.

James Abbott McNeill Whistler's Symphony in White no. 3 *(1867)*

Whiplash, cervical sprain, or neck injury. As a result of the head accidently thrown backward then forward, the muscles and ligaments in the head, neck, and shoulder area may become strained. This strain causes pain and stiffness that may be treated with a neck brace, heat, massage, or pain medicine. It happens most often through automobile accidents, although automobile headrests and shoulder harnesses help prevent or lessen the severity of this injury.

Whippet, greyhoundlike dog possessing great speed. It can run as fast as 35 mph (56 kmph). Whippets weigh 18-23 lb (8-10 kg) and stand 18-22 in (44-57 cm) high. They have short coats of tan, gray, or white, and are used for racing and for rabbit hunting.

Whipple, Abraham (1733-1819), naval officer noted for his successes in the American Revolutionary War. In 1779 he captured 11 ships of the British Jamaica fleet. In 1780 he defended Charleston, S.C., but was captured when the city fell.
See also: Revolutionary War in America.

Whipple, William (1730-85), colonial politician from New Hampshire. He was a signer of the Declaration of Independence and a member of the provincial congress (1775) as well as the Continental Congress (1775-76, 1778). During the Revolution he served as a brigadier general. Afterwards he served his state as a member of its assembly (1780-84), a financial receiver (1782-84), and an associate justice of the superior court (1782-85).

Whippoorwill, nocturnal North American bird (*Caprimulgus vociferus*) known for its odd, deliberate call. They are found in southeastern Canada, the United States, Mexico, and Central America. Whippoorwills are about 10 in (25 cm) long with brown spotted feathers. They assist farmers by feeding on crop-damaging insects.

Whirlaway (1938-53), U.S. Thoroughbred winner of the U.S. Triple Crown (1941). Whirlaway was the winner of 32 of his 60 races; established a Kentucky Derby record for speed; and broke earnings records for racehorses when awarded $500,000. Whirlaway was retired in 1943 after a leg injury.

Whirligig *see:* Water beetle.

Whirlpool, rotary current in water. Permanent whirlpools may arise in the ocean from the interactions of the tides. They occur also in streams or rivers where 2 currents meet or the shape of the channel dictates. Short-lived whirlpools may be created by wind.

Whiskey, strong, distilled spirituous liquor made from grain. When from Scotland or Canada, *whiskey* is spelled without an *e* (whisky). The ingredients and preparation vary. In the United States corn and rye are commonly used: 51% corn for bourbon whiskey and 51% rye for rye whiskey. A grain mash is allowed to ferment, then distilled, diluted, and left to age. Bourbon and rye whiskey stand in oak barrels for 4 years. Irish whiskey uses barley, wheat, oats, and rye, and vessels called potstills for the distilling process. Scotch whisky is the finest form: the best types are pure barley malt or grain whiskies. The secret of its flavor is said to be the peat-flavored water of certain Scottish streams. Manufactured commercially since the 16th century, whiskey is one of the most popular of alcoholic beverages.

Whiskey Rebellion (1794), uprising of mainly Scotch-Irish farmers of western Pennsylvania against the federal excise tax imposed on whiskey by U.S. Secretary of the Treasury Alexander Hamilton in 1791. Federal officers were attacked, some were tarred and feathered, and one had his house burned down. Resistance increased when official measures were taken to obtain the tax. At Hamilton's insistence, President George Washington sent in 13,000 militia to suppress the insurgents. They met no resistance, and Washington pardoned 2 ringleaders convicted of treason. Although Federalists claimed a victory—the federal government had demonstrated the power to enforce its law—the party suffered politically.

Whiskey Ring, U.S. scandal exposed in 1875. Distillers in St. Louis, Chicago, Milwaukee, and elsewhere had evaded taxes through payments to Republican Party funds and individuals. The investigations of Secretary of the Treasury Benjamin Bristow led to 237 indictments (including the chief treasury clerk and the president's private secretary), 110 convictions, and the recovery of over $4 million in taxes. Pres. Ulysses S. Grant was cleared personally, but his party was damaged.

Whistle, device used for signaling, consisting of a tube with a sharp edge or lip that makes a sound when air or steam is blown through it.

Whistler, James Abbott McNeill (1834-1903), U.S. artist. Born in Lowell, Mass., in his youth he lived with his family in Russia. Later he attended the U.S. Military Academy at West Point but failed academically after 3 years. He resumed his art studies in Paris and moved to London, where he lived until his death. His best-known painting is *Arrangement in Gray and Black No. 1: Portrait of the Artist's Mother* (1872), commonly called "Whistler's Mother." Whistler believed paintings should be abstract responses to the artist's imagination.

White, U.S. family including father and son journalists: **William Allen** (1868-1944) and **William Lindsay** (1900-73). Beginning with the editorial *What's the Matter with Kansas?* (1895) that appeared in his own newspaper, the *Gazette,* William Allen became an important voice in national politics. As a reporter for the *Emporia,* another Kansas newspaper, he won the

Pulitzer Prize (1923). His autobiography also won the Pulitzer Prize (1947). William Lindsay worked for a number of newspapers, including the *Gazette* and the *Washington Post.* He was a noted correspondent during World War II. He wrote a book about the war entitled *They Were Expendable* (1942).

White *see:* Color.

White, Andrew Dickson (1832-1918), U.S. educator and diplomat. While serving as chairman of the New York State education committee (1864-67), he founded (with Ezra Cornell) Cornell University on nonsectarian, liberal principles. White served as president of the university from 1867 to 1885.
See also: Cornell, Ezra.

White, Byron Raymond (1917-), U.S. Supreme Court justice, appointed by President John F. Kennedy (1962). The majority of his decisions have leaned more toward conservatism. These include votes against a person's right to privacy, abortion, fair treatment for criminal suspects, and lifting of the criminal status for homosexuality. Some decisions, though, are considered liberal. These include votes for school desegregation and affirmative action. He was educated in his home state of Colorado (where, as an All-American halfback, he was known as "Whizzer"), in England as a Rhodes Scholar, and at Yale University, where he graduated from the Law School (1946). He was assistant attorney general to Robert Kennedy (1961-62) before his appointment to the Supreme Court.
See also: Supreme Court of the United States.

White, E(lwyn) B(rooks) (1899-1985), U.S. writer noted for his witty, well-crafted essays in *The New Yorker* magazine. His work includes humorous poems, the satire *Is Sex Necessary?* (1929, with James Thurber), and such children's books as *Stuart Little* (1945) and *Charlotte's Web* (1952).

White, Edward Douglass (1845-1921), ninth chief justice of the U.S. Supreme Court (1910-21). He was appointed associate justice in 1894. White was known for his conservatism, and is best remembered for his anti-trust views, particularly his "rule of reason" opinions in antitrust cases that mandated the dissolution of the Standard Oil and American Tobacco companies (1911).
See also: Supreme Court of the United States.

White, Edward Higgins, II (1930-67), U.S. astronaut. On June 3, 1965 he was the first U.S. astronaut to leave his craft, taking a 21-minute walk in outer space. He died Jan. 27, 1967 when a fire occurred during a flight simulation at Cape Kennedy, Florida. Other astronauts who died in the tragedy were Virgil Grissom and Roger Chaffee.
See also: Astronaut.

White, Patrick (1912-90), Australian novelist, winner of the 1973 Nobel Prize in literature. His long novels, set mostly in Australia, include *Voss* (1957), *The Vivisector* (1970), *The Eye of the Storm* (1974), and *The Twyborn Affair* (1980).

White, Paul Dudley (1886-1973), U.S. physician, prominent cardiologist. White was an early advocate of diet and exercise for the prevention of heart attacks, and was one of the first to use electrocardiograms for diagnosis of heart disease. His book *Heart Disease* (1931), in its original and numerous revised editions, became a standard text in the field. He became well known as Dwight D. Eisenhower's cardiologist following the president's heart attack. In 1971 White visited the People's Republic of China to study medicine in that country.
See also: Cardiology.

White, Peregrine (1620-1703), first U.S. colonist born in New England. His parents travelled from England to North America on the *Mayflower.* Peregrine White was born aboard ship in Cape Cod Bay. His mother, Susanna White, became the first New England bride when after the death of Peregrine's father, William White, she married Edward Winslow.

White, Stanford (1853-1906), U.S. architect and painter in the firm of McKim, Mead & White, a renowned architectural firm. His designs include the Washington Arch (1889-95), the Judson Memorial Church (1891), the campus of Bronx Community College (1892-1901), and the Tiffany Building (1906). Born in New York City, White was shot to death by Harry Thaw, the jealous husband of his lover, Evelyn Nesbit.
See also: Architecture.

White, T(erence) H(anbury) (1906-64), English novelist, noted for *The Once and Future King* (4 vol., 1939-58), a retelling of the legends of King Arthur, and *The Goshawk* (1951).

White, Walter Francis (1893-1955), U.S. author and a secretary of the National Association for the Advancement of Colored People (1931-55). His works include *Rope and Faggot* (1929), an attack on the lynching of blacks, and his autobiography, *A Man Called White* (1948).

White ant *see:* Termite.

White-eye, common name for about 85 species of small birds (family Zosteropidae) of the Old World tropics that have a white ring around each eye. They feed on insects, flowers, and fruits, and are often pests.

Whitefish, important freshwater food fish found in the northern regions of North America, Europe, and Asia. Whitefish are related to the salmon and trout but have small scales and small, toothless mouths. Among the most valuable species are the lake whitefish (*Coregonus clupeaformis*), the lake herring, or cisco (*C. artedii*), and the mountain whitefish (*Prosopium williamsoni*).

Whitefly, any of a family (Aleyrodidae) of small insects related to the scale insects. Some whiteflies are pests, including the greenhouse whitefly and the citrus whitefly. The latter damages citrus plants by sucking sap and encouraging the growth of a mold.

Whitehead, Alfred North (1861-1947), English mathematician and philosopher. He was coauthor with Bertrand Russell of *Principia Mathematica* (3 vol., 1910-13), a major landmark in the philosophy of mathematics. While teaching at Harvard University (from 1924), Whitehead developed a monumental system of metaphysics, most comprehensively expounded in his book *Process and Reality* (1929).
See also: Metaphysics.

Whitehorse (pop. 15,200), capital of the Yukon Territory, located on the west bank of the Yukon River, 111 mi (179 km) north of Skagway, Alaska. Its economy centers on mining, tourism, transportation, and government services. Whitehorse was the site of the Klondike gold rush of 1897-98.
See also: Yukon Territory.

White House, official home of the president of the United States, in Washington, D.C. It was designed in the manner of an 18th-century English gentleman's country house by James Hoban (1792). John Adams was the first president to live there. It was severely damaged by the British in 1814, but rebuilt and extended (and painted white) by 1818. In 1824 Hoban added the semicircular south portico. The grounds were landscaped in 1850 by Andrew Downing. Major renovations, including the addition of the executive office building, were carried out in the early 20th century by the architectural firm of McKim, Mead & White. From 1948 onward the building was extensively rebuilt.
See also: President of the United States.

White House conference, extended meeting called by the U.S. president in which professional experts, community leaders, and other individuals discuss a specified topic. Similar state-level conferences may be mandated by the president. The topic of the first White House conference, called by Theodore Roosevelt in 1908, was conservation. Many of the more than 60 conferences since then have dealt with children or the aging.

White House hostesses, women who act as hostesses for guests of the U.S. president in place of his wife. The role has generally been filled by daughters or other relatives. During the presidency of Thomas Jefferson (a widower), Dolley Madison, wife of James Madison, distinguished herself as a hostess.

Whiteman, Paul (1891-1967), U.S. orchestra leader known as the "King of Jazz."

He introduced a personal style called "symphonic jazz." Whiteman encouraged George Gershwin to compose *Rhapsody in Blue* (1924). Born in Denver, Colo., he spent his later years as a popular musical conductor on radio shows.
See also: Jazz.

White Mountains, section of the Appalachian Mountains covering about 1,000 sq mi (2,590 sq km) in northern New Hampshire and western Maine. They include the Presidential, Sandwich, Carter-Moriah, and Franconia ranges. The highest peak, Mt. Washington (6,288 ft/1,917 m), is in the Presidential Range. Deep canyons, called *notches*, have been carved out by glaciers. The area is noted for its scenic beauty.
See also: Appalachian Mountains.

White paper, British government report or policy statement on an important issue. The documents are called white papers because they are hastily prepared and submitted without the blue cover used for longer documents.

White Sands Missile Range, main U.S. Army missile-testing site located in south-central New Mexico. It was established as White Sands Proving Ground in 1945 and renamed in 1958. The range extends 120 mi (193 km) from north to south and 40 mi (64 km) east to west. The first atomic bomb was exploded there in 1945.
See also: Army, U.S.

White Sea, arm of the Arctic Ocean, called *Beloye More* in the Soviet Union. It is icebound Sept.-June, but heavy shipping is conducted on it during the summer months.
See also: Atlantic Ocean.

White Sulphur Springs (pop. 3,371), health resort in West Virginia known for its mineral springs, located 120 mi (193 km) east of the state capital, Charleston. It developed as a spa in the 1770s. Its President's Cottage served as the summer residence for a series of U.S. presidents.
See also: West Virginia.

White-tailed deer (*Odocoileus virginianus*), North American deer named for its long white tail, raised as a danger signal when the deer is alarmed.

White walnut *see:* Butternut.

Whitman, Marcus (1802-47), U.S. physician and Presbyterian missionary who established settlements in the Pacific Northwest and encouraged emigration to Oregon. In 1847 his settlers brought an epidemic of measles with them that caused the death of many Cayuse children. Thinking the children had been poisoned, the Native Americans killed Whitman.
See also: Westward movement.

Whitman, Walt (1819-92), major U.S. poet. His *Leaves of Grass* (1855; expanded in successive editions), one of the most influential volumes of poetry in U.S. literary history, was praised by Ralph Waldo Emerson and Henry David Thoreau, but did not achieve popular recognition at the time of its publication. Other works include *Drum-Taps* (1865), a collection of Civil War poems; *Democratic Vistas* (1871), prose studies of U.S. democracy; and the autobiographical *Specimen Days* (1882-83). Whitman rejected regular meter and rhyme in favor of flowing free verse and celebrated erotic love, rugged individualism, democracy, and equality.

Walt Whitman, by Thomas Eakins

Whitman Mission National Historic Site, landmark in southeastern Washington state, near Walla Walla, site of the first mission school in the Pacific Northwest. The mission, established 1836 by Marcus Whitman and his wife, Narcissa Prentiss Whitman, was a landmark on the Oregon Trail.
See also: Whitman, Marcus.

Whitney, Eli (1765-1825), U.S. inventor of the cotton gin (1793) and pioneer of mass production. In 1798 he contracted with the U.S. government to make 10,000 muskets: He took 8 years to fulfill the 2-year contract, but he showed that with unskilled labor muskets could be put together using parts that were precision-made and thus interchangeable, a benefit not only during production but also in later maintenance.
See also: Cotton gin.

Whitney, Gertrude Vanderbilt (1875-1942), U.S. sculptor. She is best known for her monuments commemorating the victims of World War I and for her fountain sculptures. The Whitney Studio Club, which she established in New York City (1918), was a center for U.S. avant-garde art and led to the founding of the Whitney Museum of American Art (1931).

Whitney, John Hay (1904-82), U.S. diplomat and publisher. He was active in Republican politics and served as ambassador to Great Britain (1957-61). He published the New York *Herald Tribune* (1961-67), served as chairperson of the *International Herald Tribune* (from 1967), and published several prominent U.S. magazines.

Whittier, John Greenleaf (1807-92), U.S. poet born in Haverhill, Mass., to a Quaker family. The themes of his work were the injustice of slavery and the beauty of the New England countryside. He served in the state legislature and was active in the antislavery movement. His political poem, "Ichabod" (1850), attacked Daniel Webster for his role in passing the Compromise of 1850. He attacked what he saw as hypocrisy in a nation that espoused freedom but allowed slavery.

WHO *see:* World Health Organization.

Whooping cough, or pertussis, contagious bacterial disease of children causing upper respiratory symptoms, with a characteristic whoop or inspiratory noise due to inflammation of the larynx. Whooping cough is a serious disease that can lead to pneumonia, brain damage, convulsions, and collapse of the lungs. Vaccination is widely practiced to prevent it.

Whooping crane (*Grus americana*), white wading bird with a red cap on its head. The tallest bird in North America, it reaches a height of about 5 ft (1.5 m). Once widespread, whooping cranes have for several decades been close to extinction and have been preserved only by determined conservation measures.

Wichita (pop. 485,270), city in Kansas, located on the Chisholm Trail. Cowboys used to bring their herds to Wichita on their way to Texas markets. Cattle, along with the Santa Fe Railroad, made this city an important location during 19th-century westward expansion. Today there is still a strong meat industry as well as a large aviation and oil industry. McConnell Air Force Base is located here as well as the domed Century II cultural-convention center and Wichita State University. The city was founded as a trading post (1864) where European-American settlers traded with the Wichita tribespeople. The legendary western law man Wyatt Earp worked in Wichita in the 1870s.
See also: Kansas.

Wichita Falls (pop. 122,378), city in Texas, located on the Wichita River. With the discovery of oil (1910) near this north-central city, Wichita Falls began to boom. It was founded just 28 years previously. Today it is an oil industry center, the home of North Texas Oil and Gas Association. Manufacturers of electronic components, parts for jet airplanes, jeans, plastic products, and glass also are located here. Sheppard Air Force Base is situated in Wichita Falls.
See also: Texas.

Wicker, material woven from flexible plant fiber or willow twigs. Furniture, especially in hot climates, has been made from wicker since the days of ancient Egypt. Wicker has been appreciated as a durable as well as comfortable and attractive material. Bamboo, rattan, reed, and cane are natural plant fibers used for wicker. Modern synthetic wickers have been developed from materials such as treated twisted paper fibers.

Wiclif, John *see:* Wycliffe, John.

Widgeon *see:* Wigeon.

Wien *see:* Vienna.

Wiener, Norbert (1894-1964), U.S. mathematician noted for his contributions to computer science. He developed the theory of cybernetics. His major book is *Cybernetics: Or Control and Communication in the Animal and the Machine* (1948).
See also: Cybernetics.

Wiesbaden (pop. 266,600), city in southwestern Germany, capital of the German state of Hesse. The word *wiesbaden* translates as "baths on the meadows," and this resort, located in a valley of the Taunus Mountains, is known for its hot springs. The Romans enjoyed this area since the 1st century B.C. and considered it a spa—a resort where mineral springs are often found. People today still come to Wiesbaden for its mineral springs. Tourism is the economic base of the city.
See also: Germany.

Wiesel, Elie (1938-), Romanian-born U.S. novelist. In 1944, with other Jews, he and his family were sent to Auschwitz, where his parents and sister died. He then was sent to Buchenwald, which was liberated in 1945. Wiesel later became the leading spokesperson for survivors of Nazi concentration camps. His autobiographical novel, *Night* (1958), recaptures the horrors he encountered. Other novels include *The Jews of Silence* (1966), *Souls on Fire* (1972), *The Testament* (1980), and *The Fifth Son* (1984). He won the Nobel Peace Prize in 1986.
See also: Concentration camp; Holocaust.

Wiesel, Torsten Nils (1924-), Swedish neurobiologist who shared the 1981 Nobel Prize in physiology or medicine for his research on the brain's processing of visual information.
See also: Brain.

Wiesenthal, Simon (1908-), Austrian hunter of Nazi war criminals. Having lost a large number of relatives in Nazi concentration camps during World War II, he established the Jewish Documentation Center in Vienna, Austria, through which he located more than 1,000 former Nazis accused of war crimes, including Adolf Eichmann.
See also: Holocaust.

Wig, covering for the head of real or artificial hair, worn as a cosmetic device, as a mark of rank or office, as a disguise, or for theatrical portrayals. Known since ancient times, wigs became fashionable in 17th- and 18th-century Europe, when elaborate headpieces for women and full, curled wigs for men came into wide use. The latter are still worn in British law courts. In the 1960s wigs came back into fashion for women. Small hairpieces called *toupees* are worn to conceal baldness.

Wigeon, duck in the family Anatidae. Wigeons found in the United States (*Anas americana*) and those found in northern Europe (*A. penelope*) are the same size, about 19 in (48 cm) long. The U.S. wigeon, also called the *baldpate*, is known for its call, the sound *whew* repeated a number of times. These ducks feed on water plants, using their flat, broad bills. The male heads and throats are marked with white.

Wiggin, Kate Douglas (1856-1923), U.S. author and educator. She pioneered kindergarten classes by organizing the first one on the West Coast in San Francisco (1878). *Rebecca of Sunnybrook Farm* (1903), a book about a young girl's experiences after her father's death, was her most popular novel. She also wrote other children's fiction: *The Birds' Christmas Carol* (1887) and *Mother Carey's Chickens* (1911).
See also: Kindergarten.

Wight, Isle of, diamond-shaped island, 147 sq mi (381 sq km), off the southern coast of England. Its scenery and mild climate make it a popular resort area. Cowes, the chief port, is a well-known yachting center.

Wigner, Eugene Paul (1902-), Hungarian-born U.S. physicist who worked with Enrico Fermi to produce the first nuclear chain reaction in 1942. Wigner shared the Nobel Prize in physics with J. Hans Jensen and Maria Goeppert in 1963. He was professor of mathematical physics at Princeton University.
See also: Nuclear energy.

Wigwam, kind of dwelling used by Algonquian-speaking Native Americans in the eastern part of North America. Wigwams are usually oval or round and are covered with bark. The term is sometimes used to describe any Native American home, including the conical tepee and wickiup.

Wilberforce, Samuel (1805-73), English priest of the Anglican church. He held important church offices, including bishop of Oxford, dean of Westminster, and chaplain of the House of Lords. Wilberforce mediated a dispute between the Anglo-Catholic and the Evangelical factions of the church. Politically, he fought for prison reform and measures to prevent the abuse of women and children.
See also: Anglicans.

Wilbur, Richard (1921-), U.S. poet and essayist. He won a Pulitzer Prize in poetry for *Things of This World* (1957) and *New and Collected Poems* (1989). In 1987 he received an appointment as poet laureate of the United States.

Wild barley, plant in the grass family. One kind of wild barley, squirreltail (*Hordeum jubatum*), is named because of its prickly, bearded appearance. The seeds of this grass not only spread quickly and destroy other plants, they burrow through to the hide of woolly sheep and cause irritation. In addition the rest of the plant, when chewed, often causes sheep to choke.

Wild canary *see:* Goldfinch.

Wild carrot, also called Queen Anne's lace, plant (*Daucus carota*) in the parsley family. This relative of the edible carrot has a root that looks like the domesticated carrot, but it is inedible. It displays a cluster of lacy white flowers on top of a tall, thin green stalk that grows to about 3 ft (91 cm) high. It is usually a biennial plant—one that lives for 2 years.

Simon Wiesenthal

Wildcat, name given generally to any small or medium-sized wild cat, such as the Canada lynx (*Lynx canadensis*) and bobcat (*L. rufus*), which are found in North America. The true wildcat (*Felis silvestris*) is a powerful, vicious animal found in Europe and Africa. Wildcats are longer than common house cats and have shorter tails. One type of wildcat, the Egyptian cat, is probably the ancestor of the modern domestic cat.

Wildcat bank, any of numerous unsound state-chartered U.S. banks that issued paper money (wildcat currency) without having adequate assets (1830-63). They proliferated after Pres. Andrew Jackson dismantled the Second Bank of the United States. Many collapsed after Jackson, alarmed by the inflation caused by the wildcat banks, ordered government agents to accept only gold or silver in payment for public lands. The abrupt failures of the wildcat banks resulted in the 1837 financial panic.

Oscar Wilde, after an aquarelle by C. Pellegrini

Wilde, Oscar (1854-1900), Irish author. He achieved celebrity with the novel *The Picture of Dorian Gray* (1891) and such witty society comedies as *Lady Windermere's Fan* (1892), *An Ideal Husband* (1895), and his masterpiece, *The Importance of Being Earnest* (1895).

Wildebeest *see:* Gnu.

Wilder, Billy (1906-), Austrian-born U.S. screenwriter and film director. Wilder, known for his humorous treatment of seri-

Algonquian wigwam

ous subject matter, often dealt with topics that had not previously been considered for entertainment purposes, including alcoholism in *The Lost Weekend* (Academy Award; 1945), a prisoner-of-war camp in *Stalag 17* (1953), the Cold War in *One, Two, Three* (1961), and prostitution in *Irma La Douce* (1963). Other works include *Double Indemnity* (1944), *Sunset Boulevard* (Academy Award; 1950), *Some Like It Hot* (1959), *The Apartment* (Academy Award; 1960), and *Fedora* (1979).

Wilder, Laura Ingalls (1867-1957), U.S. children's author best known for her series of 9 popular autobiographical novels, including *Little House on the Prairie* (1935), depicting pioneer life in the Midwest.

Wilder, Thornton Niven (1897-1975), U.S. novelist and playwright. His novels include *The Bridge of San Luis Rey* (1927; Pulitzer Prize) and *The Ides of March* (1948). Wilder experimented with stylized techniques in plays such as *Our Town* (1938; Pulitzer Prize), *The Skin of Our Teeth* (1942; Pulitzer Prize), and *The Matchmaker* (1954).

Wilderness, Battle of the, opening engagement—fought May 5-6, 1864, in central Virginia, 10 mi (16 km) west of Fredericksburg—of the Wilderness Campaign in the U.S. Civil War. Gen. Ulysses S. Grant's 118,000-man Army of the Potomac, advancing to annihilate the Confederate Army in open battle, was met and held in heavily wooded country by 60,000 men under Gen. Robert E. Lee. Both sides suffered heavy losses. Grant then turned to attack Spotsylvania Courthouse (May 8-19). Fighting continued until early June 1864.
See also: Civil War, U.S.

Wilderness Road, early U.S. pioneer route. It ran from Virginia through the Cumberland Gap into the Ohio Valley. Laid out in 1775 by Daniel Boone, it was the main route west until 1840. It became part of U.S. 25 (the Dixie Highway) in 1926, and is now a section of U.S. Route 1.
See also: Pioneer life in America.

Wildlife conservation, organized supervision of the environment that protects the native plant and animal life. Without good environmental management many species would become extinct (killed off) or seriously endangered (greatly diminished in number). Human activities have caused the decline of native species, including hunting and clearing land for crops. Plant life has become endangered through land development and industrial pollution. U.S. National Parks, first developed by President Theodore Roosevelt, protect wilderness areas. The International Union for the Conservation of Nature and Natural Resources (IUCN) has created the *Red Data Book*, a publication that reports the status of endangered species worldwide. Conservation of plants and animals is important for many reasons: their beauty, their importance in the ecological balance of an area, their scientific and medical value, their economic value to an area.
See also: Endangered species.

Wild rice (*Zizania aquatica*), aquatic plant of the grass family, native to the lakes and streams of North America; also, the cereal grain harvested from the plant. Wild rice is not related to rice. The grain has long been eaten by Native Americans and is now planted to feed wildfowl.

Wilhelm, name of 2 German emperors: **Wilhelm I** (1797-1888) and **Wilhelm II** (1859-1941). The elder became the first emperor of modern Germany—crowned king of Prussia and Wilhelm I (1861)—then kaiser of Germany (1871). With the help of the prime minister, Otto von Bismarck, Germany was unified into an empire with the success of the Franco-Prussian Wars (1870-71). The younger was the grandson of Wilhelm I and the last emperor (kaiser) of Germany. Not only did he make Germany prosperous through growth in manufacturing, trade, and colonization of parts of Africa and the Pacific, he also developed a powerful military force. Expansion and his disruption of an alliance with Russia resulted in World War I (1914-18). With German defeat eminent, Wilhelm II moved to the neutral Netherlands where he lived out the rest of his days in exile.
See also: Germany.

Wilhelmina (1880-1962), Queen of the Netherlands (1890-1948), having acceded to the throne after the death of her father, King William III. In 1940 she fled to London to escape the German invasion, and from there directed her country's forces against Germany and Japan. Wilhelmina returned home at the end of the war (1945), and 3 years later turned the throne over to her daughter, Juliana.
See also: Netherlands.

Wilkes, Charles (1798-1877), U.S. naval officer. He led a U.S. Navy expedition that identified Antarctica as a continent. He also seized the British ship *Trent* off Cuba (1861) to remove 2 Confederate agents from it—an action that almost caused Britain to support the South in the Civil War (1861-65). His career waned afterwards, and he completed his career writing reports of his explorations.
See also: Antarctica.

Wilkes-Barre (pop. 51,551), city in northeastern Pennsylvania in the Wyoming valley along the Susquehanna River. The area was founded by colonists from Connecticut (1769), suffered near extinction twice because of war in the 19th century, then grew because of the coal industry. The importance of the coal industry lessened in the 1930s and since then other industries have developed an economic base, including publishing, electronics, data processing, and aircraft and military missile parts production. In addition to rebuilding after two fires (1769), the city again suffered severe damage during a storm and subsequent flood (1972).
See also: Pennsylvania.

Wilkins, Maurice Hugh Frederick (1916-), British biophysicist. He shared the 1962 Nobel Prize in physiology or medicine with biologists James D. Watson of the United States and Francis H.C. Crick of Great Britain. His research on deoxyribonucleic acid (DNA) led to the model of the molecular structure of DNA. Wilkins also worked on the development of the atomic bomb as part of the Manhattan Project in World War II.
See also: Deoxyribonucleic acid.

Wilkins, Roy (1901-81), U.S. civil rights leader and executive secretary of the National Association for the Advancement of Colored People (NAACP) from 1955 to 1970. Opposed to white supremacy and black separatism, he did much to bring about school desegregation and the 1964 Civil Rights Act.
See also: Civil rights.

Will, legal document by which a person (the testator) gives instructions concerning the disposal of his or her property (bequest, or legacy) after death. Wills are generally prepared by lawyers. Under most jurisdictions a will must be attested in order to be legally valid: Independent witnesses who have nothing to gain under the will must attest that the signature on the will is in fact that of the testator. Wills may be revoked during the life of the testator or altered by codicils. Wills generally appoint executors to administer the estate of the deceased and carry out his or her instructions. When a person dies intestate (without making a will), the property is normally divided among the next of kin.

Willamette River, river located in west-central Oregon, between the Cascade and Coast mountains. It flows northward and empties into the Columbia River near Portland. An annual rainfall of 40 in (1,102 mm) makes the Willamette Valley the richest farming area in Oregon.

Willard, Emma Hart (1787-1870), first U.S. woman to publicly advocate higher education for women. Along with her husband, John Willard, she established a boarding school for girls in Middlebury, Vt. The school was moved to Troy, N.Y., and became known as the Emma Willard School. In 1854 she represented the United States at the World's Educational Convention in London.
See also: Women's movements.

Willard, Frances Elizabeth Caroline (1838-98), U.S. educator, temperance leader, and social reformer. She served as president of the Woman's Christian Temperance Union (WCTU) from 1879. She also worked for woman suffrage and helped found the Prohibition Party (1882).

Willemstad (pop. 70,000), city on the Caribbean island of Curaçao, capital of the

Above left: The giant panda is the symbol of the World Wildlife Fund.

Above center: Due to destruction of its territory and the craze for collecting it, this species of Brazilian orchid is threatened with extinction.

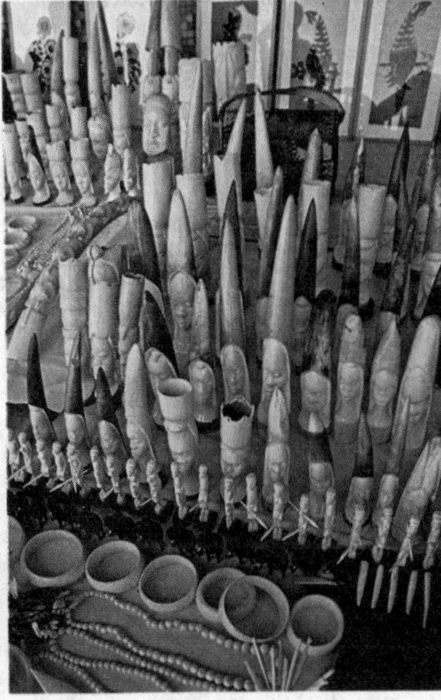

Right: The survival of wild elephants is threatened by trade in ivory objects.

Left: The kagu, native to New Caledonia, is one of the most endangered bird species.

Above: The worldwide demand for valuable tortoise shells has created a thriving business on Fiji and lead to the animals endangerment.

Left: The danger of chemical pesticides: Sprayed leaves (A) are eaten by worms (B)which, in turn, are eaten by birds (C). The poison further accumulates when the worm-eating birds are eaten by birds of prey (D).

Far left: Because of the export of exotic species, a great deal of Australian wildlife, including the koala bear, is endangered.

Netherlands Antilles. Arawak tribes inhabited this area before Dutch settlers arrived (1634). The island contains the Western Hemisphere's oldest Jewish cemetery (1659) and synagogue (1732). Its harbor is used for crude oil shipment. Oil refinement as well as banking are important to the economic base of Willemstad.

Willet, bird in the sandpiper family. This gray- to white-colored shore bird measures about 16 in (40 cm) long. It has a long, thin bill and long, thin legs. It also is known for its loud call. The eastern willet (*Catoptrophorus semipalmatus*) and the western willet (*C. semipalmatus inornatus*) live in both North and South America.

William I, prince of Orange

William, 4 kings of England. **William I**, or **William the Conqueror** (1027?-1087), duke of Normandy from 1035, became the first Norman king in 1066 by defeating Harold in the Battle of Hastings; he suppressed all opposition by 1071. William I was a harsh but capable ruler, reorganizing England's military and land-holding systems, building many castles, and creating a strong feudal government. The Domesday Book, a survey of England, was compiled by his order (1085). His son, **William II** or **Rufus** (c.1056-1100), succeeded him in 1087. Autocratic and brutal, William II put down a rebellion by his own barons in 1088 and invaded Scotland in 1097. He quarreled with St. Anselm over the independence of the Church. He was killed (probably deliberately) by an arrow while hunting. He was succeeded by his brother, Henry I. **William III**, or **William of Orange** (1650-1702), was *stadholder* (ruler) of Holland (1672-1702) and king of England (1689-1702). He married Mary, Protestant daughter of the Roman Catholic king of England, in 1677. English Protestants, unhappy with James II, invited William to invade England, which resulted in the so-called Glorious Revolution (1688). William became coruler of England with his wife after they accepted the Bill of Rights, which reduced their power (1689). William ruled alone after Mary's death (1694) and was succeeded by Queen Anne. **William IV** (1765-1837) succeeded his brother George IV in 1830. He exercised little political influence and was succeeded by his niece Victoria.
See also: United Kingdom.

Medal depicting the crowning of William III (of Orange) and Mary as king and queen of England in 1689

William and Mary, College of, coeducational, state university in Williamsburg, Va. Founded in 1693, it is the second-oldest university in the United States. William and Mary was the first college to offer law training and have separate schools of modern language and modern history. The honorary scholastic society Phi Beta Kappa was founded at the university (1776). Famous graduates include Thomas Jefferson and James Monroe.

William I (1772-1843), king of the Netherlands (1815-40) and son of William V, Prince of Orange and last governor of the Dutch Republic. After the French invaded the Dutch Republic and ousted William V in 1795, William lived in England and Prussia (northern Germany) until 1812. In 1813 the Dutch successfully rebelled against French rule, and in 1815 William was named king of the Netherlands, which then included Belgium, Liege, and the Grand Duchy of Luxembourg. In 1830 the Belgians demanded independence from the Netherlands, but William I refused to accede to the separation. Due in part to public disapproval of his handling of the Belgium question, William I abdicated in 1840.
See also: Netherlands.

William I, prince of Orange (1533-84), founder of the present dynasty of the Netherlands. Born in Germany, he supported the Spanish rule of the Netherlands, first under Charles V and then Philip II, until 1568. In that year the Protestant William led a revolt against the Catholic Philip and Spain's policies of religious and political repression in the Netherlands. He worked to unite all of the provinces of the Netherlands, and in 1579 the Dutch Republic consisting of 7 provinces was formed. He was outlawed by Philip II and subsequently assassinated.
See also: Netherlands.

William of Ockham (c.1285-1349), also spelled *Occam,* English philosopher, member of the Franciscan order. Like other great thinkers of the Middle Ages, he was a Scholastic—one who uses reason to understand faith. He broke, though, with other great Scholastics—especially the church-supported St. Thomas Aquinas. Ockham did not believe that reason could deepen understanding of faith. He did advance ideas associated with modern scientific thought in that he believed conclusions should be drawn from things observed by the senses and reasoned through logic. The saying "less is more" describes Ockham's Razor—the belief that a problem should be stated as simply as possible and supported with appropriate evidence. Pope John XXII brought charges of false theological teaching, or heresy, to William of Ockham (1324), which resulted in Ockham's self-imposed exile to Bavaria (1328).
See also: Scholasticism.

Williams, Daniel Hale (1856-1931), African-American surgeon and pioneer in the field of heart surgery. In 1893 he repaired a tear in the pericardium of a patient who then lived for more than 20 years. He founded the first interracial hospital and training school for black nurses and interns, Provident Hospital in Chicago.

Williams, Emlyn (1905-87), Welsh actor and playwright, noted for his semiautobiographical play *The Corn is Green* (1938) and for his concert readings from the works of Dylan Thomas and Charles Dickens. He also wrote *Night Must Fall* (1935).

Williams, Roger (c.1603-83), church leader and founder of the colony of Rhode Island. He came to North America (1631) because of disagreements with the doctrine of the Church of England. His disagreement with the Church became a problem for him in Salem, Mass., also. Because of this he founded Rhode Island (1636) with the help of land granted to him by the Narragansett Native American tribe. In Rhode Island he practiced the belief of religious freedom and separation of church and state—concepts later adopted by the writers of the Constitution. Williams had to journey to England several times to fight for leadership in his colony (1643, 1651). His first trip resulted in his most famous publication, *The Bloudy Tenent of Persecution* (1644). He was president of Rhode Island colony (1654-57).

Williams, Roy Lee (1915-89), U.S. labor leader, president of the International Brotherhood of Teamsters, 1981-83. A truckdriver, Williams became active in the Teamsters organization as business agent in Wichita, Kans. (1948), president of Joint Council 56 (1953-81), and director of the Central Conference (1976). He was an effective bargainer for the membership, but his connections with organized crime forced his resignation. Williams was indicted for criminal offenses 4 times, and finally convicted (1982) for attempted bribery of a U.S. senator. His 55-year prison sentence was reduced to 10 years, of which he served 3 years (1985-88) before being released because of poor health and his willingness to testify in federal crime cases.
See also: Teamsters Union; Unions, labor.

Williams, Shirley (1930-), English political leader. She served as education minister in the Labour government (1976-79), then broke with the party because of its leftward drift; she helped form the Social Democratic Party (SDP) in 1981. In that year she became the first SDP member elected to Parliament.

Williams, Ted (Theodore Samuel Williams; 1918-), U.S. baseball player. Considered one of the greatest hitters in baseball history, he was the last major leaguer to achieve a .400 season batting average (.406 in 1941), finishing with a .344 career average. Williams, an outfielder, led the American League in hitting 6 times (1941, 42, 47, 48, 57, 58) and won the Most Valuable Player award twice

(1946, 49). He played in the major leagues for the Boston Red Sox (1939-42; 1946-51; 1954-60) and was inducted into the National Baseball Hall of Fame in 1966.

Williams, Tennessee (Thomas Lanier Williams; 1911-83), U.S. playwright. His emotionally intense plays are full of brilliant, poetic dialogue and deal with the effects of failure, loneliness, and futile obsessions on human beings. His first success, *The Glass Menagerie* (1945), was followed by *A Streetcar Named Desire* (1947) and *Cat on a Hot Tin Roof* (1955), both of which received Pulitzer Prizes. Other plays include *Sweet Bird of Youth* (1959) and *The Night of the Iguana* (1961).

A scene from the film Baby Doll, *written by Tennessee Williams*

Williams, William (1731-1811), colonial politician from Connecticut, a signer of the Declaration of Independence. He served as delegate to the Continental Congress (1776-78); the Congress of Confederation (1783-84), during which time the Articles of Confederation were developed; and the convention for the ratification of the Constitution (1788).

Williams, William Carlos (1883-1963), U.S. poet. Williams was a practicing doctor and specialized in the care of children for over 40 years. He is best known for the long, reflective poem *Paterson* (1946-58) and *Pictures from Breughel* (1963), which won a Pulitzer Prize. He also wrote plays, fiction, and essays, including *In the American Grain* (1925), a study of the American character. Williams wrote hard, clear free verse emphasizing the importance of the subject matter over literary form.

Williamsburg (pop. 9,870), restored colonial city in southeastern Virginia on the James River. The city, which was the capital of Virginia from 1699 to 1779, contains over 500 original or reconstructed 18th-century buildings, including the governor's palace and the capitol, in which the Virginia assembly met. Much of the restoration work, from 1926 onward, was undertaken by the philanthropist John D. Rockefeller, Jr. Williamsburg is the site of William and Mary College, founded in 1693.
See also: Virginia.

Williamson, Hugh (1735-1819), U.S. scientist, doctor, and politician of the American Revolutionary period. A doctor in Philadelphia, Williamson actually assisted in some of Benjamin Franklin's experiments in electricity. Elected to the North Carolina legislature (1782), he served in the Congress of the Confederation (1782-85, 1787-89), and was a North Carolina delegate to the Constitutional Convention (1787) and a signer of the Constitution. After 2 terms in the U.S. House of Representatives (1789-93), he retired from politics to pursue science and writing.

William the Conqueror *see:* William (I, of England).

Willkie, Wendell Lewis (1892-1944), U.S. political leader. A lawyer, he became president of a giant utility company and led business opposition to the New Deal. A Democrat until the mid-1930s, he was the Republican presidential candidate in 1940, gaining a large popular vote but losing to Franklin D. Roosevelt. His book *One World* (1943) was a plea for international cooperation.

Will-o'-the-wisp, or jack-o-lantern, blue light caused by the natural combustion of gas from decaying matter. It is sometimes visible at night over marshes and graveyards. Also called *ignis fatuus* ("foolish fire"), it was once believed to be an evil spirit that enticed travellers with its elusive glow.

Willow, common name for about 300 species of trees of the genus *Salix*, which occur from the tropics to the Arctic. The leaves are generally swordlike, and male and female catkins are borne on separate plants. The willows of the temperate zone are large, but the dwarf willow, found beyond the tree lines of the Arctic, grows to only about 6 in (15.2 cm). The long, pliable twigs of some species are cut regularly for use in making wicker baskets and furniture. Other species are used for tannins or for their light and durable wood. The ornamental weeping willow is a native of China and southwest Asia.

Willow herb *see:* Fireweed.

Wills, Helen Newington (1906-), U.S. tennis player. Known for her strength and grace, she won 7 U.S. Open singles titles (1923-25, 27-29, 31), 8 Wimbledon championships (1927-30, 32, 33, 35, 38), and 4 French Open titles (1928-30, 32).

Wilmington (pop. 70,195), largest city in Delaware, seat of New Castle County, in the northern part of the state on the Delaware River. Wilmington, a center of the chemical industry, is the home of E. I. du Pont de Nemours & Co., one of the largest producers of chemicals, plastics, and synthetic fibers and dyes in the United States. Other industries produce leather, textiles, machinery, and paper. The city was first settled in 1638 by Swedish immigrants. The settlement later passed to the Dutch, then to the English, receiving its name in 1739, when it was incorporated as a borough. The Du Pont powder mill was established in 1802.
See also: Delaware.

Wilmot Proviso, congressional proposal to prohibit the extension of slavery into newly acquired U.S. territories. In 1846 President James K. Polk asked Congress to appropriate $2 million for Mexico to settle territorial claims. The Wilmot Proviso was the condition some members of Congress tried to impose in return for this payment. The proposal was defeated by the Senate, and the conflict was not resolved until 1862, when Congress outlawed slavery in all U.S. territories.
See also: Slavery.

Wilson, Angus (1913-91), English novelist and short-story writer who satirizes English class attitudes and social life. His novels include *Hemlock and After* (1952), *Anglo-Saxon Attitudes* (1956), *No Laughing Matter* (1967), and *Setting the World on Fire* (1980).

Wilson, Edmund (1895-1972), U.S. critic and writer who investigated the historical, sociological, and psychological background to literature. His prolific imaginative and critical output includes *Axel's Castle* (1931), a study of symbolism; *To the Finland Station* (1940), on the intellectual sources of the Russian Revolution; *The Wound and the Bow* (1941), on neurosis and literature; the explosive novel *Memoirs of Hecate County* (1949); and *Patriotic Gore* (1962), a study of Civil War literature.

Wilson, Harold (1916-), prime minister of Great Britain (1964-70, 1974-76). An Oxford economist, he entered Parliament in 1945, became president of the Board of Trade in 1947, and became leader of the Labour Party in 1963. Identified initially with the left wing and known for his tactical skill, he preserved party unity during a period of economic crisis and division over the Common Market. He resigned in 1976 and was knighted that same year. He was named a baron in 1983.
See also: United Kingdom.

Wilson, Henry (1812-75), U.S. senator from Massachusetts (1855-73), a founder of the Republican Party. He was chairperson of the Military Affairs Committee during the Civil War. Wilson devoted his life to the issue of the emancipation of slaves. He served as vice president (1873-75) in the second term of President Ulysses S. Grant.

Ted Williams

Johann Joachim Winckelmann, by Anton Raphael Mengs

Wilson, James (1742-98), Scottish-born signer of both the Declaration of Independence and the U.S. Constitution. He believed in a strong national government whose authority was rooted in the will of the people. Wilson served in the Congress of the Confederation (1783, 1785, 1786) and was appointed to the U.S. Supreme Court in 1789.

Wilson, Lanford (1937-), U.S. playwright. Known for his realistic themes, Wilson creates dramatic dialogue by combining, and at times overlapping, conversation and monologue. He was awarded the Pulitzer Prize in 1980 for *Talley's Folly* (1979), a romantic story set in World War II Missouri; the plot deals with the hero's coming to grips with the victimization of his family by anti-Semites. Other works include *The Hot l Baltimore* (1973), *Angels Fall* (1982), and *Burn This* (1987).

Wilson, Woodrow (1856-1924), 28th president of the United States. Wilson's high intellectual qualifications and idealistic fervor made him a forceful leader. Wilson is considered one of the most successful U.S. presidents. His triumphs as a war leader during World War I and his eloquence in the cause of freedom made him the idol of millions around the world. His successes form a sharp contrast to his failure to achieve a League of Nations—one of the deepest personal tragedies in U.S. politics.

Early life. Thomas Woodrow Wilson (he later dropped the first name) was born Dec. 29, 1856, in Staunton, Va. He attended Davidson College in North Carolina, then Princeton University, from which he graduated in 1879. After law school and a brief, unsuccessful law practice, he attended graduate school at Johns Hopkins University. In 1885 Wilson married Ellen Louise Axson; they had three children. Mrs. Wilson died in Aug. 1914. In 1915 Wilson married Edith Bolling Galt, a widow.

From education to politics. Wilson taught at Bryn Mawr (1885-88), Wesleyan University (1888-90), and Princeton (1890-1910), and was elected president of Princeton University in 1902. In 1910 he was elected governor of New Jersey (1911-13). In 1912 Wilson won the Democratic Party's nomination and presidential election, aided by the Republicans' split between William Howard Taft and Theodore Roosevelt.

President. In the first years of his presidency, Wilson enjoyed the support of a Democratic-controlled Congress, which led to a remarkable succession of legislative achievements, including the Underwood Tariff Act, which made significant reductions in customs duties; a graduated income tax; and the Federal Reserve Act, which overhauled the nation's banking and credit system and placed it under public control. The Clayton Antitrust Act strengthened the government's power against monopolies and exempted unions from the antitrust law; the Federal Trade Commission (FTC) was established to control "unfair business practices"; and the Adamson Act established an eight-hour work day for railroad employees, while the Child-Labor Act limited children's work hours.

In foreign affairs the United States under Wilson took control of Nicaragua's financial and foreign affairs, and U.S. troops intervened in Mexico, Haiti, and the Dominican Republic. After World War I broke out in 1914, Wilson declared the United States neutral. In 1916 he was reelected by a narrow margin with the slogan, "He kept us out of war." But after Germany sank four U.S. ships, Wilson asked Congress to declare war in Apr. 1917.

Still, Wilson pushed for peace. On Jan. 8, 1918, he proposed a basis for peace negotiations—his famous "Fourteen Points." Germany finally agreed to them and, on Nov. 11, 1918, the armistice ending the war was signed.

In 1919 Wilson attended the Versailles Peace Conference. He believed that the only hope for a lasting peace lay in a League of Nations. Back home, he campaigned hard for its establishment.

In Oct. 1919 Wilson was permanently invalided by a stroke. Yet, aided by his wife and cabinet members, he retained executive powers.

The Senate rejected the treaty that would have established the League of Nations—a bitter failure for Wilson. He did not run for reelection in 1920.

Retirement. Wilson left the presidency a sick and saddened man; winning the 1919 Nobel Peace Prize was little consolation to him. He died in Washington, D.C., on Feb. 3, 1924.

Woodrow Wilson

28th president of the United States

Born:	Staunton, Va.; Dec. 29, 1856.
Term:	Mar. 1913-Mar. 1921.
Vice president:	Thomas R. Marshall.
Political party:	Democratic.
Spouses:	Ellen Louise Axson Wilson; Edith Bolling Galt Wilson.
Children:	3.
Died:	Washington, D.C.; Feb. 3, 1924.

Wilson cloud chamber, instrument that makes radiation visible and measurable. This device is made out of a container, a piston, and water-concentrated gas. It works on the same principle as natural cloud formation—that is, when more than 100% humidity occurs and water cools, water droplets become apparent either in the form of a cloud in the sky or, in the case of the Wilson cloud chamber, as tracks of charged particles. Particles with an electric charge within the chamber join with molecules of the cooled gas to form the visible tracks. Alpha and beta rays emitted from radioactive materials form these visible streaks.
See also: Radiation.

Wilt, condition where plants droop and wither due to lack of water in their cells. This can be caused by lack of available moisture, physiological disorders, or fungi or bacteria damaging water-conducting tissues inside roots or stems.

Wimbledon *see:* Tennis.

Winch, device facilitating the hoisting or hauling of loads. It comprises a rotatable drum around which is wound a rope or cable attached to the load. The drum is turned by means of a hand-operated crank or a motor.

Winchester (pop. 93,700), English town, site of the famous 14th-century Winchester Cathedral, the longest church (556 ft/169 m) in England. During the reign of Alfred the Great (871-899) Winchester became a center of learning. It was the seat of government for the Danish king Canute (1016-35). Today Winchester is a prosperous religious, service, and light industry center.

Winckelmann, Johann Joachim (1717-68), German scholar, founder of archeology and art history. He demonstrated that art can reveal the history of a culture just as writing does. As a youngster he studied Greek and Latin in order to read Homer and other classical writers. His principal work, *The History of Ancient Art* (1764), is still used by art historians.
See also: Archeology.

Wind, body of air moving in relation to the earth's surface. The world's major wind systems are set up to counter the equal heating of the earth's surface and are modified by the rotation of the earth.

Wind Cave National Park, area of 28,292 acres (11,449 hectares) in the Black Hills in southwestern South Dakota. Established

in 1903, it surrounds a cavern with alternating air current and unusual crystal formations.
See also: National Parks.

Wind chill, index that determines the relative temperature, based on the effects of wind on exposed human flesh. An increase in wind speed increases the rate at which a person becomes chilled. Thus, the temperature will seem to be colder when there is wind than when there is not. Wind chill measurements are not exact, but they do reflect more how a person feels the cold than a thermometer reading of temperature alone.

Windermere, lake in the northwestern Cumbria section of England, better known as the Lake District. This, the largest lake in England, measures 10.5 mi (16.9 km) long and 1 mi (1.6 km) at its widest point, with a total area of 5.69 sq mi (14.7 sq km). It is a popular resort area described in the poetry of the 19th-century English romantic poets William Wordsworth and Samuel Coleridge, among others.

Windhoek (pop. 104,100), capital and largest city of Namibia, as well as its commercial, administrative, and communications center. Windhoek was originally called Aigams ("hot water")—a reference to the area's hot springs. In the late 1880s Germany occupied the city, but it was taken over by South African forces in World War I. Until Namibia's independence in 1990, the white government of South Africa ruled Namibia, and apartheid was strictly enforced. While the population of Windhoek is mostly black, the whites controlled the politics and economy of the city until 1990.
See also: Namibia.

Wind instrument, any of the musical instruments whose sound is produced by blowing air into a tube, causing a vibration within it. In *woodwind* instruments the vibration is made either by blowing across or into a specially shaped mouthpiece, as with the flute, piccolo, recorder, and flageolet, or by blowing against a single or double reed, as in the clarinet, saxophone, oboe, English horn, and bassoon. The pitch is altered by opening and closing holes set into the tube. In *brass* instruments the vibration is made by the player's lips on the mouthpiece. The bugle and various types of posthorn have a single, unbroken tube. The cornet, French horn, trumpet, and tuba have valves to vary the effective tube length and increase the range of notes; the trombone has a slide mechanism for the same purpose.

Windlass, compound machine made from a rope or chain wound around a cylinder shape attached to a crank. This wheel and axle design is commonly used to lift water from wells. A container attached to the end of the rope or chain collects the well water. Human power or machine power hoists up the container and line.

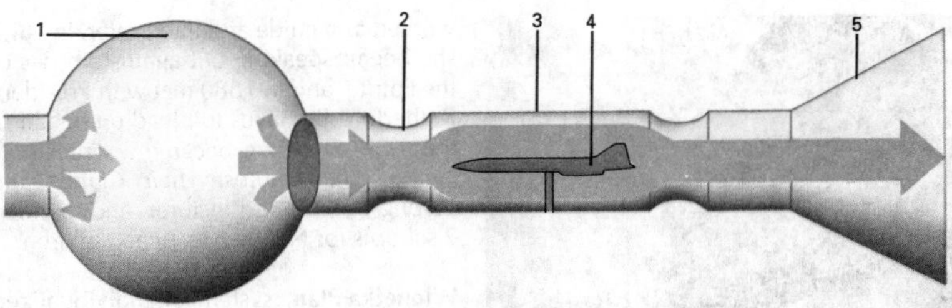

This wind tunnel is used to test the effects of high-speed air on aircraft. Air is pumped into a storage tank (1) and compressed and funneled through a sonic throat (2), which discharges it at up to six times the speed of sound. Test instruments (3) measure the effects of wind and temperature on the test model (4). A diffuser (5) slows the airstream before discharging.

Windmill, machine that performs work by harnessing wind power. In the traditional windmill the power applied to a horizontal shaft by 4 large radiating sails is transmitted to milling or pumping machinery housed in a sizable supporting structure. The windmill's modern counterpart is the wind turbine, often seen in rural areas. Here a multibladed turbine wheel mounted on a steel derrick or mast and pointed into the wind by a fantail drives a pump or electric generator.

Window, building openings for air and light. Some windows open inward or outward from the opening, and these are called *casement* or *hinged* windows. Many windows are double-hung and are opened by lifting them up or pushing them down, and these are called *double-hung* windows. Double-hung windows were a Dutch invention (1800s). The arrangement of windows—known as *fenestration*—in a building is an important part of its overall design. Stained-glass windows, in which colored bits of glass within metal frames create a picture or pattern, were an important part of church design from the Middle Ages.

Windsor (pop. 193,100), city in southern Ontario, Canada, on the opposite bank of the Detroit River from Detroit, Mich. Like Detroit, Windsor is an important automotive manufacturing center. Originally inhabited by the Huron and Iroquois tribes, it was settled by the French (early 18th century) and later the English (1790s). In its early days a ferry connected the cities of Windsor and Detroit, whereas a bridge and tunnel connect them today.

Windsor, name of the ruling dynasty of the United Kingdom of Great Britain and Northern Ireland, adopted by King George V in 1917 to replace the royal family's German name, Saxe-Coburg-Gotha (from Albert Wettin, Queen Victoria's husband), when anti-German feeling was high.
See also: United Kingdom.

Windsor, Duke of *see:* Edward (VIII).

Windsor Castle, principal residence of British sovereigns since the 11th century. Begun by William I, it stands about 20 mi (32 km) west of London. The Round Tower, built in 1180, is the castle's center, and St. George's Chapel (1528) is a fine example of English Perpendicular architecture.

Windsurfing, water sport in which an individual rides a *sailboard*, a surfboard with a central mast to which a sail is attached. The sail is turned by the rider to steer. The *sailsurfer* uses a board up to 7 ft (2.1 m) long, riding waves as in surfing. The *sailboarder* uses a longer board (up to 12 ft/3.7 m) and depends on wind as in sailing.

Wind tunnel, structure in which a controlled stream of air is produced in order to observe the effects on scale models or full-size components of airplanes, missiles, automobiles, or such structures as bridges and skyscrapers. An important research tool in aerodynamics, the wind tunnel enables a design to be accurately tested without the risks attached to full-scale trials. Hypersonic wind tunnels, operating on an impulse principle, can simulate the frictional effects of flight at over 5 times the speed of sound.
See also: Aerodynamics.

Windward Islands, group of islands in the Lesser Antilles, West Indies, stretching toward Venezuela. They include St. Lucia, St. Vincent, the Grenadines, Grenada, and Martinique. The area is about 950 sq mi (2,461 sq km) and the islands produce bananas, cacao, limes, nutmeg, and cotton. Tourism is an important industry.

Wine, alcoholic beverage made from fermented grape juice; wines made from other fruits are always named accordingly. Table wines are red, rosé, or white in color; red wines are made from dark grapes, the skins being left in the fermenting mixture; white wines may be made from dark or pale grapes, the skins being removed. The grapes—normally varieties of *Vitis vinifera*—are allowed to ripen until they attain suitable sugar content—18% or more—and acidity (in cool years or northern areas, sugar may have to be added). After crushing, they undergo fermentation in large tanks, during which time a small amount of sulfur dioxide is added to inhibit growth of wild yeasts and bacteria. When the alcohol and sugar content is right, the wine is cellared, racked off the lees (from which argol is obtained), clarified by filtration or fining (adding absorbent substances such as bentonite, gelatin, and isinglass), aged in the wood, and bottled. Sweet wines contain residual sugar; dry wines little or none. The alcohol content of table wines varies from 8% to 14% by volume. Sparkling wines—notably Champagne—are made by secondary fermentation under pressure, in bottles or in tanks. Fortified wines, or dessert wines—including sherry, port, and Madeira—have brandy added during or after fermentation and contain about 20% alcohol. Vermouth is a fortified wine flavored with wormwood and other

Grapes being harvested for wine

herbs. Major wine-producing areas of the world include France, Germany, Spain, Portugal, Italy, and California.

Winged bull, mythic beast of ancient Assyria, frequently appearing in paintings and statues. The beast, which originated c.1000 B.C., had a man's head on a winged bull's body. Enormous portal statues of winged bulls were used as guardians of palaces, to frighten away enemies and evil spirits.
See also: Mythology.

Winged lion, mythic beast of ancient Babylonia and Assyria, represented in paintings and statues. The beast had a man's head on a winged lion's body. Enormous winged lion statues were placed at a city's gate or the entranceway to a palace to frighten off harmful spirits or humans.
See also: Mythology.

Winged Victory, Greek sculpture dated c.180 B.C. depicting Nike, the goddess of victory, bringing a message of victory from the gods. The sculptor is unknown. In 1863 the statue, broken into 118 pieces, was discovered by a French archeologist. The statue was reconstructed; it stands today in the Louvre Museum in Paris.

Winnebago, Siouan-speaking Native Americans from eastern Wisconsin. Buffalo hunters and farmers, they were related to the Eastern Woodlands group. Once friendly to the French and English, they joined in the Black Hawk War (1832) against U.S. troups and were removed to reservations in Nebraska and Wisconsin. They now number about 2,000.

Winnemucca, Sarah, or Thoc-me-tony ("Shell Flower"; 1844?-91), U.S. advocate for Native American rights. A member of the Paiute tribe in the Nevada area, she worked as a guide and interpreter. In 1870 she began speaking out against abuses of the Paiute, and in 1880 met with President Rutherford B. Hayes to plead on behalf of the tribe. She then became a writer (*Life Among the Paiutes: Their Claims and Wrongs*, 1883) and lecturer, and founded 2 schools for Native American children.

Winnetka Plan, system of individualized instruction introduced in the public elementary and junior high schools of Winnetka, Ill., in 1919. It grew as a reaction to the uniform grading of students, which held them to the same rate of progress. In the plan, pupils develop particular abilities at their own pace. The curriculum is divided into 2 sections: basic tasks learned by students individually, and creative activities, such as art, literature, music, where achievement is not measured.

Winnipeg (pop. 594,600), capital city of Manitoba, Canada, on the Red and Assiniboine rivers. The Canadian transcontinental railroad goes through this city in the center of the country. Along with a network of highways, this made Winnipeg an important distribution location for Canada in the past. At the time of French settlement (1738), fur trading was the base of the Winnipeg economy. Because of its location in the wheat belt, the city became home to Canada's grain market. Early in the 20th century, with cross-continental access, the population of the area grew. At the same time it developed as a major manufacturing center. Today the city is a center for culture and finance as well as trade and industry, with a symphony orchestra, theater center, art museum, and planetarium. The city was originally inhabited by Cree and Assiniboine Native Americans, and the population of Winnipeg today contains a large number of people of Native American ancestry.
See also: Manitoba.

Winnipeg River, part of the Saskatchewan-Nelson river system that rises in western Ontario, Canada, and empties into Hudson Bay. The 140-mi (225-km)-long river was the route traveled by French explorers and fur traders to the Northwest in the 1700s. Today hydroelectric plants on the Winnipeg River provide power for most of Manitoba.

Winslow, Edward (1595-1655), one of the original settlers of Plymouth, Mass., who came from England on the *Mayflower* and served as governor of the colony for 3 years. He and his wife, Susanna White, were the first to marry in the new colony. A friend of the neighboring tribes, he arranged the first treaty with Chief Massasoit. In 1646 he returned to England, where he served in the government of Oliver Cromwell until his death.

Winterberry, shrub in the holly family. The winterberry (*Ilex verticillata*) displays red berries in November. It grows between 6 and 12 ft (2 and 4 m), usually in swampy areas in the eastern United States.

Wintergreen, plant in the heath family. This ground creeper shows pink globe-shaped flowers or bright red berries. The shiny leaves are grouped at the end of upright red-colored branches, whose leaves remain green year round. Oil extracted from the plant is used as flavoring in foods, medicines, and chewing gum.

Winthrop, name of 3 distinguished American colonists. **John Winthrop** (1588-1649), led the English Great Migration to Salem in 1630, founded Boston, and was 12 times elected governor of the Massachusetts Bay Colony. His journal, *The History of New England*, is an important historical source. His eldest son, **John Winthrop** (1606-76), went to Massachusetts Bay in 1631. After being named commissioner general of the new colony at Saybrook in 1633, he became governor of Connecticut (1657, 1659-76), receiving in 1662 a charter from Charles II uniting New Haven and Connecticut. His son **Fitz-John Winthrop** (1638-1707), left Massachusetts to join Oliver Cromwell's army in England, returning (1663) to fight the Dutch, the French, and the Native Americans. He was Connecticut's agent in London (1693-97) and a popular governor of Connecticut (1698-1707).

Wire, length of metal that has been drawn out into a thread. Wire is usually flexible, circular in cross-section, and uniform in diameter. Wire diameters generally range from about 0.001 to 0.5 in (0.025-12.7 mm). To manufacture wire, a hot-rolled metal rod pointed at one end is coated with a lubricant, threaded through a tungsten, carbide, or diamond die, and attached to a drum called a *draw block*. The draw block is rotated and wire—its diameter (gauge) determined by the diameter of the die—is drawn until the entire metal rod is reduced to steel. Steel, iron, aluminum, copper, and bronze are the metals most widely used for wire making, although others, including gold, platinum, and silver, are used as well. Copper and aluminum are preferred for electrical wiring because they combine high ductility with low resistance to electric current.

Wire glass, glass with wire mesh embedded in it to provide reinforcement for use in doors and windows. Usually 1/4-3/4 in (6-18 mm) thick, it may be produced by pressing the wire between 2 sheets of glass (Appert process), by pressing the wire into a single sheet (Shuman process), or by pouring molten glass over the mesh.

Wirehaired pointing griffon, hunting dog first bred in the Netherlands in the late 1800s. A slow, deliberate hunter, it points its body toward the location of the game. The griffon stands 19-23 in (48-58 cm) high and weighs 50-60 lb (23-27 kg). Its rough coat is steel gray and chestnut brown in color.

Wiretapping, interception of telephone conversations without the knowledge of those communicating. Wiretapping and the use of other "bugging" devices by private citizens are prohibited by U.S., federal, and state laws, but there has always been argument about whether police and other government officials should be able to use wiretapping to detect crimes and collect evidence. In 1968 Congress passed a law allowing wiretapping to be used in cases involving national security and certain serious crimes, provided that a court order is first obtained.

Wireworm, larva of the click beetle, which is often a serious pest. Wireworms are brown and hardskinned and are found in the soil. There is a wireworm pest for nearly every crop: They eat newly planted seeds or burrow into the roots and underground parts of stems. Because they spend several years in the soil before pupating, it is difficult to free the ground of wireworms.

Wirz, Henry (d. 1865), Confederate army officer in the U.S. Civil War, director of the Andersonville prison camp, in which Northern prisoners were crowded into a too-small stockade and abused and neglected. Wirz was tried by a military tribunal and hanged, the only Confederate soldier to be executed for war crimes.
See also: Civil War, U.S.

Wisconsin

Capital:	Madison
Statehood:	May 29, 1848 (30th state)
Familiar name:	Badger State
Area:	56,153 sq mi (145,436 sq km); ranks 26th
Population:	4,906,745 (1990); ranks 16th
Elevation:	Highest—1,952 ft (595 m), Timms Hill; Lowest—581 ft (177 m), along the Lake Michigan shore
Motto:	Forward
Flower:	Wood violet
Bird:	Robin
Tree:	Sugar maple
Song:	"On, Wisconsin!"

Wisconsin, state in the Great Lakes region of north-central United States; considered a Midwestern state; bordered by Lake Superior and Michigan to the north, Lake Michigan to the east, Illinois to the south, and the Mississippi River (with Iowa and Minnesota on the opposite side), the St. Croix River, and Minnesota to the west.
Land and climate. Wisconsin has five main land regions. The Eastern Ridges and Lowlands region, in the east along Lake Michigan, is a gently rolling plain that is the state's most fertile area. The Central Plain covers much of the state's center; above it lie the Northern Highland, an area of forested hills and hundreds of small lakes, and the flat plain of the Lake Superior Lowland. Below the Central Plain lies the Western Upland, an area of steep hills, bluffs, and ridges that borders the Mississippi River. Wisconsin has about 15,000 lakes, most small, and hundreds of waterfalls. The state's major rivers are the Wisconsin, Black, St. Croix, Fox, Menominee, and Mississippi. Forests covers about 50% of the state. Wisconsin has relatively short but warm and humid summers and long, cold winters. Principal cities are Milwaukee and Madison.
Economy. Wisconsin's economy is led by manufacturing and by wholesale and retail trade and other service industries. Chief manufactured goods are nonelectrical machinery, processed foods, paper products, electrical machinery and equipment, fabricated metal products, and transportation equipment. Agriculture and mining account for a small fraction of Wisconsin's state gross product. Milk and dairy products earn the most agricultural income; other leading livestock products are beef cattle and hogs; chief crops are corn, hay, oats, barley, wheat, and soybeans. Chief mining products are crushed stone, sand and gravel, and lime.
Government. Wisconsin's constitution was adopted in 1848. The governor serves a 4-year term. The state legislature consists of 33 senators serving 4-year terms and 99 assembly members serving 2-year terms. In the U.S. Congress, Wisconsin is represented by 2 senators and 9 representatives.
History. The Wisconsin area was home to Dakota, Menominee, and Winnebago Native Americans when the first Europeans—led by French explorer Jean Nicolet—arrived in 1634. Other Native American tribes moved into the area in the late 1600s. Wisconsin's European-American settlers battled the Fox Native Americans (1690-1740); the area came under British control in 1763 and became part of the United States in 1783. In the early 1800s European-American settlement grew rapidly; resistance by the Fox and Sauk was crushed in the 1832 Black Hawk War. In 1836 Congress created the Wisconsin Territory; in 1848 Wisconsin became the 30th state. In the early 1900s Wisconsin acquired a reputation for progressivism under Governor Robert M. La Follette, Sr. (elected in 1901). In the 1920s the state became predominantly urban. In 1932 Wisconsin became the first state to pass a state unemployment-compensation act. Manufacturing and agriculture remain important in Wisconsin, although the state's economy has suffered from the auto industry's decline (1980s) and the shrinking number and size of farms. Wisconsin's leaders are seeking more diverse industries and solutions to its problems of high education costs, water pollution, conservation of natural resources, and farm debt.

Wisconsin Dells *see:* Dalles.

Wisconsin River, longest river in Wisconsin, rising in the north near the Michigan border and flowing 430 mi (692 km) south and southwest to empty into the Mississippi River near Prairie du Chien. Near the town of Wisconsin Dells, the river has carved a 7-mi (11-km) scenic canyon. The river was once an important link on the trade route between the Great Lakes and the Mississippi. Today it provides considerable hydroelectric power.

Wisdom of Solomon, book of the Old Testament Apocrypha, traditionally ascribed to Solomon but probably written in the 2nd or 1st century B.C. An example of wisdom literature (pre-Christian Jewish philosophical writings), it praises wisdom and outlines God's care for the Jews.
See also: Old Testament.

Wise, Isaac Mayer (1819-1900), religious leader, Jewish rabbi, and founder of the Reform Judaism movement in the United States. He helped organize the Union of American Hebrew Congregations (1873). Two years later Wise founded a school in Cincinnati to train rabbis, Hebrew Union College (1875), at which he served as president. The Central Conference of American Rabbis (founded in 1889) was headed by him until 1900. He came to the United States (1846) from his birthplace of Bohemia, an area of modern-day Czechoslovakia.
See also: Judaism.

Wise, Stephen Samuel (1874-1949), religious leader, Jewish rabbi, and author. He presided as rabbi at the Free Synagogue in New York City, which was founded by him (1922). As a strong supporter of *Zionism*—belief in the establishment of the Jewish state of Israel—he founded the Federation of American Zionists. Other organizations he helped establish are the Jewish Institute for Religion and the American Jewish Congress. He wrote books—*How to Face Life* (1917) and *The Challenging Years* (1949),

Wisconsin

Both wolf parents are actively involved in raising their young.

among others—and edited *Opinion,* a magazine.
See also: Zionism.

Wisteria, plant in the pea family. Blue- to white-colored clusters of flowers blossom on this lacy-looking vine, which may grow to more than 35 ft (11 m) long. The Chinese wisteria (*Wisteria sinensis*) is commonly found in gardens throughout the United States while other species of this vine are native to the eastern portion of the country.

Witchcraft, manipulation of supernatural forces, usually toward evil ends. It has existed in most cultures throughout history and still has its devotees in modern society. In the Christian West witchcraft developed from surviving pagan beliefs. Witches were held responsible for disease and misfortune and were believed to acquire their evil power from the devil, whom they worshiped in obscene ritual (satanism, or devil worship, is not synonymous with witchcraft). From the 14th to the 18th century a witch-hunting epidemic prevailed in Europe, and many thousands of innocent people were tortured and executed in fanatical and hysterical persecutions.

Witch hazel, low tree or shrub (genus *Hamamelis*) growing in eastern North America and eastern Asia. It produces its small, yellow flowers in the autumn, when the leaves have fallen. A year later the seeds ripen and are thrown 20 ft (6.2 m) or more when the pods dry up and contract suddenly. Extracts from its bark and leaves are used in aftershave lotions and lotions for treating bruises.

Detail of The Death of General Wolfe *(1770), by Benjamin West*

Witenagemot, group of counselors to the Anglo-Saxon king. Before the king's court (*curia regis*) was established by the Norman conquerors of England (1066), these men partook in decisions to make war, grant lands, make important appointments in the court or church, and so on. They even had the power to dethrone a king during conflicts involving various claims to the throne. *Thanes,* or followers, of the king along with earls, bishops, and abbots were members of the witenagemot, which in translation means "a meeting of wise men."

Witherspoon, John (1723-94), Scottish-born American educator and clergyman who was one of the signers of the Declaration of Independence. He was a member of the Continental Congress. Prior to the American Revolution, he came to America to serve as president of what is now Princeton University. He resumed his post after the end of the war.

Witness, individual who testifies under oath in a legal proceeding or acts as a signer of a legal document. In giving testimony, a witness provides a court of law with information about persons or events relating to a particular case. A witness is criminally liable if he or she fails to appear in court or lies under oath. Certain individuals, such as children, are exempted from giving testimony.

Wittgenstein, Ludwig (1889-1951), Austrian philosopher whose two chief works, *Tractatus Logico-philosophicus* (1921) and the posthumous *Philosophical Investigations* (1953), have profoundly influenced the course of much British and U.S. philosophy. The *Tractatus* dwells on the logical nature and limits of language, understood as "picturing" reality. The *Investigations* rejects the assumption in the *Tractatus* that all representations must share a common logical form and instead relates the meanings of sentences to their uses in particular contexts: Philosophical problems are attributed to misuses of language. Wittgenstein was professor of philosophy at Cambridge University, England (1929-47).
See also: Philosophy.

Witwatersrand, or the Rand, gold-bearing rocky ridge in southern Transvaal, South Africa. It produces one-third of the world's gold output and is South Africa's major industrial region, with Johannesburg located at its center. Soweto township also lies in the Rand.
See also: South Africa.

Wodehouse, P.G. (Sir Pelham Grenville Wodehouse; 1881-1975), English writer of humorous novels and short stories. His writings, set in the early 1900-1920s, portray life in the upper class. Wodehouse's best-known novels, *Carry On Jeeves* (1925) and *The Code of the Woosters* (1938), relate the humorous predicaments of the dim-witted Bertie Wooster and his ever-sensible valet, Jeeves. Other works include *A Pelican at Blandings* (1969) and lyrics for such musical comedies as *Leave It to Jane* (1917) and *Rosalie* (1928). Wodehouse became a U.S. citizen (1955) and was knighted in England (1975).

Woden *see:* Odin.

Wöhler, Friedrich (1800-82), German chemist, the first to synthesize an organic substance (urea) from inorganic chemicals. He isolated the element beryllium, and was the first to measure the gravity of aluminum. Along with chemist Justus von Liebig, he developed an early theory of the structure of organic compounds.
See also: Chemistry.

Wolcott, name of a prominent Connecticut family. **Roger Wolcott** (1679-1767) became chief justice and governor of the colony (1751-54). His *Poetical Meditations* (1725) was the first book of verse published in Connecticut. His son **Oliver Wolcott** (1726-97) served in the Continental Congress (1775-78, 1780-84), was a signer of the Declaration of Independence, and was governor of Connecticut (1796-97). **Oliver Wolcott, Jr.** (1760-1833) was U.S. comptroller (1791-95), secretary of the treasury (1795-1800), and governor of Connecticut (1817-27).

Wolf (*Canis lupus*), powerful carnivore ranging throughout the deciduous and coniferous forests and tundra of the North-

ern Hemisphere. Broad-chested, with small, pointed ears and long legs, wolves are pack hunters, preying on the huge northern moose, deer, and elk herds. In the summer, with the onset of the breeding season and with small-mammal prey more readily available, the packs break up into smaller groups. Wolf packs have distinct territories, and within the pack there is a complex social structure under a top male and female.

Wolfe, James (1727-59), British general whose capture of Quebec was the decisive victory in the last of the French and Indian Wars. He fought in the War of the Austrian Succession (1742-45) and at Falkirk and Culloden Moor in the Jacobite rebellion (1745-46). Second in command under Amherst (1758), he distinguished himself in the capture of Louisburg and was chosen to lead the attack on Quebec. By brilliant strategy, aided by good luck, he routed the French but died during the battle.
See also: French and Indian Wars; Quebec, Battle of.

Wolfe, Thomas Clayton (1900-38), U.S. novelist whose works constitute an autobiographical epic. *Look Homeward, Angel* (1929), *Of Time and the River* (1935), and the posthumous works *The Web and the Rock* (1939) and *You Can't Go Home Again* (1940) are rich in detail and characterization and capture the author's vividly felt sense of place.

Wolffish, fish belonging to the Anarhichadidae family that lives in the northern Atlantic and Pacific oceans. It is known for its strong jaws and teeth, and for attacking its capturers, causing painful injury. The Atlantic wolffish measures up to 3 ft (91 cm) in length; the Pacific variety can grow to almost 8 ft (2.4 m) in length. It is a popular eating fish, and its tough skin is sometimes used for leather-type goods.

Wolfhound, family of hunting dogs consisting of three breeds. The borzoi, or Russian wolfhound, was first used by 17th-century Russian tsars to hunt wolves. The Irish wolfhound was first bred by the Celts and later imported to Ireland by the Romans. The Scottish deerhound, a descendent of the staghound, was once used for hunting deer. Wolfhounds are fiercely loyal and can make good companion dogs if they are given enough space for long, unrestricted runs.

Wolfram *see:* Tungsten.

Wolframite, brownish-black mineral derived from tungsten. It is commonly found in the veins in and around granite. Major ore deposits are located in England, the USSR, China, and Australia. Wolframite is used commercially in the production of electronic and industrial equipment.

Wollongong (pop. 206,800), city located in the state of New South Wales on the southeast coast of Australia. Founded in 1816, it achieved status as a city in 1942. Because of nearby coal deposits, it has become a major industrial and shipping center; its industries include coal mining, iron and steel production, chemicals, and processed foods. The city includes many examples of 19th-century Victorian and Georgian architecture.

Wollstonecraft, Mary (1759-97), British author and feminist. Her influential book, *A Vindication of the Rights of Woman* (1792), was based on the egalitarian principles of the French Revolution and promoted the cause of equal rights for women. She also wrote other essays, translations, and stories that focused attention on the role of women in society. Harshly critical of the notion that women were intellectually inferior to men, she was a strong believer in equal educational opportunities for women. She died shortly after the birth of her daughter, Mary Wollstonecraft Shelley, author of the novel *Frankenstein.*

Wolsey, Thomas (1473?-1530), Roman Catholic cardinal and politician. He became a political power during the reign of King Henry VIII, wielding great influence in both church and state matters; however, he fell into sudden disrepute due to his disapproval of Henry VIII's decision to divorce Catherine of Aragon and marry Anne Boleyn. Criticisms of his opulent way of life contributed to a growing desire for clerical reform.

Wolverine (*Gulo gulo*), large terrestrial carnivore of the weasel family, weighing up to 54 lb (24.5 kg). They live in tundra regions, the males defending a home range of up to 100 sq mi (259 sq km). Fierce animals, wolverines feed on insects, fish, small mammals, and carrion, although they have been known to attack big game, such as elk.

Wolverine State *see:* Michigan.

Woman's Relief Corps, National, U.S. patriotic organization. It became the women's auxiliary of the Grand Army of the Republic (Union veterans of the Civil War) in 1883. Its purposes include memorializing the war dead, assistance to veterans, and child welfare.

Woman suffrage, women's lawful right to vote. Under the U.S. Constitution, states initially gave voting rights to land-holding white men only. By 1830, although all states had abolished property requirements for white men, no state allowed women to vote. In the 19th century, as a result of changing social conditions and new ideas about equality, the movement for woman suffrage took shape; however, the efforts of such activists as Elizabeth Cady Stanton and Susan B. Anthony were strongly opposed. The 15th Amendment, which gave the vote to black men, still did not grant voting rights to women. During the early 20th century, an extensive and highly organized campaign to win congressional support for woman suffrage began. By 1920 more than half the states had granted either full or partial voting rights to women. With the passage of the 19th Amendment in 1920, women in the United States were given full voting rights. Women in 27 countries were also granted voting rights during the period following World War I. In 1952 the United Nations Convention on the Voting Rights of Women resolved that all women be entitled to vote in all elections. *See also:* Women's movements.

Wombat, heavy, stockily built, burrowing marsupial of Australia, closely related to the koala. Wombats share many anatomical features with placental, burrowing rodents. Nocturnal animals, they emerge from their holes to feed on grasses and roots.

Women's American ORT, affiliate of ORT (Organization for Rehabilitation through Training), an international nonprofit agency established in 1880 to provide education and job skills to Jews in many countries throughout the world. The ORT, which receives private and government funding, supports more than 800 facilities in over 20 countries. The Women's American ORT has a membership of about 145,000.

Women's Bureau, agency of the U.S. Department of Labor established in 1920 to deal with working conditions, needs, and opportunities of wage-earning women. The bureau acts as an information resource, advisory body, and advocacy group, helping employees, employers, institutions, government bodies, and international organizations with such issues as job training, placement and advancement, childcare, and sex discrimination.

Women's Christian Temperance Union (WCTU), U.S. organization seeking legislation against the consumption of alcohol. Founded in 1874, it became a worldwide organization in 1883 through the efforts of Frances Willard. It also conducts research into tobacco and narcotics.

Women's movements, organized attempts to achieve political, legal, economic, and social equality for women. Following the English common law, the U.S. legal system long assigned women a special and inferior status. Although the Constitution did not use the words "men" and "women" but always "people," "persons," and "citizens," the courts did not interpret these terms to include women. Rather, they classified women with children and imbeciles as incapable of managing their own affairs. Women were denied educations, barred from certain occupations and professions, and excluded from juries and public offices. Married women were virtually the property of their husbands. They were limited in their ability to own property, sign contracts, obtain credit, go into business, control their earnings, or write wills. The law regarded home and family as the special province of women, and it did all it could to confine them there in the belief that this was in the best interests of women themselves and of society as a whole.

Early in the 19th century, educated upper-class women began to enter public life through participation in the many reform movements of the period, especially the abolitionist crusade, often in the face of male hostility. The rebuff of women at a World Antislavery Convention in London in 1840 led directly to the organization of a U.S. women's rights movement at Seneca Falls, N.Y., in 1848.

From the start, a prime objective of the movement was to win for women the right to vote. After the Civil War, the 14th Amendment, in extending the status of citizen to former slaves, introduced the word "male" into the Constitution as a qualification for voting. The 15th Amendment, which enfranchised the former slaves, provided that the right to vote should not be denied or abridged "on account of race, color, or previous condition of servitude," but not on account of sex. When women sought the right to vote on the basis of the 14th Amendment's "privileges and immunities" and "equal protection" clauses, the courts upheld the states' authority to fix voter qualifications.

The states, however, acted to improve the position of women. During the second half of the 19th century, all the states passed Married Women's Property Acts, which largely ended the subordination of women under the common law by dissolving the legal unity of husband and wife. Married women thereby acquired control over their own property and earnings. By 1900

Wolverine

Above: The first women's rights convention (1848) was held in Seneca Falls, N.Y.

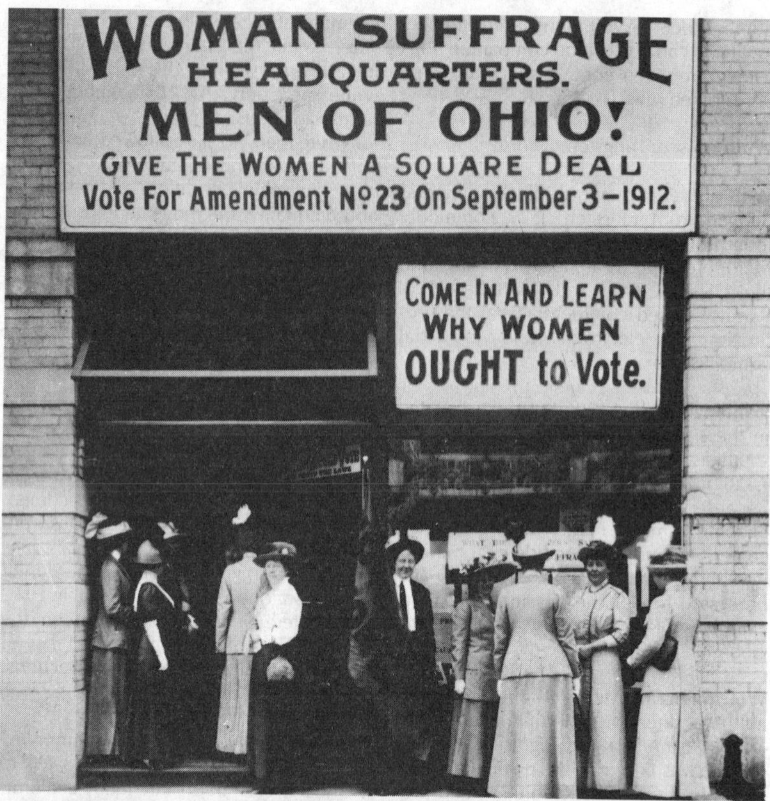

Far right: Women's suffrage was the subject of one of the amendments to Ohio's new state constitution in 1912; the amendment was not passed.

Right: Women garment workers exercising their right to better labor conditions

Below: Carrie Chapman Catt was president of the National American Women Suffrage Association in 1900.

To Mrs. Carrie Chapman Catt,
the greatest living Pioneer in the Struggle for the Rights
of Women, the sincere and grateful homage of the
Federação Brasileira pelo Progresso
Feminino
which owes its exitence to her.
Rio, November 1928.

Above center: Anna Howard Shaw was a physician, minister, and a national figure in the women suffrage movement.

Above: Women's rights has become an international issue.

Left: Gloria Steinem

women enjoyed many of the legal advantages of citizenship, the most significant exception being the right to vote. Chivalrous legislators still exempted them from certain responsibilities of citizenship, such as jury duty and poll and property taxes. This benign attitude underlay decisions of the courts early in the 20th century upholding the constitutionality of a number of state and federal laws intended to protect working women—but not men—by regulating their hours, pay, and working conditions.

In 1890 Wyoming entered the union with a state constitution providing for woman suffrage. In the next two decades many states gave women partial voting privileges. Twelve states had given women the unqualified right to vote by 1920 when ratification of the 19th Amendment secured the vote for women nationwide and established the principle of equal political rights for women.

The suffrage did not immediately bring about the removal of gender-based classifications, which, in the guise of protecting women, actually confined them to their traditional "separate place." It was, rather, the social changes resulting from 2 world wars, a major depression, and, more recently, unprecedented national affluence that revolutionized the lives of women and gave new impetus to the feminist movement. Two developments were of particular importance: The development of new and widely accessible birth-control methods liberated women from the necessity of functioning largely as child-bearers and child-rearers; and the rising flood of women into the labor force, mostly into low-paying "women's work," made women of all classes conscious of the disadvantages of their "separate place."

Feminists now perceive all gender-based classifications as discriminatory, including the legislation intended to protect women in the workplace. Not only was that legislation based on the "separate place" doctrine, but experience showed that it prevented women who wanted to do so from working overtime at premium pay, taking higher-paying jobs that required heavy work, and getting promoted to supervisory positions. A series of federal laws and executive orders has now largely nullified that protective legislation. The Equal Pay Act of 1963 legally ended discrimination on the basis of sex in the payment of wages (though in actual practice this discrimination persists). The Civil Rights Act of 1964 ended discrimination in private employment on the basis of sex as well as race, color, religion, and national origin. Executive orders have made it illegal for the federal government and for federal contractors and subcontractors to discriminate on the basis of sex.

But other legal, economic, and social inequities remain. To remove these is the goal of the modern women's movement, whose origin is usually traced to the founding of the National Organization for Women (NOW) in 1966. NOW was soon joined by numerous other women's organizations reflecting a variety of women's interests, including those of black, Hispanic, working, and poor women as well as abortion advocates and lesbians. The presence of these latter groups in the women's rights coalition provided a convenient target for opponents of the movement, who believed it to be the work of an elite of radical and professional women contemptuous of traditional values of home, family, and religion shared by many other women. As a result, by the 1970s, the women's movement in the United States was faced with a determined opposition. Progressives, following the mainstream of the traditional women's movement, continue to pursue greater individual autonomy, the elimination of all gender-based discrimination, and greater freedom and self-determination for women. Conservatives, representing a radical departure from and reversal of the goals and outlooks of the traditional women's movement, seek to maintain the traditional roles of men and women and to neutralize or reverse changes, particularly in the law, which they contend threaten the moral authority of the family. The conflict is strongest over the issue of a woman's right to have an abortion.

See also: Feminism.

Wonder, Stevie (Stevland Judkins, or Morris; 1950-), U.S. composer, keyboard player, and singer of popular music, leading Motown musician of the 1970s. "Little Stevie Wonder"'s first recorded hit, "Fingertips," became number 1 on the pop charts when he was 13. Among his many successful albums was *Songs in the Key of Life* (1976). His music combines elements of gospel, soul, jazz, and African and Jamaican music. Blind from an early age, he progressed from the harmonica to keyboards, to become a highly skilled performer on synthesizers.

Wood, hard, dead tissue obtained from the trunks and branches of trees and shrubs. Woody tissue is also found in some herbaceous plants. Botanically, wood consists of xylem tissue, which is responsible for the conduction of water around the plant. A living tree trunk is composed of (beginning from the center): the pith (remains of the primary growth); wood (xylem); cambium (a band of living cells that divide to produce new wood and phloem); phloem (conducting nutrients made in the leaves); and bark. The wood nearest the cambium is termed *sapwood* because it is capable of conducting water. However, the bulk of the wood is heartwood, in which the xylem is impregnated with lignin, which gives the cells extra strength but prevents them from conducting water. In temperate regions, a tree's age can be found by counting its annual rings. Commercially, wood is divided into hardwood (from deciduous angiosperm trees) and softwood (from gymnosperms).

Wood, Grant (1891-1942), U.S. painter, exponent of the 1930s movement known as regionalism. Influenced by Gothic and Early Renaissance painting, he realistically depicted the people and places of Iowa, as in his best-known painting, *American Gothic* (1930).

Grant Wood's American Gothic *(1930)*

Wood alcohol *see:* Methanol.

Woodcarving, old art form involving the chiseling of wood to create designs or figures. Woodcarving has played a significant role in the religious and cultural life of many of the world's great civilizations. Notable woodcarvers throughout history have achieved status as artists. Today woodcarving involves a variety of tools, including chisels of many sizes and shapes, gouges with different types of cutting edges, and parting tools for deeper cutting. Some woodcarving is done by machine on high-speed cutters.

Woodchuck, or groundhog (*Marmota monax*), familiar ground squirrel of the woodlands of North America. A large rodent, up to 2 ft (61 cm) long, with a short, bushy tail, the woodchuck is diurnal and feeds on water animals.

Woodcock, large game bird of the snipe family. One species lives in eastern North America and another in Europe and Asia. Woodcocks are very well camouflaged and are difficult to see against the forest floor. They become active at dusk, and the males fly up and down regular routes, croaking and whistling to establish a territory. They feed mainly on earthworms that they catch by thrusting their bills into the soil, opening just the tip to seize the worm.

Woodcock, Leonard (1911-), U.S. labor leader, president of the United Automobile Workers (1970-77). In 1977 he was named the first U.S. chief of mission to Communist China and served as ambassador 1979-81.

See also: United Automobile Workers.

Woodcut and wood engraving, techniques for producing pictures by incising a design on a block of wood, inking the

Detail of Four Horsemen of the Apocalypse, *one of a series, titled the* Apocalypse *(1498), of 15 woodcuts by Albrecht Dürer*

design, and then pressing the inked block onto paper. Those parts of the design that are to be white are cut away and not inked, leaving in relief the areas to be printed. Woodcut is the older method, originating in China and Japan, and used in Europe from the 14th century, particularly for book illustration. Eminent artists in the medium include Albrecht Dürer, Gauguin, and Maillol. In wood engraving the artist uses a tool called a *burin*, producing a design of white lines on a black background. It became popular in the 18th and 19th centuries.

Wood duck, bird belonging to the Anatidae family and found in the wet woodlands of southern Canada and the United States. It searches for seeds and insects in the shallow waters of swamps and ponds. It is about 20 in (51 cm) in length. The male of the species has bright multicolored feathers, while the female has feathers of yellowish brown.

Wooden, John (1910-), U.S. basketball player and coach. Between 1964-75, he led the University of California at Los Angeles (UCLA) to an unprecedented 10 National Collegiate Athletic Association (NCAA) championships, including a record 7 straight titles (1967-73) and an 88-game winning streak (1971-74). Wooden coached at Indiana State (1947-48) and UCLA (1949-75), compiling 664 career wins. A former star basketball player at the University of Purdue, he was inducted into the Basketball Hall of Fame in 1960 as both a player and a coach.

Wooden horse *see:* Trojan War.

Woodhull, Victoria Claflin (1838-1927), social reformer and first woman to run for the U.S. presidency (1872). She won support for her stand on voting rights for women, but was criticized by some suffragists for her less conventional beliefs, which included free love, communal living, and mysticism. In 1866 she and her sister Tennessee established the first female-owned brokerage firm. They also founded a weekly newspaper, which in 1872 published the first English-language translation of the *Communist Manifesto.*

Wood ibis (*Mycteria americana*), large wading bird found in the swamps of South and Central America and the southern United States. The wood ibis is not a true ibis, but a stork. It has a curved bill and feeds on water animals.

Wood louse, land-living crustacean. It has a flattened body and 7 pairs of legs. Wood lice live in moist places, under bark or stones, and come out at night to feed. Moisture is essential to wood lice, and they often bunch together to reduce evaporation. Pill wood lice can roll into a ball for protection against spiders and other predators.

Woodpecker, one of the family Picidae of birds specialized in obtaining insects from the trunks and branches of trees. The 210 species occur worldwide, except in Australasia. All have wedge-shaped tails that may be pressed against the trunk of a tree as a prop. The bill is strong and straight, and the muscles and structure of head and neck are adapted for driving the bill powerfully forward into tree bark and absorbing the shock of the blow. The tongue is long and slender for picking out insects. One group, the sapsuckers, also feeds on tree sap. Woodpeckers also use the bill during courtship "drumming" and to hack out nesting holes in tree trunks.

Woodpecker

Wood pewee, or Eastern pewee, woodland bird belonging to the flycatcher family. It lives in southern Canada and the eastern United States in the summer and migrates to Central America for the winter. It is a small, gray-brown bird with white bars on its wings. Its name is a reference to its distinctive song, which it sings at dawn and at dusk. The pewee feeds on insects that are known to destroy plants and crops.

Wood rat, or pack rat, any of 22 rat species belonging to the Cricetidae family and found in the mountains and deserts of North and Central America. It resembles the house rat but has softer fur, longer ears, and a furry tail. Its name derives from its habit of picking up small articles of interest and carrying them back to its den. Also known as *trade rat*, it will typically drop one object in favor of a more attractive one.

Woods, Granville T. (1856-1910), black U.S. inventor. Woods was largely self-taught but studied some engineering. His most important invention was a railway telegraph system (1887) for communication between moving trains and between trains and stations. Other inventions included a steam boiler furnace, an automatic air brake, and a galvanic battery. Many of his inventions were sold to General Electric and other large companies.
See also: Telegraph.

Woods Hole Oceanographic Institution, research center for marine science located at the southwest tip of Cape Cod, Mass. Its facilities include laboratories as well as deep-sea vessels. Scientists conduct research in areas such as marine biology, physics, engineering, and chemistry. Established in 1930 as a nonprofit, independent institution, it offers programs for undergraduate, doctoral, and postdoctoral students.

Woodson, Carter Goodwin (1875-1950), U.S. historian and educator who popularized African-American studies and founded the Association for the Study of Negro Life and History (1915), which trained African-American historians, collected historical documentation, and issued *The Journal of Negro History.* Woodson's works include *The Negro in Our History* (1922).

Wood sorrel *see:* Shamrock.

Woodward, Robert Burns (1917-79), U.S. chemist who won the 1965 Nobel Prize for his contributions in the field of synthetic organic chemistry. His work involved developing methods for the artificial synthesis of various chemical compounds found in nature, such as quinine, cortisone, cholesterol, and vitamin B_{12}. He was a faculty member at Harvard University from 1941 to 1979.
See also: Organic chemistry.

Woodworking, process of making objects from wood. Such objects can be of any size and may be utilitarian (houses, furniture) or

purely decorative. Many wooden objects are produced at home, and woodworking is often pursued as a hobby. By the Middle Ages the status of woodworking as a profession was formalized in organizations known as craft guilds. The use of tools to work in wood dates to about 8000 B.C. The wide variety of materials and hand tools now in use includes measuring tools (rules, squares, gauges), cutting tools (saws, chisels, planes), tools for fastening (screws, glues, hammers), and finishing tools (sandpaper, paint). Modern woodworkers such as carpenters and cabinetmakers also use power drills, saws, and other electricity-driven tools. According to the requirements of a woodworking project, wood is chosen for its hardness, pliability, durability, appearance (grain, color), and availability.
See also: Carpentry.

Wool, animal fiber that forms the fleece, or protective coat, of sheep. Coarser than most vegetable or synthetic fibers, wool fibers are wavy and vary in color from the usual white to brown or black. Wool is composed of the protein keratin, whose molecules are long, coiled chains, giving wool elasticity and resilience. Reactive side groups result in good affinity for dyes and enable new, desirable properties to be chemically imparted. Wool lasts if well cared for but is liable to be damaged by some insect larvae (which eat it), by heat, sunlight, alkalis, and hot water. It chars and smolders when burned but is not inflammable. Wool strongly absorbs moisture from the air. It is weakened when wet and liable to form felt if mechanically agitated in water. Wool has been used since ancient times to make cloth. Sheep are shorn, usually annually, and the fleeces are cleaned—the wool wax removed is the source of lanolin—and sorted, blended, carded (which disentangles the fibers and removes any foreign bodies), and combed if necessary to remove shorter fibers. A rope of woolen fibers (roving) is thus produced and is spun. The woolen yarn is woven into cloth, knitted, or made into carpets or blankets. The main wool-producing countries are Australia, New Zealand, the USSR, and India. Because the supply of new (virgin) wool is inadequate, some textiles are made of reprocessed wool.

Woolf, Virginia (1882-1941), English novelist and essayist. The daughter of Sir Leslie Stephen, she married the critic Leonard Sidney Woolf (1880-1969), and they established the Hogarth Press (1917). Their home was the center of the Bloomsbury group. Her novels *Mrs. Dalloway* (1925), *To the Lighthouse* (1927), and *The Waves* (1931) display—using the technique of stream of consciousness—her characters' thoughts and feelings about common experiences. Some of her brilliant criticism was published in *The Common Reader* (1925). She also wrote feminist tracts, including *A Room of One's Own* (1929). Subject to fits of mental instability, she drowned herself.
See also: Bloomsbury group.

Woolly monkey, or woolly spider monkey, either of two species of monkey belonging to the New World monkey family and found in the Amazon rain forest. It is a large, heavy monkey with dark, thick fur and a prehensile tail. It moves through the trees in groups of about 12, subsisting on fruit, seeds, and leaves. Its existence is threatened due to deforestation; the yellow-tailed variety is already considered very rare.

Woolworth, name of two brothers who cofounded the F.W. Woolworth Company, an extensive chain of "5-and-10-cent" stores. **Frank Winfield Woolworth** (1852-1919) was the principal founder and **Charles S. Woolworth** (1856-1947) served as vice president and later as chairman of the board. The venture, which began in Utica, N.Y., grew out of the idea that profits could be made by selling a large assortment of goods at fixed, low prices. The company later went on to operate stores in Canada, Germany, France, and Cuba.

Worcester (pop. 436,905), city in central Massachusetts on the Blackstone River. The city was established as a town in 1684, on the site of what was previously a settlement of the Nipmuc Native Americans. Colonists named the village to commemorate an English Civil War battle in which King Charles II was defeated. The city became an important industrial center in the 1800s, and its many factories attracted immigrants from all over the world. Today its hundreds of manufacturing plants produce a wide variety of products including chemicals, plastics, machinery, fabricated metals, textiles, clothing, paper, and leather. The city is also the site of many important educational, historical, and cultural institutions for the New England region.

Worden, Alfred Merrill (1932-), U.S. astronaut who piloted the *Apollo 15* command module on its journey to the moon. During the 1971 mission, he orbited the moon while astronauts David R. Scott and James B. Irwin explored its surface. On their return to earth, Worden took the first "space walk" in history, leaving the spacecraft for 20 minutes to retrieve materials from the rear of the module.
See also: Astronaut.

Word processing, use of electronic equipment to write, edit, and print documents. A word processor is basically an electronic typewriter with information storage devices similar to those of a computer and a cathode-ray-tube screen on which text is displayed. This makes it possible to edit or correct the text before it is printed out; the processor "remembers" the corrections and prints out the final version. The processor can also make the right-hand margins even (justify them) and produce documents in any desired format. The documents can be stored on magnetic disk or tape for later use. In many newspaper offices the word-processing equipment is connected directly to electronic typesetting machines.

Wordsworth, William (1770-1850), considered to be the greatest poet of the English romantic period. Known for his descriptions of nature, he derived much of his inspiration from the northern English countryside where he lived. Along with close friend and collaborator Samuel Taylor Coleridge, he believed that poetry could come out of actual experience and be written in the language of the common person. Together, they wrote *Lyrical Ballads* (1798), a collection of poems regarded as the first great works of the romantic movement. Wordsworth completed his great autobiographical poem, *The Prelude: Growth of a Poet's Mind,* in 1805, but subjected it to constant revision for the rest of his life. The author of more than 500 sonnets, he was appointed poet laureate in 1843.

Work, in physics, alternative name for energy, used particularly in discussing mechanical processes. Work of 1 joule is done when a force of 1 newton acts through a distance of 1 meter.
See also: Joule, James Prescott.

Worker's compensation, provision by employers of medical, cash, and sometimes rehabilitation benefits for workers who are injured in accidents at work. In the United States all states (Wisconsin was the first) have had worker's compensation laws since 1949, but 20% of all workers are unprotected. Railroad employees and merchant seamen are covered by other legislation. Before the first effective U.S. compensation acts, passed in 1908-11, injured employees were dependent on their employers' financial goodwill or on winning a negligence suit against them. Present laws are based on the principle of "liability without fault," which assumes that accidents are inevitable and that their costs are a legitimate business expense.

Works Progress Administration *see:* New Deal.

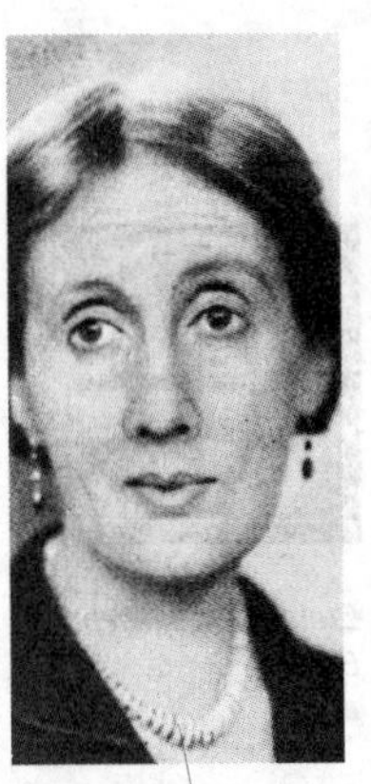
Virginia Woolf

World, term used in various ways to designate a comprehensive unity. The idea or concept of a world is ancient. Numerous cultures have proposed models for the unity of all things signified by the idea of a world. In its simplest form, the idea is suggested by the containment of a horizon, with a dome of sky above, and the ground of earth below. In pre-modern cultures, the idea of a world is never far removed from religious concerns. It is usually understood as animate and many ancient mythologies tell stories of the marriage of earth and sky. In higher cultures, animism takes on the more distinct characteristics of individual deities or spirits, gods and goddesses, and attempts are then made to explain what appears in the world, the sun and the moon, the stars, and various creatures, including humans, in terms of the workings of occult forces with which the world is understood to be infused. Another aspect of the idea of a world in its earlier forms is that it attempts to unite and explain the visible and the invisible. Most importantly, it includes a realm of the dead. In Egyptian culture, this conception took the literal form of a necropolis, or city of the dead, on the western banks of the Nile, corresponding to the city of the living on the eastern bank. Some early concepts of a world are relatively static, others dynamic and even cataclysmic. The Mayans, speculating in astronomical expanses of time, proposed the growth, fiery destruction, and birth of many worlds over the aeons. The ancient Chinese conceived of the world as the result of a ceaseless dynamic that moved according to internal laws. All of these ancient concepts of a world were graphically symbolized, many in the form of maps. Their conceptualization and elaboration was the work of many generations and inspired the arts.

The Greeks also had mythopoetic conceptions of the world peopled by gods and goddesses, but they were the first to decisively depart from the mystical and magical conceptions of the world. Greek thinkers were the first to look for reasonable answers to why the world was as it was and how things came to be. In doing so, they rejected occult explanations and put forth questions to the world, believing that the world itself was somehow reasonably organized or directed by an intelligence, resembling human intelligence. Not coincidentally, it was a Greek who worked out a reasonable approximation of the earth's circumference, and a Greek who devised star and planet charts that used to be the basis of Western astronomy until modern times. To the practical Romans, Greek concerns were too speculative. Nonetheless, the Romans further altered the content of the concept of world by conquering and organizing a vast empire. Their work as soldiers, engineers, administrators, and legislators contributed to a very practical sense of the world that was in many ways the forerunner of the modern sensibility. But the Romans were not wholly without religion; in fact, they tended to be superstitious, and as the empire aged, religion played a more and more dominant part in people's conception of the world. The most important distinction between the idea of the world in pre-modern times and the modern conception is that the Old World view had always to account for the visible and the invisible, this world and the next. The spiritualism and dualism that characterized the ancient view of the world in the West came to an end with Columbus and Copernicus.

Emblem of the World Bank

Columbus's discovery of the New World radically changed people's conception of place. It wasn't only the matter of having discovered hitherto unknown continents, but the challenge this discovery posed to all previous knowledge and the demands it made to know and measure the world as it actually was. Working within Columbus's lifetime, the Polish astronomer Nicholas Copernicus (1473-1543) reported that the earth was not the center of the universe, but rather one of several planets revolving about the central sun. The very meaning of the word *world,* in its most fundamental sense for modern peoples, begins with Columbus and Copernicus. Modern science continued to add to the concept. The idea of world retained the ancient sense of unity, but with scientific skepticism and knowledge, the world and its societal ideas were radically separated from religions and spiritual concerns. The world was no longer divided between the visible and invisible, but rather between the known and the unknown. The work of science further altered the common sense of the world thanks to Darwin. His theory of natural selection offered an explanation for the variety of life on the planet, including *Homo sapiens,* that was radically different. In absorbing the new knowledge, humans had to reconsider their position in relation to other animals.

Not only modern science but modern institutions changed people's sense of the world. Modern capital and commerce made international business possible and by the 17th century, markets in Amsterdam and London could be affected by events half a world away. Nation-states changed the way people thought of the world as well. In old Europe there had been a binding force in the ideas of a common Christendom and the Holy Roman Empire. The nation-states substituted for these ideals clearly defined territorial entities measured accurately and administered with ruthless rationalism. Printing presses and the modern printed media spread information rapidly and universally, bringing people closer to one another in their calculations and concerns.

Both the Industrial Revolution and imperialism in the 18th and 19th centuries brought to people's attention for the first time certain economic forces and conditions working on a worldwide scale. The theories of Karl Marx were an attempt to formulate the laws inherent in those forces and, combined with international socialism, to promote an understanding of the world that was opposed to the limited views and interests of nation-states and nationalism. Finally, drawing upon 2 centuries of industrial and technological development, World War I and World War II gave birth to a world united by a sense of common peril, a world with the technical capacity to utterly annihilate itself.

The modern conception of world can be considered a framework or canister for holding an ever-accumulating body of data. In 1992 there were some 5 1/3 billion people on earth and, at current rates of reproduction, there are likely to be more than 6 billion by the year 2000. Numerous species of plants and animals have become extinct, and, as pressure increases in the competition with humans for living space and food, more and more species face extinction.

Currently the world consists of 192 countries and some 45 dependencies, but boundaries are changeable and, in many places in the world, volatile. Until the early 1990s it was a common convention to divide the world's nations among the First World, consisting of the prosperous industrialized societies; the Second World, the Soviet Union; and the Third World, consisting of all the less-developed countries. Most of the Third World is concentrated in Africa, South America, and the Asian subcontinent, the southern half of the world.

Some 3,000 languages are spoken the world over, though 12 are the most widely used. The 12, in order of the numbers of people who use them, are Chinese, English, Russian, Spanish, Hindi, Arabic, Bengali, Portuguese, Japanese, German, Malay-Indonesian, and French. The 8 major religions of the world are Christianity, Islam, Buddhism, Confucianism, Hinduism, Shinto, Taoism, and Judaism. The world, as a framework or container for the data that has already been accumulated and that continues to accumulate, is virtually infinite. At the same time that it has this property of never-ending expansion, it also seems incredibly small and contracted.

Modern communications and media have made it possible to connect any 2 points on the globe instantly, for business or pleasure. Modern transport puts the entire planet within reasonable traveling distance. Common concerns suggest there may be a basis for a more genuine unity in coming to terms with overpopulation, shrinking resources, and the threat posed by a degraded environment. There are as many indications that divisions will deepen and multiply. Still we use the term *world* in numerous ways and continue to find it useful, in fact, indispensable, no matter how unstable the notion of unity it contains.

World Bank, officially the International Bank for Reconstruction and Development, specialized agency of the United Nations, founded in 1945. Its headquarters is in Washington, D.C. From capital (limited to $24 billion) it lends money to its 176 member states for investment, foreign trade, and repayment of debts. Members own shares of $100,000 and belong to the International Monetary Fund. The bank is self-sustaining and profit-making. In 1960 it set up the International Development Association.

World Council of Churches, international association of about 300 Protestant, Anglican, Eastern Orthodox, and Old Catholic

Emblem of the World Council of Churches

churches in some 90 countries. Founded 1948, with headquarters in Geneva, it promotes Christian unity, religious liberty, missionary cooperation, interfaith doctrinal study, and service projects such as refugee relief.
See also: Christianity.

World Court *see:* International Court of Justice.

World government, theoretical organization with the authority and power to maintain law order throughout the world. The idea first began in the 1300s and the massive destruction caused by World Wars I (1914-18) and II (1939-45) has led to a revival of the concept. Supporters see the creation and effective leadership of the United Nations as a positive model and test case for a world government.

World Health Organization (WHO), specialized agency of the United Nations founded in 1948 and based in Geneva. Its services are available to all nations and territories. WHO advises countries on how to develop health services, combat epidemics, and promote health education and standards of nutrition. It also coordinates the standardization of drugs and health statistics and studies pollution.

World Intellectual Property Organization (WIPO), international agency, part of the United Nations (UN), that protects the legal rights of intellectual property, such as inventions, trademarks, literary and artistic works, and other original ideas. Founded in 1967, WIPO became part of the UN in 1974 and has a membership of over 110 countries. Its headquarters are located in Geneva, Switzerland.

World Jewish Congress, international body, representing Jewish organizations from over 70 countries, whose goals are to maintain Jewish unity, culture, and religion. Founded in 1936, the congress was active during World War II (1939-45), helping Jews escape Nazi persecution, and in the 1970s, securing the release of thousands of Jews from the USSR. Its headquarters are located in New York City.
See also: Jews.

World Meteorological Organization (WMO), specialized agency of the United Nations, established in Geneva in 1951 to promote international meteorological observation and standardization.

World's fair, international exposition of science and technology, entertainment, and culture. The first such fair was the Great Exhibition of 1851 in London. World's fairs have frequently displayed new inventions and feats of engineering, such as the telephone (Philadelphia, 1876), the Eiffel Tower (Paris, 1889), the automobile (St. Louis, 1904), and television (New York, 1939). More recently, fairs have had central themes such as outer space or the oceans. World's fairs have been held all over the world.

World Trade Center, twin towers (each 110 stories) rising 1,350 ft (411 m) over lower Manhattan in New York City. Completed in 1973, they were the tallest buildings in the world until 1974, when they were surpassed by the Sears Tower in Chicago. The center was designed by Minoru Yamasaki and Emery Roth and cost $750 million to build.
See also: Skyscraper.

World War I, global conflict waged from 1914 to 1918 that caused more destruction and involved more participants than any other conflict up to that time. The war's spread was facilitated by an interlocking system of military alliances that Europe had forged during the previous decades, ostensibly to keep the peace. These alliances comprised the Central Powers (primarily Germany and Austria-Hungary) and the Allies (primarily Russia, France, and Great Britain). Later, other nations joined one or the other of the blocks.

Causes of the war. The underlying causes of the conflict involved the rise of nationalism in Europe, the military buildup pursued by parties of both alliances, and the competition among various European countries for colonies. The immediate cause of the war was the assassination of Austrian Crown Prince Francis Ferdinand at Sarajevo on June 28, 1914, by a Serbian nationalist. Austria, looking for a pretext to suppress Slavic nationalist aspirations in the Austro-Hungarian Empire, declared war on Serbia (July 28), with the approval of Germany. Russia announced full mobilization (July 30), and France rejected a German demand that she declare herself neutral.

Reconstruction of a World War I trench system

The two fronts. Germany declared war on Russia (Aug. 1) and on France (Aug. 3) and invaded neutral Belgium, the shortest route to Paris, in search of a quick victory in the west before Russia had time to muster all its forces in the east. The invasion prompted Britain to enter the war (Aug. 4) in support of Belgium and France. All the major members of the alliances were now committed to war.

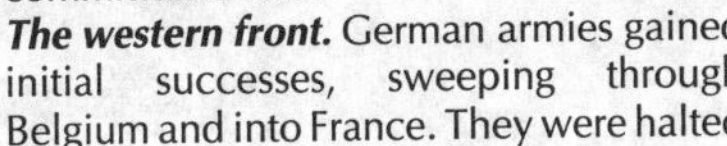

The western front. German armies gained initial successes, sweeping through Belgium and into France. They were halted

Emblem of the World Health Organization

Prelude to World War I: a cartoon of the German kaiser Wilhelm II breaking his teeth on the British-French-Russian Triple Entente (1907)

Right: British demonstration (1917) against World War I

Far right:German picture postcard of Kaiser Wilhelm II visiting the graves of German soldiers killed in World War I. The caption reads "I did not want this."

Below: British soldiers departing Victoria Station, London

During World War I barbed-wire barricades were employed for the first time on a wide scale.

World War I aerial dogfight between German and British planes

Philippe Petain, the hero of Verdun, became commander-in-chief of the French army in 1917.

at the Marne River (First Battle of the Marne, Sept. 6-9, 1914) by French forces led by Gen. Joseph Joffre. This battle ended German hopes of quickly overrunning its opponents in the west, and by late Nov. 1914 war on the western front settled into a dreadful stalemate. For the next 3½ years, terrible trench warfare raged along a 450-mile (724-km)-long front extending across Belgium and northeastern France to the Swiss border.

The eastern front. In late Aug. 1914 the Russians invaded East Prussia, but were defeated by the Germans in the battles of Tannenberg and the Masurian Lakes, suffering about 250,000 Russian casualties. Austria-Hungary was less successful, failing to capture Serbia and losing its province of Galicia to the Russians. In Oct. 1914 Turkey joined the Central Powers against Russia. In a vain attempt to aid the Russians, the Allies in early 1915 sent a fleet to the Dardanelles and ground forces to the Gallipoli Peninsula. The thrust proved unsuccessful, and troops were evacuated in Dec. 1915 with losses of about 250,000.

Outside Europe. After the Gallipoli disaster, the Allies attacked Turkey through her empire in the Middle East, and were largely successful, leaving her in possession of little more than Anatolia. Farther afield, British, French, and South African troops overran Germany's African possessions, while the Japanese (who had entered the war in Sept. 1914) and Australasian troops captured German possessions in the Far East and the Pacific.

Attrition in the West. In 1915 Italy joined the Allies and engaged the Austrian army in the Alps. In 1916 German forces were repulsed in their attempt to take the French city of Verdun with fearful losses on both sides (about 315,000 casualties for the French and 280,000 for the Germans). Paul von Hindenburg and Erich Ludendorff, the heroic leaders of German forces in the east, took command in the west, Hindenburg as chief of general staff with Ludendorff his aide.

An Allied offensive late in the year (the Battle of the Somme), led principally by the British, was also unsuccessful, and by its end it had cost the Germans over 600,000 casualties, the British over 400,000, and the French nearly 200,000. Britain maintained a naval blockade of the continent while German submarines harassed Allied mercantile shipping. An attempt by the German fleet to lift the blockade at Jutland (May 1916) failed.

The final stages. In Mar. 1917 the Russian people, sick of the war that had cost them dearly, revolted and overthrew Tsar Nicholas II. In Apr. 1917 V.I. Lenin returned to Russia from his exile in Switzerland, and 7 months later, as head of the revolutionary Bolshevik government, sued for peace with Germany. The Germans dictated a harsh peace between the 2 nations in Mar. 1918 at Brest-Litovsk. The sinking of 3 U.S. merchant ships in Mar. 1917 together with the discovery of a German plan to try to persuade Mexico to go to war against the United States (the "Zimmermann Telegram") caused the United States to declare war on the Central Powers in Apr. 1917. The American Expeditionary Forces, led by Gen. John J. Pershing, began arriving in France in mid-1917. Despite a massive final German offensive in 1918 that drove the Allies back to the Marne, Allied forces, boosted by U.S. contingents, eventually began to tell. In September the Hindenburg Line was breached. The Central Powers sued for peace, and an armistice went into effect on Nov. 11, 1918. The Treaty of Versailles (June 28, 1919), imposed on Germany, formalized the Allied victory. The dead on both sides totaled about 10 million.

Aftermath of the war. Europe had spent much of its economic resources on the war and was exhausted and in debt. The dissolution of old empires in Europe and Turkey spawned a host of new countries and allegiances, and the United States, unscathed in the war, emerged as the economic world power. An era of European dominance was clearly coming to an end, and a new, but very unsettled, world order was in the making.

World War II, second global conflict lasting from 1939 to 1945 that involved civilian populations on an unprecedented scale. Military deaths probably amounted to some 17 million, but civilian deaths were undoubtedly much higher because of mass bombing of cities, starvation, epidemics, massacres, and other war-related causes. The parties to the conflict involved nearly every major power in the world, divided into 2 groups: the Allies (principally Great Britain, the United States, the Soviet Union, and China) and the Axis Powers (principally Germany, Italy, and Japan). The development—and use—of the atomic bomb late in the war ushered in the nuclear age.

Causes of the war. The conflict arose because of the increasing military might of the aggressive, totalitarian regimes in Germany, Italy, and Japan following World War I. The harsh terms of the Treaty of Versailles after World War I had left Germany bitter and unstable, and hard economic times plagued much of the world in the 1920s and 1930s. These conditions fostered fascistic dictatorships in Germany and Italy, and Japan became aggressively militaristic and expansionist in Asia. Attempts to contain the aggressive impulses of these states through the League of Nations (which the U.S. did not join) proved ineffectual. With the rise of Hitler and Nazism to power in Germany (1933), the Versailles arrangements began to crumble. Germany rearmed and, on the pretext of defending German ethnic nationals in certain neighboring countries, laid claim to some of their territories. Hitler annexed Austria in Mar. 1938 (the *Anschluss*) and obtained the Sudetenland (in Czechoslovakia) through the Munich Pact (Sept. 1938). The policy of appeasement practiced at Munich failed, however, as Germany in Mar. 1939 occupied the rest of Czechoslovakia. On Aug. 23, 1939, Germany signed a non-aggression pact with its former arch enemy the Soviet Union, clearing the way for Hitler to move westward.

Outbreak of the war. Germany invaded Poland on Sept. 1, 1939. France and Britain responded by declaring war on Germany (Sept. 3). Germany, using the blitzkrieg strategy of speed and surprise, soon overran most of Poland, and on Sept. 17 Soviet forces invaded Poland from the east. By the end of September the Soviets had occupied the eastern third of Poland while Germany held all the rest. The Soviet Union continued with invasions of Finland and the Baltic states, as Germany went on to swift conquests of Denmark and Norway (Apr. 1940), and in May overran the Low Countries and invaded France. By June German troops had swept through France to the English Channel. British forces, almost trapped by the Germans, effected a desperate evacuation from Dunkirk back to England. France accepted an armistice on June 11, although Free French forces led by Gen. Charles de Gaulle continued the struggle. With Germany and Italy dominant on the continent, Hitler turned his sights on Britain, and attempted to bomb the nation into submission. Inspired by their leader, Winston Churchill, the British held firm and the Royal Air Force thwarted the effort in the Battle of Britain. In May 1941 Hitler broke off the massive air attack and began rebuilding his depleted air force. He continued, however, to harass British shipping with submarine warfare in the North Atlantic principally. On June 22 Germany invaded the Soviet Union, bringing that country, under its leader Joseph Stalin, into the war. Surprised, the Soviet forces initially suffered heavy losses. However, with Moscow and Leningrad surrounded and under siege, resistance stiffened. Also, a severe winter in 1941 caused enormous hardship for the German army, and they were never able to fully capture either city. Late in 1941 Germany and Italy found a new ally in Japan, whose aggressive militarism was bent on the conquest of Eastern Asia and the Western Pacific. On Dec. 7, 1941, Japan surprised and crippled the U.S. fleet at Pearl Harbor, Hawaii. President Franklin Roosevelt asked for, and obtained, an immediate U.S. declaration of war.

Turn of the tide. Though the United States initially fared badly in the Pacific, its first major victories were recorded at Coral Sea and Midway (June 1942). In North Africa, Allied supremacy was established at the Battle of El Alamein (Oct.-Nov. 1942). On the eastern front the Germans lost an army at the siege of Stalingrad (early 1943), and Soviet forces began to push the invader back. Sicily fell to Anglo-American forces in July 1943, and the Italian dictator Benito Mussolini was driven from power.

D-Day (June 6, 1944) signaled the last phase of the war in Europe, as Allied troops stormed across the Channel and invaded Normandy. By Sept. 1944 German forces, already expelled from the Soviet Union, had been driven out of France and Belgium. The Battle of the Bulge (Dec. 1944) proved to be the final German coun-

World War II U.S. fighting soldiers. From left to right: Sergeant, Army Signal Corps; Master Sergeant, U.S. Infantry; Corporal, U.S. Marine Corps; Platoon Sergeant, U.S. Marine Corps; Private, U.S. Army (Merrill's Marauders); Private First Class, U.S. Infantry.

Right: Japanese Kamikaze pilots

Far right: The USS Franklin listing after taking a hit from the Japanese (March 1945)

Below, far right: A German soldier sitting among the ruins of the Berlin Reichstag

The Mustang P51-D, considered by many the outstanding piston-engined fighter of all time

The Mitsubishi, a carrier-based fighter introduced by the Japanese in 1942

German submarines (U-boats) figured prominently in the strategies of World War II

This Russian tank played a major role in resisting the German invasion of 1941

The German 88mm gun, Germany's main air-defense weapon in World War II

The Supermarine Spitfire VB, first flown in 1936, became symbolic of British air power in World War II.

Above: U.S. troops during the landing on New Britain

Above, right: The German field marshal Erwin Rommel was known as the "desert fox" for his brilliant military strategies.

Right: Concentration camp inmates

The Messerschmitt was the most formidable German fighter in the Battle of Britain.

teroffensive. By Jan. 1945 the Allies resumed their drive into Germany; the Russians captured East Germany, and the Allies broke the Siegfried Line in March. As Russian forces at last entered Berlin, Hitler committed suicide (Apr. 30, 1945) and 8 days later all German resistance ended. The fate of conquered Europe was subsequently settled at the Yalta Conference and the Potsdam Conference, although Germany itself was not reunited into one country until 1990.

Defeat of Japan. Since 1943 Allied forces had been eroding Japanese power in the Pacific and Asia. By mid-1945 island-hopping assaults by U.S. forces, culminating in Iwo Jima and Okinawa, had largely swept Japan from the Western Pacific. The Soviet Union declared war on Japan and occupied Manchuria, and U.S. and Allied forces were massing in the Pacific for an invasion of the Japanese homeland. President Harry Truman ordered the dropping of the atomic bomb on Hiroshima and Nagasaki (Aug. 6 and 9), and on Aug. 14 Japan accepted unconditional terms of surrender.

Aftermath of the war. The stupendous destruction of World War II left much of the world in ruins, with the Soviet Union and the United States emerging as the 2 world superpowers. A struggle, known as the Cold War, soon developed between the Communist world, led by the Soviet Union, and the non-Communist world, led by the United States. Perhaps most important of all, the horror of nuclear devastation was introduced as a possibility in any future global conflict.

Worm, term used for any elongate, cylindrical invertebrate, such as the earthworm, roundworm, hairworm, or acorn worm. The word has no taxonomic validity; animals commonly referred to as worms belong to many related phyla: Chordata, Annelida, and Platyhelminthes. However, the term is sometimes restricted to the phylum Annelida.

Worms (pop. 71,827), city in southwestern Germany, situated on the Rhine River. Its main industries include the manufacture of chemicals, furniture, leather goods, and machinery. It is also a famous wine producer. Founded in 14 B.C. by Roman soldiers, Worms has a Romanesque cathedral that dates from the 1000s, and what may be Europe's oldest Jewish cemetery, also from the 1000s.

Worms, Edict of, civil decree issued at Worms, Germany, in 1521, denouncing religious reformer Martin Luther as a heretic, banning his writings, and calling for his capture. The question of whether or not to enforce the edict was a subject of great controversy until a truce was declared in 1555 with the Peace of Augsburg.
See also: Luther, Martin; Reformation.

Wormwood, group of herbs and shrubs in the composite family, found chiefly in arid regions of the Northern Hemisphere. Wormwood is grown commercially to provide an essential oil that has a variety of medicinal uses. The leaves of another type of wormwood, tarragon, is used as a seasoning. Common wormwood, or mugwort, is used in medicines and in the manufacture of absinthe.

Worsted, type of yarn known for its strength and its smooth, shiny texture. It was first produced in Worsted, England. It is made by combing the wool fibers into parallel layers before they are spun. Worsted yarns are frequently used in knitting. The term *worsted* also refers to any fabric made with worsted yarns.

Wouk, Herman (1915-), U.S. author of novels and plays. His work often draws on his own naval experiences during World War II. In 1952 he won the Pulitzer Prize in fiction for his war novel, *The Caine Mutiny* (1951), which was later adapted for stage and screen. Other popular novels that were adapted for the screen include *Marjorie Morningstar* (1955), *The Winds of War* (1971), and *War and Remembrance* (1978).

Wounded Knee, Battle of, massacre by U.S. soldiers of more than 200 Sioux men, women, and children at Wounded Knee Creek, S.D., on Dec. 29, 1890, in the last major battle of the Indian Wars. In 1973, 200 members of the American Indian Movement (AIM) occupied the Wounded Knee Reservation for 69 days, demanding a Senate investigation into the conditions of Native Americans.
See also: Indian wars.

Wovoka (1858?-1932), also known as Jack Wilson, Nevada-born Paiute Native American who originated the ghost-dance religion practiced by Native Americans of the West. In 1889, while ill with a fever, he had a prophetic vision during a solar eclipse. In the vision, the Great Spirit told him that if his people lived in harmony and performed certain rituals, the foreign settlers would leave, Paiute ancestors would be brought back to life, and they would live long, happy lives. Wovoka, the son of a Paiute prophet, was adopted as a boy by David Wilson, a European-American settler.

WPA *see:* New Deal.

Wrangel Island, island belonging to the USSR and located in the Arctic Ocean, about 90 miles north of Siberia. Whalers from the United States discovered the uninhabited island in 1867. Despite the claims of the United States and Canada, the USSR sent settlers there in 1926. The land is icy and barren during most of the year. Polar bears, walruses, and birds can be found there. It is inhabited by about 50 people who fish and hunt for a living.

Wrangell-St. Elias National Park, largest U.S. national park, located in southeastern Alaska. The park measures about 14,000 sq mi (36,000 sq km). Its terrain includes numerous glaciers and some of the tallest mountain peaks in North America. Animal life includes bears, caribou, moose, sea otters, and trumpeter swans.
See also: National Parks.

Wren, name of several groups of small birds. The true wrens are the Troglodytidae, a family of 60 species of small perching birds. The name is also used for some 80 species (family Malurinae) of warblers of Australia and New Guinea, and the New Zealand wrens (family Xenicidae). True

The Royal Navy Hospital in Greenwich, England, designed by Christopher Wren (begun in 1694)

wrens are small, compact birds with short to long tails cocked upward. They occur in Central and North America.

Wren, Sir Christopher (1632-1723), English architect, astronomer, mathematician. Wren is best remembered as architect of St. Paul's Cathedral (1710) and over 50 other churches that were rebuilt after having been destroyed by the Great Fire of London (1666). A widely respected astronomer, he was appointed professor of Gresham College, London (1657), served on the faculty of Oxford University (1661-73), and was a founder of the Royal Society (1660).
See also: Architecture; Astronomy.

Wrestling, in the West, sport in which 2 persons grapple and try to pin one another's shoulders to the floor by means of various holds. An ancient Greek sport, wrestling became a recognized Olympic sport in 1904. In the United States the preferred form is the free-style, or catch-as-catch-can. The Greco-Roman form, popular in Europe, forbids holds below the waist. Bouts are divided into 3 periods of 3 minutes each. The match is over when a wrestler pins both his opponent's shoulders for the count of 3 (a fall). Matches can also be won on points awarded by the referee for skilled maneuvers.

Wright, Frances (1795-1852), Scottish-born U.S. reformer for women's rights, public education, and the abolition of slavery. Wright lectured on women's right to divorce and birth control. She also founded the short-lived Nashoba community (1825-27) near Memphis, Tenn., where slaves worked to buy their freedom. A member of the utopian New Harmony community in Indiana, Wright was coeditor of its magazine the *Gazette* and also coedited the *Free Enquirer* of New York City.
See also: Women's movements.

Wright, Frank Lloyd (1869-1959), 20th-century U.S. architect. He studied engineering, joined the architect Louis Sullivan, and was influenced by the Arts and Crafts movement. His pioneering "prairie style" (Robie House; 1908-09)—strong, horizontal lines; low-pitched, hipped roofs; open plan; and change of internal levels—influenced De Stijl. He articulated massive forms clearly (Larkin Building, 1904) and, though he liked natural materials and locations, was innovative in his use of reinforced concrete, dramatic cantilevering, and screen walls (Kaufmann House, or Falling Water, 1936-37; Johnson's Wax Building, 1936-49; Guggenheim Museum, 1946-59).
See also: Architecture.

Wright, Quincy (1890-1970), U.S. political scientist, an expert on international law. He was a supporter of the League of Nations and United Nations. His books include *A Study of War* (2 vol., 1942) and *The Study of International Relations* (1955).

Wright, Richard (1908-60), U.S. novelist and social critic. His works include *Uncle Tom's Children* (1938), stories of Southern racial prejudice; *Native Son* (1940), about a victimized black in Chicago; and *Black Boy* (1945), his autobiography.

Wright brothers, name of two U.S. inventors; designers and builders of the world's first successful airplane (1903). Inspired by the work of Otto Lilienthal, who did pioneering work with gliders in the 1890s, the Wrights, **Wilbur** (1867-1912) and **Orville** (1871-1948), conducted experiments with kites and gliders (1899-1902) to develop and test theories of control and lift. Their powered airplane was first tested Dec. 17, 1903, at Kill Devil Hill, near Kitty Hawk, N.C. The machine weighed 750 lb (340 kg), with wings 40 ft (12 m) long. The Wrights continued experimental flights, receiving little attention in the United States but arranging for production of planes in France and Germany. After Wilbur Wright's death, his brother continued work to perfect the airplane. The Wrights were elected posthumously to the Hall of Fame for Great Americans. Their original plane is now exhibited in the National Air and Space Museum, Washington, D.C.
See also: Airplane.

Wrist, or carpus, particularly in humans, joint between the hand and forearm, along with the connecting 8 small carpal bones. The wrist joint connects the long *radius* bone of the forearm to the carpal bones of the hand. The tendons and muscles that connect the arm to the finger bones control movement of the fingers. A joint connects the *ulna* of the forearm to the parallel radius rather than to the carpal bones, allowing the free rotation of the wrist.

Writ, written order of a court of law. Under English common law, a writ had to be issued before any legal action could be initiated. Most ancient writs have been replaced by summonses and declarations, but some—such as writs of certiorari, habeas corpus, and mandamus—survive.

Writing, in business, career in such diverse areas as technical writing, journalism, fiction and poetry, and screenplay and script writing. *Staff writers* have salaried jobs with newspapers and magazines, in company public relations departments, at advertising agencies, and elsewhere. However, writing services are largely provided by *freelance writers* who are hired for particular projects (e.g., computer manuals, encyclopedia articles) or who create their own articles, scripts, and so on, which they then attempt to sell to various publishers and producers. Writers, particularly those already well established, may work through a *literary agent* to place a manuscript with a buyer. Only a small percentage of fiction writers and a handful of poets actually make a living from their creative writing.

Writing, visual representation of human language and other communication according to social convention. Early writing included marks used for counting and pictures representing situations and objects. Pictures developed into *ideographs*, symbolic representations of ideas rather than of speech. The more advanced and abstract *logographs*, which represent actual elements of speech, were first developed by the Sumerians c.3500 B.C. The Sumerians also began to develop phonetic representations, or *syllabograms*. While this *cuneiform* writing of the Sumerians spread through the Middle East, the Egyptians developed *hieroglyphics*. The complex Chinese system of writing developed c.1500 B.C. Further developments led to the Phoenician alphabet, representing consonants, the Greek alphabet, representing consonants and vowels, and the Japanese alphabet, representing consonant-vowel combinations.

Sequoyah, a Cherokee Native American, with the Cherokee script of 85 characters that he introduced in 1821. He was convinced that a written language was the key to power.

Writ of assistance, general search warrant issued to customs officers by American colonial courts from 1751. Their use to enforce import duties was imposed by the 1767 Townshend Acts and caused a major furor among the colonists. By 1772 many colonial courts were refusing to issue them. These writs were mentioned by the Declaration of Independence as one of the grievances of the colonies against England.

Wroclaw (German: *Breslau*; pop. 637,200), city in southwestern Poland, capital of Wroclaw province; located in the region of Dolny lsk (Lower Silesia) on the Oder River. The trade center of Wroclaw was established in the 10th century on the site of a Stone Age settlement. Originally Polish, the city came under control of

John Wycliffe reading the Bible to John of Ghent

Austria in 1526 and Prussia in 1742. Under the name of Breslau it was a part of Germany from 1871 to 1945, when it was returned to Poland. Modern Wroclaw is an industrial, transportation, and communication center. Manufactures include machinery, electronics, textiles, and food products.
See also: Poland.

Wryneck, jynx, or snakebird (genus *Jynx*), small, gray-brown, insect-eating bird of the Eastern Hemisphere, named for the snakelike hissing and movement of its head and neck when it is threatened. The 2 species, often considered members of the woodpecker family, are the Eurasian wryneck (*J. torquilla*) and the African red-breasted wryneck (*J. ruficollis*).

Wu, Chien-shiung (1912?-), U.S. experimental physicist. In 1957 her experiments in particle physics disproved the law of the conservation of parity, a long-held theory that the direction in which beta particles are emitted from a radioactive nucleus is not related to the direction of spin of the nucleus. Her work confirmed the theory of physicists Tsung Dao Lee and Chen Ning Yang (who shared the 1957 Nobel Prize in physics) that the direction of spin affects the predominant direction of such emissions. Her experimental work also helped confirm theoretical work of Richard P. Feynman and Murray Gell-Mann. Wu emigrated from China to study at the University of California, Berkeley. She worked at Columbia University from 1944, first in the Division of War Research and after 1957 as a professor.
See also: Parity; Physics.

Wuchang *see:* Wuhan.

Wuhan (pop. 3,340,000), city in east-central China comprised of the former cities of Hankou, Hanyang, and Wuchang. Located at the confluence of the Yangtze and Han rivers, Wuhan is a major commercial, transportation, and industrial (iron and steel production) center.
See also: China.

Wundt, Wilhelm (1832-1920), German psychologist and philosopher. He thought that research psychologists should combine laboratory work with an examination of their own thoughts and feelings. In 1879 he started a laboratory in which his ideas on experimental psychology were practiced.
See also: Psychology.

Wyatt, Sir Thomas (1503?-42), English poet of the early Renaissance. He and Henry Howard, earl of Surrey, translated and introduced Italian poetry and poetic forms to English literature. They are generally credited with having written the first sonnets in English. Wyatt, a lover of Anne Boleyn before her marriage, was known for his wit and charm in the court of King Henry VIII, and served his country as a diplomat to the European continent. In addition to sonnets, he wrote lyrics for lute accompaniment, epigrams, and satires. His poems were first published in Tottel's *Miscellany*, a famous early Renaissance collection.
See also: Renaissance.

Wycliffe, John (1328?-84), British religious reformer, created first English translation of the Latin Bible. He lived during a time that saw the roles of church and state seriously questioned. Siding with the common people against both corrupt church and civil rulers, he claimed that obedience was due only to God. For his beliefs and writings on this subject, he was tried several times, unsuccessfully. Protected by England's royal family, he wrote vehement attacks against the church, fighting in large part against its hypocrisy and in favor of the rights of the poor. Subsequent religious reformers, including the Protestants of the Reformation in the 16th century, considered Wycliffe a major influence.
See also: Reformation.

Wyeth, Andrew (1917-), U.S. painter. His work depicts scenes of strange, lonely rural life in a highly detailed style that seems almost photographic. His best-known picture is *Christina's World* (1948).

Wyler, William (1902-81), U.S. film director. He won Academy Awards for *Mrs. Miniver* (1942), *The Best Years of Our Lives (1946)*, and *Ben Hur* (1958). His other films include *Wuthering Heights* (1939), *Friendly Persuasion* (1956), and *Funny Girl* (1968).

Wylie, Elinor (1885-1928), U.S. poet and novelist. Her well-crafted verse appeared in 4 volumes during the 1920s and included *Nets to Catch the Wind* (1921), *Black Armour* (1923), *Trivial Breath* (1928), and *Angels and Earthly Creatures* (posthumously published in 1929). She usually wrote in traditional forms, including the sonnet. She also wrote 4 historical novels, including *Jennifer Lorn* (1923).

Wyoming

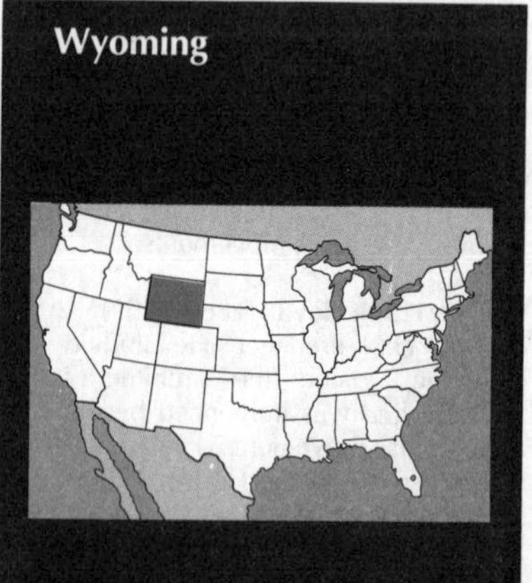

Capital:	Cheyenne
Statehood:	July 10, 1890 (44th state)
Familiar name:	Equality State
Area:	97,809 sq mi (253,326 sq km); ranks 9th
Population:	455,975 (1990); ranks 50th
Elevation:	Highest—13,804 ft (4,207 m), Gannett Peak; Lowest—3,100 ft (945 m), Belle Fourche River
Motto:	Equal Rights
Flower:	Indian paintbrush
Bird:	Meadowlark
Tree:	Cottonwood
Song:	"Wyoming"

The Great Plains in eastern Wyoming

Wyoming, state in the Rocky Mountain region of northwestern United States; bordered by Montana to the north, South Dakota and Nebraska to the east, Colorado to the south, Utah to the south and west, and Utah, Idaho, and Montana to the west.
Land and climate. Wyoming has the second-highest average elevation of any state (Colorado's is highest). Part of the Continental Divide runs northwest to southeast through central Wyoming. Wyoming has three major land regions. The Rocky Mountains in western, central, and southeastern Wyoming. The Rocky Mountains region is separated in central and northern Wyoming by the Intermontane Basins, which are relatively flat, treeless areas separating various sections of high mountain peaks. The Great Plains, in eastern Wyoming, is a region consisting of flat or gently rolling grassland. Three major river systems rise in the Rocky Mountains of Wyoming: the Missouri, the Colorado, and the Columbia. Forests cover about one-sixth of the state. Yellowstone National Park, in the state's northwestern corner, has the world's largest geyser, magnificent waterfalls, and deep canyons. Wyoming's climate is dry, with warm, brief summers and long, cold winters. Principal cities are Casper and Cheyenne.
Economy. Mining and service industries (including tourism) lead Wyoming's economy. Chief mining products are petroleum, natural gas, coal, uranium, sodium carbonate, clays, Portland cement, and crushed stone. Manufacturing and agriculture account for only a small share of the gross state product. Chief manufactured goods are chemicals, nonelectrical machinery, processed foods, lumber and wood products, refined petroleum products, and stone, clay, and glass products. Ranching is the leading agricultural activity; chief livestock products are beef cattle, milk, sheep, and wool; chief crops are hay, barley, wheat, sugar beets, corn, and beans.
Government. Wyoming's constitution was adopted in 1889. The governor serves a 4-year term. The state legislature consists of 30 senators serving 4-year terms and 64 representatives serving 2-year terms. In the U.S. Congress, Wyoming is represented by 2 senators and 1 representative.
History. Native American hunters were the area's first residents; the first Europeans—French fur trappers—arrived in the mid-1700s. John Colter, an American trapper, made the first records of the Yellowstone region in 1807. Over the next 30 years, the fur trade developed and European-American settlers passed through Wyoming on the Oregon Trail. Native Americans fought foreign encroachment on their lands (1849-76) until the U.S. Army wiped out or divided their forces. The Territory of Wyoming was created by Congress in 1868; in 1869 it became the first state or territory to give women the right to vote. Cattle and oil industries developed in the 1880s; in 1890 Wyoming became the 44th state. In 1892 the bitter Johnson County War broke out between cattle ranchers and sheep herders; tensions and occasional violence lasted into the early 1900s. Federal homestead acts brought new waves of settlers to the state in the early 1900s; 1912 brought the state's first oil boom. In 1924 Wyoming elected the nation's first woman governor, Nellie Tayloe Ross. Wyoming was hard hit by the Dust Bowl and the Great Depression of the 1930s but, since World War II, uranium and tourist industries have prospered; the state's population grew by 42% from 1970 to 1980. The 1980s brought economic decline and a drop-off in population. Wyoming's leaders are seeking more diverse industries to revive its economy.

Wyoming Valley, valley in northeastern Pennsylvania and scene of a bloody battle during the Revolutionary War. The valley, which is rich with hard coal, is about 20 mi (32 km) long and 3 mi (5 km) wide. On July 3, 1778, 200 British loyalists together with 600 Native Americans raided the valley and killed almost 200 settlers.

Wyoming Valley Massacre, event in the American Revolutionary War. A force of Loyalists, Butler's Rangers, and Iroquois led by John Butler defeated a band of 300 Connecticut settlers led by Zebulon Butler in Wyoming Valley, Pa., in July 1778. A massacre ensued in which the Iroquois butchered the survivors. The incident horrified both sides; it made the English wary of Native American allies and prompted George Washington to attack the Iroquois (1779).
See also: Revolutionary War in America.

Wyss family, authors of and models for the famous children's story *The Swiss Family Robinson*. The story of a family's life and survival alone on an island was first created and written down by **Johann David Wyss** (1743-1818) as an entertainment for his children. Many years later in 1812, one of his sons, **Johann Rudolf** (1781-1830), who was at the time a well-known Swiss editor of folklore, edited and published his father's account. The novel was an instant success and was translated into English in 1814. The book, now available in many languages, is still a popular children's book.
See also: Children's literature.

Wyszynski, Stefan Cardinal (1901-81), Polish Catholic cardinal, archbishop of Warsaw, and primate of Poland. Arrested for his attacks on the Communist government's persecution of the church in 1953, he was released after Wladyslaw Gomulka's rise to power (1956). His funeral was a national event attended by Pope John Paul II.
See also: Poland.

Wythe, George (1726-1806), judge, friend of Thomas Jefferson and first U.S. law professor at the College of William and Mary (1779-90). A member of the Second Continental Congress (1775-77) and a signer of the Declaration of Independence, he was judge of the Virginia high court of chancery (1788-1806).

X

X, 24th letter of the English alphabet, corresponding to the 21st letter of the Latin alphabet, which was itself derived from a letter of the western subdivision of the ancient Greek alphabet representing the sound "ks." The same letter in the eastern Greek alphabet represented "ch" or "kh," and as such passed into the later Greek and Cyrillic alphabets. X represents 10 in Roman numerals, and in algebra and in the sciences it is used as the symbol for an unknown quantity.

X and Y chromosomes, or sex chromosomes, cell nuclei that determine the sex of a person (as well as carrying some genetic information not related to sex determination). Sex chromosomes are inherited in the same way as the other 22 human chromosome pairs, normal persons being either XX (female) or XY (male). The Y chromosome carries little genetic information, and it is largely the properties of the X chromosome that determine sex-linked characteristics in males. Sex-linked characteristics include hemophilia and color blindness, which are carried as recessive genes in females.
See also: Chromosome.

Xavier, Saint Francis (Spanish: Francisco Javier; 1506-52), Spanish missionary. A friend of St. Ignatius of Loyola, he helped him found the order of Jesuits. In 1541 he set out as a missionary, reaching the East Indies, Goa, India, Malacca, and Ceylon. In 1549 he established a Jesuit mission in Japan and in 1552 sought to extend his work to China, but died on Shangchuan while waiting for permission to enter the country. His feast day is Dec. 3.
See also: Jesuits.

Xenakis, Yannis (1922-), Greek avant-garde composer who developed "stochastic" music using computer-programmed sequences based on mathematical probability, as in *Métastaseis* (1953-54) and *Achorripsis* (1958).

Yannis Xenakis

Xenon, chemical element, symbol Xe; for physical constants, see Periodic Table. Xenon was discovered by Sir William Ramsay and Morris W. Travers in 1898. It occurs in the atmosphere to the extent of one part in 20 million. It is obtained from liquid air residues and from the gases evolved from certain mineral springs. Xenon is a colorless, odorless, and chemically inert gas. It is a member of the noble or "inert" gases. The noble gases do not normally combine with other elements, but the existence of many xenon compounds has been established. Xenon difluoride, tetrafluoride, hexafluoride, and others have been prepared. It is used in special electric lamps.

Xenophanes (570-480 B.C.), Greek poet and pre-Socratic philosopher. An Ionian who emigrated to South Italy, he wrote satires and ridiculed the idea that the gods had human attributes, positing a single, all-embracing divine being. Only some 40 fragments of his works survive.
See also: Pre-Socratic philosophy.

Y

Xenophon (431-355 B.C.), Greek soldier and author. An Athenian and admirer of Socrates, he joined the Greek expedition supporting Cyrus the Younger (401) and after its defeat led the Greeks back in a heroic 1,500-mi (2,414-km) march recounted in his famous *Anabasis.* He later fought for Sparta, whose conservative militarism he admired. Retiring to the country, he wrote his famous volumes of Greek history, memoirs of Socrates, a romanticized account of Cyrus the Great's education, and works on horsemanship and politics.
See also: Greece, Ancient.

Xerography *see:* Photocopying.

Xerxes, name of two kings of ancient Persia. **Xerxes I** (r.486-465 B.C.) continued the war against Greece started by his father, Darius I. His vast army crossed the Hellespont in 480 B.C., and despite a defeat at Thermopylae, destroyed Athens. However, his fleet was defeated at Salamis (480), and he returned to Persia, leaving his army, which was defeated at Plataea (479). He was murdered in a court intrigue. **Xerxes II**, his grandson, was murdered by his half brother, Sogdianus, in 424 B.C., after ruling for 45 days.
See also: Persia, Ancient.

Xhosa, group of related tribes (formerly called *Kafir*) living in Transkei, South Africa. Bantu-speaking, they are mainly agriculturists, though some cattle are raised. The Xhosa are organized in patrilineal clans. Many now work as migrant laborers in Johannesburg.

Xiamen (pop. 510,700), Hsia-men, or Amoy, port city in Fujian province, southeastern China, located on Amoy and Kulang islands, on the Strait of Formosa at the mouth of the Chiu-lung Chiang (river). The city has a history of contact with Western nations, beginning in 1544 with the arrival of Portuguese traders, who were soon expelled. The port was visited by Dutch, Spanish, and British ships during the 17th and 18th centuries, but foreign trade restrictions were imposed in 1757. As a result of a treaty following the Opium War of 1839-42, Xiamen and 4 other ports were reopened to the British, and foreigners were allowed residence. During the 19th century the port was a center of the tea trade. It was held by the Japanese from 1938 to 1945. It remains a shipping center, with industries including food processing, shipbuilding, and engineering. Xiamen is now connected to the mainland by a causeway. It has had close ties with nearby Taiwan, and has a large emigrant Chinese population.
See also: China.

Xi Jiang (also Hsi Chiang), longest river of southern China. Originating in the highlands of Yunnan province, it flows some 1,500 mi (2,414 km) southeast to the South China Sea. There, along with several other rivers, it forms a delta on which is located the large Chinese city of Guangzhou.

Xinjiang, large, northwestern province of China, bordered on the northwest by the USSR. Most of the region's inhabitants are of Middle Eastern origin, including Turkish. The main religion is Islam. The region has been under Chinese rule off and on since the Han dynasty (202 B.C.-A.D. 220). It was officially made a province by the Chinese in 1884. The region's economy is based primarily on herding (cattle, sheep, and goats) and farming (corn, cotton, wheat, and rice). Ürümqi is its capital.
See also: China.

Xochimilco *see:* Lake Xochimilco.

X ray, type of radiation of higher frequency than visible light but lower than a gamma ray. Discovered by the German physicist Wilhem Conrad Roentgen in 1895, X rays are usually produced by high-energy electrons impinging upon a metal target. X rays are often used in medicine to make radiographs (X-ray pictures) of the bones and internal organs of the body.
See also: Roentgen, Wilhelm Conrad.

Xunzi, or Hsun Tzu (340?-245? B.C.), Chinese philosopher. He is considered a follower of Kongfuzi (Confucius; 551-479 B.C.). Whereas Mengzi (Mencius), the "Second Sage" (4th century B.C.), interpreted Kongfuzi in an optimistic light, teaching the intrinsic goodness of human nature, Xunzi taught that human nature is intrinsically evil and that morality must be taught and reinforced by society. His teachings are articulated in the book *Xunzi.*
See also: Philosophy.

Xylophone, percussion instrument consisting of a series of tuned wooden blocks set in a frame and struck with special hammers. Of ancient origin, it was widespread in Asia and Africa before being introduced in Europe.

XYZ Affair, diplomatic incident that nearly led to open war between the United States and France in 1798. President John Adams sent John Marshall, Elbridge Gerry, and C. C. Pinckney to settle disputes with France following Jay's Treaty. They were met by three unnamed agents, later called X, Y, and Z, who demanded U.S. loans and bribes before opening negotiations. When this was announced in Congress, there was an uproar, but Adams averted war and reopened negotiations with Talleyrand, the French foreign minister. Later, the agents were identified as Jean Conrad Hottinguer (X), a U.S. banker in Hamburg named Bellamy (Y), and Lucien Hauteval (Z).

Y, 25th letter of the English alphabet. Like *u, v,* and *w,* it derives from the ancient Semitic letter *waw* (meaning "hook"), itself adapted from an Egyptian hieroglyphic. It passed into the Greek alphabet as the letter *upsilon* and was later used in the Roman alphabet only for words of Greek origin. In Old and Middle English, *y* was often used instead of *i,* a usage that is part of our language today. In chemistry, *y* is used as the symbol for the element *yttrium.*

Yablonovyy Mountains, mountain range in northern Mongolia, USSR. The range, which extends 1,000 mi (1,600 km), is a watershed, dividing those rivers that flow into the Arctic Ocean from those that flow into the Pacific. Its highest peak is Mt. Sokhondo (8,199 ft/2,499 m). There are large tin mines in the mountains. The range is crossed by the Trans-Siberian Railroad at Yablonovo.

Yachts and yachting, popular international sport and pastime of racing or cruising in yachts. Yachting developed in the early 19th century as steam began to supplant sails in commercial vessels. It became established on an organized basis with the setting up of the New York Yacht Club in 1844. In 1851 the first race for the *America's Cup* took place, and subsequent races for the cup played a major role in the evolution of yacht design. After World War I the trend moved away from large, expensive yachts, and popular "one-design" classes emerged, with the Bermuda rig predominating. Small-keep yachts and catboats are now raced and sailed for pleasure throughout the world. Ocean racing is also popular, and recently single-handed transatlantic and round-the-world races have attracted enormous public attention.
See also: Sailing.

Yahweh *see:* Jehovah.

Yak (*Bos grunniens*), shaggy ox of the high plateau of Tibet. Yaks are distinguished by the long fringe of hair on shoulders, flanks, thighs, and tail, and the long in-curved horns. Wild yaks are large animals, up to 7 ft (2.1 m) at the shoulder, with black coats. Domestic yaks, kept as beasts of burden and for their milk, are smaller and may be any of several colors.

Yakima (pop. 188,823), city in south-central Washington state, seat of Yakima County, located on the Yakima River, at the eastern edge of Mt. Rainier National Park. The city was established as a railroad depot in 1886, and began to flourish after the introduction of irrigation (1891) made the Yakima Valley an important agricultural area. Industry includes lumber and the processing of agricultural products. Native Americans of the Yakima confederation, the group of tribes originally living in the area, now live on a nearby reservation.
See also: Washington.

Yakima, Native Americans belonging to the Sahapin-Chinook language family. They lived along the Columbia and Yakima rivers in Washington. In 1859 they were settled on a Washington reservation after a 3-year war against European-American settlers (1855-58).

Yale, Elihu (1649-1721), American-born English merchant who made a fortune in India (1670-99). In 1718 he made a donation to the collegiate school at New Haven, which was renamed Yale College (now Yale University).

Yale, Linus, Jr. (1821-68), U.S. inventor and manufacturer of locks. He developed the Yale Infallible Bank Lock (1851) and other bank locks, the combination lock (1861), and the key-operated cylinder pin-tumbler lock (patents 1861 and 1865), developed from a design used in ancient Egypt and now commonly used on doors of residences. Yale and partners Henry Towne and Henry Robinson Towne founded the Yale Lock Manufacturing Company in 1868.
See also: Lock.

Yale University, U.S. university chartered in 1701 as the Collegiate School, first at Killingworth, Milford, and Saybrook, Conn., then (1716) at New Haven, Conn., its present site. Renamed Yale College in 1718 in honor of Elihu Yale (1649-1721), it expanded greatly in the 19th century, awarded the first Ph.D. in the United States in 1861, and was renamed Yale University in 1887.

Yalow, Rosalyn Sussman (1921-), U.S. medical researcher who shared the 1977 Nobel Prize in physiology or medicine for helping develop *radioimmunoassay*, a technique for measuring minute amounts of hormones, vitamins, or enzymes that could not be detected by other means.
See also: Physiology.

Yalta (pop. 85,000), winter and health resort on the Black Sea, in southern Crimea, USSR. It was site of the 1945 Yalta Conference between U.S. president Franklin Roosevelt, British prime minister Winston Churchill, and Soviet premier Joseph Stalin.
See also: Union of Soviet Socialist Republics.

Yalta Conference, meeting held near Yalta (Crimea, USSR), Feb. 4-11, 1945, between Winston Churchill, Franklin Roosevelt, and Joseph Stalin, representing the major Allied powers in World War II. Plans were drawn up for the treatment of Germany after the war, including its division into occupation zones, the elimination of its war industries, and the prosecution of war criminals. The foundation of a new Polish state was decided upon, and the creation of the United Nations was discussed. The USSR agreed to join in the war against Japan after Germany's defeat, receiving occupation areas in eastern Europe in return.
See also: World War II.

Yalu River (Chinese: *Ya-Lu Chiang*; Korean: *Amnok-Kang*), river forming most of the boundary between North Korea and Manchuria, China. It rises in the Changbai Shan (Long White Mountains) of Manchuria and flows southeast 500 mi (800 km) to Korea Bay (Yellow Sea). The crossing of the river by Chinese Communist troops to help North Korea (Oct. 1950) was an important event of the Korean War.

Yam (genus *Dioscorea*), plant of the yam family with a flowering vine and a large tuber, similar to a sweet potato but of a different botanical family. The name "yam" often refers to the yellow- or white-fleshed tuber of edible species (e.g., *D. alata* and *D. rotundata*). The tuber is actually an enlarged underground portion of the stem, weighing as much as 100 lb (45 kg), in which the plant stores starch, water, and some sugar. Some varieties contain toxic substances that can only be eliminated by cooking, and cortisone and other drugs are derived from *saponin* compounds found in certain wild yams. Yams grow in warm, moist climates, and are an important food crop in West Africa, India, Southeast Asia, and the Caribbean area.

Yamamoto, Isoroku (1884-1943), commander of the Japanese fleet in World War II. He planned and commanded the attack on Pearl Harbor (1941) and Midway Island (1941). He was reported killed in an air ambush.
See also: World War II.

Yamasaki, Minoru (1912-86), U.S. architect. The Lambert-St. Louis air terminal (1951), the McGregor Conference Center at Wayne University, Detroit (1956), and the U.S. science pavilion at the Seattle Exposition (1962) reveal his mastery of ornamental and sculptural form. He was also the architect, with Emery Roth, of the World Trade Center in New York.
See also: Architecture.

Yamasee, Native Americans of the Muskogean language family. Living in southern Georgia and northern Florida, they were driven into South Carolina by the Spanish (1687) and back into Florida (1715) by the British, who in 1727 destroyed their village near St. Augustine. The survivors eventually assimilated with the Seminole and Creek.

Yamashita, Tomoyuki (1885-1946), Japanese army commander in World War II. His forces overran Malaya and captured Singapore (1942). He later commanded Japanese forces in the Philippines, surrendering in 1945. He was hanged by the Allies for the atrocities committed by his troops.
See also: World War II.

Yamato period, portion of Japanese history (C.A.D. 200-646) during which the imperial center was Yamato, the area around current-day Nara, near Osaka. During this time the Japanese empire included much of central Japan and parts of southern Korea. The period was characterized by the influence of Chinese culture on Japanese arts and government, and the transmission of the Buddhist religion from China to Japan (although the primary popular religion remained Shinto).
See also: Japan.

Yam bean *see:* Jicama.

Yancey, William Lowndes (1814-63), U.S. proslavery politician and advocate of secession. A lawyer and U.S. senator (1844-46), he drafted the proslavery "Alabama platform" (1848) in reply to the Wilmot proviso, became a leading "fire-eater," wrote the Alabama ordinance of secession (1860), and served the Confederate government in the Civil War as commissioner to England and France (1861-62).
See also: Civil War, U.S.; Slavery.

Yang, Chen Ning (1922-), Chinese-born U.S. physicist who shared with Tsung Dao Lee the 1957 Nobel Prize in physics for their studies of violations of the conservation of parity.
See also: Parity; Physics.

Yangon (pop. 1,316,000; formerly Rangoon), capital, largest city, and chief port of Myanmar (Burma), on the Rangoon River. It is a commercial and manufacturing center, with textile, sawmilling, food-processing, and petroleum industries. Its gold-domed Shwe Dagon Pagoda is the country's principal Buddhist shrine. Yan-

Yalta Conference (1945); from left to right: Winston Churchill, Franklin D. Roosevelt, and Joseph Stalin

gon was founded in 1753 as the Burmese capital. It was occupied by the British (1824-26) and retaken by them in 1852, after which it developed as a modern city. During World War II Yangon was occupied by the Japanese and suffered heavy damage.

Yangtze River, or Chang River, China's longest river. It rises in the Kunlun Mountains of Tibet and flows 3,434 mi (5,526 km) into the East China Sea, draining an area (about 750,000 sq mi/1,942,500 sq km) that includes China's richest agricultural land along its lower reaches. Its main tributaries are the Min, Wu, and Han. It is navigable for oceangoing ships for some 600 mi (966 km), as far as Wuhan.

Yank, World War II weekly magazine produced by U.S. Army personnel for U.S. soldiers around the world. Contributors included both soldier correspondents, photographers, and artists and enlistees, whose work for the magazine was unpaid. Information helpful to those in the armed forces as well as soldiers' comments and complaints were printed in the regular feature "Mail Call." *Yank* appeared from June 17, 1942 until the end of the war in 1945, and contained many exclusive articles on the progress of the war.
See also: World War II.

Yankee, slang term of uncertain origin, probably Dutch. Outside the United States, it refers to anyone from the United States; inside the country, it normally refers to a New Englander, especially someone descended from colonists. In the South it refers to Northerners, a tradition dating from the Civil War.

Yankee Doodle, song popular among American troops in the Revolutionary War. It probably originated among the British during the French and Indian Wars as a song making fun of the Americans, who later adopted it for themselves.

Yaoundé, or Yaunde (pop. 313,700), capital city of Cameroon, located in the south-central part of the country between the Nyong and Sanaga rivers. It was founded in 1888 by the Germans, under whom Cameroon was a protectorate. When the area was divided in 1922, the city became the capital of French East Cameroon. In 1960 it was made capital of the newly independent Republic of Cameroon. Yaoundé is a center for transportation, light industry, and education.
See also: Cameroon.

Yap Islands, in the western Pacific Ocean, part of the Caroline Islands, consisting of 4 large and 10 small islands, surrounded by a coral reef. The Micronesian population fishes and grows yams, taro, bananas, and coconuts.

Yaqui, tribe of Native Americans living in Sonora, northern Mexico, and in Arizona and California. In ancient times the Yaqui lived by farming, hunting, and gathering. They defeated the invading Spaniards (1533 and 1609). After making peace, they arranged for the Jesuit missionaries to live with them and teach them European agricultural methods. As a result, the Yaqui culture blends Roman Catholicism and ancient Yaqui custom. Starting in the 1730s the Yaqui rebelled against Spanish colonial rule. Fighting continued into the 1900s, and many Yaqui fled to the United States. Modern Yaqui are primarily subsistence farmers.

Yawning, involuntary gaping of the mouth, often accompanied by involuntary stretching of the muscles and accompanied by a deep inspiration. It usually occurs during the drowsy state produced by fatigue or boredom and is often a prelude to sleep.

Yaws, disease caused by an organism related to that which causes syphilis. Common in the tropics, it occurs often in children and consists of a local lesion on the limbs; there is also mild systemic disease. Chronic, destructive lesions of skin, bone, and cartilage may develop later. When the Wassermann test is positive, that indicates the disease is present, and penicillin is the treatment of choice.

Yazoo Fraud, 1795 scandal in which the Georgia state legislature was bribed to sell 35 million acres (14.2 million hectares) of land along the Yazoo River to 4 land companies. In 1796 a new legislature rescinded the act. In a historic 1810 decision the U.S. Supreme Court declared the rescinding unconstitutional and awarded compensation to investors who had suffered.

Yazoo River, tributary of the Mississippi River, in the state of Mississippi. It begins near Greenwood and flows southwest 188 mi (303 km) to join the Mississippi near Vicksburg. A system of dams and reservoirs on the Yazoo and its tributaries has reduced flooding in the fertile cotton-growing region.

Yeager, Chuck (Charles Elwood Yeager; 1923-), U.S. fighter pilot in World War II, test pilot, first person to fly faster than the speed of sound (Oct. 14, 1947). Yeager set a second record by flying 2 1/2 times the speed of sound, or 1,650 mph (2,655 kmph) on Dec. 12, 1953. He retired from the military as a brigadier general (1975), later serving on the presidential commission investigating the 1986 explosion of the *Challenger* space shuttle. He told his life story in *Yeager* (1985), coauthored by Leo Janos, and his exploits as a test pilot are celebrated in Tom Wolfe's *The Right Stuff* (1979).

Qutang Gorge, one of the three Tangzi Gorges on the Yangtze River

Year, name of various units of time, all depending on the revolution of the earth about the sun. The *sidereal year* (365.256636 mean solar days) is the average time the earth takes to complete one revolution measured with respect to a fixed direction in space. The *tropical year* (365.24220 mean solar days), the year measured by the changing seasons, is that in which the mean longitude of the sun moves through 360°. The *anomalistic year* (365.25964 mean solar days) is the average interval between successive terrestrial perihelions. The *civil year* is a period of variable duration, usually 365 or 366 days (leap year), depending on the type of calendar in use.

Yeast, any of single-celled plants classified with the fungi. Some cause diseases of the skin and mucous membranes, while others, notably the strains of *Saccharomyces cerevisiae* (baker's yeast), are used in baking, brewing, and winemaking. Yeasts employ either or both of 2 metabolic processes: Fermentation involves the anaerobic decomposition of hexose sugars to yield alcohol (ethanol) and carbon dioxide; "respiration" involves the exothermic decomposition of various sugars in the presence of oxygen to give carbon dioxide and water. Yeasts are also grown as a source of food rich in B-complex vitamins.

Yeats, William Butler (1865-1939), Irish poet and dramatist, leader of the Celtic Renaissance in Ireland and one of the world's greatest lyric poets. Nationalism was a major element in his early poetry, such as *The Wanderings of Oisin* (1889), which drew on Irish legend. Yeats cofounded (1898) Dublin's Irish Literary Theatre, later the Abbey Theatre. His mature poetic works, often symbolic and mystical, treated universal themes. They include *The Wild Swans at Coole* (1917), *The Tower* (1928), and *Last Poems* (1940). Yeats was awarded the Nobel Prize in literature in 1923.

Yeh Chien-Ying, or Ye Jianying (1899-1985), Chinese minister of defense (1971-78). A planner of the Long March and a Central Committee member from 1945, his seniority and military connections assured his continued position within the inner circle of leadership after the death of Mao Tse-tung (Mao Zedong).
See also: China.

Yellow *see:* Color.

Yellow daisy *see:* Black-eyed Susan.

Yellow-dog contract, pledge signed by prospective employees that they will not join a union. U.S. Supreme Court decisions (1908, 1915) upheld their legality, and they were widely used by antiunion employers in the 1920s. The Norris-La Guardia Act (1932) finally outlawed them.

Yellow fever, infectious disease caused by a virus carried by mosquitos of the genus *Aëdes* and occurring in tropical Americas and Africa. The disease consists of fever, headache, backache, prostration, and vomiting of sudden onset. Protein loss in the urine, kidney failure, and liver disorder with jaundice are also frequent. Hemorrhage from mucous membranes, especially in the gastrointestinal tract, is also common. A moderate number of cases are fatal, but a mild form of the disease is also recognized. Vaccination to induce immunity is important and effective as no specific therapy is available; mosquito control provides a similarly important preventive measure.

Yellowhammer, or yellow-shafted flicker (*Colaptes auratus auratus*), bird of the woodpecker family, subspecies of the common flicker, native to North America; also, the yellow bunting (German: *Ammer*, "bunting"; *Emberiza citrinella*), finch of Europe and Asia.

Yellow jacket, one of a genus (*Vespula*) of hornets, social wasps of the family Vespidae, common in North America. They usually construct an underground nest of paper, frequently in or near human habitation. Yellow jackets can inflict a painful sting.

Yellow journalism, vulgar and sensational newspaper reporting whose sole aim is to attract readers. The term originated with the "Yellow Kid" comic strip in the Sunday supplement of Joseph Pulitzer's New York *World* (1896). This began a "yellow journalism" circulation war in the city with William Randolph Hearst's *Journal*.It is still evident today.

Yellowknife (pop. 11,800), capital and largest city of Northwest Territories, in north-central Canada, on Yellowknife Bay of Great Slave Lake. The city was founded in 1935 after the discovery of gold nearby, and was relocated in 1945. The economy is supported by gold prospecting, mining, and tourism.
See also: Northwest Territories.

Yellowlegs (genus *Tringa*), migrating shore bird of the sandpiper family, native to the Western Hemisphere and identified by dark wings, white belly and tail, and long yellow legs. The 2 species are the greater yellowlegs (*T. melanoleuca*), measuring 13-15 in (34-38 cm), and the lesser yellowlegs (*T. flavipes*), measuring about 10 in (25 cm). The birds nest in Canada and winter in the southern United States, around the Gulf of Mexico, and as far south as Chile.

Yellow poplar, or tulip tree (*Liriodendron tulipifera*), tall hardwood tree of the magnolia family, native to eastern North America. It is the tallest broadleaf tree of eastern North America, its straight trunk growing to a height of 200 ft (60 m) and a diameter of 10 ft (3 m). The light-colored wood is widely used for furniture, veneer, plywood, and crates. Nectar from its tulip-shaped yellow and green flowers is an important source of honey.

Yellow River, or Hwang Ho, river of northern China, flowing 2,903 mi (4,672 km) from the Kunlun Mountains, generally east to the Yellow Sea. It is named for its fertile yellow silt and is often nicknamed China's Sorrow because of terrible floods and destructive changes of course. In 1955 a major 50-year flood-control and hydroelectric project was begun on the river.

Yellow Sea, or Huang Hai, western arm of the Pacific Ocean between Korea and northeast China. It opens in the south into the East China Sea. The name arises from the color of its waters, which receive yellow silt from the Yellow and other rivers.
See also: Pacific Ocean.

William Butler Yeats

Yellowstone National Park, oldest and largest U.S. national park, created in 1872 and covering 3,472 sq mi (8,992 sq km), mostly in northwestern Wyoming. It contains some of the most spectacular wonders in the United States, including Old Faithful geyser, thousands of hot springs and mud pools, petrified forests, black grass cliffs, and the Grand Canyon of the Yellowstone River. Wildlife abounds in the forests covering most of the park.
See also: National Parks.

Yellowstone River, river flowing 671 mi (1,080 km) from northwestern Wyoming north and east through Montana to join the Missouri River at the North Dakota state line. It rises in the Rocky Mountains, flowing into Yellowstone Lake in Yellowstone National Park, emptying by a dramatic drop of over 420 ft (128 m) into Yellowstone Canyon. It then flows northeast through the Great Plains of Montana. The river system, including the tributaries

Yellowstone National Park

Bighorn, Tongue, and Powder, drains 70,000 sq mi (181,000 sq km). The river is visited for its natural beauty and is used for irrigation.

Yellowthroat (*Geothlypis trichas*), small, migratory bird of the wood warbler family native to North America. Yellowthroats are olive-green with white and buff breasts and measure about 5 in (13 cm) long; males have black masks. They are found in the tall grasses of marshes and other wet areas.

Yeltsin, Boris Nikolayevich (1931-), president of the Russian Federation (1990-). He joined the Communist Party in 1961. Yeltsin was a member of the Politburo, the policy-making organ of the party, and was President Mikhail Gorbachev's chief rival. After his election to the presidency of the Russian republic, Yeltsin resigned from the Communist Party. In 1991, after a general election, he retained the presidency of the Russian Federation. In 1993 he suppressed a rebellion of communist and nationalist members of parliament. He tried to get even with the communist past.

Yemen, officially the Republic of Yemen, formerly divided into Yemen (Sana), also known as North Yemen, and Yemen (Aden), also known as South Yemen, now united into a single republic occupying the southwest corner of the Arabian peninsula and including the islands of Kamaran, Perim, and Socotra. With a combined area of 207,232 sq mi (536,870 sq km), Yemen is bordered by Saudi Arabia to the north and northeast, the Gulf of Aden to the south, Oman to the east, and the Red Sea to the west.

Land and climate. Beyond the Red Sea coast with its coral reefs and low-lying beaches is the Tihamah, a dry coastal plain, and, farther inland, a foothill region scored by valleys, known as *wadis*. The coastal plain along the Gulf of Aden is hot and arid with palm oases. The lowlands along both shores give way to a mountainous interior with some peaks exceeding 12,000 ft (3,658 m). Among the mountains is a mosaic of plateaus, upland plains, and fertile valleys. The mountains eventually give way in the north and east to the Rub'al-Khali desert. The highlands of Yemen enjoy the best climate on the Arabian peninsula, with annual rainfall of some 16-32 in (41-81 cm).

Mountain village in Yemen

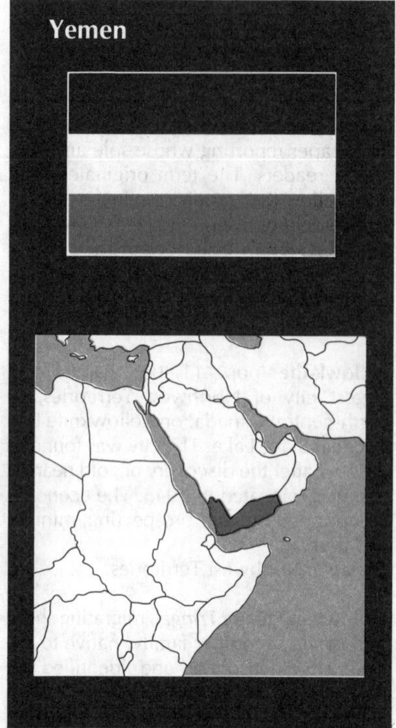

Capital:	San'a'
Area:	207,232 sq mi (536,870 sq km)
Population:	13,128,000
Government:	Republic
Independent:	since 1990 (united)
GNP:	U.S. $6,746,000,000
Per capita:	U.S. $520

People. The people of what was formerly South Yemen consist of various tribes of Arabs and are either farmers or nomads. The people of what was formerly Yemen are mostly south Arabians, but there are African influences in the people living along the Red Sea coast and toward the south. Though the people are Muslim, they are divided about equally between Sunni and Shi'te Muslims. The religious differences translated into significant social and political divisions in the former Yemen Arab Republic, and are now part of the United Republic of Yemen as well. The official language of Yemen is Arabic.

History. The histories of North Yemen and South Yemen have, since antiquity, sometimes blended, sometimes gone their separate ways, and at other times collided. Formerly known as Al-Yaman, the land of South Yemen was once home to the Minaean, Sabaean, and Himyarite kingdoms. Conquered by Arabs in the 8th century A.D., it became part of the Ottoman Empire during the 16th century. Known as Aden under British control from the 1830s, South Yemen became fully independent in 1967 following the collapse of the Federation of South Arabia. Governed by the Marxist National Liberation Front, it was known as the People's Democratic Republic of Yemen.

Neighboring North Yemen was once part of the Sabaean kingdom and was incorporated into the Muslim caliphate in the 7th century A.D. Various foreign powers have exercised nominal suzerainty over North Yemen, including the Ottoman Turks from the 1500s to 1918. But effective power from the 9th to the 20th centuries lay in the hands of competing local imams. In 1962 an army coup led to the proclamation of a republic. In the ensuing civil war, Saudi Arabia backed the royalist tribes, while Egypt supported the republicans. The conflict ended with a mediated settlement in 1970 from which the republicans emerged in control of the fledgling Yemen Arab Republic.

In 1972 war erupted between the Yemen Arab Republic and the People's Democratic Republic of Yemen. A ceasefire was followed by an agreement to unify North Yemen and South Yemen, but hostilities flared again in 1979. Finally, on May 22, 1990, the two countries were united as the Republic of Yemen under the interim presidency of Ali Abdallah Salih. Yemen abstained from a vote in the Arab League to condemn Saddam Hussein's invasion of Kuwait and earned the immediate enmity of its powerful neighbor, Saudi Arabia, at considerable cost to its already troubled economy. After the 1993 elections the tensions between the north and the south increased.

Yenisey River, major river of Siberia, flowing 2,500 mi (4,000 km) from the Sayan Mountains west and north to the Kara Sea (Arctic Ocean). The river is navigable by ocean steamers for 400 mi (640 km) to the port of Igarka, and is an important source of hydroelectric power.

Yeoman, Middle English word denoting a king's or nobleman's retainer or officer, or a freehold farmer cultivating his own land, ranking below the gentry. Yeoman now refers to a naval petty officer performing clerical duties.

Yerevan, or Erevan (pop. 1,202,000), capital city of Armenia, on the Razdan River, in southeastern Europe, near Turkey. Archeological remains indicate a settlement on the site dating from before 2000 B.C., and a fortress from the 8th century B.C.

The city was often under siege and destroyed by rival powers, particularly, during the 15th-19th centuries, the Persians and Ottomans. It was established as capital of the Armenian republic in 1920. Hydroelectric power from the Razdan River has helped the city become a center for chemical, engineering, and other industries. It is also a center for culture and higher education.

See also: Armenia.

Yerkes Observatory, observatory of the University of Chicago. It was set up in 1892 on the shores of Lake Geneva, Wis., by the

astronomer George Hale and financed by Charles Yerkes. The observatory contains the world's largest refracting telescope (built 1897), its lens 40 in (102 cm) in diameter, together with several reflecting telescopes.
See also: Astronomy; Hale, George Ellery.

Yevtushenko, Yevgeny (1933-), Russian poet who became a spokesperson for "liberal" forces in Soviet literature in the early 1960s. His best-known poems include "Babi-Yar" (1961), dealing with the Nazis' massacre of Soviet Jews in 1941, and "The Heirs of Stalin" (1962), warning of the persistence of Stalinism.

Yew, any of several species of evergreen trees and shrubs of genus *Taxus* native to the Northern Hemisphere. Yews are often grown as ornamental plants. They have flat, dark-green needles and red-brown bark. Their wood, which is hard and dense, was once valued for its use in archery bows and furniture. The bark, needles, and seeds are poisonous and can be fatal to livestock. Yews native to North America include the western, or Pacific, yew (*T. brevifolia*), used for cabinetry; the Japanese yew (*T. cuspidata*), an ornamental shrub; and the American yew, or ground hemlock (*T. canadensis*), which grows along the ground.

Yiddish, language spoken by Jewish people, developed during the A.D. 900s and 1000s. Yiddish has roots in several languages, including German, Hebrew, Aramaic, French, and Italian. After World War II (1939-45), in which the Nazis exterminated over 6 million Jews, the use of Yiddish declined considerably.

Yiddish literature, body of written works that developed in the late 1200s and remained strongly connected to Jewish religious tradition until the 1800s, when modern Jewish literature had its beginnings through a cultural literary movement called the *Haskalah* (Enlightenment). The humorist Solomon Rabinowitz, who wrote under the name Sholom Aleichem, Shalom Jacob Abramovich, whose pen name was Mendele the Bookseller, and Isaac Leibush Peretz stand out as major exponents of Yiddish literature during much of the 1800s and 1900s. Some of the common themes underlying most works of this time include the hardships involved with living in a non-Jewish world and the social conflicts within the Jewish community.
The flowering of Yiddish literature took place during the period of 1914-18 in Poland, the Soviet Union, and the United States. During this period, Sholem Asch in Poland, David Bergelson in the Soviet Union, and Moishe Leib Halpern in the United States ranked as the most important figures in Yiddish literature. During World War II (1939-45), many notable Yiddish writers perished along with the 6 million Jews that were exterminated by the Nazis. Isaac Bashevis Singer, a Polish-born U.S. author, became the first Yiddish writer to win the Nobel Prize in literature (1978).

Yin and yang, two principles in Chinese philosophy, representing the passive and the active forces of the universe. Yin stands for earth, female, passive, dark, and receiving; yang, for heaven, male, active, light, and generative. All things exist through their interaction. The symbol for yin-yang is a circle divided into 2 curved forms, one dark, the other light.
See also: Philosophy.

YMCA *see:* Young Men's Christian Association.

Yoga (Sanskrit, "union"), forms of spiritual discipline practiced in Buddhism and Hinduism. Through these disciplines the yogi (one who follows yoga) strives to free the mind from attachment to the senses and to achieve *samadhi*—or union with *Brahma*, the deity—and fusion into oneness. In Hindu tradition there are three varieties of yoga: *karma yoga*, salvation through action; *jnana yoga*, salvation through knowledge; and *bhakti yoga*, salvation through devotion. In each the student passes through 8 levels of attainment, supervised by a guru, or teacher. The practice of *hatha yoga*, based on physical postures and control, has become increasingly popular in the West.
See also: Hinduism.

Yogurt, or yoghurt, semisolid, cultured milk food made by inoculating pasteurized milk with a culture of *Streptococcus thermophilus* and *Lactobacillus bulgaricus* and incubating until the desired acidity is achieved. Various fruits can be added.

Yokohama (pop. 2,993,000), city in Japan on the western shore of Tokyo Bay, a leading national seaport and part of Tokyo's industrial belt in southern Honshu Island. It is a trading center and supports large shipbuilding, iron, steel, chemical, machinery, and oil industries. It also has several universities. Yokohama was a fishing village when visited by Commodore Matthew Perry in 1854. Its growth began in 1859, when it became a foreign-trade port.
See also: Japan.

Yom Kippur, Jewish Day of Atonement, the most sacred day in the Jewish religious calendar. It falls on the 10th day after the Jewish New Year (Rosh Hashanah) and is marked by repentance, prayers, and abstention from food, drink, sex, and work.
See also: Judaism.

Yonkers (pop. 195,351), city in southeastern New York State just north of New York City, between the Bronx and Hudson rivers. The area, once inhabited by the Manhattan tribe, was granted in 1646 to a Dutch nobleman, Adriaen Van der Donck, known as "the Young Gentleman," or De Jonkheer, thus the name Yonkers. The farming village of Yonkers developed after Frederick Philipse (who acquired land in 1693) and his heirs rented land to farmers. In the mid-19th century the area was connected by rail to New York City and the first industry, Otis Elevator, was established. Industrial development attracted immigrants during the 20th century, and the city's population peaked in 1970. Current industry includes chemicals, food products, and electronics. St. Joseph's College and Elizabeth Seton College are located in Yonkers, and the Yonkers Museum has an important collection of paintings of the Hudson River school.
See also: New York.

York (pop. 102,200), city in northern England. Built on the site of a Roman fort, it emerged during the early Middle Ages as an important religious capital and trade center. Today York, with its many museums and historic buildings and churches, thrives primarily on tourism. The Cathedral of St. Peter, known as Minster Cathedral, and the National Railway Museum are of special interest. It also supports several industries, including the manufacture of precision instruments.
See also: England.

York, ruling dynasty of England (1461-85), a branch of the Plantagenet family, whose symbol was the white rose. The three Yorkist kings were **Edward IV** (r.1461-83), his son **Edward V** (r.April-June 1483), and **Richard III** (r.1483-85), who was killed at the Battle of Bosworth Field by Henry Tudor (Henry VII), who established the House of Tudor as the ruling family.
See also: United Kingdom.

Yorkshire terrier, breed of toy dog developed in Yorkshire and Lancashire, England, in the mid-19th century to hunt rats. Yorkies stand 8-9 in (20-23 cm) at the shoulder and weigh 4-8 lb (2-2.3 kg). Their long, straight, silky coat is bluish gray, with tan on the head and chest.

Yorktown (pop. 450), town in southeastern Virginia, seat of York County, on the York River, and site of the last campaign of the Revolutionary War. In 1781, 16,000 American and French troops, led by Generals Washington and Rochambeau, laid siege to 7,000 British troops under Lord Cornwallis in Yorktown. With British naval

Yokohama

Andrew Young

reinforcements defeated by U.S. Admiral de Grasse and escape impossible, Cornwallis surrendered.
See also: Virginia.

Yorktown, Battle of *see:* Revolutionary War in America.

Yoruba, African people in southwest Nigeria, characteristically urban dwellers. Yoruba culture exists also in Cuba and Brazil because of large slave importations.

Yosemite Falls, North America's highest waterfalls, in Yosemite National Park, central California. Here Yosemite Creek descends in 2 dramatic drops: the Upper Falls (1,430 ft/436 m), and the Lower Falls (320 ft/98 m). In between the waters fall in cascades, for a total descent of 2,425 ft (739 m).

Yosemite National Park, national park in eastern California, established in 1890, 1,189 sq mi (3,000 sq km) of spectacular mountain scenery formed during the last glacial period, on the western slopes of the Sierra Nevada. Its chief attractions are the Yosemite Valley; Yosemite Falls, the highest falls in North America; and the Mariposa Grove of 200 giant sequoias.
See also: National Parks.

Youmans, Vincent (1898-1946), U.S. composer of popular musical comedies of the 1920s, among them *No, No, Nanette* and *Hit the Deck.* His songs included "Tea for Two," "Without a Song," and "I Want to Be Happy."

Young, Andrew Jackson, Jr. (1932-), U.S. clergyman and civil rights leader. He helped draft the civil rights and voting rights acts (1964, 1965) and served in the U.S. House of Representatives (1971-76). As the first black U.S. ambassador to the UN (1977-79), he stirred up frequent controversy with undiplomatic public statements. In 1981 he was elected mayor of Atlanta.
See also: Civil rights.

Lower Yosemite Falls in Yosemite National Park

Young, Brigham (1801-77), U.S. Mormon leader. He joined the Mormons in 1832 and quickly rose to prominence. After 3 years as a missionary in England, he assumed leadership of the Mormons following the death of Joseph Smith (1844) and led them to Salt Lake City, Utah, in 1846. Young established a thriving city on a sound commercial basis and became first governor of Utah in 1850. He may have had as many as 27 wives.
See also: Mormons.

Cy Young

Young, Cy (Denton True Young; 1867-1955), U.S. baseball player. Considered one of the greatest pitchers of all time, he holds the record for career wins (511) and innings pitched (7,356), he pitched no-hit games (1897 and 1908) and pitched one perfect game (May 5, 1904). Young played for the Cleveland Spiders (1890-98), St. Louis Nationals (1898-1900), Boston Red Sox (1901-08), Cleveland Indians (1909-11), and Boston Braves (1911) and was inducted into the National Baseball Hall of Fame in 1937. The Cy Young Award is given each year to the leading pitcher of each league.

Young, John Watts (1930-), U.S. astronaut. Young was a U.S. Navy test pilot (1952-62), setting 2 world altitude records, before becoming an astronaut in 1962. He made more space flights than any other astronaut. His missions included the first *Gemini* mission with Virgil I. Grissom on Mar. 23, 1965, and the command of the Apr. 1972 *Apollo 16* flight and lunar landing. Chief of the National Aeronautics and Space Administration's (NASA's) astronaut office at Johnson Space Center, Houston, Tex., Young was the commander of the *Columbia* in Apr. 1981, the first space-shuttle flight.
See also: Astronaut.

Young, Lester Willis (1909-59), U.S. tenor saxophonist, one of the most influential jazz musicians. Young grew up in New Orleans, playing in his father's carnival band, first as drummer and then saxophonist. He was active in Kansas City jazz, playing with "King" Oliver and other bands. Young (or "Prez" as he became known) played with Count Basie from 1935 to 1944 and on tour with "Jazz at the Philharmonic" in the 1940s and 1950s. He helped develop the "cool" jazz style of the 1940s, using the saxophone to create new sounds and employing expressive silences.
See also: Jazz.

Young, Owen D. (1874-1962), U.S. lawyer, industrial executive, and diplomat. An extrenely successful businessperson, he is chiefly remembered as an international diplomat. Young presided at the 1929 Paris Reparations Conference and produced the Young Plan, a schedule for German World War I reparations payments, which was considered a triumph of diplomacy.
See also: War debt.

Young, Whitney Moore, Jr. (1921-71), U.S. civil rights leader. As director of the National Urban League (1961-71), he worked for better job and housing conditions for blacks in the United States and was one of the most influential black leaders of the 1960s.
See also: Civil rights.

Young Men's Christian Association (YMCA), worldwide organization that seeks, through programs of sport, religious and current-affairs study groups, and summer camps, to promote a healthy way of life based on Christian ideals. It was begun in England in 1844.

Youngstown (pop. 115,436), city in northeastern Ohio, seat of Mahoning County, located on the Mahoning River near Pennsylvania. John Young bought the original land site in 1797. The area gradually became important for the production of iron with the opening of a nearby iron furnace (1805), the discovery of local coal for use in smelting, and the availability of Great Lakes iron ore via the Sault Ste. Marie Canal (1855). Youngstown's first steel mill opened in 1891, and the city was a leading steel center until dramatic declines in the steel industry forced closing of all its steel mills (1977-81). Aluminum, textile, and paper products, automotive parts, and other industries are still active. Among Youngstown's many city parks is its well-known Mill Creek Park.
See also: Ohio.

Young Women's Christian Association (YWCA), international organization that promotes a Christian way of life through educational and recreational activities and social work. The movement started in the United States in 1858.

Yourcenar, Marguerite (1903-87), pen name of Marguerite de Crayencour, Belgian-born French author who became a

U.S. citizen in the 1940s. The first woman elected to the Académie Française (1980), she is best known for the historical novel *Memoirs of Hadrian* (1951) and *The Abyss* (1968).

Youth hostel, inexpensive, supervised overnight lodging, particularly for young people but generally accommodating all members of such hosteling organizations as the International Youth Hostel Federation and the American Youth Hostels. Hostels provide dormitory-style sleeping and a communal kitchen, but little in the way of bedding and services. Length of stay is often limited to 1-3 nights. The first hostel was founded in Westphalia, Germany, in 1910. Hostels spread rapidly in Europe after World War I. The first U.S. hostel was founded in Northfield, Mass., in 1934.

Ypres (Flemish, "Ieper"; pop. 34,800), city in West Flanders, western Belgium, on the Yperlee River. The city was a major textile center in the Middle Ages, and the main political power of Flanders in the 13th century. It declined in the 15th-18th centuries due to a succession of civil wars, religious strife, and military domination by the French and Dutch. It was nearly destroyed during World War I (battles of Ypres) and was again the scene of fighting in World War II. The city, with many of its medieval buildings, was rebuilt, and it is now a center for linen and lace-making and agricultural products.
See also: Belgium.

Ytterbium, chemical element, symbol Yb; for physical constants, see Periodic Table. Ytterbium was discovered by Jean de Marignac in 1878. It occurs in the minerals xenotime, polycrase, gadolinite, and monazite, the principal source of the element. It is prepared by reducing the anhydrous fluoride with calcium. Ytterbium is a silvery, soft, malleable, ductile, reactive metal belonging to the series of elements known as the rare-earth metals. Ion-exchange and solvent extraction techniques have led to much easier isolation of the rare-earth elements. Ytterbium has strong magnetic properties and a characteristic spectrum. It has possible use as a stainless steel additive. Ytterbium and its compounds are used in carbon-arc lighting, glass, and ceramics. Radioactive ytterbium is used as a portable X-ray source.

Yttrium, chemical element, symbol Y; for physical constants, see Periodic Table. Yttria, an earth (oxide) containing yttrium, was discovered in 1794 by John Gadolin. Yttrium was first isolated by Friedrich Wöhler in 1828. Yttrium occurs in nature as xenotime (yttrium phosphate), and other minerals, monazite being the commercial source. It is obtained by the reduction of the fluoride with calcium metal. Yttrium is a silvery-white, soft, reactive metal. Although not a member of the rare-earth series of metals, it is chemically similar and often considered with them. Yttrium and its compounds are used in phosphors for color televisions, in yttrium aluminum garnets used in YAG-lasers, and in mantles for incandescent lamps. In 1843 Carl Gustav Mosander divided the earth yttria into three earths, which then were named yttria, erbia, and terbia.

Yüan Shih-k'ai, or Yuan Shikai (1859-1916), Chinese soldier and president of China (1912-16). His efforts to check Japan in Korea led to the Sino-Japanese War of 1894-95. He supported the dowager empress Tz'u Hsi and helped suppress the Boxer movement (1900). Supported by his army during the revolution of 1911, he emerged as president but was unable to attain his goal of establishing himself emperor.
See also: China.

Yucatán Peninsula, peninsula (c.70,000 sq mi/c.181,200 sq km) dividing the Gulf of Mexico from the Caribbean Sea. It is comprised of Belize, El Petén (part of Guatemala), and 3 Mexican states. The climate is hot and humid, and farming and forestry are the main activities. The northern region is the leading producer of henequen (fiber used for twine). The people are of Maya stock and Chichén Itza, a famed Mayan site, is on the peninsula.
See also: Mexico.

Yucca, genus of plants of the Lily family found in desert regions of Mexico and the southwestern United States. The Joshua tree is a small tree, but other yuccas are shrubs or low plants bearing clusters of sword-shaped leaves and white, waxy flowers. All depend on the yucca moth for pollination.

Yugoslavia, Until 1991 the Socialist Federal Republic of Yugoslavia, country with six constituent republics (Serbia, Croatia, Bosnia and Hercegovina, Macedonia, Slovenia and Montenegro) and two provinces, Kosovo and Vojvodina.
Land and climate. Yugoslavia, mostly mountainous, was made up of four geographical areas: an Alpine region in the northwest, fertile northern plains, the rugged mountainous south, and the island-studded Dalmatian coast. Most of the country was drained by the Danude river, which flowed southeast from the Hungarian border across the northern plains. The climate varied from continental in the north to Mediterranean in the south.
People. Yugoslavia was a federation of many different peoples, principly Serbs, Croats, Slovenes, Macedonians and Montenegrins, but also including many minority groups. The various peoples also professed several different religions. Roman Catholics comprised some 30% of the population, most of them Croats and Slovenes. Members of the Eastern Orthodox Church made up about 40% of the population; chiefly Serbs, Macedonians, and Montenegrins. The Roman Catholics used the Roman alphabet, whereas the Eastern Orthodox used the Cyrillic alphabet. Some 10% of the people were Muslims. Serbs and Croats speak Serbo-Croatian; some other groups used other languages. About 40% of the people lived in cities, the federal capital was Belgrade.
History. Once dominated by the Ottoman Empire, most of Yugoslavia subsequently came under the Austro-Hungarian monarchy, including Croatia, Slovenia, and

Plitvicka Jezera Park in Croatia, Yugoslavia

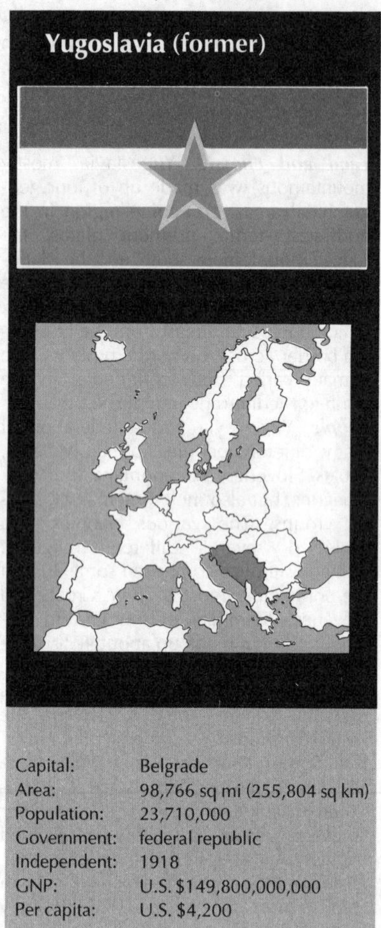

Bosnia and Hercegovina. By 1914 only Serbia and Montenegro were independent. Serbia sought unification of the country, and it was a Serbian nationalist who assassinated Archduke Francis Ferdinand of Austria and his wife, Sophie, in 1914, setting off the chain of events that led directly to World War I. In 1918 the "Kingdom of the Serbs, Croats, and Slovenes" was created. Its name was changed to Yugoslavia in 1929, but separatist pressures were strong from the very start, particularly among Croats and Macedonians. The Germans invaded in 1941, and two rival resistance groups were organized, one the royalist Draža Mihailovic and the other the communist resistance under Josip Tito. In 1943, even before the war had ended, the rival resistance groups were fighting one another; backed by Great Britain and the USSR, Tito prevailed. In 1945 he proclaimed Yugoslavia a federal republic of six states and established a communist government. Yugoslavia was expelled from the Comanform in 1948, and relations between the Yugoslavians and Soviets were strained. President Tito charted a policy of "independent national communism" for Yugoslavia and successfully withstood Soviet pressure. Tito's regime continued to have to deal with internal tensions, which were centered on the nationalist aspirations of the constituent republics, most notably from Croatia. The regime was also challenged on issues of intellectual freedom. Following Tito's death in 1980, a collective state presidency was established. Despite attempts to maintain the federal system and the country's unity, the collapse of communist regimes throughout eastern Europe, beginning in 1989, has had profound repercussions in Yugoslavia. Separatism could not be contained, and in 1991 Slovenia and Croatia were the first republics to claim independence. Macedonia and Bosnia Hercegovina followed, and Serbia and Montenegro amalgamated into a new Federal Republic of Yugoslavia. Not all inhabitants of the newly independent countries complied with the new situation, and many protested violently, resulting in civil wars in both Bosnia Hercegovina and Croatia.
See also: Tito, Josip Broz.

Yugoslavia, Federal Republic of, independent country in southeastern Europe, bordered by Croatia and Bosnia Hercegovina on the west, Hungary on the north, Romania and Bulgaria on the east, and Macedonia and Albania in the south. The Federal Republic consists of Montenegro in the south and the dominant republic Serbia in the north. About two-thirds of the population is Serbian. Although Serbia was a dominant republic in the former Socialist Federal Republic of Yugoslavia, it could not prevent the separation of the prosperous republics Slovenia and Croatia in the early 1990s. Serbia then amalgamated with Montenegro to form a new Federal Republic of Yugoslavia. Serbian troops were involved in the civil war that followed the collapse of Yugoslavia in 1991.

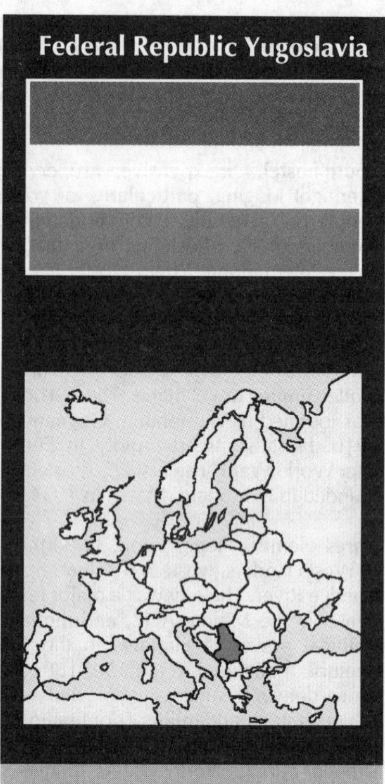

Capital:	Belgrade
Area:	39,499 sq mi (102,173 sq km)
Population:	10,597,000
Government:	federal republic
Independent:	1992
GNP:	U.S. $9,520,000,000
Per capita:	U.S. $900

Yukawa, Hideki (1907-81), Japanese physicist who postulated the meson as the agent bonding the atomic nucleus. In fact, the mu-meson (now called *muon*), discovered shortly afterward (in 1936) by Carl D. Anderson, does not fulfill this role, and Yukawa had to wait until Cecil F. Powell discovered the pi-meson (now called *pion*) in 1947 for vindication of his theory. He received the 1949 Nobel Prize in physics.
See also: Meson.

Yukon River, sixth-longest river in North America, flowing from northern British Columbia for 1,979 mi (3,185 km) through Yukon Territory into Alaska, then southwest to the Norton Sound on the Bering Sea. It is navigable for about 1,770 mi (2,848 km).

Yukon Territory, subarctic territory in northwestern Canada. Covering 207,076 sq mi (536,327 sq km), the Yukon is bordered by the Arctic Ocean to the north, the Northwest Territories to the east, British Columbia and Alaska to the south, and Alaska to the west.

Land and climate. The mountainous Yukon Territory includes the Rocky Mountains and, in the southwest, the St. Elias Range. The latter includes Canada's highest mountain, Mount Logan (19,850 ft/

Kotor, Montenegro

6,050 m). The territory has 8 other peaks over 15,000 ft (4,572 m) high. A large central basin, or plateau, is heavily forested. The Yukon River drains over one-half the region and is navigable for about 1,770 mi (2,848 km). The inhabited valleys and plateaus of the Yukon have a subarctic climate with long, cold winters and summers about 4 months long. winter temperatures can drop as low as –50°F/–°58C.
People. The Yukon is the original home of about 2,500 Native Americans, who live principally as trappers and hunters. The majority of the territory's population is concentrated in the warmer southern and central valleys. Whitehorse, the largest city, has been the capital since 1956.
Economy. Mining, the Yukon's principal industry, centers on the production of silver, lead, gold, and zinc, and provides jobs for most of the territory's inhabitants. During the 1960s, mining operations expanded to include the production of copper and asbestos; potential reserves of oil and iron ore remain to be developed.
History. The Yukon territory was first explored by the fur traders Robert Campbell and John Bell of the Hudson's Bay Company between 1840 and 1848. Canada acquired the territory from the Hudson's Bay Company in 1870. In the 1860s and 1870s prospectors began mining gold in the area. In 1897 the famous Klondike gold rush began after gold was discovered in several tributaries of the Klondike River. Between 1897 and 1904, an estimated $100 million worth of gold was obtained from deposits in the region. In 1898 the Yukon achieved separate territorial status, but the mines were soon depleted and between 1901 and 1911 the population dropped from 27,219 to 8,512. The decline of the territory was arrested during World War II. The construction of airports on the staging route to Alaska, and the Alaska Highway, brought a new influx of people to the Yukon. Since then, the expansion of mining and new transportation facilities has brought a slow but steady increase in growth to the territory.
See also: Canada.

Yuma (pop. 106,895), city in southwestern Arizona, seat of Yuma County, situated on the Colorado River at the mouth of the Gila River. The location, an important river crossing, was visited by European explorers perhaps as early as 1540, but the town (originally Colorado City) was not founded until 1854. The development of irrigation systems in the early 1900s made the region an important agricultural area. Marine and army installations and tourism help support Yuma's economy.
See also: Arizona.

Yurok, Native Americans who lived along the Klamath River and in nearby coastal aresa of nortwestn California. In 1770 their number was estimated approximately 2,500. The spoke an Algonquian language.
See also: Native Americans

YWCA *see:* Young Women's Christian Association.

Z

Z, 26th and last letter of the English alphabet, corresponding to the ancient Semitic letter *zayin,* meaning "weapon." The Greeks adopted the familiar *z* form for *zeta,* the sixth letter of their alphabet. The Romans used the letter only for words of Greek origin. In Old French, the letter was called *zède* or *zé,* hence the name *zed* used in Great Britain and Canada, and the name *zee* commonly used in the United States. In Old English, the *z* sound was represented by the letter.

Zadkine, Ossip (1890-1967), Russian-born French sculptor. Came to Paris in 1909. He was influenced by Rodin and African art. His often large works in bronze, wood, and stone include *The Destruction of Rotterdam* (1954),

Ossip Zadkine's The Drawing Lesson *(1938)*

Zagreb (pop. 706,800), capital of the republic of Croatia. Zagreb occupies the site of an early Roman settlement that was also home to Slavic tribes from C.A.D. 600. The present city of Zagreb grew from the merger of 2 earlier towns, Kaptol and Gradac, in the 16th century. It was part of the Austro-Hungarian Empire until 1918, when Croatia, Dalmatia, and Slovenia declared themselves independent. It is a cultural and industrial center, supplying machinery, leather, pharmaceuticals and chemicals, textiles, metal, and paper. Zagreb is characterized by parks and open squares, and is home to Zagreb University, a national theater, and various galleries and museums.
See also: Yugoslavia, Croatia.

Zaharias, Babe Didrikson (1913-1956), U.S. athlete. Considered the greatest woman athlete in history, between 1930-32 she won national hurdles, javelin, baseball throw, broad- and high-jump titles, and set an Olympic 80-m hurdles and javelin records (1932). A top U.S. woman golfer, she won the U.S. Women's Open 3 times (1948, 50, 54).

Zaïre (Congo), recently renamed to the Democratic Republic of the Congo, Zaïre from 1971-97, nation in west-central Africa. With an area of 905,446 sq mi (2,345,095 sq km), Congo is bordered by Angola on the southwest; Congo (Brazzaville) on the west; the Central African Republic and Sudan on the north; Uganda, Rwanda, Burundi, and Tanzania on the east; and Zambia on the southeast.
Land and climate. Central Congo, which straddles the equator, is a large, low plateau covered by rain forest. There is a higher, drier plateau in the southeast. In the east, on the border with Uganda, are the mountains of the Ruwenzori Range and lakes Albert, Edward, and Tanganyika. The Congo (Zaïre) River, one of the largest in Africa, flows west to the Atlantic, where the country narrows to a 25-mi (40-km) wide coastline. Congo has a hot, rainy climate.
People. The population is divided among many groups, among which the Kongo are

Open market in Dilolo, Congo

Congo (Zaïre)

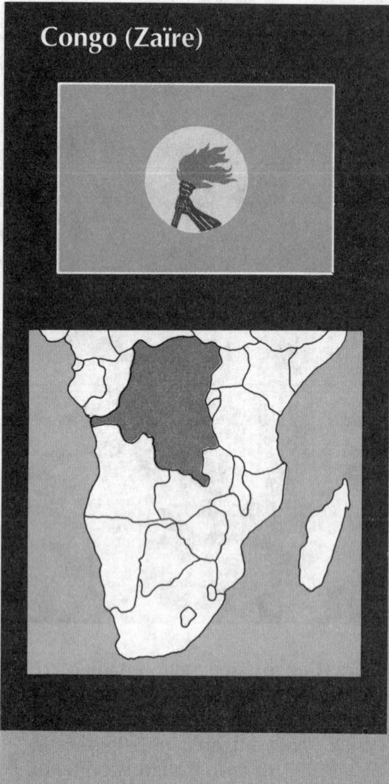

General information	
Capital:	Kinshasa
Area:	905,446 sq mi (2,345,095 sq km)
Population:	39,794,000
Official language:	French
Monetary unit:	1 zaire = 100 makuta
Main cities:	Kinshasa (2,800,000 inh.), Lubumbashi, Kananga
Government	
Form:	republic
Independent:	1960
Head of state:	President (elected every 7 years)
Head of government:	Prime minister
Legislature:	one legislative house (National Legislative Council)
Executive:	President and National Executive Council
Judiciary:	highest court is the Supreme Court
Political division:	10 provinces, 1 capital district
National economy	
Gross national product:	U.S. $8,123,000,000
Per capita income:	U.S. $220
Agriculture:	coffee, plantains, sugar cane, fruit, groundnuts, sweet potatoes
Livestock:	goats, cattle, pigs
Fisheries:	166,000 metric tons
Mining:	copper ore, cobalt ore, coal, zinc concentrates, industrial diamonds
Industries:	metal products, cement, sulphuric acid, corn flour, sugar, soap, palm oil, quicklime
Main exports:	copper, industrial products, crude petroleum, cobalt, agricultural products
Transportation:	3,265 mi (5,254 km) of railroads
Trading partners:	Belgium-Luxembourg, China, U.S., Germany, France
People	
Urban:	40%
Ethnic composition:	Luba 18%, Kongo 16%, Mongo 13.5%, Rwanda 10.5%, Azande 6%
Birth rate:	45.6 per 1,000 population
Death rate:	13.9 per 1,000 population
Infant mortality:	98 per 1,000 live births
Life expectancy:	male 51 years, female 54 years

the most numerous. Other important peoples include the Mongo, Luba, and Zande. Nilotic-speaking peoples live primarily in the north, and Pygmies live in the east. About 200 languages are spoken, most of them Bantu. French is the official language, but Lingola and Swahili are common. Most of the people are Christians, but many adhere to traditional religions. The capital of the country is Kinshasa.

Economy. The mainstay of Congo's economy is mining. The country has 65% of the world's reserves of cobalt and copper, the principal exports. It is also a major diamond producer. Industry includes food processing, chemicals, cement, and textiles. Farms produce cash crops of coffee, rubber, palm oil, cocoa, and tea.

History. First Pygmies and later Bantus were the original black African inhabitants of the region. The first Europeans in the area were Portuguese following in the wake of Diogo Cão, who came in 1482. In 1885 King Leopold II of Belgium took control of an area he called the Congo Free State; in 1908 it became the Belgian Congo and was a rich and profitable colony. The Belgian Congo became independent in 1960 and, as the Republic of the Congo, had Joseph Kasavubu as president and Patrice Lumumba as premier. The fledgling state was unable to maintain either stability or unity, and shortly after independence Moïse Tshombe urged the secession of the mineral-rich province of Katanga. Before Katanga rejoined the nation in 1963, the UN and Belgium sent troops and both the U.S. and the USSR had taken sides in the conflict. In 1965, following continuing unrest, Maj. Gen. Joseph Mobotu, later Mobuto Sese Seko, took control and has been president since 1970. The Democratic Republic of the Congo was renamed Zaïre in 1971 and adopted its current constitution in 1978. Although Zaïre was rich in mineral resources, mismanagement and decreases in world-market prices led to severe economic problems. Political liberalization in the 90s did not solve the problems. In 1997 the crisis escalated as rebels from the east captured the entire country. Their leader, Laurent Kabila, became president; Mobutu fled the country, which was again named Congo.

Zambezi River, river in southeast Africa, fourth-largest in Africa. Rising in northwest Zambia, it flows about 1,700 mi (about 2,736 km) south, then east along the Zambia-Zimbabwe border, through Mozambique to enter the Mozambique Channel of the Indian Ocean through a 2,500-sq mi (6,475-sq km) delta.

Zambia, formerly Northern Rhodesia, officially the Republic of Zambia, independent republic in south-central Africa. With an area of 290,584 sq mi (752,614 sq km), Zambia is bordered by Zaïre on the north; Tanzania on the northeast; Malawi and Mozambique on the east; Zimbabwe, Botswana, and Namibia on the south; and Angola on the west.

Land and climate. The country occupies a mostly flat plateau some 3,000 to 4,500 ft (914 to 1,372 m) above sea level and broken by deep valleys formed by the Luangwa and Zambezi rivers. The plateau is largely savanna and open woodland, and the course of the Zambezi includes Victoria Falls and Lake Kariba, formed by the Kariba Dam. Both Victoria Falls and Lake Kariba are on Zambia's border with Zimbabwe. In the northeast part of the country, the Muchinga Mountains rise some 7,000 ft (2,124 m). Zambia's climate is tropical, but its effects are moderated by altitude.

People. The Zambian people are black Africans, mostly Bantu peoples, with over 70 different tribes and a variety of languages. There are also European and Asian minorities. More than half the people follow animist beliefs. The balance profess Christianity, either Roman Catholicism or Protestantism. While English is the official language, many Bantu languages are also spoken. The capital of Zambia is Lusaka.

Economy. The majority of Zambia's people are engaged in subsistence farming, but the country is also one of the world's major producers of copper, which accounts for the bulk of its export earnings. Cobalt is the

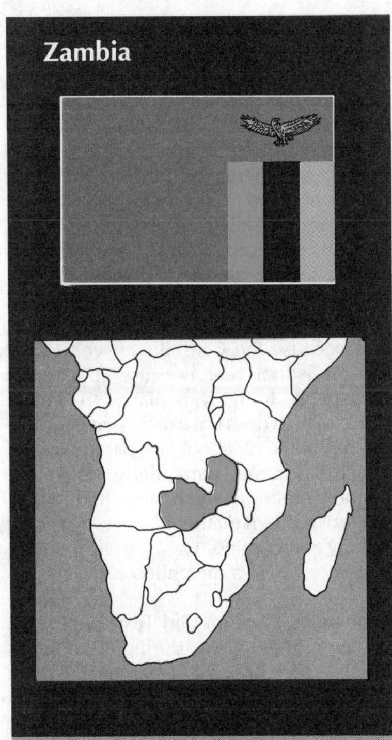

Capital:	Lusaka
Area:	290,586 sq mi (752,614 sq km)
Population:	8,148,000
Government:	republic
Independent:	1964
GNP:	U.S. $2,160,000,000
Per capita:	U.S. $290

The Kariba Dam on the Zambezi river at the border between Zimbabwe and Zambia

second-largest export earner and Zambia also supports lead, zinc, manganese, and sulfur. The agricultural sector produces cash crops, including tobacco, sugarcane, and wheat. Despite its resources, Zambia underwent considerable economic dislocation as a result of its active opposition to Southern Rhodesia in the 1960s and 1970s. In the 1980s the country faced severe food shortages principally due to drought.

History. Present-day Zambians are descendants of Bantu peoples who migrated to the region between the 16th and 18th centuries. European traders and missionaries came in the 19th century, most notably David Livingstone, who came in 1851. In 1888 Cecil Rhodes led the way for British commercial interests. As Northern Rhodesia the area became a British protectorate in 1911. Copper deposits were discovered in the 1920s, leading to rapid and lucrative development but at the expense of the native inhabitants. A nationalist movement arose in 1946, and despite its rigorous opposition to the plan, Northern Rhodesia was combined by the British into the Federation of Rhodesia and Nyasaland, which included Southern Rhodesia (now Zimbabwe) and Nyasaland (now Malawi). Northern Rhodesia and Nyasaland left the federation in 1963 and Northern Rhodesia became the independent Republic of Zambia in 1964, under the presidency of Kenneth Kaunda. The fledgling country protested against and eventually opposed the white regime of Ian Smith in Southern Rhodesia. Though contributing to the isolation of the Smith regime and the eventual emergence of Zimbabwe, the policy proved costly. Kenneth Kaunda was reelected president in 1988.

Zamboanga (pop. 343,722), Philippine city on the extreme western tip of Mindanao Island, capital of Zamboanga del Sur Province. Zamboanga is the major port and trade center of the Sulu Archipelago and exports hardwoods, rice, abaca, rubber, copra, fish, and sugar. Local seashells are exported or made into buttons. Settled by Spain in 1635, much of the city was destroyed in World War II and was subsequently rebuilt.
See also: Philippines.

Zane, Ebenezer (1747-1812), American pioneer. A Quaker, he cofounded (1769) Zanesburg (now in West Virginia; renamed Wheeling in 1806) and blazed a trail to Maysville, Ky., known as Zane's Trace.
See also: Pioneer life in America.

Zanuck, Darryl F. (1902-79), U.S. film producer. He cofounded 20th Century Pictures, which merged with Fox Films (1935) to form 20th Century-Fox, was its production head (1935-52), and its president (1962-71).

Zanzibar, island, part of Tanzania, off eastern Africa. It was a center of an Omani Arab sultanate (1700) with extensive mainland territories. Zanzibar became a British protectorate (1890-93), part of German East Africa (1893), an independent sultanate (1963), and a republic (1964). It then united (1964) with nearby Pemba and with Tanganyika to form Tanzania. The chief exports are cloves and copra.
See also: Tanzania

Zapata, Emiliano (1879?-1919), Mexican revolutionary whose chief ambition was to return Mexican land to the native population. Zapata joined the successful forces of Francisco Madero against the dictatorship of President Porfirio Díaz (1910) and led the insurrectionists of Morelos, his native state. After Díaz's overthrow, Zapata refused to recognize Madero or his successor, Victoriano Huerta, for their failure to redistribute land to the people. Together with Pancho Villa, he renewed his revolutionary endeavors. On 3 occasions (1914-15), Zapata occupied Mexico City. He was assassinated (1919).

Emiliano Zapata

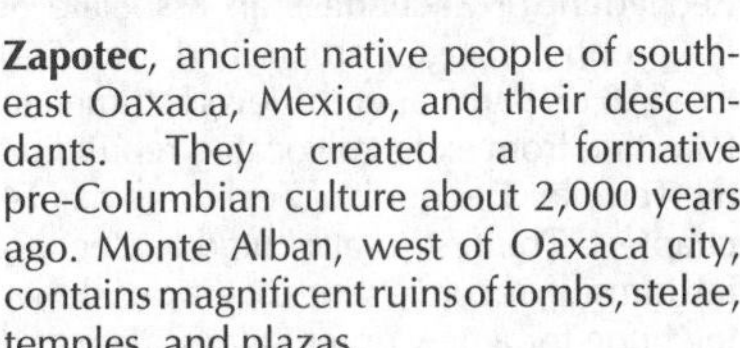

Zapotec, ancient native people of southeast Oaxaca, Mexico, and their descendants. They created a formative pre-Columbian culture about 2,000 years ago. Monte Alban, west of Oaxaca city, contains magnificent ruins of tombs, stelae, temples, and plazas.

Zarathustra *see:* Zoroastrianism.

Zealots, Jewish religious and political fanatics in Palestine about the time of Jesus. Led by Judas of Galilee and Zadock the priest, they resisted Rome and its collaborator Herod the Great, but they later perished (A.D. 70) with the destruction of Jerusalem. St. Simon the Apostle may have been a Zealot.

Zebra, 3 species of striped horses (genus *Equus*) of Africa. The zebra's black-and-white striped coat makes the animal inconspicuous at long range. The 3 species—plains zebra, mountain zebra, and Grévy's zebra—differ in stripe pattern, habitat, and behavior. Plains and mountain zebras live in permanent, nonterritorial stallion groups, but mountain zebras are adapted to life in more arid regions. Grévy's zebras, with very narrow stripes, are territorial animals.

Zebra

Zebu, or Brahman ox (*Bos indicus*), ox found in India, Africa, and Asia. It has a hump on its shoulders and a dewlap under the chin. The horns are large, up to 5 ft (1.5 m) in the *ankole* cattle of Uganda. Zebus are used as draft animals and for milk and meat. They react to heat well and have been introduced to many areas with hot climates, including the southern United States, where they are immune to the Texas fever carried by cattle ticks.

Zebulun, one of the 12 tribes of Israel and one of the 10 lost tribes removed from Palestine by the conquering Assyrians (721 B.C.) and dispersed. Zebulun was part of the Northern Kingdom of Israel and occupied lands northeast of the Plain of Jezreel. The tribe name comes from the sixth son born to Jacob and Leah (Genesis 30:20).

Zechariah, Book of, Old Testament book named for 1 of the 12 minor prophets. Zechariah (or Zacharias), an associate of the prophet Haggai, prophesied from 520 B.C.-518 B.C., and, after the Jews returned to Palestine from exile, advocated rebuilding the Temple. The Book of Zechariah has 14 chapters. The first 8, attributed to Zechariah himself, record a series of visions showing hope for a new order in Jerusalem and the plans for its establishment and organization. The last 6 chapters, attributed to a later author or group of authors, elaborate on Zechariah's themes of the restoration of the Davidic royal line, the intervention of a messiah, and Jerusalem's exiles returned and forgiven.
See also: Bible; Old Testament.

Zeeman effect, changes in the energy levels of atoms that may be observed by the splitting of spectral lines when a light source is placed in a magnetic field. The line separations are expressed as differences of frequency and increase in direct proportion to the strength of the magnetic field. They occur when an atom's electron moves from one energy level, corresponding to the concentric orbits the electron makes around the atomic nucleus, to another. The effect was discovered (1896) by Pieter Zeeman, a Dutch physicist, and was the first indication that electrons are negatively charged particles. It is used by astronomers and physicists to study the properties of nuclei, atoms, and molecules.
See also: Atom; Electron.

Zeiss, Carl (1816-88), German optical manufacturer who founded a famous workshop at Jena in 1846. Realizing that optical technology had much to gain from scientific research, in the mid-1860s he formed a fruitful association with the physicist Ernest Abbe.
See also: Optics.

Zen (Chinese: *Ch'an,* meaning "meditation"), form of Buddhism that developed in China from c.500 A.D. and spread to Japan, exerting great influence on Japanese culture. Zen differs markedly from traditional Buddhism in its abhorrance of images and ritual, scriptures and metaphysics. Rinzai Zen uses *koan* (paradoxical riddles) to shock into sudden enlightenment; Soto Zen stresses contemplation.
See also: Buddhism.

Zenger, John Peter (1697-1745), colonial publisher and journalist whose trial for libel (1735) furthered freedom of the press. As opponents of the English governor, William Cosby, and his party, Zenger and a group of colleagues established the *New York Weekly Journal* (1733) to provide a dissident political voice. The paper consistently criticized the governor, and Zenger was arrested (1734) for criminal libel. Determined to secure Zenger's conviction, the authorities disbarred his attorneys, but his case was eventually defended by Andrew Hamilton of Philadelphia, who argued that Zenger's articles were not libelous because they were based on fact. Zenger was acquitted (1735) and published a verbatim account of the trial as *A Brief Narrative of the Case and Trial of John Peter Zenger* (1736).
See also: Press.

Zenith, in astronomy, point on the celestial sphere directly above an observer and exactly 90° from the celestial horizon. It is directly opposite to the nadir.
See also: Astronomy; Nadir.

Zeno of Citium (335?-265? B.C.), Cypriot philosopher who founded the Stoic school of philosophy in Athens (301 B.C.). A wealthy merchant forced by shipwreck to remain in Athens, Zeno became fascinated with the life of Socrates and the writings of the Cynics, and abandoned trade for philosophy. After years of study he established his own school. Zeno saw the cosmos as the reference point for human ethics, with a divine intelligence guiding both nature and humanity toward "the city of Zeus," that is, toward goodness. He felt that natural law superseded civil law, and that the practice of acceptance and moderation were characteristics of a virtuous life. He defined morality as surrender to divine governance. At his death, the Athenian Assembly gave him citizenship and voted him a statue and gold crown.
See also: Stoicism.

Zeno of Elea (490?-430 B.C.), Greek philosopher who studied under Parmenides and defended his teacher's theories. Zeno used indirect argumentation to try to prove his philosophy and is considered the inventor of pre-Socratic dialectic. He based his arguments on 4 propositions: that all things belong to one unchanging reality as opposed to many; that nothing can be proved by human reason; that empty space is not real because the One fills all voids; that motion is not real because it assumes movement from someplace to empty space, which does not exist. Zeno is known for his book of about 40 paradoxes (of which 8 survive), particularly the 4 concerning motion, which were the beginnings of modern mathematical concepts of infinity and continuity.
See also: Pre-Socratic philosophy.

Zephaniah, Book of, Old Testament book written c.640-630 B.C. during the reign of Josiah (638-608 B.C.) and after the Scythian invasion of Palestine. The dominant themes of the book are condemnation of the Judeans for adopting foreign idols and customs, and a catastrophic day of judgement, the "day of the Lord," when only the few faithful will be saved. This element evolved into the popular notion of the judgement day prominent in Biblical prophecy.
See also: Bible; Old Testament.

Zeppelin *see:* Airship.

Zeppelin, Ferdinand von (1838-1917), German aeronautical engineer who designed and built almost 100 powered balloons.

Zero-base budgeting (ZBB), annual economic planning that justifies expenditure on actual cost or need rather than on increments of the previous year's budget. ZBB assumes a base of zero dollars and asks managers to prepare outlines showing expected high and low spending levels. Budgeting for the coming year is based on these outlines. Introduced in the 1960s by the electronics manufacturer, Texas Instruments, Incorporated, ZBB is used by government and business as a means of controlling spending.
See also: Sunset laws.

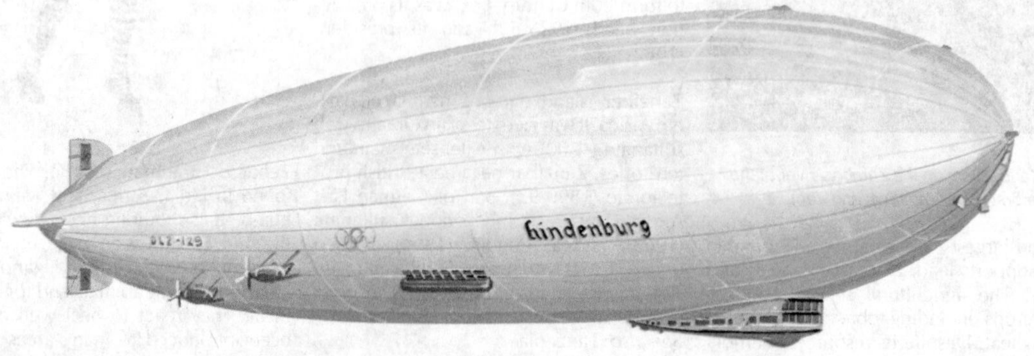

The zeppelin derives its name from its designer—Ferdinand von Zeppelin.

Zero population growth, close approximation in numbers of births and deaths needed to stabilize a nation's population and prevent annual increases. To stabilize the U.S. population at its present level, the replacement ratio for families (excluding illegitimate births) is 2.54 children per fertile married woman. Zero Population Growth is also the name of an organization formed in 1968 by Richard Bowers, Paul Ehrlich, and Charles Remington to inform the public and legislators of the disadvantages of continued population growth.

Zeus, supreme god of Greek mythology. His mother, Rhea, saved him from his jealous father, Cronus, and he was brother and husband of Hera. He led the Olympian gods in overthrowing Cronus and the other Titans. By lot he became god of earth and sky (Poseidon won the sea, Hades the underworld). Zeus's Roman counterpart is Jupiter.
See also: Mythology.

Zhao Ziyang (1919-), premier of China (1980-), successor to Hua Kuo-feng (Hua Guofeng). Purged during the Cultural Revolution, Zhao was later "rehabilitated." He was appointed governor of Szechwan (Sichuan) province in 1975 and elected to the politburo in 1979.

Zhou dynasty (also Chou), China's third and longest-ruling (1122 B.C.-256 B.C.) royal house. The Zhou people were seminomadic tribes who overturned the Shang dynasty, expanded their territory by conquering neighboring tribes, and established a feudal society of separate states ruled by a central government. Their control corresponded to the flowering of Chinese culture. Under Zhou governance, the merchant class emerged, coinage replaced trade by barter, education flourished, and the family became the focus of society. Iron implements, including the traction plow, were introduced, and irrigation improved farming. Confucius, Mencius, and Laozi lived during the Zhou dynasty, and Buddhism was introduced to China in that period.

Zhou Enlai or **Chou En Lai** (1898-1976), Chinese Communist leader, premier and foreign minister of China (1949-59). Zhou began his political activity (1919) when he was imprisoned for a year for demonstrating against the Treaty of Versailles. He was a leader in the labor revolts of Nanchang and Shanghai (1927) and helped establish the Red Army, of which he succeeded Mao Zedong as commissar (1932). In the 1940s he was a leader in the struggle for control of China and was instrumental in the ouster of Chiang Kai-shek. He became prime minister of the Chinese People's Republic (1949), and after his removal (1959) remained influential in Chinese foreign affairs.
See also: China.

Zhuangzi (Chuang Tsu or Chuang-Tzo; 377?-286 B.C.), Chinese scholar and Taoist philosopher, to whom the book *Zhuangzi*, the first Chinese book dealing only with spiritual matters, is attributed. Zhuangzi was a minor official who several times rejected public office. He advocated a life of simplicity, submissive to and at one with nature, and renounced government, science, and even education as of no help in understanding that unity. The *Zhuangzi*, an interpretation of the *Tao*, has as its primary theme unending and inevitable change. The work was important in the development of Zen Buddhism some 400 years later.
See also: Taoism.

Zhukov, Georgi Konstantinovich (1896-1974), Soviet general, hero of the battles at Stalingrad (1943) and Berlin (1945). After the death of Stalin (who had blocked his career), Zhukov was defense minister (1955-57) and briefly a full member of the Communist Party Presidium (1957).
See also: World War II.

Ziegfeld, Florenz (1869-1932), U.S. theatrical producer. In 1907 he launched the Ziegfeld Follies, an annual revue famous for its spectacular staging, beautiful women, and star performers; under his direction it ran for 24 years. Ziegfeld also produced musicals, including *Sally* (1920) and *Show Boat* (1927).

Zimbabwe, officially the Republic of Zimbabwe, formerly Southern Rhodesia under the British, and Rhodesia under Ian Smith, a landlocked republic in south central Africa. With an area of 150,803 sq mi (390,580 sq km), Zimbabwe is bordered by Zambia to the north, Mozambique to the northeast and east, and Botswana to the southwest and west.
Land and climate. Zimbabwe is situated astride a high plateau between the Zambezi and Limpopo rivers. The plateau is divided into three distinct zones. The High Veld is over 4,000 ft (1,219 m) above sea level and extends across the country from the southwest to the northeast. The Middle Veld is most extensive in the northwest and rises 3,000-4,000 ft (914-1,219 m) above sea level. The Low Veld occupies land near river basins in the north and south and is 3,000 ft (914 m) below sea level. In the east, the highlands include Mt. Inyangani which rises to 8,503 ft (2,592 m). Zimbabwe's climate varies with the altitude.
People. The people of Zimbabwe are overwhelmingly black Africans, principally Bantus of the Shona or Ndebele groups. Other important tribes include the Tonga, Sena, Hlengwe, Venda, and Sotho. About 5% of the population consists of whites, coloreds (descendants of whites and black Africans), and Asians. The majority of the people follow traditional animist beliefs, but about 20% are Christian, and there are Hindus among the small Asian minority. English is the official language, but Shona and Ndebele are widely spoken. The capital of the country is Harare.
Economy. Most of the people of Zimbabwe work as subsistence farmers. But the country's agricultural sector is a major food exporter to the South African region. The

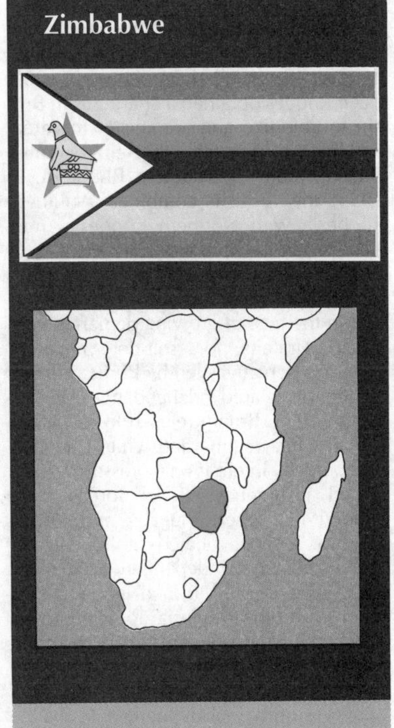

Capital:	Harare
Area:	150,873 sq mi (390,759 sq km)
Population:	9,722,000
Government:	republic
Independent:	1980
GNP:	U.S. $6,070,000,000
Per capita:	U.S. $660

Defensive constructions in Zimbabwe, stone witnesses to the fact that Rhodesia had a developed civilization during the 11th century

principal cash crop is tobacco. Zimbabwe is also rich in mineral resources. Gold is the country's major export, but other valuable minerals include iron ore, asbestos, chrome, copper, and nickel. The country also has an expanding and diversified industrial sector.
History. Bushmen paintings and tools indicate that Zimbabwe had Stone Age inhab-

itants. Bantu peoples settled the area about A.D. 400, and during the 15th century, the Shona civilization established an empire; the capital was called Zimbabwe. In 1889, Cecil Rhodes obtained a charter from Britain to colonize and administer the area, and in 1923 it became the self-governing British colony of Southern Rhodesia. In 1953 the British combined Southern Rhodesia with Northern Rhodesia (now Zambia) and Nyasaland (now Malawi) to form the Federation of Rhodesia and Nyasaland. The federation dissolved in 1963 and in the face of growing demands from black Africans for self-determination, white conservatives led by Prime Minister Ian Smith declared independence from Britain in 1965. Britain refused to recognize the all-white regime and white Rhodesia was beset by international pressure and an armed insurgency. Rebel forces were headed by Robert Mugabe and Joshua Nkomo. In a negotiated settlement, the country gained its independence and black majority rule in 1980, and its name was changed from Rhodesia to Zimbabwe. Rivalry between elements loyal to Robert Mugabe, who was elected president, and Joshua Nkomo threatened the new country's unity, but by the late 1980s the worst excesses of the internal fighting seemed to be under control.

Zimbalist, Efrem (1889-1985), Russian-born U.S. virtuoso violinist. He directed the Curtis Institute of Music in Philadelphia (1941-68) and composed several pieces for violin and orchestra.

Zinc, chemical element, symbol Zn; for physical constants, see Periodic Table. Zinc ores were used for making brass centuries before zinc was recognized as a distinct element. The metal was prepared in India in the 13th century by reducing calamine with organic substances such as wool. It occurs in nature principally as sphalerite (zinc sulfide). It is produced by reduction of the oxide with carbon. Zinc is a bluish-white, lustrous, brittle, reactive metal. It is used in many important metal alloys, including bronze, Babbitt metal, and German silver. Zinc is an essential growth element for humans and animals. The uses of the metal and its compounds are numerous, including in pigments, dry cell batteries, pharmaceuticals, and television screens.

Reconstruction of Zinjanthropus boisei. This skull dates from the Lower Pleistocene Epoch (2 million to 500,000 years ago). Despite the relatively small volume of the skull, the dentition is characteristic of a humanoid. The numerous stone implements found near the skeleton are convincing proof of an advanced people.

Zinjanthropus, humanlike creature that probably lived about 1,750,000 years ago. Its skull was discovered (1959) at Olduvai Gorge, Tanzania, by Mary D. Leakey. The skull belonged to a creature about 17 years of age with a low brow and large, flat teeth. *Zinjanthropus* was probably chiefly herbivorous and had a brain about one-third the size of a modern human. It may have used stone tools. It became extinct about 1 million years ago. *Zinjanthropus* was renamed (1967) *Australopithecus boisei.*
See also: Australopithecus.

Zinneman, Fred (1907-97), film director and winner of Academy Awards for *That Mothers Might Live* (1938), *From Here to Eternity* (1953), and *A Man for All Seasons* (1966). Zinneman studied film making in France before moving to the United States in 1929. Other works include *High Noon* (1952) and *The Nun's Story* (1958).

Zinnia, popular garden plant of the composite family that came from Mexico and has been bred in many forms, including double-flowered varieties. It has a stiff stem, thick leaves, and a single, large flower, which can be 4 in (10.2 cm) across. It is pollinated by hummingbirds, butterflies, and moths.

Zinnia

Zion, in the Old Testament, ancient citadel of David, on the southeast hill of Jerusalem. In a wider sense it symbolizes the whole of Jerusalem and the Jewish people and their aspirations.

Zionism, movement to establish a Jewish national home in Palestine. After the destruction of their state in A.D. 70, the Jews retained their identity and kept alive their dream of an eventual return from exile. The dream turned into a political movement in the 19th century, largely in response to the persecution of Jews in the USSR and Austria, and Jewish farmers and artisans began to settle in Palestine. The decisive impetus came in 1897, when Theodore Herzl organized the first World Zionist Congress, after which Zionist groups were established all over the world. In 1903 the British government offered the Jews a home in Uganda, but this was rejected. Leadership of the Zionist movement was assumed by Chaim Weizmann, who was largely responsible for the Balfour Declaration (1917).
See also: Herzl, Theodore.

Zion National Park, established in 1919 and covering 147,035 acres (59,528 hectares) in southwest Utah. It is noted for its canyons and multicolored rock formations.
See also: National Parks.

ZIP Code, acronym for Zone Improvement Plan, a 5-digit code implemented (1963) to speed sorting and delivery of domestic mail. An optional extra 4 digits were added in 1981. The first number of the code identifies 1 of 10 large geographical areas in the United States where the mail will be delivered. The second 2 numbers indicate the metropolitan area, and the last 2 numbers represent the addressee's local post office. The ZIP code facilitates mechanical mail processing.

Zipper, slide fastener having 2 rows of coils or teeth attached to strips of fabric or other material. The slide, moved in one direction, pulls the teeth together to interlock, and unlocks the teeth when moved in the opposite direction. The original slide fastener was displayed (1893) by Whitcomb L. Judson at the Chicago World's Fair Columbian Exposition and was patented that year. The B. F. Goodrich Company first used the name zipper (1922) for the slide fastener on overshoes.

Zircon, silicate mineral, zirconium silicate ($ZrSiO_4$), used chiefly as a gemstone and as the main source of the metals zirconium and hafnium, in industry and research. Zircon crystals are widespread in igneous deposits such as granite, in some metamorphic rock, and in beach sands. They occur in Australia, Asia, Europe, and North America, and may be clear, red-brown, green, yellow, or blue.

Zirconium, chemical element, symbol Zr; for physical constants, see Periodic Table. Zirconium is mentioned in biblical writings as the mineral zircon. In 1789 Martin Heinrich Klaproth isolated the oxide of zirconium from zircon. The impure metal was first isolated by Jöns J. Berzelius in 1824. Zircon (zirconium silicate) is the principal ore of zirconium. Zirconium is produced commercially by reduction of the chloride with magnesium. It is a grayish-white, lustrous metal resistant to corrosion by acids, alkalis, sea water, and other agents. It is superconductive at low temperatures. The metal has a low absorption cross section for neutrons. Most zirconium is used in nuclear reactors. Zirconium oxide is a refractory material and is used in furnaces and in the glass and ceramic industries.

Zither, stringed instrument related to the dulcimer and psaltery. It is placed across the knees, and the strings, which stretch across a shallow sound box, are plucked. The zither is a traditional folk instrument of central Europe.

Zodiac, band of the heavens whose outer limits lie 9° on each side of the ecliptic. The 12 main constellations near the eclipse, corresponding to the 12 signs of the zodiac, are Aries; Taurus; Gemini; Cancer; Leo; Virgo; Libra; Scorpio; Sagittarius; Capricorn; Aquarius; Pisces. The orbits of all the planets except Pluto lie within the zodiac, and their positions, as that of the sun, are important in astronomy and astrology. The 12 signs are each equivalent to 30° of arc along the zodiac.
See also: Astrology; Constellation.

Zodiacal light, faint cone of light visible in the night sky just before dawn or after sunset. The luminosity extends along the plane of the zodiac or ecliptic and can best be seen at a point 30° to 90° from the sun, though there is some zodiacal light in all parts of the sky. Scientists explain zodiacal light as dust particles from comets and asteroids dispersed over a vast area and reflecting sunlight.

Zog (Ahmedi Bey Zogu; 1895-1961), king of Albania (1928-46). After serving in the Austrian army he was made premier (1922-24) and president (1925-28), whereupon he proclaimed himself king. He fled when the Italians invaded, and he spent the rest of his life in exile.
See also: Albania.

Zola, Émile (1840-1902), French novelist and founder of naturalism. His works proclaim a "scientific" vision of life determined entirely by heredity and environment. His first success, *Thérèse Raquin* (1867), was followed by the *Rougon-Macquart* cycle (20 vol., 1871-93), depicting, with powerful and often lurid realism, the fortunes of a contemporary family. It includes his celebrated studies of alcoholism (*The Dram Shop*, 1877), prostitution (*Nana*, 1880), and life in a mining community (*Germinal*, 1885). In 1898 Zola threw himself into the Dreyfus affair with the pamphlet "J'accuse," attacking the army.
See also: Naturalism.

Zone melting, technique used in industry and research to remove or distribute impurities in solid materials. Zone melting uses alternate heating and freezing provided by a row of ring-shaped heaters that pass slowly along a tube of solid substance. As the rings travel, they melt bands, or zones, of the solid matter. The resulting liquid holds and carries the impurities to the end of the tube, and the melted area is then refrozen. Subsequent repetitions of the procedure improve the purification.

Zoning, control by ordinance of the uses or character of urban land or buildings, usually accomplished by confining a specific type of development, either residential, public, commercial, or industrial, to a designated area. Zoning laws are used by city and county planning departments to regulate growth and population concentration, preserve neighborhood environments, and isolate industry and commerce. The first U.S. zoning laws were enacted in New York City (1916), and until the 1950s, U.S. zoning was used chiefly in previously developed areas. Now nearly all new urban construction is controlled by zoning.

Zoo, or zoological garden, collection of wild-animal species preserved for public education, scientific research, and the breeding of endangered species. The first modern zoo (1826) was that of the Royal Zoological Society at Regent's Park, London.

Zoogeography, study of the geographical distribution of animal species and populations. Physical barriers—such as wide oceans and mountain ranges, major climatic extremes, or intense heat or cold—may prevent the spread of a species into new areas or may separate 2 previously like populations, allowing them to develop into distinct species. The effect of these barriers on movement and interbreeding, both now and in the past, are reflected in the distributions and, later, adaptive radiations of animal species, resulting in the zoogeographical distributions we find today.

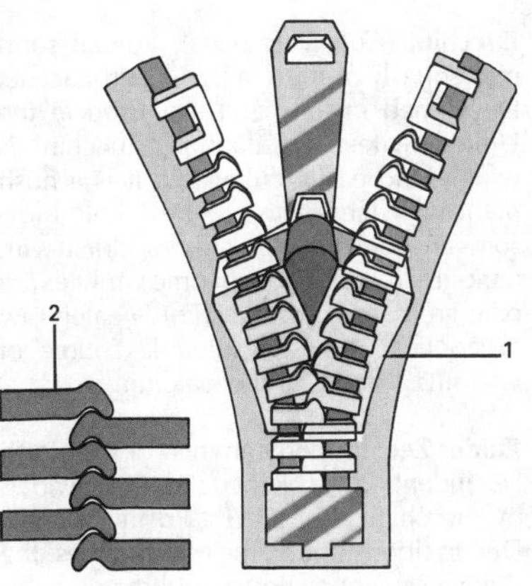

The metal zipper was patented in Germany by Catharina Kuhn-Moos in 1912.
1. The slide pulls the teeth together.
2. Each tooth has a protrusion on top and a recess underneath. These fit together alternately.

Zoology, scientific study of animal life. Originally concerned with the classification of animal groups, comparative anatomy, and physiology, the science now embraces studies of evolution, genetics, embryology, biochemistry, animal behavior, and ecology.

Zoroaster *see:* Zoroastrianism.

Zoroastrianism, Persian religion based on the teachings of Zoroaster (Greek form of *Zarathustra*), a sage who lived in the 6th century B.C. It was founded on the old Aryan folk religion but abolished its polytheism, establishing 2 predominant spirits: Ahura-Mazda (Ormazd), the spirit of light and good; and Ahriman, the spirit of evil and darkness. Zoroastrianism includes the belief in eternal reward or punishment after death according to man's deeds. Its scriptures are the *Zend-Avesta*. Almost wiped out in the 7th century by the Muslim conquest of Persia, Zoroastrianism survives among the Parsees (Parsis) of India.
See also: Persia, Ancient.

Zion National Park

Zucchini (*Cucurbita pepo*), annual summer squash of the family Cucurbitaceae. Developed in Italy and first used in the United States in California, zucchini is widely and easily cultivated. It is a bush plant with large leaves. The edible blossoms are gold; the fruits are cylindrical with dark-green skins, though some varieties are pale green or gold. Zucchini is eaten raw or cooked and is a valuable source of vitamins A and C and of calcium.

Zuider Zee, formerly an inlet of the North Sea indenting the Netherlands and divided by the chain of the West Frisian Islands. Due to floods during the Middle Ages, the Zuider Zee grew enough to threaten habitations along its shores. There were many schemes to stem the encroachment of the Zuider Zee, but the first feasible plan was developed by Cornelis Lely, a Dutch engineer, and approved by the Dutch government in 1918. He proposed constructing a heavy dike between Friesland and North Holland that would shorten the coastline and discharge the salt water. Construction began in 1920 and the 19-mi (30-km) dam, the Afsluitdijk, was completed in 1932. It separated the Zuider Zee into two areas, the Waddenzee, open to the sea, and the Ijsselmeer, in which large areas of land have been reclaimed for agricultural use.

Huldreich Zwingli

Zukerman, Pinchas (1948-), Israeli-born violinist, violist, and conductor who came to New York (1962) as a protégé of Isaac Stern. He performed with orchestras throughout the world and made his conducting debut in 1974.

Zulu, South African Bantu people who settled what is now Natal Province early in the 17th century. Under King Shaka (or Chaka), the Zulus conquered neighboring tribes and expanded their domain (1818-20). Shaka was friendly to Europeans, but his half-brother and successor, Dingaan, fought with Boer settlers (1838) in a cattle dispute. The British invaded Zulu territory (1879) and, after losing a battle at Isandhlwana, defeated the Zulus at Ulundi. There was political unrest until 1910 when the Union of South Africa absorbed the Zulu province. Traditionally cattle and grain farmers, the Zulus live in a patriarchal clan society and the clan chief is the genealogically senior male. They practice polygyny. Zulu religion was based on ancestor worship and the belief in a divine creator, though now many Zulus have adopted Christianity.

Zululand, northeastern region of Natal Province, South Africa. It borders on Mozambique, the Indian Ocean, Swaziland, and the Buffalo and Tugela rivers. It produces sugarcane, cotton, and maize. Cattle raising is the traditional occupation of the Zulus, a Bantu people who comprise most of the population. Traditionally they live in beehive-shaped huts in fenced compounds called *kraals.* Zululand was annexed by the British in 1887 after prolonged Zulu resistance to white conquest. Many Zulu men now work as migrant laborers in mines and in cities.
See also: South Africa.

Zuñi, Native Americans of the Zuñian linguistic stock, in New Mexico. The Zuñi live mainly by agriculture and produce fine jewelry and sculpture. They have retained their ancient religion, which they celebrate in magnificent festivals noted for their dancing and costumes.

Zunz, Leopold (1794-1886), German Jewish scholar and historian who made the first scientific analysis of Jewish prayers and literature. Zunz was one of the founders of the Society for Jewish Culture and Science (1819), established to analyze and explore Jewish literature, culture, and history, and he was editor of the society's periodical (1820-23). His works in German include *On Rabbinic Literature* (1818), *The Worship Sermons of the Jews, Historically Developed* (1832), and *On History and Literature* (1845).
See also: Jews.

Zurbarán, Francisco (1598-1664), Spanish painter of the Baroque period known for his religious paintings and representations of monastic life. Zurbarán's naturalistic style was stimulated by Caravaggio and Velázquez and was characterized by sculptural modeling of form created by intense contrast between shadow and light. His first known painting is dated 1616, but he produced his finest works between 1629 and 1645, including a series, *Labors of Hercules*, and *Defense of Cadiz* (1634), *Adoration of the Kings* (1638), and a number of paintings exported to Lima, Peru (1647), that influenced colonial art. His later works were more sentimental and idealized in style.
See also: Baroque.

Zürich (pop. 351,500), city in northern Switzerland, capital of Zürich canton, and the nation's financial and education center. The Romans settled Zürich C.A.D. 100 as the fortified Turicum. It joined the Swiss Confederation that became modern Switzerland (1351). Zürich is a tourist and cultural center, home to the University of Zürich; the National Museum; 2 11th-century churches, the Grossmünster and the Fraumünster; and the 15th-century Wasserkirche. Industrial products include precision machinery, textiles, food, paper, and tobacco. The world's banking and gold-trade centers are located in Zürich.
See also: Switzerland.

Zweig, Arnold (1887-1968), German novelist. He wrote an 8-volume epic that includes his best-known novel, *The Case of Sergeant Grischa* (1927), which powerfully indicted militarism in its description of World War I and its effects on German society.

Zweig, Stefan (1881-1942), Austrian biographer and novelist. He is best known for his psychological studies of such historical figures and writers as Erasmus, Mary, Queen of Scots, and Honoré Balzac. He wrote of European culture in *The Tide of Fortune* (1928).

Zwicky, Fritz (1898-1974), Swiss-born U.S. astronomer and astrophysicist best known for his studies of supernovas, which he showed to be quite distinct from, and much rarer than, novas. He also did pioneering work on jet propulsion.
See also: Astronomy; Supernova.

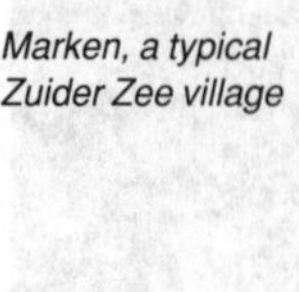
Marken, a typical Zuider Zee village

Zwingli, Huldreich (1484-1531), influential Swiss Protestant leader of the Reformation, originally a Roman Catholic priest. In 1523 the city of Zürich accepted his 67 articles demanding such reforms as the removal of religious images, simplification of the Mass, and the introduction of Bible readings. Zwingli was killed in the war between the Catholic and Protestant cantons.
See also: Reformation.

Zworykin, Vladimir Kosma (1889-1982), Russian-born U.S. electronic engineer regarded as the father of modern television: His kinescope (patented 1924), little adapted, is our modern picture tube; and his iconoscope, though now obsolete, represents the basis of the first practical television camera. He also made important contributions to the electron microscope.
See also: Television.

Earth Facts

Origin

Theories of the origin of the Earth have changed over the centuries, but recent concepts do seem to be the most plausible. It is now generally accepted that the present-day Solar System evolved slowly from a mass, or cloud, of mostly hydrogen gas. Over an enormous period of time (perhaps 10 billion years) this cloud contracted because of the force of gravity and became dense in the center. As the cloud grew denser and experienced increased luminosity, it also began to radiate. This dense cloud ultimately became a star: our Sun. As the Sun developed, gravitational forces drew in materials from surrounding areas. These materials grew in size as the force of gravity increased. Eventually, these objects assumed a spherical shape and can be considered protoplanets. This process of increasing gravitational fields and expanding planets orbiting around a stable Sun continued until the Solar System took its present shape about 5 billion years ago.

The Earth is unique among planets because of its position in the Solar System. It is the third planet from the Sun (of the nine major planets) and has been blessed with a life-supporting environment of oceans, clouds, oxygenated air, and mostly moderate temperatures. Earth's protective atmosphere, its size, and its speed of rotation are also important factors in supporting life on the planets. It is the only planet capable of supporting life without the creation of an artificial environment.

Statistics

The exact measurements of the Earth are subject to variation. The figures given are accurate approximations.

Age	45 billion years
Weight	6,6 sextillion short tons
Area	197,000,000 sq mi / 509,600,000 sq km
Land Surface	57,000,000 sq mi (29% of planet) 146,000,000 sq km
Water Surface	140,000,000 sq mi (71% of planet) 361,600,000 sq km
Circumference at Equator	24,902 mi / 40,000 km
Circumference of Meridian	24,860 mi / 40,000 km
Equatorial Diameter	7,927 mi / 12,755 km

The Continents

Name	*Area sq mi*	*Area sq km*	*% of Land Surface*
Asia	17.1	44.5	30
Africa	11.7	30.2	20
No.America	9.4	24.2	16
So.America	6.9	17.8	12
Antarctica	5.4	13.9	9.2
Europe	3.9	10.2	6.8
Oceania	3.5	8.9	6

(in millions)

Important Deserts

Name	*Continent*	*Square miles*	*Square kilometers*
Arabian	Asia	70,000	182,000
Chihuahuan	North America	140,000	364,000
Death Valley	North America	3,300	8,580
Gibson	Australia	120,000	312,000
Gobi	Asia	500,000	1,300,000
Great Sandy	Australia	150,000	390,000
Great Victoria	Australia	150,000	390,000
Kalahari	Africa	225,000	585,000
Kara-Kum	Asia	120,000	312,000
Kyzyl-Kum	Asia	100,000	260,000
Libyan	Africa	450,000	1,170,000
Lut (Dasht-e Lut)	Asia	20,000	52,000
Mojave	North America	15,000	39,000
Nafud (An Nafud)	Asia	40,000	104,000
Nubian	Africa	100,000	260,000
Rub al Khali	Asia	250,000	650,000
Sahara	Africa	3,500,000	9,100,000
Simpson	Australia	40,000	104,000
Sonoran	North America	70,000	182,000
Syrian	Asia	100,000	260,000
Taklimakan	Asia	140,000	364,000
Thar	Asia	100,000	260,000

Death Valley, California

Important Islands

Figure in parentheses shows rank among the world's 10 largest islands.

Arctic Ocean

Name	*Square Miles*	*Square Kilometers*
Axel Heiberg	16,671	43,178
Baffin (5)	195,928	507,454
Banks	27,038	70,028
Bathurst	6,194	16,042
Devon	21,331	55,247
Ellesmere (10)	75,767	196,236
Franz Joseph Land	8,000	20,720
Melville	16,274	42,150
Novaya Zemlya (two islands)	35,000	90,650
Prince of Wales	12,872	33,338
Somerset	9,570	24,786
Southampton	15,913	41,215
Svalbard	23,940	62,005
Nordaustlandet	5,410	14,012
Spitsbergen	15,060	39,005
Victoria (9)	83,896	217,291
Atlantic Ocean		
Anticosti	3,066	7,941
Ascension	34	88
Azores	888	2,300
Faial	67	174
Sao Miguel	291	754
Bahamas	5,353	13,864
Bermuda	20	521
Block	10	26
Canary Islands	2,808	7,273
Fuerteventura	668	1,730
Gran Canaria	592	1,533
Tenerife	795	2,059
Cape Breton	3,981	10,311
Cape Verde Islands	1,750	4,533
Faeroe Islands	540	1,399
Falkland Islands	4,700	12,173
Fernando de Noronha Archipelago	7	18
Greenland (1)	840,000	2,175,600
Iceland	39,769	103,002
Long Island	1,396	3,616
Bioko Island	785	2,033
Madeira Islands	307	795
Marajo	15,528	40,218
Martha's Vineyard	91	236
Mount Desert	108	280
Nantucket	46	119
Newfoundland	42,030	108,858
Prince Edward	2,184	5,659

Name	Square Miles	Square Kilometers
St. Helena	47	122
South Georgia	1,450	3,756
Tierra del Fuego	18,800	48,692
Tristan da Cunha	40	104
British Isles		
Great Britain (8)	84,200	218,078
Channel Islands	75	194
Guernsey	45	62
Jersey	24	62
Sark	2	5
Hebrides	2,744	7,107
Ireland	32,599	84,431
Irish Republic	27,136	70,282
Northern Ireland	5,463	14,149
Man	227	588
Orkney Islands	390	1,010
Scilly Islands	6	16
Shetland Islands	567	1,469
Skye	670	1,735
Wight	147	381
Baltic Sea		
Aland Islands	581	1,505
Bornholm	227	588
Gotland	1,164	3,015
Caribbean Sea		
Antigua	108	280
Aruba	75	194
Barbados	166	430
Cuba	44,218	114,525
Isle of Youth	1,182	3,061
Curaçao	171	443
Dominica	290,751	
Guadeloupe	687	1779
Hispaniola	29,530	76,483
Jamaica	4,244	10,992
Martinique	425	1,101
Puerto Rico	3,515	9,104
Tobago	116	300
Trinidad	1,864	4,828
Virgin Islands	132	342
Indian Ocean		
Andaman Islands	2,500	6,475
Madagascar (4)	226,658	587,044
Mauritius	720	1,865
Pemba	380	984
Reunion	969	2,510
Seychelles	171	443
Sri Lanka	25,332	65,610
Zanzibar	640	1,658
Persian Gulf		
Bahrain	258	668
Mediterranean Sea		
Balearic Islands	1,936	5,014
Corfu	229	593
Corsica	3,369	8,726
Crete	3,186	8,257
Cyprus	3,572	9,251
Elba	86	223
Euboea	542	1,404
Malta	1122	316
Rhodes	542	1,404
Sardinia	9,262	23,989
Sicily	9,822	25,439
Pacific Ocean		
Aleutian Islands	6,821	17,666
Adak	289	749
Amchitka	121	313
Attu	388	1,005
Kanaga	135	350
Kiska	110	285
Tanaga	209	541
Umnak	675	1,748
Unalaska	1,064	2,756
Unimak	1,600	4,144

Name	Square Miles	Square Kilometers
Canton	4	10
Caroline Islands	472	1,222
Christmas	94	243
Diomede, Big	11	28
Diomede, Little	5	
Easter	69	179
Fiji	7,056	18,275
Vanua Levu	2,242	5,807
Viti Levu	4,109	10,642
Funafuti	2	5
Galapagos Islands	3,043	7,881
Guadalcanal	2,500	6,475
Guam	209	541
Hainan	13,000	33,670
Hawaiian Islands	6,450	16,706
Hawaii	4,037	10,456
Oahu	593	1,536
Hong Kong	29	75
Japan	145,809	377,645
Hokkaido	30,144	78,073
Honshu (7)	87,805	227,415
Iwo Jima	8	21
Kyushu	14,114	36,555
Okinawa	459	1,189
Shikoku	7,049	18,257
Kodiac	3,670	9,505
Marquesas Islands	492	1,274
Marshall Islands	70	181
Bikini	2	5
Nauru	8	21
New Caledonia	6,530	16,913
New Guinea (2)	306,000	792,540
New Zealand	103,883	269,057
Chatham	372	963
North	44,035	114,051
South	58,305	151,010
Stewart	674	1,746
Northern Mariana Islands	184	479
Philippines	115,831	300,002
Leyte	2,787	7,218
Luzon	40,880	105,879
Mindanao	36,775	95,247
Mindoro	3,790	9,816
Negros	4,907	12,709
Palawan	4,554	11,795
Panay	4,446	11,515
Samar	5,050	13,080
Quemoy	56	145
Sakhalin	29,500	76,405
Samoa Islands	1,117	3,048
American Samoa	77	199
Tutuila	52	135
Samoa (Western)	1,133	2,934
Savai'i	670	1,735
Upolu	429	1,111
Santa Catalina	72	186
Tahiti	402	1041
Taiwan	13,823	35,802
Tasmania	26,178	67,801
Tonga Islands	270	699
Vancouver	12,079	31,285
Vauatu	5,700	14,763
East Indies		
Bali	2,147	5,561
Borneao (3)	280,000	725,200
Celebes	69,000	178,710
Java	48,900	126,651
Madura	2,113	5,473
Moluccas	28,766	74,504
New Britain	14,093	36,501
New Ireland	3,707	9,638
Sumatra	165,00	427,350
Timor	11,570	29,966

Important Rivers

Name	Outflow	Length Miles	Kilometers
Albany	James Bay	610	982
Amazon	Atlantic Ocean	4,000	6,437
Amu	Aral Sea	1,578	2,539
Amur	Tatar Strait	2,744	4,416
Angara	Yenisey River	1,151	1,852
Arkansas	Mississippi River	1,459	2,348
Back	Arctic Ocean	605	974
Brahmaputra	Bay of Bengal	1,800	2,897
Canadian	Arkansas River	900	1,458
Chang Jiang	East China Sea	3,964	6,379
Churchill Manitoba	Hudson Bay	1,000	1,609
Churchill Quebec	Atlantic Ocean	532	856
Colorado	Gulf of California	1,450	2,333
Columbo	Pacific Ocean	1,243	2,000
Congo	Atlantic Ocean	2,900	4,667
Danube	Black Sea	1,776	2,858
Dniepr	Black Sea	1,420	2,285
Dniester	Black Sea	877	1,411
Don	Sea of Azov	1,224	1,970
Drava	Danube River	447	719
Dvina, North	White Sea	824	1,326
Dvina, West	Gulf of Riga	634	1,020
Ebro	Mediterranean	565	909
Elbe	North Sea	724	1,165
Euphrates	Shatt-al-Arab	1,700	2,736
Fraser	Strait of Georgia	850	1,368
Gambia	Atlantic Ocean	700	1,127
Ganges	Bay of Bengal	1,560	2,511
Garonne	Bay of Biscay	357	575
Hsi	South China Sea	1,200	1,931
Huang	Yellow Sea	2,903	4,672
Indus	Arabian Sea	1,800	2,897
Irrawaddy	Bay of Bengal	1,337	2,152
Japura	Amazon River	1,750	2,816
Jordan	Dead Sea	200	322
Kootenay	Columbia River	485	781
Lena	Laptev Sea	2,734	4,400
Loire	Bay of Biscay	634	1,020
Mackenzie	Arctic Ocean	2,635	4,241
Madeira	Amazon River	2,013	3,240
Magdalena	Caribbean Sea	956	1,538
Mame	Seine River	326	552
Mekong	South China Sea	2,600	4,184
Meuse	North Sea	580	933
Mississippi	Gulf of Mexico	2,340	3,766
Missouri	Mississippi River	2,540	4,000
Murray-Darling	Indian Ocean	2,310	3,717
Negro	Amazon River	1,400	2,253
Nelson	Hudson Bay	1,410	21,269
Niger	Gulf of Guinea	2,590	4,168
Nile	Mediterranean Sea	4,160	6,695
Ob-Irtysh	Gulf of Ob	3,362	5,410
Oder	Baltic Sea	567	912
Ohio	Mississippi River	1,310	2,108
Orange	Atlantic Ocean	1,300	2,092
Orinoco	Atlantic Ocean	1,600	2,575
Ottawa	St. Lawrence River	790	1,271
Paraguay	Parana River	1,584	2,549
Parana	Rio de la Plata	2,485	3,999
Peace	Slave River	1,210	1,947
Pilcomayo	Paraguay River	1,000	1,609
Po	Adriatic Sea	405	652
Purus	Amazon River	2,100	2,380
Red	Mississippi River	1,290	2,076
Red River of North	Lake Winnipeg	545	877
Rhine	North Sea	820	1,320
Rhône	Gulf of Lions	505	813
Rio de la Plata	Atlantic Ocean	150	241
Rio Grande	Gulf of Mexico	1,760	2,832
Rio Roosevelt	Aripuana	400	644
Saguenay	St. Lawrence River	434	698
St. John	Bay of Fundy	418	673
St. Lawrence	Gulf of St. Lawrence	800	1,287
Salween	Andaman Sea	1,500	2,414
San Francisco	Atlantic Ocean	1,988	3,199
Saskatchewan	Lake Winnipeg	1,205	1,939
Seine	English Channel	496	798
Shannon	Atlantic Ocean	230	370
Snake	Columbia River	1,038	1,670
Sungari	Amur River	1,150	1,851
Syr	Aral Sea	1,370	2,205
Tajo, Tagus	Atlantic Ocean	626	1,007
Tennessee	Ohio River	652	1,049
Thames	North Sea	236	380
Tiber	Tyrrhenian	252	406
Tigris	Shatt-al-Arab	1,180	1,899
Tisza	Danube River	600	966
Tocantins	Para River	1,677	2,699
Ural	Caspian Sea	1,575	2,535
Uruguay	Rio de la Plata	1,000	1,609
Volga	Caspian Sea	2,194	3,531
Weser	North Sea	454	732
Wisla	Bay of Danzig	675	1,086
Yellow (see Huang)			
Yenisey	Kara Sea	2,543	4,092
Yukon	Bering Sea	1,979	3,185
Zambezi	Indian Ocean	1,700	2,736

Mississippi River

Highest and Lowest Continental Altitudes

Continent	Highest Point	Elevation Above Sea Level Feet	Meters
Asia	Mount Everest, Nepal-Tibet	29,028	8,708
South America	Mount Aconcagua, Argentina	22,834	6,850
North America	Mount McKinley, Alaska	20,320	6,096
Africa	Kilimanjaro, Tanzania	19,3405	5,802
Europe	Mount Elbrus, USSR	18,510	5,553
Antarctica	Vinson Massil	16,864	5,059
Australia	Mount Kosciusko, New South Wales	7,310	2,193

Continent	Lowest Point	Below Sea Level Feet	Meters
Asia	Dead Sea, Israel-Jordan	1,312	394
South America	Valdes Peninsula, Argentina	131	39
North America	Death Valley, California	282	85
Africa	Lake Assal, Djibouti	512	154
Europe	Caspian Sea, USSR	92	28
Antarctica	unknown	—	
Australia	Lake Eyre, South Australia	52	16

Important Mountains

Mount Everest

Mount Everest was considered to be 29,002 ft (8,701 m) tall when Edmund Hillary and Tenzing Norgay scaled it in 1953. This triangulation figure had been accepted since 1850. In 1954 the Surveyor General of the Republic of India set the height at 29,028 ft (8,708 m), plus or minus 10 ft (3 m) because of snow. The National Geographic Society accepts the new figure, but many mountaineering groups still use 29,002 ft (8,701 m).

In 1987 new calculations based on satellite measurements indicated that the Himalayan peak K-2 rises 29,064 ft (8,719 m) above sea level and that Mount Everest is 800 ft higher. The National Geographic Society has not yet accepted the revised figure.

North America

Name	Country	Feet	Meters
McKinley	U.S.	20,320	6,096
Logan	Canada	19,850	5,955
Citlaltepec (Orizaba)	Mexico	18,700	5,610
St. Elias	U.S.-Canada	18,008	5,402
Popocatepelt	Mexico	17,887	5,366
Foraker	U.S.	17,400	5,220
Tztaccihuatl	Mexico	17,343	5,203
Lucania	Canada	17,147	5,144
King	Canada	16,971	5,091
Steele	Canada	16,644	4,993
Bona	U.S.	16,550	4,965
Blackburn	U.S.	16,390	4,917
Kennedy	U.S.	16,286	4,886
Sanford	U.S.	16,237	4,871
South Buttress	U.S.	15,885	4,766
Wood	Canada	15,885	4,766
Vancouver	U.S.-Canada	15,700	4,710
Churchill	U.S.	15,638	4,691
Fairweather	U.S.-Canada	15,300	4,590
Zincantecatl (Toluca)	Mexico	15,016	4,505
Hubbard	U.S.-Canada	15,015	4,505

South America

Name	Country	Feet	Meters
Aconcagua	Argentina	22,834	6,850
Ojos del Salado	Argentina-Chile	22,572	6,771
Bonete	Argentina	22,546	6,764
Tupungato	Argentina-Chile	22,310	6,693
Pissis	Argentina	22,241	6,672
Mercedario	Argentina	22,211	6,663
Huascaran	Peru	22,205	6,662
Uullaillaco	Argentina-Chile	22,057	6,617
El Libertador	Argentina	22,047	6,614
Cachi	Argentina	22,047	6,614
Yerupaja	Peru	21,709	6,513
Galan	Argentina	21,654	6,496
El Muerto	Argentina-Chile	21,457	6,437
Sajama	Bolivia	21,391	6,417
Nacimiento	Argentina	21,302	6,391
Illimani	Bolivia	21,201	6,360
Coropuna	Peru	21,083	6,325

Mount Pinatubo, Philippines

The highest point in the West Indies is in the Dominican Republic, Pico Duarte (10,417 ft/3,125 m).

Africa, Australia, and Oceania

Name	Country	Feet	Meters
Kilimanjaro	Tanzania	19,340	5,802
Kenya	Kenya	17,058	5,117
Margherita Peak	Uganda-Zaire	16,763	5,029
Jaja	New Guinea	16,500	4,950
Trikora	New Guinea	15,585	4,676
Mandala	New Guinea	15,420	4,626
Ras Dashan	Ethiopia	15,158	4,547

Europe *Alps*

Name	Country	Feet	Meters
Mont Blanc	France-Italy	15,771	4,731
Monte Rosa	Switzerland	15,203	4,561
Dom	Switzerland	14,911	4,473
Liskamm	Italy-Switzerland	14,852	4,456
Weisshorn	Switzerland	14,780	4,434
Taschhorn	Switzerland	14,690	4,407
Dent Blanche	Switzerland	14,293	4,288
Nadelhorn	Switzerland	14,196	4,259
Grand Combin	Switzerland	14,154	4,246
Lenzspitze	Switzerland	14,088	4,226
Finsteraarhorn	Switzerland	14,022	4,207
Caucasus			
Elbrus	USSR	18,510	5,553
Shkara	USSR	17,064	5,119
Dykh Tau	USSR	17,054	5,116
Kashtan Tau	USSR	16,877	5,063
Dzhangi Tau	USSR	16,565	4,970
Kazbek	USSR	16,558	4,967

Asia

Name	Country	Feet	Meters
Everest	Nepal-Tibet	29,028	8,708
K2 (Godwin Austen)	Kashmir	28,250	8,475
Kanchenjunga	Nepal-Tibet	28,208	8,462
Lotse I (Everest)	Nepal-Tibet	27,923	8,377
Makalu I	Nepal-Tibet	27,824	8,347
Lhotse II (Everest)	Nepal-Tibet	27,560	8,268
Dhaulagin	Nepal	26,810	8,043
Mlanslu I	Nepal	26,760	8,028
Cho Oyu	Nepal-Tibet	26,720	8,016
Nanga Prabat	Kashmir	26,660	7,998
Annapurna I	Nepal	26,504	7,951
Gasherbrum	Kashmir	26,470	7,941
Borad	Kashmir	26,400	7,920
Gsainthan	Tibet	26,287	7,886
Annapurna II	Nepal	26,041	7,812
Gyachung Kang	Nepal-Tibet	25,910	7,773
Disteghil Sar	Kashmir	25,858	7,757
Himalchuli	Nepal	25,801	7,740
Masherbrurn	Kashmir	25,660	7,698
Nanda Devi	India	25,645	7,694
Rakaposhi	Kashmir	25,550	7,665
Kamet	India-Tibet	25,447	7,634
Namcha Barwa	Tibet	25,445	7,634
Gurla Mandhata	Tibet	25,355	7,607
Ulugh Muz Tagh	Sinkiang-Tibet	25,340	7,602
Kungur	Sinkiang	25,325	7,598
Tirich Mir	Pakistan	25,230	7,569
Makalu II	Nepal-Tibet	25,120	7,536

Antarctica

Name	*Feet*	*Meters*
Vinson Massif	16,865	5,060
Tyree	16,290	4,887
Shinn	15,750	4,725
Gardner	15,375	4,613
Epperly	15,100	4,530
Kirkpatrick	14,855	4,457
Elizabeth	14,698	4,409
Markham	14,290	4,287
Bell	14,117	4,235
Mackellar	14,098	4,229
Anderson	13,957	4,187
Bentley	13,934	4,180
Kaplan	13,877	4,163
Andrew Jackson	13,750	4,125
Sidley	13,720	4,116
Ostenso	13,710	4,113
Minto	13,668	4,100
Miller	13,650	4,095
Long Gables	13,620	4,086
Dickerson	13,517	4,055
Giovinetto	13,412	4,024
Wade	13,400	4,020
Fisher	13,386	4,016
Fridtjof Nansen	13,350	4,005
Wexler	13,202	3,961
Lister	13,200	3,960
Shear	13,100	3,930
Odishaw	13,008	3,902

Mount Machapuchare, Nepal

Important Lakes

A lake is a body of water surrounded by land. Although some lakes are called seas, they are lakes by definition.

Name	*Continent*	*Area Square miles*	*Square km*	*Length miles*	*km*	*Depth Feet*	*Meter*	*Elevation Feet*	*Meter*
Caspian Sea	Asia-Europe	143,244	371,002	760	1,223	3,363	1,025	–92	–28
Superior	North America	31,700	82,103	350	563	1,330	405	600	183
Victoria	Africa	26,828	69,485	250	402	270	82	3,720	1,134
Aral Sea	Asia	24,904	64,501	280	451	220	67	174	53
Huron	North America	23,000	59,570	206	332	750	229	579	176
Michigan	North America	22,300	57,757	307	494	923	281	579	176
Tanganyika	Africa	12,700	32,893	420	676	4,832	1,470	2,534	772
Baykal	Asia	12,162	31,500	395	636	5,315	1,620	1,493	455
Great Bear	North America	12,096	31,329	192	309	1,463	446	512	156
Malawi	Africa	11,150	28,899	360	578	2,260	695	1,550	
Great Slave	North America	11,031	28,570	298	480	2,015	614	513	156
Erie	North America	9,910	25,667	241	388	210	64	570	174
Winnipeg	North America	9,417	24,390	266	428	60	18	713	217
Ontario	North America	7,550	19,555	193	311	802	244	245	75
Balkhash	Asia	7,115	18,428	376	605	85	26	1,115	340
Ladoga	Europe	6,835	17,703	124	200	738	225	13	4
Chad	Africa	6,300	16,317	175	282	24	7	787	240
Maracaibo	South America	5,217	13,512	133	214	115	35	Sea Level	Sea Level
Onega	Europe	3,710	9,609	145	233	328	100	108	33
Eyre	Australia	3,600	9,324	90	145	4	1	–52	–16
Volta	Africa	3,276	8,485	250	402	—	—	—	—
Titicaca	South America	3,200	8,288	122	196	922	281	12,500	3,810
Nicaragua	North America	3,100	8,029	102	164	230	70	102	31
Athabasca	North America	3,064	7,936	208	335	407	124	700	213
Reindeer	North America	2,568	6,651	143	230	720	219	1,106	337
Turkana	Africa	2,473	6,405	154	248	240	73	1,230	375
Issyk Kul	Asia	2,355	6,099	115	185	2,303	702	5,279	1,609
Torrens	Australia	2,330	6,035	130	209	—	—	92	28
Vanern	Europe	2,156	5,584	90	145	328	100	144	44
Nettilling	North America	2,140	5,543	67	108	—	—	95	29
Winnipegosis	North America	2,075	5,374	141	227	38	12	830	253
Albert	Africa	2,075	5,374	100	161	168	51	2,030	619
Kariba	Africa	2,050	5,310	175	282	390	119	1,590	485
Nipigon	North America	1,872	4,848	72	116	540	165	1,050	320
Gairdner	Australia	1,840	4,766	90	145	—	—	112	34
Urmia	Asia	1,815	4,701	90	145	49	15	4,180	1,274
Manitoba	North America	1,799	4,659	140	225	12	4	813	248

The Great Lakes

The Great Lakes form the largest body of fresh water in the world, and with their connecting waterways are the largest inland water transportation unit. Draining the great north-central basin of the U.S., they enable shipping to reach the Atlantic via their outlet, the St. Lawrence River, and also the Gulf of Mexico via the Illinois Waterway, from Lake Michigan to the Mississippi River. A third outlet connects with the Hudson River, and thence the Atlantic via the N.Y State Barge Canal System. Traffic on the Illinois Waterway and the N.Y. State Barge Canal System is limited to recreational boating and small shipping vessels.

Only one of the lakes, Lake Michigan, is wholly in the United States; the others are shared with Canada. Ships carrying grain, lumber and iron ore move from the shore of Lake Superior to Whitefish Bay at the east end of the lake, thence through the Soo (Sault Ste Marie) locks, through the St. Mary's River and into Lake Huron. To reach the steel mills at Gary, and Port of Indiana and South Chicago, Ill., ore ships move west from Lake Huron to Lake Michigan through the straits of Mackinack.

Lake Huron discharges its waters into Lake Erie through a narrow waterway, the St. Clair River, Lake St. Clair (both included in the drainage basin figures) and the Detroit River. Lake St. Clair, a marshy basin, is 26 mi (42 km) long and 24 mi (38 km) wide at its maximum. A ship channel has been dredged through the lake. Lake Superior is 600 ft (180 m) above mean water level at Point-au-Père, Quebec, on the International Great Lakes Datum (1955). From Duluth, Minn., to the eastern end of Lake Ontario is 1,156 mi (1,850 km).

	Superior	Michigan	Huron	Erie	Ontario
Length					
in miles	350	307	206	241	193
in kilometers	560	491	330	386	309
Breadth					
in miles	160	118	183	57	53
in kilometers	256	189	293	91	85
Deepest Soundings					
in feet	1,330	923	750	210	802
in meters	399	211	225	63	241

Oceans and Important Gulfs

Name	*Square miles*	*Square kilometers*	*Average depth Feet*	*meters*
Pacific Ocean	64,200,000	166,920,000	19,000	4,000
Atlantic Ocean	33,400,000	86,840,000	12,000	3,700
Indian Ocean	28,400,000	73,840,000	12,600	3,800
Arctic Ocean	5,200,000	13,520,000	3,500	1,100
South China Sea	1,150,000	2,990,000	4,800	1,500
Caribbean Sea	980,000	2,548,000	8,500	2,600
Mediterranean Sea	910,000	2,366,000	5,000	1,500
Bering Sea	870,000	2,262,000	4,900	1,500
Gulf of Mexico	580,000	1,508,000	5,300	1,600
Sea of Okhotsk	538,000	1,398,800	3,200	1,000
Sea of Japan	391,000	1,016,600	5,500	1,700
East China Sea	257,000	668,200	600	180
Andaman Sea	218,000	566,800	3,700	1,100
Black Sea	196,000	509,600	3,900	1,200
Red Sea	175,000	455,000	1,800	550
North Sea	165,000	429,000	300	90
Baltic Sea	148,000	384,800	180	50
Yellow Sea	114,000	296,400	120	40
Persian Gulf	89,000	231,400	330	100
Gulf of California	59,000	153,400	2,400	730

Above: The Welland Ship Canal, which connects Lake Erie and Lake Ontario.

Below: Pacific coastline

Map Symbols

In a very real sense, the whole map is a symbol, representing the world or a part of it. It is a reduced representation of the earth; each of the world's features–cities rivers, etc.–is represented on the map by a symbol. Map symbols may take the form of points, such as dots or squares (often used for cities, capital cities, or points of interest), or lines (roads, railroads, rivers). Symbols may also occupy an area, showing extent of coverage (terrain, forests, deserts). They seldom look like the feature they represent and therefore must be identified and interpreted. For instance, the maps in this atlas define political units by colored tints. Neither the colors nor the boundary lines are actually found on the surface of the earth, but because countries and states are such important political components of the world, strong symbols are used to represent them. On the maps in this atlas the surface configuration of the earth is represented by hill-shading, which gives the three-dimensional impression of landforms. This terrain representation conveys a realistic and readily visualized impression of the surface. A complete legend to the right provides a key to the other symbols on the maps in this atlas.

In this atlas a "local-name" policy generally was used for naming cities and towns and all local topographic and water features. However, for a few major cities the Anglicized name was preferred and the local name given in parentheses, for instance, Moscow (Moskva), Vienna (Wien), Prague (Praha). In countries where more than one official language is used, a name is in the dominant local language. The generic parts of local names for topographic and water features are self-explanatory in many cases because of the associated map symbols or type styles.

Cultural Features

Political Boundaries

International

Secondary: State, Provincial, etc.
(Second order political unit)

Disputed de jure

Cities, Towns and Villages

(Note: On maps at 1:45,000,000 and smaller the town symbols do not follow the specific population classification shown below.)

PARIS	1,000,000 and over
Milwaukee	250,000 to 1,000,000
Huntsville	100,000 to 250,000
Bloomington	25,000 to 100,000
New Meadows	0 to 25,000
BUDAPEST	National Capitals
Springfield	Secondary Capitals

Other Cultural Features

Research Stations

Ruins

Transportation

Primary Roads

Secondary Roads

Railroads

Topographic Features

Nev. Sajama 21,463 — Peaks
Elevations are given in feet

Water Features

Lakes and Reservoirs

Fresh Water

Fresh Water: Intermittent

Salt Water

Other Water Features

Rivers

Rivers: Intermittent

Reefs

Ice Shelf

ARCTIC OCEAN
GREENLAND (Den.)
Baffin Bay
Hudson Bay
ALASKA (U.S.)
Dawson
Anchorage
Juneau
NORTH
CANADA
AMERICA
UNITED STATES
ICELAND
Reykjavik
ALEUTIAN IS.
Edmonton
Winnipeg
Vancouver
Seattle
NEWFOUNDLAND
St. John's
Montréal
Ottawa
Detroit
Chicago
New York
Washington
San Francisco
Los Angeles
Atlanta
Houston
New Orleans
IRELAND
PORTUGAL
AZORES (Port.)
GIBRALTAR (U.K.)
CANARY ISLANDS (Sp.)
MIDWAY IS. (U.S.)
Tropic of Cancer
HAWAIIAN ISLANDS (U.S.)
Gulf of Mexico
MEXICO
Havana
BAHAMAS
ATLANTIC
CUBA
Mexico City
Veracruz
HAITI
DOM. REP.
PUERTO RICO (U.S.)
JAMAICA
BELIZE
HOND.
GUAT.
EL SAL.
NIC.
Caribbean Sea
GUADELOUPE (Fr.)
MARTINIQUE (Fr.)
BARBADOS
CAPE VERDE
MAURITANIA
Dakar
GAMBIA
GUINEA-BISSAU
GUINEA
SIERRA LEONE
LIBERIA
PACIFIC
COSTA RICA
PANAMA
Caracas
VENEZUELA
TRINIDAD AND TOBAGO
GUYANA
Georgetown
SURINAME
FRENCH GUIANA
Bogotá
COLOMBIA
PALMYRA (U.S.)
Equator
Quito
ECUADOR
GALAPAGOS ISLANDS (Ecua.)
Belém
Manaus
KIRIBATI
Fortaleza
SOUTH
BRAZIL
Recife
MARQUESAS IS. (Fr.)
PERU
Lima
AMERICA
Salvador
OCEAN
WESTERN SAMOA
AMERICAN SAMOA
La Paz
BOLIVIA
Sucre
Brasília
TAHITI
TONGA
COOK ISLANDS (N.Z.)
FRENCH POLYNESIA
Tropic of Capricorn
PARAGUAY
Rio de Janeiro
São Paulo
Antofagasta
EASTER ISLAND (Chile)
ARGENTINA
Valparaíso
Santiago
URUGUAY
ARCH. DE JUAN FERNÁNDEZ (Chile)
Buenos Aires
Montevideo
CHILE
CHATHAM IS. (N.Z.)
FALKLAND IS. (U.K.)
Punta Arenas
TIERRA DEL FUEGO
SOUTH GEORGIA (U.K.)
SOUTH SANDWICH IS. (U.K.)
SOUTH ORKNEY IS. (U.K.)
SOUTH SHETLAND IS. (U.K.)
Antarctic Circle
Weddell Sea
Scale 1:100,000,000; one inch to 1578 miles
Robinson Projection
0 400 800 1200 1600 2000 Miles
0 600 1200 1800 2400 3000 Kilometers

ARCTIC OCEAN
ZEMLYA FRANTSA-IOSIFA
NOVAYA ZEMLYA
R U S S I A
EUROPE
FINLAND
St. Petersburg
SWEDEN
EST.
LAT.
LITH.
Moscow
Warsaw
BELARUS
POLAND
Kiev
UKRAINE
MOLD.
HUNG.
ROM.
Black Sea
Istanbul
Ankara
TURKEY
GREECE
ALB.
Athens
CRETE
CYPRUS
MEDITERRANEAN SEA
SYRIA
LEB.
ISRAEL
JORDAN
IRAQ
Baghdad
Tripoli
Cairo
LIBYA
EGYPT
KAZAKHSTAN
UZBEKISTAN
TURKMENISTAN
Caspian Sea
Tehran
IRAN
Kabol
AFGHANISTAN
PAKISTAN
Karachi
KUWAIT
QATAR
U.A.E.
SAUDI ARABIA
Riyadh
Mecca
OMAN
Red Sea
YEMEN
Aden
DJIBOUTI
SOCOTRA (Yem.)
ETHIOPIA
Addis Ababa
SOMALIA
Mogadishu
CHAD
SUDAN
AFRICA
CENTRAL AFRICAN REPUBLIC
CAMEROON
GABON
CONGO
ZAIRE
Kinshasa
RWANDA
BURUNDI
UGANDA
KENYA
Nairobi
TANZANIA
Dar es Salaam
Luanda
ANGOLA
ZAMBIA
ZIMBABWE
MOZAMBIQUE
NAMIBIA
BOTSWANA
Pretoria
SWAZILAND
Maputo
Durban
LESOTHO
SOUTH AFRICA
Cape Town
COMOROS
MADAGASCAR
Antananarivo
MAURITIUS
REUNION (Fr.)
SEYCHELLES
MALDIVES
INDIAN OCEAN
ÎLES KERGUÉLEN (Fr.)
COCOS ISLANDS (Austl.)
Novosibirsk
Irkutsk
Ulan Bator
MONGOLIA
ASIA
KYRG.
TAJIK.
CHINA
Beijing
Shanghai
Guangzhou
HONG KONG (U.K.)
MACAO (Port.)
HAINAN
New Delhi
NEPAL
BHUT.
BANGL.
INDIA
Calcutta
Bombay
Madras
ARABIAN SEA
Bay of Bengal
LAKSHADWEEP (INDIA)
SRI LANKA
Colombo
MYANMAR (BURMA)
Yangon
LAOS
Ha Noi
THAILAND
Bangkok
CAMBODIA
VIETNAM
Thanh Pho Ho Chi Minh
South China Sea
Manila
PHILIPPINES
BRUNEI
MALAYSIA
SINGAPORE
BORNEO
SUMATRA
Jakarta
JAVA
INDONESIA
NEW GUINEA
PAPUA NEW GUINEA
Okhotsk
Sea of Okhotsk
SAKHALIN
BERING SEA
Vladivostok
NORTH KOREA
SOUTH KOREA
Seoul
Sea of Japan
HOKKAIDŌ
HONSHŪ
JAPAN
Tōkyō
KYŪSHŪ
TAIWAN
PACIFIC OCEAN
Tropic of Cancer
NORTHERN MARIANA ISLANDS (U.S.)
WAKE (U.S.)
GUAM (U.S.)
PALAU
FED. STATES OF MICRONESIA
MARSHALL ISLANDS
Equator
SOLOMON ISLANDS
CORAL SEA
VANUATU
FIJI
NEW CALEDONIA (Fr.)
Tropic of Capricorn
Darwin
AUSTRALIA
Brisbane
Perth
Darling
Sydney
Canberra
Melbourne
TASMANIA
Hobart
Auckland
NORTH I.
NEW ZEALAND
Wellington
SOUTH I.
Antarctic Circle
ANTARCTICA
Copyright by Rand McNally & Co.
Made in U.S.A.
A
B
C
D
E
F
G
H
I
J
K
L
15° 14 30° 15 45° 16 60° 17 75° 18 90° 19 105° 20 120° 21 135° 22 150° 23 165° 24 180°
75°
60°
45°
30°
15°
0°
15°
30°
45°
60°
75°

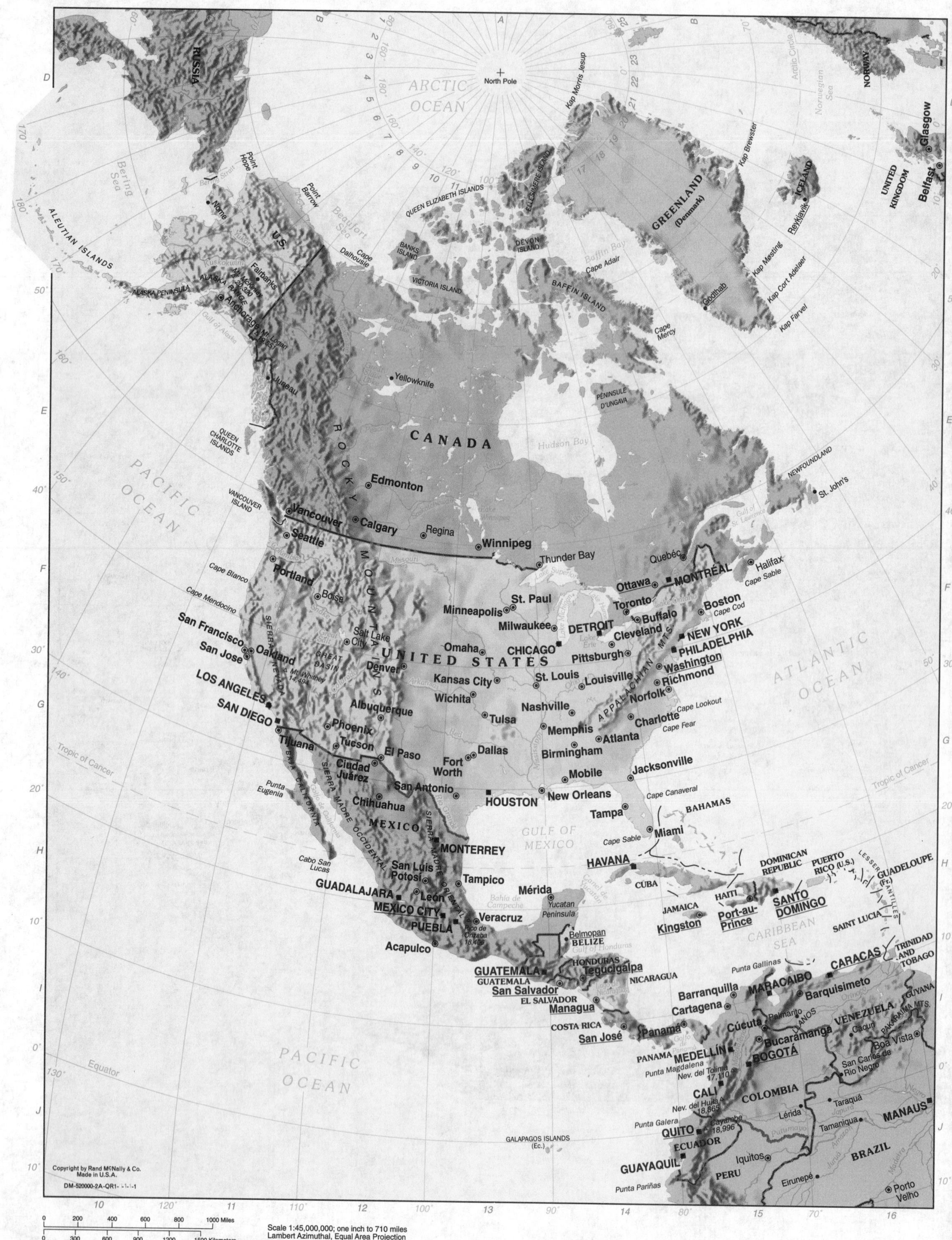
ARCTIC OCEAN
North Pole
RUSSIA
Bering Sea
Point Hope
Point Barrow
Nome
ALEUTIAN ISLANDS
ALASKA PENINSULA
U.S.
Fairbanks
Anchorage
Gulf of Alaska
Juneau
Beaufort Sea
Cape Dalhousie
QUEEN ELIZABETH ISLANDS
BANKS ISLAND
VICTORIA ISLAND
ELLESMERE ISLAND
DEVON ISLAND
BAFFIN ISLAND
Baffin Bay
Cape Adair
Kap Morris Jesup
GREENLAND (Denmark)
Kap Brewster
Kap Møsting
Kap Cort Adelaer
Kap Farvel
Godthåb
ICELAND
Reykjavík
UNITED KINGDOM
Belfast
Glasgow
NORWAY
Norwegian Sea
Arctic Circle
Cape Mercy
Yellowknife
PÉNINSULE D'UNGAVA
Hudson Bay
CANADA
QUEEN CHARLOTTE ISLANDS
VANCOUVER ISLAND
PACIFIC OCEAN
ROCKY MOUNTAINS
Edmonton
Calgary
Vancouver
Regina
Winnipeg
Seattle
Thunder Bay
Québec
NEWFOUNDLAND
St. John's
Halifax
Cape Sable
Ottawa
MONTRÉAL
Toronto
Boston
Cape Cod
Buffalo
Portland
Cape Blanco
Cape Mendocino
Boise
Minneapolis
St. Paul
Milwaukee
DETROIT
Cleveland
NEW YORK
PHILADELPHIA
San Francisco
Oakland
San Jose
Salt Lake City
GREAT BASIN
SIERRA NEVADA
Mt. Whitney 14,494
Omaha
CHICAGO
UNITED STATES
Pittsburgh
Washington
Richmond
Norfolk
ATLANTIC OCEAN
LOS ANGELES
SAN DIEGO
Denver
Kansas City
St. Louis
Louisville
Wichita
Nashville
APPALACHIAN MTS.
Albuquerque
Tulsa
Memphis
Charlotte
Cape Lookout
Cape Fear
Phoenix
Tucson
Tijuana
El Paso
Ciudad Juárez
Fort Worth
Dallas
Birmingham
Atlanta
Jacksonville
Tropic of Cancer
Punta Eugenia
San Antonio
HOUSTON
New Orleans
Mobile
Cape Canaveral
BAHAMAS
Chihuahua
Tampa
Miami
Cape Sable
MEXICO
GULF OF MEXICO
MONTERREY
SIERRA MADRE OCCIDENTAL
SIERRA MADRE ORIENTAL
Cabo San Lucas
San Luis Potosí
Tampico
HAVANA
CUBA
DOMINICAN REPUBLIC
PUERTO RICO (U.S.)
GUADELOUPE (Fr.)
LESSER ANTILLES
GUADALAJARA
León
Mérida
Yucatan Peninsula
JAMAICA
Kingston
HAITI
Port-au-Prince
SANTO DOMINGO
SAINT LUCIA
MEXICO CITY
PUEBLA
Veracruz
Pico de Orizaba 18,406
Belmopan
BELIZE
Gulf of Honduras
CARIBBEAN SEA
TRINIDAD AND TOBAGO
Acapulco
GUATEMALA
HONDURAS
Tegucigalpa
NICARAGUA
San Salvador
EL SALVADOR
Managua
Punta Gallinas
CARACAS
MARACAIBO
Barquisimeto
Barranquilla
Cartagena
GUYANA
COSTA RICA
San José
Panamá
PANAMA
Cúcuta
Bucaramanga
VENEZUELA
Boa Vista
PACIFIC OCEAN
Equator
MEDELLÍN
BOGOTÁ
Punta Magdalena
Nev. del Tolima 17,110
San Carlos de Río Negro
CALI
COLOMBIA
Nev. del Huila 18,865
Punta Galera
QUITO
Cayambe 18,996
GALAPAGOS ISLANDS (Ec.)
ECUADOR
Lérida
Tamaniqua
MANAUS
GUAYAQUIL
Iquitos
PERU
BRAZIL
Eirunepé
Porto Velho
Punta Pariñas
Copyright by Rand McNally & Co.
Made in U.S.A.
0 200 400 600 800 1000 Miles
0 300 600 900 1200 1500 Kilometers
Scale 1:45,000,000; one inch to 710 miles
Lambert Azimuthal, Equal Area Projection

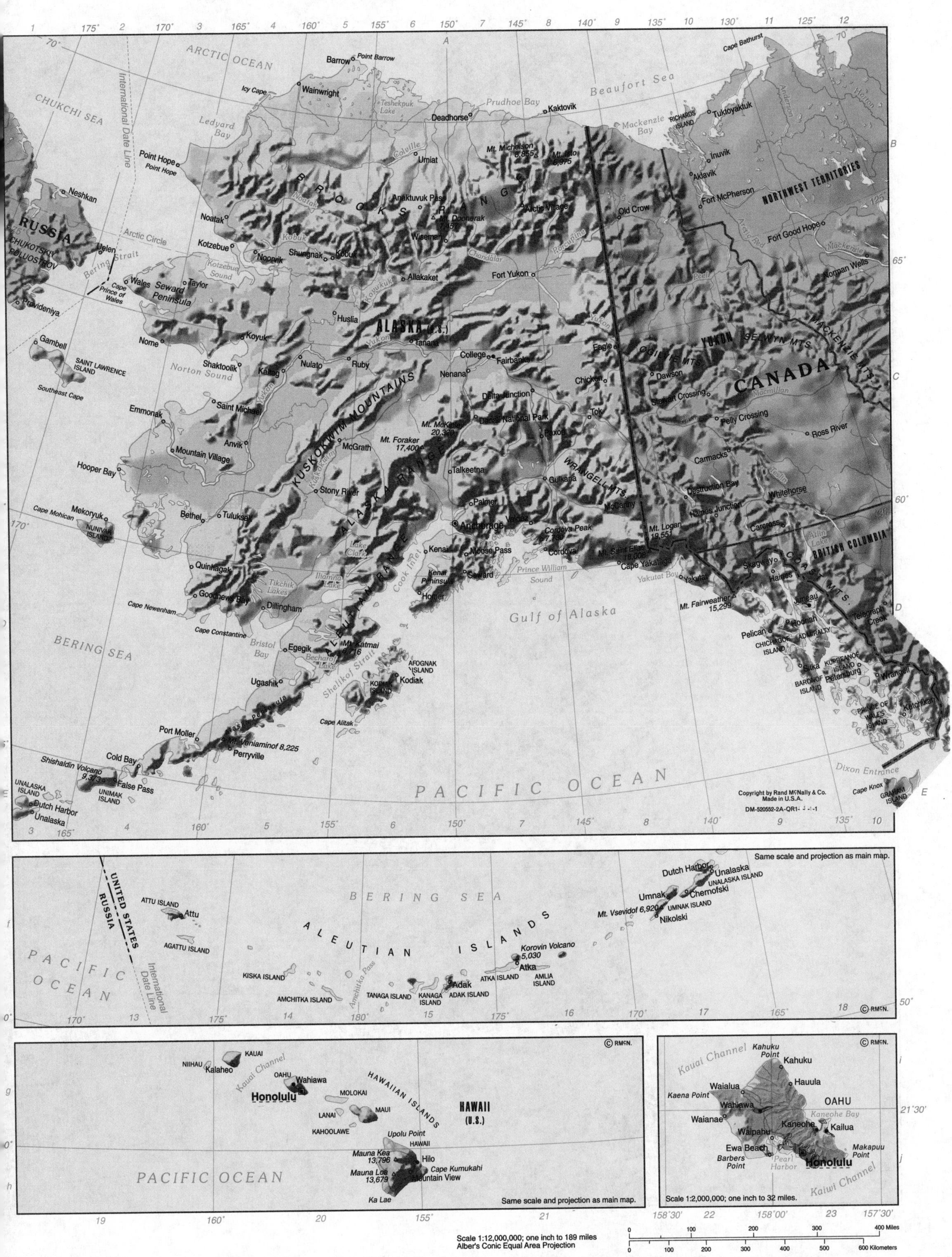

Scale 1:12,000,000; one inch to 189 miles
Alber's Conic Equal Area Projection

Beaufort Sea
Kaktovik
Cape Wrottesley
MELVILLE ISLAND
BYAM MARTIN ISLAND
BANKS ISLAND
Sachs Harbour
Cape Kellett
Viscount Melville Sound
Edé Point
STEFANSSON ISLAND
RICHARDS ISLAND
Tuktoyaktuk
Inuvik
Aklavik
Old Crow
Fort McPherson
Cape Bathurst
Cape Lambton
Amundsen Gulf
Cape Parry
Cape Baring
Holman
VICTORIA ISLAND
M'Clintock Channel
Cambridge Bay
Coppermine
NORTHWEST TERR
Bathurst Inlet
Fort Good Hope
Norman Wells
MACKENZIE MTS
Great Bear Lake
Fort Simpson
Rae
Yellowknife
Fort Providence
Great Slave Lake
Reliance
Fort Liard
Hay River
Meander River
Fort Nelson
Fond du Lac
Lake Athabasca
Fort McMurray
La Loche
ALBERTA
Fort Saint John
Grande Prairie
Athabasca
Edmonton
Lloydminster
Wainwright
Red Deer
Calgary
Banff
Lethbridge
Medicine Hat
Meadow Lake
North Battleford
SASKATCHEWAN
Prince Albert
Saskatoon
Moose Jaw
Swift Current
Regina
Yorkton
Carlyle
Brochet
Lynn Lake
Flin Flon
The Pas
Winnipegosis
Brandon
Winnipeg
Gimli
CANADA
Bethel
Ruby
Dillingham
Stony River
Mt. McKinley 20,320
ALASKA (U.S.)
Fairbanks
Fort Yukon
ALASKA RANGE
Anchorage
Palmer
Homer
Seward
Valdez
Kodiak
AFOGNAK ISLAND
KODIAK ISLAND
Gulkana
Cantwell
Tok
Chicken
Dawson
Stewart Crossing
YUKON
Carmacks
Pelly Crossing
Destruction Bay
Haines Junction
Whitehorse
Ross River
PELLY MTS
SELWYN MTS
Gulf of Alaska
Mt. Saint Elias 18,008
Yakutat
Mt. Fairweather 15,300
Skagway
Haines
Juneau
Carcross
CHICHAGOF ISLAND
BARANOF ISLAND
Sitka
Wrangell
Ketchikan
PRINCE OF WALES ISLAND
Dixon Entrance
Cape Knox
GRAHAM ISLAND
QUEEN CHARLOTTE ISLANDS
MORESBY ISLAND
Sandspit
Prince Rupert
Hazelton
Mount Sir Smythe 9,600
Dease Lake
ROCKY
BRITISH COLUMBIA
McLeod Lake
Prince George
Cape Saint James
Queen Charlotte Sound
Bella Coola
Mt. Waddington 13,163
Cape Scott
Bear Cove
Campbell River
VANCOUVER ISLAND
Tofino
Port Alberni
Powell River
100 Mile House
Kamloops
Vancouver
Burnaby
Victoria
Cape Flattery
Mt. Olympus 7,965
PACIFIC OCEAN
Everett
Seattle
Tacoma
Olympia
WASHINGTON
Spokane
Bonners Ferry
Portland
Salem
Corvallis
Albany
Eugene
Coos Bay
Cape Blanco
Roseburg
Medford
OREGON
Richland
Lewiston
Great Falls
Helena
Fort Peck
Fort Peck Lake
MONTANA
Billings
Dillon
Boise
Nampa
IDAHO
Idaho Falls
Pocatello
Twin Falls
Sheridan
WYOMING
Casper
Cape Mendocino
Eureka
Mt. Shasta 14,163
Redding
Point Arena
CALIFORNIA
Santa Rosa
Oakland
San Francisco
Sacramento
Reno
Carson City
Winnemucca
NEVADA
UTAH
Logan
Salt Lake City
Great Salt Lake
Minot
Grand Forks
NORTH DAKOTA
Bismarck
Fargo
Lake Sakakawea
Aberdeen
Lake Oahe
SOUTH DAKOTA
Pierre
Rapid City
UNITED
Lake Francis Case
Sioux Falls
Sioux City
NEBRASKA
Niobrara
Missouri
160°
155°
150°
145°
140°
135°
130°
125°
120°
115°
110°
105°
100°
55°
50°
45°
40°
1
2
3
4
5
6
7
8
9
10
11
12
13
14

BAFFIN ISLAND
Baffin Bay
Davis Strait
GREENLAND
(Denmark)
Upernavik
Umanak
Jakobshavn
Christianshåb
Egedesminde
Holsteinsborg
Sukkertoppen
Godthåb
Julianehåb
Angmagssalik
Kap Farvel
Cape Dyer
Cape Mercy
Pangnirtung
Clyde River
Pond Inlet
Arctic Bay
Cape Adair
Cape Sherard
Cape Parker
Cape Liverpool
COBURG ISLAND
DEVON ISLAND
Jones Sound
Lancaster Sound
BYLOT ISLAND
MELVILLE PENINSULA
Cape Chapman
PRINCE CHARLES ISLAND
Foxe Basin
Cape Wilson
Cape Dominion
Cape Dorchester
Repulse Bay
VANSITTART ISLAND
SOUTHAMPTON ISLAND
Coral Harbour
Cape Dorset
Seahorse Point
SALISBURY ISLAND
NOTTINGHAM ISLAND
Fair Ness
Lake Harbour
Iqaluit
Amadjuak Lake
RESOLUTION ISLAND
KILLINIQ ISLAND
Hudson Strait
Cap Hopes Advance
AKPATOK ISLAND
Cape Kendall
Chesterfield Inlet
Cape Low
Cape Pembroke
COATS ISLAND
Cape Southampton
MANSEL ISLAND
Ivujivik
Salluit
Kangiqsujuaq
PÉNINSULE D'UNGAVA
Kangirsuk
Ungava Bay
Kangiqsualujjuaq
Povungnituk
Kuujjuaq
Inukjuak
Hudson Bay
Labrador Sea
ATLANTIC OCEAN
NEWFOUNDLAND
LABRADOR
Nain
Davis Inlet
Postville
Rigolet
Cartwright
North West River
Happy Valley-Goose Bay
Battle Harbour
Saint Anthony
Port Saunders
Baie Verte
Botwood
St John's
Trepassey
Cape Race
Corner Brook
Cape Ray
Saint-Pierre
ST. PIERRE AND MIQUELON (Fr.)
Schefferville
Labrador City
Gagnon
Havre-Saint-Pierre
Port-Menier
ÎLE D'ANTICOSTI
Gulf of Saint Lawrence
Sept-Îles
Baie-Comeau
Hauterive
Matane
Gaspé
Cap Gaspé
ÎLES DE LA MADELEINE
PRINCE EDWARD ISLAND
Charlottetown
Sydney
CAPE BRETON ISLAND
Bathurst
NEW BRUNSWICK
Moncton
Fredericton
Saint John
NOVA SCOTIA
Halifax
New Glasgow
Truro
Cape Sable
Edmundston
Rivière-du-Loup
QUÉBEC
Québec
Chicoutimi
Jonquière
Chibougamau
Mistassini
Lac Mistassini
Waskaganish
Eastmain
Chisasibi
Pointe Louis-XIV
Cape Henrietta Maria
BELCHER ISLANDS
AKIMISKI I.
James Bay
Rés. La Grande Deux
Rés. Eastmain-Opinaca
Lac Sakami
Amos
Shawinigan
Trois-Rivières
Montmagny
MONTRÉAL
Laval
Granby
Sherbrooke
Maniwaki
Hull
Ottawa
Kingston
Watertown
Peterborough
Toronto
Barrie
Owen Sound
Kitchener
Hamilton
London
Buffalo
Rochester
Lake Ontario
Lake Erie
Lake Huron
Lake Michigan
Lake Superior
Georgian Bay
MANITOULIN I.
Sudbury
North Bay
Sault Sainte Marie
Wawa
Timmins
Hearst
Geraldton
Thunder Bay
International Falls
Moosonee
Pickle Crow
ONTARIO
Winisk
Fort Severn
Cape Tatnam
Keweenaw Peninsula
Marquette
Escanaba
Superior
Duluth
Wausau
WISCONSIN
Green Bay
St. Paul
MICHIGAN
Bay City
Grand Rapids
Lansing
Milwaukee
Madison
Racine
Austin
Mason City
Dubuque
ILLINOIS
DETROIT
Windsor
Toledo
Cleveland
Youngstown
Jamestown
Williamsport
PENNSYLVANIA
Harrisburg
PHILADELPHIA
Trenton
Newark
NEW YORK
LONG ISLAND
Hartford
CONN.
R.I.
Providence
MASS.
Boston
Cape Cod
Albany
VERMONT
Montpelier
N.H.
Concord
Portsmouth
Portland
Lewiston
Augusta
Bangor
MAINE
Gulf of Maine
APPALACHIAN MTS.
Copyright by Rand McNally & Co.
Made in U.S.A.
Scale 1:16,000,000; one inch to 252 miles
Lambert Conformal Conic Projection
500 Miles
800 Kilometers

BRITISH COLUMBIA
ALBERTA
SASKATCHEWAN
MANITOBA
Victoria
Bellingham
Cape Flattery
Mt. Olympus 7,965
Everett
Seattle
Tacoma
Olympia
Mt. Rainier 14,410
Mt. Saint Helens 8,365
WASHINGTON
Spokane
Coeur d'Alene
Yakima
Richland
Trail
Lethbridge
Medicine Hat
Moose Jaw
Regina
CASCADE RANGE
Portland
Salem
Albany
Eugene
Mt. Hood 11,239
Pendleton
Walla Walla
Lewiston
Moscow
OREGON
Cape Blanco
Baker
Medford
Mt. McLoughlin 9,495
ROCKY MOUNTAINS
BITTERROOT RANGE
SALMON RIVER MOUNTAINS
New Meadows
Salmon
Boise
Nampa
IDAHO
Borah Peak 12,662
Idaho Falls
Pocatello
Twin Falls
Polson
Missoula
Great Falls
Helena
MONTANA
Fort Peck
Glendive
Billings
Bozeman
Granite Peak 12,799
Minot
NORTH DAKOTA
Belfield
Bismarck
Jamestown
BADLANDS
Aberdeen
SOUTH DAKOTA
Spearfish
Pierre
BLACK HILLS
Rapid City
Harney Peak 7,247
Cody
Francs Peak 13,153
Grand Teton 13,770
Sheridan
Cloud Peak 13,167
WYOMING
Daniel
Casper
Rock Springs
Laramie
Cheyenne
Mt. Shasta 14,162
Eureka
Cape Mendocino
Alturas
Red Bluff
SIERRA NEVADA
Winnemucca
Elko
Reno
Sparks
Carson City
GREAT NEVADA BASIN
Ely
Wheeler Peak 13,063
Logan
Ogden
Great Salt Lake
Salt Lake City
WASATCH RANGE
Kings Peak 13,528
Provo
Delta
UTAH
Beaver
Cedar City
Santa Rosa
Davis
Sacramento
Berkeley
San Francisco
Oakland
Stockton
San Jose
Santa Cruz
Monterey
Merced
Fresno
Visalia
Mt. Whitney 14,494
Telescope Peak 11,050
COAST RANGES
San Luis Obispo
Bakersfield
CALIFORNIA
Las Vegas
Point Arguello
Santa Barbara
Lancaster
Barstow
Needles
Pasadena
LOS ANGELES
Long Beach
San Bernardino
Riverside
Santa Ana
SAN DIEGO
El Cajon
Tijuana
Mexicali
PACIFIC OCEAN
Ensenada
Punta Colnett
Craig
Fort Collins
Greeley
Longs Peak 14,255
Boulder
Lakewood
Aurora
Denver
Grand Junction
COLORADO
Mt. Elbert 14,433
Pikes Pk. 14,110
Colorado Springs
Cañon City
Pueblo
Durango
Mexican Hat
Page
Lake Powell
Humphrey's Peak 12,633
Flagstaff
ARIZONA
Glendale
Phoenix
Tempe
Baldy Peak 11,404
Yuma
Sonoyta
Tucson
PELONCILLO MTNS.
Nogales
Gallup
Los Alamos
Santa Fe
Mt. Taylor 11,302
Albuquerque
NEW MEXICO
Wheeler Peak 13,159
Reserve
Alamogordo
SACREMENTO MTNS.
Roswell
Clovis
Hobbs
Carlsbad
Las Cruces
El Paso
Ciudad Juárez
Agua Prieta
Janos
NEBRASKA
Gering
Grand Island
Kearney
Oakley
KANSAS
Hutchinson
Dodge City
Boise City
Oklahoma City
Amarillo
Lawton
Wichita Falls
Lubbock
Abilene
Fort Worth
Big Spring
Odessa
TEXAS
San Angelo
Pecos
Fort Stockton
Mt. Livermore 8,379
Sonora
Killeen
San Antonio
Emory Peak 7,825
Acuña
Piedras Negras
Laredo
Nuevo Laredo
Kingsville
Reynosa
SIERRA MADRE ORIENTAL
Nueva Rosita
Monclova
San Pedro de las Colonias
Gómez Palacio
MEXICO
Coyame
Chihuahua
Delicias
Cuauhtémoc
Camargo
Hidalgo del Parral
SIERRA MADRE OCCIDENTAL
Sahuaripa
Hermosillo
Puerto Libertad
Empalme
Ciudad Obregón
Navojoa
Los Mochis
Guamúchil
Golfo de California
BAJA CALIFORNIA
San Felipe
Cerro de la Encantada 10,069
Punta Prieta
Punta Eugenia
Volcan Las Tres Virgenes 6,299
ISLA GUADALUPE (Mex.)
Tropic of Cancer
Columbia
Snake
Missouri
Yellowstone
Colorado
Rio Grande
Platte
Arkansas
Canadian
Red
Pecos
Nueces

Scale 1:12,000,000; one inch to 189 miles
Alber's Conic Equal Area Projection

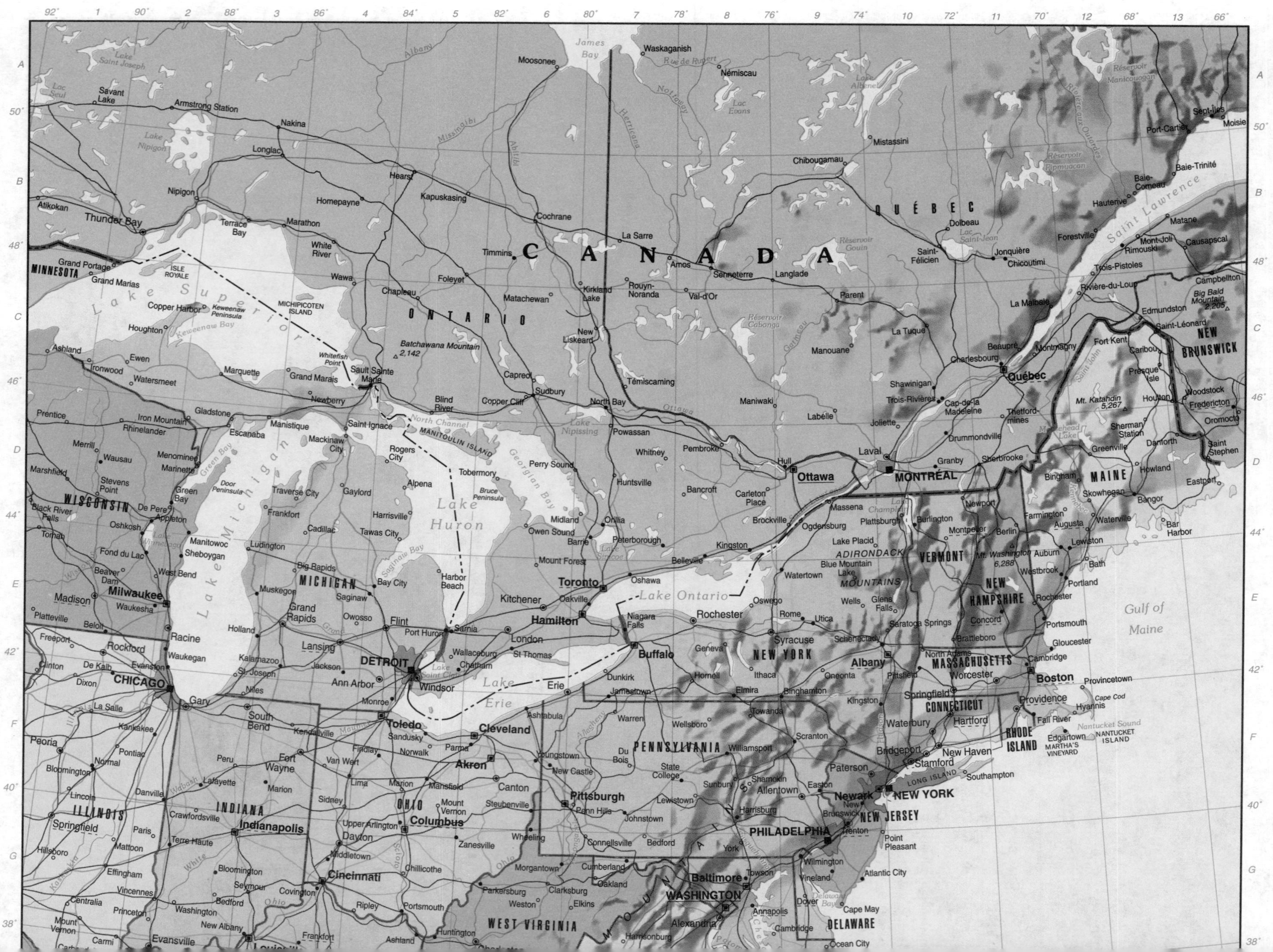
CANADA
QUÉBEC
ONTARIO
NEW BRUNSWICK
MAINE
NEW HAMPSHIRE
VERMONT
MASSACHUSETTS
CONNECTICUT
RHODE ISLAND
NEW YORK
NEW JERSEY
PENNSYLVANIA
DELAWARE
WEST VIRGINIA
OHIO
MICHIGAN
INDIANA
ILLINOIS
WISCONSIN
MINNESOTA
Lake Superior
Lake Michigan
Lake Huron
Lake Erie
Lake Ontario
Georgian Bay
James Bay
Gulf of Maine
Saint Lawrence
Ottawa
MONTRÉAL
Québec
Toronto
Hamilton
Buffalo
Rochester
Cleveland
Pittsburgh
PHILADELPHIA
NEW YORK
Boston
Providence
Hartford
Albany
DETROIT
CHICAGO
Milwaukee
Indianapolis
Columbus
Cincinnati
Baltimore
WASHINGTON
Mt. Katahdin 5,267
Mt. Washington 6,288
ADIRONDACK MOUNTAINS

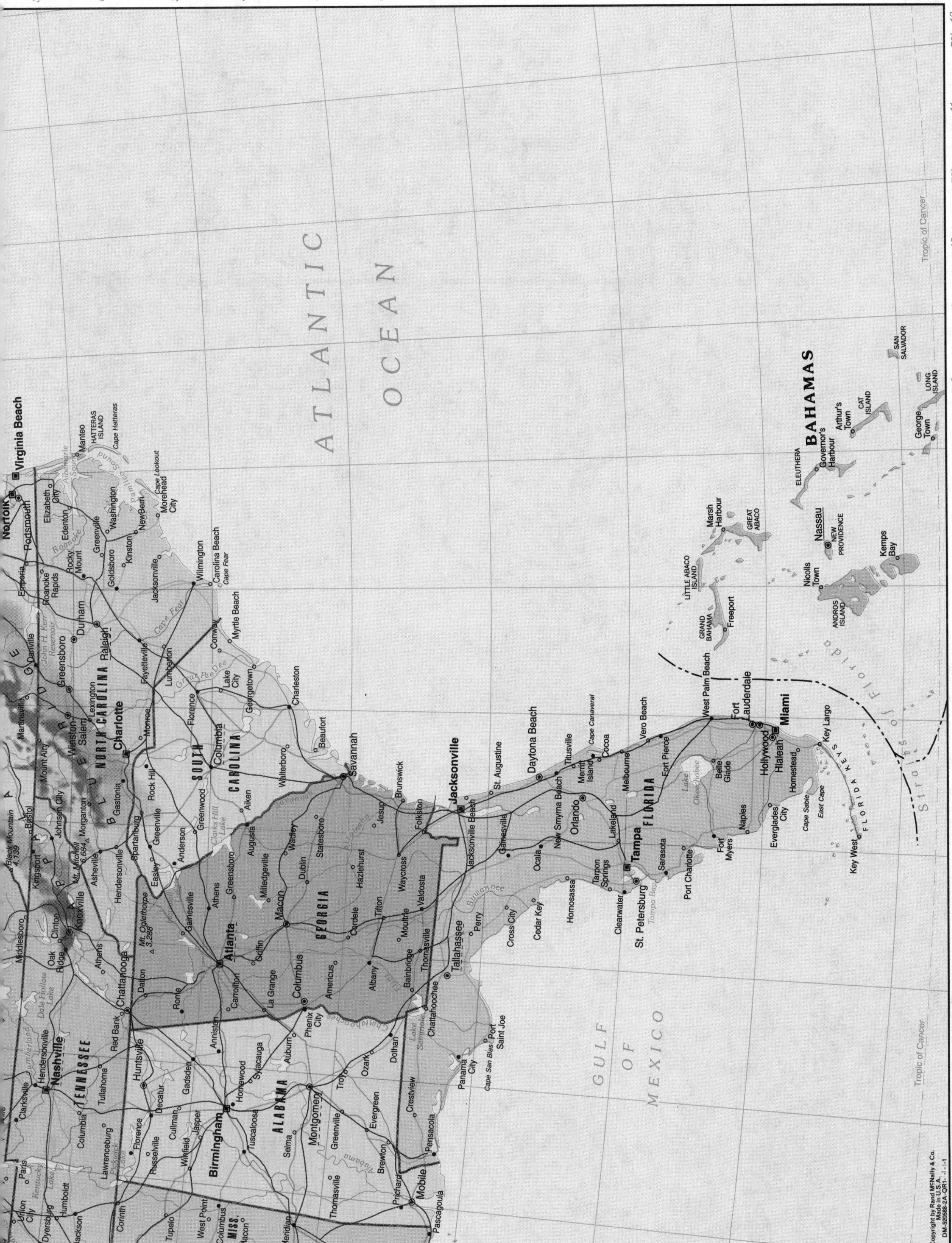

Scale 1:8,000,000; one inch to 126 miles
Lambert Conformal Conic Projection

0 50 100 150 200 250 Miles
0 100 200 300 400 Kilometers

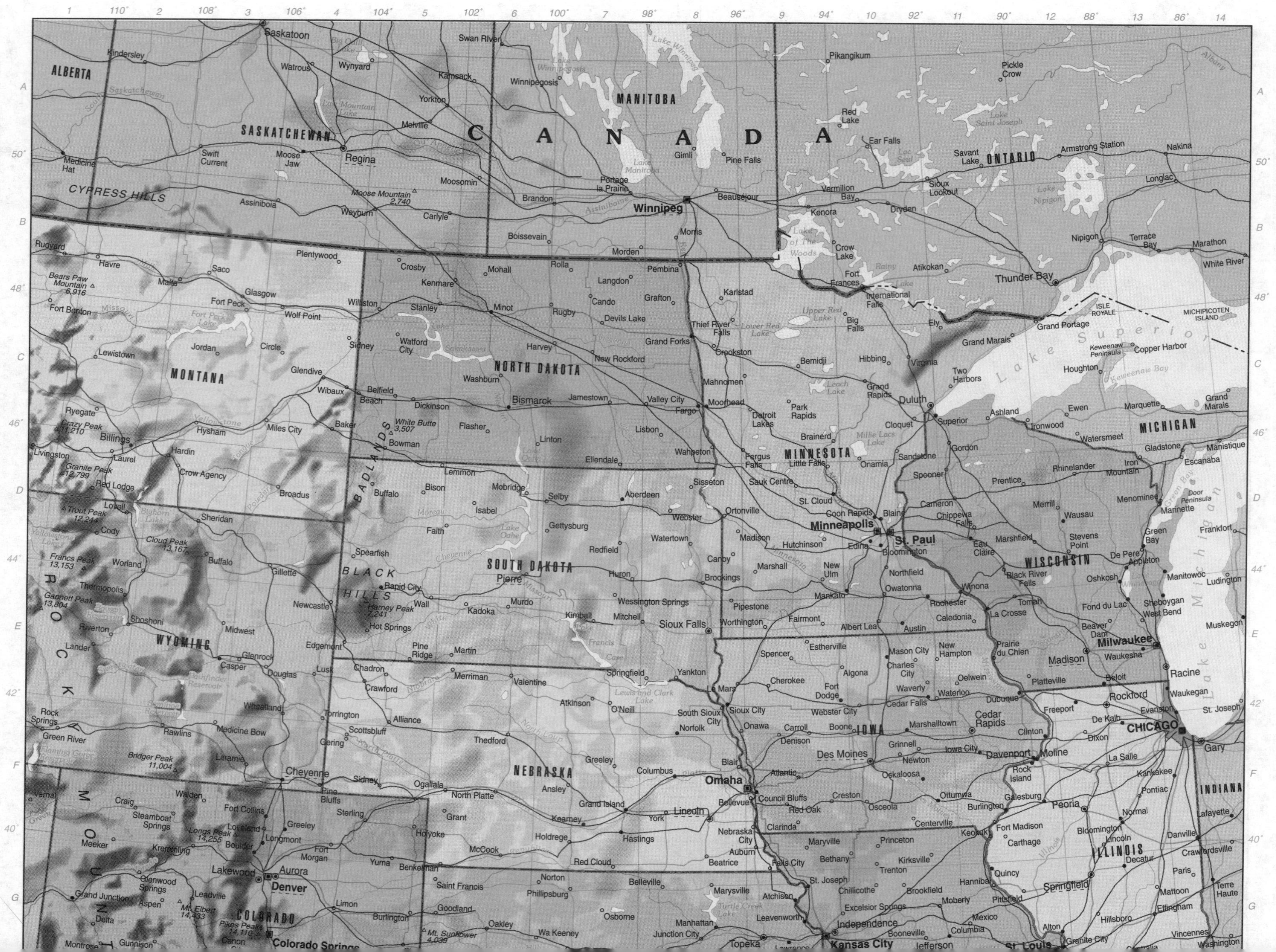

CANADA
ALBERTA
SASKATCHEWAN
MANITOBA
ONTARIO
MONTANA
NORTH DAKOTA
SOUTH DAKOTA
MINNESOTA
WISCONSIN
MICHIGAN
IOWA
ILLINOIS
INDIANA
NEBRASKA
WYOMING
COLORADO
Lake Superior
Lake Michigan
Lake Winnipeg
CYPRESS HILLS
BADLANDS
BLACK HILLS
ROCKY MOUNTAINS
Saskatoon
Regina
Moose Jaw
Swift Current
Medicine Hat
Winnipeg
Brandon
Thunder Bay
Kenora
Duluth
Minneapolis
St. Paul
Bismarck
Fargo
Grand Forks
Minot
Pierre
Sioux Falls
Rapid City
Billings
Milwaukee
Madison
CHICAGO
Des Moines
Omaha
Lincoln
Cheyenne
Denver
Kansas City
Springfield
St. Louis
Colorado Springs

Scale 1:8,000,000; one inch to 126 miles
Lambert Conformal Conic Projection

0 50 100 150 200 250 Miles
0 100 200 300 400 Kilometers

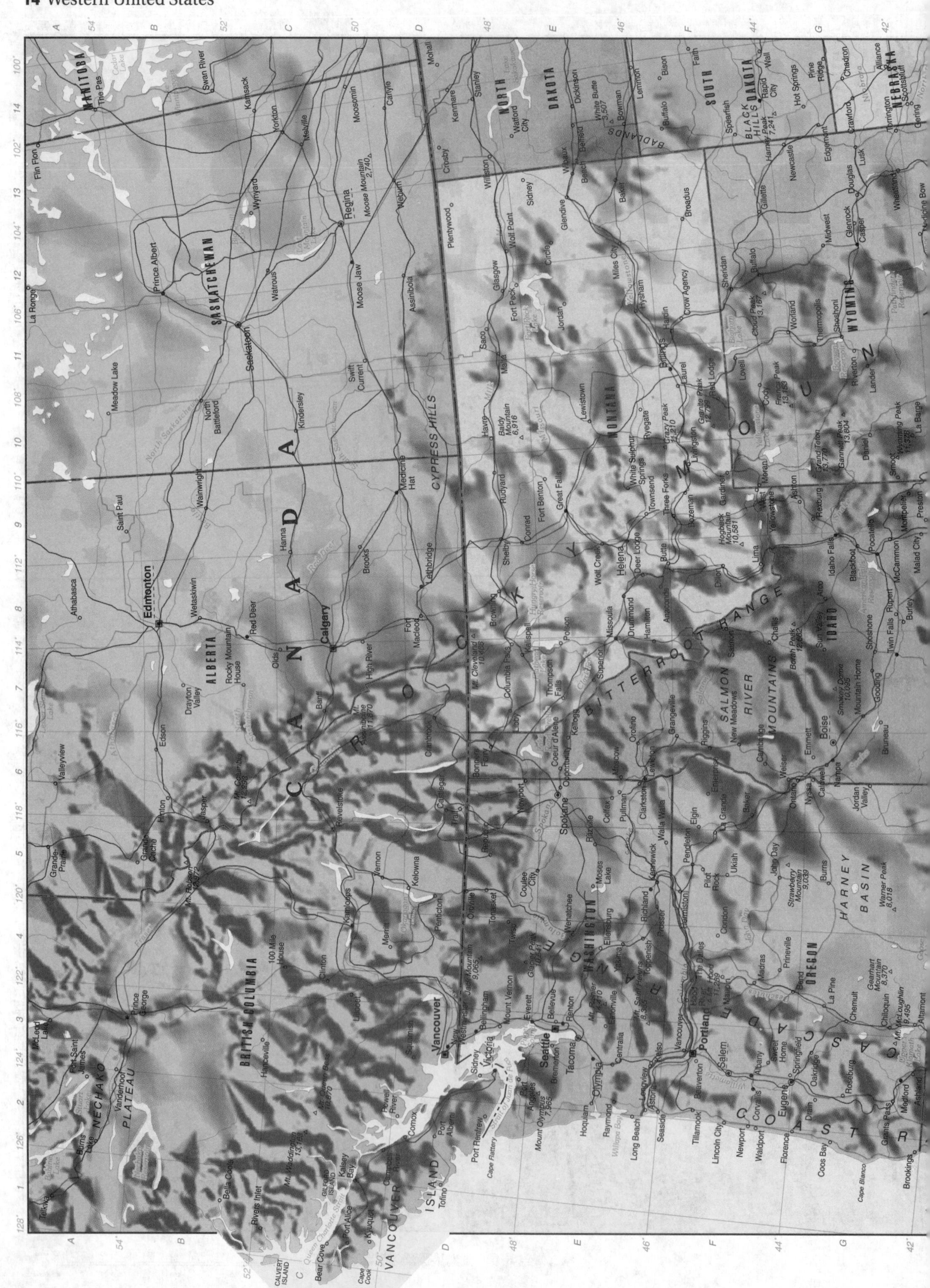

CANADA
ROCKY MOUNTAINS
CASCADE RANGE
COAST RANGES
BRITISH COLUMBIA
ALBERTA
SASKATCHEWAN
MANITOBA
WASHINGTON
OREGON
IDAHO
MONTANA
WYOMING
NORTH DAKOTA
SOUTH DAKOTA
NEBRASKA
NECHAKO PLATEAU
VANCOUVER ISLAND
CYPRESS HILLS
BITTERROOT RANGE
SALMON RIVER MOUNTAINS
HARNEY BASIN
BLACK HILLS
BADLANDS
Edmonton
Calgary
Regina
Saskatoon
Vancouver
Victoria
Seattle
Tacoma
Spokane
Portland
Salem
Eugene
Boise
Helena

Scale 1:8,000,000; one inch to 126 miles
Lambert Conformal Conic Projection

0 50 100 150 200 250 Miles
0 100 200 300 400 Kilometers

UNITED STATES
MEXICO
GULF OF MEXICO
PACIFIC OCEAN
Tropic of Cancer
LOS ANGELES
SAN DIEGO
Tijuana
Mexicali
Phoenix
Tucson
Albuquerque
El Paso
Ciudad Juárez
Chihuahua
Hermosillo
Dallas
Fort Worth
HOUSTON
San Antonio
Austin
New Orleans
Memphis
Tulsa
Oklahoma City
Corpus Christi
Laredo
Nuevo Laredo
MONTERREY
Saltillo
Torreón
Matamoros
Ciudad Victoria
Tampico
San Luis Potosí
Mazatlán
Culiacán
La Paz
Cabo San Lucas
GUADALAJARA
León
MEXICO CITY
Puebla
Veracruz
Acapulco
Mérida
YUCATÁN
Campeche
Villahermosa
BELIZE
Belize City
GUATEMALA
San Salvador
Managua
ISLAS REVILLAGIGEDO
ISLA SOCORRO
ISLAS MARÍAS
ISLA DE MALPELO (Col.)
Bahía de Campeche
Golfo de Tehuantepec
Copyright by Rand McNally & Co.
Made in U.S.A.

ATLANTIC OCEAN
CARIBBEAN SEA
WEST VIRGINIA
VIRGINIA
Lynchburg
Roanoke
Richmond
Petersburg
Norfolk
Portsmouth
Virginia Beach
Johnson City
Greensboro
Durham
Winston-Salem
Raleigh
Asheville
NORTH CAROLINA
Goldsboro
Charlotte
Fayetteville
Spartanburg
Cape Lookout
Columbia
Florence
Wilmington
Cape Fear
SOUTH CAROLINA
Augusta
Charleston
Savannah
Valdosta
Jacksonville
Gainesville
Ocala
Daytona Beach
Orlando
Merritt Island
Cape Canaveral
Melbourne
Lakeland
Fort Pierce
FLORIDA
West Palm Beach
Freeport
Lake Okeechobee
Fort Myers
Hialeah
Fort Lauderdale
Miami
Cape Sable
Key West
FLORIDA KEYS
Straits of Florida
ABACO
BAHAMA ISLANDS
BAHAMAS
Nassau
NEW PROVIDENCE
ELEUTHERA
CAT ISLAND
ANDROS
LONG ISLAND
ACKLINS
GREAT INAGUA
TURKS AND CAICOS ISLANDS (U.K.)
CAICOS ISLANDS
Grand Turk
BERMUDA (U.K.)
Tropic of Cancer
Matanzas
Cárdenas
Güines
Sagua la Grande
Santa Clara
Placetas
Morón
Cienfuegos
Ciego de Avila
Trinidad
Florida
Nuevitas
CUBA
Camagüey
Holguín
Banes
Santa Cruz del Sur
Bayamo
Manzanillo
Guantánamo
Palma Soriano
Santiago de Cuba
Cabo Cruz
GREATER ANTILLES
WEST INDIES
CAYMAN ISLANDS (U.K.)
George Town
Montego Bay
Spanish Town
Port Antonio
May Pen
Kingston
JAMAICA
Jérémie
Port-au-Prince
HAITI
HISPANIOLA
Cap-Haïtien
Gonaïves
Saint-Marc
Monte Cristi
Puerto Plata
Mao
Santiago
San Francisco de Macoris
La Vega
San Juan
La Romana
Barahona
SANTO DOMINGO
DOMINICAN REPUBLIC
Cabo Rojo
Mayagüez
San Juan
Caguas
Ponce
PUERTO RICO (U.S.)
VIRGIN ISLANDS (U.S.)
BRITISH VIRGIN ISLANDS
Road Town
Charlotte Amalie
SAINT CROIX
ANGUILLA (U.K.)
The Valley
ANTIGUA AND BARBUDA
Saint John's
Basseterre
SAINT KITTS AND NEVIS
Plymouth
MONTSERRAT (U.K.)
Pointe-à-Pitre
GUADELOUPE (Fr.)
Basse-Terre
DOMINICA
Roseau
Fort-de-France
MARTINIQUE (Fr.)
SAINT LUCIA
Castries
Bridgetown
BARBADOS
SAINT VINCENT AND THE GRENADINES
Kingstown
GRENADA
Saint George's
LESSER ANTILLES
TOBAGO
TRINIDAD AND TOBAGO
TRINIDAD
Port of Spain
San Fernando
ARUBA (Neth.)
Oranjestad
CURAÇAO
NETHERLANDS ANTILLES
BONAIRE
Willemstad
ISLA DE MARGARITA
Porlamar
Cabo de Gracias a Dios
ISLA DE SAN ANDRÉS (Col.)
Punta Gallinas
Cabo de La Vela
Punto Fijo
Golfo de Venezuela
Riohacha
Maicao
Puerto Cumarebo
Coro
Santa Marta
Cristóbal Colón 19,029
Barranquilla
Ciénaga
Sabanalarga
Soledad
Valledupar
MARACAIBO
Altagracia
Cabimas
Machiques
Puerto Cabello
Carora
Guacara
Barquisimeto
Valencia
Maracay
Teques
Petare
Guarenas
CARACAS
Cumaná
Carúpano
Güiria
Barcelona
Puerto La Cruz
Maturín
Valle de la Pascua
Anaco
San José de Guanipa
El Tigre
Tucupita
Cartagena
Turbaco
San Jacinto
Plato
San Onofre
Corozal
Lorica
Sincelejo
Cereté
Sahagún
El Banco
Montería
Lago de Maracaibo
Trujillo
Acarigua
Valera
Guanare
Mérida
Barinas
Pico Bolívar 16,427
La Fria
San Cristóbal
Cúcuta
Guasdualito
Ocaña
Calabozo
San Fernando
Ciudad Bolívar
Ciudad Guayana
Upata
Cerro Bolívar 2,631
Embalse de Guri
VENEZUELA
Cerro Mato 6,112
Auyán-tepui 9,678
LA GRAN SABANA
Cerro Yaví 8,009
Cacurí
Morawhanna
Marlborough
Charity
Suddie
Parika
Georgetown
Enmore
Bartica
New Amsterdam
Nieuw Nickerie
GUYANA
Mount Roraima 9,432
PAKARAIMA MTS.
SURINAME
Lethem
KANUKU MTS.
KAMOA MTS.
ACARAI MTS.
Boa Vista
BRAZIL
Cerro Marahuaca 8,461
SIERRA PARIMA
San Carlos de Río Negro
Puerto Ayacucho
LLANOS
Puerto Limón
Colón
Golfo de los Mosquitos
La Chorrera
Panamá
ISTMO DE PANAMA
Aguadulce
Chitre
ISLA DEL REY
Santiago
Golfo de Chiriquí
Golfo de Panamá
Península de Azuero
Punta Mala
ISLA DE COIBA
Punta Mariato
PANAMA
Punta Marzo
Turbo
Chigorodó
Barrancabermeja
Riosucio
Caucasia
Bucaramanga
Floridablanca
Yarumal
Puerto Berrío
Bello
MEDELLÍN
Itagüí
Envigado
Quibdó
Duitama
Sogamoso
La Dorada
Tunja
Yopal
Honda
Cabo Corrientes
Manizales
Pereira
COLOMBIA
BOGOTÁ
Cartago
Armenia
Ibagué
Buga
Tuluá
Espinal
Villavicencio
San Martín
Punta Magdalena
Buenaventura
CALI
Palmira
Neiva
Scale 1:16,000,000; one inch to 252 miles
Lambert Conformal Conic Projection
0 100 200 300 400 500 Miles
0 200 400 600 800 Kilometers

PACIFIC OCEAN
Golfo de California
Tropic of Cancer
BAJA CALIFORNIA
BAJA CALIFORNIA SUR
SONORA
CHIHUAHUA
SINALOA
DURANGO
NAYARIT
JALISCO
COLIMA
ARIZONA
NEW MEXICO
SIERRA MADRE OCCIDENTAL
SACRAMENTO MOUNTAINS
PELONCILLO MTS.
SIERRA SAN LÁZARO
Chula Vista
Tijuana
Tecate
Mexicali
El Centro
Yuma
Wellton
Gila Bend
Casa Grande
Coolidge
Eloy
Ajo
Tucson
Mount Lemmon 9,157
Mt. Wrightson 9,452
Benson
Willcox
Bisbee
Douglas
Nogales
Safford
Morenci
Truth or Consequences
Elephant Butte Reservoir
Silver City
Central
Lordsburg
Deming
Las Cruces
Organ Needle 8,920
Alamogordo
Mescalero
Roswell
Lovington
Artesia
Hobbs
Carlsbad
Anthony
El Paso
Ciudad Juárez
Guadalupe
Fabens
Kermit
Pecos
Sierra Blanca
Van Horn
Fort Stockton
Mt. Livermore 8,379
Alpine
Marfa
Marathon
Rodeo
Animas Peak 8,531
Ensenada
El Álamo
Punta Colnett
Villa Hidalgo
Cerro de la Encantada 10,089
San Felipe
San Simón
ISLA MONTAGUE
Sonoyta
Lukeville
Tajitos
Caborca
Altar
Santa Ana
Magdalena de Kino
Cucurpe
Cananea
Agua Prieta
Fronteras
Colonia Morelos
Nacozari de García
Bavispe
Moctezuma
Tepache
Sahuaripa
Puerto Libertad
Hermosillo
Bahía Kino
ISLA TIBURÓN
ISLA ÁNGEL DE LA GUARDA
ISLA GUADALUPE
ISLA CEDROS
Bahía Sebastián Vizcaíno
Punta Eugenia
Punta Prieta
Volcan Las Tres Vírgenes 6,299
San Ignacio
Santa Rosalía
Mulegé
Rosarito
San José de Comondú
Loreto
ISLA CARMEN
La Poza Grande
Puerto Adolfo López Mateos
ISLA MAGDALENA
ISLA SANTA MARGARITA
ISLA SAN JOSÉ
Bahía La Paz
La Paz
ISLA CERRALVO
El Triunfo
Todos Santos
San José del Cabo
Cabo San Lucas
San Lucas
ISLAS ALIJOS
Ortiz
Empalme
Guaymas
Esperanza
Ciudad Obregón
Navojoa
Huatabampo
Álamos
Ahome
Los Mochis
Topolobampo
Guasave
San Blas
Choix
Angostura
Guamúchil
Badiraguato
Pericos
Navolato
Culiacán
Altata
Quila
El Dorado
La Cruz de Elota
Mazatlán
Concordia
Rosario
Escuinapa de Hidalgo
Acaponeta
Tecuala
Rosamorada
Tuxpan
San Blas
Tepic
Volcán Ceboruco 7,598
San Marcos
Tequila
Puerto Vallarta
GUADALAJARA
Cocula
El Tuito
Tomatlán
Autlán
Ciudad Guzmán
Nevado de Colima 13,911
Chamela
Manzanillo
Colima
Armería
Tecomán
ISLAS MARÍAS
ISLA MARÍA MADRE
ISLA MARÍA MAGDALENA
ISLA MARÍA CLEOFAS
ISLAS REVILLAGIGEDO (Mex.)
ISLA SAN BENEDICTO
ISLA ROCA PARTIDA
ISLA SOCORRO
ISLA CLARIÓN (Mex.)
Janos
Nuevo Casas Grandes
Galeana
Buenaventura
Lucero
Ahumada
El Sueco
Chuhuichupa
Santa Clara
Matachic
El Sauz
Aldama
Coyame
Ojinaga
Emory Peak 7,825
Chihuahua
Adolfo López Mateos
Cuauhtémoc
General Trias
Meoqui
Julimes
Delicias
Saucillo
Camargo
Ocampo
Creel
Agua Caliente
Nonoava
Valle de Zaragoza
Batopilas
Jiménez
Sierra Mojada
Santa Bárbara
Hidalgo del Parral
Escalón
Carrillo
Ceballos
Babonoyaba
Villa Ocampo
Villa Hidalgo
Santa María del Oro
La Zarca
La Cadena
Gómez Palacio
Torreón
El Casco
Ciudad Lerdo
Nazas
Rodeo
Pedriceña
Santiago Papasquiaro
San Juan del Río
Peñón Blanco
Cuencamé
Durango
El Salto
Nombre de Dios
Juan Aldama
Sombrerete
ZACATECAS
Fresnillo
Valparaíso
Jerez
Colotlán
Jalpa
Moyahua
Tequila
Ocotlán
Los Reyes
Manzanillo
Copyright by Rand McNally & Co.
Made in U.S.A.

GULF OF MEXICO
Bahía de Campeche
Tropic of Cancer
UNITED STATES
TEXAS
LOUISIANA
MISSISSIPPI
ALABAMA
FLORIDA
TAMAULIPAS
NUEVO LEÓN
SAN LUIS POTOSÍ
QUERÉTARO
HIDALGO
MÉXICO
TLAXCALA
MORELOS
PUEBLA
VERACRUZ
GUERRERO
OAXACA
TABASCO
CHIAPAS
CAMPECHE
YUCATÁN
QUINTANA ROO
YUCATAN PENINSULA
GUATEMALA
BELIZE
SIERRA MADRE ORIENTAL
SIERRA MADRE DEL SUR
MAYA MTS.
Dallas
Fort Worth
Arlington
Waco
Austin
San Antonio
HOUSTON
Galveston
Beaumont
Port Arthur
Corpus Christi
Laredo
Nuevo Laredo
Brownsville
Matamoros
Reynosa
McAllen
Del Rio
Shreveport
Baton Rouge
New Orleans
Metairie
Lafayette
Jackson
Mobile
Pensacola
Panama City
Montgomery
MONTERREY
Ciudad Victoria
Tampico
Ciudad Madero
San Luis Potosí
Querétaro
Pachuca
Poza Rica
Tuxpan
Xalapa
Veracruz
Córdoba
Orizaba
Puebla
MEXICO CITY
Toluca
Cuernavaca
Acapulco
Oaxaca
Coatzacoalcos
Minatitlán
Villahermosa
Ciudad del Carmen
Campeche
Mérida
Progreso
Cancún
Chetumal
Belize City
Belmopan
San Pedro Sula
Tuxtla Gutiérrez
San Cristóbal de las Casas
PADRE ISLAND
MARSH ISLAND
MISSISSIPPI DELTA
ARRECÍFE ALACRÁN
CAYO ARENAS
ARRECÍFES TRIÁNGULOS
CAYOS ARCAS
ISLA COZUMEL
Cabo Catoche
Cabo Royo
Laguna Madre
Laguna de Términos
Pico de Orizaba 18,406
Volcán Popocatépetl 17,930
Volcán Tajumulco 13,845
Scale 1:8,000,000; one inch to 126 miles
Lambert Conformal Conic Projection

GULF OF MEXICO
CARIBBEAN SEA
ATLANTIC OCEAN
PACIFIC OCEAN
Tropic of Cancer
Equator
Tropic of Capricorn
Antarctic Circle
Drake Passage
HAVANA
CUBA
BAHAMAS
Miami
Cape Sable
Mérida
YUCATAN PENINSULA
MEXICO
BELIZE
Belmopan
GUATEMALA
HONDURAS
Tegucigalpa
EL SALVADOR
San Salvador
NICARAGUA
Managua
COSTA RICA
San José
PANAMA
Panamá
JAMAICA
Kingston
HAITI
Port-au-Prince
DOMINICAN REPUBLIC
SANTO DOMINGO
PUERTO RICO (U.S.)
LESSER ANTILLES
GUADELOUPE (Fr.)
SAINT LUCIA
TRINIDAD AND TOBAGO
Barranquilla
Cartagena
MARACAIBO
CARACAS
Barquisimeto
Cúcuta
VENEZUELA
Bucaramanga
MEDELLÍN
BOGOTÁ
CALI
COLOMBIA
Georgetown
GUYANA
Paramaribo
SURINAME
Cayenne
FRENCH GUIANA
GALÁPAGOS ISLANDS (Ec.)
QUITO
ECUADOR
GUAYAQUIL
Iquitos
MANAUS
Santarém
Macapá
Belém
São Luís
BRAZIL
Fortaleza
Teresina
Natal
RECIFE
PERU
Chiclayo
Lima
Callao
Cusco
Arequipa
LA PAZ
BOLIVIA
Trinidad
Santa Cruz de la Sierra
Sucre
Oruro
Cuiabá
BRASÍLIA
Goiânia
SALVADOR
Aracaju
Uberlândia
BELO HORIZONTE
RIO DE JANEIRO
SÃO PAULO
Santo André
PARAGUAY
Asunción
Antofagasta
Iquique
San Miguel de Tucumán
Santiago del Estero
CÓRDOBA
ROSARIO
Santa Fe
URUGUAY
MONTEVIDEO
BUENOS AIRES
La Plata
Mar del Plata
Porto Alegre
Florianópolis
Valparaíso
Santiago
Concepción
Valdivia
Bahía Blanca
Neuquén
CHILE
ARGENTINA
ANDES
Comodoro Rivadavia
Punta Arenas
FALKLAND ISLANDS (U.K.)
Stanley
TIERRA DEL FUEGO
Cape Horn (Cabo de Hornos)
SOUTH GEORGIA (U.K.)
SOUTH SHETLAND ISLANDS (U.K.)
SOUTH ORKNEY ISLANDS (U.K.)
SOUTH SANDWICH ISLANDS (U.K.)
ALEXANDER ISLAND
Antarctic Peninsula
TRISTAN DA CUNHA GROUP (St. Helena)
GOUGH ISLAND (St. Helena)
BOUVET (Nor.)
Copyright by Rand McNally & Co. Made in U.S.A.
Scale 1:45,000,000; one inch to 710 miles
Lambert Azimuthal, Equal Area Projection

BOLIVIA
PARAGUAY
BRAZIL
URUGUAY
ARGENTINA
CHILE
PACIFIC OCEAN
ATLANTIC OCEAN
GRAN CHACO
PAMPA
PATAGONIA
ANDES
Tropic of Capricorn
Asunción
Montevideo
Buenos Aires
Santiago
Córdoba
Rosario
Mendoza
Porto Alegre
Curitiba
São Paulo
FALKLAND ISLANDS (U.K.)
Stanley
SOUTH GEORGIA (U.K.)
TIERRA DEL FUEGO
Cape Horn (Cabo de Hornos)
Scale 1:16,000,000; one inch to 252 miles
Lambert Conformal Conic Projection

NICARAGUA

COSTA RICA

PANAMÁ

COLOMBIA

VENEZUELA

ECUADOR

PERU

BOLIVIA

CHILE

ARGENTINA

ARUBA (Neth.)

NETHERLANDS ANTILLES

CURAÇAO

BONAIRE

GALAPAGOS ISLANDS (ARCHIPIELAGO DE COLÓN) (Ecuador)

SAN CRISTOBAL

ISLA DEL COCO (Costa Rica)

ISLA DE MALPELO (Colombia)

PACIFIC OCEAN

Equator

ANDES

CORDILLERA OCCIDENTAL

CORDILLERA ORIENTAL

CORDILLERA CENTRAL

CORD. ULTRAORIENTAL

CORDILLERA DEL CONDOR

CORDILLERA DE HUANZO

CORD. REAL

ALTIPLANO

LLANOS

SIERRA DE CURUPIRA

SELVAS

ACRE

San José

Panamá

BOGOTÁ

CARACAS

QUITO

LIMA

LA PAZ

MARACAIBO

Barranquilla

Cartagena

Medellín

Cali

Guayaquil

Callao

Cochabamba

Iquitos

Leticia

Cuzco

Arequipa

Arica

Iquique

Tocopilla

Calama

Chuquicamata

Potosí

Sucre

Oruro

Santa Cruz de la Sierra

Nev. Huascarán 22,133

Chimborazo 20,702

Cotopaxi 19,347

Cayambe 18,996

Nev. Illimani 20,741

Nev. Sajama 21,463

Lago Titicaca

Lago Poopó

Golfo de Guayaquil

Golfo de Panamá

Golfo de Venezuela

Lago de Maracaibo

Amazonas

Marañón

Ucayali

Napo

Putumayo

Caquetá

Meta

Orinoco

0 100 200 300 400 500 Miles

0 200 400 600 800 Kilometers

ATLANTIC OCEAN
BRAZIL
GUYANA
SURINAME
FRENCH GUIANA
Georgetown
Paramaribo
Cayenne
AMAPÁ
PARÁ
MARANHÃO
CEARÁ
PIAUÍ
TOCANTINS
MATO GROSSO
GOIÁS
BAHIA
MINAS GERAIS
MATO GROSSO DO SUL
SÃO PAULO
RIO DE JANEIRO
PERNAMBUCO
ALAGOAS
SERGIPE
RIO GRANDE DO NORTE
PARAÍBA
DISTRITO FEDERAL
MANAUS
Belém
Macapá
Santarém
São Luís
Teresina
Fortaleza
Natal
João Pessoa
Recife
Olinda
Maceió
Aracaju
SALVADOR
Feira de Santana
BRASÍLIA
Goiânia
Cuiabá
Campo Grande
BELO HORIZONTE
RIO DE JANEIRO
SÃO PAULO
Santos
São Vicente
Niterói
Campinas
Vitória
Equator
Tropic of Capricorn
PLANALTO DO MATO GROSSO
SERRA DOS CARAJÁS
TUMUC-HUMAC MOUNTAINS
SERRA DO ESPINHAÇO
Cabo de São Roque
Cabo de São Tomé
PARAGUAY
Scale 1:16,000,000; one inch to 252 miles
Lambert Azimuthal, Equal Area Projection
Copyright by Rand McNally & Co.
Made in U.S.A.
DM-549100-2A-QR1-

ARCTIC OCEAN
North Pole
ATLANTIC OCEAN
IRELAND
UNITED KINGDOM
LONDON
NORTH SEA
NORWAY
SWEDEN
FINLAND
PORTUGAL
SPAIN
FRANCE
PARIS
GERMANY
POLAND
ITALY
EST.
LAT.
LITH.
BELARUS
HUNG.
ROMANIA
UKRAINE
KIEV (KYYIV)
MOSCOW (MOSKVA)
SAINT PETERSBURG (LENINGRAD)
NIZHNIY NOVGOROD (GORKY)
Arkhangel'sk
KAZAN'
PERM'
SAMARA
Saratov
KHARKIV
ODESA
ROSTOV-NA-DONU
VOLGOGRAD
ASTRAKHAN'
BLACK SEA
MEDITERRANEAN SEA
ALGIERS
Tunis
Tripoli
LIBYA
Banghazi
GREECE
BULG.
İSTANBUL
ANKARA
TURKEY
CYPRUS
LEBANON
SYRIA
ISRAEL
DAMASCUS
Amman
JORDAN
ALEXANDRIA
CAIRO
EGYPT
LIBYAN DESERT
IRAQ
BAGHDAD
GEORGIA
TBILISI
ARMENIA
YEREVAN
AZERBAIJAN
BAKU
Makhachkala
CASPIAN SEA
CASPIAN DEPRESSION
Atyrau
Aktau
Aktyubinsk
KAZAKHSTAN
Aral Sea
Kyzyl-Orda
Akmola
Karaganda
Semipalatinsk
Lake Balkash
TURKMENISTAN
Ashkhabad
UZBEKISTAN
TASHKENT
Bishkek
KYRGYZSTAN
ALMA-ATA
TAJIKISTAN
Dushanbe
TIEN SHAN
TARIM BASIN
ÜRÜMQI
Tabriz
TEHRĀN
MASHHAD
Eşfahān
IRAN
PLATEAU OF IRAN
ZAGROS MTS.
Kuwait
KUWAIT
Shīrāz
Bandar-e Abbās
Herāt
AFGHANISTAN
KĀBOL
Islāmābād
FAISALABAD
LAHORE
PAKISTAN
KARĀCHI
RIYADH
Ad Dammām
BAHRAIN
QATAR
Ad Dawhah
Abū Zaby
U.A.E.
SAUDI ARABIA
JIDDAH
AR RUB' AL KHĀLĪ
OMAN
Gulf of Oman
Ra's al Ḥadd
YEMEN
Sana
Aden ('Adan)
Gulf of Aden
Ra's Fartak
SOCOTRA (SUQUTRA) (Yem.)
Gees Gwardafuy
SUDAN
Khartoum
ERITREA
Asmera
ETHIOPIAN PLATEAU
ADDIS ABABA
ETHIOPIA
DJIBOUTI
SOMALIA
Mogadishu
KENYA
NAIROBI
UGANDA
TANZANIA
Mombasa
DAR ES SALAAM
MOZAMBIQUE
COMOROS
MADAGASCAR
SEYCHELLES
Red Sea
ARABIAN SEA
INDIAN OCEAN
Equator
URAL MOUNTAINS
Serov
YEKATERINBURG (SVERDLOVSK)
CHELYABINSK
OMSK
NOVOSIBIRSK
Tomsk
Surgut
Noril'sk
RUSSIA
SIBERIA
Bratsk
Irkutsk
Ulan-Ude
Yakutsk
VERKHOYANSKIY KHREBET
SAYAN KHREBET
ALTAI MTS.
Ulan Bator
MONGOLIA
GOBI DESERT
BARENTS SEA
KARA SEA
LAPTEV SEA
NOVAYA ZEMLYA
SVALBARD (Nor.)
ZEMLYA FRANTSA
SEVERNAYA ZEMLYA
NEW SIBERIAN ISLANDS
EAST SIBERIAN SEA
Arctic Circle
K2 (Qogir Feng) 28,250
ALTUN SHAN
KUNLUN SHAN
PLATEAU OF TIBET
Lhasa
Mt. Everest 29,028
NEPAL
Kathmandu
Thimphu
BHUTAN
CHINA
LANZHOU
BEIJING
TIANJIN
TAIYUAN
ZHENGZHOU
XI'AN
QIN LING
CHENGDU
CHONGQING
WUHAN
KUNMING
GUANGZHOU
GREAT INDIAN DESERT
DELHI
JAIPUR
New Delhi
Kānpur
AHMADĀBĀD
INDIA
NĀGPUR
CALCUTTA
BANGLADESH
DHAKA
CHITTAGONG
MYANMAR (BURMA)
Mandalay
BOMBAY
PUNE
HYDERABAD
DECCAN
WESTERN GHATS
EASTERN GHATS
BANGALORE
MADRAS
LAKSHADWEEP (India)
Cape Comorin
SRI LANKA
Colombo
Sri Jayawardenepura
Dondra Head
MALDIVES
Male'
BAY OF BENGAL
ANDAMAN ISLANDS (India)
NICOBAR ISLANDS (India)
Pagoda Point
YANGON
THAILAND
BANGKOK
LAOS
Viangchan
Ha Noi
Hai Phong
Gulf of Tonkin
Da Nang
CAMBODIA
Phnum Penh
Gulf of Thailand
Mui Ca Mau
MALAY PENINSULA
MALAYSIA
Kuala Lumpur
Str. of Malacca
SINGAPORE
SUMATRA
PALEMBANG
JAKARTA

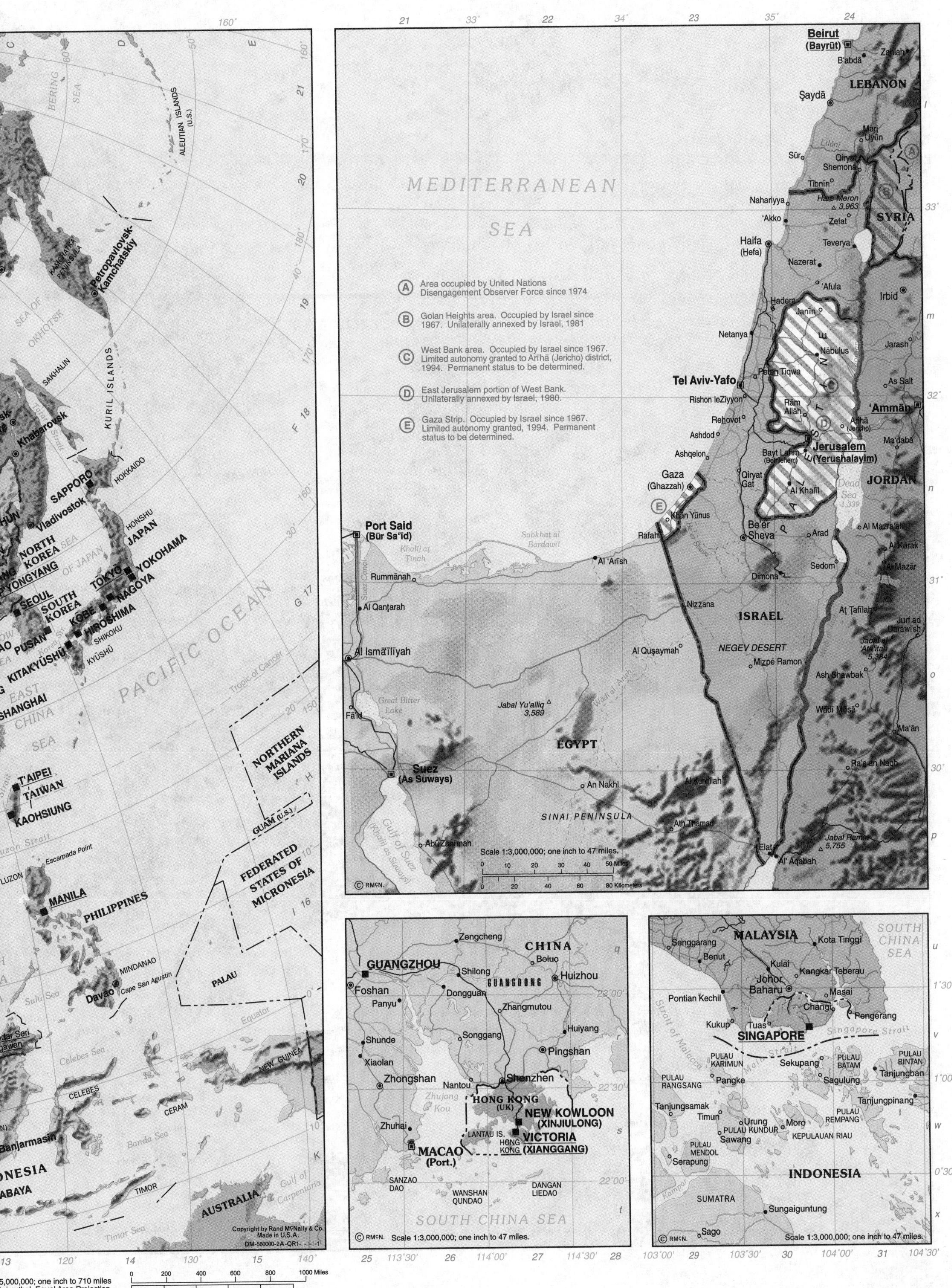

MEDITERRANEAN SEA
Area occupied by United Nations Disengagement Observer Force since 1974
Golan Heights area. Occupied by Israel since 1967. Unilaterally annexed by Israel, 1981
West Bank area. Occupied by Israel since 1967. Limited autonomy granted to Arīḥā (Jericho) district, 1994. Permanent status to be determined.
East Jerusalem portion of West Bank. Unilaterally annexed by Israel, 1980.
Gaza Strip. Occupied by Israel since 1967. Limited autonomy granted, 1994. Permanent status to be determined.
Beirut (Bayrūt)
LEBANON
SYRIA
JORDAN
ISRAEL
EGYPT
Tel Aviv-Yafo
Jerusalem (Yerushalayim)
Gaza (Ghazzah)
Port Said (Būr Sa'īd)
Suez (As Suways)
'Ammān
NEGEV DESERT
SINAI PENINSULA
Scale 1:3,000,000; one inch to 47 miles.
PACIFIC OCEAN
JAPAN
TOKYO
YOKOHAMA
NORTH KOREA
SOUTH KOREA
P'YONGYANG
SEOUL
SHANGHAI
T'AIPEI
TAIWAN
MANILA
PHILIPPINES
NORTHERN MARIANA ISLANDS
FEDERATED STATES OF MICRONESIA
AUSTRALIA
KURIL ISLANDS
ALEUTIAN ISLANDS (U.S.)
Copyright by Rand McNally & Co. Made in U.S.A.
45,000,000; one inch to 710 miles
Azimuthal, Equal Area Projection
CHINA
GUANGZHOU
HONG KONG (UK)
NEW KOWLOON (XINJIULONG)
VICTORIA (XIANGGANG)
MACAO (Port.)
SOUTH CHINA SEA
MALAYSIA
SINGAPORE
INDONESIA
SUMATRA
Johor Baharu
Singapore Strait

ICELAND
Reykjavík
Akureyri
Horn
Rifstangi
Fontur
Djúpivogur
Stokksnes
Arctic Circle
NORWEGIAN SEA
ATLANTIC OCEAN
FAEROE IS. (Den.)
Tórshavn
SHETLAND ISLANDS
Lerwick
ORKNEY ISLANDS
HEBRIDES
Wick
Duncansby Head
Kinnaird Head
Moray Firth
SCOTLAND
GRAMPIAN MTS.
Aberdeen
Dundee
Glasgow
Edinburgh
Firth of Forth
CHEVIOT HILLS
Newcastle upon Tyne
UNITED KINGDOM
Bloody Foreland
Achill Head
NORTHERN IRELAND
IRELAND
Belfast
Galway
Dublin
Loop Head
Limerick
Cork
Mizen Head
Irish Sea
Liverpool
Manchester
Kingston upon Hull
Leicester
BIRMINGHAM
WALES
St. George's Channel
Cardiff
Hartland Point
ENGLAND
Southampton
LONDON
Land's End
Plymouth
Portsmouth
Lizard Point
English Channel
Strait of Dover
CHANNEL IS. (U.K.)
Cherbourg
NORTH SEA
NETHERLANDS
Amsterdam
The Hague ('s-Gravenhage)
Rotterdam
BELGIUM
Brussels
Lille
LUX.
Luxembourg
Trondheim
NORWAY
Galdhøpiggen 8,100
Dombås
Sognefjorden
Lillehammer
Bergen
Oslo
Stavanger
Lindesnes
Skagerrak
Grenen
Ålborg
Kattegat
DENMARK
Copenhagen (København)
Malmö
LOFOTEN VESTERÅLEN
Narvik
Kebnekaise 6,926
Umeå
Örnsköldsvik
Östersund
SWEDEN
Härnösand
Bärna
Gulf
Gävle
Uppsala
Stockholm
Norrköping
Linköping
GOTLAND
Visby
Vänern
Vättern
Göteborg
ÖLAND
BALTIC SEA
Klaipėda
BORNHOLM (Den.)
Bremerhaven
Kiel
Rostock
HAMBURG
Bremen
Hannover
BERLIN
Szczecin
Gdańsk
Toruń
POLAND
Poznań
Łódź
WARSAW
Wrocław
Katowice
Kraków
GERMANY
Magdeburg
Essen
Leipzig
Bonn
Dresden
Frankfurt
Mainz
SUDETES
PRAGUE (PRAHA)
Plzeň
CZECH REPUBLIC
Ostrava
Nürnberg
Stuttgart
MUNICH (MÜNCHEN)
SLOVAKIA
Bratislava
VIENNA (WIEN)
AUSTRIA
Grossglockner 12,457
Győr
BUDAPEST
Debrecen
HUNGARY
Graz
SLOVENIA
Ljubljana
Szeged
Zagreb
CROATIA
BELGRADE (BEOGRAD)
BOSNIA AND HERZEGOVINA
Sarajevo
YUGOSLAVIA
Brest
Pointe du Raz
Rennes
Le Havre
Rouen
Reims
PARIS
Nantes
Orléans
Tours
Strasbourg
Mulhouse
FRANCE
Loire
Seine
Dijon
Saône
Bay of Biscay
Pointe de la Coubre
Limoges
Lausanne
Genève
Zürich
Bern
SWITZERLAND
LIECH.
Bordeaux
Lyon
Mont Blanc 15,771
MASSIF CENTRAL
Dordogne
Rhône
Toulouse
Nîmes
Avignon
Nice
MONACO
Marseille
Toulon
Golfe du Lion
Cap de Creus
PYRENEES
ANDORRA
Cabo Ortegal
La Coruña
Cabo de Finisterre
Gijón
Oviedo
Santander
Vigo
Bilbao
Donostia
Porto
Logroño
Cabo Mondego
PORTUGAL
Coimbra
Salamanca
Valladolid
Zaragoza
Ebro
Cabo da Roca
Lisbon (Lisboa)
MADRID
Toledo
SPAIN
BARCELONA
Tarragona
Badajoz
Cabo de São Vicente
SIERRA MORENA
València
BALEARIC ISLANDS
MENORCA
Palma
MALLORCA
EIVISSA
Cap de la Nau
Albacete
Córdoba
Faro
Sevilla
Granada
Murcia
Alacant
Cádiz
SISTEMAS BÉTICOS
Cabo de Palos
Cartagena
Málaga
Almería
Strait of Gibraltar
Tanger
GIBRALTAR (U.K.)
Ceuta (Sp.)
Tétouan
Turin (Torino)
MILAN (MILANO)
Genoa (Genova)
Venice (Venezia)
Bologna
La Spezia
Ligurian Sea
SAN MARINO
Livorno
Florence (Firenze)
Ancona
Cap Corse
CORSICA (Fr.)
Ajaccio
ROME (ROMA)
ITALY
ADRIATIC SEA
Split
Sassari
Capo Comino
SARDINIA (It.)
Cagliari
Capo Spartivento
NAPLES (NAPOLI)
Vesuvius 4,190
Bari
Taranto
Lecce
ALBANIA
Tiranë
Capo Palinuro
TYRRHENIAN SEA
Cosenza
Capo Colonna
Catanzaro
Palermo
Messina
Mt. Etna 10,902
Catania
SICILY (It.)
Capo Passero
IONIAN SEA
Cap Bon
I. DI PANTELLERIA (It.)
Valletta
MALTA
MEDITERRANEAN
Rabat
MOROCCO
Meknès
Fès
CASABLANCA
Cap Rhir
Marrakech
Beni-Mellal
ATLAS MOUNTAINS
Wahran
Melilla (Sp.)
ALGIERS (EL DJAZAÏR)
ALGERIA
Annaba
Qacentina
Tunis
Batna
El Djelfa
Laghouat
Sousse
TUNISIA
GR

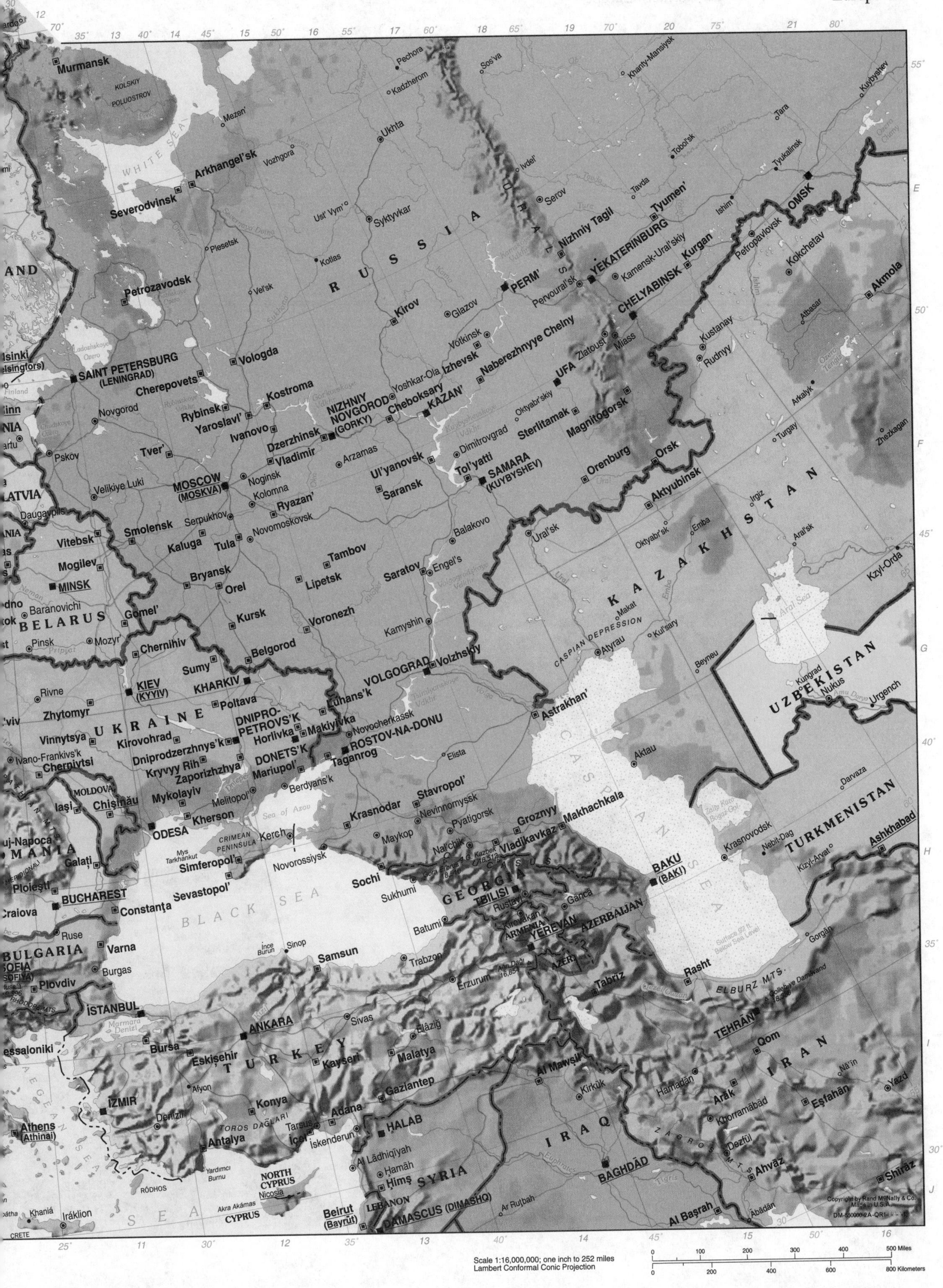
Murmansk
KOLSKIY POLUOSTROV
WHITE SEA
Mezen'
Arkhangel'sk
Severodvinsk
Vozhgora
Pechora
Kadzherom
Ukhta
Sos'va
Khanty-Mansiysk
Kuybyshev
Tara
Tobol'sk
Tyukalinsk
OMSK
Ivdel'
Serov
Ust' Vym'
Syktyvkar
Plesetsk
Kotlas
Vel'sk
Petrozavodsk
R U S S I A
URALS
Nizhniy Tagil
Tyumen'
Tavda
Ishim
Petropavlovsk
Kokchetav
Akmola
YEKATERINBURG
Kamensk-Ural'skiy
Kurgan
PERM'
Pervoural'sk
Kirov
Glazov
CHELYABINSK
Votkinsk
Izhevsk
Naberezhnyye Chelny
Zlatoust
Miass
Kustanay
Rudnyy
Atbasar
Vologda
SAINT PETERSBURG (LENINGRAD)
Cherepovets
Kostroma
Rybinsk
Yaroslavl'
Novgorod
Ivanovo
NIZHNIY NOVGOROD (GORKY)
Yoshkar-Ola
Cheboksary
KAZAN'
UFA
Oktyabr'skiy
Sterlitamak
Magnitogorsk
Arkalyk
Zhezkagan
Turgay
Pskov
Tver'
Dzerzhinsk
Vladimir
Arzamas
Dimitrovgrad
Orenburg
Orsk
MOSCOW (MOSKVA)
Noginsk
Kolomna
Velikiye Luki
Ul'yanovsk
Tol'yatti
SAMARA (KUYBYSHEV)
Saransk
LATVIA
Daugavpils
Ryazan'
Serpukhov
Smolensk
Novomoskovsk
Aktyubinsk
Irgiz
K A Z A K H S T A N
Vitebsk
Kaluga
Tula
Balakovo
Ural'sk
Oktyabr'sk
Emba
Aral'sk
Kzyl-Orda
Mogilev
MINSK
Bryansk
Orel
Tambov
Lipetsk
Saratov
Engel's
Aral Sea
BELARUS
Baranovichi
Gomel'
Pinsk
Mozyr'
Kursk
Voronezh
Kamyshin
Makat
CASPIAN DEPRESSION
Kul'sary
Atyrau
Beyneu
Chernihiv
Belgorod
Sumy
KHARKIV
KIEV (KYYIV)
VOLGOGRAD
Volzhskiy
UZBEKISTAN
Kungrad
Nukus
Urgench
Rivne
Zhytomyr
Poltava
Luhans'k
Astrakhan'
U K R A I N E
Vinnytsya
Kirovohrad
DNIPROPETROVS'K
Horlivka
Makiyivka
Novocherkassk
ROSTOV-NA-DONU
Ivano-Frankivs'k
Chernivtsi
Dniprodzerzhnys'k
Kryvyy Rih
Zaporizhzhya
DONETS'K
Mariupol'
Taganrog
Elista
Aktau
CASPIAN SEA
MOLDOVA
Iaşi
Chişinău
Mykolayiv
Melitopol'
Berdyans'k
Sea of Azov
Stavropol'
Darvaza
TURKMENISTAN
Krasnodar
Nevinnomyssk
Pyatigorsk
Groznyy
Makhachkala
ODESA
Kherson
CRIMEAN PENINSULA
Kerch
Maykop
Nal'chik
Vladikavkaz
Krasnovodsk
Nebit-Dag
Ashkhabad
Kizyl-Arvat
Galaţi
Mys Tarkhankut
Simferopol'
Novorossiysk
BAKU (BAKI)
Ploieşti
BUCHAREST
Constanţa
Sevastopol'
Sochi
Sukhumi
GEORGIA
TBILISI
Gäncä
Craiova
BLACK SEA
Rustavi
AZERBAIJAN
Ruse
BULGARIA
Varna
Batumi
ARMENIA
YEREVAN
SOFIA (SOFIYA)
Burgas
İnce Burun
Sinop
Samsun
Trabzon
Gorgān
Plovdiv
Erzurum
Ağrı Dağı 16,854
Tabriz
Rasht
ELBURZ MTS.
Qolleh-ye Damāvand 18,386
İSTANBUL
Sivas
TEHRĀN
Marmara Denizi
ANKARA
Elâzığ
Qom
Thessaloniki
Bursa
Eskişehir
TURKEY
Malatya
Kayseri
Al Mawşil
IRAN
Nā'īn
Yazd
Afyon
Gaziantep
Kirkūk
Hamadān
Arāk
Eşfahān
İZMIR
Konya
Khorramābād
Athens (Athinai)
Denizli
TOROS DAĞLARI
Tarsus
Adana
İçel
İskenderun
ḤALAB
IRAQ
ZAGROS MTS.
Dezfūl
Antalya
Al Lādhiqīyah
Ḥamāh
Ḥimş
SYRIA
BAGHDĀD
Ahvāz
Shīrāz
RÓDHOS
Yardımcı Burnu
NORTH CYPRUS
Nicosia
CYPRUS
Akra Akámas
Khaniá
Iráklion
CRETE
Beirut (Bayrūt)
LEBANON
DAMASCUS (DIMASHQ)
Ar Ruṭbah
Al Başrah
Ābādān
Copyright by Rand McNally & Co. Made in U.S.A.
Scale 1:16,000,000; one inch to 252 miles
Lambert Conformal Conic Projection
0 100 200 300 400 500 Miles
0 200 400 600 800 Kilometers

ARCTIC OCEAN
ICELAND
Reykjavík
Keflavík
Selfoss
Akureyri
Húsavík
Siglufjörður
Raufarhöfn
Fontur
GRIMSEY
Horn
Snæfellsnes
Faxaflói
Reykjanes
Vestmannaeyjar
Djúpivogur
Stokksnes
Arctic Circle
NORWEGIAN SEA
ATLANTIC OCEAN
FAEROE ISLANDS (Den.)
Tórshavn
SHETLAND ISLANDS
Lerwick
Sumburgh Head
ORKNEY ISLANDS
Kirkwall
Duncansby Head
Wick
RONA
ROCKALL (U.K.)
SAINT KILDA
HEBRIDES
Stornoway
Cape Wrath
The Minch
Moray Firth
Inverness
Kinnaird Head
Aberdeen
Tobermory
Ben Nevis 4,406
GRAMPIAN MTS.
SCOTLAND
Dundee
Perth
Stirling
Glasgow
Firth of Forth
Edinburgh
BRITISH ISLES
Malin Head
Bloody Foreland
Londonderry
Donegal Bay
Erris Head
Achill Head
NORTHERN IRELAND
Ballymena
Belfast
Bangor
North Channel
Kilmarnock
Ayr
Dumfries
Stranraer
CHEVIOT HILLS
Sligo
Clifden
IRELAND
Dundalk
Galway
ISLE OF MAN (U.K.)
Douglas
Kilkee
Loop Head
Dublin
Irish Sea
Limerick
Tipperary
Clonmel
Carlow
Waterford
Carrauntoohil 3,406
Cork
Bantry
Kinsale
Dungarvan
Mizen Head
St. George's Channel
UNITED KINGDOM
GREAT BRITAIN
Newcastle upon Tyne
Sunderland
Carlisle
Whitehaven
ENGLAND
Middlesbrough
Scarborough
York
Bradford
Liverpool
Chester
Manchester
Sheffield
Kingston upon Hull
Grimsby
Stoke on Trent
Shrewsbury
Derby
Nottingham
Leicester
Coventry
BIRMINGHAM
WALES
Hereford
Norwich
Great Yarmouth
Milford Haven
Swansea
Cardiff
Newport
Bristol
Northampton
Oxford
Cambridge
Ipswich
Reading
LONDON
Hartland Point
Exeter
Southampton
Bournemouth
Portsmouth
Brighton
Dover
Strait of Dover
CELTIC SEA
Saint Austell
Land's End
Penzance
Lizard Point
Plymouth
Start Point
ISLES OF SCILLY
English Channel
NORTH SEA
NETHERLANDS
Leeuwarden
Den Helder
Groningen
Haarlem
Leiden
Amsterdam
Utrecht
The Hague ('s-Gravenhage)
Rotterdam
Tilburg
Nijmegen
Brugge
Calais
Gent
Antwerpen
BELGIUM
Brussels (Bruxelles)
Lille
Lens
Mons
Liège
Maastricht
Namur
Charleroi
LUX.
Luxembourg
Cap de la Hague
Cherbourg
GUERNSEY (U.K.)
CHANNEL IS.
JERSEY (U.K.)
Golfe de Saint-Malo
Pointe de Saint-Mathieu
Pointe du Raz
Brest
Quimper
Lorient
Vannes
Saint-Brieuc
Saint-Malo
Rennes
Laval
Alençon
Le Mans
Chartres
Caen
Le Havre
Dieppe
Abbeville
Rouen
Évreux
Amiens
Saint-Quentin
Compiègne
Laon
Reims
Mézières
FRANCE
PARIS
Châlons-sur-Marne
Saint-Dizier
Metz
NORWAY
OSLO
Bergen
Haugesund
Stavanger
Egersund
Lindesnes
Mandal
Kristiansand
Arendal
Skien
Porsgrunn
Drammen
Lillestrøm
Lillehammer
Hamar
Halden
Sandefjord
Ålesund
Dombås
Galdhøpiggen 8,100
Trondheim
Levanger
Steinkjer
Namsos
Mosjøen
Mo
Bodø
LOFOTEN VESTERÅLEN
Sognafjorden
SWEDEN
Östersund
Strömsund
Särna
Bollnäs
Mora
Falun
Borlänge
Arvika
Karlstad
Örebro
Västerås
Eskilstuna
Katrineholm
Motala
Säffle
Uddevalla
Trollhättan
Skövde
Jönköping
Linköping
Göteborg
Borås
Varberg
Värnamo
Vetlanda
Halmstad
Ljungby
Kalmar
Karlshamn
Karlskrona
Helsingborg
Malmö
Trelleborg
Skagerrak
Kattegat
DENMARK
Frederikshavn
Grenen
Ålborg
Viborg
Randers
Holstebro
Århus
Fornæs
Kolding
Esbjerg
Odense
Copenhagen (København)
SJÆLLAND
Næstved
Nykøbing
LOLLAND
BORNHOLM (Den.)
Rønne
Kap Arkona
Flensburg
Schleswig
Kiel
Lübeck
Rostock
Stralsund
Cuxhaven
Wilhelmshaven
Itzehoe
Bremerhaven
HAMBURG
Schwerin
Neubrandenburg
Oldenburg
Bremen
Wittenberge
GERMANY
Hannover
Osnabrück
Braunschweig
BERLIN
Bielefeld
Hildesheim
Magdeburg
Potsdam
Münster
Essen
Dortmund
Wuppertal
Düsseldorf
Dessau
Göttingen
Kassel
Halle
Leipzig
Cottbus
Köln
Bonn
Siegen
Koblenz
Eisenach
Erfurt
Riesa
Chemnitz
Dresden
Wiesbaden
Mainz
Frankfurt
Offenbach
Trier
Suhl
Coburg
Zwickau
Würzburg
Mannheim
Heidelberg
Heilbronn
Saarbrücken
Karlsruhe
Nürnberg
Kołobrzeg
Świnoujście
Szczecinek
Koszalin
Szczecin
Stargard
Schwedt
Gorzów Wielkopolski
Fürstenwalde
Poznań
Zielona Góra
Głogów
Żary
Legnica
Wałbrzych
Mladá Boleslav
Liberec
Kladno
PRAGUE (PRAHA)
Hradec Králové
Cheb
Plzeň
CZECH REPUBLIC
Olomouc
Copyright by Rand McNally & Co.
Made in U.S.A.

BARENTS SEA
WHITE SEA
KOLSKIY POLUOSTROV
LAPLAND
FINLAND
RUSSIA
ESTONIA
LATVIA
LITHUANIA
BELARUS
UKRAINE
Gulf of Bothnia
Gulf of Finland
Gulf of Riga
Cheshskaya Guba
Onezhskoye Ozero
Ladozhskoye Ozero
Nordkapp
Hammerfest
Berlevåg
Vardø
Vadsø
Polmak
Kirkenes
Pechenga
Nikel'
Polyarnyy
Severomorsk
Murmansk
Verkhnetulomskiy
Olenegorsk
Monchegorsk
Kirovsk
Apatity
Kovdor
Kandalaksha
Alakurtty
Inari
Ivalo
Karasjok
Lakselv
Alta
Muonio
Lokka
Sodankylä
Kelloselkä
Kemijärvi
Pajala
Rovaniemi
Övertorneå
Tore
Torneo
Kemi
Luleå
Piteå
Skellefteå
Umeå
Pudasjärvi
Oulu
Kuusamo
Taivalkoski
Sofporog
Kalevala
Kem'
Belomorsk
Chupa
Loukhi
Sonostrov
Kanin Nos
Varzino
Mys Svyatoy Nos
Shoyna
Gremikha
Lumbovka
Ponoy
Kuzomen
Koyda
Mezen'
Megra
Indiga
Volonga
Novyy Bor
Tarasovo
Arkhangel'sk
Novodvinsk
Severodvinsk
Onega
Kodino
Obozerskiy
Plesetsk
Vozhgora
Olema
Ust'-Usa
Kozhim
Pechora
Shchel'yayur
Kadzherom
Voy-Vozh
Kedva
Sosnogorsk
Ukhta
Troitsko-Pechorsk
Zheleznodorozhnyy
Pomozdino
Ust' Un'ya
Ust'-Kulom
Ust' Vym'
Syktyvkar
Karepino
Cherdyn'
Koryazhma
Vizinga
Kotlas
Shenkursk
Bestuzhevo
Luza
Velikiy Ustyug
Pinyug
Sozimskiy
Kirs
Kudymkar
Omutninsk
Glazov
Podosinovets
Murashi
Kirov
Novovyatsk
Balezino
Kotel'nich
Nolinsk
Uva
Sovetsk
Urzhum
Yaransk
Yoshkar-Ola
Suomussalmi
Kontiomäki
Kuhmo
Kajaani
Valtimo
Iisalmi
Kokkola
Pyhäsalmi
Rautavaara
Kuopio
Polvijärvi
Joensuu
Vaasa
Seinäjoki
Suonenjoki
Heinävesi
Jyväskylä
Savonlinna
Sortavala
Mikkeli
Tampere
Pori
Rauma
Lahti
Lappeenranta
Kouvola
Hämeenlinna
Kotka
Turku (Åbo)
Espoo
Helsinki (Helsingfors)
Hanko
Yushkozero
Reboly
Lendery
Nadvoitsy
Segezha
Virandozero
Medvezh'yegorsk
Girvas
Kondopoga
Suoyarvi
Petrozavodsk
Keskozero
Pudozh
Konevo
Kargopol'
Konosha
Rovdino
Vel'sk
Vozhega
Tot'ma
Nikol'sk
Shar'ya
Vytegra
Annenskiy Most
Voznesen'ye
Lipin Bor
Lodeynoye Pole
Priozersk
Vyborg
Primorsk
Sestroretsk
SAINT PETERSBURG (LENINGRAD)
Kolpino
Kirishi
Tikhvin
Timoshino
Safronovo
Babayevo
Cherepovets
Vologda
Gryazovets
Buy
Galich
Makar'yev
Uren
Poshekhon'ye-Volodarsk
Danilov
Kostroma
Kineshma
Tutayev
Yaroslavl'
Furmanov
Ivanovo
Gorodets
NIZHNIY NOVGOROD (GORKY)
Dzerzhinsk
Cheboksary
Novocheboksarsk
Zelenodol'sk
KAZAN'
Chistopol'
Gatchina
Nebolchi
Malaya Vishera
Pestovo
Rybinskoye Vodokhranilishche
Rybinsk
Uglich
Rostov
Pereslavl'-Zalesskiy
Kovrov
Vladimir
Pavlovo
Arzamas
Shumerlya
Kanash
Buinsk
Ul'yanovsk
Dimitrovgrad
Tol'yatti
Kohtla-Järve
Slantsy
Tallinn
Haapsalu
Gdov
Luga
Novgorod
Borovichi
Bologoye
Bezhetsk
Staraya Russa
Valday
Vyshniy Volochek
Ostashkov
Torzhok
Tver'
Konakovo
Sergiyev Posad
Klin
Khimki
Noginsk
Orekhovo-Zuyevo
Elektrostal'
Murom
Vyksa
Lukoyanov
Alatyr'
Ardatov
Surskoye
Hiiumaa
Pärnu
Tartu
Võru
Valga
Pskov
Ostrov
Saaremaa
Kolkas Rags
Valmiera
Ventspils
Riga
Jūrmala
Jelgava
Rēzekne
Liepāja
Daugavpils
Opochka
Kholm
Toropets
Rzhev
Velikiye Luki
Nelidovo
MOSCOW (MOSKVA)
Lyubertsy
Kolomna
Kasimov
Saransk
Ruzayevka
Nikol'sk
Syzran'
Kuznetsk
Penza
Nevel'
Gagarin
Podol'sk
Serpukhov
Ryazan'
Sasovo
Nizhniy Lomov
Demidov
Vyaz'ma
Obninsk
Mikhaylov
Novomoskovsk
Shatsk
Morshansk
Kamenka
Yartsevo
Smolensk
Kaluga
Tula
Ryazhsk
Serdobsk
Petrovsk
Vol'sk
Balakovo
Šiauliai
Panevežys
Klaipėda
Novopolotsk
Polotsk
Vitebsk
Yelnya
Kirov
Kozelsk
Lyudinovo
Plavsk
Bogoroditsk
Yefremov
Michurinsk
Tambov
Kirsanov
Rtishchevo
Arkadak
Atkarsk
Engel's
Kaunas
Vilnius
Alytus
Molodechno
Orsha
Mogilev
Borisov
Roslavl'
Bryansk
Mtsensk
Lipetsk
Gryazi
Kotovsk
Uvarovo
Saratov
Krasnyy-Kut
Rovnoye
RUSSIA
Kaliningrad
Chernyakhovsk
Elbląg
Suwałki
Olsztyn
Ostróda
Grajewo
Łomża
Białystok
Grodno
Lida
MINSK
Bychov
Krichev
Karachev
Orel
Yelets
Livny
Voronezh
Balashov
Yelan
Kamyshin
Novogrudok
Osipovichi
Bobruysk
Baranovichi
Volkovysk
Slonim
Sluck
Svetlogorsk
Gomel'
Klintsy
Novozybkov
Trubchevsk
Zheleznogorsk
Shchigry
Semiluki
Anna
Borisoglebsk
Uryupinsk
Novoanninskiy
Mikhaylovka
Frolovo
Kursk
Staryy Oskol
L'gov
Oboyan'
Ostrogozhsk
Liski
Kalach
Dubovka
Brodnica
POLAND
WARSAW (WARSZAWA)
Włocławek
Pinsk
Mozyr'
Novhorod-Sivers'kyy
Shostka
Hlukhiv
Chernihiv
Konotop
Bilopillya
Belgorod
Alekseyevka
Rossosh
Valuyki
VOLGOGRAD
Volzhskiy
Kobrin
Brest
Siedlce
Skierniewice
Łódź
Mazowiecki
Radom
Puławy
Lublin
Sarny
Ovruch
Chornobyl'
Nizhyn
Romny
Sumy
Okhtyrka
KHARKIV
Kup'yans'k
Starobil'sk
Millerovo
Morozovsk
Kovel'
Volodymyr-Volyns'kyy
Chełm
Luts'k
Rivne
Korosten'
Novohrad-Volyns'kyy
KIEV (KYYIV)
Pryluky
Pyryatyn
Lubny
Myrhorod
Poltava
Merefa
Balakliya
Svatove
Syeverodonets'k
Luhans'k
Skarżysko Kamienna
Kielce
Częstochowa
Stalowa Wola
Rzeszów
Katowice
Sosnowiec
Kraków
Bielsko-Biała
Nowy Sącz
Krosno
Sanok
Sambir
Drohobych
L'viv
Chervonohrad
Dubno
Zhytomyr
Shepetivka
Korostyshiv
Berdychiv
Bila Tserkva
Cherkasy
Kremenchuts'ke Vodoskhovyshche
Krasnohrad
Izyum
Slov'yans'k
Kramators'k
Kostyantynivka
Stakhanov
Alchevs'k
Krasnyy Luch
Shakhty
Novocherkassk
Volgodonsk
Kozyatyn
Ternopil'
Khmel'nyts'kyy
Vinnytsya
Zhashkiv
Haysyn
Uman'
Smila
Kapitanivka
Kirovohrad
Kremenchuk
Oleksandriya
Dnipro-dzerzhyns'k
DNIPRO-PETROVS'K
Horlivka
DONETS'K
Makiyivka
Novoshakhtinsk
Taganrog
ROSTOV-NA-DONU
Elista
Scale 1:10,000,000; one inch to 158 miles
Lambert Conformal Conic Projection
0 50 100 150 200 250 300 Miles
0 100 200 300 400 500 Kilometers

IRELAND
Dublin
Limerick
Cork
Galway
Belfast
NORTHERN IRELAND
Londonderry
SCOTLAND
Glasgow
Edinburgh
UNITED KINGDOM
GREAT BRITAIN
Newcastle upon Tyne
Sunderland
Middlesbrough
Irish Sea
ISLE OF MAN (U.K.)
Liverpool
Manchester
Bradford
York
Kingston upon Hull
Sheffield
Stoke on Trent
Nottingham
BIRMINGHAM
WALES
Leicester
Coventry
Norwich
Cardiff
Bristol
LONDON
Southampton
Portsmouth
Brighton
Plymouth
Bournemouth
CELTIC SEA
ATLANTIC OCEAN
English Channel
NORTH SEA
DENMARK
NETHERLANDS
Amsterdam
The Hague ('s-Gravenhage)
Rotterdam
BELGIUM
Brussels (Bruxelles)
Antwerpen
Charleroi
LUX.
GERMANY
HAMBURG
Bremen
Hannover
Bielefeld
Essen
Dortmund
Düsseldorf
Köln
Bonn
Frankfurt
Wiesbaden
Mannheim
Stuttgart
Karlsruhe
Nürnberg
FRANCE
PARIS
Le Havre
Rouen
Caen
Brest
Rennes
Le Mans
Nantes
Orléans
Tours
Reims
Metz
Nancy
Strasbourg
Dijon
Limoges
Clermont-Ferrand
MASSIF CENTRAL
Lyon
Saint-Étienne
Grenoble
Bordeaux
Toulouse
Montpellier
Nîmes
Marseille
Toulon
Nice
MONACO
SWITZERLAND
Zürich
Bern
Genève
Lausanne
LIECHTENSTEIN
Bay of Biscay
SPAIN
PORTUGAL
La Coruña
Gijón
Oviedo
Santander
Bilbao
CORDILLERA CANTÁBRICA
Vigo
Porto
Valladolid
Zaragoza
ANDORRA
MADRID
Lisbon (Lisboa)
BARCELONA
València
Sevilla
Córdoba
Granada
Málaga
Murcia
Alacant
BALEARIC ISLANDS (Sp.)
Palma
MALLORCA
MENORCA
SIERRA MORENA
GIBRALTAR (U.K.)
Strait of Gibraltar
CORSICA (Fr.)
SARDINIA (It.)
MILAN (MILANO)
Turin (Torino)
Genoa (Genova)
Bologna
Verona
MOROCCO
Tanger
Rabat
CASABLANCA
Fès
Meknès
Oujda
ATLAS MOUNTAINS
ALGERIA
ALGIERS (EL DJAZAÏR)
Wahran
Constantine
Annaba
Tunis
TUNISIA
Sfax
Sousse
MEDITERRANEAN

BALTIC SEA
LITHUANIA
Vilnius
Kaunas
Kaliningrad
RUSSIA
BELARUS
MINSK
POLAND
WARSAW
(WARSZAWA)
CZECH REPUBLIC
PRAGUE
(PRAHA)
SLOVAKIA
Bratislava
VIENNA
(WIEN)
HUNGARY
BUDAPEST
UKRAINE
KIEV
(KYYIV)
MOLDOVA
Chişinău
ROMANIA
BUCHAREST
(BUCUREŞTI)
CARPATHIAN MOUNTAINS
CROATIA
Zagreb
BOSNIA AND HERZEGOVINA
Sarajevo
YUGOSLAVIA
BELGRADE
(BEOGRAD)
BULGARIA
SOFIA
(SOFIJA)
MACEDONIA
Skopje
ALBANIA
Tiranë
GREECE
Athens
(Athínai)
TURKEY
ANKARA
İSTANBUL
CYPRUS
Nicosia
NORTH CYPRUS
The Turkish Republic of Northern Cyprus unilaterally declared its independence on November 15, 1983.
BLACK SEA
SEA OF AZOV
CRIMEAN PENINSULA
ADRIATIC SEA
IONIAN SEA
AEGEAN SEA
MEDITERRANEAN SEA
ODESA
Copyright by Rand McNally & Co.
Made in U.S.A.
DM-559200-2A-QR1- -!-!-1
Scale 1:10,000,000; one inch to 158 miles
Lambert Conformal Conic Projection
0 50 100 150 200 250 300 Miles
0 100 200 300 400 500 Kilometers

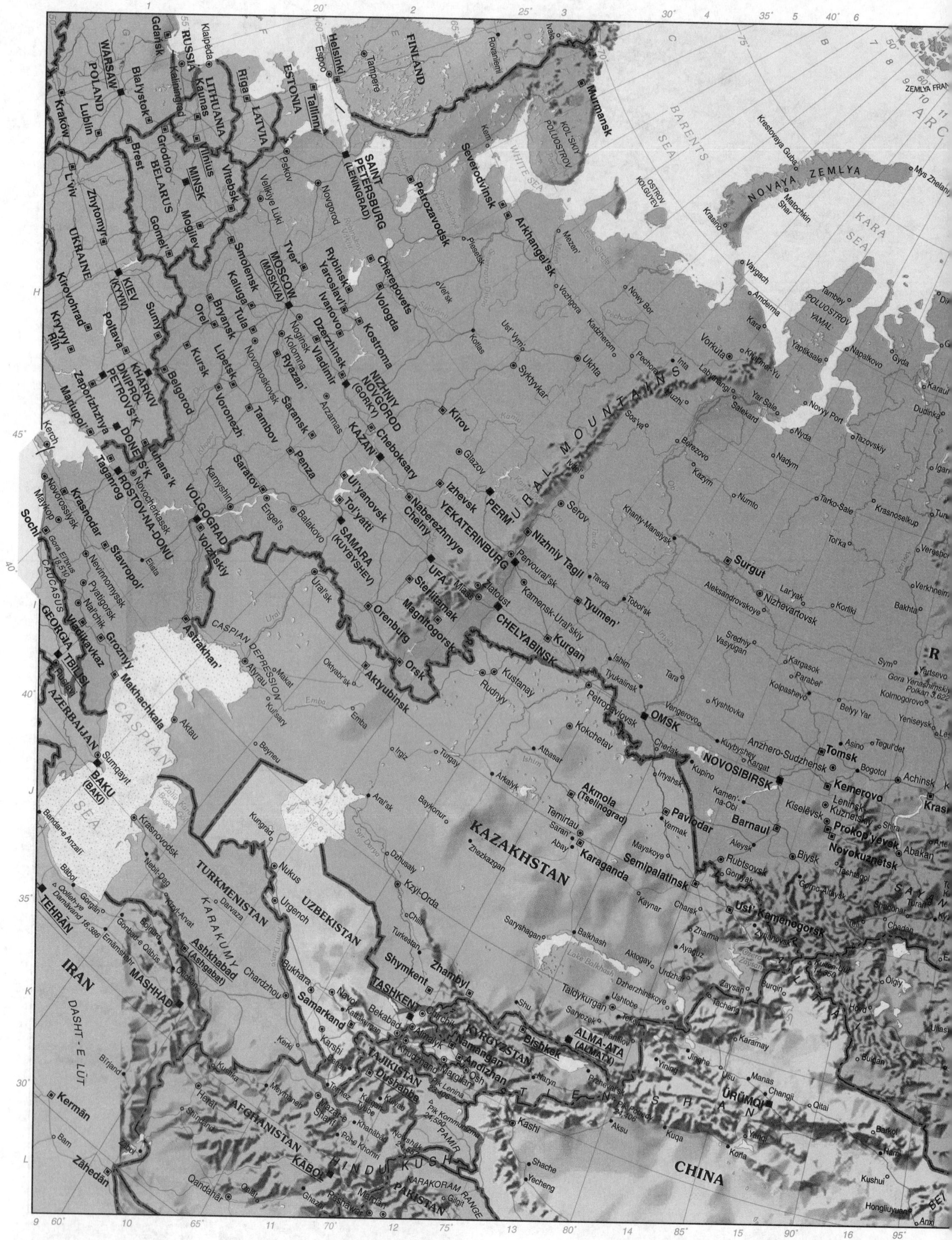
FINLAND
ESTONIA
LATVIA
LITHUANIA
RUSSIA
POLAND
BELARUS
UKRAINE
GEORGIA
AZERBAIJAN
KAZAKHSTAN
TURKMENISTAN
UZBEKISTAN
KYRGYZSTAN
TAJIKISTAN
AFGHANISTAN
IRAN
CHINA
PAKISTAN
BARENTS SEA
KARA SEA
WHITE SEA
CASPIAN SEA
NOVAYA ZEMLYA
ZEMLYA FRAN
URAL MOUNTAINS
CASPIAN DEPRESSION
CAUCASUS
KARAKUMY
DASHT-E LUT
HINDU KUSH
KARAKORAM RANGE
PAMIR
TIEN SHAN
Lake Balkhash
Aral Sea
MOSCOW (MOSKVA)
SAINT PETERSBURG (LENINGRAD)
KIEV (KYYIV)
MINSK
WARSAW
Helsinki
Tallinn
Riga
Vilnius
Murmansk
Arkhangel'sk
NIZHNIY NOVGOROD (GORKY)
KAZAN'
PERM'
YEKATERINBURG
CHELYABINSK
UFA
SAMARA (KUYBYSHEV)
VOLGOGRAD
ROSTOV-NA-DONU
KHARKIV
DONETS'K
DNIPROPETROVS'K
OMSK
NOVOSIBIRSK
Tomsk
Kemerovo
Novokuznetsk
Barnaul
Akmola (Tselinograd)
Karaganda
Semipalatinsk
ALMA-ATA (ALMATY)
Bishkek
TASHKENT
Dushanbe
Samarkand
Ashkhabad (Ashgabat)
BAKU (BAKI)
TBILISI
TEHRAN
MASHHAD
KABOL
ÜRÜMQI
Astrakhan'
Orenburg
Tyumen'
Surgut
Aktyubinsk

NEW SIBERIAN ISLANDS
(NOVOSIBIRSKIYE OSTROVA)
EAST SIBERIAN SEA
LAPTEV SEA
OCEAN
SEVERNAYA ZEMLYA
VERKHOYANSKIY KHREBET
STANOVOY KHREBET
POLUOSTROV KAMCHATKA
SEA OF OKHOTSK
SAKHALIN
KURIL ISLANDS
PACIFIC OCEAN
SEA OF JAPAN
BERING SEA
MONGOLIA
CHINA
NORTH KOREA
SOUTH KOREA
JAPAN
Yakutsk
Magadan
Petropavlovsk-Kamchatskiy
Khabarovsk
Vladivostok
Irkutsk
Ulan-Ude
Chita
Ulan Bator (Ulaanbaatar)
HARBIN
CHANGCHUN
SHENYANG
P'YŎNGYANG
SAPPORO
TŌKYŌ
YOKOHAMA
NAGOYA
KYOTO
Yuzhno-Sakhalinsk
Komsomol'sk-na-Amure
Blagoveshchensk
Bratsk
Ust'-Ilimsk
La Perouse Strait
Bering Strait
WALL OF GENGHIS KHAN
GREAT WALL
Scale 1:20,000,000; one inch to 315 miles
Lambert Azimuthal, Equal Area Projection
Copyright by Rand McNally & Co.
Made in U.S.A.

KAZAKHSTAN
KYRGYZSTAN
TAJIKISTAN
AFG.
PAKISTAN
INDIA
NEPAL
BHUTAN
BANGLADESH
MYANMAR (BURMA)
LAOS
THAILAND
VIETNAM
MONGOLIA
CHINA
Semipalatinsk
Ust'Kamenogorsk
ALMA-ATA (ALMATY)
Bishkek
Zhambyl
Namangan
Andizhan
Osh
Kashi
Aksu
ÜRÜMQI
Irkutsk
Angarsk
Ulan-Ude
SINKIANG (XINJIANG UYGUR)
TARIM PENDI
JUNGGAR PENDI
TIEN SHAN
KUNLUN SHAN
ALTUN SHAN
QAIDAM PENDI
QINGHAI
TIBET (XIZANG)
GANGDISÊ SHAN
HIMALAYAS
KARAKORAM RANGE
ZASKAR MTS.
PAMIR
BEI SHAN
GOBI
GANSU
NINGXIA HUIZU
SICHUAN
YUNNAN
GUIZHOU
GUANGXI ZHUANG
Lake Balkhash
K2 28,250
Mt. Everest 29,028
Lhasa
Xining
LANZHOU
CHENGDU
CHONGQING
KUNMING
GUIYANG
Nanning
Ha Noi
Hai Phong
Gulf of Tonkin
DELHI
New Delhi
LUDHIANA
KANPUR
LUCKNOW
Srinagar
Jalandhar
Chandigarh
Dehra Dun
Meerut
Agra
Gwalior
Allahabad
Varanasi (Benares)
Patna
Gaya
Jabalpur
Raipur
Jamshedpur
Ranchi
CALCUTTA
Haora
Khulna
DHAKA
Narayanganj
CHITTAGONG
Guwahati
Mandalay
Bhubaneshwar
Cuttack
Vishakhapatnam
Rajahmundry
Kakinada
BAY OF BENGAL
Thimphu
Kathmandu
Yinchuan
Baoji
Xi'an
Zhangye
Jiuquan
Golmud
Hotan
Xigazê
Chiang Mai
Vinh

The southern Kuril Islands are occupied by Russia pending a final peace treaty.

Scale 1:16,000,000; one inch to 252 miles
Lambert Conformal Conic Projection

MYANMAR (BURMA)
LAOS
THAILAND
CAMBODIA
VIETNAM
CHINA
MALAYSIA
BRUNEI
SINGAPORE
SOUTH CHINA SEA
Andaman Sea
Gulf of Thailand
Gulf of Tonkin
Java Sea (Laut Jawa)
INDIAN OCEAN
GREATER SUNDA ISLANDS
LESSER SUNDA ISLANDS
SUMATRA (SUMATERA)
BORNEO (KALIMANTAN)
JAVA (JAWA)
CELEBES (SULAWESI)
BANGKOK (KRUNG THEP)
Ha Noi
Vientiane
YANGON
Phnum Pénh
THANH PHO HO CHI MINH (SAIGON)
Kuala Lumpur
SINGAPORE
JAKARTA
MANILA
Bandar Seri Begawan
HONG KONG (U.K.)
MACAO (Port.)
ANDAMAN ISLANDS (India)
NICOBAR ISLANDS (India)
COCO ISLANDS (Myanmar)
PARACEL ISLANDS (XISHA QUNDAO) (Claimed by China, Taiwan, and Vietnam)
SPRATLY ISLANDS
TUNGSHA TAO (Claimed by China, Taiwan)
CHRISTMAS ISLAND (Austl.)
Equator
Copyright by Rand McNally & Co.
Made in U.S.A.

PHILIPPINE SEA
PACIFIC OCEAN
PHILIPPINES
OKINO-TORI-SHIMA (Japan)
MAUG ISLANDS
NORTHERN MARIANA ISLANDS (U.S.)
MARIANA ISLANDS
SARAGON
SAIPAN
GUAM (U.S.)
Agana
Tropic of Cancer
Legaspi
SAMAR
LEYTE
Tacloban
Cebu
Tagbilaran
Butuan
Cagayan de Oro
Bislig
MINDANAO
Davao
Mount Apo 9,692
General Santos
Cape San Agustin
Tinaca Point
YAP
SOROL
GAFEKUT
FEDERATED STATES OF MICRONESIA
PALAU ISLANDS
Koror
SONSORAL ISLANDS
PALAU (BELAU)
CAROLINE ISLANDS
KEPULAUAN TALAUD
Tahuna
MOROTAI
Wayabula
Galela
Manado
Gunung Klabat 6,634
Tondano
HALMAHERA
Weda
Molucca Sea (Laut Maluku)
Labuha
Tanjung Libobo
Laiwui
KEPULAUAN OBI
KEPULAUAN SULU
Sorong
Manokwari
Bosnik
Teba
Tanjung D'Urville
Sarmi
Serui
Waren
Teluk Cenderawasih
Jayapura
MANUS ISLAND
Patusi
BISMARCK ARCHIPELAGO
Kavieng
PULAU MISOOL
Ceram Sea (Laut Seram)
Kokas
Piru
CERAM (SERAM)
Bula
Namlea
BURU
Ambon
MOLUCCAS (MALUKU)
PEGUNUNGAN MAOKE
Puncak Jaya 16,503
Puncak Trikora 15,584
Puncak Mandala 15,617
NEW GUINEA
Wewak
Sepik
Bogia
CENTRAL RANGE
Madang
Hoskins
Aisega
Mount Hagen
Mount Wilhelm 14,793
Mount Giluwe 14,330
Goroka
Awul
NEW BRITAIN
Lae
Cape Cretin
Tual
Dobo
Birab
Kepi
Lake Murray
Banda Sea (Laut Banda)
KEPULAUAN ARU
Tanjung De Jongs
Digul
Fly
PAPUA NEW GUINEA
Kerema
KEPULAUAN BARAT DAYA
PULAU YAMDENA
Tepa
Saumlaki
PULAU YOS SUDARSO
Tanjung Vals
Merauke
Daru
Gulf of Papua
Losuia
Popondetta
Tufi
OWEN STANLEY RANGE
Port Moresby
Esa'ala
Samarai
Dili
Tutuala
Ocussi
TIMOR
ARAFURA SEA
Mari
Timor Sea
Torres Strait
Cape York
Bamaga
Equator
Scale 1:16,000,000; one inch to 252 miles
Sinusoidal Projection

Konya
Antalya
Karaman
Malatya
Elaziğ
TURKEY
Diyarbakır
Kahramanmaraş
Batman
Muş
Van
Ağrı Dağı 16,853
ARMENIA
Naxçıvan
AZERBAIJAN
AZER.
BAKU
Ali-Bajramly
Krasnovodsk
Darvaza
Tarsus
İçel
Adana
Gaziantep
Şanlıurfa
Mardin
Khvoy
Marand
Ahar
Lankāran
CASPIAN SEA
Nebit-Dag
TURKMENISTAN
Kizyl-Arvat
KARAKUM
Cardzhou
Anamur Burnu
NORTH CYPRUS
Akra Akámas
CYPRUS
Lemesós
Nicosia
Hatay (Antioch)
İskenderun
HALAB
Al Lādhiqīyah
Idlib
Buhayrat al Asad
Ar Raqqah
Al-Qāmishlī
Orūmīyeh
Tabrīz
Ardabīl
Miyāneh
Marāgheh
Mahābād
Bandar-e Anzalī
Rasht
Zanjān
Ashkhabad
Bayram
Mary
Quchān
MEDITERRANEAN SEA
Tarābulus
Tartus
Hamāh
Hims
LEBANON
Beirut
SYRIA
Saydā
Dayr az Zawr
Al-Mawşil
Irbīl
As Sulaymānīyah
Kirkūk
Tonekabon
Bābol
Āmol
Sārī
Gonbad-e Qābūs
Gorgān
Qazvīn
ELBURZ MTS.
Qolleh-ye Damavand 18,386
Emāmshahr
Sabzevār
MASHHAD
Neyshābūr
Haifa (Hefa)
ISRAEL
Netanya
Tel Aviv-Yafo
DAMASCUS (DIMASHQ)
Tiberiya
Dar'a
Irbid
Euphrates
Abū Kamāl
Tigris
Sanandaj
Hamadān
Karaj
TEHRĀN
Semnān
Port Said (Būr Sa'īd)
Al Manşūrah
CAIRO (AL QĀHIRAH)
Gaza
Az-Zarqā'
Ammān
Jerusalem (Yerushalayim)
Dead Sea
Be'er Sheva
Ar Rutbah
Ar Ramādī
BAGHDĀD
IRAQ
Karbalā'
Al Hillah
Bākhtarān
Arāk
Qom
Kāshān
Borūjerd
Khorramābād
IRAN
Torbat-e Heydarīyeh
DASHT-E LUT
PLATEAU OF IRAN
SELSELEH
Herat
JORDAN
Suez (As Suways)
Jabal Katrīnā 8,668
Jabal Ramm 5,755
Gulf of Suez
An Najaf
Ad Dīwānīyah
'Ar'ar
Dezfūl
Najafābād
Khomeynīshahr
Eşfahān
Masjed-e Soleymān
Ardakān
Qomsheh
Yazd
Birjand
AFG
An Nāşirīyah
Al 'Amārah
Ahvāz
Hawr al Hammar
Ad Duwayd
Al Jawf
Basra (Al Başrah)
Ābādān
Jabal Al Lawz 7,984
Tabūk
Ra's Muhammad
ARABIAN DESERT
KUWAIT
Būbiyān
Al Jahrah
Kuwait (Al Kuwayt)
ZAGROS MTS.
Kermān
Zābol
Daryācheh-ye Hāmūn
Shīrāz
Kāzerūn
Zāhedān
Bam
Sīrjān
Qina
Luxor
Taymā'
Hā'il
AL-HIJĀZ
Persian Gulf
Bandar-e Būshehr
Jahrom
Kawm Umbū
Aswān
Ra's Abu Madd
Umm Lajj
Buraydah
Ad Dammām
Al Khubar
BAHRAIN
Al Manāmah
Bandar-e Lengeh
Bandar-e 'Abbās
JAZIREH YE QESHM
Strait of Hormuz
EGYPT
Ra's Banās
Yanbu' al Bahr
Medina (Al Madīnah)
Shaqrā'
AD DAHNĀ
Al Mubarraz
Al Hufūf
QATAR
Ad Dawhah
Ra's al-Khaymah
Ash Shāriqah
Dubayy
OMAN
Limah
BALU
CENTRA
Tropic of Cancer
Ad Dawādimī
RIYADH (AR RIYĀD)
Abū Zaby
Gulf of Oman
Gwādar
Halā'ib
Ra's Al Hadāribah
NUBIAN DESERT
JIDDAH
Dunqunāb
ARABIAN
SAUDI ARABIA
PENINSULA
Al 'Ayn
Suhār
UNITED ARAB EMIRATES
Masqat
Mecca (Makkah)
At Tā'if
Turabah
Jabal ash-Sham 9,957
Sūr
Ra's al Hadd
RED SEA
Port Sudan (Būr Sūdān)
Sawākin
SUDAN
As Sulayyil
AR RUB' AL KHĀLĪ
OMAN
Khalūf
MAŞĪRAH
Ra's Kasr
Jabal Sawdā' 10,522
Abhā
Khamis Mushayt
'ASĪR
Khalīj Maşīrah
Ra's al Madrakha
ERITREA
Erota
Kassala
Akordat
Keren
Jīzān
Abā as Su'ūd
Şa'dah
Ghubbat Şawqirah
Şawqirah
ARA
DAHLAK ARCHIPELAGO
Mitsiwa
Asmera
Sanāw
Şalālah
Mirbāţ
Jabal an-Nabi Shu'ayb 12,008
Sana (San'ā')
Al Hudaydah
YEMEN
Al Qadārif
Ras Dashen Terara 15,158
Mekele
Zabīd
Yarīm
Ghubbat al Qamar
Ra's Fartak
Ash Shihr
Sayhūt
Gonder
Lake Tana
Ta'izz
Al Hawrah
Al Mukallā
Aseb
Bahir Dar
Bab el Mandeb
Shaykh 'Uthmān
Aden ('Adan)
Tendaho
Obock
DJIBOUTI
Djibouti
Gulf of Aden
Blue Nile
Dese
Debre Markos
Lake Abe
Hadībū
Ra's Khaanzir
Cape Sura
Qandala
Caluula
Gees Gwardafuy
SOCOTRA (SUQUTRA) (Yemen)
Fiche
(Abay)
Maydh
Berbera
Bargal
ADDIS ABABA
Akaki Beseka
Debre Zeyit
Dire Dawa
Harer
Ra's Hafun
Jima
Asela
Hargeysa
Burco
INDIA
Lake Ziway
Lake Shala
SOMALIA
Bender Beyla
RIFT VALLEY
Lake Abaya
ETHIOPIA
Imi
OGADEN
Eyl
Beyra
Shebele
Genale
Mega
KEN.
Hobyo
30° 35° 40° 45° 50° 55° 60°
35° 30° 25° 20° 15° 10° 5°
1 2 3 4 5 6 7
A B C D E F G H I

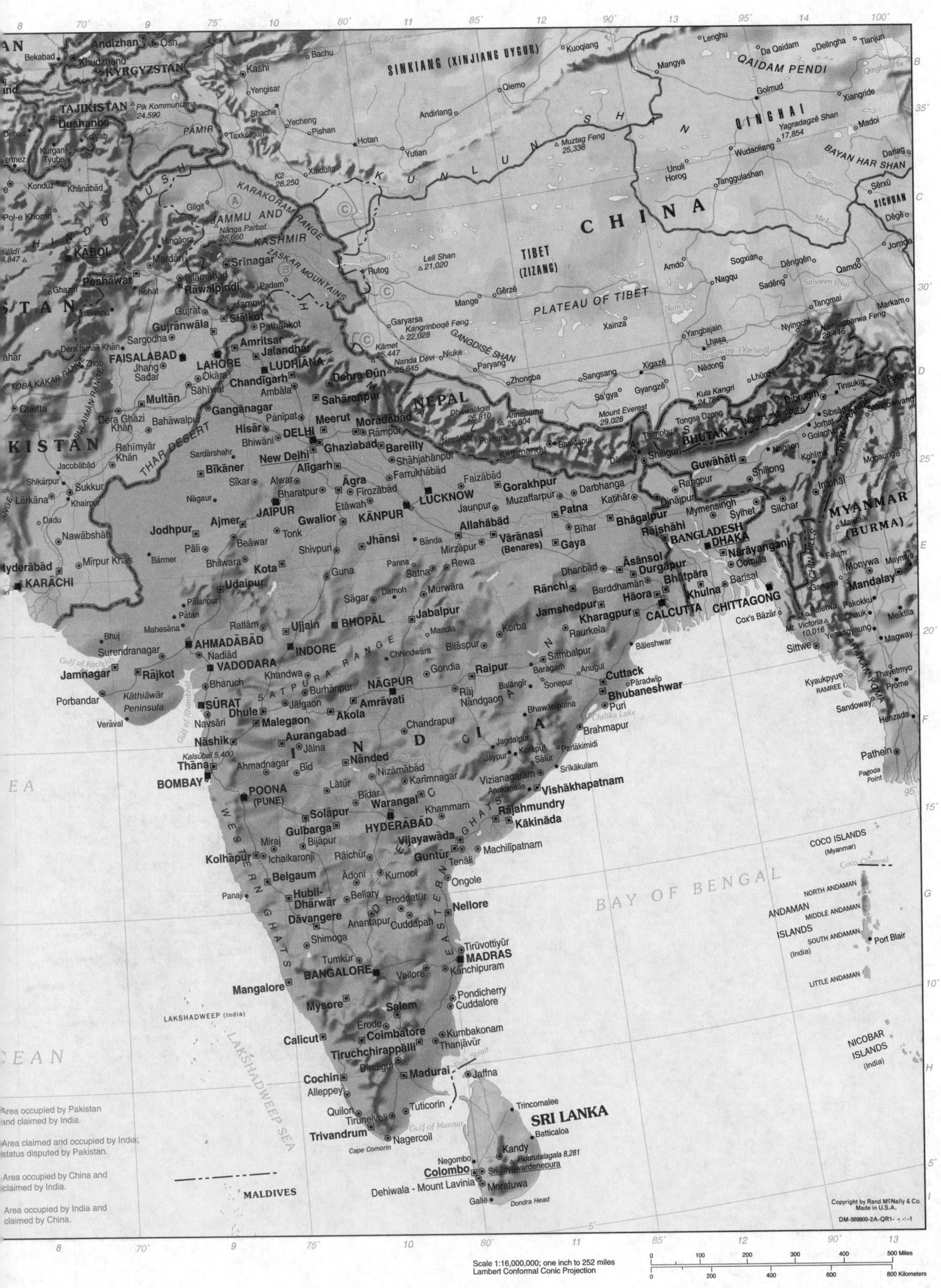

Scale 1:16,000,000; one inch to 252 miles
Lambert Conformal Conic Projection

0 100 200 300 400 500 Miles
0 200 400 600 800 Kilometers

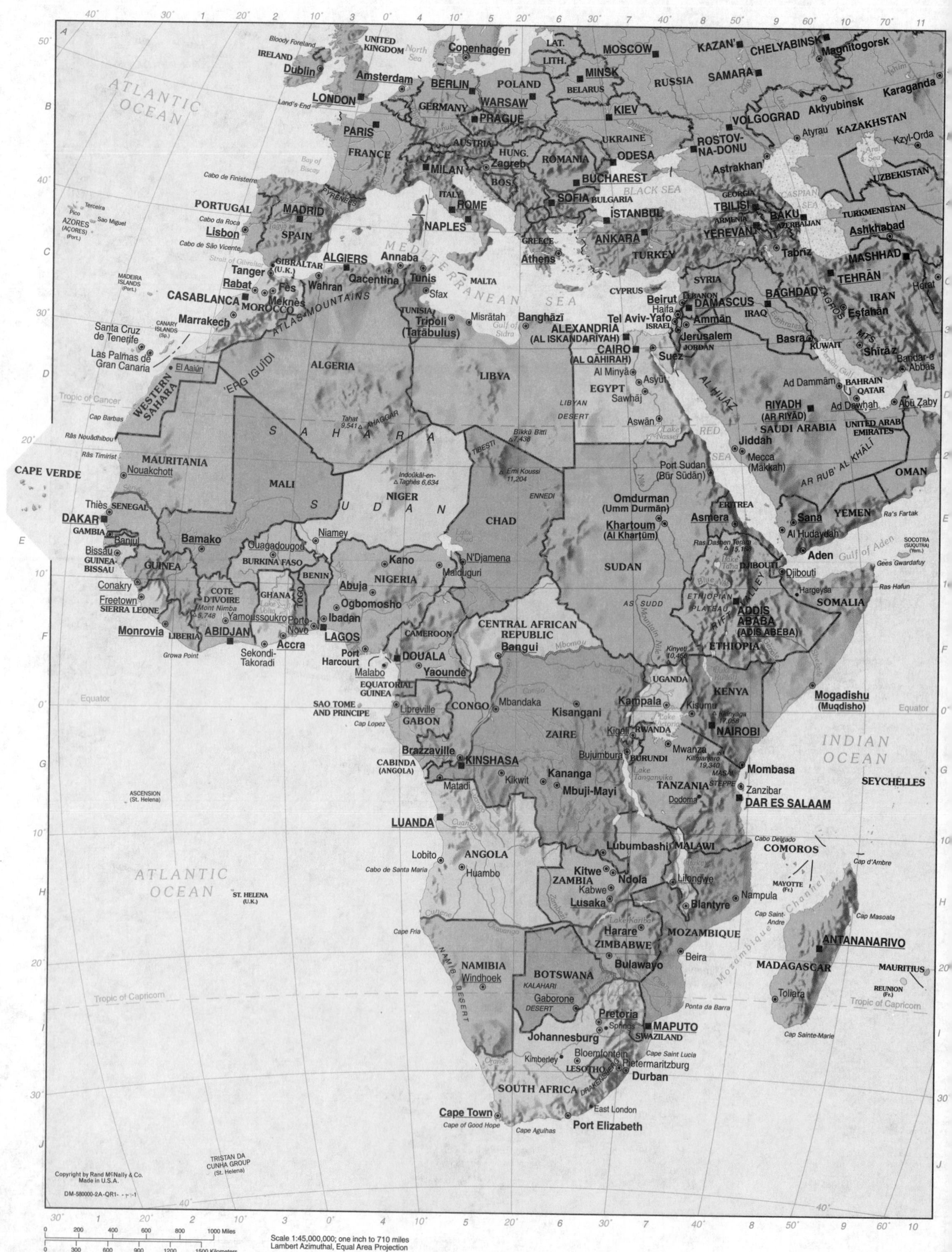

Scale 1:45,000,000; one inch to 710 miles
Lambert Azimuthal, Equal Area Projection

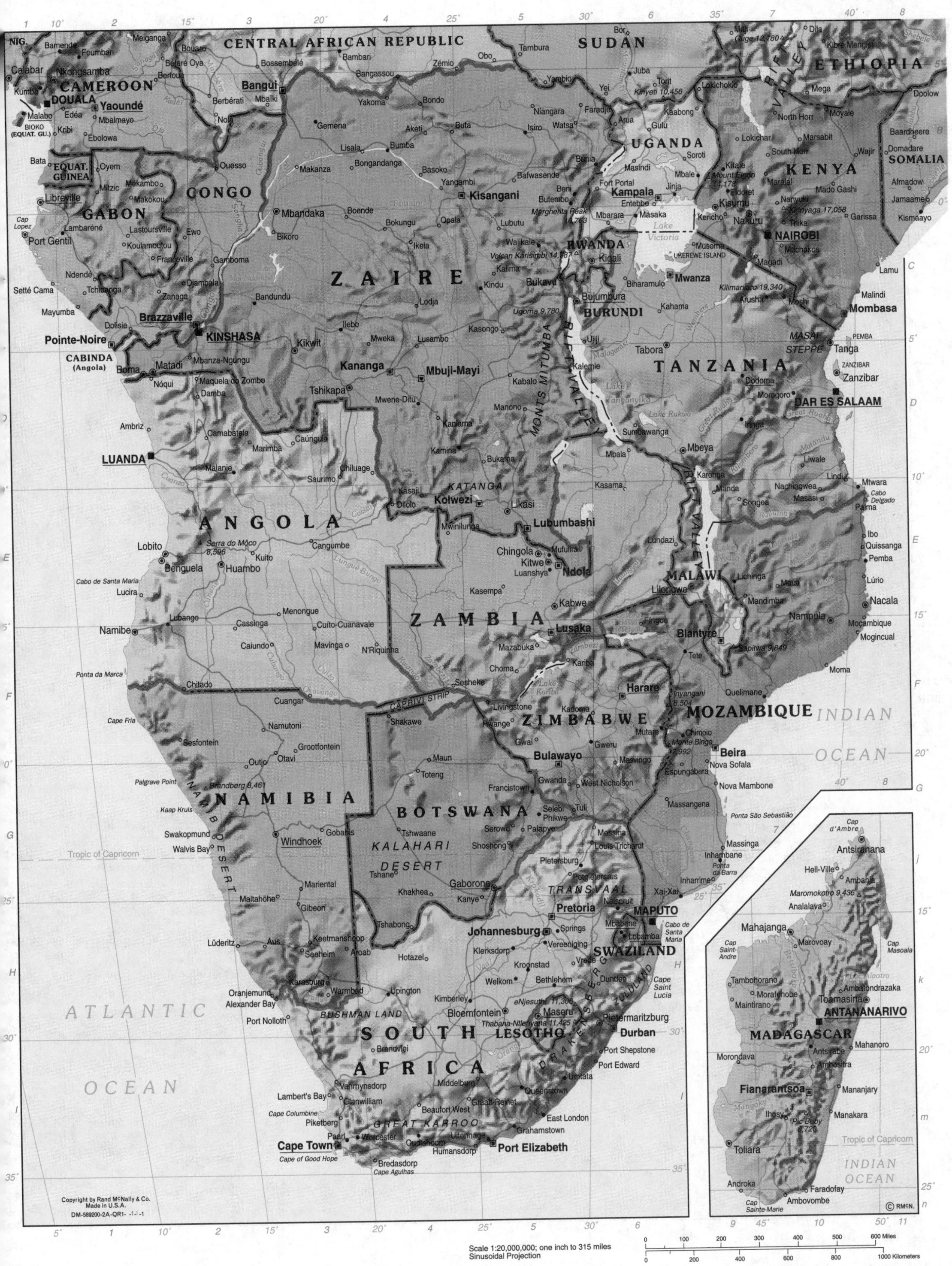

Scale 1:20,000,000; one inch to 315 miles
Sinusoidal Projection

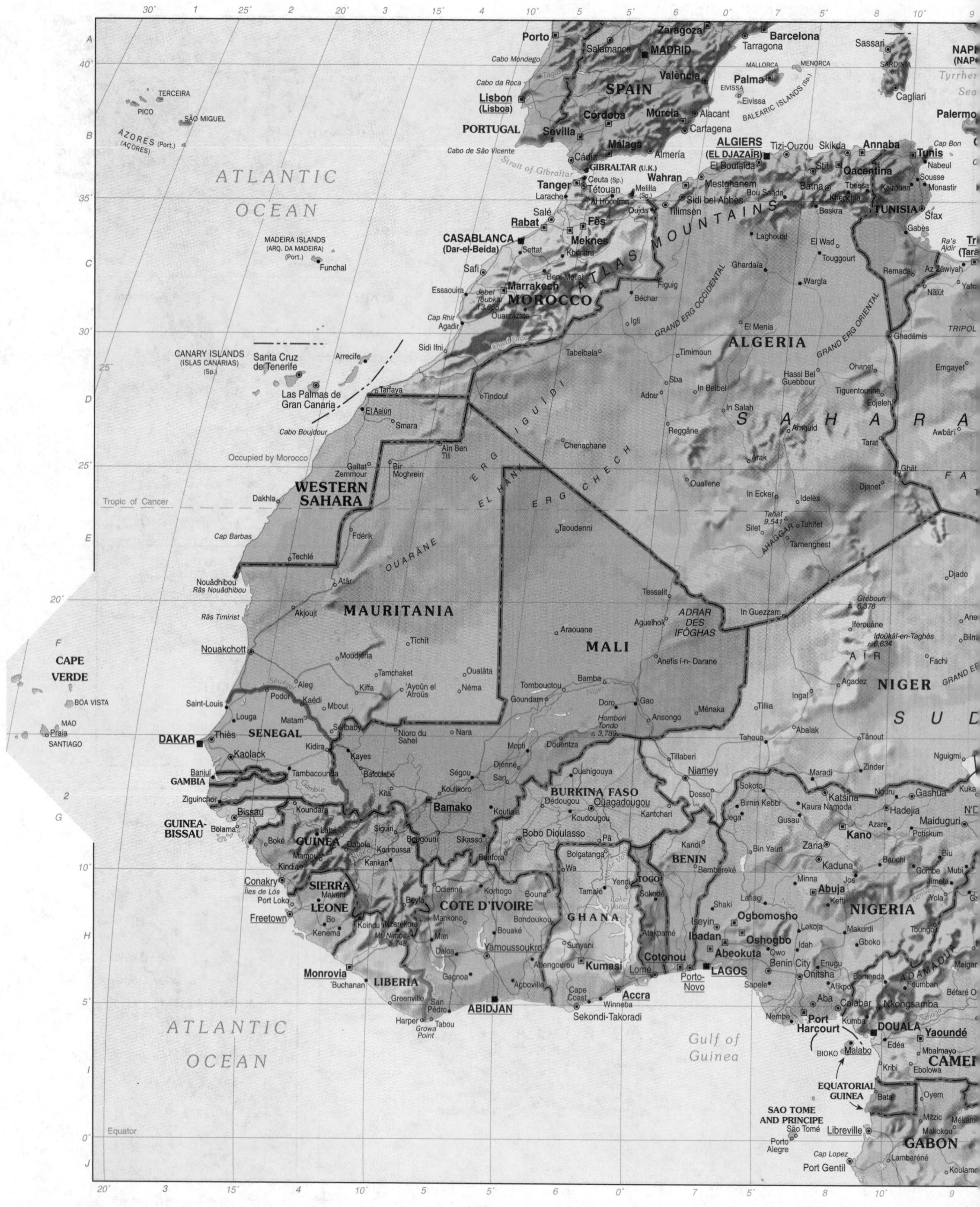

Porto
Salamanca
MADRID
Zaragoza
Barcelona
Tarragona
Cabo Mondego
Cabo da Roca
Lisbon
(Lisboa)
SPAIN
València
MALLORCA
MENORCA
Palma
EIVISSA
Eivissa
BALEARIC ISLANDS (Sp.)
Sassari
SARDINIA
Cagliari
Tyrrhenian Sea
Palermo
Córdoba
Murcia
Alacant
Cartagena
PORTUGAL
Sevilla
Málaga
Almería
Cádiz
Cabo de São Vicente
Strait of Gibraltar
GIBRALTAR (U.K.)
Ceuta (Sp.)
Tétouan
Tanger
Larache
Al Hoceima
Melilla (Sp.)
Oujda
Wahran
Tilimsen
Sidi bel Abbès
Mestghanem
ALGIERS
(EL DJAZAÏR)
El Boulaïda
Tizi-Ouzou
Skikda
Annaba
Stif
Qacentina
Batna
Tbessa
Khenchla
Bou Saâda
Tunis
Cap Bon
Nabeul
Sousse
Monastir
Kairouan
TUNISIA
Sfax
Gabès
Beskra
TERCEIRA
PICO
SÃO MIGUEL
AZORES (Port.)
(AÇORES)
ATLANTIC
OCEAN
Salé
Rabat
Fès
Meknes
Khenifra
CASABLANCA
(Dar-el-Beida)
Settat
MADEIRA ISLANDS
(ARQ. DA MADEIRA)
(Port.)
Funchal
Safi
Beni-Mellal
ATLAS MOUNTAINS
Marrakech
Essaouira
Jebel Toubkal 13,665
MOROCCO
Ouarzazate
Figuig
Béchar
Laghouat
El Wad
Touggourt
Ghardaïa
Wargla
Cap Rhir
Agadir
Igli
GRAND ERG OCCIDENTAL
GRAND ERG ORIENTAL
El Menia
ALGERIA
Remada
Az Zawiyah
Nālūt
Ghadāmis
TRIPOLI
Sidi Ifni
Oued Draa
Tabelbala
Timimoun
CANARY ISLANDS
(ISLAS CANARIAS)
(Sp.)
Santa Cruz de Tenerife
Arrecife
Las Palmas de Gran Canaria
Tarfaya
Tindouf
IGUIDI
Sba
Adrar
In Belbel
Hassi Bel Guebbour
Ohanet
Emgayet
Tiguentourine
Edjeleh
El Aaiún
Smara
Cabo Boujdour
In Salah
Reggâne
S A H A R A
Amguid
Tarat
Awbārī
Chenachane
Aïn Ben Tili
ERG CHECH
Arak
Occupied by Morocco
Galtat Zemmour
Bir Moghrein
WESTERN SAHARA
Ghât
Oualiene
Djanet
Tropic of Cancer
Dakhla
ERG EL HANK
In Ecker
Idelès
Tahat 9,541
AHAGGAR
Tahifet
Silet
Tamenghest
Cap Barbas
Fdérik
Taoudenni
Techlé
OUARÂNE
Djado
Nouâdhibou
Râs Nouâdhibou
Atâr
Tessalit
Grébouun 6,378
MAURITANIA
Akjoujt
Râs Timirist
In Guezzam
ADRAR DES IFÔGHAS
Aguelhok
Araouane
Iferouâne
Idoukâl-en-Taghès 6,634
MALI
AÏR
Tîchît
Nouakchott
CAPE VERDE
Moudjéria
Anefis i-n- Darane
Fachi
Tamchaket
Oualâta
Agadez
Aleg
Kiffa
'Ayoûn el 'Atroûs
Néma
NIGER
Tombouctou
Bamba
Ingal
Saint-Louis
Podor
Kaédi
Mbout
Goundam
Doro
Gao
Ménaka
BOA VISTA
Louga
Matam
Tillia
MAO
Praia
SANTIAGO
Thiès
SENEGAL
Sélibaby
Nioro du Sahel
Nara
Hombori Tondo 3,789
Ansongo
Abalak
Tânout
DAKAR
Kidira
Kayes
Mopti
Douentza
Tahoua
Kaolack
Tillaberi
Nguigmi
Banjul
GAMBIA
Tambacounda
Gambia
Bafoulabé
Djénné
Ouahigouya
Niamey
Maradi
Zinder
Ségou
San
Koulikoro
Kita
Bamako
Koutiala
BURKINA FASO
Dédougou
Ouagadougou
Koudougou
Kantchari
Dosso
Sokoto
Birnin Kebbi
Katsina
Kaura Namoda
Gusau
Gashua
Hadejia
Azare
Maiduguri
Potiskum
Kano
Ziguinchor
Bissau
GUINEA-BISSAU
Bolama
Koundara
Labé
GUINEA
Boké
Dabola
Siguiri
Kouroussa
Kankan
Bougouni
Sikasso
Bobo Dioulasso
Pâ
Jega
Kandi
Bin Yauri
Zaria
Bauchi
BENIN
Bembèrèké
Kaduna
Gombe
Jos
Mamou
Kindia
Banfora
Bolgatanga
Wa
TOGO
Conakry
Îles de Los
SIERRA LEONE
Makeni
Port Loko
Odienné
Korhogo
Bouna
Tamale
Yendi
Sokodé
Minna
Abuja
Keffi
Yola
Beyla
COTE D'IVOIRE
Lafiagi
Shaki
NIGERIA
Freetown
Bo
Kenema
Koindu
Nzérékoré
Mankono
Bondoukou
GHANA
Lake Volta
Iseyin
Ogbomosho
Lokoja
Makurdi
Mt. Nimba 5,748
Man
Bouaké
Atakpamé
Ibadan
Oshogbo
Idah
Gboko
Daloa
Yamoussoukro
Sunyani
Abeokuta
Owo
Benin City
Enugu
Onitsha
Abengourou
Kumasi
Lomé
Cotonou
Porto-Novo
LAGOS
Monrovia
Buchanan
LIBERIA
Gagnoa
Agboville
Sapele
Afikpo
Bamenda
Foumban
Greenville
Cape Coast
Accra
Winneba
Sekondi-Takoradi
Aba
Calabar
Nkongsamba
San Pédro
ABIDJAN
Harper
Tabou
Growa Point
Nembe
Port Harcourt
Kumba
DOUALA
Yaoundé
Edéa
ATLANTIC
OCEAN
Gulf of Guinea
BIOKO
Malabo
Kribi
Mbalmayo
Ebolowa
EQUATORIAL GUINEA
Bata
Oyem
SAO TOME AND PRINCIPE
São Tomé
Libreville
Mitzic
Makokou
Equator
Porto Alegre
GABON
Cap Lopez
Port Gentil
Lambaréné

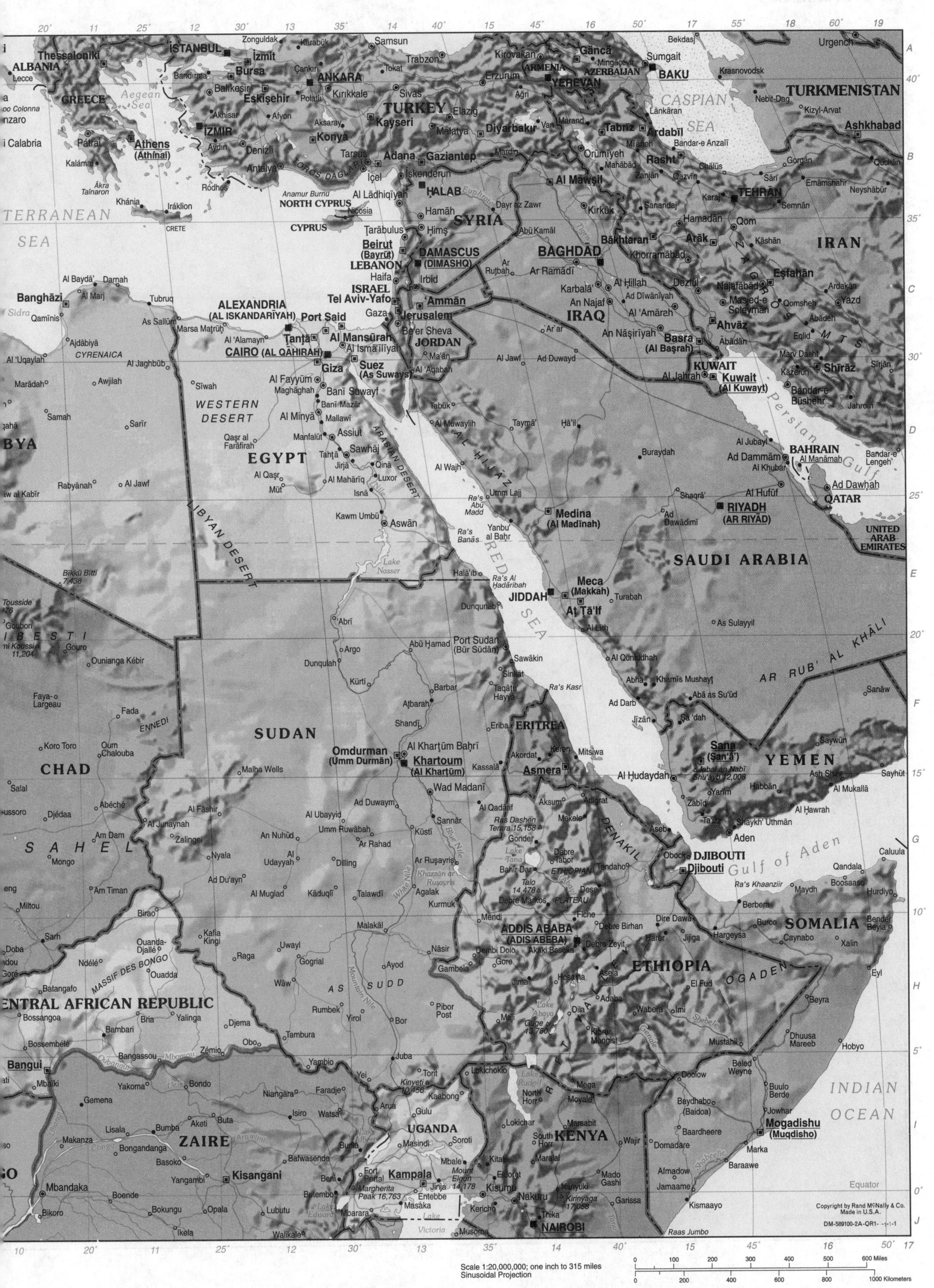

Scale 1:20,000,000; one inch to 315 miles
Sinusoidal Projection

0 100 200 300 400 500 600 Miles
0 200 400 600 800 1000 Kilometers

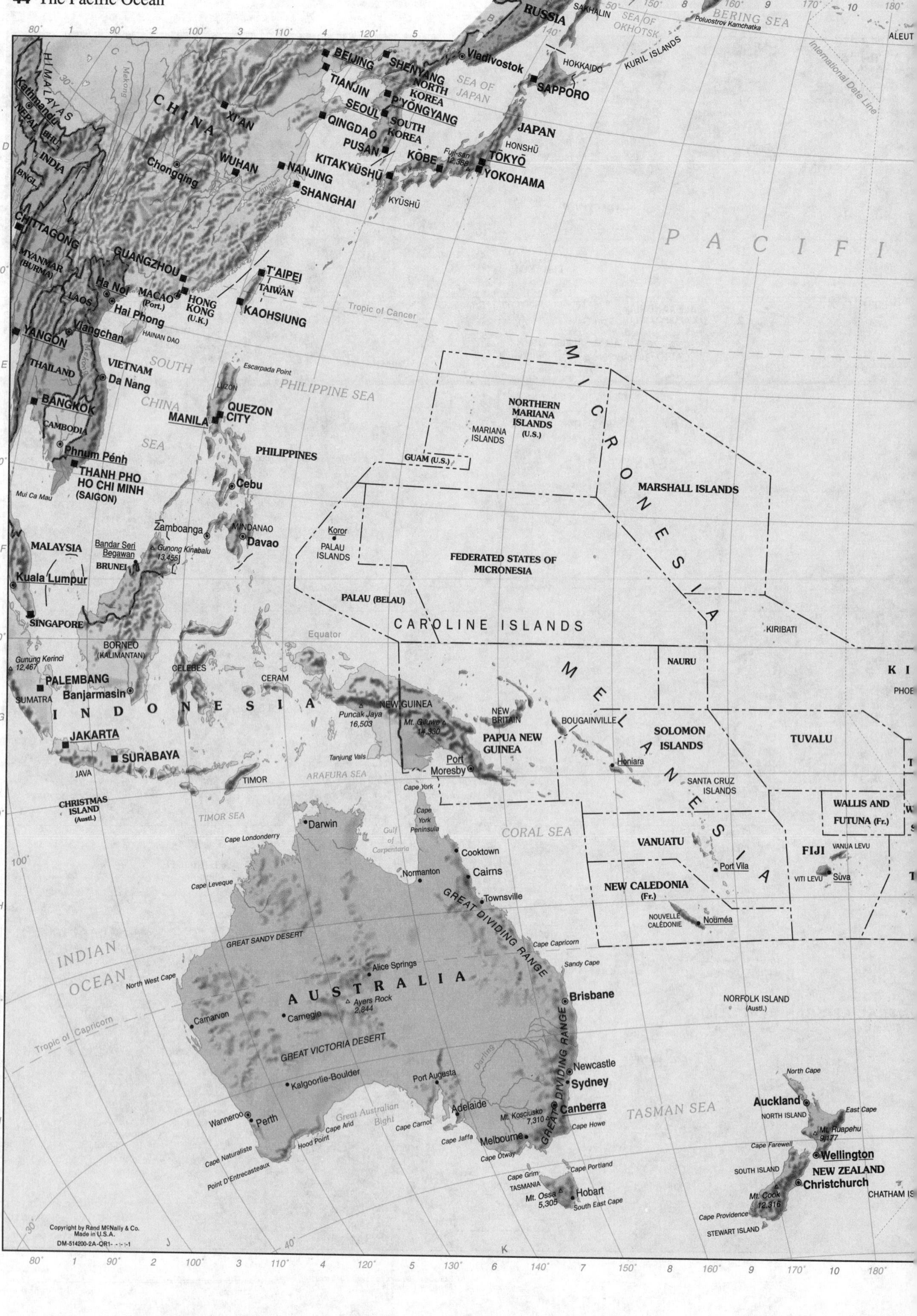
RUSSIA
SAKHALIN
SEA OF OKHOTSK
BERING SEA
Poluostrov Kamchatka
KURIL ISLANDS
ALEUT
International Date Line
HOKKAIDO
Vladivostok
SAPPORO
BEIJING
SHENYANG
TIANJIN
NORTH KOREA
SEA OF JAPAN
P'YŎNGYANG
SEOUL
SOUTH KOREA
QINGDAO
PUSAN
JAPAN
HONSHŪ
Fuji-san 12,388
TŌKYŌ
YOKOHAMA
KŌBE
KITAKYŪSHŪ
KYŪSHŪ
HIMALAYAS
Kathmandu
NEPAL
BHU.
INDIA
BNGL.
CHINA
XI'AN
Chongqing
WUHAN
NANJING
SHANGHAI
Yangtze
Mekong
CHITTAGONG
MYANMAR (BURMA)
GUANGZHOU
Ha Noi
Hai Phong
LAOS
MACAO (Port.)
HONG KONG (U.K.)
T'AIPEI
TAIWAN
KAOHSIUNG
Tropic of Cancer
YANGON
Viangchan
HAINAN DAO
PACIFIC
THAILAND
VIETNAM
Da Nang
SOUTH CHINA SEA
Escarpada Point
LUZON
PHILIPPINE SEA
BANGKOK
CAMBODIA
MANILA
QUEZON CITY
PHILIPPINES
Phnum Pénh
THANH PHO HO CHI MINH (SAIGON)
Mui Ca Mau
Cebu
Zamboanga
MINDANAO
Davao
MALAYSIA
Bandar Seri Begawan
BRUNEI
Gunong Kinabalu 13,455
Kuala Lumpur
SINGAPORE
MICRONESIA
NORTHERN MARIANA ISLANDS (U.S.)
MARIANA ISLANDS
GUAM (U.S.)
MARSHALL ISLANDS
Koror
PALAU ISLANDS
FEDERATED STATES OF MICRONESIA
PALAU (BELAU)
CAROLINE ISLANDS
KIRIBATI
Equator
BORNEO (KALIMANTAN)
Gunung Kerinci 12,467
CELEBES
CERAM
NAURU
PHOE
PALEMBANG
Banjarmasin
SUMATRA
INDONESIA
NEW GUINEA
Puncak Jaya 16,503
Mt. Giluwe 14,330
NEW BRITAIN
BOUGAINVILLE
MELANESIA
SOLOMON ISLANDS
TUVALU
JAKARTA
SURABAYA
JAVA
PAPUA NEW GUINEA
Tanjung Vals
Port Moresby
Honiara
ARAFURA SEA
TIMOR
Cape York
SANTA CRUZ ISLANDS
CHRISTMAS ISLAND (Austl.)
TIMOR SEA
Cape York Peninsula
Darwin
Gulf of Carpentaria
CORAL SEA
WALLIS AND FUTUNA (Fr.)
Cape Londonderry
Cooktown
VANUATU
FIJI
VANUA LEVU
Cairns
Normanton
Port Vila
VITI LEVU
Suva
Cape Leveque
Townsville
NEW CALEDONIA (Fr.)
GREAT DIVIDING RANGE
NOUVELLE CALÉDONIE
Nouméa
GREAT SANDY DESERT
Cape Capricorn
INDIAN OCEAN
Sandy Cape
North West Cape
Alice Springs
AUSTRALIA
Brisbane
NORFOLK ISLAND (Austl.)
Ayers Rock 2,844
Carnegie
Carnarvon
Tropic of Capricorn
GREAT VICTORIA DESERT
Darling
Newcastle
Sydney
Kalgoorlie-Boulder
Port Augusta
North Cape
Great Australian Bight
Adelaide
Canberra
TASMAN SEA
Auckland
NORTH ISLAND
East Cape
Wanneroo
Perth
Cape Arid
Cape Carnot
Mt. Kosciusko 7,310
Cape Howe
Mt. Ruapehu 9,177
Hood Point
Cape Jaffa
Melbourne
Cape Farewell
Wellington
Cape Naturaliste
Cape Otway
Cape Portland
SOUTH ISLAND
NEW ZEALAND
Point D'Entrecasteaux
Cape Grim
TASMANIA
Hobart
Christchurch
Mt. Ossa 5,305
South East Cape
Mt. Cook 12,316
CHATHAM IS
Cape Providence
STEWART ISLAND
80° 90° 100° 110° 120° 130° 140° 150° 160° 170° 180°
1 2 3 4 5 6 7 8 9 10
20° 10° 0° 10° 20° 30° 40°
B C D E F G H I J K

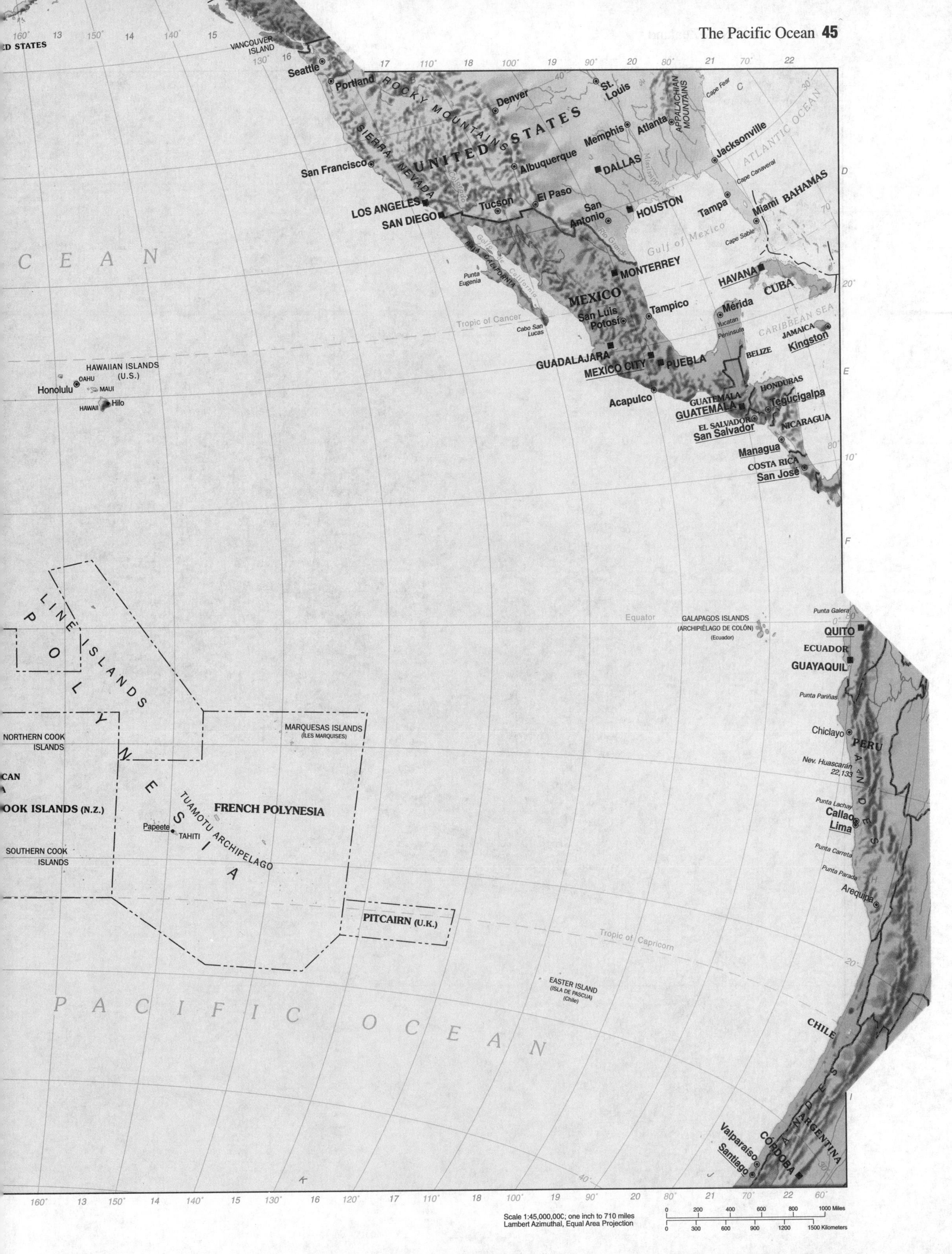

UNITED STATES
Seattle
Portland
ROCKY MOUNTAINS
Denver
St. Louis
APPALACHIAN MOUNTAINS
SIERRA NEVADA
San Francisco
Albuquerque
Memphis
Atlanta
DALLAS
Jacksonville
ATLANTIC OCEAN
LOS ANGELES
SAN DIEGO
Tucson
El Paso
San Antonio
HOUSTON
Tampa
Miami
BAHAMAS
Gulf of Mexico
MONTERREY
HAVANA
CUBA
MEXICO
San Luis Potosí
Tampico
Mérida
Tropic of Cancer
CARIBBEAN SEA
JAMAICA
Kingston
GUADALAJARA
MEXICO CITY
PUEBLA
BELIZE
HONDURAS
Acapulco
GUATEMALA
Tegucigalpa
EL SALVADOR
San Salvador
NICARAGUA
Managua
COSTA RICA
San José
HAWAIIAN ISLANDS (U.S.)
Honolulu
OAHU
MAUI
HAWAII
Hilo
O C E A N
LINE ISLANDS
POLYNESIA
Equator
GALAPAGOS ISLANDS (ARCHIPIÉLAGO DE COLÓN) (Ecuador)
QUITO
ECUADOR
GUAYAQUIL
MARQUESAS ISLANDS (ÎLES MARQUISES)
NORTHERN COOK ISLANDS
Chiclayo
PERU
COOK ISLANDS (N.Z.)
FRENCH POLYNESIA
TUAMOTU ARCHIPELAGO
Papeete
TAHITI
SOUTHERN COOK ISLANDS
Callao
Lima
ANDES
Arequipa
PITCAIRN (U.K.)
Tropic of Capricorn
EASTER ISLAND (ISLA DE PASCUA) (Chile)
P A C I F I C O C E A N
CHILE
ARGENTINA
Valparaíso
Santiago
CÓRDOBA
Scale 1:45,000,000; one inch to 710 miles
Lambert Azimuthal, Equal Area Projection

Palangkaraya
BORNEO
Banjarmasin
Martapura
Tanjung Selatan
Parepare
Singkang
CELEBES
Watampone
Sindjai
Ujungpandang
Bantaeng
Baubau
Tual
KEPULAUAN ARU
PULAU YAMDENA
Meyanodas
Birab
NEW GUINEA
Tanjung Vals
Merauke
INDONESIA
ARAFURA SEA
SEMARANG
Sumenep
Surakarta
Surabaya
Madiun
Kediri
Malang
Banyuwangi
JAVA (JAWA)
Denpasar
Mataram
SUMBAWA
Raba
Reo
FLORES
Ende
Waingapu
SUMBA
Ocussi
Dili
TIMOR
Soe
Kupang
Cape Van Diemen
TIMOR SEA
Cape Croker
Cobourg Pen.
Van Diemen Gulf
Darwin
Cape Wessel
Cape Arnhem
ARNHEM LAND
Pine Creek
GROOTE EYLANDT
Cape Beatrice
Duifken Point
Weipa
York
Bamaga
Torres Str.
Cape Londonderry
Joseph Bonaparte Gulf
Daly
Mataranka
Gulf of Carpentaria
INDIAN OCEAN
KIMBERLEY PLATEAU
Mt. Hann 2,556
Wyndham
Mt. Ord 3,074
DURACK RANGES
KING LEOPOLD RANGES
Halls Creek
Cape Leveque
Victoria
Newcastle Waters
NORTHERN TERRITORY
BARKLY TABLELAND
Hooker Creek
Burketown
Normanton
Camooweal
Cloncurry
Mount Isa
Broome
Yeeda
Fitzroy
Christmas Creek
Cape Latouche Treville
EIGHTY MILE BEACH
TANAMI DESERT
The Granites
Tennant Creek
Port Hedland
Marble Bar
GREAT SANDY DESERT
Lake Auld
Nullagine
Dampier
Yarraloola
Mt. Brockman 3,714
Mt. Bruce 4,052
Ethel Creek
Onslow
North West Cape
HAMERSLEY RANGE
Mt. Meharry 4,104
Mt. Augustus 3,625
Mt. Leisler 2,943
Mt. Liebig 5,000
Mt. Zeil 4,957
Alice Springs
MacDonnell Ranges
Lake Amadeus
AUSTRALIA
SIMPSON DESERT
GREAT ARTESIAN BASIN
WESTERN AUSTRALIA
GIBSON DESERT
Mt. Cockburn 3,734
Ayers Rock 2,844
Mt. Aloysius 3,560
Mt. Woodroffe 4,724
Minilya
Lake Carnegie
Carnegie
Cape Cuvier
Carnarvon
Tropic of Capricorn
Shark Bay
Wooramel
DIRK HARTOG ISLAND
Meekatharra
Wiluna
Innamincka
STURT STONY DESERT
Lake Eyre North
SOUTH AUSTRALIA
Marree
Sandstone
White Cliffs
Mount Magnet
Leonora
GREAT VICTORIA DESERT
Mount Eba
Lake Torrens
Bluff Point
Mullewa
Paynes Find
Kingoonya
Saint Mary Peak 3,871
BARRIER RANGE
Geraldton
Dongara
Coolgardie
Kalgoorlie-Boulder
NULLARBOR PLAIN
Eucla
Ceduna
Lake Gairdner
Port Augusta
Streaky Bay
Whyalla
Port Pirie
DARLING RANGE
Norseman
Balladonia
Great Australian Bight
Eyre Peninsula
Spencer Gulf
Wanneroo
Perth
Gosnells
Fremantle
Armadale
Newdegate
Wagin
Hopetoun
Cape Arid
Port Lincoln
Cape Carnot
Gulf Saint Vincent
Elizabeth
Adelaide
Geographe Bay
Bunbury
Cape Naturaliste
Bluff Knoll 3,596
Hood Point
ARCHIPELAGO OF THE RECHERCHE
KANGAROO ISLAND
Encounter Bay
Cape Jaffa
Horsham
Hamilton
Augusta
Cranbrook
Albany
Point D'Entrecasteaux
West Cape Hope
Mount Gambier
Portland
KING
INDIAN OCEAN

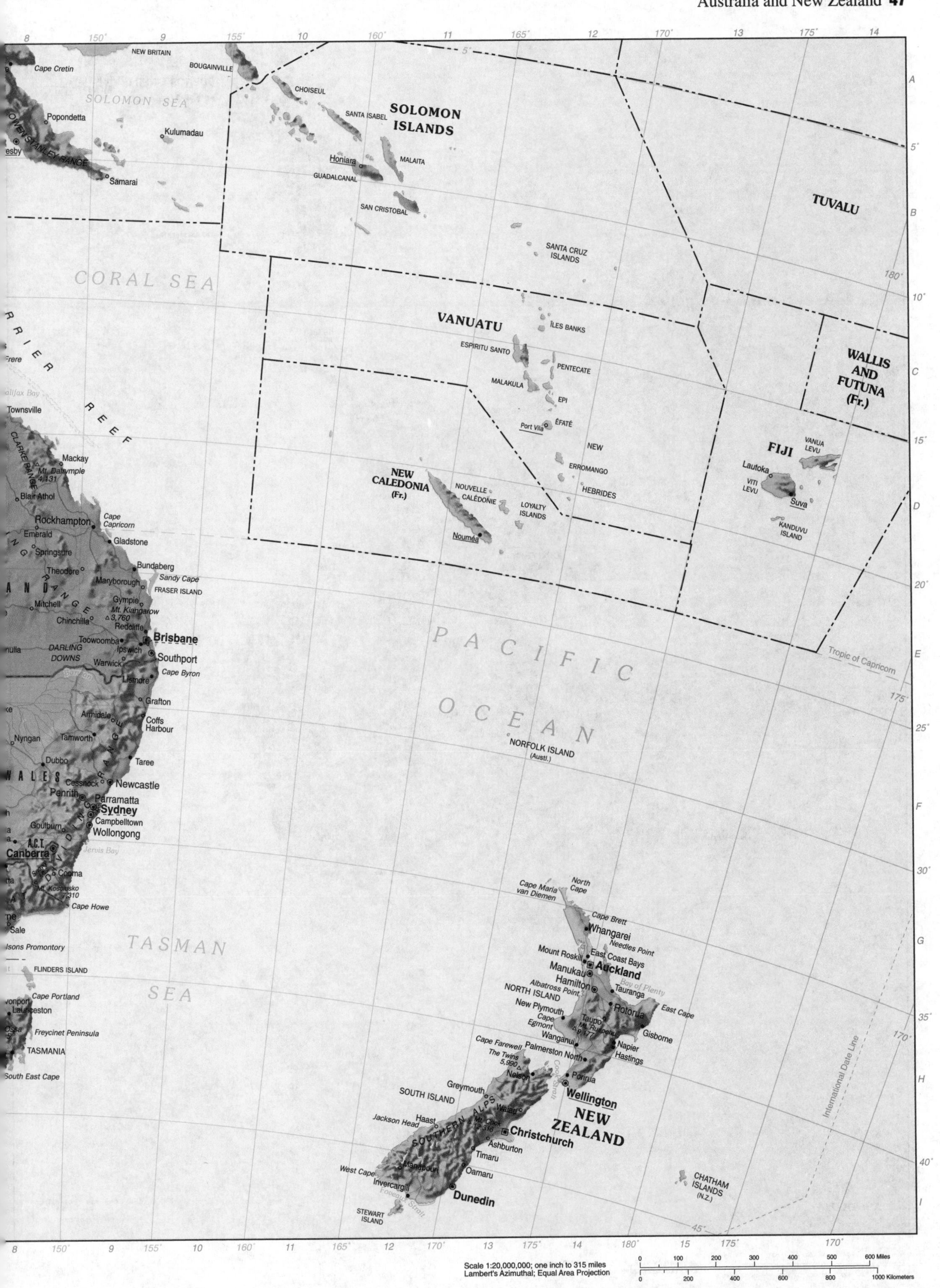

Scale 1:20,000,000; one inch to 315 miles
Lambert's Azimuthal; Equal Area Projection

PACIFIC OCEAN
ATLANTIC OCEAN
INDIAN OCEAN
ANTARCTICA
CHILE
ARGENTINA
URUGUAY
BRAZIL
Rosario
BUENOS AIRES
MONTEVIDEO
Río de la Plata
ANDES
PATAGONIA
ARCHIPIÉLAGO DE LOS CHONOS
Strait of Magellan
TIERRA DEL FUEGO
FALKLAND ISLANDS (U.K.)
Cape Horn
DRAKE PASSAGE
SOUTH SHETLAND ISLANDS (U.K.)
Palmer Station (U.S.)
ADELAIDE I.
Bellingshausen Sea
ALEXANDER I.
LARSEN ICE SHELF
ANTARCTIC PENINSULA
SOUTH GEORGIA (U.K.)
SOUTH ORKNEY ISLANDS (U.K.)
Scotia Sea
SOUTH SANDWICH ISLANDS (U.K.)
THURSTON I.
Amundsen Sea
Antarctic Circle
Mt. Rex 3,625
Mt. Siple 10,203
Mt. Sidley 13,717
Mt. Ulmer 8,996
Vinson Massif 16,066
ELLSWORTH MTS.
RONNE ICE SHELF
Weddell Sea
BERKNER I.
MARIE BYRD LAND
WHITMORE MTS.
FILCHNER ICE SHELF
ROCKEFELLER PLATEAU
THIEL MTS.
PENSACOLA MTS.
COATS LAND
Cape Norvegia
ROOSEVELT I.
QUEEN MAUD MTS.
Amundsen - Scott South Pole Station (U.S.)
South Pole
Ross Sea
ROSS ICE SHELF
QUEEN MAUD LAND
MÜHLIG-HOFMANN MTS.
Mt. Markham 14,049
Mt. Albert Markham 10,522
McMurdo Station (U.S.)
Cape Adare
Mt. Erebus 12,451
Mt. Minto 13,658
Mt. McClintock 11,457
VICTORIA LAND
TRANSANTARCTIC MOUNTAINS
CAMPBELL I. (N.Z.)
AUCKLAND IS. (N.Z.)
GEORGE V COAST
SØR RONDANE MTS.
QUEEN FABIOLA MTS.
MACQUARIE ISLAND (Austl.)
ENDERBY LAND
South Magnetic Pole
AMERICAN HIGHLAND
LAMBERT GLACIER
WILKES LAND
NAPIER MTS.
Cape Ann
AMERY ICE SHELF
Cape Darnley
Cape Poinsett
PRINCE EDWARD IS. (S. Afr.)
ARCHIPEL CROZET (Fr.)
HEARD ISLAND (Austl.)
ÎLES KERGULÉLEN (Fr.)
Great Australian Bight
AUSTRALIA
Copyright by Rand McNally & Co. Made in U.S.A.
DM-594000-2A-QR1-
0 200 400 600 800 1000 Miles
0 300 600 900 1200 1500 Kilometers
Scale 1:45,000,000; one inch to 710 miles
Polar Sterographic Projection

Index

Abbreviations of Geographical Names and Terms

Ak., U.S. . . . . Alaska
Al., U.S. . . . . . . Alabama
Ant. . . . . Antarctica
Ar., U.S. . . . . . . Arkansas
Arg. . . . . Argentina
Asia . . . . Asia
Austl. . . . . . . Australia
Az., U.S. . . . . Arizona

b. . . . . *bay, gulf*
Bah. . . . . Bahrain
B.C., Can. British Columbia
Bol. . . . . Bolivia
Braz. . . . . Brazil

c. . . . . *cape, point*
Ca., U.S. . . . . . California
Can. . . . . Canada
Cay. Is. . . Cayman Islands
Co., U.S. . . . . . . Colorado
Col. . . . . Colombia
cont. . . . . *continent*
C.R. . . . . Costa Rica
ctry. . . . . *country*

D.C., U.S. District of Columbia
De., U.S. . . . . . . Delaware
dep. . . . . *dependency*
Dom. Rep. Dominican Republic

El Sal. . . . . El Salvador
Eng., U.K. . . . . . . England

Fl., U.S. . . . . Florida

Ga., U.S. . . . . Georgia
Guad. . . . . . . Guadeloupe

hist. reg. . . *historic region*
H.K. . . . . Hong Kong
Hond. . . . . . Honduras

i. . . . . *island*
Ia., U.S. . . . . Iowa
Id., U.S. . . . . Idaho
Il., U.S. . . . . Illinois
In., U.S. . . . . Indiana
Ire. . . . . Ireland
is. . . . . *islands*

Jam. . . . . Jamaica

Ks., U.S. . . . . Kansas
Ky., U.S. . . . . . Kentucky

l. . . . . *lake*
La., U.S. . . . . . Louisiana
Leb. . . . . Lebanon

Ma., U.S. . . Massachusetts
Malay. . . . . . . Malaysia
Md., U.S. . . . . Maryland
Me., U.S. . . . . Maine
Mex. . . . . Mexico
Mi., U.S. . . . . . . Michigan
Mn., U.S. . . . . . Minnesota
Mo., U.S. . . . . . . Missouri
Monts. . . . . Montserrat
Mor. . . . . Morocco
Ms., U.S. . . . . . Mississippi
Mt., U.S. . . . . . . Montana
mtn. . . . . *mountain*
mts. . . . . *mountains*

N.A. . . . . North America
Nb., U.S. . . . . . . Nebraska
N.C., U.S. North Carolina
N.D., U.S. North Dakota
Newf., Can. Newfoundland
N.H., U.S. New Hampshire
Nic. . . . . Nicaragua
N.M., U.S. . . New Mexico
N.S., Can. . . Nova Scotia
Nv., U.S. . . . . Nevada
N.W.T., Can. Northwest Territories
N.Y., U.S. . . . . New York
N.Z. . . . . . . New Zealand

Oh., U.S. . . . . Ohio
Ok., U.S. . . . . . Oklahoma
Ont., Can. . . . . . . Ontario
Or., U.S. . . . . Oregon

Pa., U.S. . . Pennsylvania
Pak. . . . . Pakistan
Pan. . . . . Panama
Para. . . . . Paraguay
pen. . . . . *peninsula*
Phil. . . . . Philippines
plat. . . . . *plateau*
pol. div. . . *political division*
P.R. . . . . . . Puerto Rico
prov. . . . . *province*

res. . . . . *reservoir*

Sask., Can. Saskatchewan
S.C., U.S. South Carolina
Scot., U.K. . . . . Scotland
S.D., U.S. South Dakota
Sen. . . . . Senegal
Sri L. . . . . . Sri Lanka
St. K./N. St. Kitts and Nevis
stm. . . . . *river, stream*
strt. . . . . *strait*

terr. . . . . *territory*
Tn., U.S. . . . . . Tennessee
Trin. Trinidad and Tobago
Tx., U.S. . . . . Texas

U.K. . . United Kingdom
Urug. . . . . . . Uruguay
U.S. . . . . . . United States
Ut., U.S. . . . . Utah

Va., U.S. . . . . . . Virginia
Ven. . . . . Venezuela
vol. . . . . *volcano*
Vt., U.S. . . . . . . Vermont

Wa., U.S. . . . Washington
Wi., U.S. . . . . Wisconsin
W.V., U.S. West Virginia
Wy., U.S. . . . . Wyoming

A

B

C

D

E

F

I

J

K

L

M

Q

R

S

T

Illustrated Survey of World History

The intention of this survey is to indicate key developments which receive elaboration in text entries. Nonspecific dates —for example, Bayeux tapestry (c.1080)— denote approximate timings of the rise of important political or cultural developments, of significant events, and of individuals' major accomplishments.

Neolithic stone configurations in France (6000-2000 B.C.) This was probably a holy site that had use in astronomy.

10,000 - 4000 B.C.

Historic Overview: By 10,000 B.C. humans were beginning to develop agriculture and change from hunter-gatherer economies to permanent farm-based economies, which created the proper environment for the development of civilization. Between 9000 and 4000 B.C. humans had developed sophisticated farm settlements with technological advancements in the Middle East (Tigris and Euphrates rivers region), America (Mexico), and China. With the advent of agriculture human societies were transformed from egalitarian tribal societies organized by family ties into chiefdoms with hierarchical organization, which were forerunners of the ancient city-states.

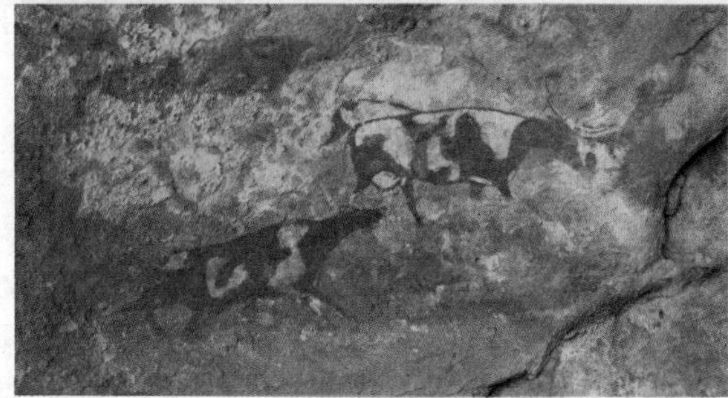

Cave paintings in North Africa (3500 B.C.)

Technology: Use of stone farm tools (axes, sickles, knives), pottery, weaving, and the development of craft. The construction of houses made of mud bricks and stone.

Religion and Philosophy: Spiritual beliefs based on the central importance of agriculture. Fertility celebrated in shrines to gods and goddesses; the bull as a recurrent theme in religious rituals.

Art: By 10,000 B.C. humans had been painting (rocks, cave walls), sculpting (walls), carving (figurines, amulets), and engraving for thousands of years. Much of prehistoric art had hunting as a central theme.

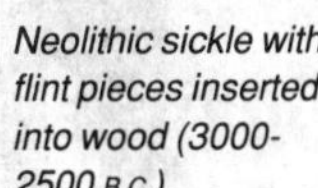

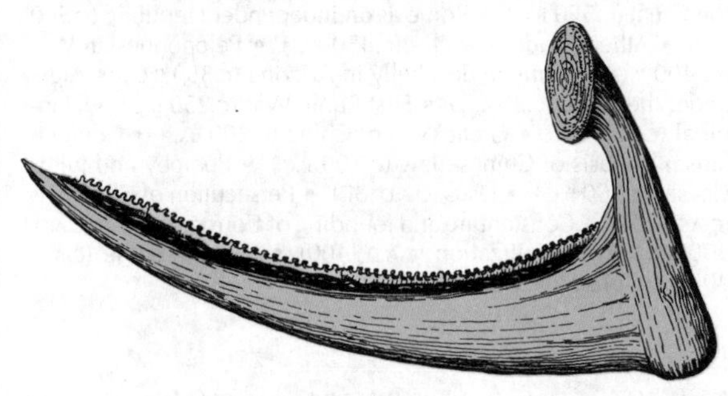

Neolithic sickle with flint pieces inserted into wood (3000-2500 B.C.)

4000-700 B.C.

Historic Overview: Development of Sumerian culture (4000-3500 B.C.) • Rise of the city-states (400-3400 B.C.) of Uruk, Ur, Kish, Lagash, Ender, and Umna • Unification of the two kingdoms of Egypt and the rise of its civilization (3200-1200 B.C.) • Cave paintings in North America (c.3000 B.C.) • First pottery in Mexico (c.2000 B.C.) • Reign of Hammurabi in Babylon (1790-50 B.C.) • Shang dynasty in China (1600-1100 B.C.) • Development of Mycenean civilization (c.1600 B.C.) • Height of Minoan civilization on Crete (c.1500 B.C.) • Olmec civilization in Mexico (c.1500 B.C.) • Moses and Jewish people leave Egypt (c.1250 B.C.) • Height of Phoenician civilization (c.1200 B.C.) • Solomon builds the temple at Jerusalem (c.950 B.C.) • Carthage established by Phoenicians (c.814 B.C.) • Rome founded (753 B.C.)

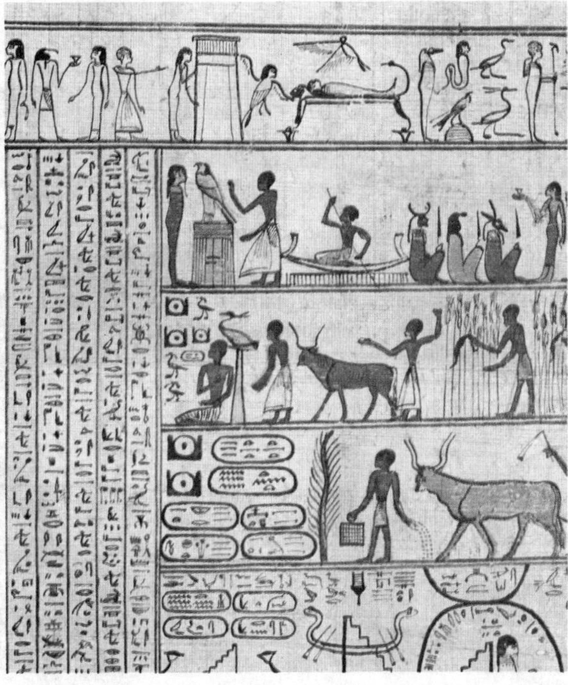

The Egyptian Book of the Dead *(1300 B.C.)*

Technology: Invention of the wheel in Mesopotamia (c.4000 B.C.) • Copper and bronze axes in Sumeria (c.3200 B.C.) • Plows in Mesopotamia and Egypt (c.3000 B.C.) • First 365-day calendar in Egypt (c.2700 B.C.) • Zoser's step pyramid (c. 2700 B.C.) and Great Pyramid and Great Sphinx (c. 2500 B.C.) in Egypt • Temple of Ur in Sumeria (c.2000 B.C.) • Iron weapons in the Middle East (c.2000 B.C.) • Minoan palace at Knossos (c.1800 B.C.) • Molten glass in Egypt (c.1500 B.C.) • Chinese bronze works (c.1500 B.C.) • Food preservation in Greece and Phoenicia (c.1200 B.C.) • Wheat, barley and cotton in the Middle East (c.750 B.C.)

Religion and Philosophy: Fertility cults based on farming in Middle East (c.4000 B.C.) • Memphite theology and concept of divine kingship in Egypt (c.3000 B.C.) • Stonehenge built (c.2000 B.C.) • Canaanite religion, based on the worship of El and Baal, in Palestine (c.1900 B.C.) • Vedas of India (c.1300 B.C.) • Worship of a single god, Yahweh, instituted by Moses (c.1200 B.C.) • Shinto religion in Japan (c.900 B.C.) • Old Testament prophets (c.750 B.C.)

Art: Painted pottery in Mesopotamia (c.4000 B.C.) • Use of gold and copper in Mesopotamian decorative arts (c.2500 B.C.) • Decorative textiles in Peru (c.1800 B.C.) • Minoan pottery flourishes (c.1600 B.C.) • First known pottery in North America (c.2400 B.C.) • Use of precious materials in Egypt (c.1500 B.C.) • Bronze casting in China (c.1300 B.C.) • Pottery flourishes in Greece (c.800 B.C.) • Jade ornaments in Mexico (c.800 B.C.)

Diorite stele with the laws of Hammurabi (1700 B.C.)

Two-handled vase from the Yangshao period in China (2500 B.C.)

Victory scene on a mosaic from Mari (c. 2500 B.C.)

---

700 B.C. - A.D. 500

Historic Overview: Etruscan cities flourished in Italy (c.700 B.C.) • Dominance of Sparta (c.650 B.C.) • Persian Empire and Cyrus the Great (c.550 B.C.) • Rome as an independent republic (c.500 B.C.) • Athens under Pericles (c.450 B.C.) • Peloponnesian War (c. 400 B.C.) • Canyon de Chelly in Arizona (c.350 B.C.) • Alexander the Great (c.30 B.C.) • First Punic War (c.250 B.C.) • Hannibal (c.200 B.C.) • Great Wall of China (c.200 B.C.) • Confucianism as basis of Chinese law (c.100 B.C.) • Pompey and Julius Caesar (c.100 B.C.) • Jesus (c.A.D. 30) • Persecution of Christians (c.A.D. 200) • Constantine and founding of Constantinople (c.A.D. 300) • Mayan civilization (c.A.D. 400) • Sack of Rome (c.A.D. 400) • Huns attack Gaul (c.A.D. 450)

Technology: Greek silver coins (c.700 B.C.) • Hanging Gardens of Babylon (c.600 B.C.) • Pythagoras (c.500 B.C.) • Iron welding in Greece (c.500 B.C.) • Parthenon (c.450 B.C.) • Hippocrates (c.400 B.C.) • Aristotle (c.350 B.C.) • Euclid (c.300 B.C.) • Colossus of Rhodes (c.280 B.C.) • Archimedes (c.250 B.C.) • Pyramid of the Sun in Mexico (c.100 B.C.) • Roman aqueducts and roads (c.A.D. 60) • Paper in China (c.A.D. 100) • Ptolemy (c.A.D. 150) • Galen (c.A.D. 200) • Abacus in China (c.A.D. 200) • Mayan mathematics and astronomy (c.A.D.350) • Boethius (c.A.D. 500)

Religion and Philosophy: Taoism in China (c.600 B.C.) • Zoroastrianism in Iran (c.600 B.C.) • Confucius (c.500 B.C.) • Buddhism in India (c.500 B.C.) • Protagoras and the Greek Sophists (c.450 B.C.) • Socrates (c.450 B.C.) • Plato (c.400 B.C.) • Aristotle (c.350 B.C.) • Yogic thought codified in India (c.150 B.C.) • The gospel of St. Mark written (c.A.D. 62) • Buddhism in China (c.A.D. 250) • Mithraism (c.A.D. 250) • Council of Nicaea (A.D. 325) • St. Augustine (c.A.D. 400)

Art: Elaborate Olmec sculptures in Mexico (c.700 B.C.) • Attic black-figure pottery (c.550 B.C.) • Celtic bronzes (c.460 B.C.) • Praxiteles (c.350 B.C.) • *Venus de Milo (c.150* B.C.) • Early Christian painting (c.A.D. 200) • Mochican art in Peru (c.A.D. 300) • Manuscript illustration (c.A.D. 500)

Temple of Zeus in Athens (2nd century B.C.)

The Cross of Justinian (A.D. 570)

Statue of Apollo (540 B.C.)

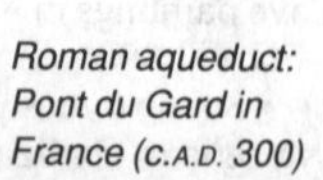

Roman aqueduct: Pont du Gard in France (c.A.D. 300)

A.D. 500 - A.D. 1500

Historic Overview: Frankish king Clovis I (c.500) • Byzantine emperor Justinian the Great (c.550) • Mayans build Palenque (c.650) • Charlemagne crowned Holy Roman Emperor (800) • Roman and Byzantine Christianity split (867) • Viking invasions of northern Europe (900-1000) • Norman conquest of England by William I; Battle of Hastings (1066) • Ottoman Empire begins (1071) • First Crusade (1096-99) • Pueblo civilizations in Americas (c.1100) • Saladin captures Jerusalem (1187) • King John signs Magna Carta (1215) • Kublai Khan establishes Yuan dynasty in China (c.1260) • Marco Polo (c.1290) • Aztecs found Tenochititlan (1325) • Hundred Years War starts (1337) • Black Death in Europe (c.1350) • Papacy split between Rome and Avignon (1378) • Rise of Moscow as political power (c.1380) • Joan of Arc leads French against English (c.1430) • Rise of the Medici (1434) • Christopher Columbus sails on first voyage (1492)

A mosaic of the emperor Justinian (C.A.D.600)

Technology: Ma'daba mosaic depicts oldest map of Holy Land (c.550) • Advancement of medical diagnosis in China (c.600) • Invention of windmill in Persia (c.640) • Mayan astronomy develops (c.740) • Jabir, father of Arabic chemistry (c.750) • Gunpowder invented in China (c.760) • Printing from relief blocks in Japan (c.800) • The word "algebra" appears in Arabic mathematical document (c.850) • Lateen sails for ships introduced to the West (c.880) • Alembic used in distilling (c.950) • Avicenna (c.1000) • • Fibonacci writes first text on algebra in West (c.1200) • Stern-mounted rudders appear on European ships (c.1250) • Roger Bacon (c.1275) • Spinning wheel and gunpowder in Europe (c.1300) • Henry the Navigator establishes school for the study of geography and navigation (1416) • Johann Gutenberg prints from moveable type (c.1450) • Leonardo da Vinci (c.1490)

Mohammed (14th century illustration)

A page from the Koran (14th century)

Religion and Philosophy: First Benedictine monastery (c.529) • Buddhism appears in Japan (552) • Pope Gregory the Great (c.590) • Mohammed receives first call (610) • Islam reaches Spain (715) • Alcuin writes vulgate text for Bible (c.780) • Rise of Sufism (c.900) • Abbey of Cluny founded (910) • Schism between Greek church and papacy (1054) • Averroes's commentaries on Aristotle (1169) • St. Thomas Aquinas's *Summa Theologica* (1266-73) • Papacy moves to Avignon (1309) • John Wycliffe (c.1380) • Papacy returns to Rome (1420) • John Huss (c.1400) • Thomas à Kempis writes *Imitation of Christ* (c.1425) • Spanish Inquisition begins (1478) • Jews expelled from Spain (1492)

Art: Manuscript illumination of early Christian era (c.500 • Cathedral of Hagia Sophia (532-37) • Great Chalice of Antioch (c.600) • Sutton Hoo treasure (c.650) • Caedmon (c.670) • Dome of the Rock construction starts (688) • *Lindisfarne Gospels* (c.700) • *Venerable Bede* (c.700) • *Beowulf* (700-1000) • Construction of Great Mosque at Cordoba begins (785) • *Book of Kells* (c.790) • The *Anglo-Saxon Chronicle* begun under Alfred the Great (c.870-99) • *The Tale of Genji* (c.1000) • Troubadours appear (c.1075) • Bayeux tapestry (c.1080) • Cathedral of Notre Dame in Paris (c.1160) • Chartres Cathedral (c.1195) • *Parzival* written by Wolfram von Eschenbach (c.1210) • Polyphony in motets and madrigals (1250-1300) • Giotto (c.1300) • Dante Alighieri begins *Divina Commedia* (c.1307) • Petrarch (c.1340) • The Japanese No play (c.1380) • Geoffrey Chaucer's *Canterbury Tales (c.1395)* • *Donatello* (c.1440) • Sir Thomas Malory writes *Morte d'Arthur* (c.1469-70) • Sandro Botticelli (c.1480)

An illustration from La cité des dames *by Christine de Pisan (c.1341-1430)*

1500 A.D. - 1992 A.D.

Historic Overview: Height of the Inca civilization (c.1500) • Amerigo Vespucci (c.1500) • African slaves introduced in the West Indies by Spain (1501) • Vasco Núñez de Balboa (1513) • Ferdinand Magellan (1520) • Hernando Cortés (1520) • Aztec Empire ends (1521) • Mogul Empire founded in India (1526) • Henry VIII (c.1530) • Suleiman the Magnificent (c.1540) • Queen Elizabeth I (c.1560) • Spanish Armada defeated (1588) • Jamestown, Va., founded (1607) • Thirty Years War begins (1618) • Pilgrims sail on *Mayflower* (1620) • English Civil War (1642-46) • Charles I of England executed (1649) • Louis XIV of France ascends to the throne (1661) • Glorious Revolution in England (1688) • Peter the Great (c.1690) • War of the Spanish Succession (1702-13) • Chinese invade Tibet (1751) • French and Indian War (1754) • Boston Tea Party (1773) • American Revolution (1775-83) • Declaration of Independence (1776) • U.S. Constitution is ratified (1788) • French Revolution begins (1789) • George Washington becomes first president of U.S. (1789) • Napoleon Bonaparte (c.1800) • Simon Bólívar (c.1810) • Holy Roman Empire ends (1806) • U.S. War of 1812 • Congress of Vienna (1814-15) • Monroe Doctrine (1823) • Battle of the Alamo (1836) • Opium Wars in China (1839) • Potato famine in Ireland (1846-47) • Gold rush in California begins (1848) • Crimean War (1854-56) • Giuseppe Garibaldi (c.1860) • U.S. Civil War (1861-65) • Karl Marx (c.1870) • Otto von Bismarck (c.1880) • All Native Americans confined to reservations (1887) • Boxer Rebellion in China (1900) • Spanish-American War (1898) • World War I (1914-18) • Russian Revolution (1917) • Chiang Kai-shek (c.1925) • Joseph Stalin begins collectivization in USSR (1929) • U.S. Wall Street crash (1929) • Mohandas Gandhi (c.1930) • Adolf Hitler made chancellor of Germany (1933) • Franklin D. Roosevelt's New Deal (1933) • World War II (1939-45) • U.N. Charter drafted (1945) • Mao Zedong establishes People's Republic of China (1949) • Korean War (1950-53) • Common Market established (1957) • Berlin Wall built (1961) • John F. Kennedy assassinated (1963) • Martin Luther King, Jr., assassinated (1968) • Height of U.S. involvement in Vietnam War (1969) • Watergate forces Richard M. Nixon to resign (1974) • Camp David Accord between Egypt and Israel (1978) • Glasnost and perestroika in USSR (1986) • Berlin Wall removed (1989) • Nelson Mandela freed in South Africa (1990) • Persian Gulf War (1991) • USSR and Eastern European Warsaw Pact dissolved (1991)

Technology: Cast iron produced on a large scale (c.1520) • Coal becomes a major fuel (c.1520) • Andreas Vesalius (c.1540) • Nicolaus Copernicus publishes his theory of astronomy (1543) • Decimals in mathematics (c.1585) • Telescope invented (1608) • Galileo (c.1610) • Francis Bacon (c.1620) • William Harvey discovers circulation of blood (1628) • Blaise Pascal (c.1640) • Isaac Newton postulates gravity (1664-66) • Christopher Wren (c.1675) • Single-lens microscope invented (c.1675) • Calculus developed (c.1675) • First steam engine (1696) • Classification of plants and animals by Carl Linnaeus (1735) • Benjamin Franklin investigates electricity (1752) • Carbon dioxide discovered (1756) • Antoine Lavoisier (c.1790) • Cotton gin invented (1793) • Edward Jenner discovers vaccination (1796) • First railroad locomotive (1804) • Gas lighting in Europe (c.1805) • Single-wire telegraph (1816) • Photography (c. 1815) • Michael Faraday (c.1830) • Morse Code invented (1838) • Sewing machine developed (1851) • Charles Darwin's theory of evolution (1858-59) • Louis Pasteur (c.1860) • Gregor Mendel (c. 1865) • Telephone invented by Alexander Graham Bell (1876) • Thomas Edison invents phonograph (1877) • Karl Benz invents automobile (1885) • X-rays discovered by Wilhelm Roentgen (1895) • Guglielmo Marconi (c.1900) • First flight by Wright brothers (1903) • Einstein publishes special (1905) and general (1915) theories of relativity • Penicillin discovered by Alexander Fleming (1928) • Frank Lloyd Wright (c.1935) • First nuclear reactor built (1942) • First nuclear bombs (1945) • Structure of DNA found (1953) • Polio

A perspective study by Leonardo Da Vinci

William Harvey

Martin Luther

John Locke

William Shakespeare

Nicolaus Copernicus

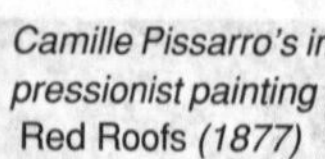

Camille Pissarro's impressionist painting Red Roofs (1877)

vaccine developed (1953-55) • Computers enter into commercial use (1955) • Sputnik launched (1957) • First manned space flight (1961) • First heart transplant (1966) • First moon landing (1969) • First test-tube baby (1978) • First artificial human heart (1982) • U.S. *Magellan* space probe reaches Venus (1990)

Religion and Philosophy : Erasmus (c.1500) • Machiavelli's *The Prince* (1513) • Martin Luther (c.1520) • Sikhism founded (c.1519) • John Calvin (c.1540) • Edict of Nantes (1598) • Hugo Grotius's *On Law* (1625) • René Descartes (c.1645) • Quakers founded in England (1652) • Thomas Hobbes's *Leviathan* (1651) • Spinoza's *Ethics* (1675) • John Locke (c.1690) • Gottfried Leibniz (c.1715) • Hasidism founded (c.1720) • Voltaire (c.1730) • David Hume (c.1735) • Methodist movement founded (c.1740) • Charles Montesquieu's *The Spirit of Laws* (1748) • Denis Diderot's *Encyclopédie* (1751) • Jean-Jacques Rousseau's *The Social Contract* (1762) • Adam Smith's *The Wealth of Nations* (1776) • Immanuel Kant's *Critique of Pure Reason* (1781) • Jeremy Bentham (c.1785) • Tom Paine's *The Rights of Man* (1791) • Mary Wollstonecraft's *Vindication of the Rights of Woman* (1792) • G.W.F. Hegel (c.1815) • Artur Schopenhauer's *The World as Will and Idea* (1819) • Alexis de Tocqueville (c.1840) • Soren Kierkegaard (c.1840) • Karl Marx and Friedrich Engels's *Communist Manifesto* (1848) • Henry David Thoreau (c.1850) • John Stewart Mill (c.1685) • Friedrich Nietzsche's *Beyond Good and Evil* (1886) • Sigmund Freud (c.1900) • Max Weber (c.1905) • Martin Heidegger (c.1930) • Jean-Paul Sartre's *Being and Nothingness* (1943) • Claude Levi-Strauss (c.1960) • John Paul II (1978) • Desmond Tutu (1984)

Art: Michelangelo's Sistine Chapel (c.1510) • Raphael (c.1515) • Titian (c.1530) • François Rabelais (c.1550) • Michel de Montaigne (c.1580) • El Greco (c.1590) • William Shakespeare (c.1600) • Miguel de Cervantes's *Don Quixote* (1605-15) • Claudio Monteverdi's *Orfeo* (1607) • Ben Jonson (c.1610) • Peter Paul Rubens (c.1620) • John Donne (c.1620) • Fugue developed (c.1630) • Molière (c.1660) • Racine (c.1670) • John Milton's *Paradise Lost* (1674) • Matsuo Basho (c.1685) • Concerto developed (c.1690) • Pianoforte invented (1709) • Jonathan Swift (c.1730) • J.S. Bach (c.1740) • George Frederick Handel (c.1740) • Joseph Haydn (c.1760) • Johann Goethe (c.1770) • W.A. Mozart (c.1785) • William Blake (c.1790) • William Wordsworth (c.1800) • Ludwig van Beethoven (c.1810) • Jane Austen (c.1810) • Percy Bysshe Shelley (c.1815) • Francisco de Goya (c.1815) • John Keats (c.1820) • James Fenimore Cooper (c.1830) • Alexander Pushkin (c.1835) • Frédéric Chopin (c.1835) • Charles Dickens (c.1845) • Herman Melville's *Moby Dick* (1851) • Walt Whitman's *Leaves of Grass* (1855) • Gustave Flaubert's *Madame Bovary* (1856) • Leo Tolstoy's *War and Peace* (1865-72) • Rise of Impressionism (1872) • Fyodor Dostoevsky (c.1875) • Richard Wagner (c.1875) • Auguste Rodin (c.1880) • Mark Twain (c.1885) • Henry James (c.1885) • Vincent van Gogh (c.1885) • Bernard Shaw (c.1900) • Pablo Picasso and Cubism (1907) • Igor Stravinsky's *The Rite of Spring* (1913) • Marcel Proust (c.1920) • James Joyce (c.1930) • Surrealism founded (c.1930) • F. Scott Fitzgerald and the Lost Generation (c.1930) • George Gershwin (c.1935) • Eugene O'Neill (c.1940) • Walt Disney (c.1940) • Orson Welles's *Citizen Kane* (1941) • Bebop emerges (c.1945) • Abstract Expressionism (c.1945) • Martha Graham (c.1950) • Beat Generation (c.1960) • Pop Art in U.S. (c.1965) • The Beatles' *Sergeant Pepper* (1967) • Gabriel Garcia Marquez (c.1970) • Michael Jackson (c.1985) • Rap music (1990s)

The signing of the Declaration of Independence, July 4, 1776

Pre-World War I automobile plant

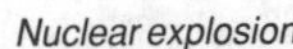

Nuclear explosion

John Hancock

In Congress, July 4, 1776

The Unanimous Declaration of the Thirteen United States of America,

When in the Course of human events, it becomes necessary for one people to dissolve the political bands which have connected them with another, and to assume among the powers of the earth, the separate and equal station to which the Laws of Nature and of Nature's God entitle them, a decent respect to the opinions of mankind requires that they should declare the causes which impel them to the separation.

We hold these truths to be self-evident, that all men are created equal, that they are endowed by their Creator with certain unalienable Rights, that among these are Life, Liberty and the pursuit of Happiness. That to secure these rights, Governments are instituted among Men, deriving their just powers from the consent of the governed. That whenever any Form of Government becomes destructive of these ends, it is the Right of the People to alter or to abolish it, and to institute new Government, laying its foundation on such principles, and organizing its powers in such form, as to them shall seem most likely to effect their Safety and Happiness. Prudence, indeed, will dictate that Governments long established should not be changed for light and transient causes; and accordingly all experience hath shewn, that mankind are more disposed to suffer, while evils are sufferable, than to right themselves by abolishing the forms to which they are accustomed. But when a long train of abuses and usurpations, pursuing invariably the same Object, evinces a design to reduce them under absolute Despotism, it is their right, it is their duty, to throw off such Government, and to provide new guards for their future security. Such has been the patient sufferance of these Colonies; and such is now the necessity which constrains them to alter their former Systems of Government. The history of the present King of Great Britain is a history of repeated injuries and usurpations, all having in direct object the establishment of an absolute Tyranny over these States. To prove this, let Facts be submitted to a candid world:

He has refused his Assent to Laws, the most wholesome and necessary for the public good.

He has forbidden his Governers to pass Laws of immediate and pressing importance, unless suspended in their operation till his Assent should be obtained; and when so suspended, he has utterly neglected to attend to them.

He has refused to pass other Laws for the accommodation of large districts of people, unless those people would relinquish the right of Representation in the Legislature, a right inestimable to them and formidable to tyrants only.

He has called together legislative bodies at places unusual, uncomfortable, and distant from the depository of their public Records, for the sole purpose of fatiguing them into compliance with his measures.

He has dissolved Representative Houses repeatedly, for opposing with manly firmness his invasions on the rights of the people.

He has refused for a long time, after such dissolutions, to cause others to be elected; whereby the Legislative powers, incapable of Annihilation, have returned to the People at large for their exercise; the State remaining in the mean time exposed to all the dangers of invasion from without, and convulsions within.

He has endeavoured to prevent the population of these States; for that purpose obstructing the Laws for Naturalization of Foreigners; refusing to pass others to encourage their migrations hither, and raising the conditions of new Appropriations of Lands.

He has obstructed the Administration of Justice, by refusing his Assent to Laws for establishing Judiciary powers.

He has made Judges dependent on his Will alone, for the tenure of their offices, and the amount and payment of their salaries.

He has erected a multitude of New Offices, and sent hither swarms of Officers to harass our people, and eat out their substance.

He has kept among us, in times of peace, Standing Armies, without the Consent of our legislatures.

He has affected to render the Military independent of and superior to the Civil power.

He has combined with others to subject us to a jurisdiction foreign to our constitution, and unacknowledged by our laws; giving his Assent to their Acts of pretended Legislation:

For quartering large bodies of armed troops among us:

For protecting them, by a mock Trial, from punishment for any Murders which they should commit on the Inhabitants of these States:

For cutting off our Trade with all parts of the world:

For imposing Taxes on us without our Consent:

For depriving us in many cases of the benefits of Trial by Jury:

For transporting us beyond Seas to be tried for pretended offences:

For abolishing the free System of English Laws in a neighbouring Province, establishing therein an Arbitrary government, and enlarging its Boundaries so as to render it at once an example and fit instrument for introducing the same absolute rule into these Colonies:

For taking away our Charters, abolishing our most valuable Laws and altering fundamentally the Forms of our Governments:

For suspending our own Legislatures, and declaring themselves invested with power to legislate for us in all cases whatsoever.

He has abdicated Government here by declaring us out of his Protection and waging War against us.

He has plundered our seas, ravaged our Coasts, burnt our towns, and destroyed the lives of our people.

He is at this time transporting large Armies of foreign Mercenaries to compleat the works of death, desolation and tyranny, already begun with circumstances of Cruelty & perfidy scarcely paralleled in the most barbarous ages, and totally unworthy the Head of a civilized nation.

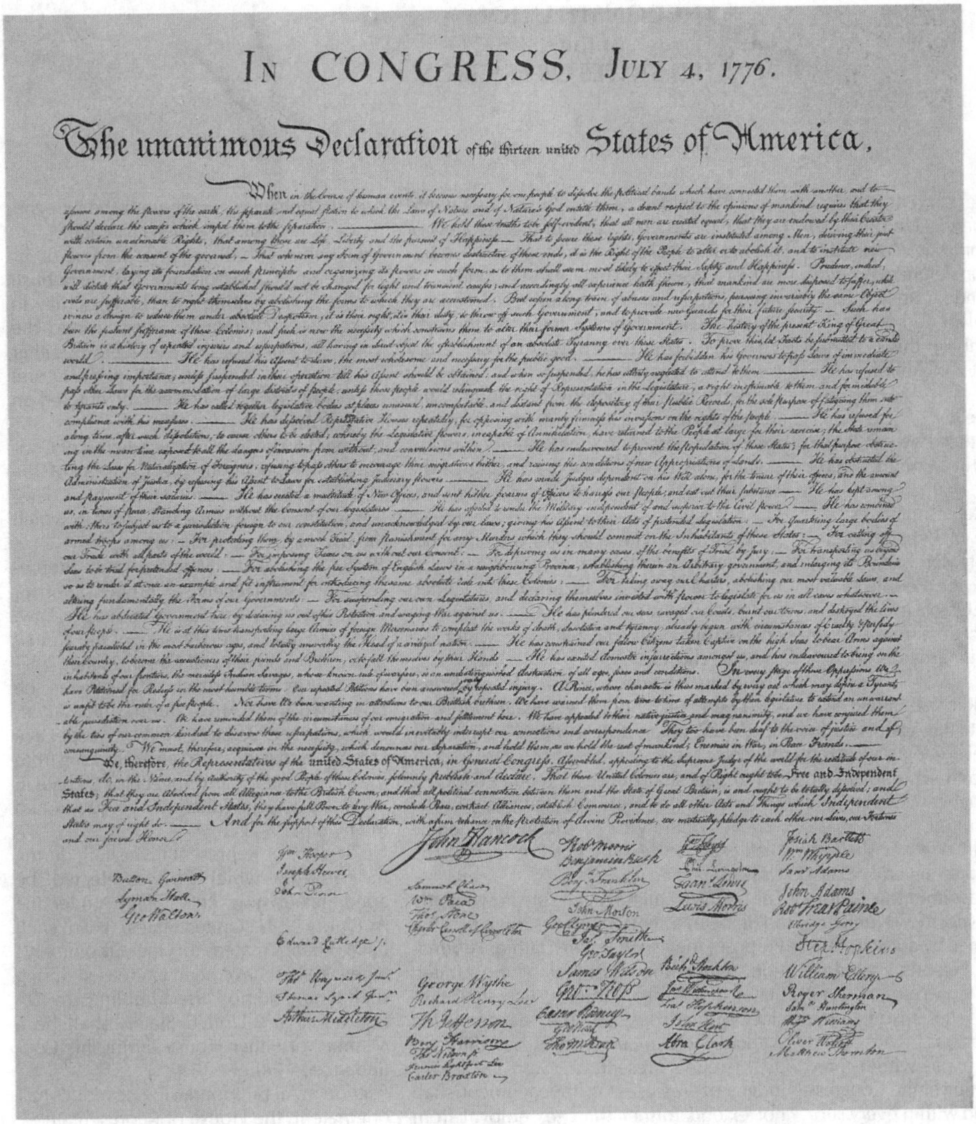

IN CONGRESS, JULY 4, 1776.

The unanimous Declaration of the thirteen united States of America,

He has constrained our fellow Citizens taken Captive on the high Seas to bear Arms against their Country, to become the executioners of their friends and Brethren, or to fall themselves by their Hands.

He has exited, domestic insurrections amongst us, and has endeavoured to bring on the inhabitants of our frontiers, the merciless Indian Savages, whose known rule of warfare is an undistinguished destruction of all ages, sexes and conditions.

In every stage of these Oppressions We have Petitioned for Redress in the most humble terms. Our repeated Petitions have been answered only by repeated injury. A Prince, whose character is thus marked by every act which may define a Tyrant, is unfit to be the ruler of a free people.

Nor have We been wanting in attentions to our British brethren. We have warned them from time to time of attempts by their legislature to extend an unwarrantable jurisdiction over us. We have reminded them of the circumstances of our emigration and settlement here. We have appealed to their native justice and magnanimity, and we have conjured them by the ties of our common kindred to disavow these usurpations,which would inevitably interrupt our connections and correspondence. They too have been deaf to the voice of justice and of consanguinity. We must, therefore, acquiesce in the necessity, which denounces our Separation, and hold them, as we hold the rest of mankind, Enemies in War, in Peace Friends.

WE, THEREFORE the Representatives of the UNITED STATES OF AMERICA, in General Congress, Assembled, appealing to the Supreme Judge of the world for the rectitude of our intentions, do, in the Name and by Authority of the good People of these Colonies, solemnly publish and declare, That these United Colonies are and of Right ought to be FREE AND INDEPENDENT STATES, that they are Absolved from all Allegiance to the British Crown, and that all political connection between them and the State of Great Britain, is and ought to be totally dissolved; and that as FREE AND INDEPENDENT STATES, they have full Power to levy War, conclude Peace, contract Alliances, establish Commerce, and to do all other Acts and Things which Independent states may of right do. AND for the support of this Declaration, with a firm reliance on the protection of divine Providence, we mutually pledge to each other our Lives, our Fortunes and our sacred Honor.

John Hancock
Button Gwinnett
Lyman Hall
Geo. Walton
Wm. Hooper
Joseph Hewes
John Penn
Edward Rutledge
Thos. Heyward, Jr.
Thomas Lynch, Jr.
Arthur Middleton
Samuel Chase
Wm. Paca
Thos. Stone
Charles Carroll of Carollton
George Wythe
Richard Henry Lee
Th. Jefferson
Benj. Harrison
Thos. Nelson, Jr.
Francis Lightfoot Lee
Carter Braxton
Robt. Morris
Benjamin Rush
Benj. Franklin
John Morton
Geo. Clymer
Jas. Smith
Geo. Taylor
James Wilson
Geo. Ross
Caesar Rodney
Geo. Read
Tho. M:Kean
Wm. Floyd
Phil. Livingston
Frans. Lewis
Lewis Morris
Richd. Stockton
Jno. Witherspoon
Fras. Hopkinson
John Hart
Abra. Clark
Josiah Bartlett
Wm. Whipple
Saml. Adams
John Adams
Robt. Treat Paine
Elbridge Gerry
Step. Hopkins
William Ellery
Roger Sherman
Sam. Huntington
Wm. Williams
Oliver Wolcott
Matthew Thornton

THE CONSTITUTION of the UNITED STATES OF AMERICA

We the People of the United States, in Order to form a more perfect Union, establish Justice, insure domestic Tranquility, provide for the common defence, promote the general Welfare, and secure the Blessings of Liberty to ourselves and our Posterity, do ordain and establish this Constitution for the United States of America.

Article I.

Section 1. All legislative Powers herein granted shall be vested in a Congress of the United States, which shall consist of a Senate and House of Representatives.

Section 2. The House of Representatives shall be composed of Members chosen every second Year by the People of the several States, and the Electors in each State shall have the Qualifications requisite for Electors of the most numerous Branch of the State Legislature.

No Person shall be a Representative who shall not have attained to the Age of twenty five Years, and been seven Years a Citizen of the United States, and who shall not, when elected, be an Inhabitant of that State in which he shall be chosen.

Representatives and direct Taxes shall be apportioned among the several States which may be included within this Union, according to their respective Numbers, which shall be determined by adding to the whole Number of free Persons, including those bound to Service for a Term of Years, and excluding Indians not taxed, three fifths of all other Persons. The actual Enumeration shall be made within three Years after the first Meeting of the Congress of the United States, and within every subsequent Term of ten Years, in such Manner as they shall by Law direct. The Number of Representatives shall not exceed one for every thirty Thousand, but each State shall have at Least one Representative; and until such enumeration shall be made, the State of New Hampshire shall be entitled to chuse three, Massachusetts eight, Rhode-Island and Providence Plantations one, Connecticut five, New-York six, New Jersey four, Pennsylvania eight, Delaware one, Maryland six, Virginia ten, North Carolina five, South Carolina five, and Georgia three.

When vacancies happen in the Representation from any State, the Executive Authority thereof shall issue Writs of Election to fill such Vacancies.

The House of Representatives shall chuse their Speaker and other Officers; and shall have the sole Power of Impeachment.

Section 3. The Senate of the United States shall be composed of two Senators from each State, chosen by the Legislature thereof, for six Years; and each Senator shall have one Vote.

Immediately after they shall be assembled in Consequence of the first Election, they shall be divided as equally as may be into three Classes. The Seats of the Senators of the first Class shall be vacated at the Expiration of the second Year, of the second Class at the Expiration of the fourth Year, and of the third Class at the Expiration of the sixth Year, so that one third may be chosen every second Year; and if Vacancies happen by Resignation, or otherwise, during the Recess of the Legislature of any State, the Executive thereof may make temporary Appointments until the next Meeting of the Legislature, which shall then fill such Vacancies.

No Person shall be a Senator who shall not have attained to the Age of thirty Years, and been nine Years a Citizen of the United States, and who shall not, when elected, be an Inhabitant of that State for which he shall be chosen.

The Vice President of the United States shall be President of the Senate, but shall have no Vote, unless they be equally divided.

The Senate shall chuse their other Officers, and also a President pro tempore, in the Absence of the Vice President, or when he shall exercise the Office of President of the United States.

The Senate shall have the sole Power to try all Impeachments. When sitting for that Purpose, they shall be on Oath or Affirmation. When the President of the United States is tried, the Chief Justice shall preside: And no Person shall be convicted without the Concurrence of two thirds of the Members present.

Judgment in Cases of Impeachment shall not extend further than to removal from Office, and disqualification to hold and enjoy any Office of honor, Trust or Profit under the United States: but the Party convicted shall nevertheless be liable and subject to Indictment, Trial, Judgment and Punishment, according to Law.

Section 4. The Times, Places and Manner of holding Elections for Senators and Representatives, shall be prescribed in each State by the Legislature thereof; but the Congress may at any time by Law make or alter such Regulations, except as to the Places of chusing Senators.

The Congress shall assemble at least once in every Year, and such Meeting shall be on the first Monday in December, unless they shall by Law appoint a different Day.

Section 5. Each House shall be the Judge of the Elections, Returns and Qualifications of its own Members, and a Majority of each shall constitute a Quorum to do Business; but a smaller Number may adjourn from day to day, and may be authorized to compel the Attendance of absent Members, in such Manner, and under such Penalties as each House may provide.

Each House may determine the Rules of its Proceedings, punish its Members for disorderly Behaviour, and, with the Concurrence of two thirds, expel a Member.

Each House shall keep a Journal of its Proceedings, and from time to time publish the same, excepting such Parts as may in their Judgment require Secrecy; and the Yeas and Nays of the Members of either House on any question shall, at the Desire of one fifth of those Present, be entered on the Journal.

Neither House, during the Session of Congress, shall, without the Consent of the other, adjourn for more than three days, nor to any other Place than that in which the two Houses shall be sitting.

Section 6. The Senators and Representatives shall receive a Compensation for their Services, to be ascertained by Law, and paid out of the Treasury of the United States. They shall in all Cases, except Treason, Felony and Breach of the Peace, be privileged from Arrest during their Attendance at the Session of their respective Houses, and in going to and returning from the same; and for any Speech or Debate in either House, they shall not be questioned in any other Place.

No Senator or Representative shall, during the Time for which he was elected, be appointed to any civil Office under the Authority of the United States, which shall have been created, or the Emoluments whereof shall have been encreased during such time; and no Person holding any Office under the United States, shall be a Member of either House during his Continuance in Office.

Section 7. All Bills for raising Revenue shall originate in the House of Representatives; but the Senate may propose or concur with Amendments as on other Bills.

Every Bill which shall have passed the House of Representatives and the Senate, shall, before it become a Law, be presented to the President of the United States; If he approve he shall sign it, but if not he shall return it, with his Objections to that House in which it shall have originated, who shall enter the Objections at large on their Journal, and proceed to reconsider it. If after such Reconsideration two thirds of that House shall agree to pass the Bill, it shall be sent, together with the Objections, to the other House, by which it shall likewise be reconsidered, and if approved by two thirds of that House, it shall become a Law. But in all such Cases the Votes of both Houses shall be determined by Yeas and Nays, and the Names of the Persons voting for and against the Bill shall be entered on the Journal of each House respectively. If any Bill shall not be returned by the President within ten Days (Sundays excepted) after it shall have been presented to him, the Same shall be a Law, in like Manner as if he had signed it, unless the Congress by their Adjournment prevents its Return, in

which Case it shall not be a Law.
Every Order, Resolution, or Vote to which the Concurrence of the Senate and House of Representatives may be necessary (except on a question of Adjournment) shall be presented to the President of the United States; and before the Same shall take Effect, shall be approved by him, or being disapproved by him, shall be repassed by two thirds of the Senate and House of Representatives, according to the Rules and Limitations prescribed in the Case of a Bill.
Section 8. The Congress shall have Power To lay and collect Taxes, Duties, Imposts and Excises, to pay the Debts and provide for the common Defence and general Welfare of the United States; but all Duties, Imposts and Excises shall be uniform throughout the United States;
To Borrow Money on the Credit of the United States;
To regulate Commerce with foreign Nations, and among the several States, and with the Indian Tribes;
To establish an uniform Rule of Naturalization, and uniform Laws on the subject of Bankruptcies throughout the United States;
To coin Money, regulate the Value thereof, and of foreign Coin, and fix the Standard of Weights and Measures;
To provide for the Punishment of counterfeiting the Securities and current Coin of the United States;
To establish Post Offices and post Roads;
To promote the Progress of Science and useful Arts, by securing for limited Times to Authors and Inventors the exclusive Right to their respective Writings and Discoveries;
To constitute Tribunals inferior to the supreme Court;
To define and punish Piracies and Felonies committed on the high Seas, and Offences against the Law of Nations;
To declare War, grant Letters of Marque and Reprisal, and make Rules concerning Captures on Land and Water;
To raise and support Armies, but no Appropriation of Money to that Use shall be for longer Term than two Years;
To provide and maintain a Navy;
To make Rules for the Government and Regulation of the land and naval Forces;
To provide for calling forth the Militia to execute the Laws of the Union, suppress Insurrections and repel Invasions;
To provide for organizing, arming, and disciplining the Militia, and for governing such Part of them as may be employed in the Service of the United States, reserving to the States respectively, the Appointment of the Officers, and the Authority of training the Militia according to the discipline prescribed by Congress;
To exercise exclusive Legislation in all Cases whatsoever, over such District (not exceeding ten Miles square) as may, by Cession of particular States, and the Acceptance of Congress, become the Seat of the Government of the United States, and to exercise like Authority over all Places purchased by the Consent of the Legislature of the State in which the Same shall be for the Erection of Forts, Magazines, Arsenals, dock-Yards, and other needful Buildings;—And
To make all Laws which shall be thereof necessary and proper for carrying into Execution the foregoing Powers, and all other Powers vested by this Constitution in the Government of the United States, or in any Department or Officer thereof.
Section 9. The Migration or Importation of such Persons as any of the States now existing shall think proper to admit, shall not be prohibited by the Congress prior to the Year one thousand eight hundred and eight, but a Tax or duty may be imposed on such Importation, not exceeding ten dollars for each Person.
The Privilege of the Writ of Habeas Corpus shall not be suspended, unless when in Cases of Rebellion or Invasion the public Safety may require it.
No Bill of Attainder or ex post facto Law shall be passed.
No Capitation or other direct, Tax shall be laid, unless in Proportion to the Census or Enumeration herein before directed to be taken.
No Tax or Duty shall be laid on Articles exported from any State.
No Preference shall be given by any Regulation of Commerce or Revenue to the Ports of one State over those of another: nor shall Vessels bound to, or from, one State, be obliged to enter, clear, or pay Duties in another.
No Money shall be drawn from the Treasury, but in Consequence of Appropriations made by Law; and a regular Statement and Account of the Receipts and Expenditures of all public Money shall be published from time to time.
No Title of Nobility shall be granted by the United States: And no Person holding any Office or Profit or Trust under them, shall, without the Consent of Congress, accept of any present, Emolument, Office, or Title, of any kind whatever, from any King, Prince, or foreign State.
Section 10. No State shall enter into any Treaty, Alliance, or Confederation; grant Letters of Marque and Reprisal; coin Money; emit Bills of Credit; make any Thing but gold and silver Coin a Tender in Payment of Debts; pass any Bill of Attainder, ex post facto Law, or Law impairing the Obligation of Contracts, or grant any Title of Nobility.
No State shall, without the Consent of the Congress, lay any Imposts or Duties on Imports or Exports, except what may be absolutely necessary for executing its inspection Laws: and the net Produce of all Duties and Imposts, laid by any State on Imports or Exports, shall be for the Use of the Treasury of the United States; and all such Laws shall be subject to the Revision and Controul of the Congress.
No State shall, without the Consent of Congress, lay any Duty of Tonnage, keep Troops, or Ships of War in time of Peace, enter into any Agreement or Compact with another State, or with a foreign Power, or engage in War, unless actually invaded, or in such imminent Danger as will not admit of delay.

Article II.

Section 1. The executive Power shall be vested in a President of the United States of America. He shall hold his Office during the Term of four Years, and, together with the Vice President, chosen for the same term, be elected, as follows
Each State shall appoint, in such Manner as the Legislature thereof may direct, a Number of Electors, equal to the whole Number of Senators and Representatives to which the State may be entitled in the Congress: but no Senator or Representative, or Person holding an Office of Trust or Profit under the United States, shall be appointed an Elector.
The Electors shall meet in their respective States, and vote by Ballot for two Persons, of whom one at least shall not be an Inhabitant of the same State with themselves. And they shall make a List of all the Persons voted for, and of the Number of Votes for each; which List they shall sign and certify, and transmit sealed to the Seat of the Government of the United States, directed to the President of the Senate. The President of the Senate shall, in the Presence of the Senate and House of Representatives, open all the Certificates, and the Votes shall then be counted. The Person having the greatest Number of Votes shall be the President, if such Number be a Majority of the whole Number of Electors appointed; and if there be more than one who have such Majority, and have an equal Number of Votes, then the House of Representives shall immediately chuse by Ballot one of them for President: and if no Person have a Majority, then from the five highest on the List the said House shall in like Manner chuse the President. But in chusing the President, the Votes shall be taken by States, the Representation from each State having one Vote; A quorum for this Purpose shall consist of a Member or Members from two thirds of the States, and a Majority of all the States shall be necessary to a Choice. In every Case, after the Choice of the President, the Person having the greatest Number of Votes of the Electors shall be the Vice President. But if there should remain two or more who have equal Votes, the Senate shall chuse from them by Ballot the Vice President.
The Congress may determine the Time of chusing the Electors, and the Day on which they shall give their Votes; which Day shall be the same throughout the United States.
No Person except a natural born Citizen, or a Citizen of the United States, at the time of the Adoption of this Constitution, shall be eligible to the Office of President; neither shall any Person be eligible to that Office who shall not have attained to the Age of thirty five Years, and been fourteen Years a Resident within the United States.
In Case of the Removal of the President from Office, or of his Death, Resignation, or Inability to discharge the Powers and Duties of the said Office, the Same shall devolve on the Vice President, and the Congress may by Law provide for the Case of Removal, Death, Resignation or Inability, both of the President and Vice President, declaring what Officer shall then act

as President, and such Officer shall act accordingly, until the Disability be removed, or a President shall be elected.

The President shall, at stated Times, receive for his Services, a Compensation, which shall neither be encreased nor diminished during the Period for which he shall have been elected, and he shall not receive within that Period any other Emolument from the United States, or any of them.

Before he enter on the Execution of his Office, he shall take the following Oath or Affirmation:- "I do solemnly swear (or affirm) that I will faithfully execute the Office of President of the United States, and will to the best of my Ability, preserve, protect and defend the Constitution of the United States."

Section 2. The President shall be Commander in Chief of the Army and Navy of the United States, and of the Militia of the several States, when called into the actual Service of the United States; he may require the Opinion in writing, of the principal Officer in each of the executive Departments, upon any Subject relating to the Duties of their respective Offices, and he shall have Power to grant Reprieves and Pardons for Offences against the United States, except in Cases of Impeachment.

He shall have Power, by and with the Advice and Consent of the Senate, to make Treaties, provided two thirds of the Senators present concur; and he shall nominate, and by and with the Advice and Consent of the Senate; shall appoint Ambassadors, other public Ministers and Consuls, Judges of the supreme Court, and all other Officers of the United States, whose Appointments are not herein otherwise provided for, and which shall be established by Law: but the Congress may by Law vest the Appointment of such inferior Officers, as they think proper, in the President alone, in the Courts of Law, or in the Heads of Departments.

The President shall have Power to fill up all Vacancies that may happen during the Recess of the Senate, by granting Commissions which shall expire at the End of their next Session.

Section 3. He shall from time to time give to the Congress Information of the State of the Union, and recommend to their Consideration such Measures as he shall judge necessary and expedient; he may, on extraordinary Occasions, convene both Houses, or either of them, and in Case of Disagreement between them, with Respect to the Time of Adjournment, he may adjourn them to such Time as he shall think proper; he shall receive Ambassadors and other public Ministers; he shall take Care that Laws be faithfully executed, and shall Commission all the Officers of the United States.

Section 4. The President, Vice President and all civil Officers of the United States, shall be removed from Office on Impeachment for, and Conviction of, Treason, Bribery, or other High Crimes and Misdemeanors.

Article III.

Section 1. The judicial Power of the United States, shall be vested in one supreme Court, and in such inferior Courts as the Congress may from time to time ordain and establish. The Judges, both of the supreme and inferior Courts, shall hold their Offices during good Behaviour, and shall, at stated Times, receive for their Services a Compensation, which shall not be diminished during their Continuance in Office.

Section 2. The judicial Power shall extend to all Cases, in Law and Equity, arising under this Constitution, the Laws of the United States, and Treaties made, or which shall be made, under their Authority; — to all Cases affecting Ambassadors, other public Ministers and Consuls;—to all Cases of admiralty and maritime Jurisdiction;—to Controversies to which the United States shall be a Party;—to Controversies between two or more States;—between a State and Citizens of another State;—between Citizens of different States;—between Citizens of the same State claiming Lands under Grants of different States, and between a State, or the Citizens thereof, and foreign States, Citizens or Subjects.

In all Cases affecting Ambassadors, other public Ministers and Consuls, and those in which a State shall be Party, the supreme Court shall have original Jurisdiction. In all the other Cases before mentioned, the supreme Court shall have appellate Jurisdiction, both as to Law and Fact, with such Exceptions, and under such Regulations as the Congress shall make.

The Trial of all Crimes, except in Cases of Impeachment, shall be by Jury; and such Trial shall be held in the State where the said Crimes shall have been committed; but when not committed within any State, the Trial shall be at such Place or Places as the Congress may by Law have directed.

Section 3. Treason against the United States, shall consist only in levying War against them, or in adhering to their Enemies, giving them Aid and Comfort. No Person shall be convicted of Treason unless on the Testimony of two Witnesses to the same overt Act, or on Confession in open Court.

The Congress shall have Power to declare the Punishment of Treason, but no Attainder of Treason shall work Corruption of Blood, or Forfeiture except during the Life of the Person attained.

Article IV.

Section 1. Full Faith and Credit shall be given in each State to the public Acts, Records, and judicial Proceedings of every other State. And the Congress may by general Laws prescribe the Manner in which such Acts, Records and Proceedings shall be proved, and the Effect thereof.

Section 2. The Citizens of each State shall be entitled to all Privileges and Immunities of Citizens in the several States.

A Person charged in any State with Treason, Felony, or other Crime, who shall flee from Justice, and be found in another State, shall on Demand of the executive Authority of the State from which he fled, be delivered up, to be removed to the State having Jurisdiction of the Crime.

No Person held to Service or Labour in one State, under the Laws thereof, escaping into another, shall, in Consequence of any Law or Regulation therein, be discharged from such Service or Labour, but shall be delivered up on Claim of the Party to whom such Service or Labour may be due.

Section 3. New States may be admitted by the Congress into this Union; but no new State shall be formed or erected within the Jurisdiction of any other State; nor any State be formed by the Junction of two or more States, or Parts of States, without the Consent of the Legislatures of the States concerned as well as of the Congress.

The Congress shall have Power to dispose of and make all needful Rules and Regulations respecting the Territory or other Property belonging to the United States; and nothing in this Constitution shall be so construed as to Prejudice any Claims of the United States, or of any particular State.

Section 4. The United States shall guarantee to every State in this Union a Republican Form of Government, and shall protect each of them against Invasion; and on Application of the Legislature, or of the Executive (when the Legislature cannot be convened) against domestic Violence.

Article V.

The Congress, whenever two thirds of both Houses shall deem it necessary, shall propose Amendments to this Constitution, or, on the Application of the Legislatures of two thirds of the several States, shall call a Convention for proposing Amendments, which, in either Case, shall be valid to all Intents and Purposes, as Part of this Constitution, when ratified by the Legislatures of three fourths of the several States, or by Conventions in three fourths thereof, as the one or the other Mode of Ratification may be proposed by the Congress; Provided that no Amendment which may be made prior to the Year One thousand eight hundred and eight shall in any Manner affect the first and fourth Clauses in the Ninth Section of the first Article; and that no State, without its Consent, shall be deprived of its equal Suffrage in the Senate.

Article VI.

All Debts contracted and Engagements entered into, before the Adoption of this Constitution, shall be as valid against the United States under this Constitution, as under the Confederation.

This Constitution, and the Laws of the United States which shall be made in Pursuance thereof; and all Treaties made, or which shall be made, under the Authority of the United States, shall be the supreme Law of the Land; and the Judges in every State shall be bound thereby, any Thing in the Constitution or Laws of any State to the Contrary notwithstanding.

The Senators and Representatives before mentioned, and the Members of the several State Legislatures, and all executive and judicial Officers, both of the United States and of the several States, shall be bound by Oath or Affirmation, to support this Constitution; but no religious Test shall ever be required as a Qualification to any Office or public Trust under the United States.

Article VII.

The Ratification of the Conventions of nine States, shall be sufficient for the Establishment of this Constitution between the States so ratifying the Same.

Done in Convention by the Unanimous Consent of the States present the Seventeenth Day of September in the Year of our Lord one thousand seven hundred and Eighty seven and of the Independence of the United States of America the Twelfth IN WITNESS WHEREOF We have hereunto subscribed our Names,

G.[O] Washington-Presid[t].
and deputy from Virginia.

Attest William Jackson Secretary

Delaware
Geo: Read
Gunning Bedford jun
John Dickinson
Richard Bassett
Jaco: Broom
Maryland
James McHenry
Dan ofSt Thos. Jenifer
Danl Carroll
Virginia
John Blair
James Madison Jr.
North Carolina
Wm. Blount
Richd. Dobbs Spaight.
Hu Williamson
South Carolina
J. Rutledge
Charles Cotesworth Pinckney
Charles Pinckney
Pierce Butler.
Georgia
William Few
Abr Baldwin
New Hampshire
John Langdon
Nicolas Gilman
Massachusetts
Nathaniel Gorham
Rufus King
Connecticut
Wm. Saml. Johnson
Roger Sherman
New York
Alexander Hamilton
New Jersey
Wil.: Livingston
David Brearley.
Wm. Paterson
Jona: Dayton
Pennsylvania
B Franklin
Thomas Mifflin
Robt Morris
Geo. Clymer
Thos. FitzSimons
Jared Ingersoll
James Wilson
Gouv Morris

Amendment I

Congress shall make no law respecting an establishment of religion, or prohibiting the free exercise thereof; or abridging the freedom of speech, or of the press; or the right of the people peaceably to assemble, and to petition the Government for a redress of grievances.

Amendment II

A well regulated Militia, being necessary to the security of a free State, the right of the people to keep and bear Arms, shall not be infringed.

Amendment III

No Soldier shall, in time of peace, be quartered in any house, without the consent of the Owner, nor in time of war, but in manner to be prescribed by law.

Amendment IV

The right of the people to be secure in their persons, houses, papers, and effects, against unreasonable searches and seizures, shall not be violated, and no Warrants shall issue, but upon probable cause, supported by Oath or affirmation, and particularly describing the place to be searched, and the persons or things to be seized.

Amendment V

No person shall be held to answer for a capital, or otherwise infamous crime, unless on a presentment or indictment of a Grand Jury, except in cases arising in the land or naval forces, or in the Militia, when in actual service in time of War or public danger; nor shall any person be subject for the same offence to be twice put in jeopardy of life or limb; nor shall be compelled in any criminal case to be a witness against himself, nor be deprived of life, liberty, or property, without due process of law; nor shall private property be taken for public use, without just compensation.

Amendment VI

In all criminal prosecutions, the accused shall enjoy the right to a speedy and public trial, by an impartial jury of the State and district wherein the crime shall have been committed, which district shall have been previously ascertained by law, and to be informed of the nature and cause of the accusation; to be confronted with the witnesses against him; to have compulsory process for obtaining witnesses in his favor, and to have the Assistance of Counsel for his defence.

Amendment VII

In Suits at common law, where the value in controversy shall exceed twenty dollars, the right of trial by jury shall be preserved, and no fact tried by a jury, shall be otherwise reexamined in any Court of the United States, than according to the rules of the common law.

Amendment VIII

Excessive bail shall not be required, nor excessive fines imposed, nor cruel and unusual punishments inflicted.

George Washington

Alexander Hamilton

Amendment IX

The enumeration in the Constitution, of certain rights, shall not be construed to deny or disparage others retained by the people.

Amendment X

The powers not delegated to the United States by the Constitution, nor prohibited by it to the States, are reserved to the States respectively, or to the people.

Amendment XI

(Adopted Jan. 8, 1798)

The Judicial power of the United States shall not be construed to extend to any suit in law or equity, commenced or prosecuted against one of the United States by Citizens of another State, or by Citizens or Subjects of any Foreign State.

Amendment XII

(Adopted Sept. 25, 1804)

The Electors shall meet in their respective states and vote by ballot for President and Vice-President, one of whom, at least, shall not be an inhabitant of the same state with themselves; they shall name in their ballots the person voted for as President, and in distinct ballots the person voted for as Vice-President, and they shall make distinct lists of all persons voted for as President, and of all persons voted for as Vice-President, and of the number of votes for each, which lists they shall sign and certify, and transmit sealed to the seat of the government of the United States, directed to the President of the Senate;—The President of the Senate shall, in presence of the Senate and House of Representatives, open all the certificates and the votes shall then be counted;—The person having the greatest number of votes for President, shall be the President, if such number be a majority of the whole number of Electors appointed; and if no person have such majority, then from the persons having the highest numbers not exceeding three on the list of those voted for as President, the House of Representatives shall choose immediately, by ballot, the President. But in choosing the President, the votes shall be taken by states, the representation from each state having one vote; a quorum for this purpose shall consist of a member or members from two-thirds of the states, and a majority of all the states shall be necessary to a choice. And if the House of Representatives shall not choose a President whenever the right of choice shall devolve upon them, before the fourth day of March next following, then the Vice-President shall act as President, as in the case of the death or other constitutional disability of the President.—The person having the greatest number of votes as Vice-President, shall be the Vice-President, if such number be a majority of the whole number of Electors appointed, and if no person have a majority, then from the two highest numbers on the list, the Senate shall choose the Vice-President; a quorum for the purpose shall consist of two-thirds of the whole number of Senators, and a majority of the whole number shall be necessary to a choice. But no person constitutionally ineligible to the office of President shall be eligible to that of Vice-President of the United States.

Amendment XIII

(Adopted Dec. 18, 1865)

Section 1. Neither slavery nor involuntary servitude, except as a punishment for crime whereof the party shall have been duly convicted, shall exist within the United States, or any place subject to their jurisdiction.

Section 2. Congress shall have power to enforce this article by appropriate legislation.

Amendment XIV

(Adopted July 28, 1868)

Section 1. All persons born or naturalized in the United States, and subject to the jurisdiction thereof, are citizens of the United States and of the State wherein they reside. No State shall make or enforce any law which shall abridge the privileges or immunities of citizens of the United States; nor shall any State deprive any person of life, liberty, or property, without due process of law; nor deny to any person within its jurisdiction the equal protection of the laws.

Section 2. Representatives shall be apportioned among the several States according to their respective numbers, counting the whole number of persons in each State, excluding Indians not taxed. But when the right to vote at any election for the choice of electors for President and Vice-President of the United States, Representatives in Congress, the Executive and Judicial officers of a State, or the members of the Legislature thereof, is denied to any of the male inhabitants of such State, being twenty-one years of age, and citizens of the United States, or in any way abridged, except for participation in rebellion, or other crime, the basis of representation therein shall be reduced in the proportion which the number of such male citizens shall bear to the whole number of male citizens twenty-one years of age in such State.

Section 3. No person shall be a Senator or Representative in Congress, or elector of President and Vice-President, or hold any office, civil or military, under the United States, or under any State, who, having previously taken an oath, as a member of Congress, or as an officer of the United States, or as a member of any State legislature, or as an executive or judicial officer of any State, to support the Constitution of the United States, shall have engaged in insurrection or rebellion against the same, or given aid or comfort to the enemies thereof. But Congress may by a vote of two-thirds of each House, remove such disability.

Section 4. The validity of the public debt of the United States, authorized by law, including debts incurred for payment of pensions and bounties for services in suppressing insurrection or rebellion, shall not be questioned. But neither the United States nor any State shall assume or pay any debt or obligation incurred in aid of insurrection or rebellion against the United States, or any claim for the loss or emancipation of any slave; but all such debts, obligations and claims shall be held illegal and void.

Section 5. The Congress shall have power to enforce, by appropriate legislation, the provisions of this article.

Amendment XV

(Adopted March 30, 1870)

*Section 1.*The right of citizens of the United States to vote shall not be denied or abridged by the United States or by any State on account of race, color, or previous condition of servitude.

Section 2. The Congress shall have power to enforce this article by appropriate legislation.

Amendment XVI

(Adopted Feb. 25, 1913)

The Congress shall have power to lay and collect taxes on incomes, from whatever source derived, without apportionment among the several States, and without regard to any census or enumeration.

Amendment XVII

(Adopted May 31, 1913)

The Senate of the United States shall be composed of two Senators from each State, elected by the people thereof, for six years; and each Senator shall have one vote. The electors in each State shall have the qualifications requisite for electors of the most numerous branch of the State legislatures.

When vacancies happen in the representation of any State in the Senate, the executive authority of such State shall issue writs of election to fill such vacancies: *Provided,* That the legislature of any State may empower the executive thereof to make temporary appointments until the people fill the vacancies by election as the legislature may direct.

This amendment shall not be so construed as to affect the election or term of any Senator chosen before it becomes valid as part of the Constitution.

Amendment XVIII

(Adopted Jan, 29, 1919)

Section 1. After one year from the ratification of this article the manufacture, sale, or transportation of intoxicating liquors within, the importation thereof into, or the exportation thereof from the United States and all territory subject to the jurisdiction thereof for beverage purposes is hereby prohibited.

Section 2. The Congress and the several States shall have concurrent power to enforce this article by appropriate legislation.

Section 3. This article shall be inoperative unless it shall have been ratified as an amendment to the Constitution by the legislatures of the several States, as provided in the Constitution, within seven years from the date of the submission hereof to the States by the Congress.

Amendment XIX

(Adopted Aug. 26, 1920)

The right of citizens of the United States to vote shall not be denied or abridged by the

United States or by any State on account of sex.

Congress shall have power to enforce this article by appropriate legislation.

Amendment XX

(Adopted Feb. 6, 1933)

Section 1. The terms of the President and Vice President shall end at noon on the 20th day of January, and the terms of Senators and Representatives at noon on the 3d day of January, of the years in which such terms would have ended if this article had not been ratified; and the terms of their successors shall then begin.

Section 2. The Congress shall assemble at least once in every year, and such meeting shall begin at noon on the 3d day of January, unless they shall by law appoint a different day.

Section 3. If, at the time fixed for the beginning of the term of the President, the President elect shall have died, the Vice President elect shall become President. If a President shall not have been chosen before the time fixed for the beginning of his term, or if the President elect shall have failed to qualify, then the Vice President elect shall act as President until a President shall have qualified; and the Congress may by law provide for the case wherein neither a President elect nor a Vice President elect shall have qualified, declaring who shall then act as President, or the manner in which one who is to act shall be selected, and such person shall act accordingly until a President or Vice President shall have qualified.

Section 4. The Congress may by law provide for the case of the death of any of the persons from whom the House of Representatives may choose a President whenever the right of choice shall have devolved upon them, and for the case of the death of any of the persons from whom the Senate may choose a Vice President whenever the right of choice shall have devolved upon them.

Section 5. Sections 1 and 2 shall take effect on the 15th day of October following the ratification of this article.

Section 6. This article shall be inoperative unless it shall have been ratified as an amendment to the Constitution by the legislatures of three-fourths of the several States within seven years from the date of its submission.

Amendment XXI

(Adopted Dec. 5, 1933)

Section 1. The eighteenth article of amendment to the Constitution of the United States is hereby repealed.

Section 2. The transportation or importation into any State, Territory, or possession of the United States for delivery or use therein of intoxicating liquors, in violation of the laws thereof, is hereby prohibited.

Section 3. This article shall be inoperative unless it shall have been ratified as an amendment to the Constitution by conventions in the several States, as provided in the Constitution, within seven years from the date of the submission hereof to the States by the Congress.

Amendment XXII

(Adopted Feb. 27, 1951)

Section 1. No person shall be elected to the office of the President more than twice, and no person who has held the office of President, or acted as President, for more than two years of a term to which some other person was elected President shall be elected to the office of the President more than once. But this Article shall not apply to any person holding the office of President when this Article was proposed by the Congress, and shall not prevent any person who may be holding the office of President, or acting as President, during the term within which this Article becomes operative from holding the office of President or acting as President during the remainder of such term.

Section 2. This article shall be inoperative unless it shall have been ratified as an amendment to the Constitution by the legislatures of three-fourths of the several States within seven years from the date of its submission to the States by the Congress.

Amendment XXIII

(Adopted Mar. 29, 1961)

Section 1. The District constituting the seat of Government of the United States shall appoint in such manner as the Congress may direct:

A number of electors of President and Vice President equal to the whole number of Senators and Representatives in Congress to which the District would be entitled if it were a State, but in no event more than the least populous State; they shall be in addition to those appointed by the States, but they shall be considered, for the purposes of the election of President and Vice President, to be electors appointed by a State; and they shall meet in the District and perform such duties as provided by the twelfth article of amendment.

Section 2. The Congress shall have power to enforce this article by appropriate legislation.

Amendment XXIV

(Adopted Jan. 23, 1964)

Section 1. The right of citizens of the United States to vote in any primary or other election for President or Vice President, for electors for President or Vice President, or for Senator or Representative in Congress, shall not be denied or abridged by the United States or any State by reason of failure to pay any poll tax or other tax.

Section 2. The Congress shall have power to enforce this article by appropriate legislation.

Amendment XXV

(Adopted Feb. 10, 1967)

Section 1. In case of the removal of the President from office or his death or resignation, the Vice President shall become President.

Section 2. Whenever there is a vacancy in the office of the Vice President, the President shall nominate a Vice President who shall take the office upon confirmation by a majority vote of both houses of Congress.

Section 3. Whenever the President transmits to the President pro tempore of the Senate and the Speaker of the House of Representatives his written declaration that he is unable to discharge the powers and duties of his office, and until he transmits to them a written declaration to the contrary, such powers and duties shall be discharged by the Vice President as Acting President.

Section 4. Whenever the Vice President and a majority of either the principal officers of the executive departments or of such other body as Congress may by law provide, transmit to the President pro tempore of the Senate and the Speaker of the House of Representatives their written declaration that the President is unable to discharge the powers and duties of his office, the Vice President shall immediately assume the powers and duties of the office as Acting President.

Thereafter, when the President transmits to the President pro tempore of the Senate and the Speaker of the House of Representatives his written declaration that no inability exists, he shall resume the powers and duties of his office unless the Vice President and a majority of either the principal officers of the executive departments or of such other body as Congress may by law provide, transmit within four days to the President pro tempore of the Senate and the Speaker of the House of Representatives their written declaration that the President is unable to discharge the powers and duties of his office. Thereupon Congress shall decide the issue, assembling within 48 hours for that purpose if not in session. If the Congress, within 21 days after receipt of the latter written declaration, or, if Congress is not in session, within 21 days after Congress is required to assemble, determines by two-thirds vote of both houses that the President is unable to discharge the powers and duties of his office, the Vice President shall continue to discharge the same as Acting President; otherwise, the President shall resume the powers and duties of his office.

Amendment XXVI

(Adopted June 30, 1971)

Section 1. The right of citizens of the United States, who are eighteen years of age or older, to vote shall not be denied or abridged by the United States or any state on account of age.

Section 2. The Congress shall have the power to enforce this article by appropriate legislation.

Presidents of the United States (with political parties, dates in office, and vice presidents)

George Washington, 1789-97
John Adams

John Adams
Federalist 1797-1801
Thomas Jefferson

Thomas Jefferson
Democratic-Republican 1801-9
Aaron Burr, 1801-5
George Clinton, 1805-9

James Madison
Democratic-Republican 1809-17
George Clinton, 1809-12
(no Vice President, April, 1812-March, 1813)
Elbridge Gerry, 1813-14
(no Vice President, Nov., 1814-March, 1817)

James Monroe
Democratic-Republican 1817-25
Daniel D. Tompkins

John Quincy Adams
Democratic-Republican 1825-29
John C. Calhoun

Andrew Jackson
Democratic 1829-37
John C. Calhoun, 1829-32
(no Vice President, Dec., 1832-March, 1833)
Martin Van Buren, 1833-37

Martin Van Buren
Democratic 1837-41
Richard M. Johnson

William Henry Harrison
Whig 1841
John Tyler

John Tyler
Whig 1841-45
(no Vice President)

James Knox Polk
Democratic 1845-49
George M. Dallas

Zachary Taylor
Whig 1849-50
Millard Fillmore

Seal of the President of the United States

Millard Fillmore
Whig 1850-53
(no Vice President)

Franklin Pierce
Democratic 1853-57
William R. King, 1853
(no Vice President, April, 1853-March, 1857)

James Buchanan
Democratic 1857-61
John C. Breckinridge

Abraham Lincoln
Republican 1861-65
Hannibal Hamlin, 1861-65
Andrew Johnson, 1865

Andrew Johnson
Democratic/National Union 1865-69
(no Vice President)

Ulysses Simpson Grant
Republican 1869-77
Schuyler Colfax, 1869-73
Henry Wilson, 1873-75
(no Vice President, Nov., 1875-March, 1877

Rutherford Birchard Hayes
Republican 1877-81
William A. Wheeler

James Abram Garfield
Republican 1881
Chester A. Arthur

Chester Alan Arthur
Republican 1881-85
(no Vice President)

Grover Cleveland
Democratic 1885-89
Thomas A. Hendricks, 1885
(no Vice President, Nov., 1885-March, 1889)

Benjamin Harrison
Republican 1889-93
Levi P. Morton

Grover Cleveland
Democratic 1893-97
Adlai E. Stevenson

William McKinley
Republican 1897-1901
Garret A. Hobart, 1897-99
(no Vice President, Nov., 1899-March, 1901)
Theodore Roosevelt, 1901

Theodore Roosevelt
Republican 1901-9
(no Vice President, Sept., 1901-March, 1905)
Charles W. Fairbanks, 1905-9

William Howard Taft
Republican 1909-13
James S. Sherman, 1902-12
(no Vice President, Oct., 1912-March, 1913)

Woodrow Wilson
Democratic 1913-21
Thomas R. Marshall

Warren Gamaliel Harding
Republican 1921-23
Calvin Coolidge

Calvin Coolidge
Republican 1923-29
(no Vice President, 1923-25)
Charles G. Dawes, 1925-29

Herbert Clark Hoover
Republican 1929-33
Charles Curtis

Franklin Delano Roosevelt
Democratic 1933-45
John N. Garner, 1933-41
Henry A. Wallace, 1941-45
Harry S. Truman, 1945

Harry S. Truman
Democratic 1945-53
(no Vice President, 1945-49)
Alben W. Barkley, 1949-53

Dwight David Eisenhower
Republican 1953-61
Richard M. Nixon

John Fitzgerald Kennedy
Democratic 1961-63
Lyndon B. Johnson

Lyndon Baines Johnson
Democratic 1963-69
(no Vice President, 1963-65)
Hubert H. Humphrey, 1965-69

Richard Milhous Nixon
Republican 1969-74
Spiro T. Agnew, 1969-73
(no Vice President, Oct. 10, 1973-Dec. 6, 1973)
Gerald R. Ford, 1973-74

Gerald Rudolph Ford
Republican 1974-77
(no Vice President, Aug. 9, 1974-Dec. 19, 1974)
Nelson A. Rockefeller, 1974-77

Jimmy Carter
Democratic 1977-81
Walter F. Mondale

Ronald Wilson Reagan
Republican 1981-89
George H. W. Bush

George H. W. Bush
Republican 1989-93
J. Danforth Quayle

William Jefferson Clinton
Democrat 1993-
Albert Gore Jr.

U.S. Supreme Court Justices (as of June 1, 1991)

Harry A. Blackmun

Thurgood Marshall

John Paul Stevens

Byron R. White

William H. Rehnquist

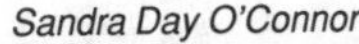
Sandra Day O'Connor

Antonin Scalia

Anthony M. Kennedy

David H. Souter

Chief Justices:

John Jay 1789-85
John Rutledge 1795
Oliver Ellsworth 1796-1800
John Marshall 1801-35
Roger B. Taney 1836-64
Salmon P. Chase 1864-73
Morrison R. Waite 1874-88
Melville W. Fuller 1888-1910
Edward D. White 1910-21
William H. Taft 1921-30
Charles E. Hughes 1930-41
Harlan F. Stone 1941-46
Fred M. Vinson 1946-53
Earl Warren 1953-69
Warren E. Burger 1969-86
William H. Rehnquist 1986-

Associate Justices:

John Rutledge 1789-91
William Cushing 1789-1810
James Wilson 1789-98
John Blair 1789-96
Robert H. Harrison 1789-90
James Iredell 1790-99
Thomas Johnson 1791-93
William Paterson 1793-1806
Samuel Chase 1796-1811
Bushrod Washington 1798-1829
Alfred Moore 1799-1804
William Johnson 1804-34
Henry Brockholst Livingston 1806-23
Thomas Todd 1807-26
Gabriel Duval 1811-36
Joseph Storey 1811-45
Smith Thompson 1823-43
Robert Trimble 1826-28
John McLean 1829-61
Henry Baldwin 1830-44
James M. Wayne 1835-67
Philip P. Barbour 1836-41
John Catron 1837-65
John McKinley 1837-52
Peter V. Daniel 1841-60
Samuel Nelson 1845-72
Levi Woodbury 1845-51
Robert C. Grier 1846-70
Benjamin R. Curtis 1851-57
John A. Campbell 1853-61
Nathan Clifford 1858-81
Noah H. Swayne 1862-81
Samuel F. Miller 1862-90
David Davis 1862-77
Stephen J. Field 1863-97
William Strong 1870-80
Joseph P. Bradley 1870-92
Ward Hunt 1873-82
John M. Harlan 1877-1911
William B. Woods 1881-87
Stanley Matthews 1881-89
Horace Gray 1882-1902
Samuel Blatchford 1882-93
Lucius G.C. Lamar 1888-93
David J. Brewer 1890-1910
Henry B. Brown 1891-1906
George Shiras Jr. 1892-1903
Howell E. Jackson 1893-95
Edward D. White 1894-1910
Rufus W. Peckham 1896-1909
Joseph McKenna 1898-1925
Oliver W. Holmes 1902-32
William R.Day 1903-22
William H. Moody 1906-10
Horace H. Lurton 1910-14
Charles E. Hughes 1910-16
Willis Van Devanter 1911-37
Joseph R. Lamar 1911-16
Mahlon Pitney 1912-22
James C. McReynolds 1914-41
Louis D. Brandeis 1916-39
John H. Clarke 1916-22
George Sutherland 1922-38
Pierce Butler 1923-39
Edward T. Sanford 1923-30
Harlan F. Stone 1925-41
Owen J. Roberts 1930-45
Benjamin N. Cardozo 1932-38
Hugo Black 1937-71
Stanley F. Reed 1938-57
Felix Frankfurter 1939-62
William O. Douglas 1939-75
Frank Murphy 1940-49
James F. Byrnes 1941-42
Robert H. Jackson 1941-54
Wiley B. Rutledge 1943-49
Harold H. Burton 1945-58
Thomas C. Clark 1949-67
Sherman Minton 1949-56
John M. Harlan 1955-71
William J. Brennan Jr. 1956-90
Charles E. Whittaker 1957-62
Potter Stewart 1958-81
Byron R. White 1962-
Arthur J. Goldberg 1962-65
Abe Fortas 1965-69
Thurgood Marshall 1967-
Harry A. Blackmun 1970-
Lewis R. Powell Jr. 1971-87
William H. Rehnquist 1971-
John Paul Stevens 1975-
Sandra Day O'Connor 1981-
Antonin Scalia 1986-
Anthony M. Kennedy 1988-
David H. Souter 1990-

National Parks

Crater Lake National Park

Acadia
Bar Harbor, Maine
Size: 38,971 acres (15,770 hectares)
Characterized by a beautiful ocean landscape with a rugged coastline, the park's interior includes a mountainous region with many glacial features. The park consists of Mount Desert Island, Schoodic Peninsula, Isle au Haut, and a group of smaller islands.

Arches
Moab, Utah
Size: 73,379 acres (29,695 hectares)
The park is famous for its large arches, windows, and pinnacles, products of natural erosion. These geological phenomena change color constantly in the sunlight, adding to the beauty of the park, which is situated above the ravine of the Colorado River.

Badlands
Interior, South Dakota
Size: 243,302 acres (98,461 hectares)
Renowned primarily for its scenery, the park also contains many prehistoric fossils. Formed by erosion, it covers large areas of prairie grasslands and is home to animals such as antelope, bighorn sheep, bison, deer, and prairie dogs.

Big Bend
Big Bend National Park, Texas
Size: 708,118 acres (286,565 hectares)
Established in a bend of the Rio Grande, the park contains many unusual geological formations. The Chisos Mountains and Desert, along with the Rio Grande, form a unique panorama of contrasting wilderness scenery.

Biscayne
Homestead, Florida
Size: 180,128 acres (72,900 hectares)
The main feature of the park is a living coral reef, with excellent skin diving and snorkeling conditions. A chain of approximately 40 islands, or keys, runs north-south through the park, with the Atlantic Ocean on the east and Biscayne Bay on the west.

Bryce Canyon
Bryce Canyon, Utah
Size: 35,835 acres (14,502 hectares)
The beauty of the park derives from its spectacular views and scenery, a result of the park's high altitude. Natural erosion has formed amphitheaters composed of pinnacles, walls, and spires, which change color constantly in the sunlight.

Canyonlands
Moab, Utah
Size: 337,570 acres (136,610 hectares)
Situated in a desert area, the park comprises canyons, mesas (some rising 7,100 ft/2,158 m), and erosion-carved pinnacles, spires, and arches. Some of the rocks contain Native American carvings that date back 1,000 years.

Capitol Reef
Torrey, Utah
Size: 241,904 acres (97,895 hectares)
The park contains a white, dome-shaped, sandstone formation that resembles the U.S. Capitol building, after which the park is named. Other features include a collection of deep canyons and arches and a 60-m (97-km) ridge, considered geologically unusual due to its size.

Carlsbad Caverns
Carlsbad, New Mexico
Size: 46,755 acres (18,921 hectares)
These immense, underground caverns, which contain striking stalactite and stalagmite formations, are among the most elaborate in the world. Home to large numbers of bats, the caves began forming c.60 million years ago and have not been fully explored.

Channel Islands
Ventura, California
Size: 249,354 acres (100,910 hectares)
Comprising Anacapa, Santa Barbara, San Miguel, Santa Rosa, and Santa Cruz Islands, the park has large rookeries of sea lions along with popular nesting grounds for many sea birds. Many fossil remains have been discovered on the islands, and the park is also a popular site for sport fishing.

Crater Lake
Crater Lake, Oregon
Size: 160,290 acres (64,869 hectares)
The park's main feature is a deep blue lake (20 sq m/52 sq km) formed by rain and snow. The second-deepest lake in North America (1,932 ft/589 m), it lies in Mount Mazama, a collapsed volcano in the Cascade Range.

Denali
Denali, Alaska
Size: 4,065,493 acres (1,645,248 hectares)
The most prominent feature of the park is Mount McKinley (20,320 ft/6,194 m), the highest mountain in North America. The park also contains huge glaciers and a variety of wildlife, including caribou, sheep, moose, grizzly bears, and wolves.

Everglades
Homestead, Florida
Size: 1,398,800 acres (566,075 hectares)
Composed of marshy, subtropical wilderness, the park has many open grasslands and mangrove forests to go along with vast water areas. Its wide variety of animal life includes alligators, crocodiles, manatees, and many types of rare birds.

Gates of the Arctic
Fairbanks, Alaska
Size: 7,052,000 acres (2,854,000 hectares)
A tundra wilderness consisting of spacious canyons and the spiked peaks of the Brooks Range, the park contains plentiful herds of caribou as well as grizzly bears, sheep, moose, and wolves.

Arches National Park

Glacier
West Glacier, Montana
Size: 1,013,595 acres (410,188 hectares)
Located in the Rocky Mountains along the Continental Divide, the park contains magnificent scenery, including over 50 glaciers and many lakes and brooks, as well as a wide array of wildlife.

Glacier Bay
Gustavus, Alaska
Size: 3,878,269 acres (1,569,481 hectares)
The park features massive glaciers—he best known being Muir Glacier (approximately 265 ft/80 m)—which move down from the mountains into the bay. The park's wildlife includes bears, eagles, seals, and whales, to go along with a wide assortment of plant life.

Grand Canyon
Grand Canyon, Arizona
Size: 1,218,375 acres (493,059 hectares)
The Grand Canyon of the Colorado River winds through the park, and there are many rock formations that illustrate the geologic history of the region. Along the southern edge of the canyon the view is striking, and there are many observatory sites as well as trails to the canyon floor.

Grand Teton
Moose, Wyoming
Size: 310,516 acres (125,661 hectares)
The park covers part of the Teton Range and consists of snow-capped mountain peaks, deep valleys, and alpine lakes. The Grand Teton (13,766 ft/4,169 m) is the most prominent feature, and the park's wildlife includes elk, moose, and swans.

Great Basin
Baker, Nevada
Size: 76,109 acres (30,801 hectares)
Home to the bristlecone pines, among the oldest living things on earth, the park contains contrasting wildlife scenery, from high desert regions to alpine tundra. The park's Lehman Caves house many intricate geologic formations.

Great Smoky Mountains
Gatlinburg, Tennessee (extends into North Carolina)
Size: 520,269 acres (210,550 hectares)
An area of high mountains and large forests, the park's prominent feature and highest point is Clingman's Dome (6,642 ft/2,024 m high). Part of the Appalachian Trail runs through the park, and the area is well known for its wide assortment of plant life.

Guadalupe Mountains
Salt Flat, Texas
Size: 76,293 acres (30,875 hectares)
Home to one of the largest Permian fossil reefs in the world, the park features a lush evergreen forest, which includes some unique forms of plant life, overlooking a desert plain. The park consists of high mountain peaks, jagged gorges, and a large fault in the earth's crust.

Glacier National Park

Haleakala
Makawao, Maui, Hawaii
Size: 28,655 acres (11,596 hectares)
Lying in the shadow of the dormant volcano Mt. Haleakala (10,023 ft/3,055 m), the park is made up of rain forests and rugged cliffs. The Haleakala Crater (2,720 ft/829 m deep) is one of its prominent features, and the park is also home to numerous rare and endangered animal species.

Hawaii Volcanoes
Hawaii Volcanoes National Park, Hawaii
Size: 229,177 acres (92,745 hectares)
Two of the world's most active volcanoes, Kilauea and Mauna Loa, are showcased in the lush tropical park. In the valleys below the volcanoes, lavish vegetation provides a habitat for many rare species of birds and animals.

Hot Springs
Hot Springs, Arkansas
Size: 5,826 acres (2,358 hectares)
The 47 hot springs located in the park are believed by many to possess extraordinary healing power. Located at the base of Hot Springs Mountain, two of the springs flow naturally, while the other spring water is collected into large reservoirs for use in bathing rooms.

Isle Royale
Houghton, Michigan
Size: 571,796 acres (231,398 hectares)
Encompassing Isle Royal and approximately 200 other islands in Lake Superior, the park retains a strong wilderness atmosphere and is home to packs of timber wolves and large moose herds. It is also known for its pre-Columbian copper mines and historic fisheries.

Katmai
King Salmon, Alaska
Size: 4,430,125 acres (1,792,810 hectares)
The park is a vast wilderness enviornment of lakes, mountains, swamps, and forests that support many types of animal life, including the Alaska brown bear. The eruption of Novarupta Volcano in 1912 shaped the park's landscape and created the "Valley of Ten Thousand Smokes," but there is little volcanic activity in the area today.

Kenai Fjords
Seward, Alaska
Size: 567,000 acres (229,457 hectares)
The most striking features of the park are Harding Icefield, one of the primary icecaps in the United States, and the majestic fjords and glaciers along the Kenai Peninsula. The park supports a wide range of animal life, including sea lions, otters, seals, mountain goats, and several species of birds.

Kings Canyon and Sequoia
Three Rivers, California
Size: Kings Canyon-460,136 acres (186,211 hectares)
Sequoia-402,488 acres (162,885 hectares)
The parks, famous for their giant sequoia groves, are dominated by the High Sierra Mountains and two large valleys of the Kings River. Another prominent feature of the parks is Mount Whitney, the highest mountain in the United States outside of Alaska (14,494 ft/4,418 m).

Kobuk Valley
Kotzebue, Alaska
Size: 1,710,000 acres (692,000 hectares)
Situated along a centuries-old trading route and home to extensive archaeological sites, the park supports a large wildlife population, including caribou, bears, and wolves. Other attractions are the Great Kobuk Sand Dunes and the Salmon River.

Lake Clark
Anchorage, Alaska
Size: 2,439,000 acres (987,000 hectares)
The park's rugged landscape features glaciers, granite spires, several lakes, two active volcanoes, and the craggy peaks of the Chigmit Mountains. Among the wildlife that inhabit the park are caribou, bears, sheep, wolves, minks, martens, and lynxes, and it is a spawning ground for red salmon.

Lassen Volcanic
Mineral, California
Size: 106,372 acres (43,047 hectares)
Lassen Peak (10,457 ft/3,187 m high) rises high above the park, which possesses many examples of volcanic activity, including steep domes of lava. Lassen Peak erupted periodically from 1914 to 1921 and there are still active hot springs and sulfurous vents around the mountain's base.

Mammoth Cave
Mammoth Cave, Kentucky
Size: 52,452 acres (21,230 hectares)
The underground caves are composed of over 300 miles (480 km) of passageways and have many stalactite and stalagmite formations. The caves, which are among the largest and most extensive in the world, also contain an underground river, waterfalls, and lakes.

Mesa Verde
Mesa Verde National Park, Colorado
Size: 52,085 acres (21,078 hectares)
The park, made up of wooded valleys and flat mesas, is famous for its pre-Columbian cliff dwellings, the best preserved in the United States. The dwellings span four archaeological time periods, from A.D. 100 to the 13th century.

Mount Ranier
Ashford, Washington
Size: 235,404 acres (95,265 hectares)
Home to the greatest single-peak glacier system in the United States, the park is dominated by Mount Ranier (14,410 ft/4,392 m), an inactive volcano. The valleys below the mountain have dense forests and alpine meadows.

North Cascades
Sedro Woolley, Washington
Size: 504,781 acres (204,277 hectares)
The park, lying in the Cascade Mountain Range, is an extensive alpine region, with waterfalls, glaciers, lakes, hanging valleys, and icefalls. In the western area, there are lush rain forests, with varied and abundant plant and animal life.

Olympic
Port Angeles, Washington
Size: 914,890 acres (370,250 hectares)
Situated in the Coast Ranges, the park has over 50 mi (80 km) of Pacific coastline as well as glaciers, lakes, and rain forests. Mount Olympus rises 7,965 ft (2,427 m), dominating the landscape, while rare Roosevelt elk graze in its shadow.

Petrified Forest
Petrified Forest National Park, Arizona
Size: 93,493 acres (37,835 hectares)
The park is renowned for its Painted Desert and its ancient trees, which have been changed or petrified into multicolored rock. The area also features Native American ruins and petroglyphs, as well as the remains of prehistoric animals.

Redwood
Crescent City, California
Size: 109,415 acres (44,280 hectares)
The park features over 40 mi (64 km) of scenic Pacific coastline and a coastal redwood forest. It is also home to the world's tallest tree (367 ft/112 m). The area's wildlife includes seals, sea lions, and sea birds.

Rocky Mountain
Estes Park, Colorado
Size: 263,809 acres (106,762 hectares)
Dotted with over 100 peaks that tower over 11,000 ft (3,353 m), the park also contains numerous lakes and several spectacular waterfalls. Located in the Front Range of the Rocky Mountains, the park sits astride the Continental Divide and possesses a wide range of wildlife.

Shenandoah
Luray, Virginia
Size: 194,826 acres (78,845 hectares)
Lying in the Blue Ridge section of the Appalachian Mountains, the park is heavily forested and offers magnificent views of the Shenandoah Valley. The Appalachian Trail runs through the park, as does Skyline Drive.

Theodore Roosevelt
Medora, North Dakota
Size: 70,416 acres (28,497 hectares)
Located along the banks of the Little Missouri River, the park's landscape consists of scenic badlands and open prairies. It was part of Theodore Roosevelt's Elkhorn Ranch and is now home to small herds of bison.

Virgin Islands
St. John, Virgin Islands
Size: 14,695 acres (5,947 hectares)
Situated on the Caribbean island of St. John, the park has white sandy beaches and blue-green water, with extensive reefs and marine gardens in the shallows. There are many isolated coves dotting the shoreline of the park, it is also the site of several ancient Dutch colonial sugar plantations.

Voyageurs
International Falls, Minnesota
Size: 219,128 acres (88,678 hectares)
Used in the 18th century as a trade route for French-Canadian voyageurs (fur traders), the park is heavily forested with aspen, birch, pine, and spruce trees and has many glacial features and scenic lakes.

Wind Cave
Hot Springs, South Dakota
Size: 28,292 acres (11,449 hectares)
The park's main attraction is a series of limestone caverns containing intricate calcite crystal and boxwork formations. Situated in the Black Hills, the park houses colonies of prairie dogs and herds of bison and elk.

Wrangell-St. Elias
Glennallen, Alaska
Size: 8,147,000 acres (3,297,000)
Populated by caribou, dall sheep, bears, wolves, wolverines, mountain goats, and moose, the park has the largest collection of peaks and glaciers above 16,000 ft (4,879 m) in the United States, the highest being Mt. Saint Elias (18,008 ft/5,489 m).

Yellowstone
Yellowstone National Park, Wyoming
Size: 2,219,823 acres (898,350 hectares)
The oldest national park in the United States, it has the world's greatest geyser area, with approximately 200 geysers and 10,000 hot springs. The park's main attraction is the geyser Old Faithful, which erupts at regular intervals, and the Grand Canyon of the Yellowstone River. There are many beautiful lakes and waterfalls, and the park's wildlife includes bears, moose, and bison.

Yosemite
Yosemite National Park, California
Size: 760,917 acres (307,932 hectares)
Amid majestic mountain landscape with deep canyons and numerous lakes, the park is the site of Yosemite Falls, the highest waterfall in North America (2,425 ft/739 m). Located in the center of the Sierra Nevada Mountains, the park also contains sprawling meadows filled with wildflowers and groves of giant sequoias.

Zion
Springdale, Utah
Size: 146,551 acres (59,308 hectares)
The most striking feature of the park, Zion Canyon, is nearly half a mile deep and has multicolored cliffs and unique rock formations. Kolob Canyons has multicolored cliffs as well, rising 1,500 ft (457 m).

Zion National Park

Chemical Elements

Name	Symbol	Atomic No.	Name	Symbol	Atomic No.	Name	Symbol	Atomic No.
Actinium	Ac	89	Hafnium	Hf	72	Promethium	Pm	61
Aluminum	Al	13	Helium	He	2	Protactinium	Pa	91
Americium	Am	95	Holmium	Ho	67	Radium	Ra	88
Antimony	Sb	51	Hydrogen	H	1	Radon	Rn	86
Argon	Ar	18	Indium	In	49	Rhenium	Re	75
Arsenic	As	33	Iodine	I	53	Rhodium	Rh	45
Astatine	At	85	Iridium	Ir	77	Rubidium	Rb	37
Barium	Ba	56	Iron (Ferrum)	Fe	26	Ruthenium	Ru	44
Berkelium	Bk	97	Krypton	Kr	36	Samarium	Sm	62
Beryllium	Be	4	Lanthanum	La	57	Scandium	Sc	21
Bismuth	Bi	83	Lead (Plumbum)	Pb	82	Selenium	Se	34
Boron	B	5	Lithium	Li	3	Silicon	Si	14
Bromine	Br	35	Lutetium	Lu	71	Silver (Argentum)	Ag	47
Cadmium	Cd	48	Magnesium	Mg	12	Sodium	Na	11
Californium	Cf	98	Manganese	Mn	25	Strontium	Sr	38
Carbon	C	6	Mendelevium	Md	101	Sulfur	S	16
Cerium	Ce	58	Mercury	Hg	80	Tentalum	Ta	73
Cesium	Cs	55	Molybdenum	Mo	42	Technetium	Tc	43
Chlorine	Cl	17	Neodymium	Nd	60	Tellurium	Te	52
Chromium	Cr	24	Neon	Ne	10	Terbium	Tb	65
Cobalt	Co	27	Neptunium	Np	93	Thallium	Tl	81
Copper (Cuprum)	Cu	29	Nickel	Ni	28	Throrium	Th	90
Curium	Cm	96	Niobium	Nb	41	Thulium	Tm	69
Dysprosium	Dy	66	Nitrogen	N	7	Tin (Stannum)	Sn	50
Einsteinium	Es	99	Nobelium	No	102	Titanium	Ti	22
Erbium	Er	68	Osmium	Os	76	Tungsten (Wolfram)	W	74
Europium	Eu	63	Oxygen	O	8	Uranium	U	92
Fermium	Fm	100	Palladium	Pd	46	Vanadium	V	23
Fluorine	F	9	Phosphorus	P	15	Xenon	Xe	54
Francium	Fr	87	Platinum	Pt	78	Ytterbium	Yb	70
Gadolinium	Gd	64	Plutonium	Pu	94	Yttrium	Y	39
Gallium	Ga	31	Polonium	Po	84	Zinc	Zn	30
Germanium	Ge	32	Potassium	K	19	Zirconium	Zr	40
Gold (Aurum)	Au	79	Praseodymium	Pr	59			

Electrical Resistivity and Temperature Coefficients of Elements

Element	Temp. °C	Temp. Microhm-cm	Coefficient per °C	Element	Temp. °C	Temp. Microhm-cm	Coefficient per °C
Aluminum, 99.996%	20	2.6548	0.00429^{20}	Nickel	20	6.84	0.0069^{0-100}
Antimony	0	39.0		Niobium	0	12.5	
Arsenic	20	33.3		Osmium	20	9.5	0.0042^{0-100}
Beryllium	20	4.0	0.025^{20}	Paladium	20	10.8	0.00377^{0-100}
Bismuth	0	106.8		Phosphorus, white	11	1×10^{17}	
Boron	0	1.8×10^{12}		Platinum, 99.85%	20	10.6	0.003927^{0-100}
Cadmium	0	6.83	0.0042^{0}	Plutonium	107	141.4	
Calcium	0	3.91	0.00416^{0}	Potassium	0	6.15	
Carbon	0	1375.0		Praseodymium	25	68	0.00171^{0-25}
Cerium	25	75.0	0.00087^{0-25}	Rhenium	20	19.3	0.00395^{0-100}
Cesium	20	20.		Rhodium	20	4.51	0.0042^{0-100}
Chromium	0	12.9	0.003^{0}	Rubidium	20	12.5	
Cobalt	20	6.24	0.00604^{0-100}	Ruthenium	0	7.6	
Copper	20	1.6730	0.0068^{20}	Samarium	25	88.0	0.00184^{0-25}
Dysprosium	25	57.0	0.00119^{0-25}	Scandium	22	61.0	0.00282^{0-25}
Erbium	25	107.0	0.00201^{0-25}	Selenium	0	12.0	
Europium	25	90.0		Silicon	0	10.0	
Gadolinium	25	140.5	0.00176^{0-25}	Silver	20	1.59	0.0041^{0-100}
Gallium	20	17.4		Sodium	0	4.2	
Germanium	22	46×10^{6}		Strontium	20	23.0	
Gold	20	2.35	0.004^{0-100}	Sulfur, Yellow	20	2×10^{23}	
Hafnium	25	35.1	0.0038^{25}	Tantalum	25	12.45	0.00383-^{0-100}
Holmium	25	87.0	0.00171^{0-25}	Tellurium	25	4.36×10^{5}	
Indium	20	8.37		Thallium	0	18.0	
Iodine	20	1.3×10^{15}		Thorium	0	13.0	0.0038^{0-100}
Iridium	20	5.3	0.003925^{0-100}	Thulium	25	79.0	0.00195^{0-25}
Iron, 99.99%	20	9.71	0.00651^{20}	Tin	0	11.0	0.0047^{0-100}
Lanthanum	25	5.70	0.00218^{0-25}	Titanium	20	42.0	
Lead	20	20.648	0.00336^{20-40}	Tungsten	27	5.65	
Lithium	0	8.55		Uranium	30.0		
Lutetium	25	79.0	0.00240^{0-25}	Vanadium	20	24.8-26.0	
Magnesium	20	4.45	0.0165^{20}	Ytterbium	25	29.0	0.0013^{0-25}
Mercury	50	98.4		Yttrium	25	57.0	0.0027^{0-25}
Molybdenum	0	5.2		Zinc	20	5.916	0.00419^{0-100}
Neodymium	25	64.0	0.00164^{0-25}	Zirconium	20	40.0	0.0044^{20}

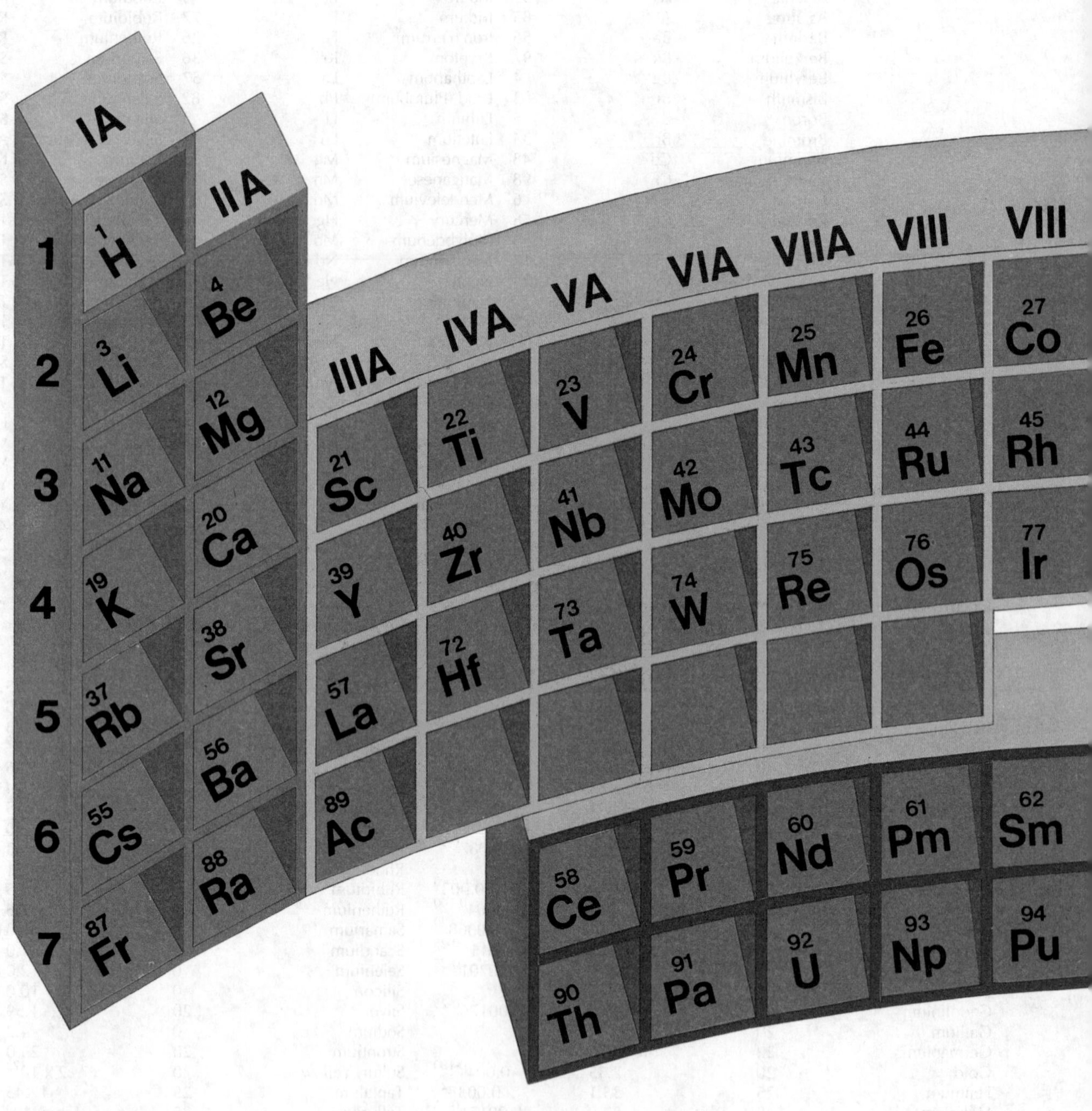

The periodic table shows an arrangement of elements according to atomic number. The vertical columns (with Roman numerals) contain elements with similar properties. The horizontal rows (with arabic numbers) relate to the build-up of the atomic constituents of each element. Metallic elements are in yellow boxes, while non-metallic are in blue. The two series of elements shown separately (in purple) are the lanthanide and actinide series. The colored edges of the boxes indicate the main groups of elements: alkaline and alkaline earth (green), transition metals (yellow), and main group elements (red). Hydrogen can be considered either as a metal or as a non-metal.

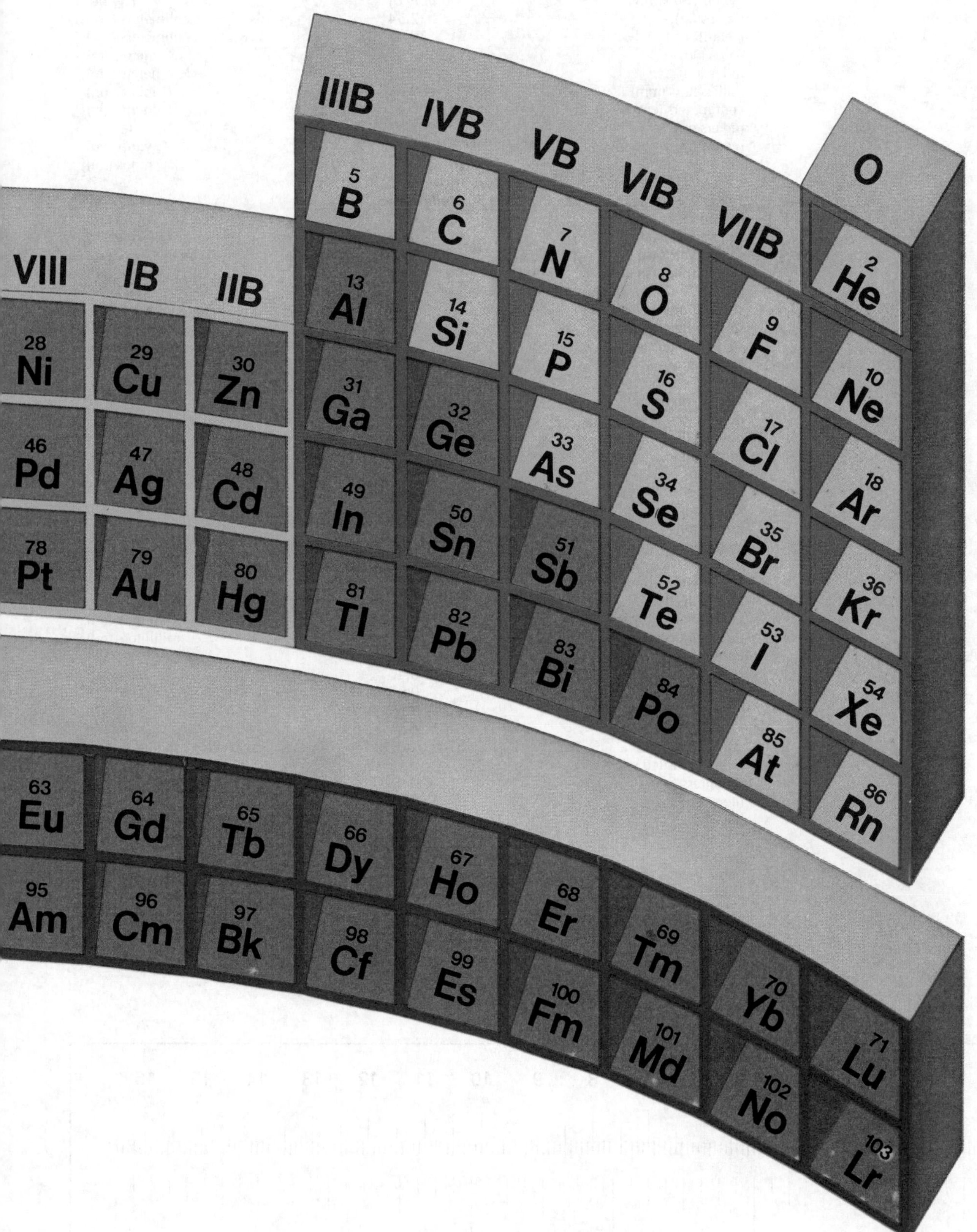
IIIB
IVB
VB
VIB
VIIB
O
VIII
IB
IIB
5 B
6 C
7 N
8 O
9 F
2 He
10 Ne
13 Al
14 Si
15 P
16 S
17 Cl
18 Ar
28 Ni
29 Cu
30 Zn
31 Ga
32 Ge
33 As
34 Se
35 Br
36 Kr
46 Pd
47 Ag
48 Cd
49 In
50 Sn
51 Sb
52 Te
53 I
54 Xe
78 Pt
79 Au
80 Hg
81 Tl
82 Pb
83 Bi
84 Po
85 At
86 Rn
63 Eu
64 Gd
65 Tb
66 Dy
67 Ho
68 Er
69 Tm
70 Yb
71 Lu
95 Am
96 Cm
97 Bk
98 Cf
99 Es
100 Fm
101 Md
102 No
103 Lr

Metric Measurement Conversions

	When you know:	Multiply by:	To find:
Length	inches (in)	2.54	centimeters (cm)
	feet (ft)	30	centimeters (cm)
	yards (yd)	0.9	meters (m)
	miles (mi)	1.6	kilometers (km)
	millimeters (mm)	0.04	inches (in)
	centimeters (cm)	0.4	inches (in)
	meters (m)	3.3	feet (ft)
	meters (m)	1.1	yards (yd)
	kilometers (km)	0.6	miles (mi)
	When you know:	*Multiply by:*	*To find:*
Area	square inches (sq in)	6.5	sq. centimeters (sq cm)
	square feet (sq ft)	0.09	square meters (sq m)
	square yards (sq yd)	0.8	square meters (sq m)
	square miles (sq mi)	2.6	sq. kilometers (sq km)
	acres	0.4	hectares
	sq. centimeters (sq cm)	0.16	square inches (sq in)
	square meters (sq m)	1.2	square yards (sq yd)
	sq. kilometers (sq km)	0.4	square miles (sq mi)
	hectares	2.5	acres
	When you know:	*Multiply by:*	*To find:*
Weight	ounces (oz)	28	grams (g)
	pounds (lb)	0.45	kilograms (kg)
	short tons	0.9	metric tons
	long tons	1.01	metric tons
	grams (g)	0.035	ounces (oz)
	kilograms (kg)	2.2	pounds (lb)
	metric tons	1.1	short tons
	metric tons	0.98	long tons
	When you know:	*Multiply by:*	*To find:*
Volume	teaspoons (tsp)	5	milliliters (ml)
	tablespoons (tbsp)	15	milliliters (ml)
	fluid ounces (fl oz)	30	milliliters (ml)
	cups (c)	0.24	liters (l)
	pints (pt)	0.47	liters (l)
	quarts (qt)	0.95	liters (l)
	gallons-U.S. (gal)	3.8	liters (l)
	gallons-imperial (gal)	4.5	liters (l)
	cubic feet (cu ft)	.028	cubic meters (cu m)
	cubic yards (cu yd)	0.76	cubic meters (cu m)
	milliliters (ml)	0.03	fluid ounces (fl oz)
	liters (l)	2.1	pints (pt)
	liters (l)	1.06	quarts (qt)
	liters (l)	0.26	gallons-U.S. (gal)
	liters (l)	0.22	gallons-imperial (gal)
	cubic meters (cu m)	35	cubic feet (cu ft)
	cubic meters (cu m)	1.3	cubic yards (cu yd)
Temperature	°C = (°F – 32) x .555		
	°F = (°C x 1.8) + 32		

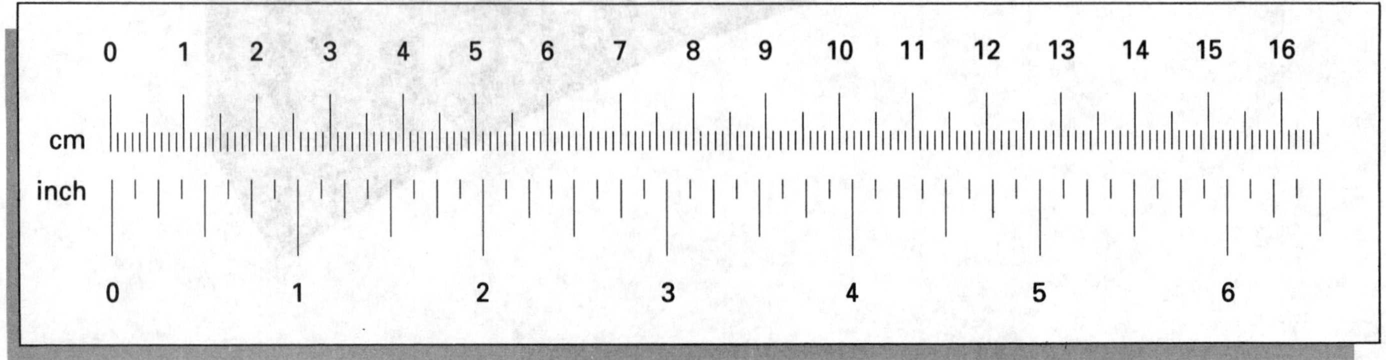

Publisher's Note: While every effort has been made to contact the copyrightholders of illustrations contained in this book, we apologize for any inadvertent omissions and offer to correct any errors in future printings.

Artworks: ©1991 International Visual Resource

Situation maps: R & R Design, De Meern

Map section: ©1995 Rand McNally & Company

All U.S. presidential portraits are copyrighted by the White House Historical Association, Washington; Photography by the National Geographic Society.

AAA-Photo Paris, 75g *(Drachoussoff)*, 124c *(Naud)*, 435a *(Fievet)*, 595b *(N. Myers)*, 612 *(A. Picou)*, 740b, 770d *(Aroulaudom)*
ABC-Press Amsterdam, 292a *(Sheldon)*, 421b *(Sheldon)*, 526c, 527a, 566a, 599b, 622a *(Paul von Stroheim)*, 693 *(Rizzoli)*, 721b *(Craig Aurness)*, 816, 840c *(M. Friedel)*, 1053b *(Intha Rona)*, 1072b *(Bellapart)*, 1086b *(H. Suying)*, 1118a *(Studio Dera)*, 1125b *(Aurness)*, 1154a *(Ingrid Claesen)*, 1170 *(Sheldon)*
Action Press Photographers International/Rob Brijker Press-Service RBP Amsterdam, 214a, 1076a
Agence International 'Actualit', Bruxelles, 370
Adams, Joe, 214b
AeroCamera-Bart Hofmeester bv Rotterdam, 780b
Aerophoto Schiphol bv Schiphol, 203a
AFP-Photo/ANP-Foto Amsterdam, 74b, 444b, 1009a, 1065b *(Vincent Amaly)*
AGE FotoStock Barcelona, 47b *(E. Gelpi)*, 65c *(G. Carles)*, 86b *(F. Forester)*, 124a, 169a, 556a *(F. Forester)*, 678a *(X. Miserachs)*, 823a *(G. Carles)*, 894b, 1022 *(X. Miserachs)*, 1058 *(F. Forester)*, 1131
AGE FotoStock/Picturepoint Ltd East Molesey, Surrey, 420b, 462a, 462b, 553a, 580b, 679b, 973
Alan Hutchison Library London, 191b *(F. Willoughby)*, 615b *(J. Baldwin)*, 634c, 635a *(B. Regent)*, 664d *(B. Moser)*, 666a *(R.I. Loyd)*, 771a *(J. Baldwin)*, 896d, 896e
Alusuisse Zürich, 114b
Amnesty International Amsterdam, 44a
Agence ANA/ABC-Press Amsterdam, 534a *(Michelangelo Durazzo)*
Agence Daniel Angeli/Rob Brijker Press-Service RBP Amsterdam, 128c
ANP-Foto Amsterdam, 47a, 271, 287b, 497d, 598b, 664b, 690a, 737a, 795b, 898b, 957b, 1031b, 1038a
Ansel Adams Carmel, 15
Anthony-Verlag Starnberg, 75d *(W. Scharf)*, 496 *(W. Scharf)*
Ardea London Ltd London, 41a *(W. Weisser)*, 85c *(H. & J. Beste)*, 264b *(V. Taylor)*, 412 *(H. & J. Beste)*, 517c *(M.D. England)*, 640c *(Wightman)*, 815b *(I.R. Beames)*, 884 *(K.W. Fink)*, 1196b *(W. Weisser)*
Art Institute of Chicago, The/Koninklijke Smeets Offset bv Weert, 983
Aspect Picture Library Ltd London, 29c *(J.A. Langley)*, 165d *(P. Carmichael)*, 730b *(T. Okuda)*, 1221b *(T. Nebbia)*
Aspect Picture Library Ltd/ABC-Press Amsterdam, 570a *(Gossler)*
Associated Newspaper/Spaarnestad Fotoarchief Haarlem, 722b, 928b
The Associated Press Amsterdam, 161b
Avena SA/Sunshine International Photo-Agency Almere-haven, 769a
B & U International Picture Service Amsterdam, 62, 67b, 96b *(L. Kuipers)*, 180c, 216, 246b, 246c, 318, 327, 384c *(L. Kuipers)*, 392, 393, 400, 435b, 451 *(L. Kuipers)*, 453a, 481c, 507, 511, 604b *(Marjo Visser)*, 616b, 645b, 653b, 664c, 682b *(David Simson)*, 717b, 746, 755b, 759, 764c, 766b, 776b, 778b, 781b, 793a, 793c, 802a, 805c, 824, 830a *(L. Kuipers)*, 920b, 921a, 926a, 955a, 958, 1020b, 1040, 1042c, 1056c, 1075, 1078b, 1116c, 1139, 1211b, 1214c
Greta Baars-Jelgersma Auteursbureau Velp, 494c
James Balog/Black Star New York, cover a
Ernst Barlach Haus/Adelheid Cordez-Beitz Hamburg, 106b
Foto Baudert Amstelveen, 1028b
BBC Hulton Picture Library London, 276, 926b
Hans Beerekamp Amsterdam, 36a
Belga Bruxelles, 60a, 561b
Belgisch Instituut voor Voorlichting en Documentatie INBEL Brussel, 369e, 701
Benelux Press bv Voorburg, 1191b, 1304a, 1304b *(Bavaria)*, 1305, 1306 *(Index Stock)*
Kors van Bennekom Schellingwoude - Ams, 643c
The Bettmann Archive Inc. New York, 132, 153a, 419c, 729d, 879, 1003, 1042b, 1045, 1050, 1073a, 1084b, 1126, 1141b, 1155a, 1157b, 1169, 1172a, 1172b, 1172c, 1173a, 1173b, 1173c, 1177a, 1177b, 1178, 1182, 1194b, 1194c, 1292d, 1293a, 1293b
Uitgeverij De Bezige Bij Amsterdam, 123a
Bibliotheque Nationale Paris, 279, 369a, 501c, 517a, 531, 603b, 619b, 707b, 707c, 712a, 1291d
Biofotos Surrey, 341
Black Star New York, cover b *(Bruno Barbey)*, 834a *(Dennis Brack)*, 834f *(Christopher Morris)*
Black Star/Transworld Features Holland bv Haarlem, 75c *(Bonway)*, 500a *(Bonway)*, 744 *(D. Break)*
Blauel Kunst-Dias/Bayerische Staatsgemäldesammlungen München, 857b
Ira Block/Image Bank, The New York, cover d
Uitgeversmaatschappij Bonaventura bv Amsterdam, 468, 482c, 560b, 676a
H. ter Borg Amsterdam, 550b
Boston Red Sox Boston, 1187a
Jak Boumans Utrecht, 705b
Museum Boymans-van Beuningen Rotterdam, 90, 912
The Bridgeman Art Library Ltd London, 288a, 330, 416a, 452a
Paul Brierley Harlow - Essex, 854b
Rob Brijker Press-Service RBP Amsterdam, 88.h, 105b, 111d, 261a, 626a
The British Council Amsterdam, 214c
The British Museum London, 986, 1292e
Ets J.E. Bulloz Paris, 289, 472a, 651a, 809b, 837b, 1166b
Roel Burgler Amsterdam, 351, 357, 670b, 681a, 699a, 776a
California Institute of Technology and Carnegie Institution of Washington/Chriet Titulaer Produkties bv Houten, 47c, 471b
Camera Press Ltd London, cover c + n
Camera Press Ltd/ABC-Press Amsterdam, 58c, 83b *(P. Mitchell)*, 99b *(M. Gershon)*, 126c *(Gyberg)*, 162a, 184d *(Hunter)*, 192b *(C. Beaton)*, 200a *(Karsh of Ottawa)*, 273a *(Tappe)*, 305b *(Bachrach)*, 344b, 353a *(Halsma)*, 387 *(Curtis)*, 420a, 498a *(Curtis)*, 575 *(Karsh of Ottawa)*, 590b *(J. Cowan)*, 618a *(Cowell)*, 621a *(Alexander)*, 643a *(P. Harrison)*, 657 *(Slade)*, 668b *(Clark)*, 674 *(C/Que)*, 715b *(S. Errington)*, 719c *(Marshall)*, 729b *(Cortez)*, 739b, 801, 849 *(Cooper)*, 871a, 972 *(Hatami)*, 1015a, 1062 *(Williams)*, 1069a *(Parkinson)*, 1073b, 1102a *(Philip Herxe)*, 1125c *(Gerald Taylor)*, 1158a *(W. Braun)*, 1175c *(John Moss)*, 1207 *(Jane Bown)*, 1225 *(Gerald Taylor)*
Peter Carmichael (Reflex) Ltd Richmond - Surrey, 34b, 102b, 104b, 118c
Carol Color Lab. Inc./Duomo Photography Inc New York, 396b *(David Madison)*
Centraal Dansberaad Den Haag, 98b
Soenar Chamid Sportfotografie Almere, 1009b
Churchill Downs Incorporated ©1991, 595a
Cinematheque Française Paris, 619a
City Film Distribution bv Amsterdam, 611a, 764b
City of Boston/Museum of Fine Arts Boston-Massachusetts, 1294
CNN Inc./Sunshine International Photo-Agency Almere-haven, 581b
Bruce Coleman Ltd Uxbridge -Middlesex, 22b *(N. Myers)*, 22c *(N. Myers)*, 36c, 41e *(M. Freeman)*, 53b *(F. Erize)*, 53c *(J.D. Drysdale)*, 58a *(J. Shaw)*, 65a *(G. Ziesler)*, 99a *(Steve Kaufman)*, 141 *(Jack Dermid)*, 148c *(S. Gillsäter)*, 193 *(Hans Reinhard)*, 195b *(Jack Dermid)*, 204a *(H. Reinhard)*, 205 *(C.&.D. Frith)*, 222 *(Hans Reinhard)*, 225a *(Jeff Foott)*, 254 *(Hoe van Wormes)*, 273b *(Charlie Ott)*, 274b *(T. Wood)*, 308a *(Hans Reinhard)*, 313b *(Gunter Ziesler)*, 317c *(N. Devore)*, 376b *(H. Reinhard)*, 411a *(Frans Lanting)*, 425a *(Jane Burton)*, 446b *(S. Nielsen)*, 460 *(Jack Stein Greve)*, 473 *(Burton)*, 482a *(Hans Reinhard)*, 486c *(H. Reinhard)*, 523 *(N. Myers)*, 529b *(Burton)*, 571 *(J. Burton)*, 600b *(Bob&Clara Calhoun)*, 618b *(R. Tidman)*, 647b *(D. Green)*, 691a *(John Shaw)*, 710b *(Jane Burton)*, 802b *(Scott Nielsen)*, 805b *(J. Wallis)*, 870a *(S.C. Bisserot)*, 975a *(J. Burton)*, 975b *(J. & D. Bartlett)*, 977 *(J. Burton)*, 994b *(Hans Reinhard)*, 1002a *(J. van Wormer)*, 1030 *(U. Hirsch)*, 1031a *(C. Laubscher)*, 1032c *(Jen&Des Bartlett)*, 1162a *(Burton)*, 1185b *(E. Crichton)*, 1185d *(Zuber)*, 1185e *(V. Serventy)*, 1185g *(E. Crichton)*, 1222b *(F. Erize)*
College Football Hall of Fame, 448b
Collegium Wilhelmitanum Strasbourg, 67, 80a
Colorific Photo Library Ltd Gloucester Terrace -, 145a *(G. Tortoli)*, 190 *(T. Spencer)*, 519b, 789a *(D. Moore)*, 951b *(S. Young)*, 960b *(L. Bartlett)*, 1014b *(D. Moore)*, 1068b *(Joyce)*, 1140b *(J.H. Pickerell)*, 1143c *(J.H. Pickerell)*, 1175a *(D. Moore)*, 1185a *(D. Wayman)*
Combi-Press Service Amsterdam, 292b
Comet-Photo AG Zürich, 386b
Contact/ABC-Press Amsterdam, 948a *(D.H. Kennerly)*
Contact/Colorific Photo Library Ltd Gloucester Terrace -, 354b *(A. Reininger)*, 361a *(B. Pierle)*
Culver Pictures Inc. New York, 1122c, 1187b, 1197
Dehler Yachtbau/Markt & Werbung GmbH Meschede-Freienohl, 862
Detroit Tigers Detroit, 240a
Deutsche Grammophon GmbH , 509a
Frans Duivis Almere, 178, 1087b, 1132b
Duomo Photography Inc New York, 458b *(Rick Rickman)*, 825 *(Dan Helms)*
Dupont de Nemours Dordrecht, 299b
F.N. Eisenloeffel Amsterdam, 464a
Uitgeverij Elsevier Sequoia/Flor Peeters Antwerpen, 405a
Encyclopaedia Universalis France Parijs Cédex 14, 1013a
Etévé Paris, 1151
European Southern Observatory/Chriet Titulaer Produkties bv, Houten 660b, 788b
Mary Evans Picture Library London, 95a, 189b, 196, 314, 323, 339a, 383, 407b, 772a, 780a, 891b, 1200c
Explorer Paris, 21b *(J. Prevost)*, 29a *(M. Brosselin)*, 275 *(J. Lelievre)*, 376a, 586b *(Hug)*, 658b *(A. Cormontagne)*, 694 *(P. Tatopoulos)*, 761b *(G. Boutin)*, 859b *(Sebert)*, 896b *(J. Valentin)*, 950a *(M. Moisnard)*, 953b *(M. Moisnard)*, 959b *(P. Tetrel)*, 1006, 1023b *(Edouard)*, 1061a *(C. Santos)*
Explorer/Sunshine International Photo-Agency Almere-haven, 316b *(Yves Lanceau)*, 389b *(Cristina Hoyos)*, 518c *(G. Boutin)*, 649a *(N. Thibaut)*, 684 *(Francois Gohier)*, 738a *(J. Perno C.D. Tetrel)*, 752b *(Francois Gohier)*, 800b *(Koene)*, 803d *(Adina Tory)*, 1046a *(Gladu Eis)*, 1104a *(Francois Gohier)*, 1230b *(Alain Thomas)*
Express Film Amstelveen, 624a
FIALHO/ABC-Press Amsterdam, 1017a
Fotocolor Fiore Torino, 617
Focus on Sports New York, 09b, 366b, 803b, 945c *(Tom Dipace)*, 998a, 1116b
Focus on Sports/Thearon , 109b
Ford Motor Company Dearborn - Michigan, 77a, 398b
Bedrich Forman , 479b
Werner Forman Archive Ltd London, 839
Agence Photographique Fotogram Paris, 187 *(Y. Bruneau)*, 201 *(Bernard Gérard)*
Fox Photos London, 339b
Sigmund Freud Copyrights Ltd Colchester, 411b
The Image Bank France Paris, 244b *(R. Phillips)*
Klaus D. Francke Hamburg, 453e, 795a
Oliver Gamgee London, 105a
Gamma/Rob Brijker Press-Service RBP Amsterdam, 10 *(L. Favorite)*, 20b *(Flori)*, 77b, 93d *(John Barr/Liaison)*, 98a *(K. Kurita)*, 149 *(C. Gerritsen)*, 153b *(Lee Waite)*, 176, 218 *(R. Depardon)*, 280b *(Aldo Payan)*, 313a *(Guerrini)*, 456b, 456c *(Pozarik)*, 510, 527b, 554 *(Alain Keler)*, 560a *(Willets- Camerapix)*, 563a *(D. Walker)*, 593b *(Breese)*, 663b, 715a *(J.C. Francolon)*, 720a, 732c *(B. Iverson)*, 733 *(Francolon)*, 751b, 820a *(Gaillarde, R)*, 834d *(Laurent v.d. Stockt)*, 834e *(Markel)* 865, 890b *(C. Vioujard)*, 969a *(F. Apesteguy)*, 990a *(Borrel)*, 996a *(Bartholomew)*, 1039a *(F. Lochon)*, 1109c *(Ellsen, I.)*, 1145a, 1166a *(R. Depardon)*
Gemeentemuseum 's-Gravenhage Den Haag, 287c
General Aniline & Film Corporation/Spaarnestad Fotoarchief Haarlem, 283c *Brady, Matthew B.*
Geocom bv Arnhem, 237b, 654b
Frits Gerritsen Amsterdam, 583, 853b
Georg Gerster Zumikon-Zürich, 263b, 367c, 369d, 391b, 404c, 505c, 647c, 787b
Gesellschaft für Strahlen- und Umweltforschung mbh München Neuherberg, 622b
Agenzia Giornalistca Italia/ANEFO bv Amsterdam, 576a
Photographie Giraudon Paris, 32a, 37b, 73d, 96a, 100a, 126b, 148a, 148b, 180a, 223 *(Garanger)*, 258, 309a *(Telarci)*, 363b *(Lauros)*, 373b, 390, 405c *(Lauros)*, 436 *(Lauros)*, 471a, *(Musée Condé, Paris)* 490, 501a, 513c, 615a *(Lauros)*, 671a, 675a, 698a, *(Musée Condé, Paris)* 736a, 742a, 748e, 822a, 829b, 854a, 871c, 882b, 914d *(Lauros)*, 992, 1037b, 1081, 1086a, 1088a, 1158b, 1217a, 1219b, 1290a *(Lauros)*, 1290b, 1290b, 1290.j *(Lauros)*
Globe Photos Inc./ABC-Press Amsterdam, 558 *(Rangefinders)*, 830b *(Slade)*
Gabriele Gossner Gauting bei München, 1222a
Granada Television International Ltd./Alan Hutchison Library London, 817b *(C. Naim)*, 896.h *(B. Moser)*
Granger Collection, The New York, cover h, cover i
Greek National Tourist Office , cover e
Richard & Sally Greenhill London, 745
Susan Griggs Agency Ltd London, 29b *(D. Fordham)*, 41b *(L. McIntyre)*, 75f *(Reflejo)*, 85f *(R.I. Lloyd)*, 85g *(R.I. Lloyd)*, 97b *(A. Howarth)*, 179a *(John G. Ross)*, 245 *(V. Englebert)*, 256b, 320a *(A. Woolfitt)*, 530b *(Dimitri Ilic)*, 535c *(William Strode)*, 549b *(Nathan Benn)*, 589a *(Cotton Coulsen)*, 743a *(J. Cobb)*, 761a *(M.St. Maur Sheil)*, 792b, 885 *(A. Woolfitt)*, 896f *(T. Eigeland)*, 1143a *(I. Murphy)*, 1227 *(N. Benn)*
Agence Photographique Guyaux Bruxelles, 294a
Foto Emile de Haas Haarlem, 807
Ray Halin Paris, 1091a
Gijsbert Hanekroot Amsterdam, 332b, 929b
Robert Harding Picture Library Ltd London, 337 *(Y. Lehmann)*, 340 *(R. Cundy)*, 342 *(J. Ross)*, 556b *(J. Gardey)*, 564c *(G.A. Mather)*, 596b *(J. Rufus)*, 627b *(I.G. Ross)*, 632c *(L. Garner)*, 686c *(T. Sheppard)*, 754 *(J. Gardey)*, 810 *(R. Cundy)*, 965 *(D. Holden)*, 1065a, 1072a, 1129c *(W. Rawlings)*, 1136b
Harkavy Press New York City, 109a, 109c, 111a, 111c
Hayward Art Group Maidstone - Kent, 22a, 53d, 75e, 85e, 239, 363c, 671b, 708b, 798a, 852a, 1013b, 1018, 1185f
Henson Associates Inc. 1985 , cover f
Taeke Henstra Haarlem, 1066a, 1137c
Hans Heus Alphen aan den Rijn, 897
HOA-QUI Paris, 172b *(André)*, 210d, 463b, 466a, 945b *(Richer)*
Michael Holford Photographs Essex, 261b
Hollandse Signaalapparaten bv Hengelo, 898a
Holle Bildarchiv Baden-Baden, 84a
H. Hovinga Blaricum, 158b
Peter Hunter Press Features/Rob Brijker Press-Service RBP Amsterdam, 381a, 416b, 826b, 1292b
I.I.A.V. Amsterdam, 54a, 1194d, 1194e, 1194f
Icelandic Photo & Press Service Reykjavik, 1150a
Image Bank, The New York/**Kelly, John P.**, 930a, 1053c *(Don King)*
Institut für Plasmaphysik - Max Planck Garching bei München, 81c *(H.U. Keller)*
Inter Nationes/United States Information Service USIS Den Haag, 306
Intercontinental Media Production Aps. Tisvilde, 464b, 881, 988, 1192a *(B. Rothausen)*
Interfoto Pressebild/Agence de Presse Photographique Rapho Paris, 361c
International Communication Agency 's-Gravenhage, 820b *(George Platt Lines)*
International Picture Research Office IPRO Landsmeer, 625a
Jacana Paris, 94b, 116 *(R. Volot)*, 119a, 186 *(Schraml)*, 212a, 296 *(R. Ruffier-Lanche)*, 328b *(Aldebert)*, 476, 505b *(Col Varin Visage)*, 524 *(A. Bert)*, 605a *(Frederic)*, 630b *(Volot)*, 688c, 799a *(Grossa)*, 860, 993, 1146b *(Y. Gillon)*, 1179, 1193 *(Varin-Varin)*
Frans Janssen Utrecht, 620b
JB Pictures/Sunshine International Photo-Agency Almere-haven, 607b *(John Nordell)*
J.E. Jongert Amsterdam, 131a
Bildarchiv Jürgens Ost-Europa-Photo Köln, 432b
Pieter Kalma Amsterdam, 215a, 715c
Jan van de Kam Griendtsveen, 402, 895b
Kant-Gymnasium Berlin, 590a
Keats-Shelley Memorial Association Rome, 989a
Keter Publishing House Jerusalem, 582 *(D. Harris)*
Keystone Pressedienst Gmbh/Universal News Organization UNO Haarlem, 95b, 118b
Kitt Peak National Observatory Tucson, 887b
Ralph Kleinhempel/Hamburger Kunsthalle Hamburg, 486b
Paolo Koch Zollikon, 49b, 93a, 160b, 220b, 361.h, 361.i, 518d, 567, 591a, 711b, 719a, 727, 1056b, 1097b, 1115a
Koninklijk Instituut voor de Tropen Amsterdam, 798b
Koninklijke Smeets Offset bv Weert, 11, 18b, 39a, 70, 73a, 83a, 91a, 102c, 164b, 200b, 377, 437a, 503a, 508, 513a, 603a, 633a, 636b, 662a, 685, 704b, 712b, 716a, 724, 728, 763c, 791a, 792a, 805a, 845a, 863b, 903a, 914c, 938b, 940, 968, 1054, 1089c, 1094b, 1137a, 1148, 1180, 1195, 1290f, 1292a
R. Korthals Altes Amsterdam, 901
Pieter Paul Koster Den Haag, 826a
Kunsthistorisches Museum Wien, 687b
Kövesdi International Press & Photo Agency KIPPA Amsterdam, 117b, 212b, 268a, 437c, 489b
Leger des Heils Amsterdam, 955b
Studio Lemaire Amsterdam, 525a
Erich Lessing/ABC-Press Amsterdam, 732b
London Express News and Features Service/ABC-Press Amsterdam, 144a, 184a, 927a
Lumen Bros./Spaarnestad Fotoarchief Haarlem, 45
Magnum Photos/ABC-Press Amsterdam, 17b *(B. Barbey)*, 20a *(M. Riboud)*, 30c *(B. Glinn)*, 40b *(B. Barbey)*, 75b *(B. Campbell)*, 119b *(E. Lessing)*, 130c *(M. Silverstone)*, 202b *(B. Barbey)*, 203d *(B. Barbey)*, 204b *(B. Glinn)*, 208a *(E. Lessing)*, 220c *(M. Riboud)*, 221 *(M. Riboud)*, 268b *(B. Barbey)*, 286b *(E. Erwitt)*, 299c, 358b *(G. Rodger)*, 361d *(I. Berry)*, 432a *(H. Cartier-Bresson)*, 432c *(E. Lessing)*, 448a *(E. Haas)*, 453b *(L. Maous)*, 469c *(B. Glinn)*, 469d *(B. Glinn)*, 489a *(R. Capa)*, 528b *(B. Barbey)*, 535a *(Harry Gruyaert)*, 551a *(Steve McCurry)*, 592b *(K. Taconis)*, 610b *(B. Barbey)*, 649b *(B. Barbey)*, 700c *(E. Haas)*, 708a *(Morath)*, 725 *(R. Jones)*, 743b *(B. Barbey)*, 767b, 786a *(E. Lessing)*, 942b *(M. Riboud)*, 980b *(I. Berry)*, 1019d *(Erich Hartmann)*, 1032b *(B. Barbey)*, 1043a *(M. Silverstone)*, 1049 *(K. Taconis)*, 1089b *(E. Lessing)*, 1109b *(Erich Lessing)*, 1115b *(B. Glinn)*, 1115c *(F. Mayer)*, 1118c *(Ian Berry)*, 1119 *(David Hurn)*, 1157a *(Halsman)*, 1200e, 1214a *(A. Webb)*
Magnum Photos/Bruce Coleman Ltd Uxbridge -Middlesex, 614b *(bisserot)*
The Mansell Collection London, 283a, 741a, 857a
Massachusetts Institute of Technology - Department of Physics Cambridge - Massachu, 892b
Peter P. Massee Brakel, 160a, 302c, 310c
Mega-Produktions Inc./Rob Brijker Press-Service RBP Amsterdam, 93b *(F. Duhamel)*, 395 *(Weber)*, 491a *(Weber)*
Melbourne Brindle/Spaarnestad Fotoarchief Haarlem, 92a
Fotostudio Vincent Mentzel Rotterdam, 1092c
The Metropolitan Museum of Art New York, 1188a *(H. Brisbane)*
Mexican Government Tourist Office , cover j
Middle East Photographic Archive/Robert Harding Picture Library Ltd London, 585 *(J. Dickie)*
Milano Press/Maurizio Leigheb Novara, 40a, 796b
Mondadori/Uitgeverij Het Spectrum B.V. Utrecht, 1202e
The Museum of Modern Art New York, 115c
Nico Naeff Den Haag, 1088b
Nationaal Fotopersbureau nv/Spaarnestad Fotoarchief Haarlem, 942a
National Aeronautics and Space Administration NASA Washington, cover p, 61a, 334c, 584b, 679a, 743c
National Aeronautics and Space Administration NASA/AGE FotoStock Barcelona, 723e
National Baseball Library Cooperstown NY, 608a, 927b, 1214b
The National Gallery of Canada Ottawa, 1192b
The National Gallery of Ireland Dublin, 1211
National Geographic Society/Supreme court Historical Society, the Washington, 1303a, 1303b, 1303c, 1303d, 1303e, 1303f, 1303g, 1303.h, 1303.i
Independence National Historical Park Collection , 1299b
The National Maritime Museum London, 919
The National Portrait Gallery London, 22e, 84b, 162b, 291a, 499c, 597, 831, 888, 1039b, 1156, 1165a, 1183b
The National Portrait Gallery/Uitgeverij Spaarnestad bv Haarlem, 1039b, 1156
Nederlands Filmmuseum Utrecht, 578, 729a
Nederlandse Aardolie Maatschappij bv NAM/Uitgeverij Spaarnestad bv Haarlem, 933b
Nederlandse Stichting voor Arctisch Natuurwetenschappelijk Onderzoek/Uitgeverij Haarlem, 384a
New York Times/Stichting World Press Photo Holland/ANP-Foto Amsterdam, 36b
New York Times/Spaarnestad Fotoarchief Haarlem/**Wide World Photos**, 108b
New York Yankees New York, 310b, 425b, 944
Chris Niedenthal Warszawa, 859c
Peter Nielsen Broek in Waterland, 1224b
A. van den Nieuwenhuizen Zevenaar, 177a, 240b, 1098
North Atlantic Treaty Organization NATO Bruxelles, 777b
Nova-Film Amsterdam, 381b
Novosti-press Den Haag, 251a, 322, 889, 1009c
Raymond O'Shea Gallery London, 22d
Onyx/Sunshine International Photo-Agency Almere-haven, 286a *(Rob Brown)*, 574 *(George Steinmetz)*, 602b *(J. Abbot)*, 953c *(Richard Sobol)*, 1194g *(E.J. Camp)*
Oslo Kommunes Kunstsamlinger Oslo, 525b
Paris-Match/Spaarnestad Fotoarchief Haarlem, 181b
Paul Mellon Collection/National Gallery of Art Washington, 749f
Pepsi Cola Nederland Bussum, 19b
Paul C. Pet Amsterdam, 65b, 82, 237e, 264a, 285b, 361g, 369c, 537, 608b, 637c, 688a, 703a, 703b, 726a, 757a, 819, 894a, 896g, 922, 932, 1057c, 1105b, 1130b, 1212b, 1289a, 1290d
Phonogram International Baarn, 164a
Photographers International/Rob Brijker Press-Service RBP Amsterdam, 591b *(G. Leonard)*
Photri Alexandria, Virginia, 315, 1079a, 1099b
Pictor International Ltd London, 53a
Pictorial Press Ltd/Sunshine International Photo-Agency Almere-haven, 593d, 929d
Picture Group/Rob Brijker Press-Service RBP Amsterdam, 871b *(Pamela Price)*

Acknowledgements

Picturepoint Ltd East Molesey, Surrey, 56, 229, 513, 522a, 628, 714b, 768a, 789b, 797b, 892c, 1042a, 1206a

Picturepoint Ltd/AGE FotoStock Barcelona, 217a

Popperfoto - Paul Popper Ltd London, 18a, 126a, 225b, 1095a, 1200a

Toine Post Ankeveen, 502a

Eddy Posthuma de Boer Amsterdam, 1019b

Thijs Postma Hoofddorp, 93c

Pressefoto Willy Pragher Freiburg im Breisgau, 177c

Sem Presser Amsterdam, 85d, 86a, 131b, 154, 167, 168, 175c, 210b, 263a, 300, 311a, 324, 344c, 358c, 367b, 391c, 410, 419b, 422c, 446a, 462c, 499a, 532a, 581a, 605b, 605c, 630a, 632b, 639b, 643b, 651b, 653a, 660a, 722a, 741b, 742b, 748b, 765a, 765b, 774a, 812, 823c, 828a, 833, 837a, 851, 852b, 895a, 903b, 904a, 913, 923, 925b, 933a, 939, 948b, 949, 970b, 1033b, 1084a, 1101b, 1165b, 1190, 1199b, 1289b, 1291b, 1291c, 1292c, 1292f

Bildarchiv Preussischer Kulturbesitz Berlin, 136a, 539b, 586a, 629b, 695a, 1043b, 1091c, 1106, 1200b, 1200d

Galerie Ra Amsterdam, 573a

Rainbird Picture Library/Robert Harding Picture Library Ltd/Akademie der Wissen Berlin, 516a

Agence de Presse Rapho Paris, 120 *(Brake)*, 183c *(K. Lawson)*, 217b *(Butler)*, 297a *(D. Berretty)*, 404a, 404b *(Dailloux)*, 559b *(T. Spiegel)*, 611b *(Charliat)*, 654a *(Garnet)*, 666d, 753b *(Brake)*, 863a *(Bernett)*, 872 *(Segalat)*, 957a *(monty)*, 1015c *(Delanne)*, 1171, 1230a *(P. McArdell)*

Photofest , 592a

Retna Pictures Ltd./Sunshine International Photo-Agency Almere, 929a

Rex Features Ltd/Rob Brijker Press-Service RBP Amsterdam, 127b, 128b, 151a *(Cath. Rebois)*, 569b, 834b, 908, 1122b

Paul van Riel Amsterdam, 361e, 602a, 1185c

Rijksinstituut voor Oorlogsdocumentatie Amsterdam, 253

Rijksmuseum voor Volkenkunde Leiden, 365b

Jan Rijsterborgh Haarlem, 1290g, 1290g

Rizzoli Press Service/ABC-Press Amsterdam, 470

Roger-Viollet Paris, 307, 366a, 382, 971

Ann Ronan Picture Library Loughton, Essex, 493b

L. Le Roy Oranjewoud, 866b

SCALA Istituto Fotografico Editoriale Antella - Firenze, 14c *(M. Wolf)*, 19a, 31, 33, 43b, 46a, 50, 54b, 60c, 67c, 73e, 97d, 101, 115e, 123b, 127a, 128a, 139b, 152, 158c, 175a, 175b, 177b, 197b, 198, 211, 232a *(J. Martin)*, 232b *(J. Martin)*, 233b *(J. Martin)*, 233c *(H. Jensen)*, 233e *(J. Martin)*, 233f *(J. Martin)*, 248, 249, 267, 274a, 291b, 295, 297b, 298 *(J. Martin)*, 311b, 321, 356b, 417b, 424b, 437b, 445a, 453c, 453d, 467b, 488a, 495b *(E. Lacey)*, 503b, 532b, 541, 588b, 648a, 650, 692a, 697b, 718a, 736c, 739a, 822b, 838b, 840a, 858, 914a, 914e, 914f, 918 *(J. Martin)*, 938a *(J. Martin)*, 962b, 989b *(J. Martin)*, 995b, 1135a, 1141a, 1149, 1155b *(J. Martin)*, 1196a, 1289d, 1290e, 1291a, 1292a *(J. Martin)*, 1292g, 1299a *(J. Martin)*

SCALA Istituto Fotografico Editoriale/The Mansell Collection London, 122a, 352, 613a

Kees Scherer Medemblik, 14b, 121b, 165a, 181a, 195a, 1057b, 1091b

Govert Schilling Utrecht, 512, 1128

A.J.M. van Schoonhoven Amsterdam, 23a

Heinz Schrempp Breisach-Oberrimsing, 799b

Schweiz Landesmuseum Zürich, 1224a

F & N Schwitter Photo-Library Lieli, Aargau, 98c

Peter Schütte Utrecht, 192a, 294c, 466b, 867, 1125a, 1159b, 1160a, 1206c, 1223b

Science Museum London, 94a, 252, 287a, 645a, 770c, 844b, 991f

Randal Scobie Photodesign Amsterdam, 547

Scottish National Portrait Gallery Edinburgh, 172c

Seaphot Ltd Bristol, 1035b *(P. Scoones)*

Servizio Editoriale Fotografico SEF Torino, 64b, 281, 409 *(A. Regaldi)*, 455b, 504b, 521a, 869, 886a, 996b, 1097a, 1215, 1216

Ronald Sheridan's Photo Library Harrow-on-the-Hill, 493a

Shostal Associates Inc. New York, 26b, 433, 518b, 533a, 576d, 663c, 749a, 749c, 840b *(E. Carle)*, 1147b, 1219c

Siemens Nederland nv/Natuur en Techniek Maastricht, 661

A.J.E. Simons Amsterdam, 497c

SIPA Paris, cover q *(An. Hussein)*, 369b *(An. Hussein)*

SIPA/Sunshine International Photo-Agency Almere-haven, 61b *(Kara, l.)*, 302a, 396a, 396c *(Win McNamee)*, 455a *(Minamikawa)*, 494a, 528c, 568 *(Laski)*, 593a *(Warner)*, 600a *(Dalmas)*, 606a, 962a *(Marquis)*, 1121 *(Trippett)*, 1228 *(Antonio Emerito)*

SIPA/Sunshine International Photo-Agency/Rijksmuseum Vincent van Gogh Amsterdam, cover r

SIPA/Sunshine International Photo-Agency/White House Press Office , 173b *(Valdez)*

G. Sirot Paris, 640.B

Photographies Jacques Six Paris, 882c

Pim Smit Koog aan de Zaan, 818b, 1217b

Pim Smit/ABC-Press Amsterdam, 1074b *(Löwe)*

Smithsonian Institution Washington, 749e

Snark International Paris, 75a, 427, 527c, 581c, 681b, 707a, 718b, 734, 736b, 772b, 1011, 1064, 1127, 1145b, 1290c

Howard Sochurek Inc. Delray Beach (Fl.), cover g

Spaarnestad Fotoarchief Haarlem, 46c, 57a, 85b, 142a, 155a, 179b, 184b, 207b, 232d, 233d *(ANP)*, 234 *(ANP)*, 282, 294b, 301, 329, 336a, 389a, 405b, 406, 444a, 450, 569a, 594a *(ANEFO)*, 625b, 666b, 696, 730a *(APIS)*, 804, 806a, 817c, 876a, 930b, 937a, 987b *(Keystone)*, 1070, 1109d, 1122e *(ANEFO)*, 1201c, 1202d, 1209, 1292d

Uitgeverij Het Spectrum B.V. Utrecht, cover m, 09a, 12, 13, 19c, 23b, 37a, 43a, 48, 57b, 59, 60b, 67a, 68, 74c, 77a, 79, 80b, 80d, 80e, 89, 112a, 134, 142b, 155b, 161a, 183a, 204c, 232c, 237, 278, 293, 308c, 310a, 346, 353b, 369f, 374, 388, 399, 407a, 415b, 422b, 430, 458a, 469a, 482b, 484, 486a, 494b, 497a, 500b, 501b, 502b, 515a, 515b, 516b, 520b, 521b, 536, 539a, 543, 548b, 563c, 598c, 613b, 637a, 637b, 640a, 642, 697b, 709a, 729c, 735a, 735b, 769b, 782a, 786b, 797b, 809a, 823b, 850a, 877, 880a, 882a, 899, 911, 916, 921b, 954, 956, 961a, 963, 964a, 969b, 1001, 1002b, 1012, 1016, 1021, 1029, 1033a, 1035a, 1039c, 1041, 1044, 1068a, 1083, 1085, 1087c, 1092b, 1094a, 1095b, 1108a, 1122a, 1122d, 1133b, 1137b, 1150c, 1152a, 1153, 1163, 1186a, 1186b, 1201b, 1201d, 1295

Nico van der Stam Amsterdam, 110, 481b, 563b, 569c

Stedelijk Museum Amsterdam Amsterdam, 115a, 864, 1024, 1038b

Stern/ABC-Press Amsterdam, 106a, 522b, 1293b, 1293c

Stichting Technische en Fysische Dienst voor de Landbouw Wageningen, 350

Stills Agency/Rob Brijker Press-Service RBP Amsterdam, 189a *(Burli/Arnal/Garcia)*

Stockcolor International Monte Carlo, 146b

Tony Stone Associates Ltd London, 88e, 88f

Sunshine International Photo-Agency Almere-haven, cover l, 111b, 520a, 553b, 646, 762b, 892a, 896c *(Marais Gaussen)*, 929c *Michael Putland)*, 953c *(Richard Sobol)*, 1077

SYGMA/ABC-Press Amsterdam, 41c *(Collart, H.)*, 119c *(W. Karel)*, 432d *(Regis Bossu)*, 447 *(D. Goldberg)*, 576b, 587a *(J. Bryson)*, 670a *(Mathew Polak)*, 676b *(Cachero, J.)*, 788a *(J.A. Pavlovsky)*, 803d, 994a, 1118b *(Derek Hudson)*, 1154b *(J.L. Atlan)*, 1154c *(Diego Goldberg)*

Syndication International Ltd/ABC-Press Amsterdam, 499b, 770a, 875, 1089a, 1210

Süddeutscher Verlag München, 1202g

Kees Tabak/Sunshine International Photo-Agency Almere-haven, 659b

Tass/ANP-Foto Amsterdam, 526b

The Tate Gallery London, 686b

Thames and Hudson Ltd London, cover s

Patrick Thurstone/SCALA Istituto Fotografico Editoriale Antella - Firenze, 358a, 616a

Chriet Titulaer Produkties bv Houten, 80c, 80f, 81d, 723b

Agence Top Paris, 584a, 633b *(E. Baubart)*, 691b

Transworld Features Holland bv Haarlem, 41d, 361f

Travel Pictures/Sunshine International Photo-Agency Almere-haven, 305a

J.W.H.N. Uijttendaal Den Haag, 326

Ullstein Bilderdienst Berlin, 165b, 459a, 609, 673

United Nations Office at Geneva Geneve, 1120

United Press International/ANP-Foto Amsterdam, 27a, 27b, 35, 69c, 117a, 344a, 472c, 517b *(R.T. Bennett)*, 598a, 689, 787a, 798c, 846a, 876b, 1183a

United Press International/The Bettmann Archive Inc. New York, 1194a

United States Information Service USIS Den Haag, 379

Universal News Organization UNO Haarlem, 928a

Universiteits-Bibliotheek van Amsterdam Amsterdam, 495a, 695b

University of California - Lick Observatory California, 753a

University of London - College London, 634a

University of Notre Dame , 928c

V-Dia-Verlag GmbH Heidelberg, 317a, 317b

Vandaag bv/Spectrum Colour Library London, 108a

Mireille Vautier Paris, 335 *(De Cool)*, 498b, 538b, 748a *(De Cool)*, 748c *(De Cool)*, 748d, 815a, 873, 896a *(De Cool)*, 906, 907 *(De Nanxe)*, 925a *(De Nanxe)*, 999a *(De Nanxe)*, 1079b, 1205

V-Dia-Verlag GmbH Heidelberg, 55a

Victoria & Albert Museum London, 1167

Vision International London, 467a *(J. Sims)*, 1047a *(J. Goldblatt)*, 1055a *(S. Rosenlund)*, 1059b *(P. McArdell)*

N. Visjager Edam, 794, 1107b

Vison/Filmbureau Niestadt Hilversum, 573c

Voorlichtingsdienst voor de Verenigde Naties Den Haag, 472b, 1198a, 1199a

Leo Vrooman Taplow, Buckinghamsh, 81b, 710a

Museen der Stadt Köl Wallraf Richartz Museum Koln, 978

Walt Disney Company, The/Uitgeverij Spaarnestad bv Haarlem, 314b

Fred Ward Product Inc./Black Star New York, cover o

Cor van Weele Amsterdam, 358d

Werner Söderström Osakeyhtiö Helsinki, 488b

West Light/ABC-Press Amsterdam, 713a *(C. O'Rear)*, 1229 *(John Gardey)*

White House Press Office , 1142, 1302

Whitney Museum of American Art New York, 947

Ken Wilkie Amsterdam, 757c

W. van Willegen Zaltbommel, 422a, 763b, 775, 842

Andreas Wolfensberger Winterthur, 961b

Woodmansterne Publications Ltd Watford, Herts, 1204

World Photo Service International/AGE FotoStock Barcelona, 144b, 146a, 158a, 184c, 185b, 269a, 438, 704a, 1019a, 1134

Zentrale Farbbild Agentur GmbH ZEFA Düsseldorf, 87 *(R. Everts)*, 533b, 533c, 731 *(J. McGeorge)*, 808 *(andres)*, 1048 *(K. Scholz)*, 1143b *(R. Everts)*

Zentrale Farbbild Agentur GmbH ZEFA/Benelux Press bv Voorburg, 931b *(H. Kramarz)*, 1213

Joseph P. Ziolo Paris, 952